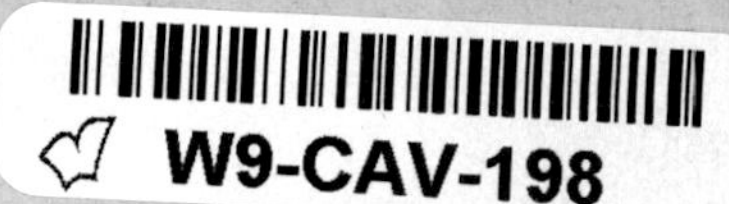

Peterson's Four-Year Colleges 2009

PETERSON'S

A nelnet COMPANY

PETERSON'S

A nelnet COMPANY

About Peterson's, a Nelnet company

Peterson's (www.petersons.com) is a leading provider of education information and advice, with books and online resources focusing on education search, test preparation, and financial aid. Its Web site offers searchable databases and interactive tools for contacting educational institutions, online practice tests and instruction, and planning tools for securing financial aid. Peterson's serves 110 million education consumers annually.

For more information, contact Peterson's, 2000 Lenox Drive, Lawrenceville, NJ 08648; 800-338-3282; or find us on the World Wide Web at www.petersons.com/about.

Peterson's makes every reasonable effort to obtain accurate, complete, and timely data from reliable sources. Nevertheless, Peterson's and the third-party data suppliers make no representation or warranty, either expressed or implied, as to the accuracy, timeliness, or completeness of the data or the results to be obtained from using the data, including, but not limited to, its quality, performance, merchantability, or fitness for a particular purpose, non-infringement or otherwise.

President: Stephen Clemente; Sales and Marketing: Roger S. Williams; Operations Director: Bernadette Webster; Content Director: Fern A. Oram; Production Editor: Mark D. Snider; Copy Editors: Bret Bollmann, Michael Haines, Sally Ross, Pam Sullivan, Valerie Bolus Vaughan; Research Project Manager: Daniel Margolin; Research Associate: Cathleen Fee; Programmer: Phyllis Johnson; Manufacturing Manager: Ray Golaszewski; Composition Manager: Linda M. Williams; Client Relations Representatives: Janet Garwo, Mimi Kaufman, Danielle Vreeland; Contributing Authors: Charlotte Thomas and Richard Woodland

Neither Peterson's nor the third-party data suppliers warrant, guarantee, or make any representations that the results from using the data will be successful or will satisfy users' requirements. The entire risk to the results and performance is assumed by the user.

ISSN 1544-2330
ISBN-13: 978-0-7689-2544-9
ISBN-10: 0-7689-2544-4

Printed in the United States of America

10 9 8 7 6 5 4 3 2 1 10 09 08

Thirty-ninth Edition

Contents

A Note from the Peterson's Editors

For nearly forty years, Peterson's has given students and parents the most comprehensive, up-to-date information on undergraduate institutions in the United States and Canada. *Peterson's Four-Year Colleges 2009* features advice and tips on the college search and selection process, such as how to consider the factors that truly make a difference during your search, how to understand the application process, and how to get financial aid. Each year, Peterson's researches the data published in *Peterson's Four-Year Colleges*. The information is furnished by the colleges and is accurate at the time of publishing.

Opportunities abound for students, and this guide can help you find what you want in a number of ways:

- For application and admissions advice and guidance, just head to **THE ADVICE CENTER**. Within the **Search, Find, Select** section, the "College Admissions Countdown Calendar" outlines pertinent month-by-month milestones. "Choosing Your Top Ten Colleges" gets you started on putting together the most important top ten list you have ever made. "Surviving Standardized Tests" describes frequently used tests and what you need to know to succeed on them. Of course, part of the college selection process involves visiting the schools themselves, and "The Whys and Whats of College Visits" is just the planner you need to make those trips well worth your while. Next, "Applying 101" provides advice on how best to approach the application phase of the process. If you can't make sense out of the early decision/early action conundrum, "The Early Decision Decision" clarifies it for you. "What International Students Need to Know About Admission to U.S. Colleges and Universities" has tips on college admissions for non–U.S. citizens and can also be useful to U.S. citizens. Finally, "Searching for Four-Year Colleges Online" outlines why you'll want to visit **www.petersons.com/colleges** for even more college search-and-selection resources. Up next is the **Money, Money, Money** section, which provides all the essential information on how to meet your education expenses, starting with the "Financial Aid Countdown Calendar" and followed by articles covering "Who's Paying for This? Financial Aid Basics" and "Middle Income Families: Making the Financial Aid Process Work." And be sure to check out our **Options, Options, Options** section for some sneak peeks into specific institutions and programs that may be just right for you, including the latest on honors programs, public versus private colleges, women's colleges, online learning, and the military and higher education! Finally, you'll want to read through the How to Use This Guide section which explains the information presented for each individual college, how we collect our data, and how we determine eligibility for inclusion in this guide.
- If you already have specifics in mind, such as a particular major or institution, turn to the **MAJORS AND MORE** section. Here you can search for a school based on major, entrance difficulty, cost ranges, and geography. If you already have colleges in mind that pique your interest, you can use the "Alphabetical Listing of Colleges and Universities" to search for these schools. Page numbers referring to all information presented about a college are conveniently referenced.
- Next up is the **COLLEGE DATA CENTER.** Here you'll find our unparalleled college descriptions, arranged alphabetically by state. They provide a complete picture of need-to-know information about accredited four-year colleges—including admission rates, majors, current expenses, financial aid, student life, and campus safety. All the information you need to apply is placed together at the conclusion of each college description. And if you still thirst for even more information, more than 700 two-page narrative descriptions appear as **College Close-Ups**—descriptions written by admissions deans that provide great detail about each college. They are edited to provide a consistent format across entries for your ease of comparison.

Peterson's publishes a full line of resources to guide you and your family through the admissions process. Peterson's publications can be found at your local bookstore, library, and high school guidance office—or visit us on the Web at **www.petersons.com/colleges**.

We welcome any comments or suggestions you may have about this publication and invite you to complete our online survey at **www.petersons.com/booksurvey**. Or you can fill out the survey at the back of this book, tear it out, and mail it to us at:

Publishing Department
Peterson's, a Nelnet company
2000 Lenox Drive
Lawrenceville, NJ 08648

Your feedback will help us make your educational dreams possible.

Colleges will be pleased to know that Peterson's helped you in your selection. Admissions staff members are more than happy to answer questions, address specific problems, and help in any way they can. The editors at Peterson's wish you great success in your college search!

The Advice Center

College Admissions Countdown Calendar

This practical month-by-month calendar is designed to help you stay on top of the process of applying to college. For most students, the process begins in September of the junior year of high school and ends in June of the senior year. You may want to begin considering financial aid options, reviewing your academic schedule, and attending college fairs before your junior year.

JUNIOR YEAR

September

- ❒ Check with your counselor to make sure your course credits will meet college requirements.
- ❒ Be sure you are involved in one or two extracurricular activities.
- ❒ Begin building your personal list of colleges at Petersons.com.

October

- ❒ Register for and take the PSAT.

November

- ❒ Strive to get the best grades you can. A serious effort will provide you with the most options during the application process.

December

- ❒ Get involved in a community service activity.
- ❒ Begin to read newspapers and a weekly news magazine.
- ❒ Buy **Peterson's Master the SAT, Peterson's Ultimate ACT Tool Kit,** or **The Real ACT Prep Guide** (published by Peterson's) and begin to study for the tests.

January

- ❒ With your school counselor, decide when to take the ACT, SAT, and SAT Subject Tests (and which Subject Tests to take). If English is not your primary language and you are planning on attending a college in North America, decide when to take the TOEFL.
- ❒ Keep your grades up!

February

- ❒ Plan a challenging schedule of classes for your senior year.
- ❒ Think about which teachers you will ask to write recommendations.
- ❒ Check http://test.nacacnet.org/MemberPortal/Events/CollegeFairs for schedules and locations of college fairs.

March

- ❒ Register for the tests you will take in the spring (ACT, SAT, SAT Subject Tests, or the TOEFL).
- ❒ Meet with your school counselor to discuss college choices.
- ❒ Review your transcript and test scores with your counselor to determine how competitive your range of choices should be.
- ❒ Visit www.petersons.com/colleges to do college research and develop a preliminary list of fifteen to twenty colleges and universities.
- ❒ Start scheduling campus visits. When school is in session (but never during final exams) is the best time. Summers are OK but will not show you what the college is really like. If possible, save your top college choices for the fall. Be aware, however, that fall is the busiest visit season and you will need advance planning. Don't forget to write thank-you letters to your interviewers.

April

- ❒ Take any standardized tests for which you have registered.
- ❒ Create a list of your potential college choices and begin to record personal and academic information that can be later transferred to your college applications.

May

- ❒ Plan college visits and make appointments.
- ❒ Structure your summer plans to include advanced academic work, travel, volunteer work, or a job.
- ❒ Confirm your academic schedule for the fall.

Summer

- ❒ Write to any colleges on your list that do not accept the Common Application to request application forms.
- ❒ Begin working on your application essays.

SENIOR YEAR

September

- ❒ Register for the ACT, SAT, SAT Subject Tests, or TOEFL, as necessary.
- ❒ Check with your school counselor for the fall visiting schedule of college reps.
- ❒ Ask appropriate teachers if they would write recommendations for you. Don't forget to write thank-you letters when they accept.
- ❒ Meet with your counselor to compile your final list of colleges.

October

- ❒ Mail or send early applications electronically after carefully checking them to be sure they are completely filled out.
- ❒ Photocopy or print extra copies of your applications to use as a backup.
- ❒ Take the tests for which you have registered.
- ❒ Don't be late! Keep track of all deadlines for transcripts, recommendations, financial aid, etc.

November

- ❒ Be sure that you have requested your ACT and SAT scores be sent to your colleges of choice.
- ❒ Complete and submit all applications. Print or photocopy an extra copy for your records.

December

- ❒ Take any necessary tests: ACT, SAT, SAT Subject Tests, or TOEFL.
- ❒ Meet with your counselor to verify that all is in order and that transcripts are out to colleges.

January

- ❒ Prepare the Free Application for Federal Student Aid (FAFSA), available at www.fafsa.ed.gov or through your school counseling office. An estimated income tax statement (which can be corrected later) can be used. The sooner you apply for financial aid, the better your chances.

February

- ❒ Send in your FAFSA via the Web or U.S. mail.
- ❒ Be sure your midyear report has gone out to the colleges to which you've applied.
- ❒ Let colleges know of any new honors or accomplishments that were not in your original application.

March

- ❒ Register for any Advanced Placement (AP) tests you might take.
- ❒ Be sure you have received a FAFSA acknowledgment.

April

- ❒ Review the acceptances and financial aid offers you receive.
- ❒ Go back to visit one or two of your top-choice colleges.
- ❒ Notify your college of choice that you have accepted its offer (and send in a deposit by May 1).
- ❒ Notify the colleges you have chosen not to attend of your decision.

May

- ❒ Take AP tests.

June

- ❒ Graduate! Congratulations and best of luck.

Choosing Your Top Ten Colleges

By using all the information in the various sections of this guide, you will find the colleges worthy of the most important top-ten list on the planet—yours.

The first thing you will need to do is decide what type of institution of higher learning you want to attend. Each of the thousands of four-year colleges and universities in the United States is as unique as the people applying to it. Although listening to the voices and media hype around you can make it sound as though there are only a few elite schools worth attending, this simply is not true. By considering some of the following criteria, you will soon find that the large pool of interesting colleges can be narrowed down to a more reasonable number.

SIZE AND CATEGORY

Schools come in all shapes and sizes, from tiny rural colleges of 400 students to massive state university systems serving 100,000 students or more. If you are coming from a small high school, a college with 3,500 students may seem large to you. If you are currently attending a high school with 3,000 students, selecting a college of a similar size may not feel like a new enough experience. Some students coming from very large impersonal high schools are looking for a place where they will be recognized from the beginning and offered a more personal approach. If you don't have a clue about what size might feel right to you, try visiting a couple of nearby colleges of varying sizes. You do not have to be seriously interested in them; just feel what impact the number of students on campus has on you.

Large Universities

Large universities offer a wide range of educational, athletic, and social experiences. Universities offer a full scope of undergraduate majors and award master's and doctoral degrees as well. Universities are usually composed of several smaller colleges. Depending on your interest in a major field or area of study, you would likely apply to a specific college within the university. Each college has the flexibility to set its own standards for admission, which may differ from the overall average of the university. The colleges within a university system also set their own course requirements for earning a degree.

Universities may be public or private. Some large private universities, such as Harvard, Yale, Princeton, University of Pennsylvania, New York University, Northwestern, and Stanford, are well-known for their high entrance standards, the excellence of their education, and the success rates of their graduates. These institutions place a great deal of emphasis on research and compete aggressively for grants from the federal government to fund these projects. Large public universities, such as the State University of New York (SUNY) System, University of Michigan, University of Texas, University of Illinois, University of Washington, and University of North Carolina, also support excellent educational programs, compete for and win research funding, and have successful graduates. Public universities usually offer substantially lower tuition rates to in-state students, although their tuition rates for out-of-state residents are often comparable to those of private institutions.

At many large universities, sports play a major role on campus. Athletics can dominate the calendar and set the tone year-round at some schools. Alumni travel from far and wide to attend their alma mater's football or basketball games, and the campus, and frequently the entire town, grinds to a halt when there is a home game. Athletes are heroes and dominate campus social life.

What are some other features of life on a university campus? Every kind of club imaginable, from literature to bioengineering and chorus to politics, can be found on most college campuses. You will be able to play the intramural version of almost every sport in which the university fields interscholastic teams and join fraternities, sororities, and groups dedicated to social action. You can become a member of a band, an orchestra, or perhaps a chamber music group or work on the newspaper, the literary magazine, or the Web site. The list can go on and on. You may want to try out a new interest or two or pursue what you have always been interested in and make like-minded friends along the way.

Take a look at the size of the classrooms in the larger universities and envision yourself sitting in that atmosphere. Would this offer a learning environment that would benefit you?

Liberal Arts Colleges

If you have considered large universities and come to the conclusion that all that action could be a distraction, a small liberal arts college might be right for you. Ideally tucked away on a picture-perfect campus, a liberal arts college generally has fewer than 5,000 students. The mission of most liberal arts schools is learning for the sake of learning, with a strong emphasis on creating lifelong learners who will be able to apply their education to any number of careers. This contrasts with objectives of the profession-based preparation of specialized colleges.

Liberal arts colleges cannot offer the breadth of courses provided by the large universities. As a result, liberal arts colleges try to create a niche for themselves. For instance, a college may place its emphasis on its humanities departments, whose professors are all well-known published authors and international presenters in their areas of expertise. A college may highlight its science departments by providing state-of-the-art facilities where undergraduates conduct research side by side with top-notch professors and copublish their findings in the most prestigious scientific journals in the country. The personal approach is very important at liberal arts colleges. Whether in advisement, course selection, athletic programs tailored to students' interests, or dinner with the department head at her home, liberal arts colleges emphasize that they get to know their students.

If they are so perfect, why doesn't everyone choose a liberal arts college? Well, the small size limits options. Fewer people may mean less diversity. The fact that many of these colleges encourage a study-abroad option (a student elects to spend a semester or a year studying in another country) reduces the number of students on campus even further. Some liberal arts colleges have a certain reputation that does not appeal to some students. You should ask yourself questions about the campus life that most appeals to you. Will you fit in with the campus culture? Will the small size mean that you go through your social options quickly? Check out the activities listed on the Student Center bulletin board. Does the student body look diverse enough for you? Will what is happening keep you busy and interested? Do the students have input into decision making? Do they create the social climate of the school?

Small Universities

Smaller universities often combine stringent admissions policies, handpicked faculty members, and attractive scholarship packages. These institutions generally have undergraduate enrollments of about 4,000 students. Some are more famous for their graduate and professional schools but have also established strong undergraduate colleges. Smaller universities balance the great majors options of large universities with a smaller campus community. They offer choices but not to the same extent as large universities. On the other hand, by limiting admissions and enrollment, they manage to cultivate some of the characteristics of a liberal arts college. Like a liberal arts college, a small university may emphasize a particular program and go out of its way to draw strong candidates in a specific area, such as premed, to its campus. Universities such as The Johns Hopkins University, University of Notre Dame, Vanderbilt University, Washington University in St. Louis, and Wesleyan University in Connecticut are a few examples of this category.

Technical or Specialized Colleges

Another alternative to the liberal arts college or large university is the technical or otherwise specialized college. Their goal is to offer a specialized and saturated experience in a particular field of study. Such an institution might limit its course offerings to engineering and science, the performing or fine arts, or business. Schools such as California Institute of Technology, Carnegie Mellon University, Massachusetts Institute of Technology, and Rensselaer Polytechnic Institute concentrate on attracting the finest math and science students in the country. At other schools, like Bentley College in Massachusetts or Bryant College in Rhode Island, students eat, sleep, and breathe business. These institutions are purists at heart and strong believers in the necessity of focused, specialized study to produce excellence in their graduates' achievements. If you are certain about your chosen path in life and want to immerse yourself in subjects such as math, music, or business, you will fit right in.

Religious Colleges

Many private colleges have religious origins, and many of these have become secular institutions with virtually no trace of their religious roots. Others remain dedicated to a religious way of education. What sets religious colleges apart is the way they combine faith, learning, and student life. Faculty members and administrators are hired with faith as a criterion as much as their academic credentials.

Single-Gender Colleges

There are strong arguments that being able to pursue one's education without the distraction, competition, and stress caused by the presence of the opposite sex helps a student evolve a stronger sense of her or his self-worth; achieve more academically; have a more fulfilling, less pressured social life; and achieve more later in life. For various historic, social, and psychological reasons, there are many more all-women than all-men colleges. A strict single-sex environment is rare. Even though the undergraduate day college adheres to an all-female or all-male admissions policy, coeducational evening classes or graduate programs and coordinate facilities and classes shared with nearby coed or opposite-sex institutions can result in a good number of students of the opposite sex being found on campus. If you want to concentrate on your studies and hone your leadership qualities, a single-gender school is an option.

LOCATION

Location and distance from home are two other important considerations. If you have always lived in the suburbs, choosing an urban campus can be an adventure, but after a week of the urban experience, will you long for a grassy campus and open space? On the other hand, if you choose a college in a rural area, will you run screaming into the Student Center some night looking for noise, lights, and people? The location—urban, rural, or suburban—can directly affect how easy or how difficult adjusting to college life will be for you.

Don't forget to factor in distance from home. Everyone going off to college wants to think he or she won't be homesick, but sometimes it's nice to get a home-cooked meal or to do the laundry in a place that does not require quarters. Even your kid sister may seem like less of a nuisance after a couple of months away.

Here are some questions you might ask yourself as you go through the selection process: In what part of the country do I want to be? How far away from home do I want to be? What is the cost of returning home? Do I need to be close to a city? How close? How large of a city? Would city life distract me? Would I concentrate better in a setting that is more rural or more suburban?

ENTRANCE DIFFICULTY

Many students will look at a college's entrance difficulty as an indicator of whether or not they will be admitted. For instance, if you have an excellent academic record, you might wish to primarily consider those colleges that are highly competitive. Although entrance difficulty does not translate directly to quality of education, it indicates which colleges are attracting large numbers of high-achieving students. A high-achieving student body usually translates into prestige for the college and its graduates. Prestige has some advantages but should definitely be viewed as a secondary factor that might tip the scales when all the other important factors are equal. Never base your decision on prestige alone!

The other principle to keep in mind when considering this factor is to not sell yourself short. If everything else tells you that a college might be right for you, but your numbers just miss that college's average range, apply there anyway. Your numbers—grades and test scores—are undeniably important in the admissions decision, but there are other considerations. First, lower grades in honors or AP courses will impress colleges more than top grades in regular-track courses because they demonstrate that you are the kind of student willing to accept challenges. Second, admissions directors are looking for different qualities in students that can be combined to create a multifaceted class. For example, if you did poorly in your freshman and sophomore years but made a great improvement in your grades in later years, this usually will impress a college. If you are likely to contribute to your class because of your special personal qualities, a strong sense of commitment and purpose, unusual and valuable experiences, or special interests and talents, these factors can outweigh numbers that are weaker than average. Nevertheless, be practical. Overreach yourself in a few applications, but put the bulk of your effort into gaining admission to colleges where you have a realistic chance for admission.

THE PRICE OF AN EDUCATION

The price tag for higher education continues to rise, and it has become an increasingly important factor for people. While it is necessary to consider your family's resources when choosing a list of colleges to which you might apply, never eliminate a college solely because of cost. There are many ways to pay for college, including loans, and a college education will never depreciate in value, unlike other purchases. It is an investment in yourself and will pay back the expense many times over in your lifetime.

Surviving Standardized Tests

WHAT ARE STANDARDIZED TESTS?

Colleges and universities in the United States use tests to help evaluate applicants' readiness for admission or to place them in appropriate courses. The tests that are most frequently used by colleges are the ACT of American College Testing, Inc., and the College Board's SAT. In addition, the Educational Testing Service (ETS) offers the TOEFL test, which evaluates the English-language proficiency of nonnative speakers. The tests are offered at designated testing centers located at high schools and colleges throughout the United States and U.S. territories and at testing centers in various countries throughout the world.

Upon request, special accommodations for students with documented visual, hearing, physical, or learning disabilities are available. Examples of special accommodations include tests in Braille or large print and such aids as a reader, recorder, magnifying glass, or sign language interpreter. Additional testing time may be allowed in some instances. Contact the appropriate testing program or your guidance counselor for details on how to request special accommodations.

THE ACT

The ACT is a standardized college entrance examination that measures knowledge and skills in English, mathematics, reading, and science reasoning and the application of these skills to future academic tasks. The ACT consists of four multiple-choice tests.

Test 1: English
- 75 questions, 45 minutes
- Usage and mechanics
- Rhetorical skills

Test 2: Mathematics
- 60 questions, 60 minutes
- Pre-algebra
- Elementary algebra
- Intermediate algebra
- Coordinate geometry
- Plane geometry
- Trigonometry

Test 3: Reading
- 40 questions, 35 minutes
- Prose fiction
- Humanities
- Social studies
- Natural sciences

Test 4: Science
- 40 questions, 35 minutes
- Data representation
- Research summary
- Conflicting viewpoints

Each section is scored from 1 to 36 and is scaled for slight variations in difficulty. Students are not penalized for incorrect responses. The composite score is the average of the four scaled scores. There is also a 30-minute Writing Test that is an optional component of the ACT.

To prepare for the ACT, ask your guidance counselor for a free guidebook called *Preparing for the ACT*. Besides providing general test-preparation information and additional test-taking strategies, this guidebook describes the content and format of the four ACT subject area tests, summarizes test administration procedures followed at ACT test centers, and includes a practice test. Peterson's publishes *The Real ACT Prep Guide* that includes three official ACT tests.

THE SAT

The SAT measures developed verbal and mathematical reasoning abilities as they relate to successful performance in college. It is intended to supplement the secondary school record and other information about the student in assessing readiness for college. There is one unscored, experimental section on the exam, which is used for equating and/or pretesting purposes and can cover either the mathematics or verbal subject area.

Critical Reading
- 67 questions, 70 minutes
- Sentence completion
- Passage-based reading

DON'T FORGET TO . . .

- Take the SAT or ACT before application deadlines.
- Note that test registration deadlines precede test dates by about six weeks.
- Register to take the TOEFL test if English is not your native language and you are planning on studying at a North American college.
- Practice your test-taking skills with **Peterson's Master the SAT, Peterson's Ultimate ACT Tool Kit, The Real ACT Prep Guide** (published by Peterson's), **Peterson's Master TOEFL Reading Skills, Peterson's Master TOEFL Vocabulary,** and **Peterson's Master TOEFL Writing Skills.**
- Contact the College Board or American College Testing, Inc., in advance if you need special accommodations when taking tests.

Mathematics

- 54 questions, 70 minutes
- Multiple-choice
- Student-produced response (grid-ins)

Writing

- 49 questions plus essay, 60 minutes
- Identifying sentence errors
- Improving paragraphs
- Improving sentences
- Essay

Students receive one point for each correct response and lose a fraction of a point for each incorrect response (except for student-produced responses). These points are totaled to produce the raw scores, which are then scaled to equalize the scores for slight variations in difficulty for various editions of the test. The critical reading, writing, and mathematics scaled scores range from 200–800 per section. The total scaled score range is from 600–2400.

SAT SUBJECT TESTS

Subject Tests are required by some institutions for admission and/or placement in freshman-level courses. Each Subject Test measures one's knowledge of a specific subject and the ability to apply that knowledge. Students should check with each institution for its specific requirements. In general, students are required to take three Subject Tests (one English, one mathematics, and one of their choice).

Subject Tests are given in the following areas: biology, chemistry, Chinese, French, German, Italian, Japanese, Korean, Latin, literature, mathematics, modern Hebrew, physics, Spanish, U.S. history, and world history. These tests are 1 hour long and are primarily multiple-choice tests. Three Subject Tests may be taken on one test date.

Scored like the SAT, students gain a point for each correct answer and lose a fraction of a point for each incorrect answer. The raw scores are then converted to scaled scores that range from 200 to 800.

THE TOEFL INTERNET-BASED TEST (IBT)

The Test of English as a Foreign Language Internet-Based Test (TOEFL iBT) is designed to help assess a student's grasp of English if it is not the student's first language. Performance on the TOEFL test may help interpret scores on the verbal sections of the SAT. The test consists of four integrated sections: speaking, listening, reading, and writing. The TOEFL iBT emphasizes integrated skills. The paper-based versions of the TOEFL will continue to be administered in certain countries until the Internet-based version is fully administered by Educational Testing Service (ETS). For further information, visit www.toefl.org.

WHAT OTHER TESTS SHOULD I KNOW ABOUT?

The AP Program

This program allows high school students to try college-level work and build valuable skills and study habits in the process. Subject matter is explored in more depth in AP courses than in other high school classes. A qualifying score on an AP test—which varies from school to school—can earn you college credit or advanced placement. Getting qualifying grades on enough exams can even earn you a full year's credit and sophomore standing at more than 1,500 higher-education institutions. There are currently thirty-seven AP courses in twenty-two different subject areas, including art history, biology, and computer science. Speak to your guidance counselor for information about your school's offerings.

College-Level Examination Program (CLEP)

The CLEP enables students to earn college credit for what they already know, whether it was learned in school, through independent study, or through other experiences outside of the classroom. Approximately 2,900 colleges and universities now award credit for qualifying scores on one or more of the 34 CLEP exams. The exams, which are 90 minutes in length and are primarily multiple choice, are administered at participating colleges and universities. For more information, check out the Web site at www.collegeboard. com/clep.

WHAT CAN I DO TO PREPARE FOR THESE TESTS?

Know what to expect. Get familiar with how the tests are structured, how much time is allowed, and the directions for each type of question. Get plenty of rest the night before the test and eat breakfast that morning.

There are a variety of products, from books to software to videos, available to help you prepare for most standardized tests. Find the learning style that suits you best. As for which products to buy, there are two major categories—those created by the test makers and those created by private companies. The best approach is to talk to someone who has been through the process and find out which product or products he or she recommends.

Some students report significant increases in scores after participating in coaching programs. Longer-term programs (40 hours) seem to raise scores more than short-term programs (20 hours), but beyond 40 hours, score gains are minor. Math scores appear to benefit more from coaching than verbal scores.

Resources

There are a variety of ways to prepare for standardized tests—find a method that fits your schedule and your budget. But you should definitely prepare. Far too many students walk into these tests cold, either because they find standardized tests frightening or annoying or they just haven't found the time to study. The key is that these exams are standardized. That means these tests are largely the same from administration to administration; they always test the same concepts. They have to, or else you couldn't compare the scores of people who took the tests on different dates. The numbers or words may change, but the underlying content doesn't.

So how do you prepare? At the very least, you should review relevant material, such as math formulas and commonly used vocabulary words, and know the directions for

TOP 10 WAYS NOT TO TAKE THE TEST

10. Cramming the night before the test.
9. Not becoming familiar with the directions before you take the test.
8. Not becoming familiar with the format of the test before you take it.
7. Not knowing how the test is graded.
6. Spending too much time on any one question.
5. Not checking spelling, grammar, and sentence structure in essays.
4. Second-guessing yourself.
3. Forgetting to take a deep breath to keep from—
2. Losing It!
1. Writing a one-paragraph essay.

each question type or test section. You should take at least one practice test and review your mistakes so you don't make them again on the test day. Beyond that, you know best how much preparation you need. You'll also find lots of material in libraries or bookstores to help you: books and software from the test makers and from other publishers (including Peterson's) or live courses that range from national test-preparation companies to teachers at your high school who offer classes.

The Whys and Whats of College Visits

Dawn B. Sova, Ph.D.

The campus visit should not be a passive activity for you and your parents. Take the initiative and gather information beyond that provided in the official tour. You will see many important indicators during your visit that will tell you more about the true character of a college and its students than the tour guide will reveal. Know what to look for and how to assess the importance of such indicators.

WHAT SHOULD YOU ASK AND WHAT SHOULD YOU LOOK FOR?

Your first stop on a campus visit is the visitor center or admissions office, where you will probably have to wait to meet with a counselor. Colleges usually plan to greet visitors later than the appointed time in order to give them the opportunity to review some of the campus information that is liberally scattered throughout the visitor waiting room. Take advantage of the time to become even more familiar with the college by arriving 15 to 30 minutes before your appointment to observe the behavior of staff members and to browse through the yearbooks and student newspapers that will be available.

If you prepare in advance, you will have already reviewed the college catalog and map of the campus. These materials familiarize you with the academic offerings and the physical layout of the campus, but the true character of the college and its students emerges in other ways.

Begin your investigation with the visitor center staff members. As a student's first official contact with the college, they should make every effort to welcome prospective students and project a friendly image.

- How do they treat you and other prospective students who are waiting? Are they friendly and willing to speak with you, or do they try their hardest to avoid eye contact and conversation?
- Are they friendly with each other and with students who enter the office, or are they curt and unwilling to help?
- Does the waiting room have a friendly feeling or is it cold and sterile?

If the visitor center staff members seem indifferent to *prospective* students, there is little reason to believe that they will be warm and welcoming to current students. View such behavior as a warning to watch very carefully the interaction of others with you during the tour. An indifferent or unfriendly reception in the admissions office may be simply the first of many signs that attending this college will not be a pleasant experience.

Look through several yearbooks and see the types of activities that are actually photographed, as opposed to the activities that colleges promise in their promotional literature. Some questions are impossible to answer if the college is very large, but for small and moderately sized colleges the yearbook is a good indicator of campus activity.

- Has the number of clubs and organizations increased or decreased in the past five years?
- Do the same students appear repeatedly in activities?
- Do sororities and fraternities dominate campus activities?
- Are participants limited to one sex or one ethnic group, or is there diversity?
- Are all activities limited to the campus, or are students involved in activities in the community?

Use what you observe in the yearbooks as a means of forming a more complete understanding of the college, but don't base your entire impression on just one facet. If time permits, look through several copies of the school newspaper, which should reflect the major concerns and interests of the students. The paper is also a good way to learn about the campus social life.

- Does the paper contain a mix of national and local news?
- What products or services are advertised?
- How assertive are the editorials?
- With what topics are the columnists concerned?
- Are movies and concerts that meet your tastes advertised or reviewed?
- What types of ads appear in the classified section?

The newspaper should be a public forum for students, and, as such, should reflect the character of the campus and of the student body. A paper that deals only with seemingly safe and well-edited topics on the editorial page and in regular feature columns might indicate administrative censorship. A lack of ads for restaurants might indicate either a lack of good places to eat or that area restaurants do not welcome student business. A limited mention of movies, concerts, or other entertainment might reveal a severely limited campus social life. Even if ads and reviews are included, you should still balance how such activities reflect your tastes.

You will have only a limited amount of time to ask questions during your initial meeting with the admissions counselor, for very few schools include a formal interview in the initial campus visit or tour. Instead, this brief meeting is often just a nicety that allows the admissions office to begin a file for the student and to record some initial impressions. Save your questions for the tour guide and for students on campus you meet along the way.

HOW CAN YOU ASSESS THE TRUE CHARACTER OF A COLLEGE AND ITS STUDENTS?

Colleges do not train their tour guides to deceive prospective students, but they do caution guides to avoid unflattering topics and campus sites. Does this mean that you will see only a sugarcoated version of life on a particular college campus? Not at all, especially not if you are observant.

Most organized campus visits include such campus facilities as dormitories, dining halls, libraries, student activity and recreation centers, and the health and student services centers. Some may only be pointed out, while you will walk through others. Either way, you will find that many signs of the true character of the college emerge if you keep your eyes open.

Bulletin boards in dormitories and student centers contain a wealth of information about campus activities, student concerns, and campus groups. Read the posters, notices, and messages to learn what *really* interests students. Unlike ads in the school newspaper, posters put up by students advertise both on- and off-campus events, so they will give you an idea of what is also available in the surrounding community.

Review the notices, which may cover either campus-wide events or events that concern only small groups of students. The catalog may not mention a performance group, but an individual dormitory with its own small theater may offer regular productions. Poetry readings, jam sessions, writers' groups, and other activities may be announced and show diversity of student interests.

Even the brief bulletin board messages offering objects for sale and noting objects that people want to purchase reveal a lot about a campus. Are most of the items computer related? Or do the messages specify CDs, audio equipment, or musical instruments? Are offers to trade goods or services posted? Don't ignore the "ride wanted" messages. Students who want to share rides home during a break may specify widely diverse geographical locations. If so, then you know that the student body is not limited to only the immediate area or one locale. Other messages can also enhance your knowledge of the true character of the campus and its students.

As you walk through various buildings, examine their condition carefully.

- Is the paint peeling, and do the exteriors look worn?
- Are the exteriors and interiors of the building clean?
- Is the equipment in the classrooms up-to-date or outdated?

Pay particular attention to the dormitories, especially to factors that might affect your safety. Observe the appearance of the structure, and ask about the security measures in and around the dormitories.

- Are the dormitories noisy or quiet?
- Do they seem crowded?
- How good is the lighting around each dormitory?
- Are the dormitories spread throughout the campus or are they clustered in one main area?
- Who has access to the dormitories in addition to students?
- How secure are the means by which students enter and leave the dormitory?

While you are on the subject of dormitory safety, you should also ask about campus safety. Don't expect that the guide will rattle off a list of crimes that have been committed in the past year. To obtain that information, access the recent year of issues of *The Chronicle of Higher Education* and locate its yearly report on campus crime. Also ask the guide about safety measures that the campus police take and those that students have initiated.

- Can students request escorts to their residences late at night?
- Do campus shuttle buses run at frequent intervals all night?
- Are "blue-light" telephones liberally placed throughout the campus for students to use to call for help?
- Do the campus police patrol the campus regularly?

If the guide does not answer your questions satisfactorily, wait until after the tour to contact the campus police or traffic office for answers.

Campus tours usually just point out the health services center without taking the time to walk through. Even if you don't see the inside of the building, you should take a close look at the location of the health services center and ask the guide questions about services.

- How far is the health center from the dormitories?
- Is a doctor always on call?
- Does the campus transport sick students from their dormitories or must they walk?
- What are the operating hours of the health center?
- Does the health center refer students to a nearby hospital?

If the guide can't answer your questions, visit the health center later and ask someone there.

Most campus tours take pride in showing students their activities centers, which may contain snack bars, game rooms, workout facilities, and other means of entertainment. Should you scrutinize this building as carefully as the rest? Of course. Outdated and poorly maintained activity equipment contributes to your total impression of the college. You should also ask about the hours, availability, and cost (no, the activities are usually *not* free) of using the bowling alleys, pool tables, air hockey tables, and other ammenities.

As you walk through campus with the tour, also look carefully at the appearance of the students who pass. The way in which both men and women groom themselves, the way they dress, and even their physical bearing communicate a lot more than any guidebook can. If everyone seems to conform to the same look, you might feel that you would be uncomfortable at the college, however nonconformist that look might be. On the other hand, you might not feel comfortable on a campus that stresses diversity of dress and behavior, and your observations now can save you discomfort later.

- Does every student seem to wear a sorority or fraternity t-shirt or jacket?
- Is everyone of your sex sporting the latest fad haircut?
- Do all of the men or the women seem to be wearing expensive name-brand clothes?
- Do most of the students seem to be working hard to look outrageous with regards to clothing, hair color, and body art?
- Would you feel uncomfortable in a room full of these students?

Is appearance important to you? If it is, then you should consider very seriously if you answer *yes* to any of the above questions. You don't have to be the same as everyone else on campus, but standing out too much may make you unhappy.

As you observe the physical appearance of the students, also listen to their conversations as you pass them. What are they talking about? How are they speaking? Are their voices and accents all the same, or do you hear diversity in their speech? Are you offended by their language? Think how you will feel if surrounded by the same speech habits and patterns for four years.

WHERE SHOULD YOU VISIT ON YOUR OWN?

Your campus visit is not over when the tour ends because you will probably have many questions yet to be answered and many places to still be seen. Where you go depends upon the extent to which the organized tour covers the campus. Your tour should take you to view residential halls, health and student services centers, the gymnasium or field house, dining halls, the library, and recreational centers. If any of the facilities on this list have been omitted, visit them on your own and ask questions of the students and staff members you meet. In addition, you should step off campus and gain an impression of the surrounding community. You will probably become bored with life on campus and spend at least some time off campus. Make certain that you know what the surrounding area is like.

The campus tour leaves little time to ask impromptu questions of current students, but you can do so after the tour. Eat lunch in one of the dining halls. Most will allow visitors to pay cash to experience a typical student meal. Food may not be important to you now while you are living at home and can simply take anything you want from the refrigerator at any time, but it will be when you are away at college with only a meal ticket to feed you.

- How clean is the dining hall? Consider serving tables, floors, and seating.
- What is the quality of the food?
- How big are the portions?
- How much variety do students have at each meal?
- How healthy are the food choices?

While you are eating, try to strike up a conversation with students and tell them that you are considering attending their college. Their reactions and advice can be eye-opening. Ask them questions about the academic atmosphere and the professors.

- Are the classes large or small?
- Do the majority of the professors only lecture or are tutorials and seminars common?
- Is the emphasis of the faculty career-oriented or abstract?
- Are the teaching methods innovative and stimulating or boring and dull?
- Is the academic atmosphere pressured, lax, or somewhere in between?
- Which are the strong majors? The weak majors?
- Is the emphasis on grades or social life or a mix of both at the college?
- How hard do students have to work to receive high grades?

Current students can also give you the inside line on the true nature of the college social life. You may gain some idea through looking in the yearbook, in the newspaper, and on the bulletin boards, but students will reveal the true highs and lows of campus life. Ask them about drug use, partying, dating, drinking, and anything else that may affect your life as a student.

- Which are the most popular club activities?
- What do students do on weekends? Do most go home?
- How frequently do concerts occur on campus? Who has recently performed?
- How can you become involved in specific activities (name them)?
- How strictly are campus rules enforced and how severe are penalties?
- What counseling services are available?
- Are academic tutoring services available?
- Do they feel that the faculty really cares about students, especially freshmen?

You will receive the most valuable information from current students, but you will only be able to speak with them after the tour is over. And you might have to risk rejection as you try to initiate conversations with students who might not want to reveal how they feel about the campus. Still, the value of this information is worth the chance.

If you have the time, you should also visit the library to see just how accessible research materials are and to observe the physical layout. The catalog usually specifies the days and hours of operation, as well as the number of volumes contained in the library and the number of periodicals to which it subscribes. A library also requires accessibility, good lighting, an adequate number of study carrels, and lounge areas for students. Many colleges have created 24-hour study lounges for students who find the residence halls too noisy for studying, although most colleges claim that they designate areas of the residences as "quiet study" areas. You may not be interested in any of this information, but when you are a student you will have to make frequent use of the campus library so you should know what is available. You should at least ask how extensive their holdings are in your proposed major area. If they have virtually nothing, you will have to spend a lot of time ordering items via interlibrary loan or making copies, which can become expensive. The ready answer of students that they will obtain their information from the Internet is unpleasantly countered by professors who demand journal articles with documentation.

Make a point of at least driving through the community surrounding the college because you will be spending time there shopping, dining, working in a part-time job, or attending events. Even the largest and best-stocked campus will not meet all of your social and personal needs. If you can spare the time, stop in several stores to see if they welcome college students.

- Is the surrounding community suburban, urban, or rural?
- Does the community offer stores of interest, such as bookstores, craft shops, and boutiques?
- Do the businesses employ college students?
- Does the community have a movie or stage theater?
- Are there several types of interesting restaurants?
- Do there seem to be any clubs that court a college clientele?
- Is the center of activity easy to walk to, or do you need other transportation?

You might feel that a day is not enough to answer all of your questions, but even answering some questions will provide you with a stronger basis for choosing a college. Many students visit a college campus several times before making their decision. Keep in mind that for the rest of your life you will be associated with the college that you attend. You will spend four years of your life at this college. The effort of spending several days to obtain the information to make your decision is worthwhile.

Dawn B. Sova, Ph.D., is a former newspaper reporter and columnist, as well as the author of more than eight books and numerous magazine articles. She teaches creative and research writing, as well as scientific and technical writing, newswriting, and journalism.

Applying 101

The words "applying yourself" have several important meanings in the college application process. One meaning refers to the fact that you need to keep focused during this important time in your life, keep your priorities straight, and know the dates that your applications are due so you can apply on time. The phrase might also refer to the person who is really responsible for your application—you.

You are the only person who should compile your college application. You need to take ownership of this process. The guidance counselor is not responsible for completing your applications, and neither are your parents. College applications must be completed in addition to your normal workload at school, college visits, and SAT, ACT, or TOEFL testing.

THE APPLICATION

The application is your way of introducing yourself to a college admissions office. As with any introduction, you want to make a good first impression. The first thing you should do in presenting your application is to find out what the college or university needs from you. Read the application carefully to find out the application fee and deadline, required standardized tests, number of essays, interview requirements, and anything else you can do or submit to help improve your chances for acceptance.

Completing college applications yourself helps you learn more about the schools to which you are applying. The information a college asks for in its application can tell you much about the school. State university applications often tell you how they are going to view their applicants. Usually, they select students based on GPAs and test scores. Colleges that request an interview, ask you to respond to a few open-ended questions, or require an essay are interested in a more personal approach to the application process and may be looking for different types of students than those sought by a state school.

In addition to submitting the actual application, there are several other items that are commonly required. You will be responsible for ensuring that your standardized test scores and your high school transcript arrive at the colleges to which you apply. Most colleges will ask that you submit teacher recommendations as well. Select teachers who know you and your abilities well and allow them plenty of time to complete the recommendations. When all portions of the application have been completed and sent in, whether electronically or by mail, make sure you follow up with the college to ensure their receipt.

FOLLOW THESE TIPS WHEN FILLING OUT YOUR APPLICATION

- **Follow the directions to the letter.** You don't want to be in a position to ask an admissions officer for exceptions due to your inattentiveness.
- **Proofread all parts of your application,** including your essay. Again, the final product indicates to the admissions staff how meticulous and careful you are in your work.
- **Submit your application as early as possible,** provided all of the pieces are available. If there is a problem with your application, this will allow you to work through it with the admissions staff in plenty of time. If you wait until the last minute, it not only takes away that cushion but also reflects poorly on your sense of priorities.
- **Keep a copy of the completed application,** whether it is a photocopy or a copy saved on your computer.

THE APPLICATION ESSAY

Whereas the other portions of your application—your transcript, test scores, and involvement in extracurricular activities—are a reflection of what you've accomplished up to this point, your application essay is an opportunity to present yourself in the here and now. The essay shows your originality and verbal skills and how you approach a topic or problem and express your opinion.

Some colleges may request one essay or a combination of essays and short-answer topics to learn more about who you are and how well you can communicate your thoughts. Common essay topics cover such simple themes as writing about yourself and your experiences or why you want to attend that particular school. Other colleges will ask that you show your imaginative or creative side by writing about a favorite author, for instance, or commenting on a hypothetical situation. In such cases, they will be looking at your thought processes and level of creativity.

Admissions officers, particularly those at small or mid-size colleges, use the essay to determine how you, as a student, will fit into life at that college. The essay, therefore, is a critical component of the application process. Here are some tips for writing a winning essay:

- Colleges are looking for an honest representation of who you are and what you think. Make sure that the tone of the essay reflects enthusiasm, maturity, creativity, the ability to communicate, talent, and your leadership skills.
- Be sure you set aside enough time to write the essay, revise it, and revise it *again*. Running "spell check" will

only detect a fraction of the errors you probably made on your first pass at writing it. Take a break and then come back to it and reread it. You will probably notice other style, content, and grammar problems—and ways that you can improve the essay overall.

- Always answer the question that is being asked, making sure that you are specific, clear, and true to your personality.
- Enlist the help of reviewers who know you well—friends, parents, teachers—since they are likely to be the most honest and will keep you on track in the presentation of your true self.

THE PERSONAL INTERVIEW

Although it is relatively rare that a personal interview is required, many colleges recommend that you take this opportunity for a face-to-face discussion with a member of the admissions staff. Read through the application materials to determine whether or not a college places great emphasis on the interview. If they strongly recommend that you have one, it may work against you to forego it.

In contrast to a group interview and some alumni interviews, which are intended to provide information about a college, the personal interview is viewed both as an information session and as further evaluation of your skills and strengths. You will meet with a member of the admissions staff who will be assessing your personal qualities, high school preparation, and your capacity to contribute to undergraduate life at the institution. On average, these meetings last about 45 minutes—a relatively short amount of time in which to gather information and leave the desired impression—so here are some suggestions on how to make the most of it.

Scheduling Your Visit

Generally, students choose to visit campuses in the summer or fall of their senior year. Both times have their advantages. A summer visit, when the campus is not in session, generally allows for a less hectic visit and interview. Visiting in the fall, on the other hand, provides the opportunity to see what campus life is like in full swing. If you choose the fall, consider arranging an overnight trip so that you can stay in one of the college dormitories. At the very least, you should make your way around campus to take part in classes, athletic events, and social activities. Always make an appointment and avoid scheduling more than two college interviews on any given day. Multiple interviews in a single day hinder your chances of making a good impression, and your impressions of the colleges will blur into each other as you hurriedly make your way from place to place.

Preparation

Know the basics about the college before going for your interview. Read the college catalog and Web site in addition to this guide. You will be better prepared to ask questions that are not answered in the literature and that will give you a better understanding of what the college has to offer. You should also spend some time thinking about your strengths and weaknesses and, in particular, what you are looking for in a college education. You will find that as you get a few interviews under your belt, they will get easier. You might consider starting with a college that is not a top contender on your list, so that the stakes are not as high.

Asking Questions

Inevitably, your interviewer will ask you, "Do you have any questions?" Not having one may suggest that you're unprepared or, even worse, not interested. When you do ask questions, make sure that they are ones that matter to you and that have a bearing on your decision about whether or not to attend that college. The questions that you ask will give the interviewer some insight into your personality and priorities. Avoid asking questions that are answered in the college literature—again, a sign of unpreparedness. Although the interviewer will undoubtedly pose questions to you, the interview should not be viewed merely as a question-and-answer session. If a conversation evolves out of a particular question, so much the better. Your interviewer can learn a great deal about you from how you sustain a conversation. Similarly, you will be able to learn a great deal about the college in a conversational format.

Separate the Interview from the Interviewer

Many students base their feelings about a college solely on their impressions of the interviewer. Try not to characterize a college based only on your personal reaction, however, since your impressions can be skewed by whether you and your interviewer hit it off. Pay lots of attention to everything else that you see, hear, and learn about a college. Once on campus, you may never see your interviewer again.

In the end, remember to relax and be yourself. Your interviewer will expect you to be somewhat nervous, which will relieve some of the pressure. Don't drink jitters-producing caffeinated beverages prior to the interview, and suppress nervous fidgets like leg-wagging, finger-drumming, or bracelet-jangling. Consider your interview an opportunity to put forth your best effort and to enhance everything that the college knows about you up to this point.

THE FINAL DECISION

Once you have received your acceptance letters, it is time to go back and look at the whole picture. Provided you received more than one acceptance, you are now in a position to compare your options. The best way to do this is to compare your original list of important college-ranking criteria with what you've discovered about each college along the way. In addition, you and your family will need to factor in the financial aid component. You will need to look beyond these cost issues and the quantifiable pros and cons of each college, however, and know that you have a good feeling about your final choice. Before sending off your acceptance letter, you need to feel confident that the college will feel like home for the next four years. Once the choice is made, the only hard part will be waiting for an entire summer before heading off to college!

The Early Decision Decision

Maybe a senior you knew last year didn't get into the college he wanted. He said it was because he didn't apply early decision. Maybe your friend's mom told your mom that unless students apply early decision, their chances of getting into top schools are slim to none, even though they have great grades and spectacular essays. Maybe you figure you'd better get in on the early decision action.

All of the above are true—well, sort of—because many students applying to college get the term "early decision" backwards. High school guidance and college counselors run into this kind of thinking all the time and suggest putting "decision" before "early"—as in making a wise decision about committing to a college before applying early. For some students, early decision is a great option. For others, early decision is loaded with pitfalls and dangers.

"When students come back in the fall of their senior year, I often hear 'I know I want to apply early. Can you help me choose the school?'" says Kathy Cleaver, Co-Director of College Counseling at Durham Academy in Durham, North Carolina. She compares that to saying, "I know I want to get married, please help me pick the man." Continues Cleaver, "First you have to fall in love with the school and know it's your first choice and then join the circus for early decision." She's referring to the media hype flying around high school halls about early decision—it's easy to fall prey to the early decision madness. Hot competition to get into "top" schools creates early decision anxiety. Mickey Gilbert, Guidance Counselor at Passaic High School in Passaic, New Jersey, throws out some scary numbers that confirm that, yes, the competition for admittance to top schools is white-hot. There are about 30,000 high schools in the United States, and although the majority of high school seniors apply to institutions in their own states, there are still limited spaces in the "top" schools and the eight Ivy League schools. "No wonder kids think that early decision is the way to go," speculates Gilbert. Early decision panic sets in because students are convinced that if they get their applications in early, they have an edge. Sometimes early decision might make the difference, but there are many issues to consider before taking the early decision leap.

EARLY THIS, EARLY THAT

With all the buzz about early decision, do you really know what it means along with all the other early options, such as early action and early notification? And what about the variations of early decision? Each institution can have its own version of early decision, meaning that deadlines and criteria are different. There's the early decision that notifies students by December, there's the early decision round two, and then there is the early action/single choice.

Seeing the confusion, the National Association for College Admission Counseling (NACAC) developed a standard set of definitions. NACAC is an education association of secondary school counselors, college and university admissions and financial aid officers, counselors, and other individuals who work with students as they transition from high school to college. While each institution has its own variations of each early option, an understanding of the basic differences can help. The list that follows was adapted from the definitions found on the NACAC Web site.

Early Decision

- Early decision is the application process in which students make a commitment to a first-choice institution where, if admitted, they definitely will enroll. Should a student who applies for financial aid not be offered an award that makes attendance possible, the student may decline the offer of admission and be released from the early decision commitment.
- While pursuing admission under an early decision plan, students may apply to other institutions, but may have only one early decision application pending at any time.
- The institution must notify the applicant of the decision within a reasonable and clearly stated period of time after the early decision deadline. Usually, a nonrefundable deposit must be made well in advance of May 1.
- A student applying for financial aid must adhere to institutional early decision aid application deadlines.
- The institution will respond to an application for financial aid at or near the time of an offer of admission.
- The early decision application supercedes all other applications. Immediately upon acceptance of an offer of admission, a student must withdraw all other applications and make no subsequent applications.
- The application form will include a request for a parent and a counselor signature, in addition to the student's signature, indicating an understanding of the early decision commitment and agreement to abide by its terms.

Early Action

- Early action is the application process in which students make application to an institution of preference and receive a decision well in advance of the institution's regular response date. Students who are admitted under early action are not obligated to accept the institution's offer of admission or to submit a deposit until the regular reply date (not prior to May 1).
- A student may apply to other colleges without restriction.

- The institution must notify the applicant of the decision within a reasonable and clearly stated period of time after the early action deadline.
- A student applying for financial aid must adhere to institutional aid application deadlines.
- A student admitted under an early action plan may not be required to make a commitment prior to May 1, but may be encouraged to do so as soon as a final college choice is made. Colleges that solicit commitments to offers of early action admission and/or financial assistance prior to May 1 may do so provided those offers include a clear statement that written requests for extensions until May 1 will be granted, and that such requests will not jeopardize a student's status for admission or financial aid.

Regular Decision

- Regular decision is the application process in which a student submits an application to an institution by a specified date and receives a decision within a reasonable and clearly stated period of time, but not later than April 15.
- A student may apply to other colleges without restriction.
- The institution will state a deadline for completion of applications and will respond to completed applications by a specified date.
- A student applying for financial aid must adhere to institutional aid application deadlines.
- A student admitted under a regular decision plan may not be required to make a commitment prior to May 1, but may be encouraged to do so as soon as a final college choice is made. Colleges that solicit commitments to offers of admission and/or financial assistance prior to May 1 may do so provided those offers include a clear statement that written requests for extensions until May 1 will be granted, and that such requests will not jeopardize a student's status for admission or financial aid.

Rolling Admission

- Rolling admission is the application process in which an institution reviews applications as they are completed and renders admission decisions to students throughout the admission cycle.
- A student may apply to other colleges without restriction.
- The institution will respond to completed applications in a timely manner.
- A student applying for financial aid must adhere to institutional aid application deadlines.
- A student admitted under a rolling admission plan may not be required to make a commitment prior to May 1, but may be encouraged to do so as soon as a final college choice is made. Colleges that solicit commitments to offers of admission and/or financial assistance prior to May 1 may do so provided those offers include a clear statement that written requests for extensions until May 1 will be granted, and that such requests will not jeopardize a student's status for admission or financial aid.

Wait List

- Wait list is an admission decision option utilized by institutions to protect against shortfalls in enrollment. Wait lists are sometimes made necessary because of the uncertainty of the admission process, as students submit applications for admission to multiple institutions and may receive several offers of admission. By placing a student on the wait list, an institution does not initially offer or deny admission, but extends to a candidate the possibility of admission in the future before the institution's admission cycle is concluded.
- The institution will ensure that a wait list, if necessary, is of reasonable length and is maintained for a reasonable period of time, but never later than August 1.
- In the letter offering a wait list position, the institution should provide a past wait list history, which describes the number of students placed on the wait list(s), the number offered admission from the wait list, and the availability of financial aid. Students should be given an indication of when they can expect to be notified of a final admission decision.
- An institution must resolve final status and notify wait list candidates as soon after May 1 as possible.
- The institution will not require students to submit deposits to remain on a wait list or pressure students for a commitment to enroll prior to sending an official offer of admission in writing.

There is one more option, called early action/single choice (EASC), that some highly selective schools such as Harvard, Yale, and Stanford have begun using. Early action/single choice is a nonbinding early admission option for freshman applicants that replaces early decision. With this change, students learn about their admission decision in December without being required to reply until May 1. This option allows students to apply to as many colleges as they want under a regular admission time frame. The difference is that the early action/single choice option does not allow a candidate to apply to other schools under any type of early action, early decision, or early notification program. Students are asked to sign a statement in their application agreeing to file only one early application.

Each of these options has variations, depending on the institution using them. Some schools have a November 1 deadline for early decision round one. Smaller schools have a deadline of November 15, while others have a December 1 deadline. Then there's an early decision round two. To make matters even more complicated, some schools with early decision say that students can't apply to other institutions if they've sent in an early decision application to their admissions office. Others say it's okay to apply to other schools at the same time you're applying early decision to them, but if they send you an acceptance, you must withdraw the other applications.

Just because two institutions have an application process called early decision or early action doesn't mean that their policies are identical. "There is no common terminology, even among the colleges that have early decision," says Christoph Guttentag, Dean of Undergraduate Admissions at Duke University in Durham, North

PARENTS, SOME ADVICE FOR YOU

Though guidance counselors stress that high school students should make the final decision about which college to attend, they also say that parents are a very important part of the decision equation. Parents can help as organizers of all the information and provide the support needed to make a good choice. "Little things like setting up file folders and keeping track of deadlines can keep a student on track," advises Gibson.

Along with their children, parents also need to understand the basics of early option terminology as it applies to each institution being considered. Five different colleges might have five different early decision criteria. Read the fine print, and make note of deadlines.

What really will help—you, your child, and your wallet—is to understand the basics about financial aid. Says Leftwich, "Have an in-depth discussion with the financial aid officer so that you are aware of the ramifications, restrictions, and implications of the financial aid offer."

If possible, make an appointment to visit with a financial aid officer at the college while your child is visiting the campus. Bring your tax forms and discuss the prospects of financial aid. "Financial aid people are straight shooters. It's not in their best interest to tell you one thing to get your foot in the door and then turn around and pull the rug out from under you," says McClintick. "Parents might not like the answer they get from the financial aid officer, but they will get a candid assessment of their eligibility for financial aid."

Leftwich suggests having an honest discussion with your child early in the college selection process. Talk about what you can realistically afford, what colleges will appropriately challenge him or her, if location is a factor, and what kind of environment best suits your child. Whichever option your child uses to apply, you both will know the decision is an informed one.

Carolina. He also points out that just when you think you've got the definitions figured out, institutions change them. "Colleges are always balancing the needs of their institution and the needs of students," he comments.

EARLY DECISION: A MATCHMAKING TOOL OR A CLEVER STRATEGY?

Despite the differences in what actually constitutes early decision, it has become more of a strategy than a matchmaking tool, according to Bill McClintick, Director of College Counseling at Mercersburg Academy in Mercersburg, Pennsylvania. He also chairs the national steering committee on admissions standards for NACAC. The focus of early decision used to be on matching the student with the college and letting the admissions office know that that institution is where the student wants to be above all others. Today, early decision is misunderstood and misused. High school seniors think that they must use the early decision tactic to get an edge. The result, says McClintick is "at many of the top places, early decision applications have gone through the roof."

Though high school students may have exaggerated ideas of how much early decision can really help them, it is true that it does give a small segment of students applying at highly selective schools an advantage. Generally, the more selective the institution, the more small differences matter. "Even if it's a small increase, you need everything you can get," states John Latting, Director of Undergraduate Admissions at The Johns Hopkins University in Baltimore, Maryland.

"Remember," cautions McClintick, "we're only talking about a small slice of kids in the grand scheme of things." He mentions 5 percent of high school seniors nationally who aspire to the "top" institutions. State colleges and universities fill a much lower percentage of their freshman class with early decision applications. "I don't believe that more kids are chasing the same number of spots," says Jon Reider, Director of College Counseling at San Francisco University High School in San Francisco, California. "Students are applying to more and more schools, even with the early decision option on the side. This is inflating the selectivity of some colleges beyond what it used to be." In reality, 90 percent of students apply regular admission. Interest in early decision comes from a relatively small segment of the college applicant pool.

THE BENEFITS OF EARLY DECISION

There are clear benefits to students. Aside from the fact that early decision does play a role in acceptance rates for a relatively small percentage of students at a small number of schools, early decision is a good option. The caveat is that students must know, without a shred of doubt, that one institution, above all others, is the best match for their goals and their likes and dislikes, and that based on grades and test scores, they solidly match the institution's criteria for admission. The option to go early decision should be taken after extensive research, multiple visits to the campus, and talking to a lot of people. "Early decision is for those who can put their hearts and souls into one application," advises Cleaver.

There are other advantages. You have to make only one choice, and you will know by December if you've been accepted. You have to fill out only one application. You are not chewing your nails over your list of possibilities during the Christmas holiday. Instead, you know where you're going and can sit back and enjoy the rest of your senior year, while others in your class are madly filling out applications, writing essays, and agonizing over the thin envelopes that arrive in the mail. Says Guttentag, "The advantage of having that challenging process over with is not insignificant."

Early decision is helpful for admissions officers at selective colleges because it allows them to make decisions between well-qualified students and select those who really want to be at their institution. As Shawn Leftwich, Director of Undergraduate Admissions at Wheaton College in Illinois, points out, early decision is for the students who are strongly committed. "We like you. You like us. We know you're coming, and we can fill our freshman class." However, on the flip side, she adds that some students aren't so sure about which college they want to attend, and early decision only makes the process more stressful.

Before you decide early decision, consider early action. Many high school counselors lean toward early action, which is another good option. With early action you're able to apply later in the process. This means you will be able to take the SATs again. Your first-semester grades and AP classes taken in the first semester of your senior year can be used to evaluate your eligibility. You have September and October to visit several campuses while they are in session and plenty of time to do the research to put more than one school on your list.

THE PITFALLS OF EARLY DECISION

Though early decision has benefits, before you jump into it, look at the ramifications of that option. Advises Gilbert, "Early decision might give you an edge, but the tradeoff is not so great."

Perhaps the most compelling reason why students should seriously examine early decision before jumping at it is because they are bound by an agreement to attend that school if accepted. Students sign a pledge to attend that institution and are required to withdraw applications from all other schools. They also are obligated to accept the financial aid award that the institution gives them. An early decision is a binding decision. "Regardless," advises David Gibson, College Advisor at St. Mary's Parish in Annapolis, Maryland, "students don't learn about their financial aid awards until March or April, and if the award funding is not at all acceptable because the family's financial need was not met, they need to decline the offer and begin searching for a new college. March or April is not a good time to start applying to new colleges."

How binding is binding? Though no school can force a student to attend if they've signed an early action agreement, students who decide not to attend that school hurt others with that decision. High school counselors have to sign the binding agreement, along with parents, and must state that they will not send out transcripts to other institutions. Many institutions will not accept the application of a student who applied early decision elsewhere and backed out of the agreement. Admissions officers may find out in May that an early decision student is not coming, so they'll call the counselor and ask if the student applied to another school. If so, often a phone call to the other institution is made and acceptance denied. Sometimes the counselor loses a good reputation with that institution, putting applicants who follow in subsequent years at a disadvantage.

After the consequences of signing a binding agreement, the financial aspect of early decision is the next biggest pitfall. "You can't compare financial aid offers," says Latting. "You have only one offer." Students won't know if they're eligible for Pell grants or merit scholarships. Government FAFSA forms are not submitted until January, and students might not find out how much aid they can get until March or April, long after the early decision agreement was signed and sealed. "This means that if they are accepted, they are then obligated to a college that might not fund them to the level of their financial need," says Gibson. Students who apply early action or regular decision are in a better position to negotiate financial aid packages.

QUESTIONS TO ASK YOURSELF BEFORE APPLYING EARLY DECISION

What if you don't get accepted early decision—then what? Speaking from the experience of seeing students deal with early decision rejection letters, Reider says, "Some of your friends are getting acceptance letters, and you get one thin envelope and the pain of rejection. You've given the early decision institution your best shot and you lost." Cleaver has seen kids in her high school end up thinking they won't get in anywhere. "This is the first time they've faced a big rejection and news they don't want to hear," she says, noting that because of the timetable of early decision, letters often come right around exam time in December.

When students apply regular decision, meaning they wait until well into their senior year and apply to several different institutions, it's "all or some," quips Latting. "With early decision, it's all or nothing." Many application deadlines for regular decision are in January. If you get that rejection letter from the school you were counting on, that doesn't give you much time to apply to other schools, much less visit them.

Are you ready to make such a drastic decision so early in your senior year? A lot can change in how you think about your future between the beginning of your senior year and graduation. With six or seven months behind you as a senior, you might be in a better position to compare colleges in April than you were back in September. Think about it—you're making the decision about where you want to spend the next four years of your life in early October of your senior year!

Have you given yourself enough time to pick one college above all others? If you want to apply early decision, you should start making plans to do so in your junior year. In order to apply early decision, you must have your ACTs or SATs taken, campus visits done, a final choice made, a dynamite essay written, a stellar application filled out, and teacher recommendation letters collected. That's a lot to cram into the end of your junior year and a few months into your senior year.

Have you given an admissions office enough information to make a decision about you? The more information the admissions office has about grades and classes you took and activities and leadership positions you held, the better they can decide if you're a good match for them. Do you really want decisions being made about you based on sophomore and junior grades and activities? What happens to that AP English class you finally felt ready to take the beginning of your senior year? What about that calculus class you kicked in the first semester of your senior year? Admissions won't be able to assess that on an early decision application.

EARLY DECISION REJECTION

In case you haven't heard, fat is good, thin is bad. Thin envelopes from college admissions offices usually mean a single-page letter saying good luck, we wish you the best, but you're not going to be attending our school next fall. However stated, it's hard to be rejected, especially when you've applied early decision, which states to the college and to yourself that this is the college you've decided is the only one you really, really want to attend above all others.

But thin envelopes don't mean the end of the world. Cleaver advises to not let early decision get control of you. "There are too many choices of colleges for you not to get into college. You might not get into Princeton, but there are many other wonderful schools if you do the research to look for a good match. Early decision is a tool to use to apply, but it is not always the best tool."

Objecting to the term "perfect match," Reider asks, "Does it really matter what kind of car you drive? There are twenty different colleges that can get you where you want to go. You'll be successful in most places."

HOW TO DO EARLY DECISION THE RIGHT WAY

Taking the early decision option requires more than gathering information, filling out an application, writing an essay, and waiting for an envelope to come in the mail. If you're going to be serious about early decision, the time to start is in your junior year.

Research the institutions at the top of your list. Think through what you want out of college—not just in terms of a future career, but also factors such as location, size, distance from home, sports, and other activities. Think about who you want to be. "It has to be a love connection," says Cleaver. Tune out all the early decision talk and do your homework about each college. Then ask yourself if one stands out above all the others you've researched. Is this the one to which you can commit to a binding agreement? Are you in the competition to be admitted? Will you have the funds to attend this college?

"Admissions can tell if your application is from the heart," Cleaver cautions. Students ask her how to make their applications "look like they want to go there." She replies that what they put on an application and in an essay has to pour out of their hearts. Students who visit the campus and sit in on a class or a campus organization have the edge if something really clicked with them. They will write a convincing application. Perhaps they'll tell about how exciting the professor they heard was or how wonderful it is that the college has a chess club. Cleaver observes that kids usually write about an institution's sports team or about the ivy-covered walls of the campus on their application essay instead of writing about some interesting aspect of the university that spoke to them, which takes research, time, and reflection. "Don't make the mistake of chasing a name and not being a good consumer," cautions McClintick. Part of being a good consumer is to make sure you are a reasonably competitive applicant. This means looking at the school's admission criteria and statistics. What percentage of the freshman class is filled with early decision and early action students? If it's a high percentage, then you might want to reconsider where that school falls on your wish list. How many students return for their sophomore year? If more than 10 percent leave after their freshman year, that should tell you something about student satisfaction—and ultimately yours.

One of the most important ways to choose the right school is to visit the campus, perhaps multiple times and preferably with students on campus. "Campus visits are a critical time to talk with undergraduates and to find out what the academic, social, and physical climate is like," advises Guttentag. If you're staying in a dorm on Tuesday night during a visit, you can tell how serious kids are about their work. What kinds of conversations are they having? "Are these the kind of kids you want to spend four years of your life with?" asks McClintick.

After you've thoroughly investigated all the aspects of a college and decided it's at the absolute top of your list, after you are familiar with the early decision requirements at that institution, after you've determined that you have a good chance of getting into that institution, then you can say early decision is for you. For those who are not so sure, fortunately, colleges and universities have plenty of other options for admission.

What International Students Need to Know About Admission to U.S. Colleges and Universities

Kitty M. Villa

There are two principles to remember about admission to a university in the United States. First, applying is almost never a one-time request for admission but an ongoing process that may involve several exchanges of information between applicant and institution. "Admission process" or "application process" means that a "yes" or "no" is usually not immediate, and requests for additional information are to be expected. To successfully manage this process, you must be prepared to send additional information when requested and then wait for replies. You need a thoughtful balance of persistence to communicate regularly and effectively with your selected universities and patience to endure what can be a very long process.

The second principle involves a marketplace analogy. The most successful applicants are alert to opportunities to create a positive impression that sets them apart from other applicants. They are able to market themselves to their target institution. Institutions are also trying to attract the highest-quality student that they can. The admissions process presents you with the opportunity to analyze your strengths and weaknesses as a student and to look for ways to present yourself in the most marketable manner.

FIRST STEP—SELECTING INSTITUTIONS

With thousands of institutions of higher education in the U.S., how do you begin to narrow your choices down to the institutions that are best for you? There are many factors to consider, and you must ultimately decide which factors are most important to you.

Location

You may spend several years studying in the U.S. Do you prefer an urban or rural campus? Large or small metropolitan area? If you need to live on campus, will you be unhappy at a university where most students commute from off-campus housing? How do you feel about extremely hot summers or cold winters? Eliminating institutions that do not match your preferences in terms of location will narrow your choices.

Recommendations from Friends, Professors, or Others

There are valid academic reasons to consider the recommendations of people who know you well and have firsthand knowledge about particular institutions. Friends and contacts may be able to provide you with "inside information" about the campus or its academic programs to which published sources have no access. You should carefully balance anecdotal information with your own research and your own impressions. However, current and former students, professors, and others may provide excellent information during the application process.

Your Own Academic and Career Goals

Consideration of your academic goals is more complex than it may seem at first glance. All institutions do not offer the same academic programs. The application form usually provides a definitive listing of the academic programs offered by an institution. A course catalog describes the degree program and all the courses offered. In addition to printed sources, there is a tremendous amount of institutional information available on the Web. Program descriptions, even course descriptions and course syllabi, are often available to peruse online.

You may be interested in the rankings of either the university or of a program of study. Keep in mind, however, that rankings usually assume that quality is quantifiable. Rankings are usually based on presumptions about how data relate to quality and are likely to be unproven. It is important to carefully consider the source and the criteria of any ranking information before believing and acting upon it.

Your Own Educational Background

You may be concerned about the interpretation of your educational credentials, since your country's degree nomenclature and the grading scale may differ from those in the U.S. Universities use reference books about the educational systems of other countries to help them understand specific educational credentials. Generally, these credentials are interpreted by each institution; there is not a single interpretation that applies to every institution. The lack of uniformity is good news for most students, since it means that students from a wide variety of educational backgrounds can find a U.S. university that is appropriate to their needs.

To choose an appropriate institution, you can and should do an informal self-evaluation of your educational background. This self-analysis involves three important questions:

1. How Many Years of Study Have You Completed?
Completion of secondary school with at least twelve total years of education usually qualifies students to apply for undergraduate (bachelor's) degree programs. Completion of a university degree program that involves at least sixteen years of total education qualifies one to apply for admission to graduate (master's) degree programs in the U.S.

2. Does the Education That You Have Completed in Your Country Provide Access to Further Study in the U.S.?
Consider the kind of institution where you completed your previous studies. If educational opportunities in your country are limited, it may be necessary to investigate many U.S. institutions and programs in order to find a match.

3. Are Your Previous Marks or Grades Excellent, Average, or Poor?
Your educational record influences your choice of U.S. institutions. If your grades are average or poor, it may be advisable to apply to several institutions with minimally difficult or noncompetitive entrance levels.

YOU are one of the best sources of information about the level and quality of your previous studies. Awareness of your educational assets and liabilities will serve you well throughout the application process.

SECOND STEP—PLANNING AND ASSEMBLING THE APPLICATION

Planning and assembling a university application can be compared to the construction of a building. First, you must start with a solid foundation, which is the application form itself. The application, often available online as well as in paper form, usually contains a wealth of useful information, such as deadlines, fees, and degree programs available at that institution. To build a solid application, it is best to begin well in advance of the application deadline.

How to Obtain the Application Form

Application forms and links to institutional Web sites may also be available at a U.S. educational advising center associated with the American Embassy or Consulate in your country. These centers are excellent resources for international students and provide information about standardized test administration, scholarships, and other matters to students who are interested in studying in the U.S. Your local U.S. Embassy or Consulate can guide you to the nearest educational advising center.

What Are the Key Components of a Complete Application?

Institutional requirements vary, but the standard components of a complete application include the following:

- Transcript
- Required standardized examination scores
- Evidence of financial support
- Letters of recommendation
- Application fee

Transcript
A complete academic record or transcript includes all courses completed, grades earned, and degrees awarded. Most universities require an official transcript to be sent directly from the school or university. In many other countries, however, the practice is to issue official transcripts and degree certificates directly to the student. If you have only one official copy of your transcript, it may be a challenge to get additional certified copies that are acceptable to U.S. universities. Some institutions will issue additional official copies for application purposes.

If your institution does not provide this service, you may have to seek an alternate source of certification. As a last resort, you may send a photocopy of your official transcript, explain that you have only one original, and ask the university for advice on how to deal with this situation.

Required Standardized Examination Scores
Arranging to take standardized examinations and earning the required scores seem to cause the most anxiety for international students.

The university application form usually indicates which examinations are required. The standardized examination required most often for undergraduate admission is the Test of English as a Foreign Language (TOEFL). Institutions may also require the SAT of undergraduate applicants. These standardized examinations are administered by the Educational Testing Service (ETS).

These examinations are offered in almost every country of the world. It is advisable to begin planning for standardized examinations at least six months prior to the application deadline of your desired institutions. Test centers fill up quickly, so it is important to register as soon as possible. Information about the examinations is available at U.S. educational advising centers associated with embassies or consulates.

FOR MORE INFORMATION

Questions about test formats, locations, dates, and registration may be addressed to:

ETS Corporate Headquarters
Rosedale Road
Princeton, New Jersey 08541
Web sites: http://www.ets.org
http://www.toefl.org
Phone: 609-921-9000
Fax: 609-734-5410

Most universities require that the original test scores, not a student copy, be sent directly by the testing service. When you register for the test, be sure to indicate that the testing service should send the test scores directly to the universities.

You should begin your application process before you receive your test scores. Delaying submission of your application until the test scores arrive may cause you to miss deadlines and negatively affect the outcome of your application. If you want to know your scores in order to assess your chances of admission to an institution with rigorous admission standards, you should take the tests early.

Many universities in the U.S. set minimum required scores on the TOEFL or other standardized examinations. Test scores are an important factor, but most institutions also look at a number of other factors in their consideration of a candidate for admission.

Evidence of Financial Support

Evidence of financial support is required to issue immigration documents to admitted students. This is part of a complete application package but usually plays no role in determining admission. Most institutions make admissions decisions without regard to the source and amount of financial support.

Letters of Recommendation

Most institutions require one or more letters of recommendation. The best letters are written by former professors, employers, or others who can comment on your academic achievements or professional potential.

Some universities provide a special form for the letters of recommendation. If possible, use the forms provided. If you are applying to a large number of universities, however, or if your recommenders are not available to complete several forms, it may be necessary for you to duplicate a general recommendation letter.

Application Fee

Most universities also require an application fee, ranging from $25 to $100, which must be paid to initiate consideration of the application.

Completing the Application Form

Whether sent by mail or electronically, the application form must be neat and thoroughly filled out. Although parts of the application may not seem to apply to you or your situation, do your best to answer all the questions.

Remember that this is a process. You provide information, and your proposed university then may request clarification and further information. If you have questions, it is better to initiate the entire process by submitting the application form rather than asking questions before you apply. The university will be better able to respond to you after it has your application. Always complete as much as you can. Do not permit uncertainty about the completion of the application form to cause unnecessary delays.

THIRD STEP—DISTINGUISH YOUR APPLICATION

To distinguish your application—to market yourself successfully—is ultimately the most important part of the application process. As you select your prospective universities, begin to analyze your strengths and weaknesses as a prospective student. As you complete your application, you should strive to create a positive impression and set yourself apart from other applicants, to highlight your assets and bring these qualities to the attention of the appropriate university administrators and professors. Applying early is a very easy way to distinguish your application.

Deadline or Guideline?

The application deadline is the last date that an application for a given semester will be accepted. Often, the application will specify that all required documents and information be submitted before the deadline date. To meet the deadlines, start the application process early. This also gives you more time to take—and perhaps retake and improve—the required standardized tests.

Admissions deliberations may take several weeks or months. In the meantime, most institutions accept additional information, including improved test scores, after the posted deadline.

Even if your application is initially rejected, you may be able to provide additional information to change the decision. You can request reconsideration based on additional information, such as improved test scores, strong letters of recommendation, or information about your class rank. Applying early allows more time to improve your application. Also, some students may decide not to accept their offers of admission, leaving room for offers to students on a waiting list. Reconsideration of the admission decisions can occur well beyond the application deadline.

Think of the deadline as a guideline rather than an impermeable barrier. Many factors—the strength of the application, your research interests, the number of spaces available at the proposed institution—can override the enforcement of an application deadline. So, if you lack a test score or transcript by the official deadline, you may still be able to apply and be accepted.

Statement of Purpose

The statement of purpose is your first and perhaps best opportunity to present yourself as an excellent candidate for admission. Whether or not a personal history essay or statement of purpose is required, always include a carefully written statement of purpose with your applications. A compelling statement of purpose does not have to be lengthy, but it should include some basic components:

- Part One—Introduce yourself and describe your educational background. This is your opportunity to describe any facet of your educational experience that you wish to emphasize. Perhaps you attended a highly ranked secondary school or university in your home country. Mention the name and any noteworthy characteristics of the secondary school or university from which you graduated. Explain the grading scale used at your university. Do not forget to mention your rank in your graduating class and any honors you may have received. This is not the time to be modest.

- Part Two—Describe your current academic and career interests and goals. Think about how these will fit into those of the institution to which you are applying, and mention the reasons why you have selected that institution.
- Part Three—Describe your long-term goals. When you finish your program of study, what do you plan to do next? If you already have a job offer or a career plan, describe it. Give some thought to how you'll demonstrate that studying in the U.S. will ultimately benefit others.

Use Personal Contacts When Possible

Appropriate and judicious use of your own network of contacts can be very helpful. Friends, former professors, former students of your selected institutions, and others may be willing to advise you during the application process and provide you with introductions to key administrators or professors. If suggested, you may wish to contact certain professors or administrators by mail, telephone, or e-mail. A personal visit to discuss your interest in the institution may be appropriate. Whatever your choice of communication, try to make the encounter pleasant and personal. Your goal is to make a positive impression, not to rush the admission decision.

There is no single right way to be admitted to U.S. universities. The same characteristics that make the educational choice in the U.S. so difficult—the number of institutions and the variety of programs of study—are the same attributes that allow so many international students to find the institution that's right for them.

Kitty M. Villa is the former Assistant Director, International Office, at the University of Texas at Austin.

Searching for Four-Year Colleges Online

The Internet can be a great tool for gathering information about four-year colleges and universities. There are many worthwhile sites that are ready to help guide you through the various aspects of the selection process, including Peterson's College Search at www.petersons.com/colleges.

HOW PETERSON'S COLLEGE SEARCH CAN HELP

Peterson's College Search is a comprehensive information resource that will help you make sense of the college admissions process and is a great place to start your college search-and-selection journey—it's as easy as these three steps:

1. Decide what's important
2. Define your criteria
3. Get results

Decide What's Important

There's no such thing as a best college—there's only the best college *for you*! Peterson's College Search site is organized into various sections and offers you enhanced search criteria—and it's easy to use! You can find colleges by name or keyword for starters, or do a detailed search based on the following:

- The Basics (location, setting, size, cost, type, religious and ethnic affiliation)
- Student Body (male-female ratio, diversity, in-state vs. out-of-state)
- Getting In (selectivity, GPA)
- Academics (degree type, majors, special programs and services)
- Campus Life (sports, clubs, fraternities and sororities, housing)

Define Your Criteria

Now it's time to take to define your criteria by taking a closer look at some more specific details. Here you are able to answer questions about what is important to you, skip questions that aren't important, and click for instant results. You'll be prompted to think about criteria:

- Where do you want to study?
- What range of tuition are you willing to consider?
- How many people do you want to go to school with?

Get Results

Once you have gotten your results, simply click on any school to get information about the institution, including school type, setting, degrees offered, comprehensive cost, entrance difficulty, application deadline, undergraduate student population, minority breakdown, international population, housing info, freshman details, faculty, majors, academic programs, student life, athletics, facilities/endowments, costs, financial aid, and applying. Keep reading but take a peek at all the great info you'll see on Petersons.com on the next page!

Get Free Info

If, after looking at the information provided on Peterson's College Search, you still have questions, you can send an e-mail directly to the admissions department of the school. Just click on the "Get Free Info" button and send your message!

Visit School Site

For institutions that have provided information about their Web sites, simply click on the "Visit School Site" button and you will be taken directly to that institution's Web page. Once you arrive at the school's Web site, look around and get a feel for the place. Often, schools offer virtual tours of the campus, complete with photos and commentary.

College Close-Up

If the schools you are interested in have provided Peterson's with a **College Close-Up,** you can do a keyword search on that description. Here, schools are given the opportunity to communicate unique features of their programs to prospective students.

Add to My Saved Schools/Add Notes/Apply

The "Add to My Saved Schools" features are designed to help you with your college planning with management tools to create notes about and track the school. The Apply link gives you the ability to directly apply to the school online.

WRITE ADMISSIONS ESSAYS

This year, 500,000 college applicants will write 500,000 different admissions essays. Half will be rejected by their first-choice school, while only 11 percent will gain admission to the nation's most selective colleges. With acceptance rates at all-time lows, setting yourself apart requires more than just blockbuster SAT scores and impeccable transcripts—it requires the perfect application essay. Named "the world's premier

SEARCH, FIND, SELECT

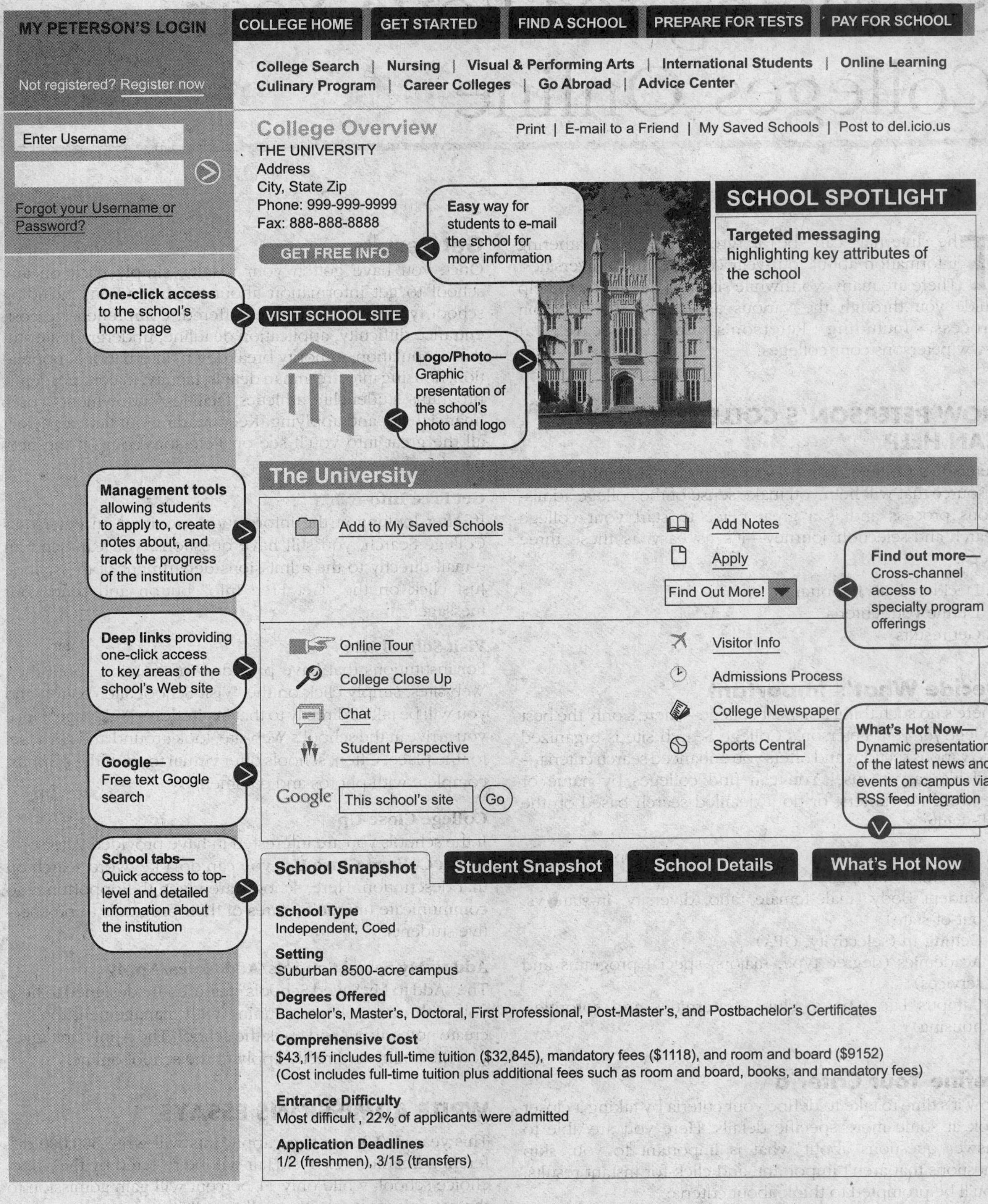

application essay editing service" by the *New York Times* Learning Network and "one of the best essay services on the Internet" by the *Washington Post*, EssayEdge (www.essayedge.com) has helped more applicants write successful personal statements than any other company in the world. Learn more about EssayEdge and how it can give you an edge over hundreds of applicants with comparable academic credentials.

PRACTICE FOR YOUR TEST

At Peterson's, we understand that the college admissions process can be very stressful. With the stakes so high and the competition getting tighter every year, it's easy to feel like the process is out of your control. Fortunately, preparing for college admissions tests, like the PSAT, SAT, and ACT, helps you exert some control over the options you will have available to you. You can visit Peterson's Prep Central (click on the "Prepare for Tests" tab at the top of the screen) to learn more about how Peterson's can help you maximize your scores—and your options.

USE THE TOOLS TO YOUR ADVANTAGE

Choosing a college is an involved and complicated process. The tools available to you on www.petersons.com can help you to be more productive in this process. So, what are you waiting for? Fire up your computer; your future alma mater may be just a click away!

Financial Aid Countdown Calendar

JUNIOR YEAR

Fall

Now is the time to get serious about the colleges in which you are interested. Meet with your guidance counselor to help you narrow down your choices. Hopefully by the spring, your list will have five to ten solid choices. College visits are always a great idea—remember this will be the place you will call home for four years, so start your campus visits soon!

- ❒ Register for the PSAT.
- ❒ Check out local financial aid nights in the area. Be sure to attend these valuable sessions, especially if this is the first time your family is sending someone off to college. Try to become familiar with common financial aid terms. Start reviewing the literature available and begin to familiarize yourself with the various programs. A good booklet is published by the U.S. Department of Education, "The Guide to Federal Student Aid" and is available at any financial aid office or on the Web at http://studentaid.ed.gov/students/publications/student_guide/index.html.
- ❒ In October, take the PSAT/NMSQT.
- ❒ Do some Web browsing! There are many free scholarship search engines, such as Petersons.com. Also, head to the bookstore or library and pick up a copy of **Peterson's Scholarships, Grants & Prizes**. It features details on billions of dollars of aid from private sources.
- ❒ Ask your parents to contact their employers, unions, and any church and fraternal organizations with which they have a connection to learn about possible scholarship opportunities.
- ❒ Check with your high school guidance counselor for the qualifications and deadlines of local scholarship awards. Many guidance counselors report that there are few applicants for these awards.

Winter

- ❒ Keep checking for scholarships! Remember that this is the one area over which you have control. The harder you work, the better your chances for success!
- ❒ Register and study for the SAT and SAT Subject Tests.

Spring

- ❒ Spring Break—a great time to visit colleges. Remember your top ten list? Time to start narrowing it down.
- ❒ Review the requirements for local scholarships. What can you do now and over the summer to improve your chances?
- ❒ Take the SATs. Good luck!
- ❒ Look for a summer job, especially one that ties in with your college plans. For example, if you want to major in premed, why not try to get a job at a hospital or with a laboratory?

Summer

- ❒ College visit time! Ask: Is this where I see myself getting my undergraduate degree? Can I adjust to the seasons, the town surrounding the campus, the distance from home, the college size? Does this school feel right for me?
- ❒ Why not get a jump on college (and maybe save some money!) and enroll for a college course at the local community college? Or, better yet, do some extra prep work for the SAT!

SENIOR YEAR

Fall

How's the college list coming? Can you get your list down to five or six choices? Your guidance counselor can help with this process. Once you have your top choices, make a list of what each college requires for admission and financial aid. Be sure your list includes all deadlines. Attend a financial aid night presentation with your parents. Some of these sessions offer help in completing forms; others offer a broader view of the process. Contact the presenter (usually a local college financial aid professional) to be sure you are getting the information you need.

- ❒ Do any of these colleges require the PROFILE® financial aid application? Many private colleges use this form for institutional aid. You need to file this comprehensive form in late September or early October. For more information or to find out which colleges use this supplemental form, go to http://profileonline.collegeboard.com/index.jsp. (Web site registration is free; however, PROFILE is a fee-based application).
- ❒ Don't falter now in your scholarship search. Get the applications filed by the published deadlines.
- ❒ Register now if you are planning to retake the SAT.
- ❒ Most important, start completing your college applications—the earlier, the better! If you are interested in early decision or early action, now is the time! Remember, accuracy and completeness are a must!

Winter

- ❒ Ensure all college applications are completed.
- ❒ Get the Free Application for Federal Student Aid (FAFSA). This is the key form for financial aid for every school across the country. Remember, watch your deadlines, but do not file until after January 1. Be sure to keep a copy of the form, whether you file electronically or with the paper application. Do you have some questions? Call the local financial aid office. Many states have special toll-free call-in programs in January and February, Financial Aid Awareness Month. Be sure that you have completed each school's required forms.
- ❒ As the letters of admission start to arrive, the financial aid award letters should be right behind them. Important question for parents: What is the bottom line? Remember, aid at a lower-cost state school will be less than a higher-cost private college. But what will you be required to pay? This can be confusing, so consider gift aid (scholarships and grants), student loans, and parent loans. The school with the lowest sticker price (tuition, fees, and room and board) might not be the best bargain when you look at the overall financial aid package.

Spring

- ❒ Still not sure where to go? The financial aid package at your top choice just not enough? Call the financial aid office and the admissions office. Talk it over. While schools don't like to bargain, they are usually willing to take a second look. Is there something unusual about your family's financial situation that might impact your parents' ability to pay?
- ❒ By May 1, you must make your final decision. Notify your chosen college and find out what you need to do next. Tell the other colleges you are not accepting their offers of admission and financial aid.

Summer

- ❒ Time to crunch the numbers. Parents, get information from the college on the total charges for the coming fall term. Deduct the aid package and then plan for how the balance will be paid. Contact the college financial aid office for the best parental loan program. If you want to arrange for a payment plan, contact the Business Office for further information. Most schools have deferred payment plans available for a nominal fee.

Congratulations! Remember that you need to reapply for aid every year!

Who's Paying for This? Financial Aid Basics

A college education can be expensive—costing more than $150,000 for four years at some of the higher priced private colleges and universities. Even at the lower cost state colleges and universities, the cost of a four-year education can approach $60,000. Determining how you and your family will come up with the necessary funds to pay for your education requires planning, perseverance, and learning as much as you can about the options that are available to you. But before you get discouraged, College Board statistics show that 42 percent of full-time students attend four-year public and private colleges with tuition and fees less than $6000, while 13 percent attend colleges that have tuition and fees more than $24,000. College costs tend to be less in the western states and higher in New England.

Paying for college should not be looked at as a four-year financial commitment. For many families, paying the total cost of a student's college education out of current income and savings is usually not realistic. For families that have planned ahead and have financial savings established for higher education, the burden is a lot easier. But for most, meeting the cost of college requires the pooling of current income and assets and investing in longer-term loan options. These family resources, together with financial assistance from state, federal, and institutional sources, enable millions of students each year to attend the institution of their choice.

FINANCIAL AID PROGRAMS

There are three types of financial aid:

1. Gift-aid—Scholarships and grants are funds that do not have to be repaid.
2. Loans—Loans must be repaid, usually after graduation; the amount you have to pay back is the total you've borrowed plus any accrued interest. This is considered a source of self-help aid.
3. Student employment—Student employment is a job arranged for you by the financial aid office. This is another source of self-help aid.

The federal government has four major grant programs—the Federal Pell Grant, the Federal Supplemental Educational Opportunity Grant, Academic Competitiveness Grants (ACG), and SMART grants. ACG and SMART grants are limited to students who qualify for a Pell grant and are awarded to a select group of students. Overall, these grants are targeted to low-to-moderate income families with significant financial need. The federal government also sponsors a student employment program called the Federal Work-Study Program, which offers jobs both on and off campus, and several loan programs, including those for students and for parents of undergraduate students.

There are two types of student loan programs: subsidized and unsubsidized. The subsidized Federal Stafford Student Loan and the Federal Perkins Loan are need-based, government-subsidized loans. Students who borrow through these programs do not have to pay interest on the loan until after they graduate or leave school. The unsubsidized Federal Stafford Student Loan and the Federal PLUS Loan Program are not based on need, and borrowers are responsible for the interest while the student is in school. These loans are administered by different methods. Once you choose your college, the financial aid office will guide you through this process.

After you've submitted your financial aid application and you've been accepted for admission, each college will send you a letter describing your financial aid award. Most award letters show estimated college costs, how much you and your family are expected to contribute, and the amount and types of aid you have been awarded. Most students are awarded aid from a combination of sources and programs. Hence, your award is often called a financial aid "package."

SOURCES OF FINANCIAL AID

More than 12 million students and family apply for financial aid each year. Financial aid from all sources exceeds $152 billion per year. The largest single source of aid is the federal government, which will award more than $483 billion this year.

The next largest source of financial aid is found in the college and university community. Most of this aid is awarded to students who have a demonstrated need based on the Federal Methodology. Some institutions use a different formula, the Institutional Methodology (IM), to award their own funds in conjunction with other forms of aid. Institutional aid may be either need-based or non-need based. Aid that is not based on need is usually awarded for a student's academic performance (merit awards), specific talents or abilities, or to attract the type of students a college seeks to enroll.

Another source of financial aid is from state government. All states offer grant and/or scholarship aid, most of which is need-based. However, more and more states are offering substantial merit-based aid programs. Most state programs award aid only to students attending college in their home state.

Other sources of financial aid include:

- Private agencies
- Foundations
- Corporations
- Clubs
- Fraternal and service organizations
- Civic associations
- Unions
- Religious groups that award grants, scholarships, and low-interest loans
- Employers that provide tuition reimbursement benefits for employees and their children

More information about these different sources of aid is available from high school guidance offices, public libraries, college financial aid offices, directly from the sponsoring organizations, and on the Web at www.petersons.com and www.finaid.org.

HOW NEED-BASED FINANCIAL AID IS AWARDED

When you apply for aid, your family's financial situation is analyzed using a government-approved formula called the Federal Methodology. This formula looks at five items:

1. Demographic information of the family
2. Income of the parents
3. Assets of the parents
4. Income of the student
5. Assets of the student

This analysis determines the amount you and your family are expected to contribute toward your college expenses, called your Expected Family Contribution or EFC. If the EFC is equal to or more than the cost of attendance at a particular college, then you do not demonstrate financial need. However, even if you don't have financial need, you may still qualify for aid, as there are grants, scholarships, and loan programs that are not need-based.

If the cost of your education is greater than your EFC, then you do demonstrate financial need and qualify for assistance. The amount of your financial need that can be met varies from school to school. Some are able to meet your full need, while others can only cover a certain percentage of need. Here's the formula:

Cost of Attendance
− Expected Family Contribution
= Financial Need

The EFC remains constant, but your need will vary according to the costs of attendance at a particular college. In general, the higher the tuition and fees at a particular college, the higher the cost of attendance will be. Expenses for books and supplies, room and board, transportation, and other miscellaneous items are included in the overall cost of attendance. It is important to remember that you do not have to be "needy" to qualify for financial aid. Many middle and upper-middle income families qualify for need-based financial aid.

APPLYING FOR FINANCIAL AID

Every student must complete the Free Application for Federal Student Aid (FAFSA) to be considered for financial aid. The FAFSA is available from your high school guidance office, many public libraries, colleges in your area, or directly from the U.S. Department of Education.

Students are encouraged to apply for federal student aid on the Web. The electronic version of the FAFSA can be accessed at http://www.fafsa.ed.gov. Both the student and at least one parent must apply for a federal pin number at http://www.pin.ed.gov. The pin number serves as your electronic signature when applying for aid on the Web.

To award their own funds, some colleges require an additional application, the Financial Aid PROFILE® form. The PROFILE asks supplemental questions that some colleges and awarding agencies feel provide a more accurate assessment of the family's ability to pay for college. It is up to the college to decide whether it will use only the FAFSA or both the FAFSA and the PROFILE. PROFILE applications are available from the high school guidance office and on the Web. Both the paper application and the Web site list those colleges and programs that require the PROFILE application.

If Every College You're Applying to for Fall 2009 Requires the FAFSA

. . . then it's pretty simple: Complete the FAFSA after January 1, 2009, being certain to send it in before any college-imposed deadlines. (You are not permitted to send in the 2009–10 FAFSA before January 1, 2009.) Most college FAFSA application deadlines are in February or early March. It is easier if you have all your financial records for the previous year available, but if that is not possible, you are strongly encouraged to use estimated figures.

After you send in your FAFSA, either with the paper application or electronically, you'll receive a Student Aid Report (SAR) that includes all of the information you reported and shows your EFC. If you provided an e-mail address, the SAR is sent to you electronically; otherwise, you will receive a paper copy in the mail. Be sure to review the SAR, checking to see if the information you reported is accurately represented. If you used estimated numbers to complete the FAFSA, you may have to resubmit the SAR with any corrections to the data. The college(s) you have designated on the FAFSA will receive the information you reported and will use that data to make their decision. In many instances, the colleges to which you've applied will ask you to send copies of your and your parents' federal income tax returns for 2008, plus any other documents needed to verify the information you reported.

If a College Requires the PROFILE

Step 1: Register for the Financial Aid PROFILE in the fall of your senior year in high school.

You can apply for the PROFILE online at http://profileonline.collegeboard.com/index.jsp. Registration information with a list of the colleges that require the PROFILE is available in most high school guidance offices. There is a fee for using the Financial Aid PROFILE application ($25 for the first college and $16 for each additional college). You must pay for the service by credit card when you register. If you do not have a credit card, you will be billed. A limited number of fee waivers are automatically granted to first-time applicants based on the financial information provided on the PROFILE.

Step 2: Fill out your customized Financial Aid PROFILE.

Once you register, your application will be immediately available online and will have questions which all students must complete, questions which must be completed by the student's parents (unless the student is independent and the colleges or programs selected do not require parental information), and *may* have supplemental questions needed by one or more of your schools or programs. If required, those will be found in Section Q of the application.

In addition to the PROFILE Application you complete online, you may also be required to complete a Business/Farm Supplement via traditional paper format. Completion of this form is not a part of the online process. If this form is required, instructions on how to download and print the supplemental form are provided. If your biological or adoptive parents are separated or divorced and your colleges and programs require it, your noncustodial parent may be asked to complete the Noncustodial PROFILE.

Once you complete and submit your PROFILE Application, it will be processed and sent directly to your requested colleges and programs.

IF YOU DON'T QUALIFY FOR NEED-BASED AID

If you are not eligible for need-based aid, you can still find ways to lessen the burden on your parents.

Here are some suggestions:

- Search for merit scholarships. You can start at the initial stages of your application process. College merit awards are increasingly important as more and more colleges award these grants to students they especially want to attract. As a result, applying to a college at which your qualifications put you at the top of the entering class may give you a larger merit award. Another source of aid to look for is private scholarships that are given for special skills and talents. Additional information can be found at www.petersons.com and at www.finaid.org.
- Seek employment during the summer and the academic year. The student employment office at your college can help you locate a school-year job. Many colleges and local businesses have vacancies remaining after they have hired students who are receiving Federal Work-Study Program financial aid.
- Borrow through the unsubsidized Federal Stafford Student Loan programs. These are generally available to all students. The terms and conditions are similar to the subsidized loans. The biggest difference is that the borrower is responsible for the interest while still in college, although most lenders permit students to delay paying the interest right away and add the accrued interest to the total amount owed. You must file the FAFSA to be considered.
- After you've secured what you can through scholarships, working, and borrowing, your parents will be expected to meet their share of the college bill (the Expected Family Contribution). Many colleges offer monthly payment plans that spread the cost over the academic year. If the monthly payments are too high, parents can borrow through the Federal PLUS Loan Program, through one of the many private education loan programs available, or through home equity loans and lines of credit. Families seeking assistance in financing college expenses should inquire at the financial aid office about what programs are available at the college. Some families seek the advice of professional financial advisers and tax consultants.

HOW IS YOUR EXPECTED FAMILY CONTRIBUTION CALCULATED?

The chart on the next page makes the following assumptions:

- Two parent family where age of older parent is 45
- Lower income families (under $30,000) will file the 1040A or 1040EZ tax form
- Student income is less than $2300
- There are no student assets
- There is only one family member attending college

All figures are estimates and may vary when the complete FAFSA or PROFILE application is submitted.

Approximate Expected Family Contribution

ASSETS	FAMILY SIZE	INCOME BEFORE TAXES $20,000	30,000	40,000	50,000	60,000	70,000	80,000	90,000	100,000
$ 20,000										
	3	$ 0	160	1,800	3,500	5,800	9,100	12,600	14,100	17,400
	4	0	0	850	2,500	4,400	7,100	10,600	12,000	15,300
	5	0	0	0	1,600	3,300	5,500	8,600	10,100	13,400
	6	0	0	0	600	2,200	4,100	6,600	7,900	11,200
$ 30,000										
	3	$ 0	160	1,800	3,500	5,800	9,100	12,600	14,100	17,400
	4	0	0	850	2,500	4,400	7,100	10,600	12,000	15,300
	5	0	0	0	1,600	3,300	5,500	8,600	10,100	13,400
	6	0	0	0	600	2,200	4,100	6,600	7,900	11,200
$ 40,000										
	3	$ 0	160	1,800	3,500	5,800	9,100	12,600	14,100	17,400
	4	0	0	850	2,500	4,400	7,100	10,600	12,000	15,300
	5	0	0	0	1,600	3,300	5,500	8,600	10,100	13,400
	6	0	0	0	600	2,200	4,100	6,600	7,900	11,200
$ 50,000										
	3	$ 0	340	2,000	3,800	6,200	9,500	13,000	14,500	17,800
	4	0	0	1,100	2,700	4,700	7,400	11,000	12,400	15,700
	5	0	0	0	1,800	3,500	5,800	9,000	10,400	13,750
	6	0	0	0	800	2,400	4,300	6,900	8,300	11,600
$ 60,000										
	3	$ 0	600	2,300	4,100	6,600	10,000	13,600	15,000	18,300
	4	0	0	1,300	3,000	5,000	8,000	11,500	13,000	16,300
	5	0	0	400	2,050	3,800	6,200	9,600	11,000	14,300
	6	0	0	0	1,000	2,700	4,600	7,400	8,800	12,150
$ 80,000										
	3	$ 0	1,130	2,800	4,800	7,600	11,200	14,700	16,150	19,500
	4	0	170	1,800	3,600	5,900	9,100	9,600	14,100	17,400
	5	0	0	900	2,600	4,500	7,200	10,700	12,100	15,450
	6	0	0	0	1,600	3,200	5,400	8,500	10,000	13,300
$ 100,000										
	3	$ 0	1,660	3,400	5,600	8,800	12,300	15,900	17,300	20,600
	4	0	700	2,400	4,200	6,800	10,250	13,800	15,200	18,500
	5	0	0	1,400	3,100	5,300	8,300	11,800	13,300	16,600
	6	0	0	400	2,100	3,900	6,300	9,700	11,100	14,400
$ 120,000										
	3	$ 0	2,190	4,000	6,500	9,900	13,400	17,000	18,400	21,700
	4	0	1,220	3,000	4,900	7,800	11,400	14,900	16,350	19,650
	5	0	310	2,000	3,700	6,100	9,500	13,000	14,400	17,700
	6	0	0	1,000	2,600	4,600	7,300	10,800	12,200	15,550
$ 140,000										
	3	$ 0	2,700	4,700	7,500	11,000	13,400	18,100	19,500	22,850
	4	0	1,750	3,500	5,700	9,000	12,500	16,000	17,750	20,800
	5	0	850	2,500	4,400	7,100	10,500	14,100	15,500	18,850
	6	0	0	1,500	3,200	5,300	8,400	11,900	13,350	16,650

Middle-Income Families: Making the Financial Aid Process Work

Richard Woodland

A report from the U.S. Department of Education's National Center for Education Statistics took a close look at how middle-income families finance a college education. The report, *Middle Income Undergraduates: Where They Enroll and How They Pay for Their Education,* was one of the first detailed studies of these families. Even though 31 percent of middle-income families have the entire cost of attendance covered by financial aid, there is widespread angst among middle-income families that, while they earn too much to qualify for grant assistance, they are financially unable to pay the spiraling costs of higher education.

First, we have to agree on what constitutes a "middle-income" family. For the purposes of the federal study, middle income is defined as those families with incomes between $35,000 and $70,000. The good news is that 52 percent of these families received grants, while the balance received loans. Other sources of aid, including work-study, also helped close the gap.

So how do these families do it? Is there a magic key that will open the door to significant amounts of grants and scholarships?

The report found some interesting trends. One way families can make college more affordable is by choosing a less expensive college. In fact, in this income group, 29 percent choose to enroll in low- to moderate-cost schools. These include schools where the total cost is less than $8,500 per year. In this sector, we find the community colleges and lower-priced state colleges and universities. But almost half of these middle-income families choose schools in the upper-level tier, with costs ranging from $8,500 to $16,000. The remaining 23 percent enrolled at the highest-tier schools, with costs above $16,000. Clearly, while cost is a factor, middle-income families are not limiting their choices based on costs alone.

The report shows that families pay these higher costs with a combination of family assets, current income, and long-term borrowing. This is often referred to as the "past-present-future" model of financing. In fact, just by looking at the Expected Family Contributions, it is clear that there is a significant gap in what families need and what the financial aid process can provide. Families are closing this gap by making the financial sacrifices necessary to pay the price at higher-cost schools, especially if they think their child is academically strong. The report concludes that parents are more likely to pay for a higher-priced education if their child scores high on the SAT.

The best place for middle-income families to start is with the high school guidance office. This office has information on financial aid and valuable leads on local scholarships. Most guidance officers report that there are far fewer applicants for these locally based scholarships than one would expect. So read the information they send home and check on the application process. A few of those $500–$1000 scholarships can add up!

Plan to attend a financial aid awareness program. If your school does not offer one, contact your local college financial aid office and see when and where they will be speaking. You can get a lot of "inside" information on how the financial aid process works.

Next, be sure to file the correct applications for aid. Remember, each school can have a different set of requirements. For example, many higher-cost private colleges will require the PROFILE, filed in September or October of the senior year. Other schools may have their own institutional aid application. All schools will require the Free Application for Federal Student Aid (FAFSA). Watch the deadlines! It is imperative that you meet the school's published application deadline. Generally, schools are not flexible about this, so be sure to double-check the due date of all applications.

Finally, become a smart educational consumer. Peterson's has a wide range of resources available to help you understand the process. Be sure to also check your local library, bookstore, and of course, the Internet. Two great Web sites to check are www.petersons.com and www.finaid.org.

Once admitted to the various colleges and universities, you will receive an award notice outlining the aid you are eligible to receive. If you feel the offer is not sufficient, or if you have some unique financial circumstances, call the school's financial aid office to see if you can have your application reviewed again. The financial aid office is your best source for putting the pieces together and finding financial solutions.

The financial aid office will help you determine the "net price." This is the actual out-of-pocket cost that you will need to cover. Through a combination of student and parent loans, most families are able to meet these expenses with other forms of financial aid and family resources.

Many students help meet their educational expenses by working while in school. While this works for many students, research shows that too many hours spent away from your studies will negatively impact your academic success. Most experts feel that working 10 to 15 hours a week is optimal.

An overlooked source of aid is the tax credits given to middle-income families. Rather than extending eligibility for traditional sources of grant assistance to middle-income families, the federal tax system has built in a number of significant tax benefits, known as the Hope Scholarship and Lifetime Learning tax credit, for middle-income families. While it may be seven or eight months before you see the tax credit, most families in this income group can count on this benefit, usually between $1500 to $2000 per student. This is real money in your pocket. You do not need to itemize your deductions to qualify for this tax credit.

A tool to help families get a handle on the ever-rising costs of college is to assume that you can pay one third of the "net charges" from savings, another third from available (non-retirement) assets, and the rest from parent borrowing. If any one of these "thirds" is not available, shift that amount to one of the other resources. However, if it looks like you will be financing most or all of the costs from future income (borrowing), it may be wise to consider a lower-cost college.

Millions of middle-income families send their children to colleges and universities every year. Only 8 percent attend the lowest-priced schools. By using the concept of past-present-future financing, institutional assistance, federal and state aid, meaningful targeted tax relief, and student earnings, you can afford even the highest-cost schools.

Richard Woodland is the former Director of Financial Aid at Rutgers University–Camden and the current Director of Student Services and Financial Aid at the Curtis Institute of Music in Philadelphia, Pennsylvania.

Honors Programs and Colleges: Smart Choices for an Undergraduate Education

Dr. Joan Digby

In general, students and their parents are guided toward a narrow selection of colleges and universities based on reputation, conversations with friends, or promotional material. Few people think to approach the college search focused on honors opportunities. As a result, students with extraordinary talents and interests miss out on a rich variety of untapped financial resources and exciting college experiences.

The smarter approach is to seek out a distinctive education that caters to students' great diversity of intellectual and creative strengths. If you are a strong student filled with ideas, longing for creative expression and ready to take on career-shaping challenges, then an honors education is just for you. Honors programs and colleges offer some of the finest undergraduate degrees available at U.S. colleges and do it with students in mind. The essence of honors is personal attention, top faculty, enlightening seminars, illuminating study-travel experiences, research options, and career-building internships—all designed to enhance a classic education and prepare you for life achievements. And here is an eye-opening bonus: honors program and colleges may reward your past academic performance by giving you scholarships that will help you pay for your higher education!

Take your choice of institutions: community college, state or private, two- or four-year, college or large research university. There are honors opportunities in each. What they share is an unqualified commitment to academic excellence. Honors education teaches students to think and write clearly, be excited by ideas, and become independent, creative, self-confident learners. It prepares exceptional students for professional choices in every imaginable sphere of life: arts and sciences, engineering, business, health, education, medicine, theater, music, film, journalism, media, law, politics—invent your own professional goal and honors will guide you to it! Whichever honors program or college you choose, you can be sure to enjoy an extraordinarily fulfilling undergraduate education.

WHO ARE HONORS STUDENTS?

Who are you? Perhaps a high school junior filling out your first college application, a community college student seeking to transfer to a four-year college, or possibly a four-year college student doing better than you had expected. You might be an international student, a varsity athlete, captain of the debate team, or second violin in the orchestra. Whether you are the first person in your family to attend college or an adult with a grown family seeking a new career, honors might well be right for you. Honors programs admit students with every imaginable background and educational goal.

How does honors satisfy students and give them something special? Read what students in some honors programs and colleges say. Although they refer to particular honors colleges or programs, their experiences are typical of what students find exciting about honors education on hundreds of campuses around the country.

> "Being an honors program student has been a life-changing experience for me. I have gained tremendously in knowledge, experience, and self-esteem. I have learned so much more in the program than any textbook could teach about the value of encouraging support and positive thinking."
>
> —*Cheri Becker, Mount Wachusett Community College*

> "I've been in a healing ceremony in Ecuador and have performed music on stage. I've guided my peers and Navajo children, hiked the Grand Canyon, and so much more. Sometimes, experience speaks for itself; always, it creates paths, opens eyes, and helps us find our places. Thanks to my honors program, I've experienced these wonders and accomplishments. Now I know that there are no greater lessons than how to learn and love discovery."
>
> —*April Fisher, University of North Florida*

> "The Honors College has been my home away from home. In the midst of a diverse, fairly large university, it has provided me with the intimacy that I needed . . . My freshman-year living situation on the honors floor . . . allowed me to find like-minded students early in my college career."
>
> —*Brian Leech, Davidson Honors College, University of Montana*

"I was able to transition from an honors program at a two-year institution into an honors program at a four-year institution without any reservations or tribulations."

—Rachel Jones Williams, Harrisburg Area Community College

"Every single professor is in love with what they do and it shows in their research, their amazing teaching, and their interaction with students outside of the classroom. The undergraduate journey can be very difficult at times, but as an Honors College student, you're sure to have plenty of support every step of the way."

—Walteria Tucker, Wilkes Honors College, Florida Atlantic University

"The class size is perfect and I've been able to make some of my closest relationships with students and teachers through the program. The majority of honors faculty I have encountered have been overwhelmingly helpful . . . and my favorite courses have been honors classes."

—Ellen Daschler, Eastern Illinois University

"Our professor met us at a local restaurant the last evening of class and we shared a wonderful dinner. It had such a familiar feel to it because these are students I have known throughout my four years in the program."

—Betsy Porter, University of La Verne

"For the last two years, I have investigated new synthetic methods under the direction of a professor emeritus. Through the University Honors College, I am able to pursue this interest in chemistry and other academic endeavors . . . that have allowed me to develop my academic potential and contribute to the scientific body of knowledge."

—Justin Chalker, University of Pittsburgh

"The most rewarding part of being a member of the honors program is the joy of doing creative, meaningful projects with faculty I love."

—Meleia Egger, Hartwick College

"I would . . . like to add a word of praise for the way the curriculum is structured. It has deepened and enriched my thinking and helped me develop tools to negotiate the complex world we live in."

—Monideepa Talukdar, Southeastern Louisiana University

"We have a better time . . . our discussions get rather heated. In a lot of classes, only one or two students will speak up, but in the honors classes, it's a free-for-all."

—Jonathan Post, Reinhardt College

"My internship at a major international bank gave me an in-depth look into the world of investment and accounting. Funded by the Honors College, I was able to study business and culture in Shanghai, China, for a month. These valuable experiences are helping me to develop professionally, academically, and personally."

—Jenny Lam, Honors College, The College of Staten Island, CUNY

"The honors thesis was the key factor during the selection process at my future employer. . . . It helped me to get the job and have an advantage over others. It is a lot of work but, in the end, it is worth it."

—Olgierd Hinz, Lee Honors College, Western Michigan University

These portraits don't tell the whole story, but they should give you a sense of what it means to be part of an honors program or college. One of the great strengths of honors programs and colleges is that they are nurturing environments that encourage students to be well-rounded and help students make life choices.

WHAT IS AN HONORS PROGRAM?

An honors program is a sequence of courses designed specifically to encourage independent and creative learning. For more than half a century, honors education—given definition by the National Collegiate Honors Council—has been an institution on U.S. campuses. Although honors programs have many different designs, there are typical components. At two-year colleges, the programs often concentrate on special versions of general education courses and may have individual capstone projects that come out of students' special interests. At four-year colleges and universities, honors programs are generally designed for students of almost every major in every college on campus. In growing numbers, they are given additional prominence as honors colleges. Whether a program or a college, honors often includes a general education or "core" component followed by advanced courses (often called colloquia or seminars). Some programs have honors contracts that shape existing courses into honors components to suit the needs of individual students. Many have interdisciplinary or collaborative seminars that bring students of different majors together to discuss a complex topic with faculty members from different disciplines. A good number have final thesis, capstone, or creative projects, which may or may not be in the departmental major. Almost always, honors curriculum is incorporated within whatever number of credits is required of every student for graduation. Honors very rarely requires students to take additional credits. Students who complete an honors program or honors college curriculum frequently receive transcript and diploma notations as well as certificates, medallions, or other citations at graduation ceremonies.

In every case, catering to the student as an individual plays a central role in honors course design. Most honors classes are small (fewer than 20 students); most are discussion-oriented, giving students a chance to present their own interpretations of ideas and even teach a part of the course. Many classes are interdisciplinary, which means they are taught by faculty members from two or more departments, providing different perspectives on a subject. All honors classes help students develop and articulate their own perspectives by cultivating both verbal and written style. They help students mature intellectually, preparing them to engage in their own explorations and research. Some programs even extend the options for self-growth to study abroad and internships in science, government, the arts, or business related to the major. Other programs encourage or require community service as part of the honors experience. In every case, honors is an experiential education that deepens classroom learning and extends far beyond.

Despite their individual differences, all honors programs and honors colleges rely on faculty members who enjoy working with bright, independent students. The ideal honors faculty members are open-minded, encouraging master teachers. They want to see their students achieve at their highest capacity and are glad to spend time with students in discussions and laboratories, on field trips and at conferences, or online in e-mail. They often influence career decisions, are inspiring role models, and remain friends long after they have served as thesis advisers.

WHERE ARE HONORS PROGRAMS AND HONORS COLLEGES LOCATED?

Because honors programs and honors colleges include students from many different departments or colleges, they usually have their own offices and space on campus. Some have their own buildings. Most programs have honors centers or lounges, where students gather together for informal conversations, luncheons, discussions, lectures, and special projects.

Many honors students have cultivated strong personal interests that have nothing to do with classes. They may be multilingual; they may be fine artists or poets, musicians or racing car enthusiasts, mothers or fathers. Some volunteer in hospitals or do landscape gardening to pay for college. Many work in retail stores and catering. Some are avid sports enthusiasts, while others collect antiques. When they get together in honors lounges, there is always an interesting mixture of ideas!

In the honors center, you will also find the honors director or dean. The honors director often serves as a personal adviser to all of the students in the program. Many programs also have peer counselors and mentors who are upperclass honors students and know the ropes from a student's perspective and experience. Some have specially assigned honors advisers who guide honors students through their degrees, assist in registration, and answer every imaginable question. The honors office area usually is a good place to meet people, ask questions, and solve problems.

In general, honors provides an environment in which students feel free to talk about their passionate interests and ideas knowing that they will find good listeners and, sometimes, even arguers. There is no end to conversations among honors students. Like many students in honors, you may feel a great relief in finding a sympathetic group that respects your intelligence and creativity. In honors, you can be eccentric; you can be yourself! Some lifelong friendships, even marriages, are the result of social relationships developed in honors programs.

ARE YOU READY FOR HONORS?

Admission to honors programs and honors colleges is generally based on a combination of several factors: high school or previous college grades, experience taking AP or IB courses, SAT or ACT scores, personal essay, and extra-curricular achievements. To stay in honors, students need to maintain a certain grade point average (GPA) and show progress toward the completion of the specific honors program or college requirements. Since you have probably exceeded admissions standards all along, maintaining your GPA will not be as big a problem as it sounds. Your professors and your honors director are there to help you succeed in the program. Most honors programs have very low attrition rates because students enjoy classes and do well.

Of course, you must be careful about how you budget your time for studying. Honors encourages well-rounded, diversified students, so you should play a sport, work at the radio station, join clubs of interest, or pledge a sorority or fraternity. You might find a job in the student center or library that will help you pay for your car expenses and that also is reasonable. But remember, each activity takes time, and you must strike the balance that leaves you enough time to do your homework, write papers, prepare for seminar discussions, do your research, and do well on exams. Choose the jobs and activities that attract you, but never let them overshadow your primary purpose—which is to be a student.

Sometimes even the very best students who apply for admission into an honors program or college are frightened by the thought of speaking in front of a group, giving seminar papers, or writing a thesis. But if you understand how the programs work, you will see that there is nothing to fear. The basis of honors is confidence in the student and building the student's self-confidence. Admittance to an honors program means you have already demonstrated your academic achievement in high school or college classes. Once in the honors environment, you learn how to formulate and structure ideas so that you can apply critical judgment to sets of facts and opinions. In small seminar classes, you practice discussion and arguments, so by the time you come to the senior thesis or project, the method is second nature. For most honors students, the senior thesis, performance, or portfolio presentation is the project that gives them the greatest fulfillment and pride. In many honors programs and colleges, students present their work either to other students or to faculty members in their major departments. Students often present their work at regional and national honors conferences. Some students even publish their work jointly with their faculty mentors. These are great achievements, and they come naturally with the training. There is nothing to fear. Honors will prepare you for life.

Dr. Joan Digby is Director of the Honors Program and Merit Fellowship at Long Island University, C.W. Post Campus. She was also President of the National Collegiate Honors Council from 1999 to 2000.

ciprocates by nurturing both oral and written style. They help students to grow intellectually, preparing them to engage in their own explorations and research. Some programs even extend the options for self-growth to study abroad and internships in science, government, the arts, or business related to the major. Other programs encourage or require community service as part of the honors experience. In every case, honors is an expansive undergraduate option that deepens classroom learning and extends far beyond.

Despite their institutional differences, all honors programs and honors colleges rely on faculty members who enjoy working with bright, independent students. The best honors faculty members are open-minded, encouraging mentors. They want to see their students achieve at the highest levels and are glad to spend time with students in discussions and conferences, field trips and at conferences, or online in e-mail. They often influence students' lifelong goals, becoming role models and lifelong friends long after they have served as thesis advisers.

WHERE ARE HONORS PROGRAMS AND HONORS COLLEGES LOCATED?

Because honors programs and honors colleges include students from many different departments or colleges, they usually have their own offices and space on campus. Some have their own buildings. Most programs have an honors center or lounge, a place study or gather together for informal conversations, luncheons, discussions, lectures, and special projects.

Many honors students have cultivated strong personal interests that have nothing to do with classes. They may be athletes; they may be fine musicians, poets, or actors, or belong to many clubs. Others may be busy earning money or volunteering. Some students may be working part time to help pay for college. Many love math, art, and computers. Some are avid sports enthusiasts, while others collect antiques. When they get together in honors lounges, there is always an interesting mixture of ideas.

In the honors center, you will also find the honors administration. The honors director often serves as a personal adviser to all of the students in the program. Many programs also have peer counselors or mentors who are upperclass honors students and know the ropes from a student's perspective and experience. Some have specially assigned honors advisers who guide honors students through their degree requirements and answer every imaginable question. The honors office in a college is a good place to meet people, ask questions, and solve problems.

In general, honors provides an environment in which students feel free to talk about their passionate interests and ideas, knowing that they will find good listeners and, sometimes, even great friends. There is no end to conversations in and out of class. If you are a student in honors, you may feel a part of a unique environment, a group. That respects your intelligence and creativity. In honors, you can be yourself and you can be yourself in some friendships. Often, friendships are the result of social relationships developed in honors programs.

ARE YOU READY FOR HONORS?

Admission to honors programs and honors colleges is generally based on a combination of several factors: high school or community college grades, high school rank, SAT or ACT scores, personal essays, and extracurricular achievements. To stay in honors, students need to maintain a certain grade point average (GPA) and show progress toward the completion of the specific honors program or college requirements. Since you have probably exceeded admissions standards all along, maintaining your GPA will not be as big a problem as it sounds. Your professors and your honors director are there to help you succeed. In fact, most honors programs have very low attrition rates because students enjoy classes and do well.

Of course, you must be a good manager of how you budget your time for studying. Honors encourages well-rounded, diversified students, so you should play a sport, work at the radio station, join clubs of interest, or pledge a sorority or fraternity. You might find a job in the student center or library that will help you pay for your expenses and that is also reasonable. Just remember, each activity takes time, and you must strike the balance that leaves you enough time to do your homework, write papers, prepare for seminar discussions, do your research, and do well on exams. Choose the jobs and activities that attract you, but never let them overshadow your primary purpose—which is to be a student.

Sometimes even the very best students who apply for admission into an honors program or college are frightened by the thought of speaking in front of a group, giving seminar papers, or writing a thesis. But if you understand how the programs work, you will see that there is nothing to fear. The basis of honors is confidence in the student and building the student's self-confidence. Admittance to an honors program means you have already demonstrated your academic achievement in high school or college classes. Once in the honors environment, you learn how to formulate and structure ideas so that you can apply critical thinking to assorted facts and opinions. In small seminar classes, you practice discussion and arguments, so by the time you come to the senior thesis or project, the method is second nature. For most honors students, the senior thesis, performance, or portfolio presentation is the project that gives them the greatest fulfillment and pride. In many honors programs and colleges, students present their work either to each other or to faculty members in their major departments. Students often present their work at regional and national honors conferences. Some students even publish their work jointly with their faculty mentors. These are great achievements, and they come naturally with the training that is part of honors. Honors will prepare you for life.

Dr. Joan Digby is Director of the Honors Program and a Professor of English at Long Island University, C.W. Post Campus. She was also President of the National Collegiate Honors Council from 1999 to 2000.

Public and Private Colleges and Universities—How to Choose

Debra Humphreys

As you survey the thousands of four-year colleges in the country and weigh the options before you, it is important to be aware of how colleges differ and what kind of educational experience each college offers you. In every state in the country, you will find both public and private colleges and universities. What are the differences between public and private colleges, and how should you approach the decision to attend one or the other? What are some common misconceptions regarding both public and private colleges that you should know about before you eliminate an entire category of institution from your list of prospective schools?

WHAT ARE THE BASIC CHARACTERISTICS OF PUBLIC AND PRIVATE INSTITUTIONS?

Over the course of the nation's history, what began as a small group of mostly church-affiliated colleges has grown in both size and complexity. Over the years, education in the United States became increasingly democratized, and more and more state-sponsored institutions and state systems of higher education emerged. These included small colleges, sometimes called "normal schools," designed to train school teachers for the expanding public school system; land-grant colleges and universities brought into existence with federal support in the mid-nineteenth century in order to prepare workers to expand the nation's agricultural and technological capacity; and large state systems that evolved in the twentieth century and now include two-year colleges, basic four-year institutions, and large research universities, all supported at least in part by state revenues.

While there are some clear distinctions to be made, even some of the core characteristics of public and private colleges vary from state to state. In general, a public institution receives at least part of its operating budget from state tax revenues, operates with a mandate and mission from the state where it is located, and is accountable to the elected officials of that state. Most private colleges and universities are independent, not-for-profit institutions. They operate with revenues from tuition, income from endowments, private gifts and bequests, and federal, private, or corporate foundation grants. These institutions are primarily accountable to a board of trustees, usually made up of local or national business and community leaders and esteemed alumni.

There are also a small but growing number of for-profit colleges whose operating revenues include tuition dollars but also might include investor financing. Some of these colleges are owned and operated by publicly traded corporations. Most of the following generalizations about private institutions however refer to the more familiar not-for-profit independent college previously described.

While the distinction between public and private institutions might seem clear at first, these two kinds of colleges and universities actually share many characteristics. All accredited colleges and universities in the country—whether public or private, for profit or not—are entitled to receive public funds from the federal government in the form of direct grants and loans for eligible students, support for student work-study programs, and competitive grants to support research or campus programs. In exchange for this federal support, all schools undergo a peer-reviewed accreditation process by a regional accreditor authorized by the federal government's Department of Education.

Whether a college is public or private, you should know if it is accredited and therefore an institution whose students are eligible for all available federal financial aid. Accreditation status also provides you with assurance that the school operates in a fiscally responsible manner and that its academic programs have been deemed sound by an outside group of educators from its peer institutions.

HOW ARE PUBLIC AND PRIVATE COLLEGES AND UNIVERSITIES RUN?

In many ways, your experience as a student will not differ significantly based on what type of governance system a college or university uses. However, some knowledge of this might be useful in making choices among the various options. Private colleges and universities tend to have more independence and autonomy in how they are run, with boards of trustees that oversee financial and other broad matters of governance. Academic and student services leaders determine the nature of the academic program and life on campus at these schools. Public colleges and universities often have more complex governing structures with boards of regents or other types of oversight committees made up of politically appointed or elected officials exercising more or less oversight and intrusion into their day-to-day operations. New York, for instance, has a board of regents that oversees the system's campuses and is more actively involved in reviewing and revising curricular requirements that apply to institutions throughout the system. Other states have multiple public colleges, each with its own board overseeing each campus' operations with more or less intrusion into day-to-day operations.

Whether an institution is public or private, you will want to ask lots of questions about campus climate and academic programs in order to help you determine if a school is right for you. Being aware of some facts about public and private institutions will help you frame these questions to get truly useful answers.

ARE ALL PUBLIC COLLEGES AND UNIVERSITIES BIG AND IMPERSONAL?

Like private institutions, public colleges come in all shapes and sizes. Some are large institutions offering multiple degrees and majors to both undergraduate and graduate students alike. These institutions offer students many curricular options as well as access to leading scholars and an environment where cutting-edge academic research is conducted. While an institution of this size and scope might seem intimidating at first, remember that there are large institutions that do take very seriously their undergraduate programs. While you may receive less customized attention at a larger institution, many large public and private research universities offer options such as smaller honors programs, academic learning communities with smaller cohorts of students, or theme residence halls that can minimize the potential that you will get lost in the crowd.

If you are considering a large research institution—whether it is public or private—you should ask questions about the undergraduate program. What is the student-faculty ratio for undergraduates? What is the average class size, especially for introductory first-year courses? How many courses are taught by graduate students, and what sort of teacher training do those students receive? Are there opportunities for undergraduate students to participate in research projects with university faculty members?

In addition to the large, public research universities, there are many other smaller, state-funded regional institutions that still offer a wide range of both liberal arts and sciences fields as well as professional fields of study. Many states also offer small, public liberal arts colleges that share many of the defining characteristics of traditional, private liberal arts colleges. In 1987, some of these institutions formed the Council of Public Liberal Arts Colleges (COPLAC). Now numbering twenty-five institutions, COPLAC schools pride themselves on providing students of high ability and from all backgrounds access to a quality liberal education. These colleges and universities have been nationally recognized as outstanding in many ways. They offer small classes, innovations in teaching, personal interactions with faculty members, opportunities for faculty-supervised research, and supportive atmospheres. Most of them are located on campuses in rural or small-town settings. In addition to offering rigorous and well-integrated undergraduate programs, these institutions often charge far less tuition than many private colleges do. More information can be found at http://www.coplac.org.

These public liberal arts colleges, along with more traditional private liberal arts institutions, do offer unique learning environments that research suggests often lead to higher levels of student achievement. Liberal arts colleges tend to offer a high degree of student-faculty interaction, high levels of student engagement with both in-class and out-of-class experiences, and lots of opportunities for collaborative and innovative learning practices. Businesses are also increasingly asking for exactly the set of skills and capacities that a liberal education provides, whether offered in a traditional liberal arts college setting or within a larger university that grants degrees in both liberal arts and other fields. Many public liberal arts and more comprehensive colleges and universities also now offer students a rigorous liberal education while integrating liberal learning into professional degree programs, for instance in health sciences, engineering, or education.

ARE PUBLIC COLLEGES CHEAPER THAN PRIVATE COLLEGES?

The cost of college is not easy to calculate and is not limited simply to the advertised price of tuition. It is absolutely not the case that attending a public college will always cost a student less money than attending a private institution. It is true that the basic tuition for in-state or out-of-state students attending public colleges is on average less expensive than the advertised tuition rate at private institutions. It is very important, however, to note that many private colleges and universities offer significant amounts of financial aid—often beyond the basic federal loans and grants available to all students. Many, but not all, private colleges have large endowments that allow them to effectively discount the standard, published tuition rates for a great number of their students. The National Association of College and University Business Officers sampled a small group of private colleges and discovered that only 10 percent of entering students were paying the full, advertised tuition. Ninety percent of their students received price discounts in the form of scholarships or financial aid. In other words, don't write off a college simply because its tuition looks extremely high relative to other institutions.

Both private and public institutions, however, have been fiscally stressed in recent years because of declining values of stock portfolios in endowments or because of declining state revenues resulting from the deteriorating economy. It is safe to say that for many students in the coming years, it will become increasingly difficult to get large amounts of financial aid. Many institutions, however, remain committed to widening access to more students from less economically privileged backgrounds. In addition, students demonstrating high levels of academic achievement are being rewarded at both private and public institutions—both in terms of admission and financial aid.

It is important to look carefully at the tuition and the financial aid requirements and availability at each school you are considering, private or public. In-state and out-of-state tuitions and the difference between them varies substantially from state to state. Out-of-state tuition also varies from state to state but still tends to be lower than average private tuition levels.

Policies vary as well for determining state residency status. In many states, the policy for dependent students requires that their parents must have lived in the state for at least twelve months prior to attendance in order to qualify for in-state tuition. For independent students, the requirement of twelve months residence prior to enrollment applies to the student. Independent status must be verified and generally entails proof that a student receives no support from parents or other relatives living in or out of the state in question. As budgets have increasingly tightened, states have over the past several years made it increasingly difficult to establish in-state residence after matriculating at a school. Exceptions are sometimes made, however, for students from migrant, refugee, or military families.

IS IT EASIER TO GAIN ADMISSION TO A PUBLIC INSTITUTION ESPECIALLY AS A STATE RESIDENT?

Few public colleges and universities automatically admit students who graduate from a public high school in their state. Many, however, give preference in admissions and financial assistance to in-state residents. Moreover, some states have implemented policies that guarantee admission to at least one of the state's public institutions for all students graduating in a top percentage of their high school classes.

There are, indeed, more highly selective private than public institutions. Many public colleges and universities, however, do admit very few applicants. These highly selective institutions might draw their students from a national pool of applicants and can be among the most selective in the country. However, the national universities and liberal arts colleges with the lowest acceptance rates in the country are mostly all private institutions.

While some public institutions offer virtually open admissions to state residents, it is important for all prospective students to realize that even an open-admission institution will require incoming students to meet certain academic standards before being admitted to credit-bearing courses. In most cases, public and private institutions give incoming students a series of placement exams that determines at what level the student can begin his or her course work. Depending on the results of these exams, a student may be required to take and pass one or more remedial courses before being admitted to courses that will actually count towards a degree.

Since each state's requirements are different and shift often, you should not assume that, regardless of your academic background, admission is automatic to your local state college. In the current climate—with costs rising and competition across systems tightening—admission rates are dropping at many public institutions.

IS THE CLIMATE ON A PUBLIC COLLEGE CAMPUS SIGNIFICANTLY DIFFERENT THAN THAT ON A PRIVATE COLLEGE CAMPUS?

The social and academic climate at colleges and universities varies substantially and public institutions do not necessarily offer a distinctively different climate than private institutions do. You can find, at some public institutions, the small, residential environment traditionally associated with private liberal arts colleges. You will also find the presence of fraternities and sororities at both public and private institutions. You should look carefully at whether a school in which you are interested has fraternities and sororities and how much influence the Greek system has on college life. At some institutions, fraternities and sororities dominate the entire social life of the campus.

One campus environment that can only be found at a private institution is a highly religious environment. Many early colleges and universities were founded by churches or religious orders. Some of these institutions no longer retain a strong affiliation with one church or denomination. Others do retain a strong affiliation, and church traditions can heavily influence the climate of these institutions. Usually, these campuses will admit a student from any religious background, but they may require students to attend chapel services and/or take religion or theology courses to graduate. In addition, some college missions and curricula are influenced by their religious affiliations. For instance, many Catholic institutions have a strong commitment to community service and social justice. Students may find, at these institutions, curricula related to social justice issues and requirements that they complete a community-service learning activity or course to graduate. Institutions with a strong mission are also often able to develop more coherent, cohesive, and innovative curricula for their students.

Finally, other important climate factors to consider include whether a college or university is in an urban or rural setting; what the diversity of the student body is in terms of geographic, religious, or racial/ethnic background; if most students live on campus or commute from home; and finally if the college dominates the life of the community in which it is located. Each of these options has advantages and disadvantages you will want to weigh in making your decisions.

ARE PRIVATE COLLEGES MORE ACADEMICALLY RIGOROUS THAN PUBLIC COLLEGES?

Private colleges and universities are not necessarily more academically rigorous than public institutions. You will find rigorous, intellectually challenging, and innovative academic programs at both private and public institutions. There is also a common misconception that schools that are more highly

QUESTIONS TO ASK AS YOU EVALUATE PROSPECTIVE COLLEGES AND UNIVERSITIES

- Does the college offer a distinctive first-year experience?
- Does the college offer a small-size freshman seminar for all students?
- Are all students required to complete a senior project or assignment that allows them to integrate all that they have learned and demonstrate acquired skills and knowledge?
- Are students encouraged or required to complete internships and/or service learning courses?
- Are students encouraged to study abroad? Is support for study abroad provided to all students and are study abroad experiences integrated into a student's overall curricula?
- Does the college offer learning communities, especially in the student's early years?
- Are students required to complete rigorous writing courses not only in the freshman year but also across the curriculum in whatever major he or she chooses to pursue?
- Are there opportunities for students to pursue independent research or creative projects under the supervision of a senior faculty member?

selective have the most effective or engaging academic programs. Research suggests that there is no connection between the selectivity of an institution and the presence of effective or innovative teaching and learning practices. There is, however, preliminary research that suggests that the academic quality of one's peers does seem to have an impact on the grade point averages of fellow students.

Nothing could be more important in your decision-making process than evaluating the nature of academic programs at prospective colleges or universities. Across both public and private institutions, there have been exciting and important changes in how colleges and universities are organizing undergraduate curricula. Many promising programs have been proven to result in higher levels of student retention, graduation, satisfaction, and academic achievement.

Many colleges and universities also now participate in the National Survey of Student Engagement. This survey asks students in both their first and last years about a series of effective educational practices and the degree to which they are engaged in the academic life of their school. Issues that are examined in the survey include the level of academic challenge, active and collaborative learning opportunities, the nature of student-faculty interactions, the number of enriching educational experiences available, and the supportive nature of the campus environment. Ask if the school you are considering participates in this survey and if you can see the results from recent classes of students.

THE PRIVATE/PUBLIC CHOICE

While there are distinct differences between public and private colleges and universities you should not limit your choice—whatever your background—to only one type of institution. There are wonderful opportunities at many different kinds of schools. The availability of many kinds of financial aid may bring private institutions with high-tuition levels within reach for you, whatever your financial background. Whether a school is highly selective or has open admissions, you should also be able to find a college or university that will challenge you academically and provide you with a supportive environment in which to live, learn, and pursue a college degree of lasting value.

Debra Humphreys is Vice President for Communications and Public Affairs for the Association of American Colleges and Universities.

Distance Education—It's Closer Than You Think

You may not realize it, but as an incoming college student, you are joining a revolution that is radically changing education. It's called distance learning. From kindergarten up to postgraduate degrees, distance learning is fast becoming an essential teaching tool. Most of the colleges and universities you are considering for a bachelor's degree offer distance learning in one form or another. Most likely you will be a distance learner at some point, whether during college or graduate school or throughout your career.

In case you're not familiar with distance learning—or asynchronous learning, online learning, or distance education—it means you don't sit in a classroom facing a teacher. You can be hundreds of miles or minutes from the teacher and other students. Most often you connect through the Internet to the teacher, fellow students, and study materials. However, increasingly sophisticated technologies, such as virtual laboratories, simulations, and interactive multimedia, are also used. You may run across the term "blended learning." Many institutions incorporate online learning into their face-to-face classes. In fact, a number of colleges require that a part of all classes is online.

FROM SNAIL-MAIL COURSES TO LEADING-EDGE TECHNOLOGY

Talk about change. Distance education began in the late 1800s, when schools mailed correspondence courses to farmers who wanted to learn how to grow better crops. Since technology came along, distance learning has become accessible and widespread. At first educators were skeptical, but as name-plate universities began to incorporate it into their teaching methodology, distance education became accepted.

When brick-and-mortar colleges and universities first considered distance education, the goal was to make it as good as face-to-face education. Now, says Ray Schroeder, Professor Emeritus of Communication and Director of the Office of Technology-Enhanced Learning (OTEL), at the University of Illinois at Springfield, "Field research shows that online learning technologies are better than face-to-face learning in a number of ways." Having taught online, he has seen firsthand how students participate more in discussions and learn from one another. Peg Miller, Ph.D., former Coordinator of Academic Support for Distributed Learning, University of Central Florida, cites a survey she conducted every other semester that compares face-to-face and distance learners at her institution. She has found that students from face-to-face and online classes were almost identical in the grades they earned and in their satisfaction with the classes.

ON THE UPSWING

Many reasons have caused the phenomenal growth of distance education. It's convenient and user-friendly, plus the scope of classes is stunning. Not that you'll likely begin your college years with classes in forensics or grading diamonds, but they are offered and indicate the enormous variety of courses. Along with many others in education, Michael P. Lambert, CEO of the Distance Education Training Council, feels that online learning has transformed how people learn. "You no longer sit in a box with 35 other people where you might never raise your hand," he says. Adds Gerald Heeger, President of the University of Maryland University College (UMUC), "Online learning gets rid of the limitations of geography and time. And as bandwidth increases, we will do more and more."

PROCEED WITH CAUTION

Now that you're convinced that distance education sounds great, sign me up, it's only fair to warn you that perhaps you shouldn't start your bachelor's degree totally online. Distance learning changes how you study, respond to your teachers, participate in class discussions, and take exams. If you're not prepared for the differences, you can easily fall behind and even fail. Though the age of online students continues to drop, most are older, have had some life experience since graduating from high school, and have the self-discipline, self-motivation, and maturity that distance education demands. The average age of distance students is in the mid-30s, and 95 percent of them work full-time. They know what they want from college and are willing to meet the rigors of online learning, which are considerable.

Of course, some students straight from high school do successfully start college as distance learners because they've already had some online learning experience. Some take online classes in high school or advanced-placement and college courses. At Stevens Institute of Technology's Web Campus, incoming freshmen brush up on math and precalculus online before their first fall semester. At first, Nathan Kahl, former instructor for the Euclid Program at Stevens Institute of Technology Web Campus, was skeptical that high school graduates could succeed in the online courses he taught, but he saw that "everyone quickly got into the swing of things." He admits that he underestimated the students' ability to learn online. Heeger agrees: "There's no reason why a bright junior in high school who is ready to take college freshmen courses can't do it."

The University of Phoenix Online (parent company: Apollo Group, Inc.) has developed a bachelor's degree program specifically for incoming freshmen of any age—including those just out of high school. In today's job market, a college education is a necessity, yet many students have life situations that prevent them from attending. Notes Apollo Group, Inc., President Brian Muller about the accommodations their program makes for students who are new to higher education, "It is our experience that if you create an online classroom, it must have all the features that incoming students need, which are small, highly interactive, and collaborative classes." Their freshman classes average 15 and require that the instructor has consistent contact with the students. New freshmen also get a tremendous amount of support in writing, math, and online research skills and have the help of an academic counselor who closely tracks them for ten weeks into their first semester. "We think there are more students coming out of high school who must have jobs, so we took the model for working adults and created an environment for traditional students that combines education and work," says Muller.

However, not all educators have the same experience with incoming freshmen. Jimmy Reeves, Ph.D., Professor and Chair, Department of Chemistry and Biochemistry at the University of North Carolina at Wilmington, teaches both online and face-to-face classes and knows how students can react. Freshmen who fail his face-to-face class sometimes ask to take his class online. He says no because the discipline required is rare among 19-year-old students. "Junior and senior college students do well, but it has more to do with their level of maturity and the reasons why they're in college," he says, referring to the fact that many incoming college students want to experiment or come because their parents demand it. "Without any real desire to learn or sense of why they're in college, it's easy to get distracted in online classes," he notes. You can't hide in the back of a lecture hall half asleep on Monday morning and hope for the best on multiple-choice questions. In online classes, your active participation is noticed and taken into account for final grades.

Attending college isn't just about acquiring knowledge in a particular field in order to get a job. It's also about learning social skills and meeting people with different ideas from diverse backgrounds. "If you want to live in a dorm and have bull sessions on the meaning of life with the kids down the hall, then being a fully online freshman student isn't for you," advises Cynthia Davis, Associate Dean of Academic Affairs in the School of Undergraduate Studies at the University of Maryland University College. She adds that sometimes students mistakenly think getting a bachelor's degree online will take less time than physically attending classes or won't require as much work. But as she points out, online classes demand the same amount of effort, if not more than face-to-face classes.

WHAT'S IT GOING TO BE LIKE?

Blended learning or mixed-mode classes, combining face-to-face and online instruction, are becoming a permanent fixture in higher education. Students might sit in a classroom on Monday but take the remaining two classes for that week online. Professors routinely post the syllabus, class calendar, or PowerPoint lectures. Reeves says that it's rare to see college classes without some Web-based materials. Davis comments that UMUC routinely Web-enhances all their face-to-face classes with companion Web classrooms. Students can have optional online discussions or print copies of class materials.

"We find more students use online technology to enhance their studies and get better grades," comments Schroeder. Educators see a trend of students enrolling in one university and taking courses from other institutions. For instance, say you're in an art class but want to study German cathedral architecture, which your university doesn't have but another one offers online. It's only a matter of time before this will be a standard option for college students.

LOTS TO LOOK FOR, LOTS TO AVOID, LOTS TO ASK

Though much of distance education depends on the Internet, you can't just type in "distance education" and see what comes up in a search for a college. You must seriously research and do background checks to make sure a diploma mill doesn't hand you a bachelor's degree that isn't credible. There are plenty of places to get information. Petersons.com offers a database of colleges and universities that have online courses, as well as totally online distance education providers. "You have to be a good consumer," recommends Heeger. "It's no different from getting a loan. You don't borrow money from people you never heard of. You shouldn't get degrees from people you never heard of." Schroeder suggests checking the course completion of online programs, their enrollment, and growth of programs. "Just as one checks with friends and colleagues about the quality of consumer services, such as computers and cars, one should check with students who are enrolled in online programs," he advises.

Is the Institution Accredited by a Valid Accrediting Body?

There are several kinds of accrediting organizations:

- The six regional accrediting agencies recognized by the U.S. Department of Education
- The Council for Higher Education Accreditation (www.chea.org)
- Other institutional accrediting agencies, such as the Accrediting Council for Independent Colleges and Schools and the Distance Education and Training Council
- Specialized accrediting agencies that cover schools offering everything from acupuncture to veterinary medicine
- Other discipline-based accrediting organizations, such as those for law and business schools

TEST-DRIVE AN ONLINE CLASS

Just like face-to-face instruction, online classes are different, depending on the course material and how each teacher chooses to structure the course, but here's a typical scenario of what it's like to be a distance learner.

Getting started. First you'll want to get to the general information page for the class, which you'll visit often. The professor's contact information, the class calendar, the syllabus, and announcements on quizzes and tests or links to other pages on which you'll find posted discussion questions may be found here. Some teachers will ask you to tell something about yourself to the other students in the class. Be sure to read the syllabus, which will outline the course and tell you when assignments are due and how grades are determined.

Responding to discussion questions. Those students who never raised their hands will get a shock in online courses. Responding with thoughtful answers to online discussion groups is mandatory. Usually the teacher will assign reading material and then post a discussion question. The material might be from your textbook or Web sites. You must respond to the question and possibly to the postings of other students in the class. Teachers will gauge your participation in the class and how well you learn the material.

Interacting with fellow students and your teacher. Ray Schroeder, Professor Emeritus of Communication and Director of the Office of Technology-Enhanced Learning (OTEL) at the University of Illinois at Springfield, gives talks about distance education. Often he'll ask his audience to recall their favorite class from elementary school up to college and what made it so memorable. Was it the textbook? The actual classroom? The view out the window? When he asks if it was the interaction among students and with the teacher, the audience realizes that's what made the class good. "Both in person and online, learning takes place in the interaction," says Schroeder. "Otherwise, we would do just as well to read a book or watch a video to learn." In online classes, interaction between you and the professor and other students is an enormous part of your success.

Nathan Kahl, former instructor for the Euclid Program at Stevens Institute of Technology Web Campus, explains, "Distance students expect that their teachers will be online at least as much as they are." The level of interaction expected from you will vary by school and course, but you should know that in online courses, you must be an active participant. On the flip side, teachers carefully monitor discussions to make sure the more talkative students don't dominate. Keith W. Miller, Professor of Computer Science at the University of Illinois at Springfield, interacts with his students in a variety of ways. "I make announcements to the whole class on the homepage. I send e-mails to the whole class. I enter into the electronic discussions on the bulletin board forums, and post daily reminders and assignments to the course calendar. The students interact with me using e-mail, notes in their assignments, and via the bulletin boards. Now and then someone calls me at my office on the phone, but that's rare." He likes to answer his e-mails at least once a day, which means that his students get much more feedback than they would if he were physically in a classroom with them.

As do most online teachers, Cynthia Davis, Associate Dean of Academic Affairs in the School of Undergraduate Studies at the University of Maryland University College, gets students to participate with a weekly discussion topic. "If we're reading a novel," she says, "I ask them to discuss the role of the narrator or analyze a passage. The students respond individually and then respond to other students' comments."

Attending virtual lectures. Some online courses allow you to hear and see the professor or other guest speakers who are also online. If you want to ask a question, there's a button to indicate you want to speak. Everyone else can hear you as if you all were in the same room. Other professors add voice to PowerPoint lectures, which you can view when you want to, not at some prearranged time.

Taking quizzes and tests. No more waiting weeks to get your tests back. Online technology in some courses instantly zaps back the corrected test and notes that you missed question six and need to study page 54 of the textbook. Just like in face-to-face classes, you have an allotted amount of time to take the quiz. Some online courses may have automated components, such as instant quizzes and animated and interactive practice sessions. Others have mandatory proctored exams at a nearby community college or learning center for students who are off campus.

Can You Transfer Credits Received Online from One Institution to Another?

Policies vary greatly among universities and colleges. Though distance education is widely accepted, there are so many places where students can take bogus online courses that institutions are justifiably cautious. If students do decide they want to get a bachelor's degree completely online, they need to be sure the campus-based program and distance education program offer the same degree. At most institutions both on-campus and online degrees are the same, but others do differentiate in the degrees conferred, and it will show up on your diploma.

What Kind of Refund Policy Does the University Have for Distance Learners?

It might become painfully apparent for students that online learning is not for them, and they want to drop out. Find out ahead of time about the refund policy for online classes. What happens if you're ill during an online class? How can you make up the work? Even before taking any classes, you should find out if you're suited for online learning. Many institutions offer self-assessment tests on their Web sites.

What Online Services Does the College Provide?

Is the dorm wired? Can you get an e-mail address from the university? What about browsers and computer compatibility? Ask how the Internet is part of face-to-face classes. To what extent is the library online, and is it available 24/7 for research? Ask about writing and math labs and help-desk support. Look for online tutorials that show students how to use the school's specific software. Is there a tech fee?

IF YOU'RE LEARNING ONLINE, YOU BETTER HAVE THESE

Since online learning is part of college, it's helpful to know what to expect ahead of time, rather than three weeks into the class, when you feel like throwing your laptop out the window and would happily settle for sitting in the back row of the nearest classroom. Here are the five skills and abilities that successful online students must have.

1. You must have the self-discipline to do things you don't want to do when you don't want to do them. If you're a procrastinator, you'll find the catch-up tactics that served you well in face-to-face classes won't work online. "Students get the idea they can whiz by without studying, or they came from high schools where they weren't pushed," cautions Heeger. "Maybe they never got Fs in high school, but they do here." That's because they don't realize they're responsible for learning the material on their own. The burden is on you to keep up with the homework. It doesn't take long to fall far behind in online classes.

Typically, students in face-to-face and online classes need 2 hours for work outside of class for every hour in class. But online students often forget to add that hour. For every hour they would have to sit in a traditional classroom, they should be listening, studying, thinking, writing, responding to discussions, and getting ready for tests, plus the 2 hours outside of class. Three classes a week—that's 9 to 10 hours for one class. Online teachers keep students on track with weekly quizzes and homework assignments. If students start lagging, they're likely to get an e-mail from the professor asking what's going on. Claudine SchWeber, Ph.D., Chair of the Doctor of Management Program at the University of Maryland University College, has taught online for years and states, "My classes are structured by weekly readings, activities, and discussions. Students can't decide to get around to doing the work when they feel like it. It must be done at the instructor's pace. The first shot of online can be a shock to their system."

2. You must have the ability to manage your time without anyone telling you do your homework NOW. In high school, students usually can put off studying until the weekend. "That doesn't work in college. You can't write complex papers the night before," says Karen L. Kirkendall, Ph.D., Associate Professor of Liberal Studies at the University of Illinois at Springfield. She teaches both online and face-to-face classes and has seen first-time online students who have never failed before start to slip and suddenly realize they are in big trouble. "My online classes are extraordinarily structured so I pretty much know when students aren't engaged, which I monitor by seeing how much they participate in online discussions," she notes.

3. You must have the skills to communicate your thoughts in writing. "Online participation in class discussions isn't instant messaging. You are what you write in

THE TRUTH IS . . .

As distance education becomes more accepted, people will readily discard some of the myths on this list. But for now, they persist.

Distance learning is for people on ranches 200 miles from the nearest freeway. Geography is not a factor. Many distance learners who are located across the campus or a few miles away just don't want to deal with the commute or have a work schedule that conflicts with being in a class at a certain time. They appreciate the flexibility that distance education gives them.

Distance learning is easier than face-to-face classes. Once you start an online class, you'll knock that myth off the list. Still, some students think it will be easier. When they realize they must not only respond to discussion questions but also comment on the responses from other students, they wonder why they ever thought distance education was going to be easy. Online teachers normally keep track of how their students progress with frequent monitoring and quizzes.

I'll get a better education in face-to-face classes. Much research has been conducted comparing the two and consistently, online learning is equivalent or better. Teachers of online courses now have plenty of precedents to follow, training and research to help them teach better, and technology to prepare for classes and keep up with their students' progress.

I'll talk to a computer all day. Yes, you are in front of a computer as a distance learner, but you also interact with professors and other students much more than you ever would in a core freshman class of 200. Teachers have sophisticated software to facilitate interaction. Even though you don't physically see your teachers, they put a great deal of effort into class preparation and reading e-mails. Some get as many as 3,000 e-mails in a ten-week class. Distance learners often get to know fellow students much more easily online than they would walking in and out of a class.

I need to be a computer geek. If you can handle the simplest maneuvers around a computer, such as attaching documents to e-mails or going to a specified Web address, you can be a distance learner. And you'll have tech support to help out if you run into problems.

Distance education is cheaper than face-to-face. Too bad this isn't a myth. But it costs the same as a traditional college if you attend a recognized institution. Most students pay for distance education through student loans.

online classes," advises SchWeber. Most of the work in online classes is written, whether it's participation in discussions, homework, quizzes, papers, or tests.

Since you'll communicate by e-mail and post your thoughts, netiquette is essential. You need to think differently online than when speaking on the phone or face-to-face. "You can't write a report that sounds like you are hanging out with friends," advises SchWeber. "When you are totally online, the only image people (including your professor) have of you is how you write." Kirkendall has reprimanded students who sent e-mails showing disrespect to the teacher because they were upset about something. Probably they would never respond that way if face-to-face. "Never hit the submit button when you're angry," Kirkendall cautions.

4. You must have the ability to research worthwhile information on the Web. You need to know what's junk and what's reliable. In addition, professors take plagiarism very seriously, especially because it's so easy to do.

5. You must have some computer skills and know some computer-speak. Those who design the software and set up how a distance learning class is taught are careful to make sure the technology doesn't get in the way of learning; however, you should know the basics. "In some classes, certain downloads are required, such as Adobe Acrobat, but in general, the skills are not beyond the abilities used daily by most elementary school children," says Schroeder, pointing out that if distance programs use expensive or exotic technology, they defeat the purpose. He reports that most computers that are five years old have the speed, memory, and capability to support online learning. Some classes might require a microphone. You should be familiar with some of the computer jargon so that if you're asked to post something or use a drop box, add an attachment, or take part in a threaded discussion, you'll know what what you need to do. Just about every distance learning provider has online tutorials to familiarize you with their particular online software. If you run into technical problems, help-desk support is available.

Why Not Women's Colleges?

Before we start talking about the many advantages that women's colleges offer, let's get some myths out of the way. It is almost certain that the minute you hear "women's colleges" in the same sentence with "choosing colleges" you immediately think: no boys, no fun, no way!

Maybe that is why some girls who visit Joan Jaffe's office at Mills College in San Francisco, California, rush in to tell her that they just saw some guys on the campus of this women's college. Jaffe, Associate Dean of Admission, frequently gets this reaction from the young women who visit the campus. That's because many think that if they go to a women's college they are never going to see a guy within 2 miles of the campus gates, which, by the way, will clang shut behind them, leaving them secluded inside a heavily guarded male-free zone.

KISS MYTH NUMBER ONE GOOD-BYE

Forget iron gates. The first myth to get rid of is the one that assumes attending a women's college means kissing your social life good-bye. In fact, as Patricia Gibbs, Vice President for Enrollment Services and Student Affairs at Wesleyan College in Macon, Georgia, points out, "If you were a guy looking for a date, where would you go?" Not only that, the majority of women's colleges are near, if not next to, coed campuses. Most share activities with other colleges and universities, and many have reciprocal agreements so that guys can take classes at the women's college and vice versa.

When it comes to dating, women's colleges offer the best of both worlds. You can hang out with guys when you want to and then retreat to your own lovely environment (women's dorms usually are beautiful) and hang out with the girls. Julie Binder, who transferred from the University of Wisconsin to all-women's Barnard College in New York City, notes that there is open registration with Columbia University, which just happens to be right next door. "Campus life is shared. Sports are shared," she says.

As you dig deeper into this myth, you will find that attending a women's college is not about isolation, it's about options. You get to choose if you want to be in classes, clubs, and organizations only with women or mingle with the men.

SCRATCH MYTH NUMBER TWO

On to myth number two. Women's colleges are just a bunch of catty, competitive females waiting for the right moment to scratch each other's eyes out. Scratch that myth, too. Instead, women's colleges cultivate an environment of sisterhood-women looking out for each other and helping each other. Most women's colleges encourage women in the upper-level classes to help their younger classmates. Talking to their "big sisters," newcomers find out what classes to take, which professors are the best, and have sympathetic ears for the problems that most first-year college students face.

"The sense of community is very strong at women's colleges," observes Fran Samuels, former Director of College

THE RICH TRADITIONS IN WOMEN'S COLLEGES

Tradition plays an important part of the experience women have in women's colleges. They run the gamut from solemn ceremonies of passing along the bond of sisterhood to the fun of secret surprises. "Women's colleges have a strong sense of tradition," says Amy Shaver, former Dean of Student Services at Stephens College in Columbia, Missouri. It's also a wonderful way to help women from all social, economic, religious, and ethnic backgrounds to share a common experience and pass it on to the next generation of students. "Traditions bond women over the generations," says Jennifer Rickard, Dean of Admissions and Financial Aid at Bryn Mawr College, who notes that it's not unusual at all to have students today singing songs and participating in ceremonies that the class of 1945 did and which will be the same when today's students have their twenty-year reunion.

Here's a sampling of the many traditions you'll find on women's college campuses:

Lantern Night At Bryn Mawr's Lantern Night, women gather around a fountain on campus. Each woman is given a lantern as a symbol of knowledge and learning. Each class has a color, and as the lanterns are passed from the sophomores to the first-year students, songs are sung in Greek that are the same as the ones sung 100 years ago around the same fountain.

Senior Paint Night Mills College seniors get the okay to paint the campus in their class color. Along with brushes and cans of paint, they are given a few guidelines as to what can and cannot be painted, but the rest is up to them.

The Crossing of the Bridge As women students come to Stephens to begin their college education, they cross over a bridge on campus in a ceremony symbolizing their entrance into the world of academia. At graduation, they cross over another bridge on campus and are welcomed into the alumnae society.

Candlelight Induction Ceremony Spelman students dressed in white dresses and black shoes light candles and hear the charge to be the best they can be. While the candles are still lit, they sing the Spelman hymn.

Midnight Breakfast At Barnard, the night before finals, the president of the college, deans, and professors make breakfast for the students.

Counseling at The Master's School in Dobbs Ferry, New York. "The myth is that a women's college will be cliquish. In truth, the women are supportive of each other." The strong bonds of sisterhood that naturally develop connect students to their college, its history, and its students, past, present, and future. Many women's colleges designate a rotating color for each incoming class. For example, if the freshman class you enter is dubbed the golden hearts, by the time you graduate, you are connected to all the golden hearts who graduated ahead of you and all the golden hearts who will graduate after you.

TOSS MYTH NUMBER THREE

Another myth that should be tossed out is that women's colleges don't prepare you for the "real world." Well, try saying that to the 12 women members of Congress who graduated from women's colleges. Or to the 15 women on *Business Week*'s list of the rising stars in corporate America. Although you are not in a totally coed situation, on the other hand you are in an environment in which you can gain skills to think critically and learn to meet challenges. Becky Marsh, Director of Advancement at Whitfield School, in St. Louis, Missouri, points out that when you first ride a bike, training wheels allow you to learn how to balance. Once you are ready to race down the street, you take them off. Same with women's colleges. The focus is on your education and your strengths, and who you are. You graduate ready to take on the obstacles of the real world. "In high school, I had the feeling that boys were given more opportunities to share their knowledge. It was harder and more intimidating for me to share my opinions in a coed class," says Brittany Johnson, from Spelman College in Atlanta, Georgia. "Now I feel like I can do anything."

Graduates of women's colleges feel empowered and willing to confront any limits to their abilities. While in college, they have many opportunities to assume leadership roles and see women in leadership positions as professors and deans. "They don't doubt whether they can do anything. Instead, they ask, 'Why can't I do it now?'" reports Amy Shaver, former Dean of Student Services at Stephens College in Columbia, Missouri. Women can find their own voices and establish their own ways of approaching things that will ultimately make them successful in a male-dominated world. They learn from seeing other women students and professors engaged in the intellectual process.

THE ADVANTAGES

As more young women find out about the advantages that women's colleges offer them, they like what they see. Maybe that is why attendance at women's colleges is growing. Learning leadership skills tops the list of advantages. Says Shaver, "Women in a same-sex environment are more likely to take risks and speak up in class. They are more willing to stand up and voice an opinion." If you think about it, students get plenty of practice at a women's college because all the leadership roles go to women. From day one on a women's campus, you will see women leading the entire college or involved in interesting and significant research. You get more exposure to what leadership is and what to expect as a leader. "Leadership becomes ingrained," notes Jennifer Fondiller, Dean of Admissions at Barnard College in New York City.

You might not realize it, but women react differently in classrooms with all women. They tend to speak up with confidence and to test their ideas more readily when they are not competing with men. Researchers find that even as early as the fifth grade, girls are taught differently than boys. Teachers call on boys more frequently and don't ask girls the more thought-provoking questions or to critically analyze problems. In coed situations, the more aggressive and competitive guys take over, whereas in all-female classes, research indicates there is much more give-and-take and exchange of ideas.

Coming from a coed public school, Johnson realized that more attention was given to the guys in her classes, but at Spelman, she says, "Everyone is on the same path." Arlene Cash, Vice President for Enrollment Management at Spelman, notes that women don't have to vie for attention or retreat into the intellectual background in all-women classes. In a coed class, the environment becomes more adversarial. "Women feel they have to perform. In women's colleges they become more academically involved and interact with faculty members more frequently," says Debbie Greenberg, College Counselor at Whitfield School. Speaking of the rich interaction that occurs in her classes at Barnard, Binder says, "The diversity of experience around the discussion table is unparalleled."

YOU CAN SUCCEED

Shaver characterizes the environment in women's colleges as one in which there is no fear of failing when the social pressures and dynamics of men and women are removed from the classroom. Women's colleges give women the opportunity to explore different avenues without the fear of failing. "We challenge them to become what they want to become," says Gibbs from Wesleyan. "No one says, 'You can't do that because you are a woman.'" At the same time, you are interacting with other women who have the same goals as you, which reinforces who you are. Or, as Jennifer Rickard, Dean of Admissions and Financial Aid at Bryn Mawr College, in Bryn Mawr, Pennsylvania, points out, women are not just sitting in classes to do well on exams and get good grades. They also are figuring out what they want to do with their education. "There's less expectation to conform to an external measure," she says.

Many women's colleges foster self-government and give their students responsibilities they might not find in a coed institution. At Bryn Mawr, for instance, students pay a self-government association fee as part of their tuition. This is put into a fund that is controlled by a student government that takes ownership of how the students want to govern themselves. "This isn't student government making only recommendations to the administration as to how to allocate the budget to the different student groups vying for funds," notes Rickard. "You have students dealing with real-world management issues, such as resource allocation."

Since women's colleges are smaller than big coed universities, women receive all the benefits that students get from a

WHAT MADE YOU CHOOSE A WOMEN'S COLLEGE?

When she got to the point of choosing which college to attend, Wisambi Loundu had plenty of options. Coming from San Diego, the California universities were a logical choice. Women's colleges were not on her list. In fact, she hardly knew they existed. Her first thought when someone suggested a women's college to her was, "I'm not going to a school full of girls minus boys." Her second thought was just as negative. "If it's all girls, they will always be fighting." The third and fourth thoughts assumed that a women's college wouldn't prepare her for the real world, plus she would be isolated.

But then her math teacher's daughter told her about Bryn Mawr, and as Wisambi started exploring the possibility, the advantages of a women's college started lining up. However, it wasn't until she visited Bryn Mawr that she really began to see herself there. "I fell in love with the campus," says Wisambi. "It was like nothing I'd ever seen before." Her stay in the dorm added to her steadily growing thoughts that Bryn Mawr might be it. "The girls I stayed with in the dorm were so friendly. At first I was suspicious, but I saw it was not a front. Plus, there were girls from all over the world."

But Wisambi didn't make her final decision just yet. She decided to look at other schools, like Wellesley and the University of California schools, as well as Stanford. Meanwhile, her friend told her more about Bryn Mawr. "She said I'd make lasting friends and she talked about how the academics would train me for the outside world even if there were no men on campus. Bryn Mawr would build my identity as a woman."

She still wasn't convinced and made a second visit, along with visits to Wellesley and Stanford, which she says were nice, but too big. It would be too hard to make friends there, she thought. When the time came to make her final selection, she chose Bryn Mawr.

Now at Bryn Mawr, how does Wisambi feel about her choice? The academics are more challenging than she anticipated but doable, and she is excited about the internships she will be able to access. She also finds that the staff and teachers at Bryn Mawr go out of their way to make her feel at home. "They match us up with a mentor and professor," she says.

How about dating? Since Bryn Mawr is part of a tri-college community, guys are around, though Wisambi says you have to make an effort to meet people on other campuses.

Talking to seniors who are getting ready to head out to the "real world," Wisambi can see that they are full of confidence and don't think for a minute that they won't do well. "And that's a positive," she says.

small liberal arts college in addition to the advantages that only a women's college offers. A big plus is interaction with professors and staff, which is hard to achieve when you are one of 200 students in a lecture hall taught by a graduate student. Women's colleges tend to foster seminar-style classes taught by full professors, many of them women. "You have an expert teaching you," says Gibbs. Faculty members get to know their students and can challenge them intellectually on an individual basis. "Within two days, all my teachers knew my name," recalls Johnson, who says she was given each professor's e-mail address, home phone number, and all the contact information she needed and was encouraged to reach out to them.

Women are encouraged to achieve their intellectual goals. Professors often will point out specific programs that they know suit the student's interests. Add to this the opportunities to conduct research with a professor, and in many cases actually present research findings to a professional society, and you can see why women graduate with a terrific resume before they even start their careers. Rickard mentions the opportunity that Bryn Mawr students have to work on funded projects with professors during the summer and then present the results along with them at conferences. "It's a window into the academic world and the world of the intellectual," she notes. It's no surprise that women in women's colleges major in math and science at a higher national average than women in coed institutions.

Paid and unpaid internships, too, are more available for women at women's colleges, mainly because of the network of women graduates in business and industry who want to help their "sisters" at their alma maters. "I'm getting my professional edge now," says Binder, who is interested in TV production and had a paid internship as a production assistant while a sophomore at Barnard. "You will have an amazing resume by the time you graduate," she says.

Peggy Hock, Ph.D., College Counselor at Notre Dame High School in San Jose, California, points out that colleges naturally rely on their alumni to come forward with networking opportunities for students; however, the alumnae of women's colleges tend to be more loyal and willing to give of their time. This translates into many more opportunities for internships, mentoring, and job possibilities. At Barnard, for example, the career office has an alumna mentor network. Students can call, ask questions, and get advice about career choices. At alumnae events, current students mix with the graduates. Binder takes full advantage of the Web log of women who are working all over the world and willing to spend time online with Barnard students. She applied for a job at a public relations firm in New York after contacting a fellow Barnard graduate working there. She met with her and subsequently got a letter of recommendation.

HOW TO CHOOSE

Choosing a women's college isn't any different from choosing a coed college. You should definitely visit the campus and don't be afraid to ask lots of questions—even the ones that might make you uncomfortable. Because women's colleges are similar to small coed liberal arts colleges, make sure that you don't compare a women's campus to a big university.

Janet Ashley, Interim Director for Admission and Orientation Services at Spelman College, advises high school women to ask what a women's college can give them academically. "Their choice depends on what their goals are," she says.

If you're worried about the dating scene, ask about the levels of interaction with guys and how close the relationships are with neighboring institutions.

"Look at the individuality of each women's college," suggests Rickard, "because each has its own personality." Look at the school before looking at the fact that it's a women's college, and on the flip side, don't rule out a school just because it is a women's college. "So many students make quick decisions about where to apply," warns Fondiller, noting that sometimes the decision hinges on what schools a friend is applying to rather than if that institution really fits the student. Many women's colleges specialize in certain fields like science, math, or theater.

FAMOUS FIRSTS FROM WOMEN'S COLLEGES

Quick, from where did the first woman to be named Secretary of State graduate? Or the woman scientist who identified Hong Kong flu? Or the first woman executive vice president of the American Stock Exchange? Here's a big clue. They were all graduates of women's colleges.

SENATORS

- Hillary Rodham Clinton (NY)—Wellesley College
- Blanche Lambert Lincoln (AR)—Randolph-Macon Woman's College
- Barbara Mikulski (MD)—Mount Saint Agnes College

REPRESENTATIVES

- Tammy Baldwin (WI)—Smith College
- Donna Christian-Christensen (VI)—St. Mary's College
- Rosa DeLauro (CT)—Marymount College
- Jane Harman (CA)—Smith College
- Gabrielle Giffords (AZ)—Scripps College
- Eddie Bernice Johnson (TX)—Saint Mary's College
- Sue Kelly (NY)—Sarah Lawrence College
- Barbara Lee (CA)—Mills College
- Nita Lowey (NY)—Mount Holyoke College
- Betty McCollum (MN)—College of Saint Catherine
- Nancy Pelosi (CA), first woman elected as Speaker of the House of Representatives—Trinity College
- Allyson Schwartz (PA)—Simmons College

OTHER FAMOUS WOMEN FIRSTS

- Madeleine Albright, first woman to be named Secretary of State in the U.S., appointed in 1997—Wellesley
- Jane Amsterdam, first woman editor, the *New York Post*—Cedar Crest
- Emily Green Balch, first woman to receive the Nobel Peace Prize in 1946—Bryn Mawr
- Catherine Brewer Benson, first woman to receive a college bachelor's degree—Wesleyan
- Earla Biekert, first scientist to identify the Hong Kong flu virus—Wesleyan
- Cathleen Black, first woman leader of the American Newspaper Publishers Association—Trinity, Washington, D.C.
- Sarah Porter Boehmler, first woman executive vice president of American Stock Exchange—Sweet Briar
- Jane Matilda Bolin, first African-American woman judge in the U.S.—Wellesley
- Dorothy L. Brown, first African-American woman general surgeon in the South—Bennett
- Pearl S. Buck, first American woman to win the Nobel Prize in Literature—Randolph-Macon Woman's College
- Ila Burdett, Georgia's first female Rhodes Scholar—Agnes Scott
- Dorothy Vredenburgh Bush, first woman secretary of the Democratic National Party—Mississippi University for Women
- Hon. Audrey J. S. Carrion, first Hispanic woman judge Circuit Court for Baltimore City—College of Notre Dame of Maryland
- Barbara Cassani, first female and CEO of a commercial airline—Mount Holyoke
- Elaine L. Chao, U.S. Secretary of Labor, 2001; First Asian-American woman appointed to a President's cabinet in U.S. history—Mount Holyoke

Adapted from the Web site of the Women's College Coalition at http://www.womenscolleges.org.

The Military and Higher Education

The first part of this section offers an overview of the opportunities that exist today for students who wish to explore the possibility of financing their higher education by participating in ROTC or attending a service academy. This information is provided in order to help students and families make well-informed decisions about this important investment. The second part of this section presents, in the Army's own words and photos, a detailed description of one military financial aid option—the Army ROTC Program.

The Military as a Source of Financial Aid

One of the major problems facing families today is how to come up with the money to meet college expenses. Many people are unaware that the military is a source of financial aid. Its focus, however, is quite different from that of other sources: military financial aid programs do not consider need but are either a payment for training or a reward for service. This large source of money (about $1 billion each year) can prove quite helpful in assisting a wide range of students. The military financial aid programs are by far the largest source of college money that is not based on need.

HOW THE MILITARY PROVIDES FINANCIAL AID

One form of military financial aid is college money for Officer candidates: tuition assistance and monthly pay in return for the student's promise to serve as an Officer in the Army, Navy, Air Force, Marine Corps, Coast Guard, or Merchant Marine. Most of this money is awarded to high school seniors who go directly to college. The main benefits are reduced or free tuition and up to $200 per month. ROTC units are located on college campuses and provide military training for a few hours a week. The five service academies (West Point, Annapolis, the Air Force Academy, the Coast Guard Academy, and the Merchant Marine Academy) are military establishments that combine education and training for the armed forces. For those already in college, financial aid is obtainable through ROTC scholarships for enrolled students or special commissioning programs.

By participating in ROTC, attending a service academy, or enrolling in a special program for military commissioning, a student not only can become an Officer but also can become eligible for financial aid, thus turning the dream of an affordable college education into a reality. The military trains students to become Officers and pays them to learn at the same time. (A detailed look at one such program, that of the Army ROTC, appears following this article.)

IS OFFICER TRAINING RIGHT FOR YOU?

Military scholarship programs exist largely to provide money to college students as they go through Officer training, and, in return, the military receives from the students a commitment to serve in the armed forces. The military's goal is to produce, through this method of attracting outstanding young men and women, "entry-level" Officers who are well educated both academically and in the workings of the military itself. Obviously, you would not be the ideal candidate for one of these programs if you had moral or religious reservations about serving your country as a military Officer. You also should not apply if the program's main appeal for you is the money. The financial benefits may be very important, but their attraction should be balanced by genuine feelings on your part that you will seriously consider becoming an Officer, you will undertake military training with a positive attitude, and you will be flexible and open-minded about your plans. Applicants are typically young men or women who are willing to serve at least four or five years as Officers in exchange for four years of a good education at little or no cost.

Are You the Military Type?

At the outset, it is essential that you determine whether or not you are cut out to be in the military. Take a personal inventory: What are you like? How do you relate to others? Of what kind of organization do you want to be a part?

- Do you consider yourself intelligent, well-rounded, energetic, organized, and somewhat athletic? Are you a serious student with good grades in precollege courses and an aptitude for science and math?
- Are you outgoing? Does leadership appeal to you? Do you work well with others, both in groups and in one-on-one situations? Can you willingly take direction from others?
- Can you exist in a structured and disciplined environment? Do you have strong feelings of patriotism? Are you willing to defend your country in a time of war?

If "yes" is your answer to most of these questions, you are the type of individual in whom the military services are interested. Even more important, you may be the type of person who can be comfortable with the military's lifestyle. Although there are many different types of military Officers—from the quiet intellectual to the extroverted athlete—the average Officer usually conforms to a set of general characteristics: a mixture of certain personal traits and a willingness to be part of and contribute to a large and very structured organization.

What Kind of Military Training Might Be Appropriate for You?

If your personal inventory revealed you to be at least somewhat the "military type," your next step is to see which of the programs offered by the different services is best for you. So, ask yourself which of the following four descriptions most closely describes your feelings at present.

1. I have firsthand knowledge of military service. I can picture myself as an Officer, perhaps even a career Officer. I have experience with discipline, both in taking and in giving orders. I plan to major in science or engineering while I'm in college. Obtaining a top-quality education at very low cost is very important to me.
2. Service in the military is of interest to me. I don't have much direct experience, but I'm willing to learn more. I'm not sure whether I'm ready to immerse myself completely in a military environment as a college student. I've done well in math and science, but I may decide to major in another field. I can look forward to the prospect of four years of service as an Officer before deciding whether to stay on. A tuition scholarship is appealing, and it would widen the range of colleges that are within my reach.
3. I don't have a negative attitude toward the military, but it's not something I know much about. I might be interested in giving it a look. Studying math and science may not be for me; my interests are probably in other areas. I'm concerned about paying for college, but my parents could help me for at least one or two years.
4. I don't think I'm the military type, but actually I haven't thought that much about it. I doubt if I would go for the discipline. I wouldn't want to commit to anything until I've been in college for a few years and can see my choices more clearly. I might be able to see myself serving in the military—if I could get duty that matches my academic interests. I could use a scholarship, but I plan to seek financial aid through other sources.

When you've determined which of the foregoing paragraphs mostly closely describes your attitude toward military service, review the following four items, the numbers of which generally relate to the numbers above.

1. Think seriously about competing for an appointment to a service academy. You must be nominated by an official source, usually your congressional representative. Each member of Congress has a set number of nominees he or she can recommend for admission. Neither political influence nor a personal relationship with the member of Congress is necessary.
2. Plan to enter the national ROTC four-year scholarship competition.
3. Join an ROTC unit in college and see what the military is like. Scholarship opportunities are available if you decide to stay on.
4. Don't get involved with a military program yet, but keep the service in mind for possible entrance after two years of college.

It should go without saying that it's best to avoid extreme discrepancies between the two lists. For example, if description number 4 applies, a military academy or even the four-year scholarship is probably not right for you. It would be far wiser to choose item number 3 or 4. Later on, after you are enrolled in college, you might find that certain aspects of the military complement your academic interests and that the military lifestyle is something to which you can adapt. If, on the other hand, description number 1 suits you, it will be worth your while to pursue either the ROTC scholarship or service academy option when you graduate from high school. If you are this far along in your thinking about a possible future in the military, you can take advantage of both the financial benefits the services offer and the head start you will get toward a possible military career by trying for an Officer training program.

Preparation While in High School

Enrolling in a precollege program while you're attending high school will improve your chances of winning a four-year ROTC scholarship or receiving an appointment to a service academy. For the most part, the services don't require that you take specific subjects (the exceptions are the Coast Guard Academy and the Merchant Marine Academy). Nonetheless, the Army, Navy, Air Force, and Marine Corps all stress the importance of a good high school curriculum. They suggest the following: 4 years of English, 4 years of math (through calculus), 2 years of a foreign language, 2 years of laboratory science, and 1 year of American history.

Being an active member of your school and community is also important, as is holding leadership positions in sports and/or other extracurricular activities. If your high school has a Junior ROTC unit, join the detachment; doing so could improve your chances of being selected for an ROTC scholarship or admitted to a service academy. For entrance into the academies and most other colleges, be prepared to take the SAT or ACT, used by college admission offices as one of the measures of a prospective college student's academic potential.

WHO IS A SUCCESSFUL CANDIDATE?

A fictional though typical winner of a four-year ROTC scholarship or an appointment to a service academy (who we will call John Doe) exhibits certain kinds of characteristics:

- He follows a curriculum that includes 4 years of English, 4 years of math, 3 or 4 years of a foreign language, 2 years of laboratory science, and 2 years of history—with some of the courses at the honors level. John maintains a B+ average and ranks in the top 15 percent of his class.
- He is a member of the National Honor Society. He holds an office in student government and is a candidate for Boys State. John has a leadership position on the student newspaper and is a member of both the debate panel and math club. He is active in varsity athletics and is cocaptain of the basketball team.
- He is one of the top all-around students in his class and makes a positive contribution to both his school and community. He is described as intelligent, industrious, well-organized, self-confident, concerned, and emotionally mature.

The services believe and expect that a person with John Doe's abilities and traits will do well in college—in both academic and military training—and will also have great potential to become a productive Officer after graduation.

FACTS ABOUT THE OFFICER TRAINING PROGRAMS

Officer Pay and Benefits

As a military Officer, you will be paid the standard rate for all members of the armed forces of your rank and length of service. In addition to your salary, significant fringe benefits include free medical care and a generous retirement plan.

The Difference Between a Regular and a Reserve Officer

Officer training programs offer Regular and Reserve commissions. However, all initial commissions after September 30, 1996, have been Reserve only. You should be aware of the difference between the two designations.

When commissioned as a Regular Officer, you are on a career path in the military. In the event that you choose not to serve at least twenty years, you must write a letter asking if you can resign your commission. Such requests are normally accepted once you have completed your minimum service obligation. If you plan to make the military your career, it is a definite advantage to be a Regular Officer.

As a Reserve Officer, you contract for a specific term, for example, four years of active duty in the case of an ROTC scholarship. Nearly all Air Force ROTC second lieutenants are in this category, along with about 85 percent of Army ROTC graduates. If you want to remain on active duty after your initial obligation, you must request to sign on for a second term.

There is another category of Reserve Officer—those who are assigned to the Reserve Forces rather than to active duty. About 50 percent of the Officers who are commissioned through the Army ROTC are given orders to the National Guard or Army Reserve. After attending the Basic Course for six months, these Officers join the Reserve Forces to finish their obligated service as "weekend warriors." In this case, the time commitment is 7½ years in the Reserve, the first 5½ years involving drills one weekend per month and two weeks of active duty per year. During the last two years of obligated service, these Officers are transferred to inactive Reserve status, in which drills are not required.

Women Officers

Virtually all of the Officer training programs are open to women. With the exception of differences in height and weight standards and lower minimums on the physical fitness test, the eligibility rules, benefits, and obligations are the same for both genders. When it comes to duty assignments, however, there is a notable difference between men and women. Depending on the branch of the service, the law restricts the types of jobs women can choose. Other than the limits imposed by certain combat restrictions for women, the position of women within the military has improved considerably in the past ten years. There are variations among the services, but overall, women make up between 8 and 20 percent of the Officers, and they are gradually but steadily moving into higher-ranking positions.

Medical Requirements

Candidates for an ROTC scholarship must pass a medical examination. You need take only one physical, even if you apply for more than one type of scholarship. Medical standards vary considerably and can be quite complicated. Nevertheless, it is worth having an idea of the general medical requirements at the outset, particularly the eyesight and height and weight rules. Keep in mind, too, that medical standards change periodically, and some of them may be waived under certain conditions.

THE ROTC PROGRAMS

The predominant way for a college student to become a military Officer is through the Reserve Officers' Training Corps program. ROTC is offered by the Army, Navy, and Air Force, while students taking the Marine Corps option participate in Naval ROTC. (The Coast Guard and Merchant Marine do not sponsor ROTC programs.)

Each service that has an ROTC program signs an agreement with a number of colleges to host a unit on their campuses. Each of these units has a commanding Officer supervising a staff of active-duty Officers and enlisted servicemembers who conduct the military training of Cadets and midshipmen. This instruction includes regular class periods in which military science is taught as well as longer drill sessions in which students concentrate on developing leadership qualities through participation in military formations, physical fitness routines, and field exercises.

It is not necessary for you to attend a college that hosts a unit to participate in ROTC. You may attend any of the approved colleges that have a cross-enrollment contract and participate in ROTC at the host institution, provided you are accepted into the unit and you are able to arrange your schedule so that you have time to commute to the ROTC classes and drill sessions.

As a member of an ROTC unit, you are a part-time Cadet or midshipman. You are required to wear a uniform and adhere to military discipline when you attend an ROTC class or drill, but not at other times. Since this involvement averages only about 4 hours per week, most of the time you will enjoy the same lifestyle as a typical college student. You must realize, however, that while you are an undergraduate, you are being trained to become an Officer when you graduate. You therefore will have a number of obligations and responsibilities your classmates do not face. Nevertheless, the part-time nature of your military training is the major difference between participating in ROTC and enrolling at a service academy, where you are in a military environment 24 hours a day.

In each ROTC unit there are two types of student—scholarship and nonscholarship. Although the focus of this section is on military programs that provide tuition aid, it should be pointed out that you may join an ROTC unit after you get to college even if you don't receive a scholarship. You take the same ROTC courses as a scholarship student, and you may major in nearly any subject. You can drop out at any time prior to the start of your junior year. If you continue, you will be paid a monthly stipend for your last two years of college and be required to attend a summer training session between your junior and senior years. Upon graduation, you will be commissioned as a second lieutenant or ensign. For the Army, your minimum active-duty obligation is six months; four years if you are in the Air Force or Navy.

The major source of scholarships is the four-year tuition scholarship program. Four-year scholarships are awarded to high school seniors on the basis of a national competition. Each year, more than 4,000 winners are selected (roughly 2,000 Army, 1,300 Navy, and 1,300 Air Force) from about 25,000 applicants. Recipients of four-year Army, Air Force, and Naval ROTC scholarships may attend either a host college or approved cross-enrollment college. In return for an Army ROTC scholarship, you must serve eight years in the Active Army, Army Reserve, or Army National Guard or a combination thereof. For scholarships from other services, four years' active duty service is required. After you accept the scholarship, you have a one-year grace period before you incur a military obligation. Prior to beginning your sophomore year, you may simply withdraw from the program. If you drop out after that time, you may be permitted to leave without penalty, ordered to active duty as an enlisted servicemember, or required to repay the financial aid you have received. The military will choose one of these three options, depending on the circumstances of your withdrawal.

Should you decide to try for a four-year ROTC scholarship, it is important that you apply to a college to which you can bring an ROTC scholarship. Because there is always the possibility you may not be accepted at your first choice, it is a good idea to apply to more than one college with an ROTC affiliation. In the case of Army and Air Force ROTC scholarships, both of which may require you to major in a specified area, you also need to be admitted to the particular program for which the scholarship is offered. For example, if you win an Air Force ROTC scholarship designated for an engineering major, you must be accepted into the engineering program as well as to the college as a whole.

While the majority of new ROTC scholarships are four-year awards given to high school seniors, each service sets aside scholarships for students who are already enrolled in college and want to try for this kind of military financial aid for their last two or three years. These in-college scholarships are a rapidly growing area within the ROTC program, since the services are finding they can do a better job of selecting Officer candidates after observing one or two years of college performance. Of further interest to applicants is the fact that for some of the services, the selection rate is quite a bit higher for the two- and three-year awards than it is for the four-year scholarship. For example, in a recent year, Air Force ROTC accepted 37 percent of its candidates for four-year awards and 63 percent of its candidates for two- and three-year awards. Most of these in-college scholarships are given to students who join an ROTC unit without a scholarship and then decide to try for a tuition grant. Since a Cadet or midshipman takes the same ROTC courses whether on scholarship or not, it makes good sense for those who are not receiving aid to apply for an in-college award.

Even if you have not been a member of an ROTC unit during your first two years in college, it is possible to receive a two-year scholarship, provided you apply by the spring of your sophomore year. If you win a two-year scholarship, you will go to a military summer camp where you will receive training equivalent to the first two years of ROTC courses. You then join the ROTC unit for your junior and senior years. (There are also limited opportunities for non-ROTC members to try for a three-year in-college scholarship; interested students should check with an ROTC unit.)

If you receive a two- or three-year scholarship, your active-duty obligation is two to eight years. You will not have the one-year grace period four-year scholarship winners have in which to decide whether they want to remain in ROTC. You must make up your mind whether or not you want to stay when you attend your first military science class as a scholarship student.

You may be married and still receive an ROTC scholarship (you may not be married in the service academies). The benefits are the same regardless of whether you are married or single.

In summary, there are four ways to participate in ROTC: as a winner of a four-year scholarship (or, in some cases, a three-year award) for high school seniors; as a recipient of a two- or three-year scholarship for ROTC members who are not initially on scholarship; by receiving an in-college scholarship (usually for two years) designated for students who have not yet joined an ROTC unit; or as a nonscholarship student.

This section, adapted from *How the Military Will Help You Pay for College: The High School Student's Guide to ROTC, the Academies, and Special Programs,* second edition, by Don M. Betterton (Peterson's), has provided an overview of the options available if you choose to turn to the military as a source of financial aid. One such option, Army ROTC, is discussed in detail in the following pages.

The Army ROTC Program

WHAT IS ROTC?

Army ROTC is a college program that enables students not only to graduate with a degree in their chosen college majors but also to receive Officers' commissions in the U.S. Army, the Army National Guard, or the Army Reserve.

ROTC courses are like any other college elective. And most college students can try ROTC for a year without incurring any military service obligation.

ROTC Cadets are eligible for numerous financial benefits, including full-tuition scholarships, allowances for books and fees, and even stipends worth up to $5000 annually.

ROTC graduates have the opportunity to serve full time as Officers in the active Army or serve part time in the Army National Guard or Army Reserve while pursuing regular civilian careers or continuing their education.

Students at hundreds of colleges and universities nationwide have access to Army ROTC programs, and about 40,000 students participate each year.

WHAT ARE THE BENEFITS OF ARMY ROTC?

Army ROTC helps ensure a young person's success in college and in life. It builds confidence and teaches the planning and time-management skills needed to succeed in college and the leadership, management, and motivational skills critical to success in life. These skills are not just taught in class. ROTC Cadets can practice them in special ROTC activities and summer training. ROTC classes last just a few hours a week and at most colleges fulfill elective requirements.

Army ROTC provides a competitive edge that will be of value in either a military or a civilian career. In fact, many civilian employers place a premium on the skills and experience gained through ROTC.

According to its headquarters at Fort Monroe, Virginia, Army ROTC describes the type of Cadets it is seeking as, "scholars, athletes, and leaders." In other words, Army ROTC wants students who are:

- Athletically inclined (even if they have not played team sports)

- Attracted to physical challenge
- At least a B student
- Serving in or have served in leadership positions in community or student organizations
- Motivated by serving and doing for others

Such young people, according to Army ROTC, are most likely to exhibit the personal and professional integrity and the ability to work as a team that are so critical to today's Army Officer.

WHAT TYPES OF FINANCIAL BENEFITS ARE AVAILABLE?

In the face of today's growing college costs, Army ROTC offers merit-based scholarships that can help pay tuition and on-campus educational expenses.

Juniors and seniors in ROTC, plus certain other ROTC Cadets, receive allowances ranging from $3000 to $5000 each school year and are paid to attend a special summer leadership training course.

Students who enroll in Army ROTC at college and who also join the National Guard or Army Reserve are eligible for other financial benefits. For more information, students should contact the Professor of Military Science at the college they plan to attend.

WHAT IS THE COMMITMENT?

College freshmen can try Army ROTC without making any commitment to join the Army. That commitment does not usually come until the junior year.

When students graduate with Officers' commissions, they serve in the active Army, the Army National Guard, the Army Reserve, or a combination for a total of eight years.

In the active Army, they serve full time as Army Officers. In the Guard or Reserve, they generally serve part time.

THE FOUR-YEAR PROGRAM

Army ROTC is traditionally a four-year college program consisting of a two-year Basic Course and a two-year Advanced Course.

The Basic Course is usually taken during a college student's freshman and sophomore years. The subjects taught cover such areas as management principles, military history and tactics, leadership development, communication skills, first aid, land navigation, and rappelling.

Most students incur no military obligation by participating in the Basic Course, and most necessary ROTC textbooks, materials, and uniforms are furnished without cost.

After completing the Basic Course, only students who have demonstrated leadership potential and who meet scholastic, physical, and moral standards are eligible to enroll in the Advanced Course.

The Advanced Course is normally taken during a college student's junior and senior years. Types of instruction include: leadership, organization theory, management, military tactics, strategic thinking, and professional ethics.

ROTC Cadets in the Advanced Course attend a paid leadership development course during the summer between their junior and senior years called the Leaders Development & Assessment Course (LDAC). This course further permits Cadets to put into practice the principles and theories they have learned in the classroom. It also exposes them to Army life in a tactical and field environment.

All ROTC Cadets in the Advanced Course receive an allowance of $4500 to $5000 each school year and are paid to attend the summer leadership development course. They are

also furnished, without cost, most necessary ROTC textbooks, materials, and uniforms.

Before entering the Advanced Course, ROTC Cadets must sign contracts that certify an understanding of their future Army service obligation, which is for eight years. This obligation may be fulfilled through various combinations of full-time active duty and part-time reserve forces duty depending upon a Cadet's personal preference and the needs of the Army at the time of commissioning.

ROTC Cadets selected for reserve forces duty actually serve on active duty for three to six months before they join a National Guard or Army Reserve unit. This is so that they can attend an Officer Basic Course to receive additional Army training. Reserve Officers generally serve when needed in the National Guard or Army Reserve while they pursue regular full-time civilian careers.

THE TWO-YEAR PROGRAM

Students can also be commissioned after only two years of ROTC instruction.

This program is open to students who did not take Army ROTC during their first two years of college. Two-year program Cadets include community and junior college graduates who have transferred to a four-year institution, graduate students, high school students planning to attend a Military Junior College, veterans, and members of the National Guard or the Army Reserve.

Students can take advantage of the two-year program by successfully completing a paid Leaders Training Course (usually attended between the sophomore and junior years of college) and entering the Advanced Course.

Veterans and members of the National Guard and Army Reserve do not have to attend the Leaders Training Course since their prior military service serves as the prerequisite for entering the Advanced Course.

Students interested in the two-year ROTC program should contact the nearest on-campus Army ROTC office for information before the end of their sophomore year of college.

EXTRACURRICULAR ACTIVITIES

Like regular college students, ROTC Cadets participate in a wide variety of social, educational, professional, and athletic activities. Most of these activities are sponsored by the colleges hosting Army ROTC, but some are sponsored by ROTC itself.

Ranger Challenge is sponsored by Army ROTC and includes competition in patrolling, marksmanship, rope-bridge building, and a 10-kilometer run. Each ROTC unit fields a Ranger Challenge team that competes against teams from ROTC units at other colleges and universities.

These and other challenging activities offer leadership opportunities that increase self-confidence.

THE SCHOLARSHIP PROGRAM

Army ROTC offers valuable four-year scholarships to students entering college as freshmen and two- or three-year scholarships to students with two or three years remaining toward their bachelor's degrees.

These scholarships pay for full tuition and have available allowances for books and required educational fees. Each scholarship recipient also receives a personal allowance of $3000 to $5000 for each school year the scholarship is in effect.

Army ROTC scholarships are merit-based scholarships awarded on a competitive basis. Selection is based on high school or college grades, SAT or ACT scores, personal rec-

ommendations, physical fitness, athletic and extracurricular activities, leadership potential, a personal interview, and other criteria as prescribed by regulation.

Many of these scholarships are specifically targeted to students pursuing degrees in engineering, nursing, the physical sciences, or other technical programs.

Army ROTC scholarship winners who fail to complete the ROTC program or do not accept commissions as Army Officers will be required to pay back the amount of their scholarships or serve as enlisted soldiers in the Army. This provision is binding for three- and four-year scholarship winners when they enter their sophomore year and for two-year scholarship winners when they enter their junior year.

Completed applications for four-year Army ROTC scholarships must be postmarked by November 15 of a high school student's senior year. Applications for two- and three-year scholarships are usually due by March of a college student's freshman and sophomore years. Since special application forms and procedures are required, interested students should contact Army ROTC for information well before these deadlines.

ARMY NURSE CORPS

Army ROTC offers two-, three-, and four-year scholarships to qualified students who are seeking bachelor's degrees in nursing. Army ROTC nurse candidates join the Army Nurse Corps upon graduation from an accredited nursing program, successful completion of a state board examination, and commissioning as Army Officers.

The management training provided through Army ROTC is just as important to a nursing career as it is to any other career, and nursing students enrolled in Army ROTC can receive special nursing leadership experiences.

In the summer between their junior and senior years, ROTC nursing Cadets attend the ROTC Nurse Summer Training Program (NSTP). NSTP allows ROTC nurse Cadets to develop both leadership and nursing skills. It introduces the Cadets to the Army Medical Department and the roles and responsibilities of an Army Nurse Corps Officer. NSTP Cadets report to Army hospitals for clinical training under the supervision of Army Nurse Corps office "preceptors." These professionals work one-on-one with the Cadets throughout the training, which concentrates on "hands-on" experiences in areas like medical-surgical wards and intensive care units.

The Army also provides Army nurses specialty training. Army nurses can apply for clinical specialty courses in such areas as obstetrics/gynecology, critical care, perioperative, and psychiatric health nursing. They can also become nurse anesthetists.

In addition to training, the Army offers nurses many unique benefits. Army nurses serve around the world, get thirty days paid vacation from the start of their career, and don't lose seniority when changing geographical areas or specialties.

OPPORTUNITIES FOR SCIENCE OR ENGINEERING STUDENTS

Army scientists designed America's first earth satellite, developed the first operational computer, and devised innovative production methods for transistors and titanium, among other scientific discoveries. All this was accomplished by giving priority to scientific knowledge and investing in students who put their scientific skills to work while serving the nation.

As Army Officers, students have exciting opportunities to be a part of world-class science from the very beginning of their careers. The Army also provides many students fully funded graduate tuition programs for approved courses of study. No matter which scientific or technical course of college study students choose, the Army offers them a chance to gain technical skills and leadership experience sooner and in more fields than any other employer.

THE SIMULTANEOUS MEMBERSHIP PROGRAM

The Simultaneous Membership Program (SMP) allows students to attend college, participate in Army ROTC, serve part time in the Army National Guard or Army Reserve, and receive generous Army benefits.

SMP Cadets receive their Guard or Reserve pay; G.I. Bill benefits, if eligible; and a monthly ROTC allowance. In many states, Guard and Reserve members are eligible for additional state benefits. In some states, this includes free tuition at state-supported colleges and universities.

OPPORTUNITIES FOR VETERANS

Veterans who attend college may enroll in Army ROTC and participate in the two-year program. Their prior military service could fulfill the requirements for the Basic Course, so they could start ROTC in the Advanced Course.

In addition to the Veterans Administration benefits to which they are already entitled, veterans in ROTC receive the annual ROTC allowance each school year and may apply for ROTC scholarships.

Soldiers who have two years of active duty may be eligible for an Army ROTC scholarship. These "Green-to-Gold" scholarships allow selected soldiers to be released from the Army in order to attend college. Interested soldiers should contact the nearest on-campus Army ROTC office or their installation Education Offices for details.

WHAT DOES BECOMING AN ARMY OFFICER MEAN?

Army Officers are leaders, thinkers, doers, and decision makers, proudly serving their country in a role that is vital to the national defense. They are required to have traits such as courage, confidence, integrity, and self-discipline.

In Army, ROTC graduates start out as Second Lieutenants. Most become eligible for promotion and new job assignments at regular intervals.

In addition to their pay, they qualify for excellent medical, educational, and retirement benefits as well as other entitlements.

In the active Army, ROTC graduates have the opportunity to serve on Army posts located across the nation as well as abroad. In the Army National Guard or Army Reserve, they are able to serve close to where they live and work.

ADDITIONAL INFORMATION

To get more information about Army ROTC and any of the specific programs described here, students should call 800-USA-ROTC (toll-free) or contact the Professor of Military Science at a college hosting Army ROTC. Students can also write: Army ROTC Opportunities, P.O. Box 171045, Salt Lake City, Utah 84117-9943. Information about Army ROTC is also available at www.armyrotc.com.

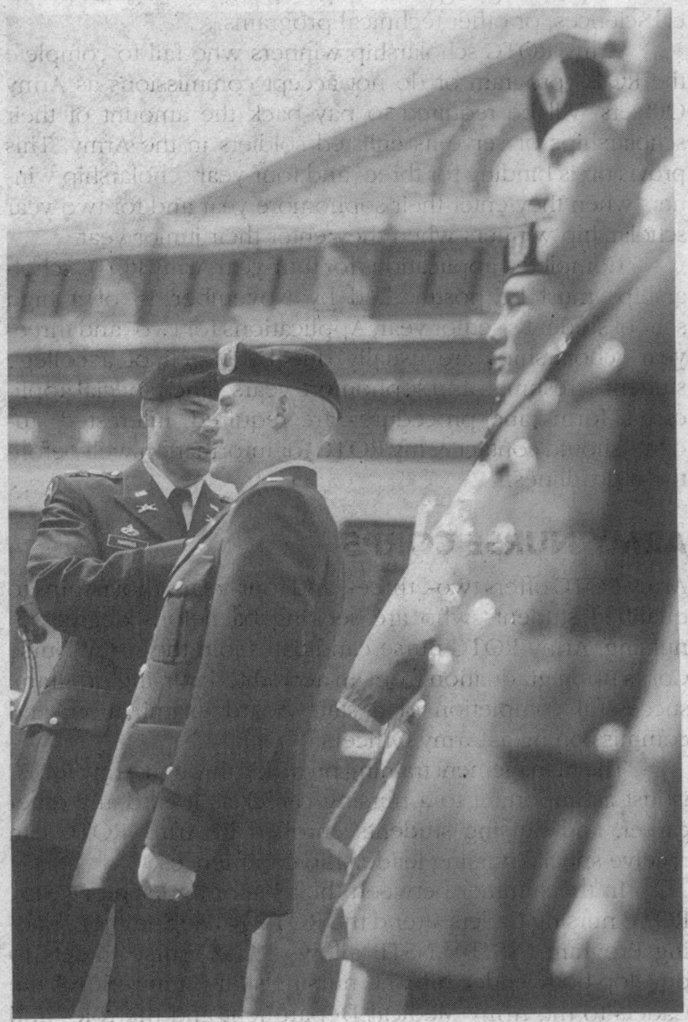

Army ROTC Colleges and Universities

Army ROTC is offered at the following colleges and universities. Students at other institutions can often take ROTC at a nearby college campus; note that affiliated schools may cross state boundaries. The four-digit code that follows each institution name should be used to identify the college when seeking further information.

ALABAMA

†• Alabama Agricultural and Mechanical University, Normal (1002)
■ Auburn University, Auburn (1009)
‡ Auburn University at Montgomery, Montgomery (8310)
‡ Jacksonville State University, Jacksonville (1020)
○ Marion Military Institute, Marion (1026)
■• Tuskegee University, Tuskegee (1050)
■ University of Alabama, Tuscaloosa (1051)
■ University of Alabama at Birmingham, Birmingham (1052)
‡ University of North Alabama, Florence (1016)
■ University of South Alabama, Mobile (1057)

ALASKA

† University of Alaska Fairbanks, Fairbanks (1063)

ARIZONA

■ Arizona State University, Tempe (1081)
■ Northern Arizona University, Flagstaff (2082)
■ University of Arizona, Tucson (1083)

ARKANSAS

■ Arkansas State University, State University (1090)
■ University of Arkansas, Fayetteville (1108)
‡• University of Arkansas at Pine Bluff, Pine Bluff (1086)
‡ University of Central Arkansas, Conway (1092)

CALIFORNIA

† California Polytechnic State University, San Luis Obispo (1143)
■ California State University, Fresno (1147)
California State University, Fullerton (1137)
† Claremont-McKenna College, Claremont (1168)
■ San Diego State University, San Diego (1151)
† Santa Clara University, Santa Clara (1326)
† University of California, Berkeley (1312)
† University of California, Davis (1313)
■ University of California, Los Angeles (1315)
† University of California, Santa Barbara (1320)
‡ University of San Francisco, San Francisco (1325)
■ University of Southern California, Los Angeles (1328)

COLORADO

† Colorado State University, Fort Collins (1350)
† University of Colorado at Boulder, Boulder (1370)
† University of Colorado at Colorado Springs, Colorado Springs (4509)

CONNECTICUT

■ University of Connecticut, Storrs (1417)

DELAWARE

■ University of Delaware, Newark (1431)

DISTRICT OF COLUMBIA

‡ Georgetown University, Washington (1445)
■• Howard University, Washington (1448)

FLORIDA

† Embry-Riddle Aeronautical University, Daytona (1479)
■• Florida Agricultural and Mechanical University, Tallahassee (1480)
† Florida Institute of Technology, Melbourne (1469)
Florida International University, Miami (9635)
Florida Southern College, Lakeland (1488)
‡ Florida State University, Tallahassee (1489)
■ University of Central Florida, Orlando (3954)
■ University of Florida, Gainesville (1535)
■ University of South Florida, Tampa (1537)
University of Tampa, Tampa (1538)
University of West Florida, Pensacola (3955)

GEORGIA

Augusta State University, Augusta (1552)
‡ Columbus State University, Columbus (1561)
†• Fort Valley State University, Fort Valley (1566)
† Georgia Institute of Technology, Atlanta (1569)
○ Georgia Military College, Milledgeville (1571)
■ Georgia Southern University, Statesboro (1572)
‡ Georgia State University, Atlanta (1574)
‡* North Georgia College, Dahlonega (1585)
† University of Georgia, Athens (1598)

GUAM

University of Guam, Mangilao (3935)

HAWAII

■ University of Hawaii, Honolulu (1610)

IDAHO

‡ Boise State University, Boise (1616)
† University of Idaho, Moscow (1626)

ILLINOIS

Eastern Illinois University, Charleston (1674)
Illinois State University, Normal (1692)
■ Northern Illinois University, DeKalb (1737)
† Southern Illinois University Carbondale, Carbondale (1758)
Southern Illinois University Edwardsville, Edwardsville (1759)
■ University of Illinois at Chicago, Chicago (1776)
‡ University of Illinois at Urbana-Champaign, Champaign (1775)
Western Illinois University, Macomb (1780)
Wheaton College, Wheaton (1781)

INDIANA

‡ Ball State University, Muncie (1786)
‡ Indiana University Bloomington, Bloomington (1809)
■ Indiana University-Purdue University Indianapolis, Indianapolis (1813)
■ Purdue University, West Lafayette (1825)
† Rose-Hulman Institute of Technology, Terre Haute (1830)
† University of Notre Dame, Notre Dame (1840)

IOWA

† Iowa State University of Science and Technology, Ames (1869)
■ University of Iowa, Iowa City (1892)
University of Northern Iowa, Cedar Falls (1890)

KANSAS

† Kansas State University, Manhattan (1928)
■ Pittsburg State University, Pittsburg (1926)
■ University of Kansas, Lawrence (1948)

KENTUCKY

‡ Eastern Kentucky University, Richmond (1963)

* Military College or University
○ Military Junior College
• Historically Black College/University
† Accredited engineering
‡ Accredited nursing
■ Accredited both engineering and nursing

Morehead State University, Morehead (1976)
■University of Kentucky, Lexington (1989)
■University of Louisville, Louisville (1999)
■Western Kentucky University, Bowling Green (2002)

LOUISIANA

‡•Grambling State University, Grambling (2006)
†Louisiana State University and Agricultural and Mechanical College, Baton Rouge (2010)
‡Northwestern State University of Louisiana, Natchitoches (2021)
‡•Southern University and Agricultural and Mechanical College, Baton Rouge (9636)
†Tulane University, New Orleans (2029)

MAINE

■University of Maine, Orono (2053)

MARYLAND

Bowie State College, Bowie (2062)
■Johns Hopkins University, Baltimore (2077)
†Loyola College in Maryland, Baltimore (2078)
McDaniel College, Westminster (2109)
•Morgan State University, Baltimore (2083)
University of Maryland, College Park (2103)

MASSACHUSETTS

†Boston University, Boston (2130)
†Massachusetts Institute of Technology, Cambridge (2178)
■Northeastern University, Boston (2199)
■University of Massachusetts, Amherst (2221)
†Worcester Polytechnic Institute, Worcester (2233)

MICHIGAN

Central Michigan University, Mount Pleasant (2243)
‡Eastern Michigan University, Ypsilanti (2259)
■Michigan State University, East Lansing (2290)
†Michigan Technological University, Houghton (2292)
‡Northern Michigan University, Marquette (2301)
■University of Michigan, Ann Arbor (9092)
†Western Michigan University, Kalamazoo (2330)

MINNESOTA

■Minnesota State University, Mankato, Mankato (2360)
St. John's University, Collegeville (2379)
■University of Minnesota, Minneapolis (3969)

MISSISSIPPI

‡•Alcorn State University, Lorman (2396)
•Jackson State University, Jackson (2410)
†Mississippi State University, Mississippi State (2423)
†University of Mississippi, University (2440)
■University of Southern Mississippi, Hattiesburg (2441)

MISSOURI

‡Central Missouri State University, Warrensburg (2454)
•Lincoln University, Jefferson City (2479)
Missouri Western State College, St. Joseph (2490)
Southwest Missouri State University, Springfield (2503)
‡Truman State University, Kirksville (2495)
■University of Missouri-Columbia, Columbia (2516)
†University of Missouri-Rolla, Rolla (2517)
†Washington University in St. Louis, St. Louis (2520)
○Wentworth Military Academy and Junior College, Lexington (2522)

MONTANA

■Montana State University, Bozeman (2532)
University of Montana, Missoula (2536)

NEBRASKA

‡Creighton University, Omaha (2542)
■University of Nebraska, Lincoln (2565)

NEVADA

■University of Nevada, Reno (2568)

NEW HAMPSHIRE

■University of New Hampshire, Durham (2589)

NEW JERSEY

■Princeton University, Princeton (2627)
†Rutgers, The State University of New Jersey, New Brunswick (6963)
‡Seton Hall University, South Orange (3632)

NEW MEXICO

○New Mexico Military Institute, Roswell (2656)
■New Mexico State University, Las Cruces (2657)
University of New Mexico, Albuquerque (2663)

NEW YORK

Canisius College, Buffalo (2681)
†Clarkson University, Potsdam (2699)
†Cornell University, Ithaca (2711)
Fordham University, Bronx (2722)
†Hofstra University, Hempstead (2732)
‡Niagara University, Niagara (2788)
†Rochester Institute of Technology, Rochester (2806)
St. Bonaventure University, St. Bonaventure (2817)
St. John's University, Jamaica (2823)
Siena College, Loudonville (2816)
State University of New York College at Brockport, Brockport (2841)
■Syracuse University, Syracuse (2882)

NORTH CAROLINA

Appalachian State University, Boone (2906)
Campbell University, Buies Creek (2913)
■Duke University, Durham (2920)
‡East Carolina University, Greenville (2923)
Elizabeth City State University, Elizabeth City (2926)
■•North Carolina Agricultural and Technical State University, Greensboro (2905)
†North Carolina State University at Raleigh, Raleigh (2972)
•St. Augustine's College, Raleigh (2968)
■University of North Carolina at Chapel Hill (2974)
■University of North Carolina at Charlotte, Charlotte (2975)
Wake Forest University, Winston-Salem (2978)

NORTH DAKOTA

†North Dakota State University, Fargo (9265)
■University of North Dakota, Grand Forks (3005)

OHIO

‡Bowling Green State University, Bowling Green (3018)
‡Capital University, Columbus (3023)
•Central State University, Wilberforce (3026)
John Carroll University, Cleveland (3050)
‡Kent University, Kent (3051)
■Ohio State University, Columbus (6883)
†Ohio University, Athens (3100)
■University of Akron, Akron (3123)
■University of Cincinnati, Cincinnati (3125)
†University of Dayton, Dayton (3127)
■University of Toledo, Toledo (3131)
‡Wright State University, Dayton (9168)
Xavier University, Cincinnati (3144)

OKLAHOMA

Cameron University, Lawton (3150)
†Oklahoma State University, Stillwater (3170)
‡University of Central Oklahoma, Edmond (3152)
■University of Oklahoma, Norman (3184)

OREGON

†Oregon State University, Corvallis (3210)
University of Oregon, Eugene (3223)
■University of Portland, Portland (3224)

PENNSYLVANIA

†Bucknell University, Lewisburg (3238)
Dickinson College, Carlisle (3253)
†Drexel University, Philadelphia (3256)
Edinboro University of Pennsylvania, Edinboro (3321)
■Gannon University, Erie (3266)
‡Indiana University of Pennsylvania, Indiana (8810)
†Lehigh University, Bethlehem (3289)
Lock Haven University of Pennsylvania, Lock Haven (3323)
■Pennsylvania State University, University Park Campus, University Park (6965)
Shippensburg University of Pennsylvania, Shippensburg (3326)
‡Slippery Rock University of Pennsylvania, Slippery Rock (3327)
‡Temple University, Pennsylvania (3371)
■University of Pittsburgh, Pittsburgh (3379)
‡University of Scranton, Scranton (3384)
○Valley Forge Military Academy and Junior College, Wayne (3386)
■Widener University, Chester (3313)

---

* Military College or University
○ Military Junior College
• Historically Black College/University
† Accredited engineering
‡ Accredited nursing
■ Accredited both engineering and nursing

PUERTO RICO

■University of Puerto Rico, Mayaguez (3944)
University of Puerto Rico, Rio Piedras Campus, Rio Piedras (7108)

RHODE ISLAND

Providence College, Providence (3406)
■University of Rhode Island, Kingston (3414)

SOUTH CAROLINA

†* The Citadel, Charleston (3423)
■Clemson University, Clemson (3425)
Furman University, Greenville (3434)
Presbyterian College, Clinton (3445)
• South Carolina State University, Orangeburg (3446)
■University of South Carolina, Columbia (3448)
Wofford College, Spartanburg (3457)

SOUTH DAKOTA

† South Dakota School of Mines and Technology, Rapid City (3470)
■South Dakota State University, Brookings (3471)
University of South Dakota, Vermillion (10300)

TENNESSEE

‡ Austin Peay State University, Clarksville (3478)
‡ Carson-Newman College, Jefferson City (3481)
■East Tennessee State University, Johnson City (3487)
‡ Middle Tennessee State University, Murfreesboro (3510)
■Tennessee Technological University, Cookeville (3523)
■The University of Memphis, Memphis (3509)
■University of Tennessee, Knoxville, Knoxville (3530)
† University of Tennessee at Martin, Martin (3531)
■Vanderbilt University, Nashville (3535)

TEXAS

■• Prairie View Agricultural and Mechanical University, Prairie View (3630)
† St. Mary's University of San Antonio, San Antonio (3623)
Sam Houston State University, Huntsville (3606)
‡ Stephen F. Austin State University, Nacogdoches (3624)
Tarleton State University, Stephenville (3631)
† Texas Agricultural and Mechanical University, College Station (10366)
† Texas Agricultural and Mechanical University, Kingsville (3639)
‡ Texas Christian University, Fort Worth (3636)
■Texas State University, San Marcos (3615)
■Texas Tech University, Lubbock (3644)
† University of Houston, Houston (3652)
■University of Texas at Arlington, Arlington (3656)
■University of Texas at Austin, Austin (3658)
■University of Texas at El Paso, El Paso (3661)
‡ University of Texas-Pan American, Edinburg (3599)
■University of Texas at San Antonio, San Antonio (10115)

UTAH

■Brigham Young University, Provo (3670)
■University of Utah, Salt Lake City (3675)
‡ Weber State University, Ogden (3680)

VERMONT

■* Norwich University, Northfield (3692)
■University of Vermont, Burlington (3696)

VIRGINIA

College of William and Mary, Williamsburg (3705)
George Mason University, Fairfax (3749)
‡• Hampton University, Hampton (3714)
‡ James Madison University, Harrisonburg (3721)
‡• Norfolk State University, Norfolk (3765)
■Old Dominion University, Norfolk (3728)
University of Richmond, Richmond (3744)
■University of Virginia, Charlottesville (6968)
†* Virginia Military Institute, Lexington (3753)
† Virginia Polytechnic Institute and State University, Blacksburg (3754)
• Virginia State University, Petersburg (3764)

WASHINGTON

Central Washington University, Ellensburg (3771)
■Eastern Washington University, Cheney (3775)
■Gonzaga University, Spokane (3778)
Pacific Lutheran University, Tacoma (3785)
■Seattle University, Seattle (3790)
■University of Washington, Seattle (3798)
■Washington State University, Pullman (3800)

WEST VIRGINIA

‡ Marshall University, Huntington (3815)
• West Virginia State College, Institute (3826)
■West Virginia University, Morgantown (3827)

WISCONSIN

■Marquette University, Milwaukee (3863)
University of Wisconsin-LaCrosse, LaCrosse (3919)
■University of Wisconsin-Madison, Madison (3895)
‡ University of Wisconsin-Oshkosh, Oshkosh (9630)
University of Wisconsin-Stevens Point, Stevens Point (3924)

WYOMING

■University of Wyoming, Laramie (3932)

* Military College or University
○ Military Junior College
• Historically Black College/University
† Accredited engineering
‡ Accredited nursing
■ Accredited both engineering and nursing

Becoming an Army Officer is an exciting opportunity. And the best part is that, through Army ROTC, a student can become an Officer while pursuing a regular college degree.

There are many ways to obtain a scholarship application or simply more information about Army ROTC. Here are five ways listed below:

1. Contact the Professor of Military Science at one of the colleges or universities listed on the previous pages.
2. Write to: Army ROTC Opportunities
   P.O. Box 171045
   Salt Lake City, UT 84117-9943
3. Call 800-USA-ROTC (toll-free).
4. Call the Army ROTC Adviser nearest you

1st Brigade, Fort Devens, MA	978-796-2243
2nd Brigade, Fort Dix, NJ	609-562-3275
3rd Brigade, Fort Belvoir, VA	703-805-4040
4th Brigade, Fort Bragg, NC	910-396-9652
5th Brigade, Fort Jackson, SC	803-751-2769
6th Brigade, Savannah, GA	912-692-8544
7th Brigade, Fort Knox, KY	502-624-1864
8th Brigade, Redstone Arsenal, AL	256-955-7577
9th Brigade, Great Lakes Naval Station, IL	847-688-3452
10th Brigade, Fort Leonard Wood, MO	573-596-0131 Ext. 6-7217
11th Brigade, Fort Carson, CO	719-526-9261
12th Brigade, Fort Sam Houston, TX	210-295-2006
13th Brigade, Fort Lewis, WA	253-966-7183
14th Brigade, Presidio of Monterey, CA	831-242-7816

5. Check out Army ROTC at www.armyrotc.com.

* Military College or University
○ Military Junior College
• Historically Black College/University
† Accredited engineering
‡ Accredited nursing
■ Accredited both engineering and nursing

How to Use This Guide

MAJORS AND MORE

Here you'll find easy-to-use breakdowns of schools' majors, entrance difficulty, and cost ranges. For a quick look-up, we've also provided a **Geographical Listing of College Close-Ups** and an **Alphabetical Listing of Colleges and Universities.**

Majors

This listing presents hundreds of undergraduate fields of study that are currently offered most widely, according to the colleges' responses on *Peterson's Annual Survey of Undergraduate Institutions*. The majors appear in alphabetical order, each followed by an alphabetical list of the schools that offer a bachelor's-level program in that field. Liberal Arts and Studies indicates a general program with no specified major.

The terms used for the majors are those of the U.S. Department of Education Classification of Instructional Programs (CIP). Many institutions, however, use different terms. Readers should visit www.petersons.com/colleges in order to contact a college and ask for its catalog or refer to the **College Close-Up** in this book for the school's exact terminology. In addition, although the term "major" is used in this guide, some colleges may use other terms, such as "concentration," "program of study," or "field."

Entrance Difficulty

This listing groups colleges by their own assessment of their entrance difficulty level. The colleges were asked to select the level that most closely corresponds to their entrance difficulty. Institutions for which high school class rank and/or standardized test scores do not apply as admission criteria were asked to select the level that best indicates their entrance difficulty as compared to other institutions.

Cost Ranges

Colleges are grouped into thirteen price ranges, from under $2000 to $30,000 and over.

COLLEGE DATA CENTER

The **COLLEGE DATA CENTER** contains basic data in capsule form for quick review and comparison. The following outline of the format shows the section headings and the items that each section covers. Any item that does not apply to a particular college or for which no information was supplied is omitted from that college's listing. **Special Messages,** which appear just below the bulleted highlights, have been written by those colleges that chose to supplement their data with additional information.

Bulleted Highlights

The bulleted highlights section features important information, including the institution's Web site, for quick reference and comparison. The number of possible bulleted highlights that an ideal college listing would have if all survey questions were answered in a timely manner follows. However, not every institution provides all of the information necessary to fill out every bulleted line. In such instances, the line will not appear.

First bullet

Institutional control: ***Private*** institutions are designated as *Private, Independent* (nonprofit), *Proprietary* (profit-making), *Independent religious,* or *Independent* (with a specific religious denomination or affiliation). *Nondenominational* or *denominational* religious orientation is possible and would be indicated. ***Public*** institutions are designated by the source of funding. Designations include *Public, Federally supported, State and locally supported* (local may refer to county, district, or city), *State-related* (funded primarily by the state but administratively autonomous), or *State-, Province-, Commonwealth-* (Puerto Rico), *Territory-* (U.S. territories), *County-, District-* (an educational administrative unit often having boundaries different from units of local government), or *City-supported*.

Religious affiliation is also noted here.

Institutional type: Each institution is classified as one of the following:

Primarily two-year college: Awards baccalaureate degrees, but the vast majority of students are enrolled in two-year programs.

Four-year college: Awards baccalaureate degrees; may also award associate degrees; does not award graduate (postbaccalaureate) degrees.

Five-year college: Awards a five-year baccalaureate in a professional field such as architecture or pharmacy; does not award graduate degrees.

Upper-level institution: Awards baccalaureate degrees, but entering students must have at least two years of previous college-level credit; may also offer graduate degrees.

Comprehensive institution: Awards baccalaureate degrees; may also award associate degrees; offers graduate degree programs, primarily at the master's, specialist's, or professional level, although one or two doctoral programs may be offered.

University: Offers four years of undergraduate work plus graduate degrees through the doctorate in more than two academic or professional fields.

Founding date: If the year an institution was chartered differs from the year when instruction actually began, the earlier date is given.

System or administrative affiliation: Any coordinate institutions or system affiliations are indicated. An institution that has separate colleges or campuses for men and women but shares facilities and courses is termed a coordinate institution. A formal administrative grouping of institutions, either private or public, of which the college is a part, or the name of a single institution with which the college is administratively affiliated, is a system.

Second bullet

Setting: Schools are designated as *urban* (located within a major city), *suburban* (a residential area within commuting distance of a major city), *small-town* (a small but compactly settled area not within commuting distance of a major city), or *rural* (a remote and sparsely populated area). The phrase "easy access to . . ." indicates that the campus is within an hour's drive of the nearest major metropolitan area that has a population greater than 500,000.

Third bullet

Endowment: The total dollar value of funds and/or property donated to the institution or the multicampus educational system of which the institution is a part.

Fourth bullet

Student body: An institution is *coed* (coeducational—admits men and women), *primarily* (80 percent or more) *women, primarily men, women only,* or *men only.* A few schools are designated as *undergraduate: women only; graduate: coed* or *undergraduate: men only; graduate: coed.*

Undergraduate students: Represents the number of full-time and part-time students enrolled in undergraduate degree programs as of fall 2007. The percentage of full-time undergraduates and the percentages of men and women are given.

Fifth bullet

Entrance level: As reported by each school, classifications of levels of entrance difficulty are as follows: *most difficult, very difficult, moderately difficult, minimally difficult,* and *noncompetitive.*

Percent of applicants admitted: The percentage of applicants who were offered admission.

Special Messages

These messages have been written by those colleges that chose to supplement their data with additional, timely, important information.

Category Overviews

Undergraduates

For fall 2007, the number of full- and part-time undergraduate students is listed. This list provides the number of states and U.S. territories, including the District of Columbia and Puerto Rico (or, for Canadian institutions, provinces and territories), and other countries from which undergraduates come. Percentages are given of undergraduates who are from out of state; Native American, African American, and Asian American or Pacific Islander; international students; transfer students; and living on campus.

Retention: The percentage of freshmen (or, for upper-level institutions, entering students) who returned the following year for the fall term.

Freshmen

Admission: Figures are given for the number of students who applied for fall 2007 admission, the number of those who were admitted, and the number who enrolled.

Average high school GPA: Freshman statistics include the average high school GPA.

Test scores: The percentage of freshmen who took the SAT and received critical reading, math, and writing scores above 500, above 600, and above 700; as well as the percentage of freshmen taking the ACT who received a composite score of 18 or higher, 24 or higher, and 30 or higher.

Faculty

Total: The total number of faculty members; the percentage of full-time faculty members as of fall 2007; and the percentage of total faculty members who hold doctoral/first professional/terminal degrees.

Student-faculty ratio: The school's estimate of the ratio of matriculated undergraduate students to faculty members teaching undergraduate courses.

Majors

This section lists the major fields of study offered by the college.

Academics

Calendar: Most colleges indicate one of the following: 4-1-4, 4-4-1, or a similar arrangement (two terms of equal length plus an abbreviated winter or spring term, with the numbers referring to months); semesters; trimesters; quarters; 3-3 (three courses for each of three terms); modular (the academic year is divided into small blocks of time; courses of varying lengths are assembled according to individual programs); or standard year (for most Canadian institutions).

Degrees: This names the full range of levels of certificates, diplomas, and degrees, including prebaccalaureate, graduate, and professional, that are offered by this institution:

Associate degree: Normally requires at least two but fewer than four years of full-time college work or its equivalent.

Bachelor's degree (baccalaureate): Requires at least four years but not more than five years of full-time college-level work or its equivalent. This includes all bachelor's degrees in which the normal four years of work are completed in three years and bachelor's degrees conferred in a five-year cooperative (work-study plan) program. A cooperative plan provides for alternate class attendance and employment in business, industry, or government. This allows students to combine actual work experience with their college studies.

Master's degree: Requires the successful completion of a program of study of at least the full-time equivalent of one but not more than two years of work beyond the bachelor's degree.
Doctoral degree (doctorate): The highest degree in graduate study. The doctoral degree classification includes Doctor of Education, Doctor of Juridical Science, Doctor of Public Health, and the Doctor of Philosophy in any nonprofessional field.
First professional degree: The first postbaccalaureate degree in one of the following fields: chiropractic (DC, DCM), dentistry (DDS, DMD), medicine (MD), optometry (OD), osteopathic medicine (DO), rabbinical and Talmudic studies (MHL, Rav), pharmacy (BPharm, PharmD), podiatry (PodD, DP, DPM), veterinary medicine (DVM), law (JD), or divinity/ministry (BD, MDiv).
First professional certificate (postdegree): Requires completion of an organized program of study after completion of the first professional degree. Examples are refresher courses or additional units of study in a specialty or subspecialty.
Post-master's certificate: Requires completion of an organized program of study of 24 credit hours beyond the master's degree but does not meet the requirements of academic degrees at the doctoral level.

Special study options: Details are next given here on study options available at each college:
Accelerated degree program: Students may earn a bachelor's degree in three academic years.
Academic remediation for entering students: Instructional courses designed for students deficient in the general competencies necessary for a regular postsecondary curriculum and educational setting.
Adult/continuing education programs: Courses offered for nontraditional students who are currently working or are returning to formal education.
Advanced placement: Credit toward a degree awarded for acceptable scores on College Board Advanced Placement (AP) tests.
Cooperative (co-op) education programs: Formal arrangements with off-campus employers allowing students to combine work and study in order to gain degree-related experience, usually extending the time required to complete a degree.
Distance learning: For-credit courses that can be accessed off-campus via cable television, the Internet, satellite, videotape, correspondence course, or other media.
Double major: A program of study in which a student concurrently completes the requirements of two majors.
English as a second language (ESL): A course of study designed specifically for students whose native language is not English.
External degree programs: A program of study in which students earn credits toward a degree through a combination of independent study, college courses, proficiency examinations, and personal experience. External degree programs require minimal or no classroom attendance.
Freshmen honors college: A separate academic program for talented freshmen.
Honors programs: Any special program for very able students offering the opportunity for educational enrichment, independent study, acceleration, or some combination of these.
Independent study: Academic work, usually undertaken outside the regular classroom structure, chosen or designed by the student with departmental approval and instructor supervision.
Internships: Any short-term, supervised work experience usually related to a student's major field, for which the student earns academic credit. The work can be full- or part-time, on or off-campus, paid or unpaid.
Off-campus study: A formal arrangement with one or more domestic institutions under which students may take courses at the other institution(s) for credit.
Part-time degree programs: Students may earn a degree through part-time enrollment in regular session (daytime) classes or evening, weekend, or summer classes.
Self-designed major: Program of study based on individual interests, designed by the student with the assistance of an adviser.
Services for LD students: Special help for learning-disabled students with resolvable difficulties, such as dyslexia.
Study abroad: An arrangement by which a student completes part of the academic program studying in another country. A college may operate a campus abroad or it may have a cooperative agreement with other U.S. institutions or institutions in other countries.
Summer session for credit: Summer courses through which students may make up degree work or accelerate their program.

ROTC: Army, Naval, or Air Force Reserve Officers' Training Corps programs offered either on campus, at a branch campus [designated by a (b)], or at a cooperating host institution [designated by (c)].

Unusual degree programs: Nontraditional programs such as a 3-2 degree program, in which 3 years of liberal arts study is followed by 2 years of study in a professional field at another institution (or in a professional division of the same institution), resulting in two bachelor's degrees or a bachelor's and a master's degree.

Computers on Campus

This paragraph includes information on the numbers of computers/terminals and ports available on campus for general student use and what computer technology is accessible to students. Information is also given on the availability of a campuswide network, the percentage of college-owned or -operated housing units wired for high-speed Internet access, and the availability of a wireless campus network.

Student Life

Housing options: The institution's policy about whether students are permitted to live off-campus or are required to live on campus for a specified period; whether freshmen-only, coed, single-sex, cooperative, and disabled student housing options are available; whether campus housing is leased by the school and/or provided by a third party; whether freshman applicants are given priority for college housing. The phrase "college housing not available" indicates that no college-owned or -operated housing facilities are provided for undergraduates and that noncommuting students must arrange for their own accommodations.

Activities and organizations: Lists information on drama/theater groups, choral groups, marching bands, student-run campus newspapers, student-run radio stations, and social organizations (sororities, fraternities, eating clubs, etc.) and how many are represented on campus.

Campus security: Campus safety measures including 24-hour emergency response devices (telephones and alarms) and patrols by trained security personnel, student patrols, late-night transport-escort service, and controlled dormitory access (key, security card, etc.).

Student services: Information provided indicates services offered to students by the college, such as legal services, health clinics, personal-psychological counseling, and women's centers.

Athletics

Membership in one or more of the following athletic associations is indicated by initials.

NCAA: National Collegiate Athletic Association

NAIA: National Association of Intercollegiate Athletics

NCCAA: National Christian College Athletic Association

NSCAA: National Small College Athletic Association

NJCAA: National Junior College Athletic Association

CIS: Canadian Interuniversity Sport

The overall NCAA division in which all or most intercollegiate teams compete is designated by a roman numeral I, II, or III. All teams that do not compete in this division are listed as exceptions.

Sports offered by the college are divided into two groups: **Intercollegiate** ("M" or "W" following the name of each sport indicates that it is offered for men or women) and **Intramural.** An "s" in parentheses following an "M" or "W" for an intercollegiate sport indicates that athletic scholarships (or grants-in-aid) are offered for men or women in that sport, and a "c" indicates a club team as opposed to a varsity team.

Standardized Tests

The most commonly required standardized tests are the ACT, SAT, and SAT Subject Tests. These and other standardized tests may be used for selective admission, as a basis for counseling or course placement, or for both purposes. This section notes if a test is used for admission or placement and whether it is required, required for some, or recommended.

In addition to the ACT and SAT, the following standardized entrance and placement examinations are referred to by their initials:

ABLE: Adult Basic Learning Examination

ACT ASSET: ACT Assessment of Skills for Successful Entry and Transfer

ACT PEP: ACT Proficiency Examination Program

CAT: California Achievement Tests

CELT: Comprehensive English Language Test

CPAt: Career Programs Assessment

CPT: Computerized Placement Test

DAT: Differential Aptitude Test

LSAT: Law School Admission Test

MAPS: Multiple Assessment Program Service

MCAT: Medical College Admission Test

MMPI: Minnesota Multiphasic Personality Inventory

OAT: Optometry Admission Test

PAA: Prueba de Aptitud Académica (Spanish-language version of the SAT)

PCAT: Pharmacy College Admission Test

PSAT: Preliminary SAT

SCAT: Scholastic College Aptitude Test

TABE: Test of Adult Basic Education

TASP: Texas Academic Skills Program

TOEFL: Test of English as a Foreign Language (for international students whose native language is not English)

WPCT: Washington Pre-College Test

Costs

Costs are given for the 2008–09 academic year or for the 2007–08 academic year if 2008–09 figures were not yet available. Annual expenses may be expressed as a comprehensive fee (including full-time tuition, mandatory fees, and college room and board) or as separate figures for full-time tuition, fees, room and board, or room only. For public institutions where tuition differs according to residence, separate figures are given for area or state residents and for nonresidents. Part-time tuition is expressed in terms of a per-unit rate (per credit, per semester hour, etc.) as specified by the institution.

The tuition structure at some institutions is complex in that freshmen and sophomores may be charged a different rate from that for juniors and seniors, a professional or vocational division may have a different fee structure from the liberal arts division of the same institution, or part-time tuition may be prorated on a sliding scale according to the number of credit hours taken. Tuition and fees may vary according to academic program, campus/location, class time (day, evening, weekend), course/credit load, course level, degree level, reciprocity agreements, and student level. Room and board charges are reported as an average for one academic year and may vary according to the board plan selected, campus/location, type of housing facility, or student level. If no college-owned or -operated housing facilities are offered, the phrase "college housing not available" will appear in the Housing section of the Student Life paragraph.

Tuition payment plans that may be offered to undergraduates include tuition prepayment, installment payments, and deferred payment. A tuition prepayment plan gives a student the option of locking in the current tuition rate for the entire term of enrollment by paying the full amount in advance rather than year by year. Colleges that offer such a prepayment plan may also help the student to arrange financing.

The availability of full or partial undergraduate tuition waivers to minority students, children of alumni, employees or their children, adult students, and senior citizens may be listed.

Financial Aid

Financial aid information presented represents aid awarded to undergraduates for the available academic year. Figures are given for the number of undergraduates who applied for aid, the number who were judged to have need, and the number who had their need met. The number of Federal Work-Study Programs and/or part-time jobs and average earnings are listed, as well as the number of non-need-based awards that were made. Non-need-based awards are college-administered scholarships for which the college determines the recipient and amount of each award. These scholarships are awarded to full-time undergraduates on the basis of merit or personal attributes without regard to need, although they many certainly be given to students who also happen to need aid. The **Average percent of need met** for those determined to have need, **Average financial aid package** awarded to undergraduates (the amount of scholarships, grants, work-study payments, or loans in the institutionally administered financial aid package divided by the number of students who received any financial aid-amounts used to pay the officially designated Expected Family Contribution (EFC), such as PLUS or other alternative loans, are excluded from the amounts reported), **Average need-based loan, Average need-based gift aid,** and **Average non-need-based aid** are given. **Average indebtedness upon graduation,** which is the average per-borrower indebtedness of the last graduating undergraduate class from amounts borrowed at this institution through any loan programs, excluding parent loans, is listed last.

Applying

Application and admission **Options** include the following:

Early admission: Highly qualified students may matriculate before graduating from high school.

Early action plan: An admission plan that allows students to apply and be notified of an admission decision well in advance of the regular notification dates. If accepted, the candidate is not committed to enroll; students may reply to the offer under the college's regular reply policy.

Deferred entrance: The practice of permitting accepted students to postpone enrollment, usually for a period of one academic term or year.

Early decision deadline: A plan that permits students to apply and be notified of an admission decision (and financial aid offer, if applicable) well in advance of the regular notification date. Applicants agree to accept an offer of admission and to withdraw their applications from other colleges. Candidates who are not accepted under early decision are automatically considered with the regular applicant pool, without prejudice.

Application fee: The fee required with an application is noted. This is typically nonrefundable, although under certain specified conditions it may be waived or returned.

Required, Required for some, and Recommended: Other application requirements are grouped into three categories: Required, Required for some, and Recommended. They may include an essay, standardized test scores, a high school transcript, a minimum high school grade point average (expressed as a number on a scale of 0 to 4.0, where 4.0 equals A, 3.0 equals B, etc.), letters of recommendation, an interview on campus or with local alumni, and, for certain types of schools or programs, special requirements such as a musical audition or an art portfolio.

Application deadlines and Notification: Admission application deadlines and dates for notification of acceptance or rejection are given either as specific dates or as rolling and continuous. *Rolling* means that applications are processed as they are received, and qualified students are accepted as long as there are openings. *Continuous* means that applicants are notified of acceptance or rejection as applications are processed up until the date indicated or the actual beginning of classes. The application deadline and the notification date for transfers are given if they differ from the dates for freshmen. Early decision and early action application deadlines and notification dates are also indicated when relevant.

Admissions Contact

The name, title, and telephone number of the person to contact for application information are given. The admission office address is listed. Toll-free telephone numbers may also be included. The admission office fax number and e-mail address, if available, are listed, provided the school wanted them printed for use by prospective students.

Additional Information

Each college that has a **College Close-Up** in the guide will have a cross-reference referring you directly to that **College Close-Up.**

College Close-Ups

More than 700 two-page narrative descriptions provide an inside look at colleges and universities, shifting the focus to a variety of other factors, some of them intangible, that should also be considered. The descriptions provide a wealth of statistics that are crucial components in the college decision-making equation—components such as tuition, financial aid, and major fields of study. Prepared exclusively by college officials, the descriptions are designed to help give students a better sense of the individuality of each institution, in terms that include campus environment, student activities, and lifestyle. Such quality-of-life intangibles can be the deciding factors in the college selection process. The absence of any college or university does not constitute an editorial decision on the part of Peterson's. In essence, these descriptions are an open forum for colleges and universities, on a voluntary basis, to communicate their particular message to prospective college students. The colleges included have paid a fee to Peterson's to provide this information. The **College Close-Ups** are edited to provide a consistent format across entries for your ease of comparison.

2008–09 CHANGES IN INSTITUTIONS

Following is an alphabetical listing of institutions that have recently closed, merged with other institutions, or changed their name or status. In the case of a name change, the former name appears first, followed by the new name.

Aakers College (Fargo, ND): name changed to Rasmussen College Fargo.

Albertson College of Idaho (Caldwell, ID): name changed to The College of Idaho.

Alliance University College (Calgary, AB): name changed to Ambrose University College.

American InterContinental University (Atlanta, GA): name changed to American InterContinental University Buckhead Campus.

American InterContinental University (Atlanta, GA): name changed to American InterContinental University Dunwoody Campus.

Barnes-Jewish College of Nursing and Allied Health (St. Louis, MO): name changed to Barnes-Jewish College, Goldfarb School of Nursing.

Bethune-Cookman College (Daytona Beach, FL): name changed to Bethune-Cookman University.

Beulah Heights Bible College (Atlanta, GA): name changed to Beulah Heights University.

California College for Health Sciences (Salt Lake City, UT): name changed to Independence University.

Central Pentecostal College (Saskatoon, SK): name changed to Horizon College & Seminary.

City University (Bellevue, WA): name changed to City University of Seattle.

College Misericordia (Dallas, PA): name changed to Misericordia University.

Colorado Technical University (Colorado Springs, CO): name changed to Colorado Technical University–Colorado Springs.

Colorado Technical University Denver Campus (Greenwood Village, CO): name changed to Colorado Technical University–Denver.

Colorado Technical University Sioux Falls Campus (Sioux Falls, SD): name changed to Colorado Technical University–Sioux Falls.

Columbia College (New York, NY) now reporting as Columbia University.

Concordia University (River Forest, IL): name changed to Concordia University Chicago.

Concordia University (Seward, NE): name changed to Concordia University, Nebraska.

Concordia University at Austin (Austin, TX): name changed to Concordia University Texas.

Columbia University, The Fu Foundation School of Engineering and Applied Science (New York, NY): now reporting as Columbia University.

Crown College (Tacoma, WA): no longer eligible.

DeVry Institute of Technology (Long Island City, NY): name changed to DeVry College of New York.

DeVry University (Broomfield, CO): closed.

ECPI College of Technology (Newport News, VA): closed.

Florida Memorial College (Miami-Dade, FL): name changed to Florida Memorial University.

Florida Metropolitan University–Brandon Campus (Tampa, FL): name changed to Everest University.

Florida Metropolitan University–Jacksonville Campus (Jacksonville, FL): name changed to Everest University.

Florida Metropolitan University–Lakeland Campus (Lakeland, FL): name changed to Everest University.

Florida Metropolitan University–Melbourne Campus (Melbourne, FL): name changed to Everest University.

Florida Metropolitan University–North Orlando Campus (Orlando, FL): name changed to Everest University.

Florida Metropolitan University–Pinellas Campus (Clearwater, FL): name changed to Everest University.

Florida Metropolitan University–Pompano Beach Campus (Pompano Beach, FL): name changed to Everest University.

Florida Metropolitan University–South Orlando Campus (Orlando, FL): name changed to Everest University.

Florida Metropolitan University–Tampa Campus (Tampa, FL): name changed to Everest University.

Full Sail Real World Education (Winter Park, FL): name changed to Full Sail University.

Hamilton College (Cedar Falls, IA): name changed to Kaplan University-Cedar Falls.

Hamilton College (Cedar Rapids, IA): name changed to Kaplan University-Cedar Rapids.

Hamilton College-Omaha (Omaha, NE): name changed to Kaplan University-Omaha.

Hawai'i Theological Seminary (Honolulu, HI): no longer eligible.

International Academy of Design & Technology (Fairmont, WV): closed.

International Institute of the Americas (Phoenix, AZ): closed.

Judson College (Elgin, IL): name changed to Judson University.

Kaplan University (Davenport, IA): name changed to Kaplan University-Davenport.

Long Island University, Global College (Brooklyn, NY): name changed to Global College of Long Island University.

Massachusetts College of Art (Boston, MA): name changed to Massachusetts College of Art and Design.

McKendree College (Lebanon, IL): name changed to McKendree University.

New College of California (San Francisco, CA): no longer eligible.

Open Learning Agency (Burnaby, BC): name changed to Thompson Rivers University, Open Learning.

Paul Smith's College of Arts and Sciences (Paul Smiths, NY): name changed to Paul Smith's College.

Puget Sound Christian College (Everett, WA): closed.

Regions University (Montgomery, AL): name changed to Amridge University.

Remington College–Denver Campus (Lakewood, CO): closed.

Remington College–Tempe Campus (Tempe, AZ): closed.

Sheldon Jackson College (Sitka, AK): closed.

Simon's Rock College of Bard (Great Barrington, MA): name changed to Bard College at Simon's Rock.

St. Mary's University of San Antonio (San Antonio, TX): name changed to St. Mary's University.

State University of New York College at Brockport (Brockport, NY): name changed to The College at Brockport, State University of New York.

Touro University International (Cypress, CA): name changed to TUI University.

University of Colorado at Denver and Health Sciences Center (Denver, CO): closed.

University of Colorado at Denver and Health Sciences Center (Denver, CO): name changed to University of Colorado Denver.

University of Judaism (Bel Air, CA): name changed to American Jewish University.

University of Missouri–Rolla (Rolla, MO): name changed to Missouri University of Science and Technology.

University of Phoenix Online Campus (Phoenix, AZ): name changed to University of Phoenix.

Walla Walla College (College Place, WA): name changed to Walla Walla University.

Waynesburg College (Waynesburg, PA): name changed to Waynesburg University.

Webster College (Holiday, FL): name changed to Rasmussen College Pasco County.

Wilmington College (New Castle, DE): name changed to Wilmington University.

Winston-Salem Bible College (Winston-Salem, NC): name changed to Carolina Christian College.

Zion Bible Institute (Barrington, RI): name changed to Zion Bible College.

DATA COLLECTION PROCEDURES

The data contained in the **COLLEGE DATA CENTER** and **MAJORS AND MORE** sections were researched between fall 2007 and spring 2008 through *Peterson's Annual Survey of Undergraduate Institutions*. Questionnaires were sent to the more than 2,000 colleges and universities that met the outlined inclusion criteria. All data included in this edition have been submitted by officials (usually admissions and financial aid officers, registrars, or institutional research personnel) at the colleges. In addition, many of the institutions that submitted data were contacted directly by the Peterson's research staff to verify unusual figures, resolve discrepancies, or obtain additional data. All usable information received in time for publication has been included. The omission of any particular item from the **COLLEGE DATA CENTER** and **MAJORS AND MORE** sections signifies that the information is either not applicable to that institution or not available. Because of Peterson's comprehensive editorial review and because all material comes directly from college officials, we believe that the information presented in this guide is accurate. You should check with a specific college or university at the time of application to verify such figures as tuition and fees, which may have changed since the publication of this volume.

CRITERIA FOR INCLUSION IN THIS BOOK

The term "four-year college" is the commonly used designation for institutions that grant the baccalaureate degree. Four years is the expected amount of time required to earn this degree, although some bachelor's degree programs may be completed in three years, others require five years, and part-time programs may take considerably longer. Upper-level institutions offer only the junior and senior years and accept only students with two years of college-level credit. Therefore, "four-year college" is a conventional term that accurately describes most of the institutions included in this guide, but should not be taken literally in all cases.

To be included in this guide, an institution must have full accreditation or be a candidate for accreditation (preaccreditation) status by an institutional or specialized accrediting body recognized by the U.S. Department of Education or the Council for Higher Education Accreditation (CHEA). Institutional accrediting bodies, which review each institution as a whole, include the six regional associations of schools and colleges (Middle States, New England, North Central, Northwest, Southern, and Western), each of which is responsible for a specified portion of the United States and its territories. Other institutional accrediting bodies are national in scope and accredit specific kinds of institutions (e.g., Bible colleges, independent colleges, and rabbinical and Talmudic schools). Program registration by the New York State Board of Regents is considered to be the equivalent of institutional accreditation, since the board requires that all programs offered by an institution meet its standards before recognition is granted. A Canadian institution must be chartered and authorized to grant degrees by the provincial government, affiliated with a chartered institution, or accredited by a recognized U.S. accrediting body. This guide also includes institutions outside the United States that are accredited by these U.S. accrediting bodies. There are recognized specialized or professional accrediting bodies in more than forty different fields, each of which is authorized to accredit institutions or specific programs in its particular field. For specialized institutions that offer programs in one field only, we designate this to be the equivalent of institutional accreditation. A full explanation of the accrediting process and complete information on recognized, institutional (regional and national) and specialized accrediting bodies can be found online at www.chea.org or at www.ed.gov/admins/finaid/accred/index.html.

Majors and More

Majors

ACCOUNTING

Abilene Christian U (TX)
Adelphi U (NY)
Adrian Coll (MI)
Alabama Ag and Mech U (AL)
Alabama State U (AL)
Albertus Magnus Coll (CT)
Albright Coll (PA)
Alcorn State U (MS)
Alderson-Broaddus Coll (WV)
Alfred U (NY)
Alma Coll (MI)
Alvernia Coll (PA)
Amberton U (TX)
The American U of Athens (Greece)
Anderson U (IN)
Anderson U (SC)
Andrews U (MI)
Angelo State U (TX)
Appalachian State U (NC)
Aquinas Coll (MI)
Arizona State U (AZ)
Arizona State U at the West campus (AZ)
Arkansas State U (AR)
Asbury Coll (KY)
Ashford U (IA)
Ashland U (OH)
Assumption Coll (MA)
Athabasca U (AB, Canada)
Athens State U (AL)
Atlantic Union Coll (MA)
Auburn U (AL)
Auburn U Montgomery (AL)
Augsburg Coll (MN)
Augustana Coll (IL)
Augustana Coll (SD)
Augusta State U (GA)
Averett U (VA)
Avila U (MO)
Azusa Pacific U (CA)
Babson Coll (MA)
Baker Coll of Auburn Hills (MI)
Baker Coll of Owosso (MI)
Baker U (KS)
Baldwin-Wallace Coll (OH)
Ball State U (IN)
Barry U (FL)
Barton Coll (NC)
Baylor U (TX)
Belhaven Coll (MS)
Bellarmine U (KY)
Belmont Abbey Coll (NC)
Belmont U (TN)
Bemidji State U (MN)
Benedictine Coll (KS)
Benedictine U (IL)
Bentley Coll (MA)
Bernard M. Baruch Coll of the City U of New York (NY)
Berry Coll (GA)
Bethany Coll (KS)
Bethany Coll (WV)
Bethune-Cookman U (FL)
Bishop's U (QC, Canada)
Blackburn Coll (IL)
Bloomfield Coll (NJ)
Bloomsburg U of Pennsylvania (PA)
Bluefield Coll (VA)
Bluefield State Coll (WV)
Bluffton U (OH)
Bob Jones U (SC)
Boise State U (ID)
Boston Coll (MA)
Boston U (MA)
Bowling Green State U (OH)
Bradley U (IL)
Brenau U (GA)
Brewton-Parker Coll (GA)
Bridgewater State Coll (MA)
Brigham Young U (UT)
British Columbia Inst of Technology (BC, Canada)
Brock U (ON, Canada)
Brown Mackie Coll–Tucson (AZ)
Bucknell U (PA)
Butler U (IN)
Cabrini Coll (PA)
California Baptist U (CA)
California Lutheran U (CA)
California State Polytechnic U, Pomona (CA)
California State U, Chico (CA)
California State U, Dominguez Hills (CA)
California State U, East Bay (CA)
California State U, Fresno (CA)
California State U, Fullerton (CA)
California State U, Long Beach (CA)
California State U, San Bernardino (CA)
California State U, San Marcos (CA)
Calumet Coll of Saint Joseph (IN)
Calvin Coll (MI)
Cameron U (OK)
Canisius Coll (NY)
Capital U (OH)
Carlow U (PA)
Carroll Coll (WI)
Carson-Newman Coll (TN)
Case Western Reserve U (OH)
Castleton State Coll (VT)
The Catholic U of America (DC)
Cedar Crest Coll (PA)
Cedarville U (OH)
Centenary Coll (NJ)
Centenary Coll of Louisiana (LA)
Central Christian Coll of Kansas (KS)
Central Coll (IA)
Central Connecticut State U (CT)
Central Michigan U (MI)
Central State U (OH)
Central Washington U (WA)
Chaminade U of Honolulu (HI)
Chapman U (CA)
Chatham U (PA)
Chestnut Hill Coll (PA)
Christopher Newport U (VA)
City U of Seattle (WA)
Claremont McKenna Coll (CA)
Clarion U of Pennsylvania (PA)
Clark Atlanta U (GA)
Clarke Coll (IA)
Clarkson U (NY)
Clayton State U (GA)
Clearwater Christian Coll (FL)
Cleary U (MI)
Clemson U (SC)
Cleveland State U (OH)
Coastal Carolina U (SC)
The Coll at Brockport, State U of New York (NY)
Coll of Charleston (SC)
The Coll of Idaho (ID)
Coll of Mount St. Joseph (OH)
The Coll of New Jersey (NJ)
Coll of Saint Benedict (MN)
Coll of St. Joseph (VT)
The Coll of Saint Rose (NY)
The Coll of St. Scholastica (MN)
Coll of Staten Island of the City U of New York (NY)
Coll of the Holy Cross (MA)
Coll of the Ozarks (MO)
Coll of the Southwest (NM)
Colorado State U (CO)
Colorado State U-Pueblo (CO)
Colorado Tech U—Colorado Springs (CO)
Colorado Tech U—Denver (CO)
Colorado Tech U—North Kansas City (MO)
Colorado Tech U—Online (CO)
Colorado Tech U—Sioux Falls (SD)
Columbia Coll (SC)
Columbus State U (GA)
Concordia Coll (MN)
Concordia U (QC, Canada)
Concordia U Chicago (IL)
Concordia U, Nebraska (NE)
Concordia U, St. Paul (MN)
Concordia U Wisconsin (WI)
Concord U (WV)
Converse Coll (SC)
Cornerstone U (MI)
Creighton U (NE)
Culver-Stockton Coll (MO)
Daemen Coll (NY)
Dakota State U (SD)
Dakota Wesleyan U (SD)
Dallas Baptist U (TX)
Dana Coll (NE)
Davenport U, Dearborn (MI)
Davenport U, Grand Rapids (MI)
Davis & Elkins Coll (WV)
Defiance Coll (OH)
Delaware Valley Coll (PA)
Delta State U (MS)
DePaul U (IL)
DeSales U (PA)
Dillard U (LA)
Dixie State Coll of Utah (UT)
Doane Coll (NE)
Dominican Coll (NY)
Dominican U (IL)
Dordt Coll (IA)
Dowling Coll (NY)
Drake U (IA)
Drexel U (PA)
Drury U (MO)
Duquesne U (PA)
D'Youville Coll (NY)
East Carolina U (NC)
East Central U (OK)
Eastern Connecticut State U (CT)
Eastern Illinois U (IL)
Eastern Kentucky U (KY)
Eastern Mennonite U (VA)
Eastern Michigan U (MI)
Eastern New Mexico U (NM)
East Tennessee State U (TN)
East Texas Baptist U (TX)
East-West U (IL)
Elizabethtown Coll (PA)
Elon U (NC)
Emory & Henry Coll (VA)
Emory U (GA)
Emporia State U (KS)
Everest U, Tampa (FL)
Everest U, Tampa (FL)
Excelsior Coll (NY)
Fairfield U (CT)
Fairleigh Dickinson U, Coll at Florham (NJ)
Fairleigh Dickinson U, Metropolitan Campus (NJ)
Fairmont State U (WV)
Faulkner U (AL)
Fayetteville State U (NC)
Felician Coll (NJ)
Ferrum Coll (VA)
Fitchburg State Coll (MA)
Flagler Coll (FL)
Florida Ag and Mech U (FL)
Florida Atlantic U (FL)
Florida Gulf Coast U (FL)
Florida Inst of Technology (FL)
Florida Intl U (FL)
Florida Memorial U (FL)
Florida Southern Coll (FL)
Florida State U (FL)
Fontbonne U (MO)
Fort Lewis Coll (CO)
Franciscan U of Steubenville (OH)
Francis Marion U (SC)
Franklin Coll (IN)
Freed-Hardeman U (TN)
Fresno Pacific U (CA)
Frostburg State U (MD)
Furman U (SC)
Gannon U (PA)
Gardner-Webb U (NC)
George Mason U (VA)
Georgetown Coll (KY)
Georgetown U (DC)
The George Washington U (DC)
Georgia Coll & State U (GA)
Georgian Court U (NJ)
Georgia Southern U (GA)
Georgia Southwestern State U (GA)
Georgia State U (GA)
Gettysburg Coll (PA)
Golden Gate U (CA)
Goldey-Beacom Coll (DE)
Gonzaga U (WA)
Gordon Coll (MA)
Grace Bible Coll (MI)
Grace Coll (IN)
Grace U (NE)
Grambling State U (LA)
Grand Canyon U (AZ)
Grand Valley State U (MI)
Grand View Coll (IA)
Greensboro Coll (NC)
Greenville Coll (IL)
Grove City Coll (PA)
Guilford Coll (NC)
Gustavus Adolphus Coll (MN)
Gwynedd-Mercy Coll (PA)
Hampton U (VA)
Hannibal-LaGrange Coll (MO)
Harding U (AR)
Hardin-Simmons U (TX)
Harris-Stowe State U (MO)
Hartwick Coll (NY)
Hastings Coll (NE)
Hawai'i Pacific U (HI)
HEC Montreal (QC, Canada)
Heidelberg Coll (OH)
Henderson State U (AR)
Hendrix Coll (AR)
High Point U (NC)
Hilbert Coll (NY)
Hillsdale Coll (MI)
Hofstra U (NY)
Holy Family U (PA)
Hope Coll (MI)
Houghton Coll (NY)
Houston Baptist U (TX)
Howard Payne U (TX)
Humboldt State U (CA)
Hunter Coll of the City U of New York (NY)
Huntingdon Coll (AL)
Huntington U (IN)
Husson Coll (ME)
Huston-Tillotson U (TX)
Idaho State U (ID)
Illinois Coll (IL)
Illinois State U (IL)
Illinois Wesleyan U (IL)
Immaculata U (PA)
Indiana State U (IN)
Indiana U of Pennsylvania (PA)
Indiana U–Purdue U Fort Wayne (IN)
Indiana Wesleyan U (IN)
Inter American U of Puerto Rico, Bayamón Campus (PR)
Iona Coll (NY)
Iowa State U of Science and Technology (IA)
Iowa Wesleyan Coll (IA)
Ithaca Coll (NY)
Jackson State U (MS)
Jacksonville State U (AL)
Jacksonville U (FL)
James Madison U (VA)
Jamestown Coll (ND)
Jarvis Christian Coll (TX)
John Brown U (AR)
John Carroll U (OH)
John F. Kennedy U (CA)
Johnson State Coll (VT)
Judson U (IL)
Juniata Coll (PA)
Kansas State U (KS)
Kean U (NJ)
Keiser U, Fort Lauderdale (FL)
Kennesaw State U (GA)
Kent State U (OH)
Kentucky Wesleyan Coll (KY)
Keuka Coll (NY)
Keystone Coll (PA)
King Coll (TN)
King's Coll (PA)
Kutztown U of Pennsylvania (PA)
Kuyper Coll (MI)
Kwantlen U Coll (BC, Canada)
LaGrange Coll (GA)
Lakehead U (ON, Canada)
Lake Superior State U (MI)
Lambuth U (TN)
La Roche Coll (PA)
La Salle U (PA)
La Sierra U (CA)
Lebanon Valley Coll (PA)
Lee U (TN)
Lehigh U (PA)
Lehman Coll of the City U of New York (NY)
Le Moyne Coll (NY)
Lenoir-Rhyne Coll (NC)
LeTourneau U (TX)
Lewis U (IL)
Liberty U (VA)
Limestone Coll (SC)
Lincoln U (MO)
Lincoln U (PA)
Lindenwood U (MO)
Linfield Coll (OR)
Lipscomb U (TN)
Livingstone Coll (NC)
Lock Haven U of Pennsylvania (PA)
Longwood U (VA)
Loras Coll (IA)
Louisiana Coll (LA)
Louisiana State U and Ag and Mech Coll (LA)
Lourdes Coll (OH)
Loyola Coll in Maryland (MD)
Loyola Marymount U (CA)
Loyola U Chicago (IL)
Loyola U New Orleans (LA)
Lubbock Christian U (TX)
Luther Coll (IA)
Lycoming Coll (PA)
Lynchburg Coll (VA)
Lyndon State Coll (VT)
Lyon Coll (AR)
Madonna U (MI)
Malone Coll (OH)
Manchester Coll (IN)
Mansfield U of Pennsylvania (PA)
Marian Coll (IN)
Marian Coll of Fond du Lac (WI)
Marietta Coll (OH)
Marist Coll (NY)
Marquette U (WI)
Marshall U (WV)
Martin U (IN)
Marymount Manhattan Coll (NY)
Maryville U of Saint Louis (MO)
Marywood U (PA)
The Master's Coll and Sem (CA)
McGill U (QC, Canada)
McKendree U (IL)
McMurry U (TX)
McNeese State U (LA)
Medaille Coll (NY)
Medgar Evers Coll of the City U of New York (NY)
Memorial U of Newfoundland (NL, Canada)
Mercy Coll (NY)
Mercyhurst Coll (PA)
Meredith Coll (NC)
Mesa State Coll (CO)
Messiah Coll (PA)
Methodist U (NC)
Metropolitan State U (MN)
Miami U (OH)
Miami U Hamilton (OH)
Michigan State U (MI)
Michigan Technological U (MI)
MidAmerica Nazarene U (KS)
Middle Tennessee State U (TN)
Midland Lutheran Coll (NE)
Midway Coll (KY)
Midwestern State U (TX)
Milligan Coll (TN)
Millikin U (IL)
Millsaps Coll (MS)
Minnesota State U Mankato (MN)
Minot State U (ND)
Misericordia U (PA)
Mississippi Coll (MS)
Mississippi State U (MS)
Mississippi U for Women (MS)
Mississippi Valley State U (MS)
Missouri Baptist U (MO)
Missouri State U (MO)
Missouri Valley Coll (MO)
Molloy Coll (NY)
Monmouth Coll (IL)
Monroe Coll, Bronx (NY)
Montana State U–Billings (MT)

Montana Tech of The U of Montana (MT)
Moravian Coll (PA)
Morehead State U (KY)
Morgan State U (MD)
Morningside Coll (IA)
Mountain State U (WV)
Mount Allison U (NB, Canada)
Mount Aloysius Coll (PA)
Mount Marty Coll (SD)
Mount Mary Coll (WI)
Mount Mercy Coll (IA)
Mount Olive Coll (NC)
Mount Saint Mary Coll (NY)
Mount St. Mary's Coll (CA)
Mount St. Mary's U (MD)
Mount Saint Vincent U (NS, Canada)
Mount Vernon Nazarene U (OH)
Muhlenberg Coll (PA)
Murray State U (KY)
National American U–Sioux Falls Branch (SD)
National-Louis U (IL)
National U (CA)
Nazareth Coll of Rochester (NY)
Nebraska Wesleyan U (NE)
Neumann Coll (PA)
New England Coll (NH)
Newman U (KS)
New Mexico Highlands U (NM)
New York Inst of Technology (NY)
New York U (NY)
Niagara U (NY)
Nichols Coll (MA)
North Carolina Ag and Tech State U (NC)
North Carolina Central U (NC)
North Carolina State U (NC)
North Carolina Wesleyan Coll (NC)
North Central Coll (IL)
North Dakota State U (ND)
Northeastern Illinois U (IL)
Northeastern State U (OK)
Northeastern U (MA)
Northern Arizona U (AZ)
Northern Illinois U (IL)
Northern Michigan U (MI)
Northern State U (SD)
North Georgia Coll & State U (GA)
North Greenville U (SC)
Northwest Christian Coll (OR)
Northwestern Coll (IA)
Northwestern Coll (MN)
Northwestern Oklahoma State U (OK)
Northwestern State U of Louisiana (LA)
Northwest Missouri State U (MO)
Northwest Nazarene U (ID)
Northwood U (MI)
Northwood U, Florida Campus (FL)
Northwood U, Texas Campus (TX)
Norwich U (VT)
Nova Southeastern U (FL)
Nyack Coll (NY)
Oakland U (MI)
Oakwood Coll (AL)
Oglethorpe U (GA)
Ohio Dominican U (OH)
Ohio Northern U (OH)
Ohio Valley U (WV)
Ohio Wesleyan U (OH)
Oklahoma Christian U (OK)
Oklahoma City U (OK)
Oklahoma Panhandle State U (OK)
Oklahoma State U (OK)
Oklahoma Wesleyan U (OK)
Old Dominion U (VA)
Oral Roberts U (OK)
Oregon Inst of Technology (OR)
Otterbein Coll (OH)
Ouachita Baptist U (AR)
Pace U (NY)
Pacific Union Coll (CA)
Pacific U (OR)
Paine Coll (GA)
Park U (MO)
Penn State Abington (PA)
Penn State Altoona (PA)
Penn State Berks (PA)
Penn State Erie, The Behrend Coll (PA)
Penn State U Park (PA)
Pepperdine U, Malibu (CA)
Peru State Coll (NE)
Pfeiffer U (NC)
Philadelphia U (PA)
Pittsburg State U (KS)
Plymouth State U (NH)
Point Loma Nazarene U (CA)
Point Park U (PA)
Portland State U (OR)
Prairie View A&M U (TX)
Prescott Coll (AZ)
Providence Coll (RI)
Purdue U (IN)
Purdue U Calumet (IN)
Queens Coll of the City U of New York (NY)
Quincy U (IL)
Quinnipiac U (CT)
Radford U (VA)
Ramapo Coll of New Jersey (NJ)
Randolph-Macon Coll (VA)
Redeemer U Coll (ON, Canada)
Regis U (CO)
Rhode Island Coll (RI)
Rider U (NJ)
Robert Morris U (PA)
Roberts Wesleyan Coll (NY)
Rochester Coll (MI)
Rochester Inst of Technology (NY)
Rockford Coll (IL)
Roger Williams U (RI)
Roosevelt U (IL)
Rosemont Coll (PA)
Rutgers, The State U of New Jersey, Camden (NJ)
Rutgers, The State U of New Jersey, Newark (NJ)
Rutgers, The State U of New Jersey, New Brunswick (NJ)
Sage Coll of Albany (NY)
Saginaw Valley State U (MI)
St. Ambrose U (IA)
St. Cloud State U (MN)
St. Edward's U (TX)
Saint Francis U (PA)
St. Francis Xavier U (NS, Canada)
St. John Fisher Coll (NY)
Saint John's U (MN)
St. John's U (NY)
Saint Joseph Coll (CT)
Saint Joseph's Coll (IN)
St. Joseph's Coll, New York (NY)
St. Joseph's Coll, Suffolk Campus (NY)
Saint Joseph's U (PA)
Saint Leo U (FL)
Saint Martin's U (WA)
Saint Mary-of-the-Woods Coll (IN)
Saint Mary's Coll (IN)
Saint Mary's Coll of California (CA)
St. Mary's U (TX)
Saint Mary's U of Minnesota (MN)
Saint Michael's Coll (VT)
St. Norbert Coll (WI)
St. Thomas Aquinas Coll (NY)
St. Thomas U (FL)
Saint Vincent Coll (PA)
Saint Xavier U (IL)
Salem Coll (NC)
Salem State Coll (MA)
Salisbury U (MD)
Salve Regina U (RI)
Samford U (AL)
Sam Houston State U (TX)
San Diego State U (CA)
San Francisco State U (CA)
Santa Clara U (CA)
Schreiner U (TX)
Seattle Pacific U (WA)
Seattle U (WA)
Seton Hill U (PA)
Shaw U (NC)
Shepherd U (WV)
Shippensburg U of Pennsylvania (PA)
Shorter Coll (GA)
Siena Coll (NY)
Siena Heights U (MI)
Simmons Coll (MA)
Simpson Coll (IA)
South Carolina State U (SC)
Southeastern Louisiana U (LA)
Southeastern Oklahoma State U (OK)
Southeastern U (FL)
Southeast Missouri State U (MO)
Southern Arkansas U–Magnolia (AR)
Southern Connecticut State U (CT)
Southern Illinois U Carbondale (IL)
Southern Illinois U Edwardsville (IL)
Southern Methodist U (TX)
Southern New Hampshire U (NH)
Southern Oregon U (OR)
Southern U and Ag and Mech Coll (LA)
Southern Utah U (UT)
Southern Wesleyan U (SC)
Southwest Baptist U (MO)
Southwestern Adventist U (TX)
Southwestern Oklahoma State U (OK)
Southwestern U (TX)
Southwest Minnesota State U (MN)
Spring Arbor U (MI)
Spring Hill Coll (AL)
State U of New York at Binghamton (NY)
State U of New York at Fredonia (NY)
State U of New York at New Paltz (NY)
State U of New York at Oswego (NY)
State U of New York at Plattsburgh (NY)
State U of New York Coll at Geneseo (NY)
State U of New York Coll at Old Westbury (NY)
State U of New York Coll at Oneonta (NY)
State U of New York Inst of Technology (NY)
Stephen F. Austin State U (TX)
Stephens Coll (MO)
Stetson U (FL)
Stonehill Coll (MA)
Suffolk U (MA)
Sullivan U (KY)
Susquehanna U (PA)
Syracuse U (NY)
Tabor Coll (KS)
Tarleton State U (TX)
Taylor U (IN)
Temple U (PA)
Tennessee State U (TN)
Tennessee Technological U (TN)
Tennessee Wesleyan Coll (TN)
Texas A&M Intl U (TX)
Texas A&M U (TX)
Texas A&M U–Commerce (TX)
Texas Christian U (TX)
Texas Lutheran U (TX)
Texas Southern U (TX)
Texas State U-San Marcos (TX)
Texas Tech U (TX)
Texas Woman's U (TX)
Thiel Coll (PA)
Thomas Coll (ME)
Thomas Edison State Coll (NJ)
Thomas More Coll (KY)
Thomas U (GA)
Thompson Rivers U (BC, Canada)
Tiffin U (OH)
Tougaloo Coll (MS)
Towson U (MD)
Transylvania U (KY)
Trevecca Nazarene U (TN)
Trinity Christian Coll (IL)
Trinity Intl U (IL)
Trinity U (TX)
Tri-State U (IN)
Troy U (AL)
Truman State U (MO)
Tulane U (LA)
Tuskegee U (AL)
Union Coll (KY)
Union Coll (NE)
Union U (TN)
Université de Sherbrooke (QC, Canada)
Université du Québec en Outaouais (QC, Canada)
U at Albany, State U of New York (NY)
The U of Akron (OH)
The U of Alabama (AL)
The U of Alabama at Birmingham (AL)
The U of Alabama in Huntsville (AL)
U of Alaska Fairbanks (AK)
The U of Arizona (AZ)
U of Arkansas (AR)
U of Arkansas at Fort Smith (AR)
U of Arkansas at Monticello (AR)
U of Arkansas at Pine Bluff (AR)
U of Baltimore (MD)
U of Bridgeport (CT)
The U of British Columbia (BC, Canada)
The U of British Columbia–Okanagan (BC, Canada)
U of Central Arkansas (AR)
U of Central Florida (FL)
U of Central Oklahoma (OK)
U of Charleston (WV)
U of Cincinnati (OH)
U of Colorado at Boulder (CO)
U of Connecticut (CT)
U of Dayton (OH)
U of Delaware (DE)
U of Denver (CO)
U of Evansville (IN)
The U of Findlay (OH)
U of Florida (FL)
U of Georgia (GA)
U of Great Falls (MT)
U of Guam (GU)
U of Hartford (CT)
U of Hawaii at Manoa (HI)
U of Houston (TX)
U of Houston–Clear Lake (TX)
U of Houston–Downtown (TX)
U of Houston–Victoria (TX)
U of Idaho (ID)
U of Illinois at Chicago (IL)
U of Illinois at Springfield (IL)
U of Illinois at Urbana–Champaign (IL)
U of Indianapolis (IN)
The U of Iowa (IA)
U of Kansas (KS)
U of La Verne (CA)
U of Lethbridge (AB, Canada)
U of Louisiana at Lafayette (LA)
U of Louisiana at Monroe (LA)
U of Louisville (KY)
The U of Maine at Augusta (ME)
U of Maine at Machias (ME)
U of Mary (ND)
U of Mary Hardin-Baylor (TX)
U of Maryland, Coll Park (MD)
U of Maryland Eastern Shore (MD)
U of Maryland U Coll (MD)
U of Massachusetts Amherst (MA)
U of Massachusetts Dartmouth (MA)
U of Memphis (TN)
U of Miami (FL)
U of Michigan–Dearborn (MI)
U of Michigan–Flint (MI)
U of Minnesota, Crookston (MN)
U of Minnesota, Duluth (MN)
U of Minnesota, Twin Cities Campus (MN)
U of Mississippi (MS)
U of Missouri–Columbia (MO)
U of Missouri–Kansas City (MO)
U of Missouri–St. Louis (MO)
The U of Montana (MT)
U of Montevallo (AL)
U of Nebraska at Omaha (NE)
U of Nebraska–Lincoln (NE)
U of Nevada, Las Vegas (NV)
U of Nevada, Reno (NV)
U of New Brunswick Fredericton (NB, Canada)
U of New Hampshire (NH)
U of New Haven (CT)
U of New Orleans (LA)
U of North Alabama (AL)
The U of North Carolina at Asheville (NC)
The U of North Carolina at Charlotte (NC)
The U of North Carolina at Greensboro (NC)
The U of North Carolina at Pembroke (NC)
The U of North Carolina Wilmington (NC)
U of North Dakota (ND)
U of Northern Iowa (IA)
U of North Florida (FL)
U of North Texas (TX)
U of Notre Dame (IN)
U of Oklahoma (OK)
U of Oregon (OR)
U of Ottawa (ON, Canada)
U of Pennsylvania (PA)
U of Pittsburgh (PA)
U of Pittsburgh at Bradford (PA)
U of Pittsburgh at Johnstown (PA)
U of Portland (OR)
U of Puerto Rico at Utuado (PR)
U of Puerto Rico, Cayey U Coll (PR)
U of Redlands (CA)
U of Regina (SK, Canada)
U of Rhode Island (RI)
U of Richmond (VA)
U of Rio Grande (OH)
U of St. Francis (IL)
U of Saint Francis (IN)
U of Saint Mary (KS)
U of St. Thomas (MN)
U of St. Thomas (TX)
U of San Diego (CA)
The U of Scranton (PA)
U of Sioux Falls (SD)
U of South Alabama (AL)
U of South Carolina (SC)
The U of South Dakota (SD)
U of Southern California (CA)
U of Southern Indiana (IN)
U of Southern Maine (ME)
U of Southern Mississippi (MS)
U of South Florida (FL)
The U of Tampa (FL)
The U of Tennessee (TN)
The U of Tennessee at Martin (TN)
The U of Texas at Arlington (TX)
The U of Texas at Austin (TX)
The U of Texas at Brownsville (TX)
The U of Texas at Dallas (TX)
The U of Texas at El Paso (TX)
The U of Texas at San Antonio (TX)
The U of Texas at Tyler (TX)
The U of Texas of the Permian Basin (TX)
The U of Texas–Pan American (TX)
U of the Ozarks (AR)
U of the Sacred Heart (PR)
U of the Virgin Islands (VI)
The U of Toledo (OH)
U of Toronto (ON, Canada)
U of Tulsa (OK)
U of Utah (UT)
The U of Virginia's Coll at Wise (VA)
The U of Western Ontario (ON, Canada)
U of West Florida (FL)
U of West Georgia (GA)
U of Windsor (ON, Canada)
U of Wisconsin–Eau Claire (WI)
U of Wisconsin–Green Bay (WI)
U of Wisconsin–La Crosse (WI)
U of Wisconsin–Madison (WI)
U of Wisconsin–Milwaukee (WI)
U of Wisconsin–Oshkosh (WI)
U of Wisconsin–Parkside (WI)
U of Wisconsin–Platteville (WI)
U of Wisconsin–Stevens Point (WI)
U of Wisconsin–Superior (WI)
U of Wisconsin–Whitewater (WI)
U of Wyoming (WY)
Ursuline Coll (OH)
Utah State U (UT)
Utah Valley State Coll (UT)
Utica Coll (NY)
Valdosta State U (GA)
Valparaiso U (IN)
Vanguard U of Southern California (CA)
Villa Julie Coll (MD)
Villanova U (PA)
Virginia Commonwealth U (VA)
Virginia Polytechnic Inst and State U (VA)
Virginia State U (VA)
Viterbo U (WI)
Voorhees Coll (SC)
Wagner Coll (NY)
Wake Forest U (NC)
Walla Walla U (WA)
Walsh U (OH)
Wartburg Coll (IA)
Washburn U (KS)
Washington & Jefferson Coll (PA)
Washington and Lee U (VA)
Washington State U (WA)
Washington U in St. Louis (MO)
Waynesburg U (PA)
Wayne State U (MI)
Webber Intl U (FL)
Weber State U (UT)
Webster U (MO)
Wesley Coll (DE)
West Chester U of Pennsylvania (PA)
Western Carolina U (NC)
Western Connecticut State U (CT)
Western Illinois U (IL)
Western Intl U (AZ)
Western Kentucky U (KY)
Western Michigan U (MI)
Western New England Coll (MA)
Western New Mexico U (NM)
Western State Coll of Colorado (CO)
Western Washington U (WA)
West Liberty State Coll (WV)
Westminster Coll (MO)
Westminster Coll (UT)
West Texas A&M U (TX)
West Virginia U (WV)
West Virginia Wesleyan Coll (WV)
Wheeling Jesuit U (WV)
Whitworth U (WA)
Wichita State U (KS)
Widener U (PA)
Wilkes U (PA)
William Jewell Coll (MO)
William Paterson U of New Jersey (NJ)
William Woods U (MO)
Wilmington Coll (OH)
Wilmington U (DE)
Wilson Coll (PA)
Wingate U (NC)
Winona State U (MN)
Wofford Coll (SC)
Woodbury U (CA)
Wright State U (OH)
Xavier U (OH)
Xavier U of Louisiana (LA)
York Coll (NE)
York Coll of Pennsylvania (PA)
York Coll of the City U of New York (NY)
York U (ON, Canada)
Youngstown State U (OH)

ACCOUNTING AND BUSINESS/MANAGEMENT

Alaska Pacific U (AK)
Babson Coll (MA)
Bethel Coll (TN)
Chestnut Hill Coll (PA)
Florida Ag and Mech U (FL)
Illinois State U (IL)
Keystone Coll (PA)
Maranatha Baptist Bible Coll (WI)
Miles Coll (AL)
Mount Aloysius Coll (PA)

Presbyterian Coll (SC)
Purdue U (IN)
Santa Clara U (CA)
U of Great Falls (MT)
U of Illinois at Urbana–Champaign (IL)
The U of Western Ontario (ON, Canada)
Western State Coll of Colorado (CO)

ACCOUNTING AND COMPUTER SCIENCE

California State U, Chico (CA)
Husson Coll (ME)
Southern New Hampshire U (NH)
Western Washington U (WA)

ACCOUNTING AND FINANCE

Adams State Coll (CO)
Albertus Magnus Coll (CT)
Babson Coll (MA)
Canisius Coll (NY)
Central Christian Coll of Kansas (KS)
Colorado Tech U—Colorado Springs (CO)
Colorado Tech U—Denver (CO)
Colorado Tech U—North Kansas City (MO)
Colorado Tech U—Online (CO)
Colorado Tech U—Sioux Falls (SD)
Drake U (IA)
McGill U (QC, Canada)
Northern Michigan U (MI)
Palm Beach Atlantic U (FL)
Purdue U (IN)
Saint Francis U (PA)
Southern New Hampshire U (NH)
U of North Dakota (ND)
The U of Western Ontario (ON, Canada)
U of Windsor (ON, Canada)
Western State Coll of Colorado (CO)

ACCOUNTING RELATED

Brigham Young U (UT)
Central Michigan U (MI)
Duquesne U (PA)
Keystone Coll (PA)
Maryville U of Saint Louis (MO)
Northern Michigan U (MI)
Saint Mary-of-the-Woods Coll (IN)
Saint Mary's Coll of California (CA)
State U of New York at Oswego (NY)
Washington State U (WA)

ACCOUNTING TECHNOLOGY AND BOOKKEEPING

Canisius Coll (NY)
Ferris State U (MI)
Lewis-Clark State Coll (ID)
Rowan U (NJ)

ACTING

Bard Coll (NY)
Bard Coll at Simon's Rock (MA)
Barry U (FL)
Baylor U (TX)
Bennington Coll (VT)
Boston U (MA)
Bowling Green State U (OH)
Bradley U (IL)
Brigham Young U (UT)
California Inst of the Arts (CA)
California State U, Long Beach (CA)
Central Christian Coll of Kansas (KS)
Central Michigan U (MI)
Coker Coll (SC)
The Coll at Brockport, State U of New York (NY)
Coll of Santa Fe (NM)
Coll of the Ozarks (MO)
Columbia Coll Chicago (IL)
DePaul U (IL)
Drake U (IA)
Emerson Coll (MA)
Florida State U (FL)
George Fox U (OR)
Greensboro Coll (NC)
Hofstra U (NY)
Illinois Wesleyan U (IL)
Ithaca Coll (NY)
Johnson State Coll (VT)
Kean U (NJ)
Keene State Coll (NH)
Kent State U (OH)
Marymount Manhattan Coll (NY)
Memorial U of Newfoundland (NL, Canada)
New World School of the Arts (FL)
Oakland U (MI)
Ohio U (OH)
Old Dominion U (VA)
Oral Roberts U (OK)
Palm Beach Atlantic U (FL)
Penn State Abington (PA)
Penn State Altoona (PA)
Penn State Berks (PA)
Penn State Erie, The Behrend Coll (PA)
Penn State U Park (PA)
Point Park U (PA)
Purdue U (IN)
St. Cloud State U (MN)
Sarah Lawrence Coll (NY)
Seton Hill U (PA)
Shenandoah U (VA)
Temple U (PA)
Texas Tech U (TX)
Trinity U (TX)
U of Connecticut (CT)
U of Miami (FL)
U of Northern Iowa (IA)
U of Regina (SK, Canada)
U of Southern California (CA)
U of Windsor (ON, Canada)
York U (ON, Canada)

ACTING/DIRECTING

Berea Coll (KY)
Bradley U (IL)
California Baptist U (CA)

ACTUARIAL SCIENCE

Appalachian State U (NC)
Ball State U (IN)
Bellarmine U (KY)
Bernard M. Baruch Coll of the City U of New York (NY)
Bob Jones U (SC)
Bradley U (IL)
Brigham Young U (UT)
Butler U (IN)
Carroll Coll (WI)
Central Michigan U (MI)
Concordia U (QC, Canada)
Drake U (IA)
Eastern Michigan U (MI)
Florida Ag and Mech U (FL)
Georgia State U (GA)
Hofstra U (NY)
Indiana U Northwest (IN)
Indiana U South Bend (IN)
Jamestown Coll (ND)
Lebanon Valley Coll (PA)
Lincoln U (PA)
Lycoming Coll (PA)
Maryville U of Saint Louis (MO)
The Master's Coll and Sem (CA)
Michigan Technological U (MI)
New Jersey Inst of Technology (NJ)
New York U (NY)
North Central Coll (IL)
Northwestern Coll (IA)
Oregon State U (OR)
Penn State Abington (PA)
Penn State Altoona (PA)
Penn State Berks (PA)
Penn State Erie, The Behrend Coll (PA)
Penn State U Park (PA)
Pittsburg State U (KS)
Purdue U (IN)
Queens Coll of the City U of New York (NY)
Quinnipiac U (CT)
Rider U (NJ)
Robert Morris U (PA)
Roosevelt U (IL)
St. John's U (NY)
Saint Joseph's U (PA)
Seton Hill U (PA)
Simon Fraser U (BC, Canada)
Southern Adventist U (TN)
Spring Arbor U (MI)
Tabor Coll (KS)
Temple U (PA)
Thiel Coll (PA)
U at Albany, State U of New York (NY)
U of Central Florida (FL)
U of Central Oklahoma (OK)
U of Connecticut (CT)
U of Illinois at Urbana–Champaign (IL)
The U of Iowa (IA)
U of Michigan (MI)
U of Michigan–Flint (MI)
U of Minnesota, Duluth (MN)
U of Minnesota, Twin Cities Campus (MN)
U of Nebraska–Lincoln (NE)
U of Northern Iowa (IA)
U of Pennsylvania (PA)
U of Regina (SK, Canada)
U of St. Thomas (MN)
The U of Texas at San Antonio (TX)
U of Toronto (ON, Canada)
The U of Western Ontario (ON, Canada)
U of Wisconsin–Madison (WI)
U of Wisconsin–Stevens Point (WI)
Valparaiso U (IN)
Worcester Polytechnic Inst (MA)
York U (ON, Canada)

ADAPTED PHYSICAL EDUCATION

Slippery Rock U of Pennsylvania (PA)

ADMINISTRATIVE ASSISTANT AND SECRETARIAL SCIENCE

Alabama State U (AL)
Baker Coll of Muskegon (MI)
Baker Coll of Owosso (MI)
Bluefield State Coll (WV)
Cedarville U (OH)
East-West U (IL)
Florida Ag and Mech U (FL)
Grace Coll (IN)
Inter American U of Puerto Rico, Bayamón Campus (PR)
Inter American U of Puerto Rico, Fajardo Campus (PR)
Lewis-Clark State Coll (ID)
Maranatha Baptist Bible Coll (WI)
Mayville State U (ND)
Miami U (OH)
Midland Lutheran Coll (NE)
North Carolina Ag and Tech State U (NC)
Northwest Missouri State U (MO)
Oakwood Coll (AL)
Pillsbury Baptist Bible Coll (MN)
Salem State Coll (MA)
Southeast Missouri State U (MO)
Southwestern Adventist U (TX)
Tabor Coll (KS)
Tennessee State U (TN)
The U of Montana (MT)
U of Puerto Rico, Cayey U Coll (PR)
U of the Sacred Heart (PR)
Valdosta State U (GA)
Wiley Coll (TX)

ADULT AND CONTINUING EDUCATION

Atlantic Union Coll (MA)
Auburn U (AL)
Biola U (CA)
Brock U (ON, Canada)
California Baptist U (CA)
Concordia U (QC, Canada)
Dakota Wesleyan U (SD)
Iowa Wesleyan Coll (IA)
Kentucky Christian U (KY)
Laurentian U (ON, Canada)
Lenoir-Rhyne Coll (NC)
Louisiana Coll (LA)
Louisiana State U and Ag and Mech Coll (LA)
Lourdes Coll (OH)
Martin U (IN)
Memorial U of Newfoundland (NL, Canada)
Ohio Valley U (WV)
St. Joseph's Coll, Suffolk Campus (NY)
San Diego Christian Coll (CA)
Tabor Coll (KS)
Tennessee State U (TN)
U of Central Oklahoma (OK)
U of Nevada, Las Vegas (NV)
U of New Brunswick Fredericton (NB, Canada)
U of New Hampshire (NH)
U of Regina (SK, Canada)
The U of Toledo (OH)

ADULT AND CONTINUING EDUCATION ADMINISTRATION

Marshall U (WV)
Penn State Abington (PA)
Penn State Altoona (PA)
Penn State Berks (PA)
Penn State Erie, The Behrend Coll (PA)
Penn State U Park (PA)

ADULT DEVELOPMENT AND AGING

Bowling Green State U (OH)
Coll of Mount St. Joseph (OH)
Madonna U (MI)
Mount Saint Vincent U (NS, Canada)
St. Thomas U (NB, Canada)
U of Northern Colorado (CO)

ADULT HEALTH NURSING

Pennsylvania Coll of Technology (PA)
Worcester State Coll (MA)
Wright State U (OH)

ADVERTISING

Acad of Art U (CA)
The American U of Athens (Greece)
Appalachian State U (NC)
The Art Inst of Atlanta (GA)
The Art Inst of Atlanta–Decatur (GA)
The Art Inst of California–Orange County (CA)
The Art Inst of California–San Diego (CA)
The Art Inst of California–San Francisco (CA)
The Art Inst of Michigan (MI)
The Art Inst of Phoenix (AZ)
The Art Inst of Pittsburgh (PA)
The Art Inst of Portland (OR)
The Art Inst of Tampa (FL)
The Art Inst of Tucson (AZ)
The Art Inst of Washington (VA)
The Art Insts Intl Minnesota (MN)
Ball State U (IN)
Barry U (FL)
Belmont U (TN)
Bernard M. Baruch Coll of the City U of New York (NY)
Boise State U (ID)
Bradley U (IL)
Brigham Young U (UT)
California State U, East Bay (CA)
California State U, Fullerton (CA)
Central Michigan U (MI)
Clarke Coll (IA)
Columbia Coll Chicago (IL)
Concordia Coll (MN)
Drake U (IA)
Drury U (MO)
East Central U (OK)
Emerson Coll (MA)
Fashion Inst of Technology (NY)
Ferris State U (MI)
Florida Southern Coll (FL)
Florida State U (FL)
Fontbonne U (MO)
Gannon U (PA)
Grand Valley State U (MI)
Hampton U (VA)
Harding U (AR)
Hastings Coll (NE)
Hawai'i Pacific U (HI)
The Illinois Inst of Art–Chicago (IL)
The Illinois Inst of Art–Schaumburg (IL)
Iona Coll (NY)
Iowa State U of Science and Technology (IA)
Kent State U (OH)
Louisiana Coll (LA)
Loyola U Chicago (IL)
Marist Coll (NY)
Marquette U (WI)
Memphis Coll of Art (TN)
Metropolitan State U (MN)
Miami Intl U of Art & Design (FL)
Michigan State U (MI)
New England School of Communications (ME)
New York Inst of Technology (NY)
Northeastern State U (OK)
Northern Arizona U (AZ)
Northwest Missouri State U (MO)
Northwood U, Florida Campus (FL)
Ohio U (OH)
Oklahoma Christian U (OK)
Oklahoma City U (OK)
Pace U (NY)
Penn State Abington (PA)
Penn State Altoona (PA)
Penn State Berks (PA)
Penn State Erie, The Behrend Coll (PA)
Penn State U Park (PA)
Pepperdine U, Malibu (CA)
Pittsburg State U (KS)
Point Park U (PA)
Portland State U (OR)
Purdue U (IN)
Quinnipiac U (CT)
Rider U (NJ)
Rochester Inst of Technology (NY)
St. Ambrose U (IA)
St. Cloud State U (MN)
St. John's U (NY)
Sam Houston State U (TX)
San Diego State U (CA)
Simmons Coll (MA)
Simpson Coll (IA)
Southern Adventist U (TN)
Southern Methodist U (TX)
Southern New Hampshire U (NH)
Stephens Coll (MO)
Syracuse U (NY)
Temple U (PA)
Texas Christian U (TX)
Texas State U-San Marcos (TX)
Texas Tech U (TX)
Union U (TN)
The U of Alabama (AL)
U of Central Florida (FL)
U of Central Oklahoma (OK)
U of Colorado at Boulder (CO)
U of Florida (FL)
U of Georgia (GA)
U of Idaho (ID)
U of Illinois at Urbana–Champaign (IL)
U of Miami (FL)
U of Mississippi (MS)
U of Missouri–Columbia (MO)
U of Nebraska–Lincoln (NE)
U of Nevada, Reno (NV)
U of Oklahoma (OK)
U of Oregon (OR)
U of South Carolina (SC)
U of Southern Indiana (IN)
U of Southern Mississippi (MS)
The U of Tampa (FL)
The U of Tennessee (TN)
The U of Texas at Arlington (TX)
The U of Texas at Austin (TX)
U of the Sacred Heart (PR)
U of Wisconsin–Madison (WI)
Washington U in St. Louis (MO)
Waynesburg U (PA)
Webster U (MO)
Wesleyan Coll (GA)
Western Kentucky U (KY)
Western Michigan U (MI)
Western New England Coll (MA)
West Texas A&M U (TX)
West Virginia U (WV)
Widener U (PA)
William Woods U (MO)
Winona State U (MN)
Xavier U (OH)
Youngstown State U (OH)

AERONAUTICAL/ AEROSPACE ENGINEERING TECHNOLOGY

American Public U System (WV)
Bowling Green State U (OH)
New York Inst of Technology (NY)
Northeastern U (MA)
Ohio U (OH)
Saint Louis U (MO)
U of Central Missouri (MO)
Utah State U (UT)

AERONAUTICS/AVIATION/ AEROSPACE SCIENCE AND TECHNOLOGY

Augsburg Coll (MN)
Central Washington U (WA)
Delta State U (MS)
Embry-Riddle Aeronautical U (AZ)
Embry-Riddle Aeronautical U (FL)
Embry-Riddle Aeronautical U Worldwide (FL)
Henderson State U (AR)
Inter American U of Puerto Rico, Bayamón Campus (PR)
Kansas State U (KS)
Kent State U (OH)
Liberty U (VA)
Middle Tennessee State U (TN)
Ohio U (OH)
Oklahoma State U (OK)
Purdue U (IN)
South Dakota State U (SD)
U of Louisiana at Monroe (LA)
U of Minnesota, Crookston (MN)
U of Nebraska at Omaha (NE)
U of Oklahoma (OK)
U of the District of Columbia (DC)
York U (ON, Canada)

AEROSPACE, AERONAUTICAL AND ASTRONAUTICAL ENGINEERING

American Public U System (WV)
Arizona State U (AZ)
Auburn U (AL)
Boston U (MA)
California Polytechnic State U, San Luis Obispo (CA)
California State Polytechnic U, Pomona (CA)
California State U, Long Beach (CA)
Case Western Reserve U (OH)
Clarkson U (NY)
Dowling Coll (NY)

Embry-Riddle Aeronautical U (AZ)
Embry-Riddle Aeronautical U (FL)
Florida Inst of Technology (FL)
Georgia Inst of Technology (GA)
Illinois Inst of Technology (IL)
Inter American U of Puerto Rico, Bayamón Campus (PR)
Iowa State U of Science and Technology (IA)
Massachusetts Inst of Technology (MA)
Miami U (OH)
Mississippi State U (MS)
Missouri U of Science and Technology (MO)
North Carolina State U (NC)
Oklahoma State U (OK)
Penn State Abington (PA)
Penn State Altoona (PA)
Penn State Berks (PA)
Penn State Erie, The Behrend Coll (PA)
Penn State U Park (PA)
Purdue U (IN)
Rensselaer Polytechnic Inst (NY)
Rochester Inst of Technology (NY)
Saint Louis U (MO)
San Diego State U (CA)
Stanford U (CA)
Syracuse U (NY)
Texas A&M U (TX)
Tuskegee U (AL)
United States Air Force Acad (CO)
United States Naval Acad (MD)
U at Buffalo, the State U of New York (NY)
The U of Alabama (AL)
The U of Arizona (AZ)
U of California, Davis (CA)
U of California, Irvine (CA)
U of California, Los Angeles (CA)
U of California, San Diego (CA)
U of Central Florida (FL)
U of Cincinnati (OH)
U of Colorado at Boulder (CO)
U of Florida (FL)
U of Illinois at Urbana–Champaign (IL)
U of Kansas (KS)
U of Maryland, Coll Park (MD)
U of Miami (FL)
U of Michigan (MI)
U of Minnesota, Twin Cities Campus (MN)
U of Notre Dame (IN)
U of Oklahoma (OK)
U of Southern California (CA)
The U of Tennessee (TN)
The U of Texas at Arlington (TX)
The U of Texas at Austin (TX)
U of Toronto (ON, Canada)
U of Virginia (VA)
Utah State U (UT)
Virginia Polytechnic Inst and State U (VA)
Weber State U (UT)
Western Michigan U (MI)
West Virginia U (WV)
Wichita State U (KS)
Worcester Polytechnic Inst (MA)
York U (ON, Canada)

AEROSPACE SCIENCE
Dallas Baptist U (TX)
Florida Inst of Technology (FL)

AFRICAN-AMERICAN/ BLACK STUDIES
Amherst Coll (MA)
Arizona State U (AZ)
Bard Coll at Simon's Rock (MA)
Bates Coll (ME)
Berea Coll (KY)
Brandeis U (MA)
Brown U (RI)
California State U, Dominguez Hills (CA)
California State U, East Bay (CA)
California State U, Fresno (CA)
California State U, Fullerton (CA)
California State U, Long Beach (CA)
California State U, Los Angeles (CA)
Chicago State U (IL)
City Coll of the City U of New York (NY)
Claflin U (SC)
Claremont McKenna Coll (CA)
Colby Coll (ME)
Colgate U (NY)
The Coll at Brockport, State U of New York (NY)
Coll of Staten Island of the City U of New York (NY)
The Coll of William and Mary (VA)
Cornell U (NY)
Dartmouth Coll (NH)
Denison U (OH)
DePaul U (IL)
DePauw U (IN)
Dillard U (LA)
Duke U (NC)
Earlham Coll (IN)
East Carolina U (NC)
Eastern Illinois U (IL)
Eastern Michigan U (MI)
Emory U (GA)
Florida Ag and Mech U (FL)
Georgia State U (GA)
Gettysburg Coll (PA)
Guilford Coll (NC)
Hampshire Coll (MA)
Harvard U (MA)
Hobart and William Smith Colls (NY)
Hunter Coll of the City U of New York (NY)
Indiana State U (IN)
Indiana U Bloomington (IN)
Indiana U Northwest (IN)
Kent State U (OH)
Kenyon Coll (OH)
Knox Coll (IL)
Lehigh U (PA)
Lehman Coll of the City U of New York (NY)
Loyola Marymount U (CA)
Luther Coll (IA)
Marquette U (WI)
Martin U (IN)
Mercer U (GA)
Miami U (OH)
Morehouse Coll (GA)
Morgan State U (MD)
Mount Holyoke Coll (MA)
New York U (NY)
Northeastern U (MA)
Northwestern U (IL)
Oberlin Coll (OH)
Ohio U (OH)
Ohio Wesleyan U (OH)
Penn State Abington (PA)
Penn State Altoona (PA)
Penn State Berks (PA)
Penn State Erie, The Behrend Coll (PA)
Penn State U Park (PA)
Pitzer Coll (CA)
Pomona Coll (CA)
Purdue U (IN)
Rhode Island Coll (RI)
Roosevelt U (IL)
Rutgers, The State U of New Jersey, Camden (NJ)
Rutgers, The State U of New Jersey, Newark (NJ)
San Diego State U (CA)
San Francisco State U (CA)
Sarah Lawrence Coll (NY)
Scripps Coll (CA)
Simmons Coll (MA)
Smith Coll (MA)
Sonoma State U (CA)
Southern Methodist U (TX)
Stanford U (CA)
State U of New York at Binghamton (NY)
State U of New York at New Paltz (NY)
State U of New York Coll at Geneseo (NY)
State U of New York Coll at Oneonta (NY)
Stony Brook U, State U of New York (NY)
Suffolk U (MA)
Syracuse U (NY)
Temple U (PA)
Tougaloo Coll (MS)
Tufts U (MA)
U at Albany, State U of New York (NY)
U at Buffalo, the State U of New York (NY)
The U of Alabama at Birmingham (AL)
U of California, Berkeley (CA)
U of California, Davis (CA)
U of California, Irvine (CA)
U of California, Los Angeles (CA)
U of California, Riverside (CA)
U of California, Santa Barbara (CA)
U of Central Arkansas (AR)
U of Chicago (IL)
U of Cincinnati (OH)
U of Georgia (GA)
U of Illinois at Chicago (IL)
The U of Iowa (IA)
U of Kansas (KS)
U of Louisville (KY)
U of Maryland, Baltimore County (MD)
U of Maryland, Coll Park (MD)
U of Massachusetts Amherst (MA)
U of Massachusetts Boston (MA)
U of Memphis (TN)
U of Miami (FL)
U of Michigan (MI)
U of Michigan–Flint (MI)
U of Minnesota, Twin Cities Campus (MN)
The U of Montana (MT)
U of Nebraska at Omaha (NE)
U of Nevada, Las Vegas (NV)
U of New Mexico (NM)
The U of North Carolina at Chapel Hill (NC)
The U of North Carolina at Charlotte (NC)
The U of North Carolina at Greensboro (NC)
U of Northern Colorado (CO)
U of Notre Dame (IN)
U of Oklahoma (OK)
U of Pennsylvania (PA)
U of Pittsburgh (PA)
U of Rochester (NY)
U of South Carolina (SC)
U of Southern California (CA)
U of South Florida (FL)
The U of Toledo (OH)
U of Virginia (VA)
U of Wisconsin–Madison (WI)
U of Wisconsin–Milwaukee (WI)
Vanderbilt U (TN)
Virginia Commonwealth U (VA)
Washington U in St. Louis (MO)
Wayne State U (MI)
Wellesley Coll (MA)
Wells Coll (NY)
Wesleyan U (CT)
Western Illinois U (IL)
William Paterson U of New Jersey (NJ)
Wright State U (OH)
Yale U (CT)
York Coll of the City U of New York (NY)
Youngstown State U (OH)

AFRICAN LANGUAGES
Harvard U (MA)
Ohio U (OH)
U of California, Los Angeles (CA)
U of Wisconsin–Madison (WI)

AFRICAN STUDIES
Agnes Scott Coll (GA)
American Public U System (WV)
Bard Coll (NY)
Barnard Coll (NY)
Bowdoin Coll (ME)
Bowling Green State U (OH)
Colgate U (NY)
The Coll at Brockport, State U of New York (NY)
Connecticut Coll (CT)
Dartmouth Coll (NH)
Drew U (NJ)
Emory U (GA)
Franklin & Marshall Coll (PA)
Hamilton Coll (NY)
Harvard U (MA)
Haverford Coll (PA)
Hobart and William Smith Colls (NY)
Hofstra U (NY)
Illinois Wesleyan U (IL)
Indiana U Bloomington (IN)
Kennesaw State U (GA)
Kenyon Coll (OH)
Marlboro Coll (VT)
McGill U (QC, Canada)
Miles Coll (AL)
Morgan State U (MD)
Northwestern U (IL)
Oakland U (MI)
Ohio U (OH)
Portland State U (OR)
Queens Coll of the City U of New York (NY)
Rutgers, The State U of New Jersey, New Brunswick (NJ)
St. Lawrence U (NY)
Sarah Lawrence Coll (NY)
Stanford U (CA)
Tennessee State U (TN)
Tulane U (LA)
U of Chicago (IL)
The U of Iowa (IA)
U of Kansas (KS)
U of Maryland, Baltimore County (MD)
U of Minnesota, Twin Cities Campus (MN)
U of Pennsylvania (PA)
U of Toronto (ON, Canada)
U of Wisconsin–Madison (WI)
Vanderbilt U (TN)
Vassar Coll (NY)
Washington U in St. Louis (MO)
Wellesley Coll (MA)
Western Michigan U (MI)
Wheaton Coll (MA)
William Paterson U of New Jersey (NJ)
Yale U (CT)
York U (ON, Canada)

AGRIBUSINESS
Abilene Christian U (TX)
Adams State Coll (CO)
Andrews U (MI)
Arkansas State U (AR)
Brigham Young U (UT)
Coll of the Ozarks (MO)
Colorado State U (CO)
Cornell U (NY)
Delaware Valley Coll (PA)
Illinois State U (IL)
Middle Tennessee State U (TN)
Mississippi State U (MS)
Missouri State U (MO)
North Carolina State U (NC)
North Dakota State U (ND)
Penn State Abington (PA)
Penn State Altoona (PA)
Penn State Berks (PA)
Penn State Erie, The Behrend Coll (PA)
Penn State U Park (PA)
Sam Houston State U (TX)
South Dakota State U (SD)
Southeast Missouri State U (MO)
Southwest Minnesota State U (MN)
State U of New York Coll of Agriculture and Technology at Cobleskill (NY)
Stephen F. Austin State U (TX)
Texas A&M U (TX)
Texas State U-San Marcos (TX)
U of Arkansas (AR)
U of Central Missouri (MO)
U of Delaware (DE)
U of Louisiana at Lafayette (LA)
U of Maine (ME)
U of Minnesota, Crookston (MN)
U of Wyoming (WY)
West Texas A&M U (TX)

AGRICULTURAL AND DOMESTIC ANIMALS SERVICES RELATED
Sterling Coll (VT)
Tarleton State U (TX)

AGRICULTURAL AND EXTENSION EDUCATION
Colorado State U (CO)
North Carolina State U (NC)
Penn State Abington (PA)
Penn State Altoona (PA)
Penn State Berks (PA)
Penn State Erie, The Behrend Coll (PA)
Penn State U Park (PA)
U of Illinois at Urbana–Champaign (IL)

AGRICULTURAL AND FOOD PRODUCTS PROCESSING
Kansas State U (KS)
Purdue U (IN)
Texas A&M U (TX)
The U of British Columbia (BC, Canada)
U of Florida (FL)
U of Nebraska–Lincoln (NE)

AGRICULTURAL AND HORTICULTURAL PLANT BREEDING
Colorado State U (CO)
Cornell U (NY)
Sterling Coll (VT)

AGRICULTURAL ANIMAL BREEDING
State U of New York Coll of Agriculture and Technology at Cobleskill (NY)
Sterling Coll (VT)
Texas A&M U (TX)
U of Nevada, Reno (NV)

AGRICULTURAL/ BIOLOGICAL ENGINEERING AND BIOENGINEERING
Auburn U (AL)
California Polytechnic State U, San Luis Obispo (CA)
California State Polytechnic U, Pomona (CA)
Clemson U (SC)
Cornell U (NY)
Dordt Coll (IA)
Iowa State U of Science and Technology (IA)
Kansas State U (KS)
McGill U (QC, Canada)
Michigan State U (MI)
Mississippi State U (MS)
Missouri U of Science and Technology (MO)
North Carolina State U (NC)
North Dakota State U (ND)
Oregon State U (OR)
Penn State Abington (PA)
Penn State Altoona (PA)
Penn State Berks (PA)
Penn State Erie, The Behrend Coll (PA)
Penn State U Park (PA)
Polytechnic U, Brooklyn Campus (NY)
Purdue U (IN)
Rutgers, The State U of New Jersey, New Brunswick (NJ)
South Dakota State U (SD)
State U of New York Coll of Environmental Science and Forestry (NY)
Tennessee Technological U (TN)
Texas A&M U (TX)
The U of Arizona (AZ)
U of Arkansas (AR)
U of California, Los Angeles (CA)
U of California, Santa Cruz (CA)
U of Delaware (DE)
U of Florida (FL)
U of Georgia (GA)
U of Idaho (ID)
U of Illinois at Urbana–Champaign (IL)
U of Maine (ME)
U of Maryland, Coll Park (MD)
U of Minnesota, Twin Cities Campus (MN)
U of Nebraska–Lincoln (NE)
The U of Tennessee (TN)
U of Wisconsin–Madison (WI)
Utah State U (UT)

AGRICULTURAL BUSINESS AND MANAGEMENT
Alcorn State U (MS)
Bard Coll at Simon's Rock (MA)
Brigham Young U (UT)
California Polytechnic State U, San Luis Obispo (CA)
California State Polytechnic U, Pomona (CA)
California State U, Chico (CA)
California State U, Fresno (CA)
Capital U (OH)
Clemson U (SC)
Cornell U (NY)
Eastern Kentucky U (KY)
Eastern New Mexico U (NM)
Florida Ag and Mech U (FL)
Florida Southern Coll (FL)
Fort Lewis Coll (CO)
Freed-Hardeman U (TN)
Grace U (NE)
Hardin-Simmons U (TX)
Iowa State U of Science and Technology (IA)
Kansas State U (KS)
Lincoln U (MO)
Louisiana State U and Ag and Mech Coll (LA)
Lubbock Christian U (TX)
McGill U (QC, Canada)
Michigan State U (MI)
Montana State U (MT)
Murray State U (KY)
Nicholls State U (LA)
North Carolina Ag and Tech State U (NC)
North Dakota State U (ND)
Northwestern Oklahoma State U (OK)
Northwest Missouri State U (MO)
Nova Scotia Ag Coll (NS, Canada)
Oklahoma Panhandle State U (OK)
Oklahoma State U (OK)
Oregon State U (OR)
Sam Houston State U (TX)
San Diego State U (CA)
South Carolina State U (SC)
Southern Arkansas U–Magnolia (AR)
Southwest Minnesota State U (MN)
State U of New York Coll of Agriculture and Technology at Cobleskill (NY)
Sterling Coll (VT)
Tabor Coll (KS)
Tennessee Technological U (TN)
Texas A&M U (TX)
Texas A&M U–Commerce (TX)
Texas Tech U (TX)
Truman State U (MO)
Tuskegee U (AL)
U of Central Missouri (MO)

U of Delaware (DE)
U of Georgia (GA)
U of Idaho (ID)
U of Illinois at Urbana–Champaign (IL)
U of Lethbridge (AB, Canada)
U of Louisiana at Monroe (LA)
U of Maryland Eastern Shore (MD)
U of Minnesota, Crookston (MN)
U of Minnesota, Twin Cities Campus (MN)
U of Missouri–Columbia (MO)
U of Nebraska at Kearney (NE)
U of Nebraska–Lincoln (NE)
U of New Hampshire (NH)
The U of Tennessee at Martin (TN)
U of Wisconsin–Madison (WI)
U of Wisconsin–Platteville (WI)
Utah State U (UT)
Washington State U (WA)
West Texas A&M U (TX)
Wilmington Coll (OH)

AGRICULTURAL BUSINESS AND MANAGEMENT RELATED

Sterling Coll (VT)
U of California, Davis (CA)
The U of Tennessee (TN)
Utah State U (UT)

AGRICULTURAL COMMUNICATION/ JOURNALISM

Michigan State U (MI)
Oklahoma State U (OK)
Purdue U (IN)
Sterling Coll (VT)
Texas Tech U (TX)
U of Arkansas (AR)
U of Georgia (GA)
U of Illinois at Urbana–Champaign (IL)
U of Missouri–Columbia (MO)
U of Nebraska–Lincoln (NE)
U of Wyoming (WY)
Washington State U (WA)

AGRICULTURAL ECONOMICS

Alabama Ag and Mech U (AL)
Alcorn State U (MS)
Auburn U (AL)
Brigham Young U (UT)
Clemson U (SC)
Colorado State U (CO)
Cornell U (NY)
Kansas State U (KS)
McGill U (QC, Canada)
Michigan State U (MI)
Mississippi State U (MS)
North Carolina Ag and Tech State U (NC)
North Carolina State U (NC)
North Dakota State U (ND)
Northwest Missouri State U (MO)
Nova Scotia Ag Coll (NS, Canada)
Oklahoma State U (OK)
Oregon State U (OR)
Purdue U (IN)
South Dakota State U (SD)
Southern Illinois U Carbondale (IL)
Southern U and Ag and Mech Coll (LA)
Tarleton State U (TX)
Texas A&M U (TX)
Texas A&M U–Commerce (TX)
Texas Tech U (TX)
The U of Arizona (AZ)
U of Arkansas at Pine Bluff (AR)
U of Central Missouri (MO)
U of Connecticut (CT)
U of Delaware (DE)
U of Florida (FL)
U of Georgia (GA)
U of Hawaii at Manoa (HI)
U of Idaho (ID)
U of Illinois at Urbana–Champaign (IL)
U of Maine (ME)
U of Maryland, Coll Park (MD)
U of Missouri–Columbia (MO)
U of Nebraska–Lincoln (NE)
U of Nevada, Reno (NV)
The U of Tennessee (TN)
U of Wisconsin–Madison (WI)
Utah State U (UT)
Virginia Polytechnic Inst and State U (VA)
Washington State U (WA)
West Virginia U (WV)

AGRICULTURAL/FARM SUPPLIES RETAILING AND WHOLESALING

Texas A&M U (TX)

AGRICULTURAL MECHANIZATION

Clemson U (SC)
Coll of the Ozarks (MO)
Iowa State U of Science and Technology (IA)
Kansas State U (KS)
Montana State U (MT)
North Carolina Ag and Tech State U (NC)
North Dakota State U (ND)
Northwest Missouri State U (MO)
Nova Scotia Ag Coll (NS, Canada)
Penn State Abington (PA)
Penn State Altoona (PA)
Penn State Berks (PA)
Penn State Erie, The Behrend Coll (PA)
Penn State U Park (PA)
Purdue U (IN)
Sam Houston State U (TX)
South Dakota State U (SD)
State U of New York Coll of Agriculture and Technology at Cobleskill (NY)
Stephen F. Austin State U (TX)
U of Idaho (ID)
U of Illinois at Urbana–Champaign (IL)
U of Missouri–Columbia (MO)
U of Nebraska–Lincoln (NE)
Washington State U (WA)

AGRICULTURAL MECHANIZATION RELATED

Coll of the Ozarks (MO)

AGRICULTURAL PRODUCTION

Eastern Kentucky U (KY)
Purdue U (IN)
Stephen F. Austin State U (TX)
Texas A&M U (TX)
U of Hawaii at Manoa (HI)

AGRICULTURAL PRODUCTION RELATED

Sterling Coll (VT)
Tarleton State U (TX)

AGRICULTURAL PUBLIC SERVICES RELATED

Sterling Coll (VT)
U of Illinois at Urbana–Champaign (IL)

AGRICULTURAL SCIENCES

Cameron U (OK)
Texas A&M U–Commerce (TX)
U of Georgia (GA)
The U of Tennessee at Martin (TN)

AGRICULTURAL SCIENCES RELATED

U of Georgia (GA)

AGRICULTURAL TEACHER EDUCATION

Arkansas State U (AR)
Auburn U (AL)
California State Polytechnic U, Pomona (CA)
California State U, Chico (CA)
California State U, Fresno (CA)
Clemson U (SC)
Coll of the Ozarks (MO)
Colorado State U (CO)
Cornell U (NY)
Dordt Coll (IA)
Eastern New Mexico U (NM)
Iowa State U of Science and Technology (IA)
McNeese State U (LA)
Mississippi State U (MS)
Missouri State U (MO)
Montana State U (MT)
Murray State U (KY)
North Carolina Ag and Tech State U (NC)
North Carolina State U (NC)
North Dakota State U (ND)
Northwest Missouri State U (MO)
Oklahoma Panhandle State U (OK)
Oklahoma State U (OK)
Prairie View A&M U (TX)
Purdue U (IN)
Sam Houston State U (TX)
Southern Arkansas U–Magnolia (AR)
Southern U and Ag and Mech Coll (LA)
State U of New York at Oswego (NY)
Sterling Coll (VT)
Tarleton State U (TX)
Tennessee Technological U (TN)
Texas A&M U–Commerce (TX)
The U of Arizona (AZ)
U of Arkansas (AR)
U of Arkansas at Pine Bluff (AR)
U of Connecticut (CT)
U of Delaware (DE)
U of Florida (FL)
U of Georgia (GA)
U of Idaho (ID)
U of Illinois at Urbana–Champaign (IL)
U of Maryland Eastern Shore (MD)
U of Minnesota, Crookston (MN)
U of Minnesota, Twin Cities Campus (MN)
U of Missouri–Columbia (MO)
U of Nebraska–Lincoln (NE)
U of Nevada, Reno (NV)
U of New Hampshire (NH)
The U of Tennessee (TN)
The U of Tennessee at Martin (TN)
U of Wisconsin–Madison (WI)
U of Wisconsin–Platteville (WI)
U of Wyoming (WY)
Utah State U (UT)
Washington State U (WA)
West Virginia U (WV)
Wilmington Coll (OH)

AGRICULTURE

Alcorn State U (MS)
American U of Beirut (Lebanon)
Arkansas State U (AR)
Auburn U (AL)
Austin Peay State U (TN)
Berea Coll (KY)
California Polytechnic State U, San Luis Obispo (CA)
California State Polytechnic U, Pomona (CA)
California State U, Stanislaus (CA)
Cornell U (NY)
Dordt Coll (IA)
Eastern Kentucky U (KY)
Ferrum Coll (VA)
Florida Ag and Mech U (FL)
Hampshire Coll (MA)
Illinois State U (IL)
Iowa State U of Science and Technology (IA)
Lincoln U (MO)
Lubbock Christian U (TX)
McGill U (QC, Canada)
McNeese State U (LA)
Mississippi State U (MS)
Missouri State U (MO)
Morehead State U (KY)
Murray State U (KY)
North Carolina Ag and Tech State U (NC)
North Dakota State U (ND)
Northwestern Oklahoma State U (OK)
Northwest Missouri State U (MO)
Nova Scotia Ag Coll (NS, Canada)
Oklahoma State U (OK)
Oregon State U (OR)
Penn State Abington (PA)
Penn State Altoona (PA)
Penn State Berks (PA)
Penn State Erie, The Behrend Coll (PA)
Penn State U Park (PA)
Prairie View A&M U (TX)
Purdue U (IN)
Rutgers, The State U of New Jersey, New Brunswick (NJ)
Sam Houston State U (TX)
South Dakota State U (SD)
Southeast Missouri State U (MO)
Southern Arkansas U–Magnolia (AR)
Southern Illinois U Carbondale (IL)
Stephen F. Austin State U (TX)
Sterling Coll (VT)
Tennessee State U (TN)
Texas A&M U (TX)
Texas A&M U–Commerce (TX)
Texas State U-San Marcos (TX)
Texas Tech U (TX)
Truman State U (MO)
Tuskegee U (AL)
The U of Arizona (AZ)
U of Arkansas at Monticello (AR)
U of Arkansas at Pine Bluff (AR)
The U of British Columbia (BC, Canada)
U of Connecticut (CT)
U of Delaware (DE)
U of Guam (GU)
U of Idaho (ID)
U of Lethbridge (AB, Canada)
U of Louisiana at Lafayette (LA)
U of Maryland, Coll Park (MD)
U of Maryland Eastern Shore (MD)
U of Minnesota, Twin Cities Campus (MN)
U of Missouri–Columbia (MO)
U of Nebraska–Lincoln (NE)
U of New Hampshire (NH)
The U of Tennessee at Martin (TN)
U of Vermont (VT)
U of Wisconsin–Madison (WI)
Utah State U (UT)
Virginia State U (VA)
Washington State U (WA)
Western Illinois U (IL)
Western Kentucky U (KY)
West Texas A&M U (TX)
Wilmington Coll (OH)

AGRICULTURE AND AGRICULTURE OPERATIONS RELATED

Michigan State U (MI)
Sterling Coll (VT)
Tarleton State U (TX)
U of California, Davis (CA)
U of Maryland, Coll Park (MD)

AGRONOMY AND CROP SCIENCE

Auburn U (AL)
California Polytechnic State U, San Luis Obispo (CA)
California State Polytechnic U, Pomona (CA)
California State U, Chico (CA)
California State U, Fresno (CA)
Coll of the Ozarks (MO)
Colorado State U (CO)
Cornell U (NY)
Delaware Valley Coll (PA)
Hardin-Simmons U (TX)
Iowa State U of Science and Technology (IA)
Kansas State U (KS)
McGill U (QC, Canada)
Mississippi State U (MS)
Missouri State U (MO)
North Carolina State U (NC)
Northwest Missouri State U (MO)
Oklahoma Panhandle State U (OK)
Oregon State U (OR)
Penn State Abington (PA)
Penn State Altoona (PA)
Penn State Berks (PA)
Penn State Erie, The Behrend Coll (PA)
Penn State U Park (PA)
Purdue U (IN)
South Dakota State U (SD)
State U of New York Coll of Agriculture and Technology at Cobleskill (NY)
Stephen F. Austin State U (TX)
Tarleton State U (TX)
Tennessee Technological U (TN)
Texas A&M U (TX)
Texas A&M U–Commerce (TX)
Texas Tech U (TX)
Truman State U (MO)
Tuskegee U (AL)
U of Arkansas at Pine Bluff (AR)
U of Connecticut (CT)
U of Delaware (DE)
U of Florida (FL)
U of Idaho (ID)
U of Illinois at Urbana–Champaign (IL)
U of Maryland, Coll Park (MD)
U of Minnesota, Crookston (MN)
U of Minnesota, Twin Cities Campus (MN)
U of Nebraska–Lincoln (NE)
U of New Hampshire (NH)
The U of Tennessee at Martin (TN)
U of Vermont (VT)
U of Wisconsin–Madison (WI)
U of Wisconsin–Platteville (WI)
Utah State U (UT)
Virginia Polytechnic Inst and State U (VA)
Washington State U (WA)
West Texas A&M U (TX)

AIRCRAFT POWERPLANT TECHNOLOGY

Embry-Riddle Aeronautical U (FL)
Embry-Riddle Aeronautical U Worldwide (FL)

AIR FORCE R.O.T.C./AIR SCIENCE

La Salle U (PA)
Rensselaer Polytechnic Inst (NY)
The U of Iowa (IA)
Weber State U (UT)

AIRFRAME MECHANICS AND AIRCRAFT MAINTENANCE TECHNOLOGY

LeTourneau U (TX)
Lewis U (IL)
Thomas Edison State Coll (NJ)
Wilmington U (DE)

AIRLINE PILOT AND FLIGHT CREW

Auburn U (AL)
Baylor U (TX)
Bridgewater State Coll (MA)
Cornerstone U (MI)
Delta State U (MS)
Eastern Kentucky U (KY)
Eastern Michigan U (MI)
Embry-Riddle Aeronautical U (AZ)
Embry-Riddle Aeronautical U (FL)
Farmingdale State Coll (NY)
Grace U (NE)
Indiana State U (IN)
Inter American U of Puerto Rico, Bayamón Campus (PR)
Jacksonville U (FL)
Kansas State U (KS)
LeTourneau U (TX)
Purdue U (IN)
Quincy U (IL)
St. Cloud State U (MN)
Saint Louis U (MO)
Southeastern Oklahoma State U (OK)
U of Illinois at Urbana–Champaign (IL)
U of North Dakota (ND)
Utah Valley State Coll (UT)
Western Michigan U (MI)
Westminster Coll (UT)

AIR TRAFFIC CONTROL

Daniel Webster Coll (NH)
Embry-Riddle Aeronautical U (FL)
Florida Memorial U (FL)
Hampton U (VA)
Inter American U of Puerto Rico, Bayamón Campus (PR)
Lewis U (IL)
Purdue U (IN)
St. Cloud State U (MN)
Thomas Edison State Coll (NJ)
U of Maryland Eastern Shore (MD)
U of North Dakota (ND)

AIR TRANSPORTATION RELATED

Thomas Edison State Coll (NJ)

ALLIED HEALTH AND MEDICAL ASSISTING SERVICES RELATED

Ramapo Coll of New Jersey (NJ)
Widener U (PA)

ALLIED HEALTH DIAGNOSTIC, INTERVENTION, AND TREATMENT PROFESSIONS RELATED

Bloomfield Coll (NJ)
Fairleigh Dickinson U, Coll at Florham (NJ)
Fairleigh Dickinson U, Metropolitan Campus (NJ)
Georgian Court U (NJ)
Gwynedd-Mercy Coll (PA)
Hofstra U (NY)
Rutgers, The State U of New Jersey, Newark (NJ)
Tennessee Wesleyan Coll (TN)
U of Connecticut (CT)
The U of Toledo (OH)

ALTERNATIVE AND COMPLEMENTARY MEDICINE RELATED

Johnson State Coll (VT)

AMERICAN GOVERNMENT AND POLITICS

Ave Maria U (FL)
Bard Coll (NY)
Bennington Coll (VT)
Bridgewater State Coll (MA)
Claremont McKenna Coll (CA)
Huston-Tillotson U (TX)
The Master's Coll and Sem (CA)
North Carolina State U (NC)
Northern Arizona U (AZ)
Oklahoma Christian U (OK)
The U of Akron (OH)
The U of Montana (MT)

AMERICAN HISTORY

Bard Coll (NY)
Bennington Coll (VT)
Chapman U (CA)
Gettysburg Coll (PA)

Sarah Lawrence Coll (NY)
U of Regina (SK, Canada)

AMERICAN INDIAN/NATIVE AMERICAN STUDIES
Arizona State U (AZ)
Bemidji State U (MN)
California State U, East Bay (CA)
Colgate U (NY)
Creighton U (NE)
Dartmouth Coll (NH)
The Evergreen State Coll (WA)
Fort Lewis Coll (CO)
Humboldt State U (CA)
Laurentian U (ON, Canada)
Northeastern State U (OK)
Northern Arizona U (AZ)
Northland Coll (WI)
Portland State U (OR)
St. Thomas U (NB, Canada)
San Diego State U (CA)
Sonoma State U (CA)
Stanford U (CA)
Trent U (ON, Canada)
U of Alaska Fairbanks (AK)
U of California, Berkeley (CA)
U of California, Davis (CA)
U of California, Los Angeles (CA)
U of California, Riverside (CA)
The U of Iowa (IA)
U of Lethbridge (AB, Canada)
U of Minnesota, Duluth (MN)
U of Minnesota, Twin Cities Campus (MN)
The U of Montana (MT)
The U of North Carolina at Pembroke (NC)
U of North Dakota (ND)
U of Oklahoma (OK)
U of Ottawa (ON, Canada)
U of Regina (SK, Canada)
U of Science and Arts of Oklahoma (OK)
The U of South Dakota (SD)
U of Toronto (ON, Canada)
The U of Western Ontario (ON, Canada)
U of Wisconsin–Eau Claire (WI)
U of Wisconsin–Green Bay (WI)
U of Wisconsin–Milwaukee (WI)

AMERICAN LITERATURE
Bard Coll at Simon's Rock (MA)
Bennington Coll (VT)
Castleton State Coll (VT)
Clarkson U (NY)
The Coll at Brockport, State U of New York (NY)
Middlebury Coll (VT)
Queens U of Charlotte (NC)
St. Lawrence U (NY)
Sarah Lawrence Coll (NY)
U of California, Los Angeles (CA)
U of Great Falls (MT)
U of Southern California (CA)
Washington U in St. Louis (MO)

AMERICAN NATIVE/NATIVE AMERICAN EDUCATION
Bard Coll at Simon's Rock (MA)
The Coll of St. Scholastica (MN)
Concordia U (QC, Canada)
Northeastern State U (OK)
Queen's U at Kingston (ON, Canada)
U of Lethbridge (AB, Canada)
U of Regina (SK, Canada)

AMERICAN NATIVE/NATIVE AMERICAN LANGUAGES
Bemidji State U (MN)
U of Lethbridge (AB, Canada)
U of Regina (SK, Canada)

AMERICAN SIGN LANGUAGE (ASL)
Augustana Coll (SD)
California State U, Sacramento (CA)
Gardner-Webb U (NC)
Madonna U (MI)
Maryville Coll (TN)
U of Rochester (NY)
Utah Valley State Coll (UT)

AMERICAN SIGN LANGUAGE RELATED
The U of Iowa (IA)

AMERICAN STUDIES
Albion Coll (MI)
Albright Coll (PA)
American Public U System (WV)
American U (DC)
Amherst Coll (MA)
Arizona State U at the West campus (AZ)
Ashland U (OH)
Bard Coll (NY)
Bard Coll at Simon's Rock (MA)
Barnard Coll (NY)
Bates Coll (ME)
Baylor U (TX)
Bennington Coll (VT)
Boston U (MA)
Bowling Green State U (OH)
Brandeis U (MA)
Brigham Young U (UT)
Brown U (RI)
Cabrini Coll (PA)
California State U, Chico (CA)
California State U, Fullerton (CA)
California State U, Long Beach (CA)
California State U, San Bernardino (CA)
Case Western Reserve U (OH)
Cedarville U (OH)
Claflin U (SC)
Claremont McKenna Coll (CA)
Clarkson U (NY)
Colby Coll (ME)
Coll of Saint Elizabeth (NJ)
The Coll of Saint Rose (NY)
Coll of Staten Island of the City U of New York (NY)
The Coll of William and Mary (VA)
Colorado State U (CO)
Connecticut Coll (CT)
Cornell U (NY)
Creighton U (NE)
DePaul U (IL)
Dickinson Coll (PA)
Dominican Coll (NY)
Dominican U (IL)
Eckerd Coll (FL)
Emmanuel Coll (MA)
Emory U (GA)
Erskine Coll (SC)
Fairfield U (CT)
Florida State U (FL)
Franklin & Marshall Coll (PA)
Franklin Coll (IN)
Georgetown Coll (KY)
Georgetown U (DC)
The George Washington U (DC)
Gettysburg Coll (PA)
Goucher Coll (MD)
Hamilton Coll (NY)
Hampshire Coll (MA)
Harvard U (MA)
Hawai'i Pacific U (HI)
Hendrix Coll (AR)
High Point U (NC)
Hillsdale Coll (MI)
Hobart and William Smith Colls (NY)
Hofstra U (NY)
Howard Payne U (TX)
Idaho State U (ID)
Illinois Wesleyan U (IL)
Indiana U Bloomington (IN)
Keene State Coll (NH)
Kent State U (OH)
Kenyon Coll (OH)
King Coll (TN)
Knox Coll (IL)
Lafayette Coll (PA)
Lake Forest Coll (IL)
Lebanon Valley Coll (PA)
Lehigh U (PA)
Lehman Coll of the City U of New York (NY)
Lesley U (MA)
Lewis U (IL)
Lindsey Wilson Coll (KY)
Lipscomb U (TN)
Lycoming Coll (PA)
Manhattanville Coll (NY)
Marist Coll (NY)
Marlboro Coll (VT)
Miami U (OH)
Miami U Hamilton (OH)
Michigan State U (MI)
Middlebury Coll (VT)
Mills Coll (CA)
Mount Allison U (NB, Canada)
Mount Holyoke Coll (MA)
Mount Ida Coll (MA)
Mount St. Mary's Coll (CA)
Muhlenberg Coll (PA)
Nazareth Coll of Rochester (NY)
Northwestern U (IL)
Nova Southeastern U (FL)
Occidental Coll (CA)
Oglethorpe U (GA)
Oklahoma City U (OK)
Oklahoma State U (OK)
Oregon State U (OR)
Penn State Abington (PA)
Penn State Altoona (PA)
Penn State Berks (PA)
Penn State Erie, The Behrend Coll (PA)
Penn State Harrisburg (PA)
Pitzer Coll (CA)
Pomona Coll (CA)
Providence Coll (RI)
Queens Coll of the City U of New York (NY)
Queens U of Charlotte (NC)
Ramapo Coll of New Jersey (NJ)
Reed Coll (OR)
Rider U (NJ)
Roger Williams U (RI)
Rutgers, The State U of New Jersey, Newark (NJ)
Rutgers, The State U of New Jersey, New Brunswick (NJ)
St. Cloud State U (MN)
Saint Francis U (PA)
St. John Fisher Coll (NY)
Saint Joseph Coll (CT)
Saint Louis U (MO)
Saint Mary's Coll of California (CA)
Saint Michael's Coll (VT)
St. Olaf Coll (MN)
Salem Coll (NC)
Salve Regina U (RI)
San Diego State U (CA)
San Francisco State U (CA)
Sarah Lawrence Coll (NY)
Scripps Coll (CA)
Sewanee: The U of the South (TN)
Shenandoah U (VA)
Siena Coll (NY)
Skidmore Coll (NY)
Smith Coll (MA)
Sonoma State U (CA)
Southwestern U (TX)
Stanford U (CA)
State U of New York at Fredonia (NY)
State U of New York at Oswego (NY)
State U of New York Coll at Geneseo (NY)
State U of New York Coll at Old Westbury (NY)
Stetson U (FL)
Stonehill Coll (MA)
Stony Brook U, State U of New York (NY)
Syracuse U (NY)
Temple U (PA)
Tennessee Wesleyan Coll (TN)
Texas A&M U (TX)
Texas State U-San Marcos (TX)
Trinity Coll (CT)
Tufts U (MA)
Tulane U (LA)
Union Coll (NY)
U at Buffalo, the State U of New York (NY)
The U of Alabama (AL)
U of Arkansas (AR)
U of California, Berkeley (CA)
U of California, Davis (CA)
U of California, Santa Cruz (CA)
U of Chicago (IL)
U of Connecticut (CT)
U of Dayton (OH)
U of Florida (FL)
U of Hawaii at Manoa (HI)
U of Idaho (ID)
The U of Iowa (IA)
U of Kansas (KS)
U of Mary Hardin-Baylor (TX)
U of Maryland, Baltimore County (MD)
U of Maryland, Coll Park (MD)
U of Mary Washington (VA)
U of Massachusetts Boston (MA)
U of Massachusetts Lowell (MA)
U of Miami (FL)
U of Michigan (MI)
U of Michigan–Dearborn (MI)
U of Minnesota, Twin Cities Campus (MN)
U of Mississippi (MS)
U of Missouri–Kansas City (MO)
U of New England (ME)
U of New Mexico (NM)
The U of North Carolina at Chapel Hill (NC)
The U of North Carolina at Pembroke (NC)
U of Northern Iowa (IA)
U of Notre Dame (IN)
U of Pennsylvania (PA)
U of Pittsburgh at Johnstown (PA)
U of Richmond (VA)
U of Rio Grande (OH)
U of Saint Francis (IN)
U of Southern California (CA)
U of Southern Mississippi (MS)
U of South Florida (FL)
The U of Texas at Austin (TX)
The U of Texas at Dallas (TX)
The U of Texas at San Antonio (TX)
The U of Texas–Pan American (TX)
The U of Toledo (OH)
U of Toronto (ON, Canada)
The U of Western Ontario (ON, Canada)
U of Wisconsin–Madison (WI)
U of Wyoming (WY)
Ursinus Coll (PA)
Ursuline Coll (OH)
Utah State U (UT)
Valparaiso U (IN)
Vanderbilt U (TN)
Vassar Coll (NY)
Virginia Wesleyan Coll (VA)
Warner Pacific Coll (OR)
Washington Coll (MD)
Washington State U (WA)
Washington U in St. Louis (MO)
Wayne State U (MI)
Wellesley Coll (MA)
Wells Coll (NY)
Wesleyan Coll (GA)
Wesleyan U (CT)
Wesley Coll (DE)
West Chester U of Pennsylvania (PA)
Western Connecticut State U (CT)
Western Washington U (WA)
Wheaton Coll (MA)
Whitworth U (WA)
Willamette U (OR)
Williams Coll (MA)
Wingate U (NC)
Wittenberg U (OH)
Yale U (CT)
Youngstown State U (OH)

ANALYTICAL CHEMISTRY
McGill U (QC, Canada)
The U of Western Ontario (ON, Canada)
West Chester U of Pennsylvania (PA)

ANATOMY
Andrews U (MI)
Duke U (NC)
McGill U (QC, Canada)
Minnesota State U Mankato (MN)
Tulane U (LA)
The U of Western Ontario (ON, Canada)
Wright State U (OH)

ANCIENT/CLASSICAL GREEK
Amherst Coll (MA)
Bard Coll (NY)
Barnard Coll (NY)
Baylor U (TX)
Boston Coll (MA)
Boston U (MA)
Brandeis U (MA)
Brigham Young U (UT)
Brock U (ON, Canada)
Bryn Mawr Coll (PA)
California State U, Long Beach (CA)
Concordia U (MI)
Creighton U (NE)
Dartmouth Coll (NH)
DePauw U (IN)
Duke U (NC)
Duquesne U (PA)
Franklin & Marshall Coll (PA)
Gettysburg Coll (PA)
Hampden-Sydney Coll (VA)
Hobart and William Smith Colls (NY)
Hunter Coll of the City U of New York (NY)
Kenyon Coll (OH)
Lawrence U (WI)
Loyola U Chicago (IL)
Miami U (OH)
Mount Allison U (NB, Canada)
Mount Holyoke Coll (MA)
Multnomah Bible Coll and Biblical Sem (OR)
Ohio U (OH)
Queens Coll of the City U of New York (NY)
Randolph Coll (VA)
Randolph-Macon Coll (VA)
Rice U (TX)
Rockford Coll (IL)
Rutgers, The State U of New Jersey, New Brunswick (NJ)
St. John's Coll (NM)
St. Olaf Coll (MN)
Santa Clara U (CA)
Smith Coll (MA)
Stanford U (CA)
State U of New York at Binghamton (NY)
Swarthmore Coll (PA)
U of California, Berkeley (CA)
U of California, Los Angeles (CA)
U of Chicago (IL)
U of Georgia (GA)
The U of Iowa (IA)
U of Nebraska–Lincoln (NE)
U of Notre Dame (IN)
U of Oregon (OR)
U of St. Thomas (MN)
The U of Scranton (PA)
The U of Texas at Austin (TX)
U of Vermont (VT)
U of Victoria (BC, Canada)
The U of Western Ontario (ON, Canada)
Vassar Coll (NY)
Wake Forest U (NC)
Washington U in St. Louis (MO)
Wellesley Coll (MA)
Wheaton Coll (MA)
Yale U (CT)

ANCIENT NEAR EASTERN AND BIBLICAL LANGUAGES
Asbury Coll (KY)
Baylor U (TX)
Belmont U (TN)
Bethany U (CA)
Brigham Young U (UT)
Carson-Newman Coll (TN)
Concordia U (MI)
Concordia U Chicago (IL)
Concordia U Wisconsin (WI)
Cornerstone U (MI)
Harvard U (MA)
Hope Coll (MI)
Howard Payne U (TX)
Indiana Wesleyan U (IN)
List Coll, The Jewish Theological Sem (NY)
Lubbock Christian U (TX)
Luther Coll (IA)
The Master's Coll and Sem (CA)
Mid-Continent U (KY)
Northwest Nazarene U (ID)
Ozark Christian Coll (MO)
Taylor U (IN)
Union U (TN)
U of Chicago (IL)
U of Toronto (ON, Canada)
Walla Walla U (WA)
York Coll (NE)
York U (ON, Canada)

ANCIENT STUDIES
Bowdoin Coll (ME)
Concordia U (QC, Canada)
Michigan State U (MI)
Missouri State U (MO)
Mount Holyoke Coll (MA)
Ohio Wesleyan U (OH)
Rockford Coll (IL)
St. Olaf Coll (MN)
Santa Clara U (CA)
Stanford U (CA)
Swarthmore Coll (PA)
The U of Iowa (IA)
U of Kansas (KS)
U of Maryland, Baltimore County (MD)
U of Nebraska–Lincoln (NE)
U of Oregon (OR)
The U of Texas at Austin (TX)
Washington U in St. Louis (MO)
Wheaton Coll (MA)

ANIMAL BEHAVIOR AND ETHOLOGY
Bucknell U (PA)
Carroll Coll (WI)
Franklin & Marshall Coll (PA)
McGill U (QC, Canada)
Southwestern U (TX)
U of Toronto (ON, Canada)

ANIMAL GENETICS
Ball State U (IN)
Cornell U (NY)
Dartmouth Coll (NH)
Harvard U (MA)
Jacksonville State U (AL)
Ohio Wesleyan U (OH)
Rutgers, The State U of New Jersey, New Brunswick (NJ)
Sarah Lawrence Coll (NY)
The U of British Columbia (BC, Canada)
U of Minnesota, Twin Cities Campus (MN)
U of Toronto (ON, Canada)
The U of Western Ontario (ON, Canada)
U of Wisconsin–Madison (WI)
Worcester Polytechnic Inst (MA)

ANIMAL HEALTH
Sterling Coll (VT)
U of Georgia (GA)

ANIMAL/LIVESTOCK HUSBANDRY AND PRODUCTION
Dordt Coll (IA)
Rutgers, The State U of New Jersey, New Brunswick (NJ)
Sterling Coll (VT)
Tarleton State U (TX)
Texas A&M U (TX)
The U of British Columbia (BC, Canada)
U of Illinois at Urbana–Champaign (IL)
U of New Hampshire (NH)

ANIMAL NUTRITION
Sterling Coll (VT)

ANIMAL PHYSIOLOGY
Boston U (MA)
California State U, Fresno (CA)
Cornell U (NY)
Minnesota State U Mankato (MN)
Rutgers, The State U of New Jersey, New Brunswick (NJ)
San Francisco State U (CA)
Sonoma State U (CA)
Texas State U-San Marcos (TX)
The U of Akron (OH)
U of California, San Diego (CA)
U of Connecticut (CT)
U of Minnesota, Twin Cities Campus (MN)
U of New Brunswick Fredericton (NB, Canada)
U of Toronto (ON, Canada)
The U of Western Ontario (ON, Canada)
Utah State U (UT)

ANIMAL SCIENCES
Abilene Christian U (TX)
Alabama Ag and Mech U (AL)
Angelo State U (TX)
Arkansas State U (AR)
Auburn U (AL)
Berry Coll (GA)
California Polytechnic State U, San Luis Obispo (CA)
California State Polytechnic U, Pomona (CA)
California State U, Chico (CA)
California State U, Fresno (CA)
Clemson U (SC)
Coll of the Ozarks (MO)
Colorado State U (CO)
Cornell U (NY)
Delaware Valley Coll (PA)
Dordt Coll (IA)
Florida Ag and Mech U (FL)
Hardin-Simmons U (TX)
Iowa State U of Science and Technology (IA)
Kansas State U (KS)
Louisiana State U and Ag and Mech Coll (LA)
Lubbock Christian U (TX)
McGill U (QC, Canada)
Mercy Coll (NY)
Michigan State U (MI)
Middle Tennessee State U (TN)
Mississippi State U (MS)
Missouri State U (MO)
Montana State U (MT)
Mount Ida Coll (MA)
North Carolina Ag and Tech State U (NC)
North Carolina State U (NC)
North Dakota State U (ND)
Northwest Missouri State U (MO)
Nova Scotia Ag Coll (NS, Canada)
Oklahoma Panhandle State U (OK)
Oklahoma State U (OK)
Oregon State U (OR)
Penn State Abington (PA)
Penn State Altoona (PA)
Penn State Berks (PA)
Penn State Erie, The Behrend Coll (PA)
Penn State U Park (PA)
Purdue U (IN)
Rutgers, The State U of New Jersey, New Brunswick (NJ)
Sam Houston State U (TX)
South Dakota State U (SD)
Southeast Missouri State U (MO)
Southern Illinois U Carbondale (IL)
Stephen F. Austin State U (TX)
Sterling Coll (VT)
Tarleton State U (TX)
Tennessee State U (TN)
Tennessee Technological U (TN)
Texas A&M U (TX)
Texas A&M U–Commerce (TX)
Texas State U-San Marcos (TX)
Texas Tech U (TX)
Thompson Rivers U (BC, Canada)
Truman State U (MO)
Tuskegee U (AL)
The U of Arizona (AZ)
U of Arkansas (AR)
U of Arkansas at Pine Bluff (AR)
The U of British Columbia (BC, Canada)
U of California, Davis (CA)
U of Connecticut (CT)
U of Delaware (DE)
U of Denver (CO)
U of Florida (FL)
U of Georgia (GA)
U of Hawaii at Manoa (HI)
U of Idaho (ID)
U of Illinois at Urbana–Champaign (IL)
U of Louisiana at Lafayette (LA)
U of Maine (ME)
U of Maryland, Coll Park (MD)
U of Massachusetts Amherst (MA)
U of Minnesota, Twin Cities Campus (MN)
U of Missouri–Columbia (MO)
U of Nebraska–Lincoln (NE)
U of Nevada, Reno (NV)
U of New Hampshire (NH)
U of Rhode Island (RI)
The U of Tennessee (TN)
The U of Tennessee at Martin (TN)
U of Vermont (VT)
U of Wisconsin–Madison (WI)
U of Wisconsin–Platteville (WI)
U of Wyoming (WY)
Utah State U (UT)
Virginia Polytechnic Inst and State U (VA)
Washington State U (WA)
West Texas A&M U (TX)
West Virginia U (WV)

ANIMAL SCIENCES RELATED
Delaware Valley Coll (PA)
Penn State Abington (PA)
Penn State Altoona (PA)
Penn State Berks (PA)
Penn State Erie, The Behrend Coll (PA)
Penn State U Park (PA)
Southern U and Ag and Mech Coll (LA)
Sterling Coll (VT)
U of California, Davis (CA)
U of Illinois at Urbana–Champaign (IL)
U of Minnesota, Crookston (MN)

ANIMAL TRAINING
Sterling Coll (VT)

ANIMATION, INTERACTIVE TECHNOLOGY, VIDEO GRAPHICS AND SPECIAL EFFECTS
Acad of Art U (CA)
American InterContinental U (CA)
American InterContinental U (FL)
American InterContinental U (TX)
American InterContinental U Buckhead Campus (GA)
American InterContinental U Dunwoody Campus (GA)
American InterContinental U-London (United Kingdom)
American InterContinental U Online (IL)
The Art Inst of Atlanta (GA)
The Art Inst of Atlanta–Decatur (GA)
The Art Inst of Austin (TX)
The Art Inst of California–Inland Empire (CA)
The Art Inst of California–Los Angeles (CA)
The Art Inst of California–Orange County (CA)
The Art Inst of California–Sacramento (CA)
The Art Inst of California–San Diego (CA)
The Art Inst of California–San Francisco (CA)
The Art Inst of Dallas (TX)
The Art Inst of Houston (TX)
The Art Inst of Indianapolis (IN)
The Art Inst of Las Vegas (NV)
The Art Inst of Phoenix (AZ)
The Art Inst of Portland (OR)
The Art Inst of Seattle (WA)
The Art Inst of Tucson (AZ)
The Art Insts Intl Minnesota (MN)
Bennington Coll (VT)
Bradley U (IL)
Brigham Young U (UT)
California Design Coll (CA)
Cogswell Polytechnical Coll (CA)
Concordia U (QC, Canada)
Davenport U, Grand Rapids (MI)
Fashion Inst of Technology (NY)
Ferris State U (MI)
Full Sail U (FL)
The Illinois Inst of Art–Chicago (IL)
The Illinois Inst of Art–Schaumburg (IL)
Kansas City Art Inst (MO)
Massachusetts Coll of Art and Design (MA)
Miami Intl U of Art & Design (FL)
Montclair State U (NJ)
The New England Inst of Art (MA)
New England School of Communications (ME)
Northwestern Coll (MN)
Ringling Coll of Art and Design (FL)
Rochester Inst of Technology (NY)
Rocky Mountain Coll of Art + Design (CO)
Savannah Coll of Art and Design (GA)
School of the Art Inst of Chicago (IL)
Southern Adventist U (TN)
Westwood Coll–Atlanta Northlake (GA)

ANTHROPOLOGY
Adelphi U (NY)
Agnes Scott Coll (GA)
Albion Coll (MI)
Alma Coll (MI)
American U (DC)
American U of Beirut (Lebanon)
Amherst Coll (MA)
Appalachian State U (NC)
Arizona State U (AZ)
Athabasca U (AB, Canada)
Auburn U (AL)
Augustana Coll (IL)
Ball State U (IN)
Bard Coll (NY)
Bard Coll at Simon's Rock (MA)
Barnard Coll (NY)
Bates Coll (ME)
Baylor U (TX)
Beloit Coll (WI)
Bennington Coll (VT)
Biola U (CA)
Bloomsburg U of Pennsylvania (PA)
Boise State U (ID)
Boston U (MA)
Bowdoin Coll (ME)
Brandeis U (MA)
Brigham Young U (UT)
Brown U (RI)
Bryn Mawr Coll (PA)
Bucknell U (PA)
Buffalo State Coll, State U of New York (NY)
Butler U (IN)
California State Polytechnic U, Pomona (CA)
California State U, Chico (CA)
California State U, Dominguez Hills (CA)
California State U, East Bay (CA)
California State U, Fresno (CA)
California State U, Fullerton (CA)
California State U, Long Beach (CA)
California State U, Los Angeles (CA)
California State U, Sacramento (CA)
California State U, San Bernardino (CA)
California State U, Stanislaus (CA)
Canisius Coll (NY)
Case Western Reserve U (OH)
The Catholic U of America (DC)
Central Connecticut State U (CT)
Central Michigan U (MI)
Central Washington U (WA)
Centre Coll (KY)
City Coll of the City U of New York (NY)
Claremont McKenna Coll (CA)
Clarion U of Pennsylvania (PA)
Cleveland State U (OH)
Colby Coll (ME)
Colgate U (NY)
The Coll at Brockport, State U of New York (NY)
Coll of Charleston (SC)
The Coll of Idaho (ID)
Coll of the Holy Cross (MA)
The Coll of William and Mary (VA)
The Colorado Coll (CO)
Colorado State U (CO)
Concordia U (QC, Canada)
Connecticut Coll (CT)
Cornell Coll (IA)
Cornell U (NY)
Creighton U (NE)
Dartmouth Coll (NH)
Davidson Coll (NC)
Denison U (OH)
DePaul U (IL)
DePauw U (IN)
Dickinson Coll (PA)
Dowling Coll (NY)
Drake U (IA)
Drew U (NJ)
Duke U (NC)
Earlham Coll (IN)
East Carolina U (NC)
Eastern Kentucky U (KY)
Eastern Michigan U (MI)
Eastern New Mexico U (NM)
Eckerd Coll (FL)
Edinboro U of Pennsylvania (PA)
Elizabethtown Coll (PA)
Elon U (NC)
Emory U (GA)
Eugene Lang Coll The New School for Liberal Arts (NY)
Florida Atlantic U (FL)
Florida Gulf Coast U (FL)
Florida State U (FL)
Fort Lewis Coll (CO)
Franciscan U of Steubenville (OH)
Franklin & Marshall Coll (PA)
George Mason U (VA)
Georgetown U (DC)
The George Washington U (DC)
Georgia Southern U (GA)
Georgia State U (GA)
Gettysburg Coll (PA)
Grand Valley State U (MI)
Green Mountain Coll (VT)
Grinnell Coll (IA)
Gustavus Adolphus Coll (MN)
Hamilton Coll (NY)
Hamline U (MN)
Hampshire Coll (MA)
Hanover Coll (IN)
Hartwick Coll (NY)
Harvard U (MA)
Haverford Coll (PA)
Hawai'i Pacific U (HI)
Heidelberg Coll (OH)
Hendrix Coll (AR)
Hobart and William Smith Colls (NY)
Hofstra U (NY)
Humboldt State U (CA)
Hunter Coll of the City U of New York (NY)
Idaho State U (ID)
Illinois State U (IL)
Illinois Wesleyan U (IL)
Indiana State U (IN)
Indiana U Bloomington (IN)
Indiana U of Pennsylvania (PA)
Indiana U–Purdue U Fort Wayne (IN)
Indiana U–Purdue U Indianapolis (IN)
Iowa State U of Science and Technology (IA)
Ithaca Coll (NY)
Jacksonville State U (AL)
James Madison U (VA)
The Johns Hopkins U (MD)
Johnson State Coll (VT)
Juniata Coll (PA)
Kalamazoo Coll (MI)
Kansas State U (KS)
Kennesaw State U (GA)
Kent State U (OH)
Kenyon Coll (OH)
Knox Coll (IL)
Kutztown U of Pennsylvania (PA)
Lafayette Coll (PA)
Lake Forest Coll (IL)
Lakehead U (ON, Canada)
Laurentian U (ON, Canada)
Lawrence U (WI)
Lee U (TN)
Lehigh U (PA)
Lehman Coll of the City U of New York (NY)
Lewis & Clark Coll (OR)
Lincoln U (PA)
Linfield Coll (OR)
Lock Haven U of Pennsylvania (PA)
Longwood U (VA)
Louisiana State U and Ag and Mech Coll (LA)
Loyola U Chicago (IL)
Luther Coll (IA)
Lycoming Coll (PA)
Macalester Coll (MN)
Mansfield U of Pennsylvania (PA)
Marlboro Coll (VT)
Marquette U (WI)
Marylhurst U (OR)
Massachusetts Inst of Technology (MA)
McGill U (QC, Canada)
Memorial U of Newfoundland (NL, Canada)
Mercyhurst Coll (PA)
Miami U (OH)
Miami U Hamilton (OH)
Michigan State U (MI)
Middle Tennessee State U (TN)
Millersville U of Pennsylvania (PA)
Millsaps Coll (MS)
Mills Coll (CA)
Minnesota State U Mankato (MN)
Mississippi State U (MS)
Missouri State U (MO)
Monmouth U (NJ)
Montana State U (MT)
Montclair State U (NJ)
Mount Allison U (NB, Canada)
Mount Holyoke Coll (MA)
Mount Saint Vincent U (NS, Canada)
Muhlenberg Coll (PA)
National-Louis U (IL)
Nazareth Coll of Rochester (NY)
New Coll of Florida (FL)
New York U (NY)
North Carolina State U (NC)
North Carolina Wesleyan Coll (NC)
Northeastern Illinois U (IL)
Northeastern U (MA)
Northern Arizona U (AZ)
Northern Illinois U (IL)
Northwestern State U of Louisiana (LA)
Northwestern U (IL)
Oakland U (MI)
Oberlin Coll (OH)
Occidental Coll (CA)
Ohio U (OH)
Ohio Wesleyan U (OH)
Oregon State U (OR)
Pacific Lutheran U (WA)
Penn State Abington (PA)
Penn State Altoona (PA)
Penn State Berks (PA)
Penn State Erie, The Behrend Coll (PA)
Penn State U Park (PA)
Pitzer Coll (CA)
Pomona Coll (CA)
Portland State U (OR)
Prescott Coll (AZ)
Princeton U (NJ)
Purchase Coll, State U of New York (NY)
Purdue U (IN)
Queens Coll of the City U of New York (NY)
Radford U (VA)
Reed Coll (OR)
Rhode Island Coll (RI)
Rhodes Coll (TN)
Rice U (TX)
Ripon Coll (WI)
Rockford Coll (IL)
Roger Williams U (RI)
Rollins Coll (FL)
Rutgers, The State U of New Jersey, Newark (NJ)
Rutgers, The State U of New Jersey, New Brunswick (NJ)
St. Cloud State U (MN)
Saint Francis U (PA)
St. Francis Xavier U (NS, Canada)
St. John Fisher Coll (NY)
St. John's U (NY)
St. Lawrence U (NY)
Saint Mary's Coll of California (CA)
St. Mary's Coll of Maryland (MD)
St. Thomas U (NB, Canada)
Saint Vincent Coll (PA)
Salve Regina U (RI)
San Diego State U (CA)
San Francisco State U (CA)
Santa Clara U (CA)
Sarah Lawrence Coll (NY)
Scripps Coll (CA)
Sewanee: The U of the South (TN)
Skidmore Coll (NY)
Slippery Rock U of Pennsylvania (PA)
Smith Coll (MA)
Sonoma State U (CA)
Southeast Missouri State U (MO)
Southern Connecticut State U (CT)
Southern Illinois U Carbondale (IL)
Southern Illinois U Edwardsville (IL)
Southern Methodist U (TX)
Southern Oregon U (OR)
Southwestern U (TX)
Spelman Coll (GA)
Stanford U (CA)
State U of New York at Binghamton (NY)
State U of New York at New Paltz (NY)
State U of New York at Oswego (NY)
State U of New York at Plattsburgh (NY)

MAJORS AND MORE

State U of New York Coll at Geneseo (NY)
State U of New York Coll at Oneonta (NY)
State U of New York Coll at Potsdam (NY)
Stony Brook U, State U of New York (NY)
Swarthmore Coll (PA)
Sweet Briar Coll (VA)
Syracuse U (NY)
Temple U (PA)
Texas A&M U (TX)
Texas Christian U (TX)
Texas State U-San Marcos (TX)
Texas Tech U (TX)
Transylvania U (KY)
Trent U (ON, Canada)
Trinity Coll (CT)
Trinity U (TX)
Tufts U (MA)
Tulane U (LA)
Union Coll (NY)
U at Albany, State U of New York (NY)
U at Buffalo, the State U of New York (NY)
The U of Alabama (AL)
The U of Alabama at Birmingham (AL)
U of Alaska Fairbanks (AK)
The U of Arizona (AZ)
U of Arkansas (AR)
The U of British Columbia (BC, Canada)
The U of British Columbia–Okanagan (BC, Canada)
U of California, Berkeley (CA)
U of California, Davis (CA)
U of California, Irvine (CA)
U of California, Los Angeles (CA)
U of California, Riverside (CA)
U of California, San Diego (CA)
U of California, Santa Barbara (CA)
U of California, Santa Cruz (CA)
U of Central Florida (FL)
U of Chicago (IL)
U of Cincinnati (OH)
U of Colorado at Boulder (CO)
U of Colorado Denver (CO)
U of Connecticut (CT)
U of Delaware (DE)
U of Denver (CO)
U of Florida (FL)
U of Georgia (GA)
U of Guam (GU)
U of Hawaii at Manoa (HI)
U of Hawaii–West Oahu (HI)
U of Houston (TX)
U of Houston–Clear Lake (TX)
U of Idaho (ID)
U of Illinois at Chicago (IL)
U of Illinois at Urbana–Champaign (IL)
U of Indianapolis (IN)
The U of Iowa (IA)
U of Kansas (KS)
U of King's Coll (NS, Canada)
U of La Verne (CA)
U of Lethbridge (AB, Canada)
U of Louisiana at Lafayette (LA)
U of Louisville (KY)
U of Maine (ME)
U of Maine at Farmington (ME)
U of Maryland, Baltimore County (MD)
U of Maryland, Coll Park (MD)
U of Massachusetts Amherst (MA)
U of Massachusetts Boston (MA)
U of Memphis (TN)
U of Miami (FL)
U of Michigan (MI)
U of Michigan–Dearborn (MI)
U of Michigan–Flint (MI)
U of Minnesota, Duluth (MN)
U of Minnesota, Twin Cities Campus (MN)
U of Mississippi (MS)
U of Missouri–Columbia (MO)
U of Missouri–St. Louis (MO)
The U of Montana (MT)
U of Nebraska–Lincoln (NE)
U of Nevada, Las Vegas (NV)
U of Nevada, Reno (NV)
U of New Brunswick Fredericton (NB, Canada)
U of New Hampshire (NH)
U of New Mexico (NM)
U of New Orleans (LA)
The U of North Carolina at Chapel Hill (NC)
The U of North Carolina at Charlotte (NC)
The U of North Carolina at Greensboro (NC)
The U of North Carolina Wilmington (NC)
U of North Dakota (ND)
U of Northern Iowa (IA)
U of North Florida (FL)
U of North Texas (TX)
U of Notre Dame (IN)
U of Oklahoma (OK)
U of Oregon (OR)
U of Ottawa (ON, Canada)
U of Pennsylvania (PA)
U of Pittsburgh (PA)
U of Prince Edward Island (PE, Canada)
U of Redlands (CA)
U of Regina (SK, Canada)
U of Rhode Island (RI)
U of Rochester (NY)
U of San Diego (CA)
U of South Alabama (AL)
U of South Carolina (SC)
The U of South Dakota (SD)
U of Southern California (CA)
U of Southern Maine (ME)
U of Southern Mississippi (MS)
U of South Florida (FL)
The U of Tennessee (TN)
The U of Texas at Arlington (TX)
The U of Texas at Austin (TX)
The U of Texas at El Paso (TX)
The U of Texas at San Antonio (TX)
The U of Texas–Pan American (TX)
U of the District of Columbia (DC)
The U of Toledo (OH)
U of Toronto (ON, Canada)
U of Tulsa (OK)
U of Utah (UT)
U of Vermont (VT)
U of Victoria (BC, Canada)
U of Virginia (VA)
The U of Western Ontario (ON, Canada)
U of West Florida (FL)
U of West Georgia (GA)
U of Windsor (ON, Canada)
The U of Winnipeg (MB, Canada)
U of Wisconsin–Madison (WI)
U of Wisconsin–Milwaukee (WI)
U of Wisconsin–Oshkosh (WI)
U of Wyoming (WY)
Ursinus Coll (PA)
Utah State U (UT)
Vanderbilt U (TN)
Vanguard U of Southern California (CA)
Vassar Coll (NY)
Virginia Commonwealth U (VA)
Wagner Coll (NY)
Wake Forest U (NC)
Washburn U (KS)
Washington and Lee U (VA)
Washington Coll (MD)
Washington State U (WA)
Washington U in St. Louis (MO)
Wayne State U (MI)
Webster U (MO)
Wellesley Coll (MA)
Wells Coll (NY)
Wesleyan U (CT)
West Chester U of Pennsylvania (PA)
Western Carolina U (NC)
Western Connecticut State U (CT)
Western Kentucky U (KY)
Western Michigan U (MI)
Western State Coll of Colorado (CO)
Western Washington U (WA)
Westminster Coll (MO)
Westmont Coll (CA)
West Virginia U (WV)
Wheaton Coll (IL)
Wheaton Coll (MA)
Whitman Coll (WA)
Wichita State U (KS)
Widener U (PA)
Wilfrid Laurier U (ON, Canada)
Willamette U (OR)
William Paterson U of New Jersey (NJ)
Williams Coll (MA)
Wright State U (OH)
Yale U (CT)
York Coll of the City U of New York (NY)
York U (ON, Canada)
Youngstown State U (OH)

ANTHROPOLOGY RELATED

Bridgewater State Coll (MA)
Carnegie Mellon U (PA)
U of California, Riverside (CA)
U of Southern California (CA)
The U of Western Ontario (ON, Canada)

APPAREL AND ACCESSORIES MARKETING

The Art Inst of Atlanta (GA)
The Art Inst of Charleston (SC)
The Art Inst of Houston (TX)
The Art Inst of Tampa (FL)
Bluffton U (OH)
Philadelphia U (PA)
U of Rhode Island (RI)

APPAREL AND TEXTILE MANUFACTURING

Fashion Inst of Technology (NY)
North Carolina State U (NC)

APPAREL AND TEXTILE MARKETING MANAGEMENT

The Art Inst of Michigan (MI)
Colorado State U (CO)
Florida State U (FL)
North Carolina State U (NC)
South Dakota State U (SD)
Wayne State U (MI)

APPAREL AND TEXTILES

Albright Coll (PA)
Appalachian State U (NC)
Auburn U (AL)
Bob Jones U (SC)
California State U, Long Beach (CA)
Coll of the Ozarks (MO)
Colorado State U (CO)
Fashion Inst of Technology (NY)
Florida State U (FL)
Framingham State Coll (MA)
Freed-Hardeman U (TN)
Georgia Southern U (GA)
Indiana State U (IN)
Iowa State U of Science and Technology (IA)
Kansas State U (KS)
Liberty U (VA)
Lipscomb U (TN)
Michigan State U (MI)
Middle Tennessee State U (TN)
Missouri State U (MO)
Murray State U (KY)
North Dakota State U (ND)
Northern Illinois U (IL)
Ohio U (OH)
Purdue U (IN)
Seattle Pacific U (WA)
Southern Illinois U Carbondale (IL)
Syracuse U (NY)
Texas Tech U (TX)
The U of Akron (OH)
The U of Alabama (AL)
U of Arkansas (AR)
U of California, Davis (CA)
U of Central Missouri (MO)
U of Georgia (GA)
U of Missouri–Columbia (MO)
U of Nebraska–Lincoln (NE)
The U of North Carolina at Greensboro (NC)
U of Northern Iowa (IA)
U of Rhode Island (RI)
U of Southern Mississippi (MS)
The U of Texas at Austin (TX)
Washington State U (WA)
Western Kentucky U (KY)
Western Michigan U (MI)

APPAREL AND TEXTILES RELATED

U of Louisiana at Lafayette (LA)

APPAREL MARKETING

Intl Acad of Design & Technology (FL)

APPLIED ART

Athabasca U (AB, Canada)
Azusa Pacific U (CA)
Bemidji State U (MN)
Buffalo State Coll, State U of New York (NY)
California Coll of the Arts (CA)
California Polytechnic State U, San Luis Obispo (CA)
California State U, Dominguez Hills (CA)
Cleveland State U (OH)
Columbia Coll (SC)
Converse Coll (SC)
Daemen Coll (NY)
Dowling Coll (NY)
Hampshire Coll (MA)
Howard Payne U (TX)
Inter American U of Puerto Rico, San Germán Campus (PR)
Lindenwood U (MO)
Lubbock Christian U (TX)
Mansfield U of Pennsylvania (PA)
McNeese State U (LA)
Memphis Coll of Art (TN)
Midwestern State U (TX)
Minnesota State U Mankato (MN)
Oregon State U (OR)
Otis Coll of Art and Design (CA)
Paier Coll of Art, Inc. (CT)
Peru State Coll (NE)
Portland State U (OR)
Pratt Inst (NY)
St. Cloud State U (MN)
School of the Museum of Fine Arts, Boston (MA)
Sewanee: The U of the South (TN)
State U of New York at Fredonia (NY)
Truman State U (MO)
U of Dayton (OH)
The U of Toledo (OH)
U of Wisconsin–Madison (WI)
Washington U in St. Louis (MO)
William Paterson U of New Jersey (NJ)
Winona State U (MN)
York U (ON, Canada)

APPLIED ECONOMICS

Allegheny Coll (PA)
Brigham Young U (UT)
The Coll of St. Scholastica (MN)
Concordia U (QC, Canada)
Farmingdale State Coll (NY)
Florida State U (FL)
HEC Montreal (QC, Canada)
Ithaca Coll (NY)
Michigan State U (MI)
Penn State Abington (PA)
Penn State Altoona (PA)
Penn State Berks (PA)
Penn State Erie, The Behrend Coll (PA)
Penn State U Park (PA)
Plymouth State U (NH)
Southern Methodist U (TX)
U of Northern Iowa (IA)
U of Rhode Island (RI)
Western New England Coll (MA)

APPLIED HISTORY

Villa Julie Coll (MD)

APPLIED HORTICULTURE

Coll of the Ozarks (MO)
Colorado State U (CO)
Farmingdale State Coll (NY)
Ferrum Coll (VA)
Iowa State U of Science and Technology (IA)
McGill U (QC, Canada)
Nova Scotia Ag Coll (NS, Canada)
Purdue U (IN)
South Dakota State U (SD)
Stephen F. Austin State U (TX)
Sterling Coll (VT)
Texas A&M U (TX)
Texas Tech U (TX)
Thomas Edison State Coll (NJ)
U of Georgia (GA)
U of Illinois at Urbana–Champaign (IL)

APPLIED HORTICULTURE/ HORTICULTURAL BUSINESS SERVICES RELATED

Delaware Valley Coll (PA)

APPLIED MATHEMATICS

American U (DC)
Asbury Coll (KY)
Auburn U (AL)
Bard Coll at Simon's Rock (MA)
Barnard Coll (NY)
Baylor U (TX)
Belmont U (TN)
Bloomfield Coll (NJ)
Bowling Green State U (OH)
Brock U (ON, Canada)
Brown U (RI)
California Inst of Technology (CA)
California State Polytechnic U, Pomona (CA)
California State U, Chico (CA)
California State U, East Bay (CA)
California State U, Fullerton (CA)
California State U, Long Beach (CA)
Carnegie Mellon U (PA)
Carroll Coll (WI)
Case Western Reserve U (OH)
Clarkson U (NY)
Coastal Carolina U (SC)
Colorado State U (CO)
Creighton U (NE)
DePaul U (IL)
Dowling Coll (NY)
Eastern Kentucky U (KY)
Emory & Henry Coll (VA)
Farmingdale State Coll (NY)
Ferris State U (MI)
Florida Inst of Technology (FL)
Florida Intl U (FL)
Florida State U (FL)
Fresno Pacific U (CA)
The George Washington U (DC)
Georgia Inst of Technology (GA)
Grand Valley State U (MI)
Grand View Coll (IA)
Hampden-Sydney Coll (VA)
Harvard U (MA)
Hawai'i Pacific U (HI)
Hofstra U (NY)
Humboldt State U (CA)
Illinois Inst of Technology (IL)
Indiana U of Pennsylvania (PA)
Indiana U South Bend (IN)
Inter American U of Puerto Rico, Bayamón Campus (PR)
Inter American U of Puerto Rico, San Germán Campus (PR)
Iona Coll (NY)
Ithaca Coll (NY)
Jamestown Coll (ND)
The Johns Hopkins U (MD)
Keene State Coll (NH)
Kent State U (OH)
Kettering U (MI)
King Coll (TN)
La Salle U (PA)
Longwood U (VA)
Loyola Coll in Maryland (MD)
Marist Coll (NY)
Marlboro Coll (VT)
Mary Baldwin Coll (VA)
Maryville U of Saint Louis (MO)
The Master's Coll and Sem (CA)
McGill U (QC, Canada)
Memorial U of Newfoundland (NL, Canada)
Metropolitan State U (MN)
Michigan State U (MI)
Michigan Technological U (MI)
Millikin U (IL)
Missouri U of Science and Technology (MO)
Montana Tech of The U of Montana (MT)
Mount Allison U (NB, Canada)
Mount Saint Vincent U (NS, Canada)
New Jersey Inst of Technology (NJ)
North Carolina Ag and Tech State U (NC)
North Carolina State U (NC)
North Central Coll (IL)
Northern Illinois U (IL)
Northland Coll (WI)
Northwestern U (IL)
Oakland City U (IN)
Oakwood Coll (AL)
Ohio U (OH)
Oregon State U (OR)
Pacific Union Coll (CA)
Penn State Harrisburg (PA)
Purdue U (IN)
Queens U of Charlotte (NC)
Quinnipiac U (CT)
Rensselaer Polytechnic Inst (NY)
Rice U (TX)
Robert Morris U (PA)
Rutgers, The State U of New Jersey, Newark (NJ)
Saginaw Valley State U (MI)
St. Thomas Aquinas Coll (NY)
Salem State Coll (MA)
San Diego State U (CA)
San Francisco State U (CA)
Seattle U (WA)
Shawnee State U (OH)
Siena Heights U (MI)
Simon Fraser U (BC, Canada)
Sonoma State U (CA)
State U of New York at Oswego (NY)
State U of New York Inst of Technology (NY)
Stony Brook U, State U of New York (NY)
Texas A&M U (TX)
Texas State U-San Marcos (TX)
Trent U (ON, Canada)
U at Albany, State U of New York (NY)
The U of Akron (OH)
U of Alaska Fairbanks (AK)
The U of British Columbia (BC, Canada)
U of California, Berkeley (CA)
U of California, Davis (CA)
U of California, Los Angeles (CA)
U of California, San Diego (CA)
U of Central Oklahoma (OK)
U of Chicago (IL)
U of Colorado at Boulder (CO)
U of Connecticut (CT)
U of Houston (TX)
U of Houston–Downtown (TX)
U of Idaho (ID)
U of Massachusetts Lowell (MA)
U of Miami (FL)

MAJORS AND MORE

U of Michigan (MI)
U of Missouri–St. Louis (MO)
The U of Montana (MT)
U of Nevada, Las Vegas (NV)
U of New Brunswick Fredericton (NB, Canada)
U of New Haven (CT)
The U of North Carolina at Chapel Hill (NC)
The U of North Carolina at Greensboro (NC)
U of Northern Iowa (IA)
U of Pittsburgh (PA)
U of Pittsburgh at Bradford (PA)
U of Rochester (NY)
U of Sioux Falls (SD)
U of South Carolina Aiken (SC)
The U of Tennessee at Chattanooga (TN)
The U of Texas at Dallas (TX)
The U of Texas at El Paso (TX)
U of Toronto (ON, Canada)
U of Tulsa (OK)
The U of Western Ontario (ON, Canada)
U of Windsor (ON, Canada)
The U of Winnipeg (MB, Canada)
U of Wisconsin–Madison (WI)
U of Wisconsin–Milwaukee (WI)
Valdosta State U (GA)
Washington U in St. Louis (MO)
Weber State U (UT)
William Paterson U of New Jersey (NJ)
Winona State U (MN)
Worcester Polytechnic Inst (MA)
Wright State U (OH)
Yale U (CT)
York U (ON, Canada)

APPLIED MATHEMATICS RELATED

Averett U (VA)
Carroll Coll (WI)
DePaul U (IL)
Georgia Inst of Technology (GA)
Lycoming Coll (PA)
Saint Mary's Coll (IN)
U of California, Santa Barbara (CA)
U of Dayton (OH)
The U of Iowa (IA)
U of Wyoming (WY)

AQUACULTURE

Auburn U (AL)
Texas A&M U (TX)
U of New England (ME)

AQUATIC BIOLOGY/ LIMNOLOGY

Florida Inst of Technology (FL)
McGill U (QC, Canada)
Stetson U (FL)
Texas State U-San Marcos (TX)
U of California, Santa Barbara (CA)
U of South Carolina (SC)

ARABIC

American U of Beirut (Lebanon)
Bard Coll (NY)
Brigham Young U (UT)
Concordia U (QC, Canada)
Dartmouth Coll (NH)
Georgetown U (DC)
Harvard U (MA)
State U of New York at Binghamton (NY)
United States Naval Acad (MD)
U of California, Los Angeles (CA)
U of Chicago (IL)
U of Michigan (MI)
U of Notre Dame (IN)
U of Ottawa (ON, Canada)
The U of Texas at Austin (TX)
U of Toronto (ON, Canada)
U of Utah (UT)
Washington U in St. Louis (MO)

ARCHEOLOGY

The American U of Athens (Greece)
American U of Beirut (Lebanon)
Bard Coll (NY)
Bates Coll (ME)
Baylor U (TX)
Boston U (MA)
Bowdoin Coll (ME)
Bridgewater State Coll (MA)
Brock U (ON, Canada)
Brown U (RI)
Bryn Mawr Coll (PA)
Claremont McKenna Coll (CA)
Concordia U (QC, Canada)
Cornell U (NY)
Dartmouth Coll (NH)
Dickinson Coll (PA)
The George Washington U (DC)
Hamilton Coll (NY)
Harvard U (MA)
Haverford Coll (PA)
Hunter Coll of the City U of New York (NY)
Lawrence U (WI)
Lycoming Coll (PA)
Memorial U of Newfoundland (NL, Canada)
Mercyhurst Coll (PA)
New York U (NY)
Oberlin Coll (OH)
Penn State Abington (PA)
Penn State Altoona (PA)
Penn State Berks (PA)
Penn State Erie, The Behrend Coll (PA)
Penn State U Park (PA)
Saint Mary's Coll of California (CA)
Sarah Lawrence Coll (NY)
Simon Fraser U (BC, Canada)
Southern Adventist U (TN)
Stanford U (CA)
State U of New York Coll at Potsdam (NY)
Sweet Briar Coll (VA)
Tufts U (MA)
The U of British Columbia (BC, Canada)
U of California, San Diego (CA)
U of Evansville (IN)
U of Indianapolis (IN)
U of Missouri–Columbia (MO)
The U of North Carolina at Greensboro (NC)
The U of Texas at Austin (TX)
U of Toronto (ON, Canada)
The U of Western Ontario (ON, Canada)
U of Wisconsin–La Crosse (WI)
Washington and Lee U (VA)
Washington U in St. Louis (MO)
Wellesley Coll (MA)
Wesleyan U (CT)
Western Washington U (WA)
Wheaton Coll (IL)
Wilfrid Laurier U (ON, Canada)
Yale U (CT)

ARCHITECTURAL DRAFTING AND CAD/CADD

The Art Inst of Pittsburgh (PA)
Thomas Edison State Coll (NJ)

ARCHITECTURAL ENGINEERING

The American U of Athens (Greece)
Andrews U (MI)
Auburn U (AL)
California Polytechnic State U, San Luis Obispo (CA)
Drexel U (PA)
Harvard U (MA)
Illinois Inst of Technology (IL)
Kansas State U (KS)
Milwaukee School of Eng (WI)
Missouri U of Science and Technology (MO)
North Carolina Ag and Tech State U (NC)
Oklahoma State U (OK)
Penn State Abington (PA)
Penn State Altoona (PA)
Penn State Berks (PA)
Penn State Erie, The Behrend Coll (PA)
Penn State U Park (PA)
Tennessee State U (TN)
Tufts U (MA)
U of Cincinnati (OH)
U of Colorado at Boulder (CO)
U of Kansas (KS)
U of Miami (FL)
U of Nebraska at Omaha (NE)
U of Nebraska–Lincoln (NE)
The U of Texas at Austin (TX)
U of Wyoming (WY)

ARCHITECTURAL ENGINEERING TECHNOLOGY

Bluefield State Coll (WV)
Eastern Kentucky U (KY)
Farmingdale State Coll (NY)
Florida Ag and Mech U (FL)
Grambling State U (LA)
Indiana State U (IN)
Indiana U–Purdue U Indianapolis (IN)
Purdue U (IN)
Southern Polytechnic State U (GA)
Texas Tech U (TX)
U of Cincinnati (OH)
U of Hartford (CT)
U of Southern Mississippi (MS)
Vermont Tech Coll (VT)
Washington U in St. Louis (MO)

ARCHITECTURAL HISTORY AND CRITICISM

Barnard Coll (NY)
Brown U (RI)
Carnegie Mellon U (PA)
Miami U Hamilton (OH)
Sarah Lawrence Coll (NY)
Savannah Coll of Art and Design (GA)
U of Kansas (KS)
U of Virginia (VA)

ARCHITECTURAL TECHNOLOGY

Carnegie Mellon U (PA)
Fitchburg State Coll (MA)
Keene State Coll (NH)
U of Idaho (ID)
Washington U in St. Louis (MO)
Western Kentucky U (KY)

ARCHITECTURE

American U of Beirut (Lebanon)
Andrews U (MI)
Arizona State U (AZ)
Auburn U (AL)
Ball State U (IN)
Barnard Coll (NY)
Baylor U (TX)
Bennington Coll (VT)
Boston Architectural Coll (MA)
California Coll of the Arts (CA)
California Polytechnic State U, San Luis Obispo (CA)
California State Polytechnic U, Pomona (CA)
Carnegie Mellon U (PA)
The Catholic U of America (DC)
City Coll of the City U of New York (NY)
Clemson U (SC)
Connecticut Coll (CT)
Cooper Union for the Advancement of Science and Art (NY)
Cornell Coll (IA)
Cornell U (NY)
Drexel U (PA)
Drury U (MO)
Eastern Michigan U (MI)
Florida Ag and Mech U (FL)
Florida Atlantic U (FL)
Georgia Inst of Technology (GA)
Hampton U (VA)
Hobart and William Smith Colls (NY)
Illinois Inst of Technology (IL)
Inter American U of Puerto Rico, San Germán Campus (PR)
Iowa State U of Science and Technology (IA)
Judson U (IL)
Kansas State U (KS)
Kent State U (OH)
Lawrence Technological U (MI)
Lehigh U (PA)
Louisiana State U and Ag and Mech Coll (LA)
Massachusetts Coll of Art and Design (MA)
Massachusetts Inst of Technology (MA)
McGill U (QC, Canada)
Miami U (OH)
Miami U Hamilton (OH)
Mississippi State U (MS)
New Jersey Inst of Technology (NJ)
North Carolina State U (NC)
North Dakota State U (ND)
Northeastern U (MA)
Norwich U (VT)
Oklahoma State U (OK)
Parsons The New School for Design (NY)
Penn State U Park (PA)
Philadelphia U (PA)
Polytechnic U of Puerto Rico (PR)
Portland State U (OR)
Prairie View A&M U (TX)
Pratt Inst (NY)
Princeton U (NJ)
Rensselaer Polytechnic Inst (NY)
Rice U (TX)
Roger Williams U (RI)
Savannah Coll of Art and Design (GA)
Smith Coll (MA)
Southern Illinois U Carbondale (IL)
Southern Polytechnic State U (GA)
Southern U and Ag and Mech Coll (LA)
Syracuse U (NY)
Temple U (PA)
Texas A&M U (TX)
Texas Tech U (TX)
Tulane U (LA)
Tuskegee U (AL)
U at Buffalo, the State U of New York (NY)
The U of Arizona (AZ)
U of Arkansas (AR)
U of California, Berkeley (CA)
U of California, Los Angeles (CA)
U of Cincinnati (OH)
U of Florida (FL)
U of Hawaii at Manoa (HI)
U of Houston (TX)
U of Idaho (ID)
U of Illinois at Chicago (IL)
U of Illinois at Urbana–Champaign (IL)
U of Kansas (KS)
U of Louisiana at Lafayette (LA)
U of Maryland, Coll Park (MD)
U of Memphis (TN)
U of Miami (FL)
U of Michigan (MI)
U of Minnesota, Twin Cities Campus (MN)
U of Nebraska–Lincoln (NE)
U of Nevada, Las Vegas (NV)
U of New Mexico (NM)
The U of North Carolina at Charlotte (NC)
U of Notre Dame (IN)
U of Oklahoma (OK)
U of Oregon (OR)
U of Pennsylvania (PA)
U of Southern California (CA)
The U of Tennessee (TN)
The U of Texas at Arlington (TX)
The U of Texas at Austin (TX)
The U of Texas at San Antonio (TX)
U of the District of Columbia (DC)
U of Toronto (ON, Canada)
U of Utah (UT)
U of Virginia (VA)
U of Wisconsin–Milwaukee (WI)
Virginia Polytechnic Inst and State U (VA)
Washington State U (WA)
Washington U in St. Louis (MO)
Wellesley Coll (MA)
Wentworth Inst of Technology (MA)
Woodbury U (CA)
Yale U (CT)

ARCHITECTURE RELATED

Carnegie Mellon U (PA)
Florida Intl U (FL)
Georgia Inst of Technology (GA)
La Roche Coll (PA)
Lipscomb U (TN)
Mount Holyoke Coll (MA)
New York Inst of Technology (NY)
Northern Michigan U (MI)
Rensselaer Polytechnic Inst (NY)
School of the Art Inst of Chicago (IL)
U of Houston (TX)
U of Illinois at Urbana–Champaign (IL)
U of Louisiana at Lafayette (LA)
U of Oklahoma (OK)
U of Utah (UT)
Washington U in St. Louis (MO)

AREA, ETHNIC, CULTURAL, AND GENDER STUDIES RELATED

Bennington Coll (VT)
Bethel U (MN)
Brandeis U (MA)
Chatham U (PA)
Claremont McKenna Coll (CA)
Columbia Coll Chicago (IL)
Connecticut Coll (CT)
The Evergreen State Coll (WA)
Gettysburg Coll (PA)
Kent State U (OH)
Linfield Coll (OR)
Mount Holyoke Coll (MA)
New York U (NY)
Northwest Christian Coll (OR)
Point Park U (PA)
Queens Coll of the City U of New York (NY)
Saint Mary's Coll of California (CA)
Skidmore Coll (NY)
Sterling Coll (VT)
Syracuse U (NY)
U of California, Irvine (CA)
U of California, Los Angeles (CA)
U of Chicago (IL)
U of Denver (CO)
U of Maryland, Baltimore County (MD)
The U of North Carolina at Chapel Hill (NC)
The U of North Carolina at Charlotte (NC)
U of Oregon (OR)
The U of Tennessee (TN)
U of the Incarnate Word (TX)
The U of Western Ontario (ON, Canada)
Washington U in St. Louis (MO)

AREA STUDIES

Bard Coll (NY)
Bucknell U (PA)
Denison U (OH)
Excelsior Coll (NY)
Gettysburg Coll (PA)
Memorial U of Newfoundland (NL, Canada)
Millersville U of Pennsylvania (PA)
United States Air Force Acad (CO)
The U of Montana (MT)
U of Oklahoma (OK)
Wilfrid Laurier U (ON, Canada)

AREA STUDIES RELATED

Boston U (MA)
Bridgewater State Coll (MA)
Claremont McKenna Coll (CA)
Drexel U (PA)
Gannon U (PA)
Gettysburg Coll (PA)
Hofstra U (NY)
Illinois Wesleyan U (IL)
Kent State U (OH)
Lewis U (IL)
Lycoming Coll (PA)
Northwestern U (IL)
Ramapo Coll of New Jersey (NJ)
U of Alaska Fairbanks (AK)
U of California, Los Angeles (CA)
U of California, Santa Barbara (CA)
U of Illinois at Urbana–Champaign (IL)
U of Michigan–Dearborn (MI)
U of Oklahoma (OK)
U of Virginia (VA)
Utah State U (UT)
Virginia Commonwealth U (VA)
Washington U in St. Louis (MO)
Wayne State U (MI)
Wright State U (OH)

ARMY R.O.T.C./MILITARY SCIENCE

Dallas Baptist U (TX)
Hampton U (VA)
Jacksonville State U (AL)
La Salle U (PA)
Longwood U (VA)
Minnesota State U Mankato (MN)
Northwest Missouri State U (MO)
Rensselaer Polytechnic Inst (NY)
The U of Iowa (IA)

ART

Adams State Coll (CO)
Adrian Coll (MI)
Agnes Scott Coll (GA)
Alabama State U (AL)
Alberta Coll of Art & Design (AB, Canada)
Albertus Magnus Coll (CT)
Albion Coll (MI)
Albright Coll (PA)
Alfred U (NY)
Allegheny Coll (PA)
Alma Coll (MI)
American InterContinental U (CA)
American InterContinental U (FL)
American InterContinental U Buckhead Campus (GA)
American InterContinental U Dunwoody Campus (GA)
American InterContinental U-London (United Kingdom)
American InterContinental U Online (IL)
Amherst Coll (MA)
Anderson U (SC)
Andrews U (MI)
Angelo State U (TX)
Anna Maria Coll (MA)
Appalachian State U (NC)
Aquinas Coll (MI)
Arizona State U (AZ)
Arkansas State U (AR)
Armstrong Atlantic State U (GA)
Athens State U (AL)
Atlantic Union Coll (MA)
Auburn U Montgomery (AL)
Augsburg Coll (MN)
Augustana Coll (IL)
Augustana Coll (SD)
Austin Coll (TX)
Austin Peay State U (TN)
Averett U (VA)
Avila U (MO)
Baldwin-Wallace Coll (OH)
Ball State U (IN)
Bard Coll (NY)
Bates Coll (ME)

MAJORS AND MORE

Baylor U (TX)
Belhaven Coll (MS)
Belmont U (TN)
Bemidji State U (MN)
Benedictine Coll (KS)
Berea Coll (KY)
Berry Coll (GA)
Bethany Coll (KS)
Bethany Coll (WV)
Bethany Lutheran Coll (MN)
Bethel U (MN)
Bishop's U (QC, Canada)
Blackburn Coll (IL)
Bluefield Coll (VA)
Bluffton U (OH)
Bob Jones U (SC)
Boise State U (ID)
Bowdoin Coll (ME)
Bowling Green State U (OH)
Bradley U (IL)
Brigham Young U (UT)
Brock U (ON, Canada)
Brown U (RI)
Bryn Mawr Coll (PA)
Bucknell U (PA)
Buffalo State Coll, State U of New York (NY)
Burlington Coll (VT)
California Coll of the Arts (CA)
California Inst of the Arts (CA)
California Lutheran U (CA)
California State Polytechnic U, Pomona (CA)
California State U, Chico (CA)
California State U, Dominguez Hills (CA)
California State U, Fresno (CA)
California State U, Fullerton (CA)
California State U, Long Beach (CA)
California State U, Los Angeles (CA)
California State U, Monterey Bay (CA)
California State U, Sacramento (CA)
California State U, San Bernardino (CA)
California State U, Stanislaus (CA)
Calvin Coll (MI)
Cameron U (OK)
Capital U (OH)
Carlow U (PA)
Carnegie Mellon U (PA)
Carroll Coll (WI)
Carson-Newman Coll (TN)
Castleton State Coll (VT)
The Catholic U of America (DC)
Cedar Crest Coll (PA)
Centenary Coll of Louisiana (LA)
Central Christian Coll of Kansas (KS)
Central Coll (IA)
Central Connecticut State U (CT)
Central Michigan U (MI)
Central State U (OH)
Central Washington U (WA)
Centre Coll (KY)
Chapman U (CA)
Cheyney U of Pennsylvania (PA)
Chicago State U (IL)
City Coll of the City U of New York (NY)
Claflin U (SC)
Claremont McKenna Coll (CA)
Clarion U of Pennsylvania (PA)
Clark Atlanta U (GA)
Clarke Coll (IA)
Cleveland State U (OH)
Colby Coll (ME)
Colby-Sawyer Coll (NH)
Colgate U (NY)
The Coll at Brockport, State U of New York (NY)
The Coll of Idaho (ID)
Coll of Mount St. Joseph (OH)
The Coll of New Jersey (NJ)
Coll of Saint Benedict (MN)
Coll of Saint Elizabeth (NJ)
Coll of Saint Mary (NE)
Coll of the Atlantic (ME)
Coll of the Ozarks (MO)
The Coll of William and Mary (VA)
Columbia Coll Chicago (IL)
Concordia Coll (MN)
Concordia U (CA)
Concordia U (MI)
Concordia U Chicago (IL)
Concordia U, Nebraska (NE)
Concordia U Wisconsin (WI)
Connecticut Coll (CT)
Converse Coll (SC)
Cornell Coll (IA)
Creighton U (NE)
Culver-Stockton Coll (MO)
Daemen Coll (NY)
Dakota Wesleyan U (SD)
Dallas Baptist U (TX)
Dana Coll (NE)
Davidson Coll (NC)
Davis & Elkins Coll (WV)
Defiance Coll (OH)
Denison U (OH)
DePaul U (IL)
Dillard U (LA)
Doane Coll (NE)
Dominican U of California (CA)
Drake U (IA)
Drew U (NJ)
Duke U (NC)
Earlham Coll (IN)
East Carolina U (NC)
East Central U (OK)
Eastern Connecticut State U (CT)
Eastern Illinois U (IL)
Eastern Kentucky U (KY)
Eastern Mennonite U (VA)
Eastern Michigan U (MI)
East Tennessee State U (TN)
Edinboro U of Pennsylvania (PA)
Elizabethtown Coll (PA)
Elon U (NC)
Emmanuel Coll (MA)
Emory & Henry Coll (VA)
Emporia State U (KS)
Erskine Coll (SC)
Evangel U (MO)
The Evergreen State Coll (WA)
Fayetteville State U (NC)
Felician Coll (NJ)
Ferrum Coll (VA)
Finlandia U (MI)
Florida Ag and Mech U (FL)
Florida Atlantic U (FL)
Florida Gulf Coast U (FL)
Florida Southern Coll (FL)
Fontbonne U (MO)
Fort Lewis Coll (CO)
Framingham State Coll (MA)
Francis Marion U (SC)
Freed-Hardeman U (TN)
Furman U (SC)
Gardner-Webb U (NC)
George Fox U (OR)
George Mason U (VA)
The George Washington U (DC)
Georgia Coll & State U (GA)
Georgian Court U (NJ)
Georgia Southern U (GA)
Georgia Southwestern State U (GA)
Georgia State U (GA)
Gettysburg Coll (PA)
Gonzaga U (WA)
Gordon Coll (MA)
Goucher Coll (MD)
Grambling State U (LA)
Grand Valley State U (MI)
Grand View Coll (IA)
Green Mountain Coll (VT)
Greensboro Coll (NC)
Greenville Coll (IL)
Grinnell Coll (IA)
Guilford Coll (NC)
Gustavus Adolphus Coll (MN)
Hamilton Coll (NY)
Hamline U (MN)
Hampton U (VA)
Hannibal-LaGrange Coll (MO)
Hanover Coll (IN)
Hartwick Coll (NY)
Harvard U (MA)
Hastings Coll (NE)
Haverford Coll (PA)
Henderson State U (AR)
Hendrix Coll (AR)
Hillsdale Coll (MI)
Hobart and William Smith Colls (NY)
Hollins U (VA)
Holy Family U (PA)
Houghton Coll (NY)
Howard Payne U (TX)
Humboldt State U (CA)
Hunter Coll of the City U of New York (NY)
Huntingdon Coll (AL)
Huntington U (IN)
Idaho State U (ID)
Illinois Coll (IL)
Illinois State U (IL)
Illinois Wesleyan U (IL)
Indiana State U (IN)
Indiana U Bloomington (IN)
Indiana U East (IN)
Indiana U Northwest (IN)
Indiana U of Pennsylvania (PA)
Indiana U South Bend (IN)
Indiana U Southeast (IN)
Indiana Wesleyan U (IN)
Inter American U of Puerto Rico, San Germán Campus (PR)
Iowa State U of Science and Technology (IA)
Iowa Wesleyan Coll (IA)
Ithaca Coll (NY)
Jacksonville State U (AL)
Jacksonville U (FL)
James Madison U (VA)
Jamestown Coll (ND)
Johnson State Coll (VT)
Judson Coll (AL)
Judson U (IL)
Kalamazoo Coll (MI)
Kansas State U (KS)
Kean U (NJ)
Keene State Coll (NH)
Kennesaw State U (GA)
Kenyon Coll (OH)
Keystone Coll (PA)
Knox Coll (IL)
Lafayette Coll (PA)
Laguna Coll of Art & Design (CA)
Lakehead U (ON, Canada)
Lambuth U (TN)
Lander U (SC)
La Sierra U (CA)
Lehigh U (PA)
Lehman Coll of the City U of New York (NY)
LeMoyne-Owen Coll (TN)
Lesley U (MA)
Lewis & Clark Coll (OR)
Lindenwood U (MO)
Linfield Coll (OR)
Lock Haven U of Pennsylvania (PA)
Longwood U (VA)
Louisiana Coll (LA)
Lourdes Coll (OH)
Loyola Coll in Maryland (MD)
Loyola U New Orleans (LA)
Luther Coll (IA)
Lycoming Coll (PA)
Lynchburg Coll (VA)
Lyon Coll (AR)
Madonna U (MI)
Manchester Coll (IN)
Mansfield U of Pennsylvania (PA)
Marietta Coll (OH)
Marist Coll (NY)
Marlboro Coll (VT)
Marshall U (WV)
Mary Baldwin Coll (VA)
Maryland Inst Coll of Art (MD)
Marylhurst U (OR)
Marymount Manhattan Coll (NY)
McDaniel Coll (MD)
McKendree U (IL)
McNeese State U (LA)
Memorial U of Newfoundland (NL, Canada)
Memphis Coll of Art (TN)
Mercer U (GA)
Mercyhurst Coll (PA)
Mesa State Coll (CO)
Methodist U (NC)
Miami U (OH)
Miami U Hamilton (OH)
Michigan State U (MI)
Middle Tennessee State U (TN)
Midland Lutheran Coll (NE)
Midwestern State U (TX)
Millersville U of Pennsylvania (PA)
Mills Coll (CA)
Minnesota State U Mankato (MN)
Minot State U (ND)
Mississippi Coll (MS)
Mississippi U for Women (MS)
Mississippi Valley State U (MS)
Missouri Southern State U (MO)
Missouri State U (MO)
Missouri Valley Coll (MO)
Molloy Coll (NY)
Monmouth Coll (IL)
Monmouth U (NJ)
Montana State U (MT)
Montana State U–Billings (MT)
Moravian Coll (PA)
Morehouse Coll (GA)
Morgan State U (MD)
Morningside Coll (IA)
Mount Mary Coll (WI)
Mount Mercy Coll (IA)
Mount Olive Coll (NC)
Mount St. Mary's Coll (CA)
Mount St. Mary's U (MD)
Mount Vernon Nazarene U (OH)
Muhlenberg Coll (PA)
National-Louis U (IL)
Nazareth Coll of Rochester (NY)
Nebraska Wesleyan U (NE)
New England Coll (NH)
New Jersey City U (NJ)
Newman U (KS)
New Mexico Highlands U (NM)
New York U (NY)
Nicholls State U (LA)
North Carolina Central U (NC)
North Central Coll (IL)
North Dakota State U (ND)
Northeastern Illinois U (IL)
Northeastern State U (OK)
Northeastern U (MA)
Northern Arizona U (AZ)
Northern Illinois U (IL)
Northern Michigan U (MI)
Northern State U (SD)
North Georgia Coll & State U (GA)
Northland Coll (WI)
Northwestern Coll (IA)
Northwestern U (IL)
Northwest Missouri State U (MO)
Northwest Nazarene U (ID)
Notre Dame de Namur U (CA)
NSCAD U (NS, Canada)
Oakland City U (IN)
Oberlin Coll (OH)
Oglethorpe U (GA)
Ohio Northern U (OH)
Oklahoma Christian U (OK)
Oklahoma Panhandle State U (OK)
Oklahoma State U (OK)
Old Dominion U (VA)
Oregon State U (OR)
Otis Coll of Art and Design (CA)
Otterbein Coll (OH)
Pace U (NY)
Pacific Lutheran U (WA)
Pacific Union Coll (CA)
Pacific U (OR)
Paier Coll of Art, Inc. (CT)
Parsons The New School for Design (NY)
Penn State Abington (PA)
Penn State Altoona (PA)
Penn State Berks (PA)
Penn State Erie, The Behrend Coll (PA)
Penn State U Park (PA)
Pepperdine U, Malibu (CA)
Peru State Coll (NE)
Piedmont Coll (GA)
Pikeville Coll (KY)
Pittsburg State U (KS)
Pitzer Coll (CA)
Plymouth State U (NH)
Point Loma Nazarene U (CA)
Pomona Coll (CA)
Portland State U (OR)
Pratt Inst (NY)
Presbyterian Coll (SC)
Prescott Coll (AZ)
Purchase Coll, State U of New York (NY)
Purdue U (IN)
Queens U of Charlotte (NC)
Radford U (VA)
Randolph Coll (VA)
Redeemer U Coll (ON, Canada)
Reed Coll (OR)
Rhodes Coll (TN)
Rice U (TX)
Ripon Coll (WI)
Roanoke Coll (VA)
Roberts Wesleyan Coll (NY)
Roger Williams U (RI)
Roosevelt U (IL)
Rowan U (NJ)
Rutgers, The State U of New Jersey, Camden (NJ)
Rutgers, The State U of New Jersey, Newark (NJ)
Rutgers, The State U of New Jersey, New Brunswick (NJ)
Saginaw Valley State U (MI)
St. Ambrose U (IA)
St. Andrews Presbyterian Coll (NC)
St. Cloud State U (MN)
St. Edward's U (TX)
Saint John's U (MN)
St. Lawrence U (NY)
Saint Mary-of-the-Woods Coll (IN)
Saint Mary's Coll (IN)
Saint Mary's Coll of California (CA)
St. Mary's Coll of Maryland (MD)
Saint Michael's Coll (VT)
St. Norbert Coll (WI)
St. Olaf Coll (MN)
St. Thomas Aquinas Coll (NY)
Saint Xavier U (IL)
Salem State Coll (MA)
Salisbury U (MD)
Sam Houston State U (TX)
San Francisco State U (CA)
Sarah Lawrence Coll (NY)
School of the Art Inst of Chicago (IL)
School of the Museum of Fine Arts, Boston (MA)
Scripps Coll (CA)
Seattle Pacific U (WA)
Seattle U (WA)
Sewanee: The U of the South (TN)
Shawnee State U (OH)
Shepherd U (WV)
Shippensburg U of Pennsylvania (PA)
Shorter Coll (GA)
Siena Heights U (MI)
Simmons Coll (MA)
Simon Fraser U (BC, Canada)
Simpson Coll (IA)
Skidmore Coll (NY)
Slippery Rock U of Pennsylvania (PA)
Smith Coll (MA)
Sonoma State U (CA)
Southeastern Louisiana U (LA)
Southeastern Oklahoma State U (OK)
Southeast Missouri State U (MO)
Southern Adventist U (TN)
Southern Arkansas U–Magnolia (AR)
Southern Illinois U Carbondale (IL)
Southern Illinois U Edwardsville (IL)
Southern Oregon U (OR)
Southern Utah U (UT)
Southwest Baptist U (MO)
Southwestern U (TX)
Southwest Minnesota State U (MN)
Spelman Coll (GA)
Spring Arbor U (MI)
Stanford U (CA)
State U of New York at Binghamton (NY)
State U of New York at Fredonia (NY)
State U of New York at New Paltz (NY)
State U of New York at Oswego (NY)
State U of New York at Plattsburgh (NY)
State U of New York Coll at Geneseo (NY)
State U of New York Coll at Old Westbury (NY)
State U of New York Coll at Oneonta (NY)
State U of New York Coll at Potsdam (NY)
State U of New York Empire State Coll (NY)
Stephen F. Austin State U (TX)
Sterling Coll (KS)
Stetson U (FL)
Stillman Coll (AL)
Susquehanna U (PA)
Syracuse U (NY)
Tarleton State U (TX)
Taylor U (IN)
Temple U (PA)
Tennessee State U (TN)
Tennessee Technological U (TN)
Texas A&M U–Commerce (TX)
Texas Coll (TX)
Texas Lutheran U (TX)
Texas Southern U (TX)
Texas State U-San Marcos (TX)
Texas Tech U (TX)
Texas Woman's U (TX)
Thiel Coll (PA)
Thomas Edison State Coll (NJ)
Tougaloo Coll (MS)
Towson U (MD)
Transylvania U (KY)
Trinity Christian Coll (IL)
Trinity Coll (CT)
Trinity U (TX)
Troy U (AL)
Truman State U (MO)
Tulane U (LA)
Union U (TN)
Université du Québec en Outaouais (QC, Canada)
U at Albany, State U of New York (NY)
U at Buffalo, the State U of New York (NY)
The U of Alabama in Huntsville (AL)
U of Alaska Fairbanks (AK)
U of Arkansas (AR)
U of Arkansas at Monticello (AR)
U of Arkansas at Pine Bluff (AR)
U of California, Berkeley (CA)
U of California, Los Angeles (CA)
U of California, Riverside (CA)
U of California, San Diego (CA)
U of California, Santa Cruz (CA)
U of Central Arkansas (AR)
U of Central Florida (FL)
U of Central Oklahoma (OK)
U of Charleston (WV)
U of Chicago (IL)
U of Cincinnati (OH)
U of Dallas (TX)
U of Delaware (DE)
U of Denver (CO)
U of Evansville (IN)
The U of Findlay (OH)
U of Georgia (GA)
U of Great Falls (MT)
U of Guam (GU)
U of Hawaii at Manoa (HI)
U of Houston (TX)
U of Houston–Clear Lake (TX)
U of Idaho (ID)
U of Indianapolis (IN)
The U of Iowa (IA)
U of La Verne (CA)
U of Lethbridge (AB, Canada)
U of Louisiana at Lafayette (LA)

U of Louisiana at Monroe (LA)
U of Louisville (KY)
U of Maine (ME)
U of Maine at Farmington (ME)
U of Maine at Machias (ME)
U of Mary Hardin-Baylor (TX)
U of Maryland, Baltimore County (MD)
U of Mary Washington (VA)
U of Massachusetts Boston (MA)
U of Memphis (TN)
U of Miami (FL)
U of Minnesota, Duluth (MN)
U of Minnesota, Twin Cities Campus (MN)
U of Mississippi (MS)
U of Missouri–Columbia (MO)
U of Missouri–Kansas City (MO)
The U of Montana (MT)
U of Montevallo (AL)
U of Nebraska at Kearney (NE)
U of Nebraska at Omaha (NE)
U of Nevada, Las Vegas (NV)
U of Nevada, Reno (NV)
U of New Hampshire (NH)
U of New Mexico (NM)
The U of North Carolina at Asheville (NC)
The U of North Carolina at Charlotte (NC)
The U of North Carolina at Greensboro (NC)
U of North Dakota (ND)
U of Northern Iowa (IA)
U of North Florida (FL)
U of North Texas (TX)
U of Oklahoma (OK)
U of Oregon (OR)
U of Puget Sound (WA)
U of Regina (SK, Canada)
U of Rhode Island (RI)
U of Richmond (VA)
U of Rio Grande (OH)
U of Saint Francis (IN)
U of Saint Mary (KS)
U of San Diego (CA)
U of Science and Arts of Oklahoma (OK)
U of Sioux Falls (SD)
U of South Alabama (AL)
The U of South Dakota (SD)
U of Southern California (CA)
U of Southern Indiana (IN)
U of Southern Maine (ME)
U of South Florida (FL)
The U of Tampa (FL)
The U of Tennessee at Chattanooga (TN)
The U of Texas at Arlington (TX)
The U of Texas at Austin (TX)
The U of Texas at Brownsville (TX)
The U of Texas at San Antonio (TX)
The U of Texas at Tyler (TX)
The U of Texas of the Permian Basin (TX)
The U of Texas–Pan American (TX)
U of the District of Columbia (DC)
U of the Incarnate Word (TX)
U of the Ozarks (AR)
U of the Pacific (CA)
The U of Toledo (OH)
U of Toronto (ON, Canada)
U of Utah (UT)
U of Virginia (VA)
The U of Virginia's Coll at Wise (VA)
The U of Western Ontario (ON, Canada)
U of West Florida (FL)
U of West Georgia (GA)
U of Windsor (ON, Canada)
U of Wisconsin–Eau Claire (WI)
U of Wisconsin–Green Bay (WI)
U of Wisconsin–La Crosse (WI)
U of Wisconsin–Madison (WI)
U of Wisconsin–Milwaukee (WI)
U of Wisconsin–Oshkosh (WI)
U of Wisconsin–Parkside (WI)
U of Wisconsin–Platteville (WI)
U of Wisconsin–Whitewater (WI)
U of Wyoming (WY)
Ursinus Coll (PA)
Utah State U (UT)
Valdosta State U (GA)
Valley City State U (ND)
Valparaiso U (IN)
Vanderbilt U (TN)
Virginia Intermont Coll (VA)
Virginia Polytechnic Inst and State U (VA)
Virginia Wesleyan Coll (VA)
Viterbo U (WI)
Wabash Coll (IN)
Wagner Coll (NY)
Walla Walla U (WA)
Warren Wilson Coll (NC)
Wartburg Coll (IA)
Washburn U (KS)
Washington & Jefferson Coll (PA)
Washington Coll (MD)
Washington U in St. Louis (MO)
Watkins Coll of Art and Design (TN)
Wayland Baptist U (TX)
Waynesburg U (PA)
Wayne State Coll (NE)
Wayne State U (MI)
Weber State U (UT)
Webster U (MO)
Wells Coll (NY)
Wesleyan U (CT)
West Chester U of Pennsylvania (PA)
Western Carolina U (NC)
Western Connecticut State U (CT)
Western Illinois U (IL)
Western Michigan U (MI)
Western New Mexico U (NM)
Western State Coll of Colorado (CO)
Western Washington U (WA)
Westfield State Coll (MA)
Westminster Coll (UT)
Westmont Coll (CA)
West Texas A&M U (TX)
West Virginia U (WV)
West Virginia Wesleyan Coll (WV)
Wheaton Coll (IL)
Whitman Coll (WA)
Whittier Coll (CA)
Whitworth U (WA)
Wichita State U (KS)
Willamette U (OR)
William Jewell Coll (MO)
William Paterson U of New Jersey (NJ)
William Woods U (MO)
Wilson Coll (PA)
Wingate U (NC)
Winona State U (MN)
Winthrop U (SC)
Wittenberg U (OH)
Wright State U (OH)
Xavier U (OH)
Xavier U of Louisiana (LA)
Yale U (CT)
York Coll of the City U of New York (NY)
York U (ON, Canada)
Youngstown State U (OH)

ART HISTORY, CRITICISM AND CONSERVATION

Adelphi U (NY)
Albertus Magnus Coll (CT)
Allegheny Coll (PA)
American U (DC)
The American U of Athens (Greece)
American U of Beirut (Lebanon)
The American U of Paris (France)
Aquinas Coll (MI)
Art Acad of Cincinnati (OH)
Augsburg Coll (MN)
Augustana Coll (IL)
Baker U (KS)
Baldwin-Wallace Coll (OH)
Bard Coll at Simon's Rock (MA)
Barnard Coll (NY)
Baylor U (TX)
Beloit Coll (WI)
Bloomsburg U of Pennsylvania (PA)
Boise State U (ID)
Boston Coll (MA)
Boston U (MA)
Bowdoin Coll (ME)
Bowling Green State U (OH)
Bradley U (IL)
Brandeis U (MA)
Bridgewater State Coll (MA)
Brigham Young U (UT)
Brown U (RI)
Bryn Mawr Coll (PA)
Bucknell U (PA)
Buffalo State Coll, State U of New York (NY)
California State U, Chico (CA)
California State U, Dominguez Hills (CA)
California State U, East Bay (CA)
California State U, Fullerton (CA)
California State U, Long Beach (CA)
California State U, San Bernardino (CA)
Calvin Coll (MI)
Canisius Coll (NY)
Carlow U (PA)
Case Western Reserve U (OH)
The Catholic U of America (DC)
Centre Coll (KY)
Chapman U (CA)
Chatham U (PA)
City Coll of the City U of New York (NY)
Claremont McKenna Coll (CA)
Clarke Coll (IA)
Clark U (MA)
Colby Coll (ME)
Colgate U (NY)
Coll of Charleston (SC)
The Coll of New Rochelle (NY)
Coll of Santa Fe (NM)
Coll of the Holy Cross (MA)
The Coll of William and Mary (VA)
The Colorado Coll (CO)
Colorado State U (CO)
Concordia Coll (MN)
Concordia U (QC, Canada)
Connecticut Coll (CT)
Converse Coll (SC)
Cornell Coll (IA)
Cornell U (NY)
Dartmouth Coll (NH)
Denison U (OH)
DePaul U (IL)
DePauw U (IN)
Dominican U (IL)
Dominican U of California (CA)
Drake U (IA)
Drew U (NJ)
Drury U (MO)
Duke U (NC)
Duquesne U (PA)
East Carolina U (NC)
Eastern Michigan U (MI)
Elon U (NC)
Emory U (GA)
Fairfield U (CT)
Fashion Inst of Technology (NY)
Ferris State U (MI)
Florida Intl U (FL)
Florida State U (FL)
Franklin & Marshall Coll (PA)
Franklin Coll Switzerland (Switzerland)
Furman U (SC)
George Mason U (VA)
Georgetown U (DC)
The George Washington U (DC)
Georgian Court U (NJ)
Gettysburg Coll (PA)
Grand Valley State U (MI)
Gustavus Adolphus Coll (MN)
Hamilton Coll (NY)
Hamline U (MN)
Hanover Coll (IN)
Hartwick Coll (NY)
Harvard U (MA)
Hastings Coll (NE)
Haverford Coll (PA)
Hobart and William Smith Colls (NY)
Hofstra U (NY)
Hollins U (VA)
Hope Coll (MI)
Humboldt State U (CA)
Hunter Coll of the City U of New York (NY)
Indiana U Bloomington (IN)
Indiana U–Purdue U Indianapolis (IN)
Inter American U of Puerto Rico, San Germán Campus (PR)
Ithaca Coll (NY)
Jacksonville U (FL)
James Madison U (VA)
John Carroll U (OH)
The Johns Hopkins U (MD)
Juniata Coll (PA)
Kalamazoo Coll (MI)
Kansas City Art Inst (MO)
Kean U (NJ)
Kent State U (OH)
Kenyon Coll (OH)
Knox Coll (IL)
Lafayette Coll (PA)
Lake Forest Coll (IL)
Lambuth U (TN)
La Salle U (PA)
Lawrence U (WI)
Lebanon Valley Coll (PA)
Lehigh U (PA)
Lehman Coll of the City U of New York (NY)
Lindenwood U (MO)
Longwood U (VA)
Lourdes Coll (OH)
Loyola Marymount U (CA)
Lycoming Coll (PA)
Macalester Coll (MN)
Madonna U (MI)
Manhattanville Coll (NY)
Marian Coll (IN)
Marist Coll (NY)
Marlboro Coll (VT)
Maryland Inst Coll of Art (MD)
Marymount Manhattan Coll (NY)
Maryville Coll (TN)
Massachusetts Coll of Art and Design (MA)
McDaniel Coll (MD)
McGill U (QC, Canada)
Memorial U of Newfoundland (NL, Canada)
Messiah Coll (PA)
Miami U (OH)
Michigan State U (MI)
Middlebury Coll (VT)
Millsaps Coll (MS)
Mills Coll (CA)
Minnesota State U Mankato (MN)
Mississippi Coll (MS)
Missouri State U (MO)
Moravian Coll (PA)
Morgan State U (MD)
Mount Allison U (NB, Canada)
Mount Holyoke Coll (MA)
Nazareth Coll of Rochester (NY)
New Coll of Florida (FL)
New England Coll (NH)
New York U (NY)
Northern Arizona U (AZ)
Northern Illinois U (IL)
Northwestern U (IL)
NSCAD U (NS, Canada)
Oakland U (MI)
Oberlin Coll (OH)
Occidental Coll (CA)
Oglethorpe U (GA)
Ohio U (OH)
Ohio Wesleyan U (OH)
Oklahoma City U (OK)
Old Dominion U (VA)
Oregon State U (OR)
Pace U (NY)
Pacific Union Coll (CA)
Penn State Abington (PA)
Penn State Altoona (PA)
Penn State Berks (PA)
Penn State Erie, The Behrend Coll (PA)
Penn State U Park (PA)
Pepperdine U, Malibu (CA)
Pitzer Coll (CA)
Pomona Coll (CA)
Portland State U (OR)
Pratt Inst (NY)
Presbyterian Coll (SC)
Princeton U (NJ)
Providence Coll (RI)
Purchase Coll, State U of New York (NY)
Purdue U (IN)
Queens Coll of the City U of New York (NY)
Queen's U at Kingston (ON, Canada)
Randolph Coll (VA)
Rhode Island Coll (RI)
Rhodes Coll (TN)
Rice U (TX)
Roanoke Coll (VA)
Rockford Coll (IL)
Roger Williams U (RI)
Rollins Coll (FL)
Roosevelt U (IL)
Rosemont Coll (PA)
Rutgers, The State U of New Jersey, New Brunswick (NJ)
St. Cloud State U (MN)
Saint Joseph Coll (CT)
St. Lawrence U (NY)
Saint Louis U (MO)
Saint Mary's Coll of California (CA)
St. Olaf Coll (MN)
Saint Vincent Coll (PA)
Salem Coll (NC)
Salve Regina U (RI)
San Diego State U (CA)
Santa Clara U (CA)
Sarah Lawrence Coll (NY)
Savannah Coll of Art and Design (GA)
School of the Art Inst of Chicago (IL)
Scripps Coll (CA)
Seattle U (WA)
Seton Hill U (PA)
Sewanee: The U of the South (TN)
Siena Heights U (MI)
Skidmore Coll (NY)
Smith Coll (MA)
Sonoma State U (CA)
Southern Connecticut State U (CT)
Southern Methodist U (TX)
Southwestern U (TX)
Stanford U (CA)
State U of New York at Binghamton (NY)
State U of New York at Fredonia (NY)
State U of New York at New Paltz (NY)
State U of New York at Plattsburgh (NY)
State U of New York Coll at Geneseo (NY)
State U of New York Coll at Oneonta (NY)
State U of New York Coll at Potsdam (NY)
Stephen F. Austin State U (TX)
Stony Brook U, State U of New York (NY)
Susquehanna U (PA)
Swarthmore Coll (PA)
Sweet Briar Coll (VA)
Syracuse U (NY)
Temple U (PA)
Texas Christian U (TX)
Texas Tech U (TX)
Towson U (MD)
Transylvania U (KY)
Trinity Coll (CT)
Trinity U (TX)
Truman State U (MO)
Tufts U (MA)
Tulane U (LA)
U at Albany, State U of New York (NY)
U at Buffalo, the State U of New York (NY)
The U of Akron (OH)
The U of Alabama (AL)
The U of Arizona (AZ)
The U of British Columbia (BC, Canada)
The U of British Columbia–Okanagan (BC, Canada)
U of California, Berkeley (CA)
U of California, Davis (CA)
U of California, Irvine (CA)
U of California, Los Angeles (CA)
U of California, Riverside (CA)
U of California, San Diego (CA)
U of California, Santa Barbara (CA)
U of California, Santa Cruz (CA)
U of Chicago (IL)
U of Cincinnati (OH)
U of Connecticut (CT)
U of Dallas (TX)
U of Dayton (OH)
U of Delaware (DE)
U of Denver (CO)
U of Evansville (IN)
U of Florida (FL)
U of Georgia (GA)
U of Hartford (CT)
U of Houston (TX)
U of Illinois at Chicago (IL)
U of Illinois at Urbana–Champaign (IL)
The U of Iowa (IA)
U of Kansas (KS)
U of La Verne (CA)
U of Louisville (KY)
U of Maine (ME)
U of Maryland, Baltimore County (MD)
U of Maryland, Coll Park (MD)
U of Mary Washington (VA)
U of Massachusetts Amherst (MA)
U of Massachusetts Dartmouth (MA)
U of Memphis (TN)
U of Miami (FL)
U of Michigan (MI)
U of Michigan–Dearborn (MI)
U of Minnesota, Duluth (MN)
U of Minnesota, Twin Cities Campus (MN)
U of Mississippi (MS)
U of Missouri–Columbia (MO)
U of Missouri–Kansas City (MO)
U of Missouri–St. Louis (MO)
The U of Montana (MT)
U of Nebraska at Omaha (NE)
U of Nebraska–Lincoln (NE)
U of Nevada, Las Vegas (NV)
U of Nevada, Reno (NV)
U of New Hampshire (NH)
U of New Mexico (NM)
U of New Orleans (LA)
The U of North Carolina at Chapel Hill (NC)
The U of North Carolina Wilmington (NC)
U of Northern Iowa (IA)
U of North Texas (TX)
U of Notre Dame (IN)
U of Oklahoma (OK)
U of Oregon (OR)
U of Ottawa (ON, Canada)
U of Pennsylvania (PA)
U of Pittsburgh (PA)
U of Redlands (CA)
U of Regina (SK, Canada)
U of Rhode Island (RI)
U of Richmond (VA)
U of Rochester (NY)
U of St. Thomas (MN)
U of San Diego (CA)
U of South Carolina (SC)
U of Southern California (CA)
The U of Tennessee (TN)
The U of Texas at Arlington (TX)
The U of Texas at Austin (TX)
The U of Texas at San Antonio (TX)
U of the Pacific (CA)
The U of Toledo (OH)

U of Toronto (ON, Canada)
U of Tulsa (OK)
U of Utah (UT)
U of Vermont (VT)
U of Victoria (BC, Canada)
The U of Western Ontario (ON, Canada)
U of Windsor (ON, Canada)
The U of Winnipeg (MB, Canada)
U of Wisconsin–Madison (WI)
U of Wisconsin–Milwaukee (WI)
U of Wisconsin–Superior (WI)
U of Wisconsin–Whitewater (WI)
Ursuline Coll (OH)
Vassar Coll (NY)
Villanova U (PA)
Virginia Commonwealth U (VA)
Wake Forest U (NC)
Washburn U (KS)
Washington and Lee U (VA)
Washington State U (WA)
Washington U in St. Louis (MO)
Wayne State U (MI)
Webster U (MO)
Wellesley Coll (MA)
Wells Coll (NY)
Wesleyan Coll (GA)
Wesleyan U (CT)
Western Michigan U (MI)
Western Washington U (WA)
West Virginia U (WV)
West Virginia Wesleyan Coll (WV)
Wheaton Coll (MA)
Whitman Coll (WA)
Wichita State U (KS)
Willamette U (OR)
William Paterson U of New Jersey (NJ)
Williams Coll (MA)
Winthrop U (SC)
Wofford Coll (SC)
Wright State U (OH)
Yale U (CT)
York U (ON, Canada)
Youngstown State U (OH)

ARTIFICIAL INTELLIGENCE AND ROBOTICS
Harvard U (MA)
Montana Tech of The U of Montana (MT)
U of Windsor (ON, Canada)

ARTS MANAGEMENT
Adrian Coll (MI)
Appalachian State U (NC)
Aquinas Coll (MI)
Belhaven Coll (MS)
Benedictine Coll (KS)
Benedictine U (IL)
Bernard M. Baruch Coll of the City U of New York (NY)
Bethany Coll (KS)
Bishop's U (QC, Canada)
Brenau U (GA)
Butler U (IN)
California State U, East Bay (CA)
Chatham U (PA)
Coll of Charleston (SC)
Coll of Santa Fe (NM)
Columbia Coll Chicago (IL)
Culver-Stockton Coll (MO)
DePaul U (IL)
Dillard U (LA)
Drury U (MO)
Eastern Michigan U (MI)
Fashion Inst of Technology (NY)
Fontbonne U (MO)
Fort Lewis Coll (CO)
Hollins U (VA)
Indiana U Bloomington (IN)
Ithaca Coll (NY)
Lenoir-Rhyne Coll (NC)
Marian Coll (IN)
Mary Baldwin Coll (VA)
Marywood U (PA)
Mercyhurst Coll (PA)
Millikin U (IL)
North Carolina State U (NC)
Northern Arizona U (AZ)
Oklahoma City U (OK)
Parsons The New School for Design (NY)
Pfeiffer U (NC)
Point Park U (PA)
Quincy U (IL)
Randolph-Macon Coll (VA)
Salem Coll (NC)
Savannah Coll of Art and Design (GA)
Seton Hill U (PA)
Shenandoah U (VA)
Simmons Coll (MA)
Southeastern Louisiana U (LA)
Spring Hill Coll (AL)
State U of New York at Fredonia (NY)
Tiffin U (OH)
The U of Iowa (IA)
U of Portland (OR)
U of Toronto (ON, Canada)
U of Tulsa (OK)
The U of Western Ontario (ON, Canada)
U of Windsor (ON, Canada)
U of Wisconsin–Stevens Point (WI)
Viterbo U (WI)
Wagner Coll (NY)
Wartburg Coll (IA)
Waynesburg U (PA)
Westminster Coll (UT)
Whitworth U (WA)
Wright State U (OH)

ART TEACHER EDUCATION
Abilene Christian U (TX)
Adelphi U (NY)
Adrian Coll (MI)
Alabama State U (AL)
Albright Coll (PA)
Alfred U (NY)
Alma Coll (MI)
Anderson U (IN)
Anderson U (SC)
Andrews U (MI)
Anna Maria Coll (MA)
Appalachian State U (NC)
Aquinas Coll (MI)
Arkansas State U (AR)
Armstrong Atlantic State U (GA)
Asbury Coll (KY)
Ashland U (OH)
Assumption Coll (MA)
Augsburg Coll (MN)
Augustana Coll (IL)
Augustana Coll (SD)
Averett U (VA)
Baker U (KS)
Ball State U (IN)
Barton Coll (NC)
Baylor U (TX)
Belmont U (TN)
Beloit Coll (WI)
Bemidji State U (MN)
Bethany Coll (KS)
Bethel U (MN)
Bishop's U (QC, Canada)
Bob Jones U (SC)
Boise State U (ID)
Boston U (MA)
Bowling Green State U (OH)
Brenau U (GA)
Bridgewater State Coll (MA)
Brigham Young U (UT)
Buffalo State Coll, State U of New York (NY)
California Lutheran U (CA)
California State U, Chico (CA)
California State U, Long Beach (CA)
Calumet Coll of Saint Joseph (IN)
Calvin Coll (MI)
Capital U (OH)
Carlow U (PA)
Carroll Coll (WI)
Carson-Newman Coll (TN)
Case Western Reserve U (OH)
The Catholic U of America (DC)
Centenary Coll of Louisiana (LA)
Central Connecticut State U (CT)
Central Michigan U (MI)
Central Washington U (WA)
City Coll of the City U of New York (NY)
Claflin U (SC)
Clarke Coll (IA)
Coker Coll (SC)
Colby-Sawyer Coll (NH)
Coll of Mount St. Joseph (OH)
The Coll of New Jersey (NJ)
The Coll of New Rochelle (NY)
The Coll of Saint Rose (NY)
Coll of the Ozarks (MO)
Colorado State U (CO)
Columbus State U (GA)
Concordia Coll (MN)
Concordia U (MI)
Concordia U (QC, Canada)
Concordia U Chicago (IL)
Concordia U, Nebraska (NE)
Concordia U, St. Paul (MN)
Concordia U Wisconsin (WI)
Concord U (WV)
Converse Coll (SC)
Culver-Stockton Coll (MO)
Daemen Coll (NY)
Dakota Wesleyan U (SD)
Dana Coll (NE)
Davis & Elkins Coll (WV)
Defiance Coll (OH)
DePaul U (IL)
Dillard U (LA)
Dowling Coll (NY)
East Carolina U (NC)
East Central U (OK)
Eastern Kentucky U (KY)
Eastern Mennonite U (VA)
Eastern Michigan U (MI)
Evangel U (MO)
Fairmont State U (WV)
Fayetteville State U (NC)
Ferris State U (MI)
Flagler Coll (FL)
Florida Ag and Mech U (FL)
Florida Intl U (FL)
Florida Southern Coll (FL)
Florida State U (FL)
Fontbonne U (MO)
Francis Marion U (SC)
Freed-Hardeman U (TN)
Georgia State U (GA)
Grace Coll (IN)
Grambling State U (LA)
Grand Valley State U (MI)
Greensboro Coll (NC)
Gustavus Adolphus Coll (MN)
Hampton U (VA)
Hannibal-LaGrange Coll (MO)
Harding U (AR)
Hardin-Simmons U (TX)
Hastings Coll (NE)
Henderson State U (AR)
High Point U (NC)
Hofstra U (NY)
Hope Coll (MI)
Houston Baptist U (TX)
Howard Payne U (TX)
Humboldt State U (CA)
Huntington U (IN)
Indiana State U (IN)
Indiana U Bloomington (IN)
Indiana U of Pennsylvania (PA)
Indiana U–Purdue U Fort Wayne (IN)
Indiana U–Purdue U Indianapolis (IN)
Indiana Wesleyan U (IN)
Inter American U of Puerto Rico, Fajardo Campus (PR)
Inter American U of Puerto Rico, San Germán Campus (PR)
Iowa Wesleyan Coll (IA)
Ithaca Coll (NY)
Johnson State Coll (VT)
Kennesaw State U (GA)
Kent State U (OH)
Kentucky Wesleyan Coll (KY)
Keystone Coll (PA)
Kutztown U of Pennsylvania (PA)
Lambuth U (TN)
Lawrence U (WI)
Lehman Coll of the City U of New York (NY)
Lenoir-Rhyne Coll (NC)
Limestone Coll (SC)
Lincoln U (MO)
Lincoln U (PA)
Lindenwood U (MO)
Lindsey Wilson Coll (KY)
Lipscomb U (TN)
Longwood U (VA)
Loras Coll (IA)
Louisiana Coll (LA)
Lubbock Christian U (TX)
Malone Coll (OH)
Manchester Coll (IN)
Manhattanville Coll (NY)
Mansfield U of Pennsylvania (PA)
Marian Coll (IN)
Marian Coll of Fond du Lac (WI)
Maryland Inst Coll of Art (MD)
Maryville Coll (TN)
Maryville U of Saint Louis (MO)
Marywood U (PA)
Massachusetts Coll of Art and Design (MA)
McKendree U (IL)
McMurry U (TX)
McNeese State U (LA)
Mercyhurst Coll (PA)
Meredith Coll (NC)
Messiah Coll (PA)
Methodist U (NC)
Miami U (OH)
Miami U Hamilton (OH)
Michigan State U (MI)
Middle Tennessee State U (TN)
Midland Lutheran Coll (NE)
Millersville U of Pennsylvania (PA)
Millikin U (IL)
Minnesota State U Mankato (MN)
Minot State U (ND)
Mississippi Coll (MS)
Mississippi U for Women (MS)
Missouri State U (MO)
Montana State U–Billings (MT)
Montserrat Coll of Art (MA)
Moravian Coll (PA)
Morningside Coll (IA)
Mount Mary Coll (WI)
Mount Mercy Coll (IA)
Mount Saint Vincent U (NS, Canada)
Mount Vernon Nazarene U (OH)
Murray State U (KY)
Nazareth Coll of Rochester (NY)
New Jersey City U (NJ)
New York Inst of Technology (NY)
Nicholls State U (LA)
North Carolina Ag and Tech State U (NC)
North Carolina Central U (NC)
North Central Coll (IL)
Northeastern State U (OK)
Northern Arizona U (AZ)
Northern Illinois U (IL)
Northern Michigan U (MI)
Northern State U (SD)
North Georgia Coll & State U (GA)
Northland Coll (WI)
Northwestern Coll (IA)
Northwestern Coll (MN)
Northwest Missouri State U (MO)
Northwest Nazarene U (ID)
Oakland City U (IN)
Ohio Dominican U (OH)
Ohio Northern U (OH)
Ohio U (OH)
Ohio Wesleyan U (OH)
Oklahoma City U (OK)
Old Dominion U (VA)
Oral Roberts U (OK)
Otterbein Coll (OH)
Ouachita Baptist U (AR)
Pacific U (OR)
Palm Beach Atlantic U (FL)
Penn State Abington (PA)
Penn State Altoona (PA)
Penn State Berks (PA)
Penn State Erie, The Behrend Coll (PA)
Penn State U Park (PA)
Peru State Coll (NE)
Pittsburg State U (KS)
Plymouth State U (NH)
Point Loma Nazarene U (CA)
Pratt Inst (NY)
Purdue U (IN)
Queens Coll of the City U of New York (NY)
Rhode Island Coll (RI)
Roberts Wesleyan Coll (NY)
Rocky Mountain Coll of Art + Design (CO)
Saginaw Valley State U (MI)
St. Ambrose U (IA)
St. Cloud State U (MN)
St. Edward's U (TX)
Saint Joseph's Coll (IN)
Saint Mary-of-the-Woods Coll (IN)
Saint Mary's Coll (IN)
St. Mary's U (TX)
Saint Michael's Coll (VT)
Saint Vincent Coll (PA)
Saint Xavier U (IL)
Salem State Coll (MA)
Sam Houston State U (TX)
School of the Art Inst of Chicago (IL)
School of the Museum of Fine Arts, Boston (MA)
Seattle Pacific U (WA)
Shawnee State U (OH)
Shorter Coll (GA)
Siena Heights U (MI)
Simpson Coll (IA)
South Carolina State U (SC)
Southeastern Louisiana U (LA)
Southeastern Oklahoma State U (OK)
Southeast Missouri State U (MO)
Southern Arkansas U–Magnolia (AR)
Southern Connecticut State U (CT)
Southern U and Ag and Mech Coll (LA)
Southern Utah U (UT)
Southwest Baptist U (MO)
Southwestern Oklahoma State U (OK)
Southwest Minnesota State U (MN)
State U of New York at New Paltz (NY)
Syracuse U (NY)
Tabor Coll (KS)
Taylor U (IN)
Temple U (PA)
Tennessee Technological U (TN)
Texas A&M U–Commerce (TX)
Texas Christian U (TX)
Texas Lutheran U (TX)
Thomas More Coll (KY)
Towson U (MD)
Transylvania U (KY)
Trinity Christian Coll (IL)
Tusculum Coll (TN)
Union Coll (NE)
Union U (TN)
The U of Akron (OH)
The U of Arizona (AZ)
U of Arkansas at Pine Bluff (AR)
The U of British Columbia (BC, Canada)
U of Central Florida (FL)
U of Central Missouri (MO)
U of Central Oklahoma (OK)
U of Cincinnati (OH)
U of Dayton (OH)
U of Denver (CO)
U of Evansville (IN)
The U of Findlay (OH)
U of Florida (FL)
U of Georgia (GA)
U of Great Falls (MT)
U of Guam (GU)
U of Idaho (ID)
U of Illinois at Chicago (IL)
U of Illinois at Urbana–Champaign (IL)
U of Indianapolis (IN)
The U of Iowa (IA)
U of Kansas (KS)
U of Lethbridge (AB, Canada)
U of Maine (ME)
U of Maryland, Coll Park (MD)
U of Maryland Eastern Shore (MD)
U of Massachusetts Dartmouth (MA)
U of Michigan (MI)
U of Michigan–Flint (MI)
U of Minnesota, Duluth (MN)
U of Minnesota, Twin Cities Campus (MN)
U of Missouri–Columbia (MO)
The U of Montana (MT)
The U of Montana–Western (MT)
U of Nebraska–Lincoln (NE)
U of Nevada, Reno (NV)
U of New Brunswick Fredericton (NB, Canada)
U of New Hampshire (NH)
U of New Mexico (NM)
The U of North Carolina at Charlotte (NC)
The U of North Carolina at Greensboro (NC)
The U of North Carolina at Pembroke (NC)
U of Northern Iowa (IA)
U of North Florida (FL)
U of Regina (SK, Canada)
U of Richmond (VA)
U of Rio Grande (OH)
U of Saint Francis (IN)
U of Sioux Falls (SD)
U of South Carolina (SC)
U of South Carolina Upstate (SC)
The U of South Dakota (SD)
U of Southern Maine (ME)
U of South Florida (FL)
The U of Tennessee (TN)
The U of Tennessee at Chattanooga (TN)
The U of Texas at El Paso (TX)
U of the District of Columbia (DC)
U of the Ozarks (AR)
The U of Toledo (OH)
U of Vermont (VT)
U of Victoria (BC, Canada)
The U of Western Ontario (ON, Canada)
U of Windsor (ON, Canada)
U of Wisconsin–Madison (WI)
U of Wisconsin–Milwaukee (WI)
U of Wisconsin–Oshkosh (WI)
U of Wisconsin–Superior (WI)
U of Wisconsin–Whitewater (WI)
Ursuline Coll (OH)
Valdosta State U (GA)
Valley City State U (ND)
Valparaiso U (IN)
Virginia Commonwealth U (VA)
Virginia Intermont Coll (VA)
Virginia Wesleyan Coll (VA)
Viterbo U (WI)
Walla Walla U (WA)
Wartburg Coll (IA)
Washburn U (KS)
Washington & Jefferson Coll (PA)
Washington U in St. Louis (MO)
Wayne State Coll (NE)
Wayne State U (MI)
Weber State U (UT)
Western Carolina U (NC)
Western New Mexico U (NM)
Western State Coll of Colorado (CO)
Western Washington U (WA)
Westfield State Coll (MA)
West Liberty State Coll (WV)
Westmont Coll (CA)
West Virginia Wesleyan Coll (WV)
Whitworth U (WA)
Wichita State U (KS)
William Jewell Coll (MO)
William Paterson U of New Jersey (NJ)
William Woods U (MO)
Wilmington Coll (OH)
Wingate U (NC)
Winona State U (MN)
Wright State U (OH)
Xavier U of Louisiana (LA)
York Coll (NE)

York U (ON, Canada)
Youngstown State U (OH)

ART THERAPY
Albertus Magnus Coll (CT)
Anna Maria Coll (MA)
Capital U (OH)
Carlow U (PA)
The Coll of New Rochelle (NY)
Coll of Santa Fe (NM)
Converse Coll (SC)
DePaul U (IL)
Emmanuel Coll (MA)
Endicott Coll (MA)
Harding U (AR)
Lesley U (MA)
Marian Coll of Fond du Lac (WI)
Marywood U (PA)
Mercyhurst Coll (PA)
Millikin U (IL)
Mount Mary Coll (WI)
Nazareth Coll of Rochester (NY)
Ohio Wesleyan U (OH)
Prescott Coll (AZ)
Russell Sage Coll (NY)
St. Thomas Aquinas Coll (NY)
Seton Hill U (PA)
Spring Hill Coll (AL)
U of Indianapolis (IN)
U of Wisconsin–Superior (WI)
Webster U (MO)
Wright State U (OH)

ASIAN-AMERICAN STUDIES
California State U, East Bay (CA)
California State U, Fullerton (CA)
California State U, Long Beach (CA)
California State U, Los Angeles (CA)
Claremont McKenna Coll (CA)
Colorado State U (CO)
Emory U (GA)
Hampshire Coll (MA)
Loyola Marymount U (CA)
Pitzer Coll (CA)
Pomona Coll (CA)
San Francisco State U (CA)
Scripps Coll (CA)
State U of New York at Binghamton (NY)
Stony Brook U, State U of New York (NY)
U of California, Berkeley (CA)
U of California, Davis (CA)
U of California, Irvine (CA)
U of California, Los Angeles (CA)
U of California, Riverside (CA)
U of California, Santa Barbara (CA)
U of Denver (CO)
U of Southern California (CA)

ASIAN HISTORY
Bard Coll (NY)
Gettysburg Coll (PA)
McGill U (QC, Canada)
Sarah Lawrence Coll (NY)
U of Regina (SK, Canada)
U of the West (CA)

ASIAN STUDIES
American Public U System (WV)
Amherst Coll (MA)
Augustana Coll (IL)
Bard Coll (NY)
Bard Coll at Simon's Rock (MA)
Barnard Coll (NY)
Baylor U (TX)
Beloit Coll (WI)
Bennington Coll (VT)
Bowdoin Coll (ME)
Bowling Green State U (OH)
Brigham Young U (UT)
California State U, Chico (CA)
California State U, Long Beach (CA)
California State U, Los Angeles (CA)
California State U, Sacramento (CA)
Calvin Coll (MI)
Case Western Reserve U (OH)
Central Washington U (WA)
City Coll of the City U of New York (NY)
Claremont McKenna Coll (CA)
Clark U (MA)
Colgate U (NY)
The Coll at Brockport, State U of New York (NY)
Coll of the Holy Cross (MA)
The Colorado Coll (CO)
Colorado State U (CO)
Cornell U (NY)
Dartmouth Coll (NH)
Duke U (NC)
Emory U (GA)
Florida Intl U (FL)
Florida State U (FL)
Fort Lewis Coll (CO)
Furman U (SC)
The George Washington U (DC)
Gonzaga U (WA)
Hamilton Coll (NY)
Hamline U (MN)
Hampshire Coll (MA)
Harvard U (MA)
Hawai'i Pacific U (HI)
Hobart and William Smith Colls (NY)
Hofstra U (NY)
Illinois Wesleyan U (IL)
Indiana U Bloomington (IN)
John Carroll U (OH)
Kenyon Coll (OH)
Knox Coll (IL)
Lake Forest Coll (IL)
Lehigh U (PA)
Macalester Coll (MN)
Manhattanville Coll (NY)
Marlboro Coll (VT)
Mary Baldwin Coll (VA)
Mount Holyoke Coll (MA)
Northwestern U (IL)
Occidental Coll (CA)
Ohio U (OH)
Old Dominion U (VA)
Pitzer Coll (CA)
Pomona Coll (CA)
Purdue U (IN)
Rice U (TX)
St. John's U (NY)
St. Lawrence U (NY)
St. Olaf Coll (MN)
Samford U (AL)
San Diego State U (CA)
Sarah Lawrence Coll (NY)
Scripps Coll (CA)
Sewanee: The U of the South (TN)
Skidmore Coll (NY)
Stanford U (CA)
State U of New York at New Paltz (NY)
Swarthmore Coll (PA)
Temple U (PA)
Texas State U-San Marcos (TX)
Trinity U (TX)
Tufts U (MA)
Tulane U (LA)
U at Albany, State U of New York (NY)
U at Buffalo, the State U of New York (NY)
The U of Alabama (AL)
The U of British Columbia (BC, Canada)
U of California, Berkeley (CA)
U of California, Los Angeles (CA)
U of California, Riverside (CA)
U of California, Santa Barbara (CA)
U of Chicago (IL)
U of Cincinnati (OH)
U of Colorado at Boulder (CO)
U of Florida (FL)
U of Hawaii at Manoa (HI)
The U of Iowa (IA)
U of Michigan (MI)
The U of Montana (MT)
U of New Mexico (NM)
The U of North Carolina at Chapel Hill (NC)
U of Northern Iowa (IA)
U of Oregon (OR)
U of Puget Sound (WA)
U of Redlands (CA)
The U of Texas at Austin (TX)
The U of Toledo (OH)
U of Toronto (ON, Canada)
U of Utah (UT)
U of Vermont (VT)
U of Victoria (BC, Canada)
The U of Western Ontario (ON, Canada)
U of Wisconsin–Madison (WI)
Utah State U (UT)
Vassar Coll (NY)
Warren Wilson Coll (NC)
Washington State U (WA)
Washington U in St. Louis (MO)
Wayne State U (MI)
Western Michigan U (MI)
Western Washington U (WA)
Wheaton Coll (MA)
Whitman Coll (WA)
Willamette U (OR)
Williams Coll (MA)

ASIAN STUDIES (EAST)
Augsburg Coll (MN)
Bates Coll (ME)
Boston U (MA)
Brandeis U (MA)
Brown U (RI)
Bryn Mawr Coll (PA)
Bucknell U (PA)
Colby Coll (ME)
Colgate U (NY)
The Coll of William and Mary (VA)
Connecticut Coll (CT)
Denison U (OH)
DePaul U (IL)
DePauw U (IN)
Dickinson Coll (PA)
Dillard U (LA)
Emory & Henry Coll (VA)
The George Washington U (DC)
Gettysburg Coll (PA)
Hamilton Coll (NY)
Hamline U (MN)
Harvard U (MA)
Haverford Coll (PA)
Indiana U Bloomington (IN)
John Carroll U (OH)
The Johns Hopkins U (MD)
Lawrence U (WI)
Lewis & Clark Coll (OR)
Marlboro Coll (VT)
McGill U (QC, Canada)
Miami U (OH)
Middlebury Coll (VT)
New York U (NY)
North Central Coll (IL)
Oakland U (MI)
Oberlin Coll (OH)
Ohio Wesleyan U (OH)
Penn State Abington (PA)
Penn State Altoona (PA)
Penn State Berks (PA)
Penn State Erie, The Behrend Coll (PA)
Penn State U Park (PA)
Pomona Coll (CA)
Portland State U (OR)
Princeton U (NJ)
Queens Coll of the City U of New York (NY)
Rutgers, The State U of New Jersey, New Brunswick (NJ)
Sarah Lawrence Coll (NY)
Scripps Coll (CA)
Seattle U (WA)
Simmons Coll (MA)
Smith Coll (MA)
Stanford U (CA)
U at Albany, State U of New York (NY)
The U of Arizona (AZ)
U of California, Davis (CA)
U of California, Irvine (CA)
U of California, Los Angeles (CA)
U of Chicago (IL)
U of Delaware (DE)
U of Guam (GU)
U of Illinois at Urbana–Champaign (IL)
U of Minnesota, Twin Cities Campus (MN)
U of Missouri–Columbia (MO)
The U of Montana (MT)
U of Pennsylvania (PA)
U of St. Thomas (MN)
U of Southern California (CA)
U of Toronto (ON, Canada)
The U of Western Ontario (ON, Canada)
Ursinus Coll (PA)
Valparaiso U (IN)
Vanderbilt U (TN)
Washington and Lee U (VA)
Washington U in St. Louis (MO)
Wellesley Coll (MA)
Wesleyan U (CT)
Western Washington U (WA)
Wittenberg U (OH)
Yale U (CT)
York U (ON, Canada)

ASIAN STUDIES (SOUTH)
Brown U (RI)
Concordia U (QC, Canada)
Gettysburg Coll (PA)
Harvard U (MA)
Indiana U Bloomington (IN)
Oakland U (MI)
Sarah Lawrence Coll (NY)
The U of British Columbia (BC, Canada)
U of Chicago (IL)
U of Michigan (MI)
U of Minnesota, Twin Cities Campus (MN)
U of Missouri–Columbia (MO)
U of Pennsylvania (PA)
U of Toronto (ON, Canada)

ASIAN STUDIES (SOUTHEAST)
Concordia U (QC, Canada)
Harvard U (MA)
Ohio U (OH)
Tufts U (MA)
U of California, Berkeley (CA)
U of California, Los Angeles (CA)
U of Chicago (IL)
U of Michigan (MI)
U of Wisconsin–Madison (WI)

ASTRONOMY
Amherst Coll (MA)
Benedictine Coll (KS)
Bennington Coll (VT)
Boston U (MA)
Brigham Young U (UT)
Bryn Mawr Coll (PA)
Case Western Reserve U (OH)
Central Michigan U (MI)
Colgate U (NY)
The Coll at Brockport, State U of New York (NY)
Cornell U (NY)
Dartmouth Coll (NH)
Drake U (IA)
Franklin & Marshall Coll (PA)
George Mason U (VA)
Harvard U (MA)
Haverford Coll (PA)
Laurentian U (ON, Canada)
Lehigh U (PA)
Lycoming Coll (PA)
Marlboro Coll (VT)
Minnesota State U Mankato (MN)
Mount Holyoke Coll (MA)
Northern Arizona U (AZ)
Northwestern U (IL)
Ohio Wesleyan U (OH)
Penn State Abington (PA)
Penn State Altoona (PA)
Penn State Berks (PA)
Penn State Erie, The Behrend Coll (PA)
Penn State U Park (PA)
Pomona Coll (CA)
Rice U (TX)
Royal Military Coll of Canada (ON, Canada)
San Diego State U (CA)
San Francisco State U (CA)
Sarah Lawrence Coll (NY)
Smith Coll (MA)
Stony Brook U, State U of New York (NY)
Swarthmore Coll (PA)
Tufts U (MA)
Union Coll (NY)
The U of Arizona (AZ)
The U of British Columbia (BC, Canada)
U of Colorado at Boulder (CO)
U of Florida (FL)
U of Illinois at Urbana–Champaign (IL)
The U of Iowa (IA)
U of Kansas (KS)
U of Maryland, Coll Park (MD)
U of Massachusetts Amherst (MA)
U of Michigan (MI)
U of Minnesota, Twin Cities Campus (MN)
The U of Montana (MT)
U of New Hampshire (NH)
The U of North Carolina at Chapel Hill (NC)
U of Oklahoma (OK)
U of Southern California (CA)
The U of Texas at Austin (TX)
The U of Toledo (OH)
U of Toronto (ON, Canada)
U of Victoria (BC, Canada)
U of Virginia (VA)
The U of Western Ontario (ON, Canada)
U of Wisconsin–Madison (WI)
Valdosta State U (GA)
Vanderbilt U (TN)
Vassar Coll (NY)
Villanova U (PA)
Wellesley Coll (MA)
Wesleyan U (CT)
Wheaton Coll (MA)
Whitman Coll (WA)
Williams Coll (MA)
Yale U (CT)
York U (ON, Canada)
Youngstown State U (OH)

ASTRONOMY AND ASTROPHYSICS RELATED
Coll of Charleston (SC)
Texas Christian U (TX)
U of Wyoming (WY)

ASTROPHYSICS
Agnes Scott Coll (GA)
Augsburg Coll (MN)
Boston U (MA)
California Inst of Technology (CA)
Carnegie Mellon U (PA)
Colgate U (NY)
Connecticut Coll (CT)
Florida Inst of Technology (FL)
Franklin & Marshall Coll (PA)
Harvard U (MA)
Lehigh U (PA)
Marlboro Coll (VT)
Michigan State U (MI)
Ohio U (OH)
Ohio Wesleyan U (OH)
Princeton U (NJ)
Rice U (TX)
Rutgers, The State U of New Jersey, New Brunswick (NJ)
San Francisco State U (CA)
Swarthmore Coll (PA)
U of California, Berkeley (CA)
U of California, Los Angeles (CA)
U of Minnesota, Twin Cities Campus (MN)
U of New Mexico (NM)
U of Oklahoma (OK)
The U of Western Ontario (ON, Canada)
Villanova U (PA)
Wellesley Coll (MA)
Whitman Coll (WA)
Williams Coll (MA)
Yale U (CT)

ATHLETIC TRAINING
Alcorn State U (MS)
Alderson-Broaddus Coll (WV)
Alfred U (NY)
Alvernia Coll (PA)
Anderson U (IN)
Angelo State U (TX)
Appalachian State U (NC)
Aquinas Coll (MI)
Arkansas State U (AR)
Ashford U (IA)
Ashland U (OH)
Augsburg Coll (MN)
Augustana Coll (SD)
Averett U (VA)
Azusa Pacific U (CA)
Baldwin-Wallace Coll (OH)
Ball State U (IN)
Barton Coll (NC)
Baylor U (TX)
Belhaven Coll (MS)
Benedictine Coll (KS)
Bethany Coll (KS)
Bethel Coll (KS)
Bethel U (MN)
Boise State U (ID)
Boston U (MA)
Bowling Green State U (OH)
Bridgewater Coll (VA)
Bridgewater State Coll (MA)
Brigham Young U (UT)
California Lutheran U (CA)
California State U, East Bay (CA)
California State U, Long Beach (CA)
California State U, Monterey Bay (CA)
Canisius Coll (NY)
Capital U (OH)
Carroll Coll (WI)
Carson-Newman Coll (TN)
Castleton State Coll (VT)
Catawba Coll (NC)
Cedarville U (OH)
Central Connecticut State U (CT)
Central Michigan U (MI)
Chapman U (CA)
Clarke Coll (IA)
Colby-Sawyer Coll (NH)
The Coll at Brockport, State U of New York (NY)
Coll of Charleston (SC)
Coll of Mount St. Joseph (OH)
Colorado State U (CO)
Concordia U Wisconsin (WI)
Creighton U (NE)
Culver-Stockton Coll (MO)
Dakota Wesleyan U (SD)
Defiance Coll (OH)
DePauw U (IN)
Dominican Coll (NY)
Duquesne U (PA)
East Carolina U (NC)
Eastern Michigan U (MI)
East Stroudsburg U of Pennsylvania (PA)
East Texas Baptist U (TX)
Elon U (NC)
Emporia State U (KS)
Endicott Coll (MA)
Erskine Coll (SC)
Faulkner U (AL)
Florida Southern Coll (FL)
Florida State U (FL)
Fort Lewis Coll (CO)
Franklin Coll (IN)
Free Will Baptist Bible Coll (TN)
Fresno Pacific U (CA)
Gardner-Webb U (NC)
George Fox U (OR)
Georgetown Coll (KY)
Georgia Southern U (GA)
Grand Canyon U (AZ)
Grand Valley State U (MI)

Greensboro Coll (NC)
Guilford Coll (NC)
Gustavus Adolphus Coll (MN)
Hamline U (MN)
Harding U (AR)
Hardin-Simmons U (TX)
Heidelberg Coll (OH)
Henderson State U (AR)
High Point U (NC)
Hofstra U (NY)
Hope Coll (MI)
Hope Intl U (CA)
Howard Payne U (TX)
Huntingdon Coll (AL)
Illinois State U (IL)
Indiana State U (IN)
Indiana Wesleyan U (IN)
Ithaca Coll (NY)
James Madison U (VA)
Jefferson Coll of Health Sciences (VA)
John Brown U (AR)
Johnson State Coll (VT)
Kansas State U (KS)
Kean U (NJ)
Keene State Coll (NH)
Kent State U (OH)
King Coll (TN)
King's Coll (PA)
Lakehead U (ON, Canada)
Lake Superior State U (MI)
Lander U (SC)
Lees-McRae Coll (NC)
Lee U (TN)
Lenoir-Rhyne Coll (NC)
Lewis U (IL)
Liberty U (VA)
Limestone Coll (SC)
Lindenwood U (MO)
Linfield Coll (OR)
Lipscomb U (TN)
Lock Haven U of Pennsylvania (PA)
Longwood U (VA)
Loras Coll (IA)
Louisiana Coll (LA)
Luther Coll (IA)
Lynchburg Coll (VA)
Lyndon State Coll (VT)
Manchester Coll (IN)
Marietta Coll (OH)
Marist Coll (NY)
Marquette U (WI)
Marywood U (PA)
McKendree U (IL)
McMurry U (TX)
Memorial U of Newfoundland (NL, Canada)
Mercyhurst Coll (PA)
Merrimack Coll (MA)
Mesa State Coll (CO)
Messiah Coll (PA)
Methodist U (NC)
Miami U (OH)
Miami U Hamilton (OH)
MidAmerica Nazarene U (KS)
Middle Tennessee State U (TN)
Midland Lutheran Coll (NE)
Midwestern State U (TX)
Millikin U (IL)
Minnesota State U Mankato (MN)
Missouri State U (MO)
Missouri Valley Coll (MO)
Montclair State U (NJ)
Mount Olive Coll (NC)
National American U, Rapid City (SD)
Nebraska Wesleyan U (NE)
North Carolina Central U (NC)
North Central Coll (IL)
North Dakota State U (ND)
Northeastern U (MA)
Northern Michigan U (MI)
Northwestern Coll (IA)
Northwest Nazarene U (ID)
Norwich U (VT)
Nova Southeastern U (FL)
Ohio Northern U (OH)
Oklahoma State U (OK)
Oklahoma Wesleyan U (OK)
Oregon State U (OR)
Otterbein Coll (OH)
Ouachita Baptist U (AR)
Pacific U (OR)
Park U (MO)
Pepperdine U, Malibu (CA)
Pfeiffer U (NC)
Plymouth State U (NH)
Point Loma Nazarene U (CA)
Purdue U (IN)
Quinnipiac U (CT)
Roanoke Coll (VA)
Sacred Heart U (CT)
Saginaw Valley State U (MI)
Salisbury U (MD)
Samford U (AL)
San Diego Christian Coll (CA)
Shawnee State U (OH)
Shaw U (NC)
Simpson Coll (IA)
Slippery Rock U of Pennsylvania (PA)
South Dakota State U (SD)
Southeastern Louisiana U (LA)
Southwest Baptist U (MO)
Southwestern Coll (KS)
Sterling Coll (KS)
Stony Brook U, State U of New York (NY)
Tabor Coll (KS)
Taylor U (IN)
Texas A&M U–Commerce (TX)
Texas Christian U (TX)
Texas Lutheran U (TX)
Texas State U-San Marcos (TX)
Towson U (MD)
Trinity Intl U (IL)
Troy U (AL)
Truman State U (MO)
Tusculum Coll (TN)
Union U (TN)
Université de Sherbrooke (QC, Canada)
The U of Akron (OH)
The U of Alabama (AL)
U of Central Arkansas (AR)
U of Charleston (WV)
U of Delaware (DE)
U of Evansville (IN)
The U of Findlay (OH)
U of Florida (FL)
U of Idaho (ID)
U of Illinois at Urbana–Champaign (IL)
U of Indianapolis (IN)
The U of Iowa (IA)
U of La Verne (CA)
U of Louisiana at Lafayette (LA)
U of Mary (ND)
U of Mary Hardin-Baylor (TX)
U of Miami (FL)
U of Michigan (MI)
U of Nebraska–Lincoln (NE)
U of Nevada, Las Vegas (NV)
U of New England (ME)
U of New Hampshire (NH)
The U of North Carolina at Pembroke (NC)
The U of North Carolina Wilmington (NC)
U of North Dakota (ND)
U of Northern Iowa (IA)
U of North Florida (FL)
U of Pittsburgh at Bradford (PA)
U of Southern Maine (ME)
U of Southern Mississippi (MS)
U of South Florida (FL)
The U of Tennessee at Martin (TN)
The U of Texas at Arlington (TX)
The U of Texas at Austin (TX)
U of the Incarnate Word (TX)
U of Tulsa (OK)
U of Vermont (VT)
U of Windsor (ON, Canada)
U of Wisconsin–Eau Claire (WI)
U of Wisconsin–La Crosse (WI)
U of Wisconsin–Stevens Point (WI)
Vanguard U of Southern California (CA)
Washburn U (KS)
Washington State U (WA)
Waynesburg U (PA)
Wayne State Coll (NE)
Weber State U (UT)
West Chester U of Pennsylvania (PA)
Western Michigan U (MI)
West Virginia Wesleyan Coll (WV)
Wheeling Jesuit U (WV)
Whitworth U (WA)
William Woods U (MO)
Wilmington Coll (OH)
Wingate U (NC)
Winona State U (MN)
Xavier U (OH)
Youngstown State U (OH)

ATHLETIC TRAINING/ SPORTS MEDICINE

Bryan Coll (TN)
Delta State U (MS)
Florida Gulf Coast U (FL)
George Mason U (VA)
Neumann Coll (PA)
U of Georgia (GA)
The U of North Carolina at Charlotte (NC)
The U of North Carolina at Pembroke (NC)
U of Pittsburgh at Bradford (PA)
The U of Tampa (FL)
Valdosta State U (GA)

ATMOSPHERIC PHYSICS AND DYNAMICS

McGill U (QC, Canada)

ATMOSPHERIC SCIENCES AND METEOROLOGY

The Coll at Brockport, State U of New York (NY)
Cornell U (NY)
Creighton U (NE)
Embry-Riddle Aeronautical U (AZ)
Embry-Riddle Aeronautical U (FL)
Florida State U (FL)
Harvard U (MA)
Iowa State U of Science and Technology (IA)
Jackson State U (MS)
Lyndon State Coll (VT)
McGill U (QC, Canada)
Millersville U of Pennsylvania (PA)
Northern Illinois U (IL)
Northland Coll (WI)
Ohio U (OH)
Penn State Abington (PA)
Penn State Altoona (PA)
Penn State Berks (PA)
Penn State Erie, The Behrend Coll (PA)
Penn State U Park (PA)
Plymouth State U (NH)
Purdue U (IN)
Rutgers, The State U of New Jersey, New Brunswick (NJ)
St. Cloud State U (MN)
Saint Louis U (MO)
San Francisco State U (CA)
State U of New York at Oswego (NY)
State U of New York Coll at Oneonta (NY)
Stony Brook U, State U of New York (NY)
Texas A&M U (TX)
United States Air Force Acad (CO)
U at Albany, State U of New York (NY)
The U of Arizona (AZ)
The U of British Columbia (BC, Canada)
U of California, Berkeley (CA)
U of California, Davis (CA)
U of California, Los Angeles (CA)
U of Illinois at Urbana–Champaign (IL)
U of Kansas (KS)
U of Louisiana at Monroe (LA)
U of Michigan (MI)
U of Missouri–Columbia (MO)
U of Nebraska–Lincoln (NE)
The U of North Carolina at Asheville (NC)
U of North Dakota (ND)
U of Oklahoma (OK)
U of South Alabama (AL)
U of Victoria (BC, Canada)
U of Wisconsin–Milwaukee (WI)
Valparaiso U (IN)
Western Connecticut State U (CT)
York U (ON, Canada)

ATMOSPHERIC SCIENCES AND METEOROLOGY RELATED

U of California, Los Angeles (CA)

ATOMIC/MOLECULAR PHYSICS

The Catholic U of America (DC)
Maryville Coll (TN)
Ohio U (OH)
San Diego State U (CA)
U of California, San Diego (CA)

AUDIO ENGINEERING

American U (DC)
Berklee Coll of Music (MA)
Cogswell Polytechnical Coll (CA)
Five Towns Coll (NY)
Michigan Technological U (MI)
New England School of Communications (ME)
Peabody Conservatory of Music of The Johns Hopkins U (MD)
State U of New York at Fredonia (NY)
U of Hartford (CT)

AUDIOLOGY AND HEARING SCIENCES

California State U, Long Beach (CA)
Cleveland State U (OH)
Indiana U–Purdue U Fort Wayne (IN)
Northwestern U (IL)
Purdue U (IN)
Stephen F. Austin State U (TX)
U of Colorado at Boulder (CO)
U of Illinois at Urbana–Champaign (IL)
The U of Iowa (IA)
U of Montevallo (AL)
U of Nebraska–Lincoln (NE)
U of Northern Colorado (CO)
U of Oklahoma Health Sciences Center (OK)
The U of Tennessee (TN)
The U of Western Ontario (ON, Canada)

AUDIOLOGY AND SPEECH-LANGUAGE PATHOLOGY

Adelphi U (NY)
Andrews U (MI)
Arkansas State U (AR)
Auburn U (AL)
Augustana Coll (SD)
Ball State U (IN)
Bloomsburg U of Pennsylvania (PA)
Brigham Young U (UT)
Buffalo State Coll, State U of New York (NY)
Butler U (IN)
California State U, East Bay (CA)
California State U, Fresno (CA)
California State U, Long Beach (CA)
California State U, Sacramento (CA)
Calvin Coll (MI)
Clarion U of Pennsylvania (PA)
The Coll of Saint Rose (NY)
Delta State U (MS)
Eastern Kentucky U (KY)
Eastern New Mexico U (NM)
East Stroudsburg U of Pennsylvania (PA)
Emerson Coll (MA)
Fontbonne U (MO)
The George Washington U (DC)
Hampton U (VA)
Hardin-Simmons U (TX)
Hofstra U (NY)
Hunter Coll of the City U of New York (NY)
Illinois State U (IL)
Indiana State U (IN)
Indiana U Bloomington (IN)
Indiana U of Pennsylvania (PA)
Iona Coll (NY)
Ithaca Coll (NY)
Kent State U (OH)
Lambuth U (TN)
La Salle U (PA)
Lehman Coll of the City U of New York (NY)
Loma Linda U (CA)
Louisiana State U and Ag and Mech Coll (LA)
Marquette U (WI)
Marywood U (PA)
Miami U (OH)
Miami U Hamilton (OH)
Michigan State U (MI)
Minnesota State U Mankato (MN)
Mississippi U for Women (MS)
Missouri State U (MO)
Molloy Coll (NY)
Murray State U (KY)
Nazareth Coll of Rochester (NY)
Nicholls State U (LA)
Northeastern State U (OK)
Northeastern U (MA)
Northern State U (SD)
Northwestern U (IL)
Ohio U (OH)
Old Dominion U (VA)
Otterbein Coll (OH)
Purdue U (IN)
Queens Coll of the City U of New York (NY)
The Richard Stockton Coll of New Jersey (NJ)
St. Cloud State U (MN)
St. John's U (NY)
Saint Louis U (MO)
San Francisco State U (CA)
Shaw U (NC)
South Carolina State U (SC)
Southeastern Louisiana U (LA)
Southern Illinois U Edwardsville (IL)
Southern U and Ag and Mech Coll (LA)
State U of New York at Fredonia (NY)
Stephen F. Austin State U (TX)
Syracuse U (NY)
Temple U (PA)
Tennessee State U (TN)
Texas State U-San Marcos (TX)
Texas Woman's U (TX)
Thiel Coll (PA)
U at Buffalo, the State U of New York (NY)
The U of Akron (OH)
The U of Alabama (AL)
U of Central Arkansas (AR)
U of Central Florida (FL)
U of Central Oklahoma (OK)
U of Cincinnati (OH)
U of Florida (FL)
U of Houston (TX)
U of Illinois at Urbana–Champaign (IL)
The U of Iowa (IA)
U of Louisiana at Lafayette (LA)
U of Louisiana at Monroe (LA)
U of Minnesota, Duluth (MN)
U of Minnesota, Twin Cities Campus (MN)
U of Mississippi (MS)
The U of Montana (MT)
U of New Hampshire (NH)
U of New Mexico (NM)
The U of North Carolina at Greensboro (NC)
U of North Texas (TX)
U of Oklahoma Health Sciences Center (OK)
U of Pittsburgh (PA)
U of Redlands (CA)
U of South Alabama (AL)
U of Southern Mississippi (MS)
U of South Florida (FL)
The U of Texas at Dallas (TX)
The U of Texas at El Paso (TX)
The U of Texas–Pan American (TX)
U of the District of Columbia (DC)
U of the Pacific (CA)
The U of Toledo (OH)
U of Tulsa (OK)
U of Utah (UT)
U of Virginia (VA)
The U of Western Ontario (ON, Canada)
U of Wisconsin–Milwaukee (WI)
U of Wisconsin–Oshkosh (WI)
U of Wisconsin–Stevens Point (WI)
U of Wyoming (WY)
Utah State U (UT)
Washington State U (WA)
West Chester U of Pennsylvania (PA)
Western Michigan U (MI)
Western Washington U (WA)
West Virginia U (WV)
Wichita State U (KS)

AUDIOVISUAL COMMUNICATIONS TECHNOLOGIES RELATED

American InterContinental U (CA)
American InterContinental U (FL)
American InterContinental U (TX)
American InterContinental U Buckhead Campus (GA)
American InterContinental U Dunwoody Campus (GA)
American InterContinental U-London (United Kingdom)
American InterContinental U Online (IL)
Greenville Coll (IL)

AUDITING

Babson Coll (MA)
Carlow U (PA)
McGill U (QC, Canada)
U of Illinois at Urbana–Champaign (IL)

AUTOBODY/COLLISION AND REPAIR TECHNOLOGY

Lewis-Clark State Coll (ID)

AUTOMOBILE/AUTOMOTIVE MECHANICS TECHNOLOGY

Lewis-Clark State Coll (ID)
Pittsburg State U (KS)
U of Arkansas at Pine Bluff (AR)

AUTOMOTIVE ENGINEERING TECHNOLOGY

Central Michigan U (MI)
Colorado State U-Pueblo (CO)
Ferris State U (MI)
Indiana State U (IN)
Minnesota State U Mankato (MN)
Pittsburg State U (KS)
Southern Illinois U Carbondale (IL)
Weber State U (UT)

AVIATION/AIRWAY MANAGEMENT

Auburn U (AL)
Averett U (VA)
Baker Coll of Muskegon (MI)
Bob Jones U (SC)
Bowling Green State U (OH)
Bridgewater State Coll (MA)

California State U, Los Angeles (CA)
Eastern Michigan U (MI)
Eastern New Mexico U (NM)
Embry-Riddle Aeronautical U (FL)
Embry-Riddle Aeronautical U Worldwide (FL)
Fairmont State U (WV)
Farmingdale State Coll (NY)
Florida Inst of Technology (FL)
Florida Memorial U (FL)
Hampton U (VA)
Indiana State U (IN)
Inter American U of Puerto Rico, Bayamón Campus (PR)
Inter American U of Puerto Rico, Fajardo Campus (PR)
Jacksonville U (FL)
Kent State U (OH)
Lewis U (IL)
Marywood U (PA)
Minnesota State U Mankato (MN)
Mountain State U (WV)
Ohio U (OH)
Purdue U (IN)
Quincy U (IL)
St. Cloud State U (MN)
Saint Louis U (MO)
Salem State Coll (MA)
South Dakota State U (SD)
Southeastern Oklahoma State U (OK)
Southern Illinois U Carbondale (IL)
Tarleton State U (TX)
Texas Southern U (TX)
U of Illinois at Urbana–Champaign (IL)
U of Nebraska at Kearney (NE)
U of North Dakota (ND)
The U of Western Ontario (ON, Canada)
Westminster Coll (UT)
Wilmington U (DE)
Winona State U (MN)

AVIONICS MAINTENANCE TECHNOLOGY
Averett U (VA)
Fairmont State U (WV)
Grace U (NE)
Inter American U of Puerto Rico, Fajardo Campus (PR)
LeTourneau U (TX)
Southern Illinois U Carbondale (IL)
Wilmington U (DE)

AYURVEDIC MEDICINE
Maharishi U of Management (IA)

BALKANS STUDIES
American Coll of Thessaloniki (Greece)

BALLET
Brigham Young U (UT)
Indiana U Bloomington (IN)
Texas Christian U (TX)
U of Utah (UT)

BANKING AND FINANCIAL SUPPORT SERVICES
Emory U (GA)
Husson Coll (ME)
National U (CA)
Northwood U, Florida Campus (FL)
Providence Coll (RI)
Texas Southern U (TX)
U of Illinois at Urbana–Champaign (IL)
U of Nebraska at Omaha (NE)
U of North Florida (FL)
U of North Texas (TX)
The U of Texas at Arlington (TX)
West Liberty State Coll (WV)

BEHAVIORAL SCIENCES
Andrews U (MI)
Athens State U (AL)
Augsburg Coll (MN)
Bemidji State U (MN)
Brown U (RI)
California Baptist U (CA)
California State Polytechnic U, Pomona (CA)
California State U, Dominguez Hills (CA)
California State U, Monterey Bay (CA)
Carnegie Mellon U (PA)
Chaminade U of Honolulu (HI)
Columbia Coll (SC)
Concordia U (CA)
Concordia U, Nebraska (NE)
Dakota Wesleyan U (SD)
Drew U (NJ)
East-West U (IL)
Erskine Coll (SC)
Evangel U (MO)
Felician Coll (NJ)
Freed-Hardeman U (TN)
George Fox U (OR)
Glenville State Coll (WV)
Grand Valley State U (MI)
Granite State Coll (NH)
Harvard U (MA)
Howard Payne U (TX)
Indiana U Kokomo (IN)
Inter American U of Puerto Rico, San Germán Campus (PR)
The Johns Hopkins U (MD)
Laurentian U (ON, Canada)
Loyola U New Orleans (LA)
Marlboro Coll (VT)
Mercy Coll (NY)
Methodist U (NC)
Midland Lutheran Coll (NE)
Miles Coll (AL)
Minnesota State U Mankato (MN)
Missouri Baptist U (MO)
Morgan State U (MD)
Mountain State U (WV)
Mount Aloysius Coll (PA)
Mount Mary Coll (WI)
National-Louis U (IL)
National U (CA)
Northeastern U (MA)
Northern Michigan U (MI)
Northwest Missouri State U (MO)
Oklahoma Wesleyan U (OK)
Pacific Union Coll (CA)
Point Park U (PA)
Purdue U Calumet (IN)
Purdue U North Central (IN)
Rochester Coll (MI)
St. Cloud State U (MN)
St. Joseph's Coll, Suffolk Campus (NY)
Sterling Coll (KS)
Tennessee Wesleyan Coll (TN)
Trevecca Nazarene U (TN)
Tufts U (MA)
United States Air Force Acad (CO)
U of Chicago (IL)
U of Houston–Clear Lake (TX)
U of Kansas (KS)
U of La Verne (CA)
U of Maine at Fort Kent (ME)
U of Maine at Machias (ME)
U of Missouri–Columbia (MO)
U of North Texas (TX)
U of Ottawa (ON, Canada)
Walsh U (OH)
Western Intl U (AZ)
Widener U (PA)
William Paterson U of New Jersey (NJ)
Wilmington U (DE)
Wilson Coll (PA)
York U (ON, Canada)

BENGALI
U of Chicago (IL)

BIBLICAL LANGUAGES/ LITERATURES
Concordia U (CA)
Lipscomb U (TN)

BIBLICAL STUDIES
Abilene Christian U (TX)
Anderson U (IN)
Andrews U (MI)
Appalachian Bible Coll (WV)
Arlington Baptist Coll (TX)
Asbury Coll (KY)
Azusa Pacific U (CA)
Baptist Bible Coll of Pennsylvania (PA)
The Baptist Coll of Florida (FL)
Barclay Coll (KS)
Belhaven Coll (MS)
Belmont U (TN)
Bethany Bible Coll (NB, Canada)
Bethany U (CA)
Bethel U (MN)
Beulah Heights U (GA)
Biola U (CA)
Bluefield Coll (VA)
Bob Jones U (SC)
Boston Baptist Coll (MA)
Bryan Coll (TN)
California Baptist U (CA)
Calvin Coll (MI)
Canadian Mennonite U (MB, Canada)
Carson-Newman Coll (TN)
Cascade Coll (OR)
Cedarville U (OH)
Central Christian Coll of Kansas (KS)
Clearwater Christian Coll (FL)
Coll of Biblical Studies–Houston (TX)
Cornerstone U (MI)
Covenant Coll (GA)
Crossroads Coll (MN)
Dallas Christian Coll (TX)
Davis Coll (NY)
Eastern Mennonite U (VA)
East Texas Baptist U (TX)
Erskine Coll (SC)
Eugene Bible Coll (OR)
Evangel U (MO)
Faith Baptist Bible Coll and Theological Sem (IA)
Faulkner U (AL)
Florida Coll (FL)
Freed-Hardeman U (TN)
Free Will Baptist Bible Coll (TN)
Fresno Pacific U (CA)
George Fox U (OR)
Grace Bible Coll (MI)
Grace Coll (IN)
Grace U (NE)
Grand Canyon U (AZ)
Great Lakes Christian Coll (MI)
Hannibal-LaGrange Coll (MO)
Harding U (AR)
Hardin-Simmons U (TX)
Harvard U (MA)
Heritage Baptist Coll and Heritage Theological Sem (ON, Canada)
Heritage Christian U (AL)
Hope Intl U (CA)
Horizon Coll & Sem (SK, Canada)
Houghton Coll (NY)
Houston Baptist U (TX)
Howard Payne U (TX)
Huntington U (IN)
Indiana Wesleyan U (IN)
John Brown U (AR)
Johnson Bible Coll (TN)
John Wesley Coll (NC)
Judson U (IL)
Kentucky Christian U (KY)
King Coll (TN)
Kuyper Coll (MI)
Lee U (TN)
LeTourneau U (TX)
Lipscomb U (TN)
List Coll, The Jewish Theological Sem (NY)
Lubbock Christian U (TX)
Magnolia Bible Coll (MS)
Malone Coll (OH)
Maranatha Baptist Bible Coll (WI)
Marlboro Coll (VT)
The Master's Coll and Sem (CA)
Master's Coll and Sem (ON, Canada)
Messiah Coll (PA)
Methodist U (NC)
Mid-Continent U (KY)
Milligan Coll (TN)
Mount Vernon Nazarene U (OH)
Multnomah Bible Coll and Biblical Sem (OR)
Nazarene Bible Coll (CO)
North Greenville U (SC)
Northwest Christian Coll (OR)
Northwestern Coll (MN)
Northwest Nazarene U (ID)
Nyack Coll (NY)
Oakland City U (IN)
Ohio Valley U (WV)
Oklahoma Christian U (OK)
Oral Roberts U (OK)
Ouachita Baptist U (AR)
Ozark Christian Coll (MO)
Palm Beach Atlantic U (FL)
Philadelphia Biblical U (PA)
Pillsbury Baptist Bible Coll (MN)
Point Loma Nazarene U (CA)
Redeemer U Coll (ON, Canada)
Roanoke Bible Coll (NC)
Rochester Coll (MI)
St. Louis Christian Coll (MO)
San Diego Christian Coll (CA)
Shasta Bible Coll (CA)
Simpson U (CA)
Southeastern Bible Coll (AL)
Southeastern U (FL)
Southern Baptist Theological Sem (KY)
Southern California Sem (CA)
Southwest Baptist U (MO)
Southwestern Coll (AZ)
Spring Arbor U (MI)
Steinbach Bible Coll (MB, Canada)
Tabor Coll (KS)
Talmudic Coll of Florida (FL)
Taylor U (IN)
Taylor U Coll and Sem (AB, Canada)
Taylor U Fort Wayne (IN)
Toccoa Falls Coll (GA)
Trinity Coll of Florida (FL)
Trinity Intl U (IL)
Tyndale U Coll & Sem (ON, Canada)
Union U (TN)
U of Evansville (IN)
U of Mary Hardin-Baylor (TX)
The U of Western Ontario (ON, Canada)
Vanguard U of Southern California (CA)
Vennard Coll (IA)
Wheaton Coll (IL)
Williamson Christian Coll (TN)
York Coll (NE)

BILINGUAL AND MULTILINGUAL EDUCATION
Belmont U (TN)
Biola U (CA)
Boise State U (ID)
Boston U (MA)
California State Polytechnic U, Pomona (CA)
California State U, Dominguez Hills (CA)
Calvin Coll (MI)
Chicago State U (IL)
Coll of the Southwest (NM)
Florida State U (FL)
Fresno Pacific U (CA)
Houston Baptist U (TX)
Indiana U Bloomington (IN)
Loyola U Chicago (IL)
McGill U (QC, Canada)
Mount Mary Coll (WI)
Northeastern Illinois U (IL)
Prescott Coll (AZ)
Rider U (NJ)
State U of New York Coll at Old Westbury (NY)
Texas A&M Intl U (TX)
Texas Christian U (TX)
Texas Southern U (TX)
U of Delaware (DE)
The U of Findlay (OH)
U of Houston (TX)
U of Maine at Fort Kent (ME)
U of Regina (SK, Canada)
U of the Sacred Heart (PR)
U of Wisconsin–Milwaukee (WI)
Washington State U (WA)
Weber State U (UT)
Western Illinois U (IL)
York U (ON, Canada)

BILINGUAL, MULTILINGUAL, AND MULTICULTURAL EDUCATION RELATED
The Coll at Brockport, State U of New York (NY)
Florida State U (FL)

BIOCHEMICAL TECHNOLOGY
Norwich U (VT)
U of Windsor (ON, Canada)

BIOCHEMISTRY
Abilene Christian U (TX)
Adelphi U (NY)
Agnes Scott Coll (GA)
Albright Coll (PA)
Allegheny Coll (PA)
Alma Coll (MI)
Alvernia Coll (PA)
American U (DC)
The American U of Athens (Greece)
Anderson U (IN)
Andrews U (MI)
Angelo State U (TX)
Arizona State U (AZ)
Asbury Coll (KY)
Auburn U (AL)
Augustana Coll (IL)
Austin Coll (TX)
Azusa Pacific U (CA)
Barnard Coll (NY)
Bates Coll (ME)
Baylor U (TX)
Belmont U (TN)
Beloit Coll (WI)
Benedictine Coll (KS)
Benedictine U (IL)
Bennington Coll (VT)
Biola U (CA)
Bishop's U (QC, Canada)
Boston Coll (MA)
Boston U (MA)
Bowdoin Coll (ME)
Bradley U (IL)
Brandeis U (MA)
Bridgewater State Coll (MA)
Brigham Young U (UT)
Brock U (ON, Canada)
Brown U (RI)
Bucknell U (PA)
California Lutheran U (CA)
California Polytechnic State U, San Luis Obispo (CA)
California State U, Chico (CA)
California State U, Dominguez Hills (CA)
California State U, East Bay (CA)
California State U, Fullerton (CA)
California State U, Long Beach (CA)
California State U, Los Angeles (CA)
California State U, San Bernardino (CA)
California State U, San Marcos (CA)
Calvin Coll (MI)
Canisius Coll (NY)
Capital U (OH)
Carroll Coll (WI)
Case Western Reserve U (OH)
The Catholic U of America (DC)
Cedar Crest Coll (PA)
Central Connecticut State U (CT)
Central Michigan U (MI)
Centre Coll (KY)
Chatham U (PA)
Chestnut Hill Coll (PA)
City Coll of the City U of New York (NY)
Claflin U (SC)
Claremont McKenna Coll (CA)
Clarkson U (NY)
Clark U (MA)
Clemson U (SC)
Colby Coll (ME)
Colgate U (NY)
The Coll at Brockport, State U of New York (NY)
Coll of Charleston (SC)
Coll of Mount St. Joseph (OH)
Coll of Mount Saint Vincent (NY)
Coll of Saint Benedict (MN)
Coll of Saint Elizabeth (NJ)
The Coll of Saint Rose (NY)
The Coll of St. Scholastica (MN)
Coll of Staten Island of the City U of New York (NY)
The Colorado Coll (CO)
Colorado State U (CO)
Connecticut Coll (CT)
Converse Coll (SC)
Cornell Coll (IA)
Cornell U (NY)
Daemen Coll (NY)
Dakota Wesleyan U (SD)
Dartmouth Coll (NH)
Denison U (OH)
DePauw U (IN)
DeSales U (PA)
Dickinson Coll (PA)
Doane Coll (NE)
Dominican U (IL)
Drake U (IA)
Drew U (NJ)
Duquesne U (PA)
Earlham Coll (IN)
East Carolina U (NC)
Eastern Connecticut State U (CT)
Eastern Mennonite U (VA)
Eastern Michigan U (MI)
East Stroudsburg U of Pennsylvania (PA)
Eckerd Coll (FL)
Edinboro U of Pennsylvania (PA)
Elizabethtown Coll (PA)
Emmanuel Coll (MA)
Fairleigh Dickinson U, Metropolitan Campus (NJ)
Felician Coll (NJ)
Ferris State U (MI)
Florida Inst of Technology (FL)
Florida State U (FL)
Fort Lewis Coll (CO)
Franklin & Marshall Coll (PA)
Freed-Hardeman U (TN)
Furman U (SC)
Georgetown U (DC)
Georgia Inst of Technology (GA)
Georgian Court U (NJ)
Gettysburg Coll (PA)
Gonzaga U (WA)
Grand Valley State U (MI)
Grinnell Coll (IA)
Grove City Coll (PA)
Gustavus Adolphus Coll (MN)
Hamilton Coll (NY)
Hamline U (MN)
Hampden-Sydney Coll (VA)
Harding U (AR)
Hartwick Coll (NY)
Harvard U (MA)
Haverford Coll (PA)
Hobart and William Smith Colls (NY)
Hofstra U (NY)
Holy Family U (PA)
Hood Coll (MD)
Houghton Coll (NY)
Humboldt State U (CA)
Idaho State U (ID)
Illinois State U (IL)
Immaculata U (PA)

Indiana U Bloomington (IN)
Indiana U of Pennsylvania (PA)
Indiana U South Bend (IN)
Inter American U of Puerto Rico, Bayamón Campus (PR)
Iona Coll (NY)
Iowa State U of Science and Technology (IA)
Ithaca Coll (NY)
Jamestown Coll (ND)
John Brown U (AR)
Juniata Coll (PA)
Kansas State U (KS)
Kennesaw State U (GA)
Kenyon Coll (OH)
Kettering U (MI)
Keuka Coll (NY)
King Coll (TN)
Knox Coll (IL)
Kutztown U of Pennsylvania (PA)
Lafayette Coll (PA)
LaGrange Coll (GA)
La Salle U (PA)
La Sierra U (CA)
Laurentian U (ON, Canada)
Lawrence Technological U (MI)
Lawrence U (WI)
Lebanon Valley Coll (PA)
Lee U (TN)
Lehigh U (PA)
Lehman Coll of the City U of New York (NY)
Le Moyne Coll (NY)
Lewis & Clark Coll (OR)
Lewis U (IL)
Lipscomb U (TN)
Loras Coll (IA)
Louisiana State U and Ag and Mech Coll (LA)
Loyola Marymount U (CA)
Lyon Coll (AR)
Madonna U (MI)
Manhattanville Coll (NY)
Mansfield U of Pennsylvania (PA)
Marietta Coll (OH)
Marist Coll (NY)
Marlboro Coll (VT)
Marquette U (WI)
Mary Baldwin Coll (VA)
Maryville Coll (TN)
McDaniel Coll (MD)
McGill U (QC, Canada)
McMurry U (TX)
Memorial U of Newfoundland (NL, Canada)
Mercer U (GA)
Mercyhurst Coll (PA)
Merrimack Coll (MA)
Messiah Coll (PA)
Miami U (OH)
Miami U Hamilton (OH)
Michigan State U (MI)
Michigan Technological U (MI)
Middlebury Coll (VT)
Mills Coll (CA)
Minnesota State U Mankato (MN)
Misericordia U (PA)
Mississippi Coll (MS)
Mississippi State U (MS)
Missouri Southern State U (MO)
Monmouth Coll (IL)
Montclair State U (NJ)
Moravian Coll (PA)
Mount Allison U (NB, Canada)
Mount Holyoke Coll (MA)
Mount St. Mary's Coll (CA)
Mount St. Mary's U (MD)
Muhlenberg Coll (PA)
Nazareth Coll of Rochester (NY)
Nebraska Wesleyan U (NE)
New York U (NY)
Niagara U (NY)
North Carolina State U (NC)
North Central Coll (IL)
Northeastern U (MA)
Northern Michigan U (MI)
Northwestern U (IL)
Northwest Nazarene U (ID)
Notre Dame de Namur U (CA)
Oakland U (MI)
Oakwood Coll (AL)
Oberlin Coll (OH)
Occidental Coll (CA)
Ohio Northern U (OH)
Oklahoma Christian U (OK)
Oklahoma City U (OK)
Oklahoma State U (OK)
Old Dominion U (VA)
Oregon State U (OR)
Otterbein Coll (OH)
Pace U (NY)
Pacific Union Coll (CA)
Penn State Abington (PA)
Penn State Altoona (PA)
Penn State Berks (PA)
Penn State Erie, The Behrend Coll (PA)
Penn State U Park (PA)
Philadelphia U (PA)
Pittsburg State U (KS)
Pitzer Coll (CA)
Point Loma Nazarene U (CA)
Pomona Coll (CA)
Portland State U (OR)
Providence Coll (RI)
Purdue U (IN)
Queen's U at Kingston (ON, Canada)
Queens U of Charlotte (NC)
Quinnipiac U (CT)
Ramapo Coll of New Jersey (NJ)
Reed Coll (OR)
Regis Coll (MA)
Regis U (CO)
Rensselaer Polytechnic Inst (NY)
Rhodes Coll (TN)
Rice U (TX)
The Richard Stockton Coll of New Jersey (NJ)
Rider U (NJ)
Ripon Coll (WI)
Roanoke Coll (VA)
Roberts Wesleyan Coll (NY)
Rochester Inst of Technology (NY)
Rockford Coll (IL)
Rockhurst U (MO)
Rollins Coll (FL)
Rosemont Coll (PA)
Rowan U (NJ)
Russell Sage Coll (NY)
Rutgers, The State U of New Jersey, New Brunswick (NJ)
Sacred Heart U (CT)
Saginaw Valley State U (MI)
St. Edward's U (TX)
St. John Fisher Coll (NY)
Saint John's U (MN)
Saint Joseph Coll (CT)
Saint Joseph's Coll (IN)
Saint Joseph's U (PA)
St. Lawrence U (NY)
Saint Louis U (MO)
Saint Mary's Coll of California (CA)
St. Mary's Coll of Maryland (MD)
St. Mary's U (TX)
Saint Mary's U of Minnesota (MN)
Saint Michael's Coll (VT)
Saint Vincent Coll (PA)
Samford U (AL)
San Francisco State U (CA)
Santa Clara U (CA)
Schreiner U (TX)
Scripps Coll (CA)
Seattle Pacific U (WA)
Seattle U (WA)
Seton Hill U (PA)
Simmons Coll (MA)
Simon Fraser U (BC, Canada)
Simpson Coll (IA)
Smith Coll (MA)
South Dakota State U (SD)
Southern Adventist U (TN)
Southern Methodist U (TX)
Southern Oregon U (OR)
Southwestern Coll (KS)
Southwestern U (TX)
Spelman Coll (GA)
Spring Arbor U (MI)
Spring Hill Coll (AL)
State U of New York at Binghamton (NY)
State U of New York at Fredonia (NY)
State U of New York at Plattsburgh (NY)
State U of New York Coll at Geneseo (NY)
State U of New York Coll at Old Westbury (NY)
State U of New York Coll at Oneonta (NY)
State U of New York Coll at Potsdam (NY)
State U of New York Coll of Environmental Science and Forestry (NY)
Stetson U (FL)
Stonehill Coll (MA)
Stony Brook U, State U of New York (NY)
Suffolk U (MA)
Susquehanna U (PA)
Swarthmore Coll (PA)
Syracuse U (NY)
Temple U (PA)
Tennessee Technological U (TN)
Texas A&M U (TX)
Texas Christian U (TX)
Texas State U-San Marcos (TX)
Texas Tech U (TX)
Texas Woman's U (TX)
Thompson Rivers U (BC, Canada)
Trent U (ON, Canada)
Trinity Coll (CT)
Trinity U (TX)
Tulane U (LA)
Union Coll (NE)
Union Coll (NY)
United States Air Force Acad (CO)
Université de Sherbrooke (QC, Canada)
U at Albany, State U of New York (NY)
U at Buffalo, the State U of New York (NY)
The U of Akron (OH)
The U of Arizona (AZ)
The U of British Columbia (BC, Canada)
The U of British Columbia–Okanagan (BC, Canada)
U of California, Los Angeles (CA)
U of California, Riverside (CA)
U of California, San Diego (CA)
U of California, Santa Barbara (CA)
U of California, Santa Cruz (CA)
U of Chicago (IL)
U of Cincinnati (OH)
U of Colorado at Boulder (CO)
U of Dallas (TX)
U of Dayton (OH)
U of Delaware (DE)
U of Denver (CO)
U of Evansville (IN)
U of Georgia (GA)
U of Houston (TX)
U of Idaho (ID)
U of Illinois at Chicago (IL)
U of Illinois at Urbana–Champaign (IL)
The U of Iowa (IA)
U of King's Coll (NS, Canada)
U of Lethbridge (AB, Canada)
U of Maine (ME)
U of Maryland, Coll Park (MD)
U of Massachusetts Boston (MA)
U of Miami (FL)
U of Michigan (MI)
U of Michigan–Dearborn (MI)
U of Minnesota, Duluth (MN)
U of Minnesota, Twin Cities Campus (MN)
U of Missouri–Columbia (MO)
U of Missouri–St. Louis (MO)
The U of Montana (MT)
U of Nebraska–Lincoln (NE)
U of Nevada, Las Vegas (NV)
U of Nevada, Reno (NV)
U of New Brunswick Fredericton (NB, Canada)
U of New England (ME)
U of New Hampshire (NH)
U of New Mexico (NM)
The U of North Carolina at Greensboro (NC)
U of Northern Iowa (IA)
U of North Texas (TX)
U of Notre Dame (IN)
U of Oregon (OR)
U of Ottawa (ON, Canada)
U of Pennsylvania (PA)
U of Puget Sound (WA)
U of Regina (SK, Canada)
U of St. Thomas (MN)
U of San Diego (CA)
U of Southern California (CA)
The U of Tampa (FL)
The U of Tennessee (TN)
The U of Texas at Arlington (TX)
The U of Texas at Austin (TX)
The U of Texas at Dallas (TX)
U of the Pacific (CA)
U of the Sciences in Philadelphia (PA)
U of Toronto (ON, Canada)
U of Tulsa (OK)
U of Vermont (VT)
U of Victoria (BC, Canada)
The U of Western Ontario (ON, Canada)
U of Windsor (ON, Canada)
The U of Winnipeg (MB, Canada)
U of Wisconsin–Madison (WI)
U of Wisconsin–Milwaukee (WI)
Valparaiso U (IN)
Vassar Coll (NY)
Virginia Polytechnic Inst and State U (VA)
Viterbo U (WI)
Wartburg Coll (IA)
Washburn U (KS)
Washington & Jefferson Coll (PA)
Washington and Lee U (VA)
Washington State U (WA)
Washington U in St. Louis (MO)
Wellesley Coll (MA)
Wells Coll (NY)
Wesleyan U (CT)
West Chester U of Pennsylvania (PA)
Western Kentucky U (KY)
Western Michigan U (MI)
Western State Coll of Colorado (CO)
Western Washington U (WA)
Westminster Coll (MO)
Wheaton Coll (MA)
Whitman Coll (WA)
Whittier Coll (CA)
Widener U (PA)
Wilkes U (PA)
William Jewell Coll (MO)
Worcester Polytechnic Inst (MA)
Wright State U (OH)
Xavier U of Louisiana (LA)

BIOCHEMISTRY/ BIOPHYSICS AND MOLECULAR BIOLOGY

Bellarmine U (KY)
California State U, Long Beach (CA)
Hardin-Simmons U (TX)
Hendrix Coll (AR)
Illinois Inst of Technology (IL)
Lebanon Valley Coll (PA)
Liberty U (VA)
Michigan State U (MI)
Monmouth Coll (IL)
Nebraska Wesleyan U (NE)
North Dakota State U (ND)
Purdue U (IN)
The U of British Columbia (BC, Canada)
U of California, Irvine (CA)
U of Kansas (KS)
U of Maryland, Baltimore County (MD)
U of Massachusetts Amherst (MA)
U of Memphis (TN)
U of Michigan–Flint (MI)
The U of Western Ontario (ON, Canada)
Whitman Coll (WA)
Wittenberg U (OH)

BIOCHEMISTRY, BIOPHYSICS AND MOLECULAR BIOLOGY RELATED

Oklahoma State U (OK)
Sweet Briar Coll (VA)
Towson U (MD)
U of California, Santa Barbara (CA)

BIOETHICS/MEDICAL ETHICS

Cleveland State U (OH)

BIOINFORMATICS

Baylor U (TX)
Brigham Young U (UT)
Canisius Coll (NY)
Chatham U (PA)
Claflin U (SC)
Davenport U, Dearborn (MI)
Davenport U, Grand Rapids (MI)
Gannon U (PA)
Loyola U Chicago (IL)
Michigan Technological U (MI)
Polytechnic U, Brooklyn Campus (NY)
Ramapo Coll of New Jersey (NJ)
Rensselaer Polytechnic Inst (NY)
Rochester Inst of Technology (NY)
Rockhurst U (MO)
St. Edward's U (TX)
Saint Vincent Coll (PA)
U at Buffalo, the State U of New York (NY)
U of California, Santa Cruz (CA)
U of Denver (CO)
U of Maryland, Baltimore County (MD)
U of New Hampshire (NH)
U of Northern Iowa (IA)
U of Pennsylvania (PA)
U of the Sciences in Philadelphia (PA)
The U of Western Ontario (ON, Canada)
U of Windsor (ON, Canada)
Virginia Commonwealth U (VA)
Wheaton Coll (MA)

BIOLOGICAL AND BIOMEDICAL SCIENCES RELATED

Boston U (MA)
Capital U (OH)
Carlow U (PA)
Carnegie Mellon U (PA)
Central Michigan U (MI)
Cornell U (NY)
Davis & Elkins Coll (WV)
Farmingdale State Coll (NY)
Guilford Coll (NC)
Holy Names U (CA)
Indiana U Bloomington (IN)
Inter American U of Puerto Rico, Bayamón Campus (PR)
Kent State U (OH)
Lehigh U (PA)
Logan U-Coll of Chiropractic (MO)
Lynchburg Coll (VA)
Monmouth Coll (IL)
Our Lady of the Lake Coll (LA)
Park U (MO)
Penn State Abington (PA)
Penn State Altoona (PA)
Penn State Berks (PA)
Penn State Erie, The Behrend Coll (PA)
Penn State U Park (PA)
Rensselaer Polytechnic Inst (NY)
Rochester Inst of Technology (NY)
Rutgers, The State U of New Jersey, Newark (NJ)
Sage Coll of Albany (NY)
Saint Mary's Coll of California (CA)
Syracuse U (NY)
Union Coll (NY)
U at Buffalo, the State U of New York (NY)
U of Illinois at Urbana–Champaign (IL)
U of Kansas (KS)
U of North Alabama (AL)
U of North Dakota (ND)
U of Ottawa (ON, Canada)
U of Puerto Rico at Utuado (PR)
U of Wisconsin–Parkside (WI)
Ursuline Coll (OH)
Washington U in St. Louis (MO)
Western State Coll of Colorado (CO)

BIOLOGICAL AND PHYSICAL SCIENCES

Adams State Coll (CO)
Alfred U (NY)
Alice Lloyd Coll (KY)
Alma Coll (MI)
Alvernia Coll (PA)
Angelo State U (TX)
Athabasca U (AB, Canada)
Augsburg Coll (MN)
Averett U (VA)
Belmont U (TN)
Bemidji State U (MN)
Bishop's U (QC, Canada)
Bluefield State Coll (WV)
Brevard Coll (NC)
Brigham Young U (UT)
Brock U (ON, Canada)
California State U, Fresno (CA)
Calvin Coll (MI)
Canisius Coll (NY)
Castleton State Coll (VT)
Cedarville U (OH)
Cheyney U of Pennsylvania (PA)
Clarion U of Pennsylvania (PA)
Coll of Saint Benedict (MN)
Coll of the Atlantic (ME)
Concordia U (MI)
Concordia U (OR)
Concordia U Chicago (IL)
Covenant Coll (GA)
DePaul U (IL)
Dowling Coll (NY)
Drexel U (PA)
Eastern Michigan U (MI)
East Stroudsburg U of Pennsylvania (PA)
Erskine Coll (SC)
The Evergreen State Coll (WA)
Fairleigh Dickinson U, Metropolitan Campus (NJ)
Florida Inst of Technology (FL)
Freed-Hardeman U (TN)
Gettysburg Coll (PA)
Grand Valley State U (MI)
Harvard U (MA)
Houghton Coll (NY)
Huntington U (IN)
Indiana U Kokomo (IN)
Indiana U of Pennsylvania (PA)
Indiana U–Purdue U Indianapolis (IN)
Iowa Wesleyan Coll (IA)
John Carroll U (OH)
The Johns Hopkins U (MD)
Johnson C. Smith U (NC)
Keystone Coll (PA)
King Coll (TN)
King's Coll (PA)
Lakehead U (ON, Canada)
Lees-McRae Coll (NC)
Lee U (TN)
Lehigh U (PA)
Le Moyne Coll (NY)
Lock Haven U of Pennsylvania (PA)
Lyndon State Coll (VT)
Madonna U (MI)
Mansfield U of Pennsylvania (PA)
Maryville U of Saint Louis (MO)
The Master's Coll and Sem (CA)
McGill U (QC, Canada)
Memorial U of Newfoundland (NL, Canada)

Methodist U (NC)
Michigan State U (MI)
Middle Tennessee State U (TN)
Midland Lutheran Coll (NE)
Minnesota State U Mankato (MN)
Mississippi State U (MS)
Mississippi U for Women (MS)
Montana Tech of The U of Montana (MT)
Mount Allison U (NB, Canada)
Mount Saint Vincent U (NS, Canada)
Mount Vernon Nazarene U (OH)
National-Louis U (IL)
North Central Coll (IL)
Northern State U (SD)
Northland Coll (WI)
Northwestern U (IL)
Northwest Missouri State U (MO)
Oakland City U (IN)
Oklahoma City U (OK)
Oklahoma Panhandle State U (OK)
Oklahoma Wesleyan U (OK)
Oregon State U (OR)
Palmer Coll of Chiropractic (IA)
Penn State Abington (PA)
Penn State Altoona (PA)
Penn State Berks (PA)
Penn State Erie, The Behrend Coll (PA)
Penn State U Park (PA)
Peru State Coll (NE)
Portland State U (OR)
Purdue U (IN)
Purdue U Calumet (IN)
Quinnipiac U (CT)
Ramapo Coll of New Jersey (NJ)
Redeemer U Coll (ON, Canada)
Rensselaer Polytechnic Inst (NY)
Roberts Wesleyan Coll (NY)
Rochester Coll (MI)
Rockford Coll (IL)
St. Francis Xavier U (NS, Canada)
St. Mary's Coll of Maryland (MD)
St. Norbert Coll (WI)
Saint Xavier U (IL)
Sam Houston State U (TX)
San Francisco State U (CA)
Santa Clara U (CA)
Sarah Lawrence Coll (NY)
Seattle U (WA)
Shawnee State U (OH)
Simon Fraser U (BC, Canada)
Simpson Coll (IA)
Southern Arkansas U–Magnolia (AR)
State U of New York at Fredonia (NY)
State U of New York Coll of Environmental Science and Forestry (NY)
State U of New York Empire State Coll (NY)
Sterling Coll (VT)
Tabor Coll (KS)
Texas A&M U at Galveston (TX)
Texas Southern U (TX)
Texas Tech U (TX)
Trent U (ON, Canada)
Trevecca Nazarene U (TN)
Union Coll (NY)
Union U (TN)
United States Air Force Acad (CO)
The U of Alabama at Birmingham (AL)
U of Alaska Fairbanks (AK)
U of Arkansas at Monticello (AR)
U of Central Arkansas (AR)
U of Denver (CO)
The U of Findlay (OH)
U of Georgia (GA)
U of Guam (GU)
U of Houston–Downtown (TX)
U of Lethbridge (AB, Canada)
U of Massachusetts Amherst (MA)
U of New Brunswick Fredericton (NB, Canada)
U of New Hampshire (NH)
U of Northern Iowa (IA)
U of Notre Dame (IN)
U of Oregon (OR)
U of Pittsburgh (PA)
U of Regina (SK, Canada)
U of Rochester (NY)
U of Saint Francis (IN)
U of Southern Indiana (IN)
U of Southern Mississippi (MS)
U of South Florida (FL)
The U of Texas at Austin (TX)
The U of Texas at San Antonio (TX)
The U of Toledo (OH)
U of Toronto (ON, Canada)
The U of Western Ontario (ON, Canada)
U of West Florida (FL)
U of Windsor (ON, Canada)
U of Wisconsin–Platteville (WI)
U of Wisconsin–Superior (WI)
U of Wisconsin–Whitewater (WI)
Ursinus Coll (PA)
Vanguard U of Southern California (CA)
Villa Julie Coll (MD)
Virginia Commonwealth U (VA)
Walsh U (OH)
Warner Pacific Coll (OR)
Washington U in St. Louis (MO)
Western New Mexico U (NM)
Western Washington U (WA)
Wilmington Coll (OH)
Winona State U (MN)
Worcester State Coll (MA)
Wright State U (OH)
Xavier U (OH)
York Coll (NE)
York U (ON, Canada)

BIOLOGICAL SPECIALIZATIONS RELATED

Frostburg State U (MD)
King Coll (TN)
U of Louisiana at Lafayette (LA)
Utah State U (UT)

BIOLOGY/BIOLOGICAL SCIENCES

Abilene Christian U (TX)
Acadia U (NS, Canada)
Adams State Coll (CO)
Adelphi U (NY)
Adrian Coll (MI)
Agnes Scott Coll (GA)
Alabama Ag and Mech U (AL)
Alabama State U (AL)
Albertus Magnus Coll (CT)
Albion Coll (MI)
Albright Coll (PA)
Alcorn State U (MS)
Alderson-Broaddus Coll (WV)
Alfred U (NY)
Alice Lloyd Coll (KY)
Allegheny Coll (PA)
Alma Coll (MI)
Alvernia Coll (PA)
American U (DC)
The American U of Athens (Greece)
American U of Beirut (Lebanon)
Amherst Coll (MA)
Anderson U (IN)
Anderson U (SC)
Andrews U (MI)
Angelo State U (TX)
Appalachian State U (NC)
Aquinas Coll (MI)
Arizona State U (AZ)
Arizona State U at the West campus (AZ)
Arkansas State U (AR)
Armstrong Atlantic State U (GA)
Asbury Coll (KY)
Ashford U (IA)
Ashland U (OH)
Assumption Coll (MA)
Athens State U (AL)
Atlantic Union Coll (MA)
Auburn U (AL)
Auburn U Montgomery (AL)
Augsburg Coll (MN)
Augustana Coll (IL)
Augustana Coll (SD)
Augusta State U (GA)
Austin Coll (TX)
Austin Peay State U (TN)
Ave Maria U (FL)
Averett U (VA)
Avila U (MO)
Azusa Pacific U (CA)
Baker U (KS)
Baldwin-Wallace Coll (OH)
Ball State U (IN)
Bard Coll (NY)
Bard Coll at Simon's Rock (MA)
Barnard Coll (NY)
Barry U (FL)
Barton Coll (NC)
Bates Coll (ME)
Baylor U (TX)
Bay Path Coll (MA)
Belhaven Coll (MS)
Bellarmine U (KY)
Belmont Abbey Coll (NC)
Belmont U (TN)
Beloit Coll (WI)
Bemidji State U (MN)
Benedictine Coll (KS)
Benedictine U (IL)
Bennington Coll (VT)
Berea Coll (KY)
Berry Coll (GA)
Bethany Coll (KS)
Bethany Coll (WV)
Bethany Lutheran Coll (MN)
Bethel Coll (KS)
Bethel Coll (TN)
Bethel U (MN)
Bethune-Cookman U (FL)
Biola U (CA)
Bishop's U (QC, Canada)
Blackburn Coll (IL)
Bloomfield Coll (NJ)
Bloomsburg U of Pennsylvania (PA)
Bluefield Coll (VA)
Bluffton U (OH)
Bob Jones U (SC)
Boise State U (ID)
Boston Coll (MA)
Boston U (MA)
Bowdoin Coll (ME)
Bowling Green State U (OH)
Bradley U (IL)
Brandeis U (MA)
Brenau U (GA)
Brewton-Parker Coll (GA)
Bridgewater Coll (VA)
Bridgewater State Coll (MA)
Brigham Young U (UT)
Brock U (ON, Canada)
Brown U (RI)
Bryan Coll (TN)
Bryn Athyn Coll of the New Church (PA)
Bryn Mawr Coll (PA)
Bucknell U (PA)
Buffalo State Coll, State U of New York (NY)
Butler U (IN)
Cabrini Coll (PA)
California Baptist U (CA)
California Inst of Technology (CA)
California Lutheran U (CA)
California Polytechnic State U, San Luis Obispo (CA)
California State Polytechnic U, Pomona (CA)
California State U, Chico (CA)
California State U, Dominguez Hills (CA)
California State U, East Bay (CA)
California State U, Fresno (CA)
California State U, Fullerton (CA)
California State U, Long Beach (CA)
California State U, Los Angeles (CA)
California State U, Monterey Bay (CA)
California State U, Sacramento (CA)
California State U, San Bernardino (CA)
California State U, San Marcos (CA)
California State U, Stanislaus (CA)
Calvin Coll (MI)
Cameron U (OK)
Capital U (OH)
Carlow U (PA)
Carnegie Mellon U (PA)
Carroll Coll (WI)
Carson-Newman Coll (TN)
Case Western Reserve U (OH)
Castleton State Coll (VT)
Catawba Coll (NC)
The Catholic U of America (DC)
Cedar Crest Coll (PA)
Cedarville U (OH)
Centenary Coll (NJ)
Centenary Coll of Louisiana (LA)
Central Coll (IA)
Central Connecticut State U (CT)
Central Michigan U (MI)
Central State U (OH)
Central Washington U (WA)
Centre Coll (KY)
Chaminade U of Honolulu (HI)
Chapman U (CA)
Chatham U (PA)
Chestnut Hill Coll (PA)
Cheyney U of Pennsylvania (PA)
Chicago State U (IL)
Christopher Newport U (VA)
The Citadel, The Military Coll of South Carolina (SC)
City Coll of the City U of New York (NY)
Claflin U (SC)
Claremont McKenna Coll (CA)
Clarion U of Pennsylvania (PA)
Clark Atlanta U (GA)
Clarke Coll (IA)
Clarkson U (NY)
Clark U (MA)
Clayton State U (GA)
Clearwater Christian Coll (FL)
Clemson U (SC)
Cleveland Chiropractic Coll-Kansas City Campus (KS)
Cleveland Chiropractic Coll-Los Angeles Campus (CA)
Cleveland State U (OH)
Coastal Carolina U (SC)
Coker Coll (SC)
Colby Coll (ME)
Colby-Sawyer Coll (NH)
Colgate U (NY)
The Coll at Brockport, State U of New York (NY)
Coll of Charleston (SC)
The Coll of Idaho (ID)
Coll of Mount St. Joseph (OH)
Coll of Mount Saint Vincent (NY)
The Coll of New Jersey (NJ)
The Coll of New Rochelle (NY)
Coll of Saint Benedict (MN)
Coll of Saint Elizabeth (NJ)
Coll of Saint Mary (NE)
The Coll of Saint Rose (NY)
The Coll of St. Scholastica (MN)
Coll of Staten Island of the City U of New York (NY)
Coll of the Atlantic (ME)
Coll of the Holy Cross (MA)
Coll of the Ozarks (MO)
Coll of the Southwest (NM)
The Coll of William and Mary (VA)
The Colorado Coll (CO)
Colorado State U (CO)
Colorado State U-Pueblo (CO)
Columbia Coll (SC)
Columbus State U (GA)
Concordia Coll (MN)
Concordia Coll–New York (NY)
Concordia U (CA)
Concordia U (MI)
Concordia U (OR)
Concordia U (QC, Canada)
Concordia U Chicago (IL)
Concordia U, Nebraska (NE)
Concordia U, St. Paul (MN)
Concordia U Texas (TX)
Concordia U Wisconsin (WI)
Concord U (WV)
Connecticut Coll (CT)
Converse Coll (SC)
Cornell Coll (IA)
Cornell U (NY)
Cornerstone U (MI)
Covenant Coll (GA)
Creighton U (NE)
Culver-Stockton Coll (MO)
Curry Coll (MA)
Daemen Coll (NY)
Dakota State U (SD)
Dakota Wesleyan U (SD)
Dallas Baptist U (TX)
Dana Coll (NE)
Dartmouth Coll (NH)
Davidson Coll (NC)
Defiance Coll (OH)
Delaware Valley Coll (PA)
Delta State U (MS)
Denison U (OH)
DePaul U (IL)
DePauw U (IN)
DeSales U (PA)
Dickinson Coll (PA)
Dillard U (LA)
Dixie State Coll of Utah (UT)
Doane Coll (NE)
Dominican Coll (NY)
Dominican U (IL)
Dominican U of California (CA)
Dordt Coll (IA)
Dowling Coll (NY)
Drake U (IA)
Drew U (NJ)
Drexel U (PA)
Drury U (MO)
Duke U (NC)
Duquesne U (PA)
D'Youville Coll (NY)
Earlham Coll (IN)
East Carolina U (NC)
East Central U (OK)
Eastern Connecticut State U (CT)
Eastern Illinois U (IL)
Eastern Kentucky U (KY)
Eastern Mennonite U (VA)
Eastern Michigan U (MI)
Eastern New Mexico U (NM)
East Stroudsburg U of Pennsylvania (PA)
East Tennessee State U (TN)
East Texas Baptist U (TX)
East-West U (IL)
Eckerd Coll (FL)
Edinboro U of Pennsylvania (PA)
Elizabethtown Coll (PA)
Elon U (NC)
Emmanuel Coll (GA)
Emmanuel Coll (MA)
Emory & Henry Coll (VA)
Emory U (GA)
Emporia State U (KS)
Erskine Coll (SC)
Evangel U (MO)
The Evergreen State Coll (WA)
Excelsior Coll (NY)
Fairfield U (CT)
Fairleigh Dickinson U, Coll at Florham (NJ)
Fairleigh Dickinson U, Metropolitan Campus (NJ)
Fairmont State U (WV)
Faulkner U (AL)
Fayetteville State U (NC)
Felician Coll (NJ)
Ferris State U (MI)
Ferrum Coll (VA)
Fitchburg State Coll (MA)
Florida Ag and Mech U (FL)
Florida Atlantic U (FL)
Florida Gulf Coast U (FL)
Florida Inst of Technology (FL)
Florida Intl U (FL)
Florida Memorial U (FL)
Florida Southern Coll (FL)
Florida State U (FL)
Fontbonne U (MO)
Fort Lewis Coll (CO)
Framingham State Coll (MA)
Franciscan U of Steubenville (OH)
Francis Marion U (SC)
Franklin & Marshall Coll (PA)
Franklin Coll (IN)
Freed-Hardeman U (TN)
Fresno Pacific U (CA)
Frostburg State U (MD)
Furman U (SC)
Gannon U (PA)
Gardner-Webb U (NC)
George Fox U (OR)
George Mason U (VA)
Georgetown Coll (KY)
Georgetown U (DC)
The George Washington U (DC)
Georgia Coll & State U (GA)
Georgia Inst of Technology (GA)
Georgian Court U (NJ)
Georgia Southern U (GA)
Georgia Southwestern State U (GA)
Georgia State U (GA)
Gettysburg Coll (PA)
Glenville State Coll (WV)
Gonzaga U (WA)
Gordon Coll (MA)
Goucher Coll (MD)
Grace Coll (IN)
Grambling State U (LA)
Grand Canyon U (AZ)
Grand Valley State U (MI)
Grand View Coll (IA)
Green Mountain Coll (VT)
Greensboro Coll (NC)
Greenville Coll (IL)
Grinnell Coll (IA)
Grove City Coll (PA)
Guilford Coll (NC)
Gustavus Adolphus Coll (MN)
Gwynedd-Mercy Coll (PA)
Hamilton Coll (NY)
Hamline U (MN)
Hampden-Sydney Coll (VA)
Hampshire Coll (MA)
Hampton U (VA)
Hannibal-LaGrange Coll (MO)
Hanover Coll (IN)
Harding U (AR)
Hardin-Simmons U (TX)
Harrisburg U of Science and Technology (PA)
Hartwick Coll (NY)
Harvard U (MA)
Harvey Mudd Coll (CA)
Hastings Coll (NE)
Haverford Coll (PA)
Hawai'i Pacific U (HI)
Heidelberg Coll (OH)
Henderson State U (AR)
Hendrix Coll (AR)
High Point U (NC)
Hillsdale Coll (MI)
Hobart and William Smith Colls (NY)
Hofstra U (NY)
Hollins U (VA)
Holy Family U (PA)
Holy Names U (CA)
Hood Coll (MD)
Hope Coll (MI)
Houghton Coll (NY)
Houston Baptist U (TX)
Howard Payne U (TX)
Humboldt State U (CA)
Hunter Coll of the City U of New York (NY)
Huntingdon Coll (AL)
Huntington U (IN)
Husson Coll (ME)
Huston-Tillotson U (TX)
Idaho State U (ID)
Illinois Coll (IL)
Illinois Inst of Technology (IL)
Illinois State U (IL)
Illinois Wesleyan U (IL)
Immaculata U (PA)
Indiana State U (IN)
Indiana U Bloomington (IN)
Indiana U East (IN)

Indiana U Kokomo (IN)
Indiana U Northwest (IN)
Indiana U of Pennsylvania (PA)
Indiana U–Purdue U Fort Wayne (IN)
Indiana U–Purdue U Indianapolis (IN)
Indiana U South Bend (IN)
Indiana U Southeast (IN)
Indiana Wesleyan U (IN)
Inter American U of Puerto Rico, Aguadilla Campus (PR)
Inter American U of Puerto Rico, Bayamón Campus (PR)
Inter American U of Puerto Rico, Fajardo Campus (PR)
Inter American U of Puerto Rico, San Germán Campus (PR)
Iona Coll (NY)
Iowa State U of Science and Technology (IA)
Iowa Wesleyan Coll (IA)
Ithaca Coll (NY)
Jackson State U (MS)
Jacksonville State U (AL)
Jacksonville U (FL)
James Madison U (VA)
Jamestown Coll (ND)
Jarvis Christian Coll (TX)
John Brown U (AR)
John Carroll U (OH)
The Johns Hopkins U (MD)
Johnson C. Smith U (NC)
Johnson State Coll (VT)
Judson Coll (AL)
Judson U (IL)
Juniata Coll (PA)
Kalamazoo Coll (MI)
Kansas State U (KS)
Kean U (NJ)
Keene State Coll (NH)
Kennesaw State U (GA)
Kent State U (OH)
Kentucky State U (KY)
Kentucky Wesleyan Coll (KY)
Kenyon Coll (OH)
Keuka Coll (NY)
Keystone Coll (PA)
King Coll (TN)
King's Coll (PA)
The King's U Coll (AB, Canada)
Knox Coll (IL)
Kutztown U of Pennsylvania (PA)
Lafayette Coll (PA)
LaGrange Coll (GA)
Lake Forest Coll (IL)
Lakehead U (ON, Canada)
Lambuth U (TN)
Lander U (SC)
La Roche Coll (PA)
La Salle U (PA)
La Sierra U (CA)
Laurentian U (ON, Canada)
Lawrence U (WI)
Lebanon Valley Coll (PA)
Lees-McRae Coll (NC)
Lee U (TN)
Lehigh U (PA)
Lehman Coll of the City U of New York (NY)
Le Moyne Coll (NY)
LeMoyne-Owen Coll (TN)
Lenoir-Rhyne Coll (NC)
LeTourneau U (TX)
Lewis & Clark Coll (OR)
Lewis-Clark State Coll (ID)
Lewis U (IL)
Liberty U (VA)
Life U (GA)
Limestone Coll (SC)
Lincoln U (MO)
Lincoln U (PA)
Lindenwood U (MO)
Lindsey Wilson Coll (KY)
Linfield Coll (OR)
Lipscomb U (TN)
Livingstone Coll (NC)
Lock Haven U of Pennsylvania (PA)
Logan U-Coll of Chiropractic (MO)
Longwood U (VA)
Loras Coll (IA)
Louisiana Coll (LA)
Louisiana State U and Ag and Mech Coll (LA)
Lourdes Coll (OH)
Loyola Coll in Maryland (MD)
Loyola Marymount U (CA)
Loyola U Chicago (IL)
Loyola U New Orleans (LA)
Lubbock Christian U (TX)
Luther Coll (IA)
Lycoming Coll (PA)
Lynchburg Coll (VA)
Lyon Coll (AR)
Macalester Coll (MN)
Madonna U (MI)
Malone Coll (OH)
Manchester Coll (IN)
Manhattanville Coll (NY)
Mansfield U of Pennsylvania (PA)
Maranatha Baptist Bible Coll (WI)
Marian Coll (IN)
Marian Coll of Fond du Lac (WI)
Marietta Coll (OH)
Marist Coll (NY)
Marlboro Coll (VT)
Marquette U (WI)
Marshall U (WV)
Martin U (IN)
Mary Baldwin Coll (VA)
Marymount Manhattan Coll (NY)
Marymount U (VA)
Maryville Coll (TN)
Maryville U of Saint Louis (MO)
Marywood U (PA)
Massachusetts Coll of Liberal Arts (MA)
Massachusetts Inst of Technology (MA)
The Master's Coll and Sem (CA)
Mayville State U (ND)
McDaniel Coll (MD)
McGill U (QC, Canada)
McKendree U (IL)
McMurry U (TX)
McNeese State U (LA)
Medaille Coll (NY)
Medgar Evers Coll of the City U of New York (NY)
Memorial U of Newfoundland (NL, Canada)
Mercer U (GA)
Mercy Coll (NY)
Mercyhurst Coll (PA)
Meredith Coll (NC)
Merrimack Coll (MA)
Mesa State Coll (CO)
Messiah Coll (PA)
Methodist U (NC)
Metropolitan State U (MN)
Miami U (OH)
Michigan State U (MI)
Michigan Technological U (MI)
MidAmerica Nazarene U (KS)
Middlebury Coll (VT)
Middle Tennessee State U (TN)
Midland Lutheran Coll (NE)
Midway Coll (KY)
Midwestern State U (TX)
Miles Coll (AL)
Millersville U of Pennsylvania (PA)
Milligan Coll (TN)
Millikin U (IL)
Millsaps Coll (MS)
Mills Coll (CA)
Minnesota State U Mankato (MN)
Minot State U (ND)
Misericordia U (PA)
Mississippi Coll (MS)
Mississippi State U (MS)
Mississippi U for Women (MS)
Mississippi Valley State U (MS)
Missouri Baptist U (MO)
Missouri Southern State U (MO)
Missouri State U (MO)
Missouri U of Science and Technology (MO)
Missouri Valley Coll (MO)
Molloy Coll (NY)
Monmouth Coll (IL)
Monmouth U (NJ)
Montana State U (MT)
Montana State U–Billings (MT)
Montana Tech of The U of Montana (MT)
Montclair State U (NJ)
Moravian Coll (PA)
Morehead State U (KY)
Morehouse Coll (GA)
Morgan State U (MD)
Morningside Coll (IA)
Morris Coll (SC)
Mount Allison U (NB, Canada)
Mount Holyoke Coll (MA)
Mount Marty Coll (SD)
Mount Mary Coll (WI)
Mount Mercy Coll (IA)
Mount Olive Coll (NC)
Mount Saint Mary Coll (NY)
Mount St. Mary's Coll (CA)
Mount St. Mary's U (MD)
Mount Saint Vincent U (NS, Canada)
Mount Vernon Nazarene U (OH)
Muhlenberg Coll (PA)
Murray State U (KY)
National-Louis U (IL)
National U (CA)
Nazareth Coll of Rochester (NY)
Nebraska Wesleyan U (NE)
Neumann Coll (PA)
New Coll of Florida (FL)
New England Coll (NH)
New Jersey City U (NJ)
New Jersey Inst of Technology (NJ)
Newman U (KS)
New Mexico Highlands U (NM)
New Mexico Inst of Mining and Technology (NM)
New York Inst of Technology (NY)
New York U (NY)
Niagara U (NY)
Nicholls State U (LA)
North Carolina Ag and Tech State U (NC)
North Carolina Central U (NC)
North Carolina State U (NC)
North Carolina Wesleyan Coll (NC)
North Central Coll (IL)
North Dakota State U (ND)
Northeastern Illinois U (IL)
Northeastern State U (OK)
Northeastern U (MA)
Northern Arizona U (AZ)
Northern Illinois U (IL)
Northern Michigan U (MI)
Northern State U (SD)
North Georgia Coll & State U (GA)
North Greenville U (SC)
Northland Coll (WI)
Northwestern Coll (IA)
Northwestern Coll (MN)
Northwestern Oklahoma State U (OK)
Northwestern State U of Louisiana (LA)
Northwestern U (IL)
Northwest Missouri State U (MO)
Northwest Nazarene U (ID)
Norwich U (VT)
Notre Dame de Namur U (CA)
Nova Southeastern U (FL)
Oakland City U (IN)
Oakland U (MI)
Oakwood Coll (AL)
Oberlin Coll (OH)
Occidental Coll (CA)
Oglethorpe U (GA)
Ohio Dominican U (OH)
Ohio Northern U (OH)
Ohio U (OH)
Ohio Wesleyan U (OH)
Oklahoma Christian U (OK)
Oklahoma City U (OK)
Oklahoma Panhandle State U (OK)
Oklahoma State U (OK)
Oklahoma Wesleyan U (OK)
Old Dominion U (VA)
Oral Roberts U (OK)
Oregon State U (OR)
Otterbein Coll (OH)
Ouachita Baptist U (AR)
Our Lady of the Lake Coll (LA)
Pace U (NY)
Pacific Lutheran U (WA)
Pacific Union Coll (CA)
Pacific U (OR)
Paine Coll (GA)
Palm Beach Atlantic U (FL)
Park U (MO)
Peace Coll (NC)
Penn State Abington (PA)
Penn State Altoona (PA)
Penn State Berks (PA)
Penn State Erie, The Behrend Coll (PA)
Penn State U Park (PA)
Pepperdine U, Malibu (CA)
Peru State Coll (NE)
Pfeiffer U (NC)
Philadelphia U (PA)
Piedmont Coll (GA)
Pikeville Coll (KY)
Pittsburg State U (KS)
Pitzer Coll (CA)
Plymouth State U (NH)
Point Loma Nazarene U (CA)
Point Park U (PA)
Pomona Coll (CA)
Portland State U (OR)
Prairie View A&M U (TX)
Presbyterian Coll (SC)
Prescott Coll (AZ)
Presentation Coll (SD)
Providence Coll (RI)
Purchase Coll, State U of New York (NY)
Purdue U (IN)
Purdue U Calumet (IN)
Purdue U North Central (IN)
Queens Coll of the City U of New York (NY)
Queen's U at Kingston (ON, Canada)
Queens U of Charlotte (NC)
Quincy U (IL)
Quinnipiac U (CT)
Radford U (VA)
Ramapo Coll of New Jersey (NJ)
Randolph Coll (VA)
Randolph-Macon Coll (VA)
Redeemer U Coll (ON, Canada)
Reed Coll (OR)
Regis Coll (MA)
Regis U (CO)
Rensselaer Polytechnic Inst (NY)
Rhode Island Coll (RI)
Rhodes Coll (TN)
Rice U (TX)
The Richard Stockton Coll of New Jersey (NJ)
Rider U (NJ)
Ripon Coll (WI)
Roanoke Coll (VA)
Roberts Wesleyan Coll (NY)
Rockford Coll (IL)
Rockhurst U (MO)
Rogers State U (OK)
Roger Williams U (RI)
Rollins Coll (FL)
Roosevelt U (IL)
Rose-Hulman Inst of Technology (IN)
Rosemont Coll (PA)
Rowan U (NJ)
Russell Sage Coll (NY)
Rutgers, The State U of New Jersey, Camden (NJ)
Rutgers, The State U of New Jersey, Newark (NJ)
Rutgers, The State U of New Jersey, New Brunswick (NJ)
Saginaw Valley State U (MI)
St. Ambrose U (IA)
St. Andrews Presbyterian Coll (NC)
St. Cloud State U (MN)
St. Edward's U (TX)
Saint Francis U (PA)
St. Francis Xavier U (NS, Canada)
St. Gregory's U, Shawnee (OK)
St. John Fisher Coll (NY)
Saint John's U (MN)
St. John's U (NY)
Saint Joseph Coll (CT)
Saint Joseph's Coll (IN)
St. Joseph's Coll, New York (NY)
St. Joseph's Coll, Suffolk Campus (NY)
Saint Joseph's U (PA)
St. Lawrence U (NY)
Saint Leo U (FL)
Saint Louis U (MO)
Saint Martin's U (WA)
Saint Mary-of-the-Woods Coll (IN)
Saint Mary's Coll (IN)
Saint Mary's Coll of California (CA)
St. Mary's Coll of Maryland (MD)
St. Mary's U (TX)
Saint Mary's U of Minnesota (MN)
Saint Michael's Coll (VT)
St. Norbert Coll (WI)
St. Olaf Coll (MN)
St. Thomas Aquinas Coll (NY)
St. Thomas U (FL)
Saint Vincent Coll (PA)
Saint Xavier U (IL)
Salem Coll (NC)
Salem Intl U (WV)
Salem State Coll (MA)
Salisbury U (MD)
Salve Regina U (RI)
Samford U (AL)
Sam Houston State U (TX)
San Diego Christian Coll (CA)
San Diego State U (CA)
San Francisco State U (CA)
Santa Clara U (CA)
Sarah Lawrence Coll (NY)
Schreiner U (TX)
Scripps Coll (CA)
Seattle Pacific U (WA)
Seattle U (WA)
Seton Hill U (PA)
Sewanee: The U of the South (TN)
Shawnee State U (OH)
Shaw U (NC)
Shenandoah U (VA)
Shepherd U (WV)
Shippensburg U of Pennsylvania (PA)
Shorter Coll (GA)
Siena Coll (NY)
Siena Heights U (MI)
Simmons Coll (MA)
Simon Fraser U (BC, Canada)
Simpson Coll (IA)
Skidmore Coll (NY)
Slippery Rock U of Pennsylvania (PA)
Smith Coll (MA)
Sonoma State U (CA)
South Carolina State U (SC)
South Dakota State U (SD)
Southeastern Louisiana U (LA)
Southeastern Oklahoma State U (OK)
Southeastern U (FL)
Southeast Missouri State U (MO)
Southern Adventist U (TN)
Southern Arkansas U–Magnolia (AR)
Southern Connecticut State U (CT)
Southern Illinois U Carbondale (IL)
Southern Illinois U Edwardsville (IL)
Southern Methodist U (TX)
Southern Oregon U (OR)
Southern Polytechnic State U (GA)
Southern U and Ag and Mech Coll (LA)
Southern Utah U (UT)
Southern Wesleyan U (SC)
Southwest Baptist U (MO)
Southwestern Adventist U (TX)
Southwestern Coll (KS)
Southwestern Oklahoma State U (OK)
Southwestern U (TX)
Southwest Minnesota State U (MN)
Spelman Coll (GA)
Spring Arbor U (MI)
Spring Hill Coll (AL)
Stanford U (CA)
State U of New York at Binghamton (NY)
State U of New York at Fredonia (NY)
State U of New York at New Paltz (NY)
State U of New York at Oswego (NY)
State U of New York at Plattsburgh (NY)
State U of New York Coll at Geneseo (NY)
State U of New York Coll at Old Westbury (NY)
State U of New York Coll at Oneonta (NY)
State U of New York Coll at Potsdam (NY)
State U of New York Coll of Environmental Science and Forestry (NY)
Stephen F. Austin State U (TX)
Stephens Coll (MO)
Sterling Coll (KS)
Stetson U (FL)
Stillman Coll (AL)
Stonehill Coll (MA)
Stony Brook U, State U of New York (NY)
Suffolk U (MA)
Susquehanna U (PA)
Swarthmore Coll (PA)
Sweet Briar Coll (VA)
Syracuse U (NY)
Tabor Coll (KS)
Tarleton State U (TX)
Taylor U (IN)
Temple U (PA)
Tennessee State U (TN)
Tennessee Technological U (TN)
Tennessee Wesleyan Coll (TN)
Texas A&M Intl U (TX)
Texas A&M U (TX)
Texas A&M U–Commerce (TX)
Texas Christian U (TX)
Texas Coll (TX)
Texas Lutheran U (TX)
Texas Southern U (TX)
Texas State U-San Marcos (TX)
Texas Tech U (TX)
Texas Woman's U (TX)
Thiel Coll (PA)
Thomas Edison State Coll (NJ)
Thomas More Coll (KY)
Thomas U (GA)
Thompson Rivers U (BC, Canada)
Toccoa Falls Coll (GA)
Tougaloo Coll (MS)
Towson U (MD)
Transylvania U (KY)
Trent U (ON, Canada)
Trevecca Nazarene U (TN)
Trinity Christian Coll (IL)
Trinity Coll (CT)
Trinity Intl U (IL)
Trinity U (TX)
Tri-State U (IN)
Troy U (AL)
Truman State U (MO)
Tufts U (MA)
Tulane U (LA)
Tusculum Coll (TN)
Tuskegee U (AL)
Union Coll (KY)
Union Coll (NE)
Union Coll (NY)
Union U (TN)
United States Air Force Acad (CO)
Université de Sherbrooke (QC, Canada)
U at Albany, State U of New York (NY)
U at Buffalo, the State U of New York (NY)
The U of Akron (OH)
The U of Alabama (AL)
The U of Alabama at Birmingham (AL)
The U of Alabama in Huntsville (AL)
U of Alaska Fairbanks (AK)
U of Alaska Southeast (AK)

The U of Arizona (AZ)
U of Arkansas (AR)
U of Arkansas at Fort Smith (AR)
U of Arkansas at Monticello (AR)
U of Arkansas at Pine Bluff (AR)
U of Bridgeport (CT)
The U of British Columbia (BC, Canada)
The U of British Columbia–Okanagan (BC, Canada)
U of California, Berkeley (CA)
U of California, Davis (CA)
U of California, Irvine (CA)
U of California, Los Angeles (CA)
U of California, Riverside (CA)
U of California, San Diego (CA)
U of California, Santa Barbara (CA)
U of California, Santa Cruz (CA)
U of Central Arkansas (AR)
U of Central Florida (FL)
U of Central Missouri (MO)
U of Central Oklahoma (OK)
U of Charleston (WV)
U of Chicago (IL)
U of Cincinnati (OH)
U of Colorado Denver (CO)
U of Connecticut (CT)
U of Dallas (TX)
U of Dayton (OH)
U of Delaware (DE)
U of Denver (CO)
U of Evansville (IN)
The U of Findlay (OH)
U of Florida (FL)
U of Georgia (GA)
U of Great Falls (MT)
U of Guam (GU)
U of Hartford (CT)
U of Hawaii at Manoa (HI)
U of Houston (TX)
U of Houston–Clear Lake (TX)
U of Houston–Downtown (TX)
U of Houston–Victoria (TX)
U of Idaho (ID)
U of Illinois at Chicago (IL)
U of Illinois at Springfield (IL)
U of Illinois at Urbana–Champaign (IL)
U of Indianapolis (IN)
The U of Iowa (IA)
U of Kansas (KS)
U of King's Coll (NS, Canada)
U of La Verne (CA)
U of Lethbridge (AB, Canada)
U of Louisiana at Lafayette (LA)
U of Louisiana at Monroe (LA)
U of Louisville (KY)
U of Maine (ME)
U of Maine at Farmington (ME)
U of Maine at Fort Kent (ME)
U of Maine at Machias (ME)
U of Mary (ND)
U of Mary Hardin-Baylor (TX)
U of Maryland, Baltimore County (MD)
U of Maryland, Coll Park (MD)
U of Maryland Eastern Shore (MD)
U of Mary Washington (VA)
U of Massachusetts Amherst (MA)
U of Massachusetts Boston (MA)
U of Massachusetts Dartmouth (MA)
U of Massachusetts Lowell (MA)
U of Memphis (TN)
U of Miami (FL)
U of Michigan (MI)
U of Michigan–Dearborn (MI)
U of Michigan–Flint (MI)
U of Minnesota, Crookston (MN)
U of Minnesota, Duluth (MN)
U of Minnesota, Twin Cities Campus (MN)
U of Mississippi (MS)
U of Missouri–Columbia (MO)
U of Missouri–Kansas City (MO)
U of Missouri–St. Louis (MO)
The U of Montana (MT)
U of Montevallo (AL)
U of Nebraska at Kearney (NE)
U of Nebraska at Omaha (NE)
U of Nebraska–Lincoln (NE)
U of Nevada, Las Vegas (NV)
U of Nevada, Reno (NV)
U of New Brunswick Fredericton (NB, Canada)
U of New England (ME)
U of New Hampshire (NH)
U of New Haven (CT)
U of New Mexico (NM)
U of New Orleans (LA)
U of North Alabama (AL)
The U of North Carolina at Asheville (NC)
The U of North Carolina at Chapel Hill (NC)
The U of North Carolina at Charlotte (NC)
The U of North Carolina at Greensboro (NC)
The U of North Carolina at Pembroke (NC)
The U of North Carolina Wilmington (NC)
U of North Dakota (ND)
U of Northern Colorado (CO)
U of Northern Iowa (IA)
U of North Florida (FL)
U of North Texas (TX)
U of Notre Dame (IN)
U of Oregon (OR)
U of Ottawa (ON, Canada)
U of Pennsylvania (PA)
U of Pittsburgh (PA)
U of Pittsburgh at Bradford (PA)
U of Pittsburgh at Johnstown (PA)
U of Portland (OR)
U of Prince Edward Island (PE, Canada)
U of Puerto Rico at Humacao (PR)
U of Puerto Rico at Utuado (PR)
U of Puerto Rico, Cayey U Coll (PR)
U of Puget Sound (WA)
U of Redlands (CA)
U of Regina (SK, Canada)
U of Rhode Island (RI)
U of Richmond (VA)
U of Rio Grande (OH)
U of Rochester (NY)
U of St. Francis (IL)
U of Saint Mary (KS)
U of St. Thomas (MN)
U of St. Thomas (TX)
U of San Diego (CA)
U of Science and Arts of Oklahoma (OK)
The U of Scranton (PA)
U of Sioux Falls (SD)
U of South Alabama (AL)
U of South Carolina (SC)
U of South Carolina Aiken (SC)
U of South Carolina Beaufort (SC)
U of South Carolina Upstate (SC)
The U of South Dakota (SD)
U of Southern California (CA)
U of Southern Indiana (IN)
U of Southern Maine (ME)
U of Southern Mississippi (MS)
U of South Florida (FL)
The U of Tampa (FL)
The U of Tennessee (TN)
The U of Tennessee at Chattanooga (TN)
The U of Tennessee at Martin (TN)
The U of Texas at Arlington (TX)
The U of Texas at Austin (TX)
The U of Texas at Brownsville (TX)
The U of Texas at Dallas (TX)
The U of Texas at El Paso (TX)
The U of Texas at San Antonio (TX)
The U of Texas at Tyler (TX)
The U of Texas of the Permian Basin (TX)
The U of Texas–Pan American (TX)
U of the District of Columbia (DC)
U of the Incarnate Word (TX)
U of the Ozarks (AR)
U of the Pacific (CA)
U of the Sacred Heart (PR)
U of the Sciences in Philadelphia (PA)
U of the Virgin Islands (VI)
The U of Toledo (OH)
U of Toronto (ON, Canada)
U of Tulsa (OK)
U of Utah (UT)
U of Vermont (VT)
U of Victoria (BC, Canada)
U of Virginia (VA)
The U of Virginia's Coll at Wise (VA)
The U of Western Ontario (ON, Canada)
U of West Florida (FL)
U of West Georgia (GA)
U of Windsor (ON, Canada)
The U of Winnipeg (MB, Canada)
U of Wisconsin–Green Bay (WI)
U of Wisconsin–La Crosse (WI)
U of Wisconsin–Madison (WI)
U of Wisconsin–Milwaukee (WI)
U of Wisconsin–Oshkosh (WI)
U of Wisconsin–Platteville (WI)
U of Wisconsin–Stevens Point (WI)
U of Wisconsin–Superior (WI)
U of Wisconsin–Whitewater (WI)
U of Wyoming (WY)
Ursinus Coll (PA)
Ursuline Coll (OH)
Utah State U (UT)
Utah Valley State Coll (UT)
Utica Coll (NY)
Valdosta State U (GA)
Valley City State U (ND)
Valparaiso U (IN)
Vanderbilt U (TN)
Vanguard U of Southern California (CA)
Vassar Coll (NY)
Villa Julie Coll (MD)
Villanova U (PA)
Virginia Commonwealth U (VA)
Virginia Intermont Coll (VA)
Virginia Military Inst (VA)
Virginia Polytechnic Inst and State U (VA)
Virginia State U (VA)
Virginia Wesleyan Coll (VA)
Viterbo U (WI)
Voorhees Coll (SC)
Wabash Coll (IN)
Wagner Coll (NY)
Wake Forest U (NC)
Walla Walla U (WA)
Walsh U (OH)
Warner Pacific Coll (OR)
Warren Wilson Coll (NC)
Wartburg Coll (IA)
Washburn U (KS)
Washington & Jefferson Coll (PA)
Washington and Lee U (VA)
Washington Coll (MD)
Washington State U (WA)
Washington U in St. Louis (MO)
Wayland Baptist U (TX)
Waynesburg U (PA)
Wayne State Coll (NE)
Wayne State U (MI)
Webster U (MO)
Wellesley Coll (MA)
Wells Coll (NY)
Wesleyan Coll (GA)
Wesleyan U (CT)
Wesley Coll (DE)
West Chester U of Pennsylvania (PA)
Western Carolina U (NC)
Western Connecticut State U (CT)
Western Illinois U (IL)
Western Kentucky U (KY)
Western Michigan U (MI)
Western New England Coll (MA)
Western New Mexico U (NM)
Western State Coll of Colorado (CO)
Western Washington U (WA)
Westfield State Coll (MA)
West Liberty State Coll (WV)
Westminster Coll (MO)
Westminster Coll (UT)
Westmont Coll (CA)
West Texas A&M U (TX)
West Virginia U (WV)
West Virginia Wesleyan Coll (WV)
Wheaton Coll (IL)
Wheaton Coll (MA)
Wheeling Jesuit U (WV)
Whitman Coll (WA)
Whittier Coll (CA)
Whitworth U (WA)
Wichita State U (KS)
Widener U (PA)
Wiley Coll (TX)
Wilfrid Laurier U (ON, Canada)
Wilkes U (PA)
Willamette U (OR)
William Jewell Coll (MO)
William Paterson U of New Jersey (NJ)
Williams Coll (MA)
William Woods U (MO)
Wilmington Coll (OH)
Wilson Coll (PA)
Wingate U (NC)
Winona State U (MN)
Winthrop U (SC)
Wittenberg U (OH)
Wofford Coll (SC)
Worcester Polytechnic Inst (MA)
Worcester State Coll (MA)
Wright State U (OH)
Xavier U (OH)
Xavier U of Louisiana (LA)
Yale U (CT)
York Coll (NE)
York Coll of Pennsylvania (PA)
York Coll of the City U of New York (NY)
York U (ON, Canada)
Youngstown State U (OH)

BIOLOGY/ BIOTECHNOLOGY LABORATORY TECHNICIAN

California State Polytechnic U, Pomona (CA)
Cleveland State U (OH)
The Coll at Brockport, State U of New York (NY)
Gannon U (PA)
Harvard U (MA)
Michigan Technological U (MI)
Minnesota State U Mankato (MN)
Niagara U (NY)
Northeastern U (MA)
Penn State Abington (PA)
Penn State Altoona (PA)
Penn State Berks (PA)
Penn State Erie, The Behrend Coll (PA)
Penn State U Park (PA)
Point Park U (PA)
Purdue U Calumet (IN)
St. Cloud State U (MN)
State U of New York at Fredonia (NY)
State U of New York Coll at Oneonta (NY)
Suffolk U (MA)
Tusculum Coll (TN)
U of Delaware (DE)
U of New Haven (CT)
U of Ottawa (ON, Canada)
Villa Julie Coll (MD)
Washburn U (KS)
Worcester Polytechnic Inst (MA)
York Coll of the City U of New York (NY)

BIOLOGY TEACHER EDUCATION

Abilene Christian U (TX)
Alma Coll (MI)
Alvernia Coll (PA)
Anderson U (SC)
Appalachian State U (NC)
Arkansas State U (AR)
Assumption Coll (MA)
Averett U (VA)
Baylor U (TX)
Bethany Coll (KS)
Bethel U (MN)
Bethune-Cookman U (FL)
Bishop's U (QC, Canada)
Bluefield Coll (VA)
Bowling Green State U (OH)
Brewton-Parker Coll (GA)
Bridgewater State Coll (MA)
Cabrini Coll (PA)
California State U, Chico (CA)
California State U, Long Beach (CA)
Capital U (OH)
Carroll Coll (WI)
The Catholic U of America (DC)
Cedarville U (OH)
Centenary Coll of Louisiana (LA)
Central Michigan U (MI)
Central Washington U (WA)
Christian Brothers U (TN)
City Coll of the City U of New York (NY)
Clearwater Christian Coll (FL)
Coker Coll (SC)
The Coll at Brockport, State U of New York (NY)
The Coll of New Jersey (NJ)
The Coll of Saint Rose (NY)
Coll of the Ozarks (MO)
Colorado State U (CO)
Concordia Coll (MN)
Concordia U (MI)
Concordia U Chicago (IL)
Concordia U, Nebraska (NE)
Concordia U, St. Paul (MN)
Cornell U (NY)
Cornerstone U (MI)
Daemen Coll (NY)
Dakota State U (SD)
Dakota Wesleyan U (SD)
Delta State U (MS)
DePaul U (IL)
Dillard U (LA)
Dominican Coll (NY)
Dordt Coll (IA)
Dowling Coll (NY)
East Central U (OK)
Eastern Mennonite U (VA)
Eastern Michigan U (MI)
East Texas Baptist U (TX)
Evangel U (MO)
Fayetteville State U (NC)
Ferris State U (MI)
Fitchburg State Coll (MA)
Florida Inst of Technology (FL)
Fort Lewis Coll (CO)
Franklin Coll (IN)
Freed-Hardeman U (TN)
Glenville State Coll (WV)
Grand Canyon U (AZ)
Greensboro Coll (NC)
Greenville Coll (IL)
Gustavus Adolphus Coll (MN)
Harding U (AR)
Hastings Coll (NE)
Hofstra U (NY)
Hope Coll (MI)
Houston Baptist U (TX)
Howard Payne U (TX)
Hunter Coll of the City U of New York (NY)
Husson Coll (ME)
Indiana U Bloomington (IN)
Indiana U–Purdue U Fort Wayne (IN)
Indiana U South Bend (IN)
Inter American U of Puerto Rico, Aguadilla Campus (PR)
Inter American U of Puerto Rico, San Germán Campus (PR)
Iona Coll (NY)
Ithaca Coll (NY)
Jamestown Coll (ND)
John Brown U (AR)
Johnson State Coll (VT)
Juniata Coll (PA)
Keene State Coll (NH)
Kennesaw State U (GA)
Kentucky Wesleyan Coll (KY)
Keuka Coll (NY)
King Coll (TN)
Kutztown U of Pennsylvania (PA)
Lambuth U (TN)
Le Moyne Coll (NY)
Lenoir-Rhyne Coll (NC)
Liberty U (VA)
Limestone Coll (SC)
Lincoln U (MO)
Lindenwood U (MO)
Lindsey Wilson Coll (KY)
Lipscomb U (TN)
Manhattanville Coll (NY)
Mansfield U of Pennsylvania (PA)
Marian Coll of Fond du Lac (WI)
Marist Coll (NY)
Maryville Coll (TN)
Maryville U of Saint Louis (MO)
Marywood U (PA)
Mayville State U (ND)
McGill U (QC, Canada)
McKendree U (IL)
McNeese State U (LA)
Mercyhurst Coll (PA)
Messiah Coll (PA)
Metropolitan State U (MN)
Miami U (OH)
Michigan Technological U (MI)
Millikin U (IL)
Minot State U (ND)
Misericordia U (PA)
Missouri State U (MO)
Molloy Coll (NY)
Montana State U–Billings (MT)
Moravian Coll (PA)
Morris Coll (SC)
Mount Mary Coll (WI)
Murray State U (KY)
Nazareth Coll of Rochester (NY)
New York Inst of Technology (NY)
New York U (NY)
Niagara U (NY)
North Carolina Central U (NC)
North Carolina State U (NC)
North Dakota State U (ND)
Northeastern State U (OK)
Northern Arizona U (AZ)
Northern Michigan U (MI)
North Greenville U (SC)
Northwestern Coll (IA)
Northwestern State U of Louisiana (LA)
Northwest Nazarene U (ID)
Oakland City U (IN)
Ohio Northern U (OH)
Ohio U (OH)
Ohio Wesleyan U (OH)
Old Dominion U (VA)
Pace U (NY)
Paine Coll (GA)
Pittsburg State U (KS)
Point Park U (PA)
Purdue U (IN)
Queens Coll of the City U of New York (NY)
Rhode Island Coll (RI)
Roberts Wesleyan Coll (NY)
Rochester Coll (MI)
Sacred Heart U (CT)
Saginaw Valley State U (MI)
St. Ambrose U (IA)
St. Edward's U (TX)
Saint Francis U (PA)
St. John's U (NY)
St. Joseph's Coll, Suffolk Campus (NY)
Saint Mary's U of Minnesota (MN)
Saint Xavier U (IL)
Salve Regina U (RI)
Samford U (AL)
Seattle Pacific U (WA)
Seton Hill U (PA)
Southeastern U (FL)
Southern Arkansas U–Magnolia (AR)
Southern U and Ag and Mech Coll (LA)
Southwest Baptist U (MO)
Southwest Minnesota State U (MN)
State U of New York at Plattsburgh (NY)
State U of New York Coll at Old Westbury (NY)

State U of New York Coll at Oneonta (NY)
State U of New York Coll at Potsdam (NY)
State U of New York Coll of Environmental Science and Forestry (NY)
Taylor U (IN)
Texas A&M Intl U (TX)
Trevecca Nazarene U (TN)
Trinity Christian Coll (IL)
Tusculum Coll (TN)
Union Coll (NE)
The U of Arizona (AZ)
U of Arkansas at Fort Smith (AR)
U of Charleston (WV)
U of Delaware (DE)
U of Evansville (IN)
U of Great Falls (MT)
U of Illinois at Chicago (IL)
The U of Iowa (IA)
U of Louisiana at Lafayette (LA)
U of Louisiana at Monroe (LA)
U of Maine (ME)
U of Maine at Farmington (ME)
U of Maine at Machias (ME)
U of Mary (ND)
U of Michigan–Flint (MI)
U of Missouri–Columbia (MO)
U of Missouri–St. Louis (MO)
The U of Montana–Western (MT)
U of Nebraska–Lincoln (NE)
U of New Orleans (LA)
The U of North Carolina at Greensboro (NC)
The U of North Carolina at Pembroke (NC)
The U of North Carolina Wilmington (NC)
U of Pittsburgh at Johnstown (PA)
U of Regina (SK, Canada)
U of Rio Grande (OH)
U of Saint Francis (IN)
U of St. Thomas (MN)
The U of South Dakota (SD)
The U of Tampa (FL)
The U of Tennessee at Martin (TN)
U of West Georgia (GA)
U of Windsor (ON, Canada)
U of Wisconsin–Superior (WI)
Utah State U (UT)
Utah Valley State Coll (UT)
Utica Coll (NY)
Valley City State U (ND)
Valparaiso U (IN)
Virginia Intermont Coll (VA)
Viterbo U (WI)
Washington State U (WA)
Washington U in St. Louis (MO)
Waynesburg U (PA)
Wayne State Coll (NE)
Weber State U (UT)
Western State Coll of Colorado (CO)
Westminster Coll (UT)
Wheeling Jesuit U (WV)
Widener U (PA)
Wingate U (NC)
Xavier U (OH)
Xavier U of Louisiana (LA)
York Coll (NE)
York Coll of Pennsylvania (PA)
York U (ON, Canada)

BIOMATHEMATICS AND BIOINFORMATICS RELATED
Case Western Reserve U (OH)
Florida State U (FL)
U of California, Los Angeles (CA)
The U of Scranton (PA)

BIOMEDICAL/MEDICAL ENGINEERING
Alfred U (NY)
Arizona State U (AZ)
Boston U (MA)
Brown U (RI)
Bucknell U (PA)
California Lutheran U (CA)
California Polytechnic State U, San Luis Obispo (CA)
California State U, Long Beach (CA)
Carnegie Mellon U (PA)
Case Western Reserve U (OH)
The Catholic U of America (DC)
City Coll of the City U of New York (NY)
Clemson U (SC)
The Coll of New Jersey (NJ)
Drexel U (PA)
Duke U (NC)
Florida Gulf Coast U (FL)
Florida Intl U (FL)
Florida State U (FL)
Georgia Inst of Technology (GA)
Harvard U (MA)
Hofstra U (NY)
Illinois Inst of Technology (IL)
Indiana U–Purdue U Indianapolis (IN)
The Johns Hopkins U (MD)
Lawrence Technological U (MI)
Lehigh U (PA)
LeTourneau U (TX)
Louisiana State U and Ag and Mech Coll (LA)
Marquette U (WI)
Massachusetts Inst of Technology (MA)
Michigan State U (MI)
Michigan Technological U (MI)
Milwaukee School of Eng (WI)
Mississippi State U (MS)
New Jersey Inst of Technology (NJ)
North Carolina State U (NC)
Northwestern U (IL)
Oklahoma State U (OK)
Oral Roberts U (OK)
Penn State Abington (PA)
Penn State Altoona (PA)
Penn State Berks (PA)
Penn State Erie, The Behrend Coll (PA)
Penn State U Park (PA)
Purdue U (IN)
Rensselaer Polytechnic Inst (NY)
Rice U (TX)
Rochester Inst of Technology (NY)
Rose-Hulman Inst of Technology (IN)
Rutgers, The State U of New Jersey, New Brunswick (NJ)
Saint Louis U (MO)
Stanford U (CA)
State U of New York at Binghamton (NY)
Stony Brook U, State U of New York (NY)
Syracuse U (NY)
Texas A&M U (TX)
Trinity Coll (CT)
Tulane U (LA)
The U of Akron (OH)
The U of Alabama at Birmingham (AL)
The U of British Columbia (BC, Canada)
U of California, Berkeley (CA)
U of California, Davis (CA)
U of California, Irvine (CA)
U of California, Riverside (CA)
U of California, San Diego (CA)
U of Central Oklahoma (OK)
U of Connecticut (CT)
U of Hartford (CT)
U of Houston (TX)
U of Illinois at Chicago (IL)
U of Illinois at Urbana–Champaign (IL)
The U of Iowa (IA)
U of Memphis (TN)
U of Miami (FL)
U of Nebraska–Lincoln (NE)
U of Oklahoma (OK)
U of Ottawa (ON, Canada)
U of Pennsylvania (PA)
U of Pittsburgh (PA)
U of Rhode Island (RI)
U of Rochester (NY)
U of Southern California (CA)
The U of Texas at Austin (TX)
U of the Pacific (CA)
The U of Toledo (OH)
U of Toronto (ON, Canada)
U of Utah (UT)
U of Virginia (VA)
U of Wisconsin–Madison (WI)
Vanderbilt U (TN)
Virginia Commonwealth U (VA)
Walla Walla U (WA)
Washington U in St. Louis (MO)
Western New England Coll (MA)
Worcester Polytechnic Inst (MA)
Wright State U (OH)
Yale U (CT)

BIOMEDICAL SCIENCES
Auburn U (AL)
Bridgewater State Coll (MA)
Brigham Young U (UT)
Brock U (ON, Canada)
Brown U (RI)
Central Michigan U (MI)
Christian Brothers U (TN)
City Coll of the City U of New York (NY)
Colorado State U (CO)
Emory U (GA)
Florida Inst of Technology (FL)
Grand Valley State U (MI)
Harvard U (MA)
Inter American U of Puerto Rico, San Germán Campus (PR)
Jefferson Coll of Health Sciences (VA)
Keuka Coll (NY)
Marist Coll (NY)
Marquette U (WI)
Maryville U of Saint Louis (MO)
McGill U (QC, Canada)
North Carolina Central U (NC)
Our Lady of the Lake Coll (LA)
Rutgers, The State U of New Jersey, New Brunswick (NJ)
St. Cloud State U (MN)
State U of New York at Fredonia (NY)
Stephens Coll (MO)
Suffolk U (MA)
Texas A&M U (TX)
U of California, Riverside (CA)
U of Colorado Denver (CO)
U of Maine (ME)
U of Michigan (MI)
U of Michigan–Flint (MI)
U of Mississippi (MS)
U of New England (ME)
U of Ottawa (ON, Canada)
U of Pennsylvania (PA)
U of South Alabama (AL)
U of Wisconsin–Eau Claire (WI)
U of Wisconsin–Green Bay (WI)
Western Michigan U (MI)
Worcester Polytechnic Inst (MA)

BIOMEDICAL TECHNOLOGY
Andrews U (MI)
California State U, East Bay (CA)
DeVry Coll of New York (NY)
DeVry U, Fremont (CA)
DeVry U, Pomona (CA)
DeVry U, Miramar (FL)
DeVry U, Orlando (FL)
DeVry U, Decatur (GA)
DeVry U, Addison (IL)
DeVry U, Chicago (IL)
DeVry U, Tinley Park (IL)
DeVry U, Kansas City (MO)
DeVry U (NJ)
DeVry U, Columbus (OH)
DeVry U (OR)
DeVry U, Fort Washington (PA)
DeVry U, Houston (TX)
DeVry U, Irving (TX)
DeVry U, Federal Way (WA)
New York Inst of Technology (NY)
Northwest Missouri State U (MO)
Rutgers, The State U of New Jersey, Camden (NJ)
Suffolk U (MA)
Texas Southern U (TX)
Thomas Edison State Coll (NJ)
U of New Hampshire (NH)
Walla Walla U (WA)
Wright State U (OH)

BIOMETRY/BIOMETRICS
Cornell U (NY)
Harvard U (MA)
Rutgers, The State U of New Jersey, New Brunswick (NJ)

BIOPHYSICS
Andrews U (MI)
Bob Jones U (SC)
Brandeis U (MA)
Brigham Young U (UT)
Brown U (RI)
Carnegie Mellon U (PA)
Centenary Coll of Louisiana (LA)
Claremont McKenna Coll (CA)
Clarkson U (NY)
Freed-Hardeman U (TN)
Hampden-Sydney Coll (VA)
Harvard U (MA)
Haverford Coll (PA)
Illinois Inst of Technology (IL)
Iowa State U of Science and Technology (IA)
The Johns Hopkins U (MD)
King Coll (TN)
La Sierra U (CA)
Laurentian U (ON, Canada)
Longwood U (VA)
Oakland U (MI)
Oklahoma City U (OK)
Oregon State U (OR)
Pacific Union Coll (CA)
Rensselaer Polytechnic Inst (NY)
St. Lawrence U (NY)
Saint Mary's U of Minnesota (MN)
Southwestern Oklahoma State U (OK)
State U of New York Coll at Geneseo (NY)
Suffolk U (MA)
Temple U (PA)
U at Buffalo, the State U of New York (NY)
The U of British Columbia (BC, Canada)
U of California, Los Angeles (CA)
U of California, San Diego (CA)
U of Connecticut (CT)
U of Illinois at Urbana–Champaign (IL)
U of Miami (FL)
U of Michigan (MI)
U of New Brunswick Fredericton (NB, Canada)
U of Pennsylvania (PA)
The U of Scranton (PA)
U of Southern California (CA)
U of Southern Indiana (IN)
U of Toronto (ON, Canada)
The U of Western Ontario (ON, Canada)
U of Windsor (ON, Canada)
Walla Walla U (WA)
Washington & Jefferson Coll (PA)
Washington U in St. Louis (MO)
Whitman Coll (WA)

BIOPSYCHOLOGY
Bucknell U (PA)
Carnegie Mellon U (PA)
Chapman U (CA)
The Coll of William and Mary (VA)
Hastings Coll (NE)
Immaculata U (PA)
Lehigh U (PA)
Messiah Coll (PA)
Morningside Coll (IA)
Mount Allison U (NB, Canada)
Nebraska Wesleyan U (NE)
Oglethorpe U (GA)
Philadelphia U (PA)
Rider U (NJ)
Rochester Inst of Technology (NY)
Russell Sage Coll (NY)
Spring Hill Coll (AL)
U of California, Santa Barbara (CA)
U of Michigan (MI)
U of Pittsburgh at Johnstown (PA)
U of Windsor (ON, Canada)
Viterbo U (WI)
Washington U in St. Louis (MO)

BIOSTATISTICS
Brigham Young U (UT)
Emmanuel Coll (MA)
Tulane U (LA)
U at Buffalo, the State U of New York (NY)
The U of North Carolina at Chapel Hill (NC)

BIOTECHNOLOGY
Bay Path Coll (MA)
Brigham Young U (UT)
British Columbia Inst of Technology (BC, Canada)
Brock U (ON, Canada)
Calvin Coll (MI)
Clarkson U (NY)
The Coll at Brockport, State U of New York (NY)
East Stroudsburg U of Pennsylvania (PA)
Elizabethtown Coll (PA)
Fayetteville State U (NC)
Ferris State U (MI)
Fitchburg State Coll (MA)
Florida Gulf Coast U (FL)
Indiana U Bloomington (IN)
Indiana U East (IN)
Indiana U–Purdue U Indianapolis (IN)
Kent State U (OH)
Marywood U (PA)
Missouri Baptist U (MO)
Montana State U (MT)
North Dakota State U (ND)
Plymouth State U (NH)
Point Park U (PA)
Rochester Inst of Technology (NY)
Roosevelt U (IL)
Rutgers, The State U of New Jersey, New Brunswick (NJ)
Southeastern Oklahoma State U (OK)
State U of New York Coll of Environmental Science and Forestry (NY)
U at Buffalo, the State U of New York (NY)
The U of British Columbia (BC, Canada)
U of California, Davis (CA)
U of California, Los Angeles (CA)
U of California, San Diego (CA)
U of Delaware (DE)
U of Houston–Downtown (TX)
U of Illinois at Urbana–Champaign (IL)
U of Lethbridge (AB, Canada)
U of Nebraska at Omaha (NE)
U of Nevada, Reno (NV)
The U of North Carolina at Pembroke (NC)
U of Northern Iowa (IA)
U of Southern Maine (ME)
U of Windsor (ON, Canada)
Ursuline Coll (OH)
Utah Valley State Coll (UT)
Washington State U (WA)
West Texas A&M U (TX)
Wilfrid Laurier U (ON, Canada)
Worcester State Coll (MA)
York U (ON, Canada)

BIOTECHNOLOGY RESEARCH
Hunter Coll of the City U of New York (NY)
Inter American U of Puerto Rico, Aguadilla Campus (PR)
Kennesaw State U (GA)

BOTANY/PLANT BIOLOGY
Andrews U (MI)
Arizona State U (AZ)
Auburn U (AL)
Ball State U (IN)
Bennington Coll (VT)
Brigham Young U (UT)
California State Polytechnic U, Pomona (CA)
California State U, Long Beach (CA)
Coll of the Atlantic (ME)
Colorado State U (CO)
Connecticut Coll (CT)
Goddard Coll (VT)
Humboldt State U (CA)
Idaho State U (ID)
Iowa State U of Science and Technology (IA)
Juniata Coll (PA)
Kent State U (OH)
Marlboro Coll (VT)
McGill U (QC, Canada)
Miami U (OH)
Michigan State U (MI)
Minnesota State U Mankato (MN)
North Carolina State U (NC)
North Dakota State U (ND)
Northern Arizona U (AZ)
Northwest Missouri State U (MO)
Ohio U (OH)
Ohio Wesleyan U (OH)
Oklahoma State U (OK)
Oregon State U (OR)
Purdue U (IN)
Rutgers, The State U of New Jersey, Newark (NJ)
St. Cloud State U (MN)
Saint Xavier U (IL)
San Francisco State U (CA)
Sonoma State U (CA)
Southeastern Oklahoma State U (OK)
Southern Illinois U Carbondale (IL)
Southern Utah U (UT)
State U of New York Coll of Environmental Science and Forestry (NY)
Texas A&M U (TX)
Texas State U-San Marcos (TX)
The U of Akron (OH)
U of California, Berkeley (CA)
U of California, Davis (CA)
U of California, Los Angeles (CA)
U of California, Riverside (CA)
U of Delaware (DE)
U of Florida (FL)
U of Georgia (GA)
U of Great Falls (MT)
U of Hawaii at Manoa (HI)
U of Illinois at Urbana–Champaign (IL)
U of Maine (ME)
U of Michigan (MI)
U of Minnesota, Twin Cities Campus (MN)
The U of Montana (MT)
U of Nebraska–Lincoln (NE)
U of New Brunswick Fredericton (NB, Canada)
U of New Hampshire (NH)
U of Oklahoma (OK)
The U of Tennessee (TN)
The U of Texas at Austin (TX)
The U of Texas at El Paso (TX)
U of Toronto (ON, Canada)
U of Vermont (VT)
U of Victoria (BC, Canada)
U of Wisconsin–Madison (WI)
U of Wyoming (WY)
Utah State U (UT)
Weber State U (UT)
Western New Mexico U (NM)

BOTANY/PLANT BIOLOGY RELATED
Frostburg State U (MD)
Miami U Hamilton (OH)

MAJORS AND MORE

BROADCAST JOURNALISM
Auburn U (AL)
Baldwin-Wallace Coll (OH)
Barry U (FL)
Belmont U (TN)
Bemidji State U (MN)
Bob Jones U (SC)
Bowling Green State U (OH)
Bradley U (IL)
Brigham Young U (UT)
Buffalo State Coll, State U of New York (NY)
California State U, East Bay (CA)
California State U, Long Beach (CA)
Carson-Newman Coll (TN)
Cedarville U (OH)
Central State U (OH)
Chapman U (CA)
Chatham U (PA)
The Coll at Brockport, State U of New York (NY)
The Coll of New Rochelle (NY)
Coll of the Ozarks (MO)
Columbia Coll Chicago (IL)
Concordia Coll (MN)
Drake U (IA)
East Carolina U (NC)
Eastern Kentucky U (KY)
Edinboro U of Pennsylvania (PA)
Elon U (NC)
Emerson Coll (MA)
Evangel U (MO)
Florida Intl U (FL)
Florida Southern Coll (FL)
Fontbonne U (MO)
George Fox U (OR)
Gettysburg Coll (PA)
Gonzaga U (WA)
Grace U (NE)
Grand Valley State U (MI)
Hampton U (VA)
Harding U (AR)
Hardin-Simmons U (TX)
Hastings Coll (NE)
Hawai'i Pacific U (HI)
Hofstra U (NY)
Humboldt State U (CA)
Huntington U (IN)
Ithaca Coll (NY)
John Brown U (AR)
Kuyper Coll (MI)
La Salle U (PA)
Lewis U (IL)
Lindenwood U (MO)
Louisiana Coll (LA)
Marquette U (WI)
Midland Lutheran Coll (NE)
Montclair State U (NJ)
Mount Vernon Nazarene U (OH)
New England School of Communications (ME)
Northwest Missouri State U (MO)
Ohio U (OH)
Ohio Wesleyan U (OH)
Oklahoma Christian U (OK)
Oklahoma City U (OK)
Oklahoma State U (OK)
Pacific U (OR)
Paine Coll (GA)
Palm Beach Atlantic U (FL)
Point Loma Nazarene U (CA)
Point Park U (PA)
Purdue U (IN)
Quinnipiac U (CT)
St. Cloud State U (MN)
Southeastern U (FL)
Southern Adventist U (TN)
Southern Arkansas U–Magnolia (AR)
Southwestern Adventist U (TX)
State U of New York at Fredonia (NY)
State U of New York at Oswego (NY)
State U of New York at Plattsburgh (NY)
Stephens Coll (MO)
Suffolk U (MA)
Susquehanna U (PA)
Texas Christian U (TX)
Troy U (AL)
Union U (TN)
U of Central Oklahoma (OK)
U of Cincinnati (OH)
U of Colorado at Boulder (CO)
U of Dayton (OH)
The U of Findlay (OH)
U of Georgia (GA)
U of Illinois at Urbana–Champaign (IL)
U of La Verne (CA)
U of Miami (FL)
U of Missouri–Columbia (MO)
U of Nebraska at Omaha (NE)
U of Nebraska–Lincoln (NE)
U of Nevada, Reno (NV)
U of Northern Iowa (IA)
U of North Texas (TX)
U of Oklahoma (OK)
U of St. Thomas (MN)
U of South Carolina (SC)
U of Southern California (CA)
The U of Texas at El Paso (TX)
U of the Ozarks (AR)
U of Windsor (ON, Canada)
U of Wisconsin–Madison (WI)
U of Wisconsin–Milwaukee (WI)
U of Wisconsin–Oshkosh (WI)
U of Wisconsin–Platteville (WI)
U of Wisconsin–Superior (WI)
Wartburg Coll (IA)
Webster U (MO)
West Texas A&M U (TX)
William Woods U (MO)
Winona State U (MN)

BUDDHIST STUDIES
U of the West (CA)

BUILDING/CONSTRUCTION FINISHING, MANAGEMENT, AND INSPECTION RELATED
Central Connecticut State U (CT)
Rensselaer Polytechnic Inst (NY)

BUILDING/CONSTRUCTION SITE MANAGEMENT
Bob Jones U (SC)

BUILDING/HOME/ CONSTRUCTION INSPECTION
Tuskegee U (AL)

BUSINESS ADMINISTRATION AND MANAGEMENT
Acadia U (NS, Canada)
Adams State Coll (CO)
Adelphi U (NY)
Adrian Coll (MI)
Alabama Ag and Mech U (AL)
Alabama State U (AL)
Alaska Pacific U (AK)
Albion Coll (MI)
Albright Coll (PA)
Alcorn State U (MS)
Alderson-Broaddus Coll (WV)
Alfred U (NY)
Alice Lloyd Coll (KY)
Alliant Intl U (CA)
Alliant Intl U–México City (Mexico)
Alma Coll (MI)
Alvernia Coll (PA)
Amberton U (TX)
American Coll of Thessaloniki (Greece)
American InterContinental U (CA)
American InterContinental U (FL)
American InterContinental U (TX)
American InterContinental U Buckhead Campus (GA)
American InterContinental U Dunwoody Campus (GA)
American InterContinental U Online (IL)
American Public U System (WV)
American U (DC)
The American U of Athens (Greece)
American U of Beirut (Lebanon)
Anderson U (IN)
Anderson U (SC)
Angelo State U (TX)
Anna Maria Coll (MA)
Antioch U McGregor (OH)
Appalachian State U (NC)
Aquinas Coll (MI)
Argosy U, Atlanta (GA)
Argosy U, Chicago (IL)
Argosy U, Denver (CO)
Argosy U, Hawai'i (HI)
Argosy U, Inland Empire (CA)
Argosy U, Nashville (TN)
Argosy U, Orange County (CA)
Argosy U, Phoenix (AZ)
Argosy U, San Diego (CA)
Argosy U, San Francisco Bay Area (CA)
Argosy U, Santa Monica (CA)
Argosy U, Sarasota (FL)
Argosy U, Schaumburg (IL)
Argosy U, Seattle (WA)
Argosy U, Tampa (FL)
Argosy U, Twin Cities (MN)
Argosy U, Washington DC (VA)
Arizona State U (AZ)
Arkansas State U (AR)
Ashford U (IA)
Ashland U (OH)
Assumption Coll (MA)
Athabasca U (AB, Canada)
Athens State U (AL)
Atlantic Union Coll (MA)
Auburn U (AL)
Auburn U Montgomery (AL)
Augsburg Coll (MN)
Augustana Coll (IL)
Augustana Coll (SD)
Augusta State U (GA)
Austin Coll (TX)
Austin Peay State U (TN)
Avila U (MO)
Azusa Pacific U (CA)
Babson Coll (MA)
Baker Coll of Auburn Hills (MI)
Baker Coll of Owosso (MI)
Baldwin-Wallace Coll (OH)
Ball State U (IN)
Barclay Coll (KS)
Barry U (FL)
Barton Coll (NC)
Baylor U (TX)
Becker Coll (MA)
Belhaven Coll (MS)
Belmont Abbey Coll (NC)
Belmont U (TN)
Beloit Coll (WI)
Bemidji State U (MN)
Benedictine Coll (KS)
Bentley Coll (MA)
Berea Coll (KY)
Bernard M. Baruch Coll of the City U of New York (NY)
Bethany Coll (KS)
Bethany Lutheran Coll (MN)
Bethel Coll (TN)
Bethel U (MN)
Bethune-Cookman U (FL)
Biola U (CA)
Bishop's U (QC, Canada)
Blackburn Coll (IL)
Bloomfield Coll (NJ)
Bloomsburg U of Pennsylvania (PA)
Bluefield Coll (VA)
Bluefield State Coll (WV)
Bluffton U (OH)
Bob Jones U (SC)
Boise State U (ID)
Boricua Coll (NY)
Boston Coll (MA)
Boston U (MA)
Bradley U (IL)
Brenau U (GA)
Brewton-Parker Coll (GA)
Bridgewater Coll (VA)
Bridgewater State Coll (MA)
Brigham Young U (UT)
British Columbia Inst of Technology (BC, Canada)
Brock U (ON, Canada)
Brown Mackie Coll–Fort Wayne (IN)
Brown Mackie Coll–Indianapolis (IN)
Brown Mackie Coll–Merrillville (IN)
Brown Mackie Coll–Michigan City (IN)
Brown Mackie Coll–South Bend (IN)
Brown Mackie Coll–Tucson (AZ)
Bryan Coll (TN)
Bucknell U (PA)
Buffalo State Coll, State U of New York (NY)
Cabrini Coll (PA)
California Baptist U (CA)
California Lutheran U (CA)
California Maritime Acad (CA)
California Polytechnic State U, San Luis Obispo (CA)
California State Polytechnic U, Pomona (CA)
California State U, Chico (CA)
California State U, Dominguez Hills (CA)
California State U, East Bay (CA)
California State U, Fresno (CA)
California State U, Fullerton (CA)
California State U, Long Beach (CA)
California State U, Los Angeles (CA)
California State U, Monterey Bay (CA)
California State U, Sacramento (CA)
California State U, San Bernardino (CA)
California State U, San Marcos (CA)
California State U, Stanislaus (CA)
Calumet Coll of Saint Joseph (IN)
Calvin Coll (MI)
Cameron U (OK)
Canisius Coll (NY)
Capital U (OH)
Carnegie Mellon U (PA)
Carroll Coll (WI)
Carson-Newman Coll (TN)
Cascade Coll (OR)
Case Western Reserve U (OH)
Castleton State Coll (VT)
Catawba Coll (NC)
The Catholic U of America (DC)
Cedar Crest Coll (PA)
Cedarville U (OH)
Centenary Coll (NJ)
Centenary Coll of Louisiana (LA)
Central Coll (IA)
Central Connecticut State U (CT)
Central Michigan U (MI)
Central Pennsylvania Coll (PA)
Central State U (OH)
Central Washington U (WA)
Chaminade U of Honolulu (HI)
Chapman U (CA)
Chatham U (PA)
Chestnut Hill Coll (PA)
Cheyney U of Pennsylvania (PA)
Chicago State U (IL)
Christian Brothers U (TN)
Christopher Newport U (VA)
The Citadel, The Military Coll of South Carolina (SC)
City Coll of the City U of New York (NY)
City U of Seattle (WA)
Claflin U (SC)
Clarion U of Pennsylvania (PA)
Clark Atlanta U (GA)
Clarke Coll (IA)
Clarkson Coll (NE)
Clarkson U (NY)
Clark U (MA)
Clayton State U (GA)
Clearwater Christian Coll (FL)
Cleary U (MI)
Clemson U (SC)
Cleveland State U (OH)
Coastal Carolina U (SC)
Coker Coll (SC)
Colby-Sawyer Coll (NH)
The Coll at Brockport, State U of New York (NY)
Coll of Charleston (SC)
The Coll of Idaho (ID)
Coll of Mount St. Joseph (OH)
The Coll of New Jersey (NJ)
The Coll of New Rochelle (NY)
Coll of Saint Benedict (MN)
Coll of Saint Elizabeth (NJ)
Coll of St. Joseph (VT)
Coll of Saint Mary (NE)
The Coll of Saint Rose (NY)
The Coll of St. Scholastica (MN)
Coll of the Ozarks (MO)
Coll of the Southwest (NM)
The Coll of William and Mary (VA)
Colorado State U (CO)
Colorado Tech U—Colorado Springs (CO)
Colorado Tech U—Denver (CO)
Colorado Tech U—North Kansas City (MO)
Colorado Tech U—Online (CO)
Colorado Tech U—Sioux Falls (SD)
Columbia Coll (SC)
Columbia Coll Chicago (IL)
Columbia Southern U (AL)
Columbus State U (GA)
Concordia Coll (MN)
Concordia Coll–New York (NY)
Concordia U (CA)
Concordia U (MI)
Concordia U (OR)
Concordia U (QC, Canada)
Concordia U Chicago (IL)
Concordia U, Nebraska (NE)
Concordia U, St. Paul (MN)
Concordia U Texas (TX)
Concordia U Wisconsin (WI)
Concord U (WV)
Converse Coll (SC)
Cornerstone U (MI)
Crossroads Coll (MN)
Culver-Stockton Coll (MO)
Curry Coll (MA)
Daemen Coll (NY)
Dakota Wesleyan U (SD)
Dallas Baptist U (TX)
Dallas Christian Coll (TX)
Dana Coll (NE)
Davenport U, Dearborn (MI)
Davenport U, Grand Rapids (MI)
Davis & Elkins Coll (WV)
Defiance Coll (OH)
Delaware Valley Coll (PA)
Delta State U (MS)
DePaul U (IL)
DeSales U (PA)
DeVry Coll of New York (NY)
DeVry U, Phoenix (AZ)
DeVry U, Fremont (CA)
DeVry U, Long Beach (CA)
DeVry U, Pomona (CA)
DeVry U, Sherman Oaks (CA)
DeVry U, Westminster (CO)
DeVry U, Miramar (FL)
DeVry U, Orlando (FL)
DeVry U, Alpharetta (GA)
DeVry U, Decatur (GA)
DeVry U, Addison (IL)
DeVry U, Chicago (IL)
DeVry U, Tinley Park (IL)
DeVry U, Indianapolis (IN)
DeVry U (MD)
DeVry U, Edina (MN)
DeVry U, Kansas City (MO)
DeVry U (NV)
DeVry U (NJ)
DeVry U, Charlotte (NC)
DeVry U, Columbus (OH)
DeVry U (OK)
DeVry U, Fort Washington (PA)
DeVry U (TN)
DeVry U, Houston (TX)
DeVry U, Irving (TX)
DeVry U (UT)
DeVry U, Arlington (VA)
DeVry U, Federal Way (WA)
DeVry U, Milwaukee (WI)
DeVry U Online (IL)
Dillard U (LA)
Dixie State Coll of Utah (UT)
Doane Coll (NE)
Dominican Coll (NY)
Dominican U (IL)
Dominican U of California (CA)
Dordt Coll (IA)
Dowling Coll (NY)
Drake U (IA)
Drury U (MO)
D'Youville Coll (NY)
Earlham Coll (IN)
East Carolina U (NC)
East Central U (OK)
Eastern Connecticut State U (CT)
Eastern Illinois U (IL)
Eastern Kentucky U (KY)
Eastern Mennonite U (VA)
Eastern Michigan U (MI)
Eastern New Mexico U (NM)
East Stroudsburg U of Pennsylvania (PA)
East Tennessee State U (TN)
East-West U (IL)
Eckerd Coll (FL)
Edinboro U of Pennsylvania (PA)
Electronic Data Processing Coll of Puerto Rico (PR)
Elizabethtown Coll (PA)
Elon U (NC)
Emmanuel Coll (MA)
Emory & Henry Coll (VA)
Emory U (GA)
Emporia State U (KS)
Endicott Coll (MA)
Erskine Coll (SC)
Evangel U (MO)
Everest U, Tampa (FL)
Everest U, Tampa (FL)
The Evergreen State Coll (WA)
Fairfield U (CT)
Fairleigh Dickinson U, Coll at Florham (NJ)
Fairleigh Dickinson U, Metropolitan Campus (NJ)
Fairmont State U (WV)
Faulkner U (AL)
Fayetteville State U (NC)
Felician Coll (NJ)
Ferris State U (MI)
Ferrum Coll (VA)
Finlandia U (MI)
Fitchburg State Coll (MA)
Five Towns Coll (NY)
Flagler Coll (FL)
Florida Ag and Mech U (FL)
Florida Atlantic U (FL)
Florida Coll (FL)
Florida Gulf Coast U (FL)
Florida Inst of Technology (FL)
Florida Intl U (FL)
Florida Memorial U (FL)
Florida Southern Coll (FL)
Florida State U (FL)
Fontbonne U (MO)
Fort Lewis Coll (CO)
Franciscan U of Steubenville (OH)
Francis Marion U (SC)
Franklin & Marshall Coll (PA)
Freed-Hardeman U (TN)
Free Will Baptist Bible Coll (TN)
Fresno Pacific U (CA)
Frostburg State U (MD)
Furman U (SC)
Gannon U (PA)
Gardner-Webb U (NC)
George Fox U (OR)
George Mason U (VA)
Georgetown Coll (KY)
Georgetown U (DC)
The George Washington U (DC)
Georgia Coll & State U (GA)
Georgia Inst of Technology (GA)
Georgian Court U (NJ)
Georgia Southern U (GA)

Georgia Southwestern State U (GA)
Georgia State U (GA)
Gettysburg Coll (PA)
Glenville State Coll (WV)
Golden Gate U (CA)
Goldey-Beacom Coll (DE)
Gonzaga U (WA)
Gordon Coll (MA)
Goucher Coll (MD)
Grace Bible Coll (MI)
Grace Coll (IN)
Grace U (NE)
Grambling State U (LA)
Grand Canyon U (AZ)
Grand Valley State U (MI)
Grand View Coll (IA)
Granite State Coll (NH)
Grantham U (MO)
Greensboro Coll (NC)
Greenville Coll (IL)
Grove City Coll (PA)
Guilford Coll (NC)
Gustavus Adolphus Coll (MN)
Gwynedd-Mercy Coll (PA)
Hamline U (MN)
Hampton U (VA)
Hannibal-LaGrange Coll (MO)
Hanover Coll (IN)
Harding U (AR)
Hardin-Simmons U (TX)
Harris-Stowe State U (MO)
Hartwick Coll (NY)
Hastings Coll (NE)
Hawai'i Pacific U (HI)
HEC Montreal (QC, Canada)
Heidelberg Coll (OH)
Hellenic Coll (MA)
High Point U (NC)
Hillsdale Coll (MI)
Hofstra U (NY)
Holy Family U (PA)
Holy Names U (CA)
Hood Coll (MD)
Hope Coll (MI)
Hope Intl U (CA)
Houghton Coll (NY)
Houston Baptist U (TX)
Howard Payne U (TX)
Humboldt State U (CA)
Huntington U (IN)
Husson Coll (ME)
Huston-Tillotson U (TX)
Idaho State U (ID)
Illinois Coll (IL)
Illinois State U (IL)
Illinois Wesleyan U (IL)
Immaculata U (PA)
Indiana State U (IN)
Indiana U Bloomington (IN)
Indiana U of Pennsylvania (PA)
Indiana U–Purdue U Fort Wayne (IN)
Indiana Wesleyan U (IN)
Inter American U of Puerto Rico, Bayamón Campus (PR)
Inter American U of Puerto Rico, Fajardo Campus (PR)
Intl U in Geneva (Switzerland)
Iona Coll (NY)
Iowa State U of Science and Technology (IA)
Iowa Wesleyan Coll (IA)
Ithaca Coll (NY)
Jackson State U (MS)
Jacksonville State U (AL)
Jacksonville U (FL)
James Madison U (VA)
Jamestown Coll (ND)
Jarvis Christian Coll (TX)
John Brown U (AR)
John Carroll U (OH)
John F. Kennedy U (CA)
Johnson C. Smith U (NC)
Johnson State Coll (VT)
John Wesley Coll (NC)
Jones Coll, Miami (FL)
Judson U (IL)
Juniata Coll (PA)
Kansas State U (KS)
Kean U (NJ)
Keene State Coll (NH)
Keiser U, Fort Lauderdale (FL)
Kennesaw State U (GA)
Kent State U (OH)
Kentucky Christian U (KY)
Kentucky Wesleyan Coll (KY)
Keuka Coll (NY)
Keystone Coll (PA)
King Coll (TN)
The King's Coll (NY)
The King's U Coll (AB, Canada)
Kutztown U of Pennsylvania (PA)
Kuyper Coll (MI)
LA Coll Intl (CA)
LaGrange Coll (GA)
Lakehead U (ON, Canada)
Lake Superior State U (MI)
Lambuth U (TN)
Lander U (SC)
La Salle U (PA)
La Sierra U (CA)
Laurentian U (ON, Canada)
Lawrence Technological U (MI)
Lebanon Valley Coll (PA)
Lees-McRae Coll (NC)
Lee U (TN)
Lehigh U (PA)
Lehman Coll of the City U of New York (NY)
Le Moyne Coll (NY)
LeMoyne-Owen Coll (TN)
Lenoir-Rhyne Coll (NC)
Lesley U (MA)
LeTourneau U (TX)
Lewis-Clark State Coll (ID)
Lewis U (IL)
Liberty U (VA)
Life U (GA)
Limestone Coll (SC)
Lincoln U (CA)
Lincoln U (MO)
Lincoln U (PA)
Lindenwood U (MO)
Lipscomb U (TN)
Livingstone Coll (NC)
Lock Haven U of Pennsylvania (PA)
Longwood U (VA)
Loras Coll (IA)
Louisiana Coll (LA)
Louisiana State U and Ag and Mech Coll (LA)
Lourdes Coll (OH)
Loyola Marymount U (CA)
Loyola U Chicago (IL)
Loyola U New Orleans (LA)
Lubbock Christian U (TX)
Luther Coll (IA)
Lycoming Coll (PA)
Lynchburg Coll (VA)
Lyon Coll (AR)
Madonna U (MI)
Maharishi U of Management (IA)
Maine Maritime Acad (ME)
Malone Coll (OH)
Manchester Coll (IN)
Manhattanville Coll (NY)
Mansfield U of Pennsylvania (PA)
Maranatha Baptist Bible Coll (WI)
Marian Coll (IN)
Marian Coll of Fond du Lac (WI)
Marietta Coll (OH)
Marist Coll (NY)
Marquette U (WI)
Marshall U (WV)
Martin U (IN)
Mary Baldwin Coll (VA)
Marylhurst U (OR)
Marymount Manhattan Coll (NY)
Marymount U (VA)
Maryville Coll (TN)
Maryville U of Saint Louis (MO)
Marywood U (PA)
Massachusetts Coll of Liberal Arts (MA)
The Master's Coll and Sem (CA)
Mayville State U (ND)
McDaniel Coll (MD)
McKendree U (IL)
McMurry U (TX)
McNeese State U (LA)
Medaille Coll (NY)
Memorial U of Newfoundland (NL, Canada)
Mercy Coll (NY)
Meredith Coll (NC)
Messiah Coll (PA)
Methodist U (NC)
Metropolitan Coll of New York (NY)
Metropolitan State U (MN)
Miami U (OH)
Michigan State U (MI)
Michigan Technological U (MI)
MidAmerica Nazarene U (KS)
Mid-Continent U (KY)
Middle Tennessee State U (TN)
Midland Lutheran Coll (NE)
Midway Coll (KY)
Midwestern State U (TX)
Miles Coll (AL)
Millersville U of Pennsylvania (PA)
Milligan Coll (TN)
Millsaps Coll (MS)
Milwaukee School of Eng (WI)
Minnesota State U Mankato (MN)
Minot State U (ND)
Misericordia U (PA)
Mississippi Coll (MS)
Mississippi State U (MS)
Mississippi U for Women (MS)
Mississippi Valley State U (MS)
Missouri Baptist U (MO)
Missouri State U (MO)
Missouri U of Science and Technology (MO)
Mitchell Coll (CT)
Molloy Coll (NY)
Monmouth Coll (IL)
Monmouth U (NJ)
Monroe Coll, Bronx (NY)
Monroe Coll, New Rochelle (NY)
Montana State U–Billings (MT)
Montana Tech of The U of Montana (MT)
Montclair State U (NJ)
Moravian Coll (PA)
Morehead State U (KY)
Morehouse Coll (GA)
Morgan State U (MD)
Morningside Coll (IA)
Morris Coll (SC)
Mount Allison U (NB, Canada)
Mount Aloysius Coll (PA)
Mount Ida Coll (MA)
Mount Marty Coll (SD)
Mount Mary Coll (WI)
Mount Mercy Coll (IA)
Mount Olive Coll (NC)
Mount Saint Mary Coll (NY)
Mount Saint Vincent U (NS, Canada)
Muhlenberg Coll (PA)
Murray State U (KY)
National American U–Sioux Falls Branch (SD)
National-Louis U (IL)
National U (CA)
Nazareth Coll of Rochester (NY)
Nebraska Wesleyan U (NE)
Neumann Coll (PA)
New England Coll (NH)
New Jersey City U (NJ)
New Jersey Inst of Technology (NJ)
Newman U (KS)
New Mexico Highlands U (NM)
New Mexico Inst of Mining and Technology (NM)
New York U (NY)
Niagara U (NY)
Nicholls State U (LA)
Nichols Coll (MA)
North Carolina Ag and Tech State U (NC)
North Carolina Central U (NC)
North Carolina State U (NC)
North Carolina Wesleyan Coll (NC)
North Central Coll (IL)
Northcentral U (AZ)
North Dakota State U (ND)
Northeastern Illinois U (IL)
Northeastern State U (OK)
Northeastern U (MA)
Northern Arizona U (AZ)
Northern Illinois U (IL)
Northern Michigan U (MI)
North Georgia Coll & State U (GA)
North Greenville U (SC)
Northland Coll (WI)
Northwestern Coll (IA)
Northwestern Coll (MN)
Northwestern Oklahoma State U (OK)
Northwestern State U of Louisiana (LA)
Northwest Missouri State U (MO)
Northwest Nazarene U (ID)
Northwood U (MI)
Northwood U, Florida Campus (FL)
Norwich U (VT)
Notre Dame de Namur U (CA)
Nova Southeastern U (FL)
Nyack Coll (NY)
Oakland City U (IN)
Oakwood Coll (AL)
Oglethorpe U (GA)
Ohio Dominican U (OH)
Ohio Northern U (OH)
Ohio U (OH)
Ohio Valley U (WV)
Ohio Wesleyan U (OH)
Okanagan Coll (BC, Canada)
Oklahoma Christian U (OK)
Oklahoma City U (OK)
Oklahoma Panhandle State U (OK)
Oklahoma Wesleyan U (OK)
Old Dominion U (VA)
Oral Roberts U (OK)
Oregon Inst of Technology (OR)
Oregon State U (OR)
Otterbein Coll (OH)
Ouachita Baptist U (AR)
Pace U (NY)
Pacific Lutheran U (WA)
Pacific States U (CA)
Pacific Union Coll (CA)
Pacific U (OR)
Paine Coll (GA)
Palm Beach Atlantic U (FL)
Park U (MO)
Parsons Paris (France)
Patricia Stevens Coll (MO)
Paul Smith's Coll (NY)
Peace Coll (NC)
Peirce Coll (PA)
Penn State Altoona (PA)
Penn State Berks (PA)
Penn State Erie, The Behrend Coll (PA)
Penn State Harrisburg (PA)
Pennsylvania Coll of Technology (PA)
Pepperdine U, Malibu (CA)
Peru State Coll (NE)
Pfeiffer U (NC)
Philadelphia Biblical U (PA)
Philadelphia U (PA)
Piedmont Coll (GA)
Pikeville Coll (KY)
Pillsbury Baptist Bible Coll (MN)
Pittsburg State U (KS)
Plymouth State U (NH)
Point Loma Nazarene U (CA)
Point Park U (PA)
Polytechnic U of Puerto Rico (PR)
Portland State U (OR)
Prairie View A&M U (TX)
Presbyterian Coll (SC)
Presentation Coll (SD)
Providence Coll (RI)
Purdue U (IN)
Purdue U Calumet (IN)
Queens U of Charlotte (NC)
Quincy U (IL)
Quinnipiac U (CT)
Radford U (VA)
Ramapo Coll of New Jersey (NJ)
Redeemer U Coll (ON, Canada)
Regis U (CO)
Rensselaer Polytechnic Inst (NY)
Rhode Island Coll (RI)
Rhodes Coll (TN)
Rice U (TX)
The Richard Stockton Coll of New Jersey (NJ)
Rider U (NJ)
Ripon Coll (WI)
Roanoke Coll (VA)
Robert Morris Coll (IL)
Robert Morris U (PA)
Roberts Wesleyan Coll (NY)
Rochester Coll (MI)
Rockford Coll (IL)
Rockhurst U (MO)
Rogers State U (OK)
Roger Williams U (RI)
Roosevelt U (IL)
Rosemont Coll (PA)
Rowan U (NJ)
Royal Military Coll of Canada (ON, Canada)
Russell Sage Coll (NY)
Rutgers, The State U of New Jersey, Camden (NJ)
Rutgers, The State U of New Jersey, Newark (NJ)
Rutgers, The State U of New Jersey, New Brunswick (NJ)
Saginaw Valley State U (MI)
St. Ambrose U (IA)
St. Andrews Presbyterian Coll (NC)
St. Cloud State U (MN)
St. Edward's U (TX)
Saint Francis U (PA)
St. Francis Xavier U (NS, Canada)
St. Gregory's U, Shawnee (OK)
St. John Fisher Coll (NY)
Saint John's U (MN)
St. John's U (NY)
Saint Joseph Coll (CT)
St. Joseph's Coll, New York (NY)
St. Joseph's Coll, Suffolk Campus (NY)
Saint Joseph's U (PA)
Saint Leo U (FL)
Saint Louis U (MO)
Saint Martin's U (WA)
Saint Mary-of-the-Woods Coll (IN)
Saint Mary's Coll (IN)
Saint Mary's Coll of California (CA)
St. Mary's Coll of Maryland (MD)
St. Mary's U (TX)
Saint Mary's U of Minnesota (MN)
Saint Michael's Coll (VT)
St. Norbert Coll (WI)
St. Thomas Aquinas Coll (NY)
St. Thomas U (FL)
Saint Vincent Coll (PA)
Salem Coll (NC)
Salem Intl U (WV)
Salem State Coll (MA)
Salisbury U (MD)
Salve Regina U (RI)
Samford U (AL)
Sam Houston State U (TX)
San Diego Christian Coll (CA)
San Francisco State U (CA)
Schiller Intl U (France)
Seattle Pacific U (WA)
Seattle U (WA)
Seton Hill U (PA)
Shawnee State U (OH)
Shaw U (NC)
Shenandoah U (VA)
Shepherd U (WV)
Shippensburg U of Pennsylvania (PA)
Shorter Coll (GA)
Siena Heights U (MI)
Simmons Coll (MA)
Simon Fraser U (BC, Canada)
Simpson Coll (IA)
Simpson U (CA)
Slippery Rock U of Pennsylvania (PA)
Sonoma State U (CA)
South Carolina State U (SC)
Southeastern Louisiana U (LA)
Southeastern Oklahoma State U (OK)
Southeastern U (FL)
Southeast Missouri State U (MO)
Southern Adventist U (TN)
Southern Connecticut State U (CT)
Southern Illinois U Carbondale (IL)
Southern Illinois U Edwardsville (IL)
Southern Methodist U (TX)
Southern New Hampshire U (NH)
Southern Oregon U (OR)
Southern U and Ag and Mech Coll (LA)
Southern Utah U (UT)
Southern Vermont Coll (VT)
South U (AL)
South U, Tampa (FL)
South U, West Palm Beach (FL)
South U (GA)
South U (SC)
Southwest Baptist U (MO)
Southwestern Adventist U (TX)
Southwestern Coll (AZ)
Southwestern Coll (KS)
Southwestern Oklahoma State U (OK)
Southwest Minnesota State U (MN)
Spring Arbor U (MI)
Spring Hill Coll (AL)
State U of New York at Binghamton (NY)
State U of New York at Fredonia (NY)
State U of New York at New Paltz (NY)
State U of New York at Oswego (NY)
State U of New York at Plattsburgh (NY)
State U of New York Coll at Geneseo (NY)
State U of New York Coll at Old Westbury (NY)
State U of New York Coll at Potsdam (NY)
State U of New York Empire State Coll (NY)
State U of New York Inst of Technology (NY)
Stephen F. Austin State U (TX)
Stephens Coll (MO)
Sterling Coll (KS)
Stetson U (FL)
Stillman Coll (AL)
Stonehill Coll (MA)
Stony Brook U, State U of New York (NY)
Suffolk U (MA)
Sullivan U (KY)
Susquehanna U (PA)
Syracuse U (NY)
Tabor Coll (KS)
Tarleton State U (TX)
Taylor U (IN)
Taylor U Fort Wayne (IN)
Temple U (PA)
Tennessee State U (TN)
Tennessee Technological U (TN)
Tennessee Wesleyan Coll (TN)
Texas A&M Intl U (TX)
Texas A&M U (TX)
Texas A&M U at Galveston (TX)
Texas A&M U–Commerce (TX)
Texas Coll (TX)
Texas Lutheran U (TX)
Texas Southern U (TX)
Texas State U-San Marcos (TX)
Texas Tech U (TX)
Texas Woman's U (TX)
Thiel Coll (PA)
Thomas Coll (ME)
Thomas Edison State Coll (NJ)
Thomas U (GA)
Thompson Rivers U (BC, Canada)
Tiffin U (OH)
Toccoa Falls Coll (GA)
Tougaloo Coll (MS)
Towson U (MD)
Transylvania U (KY)
Trent U (ON, Canada)
Trevecca Nazarene U (TN)
Trinity Christian Coll (IL)
Trinity Intl U (IL)
Trinity Lutheran Coll (WA)
Trinity U (TX)
Tri-State U (IN)

Troy U (AL)
Truman State U (MO)
Tulane U (LA)
Tusculum Coll (TN)
Tuskegee U (AL)
Union Coll (KY)
Union Coll (NE)
Union U (TN)
United States Air Force Acad (CO)
Université de Sherbrooke (QC, Canada)
Université du Québec en Outaouais (QC, Canada)
U at Albany, State U of New York (NY)
U at Buffalo, the State U of New York (NY)
The U of Akron (OH)
The U of Alabama (AL)
The U of Alabama at Birmingham (AL)
The U of Alabama in Huntsville (AL)
U of Alaska Fairbanks (AK)
U of Alaska Southeast (AK)
U of Arkansas (AR)
U of Arkansas at Fort Smith (AR)
U of Arkansas at Monticello (AR)
U of Arkansas at Pine Bluff (AR)
U of Baltimore (MD)
U of Bridgeport (CT)
The U of British Columbia (BC, Canada)
U of California, Berkeley (CA)
U of California, Riverside (CA)
U of Central Arkansas (AR)
U of Central Florida (FL)
U of Central Missouri (MO)
U of Central Oklahoma (OK)
U of Charleston (WV)
U of Cincinnati (OH)
U of Colorado Denver (CO)
U of Dallas (TX)
U of Dayton (OH)
U of Delaware (DE)
U of Denver (CO)
U of Evansville (IN)
The U of Findlay (OH)
U of Florida (FL)
U of Great Falls (MT)
U of Guam (GU)
U of Hartford (CT)
U of Hawaii–West Oahu (HI)
U of Houston (TX)
U of Houston–Clear Lake (TX)
U of Houston–Downtown (TX)
U of Houston–Victoria (TX)
U of Illinois at Chicago (IL)
U of Illinois at Springfield (IL)
U of Illinois at Urbana–Champaign (IL)
The U of Iowa (IA)
U of La Verne (CA)
U of Lethbridge (AB, Canada)
U of Louisiana at Lafayette (LA)
U of Louisiana at Monroe (LA)
U of Louisville (KY)
U of Maine (ME)
The U of Maine at Augusta (ME)
U of Maine at Fort Kent (ME)
U of Maine at Machias (ME)
U of Management and Technology (VA)
U of Mary (ND)
U of Mary Hardin-Baylor (TX)
U of Maryland, Baltimore County (MD)
U of Maryland, Coll Park (MD)
U of Maryland Eastern Shore (MD)
U of Maryland U Coll (MD)
U of Mary Washington (VA)
U of Massachusetts Amherst (MA)
U of Massachusetts Boston (MA)
U of Massachusetts Dartmouth (MA)
U of Massachusetts Lowell (MA)
U of Miami (FL)
U of Michigan (MI)
U of Michigan–Dearborn (MI)
U of Michigan–Flint (MI)
U of Minnesota, Crookston (MN)
U of Minnesota, Duluth (MN)
U of Mississippi (MS)
U of Missouri–Columbia (MO)
U of Missouri–Kansas City (MO)
U of Missouri–St. Louis (MO)
U of Montevallo (AL)
U of Nebraska at Kearney (NE)
U of Nebraska at Omaha (NE)
U of Nebraska–Lincoln (NE)
U of Nevada, Las Vegas (NV)
U of New Brunswick Fredericton (NB, Canada)
U of New England (ME)
U of New Hampshire (NH)
U of New Hampshire at Manchester (NH)
U of New Haven (CT)
U of New Mexico (NM)
U of New Orleans (LA)
U of North Alabama (AL)
The U of North Carolina at Asheville (NC)
The U of North Carolina at Chapel Hill (NC)
The U of North Carolina at Charlotte (NC)
The U of North Carolina at Greensboro (NC)
The U of North Carolina at Pembroke (NC)
The U of North Carolina Wilmington (NC)
U of North Dakota (ND)
U of Northern Colorado (CO)
U of Northern Iowa (IA)
U of North Florida (FL)
U of Oklahoma (OK)
U of Oregon (OR)
U of Pennsylvania (PA)
U of Pittsburgh at Bradford (PA)
U of Pittsburgh at Johnstown (PA)
U of Portland (OR)
U of Prince Edward Island (PE, Canada)
U of Redlands (CA)
U of Regina (SK, Canada)
U of Rhode Island (RI)
U of Richmond (VA)
U of Rio Grande (OH)
U of St. Francis (IL)
U of Saint Francis (IN)
U of Saint Mary (KS)
U of St. Thomas (MN)
U of St. Thomas (TX)
U of San Diego (CA)
The U of Scranton (PA)
U of South Alabama (AL)
U of South Carolina (SC)
U of South Carolina Aiken (SC)
U of South Carolina Beaufort (SC)
U of South Carolina Upstate (SC)
The U of South Dakota (SD)
U of Southern California (CA)
U of Southern Indiana (IN)
U of Southern Maine (ME)
U of Southern Mississippi (MS)
U of South Florida (FL)
The U of Tampa (FL)
The U of Tennessee (TN)
The U of Tennessee at Chattanooga (TN)
The U of Tennessee at Martin (TN)
The U of Texas at Arlington (TX)
The U of Texas at Austin (TX)
The U of Texas at Brownsville (TX)
The U of Texas at El Paso (TX)
The U of Texas at San Antonio (TX)
The U of Texas at Tyler (TX)
The U of Texas of the Permian Basin (TX)
The U of Texas–Pan American (TX)
U of the District of Columbia (DC)
U of the Incarnate Word (TX)
U of the Ozarks (AR)
U of the Pacific (CA)
U of the Sacred Heart (PR)
U of the Virgin Islands (VI)
U of the West (CA)
The U of Toledo (OH)
U of Toronto (ON, Canada)
U of Tulsa (OK)
U of Utah (UT)
U of Vermont (VT)
The U of Virginia's Coll at Wise (VA)
U of Washington, Bothell (WA)
U of Washington, Tacoma (WA)
The U of Western Ontario (ON, Canada)
U of West Florida (FL)
U of West Georgia (GA)
U of Windsor (ON, Canada)
The U of Winnipeg (MB, Canada)
U of Wisconsin–Eau Claire (WI)
U of Wisconsin–Green Bay (WI)
U of Wisconsin–La Crosse (WI)
U of Wisconsin–Madison (WI)
U of Wisconsin–Milwaukee (WI)
U of Wisconsin–Oshkosh (WI)
U of Wisconsin–Parkside (WI)
U of Wisconsin–Platteville (WI)
U of Wisconsin–Stevens Point (WI)
U of Wisconsin–Superior (WI)
U of Wisconsin–Whitewater (WI)
U of Wyoming (WY)
Ursinus Coll (PA)
Ursuline Coll (OH)
Utah State U (UT)
Utah Valley State Coll (UT)
Utica Coll (NY)
Valdosta State U (GA)
Valley City State U (ND)
Vanguard U of Southern California (CA)
Vennard Coll (IA)
Vermont Tech Coll (VT)
Villa Julie Coll (MD)
Villanova U (PA)
Virginia Commonwealth U (VA)
Virginia Intermont Coll (VA)
Virginia Polytechnic Inst and State U (VA)
Virginia State U (VA)
Virginia U of Lynchburg (VA)
Virginia Wesleyan Coll (VA)
Viterbo U (WI)
Voorhees Coll (SC)
Wagner Coll (NY)
Walsh U (OH)
Warner Pacific Coll (OR)
Warren Wilson Coll (NC)
Wartburg Coll (IA)
Washburn U (KS)
Washington and Lee U (VA)
Washington Coll (MD)
Washington State U (WA)
Washington U in St. Louis (MO)
Wayland Baptist U (TX)
Waynesburg U (PA)
Wayne State Coll (NE)
Webber Intl U (FL)
Weber State U (UT)
Webster U (MO)
Wells Coll (NY)
Wesleyan Coll (GA)
Wesley Coll (DE)
West Chester U of Pennsylvania (PA)
Western Carolina U (NC)
Western Connecticut State U (CT)
Western Illinois U (IL)
Western Intl U (AZ)
Western Kentucky U (KY)
Western New England Coll (MA)
Western New Mexico U (NM)
Western State Coll of Colorado (CO)
Western Washington U (WA)
Westfield State Coll (MA)
West Liberty State Coll (WV)
Westminster Coll (MO)
Westminster Coll (UT)
West Texas A&M U (TX)
West Virginia U (WV)
West Virginia Wesleyan Coll (WV)
Wheeling Jesuit U (WV)
Whittier Coll (CA)
Whitworth U (WA)
Wichita State U (KS)
Widener U (PA)
Wiley Coll (TX)
Wilfrid Laurier U (ON, Canada)
Wilkes U (PA)
William Jewell Coll (MO)
William Paterson U of New Jersey (NJ)
William Woods U (MO)
Wilmington Coll (OH)
Wilmington U (DE)
Wilson Coll (PA)
Wingate U (NC)
Winona State U (MN)
Winthrop U (SC)
Wittenberg U (OH)
Woodbury U (CA)
Worcester Polytechnic Inst (MA)
Worcester State Coll (MA)
Wright State U (OH)
Xavier U (OH)
Xavier U of Louisiana (LA)
York Coll (NE)
York Coll of Pennsylvania (PA)
York Coll of the City U of New York (NY)
York U (ON, Canada)
Youngstown State U (OH)

BUSINESS ADMINISTRATION, MANAGEMENT AND OPERATIONS RELATED

Babson Coll (MA)
Becker Coll (MA)
Bethel Coll (TN)
California State U, Chico (CA)
Canisius Coll (NY)
Capital U (OH)
Central Michigan U (MI)
Cleveland State U (OH)
Cornerstone U (MI)
Crossroads Coll (MN)
Culver-Stockton Coll (MO)
Davenport U, Dearborn (MI)
Davenport U, Grand Rapids (MI)
DePaul U (IL)
DeVry Coll of New York (NY)
DeVry U, Phoenix (AZ)
DeVry U, Fremont (CA)
DeVry U, Long Beach (CA)
DeVry U, Pomona (CA)
DeVry U, Sherman Oaks (CA)
DeVry U, Westminster (CO)
DeVry U, Miramar (FL)
DeVry U, Orlando (FL)
DeVry U, Alpharetta (GA)
DeVry U, Decatur (GA)
DeVry U, Addison (IL)
DeVry U, Chicago (IL)
DeVry U, Tinley Park (IL)
DeVry U, Indianapolis (IN)
DeVry U (MD)
DeVry U, Edina (MN)
DeVry U, Kansas City (MO)
DeVry U (NV)
DeVry U (NJ)
DeVry U, Charlotte (NC)
DeVry U, Columbus (OH)
DeVry U (OK)
DeVry U (OR)
DeVry U, Fort Washington (PA)
DeVry U (TN)
DeVry U, Houston (TX)
DeVry U, Irving (TX)
DeVry U (UT)
DeVry U, Arlington (VA)
DeVry U, Federal Way (WA)
DeVry U, Milwaukee (WI)
DeVry U Online (IL)
Dominican U of California (CA)
Duquesne U (PA)
Eastern New Mexico U (NM)
Embry-Riddle Aeronautical U (AZ)
Embry-Riddle Aeronautical U (FL)
Embry-Riddle Aeronautical U Worldwide (FL)
Gettysburg Coll (PA)
Hodges U (FL)
Hofstra U (NY)
Kettering U (MI)
La Roche Coll (PA)
Le Moyne Coll (NY)
Malone Coll (OH)
Mayville State U (ND)
Mercer U (GA)
Mesa State Coll (CO)
Miami U Hamilton (OH)
Millikin U (IL)
Missouri Baptist U (MO)
Missouri State U (MO)
Morris Coll (SC)
Northern Arizona U (AZ)
Northwest Christian Coll (OR)
Oakland City U (IN)
Palm Beach Atlantic U (FL)
Pennsylvania Coll of Technology (PA)
Point Park U (PA)
Purdue U North Central (IN)
Saint Mary-of-the-Woods Coll (IN)
Texas Christian U (TX)
Texas Tech U (TX)
Towson U (MD)
Trinity Christian Coll (IL)
U of Charleston (WV)
U of Houston–Clear Lake (TX)
U of Illinois at Springfield (IL)
U of Louisville (KY)
U of Maryland, Baltimore County (MD)
U of Miami (FL)
U of Michigan–Dearborn (MI)
U of Notre Dame (IN)
U of Pennsylvania (PA)
U of St. Thomas (MN)
The U of Scranton (PA)
U of Southern California (CA)
The U of Texas at Austin (TX)
U of the Incarnate Word (TX)
The U of Toledo (OH)
The U of Western Ontario (ON, Canada)
U of Wyoming (WY)
Ursuline Coll (OH)
Viterbo U (WI)
Washington U in St. Louis (MO)
Widener U (PA)
William Jessup U (CA)
Woodbury U (CA)

BUSINESS AUTOMATION/ TECHNOLOGY/DATA ENTRY

East Central U (OK)
Inter American U of Puerto Rico, Bayamón Campus (PR)

BUSINESS/COMMERCE

Alabama Ag and Mech U (AL)
Alice Lloyd Coll (KY)
Alvernia Coll (PA)
The American U of Athens (Greece)
Anderson U (SC)
Asbury Coll (KY)
Auburn U Montgomery (AL)
Avila U (MO)
Baker Coll of Jackson (MI)
Baker U (KS)
Baylor U (TX)
Bay Path Coll (MA)
Bellarmine U (KY)
Benedictine U (IL)
Bethel Coll (KS)
Bloomsburg U of Pennsylvania (PA)
Bowling Green State U (OH)
Brigham Young U (UT)
Brock U (ON, Canada)
Capital U (OH)
Carlow U (PA)
The Catholic U of America (DC)
Central Christian Coll of Kansas (KS)
Coll of Staten Island of the City U of New York (NY)
Columbia Coll, Caguas (PR)
Columbia Coll, Yauco (PR)
Columbus State U (GA)
Concordia Coll (MN)
Concordia U, Nebraska (NE)
Concordia U Texas (TX)
Covenant Coll (GA)
Davenport U, Dearborn (MI)
Davenport U, Grand Rapids (MI)
Delta State U (MS)
Drake U (IA)
Drexel U (PA)
Duquesne U (PA)
Earlham Coll (IN)
Eastern Connecticut State U (CT)
Eastern Kentucky U (KY)
Eastern Michigan U (MI)
East Texas Baptist U (TX)
Florida Southern Coll (FL)
Florida State U (FL)
Framingham State Coll (MA)
Franklin Coll (IN)
Georgia Coll & State U (GA)
Glenville State Coll (WV)
Grace Coll (IN)
Harris-Stowe State U (MO)
Hawai'i Pacific U (HI)
HEC Montreal (QC, Canada)
Henderson State U (AR)
Hillsdale Free Will Baptist Coll (OK)
Hofstra U (NY)
Hollins U (VA)
Houston Baptist U (TX)
Howard Payne U (TX)
Huntingdon Coll (AL)
Idaho State U (ID)
Illinois Inst of Technology (IL)
Indiana U Bloomington (IN)
Indiana U East (IN)
Indiana U Kokomo (IN)
Indiana U Northwest (IN)
Indiana U–Purdue U Indianapolis (IN)
Indiana U South Bend (IN)
Indiana U Southeast (IN)
Ithaca Coll (NY)
Jacksonville U (FL)
The Johns Hopkins U (MD)
Johnson State Coll (VT)
Judson Coll (AL)
Juniata Coll (PA)
Kentucky State U (KY)
Keystone Coll (PA)
Laboratory Inst of Merchandising (NY)
Lehigh U (PA)
Liberty U (VA)
Limestone Coll (SC)
Linfield Coll (OR)
Loras Coll (IA)
Loyola Coll in Maryland (MD)
Manchester Coll (IN)
Marian Coll of Fond du Lac (WI)
Maryville U of Saint Louis (MO)
Massachusetts Inst of Technology (MA)
McGill U (QC, Canada)
McMurry U (TX)
Medgar Evers Coll of the City U of New York (NY)
Mercer U (GA)
Mesa State Coll (CO)
Miami U (OH)
Miami U Hamilton (OH)
Midway Coll (KY)
Midwestern State U (TX)
Milwaukee School of Eng (WI)
Missouri Southern State U (MO)
Missouri State U (MO)
Missouri U of Science and Technology (MO)
Montana State U (MT)
Montana State U–Billings (MT)
Montana Tech of The U of Montana (MT)
Mountain State U (WV)
Mount Allison U (NB, Canada)
Mount St. Mary's U (MD)
Mount Vernon Nazarene U (OH)
Murray State U (KY)
Niagara U (NY)
Nichols Coll (MA)
Northeastern Illinois U (IL)
Northeastern State U (OK)
Northeastern U (MA)
Northern Arizona U (AZ)
Northern Illinois U (IL)

Northern Michigan U (MI)
Oakland U (MI)
Ohio Northern U (OH)
Ohio U (OH)
Ohio Valley U (WV)
Oklahoma Christian U (OK)
Oklahoma City U (OK)
Oklahoma State U (OK)
Pace U (NY)
Penn State Abington (PA)
Penn State Altoona (PA)
Penn State Berks (PA)
Plymouth State U (NH)
Purdue U (IN)
Purdue U North Central (IN)
Queen's U at Kingston (ON, Canada)
Randolph Coll (VA)
Regis Coll (MA)
Roosevelt U (IL)
Saginaw Valley State U (MI)
St. Ambrose U (IA)
Saint Joseph's Coll (IN)
Saint Leo U (FL)
Saint Mary's Coll of California (CA)
St. Mary's Coll of Maryland (MD)
Saint Mary's U of Minnesota (MN)
Saint Xavier U (IL)
Sam Houston State U (TX)
San Diego State U (CA)
Schreiner U (TX)
Shippensburg U of Pennsylvania (PA)
Skidmore Coll (NY)
Southern Arkansas U–Magnolia (AR)
Southern Methodist U (TX)
Southwestern U (TX)
State U of New York at Binghamton (NY)
Stephen F. Austin State U (TX)
Tarleton State U (TX)
Temple U (PA)
Texas Tech U (TX)
Thomas More Coll (KY)
Thompson Rivers U (BC, Canada)
Transylvania U (KY)
Trinity Christian Coll (IL)
TUI U (CA)
Tyndale U Coll & Sem (ON, Canada)
The U of Arizona (AZ)
U of Arkansas (AR)
The U of British Columbia (BC, Canada)
U of Central Arkansas (AR)
U of Central Florida (FL)
U of Central Oklahoma (OK)
U of Colorado Denver (CO)
U of Connecticut (CT)
U of Denver (CO)
U of Hawaii at Manoa (HI)
U of Houston–Clear Lake (TX)
U of Houston–Downtown (TX)
U of Illinois at Urbana–Champaign (IL)
U of Kansas (KS)
U of Louisiana at Lafayette (LA)
U of Maine (ME)
U of Mary Hardin-Baylor (TX)
U of Maryland, Coll Park (MD)
U of Mississippi (MS)
U of Missouri–St. Louis (MO)
The U of Montana (MT)
The U of Montana–Western (MT)
U of Nebraska at Omaha (NE)
U of Nevada, Reno (NV)
U of North Texas (TX)
U of Notre Dame (IN)
U of Oregon (OR)
U of Pittsburgh (PA)
U of Puerto Rico at Humacao (PR)
U of Puerto Rico, Cayey U Coll (PR)
U of Puget Sound (WA)
U of Redlands (CA)
U of Regina (SK, Canada)
U of Science and Arts of Oklahoma (OK)
U of South Alabama (AL)
U of Southern Indiana (IN)
U of South Florida (FL)
The U of Tennessee (TN)
The U of Texas at Austin (TX)
The U of Texas at Dallas (TX)
The U of Texas at San Antonio (TX)
The U of Toledo (OH)
U of Tulsa (OK)
U of Utah (UT)
U of Victoria (BC, Canada)
U of Virginia (VA)
The U of Western Ontario (ON, Canada)
U of Windsor (ON, Canada)
U of Wisconsin–Whitewater (WI)
Utah State U (UT)
Wake Forest U (NC)
Washburn U (KS)
Washington & Jefferson Coll (PA)
Washington State U (WA)
Washington U in St. Louis (MO)
Webber Intl U (FL)
Webster U (MO)
West Chester U of Pennsylvania (PA)
Western Michigan U (MI)
Western New England Coll (MA)
Westminster Coll (UT)
Westmont Coll (CA)
West Texas A&M U (TX)
Wright State U (OH)
York Coll of Pennsylvania (PA)
York U (ON, Canada)
Youngstown State U (OH)

BUSINESS/CORPORATE COMMUNICATIONS

Aquinas Coll (MI)
Augustana Coll (SD)
Babson Coll (MA)
Bentley Coll (MA)
Brock U (ON, Canada)
Bryan Coll (TN)
Calvin Coll (MI)
Central Pennsylvania Coll (PA)
Chestnut Hill Coll (PA)
Duquesne U (PA)
Elon U (NC)
Harding U (AR)
Hawai'i Pacific U (HI)
Holy Names U (CA)
Marietta Coll (OH)
Mercy Coll (NY)
Morningside Coll (IA)
Ohio Dominican U (OH)
Penn State Abington (PA)
Point Loma Nazarene U (CA)
Point Park U (PA)
Rochester Coll (MI)
Rockhurst U (MO)
Simpson Coll (IA)
Southwestern Coll (KS)
The U of Findlay (OH)
U of Houston (TX)
U of Mary (ND)
U of Rio Grande (OH)
U of St. Thomas (MN)
The U of Western Ontario (ON, Canada)

BUSINESS FAMILY AND CONSUMER SCIENCES/ HUMAN SCIENCES

Brigham Young U (UT)
U of Houston (TX)
Virginia Polytechnic Inst and State U (VA)

BUSINESS, MANAGEMENT, AND MARKETING RELATED

Adelphi U (NY)
Athens State U (AL)
Baylor U (TX)
Benedictine U (IL)
Bowling Green State U (OH)
Bridgewater State Coll (MA)
Cabrini Coll (PA)
California State U, Stanislaus (CA)
Carlow U (PA)
Claflin U (SC)
Clemson U (SC)
Dowling Coll (NY)
Drexel U (PA)
Duquesne U (PA)
Full Sail U (FL)
George Mason U (VA)
Greenville Coll (IL)
Inter American U of Puerto Rico, Bayamón Campus (PR)
Iowa State U of Science and Technology (IA)
Loyola U Chicago (IL)
Mercyhurst Coll (PA)
Messiah Coll (PA)
Mount Vernon Nazarene U (OH)
Nebraska Wesleyan U (NE)
New York U (NY)
Ohio U (OH)
Park U (MO)
Point Park U (PA)
Saint Vincent Coll (PA)
Skidmore Coll (NY)
Southern New Hampshire U (NH)
State U of New York at Plattsburgh (NY)
State U of New York Coll of Agriculture and Technology at Cobleskill (NY)
Sweet Briar Coll (VA)
Syracuse U (NY)
Troy U (AL)
U of Georgia (GA)
U of Maryland, Coll Park (MD)
U of Southern California (CA)
The U of Toledo (OH)
U of Utah (UT)
The U of Western Ontario (ON, Canada)
Utica Coll (NY)
Western State Coll of Colorado (CO)
York Coll of Pennsylvania (PA)

BUSINESS/MANAGERIAL ECONOMICS

Alabama Ag and Mech U (AL)
Albertus Magnus Coll (CT)
Allegheny Coll (PA)
American Jewish U (CA)
The American U of Athens (Greece)
Anderson U (IN)
Andrews U (MI)
Arkansas State U (AR)
Auburn U (AL)
Auburn U Montgomery (AL)
Augsburg Coll (MN)
Ball State U (IN)
Baylor U (TX)
Belmont U (TN)
Beloit Coll (WI)
Benedictine U (IL)
Bentley Coll (MA)
Bernard M. Baruch Coll of the City U of New York (NY)
Bethany Coll (KS)
Bethany Coll (WV)
Bishop's U (QC, Canada)
Bloomsburg U of Pennsylvania (PA)
Boise State U (ID)
Boston Coll (MA)
Bowling Green State U (OH)
Bradley U (IL)
Brock U (ON, Canada)
California Inst of Technology (CA)
California State U, East Bay (CA)
California State U, Fullerton (CA)
California State U, Long Beach (CA)
California State U, San Bernardino (CA)
Capital U (OH)
Carnegie Mellon U (PA)
Carson-Newman Coll (TN)
Catawba Coll (NC)
Centenary Coll of Louisiana (LA)
Chapman U (CA)
Chatham U (PA)
Christopher Newport U (VA)
Clarion U of Pennsylvania (PA)
Clark Atlanta U (GA)
Cleveland State U (OH)
Coll of Mount Saint Vincent (NY)
The Coll of New Jersey (NJ)
Coll of the Ozarks (MO)
Colorado State U-Pueblo (CO)
Dallas Baptist U (TX)
DePaul U (IL)
Drexel U (PA)
Duquesne U (PA)
East Central U (OK)
Eastern Kentucky U (KY)
Eastern Michigan U (MI)
East Tennessee State U (TN)
Emmanuel Coll (MA)
Emory U (GA)
Fairleigh Dickinson U, Coll at Florham (NJ)
Fairleigh Dickinson U, Metropolitan Campus (NJ)
Ferris State U (MI)
Fort Lewis Coll (CO)
Freed-Hardeman U (TN)
The George Washington U (DC)
Georgia Coll & State U (GA)
Georgia Inst of Technology (GA)
Georgia Southern U (GA)
Georgia State U (GA)
Gonzaga U (WA)
Grambling State U (LA)
Green Mountain Coll (VT)
Greensboro Coll (NC)
Grove City Coll (PA)
Gustavus Adolphus Coll (MN)
Hampden-Sydney Coll (VA)
HEC Montreal (QC, Canada)
Hendrix Coll (AR)
Hofstra U (NY)
Hope Coll (MI)
Houston Baptist U (TX)
Huntington U (IN)
Illinois Coll (IL)
Indiana U–Purdue U Fort Wayne (IN)
Inter American U of Puerto Rico, Bayamón Campus (PR)
Inter American U of Puerto Rico, San Germán Campus (PR)
Ithaca Coll (NY)
Jackson State U (MS)
James Madison U (VA)
Jamestown Coll (ND)
Kalamazoo Coll (MI)
Kent State U (OH)
Lafayette Coll (PA)
Lake Forest Coll (IL)
Lake Superior State U (MI)
La Salle U (PA)
Lehigh U (PA)
Lewis U (IL)
Limestone Coll (SC)
Lipscomb U (TN)
Lock Haven U of Pennsylvania (PA)
Longwood U (VA)
Louisiana State U and Ag and Mech Coll (LA)
Loyola U Chicago (IL)
Loyola U New Orleans (LA)
Marian Coll of Fond du Lac (WI)
Marquette U (WI)
Marshall U (WV)
McGill U (QC, Canada)
Mercy Coll (NY)
Merrimack Coll (MA)
Messiah Coll (PA)
Miami U (OH)
Miami U Hamilton (OH)
Michigan Technological U (MI)
Middle Tennessee State U (TN)
Midwestern State U (TX)
Mills Coll (CA)
Mississippi State U (MS)
Montana State U–Billings (MT)
Morehead State U (KY)
Morgan State U (MD)
Mount Allison U (NB, Canada)
New York U (NY)
Niagara U (NY)
Northern Arizona U (AZ)
Northern State U (SD)
North Georgia Coll & State U (GA)
Northland Coll (WI)
Northwest Missouri State U (MO)
Oakland U (MI)
Occidental Coll (CA)
Oglethorpe U (GA)
Ohio Wesleyan U (OH)
Oklahoma City U (OK)
Oklahoma State U (OK)
Old Dominion U (VA)
Otterbein Coll (OH)
Park U (MO)
Penn State Abington (PA)
Penn State Altoona (PA)
Penn State Berks (PA)
Penn State Erie, The Behrend Coll (PA)
Penn State U Park (PA)
Pfeiffer U (NC)
Presbyterian Coll (SC)
Quinnipiac U (CT)
Randolph-Macon Coll (VA)
Rider U (NJ)
Roosevelt U (IL)
Sacred Heart U (CT)
Saginaw Valley State U (MI)
Salem State Coll (MA)
Sam Houston State U (TX)
Santa Clara U (CA)
Seattle U (WA)
Seton Hill U (PA)
Shorter Coll (GA)
Sonoma State U (CA)
South Carolina State U (SC)
Southern Connecticut State U (CT)
Southern Illinois U Carbondale (IL)
Southern Illinois U Edwardsville (IL)
Southern U and Ag and Mech Coll (LA)
State U of New York at New Paltz (NY)
State U of New York at Plattsburgh (NY)
State U of New York Coll at Oneonta (NY)
State U of New York Coll at Potsdam (NY)
Stephen F. Austin State U (TX)
Stetson U (FL)
Susquehanna U (PA)
Tennessee State U (TN)
Texas A&M Intl U (TX)
Texas State U-San Marcos (TX)
Union U (TN)
The U of Alabama (AL)
The U of Alabama at Birmingham (AL)
The U of Arizona (AZ)
U of Arkansas (AR)
U of Arkansas at Pine Bluff (AR)
U of California, Irvine (CA)
U of California, Los Angeles (CA)
U of California, Riverside (CA)
U of California, Santa Barbara (CA)
U of California, Santa Cruz (CA)
U of Central Florida (FL)
U of Central Oklahoma (OK)
U of Dayton (OH)
U of Delaware (DE)
U of Denver (CO)
U of Evansville (IN)
U of Hartford (CT)
U of Hawaii at Manoa (HI)
U of Idaho (ID)
U of Indianapolis (IN)
The U of Iowa (IA)
U of Louisiana at Lafayette (LA)
U of Louisiana at Monroe (LA)
U of Louisville (KY)
U of Maine at Farmington (ME)
U of Memphis (TN)
U of Miami (FL)
U of Mississippi (MS)
U of Missouri–Columbia (MO)
U of Nebraska at Omaha (NE)
U of Nebraska–Lincoln (NE)
U of Nevada, Reno (NV)
U of New Brunswick Fredericton (NB, Canada)
U of New Haven (CT)
U of New Orleans (LA)
U of North Alabama (AL)
The U of North Carolina at Charlotte (NC)
The U of North Carolina Wilmington (NC)
U of North Dakota (ND)
U of North Florida (FL)
U of North Texas (TX)
U of Oklahoma (OK)
U of Pittsburgh at Johnstown (PA)
U of Richmond (VA)
U of San Diego (CA)
U of South Carolina (SC)
The U of South Dakota (SD)
U of Southern Mississippi (MS)
U of South Florida (FL)
The U of Tennessee (TN)
The U of Tennessee at Martin (TN)
The U of Texas at Arlington (TX)
The U of Texas at San Antonio (TX)
The U of Toledo (OH)
The U of Western Ontario (ON, Canada)
U of West Florida (FL)
U of West Georgia (GA)
U of Windsor (ON, Canada)
U of Wisconsin–Platteville (WI)
U of Wisconsin–Superior (WI)
U of Wisconsin–Whitewater (WI)
U of Wyoming (WY)
Utica Coll (NY)
Valdosta State U (GA)
Villanova U (PA)
Virginia Commonwealth U (VA)
Virginia Polytechnic Inst and State U (VA)
Virginia State U (VA)
Washburn U (KS)
Washington State U (WA)
Washington U in St. Louis (MO)
Weber State U (UT)
West Chester U of Pennsylvania (PA)
Western Illinois U (IL)
Western Kentucky U (KY)
Western State Coll of Colorado (CO)
West Liberty State Coll (WV)
Westminster Coll (UT)
Westmont Coll (CA)
West Texas A&M U (TX)
West Virginia U (WV)
West Virginia Wesleyan Coll (WV)
Wheaton Coll (IL)
Widener U (PA)
William Jewell Coll (MO)
William Paterson U of New Jersey (NJ)
William Woods U (MO)
Wilmington Coll (OH)
Winona State U (MN)
Wofford Coll (SC)
Wright State U (OH)
Xavier U (OH)
York U (ON, Canada)
Youngstown State U (OH)

BUSINESS STATISTICS

Alabama Ag and Mech U (AL)
Baylor U (TX)
Brigham Young U (UT)
Cleveland State U (OH)
HEC Montreal (QC, Canada)
Southern Oregon U (OR)
U of Central Missouri (MO)
U of Denver (CO)
U of Houston (TX)
York U (ON, Canada)

BUSINESS SYSTEMS ANALYSIS/DESIGN

U of Louisiana at Monroe (LA)

BUSINESS TEACHER EDUCATION

Alabama State U (AL)
Alfred U (NY)
Appalachian State U (NC)
Arkansas State U (AR)
Armstrong Atlantic State U (GA)
Ashford U (IA)
Auburn U (AL)
Ball State U (IN)
Baylor U (TX)
Belmont U (TN)
Bethany Coll (KS)
Bethune-Cookman U (FL)
Bluefield Coll (VA)
Boise State U (ID)
Bowling Green State U (OH)
Buffalo State Coll, State U of New York (NY)
Calumet Coll of Saint Joseph (IN)
Carson-Newman Coll (TN)
Centenary Coll of Louisiana (LA)
Central Michigan U (MI)
Central Washington U (WA)
Chicago State U (IL)
Coll of the Ozarks (MO)
Coll of the Southwest (NM)
Colorado State U (CO)
Concordia Coll (MN)
Concordia U, Nebraska (NE)
Concordia U Wisconsin (WI)
Concord U (WV)
Dakota State U (SD)
Dakota Wesleyan U (SD)
Dana Coll (NE)
Davis & Elkins Coll (WV)
Defiance Coll (OH)
Doane Coll (NE)
Dordt Coll (IA)
Dowling Coll (NY)
East Carolina U (NC)
East Central U (OK)
Eastern Kentucky U (KY)
Eastern Michigan U (MI)
Eastern New Mexico U (NM)
Emmanuel Coll (GA)
Evangel U (MO)
Fairmont State U (WV)
Fayetteville State U (NC)
Ferris State U (MI)
Florida Ag and Mech U (FL)
Gannon U (PA)
Glenville State Coll (WV)
Grace Coll (IN)
Grace U (NE)
Grambling State U (LA)
Gwynedd-Mercy Coll (PA)
Hampton U (VA)
Hannibal-LaGrange Coll (MO)
Hardin-Simmons U (TX)
Hastings Coll (NE)
Henderson State U (AR)
Hofstra U (NY)
Howard Payne U (TX)
Huntington U (IN)
Illinois State U (IL)
Indiana State U (IN)
Inter American U of Puerto Rico, Fajardo Campus (PR)
Jarvis Christian Coll (TX)
John Brown U (AR)
Kent State U (OH)
Lambuth U (TN)
La Salle U (PA)
Lee U (TN)
Lehman Coll of the City U of New York (NY)
Lenoir-Rhyne Coll (NC)
Liberty U (VA)
Lincoln U (MO)
Lindenwood U (MO)
Louisiana Coll (LA)
Maranatha Baptist Bible Coll (WI)
McKendree U (IL)
McNeese State U (LA)
Mercyhurst Coll (PA)
Michigan Technological U (MI)
MidAmerica Nazarene U (KS)
Middle Tennessee State U (TN)
Midland Lutheran Coll (NE)
Minot State U (ND)
Mississippi Coll (MS)
Mississippi State U (MS)
Missouri Baptist U (MO)
Missouri State U (MO)
Morehead State U (KY)
Morgan State U (MD)
Morningside Coll (IA)
Mount Mary Coll (WI)
Mount Vernon Nazarene U (OH)
Murray State U (KY)
Nazareth Coll of Rochester (NY)
New York Inst of Technology (NY)
Niagara U (NY)
Nicholls State U (LA)
North Carolina Ag and Tech State U (NC)
Northeastern State U (OK)
Northern State U (SD)
Northwestern Coll (IA)
Northwestern Oklahoma State U (OK)
Northwestern State U of Louisiana (LA)
Northwest Missouri State U (MO)
Oakland City U (IN)
Oakwood Coll (AL)
Ohio Wesleyan U (OH)
Oklahoma Panhandle State U (OK)
Oklahoma Wesleyan U (OK)
Oral Roberts U (OK)
Pace U (NY)
Pacific Union Coll (CA)
Pillsbury Baptist Bible Coll (MN)
Rider U (NJ)
Robert Morris U (PA)
St. Ambrose U (IA)
Saint Mary's Coll (IN)
St. Mary's U (TX)
Saint Vincent Coll (PA)
Salem State Coll (MA)
Sam Houston State U (TX)
South Carolina State U (SC)
Southeast Missouri State U (MO)
Southern Arkansas U–Magnolia (AR)
Southern Utah U (UT)
Suffolk U (MA)
Tabor Coll (KS)
Temple U (PA)
Tennessee State U (TN)
Texas A&M U–Commerce (TX)
Texas Southern U (TX)
Thomas More Coll (KY)
Trinity Christian Coll (IL)
Tusculum Coll (TN)
Union Coll (KY)
Union Coll (NE)
Union U (TN)
U of Arkansas at Monticello (AR)
U of Arkansas at Pine Bluff (AR)
The U of British Columbia (BC, Canada)
U of Central Arkansas (AR)
U of Central Florida (FL)
U of Central Missouri (MO)
U of Central Oklahoma (OK)
The U of Findlay (OH)
U of Idaho (ID)
U of Illinois at Urbana–Champaign (IL)
U of Indianapolis (IN)
U of Lethbridge (AB, Canada)
U of Maine at Fort Kent (ME)
U of Maine at Machias (ME)
U of Mary (ND)
U of Maryland Eastern Shore (MD)
U of Minnesota, Twin Cities Campus (MN)
U of Missouri–Columbia (MO)
U of Missouri–St. Louis (MO)
The U of Montana (MT)
The U of Montana–Western (MT)
U of Nebraska at Kearney (NE)
U of Nebraska–Lincoln (NE)
U of Nevada, Reno (NV)
U of New Brunswick Fredericton (NB, Canada)
The U of North Carolina at Greensboro (NC)
U of North Dakota (ND)
U of Northern Iowa (IA)
U of Regina (SK, Canada)
U of Rio Grande (OH)
U of Saint Francis (IN)
U of Southern Indiana (IN)
U of Southern Mississippi (MS)
U of South Florida (FL)
The U of Tennessee (TN)
The U of Tennessee at Martin (TN)
U of the Ozarks (AR)
The U of Toledo (OH)
The U of Western Ontario (ON, Canada)
U of West Georgia (GA)
U of Wisconsin–Superior (WI)
U of Wisconsin–Whitewater (WI)
Utah State U (UT)
Utah Valley State Coll (UT)
Utica Coll (NY)
Valdosta State U (GA)
Valley City State U (ND)
Virginia State U (VA)
Viterbo U (WI)
Walla Walla U (WA)
Wayne State Coll (NE)
Weber State U (UT)
Western Kentucky U (KY)
Western Michigan U (MI)
Western New Mexico U (NM)
Westfield State Coll (MA)
Wiley Coll (TX)
Wilmington Coll (OH)
Winona State U (MN)
Winthrop U (SC)
Wright State U (OH)
York Coll (NE)
Youngstown State U (OH)

CAD/CADD DRAFTING/ DESIGN TECHNOLOGY

The Art Inst of Pittsburgh (PA)
Eastern Michigan U (MI)

CANADIAN GOVERNMENT AND POLITICS

The U of British Columbia (BC, Canada)

CANADIAN HISTORY

McGill U (QC, Canada)
U of Regina (SK, Canada)

CANADIAN STUDIES

Acadia U (NS, Canada)
Athabasca U (AB, Canada)
Bishop's U (QC, Canada)
Brock U (ON, Canada)
Duke U (NC)
Franklin Coll (IN)
McGill U (QC, Canada)
Memorial U of Newfoundland (NL, Canada)
Mount Allison U (NB, Canada)
Queen's U at Kingston (ON, Canada)
St. Francis Xavier U (NS, Canada)
St. Lawrence U (NY)
Simon Fraser U (BC, Canada)
State U of New York at Plattsburgh (NY)
Sterling Coll (VT)
Thompson Rivers U (BC, Canada)
Trent U (ON, Canada)
The U of British Columbia (BC, Canada)
U of Lethbridge (AB, Canada)
U of New Brunswick Fredericton (NB, Canada)
U of Ottawa (ON, Canada)
U of Prince Edward Island (PE, Canada)
U of Regina (SK, Canada)
U of Toronto (ON, Canada)
U of Vermont (VT)
The U of Western Ontario (ON, Canada)
The U of Winnipeg (MB, Canada)
Western Washington U (WA)
Wilfrid Laurier U (ON, Canada)
York U (ON, Canada)

CARDIOVASCULAR TECHNOLOGY

Gwynedd-Mercy Coll (PA)
Louisiana State U Health Sciences Center (LA)
Nebraska Methodist Coll (NE)
Pennsylvania Coll of Technology (PA)
Rochester Inst of Technology (NY)
State U of New York Upstate Medical U (NY)
U of Central Arkansas (AR)

CARIBBEAN STUDIES

Florida State U (FL)
Hofstra U (NY)
McGill U (QC, Canada)
Northwestern U (IL)

CARTOGRAPHY

Ball State U (IN)
Brigham Young U (UT)
East Central U (OK)
Kennesaw State U (GA)
Memorial U of Newfoundland (NL, Canada)
Missouri State U (MO)
Northern Michigan U (MI)
Queen's U at Kingston (ON, Canada)
Salem State Coll (MA)
Samford U (AL)
State U of New York Coll at Oneonta (NY)
Texas A&M U (TX)
Texas State U-San Marcos (TX)
The U of Akron (OH)
U of Wisconsin–Madison (WI)
U of Wisconsin–Platteville (WI)
Western Kentucky U (KY)

CELL AND MOLECULAR BIOLOGY

Bennington Coll (VT)
Bradley U (IL)
Bridgewater State Coll (MA)
Bucknell U (PA)
The Coll at Brockport, State U of New York (NY)
Concordia U (QC, Canada)
Connecticut Coll (CT)
Florida State U (FL)
Fort Lewis Coll (CO)
Grand Valley State U (MI)
Missouri State U (MO)
Northwest Nazarene U (ID)
Oklahoma State U (OK)
Pittsburg State U (KS)
Purdue U (IN)
State U of New York at Binghamton (NY)
Texas A&M U (TX)
Texas Tech U (TX)
Thompson Rivers U (BC, Canada)
U of California, Berkeley (CA)
U of California, Los Angeles (CA)
U of Colorado at Boulder (CO)
U of Illinois at Urbana–Champaign (IL)
The U of Tennessee at Martin (TN)
Western Washington U (WA)

CELL BIOLOGY AND ANATOMICAL SCIENCES RELATED

Northern Arizona U (AZ)
Rutgers, The State U of New Jersey, New Brunswick (NJ)
Tulane U (LA)
U of Arkansas (AR)
U of Connecticut (CT)
Washington & Jefferson Coll (PA)
Western Kentucky U (KY)
Yale U (CT)

CELL BIOLOGY AND ANATOMY

McGill U (QC, Canada)
Montana State U (MT)
The U of Western Ontario (ON, Canada)
Western State Coll of Colorado (CO)

CELL BIOLOGY AND HISTOLOGY

Ball State U (IN)
Beloit Coll (WI)
California State U, Fresno (CA)
California State U, Long Beach (CA)
California State U, San Marcos (CA)
Clarkson U (NY)
Colby Coll (ME)
The Coll at Brockport, State U of New York (NY)
The Coll of Saint Rose (NY)
Harvard U (MA)
Humboldt State U (CA)
Huntingdon Coll (AL)
Juniata Coll (PA)
Lindenwood U (MO)
Mansfield U of Pennsylvania (PA)
Marlboro Coll (VT)
McGill U (QC, Canada)
Memorial U of Newfoundland (NL, Canada)
Northeastern State U (OK)
Northwestern U (IL)
Ohio U (OH)
Oregon State U (OR)
Rutgers, The State U of New Jersey, New Brunswick (NJ)
San Francisco State U (CA)
Sonoma State U (CA)
Thompson Rivers U (BC, Canada)
Tulane U (LA)
The U of Arizona (AZ)
The U of British Columbia (BC, Canada)
U of California, Davis (CA)
U of California, Irvine (CA)
U of California, San Diego (CA)
U of California, Santa Barbara (CA)
U of California, Santa Cruz (CA)
U of Georgia (GA)
U of Illinois at Urbana–Champaign (IL)
U of Maine (ME)
U of Minnesota, Duluth (MN)
U of Minnesota, Twin Cities Campus (MN)
U of New Hampshire (NH)
U of Utah (UT)
The U of Western Ontario (ON, Canada)
U of Wisconsin–Madison (WI)
Western Washington U (WA)
William Jewell Coll (MO)
Worcester Polytechnic Inst (MA)

CELTIC LANGUAGES

U of California, Berkeley (CA)

CERAMIC ARTS AND CERAMICS

Alberta Coll of Art & Design (AB, Canada)
Alfred U (NY)
Aquinas Coll (MI)
Ball State U (IN)
Bard Coll at Simon's Rock (MA)
Bennington Coll (VT)
Bethany Coll (KS)
Bradley U (IL)
Brigham Young U (UT)
California Coll of the Arts (CA)
California State U, East Bay (CA)
California State U, Long Beach (CA)
The Cleveland Inst of Art (OH)
The Coll at Brockport, State U of New York (NY)
Coll of the Atlantic (ME)
Colorado State U (CO)
Concordia U (QC, Canada)
Concord U (WV)
Finlandia U (MI)
Grand Valley State U (MI)
Hampton U (VA)
Hofstra U (NY)
Indiana Wesleyan U (IN)
Inter American U of Puerto Rico, San Germán Campus (PR)
Kansas City Art Inst (MO)
Kent State U (OH)
Marlboro Coll (VT)
Maryland Inst Coll of Art (MD)
Marywood U (PA)
Massachusetts Coll of Art and Design (MA)
McNeese State U (LA)
Memphis Coll of Art (TN)
Minnesota State U Mankato (MN)
Nazareth Coll of Rochester (NY)
Northern Michigan U (MI)
Northwest Nazarene U (ID)
NSCAD U (NS, Canada)
Ohio Northern U (OH)
Ohio U (OH)
Pittsburg State U (KS)
Pratt Inst (NY)
Providence Coll (RI)
Rutgers, The State U of New Jersey, New Brunswick (NJ)
St. Cloud State U (MN)
Salve Regina U (RI)
School of the Art Inst of Chicago (IL)
School of the Museum of Fine Arts, Boston (MA)
Seton Hill U (PA)
Shawnee State U (OH)
State U of New York at New Paltz (NY)
Temple U (PA)
Trinity Christian Coll (IL)
The U of Akron (OH)
U of Dallas (TX)
U of Hartford (CT)
The U of Iowa (IA)
U of Kansas (KS)
U of Massachusetts Dartmouth (MA)
U of Miami (FL)
U of Michigan (MI)
U of Oregon (OR)
U of Regina (SK, Canada)
The U of Texas at El Paso (TX)
U of the District of Columbia (DC)
U of Wisconsin–Milwaukee (WI)
Washington U in St. Louis (MO)
Western State Coll of Colorado (CO)
Western Washington U (WA)
West Virginia Wesleyan Coll (WV)

CERAMIC SCIENCES AND ENGINEERING

Alfred U (NY)
Clemson U (SC)
Missouri U of Science and Technology (MO)
Rutgers, The State U of New Jersey, New Brunswick (NJ)
U of Georgia (GA)
U of Illinois at Urbana–Champaign (IL)

CHEMICAL ENGINEERING

Arizona State U (AZ)
Auburn U (AL)
Brigham Young U (UT)
Brown U (RI)
Bucknell U (PA)
California Inst of Technology (CA)
California State Polytechnic U, Pomona (CA)
California State U, Long Beach (CA)
Calvin Coll (MI)
Carnegie Mellon U (PA)

Case Western Reserve U (OH)
Christian Brothers U (TN)
City Coll of the City U of New York (NY)
Clarkson U (NY)
Clemson U (SC)
Cleveland State U (OH)
Colorado School of Mines (CO)
Colorado State U (CO)
Cooper Union for the Advancement of Science and Art (NY)
Cornell U (NY)
Drexel U (PA)
Elon U (NC)
Florida Ag and Mech U (FL)
Florida Inst of Technology (FL)
Florida Intl U (FL)
Florida State U (FL)
Gannon U (PA)
Georgia Inst of Technology (GA)
Hampton U (VA)
Harvard U (MA)
Illinois Inst of Technology (IL)
Iowa State U of Science and Technology (IA)
The Johns Hopkins U (MD)
Kansas State U (KS)
Lafayette Coll (PA)
Lakehead U (ON, Canada)
Lehigh U (PA)
Louisiana State U and Ag and Mech Coll (LA)
Massachusetts Inst of Technology (MA)
McGill U (QC, Canada)
Memorial U of Newfoundland (NL, Canada)
Miami U (OH)
Michigan State U (MI)
Michigan Technological U (MI)
Mississippi State U (MS)
Missouri U of Science and Technology (MO)
Montana State U (MT)
Murray State U (KY)
New Jersey Inst of Technology (NJ)
New Mexico Inst of Mining and Technology (NM)
North Carolina Ag and Tech State U (NC)
North Carolina State U (NC)
Northeastern U (MA)
Northwestern U (IL)
Ohio U (OH)
Oklahoma State U (OK)
Oregon State U (OR)
Penn State Abington (PA)
Penn State Altoona (PA)
Penn State Berks (PA)
Penn State Erie, The Behrend Coll (PA)
Penn State U Park (PA)
Polytechnic U of Puerto Rico (PR)
Prairie View A&M U (TX)
Princeton U (NJ)
Purdue U (IN)
Queen's U at Kingston (ON, Canada)
Rensselaer Polytechnic Inst (NY)
Rice U (TX)
Rose-Hulman Inst of Technology (IN)
Rowan U (NJ)
Royal Military Coll of Canada (ON, Canada)
Rutgers, The State U of New Jersey, New Brunswick (NJ)
South Dakota School of Mines and Technology (SD)
Stanford U (CA)
State U of New York Coll of Environmental Science and Forestry (NY)
Syracuse U (NY)
Tennessee Technological U (TN)
Texas A&M U (TX)
Texas Tech U (TX)
Thiel Coll (PA)
Tri-State U (IN)
Tufts U (MA)
Tulane U (LA)
Tuskegee U (AL)
Université de Sherbrooke (QC, Canada)
U at Buffalo, the State U of New York (NY)
The U of Akron (OH)
The U of Alabama (AL)
The U of Alabama in Huntsville (AL)
The U of Arizona (AZ)
U of Arkansas (AR)
The U of British Columbia (BC, Canada)
U of California, Berkeley (CA)
U of California, Davis (CA)
U of California, Irvine (CA)
U of California, Los Angeles (CA)
U of California, Riverside (CA)
U of California, San Diego (CA)
U of California, Santa Barbara (CA)
U of Cincinnati (OH)
U of Colorado at Boulder (CO)
U of Connecticut (CT)
U of Dayton (OH)
U of Delaware (DE)
U of Florida (FL)
U of Houston (TX)
U of Idaho (ID)
U of Illinois at Chicago (IL)
U of Illinois at Urbana–Champaign (IL)
The U of Iowa (IA)
U of Kansas (KS)
U of Louisiana at Lafayette (LA)
U of Louisville (KY)
U of Maine (ME)
U of Maryland, Baltimore County (MD)
U of Maryland, Coll Park (MD)
U of Massachusetts Amherst (MA)
U of Massachusetts Lowell (MA)
U of Michigan (MI)
U of Minnesota, Duluth (MN)
U of Minnesota, Twin Cities Campus (MN)
U of Mississippi (MS)
U of Missouri–Columbia (MO)
U of Nebraska–Lincoln (NE)
U of Nevada, Reno (NV)
U of New Brunswick Fredericton (NB, Canada)
U of New Hampshire (NH)
U of New Haven (CT)
U of New Mexico (NM)
U of North Dakota (ND)
U of Notre Dame (IN)
U of Oklahoma (OK)
U of Ottawa (ON, Canada)
U of Pennsylvania (PA)
U of Pittsburgh (PA)
U of Rhode Island (RI)
U of Rochester (NY)
U of South Alabama (AL)
U of South Carolina (SC)
U of Southern California (CA)
U of South Florida (FL)
The U of Tennessee (TN)
The U of Texas at Austin (TX)
The U of Toledo (OH)
U of Toronto (ON, Canada)
U of Tulsa (OK)
U of Utah (UT)
U of Virginia (VA)
The U of Western Ontario (ON, Canada)
U of Wisconsin–Madison (WI)
U of Wyoming (WY)
Vanderbilt U (TN)
Villanova U (PA)
Virginia Commonwealth U (VA)
Virginia Polytechnic Inst and State U (VA)
Washington and Lee U (VA)
Washington State U (WA)
Washington U in St. Louis (MO)
Wayne State U (MI)
Western Michigan U (MI)
West Virginia U (WV)
Widener U (PA)
Winona State U (MN)
Worcester Polytechnic Inst (MA)
Xavier U (OH)
Yale U (CT)
Youngstown State U (OH)

CHEMICAL ENGINEERING TECHNOLOGY

Lakehead U (ON, Canada)

CHEMICAL PHYSICS

Bowdoin Coll (ME)
Carnegie Mellon U (PA)
Hendrix Coll (AR)
Michigan State U (MI)
Michigan Technological U (MI)
Saginaw Valley State U (MI)
Simon Fraser U (BC, Canada)
Swarthmore Coll (PA)

CHEMICAL TECHNOLOGY

Dakota State U (SD)
Inter American U of Puerto Rico, Bayamón Campus (PR)
Lenoir-Rhyne Coll (NC)
Miami U (OH)
Murray State U (KY)
U of Regina (SK, Canada)

CHEMISTRY

Abilene Christian U (TX)
Acadia U (NS, Canada)
Adams State Coll (CO)
Adelphi U (NY)
Adrian Coll (MI)
Agnes Scott Coll (GA)
Alabama Ag and Mech U (AL)
Alabama State U (AL)
Albertus Magnus Coll (CT)
Albion Coll (MI)
Albright Coll (PA)
Alcorn State U (MS)
Alderson-Broaddus Coll (WV)
Alfred U (NY)
Allegheny Coll (PA)
Alma Coll (MI)
Alvernia Coll (PA)
American U (DC)
The American U of Athens (Greece)
American U of Beirut (Lebanon)
Amherst Coll (MA)
Anderson U (IN)
Andrews U (MI)
Angelo State U (TX)
Appalachian State U (NC)
Aquinas Coll (MI)
Arizona State U (AZ)
Arkansas State U (AR)
Armstrong Atlantic State U (GA)
Asbury Coll (KY)
Ashland U (OH)
Assumption Coll (MA)
Athens State U (AL)
Auburn U (AL)
Augsburg Coll (MN)
Augustana Coll (IL)
Augustana Coll (SD)
Augusta State U (GA)
Austin Coll (TX)
Austin Peay State U (TN)
Averett U (VA)
Azusa Pacific U (CA)
Baker U (KS)
Baldwin-Wallace Coll (OH)
Ball State U (IN)
Bard Coll (NY)
Bard Coll at Simon's Rock (MA)
Barnard Coll (NY)
Barry U (FL)
Barton Coll (NC)
Bates Coll (ME)
Baylor U (TX)
Belhaven Coll (MS)
Bellarmine U (KY)
Belmont U (TN)
Beloit Coll (WI)
Bemidji State U (MN)
Benedictine Coll (KS)
Benedictine U (IL)
Bennington Coll (VT)
Berea Coll (KY)
Berry Coll (GA)
Bethany Coll (KS)
Bethany Coll (WV)
Bethany Lutheran Coll (MN)
Bethel Coll (KS)
Bethel Coll (TN)
Bethel U (MN)
Bethune-Cookman U (FL)
Bishop's U (QC, Canada)
Blackburn Coll (IL)
Bloomfield Coll (NJ)
Bloomsburg U of Pennsylvania (PA)
Bluefield Coll (VA)
Bluffton U (OH)
Bob Jones U (SC)
Boise State U (ID)
Boston Coll (MA)
Boston U (MA)
Bowdoin Coll (ME)
Bowling Green State U (OH)
Bradley U (IL)
Brandeis U (MA)
Bridgewater Coll (VA)
Bridgewater State Coll (MA)
Brigham Young U (UT)
Brock U (ON, Canada)
Brown U (RI)
Bryn Mawr Coll (PA)
Bucknell U (PA)
Buffalo State Coll, State U of New York (NY)
Butler U (IN)
Cabrini Coll (PA)
California Inst of Technology (CA)
California Lutheran U (CA)
California Polytechnic State U, San Luis Obispo (CA)
California State Polytechnic U, Pomona (CA)
California State U, Chico (CA)
California State U, Dominguez Hills (CA)
California State U, East Bay (CA)
California State U, Fresno (CA)
California State U, Fullerton (CA)
California State U, Long Beach (CA)
California State U, Los Angeles (CA)
California State U, Sacramento (CA)
California State U, San Bernardino (CA)
California State U, San Marcos (CA)
California State U, Stanislaus (CA)
Calvin Coll (MI)
Cameron U (OK)
Canisius Coll (NY)
Capital U (OH)
Carlow U (PA)
Carnegie Mellon U (PA)
Carroll Coll (WI)
Carson-Newman Coll (TN)
Case Western Reserve U (OH)
Catawba Coll (NC)
The Catholic U of America (DC)
Cedar Crest Coll (PA)
Cedarville U (OH)
Centenary Coll of Louisiana (LA)
Central Coll (IA)
Central Connecticut State U (CT)
Central Michigan U (MI)
Central State U (OH)
Central Washington U (WA)
Centre Coll (KY)
Chapman U (CA)
Chatham U (PA)
Chestnut Hill Coll (PA)
Cheyney U of Pennsylvania (PA)
Chicago State U (IL)
Christian Brothers U (TN)
Christopher Newport U (VA)
The Citadel, The Military Coll of South Carolina (SC)
City Coll of the City U of New York (NY)
Claflin U (SC)
Claremont McKenna Coll (CA)
Clarion U of Pennsylvania (PA)
Clark Atlanta U (GA)
Clarke Coll (IA)
Clarkson U (NY)
Clark U (MA)
Clemson U (SC)
Cleveland State U (OH)
Coastal Carolina U (SC)
Coker Coll (SC)
Colby Coll (ME)
Colgate U (NY)
The Coll at Brockport, State U of New York (NY)
Coll of Charleston (SC)
The Coll of Idaho (ID)
Coll of Mount St. Joseph (OH)
Coll of Mount Saint Vincent (NY)
The Coll of New Jersey (NJ)
The Coll of New Rochelle (NY)
Coll of Saint Benedict (MN)
Coll of Saint Elizabeth (NJ)
Coll of Saint Mary (NE)
The Coll of Saint Rose (NY)
The Coll of St. Scholastica (MN)
Coll of Staten Island of the City U of New York (NY)
Coll of the Holy Cross (MA)
Coll of the Ozarks (MO)
The Coll of William and Mary (VA)
The Colorado Coll (CO)
Colorado School of Mines (CO)
Colorado State U (CO)
Colorado State U-Pueblo (CO)
Columbia Coll (SC)
Columbus State U (GA)
Concordia Coll (MN)
Concordia U (CA)
Concordia U (MI)
Concordia U (OR)
Concordia U (QC, Canada)
Concordia U Chicago (IL)
Concordia U, Nebraska (NE)
Concord U (WV)
Connecticut Coll (CT)
Converse Coll (SC)
Cornell Coll (IA)
Cornell U (NY)
Covenant Coll (GA)
Creighton U (NE)
Dana Coll (NE)
Dartmouth Coll (NH)
Davidson Coll (NC)
Davis & Elkins Coll (WV)
Delaware Valley Coll (PA)
Delta State U (MS)
Denison U (OH)
DePaul U (IL)
DePauw U (IN)
DeSales U (PA)
Dickinson Coll (PA)
Dillard U (LA)
Doane Coll (NE)
Dominican U (IL)
Dordt Coll (IA)
Drake U (IA)
Drew U (NJ)
Drexel U (PA)
Drury U (MO)
Duke U (NC)
Duquesne U (PA)
Earlham Coll (IN)
East Carolina U (NC)
East Central U (OK)
Eastern Illinois U (IL)
Eastern Kentucky U (KY)
Eastern Mennonite U (VA)
Eastern Michigan U (MI)
Eastern New Mexico U (NM)
East Stroudsburg U of Pennsylvania (PA)
East Tennessee State U (TN)
East Texas Baptist U (TX)
Eckerd Coll (FL)
Edinboro U of Pennsylvania (PA)
Elizabethtown Coll (PA)
Elon U (NC)
Emmanuel Coll (MA)
Emory & Henry Coll (VA)
Emory U (GA)
Emporia State U (KS)
Erskine Coll (SC)
Evangel U (MO)
Excelsior Coll (NY)
Fairfield U (CT)
Fairleigh Dickinson U, Coll at Florham (NJ)
Fairleigh Dickinson U, Metropolitan Campus (NJ)
Fairmont State U (WV)
Fayetteville State U (NC)
Ferris State U (MI)
Ferrum Coll (VA)
Florida Ag and Mech U (FL)
Florida Atlantic U (FL)
Florida Gulf Coast U (FL)
Florida Inst of Technology (FL)
Florida Intl U (FL)
Florida Southern Coll (FL)
Florida State U (FL)
Fort Lewis Coll (CO)
Framingham State Coll (MA)
Franciscan U of Steubenville (OH)
Francis Marion U (SC)
Franklin & Marshall Coll (PA)
Franklin Coll (IN)
Freed-Hardeman U (TN)
Fresno Pacific U (CA)
Frostburg State U (MD)
Furman U (SC)
Gannon U (PA)
Gardner-Webb U (NC)
George Fox U (OR)
George Mason U (VA)
Georgetown Coll (KY)
Georgetown U (DC)
The George Washington U (DC)
Georgia Coll & State U (GA)
Georgia Inst of Technology (GA)
Georgian Court U (NJ)
Georgia Southern U (GA)
Georgia Southwestern State U (GA)
Georgia State U (GA)
Gettysburg Coll (PA)
Glenville State Coll (WV)
Gonzaga U (WA)
Gordon Coll (MA)
Goucher Coll (MD)
Grambling State U (LA)
Grand Valley State U (MI)
Greensboro Coll (NC)
Greenville Coll (IL)
Grinnell Coll (IA)
Grove City Coll (PA)
Guilford Coll (NC)
Gustavus Adolphus Coll (MN)
Hamilton Coll (NY)
Hamline U (MN)
Hampden-Sydney Coll (VA)
Hampshire Coll (MA)
Hampton U (VA)
Hanover Coll (IN)
Harding U (AR)
Hardin-Simmons U (TX)
Hartwick Coll (NY)
Harvard U (MA)
Harvey Mudd Coll (CA)
Hastings Coll (NE)
Haverford Coll (PA)
Heidelberg Coll (OH)
Henderson State U (AR)
Hendrix Coll (AR)
High Point U (NC)
Hillsdale Coll (MI)
Hobart and William Smith Colls (NY)
Hofstra U (NY)
Hollins U (VA)
Holy Family U (PA)
Hood Coll (MD)
Hope Coll (MI)
Houghton Coll (NY)
Houston Baptist U (TX)
Howard Payne U (TX)
Humboldt State U (CA)
Hunter Coll of the City U of New York (NY)
Huntingdon Coll (AL)
Huntington U (IN)
Husson Coll (ME)

MAJORS AND MORE

Huston-Tillotson U (TX)
Idaho State U (ID)
Illinois Coll (IL)
Illinois Inst of Technology (IL)
Illinois State U (IL)
Illinois Wesleyan U (IL)
Immaculata U (PA)
Indiana State U (IN)
Indiana U Bloomington (IN)
Indiana U Kokomo (IN)
Indiana U Northwest (IN)
Indiana U of Pennsylvania (PA)
Indiana U–Purdue U Fort Wayne (IN)
Indiana U–Purdue U Indianapolis (IN)
Indiana U South Bend (IN)
Indiana U Southeast (IN)
Indiana Wesleyan U (IN)
Inter American U of Puerto Rico, Bayamón Campus (PR)
Inter American U of Puerto Rico, San Germán Campus (PR)
Iona Coll (NY)
Iowa State U of Science and Technology (IA)
Iowa Wesleyan Coll (IA)
Ithaca Coll (NY)
Jackson State U (MS)
Jacksonville State U (AL)
Jacksonville U (FL)
James Madison U (VA)
Jamestown Coll (ND)
Jarvis Christian Coll (TX)
John Brown U (AR)
John Carroll U (OH)
The Johns Hopkins U (MD)
Johnson C. Smith U (NC)
Judson Coll (AL)
Judson U (IL)
Juniata Coll (PA)
Kalamazoo Coll (MI)
Kansas State U (KS)
Kean U (NJ)
Keene State Coll (NH)
Kennesaw State U (GA)
Kent State U (OH)
Kentucky State U (KY)
Kentucky Wesleyan Coll (KY)
Kenyon Coll (OH)
Kettering U (MI)
King Coll (TN)
King's Coll (PA)
The King's U Coll (AB, Canada)
Knox Coll (IL)
Kutztown U of Pennsylvania (PA)
Lafayette Coll (PA)
LaGrange Coll (GA)
Lake Forest Coll (IL)
Lakehead U (ON, Canada)
Lambuth U (TN)
Lander U (SC)
La Roche Coll (PA)
La Salle U (PA)
La Sierra U (CA)
Laurentian U (ON, Canada)
Lawrence Technological U (MI)
Lawrence U (WI)
Lebanon Valley Coll (PA)
Lee U (TN)
Lehigh U (PA)
Lehman Coll of the City U of New York (NY)
Le Moyne Coll (NY)
LeMoyne-Owen Coll (TN)
Lenoir-Rhyne Coll (NC)
LeTourneau U (TX)
Lewis & Clark Coll (OR)
Lewis-Clark State Coll (ID)
Lewis U (IL)
Limestone Coll (SC)
Lincoln U (MO)
Lincoln U (PA)
Lindenwood U (MO)
Linfield Coll (OR)
Lipscomb U (TN)
Livingstone Coll (NC)
Lock Haven U of Pennsylvania (PA)
Longwood U (VA)
Loras Coll (IA)
Louisiana Coll (LA)
Louisiana State U and Ag and Mech Coll (LA)
Lourdes Coll (OH)
Loyola Coll in Maryland (MD)
Loyola Marymount U (CA)
Loyola U Chicago (IL)
Loyola U New Orleans (LA)
Lubbock Christian U (TX)
Luther Coll (IA)
Lycoming Coll (PA)
Lynchburg Coll (VA)
Lyon Coll (AR)
Macalester Coll (MN)
Madonna U (MI)
Malone Coll (OH)
Manchester Coll (IN)
Manhattanville Coll (NY)
Mansfield U of Pennsylvania (PA)
Marian Coll (IN)
Marian Coll of Fond du Lac (WI)
Marietta Coll (OH)
Marist Coll (NY)
Marlboro Coll (VT)
Marquette U (WI)
Marshall U (WV)
Martin U (IN)
Mary Baldwin Coll (VA)
Maryville Coll (TN)
Maryville U of Saint Louis (MO)
Massachusetts Coll of Pharmacy and Health Sciences (MA)
Massachusetts Inst of Technology (MA)
Mayville State U (ND)
McDaniel Coll (MD)
McGill U (QC, Canada)
McKendree U (IL)
McMurry U (TX)
McNeese State U (LA)
Memorial U of Newfoundland (NL, Canada)
Mercer U (GA)
Mercyhurst Coll (PA)
Meredith Coll (NC)
Merrimack Coll (MA)
Messiah Coll (PA)
Methodist U (NC)
Miami U (OH)
Miami U Hamilton (OH)
Michigan State U (MI)
Michigan Technological U (MI)
MidAmerica Nazarene U (KS)
Middlebury Coll (VT)
Middle Tennessee State U (TN)
Midland Lutheran Coll (NE)
Midwestern State U (TX)
Miles Coll (AL)
Millersville U of Pennsylvania (PA)
Milligan Coll (TN)
Millikin U (IL)
Millsaps Coll (MS)
Mills Coll (CA)
Minnesota State U Mankato (MN)
Minot State U (ND)
Misericordia U (PA)
Mississippi Coll (MS)
Mississippi State U (MS)
Mississippi U for Women (MS)
Mississippi Valley State U (MS)
Missouri Baptist U (MO)
Missouri Southern State U (MO)
Missouri State U (MO)
Missouri U of Science and Technology (MO)
Monmouth Coll (IL)
Monmouth U (NJ)
Montana State U (MT)
Montana State U–Billings (MT)
Montana Tech of The U of Montana (MT)
Montclair State U (NJ)
Moravian Coll (PA)
Morehead State U (KY)
Morehouse Coll (GA)
Morgan State U (MD)
Morningside Coll (IA)
Mount Allison U (NB, Canada)
Mount Holyoke Coll (MA)
Mount Marty Coll (SD)
Mount Mary Coll (WI)
Mount Saint Mary Coll (NY)
Mount St. Mary's Coll (CA)
Mount St. Mary's U (MD)
Mount Saint Vincent U (NS, Canada)
Mount Vernon Nazarene U (OH)
Muhlenberg Coll (PA)
Murray State U (KY)
Nazareth Coll of Rochester (NY)
Nebraska Wesleyan U (NE)
New Coll of Florida (FL)
New Jersey City U (NJ)
New Jersey Inst of Technology (NJ)
Newman U (KS)
New Mexico Highlands U (NM)
New Mexico Inst of Mining and Technology (NM)
New York Inst of Technology (NY)
New York U (NY)
Niagara U (NY)
Nicholls State U (LA)
North Carolina Ag and Tech State U (NC)
North Carolina Central U (NC)
North Carolina State U (NC)
North Carolina Wesleyan Coll (NC)
North Central Coll (IL)
North Dakota State U (ND)
Northeastern Illinois U (IL)
Northeastern State U (OK)
Northeastern U (MA)
Northern Arizona U (AZ)
Northern Illinois U (IL)
Northern Michigan U (MI)
Northern State U (SD)
North Georgia Coll & State U (GA)
Northland Coll (WI)
Northwestern Coll (IA)
Northwestern Oklahoma State U (OK)
Northwestern State U of Louisiana (LA)
Northwestern U (IL)
Northwest Missouri State U (MO)
Northwest Nazarene U (ID)
Norwich U (VT)
Oakland City U (IN)
Oakland U (MI)
Oakwood Coll (AL)
Oberlin Coll (OH)
Occidental Coll (CA)
Oglethorpe U (GA)
Ohio Dominican U (OH)
Ohio Northern U (OH)
Ohio U (OH)
Ohio Wesleyan U (OH)
Oklahoma Christian U (OK)
Oklahoma City U (OK)
Oklahoma Panhandle State U (OK)
Oklahoma State U (OK)
Oklahoma Wesleyan U (OK)
Old Dominion U (VA)
Oral Roberts U (OK)
Oregon State U (OR)
Otterbein Coll (OH)
Ouachita Baptist U (AR)
Pace U (NY)
Pacific Lutheran U (WA)
Pacific Union Coll (CA)
Pacific U (OR)
Paine Coll (GA)
Park U (MO)
Penn State Abington (PA)
Penn State Altoona (PA)
Penn State Berks (PA)
Penn State Erie, The Behrend Coll (PA)
Penn State U Park (PA)
Pepperdine U, Malibu (CA)
Peru State Coll (NE)
Pfeiffer U (NC)
Philadelphia U (PA)
Piedmont Coll (GA)
Pikeville Coll (KY)
Pittsburg State U (KS)
Pitzer Coll (CA)
Plymouth State U (NH)
Point Loma Nazarene U (CA)
Polytechnic U, Brooklyn Campus (NY)
Pomona Coll (CA)
Portland State U (OR)
Prairie View A&M U (TX)
Presbyterian Coll (SC)
Princeton U (NJ)
Providence Coll (RI)
Purchase Coll, State U of New York (NY)
Purdue U (IN)
Purdue U Calumet (IN)
Queens Coll of the City U of New York (NY)
Queen's U at Kingston (ON, Canada)
Queens U of Charlotte (NC)
Quincy U (IL)
Quinnipiac U (CT)
Radford U (VA)
Ramapo Coll of New Jersey (NJ)
Randolph Coll (VA)
Randolph-Macon Coll (VA)
Reed Coll (OR)
Regis Coll (MA)
Regis U (CO)
Rensselaer Polytechnic Inst (NY)
Rhode Island Coll (RI)
Rhodes Coll (TN)
Rice U (TX)
The Richard Stockton Coll of New Jersey (NJ)
Rider U (NJ)
Ripon Coll (WI)
Roanoke Coll (VA)
Roberts Wesleyan Coll (NY)
Rockford Coll (IL)
Rockhurst U (MO)
Roger Williams U (RI)
Rollins Coll (FL)
Roosevelt U (IL)
Rose-Hulman Inst of Technology (IN)
Rosemont Coll (PA)
Rowan U (NJ)
Royal Military Coll of Canada (ON, Canada)
Russell Sage Coll (NY)
Rutgers, The State U of New Jersey, Camden (NJ)
Rutgers, The State U of New Jersey, Newark (NJ)
Rutgers, The State U of New Jersey, New Brunswick (NJ)
Saginaw Valley State U (MI)
St. Ambrose U (IA)
St. Andrews Presbyterian Coll (NC)
St. Cloud State U (MN)
St. Edward's U (TX)
Saint Francis U (PA)
St. Francis Xavier U (NS, Canada)
St. John Fisher Coll (NY)
Saint John's U (MN)
St. John's U (NY)
Saint Joseph Coll (CT)
Saint Joseph's Coll (IN)
St. Joseph's Coll, New York (NY)
Saint Joseph's U (PA)
St. Lawrence U (NY)
Saint Louis U (MO)
Saint Martin's U (WA)
Saint Mary's Coll (IN)
Saint Mary's Coll of California (CA)
St. Mary's Coll of Maryland (MD)
St. Mary's U (TX)
Saint Mary's U of Minnesota (MN)
Saint Michael's Coll (VT)
St. Norbert Coll (WI)
St. Olaf Coll (MN)
St. Thomas U (FL)
Saint Vincent Coll (PA)
Saint Xavier U (IL)
Salem Coll (NC)
Salem State Coll (MA)
Salisbury U (MD)
Salve Regina U (RI)
Samford U (AL)
Sam Houston State U (TX)
San Diego State U (CA)
San Francisco State U (CA)
Santa Clara U (CA)
Sarah Lawrence Coll (NY)
Schreiner U (TX)
Scripps Coll (CA)
Seattle Pacific U (WA)
Seattle U (WA)
Seton Hill U (PA)
Sewanee: The U of the South (TN)
Shawnee State U (OH)
Shaw U (NC)
Shenandoah U (VA)
Shepherd U (WV)
Shippensburg U of Pennsylvania (PA)
Shorter Coll (GA)
Siena Coll (NY)
Siena Heights U (MI)
Simmons Coll (MA)
Simon Fraser U (BC, Canada)
Simpson Coll (IA)
Skidmore Coll (NY)
Slippery Rock U of Pennsylvania (PA)
Smith Coll (MA)
Sonoma State U (CA)
South Carolina State U (SC)
South Dakota School of Mines and Technology (SD)
South Dakota State U (SD)
Southeastern Louisiana U (LA)
Southeastern Oklahoma State U (OK)
Southeast Missouri State U (MO)
Southern Adventist U (TN)
Southern Arkansas U–Magnolia (AR)
Southern Connecticut State U (CT)
Southern Illinois U Carbondale (IL)
Southern Illinois U Edwardsville (IL)
Southern Methodist U (TX)
Southern Oregon U (OR)
Southern Polytechnic State U (GA)
Southern U and Ag and Mech Coll (LA)
Southern Utah U (UT)
Southern Wesleyan U (SC)
Southwest Baptist U (MO)
Southwestern Adventist U (TX)
Southwestern Coll (KS)
Southwestern Oklahoma State U (OK)
Southwestern U (TX)
Southwest Minnesota State U (MN)
Spelman Coll (GA)
Spring Arbor U (MI)
Spring Hill Coll (AL)
Stanford U (CA)
State U of New York at Binghamton (NY)
State U of New York at Fredonia (NY)
State U of New York at New Paltz (NY)
State U of New York at Oswego (NY)
State U of New York at Plattsburgh (NY)
State U of New York Coll at Geneseo (NY)
State U of New York Coll at Old Westbury (NY)
State U of New York Coll at Oneonta (NY)
State U of New York Coll at Potsdam (NY)
State U of New York Coll of Environmental Science and Forestry (NY)
Stephen F. Austin State U (TX)
Stetson U (FL)
Stonehill Coll (MA)
Stony Brook U, State U of New York (NY)
Suffolk U (MA)
Susquehanna U (PA)
Swarthmore Coll (PA)
Sweet Briar Coll (VA)
Syracuse U (NY)
Tabor Coll (KS)
Tarleton State U (TX)
Taylor U (IN)
Temple U (PA)
Tennessee State U (TN)
Tennessee Technological U (TN)
Tennessee Wesleyan Coll (TN)
Texas A&M Intl U (TX)
Texas A&M U (TX)
Texas A&M U–Commerce (TX)
Texas Christian U (TX)
Texas Lutheran U (TX)
Texas Southern U (TX)
Texas State U-San Marcos (TX)
Texas Tech U (TX)
Texas Woman's U (TX)
Thiel Coll (PA)
Thomas More Coll (KY)
Thompson Rivers U (BC, Canada)
Tougaloo Coll (MS)
Towson U (MD)
Transylvania U (KY)
Trent U (ON, Canada)
Trevecca Nazarene U (TN)
Trinity Christian Coll (IL)
Trinity Coll (CT)
Trinity Intl U (IL)
Trinity U (TX)
Tri-State U (IN)
Troy U (AL)
Truman State U (MO)
Tufts U (MA)
Tulane U (LA)
Tuskegee U (AL)
Union Coll (KY)
Union Coll (NE)
Union Coll (NY)
Union U (TN)
United States Air Force Acad (CO)
United States Naval Acad (MD)
Université de Sherbrooke (QC, Canada)
U at Albany, State U of New York (NY)
U at Buffalo, the State U of New York (NY)
The U of Akron (OH)
The U of Alabama (AL)
The U of Alabama at Birmingham (AL)
The U of Alabama in Huntsville (AL)
U of Alaska Fairbanks (AK)
The U of Arizona (AZ)
U of Arkansas (AR)
U of Arkansas at Fort Smith (AR)
U of Arkansas at Monticello (AR)
U of Arkansas at Pine Bluff (AR)
The U of British Columbia (BC, Canada)
The U of British Columbia–Okanagan (BC, Canada)
U of California, Berkeley (CA)
U of California, Davis (CA)
U of California, Irvine (CA)
U of California, Los Angeles (CA)
U of California, Riverside (CA)
U of California, San Diego (CA)
U of California, Santa Barbara (CA)
U of California, Santa Cruz (CA)
U of Central Arkansas (AR)
U of Central Florida (FL)
U of Central Missouri (MO)
U of Central Oklahoma (OK)
U of Charleston (WV)
U of Chicago (IL)
U of Cincinnati (OH)
U of Colorado at Boulder (CO)
U of Colorado Denver (CO)
U of Connecticut (CT)
U of Dallas (TX)
U of Dayton (OH)
U of Delaware (DE)
U of Denver (CO)
U of Evansville (IN)
U of Florida (FL)
U of Georgia (GA)
U of Great Falls (MT)
U of Guam (GU)
U of Hartford (CT)
U of Hawaii at Manoa (HI)
U of Houston (TX)
U of Houston–Clear Lake (TX)
U of Houston–Downtown (TX)
U of Idaho (ID)
U of Illinois at Chicago (IL)

U of Illinois at Springfield (IL)
U of Illinois at Urbana–Champaign (IL)
The U of Iowa (IA)
U of Kansas (KS)
U of King's Coll (NS, Canada)
U of La Verne (CA)
U of Lethbridge (AB, Canada)
U of Louisiana at Lafayette (LA)
U of Louisiana at Monroe (LA)
U of Louisville (KY)
U of Maine (ME)
U of Mary Hardin-Baylor (TX)
U of Maryland, Baltimore County (MD)
U of Maryland, Coll Park (MD)
U of Maryland Eastern Shore (MD)
U of Mary Washington (VA)
U of Massachusetts Amherst (MA)
U of Massachusetts Boston (MA)
U of Massachusetts Dartmouth (MA)
U of Massachusetts Lowell (MA)
U of Memphis (TN)
U of Miami (FL)
U of Michigan (MI)
U of Michigan–Dearborn (MI)
U of Michigan–Flint (MI)
U of Minnesota, Duluth (MN)
U of Minnesota, Twin Cities Campus (MN)
U of Mississippi (MS)
U of Missouri–Columbia (MO)
U of Missouri–Kansas City (MO)
U of Missouri–St. Louis (MO)
The U of Montana (MT)
U of Montevallo (AL)
U of Nebraska at Kearney (NE)
U of Nebraska at Omaha (NE)
U of Nebraska–Lincoln (NE)
U of Nevada, Las Vegas (NV)
U of Nevada, Reno (NV)
U of New Brunswick Fredericton (NB, Canada)
U of New England (ME)
U of New Hampshire (NH)
U of New Haven (CT)
U of New Mexico (NM)
U of New Orleans (LA)
U of North Alabama (AL)
The U of North Carolina at Asheville (NC)
The U of North Carolina at Chapel Hill (NC)
The U of North Carolina at Charlotte (NC)
The U of North Carolina at Greensboro (NC)
The U of North Carolina at Pembroke (NC)
The U of North Carolina Wilmington (NC)
U of North Dakota (ND)
U of Northern Colorado (CO)
U of Northern Iowa (IA)
U of North Florida (FL)
U of North Texas (TX)
U of Notre Dame (IN)
U of Oklahoma (OK)
U of Oregon (OR)
U of Ottawa (ON, Canada)
U of Pennsylvania (PA)
U of Pittsburgh (PA)
U of Pittsburgh at Bradford (PA)
U of Pittsburgh at Johnstown (PA)
U of Portland (OR)
U of Prince Edward Island (PE, Canada)
U of Puerto Rico at Humacao (PR)
U of Puerto Rico at Utuado (PR)
U of Puerto Rico, Cayey U Coll (PR)
U of Puget Sound (WA)
U of Redlands (CA)
U of Regina (SK, Canada)
U of Rhode Island (RI)
U of Richmond (VA)
U of Rio Grande (OH)
U of Rochester (NY)
U of Saint Francis (IN)
U of Saint Mary (KS)
U of St. Thomas (MN)
U of St. Thomas (TX)
U of San Diego (CA)
U of Science and Arts of Oklahoma (OK)
The U of Scranton (PA)
U of Sioux Falls (SD)
U of South Alabama (AL)
U of South Carolina (SC)
U of South Carolina Aiken (SC)
U of South Carolina Upstate (SC)
The U of South Dakota (SD)
U of Southern California (CA)
U of Southern Indiana (IN)
U of Southern Maine (ME)
U of Southern Mississippi (MS)
U of South Florida (FL)
The U of Tampa (FL)
The U of Tennessee (TN)
The U of Tennessee at Chattanooga (TN)
The U of Tennessee at Martin (TN)
The U of Texas at Arlington (TX)
The U of Texas at Austin (TX)
The U of Texas at Brownsville (TX)
The U of Texas at Dallas (TX)
The U of Texas at El Paso (TX)
The U of Texas at San Antonio (TX)
The U of Texas at Tyler (TX)
The U of Texas of the Permian Basin (TX)
The U of Texas–Pan American (TX)
U of the District of Columbia (DC)
U of the Incarnate Word (TX)
U of the Ozarks (AR)
U of the Pacific (CA)
U of the Sacred Heart (PR)
U of the Sciences in Philadelphia (PA)
U of the Virgin Islands (VI)
The U of Toledo (OH)
U of Toronto (ON, Canada)
U of Tulsa (OK)
U of Utah (UT)
U of Vermont (VT)
U of Victoria (BC, Canada)
U of Virginia (VA)
The U of Virginia's Coll at Wise (VA)
The U of Western Ontario (ON, Canada)
U of West Florida (FL)
U of West Georgia (GA)
U of Windsor (ON, Canada)
The U of Winnipeg (MB, Canada)
U of Wisconsin–Eau Claire (WI)
U of Wisconsin–Green Bay (WI)
U of Wisconsin–La Crosse (WI)
U of Wisconsin–Madison (WI)
U of Wisconsin–Milwaukee (WI)
U of Wisconsin–Oshkosh (WI)
U of Wisconsin–Parkside (WI)
U of Wisconsin–Stevens Point (WI)
U of Wisconsin–Superior (WI)
U of Wisconsin–Whitewater (WI)
U of Wyoming (WY)
Ursinus Coll (PA)
Utah State U (UT)
Utah Valley State Coll (UT)
Utica Coll (NY)
Valdosta State U (GA)
Valley City State U (ND)
Valparaiso U (IN)
Vanderbilt U (TN)
Vanguard U of Southern California (CA)
Vassar Coll (NY)
Villa Julie Coll (MD)
Villanova U (PA)
Virginia Commonwealth U (VA)
Virginia Military Inst (VA)
Virginia Polytechnic Inst and State U (VA)
Virginia State U (VA)
Virginia Wesleyan Coll (VA)
Viterbo U (WI)
Voorhees Coll (SC)
Wabash Coll (IN)
Wagner Coll (NY)
Wake Forest U (NC)
Walla Walla U (WA)
Walsh U (OH)
Warren Wilson Coll (NC)
Wartburg Coll (IA)
Washburn U (KS)
Washington & Jefferson Coll (PA)
Washington and Lee U (VA)
Washington Coll (MD)
Washington State U (WA)
Washington U in St. Louis (MO)
Wayland Baptist U (TX)
Waynesburg U (PA)
Wayne State Coll (NE)
Wayne State U (MI)
Weber State U (UT)
Wellesley Coll (MA)
Wells Coll (NY)
Wesleyan Coll (GA)
Wesleyan U (CT)
West Chester U of Pennsylvania (PA)
Western Carolina U (NC)
Western Connecticut State U (CT)
Western Illinois U (IL)
Western Kentucky U (KY)
Western Michigan U (MI)
Western New England Coll (MA)
Western New Mexico U (NM)
Western State Coll of Colorado (CO)
Western Washington U (WA)
West Liberty State Coll (WV)
Westminster Coll (MO)
Westminster Coll (UT)
Westmont Coll (CA)
West Texas A&M U (TX)
West Virginia U (WV)
West Virginia Wesleyan Coll (WV)
Wheaton Coll (IL)
Wheaton Coll (MA)
Wheeling Jesuit U (WV)
Whitman Coll (WA)
Whittier Coll (CA)
Whitworth U (WA)
Wichita State U (KS)
Widener U (PA)
Wiley Coll (TX)
Wilfrid Laurier U (ON, Canada)
Wilkes U (PA)
Willamette U (OR)
William Jewell Coll (MO)
Williams Coll (MA)
Wilmington Coll (OH)
Wilson Coll (PA)
Wingate U (NC)
Winona State U (MN)
Winthrop U (SC)
Wittenberg U (OH)
Wofford Coll (SC)
Worcester Polytechnic Inst (MA)
Worcester State Coll (MA)
Wright State U (OH)
Xavier U (OH)
Xavier U of Louisiana (LA)
Yale U (CT)
York Coll of Pennsylvania (PA)
York Coll of the City U of New York (NY)
York U (ON, Canada)
Youngstown State U (OH)

CHEMISTRY RELATED

Bridgewater State Coll (MA)
California State U, Chico (CA)
Carlow U (PA)
Carnegie Mellon U (PA)
Connecticut Coll (CT)
Dartmouth Coll (NH)
Duquesne U (PA)
Edinboro U of Pennsylvania (PA)
Florida State U (FL)
Keene State Coll (NH)
Kettering U (MI)
Lawrence Technological U (MI)
Lehigh U (PA)
Northern Arizona U (AZ)
Northern Michigan U (MI)
Ohio Northern U (OH)
Saginaw Valley State U (MI)
St. Edward's U (TX)
Saint Mary's Coll of California (CA)
Stony Brook U, State U of New York (NY)
Towson U (MD)
U at Buffalo, the State U of New York (NY)
U of California, Berkeley (CA)
U of California, Santa Barbara (CA)
U of Denver (CO)
U of Houston–Downtown (TX)
U of Massachusetts Dartmouth (MA)
U of Miami (FL)
U of Northern Iowa (IA)
U of Notre Dame (IN)
The U of Scranton (PA)
U of Southern Mississippi (MS)
U of the Pacific (CA)
U of Wisconsin–Eau Claire (WI)
U of Wisconsin–Whitewater (WI)
Washington & Jefferson Coll (PA)
Washington U in St. Louis (MO)
Western Illinois U (IL)
Western Michigan U (MI)
Western State Coll of Colorado (CO)
Whitman Coll (WA)

CHEMISTRY TEACHER EDUCATION

Alma Coll (MI)
Alvernia Coll (PA)
Appalachian State U (NC)
Arkansas State U (AR)
Assumption Coll (MA)
Averett U (VA)
Baylor U (TX)
Bethany Coll (KS)
Bethel U (MN)
Bethune-Cookman U (FL)
Bishop's U (QC, Canada)
Bluefield Coll (VA)
Boston U (MA)
Bridgewater Coll (VA)
Brigham Young U (UT)
Cabrini Coll (PA)
California State U, Chico (CA)
Capital U (OH)
Carroll Coll (WI)
The Catholic U of America (DC)
Centenary Coll of Louisiana (LA)
Central Michigan U (MI)
Central Washington U (WA)
Christian Brothers U (TN)
City Coll of the City U of New York (NY)
Coker Coll (SC)
The Coll at Brockport, State U of New York (NY)
The Coll of New Jersey (NJ)
The Coll of Saint Rose (NY)
Coll of the Ozarks (MO)
Colorado State U (CO)
Concordia Coll (MN)
Concordia U (MI)
Concordia U, Nebraska (NE)
Concordia U, St. Paul (MN)
Cornell U (NY)
Delta State U (MS)
DePaul U (IL)
Dordt Coll (IA)
East Central U (OK)
Eastern Mennonite U (VA)
Eastern Michigan U (MI)
East Texas Baptist U (TX)
Evangel U (MO)
Ferris State U (MI)
Florida Inst of Technology (FL)
Fort Lewis Coll (CO)
Franklin Coll (IN)
Glenville State Coll (WV)
Grand Canyon U (AZ)
Greenville Coll (IL)
Gustavus Adolphus Coll (MN)
Hastings Coll (NE)
Hofstra U (NY)
Hope Coll (MI)
Husson Coll (ME)
Indiana U Bloomington (IN)
Indiana U–Purdue U Fort Wayne (IN)
Indiana U South Bend (IN)
Indiana U Southeast (IN)
Inter American U of Puerto Rico, San Germán Campus (PR)
Ithaca Coll (NY)
John Brown U (AR)
Juniata Coll (PA)
Keene State Coll (NH)
Kent State U (OH)
Kentucky Wesleyan Coll (KY)
King Coll (TN)
Kutztown U of Pennsylvania (PA)
Lambuth U (TN)
Le Moyne Coll (NY)
Lenoir-Rhyne Coll (NC)
Lincoln U (MO)
Lindenwood U (MO)
Lipscomb U (TN)
Manhattanville Coll (NY)
Mansfield U of Pennsylvania (PA)
Marian Coll of Fond du Lac (WI)
Marist Coll (NY)
Maryville Coll (TN)
Maryville U of Saint Louis (MO)
Mayville State U (ND)
McGill U (QC, Canada)
McNeese State U (LA)
Mercyhurst Coll (PA)
Messiah Coll (PA)
Miami U Hamilton (OH)
Michigan State U (MI)
Millikin U (IL)
Minot State U (ND)
Missouri State U (MO)
Montana State U–Billings (MT)
Moravian Coll (PA)
Mount Marty Coll (SD)
Mount Mary Coll (WI)
Murray State U (KY)
Nazareth Coll of Rochester (NY)
New York Inst of Technology (NY)
New York U (NY)
Niagara U (NY)
North Carolina Central U (NC)
North Carolina State U (NC)
North Dakota State U (ND)
Northeastern State U (OK)
Northern Michigan U (MI)
Northwestern State U of Louisiana (LA)
Northwest Nazarene U (ID)
Ohio Dominican U (OH)
Ohio Northern U (OH)
Ohio Wesleyan U (OH)
Old Dominion U (VA)
Pace U (NY)
Pittsburg State U (KS)
Purdue U (IN)
Rhode Island Coll (RI)
Roberts Wesleyan Coll (NY)
Sacred Heart U (CT)
Saginaw Valley State U (MI)
St. Ambrose U (IA)
Saint Francis U (PA)
Saint Mary's U of Minnesota (MN)
Seton Hill U (PA)
Southern Arkansas U–Magnolia (AR)
Southern U and Ag and Mech Coll (LA)
Southwest Baptist U (MO)
Southwest Minnesota State U (MN)
State U of New York at Plattsburgh (NY)
State U of New York Coll at Old Westbury (NY)
State U of New York Coll at Oneonta (NY)
State U of New York Coll at Potsdam (NY)
State U of New York Coll of Environmental Science and Forestry (NY)
Syracuse U (NY)
Taylor U (IN)
Transylvania U (KY)
Trevecca Nazarene U (TN)
Trinity Christian Coll (IL)
Union Coll (NE)
The U of Arizona (AZ)
U of California, San Diego (CA)
U of Delaware (DE)
U of Evansville (IN)
U of Great Falls (MT)
U of Illinois at Chicago (IL)
U of Illinois at Urbana–Champaign (IL)
The U of Iowa (IA)
U of Louisiana at Lafayette (LA)
U of Louisiana at Monroe (LA)
U of Maine (ME)
U of Mary Hardin-Baylor (TX)
U of Michigan–Dearborn (MI)
U of Michigan–Flint (MI)
U of Missouri–Columbia (MO)
U of Missouri–St. Louis (MO)
U of Nebraska–Lincoln (NE)
U of New Hampshire (NH)
U of New Orleans (LA)
The U of North Carolina at Charlotte (NC)
The U of North Carolina Wilmington (NC)
U of Pittsburgh at Johnstown (PA)
U of Regina (SK, Canada)
U of Saint Francis (IN)
U of St. Thomas (MN)
The U of Tennessee at Martin (TN)
U of West Georgia (GA)
U of Windsor (ON, Canada)
U of Wisconsin–Superior (WI)
Utah State U (UT)
Utah Valley State Coll (UT)
Utica Coll (NY)
Valley City State U (ND)
Valparaiso U (IN)
Viterbo U (WI)
Washington State U (WA)
Washington U in St. Louis (MO)
Waynesburg U (PA)
Wayne State Coll (NE)
Weber State U (UT)
Western Michigan U (MI)
Western State Coll of Colorado (CO)
Western Washington U (WA)
Westminster Coll (UT)
Wheeling Jesuit U (WV)
Widener U (PA)
William Jewell Coll (MO)
Xavier U (OH)
Xavier U of Louisiana (LA)
York U (ON, Canada)

CHILD CARE AND SUPPORT SERVICES MANAGEMENT

Brigham Young U (UT)
Chestnut Hill Coll (PA)
Pacific Union Coll (CA)
Saint Mary-of-the-Woods Coll (IN)
Seton Hill U (PA)
Siena Heights U (MI)
State U of New York Coll of Agriculture and Technology at Cobleskill (NY)

CHILD CARE/GUIDANCE

Coll of the Ozarks (MO)

CHILD CARE PROVISION

Brigham Young U (UT)
Wayne State Coll (NE)

CHILD DEVELOPMENT

Albertus Magnus Coll (CT)
Alcorn State U (MS)
Appalachian State U (NC)
Ashland U (OH)
Auburn U (AL)
Bennington Coll (VT)
Bowling Green State U (OH)
Brigham Young U (UT)
California Polytechnic State U, San Luis Obispo (CA)
California State U, Dominguez Hills (CA)
California State U, East Bay (CA)
California State U, Fresno (CA)

California State U, Long Beach (CA)
California State U, Los Angeles (CA)
California State U, Sacramento (CA)
Carson-Newman Coll (TN)
Central Michigan U (MI)
Coll of the Ozarks (MO)
Concordia Coll (MN)
Concordia U, St. Paul (MN)
East Carolina U (NC)
East Tennessee State U (TN)
Florida State U (FL)
Freed-Hardeman U (TN)
Hampton U (VA)
Hope Intl U (CA)
Houston Baptist U (TX)
Humboldt State U (CA)
Kansas State U (KS)
Kuyper Coll (MI)
Lenoir-Rhyne Coll (NC)
Lesley U (MA)
Lewis-Clark State Coll (ID)
Madonna U (MI)
Meredith Coll (NC)
Miami U (OH)
Michigan State U (MI)
Minnesota State U Mankato (MN)
Missouri Baptist U (MO)
Mitchell Coll (CT)
Mount Ida Coll (MA)
Mount Saint Vincent U (NS, Canada)
National U (CA)
North Carolina Ag and Tech State U (NC)
Northwest Missouri State U (MO)
Ohio U (OH)
Oklahoma Christian U (OK)
Pittsburg State U (KS)
Point Loma Nazarene U (CA)
Portland State U (OR)
Quinnipiac U (CT)
St. Cloud State U (MN)
Saint Joseph Coll (CT)
San Diego State U (CA)
Seton Hill U (PA)
Southern New Hampshire U (NH)
State U of New York Coll at Oneonta (NY)
Tennessee Technological U (TN)
Texas Southern U (TX)
Texas Tech U (TX)
Texas Woman's U (TX)
Tufts U (MA)
The U of Akron (OH)
U of Alaska Fairbanks (AK)
U of Central Oklahoma (OK)
U of Georgia (GA)
U of Idaho (ID)
U of Illinois at Urbana–Champaign (IL)
U of La Verne (CA)
U of Maine (ME)
U of Maryland Eastern Shore (MD)
U of Nevada, Reno (NV)
U of New Hampshire (NH)
The U of North Carolina at Greensboro (NC)
U of Saint Mary (KS)
The U of Tennessee at Martin (TN)
The U of Texas at Arlington (TX)
U of the Incarnate Word (TX)
U of Victoria (BC, Canada)
The U of Western Ontario (ON, Canada)
U of Wisconsin–Madison (WI)
West Virginia U (WV)
Wheelock Coll (MA)
Youngstown State U (OH)

CHILD GUIDANCE

Coll of the Ozarks (MO)
St. Joseph's Coll, New York (NY)
Tougaloo Coll (MS)
U of Central Oklahoma (OK)
The U of North Carolina at Charlotte (NC)

CHINESE

Augustana Coll (IL)
Bard Coll (NY)
Bard Coll at Simon's Rock (MA)
Bates Coll (ME)
Bennington Coll (VT)
Brigham Young U (UT)
California State U, Long Beach (CA)
California State U, Los Angeles (CA)
Carnegie Mellon U (PA)
Claremont McKenna Coll (CA)
Colgate U (NY)
Concordia U (QC, Canada)
Connecticut Coll (CT)
Dartmouth Coll (NH)
Emory U (GA)
Georgetown U (DC)
The George Washington U (DC)
Grinnell Coll (IA)
Harvard U (MA)
Hobart and William Smith Colls (NY)
Hofstra U (NY)
Hunter Coll of the City U of New York (NY)
Lawrence U (WI)
Lincoln U (PA)
Middlebury Coll (VT)
Pacific Lutheran U (WA)
Pacific U (OR)
Pomona Coll (CA)
Portland State U (OR)
Reed Coll (OR)
Rutgers, The State U of New Jersey, New Brunswick (NJ)
San Francisco State U (CA)
Scripps Coll (CA)
Southwestern U (TX)
Stanford U (CA)
Swarthmore Coll (PA)
Trinity Coll (CT)
Trinity U (TX)
Tufts U (MA)
U at Albany, State U of New York (NY)
The U of British Columbia (BC, Canada)
U of California, Berkeley (CA)
U of California, Davis (CA)
U of California, Irvine (CA)
U of California, Los Angeles (CA)
U of California, Riverside (CA)
U of California, San Diego (CA)
U of California, Santa Barbara (CA)
U of Chicago (IL)
U of Colorado at Boulder (CO)
U of Hawaii at Manoa (HI)
The U of Iowa (IA)
U of Maryland, Coll Park (MD)
U of Massachusetts Amherst (MA)
U of Michigan (MI)
U of Minnesota, Twin Cities Campus (MN)
The U of Montana (MT)
U of Notre Dame (IN)
U of Oklahoma (OK)
U of Oregon (OR)
U of Pittsburgh (PA)
U of Regina (SK, Canada)
U of Utah (UT)
U of Vermont (VT)
U of Victoria (BC, Canada)
The U of Western Ontario (ON, Canada)
U of Wisconsin–Madison (WI)
Vassar Coll (NY)
Wake Forest U (NC)
Washington U in St. Louis (MO)
Wellesley Coll (MA)
Williams Coll (MA)
Wofford Coll (SC)
Yale U (CT)

CHINESE STUDIES

Bard Coll at Simon's Rock (MA)
Claremont McKenna Coll (CA)
Drew U (NJ)
Pacific Lutheran U (WA)
Sarah Lawrence Coll (NY)
U of the West (CA)

CHIROPRACTIC ASSISTANT

Hawai'i Pacific U (HI)

CHRISTIAN STUDIES

Alderson-Broaddus Coll (WV)
Bethany Coll (KS)
Bethel Coll (TN)
Bryan Coll (TN)
California Baptist U (CA)
Coll of Biblical Studies–Houston (TX)
The Coll of St. Scholastica (MN)
Crown Coll (MN)
Dallas Baptist U (TX)
Gordon Coll (MA)
Harding U (AR)
Hillsdale Coll (MI)
Horizon Coll & Sem (SK, Canada)
Houston Baptist U (TX)
Lindenwood U (MO)
Marian Coll (IN)
Mercer U (GA)
Mississippi Coll (MS)
Missouri Baptist U (MO)
Southern Baptist Theological Sem (KY)
Tennessee Wesleyan Coll (TN)
Truett-McConnell Coll (GA)
U of Mary Hardin-Baylor (TX)
Ursuline Coll (OH)
Vennard Coll (IA)
Wayland Baptist U (TX)

CINEMATOGRAPHY AND FILM/VIDEO PRODUCTION

Acad of Art U (CA)
The Art Inst of Atlanta (GA)
The Art Inst of California–Los Angeles (CA)
The Art Inst of California–Sacramento (CA)
The Art Inst of California–San Francisco (CA)
The Art Inst of California–Sunnyvale (CA)
The Art Inst of Charleston (SC)
The Art Inst of Dallas (TX)
The Art Inst of Houston (TX)
The Art Inst of Jacksonville (FL)
The Art Inst of Las Vegas (NV)
The Art Inst of Phoenix (AZ)
The Art Inst of Salt Lake City (UT)
The Art Inst of Seattle (WA)
The Art Inst of Tampa (FL)
The Art Inst of Tucson (AZ)
Bard Coll (NY)
Bennington Coll (VT)
Bob Jones U (SC)
Boston U (MA)
Bowling Green State U (OH)
Brigham Young U (UT)
Burlington Coll (VT)
California State U, Long Beach (CA)
Chapman U (CA)
City Coll of the City U of New York (NY)
Coll of Staten Island of the City U of New York (NY)
Collins Coll: A School of Design and Technology (AZ)
Columbia Coll Chicago (IL)
Concordia U (QC, Canada)
DeSales U (PA)
Drexel U (PA)
Emerson Coll (MA)
The Evergreen State Coll (WA)
Fairleigh Dickinson U, Coll at Florham (NJ)
Fitchburg State Coll (MA)
Five Towns Coll (NY)
Florida State U (FL)
George Fox U (OR)
Grand Valley State U (MI)
Hawai'i Pacific U (HI)
Hunter Coll of the City U of New York (NY)
The Illinois Inst of Art–Chicago (IL)
The Illinois Inst of Art–Schaumburg (IL)
Ithaca Coll (NY)
Keene State Coll (NH)
Loyola Marymount U (CA)
Maharishi U of Management (IA)
Massachusetts Coll of Art and Design (MA)
Miami Intl U of Art & Design (FL)
Middlebury Coll (VT)
Montana State U (MT)
Montclair State U (NJ)
New England School of Communications (ME)
New Mexico Highlands U (NM)
New York U (NY)
North Carolina School of the Arts (NC)
Northern Michigan U (MI)
Northwestern Coll (IA)
Ohio U (OH)
Oklahoma City U (OK)
Point Park U (PA)
Pratt Inst (NY)
Purchase Coll, State U of New York (NY)
Quinnipiac U (CT)
Sacred Heart U (CT)
Sarah Lawrence Coll (NY)
Savannah Coll of Art and Design (GA)
School of the Art Inst of Chicago (IL)
School of the Museum of Fine Arts, Boston (MA)
School of Visual Arts (NY)
Southern Illinois U Carbondale (IL)
State U of New York at Binghamton (NY)
Syracuse U (NY)
U of Advancing Technology (AZ)
U of Central Arkansas (AR)
U of Central Florida (FL)
U of Hartford (CT)
U of Illinois at Chicago (IL)
The U of Iowa (IA)
U of Miami (FL)
The U of North Carolina Wilmington (NC)
U of Oklahoma (OK)
U of Regina (SK, Canada)
U of Southern California (CA)
Vanguard U of Southern California (CA)
Virginia Commonwealth U (VA)
Wayne State U (MI)
Webster U (MO)
York U (ON, Canada)

CITY/URBAN, COMMUNITY AND REGIONAL PLANNING

Alabama Ag and Mech U (AL)
Appalachian State U (NC)
Arizona State U (AZ)
Ball State U (IN)
Bridgewater State Coll (MA)
Buffalo State Coll, State U of New York (NY)
California Polytechnic State U, San Luis Obispo (CA)
California State Polytechnic U, Pomona (CA)
California State U, Chico (CA)
Concordia U (QC, Canada)
Cornell U (NY)
East Carolina U (NC)
Eastern Michigan U (MI)
Florida Atlantic U (FL)
Frostburg State U (MD)
Harvard U (MA)
Indiana U of Pennsylvania (PA)
Iowa State U of Science and Technology (IA)
Mansfield U of Pennsylvania (PA)
Massachusetts Inst of Technology (MA)
Miami U (OH)
Miami U Hamilton (OH)
Michigan State U (MI)
Minnesota State U Mankato (MN)
Missouri State U (MO)
New York U (NY)
Plymouth State U (NH)
Portland State U (OR)
St. Cloud State U (MN)
Saint Louis U (MO)
Salem State Coll (MA)
Savannah Coll of Art and Design (GA)
State U of New York Coll of Environmental Science and Forestry (NY)
Temple U (PA)
Texas State U-San Marcos (TX)
The U of Akron (OH)
The U of Arizona (AZ)
U of California, Davis (CA)
U of Cincinnati (OH)
U of Illinois at Urbana–Champaign (IL)
The U of Montana (MT)
U of Nevada, Las Vegas (NV)
U of New Hampshire (NH)
U of Southern California (CA)
U of Virginia (VA)
The U of Western Ontario (ON, Canada)
U of Windsor (ON, Canada)
Westfield State Coll (MA)
Wright State U (OH)

CIVIL ENGINEERING

Alabama Ag and Mech U (AL)
The American U of Athens (Greece)
American U of Beirut (Lebanon)
Arizona State U (AZ)
Auburn U (AL)
Boise State U (ID)
Bradley U (IL)
Brigham Young U (UT)
Brown U (RI)
Bucknell U (PA)
California Baptist U (CA)
California Polytechnic State U, San Luis Obispo (CA)
California State Polytechnic U, Pomona (CA)
California State U, Chico (CA)
California State U, Fresno (CA)
California State U, Fullerton (CA)
California State U, Long Beach (CA)
California State U, Los Angeles (CA)
California State U, Sacramento (CA)
Calvin Coll (MI)
Carnegie Mellon U (PA)
Case Western Reserve U (OH)
The Catholic U of America (DC)
Christian Brothers U (TN)
The Citadel, The Military Coll of South Carolina (SC)
City Coll of the City U of New York (NY)
Clarkson U (NY)
Clemson U (SC)
Cleveland State U (OH)
Colorado School of Mines (CO)
Colorado State U (CO)
Concordia U (QC, Canada)
Cooper Union for the Advancement of Science and Art (NY)
Cornell U (NY)
Dordt Coll (IA)
Drexel U (PA)
Duke U (NC)
Florida Ag and Mech U (FL)
Florida Atlantic U (FL)
Florida Gulf Coast U (FL)
Florida Inst of Technology (FL)
Florida Intl U (FL)
Florida State U (FL)
The George Washington U (DC)
Georgia Inst of Technology (GA)
Georgia Southern U (GA)
Gonzaga U (WA)
Harvard U (MA)
Hofstra U (NY)
Idaho State U (ID)
Illinois Inst of Technology (IL)
Indiana U–Purdue U Fort Wayne (IN)
Iowa State U of Science and Technology (IA)
Jackson State U (MS)
The Johns Hopkins U (MD)
Kansas State U (KS)
Lafayette Coll (PA)
Lakehead U (ON, Canada)
Lawrence Technological U (MI)
Lehigh U (PA)
Lincoln U (MO)
Louisiana State U and Ag and Mech Coll (LA)
Loyola Marymount U (CA)
Marquette U (WI)
Massachusetts Inst of Technology (MA)
McGill U (QC, Canada)
Memorial U of Newfoundland (NL, Canada)
Merrimack Coll (MA)
Messiah Coll (PA)
Michigan State U (MI)
Michigan Technological U (MI)
Minnesota State U Mankato (MN)
Mississippi State U (MS)
Missouri U of Science and Technology (MO)
Montana State U (MT)
Montana Tech of The U of Montana (MT)
Morgan State U (MD)
New Jersey Inst of Technology (NJ)
New Mexico Inst of Mining and Technology (NM)
North Carolina Ag and Tech State U (NC)
North Carolina State U (NC)
North Dakota State U (ND)
Northeastern U (MA)
Northern Arizona U (AZ)
Northwestern U (IL)
Norwich U (VT)
Ohio Northern U (OH)
Ohio U (OH)
Oklahoma State U (OK)
Old Dominion U (VA)
Oregon Inst of Technology (OR)
Oregon State U (OR)
Penn State Abington (PA)
Penn State Altoona (PA)
Penn State Berks (PA)
Penn State Erie, The Behrend Coll (PA)
Penn State U Park (PA)
Polytechnic U, Brooklyn Campus (NY)
Polytechnic U of Puerto Rico (PR)
Portland State U (OR)
Prairie View A&M U (TX)
Princeton U (NJ)
Purdue U (IN)
Queen's U at Kingston (ON, Canada)
Rensselaer Polytechnic Inst (NY)
Rice U (TX)
Rose-Hulman Inst of Technology (IN)
Rowan U (NJ)
Royal Military Coll of Canada (ON, Canada)
Rutgers, The State U of New Jersey, New Brunswick (NJ)
Saint Martin's U (WA)
San Diego State U (CA)
San Francisco State U (CA)
Santa Clara U (CA)
Seattle U (WA)
South Dakota School of Mines and Technology (SD)
South Dakota State U (SD)
Southern Illinois U Carbondale (IL)
Southern Illinois U Edwardsville (IL)
Southern Methodist U (TX)
Southern U and Ag and Mech Coll (LA)
Stanford U (CA)
Syracuse U (NY)

Temple U (PA)
Tennessee State U (TN)
Tennessee Technological U (TN)
Texas A&M U (TX)
Texas Tech U (TX)
Tri-State U (IN)
Tufts U (MA)
Tulane U (LA)
United States Air Force Acad (CO)
United States Coast Guard Acad (CT)
Université de Sherbrooke (QC, Canada)
U at Buffalo, the State U of New York (NY)
The U of Akron (OH)
The U of Alabama (AL)
The U of Alabama at Birmingham (AL)
The U of Alabama in Huntsville (AL)
U of Alaska Fairbanks (AK)
The U of Arizona (AZ)
U of Arkansas (AR)
The U of British Columbia (BC, Canada)
The U of British Columbia–Okanagan (BC, Canada)
U of California, Berkeley (CA)
U of California, Davis (CA)
U of California, Irvine (CA)
U of California, Los Angeles (CA)
U of Central Florida (FL)
U of Cincinnati (OH)
U of Colorado at Boulder (CO)
U of Colorado Denver (CO)
U of Connecticut (CT)
U of Dayton (OH)
U of Delaware (DE)
U of Evansville (IN)
U of Florida (FL)
U of Hartford (CT)
U of Hawaii at Manoa (HI)
U of Houston (TX)
U of Idaho (ID)
U of Illinois at Chicago (IL)
U of Illinois at Urbana–Champaign (IL)
The U of Iowa (IA)
U of Kansas (KS)
U of Louisiana at Lafayette (LA)
U of Louisville (KY)
U of Maine (ME)
U of Maryland, Coll Park (MD)
U of Massachusetts Amherst (MA)
U of Massachusetts Dartmouth (MA)
U of Massachusetts Lowell (MA)
U of Memphis (TN)
U of Miami (FL)
U of Michigan (MI)
U of Minnesota, Twin Cities Campus (MN)
U of Mississippi (MS)
U of Missouri–Columbia (MO)
U of Missouri–Kansas City (MO)
U of Missouri–St. Louis (MO)
U of Nebraska at Omaha (NE)
U of Nebraska–Lincoln (NE)
U of Nevada, Las Vegas (NV)
U of Nevada, Reno (NV)
U of New Brunswick Fredericton (NB, Canada)
U of New Hampshire (NH)
U of New Haven (CT)
U of New Mexico (NM)
U of New Orleans (LA)
The U of North Carolina at Charlotte (NC)
U of North Dakota (ND)
U of North Florida (FL)
U of Notre Dame (IN)
U of Oklahoma (OK)
U of Ottawa (ON, Canada)
U of Pittsburgh (PA)
U of Portland (OR)
U of Rhode Island (RI)
U of South Alabama (AL)
U of South Carolina (SC)
U of Southern California (CA)
U of South Florida (FL)
The U of Tennessee (TN)
The U of Texas at Arlington (TX)
The U of Texas at Austin (TX)
The U of Texas at El Paso (TX)
The U of Texas at San Antonio (TX)
The U of Texas at Tyler (TX)
U of the District of Columbia (DC)
U of the Pacific (CA)
The U of Toledo (OH)
U of Toronto (ON, Canada)
U of Utah (UT)
U of Vermont (VT)
U of Virginia (VA)
The U of Western Ontario (ON, Canada)
U of Windsor (ON, Canada)
U of Wisconsin–Madison (WI)
U of Wisconsin–Milwaukee (WI)
U of Wisconsin–Platteville (WI)
U of Wyoming (WY)
Ursinus Coll (PA)
Utah State U (UT)
Valparaiso U (IN)
Vanderbilt U (TN)
Villanova U (PA)
Virginia Military Inst (VA)
Virginia Polytechnic Inst and State U (VA)
Walla Walla U (WA)
Washington State U (WA)
Washington U in St. Louis (MO)
Wayne State U (MI)
Western Kentucky U (KY)
Western Michigan U (MI)
West Virginia U (WV)
Widener U (PA)
Worcester Polytechnic Inst (MA)
Youngstown State U (OH)

CIVIL ENGINEERING RELATED

Drexel U (PA)
Embry-Riddle Aeronautical U (FL)
George Mason U (VA)
Ohio Northern U (OH)

CIVIL ENGINEERING TECHNOLOGY

Alabama Ag and Mech U (AL)
Bluefield State Coll (WV)
Central Connecticut State U (CT)
Colorado State U-Pueblo (CO)
Fairleigh Dickinson U, Metropolitan Campus (NJ)
Fairmont State U (WV)
Florida Ag and Mech U (FL)
Fontbonne U (MO)
Georgia Southern U (GA)
Lakehead U (ON, Canada)
Murray State U (KY)
Old Dominion U (VA)
Point Park U (PA)
Rochester Inst of Technology (NY)
South Carolina State U (SC)
Southern Polytechnic State U (GA)
State U of New York Inst of Technology (NY)
Temple U (PA)
Texas Southern U (TX)
U of Cincinnati (OH)
U of Houston (TX)
U of Houston–Downtown (TX)
U of Massachusetts Lowell (MA)
The U of North Carolina at Charlotte (NC)
U of North Texas (TX)
U of Pittsburgh at Johnstown (PA)
The U of Toledo (OH)
Western Kentucky U (KY)
Youngstown State U (OH)

CLASSICAL, ANCIENT MEDITERRANEAN AND NEAR EASTERN STUDIES AND ARCHAEOLOGY

Bates Coll (ME)
Bowdoin Coll (ME)
Brigham Young U (UT)
Creighton U (NE)
Lycoming Coll (PA)
Samford U (AL)
U of California, Berkeley (CA)
U of California, Davis (CA)
U of California, Irvine (CA)
U of California, Los Angeles (CA)
U of Ottawa (ON, Canada)
U of Toronto (ON, Canada)

CLASSICS

Barnard Coll (NY)
Emory U (GA)
Furman U (SC)
Hunter Coll of the City U of New York (NY)
Montclair State U (NJ)
Pitzer Coll (CA)
Pontifical Coll Josephinum (OH)
Rockford Coll (IL)
The U of Arizona (AZ)
U of Hawaii at Manoa (HI)
The U of North Carolina at Greensboro (NC)
The U of Western Ontario (ON, Canada)
Ursinus Coll (PA)
Virginia Wesleyan Coll (VA)
Washington and Lee U (VA)
York U (ON, Canada)

CLASSICS AND CLASSICAL LANGUAGES RELATED

Austin Coll (TX)
Bryn Mawr Coll (PA)
California State U, Long Beach (CA)
The Catholic U of America (DC)
Concordia Coll (MN)
Lawrence U (WI)
New Coll of Florida (FL)
Rutgers, The State U of New Jersey, Newark (NJ)
Saint Louis U (MO)
San Diego State U (CA)
State U of New York at Binghamton (NY)
Tulane U (LA)
U of California, Los Angeles (CA)
U of St. Thomas (MN)
Wheaton Coll (IL)

CLASSICS AND LANGUAGES, LITERATURES AND LINGUISTICS

Acadia U (NS, Canada)
Agnes Scott Coll (GA)
Albertus Magnus Coll (CT)
Amherst Coll (MA)
Assumption Coll (MA)
Augustana Coll (IL)
Austin Coll (TX)
Ave Maria U (FL)
Ball State U (IN)
Baylor U (TX)
Beloit Coll (WI)
Bishop's U (QC, Canada)
Boston Coll (MA)
Boston U (MA)
Bowdoin Coll (ME)
Bowling Green State U (OH)
Brigham Young U (UT)
Brown U (RI)
Bryn Mawr Coll (PA)
Bucknell U (PA)
Calvin Coll (MI)
Case Western Reserve U (OH)
The Catholic U of America (DC)
Centre Coll (KY)
Christendom Coll (VA)
Claremont McKenna Coll (CA)
Clark U (MA)
Colby Coll (ME)
Colgate U (NY)
Coll of Charleston (SC)
The Coll of New Rochelle (NY)
Coll of Saint Benedict (MN)
Coll of the Holy Cross (MA)
The Coll of William and Mary (VA)
The Colorado Coll (CO)
Concordia U (QC, Canada)
Connecticut Coll (CT)
Cornell Coll (IA)
Cornell U (NY)
Dartmouth Coll (NH)
Davidson Coll (NC)
Denison U (OH)
DePauw U (IN)
Dickinson Coll (PA)
Drew U (NJ)
Duke U (NC)
Duquesne U (PA)
Earlham Coll (IN)
Emory U (GA)
The Evergreen State Coll (WA)
Florida State U (FL)
Franciscan U of Steubenville (OH)
Franklin & Marshall Coll (PA)
Georgetown U (DC)
The George Washington U (DC)
Gettysburg Coll (PA)
Grand Valley State U (MI)
Grinnell Coll (IA)
Gustavus Adolphus Coll (MN)
Hamilton Coll (NY)
Hampden-Sydney Coll (VA)
Hanover Coll (IN)
Harvard U (MA)
Haverford Coll (PA)
Hellenic Coll (MA)
Hillsdale Coll (MI)
Hobart and William Smith Colls (NY)
Hofstra U (NY)
Hollins U (VA)
Hope Coll (MI)
Hunter Coll of the City U of New York (NY)
Illinois Wesleyan U (IL)
Indiana U Bloomington (IN)
John Carroll U (OH)
The Johns Hopkins U (MD)
Kalamazoo Coll (MI)
Kent State U (OH)
Kenyon Coll (OH)
Knox Coll (IL)
La Salle U (PA)
Laurentian U (ON, Canada)
Lawrence U (WI)
Lehigh U (PA)
Lehman Coll of the City U of New York (NY)
Loyola Coll in Maryland (MD)
Loyola Marymount U (CA)
Loyola U Chicago (IL)
Loyola U New Orleans (LA)
Macalester Coll (MN)
Manhattanville Coll (NY)
Marlboro Coll (VT)
Marquette U (WI)
McGill U (QC, Canada)
Memorial U of Newfoundland (NL, Canada)
Mercer U (GA)
Miami U (OH)
Miami U Hamilton (OH)
Middlebury Coll (VT)
Millsaps Coll (MS)
Monmouth Coll (IL)
Moravian Coll (PA)
Mount Allison U (NB, Canada)
Mount Holyoke Coll (MA)
New York U (NY)
North Central Coll (IL)
North Dakota State U (ND)
Northwestern U (IL)
Oberlin Coll (OH)
Ohio U (OH)
Ohio Wesleyan U (OH)
Pacific Lutheran U (WA)
Penn State Abington (PA)
Penn State Altoona (PA)
Penn State Berks (PA)
Penn State Erie, The Behrend Coll (PA)
Penn State U Park (PA)
Pitzer Coll (CA)
Pomona Coll (CA)
Princeton U (NJ)
Purdue U (IN)
Randolph Coll (VA)
Reed Coll (OR)
Rhodes Coll (TN)
Rice U (TX)
Rockford Coll (IL)
Rollins Coll (FL)
Rutgers, The State U of New Jersey, Newark (NJ)
Rutgers, The State U of New Jersey, New Brunswick (NJ)
St. Francis Xavier U (NS, Canada)
St. John's Coll (NM)
Saint John's U (MN)
Saint Michael's Coll (VT)
St. Olaf Coll (MN)
Samford U (AL)
San Diego State U (CA)
San Francisco State U (CA)
Santa Clara U (CA)
Sarah Lawrence Coll (NY)
Scripps Coll (CA)
Seattle Pacific U (WA)
Sewanee: The U of the South (TN)
Siena Coll (NY)
Skidmore Coll (NY)
Smith Coll (MA)
Southern Illinois U Carbondale (IL)
Southwestern U (TX)
Stanford U (CA)
State U of New York at Binghamton (NY)
Swarthmore Coll (PA)
Sweet Briar Coll (VA)
Syracuse U (NY)
Temple U (PA)
Texas Tech U (TX)
Transylvania U (KY)
Trent U (ON, Canada)
Trinity Coll (CT)
Trinity U (TX)
Truman State U (MO)
Tufts U (MA)
Tulane U (LA)
Union Coll (NY)
U at Albany, State U of New York (NY)
U at Buffalo, the State U of New York (NY)
The U of Akron (OH)
U of Arkansas (AR)
The U of British Columbia (BC, Canada)
U of California, Berkeley (CA)
U of California, Irvine (CA)
U of California, Riverside (CA)
U of California, San Diego (CA)
U of California, Santa Barbara (CA)
U of California, Santa Cruz (CA)
U of Chicago (IL)
U of Cincinnati (OH)
U of Colorado at Boulder (CO)
U of Connecticut (CT)
U of Dallas (TX)
U of Evansville (IN)
U of Florida (FL)
U of Georgia (GA)
U of Houston (TX)
U of Idaho (ID)
U of Illinois at Chicago (IL)
U of Illinois at Urbana–Champaign (IL)
The U of Iowa (IA)
U of Kansas (KS)
U of King's Coll (NS, Canada)
U of Maine (ME)
U of Maryland, Coll Park (MD)
U of Mary Washington (VA)
U of Massachusetts Amherst (MA)
U of Massachusetts Boston (MA)
U of Miami (FL)
U of Michigan (MI)
U of Missouri–Columbia (MO)
The U of Montana (MT)
U of Nebraska–Lincoln (NE)
U of New Brunswick Fredericton (NB, Canada)
U of New Hampshire (NH)
U of New Mexico (NM)
The U of North Carolina at Asheville (NC)
The U of North Carolina at Chapel Hill (NC)
The U of North Carolina at Greensboro (NC)
U of North Dakota (ND)
U of Notre Dame (IN)
U of Oklahoma (OK)
U of Oregon (OR)
U of Ottawa (ON, Canada)
U of Pennsylvania (PA)
U of Pittsburgh (PA)
U of Puget Sound (WA)
U of Regina (SK, Canada)
U of Rhode Island (RI)
U of Richmond (VA)
U of Rochester (NY)
U of St. Thomas (MN)
U of South Carolina (SC)
The U of South Dakota (SD)
U of Southern California (CA)
U of Southern Maine (ME)
U of South Florida (FL)
The U of Tennessee (TN)
The U of Texas at Arlington (TX)
The U of Texas at Austin (TX)
The U of Texas at San Antonio (TX)
U of the Pacific (CA)
The U of Toledo (OH)
U of Toronto (ON, Canada)
U of Utah (UT)
U of Vermont (VT)
U of Victoria (BC, Canada)
U of Virginia (VA)
The U of Western Ontario (ON, Canada)
U of Windsor (ON, Canada)
The U of Winnipeg (MB, Canada)
U of Wisconsin–Madison (WI)
U of Wisconsin–Milwaukee (WI)
Ursinus Coll (PA)
Valparaiso U (IN)
Vanderbilt U (TN)
Vassar Coll (NY)
Villanova U (PA)
Wabash Coll (IN)
Wake Forest U (NC)
Washington U in St. Louis (MO)
Wayne State U (MI)
Wellesley Coll (MA)
Wesleyan U (CT)
Western Washington U (WA)
Wheaton Coll (MA)
Whitman Coll (WA)
Wilfrid Laurier U (ON, Canada)
Willamette U (OR)
Williams Coll (MA)
Wright State U (OH)
Xavier U (OH)
Yale U (CT)
York U (ON, Canada)

CLINICAL CHILD PSYCHOLOGY

St. John's U (NY)
U of Windsor (ON, Canada)

CLINICAL LABORATORY SCIENCE/MEDICAL TECHNOLOGY

Abilene Christian U (TX)
Albany Coll of Pharmacy of Union U (NY)
Anderson U (IN)
Andrews U (MI)
Angelo State U (TX)
Appalachian State U (NC)
Aquinas Coll (MI)
Arizona State U (AZ)
Arkansas State U (AR)
Armstrong Atlantic State U (GA)
Atlantic Union Coll (MA)
Auburn U (AL)
Augustana Coll (SD)
Augusta State U (GA)
Austin Peay State U (TN)
Averett U (VA)
Ball State U (IN)
Barry U (FL)

MAJORS AND MORE

Baylor U (TX)
Bellarmine U (KY)
Belmont Abbey Coll (NC)
Belmont U (TN)
Bemidji State U (MN)
Benedictine U (IL)
Bethune-Cookman U (FL)
Blackburn Coll (IL)
Bloomsburg U of Pennsylvania (PA)
Boise State U (ID)
Boston U (MA)
Bowling Green State U (OH)
Bradley U (IL)
Bridgewater Coll (VA)
Brigham Young U (UT)
California State U, Chico (CA)
California State U, Dominguez Hills (CA)
Cameron U (OK)
Carroll Coll (WI)
Carson-Newman Coll (TN)
Catawba Coll (NC)
The Catholic U of America (DC)
Cedarville U (OH)
Central Michigan U (MI)
Cheyney U of Pennsylvania (PA)
Clarion U of Pennsylvania (PA)
Coker Coll (SC)
The Coll at Brockport, State U of New York (NY)
Coll of Saint Elizabeth (NJ)
Coll of Saint Mary (NE)
The Coll of Saint Rose (NY)
Coll of Staten Island of the City U of New York (NY)
Coll of the Ozarks (MO)
Concordia Coll (MN)
Concord U (WV)
Defiance Coll (OH)
DePaul U (IL)
DeSales U (PA)
Dominican U (IL)
Dordt Coll (IA)
East Carolina U (NC)
Eastern Illinois U (IL)
Eastern Kentucky U (KY)
Eastern Mennonite U (VA)
Eastern Michigan U (MI)
Eastern New Mexico U (NM)
East Stroudsburg U of Pennsylvania (PA)
Elon U (NC)
Emory & Henry Coll (VA)
Erskine Coll (SC)
Evangel U (MO)
Fairleigh Dickinson U, Coll at Florham (NJ)
Fairleigh Dickinson U, Metropolitan Campus (NJ)
Felician Coll (NJ)
Ferris State U (MI)
Ferrum Coll (VA)
Florida Atlantic U (FL)
Florida Gulf Coast U (FL)
Florida Memorial U (FL)
Gannon U (PA)
Gardner-Webb U (NC)
George Mason U (VA)
The George Washington U (DC)
Georgia Southern U (GA)
Grand Valley State U (MI)
Greensboro Coll (NC)
Gwynedd-Mercy Coll (PA)
Harding U (AR)
Hartwick Coll (NY)
Henderson State U (AR)
High Point U (NC)
Houghton Coll (NY)
Humboldt State U (CA)
Idaho State U (ID)
Illinois Coll (IL)
Illinois State U (IL)
Indiana State U (IN)
Indiana U Kokomo (IN)
Indiana U of Pennsylvania (PA)
Indiana U–Purdue U Fort Wayne (IN)
Indiana U–Purdue U Indianapolis (IN)
Indiana U South Bend (IN)
Indiana U Southeast (IN)
Indiana Wesleyan U (IN)
Inter American U of Puerto Rico, Fajardo Campus (PR)
Inter American U of Puerto Rico, San Germán Campus (PR)
Iona Coll (NY)
Jamestown Coll (ND)
Kansas State U (KS)
Kean U (NJ)
Kent State U (OH)
Kentucky Wesleyan Coll (KY)
Keuka Coll (NY)
King Coll (TN)
King's Coll (PA)
Kutztown U of Pennsylvania (PA)
Lake Superior State U (MI)
Lee U (TN)
Lenoir-Rhyne Coll (NC)
Lincoln U (MO)
Lindenwood U (MO)
Loma Linda U (CA)
Longwood U (VA)
Loras Coll (IA)
Louisiana Coll (LA)
Louisiana State U Health Sciences Center (LA)
Lubbock Christian U (TX)
Madonna U (MI)
Malone Coll (OH)
Manchester Coll (IN)
Mansfield U of Pennsylvania (PA)
Marian Coll of Fond du Lac (WI)
Marist Coll (NY)
Marshall U (WV)
Mary Baldwin Coll (VA)
Maryville U of Saint Louis (MO)
Marywood U (PA)
McKendree U (IL)
McNeese State U (LA)
Mercyhurst Coll (PA)
Miami U (OH)
Miami U Hamilton (OH)
Michigan State U (MI)
Michigan Technological U (MI)
Midwestern State U (TX)
Minnesota State U Mankato (MN)
Minot State U (ND)
Misericordia U (PA)
Mississippi State U (MS)
Missouri Southern State U (MO)
Missouri State U (MO)
Monmouth U (NJ)
Moravian Coll (PA)
Morgan State U (MD)
Morningside Coll (IA)
Mount Marty Coll (SD)
Mount Mercy Coll (IA)
Mount Saint Mary Coll (NY)
Mount Vernon Nazarene U (OH)
Murray State U (KY)
National-Louis U (IL)
North Dakota State U (ND)
Northeastern State U (OK)
Northern Illinois U (IL)
Northern Michigan U (MI)
Northern State U (SD)
Northwestern Coll (IA)
Northwest Missouri State U (MO)
Oakland U (MI)
Oakwood Coll (AL)
Ohio Northern U (OH)
Oklahoma Christian U (OK)
Oklahoma Panhandle State U (OK)
Old Dominion U (VA)
Oral Roberts U (OK)
Oregon State U (OR)
Our Lady of the Lake Coll (LA)
Pace U (NY)
Pacific Union Coll (CA)
Peru State Coll (NE)
Prairie View A&M U (TX)
Purdue U (IN)
Purdue U Calumet (IN)
Quincy U (IL)
Radford U (VA)
Ramapo Coll of New Jersey (NJ)
Rhode Island Coll (RI)
Roanoke Coll (VA)
Roberts Wesleyan Coll (NY)
Rochester Inst of Technology (NY)
Roosevelt U (IL)
Rutgers, The State U of New Jersey, Camden (NJ)
Rutgers, The State U of New Jersey, Newark (NJ)
Rutgers, The State U of New Jersey, New Brunswick (NJ)
Sage Coll of Albany (NY)
Saginaw Valley State U (MI)
St. Cloud State U (MN)
Saint Francis U (PA)
St. John's U (NY)
Saint Joseph's Coll (IN)
Saint Leo U (FL)
Saint Louis U (MO)
Saint Mary-of-the-Woods Coll (IN)
Saint Mary's Coll (IN)
Saint Mary's U of Minnesota (MN)
St. Thomas Aquinas Coll (NY)
Salem Coll (NC)
Salem State Coll (MA)
Salisbury U (MD)
Salve Regina U (RI)
Sam Houston State U (TX)
San Francisco State U (CA)
Seattle U (WA)
Seton Hill U (PA)
Simpson Coll (IA)
South Dakota State U (SD)
Southeast Missouri State U (MO)
Southern Adventist U (TN)
Southern Arkansas U–Magnolia (AR)
Southern Wesleyan U (SC)
Southwest Baptist U (MO)
Southwestern Adventist U (TX)
Southwestern Oklahoma State U (OK)
State U of New York at Fredonia (NY)
State U of New York at Plattsburgh (NY)
State U of New York Upstate Medical U (NY)
Stephen F. Austin State U (TX)
Stetson U (FL)
Stony Brook U, State U of New York (NY)
Suffolk U (MA)
Tabor Coll (KS)
Tarleton State U (TX)
Taylor U (IN)
Tennessee State U (TN)
Texas Southern U (TX)
Texas State U-San Marcos (TX)
Texas Woman's U (TX)
Thiel Coll (PA)
Thomas More Coll (KY)
Trevecca Nazarene U (TN)
Tuskegee U (AL)
Union Coll (NE)
Union U (TN)
U at Buffalo, the State U of New York (NY)
The U of Alabama at Birmingham (AL)
The U of Arizona (AZ)
U of Arkansas for Medical Sciences (AR)
U of Central Arkansas (AR)
U of Central Florida (FL)
U of Central Missouri (MO)
U of Central Oklahoma (OK)
U of Cincinnati (OH)
U of Connecticut (CT)
U of Delaware (DE)
U of Evansville (IN)
The U of Findlay (OH)
U of Hartford (CT)
U of Houston (TX)
U of Illinois at Springfield (IL)
U of Indianapolis (IN)
The U of Iowa (IA)
U of Kansas (KS)
U of Louisiana at Monroe (LA)
U of Maine (ME)
U of Mary (ND)
U of Mary Hardin-Baylor (TX)
U of Maryland Eastern Shore (MD)
U of Massachusetts Boston (MA)
U of Massachusetts Dartmouth (MA)
U of Massachusetts Lowell (MA)
U of Michigan (MI)
U of Michigan–Flint (MI)
U of Minnesota, Twin Cities Campus (MN)
U of Mississippi (MS)
U of Mississippi Medical Center (MS)
The U of Montana (MT)
U of Nebraska Medical Center (NE)
U of Nevada, Las Vegas (NV)
U of New England (ME)
U of New Orleans (LA)
The U of North Carolina at Chapel Hill (NC)
The U of North Carolina at Charlotte (NC)
The U of North Carolina at Greensboro (NC)
U of North Dakota (ND)
U of North Texas (TX)
U of Rhode Island (RI)
U of Rio Grande (OH)
U of St. Francis (IL)
U of Saint Francis (IN)
The U of Scranton (PA)
U of Sioux Falls (SD)
U of South Alabama (AL)
U of Southern Mississippi (MS)
U of South Florida (FL)
The U of Tennessee (TN)
The U of Tennessee at Chattanooga (TN)
The U of Texas at Arlington (TX)
The U of Texas at Austin (TX)
The U of Texas at El Paso (TX)
The U of Texas at San Antonio (TX)
The U of Texas at Tyler (TX)
The U of Texas Medical Branch (TX)
The U of Texas–Pan American (TX)
The U of Texas Southwestern Medical Center at Dallas (TX)
U of the District of Columbia (DC)
U of the Sacred Heart (PR)
U of the Sciences in Philadelphia (PA)
The U of Toledo (OH)
U of Vermont (VT)
The U of Virginia's Coll at Wise (VA)
U of West Florida (FL)
U of Wisconsin–La Crosse (WI)
U of Wisconsin–Madison (WI)
U of Wisconsin–Milwaukee (WI)
U of Wisconsin–Oshkosh (WI)
U of Wisconsin–Stevens Point (WI)
Utah State U (UT)
Virginia Commonwealth U (VA)
Wake Forest U (NC)
Walla Walla U (WA)
Wartburg Coll (IA)
Wayne State U (MI)
Wesley Coll (DE)
Western Carolina U (NC)
Western Connecticut State U (CT)
Western Illinois U (IL)
Western Kentucky U (KY)
Western New Mexico U (NM)
West Liberty State Coll (WV)
West Texas A&M U (TX)
West Virginia U (WV)
Wichita State U (KS)
Wilkes U (PA)
William Jewell Coll (MO)
Winona State U (MN)
Winthrop U (SC)
Wright State U (OH)
Xavier U (OH)
York Coll of Pennsylvania (PA)
York Coll of the City U of New York (NY)
Youngstown State U (OH)

CLINICAL/MEDICAL LABORATORY ASSISTANT

Coll of Saint Benedict (MN)
Edinboro U of Pennsylvania (PA)

CLINICAL/MEDICAL LABORATORY SCIENCE AND ALLIED PROFESSIONS RELATED

Bellarmine U (KY)
Bloomfield Coll (NJ)
Carlow U (PA)
Hunter Coll of the City U of New York (NY)
Lebanon Valley Coll (PA)
Roosevelt U (IL)
Saint Louis U (MO)
U of Regina (SK, Canada)

CLINICAL/MEDICAL LABORATORY TECHNOLOGY

Alabama State U (AL)
Argosy U, Twin Cities (MN)
Auburn U (AL)
Barry U (FL)
California State U, Dominguez Hills (CA)
California State U, East Bay (CA)
Cameron U (OK)
East Central U (OK)
Edinboro U of Pennsylvania (PA)
Fairleigh Dickinson U, Metropolitan Campus (NJ)
Gardner-Webb U (NC)
Holy Family U (PA)
Longwood U (VA)
Madonna U (MI)
Marquette U (WI)
Morgan State U (MD)
Mount Saint Mary Coll (NY)
Northeastern U (MA)
Northern State U (SD)
Northwest Missouri State U (MO)
Our Lady of the Lake Coll (LA)
Pittsburg State U (KS)
Purdue U Calumet (IN)
St. Thomas Aquinas Coll (NY)
Slippery Rock U of Pennsylvania (PA)
Sonoma State U (CA)
The U of British Columbia (BC, Canada)
U of Maryland Eastern Shore (MD)
U of Missouri–Kansas City (MO)
The U of Montana (MT)
U of New Hampshire (NH)
U of New Mexico (NM)
U of Oklahoma (OK)
U of Science and Arts of Oklahoma (OK)
Washburn U (KS)
Winona State U (MN)

CLINICAL/MEDICAL SOCIAL WORK

New Mexico Highlands U (NM)
Slippery Rock U of Pennsylvania (PA)
U of St. Thomas (MN)
The U of Western Ontario (ON, Canada)

CLINICAL NUTRITION

Loyola U Chicago (IL)
Messiah Coll (PA)
U of North Dakota (ND)
West Chester U of Pennsylvania (PA)

CLINICAL PASTORAL COUNSELING/PATIENT COUNSELING

The U of Western Ontario (ON, Canada)

CLINICAL PSYCHOLOGY

Averett U (VA)
Biola U (CA)
Florida Inst of Technology (FL)
George Fox U (OR)
Husson Coll (ME)
Lakehead U (ON, Canada)
Mansfield U of Pennsylvania (PA)
Moravian Coll (PA)
Sam Houston State U (TX)
Simon Fraser U (BC, Canada)
Tennessee State U (TN)
The U of British Columbia (BC, Canada)
U of Michigan–Flint (MI)
U of New Brunswick Fredericton (NB, Canada)
U of Windsor (ON, Canada)
Western State Coll of Colorado (CO)

CLOTHING/TEXTILES

Bluffton U (OH)
Cheyney U of Pennsylvania (PA)
Jacksonville State U (AL)
Minnesota State U Mankato (MN)
Mississippi U for Women (MS)
North Carolina Ag and Tech State U (NC)
Northwest Missouri State U (MO)
Oregon State U (OR)
Philadelphia U (PA)
Tennessee Technological U (TN)
Texas Southern U (TX)
U of Arkansas at Pine Bluff (AR)
U of Central Oklahoma (OK)
U of Idaho (ID)
U of Minnesota, Twin Cities Campus (MN)
U of the District of Columbia (DC)
U of Wisconsin–Madison (WI)
Virginia Polytechnic Inst and State U (VA)

COGNITIVE PSYCHOLOGY AND PSYCHOLINGUISTICS

Averett U (VA)
Bard Coll at Simon's Rock (MA)
Brown U (RI)
California State U, Stanislaus (CA)
Dartmouth Coll (NH)
George Fox U (OR)
Harvard U (MA)
The Johns Hopkins U (MD)
Lawrence U (WI)
Massachusetts Inst of Technology (MA)
Northwestern U (IL)
Occidental Coll (CA)
State U of New York at Oswego (NY)
Tulane U (LA)
U of California, San Diego (CA)
U of California, Santa Cruz (CA)
U of Georgia (GA)
U of Kansas (KS)
U of Southern California (CA)
The U of Texas at Dallas (TX)
Vanderbilt U (TN)
Vassar Coll (NY)
Washington U in St. Louis (MO)
Wellesley Coll (MA)
Wilfrid Laurier U (ON, Canada)
Yale U (CT)

COGNITIVE SCIENCE

California State U, Fresno (CA)
Carnegie Mellon U (PA)
Case Western Reserve U (OH)
Central Michigan U (MI)
George Fox U (OR)
Hampshire Coll (MA)
Harvard U (MA)
Indiana U Bloomington (IN)
Lawrence U (WI)
McGill U (QC, Canada)
Occidental Coll (CA)
Pomona Coll (CA)
Queen's U at Kingston (ON, Canada)
Simon Fraser U (BC, Canada)
State U of New York at Oswego (NY)

The U of British Columbia (BC, Canada)
U of California, Berkeley (CA)
U of California, Los Angeles (CA)
U of Connecticut (CT)
U of Evansville (IN)
U of Pennsylvania (PA)
U of Rochester (NY)

COLLEGE STUDENT COUNSELING AND PERSONNEL SERVICES

The U of North Carolina at Pembroke (NC)

COMMERCIAL AND ADVERTISING ART

Alberta Coll of Art & Design (AB, Canada)
Albertus Magnus Coll (CT)
Anderson U (IN)
Anderson U (SC)
Arkansas State U (AR)
The Art Inst of Atlanta (GA)
Ashland U (OH)
Auburn U (AL)
Baker Coll of Owosso (MI)
Ball State U (IN)
Bemidji State U (MN)
Biola U (CA)
Bob Jones U (SC)
Boise State U (ID)
Boston U (MA)
Buffalo State Coll, State U of New York (NY)
California Coll of the Arts (CA)
California Inst of the Arts (CA)
California Polytechnic State U, San Luis Obispo (CA)
California State Polytechnic U, Pomona (CA)
California State U, Dominguez Hills (CA)
California State U, East Bay (CA)
California State U, Fresno (CA)
California State U, Long Beach (CA)
Carlow U (PA)
Carroll Coll (WI)
Carson-Newman Coll (TN)
Centenary Coll (NJ)
Clark U (MA)
The Cleveland Inst of Art (OH)
The Coll of New Jersey (NJ)
The Coll of Saint Rose (NY)
Colorado State U (CO)
Columbia Coll Chicago (IL)
Columbus Coll of Art & Design (OH)
Concordia U Chicago (IL)
Concordia U, Nebraska (NE)
Concordia U Wisconsin (WI)
Concord U (WV)
Curry Coll (MA)
Dominican U (IL)
Dordt Coll (IA)
Dowling Coll (NY)
Drake U (IA)
Drexel U (PA)
Eastern Kentucky U (KY)
Emmanuel Coll (MA)
Fairmont State U (WV)
Fashion Inst of Technology (NY)
Felician Coll (NJ)
Ferris State U (MI)
Florida Ag and Mech U (FL)
Florida Southern Coll (FL)
Florida State U (FL)
Fontbonne U (MO)
Freed-Hardeman U (TN)
Grand Valley State U (MI)
Hampton U (VA)
Huntington U (IN)
Indiana U Bloomington (IN)
Indiana U–Purdue U Fort Wayne (IN)
Intl Acad of Design & Technology (FL)
Intl Acad of Design & Technology (IL)
Iowa State U of Science and Technology (IA)
Keene State Coll (NH)
Kent State U (OH)
Kutztown U of Pennsylvania (PA)
Laguna Coll of Art & Design (CA)
La Roche Coll (PA)
Lipscomb U (TN)
Longwood U (VA)
Louisiana Coll (LA)
Loyola U New Orleans (LA)
Lycoming Coll (PA)
Lyndon State Coll (VT)
Marian Coll (IN)
Marietta Coll (OH)
Marymount Manhattan Coll (NY)
Massachusetts Coll of Art and Design (MA)
Memphis Coll of Art (TN)
Mercy Coll (NY)
Millikin U (IL)
Minnesota State U Mankato (MN)
Morningside Coll (IA)
Mount Ida Coll (MA)
Mount Mary Coll (WI)
Mount Olive Coll (NC)
Nazareth Coll of Rochester (NY)
The New England Inst of Art (MA)
New York Inst of Technology (NY)
Northeastern State U (OK)
Northeastern U (MA)
Northwest Missouri State U (MO)
Northwest Nazarene U (ID)
NSCAD U (NS, Canada)
Ohio Northern U (OH)
Ohio U (OH)
Oklahoma Christian U (OK)
Oklahoma City U (OK)
Oral Roberts U (OK)
Otis Coll of Art and Design (CA)
Paier Coll of Art, Inc. (CT)
Peru State Coll (NE)
Philadelphia U (PA)
Pittsburg State U (KS)
Portland State U (OR)
Pratt Inst (NY)
Purchase Coll, State U of New York (NY)
Queens Coll of the City U of New York (NY)
Rutgers, The State U of New Jersey, New Brunswick (NJ)
St. Norbert Coll (WI)
St. Thomas Aquinas Coll (NY)
Salem State Coll (MA)
Samford U (AL)
Sam Houston State U (TX)
Savannah Coll of Art and Design (GA)
School of Visual Arts (NY)
Seton Hill U (PA)
Simmons Coll (MA)
Southwest Baptist U (MO)
Southwestern Oklahoma State U (OK)
State U of New York at Fredonia (NY)
State U of New York at New Paltz (NY)
State U of New York at Oswego (NY)
Suffolk U (MA)
Syracuse U (NY)
Taylor U (IN)
Texas A&M U–Commerce (TX)
Trinity Christian Coll (IL)
Truman State U (MO)
Union Coll (NE)
U of Advancing Technology (AZ)
U of Central Missouri (MO)
U of Central Oklahoma (OK)
U of Cincinnati (OH)
U of Dayton (OH)
U of Delaware (DE)
U of Denver (CO)
U of Illinois at Chicago (IL)
U of Indianapolis (IN)
U of Massachusetts Dartmouth (MA)
U of Michigan (MI)
U of Minnesota, Duluth (MN)
U of Minnesota, Twin Cities Campus (MN)
U of New Haven (CT)
U of North Texas (TX)
U of Saint Francis (IN)
U of Sioux Falls (SD)
The U of Tennessee (TN)
The U of Texas at El Paso (TX)
U of the Pacific (CA)
U of Wisconsin–Platteville (WI)
U of Wisconsin–Stevens Point (WI)
Wartburg Coll (IA)
Washington U in St. Louis (MO)
Waynesburg U (PA)
Weber State U (UT)
West Liberty State Coll (WV)
West Texas A&M U (TX)
West Virginia Wesleyan Coll (WV)
Wichita State U (KS)
William Paterson U of New Jersey (NJ)
William Woods U (MO)
Winona State U (MN)
Woodbury U (CA)
York U (ON, Canada)

COMMERCIAL PHOTOGRAPHY

The Art Inst of Atlanta (GA)
The Art Inst of Tampa (FL)
Fashion Inst of Technology (NY)
Memphis Coll of Art (TN)
Rochester Inst of Technology (NY)
Savannah Coll of Art and Design (GA)
School of Visual Arts (NY)

COMMUNICATION AND JOURNALISM RELATED

Abilene Christian U (TX)
Anna Maria Coll (MA)
Arkansas State U (AR)
Ashford U (IA)
Auburn U (AL)
Berry Coll (GA)
Bowling Green State U (OH)
Brigham Young U (UT)
California Baptist U (CA)
California State U, Chico (CA)
Carlow U (PA)
Centenary Coll of Louisiana (LA)
Chestnut Hill Coll (PA)
Clemson U (SC)
The Coll at Brockport, State U of New York (NY)
Coll of the Ozarks (MO)
Columbia Coll (SC)
Concordia U (QC, Canada)
Drexel U (PA)
The Evergreen State Coll (WA)
Flagler Coll (FL)
Hannibal-LaGrange Coll (MO)
Hawai'i Pacific U (HI)
Illinois Inst of Technology (IL)
Indiana U Bloomington (IN)
Indiana U Kokomo (IN)
Ithaca Coll (NY)
Juniata Coll (PA)
Lehigh U (PA)
Lehman Coll of the City U of New York (NY)
Malone Coll (OH)
Marquette U (WI)
Mary Baldwin Coll (VA)
Mercer U (GA)
Mercy Coll (NY)
Milwaukee School of Eng (WI)
Mississippi Coll (MS)
Mount Mercy Coll (IA)
New England School of Communications (ME)
Northern Arizona U (AZ)
Northern Michigan U (MI)
Northwest Christian Coll (OR)
Notre Dame de Namur U (CA)
Ohio Northern U (OH)
Ohio U (OH)
Old Dominion U (VA)
Penn State Abington (PA)
Penn State Berks (PA)
Penn State Erie, The Behrend Coll (PA)
Penn State U Park (PA)
Point Park U (PA)
Quinnipiac U (CT)
Saint Mary's Coll of California (CA)
San Diego State U (CA)
Siena Heights U (MI)
Southeastern Oklahoma State U (OK)
State U of New York Inst of Technology (NY)
Sterling Coll (KS)
Syracuse U (NY)
U of Evansville (IN)
U of Illinois at Urbana–Champaign (IL)
U of Oklahoma (OK)
U of Wisconsin–Green Bay (WI)
Valparaiso U (IN)
Washington U in St. Louis (MO)
Webster U (MO)
Western Michigan U (MI)
West Virginia U (WV)
Wheeling Jesuit U (WV)

COMMUNICATION AND MEDIA RELATED

Alma Coll (MI)
Athabasca U (AB, Canada)
Calumet Coll of Saint Joseph (IN)
Canisius Coll (NY)
Carnegie Mellon U (PA)
Cascade Coll (OR)
Centenary Coll of Louisiana (LA)
Clayton State U (GA)
The Coll at Brockport, State U of New York (NY)
Coll of Santa Fe (NM)
Concordia U (QC, Canada)
Crown Coll (MN)
East Texas Baptist U (TX)
Eugene Lang Coll The New School for Liberal Arts (NY)
Fairleigh Dickinson U, Metropolitan Campus (NJ)
Florida State U (FL)
Franklin Coll Switzerland (Switzerland)
Georgetown Coll (KY)
Green Mountain Coll (VT)
Greenville Coll (IL)
Hood Coll (MD)
Houston Baptist U (TX)
Indiana U–Purdue U Fort Wayne (IN)
King's Coll (PA)
La Roche Coll (PA)
Loyola U Chicago (IL)
Miles Coll (AL)
Milligan Coll (TN)
Northwestern U (IL)
Penn State Erie, The Behrend Coll (PA)
Point Park U (PA)
Rochester Inst of Technology (NY)
Roger Williams U (RI)
St. Edward's U (TX)
Saint Leo U (FL)
Southern New Hampshire U (NH)
Southern Polytechnic State U (GA)
Southwestern Coll (KS)
Trinity Intl U (IL)
Université de Sherbrooke (QC, Canada)
U of Central Missouri (MO)
U of Colorado at Boulder (CO)
U of Evansville (IN)
U of Illinois at Springfield (IL)
The U of Western Ontario (ON, Canada)
Virginia Wesleyan Coll (VA)
Walsh U (OH)
Wilmington U (DE)

COMMUNICATION DISORDERS

Appalachian State U (NC)
Arizona State U (AZ)
Baldwin-Wallace Coll (OH)
Baylor U (TX)
Biola U (CA)
Bob Jones U (SC)
Boston U (MA)
Bowling Green State U (OH)
Bridgewater State Coll (MA)
Brock U (ON, Canada)
Butler U (IN)
California State U, Chico (CA)
California State U, Fresno (CA)
California State U, Fullerton (CA)
California State U, Long Beach (CA)
California State U, Los Angeles (CA)
Case Western Reserve U (OH)
Central Michigan U (MI)
The Coll of Saint Rose (NY)
Eastern Illinois U (IL)
Edinboro U of Pennsylvania (PA)
Emerson Coll (MA)
Harding U (AR)
Kansas State U (KS)
Longwood U (VA)
Mercy Coll (NY)
Minnesota State U Mankato (MN)
Minot State U (ND)
Northern Illinois U (IL)
Northwestern U (IL)
Oklahoma State U (OK)
Pace U (NY)
Penn State Abington (PA)
Penn State Altoona (PA)
Penn State Berks (PA)
Penn State Erie, The Behrend Coll (PA)
Penn State U Park (PA)
Radford U (VA)
St. Cloud State U (MN)
St. Mary's Coll of Maryland (MD)
San Diego State U (CA)
Southeast Missouri State U (MO)
Southern Illinois U Carbondale (IL)
State U of New York at Fredonia (NY)
State U of New York at Plattsburgh (NY)
Truman State U (MO)
The U of Akron (OH)
The U of Arizona (AZ)
U of Georgia (GA)
U of Houston (TX)
U of Kansas (KS)
U of Maine (ME)
U of Massachusetts Amherst (MA)
U of Nebraska at Kearney (NE)
U of North Dakota (ND)
U of Oregon (OR)
U of Rhode Island (RI)
The U of South Dakota (SD)
The U of Texas at Austin (TX)
U of Vermont (VT)
The U of Western Ontario (ON, Canada)
U of Wisconsin–Eau Claire (WI)
Wayne State U (MI)
Western Carolina U (NC)
Western Illinois U (IL)
West Texas A&M U (TX)
Winthrop U (SC)
Worcester State Coll (MA)

COMMUNICATION DISORDERS SCIENCES AND SERVICES RELATED

Ohio U (OH)
Ouachita Baptist U (AR)
St. Cloud State U (MN)
U of Missouri–Columbia (MO)
U of Oklahoma Health Sciences Center (OK)
The U of Western Ontario (ON, Canada)

COMMUNICATION/SPEECH COMMUNICATION AND RHETORIC

Abilene Christian U (TX)
Adams State Coll (CO)
Adrian Coll (MI)
Albright Coll (PA)
Alderson-Broaddus Coll (WV)
Alfred U (NY)
Allegheny Coll (PA)
Alvernia Coll (PA)
Anderson U (SC)
Angelo State U (TX)
Aquinas Coll (MI)
Arizona State U (AZ)
Arizona State U at the West campus (AZ)
Auburn U Montgomery (AL)
Augustana Coll (SD)
Augusta State U (GA)
Austin Coll (TX)
Avila U (MO)
Azusa Pacific U (CA)
Baker U (KS)
Baldwin-Wallace Coll (OH)
Baptist Bible Coll of Pennsylvania (PA)
Barry U (FL)
Baylor U (TX)
Belhaven Coll (MS)
Bellarmine U (KY)
Benedictine U (IL)
Bethany Coll (KS)
Bethany Coll (WV)
Bethany Lutheran Coll (MN)
Bethel U (MN)
Blackburn Coll (IL)
Bloomsburg U of Pennsylvania (PA)
Bluffton U (OH)
Bob Jones U (SC)
Boston Coll (MA)
Boston U (MA)
Bowling Green State U (OH)
Bradley U (IL)
Brewton-Parker Coll (GA)
Bridgewater State Coll (MA)
Brock U (ON, Canada)
Bryan Coll (TN)
Buffalo State Coll, State U of New York (NY)
Cabrini Coll (PA)
California Baptist U (CA)
California State U, Chico (CA)
California State U, Fresno (CA)
California State U, Fullerton (CA)
California State U, Los Angeles (CA)
California State U, Monterey Bay (CA)
California State U, Sacramento (CA)
California State U, San Marcos (CA)
California State U, Stanislaus (CA)
Calumet Coll of Saint Joseph (IN)
Calvin Coll (MI)
Capital U (OH)
Carlow U (PA)
Carroll Coll (WI)
The Catholic U of America (DC)
Cedar Crest Coll (PA)
Cedarville U (OH)
Central Coll (IA)
Central Connecticut State U (CT)
Central Michigan U (MI)
Chapman U (CA)
Chatham U (PA)
Christopher Newport U (VA)
Clarion U of Pennsylvania (PA)
Clarkson U (NY)
Clearwater Christian Coll (FL)
Cleveland State U (OH)
Coastal Carolina U (SC)
Coker Coll (SC)
The Coll at Brockport, State U of New York (NY)
Coll of Charleston (SC)
Coll of Mount St. Joseph (OH)
Coll of Saint Elizabeth (NJ)
The Coll of Saint Rose (NY)
The Coll of St. Scholastica (MN)
Coll of Santa Fe (NM)
Coll of Staten Island of the City U of New York (NY)
Colorado State U (CO)

MAJORS AND MORE

Columbia Coll (SC)
Concordia Coll (MN)
Concordia U (CA)
Concordia U (MI)
Concordia U (QC, Canada)
Concordia U Chicago (IL)
Concordia U, Nebraska (NE)
Cornell U (NY)
Creighton U (NE)
Dallas Baptist U (TX)
Davis & Elkins Coll (WV)
Delta State U (MS)
DePaul U (IL)
Dixie State Coll of Utah (UT)
Dominican U of California (CA)
Dowling Coll (NY)
Drury U (MO)
Duquesne U (PA)
East Carolina U (NC)
Eastern Connecticut State U (CT)
Eastern Mennonite U (VA)
Eastern New Mexico U (NM)
East Stroudsburg U of Pennsylvania (PA)
Eckerd Coll (FL)
Edinboro U of Pennsylvania (PA)
Elizabethtown Coll (PA)
Elon U (NC)
Embry-Riddle Aeronautical U (FL)
Emerson Coll (MA)
Emmanuel Coll (MA)
Emporia State U (KS)
The Evergreen State Coll (WA)
Fairleigh Dickinson U, Coll at Florham (NJ)
Fairleigh Dickinson U, Metropolitan Campus (NJ)
Fayetteville State U (NC)
Ferris State U (MI)
Fitchburg State Coll (MA)
Florida Atlantic U (FL)
Florida Inst of Technology (FL)
Florida Intl U (FL)
Florida Southern Coll (FL)
Florida State U (FL)
Fontbonne U (MO)
Franciscan U of Steubenville (OH)
Frostburg State U (MD)
Furman U (SC)
George Fox U (OR)
Georgian Court U (NJ)
Georgia Southern U (GA)
Gordon Coll (MA)
Grace Coll (IN)
Grace U (NE)
Grand Canyon U (AZ)
Great Lakes Christian Coll (MI)
Greensboro Coll (NC)
Hannibal-LaGrange Coll (MO)
Hardin-Simmons U (TX)
Hastings Coll (NE)
Hawai'i Pacific U (HI)
Hillsdale Coll (MI)
Hillsdale Free Will Baptist Coll (OK)
Hofstra U (NY)
Holy Family U (PA)
Hope Coll (MI)
Houston Baptist U (TX)
Howard Payne U (TX)
Humboldt State U (CA)
Huntingdon Coll (AL)
Huntington U (IN)
Idaho State U (ID)
Immaculata U (PA)
Indiana State U (IN)
Indiana U Bloomington (IN)
Indiana U East (IN)
Indiana U Kokomo (IN)
Indiana U Northwest (IN)
Indiana U of Pennsylvania (PA)
Indiana U–Purdue U Fort Wayne (IN)
Indiana U–Purdue U Indianapolis (IN)
Indiana U Southeast (IN)
Indiana Wesleyan U (IN)
Inter American U of Puerto Rico, Bayamón Campus (PR)
Iona Coll (NY)
Jacksonville State U (AL)
Jacksonville U (FL)
Jamestown Coll (ND)
Juniata Coll (PA)
Kansas State U (KS)
Kean U (NJ)
Keene State Coll (NH)
Kennesaw State U (GA)
Kentucky Wesleyan Coll (KY)
Keuka Coll (NY)
Keystone Coll (PA)
Kuyper Coll (MI)
Lake Forest Coll (IL)
La Sierra U (CA)
Le Moyne Coll (NY)
Lenoir-Rhyne Coll (NC)
Lewis & Clark Coll (OR)
Lewis-Clark State Coll (ID)
Liberty U (VA)
Lincoln U (PA)
Linfield Coll (OR)
Longwood U (VA)
Loyola Coll in Maryland (MD)
Loyola U Chicago (IL)
Loyola U New Orleans (LA)
Luther Coll (IA)
Lycoming Coll (PA)
Lynchburg Coll (VA)
Macalester Coll (MN)
Madonna U (MI)
Marian Coll (IN)
Marian Coll of Fond du Lac (WI)
Marietta Coll (OH)
Marquette U (WI)
Martin U (IN)
Mary Baldwin Coll (VA)
Marylhurst U (OR)
Marymount Manhattan Coll (NY)
Marymount U (VA)
McDaniel Coll (MD)
Mercyhurst Coll (PA)
Meredith Coll (NC)
Merrimack Coll (MA)
Messiah Coll (PA)
Metropolitan State U (MN)
Miami U Hamilton (OH)
Michigan State U (MI)
Michigan Technological U (MI)
Millersville U of Pennsylvania (PA)
Millikin U (IL)
Misericordia U (PA)
Mississippi Coll (MS)
Mississippi State U (MS)
Mississippi U for Women (MS)
Missouri Baptist U (MO)
Missouri Southern State U (MO)
Missouri State U (MO)
Molloy Coll (NY)
Monmouth U (NJ)
Montana Tech of The U of Montana (MT)
Montclair State U (NJ)
Morehead State U (KY)
Mount Mary Coll (WI)
Mount Mercy Coll (IA)
Mount St. Mary's U (MD)
Mount Vernon Nazarene U (OH)
Multnomah Bible Coll and Biblical Sem (OR)
Nazareth Coll of Rochester (NY)
Nebraska Wesleyan U (NE)
Neumann Coll (PA)
New Jersey City U (NJ)
New Mexico Highlands U (NM)
New York U (NY)
North Carolina State U (NC)
Northeastern U (MA)
Northern Arizona U (AZ)
Northern Illinois U (IL)
Northern Michigan U (MI)
Northwest Christian Coll (OR)
Northwestern Coll (MN)
Northwestern U (IL)
Northwest Nazarene U (ID)
Norwich U (VT)
Notre Dame de Namur U (CA)
Nova Southeastern U (FL)
Nyack Coll (NY)
Oakland U (MI)
Oglethorpe U (GA)
Ohio Dominican U (OH)
Ohio Northern U (OH)
Ohio U (OH)
Oral Roberts U (OK)
Oregon Inst of Technology (OR)
Ouachita Baptist U (AR)
Pace U (NY)
Palm Beach Atlantic U (FL)
Park U (MO)
Peace Coll (NC)
Penn State Abington (PA)
Penn State Altoona (PA)
Penn State Berks (PA)
Penn State Erie, The Behrend Coll (PA)
Penn State Harrisburg (PA)
Penn State U Park (PA)
Pepperdine U, Malibu (CA)
Pfeiffer U (NC)
Pikeville Coll (KY)
Pittsburg State U (KS)
Plymouth State U (NH)
Point Loma Nazarene U (CA)
Prescott Coll (AZ)
Purchase Coll, State U of New York (NY)
Purdue U (IN)
Purdue U North Central (IN)
Quincy U (IL)
Radford U (VA)
Ramapo Coll of New Jersey (NJ)
Randolph Coll (VA)
Regent U (VA)
Regis Coll (MA)
Regis U (CO)
Rensselaer Polytechnic Inst (NY)
Rhode Island Coll (RI)
The Richard Stockton Coll of New Jersey (NJ)
Ripon Coll (WI)
Roberts Wesleyan Coll (NY)
Rochester Coll (MI)
Rockhurst U (MO)
Roosevelt U (IL)
Rosemont Coll (PA)
Rowan U (NJ)
Rutgers, The State U of New Jersey, New Brunswick (NJ)
Saginaw Valley State U (MI)
St. John's U (NY)
St. Joseph's Coll, Suffolk Campus (NY)
Saint Joseph's U (PA)
Saint Louis U (MO)
Saint Mary's Coll (IN)
Saint Mary's Coll of California (CA)
St. Mary's Coll of Maryland (MD)
St. Mary's U (TX)
St. Norbert Coll (WI)
Saint Vincent Coll (PA)
Saint Xavier U (IL)
Salisbury U (MD)
San Diego Christian Coll (CA)
Santa Clara U (CA)
Seattle Pacific U (WA)
Seton Hill U (PA)
Shenandoah U (VA)
Shepherd U (WV)
Simon Fraser U (BC, Canada)
Simpson U (CA)
Slippery Rock U of Pennsylvania (PA)
Sonoma State U (CA)
Southeastern Louisiana U (LA)
Southeastern Oklahoma State U (OK)
Southeastern U (FL)
Southeast Missouri State U (MO)
Southern Connecticut State U (CT)
Southern Oregon U (OR)
Southern U and Ag and Mech Coll (LA)
Southern Vermont Coll (VT)
Southwest Baptist U (MO)
Southwestern U (TX)
Southwest Minnesota State U (MN)
Spring Arbor U (MI)
Stanford U (CA)
State U of New York at New Paltz (NY)
State U of New York Coll at Geneseo (NY)
State U of New York Coll at Old Westbury (NY)
Stephen F. Austin State U (TX)
Stetson U (FL)
Stonehill Coll (MA)
Susquehanna U (PA)
Syracuse U (NY)
Tabor Coll (KS)
Taylor U (IN)
Texas A&M Intl U (TX)
Texas A&M U–Commerce (TX)
Texas Christian U (TX)
Texas Lutheran U (TX)
Texas Southern U (TX)
Thiel Coll (PA)
Thomas More Coll (KY)
Thomas U (GA)
Tiffin U (OH)
Towson U (MD)
Trevecca Nazarene U (TN)
Trinity Christian Coll (IL)
Trinity Lutheran Coll (WA)
Trinity U (TX)
Tri-State U (IN)
Truman State U (MO)
Union Coll (KY)
U at Buffalo, the State U of New York (NY)
The U of Akron (OH)
The U of Alabama (AL)
The U of Alabama at Birmingham (AL)
U of Alaska Fairbanks (AK)
The U of Arizona (AZ)
U of Arkansas (AR)
U of California, Davis (CA)
U of California, Los Angeles (CA)
U of California, Santa Barbara (CA)
U of Central Oklahoma (OK)
U of Colorado at Boulder (CO)
U of Colorado Denver (CO)
U of Connecticut (CT)
U of Delaware (DE)
U of Denver (CO)
U of Hartford (CT)
U of Hawaii at Manoa (HI)
U of Houston (TX)
U of Houston–Clear Lake (TX)
U of Idaho (ID)
U of Illinois at Urbana–Champaign (IL)
U of Indianapolis (IN)
The U of Iowa (IA)
U of La Verne (CA)
U of Louisiana at Lafayette (LA)
U of Louisville (KY)
U of Maine (ME)
U of Mary Hardin-Baylor (TX)
U of Maryland, Coll Park (MD)
U of Maryland U Coll (MD)
U of Massachusetts Amherst (MA)
U of Memphis (TN)
U of Miami (FL)
U of Michigan–Dearborn (MI)
U of Minnesota, Crookston (MN)
U of Missouri–Columbia (MO)
U of Missouri–Kansas City (MO)
U of Missouri–St. Louis (MO)
The U of Montana (MT)
U of Nebraska at Omaha (NE)
U of Nebraska–Lincoln (NE)
U of Nevada, Las Vegas (NV)
U of Nevada, Reno (NV)
U of New Haven (CT)
U of New Orleans (LA)
The U of North Carolina at Chapel Hill (NC)
The U of North Carolina at Charlotte (NC)
The U of North Carolina Wilmington (NC)
U of North Dakota (ND)
U of Northern Colorado (CO)
U of Northern Iowa (IA)
U of Oklahoma (OK)
U of Ottawa (ON, Canada)
U of Pennsylvania (PA)
U of Puget Sound (WA)
U of Rhode Island (RI)
U of Rio Grande (OH)
U of Saint Francis (IN)
U of St. Thomas (MN)
U of St. Thomas (TX)
U of San Diego (CA)
U of Science and Arts of Oklahoma (OK)
The U of Scranton (PA)
U of Sioux Falls (SD)
U of South Alabama (AL)
U of South Carolina Aiken (SC)
U of South Carolina Upstate (SC)
U of Southern California (CA)
U of Southern Indiana (IN)
U of Southern Maine (ME)
U of Southern Mississippi (MS)
U of South Florida (FL)
The U of Tampa (FL)
The U of Texas at Austin (TX)
The U of Texas at Brownsville (TX)
The U of Texas at San Antonio (TX)
The U of Texas–Pan American (TX)
U of the Incarnate Word (TX)
U of the Pacific (CA)
U of the Sacred Heart (PR)
The U of Toledo (OH)
U of Tulsa (OK)
U of Utah (UT)
The U of Virginia's Coll at Wise (VA)
U of West Florida (FL)
U of Windsor (ON, Canada)
U of Wisconsin–Eau Claire (WI)
U of Wisconsin–La Crosse (WI)
U of Wisconsin–Parkside (WI)
U of Wisconsin–Stevens Point (WI)
U of Wisconsin–Whitewater (WI)
U of Wyoming (WY)
Utica Coll (NY)
Valdosta State U (GA)
Vanguard U of Southern California (CA)
Virginia Polytechnic Inst and State U (VA)
Wake Forest U (NC)
Washburn U (KS)
Washington State U (WA)
Washington U in St. Louis (MO)
Waynesburg U (PA)
Wayne State Coll (NE)
Wayne State U (MI)
Wesleyan Coll (GA)
West Chester U of Pennsylvania (PA)
Western Carolina U (NC)
Western Connecticut State U (CT)
Western Illinois U (IL)
Western Kentucky U (KY)
Western Michigan U (MI)
Western New England Coll (MA)
Western Washington U (WA)
Westminster Coll (UT)
Westmont Coll (CA)
West Virginia Wesleyan Coll (WV)
Wheaton Coll (IL)
Whitman Coll (WA)
Wichita State U (KS)
Wilkes U (PA)
William Woods U (MO)
Wittenberg U (OH)
Woodbury U (CA)
Worcester State Coll (MA)
Wright State U (OH)
York Coll of Pennsylvania (PA)
York U (ON, Canada)

COMMUNICATIONS TECHNOLOGIES AND SUPPORT SERVICES RELATED

Chestnut Hill Coll (PA)
Framingham State Coll (MA)
Lesley U (MA)
New England School of Communications (ME)
Saint Mary-of-the-Woods Coll (IN)
The U of Scranton (PA)
U of Windsor (ON, Canada)

COMMUNICATIONS TECHNOLOGY

Cedarville U (OH)
Cheyney U of Pennsylvania (PA)
The Coll of Saint Rose (NY)
Eastern Michigan U (MI)
East Stroudsburg U of Pennsylvania (PA)
Hastings Coll (NE)
Inter American U of Puerto Rico, Bayamón Campus (PR)
Lawrence Technological U (MI)
Lewis U (IL)
Saint Mary-of-the-Woods Coll (IN)
Salve Regina U (RI)
U of Massachusetts Boston (MA)
U of Puerto Rico at Humacao (PR)

COMMUNITY HEALTH AND PREVENTIVE MEDICINE

Florida Gulf Coast U (FL)
Hofstra U (NY)
Northern Arizona U (AZ)
Tufts U (MA)
U of Illinois at Urbana–Champaign (IL)
U of Massachusetts Lowell (MA)

COMMUNITY HEALTH LIAISON

Eastern Kentucky U (KY)
Texas Woman's U (TX)

COMMUNITY HEALTH SERVICES COUNSELING

Bethel U (MN)
Central Washington U (WA)
Cleveland State U (OH)
Eastern Kentucky U (KY)
Florida State U (FL)
Indiana State U (IN)
Indiana U–Purdue U Fort Wayne (IN)
James Madison U (VA)
Longwood U (VA)
Morris Coll (SC)
Northeastern Illinois U (IL)
Northern Michigan U (MI)
Prairie View A&M U (TX)
Sam Houston State U (TX)
Seton Hill U (PA)
Stephen F. Austin State U (TX)
Texas A&M U (TX)
U of Central Arkansas (AR)
U of Florida (FL)
U of Houston (TX)
U of Kansas (KS)
U of Nebraska at Omaha (NE)
U of Nebraska–Lincoln (NE)
U of Northern Iowa (IA)
U of Pennsylvania (PA)
The U of Western Ontario (ON, Canada)
U of West Florida (FL)
Western Connecticut State U (CT)
Western Kentucky U (KY)
Western Washington U (WA)
Worcester State Coll (MA)
Youngstown State U (OH)

COMMUNITY ORGANIZATION AND ADVOCACY

Bemidji State U (MN)
Central Michigan U (MI)
Cleveland State U (OH)
Cornell U (NY)
DePaul U (IL)
Eastern Michigan U (MI)
Emory & Henry Coll (VA)
High Point U (NC)
Mercer U (GA)
Northern State U (SD)
Northwestern U (IL)
Pace U (NY)
Providence Coll (RI)
Rockhurst U (MO)
Roosevelt U (IL)
Saint Leo U (FL)
Saint Martin's U (WA)
Samford U (AL)

MAJORS AND MORE

Siena Heights U (MI)
Southern Arkansas U–Magnolia (AR)
State U of New York Empire State Coll (NY)
Thomas Edison State Coll (NJ)
U of Alaska Fairbanks (AK)
U of Baltimore (MD)
U of Delaware (DE)
U of Massachusetts Boston (MA)
U of Saint Mary (KS)
The U of Texas at El Paso (TX)
The U of Toledo (OH)
Woodbury Coll (VT)

COMMUNITY PSYCHOLOGY

Kwantlen U Coll (BC, Canada)
Montana State U–Billings (MT)
New York Inst of Technology (NY)
Northwestern U (IL)
Rogers State U (OK)
Seton Hill U (PA)
U of Saint Mary (KS)
Wilfrid Laurier U (ON, Canada)
Wright State U (OH)

COMPARATIVE LITERATURE

The American U of Paris (France)
Bard Coll (NY)
Barnard Coll (NY)
Beloit Coll (WI)
Benedictine U (IL)
Brandeis U (MA)
Brigham Young U (UT)
Brown U (RI)
Bryn Mawr Coll (PA)
California State U, Fullerton (CA)
California State U, Long Beach (CA)
Case Western Reserve U (OH)
Clark U (MA)
Coll of the Holy Cross (MA)
The Colorado Coll (CO)
Cornell U (NY)
Dartmouth Coll (NH)
Earlham Coll (IN)
Eckerd Coll (FL)
Emory U (GA)
Georgetown U (DC)
Hamilton Coll (NY)
Hampshire Coll (MA)
Harvard U (MA)
Haverford Coll (PA)
Hillsdale Coll (MI)
Hobart and William Smith Colls (NY)
Hofstra U (NY)
Hunter Coll of the City U of New York (NY)
Indiana U Bloomington (IN)
Marlboro Coll (VT)
Mills Coll (CA)
New Coll of Florida (FL)
New England Coll (NH)
New York U (NY)
Northwestern U (IL)
Oakland U (MI)
Oberlin Coll (OH)
Occidental Coll (CA)
Oregon State U (OR)
Penn State Abington (PA)
Penn State Altoona (PA)
Penn State Berks (PA)
Penn State Erie, The Behrend Coll (PA)
Penn State U Park (PA)
Princeton U (NJ)
Queens Coll of the City U of New York (NY)
Ramapo Coll of New Jersey (NJ)
Roosevelt U (IL)
Rutgers, The State U of New Jersey, New Brunswick (NJ)
St. Cloud State U (MN)
Salem State Coll (MA)
San Diego State U (CA)
San Francisco State U (CA)
Sarah Lawrence Coll (NY)
Sewanee: The U of the South (TN)
Simmons Coll (MA)
Smith Coll (MA)
Stanford U (CA)
State U of New York at Binghamton (NY)
State U of New York Coll at Geneseo (NY)
Stony Brook U, State U of New York (NY)
Swarthmore Coll (PA)
Trinity Coll (CT)
U of California, Berkeley (CA)
U of California, Davis (CA)
U of California, Irvine (CA)
U of California, Los Angeles (CA)
U of California, Riverside (CA)
U of California, Santa Barbara (CA)
U of Chicago (IL)
U of Cincinnati (OH)
U of Delaware (DE)
U of Georgia (GA)
U of Illinois at Urbana–Champaign (IL)
The U of Iowa (IA)
U of La Verne (CA)
U of Massachusetts Amherst (MA)
U of Michigan (MI)
U of Minnesota, Twin Cities Campus (MN)
U of Nevada, Las Vegas (NV)
U of New Brunswick Fredericton (NB, Canada)
U of New Mexico (NM)
The U of North Carolina at Chapel Hill (NC)
U of Oregon (OR)
U of Pennsylvania (PA)
U of Rhode Island (RI)
U of Rochester (NY)
U of Southern California (CA)
U of Virginia (VA)
The U of Western Ontario (ON, Canada)
U of Windsor (ON, Canada)
U of Wisconsin–Madison (WI)
U of Wisconsin–Milwaukee (WI)
Washington U in St. Louis (MO)
Wellesley Coll (MA)
Willamette U (OR)
William Woods U (MO)

COMPUTATIONAL MATHEMATICS

Arizona State U (AZ)
California Inst of Technology (CA)
Carnegie Mellon U (PA)
Indiana U–Purdue U Fort Wayne (IN)
Marist Coll (NY)
Marquette U (WI)
Michigan State U (MI)
Michigan Technological U (MI)
Northern Illinois U (IL)
U of California, Davis (CA)
U of California, Los Angeles (CA)
U of Illinois at Urbana–Champaign (IL)
U of Puerto Rico at Utuado (PR)

COMPUTER AND INFORMATION SCIENCES

Adelphi U (NY)
Alabama Ag and Mech U (AL)
Alcorn State U (MS)
Alvernia Coll (PA)
Amberton U (TX)
American InterContinental U (TX)
The American U of Athens (Greece)
Andrews U (MI)
Angelo State U (TX)
Anna Maria Coll (MA)
Aquinas Coll (MI)
Arizona State U at the West campus (AZ)
Arkansas State U (AR)
Ashford U (IA)
Assumption Coll (MA)
Athabasca U (AB, Canada)
Auburn U (AL)
Augusta State U (GA)
Austin Peay State U (TN)
Avila U (MO)
Baker Coll of Muskegon (MI)
Bard Coll at Simon's Rock (MA)
Barnard Coll (NY)
Barton Coll (NC)
Belhaven Coll (MS)
Bellarmine U (KY)
Bennington Coll (VT)
Bentley Coll (MA)
Bethel U (MN)
Bethune-Cookman U (FL)
Biola U (CA)
Bishop's U (QC, Canada)
Bloomfield Coll (NJ)
Bloomsburg U of Pennsylvania (PA)
Bluefield State Coll (WV)
Bob Jones U (SC)
Boise State U (ID)
Boston Coll (MA)
Bowling Green State U (OH)
Brewton-Parker Coll (GA)
Bucknell U (PA)
Butler U (IN)
Cabrini Coll (PA)
California Lutheran U (CA)
California State Polytechnic U, Pomona (CA)
California State U, Fresno (CA)
California State U, Los Angeles (CA)
California State U, San Bernardino (CA)
California State U, Stanislaus (CA)
Cameron U (OK)
Carroll Coll (WI)
Castleton State Coll (VT)
Cedar Crest Coll (PA)
Cedarville U (OH)
Central Connecticut State U (CT)
Central State U (OH)
Central Washington U (WA)
Chaminade U of Honolulu (HI)
Chapman U (CA)
Chatham U (PA)
Chestnut Hill Coll (PA)
Christopher Newport U (VA)
Claremont McKenna Coll (CA)
Clarion U of Pennsylvania (PA)
Clark Atlanta U (GA)
Clarkson U (NY)
Clemson U (SC)
Cleveland State U (OH)
Coastal Carolina U (SC)
Coll of Charleston (SC)
Coll of Mount St. Joseph (OH)
The Coll of New Jersey (NJ)
Coll of Saint Elizabeth (NJ)
Coll of Saint Mary (NE)
The Coll of Saint Rose (NY)
The Coll of St. Scholastica (MN)
Coll of the Ozarks (MO)
The Coll of William and Mary (VA)
Colorado State U (CO)
Columbus State U (GA)
Concordia U, Nebraska (NE)
Dakota State U (SD)
Dallas Baptist U (TX)
Davenport U, Dearborn (MI)
Davenport U, Grand Rapids (MI)
Dixie State Coll of Utah (UT)
Doane Coll (NE)
Dominican Coll (NY)
Dowling Coll (NY)
Drury U (MO)
Eastern Connecticut State U (CT)
Eastern Kentucky U (KY)
Eastern Michigan U (MI)
Eastern New Mexico U (NM)
East Stroudsburg U of Pennsylvania (PA)
East Tennessee State U (TN)
Edinboro U of Pennsylvania (PA)
Elon U (NC)
Emmanuel Coll (GA)
Emporia State U (KS)
The Evergreen State Coll (WA)
Fairleigh Dickinson U, Coll at Florham (NJ)
Fitchburg State Coll (MA)
Florida Ag and Mech U (FL)
Florida Atlantic U (FL)
Florida Gulf Coast U (FL)
Florida Intl U (FL)
Framingham State Coll (MA)
Franciscan U of Steubenville (OH)
Francis Marion U (SC)
Franklin Coll (IN)
Freed-Hardeman U (TN)
Fresno Pacific U (CA)
Frostburg State U (MD)
Gannon U (PA)
George Fox U (OR)
George Mason U (VA)
Georgetown Coll (KY)
The George Washington U (DC)
Georgia Coll & State U (GA)
Georgia Inst of Technology (GA)
Georgian Court U (NJ)
Georgia Southern U (GA)
Georgia Southwestern State U (GA)
Georgia State U (GA)
Grace Bible Coll (MI)
Grace U (NE)
Grand Valley State U (MI)
Greenville Coll (IL)
Grove City Coll (PA)
Guilford Coll (NC)
Gwynedd-Mercy Coll (PA)
Hannibal-LaGrange Coll (MO)
Harding U (AR)
Harrisburg U of Science and Technology (PA)
Hartwick Coll (NY)
Harvard U (MA)
Hastings Coll (NE)
Hawai'i Pacific U (HI)
Henderson State U (AR)
High Point U (NC)
Holy Family U (PA)
Houston Baptist U (TX)
Idaho State U (ID)
Indiana State U (IN)
Indiana U Bloomington (IN)
Indiana U Kokomo (IN)
Indiana U Northwest (IN)
Indiana U of Pennsylvania (PA)
Indiana U–Purdue U Indianapolis (IN)
Indiana U South Bend (IN)
Indiana U Southeast (IN)
Indiana Wesleyan U (IN)
Iowa State U of Science and Technology (IA)
Ithaca Coll (NY)
Jackson State U (MS)
Jacksonville State U (AL)
Jacksonville U (FL)
James Madison U (VA)
The Johns Hopkins U (MD)
Johnson C. Smith U (NC)
Jones Coll, Miami (FL)
Juniata Coll (PA)
Kansas State U (KS)
Kean U (NJ)
Keene State Coll (NH)
Kennesaw State U (GA)
Kentucky State U (KY)
Kentucky Wesleyan Coll (KY)
Knox Coll (IL)
Kuyper Coll (MI)
LaGrange Coll (GA)
Lambuth U (TN)
Lander U (SC)
La Roche Coll (PA)
La Salle U (PA)
Lehman Coll of the City U of New York (NY)
Le Moyne Coll (NY)
Lenoir-Rhyne Coll (NC)
Lewis-Clark State Coll (ID)
Lewis U (IL)
Liberty U (VA)
Lincoln U (PA)
Lock Haven U of Pennsylvania (PA)
Loyola Coll in Maryland (MD)
Loyola U Chicago (IL)
Loyola U New Orleans (LA)
Lubbock Christian U (TX)
Lycoming Coll (PA)
Madonna U (MI)
Mansfield U of Pennsylvania (PA)
Marshall U (WV)
Mary Baldwin Coll (VA)
Massachusetts Coll of Liberal Arts (MA)
The Master's Coll and Sem (CA)
Mayville State U (ND)
McDaniel Coll (MD)
McGill U (QC, Canada)
McMurry U (TX)
Mercy Coll (NY)
Mercyhurst Coll (PA)
Meredith Coll (NC)
Mesa State Coll (CO)
Miami U (OH)
Michigan Jewish Inst (MI)
Michigan State U (MI)
Midway Coll (KY)
Miles Coll (AL)
Millersville U of Pennsylvania (PA)
Milligan Coll (TN)
Mississippi Coll (MS)
Mississippi State U (MS)
Missouri Baptist U (MO)
Missouri Southern State U (MO)
Monmouth U (NJ)
Montana Tech of The U of Montana (MT)
Morehead State U (KY)
Morehouse Coll (GA)
Mount Mercy Coll (IA)
Mount Saint Mary Coll (NY)
Mount St. Mary's U (MD)
Mount Saint Vincent U (NS, Canada)
Mount Vernon Nazarene U (OH)
Murray State U (KY)
Neumann Coll (PA)
Neumont U (UT)
New Jersey City U (NJ)
New Jersey Inst of Technology (NJ)
New Mexico Highlands U (NM)
New York Inst of Technology (NY)
New York U (NY)
Northeastern Illinois U (IL)
Northern Arizona U (AZ)
Northern Michigan U (MI)
North Georgia Coll & State U (GA)
Northwest Christian Coll (OR)
Northwestern U (IL)
Northwood U (MI)
Northwood U, Florida Campus (FL)
Notre Dame de Namur U (CA)
Nova Southeastern U (FL)
Oakland U (MI)
Okanagan Coll (BC, Canada)
Old Dominion U (VA)
Oral Roberts U (OK)
Oregon Inst of Technology (OR)
Pace U (NY)
Pacific Union Coll (CA)
Palm Beach Atlantic U (FL)
Park U (MO)
Penn State Abington (PA)
Penn State Altoona (PA)
Penn State Berks (PA)
Penn State Erie, The Behrend Coll (PA)
Penn State Harrisburg (PA)
Penn State U Park (PA)
Philadelphia U (PA)
Pikeville Coll (KY)
Portland State U (OR)
Prescott Coll (AZ)
Purdue U (IN)
Purdue U Calumet (IN)
Queens Coll of the City U of New York (NY)
Quincy U (IL)
Ramapo Coll of New Jersey (NJ)
Regis Coll (MA)
Rensselaer Polytechnic Inst (NY)
Rhode Island Coll (RI)
Rice U (TX)
The Richard Stockton Coll of New Jersey (NJ)
Rochester Inst of Technology (NY)
Rowan U (NJ)
Rutgers, The State U of New Jersey, Camden (NJ)
Rutgers, The State U of New Jersey, Newark (NJ)
Saginaw Valley State U (MI)
St. Edward's U (TX)
St. Francis Xavier U (NS, Canada)
St. John's U (NY)
Saint Joseph's Coll (IN)
Saint Joseph's U (PA)
Saint Louis U (MO)
Saint Mary-of-the-Woods Coll (IN)
St. Mary's Coll of Maryland (MD)
St. Norbert Coll (WI)
Saint Vincent Coll (PA)
Saint Xavier U (IL)
Salisbury U (MD)
Sam Houston State U (TX)
Shaw U (NC)
Shepherd U (WV)
Shippensburg U of Pennsylvania (PA)
Shorter Coll (GA)
Siena Coll (NY)
Siena Heights U (MI)
Skidmore Coll (NY)
Slippery Rock U of Pennsylvania (PA)
South Dakota State U (SD)
Southeastern Oklahoma State U (OK)
Southeast Missouri State U (MO)
Southern Arkansas U–Magnolia (AR)
Southern New Hampshire U (NH)
Southern Polytechnic State U (GA)
Southern Wesleyan U (SC)
Southwest Baptist U (MO)
Southwestern Oklahoma State U (OK)
Southwestern U (TX)
Spring Hill Coll (AL)
State U of New York at Binghamton (NY)
State U of New York at New Paltz (NY)
State U of New York Coll at Old Westbury (NY)
State U of New York Coll at Potsdam (NY)
State U of New York Inst of Technology (NY)
Stephen F. Austin State U (TX)
Sterling Coll (KS)
Stillman Coll (AL)
Suffolk U (MA)
Swarthmore Coll (PA)
Syracuse U (NY)
Tarleton State U (TX)
Temple U (PA)
Tennessee Wesleyan Coll (TN)
Texas Christian U (TX)
Texas Southern U (TX)
Texas State U-San Marcos (TX)
Texas Tech U (TX)
Texas Woman's U (TX)
Thomas Coll (ME)
Thomas More Coll (KY)
Thompson Rivers U (BC, Canada)
Towson U (MD)
Transylvania U (KY)
Trinity U (TX)
Troy U (AL)
Truman State U (MO)
Tulane U (LA)
Union Coll (NY)
United States Naval Acad (MD)
U at Albany, State U of New York (NY)
The U of Alabama at Birmingham (AL)
The U of Alabama in Huntsville (AL)
U of Alaska Fairbanks (AK)
The U of Arizona (AZ)
U of Arkansas (AR)
U of Arkansas at Fort Smith (AR)
U of Baltimore (MD)
U of California, Irvine (CA)
U of California, Los Angeles (CA)

U of Central Arkansas (AR)
U of Central Florida (FL)
U of Central Missouri (MO)
U of Charleston (WV)
U of Cincinnati (OH)
U of Colorado Denver (CO)
U of Delaware (DE)
U of Evansville (IN)
U of Florida (FL)
U of Georgia (GA)
U of Great Falls (MT)
U of Hartford (CT)
U of Hawaii at Manoa (HI)
U of Houston (TX)
U of Houston–Clear Lake (TX)
U of Illinois at Chicago (IL)
U of Illinois at Urbana–Champaign (IL)
The U of Iowa (IA)
U of Kansas (KS)
U of Louisiana at Lafayette (LA)
The U of Maine at Augusta (ME)
U of Mary (ND)
U of Mary Hardin-Baylor (TX)
U of Maryland, Coll Park (MD)
U of Maryland U Coll (MD)
U of Massachusetts Dartmouth (MA)
U of Michigan–Dearborn (MI)
U of Michigan–Flint (MI)
U of Mississippi (MS)
U of Missouri–Columbia (MO)
U of Missouri–St. Louis (MO)
The U of Montana (MT)
U of Nebraska at Kearney (NE)
U of Nebraska–Lincoln (NE)
U of Nevada, Reno (NV)
U of New Haven (CT)
U of New Mexico (NM)
U of North Alabama (AL)
The U of North Carolina at Greensboro (NC)
U of North Dakota (ND)
U of North Florida (FL)
U of North Texas (TX)
U of Notre Dame (IN)
U of Oklahoma (OK)
U of Oregon (OR)
U of Ottawa (ON, Canada)
U of Rhode Island (RI)
U of Saint Mary (KS)
U of St. Thomas (MN)
U of Science and Arts of Oklahoma (OK)
U of Sioux Falls (SD)
U of South Alabama (AL)
U of South Carolina (SC)
U of South Carolina Upstate (SC)
The U of South Dakota (SD)
U of Southern California (CA)
U of Southern Indiana (IN)
U of Southern Mississippi (MS)
U of South Florida (FL)
The U of Texas at Arlington (TX)
The U of Texas at Austin (TX)
The U of Texas at Brownsville (TX)
The U of Texas at Dallas (TX)
The U of Texas at Tyler (TX)
The U of Texas–Pan American (TX)
U of the Incarnate Word (TX)
U of Vermont (VT)
U of Virginia (VA)
The U of Virginia's Coll at Wise (VA)
U of Washington, Bothell (WA)
U of Washington, Tacoma (WA)
The U of Western Ontario (ON, Canada)
U of West Florida (FL)
U of West Georgia (GA)
U of Windsor (ON, Canada)
U of Wisconsin–Eau Claire (WI)
U of Wisconsin–La Crosse (WI)
U of Wisconsin–Stevens Point (WI)
U of Wisconsin–Superior (WI)
U of Wisconsin–Whitewater (WI)
Utah State U (UT)
Utica Coll (NY)
Valdosta State U (GA)
Valley City State U (ND)
Vassar Coll (NY)
Villa Julie Coll (MD)
Virginia Commonwealth U (VA)
Virginia Intermont Coll (VA)
Virginia Polytechnic Inst and State U (VA)
Viterbo U (WI)
Wake Forest U (NC)
Washburn U (KS)
Washington and Lee U (VA)
Washington U in St. Louis (MO)
Waynesburg U (PA)
Wayne State Coll (NE)
Wayne State U (MI)
Wesleyan Coll (GA)
West Chester U of Pennsylvania (PA)
Western Illinois U (IL)
Western Kentucky U (KY)
Western Michigan U (MI)
West Texas A&M U (TX)
West Virginia Wesleyan Coll (WV)
Wichita State U (KS)
Widener U (PA)
Wiley Coll (TX)
Wilkes U (PA)
William Woods U (MO)
Winona State U (MN)
Worcester Polytechnic Inst (MA)
Worcester State Coll (MA)
Wright State U (OH)
Xavier U of Louisiana (LA)
Yale U (CT)
York Coll of Pennsylvania (PA)
York U (ON, Canada)

COMPUTER AND INFORMATION SCIENCES AND SUPPORT SERVICES RELATED

Bloomsburg U of Pennsylvania (PA)
Cabrini Coll (PA)
California State U, Chico (CA)
California State U, Los Angeles (CA)
City U of Seattle (WA)
Coll of Staten Island of the City U of New York (NY)
Columbia Coll (SC)
Columbia Coll Chicago (IL)
Delaware Valley Coll (PA)
DePaul U (IL)
Dowling Coll (NY)
Hofstra U (NY)
Indiana U East (IN)
Indiana U–Purdue U Indianapolis (IN)
Inter American U of Puerto Rico, Bayamón Campus (PR)
Intl Acad of Design & Technology (IL)
Lehigh U (PA)
Mayville State U (ND)
Missouri U of Science and Technology (MO)
New Jersey Inst of Technology (NJ)
Park U (MO)
Purdue U (IN)
Regis Coll (MA)
Roberts Wesleyan Coll (NY)
Southern Polytechnic State U (GA)
State U of New York Coll of Agriculture and Technology at Cobleskill (NY)
Syracuse U (NY)
Tiffin U (OH)
U of California, Irvine (CA)
U of Evansville (IN)
U of Great Falls (MT)
U of Michigan–Flint (MI)
U of Northern Iowa (IA)
U of Notre Dame (IN)
U of Pittsburgh (PA)
The U of Scranton (PA)
Utah State U (UT)
Valley City State U (ND)
Washington U in St. Louis (MO)
West Virginia U (WV)
York Coll of Pennsylvania (PA)

COMPUTER AND INFORMATION SCIENCES RELATED

The Colorado Coll (CO)
DigiPen Inst of Technology (WA)
Eastern Illinois U (IL)
George Mason U (VA)
Grace U (NE)
Maryville Coll (TN)
Miami U Hamilton (OH)
Neumont U (UT)
Northern Arizona U (AZ)
Texas Christian U (TX)
Université de Sherbrooke (QC, Canada)
U of Great Falls (MT)
U of Lethbridge (AB, Canada)
U of Northern Iowa (IA)
U of Windsor (ON, Canada)
Wagner Coll (NY)
West Virginia U (WV)
Wilfrid Laurier U (ON, Canada)

COMPUTER AND INFORMATION SYSTEMS SECURITY

Dakota State U (SD)
Davenport U, Dearborn (MI)
Davenport U, Grand Rapids (MI)
DePaul U (IL)
East Stroudsburg U of Pennsylvania (PA)
Emporia State U (KS)
Kennesaw State U (GA)
Loyola U Chicago (IL)
Metropolitan State U (MN)
Pennsylvania Coll of Technology (PA)
Pittsburg State U (KS)
Rochester Inst of Technology (NY)
St. John's U (NY)
U of Great Falls (MT)
U of Illinois at Urbana–Champaign (IL)
U of Miami (FL)
World Coll (VA)

COMPUTER ENGINEERING

American U of Beirut (Lebanon)
Arizona State U (AZ)
Auburn U (AL)
Bellarmine U (KY)
Bethune-Cookman U (FL)
Bob Jones U (SC)
Boston U (MA)
Bradley U (IL)
Brigham Young U (UT)
Brown U (RI)
Bucknell U (PA)
California Inst of Technology (CA)
California Polytechnic State U, San Luis Obispo (CA)
California State Polytechnic U, Pomona (CA)
California State U, Chico (CA)
California State U, Fresno (CA)
California State U, Fullerton (CA)
California State U, Long Beach (CA)
California State U, Sacramento (CA)
Capital U (OH)
Case Western Reserve U (OH)
The Catholic U of America (DC)
Cedarville U (OH)
Christopher Newport U (VA)
Clarkson U (NY)
Clemson U (SC)
Cleveland State U (OH)
The Coll of New Jersey (NJ)
Colorado State U (CO)
Colorado Tech U—Colorado Springs (CO)
Colorado Tech U—Denver (CO)
Colorado Tech U—North Kansas City (MO)
Colorado Tech U—Online (CO)
Colorado Tech U—Sioux Falls (SD)
Concordia U (QC, Canada)
Dominican U (IL)
Dordt Coll (IA)
Drexel U (PA)
Elizabethtown Coll (PA)
Embry-Riddle Aeronautical U (AZ)
Embry-Riddle Aeronautical U (FL)
Fairfield U (CT)
Florida Ag and Mech U (FL)
Florida Atlantic U (FL)
Florida Inst of Technology (FL)
Florida Intl U (FL)
Florida State U (FL)
Franklin W. Olin Coll of Eng (MA)
George Mason U (VA)
The George Washington U (DC)
Georgia Inst of Technology (GA)
Georgia Southern U (GA)
Gonzaga U (WA)
Grand Valley State U (MI)
Harding U (AR)
Harvard U (MA)
Hofstra U (NY)
Illinois Inst of Technology (IL)
Indiana Tech (IN)
Indiana U–Purdue U Fort Wayne (IN)
Indiana U–Purdue U Indianapolis (IN)
Iowa State U of Science and Technology (IA)
Jackson State U (MS)
The Johns Hopkins U (MD)
Johnson C. Smith U (NC)
Kansas State U (KS)
Kettering U (MI)
Lakehead U (ON, Canada)
Lawrence Technological U (MI)
Lehigh U (PA)
LeTourneau U (TX)
Liberty U (VA)
Lipscomb U (TN)
Louisiana State U and Ag and Mech Coll (LA)
Loyola Marymount U (CA)
Marquette U (WI)
McGill U (QC, Canada)
Merrimack Coll (MA)
Miami U (OH)
Miami U Hamilton (OH)
Michigan State U (MI)
Michigan Technological U (MI)
Midwestern State U (TX)
Milwaukee School of Eng (WI)
Minnesota State U Mankato (MN)
Mississippi State U (MS)
Missouri U of Science and Technology (MO)
Montana State U (MT)
Montana Tech of The U of Montana (MT)
New Jersey Inst of Technology (NJ)
North Carolina State U (NC)
North Dakota State U (ND)
Northeastern U (MA)
Northwestern U (IL)
Norwich U (VT)
Oakland U (MI)
Ohio Northern U (OH)
Ohio U (OH)
Oklahoma Christian U (OK)
Old Dominion U (VA)
Oral Roberts U (OK)
Oregon State U (OR)
Penn State Abington (PA)
Penn State Altoona (PA)
Penn State Berks (PA)
Penn State Erie, The Behrend Coll (PA)
Penn State U Park (PA)
Polytechnic U, Brooklyn Campus (NY)
Polytechnic U of Puerto Rico (PR)
Portland State U (OR)
Princeton U (NJ)
Purdue U (IN)
Purdue U Calumet (IN)
Queen's U at Kingston (ON, Canada)
Rensselaer Polytechnic Inst (NY)
Rice U (TX)
Rochester Inst of Technology (NY)
Rose-Hulman Inst of Technology (IN)
Royal Military Coll of Canada (ON, Canada)
Rutgers, The State U of New Jersey, New Brunswick (NJ)
St. Cloud State U (MN)
Saint Louis U (MO)
St. Mary's U (TX)
Saint Mary's U of Minnesota (MN)
San Diego State U (CA)
Santa Clara U (CA)
South Dakota School of Mines and Technology (SD)
Southern Illinois U Carbondale (IL)
Southern Illinois U Edwardsville (IL)
Southern Methodist U (TX)
Stanford U (CA)
State U of New York at Binghamton (NY)
State U of New York at New Paltz (NY)
Stonehill Coll (MA)
Syracuse U (NY)
Taylor U (IN)
Tennessee Technological U (TN)
Texas A&M U (TX)
Texas Tech U (TX)
Trinity Coll (CT)
Tri-State U (IN)
Tufts U (MA)
Tulane U (LA)
Université de Sherbrooke (QC, Canada)
Université du Québec en Outaouais (QC, Canada)
U at Buffalo, the State U of New York (NY)
The U of Akron (OH)
The U of Alabama in Huntsville (AL)
U of Alaska Fairbanks (AK)
The U of Arizona (AZ)
U of Arkansas (AR)
U of Bridgeport (CT)
The U of British Columbia (BC, Canada)
U of California, Irvine (CA)
U of California, Los Angeles (CA)
U of California, Riverside (CA)
U of California, San Diego (CA)
U of California, Santa Barbara (CA)
U of California, Santa Cruz (CA)
U of Central Florida (FL)
U of Cincinnati (OH)
U of Colorado at Boulder (CO)
U of Connecticut (CT)
U of Dayton (OH)
U of Delaware (DE)
U of Denver (CO)
U of Evansville (IN)
U of Florida (FL)
U of Hartford (CT)
U of Houston (TX)
U of Houston–Clear Lake (TX)
U of Idaho (ID)
U of Illinois at Chicago (IL)
U of Illinois at Urbana–Champaign (IL)
U of Indianapolis (IN)
U of Kansas (KS)
U of La Verne (CA)
U of Louisiana at Lafayette (LA)
U of Louisville (KY)
U of Maine (ME)
U of Maryland, Baltimore County (MD)
U of Maryland, Coll Park (MD)
U of Massachusetts Amherst (MA)
U of Massachusetts Dartmouth (MA)
U of Massachusetts Lowell (MA)
U of Memphis (TN)
U of Miami (FL)
U of Michigan (MI)
U of Minnesota, Duluth (MN)
U of Missouri–Columbia (MO)
U of Nebraska at Omaha (NE)
U of Nebraska–Lincoln (NE)
U of Nevada, Las Vegas (NV)
U of Nevada, Reno (NV)
U of New Brunswick Fredericton (NB, Canada)
U of New Hampshire (NH)
U of New Haven (CT)
U of New Mexico (NM)
The U of North Carolina at Charlotte (NC)
U of North Texas (TX)
U of Notre Dame (IN)
U of Oklahoma (OK)
U of Ottawa (ON, Canada)
U of Pennsylvania (PA)
U of Pittsburgh (PA)
U of Portland (OR)
U of Rhode Island (RI)
The U of Scranton (PA)
U of South Alabama (AL)
U of South Carolina (SC)
U of Southern California (CA)
U of South Florida (FL)
The U of Tennessee (TN)
The U of Texas at Arlington (TX)
The U of Texas at Dallas (TX)
The U of Texas at San Antonio (TX)
The U of Texas–Pan American (TX)
U of the Pacific (CA)
The U of Toledo (OH)
U of Toronto (ON, Canada)
U of Utah (UT)
U of Victoria (BC, Canada)
U of Virginia (VA)
The U of Western Ontario (ON, Canada)
U of West Florida (FL)
U of Windsor (ON, Canada)
U of Wisconsin–Madison (WI)
U of Wyoming (WY)
Utah State U (UT)
Valparaiso U (IN)
Vanderbilt U (TN)
Villanova U (PA)
Virginia Commonwealth U (VA)
Virginia Polytechnic Inst and State U (VA)
Virginia State U (VA)
Washington State U (WA)
Washington U in St. Louis (MO)
Western Michigan U (MI)
West Virginia U (WV)
Wichita State U (KS)
Worcester Polytechnic Inst (MA)
Wright State U (OH)
Xavier U of Louisiana (LA)
York Coll of Pennsylvania (PA)
York U (ON, Canada)

COMPUTER ENGINEERING RELATED

Auburn U (AL)
Carnegie Mellon U (PA)
DigiPen Inst of Technology (WA)
Ohio Northern U (OH)
U of Southern California (CA)

COMPUTER ENGINEERING TECHNOLOGIES RELATED

Old Dominion U (VA)
Thomas Edison State Coll (NJ)

COMPUTER ENGINEERING TECHNOLOGY

Brock U (ON, Canada)
California State U, Long Beach (CA)
DeVry Coll of New York (NY)
DeVry U, Phoenix (AZ)
DeVry U, Fremont (CA)
DeVry U, Long Beach (CA)
DeVry U, Pomona (CA)
DeVry U, Sherman Oaks (CA)
DeVry U, Westminster (CO)
DeVry U, Miramar (FL)
DeVry U, Orlando (FL)
DeVry U, Alpharetta (GA)
DeVry U, Decatur (GA)
DeVry U, Addison (IL)
DeVry U, Chicago (IL)

DeVry U, Tinley Park (IL)
DeVry U, Kansas City (MO)
DeVry U, Columbus (OH)
DeVry U, Fort Washington (PA)
DeVry U, Houston (TX)
DeVry U, Irving (TX)
DeVry U, Arlington (VA)
DeVry U, Federal Way (WA)
East Carolina U (NC)
Eastern Michigan U (MI)
East-West U (IL)
Farmingdale State Coll (NY)
Georgia Southwestern State U (GA)
Grantham U (MO)
Harvard U (MA)
Indiana State U (IN)
Indiana U–Purdue U Fort Wayne (IN)
Indiana U–Purdue U Indianapolis (IN)
Lake Superior State U (MI)
LeTourneau U (TX)
Marshall U (WV)
Martin U (IN)
Minnesota State U Mankato (MN)
Murray State U (KY)
Northeastern U (MA)
Oregon Inst of Technology (OR)
Purdue U (IN)
Purdue U Calumet (IN)
Purdue U North Central (IN)
Rochester Inst of Technology (NY)
Shawnee State U (OH)
Southern Polytechnic State U (GA)
State U of New York Inst of Technology (NY)
Texas Southern U (TX)
U of Dayton (OH)
U of Houston (TX)
U of Memphis (TN)
U of Minnesota, Crookston (MN)
U of Southern Mississippi (MS)
Utah State U (UT)
Vermont Tech Coll (VT)

COMPUTER GRAPHICS

Acad of Art U (CA)
Alberta Coll of Art & Design (AB, Canada)
American InterContinental U (CA)
American InterContinental U (FL)
American InterContinental U (TX)
American InterContinental U Buckhead Campus (GA)
American InterContinental U Dunwoody Campus (GA)
American InterContinental U-London (United Kingdom)
American InterContinental U Online (IL)
The American U of Athens (Greece)
The Art Inst of Atlanta (GA)
The Art Inst of Fort Lauderdale (FL)
The Art Inst of Tampa (FL)
The Art Insts Intl Minnesota (MN)
Baker Coll of Flint (MI)
Bard Coll at Simon's Rock (MA)
Becker Coll (MA)
California Inst of the Arts (CA)
California State U, Chico (CA)
California State U, East Bay (CA)
Cogswell Polytechnical Coll (CA)
Coll of the Atlantic (ME)
Dakota State U (SD)
DePaul U (IL)
Dominican U of California (CA)
Full Sail U (FL)
Hampshire Coll (MA)
Harvard U (MA)
Indiana Wesleyan U (IN)
John Brown U (AR)
Lewis U (IL)
Memphis Coll of Art (TN)
The New England Inst of Art (MA)
New England School of Communications (ME)
Oakland City U (IN)
Pratt Inst (NY)
Purdue U (IN)
Rochester Inst of Technology (NY)
Rogers State U (OK)
Savannah Coll of Art and Design (GA)
School of the Art Inst of Chicago (IL)
School of the Museum of Fine Arts, Boston (MA)
Southern Adventist U (TN)
State U of New York at Fredonia (NY)
State U of New York Coll at Oneonta (NY)
Taylor U (IN)
U of Advancing Technology (AZ)
U of California, Santa Cruz (CA)
U of Great Falls (MT)
U of Mary Hardin-Baylor (TX)
U of Miami (FL)
U of Pennsylvania (PA)
The U of Tampa (FL)
Wingate U (NC)

COMPUTER HARDWARE ENGINEERING

Auburn U (AL)
Stony Brook U, State U of New York (NY)
United States Naval Acad (MD)
York U (ON, Canada)

COMPUTER/INFORMATION TECHNOLOGY SERVICES ADMINISTRATION RELATED

American InterContinental U (CA)
American InterContinental U (FL)
American InterContinental U (TX)
American InterContinental U Buckhead Campus (GA)
American InterContinental U Dunwoody Campus (GA)
American InterContinental U-London (United Kingdom)
American InterContinental U Online (IL)
Chestnut Hill Coll (PA)
Clayton State U (GA)
Concordia U, St. Paul (MN)
Dordt Coll (IA)
Eastern Illinois U (IL)
Hodges U (FL)
Holy Names U (CA)
Lindenwood U (MO)
Marywood U (PA)
Point Park U (PA)
Queens U of Charlotte (NC)
Robert Morris U (PA)
Saint Mary's U of Minnesota (MN)
Seattle Pacific U (WA)
U of Great Falls (MT)
U of Maryland, Baltimore County (MD)
U of South Florida (FL)
Washington U in St. Louis (MO)
Western Kentucky U (KY)

COMPUTER INSTALLATION AND REPAIR TECHNOLOGY

Inter American U of Puerto Rico, Bayamón Campus (PR)

COMPUTER MANAGEMENT

Belmont U (TN)
Faulkner U (AL)
Grove City Coll (PA)
HEC Montreal (QC, Canada)
Holy Family U (PA)
Lehman Coll of the City U of New York (NY)
National American U, Rapid City (SD)
National-Louis U (IL)
New England Coll (NH)
Northwest Missouri State U (MO)
Oklahoma State U (OK)
Pacific Union Coll (CA)
Rochester Coll (MI)
St. Mary's U (TX)
Thomas Coll (ME)
Université de Sherbrooke (QC, Canada)
U of Cincinnati (OH)
U of Great Falls (MT)
Webber Intl U (FL)
Western Intl U (AZ)
York Coll of the City U of New York (NY)

COMPUTER PROGRAMMING

Andrews U (MI)
The Art Inst of Tampa (FL)
Baker Coll of Owosso (MI)
Belmont U (TN)
Bishop's U (QC, Canada)
Bloomfield Coll (NJ)
Brock U (ON, Canada)
City U of Seattle (WA)
Clemson U (SC)
DePaul U (IL)
Dordt Coll (IA)
East-West U (IL)
Electronic Data Processing Coll of Puerto Rico (PR)
Everest U, Tampa (FL)
Farmingdale State Coll (NY)
Florida State U (FL)
Gannon U (PA)
Grace U (NE)
Grand Valley State U (MI)
Granite State Coll (NH)
Hardin-Simmons U (TX)
Harvard U (MA)
Husson Coll (ME)
Inter American U of Puerto Rico, Bayamón Campus (PR)
Inter American U of Puerto Rico, San Germán Campus (PR)
Iowa Wesleyan Coll (IA)
Kent State U (OH)
La Salle U (PA)
Limestone Coll (SC)
Marist Coll (NY)
Memorial U of Newfoundland (NL, Canada)
Michigan Technological U (MI)
Midland Lutheran Coll (NE)
Minnesota State U Mankato (MN)
Montana Tech of The U of Montana (MT)
National American U–Sioux Falls Branch (SD)
Neumont U (UT)
Northwest Christian Coll (OR)
Northwest Missouri State U (MO)
Oregon Inst of Technology (OR)
Pacific Union Coll (CA)
Rockhurst U (MO)
Saint Francis U (PA)
Southwestern Coll (KS)
Taylor U (IN)
Thompson Rivers U (BC, Canada)
Université de Sherbrooke (QC, Canada)
U of Advancing Technology (AZ)
U of Cincinnati (OH)
U of Great Falls (MT)
U of Illinois at Urbana–Champaign (IL)
U of Michigan–Dearborn (MI)
The U of Tampa (FL)
The U of Toledo (OH)
The U of Western Ontario (ON, Canada)
Wheeling Jesuit U (WV)
Winona State U (MN)
York U (ON, Canada)
Youngstown State U (OH)

COMPUTER PROGRAMMING RELATED

Farmingdale State Coll (NY)
Neumont U (UT)

COMPUTER PROGRAMMING (SPECIFIC APPLICATIONS)

The Art Inst of California–San Francisco (CA)
The Art Inst of Portland (OR)
DePaul U (IL)
Georgia Southwestern State U (GA)
Husson Coll (ME)
Kent State U (OH)
Neumont U (UT)
U of Puget Sound (WA)
U of Windsor (ON, Canada)

COMPUTER PROGRAMMING (VENDOR/ PRODUCT CERTIFICATION)

Marist Coll (NY)
National American U–Sioux Falls Branch (SD)
Neumont U (UT)

COMPUTER SCIENCE

Abilene Christian U (TX)
Acadia U (NS, Canada)
Alabama State U (AL)
Albion Coll (MI)
Albright Coll (PA)
Alderson-Broaddus Coll (WV)
Allegheny Coll (PA)
Alma Coll (MI)
American Coll of Thessaloniki (Greece)
American U (DC)
The American U of Athens (Greece)
American U of Beirut (Lebanon)
The American U of Paris (France)
Amherst Coll (MA)
Anderson U (IN)
Andrews U (MI)
Appalachian State U (NC)
Aquinas Coll (MI)
Arizona State U (AZ)
Arkansas State U (AR)
Armstrong Atlantic State U (GA)
Ashland U (OH)
Athens State U (AL)
Atlantic Union Coll (MA)
Augsburg Coll (MN)
Augustana Coll (IL)
Augustana Coll (SD)
Austin Coll (TX)
Azusa Pacific U (CA)
Baker Coll of Muskegon (MI)
Baker Coll of Owosso (MI)
Baker U (KS)
Baldwin-Wallace Coll (OH)
Ball State U (IN)
Bard Coll (NY)
Bard Coll at Simon's Rock (MA)
Barry U (FL)
Baylor U (TX)
Belhaven Coll (MS)
Belmont U (TN)
Beloit Coll (WI)
Bemidji State U (MN)
Benedictine Coll (KS)
Benedictine U (IL)
Bennington Coll (VT)
Berry Coll (GA)
Bethany Coll (WV)
Bethel Coll (KS)
Bethune-Cookman U (FL)
Bishop's U (QC, Canada)
Blackburn Coll (IL)
Bloomsburg U of Pennsylvania (PA)
Bluefield Coll (VA)
Bluffton U (OH)
Boise State U (ID)
Boston Coll (MA)
Boston U (MA)
Bowdoin Coll (ME)
Bradley U (IL)
Brandeis U (MA)
Bridgewater Coll (VA)
Bridgewater State Coll (MA)
Brigham Young U (UT)
British Columbia Inst of Technology (BC, Canada)
Brock U (ON, Canada)
Brown Mackie Coll–Tucson (AZ)
Brown U (RI)
Bryan Coll (TN)
California Inst of Technology (CA)
California Lutheran U (CA)
California Polytechnic State U, San Luis Obispo (CA)
California State Polytechnic U, Pomona (CA)
California State U, Chico (CA)
California State U, Dominguez Hills (CA)
California State U, East Bay (CA)
California State U, Fresno (CA)
California State U, Fullerton (CA)
California State U, Long Beach (CA)
California State U, Los Angeles (CA)
California State U, Sacramento (CA)
California State U, San Bernardino (CA)
California State U, San Marcos (CA)
Calumet Coll of Saint Joseph (IN)
Calvin Coll (MI)
Cameron U (OK)
Canadian Mennonite U (MB, Canada)
Canisius Coll (NY)
Capital U (OH)
Carnegie Mellon U (PA)
Carson-Newman Coll (TN)
Case Western Reserve U (OH)
Catawba Coll (NC)
The Catholic U of America (DC)
Cedarville U (OH)
Central Coll (IA)
Central Michigan U (MI)
Centre Coll (KY)
Chaminade U of Honolulu (HI)
Chapman U (CA)
Chestnut Hill Coll (PA)
Cheyney U of Pennsylvania (PA)
Chicago State U (IL)
Christian Brothers U (TN)
Christopher Newport U (VA)
The Citadel, The Military Coll of South Carolina (SC)
City Coll of the City U of New York (NY)
Claflin U (SC)
Claremont McKenna Coll (CA)
Clark Atlanta U (GA)
Clarke Coll (IA)
Clarkson U (NY)
Clark U (MA)
Clemson U (SC)
Cleveland State U (OH)
Coker Coll (SC)
Colby Coll (ME)
The Coll at Brockport, State U of New York (NY)
Coll of Saint Benedict (MN)
Coll of Saint Elizabeth (NJ)
Coll of the Holy Cross (MA)
Coll of the Ozarks (MO)
Coll of the Southwest (NM)
Colorado School of Mines (CO)
Colorado State U (CO)
Colorado Tech U—Colorado Springs (CO)
Colorado Tech U—Denver (CO)
Colorado Tech U—North Kansas City (MO)
Colorado Tech U—Online (CO)
Colorado Tech U—Sioux Falls (SD)
Concordia Coll (MN)
Concordia U (QC, Canada)
Concordia U Chicago (IL)
Concordia U, Nebraska (NE)
Concordia U Texas (TX)
Concordia U Wisconsin (WI)
Concord U (WV)
Connecticut Coll (CT)
Converse Coll (SC)
Cornell Coll (IA)
Cornell U (NY)
Covenant Coll (GA)
Creighton U (NE)
Dallas Baptist U (TX)
Daniel Webster Coll (NH)
Dartmouth Coll (NH)
Davis & Elkins Coll (WV)
Defiance Coll (OH)
Denison U (OH)
DePaul U (IL)
DePauw U (IN)
DeSales U (PA)
Dickinson Coll (PA)
Dillard U (LA)
Doane Coll (NE)
Dominican U (IL)
Dordt Coll (IA)
Drake U (IA)
Drew U (NJ)
Drexel U (PA)
Drury U (MO)
Duke U (NC)
Duquesne U (PA)
Earlham Coll (IN)
East Carolina U (NC)
East Central U (OK)
Eastern Kentucky U (KY)
Eastern Mennonite U (VA)
Eastern Michigan U (MI)
East-West U (IL)
Eckerd Coll (FL)
Elizabethtown Coll (PA)
Elon U (NC)
Emory & Henry Coll (VA)
Emory U (GA)
Evangel U (MO)
Everest U, Tampa (FL)
Fairfield U (CT)
Fairleigh Dickinson U, Metropolitan Campus (NJ)
Fairmont State U (WV)
Fayetteville State U (NC)
Felician Coll (NJ)
Ferrum Coll (VA)
Fitchburg State Coll (MA)
Florida Inst of Technology (FL)
Florida Intl U (FL)
Florida Memorial U (FL)
Florida Southern Coll (FL)
Florida State U (FL)
Fontbonne U (MO)
Fort Lewis Coll (CO)
Franciscan U of Steubenville (OH)
Franklin Coll (IN)
Freed-Hardeman U (TN)
Furman U (SC)
Gardner-Webb U (NC)
Georgetown U (DC)
The George Washington U (DC)
Georgia Southwestern State U (GA)
Gettysburg Coll (PA)
Glenville State Coll (WV)
Gonzaga U (WA)
Gordon Coll (MA)
Goucher Coll (MD)
Grace U (NE)
Grambling State U (LA)
Grand Valley State U (MI)
Grand View Coll (IA)
Grantham U (MO)
Grinnell Coll (IA)
Gustavus Adolphus Coll (MN)
Hamilton Coll (NY)
Hampden-Sydney Coll (VA)
Hampshire Coll (MA)
Hampton U (VA)
Hanover Coll (IN)
Harding U (AR)
Hartwick Coll (NY)
Harvard U (MA)
Harvey Mudd Coll (CA)
Hastings Coll (NE)
Haverford Coll (PA)
Hawai'i Pacific U (HI)
Heidelberg Coll (OH)
Hendrix Coll (AR)
High Point U (NC)
Hillsdale Coll (MI)
Hobart and William Smith Colls (NY)
Hofstra U (NY)
Hood Coll (MD)
Hope Coll (MI)

MAJORS AND MORE

Houghton Coll (NY)
Houston Baptist U (TX)
Howard Payne U (TX)
Humboldt State U (CA)
Hunter Coll of the City U of New York (NY)
Huntington U (IN)
Huston-Tillotson U (TX)
Illinois Coll (IL)
Illinois Inst of Technology (IL)
Illinois Wesleyan U (IL)
Immaculata U (PA)
Indiana Tech (IN)
Indiana U–Purdue U Fort Wayne (IN)
Inter American U of Puerto Rico, Bayamón Campus (PR)
Inter American U of Puerto Rico, Fajardo Campus (PR)
Inter American U of Puerto Rico, San Germán Campus (PR)
Iona Coll (NY)
Iowa Wesleyan Coll (IA)
Ithaca Coll (NY)
Jamestown Coll (ND)
Jarvis Christian Coll (TX)
John Carroll U (OH)
Kalamazoo Coll (MI)
Keene State Coll (NH)
Kennesaw State U (GA)
Kent State U (OH)
Kentucky Wesleyan Coll (KY)
Kettering U (MI)
King Coll (TN)
King's Coll (PA)
The King's U Coll (AB, Canada)
Kutztown U of Pennsylvania (PA)
LA Coll Intl (CA)
Lafayette Coll (PA)
LaGrange Coll (GA)
Lake Forest Coll (IL)
Lakehead U (ON, Canada)
Lake Superior State U (MI)
La Roche Coll (PA)
La Salle U (PA)
La Sierra U (CA)
Laurentian U (ON, Canada)
Lawrence Technological U (MI)
Lawrence U (WI)
Lebanon Valley Coll (PA)
Lehigh U (PA)
Lehman Coll of the City U of New York (NY)
LeMoyne-Owen Coll (TN)
LeTourneau U (TX)
Lewis & Clark Coll (OR)
Lewis-Clark State Coll (ID)
Lewis U (IL)
Limestone Coll (SC)
Lindenwood U (MO)
Linfield Coll (OR)
Lipscomb U (TN)
Livingstone Coll (NC)
Lock Haven U of Pennsylvania (PA)
Longwood U (VA)
Loras Coll (IA)
Louisiana State U and Ag and Mech Coll (LA)
Loyola Marymount U (CA)
Loyola U Chicago (IL)
Lubbock Christian U (TX)
Luther Coll (IA)
Lynchburg Coll (VA)
Lyon Coll (AR)
Macalester Coll (MN)
Madonna U (MI)
Maharishi U of Management (IA)
Malone Coll (OH)
Manchester Coll (IN)
Manhattanville Coll (NY)
Mansfield U of Pennsylvania (PA)
Marietta Coll (OH)
Marist Coll (NY)
Marlboro Coll (VT)
Marquette U (WI)
Maryville Coll (TN)
Maryville U of Saint Louis (MO)
Massachusetts Coll of Liberal Arts (MA)
Massachusetts Inst of Technology (MA)
McGill U (QC, Canada)
McKendree U (IL)
Memorial U of Newfoundland (NL, Canada)
Mercer U (GA)
Mercy Coll (NY)
Mercyhurst Coll (PA)
Meredith Coll (NC)
Messiah Coll (PA)
Methodist U (NC)
Metropolitan State U (MN)
Miami U Hamilton (OH)
Michigan Technological U (MI)
MidAmerica Nazarene U (KS)
Middlebury Coll (VT)
Middle Tennessee State U (TN)
Midland Lutheran Coll (NE)
Milligan Coll (TN)
Millikin U (IL)
Millsaps Coll (MS)
Mills Coll (CA)
Minnesota State U Mankato (MN)
Minot State U (ND)
Misericordia U (PA)
Mississippi Coll (MS)
Mississippi Valley State U (MS)
Missouri State U (MO)
Missouri U of Science and Technology (MO)
Missouri Valley Coll (MO)
Molloy Coll (NY)
Monroe Coll, Bronx (NY)
Monroe Coll, New Rochelle (NY)
Montana State U (MT)
Montana Tech of The U of Montana (MT)
Montclair State U (NJ)
Moravian Coll (PA)
Morgan State U (MD)
Morningside Coll (IA)
Mountain State U (WV)
Mount Allison U (NB, Canada)
Mount Holyoke Coll (MA)
Mount Marty Coll (SD)
Mount Mary Coll (WI)
Mount Mercy Coll (IA)
Mount Saint Mary Coll (NY)
Mount Vernon Nazarene U (OH)
National U (CA)
Nebraska Wesleyan U (NE)
Neumont U (UT)
New Mexico Inst of Mining and Technology (NM)
New York U (NY)
Niagara U (NY)
Nicholls State U (LA)
North Carolina Ag and Tech State U (NC)
North Carolina Central U (NC)
North Carolina State U (NC)
North Dakota State U (ND)
Northeastern Illinois U (IL)
Northeastern State U (OK)
Northeastern U (MA)
Northern Illinois U (IL)
North Georgia Coll & State U (GA)
Northwestern Coll (IA)
Northwestern Oklahoma State U (OK)
Northwestern U (IL)
Northwest Missouri State U (MO)
Northwest Nazarene U (ID)
Norwich U (VT)
Nova Southeastern U (FL)
Nyack Coll (NY)
Oakwood Coll (AL)
Oberlin Coll (OH)
Ohio Northern U (OH)
Ohio U (OH)
Ohio Wesleyan U (OH)
Oklahoma Christian U (OK)
Oklahoma City U (OK)
Oklahoma State U (OK)
Oral Roberts U (OK)
Oregon State U (OR)
Otterbein Coll (OH)
Ouachita Baptist U (AR)
Pace U (NY)
Pacific Lutheran U (WA)
Pacific States U (CA)
Pacific Union Coll (CA)
Pacific U (OR)
Park U (MO)
Penn State Erie, The Behrend Coll (PA)
Pepperdine U, Malibu (CA)
Philadelphia U (PA)
Piedmont Coll (GA)
Pittsburg State U (KS)
Plymouth State U (NH)
Point Loma Nazarene U (CA)
Polytechnic U, Brooklyn Campus (NY)
Pomona Coll (CA)
Portland State U (OR)
Prairie View A&M U (TX)
Presbyterian Coll (SC)
Providence Coll (RI)
Purdue U (IN)
Purdue U Calumet (IN)
Queen's U at Kingston (ON, Canada)
Quincy U (IL)
Quinnipiac U (CT)
Radford U (VA)
Randolph-Macon Coll (VA)
Redeemer U Coll (ON, Canada)
Regis U (CO)
Rensselaer Polytechnic Inst (NY)
Rhodes Coll (TN)
The Richard Stockton Coll of New Jersey (NJ)
Rider U (NJ)
Ripon Coll (WI)
Roanoke Coll (VA)
Roberts Wesleyan Coll (NY)
Rockford Coll (IL)
Rockhurst U (MO)
Roger Williams U (RI)
Rollins Coll (FL)
Roosevelt U (IL)
Rose-Hulman Inst of Technology (IN)
Royal Military Coll of Canada (ON, Canada)
Rutgers, The State U of New Jersey, New Brunswick (NJ)
Saginaw Valley State U (MI)
St. Ambrose U (IA)
St. Cloud State U (MN)
St. Edward's U (TX)
Saint Francis U (PA)
St. John Fisher Coll (NY)
Saint John's U (MN)
St. Joseph's Coll, Suffolk Campus (NY)
St. Lawrence U (NY)
Saint Martin's U (WA)
St. Mary's U (TX)
Saint Mary's U of Minnesota (MN)
Saint Michael's Coll (VT)
St. Olaf Coll (MN)
St. Thomas U (FL)
Saint Xavier U (IL)
Salem Intl U (WV)
Salem State Coll (MA)
Samford U (AL)
San Diego State U (CA)
San Francisco State U (CA)
Santa Clara U (CA)
Sarah Lawrence Coll (NY)
Scripps Coll (CA)
Seattle Pacific U (WA)
Seattle U (WA)
Seton Hill U (PA)
Sewanee: The U of the South (TN)
Shaw U (NC)
Simmons Coll (MA)
Simon Fraser U (BC, Canada)
Simpson Coll (IA)
Smith Coll (MA)
Sonoma State U (CA)
South Carolina State U (SC)
South Dakota School of Mines and Technology (SD)
Southeastern Louisiana U (LA)
Southern Connecticut State U (CT)
Southern Illinois U Carbondale (IL)
Southern Illinois U Edwardsville (IL)
Southern Methodist U (TX)
Southern Oregon U (OR)
Southern U and Ag and Mech Coll (LA)
Southern Utah U (UT)
Southwest Baptist U (MO)
Southwestern Adventist U (TX)
Southwestern Coll (KS)
Southwestern Oklahoma State U (OK)
Southwest Minnesota State U (MN)
Spelman Coll (GA)
Spring Arbor U (MI)
Stanford U (CA)
State U of New York at Binghamton (NY)
State U of New York at Fredonia (NY)
State U of New York at Oswego (NY)
State U of New York at Plattsburgh (NY)
State U of New York Coll at Geneseo (NY)
State U of New York Coll at Old Westbury (NY)
State U of New York Coll at Oneonta (NY)
State U of New York Inst of Technology (NY)
Stetson U (FL)
Stillman Coll (AL)
Stonehill Coll (MA)
Stony Brook U, State U of New York (NY)
Suffolk U (MA)
Susquehanna U (PA)
Sweet Briar Coll (VA)
Tabor Coll (KS)
Taylor U (IN)
Tennessee State U (TN)
Tennessee Technological U (TN)
Texas A&M U (TX)
Texas A&M U–Commerce (TX)
Texas Coll (TX)
Texas Lutheran U (TX)
Texas Southern U (TX)
Thiel Coll (PA)
Thomas Coll (ME)
Thomas Edison State Coll (NJ)
Thompson Rivers U (BC, Canada)
Tougaloo Coll (MS)
Transylvania U (KY)
Trent U (ON, Canada)
Trinity Christian Coll (IL)
Trinity Coll (CT)
Trinity Intl U (IL)
Tri-State U (IN)
Tufts U (MA)
Tulane U (LA)
Tuskegee U (AL)
Union Coll (NE)
Union U (TN)
United States Air Force Acad (CO)
United States Naval Acad (MD)
Université de Sherbrooke (QC, Canada)
Université du Québec en Outaouais (QC, Canada)
U at Albany, State U of New York (NY)
U at Buffalo, the State U of New York (NY)
The U of Akron (OH)
The U of Alabama (AL)
U of Alaska Fairbanks (AK)
U of Arkansas at Pine Bluff (AR)
U of Bridgeport (CT)
The U of British Columbia (BC, Canada)
The U of British Columbia–Okanagan (BC, Canada)
U of California, Berkeley (CA)
U of California, Irvine (CA)
U of California, Riverside (CA)
U of California, San Diego (CA)
U of California, Santa Barbara (CA)
U of California, Santa Cruz (CA)
U of Central Oklahoma (OK)
U of Chicago (IL)
U of Cincinnati (OH)
U of Colorado at Boulder (CO)
U of Connecticut (CT)
U of Dayton (OH)
U of Delaware (DE)
U of Denver (CO)
The U of Findlay (OH)
U of Great Falls (MT)
U of Guam (GU)
U of Hawaii at Manoa (HI)
U of Houston–Downtown (TX)
U of Houston–Victoria (TX)
U of Idaho (ID)
U of Illinois at Springfield (IL)
U of Illinois at Urbana–Champaign (IL)
U of Indianapolis (IN)
The U of Iowa (IA)
U of King's Coll (NS, Canada)
U of La Verne (CA)
U of Lethbridge (AB, Canada)
U of Louisiana at Lafayette (LA)
U of Louisiana at Monroe (LA)
U of Maine (ME)
U of Maine at Farmington (ME)
U of Maine at Fort Kent (ME)
U of Management and Technology (VA)
U of Mary Hardin-Baylor (TX)
U of Maryland, Baltimore County (MD)
U of Maryland Eastern Shore (MD)
U of Maryland U Coll (MD)
U of Mary Washington (VA)
U of Massachusetts Amherst (MA)
U of Massachusetts Boston (MA)
U of Massachusetts Lowell (MA)
U of Memphis (TN)
U of Miami (FL)
U of Michigan (MI)
U of Michigan–Flint (MI)
U of Minnesota, Duluth (MN)
U of Minnesota, Twin Cities Campus (MN)
U of Missouri–Columbia (MO)
U of Missouri–Kansas City (MO)
The U of Montana (MT)
U of Nebraska at Omaha (NE)
U of Nevada, Las Vegas (NV)
U of Nevada, Reno (NV)
U of New Brunswick Fredericton (NB, Canada)
U of New Hampshire (NH)
U of New Orleans (LA)
The U of North Carolina at Asheville (NC)
The U of North Carolina at Chapel Hill (NC)
The U of North Carolina at Charlotte (NC)
The U of North Carolina at Pembroke (NC)
The U of North Carolina Wilmington (NC)
U of Northern Iowa (IA)
U of Pittsburgh (PA)
U of Pittsburgh at Bradford (PA)
U of Pittsburgh at Johnstown (PA)
U of Portland (OR)
U of Prince Edward Island (PE, Canada)
U of Puget Sound (WA)
U of Redlands (CA)
U of Regina (SK, Canada)
U of Richmond (VA)
U of Rio Grande (OH)
U of Rochester (NY)
U of St. Francis (IL)
U of San Diego (CA)
The U of Scranton (PA)
U of Sioux Falls (SD)
U of South Carolina Aiken (SC)
U of Southern California (CA)
U of Southern Maine (ME)
The U of Tennessee (TN)
The U of Tennessee at Chattanooga (TN)
The U of Tennessee at Martin (TN)
The U of Texas at Arlington (TX)
The U of Texas at Dallas (TX)
The U of Texas at El Paso (TX)
The U of Texas at Tyler (TX)
The U of Texas of the Permian Basin (TX)
The U of Texas–Pan American (TX)
U of the District of Columbia (DC)
U of the Pacific (CA)
U of the Sacred Heart (PR)
U of the Sciences in Philadelphia (PA)
The U of Toledo (OH)
U of Toronto (ON, Canada)
U of Tulsa (OK)
U of Utah (UT)
U of Vermont (VT)
U of Victoria (BC, Canada)
The U of Western Ontario (ON, Canada)
U of Windsor (ON, Canada)
U of Wisconsin–Green Bay (WI)
U of Wisconsin–Madison (WI)
U of Wisconsin–Milwaukee (WI)
U of Wisconsin–Oshkosh (WI)
U of Wisconsin–Parkside (WI)
U of Wisconsin–Platteville (WI)
U of Wisconsin–Superior (WI)
U of Wyoming (WY)
Ursinus Coll (PA)
Utah Valley State Coll (UT)
Valdosta State U (GA)
Valparaiso U (IN)
Vanderbilt U (TN)
Villanova U (PA)
Virginia Military Inst (VA)
Virginia Polytechnic Inst and State U (VA)
Virginia State U (VA)
Virginia Wesleyan Coll (VA)
Voorhees Coll (SC)
Wagner Coll (NY)
Walla Walla U (WA)
Walsh U (OH)
Wartburg Coll (IA)
Washington and Lee U (VA)
Washington Coll (MD)
Washington State U (WA)
Washington U in St. Louis (MO)
Waynesburg U (PA)
Webster U (MO)
Wellesley Coll (MA)
Wells Coll (NY)
Wesleyan U (CT)
Western Carolina U (NC)
Western Connecticut State U (CT)
Western Michigan U (MI)
Western New England Coll (MA)
Western New Mexico U (NM)
Western State Coll of Colorado (CO)
Western Washington U (WA)
Westfield State Coll (MA)
Westminster Coll (MO)
Westminster Coll (UT)
Westmont Coll (CA)
West Virginia U (WV)
West Virginia Wesleyan Coll (WV)
Wheaton Coll (IL)
Wheaton Coll (MA)
Wheeling Jesuit U (WV)
Whitworth U (WA)
Widener U (PA)
Wiley Coll (TX)
Wilfrid Laurier U (ON, Canada)
Willamette U (OR)
William Jewell Coll (MO)
William Paterson U of New Jersey (NJ)
Williams Coll (MA)
Wilmington Coll (OH)
Winona State U (MN)
Winthrop U (SC)
Wittenberg U (OH)
Wofford Coll (SC)
Worcester Polytechnic Inst (MA)
Wright State U (OH)
Xavier U (OH)
Xavier U of Louisiana (LA)
York Coll of Pennsylvania (PA)
York U (ON, Canada)
Youngstown State U (OH)

COMPUTER SOFTWARE AND MEDIA APPLICATIONS RELATED
Baldwin-Wallace Coll (OH)
Dakota Wesleyan U (SD)
Duquesne U (PA)
Florida State U (FL)
Holy Names U (CA)
Indiana U–Purdue U Fort Wayne (IN)
Neumont U (UT)
New England School of Communications (ME)
U of Denver (CO)
U of Great Falls (MT)
U of Massachusetts Boston (MA)
The U of Western Ontario (ON, Canada)
U of Windsor (ON, Canada)

COMPUTER SOFTWARE ENGINEERING
Allegheny Coll (PA)
Auburn U (AL)
Brock U (ON, Canada)
California Polytechnic State U, San Luis Obispo (CA)
Carroll Coll (WI)
Claflin U (SC)
Clarkson U (NY)
Cogswell Polytechnical Coll (CA)
Concordia U (QC, Canada)
DeVry U, Phoenix (AZ)
DeVry U, Fremont (CA)
DeVry U, Long Beach (CA)
DeVry U, Pomona (CA)
DeVry U, Westminster (CO)
DeVry U, Orlando (FL)
DeVry U, Alpharetta (GA)
DeVry U, Decatur (GA)
DeVry U, Addison (IL)
DeVry U, Tinley Park (IL)
DeVry U, Edina (MN)
DeVry U, Irving (TX)
DeVry U, Arlington (VA)
DeVry U, Federal Way (WA)
DeVry U Online (IL)
Embry-Riddle Aeronautical U (AZ)
Embry-Riddle Aeronautical U (FL)
Fairfield U (CT)
Florida Inst of Technology (FL)
Florida State U (FL)
Liberty U (VA)
McGill U (QC, Canada)
Michigan Technological U (MI)
Milwaukee School of Eng (WI)
Monmouth U (NJ)
National U (CA)
Penn State Erie, The Behrend Coll (PA)
Robert Morris U (PA)
Rochester Inst of Technology (NY)
Rose-Hulman Inst of Technology (IN)
South Dakota State U (SD)
Southern Polytechnic State U (GA)
U of Illinois at Urbana–Champaign (IL)
U of Management and Technology (VA)
U of Ottawa (ON, Canada)
U of Regina (SK, Canada)
The U of Texas at Arlington (TX)
The U of Texas at Dallas (TX)
U of Toronto (ON, Canada)
U of Victoria (BC, Canada)
The U of Western Ontario (ON, Canada)
U of Wisconsin–Platteville (WI)
Utah Valley State Coll (UT)
Vermont Tech Coll (VT)
York U (ON, Canada)

COMPUTER SOFTWARE TECHNOLOGY
Colorado Tech U—Colorado Springs (CO)
Colorado Tech U—Denver (CO)
Colorado Tech U—North Kansas City (MO)
Colorado Tech U—Online (CO)
Colorado Tech U—Sioux Falls (SD)

COMPUTER SYSTEMS ANALYSIS
Baldwin-Wallace Coll (OH)
British Columbia Inst of Technology (BC, Canada)
Concordia U (QC, Canada)
DeVry Coll of New York (NY)
DeVry U, Phoenix (AZ)
DeVry U, Fremont (CA)
DeVry U, Long Beach (CA)
DeVry U, Pomona (CA)
DeVry U, Sherman Oaks (CA)
DeVry U, Westminster (CO)
DeVry U, Miramar (FL)
DeVry U, Orlando (FL)
DeVry U, Alpharetta (GA)
DeVry U, Decatur (GA)
DeVry U, Addison (IL)
DeVry U, Chicago (IL)
DeVry U, Tinley Park (IL)
DeVry U, Indianapolis (IN)
DeVry U (MD)
DeVry U, Edina (MN)
DeVry U, Kansas City (MO)
DeVry U (NJ)
DeVry U, Charlotte (NC)
DeVry U, Columbus (OH)
DeVry U (OK)
DeVry U (OR)
DeVry U, Fort Washington (PA)
DeVry U, Houston (TX)
DeVry U, Irving (TX)
DeVry U, Arlington (VA)
DeVry U, Federal Way (WA)
DeVry U, Milwaukee (WI)
DeVry U Online (IL)
Granite State Coll (NH)
HEC Montreal (QC, Canada)
Inter American U of Puerto Rico, Bayamón Campus (PR)
Kent State U (OH)
Metropolitan State U (MN)
Miami U (OH)
Miami U Hamilton (OH)
Montana Tech of The U of Montana (MT)
Mount Saint Vincent U (NS, Canada)
Pace U (NY)
Pennsylvania Coll of Technology (PA)
Rochester Inst of Technology (NY)
St. Ambrose U (IA)
Seattle Pacific U (WA)
Shippensburg U of Pennsylvania (PA)
Thompson Rivers U (BC, Canada)
U of Advancing Technology (AZ)
U of Denver (CO)
U of Great Falls (MT)
U of Houston (TX)
U of Louisiana at Lafayette (LA)
U of North Dakota (ND)
U of Vermont (VT)

COMPUTER SYSTEMS NETWORKING AND TELECOMMUNICATIONS
The American U of Athens (Greece)
Baldwin-Wallace Coll (OH)
Bloomfield Coll (NJ)
Boise State U (ID)
California State U, East Bay (CA)
Davenport U, Dearborn (MI)
Davenport U, Grand Rapids (MI)
DePaul U (IL)
DeVry Coll of New York (NY)
DeVry U, Phoenix (AZ)
DeVry U, Fremont (CA)
DeVry U, Long Beach (CA)
DeVry U, Pomona (CA)
DeVry U, Sherman Oaks (CA)
DeVry U, Westminster (CO)
DeVry U, Miramar (FL)
DeVry U, Orlando (FL)
DeVry U, Alpharetta (GA)
DeVry U, Decatur (GA)
DeVry U, Addison (IL)
DeVry U, Chicago (IL)
DeVry U, Tinley Park (IL)
DeVry U, Edina (MN)
DeVry U, Kansas City (MO)
DeVry U (NJ)
DeVry U, Columbus (OH)
DeVry U, Fort Washington (PA)
DeVry U, Houston (TX)
DeVry U, Irving (TX)
DeVry U, Arlington (VA)
DeVry U, Federal Way (WA)
DeVry U Online (IL)
Electronic Data Processing Coll of Puerto Rico (PR)
Iona Coll (NY)
Kean U (NJ)
Michigan Technological U (MI)
Mountain State U (WV)
Northern Michigan U (MI)
Northwestern Oklahoma State U (OK)
Purdue U (IN)
Rochester Inst of Technology (NY)
Roosevelt U (IL)
St. Ambrose U (IA)
The U of Akron (OH)
The U of Findlay (OH)
U of Great Falls (MT)
The U of North Carolina at Greensboro (NC)
U of Pennsylvania (PA)
U of Toronto (ON, Canada)
U of Windsor (ON, Canada)
Weber State U (UT)
Western Illinois U (IL)
Western State Coll of Colorado (CO)

COMPUTER TEACHER EDUCATION
Alma Coll (MI)
Baylor U (TX)
Bishop's U (QC, Canada)
Bridgewater Coll (VA)
Capital U (OH)
Concordia U Chicago (IL)
Concordia U, Nebraska (NE)
Dakota State U (SD)
DePaul U (IL)
Dordt Coll (IA)
Eastern Michigan U (MI)
Hardin-Simmons U (TX)
Immaculata U (PA)
Keene State Coll (NH)
Liberty U (VA)
Michigan Technological U (MI)
Pace U (NY)
Pillsbury Baptist Bible Coll (MN)
Southeastern Louisiana U (LA)
Southern U and Ag and Mech Coll (LA)
Union Coll (NE)
U of Nebraska–Lincoln (NE)
Utica Coll (NY)
Wright State U (OH)

COMPUTER TECHNOLOGY/ COMPUTER SYSTEMS TECHNOLOGY
Bob Jones U (SC)
Central Michigan U (MI)
Colorado Tech U—Colorado Springs (CO)
Colorado Tech U—Denver (CO)
Colorado Tech U—North Kansas City (MO)
Colorado Tech U—Online (CO)
Colorado Tech U—Sioux Falls (SD)
Florida Atlantic U (FL)
Prairie View A&M U (TX)
Southwestern Coll (KS)
U of Central Florida (FL)
Wayne State U (MI)

CONDUCTING
Calvin Coll (MI)
Canadian Mennonite U (MB, Canada)
Chapman U (CA)
Loyola Marymount U (CA)
Mannes Coll The New School for Music (NY)
Ohio U (OH)
Sam Houston State U (TX)
U of Miami (FL)

CONSERVATION BIOLOGY
Arizona State U (AZ)
Brigham Young U (UT)
Philadelphia U (PA)
Sterling Coll (VT)
U of Idaho (ID)
U of Maine at Machias (ME)
The U of Western Ontario (ON, Canada)

CONSTRUCTION ENGINEERING
Bradley U (IL)
California State U, Long Beach (CA)
Clarkson U (NY)
Concordia U (QC, Canada)
John Brown U (AR)
Michigan Technological U (MI)
National U (CA)
North Carolina State U (NC)
North Dakota State U (ND)
Oregon State U (OR)
Purdue U (IN)
Southern Polytechnic State U (GA)
State U of New York Coll of Environmental Science and Forestry (NY)
Texas A&M U–Commerce (TX)
The U of Alabama (AL)
U of Cincinnati (OH)
U of Illinois at Urbana–Champaign (IL)
U of Nevada, Las Vegas (NV)
U of New Brunswick Fredericton (NB, Canada)
U of Southern California (CA)

CONSTRUCTION ENGINEERING TECHNOLOGY
Bemidji State U (MN)
Bowling Green State U (OH)
California State Polytechnic U, Pomona (CA)
California State U, Chico (CA)
California State U, Fresno (CA)
California State U, Long Beach (CA)
California State U, Sacramento (CA)
Central Michigan U (MI)
Eastern Kentucky U (KY)
Eastern Michigan U (MI)
Fairleigh Dickinson U, Metropolitan Campus (NJ)
Farmingdale State Coll (NY)
Fitchburg State Coll (MA)
Florida Ag and Mech U (FL)
Florida Inst of Technology (FL)
Florida Intl U (FL)
Georgia Southern U (GA)
Hampton U (VA)
Indiana U–Purdue U Fort Wayne (IN)
Montana State U (MT)
Northern Arizona U (AZ)
Northern Michigan U (MI)
Pittsburg State U (KS)
Purdue U (IN)
Purdue U Calumet (IN)
Sam Houston State U (TX)
San Diego State U (CA)
South Dakota State U (SD)
Southern Illinois U Edwardsville (IL)
Southern Utah U (UT)
Texas A&M U (TX)
Texas Southern U (TX)
Texas State U-San Marcos (TX)
Thomas Edison State Coll (NJ)
Tuskegee U (AL)
The U of Akron (OH)
U of Cincinnati (OH)
U of Florida (FL)
U of Houston (TX)
U of Louisiana at Monroe (LA)
U of Maine (ME)
U of Maryland Eastern Shore (MD)
U of Nebraska at Omaha (NE)
U of Nebraska–Lincoln (NE)
U of Nevada, Reno (NV)
U of North Florida (FL)
U of North Texas (TX)
The U of Toledo (OH)

CONSTRUCTION MANAGEMENT
Appalachian State U (NC)
Arizona State U (AZ)
Boise State U (ID)
California Polytechnic State U, San Luis Obispo (CA)
California State U, Fresno (CA)
California State U, Long Beach (CA)
Clemson U (SC)
Eastern Michigan U (MI)
Farmingdale State Coll (NY)
Ferris State U (MI)
Hampton U (VA)
John Brown U (AR)
Lawrence Technological U (MI)
Louisiana State U and Ag and Mech Coll (LA)
Michigan State U (MI)
Milwaukee School of Eng (WI)
Minnesota State U Mankato (MN)
Mississippi State U (MS)
Missouri State U (MO)
North Carolina Ag and Tech State U (NC)
North Carolina State U (NC)
North Dakota State U (ND)
Oklahoma State U (OK)
Oregon State U (OR)
Pennsylvania Coll of Technology (PA)
Pittsburg State U (KS)
Polytechnic U, Brooklyn Campus (NY)
Pratt Inst (NY)
Roger Williams U (RI)
Sam Houston State U (TX)
Southern Polytechnic State U (GA)
State U of New York Coll of Environmental Science and Forestry (NY)
U of Cincinnati (OH)
U of Denver (CO)
U of Maryland Eastern Shore (MD)
U of Minnesota, Twin Cities Campus (MN)
U of Northern Iowa (IA)
U of the District of Columbia (DC)
U of Wisconsin–Madison (WI)
U of Wisconsin–Platteville (WI)
Virginia Polytechnic Inst and State U (VA)
Western Carolina U (NC)
Western Illinois U (IL)

CONSUMER ECONOMICS
Cornell U (NY)
Indiana U of Pennsylvania (PA)
South Dakota State U (SD)
The U of Arizona (AZ)
U of Delaware (DE)
U of Georgia (GA)
U of Illinois at Urbana–Champaign (IL)
U of Rhode Island (RI)
The U of Tennessee (TN)

CONSUMER/HOMEMAKING EDUCATION
California State U, Monterey Bay (CA)
Virginia Polytechnic Inst and State U (VA)

CONSUMER MERCHANDISING/ RETAILING MANAGEMENT
Belmont U (TN)
Bradley U (IL)
East Central U (OK)
Eastern Kentucky U (KY)
Fontbonne U (MO)
HEC Montreal (QC, Canada)
John F. Kennedy U (CA)
Lindenwood U (MO)
Madonna U (MI)
Mount Ida Coll (MA)
Northwest Missouri State U (MO)
Salem State Coll (MA)
San Francisco State U (CA)
Simmons Coll (MA)
U of Central Oklahoma (OK)
U of Memphis (TN)
Winona State U (MN)

CONSUMER SERVICES AND ADVOCACY
Carson-Newman Coll (TN)
Coll of the Ozarks (MO)
State U of New York Coll at Oneonta (NY)
Tennessee State U (TN)
U of Wisconsin–Madison (WI)

CORRECTIONS
Bluefield State Coll (WV)
California State U, East Bay (CA)
Coker Coll (SC)
The Coll at Brockport, State U of New York (NY)
Coll of the Ozarks (MO)
East Central U (OK)
Hardin-Simmons U (TX)
Jacksonville State U (AL)
Lake Superior State U (MI)
Lewis-Clark State Coll (ID)
Limestone Coll (SC)
Mercyhurst Coll (PA)
Minnesota State U Mankato (MN)
Northeastern U (MA)
Oklahoma City U (OK)
Saint Louis U (MO)
Saint Mary's U of Minnesota (MN)
Sam Houston State U (TX)
Southeast Missouri State U (MO)
Stephen F. Austin State U (TX)
Texas State U-San Marcos (TX)
Tiffin U (OH)
Troy U (AL)
Tulane U (LA)
U of Arkansas at Pine Bluff (AR)
U of Great Falls (MT)
U of New Mexico (NM)
U of Pittsburgh (PA)
The U of Texas at Brownsville (TX)
Washburn U (KS)
Winona State U (MN)
York Coll of Pennsylvania (PA)

CORRECTIONS ADMINISTRATION
American Public U System (WV)
U of Great Falls (MT)

CORRECTIONS AND CRIMINAL JUSTICE RELATED
American InterContinental U (CA)
American InterContinental U (FL)
American InterContinental U Buckhead Campus (GA)
American InterContinental U Dunwoody Campus (GA)

American InterContinental U Online (IL)
Averett U (VA)
Bethune-Cookman U (FL)
Bob Jones U (SC)
Coker Coll (SC)
The Coll at Brockport, State U of New York (NY)
Emporia State U (KS)
Granite State Coll (NH)
Harding U (AR)
Hastings Coll (NE)
La Roche Coll (PA)
Limestone Coll (SC)
Mercyhurst Coll (PA)
Mount Mary Coll (WI)
North Dakota State U (ND)
Russell Sage Coll (NY)
Sam Houston State U (TX)
Southern New Hampshire U (NH)
The U of Alabama at Birmingham (AL)
U of Alaska Fairbanks (AK)
U of Great Falls (MT)
U of Michigan–Flint (MI)

COUNSELING PSYCHOLOGY

Bob Jones U (SC)
Coker Coll (SC)
Coll of Santa Fe (NM)
Crossroads Coll (MN)
Grace Coll (IN)
Great Lakes Christian Coll (MI)
Jamestown Coll (ND)
Kentucky Christian U (KY)
Lesley U (MA)
Mid-Continent U (KY)
Morningside Coll (IA)
Newman U (KS)
Northwestern U (IL)
Oak Hills Christian Coll (MN)
Oregon Inst of Technology (OR)
Paine Coll (GA)
Pittsburg State U (KS)
Rochester Coll (MI)
Saint Xavier U (IL)
Samford U (AL)
Sam Houston State U (TX)
San Diego Christian Coll (CA)
Southwestern Coll (AZ)
Taylor U Fort Wayne (IN)
Toccoa Falls Coll (GA)
Trinity Coll of Florida (FL)
U of Great Falls (MT)
U of Lethbridge (AB, Canada)
U of North Alabama (AL)
Wayne State Coll (NE)

COUNSELOR EDUCATION/ SCHOOL COUNSELING AND GUIDANCE

Amberton U (TX)
Belmont U (TN)
California State Polytechnic U, Pomona (CA)
Clemson U (SC)
East Central U (OK)
Edinboro U of Pennsylvania (PA)
Florida Gulf Coast U (FL)
Harding U (AR)
Houston Baptist U (TX)
Keene State Coll (NH)
Lenoir-Rhyne Coll (NC)
Marshall U (WV)
Martin U (IN)
Memorial U of Newfoundland (NL, Canada)
Northern Arizona U (AZ)
Northwest Missouri State U (MO)
St. Cloud State U (MN)
Sam Houston State U (TX)
Slippery Rock U of Pennsylvania (PA)
Tarleton State U (TX)
Texas A&M U–Commerce (TX)
Texas Christian U (TX)
Texas Southern U (TX)
Université de Sherbrooke (QC, Canada)
The U of British Columbia (BC, Canada)
U of Central Oklahoma (OK)
U of Hawaii at Manoa (HI)
U of Houston–Clear Lake (TX)
U of Montevallo (AL)
U of New Brunswick Fredericton (NB, Canada)
The U of North Carolina at Pembroke (NC)
U of Windsor (ON, Canada)
West Chester U of Pennsylvania (PA)
Western Washington U (WA)
Westfield State Coll (MA)
Wright State U (OH)

COURT REPORTING

U of Mississippi (MS)

CRAFTS, FOLK ART AND ARTISANRY

Bridgewater State Coll (MA)
Brigham Young U (UT)
The Cleveland Inst of Art (OH)
Indiana U–Purdue U Fort Wayne (IN)
Kent State U (OH)
Kutztown U of Pennsylvania (PA)
North Georgia Coll & State U (GA)
NSCAD U (NS, Canada)
Rochester Inst of Technology (NY)
U of Illinois at Urbana–Champaign (IL)
Virginia Commonwealth U (VA)

CREATIVE WRITING

Agnes Scott Coll (GA)
Alderson-Broaddus Coll (WV)
Allegheny Coll (PA)
Ashland U (OH)
Augustana Coll (IL)
Baldwin-Wallace Coll (OH)
Bard Coll (NY)
Bard Coll at Simon's Rock (MA)
Belhaven Coll (MS)
Beloit Coll (WI)
Bennington Coll (VT)
Bernard M. Baruch Coll of the City U of New York (NY)
Bluffton U (OH)
Bob Jones U (SC)
Bowling Green State U (OH)
Bradley U (IL)
Brandeis U (MA)
Bridgewater State Coll (MA)
Brown U (RI)
Bucknell U (PA)
California State U, East Bay (CA)
California State U, Long Beach (CA)
California State U, San Bernardino (CA)
Canisius Coll (NY)
Capital U (OH)
Carlow U (PA)
Carnegie Mellon U (PA)
Carroll Coll (WI)
Carson-Newman Coll (TN)
Central Michigan U (MI)
Chapman U (CA)
Chatham U (PA)
City Coll of the City U of New York (NY)
Colby Coll (ME)
The Coll at Brockport, State U of New York (NY)
The Coll of Idaho (ID)
Coll of Santa Fe (NM)
The Colorado Coll (CO)
Colorado State U (CO)
Columbia Coll Chicago (IL)
Concordia Coll (MN)
Concordia U (QC, Canada)
Cornerstone U (MI)
Dartmouth Coll (NH)
Denison U (OH)
Dominican U of California (CA)
Eastern Michigan U (MI)
Eckerd Coll (FL)
Emerson Coll (MA)
Emory & Henry Coll (VA)
Emory U (GA)
Eugene Lang Coll The New School for Liberal Arts (NY)
Fairleigh Dickinson U, Coll at Florham (NJ)
Fitchburg State Coll (MA)
Florida State U (FL)
Franklin & Marshall Coll (PA)
Gettysburg Coll (PA)
Grand Valley State U (MI)
Green Mountain Coll (VT)
Hamilton Coll (NY)
Harvard U (MA)
Hastings Coll (NE)
High Point U (NC)
Hofstra U (NY)
Hollins U (VA)
Houghton Coll (NY)
Indiana Wesleyan U (IN)
Ithaca Coll (NY)
The Johns Hopkins U (MD)
Johnson State Coll (VT)
Kansas City Art Inst (MO)
Kenyon Coll (OH)
Knox Coll (IL)
Lehman Coll of the City U of New York (NY)
Lewis-Clark State Coll (ID)
Linfield Coll (OR)
Loras Coll (IA)
Loyola Coll in Maryland (MD)
Loyola U New Orleans (LA)
Lycoming Coll (PA)
Lynchburg Coll (VA)
Marlboro Coll (VT)
Marquette U (WI)
Massachusetts Inst of Technology (MA)
McMurry U (TX)
Mercyhurst Coll (PA)
Methodist U (NC)
Miami U (OH)
Miami U Hamilton (OH)
Mills Coll (CA)
Minnesota State U Mankato (MN)
Moravian Coll (PA)
Nazareth Coll of Rochester (NY)
New England Coll (NH)
North Carolina State U (NC)
North Central Coll (IL)
Northland Coll (WI)
Northwestern Coll (MN)
Oberlin Coll (OH)
Ohio Northern U (OH)
Ohio U (OH)
Ohio Wesleyan U (OH)
Oklahoma Christian U (OK)
Pacific U (OR)
Pittsburg State U (KS)
Pitzer Coll (CA)
Pratt Inst (NY)
Purchase Coll, State U of New York (NY)
Purdue U (IN)
Randolph Coll (VA)
Rockhurst U (MO)
Roger Williams U (RI)
St. Andrews Presbyterian Coll (NC)
St. Cloud State U (MN)
Saint Joseph's Coll (IN)
St. Lawrence U (NY)
Saint Mary's Coll (IN)
Salem Coll (NC)
San Diego State U (CA)
San Francisco State U (CA)
Sarah Lawrence Coll (NY)
Savannah Coll of Art and Design (GA)
School of the Art Inst of Chicago (IL)
Seattle U (WA)
Seton Hill U (PA)
Siena Heights U (MI)
Southern Methodist U (TX)
Southern New Hampshire U (NH)
Southern Vermont Coll (VT)
Southwest Minnesota State U (MN)
State U of New York at Binghamton (NY)
State U of New York at New Paltz (NY)
State U of New York at Oswego (NY)
Stephens Coll (MO)
Susquehanna U (PA)
Sweet Briar Coll (VA)
Syracuse U (NY)
Taylor U (IN)
Taylor U Fort Wayne (IN)
Texas Christian U (TX)
Trinity Coll (CT)
The U of Arizona (AZ)
The U of British Columbia (BC, Canada)
The U of British Columbia–Okanagan (BC, Canada)
U of California, Riverside (CA)
U of California, San Diego (CA)
U of California, Santa Cruz (CA)
U of Chicago (IL)
U of Denver (CO)
U of Evansville (IN)
The U of Findlay (OH)
U of Great Falls (MT)
U of Houston (TX)
U of Maine at Farmington (ME)
U of Maine at Machias (ME)
U of Miami (FL)
U of Michigan (MI)
The U of Montana (MT)
U of Nebraska at Omaha (NE)
The U of North Carolina Wilmington (NC)
U of Pittsburgh (PA)
U of Pittsburgh at Bradford (PA)
U of Pittsburgh at Johnstown (PA)
U of Puget Sound (WA)
U of Redlands (CA)
U of St. Thomas (MN)
U of Southern California (CA)
The U of Tampa (FL)
The U of Texas at El Paso (TX)
U of Victoria (BC, Canada)
U of Windsor (ON, Canada)
U of Wisconsin–Parkside (WI)
Warren Wilson Coll (NC)
Washington U in St. Louis (MO)
Waynesburg U (PA)
Wells Coll (NY)
Western New England Coll (MA)
Western State Coll of Colorado (CO)
Western Washington U (WA)
West Virginia Wesleyan Coll (WV)
Wofford Coll (SC)
York U (ON, Canada)

CRIMINALISTICS AND CRIMINAL SCIENCE

Florida Gulf Coast U (FL)
West Virginia U (WV)
York Coll of Pennsylvania (PA)

CRIMINAL JUSTICE/LAW ENFORCEMENT ADMINISTRATION

Adelphi U (NY)
Adrian Coll (MI)
Alabama State U (AL)
Albertus Magnus Coll (CT)
Alfred U (NY)
Alvernia Coll (PA)
American InterContinental U (CA)
American InterContinental U (FL)
American InterContinental U Buckhead Campus (GA)
American InterContinental U Dunwoody Campus (GA)
American InterContinental U Online (IL)
American Public U System (WV)
Anderson U (IN)
Anderson U (SC)
Argosy U, Atlanta (GA)
Argosy U, Inland Empire (CA)
Argosy U, Nashville (TN)
Argosy U, Orange County (CA)
Argosy U, San Diego (CA)
Argosy U, San Francisco Bay Area (CA)
Argosy U, Santa Monica (CA)
Argosy U, Sarasota (FL)
Argosy U, Schaumburg (IL)
Argosy U, Twin Cities (MN)
Argosy U, Washington DC (VA)
Arizona State U at the West campus (AZ)
Athens State U (AL)
Austin Peay State U (TN)
Averett U (VA)
Ball State U (IN)
Barton Coll (NC)
Bay Path Coll (MA)
Bemidji State U (MN)
Blackburn Coll (IL)
Bluefield Coll (VA)
Bradley U (IL)
Brevard Coll (NC)
Brown Mackie Coll–Fort Wayne (IN)
Brown Mackie Coll–Indianapolis (IN)
Brown Mackie Coll–Merrillville (IN)
Brown Mackie Coll–Michigan City (IN)
Brown Mackie Coll–South Bend (IN)
Buffalo State Coll, State U of New York (NY)
California Baptist U (CA)
California Lutheran U (CA)
California State U, Dominguez Hills (CA)
California State U, East Bay (CA)
California State U, Long Beach (CA)
California State U, Sacramento (CA)
California State U, San Bernardino (CA)
California State U, Stanislaus (CA)
Calumet Coll of Saint Joseph (IN)
Canisius Coll (NY)
Castleton State Coll (VT)
Cedarville U (OH)
Central Pennsylvania Coll (PA)
Central Washington U (WA)
Chestnut Hill Coll (PA)
The Citadel, The Military Coll of South Carolina (SC)
Claflin U (SC)
Coker Coll (SC)
The Coll at Brockport, State U of New York (NY)
The Coll of New Jersey (NJ)
Coll of St. Joseph (VT)
The Coll of Saint Rose (NY)
Coll of the Ozarks (MO)
Colorado Tech U—Colorado Springs (CO)
Colorado Tech U—Denver (CO)
Colorado Tech U—North Kansas City (MO)
Colorado Tech U—Online (CO)
Colorado Tech U—Sioux Falls (SD)
Concordia U (MI)
Concordia U Texas (TX)
Concordia U Wisconsin (WI)
Culver-Stockton Coll (MO)
Curry Coll (MA)
Dakota Wesleyan U (SD)
Dallas Baptist U (TX)
Dana Coll (NE)
Defiance Coll (OH)
Delaware Valley Coll (PA)
DeSales U (PA)
Dordt Coll (IA)
East Central U (OK)
East Tennessee State U (TN)
Evangel U (MO)
Everest U, Tampa (FL)
Everest U, Tampa (FL)
Excelsior Coll (NY)
Faulkner U (AL)
Fayetteville State U (NC)
Florida Ag and Mech U (FL)
Florida Memorial U (FL)
Frostburg State U (MD)
The George Washington U (DC)
Georgia Coll & State U (GA)
Georgian Court U (NJ)
Gonzaga U (WA)
Grace Coll (IN)
Grambling State U (LA)
Grand Valley State U (MI)
Grand View Coll (IA)
Granite State Coll (NH)
Grantham U (MO)
Greenville Coll (IL)
Gustavus Adolphus Coll (MN)
Hamline U (MN)
Hampton U (VA)
Hannibal-LaGrange Coll (MO)
Harris-Stowe State U (MO)
Hawai'i Pacific U (HI)
Holy Family U (PA)
Indiana U–Purdue U Fort Wayne (IN)
Inter American U of Puerto Rico, Fajardo Campus (PR)
Iona Coll (NY)
Iowa Wesleyan Coll (IA)
Jacksonville State U (AL)
Judson Coll (AL)
Kean U (NJ)
Keiser U, Fort Lauderdale (FL)
Keuka Coll (NY)
Keystone Coll (PA)
Lake Superior State U (MI)
Lambuth U (TN)
Lees-McRae Coll (NC)
LeMoyne-Owen Coll (TN)
Lewis U (IL)
Liberty U (VA)
Lincoln U (MO)
Lindenwood U (MO)
Lindsey Wilson Coll (KY)
Lock Haven U of Pennsylvania (PA)
Longwood U (VA)
Lourdes Coll (OH)
Mansfield U of Pennsylvania (PA)
Marian Coll of Fond du Lac (WI)
Marist Coll (NY)
Martin U (IN)
McKendree U (IL)
Mercy Coll (NY)
Methodist U (NC)
Michigan State U (MI)
MidAmerica Nazarene U (KS)
Middle Tennessee State U (TN)
Midland Lutheran Coll (NE)
Midwestern State U (TX)
Miles Coll (AL)
Millikin U (IL)
Mississippi Coll (MS)
Mississippi Valley State U (MS)
Missouri Southern State U (MO)
Missouri Valley Coll (MO)
Mitchell Coll (CT)
Monroe Coll, Bronx (NY)
Moravian Coll (PA)
Morris Coll (SC)
Mountain State U (WV)
Mount Ida Coll (MA)
Mount Mercy Coll (IA)
Mount Olive Coll (NC)
Mount Vernon Nazarene U (OH)
National U (CA)
New England Coll (NH)
Newman U (KS)
New York Inst of Technology (NY)
Niagara U (NY)
North Carolina Wesleyan Coll (NC)
Northeastern State U (OK)
Northern Arizona U (AZ)
North Georgia Coll & State U (GA)
Norwich U (VT)
Oakland City U (IN)
Ohio Dominican U (OH)
Ohio Northern U (OH)
Ohio U (OH)
Ohio U–Zanesville (OH)
Oklahoma City U (OK)
Pace U (NY)
Penn State Abington (PA)
Penn State Altoona (PA)
Penn State Berks (PA)

Penn State Erie, The Behrend Coll (PA)
Penn State U Park (PA)
Peru State Coll (NE)
Pfeiffer U (NC)
Piedmont Coll (GA)
Point Park U (PA)
Portland State U (OR)
Purdue U (IN)
Purdue U Calumet (IN)
Radford U (VA)
Regis U (CO)
Remington Coll–Colorado Springs Campus (CO)
Remington Coll–Honolulu Campus (HI)
Remington Coll–Largo Campus (FL)
Remington Coll–San Diego Campus (CA)
Remington Coll–Tampa Campus (FL)
Roberts Wesleyan Coll (NY)
Rochester Inst of Technology (NY)
Rogers State U (OK)
Roger Williams U (RI)
Rutgers, The State U of New Jersey, New Brunswick (NJ)
Sacred Heart U (CT)
St. Cloud State U (MN)
Saint Francis U (PA)
St. John's U (NY)
Saint Louis U (MO)
Saint Martin's U (WA)
St. Mary's U (TX)
Saint Mary's U of Minnesota (MN)
St. Thomas Aquinas Coll (NY)
St. Thomas U (FL)
Salem Intl U (WV)
Salem State Coll (MA)
Salve Regina U (RI)
Samford U (AL)
Sam Houston State U (TX)
San Diego State U (CA)
San Francisco State U (CA)
Seattle U (WA)
Seton Hill U (PA)
Shenandoah U (VA)
Simpson Coll (IA)
Sonoma State U (CA)
South Carolina State U (SC)
Southeastern U (FL)
Southern Illinois U Carbondale (IL)
Southern Vermont Coll (VT)
South U (AL)
South U (GA)
South U (SC)
Southwest Baptist U (MO)
Southwestern Adventist U (TX)
Southwestern Coll (KS)
Southwestern Oklahoma State U (OK)
Southwest Minnesota State U (MN)
State U of New York at Fredonia (NY)
State U of New York at Oswego (NY)
Suffolk U (MA)
Taylor U Fort Wayne (IN)
Tennessee State U (TN)
Texas A&M U–Commerce (TX)
Texas Southern U (TX)
Thomas Coll (ME)
Thomas Edison State Coll (NJ)
Thomas More Coll (KY)
Thomas U (GA)
Tiffin U (OH)
Tri-State U (IN)
Union Coll (KY)
U at Albany, State U of New York (NY)
The U of Arizona (AZ)
U of Arkansas at Pine Bluff (AR)
U of Baltimore (MD)
U of Central Missouri (MO)
U of Central Oklahoma (OK)
U of Cincinnati (OH)
U of Colorado Denver (CO)
U of Dayton (OH)
U of Delaware (DE)
The U of Findlay (OH)
U of Great Falls (MT)
U of Guam (GU)
U of Hawaii–West Oahu (HI)
U of Louisville (KY)
The U of Maine at Augusta (ME)
U of Mary Hardin-Baylor (TX)
U of Maryland Eastern Shore (MD)
U of Maryland U Coll (MD)
U of Massachusetts Lowell (MA)
U of Memphis (TN)
U of Missouri–Kansas City (MO)
U of Nevada, Las Vegas (NV)
U of New Hampshire (NH)
U of New Haven (CT)
U of North Alabama (AL)
U of Pittsburgh at Bradford (PA)
U of Regina (SK, Canada)
U of Richmond (VA)
U of South Alabama (AL)
U of South Carolina (SC)
U of South Carolina Upstate (SC)
The U of South Dakota (SD)
The U of Tennessee at Chattanooga (TN)
The U of Tennessee at Martin (TN)
The U of Texas at Brownsville (TX)
The U of Texas at El Paso (TX)
The U of Texas–Pan American (TX)
U of Wisconsin–Milwaukee (WI)
U of Wisconsin–Oshkosh (WI)
U of Wisconsin–Parkside (WI)
U of Wisconsin–Platteville (WI)
Utah Valley State Coll (UT)
Utica Coll (NY)
Villanova U (PA)
Virginia Commonwealth U (VA)
Virginia Intermont Coll (VA)
Voorhees Coll (SC)
Washburn U (KS)
Washington State U (WA)
Waynesburg U (PA)
Western Illinois U (IL)
Western Intl U (AZ)
Western New Mexico U (NM)
West Liberty State Coll (WV)
West Texas A&M U (TX)
West Virginia Wesleyan Coll (WV)
Wheeling Jesuit U (WV)
Widener U (PA)
Wilmington Coll (OH)
Wilmington U (DE)
Winona State U (MN)

CRIMINAL JUSTICE/POLICE SCIENCE

Athabasca U (AB, Canada)
Bemidji State U (MN)
California State U, East Bay (CA)
Central Pennsylvania Coll (PA)
The Coll at Brockport, State U of New York (NY)
Coll of the Ozarks (MO)
Defiance Coll (OH)
East Central U (OK)
Fairmont State U (WV)
Ferris State U (MI)
Frostburg State U (MD)
George Mason U (VA)
Grambling State U (LA)
Grand Valley State U (MI)
Hardin-Simmons U (TX)
Hilbert Coll (NY)
Husson Coll (ME)
Jacksonville State U (AL)
Lake Superior State U (MI)
Louisiana Coll (LA)
Memorial U of Newfoundland (NL, Canada)
Metropolitan State U (MN)
Minnesota State U Mankato (MN)
Monroe Coll, Bronx (NY)
Monroe Coll, New Rochelle (NY)
Northeastern U (MA)
Northern State U (SD)
Northwestern Oklahoma State U (OK)
Ohio Northern U (OH)
Oklahoma City U (OK)
Purdue U Calumet (IN)
Rowan U (NJ)
St. Gregory's U, Shawnee (OK)
Saint Mary's U of Minnesota (MN)
Sam Houston State U (TX)
Stephen F. Austin State U (TX)
Texas A&M U–Commerce (TX)
Texas State U-San Marcos (TX)
Tiffin U (OH)
Truman State U (MO)
U of Cincinnati (OH)
U of Great Falls (MT)
U of Guam (GU)
U of Hartford (CT)
U of Mary (ND)
U of Regina (SK, Canada)
The U of Tennessee at Chattanooga (TN)
U of Toronto (ON, Canada)
The U of Winnipeg (MB, Canada)
U of Wisconsin–Milwaukee (WI)
Washburn U (KS)
Western Connecticut State U (CT)
Western New Mexico U (NM)
Winona State U (MN)
Wright State U (OH)

CRIMINAL JUSTICE/SAFETY

Alcorn State U (MS)
Angelo State U (TX)
Anna Maria Coll (MA)
Appalachian State U (NC)
Arizona State U (AZ)
Ashford U (IA)
Auburn U Montgomery (AL)
Augsburg Coll (MN)
Augusta State U (GA)
Baldwin-Wallace Coll (OH)
Becker Coll (MA)
Bellarmine U (KY)
Bethany Coll (KS)
Bloomsburg U of Pennsylvania (PA)
Bluefield State Coll (WV)
Bluffton U (OH)
Bowling Green State U (OH)
Bridgewater State Coll (MA)
Brown Mackie Coll–Tucson (AZ)
California State U, Chico (CA)
California State U, Fullerton (CA)
California State U, Los Angeles (CA)
Capital U (OH)
Central State U (OH)
Chicago State U (IL)
Clark Atlanta U (GA)
Coll of the Southwest (NM)
Colorado State U (CO)
Columbia Southern U (AL)
Columbus State U (GA)
Concordia U, St. Paul (MN)
Delta State U (MS)
DeSales U (PA)
Dominican Coll (NY)
East Carolina U (NC)
Eastern New Mexico U (NM)
Edinboro U of Pennsylvania (PA)
Elizabethtown Coll (PA)
Endicott Coll (MA)
Fairleigh Dickinson U, Metropolitan Campus (NJ)
Ferrum Coll (VA)
Fitchburg State Coll (MA)
Florida Atlantic U (FL)
Florida Gulf Coast U (FL)
Florida Intl U (FL)
Florida Southern Coll (FL)
Florida State U (FL)
Gannon U (PA)
Georgia Southern U (GA)
Georgia State U (GA)
Grace Coll (IN)
Grand Canyon U (AZ)
Grantham U (MO)
Guilford Coll (NC)
High Point U (NC)
Husson Coll (ME)
Huston-Tillotson U (TX)
Illinois State U (IL)
Indiana U Bloomington (IN)
Indiana U East (IN)
Indiana U Kokomo (IN)
Indiana U Northwest (IN)
Indiana U–Purdue U Fort Wayne (IN)
Indiana U–Purdue U Indianapolis (IN)
Indiana U South Bend (IN)
Indiana U Southeast (IN)
Indiana Wesleyan U (IN)
Inter American U of Puerto Rico, Aguadilla Campus (PR)
Jackson State U (MS)
Jamestown Coll (ND)
Judson U (IL)
Juniata Coll (PA)
Kennesaw State U (GA)
Kentucky State U (KY)
Kentucky Wesleyan Coll (KY)
Kutztown U of Pennsylvania (PA)
La Roche Coll (PA)
La Salle U (PA)
Lewis U (IL)
Limestone Coll (SC)
Lincoln U (PA)
Loras Coll (IA)
Lourdes Coll (OH)
Loyola U Chicago (IL)
Loyola U New Orleans (LA)
Lubbock Christian U (TX)
Madonna U (MI)
Marshall U (WV)
Marymount U (VA)
Marywood U (PA)
McNeese State U (LA)
Medaille Coll (NY)
Mercer U (GA)
Mercyhurst Coll (PA)
Mesa State Coll (CO)
Messiah Coll (PA)
Metropolitan State U (MN)
Michigan State U (MI)
Minot State U (ND)
Missouri Baptist U (MO)
Mitchell Coll (CT)
Molloy Coll (NY)
Monmouth U (NJ)
Montclair State U (NJ)
Mountain State U (WV)
Mount Aloysius Coll (PA)
Mount Marty Coll (SD)
Mount Saint Mary Coll (NY)
Mount St. Mary's U (MD)
Murray State U (KY)
Neumann Coll (PA)
New Jersey City U (NJ)
New Mexico Highlands U (NM)
North Carolina Central U (NC)
Northeastern Illinois U (IL)
Northeastern U (MA)
Northern Michigan U (MI)
North Georgia Coll & State U (GA)
Northwestern Coll (MN)
Northwestern State U of Louisiana (LA)
Ohio Northern U (OH)
Ohio U (OH)
Penn State Abington (PA)
Penn State Altoona (PA)
Penn State Berks (PA)
Penn State Erie, The Behrend Coll (PA)
Penn State Harrisburg (PA)
Pikeville Coll (KY)
Plymouth State U (NH)
Point Park U (PA)
Prairie View A&M U (TX)
Prescott Coll (AZ)
Quincy U (IL)
Quinnipiac U (CT)
Rhode Island Coll (RI)
Roanoke Coll (VA)
Rochester Inst of Technology (NY)
Rosemont Coll (PA)
Rutgers, The State U of New Jersey, Camden (NJ)
Rutgers, The State U of New Jersey, Newark (NJ)
Saginaw Valley State U (MI)
St. Ambrose U (IA)
St. Edward's U (TX)
Saint Joseph's Coll (IN)
Saint Leo U (FL)
Saint Xavier U (IL)
Sam Houston State U (TX)
Shaw U (NC)
Shippensburg U of Pennsylvania (PA)
Siena Heights U (MI)
Southeastern Louisiana U (LA)
Southeastern Oklahoma State U (OK)
Southern Arkansas U–Magnolia (AR)
Southern Illinois U Edwardsville (IL)
Southern U and Ag and Mech Coll (LA)
Southwest Minnesota State U (MN)
State U of New York at Plattsburgh (NY)
State U of New York Coll at Oneonta (NY)
State U of New York Coll at Potsdam (NY)
State U of New York Inst of Technology (NY)
Stephen F. Austin State U (TX)
Sullivan U (KY)
Tarleton State U (TX)
Taylor U Fort Wayne (IN)
Temple U (PA)
Texas A&M Intl U (TX)
Texas Christian U (TX)
Texas Coll (TX)
Texas State U-San Marcos (TX)
Texas Woman's U (TX)
Thiel Coll (PA)
Tiffin U (OH)
Troy U (AL)
Truman State U (MO)
Tulane U (LA)
The U of Akron (OH)
The U of Alabama (AL)
U of Arkansas (AR)
U of Arkansas at Fort Smith (AR)
U of Arkansas at Monticello (AR)
U of Central Florida (FL)
U of Central Oklahoma (OK)
U of Georgia (GA)
U of Great Falls (MT)
U of Houston–Downtown (TX)
U of Houston–Victoria (TX)
U of Idaho (ID)
U of Illinois at Chicago (IL)
U of Illinois at Springfield (IL)
U of Louisiana at Lafayette (LA)
U of Louisiana at Monroe (LA)
U of Mary (ND)
U of Massachusetts Boston (MA)
U of Michigan–Dearborn (MI)
U of Nebraska at Kearney (NE)
U of Nebraska at Omaha (NE)
The U of North Carolina at Charlotte (NC)
The U of North Carolina at Pembroke (NC)
The U of North Carolina Wilmington (NC)
U of North Dakota (ND)
U of Northern Colorado (CO)
U of North Florida (FL)
U of North Texas (TX)
U of Portland (OR)
U of Regina (SK, Canada)
The U of Scranton (PA)
U of Southern Mississippi (MS)
U of South Florida (FL)
The U of Texas at Arlington (TX)
The U of Texas at Brownsville (TX)
The U of Texas at San Antonio (TX)
The U of Texas at Tyler (TX)
U of the Sacred Heart (PR)
The U of Toledo (OH)
The U of Virginia's Coll at Wise (VA)
U of West Florida (FL)
U of Windsor (ON, Canada)
U of Wisconsin–Eau Claire (WI)
U of Wisconsin–Superior (WI)
U of Wyoming (WY)
Valdosta State U (GA)
Virginia State U (VA)
Viterbo U (WI)
Washburn U (KS)
Wayland Baptist U (TX)
Wayne State Coll (NE)
Wayne State U (MI)
West Chester U of Pennsylvania (PA)
Western Carolina U (NC)
Western Michigan U (MI)
Western New England Coll (MA)
Westfield State Coll (MA)
Wichita State U (KS)
Wiley Coll (TX)
Wilfrid Laurier U (ON, Canada)
Wilkes U (PA)
Worcester State Coll (MA)
Xavier U (OH)
Youngstown State U (OH)

CRIMINOLOGY

Adams State Coll (CO)
Albright Coll (PA)
Arkansas State U (AR)
Auburn U (AL)
Ball State U (IN)
Barry U (FL)
Butler U (IN)
Cabrini Coll (PA)
California State U, Fresno (CA)
Capital U (OH)
Castleton State Coll (VT)
Cedar Crest Coll (PA)
Centenary Coll (NJ)
Central Connecticut State U (CT)
Chaminade U of Honolulu (HI)
Coker Coll (SC)
The Coll at Brockport, State U of New York (NY)
Coll of Mount St. Joseph (OH)
Coll of the Ozarks (MO)
Davis & Elkins Coll (WV)
Dominican U (IL)
Drury U (MO)
Eastern Michigan U (MI)
Florida State U (FL)
Husson Coll (ME)
Immaculata U (PA)
Indiana State U (IN)
Indiana U of Pennsylvania (PA)
Johnson C. Smith U (NC)
Juniata Coll (PA)
Kwantlen U Coll (BC, Canada)
Lebanon Valley Coll (PA)
Le Moyne Coll (NY)
Lindenwood U (MO)
Marquette U (WI)
Marymount U (VA)
Maryville U of Saint Louis (MO)
Memorial U of Newfoundland (NL, Canada)
Midland Lutheran Coll (NE)
Mount Aloysius Coll (PA)
Niagara U (NY)
North Carolina State U (NC)
Ohio U (OH)
Old Dominion U (VA)
Paine Coll (GA)
The Richard Stockton Coll of New Jersey (NJ)
Sage Coll of Albany (NY)
St. Cloud State U (MN)
St. Edward's U (TX)
Saint Francis U (PA)
St. John's U (NY)
Saint Joseph's U (PA)
St. Mary's U (TX)
St. Thomas U (NB, Canada)
Simon Fraser U (BC, Canada)
Southern Oregon U (OR)
State U of New York Coll at Old Westbury (NY)
Stonehill Coll (MA)
Texas A&M U–Commerce (TX)
Thomas U (GA)
The U of Akron (OH)
U of California, Irvine (CA)
U of Denver (CO)
U of Florida (FL)
U of Houston–Clear Lake (TX)
U of La Verne (CA)
U of Maryland, Coll Park (MD)

U of Massachusetts Dartmouth (MA)
U of Memphis (TN)
U of Miami (FL)
U of Minnesota, Duluth (MN)
U of Missouri–Kansas City (MO)
U of Missouri–St. Louis (MO)
U of Nevada, Reno (NV)
U of Northern Iowa (IA)
U of Oklahoma (OK)
U of Ottawa (ON, Canada)
U of Saint Mary (KS)
U of St. Thomas (MN)
U of Southern Maine (ME)
The U of Tampa (FL)
The U of Texas at Dallas (TX)
The U of Texas of the Permian Basin (TX)
U of Toronto (ON, Canada)
The U of Western Ontario (ON, Canada)
U of West Georgia (GA)
U of Windsor (ON, Canada)
Valparaiso U (IN)
Virginia Wesleyan Coll (VA)
Western State Coll of Colorado (CO)
Wright State U (OH)

CRITICAL CARE NURSING
British Columbia Inst of Technology (BC, Canada)

CROP PRODUCTION
Colorado State U (CO)
Delaware Valley Coll (PA)
North Dakota State U (ND)
Sterling Coll (VT)
U of Arkansas (AR)
Washington State U (WA)

CULINARY ARTS
The Art Inst of Phoenix (AZ)
The Art Inst of Tampa (FL)
The Art Inst of Tucson (AZ)
Drexel U (PA)
Mississippi U for Women (MS)
Mountain State U (WV)
Nicholls State U (LA)
Paul Smith's Coll (NY)
U of Nevada, Las Vegas (NV)

CULINARY ARTS RELATED
U of Nevada, Las Vegas (NV)

CULTURAL RESOURCE MANAGEMENT AND POLICY ANALYSIS
Northwestern State U of Louisiana (LA)
Sterling Coll (VT)

CULTURAL STUDIES
Azusa Pacific U (CA)
Bard Coll at Simon's Rock (MA)
Boise State U (ID)
California Polytechnic State U, San Luis Obispo (CA)
California State Polytechnic U, Pomona (CA)
California State U, East Bay (CA)
California State U, Sacramento (CA)
Clark U (MA)
The Coll of William and Mary (VA)
Concordia U (QC, Canada)
Cornell Coll (IA)
Eugene Lang Coll The New School for Liberal Arts (NY)
Fort Lewis Coll (CO)
Harvard U (MA)
Houghton Coll (NY)
Indiana Wesleyan U (IN)
Kent State U (OH)
Marlboro Coll (VT)
Mills Coll (CA)
Minnesota State U Mankato (MN)
Ohio Wesleyan U (OH)
Oregon State U (OR)
Rutgers, The State U of New Jersey, Newark (NJ)
Rutgers, The State U of New Jersey, New Brunswick (NJ)
St. Francis Xavier U (NS, Canada)
Sonoma State U (CA)
Stanford U (CA)
The U of British Columbia (BC, Canada)
The U of British Columbia–Okanagan (BC, Canada)
U of California, Riverside (CA)
U of California, San Diego (CA)
U of Colorado at Boulder (CO)
U of Nevada, Las Vegas (NV)
U of Southern California (CA)
The U of Tampa (FL)
The U of Tennessee (TN)
U of Toronto (ON, Canada)
U of Virginia (VA)
U of Wisconsin–Milwaukee (WI)
Washington U in St. Louis (MO)
Western Washington U (WA)
Yale U (CT)
York U (ON, Canada)

CURRICULUM AND INSTRUCTION
Albertus Magnus Coll (CT)
Keene State Coll (NH)
Lock Haven U of Pennsylvania (PA)
Ohio U (OH)
Sam Houston State U (TX)
Tarleton State U (TX)
Texas A&M U (TX)
Texas Southern U (TX)
The U of Montana (MT)
U of Saint Mary (KS)
The U of South Dakota (SD)
Utah State U (UT)
Wright State U (OH)
York U (ON, Canada)

CUSTOMER SERVICE MANAGEMENT
Southwest Baptist U (MO)

CUSTOMER SERVICE SUPPORT/CALL CENTER/ TELESERVICE OPERATION
National American U–Sioux Falls Branch (SD)

CYTOGENETICS/GENETICS/ CLINICAL GENETICS TECHNOLOGY
Northern Michigan U (MI)
Saint Mary's U of Minnesota (MN)

CYTOTECHNOLOGY
Albany Coll of Pharmacy of Union U (NY)
Anderson U (SC)
Ashford U (IA)
Barry U (FL)
California State U, Dominguez Hills (CA)
The Coll of Saint Rose (NY)
Felician Coll (NJ)
Illinois Coll (IL)
Indiana U–Purdue U Indianapolis (IN)
Indiana U South Bend (IN)
Indiana U Southeast (IN)
Loma Linda U (CA)
Marian Coll of Fond du Lac (WI)
Marshall U (WV)
Michigan Technological U (MI)
Northern Michigan U (MI)
Oakland U (MI)
Old Dominion U (VA)
Saint Louis U (MO)
Saint Mary's Coll (IN)
Saint Mary's U of Minnesota (MN)
Salve Regina U (RI)
Slippery Rock U of Pennsylvania (PA)
State U of New York at Plattsburgh (NY)
State U of New York Upstate Medical U (NY)
Stony Brook U, State U of New York (NY)
Thiel Coll (PA)
The U of Alabama at Birmingham (AL)
U of Arkansas for Medical Sciences (AR)
U of Connecticut (CT)
U of Kansas (KS)
U of Mississippi Medical Center (MS)
U of North Dakota (ND)
U of North Texas (TX)
Winona State U (MN)

CZECH
The U of Texas at Austin (TX)

DAIRY HUSBANDRY AND PRODUCTION
Sterling Coll (VT)
U of Vermont (VT)

DAIRY SCIENCE
Auburn U (AL)
California Polytechnic State U, San Luis Obispo (CA)
Delaware Valley Coll (PA)
Iowa State U of Science and Technology (IA)
South Dakota State U (SD)
State U of New York Coll of Agriculture and Technology at Cobleskill (NY)
Texas A&M U (TX)
U of Florida (FL)
U of Georgia (GA)
U of New Hampshire (NH)
U of Wisconsin–Madison (WI)
Utah State U (UT)
Virginia Polytechnic Inst and State U (VA)

DANCE
Adelphi U (NY)
Alma Coll (MI)
Amherst Coll (MA)
Appalachian State U (NC)
Arizona State U (AZ)
Ball State U (IN)
Bard Coll (NY)
Bard Coll at Simon's Rock (MA)
Barnard Coll (NY)
Belhaven Coll (MS)
Bennington Coll (VT)
The Boston Conservatory (MA)
Brenau U (GA)
Brigham Young U (UT)
Butler U (IN)
California Inst of the Arts (CA)
California State U, East Bay (CA)
California State U, Fresno (CA)
California State U, Fullerton (CA)
California State U, Long Beach (CA)
California State U, Los Angeles (CA)
California State U, Sacramento (CA)
Cedar Crest Coll (PA)
Centenary Coll of Louisiana (LA)
Chapman U (CA)
Claremont McKenna Coll (CA)
Cleveland State U (OH)
The Coll at Brockport, State U of New York (NY)
The Colorado Coll (CO)
Colorado State U (CO)
Columbia Coll (SC)
Columbia Coll Chicago (IL)
Concordia U (QC, Canada)
Connecticut Coll (CT)
Cornell U (NY)
Denison U (OH)
DeSales U (PA)
Dickinson Coll (PA)
Dominican U of California (CA)
East Carolina U (NC)
Eastern Michigan U (MI)
Elon U (NC)
Emory U (GA)
Eugene Lang Coll The New School for Liberal Arts (NY)
Florida Intl U (FL)
Florida State U (FL)
Franklin & Marshall Coll (PA)
George Mason U (VA)
The George Washington U (DC)
Goucher Coll (MD)
Gustavus Adolphus Coll (MN)
Hamilton Coll (NY)
Hampshire Coll (MA)
Hobart and William Smith Colls (NY)
Hofstra U (NY)
Hollins U (VA)
Hope Coll (MI)
Hunter Coll of the City U of New York (NY)
Ithaca Coll (NY)
Jacksonville U (FL)
Johnson State Coll (VT)
The Juilliard School (NY)
Kent State U (OH)
Kenyon Coll (OH)
La Roche Coll (PA)
Lehman Coll of the City U of New York (NY)
Lindenwood U (MO)
Loyola Marymount U (CA)
Manhattanville Coll (NY)
Marlboro Coll (VT)
Marymount Manhattan Coll (NY)
Mercyhurst Coll (PA)
Meredith Coll (NC)
Middlebury Coll (VT)
Mills Coll (CA)
Missouri State U (MO)
Montclair State U (NJ)
Mount Holyoke Coll (MA)
Muhlenberg Coll (PA)
New World School of the Arts (FL)
New York U (NY)
North Carolina School of the Arts (NC)
Northwestern U (IL)
Oakland U (MI)
Oberlin Coll (OH)
Ohio U (OH)
Oklahoma City U (OK)
Old Dominion U (VA)
Oral Roberts U (OK)
Palm Beach Atlantic U (FL)
Pitzer Coll (CA)
Point Park U (PA)
Pomona Coll (CA)
Prescott Coll (AZ)
Purchase Coll, State U of New York (NY)
Radford U (VA)
Randolph Coll (VA)
Reed Coll (OR)
Rhode Island Coll (RI)
Roger Williams U (RI)
Rutgers, The State U of New Jersey, New Brunswick (NJ)
St. Gregory's U, Shawnee (OK)
Saint Mary's Coll of California (CA)
St. Olaf Coll (MN)
Sam Houston State U (TX)
San Diego State U (CA)
San Francisco State U (CA)
Sarah Lawrence Coll (NY)
Scripps Coll (CA)
Shenandoah U (VA)
Simon Fraser U (BC, Canada)
Skidmore Coll (NY)
Slippery Rock U of Pennsylvania (PA)
Smith Coll (MA)
Southern Methodist U (TX)
Southern Utah U (UT)
State U of New York at Binghamton (NY)
State U of New York at Fredonia (NY)
State U of New York Coll at Potsdam (NY)
Stephen F. Austin State U (TX)
Stephens Coll (MO)
Swarthmore Coll (PA)
Sweet Briar Coll (VA)
Temple U (PA)
Texas State U-San Marcos (TX)
Texas Tech U (TX)
Towson U (MD)
Trinity Coll (CT)
U at Buffalo, the State U of New York (NY)
The U of Akron (OH)
The U of Alabama (AL)
The U of Arizona (AZ)
U of California, Berkeley (CA)
U of California, Irvine (CA)
U of California, Riverside (CA)
U of California, San Diego (CA)
U of California, Santa Barbara (CA)
U of Central Oklahoma (OK)
U of Cincinnati (OH)
U of Colorado at Boulder (CO)
U of Florida (FL)
U of Georgia (GA)
U of Hartford (CT)
U of Hawaii at Manoa (HI)
U of Idaho (ID)
U of Illinois at Urbana–Champaign (IL)
The U of Iowa (IA)
U of Kansas (KS)
U of Maryland, Baltimore County (MD)
U of Maryland, Coll Park (MD)
U of Massachusetts Amherst (MA)
U of Michigan (MI)
U of Minnesota, Twin Cities Campus (MN)
U of Missouri–Kansas City (MO)
The U of Montana (MT)
U of Nebraska–Lincoln (NE)
U of Nevada, Las Vegas (NV)
U of New Hampshire (NH)
U of New Mexico (NM)
The U of North Carolina at Charlotte (NC)
The U of North Carolina at Greensboro (NC)
U of North Texas (TX)
U of Oklahoma (OK)
U of Oregon (OR)
U of Southern Mississippi (MS)
U of South Florida (FL)
The U of Texas at Austin (TX)
The U of Texas–Pan American (TX)
U of Utah (UT)
U of Wisconsin–Milwaukee (WI)
U of Wisconsin–Stevens Point (WI)
Utah State U (UT)
Utah Valley State Coll (UT)
Valdosta State U (GA)
Virginia Commonwealth U (VA)
Virginia Intermont Coll (VA)
Washington U in St. Louis (MO)
Wayne State U (MI)
Weber State U (UT)
Webster U (MO)
Wells Coll (NY)
Wesleyan U (CT)
Western Kentucky U (KY)
Western Michigan U (MI)
Westmont Coll (CA)
West Texas A&M U (TX)
Wheaton Coll (MA)
Winthrop U (SC)
Wright State U (OH)
York U (ON, Canada)

DANCE RELATED
Brigham Young U (UT)
California State U, Long Beach (CA)
Coker Coll (SC)
Sarah Lawrence Coll (NY)
Utah Valley State Coll (UT)

DANCE THERAPY
Columbia Coll Chicago (IL)

DATA MODELING/ WAREHOUSING AND DATABASE ADMINISTRATION
National U (CA)
Neumont U (UT)
Rochester Inst of Technology (NY)

DATA PROCESSING AND DATA PROCESSING TECHNOLOGY
Arkansas State U (AR)
Bemidji State U (MN)
Everest U, Tampa (FL)
Florida Memorial U (FL)
Miami U (OH)
Midway Coll (KY)
Minnesota State U Mankato (MN)
Northwest Missouri State U (MO)
Pace U (NY)
Pacific Union Coll (CA)
Stephen F. Austin State U (TX)
U of Advancing Technology (AZ)
U of New Brunswick Fredericton (NB, Canada)
U of Southern Indiana (IN)
U of Southern Mississippi (MS)
The U of Winnipeg (MB, Canada)
Utah Valley State Coll (UT)

DEMOGRAPHY AND POPULATION
Hampshire Coll (MA)
The U of Western Ontario (ON, Canada)

DENTAL HYGIENE
Armstrong Atlantic State U (GA)
Clayton State U (GA)
Dixie State Coll of Utah (UT)
East Tennessee State U (TN)
Farmingdale State Coll (NY)
Idaho State U (ID)
Indiana U–Purdue U Indianapolis (IN)
Indiana U South Bend (IN)
Loma Linda U (CA)
Louisiana State U Health Sciences Center (LA)
Marquette U (WI)
Massachusetts Coll of Pharmacy and Health Sciences (MA)
Medical Coll of Georgia (GA)
Metropolitan State U (MN)
Midwestern State U (TX)
Minnesota State U Mankato (MN)
New York U (NY)
Northeastern U (MA)
Northern Arizona U (AZ)
Old Dominion U (VA)
Oregon Inst of Technology (OR)
Southern Illinois U Carbondale (IL)
Tennessee State U (TN)
Texas A&M Health Science Center (TX)
Texas Woman's U (TX)
Thomas Edison State Coll (NJ)
U of Bridgeport (CT)
The U of British Columbia (BC, Canada)
U of Colorado Denver (CO)
U of Hawaii at Manoa (HI)
U of Louisiana at Lafayette (LA)
U of Louisiana at Monroe (LA)
U of Louisville (KY)
The U of Maine at Augusta (ME)
U of Michigan (MI)
U of Minnesota, Twin Cities Campus (MN)
U of Mississippi Medical Center (MS)
U of Missouri–Kansas City (MO)
U of Nebraska Medical Center (NE)
U of New England (ME)

U of New Haven (CT)
The U of North Carolina at Chapel Hill (NC)
U of Oklahoma Health Sciences Center (OK)
U of Pittsburgh (PA)
U of Rhode Island (RI)
U of Southern California (CA)
U of Southern Indiana (IN)
U of Wyoming (WY)
Utah Valley State Coll (UT)
Vermont Tech Coll (VT)
Virginia Commonwealth U (VA)
Western Kentucky U (KY)
West Liberty State Coll (WV)
West Virginia U (WV)
Wichita State U (KS)

DENTAL LABORATORY TECHNOLOGY
Boston U (MA)

DENTAL SERVICES AND ALLIED PROFESSIONS RELATED
Indiana U–Purdue U Indianapolis (IN)

DESIGN AND APPLIED ARTS RELATED
Arizona State U (AZ)
The Art Inst of California–San Diego (CA)
Coll of Santa Fe (NM)
Drexel U (PA)
Ferris State U (MI)
Full Sail U (FL)
Harding U (AR)
Hofstra U (NY)
Laguna Coll of Art & Design (CA)
Lehigh U (PA)
Maryland Inst Coll of Art (MD)
McMurry U (TX)
The New England Inst of Art (MA)
New York Inst of Technology (NY)
North Carolina State U (NC)
NSCAD U (NS, Canada)
Ohio U (OH)
Paier Coll of Art, Inc. (CT)
Point Park U (PA)
Pratt Inst (NY)
Robert Morris Coll (IL)
St. Cloud State U (MN)
Savannah Coll of Art and Design (GA)
School of the Art Inst of Chicago (IL)
School of Visual Arts (NY)
U of California, Los Angeles (CA)
U of Massachusetts Dartmouth (MA)
U of Saint Francis (IN)
U of the Incarnate Word (TX)
Virginia Commonwealth U (VA)
Washburn U (KS)

DESIGN AND VISUAL COMMUNICATIONS
Alberta Coll of Art & Design (AB, Canada)
Albright Coll (PA)
Alma Coll (MI)
American InterContinental U (CA)
American InterContinental U (FL)
American InterContinental U (TX)
American InterContinental U Buckhead Campus (GA)
American InterContinental U Dunwoody Campus (GA)
American InterContinental U-London (United Kingdom)
American InterContinental U Online (IL)
American U (DC)
Anderson U (IN)
The Art Inst of Michigan (MI)
The Art Inst of Washington (VA)
Auburn U (AL)
Bennington Coll (VT)
Bowling Green State U (OH)
Brigham Young U (UT)
Buffalo State Coll, State U of New York (NY)
California State U, Chico (CA)
Central Connecticut State U (CT)
Collins Coll: A School of Design and Technology (AZ)
Columbia Coll Chicago (IL)
Drury U (MO)
Duke U (NC)
Endicott Coll (MA)
Farmingdale State Coll (NY)
Ferris State U (MI)
Illinois Inst of Technology (IL)
Intl Acad of Design & Technology (FL)
Intl Acad of Design & Technology (IL)
Iowa State U of Science and Technology (IA)
Jacksonville U (FL)
Kean U (NJ)
Laboratory Inst of Merchandising (NY)
Laguna Coll of Art & Design (CA)
Lambuth U (TN)
Lehigh U (PA)
Liberty U (VA)
Linfield Coll (OR)
Lubbock Christian U (TX)
Memphis Coll of Art (TN)
Missouri State U (MO)
Montana State U (MT)
Mount Vernon Nazarene U (OH)
New Mexico Highlands U (NM)
North Carolina State U (NC)
Northeastern State U (OK)
NSCAD U (NS, Canada)
Ohio Northern U (OH)
Ohio U (OH)
Oral Roberts U (OK)
Paier Coll of Art, Inc. (CT)
Parsons The New School for Design (NY)
Peace Coll (NC)
Purdue U (IN)
Radford U (VA)
Robert Morris U (PA)
Rochester Inst of Technology (NY)
Saginaw Valley State U (MI)
St. Ambrose U (IA)
Saint Mary-of-the-Woods Coll (IN)
San Diego State U (CA)
Savannah Coll of Art and Design (GA)
School of the Art Inst of Chicago (IL)
Southern Illinois U Carbondale (IL)
Spring Arbor U (MI)
State U of New York at Binghamton (NY)
Texas A&M U–Commerce (TX)
Truman State U (MO)
Université du Québec en Outaouais (QC, Canada)
U of Advancing Technology (AZ)
U of Evansville (IN)
U of Kansas (KS)
U of Massachusetts Dartmouth (MA)
U of Miami (FL)
U of Michigan (MI)
U of Michigan–Flint (MI)
U of Notre Dame (IN)
U of Oklahoma (OK)
U of Oregon (OR)
The U of Tennessee at Martin (TN)
The U of Texas at Austin (TX)
Utah Valley State Coll (UT)
Villa Julie Coll (MD)
Virginia Commonwealth U (VA)
Viterbo U (WI)
Washington U in St. Louis (MO)
Weber State U (UT)
Western Washington U (WA)
Westwood Coll–Atlanta Northlake (GA)
William Woods U (MO)
York U (ON, Canada)

DESKTOP PUBLISHING AND DIGITAL IMAGING DESIGN
Texas State U-San Marcos (TX)

DEVELOPMENTAL AND CHILD PSYCHOLOGY
Bard Coll at Simon's Rock (MA)
Belmont U (TN)
Bridgewater State Coll (MA)
California Polytechnic State U, San Luis Obispo (CA)
California State U, East Bay (CA)
California State U, San Bernardino (CA)
Carson-Newman Coll (TN)
Castleton State Coll (VT)
Colby-Sawyer Coll (NH)
Eastern Connecticut State U (CT)
Emmanuel Coll (MA)
Fitchburg State Coll (MA)
Fresno Pacific U (CA)
Hampton U (VA)
Houston Baptist U (TX)
Humboldt State U (CA)
Liberty U (VA)
Longwood U (VA)
Marlboro Coll (VT)
Maryville Coll (TN)
Metropolitan State U (MN)
Mills Coll (CA)
Minnesota State U Mankato (MN)
Mount Ida Coll (MA)
Mount St. Mary's Coll (CA)
Mount Saint Vincent U (NS, Canada)
Northeastern State U (OK)
Northern Michigan U (MI)
Northwest Missouri State U (MO)
Quinnipiac U (CT)
St. Joseph's Coll, New York (NY)
St. Joseph's Coll, Suffolk Campus (NY)
Sarah Lawrence Coll (NY)
Sonoma State U (CA)
Spelman Coll (GA)
Suffolk U (MA)
Tufts U (MA)
The U of British Columbia (BC, Canada)
U of California, Santa Cruz (CA)
U of Delaware (DE)
U of Minnesota, Twin Cities Campus (MN)
U of New Brunswick Fredericton (NB, Canada)
U of the District of Columbia (DC)
The U of Toledo (OH)
U of Utah (UT)
U of Windsor (ON, Canada)
The U of Winnipeg (MB, Canada)
U of Wisconsin–Green Bay (WI)
U of Wisconsin–Madison (WI)
Utica Coll (NY)
Villa Julie Coll (MD)
Western Washington U (WA)
Whittier Coll (CA)
Wilfrid Laurier U (ON, Canada)

DEVELOPMENTAL BIOLOGY AND EMBRYOLOGY
U of Puget Sound (WA)

DEVELOPMENT ECONOMICS AND INTERNATIONAL DEVELOPMENT
Brown U (RI)
Calvin Coll (MI)
Canadian Mennonite U (MB, Canada)
Clark U (MA)
Georgia Southern U (GA)
McGill U (QC, Canada)
Point Loma Nazarene U (CA)
U of California, Los Angeles (CA)
U of King's Coll (NS, Canada)
U of Ottawa (ON, Canada)
U of Vermont (VT)
U of Windsor (ON, Canada)
The U of Winnipeg (MB, Canada)
York U (ON, Canada)

DIAGNOSTIC MEDICAL SONOGRAPHY AND ULTRASOUND TECHNOLOGY
Baptist Coll of Health Sciences (TN)
The George Washington U (DC)
Lewis U (IL)
Medical Coll of Georgia (GA)
Mountain State U (WV)
Nebraska Methodist Coll (NE)
Seattle U (WA)
State U of New York Downstate Medical Center (NY)
U of Arkansas at Fort Smith (AR)
U of Missouri–Columbia (MO)
U of Nebraska Medical Center (NE)
Washburn U (KS)
Weber State U (UT)

DIESEL MECHANICS TECHNOLOGY
Lewis-Clark State Coll (ID)
Pittsburg State U (KS)

DIETETICS
Abilene Christian U (TX)
Acadia U (NS, Canada)
Andrews U (MI)
Ashland U (OH)
Ball State U (IN)
Bastyr U (WA)
Bowling Green State U (OH)
Bradley U (IL)
Brigham Young U (UT)
Buffalo State Coll, State U of New York (NY)
California State Polytechnic U, Pomona (CA)
California State U, Chico (CA)
California State U, Fresno (CA)
California State U, Long Beach (CA)
California State U, Los Angeles (CA)
California State U, San Bernardino (CA)
Carson-Newman Coll (TN)
Case Western Reserve U (OH)
Central Michigan U (MI)
Coll of Saint Benedict (MN)
Coll of Saint Elizabeth (NJ)
Coll of the Ozarks (MO)
Colorado State U (CO)
Concordia Coll (MN)
Dominican U (IL)
D'Youville Coll (NY)
East Carolina U (NC)
Eastern Kentucky U (KY)
Eastern Michigan U (MI)
Florida Intl U (FL)
Florida State U (FL)
Fontbonne U (MO)
Gannon U (PA)
Harding U (AR)
Idaho State U (ID)
Immaculata U (PA)
Indiana U of Pennsylvania (PA)
Iowa State U of Science and Technology (IA)
Jacksonville State U (AL)
Kansas State U (KS)
Keene State Coll (NH)
Lehman Coll of the City U of New York (NY)
Life U (GA)
Lipscomb U (TN)
Louisiana State U and Ag and Mech Coll (LA)
Mansfield U of Pennsylvania (PA)
Marshall U (WV)
Marywood U (PA)
Memorial U of Newfoundland (NL, Canada)
Mercyhurst Coll (PA)
Meredith Coll (NC)
Miami U (OH)
Miami U Hamilton (OH)
Michigan State U (MI)
Minnesota State U Mankato (MN)
Missouri State U (MO)
Morgan State U (MD)
Mount Mary Coll (WI)
Mount Saint Vincent U (NS, Canada)
Nicholls State U (LA)
North Carolina Ag and Tech State U (NC)
North Dakota State U (ND)
Northwest Missouri State U (MO)
Oakwood Coll (AL)
Ouachita Baptist U (AR)
Point Loma Nazarene U (CA)
Saint John's U (MN)
San Diego State U (CA)
San Francisco State U (CA)
Seton Hill U (PA)
Simmons Coll (MA)
State U of New York Coll at Oneonta (NY)
Tennessee Technological U (TN)
Texas Christian U (TX)
Texas Southern U (TX)
Texas Tech U (TX)
Texas Woman's U (TX)
Tuskegee U (AL)
The U of Alabama (AL)
U of Arkansas at Pine Bluff (AR)
The U of British Columbia (BC, Canada)
U of Central Missouri (MO)
U of Central Oklahoma (OK)
U of Connecticut (CT)
U of Dayton (OH)
U of Delaware (DE)
U of Georgia (GA)
U of Hawaii at Manoa (HI)
U of Illinois at Chicago (IL)
U of Illinois at Urbana–Champaign (IL)
U of Louisiana at Lafayette (LA)
U of Maryland, Coll Park (MD)
U of Maryland Eastern Shore (MD)
U of Missouri–Columbia (MO)
U of Nebraska at Kearney (NE)
U of New Hampshire (NH)
U of New Haven (CT)
U of North Dakota (ND)
U of Northern Colorado (CO)
U of Oklahoma Health Sciences Center (OK)
U of Pittsburgh (PA)
U of Rhode Island (RI)
U of Southern Mississippi (MS)
The U of Tennessee at Martin (TN)
The U of Texas–Pan American (TX)
The U of Texas Southwestern Medical Center at Dallas (TX)
U of Vermont (VT)
The U of Western Ontario (ON, Canada)
U of Wisconsin–Madison (WI)
U of Wisconsin–Stevens Point (WI)
Viterbo U (WI)
Wayne State U (MI)
West Chester U of Pennsylvania (PA)
Western Carolina U (NC)
Western Michigan U (MI)
Youngstown State U (OH)

DIETETICS AND CLINICAL NUTRITION SERVICES RELATED
Madonna U (MI)
Texas Christian U (TX)

DIETETIC TECHNICIAN
Purdue U (IN)

DIGITAL COMMUNICATION AND MEDIA/MULTIMEDIA
Abilene Christian U (TX)
Acad of Art U (CA)
The Art Inst of California–San Diego (CA)
The Art Inst of Washington (VA)
Baylor U (TX)
California Baptist U (CA)
California Lutheran U (CA)
Calvin Coll (MI)
Canisius Coll (NY)
Clarkson U (NY)
Cogswell Polytechnical Coll (CA)
Eastern Mennonite U (VA)
Electronic Data Processing Coll of Puerto Rico (PR)
Fitchburg State Coll (MA)
Florida Atlantic U (FL)
Georgia Inst of Technology (GA)
Grace Bible Coll (MI)
Harding U (AR)
Hilbert Coll (NY)
Huntington U (IN)
Indiana U–Purdue U Indianapolis (IN)
Kent State U (OH)
Kutztown U of Pennsylvania (PA)
Lebanon Valley Coll (PA)
Lindenwood U (MO)
Marist Coll (NY)
Marywood U (PA)
Michigan Technological U (MI)
Minot State U (ND)
Mount Marty Coll (SD)
The New England Inst of Art (MA)
New York U (NY)
Northern Michigan U (MI)
Sam Houston State U (TX)
Savannah Coll of Art and Design (GA)
School of the Art Inst of Chicago (IL)
Southern New Hampshire U (NH)
Texas A&M U (TX)
U of Baltimore (MD)
U of Denver (CO)
U of Georgia (GA)
U of Lethbridge (AB, Canada)
U of Northern Iowa (IA)
U of Oregon (OR)
The U of Texas at Arlington (TX)
U of Toronto (ON, Canada)
The U of Western Ontario (ON, Canada)
Washington State U (WA)
Wellesley Coll (MA)
Wheeling Jesuit U (WV)
Wilkes U (PA)
York Coll of Pennsylvania (PA)

DIRECT ENTRY MIDWIFERY
Midwives Coll of Utah (UT)

DIRECTING AND THEATRICAL PRODUCTION
Bennington Coll (VT)
Brigham Young U (UT)
California State U, Long Beach (CA)
Drake U (IA)
Elizabethtown Coll (PA)
George Fox U (OR)
Hofstra U (NY)
Ohio U (OH)
Sarah Lawrence Coll (NY)
State U of New York at Binghamton (NY)
U of Illinois at Urbana–Champaign (IL)
U of Southern California (CA)

DIVINITY/MINISTRY
Atlantic Union Coll (MA)
Azusa Pacific U (CA)
Baptist Bible Coll of Pennsylvania (PA)

Barclay Coll (KS)
Belmont U (TN)
Bethany Bible Coll (NB, Canada)
Bethany U (CA)
Biola U (CA)
Bluefield Coll (VA)
Canadian Mennonite U (MB, Canada)
Central Christian Coll of Kansas (KS)
Crown Coll (MN)
Dallas Baptist U (TX)
Davis Coll (NY)
Eugene Bible Coll (OR)
Faith Baptist Bible Coll and Theological Sem (IA)
Faulkner U (AL)
Fresno Pacific U (CA)
Grace U (NE)
Great Lakes Christian Coll (MI)
Grove City Coll (PA)
Harding U (AR)
Huntington U (IN)
John Brown U (AR)
John Wesley Coll (NC)
Kuyper Coll (MI)
The Master's Coll and Sem (CA)
Master's Coll and Sem (ON, Canada)
Mount Olive Coll (NC)
Nebraska Christian Coll (NE)
Northwest Nazarene U (ID)
Oak Hills Christian Coll (MN)
Oakland City U (IN)
Oklahoma Wesleyan U (OK)
Providence Coll (RI)
Regent U (VA)
Roberts Wesleyan Coll (NY)
San Diego Christian Coll (CA)
Shorter Coll (GA)
Southern Baptist Theological Sem (KY)
Southern Wesleyan U (SC)
Tabor Coll (KS)
Taylor U Coll and Sem (AB, Canada)
Tyndale U Coll & Sem (ON, Canada)
U of Mary (ND)
The U of Western Ontario (ON, Canada)
Viterbo U (WI)

DRAFTING AND DESIGN TECHNOLOGY

Baker Coll of Owosso (MI)
Cameron U (OK)
East Central U (OK)
Grambling State U (LA)
Keene State Coll (NH)
Lewis-Clark State Coll (ID)
Pacific Union Coll (CA)
Prairie View A&M U (TX)
Sam Houston State U (TX)
Texas Southern U (TX)
Tri-State U (IN)
U of Houston (TX)
U of Maine (ME)
U of Rio Grande (OH)

DRAFTING/DESIGN ENGINEERING TECHNOLOGIES RELATED

National U (CA)
Thomas Edison State Coll (NJ)

DRAFTING/DESIGN TECHNOLOGY

U of North Dakota (ND)

DRAMA AND DANCE TEACHER EDUCATION

Appalachian State U (NC)
Baylor U (TX)
Bishop's U (QC, Canada)
Boston U (MA)
Bowling Green State U (OH)
Brenau U (GA)
Bridgewater State Coll (MA)
Brigham Young U (UT)
Capital U (OH)
The Catholic U of America (DC)
Centenary Coll of Louisiana (LA)
Central Washington U (WA)
Columbia Coll (SC)
Columbus State U (GA)
Concordia U, Nebraska (NE)
Dordt Coll (IA)
East Carolina U (NC)
East Texas Baptist U (TX)
Emerson Coll (MA)
Greensboro Coll (NC)
Hardin-Simmons U (TX)
Hastings Coll (NE)
Hope Coll (MI)
Howard Payne U (TX)
Huntington U (IN)
Jacksonville U (FL)
Johnson State Coll (VT)
Lipscomb U (TN)
Meredith Coll (NC)
Montclair State U (NJ)
North Carolina Central U (NC)
Northern Arizona U (AZ)
Ohio Wesleyan U (OH)
Old Dominion U (VA)
Point Park U (PA)
St. Edward's U (TX)
Salve Regina U (RI)
Shenandoah U (VA)
The U of Akron (OH)
The U of Arizona (AZ)
U of Evansville (IN)
U of Georgia (GA)
The U of Iowa (IA)
U of Lethbridge (AB, Canada)
The U of North Carolina at Charlotte (NC)
The U of North Carolina at Greensboro (NC)
U of St. Thomas (MN)
The U of South Dakota (SD)
U of South Florida (FL)
U of Windsor (ON, Canada)
Utah Valley State Coll (UT)
Valparaiso U (IN)
Viterbo U (WI)
Washington U in St. Louis (MO)
Wayne State Coll (NE)
Weber State U (UT)
William Jewell Coll (MO)
York U (ON, Canada)
Youngstown State U (OH)

DRAMATIC/THEATER ARTS

Abilene Christian U (TX)
Acadia U (NS, Canada)
Adams State Coll (CO)
Adelphi U (NY)
Adrian Coll (MI)
Agnes Scott Coll (GA)
Alabama State U (AL)
Albertus Magnus Coll (CT)
Albion Coll (MI)
Albright Coll (PA)
Alfred U (NY)
Allegheny Coll (PA)
Alma Coll (MI)
American U (DC)
Amherst Coll (MA)
Anderson U (IN)
Anderson U (SC)
Angelo State U (TX)
Appalachian State U (NC)
Aquinas Coll (MI)
Arizona State U (AZ)
Arkansas State U (AR)
Armstrong Atlantic State U (GA)
Asbury Coll (KY)
Ashland U (OH)
Auburn U (AL)
Augsburg Coll (MN)
Augustana Coll (IL)
Augustana Coll (SD)
Averett U (VA)
Avila U (MO)
Baker U (KS)
Ball State U (IN)
Bard Coll (NY)
Bard Coll at Simon's Rock (MA)
Barnard Coll (NY)
Barry U (FL)
Barton Coll (NC)
Bates Coll (ME)
Baylor U (TX)
Belhaven Coll (MS)
Belmont U (TN)
Beloit Coll (WI)
Bemidji State U (MN)
Benedictine Coll (KS)
Bennington Coll (VT)
Bethany Coll (WV)
Bethany Lutheran Coll (MN)
Bethany U (CA)
Bethel U (MN)
Bishop's U (QC, Canada)
Bloomsburg U of Pennsylvania (PA)
Bluefield Coll (VA)
Bob Jones U (SC)
Boise State U (ID)
Boston Coll (MA)
The Boston Conservatory (MA)
Bowling Green State U (OH)
Bradley U (IL)
Brandeis U (MA)
Brenau U (GA)
Brevard Coll (NC)
Bridgewater State Coll (MA)
Brigham Young U (UT)
Brock U (ON, Canada)
Brown U (RI)
Bucknell U (PA)
Buffalo State Coll, State U of New York (NY)
Butler U (IN)
California Baptist U (CA)
California Inst of the Arts (CA)
California Lutheran U (CA)
California State Polytechnic U, Pomona (CA)
California State U, Chico (CA)
California State U, Dominguez Hills (CA)
California State U, East Bay (CA)
California State U, Fresno (CA)
California State U, Fullerton (CA)
California State U, Long Beach (CA)
California State U, Los Angeles (CA)
California State U, Monterey Bay (CA)
California State U, Sacramento (CA)
California State U, San Bernardino (CA)
California State U, Stanislaus (CA)
Calvin Coll (MI)
Canisius Coll (NY)
Capital U (OH)
Carnegie Mellon U (PA)
Carroll Coll (WI)
Carson-Newman Coll (TN)
Case Western Reserve U (OH)
Castleton State Coll (VT)
Catawba Coll (NC)
The Catholic U of America (DC)
Cedar Crest Coll (PA)
Cedarville U (OH)
Centenary Coll of Louisiana (LA)
Central Coll (IA)
Central Connecticut State U (CT)
Central Michigan U (MI)
Central Washington U (WA)
Centre Coll (KY)
Chapman U (CA)
Chatham U (PA)
Cheyney U of Pennsylvania (PA)
Christopher Newport U (VA)
City Coll of the City U of New York (NY)
Claremont McKenna Coll (CA)
Clarion U of Pennsylvania (PA)
Clarke Coll (IA)
Clark U (MA)
Cleveland State U (OH)
Coastal Carolina U (SC)
Coker Coll (SC)
Colby Coll (ME)
Colgate U (NY)
The Coll at Brockport, State U of New York (NY)
Coll of Charleston (SC)
The Coll of Idaho (ID)
Coll of Saint Benedict (MN)
Coll of Santa Fe (NM)
Coll of Staten Island of the City U of New York (NY)
Coll of the Holy Cross (MA)
Coll of the Ozarks (MO)
Coll of the Southwest (NM)
The Coll of William and Mary (VA)
The Colorado Coll (CO)
Colorado State U (CO)
Columbia Coll Chicago (IL)
Columbus State U (GA)
Concordia Coll (MN)
Concordia U (CA)
Concordia U (MI)
Concordia U (OR)
Concordia U (QC, Canada)
Concordia U Chicago (IL)
Concordia U, Nebraska (NE)
Concordia U, St. Paul (MN)
Connecticut Coll (CT)
Converse Coll (SC)
Cornell Coll (IA)
Cornell U (NY)
Covenant Coll (GA)
Creighton U (NE)
Culver-Stockton Coll (MO)
Dakota Wesleyan U (SD)
Dartmouth Coll (NH)
Davidson Coll (NC)
Davis & Elkins Coll (WV)
Denison U (OH)
DePaul U (IL)
DePauw U (IN)
DeSales U (PA)
Dickinson Coll (PA)
Dillard U (LA)
Doane Coll (NE)
Dominican U (IL)
Dordt Coll (IA)
Drake U (IA)
Drew U (NJ)
Drury U (MO)
Duke U (NC)
Duquesne U (PA)
Earlham Coll (IN)
East Carolina U (NC)
Eastern Illinois U (IL)
Eastern Kentucky U (KY)
Eastern Mennonite U (VA)
Eastern Michigan U (MI)
Eastern New Mexico U (NM)
East Stroudsburg U of Pennsylvania (PA)
East Texas Baptist U (TX)
Eckerd Coll (FL)
Edinboro U of Pennsylvania (PA)
Elon U (NC)
Emerson Coll (MA)
Emory & Henry Coll (VA)
Emory U (GA)
Emporia State U (KS)
Eugene Lang Coll The New School for Liberal Arts (NY)
The Evergreen State Coll (WA)
Fairleigh Dickinson U, Coll at Florham (NJ)
Fairleigh Dickinson U, Metropolitan Campus (NJ)
Fairmont State U (WV)
Faulkner U (AL)
Ferrum Coll (VA)
Fitchburg State Coll (MA)
Five Towns Coll (NY)
Flagler Coll (FL)
Florida Ag and Mech U (FL)
Florida Atlantic U (FL)
Florida Gulf Coast U (FL)
Florida Intl U (FL)
Florida Southern Coll (FL)
Florida State U (FL)
Fontbonne U (MO)
Fort Lewis Coll (CO)
Franciscan U of Steubenville (OH)
Francis Marion U (SC)
Franklin & Marshall Coll (PA)
Franklin Coll (IN)
Freed-Hardeman U (TN)
Frostburg State U (MD)
Furman U (SC)
Gannon U (PA)
Gardner-Webb U (NC)
George Fox U (OR)
George Mason U (VA)
Georgetown Coll (KY)
The George Washington U (DC)
Georgia Coll & State U (GA)
Georgia Southern U (GA)
Georgia Southwestern State U (GA)
Gettysburg Coll (PA)
Gonzaga U (WA)
Goucher Coll (MD)
Grambling State U (LA)
Grand Valley State U (MI)
Grand View Coll (IA)
Greensboro Coll (NC)
Greenville Coll (IL)
Grinnell Coll (IA)
Guilford Coll (NC)
Gustavus Adolphus Coll (MN)
Hamilton Coll (NY)
Hamline U (MN)
Hampshire Coll (MA)
Hampton U (VA)
Hannibal-LaGrange Coll (MO)
Hanover Coll (IN)
Harding U (AR)
Hardin-Simmons U (TX)
Hartwick Coll (NY)
Harvard U (MA)
Hastings Coll (NE)
Heidelberg Coll (OH)
Henderson State U (AR)
High Point U (NC)
Hillsdale Coll (MI)
Hobart and William Smith Colls (NY)
Hofstra U (NY)
Hollins U (VA)
Hope Coll (MI)
Howard Payne U (TX)
Humboldt State U (CA)
Hunter Coll of the City U of New York (NY)
Huntington U (IN)
Idaho State U (ID)
Illinois Coll (IL)
Illinois State U (IL)
Illinois Wesleyan U (IL)
Indiana State U (IN)
Indiana U Bloomington (IN)
Indiana U Northwest (IN)
Indiana U of Pennsylvania (PA)
Indiana U–Purdue U Fort Wayne (IN)
Indiana U South Bend (IN)
Iona Coll (NY)
Iowa State U of Science and Technology (IA)
Ithaca Coll (NY)
Jacksonville State U (AL)
Jacksonville U (FL)
James Madison U (VA)
Jamestown Coll (ND)
Johnson State Coll (VT)
The Juilliard School (NY)
Kalamazoo Coll (MI)
Kansas State U (KS)
Kean U (NJ)
Keene State Coll (NH)
Kennesaw State U (GA)
Kent State U (OH)
Kenyon Coll (OH)
King's Coll (PA)
Knox Coll (IL)
Kutztown U of Pennsylvania (PA)
Kuyper Coll (MI)
LaGrange Coll (GA)
Lake Forest Coll (IL)
Lambuth U (TN)
Laurentian U (ON, Canada)
Lawrence U (WI)
Lees-McRae Coll (NC)
Lehigh U (PA)
Lehman Coll of the City U of New York (NY)
Le Moyne Coll (NY)
Lenoir-Rhyne Coll (NC)
Lewis & Clark Coll (OR)
Lewis U (IL)
Limestone Coll (SC)
Lindenwood U (MO)
Linfield Coll (OR)
Lipscomb U (TN)
Lock Haven U of Pennsylvania (PA)
Longwood U (VA)
Louisiana Coll (LA)
Louisiana State U and Ag and Mech Coll (LA)
Loyola Marymount U (CA)
Loyola U Chicago (IL)
Loyola U New Orleans (LA)
Luther Coll (IA)
Lycoming Coll (PA)
Lynchburg Coll (VA)
Lyon Coll (AR)
Macalester Coll (MN)
Manchester Coll (IN)
Marietta Coll (OH)
Marist Coll (NY)
Marlboro Coll (VT)
Marquette U (WI)
Mary Baldwin Coll (VA)
Marymount Manhattan Coll (NY)
Maryville Coll (TN)
Marywood U (PA)
McDaniel Coll (MD)
McGill U (QC, Canada)
McMurry U (TX)
McNeese State U (LA)
Memorial U of Newfoundland (NL, Canada)
Mercer U (GA)
Meredith Coll (NC)
Mesa State Coll (CO)
Messiah Coll (PA)
Methodist U (NC)
Metropolitan State U (MN)
Miami U (OH)
Michigan State U (MI)
Middlebury Coll (VT)
Middle Tennessee State U (TN)
Midland Lutheran Coll (NE)
Midwestern State U (TX)
Millikin U (IL)
Millsaps Coll (MS)
Minnesota State U Mankato (MN)
Mississippi U for Women (MS)
Missouri Southern State U (MO)
Missouri State U (MO)
Missouri Valley Coll (MO)
Monmouth Coll (IL)
Monmouth U (NJ)
Montana State U (MT)
Montana State U–Billings (MT)
Montclair State U (NJ)
Moravian Coll (PA)
Morehead State U (KY)
Morehouse Coll (GA)
Morgan State U (MD)
Morningside Coll (IA)
Mount Allison U (NB, Canada)
Mount Holyoke Coll (MA)
Mount Marty Coll (SD)
Mount Vernon Nazarene U (OH)
Muhlenberg Coll (PA)
Murray State U (KY)
Naropa U (CO)
National-Louis U (IL)
Nazareth Coll of Rochester (NY)
Nebraska Wesleyan U (NE)
New England Coll (NH)
New World School of the Arts (FL)
New York U (NY)
Niagara U (NY)
North Carolina Ag and Tech State U (NC)
North Carolina Central U (NC)
North Carolina School of the Arts (NC)
North Carolina Wesleyan Coll (NC)
North Central Coll (IL)
North Dakota State U (ND)
Northeastern State U (OK)
Northeastern U (MA)

Northern Arizona U (AZ)
Northern Illinois U (IL)
Northern Michigan U (MI)
Northern State U (SD)
Northwestern Coll (IA)
Northwestern Coll (MN)
Northwestern State U of Louisiana (LA)
Northwestern U (IL)
Northwest Missouri State U (MO)
Notre Dame de Namur U (CA)
Nova Southeastern U (FL)
Oakland U (MI)
Oberlin Coll (OH)
Occidental Coll (CA)
Ohio Northern U (OH)
Ohio U (OH)
Ohio Wesleyan U (OH)
Oklahoma Christian U (OK)
Oklahoma City U (OK)
Oklahoma State U (OK)
Old Dominion U (VA)
Oral Roberts U (OK)
Otterbein Coll (OH)
Ouachita Baptist U (AR)
Pace U (NY)
Pacific U (OR)
Paine Coll (GA)
Palm Beach Atlantic U (FL)
Park U (MO)
Pepperdine U, Malibu (CA)
Piedmont Coll (GA)
Pitzer Coll (CA)
Plymouth State U (NH)
Point Loma Nazarene U (CA)
Point Park U (PA)
Pomona Coll (CA)
Portland State U (OR)
Prairie View A&M U (TX)
Presbyterian Coll (SC)
Prescott Coll (AZ)
Purchase Coll, State U of New York (NY)
Purdue U (IN)
Queens Coll of the City U of New York (NY)
Queen's U at Kingston (ON, Canada)
Queens U of Charlotte (NC)
Quinnipiac U (CT)
Radford U (VA)
Ramapo Coll of New Jersey (NJ)
Randolph Coll (VA)
Randolph-Macon Coll (VA)
Redeemer U Coll (ON, Canada)
Reed Coll (OR)
Regis Coll (MA)
Rhode Island Coll (RI)
Rhodes Coll (TN)
Ripon Coll (WI)
Roanoke Coll (VA)
Rockford Coll (IL)
Roger Williams U (RI)
Rollins Coll (FL)
Roosevelt U (IL)
Rowan U (NJ)
Russell Sage Coll (NY)
Rutgers, The State U of New Jersey, Camden (NJ)
Rutgers, The State U of New Jersey, Newark (NJ)
Rutgers, The State U of New Jersey, New Brunswick (NJ)
Sacred Heart U (CT)
Saginaw Valley State U (MI)
St. Ambrose U (IA)
St. Cloud State U (MN)
St. Edward's U (TX)
Saint John's U (MN)
Saint Joseph's Coll (IN)
St. Lawrence U (NY)
Saint Louis U (MO)
Saint Martin's U (WA)
Saint Mary-of-the-Woods Coll (IN)
Saint Mary's Coll (IN)
Saint Mary's Coll of California (CA)
St. Mary's Coll of Maryland (MD)
Saint Mary's U of Minnesota (MN)
Saint Michael's Coll (VT)
St. Olaf Coll (MN)
Saint Vincent Coll (PA)
Salem State Coll (MA)
Salisbury U (MD)
Salve Regina U (RI)
Samford U (AL)
Sam Houston State U (TX)
San Diego State U (CA)
San Francisco State U (CA)
Santa Clara U (CA)
Sarah Lawrence Coll (NY)
Savannah Coll of Art and Design (GA)
Schreiner U (TX)
Scripps Coll (CA)
Seattle Pacific U (WA)
Seattle U (WA)
Seton Hill U (PA)
Sewanee: The U of the South (TN)
Shawnee State U (OH)
Shaw U (NC)
Shenandoah U (VA)
Shorter Coll (GA)
Siena Heights U (MI)
Simon Fraser U (BC, Canada)
Simpson Coll (IA)
Skidmore Coll (NY)
Slippery Rock U of Pennsylvania (PA)
Smith Coll (MA)
Sonoma State U (CA)
South Carolina State U (SC)
Southeastern Oklahoma State U (OK)
Southeastern U (FL)
Southeast Missouri State U (MO)
Southern Arkansas U–Magnolia (AR)
Southern Connecticut State U (CT)
Southern Illinois U Carbondale (IL)
Southern Illinois U Edwardsville (IL)
Southern Methodist U (TX)
Southern Oregon U (OR)
Southern U and Ag and Mech Coll (LA)
Southern Utah U (UT)
Southwest Baptist U (MO)
Southwestern U (TX)
Southwest Minnesota State U (MN)
Spelman Coll (GA)
Spring Arbor U (MI)
Spring Hill Coll (AL)
Stanford U (CA)
State U of New York at Binghamton (NY)
State U of New York at Fredonia (NY)
State U of New York at New Paltz (NY)
State U of New York at Oswego (NY)
State U of New York at Plattsburgh (NY)
State U of New York Coll at Geneseo (NY)
State U of New York Coll at Oneonta (NY)
State U of New York Coll at Potsdam (NY)
Stephen F. Austin State U (TX)
Stephens Coll (MO)
Sterling Coll (KS)
Stetson U (FL)
Stony Brook U, State U of New York (NY)
Suffolk U (MA)
Susquehanna U (PA)
Swarthmore Coll (PA)
Sweet Briar Coll (VA)
Syracuse U (NY)
Tarleton State U (TX)
Taylor U (IN)
Temple U (PA)
Tennessee Wesleyan Coll (TN)
Texas A&M U (TX)
Texas A&M U–Commerce (TX)
Texas Christian U (TX)
Texas Lutheran U (TX)
Texas Southern U (TX)
Texas State U-San Marcos (TX)
Texas Tech U (TX)
Texas Woman's U (TX)
Thomas More Coll (KY)
Thompson Rivers U (BC, Canada)
Towson U (MD)
Transylvania U (KY)
Trevecca Nazarene U (TN)
Trinity Coll (CT)
Trinity U (TX)
Troy U (AL)
Truman State U (MO)
Tufts U (MA)
Tulane U (LA)
Union U (TN)
U at Albany, State U of New York (NY)
U at Buffalo, the State U of New York (NY)
The U of Akron (OH)
The U of Alabama (AL)
The U of Arizona (AZ)
U of Arkansas (AR)
U of Arkansas at Pine Bluff (AR)
The U of British Columbia (BC, Canada)
The U of British Columbia–Okanagan (BC, Canada)
U of California, Berkeley (CA)
U of California, Irvine (CA)
U of California, Los Angeles (CA)
U of California, Riverside (CA)
U of California, San Diego (CA)
U of California, Santa Barbara (CA)
U of California, Santa Cruz (CA)
U of Central Arkansas (AR)
U of Central Florida (FL)
U of Central Missouri (MO)
U of Central Oklahoma (OK)
U of Cincinnati (OH)
U of Colorado at Boulder (CO)
U of Colorado Denver (CO)
U of Connecticut (CT)
U of Dallas (TX)
U of Dayton (OH)
U of Denver (CO)
U of Evansville (IN)
The U of Findlay (OH)
U of Florida (FL)
U of Georgia (GA)
U of Hartford (CT)
U of Hawaii at Manoa (HI)
U of Houston (TX)
U of Illinois at Chicago (IL)
U of Illinois at Urbana–Champaign (IL)
U of Indianapolis (IN)
The U of Iowa (IA)
U of Kansas (KS)
U of King's Coll (NS, Canada)
U of La Verne (CA)
U of Lethbridge (AB, Canada)
U of Louisiana at Lafayette (LA)
U of Louisville (KY)
U of Maine (ME)
U of Maine at Farmington (ME)
U of Maine at Machias (ME)
U of Mary Hardin-Baylor (TX)
U of Maryland, Baltimore County (MD)
U of Maryland, Coll Park (MD)
U of Mary Washington (VA)
U of Massachusetts Amherst (MA)
U of Massachusetts Boston (MA)
U of Memphis (TN)
U of Miami (FL)
U of Michigan (MI)
U of Michigan–Flint (MI)
U of Minnesota, Duluth (MN)
U of Minnesota, Twin Cities Campus (MN)
U of Mississippi (MS)
U of Missouri–Columbia (MO)
U of Missouri–Kansas City (MO)
The U of Montana (MT)
The U of Montana–Western (MT)
U of Montevallo (AL)
U of Nebraska at Kearney (NE)
U of Nebraska at Omaha (NE)
U of Nebraska–Lincoln (NE)
U of Nevada, Las Vegas (NV)
U of Nevada, Reno (NV)
U of New Brunswick Fredericton (NB, Canada)
U of New Hampshire (NH)
U of New Mexico (NM)
The U of North Carolina at Asheville (NC)
The U of North Carolina at Chapel Hill (NC)
The U of North Carolina at Charlotte (NC)
The U of North Carolina at Greensboro (NC)
The U of North Carolina at Pembroke (NC)
The U of North Carolina Wilmington (NC)
U of North Dakota (ND)
U of Northern Colorado (CO)
U of Northern Iowa (IA)
U of North Texas (TX)
U of Notre Dame (IN)
U of Oklahoma (OK)
U of Oregon (OR)
U of Ottawa (ON, Canada)
U of Pennsylvania (PA)
U of Pittsburgh (PA)
U of Pittsburgh at Johnstown (PA)
U of Portland (OR)
U of Puget Sound (WA)
U of Regina (SK, Canada)
U of Richmond (VA)
U of Saint Mary (KS)
U of St. Thomas (MN)
U of St. Thomas (TX)
U of San Diego (CA)
U of Science and Arts of Oklahoma (OK)
The U of Scranton (PA)
U of South Alabama (AL)
U of South Carolina (SC)
The U of South Dakota (SD)
U of Southern California (CA)
U of Southern Indiana (IN)
U of Southern Maine (ME)
U of Southern Mississippi (MS)
U of South Florida (FL)
The U of Tampa (FL)
The U of Tennessee (TN)
The U of Tennessee at Chattanooga (TN)
The U of Tennessee at Martin (TN)
The U of Texas at Arlington (TX)
The U of Texas at Austin (TX)
The U of Texas at El Paso (TX)
The U of Texas at Tyler (TX)
The U of Texas–Pan American (TX)
U of the District of Columbia (DC)
U of the Incarnate Word (TX)
U of the Ozarks (AR)
U of the Pacific (CA)
U of the Sacred Heart (PR)
U of the Virgin Islands (VI)
The U of Toledo (OH)
U of Toronto (ON, Canada)
U of Tulsa (OK)
U of Utah (UT)
U of Vermont (VT)
U of Victoria (BC, Canada)
U of Virginia (VA)
The U of Virginia's Coll at Wise (VA)
U of West Florida (FL)
U of West Georgia (GA)
U of Windsor (ON, Canada)
The U of Winnipeg (MB, Canada)
U of Wisconsin–Eau Claire (WI)
U of Wisconsin–Green Bay (WI)
U of Wisconsin–La Crosse (WI)
U of Wisconsin–Madison (WI)
U of Wisconsin–Milwaukee (WI)
U of Wisconsin–Oshkosh (WI)
U of Wisconsin–Parkside (WI)
U of Wisconsin–Stevens Point (WI)
U of Wisconsin–Superior (WI)
U of Wisconsin–Whitewater (WI)
U of Wyoming (WY)
Utah State U (UT)
Utah Valley State Coll (UT)
Valdosta State U (GA)
Valparaiso U (IN)
Vanderbilt U (TN)
Vanguard U of Southern California (CA)
Vassar Coll (NY)
Virginia Commonwealth U (VA)
Virginia Intermont Coll (VA)
Virginia Polytechnic Inst and State U (VA)
Virginia Wesleyan Coll (VA)
Viterbo U (WI)
Wabash Coll (IN)
Wagner Coll (NY)
Wake Forest U (NC)
Washburn U (KS)
Washington and Lee U (VA)
Washington Coll (MD)
Washington State U (WA)
Washington U in St. Louis (MO)
Wayland Baptist U (TX)
Wayne State Coll (NE)
Wayne State U (MI)
Weber State U (UT)
Webster U (MO)
Wellesley Coll (MA)
Wells Coll (NY)
Wesleyan U (CT)
West Chester U of Pennsylvania (PA)
Western Carolina U (NC)
Western Connecticut State U (CT)
Western Illinois U (IL)
Western Kentucky U (KY)
Western State Coll of Colorado (CO)
Western Washington U (WA)
Westfield State Coll (MA)
Westmont Coll (CA)
West Texas A&M U (TX)
West Virginia U (WV)
West Virginia Wesleyan Coll (WV)
Wheaton Coll (MA)
Whitman Coll (WA)
Whittier Coll (CA)
Whitworth U (WA)
Wichita State U (KS)
Wilkes U (PA)
Willamette U (OR)
William Jewell Coll (MO)
William Paterson U of New Jersey (NJ)
Williams Coll (MA)
William Woods U (MO)
Wilmington Coll (OH)
Winona State U (MN)
Winthrop U (SC)
Wittenberg U (OH)
Wofford Coll (SC)
Wright State U (OH)
Yale U (CT)
York Coll of Pennsylvania (PA)
York Coll of the City U of New York (NY)
York U (ON, Canada)

DRAMATIC/THEATER ARTS AND STAGECRAFT RELATED

Baldwin-Wallace Coll (OH)
Bowling Green State U (OH)
Brigham Young U (UT)
California Inst of the Arts (CA)
California State U, Chico (CA)
Coastal Carolina U (SC)
Coll of Santa Fe (NM)
DePaul U (IL)
Drake U (IA)
Fayetteville State U (NC)
Indiana U South Bend (IN)
Lehigh U (PA)
Meredith Coll (NC)
Nebraska Wesleyan U (NE)
North Central Coll (IL)
North Greenville U (SC)
Oakland U (MI)
Ohio U (OH)
Pepperdine U, Malibu (CA)
St. Cloud State U (MN)
Seton Hill U (PA)
Shenandoah U (VA)
Southwest Minnesota State U (MN)
Thompson Rivers U (BC, Canada)
U at Buffalo, the State U of New York (NY)
U of Connecticut (CT)
U of Miami (FL)
U of Michigan–Flint (MI)
U of Nevada, Las Vegas (NV)
U of Northern Colorado (CO)
U of Regina (SK, Canada)

DRAWING

Alberta Coll of Art & Design (AB, Canada)
Aquinas Coll (MI)
Art Acad of Cincinnati (OH)
Ball State U (IN)
Bard Coll at Simon's Rock (MA)
Bennington Coll (VT)
Bethany Coll (KS)
Biola U (CA)
Boise State U (ID)
Boston U (MA)
Bradley U (IL)
Brigham Young U (UT)
Buffalo State Coll, State U of New York (NY)
California Coll of the Arts (CA)
California State U, East Bay (CA)
California State U, Long Beach (CA)
Carson-Newman Coll (TN)
The Cleveland Inst of Art (OH)
The Coll at Brockport, State U of New York (NY)
Coll of the Atlantic (ME)
Coll of Visual Arts (MN)
Colorado State U (CO)
Columbus State U (GA)
Drake U (IA)
Grace Coll (IN)
Grand Valley State U (MI)
Hampton U (VA)
Indiana U–Purdue U Fort Wayne (IN)
Inter American U of Puerto Rico, San Germán Campus (PR)
Laguna Coll of Art & Design (CA)
Lewis U (IL)
Lindenwood U (MO)
Longwood U (VA)
Marlboro Coll (VT)
Maryland Inst Coll of Art (MD)
McNeese State U (LA)
Memorial U of Newfoundland (NL, Canada)
Memphis Coll of Art (TN)
Minnesota State U Mankato (MN)
Mississippi U for Women (MS)
Montserrat Coll of Art (MA)
Mount Allison U (NB, Canada)
Nazareth Coll of Rochester (NY)
New England Coll (NH)
Northern Michigan U (MI)
North Georgia Coll & State U (GA)
Northwest Missouri State U (MO)
NSCAD U (NS, Canada)
Oakland U (MI)
Ohio U (OH)
Otis Coll of Art and Design (CA)
Paier Coll of Art, Inc. (CT)
Portland State U (OR)
Pratt Inst (NY)
Providence Coll (RI)
Rutgers, The State U of New Jersey, New Brunswick (NJ)
St. Cloud State U (MN)
Salem State Coll (MA)
Sarah Lawrence Coll (NY)
Savannah Coll of Art and Design (GA)
School of the Art Inst of Chicago (IL)
School of the Museum of Fine Arts, Boston (MA)
School of Visual Arts (NY)
Seton Hill U (PA)
Sewanee: The U of the South (TN)
Shawnee State U (OH)
Sonoma State U (CA)
State U of New York at Fredonia (NY)
Trinity Christian Coll (IL)
U of Georgia (GA)
U of Hartford (CT)

MAJORS AND MORE

The U of Iowa (IA)
U of Michigan (MI)
U of Missouri–St. Louis (MO)
The U of Montana (MT)
U of Regina (SK, Canada)
The U of Texas at El Paso (TX)
The U of Toledo (OH)
U of Windsor (ON, Canada)
Washington U in St. Louis (MO)
Western Washington U (WA)
West Virginia Wesleyan Coll (WV)
Winona State U (MN)
Wright State U (OH)
York U (ON, Canada)

DRIVER AND SAFETY TEACHER EDUCATION
U of Northern Iowa (IA)

DUTCH/FLEMISH
U of California, Berkeley (CA)

EARLY CHILDHOOD EDUCATION
Alma Coll (MI)
Alvernia Coll (PA)
Arizona State U (AZ)
Arizona State U at the West campus (AZ)
Arkansas State U (AR)
Arlington Baptist Coll (TX)
Auburn U (AL)
Baldwin-Wallace Coll (OH)
Baylor U (TX)
Becker Coll (MA)
Bennington Coll (VT)
Berry Coll (GA)
Bethel U (MN)
Bloomsburg U of Pennsylvania (PA)
Bob Jones U (SC)
Bradley U (IL)
Brenau U (GA)
Brewton-Parker Coll (GA)
Bridgewater State Coll (MA)
Brigham Young U (UT)
Bucknell U (PA)
California State U, Chico (CA)
California State U, Fullerton (CA)
California State U, Los Angeles (CA)
Canisius Coll (NY)
Capital U (OH)
Carlow U (PA)
Carroll Coll (WI)
Cascade Coll (OR)
Cedarville U (OH)
Central Michigan U (MI)
Central Washington U (WA)
Chaminade U of Honolulu (HI)
Chatham U (PA)
Chestnut Hill Coll (PA)
Chicago State U (IL)
City Coll of the City U of New York (NY)
Claflin U (SC)
Clemson U (SC)
Cleveland State U (OH)
Coastal Carolina U (SC)
Coker Coll (SC)
Colby-Sawyer Coll (NH)
The Coll at Brockport, State U of New York (NY)
Coll of Charleston (SC)
Coll of Mount St. Joseph (OH)
Coll of Saint Mary (NE)
Columbia Coll Chicago (IL)
Columbus State U (GA)
Concordia Coll–New York (NY)
Concordia U (CA)
Concordia U (MI)
Concordia U, Nebraska (NE)
Concordia U, St. Paul (MN)
Cornerstone U (MI)
Curry Coll (MA)
Daemen Coll (NY)
DePaul U (IL)
Duquesne U (PA)
East Central U (OK)
Eastern Connecticut State U (CT)
Eastern Mennonite U (VA)
East Stroudsburg U of Pennsylvania (PA)
Edinboro U of Pennsylvania (PA)
Endicott Coll (MA)
Evangel U (MO)
Fayetteville State U (NC)
Ferris State U (MI)
Fitchburg State Coll (MA)
Florida Atlantic U (FL)
Florida Gulf Coast U (FL)
Florida State U (FL)
Fort Lewis Coll (CO)
Francis Marion U (SC)
Gannon U (PA)
Gardner-Webb U (NC)
Georgia Coll & State U (GA)
Georgia State U (GA)
Grace Bible Coll (MI)
Grand Canyon U (AZ)
Granite State Coll (NH)
Greensboro Coll (NC)
Greenville Coll (IL)
Hannibal-LaGrange Coll (MO)
Harding U (AR)
Hardin-Simmons U (TX)
Harris-Stowe State U (MO)
Hastings Coll (NE)
Henderson State U (AR)
Hendrix Coll (AR)
Hillsdale Coll (MI)
Hofstra U (NY)
Hood Coll (MD)
Houston Baptist U (TX)
Idaho State U (ID)
Illinois Coll (IL)
Illinois State U (IL)
Indiana State U (IN)
Indiana U Kokomo (IN)
Indiana U of Pennsylvania (PA)
Indiana U–Purdue U Indianapolis (IN)
Inter American U of Puerto Rico, Aguadilla Campus (PR)
Inter American U of Puerto Rico, San Germán Campus (PR)
Iona Coll (NY)
Iowa State U of Science and Technology (IA)
John Brown U (AR)
Juniata Coll (PA)
Kentucky Christian U (KY)
Keystone Coll (PA)
King's Coll (PA)
LaGrange Coll (GA)
Lake Superior State U (MI)
Lander U (SC)
LeMoyne-Owen Coll (TN)
Lincoln U (MO)
Loras Coll (IA)
Louisiana State U and Ag and Mech Coll (LA)
Lourdes Coll (OH)
Lubbock Christian U (TX)
Lyon Coll (AR)
Madonna U (MI)
Malone Coll (OH)
Maranatha Baptist Bible Coll (WI)
Marywood U (PA)
Mayville State U (ND)
McGill U (QC, Canada)
McNeese State U (LA)
Messiah Coll (PA)
Miami U (OH)
Miami U Hamilton (OH)
Midwestern State U (TX)
Miles Coll (AL)
Millersville U of Pennsylvania (PA)
Milligan Coll (TN)
Millikin U (IL)
Missouri State U (MO)
Mitchell Coll (CT)
Morris Coll (SC)
Mount Vernon Nazarene U (OH)
Murray State U (KY)
Naropa U (CO)
Nicholls State U (LA)
Northeastern Illinois U (IL)
Northeastern State U (OK)
Northern Arizona U (AZ)
Northwestern Coll (MN)
Northwestern Oklahoma State U (OK)
Northwestern State U of Louisiana (LA)
Ohio Dominican U (OH)
Ohio Northern U (OH)
Ohio U (OH)
Ohio Wesleyan U (OH)
Oklahoma Christian U (OK)
Oral Roberts U (OK)
Ouachita Baptist U (AR)
Pace U (NY)
Park U (MO)
Plymouth State U (NH)
Point Park U (PA)
Presbyterian Coll (SC)
Purdue U (IN)
Purdue U North Central (IN)
Rhode Island Coll (RI)
Ripon Coll (WI)
Rochester Coll (MI)
St. Ambrose U (IA)
Saint Joseph Coll (CT)
St. Joseph's Coll, Suffolk Campus (NY)
Salve Regina U (RI)
San Diego State U (CA)
San Francisco State U (CA)
Sarah Lawrence Coll (NY)
Schreiner U (TX)
Seton Hill U (PA)
Shawnee State U (OH)
South Carolina State U (SC)
South Dakota State U (SD)
Southeastern Louisiana U (LA)
Southern Connecticut State U (CT)
Southern Illinois U Carbondale (IL)
Southern Illinois U Edwardsville (IL)
Southern New Hampshire U (NH)
Southern U and Ag and Mech Coll (LA)
Southwest Baptist U (MO)
Southwestern Coll (KS)
Spring Hill Coll (AL)
State U of New York Coll at Geneseo (NY)
State U of New York Coll at Old Westbury (NY)
State U of New York Coll at Oneonta (NY)
Stephens Coll (MO)
Stonehill Coll (MA)
Tennessee Wesleyan Coll (TN)
Texas A&M U–Commerce (TX)
Texas Christian U (TX)
Thomas U (GA)
Toccoa Falls Coll (GA)
Towson U (MD)
Trinity Lutheran Coll (WA)
Troy U (AL)
Truett-McConnell Coll (GA)
Tusculum Coll (TN)
The U of Akron (OH)
The U of Alabama (AL)
The U of Arizona (AZ)
U of Arkansas (AR)
U of Arkansas at Fort Smith (AR)
U of Central Florida (FL)
U of Cincinnati (OH)
U of Georgia (GA)
U of Hartford (CT)
U of Idaho (ID)
U of Illinois at Urbana–Champaign (IL)
U of Maine at Farmington (ME)
U of Mary (ND)
U of Michigan–Dearborn (MI)
U of Michigan–Flint (MI)
U of Minnesota, Crookston (MN)
U of Missouri–Columbia (MO)
U of Missouri–Kansas City (MO)
U of Missouri–St. Louis (MO)
U of Montevallo (AL)
U of New Mexico (NM)
U of New Orleans (LA)
The U of North Carolina at Chapel Hill (NC)
The U of North Carolina at Greensboro (NC)
The U of North Carolina at Pembroke (NC)
U of North Dakota (ND)
U of North Florida (FL)
U of Oklahoma (OK)
U of Regina (SK, Canada)
U of Science and Arts of Oklahoma (OK)
The U of Scranton (PA)
U of South Alabama (AL)
U of South Carolina Aiken (SC)
U of South Carolina Upstate (SC)
U of Tulsa (OK)
U of Vermont (VT)
U of West Florida (FL)
U of Wisconsin–Whitewater (WI)
Ursuline Coll (OH)
Utah Valley State Coll (UT)
Valdosta State U (GA)
Villa Julie Coll (MD)
Walsh U (OH)
Warner Pacific Coll (OR)
Washington State U (WA)
Wayne State Coll (NE)
Wesleyan Coll (GA)
West Chester U of Pennsylvania (PA)
Western Kentucky U (KY)
Western New Mexico U (NM)
Widener U (PA)
Wilmington U (DE)
Xavier U of Louisiana (LA)
Youngstown State U (OH)

EARTH SCIENCES
Florida Inst of Technology (FL)
Millersville U of Pennsylvania (PA)
Stanford U (CA)
U of Arkansas (AR)
The U of North Carolina at Charlotte (NC)
The U of Western Ontario (ON, Canada)

EAST ASIAN LANGUAGES
Eckerd Coll (FL)
Indiana U Bloomington (IN)
McGill U (QC, Canada)
Smith Coll (MA)
U of Illinois at Urbana–Champaign (IL)
U of Kansas (KS)
U of Pennsylvania (PA)
U of Southern California (CA)
The U of Texas at Austin (TX)
The U of Western Ontario (ON, Canada)

EAST ASIAN LANGUAGES RELATED
Arizona State U (AZ)
Claremont McKenna Coll (CA)
Dartmouth Coll (NH)
Michigan State U (MI)
Northwestern U (IL)
U of California, Los Angeles (CA)
U of Florida (FL)
Washington U in St. Louis (MO)

ECOLOGY
Appalachian State U (NC)
Averett U (VA)
Ball State U (IN)
Bard Coll at Simon's Rock (MA)
Barry U (FL)
Bemidji State U (MN)
Bennington Coll (VT)
Boston U (MA)
Bowling Green State U (OH)
Bradley U (IL)
Brevard Coll (NC)
California State U, Chico (CA)
California State U, East Bay (CA)
California State U, Fresno (CA)
California State U, Long Beach (CA)
California State U, San Marcos (CA)
Clarkson U (NY)
Clark U (MA)
Concordia Coll–New York (NY)
Concordia U (QC, Canada)
Connecticut Coll (CT)
Cornell U (NY)
Dartmouth Coll (NH)
Defiance Coll (OH)
East Central U (OK)
Eastern Kentucky U (KY)
Florida Inst of Technology (FL)
Florida State U (FL)
Georgetown Coll (KY)
Harvard U (MA)
Idaho State U (ID)
Iowa State U of Science and Technology (IA)
Jacksonville State U (AL)
Juniata Coll (PA)
Keene State Coll (NH)
Kent State U (OH)
Lawrence U (WI)
Lehigh U (PA)
Le Moyne Coll (NY)
Manchester Coll (IN)
Marlboro Coll (VT)
McGill U (QC, Canada)
Medgar Evers Coll of the City U of New York (NY)
Memorial U of Newfoundland (NL, Canada)
Michigan Technological U (MI)
Minnesota State U Mankato (MN)
Morehead State U (KY)
North Carolina State U (NC)
Northern Arizona U (AZ)
Northern Michigan U (MI)
Northland Coll (WI)
Northwestern U (IL)
Northwest Missouri State U (MO)
Oberlin Coll (OH)
Oklahoma State U (OK)
Paul Smith's Coll (NY)
Pitzer Coll (CA)
Pomona Coll (CA)
Prescott Coll (AZ)
Princeton U (NJ)
Rice U (TX)
Rutgers, The State U of New Jersey, New Brunswick (NJ)
St. Cloud State U (MN)
San Francisco State U (CA)
Sarah Lawrence Coll (NY)
Siena Coll (NY)
Sonoma State U (CA)
State U of New York at Binghamton (NY)
State U of New York at Plattsburgh (NY)
State U of New York Coll of Environmental Science and Forestry (NY)
Sterling Coll (VT)
Susquehanna U (PA)
Texas A&M U (TX)
Thompson Rivers U (BC, Canada)
Towson U (MD)
Tufts U (MA)
Tulane U (LA)
Université de Sherbrooke (QC, Canada)
The U of Akron (OH)
U of California, Irvine (CA)
U of California, Los Angeles (CA)
U of California, San Diego (CA)
U of California, Santa Cruz (CA)
U of Connecticut (CT)
U of Delaware (DE)
U of Denver (CO)
U of Georgia (GA)
U of Idaho (ID)
U of Illinois at Urbana–Champaign (IL)
U of Maine (ME)
U of Maine at Machias (ME)
U of Maryland, Coll Park (MD)
U of Maryland Eastern Shore (MD)
U of Michigan–Flint (MI)
U of Minnesota, Twin Cities Campus (MN)
U of New Brunswick Fredericton (NB, Canada)
U of New Hampshire (NH)
U of New Haven (CT)
U of Northern Iowa (IA)
U of Pittsburgh (PA)
U of Pittsburgh at Johnstown (PA)
U of Rio Grande (OH)
The U of Tennessee (TN)
The U of Texas at Austin (TX)
U of Toronto (ON, Canada)
U of Victoria (BC, Canada)
The U of Western Ontario (ON, Canada)
The U of Winnipeg (MB, Canada)
U of Wisconsin–Milwaukee (WI)
Utah State U (UT)
Vanderbilt U (TN)
Washington Coll (MD)
Washington State U (WA)
William Paterson U of New Jersey (NJ)
Winona State U (MN)
Yale U (CT)
York U (ON, Canada)

ECOLOGY, EVOLUTION, SYSTEMATICS AND POPULATION BIOLOGY RELATED
Angelo State U (TX)
Brigham Young U (UT)
Sterling Coll (VT)
The U of British Columbia–Okanagan (BC, Canada)
U of California, Davis (CA)
U of California, Irvine (CA)
U of California, Santa Barbara (CA)
U of Colorado at Boulder (CO)

E-COMMERCE
Clarkson U (NY)
Colorado Tech U—Colorado Springs (CO)
Colorado Tech U—Denver (CO)
Colorado Tech U—North Kansas City (MO)
Colorado Tech U—Online (CO)
Colorado Tech U—Sioux Falls (SD)
DePaul U (IL)
DeSales U (PA)
Dominican U of California (CA)
Florida Inst of Technology (FL)
Harrisburg U of Science and Technology (PA)
Maryville U of Saint Louis (MO)
McGill U (QC, Canada)
Messiah Coll (PA)
Mountain State U (WV)
National U (CA)
Northwestern Oklahoma State U (OK)
Philadelphia U (PA)
Southern U and Ag and Mech Coll (LA)
Stetson U (FL)
Texas Christian U (TX)
Thiel Coll (PA)
The U of Akron (OH)
U of La Verne (CA)
U of North Texas (TX)
U of Ottawa (ON, Canada)
U of Pennsylvania (PA)
U of South Alabama (AL)
U of Southern Indiana (IN)
U of Toronto (ON, Canada)
Washington State U (WA)
Western Michigan U (MI)
Westwood Coll–Atlanta Northlake (GA)
Winthrop U (SC)

ECONOMETRICS AND QUANTITATIVE ECONOMICS
Baldwin-Wallace Coll (OH)
Bowdoin Coll (ME)
The Colorado Coll (CO)
Hampden-Sydney Coll (VA)
Haverford Coll (PA)

Hofstra U (NY)
Miami U Hamilton (OH)
Southern Methodist U (TX)
State U of New York at Oswego (NY)
United States Naval Acad (MD)
U of California, Irvine (CA)
U of California, San Diego (CA)
U of California, Santa Barbara (CA)
U of Rhode Island (RI)
U of St. Thomas (MN)
Wake Forest U (NC)

ECONOMICS

Acadia U (NS, Canada)
Adelphi U (NY)
Adrian Coll (MI)
Agnes Scott Coll (GA)
Alabama Ag and Mech U (AL)
Alabama State U (AL)
Albertus Magnus Coll (CT)
Albion Coll (MI)
Albright Coll (PA)
Alcorn State U (MS)
Alfred U (NY)
Allegheny Coll (PA)
Alma Coll (MI)
American U (DC)
American U of Beirut (Lebanon)
The American U of Paris (France)
Amherst Coll (MA)
Andrews U (MI)
Appalachian State U (NC)
Aquinas Coll (MI)
Arizona State U (AZ)
Arkansas State U (AR)
Armstrong Atlantic State U (GA)
Ashland U (OH)
Assumption Coll (MA)
Auburn U (AL)
Augsburg Coll (MN)
Augustana Coll (IL)
Augustana Coll (SD)
Austin Coll (TX)
Ave Maria U (FL)
Babson Coll (MA)
Baker U (KS)
Baldwin-Wallace Coll (OH)
Ball State U (IN)
Bard Coll (NY)
Barnard Coll (NY)
Barry U (FL)
Barton Coll (NC)
Bates Coll (ME)
Baylor U (TX)
Bellarmine U (KY)
Belmont Abbey Coll (NC)
Belmont U (TN)
Beloit Coll (WI)
Bemidji State U (MN)
Benedictine Coll (KS)
Benedictine U (IL)
Berea Coll (KY)
Bernard M. Baruch Coll of the City U of New York (NY)
Berry Coll (GA)
Bethany Coll (WV)
Bethel U (MN)
Bishop's U (QC, Canada)
Bloomsburg U of Pennsylvania (PA)
Bluffton U (OH)
Boise State U (ID)
Boston Coll (MA)
Boston U (MA)
Bowdoin Coll (ME)
Bowling Green State U (OH)
Bradley U (IL)
Brandeis U (MA)
Bridgewater Coll (VA)
Bridgewater State Coll (MA)
Brigham Young U (UT)
Brock U (ON, Canada)
Brown U (RI)
Bryn Mawr Coll (PA)
Bucknell U (PA)
Buffalo State Coll, State U of New York (NY)
Butler U (IN)
California Inst of Technology (CA)
California Lutheran U (CA)
California Polytechnic State U, San Luis Obispo (CA)
California State Polytechnic U, Pomona (CA)
California State U, Chico (CA)
California State U, Dominguez Hills (CA)
California State U, East Bay (CA)
California State U, Fresno (CA)
California State U, Fullerton (CA)
California State U, Long Beach (CA)
California State U, Los Angeles (CA)
California State U, Sacramento (CA)
California State U, San Bernardino (CA)
California State U, San Marcos (CA)
California State U, Stanislaus (CA)
Calvin Coll (MI)
Canadian Mennonite U (MB, Canada)
Canisius Coll (NY)
Capital U (OH)
Carnegie Mellon U (PA)
Carson-Newman Coll (TN)
Case Western Reserve U (OH)
The Catholic U of America (DC)
Centenary Coll of Louisiana (LA)
Central Coll (IA)
Central Connecticut State U (CT)
Central Michigan U (MI)
Central State U (OH)
Central Washington U (WA)
Centre Coll (KY)
Chatham U (PA)
Cheyney U of Pennsylvania (PA)
Chicago State U (IL)
Christopher Newport U (VA)
City Coll of the City U of New York (NY)
Claremont McKenna Coll (CA)
Clarion U of Pennsylvania (PA)
Clarke Coll (IA)
Clark U (MA)
Clemson U (SC)
Cleveland State U (OH)
Coastal Carolina U (SC)
Colby Coll (ME)
Colgate U (NY)
The Coll at Brockport, State U of New York (NY)
Coll of Charleston (SC)
The Coll of Idaho (ID)
Coll of Mount Saint Vincent (NY)
The Coll of New Jersey (NJ)
The Coll of New Rochelle (NY)
Coll of Saint Benedict (MN)
Coll of Saint Elizabeth (NJ)
Coll of Staten Island of the City U of New York (NY)
Coll of the Atlantic (ME)
Coll of the Holy Cross (MA)
The Coll of William and Mary (VA)
The Colorado Coll (CO)
Colorado School of Mines (CO)
Colorado State U (CO)
Concordia Coll (MN)
Concordia U (QC, Canada)
Concordia U Wisconsin (WI)
Connecticut Coll (CT)
Converse Coll (SC)
Cornell Coll (IA)
Cornell U (NY)
Covenant Coll (GA)
Creighton U (NE)
Dartmouth Coll (NH)
Davidson Coll (NC)
Davis & Elkins Coll (WV)
Denison U (OH)
DePaul U (IL)
DePauw U (IN)
Dickinson Coll (PA)
Dillard U (LA)
Doane Coll (NE)
Dominican Coll (NY)
Dominican U (IL)
Dowling Coll (NY)
Drew U (NJ)
Drury U (MO)
Duke U (NC)
Duquesne U (PA)
Earlham Coll (IN)
East Carolina U (NC)
Eastern Connecticut State U (CT)
Eastern Illinois U (IL)
Eastern Kentucky U (KY)
Eastern Mennonite U (VA)
Eastern Michigan U (MI)
East Stroudsburg U of Pennsylvania (PA)
East Tennessee State U (TN)
Eckerd Coll (FL)
Edinboro U of Pennsylvania (PA)
Elizabethtown Coll (PA)
Elon U (NC)
Emmanuel Coll (MA)
Emory & Henry Coll (VA)
Emory U (GA)
Emporia State U (KS)
Eugene Lang Coll The New School for Liberal Arts (NY)
Excelsior Coll (NY)
Fairfield U (CT)
Fairleigh Dickinson U, Coll at Florham (NJ)
Fairleigh Dickinson U, Metropolitan Campus (NJ)
Fairmont State U (WV)
Fitchburg State Coll (MA)
Florida Ag and Mech U (FL)
Florida Atlantic U (FL)
Florida Intl U (FL)
Florida Southern Coll (FL)
Florida State U (FL)
Fort Lewis Coll (CO)
Framingham State Coll (MA)
Franciscan U of Steubenville (OH)
Francis Marion U (SC)
Franklin & Marshall Coll (PA)
Franklin Coll (IN)
Frostburg State U (MD)
Furman U (SC)
George Fox U (OR)
George Mason U (VA)
Georgetown Coll (KY)
Georgetown U (DC)
The George Washington U (DC)
Georgia Southern U (GA)
Georgia State U (GA)
Gettysburg Coll (PA)
Gonzaga U (WA)
Gordon Coll (MA)
Goucher Coll (MD)
Grand Valley State U (MI)
Grove City Coll (PA)
Guilford Coll (NC)
Gustavus Adolphus Coll (MN)
Hamilton Coll (NY)
Hamline U (MN)
Hampden-Sydney Coll (VA)
Hampshire Coll (MA)
Hampton U (VA)
Hanover Coll (IN)
Harding U (AR)
Hardin-Simmons U (TX)
Hartwick Coll (NY)
Harvard U (MA)
Hastings Coll (NE)
Haverford Coll (PA)
Hawai'i Pacific U (HI)
Heidelberg Coll (OH)
Hendrix Coll (AR)
Hillsdale Coll (MI)
Hobart and William Smith Colls (NY)
Hofstra U (NY)
Hollins U (VA)
Holy Family U (PA)
Hood Coll (MD)
Hope Coll (MI)
Houston Baptist U (TX)
Humboldt State U (CA)
Hunter Coll of the City U of New York (NY)
Huntington U (IN)
Idaho State U (ID)
Illinois Coll (IL)
Illinois State U (IL)
Illinois Wesleyan U (IL)
Immaculata U (PA)
Indiana State U (IN)
Indiana U Bloomington (IN)
Indiana U Northwest (IN)
Indiana U of Pennsylvania (PA)
Indiana U–Purdue U Fort Wayne (IN)
Indiana U–Purdue U Indianapolis (IN)
Indiana U South Bend (IN)
Indiana U Southeast (IN)
Indiana Wesleyan U (IN)
Inter American U of Puerto Rico, Fajardo Campus (PR)
Inter American U of Puerto Rico, San Germán Campus (PR)
Iona Coll (NY)
Iowa State U of Science and Technology (IA)
Ithaca Coll (NY)
Jacksonville State U (AL)
Jacksonville U (FL)
James Madison U (VA)
Jarvis Christian Coll (TX)
John Carroll U (OH)
The Johns Hopkins U (MD)
Johnson C. Smith U (NC)
Juniata Coll (PA)
Kansas State U (KS)
Kean U (NJ)
Keene State Coll (NH)
Kennesaw State U (GA)
Kent State U (OH)
Kenyon Coll (OH)
King Coll (TN)
King's Coll (PA)
Knox Coll (IL)
Lafayette Coll (PA)
Lake Forest Coll (IL)
Lakehead U (ON, Canada)
Lambuth U (TN)
La Salle U (PA)
Laurentian U (ON, Canada)
Lawrence U (WI)
Lebanon Valley Coll (PA)
Lehman Coll of the City U of New York (NY)
Le Moyne Coll (NY)
Lenoir-Rhyne Coll (NC)
Lewis & Clark Coll (OR)
Lewis U (IL)
Liberty U (VA)
Lincoln U (CA)
Lincoln U (MO)
Lincoln U (PA)
Lindenwood U (MO)
Linfield Coll (OR)
Lock Haven U of Pennsylvania (PA)
Longwood U (VA)
Loras Coll (IA)
Louisiana Coll (LA)
Louisiana State U and Ag and Mech Coll (LA)
Loyola Coll in Maryland (MD)
Loyola Marymount U (CA)
Loyola U New Orleans (LA)
Luther Coll (IA)
Lycoming Coll (PA)
Lynchburg Coll (VA)
Lyon Coll (AR)
Macalester Coll (MN)
Manchester Coll (IN)
Manhattanville Coll (NY)
Mansfield U of Pennsylvania (PA)
Marian Coll (IN)
Marietta Coll (OH)
Marist Coll (NY)
Marlboro Coll (VT)
Marquette U (WI)
Marshall U (WV)
Mary Baldwin Coll (VA)
Marymount U (VA)
Maryville Coll (TN)
Massachusetts Inst of Technology (MA)
McDaniel Coll (MD)
McGill U (QC, Canada)
McKendree U (IL)
Memorial U of Newfoundland (NL, Canada)
Mercer U (GA)
Meredith Coll (NC)
Merrimack Coll (MA)
Messiah Coll (PA)
Methodist U (NC)
Metropolitan State U (MN)
Miami U (OH)
Miami U Hamilton (OH)
Michigan State U (MI)
Michigan Technological U (MI)
Middlebury Coll (VT)
Middle Tennessee State U (TN)
Midland Lutheran Coll (NE)
Midwestern State U (TX)
Millersville U of Pennsylvania (PA)
Millsaps Coll (MS)
Mills Coll (CA)
Minnesota State U Mankato (MN)
Minot State U (ND)
Mississippi State U (MS)
Missouri State U (MO)
Missouri U of Science and Technology (MO)
Missouri Valley Coll (MO)
Monmouth Coll (IL)
Montana State U (MT)
Montclair State U (NJ)
Moravian Coll (PA)
Morehouse Coll (GA)
Morgan State U (MD)
Mount Allison U (NB, Canada)
Mount Holyoke Coll (MA)
Mount St. Mary's U (MD)
Mount Saint Vincent U (NS, Canada)
Muhlenberg Coll (PA)
Murray State U (KY)
National U (CA)
Nazareth Coll of Rochester (NY)
Nebraska Wesleyan U (NE)
New Coll of Florida (FL)
New Jersey City U (NJ)
New York Inst of Technology (NY)
New York U (NY)
Niagara U (NY)
Nichols Coll (MA)
North Carolina Ag and Tech State U (NC)
North Carolina State U (NC)
North Central Coll (IL)
Northeastern Illinois U (IL)
Northeastern U (MA)
Northern Arizona U (AZ)
Northern Illinois U (IL)
Northern Michigan U (MI)
Northern State U (SD)
Northland Coll (WI)
Northwestern Coll (IA)
Northwestern U (IL)
Northwest Missouri State U (MO)
Norwich U (VT)
Nova Southeastern U (FL)
Oakland U (MI)
Oakwood Coll (AL)
Oberlin Coll (OH)
Occidental Coll (CA)
Oglethorpe U (GA)
Ohio Dominican U (OH)
Ohio U (OH)
Ohio Wesleyan U (OH)
Oklahoma State U (OK)
Old Dominion U (VA)
Oregon State U (OR)
Otterbein Coll (OH)
Pace U (NY)
Pacific Lutheran U (WA)
Pacific U (OR)
Park U (MO)
Penn State Abington (PA)
Penn State Altoona (PA)
Penn State Berks (PA)
Penn State Erie, The Behrend Coll (PA)
Penn State U Park (PA)
Pepperdine U, Malibu (CA)
Pfeiffer U (NC)
Pittsburg State U (KS)
Pitzer Coll (CA)
Pomona Coll (CA)
Portland State U (OR)
Presbyterian Coll (SC)
Princeton U (NJ)
Providence Coll (RI)
Purchase Coll, State U of New York (NY)
Purdue U Calumet (IN)
Queens Coll of the City U of New York (NY)
Queen's U at Kingston (ON, Canada)
Quinnipiac U (CT)
Radford U (VA)
Ramapo Coll of New Jersey (NJ)
Randolph Coll (VA)
Randolph-Macon Coll (VA)
Reed Coll (OR)
Regis U (CO)
Rensselaer Polytechnic Inst (NY)
Rhode Island Coll (RI)
Rhodes Coll (TN)
Rice U (TX)
The Richard Stockton Coll of New Jersey (NJ)
Rider U (NJ)
Ripon Coll (WI)
Roanoke Coll (VA)
Robert Morris U (PA)
Rochester Inst of Technology (NY)
Rockford Coll (IL)
Rockhurst U (MO)
Rollins Coll (FL)
Roosevelt U (IL)
Rose-Hulman Inst of Technology (IN)
Rosemont Coll (PA)
Rowan U (NJ)
Rutgers, The State U of New Jersey, Camden (NJ)
Rutgers, The State U of New Jersey, Newark (NJ)
Rutgers, The State U of New Jersey, New Brunswick (NJ)
Saginaw Valley State U (MI)
St. Ambrose U (IA)
St. Cloud State U (MN)
St. Edward's U (TX)
Saint Francis U (PA)
St. Francis Xavier U (NS, Canada)
St. John Fisher Coll (NY)
Saint John's U (MN)
St. John's U (NY)
Saint Joseph Coll (CT)
Saint Joseph's Coll (IN)
St. Joseph's Coll, Suffolk Campus (NY)
Saint Joseph's U (PA)
St. Lawrence U (NY)
Saint Louis U (MO)
Saint Martin's U (WA)
Saint Mary's Coll (IN)
Saint Mary's Coll of California (CA)
St. Mary's Coll of Maryland (MD)
St. Mary's U (TX)
Saint Michael's Coll (VT)
St. Norbert Coll (WI)
St. Olaf Coll (MN)
St. Thomas U (NB, Canada)
Saint Vincent Coll (PA)
Salem Coll (NC)
Salem State Coll (MA)
Salisbury U (MD)
Salve Regina U (RI)
San Diego State U (CA)
San Francisco State U (CA)
Santa Clara U (CA)
Sarah Lawrence Coll (NY)
Schiller Intl U (United Kingdom)
Scripps Coll (CA)
Seattle Pacific U (WA)
Seattle U (WA)
Seton Hill U (PA)
Sewanee: The U of the South (TN)
Shepherd U (WV)
Shippensburg U of Pennsylvania (PA)
Shorter Coll (GA)
Siena Coll (NY)
Simmons Coll (MA)
Simon Fraser U (BC, Canada)
Simpson Coll (IA)
Skidmore Coll (NY)

Slippery Rock U of Pennsylvania (PA)
Smith Coll (MA)
Sonoma State U (CA)
South Dakota State U (SD)
Southeastern Oklahoma State U (OK)
Southeast Missouri State U (MO)
Southern Connecticut State U (CT)
Southern Illinois U Carbondale (IL)
Southern Illinois U Edwardsville (IL)
Southern Methodist U (TX)
Southern New Hampshire U (NH)
Southern Oregon U (OR)
Southern Utah U (UT)
Southwestern U (TX)
Spelman Coll (GA)
Stanford U (CA)
State U of New York at Binghamton (NY)
State U of New York at Fredonia (NY)
State U of New York at New Paltz (NY)
State U of New York at Oswego (NY)
State U of New York at Plattsburgh (NY)
State U of New York Coll at Geneseo (NY)
State U of New York Coll at Old Westbury (NY)
State U of New York Coll at Oneonta (NY)
State U of New York Coll at Potsdam (NY)
State U of New York Empire State Coll (NY)
Stephen F. Austin State U (TX)
Stetson U (FL)
Stonehill Coll (MA)
Stony Brook U, State U of New York (NY)
Suffolk U (MA)
Susquehanna U (PA)
Swarthmore Coll (PA)
Sweet Briar Coll (VA)
Syracuse U (NY)
Tarleton State U (TX)
Taylor U (IN)
Temple U (PA)
Tennessee Technological U (TN)
Texas A&M U (TX)
Texas A&M U–Commerce (TX)
Texas Christian U (TX)
Texas Lutheran U (TX)
Texas Southern U (TX)
Texas State U-San Marcos (TX)
Texas Tech U (TX)
Thomas More Coll (KY)
Thompson Rivers U (BC, Canada)
Tougaloo Coll (MS)
Towson U (MD)
Transylvania U (KY)
Trent U (ON, Canada)
Trinity Coll (CT)
Trinity U (TX)
Truman State U (MO)
Tufts U (MA)
Tulane U (LA)
Tuskegee U (AL)
Union Coll (NY)
Union U (TN)
United States Air Force Acad (CO)
United States Naval Acad (MD)
U at Albany, State U of New York (NY)
U at Buffalo, the State U of New York (NY)
The U of Akron (OH)
U of Alaska Fairbanks (AK)
The U of Arizona (AZ)
U of Arkansas (AR)
U of Arkansas at Pine Bluff (AR)
U of Baltimore (MD)
The U of British Columbia (BC, Canada)
The U of British Columbia–Okanagan (BC, Canada)
U of California, Berkeley (CA)
U of California, Davis (CA)
U of California, Irvine (CA)
U of California, Los Angeles (CA)
U of California, Riverside (CA)
U of California, San Diego (CA)
U of California, Santa Barbara (CA)
U of California, Santa Cruz (CA)
U of Central Arkansas (AR)
U of Central Florida (FL)
U of Central Missouri (MO)
U of Central Oklahoma (OK)
U of Chicago (IL)
U of Cincinnati (OH)
U of Colorado at Boulder (CO)
U of Colorado Denver (CO)
U of Connecticut (CT)
U of Dallas (TX)
U of Dayton (OH)
U of Delaware (DE)
U of Denver (CO)
U of Evansville (IN)
The U of Findlay (OH)
U of Florida (FL)
U of Georgia (GA)
U of Guam (GU)
U of Hartford (CT)
U of Hawaii at Manoa (HI)
U of Hawaii–West Oahu (HI)
U of Houston (TX)
U of Idaho (ID)
U of Illinois at Chicago (IL)
U of Illinois at Springfield (IL)
U of Illinois at Urbana–Champaign (IL)
The U of Iowa (IA)
U of Kansas (KS)
U of King's Coll (NS, Canada)
U of La Verne (CA)
U of Lethbridge (AB, Canada)
U of Louisville (KY)
U of Maine (ME)
U of Mary Hardin-Baylor (TX)
U of Maryland, Baltimore County (MD)
U of Maryland, Coll Park (MD)
U of Mary Washington (VA)
U of Massachusetts Amherst (MA)
U of Massachusetts Boston (MA)
U of Massachusetts Dartmouth (MA)
U of Massachusetts Lowell (MA)
U of Memphis (TN)
U of Miami (FL)
U of Michigan (MI)
U of Michigan–Dearborn (MI)
U of Michigan–Flint (MI)
U of Minnesota, Duluth (MN)
U of Minnesota, Twin Cities Campus (MN)
U of Mississippi (MS)
U of Missouri–Columbia (MO)
U of Missouri–Kansas City (MO)
U of Missouri–St. Louis (MO)
The U of Montana (MT)
U of Nebraska at Kearney (NE)
U of Nebraska–Lincoln (NE)
U of Nevada, Las Vegas (NV)
U of New Brunswick Fredericton (NB, Canada)
U of New Hampshire (NH)
U of New Mexico (NM)
U of New Orleans (LA)
The U of North Carolina at Asheville (NC)
The U of North Carolina at Chapel Hill (NC)
The U of North Carolina at Charlotte (NC)
The U of North Carolina at Greensboro (NC)
The U of North Carolina Wilmington (NC)
U of North Dakota (ND)
U of Northern Colorado (CO)
U of Northern Iowa (IA)
U of North Florida (FL)
U of North Texas (TX)
U of Notre Dame (IN)
U of Oklahoma (OK)
U of Oregon (OR)
U of Ottawa (ON, Canada)
U of Pennsylvania (PA)
U of Pittsburgh (PA)
U of Pittsburgh at Bradford (PA)
U of Pittsburgh at Johnstown (PA)
U of Prince Edward Island (PE, Canada)
U of Puerto Rico, Cayey U Coll (PR)
U of Puget Sound (WA)
U of Redlands (CA)
U of Regina (SK, Canada)
U of Rhode Island (RI)
U of Richmond (VA)
U of Rio Grande (OH)
U of Rochester (NY)
U of St. Thomas (MN)
U of St. Thomas (TX)
U of San Diego (CA)
U of Science and Arts of Oklahoma (OK)
The U of Scranton (PA)
U of South Carolina (SC)
The U of South Dakota (SD)
U of Southern California (CA)
U of Southern Indiana (IN)
U of Southern Maine (ME)
U of South Florida (FL)
The U of Tampa (FL)
The U of Tennessee (TN)
The U of Tennessee at Chattanooga (TN)
The U of Tennessee at Martin (TN)
The U of Texas at Arlington (TX)
The U of Texas at Austin (TX)
The U of Texas at Dallas (TX)
The U of Texas at El Paso (TX)
The U of Texas at Tyler (TX)
The U of Texas of the Permian Basin (TX)
The U of Texas–Pan American (TX)
U of the District of Columbia (DC)
U of the Ozarks (AR)
U of the Pacific (CA)
The U of Toledo (OH)
U of Toronto (ON, Canada)
U of Tulsa (OK)
U of Utah (UT)
U of Vermont (VT)
U of Victoria (BC, Canada)
U of Virginia (VA)
The U of Virginia's Coll at Wise (VA)
The U of Western Ontario (ON, Canada)
U of West Florida (FL)
U of West Georgia (GA)
U of Windsor (ON, Canada)
The U of Winnipeg (MB, Canada)
U of Wisconsin–Eau Claire (WI)
U of Wisconsin–Green Bay (WI)
U of Wisconsin–La Crosse (WI)
U of Wisconsin–Milwaukee (WI)
U of Wisconsin–Oshkosh (WI)
U of Wisconsin–Parkside (WI)
U of Wisconsin–Platteville (WI)
U of Wisconsin–Stevens Point (WI)
U of Wisconsin–Superior (WI)
U of Wisconsin–Whitewater (WI)
Ursinus Coll (PA)
Utah State U (UT)
Utah Valley State Coll (UT)
Utica Coll (NY)
Valparaiso U (IN)
Vanderbilt U (TN)
Vassar Coll (NY)
Villanova U (PA)
Virginia Military Inst (VA)
Virginia Polytechnic Inst and State U (VA)
Wabash Coll (IN)
Wagner Coll (NY)
Wake Forest U (NC)
Walla Walla U (WA)
Warren Wilson Coll (NC)
Wartburg Coll (IA)
Washburn U (KS)
Washington & Jefferson Coll (PA)
Washington and Lee U (VA)
Washington Coll (MD)
Washington State U (WA)
Washington U in St. Louis (MO)
Wayne State U (MI)
Weber State U (UT)
Webster U (MO)
Wellesley Coll (MA)
Wells Coll (NY)
Wesleyan Coll (GA)
Wesleyan U (CT)
Western Connecticut State U (CT)
Western Illinois U (IL)
Western Kentucky U (KY)
Western Michigan U (MI)
Western New England Coll (MA)
Western State Coll of Colorado (CO)
Western Washington U (WA)
Westfield State Coll (MA)
Westminster Coll (MO)
Westminster Coll (UT)
Westmont Coll (CA)
West Texas A&M U (TX)
West Virginia U (WV)
West Virginia Wesleyan Coll (WV)
Wheaton Coll (IL)
Wheaton Coll (MA)
Whitman Coll (WA)
Whittier Coll (CA)
Whitworth U (WA)
Wichita State U (KS)
Widener U (PA)
Wilfrid Laurier U (ON, Canada)
Willamette U (OR)
William Jewell Coll (MO)
Williams Coll (MA)
Wilmington Coll (OH)
Wingate U (NC)
Winona State U (MN)
Wittenberg U (OH)
Wofford Coll (SC)
Worcester Polytechnic Inst (MA)
Worcester State Coll (MA)
Wright State U (OH)
Xavier U (OH)
Yale U (CT)
York Coll of the City U of New York (NY)
York U (ON, Canada)
Youngstown State U (OH)

ECONOMICS RELATED

Bard Coll at Simon's Rock (MA)
Bloomsburg U of Pennsylvania (PA)
California State U, Chico (CA)
Claremont McKenna Coll (CA)
The Colorado Coll (CO)
Eastern Michigan U (MI)
Marymount U (VA)
Muhlenberg Coll (PA)
The U of Akron (OH)
U of California, Riverside (CA)
U of Hartford (CT)
U of Illinois at Urbana–Champaign (IL)
U of West Georgia (GA)
Valparaiso U (IN)
Wright State U (OH)

EDUCATION

Acadia U (NS, Canada)
Adelphi U (NY)
Adrian Coll (MI)
Alabama State U (AL)
Albertus Magnus Coll (CT)
Albion Coll (MI)
Allegheny Coll (PA)
Alma Coll (MI)
Alvernia Coll (PA)
Anderson U (IN)
Anderson U (SC)
Andrews U (MI)
Aquinas Coll (MI)
Arlington Baptist Coll (TX)
Ashford U (IA)
Ashland U (OH)
Atlantic Union Coll (MA)
Augsburg Coll (MN)
Augustana Coll (IL)
Ball State U (IN)
Baptist Bible Coll of Pennsylvania (PA)
The Baptist Coll of Florida (FL)
Barnard Coll (NY)
Barry U (FL)
Baylor U (TX)
Becker Coll (MA)
Belmont Abbey Coll (NC)
Belmont U (TN)
Beloit Coll (WI)
Bemidji State U (MN)
Benedictine U (IL)
Bennington Coll (VT)
Berea Coll (KY)
Bernard M. Baruch Coll of the City U of New York (NY)
Bethany Coll (KS)
Bethany Coll (WV)
Bethany U (CA)
Biola U (CA)
Bishop's U (QC, Canada)
Bloomfield Coll (NJ)
Bluefield Coll (VA)
Boise State U (ID)
Boston U (MA)
Bowling Green State U (OH)
Brewton-Parker Coll (GA)
Brock U (ON, Canada)
Brown U (RI)
Bryan Coll (TN)
Bucknell U (PA)
Cabrini Coll (PA)
California Baptist U (CA)
Cameron U (OK)
Canisius Coll (NY)
Capital U (OH)
Carroll Coll (WI)
Carson-Newman Coll (TN)
Catawba Coll (NC)
The Catholic U of America (DC)
Cedar Crest Coll (PA)
Centenary Coll (NJ)
Cheyney U of Pennsylvania (PA)
Christian Brothers U (TN)
Christopher Newport U (VA)
City Coll of the City U of New York (NY)
Clarion U of Pennsylvania (PA)
Clark Atlanta U (GA)
Clarke Coll (IA)
Clark U (MA)
Cleveland State U (OH)
Coker Coll (SC)
Colgate U (NY)
The Coll at Brockport, State U of New York (NY)
Coll of Mount Saint Vincent (NY)
The Coll of New Jersey (NJ)
The Coll of New Rochelle (NY)
Coll of Saint Benedict (MN)
Coll of Saint Mary (NE)
Coll of the Atlantic (ME)
Coll of the Ozarks (MO)
Coll of the Southwest (NM)
Concordia Coll (MN)
Concordia Coll–New York (NY)
Concordia U (OR)
Concordia U (QC, Canada)
Concordia U Chicago (IL)
Concordia U, Nebraska (NE)
Concordia U, St. Paul (MN)
Concordia U Wisconsin (WI)
Concord U (WV)
Converse Coll (SC)
Cornell U (NY)
Cornerstone U (MI)
Curry Coll (MA)
Dakota Wesleyan U (SD)
Dallas Baptist U (TX)
Dallas Christian Coll (TX)
Dana Coll (NE)
Davis Coll (NY)
Defiance Coll (OH)
Delta State U (MS)
Dillard U (LA)
Dominican Coll (NY)
Dordt Coll (IA)
Dowling Coll (NY)
Drury U (MO)
Duquesne U (PA)
East Central U (OK)
Eastern Kentucky U (KY)
East Texas Baptist U (TX)
Elizabethtown Coll (PA)
Elon U (NC)
Emmanuel Coll (MA)
Emory U (GA)
Eugene Lang Coll The New School for Liberal Arts (NY)
Fairmont State U (WV)
Faulkner U (AL)
Felician Coll (NJ)
Ferrum Coll (VA)
Finlandia U (MI)
Fitchburg State Coll (MA)
Florida Ag and Mech U (FL)
Florida Southern Coll (FL)
Fontbonne U (MO)
Framingham State Coll (MA)
Freed-Hardeman U (TN)
Free Will Baptist Bible Coll (TN)
Fresno Pacific U (CA)
Furman U (SC)
Gardner-Webb U (NC)
Georgia Southern U (GA)
Georgia Southwestern State U (GA)
Gettysburg Coll (PA)
Glenville State Coll (WV)
Grand Canyon U (AZ)
Grand Valley State U (MI)
Greensboro Coll (NC)
Gustavus Adolphus Coll (MN)
Hamline U (MN)
Hampshire Coll (MA)
Hampton U (VA)
Hannibal-LaGrange Coll (MO)
Hardin-Simmons U (TX)
Hastings Coll (NE)
Haverford Coll (PA)
Hebrew Coll (MA)
Heidelberg Coll (OH)
High Point U (NC)
Hillsdale Coll (MI)
Hollins U (VA)
Holy Family U (PA)
Houston Baptist U (TX)
Howard Payne U (TX)
Humboldt State U (CA)
Huntingdon Coll (AL)
Huntington U (IN)
Huston-Tillotson U (TX)
Illinois Coll (IL)
Illinois Wesleyan U (IL)
Indiana State U (IN)
Indiana U–Purdue U Fort Wayne (IN)
Indiana U–Purdue U Indianapolis (IN)
Indiana U South Bend (IN)
Indiana Wesleyan U (IN)
Inter American U of Puerto Rico, Fajardo Campus (PR)
Inter American U of Puerto Rico, San Germán Campus (PR)
Iona Coll (NY)
Iowa State U of Science and Technology (IA)
Iowa Wesleyan Coll (IA)
Jacksonville State U (AL)
John Brown U (AR)
John Carroll U (OH)
Johnson State Coll (VT)
Juniata Coll (PA)
Keene State Coll (NH)
Kent State U (OH)
King Coll (TN)
Knox Coll (IL)
Lake Forest Coll (IL)
Lakehead U (ON, Canada)
Lake Superior State U (MI)
Lambuth U (TN)
La Salle U (PA)
Laurentian U (ON, Canada)
Lees-McRae Coll (NC)
Lee U (TN)
Lehigh U (PA)
Lenoir-Rhyne Coll (NC)
Lesley U (MA)
Limestone Coll (SC)
Lincoln U (PA)
Lindenwood U (MO)
Lindsey Wilson Coll (KY)
Lipscomb U (TN)
Livingstone Coll (NC)

MAJORS AND MORE

Lock Haven U of Pennsylvania (PA)
Longwood U (VA)
Loras Coll (IA)
Loyola Coll in Maryland (MD)
Loyola U New Orleans (LA)
Lubbock Christian U (TX)
Lynchburg Coll (VA)
Madonna U (MI)
Manchester Coll (IN)
Manhattanville Coll (NY)
Mansfield U of Pennsylvania (PA)
Maranatha Baptist Bible Coll (WI)
Marian Coll (IN)
Marian Coll of Fond du Lac (WI)
Marietta Coll (OH)
Marquette U (WI)
Martin U (IN)
Maryville Coll (TN)
Massachusetts Coll of Liberal Arts (MA)
The Master's Coll and Sem (CA)
Mayville State U (ND)
McGill U (QC, Canada)
McNeese State U (LA)
Memorial U of Newfoundland (NL, Canada)
Mercyhurst Coll (PA)
Methodist U (NC)
Michigan State U (MI)
Midland Lutheran Coll (NE)
Midway Coll (KY)
Miles Coll (AL)
Milligan Coll (TN)
Millsaps Coll (MS)
Minnesota State U Mankato (MN)
Mississippi Coll (MS)
Mississippi U for Women (MS)
Mississippi Valley State U (MS)
Missouri Southern State U (MO)
Missouri Valley Coll (MO)
Molloy Coll (NY)
Monmouth Coll (IL)
Monmouth U (NJ)
Montana State U–Billings (MT)
Moravian Coll (PA)
Morehouse Coll (GA)
Morgan State U (MD)
Morningside Coll (IA)
Mount Holyoke Coll (MA)
Mount Marty Coll (SD)
Mount Mary Coll (WI)
Mount Saint Mary Coll (NY)
Mount St. Mary's Coll (CA)
Mount Saint Vincent U (NS, Canada)
Mount Vernon Nazarene U (OH)
Nazareth Coll of Rochester (NY)
New England Coll (NH)
Newman U (KS)
New York Inst of Technology (NY)
New York U (NY)
Niagara U (NY)
North Carolina Ag and Tech State U (NC)
North Carolina State U (NC)
North Carolina Wesleyan Coll (NC)
North Central Coll (IL)
Northeastern State U (OK)
Northeastern U (MA)
Northern Arizona U (AZ)
Northern Illinois U (IL)
Northern Michigan U (MI)
Northern State U (SD)
North Georgia Coll & State U (GA)
Northland Coll (WI)
Northwestern U (IL)
Northwest Missouri State U (MO)
Notre Dame de Namur U (CA)
Oakland City U (IN)
Ohio Northern U (OH)
Ohio U (OH)
Ohio Wesleyan U (OH)
Oklahoma City U (OK)
Oklahoma State U (OK)
Oklahoma Wesleyan U (OK)
Oral Roberts U (OK)
Otterbein Coll (OH)
Ouachita Baptist U (AR)
Pacific Lutheran U (WA)
Pacific Union Coll (CA)
Pacific U (OR)
Palm Beach Atlantic U (FL)
Pepperdine U, Malibu (CA)
Peru State Coll (NE)
Pfeiffer U (NC)
Pillsbury Baptist Bible Coll (MN)
Point Park U (PA)
Presbyterian Coll (SC)
Prescott Coll (AZ)
Purdue U (IN)
Purdue U Calumet (IN)
Queen's U at Kingston (ON, Canada)
Queens U of Charlotte (NC)
Quinnipiac U (CT)
Redeemer U Coll (ON, Canada)
Regis U (CO)
Ripon Coll (WI)
Roberts Wesleyan Coll (NY)
Rockford Coll (IL)
Rockhurst U (MO)
Rollins Coll (FL)
Roosevelt U (IL)
Rowan U (NJ)
Sacred Heart U (CT)
St. Ambrose U (IA)
St. Cloud State U (MN)
Saint Francis U (PA)
St. Francis Xavier U (NS, Canada)
Saint John's U (MN)
St. Joseph's Coll, New York (NY)
St. Joseph's Coll, Suffolk Campus (NY)
Saint Louis U (MO)
Saint Martin's U (WA)
Saint Mary-of-the-Woods Coll (IN)
Saint Mary's Coll (IN)
St. Mary's U (TX)
Saint Michael's Coll (VT)
St. Thomas Aquinas Coll (NY)
St. Thomas U (NB, Canada)
Salem Coll (NC)
Salem Intl U (WV)
Salem State Coll (MA)
Salisbury U (MD)
Sam Houston State U (TX)
San Diego Christian Coll (CA)
Sarah Lawrence Coll (NY)
Schreiner U (TX)
Shasta Bible Coll (CA)
Shawnee State U (OH)
Simmons Coll (MA)
Simon Fraser U (BC, Canada)
Simpson Coll (IA)
Smith Coll (MA)
Southeastern Bible Coll (AL)
Southeastern Oklahoma State U (OK)
Southeastern U (FL)
Southeast Missouri State U (MO)
Southern New Hampshire U (NH)
Southern Utah U (UT)
Southern Wesleyan U (SC)
Southwestern Oklahoma State U (OK)
Southwestern U (TX)
Southwest Minnesota State U (MN)
State U of New York at Fredonia (NY)
State U of New York at New Paltz (NY)
State U of New York at Oswego (NY)
State U of New York at Plattsburgh (NY)
State U of New York Coll at Geneseo (NY)
State U of New York Coll at Oneonta (NY)
State U of New York Empire State Coll (NY)
Stetson U (FL)
Stillman Coll (AL)
Suffolk U (MA)
Tabor Coll (KS)
Tarleton State U (TX)
Taylor U (IN)
Taylor U Fort Wayne (IN)
Tennessee State U (TN)
Tennessee Technological U (TN)
Tennessee Wesleyan Coll (TN)
Texas A&M U–Commerce (TX)
Texas Lutheran U (TX)
Texas Southern U (TX)
Tougaloo Coll (MS)
Trent U (ON, Canada)
Trinity Christian Coll (IL)
Trinity Coll (CT)
Trinity Intl U (IL)
Tri-State U (IN)
Troy U (AL)
Union Coll (KY)
Union Coll (NE)
Union U (TN)
Université de Sherbrooke (QC, Canada)
Université du Québec en Outaouais (QC, Canada)
U of Alaska Southeast (AK)
U of Arkansas at Monticello (AR)
The U of British Columbia (BC, Canada)
The U of British Columbia–Okanagan (BC, Canada)
U of California, Santa Cruz (CA)
U of Central Missouri (MO)
U of Charleston (WV)
U of Cincinnati (OH)
U of Dallas (TX)
U of Dayton (OH)
U of Delaware (DE)
U of Evansville (IN)
The U of Findlay (OH)
U of Guam (GU)
U of Hawaii at Manoa (HI)
U of Houston (TX)
U of Houston–Victoria (TX)
U of Indianapolis (IN)
U of Lethbridge (AB, Canada)
U of Louisiana at Lafayette (LA)
U of Maine (ME)
U of Maine at Fort Kent (ME)
U of Maine at Machias (ME)
U of Mary Hardin-Baylor (TX)
U of Maryland, Coll Park (MD)
U of Maryland Eastern Shore (MD)
U of Miami (FL)
U of Michigan (MI)
U of Michigan–Dearborn (MI)
U of Minnesota, Duluth (MN)
U of Minnesota, Twin Cities Campus (MN)
U of Missouri–Columbia (MO)
U of Missouri–St. Louis (MO)
The U of Montana (MT)
The U of Montana–Western (MT)
U of Montevallo (AL)
U of Nevada, Las Vegas (NV)
U of New Brunswick Fredericton (NB, Canada)
The U of North Carolina at Greensboro (NC)
U of Oregon (OR)
U of Pittsburgh at Johnstown (PA)
U of Portland (OR)
U of Prince Edward Island (PE, Canada)
U of Redlands (CA)
U of Regina (SK, Canada)
U of Rio Grande (OH)
U of Saint Francis (IN)
U of Saint Mary (KS)
U of St. Thomas (TX)
U of Sioux Falls (SD)
U of South Carolina Beaufort (SC)
The U of South Dakota (SD)
U of Southern Indiana (IN)
U of South Florida (FL)
U of the Pacific (CA)
U of the Sacred Heart (PR)
The U of Toledo (OH)
U of Toronto (ON, Canada)
U of Tulsa (OK)
U of Utah (UT)
U of Vermont (VT)
U of Victoria (BC, Canada)
U of Washington, Bothell (WA)
U of Washington, Tacoma (WA)
The U of Western Ontario (ON, Canada)
U of Windsor (ON, Canada)
The U of Winnipeg (MB, Canada)
U of Wisconsin–Green Bay (WI)
U of Wisconsin–Milwaukee (WI)
U of Wisconsin–Oshkosh (WI)
U of Wisconsin–Platteville (WI)
U of Wisconsin–Stevens Point (WI)
U of Wisconsin–Superior (WI)
U of Wisconsin–Whitewater (WI)
Valley City State U (ND)
Vanderbilt U (TN)
Vanguard U of Southern California (CA)
Villanova U (PA)
Virginia Intermont Coll (VA)
Voorhees Coll (SC)
Wagner Coll (NY)
Walsh U (OH)
Warren Wilson Coll (NC)
Washburn U (KS)
Washington & Jefferson Coll (PA)
Washington State U (WA)
Washington U in St. Louis (MO)
Webster U (MO)
Wells Coll (NY)
Wesleyan Coll (GA)
Wesley Coll (DE)
Western New Mexico U (NM)
Western Washington U (WA)
Westfield State Coll (MA)
West Liberty State Coll (WV)
Westmont Coll (CA)
West Virginia Wesleyan Coll (WV)
Wheeling Jesuit U (WV)
Wheelock Coll (MA)
Wilfrid Laurier U (ON, Canada)
Wilkes U (PA)
William Jessup U (CA)
William Paterson U of New Jersey (NJ)
William Woods U (MO)
Wilmington Coll (OH)
Winona State U (MN)
Wittenberg U (OH)
Wright State U (OH)
Xavier U (OH)
Xavier U of Louisiana (LA)
York Coll (NE)
York U (ON, Canada)
Youngstown State U (OH)

EDUCATIONAL ADMINISTRATION AND SUPERVISION RELATED

U of the Incarnate Word (TX)

EDUCATIONAL, INSTRUCTIONAL, AND CURRICULUM SUPERVISION

Sterling Coll (VT)
Texas A&M U–Commerce (TX)
Wright State U (OH)

EDUCATIONAL/ INSTRUCTIONAL MEDIA DESIGN

Ball State U (IN)
California State U, Chico (CA)
Capital U (OH)
Ithaca Coll (NY)
Jackson State U (MS)
Jacksonville State U (AL)
Lindenwood U (MO)
St. Cloud State U (MN)
Seton Hill U (PA)
U of Central Oklahoma (OK)
U of Maine (ME)
The U of Toledo (OH)
Western Illinois U (IL)
Widener U (PA)

EDUCATIONAL LEADERSHIP AND ADMINISTRATION

Cleveland State U (OH)
Edinboro U of Pennsylvania (PA)
Harding U (AR)
Jamestown Coll (ND)
Keene State Coll (NH)
Lindenwood U (MO)
McNeese State U (LA)
Northern Arizona U (AZ)
North Georgia Coll & State U (GA)
Northwest Missouri State U (MO)
Nova Southeastern U (FL)
Ohio U (OH)
Oral Roberts U (OK)
St. Cloud State U (MN)
Sterling Coll (VT)
Tarleton State U (TX)
Tennessee State U (TN)
Texas A&M U–Commerce (TX)
Texas Christian U (TX)
Texas Southern U (TX)
The U of British Columbia (BC, Canada)
U of Central Oklahoma (OK)
U of Illinois at Springfield (IL)
U of Lethbridge (AB, Canada)
U of Montevallo (AL)
U of Windsor (ON, Canada)
U of Wisconsin–Superior (WI)
Western Washington U (WA)
Wright State U (OH)

EDUCATIONAL PSYCHOLOGY

Alcorn State U (MS)
The Catholic U of America (DC)
Cornell U (NY)
DePaul U (IL)
Edinboro U of Pennsylvania (PA)
Indiana U of Pennsylvania (PA)
Jacksonville State U (AL)
Mississippi State U (MS)
Shenandoah U (VA)
Texas A&M U–Commerce (TX)
U of Pittsburgh (PA)
U of Regina (SK, Canada)

EDUCATIONAL STATISTICS AND RESEARCH METHODS

Bucknell U (PA)

EDUCATIONAL SYSTEM ADMINISTRATION AND SUPERINTENDENCY

Dordt Coll (IA)

EDUCATION (K-12)

Adrian Coll (MI)
Augustana Coll (SD)
Biola U (CA)
Centenary Coll of Louisiana (LA)
Coll of Saint Mary (NE)
The Coll of St. Scholastica (MN)
Dominican U (IL)
Dordt Coll (IA)
Felician Coll (NJ)
Finlandia U (MI)
Grace U (NE)
Hamline U (MN)
Hillsdale Coll (MI)
Illinois Coll (IL)
Indiana Wesleyan U (IN)
Ithaca Coll (NY)
Jamestown Coll (ND)
John Carroll U (OH)
Keystone Coll (PA)
Lambuth U (TN)
Lindenwood U (MO)
McKendree U (IL)
Methodist U (NC)
Midland Lutheran Coll (NE)
Mount Saint Mary Coll (NY)
New England Coll (NH)
Northwestern Coll (IA)
Ohio Dominican U (OH)
Ohio Wesleyan U (OH)
Pacific Union Coll (CA)
Redeemer U Coll (ON, Canada)
St. Ambrose U (IA)
St. Cloud State U (MN)
Saint Mary-of-the-Woods Coll (IN)
Salem Intl U (WV)
San Diego Christian Coll (CA)
Tabor Coll (KS)
Tennessee Wesleyan Coll (TN)
Trevecca Nazarene U (TN)
Trinity Intl U (IL)
U of Lethbridge (AB, Canada)
U of Maine at Fort Kent (ME)
The U of Montana–Western (MT)
U of St. Thomas (MN)
The U of Tampa (FL)
The U of Tennessee at Martin (TN)
U of Windsor (ON, Canada)
Virginia Wesleyan Coll (VA)
Walla Walla U (WA)
Washington U in St. Louis (MO)
West Virginia Wesleyan Coll (WV)
York U (ON, Canada)

EDUCATION (MULTIPLE LEVELS)

Averett U (VA)
Baptist Bible Coll of Pennsylvania (PA)
Central State U (OH)
Chestnut Hill Coll (PA)
Coll of Saint Elizabeth (NJ)
Concordia U Wisconsin (WI)
Connecticut Coll (CT)
Dakota Wesleyan U (SD)
Duquesne U (PA)
Edinboro U of Pennsylvania (PA)
Gannon U (PA)
Grambling State U (LA)
Harding U (AR)
Hofstra U (NY)
Howard Payne U (TX)
Indiana U Bloomington (IN)
Iona Coll (NY)
Ithaca Coll (NY)
Juniata Coll (PA)
Lake Superior State U (MI)
Liberty U (VA)
Miami U Hamilton (OH)
Northwest Christian Coll (OR)
Ohio Northern U (OH)
Ohio Wesleyan U (OH)
Queen's U at Kingston (ON, Canada)
Rhode Island Coll (RI)
The Richard Stockton Coll of New Jersey (NJ)
Saint Louis U (MO)
Shawnee State U (OH)
Tarleton State U (TX)
Tennessee Wesleyan Coll (TN)
Texas Lutheran U (TX)
Troy U (AL)
U of Great Falls (MT)
U of Illinois at Urbana–Champaign (IL)
U of Memphis (TN)
U of Nebraska–Lincoln (NE)
U of North Alabama (AL)
U of Rio Grande (OH)
Utah State U (UT)
Wake Forest U (NC)
Western Washington U (WA)
Wright State U (OH)
York Coll (NE)

EDUCATION RELATED

Alliant Intl U (CA)
Arizona State U (AZ)
Bowling Green State U (OH)
Brigham Young U (UT)
Centenary Coll of Louisiana (LA)
Central State U (OH)
Cleveland State U (OH)
Concordia U, St. Paul (MN)
DePaul U (IL)
Gannon U (PA)
Georgia Coll & State U (GA)
Grace Coll (IN)
Jackson State U (MS)
Madonna U (MI)
McNeese State U (LA)
Mercer U (GA)
Mount Holyoke Coll (MA)
Northern Michigan U (MI)
Ohio Northern U (OH)
Park U (MO)

Point Park U (PA)
Rhode Island Coll (RI)
Roosevelt U (IL)
Saginaw Valley State U (MI)
State U of New York Coll at Potsdam (NY)
Sterling Coll (VT)
Swarthmore Coll (PA)
Syracuse U (NY)
Texas Southern U (TX)
Towson U (MD)
U of Alaska Fairbanks (AK)
U of Missouri–Columbia (MO)
U of Puerto Rico at Utuado (PR)
Wayland Baptist U (TX)
Wright State U (OH)
York Coll of Pennsylvania (PA)

EDUCATION (SPECIFIC LEVELS AND METHODS) RELATED

Anderson U (SC)
Boston U (MA)
Brigham Young U (UT)
Columbia Coll Chicago (IL)
Rhode Island Coll (RI)
Rowan U (NJ)
St. Cloud State U (MN)
The U of North Carolina at Pembroke (NC)
U of Ottawa (ON, Canada)
The U of Toledo (OH)
Washington U in St. Louis (MO)
Wright State U (OH)
Xavier U (OH)

EDUCATION (SPECIFIC SUBJECT AREAS) RELATED

Appalachian State U (NC)
Averett U (VA)
Avila U (MO)
Baylor U (TX)
Bowling Green State U (OH)
Bradley U (IL)
Brigham Young U (UT)
Cameron U (OK)
Central Michigan U (MI)
Columbia Coll Chicago (IL)
DePaul U (IL)
Drexel U (PA)
Eastern Kentucky U (KY)
Henderson State U (AR)
Hope Coll (MI)
Indiana U Bloomington (IN)
Keene State Coll (NH)
Madonna U (MI)
Marquette U (WI)
Marywood U (PA)
Minot State U (ND)
Missouri State U (MO)
Northern Arizona U (AZ)
Ohio U (OH)
Old Dominion U (VA)
Plymouth State U (NH)
Point Park U (PA)
St. Edward's U (TX)
Schreiner U (TX)
State U of New York Coll at Potsdam (NY)
Syracuse U (NY)
Thomas More Coll (KY)
Tusculum Coll (TN)
The U of Akron (OH)
The U of Arizona (AZ)
U of Central Oklahoma (OK)
U of Louisiana at Lafayette (LA)
U of Louisiana at Monroe (LA)
U of Michigan–Flint (MI)
U of Nebraska–Lincoln (NE)
U of Nevada, Reno (NV)
U of New Orleans (LA)
The U of North Carolina Wilmington (NC)
U of Oklahoma (OK)
U of St. Thomas (MN)
The U of Toledo (OH)
U of Wisconsin–Eau Claire (WI)
Utah State U (UT)
Wayne State Coll (NE)
Wright State U (OH)

ELECTRICAL AND ELECTRONIC ENGINEERING TECHNOLOGIES RELATED

Embry-Riddle Aeronautical U (FL)
Grove City Coll (PA)
Indiana U of Pennsylvania (PA)
Northern Michigan U (MI)
Old Dominion U (VA)
Point Park U (PA)
Rochester Inst of Technology (NY)
Southern Illinois U Carbondale (IL)
Virginia State U (VA)
Western Carolina U (NC)

ELECTRICAL, ELECTRONIC AND COMMUNICATIONS ENGINEERING TECHNOLOGY

Baker Coll of Owosso (MI)
Bluefield State Coll (WV)
Bowling Green State U (OH)
Bradley U (IL)
British Columbia Inst of Technology (BC, Canada)
Buffalo State Coll, State U of New York (NY)
California State Polytechnic U, Pomona (CA)
California State U, Long Beach (CA)
Cameron U (OK)
Central Michigan U (MI)
Central Washington U (WA)
Cleveland State U (OH)
Colorado Tech U—Colorado Springs (CO)
Colorado Tech U—Denver (CO)
Colorado Tech U—North Kansas City (MO)
Colorado Tech U—Online (CO)
Colorado Tech U—Sioux Falls (SD)
DeVry Coll of New York (NY)
DeVry U, Phoenix (AZ)
DeVry U, Fremont (CA)
DeVry U, Long Beach (CA)
DeVry U, Pomona (CA)
DeVry U, Sherman Oaks (CA)
DeVry U, Westminster (CO)
DeVry U, Miramar (FL)
DeVry U, Orlando (FL)
DeVry U, Alpharetta (GA)
DeVry U, Decatur (GA)
DeVry U, Addison (IL)
DeVry U, Tinley Park (IL)
DeVry U, Kansas City (MO)
DeVry U (NJ)
DeVry U, Columbus (OH)
DeVry U, Fort Washington (PA)
DeVry U, Houston (TX)
DeVry U, Irving (TX)
DeVry U, Arlington (VA)
DeVry U, Federal Way (WA)
East Central U (OK)
Eastern Michigan U (MI)
East-West U (IL)
Fairleigh Dickinson U, Metropolitan Campus (NJ)
Fairmont State U (WV)
Farmingdale State Coll (NY)
Ferris State U (MI)
Fitchburg State Coll (MA)
Florida Ag and Mech U (FL)
Georgia Southern U (GA)
Grambling State U (LA)
Grantham U (MO)
Hampton U (VA)
Indiana State U (IN)
Indiana U–Purdue U Fort Wayne (IN)
Indiana U–Purdue U Indianapolis (IN)
Inter American U of Puerto Rico, Aguadilla Campus (PR)
Inter American U of Puerto Rico, Bayamón Campus (PR)
Inter American U of Puerto Rico, San Germán Campus (PR)
Jacksonville State U (AL)
Kean U (NJ)
Keene State Coll (NH)
Lakehead U (ON, Canada)
Lake Superior State U (MI)
LeTourneau U (TX)
McNeese State U (LA)
Miami U (OH)
Michigan Technological U (MI)
Milwaukee School of Eng (WI)
Minnesota State U Mankato (MN)
New York Inst of Technology (NY)
Northeastern State U (OK)
Northwestern State U of Louisiana (LA)
Oklahoma State U (OK)
Oregon Inst of Technology (OR)
Pacific Union Coll (CA)
Penn State Erie, The Behrend Coll (PA)
Pittsburg State U (KS)
Point Park U (PA)
Prairie View A&M U (TX)
Purdue U (IN)
Purdue U Calumet (IN)
Roosevelt U (IL)
St. Cloud State U (MN)
Sam Houston State U (TX)
South Carolina State U (SC)
South Dakota State U (SD)
Southern Polytechnic State U (GA)
Southern U and Ag and Mech Coll (LA)
Southern Utah U (UT)
State U of New York Inst of Technology (NY)
Texas A&M U (TX)
Texas Southern U (TX)
Texas Tech U (TX)
Thomas Edison State Coll (NJ)
Troy U (AL)
The U of Akron (OH)
U of Central Florida (FL)
U of Central Missouri (MO)
U of Cincinnati (OH)
U of Dayton (OH)
U of Hartford (CT)
U of Maine (ME)
U of Maryland Eastern Shore (MD)
U of Massachusetts Dartmouth (MA)
U of Massachusetts Lowell (MA)
U of Memphis (TN)
U of New Hampshire at Manchester (NH)
U of North Texas (TX)
U of Pittsburgh at Johnstown (PA)
U of Regina (SK, Canada)
U of Southern Mississippi (MS)
The U of Texas at Brownsville (TX)
The U of Toledo (OH)
Wayne State U (MI)
Western Carolina U (NC)
Western Washington U (WA)
World Coll (VA)
Youngstown State U (OH)

ELECTRICAL, ELECTRONICS AND COMMUNICATIONS ENGINEERING

Alabama Ag and Mech U (AL)
Alfred U (NY)
The American U of Athens (Greece)
American U of Beirut (Lebanon)
Arizona State U (AZ)
Auburn U (AL)
Baylor U (TX)
Bloomsburg U of Pennsylvania (PA)
Bob Jones U (SC)
Boise State U (ID)
Boston U (MA)
Bradley U (IL)
Brigham Young U (UT)
Brown U (RI)
Bucknell U (PA)
California Baptist U (CA)
California Inst of Technology (CA)
California Polytechnic State U, San Luis Obispo (CA)
California State Polytechnic U, Pomona (CA)
California State U, Chico (CA)
California State U, Fresno (CA)
California State U, Fullerton (CA)
California State U, Long Beach (CA)
California State U, Los Angeles (CA)
California State U, Sacramento (CA)
Calvin Coll (MI)
Case Western Reserve U (OH)
The Catholic U of America (DC)
Cedarville U (OH)
Central Connecticut State U (CT)
Central Michigan U (MI)
Christian Brothers U (TN)
The Citadel, The Military Coll of South Carolina (SC)
City Coll of the City U of New York (NY)
Clarkson U (NY)
Clemson U (SC)
Cleveland State U (OH)
Cogswell Polytechnical Coll (CA)
The Coll of New Jersey (NJ)
Colorado School of Mines (CO)
Colorado State U (CO)
Colorado Tech U—Colorado Springs (CO)
Colorado Tech U—Denver (CO)
Colorado Tech U—North Kansas City (MO)
Colorado Tech U—Online (CO)
Colorado Tech U—Sioux Falls (SD)
Concordia U (QC, Canada)
Cooper Union for the Advancement of Science and Art (NY)
Cornell U (NY)
Dominican U (IL)
Dordt Coll (IA)
Drexel U (PA)
Duke U (NC)
East-West U (IL)
Embry-Riddle Aeronautical U (AZ)
Embry-Riddle Aeronautical U (FL)
Fairfield U (CT)
Fairleigh Dickinson U, Metropolitan Campus (NJ)
Florida Ag and Mech U (FL)
Florida Atlantic U (FL)
Florida Inst of Technology (FL)
Florida Intl U (FL)
Florida State U (FL)
Frostburg State U (MD)
Gannon U (PA)
George Fox U (OR)
George Mason U (VA)
The George Washington U (DC)
Georgia Inst of Technology (GA)
Georgia Southern U (GA)
Gonzaga U (WA)
Grand Valley State U (MI)
Grove City Coll (PA)
Hampton U (VA)
Harding U (AR)
Harvard U (MA)
Hofstra U (NY)
Idaho State U (ID)
Illinois Inst of Technology (IL)
Indiana Tech (IN)
Indiana U–Purdue U Fort Wayne (IN)
Indiana U–Purdue U Indianapolis (IN)
Inter American U of Puerto Rico, Bayamón Campus (PR)
Inter American U of Puerto Rico, Fajardo Campus (PR)
Iowa State U of Science and Technology (IA)
Jackson State U (MS)
Jacksonville U (FL)
John Brown U (AR)
The Johns Hopkins U (MD)
Kansas State U (KS)
Kettering U (MI)
Lafayette Coll (PA)
Lakehead U (ON, Canada)
Lake Superior State U (MI)
Lawrence Technological U (MI)
Lehigh U (PA)
LeTourneau U (TX)
Louisiana State U and Ag and Mech Coll (LA)
Loyola Coll in Maryland (MD)
Loyola Marymount U (CA)
Marquette U (WI)
Massachusetts Inst of Technology (MA)
McGill U (QC, Canada)
Memorial U of Newfoundland (NL, Canada)
Merrimack Coll (MA)
Miami U (OH)
Michigan State U (MI)
Michigan Technological U (MI)
Milwaukee School of Eng (WI)
Minnesota State U Mankato (MN)
Mississippi State U (MS)
Missouri U of Science and Technology (MO)
Montana State U (MT)
Montana Tech of The U of Montana (MT)
Morgan State U (MD)
New Jersey Inst of Technology (NJ)
New Mexico Highlands U (NM)
New Mexico Inst of Mining and Technology (NM)
New York Inst of Technology (NY)
North Carolina Ag and Tech State U (NC)
North Carolina State U (NC)
North Dakota State U (ND)
Northeastern U (MA)
Northern Arizona U (AZ)
Northern Illinois U (IL)
Northwestern U (IL)
Norwich U (VT)
Oakland U (MI)
Ohio Northern U (OH)
Ohio U (OH)
Oklahoma Christian U (OK)
Oklahoma State U (OK)
Old Dominion U (VA)
Oral Roberts U (OK)
Oregon State U (OR)
Pacific States U (CA)
Penn State Abington (PA)
Penn State Altoona (PA)
Penn State Berks (PA)
Penn State Erie, The Behrend Coll (PA)
Penn State Harrisburg (PA)
Penn State U Park (PA)
Polytechnic U, Brooklyn Campus (NY)
Polytechnic U of Puerto Rico (PR)
Portland State U (OR)
Prairie View A&M U (TX)
Princeton U (NJ)
Purdue U (IN)
Purdue U Calumet (IN)
Queen's U at Kingston (ON, Canada)
Rensselaer Polytechnic Inst (NY)
Rice U (TX)
Rochester Inst of Technology (NY)
Rose-Hulman Inst of Technology (IN)
Rowan U (NJ)
Royal Military Coll of Canada (ON, Canada)
Rutgers, The State U of New Jersey, New Brunswick (NJ)
Saginaw Valley State U (MI)
St. Cloud State U (MN)
Saint Louis U (MO)
St. Mary's U (TX)
San Diego State U (CA)
San Francisco State U (CA)
Santa Clara U (CA)
Seattle Pacific U (WA)
Seattle U (WA)
South Dakota School of Mines and Technology (SD)
South Dakota State U (SD)
Southern Illinois U Carbondale (IL)
Southern Illinois U Edwardsville (IL)
Southern Methodist U (TX)
Southern U and Ag and Mech Coll (LA)
Stanford U (CA)
State U of New York at Binghamton (NY)
State U of New York at New Paltz (NY)
Stony Brook U, State U of New York (NY)
Suffolk U (MA)
Syracuse U (NY)
Temple U (PA)
Tennessee State U (TN)
Tennessee Technological U (TN)
Texas A&M U (TX)
Texas Tech U (TX)
Trinity Coll (CT)
Tri-State U (IN)
Tufts U (MA)
Tulane U (LA)
Tuskegee U (AL)
Union Coll (NY)
United States Air Force Acad (CO)
United States Coast Guard Acad (CT)
United States Naval Acad (MD)
Université de Sherbrooke (QC, Canada)
U at Buffalo, the State U of New York (NY)
The U of Akron (OH)
The U of Alabama (AL)
The U of Alabama at Birmingham (AL)
The U of Alabama in Huntsville (AL)
U of Alaska Fairbanks (AK)
The U of Arizona (AZ)
U of Arkansas (AR)
The U of British Columbia (BC, Canada)
The U of British Columbia–Okanagan (BC, Canada)
U of California, Berkeley (CA)
U of California, Davis (CA)
U of California, Irvine (CA)
U of California, Los Angeles (CA)
U of California, Riverside (CA)
U of California, San Diego (CA)
U of California, Santa Barbara (CA)
U of California, Santa Cruz (CA)
U of Central Florida (FL)
U of Colorado at Boulder (CO)
U of Colorado Denver (CO)
U of Connecticut (CT)
U of Dayton (OH)
U of Delaware (DE)
U of Denver (CO)
U of Evansville (IN)
U of Florida (FL)
U of Hartford (CT)
U of Hawaii at Manoa (HI)
U of Houston (TX)
U of Idaho (ID)
U of Illinois at Chicago (IL)
U of Illinois at Urbana–Champaign (IL)
The U of Iowa (IA)
U of Kansas (KS)
U of Louisiana at Lafayette (LA)
U of Louisville (KY)
U of Maine (ME)
U of Maryland, Coll Park (MD)
U of Massachusetts Amherst (MA)
U of Massachusetts Dartmouth (MA)
U of Massachusetts Lowell (MA)
U of Memphis (TN)
U of Miami (FL)
U of Michigan (MI)
U of Michigan–Dearborn (MI)
U of Minnesota, Duluth (MN)
U of Minnesota, Twin Cities Campus (MN)
U of Mississippi (MS)
U of Missouri–Columbia (MO)

U of Missouri–Kansas City (MO)
U of Missouri–St. Louis (MO)
U of Nebraska at Omaha (NE)
U of Nebraska–Lincoln (NE)
U of Nevada, Las Vegas (NV)
U of Nevada, Reno (NV)
U of New Brunswick Fredericton (NB, Canada)
U of New Hampshire (NH)
U of New Haven (CT)
U of New Mexico (NM)
U of New Orleans (LA)
The U of North Carolina at Charlotte (NC)
U of North Dakota (ND)
U of North Florida (FL)
U of North Texas (TX)
U of Notre Dame (IN)
U of Oklahoma (OK)
U of Ottawa (ON, Canada)
U of Pennsylvania (PA)
U of Pittsburgh (PA)
U of Portland (OR)
U of Regina (SK, Canada)
U of Rhode Island (RI)
U of Rochester (NY)
U of St. Thomas (MN)
U of San Diego (CA)
The U of Scranton (PA)
U of South Alabama (AL)
U of South Carolina (SC)
U of Southern California (CA)
U of Southern Maine (ME)
U of South Florida (FL)
The U of Tennessee (TN)
The U of Texas at Arlington (TX)
The U of Texas at Austin (TX)
The U of Texas at Dallas (TX)
The U of Texas at El Paso (TX)
The U of Texas at San Antonio (TX)
The U of Texas at Tyler (TX)
The U of Texas–Pan American (TX)
U of the District of Columbia (DC)
U of the Pacific (CA)
The U of Toledo (OH)
U of Toronto (ON, Canada)
U of Tulsa (OK)
U of Utah (UT)
U of Vermont (VT)
U of Victoria (BC, Canada)
U of Virginia (VA)
The U of Western Ontario (ON, Canada)
U of West Florida (FL)
U of Windsor (ON, Canada)
U of Wisconsin–Madison (WI)
U of Wisconsin–Milwaukee (WI)
U of Wisconsin–Platteville (WI)
U of Wyoming (WY)
Ursinus Coll (PA)
Utah State U (UT)
Valparaiso U (IN)
Vanderbilt U (TN)
Villanova U (PA)
Virginia Commonwealth U (VA)
Virginia Military Inst (VA)
Virginia Polytechnic Inst and State U (VA)
Walla Walla U (WA)
Washington State U (WA)
Washington U in St. Louis (MO)
Wayne State U (MI)
Wentworth Inst of Technology (MA)
Western Carolina U (NC)
Western Kentucky U (KY)
Western Michigan U (MI)
Western New England Coll (MA)
West Virginia U (WV)
Wichita State U (KS)
Widener U (PA)
Wilkes U (PA)
Worcester Polytechnic Inst (MA)
Wright State U (OH)
Yale U (CT)
York Coll of Pennsylvania (PA)
Youngstown State U (OH)

ELECTRICAL/ ELECTRONICS EQUIPMENT INSTALLATION AND REPAIR
Lewis-Clark State Coll (ID)

ELECTROMECHANICAL AND INSTRUMENTATION AND MAINTENANCE TECHNOLOGIES RELATED
Keene State Coll (NH)

ELECTROMECHANICAL TECHNOLOGY
Bowling Green State U (OH)
Buffalo State Coll, State U of New York (NY)
Miami U Hamilton (OH)
Murray State U (KY)
Rochester Inst of Technology (NY)
U of Houston (TX)
U of Northern Iowa (IA)
The U of Toledo (OH)
Vermont Tech Coll (VT)
Wayne State U (MI)

ELECTRONEURO-DIAGNOSTIC/ ELECTROENCEPHALO-GRAPHIC TECHNOLOGY
The Johns Hopkins U (MD)

ELEMENTARY AND MIDDLE SCHOOL ADMINISTRATION/ PRINCIPALSHIP
Ohio U (OH)
Piedmont Coll (GA)

ELEMENTARY EDUCATION
Abilene Christian U (TX)
Acadia U (NS, Canada)
Adams State Coll (CO)
Adrian Coll (MI)
Alabama Ag and Mech U (AL)
Alabama State U (AL)
Albertus Magnus Coll (CT)
Albion Coll (MI)
Albright Coll (PA)
Alcorn State U (MS)
Alderson-Broaddus Coll (WV)
Alfred U (NY)
Alice Lloyd Coll (KY)
Alma Coll (MI)
Alvernia Coll (PA)
American U (DC)
American U of Beirut (Lebanon)
Anderson U (IN)
Anderson U (SC)
Andrews U (MI)
Appalachian State U (NC)
Aquinas Coll (MI)
Arizona State U (AZ)
Arizona State U at the West campus (AZ)
Arlington Baptist Coll (TX)
Asbury Coll (KY)
Ashford U (IA)
Ashland U (OH)
Assumption Coll (MA)
Athens State U (AL)
Atlantic Union Coll (MA)
Auburn U (AL)
Auburn U Montgomery (AL)
Augsburg Coll (MN)
Augustana Coll (IL)
Augustana Coll (SD)
Augusta State U (GA)
Avila U (MO)
Baker U (KS)
Ball State U (IN)
Baptist Bible Coll of Pennsylvania (PA)
The Baptist Coll of Florida (FL)
Barclay Coll (KS)
Barry U (FL)
Barton Coll (NC)
Baylor U (TX)
Bay Path Coll (MA)
Becker Coll (MA)
Belhaven Coll (MS)
Bellarmine U (KY)
Belmont Abbey Coll (NC)
Belmont U (TN)
Beloit Coll (WI)
Bemidji State U (MN)
Benedictine Coll (KS)
Benedictine U (IL)
Bennington Coll (VT)
Berea Coll (KY)
Bethany Bible Coll (NB, Canada)
Bethany Coll (KS)
Bethany Lutheran Coll (MN)
Bethany U (CA)
Bethel Coll (KS)
Bethel Coll (TN)
Bethel U (MN)
Bethune-Cookman U (FL)
Biola U (CA)
Bishop's U (QC, Canada)
Blackburn Coll (IL)
Bloomsburg U of Pennsylvania (PA)
Bluefield Coll (VA)
Bluefield State Coll (WV)
Bluffton U (OH)
Bob Jones U (SC)
Boise State U (ID)
Boricua Coll (NY)
Boston Coll (MA)
Boston U (MA)
Bradley U (IL)
Brevard Coll (NC)
Bridgewater Coll (VA)
Bridgewater State Coll (MA)
Brigham Young U (UT)
Brock U (ON, Canada)
Bryan Coll (TN)
Bryn Athyn Coll of the New Church (PA)
Bucknell U (PA)
Buffalo State Coll, State U of New York (NY)
Butler U (IN)
Cabrini Coll (PA)
Calumet Coll of Saint Joseph (IN)
Calvin Coll (MI)
Cameron U (OK)
Capital U (OH)
Carlow U (PA)
Carroll Coll (WI)
Carson-Newman Coll (TN)
Cascade Coll (OR)
Catawba Coll (NC)
The Catholic U of America (DC)
Cedar Crest Coll (PA)
Centenary Coll (NJ)
Centenary Coll of Louisiana (LA)
Central Coll (IA)
Central Connecticut State U (CT)
Central Michigan U (MI)
Central Washington U (WA)
Centre Coll (KY)
Chaminade U of Honolulu (HI)
Chatham U (PA)
Chestnut Hill Coll (PA)
Cheyney U of Pennsylvania (PA)
Chicago State U (IL)
Christian Brothers U (TN)
City Coll of the City U of New York (NY)
City U of Seattle (WA)
Claflin U (SC)
Clarion U of Pennsylvania (PA)
Clarke Coll (IA)
Clark U (MA)
Clearwater Christian Coll (FL)
Clemson U (SC)
Cleveland State U (OH)
Coastal Carolina U (SC)
Coker Coll (SC)
The Coll at Brockport, State U of New York (NY)
Coll of Charleston (SC)
Coll of Mount Saint Vincent (NY)
The Coll of New Jersey (NJ)
The Coll of New Rochelle (NY)
Coll of Saint Benedict (MN)
Coll of St. Joseph (VT)
Coll of Saint Mary (NE)
The Coll of Saint Rose (NY)
The Coll of St. Scholastica (MN)
Coll of the Atlantic (ME)
Coll of the Ozarks (MO)
Coll of the Southwest (NM)
Columbia Coll (SC)
Concordia Coll (MN)
Concordia Coll–New York (NY)
Concordia U (MI)
Concordia U (OR)
Concordia U (QC, Canada)
Concordia U Chicago (IL)
Concordia U, Nebraska (NE)
Concordia U, St. Paul (MN)
Concordia U Texas (TX)
Concordia U Wisconsin (WI)
Concord U (WV)
Connecticut Coll (CT)
Converse Coll (SC)
Cornell Coll (IA)
Cornerstone U (MI)
Covenant Coll (GA)
Creighton U (NE)
Crown Coll (MN)
Culver-Stockton Coll (MO)
Curry Coll (MA)
Daemen Coll (NY)
Dakota State U (SD)
Dakota Wesleyan U (SD)
Dallas Baptist U (TX)
Dana Coll (NE)
Davis & Elkins Coll (WV)
Defiance Coll (OH)
Delta State U (MS)
DePaul U (IL)
DePauw U (IN)
DeSales U (PA)
Dillard U (LA)
Dixie State Coll of Utah (UT)
Doane Coll (NE)
Dominican Coll (NY)
Dominican U (IL)
Dordt Coll (IA)
Dowling Coll (NY)
Drake U (IA)
Drury U (MO)
Duquesne U (PA)
East Carolina U (NC)
East Central U (OK)
Eastern Connecticut State U (CT)
Eastern Illinois U (IL)
Eastern Kentucky U (KY)
Eastern Mennonite U (VA)
Eastern Michigan U (MI)
Eastern New Mexico U (NM)
East Stroudsburg U of Pennsylvania (PA)
East Texas Baptist U (TX)
Edinboro U of Pennsylvania (PA)
Elizabethtown Coll (PA)
Elon U (NC)
Emmanuel Coll (GA)
Emmanuel Coll (MA)
Emporia State U (KS)
Endicott Coll (MA)
Erskine Coll (SC)
Evangel U (MO)
Fairmont State U (WV)
Faith Baptist Bible Coll and Theological Sem (IA)
Faulkner U (AL)
Fayetteville State U (NC)
Felician Coll (NJ)
Ferris State U (MI)
Fitchburg State Coll (MA)
Five Towns Coll (NY)
Flagler Coll (FL)
Florida Ag and Mech U (FL)
Florida Atlantic U (FL)
Florida Coll (FL)
Florida Gulf Coast U (FL)
Florida Intl U (FL)
Florida Memorial U (FL)
Florida Southern Coll (FL)
Florida State U (FL)
Fontbonne U (MO)
Fort Lewis Coll (CO)
Franciscan U of Steubenville (OH)
Francis Marion U (SC)
Franklin Coll (IN)
Freed-Hardeman U (TN)
Free Will Baptist Bible Coll (TN)
Fresno Pacific U (CA)
Frostburg State U (MD)
Furman U (SC)
Gannon U (PA)
Gardner-Webb U (NC)
George Fox U (OR)
Georgetown Coll (KY)
Georgian Court U (NJ)
Georgia Southern U (GA)
Georgia Southwestern State U (GA)
Georgia State U (GA)
Gettysburg Coll (PA)
Glenville State Coll (WV)
Gonzaga U (WA)
Gordon Coll (MA)
Goucher Coll (MD)
Grace Bible Coll (MI)
Grace Coll (IN)
Grace U (NE)
Grambling State U (LA)
Grand Canyon U (AZ)
Grand Valley State U (MI)
Grand View Coll (IA)
Green Mountain Coll (VT)
Greensboro Coll (NC)
Greenville Coll (IL)
Grove City Coll (PA)
Guilford Coll (NC)
Gustavus Adolphus Coll (MN)
Gwynedd-Mercy Coll (PA)
Hamline U (MN)
Hampton U (VA)
Hannibal-LaGrange Coll (MO)
Harding U (AR)
Harris-Stowe State U (MO)
Hastings Coll (NE)
Heidelberg Coll (OH)
Hellenic Coll (MA)
High Point U (NC)
Hillsdale Coll (MI)
Hofstra U (NY)
Holy Family U (PA)
Hope Coll (MI)
Hope Intl U (CA)
Houghton Coll (NY)
Houston Baptist U (TX)
Howard Payne U (TX)
Humboldt State U (CA)
Hunter Coll of the City U of New York (NY)
Huntington U (IN)
Husson Coll (ME)
Huston-Tillotson U (TX)
Idaho State U (ID)
Illinois Coll (IL)
Illinois State U (IL)
Illinois Wesleyan U (IL)
Immaculata U (PA)
Indiana State U (IN)
Indiana U Bloomington (IN)
Indiana U East (IN)
Indiana U Kokomo (IN)
Indiana U Northwest (IN)
Indiana U of Pennsylvania (PA)
Indiana U–Purdue U Fort Wayne (IN)
Indiana U–Purdue U Indianapolis (IN)
Indiana U South Bend (IN)
Indiana U Southeast (IN)
Indiana Wesleyan U (IN)
Inter American U of Puerto Rico, Aguadilla Campus (PR)
Inter American U of Puerto Rico, Fajardo Campus (PR)
Inter American U of Puerto Rico, San Germán Campus (PR)
Iona Coll (NY)
Iowa State U of Science and Technology (IA)
Iowa Wesleyan Coll (IA)
Jackson State U (MS)
Jacksonville State U (AL)
Jacksonville U (FL)
Jamestown Coll (ND)
Jarvis Christian Coll (TX)
John Brown U (AR)
John Carroll U (OH)
Johnson Bible Coll (TN)
Johnson C. Smith U (NC)
Johnson State Coll (VT)
John Wesley Coll (NC)
Judson Coll (AL)
Judson U (IL)
Juniata Coll (PA)
Kansas State U (KS)
Kean U (NJ)
Keene State Coll (NH)
Keiser U, Fort Lauderdale (FL)
Kennesaw State U (GA)
Kentucky State U (KY)
Kentucky Wesleyan Coll (KY)
Keuka Coll (NY)
Keystone Coll (PA)
King's Coll (PA)
The King's U Coll (AB, Canada)
Kutztown U of Pennsylvania (PA)
Kuyper Coll (MI)
LaGrange Coll (GA)
Lake Forest Coll (IL)
Lakehead U (ON, Canada)
Lake Superior State U (MI)
Lambuth U (TN)
Lander U (SC)
La Roche Coll (PA)
La Salle U (PA)
La Sierra U (CA)
Lebanon Valley Coll (PA)
Lees-McRae Coll (NC)
Lee U (TN)
Le Moyne Coll (NY)
Lenoir-Rhyne Coll (NC)
Lesley U (MA)
LeTourneau U (TX)
Lewis-Clark State Coll (ID)
Lewis U (IL)
Liberty U (VA)
Limestone Coll (SC)
Lincoln U (MO)
Lincoln U (PA)
Lindenwood U (MO)
Lindsey Wilson Coll (KY)
Linfield Coll (OR)
Lipscomb U (TN)
Livingstone Coll (NC)
Lock Haven U of Pennsylvania (PA)
Longwood U (VA)
Loras Coll (IA)
Louisiana Coll (LA)
Louisiana State U and Ag and Mech Coll (LA)
Loyola Coll in Maryland (MD)
Loyola U Chicago (IL)
Loyola U New Orleans (LA)
Lubbock Christian U (TX)
Luther Coll (IA)
Lynchburg Coll (VA)
Lyndon State Coll (VT)
Madonna U (MI)
Maharishi U of Management (IA)
Manchester Coll (IN)
Manhattanville Coll (NY)
Mansfield U of Pennsylvania (PA)
Maranatha Baptist Bible Coll (WI)
Marian Coll (IN)
Marian Coll of Fond du Lac (WI)
Marietta Coll (OH)
Marquette U (WI)
Marshall U (WV)
Martin U (IN)
Maryville U of Saint Louis (MO)
Marywood U (PA)
The Master's Coll and Sem (CA)
Mayville State U (ND)
McGill U (QC, Canada)
McKendree U (IL)
McMurry U (TX)
McNeese State U (LA)
Medaille Coll (NY)
Medgar Evers Coll of the City U of New York (NY)
Memorial U of Newfoundland (NL, Canada)
Mercer U (GA)
Mercyhurst Coll (PA)
Merrimack Coll (MA)
Messiah Coll (PA)
Methodist U (NC)

MAJORS AND MORE

Metropolitan State U (MN)
Miami U (OH)
Michigan State U (MI)
MidAmerica Nazarene U (KS)
Mid-Continent U (KY)
Midland Lutheran Coll (NE)
Midway Coll (KY)
Miles Coll (AL)
Millersville U of Pennsylvania (PA)
Millikin U (IL)
Minnesota State U Mankato (MN)
Minot State U (ND)
Misericordia U (PA)
Mississippi Coll (MS)
Mississippi State U (MS)
Mississippi U for Women (MS)
Mississippi Valley State U (MS)
Missouri Baptist U (MO)
Missouri Southern State U (MO)
Missouri State U (MO)
Missouri Valley Coll (MO)
Molloy Coll (NY)
Monmouth Coll (IL)
Montana State U (MT)
Montana State U–Billings (MT)
Moravian Coll (PA)
Morehead State U (KY)
Morgan State U (MD)
Morningside Coll (IA)
Morris Coll (SC)
Mount Marty Coll (SD)
Mount Mary Coll (WI)
Mount Mercy Coll (IA)
Mount Saint Mary Coll (NY)
Mount St. Mary's Coll (CA)
Mount St. Mary's U (MD)
Mount Saint Vincent U (NS, Canada)
Mount Vernon Nazarene U (OH)
Murray State U (KY)
National-Louis U (IL)
Nazareth Coll of Rochester (NY)
Nebraska Christian Coll (NE)
Nebraska Wesleyan U (NE)
Neumann Coll (PA)
New England Coll (NH)
New Jersey City U (NJ)
Newman U (KS)
New Mexico Highlands U (NM)
New York Inst of Technology (NY)
New York U (NY)
Niagara U (NY)
Nicholls State U (LA)
North Carolina Ag and Tech State U (NC)
North Carolina Central U (NC)
North Carolina Wesleyan Coll (NC)
North Central Coll (IL)
North Dakota State U (ND)
Northeastern Illinois U (IL)
Northeastern State U (OK)
Northeastern U (MA)
Northern Arizona U (AZ)
Northern Illinois U (IL)
Northern Michigan U (MI)
Northern State U (SD)
North Georgia Coll & State U (GA)
North Greenville U (SC)
Northland Coll (WI)
Northwestern Coll (IA)
Northwestern Coll (MN)
Northwestern Oklahoma State U (OK)
Northwestern State U of Louisiana (LA)
Northwest Missouri State U (MO)
Northwest Nazarene U (ID)
Notre Dame de Namur U (CA)
Nova Southeastern U (FL)
Nyack Coll (NY)
Oakland City U (IN)
Oakland U (MI)
Oakwood Coll (AL)
Ohio Northern U (OH)
Ohio U (OH)
Ohio U–Zanesville (OH)
Ohio Wesleyan U (OH)
Oklahoma Christian U (OK)
Oklahoma City U (OK)
Oklahoma Panhandle State U (OK)
Oklahoma State U (OK)
Oklahoma Wesleyan U (OK)
Oral Roberts U (OK)
Otterbein Coll (OH)
Pace U (NY)
Pacific Union Coll (CA)
Pacific U (OR)
Paine Coll (GA)
Palm Beach Atlantic U (FL)
Park U (MO)
Penn State Abington (PA)
Penn State Altoona (PA)
Penn State Berks (PA)
Penn State Erie, The Behrend Coll (PA)
Penn State Harrisburg (PA)
Penn State U Park (PA)
Pepperdine U, Malibu (CA)
Peru State Coll (NE)
Pfeiffer U (NC)
Philadelphia Biblical U (PA)
Pikeville Coll (KY)
Pillsbury Baptist Bible Coll (MN)
Pittsburg State U (KS)
Plymouth State U (NH)
Point Park U (PA)
Prescott Coll (AZ)
Purdue U (IN)
Purdue U Calumet (IN)
Purdue U North Central (IN)
Queens Coll of the City U of New York (NY)
Queen's U at Kingston (ON, Canada)
Queens U of Charlotte (NC)
Quincy U (IL)
Randolph Coll (VA)
Redeemer U Coll (ON, Canada)
Regis U (CO)
Rhode Island Coll (RI)
Rider U (NJ)
Ripon Coll (WI)
Robert Morris U (PA)
Roberts Wesleyan Coll (NY)
Rochester Coll (MI)
Rockford Coll (IL)
Rockhurst U (MO)
Roger Williams U (RI)
Roosevelt U (IL)
Rowan U (NJ)
Russell Sage Coll (NY)
Sacred Heart U (CT)
Saginaw Valley State U (MI)
St. Ambrose U (IA)
St. Andrews Presbyterian Coll (NC)
St. Cloud State U (MN)
Saint Francis U (PA)
St. Francis Xavier U (NS, Canada)
St. John Fisher Coll (NY)
Saint John's U (MN)
St. John's U (NY)
Saint Joseph Coll (CT)
Saint Joseph's Coll (IN)
St. Joseph's Coll, Suffolk Campus (NY)
Saint Joseph's U (PA)
Saint Leo U (FL)
Saint Martin's U (WA)
Saint Mary-of-the-Woods Coll (IN)
Saint Mary's Coll (IN)
St. Mary's Coll of Maryland (MD)
Saint Mary's U of Minnesota (MN)
Saint Michael's Coll (VT)
St. Norbert Coll (WI)
St. Thomas Aquinas Coll (NY)
St. Thomas U (FL)
Saint Xavier U (IL)
Salem State Coll (MA)
Salisbury U (MD)
Salve Regina U (RI)
San Diego Christian Coll (CA)
Sarah Lawrence Coll (NY)
Schreiner U (TX)
Seton Hill U (PA)
Shawnee State U (OH)
Shaw U (NC)
Shepherd U (WV)
Shippensburg U of Pennsylvania (PA)
Shorter Coll (GA)
Siena Heights U (MI)
Simmons Coll (MA)
Simpson Coll (IA)
Skidmore Coll (NY)
Slippery Rock U of Pennsylvania (PA)
South Carolina State U (SC)
Southeastern Louisiana U (LA)
Southeastern Oklahoma State U (OK)
Southeastern U (FL)
Southeast Missouri State U (MO)
Southern Adventist U (TN)
Southern Arkansas U–Magnolia (AR)
Southern Connecticut State U (CT)
Southern Illinois U Carbondale (IL)
Southern Illinois U Edwardsville (IL)
Southern New Hampshire U (NH)
Southern U and Ag and Mech Coll (LA)
Southern Utah U (UT)
Southern Wesleyan U (SC)
Southwest Baptist U (MO)
Southwestern Adventist U (TX)
Southwestern Coll (AZ)
Southwestern Coll (KS)
Southwestern Oklahoma State U (OK)
Southwestern U (TX)
Southwest Minnesota State U (MN)
Spring Arbor U (MI)
Spring Hill Coll (AL)
State U of New York at Fredonia (NY)
State U of New York at New Paltz (NY)
State U of New York at Oswego (NY)
State U of New York at Plattsburgh (NY)
State U of New York Coll at Geneseo (NY)
State U of New York Coll at Old Westbury (NY)
State U of New York Coll at Oneonta (NY)
State U of New York Coll at Potsdam (NY)
Stephens Coll (MO)
Sterling Coll (KS)
Stetson U (FL)
Stonehill Coll (MA)
Suffolk U (MA)
Susquehanna U (PA)
Tabor Coll (KS)
Tarleton State U (TX)
Taylor U (IN)
Temple U (PA)
Tennessee State U (TN)
Tennessee Technological U (TN)
Tennessee Wesleyan Coll (TN)
Texas A&M U–Commerce (TX)
Texas Christian U (TX)
Texas Coll (TX)
Texas Lutheran U (TX)
Texas Southern U (TX)
Thiel Coll (PA)
Thomas Coll (ME)
Thomas More Coll (KY)
Thompson Rivers U (BC, Canada)
Tougaloo Coll (MS)
Towson U (MD)
Transylvania U (KY)
Trent U (ON, Canada)
Trinity Christian Coll (IL)
Trinity Coll of Florida (FL)
Trinity Intl U (IL)
Trinity Lutheran Coll (WA)
Tri-State U (IN)
Troy U (AL)
Tufts U (MA)
Tusculum Coll (TN)
Tuskegee U (AL)
Union Coll (KY)
Union Coll (NE)
Union U (TN)
Université de Sherbrooke (QC, Canada)
Université du Québec en Outaouais (QC, Canada)
The U of Alabama (AL)
The U of Alabama at Birmingham (AL)
The U of Alabama in Huntsville (AL)
U of Alaska Fairbanks (AK)
The U of Arizona (AZ)
U of Arkansas (AR)
U of Arkansas at Monticello (AR)
U of Arkansas at Pine Bluff (AR)
The U of British Columbia (BC, Canada)
U of Central Florida (FL)
U of Central Missouri (MO)
U of Central Oklahoma (OK)
U of Charleston (WV)
U of Cincinnati (OH)
U of Connecticut (CT)
U of Dallas (TX)
U of Dayton (OH)
U of Delaware (DE)
U of Evansville (IN)
The U of Findlay (OH)
U of Florida (FL)
U of Great Falls (MT)
U of Guam (GU)
U of Hartford (CT)
U of Hawaii at Manoa (HI)
U of Hawaii–West Oahu (HI)
U of Idaho (ID)
U of Illinois at Chicago (IL)
U of Illinois at Urbana–Champaign (IL)
U of Indianapolis (IN)
The U of Iowa (IA)
U of Kansas (KS)
U of Louisiana at Lafayette (LA)
U of Louisiana at Monroe (LA)
U of Louisville (KY)
U of Maine (ME)
U of Maine at Farmington (ME)
U of Maine at Fort Kent (ME)
U of Maine at Machias (ME)
U of Mary (ND)
U of Mary Hardin-Baylor (TX)
U of Maryland, Coll Park (MD)
U of Maryland Eastern Shore (MD)
U of Mary Washington (VA)
U of Miami (FL)
U of Michigan (MI)
U of Michigan–Dearborn (MI)
U of Michigan–Flint (MI)
U of Minnesota, Duluth (MN)
U of Minnesota, Twin Cities Campus (MN)
U of Mississippi (MS)
U of Missouri–Columbia (MO)
U of Missouri–Kansas City (MO)
U of Missouri–St. Louis (MO)
The U of Montana (MT)
The U of Montana–Western (MT)
U of Montevallo (AL)
U of Nebraska at Kearney (NE)
U of Nebraska at Omaha (NE)
U of Nebraska–Lincoln (NE)
U of Nevada, Las Vegas (NV)
U of Nevada, Reno (NV)
U of New Brunswick Fredericton (NB, Canada)
U of New England (ME)
U of New Hampshire (NH)
U of New Mexico (NM)
U of New Orleans (LA)
U of North Alabama (AL)
The U of North Carolina at Chapel Hill (NC)
The U of North Carolina at Charlotte (NC)
The U of North Carolina at Greensboro (NC)
The U of North Carolina at Pembroke (NC)
The U of North Carolina Wilmington (NC)
U of North Dakota (ND)
U of Northern Iowa (IA)
U of North Florida (FL)
U of Oklahoma (OK)
U of Pennsylvania (PA)
U of Pittsburgh at Bradford (PA)
U of Pittsburgh at Johnstown (PA)
U of Portland (OR)
U of Prince Edward Island (PE, Canada)
U of Puerto Rico at Humacao (PR)
U of Puerto Rico at Utuado (PR)
U of Redlands (CA)
U of Regina (SK, Canada)
U of Rhode Island (RI)
U of Rio Grande (OH)
U of St. Francis (IL)
U of Saint Francis (IN)
U of Saint Mary (KS)
U of St. Thomas (MN)
U of St. Thomas (TX)
U of Science and Arts of Oklahoma (OK)
The U of Scranton (PA)
U of Sioux Falls (SD)
U of South Alabama (AL)
U of South Carolina Aiken (SC)
U of South Carolina Upstate (SC)
The U of South Dakota (SD)
U of Southern Indiana (IN)
U of Southern Mississippi (MS)
U of South Florida (FL)
The U of Tampa (FL)
The U of Tennessee at Martin (TN)
U of the District of Columbia (DC)
U of the Incarnate Word (TX)
U of the Ozarks (AR)
U of the Sacred Heart (PR)
U of the Virgin Islands (VI)
The U of Toledo (OH)
U of Tulsa (OK)
U of Utah (UT)
U of Vermont (VT)
U of Victoria (BC, Canada)
The U of Western Ontario (ON, Canada)
U of West Florida (FL)
U of West Georgia (GA)
U of Windsor (ON, Canada)
The U of Winnipeg (MB, Canada)
U of Wisconsin–Eau Claire (WI)
U of Wisconsin–La Crosse (WI)
U of Wisconsin–Madison (WI)
U of Wisconsin–Milwaukee (WI)
U of Wisconsin–Oshkosh (WI)
U of Wisconsin–Platteville (WI)
U of Wisconsin–Stevens Point (WI)
U of Wisconsin–Superior (WI)
U of Wisconsin–Whitewater (WI)
U of Wyoming (WY)
Utah State U (UT)
Utah Valley State Coll (UT)
Utica Coll (NY)
Valley City State U (ND)
Valparaiso U (IN)
Vanderbilt U (TN)
Vennard Coll (IA)
Villa Julie Coll (MD)
Villanova U (PA)
Virginia Intermont Coll (VA)
Virginia Wesleyan Coll (VA)
Viterbo U (WI)
Voorhees Coll (SC)
Wagner Coll (NY)
Walla Walla U (WA)
Warner Pacific Coll (OR)
Warren Wilson Coll (NC)
Wartburg Coll (IA)
Washburn U (KS)
Washington Bible Coll (MD)
Washington State U (WA)
Washington U in St. Louis (MO)
Wayland Baptist U (TX)
Waynesburg U (PA)
Wayne State Coll (NE)
Wayne State U (MI)
Weber State U (UT)
Webster U (MO)
Wells Coll (NY)
West Chester U of Pennsylvania (PA)
Western Carolina U (NC)
Western Connecticut State U (CT)
Western Illinois U (IL)
Western Kentucky U (KY)
Western New England Coll (MA)
Western New Mexico U (NM)
Western Washington U (WA)
Westfield State Coll (MA)
West Liberty State Coll (WV)
Westminster Coll (MO)
Westminster Coll (UT)
Westmont Coll (CA)
West Virginia U (WV)
West Virginia Wesleyan Coll (WV)
Wheaton Coll (IL)
Wheeling Jesuit U (WV)
Wheelock Coll (MA)
Whitworth U (WA)
Wichita State U (KS)
Widener U (PA)
Wiley Coll (TX)
Wilkes U (PA)
William Jewell Coll (MO)
William Paterson U of New Jersey (NJ)
William Woods U (MO)
Wilmington Coll (OH)
Wilson Coll (PA)
Wingate U (NC)
Winona State U (MN)
Winthrop U (SC)
Worcester State Coll (MA)
Wright State U (OH)
Xavier U (OH)
Xavier U of Louisiana (LA)
York Coll (NE)
York Coll of Pennsylvania (PA)
York U (ON, Canada)
Youngstown State U (OH)

EMERGENCY MEDICAL TECHNOLOGY (EMT PARAMEDIC)

Central Washington U (WA)
Creighton U (NE)
The George Washington U (DC)
Hannibal-LaGrange Coll (MO)
Loma Linda U (CA)
Nebraska Methodist Coll (NE)
U of Maryland, Baltimore County (MD)
U of Minnesota, Twin Cities Campus (MN)
U of Sioux Falls (SD)
Western Carolina U (NC)

ENERGY MANAGEMENT AND SYSTEMS TECHNOLOGY

Ferris State U (MI)
Fitchburg State Coll (MA)
Sterling Coll (VT)

ENGINEERING

Abilene Christian U (TX)
Arkansas State U (AR)
Auburn U (AL)
Barry U (FL)
Bates Coll (ME)
Baylor U (TX)
Beloit Coll (WI)
Bethany Lutheran Coll (MN)
Boston U (MA)
Brown U (RI)
Buffalo State Coll, State U of New York (NY)
California Baptist U (CA)
California State U, Fullerton (CA)
California State U, Long Beach (CA)
California State U, Los Angeles (CA)
Calvin Coll (MI)
Case Western Reserve U (OH)
The Catholic U of America (DC)
Claremont McKenna Coll (CA)
Clarkson U (NY)
Clark U (MA)
Cleveland State U (OH)
Coll of Staten Island of the City U of New York (NY)
Coll of the Ozarks (MO)
Colorado School of Mines (CO)
Colorado State U-Pueblo (CO)
Concordia U (MI)

Cooper Union for the Advancement of Science and Art (NY)
Cornell U (NY)
Dartmouth Coll (NH)
Dordt Coll (IA)
Drexel U (PA)
Drury U (MO)
East Carolina U (NC)
Elizabethtown Coll (PA)
Elon U (NC)
Florida Inst of Technology (FL)
Fontbonne U (MO)
Franklin W. Olin Coll of Eng (MA)
George Fox U (OR)
The George Washington U (DC)
Gonzaga U (WA)
Grand Valley State U (MI)
Harvard U (MA)
Harvey Mudd Coll (CA)
Hope Coll (MI)
Indiana U–Purdue U Indianapolis (IN)
Inter American U of Puerto Rico, Bayamón Campus (PR)
Inter American U of Puerto Rico, San Germán Campus (PR)
Iowa State U of Science and Technology (IA)
James Madison U (VA)
John Brown U (AR)
The Johns Hopkins U (MD)
Juniata Coll (PA)
King Coll (TN)
Lafayette Coll (PA)
Lakehead U (ON, Canada)
LeTourneau U (TX)
Liberty U (VA)
Lock Haven U of Pennsylvania (PA)
Loyola Coll in Maryland (MD)
Lubbock Christian U (TX)
Maine Maritime Acad (ME)
Marquette U (WI)
Marshall U (WV)
Maryville Coll (TN)
Massachusetts Maritime Acad (MA)
McNeese State U (LA)
Memorial U of Newfoundland (NL, Canada)
Mercer U (GA)
Messiah Coll (PA)
Michigan State U (MI)
Michigan Technological U (MI)
Mills Coll (CA)
Milwaukee School of Eng (WI)
Montana Tech of The U of Montana (MT)
Morehouse Coll (GA)
Morgan State U (MD)
Mount Holyoke Coll (MA)
New Mexico Highlands U (NM)
North Carolina State U (NC)
North Dakota State U (ND)
Northeastern U (MA)
Northern Arizona U (AZ)
Northwestern Coll (MN)
Northwestern U (IL)
Nova Scotia Ag Coll (NS, Canada)
Oakwood Coll (AL)
Oglethorpe U (GA)
Ohio Northern U (OH)
Ohio U (OH)
Oklahoma Christian U (OK)
Oklahoma State U (OK)
Oral Roberts U (OK)
Oregon State U (OR)
Pacific Lutheran U (WA)
Pacific Union Coll (CA)
Pfeiffer U (NC)
Pitzer Coll (CA)
Purdue U Calumet (IN)
Queen's U at Kingston (ON, Canada)
Rensselaer Polytechnic Inst (NY)
Robert Morris U (PA)
Rochester Inst of Technology (NY)
Russell Sage Coll (NY)
Rutgers, The State U of New Jersey, Camden (NJ)
Rutgers, The State U of New Jersey, Newark (NJ)
St. Cloud State U (MN)
Saint Francis U (PA)
Saint Mary's Coll of California (CA)
St. Mary's U (TX)
Saint Vincent Coll (PA)
San Diego State U (CA)
Santa Clara U (CA)
Schreiner U (TX)
Seton Hill U (PA)
Spelman Coll (GA)
Stanford U (CA)
State U of New York at Binghamton (NY)
Stony Brook U, State U of New York (NY)
Swarthmore Coll (PA)
Tennessee State U (TN)
Texas Christian U (TX)
Texas Tech U (TX)
Trinity Coll (CT)
Tufts U (MA)
United States Air Force Acad (CO)
United States Naval Acad (MD)
U at Buffalo, the State U of New York (NY)
The U of Akron (OH)
The U of Arizona (AZ)
U of California, San Diego (CA)
U of Cincinnati (OH)
U of Delaware (DE)
U of Denver (CO)
U of Hartford (CT)
U of Idaho (ID)
U of Illinois at Urbana–Champaign (IL)
The U of Iowa (IA)
U of Louisiana at Lafayette (LA)
U of Louisville (KY)
U of Maryland, Baltimore County (MD)
U of Maryland, Coll Park (MD)
U of Massachusetts Amherst (MA)
U of Michigan (MI)
U of Mississippi (MS)
U of New Brunswick Fredericton (NB, Canada)
U of New Haven (CT)
The U of North Carolina at Asheville (NC)
U of Oklahoma (OK)
U of Pittsburgh (PA)
U of Portland (OR)
U of Puerto Rico at Humacao (PR)
U of Regina (SK, Canada)
U of Southern California (CA)
U of Southern Indiana (IN)
U of South Florida (FL)
The U of Tennessee at Chattanooga (TN)
The U of Tennessee at Martin (TN)
The U of Toledo (OH)
U of Toronto (ON, Canada)
U of Utah (UT)
U of Virginia (VA)
U of Windsor (ON, Canada)
U of Wisconsin–Madison (WI)
U of Wisconsin–Milwaukee (WI)
Vanderbilt U (TN)
Wake Forest U (NC)
Walla Walla U (WA)
Wartburg Coll (IA)
Washington U in St. Louis (MO)
Wells Coll (NY)
Widener U (PA)
Wilkes U (PA)
Winona State U (MN)
Wright State U (OH)
York U (ON, Canada)
Youngstown State U (OH)

ENGINEERING/INDUSTRIAL MANAGEMENT

California State U, Chico (CA)
California State U, Long Beach (CA)
Claremont McKenna Coll (CA)
Clemson U (SC)
Farmingdale State Coll (NY)
Fort Lewis Coll (CO)
Grand Valley State U (MI)
Illinois Inst of Technology (IL)
John Brown U (AR)
Lake Superior State U (MI)
Lawrence Technological U (MI)
Massachusetts Maritime Acad (MA)
Miami U (OH)
Miami U Hamilton (OH)
Middle Tennessee State U (TN)
Missouri State U (MO)
Missouri U of Science and Technology (MO)
Purdue U (IN)
Saginaw Valley State U (MI)
Saint Louis U (MO)
South Dakota School of Mines and Technology (SD)
South Dakota State U (SD)
Tri-State U (IN)
United States Merchant Marine Acad (NY)
The U of Arizona (AZ)
U of Illinois at Chicago (IL)
U of Massachusetts Lowell (MA)
U of Portland (OR)
The U of Tennessee at Chattanooga (TN)
U of the Pacific (CA)
U of Vermont (VT)
Western Michigan U (MI)
Widener U (PA)
Wilkes U (PA)
Worcester Polytechnic Inst (MA)
York Coll of Pennsylvania (PA)

ENGINEERING MECHANICS

Clemson U (SC)
Cleveland State U (OH)
Dordt Coll (IA)
The Johns Hopkins U (MD)
Lehigh U (PA)
Lipscomb U (TN)
Michigan Technological U (MI)
New Mexico Inst of Mining and Technology (NM)
United States Air Force Acad (CO)
U of Cincinnati (OH)
U of Illinois at Urbana–Champaign (IL)
U of Windsor (ON, Canada)
U of Wisconsin–Madison (WI)
Virginia Polytechnic Inst and State U (VA)
Wentworth Inst of Technology (MA)
Worcester Polytechnic Inst (MA)

ENGINEERING PHYSICS

Augustana Coll (IL)
Augustana Coll (SD)
Bemidji State U (MN)
Bradley U (IL)
Brown U (RI)
Butler U (IN)
Carroll Coll (WI)
Case Western Reserve U (OH)
Christian Brothers U (TN)
Coll of Saint Benedict (MN)
Colorado School of Mines (CO)
Colorado State U (CO)
Connecticut Coll (CT)
Cornell U (NY)
Dartmouth Coll (NH)
Elizabethtown Coll (PA)
Embry-Riddle Aeronautical U (FL)
Fort Lewis Coll (CO)
Harvard U (MA)
Hope Coll (MI)
Jacksonville U (FL)
John Carroll U (OH)
Juniata Coll (PA)
Kettering U (MI)
Lehigh U (PA)
Loras Coll (IA)
Loyola Marymount U (CA)
Miami U (OH)
Miami U Hamilton (OH)
Michigan Technological U (MI)
Morgan State U (MD)
Morningside Coll (IA)
Murray State U (KY)
North Carolina Ag and Tech State U (NC)
Northern Arizona U (AZ)
Northwest Nazarene U (ID)
Oakland U (MI)
Oral Roberts U (OK)
Oregon State U (OR)
Point Loma Nazarene U (CA)
Providence Coll (RI)
Queen's U at Kingston (ON, Canada)
Randolph Coll (VA)
Rensselaer Polytechnic Inst (NY)
Rose-Hulman Inst of Technology (IN)
St. Ambrose U (IA)
Saint John's U (MN)
Saint Louis U (MO)
St. Mary's Coll of Maryland (MD)
Saint Mary's U of Minnesota (MN)
Samford U (AL)
Santa Clara U (CA)
South Dakota State U (SD)
Southeast Missouri State U (MO)
Southern Arkansas U–Magnolia (AR)
Southwestern Coll (KS)
Southwestern Oklahoma State U (OK)
State U of New York at New Paltz (NY)
Syracuse U (NY)
Tarleton State U (TX)
Taylor U (IN)
Texas Tech U (TX)
Thiel Coll (PA)
Tufts U (MA)
U at Buffalo, the State U of New York (NY)
The U of Arizona (AZ)
The U of British Columbia (BC, Canada)
U of California, Berkeley (CA)
U of California, San Diego (CA)
U of Colorado at Boulder (CO)
U of Connecticut (CT)
U of Illinois at Chicago (IL)
U of Illinois at Urbana–Champaign (IL)
U of Kansas (KS)
U of Maine (ME)
U of Massachusetts Boston (MA)
U of Michigan (MI)
U of Nebraska at Omaha (NE)
U of Nevada, Reno (NV)
U of Northern Iowa (IA)
U of Oklahoma (OK)
U of Pittsburgh (PA)
The U of Tennessee (TN)
The U of Texas at Brownsville (TX)
U of the Pacific (CA)
The U of Toledo (OH)
U of Tulsa (OK)
U of Wisconsin–Madison (WI)
Washington and Lee U (VA)
Westmont Coll (CA)
West Virginia Wesleyan Coll (WV)
Worcester Polytechnic Inst (MA)
Wright State U (OH)
Yale U (CT)
York U (ON, Canada)

ENGINEERING RELATED

Alfred U (NY)
Augustana Coll (IL)
Boston U (MA)
California State U, Chico (CA)
California State U, Long Beach (CA)
Canisius Coll (NY)
Carnegie Mellon U (PA)
Claremont McKenna Coll (CA)
Cleveland State U (OH)
Dowling Coll (NY)
Eastern Illinois U (IL)
George Mason U (VA)
Gettysburg Coll (PA)
Hawai'i Pacific U (HI)
Iowa State U of Science and Technology (IA)
Kentucky Wesleyan Coll (KY)
Lehigh U (PA)
Le Moyne Coll (NY)
Lipscomb U (TN)
Loras Coll (IA)
Marquette U (WI)
Massachusetts Maritime Acad (MA)
Mississippi State U (MS)
New York U (NY)
Northern Michigan U (MI)
Northwestern U (IL)
Oakland U (MI)
Ohio Northern U (OH)
Ohio U (OH)
Ohio Wesleyan U (OH)
Pacific Union Coll (CA)
Park U (MO)
Purdue U (IN)
Queen's U at Kingston (ON, Canada)
Rochester Inst of Technology (NY)
Rose-Hulman Inst of Technology (IN)
Samford U (AL)
Spring Hill Coll (AL)
Tufts U (MA)
The U of Alabama in Huntsville (AL)
The U of Arizona (AZ)
U of California, Davis (CA)
U of Connecticut (CT)
U of Houston–Downtown (TX)
U of Maryland, Coll Park (MD)
U of Michigan–Dearborn (MI)
U of Nebraska–Lincoln (NE)
U of Pennsylvania (PA)
U of the Incarnate Word (TX)
Waynesburg U (PA)
Western Washington U (WA)
Wheaton Coll (IL)
Worcester Polytechnic Inst (MA)
Wright State U (OH)

ENGINEERING-RELATED TECHNOLOGIES

Rochester Inst of Technology (NY)
United States Merchant Marine Acad (NY)

ENGINEERING SCIENCE

Abilene Christian U (TX)
The American U of Athens (Greece)
Belmont U (TN)
Benedictine U (IL)
Bethel U (MN)
Bob Jones U (SC)
California Polytechnic State U, San Luis Obispo (CA)
California State U, Fullerton (CA)
Case Western Reserve U (OH)
Claremont McKenna Coll (CA)
Cleveland State U (OH)
The Coll of New Jersey (NJ)
Colorado School of Mines (CO)
Colorado State U (CO)
Harvard U (MA)
Hofstra U (NY)
Houston Baptist U (TX)
Iowa State U of Science and Technology (IA)
Lipscomb U (TN)
Manchester Coll (IN)
Montana Tech of The U of Montana (MT)
New Jersey Inst of Technology (NJ)
Northwestern U (IL)
Ohio Wesleyan U (OH)
Penn State Abington (PA)
Penn State Altoona (PA)
Penn State Berks (PA)
Penn State Erie, The Behrend Coll (PA)
Penn State U Park (PA)
Rensselaer Polytechnic Inst (NY)
Rutgers, The State U of New Jersey, New Brunswick (NJ)
St. Mary's U (TX)
St. Thomas Aquinas Coll (NY)
Seattle Pacific U (WA)
Simon Fraser U (BC, Canada)
Smith Coll (MA)
Sonoma State U (CA)
State U of New York Coll at Oneonta (NY)
Sweet Briar Coll (VA)
Trinity U (TX)
Tufts U (MA)
Tulane U (LA)
United States Air Force Acad (CO)
U at Buffalo, the State U of New York (NY)
U of California, Berkeley (CA)
U of California, San Diego (CA)
U of Cincinnati (OH)
U of Florida (FL)
U of Mary (ND)
U of Miami (FL)
U of Michigan (MI)
U of Michigan–Flint (MI)
U of New Mexico (NM)
U of Ottawa (ON, Canada)
U of Portland (OR)
U of Rochester (NY)
The U of Tennessee (TN)
U of Toronto (ON, Canada)
The U of Western Ontario (ON, Canada)
Vanderbilt U (TN)
Wright State U (OH)
Yale U (CT)

ENGINEERING TECHNOLOGIES RELATED

Arkansas State U (AR)
California Maritime Acad (CA)
California State Polytechnic U, Pomona (CA)
East Carolina U (NC)
New Jersey Inst of Technology (NJ)
Ohio U (OH)
Old Dominion U (VA)
Pennsylvania Coll of Technology (PA)
Rogers State U (OK)
The U of British Columbia (BC, Canada)
U of Hartford (CT)
U of Southern Indiana (IN)

ENGINEERING TECHNOLOGY

Arkansas State U (AR)
Austin Peay State U (TN)
Berry Coll (GA)
Brigham Young U (UT)
Buffalo State Coll, State U of New York (NY)
California State Polytechnic U, Pomona (CA)
California State U, Long Beach (CA)
Central Connecticut State U (CT)
Cleveland State U (OH)
Dordt Coll (IA)
Eastern Michigan U (MI)
Eastern New Mexico U (NM)
East Tennessee State U (TN)
Fairmont State U (WV)
Lawrence Technological U (MI)
Lenoir-Rhyne Coll (NC)
LeTourneau U (TX)
Maine Maritime Acad (ME)
Massachusetts Maritime Acad (MA)
McNeese State U (LA)
Miami U (OH)
Miami U Hamilton (OH)
Middle Tennessee State U (TN)
Midwestern State U (TX)
Murray State U (KY)
New Jersey Inst of Technology (NJ)
Northeastern State U (OK)
Northern Illinois U (IL)
Oklahoma State U (OK)
Pacific Union Coll (CA)
Prairie View A&M U (TX)
Purdue U Calumet (IN)
Purdue U North Central (IN)
St. Cloud State U (MN)
Southeast Missouri State U (MO)

Southern Illinois U Carbondale (IL)
Southern Polytechnic State U (GA)
Southwestern Oklahoma State U (OK)
Temple U (PA)
Texas A&M U (TX)
Texas Southern U (TX)
Texas State U-San Marcos (TX)
Texas Tech U (TX)
Tuskegee U (AL)
U of Central Florida (FL)
U of Hartford (CT)
U of Maine (ME)
U of Maryland Eastern Shore (MD)
U of Pittsburgh at Johnstown (PA)
U of South Carolina Upstate (SC)
The U of Texas at Tyler (TX)
U of West Florida (FL)
Walla Walla U (WA)
Western Carolina U (NC)
Western Washington U (WA)
Youngstown State U (OH)

ENGLISH

Abilene Christian U (TX)
Acadia U (NS, Canada)
Adams State Coll (CO)
Adelphi U (NY)
Adrian Coll (MI)
Agnes Scott Coll (GA)
Alabama Ag and Mech U (AL)
Alabama State U (AL)
Albertus Magnus Coll (CT)
Albion Coll (MI)
Albright Coll (PA)
Alcorn State U (MS)
Alfred U (NY)
Alice Lloyd Coll (KY)
Allegheny Coll (PA)
Alma Coll (MI)
Alvernia Coll (PA)
American Public U System (WV)
The American U of Athens (Greece)
American U of Beirut (Lebanon)
Amherst Coll (MA)
Anderson U (IN)
Anderson U (SC)
Andrews U (MI)
Angelo State U (TX)
Anna Maria Coll (MA)
Appalachian State U (NC)
Aquinas Coll (MI)
Arizona State U (AZ)
Arizona State U at the West campus (AZ)
Arkansas State U (AR)
Armstrong Atlantic State U (GA)
Asbury Coll (KY)
Ashford U (IA)
Ashland U (OH)
Assumption Coll (MA)
Athabasca U (AB, Canada)
Athens State U (AL)
Atlantic Union Coll (MA)
Auburn U (AL)
Auburn U Montgomery (AL)
Augsburg Coll (MN)
Augustana Coll (IL)
Augustana Coll (SD)
Augusta State U (GA)
Austin Coll (TX)
Austin Peay State U (TN)
Ave Maria U (FL)
Averett U (VA)
Avila U (MO)
Azusa Pacific U (CA)
Baker U (KS)
Baldwin-Wallace Coll (OH)
Ball State U (IN)
Bard Coll (NY)
Barnard Coll (NY)
Barry U (FL)
Barton Coll (NC)
Bates Coll (ME)
Baylor U (TX)
Belhaven Coll (MS)
Bellarmine U (KY)
Belmont Abbey Coll (NC)
Belmont U (TN)
Beloit Coll (WI)
Bemidji State U (MN)
Benedictine Coll (KS)
Benedictine U (IL)
Bennington Coll (VT)
Berea Coll (KY)
Bernard M. Baruch Coll of the City U of New York (NY)
Berry Coll (GA)
Bethany Coll (KS)
Bethany Coll (WV)
Bethany Lutheran Coll (MN)
Bethany U (CA)
Bethel Coll (KS)
Bethel Coll (TN)
Bethel U (MN)
Bethune-Cookman U (FL)
Biola U (CA)
Bishop's U (QC, Canada)
Blackburn Coll (IL)
Bloomfield Coll (NJ)
Bloomsburg U of Pennsylvania (PA)
Bluefield Coll (VA)
Bluffton U (OH)
Bob Jones U (SC)
Boise State U (ID)
Boston Coll (MA)
Boston U (MA)
Bowdoin Coll (ME)
Bowling Green State U (OH)
Bradley U (IL)
Brandeis U (MA)
Brenau U (GA)
Brevard Coll (NC)
Brewton-Parker Coll (GA)
Bridgewater Coll (VA)
Bridgewater State Coll (MA)
Brigham Young U (UT)
Brock U (ON, Canada)
Brown U (RI)
Bryan Coll (TN)
Bryn Athyn Coll of the New Church (PA)
Bryn Mawr Coll (PA)
Bucknell U (PA)
Buffalo State Coll, State U of New York (NY)
Butler U (IN)
Cabrini Coll (PA)
California Baptist U (CA)
California Inst of Technology (CA)
California Lutheran U (CA)
California Polytechnic State U, San Luis Obispo (CA)
California State Polytechnic U, Pomona (CA)
California State U, Chico (CA)
California State U, Dominguez Hills (CA)
California State U, East Bay (CA)
California State U, Fresno (CA)
California State U, Fullerton (CA)
California State U, Long Beach (CA)
California State U, Los Angeles (CA)
California State U, Sacramento (CA)
California State U, San Bernardino (CA)
California State U, San Marcos (CA)
California State U, Stanislaus (CA)
Calumet Coll of Saint Joseph (IN)
Calvin Coll (MI)
Cameron U (OK)
Canadian Mennonite U (MB, Canada)
Canisius Coll (NY)
Capital U (OH)
Carlow U (PA)
Carnegie Mellon U (PA)
Carroll Coll (WI)
Carson-Newman Coll (TN)
Cascade Coll (OR)
Case Western Reserve U (OH)
Catawba Coll (NC)
The Catholic U of America (DC)
Cedar Crest Coll (PA)
Cedarville U (OH)
Centenary Coll (NJ)
Centenary Coll of Louisiana (LA)
Central Christian Coll of Kansas (KS)
Central Coll (IA)
Central Connecticut State U (CT)
Central Michigan U (MI)
Central State U (OH)
Central Washington U (WA)
Centre Coll (KY)
Chaminade U of Honolulu (HI)
Chapman U (CA)
Chatham U (PA)
Chestnut Hill Coll (PA)
Cheyney U of Pennsylvania (PA)
Christian Brothers U (TN)
Christopher Newport U (VA)
The Citadel, The Military Coll of South Carolina (SC)
City Coll of the City U of New York (NY)
Claflin U (SC)
Claremont McKenna Coll (CA)
Clarion U of Pennsylvania (PA)
Clark Atlanta U (GA)
Clarke Coll (IA)
Clark U (MA)
Clearwater Christian Coll (FL)
Clemson U (SC)
Cleveland State U (OH)
Coastal Carolina U (SC)
Coker Coll (SC)
Colby Coll (ME)
Colby-Sawyer Coll (NH)
Colgate U (NY)
The Coll at Brockport, State U of New York (NY)
Coll of Charleston (SC)
The Coll of Idaho (ID)
Coll of Mount St. Joseph (OH)
Coll of Mount Saint Vincent (NY)
The Coll of New Jersey (NJ)
The Coll of New Rochelle (NY)
Coll of Saint Benedict (MN)
Coll of Saint Elizabeth (NJ)
Coll of St. Joseph (VT)
Coll of Saint Mary (NE)
The Coll of Saint Rose (NY)
The Coll of St. Scholastica (MN)
Coll of Santa Fe (NM)
Coll of Staten Island of the City U of New York (NY)
Coll of the Atlantic (ME)
Coll of the Holy Cross (MA)
Coll of the Ozarks (MO)
Coll of the Southwest (NM)
The Coll of William and Mary (VA)
The Colorado Coll (CO)
Colorado State U (CO)
Colorado State U-Pueblo (CO)
Columbia Coll (SC)
Columbus State U (GA)
Concordia Coll (MN)
Concordia Coll–New York (NY)
Concordia U (CA)
Concordia U (MI)
Concordia U (OR)
Concordia U (QC, Canada)
Concordia U Chicago (IL)
Concordia U, Nebraska (NE)
Concordia U, St. Paul (MN)
Concordia U Texas (TX)
Concordia U Wisconsin (WI)
Concord U (WV)
Connecticut Coll (CT)
Converse Coll (SC)
Cornell Coll (IA)
Cornell U (NY)
Cornerstone U (MI)
Covenant Coll (GA)
Creighton U (NE)
Crown Coll (MN)
Culver-Stockton Coll (MO)
Curry Coll (MA)
Daemen Coll (NY)
Dakota Wesleyan U (SD)
Dallas Baptist U (TX)
Dana Coll (NE)
Dartmouth Coll (NH)
Davidson Coll (NC)
Davis & Elkins Coll (WV)
Defiance Coll (OH)
Delaware Valley Coll (PA)
Delta State U (MS)
Denison U (OH)
DePaul U (IL)
DePauw U (IN)
DeSales U (PA)
Dickinson Coll (PA)
Dillard U (LA)
Dixie State Coll of Utah (UT)
Doane Coll (NE)
Dominican Coll (NY)
Dominican U (IL)
Dominican U of California (CA)
Dordt Coll (IA)
Dowling Coll (NY)
Drake U (IA)
Drew U (NJ)
Drury U (MO)
Duke U (NC)
Duquesne U (PA)
Earlham Coll (IN)
East Carolina U (NC)
East Central U (OK)
Eastern Connecticut State U (CT)
Eastern Illinois U (IL)
Eastern Kentucky U (KY)
Eastern Mennonite U (VA)
Eastern Michigan U (MI)
Eastern New Mexico U (NM)
East Stroudsburg U of Pennsylvania (PA)
East Tennessee State U (TN)
East Texas Baptist U (TX)
East-West U (IL)
Edinboro U of Pennsylvania (PA)
Elizabethtown Coll (PA)
Elon U (NC)
Emmanuel Coll (GA)
Emmanuel Coll (MA)
Emory & Henry Coll (VA)
Emory U (GA)
Emporia State U (KS)
Endicott Coll (MA)
Erskine Coll (SC)
Eugene Lang Coll The New School for Liberal Arts (NY)
Evangel U (MO)
The Evergreen State Coll (WA)
Fairfield U (CT)
Fairleigh Dickinson U, Coll at Florham (NJ)
Fairleigh Dickinson U, Metropolitan Campus (NJ)
Fairmont State U (WV)
Faulkner U (AL)
Fayetteville State U (NC)
Felician Coll (NJ)
Ferrum Coll (VA)
Fitchburg State Coll (MA)
Flagler Coll (FL)
Florida Ag and Mech U (FL)
Florida Atlantic U (FL)
Florida Gulf Coast U (FL)
Florida Intl U (FL)
Florida Memorial U (FL)
Florida Southern Coll (FL)
Florida State U (FL)
Fontbonne U (MO)
Fort Lewis Coll (CO)
Framingham State Coll (MA)
Franciscan U of Steubenville (OH)
Francis Marion U (SC)
Franklin & Marshall Coll (PA)
Franklin Coll (IN)
Freed-Hardeman U (TN)
Free Will Baptist Bible Coll (TN)
Fresno Pacific U (CA)
Frostburg State U (MD)
Furman U (SC)
Gardner-Webb U (NC)
George Fox U (OR)
George Mason U (VA)
Georgetown Coll (KY)
Georgetown U (DC)
The George Washington U (DC)
Georgia Coll & State U (GA)
Georgian Court U (NJ)
Georgia Southern U (GA)
Georgia Southwestern State U (GA)
Georgia State U (GA)
Gettysburg Coll (PA)
Glenville State Coll (WV)
Gonzaga U (WA)
Gordon Coll (MA)
Goucher Coll (MD)
Grace Coll (IN)
Grambling State U (LA)
Grand Canyon U (AZ)
Grand Valley State U (MI)
Grand View Coll (IA)
Green Mountain Coll (VT)
Greensboro Coll (NC)
Greenville Coll (IL)
Grinnell Coll (IA)
Grove City Coll (PA)
Guilford Coll (NC)
Gustavus Adolphus Coll (MN)
Gwynedd-Mercy Coll (PA)
Hamilton Coll (NY)
Hamline U (MN)
Hampden-Sydney Coll (VA)
Hampshire Coll (MA)
Hampton U (VA)
Hannibal-LaGrange Coll (MO)
Hanover Coll (IN)
Harding U (AR)
Hardin-Simmons U (TX)
Hartwick Coll (NY)
Harvard U (MA)
Hastings Coll (NE)
Haverford Coll (PA)
Hawai'i Pacific U (HI)
Heidelberg Coll (OH)
Henderson State U (AR)
Hendrix Coll (AR)
High Point U (NC)
Hilbert Coll (NY)
Hillsdale Coll (MI)
Hobart and William Smith Colls (NY)
Hofstra U (NY)
Hollins U (VA)
Holy Family U (PA)
Holy Names U (CA)
Hood Coll (MD)
Hope Coll (MI)
Houghton Coll (NY)
Houston Baptist U (TX)
Howard Payne U (TX)
Humboldt State U (CA)
Hunter Coll of the City U of New York (NY)
Huntingdon Coll (AL)
Huntington U (IN)
Huston-Tillotson U (TX)
Idaho State U (ID)
Illinois Coll (IL)
Illinois State U (IL)
Immaculata U (PA)
Indiana State U (IN)
Indiana U Bloomington (IN)
Indiana U East (IN)
Indiana U Kokomo (IN)
Indiana U Northwest (IN)
Indiana U of Pennsylvania (PA)
Indiana U–Purdue U Fort Wayne (IN)
Indiana U–Purdue U Indianapolis (IN)
Indiana U South Bend (IN)
Indiana U Southeast (IN)
Indiana Wesleyan U (IN)
Inter American U of Puerto Rico, San Germán Campus (PR)
Iona Coll (NY)
Iowa State U of Science and Technology (IA)
Iowa Wesleyan Coll (IA)
Ithaca Coll (NY)
Jackson State U (MS)
Jacksonville State U (AL)
Jacksonville U (FL)
James Madison U (VA)
Jamestown Coll (ND)
Jarvis Christian Coll (TX)
John Brown U (AR)
John Carroll U (OH)
The Johns Hopkins U (MD)
Johnson C. Smith U (NC)
Johnson State Coll (VT)
Judson Coll (AL)
Judson U (IL)
Juniata Coll (PA)
Kalamazoo Coll (MI)
Kansas State U (KS)
Kean U (NJ)
Keene State Coll (NH)
Kennesaw State U (GA)
Kent State U (OH)
Kentucky State U (KY)
Kentucky Wesleyan Coll (KY)
Kenyon Coll (OH)
Keuka Coll (NY)
King Coll (TN)
King's Coll (PA)
The King's U Coll (AB, Canada)
Knox Coll (IL)
Kutztown U of Pennsylvania (PA)
Lafayette Coll (PA)
LaGrange Coll (GA)
Lake Forest Coll (IL)
Lakehead U (ON, Canada)
Lake Superior State U (MI)
Lambuth U (TN)
Lander U (SC)
La Roche Coll (PA)
La Salle U (PA)
La Sierra U (CA)
Laurentian U (ON, Canada)
Lawrence U (WI)
Lebanon Valley Coll (PA)
Lees-McRae Coll (NC)
Lee U (TN)
Lehigh U (PA)
Lehman Coll of the City U of New York (NY)
Le Moyne Coll (NY)
LeMoyne-Owen Coll (TN)
Lenoir-Rhyne Coll (NC)
Lesley U (MA)
LeTourneau U (TX)
Lewis & Clark Coll (OR)
Lewis-Clark State Coll (ID)
Lewis U (IL)
Liberty U (VA)
Limestone Coll (SC)
Lincoln U (MO)
Lincoln U (PA)
Lindenwood U (MO)
Lindsey Wilson Coll (KY)
Linfield Coll (OR)
Lipscomb U (TN)
Livingstone Coll (NC)
Lock Haven U of Pennsylvania (PA)
Longwood U (VA)
Loras Coll (IA)
Louisiana Coll (LA)
Louisiana State U and Ag and Mech Coll (LA)
Lourdes Coll (OH)
Loyola Coll in Maryland (MD)
Loyola Marymount U (CA)
Loyola U Chicago (IL)
Loyola U New Orleans (LA)
Luther Coll (IA)
Lycoming Coll (PA)
Lynchburg Coll (VA)
Lyndon State Coll (VT)
Lyon Coll (AR)
Macalester Coll (MN)
Madonna U (MI)
Maharishi U of Management (IA)
Malone Coll (OH)
Manchester Coll (IN)
Manhattanville Coll (NY)
Mansfield U of Pennsylvania (PA)
Maranatha Baptist Bible Coll (WI)
Marian Coll (IN)
Marian Coll of Fond du Lac (WI)
Marietta Coll (OH)
Marist Coll (NY)
Marlboro Coll (VT)
Marquette U (WI)
Marshall U (WV)
Martin U (IN)
Mary Baldwin Coll (VA)
Marylhurst U (OR)
Marymount Manhattan Coll (NY)
Marymount U (VA)
Maryville Coll (TN)

Maryville U of Saint Louis (MO)
Marywood U (PA)
Massachusetts Coll of Liberal Arts (MA)
Massachusetts Inst of Technology (MA)
The Master's Coll and Sem (CA)
Mayville State U (ND)
McDaniel Coll (MD)
McGill U (QC, Canada)
McKendree U (IL)
McMurry U (TX)
McNeese State U (LA)
Medaille Coll (NY)
Memorial U of Newfoundland (NL, Canada)
Mercer U (GA)
Mercy Coll (NY)
Mercyhurst Coll (PA)
Meredith Coll (NC)
Merrimack Coll (MA)
Mesa State Coll (CO)
Messiah Coll (PA)
Methodist U (NC)
Metropolitan State U (MN)
Miami U (OH)
Miami U Hamilton (OH)
Michigan State U (MI)
Michigan Technological U (MI)
MidAmerica Nazarene U (KS)
Mid-Continent U (KY)
Middlebury Coll (VT)
Middle Tennessee State U (TN)
Midland Lutheran Coll (NE)
Midway Coll (KY)
Midwestern State U (TX)
Miles Coll (AL)
Millersville U of Pennsylvania (PA)
Milligan Coll (TN)
Millikin U (IL)
Millsaps Coll (MS)
Mills Coll (CA)
Minnesota State U Mankato (MN)
Minot State U (ND)
Misericordia U (PA)
Mississippi Coll (MS)
Mississippi State U (MS)
Mississippi U for Women (MS)
Mississippi Valley State U (MS)
Missouri Baptist U (MO)
Missouri Southern State U (MO)
Missouri State U (MO)
Missouri U of Science and Technology (MO)
Missouri Valley Coll (MO)
Molloy Coll (NY)
Monmouth Coll (IL)
Monmouth U (NJ)
Montana State U (MT)
Montana State U–Billings (MT)
Montclair State U (NJ)
Moravian Coll (PA)
Morehead State U (KY)
Morehouse Coll (GA)
Morgan State U (MD)
Morningside Coll (IA)
Morris Coll (SC)
Mountain State U (WV)
Mount Allison U (NB, Canada)
Mount Aloysius Coll (PA)
Mount Holyoke Coll (MA)
Mount Marty Coll (SD)
Mount Mary Coll (WI)
Mount Mercy Coll (IA)
Mount Olive Coll (NC)
Mount Saint Mary Coll (NY)
Mount St. Mary's Coll (CA)
Mount St. Mary's U (MD)
Mount Saint Vincent U (NS, Canada)
Mount Vernon Nazarene U (OH)
Muhlenberg Coll (PA)
Murray State U (KY)
Naropa U (CO)
National-Louis U (IL)
National U (CA)
Nazareth Coll of Rochester (NY)
Nebraska Wesleyan U (NE)
Neumann Coll (PA)
New Coll of Florida (FL)
New England Coll (NH)
New Jersey City U (NJ)
Newman U (KS)
New Mexico Highlands U (NM)
New York U (NY)
Niagara U (NY)
Nicholls State U (LA)
Nichols Coll (MA)
North Carolina Ag and Tech State U (NC)
North Carolina Central U (NC)
North Carolina State U (NC)
North Carolina Wesleyan Coll (NC)
North Central Coll (IL)
North Dakota State U (ND)
Northeastern Illinois U (IL)
Northeastern State U (OK)
Northeastern U (MA)
Northern Arizona U (AZ)
Northern Illinois U (IL)
Northern Michigan U (MI)
Northern State U (SD)
North Georgia Coll & State U (GA)
North Greenville U (SC)
Northland Coll (WI)
Northwest Christian Coll (OR)
Northwestern Coll (IA)
Northwestern Coll (MN)
Northwestern Oklahoma State U (OK)
Northwestern State U of Louisiana (LA)
Northwestern U (IL)
Northwest Missouri State U (MO)
Northwest Nazarene U (ID)
Norwich U (VT)
Notre Dame de Namur U (CA)
Nova Southeastern U (FL)
Nyack Coll (NY)
Oakland U (MI)
Oakwood Coll (AL)
Oberlin Coll (OH)
Occidental Coll (CA)
Oglethorpe U (GA)
Ohio Dominican U (OH)
Ohio Northern U (OH)
Ohio U (OH)
Ohio Wesleyan U (OH)
Oklahoma Christian U (OK)
Oklahoma City U (OK)
Oklahoma Panhandle State U (OK)
Oklahoma State U (OK)
Oklahoma Wesleyan U (OK)
Old Dominion U (VA)
Oregon State U (OR)
Otterbein Coll (OH)
Ouachita Baptist U (AR)
Pace U (NY)
Pacific Lutheran U (WA)
Pacific Union Coll (CA)
Pacific U (OR)
Paine Coll (GA)
Palm Beach Atlantic U (FL)
Park U (MO)
Peace Coll (NC)
Penn State Abington (PA)
Penn State Altoona (PA)
Penn State Berks (PA)
Penn State Erie, The Behrend Coll (PA)
Penn State Harrisburg (PA)
Penn State U Park (PA)
Pepperdine U, Malibu (CA)
Peru State Coll (NE)
Pfeiffer U (NC)
Piedmont Coll (GA)
Pikeville Coll (KY)
Pittsburg State U (KS)
Pitzer Coll (CA)
Plymouth State U (NH)
Point Park U (PA)
Pomona Coll (CA)
Pontifical Coll Josephinum (OH)
Portland State U (OR)
Prairie View A&M U (TX)
Presbyterian Coll (SC)
Princeton U (NJ)
Providence Coll (RI)
Purdue U (IN)
Purdue U Calumet (IN)
Purdue U North Central (IN)
Queens Coll of the City U of New York (NY)
Queen's U at Kingston (ON, Canada)
Queens U of Charlotte (NC)
Quincy U (IL)
Quinnipiac U (CT)
Radford U (VA)
Randolph Coll (VA)
Randolph-Macon Coll (VA)
Redeemer U Coll (ON, Canada)
Reed Coll (OR)
Regis Coll (MA)
Regis U (CO)
Rhode Island Coll (RI)
Rhodes Coll (TN)
Rice U (TX)
The Richard Stockton Coll of New Jersey (NJ)
Rider U (NJ)
Ripon Coll (WI)
Roanoke Coll (VA)
Robert Morris U (PA)
Roberts Wesleyan Coll (NY)
Rochester Coll (MI)
Rockford Coll (IL)
Rockhurst U (MO)
Roger Williams U (RI)
Rollins Coll (FL)
Roosevelt U (IL)
Rosemont Coll (PA)
Rowan U (NJ)
Royal Military Coll of Canada (ON, Canada)
Russell Sage Coll (NY)
Rutgers, The State U of New Jersey, Camden (NJ)
Rutgers, The State U of New Jersey, Newark (NJ)
Rutgers, The State U of New Jersey, New Brunswick (NJ)
Saginaw Valley State U (MI)
St. Ambrose U (IA)
St. Andrews Presbyterian Coll (NC)
St. Cloud State U (MN)
St. Edward's U (TX)
Saint Francis U (PA)
St. Francis Xavier U (NS, Canada)
St. Gregory's U, Shawnee (OK)
St. John Fisher Coll (NY)
St. John's Coll (NM)
Saint John's U (MN)
St. John's U (NY)
Saint Joseph Coll (CT)
Saint Joseph's Coll (IN)
St. Joseph's Coll, New York (NY)
St. Joseph's Coll, Suffolk Campus (NY)
Saint Joseph's U (PA)
St. Lawrence U (NY)
Saint Leo U (FL)
Saint Louis U (MO)
Saint Martin's U (WA)
Saint Mary-of-the-Woods Coll (IN)
Saint Mary's Coll of California (CA)
St. Mary's Coll of Maryland (MD)
St. Mary's U (TX)
Saint Mary's U of Minnesota (MN)
Saint Michael's Coll (VT)
St. Norbert Coll (WI)
St. Olaf Coll (MN)
St. Thomas Aquinas Coll (NY)
St. Thomas U (FL)
St. Thomas U (NB, Canada)
Saint Vincent Coll (PA)
Saint Xavier U (IL)
Salem Coll (NC)
Salem State Coll (MA)
Salisbury U (MD)
Salve Regina U (RI)
Samford U (AL)
Sam Houston State U (TX)
San Diego Christian Coll (CA)
San Diego State U (CA)
San Francisco State U (CA)
Santa Clara U (CA)
Sarah Lawrence Coll (NY)
Schreiner U (TX)
Scripps Coll (CA)
Seattle Pacific U (WA)
Seattle U (WA)
Seton Hill U (PA)
Sewanee: The U of the South (TN)
Shawnee State U (OH)
Shaw U (NC)
Shenandoah U (VA)
Shepherd U (WV)
Shippensburg U of Pennsylvania (PA)
Shorter Coll (GA)
Siena Coll (NY)
Siena Heights U (MI)
Simmons Coll (MA)
Simon Fraser U (BC, Canada)
Simpson Coll (IA)
Simpson U (CA)
Skidmore Coll (NY)
Slippery Rock U of Pennsylvania (PA)
Smith Coll (MA)
Sonoma State U (CA)
South Carolina State U (SC)
South Dakota State U (SD)
Southeastern Louisiana U (LA)
Southeastern Oklahoma State U (OK)
Southeastern U (FL)
Southeast Missouri State U (MO)
Southern Adventist U (TN)
Southern Arkansas U–Magnolia (AR)
Southern Connecticut State U (CT)
Southern Illinois U Carbondale (IL)
Southern Illinois U Edwardsville (IL)
Southern Methodist U (TX)
Southern New Hampshire U (NH)
Southern Oregon U (OR)
Southern U and Ag and Mech Coll (LA)
Southern Utah U (UT)
Southern Vermont Coll (VT)
Southern Wesleyan U (SC)
Southwest Baptist U (MO)
Southwestern Adventist U (TX)
Southwestern Coll (KS)
Southwestern Oklahoma State U (OK)
Southwestern U (TX)
Southwest Minnesota State U (MN)
Spelman Coll (GA)
Spring Arbor U (MI)
Spring Hill Coll (AL)
Stanford U (CA)
State U of New York at Binghamton (NY)
State U of New York at Fredonia (NY)
State U of New York at New Paltz (NY)
State U of New York at Oswego (NY)
State U of New York at Plattsburgh (NY)
State U of New York Coll at Geneseo (NY)
State U of New York Coll at Oneonta (NY)
State U of New York Coll at Potsdam (NY)
Stephen F. Austin State U (TX)
Stephens Coll (MO)
Sterling Coll (KS)
Stetson U (FL)
Stillman Coll (AL)
Stonehill Coll (MA)
Stony Brook U, State U of New York (NY)
Suffolk U (MA)
Susquehanna U (PA)
Swarthmore Coll (PA)
Sweet Briar Coll (VA)
Tabor Coll (KS)
Tarleton State U (TX)
Taylor U (IN)
Taylor U Coll and Sem (AB, Canada)
Taylor U Fort Wayne (IN)
Temple U (PA)
Tennessee State U (TN)
Tennessee Technological U (TN)
Tennessee Wesleyan Coll (TN)
Texas A&M Intl U (TX)
Texas A&M U (TX)
Texas A&M U–Commerce (TX)
Texas Christian U (TX)
Texas Coll (TX)
Texas Lutheran U (TX)
Texas Southern U (TX)
Texas State U-San Marcos (TX)
Texas Tech U (TX)
Texas Woman's U (TX)
Thiel Coll (PA)
Thomas Edison State Coll (NJ)
Thomas More Coll (KY)
Thomas U (GA)
Thompson Rivers U (BC, Canada)
Tiffin U (OH)
Toccoa Falls Coll (GA)
Tougaloo Coll (MS)
Towson U (MD)
Transylvania U (KY)
Trent U (ON, Canada)
Trevecca Nazarene U (TN)
Trinity Christian Coll (IL)
Trinity Coll (CT)
Trinity Intl U (IL)
Trinity U (TX)
Tri-State U (IN)
Troy U (AL)
Truman State U (MO)
Tufts U (MA)
Tulane U (LA)
Tusculum Coll (TN)
Tuskegee U (AL)
Tyndale U Coll & Sem (ON, Canada)
Union Coll (NE)
Union Coll (NY)
Union U (TN)
United States Air Force Acad (CO)
United States Naval Acad (MD)
Université de Sherbrooke (QC, Canada)
U at Albany, State U of New York (NY)
U at Buffalo, the State U of New York (NY)
The U of Akron (OH)
The U of Alabama (AL)
The U of Alabama at Birmingham (AL)
The U of Alabama in Huntsville (AL)
U of Alaska Fairbanks (AK)
The U of Arizona (AZ)
U of Arkansas (AR)
U of Arkansas at Monticello (AR)
U of Arkansas at Pine Bluff (AR)
U of Baltimore (MD)
U of Bridgeport (CT)
The U of British Columbia (BC, Canada)
The U of British Columbia–Okanagan (BC, Canada)
U of California, Berkeley (CA)
U of California, Davis (CA)
U of California, Irvine (CA)
U of California, Los Angeles (CA)
U of California, Riverside (CA)
U of California, San Diego (CA)
U of California, Santa Barbara (CA)
U of Central Florida (FL)
U of Central Missouri (MO)
U of Central Oklahoma (OK)
U of Chicago (IL)
U of Cincinnati (OH)
U of Colorado at Boulder (CO)
U of Colorado Denver (CO)
U of Connecticut (CT)
U of Dallas (TX)
U of Dayton (OH)
U of Delaware (DE)
U of Denver (CO)
U of Evansville (IN)
The U of Findlay (OH)
U of Florida (FL)
U of Georgia (GA)
U of Great Falls (MT)
U of Guam (GU)
U of Hartford (CT)
U of Hawaii at Manoa (HI)
U of Hawaii–West Oahu (HI)
U of Houston (TX)
U of Houston–Clear Lake (TX)
U of Houston–Downtown (TX)
U of Idaho (ID)
U of Illinois at Chicago (IL)
U of Illinois at Springfield (IL)
U of Illinois at Urbana–Champaign (IL)
U of Indianapolis (IN)
The U of Iowa (IA)
U of Kansas (KS)
U of King's Coll (NS, Canada)
U of La Verne (CA)
U of Lethbridge (AB, Canada)
U of Louisiana at Lafayette (LA)
U of Louisiana at Monroe (LA)
U of Louisville (KY)
U of Maine (ME)
U of Maine at Farmington (ME)
U of Maine at Fort Kent (ME)
U of Maine at Machias (ME)
U of Mary (ND)
U of Mary Hardin-Baylor (TX)
U of Maryland, Baltimore County (MD)
U of Maryland, Coll Park (MD)
U of Maryland Eastern Shore (MD)
U of Maryland U Coll (MD)
U of Mary Washington (VA)
U of Massachusetts Amherst (MA)
U of Massachusetts Boston (MA)
U of Massachusetts Dartmouth (MA)
U of Massachusetts Lowell (MA)
U of Memphis (TN)
U of Miami (FL)
U of Michigan (MI)
U of Michigan–Dearborn (MI)
U of Michigan–Flint (MI)
U of Minnesota, Duluth (MN)
U of Minnesota, Twin Cities Campus (MN)
U of Mississippi (MS)
U of Missouri–Columbia (MO)
U of Missouri–Kansas City (MO)
U of Missouri–St. Louis (MO)
The U of Montana (MT)
The U of Montana–Western (MT)
U of Montevallo (AL)
U of Nebraska at Kearney (NE)
U of Nebraska at Omaha (NE)
U of Nebraska–Lincoln (NE)
U of Nevada, Las Vegas (NV)
U of Nevada, Reno (NV)
U of New Brunswick Fredericton (NB, Canada)
U of New England (ME)
U of New Hampshire (NH)
U of New Hampshire at Manchester (NH)
U of New Haven (CT)
U of New Mexico (NM)
U of New Orleans (LA)
U of North Alabama (AL)
The U of North Carolina at Asheville (NC)
The U of North Carolina at Chapel Hill (NC)
The U of North Carolina at Charlotte (NC)
The U of North Carolina at Greensboro (NC)
The U of North Carolina at Pembroke (NC)
The U of North Carolina Wilmington (NC)
U of North Dakota (ND)
U of Northern Colorado (CO)
U of Northern Iowa (IA)
U of North Florida (FL)
U of North Texas (TX)
U of Notre Dame (IN)
U of Oklahoma (OK)
U of Oregon (OR)
U of Ottawa (ON, Canada)
U of Pennsylvania (PA)
U of Pittsburgh (PA)
U of Pittsburgh at Bradford (PA)
U of Pittsburgh at Johnstown (PA)
U of Portland (OR)

MAJORS AND MORE

U of Prince Edward Island (PE, Canada)
U of Puerto Rico, Cayey U Coll (PR)
U of Puget Sound (WA)
U of Redlands (CA)
U of Regina (SK, Canada)
U of Rhode Island (RI)
U of Richmond (VA)
U of Rio Grande (OH)
U of Rochester (NY)
U of St. Francis (IL)
U of Saint Francis (IN)
U of Saint Mary (KS)
U of St. Thomas (MN)
U of St. Thomas (TX)
U of San Diego (CA)
U of Science and Arts of Oklahoma (OK)
The U of Scranton (PA)
U of Sioux Falls (SD)
U of South Alabama (AL)
U of South Carolina (SC)
U of South Carolina Aiken (SC)
U of South Carolina Beaufort (SC)
U of South Carolina Upstate (SC)
The U of South Dakota (SD)
U of Southern California (CA)
U of Southern Indiana (IN)
U of Southern Maine (ME)
U of Southern Mississippi (MS)
U of South Florida (FL)
The U of Tampa (FL)
The U of Tennessee (TN)
The U of Tennessee at Chattanooga (TN)
The U of Tennessee at Martin (TN)
The U of Texas at Arlington (TX)
The U of Texas at Austin (TX)
The U of Texas at Brownsville (TX)
The U of Texas at El Paso (TX)
The U of Texas at San Antonio (TX)
The U of Texas at Tyler (TX)
The U of Texas of the Permian Basin (TX)
The U of Texas–Pan American (TX)
U of the Incarnate Word (TX)
U of the Ozarks (AR)
U of the Pacific (CA)
U of the Virgin Islands (VI)
U of the West (CA)
The U of Toledo (OH)
U of Toronto (ON, Canada)
U of Tulsa (OK)
U of Utah (UT)
U of Vermont (VT)
U of Victoria (BC, Canada)
U of Virginia (VA)
The U of Virginia's Coll at Wise (VA)
The U of Western Ontario (ON, Canada)
U of West Florida (FL)
U of West Georgia (GA)
U of Windsor (ON, Canada)
The U of Winnipeg (MB, Canada)
U of Wisconsin–Eau Claire (WI)
U of Wisconsin–Green Bay (WI)
U of Wisconsin–La Crosse (WI)
U of Wisconsin–Madison (WI)
U of Wisconsin–Milwaukee (WI)
U of Wisconsin–Oshkosh (WI)
U of Wisconsin–Parkside (WI)
U of Wisconsin–Platteville (WI)
U of Wisconsin–Stevens Point (WI)
U of Wisconsin–Superior (WI)
U of Wisconsin–Whitewater (WI)
U of Wyoming (WY)
Ursinus Coll (PA)
Ursuline Coll (OH)
Utah State U (UT)
Utah Valley State Coll (UT)
Utica Coll (NY)
Valdosta State U (GA)
Valley City State U (ND)
Valparaiso U (IN)
Vanderbilt U (TN)
Vanguard U of Southern California (CA)
Vassar Coll (NY)
Villa Julie Coll (MD)
Villanova U (PA)
Virginia Commonwealth U (VA)
Virginia Intermont Coll (VA)
Virginia Military Inst (VA)
Virginia Polytechnic Inst and State U (VA)
Virginia State U (VA)
Virginia Wesleyan Coll (VA)
Viterbo U (WI)
Voorhees Coll (SC)
Wabash Coll (IN)
Wagner Coll (NY)
Wake Forest U (NC)
Walla Walla U (WA)
Walsh U (OH)
Warner Pacific Coll (OR)
Warren Wilson Coll (NC)
Wartburg Coll (IA)
Washburn U (KS)
Washington & Jefferson Coll (PA)
Washington and Lee U (VA)
Washington Coll (MD)
Washington State U (WA)
Washington U in St. Louis (MO)
Wayland Baptist U (TX)
Waynesburg U (PA)
Wayne State Coll (NE)
Wayne State U (MI)
Weber State U (UT)
Webster U (MO)
Wellesley Coll (MA)
Wells Coll (NY)
Wesleyan Coll (GA)
Wesleyan U (CT)
Wesley Coll (DE)
West Chester U of Pennsylvania (PA)
Western Carolina U (NC)
Western Connecticut State U (CT)
Western Illinois U (IL)
Western Kentucky U (KY)
Western Michigan U (MI)
Western New England Coll (MA)
Western New Mexico U (NM)
Western State Coll of Colorado (CO)
Western Washington U (WA)
Westfield State Coll (MA)
West Liberty State Coll (WV)
Westminster Coll (MO)
Westminster Coll (UT)
Westmont Coll (CA)
West Texas A&M U (TX)
West Virginia U (WV)
West Virginia Wesleyan Coll (WV)
Wheaton Coll (IL)
Wheaton Coll (MA)
Wheeling Jesuit U (WV)
Whitman Coll (WA)
Whittier Coll (CA)
Whitworth U (WA)
Wichita State U (KS)
Widener U (PA)
Wiley Coll (TX)
Wilfrid Laurier U (ON, Canada)
Wilkes U (PA)
Willamette U (OR)
William Jewell Coll (MO)
William Paterson U of New Jersey (NJ)
Williams Coll (MA)
William Woods U (MO)
Wilmington Coll (OH)
Wilson Coll (PA)
Wingate U (NC)
Winona State U (MN)
Winthrop U (SC)
Wittenberg U (OH)
Wofford Coll (SC)
Worcester State Coll (MA)
Wright State U (OH)
Xavier U (OH)
Xavier U of Louisiana (LA)
Yale U (CT)
York Coll (NE)
York Coll of Pennsylvania (PA)
York Coll of the City U of New York (NY)
York U (ON, Canada)
Youngstown State U (OH)

ENGLISH AS A SECOND/FOREIGN LANGUAGE (TEACHING)

Aquinas Coll (MI)
Auburn U (AL)
Bethel U (MN)
Brigham Young U (UT)
Brock U (ON, Canada)
Calvin Coll (MI)
Carnegie Mellon U (PA)
Concordia U (QC, Canada)
Concordia U, Nebraska (NE)
Concordia U, St. Paul (MN)
Concordia U Wisconsin (WI)
Davis Coll (NY)
Doane Coll (NE)
Eastern Mennonite U (VA)
Grand Canyon U (AZ)
Hawai'i Pacific U (HI)
Houghton Coll (NY)
Howard Payne U (TX)
Inter American U of Puerto Rico, Aguadilla Campus (PR)
Inter American U of Puerto Rico, Fajardo Campus (PR)
Inter American U of Puerto Rico, San Germán Campus (PR)
John Brown U (AR)
Le Moyne Coll (NY)
Lenoir-Rhyne Coll (NC)
Liberty U (VA)
Lipscomb U (TN)
Maryville Coll (TN)
McGill U (QC, Canada)
Mercy Coll (NY)
Murray State U (KY)
Niagara U (NY)
Northern Arizona U (AZ)
Northwestern Coll (MN)
Nyack Coll (NY)
Ohio U (OH)
Oklahoma Christian U (OK)
Oklahoma Wesleyan U (OK)
Queens Coll of the City U of New York (NY)
Simmons Coll (MA)
Tarleton State U (TX)
Union U (TN)
The U of Arizona (AZ)
The U of British Columbia (BC, Canada)
U of Delaware (DE)
The U of Findlay (OH)
U of Hawaii at Manoa (HI)
The U of Iowa (IA)
The U of Montana (MT)
U of Nebraska–Lincoln (NE)
U of New Brunswick Fredericton (NB, Canada)
U of Northern Iowa (IA)
U of Puerto Rico at Humacao (PR)
U of Victoria (BC, Canada)
U of Wisconsin–Oshkosh (WI)
Washington State U (WA)
Wright State U (OH)
York U (ON, Canada)

ENGLISH COMPOSITION

Bard Coll at Simon's Rock (MA)
Baylor U (TX)
Bennington Coll (VT)
Bethel U (MN)
Brigham Young U (UT)
DePauw U (IN)
Eastern Michigan U (MI)
Ferris State U (MI)
Florida Southern Coll (FL)
Georgia Southern U (GA)
Gettysburg Coll (PA)
Indiana U–Purdue U Fort Wayne (IN)
Jamestown Coll (ND)
La Roche Coll (PA)
Marian Coll of Fond du Lac (WI)
Metropolitan State U (MN)
Miami U Hamilton (OH)
Oral Roberts U (OK)
St. Edward's U (TX)
U of Central Arkansas (AR)
U of Colorado Denver (CO)
U of Evansville (IN)
U of Great Falls (MT)
U of Illinois at Urbana–Champaign (IL)
U of Michigan–Flint (MI)
U of Nevada, Reno (NV)
The U of Texas at Austin (TX)
Wartburg Coll (IA)
Western Michigan U (MI)
William Woods U (MO)

ENGLISH/FRENCH AS A SECOND/FOREIGN LANGUAGE (TEACHING) RELATED

Western Michigan U (MI)

ENGLISH LANGUAGE AND LITERATURE RELATED

Burlington Coll (VT)
Columbia Coll (SC)
Dakota State U (SD)
Doane Coll (NE)
Drexel U (PA)
Duquesne U (PA)
Emmanuel Coll (MA)
Ferris State U (MI)
Fort Lewis Coll (CO)
Hastings Coll (NE)
Hofstra U (NY)
Milligan Coll (TN)
Moravian Coll (PA)
Old Dominion U (VA)
Patrick Henry Coll (VA)
Point Loma Nazarene U (CA)
St. Gregory's U, Shawnee (OK)
Saint Mary-of-the-Woods Coll (IN)
Saint Mary's Coll of California (CA)
Sarah Lawrence Coll (NY)
Skidmore Coll (NY)
Southeastern U (FL)
Spring Hill Coll (AL)
U of Alaska Southeast (AK)
U of Chicago (IL)
U of Great Falls (MT)
The U of Iowa (IA)
The U of Maine at Augusta (ME)
U of Nevada, Reno (NV)
U of Oklahoma (OK)
U of Pennsylvania (PA)
The U of Western Ontario (ON, Canada)
The U of Winnipeg (MB, Canada)
Viterbo U (WI)
Washington U in St. Louis (MO)
Webster U (MO)
Western Kentucky U (KY)

ENGLISH/LANGUAGE ARTS TEACHER EDUCATION

Abilene Christian U (TX)
Alice Lloyd Coll (KY)
Alma Coll (MI)
Alvernia Coll (PA)
Anderson U (IN)
Anderson U (SC)
Anna Maria Coll (MA)
Appalachian State U (NC)
Aquinas Coll (MI)
Arkansas State U (AR)
Arlington Baptist Coll (TX)
Assumption Coll (MA)
Auburn U (AL)
Averett U (VA)
Barry U (FL)
Baylor U (TX)
Bethany Coll (KS)
Bethel U (MN)
Bethune-Cookman U (FL)
Bishop's U (QC, Canada)
Bluefield Coll (VA)
Bob Jones U (SC)
Boston U (MA)
Bowling Green State U (OH)
Brewton-Parker Coll (GA)
Bridgewater Coll (VA)
Bridgewater State Coll (MA)
Brigham Young U (UT)
Bryan Coll (TN)
Buffalo State Coll, State U of New York (NY)
Cabrini Coll (PA)
California State U, Chico (CA)
California State U, Long Beach (CA)
Calumet Coll of Saint Joseph (IN)
Capital U (OH)
Carroll Coll (WI)
The Catholic U of America (DC)
Cedarville U (OH)
Centenary Coll of Louisiana (LA)
Central Michigan U (MI)
Central Washington U (WA)
Christian Brothers U (TN)
Clearwater Christian Coll (FL)
Coker Coll (SC)
Colby-Sawyer Coll (NH)
The Coll at Brockport, State U of New York (NY)
The Coll of New Jersey (NJ)
The Coll of Saint Rose (NY)
Coll of the Ozarks (MO)
Colorado State U (CO)
Columbus State U (GA)
Concordia Coll (MN)
Concordia U (MI)
Concordia U (OR)
Concordia U Chicago (IL)
Concordia U, Nebraska (NE)
Cornerstone U (MI)
Covenant Coll (GA)
Crown Coll (MN)
Culver-Stockton Coll (MO)
Daemen Coll (NY)
Dakota State U (SD)
Dakota Wesleyan U (SD)
Dana Coll (NE)
Delta State U (MS)
DePaul U (IL)
Dillard U (LA)
Dominican Coll (NY)
Dowling Coll (NY)
Duquesne U (PA)
East Carolina U (NC)
East Central U (OK)
Eastern Mennonite U (VA)
Eastern Michigan U (MI)
East Texas Baptist U (TX)
Emmanuel Coll (GA)
Faith Baptist Bible Coll and Theological Sem (IA)
Fayetteville State U (NC)
Ferris State U (MI)
Fitchburg State Coll (MA)
Florida Atlantic U (FL)
Florida Intl U (FL)
Florida State U (FL)
Fort Lewis Coll (CO)
Franklin Coll (IN)
Freed-Hardeman U (TN)
Gardner-Webb U (NC)
Glenville State Coll (WV)
Grace Coll (IN)
Grambling State U (LA)
Grand Canyon U (AZ)
Greensboro Coll (NC)
Greenville Coll (IL)
Hannibal-LaGrange Coll (MO)
Harding U (AR)
Hardin-Simmons U (TX)
Hastings Coll (NE)
Hofstra U (NY)
Hope Coll (MI)
Hope Intl U (CA)
Houston Baptist U (TX)
Howard Payne U (TX)
Indiana U Bloomington (IN)
Indiana U Northwest (IN)
Indiana U–Purdue U Fort Wayne (IN)
Indiana U–Purdue U Indianapolis (IN)
Indiana U South Bend (IN)
Indiana U Southeast (IN)
Indiana Wesleyan U (IN)
Iona Coll (NY)
Ithaca Coll (NY)
Jamestown Coll (ND)
John Brown U (AR)
Johnson State Coll (VT)
Judson Coll (AL)
Juniata Coll (PA)
Keene State Coll (NH)
Kennesaw State U (GA)
Kent State U (OH)
Kentucky Christian U (KY)
Kentucky Wesleyan Coll (KY)
Keuka Coll (NY)
King Coll (TN)
Kutztown U of Pennsylvania (PA)
Lambuth U (TN)
La Roche Coll (PA)
Le Moyne Coll (NY)
LeMoyne-Owen Coll (TN)
Lenoir-Rhyne Coll (NC)
Lewis-Clark State Coll (ID)
Liberty U (VA)
Limestone Coll (SC)
Lincoln U (MO)
Lincoln U (PA)
Lipscomb U (TN)
Malone Coll (OH)
Manhattanville Coll (NY)
Mansfield U of Pennsylvania (PA)
Maranatha Baptist Bible Coll (WI)
Marian Coll of Fond du Lac (WI)
Marist Coll (NY)
Marquette U (WI)
Maryville Coll (TN)
Maryville U of Saint Louis (MO)
Marywood U (PA)
Mayville State U (ND)
McGill U (QC, Canada)
McKendree U (IL)
McNeese State U (LA)
Mercy Coll (NY)
Mercyhurst Coll (PA)
Messiah Coll (PA)
Metropolitan State U (MN)
Miami U (OH)
Miami U Hamilton (OH)
Michigan Technological U (MI)
MidAmerica Nazarene U (KS)
Miles Coll (AL)
Millersville U of Pennsylvania (PA)
Millikin U (IL)
Minot State U (ND)
Misericordia U (PA)
Mississippi Valley State U (MS)
Missouri State U (MO)
Molloy Coll (NY)
Montana State U–Billings (MT)
Morris Coll (SC)
Mount Marty Coll (SD)
Mount Mary Coll (WI)
Mount Vernon Nazarene U (OH)
Murray State U (KY)
Nazareth Coll of Rochester (NY)
Nebraska Wesleyan U (NE)
New York U (NY)
Nicholls State U (LA)
North Carolina Central U (NC)
North Carolina State U (NC)
North Dakota State U (ND)
Northeastern State U (OK)
Northern Arizona U (AZ)
Northern Michigan U (MI)
North Georgia Coll & State U (GA)
North Greenville U (SC)
Northwestern Coll (MN)
Northwestern Oklahoma State U (OK)
Northwestern State U of Louisiana (LA)
Northwest Nazarene U (ID)
Ohio Northern U (OH)
Oklahoma Christian U (OK)
Old Dominion U (VA)
Oral Roberts U (OK)
Pace U (NY)
Paine Coll (GA)
Philadelphia Biblical U (PA)
Pillsbury Baptist Bible Coll (MN)
Pittsburg State U (KS)
Point Park U (PA)
Prescott Coll (AZ)
Queens U of Charlotte (NC)
Rhode Island Coll (RI)

Roberts Wesleyan Coll (NY)
Rochester Coll (MI)
Sacred Heart U (CT)
Saginaw Valley State U (MI)
St. Ambrose U (IA)
Saint Francis U (PA)
St. Gregory's U, Shawnee (OK)
St. John's U (NY)
St. Joseph's Coll, Suffolk Campus (NY)
Saint Joseph's U (PA)
Saint Mary's U of Minnesota (MN)
Saint Xavier U (IL)
Salve Regina U (RI)
Samford U (AL)
Sam Houston State U (TX)
Schreiner U (TX)
Seattle Pacific U (WA)
Seton Hill U (PA)
Shawnee State U (OH)
Shaw U (NC)
Simpson U (CA)
Southeastern Louisiana U (LA)
Southeastern Oklahoma State U (OK)
Southeastern U (FL)
Southeast Missouri State U (MO)
Southern Adventist U (TN)
Southern Arkansas U–Magnolia (AR)
Southern New Hampshire U (NH)
Southern U and Ag and Mech Coll (LA)
Southwest Baptist U (MO)
Southwestern Oklahoma State U (OK)
Southwest Minnesota State U (MN)
State U of New York at Plattsburgh (NY)
State U of New York Coll at Oneonta (NY)
State U of New York Coll at Potsdam (NY)
Syracuse U (NY)
Temple U (PA)
Texas A&M Intl U (TX)
Texas Christian U (TX)
Toccoa Falls Coll (GA)
Trevecca Nazarene U (TN)
Trinity Christian Coll (IL)
Tusculum Coll (TN)
Union Coll (NE)
The U of Akron (OH)
The U of Arizona (AZ)
U of Arkansas at Fort Smith (AR)
U of Central Arkansas (AR)
U of Central Florida (FL)
U of Central Oklahoma (OK)
U of Delaware (DE)
U of Evansville (IN)
U of Georgia (GA)
U of Great Falls (MT)
U of Illinois at Chicago (IL)
U of Illinois at Urbana–Champaign (IL)
U of Indianapolis (IN)
U of Louisiana at Monroe (LA)
U of Maine (ME)
U of Maine at Farmington (ME)
U of Maine at Fort Kent (ME)
U of Maine at Machias (ME)
U of Mary (ND)
U of Mary Hardin-Baylor (TX)
U of Maryland, Coll Park (MD)
U of Michigan–Flint (MI)
U of Minnesota, Twin Cities Campus (MN)
U of Mississippi (MS)
U of Missouri–St. Louis (MO)
The U of Montana–Western (MT)
U of Nebraska–Lincoln (NE)
U of Nevada, Reno (NV)
U of New Hampshire (NH)
U of New Orleans (LA)
The U of North Carolina at Charlotte (NC)
The U of North Carolina at Greensboro (NC)
The U of North Carolina at Pembroke (NC)
The U of North Carolina Wilmington (NC)
U of Oklahoma (OK)
U of Pittsburgh at Johnstown (PA)
U of Puerto Rico at Utuado (PR)
U of Puerto Rico, Cayey U Coll (PR)
U of Regina (SK, Canada)
U of Rio Grande (OH)
U of St. Francis (IL)
U of Saint Francis (IN)
U of St. Thomas (MN)
The U of South Dakota (SD)
U of South Florida (FL)
The U of Tampa (FL)
The U of Tennessee at Martin (TN)
U of the Ozarks (AR)
The U of Toledo (OH)
U of Vermont (VT)
The U of Western Ontario (ON, Canada)
U of Windsor (ON, Canada)
U of Wisconsin–Superior (WI)
Ursuline Coll (OH)
Utah Valley State Coll (UT)
Utica Coll (NY)
Valley City State U (ND)
Valparaiso U (IN)
Virginia Intermont Coll (VA)
Viterbo U (WI)
Washington State U (WA)
Washington U in St. Louis (MO)
Waynesburg U (PA)
Wayne State Coll (NE)
Wayne State U (MI)
Weber State U (UT)
Western Carolina U (NC)
Western Michigan U (MI)
Western State Coll of Colorado (CO)
Westmont Coll (CA)
West Virginia Wesleyan Coll (WV)
Wheeling Jesuit U (WV)
Widener U (PA)
William Jewell Coll (MO)
William Woods U (MO)
Wright State U (OH)
York Coll (NE)
York Coll of Pennsylvania (PA)
York U (ON, Canada)
Youngstown State U (OH)

ENGLISH LITERATURE (BRITISH AND COMMONWEALTH)
The American U of Athens (Greece)
Bennington Coll (VT)
Concordia U (QC, Canada)
Gannon U (PA)
Hofstra U (NY)
Hunter Coll of the City U of New York (NY)
Indiana U–Purdue U Fort Wayne (IN)
Marian Coll of Fond du Lac (WI)
St. Lawrence U (NY)
Saint Mary's Coll (IN)
Sarah Lawrence Coll (NY)
Syracuse U (NY)
U of New Hampshire (NH)
U of Pittsburgh (PA)
U of Southern California (CA)
Washington U in St. Louis (MO)

ENTOMOLOGY
Colorado State U (CO)
Cornell U (NY)
Florida Ag and Mech U (FL)
Harvard U (MA)
Iowa State U of Science and Technology (IA)
Memorial U of Newfoundland (NL, Canada)
Michigan State U (MI)
Oklahoma State U (OK)
Oregon State U (OR)
Purdue U (IN)
State U of New York Coll of Environmental Science and Forestry (NY)
Texas A&M U (TX)
U of California, Davis (CA)
U of California, Riverside (CA)
U of Delaware (DE)
U of Florida (FL)
U of Georgia (GA)
U of Hawaii at Manoa (HI)
U of Idaho (ID)
U of Illinois at Urbana–Champaign (IL)
U of Nebraska–Lincoln (NE)
U of New Brunswick Fredericton (NB, Canada)
U of Wisconsin–Madison (WI)
Utah State U (UT)
Washington State U (WA)

ENTREPRENEURIAL AND SMALL BUSINESS RELATED
Babson Coll (MA)
Fairleigh Dickinson U, Metropolitan Campus (NJ)
Florida State U (FL)
Pennsylvania Coll of Technology (PA)
Saint Leo U (FL)
Stetson U (FL)
Warren Wilson Coll (NC)

ENTREPRENEURSHIP
Anderson U (IN)
Babson Coll (MA)
Baylor U (TX)
Belmont U (TN)
Bradley U (IL)
Brigham Young U (UT)
California State U, Fullerton (CA)
Canisius Coll (NY)
Central Michigan U (MI)
Clarkson U (NY)
Duquesne U (PA)
East Central U (OK)
Eastern Michigan U (MI)
Ferris State U (MI)
Grove City Coll (PA)
Hawai'i Pacific U (HI)
HEC Montreal (QC, Canada)
Hofstra U (NY)
Houston Baptist U (TX)
Inter American U of Puerto Rico, Bayamón Campus (PR)
Iowa State U of Science and Technology (IA)
Jackson State U (MS)
Kwantlen U Coll (BC, Canada)
Lees-McRae Coll (NC)
McGill U (QC, Canada)
Messiah Coll (PA)
Millikin U (IL)
Missouri State U (MO)
National U (CA)
Newman U (KS)
Northeastern State U (OK)
Northeastern U (MA)
Northern Michigan U (MI)
Pace U (NY)
Palm Beach Atlantic U (FL)
Quinnipiac U (CT)
Rider U (NJ)
St. Edward's U (TX)
Seton Hill U (PA)
Shaw U (NC)
Southern Polytechnic State U (GA)
State U of New York at Plattsburgh (NY)
Susquehanna U (PA)
Syracuse U (NY)
Temple U (PA)
Tri-State U (IN)
Union Coll (NE)
The U of Arizona (AZ)
The U of British Columbia–Okanagan (BC, Canada)
U of Illinois at Chicago (IL)
U of Illinois at Urbana–Champaign (IL)
U of Indianapolis (IN)
The U of Iowa (IA)
U of Maine at Machias (ME)
U of Miami (FL)
U of Nevada, Las Vegas (NV)
U of Nevada, Reno (NV)
U of New Orleans (LA)
U of North Dakota (ND)
U of Oklahoma (OK)
U of Pittsburgh at Bradford (PA)
U of St. Thomas (MN)
The U of Scranton (PA)
U of Southern Indiana (IN)
The U of Tampa (FL)
The U of Texas at San Antonio (TX)
The U of Toledo (OH)
U of Vermont (VT)
The U of Western Ontario (ON, Canada)
Washington State U (WA)
Washington U in St. Louis (MO)
Western Carolina U (NC)
Western State Coll of Colorado (CO)
Wichita State U (KS)
Wilkes U (PA)
Xavier U (OH)
York Coll of Pennsylvania (PA)
York U (ON, Canada)

ENVIRONMENTAL BIOLOGY
Averett U (VA)
Barnard Coll (NY)
Beloit Coll (WI)
Bennington Coll (VT)
Bridgewater State Coll (MA)
California Polytechnic State U, San Luis Obispo (CA)
California State U, Monterey Bay (CA)
Carlow U (PA)
Cedar Crest Coll (PA)
Cedarville U (OH)
Colgate U (NY)
The Coll at Brockport, State U of New York (NY)
Coll of the Atlantic (ME)
Cornerstone U (MI)
East Stroudsburg U of Pennsylvania (PA)
Fitchburg State Coll (MA)
Florida State U (FL)
Fort Lewis Coll (CO)
Greenville Coll (IL)
Harvard U (MA)
Heidelberg Coll (OH)
Houghton Coll (NY)
Humboldt State U (CA)
Inter American U of Puerto Rico, Bayamón Campus (PR)
Iona Coll (NY)
Iowa Wesleyan Coll (IA)
Jacksonville State U (AL)
Keystone Coll (PA)
Lakehead U (ON, Canada)
Marlboro Coll (VT)
The Master's Coll and Sem (CA)
McGill U (QC, Canada)
Memorial U of Newfoundland (NL, Canada)
Michigan State U (MI)
Midway Coll (KY)
Minnesota State U Mankato (MN)
Northland Coll (WI)
Northwestern Coll (IA)
Ohio U (OH)
Oregon State U (OR)
Otterbein Coll (OH)
Philadelphia U (PA)
Plymouth State U (NH)
Sacred Heart U (CT)
St. Cloud State U (MN)
Saint Mary's U of Minnesota (MN)
Simpson Coll (IA)
State U of New York Coll of Environmental Science and Forestry (NY)
Sterling Coll (VT)
Suffolk U (MA)
Tabor Coll (KS)
Taylor U (IN)
Thompson Rivers U (BC, Canada)
Tulane U (LA)
U of Arkansas at Pine Bluff (AR)
The U of British Columbia (BC, Canada)
U of Charleston (WV)
U of Dayton (OH)
U of La Verne (CA)
U of Pittsburgh at Johnstown (PA)
U of Regina (SK, Canada)
The U of Tampa (FL)
The U of Tennessee at Martin (TN)
U of Windsor (ON, Canada)
Western State Coll of Colorado (CO)
Western Washington U (WA)
Westfield State Coll (MA)
Wingate U (NC)
Winona State U (MN)
York U (ON, Canada)

ENVIRONMENTAL CONTROL TECHNOLOGIES RELATED
Davis & Elkins Coll (WV)
Florida Intl U (FL)
Inter American U of Puerto Rico, Bayamón Campus (PR)
New York Inst of Technology (NY)
U of Puerto Rico at Utuado (PR)

ENVIRONMENTAL DESIGN/ ARCHITECTURE
The American U of Athens (Greece)
Auburn U (AL)
Ball State U (IN)
Bowling Green State U (OH)
Coll of the Atlantic (ME)
Cornell U (NY)
Florida Intl U (FL)
Hampshire Coll (MA)
Harvard U (MA)
Kent State U (OH)
Lawrence Technological U (MI)
Miami U (OH)
Montana State U (MT)
North Carolina State U (NC)
North Dakota State U (ND)
Otis Coll of Art and Design (CA)
Prescott Coll (AZ)
Rutgers, The State U of New Jersey, New Brunswick (NJ)
Stanford U (CA)
State U of New York Coll of Environmental Science and Forestry (NY)
Sterling Coll (VT)
Texas A&M U (TX)
U at Buffalo, the State U of New York (NY)
U of California, Irvine (CA)
U of Colorado at Boulder (CO)
U of Houston (TX)
U of Massachusetts Amherst (MA)
U of New Mexico (NM)
U of Oklahoma (OK)
U of Pennsylvania (PA)

ENVIRONMENTAL EDUCATION
Coll of the Atlantic (ME)
Johnson State Coll (VT)
Northland Coll (WI)
Prescott Coll (AZ)
Sonoma State U (CA)
State U of New York Coll of Environmental Science and Forestry (NY)
U of Maine at Machias (ME)
The U of Montana (MT)
Western Washington U (WA)
York U (ON, Canada)

ENVIRONMENTAL ENGINEERING TECHNOLOGY
British Columbia Inst of Technology (BC, Canada)
California State U, Long Beach (CA)
City Coll of the City U of New York (NY)
East Carolina U (NC)
Eastern Kentucky U (KY)
Lake Superior State U (MI)
Middle Tennessee State U (TN)
Murray State U (KY)
Shawnee State U (OH)
Temple U (PA)
The U of British Columbia (BC, Canada)
U of Delaware (DE)
U of Wisconsin–Whitewater (WI)
Wright State U (OH)

ENVIRONMENTAL/ ENVIRONMENTAL HEALTH ENGINEERING
Bradley U (IL)
California Inst of Technology (CA)
California Polytechnic State U, San Luis Obispo (CA)
Christian Brothers U (TN)
Clarkson U (NY)
Colorado School of Mines (CO)
Colorado State U (CO)
Cornell U (NY)
Drexel U (PA)
Florida Gulf Coast U (FL)
Florida State U (FL)
Gannon U (PA)
The George Washington U (DC)
Georgia Inst of Technology (GA)
Harvard U (MA)
Hofstra U (NY)
Humboldt State U (CA)
Illinois Inst of Technology (IL)
The Johns Hopkins U (MD)
Lafayette Coll (PA)
Lehigh U (PA)
Louisiana State U and Ag and Mech Coll (LA)
Marquette U (WI)
Massachusetts Inst of Technology (MA)
Massachusetts Maritime Acad (MA)
Michigan Technological U (MI)
Missouri U of Science and Technology (MO)
Montana Tech of The U of Montana (MT)
New Jersey Inst of Technology (NJ)
New Mexico Inst of Mining and Technology (NM)
North Carolina State U (NC)
Northeastern State U (OK)
Northern Arizona U (AZ)
Northwestern U (IL)
Old Dominion U (VA)
Oregon State U (OR)
Penn State Abington (PA)
Penn State Altoona (PA)
Penn State Berks (PA)
Penn State Erie, The Behrend Coll (PA)
Penn State Harrisburg (PA)
Penn State U Park (PA)
Polytechnic U of Puerto Rico (PR)
Rensselaer Polytechnic Inst (NY)
Rice U (TX)
San Diego State U (CA)
Seattle U (WA)
South Dakota School of Mines and Technology (SD)
South Dakota State U (SD)
Southern Methodist U (TX)
Stanford U (CA)
State U of New York Coll of Environmental Science and Forestry (NY)
Syracuse U (NY)
Texas Tech U (TX)
Tufts U (MA)
Tulane U (LA)
United States Air Force Acad (CO)

MAJORS AND MORE

U at Buffalo, the State U of New York (NY)
U of California, Berkeley (CA)
U of California, Irvine (CA)
U of California, Riverside (CA)
U of Central Florida (FL)
U of Colorado at Boulder (CO)
U of Connecticut (CT)
U of Delaware (DE)
U of Florida (FL)
U of Hartford (CT)
U of Illinois at Urbana–Champaign (IL)
U of Miami (FL)
U of Michigan (MI)
U of Nevada, Reno (NV)
U of New Hampshire (NH)
U of North Dakota (ND)
U of Notre Dame (IN)
U of Oklahoma (OK)
U of Pennsylvania (PA)
U of Regina (SK, Canada)
U of Southern California (CA)
U of Vermont (VT)
The U of Western Ontario (ON, Canada)
U of Windsor (ON, Canada)
U of Wisconsin–Madison (WI)
U of Wisconsin–Platteville (WI)
Utah State U (UT)
Wentworth Inst of Technology (MA)
Wilkes U (PA)
Worcester Polytechnic Inst (MA)
Yale U (CT)

ENVIRONMENTAL HEALTH

Boise State U (ID)
Bowling Green State U (OH)
British Columbia Inst of Technology (BC, Canada)
Clarkson U (NY)
Colorado State U (CO)
East Carolina U (NC)
East Central U (OK)
Eastern Kentucky U (KY)
East Tennessee State U (TN)
Illinois State U (IL)
Indiana State U (IN)
Indiana U of Pennsylvania (PA)
Iowa Wesleyan Coll (IA)
Oakland U (MI)
Old Dominion U (VA)
Oregon State U (OR)
Salisbury U (MD)
Texas Southern U (TX)
U of Georgia (GA)
U of Illinois at Urbana–Champaign (IL)
The U of North Carolina at Chapel Hill (NC)
U of Regina (SK, Canada)
U of Southern Maine (ME)
U of Wisconsin–Eau Claire (WI)
Western Carolina U (NC)
Western Kentucky U (KY)
Wright State U (OH)
York Coll of the City U of New York (NY)

ENVIRONMENTAL PSYCHOLOGY

Embry-Riddle Aeronautical U (FL)

ENVIRONMENTAL SCIENCE

Abilene Christian U (TX)
Adrian Coll (MI)
Alaska Pacific U (AK)
Albright Coll (PA)
Alderson-Broaddus Coll (WV)
Allegheny Coll (PA)
Anna Maria Coll (MA)
Aquinas Coll (MI)
Assumption Coll (MA)
Auburn U (AL)
Averett U (VA)
Barnard Coll (NY)
Baylor U (TX)
Berry Coll (GA)
Bethel U (MN)
Blackburn Coll (IL)
Bradley U (IL)
Brevard Coll (NC)
Bridgewater Coll (VA)
Brigham Young U (UT)
Brown U (RI)
California State U, Fresno (CA)
California State U, Long Beach (CA)
Canisius Coll (NY)
Capital U (OH)
Carlow U (PA)
Carroll Coll (WI)
Central Michigan U (MI)
Chatham U (PA)
Claflin U (SC)
Colby Coll (ME)
The Colorado Coll (CO)
Concordia U (QC, Canada)
Cornell U (NY)
Delta State U (MS)
DePaul U (IL)
DeSales U (PA)
Dickinson Coll (PA)
Drake U (IA)
Duquesne U (PA)
East Central U (OK)
Eastern Connecticut State U (CT)
Eastern Mennonite U (VA)
Eastern New Mexico U (NM)
Edinboro U of Pennsylvania (PA)
The Evergreen State Coll (WA)
Fairleigh Dickinson U, Metropolitan Campus (NJ)
Florida Ag and Mech U (FL)
Florida Gulf Coast U (FL)
Florida Inst of Technology (FL)
Franklin & Marshall Coll (PA)
Gannon U (PA)
Georgia Coll & State U (GA)
Gettysburg Coll (PA)
Hardin-Simmons U (TX)
Hartwick Coll (NY)
Hawai'i Pacific U (HI)
Heidelberg Coll (OH)
Hood Coll (MD)
Hunter Coll of the City U of New York (NY)
Idaho State U (ID)
Indiana U Bloomington (IN)
Indiana U–Purdue U Indianapolis (IN)
Iowa State U of Science and Technology (IA)
John Brown U (AR)
Juniata Coll (PA)
Keene State Coll (NH)
Keuka Coll (NY)
Keystone Coll (PA)
King's Coll (PA)
Kutztown U of Pennsylvania (PA)
Lambuth U (TN)
Lander U (SC)
Lehigh U (PA)
Lincoln U (PA)
Lindenwood U (MO)
Louisiana State U and Ag and Mech Coll (LA)
Lourdes Coll (OH)
Madonna U (MI)
Marietta Coll (OH)
Marshall U (WV)
Marylhurst U (OR)
Maryville U of Saint Louis (MO)
Marywood U (PA)
Massachusetts Coll of Pharmacy and Health Sciences (MA)
Massachusetts Maritime Acad (MA)
McDaniel Coll (MD)
McGill U (QC, Canada)
McNeese State U (LA)
Mercer U (GA)
Meredith Coll (NC)
Mesa State Coll (CO)
Messiah Coll (PA)
Miami U Hamilton (OH)
Michigan State U (MI)
Michigan Technological U (MI)
Midwestern State U (TX)
Miles Coll (AL)
Mills Coll (CA)
Monmouth Coll (IL)
Montana State U (MT)
Muhlenberg Coll (PA)
National U (CA)
Nazareth Coll of Rochester (NY)
New England Coll (NH)
North Carolina Central U (NC)
North Carolina State U (NC)
Northeastern State U (OK)
Northern Michigan U (MI)
Northwestern U (IL)
Oklahoma State U (OK)
Otterbein Coll (OH)
Paine Coll (GA)
Pfeiffer U (NC)
Piedmont Coll (GA)
Pitzer Coll (CA)
Point Park U (PA)
Purdue U (IN)
Queens Coll of the City U of New York (NY)
Queen's U at Kingston (ON, Canada)
Queens U of Charlotte (NC)
Ramapo Coll of New Jersey (NJ)
Roanoke Coll (VA)
Robert Morris U (PA)
Rochester Inst of Technology (NY)
Roger Williams U (RI)
Saint Francis U (PA)
Saint Joseph Coll (CT)
Saint Leo U (FL)
Saint Louis U (MO)
Saint Michael's Coll (VT)
St. Norbert Coll (WI)
Saint Vincent Coll (PA)
Samford U (AL)
San Diego State U (CA)
Santa Clara U (CA)
Scripps Coll (CA)
Siena Heights U (MI)
Simon Fraser U (BC, Canada)
Slippery Rock U of Pennsylvania (PA)
Southeastern Oklahoma State U (OK)
Southwest Minnesota State U (MN)
Stetson U (FL)
Sweet Briar Coll (VA)
Tarleton State U (TX)
Texas A&M U (TX)
Texas A&M U–Commerce (TX)
Texas Christian U (TX)
Texas Southern U (TX)
Texas State U-San Marcos (TX)
Thomas Edison State Coll (NJ)
Trinity Coll (CT)
Troy U (AL)
U at Albany, State U of New York (NY)
The U of Alabama (AL)
The U of Arizona (AZ)
U of Arkansas (AR)
The U of British Columbia–Okanagan (BC, Canada)
U of California, Berkeley (CA)
U of California, Los Angeles (CA)
U of Charleston (WV)
U of Denver (CO)
U of Evansville (IN)
U of Florida (FL)
U of Georgia (GA)
U of Hawaii at Manoa (HI)
U of Houston–Clear Lake (TX)
U of Idaho (ID)
U of Illinois at Urbana–Champaign (IL)
The U of Iowa (IA)
U of Lethbridge (AB, Canada)
U of Maine (ME)
U of Maryland, Baltimore County (MD)
U of Massachusetts Amherst (MA)
U of Massachusetts Lowell (MA)
U of Michigan–Dearborn (MI)
U of Michigan–Flint (MI)
U of New England (ME)
U of New Hampshire (NH)
U of New Mexico (NM)
The U of North Carolina at Chapel Hill (NC)
The U of North Carolina at Pembroke (NC)
The U of North Carolina Wilmington (NC)
U of Northern Iowa (IA)
U of Notre Dame (IN)
U of Oklahoma (OK)
U of Oregon (OR)
U of Ottawa (ON, Canada)
U of Regina (SK, Canada)
U of Rochester (NY)
U of St. Francis (IL)
The U of Tampa (FL)
The U of Texas at Brownsville (TX)
The U of Texas at San Antonio (TX)
U of the Incarnate Word (TX)
U of the Sciences in Philadelphia (PA)
U of Vermont (VT)
U of Virginia (VA)
U of Washington, Bothell (WA)
U of Washington, Tacoma (WA)
The U of Western Ontario (ON, Canada)
U of West Georgia (GA)
U of Windsor (ON, Canada)
U of Wisconsin–Green Bay (WI)
Valparaiso U (IN)
Vassar Coll (NY)
Washington State U (WA)
Wayne State U (MI)
Wesleyan Coll (GA)
Western Carolina U (NC)
Western Washington U (WA)
Westminster Coll (MO)
West Texas A&M U (TX)
West Virginia Wesleyan Coll (WV)
Willamette U (OR)
Wright State U (OH)
York U (ON, Canada)

ENVIRONMENTAL STUDIES

Acadia U (NS, Canada)
Adrian Coll (MI)
Albion Coll (MI)
Alfred U (NY)
Allegheny Coll (PA)
American Public U System (WV)
American U (DC)
Aquinas Coll (MI)
Ashland U (OH)
Auburn U (AL)
Augustana Coll (IL)
Austin Peay State U (TN)
Ball State U (IN)
Bard Coll (NY)
Bard Coll at Simon's Rock (MA)
Barton Coll (NC)
Bates Coll (ME)
Baylor U (TX)
Beloit Coll (WI)
Bemidji State U (MN)
Benedictine U (IL)
Bennington Coll (VT)
Bethany Coll (WV)
Bishop's U (QC, Canada)
Boise State U (ID)
Boston U (MA)
Bowdoin Coll (ME)
Brown U (RI)
Bucknell U (PA)
California State U, East Bay (CA)
California State U, Monterey Bay (CA)
California State U, Sacramento (CA)
California State U, San Bernardino (CA)
Calvin Coll (MI)
Case Western Reserve U (OH)
Castleton State Coll (VT)
Catawba Coll (NC)
Centenary Coll of Louisiana (LA)
Central Coll (IA)
Central Michigan U (MI)
Chaminade U of Honolulu (HI)
Chatham U (PA)
Chestnut Hill Coll (PA)
Christopher Newport U (VA)
City Coll of the City U of New York (NY)
Claremont McKenna Coll (CA)
Clarion U of Pennsylvania (PA)
Clarkson U (NY)
Cleveland State U (OH)
Colby Coll (ME)
Colby-Sawyer Coll (NH)
Colgate U (NY)
The Coll at Brockport, State U of New York (NY)
The Coll of New Rochelle (NY)
Coll of Saint Benedict (MN)
The Coll of Saint Rose (NY)
Coll of the Atlantic (ME)
Coll of the Holy Cross (MA)
Coll of the Southwest (NM)
The Coll of William and Mary (VA)
Columbia Southern U (AL)
Concordia Coll (MN)
Concordia U (OR)
Concordia U Chicago (IL)
Concordia U Texas (TX)
Connecticut Coll (CT)
Cornell Coll (IA)
Creighton U (NE)
Curry Coll (MA)
Dartmouth Coll (NH)
Defiance Coll (OH)
Denison U (OH)
DePauw U (IN)
DeSales U (PA)
Dickinson Coll (PA)
Doane Coll (NE)
Dominican U (IL)
Dordt Coll (IA)
Drake U (IA)
Drexel U (PA)
Drury U (MO)
Duke U (NC)
Earlham Coll (IN)
East Central U (OK)
Eastern Kentucky U (KY)
Eckerd Coll (FL)
Elizabethtown Coll (PA)
Elon U (NC)
Emmanuel Coll (MA)
Emory & Henry Coll (VA)
Endicott Coll (MA)
The Evergreen State Coll (WA)
Felician Coll (NJ)
Ferrum Coll (VA)
Florida Intl U (FL)
Florida Southern Coll (FL)
Florida State U (FL)
Fort Lewis Coll (CO)
Franklin & Marshall Coll (PA)
Frostburg State U (MD)
Furman U (SC)
The George Washington U (DC)
Gettysburg Coll (PA)
Green Mountain Coll (VT)
Guilford Coll (NC)
Gustavus Adolphus Coll (MN)
Hamline U (MN)
Hampshire Coll (MA)
Hampton U (VA)
Harvard U (MA)
Hawai'i Pacific U (HI)
Heidelberg Coll (OH)
Hendrix Coll (AR)
Hobart and William Smith Colls (NY)
Hofstra U (NY)
Hope Coll (MI)
Humboldt State U (CA)
Illinois Coll (IL)
Illinois Wesleyan U (IL)
Immaculata U (PA)
Inter American U of Puerto Rico, San Germán Campus (PR)
Iowa State U of Science and Technology (IA)
Ithaca Coll (NY)
Jacksonville U (FL)
John Brown U (AR)
John Carroll U (OH)
The Johns Hopkins U (MD)
Johnson State Coll (VT)
Juniata Coll (PA)
Keene State Coll (NH)
Kentucky Wesleyan Coll (KY)
Kenyon Coll (OH)
Keystone Coll (PA)
King's Coll (PA)
The King's U Coll (AB, Canada)
Knox Coll (IL)
Lake Forest Coll (IL)
Lakehead U (ON, Canada)
Lake Superior State U (MI)
Lambuth U (TN)
La Salle U (PA)
Lawrence U (WI)
Lees-McRae Coll (NC)
Lehigh U (PA)
Lenoir-Rhyne Coll (NC)
Lesley U (MA)
Lewis & Clark Coll (OR)
Lewis U (IL)
Linfield Coll (OR)
Lipscomb U (TN)
Longwood U (VA)
Loyola U Chicago (IL)
Luther Coll (IA)
Lynchburg Coll (VA)
Lyon Coll (AR)
Macalester Coll (MN)
Maharishi U of Management (IA)
Manchester Coll (IN)
Mansfield U of Pennsylvania (PA)
Marietta Coll (OH)
Marist Coll (NY)
Marlboro Coll (VT)
Maryville Coll (TN)
Maryville U of Saint Louis (MO)
Massachusetts Coll of Liberal Arts (MA)
Massachusetts Maritime Acad (MA)
McGill U (QC, Canada)
Memorial U of Newfoundland (NL, Canada)
Mercer U (GA)
Meredith Coll (NC)
Messiah Coll (PA)
Miami U Hamilton (OH)
Michigan State U (MI)
Middlebury Coll (VT)
Midland Lutheran Coll (NE)
Mills Coll (CA)
Minnesota State U Mankato (MN)
Mitchell Coll (CT)
Molloy Coll (NY)
Montana State U (MT)
Montana State U–Billings (MT)
Moravian Coll (PA)
Mountain State U (WV)
Mount Allison U (NB, Canada)
Mount Holyoke Coll (MA)
Mount Olive Coll (NC)
Mount St. Mary's U (MD)
Naropa U (CO)
Nazareth Coll of Rochester (NY)
Neumann Coll (PA)
New Coll of Florida (FL)
New England Coll (NH)
New Mexico Highlands U (NM)
New Mexico Inst of Mining and Technology (NM)
North Carolina State U (NC)
North Carolina Wesleyan Coll (NC)
Northeastern Illinois U (IL)
Northeastern U (MA)
Northern Arizona U (AZ)
Northern State U (SD)
Northland Coll (WI)
Northwestern U (IL)
Norwich U (VT)
Nova Scotia Ag Coll (NS, Canada)
Nova Southeastern U (FL)
Oberlin Coll (OH)
Ohio Northern U (OH)
Ohio Wesleyan U (OH)
Oklahoma State U (OK)
Oregon Inst of Technology (OR)
Oregon State U (OR)
Pace U (NY)
Pacific Lutheran U (WA)
Pacific U (OR)
Paul Smith's Coll (NY)
Penn State Altoona (PA)
Pfeiffer U (NC)
Piedmont Coll (GA)
Pitzer Coll (CA)

MAJORS AND MORE

Pomona Coll (CA)
Portland State U (OR)
Prescott Coll (AZ)
Purchase Coll, State U of New York (NY)
Queens Coll of the City U of New York (NY)
Ramapo Coll of New Jersey (NJ)
Randolph Coll (VA)
Randolph-Macon Coll (VA)
Regis U (CO)
The Richard Stockton Coll of New Jersey (NJ)
Rider U (NJ)
Ripon Coll (WI)
Rollins Coll (FL)
Rowan U (NJ)
Rutgers, The State U of New Jersey, Newark (NJ)
Rutgers, The State U of New Jersey, New Brunswick (NJ)
Saint Francis U (PA)
St. Francis Xavier U (NS, Canada)
Saint John's U (MN)
St. John's U (NY)
Saint Joseph's U (PA)
St. Lawrence U (NY)
St. Norbert Coll (WI)
St. Olaf Coll (MN)
Saint Vincent Coll (PA)
Samford U (AL)
Sam Houston State U (TX)
San Diego State U (CA)
San Francisco State U (CA)
Sarah Lawrence Coll (NY)
Scripps Coll (CA)
Seattle U (WA)
Sewanee: The U of the South (TN)
Shaw U (NC)
Shenandoah U (VA)
Shepherd U (WV)
Shippensburg U of Pennsylvania (PA)
Shorter Coll (GA)
Simmons Coll (MA)
Skidmore Coll (NY)
Slippery Rock U of Pennsylvania (PA)
Sonoma State U (CA)
Southeast Missouri State U (MO)
Southern Methodist U (TX)
Southern New Hampshire U (NH)
Southern Oregon U (OR)
Southern Vermont Coll (VT)
Southwestern U (TX)
Spelman Coll (GA)
Stanford U (CA)
State U of New York at Binghamton (NY)
State U of New York at Fredonia (NY)
State U of New York at New Paltz (NY)
State U of New York at Plattsburgh (NY)
State U of New York Coll at Oneonta (NY)
State U of New York Coll at Potsdam (NY)
State U of New York Coll of Agriculture and Technology at Cobleskill (NY)
State U of New York Coll of Environmental Science and Forestry (NY)
Stephen F. Austin State U (TX)
Sterling Coll (VT)
Stonehill Coll (MA)
Stony Brook U, State U of New York (NY)
Suffolk U (MA)
Sweet Briar Coll (VA)
Taylor U (IN)
Temple U (PA)
Tennessee Wesleyan Coll (TN)
Texas A&M U (TX)
Thiel Coll (PA)
Thomas Edison State Coll (NJ)
Trent U (ON, Canada)
Tri-State U (IN)
Tufts U (MA)
Tulane U (LA)
Tusculum Coll (TN)
Tuskegee U (AL)
The U of Arizona (AZ)
The U of British Columbia (BC, Canada)
U of California, Berkeley (CA)
U of California, Davis (CA)
U of California, Riverside (CA)
U of California, San Diego (CA)
U of California, Santa Barbara (CA)
U of California, Santa Cruz (CA)
U of Central Arkansas (AR)
U of Chicago (IL)
U of Colorado at Boulder (CO)
U of Connecticut (CT)
U of Dayton (OH)
U of Delaware (DE)
U of Evansville (IN)
The U of Findlay (OH)
U of Hawaii at Manoa (HI)
U of Houston (TX)
U of Indianapolis (IN)
The U of Iowa (IA)
U of Kansas (KS)
U of Maine at Farmington (ME)
U of Maine at Fort Kent (ME)
U of Maine at Machias (ME)
U of Maryland, Baltimore County (MD)
U of Maryland Eastern Shore (MD)
U of Maryland U Coll (MD)
U of Mary Washington (VA)
U of Michigan (MI)
U of Michigan–Dearborn (MI)
U of Minnesota, Duluth (MN)
U of Minnesota, Twin Cities Campus (MN)
U of Missouri–Columbia (MO)
The U of Montana (MT)
The U of Montana–Western (MT)
U of Nebraska at Omaha (NE)
U of Nebraska–Lincoln (NE)
U of Nevada, Las Vegas (NV)
U of New England (ME)
U of New Hampshire (NH)
U of New Orleans (LA)
The U of North Carolina at Asheville (NC)
The U of North Carolina at Chapel Hill (NC)
The U of North Carolina Wilmington (NC)
U of Oregon (OR)
U of Ottawa (ON, Canada)
U of Pennsylvania (PA)
U of Pittsburgh at Bradford (PA)
U of Pittsburgh at Johnstown (PA)
U of Portland (OR)
U of Redlands (CA)
U of Regina (SK, Canada)
U of Rhode Island (RI)
U of Richmond (VA)
U of Rochester (NY)
U of Saint Francis (IN)
U of St. Thomas (TX)
U of Southern California (CA)
U of Southern Maine (ME)
U of South Florida (FL)
The U of Tampa (FL)
The U of Tennessee at Chattanooga (TN)
The U of Tennessee at Martin (TN)
The U of Texas of the Permian Basin (TX)
U of the District of Columbia (DC)
U of the Ozarks (AR)
U of the Pacific (CA)
The U of Toledo (OH)
U of Toronto (ON, Canada)
U of Tulsa (OK)
U of Utah (UT)
U of Vermont (VT)
U of Victoria (BC, Canada)
The U of Virginia's Coll at Wise (VA)
The U of Western Ontario (ON, Canada)
U of West Florida (FL)
U of West Georgia (GA)
U of Windsor (ON, Canada)
The U of Winnipeg (MB, Canada)
U of Wisconsin–Green Bay (WI)
U of Wyoming (WY)
Ursinus Coll (PA)
Valdosta State U (GA)
Vassar Coll (NY)
Villa Julie Coll (MD)
Virginia Commonwealth U (VA)
Virginia Intermont Coll (VA)
Virginia Polytechnic Inst and State U (VA)
Virginia Wesleyan Coll (VA)
Walla Walla U (WA)
Warren Wilson Coll (NC)
Washington & Jefferson Coll (PA)
Washington Coll (MD)
Washington U in St. Louis (MO)
Waynesburg U (PA)
Wellesley Coll (MA)
Wells Coll (NY)
Wesleyan U (CT)
Wesley Coll (DE)
Western Michigan U (MI)
Western State Coll of Colorado (CO)
Western Washington U (WA)
Westminster Coll (MO)
Westminster Coll (UT)
West Virginia U (WV)
Wheaton Coll (IL)
Wheeling Jesuit U (WV)
Widener U (PA)
William Paterson U of New Jersey (NJ)
Wilson Coll (PA)
Worcester Polytechnic Inst (MA)
Xavier U of Louisiana (LA)
Yale U (CT)
York U (ON, Canada)

ENVIRONMENTAL TOXICOLOGY
U of California, Davis (CA)

EQUESTRIAN STUDIES
Asbury Coll (KY)
Averett U (VA)
Centenary Coll (NJ)
Colorado State U (CO)
Midway Coll (KY)
Mount Ida Coll (MA)
North Dakota State U (ND)
Otterbein Coll (OH)
Rutgers, The State U of New Jersey, New Brunswick (NJ)
St. Andrews Presbyterian Coll (NC)
Stephens Coll (MO)
Truman State U (MO)
The U of Findlay (OH)
U of Minnesota, Crookston (MN)
The U of Montana–Western (MT)
U of New Hampshire (NH)
Virginia Intermont Coll (VA)
West Texas A&M U (TX)
William Woods U (MO)
Wilson Coll (PA)

ETHICS
Bridgewater State Coll (MA)
Carnegie Mellon U (PA)
Drake U (IA)
St. John's Coll (NM)
U of Michigan–Flint (MI)
U of Ottawa (ON, Canada)
U of Southern California (CA)

ETHNIC, CULTURAL MINORITY, AND GENDER STUDIES RELATED
Arizona State U at the West campus (AZ)
Bard Coll at Simon's Rock (MA)
Boston U (MA)
Bowling Green State U (OH)
Burlington Coll (VT)
California State Polytechnic U, Pomona (CA)
California State U, Chico (CA)
Carnegie Mellon U (PA)
Claremont McKenna Coll (CA)
The Colorado Coll (CO)
Connecticut Coll (CT)
Cornell Coll (IA)
Hawai'i Pacific U (HI)
Indiana U Bloomington (IN)
Kenyon Coll (OH)
Lawrence U (WI)
Metropolitan State U (MN)
Miami U Hamilton (OH)
St. Olaf Coll (MN)
Sterling Coll (VT)
Stonehill Coll (MA)
U of California, Berkeley (CA)
U of California, Riverside (CA)
U of Colorado at Boulder (CO)
U of Denver (CO)
U of Hawaii at Manoa (HI)
U of Pittsburgh (PA)
U of Regina (SK, Canada)
The U of Texas at Austin (TX)
The U of Texas at Dallas (TX)
The U of Western Ontario (ON, Canada)
Washington State U (WA)
Washington U in St. Louis (MO)
Wellesley Coll (MA)
Whitman Coll (WA)
Williams Coll (MA)
Yale U (CT)

EUROPEAN HISTORY
Bard Coll (NY)
Bennington Coll (VT)
Carnegie Mellon U (PA)
Chapman U (CA)
Gettysburg Coll (PA)
McGill U (QC, Canada)
Sarah Lawrence Coll (NY)
U of Regina (SK, Canada)

EUROPEAN STUDIES
American Public U System (WV)
American U (DC)
The American U of Paris (France)
Amherst Coll (MA)
Bard Coll (NY)
Bard Coll at Simon's Rock (MA)
Barnard Coll (NY)
Beloit Coll (WI)
Bennington Coll (VT)
Brandeis U (MA)
California State U, Fullerton (CA)
Canisius Coll (NY)
Carnegie Mellon U (PA)
Carroll Coll (WI)
Central Michigan U (MI)
Claremont McKenna Coll (CA)
The Coll at Brockport, State U of New York (NY)
The Coll of William and Mary (VA)
Emory & Henry Coll (VA)
Fort Lewis Coll (CO)
Franklin Coll Switzerland (Switzerland)
Georgetown Coll (KY)
The George Washington U (DC)
Hamline U (MN)
Harvard U (MA)
Hillsdale Coll (MI)
Hobart and William Smith Colls (NY)
Howard Payne U (TX)
Loyola Marymount U (CA)
Marlboro Coll (VT)
Middlebury Coll (VT)
Millsaps Coll (MS)
Mount Holyoke Coll (MA)
New York U (NY)
Ohio U (OH)
Pitzer Coll (CA)
Rollins Coll (FL)
Saint Joseph's U (PA)
Saint Mary's Coll of California (CA)
Salem State Coll (MA)
San Diego State U (CA)
Sarah Lawrence Coll (NY)
Scripps Coll (CA)
Seattle Pacific U (WA)
Sewanee: The U of the South (TN)
Southern Methodist U (TX)
Stony Brook U, State U of New York (NY)
Texas State U-San Marcos (TX)
Trinity U (TX)
The U of British Columbia (BC, Canada)
U of California, Irvine (CA)
U of California, Los Angeles (CA)
U of Kansas (KS)
U of Michigan (MI)
U of Minnesota, Twin Cities Campus (MN)
U of Missouri–Columbia (MO)
U of New Hampshire (NH)
U of New Mexico (NM)
U of Northern Iowa (IA)
U of Richmond (VA)
U of South Carolina (SC)
The U of Texas at Austin (TX)
The U of Toledo (OH)
U of Toronto (ON, Canada)
U of Vermont (VT)
Vanderbilt U (TN)
Washington U in St. Louis (MO)
York U (ON, Canada)

EUROPEAN STUDIES (CENTRAL AND EASTERN)
Bowdoin Coll (ME)
Brigham Young U (UT)
Connecticut Coll (CT)
Florida State U (FL)
Hamline U (MN)
Harvard U (MA)
Hawai'i Pacific U (HI)
Indiana U Bloomington (IN)
Kent State U (OH)
Marlboro Coll (VT)
Middlebury Coll (VT)
Portland State U (OR)
Rutgers, The State U of New Jersey, New Brunswick (NJ)
Salem State Coll (MA)
San Diego State U (CA)
Sarah Lawrence Coll (NY)
U at Albany, State U of New York (NY)
The U of British Columbia (BC, Canada)
U of Chicago (IL)
U of Missouri–Columbia (MO)
U of Richmond (VA)
U of Toronto (ON, Canada)
U of Victoria (BC, Canada)
Wesleyan U (CT)

EUROPEAN STUDIES (WESTERN)
Claremont McKenna Coll (CA)
Illinois Wesleyan U (IL)
Seattle U (WA)
U of Houston (TX)
U of Nebraska–Lincoln (NE)

EVOLUTIONARY BIOLOGY
Bennington Coll (VT)
Case Western Reserve U (OH)
Coll of the Atlantic (ME)
Dartmouth Coll (NH)
Florida State U (FL)
Harvard U (MA)
Oregon State U (OR)
Rice U (TX)
Rutgers, The State U of New Jersey, New Brunswick (NJ)
State U of New York at Binghamton (NY)
Tulane U (LA)
U of New Hampshire (NH)
Yale U (CT)

EXECUTIVE ASSISTANT/ EXECUTIVE SECRETARY
Inter American U of Puerto Rico, Bayamón Campus (PR)

EXERCISE PHYSIOLOGY
Baldwin-Wallace Coll (OH)
Baylor U (TX)
Berry Coll (GA)
Chapman U (CA)
The Coll at Brockport, State U of New York (NY)
The Coll of St. Scholastica (MN)
Concordia U Wisconsin (WI)
East Carolina U (NC)
Fitchburg State Coll (MA)
Miami U Hamilton (OH)
Pfeiffer U (NC)
Saint Francis U (PA)
Truman State U (MO)
U of California, Davis (CA)
West Virginia U (WV)

EXPERIMENTAL PSYCHOLOGY
Longwood U (VA)
Marlboro Coll (VT)
Moravian Coll (PA)
Northern Michigan U (MI)
Paine Coll (GA)
Tufts U (MA)
The U of British Columbia (BC, Canada)
U of South Carolina (SC)
The U of Toledo (OH)
U of Wisconsin–Madison (WI)
Wilfrid Laurier U (ON, Canada)

FACILITIES PLANNING AND MANAGEMENT
Eastern Michigan U (MI)
Georgia State U (GA)
North Dakota State U (ND)

FAMILY AND COMMUNITY SERVICES
Andrews U (MI)
East Carolina U (NC)
Eastern Kentucky U (KY)
Iowa State U of Science and Technology (IA)
Keystone Coll (PA)
Lubbock Christian U (TX)
Messiah Coll (PA)
Michigan State U (MI)
Oklahoma Christian U (OK)
Oregon State U (OR)
Point Loma Nazarene U (CA)
Prairie View A&M U (TX)
Purdue U (IN)
Southern Utah U (UT)
Texas Tech U (TX)
Union U (TN)
U of California, Santa Cruz (CA)
U of Delaware (DE)
U of Florida (FL)
U of Maryland, Coll Park (MD)
U of Minnesota, Twin Cities Campus (MN)
U of Northern Iowa (IA)
Villa Julie Coll (MD)
Youngstown State U (OH)

FAMILY AND CONSUMER ECONOMICS RELATED
Alabama Ag and Mech U (AL)
Andrews U (MI)
Ashland U (OH)
Ball State U (IN)
Bob Jones U (SC)
Brigham Young U (UT)
California State U, Fresno (CA)
Carson-Newman Coll (TN)
Fairmont State U (WV)
Florida State U (FL)
Iowa State U of Science and Technology (IA)
Louisiana Coll (LA)
Miami U (OH)
Minnesota State U Mankato (MN)
Mount Saint Vincent U (NS, Canada)

Murray State U (KY)
Northwest Missouri State U (MO)
Oregon State U (OR)
Saint Joseph Coll (CT)
Seattle Pacific U (WA)
Tennessee State U (TN)
The U of Akron (OH)
U of Delaware (DE)
U of Maryland Eastern Shore (MD)
U of Missouri–Columbia (MO)
U of Nebraska at Kearney (NE)
U of Nebraska–Lincoln (NE)
U of New Hampshire (NH)
U of Northern Iowa (IA)
U of Prince Edward Island (PE, Canada)
U of Utah (UT)
U of Windsor (ON, Canada)
U of Wisconsin–Madison (WI)
U of Wisconsin–Stevens Point (WI)
Utah State U (UT)
Virginia State U (VA)

FAMILY AND CONSUMER SCIENCES/HOME ECONOMICS TEACHER EDUCATION

Appalachian State U (NC)
Ashland U (OH)
Ball State U (IN)
Bluffton U (OH)
Bridgewater Coll (VA)
Brigham Young U (UT)
Carson-Newman Coll (TN)
Central Michigan U (MI)
Cheyney U of Pennsylvania (PA)
Coll of the Ozarks (MO)
Colorado State U (CO)
Concordia U, Nebraska (NE)
Cornell U (NY)
East Carolina U (NC)
East Central U (OK)
Eastern Kentucky U (KY)
Fairmont State U (WV)
Ferris State U (MI)
Florida Intl U (FL)
Florida State U (FL)
Fontbonne U (MO)
Georgia Southern U (GA)
Grambling State U (LA)
Hampton U (VA)
Harding U (AR)
Immaculata U (PA)
Indiana U of Pennsylvania (PA)
Iowa State U of Science and Technology (IA)
Jacksonville State U (AL)
Keene State Coll (NH)
Kent State U (OH)
Liberty U (VA)
Marywood U (PA)
McNeese State U (LA)
Mercyhurst Coll (PA)
Miami U (OH)
Michigan State U (MI)
Minnesota State U Mankato (MN)
Missouri State U (MO)
Mount Vernon Nazarene U (OH)
Murray State U (KY)
North Carolina Ag and Tech State U (NC)
North Dakota State U (ND)
Northeastern State U (OK)
Northern Illinois U (IL)
Northwestern State U of Louisiana (LA)
Northwest Missouri State U (MO)
Oakwood Coll (AL)
Pittsburg State U (KS)
Purdue U (IN)
Queens Coll of the City U of New York (NY)
Sam Houston State U (TX)
Seattle Pacific U (WA)
Seton Hill U (PA)
South Carolina State U (SC)
Southeastern Louisiana U (LA)
Southeast Missouri State U (MO)
Southern Utah U (UT)
State U of New York Coll at Oneonta (NY)
Syracuse U (NY)
Tennessee Technological U (TN)
The U of Akron (OH)
The U of Arizona (AZ)
U of Arkansas at Pine Bluff (AR)
The U of British Columbia (BC, Canada)
U of Central Arkansas (AR)
U of Central Oklahoma (OK)
U of Georgia (GA)
U of Guam (GU)
U of Louisiana at Monroe (LA)
U of Maryland Eastern Shore (MD)
U of Minnesota, Twin Cities Campus (MN)
U of Nevada, Reno (NV)
U of New Brunswick Fredericton (NB, Canada)
The U of Tennessee (TN)
The U of Tennessee at Martin (TN)
U of the District of Columbia (DC)
U of Vermont (VT)
U of Wisconsin–Madison (WI)
U of Wisconsin–Stevens Point (WI)
Utah State U (UT)
Washington State U (WA)
Wayne State Coll (NE)
Western Kentucky U (KY)
Western Michigan U (MI)
Winthrop U (SC)
Youngstown State U (OH)

FAMILY AND CONSUMER SCIENCES/HUMAN SCIENCES

Ashland U (OH)
Auburn U (AL)
Ball State U (IN)
Baylor U (TX)
Bluffton U (OH)
Bradley U (IL)
Bridgewater Coll (VA)
Brigham Young U (UT)
California State Polytechnic U, Pomona (CA)
California State U, Long Beach (CA)
Cameron U (OK)
Carson-Newman Coll (TN)
Central Washington U (WA)
Coll of the Ozarks (MO)
Colorado State U (CO)
Cornell U (NY)
Delta State U (MS)
East Central U (OK)
Eastern Illinois U (IL)
Eastern Kentucky U (KY)
Eastern New Mexico U (NM)
East Tennessee State U (TN)
Fairmont State U (WV)
Florida State U (FL)
Fontbonne U (MO)
Framingham State Coll (MA)
Freed-Hardeman U (TN)
George Fox U (OR)
Great Lakes Christian Coll (MI)
Harding U (AR)
Henderson State U (AR)
Idaho State U (ID)
Illinois State U (IL)
Indiana State U (IN)
Iowa State U of Science and Technology (IA)
Jacksonville State U (AL)
Kent State U (OH)
Lambuth U (TN)
Liberty U (VA)
Lipscomb U (TN)
Louisiana State U and Ag and Mech Coll (LA)
Madonna U (MI)
Marshall U (WV)
The Master's Coll and Sem (CA)
McNeese State U (LA)
Mercyhurst Coll (PA)
Meredith Coll (NC)
Miami U (OH)
Michigan State U (MI)
Minnesota State U Mankato (MN)
Mississippi State U (MS)
Montana State U (MT)
Montclair State U (NJ)
Morgan State U (MD)
New Mexico Highlands U (NM)
Nicholls State U (LA)
North Carolina Ag and Tech State U (NC)
North Carolina Central U (NC)
Northeastern State U (OK)
Northwestern State U of Louisiana (LA)
Northwest Missouri State U (MO)
Oakwood Coll (AL)
Ohio U (OH)
Oregon State U (OR)
Pittsburg State U (KS)
Point Loma Nazarene U (CA)
Purdue U (IN)
Queens Coll of the City U of New York (NY)
Saint Joseph Coll (CT)
Sam Houston State U (TX)
San Francisco State U (CA)
Seton Hill U (PA)
Shepherd U (WV)
South Carolina State U (SC)
Southeastern Louisiana U (LA)
Southeast Missouri State U (MO)
Southern U and Ag and Mech Coll (LA)
Southern Utah U (UT)
State U of New York Coll at Oneonta (NY)
Stephen F. Austin State U (TX)
Tarleton State U (TX)
Tennessee Technological U (TN)
Texas Southern U (TX)
Texas State U-San Marcos (TX)
Texas Tech U (TX)
Texas Woman's U (TX)
U of Arkansas at Pine Bluff (AR)
The U of British Columbia (BC, Canada)
U of Central Arkansas (AR)
U of Central Missouri (MO)
U of Central Oklahoma (OK)
U of Hawaii at Manoa (HI)
U of Houston (TX)
U of Idaho (ID)
U of Louisiana at Monroe (LA)
U of Maryland Eastern Shore (MD)
U of Mississippi (MS)
U of Montevallo (AL)
U of Nebraska at Omaha (NE)
U of New Hampshire (NH)
U of New Mexico (NM)
U of North Alabama (AL)
The U of North Carolina at Greensboro (NC)
The U of Tennessee at Martin (TN)
The U of Texas at Austin (TX)
U of the District of Columbia (DC)
The U of Western Ontario (ON, Canada)
U of Wisconsin–Madison (WI)
U of Wyoming (WY)
Wayne State Coll (NE)
Western Illinois U (IL)
West Virginia U (WV)
Youngstown State U (OH)

FAMILY AND CONSUMER SCIENCES/HUMAN SCIENCES BUSINESS SERVICES RELATED

Brigham Young U (UT)
U of Illinois at Urbana–Champaign (IL)

FAMILY AND CONSUMER SCIENCES/HUMAN SCIENCES COMMUNICATION

U of Nebraska at Omaha (NE)

FAMILY AND CONSUMER SCIENCES/HUMAN SCIENCES RELATED

California State U, Long Beach (CA)
Morehead State U (KY)
The U of Western Ontario (ON, Canada)

FAMILY/COMMUNITY STUDIES

Alderson-Broaddus Coll (WV)
Coll of the Ozarks (MO)
Curry Coll (MA)
U of California, Santa Cruz (CA)
U of Maine at Machias (ME)

FAMILY/CONSUMER STUDIES

California State U, Sacramento (CA)

FAMILY LIVING/ PARENTHOOD

The U of North Carolina at Charlotte (NC)

FAMILY PRACTICE NURSING/NURSE PRACTITIONER

Edinboro U of Pennsylvania (PA)
North Georgia Coll & State U (GA)
The U of Virginia's Coll at Wise (VA)
The U of Western Ontario (ON, Canada)
U of Windsor (ON, Canada)

FAMILY RESOURCE MANAGEMENT

Arizona State U (AZ)
Bradley U (IL)
Brigham Young U (UT)
Iowa State U of Science and Technology (IA)
Middle Tennessee State U (TN)
Ohio U (OH)
South Dakota State U (SD)
The U of Alabama (AL)
U of Nebraska at Omaha (NE)
U of Utah (UT)

FAMILY SYSTEMS

Anderson U (IN)
Brigham Young U (UT)
Central Michigan U (MI)
Connecticut Coll (CT)
Lipscomb U (TN)
Southern Adventist U (TN)
Spring Arbor U (MI)
Texas Tech U (TX)
Towson U (MD)
The U of Akron (OH)
U of Southern Mississippi (MS)
The U of Tennessee (TN)
Weber State U (UT)
Western Michigan U (MI)

FARM AND RANCH MANAGEMENT

California State Polytechnic U, Pomona (CA)
Eastern Kentucky U (KY)
Iowa State U of Science and Technology (IA)
Northwest Missouri State U (MO)
Purdue U (IN)
Sterling Coll (VT)
Tarleton State U (TX)
Texas A&M U (TX)
Texas Christian U (TX)
The U of Findlay (OH)
U of Illinois at Urbana–Champaign (IL)
U of Wisconsin–Madison (WI)

FASHION AND FABRIC CONSULTING

U of Georgia (GA)

FASHION/APPAREL DESIGN

Acad of Art U (CA)
American InterContinental U (CA)
American InterContinental U (FL)
American InterContinental U Buckhead Campus (GA)
American InterContinental U-London (United Kingdom)
The American U of Athens (Greece)
The Art Inst of California–San Francisco (CA)
The Art Inst of Dallas (TX)
The Art Inst of Indianapolis (IN)
The Art Inst of Portland (OR)
The Art Inst of Seattle (WA)
The Art Inst of Tucson (AZ)
Baylor U (TX)
Buffalo State Coll, State U of New York (NY)
California Coll of the Arts (CA)
California Design Coll (CA)
Centenary Coll (NJ)
Clark Atlanta U (GA)
Columbia Coll Chicago (IL)
Columbus Coll of Art & Design (OH)
Dominican U (IL)
Drexel U (PA)
Fashion Inst of Technology (NY)
Florida State U (FL)
Hampton U (VA)
The Illinois Inst of Art–Chicago (IL)
Intl Acad of Design & Technology (FL)
Intl Acad of Design & Technology (IL)
Iowa State U of Science and Technology (IA)
Kent State U (OH)
Kwantlen U Coll (BC, Canada)
Lindenwood U (MO)
Marist Coll (NY)
Marshall U (WV)
Marymount U (VA)
Massachusetts Coll of Art and Design (MA)
Meredith Coll (NC)
Michigan State U (MI)
Minnesota State U Mankato (MN)
Montclair State U (NJ)
Mount Ida Coll (MA)
Mount Mary Coll (WI)
Northwest Missouri State U (MO)
Oregon State U (OR)
Otis Coll of Art and Design (CA)
Parsons Paris (France)
Parsons The New School for Design (NY)
Philadelphia U (PA)
Pratt Inst (NY)
Purdue U (IN)
Savannah Coll of Art and Design (GA)
School of the Art Inst of Chicago (IL)
Stephens Coll (MO)
Texas Southern U (TX)
Texas Tech U (TX)
Texas Woman's U (TX)
U of Cincinnati (OH)
U of Delaware (DE)
U of Hawaii at Manoa (HI)
U of Louisiana at Lafayette (LA)
U of Maryland Eastern Shore (MD)
U of North Texas (TX)
Ursuline Coll (OH)
Virginia Commonwealth U (VA)
Washington U in St. Louis (MO)
Woodbury U (CA)

FASHION MERCHANDISING

American InterContinental U (CA)
American InterContinental U (FL)
American InterContinental U Buckhead Campus (GA)
American InterContinental U-London (United Kingdom)
The Art Inst of Austin (TX)
The Art Inst of California–Inland Empire (CA)
The Art Inst of California–San Francisco (CA)
The Art Inst of California–Sunnyvale (CA)
The Art Inst of Dallas (TX)
The Art Inst of Indianapolis (IN)
The Art Inst of Las Vegas (NV)
The Art Inst of Phoenix (AZ)
The Art Inst of Portland (OR)
The Art Inst of Seattle (WA)
The Art Inst of Tucson (AZ)
The Art Insts Intl Minnesota (MN)
Ashland U (OH)
Ball State U (IN)
Baylor U (TX)
Bowling Green State U (OH)
Brenau U (GA)
Buffalo State Coll, State U of New York (NY)
California Design Coll (CA)
California State U, Long Beach (CA)
Carson-Newman Coll (TN)
Central Michigan U (MI)
Central Washington U (WA)
Dominican U (IL)
East Central U (OK)
Eastern Kentucky U (KY)
Eastern Michigan U (MI)
Fashion Inst of Technology (NY)
Florida State U (FL)
Fontbonne U (MO)
Freed-Hardeman U (TN)
George Fox U (OR)
Hampton U (VA)
Harding U (AR)
The Illinois Inst of Art–Chicago (IL)
The Illinois Inst of Art–Schaumburg (IL)
Immaculata U (PA)
Indiana U of Pennsylvania (PA)
Intl Acad of Design & Technology (FL)
Intl Acad of Design & Technology (IL)
Kent State U (OH)
Laboratory Inst of Merchandising (NY)
Lambuth U (TN)
Liberty U (VA)
Lindenwood U (MO)
Lipscomb U (TN)
Louisiana State U and Ag and Mech Coll (LA)
Marist Coll (NY)
Marymount U (VA)
Mercyhurst Coll (PA)
Meredith Coll (NC)
Miami Intl U of Art & Design (FL)
Mount Ida Coll (MA)
Mount Mary Coll (WI)
The New England Inst of Art (MA)
Northwest Missouri State U (MO)
Oregon State U (OR)
Parsons The New School for Design (NY)
Philadelphia U (PA)
Pittsburg State U (KS)
Purdue U (IN)
Sam Houston State U (TX)
State U of New York Coll at Oneonta (NY)
Stephen F. Austin State U (TX)
Stephens Coll (MO)
Tennessee Technological U (TN)
Texas Christian U (TX)
Texas Southern U (TX)
Texas State U-San Marcos (TX)
Texas Tech U (TX)
Texas Woman's U (TX)
U of Arkansas at Pine Bluff (AR)
U of Bridgeport (CT)
U of Central Oklahoma (OK)
U of Delaware (DE)
U of Georgia (GA)
U of Illinois at Urbana–Champaign (IL)
U of Louisiana at Lafayette (LA)
U of Maryland Eastern Shore (MD)
The U of Montana (MT)

U of North Texas (TX)
The U of Tennessee at Martin (TN)
U of Wisconsin–Madison (WI)
Ursuline Coll (OH)
Utah State U (UT)
Woodbury U (CA)
Youngstown State U (OH)

FIBER, TEXTILE AND WEAVING ARTS

Alberta Coll of Art & Design (AB, Canada)
California Coll of the Arts (CA)
California State U, Long Beach (CA)
The Cleveland Inst of Art (OH)
Colorado State U (CO)
Cornell U (NY)
Finlandia U (MI)
Kansas City Art Inst (MO)
Maryland Inst Coll of Art (MD)
Massachusetts Coll of Art and Design (MA)
Mercyhurst Coll (PA)
Northwest Missouri State U (MO)
NSCAD U (NS, Canada)
Philadelphia U (PA)
Savannah Coll of Art and Design (GA)
School of the Art Inst of Chicago (IL)
Temple U (PA)
U of Kansas (KS)
U of Massachusetts Dartmouth (MA)
U of Michigan (MI)
U of Oregon (OR)
U of Wisconsin–Milwaukee (WI)
Western Washington U (WA)

FILIPINO/TAGALOG

U of Hawaii at Manoa (HI)

FILM/CINEMA STUDIES

The American U of Paris (France)
Baldwin-Wallace Coll (OH)
Bard Coll (NY)
Barnard Coll (NY)
Bennington Coll (VT)
Bishop's U (QC, Canada)
Boston Coll (MA)
Bowling Green State U (OH)
Brigham Young U (UT)
Brock U (ON, Canada)
Brown U (RI)
Burlington Coll (VT)
California Coll of the Arts (CA)
California Inst of the Arts (CA)
California State U, Long Beach (CA)
California State U, Sacramento (CA)
Calvin Coll (MI)
Carson-Newman Coll (TN)
Centenary Coll of Louisiana (LA)
Chapman U (CA)
Claremont McKenna Coll (CA)
Clark U (MA)
Coll of Santa Fe (NM)
The Colorado Coll (CO)
Columbia Coll Chicago (IL)
Concordia U (CA)
Concordia U (QC, Canada)
Connecticut Coll (CT)
Cornell U (NY)
Curry Coll (MA)
Dartmouth Coll (NH)
Denison U (OH)
Eastern Michigan U (MI)
Emerson Coll (MA)
Emory U (GA)
The Evergreen State Coll (WA)
Florida State U (FL)
George Fox U (OR)
Georgia State U (GA)
Grand Valley State U (MI)
Harvard U (MA)
Hunter Coll of the City U of New York (NY)
Huntington U (IN)
Ithaca Coll (NY)
The Johns Hopkins U (MD)
Kansas City Art Inst (MO)
La Salle U (PA)
Laurentian U (ON, Canada)
Marlboro Coll (VT)
Mount Holyoke Coll (MA)
New York U (NY)
North Carolina School of the Arts (NC)
North Carolina State U (NC)
Northwestern U (IL)
NSCAD U (NS, Canada)
Ohio U (OH)
Penn State Abington (PA)
Penn State Altoona (PA)
Penn State Berks (PA)
Penn State Erie, The Behrend Coll (PA)
Penn State U Park (PA)
Pitzer Coll (CA)
Pomona Coll (CA)
Prescott Coll (AZ)
Purchase Coll, State U of New York (NY)
Purdue U (IN)
Queens Coll of the City U of New York (NY)
Queen's U at Kingston (ON, Canada)
Quinnipiac U (CT)
Rhode Island Coll (RI)
Rutgers, The State U of New Jersey, New Brunswick (NJ)
Sacred Heart U (CT)
St. Cloud State U (MN)
San Francisco State U (CA)
Sarah Lawrence Coll (NY)
Savannah Coll of Art and Design (GA)
School of the Art Inst of Chicago (IL)
School of the Museum of Fine Arts, Boston (MA)
School of Visual Arts (NY)
Simon Fraser U (BC, Canada)
Southern Methodist U (TX)
Stanford U (CA)
State U of New York at Fredonia (NY)
Stephens Coll (MO)
Temple U (PA)
U at Buffalo, the State U of New York (NY)
The U of British Columbia (BC, Canada)
U of California, Berkeley (CA)
U of California, Davis (CA)
U of California, Irvine (CA)
U of California, Los Angeles (CA)
U of California, San Diego (CA)
U of California, Santa Barbara (CA)
U of California, Santa Cruz (CA)
U of Chicago (IL)
U of Colorado at Boulder (CO)
U of Georgia (GA)
U of Hartford (CT)
U of Illinois at Urbana–Champaign (IL)
The U of Iowa (IA)
U of Maryland, Baltimore County (MD)
U of Miami (FL)
U of Michigan (MI)
U of Minnesota, Twin Cities Campus (MN)
U of Nebraska–Lincoln (NE)
U of Nevada, Las Vegas (NV)
U of New Mexico (NM)
U of Pennsylvania (PA)
U of Pittsburgh (PA)
U of Regina (SK, Canada)
U of Rochester (NY)
U of Southern California (CA)
The U of Tampa (FL)
The U of Toledo (OH)
U of Toronto (ON, Canada)
U of Tulsa (OK)
U of Utah (UT)
U of Vermont (VT)
The U of Western Ontario (ON, Canada)
U of Windsor (ON, Canada)
U of Wisconsin–Milwaukee (WI)
Vassar Coll (NY)
Washington U in St. Louis (MO)
Watkins Coll of Art and Design (TN)
Wayne State U (MI)
Webster U (MO)
Wellesley Coll (MA)
Wesleyan U (CT)
Whitman Coll (WA)
Wilfrid Laurier U (ON, Canada)
Wright State U (OH)
Yale U (CT)
York U (ON, Canada)

FILM/VIDEO AND PHOTOGRAPHIC ARTS RELATED

Arizona State U (AZ)
The Art Inst of Philadelphia (PA)
Brigham Young U (UT)
California Inst of the Arts (CA)
Chatham U (PA)
Columbus Coll of Art & Design (OH)
Fairfield U (CT)
Five Towns Coll (NY)
Full Sail U (FL)
Hampshire Coll (MA)
Hollins U (VA)
La Roche Coll (PA)
Maryland Inst Coll of Art (MD)
New England School of Communications (ME)
Pratt Inst (NY)
Ringling Coll of Art and Design (FL)
Rocky Mountain Coll of Art + Design (CO)
School of the Art Inst of Chicago (IL)
School of the Museum of Fine Arts, Boston (MA)
School of Visual Arts (NY)
Scripps Coll (CA)
Spring Arbor U (MI)
Swarthmore Coll (PA)
The U of Iowa (IA)
U of Regina (SK, Canada)
Villa Julie Coll (MD)
Woodbury U (CA)

FINANCE

Abilene Christian U (TX)
Adelphi U (NY)
Alabama Ag and Mech U (AL)
Alabama State U (AL)
Albertus Magnus Coll (CT)
Albright Coll (PA)
Alfred U (NY)
American Coll of Thessaloniki (Greece)
The American U of Athens (Greece)
The American U of Paris (France)
Anderson U (IN)
Anderson U (SC)
Angelo State U (TX)
Appalachian State U (NC)
Argosy U, Atlanta (GA)
Argosy U, Chicago (IL)
Argosy U, Denver (CO)
Argosy U, Hawai'i (HI)
Argosy U, Inland Empire (CA)
Argosy U, Nashville (TN)
Argosy U, Orange County (CA)
Argosy U, Phoenix (AZ)
Argosy U, San Diego (CA)
Argosy U, San Francisco Bay Area (CA)
Argosy U, Santa Monica (CA)
Argosy U, Sarasota (FL)
Argosy U, Schaumburg (IL)
Argosy U, Seattle (WA)
Argosy U, Twin Cities (MN)
Arizona State U (AZ)
Arkansas State U (AR)
Ashland U (OH)
Auburn U (AL)
Auburn U Montgomery (AL)
Augsburg Coll (MN)
Augustana Coll (IL)
Augusta State U (GA)
Averett U (VA)
Avila U (MO)
Babson Coll (MA)
Baldwin-Wallace Coll (OH)
Ball State U (IN)
Barry U (FL)
Baylor U (TX)
Belmont U (TN)
Benedictine U (IL)
Bentley Coll (MA)
Bernard M. Baruch Coll of the City U of New York (NY)
Berry Coll (GA)
Bishop's U (QC, Canada)
Bob Jones U (SC)
Boise State U (ID)
Boston Coll (MA)
Boston U (MA)
Bowling Green State U (OH)
Bradley U (IL)
Bridgewater State Coll (MA)
Brock U (ON, Canada)
Butler U (IN)
Cabrini Coll (PA)
California State Polytechnic U, Pomona (CA)
California State U, Chico (CA)
California State U, Dominguez Hills (CA)
California State U, East Bay (CA)
California State U, Fresno (CA)
California State U, Fullerton (CA)
California State U, Long Beach (CA)
California State U, San Bernardino (CA)
Canisius Coll (NY)
Capital U (OH)
Carroll Coll (WI)
Castleton State Coll (VT)
The Catholic U of America (DC)
Cedarville U (OH)
Centenary Coll of Louisiana (LA)
Central Connecticut State U (CT)
Central Michigan U (MI)
Christopher Newport U (VA)
Clarion U of Pennsylvania (PA)
Clarkson U (NY)
Cleary U (MI)
Clemson U (SC)
Cleveland State U (OH)
Coastal Carolina U (SC)
The Coll at Brockport, State U of New York (NY)
The Coll of New Jersey (NJ)
Colorado State U (CO)
Colorado Tech U—Colorado Springs (CO)
Colorado Tech U—Denver (CO)
Colorado Tech U—North Kansas City (MO)
Colorado Tech U—Online (CO)
Colorado Tech U—Sioux Falls (SD)
Columbus State U (GA)
Concordia U (QC, Canada)
Concordia U, St. Paul (MN)
Creighton U (NE)
Culver-Stockton Coll (MO)
Dakota State U (SD)
Dakota Wesleyan U (SD)
Dallas Baptist U (TX)
Davenport U, Dearborn (MI)
Davenport U, Grand Rapids (MI)
Delta State U (MS)
DePaul U (IL)
DeSales U (PA)
Dominican Coll (NY)
Dowling Coll (NY)
Drake U (IA)
Drexel U (PA)
Drury U (MO)
Duquesne U (PA)
East Carolina U (NC)
East Central U (OK)
Eastern Illinois U (IL)
Eastern Kentucky U (KY)
Eastern Michigan U (MI)
Eastern New Mexico U (NM)
East Tennessee State U (TN)
East-West U (IL)
Emory U (GA)
Excelsior Coll (NY)
Fairfield U (CT)
Fairleigh Dickinson U, Coll at Florham (NJ)
Fairmont State U (WV)
Fayetteville State U (NC)
Ferris State U (MI)
Fitchburg State Coll (MA)
Florida Ag and Mech U (FL)
Florida Atlantic U (FL)
Florida Gulf Coast U (FL)
Florida Intl U (FL)
Florida Southern Coll (FL)
Florida State U (FL)
Fontbonne U (MO)
Fort Lewis Coll (CO)
Francis Marion U (SC)
Freed-Hardeman U (TN)
Fresno Pacific U (CA)
Gannon U (PA)
George Fox U (OR)
George Mason U (VA)
Georgetown U (DC)
The George Washington U (DC)
Georgia Southern U (GA)
Georgia State U (GA)
Golden Gate U (CA)
Goldey-Beacom Coll (DE)
Gonzaga U (WA)
Grace Coll (IN)
Grand Valley State U (MI)
Granite State Coll (NH)
Grove City Coll (PA)
Hampton U (VA)
Hardin-Simmons U (TX)
Hawai'i Pacific U (HI)
HEC Montreal (QC, Canada)
Hilbert Coll (NY)
Hillsdale Coll (MI)
Hofstra U (NY)
Houston Baptist U (TX)
Howard Payne U (TX)
Husson Coll (ME)
Idaho State U (ID)
Illinois Coll (IL)
Illinois State U (IL)
Immaculata U (PA)
Indiana State U (IN)
Indiana U Bloomington (IN)
Indiana U of Pennsylvania (PA)
Indiana U–Purdue U Fort Wayne (IN)
Indiana Wesleyan U (IN)
Inter American U of Puerto Rico, Bayamón Campus (PR)
Inter American U of Puerto Rico, San Germán Campus (PR)
Iona Coll (NY)
Iowa State U of Science and Technology (IA)
Ithaca Coll (NY)
Jackson State U (MS)
Jacksonville State U (AL)
Jacksonville U (FL)
James Madison U (VA)
John Carroll U (OH)
Juniata Coll (PA)
Kansas State U (KS)
Kean U (NJ)
Keiser U, Fort Lauderdale (FL)
Kennesaw State U (GA)
Kent State U (OH)
King Coll (TN)
King's Coll (PA)
Kutztown U of Pennsylvania (PA)
Lakehead U (ON, Canada)
Lake Superior State U (MI)
La Roche Coll (PA)
La Salle U (PA)
Lehigh U (PA)
Le Moyne Coll (NY)
Lenoir-Rhyne Coll (NC)
LeTourneau U (TX)
Lewis U (IL)
Lincoln U (PA)
Lindenwood U (MO)
Linfield Coll (OR)
Longwood U (VA)
Loras Coll (IA)
Louisiana Coll (LA)
Louisiana State U and Ag and Mech Coll (LA)
Loyola Coll in Maryland (MD)
Loyola U Chicago (IL)
Loyola U New Orleans (LA)
Lubbock Christian U (TX)
Lycoming Coll (PA)
Manchester Coll (IN)
Manhattanville Coll (NY)
Marian Coll (IN)
Marian Coll of Fond du Lac (WI)
Marquette U (WI)
Marshall U (WV)
The Master's Coll and Sem (CA)
McGill U (QC, Canada)
McKendree U (IL)
McMurry U (TX)
McNeese State U (LA)
Memorial U of Newfoundland (NL, Canada)
Mercyhurst Coll (PA)
Merrimack Coll (MA)
Methodist U (NC)
Metropolitan State U (MN)
Miami U (OH)
Miami U Hamilton (OH)
Michigan State U (MI)
Michigan Technological U (MI)
Middle Tennessee State U (TN)
Midwestern State U (TX)
Millikin U (IL)
Minnesota State U Mankato (MN)
Minot State U (ND)
Mississippi State U (MS)
Missouri State U (MO)
Montana State U–Billings (MT)
Montana Tech of The U of Montana (MT)
Morehead State U (KY)
Morgan State U (MD)
Mount Vernon Nazarene U (OH)
Murray State U (KY)
National American U, Rapid City (SD)
National U (CA)
New England Coll (NH)
Newman U (KS)
New Mexico Highlands U (NM)
New York Inst of Technology (NY)
New York U (NY)
Nicholls State U (LA)
Nichols Coll (MA)
North Carolina State U (NC)
North Central Coll (IL)
Northeastern Illinois U (IL)
Northeastern State U (OK)
Northeastern U (MA)
Northern Arizona U (AZ)
Northern Illinois U (IL)
Northern Michigan U (MI)
Northern State U (SD)
North Georgia Coll & State U (GA)
Northwestern Coll (MN)
Northwest Missouri State U (MO)
Northwest Nazarene U (ID)
Nova Southeastern U (FL)
Oakland U (MI)
Ohio Dominican U (OH)
Oklahoma City U (OK)
Oklahoma State U (OK)
Old Dominion U (VA)
Oral Roberts U (OK)
Oregon State U (OR)
Otterbein Coll (OH)
Pace U (NY)
Pacific Union Coll (CA)
Pacific U (OR)
Penn State Abington (PA)
Penn State Altoona (PA)
Penn State Berks (PA)
Penn State Erie, The Behrend Coll (PA)
Penn State Harrisburg (PA)
Penn State U Park (PA)
Pfeiffer U (NC)
Philadelphia U (PA)

MAJORS AND MORE

Pittsburg State U (KS)
Polytechnic U of Puerto Rico (PR)
Portland State U (OR)
Prairie View A&M U (TX)
Providence Coll (RI)
Queens Coll of the City U of New York (NY)
Quincy U (IL)
Quinnipiac U (CT)
Radford U (VA)
Rensselaer Polytechnic Inst (NY)
Rhode Island Coll (RI)
Rider U (NJ)
Robert Morris U (PA)
Rochester Inst of Technology (NY)
Rockford Coll (IL)
Roger Williams U (RI)
Roosevelt U (IL)
Rutgers, The State U of New Jersey, Camden (NJ)
Rutgers, The State U of New Jersey, Newark (NJ)
Rutgers, The State U of New Jersey, New Brunswick (NJ)
Saginaw Valley State U (MI)
St. Ambrose U (IA)
St. Cloud State U (MN)
St. Edward's U (TX)
Saint Francis U (PA)
St. John Fisher Coll (NY)
St. John's U (NY)
Saint Joseph's U (PA)
Saint Martin's U (WA)
Saint Mary's Coll (IN)
St. Mary's U (TX)
Saint Mary's U of Minnesota (MN)
St. Thomas Aquinas Coll (NY)
St. Thomas U (FL)
Saint Vincent Coll (PA)
Salem State Coll (MA)
Salisbury U (MD)
Salve Regina U (RI)
Sam Houston State U (TX)
San Diego State U (CA)
San Francisco State U (CA)
Santa Clara U (CA)
Seattle U (WA)
Seton Hill U (PA)
Shippensburg U of Pennsylvania (PA)
Siena Coll (NY)
Simmons Coll (MA)
Southeastern Louisiana U (LA)
Southeastern Oklahoma State U (OK)
Southeastern U (FL)
Southeast Missouri State U (MO)
Southern Connecticut State U (CT)
Southern Illinois U Carbondale (IL)
Southern Methodist U (TX)
Southern U and Ag and Mech Coll (LA)
Southwest Baptist U (MO)
Southwestern Oklahoma State U (OK)
Southwest Minnesota State U (MN)
Spring Arbor U (MI)
Spring Hill Coll (AL)
State U of New York at Fredonia (NY)
State U of New York at New Paltz (NY)
State U of New York at Oswego (NY)
State U of New York at Plattsburgh (NY)
State U of New York Coll at Old Westbury (NY)
State U of New York Inst of Technology (NY)
Stephen F. Austin State U (TX)
Stetson U (FL)
Stonehill Coll (MA)
Suffolk U (MA)
Sullivan U (KY)
Susquehanna U (PA)
Syracuse U (NY)
Tarleton State U (TX)
Taylor U (IN)
Temple U (PA)
Tennessee Technological U (TN)
Tennessee Wesleyan Coll (TN)
Texas A&M Intl U (TX)
Texas A&M U (TX)
Texas A&M U–Commerce (TX)
Texas Christian U (TX)
Texas Lutheran U (TX)
Texas Southern U (TX)
Texas State U-San Marcos (TX)
Texas Tech U (TX)
Texas Woman's U (TX)
Thomas Coll (ME)
Thompson Rivers U (BC, Canada)
Tiffin U (OH)
Trinity U (TX)
Troy U (AL)
Truman State U (MO)
Tulane U (LA)
Tuskegee U (AL)
Union U (TN)
Université de Sherbrooke (QC, Canada)
The U of Alabama (AL)
The U of Alabama at Birmingham (AL)
The U of Alabama in Huntsville (AL)
The U of Arizona (AZ)
U of Arkansas (AR)
U of Baltimore (MD)
U of Bridgeport (CT)
The U of British Columbia (BC, Canada)
The U of British Columbia–Okanagan (BC, Canada)
U of Central Arkansas (AR)
U of Central Florida (FL)
U of Central Missouri (MO)
U of Central Oklahoma (OK)
U of Charleston (WV)
U of Cincinnati (OH)
U of Colorado at Boulder (CO)
U of Connecticut (CT)
U of Dayton (OH)
U of Delaware (DE)
U of Denver (CO)
U of Evansville (IN)
U of Florida (FL)
U of Georgia (GA)
U of Guam (GU)
U of Hartford (CT)
U of Hawaii at Manoa (HI)
U of Houston (TX)
U of Houston–Clear Lake (TX)
U of Houston–Downtown (TX)
U of Idaho (ID)
U of Illinois at Chicago (IL)
U of Illinois at Urbana–Champaign (IL)
The U of Iowa (IA)
U of Kansas (KS)
U of Lethbridge (AB, Canada)
U of Louisiana at Lafayette (LA)
U of Louisiana at Monroe (LA)
U of Louisville (KY)
U of Maine (ME)
U of Mary Hardin-Baylor (TX)
U of Maryland, Coll Park (MD)
U of Massachusetts Amherst (MA)
U of Massachusetts Dartmouth (MA)
U of Memphis (TN)
U of Miami (FL)
U of Michigan–Dearborn (MI)
U of Michigan–Flint (MI)
U of Minnesota, Duluth (MN)
U of Minnesota, Twin Cities Campus (MN)
U of Mississippi (MS)
U of Missouri–Columbia (MO)
U of Missouri–St. Louis (MO)
The U of Montana (MT)
U of Montevallo (AL)
U of Nebraska at Omaha (NE)
U of Nebraska–Lincoln (NE)
U of Nevada, Las Vegas (NV)
U of Nevada, Reno (NV)
U of New Brunswick Fredericton (NB, Canada)
U of New Hampshire (NH)
U of New Haven (CT)
U of New Orleans (LA)
U of North Alabama (AL)
The U of North Carolina at Charlotte (NC)
The U of North Carolina at Greensboro (NC)
The U of North Carolina Wilmington (NC)
U of North Dakota (ND)
U of Northern Iowa (IA)
U of North Florida (FL)
U of North Texas (TX)
U of Notre Dame (IN)
U of Oklahoma (OK)
U of Ottawa (ON, Canada)
U of Pennsylvania (PA)
U of Pittsburgh (PA)
U of Pittsburgh at Johnstown (PA)
U of Portland (OR)
U of Regina (SK, Canada)
U of Rhode Island (RI)
U of Richmond (VA)
U of St. Francis (IL)
U of St. Thomas (MN)
U of St. Thomas (TX)
U of San Diego (CA)
The U of Scranton (PA)
U of South Alabama (AL)
U of South Carolina (SC)
The U of South Dakota (SD)
U of Southern Indiana (IN)
U of Southern Mississippi (MS)
U of South Florida (FL)
The U of Tampa (FL)
The U of Tennessee (TN)
The U of Tennessee at Martin (TN)
The U of Texas at Austin (TX)
The U of Texas at Brownsville (TX)
The U of Texas at Dallas (TX)
The U of Texas at El Paso (TX)
The U of Texas at San Antonio (TX)
The U of Texas at Tyler (TX)
The U of Texas of the Permian Basin (TX)
The U of Texas–Pan American (TX)
U of the District of Columbia (DC)
The U of Toledo (OH)
U of Toronto (ON, Canada)
U of Tulsa (OK)
U of Utah (UT)
The U of Western Ontario (ON, Canada)
U of West Florida (FL)
U of West Georgia (GA)
U of Windsor (ON, Canada)
U of Wisconsin–Eau Claire (WI)
U of Wisconsin–La Crosse (WI)
U of Wisconsin–Madison (WI)
U of Wisconsin–Milwaukee (WI)
U of Wisconsin–Oshkosh (WI)
U of Wisconsin–Parkside (WI)
U of Wisconsin–Superior (WI)
U of Wisconsin–Whitewater (WI)
U of Wyoming (WY)
Utah State U (UT)
Valdosta State U (GA)
Valparaiso U (IN)
Vanguard U of Southern California (CA)
Villanova U (PA)
Virginia Polytechnic Inst and State U (VA)
Wagner Coll (NY)
Wake Forest U (NC)
Walsh U (OH)
Wartburg Coll (IA)
Washburn U (KS)
Washington State U (WA)
Washington U in St. Louis (MO)
Waynesburg U (PA)
Wayne State U (MI)
Webber Intl U (FL)
Weber State U (UT)
West Chester U of Pennsylvania (PA)
Western Carolina U (NC)
Western Connecticut State U (CT)
Western Illinois U (IL)
Western Intl U (AZ)
Western Kentucky U (KY)
Western Michigan U (MI)
Western New England Coll (MA)
Western Washington U (WA)
Westminster Coll (UT)
West Texas A&M U (TX)
West Virginia U (WV)
West Virginia Wesleyan Coll (WV)
Wichita State U (KS)
Wilmington U (DE)
Wingate U (NC)
Winona State U (MN)
Wofford Coll (SC)
Wright State U (OH)
Xavier U (OH)
York Coll (NE)
York Coll of Pennsylvania (PA)
York U (ON, Canada)
Youngstown State U (OH)

FINANCE AND FINANCIAL MANAGEMENT SERVICES RELATED

Babson Coll (MA)
Florida Ag and Mech U (FL)
Grace Bible Coll (MI)
Hofstra U (NY)
James Madison U (VA)
Park U (MO)
Saint Mary's Coll of California (CA)
Southern Methodist U (TX)
The U of Akron (OH)
The U of Tampa (FL)
Virginia Commonwealth U (VA)

FINANCIAL PLANNING AND SERVICES

Baylor U (TX)
Bethany Coll (KS)
Brigham Young U (UT)
Central Michigan U (MI)
Cleary U (MI)
Jamestown Coll (ND)
Marywood U (PA)
Medaille Coll (NY)
Northern Michigan U (MI)
Purdue U (IN)
Roger Williams U (RI)
Southern Methodist U (TX)
Trinity Christian Coll (IL)
The U of Akron (OH)
U of Illinois at Urbana–Champaign (IL)
The U of Maine at Augusta (ME)
U of North Texas (TX)
Western Michigan U (MI)
Western New Mexico U (NM)
Westminster Coll (UT)
Widener U (PA)

FINE ARTS RELATED

Abilene Christian U (TX)
Adelphi U (NY)
Allegheny Coll (PA)
Bowling Green State U (OH)
Burlington Coll (VT)
California State U, Long Beach (CA)
The Catholic U of America (DC)
Coll of Staten Island of the City U of New York (NY)
Columbus Coll of Art & Design (OH)
Covenant Coll (GA)
Dowling Coll (NY)
Hood Coll (MD)
Kentucky Wesleyan Coll (KY)
Madonna U (MI)
Maryland Inst Coll of Art (MD)
Memphis Coll of Art (TN)
Monmouth U (NJ)
Montserrat Coll of Art (MA)
Northern Michigan U (MI)
Oakland U (MI)
Paier Coll of Art, Inc. (CT)
Point Loma Nazarene U (CA)
Pratt Inst (NY)
Presbyterian Coll (SC)
Purchase Coll, State U of New York (NY)
Rogers State U (OK)
Rutgers, The State U of New Jersey, Newark (NJ)
St. John's U (NY)
St. Mary's Coll of Maryland (MD)
Salisbury U (MD)
School of the Art Inst of Chicago (IL)
School of the Museum of Fine Arts, Boston (MA)
Skidmore Coll (NY)
Syracuse U (NY)
The U of Akron (OH)
U of California, Los Angeles (CA)
U of Denver (CO)
U of Hartford (CT)
U of Massachusetts Dartmouth (MA)
U of North Alabama (AL)
U of Regina (SK, Canada)
The U of Western Ontario (ON, Canada)
Ursinus Coll (PA)
Virginia Commonwealth U (VA)
Widener U (PA)
York Coll of Pennsylvania (PA)

FINE/STUDIO ARTS

Abilene Christian U (TX)
Acad of Art U (CA)
Alberta Coll of Art & Design (AB, Canada)
Albertus Magnus Coll (CT)
Alfred U (NY)
Allegheny Coll (PA)
Alma Coll (MI)
American U (DC)
Amherst Coll (MA)
Anderson U (IN)
Angelo State U (TX)
Appalachian State U (NC)
Aquinas Coll (MI)
The Art Inst of Boston at Lesley U (MA)
Asbury Coll (KY)
Ashland U (OH)
Auburn U (AL)
Augsburg Coll (MN)
Augustana Coll (IL)
Baker U (KS)
Baldwin-Wallace Coll (OH)
Ball State U (IN)
Bard Coll (NY)
Bard Coll at Simon's Rock (MA)
Barton Coll (NC)
Baylor U (TX)
Bellarmine U (KY)
Belmont U (TN)
Beloit Coll (WI)
Bemidji State U (MN)
Benedictine U (IL)
Bennington Coll (VT)
Bethany Coll (WV)
Biola U (CA)
Bishop's U (QC, Canada)
Bloomfield Coll (NJ)
Bloomsburg U of Pennsylvania (PA)
Boston Coll (MA)
Bowdoin Coll (ME)
Bowling Green State U (OH)
Bradley U (IL)
Brandeis U (MA)
Brenau U (GA)
Brevard Coll (NC)
Bridgewater Coll (VA)
Bridgewater State Coll (MA)
Brigham Young U (UT)
Brock U (ON, Canada)
Brown U (RI)
Bucknell U (PA)
Buffalo State Coll, State U of New York (NY)
Cabrini Coll (PA)
California Coll of the Arts (CA)
California Inst of the Arts (CA)
California State U, Chico (CA)
California State U, Dominguez Hills (CA)
California State U, East Bay (CA)
California State U, Fullerton (CA)
California State U, Long Beach (CA)
California State U, Stanislaus (CA)
Calvin Coll (MI)
Canisius Coll (NY)
Capital U (OH)
Carroll Coll (WI)
The Catholic U of America (DC)
Cedarville U (OH)
Centenary Coll of Louisiana (LA)
Central Michigan U (MI)
Chapman U (CA)
Chatham U (PA)
Christian Brothers U (TN)
Christopher Newport U (VA)
Claremont McKenna Coll (CA)
Clarke Coll (IA)
Clark U (MA)
Coastal Carolina U (SC)
Coker Coll (SC)
Colby-Sawyer Coll (NH)
The Coll at Brockport, State U of New York (NY)
Coll of Charleston (SC)
Coll of Mount St. Joseph (OH)
The Coll of New Jersey (NJ)
The Coll of New Rochelle (NY)
Coll of Saint Benedict (MN)
The Coll of Saint Rose (NY)
Coll of Santa Fe (NM)
Coll of the Holy Cross (MA)
Coll of the Ozarks (MO)
Coll of Visual Arts (MN)
The Colorado Coll (CO)
Colorado State U (CO)
Colorado State U-Pueblo (CO)
Columbia Coll (SC)
Columbia Coll Chicago (IL)
Concordia Coll (MN)
Concordia U (QC, Canada)
Concordia U, Nebraska (NE)
Concordia U, St. Paul (MN)
Converse Coll (SC)
Cooper Union for the Advancement of Science and Art (NY)
Cornell U (NY)
Daemen Coll (NY)
Dartmouth Coll (NH)
Denison U (OH)
DePauw U (IN)
Dickinson Coll (PA)
Dowling Coll (NY)
Drake U (IA)
Drury U (MO)
Duquesne U (PA)
East Carolina U (NC)
Eastern Kentucky U (KY)
Edinboro U of Pennsylvania (PA)
Emmanuel Coll (MA)
Emory U (GA)
Endicott Coll (MA)
The Evergreen State Coll (WA)
Fairfield U (CT)
Fashion Inst of Technology (NY)
Felician Coll (NJ)
Ferris State U (MI)
Ferrum Coll (VA)
Finlandia U (MI)
Flagler Coll (FL)
Florida Intl U (FL)
Florida Southern Coll (FL)
Florida State U (FL)
Fontbonne U (MO)
Franklin & Marshall Coll (PA)
Furman U (SC)
Gardner-Webb U (NC)
George Fox U (OR)
George Mason U (VA)
Georgetown Coll (KY)
Georgetown U (DC)
The George Washington U (DC)
Georgia State U (GA)
Gettysburg Coll (PA)
Grand Valley State U (MI)
Grand View Coll (IA)
Green Mountain Coll (VT)
Hamilton Coll (NY)
Hamline U (MN)
Hampden-Sydney Coll (VA)
Hampshire Coll (MA)
Harding U (AR)

MAJORS AND MORE

Hardin-Simmons U (TX)
Harvard U (MA)
High Point U (NC)
Hobart and William Smith Colls (NY)
Hofstra U (NY)
Hope Coll (MI)
Houston Baptist U (TX)
Howard Payne U (TX)
Humboldt State U (CA)
Hunter Coll of the City U of New York (NY)
Illinois State U (IL)
Indiana State U (IN)
Indiana U Bloomington (IN)
Indiana U of Pennsylvania (PA)
Indiana U–Purdue U Fort Wayne (IN)
Indiana U–Purdue U Indianapolis (IN)
Indiana U South Bend (IN)
Indiana U Southeast (IN)
Iowa Wesleyan Coll (IA)
Ithaca Coll (NY)
Jacksonville U (FL)
Jamestown Coll (ND)
Johnson State Coll (VT)
Judson U (IL)
Juniata Coll (PA)
Kean U (NJ)
Keene State Coll (NH)
Kent State U (OH)
Kentucky State U (KY)
Kenyon Coll (OH)
Keystone Coll (PA)
Kutztown U of Pennsylvania (PA)
Lafayette Coll (PA)
Laguna Coll of Art & Design (CA)
Lake Forest Coll (IL)
Lambuth U (TN)
La Sierra U (CA)
Lawrence U (WI)
Lebanon Valley Coll (PA)
Lewis U (IL)
Limestone Coll (SC)
Lincoln U (MO)
Lindenwood U (MO)
Linfield Coll (OR)
Lipscomb U (TN)
Longwood U (VA)
Loras Coll (IA)
Louisiana Coll (LA)
Louisiana State U and Ag and Mech Coll (LA)
Loyola Marymount U (CA)
Loyola U Chicago (IL)
Lycoming Coll (PA)
Macalester Coll (MN)
Maharishi U of Management (IA)
Malone Coll (OH)
Manchester Coll (IN)
Manhattanville Coll (NY)
Marian Coll (IN)
Marian Coll of Fond du Lac (WI)
Marietta Coll (OH)
Marist Coll (NY)
Marlboro Coll (VT)
Martin U (IN)
Maryland Inst Coll of Art (MD)
Marylhurst U (OR)
Marymount Manhattan Coll (NY)
Marymount U (VA)
Maryville Coll (TN)
Maryville U of Saint Louis (MO)
Massachusetts Coll of Art and Design (MA)
McMurry U (TX)
Memphis Coll of Art (TN)
Mercyhurst Coll (PA)
Meredith Coll (NC)
Merrimack Coll (MA)
Messiah Coll (PA)
Miami U (OH)
Middlebury Coll (VT)
Milligan Coll (TN)
Millikin U (IL)
Millsaps Coll (MS)
Mills Coll (CA)
Minnesota State U Mankato (MN)
Missouri State U (MO)
Montana State U (MT)
Montclair State U (NJ)
Montserrat Coll of Art (MA)
Moravian Coll (PA)
Morehead State U (KY)
Morningside Coll (IA)
Mount Allison U (NB, Canada)
Mount Holyoke Coll (MA)
Mount Saint Vincent U (NS, Canada)
Murray State U (KY)
Naropa U (CO)
Nazareth Coll of Rochester (NY)
New Coll of Florida (FL)
New England Coll (NH)
New York Inst of Technology (NY)
New York U (NY)
Northeastern State U (OK)
Northern Illinois U (IL)
Northland Coll (WI)
Northwestern Coll (MN)
Northwestern State U of Louisiana (LA)
Northwest Missouri State U (MO)
Notre Dame de Namur U (CA)
NSCAD U (NS, Canada)
Oakland U (MI)
Oberlin Coll (OH)
Occidental Coll (CA)
Ohio Dominican U (OH)
Ohio Northern U (OH)
Ohio U (OH)
Ohio Wesleyan U (OH)
Oklahoma City U (OK)
Old Dominion U (VA)
Oral Roberts U (OK)
Otis Coll of Art and Design (CA)
Ouachita Baptist U (AR)
Pacific Lutheran U (WA)
Pacific Union Coll (CA)
Paier Coll of Art, Inc. (CT)
Palm Beach Atlantic U (FL)
Park U (MO)
Parsons Paris (France)
Parsons The New School for Design (NY)
Pennsylvania Coll of Art & Design (PA)
Piedmont Coll (GA)
Pitzer Coll (CA)
Plymouth State U (NH)
Pomona Coll (CA)
Pratt Inst (NY)
Presbyterian Coll (SC)
Providence Coll (RI)
Purdue U (IN)
Queens Coll of the City U of New York (NY)
Queens U of Charlotte (NC)
Randolph Coll (VA)
Randolph-Macon Coll (VA)
Reed Coll (OR)
Rhode Island Coll (RI)
Rhodes Coll (TN)
Rice U (TX)
Rider U (NJ)
Ringling Coll of Art and Design (FL)
Roberts Wesleyan Coll (NY)
Rollins Coll (FL)
Rosemont Coll (PA)
Rowan U (NJ)
Saginaw Valley State U (MI)
St. Ambrose U (IA)
St. Andrews Presbyterian Coll (NC)
St. Cloud State U (MN)
St. Gregory's U, Shawnee (OK)
Saint John's U (MN)
Saint Joseph's Coll (IN)
St. Lawrence U (NY)
Saint Louis U (MO)
Saint Mary-of-the-Woods Coll (IN)
Saint Mary's U of Minnesota (MN)
St. Thomas Aquinas Coll (NY)
Saint Vincent Coll (PA)
Salem Coll (NC)
Salve Regina U (RI)
Sam Houston State U (TX)
San Diego State U (CA)
Santa Clara U (CA)
Sarah Lawrence Coll (NY)
School of the Art Inst of Chicago (IL)
School of the Museum of Fine Arts, Boston (MA)
School of Visual Arts (NY)
Scripps Coll (CA)
Seattle U (WA)
Seton Hill U (PA)
Sewanee: The U of the South (TN)
Shawnee State U (OH)
Shorter Coll (GA)
Siena Coll (NY)
Smith Coll (MA)
Sonoma State U (CA)
South Carolina State U (SC)
Southern Connecticut State U (CT)
Southern Illinois U Carbondale (IL)
Southern Illinois U Edwardsville (IL)
Southern Methodist U (TX)
Southern U and Ag and Mech Coll (LA)
Spring Hill Coll (AL)
Stanford U (CA)
State U of New York at Binghamton (NY)
State U of New York at Fredonia (NY)
State U of New York at Plattsburgh (NY)
State U of New York Coll at Geneseo (NY)
State U of New York Coll at Oneonta (NY)
Stonehill Coll (MA)
Stony Brook U, State U of New York (NY)
Swarthmore Coll (PA)
Sweet Briar Coll (VA)
Syracuse U (NY)
Tarleton State U (TX)
Texas A&M U–Commerce (TX)
Texas Christian U (TX)
Texas Southern U (TX)
Texas State U-San Marcos (TX)
Texas Tech U (TX)
Thompson Rivers U (BC, Canada)
Trinity Coll (CT)
Troy U (AL)
Truman State U (MO)
Tulane U (LA)
Union Coll (NE)
Union Coll (NY)
Université du Québec en Outaouais (QC, Canada)
U at Buffalo, the State U of New York (NY)
The U of Akron (OH)
The U of Alabama (AL)
The U of Alabama at Birmingham (AL)
The U of Arizona (AZ)
The U of British Columbia (BC, Canada)
U of California, Davis (CA)
U of California, Irvine (CA)
U of California, Riverside (CA)
U of California, San Diego (CA)
U of California, Santa Barbara (CA)
U of Central Florida (FL)
U of Central Missouri (MO)
U of Chicago (IL)
U of Colorado at Boulder (CO)
U of Colorado Denver (CO)
U of Connecticut (CT)
U of Dallas (TX)
U of Dayton (OH)
U of Florida (FL)
U of Great Falls (MT)
U of Houston (TX)
U of Idaho (ID)
U of Illinois at Chicago (IL)
U of Illinois at Springfield (IL)
U of Indianapolis (IN)
The U of Iowa (IA)
U of Kansas (KS)
U of Louisville (KY)
U of Maine (ME)
The U of Maine at Augusta (ME)
U of Mary Hardin-Baylor (TX)
U of Maryland, Coll Park (MD)
U of Mary Washington (VA)
U of Massachusetts Amherst (MA)
U of Massachusetts Lowell (MA)
U of Miami (FL)
U of Michigan–Flint (MI)
U of Minnesota, Duluth (MN)
U of Missouri–Kansas City (MO)
U of Missouri–St. Louis (MO)
U of Nebraska at Omaha (NE)
U of Nebraska–Lincoln (NE)
U of Nevada, Las Vegas (NV)
U of New Hampshire (NH)
U of New Haven (CT)
U of New Orleans (LA)
U of North Alabama (AL)
The U of North Carolina at Asheville (NC)
The U of North Carolina at Chapel Hill (NC)
The U of North Carolina at Charlotte (NC)
The U of North Carolina at Greensboro (NC)
The U of North Carolina at Pembroke (NC)
The U of North Carolina Wilmington (NC)
U of Northern Colorado (CO)
U of Northern Iowa (IA)
U of North Florida (FL)
U of North Texas (TX)
U of Notre Dame (IN)
U of Oklahoma (OK)
U of Oregon (OR)
U of Ottawa (ON, Canada)
U of Pennsylvania (PA)
U of Pittsburgh (PA)
U of Puerto Rico at Utuado (PR)
U of Redlands (CA)
U of Richmond (VA)
U of Rochester (NY)
U of St. Thomas (TX)
U of Science and Arts of Oklahoma (OK)
U of South Carolina (SC)
U of South Carolina Aiken (SC)
U of South Carolina Upstate (SC)
U of Southern California (CA)
The U of Tennessee (TN)
The U of Tennessee at Chattanooga (TN)
The U of Texas at Arlington (TX)
The U of Texas at Austin (TX)
The U of Texas at El Paso (TX)
The U of Texas–Pan American (TX)
U of the District of Columbia (DC)
U of the Ozarks (AR)
U of the Pacific (CA)
The U of Toledo (OH)
U of Toronto (ON, Canada)
U of Tulsa (OK)
U of Vermont (VT)
U of Victoria (BC, Canada)
The U of Western Ontario (ON, Canada)
U of West Florida (FL)
U of Windsor (ON, Canada)
U of Wisconsin–Milwaukee (WI)
U of Wisconsin–Oshkosh (WI)
U of Wisconsin–Stevens Point (WI)
U of Wisconsin–Superior (WI)
Ursuline Coll (OH)
Valparaiso U (IN)
Vassar Coll (NY)
Wake Forest U (NC)
Washington and Lee U (VA)
Washington State U (WA)
Washington U in St. Louis (MO)
Watkins Coll of Art and Design (TN)
Webster U (MO)
Wellesley Coll (MA)
Wells Coll (NY)
Wesleyan Coll (GA)
Wesleyan U (CT)
West Chester U of Pennsylvania (PA)
Western Carolina U (NC)
Western Illinois U (IL)
Western Kentucky U (KY)
Western State Coll of Colorado (CO)
Western Washington U (WA)
West Texas A&M U (TX)
West Virginia Wesleyan Coll (WV)
Wheaton Coll (MA)
Whitworth U (WA)
Willamette U (OR)
William Paterson U of New Jersey (NJ)
Williams Coll (MA)
William Woods U (MO)
Wingate U (NC)
Winona State U (MN)
Xavier U (OH)
York Coll of Pennsylvania (PA)
York U (ON, Canada)
Youngstown State U (OH)

FIRE PROTECTION AND SAFETY TECHNOLOGY

Columbia Southern U (AL)
Oklahoma State U (OK)
Thomas Edison State Coll (NJ)
U of Cincinnati (OH)
U of Houston–Downtown (TX)
U of New Haven (CT)

FIRE PROTECTION RELATED

The U of Akron (OH)
U of New Haven (CT)

FIRE SCIENCE

American Public U System (WV)
Anna Maria Coll (MA)
Cogswell Polytechnical Coll (CA)
Hampton U (VA)
Holy Family U (PA)
Lake Superior State U (MI)
Lewis-Clark State Coll (ID)
Madonna U (MI)
Providence Coll (RI)
U of Cincinnati (OH)
U of Florida (FL)
U of Maryland U Coll (MD)
U of New Brunswick Fredericton (NB, Canada)
Utah Valley State Coll (UT)

FIRE SERVICES ADMINISTRATION

California State U, Los Angeles (CA)
Colorado State U (CO)
Columbia Southern U (AL)
Fayetteville State U (NC)
Lewis U (IL)
Southern Illinois U Carbondale (IL)
The U of North Carolina at Charlotte (NC)
Utah Valley State Coll (UT)

FISH/GAME MANAGEMENT

Humboldt State U (CA)
Iowa State U of Science and Technology (IA)
Lake Superior State U (MI)
Northland Coll (WI)
Oregon State U (OR)
Southeastern Oklahoma State U (OK)
State U of New York Coll of Environmental Science and Forestry (NY)
Texas A&M U at Galveston (TX)
U of Arkansas at Pine Bluff (AR)
The U of British Columbia (BC, Canada)
U of Minnesota, Twin Cities Campus (MN)
U of Missouri–Columbia (MO)
U of New Brunswick Fredericton (NB, Canada)
West Virginia U (WV)

FISHING AND FISHERIES SCIENCES AND MANAGEMENT

Clemson U (SC)
Colorado State U (CO)
Humboldt State U (CA)
Mansfield U of Pennsylvania (PA)
Murray State U (KY)
North Carolina State U (NC)
Oregon State U (OR)
Purdue U (IN)
State U of New York Coll of Agriculture and Technology at Cobleskill (NY)
State U of New York Coll of Environmental Science and Forestry (NY)
Sterling Coll (VT)
Texas A&M U (TX)
Texas Tech U (TX)
U of Alaska Fairbanks (AK)
U of Georgia (GA)
U of Idaho (ID)
U of Missouri–Columbia (MO)
U of Rhode Island (RI)
The U of Tennessee at Martin (TN)

FLIGHT INSTRUCTION

South Dakota State U (SD)
U of North Dakota (ND)

FLUID/THERMAL SCIENCES

Harvard U (MA)
Worcester Polytechnic Inst (MA)

FOLKLORE

Harvard U (MA)
Laurentian U (ON, Canada)
Marlboro Coll (VT)
Memorial U of Newfoundland (NL, Canada)

FOOD/NUTRITION

Montclair State U (NJ)

FOODS AND NUTRITION RELATED

California State U, Long Beach (CA)
Kent State U (OH)
The U of British Columbia (BC, Canada)
Utah State U (UT)

FOOD SCIENCE

Acadia U (NS, Canada)
Alabama Ag and Mech U (AL)
American U of Beirut (Lebanon)
Auburn U (AL)
Brigham Young U (UT)
California Polytechnic State U, San Luis Obispo (CA)
Clemson U (SC)
Cornell U (NY)
Delaware Valley Coll (PA)
Dominican U (IL)
Framingham State Coll (MA)
Kansas State U (KS)
Louisiana State U and Ag and Mech Coll (LA)
McGill U (QC, Canada)
Memorial U of Newfoundland (NL, Canada)
Michigan State U (MI)
Mississippi State U (MS)
North Carolina Ag and Tech State U (NC)
North Carolina State U (NC)
North Dakota State U (ND)
Northwest Missouri State U (MO)
Oklahoma State U (OK)
Oregon State U (OR)
Penn State Abington (PA)
Penn State Altoona (PA)
Penn State Berks (PA)
Penn State Erie, The Behrend Coll (PA)
Penn State U Park (PA)
Purdue U (IN)
Rutgers, The State U of New Jersey, New Brunswick (NJ)

Texas A&M U (TX)
Texas Tech U (TX)
Tuskegee U (AL)
U of Arkansas (AR)
The U of British Columbia (BC, Canada)
U of California, Davis (CA)
U of Delaware (DE)
U of Florida (FL)
U of Georgia (GA)
U of Idaho (ID)
U of Illinois at Urbana–Champaign (IL)
U of Maine (ME)
U of Maryland, Coll Park (MD)
U of Massachusetts Amherst (MA)
U of Missouri–Columbia (MO)
U of Nebraska–Lincoln (NE)
The U of Tennessee (TN)
U of the District of Columbia (DC)
U of Wisconsin–Madison (WI)
Virginia Polytechnic Inst and State U (VA)
Washington State U (WA)

FOOD SCIENCE AND TECHNOLOGY RELATED

The U of British Columbia (BC, Canada)
U of Illinois at Urbana–Champaign (IL)

FOOD SERVICE AND DINING ROOM MANAGEMENT

The Art Inst of Pittsburgh (PA)

FOOD SERVICES TECHNOLOGY

Iowa State U of Science and Technology (IA)
Tennessee State U (TN)

FOODSERVICE SYSTEMS ADMINISTRATION

Central Michigan U (MI)
Dominican U (IL)
Lipscomb U (TN)
Rochester Inst of Technology (NY)
State U of New York Coll at Oneonta (NY)
Syracuse U (NY)
The U of North Carolina at Greensboro (NC)
Western Michigan U (MI)

FOODS, NUTRITION, AND WELLNESS

Acadia U (NS, Canada)
Alcorn State U (MS)
Andrews U (MI)
Appalachian State U (NC)
Ashland U (OH)
Auburn U (AL)
Bastyr U (WA)
Bluffton U (OH)
Bob Jones U (SC)
Bowling Green State U (OH)
Bridgewater Coll (VA)
California Polytechnic State U, San Luis Obispo (CA)
California State Polytechnic U, Pomona (CA)
California State U, Fresno (CA)
California State U, Los Angeles (CA)
California State U, San Bernardino (CA)
Carson-Newman Coll (TN)
Cedar Crest Coll (PA)
Central Washington U (WA)
Coll of Saint Benedict (MN)
Coll of the Ozarks (MO)
Colorado State U (CO)
Concordia Coll (MN)
Cornell U (NY)
Dominican U (IL)
Florida State U (FL)
George Fox U (OR)
Georgia Southern U (GA)
Georgia State U (GA)
Goddard Coll (VT)
Hunter Coll of the City U of New York (NY)
Immaculata U (PA)
Indiana State U (IN)
Indiana U of Pennsylvania (PA)
Iowa State U of Science and Technology (IA)
Ithaca Coll (NY)
Jacksonville State U (AL)
James Madison U (VA)
Kansas State U (KS)
Keene State Coll (NH)
Kent State U (OH)
Lambuth U (TN)
Lehman Coll of the City U of New York (NY)
Madonna U (MI)
The Master's Coll and Sem (CA)
McGill U (QC, Canada)
McNeese State U (LA)
Memorial U of Newfoundland (NL, Canada)
Middle Tennessee State U (TN)
Minnesota State U Mankato (MN)
Montclair State U (NJ)
Morgan State U (MD)
Mount Saint Vincent U (NS, Canada)
Murray State U (KY)
New York U (NY)
North Carolina Ag and Tech State U (NC)
Northeastern State U (OK)
Northern Illinois U (IL)
Northwest Missouri State U (MO)
Ohio U (OH)
Oregon State U (OR)
Pepperdine U, Malibu (CA)
Point Loma Nazarene U (CA)
Prairie View A&M U (TX)
Purdue U (IN)
Radford U (VA)
St. Francis Xavier U (NS, Canada)
Saint John's U (MN)
Saint Louis U (MO)
Sam Houston State U (TX)
Seattle Pacific U (WA)
Simmons Coll (MA)
South Carolina State U (SC)
South Dakota State U (SD)
Southern Illinois U Carbondale (IL)
State U of New York at Plattsburgh (NY)
Stephen F. Austin State U (TX)
Syracuse U (NY)
Tennessee Technological U (TN)
Texas A&M U (TX)
Texas State U-San Marcos (TX)
Texas Tech U (TX)
Texas Woman's U (TX)
Tuskegee U (AL)
U of Arkansas (AR)
The U of British Columbia (BC, Canada)
U of Central Oklahoma (OK)
U of Cincinnati (OH)
U of Dayton (OH)
U of Delaware (DE)
U of Houston (TX)
U of Idaho (ID)
U of Maine (ME)
U of Maryland, Coll Park (MD)
U of Minnesota, Twin Cities Campus (MN)
U of Missouri–Columbia (MO)
U of Nebraska–Lincoln (NE)
U of Nevada, Reno (NV)
U of New Hampshire (NH)
U of New Mexico (NM)
The U of North Carolina at Chapel Hill (NC)
U of Northern Iowa (IA)
U of Ottawa (ON, Canada)
U of Prince Edward Island (PE, Canada)
U of Rhode Island (RI)
The U of Tennessee (TN)
The U of Texas at Austin (TX)
U of Toronto (ON, Canada)
The U of Western Ontario (ON, Canada)
U of Wisconsin–Madison (WI)
Virginia Polytechnic Inst and State U (VA)
Wayne State U (MI)
Winthrop U (SC)
Youngstown State U (OH)

FOOD TECHNOLOGY AND PROCESSING

Brigham Young U (UT)
U of Illinois at Urbana–Champaign (IL)

FOREIGN LANGUAGES AND LITERATURES

American U (DC)
The American U of Athens (Greece)
Assumption Coll (MA)
Auburn U (AL)
Auburn U Montgomery (AL)
Augustana Coll (SD)
Austin Peay State U (TN)
Bard Coll at Simon's Rock (MA)
Bennington Coll (VT)
Boston U (MA)
California State U, Monterey Bay (CA)
Carnegie Mellon U (PA)
Centenary Coll of Louisiana (LA)
Central Washington U (WA)
The Citadel, The Military Coll of South Carolina (SC)
Colorado State U (CO)
Colorado State U-Pueblo (CO)
Covenant Coll (GA)
Delta State U (MS)
Dowling Coll (NY)
Duquesne U (PA)
Eastern Illinois U (IL)
East Tennessee State U (TN)
Eckerd Coll (FL)
Elon U (NC)
Emporia State U (KS)
Eugene Lang Coll The New School for Liberal Arts (NY)
Excelsior Coll (NY)
Framingham State Coll (MA)
Francis Marion U (SC)
Frostburg State U (MD)
Gannon U (PA)
George Mason U (VA)
Gordon Coll (MA)
Grace Coll (IN)
Hastings Coll (NE)
Indiana State U (IN)
Jackson State U (MS)
James Madison U (VA)
Juniata Coll (PA)
Kansas State U (KS)
Kenyon Coll (OH)
Knox Coll (IL)
Lambuth U (TN)
Lewis & Clark Coll (OR)
Lycoming Coll (PA)
Marian Coll of Fond du Lac (WI)
Marshall U (WV)
Massachusetts Inst of Technology (MA)
Mercyhurst Coll (PA)
Middle Tennessee State U (TN)
Mississippi Coll (MS)
Mississippi State U (MS)
Monmouth U (NJ)
Montana State U (MT)
New Coll of Florida (FL)
Oakland U (MI)
Old Dominion U (VA)
Pace U (NY)
Penn State Berks (PA)
Pitzer Coll (CA)
Presbyterian Coll (SC)
Purdue U (IN)
Queens U of Charlotte (NC)
Radford U (VA)
Rhode Island Coll (RI)
The Richard Stockton Coll of New Jersey (NJ)
Roger Williams U (RI)
Roosevelt U (IL)
Rutgers, The State U of New Jersey, New Brunswick (NJ)
St. John's Coll (NM)
St. Lawrence U (NY)
Saint Louis U (MO)
St. Mary's Coll of Maryland (MD)
Samford U (AL)
Sarah Lawrence Coll (NY)
Scripps Coll (CA)
South Carolina State U (SC)
Southern Adventist U (TN)
Southern Illinois U Edwardsville (IL)
State U of New York Coll at Old Westbury (NY)
Stonehill Coll (MA)
Sweet Briar Coll (VA)
Syracuse U (NY)
Thomas Edison State Coll (NJ)
Troy U (AL)
Tulane U (LA)
Union Coll (NY)
Union U (TN)
The U of Alabama (AL)
The U of Alabama in Huntsville (AL)
U of Alaska Fairbanks (AK)
U of California, Riverside (CA)
U of California, San Diego (CA)
U of California, Santa Cruz (CA)
U of Central Florida (FL)
U of Delaware (DE)
U of Georgia (GA)
U of Hartford (CT)
U of Idaho (ID)
U of Maine (ME)
U of Maryland, Coll Park (MD)
U of Massachusetts Lowell (MA)
U of Memphis (TN)
The U of Montana (MT)
U of Montevallo (AL)
U of New Mexico (NM)
U of North Alabama (AL)
U of North Dakota (ND)
U of Northern Colorado (CO)
U of Northern Iowa (IA)
The U of Scranton (PA)
U of South Alabama (AL)
U of South Carolina Beaufort (SC)
U of Southern Mississippi (MS)
The U of Texas at Arlington (TX)
The U of Texas at Austin (TX)
The U of Texas at Tyler (TX)
The U of Virginia's Coll at Wise (VA)
Utica Coll (NY)
Virginia Commonwealth U (VA)
Virginia Wesleyan Coll (VA)
Washington and Lee U (VA)
Washington Coll (MD)
Washington State U (WA)
Wayne State Coll (NE)
Wayne State U (MI)
West Virginia U (WV)
Widener U (PA)
Wright State U (OH)
Youngstown State U (OH)

FOREIGN LANGUAGES RELATED

Bellarmine U (KY)
The Coll of New Rochelle (NY)
The Evergreen State Coll (WA)
Houston Baptist U (TX)
Indiana U of Pennsylvania (PA)
Kennesaw State U (GA)
Marquette U (WI)
Mississippi Coll (MS)
Saint Mary's Coll of California (CA)
Southern Illinois U Carbondale (IL)
U of Alaska Fairbanks (AK)
U of California, Berkeley (CA)
U of California, Los Angeles (CA)
U of California, Riverside (CA)
U of Michigan–Flint (MI)
U of Northern Iowa (IA)
U of St. Thomas (MN)
U of the Sacred Heart (PR)
Yale U (CT)

FOREIGN LANGUAGE TEACHER EDUCATION

Adams State Coll (CO)
Baylor U (TX)
Boston U (MA)
Bowling Green State U (OH)
Brigham Young U (UT)
Buffalo State Coll, State U of New York (NY)
Carroll Coll (WI)
The Catholic U of America (DC)
The Coll at Brockport, State U of New York (NY)
Dana Coll (NE)
Eastern Michigan U (MI)
Florida Intl U (FL)
Florida State U (FL)
Gannon U (PA)
Gardner-Webb U (NC)
Greensboro Coll (NC)
Hastings Coll (NE)
Hofstra U (NY)
Indiana U Bloomington (IN)
Juniata Coll (PA)
Kent State U (OH)
Lincoln U (PA)
Marquette U (WI)
McNeese State U (LA)
Mercyhurst Coll (PA)
Millersville U of Pennsylvania (PA)
Moravian Coll (PA)
Murray State U (KY)
Nazareth Coll of Rochester (NY)
New York U (NY)
North Carolina State U (NC)
Ohio Dominican U (OH)
Ohio Northern U (OH)
Ohio Wesleyan U (OH)
Old Dominion U (VA)
Oral Roberts U (OK)
Penn State Abington (PA)
Penn State Altoona (PA)
Penn State Berks (PA)
Penn State Erie, The Behrend Coll (PA)
Penn State U Park (PA)
Purdue U (IN)
Saint Francis U (PA)
Saint Joseph's U (PA)
Sam Houston State U (TX)
Seton Hill U (PA)
Southeast Missouri State U (MO)
State U of New York Coll at Old Westbury (NY)
State U of New York Coll at Potsdam (NY)
Temple U (PA)
The U of Arizona (AZ)
U of Central Florida (FL)
U of Delaware (DE)
U of Georgia (GA)
U of Illinois at Chicago (IL)
U of Illinois at Urbana–Champaign (IL)
U of Lethbridge (AB, Canada)
U of Maine (ME)
U of Maryland, Coll Park (MD)
U of Minnesota, Twin Cities Campus (MN)
U of Nebraska–Lincoln (NE)
U of Nevada, Reno (NV)
U of Northern Iowa (IA)
U of Oklahoma (OK)
U of St. Thomas (MN)
The U of South Dakota (SD)
U of South Florida (FL)
U of Vermont (VT)
U of Windsor (ON, Canada)
Valparaiso U (IN)
Virginia Wesleyan Coll (VA)
Washington State U (WA)
Wayne State Coll (NE)
Wheeling Jesuit U (WV)
William Jewell Coll (MO)
Wright State U (OH)
Youngstown State U (OH)

FORENSIC PSYCHOLOGY

Bay Path Coll (MA)
Florida Inst of Technology (FL)
Gwynedd-Mercy Coll (PA)
St. Ambrose U (IA)
Sam Houston State U (TX)
Tiffin U (OH)
U of Puerto Rico at Utuado (PR)
Western State Coll of Colorado (CO)

FORENSIC SCIENCE AND TECHNOLOGY

Alvernia Coll (PA)
Arkansas State U (AR)
Baylor U (TX)
Becker Coll (MA)
Buffalo State Coll, State U of New York (NY)
Carroll Coll (WI)
Cedar Crest Coll (PA)
Cedarville U (OH)
Chaminade U of Honolulu (HI)
Chatham U (PA)
Chestnut Hill Coll (PA)
Coll of the Ozarks (MO)
Defiance Coll (OH)
Eastern Kentucky U (KY)
Eastern New Mexico U (NM)
Fayetteville State U (NC)
Hilbert Coll (NY)
Hofstra U (NY)
Indiana U–Purdue U Indianapolis (IN)
Inter American U of Puerto Rico, Bayamón Campus (PR)
Jacksonville State U (AL)
Keystone Coll (PA)
Loyola U Chicago (IL)
Loyola U New Orleans (LA)
Madonna U (MI)
Mercyhurst Coll (PA)
Mountain State U (WV)
Mount Marty Coll (SD)
New Mexico Highlands U (NM)
Northwest Nazarene U (ID)
Our Lady of the Lake Coll (LA)
Pace U (NY)
Russell Sage Coll (NY)
St. Edward's U (TX)
Saint Francis U (PA)
Sam Houston State U (TX)
Seattle U (WA)
Seton Hill U (PA)
Simpson Coll (IA)
Thomas More Coll (KY)
Tiffin U (OH)
Towson U (MD)
Tri-State U (IN)
U of Baltimore (MD)
U of Central Florida (FL)
U of Central Oklahoma (OK)
U of Great Falls (MT)
U of Mississippi (MS)
U of Nebraska–Lincoln (NE)
U of New Haven (CT)
U of North Dakota (ND)
The U of Tampa (FL)
U of Toronto (ON, Canada)
U of Windsor (ON, Canada)
Utah Valley State Coll (UT)
Virginia Commonwealth U (VA)
Washburn U (KS)
Waynesburg U (PA)
Western Carolina U (NC)
West Virginia U (WV)
York Coll of Pennsylvania (PA)
Youngstown State U (OH)

FOREST ENGINEERING

Oregon State U (OR)
State U of New York Coll of Environmental Science and Forestry (NY)
U of Maine (ME)
U of New Brunswick Fredericton (NB, Canada)

FOREST/FOREST RESOURCES MANAGEMENT

Clemson U (SC)
Louisiana State U and Ag and Mech Coll (LA)
North Carolina State U (NC)
Oregon State U (OR)
State U of New York Coll of Environmental Science and Forestry (NY)
Stephen F. Austin State U (TX)
Sterling Coll (VT)
Texas A&M U (TX)
The U of British Columbia (BC, Canada)
U of California, Berkeley (CA)
U of Idaho (ID)
U of Minnesota, Twin Cities Campus (MN)
The U of Montana (MT)
U of Toronto (ON, Canada)
West Virginia U (WV)

FOREST RESOURCES PRODUCTION AND MANAGEMENT

Oregon State U (OR)
Sterling Coll (VT)

FORESTRY

Albright Coll (PA)
Baylor U (TX)
California Polytechnic State U, San Luis Obispo (CA)
Coll of Saint Benedict (MN)
Georgia Southern U (GA)
Humboldt State U (CA)
Iowa State U of Science and Technology (IA)
Lakehead U (ON, Canada)
Lenoir-Rhyne Coll (NC)
Michigan State U (MI)
Michigan Technological U (MI)
Mississippi State U (MS)
New Mexico Highlands U (NM)
Northland Coll (WI)
Northwest Missouri State U (MO)
Oklahoma State U (OK)
Oregon State U (OR)
Paul Smith's Coll (NY)
Purdue U (IN)
Sewanee: The U of the South (TN)
Southern Illinois U Carbondale (IL)
State U of New York Coll of Environmental Science and Forestry (NY)
Stephen F. Austin State U (TX)
Sterling Coll (VT)
Texas A&M U (TX)
Thomas Edison State Coll (NJ)
U of Arkansas at Monticello (AR)
The U of British Columbia (BC, Canada)
U of California, Berkeley (CA)
U of Florida (FL)
U of Georgia (GA)
U of Idaho (ID)
U of Illinois at Urbana–Champaign (IL)
U of Maine (ME)
U of Massachusetts Amherst (MA)
U of Minnesota, Twin Cities Campus (MN)
U of Missouri–Columbia (MO)
The U of Montana (MT)
U of Nevada, Reno (NV)
U of New Brunswick Fredericton (NB, Canada)
U of New Hampshire (NH)
The U of Tennessee (TN)
U of the District of Columbia (DC)
U of Toronto (ON, Canada)
U of Vermont (VT)
U of Wisconsin–Madison (WI)
U of Wisconsin–Milwaukee (WI)
U of Wisconsin–Stevens Point (WI)
Utah State U (UT)
Virginia Polytechnic Inst and State U (VA)
Washington State U (WA)
West Virginia U (WV)

FORESTRY RELATED

Davis & Elkins Coll (WV)
Sterling Coll (VT)
Utah State U (UT)

FORESTRY TECHNOLOGY

Penn State Abington (PA)
Penn State Altoona (PA)
Penn State Berks (PA)
Penn State Erie, The Behrend Coll (PA)
Penn State U Park (PA)

FOREST SCIENCES AND BIOLOGY

Auburn U (AL)
Canisius Coll (NY)
Coll of Saint Benedict (MN)
Colorado State U (CO)
Memorial U of Newfoundland (NL, Canada)
Northern Arizona U (AZ)
Penn State Abington (PA)
Penn State Altoona (PA)
Penn State Berks (PA)
Penn State Erie, The Behrend Coll (PA)
Penn State U Park (PA)
Saint John's U (MN)
State U of New York Coll of Environmental Science and Forestry (NY)
Sterling Coll (VT)
U of Georgia (GA)
U of Idaho (ID)
U of Illinois at Urbana–Champaign (IL)

FRENCH

Acadia U (NS, Canada)
Adelphi U (NY)
Adrian Coll (MI)
Agnes Scott Coll (GA)
Alabama State U (AL)
Albertus Magnus Coll (CT)
Albion Coll (MI)
Albright Coll (PA)
Alfred U (NY)
Allegheny Coll (PA)
Alma Coll (MI)
American U (DC)
The American U of Paris (France)
Amherst Coll (MA)
Anderson U (IN)
Andrews U (MI)
Angelo State U (TX)
Appalachian State U (NC)
Aquinas Coll (MI)
Arizona State U (AZ)
Arkansas State U (AR)
Asbury Coll (KY)
Ashland U (OH)
Assumption Coll (MA)
Athabasca U (AB, Canada)
Auburn U (AL)
Augsburg Coll (MN)
Augustana Coll (IL)
Augustana Coll (SD)
Augusta State U (GA)
Austin Coll (TX)
Baker U (KS)
Baldwin-Wallace Coll (OH)
Ball State U (IN)
Bard Coll (NY)
Bard Coll at Simon's Rock (MA)
Barnard Coll (NY)
Barry U (FL)
Bates Coll (ME)
Baylor U (TX)
Beloit Coll (WI)
Benedictine Coll (KS)
Bennington Coll (VT)
Berea Coll (KY)
Berry Coll (GA)
Bethany Coll (WV)
Bethel U (MN)
Bishop's U (QC, Canada)
Bloomsburg U of Pennsylvania (PA)
Bob Jones U (SC)
Boise State U (ID)
Boston Coll (MA)
Boston U (MA)
Bowdoin Coll (ME)
Bowling Green State U (OH)
Bradley U (IL)
Brandeis U (MA)
Bridgewater Coll (VA)
Brigham Young U (UT)
Brock U (ON, Canada)
Brown U (RI)
Bryn Mawr Coll (PA)
Bucknell U (PA)
Buffalo State Coll, State U of New York (NY)
Butler U (IN)
Cabrini Coll (PA)
California Lutheran U (CA)
California State U, Chico (CA)
California State U, Dominguez Hills (CA)
California State U, East Bay (CA)
California State U, Fresno (CA)
California State U, Fullerton (CA)
California State U, Long Beach (CA)
California State U, Los Angeles (CA)
California State U, Sacramento (CA)
California State U, San Bernardino (CA)
California State U, Stanislaus (CA)
Calvin Coll (MI)
Canisius Coll (NY)
Capital U (OH)
Carnegie Mellon U (PA)
Carson-Newman Coll (TN)
Case Western Reserve U (OH)
Catawba Coll (NC)
The Catholic U of America (DC)
Centenary Coll of Louisiana (LA)
Central Coll (IA)
Central Connecticut State U (CT)
Central Michigan U (MI)
Centre Coll (KY)
Chapman U (CA)
Chatham U (PA)
Chestnut Hill Coll (PA)
Cheyney U of Pennsylvania (PA)
Christopher Newport U (VA)
City Coll of the City U of New York (NY)
Claremont McKenna Coll (CA)
Clarion U of Pennsylvania (PA)
Clark Atlanta U (GA)
Clarke Coll (IA)
Clark U (MA)
Cleveland State U (OH)
Coker Coll (SC)
Colby Coll (ME)
Colgate U (NY)
The Coll at Brockport, State U of New York (NY)
Coll of Charleston (SC)
Coll of Mount Saint Vincent (NY)
The Coll of New Rochelle (NY)
Coll of Saint Benedict (MN)
Coll of the Holy Cross (MA)
Coll of the Ozarks (MO)
The Coll of William and Mary (VA)
The Colorado Coll (CO)
Colorado State U (CO)
Columbia Coll (SC)
Columbus State U (GA)
Concordia Coll (MN)
Concordia U (QC, Canada)
Connecticut Coll (CT)
Converse Coll (SC)
Cornell Coll (IA)
Cornell U (NY)
Creighton U (NE)
Daemen Coll (NY)
Dartmouth Coll (NH)
Davidson Coll (NC)
Denison U (OH)
DePaul U (IL)
DePauw U (IN)
Dickinson Coll (PA)
Dillard U (LA)
Doane Coll (NE)
Dominican U (IL)
Drew U (NJ)
Drury U (MO)
Duke U (NC)
Earlham Coll (IN)
East Carolina U (NC)
Eastern Kentucky U (KY)
Eastern Mennonite U (VA)
Eastern Michigan U (MI)
East Stroudsburg U of Pennsylvania (PA)
Eckerd Coll (FL)
Elizabethtown Coll (PA)
Elon U (NC)
Emory & Henry Coll (VA)
Emory U (GA)
Erskine Coll (SC)
Fairfield U (CT)
Fairleigh Dickinson U, Coll at Florham (NJ)
Fairleigh Dickinson U, Metropolitan Campus (NJ)
Fairmont State U (WV)
Florida Ag and Mech U (FL)
Florida Atlantic U (FL)
Florida Intl U (FL)
Florida State U (FL)
Franciscan U of Steubenville (OH)
Francis Marion U (SC)
Franklin & Marshall Coll (PA)
Franklin Coll (IN)
Furman U (SC)
Gardner-Webb U (NC)
Georgetown Coll (KY)
Georgetown U (DC)
The George Washington U (DC)
Georgia Coll & State U (GA)
Georgia Southern U (GA)
Georgia State U (GA)
Gettysburg Coll (PA)
Gonzaga U (WA)
Gordon Coll (MA)
Goucher Coll (MD)
Grace Coll (IN)
Grambling State U (LA)
Grand Valley State U (MI)
Greensboro Coll (NC)
Grinnell Coll (IA)
Grove City Coll (PA)
Guilford Coll (NC)
Gustavus Adolphus Coll (MN)
Hamilton Coll (NY)
Hamline U (MN)
Hampden-Sydney Coll (VA)
Hanover Coll (IN)
Harding U (AR)
Hartwick Coll (NY)
Harvard U (MA)
Haverford Coll (PA)
Hendrix Coll (AR)
High Point U (NC)
Hillsdale Coll (MI)
Hobart and William Smith Colls (NY)
Hofstra U (NY)
Hollins U (VA)
Holy Family U (PA)
Hood Coll (MD)
Hope Coll (MI)
Houghton Coll (NY)
Houston Baptist U (TX)
Humboldt State U (CA)
Hunter Coll of the City U of New York (NY)
Idaho State U (ID)
Illinois Coll (IL)
Illinois State U (IL)
Illinois Wesleyan U (IL)
Immaculata U (PA)
Indiana State U (IN)
Indiana U Bloomington (IN)
Indiana U Northwest (IN)
Indiana U of Pennsylvania (PA)
Indiana U–Purdue U Fort Wayne (IN)
Indiana U–Purdue U Indianapolis (IN)
Indiana U South Bend (IN)
Indiana U Southeast (IN)
Iona Coll (NY)
Iowa State U of Science and Technology (IA)
Ithaca Coll (NY)
Jacksonville State U (AL)
Jacksonville U (FL)
John Carroll U (OH)
The Johns Hopkins U (MD)
Johnson C. Smith U (NC)
Juniata Coll (PA)
Kalamazoo Coll (MI)
Keene State Coll (NH)
Kent State U (OH)
Kenyon Coll (OH)
King Coll (TN)
King's Coll (PA)
Knox Coll (IL)
Kutztown U of Pennsylvania (PA)
Lafayette Coll (PA)
Lake Forest Coll (IL)
Lakehead U (ON, Canada)
La Salle U (PA)
Laurentian U (ON, Canada)
Lawrence U (WI)
Lebanon Valley Coll (PA)
Lehigh U (PA)
Lehman Coll of the City U of New York (NY)
Le Moyne Coll (NY)
Lenoir-Rhyne Coll (NC)
Lewis & Clark Coll (OR)
Lincoln U (PA)
Lindenwood U (MO)
Linfield Coll (OR)
Lipscomb U (TN)
Lock Haven U of Pennsylvania (PA)
Longwood U (VA)
Loras Coll (IA)
Louisiana Coll (LA)
Louisiana State U and Ag and Mech Coll (LA)
Loyola Coll in Maryland (MD)
Loyola Marymount U (CA)
Loyola U Chicago (IL)
Loyola U New Orleans (LA)
Luther Coll (IA)
Lycoming Coll (PA)
Lynchburg Coll (VA)
Macalester Coll (MN)
Manchester Coll (IN)
Manhattanville Coll (NY)
Mansfield U of Pennsylvania (PA)
Marian Coll (IN)
Marist Coll (NY)
Marlboro Coll (VT)
Marquette U (WI)
Mary Baldwin Coll (VA)
Marywood U (PA)
McDaniel Coll (MD)
McGill U (QC, Canada)
McNeese State U (LA)
Memorial U of Newfoundland (NL, Canada)
Mercer U (GA)
Meredith Coll (NC)
Merrimack Coll (MA)
Messiah Coll (PA)
Methodist U (NC)
Miami U (OH)
Miami U Hamilton (OH)
Michigan State U (MI)
Middlebury Coll (VT)
Millersville U of Pennsylvania (PA)
Millsaps Coll (MS)
Mills Coll (CA)
Minnesota State U Mankato (MN)
Minot State U (ND)
Mississippi Coll (MS)
Missouri Southern State U (MO)
Missouri State U (MO)
Molloy Coll (NY)
Monmouth Coll (IL)
Montclair State U (NJ)
Moravian Coll (PA)
Morehead State U (KY)
Morehouse Coll (GA)
Mount Allison U (NB, Canada)
Mount Holyoke Coll (MA)
Mount Mary Coll (WI)
Mount St. Mary's Coll (CA)
Mount St. Mary's U (MD)
Mount Saint Vincent U (NS, Canada)
Muhlenberg Coll (PA)
Murray State U (KY)
Nazareth Coll of Rochester (NY)
Nebraska Wesleyan U (NE)
New Coll of Florida (FL)
New York U (NY)
Niagara U (NY)
Nicholls State U (LA)
North Carolina Ag and Tech State U (NC)
North Carolina Central U (NC)
North Carolina State U (NC)
North Central Coll (IL)
North Dakota State U (ND)
Northeastern Illinois U (IL)
Northeastern U (MA)
Northern Arizona U (AZ)
Northern Illinois U (IL)
Northern Michigan U (MI)
Northern State U (SD)
North Georgia Coll & State U (GA)
Northwestern U (IL)
Northwest Missouri State U (MO)
Oakland U (MI)
Oakwood Coll (AL)
Oberlin Coll (OH)
Occidental Coll (CA)
Oglethorpe U (GA)
Ohio Northern U (OH)
Ohio U (OH)
Ohio Wesleyan U (OH)
Oklahoma City U (OK)
Oklahoma State U (OK)
Old Dominion U (VA)
Oral Roberts U (OK)
Oregon State U (OR)
Otterbein Coll (OH)
Ouachita Baptist U (AR)
Pace U (NY)
Pacific Lutheran U (WA)
Pacific U (OR)
Penn State Abington (PA)
Penn State Altoona (PA)
Penn State Berks (PA)
Penn State Erie, The Behrend Coll (PA)
Penn State U Park (PA)
Pepperdine U, Malibu (CA)
Pittsburg State U (KS)
Pitzer Coll (CA)
Plymouth State U (NH)
Pomona Coll (CA)
Portland State U (OR)
Presbyterian Coll (SC)
Princeton U (NJ)
Providence Coll (RI)
Purchase Coll, State U of New York (NY)
Purdue U Calumet (IN)
Queens Coll of the City U of New York (NY)
Queen's U at Kingston (ON, Canada)
Randolph Coll (VA)
Randolph-Macon Coll (VA)
Redeemer U Coll (ON, Canada)
Reed Coll (OR)
Regis U (CO)
Rhode Island Coll (RI)
Rhodes Coll (TN)
Rice U (TX)
Rider U (NJ)
Ripon Coll (WI)
Roanoke Coll (VA)
Rockford Coll (IL)
Rockhurst U (MO)
Rollins Coll (FL)
Rosemont Coll (PA)
Royal Military Coll of Canada (ON, Canada)
Rutgers, The State U of New Jersey, Camden (NJ)

MAJORS AND MORE

Rutgers, The State U of New Jersey, Newark (NJ)
Rutgers, The State U of New Jersey, New Brunswick (NJ)
Saginaw Valley State U (MI)
St. Ambrose U (IA)
St. Cloud State U (MN)
Saint Francis U (PA)
St. Francis Xavier U (NS, Canada)
St. John Fisher Coll (NY)
St. John's Coll (NM)
Saint John's U (MN)
St. John's U (NY)
Saint Joseph's U (PA)
St. Lawrence U (NY)
Saint Louis U (MO)
Saint Mary's Coll (IN)
Saint Mary's Coll of California (CA)
St. Mary's U (TX)
Saint Mary's U of Minnesota (MN)
Saint Michael's Coll (VT)
St. Norbert Coll (WI)
St. Olaf Coll (MN)
St. Thomas U (NB, Canada)
Saint Vincent Coll (PA)
Salem Coll (NC)
Salisbury U (MD)
Salve Regina U (RI)
Samford U (AL)
Sam Houston State U (TX)
San Diego State U (CA)
San Francisco State U (CA)
Santa Clara U (CA)
Sarah Lawrence Coll (NY)
Scripps Coll (CA)
Seattle Pacific U (WA)
Seattle U (WA)
Sewanee: The U of the South (TN)
Shippensburg U of Pennsylvania (PA)
Shorter Coll (GA)
Siena Coll (NY)
Simmons Coll (MA)
Simon Fraser U (BC, Canada)
Simpson Coll (IA)
Skidmore Coll (NY)
Slippery Rock U of Pennsylvania (PA)
Smith Coll (MA)
Sonoma State U (CA)
South Dakota State U (SD)
Southeastern Louisiana U (LA)
Southeast Missouri State U (MO)
Southern Adventist U (TN)
Southern Connecticut State U (CT)
Southern Illinois U Carbondale (IL)
Southern Methodist U (TX)
Southern Oregon U (OR)
Southern U and Ag and Mech Coll (LA)
Southern Utah U (UT)
Southwestern U (TX)
Spelman Coll (GA)
Stanford U (CA)
State U of New York at Binghamton (NY)
State U of New York at Fredonia (NY)
State U of New York at New Paltz (NY)
State U of New York at Oswego (NY)
State U of New York at Plattsburgh (NY)
State U of New York Coll at Geneseo (NY)
State U of New York Coll at Oneonta (NY)
State U of New York Coll at Potsdam (NY)
Stephen F. Austin State U (TX)
Stetson U (FL)
Stony Brook U, State U of New York (NY)
Suffolk U (MA)
Susquehanna U (PA)
Swarthmore Coll (PA)
Sweet Briar Coll (VA)
Syracuse U (NY)
Taylor U (IN)
Temple U (PA)
Tennessee State U (TN)
Tennessee Technological U (TN)
Tennessee Wesleyan Coll (TN)
Texas A&M U (TX)
Texas A&M U–Commerce (TX)
Texas Christian U (TX)
Texas Southern U (TX)
Texas State U-San Marcos (TX)
Texas Tech U (TX)
Towson U (MD)
Transylvania U (KY)
Trent U (ON, Canada)
Trinity Coll (CT)
Trinity U (TX)
Truman State U (MO)
Tufts U (MA)
Tulane U (LA)
Union Coll (NE)
Union U (TN)
United States Naval Acad (MD)
Université de Sherbrooke (QC, Canada)
U at Albany, State U of New York (NY)
U at Buffalo, the State U of New York (NY)
The U of Akron (OH)
The U of Alabama at Birmingham (AL)
The U of Arizona (AZ)
U of Arkansas (AR)
The U of British Columbia (BC, Canada)
The U of British Columbia–Okanagan (BC, Canada)
U of California, Berkeley (CA)
U of California, Davis (CA)
U of California, Irvine (CA)
U of California, Los Angeles (CA)
U of California, Riverside (CA)
U of California, San Diego (CA)
U of California, Santa Barbara (CA)
U of Central Arkansas (AR)
U of Central Florida (FL)
U of Central Missouri (MO)
U of Central Oklahoma (OK)
U of Chicago (IL)
U of Cincinnati (OH)
U of Colorado at Boulder (CO)
U of Colorado Denver (CO)
U of Connecticut (CT)
U of Dallas (TX)
U of Dayton (OH)
U of Delaware (DE)
U of Denver (CO)
U of Evansville (IN)
U of Florida (FL)
U of Georgia (GA)
U of Hawaii at Manoa (HI)
U of Houston (TX)
U of Idaho (ID)
U of Illinois at Chicago (IL)
U of Illinois at Urbana–Champaign (IL)
U of Indianapolis (IN)
The U of Iowa (IA)
U of Kansas (KS)
U of King's Coll (NS, Canada)
U of La Verne (CA)
U of Lethbridge (AB, Canada)
U of Louisiana at Lafayette (LA)
U of Louisiana at Monroe (LA)
U of Louisville (KY)
U of Maine (ME)
U of Maine at Fort Kent (ME)
U of Maryland, Coll Park (MD)
U of Mary Washington (VA)
U of Massachusetts Amherst (MA)
U of Massachusetts Boston (MA)
U of Massachusetts Dartmouth (MA)
U of Miami (FL)
U of Michigan (MI)
U of Michigan–Dearborn (MI)
U of Michigan–Flint (MI)
U of Minnesota, Twin Cities Campus (MN)
U of Mississippi (MS)
U of Missouri–Columbia (MO)
U of Missouri–Kansas City (MO)
U of Missouri–St. Louis (MO)
The U of Montana (MT)
U of Nebraska at Kearney (NE)
U of Nebraska at Omaha (NE)
U of Nebraska–Lincoln (NE)
U of Nevada, Las Vegas (NV)
U of Nevada, Reno (NV)
U of New Brunswick Fredericton (NB, Canada)
U of New Hampshire (NH)
U of New Mexico (NM)
U of New Orleans (LA)
The U of North Carolina at Asheville (NC)
The U of North Carolina at Charlotte (NC)
The U of North Carolina at Greensboro (NC)
The U of North Carolina Wilmington (NC)
U of North Dakota (ND)
U of Northern Colorado (CO)
U of Northern Iowa (IA)
U of North Texas (TX)
U of Notre Dame (IN)
U of Oklahoma (OK)
U of Oregon (OR)
U of Ottawa (ON, Canada)
U of Pennsylvania (PA)
U of Pittsburgh (PA)
U of Prince Edward Island (PE, Canada)
U of Puerto Rico at Utuado (PR)
U of Puget Sound (WA)
U of Redlands (CA)
U of Regina (SK, Canada)
U of Rhode Island (RI)
U of Richmond (VA)
U of Rochester (NY)
U of St. Thomas (MN)
U of St. Thomas (TX)
U of San Diego (CA)
The U of Scranton (PA)
U of South Carolina (SC)
The U of South Dakota (SD)
U of Southern California (CA)
U of Southern Indiana (IN)
U of Southern Maine (ME)
U.of South Florida (FL)
The U of Tennessee (TN)
The U of Tennessee at Chattanooga (TN)
The U of Tennessee at Martin (TN)
The U of Texas at Arlington (TX)
The U of Texas at Austin (TX)
The U of Texas at El Paso (TX)
The U of Texas at San Antonio (TX)
The U of Texas–Pan American (TX)
U of the District of Columbia (DC)
U of the Pacific (CA)
The U of Toledo (OH)
U of Toronto (ON, Canada)
U of Tulsa (OK)
U of Utah (UT)
U of Vermont (VT)
U of Victoria (BC, Canada)
U of Virginia (VA)
The U of Virginia's Coll at Wise (VA)
The U of Western Ontario (ON, Canada)
U of West Georgia (GA)
U of Windsor (ON, Canada)
The U of Winnipeg (MB, Canada)
U of Wisconsin–Eau Claire (WI)
U of Wisconsin–Green Bay (WI)
U of Wisconsin–La Crosse (WI)
U of Wisconsin–Madison (WI)
U of Wisconsin–Milwaukee (WI)
U of Wisconsin–Oshkosh (WI)
U of Wisconsin–Parkside (WI)
U of Wisconsin–Stevens Point (WI)
U of Wisconsin–Whitewater (WI)
U of Wyoming (WY)
Ursinus Coll (PA)
Utah State U (UT)
Valdosta State U (GA)
Valparaiso U (IN)
Vanderbilt U (TN)
Vassar Coll (NY)
Villanova U (PA)
Virginia Polytechnic Inst and State U (VA)
Virginia Wesleyan Coll (VA)
Wabash Coll (IN)
Wake Forest U (NC)
Walla Walla U (WA)
Walsh U (OH)
Wartburg Coll (IA)
Washburn U (KS)
Washington & Jefferson Coll (PA)
Washington and Lee U (VA)
Washington Coll (MD)
Washington State U (WA)
Washington U in St. Louis (MO)
Weber State U (UT)
Webster U (MO)
Wellesley Coll (MA)
Wells Coll (NY)
Wesleyan Coll (GA)
Wesleyan U (CT)
West Chester U of Pennsylvania (PA)
Western Illinois U (IL)
Western Kentucky U (KY)
Western Michigan U (MI)
Western Washington U (WA)
Westminster Coll (MO)
Westmont Coll (CA)
Wheaton Coll (IL)
Wheeling Jesuit U (WV)
Whitman Coll (WA)
Whittier Coll (CA)
Whitworth U (WA)
Wichita State U (KS)
Widener U (PA)
Wilfrid Laurier U (ON, Canada)
Wilkes U (PA)
Willamette U (OR)
William Jewell Coll (MO)
Williams Coll (MA)
Wilson Coll (PA)
Wingate U (NC)
Winona State U (MN)
Wittenberg U (OH)
Wofford Coll (SC)
Wright State U (OH)
Xavier U (OH)
Xavier U of Louisiana (LA)
Yale U (CT)
York Coll of the City U of New York (NY)
York U (ON, Canada)
Youngstown State U (OH)

FRENCH AS A SECOND/ FOREIGN LANGUAGE (TEACHING)

Bishop's U (QC, Canada)
McGill U (QC, Canada)
Saginaw Valley State U (MI)
U of Toronto (ON, Canada)
U of Windsor (ON, Canada)
Western Michigan U (MI)

FRENCH LANGUAGE TEACHER EDUCATION

Alma Coll (MI)
Anderson U (IN)
Appalachian State U (NC)
Arkansas State U (AR)
Assumption Coll (MA)
Auburn U (AL)
Baylor U (TX)
Bethel U (MN)
Bishop's U (QC, Canada)
Bridgewater Coll (VA)
Brigham Young U (UT)
California Lutheran U (CA)
California State U, Chico (CA)
The Catholic U of America (DC)
Centenary Coll of Louisiana (LA)
Central Michigan U (MI)
Central Washington U (WA)
The Coll at Brockport, State U of New York (NY)
Coll of the Ozarks (MO)
Colorado State U (CO)
Concordia Coll (MN)
Daemen Coll (NY)
DePaul U (IL)
Duquesne U (PA)
East Carolina U (NC)
Eastern Mennonite U (VA)
Eastern Michigan U (MI)
Franklin Coll (IN)
Gardner-Webb U (NC)
Grace Coll (IN)
Grambling State U (LA)
Harding U (AR)
Hofstra U (NY)
Hope Coll (MI)
Indiana U Bloomington (IN)
Indiana U–Purdue U Fort Wayne (IN)
Indiana U–Purdue U Indianapolis (IN)
Iona Coll (NY)
Ithaca Coll (NY)
Juniata Coll (PA)
Keene State Coll (NH)
Kent State U (OH)
King Coll (TN)
Kutztown U of Pennsylvania (PA)
Le Moyne Coll (NY)
Lindenwood U (MO)
Lipscomb U (TN)
Manhattanville Coll (NY)
Mansfield U of Pennsylvania (PA)
Marist Coll (NY)
Marywood U (PA)
McGill U (QC, Canada)
Messiah Coll (PA)
Miami U Hamilton (OH)
Minot State U (ND)
Missouri State U (MO)
Molloy Coll (NY)
Moravian Coll (PA)
Mount Mary Coll (WI)
Murray State U (KY)
New York U (NY)
Niagara U (NY)
Nicholls State U (LA)
North Carolina Central U (NC)
North Carolina State U (NC)
North Dakota State U (ND)
Northern Michigan U (MI)
Ohio Northern U (OH)
Ohio U (OH)
Ohio Wesleyan U (OH)
Old Dominion U (VA)
Pace U (NY)
Pittsburg State U (KS)
Purdue U (IN)
Rhode Island Coll (RI)
St. Ambrose U (IA)
Saint Francis U (PA)
Saint Mary's U of Minnesota (MN)
Salve Regina U (RI)
Seton Hill U (PA)
Southeastern Louisiana U (LA)
Southern U and Ag and Mech Coll (LA)
State U of New York at Plattsburgh (NY)
State U of New York Coll at Oneonta (NY)
State U of New York Coll at Potsdam (NY)
The U of Akron (OH)
The U of Arizona (AZ)
U of Evansville (IN)
U of Illinois at Chicago (IL)
U of Illinois at Urbana–Champaign (IL)
U of Indianapolis (IN)
The U of Iowa (IA)
U of Louisiana at Lafayette (LA)
U of Louisiana at Monroe (LA)
U of Maine (ME)
U of Maine at Fort Kent (ME)
U of Michigan–Flint (MI)
U of Minnesota, Duluth (MN)
U of Missouri–St. Louis (MO)
U of Nebraska–Lincoln (NE)
The U of North Carolina at Charlotte (NC)
The U of North Carolina at Greensboro (NC)
The U of North Carolina Wilmington (NC)
U of Regina (SK, Canada)
The U of South Dakota (SD)
The U of Tennessee at Martin (TN)
The U of Toledo (OH)
U of Toronto (ON, Canada)
U of Windsor (ON, Canada)
Valparaiso U (IN)
Washington State U (WA)
Washington U in St. Louis (MO)
Weber State U (UT)
Western Carolina U (NC)
Western Michigan U (MI)
Wheeling Jesuit U (WV)
Widener U (PA)
William Jewell Coll (MO)
William Woods U (MO)
Xavier U of Louisiana (LA)
Youngstown State U (OH)

FRENCH STUDIES

American U (DC)
Bard Coll at Simon's Rock (MA)
Barnard Coll (NY)
Brock U (ON, Canada)
Brown U (RI)
Case Western Reserve U (OH)
Claremont McKenna Coll (CA)
The Colorado Coll (CO)
Lake Superior State U (MI)
Mills Coll (CA)
New Coll of Florida (FL)
Purdue U (IN)
Saint Joseph's U (PA)
Santa Clara U (CA)
Skidmore Coll (NY)
Smith Coll (MA)
U of Victoria (BC, Canada)
U of Windsor (ON, Canada)
The U of Winnipeg (MB, Canada)
Wheaton Coll (MA)
Wilfrid Laurier U (ON, Canada)
York U (ON, Canada)

FUNERAL SERVICE AND MORTUARY SCIENCE

Gannon U (PA)
Lindenwood U (MO)
Mount Ida Coll (MA)
Point Park U (PA)
St. John's U (NY)
Southern Illinois U Carbondale (IL)
Thiel Coll (PA)
U of Central Oklahoma (OK)
U of Minnesota, Twin Cities Campus (MN)
U of the District of Columbia (DC)
Wayne State U (MI)

GAY/LESBIAN STUDIES

Bennington Coll (VT)
Cornell U (NY)
Hobart and William Smith Colls (NY)
Sarah Lawrence Coll (NY)
Trinity Coll (CT)
The U of Western Ontario (ON, Canada)

GENERAL RETAILING/ WHOLESALING

U of South Carolina (SC)

GENERAL STUDIES

Albertus Magnus Coll (CT)
Alfred U (NY)
Anderson U (IN)
Angelo State U (TX)
Antioch U Santa Barbara (CA)
Aquinas Coll (MI)
Arkansas State U (AR)
Ashford U (IA)
Athabasca U (AB, Canada)
Austin Peay State U (TN)
Avila U (MO)
Bluefield State Coll (WV)
Brenau U (GA)
Brewton-Parker Coll (GA)

Buffalo State Coll, State U of New York (NY)
Calumet Coll of Saint Joseph (IN)
Canisius Coll (NY)
The Catholic U of America (DC)
Central Coll (IA)
Chicago State U (IL)
City U of Seattle (WA)
Clearwater Christian Coll (FL)
Cleveland State U (OH)
Concordia U, St. Paul (MN)
Concordia U Wisconsin (WI)
Dallas Baptist U (TX)
Daniel Webster Coll (NH)
DePaul U (IL)
Dordt Coll (IA)
Drexel U (PA)
Duquesne U (PA)
East Central U (OK)
Eastern Connecticut State U (CT)
Eastern Kentucky U (KY)
East Tennessee State U (TN)
Emporia State U (KS)
Fairleigh Dickinson U, Coll at Florham (NJ)
Fairleigh Dickinson U, Metropolitan Campus (NJ)
Florida Gulf Coast U (FL)
Florida Inst of Technology (FL)
Georgia Southern U (GA)
Grand Canyon U (AZ)
Grantham U (MO)
Hampton U (VA)
Harding U (AR)
Howard Payne U (TX)
Idaho State U (ID)
Indiana U Bloomington (IN)
Indiana U East (IN)
Indiana U Kokomo (IN)
Indiana U Northwest (IN)
Indiana U of Pennsylvania (PA)
Indiana U–Purdue U Fort Wayne (IN)
Indiana U–Purdue U Indianapolis (IN)
Indiana U South Bend (IN)
Indiana U Southeast (IN)
Indiana Wesleyan U (IN)
Keene State Coll (NH)
Kent State U (OH)
Kutztown U of Pennsylvania (PA)
LaGrange Coll (GA)
La Roche Coll (PA)
La Salle U (PA)
Lipscomb U (TN)
Louisiana State U and Ag and Mech Coll (LA)
Loyola U Chicago (IL)
Loyola U New Orleans (LA)
Marist Coll (NY)
Marshall U (WV)
Mayville State U (ND)
McNeese State U (LA)
Metropolitan State U (MN)
Michigan Technological U (MI)
Mid-Continent U (KY)
Minot State U (ND)
Morehead State U (KY)
Morehouse Coll (GA)
Mount Marty Coll (SD)
Murray State U (KY)
National U (CA)
New Coll of Florida (FL)
New Mexico Inst of Mining and Technology (NM)
Nicholls State U (LA)
Northcentral U (AZ)
Northeastern State U (OK)
Northern Arizona U (AZ)
Northwest Christian Coll (OR)
Northwestern Oklahoma State U (OK)
Northwestern State U of Louisiana (LA)
Northwestern U (IL)
Ohio Dominican U (OH)
Ohio Northern U (OH)
Ohio U (OH)
Ohio Wesleyan U (OH)
Oklahoma State U (OK)
Pittsburg State U (KS)
Point Park U (PA)
Providence Coll (RI)
Radford U (VA)
Saginaw Valley State U (MI)
St. John's Coll (NM)
St. Joseph's Coll, New York (NY)
Samford U (AL)
Seattle Pacific U (WA)
Seton Hill U (PA)
Shawnee State U (OH)
Shepherd U (WV)
Shimer Coll (IL)
Shorter Coll (GA)
Siena Heights U (MI)
Simon Fraser U (BC, Canada)
Southeastern Louisiana U (LA)
Southeastern Oklahoma State U (OK)
Southeast Missouri State U (MO)
Southern New Hampshire U (NH)
Southwestern Coll (KS)
Southwest Minnesota State U (MN)
Spring Hill Coll (AL)
State U of New York Inst of Technology (NY)
Temple U (PA)
Texas Christian U (TX)
Texas Southern U (TX)
Texas Tech U (TX)
Texas Woman's U (TX)
Thompson Rivers U (BC, Canada)
Trinity Coll of Florida (FL)
U of Alaska Southeast (AK)
The U of British Columbia–Okanagan (BC, Canada)
U of Charleston (WV)
U of Connecticut (CT)
U of Dayton (OH)
U of Idaho (ID)
U of Illinois at Urbana–Champaign (IL)
U of Louisiana at Lafayette (LA)
U of Louisiana at Monroe (LA)
The U of Maine at Augusta (ME)
U of Maine at Farmington (ME)
U of Maine at Machias (ME)
U of Management and Technology (VA)
U of Mary (ND)
U of Mary Hardin-Baylor (TX)
U of Massachusetts Amherst (MA)
U of Memphis (TN)
U of Miami (FL)
U of Michigan (MI)
U of Michigan–Dearborn (MI)
U of Missouri–Columbia (MO)
U of Missouri–St. Louis (MO)
U of Nebraska at Kearney (NE)
U of Nebraska at Omaha (NE)
U of Nevada, Reno (NV)
U of New Mexico (NM)
U of New Orleans (LA)
U of North Alabama (AL)
U of North Dakota (ND)
U of North Texas (TX)
U of Regina (SK, Canada)
U of St. Thomas (TX)
U of Southern California (CA)
U of South Florida (FL)
The U of Texas at Tyler (TX)
The U of Texas–Pan American (TX)
U of the Ozarks (AR)
The U of Toledo (OH)
U of Windsor (ON, Canada)
U of Wisconsin–La Crosse (WI)
U of Wisconsin–Stevens Point (WI)
Valdosta State U (GA)
Western Kentucky U (KY)
Western Washington U (WA)
West Texas A&M U (TX)
West Virginia U (WV)
Widener U (PA)
York Coll (NE)
Youngstown State U (OH)

GENETICS

Cedar Crest Coll (PA)
Clemson U (SC)
Iowa State U of Science and Technology (IA)
McGill U (QC, Canada)
Ohio Wesleyan U (OH)
U of California, Davis (CA)
U of Georgia (GA)
The U of Western Ontario (ON, Canada)
Washington State U (WA)

GENETICS RELATED

The George Washington U (DC)

GEOCHEMISTRY

Bowdoin Coll (ME)
Bridgewater State Coll (MA)
Brown U (RI)
California Inst of Technology (CA)
Harvard U (MA)
Northern Arizona U (AZ)
State U of New York at Fredonia (NY)
State U of New York at Oswego (NY)
State U of New York Coll at Geneseo (NY)
U of Maine at Farmington (ME)
U of New Brunswick Fredericton (NB, Canada)
Western Michigan U (MI)

GEOGRAPHY

Appalachian State U (NC)
Aquinas Coll (MI)
Arizona State U (AZ)
Arkansas State U (AR)
Auburn U (AL)
Augustana Coll (IL)
Ball State U (IN)
Bard Coll at Simon's Rock (MA)
Bemidji State U (MN)
Bishop's U (QC, Canada)
Bloomsburg U of Pennsylvania (PA)
Boston U (MA)
Bowling Green State U (OH)
Bridgewater State Coll (MA)
Brigham Young U (UT)
Brock U (ON, Canada)
Bucknell U (PA)
Buffalo State Coll, State U of New York (NY)
California State Polytechnic U, Pomona (CA)
California State U, Chico (CA)
California State U, Dominguez Hills (CA)
California State U, East Bay (CA)
California State U, Fresno (CA)
California State U, Fullerton (CA)
California State U, Long Beach (CA)
California State U, Los Angeles (CA)
California State U, Sacramento (CA)
California State U, San Bernardino (CA)
California State U, Stanislaus (CA)
Calvin Coll (MI)
Canadian Mennonite U (MB, Canada)
Central Connecticut State U (CT)
Central Michigan U (MI)
Central Washington U (WA)
Cheyney U of Pennsylvania (PA)
Chicago State U (IL)
City Coll of the City U of New York (NY)
Clarion U of Pennsylvania (PA)
Clark U (MA)
Colgate U (NY)
Concordia U (QC, Canada)
Concordia U Chicago (IL)
Concordia U, Nebraska (NE)
Concord U (WV)
Dartmouth Coll (NH)
DePaul U (IL)
East Carolina U (NC)
Eastern Illinois U (IL)
Eastern Kentucky U (KY)
Eastern Michigan U (MI)
East Stroudsburg U of Pennsylvania (PA)
East Tennessee State U (TN)
Edinboro U of Pennsylvania (PA)
Emory & Henry Coll (VA)
Excelsior Coll (NY)
Fayetteville State U (NC)
Fitchburg State Coll (MA)
Florida Ag and Mech U (FL)
Florida Atlantic U (FL)
Florida Intl U (FL)
Florida State U (FL)
Framingham State Coll (MA)
Francis Marion U (SC)
Frostburg State U (MD)
George Mason U (VA)
The George Washington U (DC)
Georgia Southern U (GA)
Georgia State U (GA)
Gustavus Adolphus Coll (MN)
Harrisburg U of Science and Technology (PA)
Hofstra U (NY)
Humboldt State U (CA)
Hunter Coll of the City U of New York (NY)
Illinois State U (IL)
Indiana State U (IN)
Indiana U Bloomington (IN)
Indiana U of Pennsylvania (PA)
Indiana U–Purdue U Indianapolis (IN)
Indiana U Southeast (IN)
Jacksonville State U (AL)
Jacksonville U (FL)
James Madison U (VA)
The Johns Hopkins U (MD)
Kansas State U (KS)
Keene State Coll (NH)
Kennesaw State U (GA)
Kent State U (OH)
Kutztown U of Pennsylvania (PA)
Lakehead U (ON, Canada)
Laurentian U (ON, Canada)
Lehman Coll of the City U of New York (NY)
Lock Haven U of Pennsylvania (PA)
Longwood U (VA)
Louisiana State U and Ag and Mech Coll (LA)
Macalester Coll (MN)
Mansfield U of Pennsylvania (PA)
Marshall U (WV)
McGill U (QC, Canada)
Memorial U of Newfoundland (NL, Canada)
Miami U (OH)
Miami U Hamilton (OH)
Michigan State U (MI)
Middlebury Coll (VT)
Millersville U of Pennsylvania (PA)
Minnesota State U Mankato (MN)
Missouri State U (MO)
Montclair State U (NJ)
Morehead State U (KY)
Mount Allison U (NB, Canada)
Mount Holyoke Coll (MA)
Murray State U (KY)
North Carolina Central U (NC)
Northeastern Illinois U (IL)
Northeastern State U (OK)
Northern Arizona U (AZ)
Northern Illinois U (IL)
Northern Michigan U (MI)
Northwestern U (IL)
Northwest Missouri State U (MO)
Ohio U (OH)
Ohio Wesleyan U (OH)
Oklahoma State U (OK)
Old Dominion U (VA)
Oregon State U (OR)
Park U (MO)
Penn State Abington (PA)
Penn State Altoona (PA)
Penn State Berks (PA)
Penn State Erie, The Behrend Coll (PA)
Penn State U Park (PA)
Pittsburg State U (KS)
Plymouth State U (NH)
Portland State U (OR)
Queen's U at Kingston (ON, Canada)
Radford U (VA)
Rhode Island Coll (RI)
Roosevelt U (IL)
Rowan U (NJ)
Rutgers, The State U of New Jersey, New Brunswick (NJ)
St. Cloud State U (MN)
Salem State Coll (MA)
Salisbury U (MD)
Samford U (AL)
Sam Houston State U (TX)
San Diego State U (CA)
San Francisco State U (CA)
Shippensburg U of Pennsylvania (PA)
Simon Fraser U (BC, Canada)
Slippery Rock U of Pennsylvania (PA)
Sonoma State U (CA)
South Dakota State U (SD)
Southern Connecticut State U (CT)
Southern Illinois U Carbondale (IL)
Southern Illinois U Edwardsville (IL)
Southern Oregon U (OR)
State U of New York at Binghamton (NY)
State U of New York at New Paltz (NY)
State U of New York at Plattsburgh (NY)
State U of New York Coll at Geneseo (NY)
State U of New York Coll at Oneonta (NY)
Stephen F. Austin State U (TX)
Stetson U (FL)
Syracuse U (NY)
Temple U (PA)
Texas A&M U (TX)
Texas Christian U (TX)
Texas State U-San Marcos (TX)
Texas Tech U (TX)
Thompson Rivers U (BC, Canada)
Towson U (MD)
Trent U (ON, Canada)
United States Air Force Acad (CO)
U at Albany, State U of New York (NY)
U at Buffalo, the State U of New York (NY)
The U of Akron (OH)
The U of Alabama (AL)
U of Alaska Fairbanks (AK)
The U of Arizona (AZ)
The U of British Columbia (BC, Canada)
The U of British Columbia–Okanagan (BC, Canada)
U of California, Berkeley (CA)
U of California, Los Angeles (CA)
U of California, Santa Barbara (CA)
U of Central Arkansas (AR)
U of Central Missouri (MO)
U of Central Oklahoma (OK)
U of Chicago (IL)
U of Cincinnati (OH)
U of Colorado at Boulder (CO)
U of Colorado Denver (CO)
U of Connecticut (CT)
U of Delaware (DE)
U of Denver (CO)
U of Florida (FL)
U of Georgia (GA)
U of Hawaii at Manoa (HI)
U of Houston–Clear Lake (TX)
U of Idaho (ID)
U of Illinois at Urbana–Champaign (IL)
The U of Iowa (IA)
U of Kansas (KS)
U of Lethbridge (AB, Canada)
U of Louisville (KY)
U of Maine at Farmington (ME)
U of Maryland, Baltimore County (MD)
U of Maryland, Coll Park (MD)
U of Mary Washington (VA)
U of Massachusetts Amherst (MA)
U of Massachusetts Boston (MA)
U of Memphis (TN)
U of Miami (FL)
U of Minnesota, Duluth (MN)
U of Minnesota, Twin Cities Campus (MN)
U of Missouri–Columbia (MO)
U of Missouri–Kansas City (MO)
The U of Montana (MT)
U of Nebraska at Kearney (NE)
U of Nebraska at Omaha (NE)
U of Nebraska–Lincoln (NE)
U of Nevada, Reno (NV)
U of New Hampshire (NH)
U of New Mexico (NM)
U of New Orleans (LA)
U of North Alabama (AL)
The U of North Carolina at Chapel Hill (NC)
The U of North Carolina at Charlotte (NC)
The U of North Carolina at Greensboro (NC)
The U of North Carolina Wilmington (NC)
U of North Dakota (ND)
U of Northern Colorado (CO)
U of Northern Iowa (IA)
U of North Texas (TX)
U of Oklahoma (OK)
U of Oregon (OR)
U of Ottawa (ON, Canada)
U of Pittsburgh at Johnstown (PA)
U of Regina (SK, Canada)
U of St. Thomas (MN)
U of South Alabama (AL)
U of South Carolina (SC)
U of Southern California (CA)
U of Southern Maine (ME)
U of Southern Mississippi (MS)
U of South Florida (FL)
The U of Tennessee (TN)
The U of Tennessee at Martin (TN)
The U of Texas at Austin (TX)
The U of Texas at Dallas (TX)
The U of Texas at El Paso (TX)
The U of Texas at San Antonio (TX)
U of the District of Columbia (DC)
The U of Toledo (OH)
U of Toronto (ON, Canada)
U of Utah (UT)
U of Vermont (VT)
U of Victoria (BC, Canada)
The U of Western Ontario (ON, Canada)
U of West Georgia (GA)
The U of Winnipeg (MB, Canada)
U of Wisconsin–Eau Claire (WI)
U of Wisconsin–La Crosse (WI)
U of Wisconsin–Madison (WI)
U of Wisconsin–Milwaukee (WI)
U of Wisconsin–Oshkosh (WI)
U of Wisconsin–Parkside (WI)
U of Wisconsin–Stevens Point (WI)
U of Wisconsin–Whitewater (WI)
U of Wyoming (WY)
Utah State U (UT)
Valparaiso U (IN)
Vassar Coll (NY)
Villanova U (PA)
Virginia Polytechnic Inst and State U (VA)
Wayne State Coll (NE)
Wayne State U (MI)
Weber State U (UT)
West Chester U of Pennsylvania (PA)
Western Carolina U (NC)
Western Illinois U (IL)
Western Kentucky U (KY)
Western Michigan U (MI)
Western Washington U (WA)
West Texas A&M U (TX)
West Virginia U (WV)
Wilfrid Laurier U (ON, Canada)
William Paterson U of New Jersey (NJ)
Wittenberg U (OH)
Worcester State Coll (MA)

Wright State U (OH)
York U (ON, Canada)
Youngstown State U (OH)

GEOGRAPHY RELATED
Bridgewater State Coll (MA)
Brigham Young U (UT)
Central Michigan U (MI)
South Dakota State U (SD)
U of California, Los Angeles (CA)

GEOGRAPHY TEACHER EDUCATION
Bishop's U (QC, Canada)
Concordia U, Nebraska (NE)
DePaul U (IL)
Fitchburg State Coll (MA)
Keene State Coll (NH)
Mayville State U (ND)
McGill U (QC, Canada)
Northern Michigan U (MI)
Shawnee State U (OH)
The U of Iowa (IA)
The U of Tennessee at Martin (TN)
U of Windsor (ON, Canada)
Valparaiso U (IN)
Wayne State Coll (NE)
Western Michigan U (MI)

GEOLOGICAL AND EARTH SCIENCES/GEOSCIENCES RELATED
Baylor U (TX)
Bridgewater State Coll (MA)
Brigham Young U (UT)
Bucknell U (PA)
California State U, Chico (CA)
The Coll at Brockport, State U of New York (NY)
Earlham Coll (IN)
Georgia Inst of Technology (GA)
Lehigh U (PA)
Montclair State U (NJ)
Ohio U (OH)
Pacific Lutheran U (WA)
Penn State Abington (PA)
Penn State Altoona (PA)
Penn State Berks (PA)
Penn State Erie, The Behrend Coll (PA)
Penn State U Park (PA)
Princeton U (NJ)
Stanford U (CA)
Texas A&M U (TX)
The U of Akron (OH)
U of Arkansas (AR)
U of California, Los Angeles (CA)
U of Illinois at Urbana–Champaign (IL)
U of Nevada, Las Vegas (NV)
The U of North Carolina at Charlotte (NC)
U of Northern Iowa (IA)
U of Oklahoma (OK)
U of Ottawa (ON, Canada)
U of Pittsburgh (PA)
The U of Texas at Austin (TX)
U of Utah (UT)
U of West Georgia (GA)
U of Wyoming (WY)
Utah Valley State Coll (UT)
Washington and Lee U (VA)
Western State Coll of Colorado (CO)
Whitman Coll (WA)
Wittenberg U (OH)
Yale U (CT)

GEOLOGICAL ENGINEERING
The U of Arizona (AZ)
U of Toronto (ON, Canada)

GEOLOGICAL/ GEOPHYSICAL ENGINEERING
Auburn U (AL)
Colorado School of Mines (CO)
Harvard U (MA)
Laurentian U (ON, Canada)
Memorial U of Newfoundland (NL, Canada)
Michigan Technological U (MI)
Missouri U of Science and Technology (MO)
Montana Tech of The U of Montana (MT)
New Jersey Inst of Technology (NJ)
Oregon State U (OR)
Queen's U at Kingston (ON, Canada)
Rutgers, The State U of New Jersey, Newark (NJ)
South Dakota School of Mines and Technology (SD)
Tufts U (MA)
U of Alaska Fairbanks (AK)
The U of British Columbia (BC, Canada)
U of California, Berkeley (CA)
U of California, Los Angeles (CA)
U of Minnesota, Twin Cities Campus (MN)
U of Mississippi (MS)
U of Nevada, Reno (NV)
U of New Brunswick Fredericton (NB, Canada)
U of North Dakota (ND)
U of Rochester (NY)
U of Utah (UT)

GEOLOGY/EARTH SCIENCE
Acadia U (NS, Canada)
Adams State Coll (CO)
Adrian Coll (MI)
Albion Coll (MI)
Alfred U (NY)
Allegheny Coll (PA)
American U of Beirut (Lebanon)
Amherst Coll (MA)
Appalachian State U (NC)
Arizona State U (AZ)
Ashland U (OH)
Auburn U (AL)
Augustana Coll (IL)
Austin Peay State U (TN)
Ball State U (IN)
Bard Coll at Simon's Rock (MA)
Bates Coll (ME)
Baylor U (TX)
Beloit Coll (WI)
Bemidji State U (MN)
Bloomsburg U of Pennsylvania (PA)
Boise State U (ID)
Boston Coll (MA)
Boston U (MA)
Bowdoin Coll (ME)
Bowling Green State U (OH)
Bridgewater State Coll (MA)
Brigham Young U (UT)
Brock U (ON, Canada)
Brown U (RI)
Bryn Mawr Coll (PA)
Bucknell U (PA)
Buffalo State Coll, State U of New York (NY)
California Inst of Technology (CA)
California Lutheran U (CA)
California Polytechnic State U, San Luis Obispo (CA)
California State Polytechnic U, Pomona (CA)
California State U, Chico (CA)
California State U, Dominguez Hills (CA)
California State U, East Bay (CA)
California State U, Fresno (CA)
California State U, Fullerton (CA)
California State U, Long Beach (CA)
California State U, Los Angeles (CA)
California State U, Monterey Bay (CA)
California State U, Sacramento (CA)
California State U, San Bernardino (CA)
California State U, Stanislaus (CA)
Calvin Coll (MI)
Case Western Reserve U (OH)
Castleton State Coll (VT)
Centenary Coll of Louisiana (LA)
Central Connecticut State U (CT)
Central Michigan U (MI)
Central State U (OH)
Central Washington U (WA)
City Coll of the City U of New York (NY)
Clarion U of Pennsylvania (PA)
Clark U (MA)
Clemson U (SC)
Cleveland State U (OH)
Colby Coll (ME)
Colgate U (NY)
The Coll at Brockport, State U of New York (NY)
Coll of Charleston (SC)
The Coll of William and Mary (VA)
The Colorado Coll (CO)
Colorado State U (CO)
Columbus State U (GA)
Cornell Coll (IA)
Cornell U (NY)
Dartmouth Coll (NH)
Denison U (OH)
DePauw U (IN)
Dickinson Coll (PA)
Duke U (NC)
Earlham Coll (IN)
East Carolina U (NC)
Eastern Illinois U (IL)
Eastern Kentucky U (KY)
Eastern Michigan U (MI)
Eastern New Mexico U (NM)
East Stroudsburg U of Pennsylvania (PA)
Edinboro U of Pennsylvania (PA)
Emporia State U (KS)
Excelsior Coll (NY)
Florida Atlantic U (FL)
Florida Intl U (FL)
Florida State U (FL)
Fort Lewis Coll (CO)
Franklin & Marshall Coll (PA)
Furman U (SC)
George Mason U (VA)
The George Washington U (DC)
Georgia Southern U (GA)
Georgia Southwestern State U (GA)
Georgia State U (GA)
Grand Valley State U (MI)
Guilford Coll (NC)
Gustavus Adolphus Coll (MN)
Hamilton Coll (NY)
Hampshire Coll (MA)
Hanover Coll (IN)
Hardin-Simmons U (TX)
Hartwick Coll (NY)
Harvard U (MA)
Haverford Coll (PA)
Hobart and William Smith Colls (NY)
Hofstra U (NY)
Hope Coll (MI)
Humboldt State U (CA)
Idaho State U (ID)
Illinois State U (IL)
Indiana State U (IN)
Indiana U Bloomington (IN)
Indiana U Northwest (IN)
Indiana U of Pennsylvania (PA)
Indiana U–Purdue U Fort Wayne (IN)
Indiana U–Purdue U Indianapolis (IN)
Iowa State U of Science and Technology (IA)
Jackson State U (MS)
Jacksonville State U (AL)
James Madison U (VA)
The Johns Hopkins U (MD)
Juniata Coll (PA)
Kansas State U (KS)
Kean U (NJ)
Keene State Coll (NH)
Kent State U (OH)
Kutztown U of Pennsylvania (PA)
Lafayette Coll (PA)
Lakehead U (ON, Canada)
Lake Superior State U (MI)
La Salle U (PA)
Laurentian U (ON, Canada)
Lawrence U (WI)
Lehman Coll of the City U of New York (NY)
Lock Haven U of Pennsylvania (PA)
Loma Linda U (CA)
Longwood U (VA)
Louisiana State U and Ag and Mech Coll (LA)
Macalester Coll (MN)
Mansfield U of Pennsylvania (PA)
Marietta Coll (OH)
Marshall U (WV)
Massachusetts Inst of Technology (MA)
McGill U (QC, Canada)
McNeese State U (LA)
Memorial U of Newfoundland (NL, Canada)
Mercyhurst Coll (PA)
Miami U (OH)
Miami U Hamilton (OH)
Michigan State U (MI)
Michigan Technological U (MI)
Middlebury Coll (VT)
Middle Tennessee State U (TN)
Midwestern State U (TX)
Millersville U of Pennsylvania (PA)
Millsaps Coll (MS)
Minnesota State U Mankato (MN)
Minot State U (ND)
Mississippi State U (MS)
Missouri State U (MO)
Missouri U of Science and Technology (MO)
Montana State U (MT)
Montclair State U (NJ)
Moravian Coll (PA)
Morehead State U (KY)
Mount Allison U (NB, Canada)
Mount Holyoke Coll (MA)
Murray State U (KY)
National U (CA)
New Jersey City U (NJ)
New Mexico Highlands U (NM)
New Mexico Inst of Mining and Technology (NM)
North Carolina State U (NC)
North Dakota State U (ND)
Northeastern Illinois U (IL)
Northeastern U (MA)
Northern Arizona U (AZ)
Northern Illinois U (IL)
Northern Michigan U (MI)
Northland Coll (WI)
Northwestern U (IL)
Northwest Missouri State U (MO)
Norwich U (VT)
Oberlin Coll (OH)
Occidental Coll (CA)
Ohio U (OH)
Ohio Wesleyan U (OH)
Oklahoma State U (OK)
Old Dominion U (VA)
Oregon State U (OR)
Pace U (NY)
Pacific Lutheran U (WA)
Penn State Abington (PA)
Penn State Altoona (PA)
Penn State Berks (PA)
Penn State Erie, The Behrend Coll (PA)
Penn State U Park (PA)
Piedmont Coll (GA)
Pomona Coll (CA)
Portland State U (OR)
Purdue U (IN)
Queens Coll of the City U of New York (NY)
Queen's U at Kingston (ON, Canada)
Radford U (VA)
Rensselaer Polytechnic Inst (NY)
Rice U (TX)
The Richard Stockton Coll of New Jersey (NJ)
Rider U (NJ)
Rutgers, The State U of New Jersey, Newark (NJ)
Rutgers, The State U of New Jersey, New Brunswick (NJ)
St. Cloud State U (MN)
St. Francis Xavier U (NS, Canada)
St. Lawrence U (NY)
Saint Louis U (MO)
St. Mary's U (TX)
St. Norbert Coll (WI)
Salem State Coll (MA)
Sam Houston State U (TX)
San Diego State U (CA)
San Francisco State U (CA)
Sarah Lawrence Coll (NY)
Scripps Coll (CA)
Sewanee: The U of the South (TN)
Shippensburg U of Pennsylvania (PA)
Simon Fraser U (BC, Canada)
Skidmore Coll (NY)
Slippery Rock U of Pennsylvania (PA)
Smith Coll (MA)
Sonoma State U (CA)
South Dakota School of Mines and Technology (SD)
Southern Connecticut State U (CT)
Southern Illinois U Carbondale (IL)
Southern Methodist U (TX)
Southern Oregon U (OR)
Southern Utah U (UT)
Stanford U (CA)
State U of New York at Binghamton (NY)
State U of New York at Fredonia (NY)
State U of New York at New Paltz (NY)
State U of New York at Oswego (NY)
State U of New York at Plattsburgh (NY)
State U of New York Coll at Geneseo (NY)
State U of New York Coll at Oneonta (NY)
State U of New York Coll at Potsdam (NY)
Stephen F. Austin State U (TX)
Stony Brook U, State U of New York (NY)
Susquehanna U (PA)
Syracuse U (NY)
Tarleton State U (TX)
Temple U (PA)
Tennessee Technological U (TN)
Texas A&M U (TX)
Texas Christian U (TX)
Texas Tech U (TX)
Towson U (MD)
Trinity U (TX)
Tufts U (MA)
Tulane U (LA)
Union Coll (NY)
U at Albany, State U of New York (NY)
U at Buffalo, the State U of New York (NY)
The U of Akron (OH)
The U of Alabama (AL)
U of Alaska Fairbanks (AK)
The U of Arizona (AZ)
U of Arkansas (AR)
The U of British Columbia (BC, Canada)
U of California, Berkeley (CA)
U of California, Davis (CA)
U of California, Irvine (CA)
U of California, Los Angeles (CA)
U of California, Riverside (CA)
U of California, San Diego (CA)
U of California, Santa Barbara (CA)
U of California, Santa Cruz (CA)
U of Central Missouri (MO)
U of Cincinnati (OH)
U of Colorado at Boulder (CO)
U of Connecticut (CT)
U of Dayton (OH)
U of Delaware (DE)
U of Florida (FL)
U of Georgia (GA)
U of Hawaii at Manoa (HI)
U of Houston (TX)
U of Idaho (ID)
U of Illinois at Chicago (IL)
U of Illinois at Urbana–Champaign (IL)
U of Indianapolis (IN)
The U of Iowa (IA)
U of Kansas (KS)
U of King's Coll (NS, Canada)
U of Louisiana at Lafayette (LA)
U of Maine (ME)
U of Maine at Farmington (ME)
U of Maryland, Coll Park (MD)
U of Mary Washington (VA)
U of Massachusetts Amherst (MA)
U of Massachusetts Boston (MA)
U of Memphis (TN)
U of Miami (FL)
U of Michigan (MI)
U of Michigan–Dearborn (MI)
U of Minnesota, Duluth (MN)
U of Minnesota, Twin Cities Campus (MN)
U of Mississippi (MS)
U of Missouri–Columbia (MO)
U of Missouri–Kansas City (MO)
The U of Montana (MT)
U of Nebraska at Omaha (NE)
U of Nebraska–Lincoln (NE)
U of Nevada, Las Vegas (NV)
U of Nevada, Reno (NV)
U of New Brunswick Fredericton (NB, Canada)
U of New Hampshire (NH)
U of New Mexico (NM)
U of New Orleans (LA)
U of North Alabama (AL)
The U of North Carolina at Chapel Hill (NC)
The U of North Carolina at Charlotte (NC)
The U of North Carolina Wilmington (NC)
U of North Dakota (ND)
U of Northern Colorado (CO)
U of Northern Iowa (IA)
U of Oklahoma (OK)
U of Oregon (OR)
U of Pennsylvania (PA)
U of Pittsburgh (PA)
U of Pittsburgh at Johnstown (PA)
U of Puget Sound (WA)
U of Regina (SK, Canada)
U of Rhode Island (RI)
U of Rochester (NY)
U of St. Thomas (MN)
U of South Alabama (AL)
U of South Carolina (SC)
The U of South Dakota (SD)
U of Southern California (CA)
U of Southern Indiana (IN)
U of Southern Maine (ME)
U of Southern Mississippi (MS)
U of South Florida (FL)
The U of Tennessee (TN)
The U of Tennessee at Chattanooga (TN)
The U of Tennessee at Martin (TN)
The U of Texas at Arlington (TX)
The U of Texas at Austin (TX)
The U of Texas at Dallas (TX)
The U of Texas at El Paso (TX)
The U of Texas at San Antonio (TX)
The U of Texas of the Permian Basin (TX)
U of the Pacific (CA)
The U of Toledo (OH)
U of Toronto (ON, Canada)
U of Tulsa (OK)
U of Utah (UT)
U of Vermont (VT)
U of Victoria (BC, Canada)
The U of Western Ontario (ON, Canada)
U of West Georgia (GA)

MAJORS AND MORE

U of Windsor (ON, Canada)
U of Wisconsin–Eau Claire (WI)
U of Wisconsin–Green Bay (WI)
U of Wisconsin–Madison (WI)
U of Wisconsin–Milwaukee (WI)
U of Wisconsin–Oshkosh (WI)
U of Wisconsin–Parkside (WI)
U of Wisconsin–Platteville (WI)
U of Wyoming (WY)
Utah State U (UT)
Valparaiso U (IN)
Vanderbilt U (TN)
Vassar Coll (NY)
Virginia Polytechnic Inst and State U (VA)
Virginia Wesleyan Coll (VA)
Washington and Lee U (VA)
Washington State U (WA)
Washington U in St. Louis (MO)
Wayne State U (MI)
Weber State U (UT)
Wellesley Coll (MA)
Wesleyan U (CT)
West Chester U of Pennsylvania (PA)
Western Carolina U (NC)
Western Connecticut State U (CT)
Western Illinois U (IL)
Western Kentucky U (KY)
Western Michigan U (MI)
Western New Mexico U (NM)
Western State Coll of Colorado (CO)
Western Washington U (WA)
West Texas A&M U (TX)
West Virginia U (WV)
Wheaton Coll (IL)
Whitman Coll (WA)
Wichita State U (KS)
Wilkes U (PA)
Williams Coll (MA)
Winona State U (MN)
Wittenberg U (OH)
Wright State U (OH)
York Coll of the City U of New York (NY)
York U (ON, Canada)
Youngstown State U (OH)

GEOPHYSICS AND SEISMOLOGY

Baylor U (TX)
Boise State U (ID)
Boston Coll (MA)
Bowdoin Coll (ME)
Brown U (RI)
California Inst of Technology (CA)
Eastern Michigan U (MI)
Harvard U (MA)
Hope Coll (MI)
McGill U (QC, Canada)
Memorial U of Newfoundland (NL, Canada)
Michigan State U (MI)
Michigan Technological U (MI)
Missouri U of Science and Technology (MO)
New Mexico Inst of Mining and Technology (NM)
Occidental Coll (CA)
Oregon State U (OR)
Rice U (TX)
St. Lawrence U (NY)
Saint Louis U (MO)
Southern Methodist U (TX)
Stanford U (CA)
State U of New York at Binghamton (NY)
State U of New York at Fredonia (NY)
State U of New York Coll at Geneseo (NY)
Texas A&M U (TX)
Texas Tech U (TX)
The U of Akron (OH)
The U of British Columbia (BC, Canada)
U of California, Los Angeles (CA)
U of California, Riverside (CA)
U of California, Santa Barbara (CA)
U of Chicago (IL)
U of Delaware (DE)
U of Houston (TX)
U of Minnesota, Twin Cities Campus (MN)
U of Nevada, Reno (NV)
U of New Brunswick Fredericton (NB, Canada)
U of Oklahoma (OK)
U of South Carolina (SC)
The U of Texas at Austin (TX)
The U of Texas at El Paso (TX)
U of Toronto (ON, Canada)
U of Tulsa (OK)
U of Utah (UT)
U of Victoria (BC, Canada)
The U of Western Ontario (ON, Canada)
U of Wisconsin–Madison (WI)
Western Michigan U (MI)
Western Washington U (WA)
Wright State U (OH)

GEOTECHNICAL ENGINEERING

Montana Tech of The U of Montana (MT)
U of Illinois at Urbana–Champaign (IL)
York U (ON, Canada)

GERMAN

Adrian Coll (MI)
Agnes Scott Coll (GA)
Albion Coll (MI)
Alfred U (NY)
Allegheny Coll (PA)
Alma Coll (MI)
American U (DC)
Amherst Coll (MA)
Angelo State U (TX)
Aquinas Coll (MI)
Arizona State U (AZ)
Auburn U (AL)
Augsburg Coll (MN)
Augustana Coll (IL)
Augustana Coll (SD)
Austin Coll (TX)
Baker U (KS)
Baldwin-Wallace Coll (OH)
Ball State U (IN)
Bard Coll (NY)
Bard Coll at Simon's Rock (MA)
Barnard Coll (NY)
Bates Coll (ME)
Baylor U (TX)
Beloit Coll (WI)
Bemidji State U (MN)
Berea Coll (KY)
Berry Coll (GA)
Bethany Coll (WV)
Bishop's U (QC, Canada)
Bloomsburg U of Pennsylvania (PA)
Bob Jones U (SC)
Boise State U (ID)
Boston Coll (MA)
Boston U (MA)
Bowdoin Coll (ME)
Bowling Green State U (OH)
Bradley U (IL)
Brandeis U (MA)
Brigham Young U (UT)
Brock U (ON, Canada)
Brown U (RI)
Bryn Mawr Coll (PA)
Bucknell U (PA)
Butler U (IN)
California Lutheran U (CA)
California State U, Chico (CA)
California State U, Fullerton (CA)
California State U, Long Beach (CA)
Calvin Coll (MI)
Canisius Coll (NY)
Carnegie Mellon U (PA)
Case Western Reserve U (OH)
The Catholic U of America (DC)
Centenary Coll of Louisiana (LA)
Central Connecticut State U (CT)
Central Michigan U (MI)
Centre Coll (KY)
Christopher Newport U (VA)
Claremont McKenna Coll (CA)
Colby Coll (ME)
Colgate U (NY)
Coll of Charleston (SC)
Coll of Saint Benedict (MN)
Coll of the Holy Cross (MA)
Coll of the Ozarks (MO)
The Coll of William and Mary (VA)
The Colorado Coll (CO)
Colorado State U (CO)
Concordia Coll (MN)
Concordia U (QC, Canada)
Concordia U Wisconsin (WI)
Cornell Coll (IA)
Cornell U (NY)
Creighton U (NE)
Dartmouth Coll (NH)
Davidson Coll (NC)
Denison U (OH)
DePaul U (IL)
DePauw U (IN)
Dickinson Coll (PA)
Doane Coll (NE)
Dordt Coll (IA)
Drew U (NJ)
Drury U (MO)
Duke U (NC)
Earlham Coll (IN)
East Carolina U (NC)
Eastern Michigan U (MI)
Edinboro U of Pennsylvania (PA)
Elizabethtown Coll (PA)
Emory U (GA)
Fairfield U (CT)
Florida Atlantic U (FL)
Florida Intl U (FL)
Florida State U (FL)
Franciscan U of Steubenville (OH)
Franklin & Marshall Coll (PA)
Furman U (SC)
Georgetown Coll (KY)
Georgetown U (DC)
The George Washington U (DC)
Georgia Southern U (GA)
Georgia State U (GA)
Gettysburg Coll (PA)
Gonzaga U (WA)
Gordon Coll (MA)
Grace Coll (IN)
Grand Valley State U (MI)
Grinnell Coll (IA)
Guilford Coll (NC)
Gustavus Adolphus Coll (MN)
Hamilton Coll (NY)
Hamline U (MN)
Hampden-Sydney Coll (VA)
Hanover Coll (IN)
Hartwick Coll (NY)
Harvard U (MA)
Hastings Coll (NE)
Haverford Coll (PA)
Heidelberg Coll (OH)
Hendrix Coll (AR)
Hillsdale Coll (MI)
Hofstra U (NY)
Hollins U (VA)
Hood Coll (MD)
Hope Coll (MI)
Humboldt State U (CA)
Hunter Coll of the City U of New York (NY)
Idaho State U (ID)
Illinois Coll (IL)
Illinois State U (IL)
Illinois Wesleyan U (IL)
Indiana State U (IN)
Indiana U Bloomington (IN)
Indiana U of Pennsylvania (PA)
Indiana U–Purdue U Fort Wayne (IN)
Indiana U–Purdue U Indianapolis (IN)
Indiana U South Bend (IN)
Indiana U Southeast (IN)
Iowa State U of Science and Technology (IA)
Ithaca Coll (NY)
Jacksonville State U (AL)
John Carroll U (OH)
The Johns Hopkins U (MD)
Juniata Coll (PA)
Kalamazoo Coll (MI)
Kent State U (OH)
Kenyon Coll (OH)
Knox Coll (IL)
Lafayette Coll (PA)
La Salle U (PA)
Lawrence U (WI)
Lebanon Valley Coll (PA)
Lehigh U (PA)
Lenoir-Rhyne Coll (NC)
Lewis & Clark Coll (OR)
Linfield Coll (OR)
Lipscomb U (TN)
Lock Haven U of Pennsylvania (PA)
Longwood U (VA)
Louisiana State U and Ag and Mech Coll (LA)
Loyola Coll in Maryland (MD)
Loyola U Chicago (IL)
Loyola U New Orleans (LA)
Luther Coll (IA)
Lycoming Coll (PA)
Manchester Coll (IN)
Mansfield U of Pennsylvania (PA)
Marlboro Coll (VT)
Marquette U (WI)
McDaniel Coll (MD)
McGill U (QC, Canada)
Memorial U of Newfoundland (NL, Canada)
Mercer U (GA)
Messiah Coll (PA)
Miami U (OH)
Miami U Hamilton (OH)
Michigan State U (MI)
Middlebury Coll (VT)
Millersville U of Pennsylvania (PA)
Millsaps Coll (MS)
Minnesota State U Mankato (MN)
Minot State U (ND)
Missouri Southern State U (MO)
Missouri State U (MO)
Moravian Coll (PA)
Mount Allison U (NB, Canada)
Mount Holyoke Coll (MA)
Mount St. Mary's U (MD)
Mount Saint Vincent U (NS, Canada)
Muhlenberg Coll (PA)
Murray State U (KY)
Nazareth Coll of Rochester (NY)
Nebraska Wesleyan U (NE)
New Coll of Florida (FL)
New York U (NY)
North Central Coll (IL)
Northeastern U (MA)
Northern Arizona U (AZ)
Northern Illinois U (IL)
Northern State U (SD)
Northwestern U (IL)
Oakland U (MI)
Oberlin Coll (OH)
Ohio U (OH)
Ohio Wesleyan U (OH)
Oklahoma City U (OK)
Oklahoma State U (OK)
Old Dominion U (VA)
Oral Roberts U (OK)
Oregon State U (OR)
Pacific Lutheran U (WA)
Pacific U (OR)
Penn State Abington (PA)
Penn State Altoona (PA)
Penn State Berks (PA)
Penn State Erie, The Behrend Coll (PA)
Penn State U Park (PA)
Pepperdine U, Malibu (CA)
Pitzer Coll (CA)
Pomona Coll (CA)
Portland State U (OR)
Presbyterian Coll (SC)
Princeton U (NJ)
Purdue U Calumet (IN)
Queens Coll of the City U of New York (NY)
Queen's U at Kingston (ON, Canada)
Randolph Coll (VA)
Randolph-Macon Coll (VA)
Reed Coll (OR)
Rhodes Coll (TN)
Rice U (TX)
Rider U (NJ)
Ripon Coll (WI)
Rosemont Coll (PA)
Rutgers, The State U of New Jersey, Camden (NJ)
Rutgers, The State U of New Jersey, Newark (NJ)
Rutgers, The State U of New Jersey, New Brunswick (NJ)
St. Ambrose U (IA)
St. Cloud State U (MN)
St. John Fisher Coll (NY)
Saint John's U (MN)
Saint Joseph's U (PA)
St. Lawrence U (NY)
Saint Louis U (MO)
Saint Mary's Coll of California (CA)
St. Norbert Coll (WI)
St. Olaf Coll (MN)
Salem Coll (NC)
Samford U (AL)
Sam Houston State U (TX)
San Diego State U (CA)
San Francisco State U (CA)
Sarah Lawrence Coll (NY)
Scripps Coll (CA)
Seattle Pacific U (WA)
Seattle U (WA)
Sewanee: The U of the South (TN)
Simpson Coll (IA)
Skidmore Coll (NY)
Smith Coll (MA)
South Dakota State U (SD)
Southeast Missouri State U (MO)
Southern Connecticut State U (CT)
Southern Illinois U Carbondale (IL)
Southern Methodist U (TX)
Southern Oregon U (OR)
Southern Utah U (UT)
Southwestern U (TX)
Stanford U (CA)
State U of New York at Binghamton (NY)
State U of New York at New Paltz (NY)
State U of New York at Oswego (NY)
Stetson U (FL)
Stony Brook U, State U of New York (NY)
Susquehanna U (PA)
Swarthmore Coll (PA)
Sweet Briar Coll (VA)
Syracuse U (NY)
Temple U (PA)
Tennessee Technological U (TN)
Texas A&M U (TX)
Texas State U-San Marcos (TX)
Texas Tech U (TX)
Towson U (MD)
Trent U (ON, Canada)
Trinity Coll (CT)
Trinity U (TX)
Truman State U (MO)
Tufts U (MA)
Tulane U (LA)
Union Coll (NE)
U at Buffalo, the State U of New York (NY)
The U of Arizona (AZ)
U of Arkansas (AR)
The U of British Columbia (BC, Canada)
U of California, Berkeley (CA)
U of California, Davis (CA)
U of California, Irvine (CA)
U of California, Los Angeles (CA)
U of California, Riverside (CA)
U of California, San Diego (CA)
U of California, Santa Barbara (CA)
U of California, Santa Cruz (CA)
U of Central Missouri (MO)
U of Central Oklahoma (OK)
U of Chicago (IL)
U of Cincinnati (OH)
U of Connecticut (CT)
U of Dallas (TX)
U of Dayton (OH)
U of Delaware (DE)
U of Denver (CO)
U of Evansville (IN)
U of Florida (FL)
U of Georgia (GA)
U of Hawaii at Manoa (HI)
U of Houston (TX)
U of Idaho (ID)
U of Illinois at Chicago (IL)
U of Illinois at Urbana–Champaign (IL)
U of Indianapolis (IN)
The U of Iowa (IA)
U of King's Coll (NS, Canada)
U of Lethbridge (AB, Canada)
U of Maine (ME)
U of Maryland, Coll Park (MD)
U of Mary Washington (VA)
U of Massachusetts Amherst (MA)
U of Massachusetts Boston (MA)
U of Miami (FL)
U of Michigan (MI)
U of Minnesota, Twin Cities Campus (MN)
U of Mississippi (MS)
U of Missouri–Columbia (MO)
U of Missouri–Kansas City (MO)
U of Missouri–St. Louis (MO)
The U of Montana (MT)
U of Nebraska at Kearney (NE)
U of Nebraska at Omaha (NE)
U of Nebraska–Lincoln (NE)
U of Nevada, Las Vegas (NV)
U of Nevada, Reno (NV)
U of New Brunswick Fredericton (NB, Canada)
U of New Hampshire (NH)
U of New Mexico (NM)
The U of North Carolina at Asheville (NC)
The U of North Carolina at Chapel Hill (NC)
The U of North Carolina at Charlotte (NC)
The U of North Carolina at Greensboro (NC)
The U of North Carolina Wilmington (NC)
U of North Dakota (ND)
U of Northern Colorado (CO)
U of Northern Iowa (IA)
U of North Texas (TX)
U of Notre Dame (IN)
U of Oklahoma (OK)
U of Oregon (OR)
U of Ottawa (ON, Canada)
U of Pennsylvania (PA)
U of Pittsburgh (PA)
U of Prince Edward Island (PE, Canada)
U of Puget Sound (WA)
U of Redlands (CA)
U of Regina (SK, Canada)
U of Rhode Island (RI)
U of Richmond (VA)
U of Rochester (NY)
U of St. Thomas (MN)
The U of Scranton (PA)
U of South Carolina (SC)
The U of South Dakota (SD)
U of Southern California (CA)
U of Southern Indiana (IN)
U of South Florida (FL)
The U of Tennessee (TN)
The U of Texas at Arlington (TX)
The U of Texas at Austin (TX)
The U of Texas at El Paso (TX)
U of the Pacific (CA)
The U of Toledo (OH)
U of Toronto (ON, Canada)
U of Tulsa (OK)
U of Utah (UT)
U of Victoria (BC, Canada)
U of Virginia (VA)
The U of Western Ontario (ON, Canada)
U of West Georgia (GA)
U of Windsor (ON, Canada)

The U of Winnipeg (MB, Canada)
U of Wisconsin–La Crosse (WI)
U of Wisconsin–Madison (WI)
U of Wisconsin–Milwaukee (WI)
U of Wisconsin–Oshkosh (WI)
U of Wisconsin–Parkside (WI)
U of Wisconsin–Platteville (WI)
U of Wisconsin–Stevens Point (WI)
U of Wisconsin–Whitewater (WI)
U of Wyoming (WY)
Ursinus Coll (PA)
Utah State U (UT)
Valparaiso U (IN)
Vanderbilt U (TN)
Vassar Coll (NY)
Villanova U (PA)
Virginia Polytechnic Inst and State U (VA)
Virginia Wesleyan Coll (VA)
Wabash Coll (IN)
Wake Forest U (NC)
Walla Walla U (WA)
Wartburg Coll (IA)
Washburn U (KS)
Washington & Jefferson Coll (PA)
Washington and Lee U (VA)
Washington Coll (MD)
Washington State U (WA)
Washington U in St. Louis (MO)
Wayne State U (MI)
Weber State U (UT)
Webster U (MO)
Wellesley Coll (MA)
Wesleyan U (CT)
West Chester U of Pennsylvania (PA)
Western Carolina U (NC)
Western Kentucky U (KY)
Western Michigan U (MI)
Western Washington U (WA)
Wheaton Coll (IL)
Wheaton Coll (MA)
Whitman Coll (WA)
Wilfrid Laurier U (ON, Canada)
Willamette U (OR)
Williams Coll (MA)
Winona State U (MN)
Wittenberg U (OH)
Wofford Coll (SC)
Wright State U (OH)
Xavier U (OH)
Yale U (CT)
York U (ON, Canada)
Youngstown State U (OH)

GERMANIC LANGUAGES
Bethel Coll (KS)
Canisius Coll (NY)
Claremont McKenna Coll (CA)
Cleveland State U (OH)
Eastern Michigan U (MI)
New Coll of Florida (FL)
U of Colorado at Boulder (CO)
U of Kansas (KS)
The U of Texas at San Antonio (TX)
U of Wisconsin–Eau Claire (WI)
U of Wisconsin–Green Bay (WI)
Washington U in St. Louis (MO)

GERMANIC LANGUAGES RELATED
Calvin Coll (MI)
Ohio Northern U (OH)
U of Georgia (GA)

GERMAN LANGUAGE TEACHER EDUCATION
Alma Coll (MI)
Auburn U (AL)
Baylor U (TX)
Brigham Young U (UT)
California Lutheran U (CA)
California State U, Chico (CA)
The Catholic U of America (DC)
Centenary Coll of Louisiana (LA)
Central Michigan U (MI)
Central Washington U (WA)
Colorado State U (CO)
Concordia Coll (MN)
Concordia U Wisconsin (WI)
DePaul U (IL)
East Carolina U (NC)
Eastern Michigan U (MI)
Grace Coll (IN)
Hastings Coll (NE)
Hofstra U (NY)
Hope Coll (MI)
Hunter Coll of the City U of New York (NY)
Indiana U Bloomington (IN)
Indiana U–Purdue U Fort Wayne (IN)
Indiana U–Purdue U Indianapolis (IN)
Ithaca Coll (NY)
Juniata Coll (PA)
Kutztown U of Pennsylvania (PA)
Mansfield U of Pennsylvania (PA)
Messiah Coll (PA)
Miami U Hamilton (OH)
Minot State U (ND)
Missouri State U (MO)
Moravian Coll (PA)
Murray State U (KY)
Ohio Northern U (OH)
Ohio U (OH)
Ohio Wesleyan U (OH)
Old Dominion U (VA)
Purdue U (IN)
St. Ambrose U (IA)
The U of Arizona (AZ)
U of Evansville (IN)
U of Illinois at Chicago (IL)
U of Illinois at Urbana–Champaign (IL)
The U of Iowa (IA)
U of Louisiana at Lafayette (LA)
U of Minnesota, Duluth (MN)
U of Missouri–St. Louis (MO)
U of Nebraska–Lincoln (NE)
The U of North Carolina at Charlotte (NC)
The U of North Carolina at Greensboro (NC)
The U of South Dakota (SD)
The U of Tennessee at Martin (TN)
The U of Toledo (OH)
U of Windsor (ON, Canada)
Valparaiso U (IN)
Washington State U (WA)
Washington U in St. Louis (MO)
Weber State U (UT)
Western Carolina U (NC)
Western Michigan U (MI)

GERMAN STUDIES
American U (DC)
Bard Coll at Simon's Rock (MA)
Barnard Coll (NY)
Brock U (ON, Canada)
Brown U (RI)
Case Western Reserve U (OH)
Central Coll (IA)
Claremont McKenna Coll (CA)
Coll of the Holy Cross (MA)
Connecticut Coll (CT)
Cornell U (NY)
Franklin & Marshall Coll (PA)
Ithaca Coll (NY)
Kutztown U of Pennsylvania (PA)
Manhattanville Coll (NY)
McGill U (QC, Canada)
Moravian Coll (PA)
Purdue U (IN)
Queen's U at Kingston (ON, Canada)
Santa Clara U (CA)
Smith Coll (MA)
Stanford U (CA)
Swarthmore Coll (PA)
Sweet Briar Coll (VA)
U of California, Irvine (CA)
U of Houston (TX)
U of Victoria (BC, Canada)
U of Windsor (ON, Canada)
The U of Winnipeg (MB, Canada)
Wellesley Coll (MA)
Wheaton Coll (MA)
York U (ON, Canada)

GERONTOLOGY
Alfred U (NY)
Alma Coll (MI)
Bethune-Cookman U (FL)
Bishop's U (QC, Canada)
Bowling Green State U (OH)
California State U, Chico (CA)
California State U, Dominguez Hills (CA)
California State U, East Bay (CA)
California State U, Sacramento (CA)
Case Western Reserve U (OH)
Central Washington U (WA)
Cleveland State U (OH)
Coll of the Ozarks (MO)
Dominican U (IL)
Felician Coll (NJ)
Gwynedd-Mercy Coll (PA)
Indiana U Kokomo (IN)
Ithaca Coll (NY)
John Carroll U (OH)
Lakehead U (ON, Canada)
Lindenwood U (MO)
Madonna U (MI)
Miami U Hamilton (OH)
Missouri State U (MO)
Mount St. Mary's Coll (CA)
Mount Saint Vincent U (NS, Canada)
National-Louis U (IL)
Nazareth Coll of Rochester (NY)
Quinnipiac U (CT)
Roosevelt U (IL)
St. Cloud State U (MN)
St. Thomas U (NB, Canada)
San Diego State U (CA)
State U of New York at Fredonia (NY)
State U of New York Coll at Oneonta (NY)
Stephen F. Austin State U (TX)
Thomas Edison State Coll (NJ)
Towson U (MD)
U of Arkansas at Pine Bluff (AR)
U of Massachusetts Boston (MA)
U of Nebraska at Omaha (NE)
U of Nevada, Las Vegas (NV)
U of Northern Iowa (IA)
U of North Texas (TX)
The U of Scranton (PA)
U of Southern California (CA)
U of South Florida (FL)
Weber State U (UT)
Wichita State U (KS)
York Coll of the City U of New York (NY)
York U (ON, Canada)

GRAPHIC AND PRINTING EQUIPMENT OPERATION/ PRODUCTION
Appalachian State U (NC)
Fairmont State U (WV)
Ferris State U (MI)
Florida Ag and Mech U (FL)
Georgia Southern U (GA)
Lewis-Clark State Coll (ID)
Murray State U (KY)
Western Illinois U (IL)

GRAPHIC COMMUNICATIONS
Arkansas State U (AR)
California Polytechnic State U, San Luis Obispo (CA)
Carroll Coll (WI)
Clemson U (SC)
Grand View Coll (IA)
Memphis Coll of Art (TN)
New England School of Communications (ME)
New York U (NY)
Pittsburg State U (KS)
Point Loma Nazarene U (CA)
Rochester Inst of Technology (NY)
School of the Art Inst of Chicago (IL)
U of Houston (TX)
U of North Dakota (ND)
U of Northern Iowa (IA)

GRAPHIC COMMUNICATIONS RELATED
U of the District of Columbia (DC)

GRAPHIC DESIGN
Abilene Christian U (TX)
Acad of Art U (CA)
Alberta Coll of Art & Design (AB, Canada)
Albertus Magnus Coll (CT)
Alma Coll (MI)
American InterContinental U (CA)
American InterContinental U (FL)
American InterContinental U (TX)
American InterContinental U Buckhead Campus (GA)
American InterContinental U Dunwoody Campus (GA)
American InterContinental U-London (United Kingdom)
American InterContinental U Online (IL)
American U (DC)
The American U of Athens (Greece)
Anna Maria Coll (MA)
Appalachian State U (NC)
Arizona State U (AZ)
Art Acad of Cincinnati (OH)
The Art Inst of Atlanta (GA)
The Art Inst of Atlanta–Decatur (GA)
The Art Inst of Austin (TX)
The Art Inst of Boston at Lesley U (MA)
The Art Inst of California–Inland Empire (CA)
The Art Inst of California–Los Angeles (CA)
The Art Inst of California–Sacramento (CA)
The Art Inst of California–San Francisco (CA)
The Art Inst of California–Sunnyvale (CA)
The Art Inst of Charleston (SC)
The Art Inst of Dallas (TX)
The Art Inst of Houston (TX)
The Art Inst of Indianapolis (IN)
The Art Inst of Las Vegas (NV)
The Art Inst of Phoenix (AZ)
The Art Inst of Portland (OR)
The Art Inst of Salt Lake City (UT)
The Art Inst of Seattle (WA)
The Art Inst of Tampa (FL)
The Art Inst of Tucson (AZ)
The Art Insts Intl Minnesota (MN)
Auburn U (AL)
Becker Coll (MA)
Bradley U (IL)
Brenau U (GA)
Bridgewater State Coll (MA)
Brigham Young U (UT)
Cabrini Coll (PA)
California Design Coll (CA)
California Inst of the Arts (CA)
California State U, Chico (CA)
California State U, Fresno (CA)
California State U, Long Beach (CA)
California State U, Sacramento (CA)
Cedarville U (OH)
Central Michigan U (MI)
Chapman U (CA)
City Coll of the City U of New York (NY)
The Cleveland Inst of Art (OH)
Coker Coll (SC)
Colby-Sawyer Coll (NH)
Coll of Mount St. Joseph (OH)
Coll of Santa Fe (NM)
Coll of Visual Arts (MN)
Collins Coll: A School of Design and Technology (AZ)
Colorado Tech U—Colorado Springs (CO)
Colorado Tech U—Denver (CO)
Colorado Tech U—North Kansas City (MO)
Colorado Tech U—Online (CO)
Colorado Tech U—Sioux Falls (SD)
Concordia U Wisconsin (WI)
Creighton U (NE)
Daemen Coll (NY)
Dordt Coll (IA)
Drake U (IA)
East Stroudsburg U of Pennsylvania (PA)
Emmanuel Coll (MA)
Fashion Inst of Technology (NY)
Fitchburg State Coll (MA)
Flagler Coll (FL)
Florida State U (FL)
George Fox U (OR)
Grace Coll (IN)
Grand View Coll (IA)
Harding U (AR)
Hardin-Simmons U (TX)
Huntington U (IN)
The Illinois Inst of Art–Schaumburg (IL)
Indiana U–Purdue U Fort Wayne (IN)
Intl Acad of Design & Technology (FL)
Iowa State U of Science and Technology (IA)
Iowa Wesleyan Coll (IA)
Kansas City Art Inst (MO)
Keene State Coll (NH)
Kwantlen U Coll (BC, Canada)
Laguna Coll of Art & Design (CA)
Lenoir-Rhyne Coll (NC)
Limestone Coll (SC)
Madonna U (MI)
Marian Coll of Fond du Lac (WI)
Marietta Coll (OH)
Maryland Inst Coll of Art (MD)
Marymount U (VA)
Maryville U of Saint Louis (MO)
Marywood U (PA)
Memphis Coll of Art (TN)
Meredith Coll (NC)
Miami Intl U of Art & Design (FL)
Miami U (OH)
Miami U Hamilton (OH)
MidAmerica Nazarene U (KS)
Mississippi Coll (MS)
Montclair State U (NJ)
Montserrat Coll of Art (MA)
Moravian Coll (PA)
Mount Mary Coll (WI)
Mount Vernon Nazarene U (OH)
The New England Inst of Art (MA)
North Carolina State U (NC)
North Central Coll (IL)
Northern Michigan U (MI)
Northwestern Coll (IA)
Northwestern Coll (MN)
Northwest Nazarene U (ID)
NSCAD U (NS, Canada)
Ohio Dominican U (OH)
Ohio Northern U (OH)
Old Dominion U (VA)
Ouachita Baptist U (AR)
Paier Coll of Art, Inc. (CT)
Palm Beach Atlantic U (FL)
Park U (MO)
Peace Coll (NC)
Penn State Abington (PA)
Penn State Altoona (PA)
Penn State Berks (PA)
Penn State Erie, The Behrend Coll (PA)
Penn State U Park (PA)
Pennsylvania Coll of Art & Design (PA)
Pennsylvania Coll of Technology (PA)
Philadelphia U (PA)
Point Loma Nazarene U (CA)
Pratt Inst (NY)
Quincy U (IL)
Regis Coll (MA)
Ringling Coll of Art and Design (FL)
Rocky Mountain Coll of Art + Design (CO)
Roger Williams U (RI)
St. Ambrose U (IA)
St. Edward's U (TX)
St. John's U (NY)
Saint Mary's U of Minnesota (MN)
Salve Regina U (RI)
San Diego State U (CA)
Savannah Coll of Art and Design (GA)
School of the Art Inst of Chicago (IL)
School of the Museum of Fine Arts, Boston (MA)
School of Visual Arts (NY)
Schreiner U (TX)
Shawnee State U (OH)
South Dakota State U (SD)
Southern Adventist U (TN)
Southern New Hampshire U (NH)
Spring Arbor U (MI)
Spring Hill Coll (AL)
Stephens Coll (MO)
Susquehanna U (PA)
Temple U (PA)
Texas State U-San Marcos (TX)
Texas Tech U (TX)
Union Coll (NE)
The U of Akron (OH)
U of Bridgeport (CT)
U of Denver (CO)
U of Evansville (IN)
U of Florida (FL)
U of Georgia (GA)
U of Illinois at Chicago (IL)
U of Illinois at Urbana–Champaign (IL)
U of Kansas (KS)
U of Miami (FL)
U of Missouri–St. Louis (MO)
U of North Dakota (ND)
U of Rio Grande (OH)
The U of Tampa (FL)
The U of Tennessee at Martin (TN)
Ursuline Coll (OH)
Virginia Commonwealth U (VA)
Viterbo U (WI)
Washington U in St. Louis (MO)
Watkins Coll of Art and Design (TN)
Waynesburg U (PA)
Wayne State Coll (NE)
Western Michigan U (MI)
Western State Coll of Colorado (CO)
Western Washington U (WA)
York Coll of Pennsylvania (PA)
Youngstown State U (OH)

GRAPHIC/PRINTING EQUIPMENT
Coll of the Ozarks (MO)

GREENHOUSE MANAGEMENT
Sterling Coll (VT)

HAZARDOUS MATERIALS MANAGEMENT AND WASTE TECHNOLOGY
Rochester Inst of Technology (NY)

HEALTH AND MEDICAL ADMINISTRATIVE SERVICES RELATED
Kent State U (OH)
Missouri Southern State U (MO)
Mount Mercy Coll (IA)
Pennsylvania Coll of Technology (PA)
Robert Morris U (PA)
U of Baltimore (MD)
U of Miami (FL)
U of Michigan–Flint (MI)
U of Minnesota, Crookston (MN)
Ursuline Coll (OH)

HEALTH AND PHYSICAL EDUCATION

Abilene Christian U (TX)
Adrian Coll (MI)
Anderson U (IN)
Angelo State U (TX)
Arkansas State U (AR)
Asbury Coll (KY)
Austin Peay State U (TN)
Averett U (VA)
Baker U (KS)
Baldwin-Wallace Coll (OH)
Baylor U (TX)
Belmont U (TN)
Bethel Coll (KS)
Bethel Coll (TN)
Bethel U (MN)
Bluffton U (OH)
Bob Jones U (SC)
Bridgewater Coll (VA)
Brigham Young U (UT)
Bryan Coll (TN)
California State U, Chico (CA)
California State U, Fullerton (CA)
Cameron U (OK)
Capital U (OH)
Carroll Coll (WI)
Castleton State Coll (VT)
Cedarville U (OH)
Central Michigan U (MI)
Claflin U (SC)
The Coll at Brockport, State U of New York (NY)
Coll of the Ozarks (MO)
The Colorado Coll (CO)
Concordia Coll (MN)
Concordia U (MI)
Concordia U, Nebraska (NE)
Concordia U Wisconsin (WI)
DePaul U (IL)
Doane Coll (NE)
Dordt Coll (IA)
Eastern Michigan U (MI)
East Tennessee State U (TN)
East Texas Baptist U (TX)
Emory & Henry Coll (VA)
Evangel U (MO)
Florida Ag and Mech U (FL)
Freed-Hardeman U (TN)
Gardner-Webb U (NC)
George Fox U (OR)
Georgia Southern U (GA)
Georgia State U (GA)
Grace Coll (IN)
Guilford Coll (NC)
Hamline U (MN)
Hardin-Simmons U (TX)
Hastings Coll (NE)
Houghton Coll (NY)
Houston Baptist U (TX)
Howard Payne U (TX)
Indiana U of Pennsylvania (PA)
Iowa State U of Science and Technology (IA)
Ithaca Coll (NY)
Jacksonville State U (AL)
James Madison U (VA)
Jarvis Christian Coll (TX)
Johnson State Coll (VT)
Keene State Coll (NH)
La Sierra U (CA)
Liberty U (VA)
Lincoln U (PA)
Lindenwood U (MO)
Linfield Coll (OR)
Loras Coll (IA)
Lubbock Christian U (TX)
Luther Coll (IA)
Lyndon State Coll (VT)
Malone Coll (OH)
Maryville Coll (TN)
Marywood U (PA)
The Master's Coll and Sem (CA)
Mayville State U (ND)
McGill U (QC, Canada)
Miami U (OH)
Middle Tennessee State U (TN)
Milligan Coll (TN)
Mississippi Coll (MS)
Montana State U (MT)
Montana State U–Billings (MT)
Morehouse Coll (GA)
Nebraska Wesleyan U (NE)
New England Coll (NH)
North Carolina Central U (NC)
Northern Michigan U (MI)
Northwestern Coll (MN)
Northwestern State U of Louisiana (LA)
Northwest Nazarene U (ID)
Ohio Northern U (OH)
Ohio U (OH)
Oklahoma Panhandle State U (OK)
Oral Roberts U (OK)
Plymouth State U (NH)
Point Loma Nazarene U (CA)
Purdue U (IN)
Queen's U at Kingston (ON, Canada)
Redeemer U Coll (ON, Canada)
Roanoke Coll (VA)
Sage Coll of Albany (NY)
St. Ambrose U (IA)
Saint Joseph's Coll (IN)
Saint Mary's Coll of California (CA)
St. Mary's U (TX)
Salisbury U (MD)
Samford U (AL)
San Diego State U (CA)
Slippery Rock U of Pennsylvania (PA)
South Dakota State U (SD)
Southeast Missouri State U (MO)
Southern Illinois U Edwardsville (IL)
Southern Wesleyan U (SC)
Southwest Baptist U (MO)
Southwestern Adventist U (TX)
Southwestern Coll (KS)
Southwest Minnesota State U (MN)
Stephen F. Austin State U (TX)
Sterling Coll (KS)
Tennessee Wesleyan Coll (TN)
Texas A&M Intl U (TX)
Texas A&M U (TX)
Texas A&M U–Commerce (TX)
Texas Christian U (TX)
Texas Coll (TX)
Texas Southern U (TX)
Texas State U-San Marcos (TX)
Texas Tech U (TX)
Texas Woman's U (TX)
Tusculum Coll (TN)
U of Arkansas (AR)
U of Arkansas at Monticello (AR)
U of Delaware (DE)
U of Georgia (GA)
U of Great Falls (MT)
U of Hawaii at Manoa (HI)
U of Houston (TX)
U of Houston–Clear Lake (TX)
U of Kansas (KS)
U of Louisville (KY)
U of Mary (ND)
U of Montevallo (AL)
U of Nebraska at Omaha (NE)
U of New Orleans (LA)
The U of North Carolina at Chapel Hill (NC)
The U of North Carolina at Charlotte (NC)
The U of North Carolina at Pembroke (NC)
The U of North Carolina Wilmington (NC)
U of Northern Iowa (IA)
U of North Texas (TX)
U of Oklahoma (OK)
U of Ottawa (ON, Canada)
U of Rio Grande (OH)
U of St. Thomas (MN)
U of Science and Arts of Oklahoma (OK)
U of Southern Mississippi (MS)
The U of Tennessee at Martin (TN)
The U of Texas at Arlington (TX)
The U of Texas at Austin (TX)
The U of Texas at Brownsville (TX)
The U of Texas at San Antonio (TX)
The U of Texas at Tyler (TX)
The U of Texas–Pan American (TX)
U of Toronto (ON, Canada)
U of Utah (UT)
U of West Florida (FL)
U of Windsor (ON, Canada)
U of Wisconsin–Stevens Point (WI)
U of Wisconsin–Superior (WI)
Ursinus Coll (PA)
Utah Valley State Coll (UT)
Valparaiso U (IN)
Vanguard U of Southern California (CA)
Virginia Intermont Coll (VA)
Walla Walla U (WA)
Walsh U (OH)
Washington State U (WA)
Weber State U (UT)
Wesleyan U (CT)
West Chester U of Pennsylvania (PA)
West Texas A&M U (TX)
West Virginia U (WV)
West Virginia Wesleyan Coll (WV)
Wingate U (NC)
York U (ON, Canada)
Youngstown State U (OH)

HEALTH AND PHYSICAL EDUCATION RELATED

Averett U (VA)
Avila U (MO)
Bloomsburg U of Pennsylvania (PA)
Bowling Green State U (OH)
Brewton-Parker Coll (GA)
Bridgewater State Coll (MA)
Brigham Young U (UT)
California Baptist U (CA)
California State U, Long Beach (CA)
Capital U (OH)
Coker Coll (SC)
The Coll at Brockport, State U of New York (NY)
Concordia U Wisconsin (WI)
Cornell Coll (IA)
East Carolina U (NC)
East Stroudsburg U of Pennsylvania (PA)
Edinboro U of Pennsylvania (PA)
Greensboro Coll (NC)
Gustavus Adolphus Coll (MN)
Ithaca Coll (NY)
Johnson C. Smith U (NC)
Lambuth U (TN)
Limestone Coll (SC)
Lincoln U (PA)
Mayville State U (ND)
Midwestern State U (TX)
Missouri Southern State U (MO)
Naropa U (CO)
Ohio Northern U (OH)
St. John Fisher Coll (NY)
Saint Mary's Coll of California (CA)
Sam Houston State U (TX)
South Dakota State U (SD)
Texas Christian U (TX)
Texas Lutheran U (TX)
Towson U (MD)
Tusculum Coll (TN)
U of Central Oklahoma (OK)
U of Georgia (GA)
U of Minnesota, Twin Cities Campus (MN)
U of New England (ME)
U of Victoria (BC, Canada)
U of Wisconsin–Superior (WI)
Wayne State Coll (NE)

HEALTH COMMUNICATION

Juniata Coll (PA)

HEALTH/HEALTH CARE ADMINISTRATION

Adams State Coll (CO)
Alaska Pacific U (AK)
Albertus Magnus Coll (CT)
American InterContinental U Buckhead Campus (GA)
Appalachian State U (NC)
Argosy U, Atlanta (GA)
Argosy U, Chicago (IL)
Argosy U, Denver (CO)
Argosy U, Nashville (TN)
Argosy U, Orange County (CA)
Argosy U, Phoenix (AZ)
Argosy U, San Diego (CA)
Argosy U, San Francisco Bay Area (CA)
Argosy U, Santa Monica (CA)
Argosy U, Sarasota (FL)
Argosy U, Schaumburg (IL)
Argosy U, Seattle (WA)
Argosy U, Twin Cities (MN)
Ashford U (IA)
Auburn U (AL)
Augustana Coll (SD)
Baker Coll of Auburn Hills (MI)
Baker Coll of Owosso (MI)
Baker Coll of Port Huron (MI)
Baptist Coll of Health Sciences (TN)
Belhaven Coll (MS)
Belmont U (TN)
Benedictine U (IL)
Bowling Green State U (OH)
Brandeis U (MA)
British Columbia Inst of Technology (BC, Canada)
Brock U (ON, Canada)
California State U, Dominguez Hills (CA)
California State U, Long Beach (CA)
California State U, San Bernardino (CA)
Calumet Coll of Saint Joseph (IN)
Central Michigan U (MI)
Chestnut Hill Coll (PA)
Clayton State U (GA)
The Coll at Brockport, State U of New York (NY)
Colorado Tech U—Colorado Springs (CO)
Colorado Tech U—Denver (CO)
Colorado Tech U—North Kansas City (MO)
Colorado Tech U—Online (CO)
Colorado Tech U—Sioux Falls (SD)
Columbia Southern U (AL)
Concordia Coll (MN)
Concordia U (OR)
Concordia U Wisconsin (WI)
Creighton U (NE)
Dallas Baptist U (TX)
Davenport U, Dearborn (MI)
Davenport U, Grand Rapids (MI)
Dillard U (LA)
Dominican Coll (NY)
Drexel U (PA)
Duquesne U (PA)
D'Youville Coll (NY)
East Carolina U (NC)
Eastern Kentucky U (KY)
Eastern Michigan U (MI)
Ferris State U (MI)
Florida Ag and Mech U (FL)
Florida Atlantic U (FL)
Florida Intl U (FL)
Granite State Coll (NH)
Harding U (AR)
Harris-Stowe State U (MO)
Hastings Coll (NE)
Heidelberg Coll (OH)
Hodges U (FL)
Howard Payne U (TX)
Idaho State U (ID)
Immaculata U (PA)
Indiana U–Purdue U Fort Wayne (IN)
Indiana U–Purdue U Indianapolis (IN)
Iona Coll (NY)
Ithaca Coll (NY)
Jackson State U (MS)
James Madison U (VA)
Jefferson Coll of Health Sciences (VA)
LA Coll Intl (CA)
Lebanon Valley Coll (PA)
Lehman Coll of the City U of New York (NY)
Lindenwood U (MO)
Lourdes Coll (OH)
Loyola U Chicago (IL)
Madonna U (MI)
Mary Baldwin Coll (VA)
Marywood U (PA)
Mercy Coll of Health Sciences (IA)
Methodist U (NC)
Midway Coll (KY)
Misericordia U (PA)
Montana State U (MT)
Montana State U–Billings (MT)
Mountain State U (WV)
Mount St. Mary's Coll (CA)
National-Louis U (IL)
New England Coll (NH)
New York U (NY)
Northeastern State U (OK)
Northeastern U (MA)
Oregon State U (OR)
Our Lady of the Lake Coll (LA)
Penn State Abington (PA)
Penn State Altoona (PA)
Penn State Berks (PA)
Penn State Erie, The Behrend Coll (PA)
Penn State Harrisburg (PA)
Penn State U Park (PA)
Point Park U (PA)
Providence Coll (RI)
Roger Williams U (RI)
Roosevelt U (IL)
St. John's U (NY)
St. Joseph's Coll, New York (NY)
St. Joseph's Coll, Suffolk Campus (NY)
Saint Louis U (MO)
Shippensburg U of Pennsylvania (PA)
Southern Adventist U (TN)
Southern Illinois U Carbondale (IL)
South U, Tampa (FL)
South U, West Palm Beach (FL)
South U (GA)
South U (SC)
Southwestern Adventist U (TX)
Southwestern Oklahoma State U (OK)
Spring Arbor U (MI)
State U of New York at Fredonia (NY)
State U of New York Inst of Technology (NY)
Stonehill Coll (MA)
Taylor U Fort Wayne (IN)
Tennessee State U (TN)
Texas Southern U (TX)
Texas State U-San Marcos (TX)
Thomas Edison State Coll (NJ)
Towson U (MD)
TUI U (CA)
The U of Arizona (AZ)
U of Central Florida (FL)
U of Cincinnati (OH)
U of Connecticut (CT)
U of Evansville (IN)
U of Great Falls (MT)
U of Houston–Clear Lake (TX)
U of La Verne (CA)
U of Maryland, Baltimore County (MD)
U of Michigan–Dearborn (MI)
U of Michigan–Flint (MI)
U of Nevada, Las Vegas (NV)
U of New England (ME)
U of New Hampshire (NH)
The U of North Carolina at Chapel Hill (NC)
U of North Florida (FL)
U of Pennsylvania (PA)
U of Rhode Island (RI)
U of St. Francis (IL)
U of Saint Francis (IN)
The U of Scranton (PA)
The U of Texas at El Paso (TX)
U of Victoria (BC, Canada)
U of Wisconsin–Eau Claire (WI)
U of Wisconsin–Milwaukee (WI)
Ursuline Coll (OH)
Waynesburg U (PA)
Weber State U (UT)
West Chester U of Pennsylvania (PA)
Western Carolina U (NC)
Western Illinois U (IL)
Western Intl U (AZ)
Western Kentucky U (KY)
Wheeling Jesuit U (WV)
Wichita State U (KS)
Winona State U (MN)
Wright State U (OH)

HEALTH INFORMATION/ MEDICAL RECORDS ADMINISTRATION

Alabama State U (AL)
Baker Coll of Auburn Hills (MI)
Chicago State U (IL)
The Coll of St. Scholastica (MN)
Dakota State U (SD)
Davenport U, Dearborn (MI)
Davenport U, Grand Rapids (MI)
East Carolina U (NC)
East Central U (OK)
Ferris State U (MI)
Florida Ag and Mech U (FL)
Florida Intl U (FL)
Gwynedd-Mercy Coll (PA)
Illinois State U (IL)
Indiana U East (IN)
Indiana U–Purdue U Indianapolis (IN)
Indiana U South Bend (IN)
Indiana U Southeast (IN)
Kean U (NJ)
Loma Linda U (CA)
Medical Coll of Georgia (GA)
Regis U (CO)
Saint Louis U (MO)
Southwestern Oklahoma State U (OK)
State U of New York Downstate Medical Center (NY)
State U of New York Inst of Technology (NY)
Stephens Coll (MO)
Temple U (PA)
Tennessee State U (TN)
Texas Southern U (TX)
Texas State U-San Marcos (TX)
The U of Alabama at Birmingham (AL)
U of Central Florida (FL)
U of Cincinnati (OH)
U of Illinois at Chicago (IL)
U of Kansas (KS)
U of Louisiana at Lafayette (LA)
U of Mississippi Medical Center (MS)
U of Pittsburgh (PA)
The U of Toledo (OH)
The U of Western Ontario (ON, Canada)
U of Wisconsin–Milwaukee (WI)
Western Carolina U (NC)

HEALTH INFORMATION/ MEDICAL RECORDS TECHNOLOGY

Colorado Tech U—Colorado Springs (CO)
Colorado Tech U—Denver (CO)
Colorado Tech U—North Kansas City (MO)
Colorado Tech U—Online (CO)
Colorado Tech U—Sioux Falls (SD)
Gwynedd-Mercy Coll (PA)
Mercyhurst Coll (PA)

HEALTH/MEDICAL PHYSICS

Bloomsburg U of Pennsylvania (PA)
U of Nevada, Las Vegas (NV)

HEALTH/MEDICAL PREPARATORY PROGRAMS RELATED

Abilene Christian U (TX)
Allegheny Coll (PA)

MAJORS AND MORE

Asbury Coll (KY)
Avila U (MO)
Baylor U (TX)
Bob Jones U (SC)
Coll of the Ozarks (MO)
Concordia U, Nebraska (NE)
DeSales U (PA)
Gannon U (PA)
Guilford Coll (NC)
Hodges U (FL)
Ithaca Coll (NY)
Juniata Coll (PA)
Lipscomb U (TN)
Maryville U of Saint Louis (MO)
Mercer U (GA)
Mercyhurst Coll (PA)
Meredith Coll (NC)
Northern Michigan U (MI)
Roosevelt U (IL)
St. Cloud State U (MN)
Salisbury U (MD)
Tusculum Coll (TN)
The U of Akron (OH)
U of Evansville (IN)
U of Louisiana at Monroe (LA)
U of Louisville (KY)
U of Missouri–Columbia (MO)
U of Nevada, Reno (NV)
U of South Alabama (AL)
Utica Coll (NY)
Wright State U (OH)

HEALTH/MEDICAL PSYCHOLOGY

Bridgewater State Coll (MA)
Jefferson Coll of Health Sciences (VA)
Massachusetts Coll of Pharmacy and Health Sciences (MA)
U of the Sciences in Philadelphia (PA)

HEALTH OCCUPATIONS TEACHER EDUCATION

Baylor U (TX)
New York Inst of Technology (NY)
North Carolina State U (NC)
U of Central Oklahoma (OK)
U of Georgia (GA)
U of Maine at Farmington (ME)

HEALTH PROFESSIONS RELATED

Alcorn State U (MS)
Armstrong Atlantic State U (GA)
Baldwin-Wallace Coll (OH)
Bowling Green State U (OH)
Bradley U (IL)
California State U, Fullerton (CA)
California State U, Los Angeles (CA)
Clemson U (SC)
Cleveland State U (OH)
Dowling Coll (NY)
D'Youville Coll (NY)
East Tennessee State U (TN)
The Evergreen State Coll (WA)
Gannon U (PA)
George Mason U (VA)
Grand Canyon U (AZ)
King Coll (TN)
King's Coll (PA)
Massachusetts Coll of Pharmacy and Health Sciences (MA)
Mercy Coll (NY)
Missouri Southern State U (MO)
Northeastern State U (OK)
Oakland U (MI)
Pennsylvania Coll of Technology (PA)
Purdue U (IN)
Randolph Coll (VA)
Saint Mary's Coll of California (CA)
San Diego State U (CA)
Southeastern Louisiana U (LA)
State U of New York Coll at Potsdam (NY)
Stony Brook U, State U of New York (NY)
Syracuse U (NY)
Towson U (MD)
The U of Alabama (AL)
U of Central Arkansas (AR)
U of Charleston (WV)
U of Louisiana at Lafayette (LA)
U of Maryland, Baltimore County (MD)
U of Nevada, Reno (NV)
U of New England (ME)
The U of North Carolina Wilmington (NC)
U of Northern Iowa (IA)
U of Pennsylvania (PA)
U of Pittsburgh (PA)
U of Saint Francis (IN)
U of Southern Indiana (IN)
The U of Texas at Tyler (TX)
Washington U in St. Louis (MO)
Wayne State U (MI)
Worcester State Coll (MA)
Youngstown State U (OH)

HEALTH SCIENCE

Alderson-Broaddus Coll (WV)
Alma Coll (MI)
American U (DC)
American U of Beirut (Lebanon)
Armstrong Atlantic State U (GA)
Athens State U (AL)
Azusa Pacific U (CA)
Ball State U (IN)
Bastyr U (WA)
Benedictine U (IL)
Boise State U (ID)
Boston U (MA)
Bradley U (IL)
Brock U (ON, Canada)
California State U, Dominguez Hills (CA)
California State U, East Bay (CA)
California State U, Fresno (CA)
California State U, Long Beach (CA)
California State U, Los Angeles (CA)
California State U, Sacramento (CA)
California State U, San Bernardino (CA)
Castleton State Coll (VT)
Clemson U (SC)
The Coll at Brockport, State U of New York (NY)
Coll of the Ozarks (MO)
Fairmont State U (WV)
Florida Atlantic U (FL)
Florida Intl U (FL)
Georgetown U (DC)
Gettysburg Coll (PA)
Grand Valley State U (MI)
Gwynedd-Mercy Coll (PA)
Inter American U of Puerto Rico, San Germán Campus (PR)
Johnson State Coll (VT)
Kalamazoo Coll (MI)
Kansas State U (KS)
Keiser U, Fort Lauderdale (FL)
Kettering Coll of Medical Arts (OH)
Lock Haven U of Pennsylvania (PA)
Longwood U (VA)
Manchester Coll (IN)
Maryville U of Saint Louis (MO)
Merrimack Coll (MA)
Milligan Coll (TN)
Minnesota State U Mankato (MN)
Misericordia U (PA)
Montana Tech of The U of Montana (MT)
Mount Olive Coll (NC)
New Jersey City U (NJ)
Newman U (KS)
Northeastern U (MA)
Northern Arizona U (AZ)
Northern Illinois U (IL)
Northwest Missouri State U (MO)
Norwich U (VT)
Oklahoma State U (OK)
Oregon State U (OR)
Pacific U (OR)
Roosevelt U (IL)
San Francisco State U (CA)
Sonoma State U (CA)
South U, Tampa (FL)
Tennessee Wesleyan Coll (TN)
Texas A&M U–Commerce (TX)
Texas Christian U (TX)
Texas Southern U (TX)
Truman State U (MO)
U of Arkansas (AR)
The U of British Columbia–Okanagan (BC, Canada)
U of California, Santa Cruz (CA)
U of Central Florida (FL)
U of Hartford (CT)
U of Maryland, Baltimore County (MD)
U of Nevada, Las Vegas (NV)
U of New England (ME)
U of St. Thomas (MN)
U of Southern California (CA)
U of Southern Maine (ME)
The U of Tennessee at Martin (TN)
The U of Texas at El Paso (TX)
The U of Western Ontario (ON, Canada)
U of Wisconsin–Milwaukee (WI)
Walla Walla U (WA)
West Liberty State Coll (WV)
Wilfrid Laurier U (ON, Canada)
William Paterson U of New Jersey (NJ)
Winona State U (MN)
York U (ON, Canada)
Youngstown State U (OH)

HEALTH SERVICES ADMINISTRATION

East Stroudsburg U of Pennsylvania (PA)
Freed-Hardeman U (TN)
Indiana U Northwest (IN)
Indiana U–Purdue U Fort Wayne (IN)
Indiana U–Purdue U Indianapolis (IN)
Indiana U South Bend (IN)
Keiser U, Fort Lauderdale (FL)
Monroe Coll, Bronx (NY)
Northwest Christian Coll (OR)
Robert Morris U (PA)
Thomas Edison State Coll (NJ)
U of Illinois at Urbana–Champaign (IL)
Ursuline Coll (OH)

HEALTH SERVICES/ALLIED HEALTH/HEALTH SCIENCES

Anna Maria Coll (MA)
Baptist Coll of Health Sciences (TN)
Brevard Coll (NC)
California Baptist U (CA)
California State U, Chico (CA)
California State U, Fullerton (CA)
Chicago State U (IL)
The Coll of St. Scholastica (MN)
Columbus State U (GA)
D'Youville Coll (NY)
Emmanuel Coll (MA)
Fairleigh Dickinson U, Coll at Florham (NJ)
Florida Atlantic U (FL)
Florida Gulf Coast U (FL)
Florida Intl U (FL)
Gwynedd-Mercy Coll (PA)
Hendrix Coll (AR)
Idaho State U (ID)
Jones Coll, Miami (FL)
Kent State U (OH)
Lebanon Valley Coll (PA)
Liberty U (VA)
Marywood U (PA)
Monmouth U (NJ)
Monroe Coll, New Rochelle (NY)
Montclair State U (NJ)
Mount Aloysius Coll (PA)
National U (CA)
Nicholls State U (LA)
Nova Southeastern U (FL)
Old Dominion U (VA)
Purdue U (IN)
Saginaw Valley State U (MI)
St. Cloud State U (MN)
Saint Joseph's U (PA)
San Diego State U (CA)
Stetson U (FL)
Texas State U-San Marcos (TX)
Texas Tech U (TX)
Texas Woman's U (TX)
Thomas Edison State Coll (NJ)
Thompson Rivers U (BC, Canada)
Truman State U (MO)
U of Central Florida (FL)
U of Florida (FL)
U of Miami (FL)
U of Michigan–Flint (MI)
U of Minnesota, Crookston (MN)
U of North Florida (FL)
U of North Texas (TX)
U of Ottawa (ON, Canada)
U of Regina (SK, Canada)
U of Southern Mississippi (MS)
The U of Texas at Austin (TX)
The U of Texas at Brownsville (TX)
The U of Texas at San Antonio (TX)
The U of Texas–Pan American (TX)
U of the Sciences in Philadelphia (PA)
U of Utah (UT)
The U of Western Ontario (ON, Canada)
U of Wyoming (WY)
Ursuline Coll (OH)
Washburn U (KS)
Western Kentucky U (KY)
Wheaton Coll (IL)
Widener U (PA)
York U (ON, Canada)

HEALTH TEACHER EDUCATION

Alma Coll (MI)
Appalachian State U (NC)
Aquinas Coll (MI)
Armstrong Atlantic State U (GA)
Ashland U (OH)
Auburn U (AL)
Augsburg Coll (MN)
Austin Peay State U (TN)
Averett U (VA)
Ball State U (IN)
Baylor U (TX)
Belmont U (TN)
Bemidji State U (MN)
Bethel U (MN)
Bluefield Coll (VA)
Bowling Green State U (OH)
Bridgewater State Coll (MA)
California State U, Chico (CA)
California State U, San Bernardino (CA)
Capital U (OH)
Carroll Coll (WI)
Cedarville U (OH)
Central Michigan U (MI)
Central Washington U (WA)
The Coll at Brockport, State U of New York (NY)
Concordia Coll (MN)
Concordia U (MI)
Concordia U, Nebraska (NE)
Concordia U, St. Paul (MN)
Concord U (WV)
Curry Coll (MA)
Defiance Coll (OH)
DePaul U (IL)
East Central U (OK)
Eastern Illinois U (IL)
Eastern Kentucky U (KY)
Eastern Mennonite U (VA)
East Stroudsburg U of Pennsylvania (PA)
Elon U (NC)
Fayetteville State U (NC)
Ferris State U (MI)
Florida Ag and Mech U (FL)
Florida Intl U (FL)
Florida State U (FL)
Freed-Hardeman U (TN)
Gardner-Webb U (NC)
George Fox U (OR)
George Mason U (VA)
Georgia Coll & State U (GA)
Gustavus Adolphus Coll (MN)
Hamline U (MN)
Hampton U (VA)
Harding U (AR)
Heidelberg Coll (OH)
Hofstra U (NY)
Hunter Coll of the City U of New York (NY)
Idaho State U (ID)
Illinois State U (IL)
Indiana U Bloomington (IN)
Indiana U–Purdue U Indianapolis (IN)
Indiana U Southeast (IN)
Iowa State U of Science and Technology (IA)
Ithaca Coll (NY)
Jacksonville State U (AL)
John Brown U (AR)
Johnson C. Smith U (NC)
Keene State Coll (NH)
Kent State U (OH)
Lambuth U (TN)
Lee U (TN)
Lehman Coll of the City U of New York (NY)
Liberty U (VA)
Longwood U (VA)
Louisiana Coll (LA)
Lynchburg Coll (VA)
Malone Coll (OH)
Manchester Coll (IN)
Maryville Coll (TN)
Mayville State U (ND)
McGill U (QC, Canada)
Miami U (OH)
Miami U Hamilton (OH)
Middle Tennessee State U (TN)
Minnesota State U Mankato (MN)
Missouri Baptist U (MO)
Missouri Valley Coll (MO)
Montana State U–Billings (MT)
Montclair State U (NJ)
Morehead State U (KY)
Morgan State U (MD)
Mount Vernon Nazarene U (OH)
Murray State U (KY)
New Mexico Highlands U (NM)
North Carolina Ag and Tech State U (NC)
North Carolina Central U (NC)
North Dakota State U (ND)
Northeastern State U (OK)
Northern Arizona U (AZ)
Northern Illinois U (IL)
Northern Michigan U (MI)
Northern State U (SD)
Northwestern Oklahoma State U (OK)
Northwest Missouri State U (MO)
Ohio Northern U (OH)
Ohio Wesleyan U (OH)
Oral Roberts U (OK)
Otterbein Coll (OH)
Peru State Coll (NE)
Portland State U (OR)
Purdue U (IN)
Rhode Island Coll (RI)
St. Ambrose U (IA)
St. Cloud State U (MN)
Salem State Coll (MA)
Salisbury U (MD)
Sam Houston State U (TX)
San Francisco State U (CA)
South Carolina State U (SC)
Southeastern Oklahoma State U (OK)
Southern Illinois U Carbondale (IL)
Southern Illinois U Edwardsville (IL)
Southern Oregon U (OR)
Southwest Baptist U (MO)
Southwest Minnesota State U (MN)
State U of New York at Oswego (NY)
Tabor Coll (KS)
Tennessee State U (TN)
Tennessee Technological U (TN)
Texas A&M U–Commerce (TX)
Texas Southern U (TX)
TUI U (CA)
Union Coll (KY)
The U of Alabama at Birmingham (AL)
The U of Arizona (AZ)
U of Charleston (WV)
U of Cincinnati (OH)
U of Dayton (OH)
U of Delaware (DE)
U of Florida (FL)
U of Georgia (GA)
U of Great Falls (MT)
U of Lethbridge (AB, Canada)
U of Maine (ME)
U of Maine at Farmington (ME)
U of Maryland, Coll Park (MD)
U of Minnesota, Duluth (MN)
The U of Montana (MT)
The U of Montana–Western (MT)
U of Nebraska–Lincoln (NE)
U of Nevada, Las Vegas (NV)
U of Nevada, Reno (NV)
U of New Brunswick Fredericton (NB, Canada)
U of New Mexico (NM)
The U of North Carolina at Greensboro (NC)
U of Northern Iowa (IA)
U of Richmond (VA)
U of Rio Grande (OH)
U of Saint Francis (IN)
U of St. Thomas (MN)
The U of South Dakota (SD)
The U of Tennessee (TN)
U of the District of Columbia (DC)
The U of Toledo (OH)
U of Toronto (ON, Canada)
U of Windsor (ON, Canada)
U of Wisconsin–La Crosse (WI)
Utah State U (UT)
Utah Valley State Coll (UT)
Valley City State U (ND)
Virginia Commonwealth U (VA)
Washington State U (WA)
Wayne State U (MI)
West Chester U of Pennsylvania (PA)
Western Connecticut State U (CT)
Western Illinois U (IL)
Western Michigan U (MI)
Western Washington U (WA)
West Liberty State Coll (WV)
West Virginia Wesleyan Coll (WV)
William Paterson U of New Jersey (NJ)
Wilmington Coll (OH)
Winona State U (MN)
Wright State U (OH)
Xavier U of Louisiana (LA)
York Coll of the City U of New York (NY)
Youngstown State U (OH)

HEATING, AIR CONDITIONING, VENTILATION AND REFRIGERATION MAINTENANCE TECHNOLOGY

Lewis-Clark State Coll (ID)

HEAVY EQUIPMENT MAINTENANCE TECHNOLOGY

Ferris State U (MI)

HEBREW

Bard Coll (NY)
Brigham Young U (UT)
Concordia U Wisconsin (WI)
Dartmouth Coll (NH)
Harvard U (MA)
Hofstra U (NY)

Hunter Coll of the City U of New York (NY)
Lehman Coll of the City U of New York (NY)
List Coll, The Jewish Theological Sem (NY)
Multnomah Bible Coll and Biblical Sem (OR)
New York U (NY)
Queens Coll of the City U of New York (NY)
State U of New York at Binghamton (NY)
Temple U (PA)
U of California, Los Angeles (CA)
U of Illinois at Urbana–Champaign (IL)
U of Michigan (MI)
U of Minnesota, Twin Cities Campus (MN)
The U of Texas at Austin (TX)
The U of Western Ontario (ON, Canada)
U of Wisconsin–Madison (WI)
U of Wisconsin–Milwaukee (WI)
Washington U in St. Louis (MO)
York U (ON, Canada)

HERBALISM
Bastyr U (WA)

HIGHER EDUCATION/ HIGHER EDUCATION ADMINISTRATION
Wright State U (OH)

HINDI
U of Chicago (IL)

HISPANIC-AMERICAN, PUERTO RICAN, AND MEXICAN-AMERICAN/ CHICANO STUDIES
Arizona State U (AZ)
Boston Coll (MA)
Brown U (RI)
California State U, Dominguez Hills (CA)
California State U, East Bay (CA)
California State U, Fresno (CA)
California State U, Fullerton (CA)
California State U, Long Beach (CA)
California State U, Los Angeles (CA)
Cedar Crest Coll (PA)
Claremont McKenna Coll (CA)
The Colorado Coll (CO)
Connecticut Coll (CT)
Dartmouth Coll (NH)
Gettysburg Coll (PA)
Hampshire Coll (MA)
Harvard U (MA)
Hofstra U (NY)
Hunter Coll of the City U of New York (NY)
Lewis & Clark Coll (OR)
Loyola Marymount U (CA)
McGill U (QC, Canada)
Mills Coll (CA)
Pitzer Coll (CA)
Pomona Coll (CA)
Rutgers, The State U of New Jersey, Newark (NJ)
Rutgers, The State U of New Jersey, New Brunswick (NJ)
San Diego State U (CA)
San Francisco State U (CA)
Scripps Coll (CA)
Sonoma State U (CA)
Southern Methodist U (TX)
Stanford U (CA)
State U of New York Coll at Oneonta (NY)
Trent U (ON, Canada)
Tulane U (LA)
U at Albany, State U of New York (NY)
The U of Arizona (AZ)
U of California, Berkeley (CA)
U of California, Davis (CA)
U of California, Irvine (CA)
U of California, Los Angeles (CA)
U of California, Riverside (CA)
U of California, Santa Barbara (CA)
U of California, Santa Cruz (CA)
U of Minnesota, Twin Cities Campus (MN)
U of Northern Colorado (CO)
U of Southern California (CA)
U of Southern Maine (ME)
The U of Texas at El Paso (TX)
The U of Texas at San Antonio (TX)
The U of Texas–Pan American (TX)
U of Windsor (ON, Canada)
U of Wisconsin–Madison (WI)
Western New Mexico U (NM)
Wheaton Coll (MA)

HISTOLOGIC TECHNOLOGY/ HISTOTECHNOLOGIST
Michigan Technological U (MI)
Northern Michigan U (MI)
Oakland U (MI)

HISTORIC PRESERVATION AND CONSERVATION
Coll of Charleston (SC)
Roger Williams U (RI)
Saint Mary's Coll of California (CA)
Salve Regina U (RI)
Savannah Coll of Art and Design (GA)
U of Mary Washington (VA)
Ursuline Coll (OH)

HISTORY
Abilene Christian U (TX)
Acadia U (NS, Canada)
Adams State Coll (CO)
Adelphi U (NY)
Adrian Coll (MI)
Agnes Scott Coll (GA)
Alabama State U (AL)
Albertus Magnus Coll (CT)
Albion Coll (MI)
Albright Coll (PA)
Alcorn State U (MS)
Alderson-Broaddus Coll (WV)
Alfred U (NY)
Alice Lloyd Coll (KY)
Allegheny Coll (PA)
Alma Coll (MI)
Alvernia Coll (PA)
American Public U System (WV)
American U (DC)
The American U of Athens (Greece)
American U of Beirut (Lebanon)
The American U of Paris (France)
Amherst Coll (MA)
Anderson U (IN)
Anderson U (SC)
Andrews U (MI)
Angelo State U (TX)
Anna Maria Coll (MA)
Appalachian State U (NC)
Aquinas Coll (MI)
Arizona State U (AZ)
Arizona State U at the West campus (AZ)
Arkansas State U (AR)
Armstrong Atlantic State U (GA)
Asbury Coll (KY)
Ashland U (OH)
Assumption Coll (MA)
Athabasca U (AB, Canada)
Athens State U (AL)
Atlantic Union Coll (MA)
Auburn U (AL)
Auburn U Montgomery (AL)
Augsburg Coll (MN)
Augustana Coll (IL)
Augustana Coll (SD)
Augusta State U (GA)
Austin Coll (TX)
Austin Peay State U (TN)
Ave Maria U (FL)
Averett U (VA)
Avila U (MO)
Azusa Pacific U (CA)
Baker U (KS)
Baldwin-Wallace Coll (OH)
Ball State U (IN)
Bard Coll (NY)
Barnard Coll (NY)
Barry U (FL)
Barton Coll (NC)
Bates Coll (ME)
Baylor U (TX)
Belhaven Coll (MS)
Bellarmine U (KY)
Belmont Abbey Coll (NC)
Belmont U (TN)
Beloit Coll (WI)
Bemidji State U (MN)
Benedictine Coll (KS)
Benedictine U (IL)
Bennington Coll (VT)
Berea Coll (KY)
Bernard M. Baruch Coll of the City U of New York (NY)
Berry Coll (GA)
Bethany Coll (KS)
Bethany Coll (WV)
Bethany Lutheran Coll (MN)
Bethel Coll (KS)
Bethel Coll (TN)
Bethel U (MN)
Bethune-Cookman U (FL)
Biola U (CA)
Bishop's U (QC, Canada)
Blackburn Coll (IL)
Bloomfield Coll (NJ)
Bloomsburg U of Pennsylvania (PA)
Bluefield Coll (VA)
Bluffton U (OH)
Bob Jones U (SC)
Boise State U (ID)
Boston Coll (MA)
Boston U (MA)
Bowdoin Coll (ME)
Bowling Green State U (OH)
Bradley U (IL)
Brandeis U (MA)
Brenau U (GA)
Brevard Coll (NC)
Brewton-Parker Coll (GA)
Bridgewater Coll (VA)
Bridgewater State Coll (MA)
Brigham Young U (UT)
Brock U (ON, Canada)
Brown U (RI)
Bryan Coll (TN)
Bryn Athyn Coll of the New Church (PA)
Bryn Mawr Coll (PA)
Bucknell U (PA)
Buffalo State Coll, State U of New York (NY)
Butler U (IN)
Cabrini Coll (PA)
California Baptist U (CA)
California Inst of Technology (CA)
California Lutheran U (CA)
California Polytechnic State U, San Luis Obispo (CA)
California State Polytechnic U, Pomona (CA)
California State U, Chico (CA)
California State U, Dominguez Hills (CA)
California State U, East Bay (CA)
California State U, Fresno (CA)
California State U, Fullerton (CA)
California State U, Long Beach (CA)
California State U, Los Angeles (CA)
California State U, Sacramento (CA)
California State U, San Bernardino (CA)
California State U, San Marcos (CA)
California State U, Stanislaus (CA)
Calvin Coll (MI)
Cameron U (OK)
Canadian Mennonite U (MB, Canada)
Canisius Coll (NY)
Capital U (OH)
Carlow U (PA)
Carroll Coll (WI)
Carson-Newman Coll (TN)
Case Western Reserve U (OH)
Castleton State Coll (VT)
Catawba Coll (NC)
The Catholic U of America (DC)
Cedar Crest Coll (PA)
Cedarville U (OH)
Centenary Coll (NJ)
Centenary Coll of Louisiana (LA)
Central Coll (IA)
Central Connecticut State U (CT)
Central Michigan U (MI)
Central State U (OH)
Central Washington U (WA)
Centre Coll (KY)
Chaminade U of Honolulu (HI)
Chatham U (PA)
Chestnut Hill Coll (PA)
Chicago State U (IL)
Christendom Coll (VA)
Christian Brothers U (TN)
Christopher Newport U (VA)
The Citadel, The Military Coll of South Carolina (SC)
City Coll of the City U of New York (NY)
Claflin U (SC)
Claremont McKenna Coll (CA)
Clarion U of Pennsylvania (PA)
Clark Atlanta U (GA)
Clarke Coll (IA)
Clarkson U (NY)
Clark U (MA)
Clayton State U (GA)
Clearwater Christian Coll (FL)
Clemson U (SC)
Coastal Carolina U (SC)
Coker Coll (SC)
Colby Coll (ME)
Colgate U (NY)
The Coll at Brockport, State U of New York (NY)
Coll of Charleston (SC)
The Coll of Idaho (ID)
Coll of Mount St. Joseph (OH)
Coll of Mount Saint Vincent (NY)
The Coll of New Jersey (NJ)
The Coll of New Rochelle (NY)
Coll of Saint Benedict (MN)
Coll of Saint Elizabeth (NJ)
Coll of St. Joseph (VT)
The Coll of Saint Rose (NY)
The Coll of St. Scholastica (MN)
The Coll of Staten Island of the City U of New York (NY)
Coll of the Holy Cross (MA)
Coll of the Ozarks (MO)
Coll of the Southwest (NM)
The Coll of William and Mary (VA)
The Colorado Coll (CO)
Colorado State U (CO)
Colorado State U-Pueblo (CO)
Columbia Coll (SC)
Columbus State U (GA)
Concordia Coll (MN)
Concordia Coll–New York (NY)
Concordia U (CA)
Concordia U (MI)
Concordia U (QC, Canada)
Concordia U Chicago (IL)
Concordia U, Nebraska (NE)
Concordia U, St. Paul (MN)
Concordia U Texas (TX)
Concordia U Wisconsin (WI)
Concord U (WV)
Connecticut Coll (CT)
Converse Coll (SC)
Cornell Coll (IA)
Cornell U (NY)
Cornerstone U (MI)
Covenant Coll (GA)
Creighton U (NE)
Crown Coll (MN)
Culver-Stockton Coll (MO)
Curry Coll (MA)
Daemen Coll (NY)
Dakota Wesleyan U (SD)
Dallas Baptist U (TX)
Dana Coll (NE)
Dartmouth Coll (NH)
Davidson Coll (NC)
Davis & Elkins Coll (WV)
Defiance Coll (OH)
Delta State U (MS)
Denison U (OH)
DePaul U (IL)
DePauw U (IN)
DeSales U (PA)
Dickinson Coll (PA)
Dillard U (LA)
Doane Coll (NE)
Dominican Coll (NY)
Dominican U (IL)
Dominican U of California (CA)
Dordt Coll (IA)
Dowling Coll (NY)
Drake U (IA)
Drew U (NJ)
Drexel U (PA)
Drury U (MO)
Duke U (NC)
Duquesne U (PA)
D'Youville Coll (NY)
Earlham Coll (IN)
East Carolina U (NC)
East Central U (OK)
Eastern Connecticut State U (CT)
Eastern Illinois U (IL)
Eastern Kentucky U (KY)
Eastern Mennonite U (VA)
Eastern Michigan U (MI)
Eastern New Mexico U (NM)
East Stroudsburg U of Pennsylvania (PA)
East Tennessee State U (TN)
East Texas Baptist U (TX)
Eckerd Coll (FL)
Edinboro U of Pennsylvania (PA)
Elizabethtown Coll (PA)
Elon U (NC)
Emmanuel Coll (MA)
Emory & Henry Coll (VA)
Emory U (GA)
Emporia State U (KS)
Erskine Coll (SC)
Eugene Lang Coll The New School for Liberal Arts (NY)
Evangel U (MO)
Excelsior Coll (NY)
Fairfield U (CT)
Fairleigh Dickinson U, Coll at Florham (NJ)
Fairleigh Dickinson U, Metropolitan Campus (NJ)
Fairmont State U (WV)
Faulkner U (AL)
Fayetteville State U (NC)
Felician Coll (NJ)
Ferris State U (MI)
Ferrum Coll (VA)
Fitchburg State Coll (MA)
Flagler Coll (FL)
Florida Ag and Mech U (FL)
Florida Atlantic U (FL)
Florida Gulf Coast U (FL)
Florida Inst of Technology (FL)
Florida Intl U (FL)
Florida Southern Coll (FL)
Florida State U (FL)
Fontbonne U (MO)
Fort Lewis Coll (CO)
Framingham State Coll (MA)
Franciscan U of Steubenville (OH)
Francis Marion U (SC)
Franklin & Marshall Coll (PA)
Franklin Coll (IN)
Franklin Coll Switzerland (Switzerland)
Freed-Hardeman U (TN)
Fresno Pacific U (CA)
Frostburg State U (MD)
Furman U (SC)
Gannon U (PA)
Gardner-Webb U (NC)
George Fox U (OR)
George Mason U (VA)
Georgetown Coll (KY)
Georgetown U (DC)
The George Washington U (DC)
Georgia Coll & State U (GA)
Georgian Court U (NJ)
Georgia Southern U (GA)
Georgia Southwestern State U (GA)
Georgia State U (GA)
Gettysburg Coll (PA)
Glenville State Coll (WV)
Gonzaga U (WA)
Gordon Coll (MA)
Goucher Coll (MD)
Grace Coll (IN)
Grambling State U (LA)
Grand Canyon U (AZ)
Grand Valley State U (MI)
Grand View Coll (IA)
Great Lakes Christian Coll (MI)
Green Mountain Coll (VT)
Greensboro Coll (NC)
Greenville Coll (IL)
Grinnell Coll (IA)
Grove City Coll (PA)
Guilford Coll (NC)
Gustavus Adolphus Coll (MN)
Gwynedd-Mercy Coll (PA)
Hamilton Coll (NY)
Hamline U (MN)
Hampden-Sydney Coll (VA)
Hampshire Coll (MA)
Hampton U (VA)
Hannibal-LaGrange Coll (MO)
Hanover Coll (IN)
Harding U (AR)
Hardin-Simmons U (TX)
Hartwick Coll (NY)
Harvard U (MA)
Hastings Coll (NE)
Haverford Coll (PA)
Hawai'i Pacific U (HI)
Heidelberg Coll (OH)
Henderson State U (AR)
Hendrix Coll (AR)
High Point U (NC)
Hillsdale Coll (MI)
Hobart and William Smith Colls (NY)
Hofstra U (NY)
Hollins U (VA)
Holy Family U (PA)
Holy Names U (CA)
Hood Coll (MD)
Hope Coll (MI)
Houghton Coll (NY)
Houston Baptist U (TX)
Howard Payne U (TX)
Humboldt State U (CA)
Hunter Coll of the City U of New York (NY)
Huntingdon Coll (AL)
Huntington U (IN)
Huston-Tillotson U (TX)
Idaho State U (ID)
Illinois Coll (IL)
Illinois State U (IL)
Illinois Wesleyan U (IL)
Immaculata U (PA)
Indiana State U (IN)
Indiana U Bloomington (IN)
Indiana U Northwest (IN)
Indiana U of Pennsylvania (PA)
Indiana U–Purdue U Fort Wayne (IN)
Indiana U–Purdue U Indianapolis (IN)
Indiana U South Bend (IN)
Indiana U Southeast (IN)
Indiana Wesleyan U (IN)
Inter American U of Puerto Rico, Fajardo Campus (PR)
Iona Coll (NY)
Iowa State U of Science and Technology (IA)
Iowa Wesleyan Coll (IA)
Ithaca Coll (NY)

Jackson State U (MS)
Jacksonville State U (AL)
Jacksonville U (FL)
James Madison U (VA)
Jamestown Coll (ND)
Jarvis Christian Coll (TX)
John Brown U (AR)
John Carroll U (OH)
The Johns Hopkins U (MD)
Johnson C. Smith U (NC)
Johnson State Coll (VT)
Judson Coll (AL)
Judson U (IL)
Juniata Coll (PA)
Kalamazoo Coll (MI)
Kansas State U (KS)
Kean U (NJ)
Keene State Coll (NH)
Kennesaw State U (GA)
Kent State U (OH)
Kentucky Christian U (KY)
Kentucky Wesleyan Coll (KY)
Kenyon Coll (OH)
Keuka Coll (NY)
King Coll (TN)
King's Coll (PA)
The King's U Coll (AB, Canada)
Knox Coll (IL)
Kutztown U of Pennsylvania (PA)
Lafayette Coll (PA)
LaGrange Coll (GA)
Lake Forest Coll (IL)
Lakehead U (ON, Canada)
Lake Superior State U (MI)
Lambuth U (TN)
Lander U (SC)
La Roche Coll (PA)
La Salle U (PA)
La Sierra U (CA)
Laurentian U (ON, Canada)
Lawrence U (WI)
Lebanon Valley Coll (PA)
Lees-McRae Coll (NC)
Lee U (TN)
Lehigh U (PA)
Lehman Coll of the City U of New York (NY)
Le Moyne Coll (NY)
LeMoyne-Owen Coll (TN)
Lenoir-Rhyne Coll (NC)
LeTourneau U (TX)
Lewis & Clark Coll (OR)
Lewis U (IL)
Liberty U (VA)
Limestone Coll (SC)
Lincoln U (MO)
Lincoln U (PA)
Lindenwood U (MO)
Linfield Coll (OR)
Lipscomb U (TN)
List Coll, The Jewish Theological Sem (NY)
Livingstone Coll (NC)
Lock Haven U of Pennsylvania (PA)
Longwood U (VA)
Loras Coll (IA)
Louisiana Coll (LA)
Louisiana State U and Ag and Mech Coll (LA)
Lourdes Coll (OH)
Loyola Coll in Maryland (MD)
Loyola Marymount U (CA)
Loyola U Chicago (IL)
Loyola U New Orleans (LA)
Luther Coll (IA)
Lycoming Coll (PA)
Lynchburg Coll (VA)
Lyon Coll (AR)
Macalester Coll (MN)
Madonna U (MI)
Malone Coll (OH)
Manchester Coll (IN)
Manhattanville Coll (NY)
Mansfield U of Pennsylvania (PA)
Marian Coll (IN)
Marian Coll of Fond du Lac (WI)
Marietta Coll (OH)
Marist Coll (NY)
Marlboro Coll (VT)
Marquette U (WI)
Marshall U (WV)
Martin U (IN)
Mary Baldwin Coll (VA)
Marymount Manhattan Coll (NY)
Marymount U (VA)
Maryville Coll (TN)
Maryville U of Saint Louis (MO)
Marywood U (PA)
Massachusetts Coll of Liberal Arts (MA)
Massachusetts Inst of Technology (MA)
The Master's Coll and Sem (CA)
McDaniel Coll (MD)
McGill U (QC, Canada)
McKendree U (IL)
McMurry U (TX)
McNeese State U (LA)
Memorial U of Newfoundland (NL, Canada)
Mercer U (GA)
Mercy Coll (NY)
Mercyhurst Coll (PA)
Meredith Coll (NC)
Merrimack Coll (MA)
Mesa State Coll (CO)
Messiah Coll (PA)
Methodist U (NC)
Metropolitan State U (MN)
Miami U (OH)
Miami U Hamilton (OH)
Michigan State U (MI)
Michigan Technological U (MI)
MidAmerica Nazarene U (KS)
Middlebury Coll (VT)
Middle Tennessee State U (TN)
Midland Lutheran Coll (NE)
Midwestern State U (TX)
Miles Coll (AL)
Millersville U of Pennsylvania (PA)
Milligan Coll (TN)
Millikin U (IL)
Millsaps Coll (MS)
Mills Coll (CA)
Minnesota State U Mankato (MN)
Minot State U (ND)
Misericordia U (PA)
Mississippi Coll (MS)
Mississippi State U (MS)
Mississippi U for Women (MS)
Mississippi Valley State U (MS)
Missouri Baptist U (MO)
Missouri Southern State U (MO)
Missouri State U (MO)
Missouri U of Science and Technology (MO)
Missouri Valley Coll (MO)
Molloy Coll (NY)
Monmouth Coll (IL)
Monmouth U (NJ)
Montana State U (MT)
Montana State U–Billings (MT)
Montclair State U (NJ)
Moravian Coll (PA)
Morehead State U (KY)
Morehouse Coll (GA)
Morgan State U (MD)
Morningside Coll (IA)
Morris Coll (SC)
Mount Allison U (NB, Canada)
Mount Aloysius Coll (PA)
Mount Holyoke Coll (MA)
Mount Marty Coll (SD)
Mount Mary Coll (WI)
Mount Mercy Coll (IA)
Mount Olive Coll (NC)
Mount Saint Mary Coll (NY)
Mount St. Mary's Coll (CA)
Mount St. Mary's U (MD)
Mount Saint Vincent U (NS, Canada)
Mount Vernon Nazarene U (OH)
Muhlenberg Coll (PA)
Multnomah Bible Coll and Biblical Sem (OR)
Murray State U (KY)
National U (CA)
Nazareth Coll of Rochester (NY)
Nebraska Wesleyan U (NE)
New Coll of Florida (FL)
New England Coll (NH)
New Jersey City U (NJ)
New Jersey Inst of Technology (NJ)
Newman U (KS)
New Mexico Highlands U (NM)
New York U (NY)
Niagara U (NY)
Nicholls State U (LA)
Nichols Coll (MA)
North Carolina Ag and Tech State U (NC)
North Carolina Central U (NC)
North Carolina State U (NC)
North Carolina Wesleyan Coll (NC)
North Central Coll (IL)
North Dakota State U (ND)
Northeastern Illinois U (IL)
Northeastern State U (OK)
Northeastern U (MA)
Northern Arizona U (AZ)
Northern Illinois U (IL)
Northern Michigan U (MI)
Northern State U (SD)
North Georgia Coll & State U (GA)
North Greenville U (SC)
Northland Coll (WI)
Northwest Christian Coll (OR)
Northwestern Coll (IA)
Northwestern Coll (MN)
Northwestern Oklahoma State U (OK)
Northwestern State U of Louisiana (LA)
Northwestern U (IL)
Northwest Missouri State U (MO)
Northwest Nazarene U (ID)
Norwich U (VT)
Notre Dame de Namur U (CA)
Nova Southeastern U (FL)
Nyack Coll (NY)
Oakland U (MI)
Oakwood Coll (AL)
Oberlin Coll (OH)
Occidental Coll (CA)
Oglethorpe U (GA)
Ohio Dominican U (OH)
Ohio Northern U (OH)
Ohio Wesleyan U (OH)
Oklahoma Christian U (OK)
Oklahoma City U (OK)
Oklahoma Panhandle State U (OK)
Oklahoma State U (OK)
Oklahoma Wesleyan U (OK)
Old Dominion U (VA)
Oral Roberts U (OK)
Oregon State U (OR)
Otterbein Coll (OH)
Ouachita Baptist U (AR)
Pace U (NY)
Pacific Lutheran U (WA)
Pacific Union Coll (CA)
Pacific U (OR)
Paine Coll (GA)
Palm Beach Atlantic U (FL)
Park U (MO)
Patrick Henry Coll (VA)
Penn State Abington (PA)
Penn State Altoona (PA)
Penn State Berks (PA)
Penn State Erie, The Behrend Coll (PA)
Penn State U Park (PA)
Pepperdine U, Malibu (CA)
Peru State Coll (NE)
Pfeiffer U (NC)
Piedmont Coll (GA)
Pikeville Coll (KY)
Pittsburg State U (KS)
Pitzer Coll (CA)
Plymouth State U (NH)
Point Loma Nazarene U (CA)
Point Park U (PA)
Pomona Coll (CA)
Pontifical Coll Josephinum (OH)
Portland State U (OR)
Prairie View A&M U (TX)
Presbyterian Coll (SC)
Prescott Coll (AZ)
Princeton U (NJ)
Providence Coll (RI)
Purchase Coll, State U of New York (NY)
Purdue U (IN)
Purdue U Calumet (IN)
Queens Coll of the City U of New York (NY)
Queen's U at Kingston (ON, Canada)
Queens U of Charlotte (NC)
Quincy U (IL)
Quinnipiac U (CT)
Radford U (VA)
Ramapo Coll of New Jersey (NJ)
Randolph Coll (VA)
Randolph-Macon Coll (VA)
Redeemer U Coll (ON, Canada)
Reed Coll (OR)
Regis Coll (MA)
Regis U (CO)
Rhode Island Coll (RI)
Rhodes Coll (TN)
Rice U (TX)
The Richard Stockton Coll of New Jersey (NJ)
Rider U (NJ)
Ripon Coll (WI)
Roanoke Coll (VA)
Roberts Wesleyan Coll (NY)
Rochester Coll (MI)
Rockford Coll (IL)
Rockhurst U (MO)
Roger Williams U (RI)
Rollins Coll (FL)
Roosevelt U (IL)
Rosemont Coll (PA)
Rowan U (NJ)
Royal Military Coll of Canada (ON, Canada)
Russell Sage Coll (NY)
Rutgers, The State U of New Jersey, Camden (NJ)
Rutgers, The State U of New Jersey, Newark (NJ)
Rutgers, The State U of New Jersey, New Brunswick (NJ)
Saginaw Valley State U (MI)
St. Ambrose U (IA)
St. Andrews Presbyterian Coll (NC)
St. Cloud State U (MN)
St. Edward's U (TX)
Saint Francis U (PA)
St. Francis Xavier U (NS, Canada)
St. Gregory's U, Shawnee (OK)
St. John Fisher Coll (NY)
St. John's Coll (NM)
Saint John's U (MN)
St. John's U (NY)
Saint Joseph Coll (CT)
Saint Joseph's Coll (IN)
St. Joseph's Coll, New York (NY)
St. Joseph's Coll, Suffolk Campus (NY)
Saint Joseph's U (PA)
St. Lawrence U (NY)
Saint Leo U (FL)
Saint Louis U (MO)
Saint Martin's U (WA)
Saint Mary's Coll (IN)
Saint Mary's Coll of California (CA)
St. Mary's Coll of Maryland (MD)
St. Mary's U (TX)
Saint Mary's U of Minnesota (MN)
Saint Michael's Coll (VT)
St. Norbert Coll (WI)
St. Olaf Coll (MN)
St. Thomas Aquinas Coll (NY)
St. Thomas U (FL)
St. Thomas U (NB, Canada)
Saint Vincent Coll (PA)
Saint Xavier U (IL)
Salem Coll (NC)
Salem State Coll (MA)
Salisbury U (MD)
Salve Regina U (RI)
Samford U (AL)
Sam Houston State U (TX)
San Diego Christian Coll (CA)
San Diego State U (CA)
San Francisco State U (CA)
Santa Clara U (CA)
Sarah Lawrence Coll (NY)
Schreiner U (TX)
Scripps Coll (CA)
Seattle Pacific U (WA)
Seattle U (WA)
Seton Hill U (PA)
Sewanee: The U of the South (TN)
Shawnee State U (OH)
Shenandoah U (VA)
Shepherd U (WV)
Shippensburg U of Pennsylvania (PA)
Shorter Coll (GA)
Siena Coll (NY)
Siena Heights U (MI)
Simmons Coll (MA)
Simon Fraser U (BC, Canada)
Simpson Coll (IA)
Simpson U (CA)
Skidmore Coll (NY)
Slippery Rock U of Pennsylvania (PA)
Smith Coll (MA)
Sonoma State U (CA)
South Carolina State U (SC)
South Dakota State U (SD)
Southeastern Louisiana U (LA)
Southeastern Oklahoma State U (OK)
Southeastern U (FL)
Southeast Missouri State U (MO)
Southern Adventist U (TN)
Southern Arkansas U–Magnolia (AR)
Southern Connecticut State U (CT)
Southern Illinois U Carbondale (IL)
Southern Illinois U Edwardsville (IL)
Southern Methodist U (TX)
Southern New Hampshire U (NH)
Southern Oregon U (OR)
Southern U and Ag and Mech Coll (LA)
Southern Utah U (UT)
Southern Vermont Coll (VT)
Southern Wesleyan U (SC)
Southwest Baptist U (MO)
Southwestern Adventist U (TX)
Southwestern Coll (KS)
Southwestern Oklahoma State U (OK)
Southwestern U (TX)
Southwest Minnesota State U (MN)
Spelman Coll (GA)
Spring Arbor U (MI)
Spring Hill Coll (AL)
Stanford U (CA)
State U of New York at Binghamton (NY)
State U of New York at Fredonia (NY)
State U of New York at New Paltz (NY)
State U of New York at Oswego (NY)
State U of New York at Plattsburgh (NY)
State U of New York Coll at Geneseo (NY)
State U of New York Coll at Oneonta (NY)
State U of New York Coll at Potsdam (NY)
State U of New York Empire State Coll (NY)
Stephen F. Austin State U (TX)
Sterling Coll (KS)
Stetson U (FL)
Stillman Coll (AL)
Stonehill Coll (MA)
Stony Brook U, State U of New York (NY)
Suffolk U (MA)
Susquehanna U (PA)
Swarthmore Coll (PA)
Sweet Briar Coll (VA)
Syracuse U (NY)
Tabor Coll (KS)
Tarleton State U (TX)
Taylor U (IN)
Temple U (PA)
Tennessee State U (TN)
Tennessee Technological U (TN)
Tennessee Wesleyan Coll (TN)
Texas A&M Intl U (TX)
Texas A&M U (TX)
Texas A&M U–Commerce (TX)
Texas Christian U (TX)
Texas Coll (TX)
Texas Lutheran U (TX)
Texas Southern U (TX)
Texas State U-San Marcos (TX)
Texas Tech U (TX)
Texas Woman's U (TX)
Thiel Coll (PA)
Thomas Edison State Coll (NJ)
Thomas More Coll (KY)
Thompson Rivers U (BC, Canada)
Tiffin U (OH)
Tougaloo Coll (MS)
Towson U (MD)
Transylvania U (KY)
Trent U (ON, Canada)
Trevecca Nazarene U (TN)
Trinity Christian Coll (IL)
Trinity Coll (CT)
Trinity Intl U (IL)
Trinity U (TX)
Troy U (AL)
Truett-McConnell Coll (GA)
Truman State U (MO)
Tufts U (MA)
Tulane U (LA)
Tusculum Coll (TN)
Tuskegee U (AL)
Tyndale U Coll & Sem (ON, Canada)
Union Coll (KY)
Union Coll (NE)
Union Coll (NY)
Union U (TN)
United States Air Force Acad (CO)
United States Naval Acad (MD)
Université de Sherbrooke (QC, Canada)
U at Albany, State U of New York (NY)
U at Buffalo, the State U of New York (NY)
The U of Akron (OH)
The U of Alabama (AL)
The U of Alabama at Birmingham (AL)
The U of Alabama in Huntsville (AL)
U of Alaska Fairbanks (AK)
U of Alaska Southeast (AK)
The U of Arizona (AZ)
U of Arkansas (AR)
U of Arkansas at Fort Smith (AR)
U of Arkansas at Monticello (AR)
U of Arkansas at Pine Bluff (AR)
U of Baltimore (MD)
The U of British Columbia (BC, Canada)
The U of British Columbia–Okanagan (BC, Canada)
U of California, Berkeley (CA)
U of California, Davis (CA)
U of California, Irvine (CA)
U of California, Los Angeles (CA)
U of California, Riverside (CA)
U of California, San Diego (CA)
U of California, Santa Barbara (CA)
U of California, Santa Cruz (CA)
U of Central Arkansas (AR)
U of Central Florida (FL)
U of Central Missouri (MO)
U of Central Oklahoma (OK)
U of Charleston (WV)
U of Chicago (IL)
U of Cincinnati (OH)
U of Colorado at Boulder (CO)
U of Colorado Denver (CO)
U of Connecticut (CT)
U of Dallas (TX)
U of Dayton (OH)
U of Delaware (DE)
U of Denver (CO)
U of Evansville (IN)
The U of Findlay (OH)
U of Florida (FL)
U of Georgia (GA)
U of Great Falls (MT)
U of Guam (GU)

MAJORS AND MORE

U of Hartford (CT)
U of Hawaii at Manoa (HI)
U of Hawaii–West Oahu (HI)
U of Houston (TX)
U of Houston–Clear Lake (TX)
U of Houston–Downtown (TX)
U of Houston–Victoria (TX)
U of Idaho (ID)
U of Illinois at Chicago (IL)
U of Illinois at Springfield (IL)
U of Illinois at Urbana–Champaign (IL)
U of Indianapolis (IN)
The U of Iowa (IA)
U of Kansas (KS)
U of King's Coll (NS, Canada)
U of La Verne (CA)
U of Lethbridge (AB, Canada)
U of Louisiana at Lafayette (LA)
U of Louisiana at Monroe (LA)
U of Louisville (KY)
U of Maine (ME)
U of Maine at Farmington (ME)
U of Maine at Machias (ME)
U of Mary Hardin-Baylor (TX)
U of Maryland, Baltimore County (MD)
U of Maryland, Coll Park (MD)
U of Maryland Eastern Shore (MD)
U of Maryland U Coll (MD)
U of Mary Washington (VA)
U of Massachusetts Amherst (MA)
U of Massachusetts Boston (MA)
U of Massachusetts Dartmouth (MA)
U of Massachusetts Lowell (MA)
U of Memphis (TN)
U of Miami (FL)
U of Michigan (MI)
U of Michigan–Dearborn (MI)
U of Michigan–Flint (MI)
U of Minnesota, Duluth (MN)
U of Minnesota, Twin Cities Campus (MN)
U of Mississippi (MS)
U of Missouri–Columbia (MO)
U of Missouri–Kansas City (MO)
U of Missouri–St. Louis (MO)
The U of Montana (MT)
U of Montevallo (AL)
U of Nebraska at Kearney (NE)
U of Nebraska at Omaha (NE)
U of Nebraska–Lincoln (NE)
U of Nevada, Las Vegas (NV)
U of Nevada, Reno (NV)
U of New Brunswick Fredericton (NB, Canada)
U of New England (ME)
U of New Hampshire (NH)
U of New Hampshire at Manchester (NH)
U of New Haven (CT)
U of New Mexico (NM)
U of New Orleans (LA)
U of North Alabama (AL)
The U of North Carolina at Asheville (NC)
The U of North Carolina at Chapel Hill (NC)
The U of North Carolina at Charlotte (NC)
The U of North Carolina at Greensboro (NC)
The U of North Carolina at Pembroke (NC)
The U of North Carolina Wilmington (NC)
U of North Dakota (ND)
U of Northern Colorado (CO)
U of Northern Iowa (IA)
U of North Florida (FL)
U of North Texas (TX)
U of Notre Dame (IN)
U of Oklahoma (OK)
U of Oregon (OR)
U of Ottawa (ON, Canada)
U of Pennsylvania (PA)
U of Pittsburgh (PA)
U of Pittsburgh at Bradford (PA)
U of Pittsburgh at Johnstown (PA)
U of Portland (OR)
U of Prince Edward Island (PE, Canada)
U of Puerto Rico at Utuado (PR)
U of Puerto Rico, Cayey U Coll (PR)
U of Puget Sound (WA)
U of Redlands (CA)
U of Regina (SK, Canada)
U of Rhode Island (RI)
U of Richmond (VA)
U of Rio Grande (OH)
U of Rochester (NY)
U of St. Francis (IL)
U of Saint Francis (IN)
U of Saint Mary (KS)
U of St. Thomas (MN)
U of St. Thomas (TX)
U of San Diego (CA)
U of Science and Arts of Oklahoma (OK)
The U of Scranton (PA)
U of Sioux Falls (SD)
U of South Alabama (AL)
U of South Carolina (SC)
U of South Carolina Aiken (SC)
U of South Carolina Beaufort (SC)
U of South Carolina Upstate (SC)
The U of South Dakota (SD)
U of Southern California (CA)
U of Southern Indiana (IN)
U of Southern Maine (ME)
U of Southern Mississippi (MS)
U of South Florida (FL)
The U of Tampa (FL)
The U of Tennessee (TN)
The U of Tennessee at Chattanooga (TN)
The U of Tennessee at Martin (TN)
The U of Texas at Arlington (TX)
The U of Texas at Austin (TX)
The U of Texas at Brownsville (TX)
The U of Texas at Dallas (TX)
The U of Texas at El Paso (TX)
The U of Texas at San Antonio (TX)
The U of Texas at Tyler (TX)
The U of Texas of the Permian Basin (TX)
The U of Texas–Pan American (TX)
U of the Incarnate Word (TX)
U of the Ozarks (AR)
U of the Pacific (CA)
U of the West (CA)
The U of Toledo (OH)
U of Toronto (ON, Canada)
U of Tulsa (OK)
U of Utah (UT)
U of Vermont (VT)
U of Victoria (BC, Canada)
U of Virginia (VA)
The U of Virginia's Coll at Wise (VA)
The U of Western Ontario (ON, Canada)
U of West Florida (FL)
U of West Georgia (GA)
U of Windsor (ON, Canada)
The U of Winnipeg (MB, Canada)
U of Wisconsin–Eau Claire (WI)
U of Wisconsin–Green Bay (WI)
U of Wisconsin–La Crosse (WI)
U of Wisconsin–Madison (WI)
U of Wisconsin–Milwaukee (WI)
U of Wisconsin–Oshkosh (WI)
U of Wisconsin–Parkside (WI)
U of Wisconsin–Platteville (WI)
U of Wisconsin–Stevens Point (WI)
U of Wisconsin–Superior (WI)
U of Wisconsin–Whitewater (WI)
U of Wyoming (WY)
Ursinus Coll (PA)
Ursuline Coll (OH)
Utah State U (UT)
Utah Valley State Coll (UT)
Utica Coll (NY)
Valdosta State U (GA)
Valley City State U (ND)
Valparaiso U (IN)
Vanderbilt U (TN)
Vanguard U of Southern California (CA)
Vassar Coll (NY)
Villanova U (PA)
Virginia Commonwealth U (VA)
Virginia Intermont Coll (VA)
Virginia Military Inst (VA)
Virginia Polytechnic Inst and State U (VA)
Virginia State U (VA)
Virginia Wesleyan Coll (VA)
Wabash Coll (IN)
Wagner Coll (NY)
Wake Forest U (NC)
Walla Walla U (WA)
Walsh U (OH)
Warner Pacific Coll (OR)
Warren Wilson Coll (NC)
Wartburg Coll (IA)
Washburn U (KS)
Washington & Jefferson Coll (PA)
Washington and Lee U (VA)
Washington Coll (MD)
Washington State U (WA)
Washington U in St. Louis (MO)
Wayland Baptist U (TX)
Waynesburg U (PA)
Wayne State Coll (NE)
Wayne State U (MI)
Weber State U (UT)
Webster U (MO)
Wellesley Coll (MA)
Wells Coll (NY)
Wesleyan Coll (GA)
Wesleyan U (CT)
Wesley Coll (DE)
West Chester U of Pennsylvania (PA)
Western Carolina U (NC)
Western Connecticut State U (CT)
Western Illinois U (IL)
Western Kentucky U (KY)
Western Michigan U (MI)
Western New England Coll (MA)
Western New Mexico U (NM)
Western State Coll of Colorado (CO)
Western Washington U (WA)
Westfield State Coll (MA)
West Liberty State Coll (WV)
Westminster Coll (MO)
Westminster Coll (UT)
Westmont Coll (CA)
West Texas A&M U (TX)
West Virginia U (WV)
West Virginia Wesleyan Coll (WV)
Wheaton Coll (IL)
Wheaton Coll (MA)
Wheeling Jesuit U (WV)
Whitman Coll (WA)
Whittier Coll (CA)
Whitworth U (WA)
Wichita State U (KS)
Widener U (PA)
Wiley Coll (TX)
Wilfrid Laurier U (ON, Canada)
Wilkes U (PA)
Willamette U (OR)
William Jewell Coll (MO)
William Paterson U of New Jersey (NJ)
Williams Coll (MA)
William Woods U (MO)
Wilmington Coll (OH)
Wingate U (NC)
Winona State U (MN)
Winthrop U (SC)
Wittenberg U (OH)
Wofford Coll (SC)
Woodbury U (CA)
Worcester Polytechnic Inst (MA)
Worcester State Coll (MA)
Wright State U (OH)
Xavier U (OH)
Xavier U of Louisiana (LA)
Yale U (CT)
York Coll (NE)
York Coll of Pennsylvania (PA)
York Coll of the City U of New York (NY)
York U (ON, Canada)
Youngstown State U (OH)

HISTORY AND PHILOSOPHY OF SCIENCE AND TECHNOLOGY

Bard Coll (NY)
Case Western Reserve U (OH)
Farmingdale State Coll (NY)
Georgia Inst of Technology (GA)
Harvard U (MA)
The Johns Hopkins U (MD)
Oregon State U (OR)
Sarah Lawrence Coll (NY)
U of Pennsylvania (PA)
U of Pittsburgh (PA)
U of Toronto (ON, Canada)
U of Wisconsin–Madison (WI)
Worcester Polytechnic Inst (MA)

HISTORY OF PHILOSOPHY

Harvard U (MA)
Marlboro Coll (VT)
Marquette U (WI)
St. John's Coll (NM)
U of Regina (SK, Canada)
U of Toronto (ON, Canada)

HISTORY OF SCIENCE AND TECHNOLOGY

California Inst of Technology (CA)

HISTORY RELATED

American Public U System (WV)
Ashford U (IA)
Bridgewater Coll (VA)
Bridgewater State Coll (MA)
Brigham Young U (UT)
Carnegie Mellon U (PA)
Coll of the Ozarks (MO)
D'Youville Coll (NY)
Grace Coll (IN)
Hamilton Coll (NY)
Marquette U (WI)
Mercyhurst Coll (PA)
Saint Mary's U of Minnesota (MN)
Sarah Lawrence Coll (NY)
U of California, Riverside (CA)
U of Regina (SK, Canada)

HISTORY TEACHER EDUCATION

Abilene Christian U (TX)
Alma Coll (MI)
Anderson U (SC)
Anna Maria Coll (MA)
Appalachian State U (NC)
Assumption Coll (MA)
Auburn U (AL)
Averett U (VA)
Bishop's U (QC, Canada)
Bluefield Coll (VA)
Brewton-Parker Coll (GA)
Bridgewater Coll (VA)
Brigham Young U (UT)
Bryan Coll (TN)
Carroll Coll (WI)
The Catholic U of America (DC)
Central Michigan U (MI)
Central Washington U (WA)
Christian Brothers U (TN)
Coker Coll (SC)
The Coll at Brockport, State U of New York (NY)
The Coll of New Jersey (NJ)
Coll of the Ozarks (MO)
Concordia U (MI)
Concordia U Chicago (IL)
Concordia U, Nebraska (NE)
Concordia U Wisconsin (WI)
Cornerstone U (MI)
Covenant Coll (GA)
Crown Coll (MN)
Culver-Stockton Coll (MO)
Dakota Wesleyan U (SD)
Dana Coll (NE)
DePaul U (IL)
Dominican Coll (NY)
Dordt Coll (IA)
East Central U (OK)
Eastern Michigan U (MI)
East Texas Baptist U (TX)
Evangel U (MO)
Ferris State U (MI)
Fitchburg State Coll (MA)
Greenville Coll (IL)
Gwynedd-Mercy Coll (PA)
Hannibal-LaGrange Coll (MO)
Hardin-Simmons U (TX)
Hastings Coll (NE)
Hope Coll (MI)
Howard Payne U (TX)
Indiana U–Purdue U Fort Wayne (IN)
Ithaca Coll (NY)
Jamestown Coll (ND)
Johnson State Coll (VT)
Keene State Coll (NH)
King Coll (TN)
Lambuth U (TN)
Lenoir-Rhyne Coll (NC)
Liberty U (VA)
Lindenwood U (MO)
Lipscomb U (TN)
Maranatha Baptist Bible Coll (WI)
Marian Coll of Fond du Lac (WI)
Maryville Coll (TN)
Maryville U of Saint Louis (MO)
Mayville State U (ND)
McGill U (QC, Canada)
McKendree U (IL)
Minot State U (ND)
Missouri State U (MO)
Montana State U–Billings (MT)
Moravian Coll (PA)
Mount Marty Coll (SD)
Mount Mary Coll (WI)
Mount Vernon Nazarene U (OH)
Murray State U (KY)
Nazareth Coll of Rochester (NY)
North Carolina Central U (NC)
North Carolina State U (NC)
North Dakota State U (ND)
Northern Arizona U (AZ)
Northern Michigan U (MI)
Northwest Nazarene U (ID)
Ohio Northern U (OH)
Ohio Wesleyan U (OH)
Old Dominion U (VA)
Pace U (NY)
Paine Coll (GA)
Rhode Island Coll (RI)
Rochester Coll (MI)
Sacred Heart U (CT)
Saginaw Valley State U (MI)
St. Ambrose U (IA)
St. Edward's U (TX)
Saint Francis U (PA)
St. Joseph's Coll, Suffolk Campus (NY)
Saint Xavier U (IL)
Salve Regina U (RI)
Samford U (AL)
Schreiner U (TX)
Shawnee State U (OH)
Southwestern Oklahoma State U (OK)
Taylor U (IN)
Texas A&M Intl U (TX)
Texas Lutheran U (TX)
Toccoa Falls Coll (GA)
Trevecca Nazarene U (TN)
Trinity Christian Coll (IL)
Tusculum Coll (TN)
Union Coll (NE)
The U of Arizona (AZ)
U of Arkansas at Fort Smith (AR)
U of Central Oklahoma (OK)
U of Delaware (DE)
U of Great Falls (MT)
U of Illinois at Chicago (IL)
U of Illinois at Urbana–Champaign (IL)
The U of Iowa (IA)
U of Maine (ME)
U of Maine at Machias (ME)
U of Mary (ND)
U of Michigan–Flint (MI)
The U of Montana–Western (MT)
U of Nebraska–Lincoln (NE)
The U of North Carolina at Charlotte (NC)
The U of North Carolina Wilmington (NC)
U of Pittsburgh at Johnstown (PA)
U of Puerto Rico at Utuado (PR)
U of Puerto Rico, Cayey U Coll (PR)
U of Rio Grande (OH)
The U of South Dakota (SD)
The U of Tennessee at Martin (TN)
U of Windsor (ON, Canada)
U of Wisconsin–Superior (WI)
Utah Valley State Coll (UT)
Utica Coll (NY)
Valley City State U (ND)
Valparaiso U (IN)
Wartburg Coll (IA)
Washington State U (WA)
Washington U in St. Louis (MO)
Wayne State Coll (NE)
Weber State U (UT)
Western Michigan U (MI)
Western State Coll of Colorado (CO)
Wheeling Jesuit U (WV)
Widener U (PA)
Xavier U of Louisiana (LA)
York Coll (NE)
York Coll of Pennsylvania (PA)
York U (ON, Canada)

HOME FURNISHINGS AND EQUIPMENT INSTALLATION

Brigham Young U (UT)

HORSE HUSBANDRY/ EQUINE SCIENCE AND MANAGEMENT

Becker Coll (MA)
Bethany Coll (WV)
Midway Coll (KY)
Mount Ida Coll (MA)
Oklahoma Panhandle State U (OK)
Stephens Coll (MO)
Sterling Coll (VT)
Vermont Tech Coll (VT)

HORTICULTURAL SCIENCE

Auburn U (AL)
California Polytechnic State U, San Luis Obispo (CA)
California State Polytechnic U, Pomona (CA)
Christopher Newport U (VA)
Clemson U (SC)
Coll of the Ozarks (MO)
Colorado State U (CO)
Cornell U (NY)
Delaware Valley Coll (PA)
Ferrum Coll (VA)
Florida Ag and Mech U (FL)
Florida Southern Coll (FL)
Iowa State U of Science and Technology (IA)
Kansas State U (KS)
Michigan State U (MI)
Mississippi State U (MS)
Missouri State U (MO)
Montana State U (MT)
North Carolina State U (NC)
North Dakota State U (ND)
Northwest Missouri State U (MO)
Oklahoma State U (OK)
Oregon State U (OR)
Penn State Abington (PA)
Penn State Altoona (PA)
Penn State Berks (PA)
Penn State Erie, The Behrend Coll (PA)
Penn State U Park (PA)
Purdue U (IN)
Sam Houston State U (TX)
Southeastern Louisiana U (LA)
Southeast Missouri State U (MO)
State U of New York Coll of Agriculture and Technology at Cobleskill (NY)
Stephen F. Austin State U (TX)
Sterling Coll (VT)

Tarleton State U (TX)
Temple U (PA)
Tennessee Technological U (TN)
Texas A&M U (TX)
Truman State U (MO)
U of Arkansas (AR)
The U of British Columbia (BC, Canada)
U of Connecticut (CT)
U of Delaware (DE)
U of Florida (FL)
U of Idaho (ID)
U of Illinois at Urbana–Champaign (IL)
U of Louisiana at Lafayette (LA)
U of Maryland, Coll Park (MD)
U of Minnesota, Crookston (MN)
U of Nebraska–Lincoln (NE)
U of New Hampshire (NH)
U of Vermont (VT)
U of Wisconsin–Madison (WI)
Utah State U (UT)
Virginia Polytechnic Inst and State U (VA)
Washington State U (WA)

HORTICULTURE SCIENCE
U of Georgia (GA)

HOSPITAL AND HEALTH CARE FACILITIES ADMINISTRATION
Avila U (MO)
Carson-Newman Coll (TN)
Gwynedd-Mercy Coll (PA)
Ithaca Coll (NY)
Saint Joseph's U (PA)
Saint Leo U (FL)
The U of Alabama (AL)
The U of South Dakota (SD)
The U of Toledo (OH)
Ursuline Coll (OH)
York U (ON, Canada)
Youngstown State U (OH)

HOSPITALITY ADMINISTRATION
American Public U System (WV)
The American U of Athens (Greece)
Appalachian State U (NC)
The Art Insts Intl Minnesota (MN)
Becker Coll (MA)
Boston U (MA)
Bowling Green State U (OH)
Buffalo State Coll, State U of New York (NY)
Central Michigan U (MI)
Coll of Charleston (SC)
Concordia U (MI)
Concord U (WV)
Delta State U (MS)
East Carolina U (NC)
Eastern Michigan U (MI)
East Stroudsburg U of Pennsylvania (PA)
Ecole Hôtelière de Lausanne (Switzerland)
Endicott Coll (MA)
Ferris State U (MI)
Florida Atlantic U (FL)
Florida Intl U (FL)
Florida State U (FL)
Husson Coll (ME)
Indiana U of Pennsylvania (PA)
Indiana U–Purdue U Fort Wayne (IN)
James Madison U (VA)
Johnson State Coll (VT)
Lewis-Clark State Coll (ID)
Lexington Coll (IL)
Madonna U (MI)
Marywood U (PA)
Mercyhurst Coll (PA)
Metropolitan State U (MN)
Michigan State U (MI)
Missouri State U (MO)
Monroe Coll, Bronx (NY)
Monroe Coll, New Rochelle (NY)
Montclair State U (NJ)
Morgan State U (MD)
Mount Saint Vincent U (NS, Canada)
National U (CA)
New York U (NY)
North Carolina Central U (NC)
North Dakota State U (ND)
Northern Michigan U (MI)
Northwestern State U of Louisiana (LA)
Paul Smith's Coll (NY)
The Richard Stockton Coll of New Jersey (NJ)
Robert Morris U (PA)
Rochester Inst of Technology (NY)
Roosevelt U (IL)
Rutgers, The State U of New Jersey, Camden (NJ)
St. John's U (NY)
Saint Leo U (FL)
San Diego State U (CA)
San Francisco State U (CA)
Seton Hill U (PA)
Southern New Hampshire U (NH)
Stephen F. Austin State U (TX)
Temple U (PA)
Thomas Edison State Coll (NJ)
Thompson Rivers U (BC, Canada)
Tri-State U (IN)
TUI U (CA)
Tuskegee U (AL)
U of Arkansas (AR)
U of Central Florida (FL)
U of Denver (CO)
U of Illinois at Urbana–Champaign (IL)
U of Massachusetts Amherst (MA)
U of Memphis (TN)
U of Minnesota, Crookston (MN)
U of Nebraska–Lincoln (NE)
U of Nevada, Las Vegas (NV)
U of Nevada, Reno (NV)
U of New Hampshire (NH)
U of New Haven (CT)
U of New Orleans (LA)
The U of North Carolina at Greensboro (NC)
U of North Texas (TX)
U of Prince Edward Island (PE, Canada)
U of South Carolina (SC)
U of South Carolina Beaufort (SC)
U of South Florida (FL)
U of West Florida (FL)
Utah Valley State Coll (UT)
Virginia State U (VA)
Washington State U (WA)
Western Carolina U (NC)
Western Kentucky U (KY)
Youngstown State U (OH)

HOSPITALITY ADMINISTRATION RELATED
Auburn U (AL)
California State U, Fullerton (CA)
Davis & Elkins Coll (WV)
Drexel U (PA)
Florida State U (FL)
Indiana U–Purdue U Indianapolis (IN)
Kent State U (OH)
Mountain State U (WV)
Niagara U (NY)
Penn State Abington (PA)
Penn State Altoona (PA)
Penn State Berks (PA)
Penn State Erie, The Behrend Coll (PA)
Penn State U Park (PA)
Southern Illinois U Carbondale (IL)
Thompson Rivers U (BC, Canada)
U of Louisiana at Lafayette (LA)
U of Nevada, Las Vegas (NV)
U of Southern Mississippi (MS)
U of the District of Columbia (DC)
Widener U (PA)

HOSPITALITY AND RECREATION MARKETING
Ferris State U (MI)
Methodist U (NC)
Northwest Missouri State U (MO)
Rochester Inst of Technology (NY)
Tuskegee U (AL)
Tyndale U Coll & Sem (ON, Canada)
U of Delaware (DE)

HOSPITALITY/RECREATION MARKETING
Mountain State U (WV)

HOTEL AND RESTAURANT MANAGEMENT
Coll of the Ozarks (MO)
Ecole Hôtelière de Lausanne (Switzerland)
Fairleigh Dickinson U, Coll at Florham (NJ)
Northern Arizona U (AZ)

HOTEL/MOTEL ADMINISTRATION
Alliant Intl U (CA)
The American U of Athens (Greece)
Ashland U (OH)
Auburn U (AL)
Becker Coll (MA)
Bethune-Cookman U (FL)
Boston U (MA)
Buffalo State Coll, State U of New York (NY)
California State Polytechnic U, Pomona (CA)
California State U, Long Beach (CA)
Central Michigan U (MI)
Cheyney U of Pennsylvania (PA)
Colorado State U (CO)
Concord U (WV)
Cornell U (NY)
East Carolina U (NC)
Fairleigh Dickinson U, Metropolitan Campus (NJ)
Ferris State U (MI)
Florida Southern Coll (FL)
Georgia Southern U (GA)
Georgia State U (GA)
Grambling State U (LA)
Grand Valley State U (MI)
Hampton U (VA)
Inter American U of Puerto Rico, Aguadilla Campus (PR)
Inter American U of Puerto Rico, Fajardo Campus (PR)
Iowa State U of Science and Technology (IA)
Kansas State U (KS)
Keuka Coll (NY)
Michigan State U (MI)
Morgan State U (MD)
Mount Ida Coll (MA)
Mount Saint Vincent U (NS, Canada)
New York Inst of Technology (NY)
New York U (NY)
Niagara U (NY)
North Carolina Wesleyan Coll (NC)
Northern Arizona U (AZ)
Northwood U, Florida Campus (FL)
Oklahoma State U (OK)
Pace U (NY)
Paul Smith's Coll (NY)
Purdue U (IN)
Purdue U Calumet (IN)
St. Thomas U (FL)
Schiller Intl U (FL)
Schiller Intl U (United Kingdom)
South Dakota State U (SD)
Southern Oregon U (OR)
Southwest Minnesota State U (MN)
State U of New York at Plattsburgh (NY)
Texas Tech U (TX)
Thomas Coll (ME)
The U of Akron (OH)
U of Arkansas at Pine Bluff (AR)
U of Central Missouri (MO)
U of Central Oklahoma (OK)
U of Delaware (DE)
U of Denver (CO)
The U of Findlay (OH)
U of Houston (TX)
U of Maine at Machias (ME)
U of Maryland Eastern Shore (MD)
U of Missouri–Columbia (MO)
U of Nevada, Las Vegas (NV)
U of New Hampshire (NH)
U of New Haven (CT)
U of Southern Mississippi (MS)
The U of Tennessee (TN)
U of Victoria (BC, Canada)
Virginia Polytechnic Inst and State U (VA)
Webber Intl U (FL)
Widener U (PA)
Wiley Coll (TX)

HOUSING AND HUMAN ENVIRONMENTS
Eastern Kentucky U (KY)
Florida State U (FL)
Missouri State U (MO)
Ohio U (OH)
The U of Akron (OH)
U of Georgia (GA)
U of Missouri–Columbia (MO)
U of Northern Iowa (IA)
Utah State U (UT)

HOUSING AND HUMAN ENVIRONMENTS RELATED
Bob Jones U (SC)
U of Nevada, Reno (NV)

HUMAN DEVELOPMENT AND FAMILY STUDIES
Abilene Christian U (TX)
Amberton U (TX)
American Public U System (WV)
Antioch U McGregor (OH)
Ashland U (OH)
Auburn U (AL)
Baylor U (TX)
Berea Coll (KY)
Boston Coll (MA)
Bowling Green State U (OH)
Brigham Young U (UT)
California State U, East Bay (CA)
California State U, Long Beach (CA)
California State U, San Bernardino (CA)
Colorado State U (CO)
Concordia U (MI)
Concordia U, St. Paul (MN)
Connecticut Coll (CT)
Cornell U (NY)
East Carolina U (NC)
Eastern Kentucky U (KY)
Eckerd Coll (FL)
Florida State U (FL)
Georgia Southern U (GA)
Harvard U (MA)
Hellenic Coll (MA)
Hope Intl U (CA)
Indiana State U (IN)
Indiana U of Pennsylvania (PA)
Kansas State U (KS)
Kent State U (OH)
Kentucky State U (KY)
Lee U (TN)
Lesley U (MA)
Liberty U (VA)
Mercyhurst Coll (PA)
Miami U (OH)
Mississippi U for Women (MS)
Missouri State U (MO)
Mitchell Coll (CT)
Montana State U (MT)
Murray State U (KY)
National-Louis U (IL)
North Dakota State U (ND)
Northern Illinois U (IL)
Ohio U (OH)
Oklahoma State U (OK)
Oregon State U (OR)
Penn State Abington (PA)
Penn State Altoona (PA)
Penn State Berks (PA)
Penn State Erie, The Behrend Coll (PA)
Penn State U Park (PA)
Prescott Coll (AZ)
Purdue U (IN)
Samford U (AL)
San Diego Christian Coll (CA)
Sarah Lawrence Coll (NY)
South Dakota State U (SD)
State U of New York at Oswego (NY)
State U of New York at Plattsburgh (NY)
State U of New York Empire State Coll (NY)
Stephen F. Austin State U (TX)
Stephens Coll (MO)
Syracuse U (NY)
Texas State U-San Marcos (TX)
Texas Tech U (TX)
Texas Woman's U (TX)
The U of Alabama (AL)
The U of Arizona (AZ)
U of Arkansas (AR)
U of California, Davis (CA)
U of California, Riverside (CA)
U of Chicago (IL)
U of Connecticut (CT)
U of Delaware (DE)
U of Georgia (GA)
U of Hawaii at Manoa (HI)
U of Houston (TX)
U of Illinois at Urbana–Champaign (IL)
U of Maine (ME)
U of Memphis (TN)
U of Missouri–Columbia (MO)
U of Nevada, Reno (NV)
U of New Mexico (NM)
The U of North Carolina at Charlotte (NC)
The U of North Carolina at Greensboro (NC)
U of North Texas (TX)
U of Rhode Island (RI)
The U of Tennessee (TN)
The U of Texas at Austin (TX)
U of Utah (UT)
U of Vermont (VT)
Utah State U (UT)
Vanderbilt U (TN)
Virginia Polytechnic Inst and State U (VA)
Warner Pacific Coll (OR)
Washington State U (WA)
Wheelock Coll (MA)
Youngstown State U (OH)

HUMAN DEVELOPMENT AND FAMILY STUDIES RELATED
Columbia Coll (SC)
Harding U (AR)
Kent State U (OH)
Park U (MO)
State U of New York at Binghamton (NY)
The U of Alabama (AL)
U of Louisiana at Lafayette (LA)

HUMAN ECOLOGY
California State U, East Bay (CA)
Coll of the Atlantic (ME)
Connecticut Coll (CT)
Kansas State U (KS)
Mercyhurst Coll (PA)
Morgan State U (MD)
Mount Saint Vincent U (NS, Canada)
Prescott Coll (AZ)
Regis U (CO)
Rutgers, The State U of New Jersey, New Brunswick (NJ)
State U of New York Coll at Oneonta (NY)
Sterling Coll (VT)
U of California, Irvine (CA)
U of California, San Diego (CA)
U of Maryland Eastern Shore (MD)
The U of Tennessee at Chattanooga (TN)
The U of Western Ontario (ON, Canada)

HUMANITIES
Adelphi U (NY)
Albertus Magnus Coll (CT)
Alma Coll (MI)
Antioch U McGregor (OH)
Ashford U (IA)
Athens State U (AL)
Augsburg Coll (MN)
Baylor U (TX)
Belhaven Coll (MS)
Bemidji State U (MN)
Bennington Coll (VT)
Biola U (CA)
Bishop's U (QC, Canada)
Bluefield State Coll (WV)
Bob Jones U (SC)
Bradley U (IL)
Brigham Young U (UT)
Brock U (ON, Canada)
Bucknell U (PA)
Buffalo State Coll, State U of New York (NY)
Burlington Coll (VT)
California State Polytechnic U, Pomona (CA)
California State U, Chico (CA)
California State U, Dominguez Hills (CA)
California State U, Monterey Bay (CA)
California State U, Sacramento (CA)
California State U, San Bernardino (CA)
Catawba Coll (NC)
Chaminade U of Honolulu (HI)
Clarion U of Pennsylvania (PA)
Clarkson U (NY)
Clearwater Christian Coll (FL)
Colgate U (NY)
Coll of Saint Benedict (MN)
Coll of Saint Mary (NE)
The Coll of St. Scholastica (MN)
Colorado State U (CO)
Concordia Coll (MN)
Concordia U (CA)
Concordia U (OR)
Concordia U (QC, Canada)
Concordia U Wisconsin (WI)
DePaul U (IL)
Dominican Coll (NY)
Dominican U of California (CA)
Dowling Coll (NY)
Drexel U (PA)
East Stroudsburg U of Pennsylvania (PA)
Eckerd Coll (FL)
Eugene Lang Coll The New School for Liberal Arts (NY)
The Evergreen State Coll (WA)
Fairleigh Dickinson U, Coll at Florham (NJ)
Fairleigh Dickinson U, Metropolitan Campus (NJ)
Faulkner U (AL)
Felician Coll (NJ)
Florida Inst of Technology (FL)
Florida Intl U (FL)
Florida Southern Coll (FL)
Florida State U (FL)
Fort Lewis Coll (CO)
Franciscan U of Steubenville (OH)
Freed-Hardeman U (TN)
Fresno Pacific U (CA)
The George Washington U (DC)
Georgian Court U (NJ)
Grace U (NE)
Grand Valley State U (MI)
Hampden-Sydney Coll (VA)
Harding U (AR)
Harvard U (MA)

MAJORS AND MORE

Hofstra U (NY)
Holy Apostles Coll and Sem (CT)
Holy Family U (PA)
Holy Names U (CA)
Hope Coll (MI)
Houghton Coll (NY)
Hunter Coll of the City U of New York (NY)
Indiana U East (IN)
Indiana U Kokomo (IN)
Jacksonville U (FL)
John Carroll U (OH)
John F. Kennedy U (CA)
Johnson State Coll (VT)
Juniata Coll (PA)
Kansas State U (KS)
Kentucky Christian U (KY)
Kenyon Coll (OH)
Lawrence Technological U (MI)
Lees-McRae Coll (NC)
LeMoyne-Owen Coll (TN)
Lesley U (MA)
Lindsey Wilson Coll (KY)
Lock Haven U of Pennsylvania (PA)
Loyola Marymount U (CA)
Loyola U New Orleans (LA)
Lubbock Christian U (TX)
Macalester Coll (MN)
Maranatha Baptist Bible Coll (WI)
Marlboro Coll (VT)
Marshall U (WV)
Martin U (IN)
Marylhurst U (OR)
McGill U (QC, Canada)
Memorial U of Newfoundland (NL, Canada)
Mercyhurst Coll (PA)
Messiah Coll (PA)
Michigan State U (MI)
Midland Lutheran Coll (NE)
Midwestern State U (TX)
Milligan Coll (TN)
Minnesota State U Mankato (MN)
Minot State U (ND)
Monmouth Coll (IL)
Montclair State U (NJ)
Mountain State U (WV)
Mount Allison U (NB, Canada)
Mount Aloysius Coll (PA)
Mount Saint Vincent U (NS, Canada)
New Coll of Florida (FL)
New York U (NY)
North Central Coll (IL)
North Dakota State U (ND)
Northern Arizona U (AZ)
North Greenville U (SC)
Northwest Christian Coll (OR)
Northwestern Coll (IA)
Northwestern U (IL)
Northwest Missouri State U (MO)
Northwest Nazarene U (ID)
Nova Southeastern U (FL)
Oakland City U (IN)
Ohio Wesleyan U (OH)
Oklahoma City U (OK)
Our Lady of the Lake Coll (LA)
Pacific U (OR)
Penn State Harrisburg (PA)
Pepperdine U, Malibu (CA)
Plymouth State U (NH)
Pomona Coll (CA)
Pontifical Coll Josephinum (OH)
Portland State U (OR)
Prescott Coll (AZ)
Providence Coll (RI)
Purchase Coll, State U of New York (NY)
Purdue U (IN)
Quincy U (IL)
Ramapo Coll of New Jersey (NJ)
Redeemer U Coll (ON, Canada)
Regis U (CO)
Roberts Wesleyan Coll (NY)
Rockford Coll (IL)
Rosemont Coll (PA)
St. Gregory's U, Shawnee (OK)
St. John's Coll (NM)
Saint John's U (MN)
Saint Joseph's U (PA)
Saint Louis U (MO)
Saint Martin's U (WA)
Saint Mary-of-the-Woods Coll (IN)
Saint Mary's Coll (IN)
St. Norbert Coll (WI)
St. Thomas Aquinas Coll (NY)
San Diego State U (CA)
San Francisco State U (CA)
Sarah Lawrence Coll (NY)
Schreiner U (TX)
Seattle U (WA)
Shimer Coll (IL)
Siena Heights U (MI)
Simon Fraser U (BC, Canada)
Southeast Missouri State U (MO)
Southern Methodist U (TX)
Spring Hill Coll (AL)
Stanford U (CA)
State U of New York Coll at Old Westbury (NY)
State U of New York Empire State Coll (NY)
Stephen F. Austin State U (TX)
Stetson U (FL)
Stony Brook U, State U of New York (NY)
Suffolk U (MA)
Tabor Coll (KS)
Tennessee State U (TN)
Thomas Edison State Coll (NJ)
Thomas More Coll (KY)
Thomas U (GA)
Trent U (ON, Canada)
Trinity Intl U (IL)
Trinity U (TX)
Truett-McConnell Coll (GA)
Union Coll (NY)
United States Air Force Acad (CO)
U at Buffalo, the State U of New York (NY)
The U of Akron (OH)
U of Alaska Southeast (AK)
U of Bridgeport (CT)
U of California, Irvine (CA)
U of California, Riverside (CA)
U of Central Florida (FL)
U of Chicago (IL)
U of Cincinnati (OH)
U of Colorado at Boulder (CO)
U of Hawaii–West Oahu (HI)
U of Houston–Clear Lake (TX)
U of Houston–Downtown (TX)
U of Houston–Victoria (TX)
U of Illinois at Urbana–Champaign (IL)
U of Kansas (KS)
U of Lethbridge (AB, Canada)
U of Maryland U Coll (MD)
U of Massachusetts Amherst (MA)
U of Michigan (MI)
U of Michigan–Dearborn (MI)
U of New Hampshire (NH)
U of New Hampshire at Manchester (NH)
U of New Mexico (NM)
U of Northern Iowa (IA)
U of Oregon (OR)
U of Ottawa (ON, Canada)
U of Pennsylvania (PA)
U of Pittsburgh (PA)
U of Pittsburgh at Bradford (PA)
U of Pittsburgh at Johnstown (PA)
U of Puerto Rico at Utuado (PR)
U of Puerto Rico, Cayey U Coll (PR)
U of Regina (SK, Canada)
U of Rio Grande (OH)
U of San Diego (CA)
U of South Florida (FL)
The U of Tennessee at Chattanooga (TN)
The U of Texas at Austin (TX)
The U of Texas at Dallas (TX)
The U of Texas at San Antonio (TX)
The U of Texas of the Permian Basin (TX)
U of the Ozarks (AR)
U of the Sacred Heart (PR)
U of the Virgin Islands (VI)
The U of Toledo (OH)
U of Toronto (ON, Canada)
U of Utah (UT)
U of West Florida (FL)
U of Windsor (ON, Canada)
U of Wisconsin–Green Bay (WI)
U of Wisconsin–Parkside (WI)
U of Wyoming (WY)
Ursuline Coll (OH)
Valparaiso U (IN)
Villa Julie Coll (MD)
Virginia Wesleyan Coll (VA)
Walla Walla U (WA)
Warren Wilson Coll (NC)
Washington Coll (MD)
Washington State U (WA)
Washington U in St. Louis (MO)
Wesleyan Coll (GA)
Wesleyan U (CT)
Western New Mexico U (NM)
Western Washington U (WA)
Widener U (PA)
Willamette U (OR)
William Paterson U of New Jersey (NJ)
Wofford Coll (SC)
Worcester Polytechnic Inst (MA)
Wright State U (OH)
Yale U (CT)
York Coll of Pennsylvania (PA)
York U (ON, Canada)

HUMAN/MEDICAL GENETICS

Sarah Lawrence Coll (NY)

HUMAN NUTRITION

Baylor U (TX)
Case Western Reserve U (OH)
Colorado State U (CO)
Kent State U (OH)
Life U (GA)
McGill U (QC, Canada)
Penn State Abington (PA)
Penn State Altoona (PA)
Penn State Berks (PA)
Penn State Erie, The Behrend Coll (PA)
Penn State U Park (PA)
Rochester Inst of Technology (NY)
Samford U (AL)
Tarleton State U (TX)
The U of British Columbia (BC, Canada)
U of Houston (TX)
U of Illinois at Urbana–Champaign (IL)
U of Massachusetts Amherst (MA)
U of Missouri–Columbia (MO)
Washington State U (WA)

HUMAN RESOURCES DEVELOPMENT

Brigham Young U (UT)
Clemson U (SC)
Concordia U Texas (TX)
Georgia State U (GA)
Hawai'i Pacific U (HI)
Limestone Coll (SC)
Oakland U (MI)
Park U (MO)
Trinity Intl U (IL)
The U of Texas at Tyler (TX)

HUMAN RESOURCES MANAGEMENT

Alvernia Coll (PA)
Amberton U (TX)
The American U of Athens (Greece)
Anderson U (SC)
Antioch U McGregor (OH)
Athabasca U (AB, Canada)
Athens State U (AL)
Auburn U (AL)
Auburn U Montgomery (AL)
Baker Coll of Owosso (MI)
Baldwin-Wallace Coll (OH)
Ball State U (IN)
Barton Coll (NC)
Baylor U (TX)
Bernard M. Baruch Coll of the City U of New York (NY)
Bishop's U (QC, Canada)
Bob Jones U (SC)
Boise State U (ID)
Boston Coll (MA)
Bowling Green State U (OH)
Bradley U (IL)
Brigham Young U (UT)
Brock U (ON, Canada)
Cabrini Coll (PA)
California State Polytechnic U, Pomona (CA)
California State U, Chico (CA)
California State U, Dominguez Hills (CA)
California State U, East Bay (CA)
California State U, Fresno (CA)
California State U, Long Beach (CA)
Capital U (OH)
Carroll Coll (WI)
The Catholic U of America (DC)
Central Michigan U (MI)
Chestnut Hill Coll (PA)
Clarkson U (NY)
Cleary U (MI)
Coll of Saint Elizabeth (NJ)
Colorado Tech U—Colorado Springs (CO)
Colorado Tech U—Denver (CO)
Colorado Tech U—North Kansas City (MO)
Colorado Tech U—Online (CO)
Colorado Tech U—Sioux Falls (SD)
Concordia U (QC, Canada)
Concordia U, St. Paul (MN)
Davenport U, Dearborn (MI)
Davenport U, Grand Rapids (MI)
DePaul U (IL)
DeSales U (PA)
Dominican Coll (NY)
Dominican U of California (CA)
Drexel U (PA)
East Central U (OK)
Eastern New Mexico U (NM)
Eckerd Coll (FL)
Excelsior Coll (NY)
Faulkner U (AL)
Ferris State U (MI)
Florida Atlantic U (FL)
Florida Intl U (FL)
Florida Southern Coll (FL)
Florida State U (FL)
Freed-Hardeman U (TN)
The George Washington U (DC)
Georgia Southwestern State U (GA)
Golden Gate U (CA)
Goldey-Beacom Coll (DE)
Grace U (NE)
Grand Valley State U (MI)
Granite State Coll (NH)
Harding U (AR)
Hastings Coll (NE)
Hawai'i Pacific U (HI)
HEC Montreal (QC, Canada)
Holy Names U (CA)
Idaho State U (ID)
Immaculata U (PA)
Indiana State U (IN)
Indiana Tech (IN)
Indiana U of Pennsylvania (PA)
Inter American U of Puerto Rico, Bayamón Campus (PR)
Inter American U of Puerto Rico, San Germán Campus (PR)
Judson U (IL)
Juniata Coll (PA)
Keiser U, Fort Lauderdale (FL)
Kutztown U of Pennsylvania (PA)
Lakehead U (ON, Canada)
La Salle U (PA)
Le Moyne Coll (NY)
Lewis U (IL)
Lindenwood U (MO)
Lipscomb U (TN)
Loras Coll (IA)
Lourdes Coll (OH)
Loyola U Chicago (IL)
Madonna U (MI)
Mansfield U of Pennsylvania (PA)
Marian Coll (IN)
Marian Coll of Fond du Lac (WI)
Marietta Coll (OH)
Marquette U (WI)
Martin U (IN)
McGill U (QC, Canada)
Mercyhurst Coll (PA)
Messiah Coll (PA)
Metropolitan State U (MN)
Miami U (OH)
Michigan State U (MI)
MidAmerica Nazarene U (KS)
Midway Coll (KY)
National U (CA)
Nazareth Coll of Rochester (NY)
New York Inst of Technology (NY)
Niagara U (NY)
Nichols Coll (MA)
North Carolina State U (NC)
North Central Coll (IL)
Northeastern Illinois U (IL)
Northeastern State U (OK)
Northeastern U (MA)
Oakland City U (IN)
Oakland U (MI)
Ohio Valley U (WV)
Pace U (NY)
Palm Beach Atlantic U (FL)
Peace Coll (NC)
Pennsylvania Coll of Technology (PA)
Point Park U (PA)
Portland State U (OR)
Purdue U (IN)
Purdue U Calumet (IN)
Quinnipiac U (CT)
Redeemer U Coll (ON, Canada)
Rider U (NJ)
Roberts Wesleyan Coll (NY)
Roosevelt U (IL)
St. Cloud State U (MN)
Saint Francis U (PA)
St. John Fisher Coll (NY)
St. Joseph's Coll, New York (NY)
St. Joseph's Coll, Suffolk Campus (NY)
Saint Leo U (FL)
Saint Louis U (MO)
Saint Mary-of-the-Woods Coll (IN)
St. Mary's U (TX)
Saint Mary's U of Minnesota (MN)
Samford U (AL)
Sam Houston State U (TX)
San Diego State U (CA)
Seton Hill U (PA)
Simpson U (CA)
Southern Wesleyan U (SC)
Southwestern Coll (KS)
Spring Arbor U (MI)
State U of New York at Oswego (NY)
Sullivan U (KY)
Susquehanna U (PA)
Tarleton State U (TX)
Taylor U (IN)
Tennessee Wesleyan Coll (TN)
Texas A&M U–Commerce (TX)
Thomas Coll (ME)
Thomas Edison State Coll (NJ)
Thompson Rivers U (BC, Canada)
Trinity Christian Coll (IL)
Trinity Intl U (IL)
Troy U (AL)
The U of Akron (OH)
The U of Arizona (AZ)
U of Baltimore (MD)
The U of British Columbia–Okanagan (BC, Canada)
U of Central Missouri (MO)
U of Central Oklahoma (OK)
The U of Findlay (OH)
U of Hawaii at Manoa (HI)
U of Idaho (ID)
U of Illinois at Urbana–Champaign (IL)
The U of Iowa (IA)
U of Lethbridge (AB, Canada)
U of Maryland, Coll Park (MD)
U of Maryland U Coll (MD)
U of Miami (FL)
U of Michigan–Dearborn (MI)
U of Michigan–Flint (MI)
U of Minnesota, Duluth (MN)
U of Nebraska at Omaha (NE)
U of Nevada, Las Vegas (NV)
U of Nevada, Reno (NV)
U of New Brunswick Fredericton (NB, Canada)
The U of North Carolina at Chapel Hill (NC)
U of Ottawa (ON, Canada)
U of Pennsylvania (PA)
U of Puerto Rico at Humacao (PR)
U of St. Francis (IL)
U of St. Thomas (MN)
The U of Scranton (PA)
U of Southern Mississippi (MS)
The U of Tennessee at Martin (TN)
The U of Texas at San Antonio (TX)
U of the Incarnate Word (TX)
The U of Toledo (OH)
The U of Western Ontario (ON, Canada)
U of Windsor (ON, Canada)
U of Wisconsin–Milwaukee (WI)
U of Wisconsin–Whitewater (WI)
Ursuline Coll (OH)
Utah State U (UT)
Valley City State U (ND)
Vanderbilt U (TN)
Washington State U (WA)
Washington U in St. Louis (MO)
Weber State U (UT)
Western Illinois U (IL)
Western Michigan U (MI)
Western Washington U (WA)
Wichita State U (KS)
Wilmington U (DE)
Winona State U (MN)
Wright State U (OH)
Xavier U (OH)
York Coll (NE)
York U (ON, Canada)
Youngstown State U (OH)

HUMAN RESOURCES MANAGEMENT AND SERVICES RELATED

Albertus Magnus Coll (CT)
Alderson-Broaddus Coll (WV)
Becker Coll (MA)
Columbia Southern U (AL)
Grand Canyon U (AZ)
Miami U Hamilton (OH)
Mountain State U (WV)
Niagara U (NY)
Park U (MO)
Thompson Rivers U (BC, Canada)
Université du Québec en Outaouais (QC, Canada)
The U of British Columbia (BC, Canada)
U of Oklahoma (OK)
U of the District of Columbia (DC)
Widener U (PA)

HUMAN SERVICES

Alaska Pacific U (AK)
Albertus Magnus Coll (CT)
Albion Coll (MI)
Antioch U McGregor (OH)
Ashford U (IA)
Beacon Coll (FL)
Bethel Coll (TN)
Boricua Coll (NY)
Burlington Coll (VT)
California State U, Dominguez Hills (CA)
California State U, Fullerton (CA)
California State U, Monterey Bay (CA)
California State U, San Bernardino (CA)
Calumet Coll of Saint Joseph (IN)
Cambridge Coll (MA)
Carson-Newman Coll (TN)
Chestnut Hill Coll (PA)

Clayton State U (GA)
Coll of St. Joseph (VT)
Concordia U, St. Paul (MN)
Cornell U (NY)
Dakota Wesleyan U (SD)
Doane Coll (NE)
East Central U (OK)
Elon U (NC)
Endicott Coll (MA)
Fairmont State U (WV)
Finlandia U (MI)
Fitchburg State Coll (MA)
Florida Gulf Coast U (FL)
Fontbonne U (MO)
The George Washington U (DC)
Grace Bible Coll (MI)
Grand View Coll (IA)
Gwynedd-Mercy Coll (PA)
Hannibal-LaGrange Coll (MO)
Hastings Coll (NE)
Hawai'i Pacific U (HI)
High Point U (NC)
Holy Names U (CA)
Indiana Tech (IN)
Indiana U–Purdue U Fort Wayne (IN)
Kennesaw State U (GA)
Kentucky Wesleyan Coll (KY)
LaGrange Coll (GA)
Lake Superior State U (MI)
La Roche Coll (PA)
Lenoir-Rhyne Coll (NC)
Lesley U (MA)
Lincoln U (PA)
Lindenwood U (MO)
Lindsey Wilson Coll (KY)
Livingstone Coll (NC)
Loyola U Chicago (IL)
Mercer U (GA)
Merrimack Coll (MA)
Metropolitan State U (MN)
Midland Lutheran Coll (NE)
Missouri Baptist U (MO)
Missouri Valley Coll (MO)
Mount Ida Coll (MA)
Mount Marty Coll (SD)
Mount Olive Coll (NC)
Mount Saint Mary Coll (NY)
National-Louis U (IL)
Northeastern U (MA)
Northwest Christian Coll (OR)
Notre Dame de Namur U (CA)
Park U (MO)
Pfeiffer U (NC)
Quincy U (IL)
Quinnipiac U (CT)
Roosevelt U (IL)
St. John's U (NY)
St. Joseph's Coll, New York (NY)
Saint Mary-of-the-Woods Coll (IN)
Saint Mary's U of Minnesota (MN)
Seton Hill U (PA)
Siena Heights U (MI)
Simmons Coll (MA)
Southern Vermont Coll (VT)
Southwest Baptist U (MO)
State U of New York Empire State Coll (NY)
Suffolk U (MA)
Tennessee Wesleyan Coll (TN)
Thomas Edison State Coll (NJ)
Tiffin U (OH)
Tyndale U Coll & Sem (ON, Canada)
U of Baltimore (MD)
U of Bridgeport (CT)
U of Great Falls (MT)
U of Maine at Machias (ME)
U of Massachusetts Boston (MA)
U of Nevada, Las Vegas (NV)
U of Northern Colorado (CO)
U of North Texas (TX)
U of Oregon (OR)
U of Rhode Island (RI)
The U of Scranton (PA)
The U of Tennessee at Chattanooga (TN)
U of Wisconsin–Oshkosh (WI)
Villanova U (PA)
Virginia Wesleyan Coll (VA)
Walsh U (OH)
Wayland Baptist U (TX)
Western Washington U (WA)
Wingate U (NC)

HYDROLOGY AND WATER RESOURCES SCIENCE

California State U, Chico (CA)
The Coll at Brockport, State U of New York (NY)
East Central U (OK)
Grand Valley State U (MI)
Heidelberg Coll (OH)
Humboldt State U (CA)
Lakehead U (ON, Canada)
McGill U (QC, Canada)
North Carolina State U (NC)
Northland Coll (WI)
Rensselaer Polytechnic Inst (NY)
St. Francis Xavier U (NS, Canada)
State U of New York Coll at Oneonta (NY)
State U of New York Coll of Environmental Science and Forestry (NY)
Tarleton State U (TX)
U of California, Davis (CA)
U of California, Santa Barbara (CA)
U of New Hampshire (NH)
The U of Texas at Austin (TX)
U of Toronto (ON, Canada)
U of Wisconsin–Madison (WI)
U of Wisconsin–Stevens Point (WI)
Western Michigan U (MI)
Wright State U (OH)

ILLUSTRATION

Acad of Art U (CA)
Alberta Coll of Art & Design (AB, Canada)
Art Acad of Cincinnati (OH)
The Art Inst of Atlanta (GA)
The Art Inst of Boston at Lesley U (MA)
Brigham Young U (UT)
California State U, Long Beach (CA)
The Cleveland Inst of Art (OH)
Columbus Coll of Art & Design (OH)
Fashion Inst of Technology (NY)
Grace Coll (IN)
Laguna Coll of Art & Design (CA)
Lawrence Technological U (MI)
Lewis U (IL)
Maryland Inst Coll of Art (MD)
Marywood U (PA)
Memphis Coll of Art (TN)
Montserrat Coll of Art (MA)
Paier Coll of Art, Inc. (CT)
Parsons The New School for Design (NY)
Pennsylvania Coll of Art & Design (PA)
Pratt Inst (NY)
Ringling Coll of Art and Design (FL)
Rochester Inst of Technology (NY)
Rocky Mountain Coll of Art + Design (CO)
St. John's U (NY)
Savannah Coll of Art and Design (GA)
School of the Art Inst of Chicago (IL)
School of the Museum of Fine Arts, Boston (MA)
School of Visual Arts (NY)
U of Bridgeport (CT)
U of Kansas (KS)
U of Miami (FL)
Virginia Commonwealth U (VA)
Washington U in St. Louis (MO)

IMMUNOLOGY

The U of Western Ontario (ON, Canada)

INDUSTRIAL AND ORGANIZATIONAL PSYCHOLOGY

Abilene Christian U (TX)
Albright Coll (PA)
Averett U (VA)
Bridgewater State Coll (MA)
California State U, East Bay (CA)
Clarkson U (NY)
Eastern Connecticut State U (CT)
East Texas Baptist U (TX)
Farmingdale State Coll (NY)
Fitchburg State Coll (MA)
Georgia Inst of Technology (GA)
Holy Family U (PA)
Ithaca Coll (NY)
Lincoln U (PA)
Madonna U (MI)
Maryville U of Saint Louis (MO)
Marywood U (PA)
Middle Tennessee State U (TN)
Moravian Coll (PA)
Nebraska Wesleyan U (NE)
Point Loma Nazarene U (CA)
Saint Mary's Coll of California (CA)
Saint Xavier U (IL)
U of Illinois at Urbana–Champaign (IL)
The U of Tennessee at Martin (TN)
Washington U in St. Louis (MO)
Wright State U (OH)

INDUSTRIAL ARTS

Alcorn State U (MS)
Ball State U (IN)
Bemidji State U (MN)
Buffalo State Coll, State U of New York (NY)
California State U, Fresno (CA)
Chicago State U (IL)
Coll of the Ozarks (MO)
Fairmont State U (WV)
Florida Ag and Mech U (FL)
Humboldt State U (CA)
Keene State Coll (NH)
Minnesota State U Mankato (MN)
North Carolina Ag and Tech State U (NC)
Northern State U (SD)
Ohio Northern U (OH)
Pittsburg State U (KS)
St. Cloud State U (MN)
San Francisco State U (CA)
Southern Utah U (UT)
Southwestern Oklahoma State U (OK)
Tarleton State U (TX)
Tennessee State U (TN)
Texas A&M U–Commerce (TX)
U of Arkansas at Pine Bluff (AR)
U of Maryland Eastern Shore (MD)
The U of Montana–Western (MT)
U of Southern Maine (ME)
U of the District of Columbia (DC)
U of Wisconsin–Platteville (WI)
Walla Walla U (WA)

INDUSTRIAL DESIGN

Acad of Art U (CA)
Appalachian State U (NC)
Arizona State U (AZ)
The Art Inst of California–Orange County (CA)
The Art Inst of Fort Lauderdale (FL)
The Art Inst of Philadelphia (PA)
The Art Inst of Portland (OR)
The Art Inst of Tampa (FL)
Auburn U (AL)
Brigham Young U (UT)
California Coll of the Arts (CA)
California State U, Long Beach (CA)
Carnegie Mellon U (PA)
Clemson U (SC)
The Cleveland Inst of Art (OH)
Columbia Coll Chicago (IL)
Columbus Coll of Art & Design (OH)
Fashion Inst of Technology (NY)
Ferris State U (MI)
Finlandia U (MI)
George Fox U (OR)
Georgia Inst of Technology (GA)
Kean U (NJ)
Massachusetts Coll of Art and Design (MA)
North Carolina State U (NC)
Parsons The New School for Design (NY)
Philadelphia U (PA)
Pratt Inst (NY)
San Francisco State U (CA)
Savannah Coll of Art and Design (GA)
Stanford U (CA)
U of Bridgeport (CT)
U of Cincinnati (OH)
U of Illinois at Chicago (IL)
U of Illinois at Urbana–Champaign (IL)
U of Kansas (KS)
U of Louisiana at Lafayette (LA)
U of Michigan (MI)
U of Wisconsin–Platteville (WI)
Virginia Polytechnic Inst and State U (VA)
Western Michigan U (MI)
Western Washington U (WA)

INDUSTRIAL ELECTRONICS TECHNOLOGY

Lewis-Clark State Coll (ID)

INDUSTRIAL ENGINEERING

The American U of Athens (Greece)
Arizona State U (AZ)
Auburn U (AL)
Boston U (MA)
Bradley U (IL)
California Polytechnic State U, San Luis Obispo (CA)
California State Polytechnic U, Pomona (CA)
California State U, East Bay (CA)
California State U, Long Beach (CA)
Clemson U (SC)
Cleveland State U (OH)
Concordia U (QC, Canada)
Drexel U (PA)
Elizabethtown Coll (PA)
Florida Ag and Mech U (FL)
Florida State U (FL)
Gannon U (PA)
Georgia Inst of Technology (GA)
Grand Valley State U (MI)
Hofstra U (NY)
Inter American U of Puerto Rico, Bayamón Campus (PR)
Iowa State U of Science and Technology (IA)
The Johns Hopkins U (MD)
Kansas State U (KS)
Kent State U (OH)
Kettering U (MI)
Lehigh U (PA)
Liberty U (VA)
Louisiana State U and Ag and Mech Coll (LA)
Marquette U (WI)
Memorial U of Newfoundland (NL, Canada)
Miami U (OH)
Michigan Technological U (MI)
Milwaukee School of Eng (WI)
Mississippi State U (MS)
Missouri Southern State U (MO)
Missouri U of Science and Technology (MO)
Montana State U (MT)
Morgan State U (MD)
New Jersey Inst of Technology (NJ)
New York Inst of Technology (NY)
North Carolina Ag and Tech State U (NC)
North Carolina State U (NC)
North Dakota State U (ND)
Northeastern U (MA)
Northern Illinois U (IL)
Northwestern U (IL)
Oakland U (MI)
Ohio U (OH)
Oklahoma State U (OK)
Oregon State U (OR)
Penn State Abington (PA)
Penn State Altoona (PA)
Penn State Berks (PA)
Penn State Erie, The Behrend Coll (PA)
Penn State U Park (PA)
Polytechnic U of Puerto Rico (PR)
Purdue U (IN)
Rensselaer Polytechnic Inst (NY)
Rochester Inst of Technology (NY)
Rutgers, The State U of New Jersey, New Brunswick (NJ)
St. Ambrose U (IA)
St. Cloud State U (MN)
St. Mary's U (TX)
Seattle U (WA)
South Dakota School of Mines and Technology (SD)
Southern Illinois U Edwardsville (IL)
State U of New York at Binghamton (NY)
Tennessee State U (TN)
Tennessee Technological U (TN)
Texas A&M U (TX)
Texas A&M U–Commerce (TX)
Texas State U-San Marcos (TX)
Texas Tech U (TX)
Tufts U (MA)
U at Buffalo, the State U of New York (NY)
The U of Alabama in Huntsville (AL)
U of Arkansas (AR)
U of Central Florida (FL)
U of Cincinnati (OH)
U of Connecticut (CT)
U of Florida (FL)
U of Houston (TX)
U of Illinois at Chicago (IL)
U of Illinois at Urbana–Champaign (IL)
The U of Iowa (IA)
U of Louisville (KY)
U of Massachusetts Amherst (MA)
U of Miami (FL)
U of Michigan (MI)
U of Michigan–Dearborn (MI)
U of Minnesota, Crookston (MN)
U of Minnesota, Duluth (MN)
U of Minnesota, Twin Cities Campus (MN)
U of Missouri–Columbia (MO)
U of Nebraska–Lincoln (NE)
U of Oklahoma (OK)
U of Pittsburgh (PA)
U of Regina (SK, Canada)
U of Rhode Island (RI)
U of San Diego (CA)
U of South Florida (FL)
The U of Tennessee (TN)
The U of Texas at Arlington (TX)
The U of Texas at El Paso (TX)
The U of Toledo (OH)
U of Toronto (ON, Canada)
U of Vermont (VT)
U of Windsor (ON, Canada)
U of Wisconsin–Madison (WI)
U of Wisconsin–Milwaukee (WI)
U of Wisconsin–Platteville (WI)
Virginia Polytechnic Inst and State U (VA)
Wayne State U (MI)
Western Michigan U (MI)
Western New England Coll (MA)
West Virginia U (WV)
Wichita State U (KS)
Worcester Polytechnic Inst (MA)
Youngstown State U (OH)

INDUSTRIAL/ MANUFACTURING ENGINEERING

Indiana Tech (IN)
The U of Arizona (AZ)

INDUSTRIAL PRODUCTION TECHNOLOGIES RELATED

Appalachian State U (NC)
Central Connecticut State U (CT)
Central Michigan U (MI)
East Carolina U (NC)
Ferris State U (MI)
Georgia Southern U (GA)
Millersville U of Pennsylvania (PA)
Southern Polytechnic State U (GA)
Southwestern Coll (KS)
Tarleton State U (TX)
U of Nebraska–Lincoln (NE)
U of Puerto Rico at Utuado (PR)
Utah State U (UT)
Wayne State Coll (NE)
Wayne State U (MI)

INDUSTRIAL RADIOLOGIC TECHNOLOGY

Baker Coll of Owosso (MI)
Concordia U Wisconsin (WI)
Jamestown Coll (ND)
Madonna U (MI)
National-Louis U (IL)
Oregon Inst of Technology (OR)
U of Maryland Eastern Shore (MD)

INDUSTRIAL SAFETY TECHNOLOGY

Northeastern State U (OK)
Rochester Inst of Technology (NY)
South Dakota State U (SD)
U of Houston–Downtown (TX)

INDUSTRIAL TECHNOLOGY

Appalachian State U (NC)
Baker Coll of Flint (MI)
Ball State U (IN)
Bemidji State U (MN)
Berea Coll (KY)
Boise State U (ID)
Bowling Green State U (OH)
Buffalo State Coll, State U of New York (NY)
California Polytechnic State U, San Luis Obispo (CA)
California State U, Fresno (CA)
California State U, Long Beach (CA)
California State U, Los Angeles (CA)
Central State U (OH)
Central Washington U (WA)
Cheyney U of Pennsylvania (PA)
Cleveland State U (OH)
East Carolina U (NC)
Eastern Illinois U (IL)
Eastern Michigan U (MI)
Fairmont State U (WV)
Ferris State U (MI)
Fitchburg State Coll (MA)
Grambling State U (LA)
Illinois Inst of Technology (IL)
Illinois State U (IL)
Indiana State U (IN)
Indiana U–Purdue U Fort Wayne (IN)
Jackson State U (MS)
Jacksonville State U (AL)
Keene State Coll (NH)
Kent State U (OH)
Lake Superior State U (MI)
Lawrence Technological U (MI)
Middle Tennessee State U (TN)
Minnesota State U Mankato (MN)
Mississippi State U (MS)
Mississippi Valley State U (MS)
Morehead State U (KY)
Murray State U (KY)
North Carolina Ag and Tech State U (NC)
Northern Illinois U (IL)
Northern Michigan U (MI)
Northwestern State U of Louisiana (LA)
Ohio Northern U (OH)
Ohio U (OH)
Oklahoma Panhandle State U (OK)
Prairie View A&M U (TX)
Purdue U (IN)

Purdue U Calumet (IN)
Saint Mary's U of Minnesota (MN)
Sam Houston State U (TX)
South Carolina State U (SC)
Southeastern Louisiana U (LA)
Southeastern Oklahoma State U (OK)
Southeast Missouri State U (MO)
Southern Arkansas U–Magnolia (AR)
Southern Illinois U Carbondale (IL)
Southwestern Oklahoma State U (OK)
State U of New York Inst of Technology (NY)
Tennessee State U (TN)
Tennessee Technological U (TN)
Texas A&M U–Commerce (TX)
Texas Southern U (TX)
Texas State U-San Marcos (TX)
U of Arkansas at Pine Bluff (AR)
U of Dayton (OH)
U of Houston (TX)
U of Idaho (ID)
U of Louisiana at Lafayette (LA)
U of Massachusetts Lowell (MA)
U of Nebraska at Omaha (NE)
The U of North Carolina at Charlotte (NC)
U of North Dakota (ND)
U of Northern Iowa (IA)
U of Rio Grande (OH)
U of Southern Mississippi (MS)
The U of Texas at Tyler (TX)
The U of Toledo (OH)
U of Wisconsin–Platteville (WI)
Wayne State U (MI)
Western Carolina U (NC)
Western Illinois U (IL)
Western Kentucky U (KY)
Western Washington U (WA)
West Texas A&M U (TX)

INFORMATION RESOURCES MANAGEMENT

Abilene Christian U (TX)
Clarkson U (NY)
Juniata Coll (PA)
Metropolitan State U (MN)
Mount St. Mary's U (MD)
U of Wisconsin–Eau Claire (WI)
Western Michigan U (MI)

INFORMATION SCIENCE/ STUDIES

Alabama State U (AL)
Albertus Magnus Coll (CT)
Albright Coll (PA)
Anderson U (IN)
Andrews U (MI)
Armstrong Atlantic State U (GA)
Ashland U (OH)
Athabasca U (AB, Canada)
Athens State U (AL)
Averett U (VA)
Baker Coll of Owosso (MI)
Baker U (KS)
Ball State U (IN)
Barry U (FL)
Beacon Coll (FL)
Belmont Abbey Coll (NC)
Belmont U (TN)
Bemidji State U (MN)
Benedictine U (IL)
Bernard M. Baruch Coll of the City U of New York (NY)
Bethune-Cookman U (FL)
Bluffton U (OH)
Boise State U (ID)
Boston U (MA)
Bradley U (IL)
Brewton-Parker Coll (GA)
Brock U (ON, Canada)
Buffalo State Coll, State U of New York (NY)
California Baptist U (CA)
California Lutheran U (CA)
California State Polytechnic U, Pomona (CA)
California State U, Dominguez Hills (CA)
California State U, East Bay (CA)
California State U, Fullerton (CA)
California State U, Stanislaus (CA)
Calumet Coll of Saint Joseph (IN)
Carlow U (PA)
Carnegie Mellon U (PA)
Carroll Coll (WI)
Carson-Newman Coll (TN)
Catawba Coll (NC)
Cedarville U (OH)
Centenary Coll (NJ)
Central Coll (IA)
Central Pennsylvania Coll (PA)
Christopher Newport U (VA)
Clarion U of Pennsylvania (PA)
Clark Atlanta U (GA)
Clarke Coll (IA)
Clayton State U (GA)
Cleary U (MI)
Clemson U (SC)
Cleveland State U (OH)
Coll of Charleston (SC)
The Coll of Saint Rose (NY)
Coll of Staten Island of the City U of New York (NY)
Colorado State U (CO)
Colorado State U-Pueblo (CO)
Colorado Tech U—Colorado Springs (CO)
Colorado Tech U—Denver (CO)
Colorado Tech U—North Kansas City (MO)
Colorado Tech U—Online (CO)
Colorado Tech U—Sioux Falls (SD)
Concordia U Chicago (IL)
Concord U (WV)
Cornerstone U (MI)
Culver-Stockton Coll (MO)
Davis & Elkins Coll (WV)
DePaul U (IL)
Doane Coll (NE)
Dominican U (IL)
Drexel U (PA)
Eastern Kentucky U (KY)
Eastern Michigan U (MI)
Emporia State U (KS)
Everest U, Tampa (FL)
Excelsior Coll (NY)
Fairfield U (CT)
Faulkner U (AL)
Ferrum Coll (VA)
Florida Ag and Mech U (FL)
Florida Inst of Technology (FL)
Florida State U (FL)
Fort Lewis Coll (CO)
Freed-Hardeman U (TN)
Frostburg State U (MD)
George Fox U (OR)
Georgia Southern U (GA)
Glenville State Coll (WV)
Goldey-Beacom Coll (DE)
Gonzaga U (WA)
Grambling State U (LA)
Grand Valley State U (MI)
Grand View Coll (IA)
Guilford Coll (NC)
Hampton U (VA)
Harris-Stowe State U (MO)
Harvard U (MA)
HEC Montreal (QC, Canada)
Heidelberg Coll (OH)
High Point U (NC)
Houston Baptist U (TX)
Howard Payne U (TX)
Humboldt State U (CA)
Husson Coll (ME)
Idaho State U (ID)
Illinois Coll (IL)
Illinois Inst of Technology (IL)
Illinois State U (IL)
Immaculata U (PA)
Indiana U–Purdue U Fort Wayne (IN)
Inter American U of Puerto Rico, San Germán Campus (PR)
Iowa Wesleyan Coll (IA)
James Madison U (VA)
Johnson State Coll (VT)
Kansas State U (KS)
Kennesaw State U (GA)
King Coll (TN)
Lakehead U (ON, Canada)
La Salle U (PA)
La Sierra U (CA)
Lees-McRae Coll (NC)
Lee U (TN)
Lehigh U (PA)
Lenoir-Rhyne Coll (NC)
LeTourneau U (TX)
Limestone Coll (SC)
Lincoln U (MO)
Lipscomb U (TN)
Livingstone Coll (NC)
Loyola U New Orleans (LA)
Madonna U (MI)
Mansfield U of Pennsylvania (PA)
Marietta Coll (OH)
Marist Coll (NY)
Marquette U (WI)
Marymount U (VA)
McKendree U (IL)
Medgar Evers Coll of the City U of New York (NY)
Memorial U of Newfoundland (NL, Canada)
Mercer U (GA)
Mercy Coll (NY)
Mercyhurst Coll (PA)
Messiah Coll (PA)
Metropolitan State U (MN)
Michigan Jewish Inst (MI)
Michigan Technological U (MI)
Midwestern State U (TX)
Minnesota State U Mankato (MN)
Misericordia U (PA)
Mississippi U for Women (MS)
Missouri U of Science and Technology (MO)
Monroe Coll, Bronx (NY)
Montana Tech of The U of Montana (MT)
Morgan State U (MD)
Mountain State U (WV)
Mount Aloysius Coll (PA)
Mount Olive Coll (NC)
Mount Saint Vincent U (NS, Canada)
Murray State U (KY)
National American U–Sioux Falls Branch (SD)
National-Louis U (IL)
National U (CA)
Nazareth Coll of Rochester (NY)
Nebraska Wesleyan U (NE)
New Jersey Inst of Technology (NJ)
Newman U (KS)
New Mexico Highlands U (NM)
New York Inst of Technology (NY)
New York U (NY)
Niagara U (NY)
North Carolina Central U (NC)
North Carolina Wesleyan Coll (NC)
Northeastern U (MA)
North Georgia Coll & State U (GA)
Northland Coll (WI)
Northwestern Oklahoma State U (OK)
Northwestern State U of Louisiana (LA)
Northwestern U (IL)
Northwest Missouri State U (MO)
Oakland City U (IN)
Oakwood Coll (AL)
Ohio Dominican U (OH)
Oklahoma Christian U (OK)
Oklahoma Wesleyan U (OK)
Oregon State U (OR)
Pace U (NY)
Pacific Union Coll (CA)
Peirce Coll (PA)
Penn State Abington (PA)
Penn State Altoona (PA)
Penn State Berks (PA)
Penn State Erie, The Behrend Coll (PA)
Penn State Harrisburg (PA)
Penn State U Park (PA)
Philadelphia U (PA)
Purdue U Calumet (IN)
Queens U of Charlotte (NC)
Quincy U (IL)
Quinnipiac U (CT)
Radford U (VA)
Ramapo Coll of New Jersey (NJ)
Regis Coll (MA)
Rider U (NJ)
Roanoke Coll (VA)
Robert Morris U (PA)
Rutgers, The State U of New Jersey, Newark (NJ)
Rutgers, The State U of New Jersey, New Brunswick (NJ)
St. Ambrose U (IA)
St. Cloud State U (MN)
St. Francis Xavier U (NS, Canada)
St. John's U (NY)
Saint Joseph's U (PA)
Saint Martin's U (WA)
Saint Mary-of-the-Woods Coll (IN)
St. Mary's U (TX)
Saint Mary's U of Minnesota (MN)
Saint Michael's Coll (VT)
St. Thomas Aquinas Coll (NY)
St. Thomas U (FL)
Salve Regina U (RI)
San Diego State U (CA)
San Francisco State U (CA)
Simpson Coll (IA)
Southeastern Oklahoma State U (OK)
Southern Illinois U Carbondale (IL)
Southern Methodist U (TX)
Southern Polytechnic State U (GA)
South U (AL)
Southwestern Adventist U (TX)
State U of New York at Binghamton (NY)
State U of New York at Fredonia (NY)
State U of New York at Oswego (NY)
State U of New York Coll at Old Westbury (NY)
State U of New York Inst of Technology (NY)
Stony Brook U, State U of New York (NY)
Suffolk U (MA)
Susquehanna U (PA)
Syracuse U (NY)
Taylor U (IN)
Tennessee Technological U (TN)
Texas A&M Intl U (TX)
Texas A&M U–Commerce (TX)
Texas Lutheran U (TX)
Thiel Coll (PA)
Tiffin U (OH)
Towson U (MD)
Tulane U (LA)
Union Coll (NE)
Union U (TN)
Université de Sherbrooke (QC, Canada)
U at Albany, State U of New York (NY)
U at Buffalo, the State U of New York (NY)
U of Baltimore (MD)
U of Bridgeport (CT)
U of California, Irvine (CA)
U of California, Riverside (CA)
U of California, Santa Cruz (CA)
U of Charleston (WV)
U of Cincinnati (OH)
U of Dayton (OH)
U of Great Falls (MT)
U of Houston (TX)
U of Houston–Clear Lake (TX)
U of Management and Technology (VA)
U of Mary (ND)
U of Mary Hardin-Baylor (TX)
U of Maryland, Baltimore County (MD)
U of Maryland, Coll Park (MD)
U of Maryland U Coll (MD)
U of Miami (FL)
U of Michigan–Flint (MI)
The U of Montana (MT)
U of New Brunswick Fredericton (NB, Canada)
U of New Haven (CT)
The U of North Carolina at Chapel Hill (NC)
U of North Texas (TX)
U of Pittsburgh (PA)
The U of Scranton (PA)
U of South Carolina Upstate (SC)
U of South Florida (FL)
The U of Tampa (FL)
The U of Texas at Brownsville (TX)
The U of Texas at El Paso (TX)
U of the District of Columbia (DC)
U of the Pacific (CA)
U of the Sacred Heart (PR)
The U of Toledo (OH)
U of Tulsa (OK)
U of Vermont (VT)
The U of Western Ontario (ON, Canada)
U of Windsor (ON, Canada)
The U of Winnipeg (MB, Canada)
U of Wisconsin–Superior (WI)
Utah State U (UT)
Utah Valley State Coll (UT)
Valdosta State U (GA)
Villa Julie Coll (MD)
Villanova U (PA)
Virginia Commonwealth U (VA)
Virginia Polytechnic Inst and State U (VA)
Wartburg Coll (IA)
Washington U in St. Louis (MO)
Wayne State Coll (NE)
Wayne State U (MI)
Western Intl U (AZ)
Westfield State Coll (MA)
West Liberty State Coll (WV)
West Virginia Wesleyan Coll (WV)
Widener U (PA)
Wilkes U (PA)
William Jewell Coll (MO)
Winona State U (MN)
Woodbury U (CA)
Worcester Polytechnic Inst (MA)
Wright State U (OH)
York Coll of the City U of New York (NY)

INFORMATION TECHNOLOGY

Abilene Christian U (TX)
American InterContinental U (CA)
American InterContinental U (FL)
American InterContinental U (TX)
American InterContinental U Dunwoody Campus (GA)
American InterContinental U Online (IL)
American Public U System (WV)
Armstrong Atlantic State U (GA)
Bluefield Coll (VA)
Bluffton U (OH)
Brigham Young U (UT)
Cabrini Coll (PA)
California State U, Chico (CA)
California State U, Los Angeles (CA)
Canisius Coll (NY)
Central Pennsylvania Coll (PA)
Coll of the Ozarks (MO)
Collins Coll: A School of Design and Technology (AZ)
Colorado Tech U—Colorado Springs (CO)
Colorado Tech U—Denver (CO)
Colorado Tech U—North Kansas City (MO)
Colorado Tech U—Online (CO)
Colorado Tech U—Sioux Falls (SD)
Columbia Southern U (AL)
Concordia U (CA)
Cornell U (NY)
Curry Coll (MA)
Dakota State U (SD)
DePaul U (IL)
D'Youville Coll (NY)
East Carolina U (NC)
Edinboro U of Pennsylvania (PA)
Endicott Coll (MA)
Fairleigh Dickinson U, Metropolitan Campus (NJ)
Ferris State U (MI)
Florida Intl U (FL)
Furman U (SC)
Golden Gate U (CA)
Grace Coll (IN)
Harding U (AR)
Houghton Coll (NY)
Illinois Inst of Technology (IL)
Illinois State U (IL)
Indiana State U (IN)
Indiana U Bloomington (IN)
Indiana U Kokomo (IN)
Indiana U–Purdue U Indianapolis (IN)
Indiana U Southeast (IN)
Johnson C. Smith U (NC)
Juniata Coll (PA)
Keiser U, Fort Lauderdale (FL)
Keystone Coll (PA)
Kutztown U of Pennsylvania (PA)
Kwantlen U Coll (BC, Canada)
La Roche Coll (PA)
Lawrence Technological U (MI)
LeMoyne-Owen Coll (TN)
Lipscomb U (TN)
Marian Coll of Fond du Lac (WI)
Marist Coll (NY)
Montclair State U (NJ)
Mount Marty Coll (SD)
Mount Saint Mary Coll (NY)
National American U–Sioux Falls Branch (SD)
National U (CA)
Nazareth Coll of Rochester (NY)
Neumont U (UT)
New Mexico Inst of Mining and Technology (NM)
North Carolina State U (NC)
Oakland U (MI)
Plymouth State U (NH)
Point Park U (PA)
Purdue U North Central (IN)
Rensselaer Polytechnic Inst (NY)
Robert Morris Coll (IL)
Rochester Inst of Technology (NY)
Sacred Heart U (CT)
St. Joseph's Coll, Suffolk Campus (NY)
San Diego State U (CA)
Simmons Coll (MA)
Slippery Rock U of Pennsylvania (PA)
Southern Polytechnic State U (GA)
South U, West Palm Beach (FL)
South U (GA)
South U (SC)
Southwest Minnesota State U (MN)
Stephen F. Austin State U (TX)
Sullivan U (KY)
Temple U (PA)
Université de Sherbrooke (QC, Canada)
U of Arkansas (AR)
The U of British Columbia–Okanagan (BC, Canada)
U of Central Florida (FL)
U of Denver (CO)
U of Great Falls (MT)
U of Houston (TX)
U of Massachusetts Lowell (MA)
U of Missouri–Kansas City (MO)
The U of Montana (MT)
The U of North Carolina at Pembroke (NC)
U of Rio Grande (OH)
U of St. Francis (IL)
U of Saint Mary (KS)
U of Tulsa (OK)
The U of Western Ontario (ON, Canada)
U of Windsor (ON, Canada)
U of Wisconsin–Whitewater (WI)
Vermont Tech Coll (VT)
Virginia State U (VA)
Washington & Jefferson Coll (PA)
Western Kentucky U (KY)
Wilmington U (DE)
York U (ON, Canada)
Youngstown State U (OH)

INORGANIC CHEMISTRY
McGill U (QC, Canada)
The U of Western Ontario (ON, Canada)

INSURANCE
Appalachian State U (NC)
Ball State U (IN)
Baylor U (TX)
Bradley U (IL)
California State Polytechnic U, Pomona (CA)
Delta State U (MS)
Eastern Kentucky U (KY)
Excelsior Coll (NY)
Florida Intl U (FL)
Gannon U (PA)
Georgia State U (GA)
Illinois State U (IL)
Illinois Wesleyan U (IL)
Indiana State U (IN)
Martin U (IN)
McGill U (QC, Canada)
Minnesota State U Mankato (MN)
Mississippi State U (MS)
Missouri State U (MO)
Roosevelt U (IL)
St. Cloud State U (MN)
St. John's U (NY)
Seattle U (WA)
Temple U (PA)
Texas Southern U (TX)
U of Central Arkansas (AR)
U of Cincinnati (OH)
U of Connecticut (CT)
U of Florida (FL)
U of Hartford (CT)
U of Illinois at Urbana–Champaign (IL)
U of Louisiana at Lafayette (LA)
U of Memphis (TN)
U of Minnesota, Twin Cities Campus (MN)
U of Mississippi (MS)
U of North Texas (TX)
U of Pennsylvania (PA)
U of South Carolina (SC)
U of Wisconsin–Madison (WI)
Washington State U (WA)

INSURANCE/RISK MANAGEMENT
Delta State U (MS)
Illinois Wesleyan U (IL)
U of Georgia (GA)
U of Louisiana at Monroe (LA)

INTERCULTURAL/ MULTICULTURAL AND DIVERSITY STUDIES
California Baptist U (CA)
Concordia U (QC, Canada)
Evangel U (MO)
The Evergreen State Coll (WA)
Kentucky Christian U (KY)
Marquette U (WI)
Taylor U Fort Wayne (IN)
Trinity Lutheran Coll (WA)
U of San Diego (CA)
Wilfrid Laurier U (ON, Canada)
William Jessup U (CA)

INTERDISCIPLINARY STUDIES
Abilene Christian U (TX)
Agnes Scott Coll (GA)
Albertus Magnus Coll (CT)
Albright Coll (PA)
Alderson-Broaddus Coll (WV)
Alfred U (NY)
Alice Lloyd Coll (KY)
Amberton U (TX)
American Jewish U (CA)
American U (DC)
Amherst Coll (MA)
Angelo State U (TX)
Arizona State U (AZ)
Arkansas State U (AR)
Augsburg Coll (MN)
Austin Peay State U (TN)
Bard Coll (NY)
Bard Coll at Simon's Rock (MA)
Barnard Coll (NY)
Beloit Coll (WI)
Bentley Coll (MA)
Bernard M. Baruch Coll of the City U of New York (NY)
Bethany Coll (WV)
Bethany U (CA)
Blackburn Coll (IL)
Bluefield Coll (VA)
Boise State U (ID)
Boston Coll (MA)
Boston U (MA)
Bowdoin Coll (ME)
Brock U (ON, Canada)
Bryn Athyn Coll of the New Church (PA)
Bucknell U (PA)
Burlington Coll (VT)
California Baptist U (CA)
California Lutheran U (CA)
California Polytechnic State U, San Luis Obispo (CA)
California State U, Dominguez Hills (CA)
California State U, East Bay (CA)
California State U, Long Beach (CA)
California State U, Los Angeles (CA)
California State U, Monterey Bay (CA)
California State U, San Bernardino (CA)
Calvin Coll (MI)
Capital U (OH)
Carson-Newman Coll (TN)
Catawba Coll (NC)
The Catholic U of America (DC)
Cedarville U (OH)
Centenary Coll of Louisiana (LA)
Central Coll (IA)
Central Connecticut State U (CT)
Christopher Newport U (VA)
Clarkson U (NY)
Clark U (MA)
Cleveland State U (OH)
Colby Coll (ME)
The Coll at Brockport, State U of New York (NY)
The Coll of Saint Rose (NY)
Coll of the Atlantic (ME)
Coll of the Ozarks (MO)
The Coll of William and Mary (VA)
Columbia Coll Chicago (IL)
Concordia U (OR)
Connecticut Coll (CT)
Cornell Coll (IA)
Cornell U (NY)
Cornerstone U (MI)
Covenant Coll (GA)
Dallas Baptist U (TX)
Dana Coll (NE)
Delta State U (MS)
DePauw U (IN)
Dowling Coll (NY)
D'Youville Coll (NY)
Earlham Coll (IN)
Eckerd Coll (FL)
Emerson Coll (MA)
Emmanuel Coll (MA)
Emory & Henry Coll (VA)
Emory U (GA)
Felician Coll (NJ)
Florida Inst of Technology (FL)
Freed-Hardeman U (TN)
George Fox U (OR)
George Mason U (VA)
Georgetown U (DC)
The George Washington U (DC)
Gettysburg Coll (PA)
Global Coll of Long Island U (NY)
Goddard Coll (VT)
Goucher Coll (MD)
Grand Valley State U (MI)
Grantham U (MO)
Greensboro Coll (NC)
Grinnell Coll (IA)
Guilford Coll (NC)
Gustavus Adolphus Coll (MN)
Harrisburg U of Science and Technology (PA)
Harris-Stowe State U (MO)
Harvard U (MA)
Hendrix Coll (AR)
Hillsdale Coll (MI)
Hillsdale Free Will Baptist Coll (OK)
Hobart and William Smith Colls (NY)
Hollins U (VA)
Hope Coll (MI)
Hope Intl U (CA)
Houston Baptist U (TX)
Huston-Tillotson U (TX)
Illinois Coll (IL)
Illinois State U (IL)
Iona Coll (NY)
Iowa State U of Science and Technology (IA)
Ithaca Coll (NY)
Jacksonville U (FL)
John Brown U (AR)
John Carroll U (OH)
The Johns Hopkins U (MD)
Jones Coll, Jacksonville (FL)
Jones Coll, Miami (FL)
Judson Coll (AL)
Kalamazoo Coll (MI)
Kansas City Art Inst (MO)
Keene State Coll (NH)
Kentucky Christian U (KY)
Kentucky Wesleyan Coll (KY)
Kenyon Coll (OH)
Keuka Coll (NY)
The King's Coll (NY)
Kuyper Coll (MI)
Lake Superior State U (MI)
Lander U (SC)
Lees-McRae Coll (NC)
Lee U (TN)
Lehman Coll of the City U of New York (NY)
LeTourneau U (TX)
Lewis-Clark State Coll (ID)
Liberty U (VA)
Louisiana Coll (LA)
Loyola Coll in Maryland (MD)
Luther Coll (IA)
Manchester Coll (IN)
Marlboro Coll (VT)
Marquette U (WI)
Maryville U of Saint Louis (MO)
Massachusetts Coll of Liberal Arts (MA)
Merrimack Coll (MA)
Miami U (OH)
Middle Tennessee State U (TN)
Midwestern State U (TX)
Mills Coll (CA)
Misericordia U (PA)
Molloy Coll (NY)
Morningside Coll (IA)
Mount Allison U (NB, Canada)
Mount Holyoke Coll (MA)
Mount Saint Mary Coll (NY)
Mount Saint Vincent U (NS, Canada)
National U (CA)
Nazareth Coll of Rochester (NY)
Nebraska Wesleyan U (NE)
New York U (NY)
North Greenville U (SC)
Northland Coll (WI)
Northwestern U (IL)
Nyack Coll (NY)
Oakland City U (IN)
Oakwood Coll (AL)
Oberlin Coll (OH)
Oglethorpe U (GA)
Ohio U (OH)
Oregon State U (OR)
Pacific Union Coll (CA)
Pepperdine U, Malibu (CA)
Piedmont Coll (GA)
Pitzer Coll (CA)
Pomona Coll (CA)
Prairie View A&M U (TX)
Prescott Coll (AZ)
Purdue U (IN)
Queens Coll of the City U of New York (NY)
Ramapo Coll of New Jersey (NJ)
Rensselaer Polytechnic Inst (NY)
Rhodes Coll (TN)
Ripon Coll (WI)
Rochester Coll (MI)
Rochester Inst of Technology (NY)
Russell Sage Coll (NY)
Rutgers, The State U of New Jersey, New Brunswick (NJ)
St. Andrews Presbyterian Coll (NC)
St. Cloud State U (MN)
St. John's Coll (MD)
Saint Mary's Coll (IN)
Saint Mary's Coll of California (CA)
St. Thomas U (NB, Canada)
Salem Coll (NC)
San Diego Christian Coll (CA)
Santa Clara U (CA)
Sarah Lawrence Coll (NY)
Schiller Intl U (FL)
Schiller Intl U (France)
Schiller Intl U (United Kingdom)
Smith Coll (MA)
Sonoma State U (CA)
South Dakota School of Mines and Technology (SD)
Southern Oregon U (OR)
Spring Hill Coll (AL)
Stanford U (CA)
State U of New York at Fredonia (NY)
State U of New York Coll at Oneonta (NY)
State U of New York Empire State Coll (NY)
Stephen F. Austin State U (TX)
Stephens Coll (MO)
Sterling Coll (KS)
Suffolk U (MA)
Sweet Briar Coll (VA)
Tabor Coll (KS)
Tarleton State U (TX)
Tennessee Wesleyan Coll (TN)
Texas A&M U (TX)
Texas A&M U–Commerce (TX)
Texas Southern U (TX)
Texas Tech U (TX)
Texas Woman's U (TX)
Thomas Aquinas Coll (CA)
Tougaloo Coll (MS)
Towson U (MD)
Trent U (ON, Canada)
Trinity Coll (CT)
United States Air Force Acad (CO)
Université de Sherbrooke (QC, Canada)
U at Albany, State U of New York (NY)
The U of Alabama (AL)
U of Baltimore (MD)
U of Bridgeport (CT)
The U of British Columbia (BC, Canada)
U of California, San Diego (CA)
U of California, Santa Barbara (CA)
U of Chicago (IL)
U of Georgia (GA)
U of Hartford (CT)
U of Hawaii at Manoa (HI)
U of Houston (TX)
U of Houston–Downtown (TX)
U of Idaho (ID)
The U of Iowa (IA)
U of Maine at Farmington (ME)
U of Maryland, Baltimore County (MD)
U of Mary Washington (VA)
U of Massachusetts Boston (MA)
U of Massachusetts Dartmouth (MA)
U of Memphis (TN)
U of Michigan (MI)
U of Minnesota, Duluth (MN)
U of Missouri–Columbia (MO)
U of Missouri–Kansas City (MO)
The U of Montana (MT)
U of Nevada, Las Vegas (NV)
U of New Hampshire (NH)
The U of North Carolina at Greensboro (NC)
U of Northern Colorado (CO)
U of North Texas (TX)
U of Pittsburgh (PA)
U of Portland (OR)
U of Puget Sound (WA)
U of Redlands (CA)
U of Rhode Island (RI)
U of Richmond (VA)
U of Saint Mary (KS)
U of St. Thomas (MN)
U of South Carolina Upstate (SC)
U of Southern California (CA)
The U of Tennessee at Martin (TN)
The U of Texas at Arlington (TX)
The U of Texas at Dallas (TX)
The U of Texas at El Paso (TX)
The U of Texas at Tyler (TX)
The U of Texas of the Permian Basin (TX)
The U of Texas–Pan American (TX)
U of the Pacific (CA)
U of the Sacred Heart (PR)
U of Vermont (VT)
The U of Virginia's Coll at Wise (VA)
The U of Western Ontario (ON, Canada)
The U of Winnipeg (MB, Canada)
U of Wisconsin–Green Bay (WI)
U of Wisconsin–Milwaukee (WI)
U of Wisconsin–Parkside (WI)
Vanderbilt U (TN)
Vanguard U of Southern California (CA)
Vassar Coll (NY)
Villa Julie Coll (MD)
Virginia Intermont Coll (VA)
Virginia Polytechnic Inst and State U (VA)
Virginia State U (VA)
Virginia Wesleyan Coll (VA)
Warren Wilson Coll (NC)
Wayne State Coll (NE)
Webster U (MO)
Wesleyan Coll (GA)
Wesleyan U (CT)
Western Illinois U (IL)
Western New Mexico U (NM)
Western State Coll of Colorado (CO)
Western Washington U (WA)
West Liberty State Coll (WV)
West Texas A&M U (TX)
West Virginia U (WV)
William Woods U (MO)
Woodbury U (CA)
Worcester Polytechnic Inst (MA)
York U (ON, Canada)

INTERIOR ARCHITECTURE
Arizona State U (AZ)
The Art Inst of Charleston (SC)
Auburn U (AL)
Bowling Green State U (OH)
California Coll of the Arts (CA)
Central Michigan U (MI)
Chatham U (PA)
Ferris State U (MI)
Indiana State U (IN)
Kansas State U (KS)
La Roche Coll (PA)
Lawrence Technological U (MI)
Louisiana State U and Ag and Mech Coll (LA)
Philadelphia U (PA)
School of the Art Inst of Chicago (IL)
Stephen F. Austin State U (TX)
Syracuse U (NY)
Texas Tech U (TX)
U of Central Missouri (MO)
U of Houston (TX)
U of Idaho (ID)
U of Louisiana at Lafayette (LA)
U of Missouri–Columbia (MO)
U of Nebraska–Lincoln (NE)
U of Nevada, Las Vegas (NV)
U of New Haven (CT)
U of Oregon (OR)
U of Southern Mississippi (MS)
The U of Texas at Arlington (TX)
The U of Texas at San Antonio (TX)
Woodbury U (CA)

INTERIOR DESIGN
Abilene Christian U (TX)
Acad of Art U (CA)
Adrian Coll (MI)
American InterContinental U (FL)
American InterContinental U Buckhead Campus (GA)
American InterContinental U-London (United Kingdom)
Anderson U (SC)
Appalachian State U (NC)
The Art Inst of Atlanta (GA)
The Art Inst of Atlanta–Decatur (GA)
The Art Inst of Austin (TX)
The Art Inst of California–Inland Empire (CA)
The Art Inst of California–Los Angeles (CA)
The Art Inst of California–Orange County (CA)
The Art Inst of California–Sacramento (CA)
The Art Inst of California–San Diego (CA)
The Art Inst of California–San Francisco (CA)
The Art Inst of California–Sunnyvale (CA)
The Art Inst of Dallas (TX)
The Art Inst of Fort Lauderdale (FL)
The Art Inst of Houston (TX)
The Art Inst of Indianapolis (IN)
The Art Inst of Jacksonville (FL)
The Art Inst of Las Vegas (NV)
The Art Inst of Michigan (MI)
The Art Inst of Phoenix (AZ)
The Art Inst of Portland (OR)
The Art Inst of Salt Lake City (UT)
The Art Inst of Seattle (WA)
The Art Inst of Tucson (AZ)
The Art Inst of Washington (VA)
The Art Insts Intl Minnesota (MN)
Baylor U (TX)
Becker Coll (MA)
Boston Architectural Coll (MA)
Brenau U (GA)
Brigham Young U (UT)
California Design Coll (CA)
California State U, Chico (CA)
California State U, Fresno (CA)
California State U, Long Beach (CA)
California State U, Sacramento (CA)
Carson-Newman Coll (TN)
Chaminade U of Honolulu (HI)
The Cleveland Inst of Art (OH)
Coll of Mount St. Joseph (OH)
Collins Coll: A School of Design and Technology (AZ)
Colorado State U (CO)
Columbia Coll Chicago (IL)
Columbus Coll of Art & Design (OH)
Concordia U Wisconsin (WI)
Converse Coll (SC)
Drexel U (PA)
East Carolina U (NC)
Eastern Michigan U (MI)
Fashion Inst of Technology (NY)
Florida Intl U (FL)
Florida State U (FL)
Georgia Southern U (GA)
Hampton U (VA)
Harding U (AR)
High Point U (NC)
The Illinois Inst of Art–Chicago (IL)
The Illinois Inst of Art–Schaumburg (IL)
Indiana U Bloomington (IN)
Indiana U of Pennsylvania (PA)
Indiana U–Purdue U Indianapolis (IN)

Intl Acad of Design & Technology (FL)
Intl Acad of Design & Technology (IL)
Iowa State U of Science and Technology (IA)
Kansas State U (KS)
Kean U (NJ)
Kent State U (OH)
Kwantlen U Coll (BC, Canada)
Lambuth U (TN)
Longwood U (VA)
Maryland Inst Coll of Art (MD)
Marylhurst U (OR)
Marymount U (VA)
Maryville U of Saint Louis (MO)
Marywood U (PA)
Mercyhurst Coll (PA)
Meredith Coll (NC)
Miami Intl U of Art & Design (FL)
Miami U (OH)
Miami U Hamilton (OH)
Michigan State U (MI)
Middle Tennessee State U (TN)
Minnesota State U Mankato (MN)
Mississippi Coll (MS)
Mount Ida Coll (MA)
Mount Mary Coll (WI)
The New England Inst of Art (MA)
New York Inst of Technology (NY)
New York School of Interior Design (NY)
North Dakota State U (ND)
Northern Arizona U (AZ)
Northwest Missouri State U (MO)
Oklahoma Christian U (OK)
Oklahoma State U (OK)
Oregon State U (OR)
Otis Coll of Art and Design (CA)
Paier Coll of Art, Inc. (CT)
Park U (MO)
Parsons The New School for Design (NY)
Patricia Stevens Coll (MO)
Philadelphia U (PA)
Pittsburg State U (KS)
Pratt Inst (NY)
Purdue U (IN)
Ringling Coll of Art and Design (FL)
Rocky Mountain Coll of Art + Design (CO)
Salem Coll (NC)
Samford U (AL)
Sam Houston State U (TX)
San Diego State U (CA)
San Francisco State U (CA)
Savannah Coll of Art and Design (GA)
School of Visual Arts (NY)
South Dakota State U (SD)
Southern Illinois U Carbondale (IL)
Stephens Coll (MO)
Suffolk U (MA)
Texas Christian U (TX)
Texas State U-San Marcos (TX)
The U of Alabama (AL)
U of Arkansas (AR)
U of Bridgeport (CT)
U of Central Missouri (MO)
U of Central Oklahoma (OK)
U of Cincinnati (OH)
U of Florida (FL)
U of Georgia (GA)
U of Houston (TX)
U of Idaho (ID)
U of Kansas (KS)
U of Massachusetts Amherst (MA)
U of Minnesota, Twin Cities Campus (MN)
The U of North Carolina at Greensboro (NC)
U of Northern Iowa (IA)
U of North Texas (TX)
U of Oklahoma (OK)
The U of Tennessee (TN)
The U of Tennessee at Martin (TN)
The U of Texas at Austin (TX)
The U of Texas at San Antonio (TX)
U of the Incarnate Word (TX)
U of Wisconsin–Madison (WI)
U of Wisconsin–Stevens Point (WI)
Ursuline Coll (OH)
Utah State U (UT)
Valdosta State U (GA)
Virginia Commonwealth U (VA)
Virginia Polytechnic Inst and State U (VA)
Washington State U (WA)
Watkins Coll of Art and Design (TN)
Western Carolina U (NC)
Western Michigan U (MI)
Westwood Coll–Atlanta Northlake (GA)
William Woods U (MO)

INTERIOR ENVIRONMENTS

U of Georgia (GA)

INTERMEDIA/MULTIMEDIA

Alberta Coll of Art & Design (AB, Canada)
American U (DC)
Art Acad of Cincinnati (OH)
The Art Inst of California–San Diego (CA)
Augusta State U (GA)
Bennington Coll (VT)
Calumet Coll of Saint Joseph (IN)
Carlow U (PA)
City Coll of the City U of New York (NY)
The Cleveland Inst of Art (OH)
The Coll of New Jersey (NJ)
Coll of Santa Fe (NM)
Columbia Coll Chicago (IL)
Concordia U (QC, Canada)
Emerson Coll (MA)
The Evergreen State Coll (WA)
George Fox U (OR)
Hawai'i Pacific U (HI)
Indiana U of Pennsylvania (PA)
Laguna Coll of Art & Design (CA)
Lewis U (IL)
Maryland Inst Coll of Art (MD)
Massachusetts Coll of Art and Design (MA)
Memphis Coll of Art (TN)
Mills Coll (CA)
Missouri State U (MO)
National U (CA)
New England School of Communications (ME)
Ramapo Coll of New Jersey (NJ)
School of the Art Inst of Chicago (IL)
School of the Museum of Fine Arts, Boston (MA)
State U of New York at Fredonia (NY)
U of California, San Diego (CA)
U of Central Florida (FL)
U of Florida (FL)
U of Massachusetts Dartmouth (MA)
U of Michigan (MI)
U of Oregon (OR)
U of Regina (SK, Canada)
U of Windsor (ON, Canada)
Western Washington U (WA)
Worcester Polytechnic Inst (MA)

INTERNATIONAL AGRICULTURE

Cornell U (NY)
Iowa State U of Science and Technology (IA)
Sterling Coll (VT)
Tarleton State U (TX)
U of California, Davis (CA)
U of Illinois at Urbana–Champaign (IL)
U of Missouri–Columbia (MO)
Utah State U (UT)

INTERNATIONAL BUSINESS/TRADE/COMMERCE

Adrian Coll (MI)
Albertus Magnus Coll (CT)
Albright Coll (PA)
Alliant Intl U (CA)
Alliant Intl U–México City (Mexico)
Alma Coll (MI)
American Coll of Thessaloniki (Greece)
American InterContinental U-London (United Kingdom)
The American U of Athens (Greece)
The American U of Paris (France)
Anderson U (IN)
Appalachian State U (NC)
Aquinas Coll (MI)
Argosy U, Atlanta (GA)
Argosy U, Chicago (IL)
Argosy U, Denver (CO)
Argosy U, Hawai'i (HI)
Argosy U, Inland Empire (CA)
Argosy U, Nashville (TN)
Argosy U, Orange County (CA)
Argosy U, Phoenix (AZ)
Argosy U, San Diego (CA)
Argosy U, San Francisco Bay Area (CA)
Argosy U, Santa Monica (CA)
Argosy U, Sarasota (FL)
Argosy U, Schaumburg (IL)
Argosy U, Seattle (WA)
Argosy U, Twin Cities (MN)
Argosy U, Washington DC (VA)
Arizona State U at the West campus (AZ)
Arkansas State U (AR)
Assumption Coll (MA)
Auburn U (AL)
Augsburg Coll (MN)
Avila U (MO)
Babson Coll (MA)
Baker U (KS)
Barry U (FL)
Baylor U (TX)
Belmont Abbey Coll (NC)
Belmont U (TN)
Benedictine U (IL)
Bernard M. Baruch Coll of the City U of New York (NY)
Bethany Coll (KS)
Bethune-Cookman U (FL)
Bishop's U (QC, Canada)
Boise State U (ID)
Boston U (MA)
Bowling Green State U (OH)
Bradley U (IL)
Bridgewater State Coll (MA)
Brock U (ON, Canada)
Butler U (IN)
California State Polytechnic U, Pomona (CA)
California State U, Dominguez Hills (CA)
California State U, Fresno (CA)
California State U, Fullerton (CA)
California State U, Long Beach (CA)
California State U, Monterey Bay (CA)
Canisius Coll (NY)
Cedarville U (OH)
Central Coll (IA)
Central Connecticut State U (CT)
Central Michigan U (MI)
Chatham U (PA)
Chestnut Hill Coll (PA)
Christopher Newport U (VA)
City U of Seattle (WA)
Claremont McKenna Coll (CA)
Clarion U of Pennsylvania (PA)
Clarke Coll (IA)
Clarkson U (NY)
Clemson U (SC)
The Coll at Brockport, State U of New York (NY)
Coll of Charleston (SC)
The Coll of Idaho (ID)
The Coll of New Jersey (NJ)
The Coll of St. Scholastica (MN)
Coll of the Ozarks (MO)
Columbia Southern U (AL)
Concordia Coll (MN)
Concordia U (QC, Canada)
Converse Coll (SC)
Cornell Coll (IA)
Creighton U (NE)
Davenport U, Dearborn (MI)
Davenport U, Grand Rapids (MI)
Davis & Elkins Coll (WV)
Dickinson Coll (PA)
Dillard U (LA)
Dominican Coll (NY)
Dominican U (IL)
Dominican U of California (CA)
Dowling Coll (NY)
Drake U (IA)
Drexel U (PA)
Duquesne U (PA)
D'Youville Coll (NY)
Eastern Mennonite U (VA)
Eastern Michigan U (MI)
Eckerd Coll (FL)
Elizabethtown Coll (PA)
Excelsior Coll (NY)
Ferris State U (MI)
Finlandia U (MI)
Fitchburg State Coll (MA)
Florida Atlantic U (FL)
Florida Inst of Technology (FL)
Florida Intl U (FL)
Florida Southern Coll (FL)
Florida State U (FL)
Fort Lewis Coll (CO)
Franklin Coll Switzerland (Switzerland)
Fresno Pacific U (CA)
Gannon U (PA)
George Fox U (OR)
Georgetown U (DC)
The George Washington U (DC)
Georgia Coll & State U (GA)
Georgia Southern U (GA)
Georgia State U (GA)
Gettysburg Coll (PA)
Golden Gate U (CA)
Goldey-Beacom Coll (DE)
Gonzaga U (WA)
Grace Coll (IN)
Grand Valley State U (MI)
Grove City Coll (PA)
Gustavus Adolphus Coll (MN)
Hamline U (MN)
Harding U (AR)
Hawai'i Pacific U (HI)
HEC Montreal (QC, Canada)
High Point U (NC)
Hofstra U (NY)
Holy Family U (PA)
Houston Baptist U (TX)
Husson Coll (ME)
Illinois State U (IL)
Illinois Wesleyan U (IL)
Immaculata U (PA)
Indiana U of Pennsylvania (PA)
Iona Coll (NY)
Iowa State U of Science and Technology (IA)
Ithaca Coll (NY)
Jacksonville U (FL)
James Madison U (VA)
Jamestown Coll (ND)
John Brown U (AR)
Juniata Coll (PA)
Keiser U, Fort Lauderdale (FL)
Kennesaw State U (GA)
King Coll (TN)
King's Coll (PA)
Kutztown U of Pennsylvania (PA)
Kuyper Coll (MI)
La Roche Coll (PA)
Lenoir-Rhyne Coll (NC)
LeTourneau U (TX)
Lewis U (IL)
Lincoln U (CA)
Linfield Coll (OR)
Lipscomb U (TN)
Loras Coll (IA)
Louisiana State U and Ag and Mech Coll (LA)
Loyola Coll in Maryland (MD)
Loyola U Chicago (IL)
Loyola U New Orleans (LA)
Lycoming Coll (PA)
Madonna U (MI)
Maine Maritime Acad (ME)
Mansfield U of Pennsylvania (PA)
Marietta Coll (OH)
Marquette U (WI)
Maryville Coll (TN)
Marywood U (PA)
Massachusetts Maritime Acad (MA)
McGill U (QC, Canada)
Merrimack Coll (MA)
Messiah Coll (PA)
Metropolitan State U (MN)
MidAmerica Nazarene U (KS)
Midwestern State U (TX)
Millikin U (IL)
Milwaukee School of Eng (WI)
Minnesota State U Mankato (MN)
Minot State U (ND)
Monmouth U (NJ)
Moravian Coll (PA)
Mount Allison U (NB, Canada)
Mount Saint Mary Coll (NY)
Mount St. Mary's Coll (CA)
Mount Vernon Nazarene U (OH)
Murray State U (KY)
National American U, Rapid City (SD)
National-Louis U (IL)
Nebraska Wesleyan U (NE)
Neumann Coll (PA)
New York Inst of Technology (NY)
New York U (NY)
Niagara U (NY)
North Central Coll (IL)
Northeastern State U (OK)
Northeastern U (MA)
Northern State U (SD)
North Greenville U (SC)
Northwestern Coll (MN)
Northwest Missouri State U (MO)
Northwest Nazarene U (ID)
Northwood U, Florida Campus (FL)
Ohio Dominican U (OH)
Ohio Northern U (OH)
Ohio Wesleyan U (OH)
Oklahoma City U (OK)
Oklahoma State U (OK)
Old Dominion U (VA)
Oral Roberts U (OK)
Oregon State U (OR)
Otterbein Coll (OH)
Pace U (NY)
Pacific Union Coll (CA)
Paine Coll (GA)
Palm Beach Atlantic U (FL)
Penn State Erie, The Behrend Coll (PA)
Penn State Harrisburg (PA)
Penn State U Park (PA)
Pepperdine U, Malibu (CA)
Pfeiffer U (NC)
Philadelphia U (PA)
Pittsburg State U (KS)
Queens Coll of the City U of New York (NY)
Quinnipiac U (CT)
Ramapo Coll of New Jersey (NJ)
Regent U (VA)
Rhodes Coll (TN)
Rider U (NJ)
Rochester Inst of Technology (NY)
Roger Williams U (RI)
Rollins Coll (FL)
Roosevelt U (IL)
Sacred Heart U (CT)
Saginaw Valley State U (MI)
St. Ambrose U (IA)
St. Cloud State U (MN)
St. Edward's U (TX)
Saint Francis U (PA)
St. John Fisher Coll (NY)
Saint Joseph's U (PA)
Saint Louis U (MO)
Saint Mary's Coll (IN)
Saint Mary's Coll of California (CA)
St. Mary's U (TX)
Saint Mary's U of Minnesota (MN)
St. Norbert Coll (WI)
St. Thomas U (FL)
Saint Vincent Coll (PA)
Saint Xavier U (IL)
Salem Coll (NC)
Salem Intl U (WV)
Samford U (AL)
Sam Houston State U (TX)
San Diego State U (CA)
San Francisco State U (CA)
Schiller Intl U (FL)
Schiller Intl U (France)
Schiller Intl U (United Kingdom)
Seattle U (WA)
Seton Hill U (PA)
Shaw U (NC)
Simpson Coll (IA)
Southeastern U (FL)
Southern Adventist U (TN)
Southern New Hampshire U (NH)
Southwestern Adventist U (TX)
Spring Hill Coll (AL)
State U of New York at Binghamton (NY)
State U of New York at New Paltz (NY)
State U of New York at Plattsburgh (NY)
Stephen F. Austin State U (TX)
Stetson U (FL)
Tarleton State U (TX)
Taylor U (IN)
Temple U (PA)
Tennessee Technological U (TN)
Texas Christian U (TX)
Texas Tech U (TX)
Thiel Coll (PA)
Thomas Coll (ME)
Thomas Edison State Coll (NJ)
Trinity Intl U (IL)
Trinity U (TX)
Université du Québec en Outaouais (QC, Canada)
The U of Akron (OH)
U of Arkansas (AR)
U of Baltimore (MD)
U of Bridgeport (CT)
The U of British Columbia (BC, Canada)
U of Dayton (OH)
U of Denver (CO)
U of Evansville (IN)
The U of Findlay (OH)
U of Georgia (GA)
U of Guam (GU)
U of Hawaii at Manoa (HI)
U of Houston–Downtown (TX)
U of Indianapolis (IN)
U of La Verne (CA)
U of Lethbridge (AB, Canada)
U of Maryland, Coll Park (MD)
U of Memphis (TN)
U of Miami (FL)
U of Minnesota, Twin Cities Campus (MN)
U of Mississippi (MS)
U of Missouri–Columbia (MO)
U of Missouri–St. Louis (MO)
The U of Montana (MT)
U of Nebraska–Lincoln (NE)
U of Nevada, Las Vegas (NV)
U of Nevada, Reno (NV)
U of New Brunswick Fredericton (NB, Canada)
U of New Haven (CT)
The U of North Carolina at Charlotte (NC)
The U of North Carolina at Greensboro (NC)
U of North Florida (FL)
U of Oklahoma (OK)
U of Ottawa (ON, Canada)
U of Pennsylvania (PA)
U of Portland (OR)
U of Puget Sound (WA)
U of Rhode Island (RI)
U of Richmond (VA)
U of Rio Grande (OH)
U of St. Thomas (MN)
The U of Scranton (PA)
U of Southern California (CA)
U of Southern Mississippi (MS)
U of South Florida (FL)
The U of Tampa (FL)
The U of Tennessee at Martin (TN)

The U of Texas at Arlington (TX)
The U of Texas at Dallas (TX)
The U of Texas at San Antonio (TX)
The U of Texas–Pan American (TX)
The U of Toledo (OH)
U of Tulsa (OK)
U of Victoria (BC, Canada)
The U of Western Ontario (ON, Canada)
U of Wisconsin–La Crosse (WI)
Utica Coll (NY)
Valparaiso U (IN)
Vanguard U of Southern California (CA)
Villanova U (PA)
Virginia Commonwealth U (VA)
Virginia Intermont Coll (VA)
Warren Wilson Coll (NC)
Wartburg Coll (IA)
Washington & Jefferson Coll (PA)
Washington State U (WA)
Washington U in St. Louis (MO)
Waynesburg U (PA)
Webster U (MO)
Wesleyan Coll (GA)
Western Carolina U (NC)
Western Intl U (AZ)
Western New Mexico U (NM)
Western Washington U (WA)
Westminster Coll (MO)
Westminster Coll (UT)
Wheeling Jesuit U (WV)
Whitworth U (WA)
Wichita State U (KS)
Widener U (PA)
William Jewell Coll (MO)
William Paterson U of New Jersey (NJ)
William Woods U (MO)
Wofford Coll (SC)
Xavier U (OH)
York U (ON, Canada)

INTERNATIONAL ECONOMICS

Albertus Magnus Coll (CT)
The American U of Paris (France)
Austin Coll (TX)
Brock U (ON, Canada)
California State U, Chico (CA)
Carson-Newman Coll (TN)
The Catholic U of America (DC)
Claremont McKenna Coll (CA)
The Coll of Idaho (ID)
The Colorado Coll (CO)
Eastern Michigan U (MI)
Franklin Coll Switzerland (Switzerland)
Georgetown U (DC)
Gettysburg Coll (PA)
Hamline U (MN)
Harvard U (MA)
HEC Montreal (QC, Canada)
John Carroll U (OH)
Lawrence U (WI)
Longwood U (VA)
Loyola Marymount U (CA)
Marlboro Coll (VT)
Ohio U (OH)
Rhodes Coll (TN)
Rockford Coll (IL)
Seattle U (WA)
State U of New York at New Paltz (NY)
State U of New York at Oswego (NY)
Suffolk U (MA)
Taylor U (IN)
Texas Christian U (TX)
U of California, Los Angeles (CA)
U of California, Santa Cruz (CA)
U of Missouri–Columbia (MO)
U of Puget Sound (WA)
U of Richmond (VA)
U of St. Thomas (MN)
U of West Georgia (GA)
Valparaiso U (IN)
Washington U in St. Louis (MO)

INTERNATIONAL FINANCE

Babson Coll (MA)
Boston U (MA)
Brigham Young U (UT)
The Catholic U of America (DC)
Franklin Coll Switzerland (Switzerland)
HEC Montreal (QC, Canada)
McGill U (QC, Canada)
Texas Christian U (TX)
The U of Western Ontario (ON, Canada)
Washington U in St. Louis (MO)

INTERNATIONAL/GLOBAL STUDIES

Abilene Christian U (TX)
Adelphi U (NY)
Adrian Coll (MI)
Alfred U (NY)
Allegheny Coll (PA)
Arizona State U (AZ)
Assumption Coll (MA)
Baker U (KS)
Baldwin-Wallace Coll (OH)
Belhaven Coll (MS)
Bellarmine U (KY)
Bennington Coll (VT)
Brandeis U (MA)
California State U, Monterey Bay (CA)
Case Western Reserve U (OH)
Cedarville U (OH)
Central Coll (IA)
Chatham U (PA)
City Coll of the City U of New York (NY)
Colby Coll (ME)
The Coll of New Rochelle (NY)
Coll of Saint Elizabeth (NJ)
The Coll of St. Scholastica (MN)
Coll of Santa Fe (NM)
Concordia Coll (MN)
Concordia U (CA)
Davis Coll (NY)
Doane Coll (NE)
Dominican U of California (CA)
East Texas Baptist U (TX)
Emmanuel Coll (MA)
Endicott Coll (MA)
The Evergreen State Coll (WA)
George Fox U (OR)
Georgia Inst of Technology (GA)
Greenville Coll (IL)
Hampshire Coll (MA)
Hanover Coll (IN)
Harding U (AR)
Hawai'i Pacific U (HI)
Hope Coll (MI)
Iona Coll (NY)
Kenyon Coll (OH)
Lewis U (IL)
Louisiana State U and Ag and Mech Coll (LA)
Marquette U (WI)
Meredith Coll (NC)
Miami U Hamilton (OH)
Michigan State U (MI)
Midwestern State U (TX)
National U (CA)
Nebraska Wesleyan U (NE)
New Coll of Florida (FL)
North Dakota State U (ND)
Oregon State U (OR)
Pacific Lutheran U (WA)
Pittsburg State U (KS)
Pitzer Coll (CA)
Point Loma Nazarene U (CA)
Providence Coll (RI)
Randolph-Macon Coll (VA)
Rockford Coll (IL)
Russell Sage Coll (NY)
Saint Joseph Coll (CT)
St. Lawrence U (NY)
Saint Mary's U of Minnesota (MN)
South Dakota State U (SD)
Southeast Missouri State U (MO)
Spring Arbor U (MI)
State U of New York at Binghamton (NY)
Sterling Coll (VT)
Tennessee Wesleyan Coll (TN)
Texas A&M U (TX)
Texas State U-San Marcos (TX)
U of California, Irvine (CA)
U of California, Los Angeles (CA)
U of California, Riverside (CA)
U of California, Santa Barbara (CA)
U of Central Arkansas (AR)
U of Chicago (IL)
U of Colorado at Boulder (CO)
U of Colorado Denver (CO)
U of Illinois at Urbana–Champaign (IL)
The U of Iowa (IA)
U of La Verne (CA)
U of Maine at Farmington (ME)
U of Nebraska at Omaha (NE)
U of New Hampshire (NH)
U of New Orleans (LA)
U of North Dakota (ND)
U of North Florida (FL)
U of North Texas (TX)
U of Oregon (OR)
U of Ottawa (ON, Canada)
U of Pennsylvania (PA)
U of Regina (SK, Canada)
The U of Tampa (FL)
U of Utah (UT)
The U of Western Ontario (ON, Canada)
U of Wisconsin–Whitewater (WI)
Warren Wilson Coll (NC)
Washington & Jefferson Coll (PA)
Western Michigan U (MI)
Wilfrid Laurier U (ON, Canada)
Willamette U (OR)

INTERNATIONAL MARKETING

Brigham Young U (UT)
Davis & Elkins Coll (WV)
Fashion Inst of Technology (NY)
Pace U (NY)
Saint Joseph's U (PA)
Texas Christian U (TX)
York U (ON, Canada)

INTERNATIONAL PUBLIC HEALTH

Clemson U (SC)

INTERNATIONAL RELATIONS AND AFFAIRS

Adrian Coll (MI)
Agnes Scott Coll (GA)
Albion Coll (MI)
Allegheny Coll (PA)
Alliant Intl U (CA)
Alliant Intl U–México City (Mexico)
American Coll of Thessaloniki (Greece)
American Public U System (WV)
American U (DC)
The American U of Paris (France)
Aquinas Coll (MI)
Ashland U (OH)
Augsburg Coll (MN)
Augustana Coll (SD)
Austin Coll (TX)
Azusa Pacific U (CA)
Bard Coll (NY)
Barry U (FL)
Baylor U (TX)
Beloit Coll (WI)
Benedictine U (IL)
Bennington Coll (VT)
Berry Coll (GA)
Bethany Coll (WV)
Bethany U (CA)
Bethel U (MN)
Bethune-Cookman U (FL)
Bishop's U (QC, Canada)
Bob Jones U (SC)
Boston U (MA)
Bowling Green State U (OH)
Bradley U (IL)
Brenau U (GA)
Bridgewater Coll (VA)
Bridgewater State Coll (MA)
Brigham Young U (UT)
Brown U (RI)
Bucknell U (PA)
Butler U (IN)
California Lutheran U (CA)
California State U, Chico (CA)
California State U, East Bay (CA)
California State U, Long Beach (CA)
California State U, Monterey Bay (CA)
Calvin Coll (MI)
Canadian Mennonite U (MB, Canada)
Canisius Coll (NY)
Capital U (OH)
Carnegie Mellon U (PA)
Carroll Coll (WI)
Case Western Reserve U (OH)
Catawba Coll (NC)
The Catholic U of America (DC)
Cedarville U (OH)
Centenary Coll (NJ)
Central Michigan U (MI)
Centre Coll (KY)
Chaminade U of Honolulu (HI)
Chatham U (PA)
City Coll of the City U of New York (NY)
Claremont McKenna Coll (CA)
Clark U (MA)
Cleveland State U (OH)
Colby Coll (ME)
Colgate U (NY)
The Coll at Brockport, State U of New York (NY)
The Coll of New Jersey (NJ)
Coll of Staten Island of the City U of New York (NY)
The Coll of William and Mary (VA)
Concordia Coll–New York (NY)
Connecticut Coll (CT)
Cornell Coll (IA)
Creighton U (NE)
Denison U (OH)
DePaul U (IL)
Dickinson Coll (PA)
Drake U (IA)
Duke U (NC)
Duquesne U (PA)
Earlham Coll (IN)
Eckerd Coll (FL)
Embry-Riddle Aeronautical U (AZ)
Emory & Henry Coll (VA)
Emory U (GA)
Fairfield U (CT)
Fairleigh Dickinson U, Metropolitan Campus (NJ)
Ferrum Coll (VA)
Florida Intl U (FL)
Florida State U (FL)
Francis Marion U (SC)
Franklin Coll Switzerland (Switzerland)
Frostburg State U (MD)
George Mason U (VA)
Georgetown U (DC)
The George Washington U (DC)
Georgia Inst of Technology (GA)
Georgia Southern U (GA)
Gettysburg Coll (PA)
Gonzaga U (WA)
Gordon Coll (MA)
Goucher Coll (MD)
Grand Valley State U (MI)
Guilford Coll (NC)
Hamilton Coll (NY)
Hamline U (MN)
Hampden-Sydney Coll (VA)
Harvard U (MA)
Hastings Coll (NE)
Hawai'i Pacific U (HI)
Heidelberg Coll (OH)
Hendrix Coll (AR)
High Point U (NC)
Hillsdale Coll (MI)
Hobart and William Smith Colls (NY)
Hollins U (VA)
Holy Names U (CA)
Houghton Coll (NY)
Idaho State U (ID)
Illinois Coll (IL)
Illinois Wesleyan U (IL)
Immaculata U (PA)
Indiana U Bloomington (IN)
Indiana U of Pennsylvania (PA)
Indiana U–Purdue U Indianapolis (IN)
Indiana U Southeast (IN)
Intl U in Geneva (Switzerland)
Iowa State U of Science and Technology (IA)
Jacksonville U (FL)
James Madison U (VA)
John Brown U (AR)
John Carroll U (OH)
The Johns Hopkins U (MD)
Juniata Coll (PA)
Kennesaw State U (GA)
Kent State U (OH)
Kenyon Coll (OH)
Knox Coll (IL)
Lafayette Coll (PA)
Lake Forest Coll (IL)
Lambuth U (TN)
La Roche Coll (PA)
Lawrence U (WI)
Lees-McRae Coll (NC)
Lee U (TN)
Lehigh U (PA)
Lenoir-Rhyne Coll (NC)
Lewis & Clark Coll (OR)
Lincoln U (PA)
Lindenwood U (MO)
Lock Haven U of Pennsylvania (PA)
Longwood U (VA)
Loras Coll (IA)
Loyola U Chicago (IL)
Luther Coll (IA)
Lycoming Coll (PA)
Lynchburg Coll (VA)
Manhattanville Coll (NY)
Mansfield U of Pennsylvania (PA)
Marlboro Coll (VT)
Marquette U (WI)
Marshall U (WV)
Mary Baldwin Coll (VA)
Marymount Manhattan Coll (NY)
Maryville Coll (TN)
McKendree U (IL)
Mercer U (GA)
Meredith Coll (NC)
Methodist U (NC)
Miami U (OH)
Michigan State U (MI)
Middlebury Coll (VT)
Middle Tennessee State U (TN)
Millikin U (IL)
Mills Coll (CA)
Minnesota State U Mankato (MN)
Missouri Southern State U (MO)
Morehouse Coll (GA)
Mount Allison U (NB, Canada)
Mount Holyoke Coll (MA)
Mount Mary Coll (WI)
Mount Mercy Coll (IA)
Mount Saint Mary Coll (NY)
Mount St. Mary's U (MD)
Muhlenberg Coll (PA)
Murray State U (KY)
Nazareth Coll of Rochester (NY)
New York U (NY)
Niagara U (NY)
Northeastern U (MA)
Northern Arizona U (AZ)
Northern Michigan U (MI)
Northwestern U (IL)
Northwest Nazarene U (ID)
Norwich U (VT)
Nova Southeastern U (FL)
Oakland U (MI)
Occidental Coll (CA)
Oglethorpe U (GA)
Ohio Northern U (OH)
Ohio U (OH)
Ohio Wesleyan U (OH)
Old Dominion U (VA)
Oral Roberts U (OK)
Oregon State U (OR)
Otterbein Coll (OH)
Pacific U (OR)
Penn State Abington (PA)
Penn State Altoona (PA)
Penn State Berks (PA)
Penn State Erie, The Behrend Coll (PA)
Penn State U Park (PA)
Pepperdine U, Malibu (CA)
Pitzer Coll (CA)
Pomona Coll (CA)
Portland State U (OR)
Queens U of Charlotte (NC)
Quinnipiac U (CT)
Randolph Coll (VA)
Reed Coll (OR)
Regis Coll (MA)
Rhodes Coll (TN)
Rider U (NJ)
Roanoke Coll (VA)
Rochester Inst of Technology (NY)
Rockhurst U (MO)
Rollins Coll (FL)
Roosevelt U (IL)
Sacred Heart U (CT)
Saginaw Valley State U (MI)
St. Cloud State U (MN)
St. Edward's U (TX)
Saint Francis U (PA)
St. John Fisher Coll (NY)
Saint Joseph's Coll (IN)
Saint Joseph's U (PA)
Saint Leo U (FL)
Saint Louis U (MO)
Saint Mary's Coll of California (CA)
St. Norbert Coll (WI)
Saint Xavier U (IL)
Salem Coll (NC)
Samford U (AL)
San Diego State U (CA)
San Francisco State U (CA)
Sarah Lawrence Coll (NY)
Schiller Intl U (FL)
Schiller Intl U (France)
Schiller Intl U (United Kingdom)
Scripps Coll (CA)
Seattle U (WA)
Seton Hill U (PA)
Sewanee: The U of the South (TN)
Shawnee State U (OH)
Shaw U (NC)
Simmons Coll (MA)
Simpson Coll (IA)
Skidmore Coll (NY)
Sonoma State U (CA)
Southern Methodist U (TX)
Southern Oregon U (OR)
Southern Polytechnic State U (GA)
Southwestern Adventist U (TX)
Southwestern U (TX)
Spring Hill Coll (AL)
Stanford U (CA)
State U of New York at Binghamton (NY)
State U of New York at New Paltz (NY)
State U of New York at Oswego (NY)
State U of New York Coll at Geneseo (NY)
State U of New York Coll at Oneonta (NY)
Stetson U (FL)
Stonehill Coll (MA)
Susquehanna U (PA)
Sweet Briar Coll (VA)
Syracuse U (NY)
Tabor Coll (KS)
Taylor U (IN)
Texas Christian U (TX)
Texas Lutheran U (TX)
Texas State U-San Marcos (TX)
Thomas More Coll (KY)
Tiffin U (OH)
Towson U (MD)
Trent U (ON, Canada)
Trinity Coll (CT)

Tufts U (MA)
Tulane U (LA)
Union Coll (NE)
The U of Akron (OH)
The U of Alabama (AL)
U of Arkansas (AR)
U of Bridgeport (CT)
The U of British Columbia (BC, Canada)
The U of British Columbia–Okanagan (BC, Canada)
U of California, Davis (CA)
U of California, Riverside (CA)
U of Cincinnati (OH)
U of Dayton (OH)
U of Delaware (DE)
U of Denver (CO)
U of Evansville (IN)
U of Georgia (GA)
U of Idaho (ID)
U of Indianapolis (IN)
U of Kansas (KS)
U of La Verne (CA)
U of Maine (ME)
U of Mary Washington (VA)
U of Memphis (TN)
U of Miami (FL)
U of Michigan (MI)
U of Minnesota, Duluth (MN)
U of Minnesota, Twin Cities Campus (MN)
U of Mississippi (MS)
U of Nebraska at Kearney (NE)
U of Nebraska–Lincoln (NE)
U of Nevada, Reno (NV)
U of New Brunswick Fredericton (NB, Canada)
U of New Hampshire (NH)
U of North Florida (FL)
U of Ottawa (ON, Canada)
U of Pennsylvania (PA)
U of Puget Sound (WA)
U of Redlands (CA)
U of Richmond (VA)
U of St. Thomas (MN)
U of St. Thomas (TX)
U of San Diego (CA)
The U of Scranton (PA)
U of South Carolina (SC)
U of Southern California (CA)
U of Southern Indiana (IN)
U of Southern Maine (ME)
U of Southern Mississippi (MS)
U of South Florida (FL)
The U of Tampa (FL)
The U of Tennessee at Martin (TN)
U of the Pacific (CA)
The U of Toledo (OH)
U of Toronto (ON, Canada)
U of Virginia (VA)
The U of Western Ontario (ON, Canada)
U of West Florida (FL)
U of West Georgia (GA)
U of Windsor (ON, Canada)
U of Wisconsin–Madison (WI)
U of Wisconsin–Milwaukee (WI)
U of Wisconsin–Oshkosh (WI)
U of Wisconsin–Parkside (WI)
U of Wisconsin–Platteville (WI)
U of Wisconsin–Stevens Point (WI)
U of Wisconsin–Superior (WI)
U of Wisconsin–Whitewater (WI)
U of Wyoming (WY)
Ursinus Coll (PA)
Utica Coll (NY)
Valparaiso U (IN)
Vassar Coll (NY)
Virginia Military Inst (VA)
Virginia Polytechnic Inst and State U (VA)
Virginia Wesleyan Coll (VA)
Wagner Coll (NY)
Wartburg Coll (IA)
Washington Coll (MD)
Washington U in St. Louis (MO)
Webster U (MO)
Wellesley Coll (MA)
Wells Coll (NY)
Wesleyan Coll (GA)
West Chester U of Pennsylvania (PA)
Western Intl U (AZ)
Westminster Coll (MO)
West Virginia U (WV)
West Virginia Wesleyan Coll (WV)
Wheaton Coll (IL)
Wheaton Coll (MA)
Wheeling Jesuit U (WV)
Whittier Coll (CA)
Whitworth U (WA)
Widener U (PA)
Wilkes U (PA)
William Jewell Coll (MO)
William Woods U (MO)
Wilson Coll (PA)
Winona State U (MN)
Wofford Coll (SC)
Wright State U (OH)
Xavier U (OH)
York U (ON, Canada)

INVESTMENTS AND SECURITIES

Babson Coll (MA)
Duquesne U (PA)

IRANIAN/PERSIAN LANGUAGES

The U of Texas at Austin (TX)

ISLAMIC STUDIES

DePaul U (IL)
East-West U (IL)
Harvard U (MA)
U of Michigan (MI)
The U of Texas at Austin (TX)
U of Toronto (ON, Canada)
Washington U in St. Louis (MO)
Wellesley Coll (MA)

ITALIAN

Albertus Magnus Coll (CT)
Arizona State U (AZ)
Assumption Coll (MA)
Bard Coll (NY)
Barnard Coll (NY)
Bishop's U (QC, Canada)
Boston Coll (MA)
Boston U (MA)
Brigham Young U (UT)
Brock U (ON, Canada)
Brown U (RI)
Bryn Mawr Coll (PA)
California State U, Long Beach (CA)
Central Connecticut State U (CT)
Claremont McKenna Coll (CA)
Coll of the Holy Cross (MA)
The Colorado Coll (CO)
Concordia U (QC, Canada)
Connecticut Coll (CT)
Cornell U (NY)
Dartmouth Coll (NH)
DePaul U (IL)
Dickinson Coll (PA)
Dominican U (IL)
Duke U (NC)
Emory U (GA)
Fairfield U (CT)
Florida Intl U (FL)
Florida State U (FL)
Georgetown U (DC)
Gettysburg Coll (PA)
Gonzaga U (WA)
Harvard U (MA)
Haverford Coll (PA)
Hofstra U (NY)
Hunter Coll of the City U of New York (NY)
Indiana U Bloomington (IN)
Iona Coll (NY)
The Johns Hopkins U (MD)
La Salle U (PA)
Laurentian U (ON, Canada)
Lehman Coll of the City U of New York (NY)
Loyola U Chicago (IL)
Marlboro Coll (VT)
McGill U (QC, Canada)
Middlebury Coll (VT)
Montclair State U (NJ)
Mount Holyoke Coll (MA)
Nazareth Coll of Rochester (NY)
New York U (NY)
Northeastern U (MA)
Northwestern U (IL)
Penn State Abington (PA)
Penn State Altoona (PA)
Penn State Berks (PA)
Penn State Erie, The Behrend Coll (PA)
Penn State U Park (PA)
Providence Coll (RI)
Queens Coll of the City U of New York (NY)
Rosemont Coll (PA)
Rutgers, The State U of New Jersey, Newark (NJ)
Rutgers, The State U of New Jersey, New Brunswick (NJ)
St. John Fisher Coll (NY)
St. John's U (NY)
Saint Joseph's U (PA)
Saint Mary's Coll (IN)
Saint Mary's Coll of California (CA)
San Francisco State U (CA)
Santa Clara U (CA)
Sarah Lawrence Coll (NY)
Scripps Coll (CA)
Smith Coll (MA)
Southern Connecticut State U (CT)
Southern Methodist U (TX)
Stanford U (CA)
State U of New York at Binghamton (NY)
Stony Brook U, State U of New York (NY)
Sweet Briar Coll (VA)
Syracuse U (NY)
Temple U (PA)
Trinity Coll (CT)
Tulane U (LA)
U at Albany, State U of New York (NY)
U at Buffalo, the State U of New York (NY)
The U of Arizona (AZ)
The U of British Columbia (BC, Canada)
U of California, Berkeley (CA)
U of California, Davis (CA)
U of California, Los Angeles (CA)
U of California, San Diego (CA)
U of California, Santa Barbara (CA)
U of Chicago (IL)
U of Colorado at Boulder (CO)
U of Connecticut (CT)
U of Delaware (DE)
U of Denver (CO)
U of Georgia (GA)
U of Houston (TX)
U of Illinois at Chicago (IL)
U of Illinois at Urbana–Champaign (IL)
The U of Iowa (IA)
U of Maryland, Coll Park (MD)
U of Massachusetts Amherst (MA)
U of Massachusetts Boston (MA)
U of Michigan (MI)
U of Minnesota, Twin Cities Campus (MN)
U of Notre Dame (IN)
U of Oregon (OR)
U of Ottawa (ON, Canada)
U of Pennsylvania (PA)
U of Pittsburgh (PA)
U of Rhode Island (RI)
The U of Scranton (PA)
U of South Carolina (SC)
U of Southern California (CA)
U of South Florida (FL)
The U of Tennessee (TN)
The U of Texas at Austin (TX)
U of Toronto (ON, Canada)
U of Victoria (BC, Canada)
U of Virginia (VA)
The U of Western Ontario (ON, Canada)
U of Windsor (ON, Canada)
U of Wisconsin–Madison (WI)
U of Wisconsin–Milwaukee (WI)
Vassar Coll (NY)
Villanova U (PA)
Washington U in St. Louis (MO)
Wellesley Coll (MA)
Wesleyan U (CT)
Yale U (CT)
York Coll of the City U of New York (NY)
York U (ON, Canada)
Youngstown State U (OH)

ITALIAN STUDIES

Brock U (ON, Canada)
Brown U (RI)
Connecticut Coll (CT)
McGill U (QC, Canada)
Miami U (OH)
Santa Clara U (CA)
Sweet Briar Coll (VA)
U of California, Santa Cruz (CA)
U of Vermont (VT)
U of Victoria (BC, Canada)
U of Windsor (ON, Canada)
The U of Winnipeg (MB, Canada)
Wellesley Coll (MA)
Wheaton Coll (MA)
York U (ON, Canada)

JAPANESE

Aquinas Coll (MI)
Augustana Coll (IL)
Ball State U (IN)
Bates Coll (ME)
Bennington Coll (VT)
Brigham Young U (UT)
California State U, Fullerton (CA)
California State U, Long Beach (CA)
California State U, Los Angeles (CA)
Carnegie Mellon U (PA)
Claremont McKenna Coll (CA)
Colgate U (NY)
Connecticut Coll (CT)
Dartmouth Coll (NH)
Dillard U (LA)
Eastern Michigan U (MI)
Emory U (GA)
Georgetown U (DC)
Gettysburg Coll (PA)
Gustavus Adolphus Coll (MN)
Harvard U (MA)
Hobart and William Smith Colls (NY)
Hope Coll (MI)
Lawrence U (WI)
Lincoln U (PA)
Linfield Coll (OR)
Middlebury Coll (VT)
North Central Coll (IL)
Pacific U (OR)
Penn State Abington (PA)
Penn State Altoona (PA)
Penn State Berks (PA)
Penn State Erie, The Behrend Coll (PA)
Penn State U Park (PA)
Pomona Coll (CA)
Portland State U (OR)
Purdue U (IN)
San Diego State U (CA)
San Francisco State U (CA)
Sarah Lawrence Coll (NY)
Scripps Coll (CA)
Stanford U (CA)
Trinity Coll (CT)
U of Alaska Fairbanks (AK)
The U of British Columbia (BC, Canada)
U of California, Berkeley (CA)
U of California, Davis (CA)
U of California, Irvine (CA)
U of California, Los Angeles (CA)
U of California, San Diego (CA)
U of California, Santa Barbara (CA)
U of Chicago (IL)
U of Colorado at Boulder (CO)
The U of Findlay (OH)
U of Georgia (GA)
U of Hawaii at Manoa (HI)
The U of Iowa (IA)
U of Maryland, Coll Park (MD)
U of Massachusetts Amherst (MA)
U of Michigan (MI)
U of Minnesota, Twin Cities Campus (MN)
The U of Montana (MT)
U of Notre Dame (IN)
U of Oregon (OR)
U of Pittsburgh (PA)
U of Regina (SK, Canada)
U of Rochester (NY)
U of St. Thomas (MN)
U of the Pacific (CA)
U of Utah (UT)
U of Vermont (VT)
U of Victoria (BC, Canada)
The U of Western Ontario (ON, Canada)
U of Windsor (ON, Canada)
U of Wisconsin–Madison (WI)
Vassar Coll (NY)
Wake Forest U (NC)
Washington U in St. Louis (MO)
Wellesley Coll (MA)
Williams Coll (MA)
Yale U (CT)
York U (ON, Canada)

JAPANESE STUDIES

Adrian Coll (MI)
Case Western Reserve U (OH)
Claremont McKenna Coll (CA)
Earlham Coll (IN)
Gettysburg Coll (PA)
Gustavus Adolphus Coll (MN)
Purdue U (IN)
U at Albany, State U of New York (NY)
Willamette U (OR)

JAZZ

The New School for Jazz and Contemporary Music (NY)

JAZZ/JAZZ STUDIES

Augustana Coll (IL)
Bard Coll (NY)
Bard Coll at Simon's Rock (MA)
Bennington Coll (VT)
Berklee Coll of Music (MA)
Brigham Young U (UT)
California Inst of the Arts (CA)
Capital U (OH)
Central State U (OH)
City Coll of the City U of New York (NY)
Concordia U (QC, Canada)
DePaul U (IL)
Drake U (IA)
Five Towns Coll (NY)
Florida Ag and Mech U (FL)
Florida State U (FL)
Hampton U (VA)
Hofstra U (NY)
Hope Coll (MI)
Ithaca Coll (NY)
Johnson State Coll (VT)
Limestone Coll (SC)
Loyola U New Orleans (LA)
Manhattan School of Music (NY)
McGill U (QC, Canada)
Michigan State U (MI)
New England Conservatory of Music (MA)
The New School for Jazz and Contemporary Music (NY)
North Carolina Central U (NC)
North Central Coll (IL)
Northwestern U (IL)
Oberlin Coll (OH)
Peabody Conservatory of Music of The Johns Hopkins U (MD)
Roosevelt U (IL)
Rutgers, The State U of New Jersey, New Brunswick (NJ)
St. Cloud State U (MN)
St. Francis Xavier U (NS, Canada)
Sarah Lawrence Coll (NY)
Temple U (PA)
Texas Southern U (TX)
Texas State U-San Marcos (TX)
The U of Akron (OH)
U of Cincinnati (OH)
U of Hartford (CT)
U of Illinois at Urbana–Champaign (IL)
The U of Iowa (IA)
U of Louisiana at Lafayette (LA)
U of Miami (FL)
U of Michigan (MI)
U of Minnesota, Duluth (MN)
U of Nevada, Las Vegas (NV)
The U of North Carolina at Greensboro (NC)
U of North Florida (FL)
U of North Texas (TX)
U of Oregon (OR)
U of Rochester (NY)
U of Southern California (CA)
Western Michigan U (MI)
Western Washington U (WA)
William Paterson U of New Jersey (NJ)

JEWISH/JUDAIC STUDIES

American Jewish U (CA)
American U (DC)
Bard Coll (NY)
Barnard Coll (NY)
Brandeis U (MA)
Brown U (RI)
California State U, Chico (CA)
City Coll of the City U of New York (NY)
Clark U (MA)
Concordia U (QC, Canada)
DePaul U (IL)
Dickinson Coll (PA)
Emory U (GA)
Florida Atlantic U (FL)
The George Washington U (DC)
Hamline U (MN)
Harvard U (MA)
Hebrew Coll (MA)
Hofstra U (NY)
Hunter Coll of the City U of New York (NY)
Indiana U Bloomington (IN)
Lehman Coll of the City U of New York (NY)
List Coll, The Jewish Theological Sem (NY)
McGill U (QC, Canada)
Mount Holyoke Coll (MA)
New York U (NY)
Oberlin Coll (OH)
Penn State Abington (PA)
Penn State Altoona (PA)
Penn State Berks (PA)
Penn State Erie, The Behrend Coll (PA)
Penn State U Park (PA)
Queens Coll of the City U of New York (NY)
Rutgers, The State U of New Jersey, New Brunswick (NJ)
San Diego State U (CA)
San Francisco State U (CA)
Scripps Coll (CA)
State U of New York at Binghamton (NY)
Talmudic Coll of Florida (FL)
Temple U (PA)
Trinity Coll (CT)
Tufts U (MA)
Tulane U (LA)
U at Albany, State U of New York (NY)
The U of Arizona (AZ)
U of California, San Diego (CA)
U of Chicago (IL)
U of Cincinnati (OH)
U of Florida (FL)
U of Hartford (CT)
U of Maryland, Coll Park (MD)
U of Massachusetts Amherst (MA)
U of Miami (FL)
U of Michigan (MI)

U of Minnesota, Twin Cities Campus (MN)
U of Oregon (OR)
U of Pennsylvania (PA)
U of Southern California (CA)
The U of Texas at Austin (TX)
U of Toronto (ON, Canada)
The U of Western Ontario (ON, Canada)
Vassar Coll (NY)
Washington U in St. Louis (MO)
Wellesley Coll (MA)
Yale U (CT)
York U (ON, Canada)

JOURNALISM

Abilene Christian U (TX)
Adrian Coll (MI)
Alabama State U (AL)
Allegheny Coll (PA)
Alliant Intl U (CA)
American U (DC)
The American U of Athens (Greece)
Anderson U (SC)
Andrews U (MI)
Angelo State U (TX)
Appalachian State U (NC)
Arizona State U (AZ)
Arkansas State U (AR)
Asbury Coll (KY)
Ashford U (IA)
Ashland U (OH)
Auburn U (AL)
Augustana Coll (SD)
Averett U (VA)
Ball State U (IN)
Barry U (FL)
Baylor U (TX)
Belmont U (TN)
Bemidji State U (MN)
Bennington Coll (VT)
Bernard M. Baruch Coll of the City U of New York (NY)
Boston U (MA)
Bowling Green State U (OH)
Bradley U (IL)
Brigham Young U (UT)
Buffalo State Coll, State U of New York (NY)
Butler U (IN)
California Baptist U (CA)
California Lutheran U (CA)
California Polytechnic State U, San Luis Obispo (CA)
California State Polytechnic U, Pomona (CA)
California State U, Chico (CA)
California State U, East Bay (CA)
California State U, Fresno (CA)
California State U, Fullerton (CA)
California State U, Long Beach (CA)
California State U, Sacramento (CA)
Carroll Coll (WI)
Carson-Newman Coll (TN)
Castleton State Coll (VT)
Central Michigan U (MI)
Central Washington U (WA)
Chatham U (PA)
The Coll at Brockport, State U of New York (NY)
The Coll of St. Scholastica (MN)
Coll of the Ozarks (MO)
Colorado State U (CO)
Columbia Coll (SC)
Columbia Coll Chicago (IL)
Concordia Coll (MN)
Concordia U (MI)
Concordia U (QC, Canada)
Creighton U (NE)
Curry Coll (MA)
Delta State U (MS)
Doane Coll (NE)
Dordt Coll (IA)
Drake U (IA)
Duquesne U (PA)
Eastern Illinois U (IL)
Eastern Kentucky U (KY)
Eastern Michigan U (MI)
Edinboro U of Pennsylvania (PA)
Elon U (NC)
Emerson Coll (MA)
Emory U (GA)
Eugene Lang Coll The New School for Liberal Arts (NY)
Florida Ag and Mech U (FL)
Florida Southern Coll (FL)
Franklin Coll (IN)
Gannon U (PA)
Gardner-Webb U (NC)
The George Washington U (DC)
Georgia Coll & State U (GA)
Georgia Southern U (GA)
Georgia State U (GA)
Gettysburg Coll (PA)
Gonzaga U (WA)
Grace Coll (IN)
Grand Valley State U (MI)
Grand View Coll (IA)
Hampton U (VA)
Hastings Coll (NE)
Hawai'i Pacific U (HI)
Henderson State U (AR)
Hofstra U (NY)
Humboldt State U (CA)
Huntington U (IN)
Illinois State U (IL)
Indiana U Bloomington (IN)
Indiana U of Pennsylvania (PA)
Indiana U–Purdue U Indianapolis (IN)
Indiana U Southeast (IN)
Iona Coll (NY)
Iowa State U of Science and Technology (IA)
Ithaca Coll (NY)
John Brown U (AR)
Johnson State Coll (VT)
Kansas State U (KS)
Keene State Coll (NH)
Kent State U (OH)
Kwantlen U Coll (BC, Canada)
La Salle U (PA)
Lehigh U (PA)
Lewis U (IL)
Liberty U (VA)
Lincoln U (MO)
Lincoln U (PA)
Lindenwood U (MO)
Lindsey Wilson Coll (KY)
Lipscomb U (TN)
Lock Haven U of Pennsylvania (PA)
Longwood U (VA)
Loras Coll (IA)
Louisiana Coll (LA)
Loyola U Chicago (IL)
Lynchburg Coll (VA)
Lyndon State Coll (VT)
Madonna U (MI)
Mansfield U of Pennsylvania (PA)
Marietta Coll (OH)
Marist Coll (NY)
Marquette U (WI)
Marshall U (WV)
Mercer U (GA)
Mercyhurst Coll (PA)
Messiah Coll (PA)
Miami U (OH)
Miami U Hamilton (OH)
Michigan State U (MI)
Midland Lutheran Coll (NE)
Minnesota State U Mankato (MN)
Missouri State U (MO)
Mount Mercy Coll (IA)
Mount Vernon Nazarene U (OH)
Multnomah Bible Coll and Biblical Sem (OR)
Murray State U (KY)
New England Coll (NH)
New York U (NY)
North Central Coll (IL)
Northeastern State U (OK)
Northeastern U (MA)
Northern Arizona U (AZ)
Northern Illinois U (IL)
North Greenville U (SC)
Northwestern Coll (IA)
Northwestern Coll (MN)
Northwestern State U of Louisiana (LA)
Northwestern U (IL)
Northwest Missouri State U (MO)
Northwest Nazarene U (ID)
Oakland U (MI)
Ohio Northern U (OH)
Ohio U (OH)
Ohio Wesleyan U (OH)
Oklahoma Christian U (OK)
Oklahoma City U (OK)
Oklahoma State U (OK)
Otterbein Coll (OH)
Pacific Union Coll (CA)
Pacific U (OR)
Paine Coll (GA)
Palm Beach Atlantic U (FL)
Patrick Henry Coll (VA)
Penn State Abington (PA)
Penn State Altoona (PA)
Penn State Berks (PA)
Penn State Erie, The Behrend Coll (PA)
Penn State U Park (PA)
Pepperdine U, Malibu (CA)
Pfeiffer U (NC)
Pittsburg State U (KS)
Point Loma Nazarene U (CA)
Point Park U (PA)
Polytechnic U, Brooklyn Campus (NY)
Purchase Coll, State U of New York (NY)
Purdue U (IN)
Purdue U Calumet (IN)
Queens U of Charlotte (NC)
Quincy U (IL)
Quinnipiac U (CT)
Radford U (VA)
Rider U (NJ)
Roosevelt U (IL)
Rutgers, The State U of New Jersey, Newark (NJ)
Rutgers, The State U of New Jersey, New Brunswick (NJ)
Sacred Heart U (CT)
St. Ambrose U (IA)
St. Cloud State U (MN)
Saint Francis U (PA)
St. Gregory's U, Shawnee (OK)
St. John's U (NY)
Saint Mary-of-the-Woods Coll (IN)
St. Mary's Coll of Maryland (MD)
Saint Mary's U of Minnesota (MN)
Saint Michael's Coll (VT)
St. Thomas Aquinas Coll (NY)
St. Thomas U (NB, Canada)
Salem State Coll (MA)
Samford U (AL)
Sam Houston State U (TX)
San Diego State U (CA)
San Francisco State U (CA)
Seattle U (WA)
Seton Hill U (PA)
Shippensburg U of Pennsylvania (PA)
South Dakota State U (SD)
Southeastern U (FL)
Southern Adventist U (TN)
Southern Arkansas U–Magnolia (AR)
Southern Connecticut State U (CT)
Southern Illinois U Carbondale (IL)
Southern Methodist U (TX)
Southwestern Adventist U (TX)
Spring Hill Coll (AL)
State U of New York at New Paltz (NY)
State U of New York at Oswego (NY)
State U of New York at Plattsburgh (NY)
Stephen F. Austin State U (TX)
Stony Brook U, State U of New York (NY)
Suffolk U (MA)
Susquehanna U (PA)
Syracuse U (NY)
Tabor Coll (KS)
Temple U (PA)
Tennessee Technological U (TN)
Texas A&M U (TX)
Texas A&M U–Commerce (TX)
Texas Christian U (TX)
Texas Southern U (TX)
Texas State U-San Marcos (TX)
Texas Tech U (TX)
Thomas Edison State Coll (NJ)
Thompson Rivers U (BC, Canada)
Troy U (AL)
Truman State U (MO)
Union Coll (NE)
Union U (TN)
The U of Alabama (AL)
U of Alaska Fairbanks (AK)
The U of Arizona (AZ)
U of Arkansas (AR)
U of Arkansas at Monticello (AR)
U of Baltimore (MD)
U of Bridgeport (CT)
U of California, Irvine (CA)
U of Central Arkansas (AR)
U of Central Florida (FL)
U of Central Missouri (MO)
U of Central Oklahoma (OK)
U of Colorado at Boulder (CO)
U of Connecticut (CT)
U of Dayton (OH)
U of Delaware (DE)
U of Denver (CO)
The U of Findlay (OH)
U of Florida (FL)
U of Georgia (GA)
U of Hawaii at Manoa (HI)
U of Houston (TX)
U of Idaho (ID)
U of Illinois at Urbana–Champaign (IL)
The U of Iowa (IA)
U of Kansas (KS)
U of King's Coll (NS, Canada)
U of La Verne (CA)
U of Maine (ME)
U of Maryland, Coll Park (MD)
U of Massachusetts Amherst (MA)
U of Memphis (TN)
U of Miami (FL)
U of Minnesota, Twin Cities Campus (MN)
U of Mississippi (MS)
U of Missouri–Columbia (MO)
The U of Montana (MT)
U of Nebraska at Kearney (NE)
U of Nebraska at Omaha (NE)
U of Nevada, Reno (NV)
U of New Hampshire (NH)
U of New Mexico (NM)
U of Northern Colorado (CO)
U of North Texas (TX)
U of Oklahoma (OK)
U of Oregon (OR)
U of Ottawa (ON, Canada)
U of Pittsburgh at Johnstown (PA)
U of Portland (OR)
U of Regina (SK, Canada)
U of Rhode Island (RI)
U of Richmond (VA)
U of St. Thomas (MN)
U of South Carolina (SC)
U of Southern California (CA)
U of Southern Indiana (IN)
U of Southern Mississippi (MS)
The U of Tennessee (TN)
The U of Texas at Arlington (TX)
The U of Texas at Austin (TX)
The U of Texas at El Paso (TX)
The U of Texas at Tyler (TX)
The U of Texas–Pan American (TX)
U of the Sacred Heart (PR)
The U of Toledo (OH)
U of West Georgia (GA)
U of Windsor (ON, Canada)
The U of Winnipeg (MB, Canada)
U of Wisconsin–Eau Claire (WI)
U of Wisconsin–Madison (WI)
U of Wisconsin–Milwaukee (WI)
U of Wisconsin–Oshkosh (WI)
U of Wisconsin–Superior (WI)
U of Wisconsin–Whitewater (WI)
U of Wyoming (WY)
Utah State U (UT)
Utica Coll (NY)
Valparaiso U (IN)
Walla Walla U (WA)
Wartburg Coll (IA)
Washington and Lee U (VA)
Waynesburg U (PA)
Wayne State U (MI)
Weber State U (UT)
Webster U (MO)
Western Illinois U (IL)
Western Kentucky U (KY)
Western Michigan U (MI)
Western Washington U (WA)
West Texas A&M U (TX)
West Virginia U (WV)
Wheeling Jesuit U (WV)
Whitworth U (WA)
Wilfrid Laurier U (ON, Canada)
Winona State U (MN)
Youngstown State U (OH)

JOURNALISM RELATED

Arizona State U (AZ)
Bob Jones U (SC)
Boston U (MA)
California State U, Long Beach (CA)
Central State U (OH)
Columbia Coll (SC)
Dana Coll (NE)
Kent State U (OH)
Kentucky State U (KY)
Ohio U (OH)
Roosevelt U (IL)
Texas Southern U (TX)
The U of Akron (OH)
U of Nebraska–Lincoln (NE)
U of Oregon (OR)
U of St. Thomas (MN)
The U of Western Ontario (ON, Canada)

JUDAIC STUDIES

Hampshire Coll (MA)
Michigan Jewish Inst (MI)
San Diego State U (CA)
The U of Arizona (AZ)

JUVENILE CORRECTIONS

East Central U (OK)
Harris-Stowe State U (MO)

KINDERGARTEN/ PRESCHOOL EDUCATION

Alabama Ag and Mech U (AL)
Alabama State U (AL)
Albright Coll (PA)
Alma Coll (MI)
Anna Maria Coll (MA)
Appalachian State U (NC)
Armstrong Atlantic State U (GA)
Ashford U (IA)
Ashland U (OH)
Athens State U (AL)
Atlantic Union Coll (MA)
Auburn U (AL)
Augsburg Coll (MN)
Ball State U (IN)
Barry U (FL)
Baylor U (TX)
Bay Path Coll (MA)
Bethany U (CA)
Bluefield Coll (VA)
Bluffton U (OH)
Boise State U (ID)
Boston Coll (MA)
Boston U (MA)
Bowling Green State U (OH)
Bryan Coll (TN)
Bucknell U (PA)
Buffalo State Coll, State U of New York (NY)
Butler U (IN)
Cabrini Coll (PA)
Carson-Newman Coll (TN)
The Catholic U of America (DC)
Central Washington U (WA)
Cheyney U of Pennsylvania (PA)
Clarion U of Pennsylvania (PA)
Clarke Coll (IA)
The Coll of New Jersey (NJ)
Columbia Coll (SC)
Columbia Coll Chicago (IL)
Concordia Coll (MN)
Concordia U (OR)
Concordia U (QC, Canada)
Concordia U Chicago (IL)
Concordia U, Nebraska (NE)
Concordia U Wisconsin (WI)
Concord U (WV)
Converse Coll (SC)
Curry Coll (MA)
Dallas Baptist U (TX)
Dillard U (LA)
East Central U (OK)
Eastern Connecticut State U (CT)
Eastern Illinois U (IL)
Eastern Kentucky U (KY)
Eastern Mennonite U (VA)
Eastern New Mexico U (NM)
Elizabethtown Coll (PA)
Erskine Coll (SC)
Evangel U (MO)
Faulkner U (AL)
Florida Ag and Mech U (FL)
Florida Southern Coll (FL)
Florida State U (FL)
Fontbonne U (MO)
Frostburg State U (MD)
Furman U (SC)
Gardner-Webb U (NC)
Glenville State Coll (WV)
Grambling State U (LA)
Greensboro Coll (NC)
Grove City Coll (PA)
Hampton U (VA)
Hannibal-LaGrange Coll (MO)
Harris-Stowe State U (MO)
High Point U (NC)
Hillsdale Coll (MI)
Holy Family U (PA)
Houston Baptist U (TX)
Howard Payne U (TX)
Humboldt State U (CA)
Hunter Coll of the City U of New York (NY)
Indiana U of Pennsylvania (PA)
Inter American U of Puerto Rico, Aguadilla Campus (PR)
Inter American U of Puerto Rico, San Germán Campus (PR)
Iowa Wesleyan Coll (IA)
Jacksonville State U (AL)
Jarvis Christian Coll (TX)
John Brown U (AR)
John Carroll U (OH)
Juniata Coll (PA)
Kean U (NJ)
Keene State Coll (NH)
Kent State U (OH)
King Coll (TN)
Kutztown U of Pennsylvania (PA)
Lenoir-Rhyne Coll (NC)
Lesley U (MA)
Lincoln U (PA)
Lindenwood U (MO)
Livingstone Coll (NC)
Lock Haven U of Pennsylvania (PA)
Longwood U (VA)
Loras Coll (IA)
Louisiana Coll (LA)
Lourdes Coll (OH)
Lynchburg Coll (VA)
Mansfield U of Pennsylvania (PA)
Maranatha Baptist Bible Coll (WI)
Marian Coll of Fond du Lac (WI)
Martin U (IN)
Maryville U of Saint Louis (MO)
McNeese State U (LA)
Methodist U (NC)
Metropolitan State U (MN)
Miami U (OH)
Middle Tennessee State U (TN)
Midland Lutheran Coll (NE)
Minnesota State U Mankato (MN)
Mississippi Valley State U (MS)
Missouri Baptist U (MO)
Morehead State U (KY)
Mount Aloysius Coll (PA)
Mount Ida Coll (MA)

MAJORS AND MORE

Mount Mary Coll (WI)
Mount Saint Vincent U (NS, Canada)
Mount Vernon Nazarene U (OH)
National-Louis U (IL)
Neumann Coll (PA)
New Jersey City U (NJ)
New Mexico Highlands U (NM)
New York U (NY)
North Carolina Ag and Tech State U (NC)
North Carolina Central U (NC)
Northeastern Illinois U (IL)
Northeastern State U (OK)
Northeastern U (MA)
Northern Illinois U (IL)
North Georgia Coll & State U (GA)
North Greenville U (SC)
Northwestern Oklahoma State U (OK)
Northwest Missouri State U (MO)
Ohio Dominican U (OH)
Ohio Northern U (OH)
Ohio U (OH)
Ohio Wesleyan U (OH)
Oklahoma Christian U (OK)
Oklahoma City U (OK)
Oregon State U (OR)
Pacific Union Coll (CA)
Pacific U (OR)
Peru State Coll (NE)
Philadelphia Biblical U (PA)
Piedmont Coll (GA)
Prescott Coll (AZ)
Purdue U (IN)
Rhode Island Coll (RI)
Roosevelt U (IL)
Rowan U (NJ)
Sacred Heart U (CT)
St. Cloud State U (MN)
Saint Joseph Coll (CT)
St. Joseph's Coll, Suffolk Campus (NY)
Saint Mary-of-the-Woods Coll (IN)
St. Thomas Aquinas Coll (NY)
Saint Xavier U (IL)
Salem State Coll (MA)
Sarah Lawrence Coll (NY)
Seton Hill U (PA)
Shawnee State U (OH)
Shaw U (NC)
Siena Heights U (MI)
Simmons Coll (MA)
Simpson Coll (IA)
Southeastern Oklahoma State U (OK)
Southeast Missouri State U (MO)
Southern Adventist U (TN)
Southern Arkansas U–Magnolia (AR)
Southern Wesleyan U (SC)
Southwest Minnesota State U (MN)
State U of New York at Fredonia (NY)
Stephens Coll (MO)
Susquehanna U (PA)
Tabor Coll (KS)
Taylor U (IN)
Tennessee State U (TN)
Tennessee Technological U (TN)
Texas A&M Intl U (TX)
Texas A&M U–Commerce (TX)
Texas Southern U (TX)
Thomas U (GA)
Tougaloo Coll (MS)
Troy U (AL)
Tufts U (MA)
Union U (TN)
Université de Sherbrooke (QC, Canada)
Université du Québec en Outaouais (QC, Canada)
The U of Alabama at Birmingham (AL)
The U of Arizona (AZ)
U of Arkansas at Pine Bluff (AR)
The U of British Columbia (BC, Canada)
U of Central Arkansas (AR)
U of Central Oklahoma (OK)
U of Cincinnati (OH)
U of Dayton (OH)
U of Delaware (DE)
U of Great Falls (MT)
U of Guam (GU)
U of Illinois at Urbana–Champaign (IL)
U of Mary Hardin-Baylor (TX)
U of Maryland, Coll Park (MD)
U of Maryland Eastern Shore (MD)
U of Minnesota, Duluth (MN)
U of Minnesota, Twin Cities Campus (MN)
U of Missouri–Columbia (MO)
U of Nevada, Las Vegas (NV)
U of New Brunswick Fredericton (NB, Canada)
U of New Hampshire (NH)
U of North Alabama (AL)
The U of North Carolina at Charlotte (NC)
The U of North Carolina at Pembroke (NC)
The U of North Carolina Wilmington (NC)
U of Northern Iowa (IA)
U of Regina (SK, Canada)
The U of Scranton (PA)
U of South Carolina Aiken (SC)
U of South Carolina Upstate (SC)
U of South Florida (FL)
The U of Tennessee at Martin (TN)
U of the District of Columbia (DC)
The U of Toledo (OH)
U of Vermont (VT)
U of Victoria (BC, Canada)
The U of Western Ontario (ON, Canada)
U of Windsor (ON, Canada)
U of Wisconsin–Madison (WI)
U of Wisconsin–Milwaukee (WI)
U of Wisconsin–Oshkosh (WI)
U of Wisconsin–Platteville (WI)
U of Wisconsin–Stevens Point (WI)
Utah State U (UT)
Utah Valley State Coll (UT)
Vanderbilt U (TN)
Voorhees Coll (SC)
Wagner Coll (NY)
Walsh U (OH)
Wartburg Coll (IA)
Washington Bible Coll (MD)
Washington State U (WA)
Weber State U (UT)
Western New Mexico U (NM)
Western Washington U (WA)
Westfield State Coll (MA)
West Liberty State Coll (WV)
West Virginia Wesleyan Coll (WV)
Wheelock Coll (MA)
Whittier Coll (CA)
Widener U (PA)
Winona State U (MN)
Winthrop U (SC)
Worcester State Coll (MA)
Wright State U (OH)
York U (ON, Canada)

KINESIOLOGY AND EXERCISE SCIENCE

Acadia U (NS, Canada)
Adams State Coll (CO)
Adrian Coll (MI)
Alma Coll (MI)
Anderson U (SC)
Appalachian State U (NC)
Arizona State U (AZ)
Arkansas State U (AR)
Augustana Coll (SD)
Baker U (KS)
Ball State U (IN)
Barry U (FL)
Bastyr U (WA)
Becker Coll (MA)
Belhaven Coll (MS)
Bethany Lutheran Coll (MN)
Bethel U (MN)
Biola U (CA)
Bluefield Coll (VA)
Boise State U (ID)
Boston U (MA)
Brevard Coll (NC)
Bridgewater Coll (VA)
Bridgewater State Coll (MA)
Brigham Young U (UT)
Brock U (ON, Canada)
Bryan Coll (TN)
Buffalo State Coll, State U of New York (NY)
Cabrini Coll (PA)
California Baptist U (CA)
California Lutheran U (CA)
California Polytechnic State U, San Luis Obispo (CA)
California State U, Chico (CA)
California State U, East Bay (CA)
California State U, Long Beach (CA)
California State U, Los Angeles (CA)
California State U, Sacramento (CA)
Calvin Coll (MI)
Capital U (OH)
Carroll Coll (WI)
Carson-Newman Coll (TN)
Castleton State Coll (VT)
Cedarville U (OH)
Centenary Coll of Louisiana (LA)
Central Christian Coll of Kansas (KS)
Central Coll (IA)
Central Michigan U (MI)
Central Washington U (WA)
Chatham U (PA)
Clearwater Christian Coll (FL)
Cleveland State U (OH)
Coker Coll (SC)
Colby-Sawyer Coll (NH)
The Coll at Brockport, State U of New York (NY)
The Coll of Idaho (ID)
Colorado State U (CO)
Colorado State U-Pueblo (CO)
Columbus State U (GA)
Concordia Coll (MN)
Concordia U (CA)
Concordia U (QC, Canada)
Concordia U Chicago (IL)
Concordia U, Nebraska (NE)
Concordia U, St. Paul (MN)
Concordia U Texas (TX)
Cornerstone U (MI)
Creighton U (NE)
Dakota State U (SD)
Davis & Elkins Coll (WV)
Defiance Coll (OH)
DePauw U (IN)
DeSales U (PA)
Dordt Coll (IA)
Drury U (MO)
East Carolina U (NC)
East Stroudsburg U of Pennsylvania (PA)
Emmanuel Coll (GA)
Fitchburg State Coll (MA)
Florida Atlantic U (FL)
Florida Gulf Coast U (FL)
Florida Intl U (FL)
Florida State U (FL)
Fort Lewis Coll (CO)
Frostburg State U (MD)
Furman U (SC)
Gannon U (PA)
Georgetown Coll (KY)
The George Washington U (DC)
Georgia Southern U (GA)
Georgia State U (GA)
Gonzaga U (WA)
Gordon Coll (MA)
Greensboro Coll (NC)
Greenville Coll (IL)
Hamline U (MN)
Harding U (AR)
Hardin-Simmons U (TX)
Hastings Coll (NE)
Hendrix Coll (AR)
High Point U (NC)
Hope Coll (MI)
Houston Baptist U (TX)
Howard Payne U (TX)
Humboldt State U (CA)
Huntingdon Coll (AL)
Huntington U (IN)
Illinois State U (IL)
Immaculata U (PA)
Indiana Wesleyan U (IN)
Iowa Wesleyan Coll (IA)
Ithaca Coll (NY)
Jacksonville State U (AL)
Jacksonville U (FL)
Jefferson Coll of Health Sciences (VA)
John Brown U (AR)
Johnson State Coll (VT)
Kansas State U (KS)
Kennesaw State U (GA)
Kent State U (OH)
Kuyper Coll (MI)
Lake Superior State U (MI)
Lander U (SC)
La Sierra U (CA)
Laurentian U (ON, Canada)
Lenoir-Rhyne Coll (NC)
Lewis-Clark State Coll (ID)
Liberty U (VA)
Linfield Coll (OR)
Lipscomb U (TN)
Longwood U (VA)
Loras Coll (IA)
Louisiana Coll (LA)
Lubbock Christian U (TX)
Lynchburg Coll (VA)
Malone Coll (OH)
Marquette U (WI)
Marymount U (VA)
The Master's Coll and Sem (CA)
Mayville State U (ND)
McDaniel Coll (MD)
McGill U (QC, Canada)
McNeese State U (LA)
Memorial U of Newfoundland (NL, Canada)
Meredith Coll (NC)
Mesa State Coll (CO)
Messiah Coll (PA)
Miami U (OH)
Michigan State U (MI)
MidAmerica Nazarene U (KS)
Midwestern State U (TX)
Mississippi Coll (MS)
Mississippi U for Women (MS)
Morehead State U (KY)
Mount Vernon Nazarene U (OH)
Murray State U (KY)
Nebraska Wesleyan U (NE)
North Central Coll (IL)
Northeastern State U (OK)
Northern Arizona U (AZ)
Northern Michigan U (MI)
Northwestern Coll (IA)
Northwestern Coll (MN)
Northwest Nazarene U (ID)
Notre Dame de Namur U (CA)
Occidental Coll (CA)
Ohio Northern U (OH)
Ohio U (OH)
Oklahoma City U (OK)
Oklahoma Wesleyan U (OK)
Old Dominion U (VA)
Oral Roberts U (OK)
Oregon State U (OR)
Ouachita Baptist U (AR)
Pacific Union Coll (CA)
Pacific U (OR)
Penn State Abington (PA)
Penn State Altoona (PA)
Penn State Berks (PA)
Penn State Erie, The Behrend Coll (PA)
Penn State U Park (PA)
Pennsylvania Coll of Technology (PA)
Pepperdine U, Malibu (CA)
Point Loma Nazarene U (CA)
Purdue U (IN)
Queens Coll of the City U of New York (NY)
Redeemer U Coll (ON, Canada)
Rice U (TX)
Rutgers, The State U of New Jersey, New Brunswick (NJ)
Sacred Heart U (CT)
Saginaw Valley State U (MI)
St. Cloud State U (MN)
St. Edward's U (TX)
St. Francis Xavier U (NS, Canada)
Saint Louis U (MO)
Saint Mary's Coll of California (CA)
St. Mary's U (TX)
St. Olaf Coll (MN)
Salem State Coll (MA)
Samford U (AL)
Sam Houston State U (TX)
San Diego Christian Coll (CA)
Schreiner U (TX)
Seattle Pacific U (WA)
Shaw U (NC)
Shenandoah U (VA)
Shippensburg U of Pennsylvania (PA)
Simon Fraser U (BC, Canada)
Skidmore Coll (NY)
Slippery Rock U of Pennsylvania (PA)
Sonoma State U (CA)
Southern Adventist U (TN)
Southern Arkansas U–Magnolia (AR)
Southern Illinois U Carbondale (IL)
Southwestern Adventist U (TX)
Spring Arbor U (MI)
Stetson U (FL)
Tarleton State U (TX)
Tennessee Wesleyan Coll (TN)
Texas A&M U–Commerce (TX)
Texas Lutheran U (TX)
Towson U (MD)
Transylvania U (KY)
Trevecca Nazarene U (TN)
Trinity Christian Coll (IL)
Truman State U (MO)
Tulane U (LA)
Tusculum Coll (TN)
Union Coll (NE)
Union U (TN)
Université de Sherbrooke (QC, Canada)
U at Buffalo, the State U of New York (NY)
The U of Akron (OH)
U of Arkansas (AR)
The U of British Columbia (BC, Canada)
The U of British Columbia–Okanagan (BC, Canada)
U of Central Arkansas (AR)
U of Dayton (OH)
U of Delaware (DE)
U of Evansville (IN)
U of Florida (FL)
U of Hawaii at Manoa (HI)
U of Houston (TX)
U of Idaho (ID)
U of Illinois at Chicago (IL)
U of Illinois at Urbana–Champaign (IL)
U of Indianapolis (IN)
The U of Iowa (IA)
U of La Verne (CA)
U of Lethbridge (AB, Canada)
U of Mary (ND)
U of Massachusetts Amherst (MA)
U of Massachusetts Boston (MA)
U of Massachusetts Lowell (MA)
U of Memphis (TN)
U of Miami (FL)
U of Michigan (MI)
U of Minnesota, Duluth (MN)
U of Mississippi (MS)
U of Nevada, Las Vegas (NV)
U of New Brunswick Fredericton (NB, Canada)
U of New England (ME)
U of New Hampshire (NH)
The U of North Carolina at Greensboro (NC)
U of Northern Colorado (CO)
U of Puget Sound (WA)
U of Regina (SK, Canada)
The U of Scranton (PA)
U of Sioux Falls (SD)
U of South Carolina (SC)
U of South Carolina Aiken (SC)
U of Southern California (CA)
U of Southern Indiana (IN)
The U of Tampa (FL)
The U of Tennessee (TN)
The U of Tennessee at Chattanooga (TN)
The U of Texas at Tyler (TX)
The U of Texas of the Permian Basin (TX)
U of the Incarnate Word (TX)
U of the Pacific (CA)
U of the Sacred Heart (PR)
The U of Toledo (OH)
U of Tulsa (OK)
U of Utah (UT)
U of Vermont (VT)
U of Victoria (BC, Canada)
The U of Western Ontario (ON, Canada)
U of Windsor (ON, Canada)
U of Wisconsin–Eau Claire (WI)
U of Wisconsin–La Crosse (WI)
U of Wisconsin–Superior (WI)
U of Wyoming (WY)
Valdosta State U (GA)
Valparaiso U (IN)
Vanguard U of Southern California (CA)
Voorhees Coll (SC)
Wake Forest U (NC)
Walla Walla U (WA)
Warner Pacific Coll (OR)
Washington State U (WA)
Waynesburg U (PA)
Weber State U (UT)
Western Illinois U (IL)
Western Kentucky U (KY)
Western Michigan U (MI)
Western New Mexico U (NM)
Western State Coll of Colorado (CO)
Western Washington U (WA)
West Liberty State Coll (WV)
Westmont Coll (CA)
West Virginia U (WV)
West Virginia Wesleyan Coll (WV)
Wilfrid Laurier U (ON, Canada)
Willamette U (OR)
William Paterson U of New Jersey (NJ)
Wilson Coll (PA)
Winona State U (MN)
Youngstown State U (OH)

KINESIOTHERAPY

Bridgewater State Coll (MA)
California State U, Long Beach (CA)
U of Regina (SK, Canada)

KNOWLEDGE MANAGEMENT

Framingham State Coll (MA)

KOREAN

Brigham Young U (UT)
U of California, Los Angeles (CA)
U of Hawaii at Manoa (HI)

KOREAN STUDIES

Claremont McKenna Coll (CA)

LABOR AND INDUSTRIAL RELATIONS

Athabasca U (AB, Canada)
Brock U (ON, Canada)
California State U, Dominguez Hills (CA)
Clarion U of Pennsylvania (PA)
Cleveland State U (OH)
Cornell U (NY)
Grand Valley State U (MI)
Indiana U Bloomington (IN)
Indiana U–Purdue U Indianapolis (IN)
Ithaca Coll (NY)
Lakehead U (ON, Canada)
Le Moyne Coll (NY)

McGill U (QC, Canada)
Memorial U of Newfoundland (NL, Canada)
Penn State Abington (PA)
Penn State Altoona (PA)
Penn State Berks (PA)
Penn State Erie, The Behrend Coll (PA)
Penn State U Park (PA)
Rhode Island Coll (RI)
Roosevelt U (IL)
Rutgers, The State U of New Jersey, New Brunswick (NJ)
Saint Francis U (PA)
San Francisco State U (CA)
State U of New York at Fredonia (NY)
State U of New York Coll at Old Westbury (NY)
State U of New York Coll at Potsdam (NY)
State U of New York Empire State Coll (NY)
Temple U (PA)
Tennessee Technological U (TN)
Texas A&M U–Commerce (TX)
Université du Québec en Outaouais (QC, Canada)
The U of British Columbia (BC, Canada)
The U of Iowa (IA)
U of Maine (ME)
U of Massachusetts Boston (MA)
U of Toronto (ON, Canada)
U of Windsor (ON, Canada)
U of Wisconsin–Madison (WI)
U of Wisconsin–Milwaukee (WI)
Winona State U (MN)
York U (ON, Canada)

LABOR STUDIES
Eastern Michigan U (MI)
Hofstra U (NY)
Indiana U Bloomington (IN)
Indiana U Kokomo (IN)
Indiana U Northwest (IN)
Indiana U–Purdue U Fort Wayne (IN)
Indiana U South Bend (IN)
Queens Coll of the City U of New York (NY)
U of Windsor (ON, Canada)
Wayne State U (MI)

LANDSCAPE ARCHITECTURE
Arizona State U (AZ)
Auburn U (AL)
Ball State U (IN)
California Polytechnic State U, San Luis Obispo (CA)
California State Polytechnic U, Pomona (CA)
Clemson U (SC)
Coll of the Atlantic (ME)
Colorado State U (CO)
Cornell U (NY)
Florida Ag and Mech U (FL)
Iowa State U of Science and Technology (IA)
Kansas State U (KS)
Louisiana State U and Ag and Mech Coll (LA)
Michigan State U (MI)
Mississippi State U (MS)
North Carolina Ag and Tech State U (NC)
North Carolina State U (NC)
North Dakota State U (ND)
Northwest Missouri State U (MO)
Oklahoma State U (OK)
Penn State U Park (PA)
Philadelphia U (PA)
Purdue U (IN)
State U of New York Coll of Environmental Science and Forestry (NY)
Temple U (PA)
Texas A&M U (TX)
Texas Tech U (TX)
The U of Arizona (AZ)
U of Arkansas (AR)
The U of British Columbia (BC, Canada)
U of California, Berkeley (CA)
U of California, Davis (CA)
U of Connecticut (CT)
U of Florida (FL)
U of Georgia (GA)
U of Hawaii at Manoa (HI)
U of Idaho (ID)
U of Illinois at Urbana–Champaign (IL)
U of Maryland, Coll Park (MD)
U of Massachusetts Amherst (MA)
U of Michigan (MI)
U of Minnesota, Twin Cities Campus (MN)
U of Nebraska–Lincoln (NE)
U of Nevada, Las Vegas (NV)
U of Oregon (OR)
U of Rhode Island (RI)
U of Southern California (CA)
U of Wisconsin–Madison (WI)
Utah State U (UT)
Virginia Polytechnic Inst and State U (VA)
Washington State U (WA)
West Virginia U (WV)

LANDSCAPING AND GROUNDSKEEPING
American U of Beirut (Lebanon)
Andrews U (MI)
Colorado State U (CO)
Mississippi State U (MS)
Penn State Abington (PA)
Penn State Altoona (PA)
Penn State Berks (PA)
Penn State Erie, The Behrend Coll (PA)
Penn State U Park (PA)
South Dakota State U (SD)
Tennessee Technological U (TN)
U of Georgia (GA)
U of Maine (ME)
U of Nebraska–Lincoln (NE)

LAND USE PLANNING AND MANAGEMENT
Grand Valley State U (MI)
Northland Coll (WI)
State U of New York Coll of Environmental Science and Forestry (NY)
Sterling Coll (VT)
U of Wisconsin–Platteville (WI)

LANGUAGE INTERPRETATION AND TRANSLATION
Brigham Young U (UT)
Concordia U (QC, Canada)
Laurentian U (ON, Canada)
McGill U (QC, Canada)
Mississippi Coll (MS)
Quincy U (IL)
Université du Québec en Outaouais (QC, Canada)
U of Ottawa (ON, Canada)
York U (ON, Canada)

LASER AND OPTICAL TECHNOLOGY
Oregon Inst of Technology (OR)

LATIN
Acadia U (NS, Canada)
Amherst Coll (MA)
Augustana Coll (IL)
Austin Coll (TX)
Ball State U (IN)
Bard Coll (NY)
Bard Coll at Simon's Rock (MA)
Barnard Coll (NY)
Baylor U (TX)
Boston Coll (MA)
Boston U (MA)
Bowling Green State U (OH)
Brandeis U (MA)
Brigham Young U (UT)
Bryn Mawr Coll (PA)
Butler U (IN)
Calvin Coll (MI)
The Catholic U of America (DC)
Centenary Coll of Louisiana (LA)
Claremont McKenna Coll (CA)
Colgate U (NY)
The Coll of New Rochelle (NY)
The Coll of William and Mary (VA)
Concordia Coll (MN)
Cornell Coll (IA)
Creighton U (NE)
Dartmouth Coll (NH)
DePauw U (IN)
Duke U (NC)
Duquesne U (PA)
Emory U (GA)
Florida State U (FL)
Franklin & Marshall Coll (PA)
Furman U (SC)
Gettysburg Coll (PA)
Hamilton Coll (NY)
Hampden-Sydney Coll (VA)
Harvard U (MA)
Haverford Coll (PA)
Hobart and William Smith Colls (NY)
Hofstra U (NY)
Hope Coll (MI)
Hunter Coll of the City U of New York (NY)
John Carroll U (OH)
Kent State U (OH)
Kenyon Coll (OH)
Lawrence U (WI)
Lehman Coll of the City U of New York (NY)
Lenoir-Rhyne Coll (NC)
Louisiana State U and Ag and Mech Coll (LA)
Loyola Marymount U (CA)
Loyola U Chicago (IL)
Marlboro Coll (VT)
Memorial U of Newfoundland (NL, Canada)
Mercer U (GA)
Miami U (OH)
Miami U Hamilton (OH)
Missouri State U (MO)
Monmouth Coll (IL)
Montclair State U (NJ)
Mount Allison U (NB, Canada)
Mount Holyoke Coll (MA)
New York U (NY)
Oberlin Coll (OH)
Ohio U (OH)
Queens Coll of the City U of New York (NY)
Randolph Coll (VA)
Randolph-Macon Coll (VA)
Rhodes Coll (TN)
Rice U (TX)
Rockford Coll (IL)
Rutgers, The State U of New Jersey, New Brunswick (NJ)
Saint Joseph's U (PA)
Saint Mary's Coll of California (CA)
St. Olaf Coll (MN)
Samford U (AL)
Santa Clara U (CA)
Sarah Lawrence Coll (NY)
Scripps Coll (CA)
Seattle Pacific U (WA)
Sewanee: The U of the South (TN)
Smith Coll (MA)
Southwestern U (TX)
Stanford U (CA)
State U of New York at Binghamton (NY)
Swarthmore Coll (PA)
Tufts U (MA)
Tulane U (LA)
U at Albany, State U of New York (NY)
The U of British Columbia (BC, Canada)
U of California, Berkeley (CA)
U of California, Los Angeles (CA)
U of Chicago (IL)
U of Delaware (DE)
U of Georgia (GA)
U of Houston (TX)
U of Idaho (ID)
The U of Iowa (IA)
U of Maine (ME)
U of Maryland, Coll Park (MD)
U of Mary Washington (VA)
U of Michigan (MI)
U of Minnesota, Twin Cities Campus (MN)
U of Missouri–Columbia (MO)
The U of Montana (MT)
U of Nebraska–Lincoln (NE)
U of New Brunswick Fredericton (NB, Canada)
U of New Hampshire (NH)
U of Oregon (OR)
U of Ottawa (ON, Canada)
U of Richmond (VA)
U of St. Thomas (MN)
The U of Scranton (PA)
The U of Tennessee at Chattanooga (TN)
The U of Texas at Austin (TX)
U of Toronto (ON, Canada)
U of Vermont (VT)
U of Victoria (BC, Canada)
The U of Western Ontario (ON, Canada)
U of Windsor (ON, Canada)
The U of Winnipeg (MB, Canada)
U of Wisconsin–Madison (WI)
U of Wisconsin–Milwaukee (WI)
Vassar Coll (NY)
Wabash Coll (IN)
Wake Forest U (NC)
Washington U in St. Louis (MO)
Wellesley Coll (MA)
West Chester U of Pennsylvania (PA)
Western Michigan U (MI)
Wheaton Coll (MA)
Wichita State U (KS)
Wilfrid Laurier U (ON, Canada)
Yale U (CT)
York U (ON, Canada)

LATIN AMERICAN STUDIES
Adelphi U (NY)
Albright Coll (PA)
Alliant Intl U (CA)
Alliant Intl U–México City (Mexico)
American Public U System (WV)
American U (DC)
Assumption Coll (MA)
Ball State U (IN)
Bard Coll (NY)
Bard Coll at Simon's Rock (MA)
Barnard Coll (NY)
Baylor U (TX)
Beloit Coll (WI)
Boston U (MA)
Bowdoin Coll (ME)
Brandeis U (MA)
Brigham Young U (UT)
Brown U (RI)
Bucknell U (PA)
Burlington Coll (VT)
California State U, Chico (CA)
California State U, East Bay (CA)
California State U, Fullerton (CA)
California State U, Los Angeles (CA)
Carnegie Mellon U (PA)
City Coll of the City U of New York (NY)
Claremont McKenna Coll (CA)
Colby Coll (ME)
Colgate U (NY)
The Coll at Brockport, State U of New York (NY)
Coll of Charleston (SC)
The Coll of William and Mary (VA)
Colorado State U (CO)
Connecticut Coll (CT)
Cornell Coll (IA)
Dartmouth Coll (NH)
Denison U (OH)
DePaul U (IL)
Earlham Coll (IN)
Edinboro U of Pennsylvania (PA)
Emory U (GA)
Flagler Coll (FL)
Florida State U (FL)
Fort Lewis Coll (CO)
George Mason U (VA)
The George Washington U (DC)
Gettysburg Coll (PA)
Gustavus Adolphus Coll (MN)
Hamline U (MN)
Hampshire Coll (MA)
Hanover Coll (IN)
Harvard U (MA)
Haverford Coll (PA)
Hobart and William Smith Colls (NY)
Hofstra U (NY)
Hood Coll (MD)
Hunter Coll of the City U of New York (NY)
Illinois Wesleyan U (IL)
Indiana U Bloomington (IN)
The Johns Hopkins U (MD)
Kent State U (OH)
Lake Forest Coll (IL)
Lehman Coll of the City U of New York (NY)
Lock Haven U of Pennsylvania (PA)
Macalester Coll (MN)
Marlboro Coll (VT)
McGill U (QC, Canada)
Middlebury Coll (VT)
Mount Holyoke Coll (MA)
New York U (NY)
Oakland U (MI)
Oberlin Coll (OH)
Ohio U (OH)
Ohio Wesleyan U (OH)
Penn State Abington (PA)
Penn State Altoona (PA)
Penn State Berks (PA)
Penn State Erie, The Behrend Coll (PA)
Penn State U Park (PA)
Pitzer Coll (CA)
Pomona Coll (CA)
Pontifical Coll Josephinum (OH)
Portland State U (OR)
Prescott Coll (AZ)
Queens Coll of the City U of New York (NY)
Rice U (TX)
Ripon Coll (WI)
Rollins Coll (FL)
Rutgers, The State U of New Jersey, New Brunswick (NJ)
St. Cloud State U (MN)
St. Edward's U (TX)
Saint Mary's Coll of California (CA)
St. Olaf Coll (MN)
Samford U (AL)
San Diego State U (CA)
Sarah Lawrence Coll (NY)
Scripps Coll (CA)
Seattle Pacific U (WA)
Skidmore Coll (NY)
Smith Coll (MA)
Southern Methodist U (TX)
Southwestern U (TX)
State U of New York at Binghamton (NY)
State U of New York at New Paltz (NY)
State U of New York at Plattsburgh (NY)
Stetson U (FL)
Syracuse U (NY)
Temple U (PA)
Texas Christian U (TX)
Texas Tech U (TX)
Trinity U (TX)
Tulane U (LA)
U at Albany, State U of New York (NY)
The U of Alabama (AL)
The U of Arizona (AZ)
The U of British Columbia (BC, Canada)
U of California, Berkeley (CA)
U of California, Los Angeles (CA)
U of California, Riverside (CA)
U of California, San Diego (CA)
U of California, Santa Cruz (CA)
U of Chicago (IL)
U of Cincinnati (OH)
U of Connecticut (CT)
U of Delaware (DE)
U of Denver (CO)
U of Idaho (ID)
U of Illinois at Chicago (IL)
U of Illinois at Urbana–Champaign (IL)
The U of Iowa (IA)
U of Kansas (KS)
U of Michigan (MI)
U of Minnesota, Twin Cities Campus (MN)
U of Missouri–Columbia (MO)
U of Nebraska at Omaha (NE)
U of Nebraska–Lincoln (NE)
U of New Mexico (NM)
The U of North Carolina at Chapel Hill (NC)
The U of North Carolina at Charlotte (NC)
U of Northern Iowa (IA)
U of Pennsylvania (PA)
U of Rhode Island (RI)
U of Richmond (VA)
U of South Carolina (SC)
The U of Texas at Austin (TX)
The U of Texas at El Paso (TX)
The U of Toledo (OH)
U of Toronto (ON, Canada)
U of Vermont (VT)
The U of Western Ontario (ON, Canada)
U of Wisconsin–Eau Claire (WI)
U of Wisconsin–Madison (WI)
U of Wisconsin–Milwaukee (WI)
Vanderbilt U (TN)
Vassar Coll (NY)
Warren Wilson Coll (NC)
Washington Coll (MD)
Washington U in St. Louis (MO)
Wellesley Coll (MA)
Wesleyan U (CT)
Western Washington U (WA)
Willamette U (OR)
Yale U (CT)
York U (ON, Canada)

LATIN TEACHER EDUCATION
Baylor U (TX)
Brigham Young U (UT)
Centenary Coll of Louisiana (LA)
Duquesne U (PA)
Hope Coll (MI)
Kent State U (OH)
Miami U Hamilton (OH)
Ohio Wesleyan U (OH)
U of Illinois at Urbana–Champaign (IL)
The U of Iowa (IA)
Western Michigan U (MI)

LAW AND LEGAL STUDIES RELATED
Bradley U (IL)
Brenau U (GA)
Skidmore Coll (NY)
U of Nebraska–Lincoln (NE)

LEGAL ADMINISTRATIVE ASSISTANT/SECRETARY
Ball State U (IN)
Lewis-Clark State Coll (ID)
Northwest Missouri State U (MO)
South U, West Palm Beach (FL)
Tabor Coll (KS)
Texas A&M U–Commerce (TX)

LEGAL ASSISTANT/ PARALEGAL

Anna Maria Coll (MA)
Ball State U (IN)
Boston U (MA)
California State U, Chico (CA)
Calumet Coll of Saint Joseph (IN)
Coll of Mount St. Joseph (OH)
Concordia U Wisconsin (WI)
Davenport U, Dearborn (MI)
Davenport U, Grand Rapids (MI)
Eastern Michigan U (MI)
Everest U, Tampa (FL)
Faulkner U (AL)
Florida Gulf Coast U (FL)
Gannon U (PA)
Grand Valley State U (MI)
Hamline U (MN)
Hampton U (VA)
Howard Payne U (TX)
Husson Coll (ME)
Jones Coll, Miami (FL)
Lake Superior State U (MI)
Lewis-Clark State Coll (ID)
Lock Haven U of Pennsylvania (PA)
Madonna U (MI)
Maryville U of Saint Louis (MO)
Mississippi Coll (MS)
Mississippi U for Women (MS)
Morehead State U (KY)
National American U–Sioux Falls Branch (SD)
Nova Southeastern U (FL)
Peirce Coll (PA)
Quinnipiac U (CT)
Roger Williams U (RI)
Roosevelt U (IL)
Southern Illinois U Carbondale (IL)
Stephen F. Austin State U (TX)
Suffolk U (MA)
Sullivan U (KY)
Texas Woman's U (TX)
Thomas Edison State Coll (NJ)
U of Central Florida (FL)
U of Great Falls (MT)
U of Houston–Clear Lake (TX)
U of La Verne (CA)
U of Louisville (KY)
U of Maryland U Coll (MD)
U of Memphis (TN)
U of Southern Mississippi (MS)
The U of Tennessee at Chattanooga (TN)
Ursuline Coll (OH)
Utah Valley State Coll (UT)
Valdosta State U (GA)
Villa Julie Coll (MD)
Virginia Intermont Coll (VA)
Wesley Coll (DE)
Winona State U (MN)
Woodbury Coll (VT)

LEGAL PROFESSIONS AND STUDIES RELATED

Anna Maria Coll (MA)
Bethany Coll (KS)
Central Pennsylvania Coll (PA)
Hodges U (FL)
Mercy Coll (NY)
Missouri Southern State U (MO)
Montclair State U (NJ)
Pennsylvania Coll of Technology (PA)
Ramapo Coll of New Jersey (NJ)
Roger Williams U (RI)
Syracuse U (NY)
Tulane U (LA)
U of Evansville (IN)
U of Illinois at Springfield (IL)
U of Nebraska–Lincoln (NE)
U of Pennsylvania (PA)
U of Tulsa (OK)

LEGAL STUDIES

American Public U System (WV)
American U (DC)
The American U of Athens (Greece)
Amherst Coll (MA)
Bay Path Coll (MA)
Becker Coll (MA)
Bridgewater State Coll (MA)
Brown Mackie Coll–Fort Wayne (IN)
Brown Mackie Coll–Indianapolis (IN)
Brown Mackie Coll–Merrillville (IN)
Brown Mackie Coll–Michigan City (IN)
Brown Mackie Coll–South Bend (IN)
Brown Mackie Coll–Tucson (AZ)
Burlington Coll (VT)
California State U, Chico (CA)
Christopher Newport U (VA)
Claremont McKenna Coll (CA)
Coll of the Atlantic (ME)
Concordia U Chicago (IL)
Dickinson Coll (PA)
East Central U (OK)
Franciscan U of Steubenville (OH)
Grand Valley State U (MI)
Hamline U (MN)
Hampshire Coll (MA)
Harding U (AR)
Hood Coll (MD)
Keiser U, Fort Lauderdale (FL)
Kenyon Coll (OH)
Lake Superior State U (MI)
Laurentian U (ON, Canada)
Lipscomb U (TN)
Manhattanville Coll (NY)
McGill U (QC, Canada)
Methodist U (NC)
Montclair State U (NJ)
Mountain State U (WV)
National U (CA)
North Carolina Wesleyan Coll (NC)
Northwestern U (IL)
Oberlin Coll (OH)
Park U (MO)
Pennsylvania Coll of Technology (PA)
Point Park U (PA)
Quinnipiac U (CT)
Roosevelt U (IL)
St. John's U (NY)
Saint Joseph's U (PA)
Schreiner U (TX)
Scripps Coll (CA)
South U (AL)
South U, West Palm Beach (FL)
South U (GA)
South U (SC)
State U of New York at Fredonia (NY)
Suffolk U (MA)
United States Air Force Acad (CO)
Université de Sherbrooke (QC, Canada)
U of Baltimore (MD)
U of California, Berkeley (CA)
U of California, Riverside (CA)
U of California, Santa Barbara (CA)
U of California, Santa Cruz (CA)
U of Hartford (CT)
U of Massachusetts Amherst (MA)
U of Massachusetts Boston (MA)
U of Miami (FL)
The U of Montana (MT)
U of New Brunswick Fredericton (NB, Canada)
U of New Haven (CT)
U of Pittsburgh (PA)
The U of Western Ontario (ON, Canada)
U of Windsor (ON, Canada)
U of Wisconsin–Superior (WI)
Villa Julie Coll (MD)
Virginia Intermont Coll (VA)
Washburn U (KS)
Webster U (MO)
Western New England Coll (MA)
Wilmington U (DE)
Winona State U (MN)
York U (ON, Canada)

LIBERAL ARTS AND SCIENCES AND HUMANITIES RELATED

Barton Coll (NC)
Bennington Coll (VT)
Bishop's U (QC, Canada)
Brigham Young U (UT)
Central Christian Coll of Kansas (KS)
The Colorado Coll (CO)
Dominican U of California (CA)
Duquesne U (PA)
Florida Atlantic U (FL)
George Mason U (VA)
Georgia Coll & State U (GA)
Goddard Coll (VT)
Hofstra U (NY)
Howard Payne U (TX)
The Johns Hopkins U (MD)
Lambuth U (TN)
Malone Coll (OH)
Marshall U (WV)
Northern Arizona U (AZ)
Northwest Christian Coll (OR)
Ohio U (OH)
Rhode Island Coll (RI)
St. John's Coll (NM)
Saint Mary's Coll of California (CA)
Sarah Lawrence Coll (NY)
Shimer Coll (IL)
Southern Methodist U (TX)
Southwestern Coll (KS)
Southwestern U (TX)
Tulane U (LA)
The U of Akron (OH)
U of California, Los Angeles (CA)
U of California, Santa Barbara (CA)
U of Illinois at Urbana–Champaign (IL)
U of Louisville (KY)
U of Massachusetts Amherst (MA)
U of South Alabama (AL)
U of Wisconsin–Whitewater (WI)
Vassar Coll (NY)
Virginia Intermont Coll (VA)
Wright State U (OH)

LIBERAL ARTS AND SCIENCES/LIBERAL STUDIES

Abilene Christian U (TX)
Adams State Coll (CO)
Alabama State U (AL)
Alaska Pacific U (AK)
Albertus Magnus Coll (CT)
Alcorn State U (MS)
Alliant Intl U–México City (Mexico)
Alma Coll (MI)
Alvernia Coll (PA)
American Jewish U (CA)
American U (DC)
Angelo State U (TX)
Anna Maria Coll (MA)
Antioch U McGregor (OH)
Appalachian State U (NC)
Aquinas Coll (MI)
Arizona State U (AZ)
Armstrong Atlantic State U (GA)
Ashford U (IA)
Ashland U (OH)
Athabasca U (AB, Canada)
Auburn U Montgomery (AL)
Augsburg Coll (MN)
Augustana Coll (IL)
Augustana Coll (SD)
Azusa Pacific U (CA)
Ball State U (IN)
Barry U (FL)
Bay Path Coll (MA)
Beacon Coll (FL)
Becker Coll (MA)
Bellarmine U (KY)
Bemidji State U (MN)
Benedictine Coll (KS)
Bennington Coll (VT)
Bentley Coll (MA)
Bethany U (CA)
Bethune-Cookman U (FL)
Bishop's U (QC, Canada)
Bluefield Coll (VA)
Boise State U (ID)
Boricua Coll (NY)
Bowling Green State U (OH)
Bradley U (IL)
Bridgewater Coll (VA)
Brigham Young U (UT)
Brock U (ON, Canada)
Bryan Coll (TN)
Buffalo State Coll, State U of New York (NY)
Burlington Coll (VT)
Butler U (IN)
Cabrini Coll (PA)
California Baptist U (CA)
California Lutheran U (CA)
California Polytechnic State U, San Luis Obispo (CA)
California State Polytechnic U, Pomona (CA)
California State U, Chico (CA)
California State U, Dominguez Hills (CA)
California State U, East Bay (CA)
California State U, Fresno (CA)
California State U, Fullerton (CA)
California State U, Long Beach (CA)
California State U, Los Angeles (CA)
California State U, Monterey Bay (CA)
California State U, Sacramento (CA)
California State U, San Bernardino (CA)
California State U, San Marcos (CA)
California State U, Stanislaus (CA)
Calumet Coll of Saint Joseph (IN)
Capital U (OH)
Carlow U (PA)
Carnegie Mellon U (PA)
Carson-Newman Coll (TN)
Cascade Coll (OR)
Cedar Crest Coll (PA)
Centenary Coll of Louisiana (LA)
Central Christian Coll of Kansas (KS)
Chapman U (CA)
Charter Oak State Coll (CT)
Chestnut Hill Coll (PA)
Chicago State U (IL)
Christian Brothers U (TN)
Clarion U of Pennsylvania (PA)
Clarkson U (NY)
Cleveland State U (OH)
Coastal Carolina U (SC)
Coll of Mount St. Joseph (OH)
Coll of Mount Saint Vincent (NY)
The Coll of New Rochelle (NY)
Coll of Saint Benedict (MN)
Coll of St. Joseph (VT)
The Coll of Saint Rose (NY)
The Coll of St. Scholastica (MN)
Coll of Staten Island of the City U of New York (NY)
Coll of the Atlantic (ME)
Colorado State U (CO)
Colorado State U-Pueblo (CO)
Columbia Coll (SC)
Columbia Coll Chicago (IL)
Concordia Coll–New York (NY)
Concordia U (CA)
Concordia U (OR)
Concordia U Texas (TX)
Concordia U Wisconsin (WI)
Cornell Coll (IA)
Cornell U (NY)
Crossroads Coll (MN)
Dallas Baptist U (TX)
Defiance Coll (OH)
DeSales U (PA)
Dominican U of California (CA)
Dowling Coll (NY)
D'Youville Coll (NY)
East Carolina U (NC)
Eastern Illinois U (IL)
Eastern Mennonite U (VA)
Eastern New Mexico U (NM)
East Stroudsburg U of Pennsylvania (PA)
East Texas Baptist U (TX)
Edinboro U of Pennsylvania (PA)
Emmanuel Coll (MA)
Emory U (GA)
Eugene Lang Coll The New School for Liberal Arts (NY)
The Evergreen State Coll (WA)
Faulkner U (AL)
Ferrum Coll (VA)
Finlandia U (MI)
Fitchburg State Coll (MA)
Flagler Coll (FL)
Florida Atlantic U (FL)
Florida Coll (FL)
Florida Gulf Coast U (FL)
Florida Intl U (FL)
Fontbonne U (MO)
Fort Lewis Coll (CO)
Framingham State Coll (MA)
Francis Marion U (SC)
Freed-Hardeman U (TN)
Fresno Pacific U (CA)
Frostburg State U (MD)
Gannon U (PA)
George Mason U (VA)
Georgetown Coll (KY)
Georgetown U (DC)
The George Washington U (DC)
Georgian Court U (NJ)
Gettysburg Coll (PA)
Global Coll of Long Island U (NY)
Gonzaga U (WA)
Grace U (NE)
Grand Valley State U (MI)
Grand View Coll (IA)
Granite State Coll (NH)
Green Mountain Coll (VT)
Greenville Coll (IL)
Gutenberg Coll (OR)
Hannibal-LaGrange Coll (MO)
Harvard U (MA)
Hastings Coll (NE)
Hillsdale Free Will Baptist Coll (OK)
Hobart and William Smith Colls (NY)
Hofstra U (NY)
Holy Family U (PA)
Holy Names U (CA)
Houghton Coll (NY)
Houston Baptist U (TX)
Howard Payne U (TX)
Humboldt State U (CA)
Husson Coll (ME)
Illinois Coll (IL)
Illinois Wesleyan U (IL)
Indiana State U (IN)
Iona Coll (NY)
Iowa State U of Science and Technology (IA)
Iowa Wesleyan Coll (IA)
Ithaca Coll (NY)
Jacksonville U (FL)
James Madison U (VA)
John F. Kennedy U (CA)
The Johns Hopkins U (MD)
Johnson C. Smith U (NC)
Johnson State Coll (VT)
Juniata Coll (PA)
Kean U (NJ)
Keene State Coll (NH)
Kent State U (OH)
Kentucky State U (KY)
Keuka Coll (NY)
Lakehead U (ON, Canada)
Lander U (SC)
La Roche Coll (PA)
La Sierra U (CA)
Laurentian U (ON, Canada)
Lebanon Valley Coll (PA)
Lees-McRae Coll (NC)
Lenoir-Rhyne Coll (NC)
Lesley U (MA)
Lewis U (IL)
Limestone Coll (SC)
Lindenwood U (MO)
Lock Haven U of Pennsylvania (PA)
Longwood U (VA)
Louisiana Coll (LA)
Louisiana State U and Ag and Mech Coll (LA)
Lourdes Coll (OH)
Loyola Marymount U (CA)
Mansfield U of Pennsylvania (PA)
Marian Coll of Fond du Lac (WI)
Marietta Coll (OH)
Marymount Manhattan Coll (NY)
Marymount U (VA)
Maryville U of Saint Louis (MO)
Massachusetts Inst of Technology (MA)
The Master's Coll and Sem (CA)
McNeese State U (LA)
Mercer U (GA)
Mercy Coll (NY)
Mesa State Coll (CO)
Methodist U (NC)
Metropolitan State U (MN)
Miami U (OH)
Michigan Technological U (MI)
Middlebury Coll (VT)
Middle Tennessee State U (TN)
Midland Lutheran Coll (NE)
Midway Coll (KY)
Midwestern State U (TX)
Mills Coll (CA)
Minnesota State U Mankato (MN)
Misericordia U (PA)
Mississippi Coll (MS)
Mississippi State U (MS)
Mitchell Coll (CT)
Monmouth Coll (IL)
Montana State U–Billings (MT)
Montana Tech of The U of Montana (MT)
Morris Coll (SC)
Mountain State U (WV)
Mount Allison U (NB, Canada)
Mount Aloysius Coll (PA)
Mount Ida Coll (MA)
Mount Marty Coll (SD)
Mount Mary Coll (WI)
Mount Olive Coll (NC)
Mount Saint Mary Coll (NY)
Mount Saint Vincent U (NS, Canada)
Murray State U (KY)
National-Louis U (IL)
Neumann Coll (PA)
New Coll of Florida (FL)
Newman U (KS)
New Saint Andrews Coll (ID)
The New School for General Studies (NY)
New York U (NY)
Niagara U (NY)
North Carolina State U (NC)
North Central Coll (IL)
Northeastern Illinois U (IL)
Northeastern U (MA)
Northern Arizona U (AZ)
Northern Illinois U (IL)
North Greenville U (SC)
Northwestern State U of Louisiana (LA)
Northwestern U (IL)
Northwest Nazarene U (ID)
Notre Dame de Namur U (CA)
Nyack Coll (NY)
Oakland U (MI)
Ohio Dominican U (OH)
Ohio U (OH)
Oklahoma Christian U (OK)
Oklahoma City U (OK)
Oklahoma State U (OK)
Oral Roberts U (OK)
Oregon State U (OR)
Pace U (NY)
Pacific U (OR)
Park U (MO)
Patrick Henry Coll (VA)
Paul Smith's Coll (NY)
Penn State Abington (PA)
Penn State Altoona (PA)
Penn State Berks (PA)
Penn State Erie, The Behrend Coll (PA)
Penn State U Park (PA)
Pepperdine U, Malibu (CA)
Point Loma Nazarene U (CA)
Polytechnic U, Brooklyn Campus (NY)
Pomona Coll (CA)
Portland State U (OR)

Prescott Coll (AZ)
Providence Coll (RI)
Purchase Coll, State U of New York (NY)
Purdue U (IN)
Purdue U North Central (IN)
Queens Coll of the City U of New York (NY)
Quinnipiac U (CT)
Randolph Coll (VA)
Redeemer U Coll (ON, Canada)
Regis Coll (MA)
Regis U (CO)
Rhode Island Coll (RI)
The Richard Stockton Coll of New Jersey (NJ)
Rider U (NJ)
Rogers State U (OK)
Roger Williams U (RI)
Roosevelt U (IL)
Rowan U (NJ)
Rutgers, The State U of New Jersey, Camden (NJ)
Rutgers, The State U of New Jersey, New Brunswick (NJ)
Sacred Heart Major Sem (MI)
St. Andrews Presbyterian Coll (NC)
St. Cloud State U (MN)
St. Edward's U (TX)
St. Francis Xavier U (NS, Canada)
St. Gregory's U, Shawnee (OK)
St. John's Coll (MD)
St. John's Coll (NM)
St. John's U (NY)
Saint Joseph Coll (CT)
St. Joseph's Coll, Suffolk Campus (NY)
Saint Mary's Coll of California (CA)
St. Mary's Coll of Maryland (MD)
St. Olaf Coll (MN)
St. Thomas U (FL)
Saint Vincent Coll (PA)
Saint Xavier U (IL)
Salem Intl U (WV)
Salem State Coll (MA)
Salisbury U (MD)
Salve Regina U (RI)
San Diego Christian Coll (CA)
San Diego State U (CA)
San Francisco State U (CA)
Santa Clara U (CA)
Sarah Lawrence Coll (NY)
Schiller Intl U (FL)
Schreiner U (TX)
Seattle Pacific U (WA)
Seattle U (WA)
Shaw U (NC)
Shenandoah U (VA)
Shimer Coll (IL)
Shorter Coll (GA)
Simon Fraser U (BC, Canada)
Simpson U (CA)
Skidmore Coll (NY)
Soka U of America (CA)
Sonoma State U (CA)
South Dakota State U (SD)
Southeastern Louisiana U (LA)
Southern Connecticut State U (CT)
Southern Illinois U Carbondale (IL)
Southern Illinois U Edwardsville (IL)
Southern Oregon U (OR)
Southern Vermont Coll (VT)
Southwestern Coll (KS)
State U of New York at Fredonia (NY)
State U of New York at Plattsburgh (NY)
State U of New York Coll at Oneonta (NY)
Sterling Coll (VT)
Suffolk U (MA)
Sweet Briar Coll (VA)
Syracuse U (NY)
Tarleton State U (TX)
Taylor U Coll and Sem (AB, Canada)
Temple U (PA)
Tennessee State U (TN)
Texas A&M U–Commerce (TX)
Texas Christian U (TX)
Texas Coll (TX)
Texas Southern U (TX)
Texas Tech U (TX)
Thomas Aquinas Coll (CA)
Thomas Edison State Coll (NJ)
Thomas More Coll (KY)
Thomas U (GA)
Thompson Rivers U (BC, Canada)
Trent U (ON, Canada)
Trinity Intl U (IL)
Troy U (AL)
Tulane U (LA)
Tyndale U Coll & Sem (ON, Canada)
Union Coll (NY)
U at Buffalo, the State U of New York (NY)
The U of Akron (OH)
U of Alaska Fairbanks (AK)
U of Alaska Southeast (AK)
The U of Arizona (AZ)
U of Baltimore (MD)
U of Bridgeport (CT)
The U of British Columbia (BC, Canada)
U of California, Riverside (CA)
U of California, Santa Barbara (CA)
U of Central Florida (FL)
U of Central Oklahoma (OK)
U of Chicago (IL)
U of Cincinnati (OH)
U of Delaware (DE)
U of Evansville (IN)
U of Houston–Downtown (TX)
U of Illinois at Springfield (IL)
U of Illinois at Urbana–Champaign (IL)
The U of Iowa (IA)
U of Kansas (KS)
U of La Verne (CA)
U of Louisville (KY)
U of Maine (ME)
U of Maine at Farmington (ME)
U of Maine at Fort Kent (ME)
U of Maryland Eastern Shore (MD)
U of Mary Washington (VA)
U of Massachusetts Dartmouth (MA)
U of Massachusetts Lowell (MA)
U of Memphis (TN)
U of Michigan–Dearborn (MI)
U of Michigan–Flint (MI)
U of Mississippi (MS)
U of Missouri–Kansas City (MO)
U of Missouri–St. Louis (MO)
The U of Montana (MT)
The U of Montana–Western (MT)
U of Nebraska–Lincoln (NE)
U of New Brunswick Fredericton (NB, Canada)
U of New England (ME)
U of New Haven (CT)
U of New Mexico (NM)
The U of North Carolina at Asheville (NC)
The U of North Carolina at Chapel Hill (NC)
The U of North Carolina at Greensboro (NC)
U of Northern Iowa (IA)
U of North Florida (FL)
U of Notre Dame (IN)
U of Oklahoma (OK)
U of Pennsylvania (PA)
U of Pittsburgh (PA)
U of Redlands (CA)
U of Regina (SK, Canada)
U of Rhode Island (RI)
U of St. Francis (IL)
U of Saint Francis (IN)
U of St. Thomas (TX)
U of San Diego (CA)
U of Sioux Falls (SD)
U of South Carolina (SC)
U of South Carolina Aiken (SC)
U of South Carolina Beaufort (SC)
The U of South Dakota (SD)
U of Southern Indiana (IN)
U of South Florida (FL)
The U of Tampa (FL)
The U of Texas at Austin (TX)
The U of Texas at Tyler (TX)
U of the Incarnate Word (TX)
The U of Toledo (OH)
U of Tulsa (OK)
U of Vermont (VT)
U of Victoria (BC, Canada)
U of Virginia (VA)
The U of Virginia's Coll at Wise (VA)
The U of Western Ontario (ON, Canada)
U of Wisconsin–Green Bay (WI)
U of Wisconsin–Oshkosh (WI)
U of Wisconsin–Platteville (WI)
U of Wisconsin–Whitewater (WI)
Utah State U (UT)
Utica Coll (NY)
Villa Julie Coll (MD)
Villanova U (PA)
Virginia State U (VA)
Virginia Wesleyan Coll (VA)
Viterbo U (WI)
Walsh U (OH)
Warner Pacific Coll (OR)
Washburn U (KS)
Washington Coll (MD)
Washington U in St. Louis (MO)
Webster U (MO)
Wesley Coll (DE)
West Chester U of Pennsylvania (PA)
Western Carolina U (NC)
Western Connecticut State U (CT)
Western Illinois U (IL)
Western Intl U (AZ)
Western New England Coll (MA)
Western New Mexico U (NM)
Western Washington U (WA)
Westfield State Coll (MA)
Westmont Coll (CA)
West Virginia U (WV)
Wheeling Jesuit U (WV)
Whittier Coll (CA)
Wichita State U (KS)
Wilkes U (PA)
Wilmington Coll (OH)
Wingate U (NC)
Winona State U (MN)
Wittenberg U (OH)
Wright State U (OH)
Xavier U (OH)
York Coll of the City U of New York (NY)
York U (ON, Canada)
Youngstown State U (OH)

LIBRARY SCIENCE

Clarion U of Pennsylvania (PA)
Concord U (WV)
Kutztown U of Pennsylvania (PA)
Longwood U (VA)
Mountain State U (WV)
Murray State U (KY)
St. Cloud State U (MN)
Southern Connecticut State U (CT)
Syracuse U (NY)
Texas A&M U–Commerce (TX)
The U of Maine at Augusta (ME)
U of Nebraska at Omaha (NE)
U of Oklahoma (OK)
U of Southern Mississippi (MS)

LIBRARY SCIENCE RELATED

Bethel U (MN)
U of Great Falls (MT)

LINGUISTIC AND COMPARATIVE LANGUAGE STUDIES RELATED

Brigham Young U (UT)
U of California, Los Angeles (CA)

LINGUISTICS

Baylor U (TX)
Boston U (MA)
Brandeis U (MA)
Brigham Young U (UT)
Brock U (ON, Canada)
Brown U (RI)
California State U, Chico (CA)
California State U, Dominguez Hills (CA)
California State U, Fresno (CA)
California State U, Fullerton (CA)
Central Coll (IA)
City Coll of the City U of New York (NY)
Cleveland State U (OH)
The Coll of William and Mary (VA)
Concordia U (QC, Canada)
Cornell U (NY)
Crown Coll (MN)
Dartmouth Coll (NH)
Duke U (NC)
Eastern Michigan U (MI)
Florida Atlantic U (FL)
Georgetown U (DC)
Hampshire Coll (MA)
Harvard U (MA)
Hofstra U (NY)
Indiana U Bloomington (IN)
Inter American U of Puerto Rico, San Germán Campus (PR)
Iowa State U of Science and Technology (IA)
Lawrence U (WI)
Lehman Coll of the City U of New York (NY)
Liberty U (VA)
Macalester Coll (MN)
Marlboro Coll (VT)
Massachusetts Inst of Technology (MA)
McGill U (QC, Canada)
Memorial U of Newfoundland (NL, Canada)
Miami U (OH)
Miami U Hamilton (OH)
Montclair State U (NJ)
Mount Saint Vincent U (NS, Canada)
New York U (NY)
Northeastern Illinois U (IL)
Northeastern U (MA)
Northwestern U (IL)
Oakland U (MI)
Ohio U (OH)
Oklahoma Wesleyan U (OK)
Pitzer Coll (CA)
Pomona Coll (CA)
Portland State U (OR)
Queens Coll of the City U of New York (NY)
Queen's U at Kingston (ON, Canada)
Reed Coll (OR)
Rice U (TX)
Rutgers, The State U of New Jersey, New Brunswick (NJ)
St. Cloud State U (MN)
San Diego State U (CA)
Scripps Coll (CA)
Simon Fraser U (BC, Canada)
Southern Illinois U Carbondale (IL)
Stanford U (CA)
State U of New York at Binghamton (NY)
State U of New York at Oswego (NY)
Stony Brook U, State U of New York (NY)
Swarthmore Coll (PA)
Syracuse U (NY)
Temple U (PA)
Truman State U (MO)
Tulane U (LA)
U at Albany, State U of New York (NY)
U at Buffalo, the State U of New York (NY)
U of Alaska Fairbanks (AK)
The U of Arizona (AZ)
The U of British Columbia (BC, Canada)
U of California, Berkeley (CA)
U of California, Davis (CA)
U of California, Irvine (CA)
U of California, Los Angeles (CA)
U of California, Riverside (CA)
U of California, San Diego (CA)
U of California, Santa Barbara (CA)
U of California, Santa Cruz (CA)
U of Chicago (IL)
U of Cincinnati (OH)
U of Colorado at Boulder (CO)
U of Connecticut (CT)
U of Delaware (DE)
U of Florida (FL)
U of Georgia (GA)
U of Hawaii at Manoa (HI)
U of Illinois at Urbana–Champaign (IL)
The U of Iowa (IA)
U of Kansas (KS)
U of King's Coll (NS, Canada)
U of Maryland, Baltimore County (MD)
U of Maryland, Coll Park (MD)
U of Massachusetts Amherst (MA)
U of Michigan (MI)
U of Minnesota, Twin Cities Campus (MN)
U of Mississippi (MS)
U of Missouri–Columbia (MO)
The U of Montana (MT)
U of New Brunswick Fredericton (NB, Canada)
U of New Hampshire (NH)
U of New Mexico (NM)
U of Oklahoma (OK)
U of Oregon (OR)
U of Ottawa (ON, Canada)
U of Pennsylvania (PA)
U of Pittsburgh (PA)
U of Regina (SK, Canada)
U of Rochester (NY)
U of Southern California (CA)
U of Southern Maine (ME)
The U of Texas at Austin (TX)
The U of Texas at El Paso (TX)
The U of Toledo (OH)
U of Toronto (ON, Canada)
U of Utah (UT)
U of Victoria (BC, Canada)
The U of Western Ontario (ON, Canada)
U of Windsor (ON, Canada)
U of Wisconsin–Madison (WI)
U of Wisconsin–Milwaukee (WI)
Washington State U (WA)
Wayne State U (MI)
Wellesley Coll (MA)
Western Washington U (WA)
Wright State U (OH)
Yale U (CT)
York U (ON, Canada)

LINGUISTICS OF ASL AND OTHER SIGN LANGUAGES

Kent State U (OH)

LITERATURE

Agnes Scott Coll (GA)
Alfred U (NY)
American Jewish U (CA)
American U (DC)
Augustana Coll (IL)
Ave Maria U (FL)
Bard Coll (NY)
Bard Coll at Simon's Rock (MA)
Barry U (FL)
Beloit Coll (WI)
Bernard M. Baruch Coll of the City U of New York (NY)
Bishop's U (QC, Canada)
Blackburn Coll (IL)
Boise State U (ID)
Brock U (ON, Canada)
Bryan Coll (TN)
Burlington Coll (VT)
California State U, Dominguez Hills (CA)
California State U, Long Beach (CA)
Capital U (OH)
Carson-Newman Coll (TN)
Castleton State Coll (VT)
Christendom Coll (VA)
Christopher Newport U (VA)
City Coll of the City U of New York (NY)
Claremont McKenna Coll (CA)
The Coll at Brockport, State U of New York (NY)
Coll of the Atlantic (ME)
Coll of the Holy Cross (MA)
Duke U (NC)
East Central U (OK)
Emory U (GA)
Eugene Lang Coll The New School for Liberal Arts (NY)
Excelsior Coll (NY)
Florida State U (FL)
Franklin Coll Switzerland (Switzerland)
Fresno Pacific U (CA)
Gettysburg Coll (PA)
Gonzaga U (WA)
Grand Valley State U (MI)
Grove City Coll (PA)
Harvard U (MA)
Hastings Coll (NE)
High Point U (NC)
Holy Family U (PA)
Houghton Coll (NY)
Hunter Coll of the City U of New York (NY)
Inter American U of Puerto Rico, San Germán Campus (PR)
John Carroll U (OH)
The Johns Hopkins U (MD)
Johnson State Coll (VT)
Kenyon Coll (OH)
Lake Superior State U (MI)
List Coll, The Jewish Theological Sem (NY)
Lycoming Coll (PA)
Marlboro Coll (VT)
Memorial U of Newfoundland (NL, Canada)
Minnesota State U Mankato (MN)
Morningside Coll (IA)
Mount Allison U (NB, Canada)
Mount Saint Vincent U (NS, Canada)
Nazareth Coll of Rochester (NY)
Northwest Missouri State U (MO)
Ohio Wesleyan U (OH)
Oregon State U (OR)
Otterbein Coll (OH)
Pacific U (OR)
Pitzer Coll (CA)
Prescott Coll (AZ)
Purchase Coll, State U of New York (NY)
Purdue U Calumet (IN)
Quinnipiac U (CT)
Reed Coll (OR)
Rochester Coll (MI)
Rockford Coll (IL)
Roosevelt U (IL)
Saint Francis U (PA)
St. John's Coll (NM)
Saint Mary's Coll of California (CA)
Salem State Coll (MA)
Sarah Lawrence Coll (NY)
Schreiner U (TX)
Sewanee: The U of the South (TN)
Shimer Coll (IL)
Sonoma State U (CA)
Southwest Minnesota State U (MN)
State U of New York Coll at Old Westbury (NY)
Taylor U (IN)
Trent U (ON, Canada)
U of Baltimore (MD)
U of California, Irvine (CA)
U of California, San Diego (CA)
U of California, Santa Cruz (CA)
U of Cincinnati (OH)
The U of Iowa (IA)
U of Missouri–St. Louis (MO)
The U of Montana–Western (MT)
U of New Brunswick Fredericton (NB, Canada)
U of New Hampshire (NH)
U of Pittsburgh at Johnstown (PA)
U of Redlands (CA)

The U of Texas at Dallas (TX)
U of the Sacred Heart (PR)
The U of Toledo (OH)
U of Toronto (ON, Canada)
U of Victoria (BC, Canada)
U of Windsor (ON, Canada)
U of Wisconsin–Milwaukee (WI)
Washington U in St. Louis (MO)
Webster U (MO)
Western Washington U (WA)
West Virginia Wesleyan Coll (WV)
William Paterson U of New Jersey (NJ)
Williams Coll (MA)
Yale U (CT)
York U (ON, Canada)

LIVESTOCK MANAGEMENT

Sterling Coll (VT)

LOGIC

Carnegie Mellon U (PA)
U of Pennsylvania (PA)

LOGISTICS AND MATERIALS MANAGEMENT

Auburn U (AL)
Baylor U (TX)
Bowling Green State U (OH)
Brigham Young U (UT)
Central Michigan U (MI)
Clarkson U (NY)
Duquesne U (PA)
Florida Intl U (FL)
Georgia Southern U (GA)
Iowa State U of Science and Technology (IA)
Lehigh U (PA)
Maine Maritime Acad (ME)
Michigan State U (MI)
Missouri State U (MO)
Mountain State U (WV)
Niagara U (NY)
Northeastern State U (OK)
Northeastern U (MA)
Park U (MO)
Portland State U (OR)
Sullivan U (KY)
Taylor U Fort Wayne (IN)
U of Arkansas (AR)
The U of Findlay (OH)
U of Illinois at Urbana–Champaign (IL)
U of Kansas (KS)
U of Maryland, Coll Park (MD)
U of Nevada, Reno (NV)
U of North Texas (TX)
The U of Tennessee (TN)
The U of Texas at Austin (TX)
The U of Toledo (OH)
Wayne State U (MI)
Weber State U (UT)
Western Illinois U (IL)
Western Michigan U (MI)
Wright State U (OH)

MANAGEMENT INFORMATION SYSTEMS

Abilene Christian U (TX)
Albertus Magnus Coll (CT)
Alliant Intl U (CA)
Alliant Intl U–México City (Mexico)
Amberton U (TX)
American Coll of Thessaloniki (Greece)
Angelo State U (TX)
Anna Maria Coll (MA)
Appalachian State U (NC)
Arizona State U (AZ)
Auburn U (AL)
Auburn U Montgomery (AL)
Augsburg Coll (MN)
Augustana Coll (SD)
Avila U (MO)
Azusa Pacific U (CA)
Babson Coll (MA)
Baker Coll of Flint (MI)
Ball State U (IN)
Barry U (FL)
Baylor U (TX)
Bernard M. Baruch Coll of the City U of New York (NY)
Bethel Coll (TN)
Bishop's U (QC, Canada)
Boston Coll (MA)
Boston U (MA)
Bradley U (IL)
Bridgewater Coll (VA)
Bridgewater State Coll (MA)
Brigham Young U (UT)
Butler U (IN)
California State U, Chico (CA)
California State U, Dominguez Hills (CA)
California State U, East Bay (CA)
California State U, Fresno (CA)
California State U, Long Beach (CA)
California State U, San Bernardino (CA)
Calvin Coll (MI)
Carroll Coll (WI)
Carson-Newman Coll (TN)
Cedarville U (OH)
Central Connecticut State U (CT)
Central Michigan U (MI)
Claflin U (SC)
Clarke Coll (IA)
Clarkson U (NY)
Clayton State U (GA)
Cleary U (MI)
Clemson U (SC)
Colorado Tech U—Colorado Springs (CO)
Colorado Tech U—Denver (CO)
Colorado Tech U—North Kansas City (MO)
Colorado Tech U—Online (CO)
Colorado Tech U—Sioux Falls (SD)
Columbus State U (GA)
Concordia U (QC, Canada)
Concordia U, Nebraska (NE)
Cornerstone U (MI)
Creighton U (NE)
Culver-Stockton Coll (MO)
Dallas Baptist U (TX)
Dana Coll (NE)
Davis & Elkins Coll (WV)
Delaware Valley Coll (PA)
Delta State U (MS)
DePaul U (IL)
DeSales U (PA)
Dominican Coll (NY)
Dordt Coll (IA)
Drexel U (PA)
Duquesne U (PA)
East Carolina U (NC)
East Central U (OK)
Eastern Connecticut State U (CT)
Eastern Kentucky U (KY)
Eastern Michigan U (MI)
Eastern New Mexico U (NM)
East Texas Baptist U (TX)
Excelsior Coll (NY)
Fairfield U (CT)
Fayetteville State U (NC)
Florida Ag and Mech U (FL)
Florida Atlantic U (FL)
Florida Gulf Coast U (FL)
Florida Inst of Technology (FL)
Florida Intl U (FL)
Florida Southern Coll (FL)
Fontbonne U (MO)
Francis Marion U (SC)
Gannon U (PA)
Gardner-Webb U (NC)
George Fox U (OR)
Georgia Southern U (GA)
Georgia Southwestern State U (GA)
Goldey-Beacom Coll (DE)
Grace Coll (IN)
Grand Valley State U (MI)
Grand View Coll (IA)
Greenville Coll (IL)
HEC Montreal (QC, Canada)
Henderson State U (AR)
Hofstra U (NY)
Husson Coll (ME)
Illinois Coll (IL)
Indiana State U (IN)
Indiana U of Pennsylvania (PA)
Inter American U of Puerto Rico, Aguadilla Campus (PR)
Inter American U of Puerto Rico, Bayamón Campus (PR)
Iona Coll (NY)
Iowa State U of Science and Technology (IA)
Jacksonville U (FL)
Jamestown Coll (ND)
Johnson State Coll (VT)
Judson U (IL)
Keiser U, Fort Lauderdale (FL)
King Coll (TN)
Lakehead U (ON, Canada)
La Salle U (PA)
Lehigh U (PA)
Le Moyne Coll (NY)
Lenoir-Rhyne Coll (NC)
LeTourneau U (TX)
Liberty U (VA)
Lincoln U (CA)
Lindenwood U (MO)
Lipscomb U (TN)
Longwood U (VA)
Loras Coll (IA)
Loyola U Chicago (IL)
Luther Coll (IA)
Madonna U (MI)
Maranatha Baptist Bible Coll (WI)
Marquette U (WI)
Maryville U of Saint Louis (MO)
The Master's Coll and Sem (CA)
McMurry U (TX)
Mesa State Coll (CO)
Metropolitan State U (MN)
Miami U (OH)
Michigan Technological U (MI)
Middle Tennessee State U (TN)
Midland Lutheran Coll (NE)
Millikin U (IL)
Milwaukee School of Eng (WI)
Minot State U (ND)
Misericordia U (PA)
Mississippi State U (MS)
Missouri State U (MO)
Morehead State U (KY)
Morgan State U (MD)
Morningside Coll (IA)
Mount Saint Vincent U (NS, Canada)
Murray State U (KY)
National American U–Sioux Falls Branch (SD)
National U (CA)
Nazareth Coll of Rochester (NY)
Newman U (KS)
New Mexico Highlands U (NM)
New York Inst of Technology (NY)
New York U (NY)
Nicholls State U (LA)
Nichols Coll (MA)
North Central Coll (IL)
Northeastern State U (OK)
Northeastern U (MA)
Northern Arizona U (AZ)
Northern Illinois U (IL)
Northern Michigan U (MI)
Northern State U (SD)
Northwest Christian Coll (OR)
Northwestern Coll (MN)
Northwest Missouri State U (MO)
Northwood U, Florida Campus (FL)
Oakland U (MI)
Oklahoma City U (OK)
Oklahoma State U (OK)
Old Dominion U (VA)
Oral Roberts U (OK)
Oregon Inst of Technology (OR)
Oregon State U (OR)
Pacific Union Coll (CA)
Paine Coll (GA)
Park U (MO)
Penn State Abington (PA)
Penn State Altoona (PA)
Penn State Berks (PA)
Penn State Erie, The Behrend Coll (PA)
Penn State Harrisburg (PA)
Penn State U Park (PA)
Pennsylvania Coll of Technology (PA)
Peru State Coll (NE)
Pfeiffer U (NC)
Philadelphia U (PA)
Point Loma Nazarene U (CA)
Polytechnic U, Brooklyn Campus (NY)
Rensselaer Polytechnic Inst (NY)
Rhode Island Coll (RI)
Robert Morris U (PA)
Roberts Wesleyan Coll (NY)
Rochester Inst of Technology (NY)
Rockford Coll (IL)
Roger Williams U (RI)
Saint Francis U (PA)
St. Francis Xavier U (NS, Canada)
St. John Fisher Coll (NY)
St. John's U (NY)
Saint Joseph's Coll (IN)
Saint Joseph's U (PA)
Saint Leo U (FL)
Saint Louis U (MO)
Saint Martin's U (WA)
Saint Mary's Coll (IN)
Salem State Coll (MA)
Salisbury U (MD)
Santa Clara U (CA)
Schreiner U (TX)
Seattle U (WA)
Seton Hill U (PA)
Shawnee State U (OH)
Simmons Coll (MA)
Simon Fraser U (BC, Canada)
Simpson U (CA)
Southeastern U (FL)
Southern Adventist U (TN)
Southern Illinois U Edwardsville (IL)
Southwestern Coll (KS)
Spring Arbor U (MI)
State U of New York at Binghamton (NY)
State U of New York Coll at Old Westbury (NY)
Stetson U (FL)
Suffolk U (MA)
Tarleton State U (TX)
Temple U (PA)
Texas A&M U–Commerce (TX)
Texas State U-San Marcos (TX)
Texas Tech U (TX)
Thiel Coll (PA)
Thomas Coll (ME)
Tri-State U (IN)
Troy U (AL)
Truman State U (MO)
TUI U (CA)
Université du Québec en Outaouais (QC, Canada)
The U of Akron (OH)
The U of Alabama (AL)
The U of Alabama at Birmingham (AL)
The U of Alabama in Huntsville (AL)
The U of Arizona (AZ)
U of Arkansas at Monticello (AR)
U of Baltimore (MD)
The U of British Columbia (BC, Canada)
U of Central Arkansas (AR)
U of Central Florida (FL)
U of Central Missouri (MO)
U of Cincinnati (OH)
U of Connecticut (CT)
U of Dayton (OH)
U of Delaware (DE)
U of Denver (CO)
U of Evansville (IN)
U of Georgia (GA)
U of Hartford (CT)
U of Hawaii at Manoa (HI)
U of Houston (TX)
U of Houston–Clear Lake (TX)
U of Houston–Downtown (TX)
U of Idaho (ID)
U of Illinois at Chicago (IL)
U of Illinois at Urbana–Champaign (IL)
The U of Iowa (IA)
U of Kansas (KS)
U of Lethbridge (AB, Canada)
U of Louisville (KY)
U of Maine (ME)
U of Mary (ND)
U of Mary Hardin-Baylor (TX)
U of Massachusetts Dartmouth (MA)
U of Memphis (TN)
U of Michigan–Dearborn (MI)
U of Minnesota, Crookston (MN)
U of Minnesota, Twin Cities Campus (MN)
U of Mississippi (MS)
U of Missouri–Columbia (MO)
U of Missouri–St. Louis (MO)
U of Montevallo (AL)
U of Nebraska at Omaha (NE)
U of Nevada, Las Vegas (NV)
U of New Orleans (LA)
U of North Alabama (AL)
The U of North Carolina at Charlotte (NC)
The U of North Carolina at Greensboro (NC)
The U of North Carolina Wilmington (NC)
U of Northern Iowa (IA)
U of North Texas (TX)
U of Notre Dame (IN)
U of Oklahoma (OK)
U of Ottawa (ON, Canada)
U of Pennsylvania (PA)
U of Redlands (CA)
U of Rhode Island (RI)
U of Richmond (VA)
U of St. Thomas (TX)
U of Southern Mississippi (MS)
U of South Florida (FL)
The U of Tampa (FL)
The U of Tennessee at Martin (TN)
The U of Texas at Arlington (TX)
The U of Texas at Austin (TX)
The U of Texas at San Antonio (TX)
The U of Texas–Pan American (TX)
The U of Toledo (OH)
U of Tulsa (OK)
U of Utah (UT)
The U of Western Ontario (ON, Canada)
U of West Florida (FL)
U of West Georgia (GA)
U of Windsor (ON, Canada)
U of Wisconsin–Green Bay (WI)
U of Wisconsin–La Crosse (WI)
U of Wisconsin–Milwaukee (WI)
U of Wisconsin–Oshkosh (WI)
U of Wisconsin–Whitewater (WI)
Ursuline Coll (OH)
Villa Julie Coll (MD)
Villanova U (PA)
Viterbo U (WI)
Wake Forest U (NC)
Walla Walla U (WA)
Walsh U (OH)
Washington State U (WA)
Wayne State U (MI)
Western Carolina U (NC)
Western Connecticut State U (CT)
Western Illinois U (IL)
Western Kentucky U (KY)
Western New England Coll (MA)
Western State Coll of Colorado (CO)
Western Washington U (WA)
Westminster Coll (MO)
West Texas A&M U (TX)
West Virginia U (WV)
Wichita State U (KS)
William Woods U (MO)
Wingate U (NC)
Winona State U (MN)
Worcester Polytechnic Inst (MA)
Wright State U (OH)
Xavier U (OH)
York U (ON, Canada)
Youngstown State U (OH)

MANAGEMENT INFORMATION SYSTEMS AND SERVICES RELATED

Bowling Green State U (OH)
California State U, Chico (CA)
Columbia Southern U (AL)
Florida Ag and Mech U (FL)
Midwestern State U (TX)
Purdue U (IN)
Rensselaer Polytechnic Inst (NY)
Rogers State U (OK)
Southeastern Oklahoma State U (OK)
Thomas Edison State Coll (NJ)
Westminster Coll (UT)
Widener U (PA)
York Coll of Pennsylvania (PA)

MANAGEMENT SCIENCE

The American U of Athens (Greece)
Averett U (VA)
Cambridge Coll (MA)
Clarion U of Pennsylvania (PA)
DePaul U (IL)
Duquesne U (PA)
Eastern Illinois U (IL)
Fitchburg State Coll (MA)
Florida Inst of Technology (FL)
Grace Bible Coll (MI)
Hardin-Simmons U (TX)
Hawai'i Pacific U (HI)
HEC Montreal (QC, Canada)
Inter American U of Puerto Rico, Bayamón Campus (PR)
Keiser U, Fort Lauderdale (FL)
La Roche Coll (PA)
Lenoir-Rhyne Coll (NC)
Louisiana State U and Ag and Mech Coll (LA)
Lourdes Coll (OH)
Madonna U (MI)
McGill U (QC, Canada)
Miami U (OH)
Minnesota State U Mankato (MN)
Mountain State U (WV)
Northeastern U (MA)
Oakland City U (IN)
Ohio Northern U (OH)
Oklahoma State U (OK)
Oral Roberts U (OK)
Pace U (NY)
Pennsylvania Coll of Technology (PA)
Prescott Coll (AZ)
Rider U (NJ)
Roosevelt U (IL)
Rutgers, The State U of New Jersey, New Brunswick (NJ)
St. Ambrose U (IA)
St. Gregory's U, Shawnee (OK)
Saint Louis U (MO)
Salisbury U (MD)
Shippensburg U of Pennsylvania (PA)
Simon Fraser U (BC, Canada)
Southeastern Oklahoma State U (OK)
Southern Adventist U (TN)
Southern Illinois U Carbondale (IL)
Southern Methodist U (TX)
Southern Vermont Coll (VT)
Southwestern Coll (KS)
State U of New York at Binghamton (NY)
State U of New York at Oswego (NY)
Stetson U (FL)
Texas A&M U (TX)
Texas Christian U (TX)
Trinity Intl U (IL)
Trinity U (TX)
Tuskegee U (AL)
United States Coast Guard Acad (CT)
The U of Alabama (AL)
U of California, San Diego (CA)
U of Connecticut (CT)
U of Florida (FL)
U of Great Falls (MT)

U of Illinois at Urbana–Champaign (IL)
The U of Iowa (IA)
U of Mary (ND)
U of Maryland, Coll Park (MD)
U of Maryland U Coll (MD)
U of Memphis (TN)
U of Missouri–St. Louis (MO)
U of Nebraska–Lincoln (NE)
The U of Scranton (PA)
U of South Carolina (SC)
U of South Florida (FL)
The U of Tampa (FL)
The U of Tennessee at Martin (TN)
The U of Texas at San Antonio (TX)
The U of Western Ontario (ON, Canada)
U of Windsor (ON, Canada)
U of Wyoming (WY)
Valparaiso U (IN)
Virginia Polytechnic Inst and State U (VA)
Wake Forest U (NC)
Washington State U (WA)
Western Michigan U (MI)
Wheeling Jesuit U (WV)
Wright State U (OH)

MANAGEMENT SCIENCES AND QUANTITATIVE METHODS RELATED

The American U of Athens (Greece)
Duquesne U (PA)
George Mason U (VA)
Georgia Coll & State U (GA)
Indiana State U (IN)
Ohio Northern U (OH)
Penn State U Park (PA)
Rutgers, The State U of New Jersey, New Brunswick (NJ)
Southwest Minnesota State U (MN)
The U of Iowa (IA)
U of Pennsylvania (PA)
The U of Toledo (OH)
Valparaiso U (IN)

MANUFACTURING ENGINEERING

Bradley U (IL)
Brigham Young U (UT)
California Polytechnic State U, San Luis Obispo (CA)
Central Michigan U (MI)
Clarkson U (NY)
Hofstra U (NY)
Missouri U of Science and Technology (MO)
New Jersey Inst of Technology (NJ)
North Dakota State U (ND)
Northwestern U (IL)
Rensselaer Polytechnic Inst (NY)
Robert Morris U (PA)
Southern Illinois U Edwardsville (IL)
Texas State U-San Marcos (TX)
U of California, Berkeley (CA)
U of Connecticut (CT)
U of Illinois at Urbana–Champaign (IL)
U of Michigan–Dearborn (MI)
The U of Texas–Pan American (TX)
U of Toronto (ON, Canada)
Virginia State U (VA)
Western Michigan U (MI)
Wichita State U (KS)

MANUFACTURING TECHNOLOGY

Bradley U (IL)
California State U, Long Beach (CA)
Central Connecticut State U (CT)
Central Michigan U (MI)
East Carolina U (NC)
Eastern Michigan U (MI)
Farmingdale State Coll (NY)
Ferris State U (MI)
Fitchburg State Coll (MA)
Illinois Inst of Technology (IL)
Indiana State U (IN)
Kean U (NJ)
Lewis-Clark State Coll (ID)
Midwestern State U (TX)
Murray State U (KY)
Northern Michigan U (MI)
Pittsburg State U (KS)
Purdue U (IN)
Rochester Inst of Technology (NY)
Roger Williams U (RI)
South Dakota State U (SD)
Southwestern Coll (KS)
Tarleton State U (TX)
Texas A&M U (TX)
Texas State U-San Marcos (TX)
Thomas Edison State Coll (NJ)
The U of Akron (OH)
U of Memphis (TN)
U of Nebraska at Omaha (NE)
U of Northern Iowa (IA)
U of North Texas (TX)
Western Carolina U (NC)
Western Illinois U (IL)
Western Kentucky U (KY)
Western Washington U (WA)

MARINE BIOLOGY

Michigan Technological U (MI)
Monmouth U (NJ)
Rollins Coll (FL)
Stony Brook U, State U of New York (NY)
U of Hawaii at Manoa (HI)
U of South Carolina (SC)

MARINE BIOLOGY AND BIOLOGICAL OCEANOGRAPHY

Alabama State U (AL)
Alaska Pacific U (AK)
Auburn U (AL)
Ball State U (IN)
Barry U (FL)
Bemidji State U (MN)
Boston U (MA)
Brown U (RI)
California State U, Long Beach (CA)
Coastal Carolina U (SC)
Coll of Charleston (SC)
Coll of the Atlantic (ME)
Dowling Coll (NY)
East Stroudsburg U of Pennsylvania (PA)
Eckerd Coll (FL)
Fairleigh Dickinson U, Coll at Florham (NJ)
Fairleigh Dickinson U, Metropolitan Campus (NJ)
Florida Inst of Technology (FL)
Florida Intl U (FL)
Florida State U (FL)
Gettysburg Coll (PA)
Hampton U (VA)
Harvard U (MA)
Hawai'i Pacific U (HI)
Humboldt State U (CA)
Jacksonville State U (AL)
Juniata Coll (PA)
Maine Maritime Acad (ME)
McGill U (QC, Canada)
Memorial U of Newfoundland (NL, Canada)
New Coll of Florida (FL)
Northeastern U (MA)
Northern Arizona U (AZ)
Nova Southeastern U (FL)
Old Dominion U (VA)
The Richard Stockton Coll of New Jersey (NJ)
Roger Williams U (RI)
Rutgers, The State U of New Jersey, New Brunswick (NJ)
Saint Francis U (PA)
Salem State Coll (MA)
Samford U (AL)
San Francisco State U (CA)
Sarah Lawrence Coll (NY)
Sonoma State U (CA)
Southwestern Coll (KS)
Spring Hill Coll (AL)
Suffolk U (MA)
Texas A&M U at Galveston (TX)
Troy U (AL)
The U of Alabama (AL)
The U of British Columbia (BC, Canada)
U of California, Los Angeles (CA)
U of California, Santa Barbara (CA)
U of California, Santa Cruz (CA)
U of Connecticut (CT)
U of King's Coll (NS, Canada)
U of Maine (ME)
U of Maine at Machias (ME)
U of Maryland Eastern Shore (MD)
U of Miami (FL)
U of New England (ME)
U of New Hampshire (NH)
U of New Haven (CT)
U of North Alabama (AL)
The U of North Carolina Wilmington (NC)
U of Oregon (OR)
U of Puerto Rico at Humacao (PR)
U of Rhode Island (RI)
U of San Diego (CA)
U of South Carolina (SC)
U of Southern Mississippi (MS)
U of the Virgin Islands (VI)
U of Victoria (BC, Canada)
U of West Florida (FL)
Waynesburg U (PA)
Western Washington U (WA)

MARINE SCIENCE/ MERCHANT MARINE OFFICER

American U (DC)
Hampton U (VA)
Jacksonville U (FL)
Maine Maritime Acad (ME)
Massachusetts Maritime Acad (MA)
Memorial U of Newfoundland (NL, Canada)
Prescott Coll (AZ)
Salem State Coll (MA)
Texas A&M U at Galveston (TX)
United States Merchant Marine Acad (NY)
U of New Hampshire (NH)
U of South Carolina (SC)
The U of Tampa (FL)

MARINE TECHNOLOGY

California Maritime Acad (CA)

MARINE TRANSPORTATION RELATED

United States Merchant Marine Acad (NY)

MARITIME SCIENCE

Coll of the Atlantic (ME)
Massachusetts Maritime Acad (MA)
Texas A&M U at Galveston (TX)
United States Merchant Marine Acad (NY)

MARKETING/MARKETING MANAGEMENT

Abilene Christian U (TX)
Adams State Coll (CO)
Alabama Ag and Mech U (AL)
Alabama State U (AL)
Albertus Magnus Coll (CT)
Albright Coll (PA)
Alderson-Broaddus Coll (WV)
Alfred U (NY)
Alma Coll (MI)
Alvernia Coll (PA)
Amberton U (TX)
American Coll of Thessaloniki (Greece)
American InterContinental U (CA)
American InterContinental U (FL)
American InterContinental U (TX)
American InterContinental U Buckhead Campus (GA)
American InterContinental U Dunwoody Campus (GA)
American InterContinental U-London (United Kingdom)
American InterContinental U Online (IL)
American Public U System (WV)
The American U of Athens (Greece)
Anderson U (IN)
Anderson U (SC)
Andrews U (MI)
Angelo State U (TX)
Appalachian State U (NC)
Argosy U, Atlanta (GA)
Argosy U, Chicago (IL)
Argosy U, Denver (CO)
Argosy U, Hawai'i (HI)
Argosy U, Inland Empire (CA)
Argosy U, Nashville (TN)
Argosy U, Orange County (CA)
Argosy U, Phoenix (AZ)
Argosy U, San Diego (CA)
Argosy U, San Francisco Bay Area (CA)
Argosy U, Santa Monica (CA)
Argosy U, Sarasota (FL)
Argosy U, Schaumburg (IL)
Argosy U, Seattle (WA)
Argosy U, Twin Cities (MN)
Argosy U, Washington DC (VA)
Arizona State U (AZ)
Arizona State U at the West campus (AZ)
Arkansas State U (AR)
Ashland U (OH)
Assumption Coll (MA)
Athabasca U (AB, Canada)
Auburn U (AL)
Auburn U Montgomery (AL)
Augsburg Coll (MN)
Augustana Coll (IL)
Augusta State U (GA)
Averett U (VA)
Avila U (MO)
Azusa Pacific U (CA)
Babson Coll (MA)
Baker Coll of Auburn Hills (MI)
Baker Coll of Owosso (MI)
Baldwin-Wallace Coll (OH)
Ball State U (IN)
Barry U (FL)
Barton Coll (NC)
Baylor U (TX)
Becker Coll (MA)
Belmont U (TN)
Benedictine U (IL)
Bentley Coll (MA)
Bernard M. Baruch Coll of the City U of New York (NY)
Berry Coll (GA)
Bishop's U (QC, Canada)
Blackburn Coll (IL)
Bluefield State Coll (WV)
Bob Jones U (SC)
Boston Coll (MA)
Boston U (MA)
Bradley U (IL)
Brenau U (GA)
Bridgewater State Coll (MA)
Brigham Young U (UT)
Brock U (ON, Canada)
Butler U (IN)
Cabrini Coll (PA)
California Baptist U (CA)
California Lutheran U (CA)
California State Polytechnic U, Pomona (CA)
California State U, Chico (CA)
California State U, Dominguez Hills (CA)
California State U, East Bay (CA)
California State U, Fresno (CA)
California State U, Fullerton (CA)
California State U, Long Beach (CA)
California State U, Sacramento (CA)
California State U, San Bernardino (CA)
Canisius Coll (NY)
Capital U (OH)
Carroll Coll (WI)
Carson-Newman Coll (TN)
Cascade Coll (OR)
Castleton State Coll (VT)
Catawba Coll (NC)
Cedarville U (OH)
Centenary Coll (NJ)
Central Connecticut State U (CT)
Central Michigan U (MI)
Chaminade U of Honolulu (HI)
Chatham U (PA)
Chestnut Hill Coll (PA)
Christopher Newport U (VA)
Claflin U (SC)
Clarion U of Pennsylvania (PA)
Clarke Coll (IA)
Clarkson U (NY)
Cleary U (MI)
Clemson U (SC)
Cleveland State U (OH)
Coastal Carolina U (SC)
The Coll at Brockport, State U of New York (NY)
The Coll of St. Scholastica (MN)
Coll of the Ozarks (MO)
Coll of the Southwest (NM)
Colorado State U (CO)
Colorado Tech U—Colorado Springs (CO)
Colorado Tech U—Denver (CO)
Colorado Tech U—North Kansas City (MO)
Colorado Tech U—Online (CO)
Colorado Tech U—Sioux Falls (SD)
Columbia Coll Chicago (IL)
Columbia Southern U (AL)
Columbus State U (GA)
Concordia U (QC, Canada)
Concordia U, St. Paul (MN)
Concordia U Wisconsin (WI)
Converse Coll (SC)
Cornerstone U (MI)
Creighton U (NE)
Dakota State U (SD)
Dakota Wesleyan U (SD)
Dallas Baptist U (TX)
Davenport U, Dearborn (MI)
Davenport U, Grand Rapids (MI)
Davis & Elkins Coll (WV)
Delaware Valley Coll (PA)
Delta State U (MS)
DePaul U (IL)
DeSales U (PA)
Dominican Coll (NY)
Drake U (IA)
Drexel U (PA)
Drury U (MO)
Duquesne U (PA)
D'Youville Coll (NY)
East Carolina U (NC)
East Central U (OK)
Eastern Illinois U (IL)
Eastern Kentucky U (KY)
Eastern Michigan U (MI)
Eastern New Mexico U (NM)
East Tennessee State U (TN)
Emerson Coll (MA)
Emory U (GA)
Emporia State U (KS)
Evangel U (MO)
Everest U, Tampa (FL)
Excelsior Coll (NY)
Fairfield U (CT)
Fairleigh Dickinson U, Coll at Florham (NJ)
Faulkner U (AL)
Fayetteville State U (NC)
Felician Coll (NJ)
Ferris State U (MI)
Fitchburg State Coll (MA)
Florida Atlantic U (FL)
Florida Gulf Coast U (FL)
Florida Intl U (FL)
Florida Southern Coll (FL)
Fontbonne U (MO)
Fort Lewis Coll (CO)
Francis Marion U (SC)
Freed-Hardeman U (TN)
Fresno Pacific U (CA)
Gannon U (PA)
George Fox U (OR)
George Mason U (VA)
Georgetown U (DC)
The George Washington U (DC)
Georgia Coll & State U (GA)
Georgia Southern U (GA)
Georgia Southwestern State U (GA)
Georgia State U (GA)
Golden Gate U (CA)
Goldey-Beacom Coll (DE)
Gonzaga U (WA)
Grace Bible Coll (MI)
Grace Coll (IN)
Grambling State U (LA)
Grand Canyon U (AZ)
Grand Valley State U (MI)
Greenville Coll (IL)
Grove City Coll (PA)
Hampton U (VA)
Hannibal-LaGrange Coll (MO)
Harding U (AR)
Hardin-Simmons U (TX)
Harris-Stowe State U (MO)
Hastings Coll (NE)
Hawai'i Pacific U (HI)
HEC Montreal (QC, Canada)
High Point U (NC)
Hillsdale Coll (MI)
Hofstra U (NY)
Holy Family U (PA)
Holy Names U (CA)
Houston Baptist U (TX)
Howard Payne U (TX)
Humboldt State U (CA)
Husson Coll (ME)
Idaho State U (ID)
Illinois State U (IL)
Indiana State U (IN)
Indiana Tech (IN)
Indiana U of Pennsylvania (PA)
Indiana Wesleyan U (IN)
Inter American U of Puerto Rico, Aguadilla Campus (PR)
Inter American U of Puerto Rico, Bayamón Campus (PR)
Inter American U of Puerto Rico, San Germán Campus (PR)
Iona Coll (NY)
Iowa State U of Science and Technology (IA)
Ithaca Coll (NY)
Jackson State U (MS)
Jacksonville State U (AL)
Jacksonville U (FL)
James Madison U (VA)
Jamestown Coll (ND)
Jarvis Christian Coll (TX)
John Brown U (AR)
John Carroll U (OH)
Johnson State Coll (VT)
Juniata Coll (PA)
Kansas State U (KS)
Kean U (NJ)
Kennesaw State U (GA)
Kent State U (OH)
Keuka Coll (NY)
King's Coll (PA)
Kutztown U of Pennsylvania (PA)
Laboratory Inst of Merchandising (NY)
Lakehead U (ON, Canada)
Lambuth U (TN)
La Roche Coll (PA)
La Salle U (PA)
Lehigh U (PA)
Le Moyne Coll (NY)
Lenoir-Rhyne Coll (NC)
LeTourneau U (TX)
Lewis U (IL)
Limestone Coll (SC)
Lincoln U (MO)
Lindenwood U (MO)
Lipscomb U (TN)
Longwood U (VA)
Loras Coll (IA)
Louisiana Coll (LA)

Louisiana State U and Ag and Mech Coll (LA)
Lourdes Coll (OH)
Loyola U Chicago (IL)
Loyola U New Orleans (LA)
Lubbock Christian U (TX)
Lycoming Coll (PA)
Lynchburg Coll (VA)
Madonna U (MI)
Manchester Coll (IN)
Mansfield U of Pennsylvania (PA)
Maranatha Baptist Bible Coll (WI)
Marian Coll (IN)
Marian Coll of Fond du Lac (WI)
Marietta Coll (OH)
Marquette U (WI)
Marshall U (WV)
Martin U (IN)
Maryville U of Saint Louis (MO)
Marywood U (PA)
McGill U (QC, Canada)
McKendree U (IL)
McMurry U (TX)
McNeese State U (LA)
Memorial U of Newfoundland (NL, Canada)
Mercyhurst Coll (PA)
Merrimack Coll (MA)
Messiah Coll (PA)
Metropolitan State U (MN)
Miami U (OH)
Michigan State U (MI)
Michigan Technological U (MI)
MidAmerica Nazarene U (KS)
Middle Tennessee State U (TN)
Midland Lutheran Coll (NE)
Midwestern State U (TX)
Millikin U (IL)
Minnesota State U Mankato (MN)
Minot State U (ND)
Misericordia U (PA)
Mississippi Coll (MS)
Mississippi State U (MS)
Mississippi U for Women (MS)
Missouri Baptist U (MO)
Missouri State U (MO)
Missouri Valley Coll (MO)
Montana State U–Billings (MT)
Morehead State U (KY)
Morgan State U (MD)
Morningside Coll (IA)
Mountain State U (WV)
Mount Ida Coll (MA)
Mount Mary Coll (WI)
Mount Mercy Coll (IA)
Mount St. Mary's Coll (CA)
Mount Saint Vincent U (NS, Canada)
Mount Vernon Nazarene U (OH)
Murray State U (KY)
National American U, Rapid City (SD)
National U (CA)
Nazareth Coll of Rochester (NY)
Neumann Coll (PA)
New England Coll (NH)
New England School of Communications (ME)
Newman U (KS)
New Mexico Highlands U (NM)
New York Inst of Technology (NY)
New York U (NY)
Niagara U (NY)
Nicholls State U (LA)
Nichols Coll (MA)
North Carolina State U (NC)
North Central Coll (IL)
Northeastern Illinois U (IL)
Northeastern State U (OK)
Northeastern U (MA)
Northern Arizona U (AZ)
Northern Illinois U (IL)
Northern Michigan U (MI)
Northern State U (SD)
North Georgia Coll & State U (GA)
North Greenville U (SC)
Northwestern Coll (MN)
Northwest Missouri State U (MO)
Northwest Nazarene U (ID)
Northwood U (MI)
Northwood U, Florida Campus (FL)
Northwood U, Texas Campus (TX)
Nova Southeastern U (FL)
Oakland U (MI)
Oklahoma Christian U (OK)
Oklahoma City U (OK)
Oklahoma State U (OK)
Old Dominion U (VA)
Oral Roberts U (OK)
Oregon State U (OR)
Otterbein Coll (OH)
Pace U (NY)
Pacific Union Coll (CA)
Pacific U (OR)
Paine Coll (GA)
Palm Beach Atlantic U (FL)
Park U (MO)
Penn State Abington (PA)
Penn State Altoona (PA)
Penn State Berks (PA)
Penn State Erie, The Behrend Coll (PA)
Penn State Harrisburg (PA)
Penn State U Park (PA)
Pennsylvania Coll of Technology (PA)
Peru State Coll (NE)
Pfeiffer U (NC)
Philadelphia U (PA)
Pittsburg State U (KS)
Plymouth State U (NH)
Polytechnic U of Puerto Rico (PR)
Portland State U (OR)
Prairie View A&M U (TX)
Providence Coll (RI)
Purdue U (IN)
Purdue U Calumet (IN)
Quincy U (IL)
Quinnipiac U (CT)
Radford U (VA)
Rensselaer Polytechnic Inst (NY)
Rhode Island Coll (RI)
Rider U (NJ)
Robert Morris U (PA)
Roberts Wesleyan Coll (NY)
Rochester Coll (MI)
Rochester Inst of Technology (NY)
Rockford Coll (IL)
Roger Williams U (RI)
Roosevelt U (IL)
Rutgers, The State U of New Jersey, Camden (NJ)
Rutgers, The State U of New Jersey, Newark (NJ)
Rutgers, The State U of New Jersey, New Brunswick (NJ)
Sacred Heart U (CT)
Saginaw Valley State U (MI)
St. Ambrose U (IA)
St. Cloud State U (MN)
St. Edward's U (TX)
Saint Francis U (PA)
St. Gregory's U, Shawnee (OK)
St. John Fisher Coll (NY)
St. John's U (NY)
Saint Joseph's U (PA)
Saint Leo U (FL)
Saint Louis U (MO)
Saint Martin's U (WA)
Saint Mary-of-the-Woods Coll (IN)
Saint Mary's Coll (IN)
St. Mary's U (TX)
Saint Mary's U of Minnesota (MN)
St. Thomas Aquinas Coll (NY)
St. Thomas U (FL)
Saint Vincent Coll (PA)
Salem State Coll (MA)
Salisbury U (MD)
Sam Houston State U (TX)
San Diego State U (CA)
San Francisco State U (CA)
Santa Clara U (CA)
Schiller Intl U (FL)
Seattle U (WA)
Seton Hill U (PA)
Shippensburg U of Pennsylvania (PA)
Siena Coll (NY)
Simmons Coll (MA)
South Carolina State U (SC)
Southeastern Louisiana U (LA)
Southeastern Oklahoma State U (OK)
Southeastern U (FL)
Southeast Missouri State U (MO)
Southern Adventist U (TN)
Southern Connecticut State U (CT)
Southern Illinois U Carbondale (IL)
Southern Methodist U (TX)
Southern New Hampshire U (NH)
Southern Oregon U (OR)
Southern U and Ag and Mech Coll (LA)
Southwest Baptist U (MO)
Southwestern Oklahoma State U (OK)
Southwest Minnesota State U (MN)
Spring Hill Coll (AL)
State U of New York at Binghamton (NY)
State U of New York at Fredonia (NY)
State U of New York at New Paltz (NY)
State U of New York at Oswego (NY)
State U of New York at Plattsburgh (NY)
State U of New York Coll at Old Westbury (NY)
Stephen F. Austin State U (TX)
Stephens Coll (MO)
Stetson U (FL)
Stonehill Coll (MA)
Suffolk U (MA)
Sullivan U (KY)
Susquehanna U (PA)
Syracuse U (NY)
Tabor Coll (KS)
Taylor U (IN)
Taylor U Fort Wayne (IN)
Temple U (PA)
Tennessee Technological U (TN)
Texas A&M Intl U (TX)
Texas A&M U (TX)
Texas A&M U–Commerce (TX)
Texas Christian U (TX)
Texas Southern U (TX)
Texas State U-San Marcos (TX)
Texas Tech U (TX)
Texas Woman's U (TX)
Thomas Coll (ME)
Thompson Rivers U (BC, Canada)
Tiffin U (OH)
Trevecca Nazarene U (TN)
Trinity Christian Coll (IL)
Trinity Intl U (IL)
Trinity U (TX)
Tri-State U (IN)
Truman State U (MO)
Tulane U (LA)
Tuskegee U (AL)
Union U (TN)
Université de Sherbrooke (QC, Canada)
The U of Akron (OH)
The U of Alabama (AL)
The U of Alabama at Birmingham (AL)
The U of Alabama in Huntsville (AL)
The U of Arizona (AZ)
U of Arkansas (AR)
U of Baltimore (MD)
U of Bridgeport (CT)
The U of British Columbia (BC, Canada)
The U of British Columbia–Okanagan (BC, Canada)
U of Central Arkansas (AR)
U of Central Florida (FL)
U of Central Missouri (MO)
U of Central Oklahoma (OK)
U of Charleston (WV)
U of Cincinnati (OH)
U of Colorado at Boulder (CO)
U of Connecticut (CT)
U of Dayton (OH)
U of Delaware (DE)
U of Denver (CO)
U of Evansville (IN)
The U of Findlay (OH)
U of Florida (FL)
U of Georgia (GA)
U of Great Falls (MT)
U of Guam (GU)
U of Hawaii at Manoa (HI)
U of Houston (TX)
U of Houston–Clear Lake (TX)
U of Houston–Downtown (TX)
U of Houston–Victoria (TX)
U of Idaho (ID)
U of Illinois at Chicago (IL)
U of Illinois at Urbana–Champaign (IL)
U of Indianapolis (IN)
The U of Iowa (IA)
U of Kansas (KS)
U of La Verne (CA)
U of Lethbridge (AB, Canada)
U of Louisiana at Lafayette (LA)
U of Louisiana at Monroe (LA)
U of Louisville (KY)
U of Maine at Machias (ME)
U of Mary Hardin-Baylor (TX)
U of Maryland, Coll Park (MD)
U of Maryland U Coll (MD)
U of Massachusetts Amherst (MA)
U of Massachusetts Dartmouth (MA)
U of Memphis (TN)
U of Miami (FL)
U of Michigan–Dearborn (MI)
U of Michigan–Flint (MI)
U of Minnesota, Duluth (MN)
U of Minnesota, Twin Cities Campus (MN)
U of Mississippi (MS)
U of Missouri–Columbia (MO)
U of Missouri–St. Louis (MO)
The U of Montana (MT)
U of Montevallo (AL)
U of Nebraska at Omaha (NE)
U of Nebraska–Lincoln (NE)
U of Nevada, Las Vegas (NV)
U of Nevada, Reno (NV)
U of New Brunswick Fredericton (NB, Canada)
U of New Haven (CT)
U of New Orleans (LA)
U of North Alabama (AL)
The U of North Carolina Wilmington (NC)
U of North Dakota (ND)
U of Northern Iowa (IA)
U of North Florida (FL)
U of North Texas (TX)
U of Notre Dame (IN)
U of Oklahoma (OK)
U of Ottawa (ON, Canada)
U of Pennsylvania (PA)
U of Pittsburgh (PA)
U of Portland (OR)
U of Regina (SK, Canada)
U of Rhode Island (RI)
U of Richmond (VA)
U of Rio Grande (OH)
U of St. Francis (IL)
U of St. Thomas (MN)
U of St. Thomas (TX)
U of San Diego (CA)
The U of Scranton (PA)
U of South Alabama (AL)
U of South Carolina (SC)
The U of South Dakota (SD)
U of Southern Indiana (IN)
U of Southern Mississippi (MS)
U of South Florida (FL)
The U of Tampa (FL)
The U of Tennessee (TN)
The U of Tennessee at Martin (TN)
The U of Texas at Arlington (TX)
The U of Texas at Austin (TX)
The U of Texas at Brownsville (TX)
The U of Texas at El Paso (TX)
The U of Texas at San Antonio (TX)
The U of Texas at Tyler (TX)
The U of Texas of the Permian Basin (TX)
The U of Texas–Pan American (TX)
U of the Ozarks (AR)
U of the Sacred Heart (PR)
U of the Sciences in Philadelphia (PA)
The U of Toledo (OH)
U of Tulsa (OK)
U of Utah (UT)
The U of Western Ontario (ON, Canada)
U of West Florida (FL)
U of West Georgia (GA)
U of Windsor (ON, Canada)
U of Wisconsin–Eau Claire (WI)
U of Wisconsin–La Crosse (WI)
U of Wisconsin–Milwaukee (WI)
U of Wisconsin–Oshkosh (WI)
U of Wisconsin–Superior (WI)
U of Wisconsin–Whitewater (WI)
U of Wyoming (WY)
Ursuline Coll (OH)
Utah State U (UT)
Valdosta State U (GA)
Valparaiso U (IN)
Vanguard U of Southern California (CA)
Villanova U (PA)
Virginia Commonwealth U (VA)
Virginia Intermont Coll (VA)
Virginia Polytechnic Inst and State U (VA)
Virginia State U (VA)
Viterbo U (WI)
Walla Walla U (WA)
Wartburg Coll (IA)
Washburn U (KS)
Washington State U (WA)
Washington U in St. Louis (MO)
Waynesburg U (PA)
Wayne State U (MI)
Webber Intl U (FL)
Webster U (MO)
Wesley Coll (DE)
Western Carolina U (NC)
Western Connecticut State U (CT)
Western Illinois U (IL)
Western Intl U (AZ)
Western Kentucky U (KY)
Western Michigan U (MI)
Western New England Coll (MA)
Western New Mexico U (NM)
Western State Coll of Colorado (CO)
Western Washington U (WA)
West Liberty State Coll (WV)
Westminster Coll (UT)
West Texas A&M U (TX)
West Virginia U (WV)
West Virginia Wesleyan Coll (WV)
Wheeling Jesuit U (WV)
Wichita State U (KS)
Widener U (PA)
Wilmington Coll (OH)
Wilmington U (DE)
Wingate U (NC)
Winona State U (MN)
Woodbury U (CA)
Wright State U (OH)
Xavier U (OH)
Xavier U of Louisiana (LA)
York Coll of Pennsylvania (PA)
York Coll of the City U of New York (NY)
York U (ON, Canada)
Youngstown State U (OH)

MARKETING RELATED

Babson Coll (MA)
Bowling Green State U (OH)
Canisius Coll (NY)
Clayton State U (GA)
DeSales U (PA)
Duquesne U (PA)
Inter American U of Puerto Rico, San Germán Campus (PR)
Miami U Hamilton (OH)
Mount Saint Mary Coll (NY)
Troy U (AL)
The U of Akron (OH)
The U of Iowa (IA)
Washington U in St. Louis (MO)
Western Carolina U (NC)
Western Michigan U (MI)
Western New England Coll (MA)

MARKETING RESEARCH

Ashland U (OH)
Baker Coll of Jackson (MI)
Boston U (MA)
Fairleigh Dickinson U, Metropolitan Campus (NJ)
Fashion Inst of Technology (NY)
Inter American U of Puerto Rico, Bayamón Campus (PR)
Ithaca Coll (NY)
Methodist U (NC)
Mount Saint Vincent U (NS, Canada)
U of Illinois at Urbana–Champaign (IL)
The U of Toledo (OH)
U of Windsor (ON, Canada)

MARRIAGE AND FAMILY THERAPY/COUNSELING

Grace U (NE)
Harding U (AR)
Limestone Coll (SC)
Seton Hill U (PA)
U of Nevada, Las Vegas (NV)
The U of Western Ontario (ON, Canada)

MARRIAGE/FAMILY COUNSELING

Northcentral U (AZ)

MASS COMMUNICATION/ MEDIA

Alabama State U (AL)
Albertus Magnus Coll (CT)
Albion Coll (MI)
Alcorn State U (MS)
Allegheny Coll (PA)
American U (DC)
The American U of Paris (France)
Anderson U (IN)
Andrews U (MI)
Ashland U (OH)
Auburn U (AL)
Augsburg Coll (MN)
Augustana Coll (IL)
Austin Peay State U (TN)
Baker U (KS)
Baldwin-Wallace Coll (OH)
Barry U (FL)
Barton Coll (NC)
Belmont U (TN)
Beloit Coll (WI)
Bemidji State U (MN)
Benedictine Coll (KS)
Bethel Coll (KS)
Bethel U (MN)
Bethune-Cookman U (FL)
Bloomsburg U of Pennsylvania (PA)
Bluefield Coll (VA)
Boise State U (ID)
Boston U (MA)
Brenau U (GA)
Bridgewater Coll (VA)
Brigham Young U (UT)
Brock U (ON, Canada)
Buffalo State Coll, State U of New York (NY)
California Lutheran U (CA)
California State Polytechnic U, Pomona (CA)
California State U, Chico (CA)
California State U, Dominguez Hills (CA)
California State U, East Bay (CA)
California State U, Fresno (CA)
California State U, Long Beach (CA)
California State U, Sacramento (CA)
Calvin Coll (MI)
Carlow U (PA)
Carson-Newman Coll (TN)
Catawba Coll (NC)
Centenary Coll (NJ)

Central Pennsylvania Coll (PA)
Central Washington U (WA)
Chaminade U of Honolulu (HI)
Cheyney U of Pennsylvania (PA)
City Coll of the City U of New York (NY)
City U of Seattle (WA)
Claflin U (SC)
Clarke Coll (IA)
Clark U (MA)
Colby-Sawyer Coll (NH)
The Coll at Brockport, State U of New York (NY)
Coll of Mount Saint Vincent (NY)
The Coll of New Rochelle (NY)
Coll of the Ozarks (MO)
Colorado State U-Pueblo (CO)
Concordia Coll (MN)
Concordia U (QC, Canada)
Concordia U, Nebraska (NE)
Concordia U, St. Paul (MN)
Concordia U Texas (TX)
Concordia U Wisconsin (WI)
Concord U (WV)
Cornerstone U (MI)
Culver-Stockton Coll (MO)
Curry Coll (MA)
Defiance Coll (OH)
Denison U (OH)
DePauw U (IN)
DeSales U (PA)
Dillard U (LA)
Dominican U (IL)
Dordt Coll (IA)
Drake U (IA)
East Central U (OK)
Eastern Kentucky U (KY)
East Tennessee State U (TN)
Emerson Coll (MA)
Emmanuel Coll (GA)
Emmanuel Coll (MA)
Emory & Henry Coll (VA)
Endicott Coll (MA)
Excelsior Coll (NY)
Fairfield U (CT)
Felician Coll (NJ)
Five Towns Coll (NY)
Florida Ag and Mech U (FL)
Florida Gulf Coast U (FL)
Florida State U (FL)
Francis Marion U (SC)
Fresno Pacific U (CA)
Frostburg State U (MD)
Gardner-Webb U (NC)
The George Washington U (DC)
Gonzaga U (WA)
Goucher Coll (MD)
Grace U (NE)
Grambling State U (LA)
Grand Canyon U (AZ)
Grand Valley State U (MI)
Grand View Coll (IA)
Greenville Coll (IL)
Grove City Coll (PA)
Gustavus Adolphus Coll (MN)
Hamilton Coll (NY)
Hamline U (MN)
Hampshire Coll (MA)
Hampton U (VA)
Hanover Coll (IN)
Hastings Coll (NE)
Hawai'i Pacific U (HI)
Heidelberg Coll (OH)
High Point U (NC)
Hobart and William Smith Colls (NY)
Hofstra U (NY)
Hollins U (VA)
Houston Baptist U (TX)
Hunter Coll of the City U of New York (NY)
Huntington U (IN)
Idaho State U (ID)
Illinois Coll (IL)
Illinois State U (IL)
Indiana U–Purdue U Fort Wayne (IN)
Indiana U South Bend (IN)
Inter American U of Puerto Rico, Bayamón Campus (PR)
Intl U in Geneva (Switzerland)
Iona Coll (NY)
Iowa State U of Science and Technology (IA)
Iowa Wesleyan Coll (IA)
Ithaca Coll (NY)
Jackson State U (MS)
John Brown U (AR)
John Carroll U (OH)
Johnson Bible Coll (TN)
Johnson C. Smith U (NC)
Keene State Coll (NH)
Kent State U (OH)
Kuyper Coll (MI)
Lambuth U (TN)
La Salle U (PA)
Lees-McRae Coll (NC)
Lee U (TN)
Lehman Coll of the City U of New York (NY)
Lewis U (IL)
Lindenwood U (MO)
Lindsey Wilson Coll (KY)
Linfield Coll (OR)
Lipscomb U (TN)
Loras Coll (IA)
Louisiana Coll (LA)
Louisiana State U and Ag and Mech Coll (LA)
Loyola Marymount U (CA)
Loyola U Chicago (IL)
Lubbock Christian U (TX)
Lynchburg Coll (VA)
Madonna U (MI)
Manchester Coll (IN)
Mansfield U of Pennsylvania (PA)
Marian Coll (IN)
Marquette U (WI)
Marylhurst U (OR)
Maryville U of Saint Louis (MO)
Massachusetts Inst of Technology (MA)
The Master's Coll and Sem (CA)
McKendree U (IL)
McNeese State U (LA)
Medaille Coll (NY)
Mercer U (GA)
Mercyhurst Coll (PA)
Meredith Coll (NC)
Mesa State Coll (CO)
Methodist U (NC)
Miami U (OH)
Miami U Hamilton (OH)
Michigan State U (MI)
MidAmerica Nazarene U (KS)
Middle Tennessee State U (TN)
Midland Lutheran Coll (NE)
Midwestern State U (TX)
Miles Coll (AL)
Minnesota State U Mankato (MN)
Mississippi Coll (MS)
Mississippi Valley State U (MS)
Missouri State U (MO)
Missouri Valley Coll (MO)
Montana State U–Billings (MT)
Morgan State U (MD)
Morningside Coll (IA)
Morris Coll (SC)
Mountain State U (WV)
Mount Saint Mary Coll (NY)
Murray State U (KY)
New England Coll (NH)
Newman U (KS)
New York U (NY)
Niagara U (NY)
Nicholls State U (LA)
North Carolina Ag and Tech State U (NC)
North Carolina Central U (NC)
North Carolina State U (NC)
North Dakota State U (ND)
Northeastern U (MA)
North Greenville U (SC)
Northwestern Oklahoma State U (OK)
Northwest Missouri State U (MO)
Northwest Nazarene U (ID)
Oakwood Coll (AL)
Oglethorpe U (GA)
Ohio Northern U (OH)
Oklahoma Christian U (OK)
Oklahoma City U (OK)
Oklahoma Wesleyan U (OK)
Ouachita Baptist U (AR)
Pace U (NY)
Pacific Union Coll (CA)
Pacific U (OR)
Piedmont Coll (GA)
Point Loma Nazarene U (CA)
Point Park U (PA)
Purdue U Calumet (IN)
Queens Coll of the City U of New York (NY)
Queens U of Charlotte (NC)
Quinnipiac U (CT)
Robert Morris U (PA)
Russell Sage Coll (NY)
Rutgers, The State U of New Jersey, New Brunswick (NJ)
St. Ambrose U (IA)
St. Andrews Presbyterian Coll (NC)
St. Cloud State U (MN)
Saint Francis U (PA)
St. John Fisher Coll (NY)
Saint Joseph's Coll (IN)
Saint Mary-of-the-Woods Coll (IN)
St. Mary's Coll of Maryland (MD)
St. Mary's U (TX)
St. Thomas Aquinas Coll (NY)
St. Thomas U (FL)
Salem Coll (NC)
Salem Intl U (WV)
Salem State Coll (MA)
San Diego State U (CA)
Scripps Coll (CA)
Seattle U (WA)
Shaw U (NC)
Simmons Coll (MA)
Simpson Coll (IA)
Sonoma State U (CA)
Southern Adventist U (TN)
Southern Arkansas U–Magnolia (AR)
Southern Illinois U Edwardsville (IL)
Southern U and Ag and Mech Coll (LA)
Southern Utah U (UT)
Southern Vermont Coll (VT)
Southwestern Adventist U (TX)
Southwestern Oklahoma State U (OK)
Southwestern U (TX)
State U of New York at Fredonia (NY)
State U of New York at Oswego (NY)
State U of New York at Plattsburgh (NY)
State U of New York Coll at Oneonta (NY)
Stephens Coll (MO)
Stillman Coll (AL)
Suffolk U (MA)
Susquehanna U (PA)
Tabor Coll (KS)
Taylor U (IN)
Tennessee State U (TN)
Texas Christian U (TX)
Texas Southern U (TX)
Texas State U-San Marcos (TX)
Thiel Coll (PA)
Toccoa Falls Coll (GA)
Towson U (MD)
Trevecca Nazarene U (TN)
Truman State U (MO)
Tulane U (LA)
Union U (TN)
U at Albany, State U of New York (NY)
U at Buffalo, the State U of New York (NY)
U of Baltimore (MD)
U of Bridgeport (CT)
U of California, Berkeley (CA)
U of California, San Diego (CA)
U of Central Florida (FL)
U of Cincinnati (OH)
U of Dayton (OH)
U of Delaware (DE)
U of Georgia (GA)
U of Guam (GU)
U of Houston (TX)
U of Illinois at Urbana–Champaign (IL)
The U of Iowa (IA)
U of Louisiana at Lafayette (LA)
U of Maine (ME)
U of Mary (ND)
U of Mary Hardin-Baylor (TX)
U of Maryland, Baltimore County (MD)
U of Maryland Eastern Shore (MD)
U of Miami (FL)
U of Michigan (MI)
U of Minnesota, Twin Cities Campus (MN)
U of Missouri–Columbia (MO)
U of Missouri–Kansas City (MO)
U of Missouri–St. Louis (MO)
U of Nebraska at Kearney (NE)
U of Nevada, Las Vegas (NV)
U of New Hampshire (NH)
U of New Hampshire at Manchester (NH)
U of New Mexico (NM)
The U of North Carolina at Asheville (NC)
The U of North Carolina at Chapel Hill (NC)
The U of North Carolina at Greensboro (NC)
U of North Florida (FL)
U of Oregon (OR)
U of Pittsburgh at Johnstown (PA)
U of Portland (OR)
U of Rio Grande (OH)
U of St. Francis (IL)
U of Saint Mary (KS)
U of Sioux Falls (SD)
The U of South Dakota (SD)
U of Southern California (CA)
U of Southern Maine (ME)
The U of Tampa (FL)
The U of Tennessee at Chattanooga (TN)
The U of Texas at El Paso (TX)
The U of Texas at San Antonio (TX)
The U of Texas of the Permian Basin (TX)
U of the District of Columbia (DC)
U of the Ozarks (AR)
U of the Sacred Heart (PR)
The U of Toledo (OH)
U of Toronto (ON, Canada)
U of Utah (UT)
The U of Western Ontario (ON, Canada)
U of Windsor (ON, Canada)
U of Wisconsin–Eau Claire (WI)
U of Wisconsin–Madison (WI)
U of Wisconsin–Milwaukee (WI)
U of Wisconsin–Oshkosh (WI)
U of Wisconsin–Platteville (WI)
U of Wisconsin–Superior (WI)
Ursinus Coll (PA)
Valdosta State U (GA)
Valley City State U (ND)
Valparaiso U (IN)
Vanderbilt U (TN)
Vassar Coll (NY)
Villanova U (PA)
Virginia Commonwealth U (VA)
Virginia State U (VA)
Walla Walla U (WA)
Wartburg Coll (IA)
Washburn U (KS)
Wayland Baptist U (TX)
Wayne State Coll (NE)
Wesley Coll (DE)
Western New England Coll (MA)
Westfield State Coll (MA)
West Liberty State Coll (WV)
West Texas A&M U (TX)
West Virginia U (WV)
Whitworth U (WA)
Widener U (PA)
Wiley Coll (TX)
Wilfrid Laurier U (ON, Canada)
William Paterson U of New Jersey (NJ)
Wilmington Coll (OH)
Wilson Coll (PA)
Wingate U (NC)
Winona State U (MN)
Winthrop U (SC)
Worcester State Coll (MA)
Wright State U (OH)
Xavier U of Louisiana (LA)
York Coll of Pennsylvania (PA)
York U (ON, Canada)

MASS COMMUNICATIONS

Brigham Young U (UT)
Clemson U (SC)
East Central U (OK)
Mitchell Coll (CT)
Rochester Coll (MI)
U of Louisiana at Monroe (LA)
The U of North Carolina at Greensboro (NC)
The U of North Carolina at Pembroke (NC)

MATERIALS ENGINEERING

Alfred U (NY)
Arizona State U (AZ)
Auburn U (AL)
Brown U (RI)
California Polytechnic State U, San Luis Obispo (CA)
California State Polytechnic U, Pomona (CA)
California State U, Long Beach (CA)
Case Western Reserve U (OH)
Clarkson U (NY)
Clemson U (SC)
Cornell U (NY)
Drexel U (PA)
Florida State U (FL)
Georgia Inst of Technology (GA)
Harvard U (MA)
Illinois Inst of Technology (IL)
Iowa State U of Science and Technology (IA)
The Johns Hopkins U (MD)
Lehigh U (PA)
Massachusetts Inst of Technology (MA)
McGill U (QC, Canada)
Michigan Technological U (MI)
Missouri U of Science and Technology (MO)
Montana Tech of The U of Montana (MT)
New Mexico Inst of Mining and Technology (NM)
North Carolina State U (NC)
Northwestern U (IL)
Purdue U (IN)
Rensselaer Polytechnic Inst (NY)
Rice U (TX)
The U of Alabama at Birmingham (AL)
The U of British Columbia (BC, Canada)
U of California, Davis (CA)
U of California, Irvine (CA)
U of California, Los Angeles (CA)
U of Connecticut (CT)
U of Florida (FL)
U of Idaho (ID)
U of Illinois at Urbana–Champaign (IL)
U of Maryland, Coll Park (MD)
U of Michigan (MI)
U of Minnesota, Twin Cities Campus (MN)
U of Pennsylvania (PA)
U of Pittsburgh (PA)
The U of Tennessee (TN)
U of Toronto (ON, Canada)
U of Utah (UT)
The U of Western Ontario (ON, Canada)
U of Windsor (ON, Canada)
U of Wisconsin–Milwaukee (WI)
Virginia Polytechnic Inst and State U (VA)
Washington State U (WA)
Winona State U (MN)
Worcester Polytechnic Inst (MA)
Wright State U (OH)

MATERIALS SCIENCE

California Inst of Technology (CA)
Carnegie Mellon U (PA)
Case Western Reserve U (OH)
Clarkson U (NY)
Duke U (NC)
Harvard U (MA)
The Johns Hopkins U (MD)
Michigan State U (MI)
Montana Tech of The U of Montana (MT)
North Carolina State U (NC)
Northwestern U (IL)
Penn State Abington (PA)
Penn State Altoona (PA)
Penn State Berks (PA)
Penn State Erie, The Behrend Coll (PA)
Penn State U Park (PA)
Rice U (TX)
Stanford U (CA)
United States Air Force Acad (CO)
The U of Arizona (AZ)
U of California, Berkeley (CA)
U of California, Los Angeles (CA)
U of California, Riverside (CA)
U of Illinois at Urbana–Champaign (IL)
U of Michigan (MI)
U of Minnesota, Twin Cities Campus (MN)
U of Pennsylvania (PA)
U of Toronto (ON, Canada)
Washington State U (WA)
Worcester Polytechnic Inst (MA)

MATERNAL/CHILD HEALTH AND NEONATAL NURSING

U at Buffalo, the State U of New York (NY)

MATHEMATICAL STATISTICS AND PROBABILITY

Barnard Coll (NY)
Carnegie Mellon U (PA)
Concordia U (QC, Canada)
McGill U (QC, Canada)
Northern Illinois U (IL)
U of Miami (FL)
The U of Western Ontario (ON, Canada)

MATHEMATICS

Abilene Christian U (TX)
Acadia U (NS, Canada)
Adams State Coll (CO)
Adelphi U (NY)
Adrian Coll (MI)
Agnes Scott Coll (GA)
Alabama Ag and Mech U (AL)
Alabama State U (AL)
Albertus Magnus Coll (CT)
Albion Coll (MI)
Albright Coll (PA)
Alcorn State U (MS)
Alderson-Broaddus Coll (WV)
Alfred U (NY)
Allegheny Coll (PA)
Alma Coll (MI)
Alvernia Coll (PA)
American U (DC)
The American U of Athens (Greece)
American U of Beirut (Lebanon)
Amherst Coll (MA)
Anderson U (IN)
Anderson U (SC)
Andrews U (MI)
Angelo State U (TX)
Appalachian State U (NC)
Aquinas Coll (MI)
Arizona State U (AZ)
Arkansas State U (AR)

Armstrong Atlantic State U (GA)
Asbury Coll (KY)
Ashland U (OH)
Assumption Coll (MA)
Athens State U (AL)
Auburn U (AL)
Auburn U Montgomery (AL)
Augsburg Coll (MN)
Augustana Coll (IL)
Augustana Coll (SD)
Augusta State U (GA)
Austin Coll (TX)
Austin Peay State U (TN)
Ave Maria U (FL)
Averett U (VA)
Avila U (MO)
Azusa Pacific U (CA)
Baker U (KS)
Baldwin-Wallace Coll (OH)
Ball State U (IN)
Bard Coll (NY)
Bard Coll at Simon's Rock (MA)
Barnard Coll (NY)
Barry U (FL)
Barton Coll (NC)
Bates Coll (ME)
Baylor U (TX)
Belhaven Coll (MS)
Bellarmine U (KY)
Belmont U (TN)
Beloit Coll (WI)
Bemidji State U (MN)
Benedictine Coll (KS)
Benedictine U (IL)
Bennington Coll (VT)
Bentley Coll (MA)
Berea Coll (KY)
Bernard M. Baruch Coll of the City U of New York (NY)
Berry Coll (GA)
Bethany Coll (KS)
Bethany Coll (WV)
Bethany Lutheran Coll (MN)
Bethel Coll (KS)
Bethel Coll (TN)
Bethel U (MN)
Bethune-Cookman U (FL)
Biola U (CA)
Bishop's U (QC, Canada)
Blackburn Coll (IL)
Bloomfield Coll (NJ)
Bloomsburg U of Pennsylvania (PA)
Bluefield Coll (VA)
Bluffton U (OH)
Bob Jones U (SC)
Boise State U (ID)
Boston Coll (MA)
Boston U (MA)
Bowdoin Coll (ME)
Bowling Green State U (OH)
Bradley U (IL)
Brandeis U (MA)
Brevard Coll (NC)
Brewton-Parker Coll (GA)
Bridgewater Coll (VA)
Bridgewater State Coll (MA)
Brigham Young U (UT)
Brock U (ON, Canada)
Brown U (RI)
Bryan Coll (TN)
Bryn Mawr Coll (PA)
Bucknell U (PA)
Buffalo State Coll, State U of New York (NY)
Butler U (IN)
Cabrini Coll (PA)
California Baptist U (CA)
California Inst of Technology (CA)
California Lutheran U (CA)
California Polytechnic State U, San Luis Obispo (CA)
California State Polytechnic U, Pomona (CA)
California State U, Chico (CA)
California State U, Dominguez Hills (CA)
California State U, East Bay (CA)
California State U, Fresno (CA)
California State U, Fullerton (CA)
California State U, Long Beach (CA)
California State U, Los Angeles (CA)
California State U, Sacramento (CA)
California State U, San Bernardino (CA)
California State U, San Marcos (CA)
California State U, Stanislaus (CA)
Calvin Coll (MI)
Cameron U (OK)
Canadian Mennonite U (MB, Canada)
Capital U (OH)
Carlow U (PA)
Carroll Coll (WI)
Carson-Newman Coll (TN)
Case Western Reserve U (OH)
Castleton State Coll (VT)
Catawba Coll (NC)
The Catholic U of America (DC)
Cedar Crest Coll (PA)
Cedarville U (OH)
Centenary Coll (NJ)
Centenary Coll of Louisiana (LA)
Central Coll (IA)
Central Connecticut State U (CT)
Central Michigan U (MI)
Central State U (OH)
Central Washington U (WA)
Centre Coll (KY)
Chapman U (CA)
Chatham U (PA)
Cheyney U of Pennsylvania (PA)
Chicago State U (IL)
Christian Brothers U (TN)
Christopher Newport U (VA)
The Citadel, The Military Coll of South Carolina (SC)
City Coll of the City U of New York (NY)
Claflin U (SC)
Claremont McKenna Coll (CA)
Clarion U of Pennsylvania (PA)
Clark Atlanta U (GA)
Clarke Coll (IA)
Clarkson U (NY)
Clark U (MA)
Clearwater Christian Coll (FL)
Clemson U (SC)
Cleveland State U (OH)
Coker Coll (SC)
Colby Coll (ME)
Colgate U (NY)
The Coll at Brockport, State U of New York (NY)
Coll of Charleston (SC)
The Coll of Idaho (ID)
Coll of Mount St. Joseph (OH)
Coll of Mount Saint Vincent (NY)
The Coll of New Jersey (NJ)
The Coll of New Rochelle (NY)
Coll of Saint Benedict (MN)
Coll of Saint Elizabeth (NJ)
Coll of Saint Mary (NE)
The Coll of Saint Rose (NY)
The Coll of St. Scholastica (MN)
Coll of Staten Island of the City U of New York (NY)
Coll of the Holy Cross (MA)
Coll of the Ozarks (MO)
Coll of the Southwest (NM)
The Coll of William and Mary (VA)
The Colorado Coll (CO)
Colorado School of Mines (CO)
Colorado State U (CO)
Columbia Coll (SC)
Columbus State U (GA)
Concordia Coll (MN)
Concordia Coll–New York (NY)
Concordia U (CA)
Concordia U (MI)
Concordia U (QC, Canada)
Concordia U Chicago (IL)
Concordia U, Nebraska (NE)
Concordia U, St. Paul (MN)
Concordia U Texas (TX)
Concordia U Wisconsin (WI)
Concord U (WV)
Connecticut Coll (CT)
Converse Coll (SC)
Cornell Coll (IA)
Cornell U (NY)
Cornerstone U (MI)
Covenant Coll (GA)
Creighton U (NE)
Culver-Stockton Coll (MO)
Daemen Coll (NY)
Dakota Wesleyan U (SD)
Dallas Baptist U (TX)
Dana Coll (NE)
Dartmouth Coll (NH)
Davidson Coll (NC)
Davis & Elkins Coll (WV)
Defiance Coll (OH)
Delaware Valley Coll (PA)
Delta State U (MS)
Denison U (OH)
DePaul U (IL)
DePauw U (IN)
DeSales U (PA)
Dickinson Coll (PA)
Dillard U (LA)
Doane Coll (NE)
Dominican Coll (NY)
Dominican U (IL)
Dordt Coll (IA)
Dowling Coll (NY)
Drake U (IA)
Drew U (NJ)
Drexel U (PA)
Drury U (MO)
Duke U (NC)
Duquesne U (PA)
Earlham Coll (IN)
East Carolina U (NC)
East Central U (OK)
Eastern Connecticut State U (CT)
Eastern Illinois U (IL)
Eastern Kentucky U (KY)
Eastern Mennonite U (VA)
Eastern Michigan U (MI)
East Stroudsburg U of Pennsylvania (PA)
East Tennessee State U (TN)
East Texas Baptist U (TX)
East-West U (IL)
Eckerd Coll (FL)
Edinboro U of Pennsylvania (PA)
Elizabethtown Coll (PA)
Elon U (NC)
Emmanuel Coll (GA)
Emmanuel Coll (MA)
Emory & Henry Coll (VA)
Emory U (GA)
Emporia State U (KS)
Erskine Coll (SC)
Evangel U (MO)
Excelsior Coll (NY)
Fairfield U (CT)
Fairleigh Dickinson U, Coll at Florham (NJ)
Fairleigh Dickinson U, Metropolitan Campus (NJ)
Fairmont State U (WV)
Fayetteville State U (NC)
Felician Coll (NJ)
Ferris State U (MI)
Ferrum Coll (VA)
Fitchburg State Coll (MA)
Florida Ag and Mech U (FL)
Florida Atlantic U (FL)
Florida Gulf Coast U (FL)
Florida Intl U (FL)
Florida Memorial U (FL)
Florida Southern Coll (FL)
Florida State U (FL)
Fontbonne U (MO)
Fort Lewis Coll (CO)
Framingham State Coll (MA)
Franciscan U of Steubenville (OH)
Francis Marion U (SC)
Franklin & Marshall Coll (PA)
Franklin Coll (IN)
Freed-Hardeman U (TN)
Fresno Pacific U (CA)
Frostburg State U (MD)
Furman U (SC)
Gannon U (PA)
Gardner-Webb U (NC)
George Fox U (OR)
George Mason U (VA)
Georgetown Coll (KY)
Georgetown U (DC)
The George Washington U (DC)
Georgia Coll & State U (GA)
Georgian Court U (NJ)
Georgia Southern U (GA)
Georgia Southwestern State U (GA)
Georgia State U (GA)
Gettysburg Coll (PA)
Gonzaga U (WA)
Gordon Coll (MA)
Goucher Coll (MD)
Grace Coll (IN)
Grambling State U (LA)
Grand Valley State U (MI)
Greensboro Coll (NC)
Greenville Coll (IL)
Grinnell Coll (IA)
Grove City Coll (PA)
Guilford Coll (NC)
Gustavus Adolphus Coll (MN)
Gwynedd-Mercy Coll (PA)
Hamilton Coll (NY)
Hamline U (MN)
Hampden-Sydney Coll (VA)
Hampshire Coll (MA)
Hampton U (VA)
Hannibal-LaGrange Coll (MO)
Hanover Coll (IN)
Harding U (AR)
Hardin-Simmons U (TX)
Hartwick Coll (NY)
Harvard U (MA)
Harvey Mudd Coll (CA)
Hastings Coll (NE)
Haverford Coll (PA)
Heidelberg Coll (OH)
Henderson State U (AR)
Hendrix Coll (AR)
High Point U (NC)
Hillsdale Coll (MI)
Hobart and William Smith Colls (NY)
Hofstra U (NY)
Hollins U (VA)
Holy Family U (PA)
Hood Coll (MD)
Hope Coll (MI)
Houghton Coll (NY)
Houston Baptist U (TX)
Howard Payne U (TX)
Humboldt State U (CA)
Hunter Coll of the City U of New York (NY)
Huntingdon Coll (AL)
Huntington U (IN)
Huston-Tillotson U (TX)
Idaho State U (ID)
Illinois Coll (IL)
Illinois State U (IL)
Illinois Wesleyan U (IL)
Immaculata U (PA)
Indiana State U (IN)
Indiana U Bloomington (IN)
Indiana U Kokomo (IN)
Indiana U Northwest (IN)
Indiana U of Pennsylvania (PA)
Indiana U–Purdue U Fort Wayne (IN)
Indiana U–Purdue U Indianapolis (IN)
Indiana U South Bend (IN)
Indiana U Southeast (IN)
Indiana Wesleyan U (IN)
Inter American U of Puerto Rico, Bayamón Campus (PR)
Inter American U of Puerto Rico, San Germán Campus (PR)
Iona Coll (NY)
Iowa State U of Science and Technology (IA)
Iowa Wesleyan Coll (IA)
Ithaca Coll (NY)
Jackson State U (MS)
Jacksonville State U (AL)
Jacksonville U (FL)
James Madison U (VA)
Jamestown Coll (ND)
Jarvis Christian Coll (TX)
John Brown U (AR)
John Carroll U (OH)
The Johns Hopkins U (MD)
Johnson C. Smith U (NC)
Johnson State Coll (VT)
Judson Coll (AL)
Judson U (IL)
Juniata Coll (PA)
Kalamazoo Coll (MI)
Kansas State U (KS)
Kean U (NJ)
Keene State Coll (NH)
Kennesaw State U (GA)
Kent State U (OH)
Kentucky State U (KY)
Kentucky Wesleyan Coll (KY)
Kenyon Coll (OH)
Keuka Coll (NY)
King Coll (TN)
King's Coll (PA)
Knox Coll (IL)
Kutztown U of Pennsylvania (PA)
Lafayette Coll (PA)
LaGrange Coll (GA)
Lake Forest Coll (IL)
Lakehead U (ON, Canada)
Lake Superior State U (MI)
Lambuth U (TN)
Lander U (SC)
La Roche Coll (PA)
La Salle U (PA)
La Sierra U (CA)
Laurentian U (ON, Canada)
Lawrence Technological U (MI)
Lawrence U (WI)
Lebanon Valley Coll (PA)
Lees-McRae Coll (NC)
Lee U (TN)
Lehigh U (PA)
Lehman Coll of the City U of New York (NY)
Le Moyne Coll (NY)
LeMoyne-Owen Coll (TN)
Lenoir-Rhyne Coll (NC)
LeTourneau U (TX)
Lewis & Clark Coll (OR)
Lewis-Clark State Coll (ID)
Lewis U (IL)
Liberty U (VA)
Limestone Coll (SC)
Lincoln U (MO)
Lincoln U (PA)
Lindenwood U (MO)
Linfield Coll (OR)
Lipscomb U (TN)
Livingstone Coll (NC)
Lock Haven U of Pennsylvania (PA)
Longwood U (VA)
Loras Coll (IA)
Louisiana Coll (LA)
Louisiana State U and Ag and Mech Coll (LA)
Loyola Coll in Maryland (MD)
Loyola Marymount U (CA)
Loyola U Chicago (IL)
Loyola U New Orleans (LA)
Lubbock Christian U (TX)
Luther Coll (IA)
Lycoming Coll (PA)
Lynchburg Coll (VA)
Lyndon State Coll (VT)
Lyon Coll (AR)
Macalester Coll (MN)
Madonna U (MI)
Maharishi U of Management (IA)
Malone Coll (OH)
Manchester Coll (IN)
Manhattanville Coll (NY)
Mansfield U of Pennsylvania (PA)
Marian Coll (IN)
Marian Coll of Fond du Lac (WI)
Marietta Coll (OH)
Marist Coll (NY)
Marlboro Coll (VT)
Marquette U (WI)
Marshall U (WV)
Martin U (IN)
Mary Baldwin Coll (VA)
Marymount U (VA)
Maryville Coll (TN)
Maryville U of Saint Louis (MO)
Marywood U (PA)
Massachusetts Coll of Liberal Arts (MA)
Massachusetts Inst of Technology (MA)
The Master's Coll and Sem (CA)
Mayville State U (ND)
McDaniel Coll (MD)
McGill U (QC, Canada)
McKendree U (IL)
McMurry U (TX)
McNeese State U (LA)
Memorial U of Newfoundland (NL, Canada)
Mercer U (GA)
Mercy Coll (NY)
Mercyhurst Coll (PA)
Meredith Coll (NC)
Merrimack Coll (MA)
Mesa State Coll (CO)
Messiah Coll (PA)
Methodist U (NC)
Miami U (OH)
Miami U Hamilton (OH)
Michigan State U (MI)
Michigan Technological U (MI)
MidAmerica Nazarene U (KS)
Middlebury Coll (VT)
Middle Tennessee State U (TN)
Midland Lutheran Coll (NE)
Midway Coll (KY)
Midwestern State U (TX)
Miles Coll (AL)
Millersville U of Pennsylvania (PA)
Milligan Coll (TN)
Millsaps Coll (MS)
Mills Coll (CA)
Minnesota State U Mankato (MN)
Minot State U (ND)
Misericordia U (PA)
Mississippi Coll (MS)
Mississippi State U (MS)
Mississippi U for Women (MS)
Mississippi Valley State U (MS)
Missouri Baptist U (MO)
Missouri Southern State U (MO)
Missouri State U (MO)
Missouri Valley Coll (MO)
Molloy Coll (NY)
Monmouth Coll (IL)
Monmouth U (NJ)
Montana State U (MT)
Montana State U–Billings (MT)
Montana Tech of The U of Montana (MT)
Montclair State U (NJ)
Moravian Coll (PA)
Morehead State U (KY)
Morehouse Coll (GA)
Morgan State U (MD)
Morningside Coll (IA)
Morris Coll (SC)
Mount Allison U (NB, Canada)
Mount Holyoke Coll (MA)
Mount Marty Coll (SD)
Mount Mary Coll (WI)
Mount Mercy Coll (IA)
Mount Olive Coll (NC)
Mount Saint Mary Coll (NY)
Mount St. Mary's Coll (CA)
Mount St. Mary's U (MD)
Mount Saint Vincent U (NS, Canada)
Mount Vernon Nazarene U (OH)
Muhlenberg Coll (PA)
Murray State U (KY)
National-Louis U (IL)
National U (CA)
Nazareth Coll of Rochester (NY)
Nebraska Wesleyan U (NE)
New Coll of Florida (FL)
New Jersey City U (NJ)
Newman U (KS)
New Mexico Highlands U (NM)
New Mexico Inst of Mining and Technology (NM)
New York U (NY)
Niagara U (NY)
Nicholls State U (LA)

Nichols Coll (MA)
North Carolina Ag and Tech State U (NC)
North Carolina Central U (NC)
North Carolina State U (NC)
North Carolina Wesleyan Coll (NC)
North Central Coll (IL)
North Dakota State U (ND)
Northeastern Illinois U (IL)
Northeastern State U (OK)
Northeastern U (MA)
Northern Arizona U (AZ)
Northern Illinois U (IL)
Northern Michigan U (MI)
Northern State U (SD)
North Georgia Coll & State U (GA)
Northland Coll (WI)
Northwest Christian Coll (OR)
Northwestern Coll (IA)
Northwestern Coll (MN)
Northwestern Oklahoma State U (OK)
Northwestern State U of Louisiana (LA)
Northwestern U (IL)
Northwest Missouri State U (MO)
Northwest Nazarene U (ID)
Norwich U (VT)
Nyack Coll (NY)
Oakland City U (IN)
Oakland U (MI)
Oakwood Coll (AL)
Oberlin Coll (OH)
Occidental Coll (CA)
Oglethorpe U (GA)
Ohio Dominican U (OH)
Ohio Northern U (OH)
Ohio U (OH)
Ohio Wesleyan U (OH)
Oklahoma Christian U (OK)
Oklahoma City U (OK)
Oklahoma Panhandle State U (OK)
Oklahoma State U (OK)
Oklahoma Wesleyan U (OK)
Old Dominion U (VA)
Oral Roberts U (OK)
Oregon State U (OR)
Otterbein Coll (OH)
Ouachita Baptist U (AR)
Pace U (NY)
Pacific Lutheran U (WA)
Pacific Union Coll (CA)
Pacific U (OR)
Paine Coll (GA)
Palm Beach Atlantic U (FL)
Park U (MO)
Penn State Abington (PA)
Penn State Altoona (PA)
Penn State Berks (PA)
Penn State Erie, The Behrend Coll (PA)
Penn State U Park (PA)
Pepperdine U, Malibu (CA)
Peru State Coll (NE)
Pfeiffer U (NC)
Piedmont Coll (GA)
Pikeville Coll (KY)
Pittsburg State U (KS)
Pitzer Coll (CA)
Plymouth State U (NH)
Point Loma Nazarene U (CA)
Polytechnic U, Brooklyn Campus (NY)
Pomona Coll (CA)
Portland State U (OR)
Prairie View A&M U (TX)
Presbyterian Coll (SC)
Princeton U (NJ)
Providence Coll (RI)
Purchase Coll, State U of New York (NY)
Purdue U (IN)
Purdue U Calumet (IN)
Queens Coll of the City U of New York (NY)
Queen's U at Kingston (ON, Canada)
Queens U of Charlotte (NC)
Quincy U (IL)
Quinnipiac U (CT)
Radford U (VA)
Ramapo Coll of New Jersey (NJ)
Randolph Coll (VA)
Randolph-Macon Coll (VA)
Redeemer U Coll (ON, Canada)
Reed Coll (OR)
Regis U (CO)
Rensselaer Polytechnic Inst (NY)
Rhode Island Coll (RI)
Rhodes Coll (TN)
Rice U (TX)
The Richard Stockton Coll of New Jersey (NJ)
Rider U (NJ)
Ripon Coll (WI)
Roanoke Coll (VA)
Roberts Wesleyan Coll (NY)
Rochester Inst of Technology (NY)
Rockford Coll (IL)
Rockhurst U (MO)
Roger Williams U (RI)
Rollins Coll (FL)
Roosevelt U (IL)
Rose-Hulman Inst of Technology (IN)
Rosemont Coll (PA)
Rowan U (NJ)
Russell Sage Coll (NY)
Rutgers, The State U of New Jersey, Camden (NJ)
Rutgers, The State U of New Jersey, Newark (NJ)
Rutgers, The State U of New Jersey, New Brunswick (NJ)
Saginaw Valley State U (MI)
St. Ambrose U (IA)
St. Andrews Presbyterian Coll (NC)
St. Cloud State U (MN)
St. Edward's U (TX)
Saint Francis U (PA)
St. Francis Xavier U (NS, Canada)
St. Gregory's U, Shawnee (OK)
St. John Fisher Coll (NY)
St. John's Coll (NM)
Saint John's U (MN)
St. John's U (NY)
Saint Joseph Coll (CT)
Saint Joseph's Coll (IN)
St. Joseph's Coll, New York (NY)
St. Joseph's Coll, Suffolk Campus (NY)
Saint Joseph's U (PA)
St. Lawrence U (NY)
Saint Leo U (FL)
Saint Louis U (MO)
Saint Martin's U (WA)
Saint Mary-of-the-Woods Coll (IN)
Saint Mary's Coll (IN)
Saint Mary's Coll of California (CA)
St. Mary's Coll of Maryland (MD)
St. Mary's U (TX)
Saint Mary's U of Minnesota (MN)
Saint Michael's Coll (VT)
St. Norbert Coll (WI)
St. Olaf Coll (MN)
St. Thomas Aquinas Coll (NY)
St. Thomas U (NB, Canada)
Saint Vincent Coll (PA)
Saint Xavier U (IL)
Salem Coll (NC)
Salem Intl U (WV)
Salem State Coll (MA)
Salisbury U (MD)
Salve Regina U (RI)
Samford U (AL)
Sam Houston State U (TX)
San Diego Christian Coll (CA)
San Diego State U (CA)
San Francisco State U (CA)
Santa Clara U (CA)
Sarah Lawrence Coll (NY)
Schreiner U (TX)
Scripps Coll (CA)
Seattle Pacific U (WA)
Seattle U (WA)
Seton Hill U (PA)
Sewanee: The U of the South (TN)
Shawnee State U (OH)
Shaw U (NC)
Shenandoah U (VA)
Shepherd U (WV)
Shippensburg U of Pennsylvania (PA)
Shorter Coll (GA)
Siena Coll (NY)
Siena Heights U (MI)
Simmons Coll (MA)
Simon Fraser U (BC, Canada)
Simpson Coll (IA)
Simpson U (CA)
Skidmore Coll (NY)
Slippery Rock U of Pennsylvania (PA)
Smith Coll (MA)
Sonoma State U (CA)
South Carolina State U (SC)
South Dakota School of Mines and Technology (SD)
South Dakota State U (SD)
Southeastern Louisiana U (LA)
Southeastern Oklahoma State U (OK)
Southeastern U (FL)
Southeast Missouri State U (MO)
Southern Adventist U (TN)
Southern Arkansas U–Magnolia (AR)
Southern Connecticut State U (CT)
Southern Illinois U Carbondale (IL)
Southern Illinois U Edwardsville (IL)
Southern Methodist U (TX)
Southern Oregon U (OR)
Southern Polytechnic State U (GA)
Southern U and Ag and Mech Coll (LA)
Southern Utah U (UT)
Southern Wesleyan U (SC)
Southwest Baptist U (MO)
Southwestern Adventist U (TX)
Southwestern Coll (KS)
Southwestern Oklahoma State U (OK)
Southwestern U (TX)
Southwest Minnesota State U (MN)
Spelman Coll (GA)
Spring Arbor U (MI)
Spring Hill Coll (AL)
Stanford U (CA)
State U of New York at Binghamton (NY)
State U of New York at Fredonia (NY)
State U of New York at New Paltz (NY)
State U of New York at Oswego (NY)
State U of New York at Plattsburgh (NY)
State U of New York Coll at Geneseo (NY)
State U of New York Coll at Old Westbury (NY)
State U of New York Coll at Oneonta (NY)
State U of New York Coll at Potsdam (NY)
State U of New York Empire State Coll (NY)
Stephen F. Austin State U (TX)
Sterling Coll (KS)
Stetson U (FL)
Stillman Coll (AL)
Stonehill Coll (MA)
Stony Brook U, State U of New York (NY)
Suffolk U (MA)
Susquehanna U (PA)
Swarthmore Coll (PA)
Sweet Briar Coll (VA)
Syracuse U (NY)
Tabor Coll (KS)
Tarleton State U (TX)
Taylor U (IN)
Temple U (PA)
Tennessee State U (TN)
Tennessee Technological U (TN)
Tennessee Wesleyan Coll (TN)
Texas A&M Intl U (TX)
Texas A&M U (TX)
Texas A&M U–Commerce (TX)
Texas Christian U (TX)
Texas Coll (TX)
Texas Lutheran U (TX)
Texas Southern U (TX)
Texas State U-San Marcos (TX)
Texas Tech U (TX)
Texas Woman's U (TX)
Thiel Coll (PA)
Thomas Edison State Coll (NJ)
Thomas More Coll (KY)
Thompson Rivers U (BC, Canada)
Tougaloo Coll (MS)
Towson U (MD)
Transylvania U (KY)
Trent U (ON, Canada)
Trevecca Nazarene U (TN)
Trinity Christian Coll (IL)
Trinity Coll (CT)
Trinity Intl U (IL)
Trinity U (TX)
Tri-State U (IN)
Troy U (AL)
Truman State U (MO)
Tufts U (MA)
Tulane U (LA)
Tusculum Coll (TN)
Tuskegee U (AL)
Union Coll (KY)
Union Coll (NE)
Union Coll (NY)
Union U (TN)
United States Air Force Acad (CO)
United States Naval Acad (MD)
Université de Sherbrooke (QC, Canada)
U at Albany, State U of New York (NY)
U at Buffalo, the State U of New York (NY)
The U of Akron (OH)
The U of Alabama (AL)
The U of Alabama at Birmingham (AL)
The U of Alabama in Huntsville (AL)
U of Alaska Fairbanks (AK)
U of Alaska Southeast (AK)
The U of Arizona (AZ)
U of Arkansas (AR)
U of Arkansas at Fort Smith (AR)
U of Arkansas at Monticello (AR)
U of Arkansas at Pine Bluff (AR)
U of Bridgeport (CT)
The U of British Columbia (BC, Canada)
The U of British Columbia–Okanagan (BC, Canada)
U of California, Berkeley (CA)
U of California, Davis (CA)
U of California, Irvine (CA)
U of California, Los Angeles (CA)
U of California, Riverside (CA)
U of California, San Diego (CA)
U of California, Santa Barbara (CA)
U of California, Santa Cruz (CA)
U of Central Arkansas (AR)
U of Central Florida (FL)
U of Central Missouri (MO)
U of Central Oklahoma (OK)
U of Chicago (IL)
U of Cincinnati (OH)
U of Colorado at Boulder (CO)
U of Colorado Denver (CO)
U of Connecticut (CT)
U of Dallas (TX)
U of Dayton (OH)
U of Delaware (DE)
U of Denver (CO)
U of Evansville (IN)
The U of Findlay (OH)
U of Florida (FL)
U of Georgia (GA)
U of Great Falls (MT)
U of Guam (GU)
U of Hartford (CT)
U of Hawaii at Manoa (HI)
U of Houston (TX)
U of Houston–Clear Lake (TX)
U of Houston–Downtown (TX)
U of Houston–Victoria (TX)
U of Idaho (ID)
U of Illinois at Chicago (IL)
U of Illinois at Springfield (IL)
U of Illinois at Urbana–Champaign (IL)
U of Indianapolis (IN)
The U of Iowa (IA)
U of Kansas (KS)
U of King's Coll (NS, Canada)
U of La Verne (CA)
U of Lethbridge (AB, Canada)
U of Louisiana at Lafayette (LA)
U of Louisiana at Monroe (LA)
U of Louisville (KY)
U of Maine (ME)
U of Maine at Farmington (ME)
U of Mary (ND)
U of Mary Hardin-Baylor (TX)
U of Maryland, Baltimore County (MD)
U of Maryland, Coll Park (MD)
U of Maryland Eastern Shore (MD)
U of Mary Washington (VA)
U of Massachusetts Amherst (MA)
U of Massachusetts Boston (MA)
U of Massachusetts Dartmouth (MA)
U of Massachusetts Lowell (MA)
U of Memphis (TN)
U of Miami (FL)
U of Michigan (MI)
U of Michigan–Dearborn (MI)
U of Michigan–Flint (MI)
U of Minnesota, Duluth (MN)
U of Minnesota, Twin Cities Campus (MN)
U of Mississippi (MS)
U of Missouri–Columbia (MO)
U of Missouri–Kansas City (MO)
U of Missouri–St. Louis (MO)
The U of Montana (MT)
U of Montevallo (AL)
U of Nebraska at Kearney (NE)
U of Nebraska at Omaha (NE)
U of Nebraska–Lincoln (NE)
U of Nevada, Las Vegas (NV)
U of Nevada, Reno (NV)
U of New Brunswick Fredericton (NB, Canada)
U of New England (ME)
U of New Hampshire (NH)
U of New Haven (CT)
U of New Mexico (NM)
U of New Orleans (LA)
U of North Alabama (AL)
The U of North Carolina at Asheville (NC)
The U of North Carolina at Chapel Hill (NC)
The U of North Carolina at Charlotte (NC)
The U of North Carolina at Greensboro (NC)
The U of North Carolina at Pembroke (NC)
The U of North Carolina Wilmington (NC)
U of North Dakota (ND)
U of Northern Colorado (CO)
U of Northern Iowa (IA)
U of North Florida (FL)
U of North Texas (TX)
U of Notre Dame (IN)
U of Oklahoma (OK)
U of Oregon (OR)
U of Ottawa (ON, Canada)
U of Pennsylvania (PA)
U of Pittsburgh (PA)
U of Pittsburgh at Johnstown (PA)
U of Portland (OR)
U of Prince Edward Island (PE, Canada)
U of Puerto Rico, Cayey U Coll (PR)
U of Puget Sound (WA)
U of Redlands (CA)
U of Regina (SK, Canada)
U of Rhode Island (RI)
U of Richmond (VA)
U of Rio Grande (OH)
U of Rochester (NY)
U of St. Francis (IL)
U of Saint Francis (IN)
U of Saint Mary (KS)
U of St. Thomas (MN)
U of St. Thomas (TX)
U of San Diego (CA)
U of Science and Arts of Oklahoma (OK)
The U of Scranton (PA)
U of Sioux Falls (SD)
U of South Carolina (SC)
U of South Carolina Upstate (SC)
The U of South Dakota (SD)
U of Southern California (CA)
U of Southern Indiana (IN)
U of Southern Maine (ME)
U of Southern Mississippi (MS)
U of South Florida (FL)
The U of Tampa (FL)
The U of Tennessee (TN)
The U of Tennessee at Chattanooga (TN)
The U of Tennessee at Martin (TN)
The U of Texas at Arlington (TX)
The U of Texas at Austin (TX)
The U of Texas at Brownsville (TX)
The U of Texas at Dallas (TX)
The U of Texas at El Paso (TX)
The U of Texas at San Antonio (TX)
The U of Texas at Tyler (TX)
The U of Texas of the Permian Basin (TX)
The U of Texas–Pan American (TX)
U of the District of Columbia (DC)
U of the Incarnate Word (TX)
U of the Ozarks (AR)
U of the Pacific (CA)
U of the Virgin Islands (VI)
The U of Toledo (OH)
U of Toronto (ON, Canada)
U of Tulsa (OK)
U of Utah (UT)
U of Vermont (VT)
U of Victoria (BC, Canada)
U of Virginia (VA)
The U of Virginia's Coll at Wise (VA)
The U of Western Ontario (ON, Canada)
U of West Florida (FL)
U of West Georgia (GA)
U of Windsor (ON, Canada)
The U of Winnipeg (MB, Canada)
U of Wisconsin–Eau Claire (WI)
U of Wisconsin–Green Bay (WI)
U of Wisconsin–La Crosse (WI)
U of Wisconsin–Madison (WI)
U of Wisconsin–Milwaukee (WI)
U of Wisconsin–Oshkosh (WI)
U of Wisconsin–Parkside (WI)
U of Wisconsin–Platteville (WI)
U of Wisconsin–Stevens Point (WI)
U of Wisconsin–Superior (WI)
U of Wisconsin–Whitewater (WI)
U of Wyoming (WY)
Ursinus Coll (PA)
Ursuline Coll (OH)
Utah State U (UT)
Utah Valley State Coll (UT)
Utica Coll (NY)
Valdosta State U (GA)
Valley City State U (ND)
Valparaiso U (IN)
Vanderbilt U (TN)
Vanguard U of Southern California (CA)
Vassar Coll (NY)
Villanova U (PA)
Virginia Commonwealth U (VA)
Virginia Military Inst (VA)
Virginia Polytechnic Inst and State U (VA)
Virginia State U (VA)
Virginia Wesleyan Coll (VA)
Viterbo U (WI)
Voorhees Coll (SC)
Wabash Coll (IN)
Wagner Coll (NY)
Wake Forest U (NC)
Walla Walla U (WA)
Walsh U (OH)
Warren Wilson Coll (NC)
Wartburg Coll (IA)

Washburn U (KS)
Washington & Jefferson Coll (PA)
Washington and Lee U (VA)
Washington Coll (MD)
Washington State U (WA)
Washington U in St. Louis (MO)
Wayland Baptist U (TX)
Waynesburg U (PA)
Wayne State Coll (NE)
Wayne State U (MI)
Weber State U (UT)
Webster U (MO)
Wellesley Coll (MA)
Wells Coll (NY)
Wesleyan Coll (GA)
Wesleyan U (CT)
West Chester U of Pennsylvania (PA)
Western Carolina U (NC)
Western Connecticut State U (CT)
Western Illinois U (IL)
Western Kentucky U (KY)
Western Michigan U (MI)
Western New England Coll (MA)
Western New Mexico U (NM)
Western State Coll of Colorado (CO)
Western Washington U (WA)
Westfield State Coll (MA)
West Liberty State Coll (WV)
Westminster Coll (MO)
Westminster Coll (UT)
Westmont Coll (CA)
West Texas A&M U (TX)
West Virginia U (WV)
West Virginia Wesleyan Coll (WV)
Wheaton Coll (IL)
Wheaton Coll (MA)
Wheeling Jesuit U (WV)
Whitman Coll (WA)
Whittier Coll (CA)
Whitworth U (WA)
Wichita State U (KS)
Widener U (PA)
Wiley Coll (TX)
Wilfrid Laurier U (ON, Canada)
Wilkes U (PA)
Willamette U (OR)
William Jewell Coll (MO)
William Paterson U of New Jersey (NJ)
Williams Coll (MA)
William Woods U (MO)
Wilmington Coll (OH)
Wilson Coll (PA)
Wingate U (NC)
Winona State U (MN)
Winthrop U (SC)
Wittenberg U (OH)
Wofford Coll (SC)
Worcester Polytechnic Inst (MA)
Worcester State Coll (MA)
Wright State U (OH)
Xavier U (OH)
Xavier U of Louisiana (LA)
Yale U (CT)
York Coll of Pennsylvania (PA)
York Coll of the City U of New York (NY)
York U (ON, Canada)
Youngstown State U (OH)

MATHEMATICS AND COMPUTER SCIENCE

Anderson U (IN)
Augustana Coll (IL)
Boston U (MA)
Bowdoin Coll (ME)
Brown U (RI)
Bryan Coll (TN)
Central Coll (IA)
Central Michigan U (MI)
Chestnut Hill Coll (PA)
Coll of Saint Benedict (MN)
The Colorado Coll (CO)
DePaul U (IL)
Drew U (NJ)
Eastern Illinois U (IL)
George Mason U (VA)
Hampden-Sydney Coll (VA)
Harvard U (MA)
Hofstra U (NY)
Immaculata U (PA)
Indiana U–Purdue U Fort Wayne (IN)
Ithaca Coll (NY)
Keene State Coll (NH)
Lake Superior State U (MI)
Lawrence Technological U (MI)
Lawrence U (WI)
Loyola U Chicago (IL)
Maryville Coll (TN)
Massachusetts Inst of Technology (MA)
McGill U (QC, Canada)
Mountain State U (WV)
Mount Allison U (NB, Canada)
Mount Saint Vincent U (NS, Canada)
Paine Coll (GA)
Pfeiffer U (NC)
Piedmont Coll (GA)
Rochester Inst of Technology (NY)
Sacred Heart U (CT)
Saint Francis U (PA)
Saint John's U (MN)
St. Joseph's Coll, New York (NY)
St. Lawrence U (NY)
Saint Mary's Coll (IN)
Saint Mary's Coll of California (CA)
Saint Mary's U of Minnesota (MN)
Southern Oregon U (OR)
Stanford U (CA)
Tusculum Coll (TN)
U at Albany, State U of New York (NY)
U of Illinois at Chicago (IL)
U of Illinois at Urbana–Champaign (IL)
U of Oregon (OR)
U of Puerto Rico at Humacao (PR)
U of Regina (SK, Canada)
U of St. Francis (IL)
The U of Texas at Austin (TX)
U of Windsor (ON, Canada)
Washington U in St. Louis (MO)
Whitman Coll (WA)
Yale U (CT)
York U (ON, Canada)

MATHEMATICS AND STATISTICS RELATED

The American U of Paris (France)
Anderson U (IN)
Asbury Coll (KY)
Canisius Coll (NY)
Carnegie Mellon U (PA)
Dakota State U (SD)
The Evergreen State Coll (WA)
Hofstra U (NY)
Indiana U of Pennsylvania (PA)
Miami U Hamilton (OH)
New York U (NY)
Purchase Coll, State U of New York (NY)
Saint Mary's Coll of California (CA)
Seattle Pacific U (WA)
Tulane U (LA)
The U of British Columbia–Okanagan (BC, Canada)
U of Hartford (CT)
U of Miami (FL)
U of Pittsburgh (PA)
U of Regina (SK, Canada)
U of Rochester (NY)
The U of Scranton (PA)
U of South Alabama (AL)
Western State Coll of Colorado (CO)

MATHEMATICS RELATED

California State U, Monterey Bay (CA)
Carlow U (PA)
Hillsdale Coll (MI)
Ohio Northern U (OH)
Seton Hill U (PA)
U at Buffalo, the State U of New York (NY)
U of California, Los Angeles (CA)
U of Miami (FL)
U of Pittsburgh (PA)

MATHEMATICS TEACHER EDUCATION

Abilene Christian U (TX)
Albertus Magnus Coll (CT)
Alice Lloyd Coll (KY)
Alma Coll (MI)
Alvernia Coll (PA)
Anderson U (IN)
Anderson U (SC)
Appalachian State U (NC)
Arkansas State U (AR)
Assumption Coll (MA)
Auburn U (AL)
Averett U (VA)
Baptist Bible Coll of Pennsylvania (PA)
Baylor U (TX)
Berry Coll (GA)
Bethany Coll (KS)
Bethel U (MN)
Bishop's U (QC, Canada)
Bluefield Coll (VA)
Bob Jones U (SC)
Boston U (MA)
Bowling Green State U (OH)
Brewton-Parker Coll (GA)
Bridgewater Coll (VA)
Brigham Young U (UT)
Brock U (ON, Canada)
Bryan Coll (TN)
Buffalo State Coll, State U of New York (NY)
Cabrini Coll (PA)
California Lutheran U (CA)
California State U, Chico (CA)
California State U, Long Beach (CA)
Capital U (OH)
Carroll Coll (WI)
Castleton State Coll (VT)
The Catholic U of America (DC)
Cedarville U (OH)
Centenary Coll of Louisiana (LA)
Central Michigan U (MI)
Central Washington U (WA)
Christian Brothers U (TN)
City Coll of the City U of New York (NY)
Claflin U (SC)
Clearwater Christian Coll (FL)
Clemson U (SC)
Coker Coll (SC)
The Coll at Brockport, State U of New York (NY)
The Coll of New Jersey (NJ)
The Coll of Saint Rose (NY)
Coll of the Ozarks (MO)
Colorado State U (CO)
Columbus State U (GA)
Concordia Coll (MN)
Concordia U (MI)
Concordia U (OR)
Concordia U Chicago (IL)
Concordia U, Nebraska (NE)
Concordia U, St. Paul (MN)
Cornell U (NY)
Cornerstone U (MI)
Covenant Coll (GA)
Culver-Stockton Coll (MO)
Daemen Coll (NY)
Dakota State U (SD)
Dakota Wesleyan U (SD)
Dana Coll (NE)
Davis & Elkins Coll (WV)
Delta State U (MS)
DePaul U (IL)
Dillard U (LA)
Dominican Coll (NY)
Dowling Coll (NY)
Duquesne U (PA)
East Carolina U (NC)
East Central U (OK)
Eastern Mennonite U (VA)
Eastern Michigan U (MI)
East Texas Baptist U (TX)
Emmanuel Coll (GA)
Fayetteville State U (NC)
Felician Coll (NJ)
Ferris State U (MI)
Fitchburg State Coll (MA)
Florida Atlantic U (FL)
Florida Inst of Technology (FL)
Florida Intl U (FL)
Florida State U (FL)
Franklin Coll (IN)
Freed-Hardeman U (TN)
Gardner-Webb U (NC)
Glenville State Coll (WV)
Grace Coll (IN)
Grand Canyon U (AZ)
Greensboro Coll (NC)
Greenville Coll (IL)
Gustavus Adolphus Coll (MN)
Gwynedd-Mercy Coll (PA)
Hannibal-LaGrange Coll (MO)
Harding U (AR)
Hardin-Simmons U (TX)
Hastings Coll (NE)
Hawai'i Pacific U (HI)
Hofstra U (NY)
Hope Coll (MI)
Houston Baptist U (TX)
Howard Payne U (TX)
Hunter Coll of the City U of New York (NY)
Indiana U Bloomington (IN)
Indiana U Northwest (IN)
Indiana U–Purdue U Fort Wayne (IN)
Indiana U South Bend (IN)
Indiana U Southeast (IN)
Indiana Wesleyan U (IN)
Inter American U of Puerto Rico, San Germán Campus (PR)
Iona Coll (NY)
Ithaca Coll (NY)
Jackson State U (MS)
Jamestown Coll (ND)
Johnson C. Smith U (NC)
Johnson State Coll (VT)
Judson Coll (AL)
Juniata Coll (PA)
Keene State Coll (NH)
Kennesaw State U (GA)
Kentucky Wesleyan Coll (KY)
Keuka Coll (NY)
Keystone Coll (PA)
King Coll (TN)
Kutztown U of Pennsylvania (PA)
Lambuth U (TN)
Le Moyne Coll (NY)
LeMoyne-Owen Coll (TN)
Lenoir-Rhyne Coll (NC)
Lewis-Clark State Coll (ID)
Liberty U (VA)
Limestone Coll (SC)
Lincoln U (MO)
Lincoln U (PA)
Lindenwood U (MO)
Lindsey Wilson Coll (KY)
Lipscomb U (TN)
Loyola U Chicago (IL)
Lyndon State Coll (VT)
Madonna U (MI)
Manhattanville Coll (NY)
Mansfield U of Pennsylvania (PA)
Maranatha Baptist Bible Coll (WI)
Marian Coll of Fond du Lac (WI)
Marist Coll (NY)
Marquette U (WI)
Maryville Coll (TN)
Maryville U of Saint Louis (MO)
Marywood U (PA)
Mayville State U (ND)
McGill U (QC, Canada)
McKendree U (IL)
McNeese State U (LA)
Mercyhurst Coll (PA)
Messiah Coll (PA)
Metropolitan State U (MN)
Miami U Hamilton (OH)
Michigan Technological U (MI)
MidAmerica Nazarene U (KS)
Miles Coll (AL)
Millersville U of Pennsylvania (PA)
Millikin U (IL)
Minot State U (ND)
Misericordia U (PA)
Mississippi Valley State U (MS)
Missouri State U (MO)
Molloy Coll (NY)
Montana State U–Billings (MT)
Moravian Coll (PA)
Morris Coll (SC)
Mount Marty Coll (SD)
Mount Mary Coll (WI)
Mount Vernon Nazarene U (OH)
Murray State U (KY)
Nazareth Coll of Rochester (NY)
New York Inst of Technology (NY)
New York U (NY)
Niagara U (NY)
Nicholls State U (LA)
North Carolina Central U (NC)
North Carolina State U (NC)
North Dakota State U (ND)
Northeastern State U (OK)
Northern Arizona U (AZ)
Northern Michigan U (MI)
North Georgia Coll & State U (GA)
Northwestern Coll (MN)
Northwestern Oklahoma State U (OK)
Northwestern State U of Louisiana (LA)
Northwestern U (IL)
Northwest Nazarene U (ID)
Oakland City U (IN)
Oakland U (MI)
Ohio Dominican U (OH)
Ohio Northern U (OH)
Ohio U (OH)
Ohio Valley U (WV)
Ohio Wesleyan U (OH)
Oklahoma Christian U (OK)
Old Dominion U (VA)
Oral Roberts U (OK)
Pace U (NY)
Paine Coll (GA)
Pepperdine U, Malibu (CA)
Philadelphia Biblical U (PA)
Pillsbury Baptist Bible Coll (MN)
Pittsburg State U (KS)
Point Park U (PA)
Prescott Coll (AZ)
Purdue U (IN)
Queens U of Charlotte (NC)
Regis Coll (MA)
Rhode Island Coll (RI)
Roberts Wesleyan Coll (NY)
Rochester Coll (MI)
Sacred Heart U (CT)
Saginaw Valley State U (MI)
St. Ambrose U (IA)
St. Edward's U (TX)
Saint Francis U (PA)
St. Gregory's U, Shawnee (OK)
St. John Fisher Coll (NY)
St. John's U (NY)
St. Joseph's Coll, Suffolk Campus (NY)
Saint Joseph's U (PA)
Saint Mary's U of Minnesota (MN)
Saint Xavier U (IL)
Salve Regina U (RI)
Sam Houston State U (TX)
Schreiner U (TX)
Seattle Pacific U (WA)
Seton Hill U (PA)
Shawnee State U (OH)
Shaw U (NC)
Shorter Coll (GA)
Southeastern Louisiana U (LA)
Southeastern Oklahoma State U (OK)
Southeastern U (FL)
Southeast Missouri State U (MO)
Southern Arkansas U–Magnolia (AR)
Southern U and Ag and Mech Coll (LA)
Southern Wesleyan U (SC)
Southwest Baptist U (MO)
Southwest Minnesota State U (MN)
State U of New York Coll at Old Westbury (NY)
State U of New York Coll at Oneonta (NY)
State U of New York Coll at Potsdam (NY)
Syracuse U (NY)
Temple U (PA)
Texas A&M Intl U (TX)
Texas Christian U (TX)
Texas Lutheran U (TX)
Trevecca Nazarene U (TN)
Trinity Christian Coll (IL)
Tri-State U (IN)
Tusculum Coll (TN)
Union Coll (NE)
The U of Akron (OH)
The U of Arizona (AZ)
U of Arkansas at Fort Smith (AR)
U of California, San Diego (CA)
U of Central Arkansas (AR)
U of Central Florida (FL)
U of Central Oklahoma (OK)
U of Delaware (DE)
U of Evansville (IN)
U of Georgia (GA)
U of Great Falls (MT)
U of Illinois at Chicago (IL)
U of Illinois at Urbana–Champaign (IL)
U of Indianapolis (IN)
The U of Iowa (IA)
U of Lethbridge (AB, Canada)
U of Louisiana at Monroe (LA)
U of Maine (ME)
U of Maine at Farmington (ME)
U of Maine at Fort Kent (ME)
U of Maine at Machias (ME)
U of Mary (ND)
U of Mary Hardin-Baylor (TX)
U of Maryland, Coll Park (MD)
U of Michigan (MI)
U of Michigan–Dearborn (MI)
U of Michigan–Flint (MI)
U of Minnesota, Duluth (MN)
U of Minnesota, Twin Cities Campus (MN)
U of Mississippi (MS)
U of Missouri–Columbia (MO)
U of Missouri–St. Louis (MO)
The U of Montana (MT)
The U of Montana–Western (MT)
U of Nebraska–Lincoln (NE)
U of Nevada, Reno (NV)
U of New Hampshire (NH)
U of New Orleans (LA)
The U of North Carolina at Charlotte (NC)
The U of North Carolina at Greensboro (NC)
The U of North Carolina at Pembroke (NC)
The U of North Carolina Wilmington (NC)
U of North Dakota (ND)
U of Northern Iowa (IA)
U of North Florida (FL)
U of Oklahoma (OK)
U of Pittsburgh at Johnstown (PA)
U of Puerto Rico at Utuado (PR)
U of Puerto Rico, Cayey U Coll (PR)
U of Regina (SK, Canada)
U of Rio Grande (OH)
U of St. Francis (IL)
U of Saint Francis (IN)
U of St. Thomas (MN)
The U of South Dakota (SD)
U of South Florida (FL)
The U of Tampa (FL)
The U of Tennessee at Martin (TN)
The U of Toledo (OH)
U of Tulsa (OK)
U of Vermont (VT)
The U of Western Ontario (ON, Canada)
U of Windsor (ON, Canada)
U of Wisconsin–Superior (WI)
Ursuline Coll (OH)
Utah State U (UT)
Utah Valley State Coll (UT)
Utica Coll (NY)
Valley City State U (ND)
Valparaiso U (IN)
Viterbo U (WI)
Walsh U (OH)

MAJORS AND MORE

Wartburg Coll (IA)
Washington State U (WA)
Washington U in St. Louis (MO)
Waynesburg U (PA)
Wayne State Coll (NE)
Wayne State U (MI)
West Chester U of Pennsylvania (PA)
Western Carolina U (NC)
Western Michigan U (MI)
Western State Coll of Colorado (CO)
Westmont Coll (CA)
West Virginia Wesleyan Coll (WV)
Wheeling Jesuit U (WV)
Widener U (PA)
William Woods U (MO)
Wright State U (OH)
York Coll (NE)
York Coll of Pennsylvania (PA)
York U (ON, Canada)
Youngstown State U (OH)

MECHANICAL DESIGN TECHNOLOGY

Lincoln U (MO)

MECHANICAL DRAFTING AND CAD/CADD

Eastern Michigan U (MI)
Murray State U (KY)
Purdue U (IN)

MECHANICAL ENGINEERING

Alabama Ag and Mech U (AL)
Alfred U (NY)
The American U of Athens (Greece)
American U of Beirut (Lebanon)
Andrews U (MI)
Arizona State U (AZ)
Auburn U (AL)
Baker Coll of Flint (MI)
Baylor U (TX)
Boston U (MA)
Bradley U (IL)
Brigham Young U (UT)
Brown U (RI)
Bucknell U (PA)
California Baptist U (CA)
California Inst of Technology (CA)
California Maritime Acad (CA)
California Polytechnic State U, San Luis Obispo (CA)
California State Polytechnic U, Pomona (CA)
California State U, Chico (CA)
California State U, Fresno (CA)
California State U, Fullerton (CA)
California State U, Long Beach (CA)
California State U, Los Angeles (CA)
California State U, Sacramento (CA)
Calvin Coll (MI)
Carnegie Mellon U (PA)
Case Western Reserve U (OH)
The Catholic U of America (DC)
Cedarville U (OH)
Central Michigan U (MI)
Christian Brothers U (TN)
City Coll of the City U of New York (NY)
Clarkson U (NY)
Clemson U (SC)
Cleveland State U (OH)
The Coll of New Jersey (NJ)
Colorado School of Mines (CO)
Colorado State U (CO)
Concordia U (QC, Canada)
Cooper Union for the Advancement of Science and Art (NY)
Cornell U (NY)
Dordt Coll (IA)
Drexel U (PA)
Duke U (NC)
Embry-Riddle Aeronautical U (FL)
Fairfield U (CT)
Florida Ag and Mech U (FL)
Florida Atlantic U (FL)
Florida Inst of Technology (FL)
Florida Intl U (FL)
Florida State U (FL)
Franklin W. Olin Coll of Eng (MA)
Frostburg State U (MD)
Gannon U (PA)
George Fox U (OR)
The George Washington U (DC)
Georgia Inst of Technology (GA)
Georgia Southern U (GA)
Gonzaga U (WA)
Grand Valley State U (MI)
Grove City Coll (PA)
Harding U (AR)
Harvard U (MA)
Hofstra U (NY)
Idaho State U (ID)
Illinois Inst of Technology (IL)
Indiana Tech (IN)
Indiana U–Purdue U Fort Wayne (IN)
Indiana U–Purdue U Indianapolis (IN)
Inter American U of Puerto Rico, Bayamón Campus (PR)
Iowa State U of Science and Technology (IA)
Jacksonville U (FL)
John Brown U (AR)
The Johns Hopkins U (MD)
Kansas State U (KS)
Kettering U (MI)
Lafayette Coll (PA)
Lakehead U (ON, Canada)
Lake Superior State U (MI)
Lawrence Technological U (MI)
Lehigh U (PA)
LeTourneau U (TX)
Lipscomb U (TN)
Louisiana State U and Ag and Mech Coll (LA)
Loyola Marymount U (CA)
Marquette U (WI)
Massachusetts Inst of Technology (MA)
McGill U (QC, Canada)
Memorial U of Newfoundland (NL, Canada)
Miami U (OH)
Michigan State U (MI)
Michigan Technological U (MI)
Milwaukee School of Eng (WI)
Minnesota State U Mankato (MN)
Mississippi State U (MS)
Missouri U of Science and Technology (MO)
Montana State U (MT)
Montana Tech of The U of Montana (MT)
Murray State U (KY)
New Jersey Inst of Technology (NJ)
New Mexico Inst of Mining and Technology (NM)
New York Inst of Technology (NY)
North Carolina Ag and Tech State U (NC)
North Carolina State U (NC)
North Dakota State U (ND)
Northeastern U (MA)
Northern Arizona U (AZ)
Northern Illinois U (IL)
Northwestern U (IL)
Norwich U (VT)
Oakland U (MI)
Ohio Northern U (OH)
Ohio U (OH)
Oklahoma Christian U (OK)
Oklahoma State U (OK)
Old Dominion U (VA)
Oral Roberts U (OK)
Oregon State U (OR)
Penn State Abington (PA)
Penn State Altoona (PA)
Penn State Berks (PA)
Penn State Erie, The Behrend Coll (PA)
Penn State Harrisburg (PA)
Penn State U Park (PA)
Polytechnic U, Brooklyn Campus (NY)
Polytechnic U of Puerto Rico (PR)
Portland State U (OR)
Prairie View A&M U (TX)
Princeton U (NJ)
Purdue U (IN)
Purdue U Calumet (IN)
Queen's U at Kingston (ON, Canada)
Rensselaer Polytechnic Inst (NY)
Rice U (TX)
Rochester Inst of Technology (NY)
Rose-Hulman Inst of Technology (IN)
Rowan U (NJ)
Royal Military Coll of Canada (ON, Canada)
Rutgers, The State U of New Jersey, New Brunswick (NJ)
Saginaw Valley State U (MI)
St. Cloud State U (MN)
Saint Louis U (MO)
Saint Martin's U (WA)
San Diego State U (CA)
San Francisco State U (CA)
Santa Clara U (CA)
Seattle U (WA)
South Dakota School of Mines and Technology (SD)
South Dakota State U (SD)
Southern Illinois U Carbondale (IL)
Southern Illinois U Edwardsville (IL)
Southern Methodist U (TX)
Southern Polytechnic State U (GA)
Southern U and Ag and Mech Coll (LA)
Stanford U (CA)
State U of New York at Binghamton (NY)
Stony Brook U, State U of New York (NY)
Syracuse U (NY)
Temple U (PA)
Tennessee State U (TN)
Tennessee Technological U (TN)
Texas A&M U (TX)
Texas Tech U (TX)
Trinity Coll (CT)
Tri-State U (IN)
Tufts U (MA)
Tulane U (LA)
Tuskegee U (AL)
Union Coll (NY)
United States Air Force Acad (CO)
United States Coast Guard Acad (CT)
United States Naval Acad (MD)
Université de Sherbrooke (QC, Canada)
U at Buffalo, the State U of New York (NY)
The U of Akron (OH)
The U of Alabama (AL)
The U of Alabama at Birmingham (AL)
The U of Alabama in Huntsville (AL)
U of Alaska Fairbanks (AK)
The U of Arizona (AZ)
U of Arkansas (AR)
The U of British Columbia (BC, Canada)
The U of British Columbia–Okanagan (BC, Canada)
U of California, Berkeley (CA)
U of California, Davis (CA)
U of California, Irvine (CA)
U of California, Los Angeles (CA)
U of California, Riverside (CA)
U of California, San Diego (CA)
U of California, Santa Barbara (CA)
U of Central Florida (FL)
U of Cincinnati (OH)
U of Colorado at Boulder (CO)
U of Colorado Denver (CO)
U of Connecticut (CT)
U of Dayton (OH)
U of Delaware (DE)
U of Denver (CO)
U of Evansville (IN)
U of Florida (FL)
U of Hartford (CT)
U of Hawaii at Manoa (HI)
U of Houston (TX)
U of Idaho (ID)
U of Illinois at Chicago (IL)
U of Illinois at Urbana–Champaign (IL)
U of Indianapolis (IN)
The U of Iowa (IA)
U of Kansas (KS)
U of Louisiana at Lafayette (LA)
U of Louisville (KY)
U of Maine (ME)
U of Maryland, Baltimore County (MD)
U of Maryland, Coll Park (MD)
U of Massachusetts Amherst (MA)
U of Massachusetts Dartmouth (MA)
U of Massachusetts Lowell (MA)
U of Memphis (TN)
U of Miami (FL)
U of Michigan (MI)
U of Michigan–Dearborn (MI)
U of Minnesota, Twin Cities Campus (MN)
U of Mississippi (MS)
U of Missouri–Columbia (MO)
U of Missouri–Kansas City (MO)
U of Missouri–St. Louis (MO)
U of Nebraska–Lincoln (NE)
U of Nevada, Las Vegas (NV)
U of Nevada, Reno (NV)
U of New Brunswick Fredericton (NB, Canada)
U of New Hampshire (NH)
U of New Haven (CT)
U of New Mexico (NM)
U of New Orleans (LA)
The U of North Carolina at Charlotte (NC)
U of North Dakota (ND)
U of North Florida (FL)
U of North Texas (TX)
U of Notre Dame (IN)
U of Oklahoma (OK)
U of Ottawa (ON, Canada)
U of Pennsylvania (PA)
U of Pittsburgh (PA)
U of Portland (OR)
U of Rhode Island (RI)
U of Rochester (NY)
U of St. Thomas (MN)
U of San Diego (CA)
U of South Alabama (AL)
U of South Carolina (SC)
U of Southern California (CA)
U of South Florida (FL)
The U of Tennessee (TN)
The U of Texas at Arlington (TX)
The U of Texas at Austin (TX)
The U of Texas at El Paso (TX)
The U of Texas at San Antonio (TX)
The U of Texas at Tyler (TX)
The U of Texas–Pan American (TX)
U of the District of Columbia (DC)
U of the Pacific (CA)
The U of Toledo (OH)
U of Toronto (ON, Canada)
U of Tulsa (OK)
U of Utah (UT)
U of Vermont (VT)
U of Victoria (BC, Canada)
U of Virginia (VA)
The U of Western Ontario (ON, Canada)
U of Windsor (ON, Canada)
U of Wisconsin–Madison (WI)
U of Wisconsin–Milwaukee (WI)
U of Wisconsin–Platteville (WI)
U of Wyoming (WY)
Ursinus Coll (PA)
Utah State U (UT)
Valparaiso U (IN)
Vanderbilt U (TN)
Villanova U (PA)
Virginia Commonwealth U (VA)
Virginia Military Inst (VA)
Virginia Polytechnic Inst and State U (VA)
Walla Walla U (WA)
Washington State U (WA)
Washington U in St. Louis (MO)
Wayne State U (MI)
Western Kentucky U (KY)
Western Michigan U (MI)
Western New England Coll (MA)
West Texas A&M U (TX)
West Virginia U (WV)
Wichita State U (KS)
Widener U (PA)
Wilkes U (PA)
Winona State U (MN)
Worcester Polytechnic Inst (MA)
Wright State U (OH)
Yale U (CT)
York Coll of Pennsylvania (PA)
Youngstown State U (OH)

MECHANICAL ENGINEERING/ MECHANICAL TECHNOLOGY

Alabama Ag and Mech U (AL)
Bluefield State Coll (WV)
Boise State U (ID)
Bowling Green State U (OH)
British Columbia Inst of Technology (BC, Canada)
Buffalo State Coll, State U of New York (NY)
California Polytechnic State U, San Luis Obispo (CA)
California State Polytechnic U, Pomona (CA)
California State U, Long Beach (CA)
California State U, Sacramento (CA)
Central Connecticut State U (CT)
Central Michigan U (MI)
Central Washington U (WA)
Eastern Michigan U (MI)
Fairleigh Dickinson U, Metropolitan Campus (NJ)
Fairmont State U (WV)
Ferris State U (MI)
Georgia Southern U (GA)
Indiana U–Purdue U Fort Wayne (IN)
Indiana U–Purdue U Indianapolis (IN)
Lakehead U (ON, Canada)
Lake Superior State U (MI)
LeTourneau U (TX)
Miami U (OH)
Miami U Hamilton (OH)
Michigan Technological U (MI)
Midwestern State U (TX)
Milwaukee School of Eng (WI)
Montana State U (MT)
Nicholls State U (LA)
Northeastern U (MA)
Northern Michigan U (MI)
Ohio U (OH)
Oklahoma State U (OK)
Oregon Inst of Technology (OR)
Penn State Erie, The Behrend Coll (PA)
Pennsylvania Coll of Technology (PA)
Pittsburg State U (KS)
Point Park U (PA)
Purdue U (IN)
Purdue U Calumet (IN)
Purdue U North Central (IN)
South Carolina State U (SC)
Southern Polytechnic State U (GA)
State U of New York Inst of Technology (NY)
Syracuse U (NY)
Texas A&M U (TX)
Texas Tech U (TX)
Thomas Edison State Coll (NJ)
The U of Akron (OH)
The U of British Columbia (BC, Canada)
U of Cincinnati (OH)
U of Dayton (OH)
U of Houston–Downtown (TX)
U of Maine (ME)
U of Massachusetts Dartmouth (MA)
U of Massachusetts Lowell (MA)
U of New Hampshire at Manchester (NH)
The U of North Carolina at Charlotte (NC)
U of North Texas (TX)
U of Pittsburgh at Johnstown (PA)
U of Rio Grande (OH)
The U of Texas at Brownsville (TX)
The U of Toledo (OH)
Virginia State U (VA)
Wayne State U (MI)
Youngstown State U (OH)

MECHANICAL ENGINEERING TECHNOLOGIES RELATED

Cleveland State U (OH)
Grove City Coll (PA)
Indiana State U (IN)
New York Inst of Technology (NY)
Old Dominion U (VA)
Purdue U (IN)
Thomas Edison State Coll (NJ)
U of Central Florida (FL)
U of Hartford (CT)

MECHANICS AND REPAIR

Lewis-Clark State Coll (ID)

MEDICAL ADMINISTRATIVE ASSISTANT AND MEDICAL SECRETARY

Baker Coll of Auburn Hills (MI)
Mercyhurst Coll (PA)
Tabor Coll (KS)
U of Cincinnati (OH)

MEDICAL BASIC SCIENCES RELATED

Ramapo Coll of New Jersey (NJ)

MEDICAL BIOMATHEMATICS/ BIOMETRICS

Stanford U (CA)

MEDICAL/CLINICAL ASSISTANT

California State U, Dominguez Hills (CA)
Colorado Tech U—Colorado Springs (CO)
Colorado Tech U—Denver (CO)
Colorado Tech U—North Kansas City (MO)
Colorado Tech U—Sioux Falls (SD)
Pennsylvania Coll of Technology (PA)

MEDICAL/HEALTH MANAGEMENT AND CLINICAL ASSISTANT

Davenport U, Dearborn (MI)
Davenport U, Grand Rapids (MI)
Lewis-Clark State Coll (ID)

MEDICAL ILLUSTRATION

Alma Coll (MI)
The Cleveland Inst of Art (OH)
Iowa State U of Science and Technology (IA)
Rochester Inst of Technology (NY)

MEDICAL ILLUSTRATION AND INFORMATICS RELATED
Florida Ag and Mech U (FL)

MEDICAL INFORMATICS
Misericordia U (PA)
Montana Tech of The U of Montana (MT)
Montclair State U (NJ)
Slippery Rock U of Pennsylvania (PA)

MEDICAL INSURANCE CODING
Davenport U, Dearborn (MI)

MEDICAL LABORATORY TECHNOLOGY
Abilene Christian U (TX)
Auburn U (AL)
Felician Coll (NJ)
The George Washington U (DC)
Quinnipiac U (CT)
Rockhurst U (MO)
Roosevelt U (IL)
Southeastern Oklahoma State U (OK)
U of Nevada, Las Vegas (NV)
U of New England (ME)
U of Oklahoma (OK)
U of Windsor (ON, Canada)

MEDICAL MICROBIOLOGY AND BACTERIOLOGY
Auburn U (AL)
Ball State U (IN)
Bowling Green State U (OH)
California Polytechnic State U, San Luis Obispo (CA)
California State Polytechnic U, Pomona (CA)
California State U, Dominguez Hills (CA)
Central Michigan U (MI)
Colorado State U (CO)
Eastern Kentucky U (KY)
Harvard U (MA)
Humboldt State U (CA)
Inter American U of Puerto Rico, Bayamón Campus (PR)
Inter American U of Puerto Rico, San Germán Campus (PR)
McGill U (QC, Canada)
Memorial U of Newfoundland (NL, Canada)
Miami U (OH)
Michigan Technological U (MI)
Minnesota State U Mankato (MN)
Mississippi State U (MS)
Mississippi U for Women (MS)
Montana State U (MT)
Northern Arizona U (AZ)
Ohio U (OH)
Ohio Wesleyan U (OH)
Oregon State U (OR)
Penn State Abington (PA)
Penn State Altoona (PA)
Penn State Berks (PA)
Penn State Erie, The Behrend Coll (PA)
Penn State U Park (PA)
Pomona Coll (CA)
Quinnipiac U (CT)
Rutgers, The State U of New Jersey, New Brunswick (NJ)
St. Cloud State U (MN)
San Francisco State U (CA)
Sonoma State U (CA)
Université de Sherbrooke (QC, Canada)
The U of British Columbia (BC, Canada)
U of California, San Diego (CA)
U of California, Santa Barbara (CA)
U of Central Florida (FL)
U of Cincinnati (OH)
U of Florida (FL)
U of Georgia (GA)
U of Idaho (ID)
U of King's Coll (NS, Canada)
U of Louisiana at Lafayette (LA)
U of Maine (ME)
U of Maryland, Coll Park (MD)
U of Miami (FL)
U of Minnesota, Twin Cities Campus (MN)
The U of Montana (MT)
U of New Brunswick Fredericton (NB, Canada)
U of New Hampshire (NH)
U of Puerto Rico at Humacao (PR)
U of Rhode Island (RI)
U of South Florida (FL)
The U of Tennessee (TN)
The U of Texas at El Paso (TX)
U of Toronto (ON, Canada)
U of Vermont (VT)
U of Victoria (BC, Canada)
The U of Western Ontario (ON, Canada)
U of Windsor (ON, Canada)
U of Wisconsin–Madison (WI)
U of Wisconsin–Oshkosh (WI)
Utah State U (UT)
Wagner Coll (NY)
Weber State U (UT)
Worcester Polytechnic Inst (MA)
Xavier U of Louisiana (LA)

MEDICAL OFFICE ASSISTANT
Concordia U Wisconsin (WI)
Lewis-Clark State Coll (ID)
Mount Aloysius Coll (PA)

MEDICAL OFFICE MANAGEMENT
Eastern Kentucky U (KY)

MEDICAL PHARMACOLOGY AND PHARMACEUTICAL SCIENCES
South Dakota State U (SD)
The U of Montana (MT)
U of the Sciences in Philadelphia (PA)
West Chester U of Pennsylvania (PA)

MEDICAL RADIOLOGIC TECHNOLOGY
Arkansas State U (AR)
Avila U (MO)
Baptist Coll of Health Sciences (TN)
Bloomsburg U of Pennsylvania (PA)
British Columbia Inst of Technology (BC, Canada)
California State U, Long Beach (CA)
Fairleigh Dickinson U, Coll at Florham (NJ)
Gannon U (PA)
Idaho State U (ID)
Indiana U East (IN)
Indiana U Kokomo (IN)
Indiana U–Purdue U Indianapolis (IN)
Indiana U Southeast (IN)
La Roche Coll (PA)
Loma Linda U (CA)
Marian Coll of Fond du Lac (WI)
Massachusetts Coll of Pharmacy and Health Sciences (MA)
McNeese State U (LA)
Minot State U (ND)
Misericordia U (PA)
Missouri Southern State U (MO)
Morehead State U (KY)
Mount Marty Coll (SD)
North Central Coll (IL)
Oakland U (MI)
Presentation Coll (SD)
Roosevelt U (IL)
Southern Illinois U Carbondale (IL)
Southern Vermont Coll (VT)
State U of New York Upstate Medical U (NY)
Texas State U-San Marcos (TX)
The U of Alabama at Birmingham (AL)
U of Central Florida (FL)
U of Hartford (CT)
U of Louisiana at Monroe (LA)
U of Michigan–Flint (MI)
U of Missouri–Columbia (MO)
U of Nebraska Medical Center (NE)
U of Nevada, Las Vegas (NV)
U of New Mexico (NM)
The U of North Carolina at Chapel Hill (NC)
U of Prince Edward Island (PE, Canada)
U of St. Francis (IL)
U of Sioux Falls (SD)
U of Vermont (VT)
Wayne State U (MI)

MEDICAL STAFF SERVICES TECHNOLOGY
East Central U (OK)
Mount Vernon Nazarene U (OH)

MEDICAL TRANSCRIPTION
Mercyhurst Coll (PA)

MEDICINAL AND PHARMACEUTICAL CHEMISTRY
Ohio Northern U (OH)
U of California, San Diego (CA)
U of the Sciences in Philadelphia (PA)
Worcester Polytechnic Inst (MA)

MEDICINAL/ PHARMACEUTICAL CHEMISTRY
Michigan Technological U (MI)

MEDIEVAL AND RENAISSANCE STUDIES
Bard Coll (NY)
Barnard Coll (NY)
Brown U (RI)
The Catholic U of America (DC)
Coll of the Holy Cross (MA)
The Coll of William and Mary (VA)
Connecticut Coll (CT)
Cornell Coll (IA)
Dickinson Coll (PA)
Duke U (NC)
Emory U (GA)
Georgetown U (DC)
Hamilton Coll (NY)
Hanover Coll (IN)
Harvard U (MA)
Hobart and William Smith Colls (NY)
Marlboro Coll (VT)
Memorial U of Newfoundland (NL, Canada)
Mount Allison U (NB, Canada)
Mount Holyoke Coll (MA)
New Coll of Florida (FL)
New York U (NY)
Ohio Wesleyan U (OH)
Penn State Abington (PA)
Penn State Altoona (PA)
Penn State Berks (PA)
Penn State Erie, The Behrend Coll (PA)
Penn State U Park (PA)
Rutgers, The State U of New Jersey, New Brunswick (NJ)
Sewanee: The U of the South (TN)
Smith Coll (MA)
Southern Methodist U (TX)
State U of New York at Binghamton (NY)
Swarthmore Coll (PA)
Tulane U (LA)
U at Albany, State U of New York (NY)
U of California, Santa Barbara (CA)
U of Chicago (IL)
The U of Iowa (IA)
U of Michigan (MI)
U of Nebraska–Lincoln (NE)
U of Notre Dame (IN)
U of Oregon (OR)
U of Ottawa (ON, Canada)
The U of Toledo (OH)
U of Toronto (ON, Canada)
U of Victoria (BC, Canada)
Vassar Coll (NY)
Washington and Lee U (VA)
Washington U in St. Louis (MO)
Wellesley Coll (MA)
Wesleyan U (CT)
Wilfrid Laurier U (ON, Canada)

MENTAL AND SOCIAL HEALTH SERVICES AND ALLIED PROFESSIONS RELATED
Edinboro U of Pennsylvania (PA)
Old Dominion U (VA)
Pennsylvania Coll of Technology (PA)
The U of Maine at Augusta (ME)
The U of Toledo (OH)
Wright State U (OH)

MENTAL HEALTH/ REHABILITATION
Morgan State U (MD)
Newman U (KS)
Prescott Coll (AZ)
St. Cloud State U (MN)
Tufts U (MA)
U of Maine at Farmington (ME)

MERCHANDISING
Michigan State U (MI)

MERCHANDISING, SALES, AND MARKETING OPERATIONS RELATED (GENERAL)
Brigham Young U (UT)
Eastern Michigan U (MI)
Oregon State U (OR)
Washington U in St. Louis (MO)

MERCHANDISING, SALES, AND MARKETING OPERATIONS RELATED (SPECIALIZED)
Baylor U (TX)
Eastern Michigan U (MI)
Fashion Inst of Technology (NY)
Gannon U (PA)

METAL AND JEWELRY ARTS
Alberta Coll of Art & Design (AB, Canada)
Bard Coll at Simon's Rock (MA)
California Coll of the Arts (CA)
California State U, Long Beach (CA)
The Cleveland Inst of Art (OH)
The Coll at Brockport, State U of New York (NY)
Colorado State U (CO)
Edinboro U of Pennsylvania (PA)
Ferris State U (MI)
Grand Valley State U (MI)
Hofstra U (NY)
Kent State U (OH)
Massachusetts Coll of Art and Design (MA)
Memphis Coll of Art (TN)
Northern Michigan U (MI)
Northwest Missouri State U (MO)
NSCAD U (NS, Canada)
Pratt Inst (NY)
Savannah Coll of Art and Design (GA)
School of the Art Inst of Chicago (IL)
School of the Museum of Fine Arts, Boston (MA)
Seton Hill U (PA)
State U of New York at New Paltz (NY)
Temple U (PA)
The U of Akron (OH)
U of Georgia (GA)
The U of Iowa (IA)
U of Kansas (KS)
U of Massachusetts Dartmouth (MA)
U of Michigan (MI)
U of Oregon (OR)
U of Wisconsin–Milwaukee (WI)
Western State Coll of Colorado (CO)

METALLURGICAL ENGINEERING
Cleveland State U (OH)
Colorado School of Mines (CO)
Harvard U (MA)
Illinois Inst of Technology (IL)
Laurentian U (ON, Canada)
McGill U (QC, Canada)
Michigan Technological U (MI)
Missouri U of Science and Technology (MO)
Montana Tech of The U of Montana (MT)
Oregon State U (OR)
South Dakota School of Mines and Technology (SD)
The U of Alabama (AL)
The U of British Columbia (BC, Canada)
U of Cincinnati (OH)
U of Idaho (ID)
U of Illinois at Urbana–Champaign (IL)
U of Nevada, Reno (NV)
U of Pittsburgh (PA)
The U of Texas at El Paso (TX)
U of Toronto (ON, Canada)
U of Utah (UT)
U of Wisconsin–Madison (WI)
Ursinus Coll (PA)

METALLURGICAL TECHNOLOGY
U of Cincinnati (OH)

METEOROLOGY
Central Michigan U (MI)
The Coll at Brockport, State U of New York (NY)
Florida Inst of Technology (FL)
Florida State U (FL)
North Carolina State U (NC)
Purdue U (IN)
Saint Louis U (MO)
U of Hawaii at Manoa (HI)
U of Miami (FL)
The U of North Carolina at Charlotte (NC)
U of the Incarnate Word (TX)
U of Utah (UT)
Western Illinois U (IL)
Western Kentucky U (KY)

MICROBIOLOGICAL SCIENCES AND IMMUNOLOGY RELATED
U of California, Irvine (CA)
U of California, Los Angeles (CA)
The U of Western Ontario (ON, Canada)
Wright State U (OH)

MICROBIOLOGY
Arizona State U (AZ)
Auburn U (AL)
Brigham Young U (UT)
California State U, Chico (CA)
California State U, Long Beach (CA)
California State U, Los Angeles (CA)
Clemson U (SC)
Cornell U (NY)
Idaho State U (ID)
Inter American U of Puerto Rico, Aguadilla Campus (PR)
Iowa State U of Science and Technology (IA)
Juniata Coll (PA)
Louisiana State U and Ag and Mech Coll (LA)
McGill U (QC, Canada)
Miami U Hamilton (OH)
Michigan State U (MI)
Michigan Technological U (MI)
North Carolina State U (NC)
North Dakota State U (ND)
Northern Michigan U (MI)
Oklahoma State U (OK)
Oregon State U (OR)
Purdue U (IN)
San Diego State U (CA)
South Dakota State U (SD)
Southern Illinois U Carbondale (IL)
Texas A&M U (TX)
Texas State U-San Marcos (TX)
Texas Tech U (TX)
The U of Akron (OH)
The U of Alabama (AL)
The U of British Columbia–Okanagan (BC, Canada)
U of California, Berkeley (CA)
U of California, Davis (CA)
U of California, Irvine (CA)
U of California, Santa Barbara (CA)
U of Georgia (GA)
U of Hawaii at Manoa (HI)
U of Houston–Downtown (TX)
U of Idaho (ID)
U of Illinois at Urbana–Champaign (IL)
The U of Iowa (IA)
U of Kansas (KS)
U of Massachusetts Amherst (MA)
U of Memphis (TN)
U of Michigan–Dearborn (MI)
U of Missouri–Columbia (MO)
U of Northern Iowa (IA)
U of Oklahoma (OK)
U of Pittsburgh (PA)
The U of Texas at Arlington (TX)
U of the Sciences in Philadelphia (PA)
U of Toronto (ON, Canada)
U of Vermont (VT)
The U of Western Ontario (ON, Canada)
U of Wisconsin–La Crosse (WI)
U of Wyoming (WY)
Washington State U (WA)

MIDDLE/NEAR EASTERN AND SEMITIC LANGUAGES RELATED
Bryn Mawr Coll (PA)
Sarah Lawrence Coll (NY)
Wayne State U (MI)

MIDDLE SCHOOL EDUCATION
Abilene Christian U (TX)
Alaska Pacific U (AK)
Albertus Magnus Coll (CT)
Alice Lloyd Coll (KY)
Appalachian State U (NC)
Arkansas State U (AR)

MAJORS AND MORE

Arlington Baptist Coll (TX)
Armstrong Atlantic State U (GA)
Asbury Coll (KY)
Ashford U (IA)
Ashland U (OH)
Assumption Coll (MA)
Augusta State U (GA)
Avila U (MO)
Baker U (KS)
Baldwin-Wallace Coll (OH)
Barton Coll (NC)
Bellarmine U (KY)
Bennington Coll (VT)
Berea Coll (KY)
Berry Coll (GA)
Bluefield Coll (VA)
Bluffton U (OH)
Bob Jones U (SC)
Bowling Green State U (OH)
Brenau U (GA)
Brewton-Parker Coll (GA)
Bryan Coll (TN)
Butler U (IN)
Capital U (OH)
Carroll Coll (WI)
Catawba Coll (NC)
Cedarville U (OH)
Central State U (OH)
Christopher Newport U (VA)
Claflin U (SC)
Clarke Coll (IA)
Clark U (MA)
Clayton State U (GA)
Cleveland State U (OH)
Coastal Carolina U (SC)
The Coll at Brockport, State U of New York (NY)
Coll of Charleston (SC)
Coll of Mount St. Joseph (OH)
Coll of the Atlantic (ME)
Coll of the Ozarks (MO)
Coll of the Southwest (NM)
Columbia Coll (SC)
Columbus State U (GA)
Concordia Coll–New York (NY)
Concordia U, Nebraska (NE)
Concordia U, St. Paul (MN)
Concordia U Texas (TX)
Concordia U Wisconsin (WI)
Dakota Wesleyan U (SD)
East Carolina U (NC)
Eastern Illinois U (IL)
Eastern Kentucky U (KY)
Eastern Mennonite U (VA)
Elon U (NC)
Emmanuel Coll (GA)
Evangel U (MO)
Fayetteville State U (NC)
Fitchburg State Coll (MA)
Florida State U (FL)
Fontbonne U (MO)
Georgetown Coll (KY)
Georgia Coll & State U (GA)
Georgia Southern U (GA)
Georgia Southwestern State U (GA)
Gettysburg Coll (PA)
Gordon Coll (MA)
Grace U (NE)
Grambling State U (LA)
Greensboro Coll (NC)
Hampton U (VA)
Harding U (AR)
Harris-Stowe State U (MO)
Henderson State U (AR)
High Point U (NC)
Houston Baptist U (TX)
Huntington U (IN)
Indiana Wesleyan U (IN)
Ithaca Coll (NY)
Jacksonville State U (AL)
John Brown U (AR)
Johnson Bible Coll (TN)
Johnson State Coll (VT)
Kennesaw State U (GA)
Kent State U (OH)
Kentucky Christian U (KY)
Kentucky Wesleyan Coll (KY)
King Coll (TN)
LaGrange Coll (GA)
Lake Superior State U (MI)
Lambuth U (TN)
Le Moyne Coll (NY)
Lenoir-Rhyne Coll (NC)
Lesley U (MA)
Lincoln U (MO)
Lindenwood U (MO)
Lindsey Wilson Coll (KY)
Lourdes Coll (OH)
Lubbock Christian U (TX)
Malone Coll (OH)
Marian Coll of Fond du Lac (WI)
Marquette U (WI)
Maryville U of Saint Louis (MO)
The Master's Coll and Sem (CA)
McKendree U (IL)
McMurry U (TX)
Medaille Coll (NY)
Memorial U of Newfoundland (NL, Canada)
Mercer U (GA)
Merrimack Coll (MA)
Miami U (OH)
MidAmerica Nazarene U (KS)
Midland Lutheran Coll (NE)
Midway Coll (KY)
Missouri Baptist U (MO)
Missouri State U (MO)
Morehead State U (KY)
Mount Mercy Coll (IA)
Mount Olive Coll (NC)
Mount Vernon Nazarene U (OH)
Murray State U (KY)
Nebraska Wesleyan U (NE)
New York U (NY)
Nicholls State U (LA)
North Carolina Central U (NC)
North Carolina State U (NC)
North Carolina Wesleyan Coll (NC)
North Georgia Coll & State U (GA)
Northland Coll (WI)
Northwestern State U of Louisiana (LA)
Northwest Missouri State U (MO)
Oakland City U (IN)
Ohio Dominican U (OH)
Ohio Northern U (OH)
Ohio U (OH)
Ohio Wesleyan U (OH)
Otterbein Coll (OH)
Ouachita Baptist U (AR)
Paine Coll (GA)
Peru State Coll (NE)
Piedmont Coll (GA)
Pikeville Coll (KY)
Presbyterian Coll (SC)
Prescott Coll (AZ)
Sacred Heart U (CT)
St. Cloud State U (MN)
St. Joseph's Coll, Suffolk Campus (NY)
Saint Leo U (FL)
Shawnee State U (OH)
Shorter Coll (GA)
South Carolina State U (SC)
Southeastern Louisiana U (LA)
Southeast Missouri State U (MO)
Southern U and Ag and Mech Coll (LA)
Southwest Baptist U (MO)
State U of New York Coll at Old Westbury (NY)
State U of New York Coll at Oneonta (NY)
Tarleton State U (TX)
Taylor U (IN)
Texas Lutheran U (TX)
Thomas More Coll (KY)
Thomas U (GA)
Toccoa Falls Coll (GA)
Transylvania U (KY)
Trinity Christian Coll (IL)
Tusculum Coll (TN)
Union Coll (KY)
The U of Akron (OH)
U of Arkansas (AR)
U of Arkansas at Fort Smith (AR)
U of Central Arkansas (AR)
U of Central Missouri (MO)
U of Florida (FL)
U of Georgia (GA)
U of Great Falls (MT)
U of Kansas (KS)
U of Mary Hardin-Baylor (TX)
U of Minnesota, Duluth (MN)
U of Missouri–Columbia (MO)
U of Missouri–Kansas City (MO)
U of Nebraska–Lincoln (NE)
U of New Orleans (LA)
The U of North Carolina at Chapel Hill (NC)
The U of North Carolina at Charlotte (NC)
The U of North Carolina at Greensboro (NC)
The U of North Carolina at Pembroke (NC)
The U of North Carolina Wilmington (NC)
U of North Dakota (ND)
U of Northern Iowa (IA)
U of North Florida (FL)
U of Regina (SK, Canada)
U of Richmond (VA)
U of St. Thomas (MN)
U of Sioux Falls (SD)
U of South Carolina Upstate (SC)
The U of South Dakota (SD)
The U of Tennessee at Chattanooga (TN)
U of the Ozarks (AR)
U of Vermont (VT)
The U of Western Ontario (ON, Canada)
U of West Florida (FL)
U of West Georgia (GA)
U of Wisconsin–Platteville (WI)
Ursuline Coll (OH)
Valdosta State U (GA)
Valparaiso U (IN)
Villa Julie Coll (MD)
Virginia Wesleyan Coll (VA)
Walsh U (OH)
Warner Pacific Coll (OR)
Washington U in St. Louis (MO)
Wayne State Coll (NE)
Wesleyan Coll (GA)
Western Carolina U (NC)
Western Kentucky U (KY)
Westminster Coll (MO)
West Virginia Wesleyan Coll (WV)
Wheeling Jesuit U (WV)
William Jewell Coll (MO)
William Woods U (MO)
Wilmington U (DE)
Wingate U (NC)
Winona State U (MN)
Wright State U (OH)
Xavier U (OH)
Xavier U of Louisiana (LA)
York Coll (NE)
York U (ON, Canada)
Youngstown State U (OH)

MILITARY STUDIES

Florida Inst of Technology (FL)
Hawai'i Pacific U (HI)
Pacific Lutheran U (WA)
Texas Christian U (TX)
United States Air Force Acad (CO)

MILITARY TECHNOLOGIES

American Public U System (WV)
Royal Military Coll of Canada (ON, Canada)
Wright State U (OH)

MINING AND MINERAL ENGINEERING

Colorado School of Mines (CO)
Laurentian U (ON, Canada)
McGill U (QC, Canada)
Missouri U of Science and Technology (MO)
Montana Tech of The U of Montana (MT)
New Mexico Inst of Mining and Technology (NM)
Oregon State U (OR)
Penn State Abington (PA)
Penn State Altoona (PA)
Penn State Berks (PA)
Penn State Erie, The Behrend Coll (PA)
Penn State U Park (PA)
Queen's U at Kingston (ON, Canada)
South Dakota School of Mines and Technology (SD)
Southern Illinois U Carbondale (IL)
The U of Arizona (AZ)
The U of British Columbia (BC, Canada)
U of Nevada, Reno (NV)
U of Toronto (ON, Canada)
U of Utah (UT)
U of Wisconsin–Madison (WI)
Virginia Polytechnic Inst and State U (VA)
West Virginia U (WV)

MINING AND PETROLEUM TECHNOLOGIES RELATED

U of Alaska Fairbanks (AK)

MINING TECHNOLOGY

Bluefield State Coll (WV)

MISSIONARY STUDIES AND MISSIOLOGY

Abilene Christian U (TX)
Asbury Coll (KY)
Baptist Bible Coll of Pennsylvania (PA)
Biola U (CA)
California Baptist U (CA)
Canadian Mennonite U (MB, Canada)
Cedarville U (OH)
Central Christian Coll of Kansas (KS)
Concordia U, St. Paul (MN)
Concordia U Wisconsin (WI)
Crossroads Coll (MN)
Crown Coll (MN)
Dordt Coll (IA)
East Texas Baptist U (TX)
Eugene Bible Coll (OR)
Faith Baptist Bible Coll and Theological Sem (IA)
Freed-Hardeman U (TN)
Gardner-Webb U (NC)
George Fox U (OR)
Grace Bible Coll (MI)
Grace U (NE)
Harding U (AR)
Hardin-Simmons U (TX)
Hillsdale Free Will Baptist Coll (OK)
Horizon Coll & Sem (SK, Canada)
Huntington U (IN)
John Brown U (AR)
Kuyper Coll (MI)
LeTourneau U (TX)
Lipscomb U (TN)
Lubbock Christian U (TX)
Maranatha Baptist Bible Coll (WI)
Master's Coll and Sem (ON, Canada)
MidAmerica Nazarene U (KS)
Mid-Continent U (KY)
Multnomah Bible Coll and Biblical Sem (OR)
North Greenville U (SC)
Northwestern Coll (MN)
Northwest Nazarene U (ID)
Nyack Coll (NY)
Oklahoma Christian U (OK)
Oral Roberts U (OK)
Ouachita Baptist U (AR)
Pillsbury Baptist Bible Coll (MN)
Rochester Coll (MI)
Simpson U (CA)
Southeastern U (FL)
Southern Baptist Theological Sem (KY)
Southwest Baptist U (MO)
Spring Arbor U (MI)
Toccoa Falls Coll (GA)
Trinity Coll of Florida (FL)
Vanguard U of Southern California (CA)
Vennard Coll (IA)
Washington Bible Coll (MD)

MODERN GREEK

Ball State U (IN)
Belmont U (TN)
Boston U (MA)
Butler U (IN)
Calvin Coll (MI)
The Catholic U of America (DC)
Claremont McKenna Coll (CA)
Colgate U (NY)
The Coll of William and Mary (VA)
Concordia U Wisconsin (WI)
Cornell Coll (IA)
Emory U (GA)
Florida State U (FL)
Furman U (SC)
Hamilton Coll (NY)
Harvard U (MA)
Haverford Coll (PA)
John Carroll U (OH)
Kenyon Coll (OH)
Lehman Coll of the City U of New York (NY)
Loyola Marymount U (CA)
Marlboro Coll (VT)
Memorial U of Newfoundland (NL, Canada)
Miami U (OH)
Monmouth Coll (IL)
Mount Holyoke Coll (MA)
New York U (NY)
Oberlin Coll (OH)
Rhodes Coll (TN)
Saint Louis U (MO)
Saint Mary's Coll of California (CA)
Sewanee: The U of the South (TN)
Trent U (ON, Canada)
Tufts U (MA)
Tulane U (LA)
U of Georgia (GA)
U of Idaho (ID)
The U of Iowa (IA)
U of Michigan (MI)
U of Minnesota, Twin Cities Campus (MN)
U of Missouri–Columbia (MO)
U of New Brunswick Fredericton (NB, Canada)
U of New Hampshire (NH)
U of Richmond (VA)
The U of Tennessee at Chattanooga (TN)
U of Toronto (ON, Canada)
U of Windsor (ON, Canada)
The U of Winnipeg (MB, Canada)
U of Wisconsin–Madison (WI)
U of Wisconsin–Milwaukee (WI)
Wabash Coll (IN)
Wilfrid Laurier U (ON, Canada)
Wright State U (OH)
York U (ON, Canada)

MODERN LANGUAGES

Albion Coll (MI)
Alfred U (NY)
Alma Coll (MI)
Ball State U (IN)
Beloit Coll (WI)
Bemidji State U (MN)
Bishop's U (QC, Canada)
California Polytechnic State U, San Luis Obispo (CA)
Claremont McKenna Coll (CA)
Clark U (MA)
Clemson U (SC)
Coll of Mount Saint Vincent (NY)
The Coll of William and Mary (VA)
Converse Coll (SC)
Cornell Coll (IA)
Dallas Baptist U (TX)
Dillard U (LA)
Eckerd Coll (FL)
Elizabethtown Coll (PA)
Fairfield U (CT)
Florida Memorial U (FL)
Franklin Coll Switzerland (Switzerland)
Gettysburg Coll (PA)
Grove City Coll (PA)
Hamilton Coll (NY)
Hampton U (VA)
Harvard U (MA)
Hobart and William Smith Colls (NY)
Howard Payne U (TX)
Immaculata U (PA)
Judson Coll (AL)
Kennesaw State U (GA)
Kenyon Coll (OH)
King Coll (TN)
La Salle U (PA)
Laurentian U (ON, Canada)
Lee U (TN)
Lewis & Clark Coll (OR)
Longwood U (VA)
Louisiana Coll (LA)
Marlboro Coll (VT)
Middlebury Coll (VT)
Minnesota State U Mankato (MN)
Monmouth Coll (IL)
Mount Allison U (NB, Canada)
Mount Saint Vincent U (NS, Canada)
Nazareth Coll of Rochester (NY)
Northeastern U (MA)
Pacific U (OR)
Pomona Coll (CA)
Presbyterian Coll (SC)
Purchase Coll, State U of New York (NY)
Saint Francis U (PA)
St. Francis Xavier U (NS, Canada)
St. Lawrence U (NY)
Saint Mary's Coll of California (CA)
Saint Michael's Coll (VT)
St. Thomas Aquinas Coll (NY)
Sarah Lawrence Coll (NY)
Scripps Coll (CA)
Slippery Rock U of Pennsylvania (PA)
Suffolk U (MA)
Trent U (ON, Canada)
Trinity Coll (CT)
U of Chicago (IL)
U of Lethbridge (AB, Canada)
U of Louisiana at Lafayette (LA)
U of Maine (ME)
U of Maryland, Baltimore County (MD)
U of Mary Washington (VA)
U of New Brunswick Fredericton (NB, Canada)
U of New Hampshire (NH)
U of Ottawa (ON, Canada)
U of Southern Maine (ME)
U of South Florida (FL)
U of Toronto (ON, Canada)
U of Victoria (BC, Canada)
The U of Western Ontario (ON, Canada)
U of Windsor (ON, Canada)
Virginia Military Inst (VA)
Walla Walla U (WA)
Walsh U (OH)
Washington U in St. Louis (MO)
Westmont Coll (CA)
Widener U (PA)
Wilmington Coll (OH)
Winthrop U (SC)
Wright State U (OH)
York U (ON, Canada)

MOLECULAR BIOCHEMISTRY

Michigan Technological U (MI)
Polytechnic U, Brooklyn Campus (NY)
Simon Fraser U (BC, Canada)
U of California, Davis (CA)

MOLECULAR BIOLOGY

Adams State Coll (CO)
The American U of Athens (Greece)
Arizona State U (AZ)

Assumption Coll (MA)
Auburn U (AL)
Baker U (KS)
Ball State U (IN)
Beloit Coll (WI)
Benedictine U (IL)
Bethel U (MN)
Blackburn Coll (IL)
Boston U (MA)
Brigham Young U (UT)
Brown U (RI)
California Lutheran U (CA)
California State U, Fresno (CA)
California State U, San Marcos (CA)
Central Connecticut State U (CT)
Centre Coll (KY)
Chapman U (CA)
Chestnut Hill Coll (PA)
Clarion U of Pennsylvania (PA)
Clarkson U (NY)
Clark U (MA)
Colby Coll (ME)
Colgate U (NY)
The Coll at Brockport, State U of New York (NY)
Connecticut Coll (CT)
Dartmouth Coll (NH)
Florida Ag and Mech U (FL)
Florida Inst of Technology (FL)
Gettysburg Coll (PA)
Grove City Coll (PA)
Hamilton Coll (NY)
Hampton U (VA)
Harvard U (MA)
Houston Baptist U (TX)
Humboldt State U (CA)
Juniata Coll (PA)
Kenyon Coll (OH)
Lakehead U (ON, Canada)
Lehigh U (PA)
Marlboro Coll (VT)
Marquette U (WI)
McGill U (QC, Canada)
Meredith Coll (NC)
Middlebury Coll (VT)
Millikin U (IL)
Missouri State U (MO)
Montclair State U (NJ)
Northwestern U (IL)
Ohio Northern U (OH)
Otterbein Coll (OH)
Pitzer Coll (CA)
Pomona Coll (CA)
Princeton U (NJ)
Purdue U (IN)
Rutgers, The State U of New Jersey, New Brunswick (NJ)
San Francisco State U (CA)
Sarah Lawrence Coll (NY)
Scripps Coll (CA)
Simon Fraser U (BC, Canada)
Stetson U (FL)
Texas Lutheran U (TX)
Thompson Rivers U (BC, Canada)
Tulane U (LA)
U at Albany, State U of New York (NY)
The U of British Columbia–Okanagan (BC, Canada)
U of California, San Diego (CA)
U of California, Santa Barbara (CA)
U of California, Santa Cruz (CA)
U of Denver (CO)
U of Idaho (ID)
U of Kansas (KS)
U of Maine (ME)
U of Memphis (TN)
U of Michigan (MI)
U of Michigan–Flint (MI)
U of Minnesota, Duluth (MN)
U of New Brunswick Fredericton (NB, Canada)
U of New Hampshire (NH)
U of Pittsburgh (PA)
U of Puget Sound (WA)
U of Richmond (VA)
The U of Texas at Dallas (TX)
U of Toronto (ON, Canada)
U of Vermont (VT)
The U of Winnipeg (MB, Canada)
U of Wisconsin–Eau Claire (WI)
U of Wisconsin–Madison (WI)
U of Wisconsin–Parkside (WI)
U of Wyoming (WY)
Vanderbilt U (TN)
Wells Coll (NY)
Wesleyan U (CT)
Western New England Coll (MA)
Whitman Coll (WA)
William Jewell Coll (MO)
Worcester Polytechnic Inst (MA)
Yale U (CT)
York U (ON, Canada)

MOLECULAR GENETICS

Texas A&M U (TX)
U of Vermont (VT)

MONTESSORI TEACHER EDUCATION

Oklahoma City U (OK)
Siena Heights U (MI)
Xavier U (OH)

MOVEMENT THERAPY AND MOVEMENT EDUCATION

Brock U (ON, Canada)
Pacific Lutheran U (WA)
Texas Christian U (TX)
U of Vermont (VT)

MULTICULTURAL EDUCATION

Florida State U (FL)

MULTI-/INTERDISCIPLINARY STUDIES RELATED

Abilene Christian U (TX)
Adelphi U (NY)
Agnes Scott Coll (GA)
Albright Coll (PA)
Allegheny Coll (PA)
American Public U System (WV)
Anderson U (IN)
Angelo State U (TX)
Anna Maria Coll (MA)
Arizona State U (AZ)
Arizona State U at the West campus (AZ)
Arkansas State U (AR)
Ashford U (IA)
Austin Coll (TX)
Baldwin-Wallace Coll (OH)
Bates Coll (ME)
Baylor U (TX)
Berry Coll (GA)
Bethel Coll (TN)
Bethel U (MN)
Bloomfield Coll (NJ)
Bluffton U (OH)
Bowling Green State U (OH)
Brandeis U (MA)
Brevard Coll (NC)
Bucknell U (PA)
Buffalo State Coll, State U of New York (NY)
Burlington Coll (VT)
California Lutheran U (CA)
California State U, Chico (CA)
California State U, Long Beach (CA)
California State U, Los Angeles (CA)
California State U, Stanislaus (CA)
Cambridge Coll (MA)
Capital U (OH)
Central Connecticut State U (CT)
Chestnut Hill Coll (PA)
Clayton State U (GA)
Cleveland State U (OH)
The Coll of New Jersey (NJ)
The Coll of New Rochelle (NY)
Coll of Saint Elizabeth (NJ)
Coll of Santa Fe (NM)
Coll of the Ozarks (MO)
The Coll of William and Mary (VA)
The Colorado Coll (CO)
Columbia Coll Chicago (IL)
Connecticut Coll (CT)
Cornell Coll (IA)
Cornell U (NY)
Cornerstone U (MI)
Dallas Baptist U (TX)
Dartmouth Coll (NH)
Davidson Coll (NC)
DePauw U (IN)
Dickinson Coll (PA)
Dixie State Coll of Utah (UT)
Earlham Coll (IN)
Eastern Illinois U (IL)
Eastern Mennonite U (VA)
Eastern New Mexico U (NM)
East Tennessee State U (TN)
East Texas Baptist U (TX)
Emporia State U (KS)
The Evergreen State Coll (WA)
Fairleigh Dickinson U, Metropolitan Campus (NJ)
Florida Inst of Technology (FL)
Franklin & Marshall Coll (PA)
Frostburg State U (MD)
Gannon U (PA)
Georgetown Coll (KY)
Georgetown U (DC)
Georgia Inst of Technology (GA)
Georgia State U (GA)
Glenville State Coll (WV)
Global Coll of Long Island U (NY)
Grace Bible Coll (MI)
Greenville Coll (IL)
Hofstra U (NY)
Hood Coll (MD)
Hope Coll (MI)
Illinois Inst of Technology (IL)
Indiana U–Purdue U Indianapolis (IN)
Indiana U Southeast (IN)
Iowa State U of Science and Technology (IA)
Ithaca Coll (NY)
Jackson State U (MS)
Keene State Coll (NH)
Kennesaw State U (GA)
Kent State U (OH)
Kentucky Wesleyan Coll (KY)
Kenyon Coll (OH)
Knox Coll (IL)
Lambuth U (TN)
Lebanon Valley Coll (PA)
Lewis-Clark State Coll (ID)
Liberty U (VA)
Lourdes Coll (OH)
Lycoming Coll (PA)
Marian Coll of Fond du Lac (WI)
Marquette U (WI)
Marshall U (WV)
Marylhurst U (OR)
Maryville Coll (TN)
Marywood U (PA)
McDaniel Coll (MD)
Mercer U (GA)
Mercyhurst Coll (PA)
Meredith Coll (NC)
Messiah Coll (PA)
Miami U (OH)
Miami U Hamilton (OH)
Mid-Continent U (KY)
Middle Tennessee State U (TN)
Midway Coll (KY)
Midwestern State U (TX)
Millikin U (IL)
Millsaps Coll (MS)
Mississippi State U (MS)
Missouri Baptist U (MO)
Montana State U–Billings (MT)
Mount St. Mary's U (MD)
Naropa U (CO)
New York Inst of Technology (NY)
North Central Coll (IL)
North Dakota State U (ND)
Northeastern State U (OK)
North Greenville U (SC)
Northwest Christian Coll (OR)
Northwestern Coll (MN)
Northwestern Oklahoma State U (OK)
Northwestern U (IL)
Ohio Wesleyan U (OH)
Old Dominion U (VA)
Otterbein Coll (OH)
Park U (MO)
Penn State Erie, The Behrend Coll (PA)
Pikeville Coll (KY)
Plymouth State U (NH)
Princeton U (NJ)
Radford U (VA)
Ramapo Coll of New Jersey (NJ)
Regis Coll (MA)
Rice U (TX)
The Richard Stockton Coll of New Jersey (NJ)
Robert Morris U (PA)
Rochester Coll (MI)
Rogers State U (OK)
Roger Williams U (RI)
Rutgers, The State U of New Jersey, Camden (NJ)
Rutgers, The State U of New Jersey, Newark (NJ)
Sage Coll of Albany (NY)
St. Ambrose U (IA)
St. Cloud State U (MN)
St. Edward's U (TX)
St. John Fisher Coll (NY)
Saint Mary's Coll of California (CA)
St. Mary's Coll of Maryland (MD)
Saint Mary's U of Minnesota (MN)
St. Olaf Coll (MN)
Sam Houston State U (TX)
San Diego Christian Coll (CA)
San Diego State U (CA)
San Francisco State U (CA)
Scripps Coll (CA)
Shippensburg U of Pennsylvania (PA)
Sonoma State U (CA)
Southeast Missouri State U (MO)
Southern Illinois U Carbondale (IL)
Southern Methodist U (TX)
Spring Hill Coll (AL)
State U of New York at Binghamton (NY)
State U of New York Coll at Potsdam (NY)
Stephen F. Austin State U (TX)
Sterling Coll (VT)
Stonehill Coll (MA)
Stony Brook U, State U of New York (NY)
Tarleton State U (TX)
Taylor U Fort Wayne (IN)
Tennessee Wesleyan Coll (TN)
Texas A&M U (TX)
Texas A&M U at Galveston (TX)
Texas Southern U (TX)
Texas State U-San Marcos (TX)
Texas Tech U (TX)
Thomas Aquinas Coll (CA)
Truett-McConnell Coll (GA)
Truman State U (MO)
Tulane U (LA)
Tusculum Coll (TN)
U at Buffalo, the State U of New York (NY)
The U of Akron (OH)
U of Alaska Fairbanks (AK)
The U of Arizona (AZ)
U of Arkansas at Monticello (AR)
U of California, Berkeley (CA)
U of California, Davis (CA)
U of California, Irvine (CA)
U of California, Los Angeles (CA)
U of California, Riverside (CA)
U of California, Santa Barbara (CA)
U of Central Arkansas (AR)
U of Colorado Denver (CO)
U of Connecticut (CT)
U of Denver (CO)
U of Evansville (IN)
U of Florida (FL)
U of Hartford (CT)
U of Houston–Clear Lake (TX)
U of Houston–Downtown (TX)
U of Idaho (ID)
U of King's Coll (NS, Canada)
U of Maryland, Coll Park (MD)
U of Maryland U Coll (MD)
U of Massachusetts Amherst (MA)
U of Memphis (TN)
U of Michigan–Dearborn (MI)
U of Michigan–Flint (MI)
U of Minnesota, Crookston (MN)
U of Nebraska at Omaha (NE)
The U of North Carolina at Pembroke (NC)
U of North Dakota (ND)
U of Northern Colorado (CO)
U of North Texas (TX)
U of Oklahoma (OK)
U of Oregon (OR)
U of Ottawa (ON, Canada)
U of Pittsburgh (PA)
U of St. Francis (IL)
U of Saint Mary (KS)
U of St. Thomas (MN)
U of South Alabama (AL)
The U of Tennessee (TN)
The U of Texas at Arlington (TX)
The U of Texas at Austin (TX)
The U of Texas at Brownsville (TX)
The U of Texas at Tyler (TX)
The U of Texas–Pan American (TX)
U of the Incarnate Word (TX)
The U of Toledo (OH)
U of Virginia (VA)
U of Washington, Bothell (WA)
U of Washington, Tacoma (WA)
U of Wisconsin–Superior (WI)
U of Wyoming (WY)
Ursinus Coll (PA)
Ursuline Coll (OH)
Utah State U (UT)
Utah Valley State Coll (UT)
Valparaiso U (IN)
Vassar Coll (NY)
Vennard Coll (IA)
Virginia Commonwealth U (VA)
Viterbo U (WI)
Washington & Jefferson Coll (PA)
Washington and Lee U (VA)
Washington Coll (MD)
Washington U in St. Louis (MO)
Wayne State U (MI)
Western Kentucky U (KY)
West Texas A&M U (TX)
Wheaton Coll (IL)
Wilkes U (PA)
Woodbury Coll (VT)
Wright State U (OH)
Yale U (CT)
York Coll of Pennsylvania (PA)

MUSEUM STUDIES

Baylor U (TX)
Beloit Coll (WI)
Centenary Coll of Louisiana (LA)
Coll of the Atlantic (ME)
Connecticut Coll (CT)
Juniata Coll (PA)
Randolph Coll (VA)
Regis Coll (MA)
Texas A&M U (TX)
Tusculum Coll (TN)
The U of Iowa (IA)

MUSIC

Abilene Christian U (TX)
Acadia U (NS, Canada)
Adams State Coll (CO)
Adelphi U (NY)
Adrian Coll (MI)
Agnes Scott Coll (GA)
Alabama State U (AL)
Albion Coll (MI)
Albright Coll (PA)
Alderson-Broaddus Coll (WV)
Allegheny Coll (PA)
Alma Coll (MI)
American U (DC)
Amherst Coll (MA)
Anderson U (SC)
Andrews U (MI)
Angelo State U (TX)
Anna Maria Coll (MA)
Aquinas Coll (MI)
Arizona State U (AZ)
Arkansas State U (AR)
Arlington Baptist Coll (TX)
Armstrong Atlantic State U (GA)
Asbury Coll (KY)
Ashford U (IA)
Ashland U (OH)
Assumption Coll (MA)
Atlantic Union Coll (MA)
Augsburg Coll (MN)
Augustana Coll (IL)
Augustana Coll (SD)
Augusta State U (GA)
Austin Coll (TX)
Austin Peay State U (TN)
Averett U (VA)
Avila U (MO)
Azusa Pacific U (CA)
Baker U (KS)
Baldwin-Wallace Coll (OH)
Ball State U (IN)
Baptist Bible Coll of Pennsylvania (PA)
Bard Coll (NY)
Bard Coll at Simon's Rock (MA)
Barnard Coll (NY)
Bates Coll (ME)
Baylor U (TX)
Belhaven Coll (MS)
Bellarmine U (KY)
Belmont U (TN)
Beloit Coll (WI)
Bemidji State U (MN)
Benedictine Coll (KS)
Benedictine U (IL)
Bennington Coll (VT)
Berea Coll (KY)
Berklee Coll of Music (MA)
Bernard M. Baruch Coll of the City U of New York (NY)
Berry Coll (GA)
Bethany Bible Coll (NB, Canada)
Bethany Coll (KS)
Bethany Coll (WV)
Bethany Lutheran Coll (MN)
Bethel Coll (TN)
Bethel U (MN)
Biola U (CA)
Bishop's U (QC, Canada)
Blackburn Coll (IL)
Bloomsburg U of Pennsylvania (PA)
Bluefield Coll (VA)
Bluffton U (OH)
Boise State U (ID)
Boston Coll (MA)
The Boston Conservatory (MA)
Bowdoin Coll (ME)
Bowling Green State U (OH)
Bradley U (IL)
Brandeis U (MA)
Brenau U (GA)
Brevard Coll (NC)
Brewton-Parker Coll (GA)
Bridgewater State Coll (MA)
Brigham Young U (UT)
Brock U (ON, Canada)
Brown U (RI)
Bryan Coll (TN)
Bryn Mawr Coll (PA)
Bucknell U (PA)
Buffalo State Coll, State U of New York (NY)
Butler U (IN)
California Baptist U (CA)
California Inst of the Arts (CA)
California Lutheran U (CA)
California Polytechnic State U, San Luis Obispo (CA)
California State Polytechnic U, Pomona (CA)
California State U, Chico (CA)
California State U, Dominguez Hills (CA)
California State U, East Bay (CA)
California State U, Fresno (CA)
California State U, Fullerton (CA)
California State U, Long Beach (CA)
California State U, Los Angeles (CA)
California State U, Sacramento (CA)

MAJORS AND MORE

California State U, San Bernardino (CA)
California State U, Stanislaus (CA)
Calvin Coll (MI)
Cameron U (OK)
Canadian Mennonite U (MB, Canada)
Capital U (OH)
Carroll Coll (WI)
Carson-Newman Coll (TN)
Case Western Reserve U (OH)
Castleton State Coll (VT)
Catawba Coll (NC)
The Catholic U of America (DC)
Cedar Crest Coll (PA)
Cedarville U (OH)
Centenary Coll of Louisiana (LA)
Central Christian Coll of Kansas (KS)
Central Coll (IA)
Central Connecticut State U (CT)
Central Michigan U (MI)
Central Washington U (WA)
Centre Coll (KY)
Chapman U (CA)
Chatham U (PA)
Chestnut Hill Coll (PA)
Cheyney U of Pennsylvania (PA)
Chicago State U (IL)
Christopher Newport U (VA)
City Coll of the City U of New York (NY)
Claflin U (SC)
Claremont McKenna Coll (CA)
Clark Atlanta U (GA)
Clarke Coll (IA)
Clark U (MA)
Clayton State U (GA)
Clearwater Christian Coll (FL)
Cleveland State U (OH)
Coastal Carolina U (SC)
Colby Coll (ME)
Colgate U (NY)
Coll of Charleston (SC)
The Coll of Idaho (ID)
Coll of Mount St. Joseph (OH)
The Coll of New Jersey (NJ)
Coll of Saint Benedict (MN)
Coll of Saint Elizabeth (NJ)
The Coll of Saint Rose (NY)
Coll of Santa Fe (NM)
Coll of Staten Island of the City U of New York (NY)
Coll of the Atlantic (ME)
Coll of the Holy Cross (MA)
Coll of the Ozarks (MO)
The Coll of William and Mary (VA)
The Colorado Coll (CO)
Colorado State U (CO)
Colorado State U-Pueblo (CO)
Columbia Coll (SC)
Columbia Coll Chicago (IL)
Columbus State U (GA)
Concordia Coll (MN)
Concordia Coll–New York (NY)
Concordia U (CA)
Concordia U (MI)
Concordia U (QC, Canada)
Concordia U Chicago (IL)
Concordia U, Nebraska (NE)
Concordia U, St. Paul (MN)
Concordia U Wisconsin (WI)
Connecticut Coll (CT)
Converse Coll (SC)
Cornell Coll (IA)
Cornell U (NY)
Cornerstone U (MI)
Covenant Coll (GA)
Creighton U (NE)
Crossroads Coll (MN)
Culver-Stockton Coll (MO)
Dakota Wesleyan U (SD)
Dallas Baptist U (TX)
Dana Coll (NE)
Dartmouth Coll (NH)
Davidson Coll (NC)
Davis & Elkins Coll (WV)
Delta State U (MS)
Denison U (OH)
DePauw U (IN)
Dickinson Coll (PA)
Dillard U (LA)
Doane Coll (NE)
Dominican U of California (CA)
Dordt Coll (IA)
Dowling Coll (NY)
Drake U (IA)
Drew U (NJ)
Drexel U (PA)
Drury U (MO)
Duke U (NC)
Earlham Coll (IN)
East Central U (OK)
Eastern Illinois U (IL)
Eastern Kentucky U (KY)
Eastern Mennonite U (VA)
Eastern Michigan U (MI)
Eastern New Mexico U (NM)
East Tennessee State U (TN)
East Texas Baptist U (TX)
Eckerd Coll (FL)
Edinboro U of Pennsylvania (PA)
Elizabethtown Coll (PA)
Elon U (NC)
Emmanuel Coll (GA)
Emory & Henry Coll (VA)
Emory U (GA)
Emporia State U (KS)
Erskine Coll (SC)
Evangel U (MO)
Excelsior Coll (NY)
Fayetteville State U (NC)
Five Towns Coll (NY)
Florida Ag and Mech U (FL)
Florida Atlantic U (FL)
Florida Coll (FL)
Florida Intl U (FL)
Florida Southern Coll (FL)
Florida State U (FL)
Fort Lewis Coll (CO)
Franklin & Marshall Coll (PA)
Freed-Hardeman U (TN)
Fresno Pacific U (CA)
Frostburg State U (MD)
Furman U (SC)
George Fox U (OR)
Georgetown Coll (KY)
The George Washington U (DC)
Georgia Coll & State U (GA)
Georgia Southern U (GA)
Georgia Southwestern State U (GA)
Gettysburg Coll (PA)
Gonzaga U (WA)
Gordon Coll (MA)
Goucher Coll (MD)
Grace Bible Coll (MI)
Grace U (NE)
Grand Valley State U (MI)
Grand View Coll (IA)
Greensboro Coll (NC)
Greenville Coll (IL)
Grinnell Coll (IA)
Grove City Coll (PA)
Guilford Coll (NC)
Gustavus Adolphus Coll (MN)
Hamilton Coll (NY)
Hamline U (MN)
Hampshire Coll (MA)
Hampton U (VA)
Hannibal-LaGrange Coll (MO)
Hanover Coll (IN)
Harding U (AR)
Hardin-Simmons U (TX)
Hartwick Coll (NY)
Harvard U (MA)
Hastings Coll (NE)
Haverford Coll (PA)
Hebrew Coll (MA)
Heidelberg Coll (OH)
Henderson State U (AR)
Hendrix Coll (AR)
Hillsdale Coll (MI)
Hobart and William Smith Colls (NY)
Hofstra U (NY)
Hollins U (VA)
Holy Names U (CA)
Hood Coll (MD)
Hope Coll (MI)
Houghton Coll (NY)
Houston Baptist U (TX)
Howard Payne U (TX)
Humboldt State U (CA)
Hunter Coll of the City U of New York (NY)
Huntingdon Coll (AL)
Huntington U (IN)
Huston-Tillotson U (TX)
Idaho State U (ID)
Illinois Coll (IL)
Illinois State U (IL)
Illinois Wesleyan U (IL)
Immaculata U (PA)
Indiana State U (IN)
Indiana U Bloomington (IN)
Indiana U of Pennsylvania (PA)
Indiana U–Purdue U Fort Wayne (IN)
Indiana U Southeast (IN)
Indiana Wesleyan U (IN)
Inter American U of Puerto Rico, Fajardo Campus (PR)
Inter American U of Puerto Rico, San Germán Campus (PR)
Iowa State U of Science and Technology (IA)
Iowa Wesleyan Coll (IA)
Ithaca Coll (NY)
Jacksonville State U (AL)
Jacksonville U (FL)
Jamestown Coll (ND)
Jarvis Christian Coll (TX)
John Brown U (AR)
The Johns Hopkins U (MD)
Johnson C. Smith U (NC)
Johnson State Coll (VT)
Judson Coll (AL)
The Juilliard School (NY)
Kalamazoo Coll (MI)
Kansas State U (KS)
Kean U (NJ)
Keene State Coll (NH)
Kennesaw State U (GA)
Kent State U (OH)
Kentucky State U (KY)
Kenyon Coll (OH)
King Coll (TN)
The King's U Coll (AB, Canada)
Knox Coll (IL)
Kutztown U of Pennsylvania (PA)
Lafayette Coll (PA)
LaGrange Coll (GA)
Lake Forest Coll (IL)
Lakehead U (ON, Canada)
Lambuth U (TN)
Lander U (SC)
La Sierra U (CA)
Laurentian U (ON, Canada)
Lawrence U (WI)
Lee U (TN)
Lehigh U (PA)
Lehman Coll of the City U of New York (NY)
LeMoyne-Owen Coll (TN)
Lenoir-Rhyne Coll (NC)
Lewis & Clark Coll (OR)
Lewis U (IL)
Liberty U (VA)
Limestone Coll (SC)
Lincoln U (PA)
Lindenwood U (MO)
Linfield Coll (OR)
List Coll, The Jewish Theological Sem (NY)
Livingstone Coll (NC)
Lock Haven U of Pennsylvania (PA)
Longwood U (VA)
Loras Coll (IA)
Louisiana Coll (LA)
Louisiana State U and Ag and Mech Coll (LA)
Loyola Marymount U (CA)
Loyola U Chicago (IL)
Loyola U New Orleans (LA)
Lubbock Christian U (TX)
Luther Coll (IA)
Lycoming Coll (PA)
Lynchburg Coll (VA)
Lyon Coll (AR)
Macalester Coll (MN)
Madonna U (MI)
Malone Coll (OH)
Manchester Coll (IN)
Manhattan School of Music (NY)
Manhattanville Coll (NY)
Mannes Coll The New School for Music (NY)
Mansfield U of Pennsylvania (PA)
Maranatha Baptist Bible Coll (WI)
Marian Coll (IN)
Marian Coll of Fond du Lac (WI)
Marietta Coll (OH)
Marlboro Coll (VT)
Martin U (IN)
Mary Baldwin Coll (VA)
Marylhurst U (OR)
Massachusetts Inst of Technology (MA)
The Master's Coll and Sem (CA)
McDaniel Coll (MD)
McGill U (QC, Canada)
McKendree U (IL)
McMurry U (TX)
McNeese State U (LA)
Memorial U of Newfoundland (NL, Canada)
Mercer U (GA)
Mercyhurst Coll (PA)
Meredith Coll (NC)
Mesa State Coll (CO)
Messiah Coll (PA)
Methodist U (NC)
Miami U (OH)
Miami U Hamilton (OH)
Michigan State U (MI)
Middlebury Coll (VT)
Middle Tennessee State U (TN)
Midland Lutheran Coll (NE)
Midwestern State U (TX)
Millersville U of Pennsylvania (PA)
Milligan Coll (TN)
Millikin U (IL)
Millsaps Coll (MS)
Mills Coll (CA)
Minnesota State U Mankato (MN)
Minot State U (ND)
Mississippi Coll (MS)
Mississippi Valley State U (MS)
Missouri State U (MO)
Missouri Valley Coll (MO)
Molloy Coll (NY)
Monmouth Coll (IL)
Monmouth U (NJ)
Montana State U (MT)
Montana State U–Billings (MT)
Montclair State U (NJ)
Moravian Coll (PA)
Morehead State U (KY)
Morehouse Coll (GA)
Morgan State U (MD)
Morningside Coll (IA)
Mount Allison U (NB, Canada)
Mount Holyoke Coll (MA)
Mount Marty Coll (SD)
Mount Mary Coll (WI)
Mount Mercy Coll (IA)
Mount St. Mary's Coll (CA)
Mount Vernon Nazarene U (OH)
Muhlenberg Coll (PA)
Murray State U (KY)
Nazareth Coll of Rochester (NY)
Nebraska Wesleyan U (NE)
New Coll of Florida (FL)
New Jersey City U (NJ)
New Mexico Highlands U (NM)
The New School for Jazz and Contemporary Music (NY)
New York U (NY)
Nicholls State U (LA)
North Carolina Central U (NC)
North Central Coll (IL)
North Dakota State U (ND)
Northeastern Illinois U (IL)
Northeastern State U (OK)
Northeastern U (MA)
Northern Arizona U (AZ)
Northern Illinois U (IL)
Northern Michigan U (MI)
Northern State U (SD)
North Georgia Coll & State U (GA)
North Greenville U (SC)
Northland Coll (WI)
Northwest Christian Coll (OR)
Northwestern Coll (IA)
Northwestern Coll (MN)
Northwestern Oklahoma State U (OK)
Northwestern U (IL)
Northwest Missouri State U (MO)
Northwest Nazarene U (ID)
Notre Dame de Namur U (CA)
Oakland City U (IN)
Oakland U (MI)
Oakwood Coll (AL)
Oberlin Coll (OH)
Occidental Coll (CA)
Ohio Northern U (OH)
Ohio U (OH)
Ohio Wesleyan U (OH)
Oklahoma Christian U (OK)
Oklahoma City U (OK)
Oklahoma Panhandle State U (OK)
Oklahoma State U (OK)
Oklahoma Wesleyan U (OK)
Old Dominion U (VA)
Oral Roberts U (OK)
Oregon State U (OR)
Otterbein Coll (OH)
Ouachita Baptist U (AR)
Pacific Lutheran U (WA)
Pacific Union Coll (CA)
Pacific U (OR)
Palm Beach Atlantic U (FL)
Park U (MO)
Peabody Conservatory of Music of The Johns Hopkins U (MD)
Penn State U Park (PA)
Pepperdine U, Malibu (CA)
Peru State Coll (NE)
Pfeiffer U (NC)
Philadelphia Biblical U (PA)
Piedmont Coll (GA)
Pillsbury Baptist Bible Coll (MN)
Pitzer Coll (CA)
Plymouth State U (NH)
Point Loma Nazarene U (CA)
Pomona Coll (CA)
Portland State U (OR)
Prairie View A&M U (TX)
Presbyterian Coll (SC)
Princeton U (NJ)
Providence Coll (RI)
Purdue U (IN)
Queen's U at Kingston (ON, Canada)
Queens U of Charlotte (NC)
Quincy U (IL)
Radford U (VA)
Ramapo Coll of New Jersey (NJ)
Randolph-Macon Coll (VA)
Redeemer U Coll (ON, Canada)
Reed Coll (OR)
Rhode Island Coll (RI)
Rhodes Coll (TN)
Rice U (TX)
Rider U (NJ)
Ripon Coll (WI)
Roanoke Coll (VA)
Roberts Wesleyan Coll (NY)
Rochester Coll (MI)
Rockford Coll (IL)
Rollins Coll (FL)
Roosevelt U (IL)
Rowan U (NJ)
Rutgers, The State U of New Jersey, Camden (NJ)
Rutgers, The State U of New Jersey, Newark (NJ)
Rutgers, The State U of New Jersey, New Brunswick (NJ)
Saginaw Valley State U (MI)
St. Ambrose U (IA)
St. Cloud State U (MN)
St. Francis Xavier U (NS, Canada)
Saint John's U (MN)
St. Lawrence U (NY)
Saint Louis U (MO)
Saint Mary-of-the-Woods Coll (IN)
Saint Mary's Coll (IN)
Saint Mary's Coll of California (CA)
St. Mary's Coll of Maryland (MD)
St. Mary's U (TX)
Saint Mary's U of Minnesota (MN)
Saint Michael's Coll (VT)
St. Norbert Coll (WI)
St. Olaf Coll (MN)
Saint Vincent Coll (PA)
Saint Xavier U (IL)
Salem Coll (NC)
Salisbury U (MD)
Salve Regina U (RI)
Sam Houston State U (TX)
San Diego Christian Coll (CA)
San Francisco State U (CA)
Santa Clara U (CA)
Sarah Lawrence Coll (NY)
Schreiner U (TX)
Scripps Coll (CA)
Seattle Pacific U (WA)
Seton Hill U (PA)
Sewanee: The U of the South (TN)
Shaw U (NC)
Shenandoah U (VA)
Shepherd U (WV)
Shorter Coll (GA)
Simmons Coll (MA)
Simon Fraser U (BC, Canada)
Simpson Coll (IA)
Simpson U (CA)
Slippery Rock U of Pennsylvania (PA)
Smith Coll (MA)
Sonoma State U (CA)
South Dakota State U (SD)
Southeastern Bible Coll (AL)
Southeastern Oklahoma State U (OK)
Southeastern U (FL)
Southeast Missouri State U (MO)
Southern Adventist U (TN)
Southern Connecticut State U (CT)
Southern Illinois U Carbondale (IL)
Southern Illinois U Edwardsville (IL)
Southern Methodist U (TX)
Southern Oregon U (OR)
Southern Utah U (UT)
Southern Wesleyan U (SC)
Southwest Baptist U (MO)
Southwestern Adventist U (TX)
Southwestern Coll (KS)
Southwestern Oklahoma State U (OK)
Southwestern U (TX)
Southwest Minnesota State U (MN)
Spelman Coll (GA)
Spring Arbor U (MI)
Stanford U (CA)
State U of New York at Binghamton (NY)
State U of New York at Fredonia (NY)
State U of New York at New Paltz (NY)
State U of New York at Oswego (NY)
State U of New York at Plattsburgh (NY)
State U of New York Coll at Geneseo (NY)
State U of New York Coll at Oneonta (NY)
State U of New York Coll at Potsdam (NY)
Steinbach Bible Coll (MB, Canada)
Stephen F. Austin State U (TX)
Sterling Coll (KS)
Stetson U (FL)
Stillman Coll (AL)
Stony Brook U, State U of New York (NY)
Susquehanna U (PA)
Swarthmore Coll (PA)
Sweet Briar Coll (VA)
Syracuse U (NY)
Tabor Coll (KS)
Tarleton State U (TX)
Taylor U (IN)
Taylor U Coll and Sem (AB, Canada)
Temple U (PA)
Tennessee State U (TN)
Tennessee Technological U (TN)
Tennessee Wesleyan Coll (TN)

Texas A&M U (TX)
Texas A&M U–Commerce (TX)
Texas Christian U (TX)
Texas Coll (TX)
Texas Lutheran U (TX)
Texas Southern U (TX)
Texas State U-San Marcos (TX)
Texas Tech U (TX)
Texas Woman's U (TX)
Thomas Edison State Coll (NJ)
Toccoa Falls Coll (GA)
Tougaloo Coll (MS)
Towson U (MD)
Trevecca Nazarene U (TN)
Trinity Christian Coll (IL)
Trinity Coll (CT)
Trinity Intl U (IL)
Trinity U (TX)
Troy U (AL)
Truett-McConnell Coll (GA)
Truman State U (MO)
Tufts U (MA)
Tulane U (LA)
Union Coll (NE)
Union U (TN)
U at Albany, State U of New York (NY)
U at Buffalo, the State U of New York (NY)
The U of Akron (OH)
The U of Alabama (AL)
The U of Alabama at Birmingham (AL)
The U of Alabama in Huntsville (AL)
U of Alaska Fairbanks (AK)
The U of Arizona (AZ)
U of Arkansas (AR)
U of Arkansas at Fort Smith (AR)
U of Arkansas at Monticello (AR)
U of Arkansas at Pine Bluff (AR)
U of Bridgeport (CT)
The U of British Columbia (BC, Canada)
U of California, Berkeley (CA)
U of California, Davis (CA)
U of California, Irvine (CA)
U of California, Los Angeles (CA)
U of California, Riverside (CA)
U of California, San Diego (CA)
U of California, Santa Barbara (CA)
U of California, Santa Cruz (CA)
U of Central Arkansas (AR)
U of Central Missouri (MO)
U of Central Oklahoma (OK)
U of Chicago (IL)
U of Cincinnati (OH)
U of Colorado at Boulder (CO)
U of Colorado Denver (CO)
U of Connecticut (CT)
U of Dayton (OH)
U of Delaware (DE)
U of Denver (CO)
U of Evansville (IN)
U of Florida (FL)
U of Georgia (GA)
U of Hartford (CT)
U of Hawaii at Manoa (HI)
U of Houston (TX)
U of Idaho (ID)
U of Illinois at Chicago (IL)
U of Illinois at Urbana–Champaign (IL)
U of Indianapolis (IN)
The U of Iowa (IA)
U of Kansas (KS)
U of King's Coll (NS, Canada)
U of La Verne (CA)
U of Lethbridge (AB, Canada)
U of Louisiana at Lafayette (LA)
U of Louisville (KY)
U of Maine (ME)
The U of Maine at Augusta (ME)
U of Maine at Farmington (ME)
U of Maine at Machias (ME)
U of Maryland, Baltimore County (MD)
U of Maryland, Coll Park (MD)
U of Mary Washington (VA)
U of Massachusetts Amherst (MA)
U of Massachusetts Boston (MA)
U of Massachusetts Dartmouth (MA)
U of Massachusetts Lowell (MA)
U of Memphis (TN)
U of Miami (FL)
U of Michigan (MI)
U of Michigan–Flint (MI)
U of Minnesota, Duluth (MN)
U of Minnesota, Twin Cities Campus (MN)
U of Mississippi (MS)
U of Missouri–Columbia (MO)
U of Missouri–Kansas City (MO)
U of Missouri–St. Louis (MO)
The U of Montana (MT)
U of Montevallo (AL)
U of Nebraska at Kearney (NE)
U of Nebraska at Omaha (NE)
U of Nebraska–Lincoln (NE)
U of Nevada, Las Vegas (NV)
U of Nevada, Reno (NV)
U of New Hampshire (NH)
U of New Haven (CT)
U of New Orleans (LA)
U of North Alabama (AL)
The U of North Carolina at Asheville (NC)
The U of North Carolina at Chapel Hill (NC)
The U of North Carolina at Charlotte (NC)
The U of North Carolina at Greensboro (NC)
The U of North Carolina at Pembroke (NC)
The U of North Carolina Wilmington (NC)
U of North Dakota (ND)
U of Northern Colorado (CO)
U of Northern Iowa (IA)
U of North Florida (FL)
U of North Texas (TX)
U of Notre Dame (IN)
U of Oklahoma (OK)
U of Oregon (OR)
U of Ottawa (ON, Canada)
U of Pennsylvania (PA)
U of Pittsburgh (PA)
U of Portland (OR)
U of Prince Edward Island (PE, Canada)
U of Puget Sound (WA)
U of Redlands (CA)
U of Regina (SK, Canada)
U of Rhode Island (RI)
U of Richmond (VA)
U of Rio Grande (OH)
U of Rochester (NY)
U of St. Francis (IL)
U of St. Thomas (MN)
U of St. Thomas (TX)
U of San Diego (CA)
U of Science and Arts of Oklahoma (OK)
U of Sioux Falls (SD)
U of South Alabama (AL)
U of South Carolina (SC)
The U of South Dakota (SD)
U of Southern California (CA)
U of Southern Maine (ME)
U of Southern Mississippi (MS)
The U of Tampa (FL)
The U of Tennessee (TN)
The U of Tennessee at Chattanooga (TN)
The U of Tennessee at Martin (TN)
The U of Texas at Arlington (TX)
The U of Texas at Austin (TX)
The U of Texas at Brownsville (TX)
The U of Texas at El Paso (TX)
The U of Texas at San Antonio (TX)
The U of Texas at Tyler (TX)
The U of Texas–Pan American (TX)
U of the Incarnate Word (TX)
U of the Ozarks (AR)
U of the Pacific (CA)
The U of Toledo (OH)
U of Toronto (ON, Canada)
U of Tulsa (OK)
U of Utah (UT)
U of Vermont (VT)
U of Victoria (BC, Canada)
U of Virginia (VA)
The U of Western Ontario (ON, Canada)
U of Windsor (ON, Canada)
The U of Winnipeg (MB, Canada)
U of Wisconsin–Eau Claire (WI)
U of Wisconsin–Green Bay (WI)
U of Wisconsin–La Crosse (WI)
U of Wisconsin–Madison (WI)
U of Wisconsin–Milwaukee (WI)
U of Wisconsin–Oshkosh (WI)
U of Wisconsin–Parkside (WI)
U of Wisconsin–Platteville (WI)
U of Wisconsin–Stevens Point (WI)
U of Wisconsin–Superior (WI)
U of Wisconsin–Whitewater (WI)
U of Wyoming (WY)
Utah State U (UT)
Utah Valley State Coll (UT)
Valdosta State U (GA)
Valley City State U (ND)
Valparaiso U (IN)
Vanderbilt U (TN)
Vanguard U of Southern California (CA)
Vassar Coll (NY)
Virginia Polytechnic Inst and State U (VA)
Virginia State U (VA)
Virginia Wesleyan Coll (VA)
Viterbo U (WI)
Wabash Coll (IN)
Wagner Coll (NY)
Wake Forest U (NC)
Walla Walla U (WA)
Warner Pacific Coll (OR)
Wartburg Coll (IA)
Washburn U (KS)
Washington & Jefferson Coll (PA)
Washington and Lee U (VA)
Washington Bible Coll (MD)
Washington Coll (MD)
Washington State U (WA)
Washington U in St. Louis (MO)
Wayland Baptist U (TX)
Wayne State Coll (NE)
Wayne State U (MI)
Weber State U (UT)
Webster U (MO)
Wellesley Coll (MA)
Wells Coll (NY)
Wesleyan Coll (GA)
Wesleyan U (CT)
West Chester U of Pennsylvania (PA)
Western Carolina U (NC)
Western Connecticut State U (CT)
Western Illinois U (IL)
Western Kentucky U (KY)
Western Michigan U (MI)
Western New Mexico U (NM)
Western State Coll of Colorado (CO)
Western Washington U (WA)
Westfield State Coll (MA)
Westmont Coll (CA)
West Texas A&M U (TX)
West Virginia U (WV)
West Virginia Wesleyan Coll (WV)
Wheaton Coll (IL)
Wheaton Coll (MA)
Whitman Coll (WA)
Whittier Coll (CA)
Whitworth U (WA)
Wichita State U (KS)
Wiley Coll (TX)
Wilfrid Laurier U (ON, Canada)
Willamette U (OR)
William Jewell Coll (MO)
William Paterson U of New Jersey (NJ)
Williams Coll (MA)
Wingate U (NC)
Winona State U (MN)
Winthrop U (SC)
Wittenberg U (OH)
Worcester Polytechnic Inst (MA)
Wright State U (OH)
Xavier U (OH)
Xavier U of Louisiana (LA)
Yale U (CT)
York Coll (NE)
York Coll of Pennsylvania (PA)
York Coll of the City U of New York (NY)
York U (ON, Canada)
Youngstown State U (OH)

MUSICAL INSTRUMENT FABRICATION AND REPAIR

Ball State U (IN)
Barton Coll (NC)

MUSICAL INSTRUMENT TECHNOLOGY

The New School for Jazz and Contemporary Music (NY)

MUSIC HISTORY, LITERATURE, AND THEORY

Baldwin-Wallace Coll (OH)
Bard Coll (NY)
Baylor U (TX)
Belmont U (TN)
Bennington Coll (VT)
Boston U (MA)
Bowling Green State U (OH)
Bridgewater Coll (VA)
Brigham Young U (UT)
Bucknell U (PA)
Butler U (IN)
California State U, Fresno (CA)
California State U, Long Beach (CA)
Calvin Coll (MI)
Canadian Mennonite U (MB, Canada)
The Catholic U of America (DC)
Central Michigan U (MI)
Christopher Newport U (VA)
Converse Coll (SC)
Covenant Coll (GA)
Eugene Lang Coll The New School for Liberal Arts (NY)
Fairfield U (CT)
Florida State U (FL)
Hardin-Simmons U (TX)
Harvard U (MA)
Hastings Coll (NE)
Hofstra U (NY)
Indiana U Bloomington (IN)
Keene State Coll (NH)
Lafayette Coll (PA)
Loyola Marymount U (CA)
Marlboro Coll (VT)
McGill U (QC, Canada)
Memorial U of Newfoundland (NL, Canada)
Mount Allison U (NB, Canada)
Nazareth Coll of Rochester (NY)
New Coll of Florida (FL)
New England Conservatory of Music (MA)
Northeastern U (MA)
North Greenville U (SC)
Northwestern U (IL)
Oberlin Coll (OH)
Ohio U (OH)
Otterbein Coll (OH)
Ouachita Baptist U (AR)
Randolph Coll (VA)
Rice U (TX)
Roosevelt U (IL)
St. Cloud State U (MN)
Saint Joseph's Coll (IN)
Sarah Lawrence Coll (NY)
Sewanee: The U of the South (TN)
Simmons Coll (MA)
Skidmore Coll (NY)
Southwestern U (TX)
State U of New York at Binghamton (NY)
State U of New York at Fredonia (NY)
Syracuse U (NY)
Temple U (PA)
Trinity Intl U (IL)
The U of Akron (OH)
The U of British Columbia (BC, Canada)
U of California, Los Angeles (CA)
U of California, San Diego (CA)
U of Chicago (IL)
U of Cincinnati (OH)
U of Hartford (CT)
U of Idaho (ID)
U of Illinois at Urbana–Champaign (IL)
U of Michigan (MI)
The U of North Carolina at Greensboro (NC)
U of North Texas (TX)
U of Redlands (CA)
U of Regina (SK, Canada)
U of Richmond (VA)
U of the Pacific (CA)
U of Toronto (ON, Canada)
U of Vermont (VT)
U of Victoria (BC, Canada)
The U of Western Ontario (ON, Canada)
U of Windsor (ON, Canada)
U of Wisconsin–Milwaukee (WI)
Washington U in St. Louis (MO)
Western Washington U (WA)
Wheaton Coll (IL)
Whitman Coll (WA)
Wright State U (OH)
York U (ON, Canada)
Youngstown State U (OH)

MUSIC MANAGEMENT AND MERCHANDISING

Anderson U (IN)
Appalachian State U (NC)
Asbury Coll (KY)
Belmont U (TN)
Berklee Coll of Music (MA)
Berry Coll (GA)
Boise State U (ID)
Bryan Coll (TN)
Butler U (IN)
Capital U (OH)
Central Washington U (WA)
Clarion U of Pennsylvania (PA)
Coll of the Ozarks (MO)
Columbia Coll Chicago (IL)
Dallas Baptist U (TX)
DePaul U (IL)
DePauw U (IN)
Dillard U (LA)
Drake U (IA)
Ferris State U (MI)
Five Towns Coll (NY)
Florida Atlantic U (FL)
Florida Southern Coll (FL)
Georgia State U (GA)
Greenville Coll (IL)
Grove City Coll (PA)
Hardin-Simmons U (TX)
Heidelberg Coll (OH)
Hofstra U (NY)
Huntington U (IN)
Jacksonville U (FL)
Johnson C. Smith U (NC)
Johnson State Coll (VT)
Kentucky Christian U (KY)
Lebanon Valley Coll (PA)
Lewis U (IL)
Loyola U New Orleans (LA)
Mansfield U of Pennsylvania (PA)
Marian Coll of Fond du Lac (WI)
The Master's Coll and Sem (CA)
Methodist U (NC)
Middle Tennessee State U (TN)
Minnesota State U Mankato (MN)
Mississippi U for Women (MS)
New York U (NY)
Northeastern U (MA)
Northwest Christian Coll (OR)
Northwest Missouri State U (MO)
Ohio Northern U (OH)
Ohio U (OH)
Oklahoma City U (OK)
Otterbein Coll (OH)
Peru State Coll (NE)
Saint Joseph's Coll (IN)
Saint Mary's U of Minnesota (MN)
South Carolina State U (SC)
South Dakota State U (SD)
Southern Oregon U (OR)
Southwestern Oklahoma State U (OK)
Southwest Minnesota State U (MN)
State U of New York at Fredonia (NY)
State U of New York Coll at Oneonta (NY)
State U of New York Coll at Potsdam (NY)
Tabor Coll (KS)
Taylor U (IN)
Trevecca Nazarene U (TN)
Union U (TN)
U of Evansville (IN)
U of Hartford (CT)
U of Idaho (ID)
The U of Iowa (IA)
U of Memphis (TN)
U of New Haven (CT)
U of Puget Sound (WA)
U of Southern California (CA)
U of Southern Mississippi (MS)
The U of Texas at San Antonio (TX)
U of the Pacific (CA)
The U of Western Ontario (ON, Canada)
Valparaiso U (IN)
Warner Pacific Coll (OR)
Western State Coll of Colorado (CO)
William Paterson U of New Jersey (NJ)
Winona State U (MN)

MUSICOLOGY AND ETHNOMUSICOLOGY

Baldwin-Wallace Coll (OH)
Bennington Coll (VT)
Brown U (RI)
Canadian Mennonite U (MB, Canada)
Coll of Santa Fe (NM)
Loyola Marymount U (CA)
The New School for Jazz and Contemporary Music (NY)
Northwestern U (IL)
Southwestern U (TX)
U of California, Los Angeles (CA)
U of Denver (CO)
U of Kansas (KS)
U of Miami (FL)
U of Regina (SK, Canada)
The U of Western Ontario (ON, Canada)
York U (ON, Canada)

MUSIC PEDAGOGY

Baylor U (TX)
Brigham Young U (UT)
Bryan Coll (TN)
Cedarville U (OH)
Florida State U (FL)
Hastings Coll (NE)
Holy Names U (CA)
Lawrence U (WI)
Madonna U (MI)
Maranatha Baptist Bible Coll (WI)
McGill U (QC, Canada)
Meredith Coll (NC)
Michigan State U (MI)
The New School for Jazz and Contemporary Music (NY)
Roosevelt U (IL)
St. Cloud State U (MN)
St. Mary's Coll of Maryland (MD)
Spring Arbor U (MI)
Temple U (PA)
Trinity Intl U (IL)
U of Delaware (DE)
U of Louisiana at Lafayette (LA)
The U of Tennessee at Martin (TN)
The U of Western Ontario (ON, Canada)
Viterbo U (WI)

MUSIC PERFORMANCE

Adams State Coll (CO)
Alcorn State U (MS)
Alderson-Broaddus Coll (WV)
Allegheny Coll (PA)
Alma Coll (MI)
Anderson U (IN)
Anderson U (SC)
Anna Maria Coll (MA)
Appalachian State U (NC)
Aquinas Coll (MI)
Arizona State U (AZ)
Arkansas State U (AR)
Augustana Coll (IL)
Augusta State U (GA)
Averett U (VA)
Avila U (MO)
Baldwin-Wallace Coll (OH)
Bard Coll (NY)
Baylor U (TX)
Bennington Coll (VT)
Berklee Coll of Music (MA)
Bethel U (MN)
Bethune-Cookman U (FL)
Bob Jones U (SC)
Boston U (MA)
Bowling Green State U (OH)
Bradley U (IL)
Brenau U (GA)
Brewton-Parker Coll (GA)
Brigham Young U (UT)
Bryan Coll (TN)
Bucknell U (PA)
Butler U (IN)
California Baptist U (CA)
California Inst of the Arts (CA)
California State U, Chico (CA)
California State U, Fullerton (CA)
California State U, Long Beach (CA)
California State U, Los Angeles (CA)
California State U, Stanislaus (CA)
Calvin Coll (MI)
Canadian Mennonite U (MB, Canada)
Capital U (OH)
Carnegie Mellon U (PA)
The Catholic U of America (DC)
Cedarville U (OH)
Centenary Coll of Louisiana (LA)
Central State U (OH)
Chapman U (CA)
City Coll of the City U of New York (NY)
Clarion U of Pennsylvania (PA)
Clayton State U (GA)
The Colburn School Conservatory of Music (CA)
The Coll of St. Scholastica (MN)
Coll of Santa Fe (NM)
Colorado State U (CO)
Columbia Coll (SC)
Columbia Coll Chicago (IL)
Columbus State U (GA)
Concordia Coll (MN)
Concordia U (QC, Canada)
Cornerstone U (MI)
Covenant Coll (GA)
DePaul U (IL)
DePauw U (IN)
Dillard U (LA)
Dordt Coll (IA)
Drake U (IA)
Drury U (MO)
Duquesne U (PA)
East Carolina U (NC)
Eastern Michigan U (MI)
Elon U (NC)
Florida Ag and Mech U (FL)
Florida Gulf Coast U (FL)
Florida State U (FL)
Fort Lewis Coll (CO)
Gardner-Webb U (NC)
George Fox U (OR)
George Mason U (VA)
Georgia Southern U (GA)
Georgia State U (GA)
Glenville State Coll (WV)
Gordon Coll (MA)
Grace Coll (IN)
Grambling State U (LA)
Greensboro Coll (NC)
Grove City Coll (PA)
Hardin-Simmons U (TX)
Hastings Coll (NE)
Henderson State U (AR)
Hillsdale Free Will Baptist Coll (OK)
Hofstra U (NY)
Holy Names U (CA)
Hope Coll (MI)
Houghton Coll (NY)
Houston Baptist U (TX)
Howard Payne U (TX)
Idaho State U (ID)
Illinois State U (IL)
Illinois Wesleyan U (IL)
Immaculata U (PA)
Indiana U Bloomington (IN)
Indiana U of Pennsylvania (PA)
Indiana U South Bend (IN)
Ithaca Coll (NY)
Jackson State U (MS)
Jacksonville U (FL)
James Madison U (VA)
Jamestown Coll (ND)
Johnson State Coll (VT)
The Juilliard School (NY)
Kennesaw State U (GA)
Kent State U (OH)
Kentucky Christian U (KY)
Lambuth U (TN)
Lawrence U (WI)
Lebanon Valley Coll (PA)
Lenoir-Rhyne Coll (NC)
Linfield Coll (OR)
Lipscomb U (TN)
Louisiana State U and Ag and Mech Coll (LA)
Loyola U New Orleans (LA)
Lynchburg Coll (VA)
Mannes Coll The New School for Music (NY)
Mansfield U of Pennsylvania (PA)
Maranatha Baptist Bible Coll (WI)
Marylhurst U (OR)
Maryville Coll (TN)
Marywood U (PA)
McGill U (QC, Canada)
McNeese State U (LA)
Mercer U (GA)
Mercyhurst Coll (PA)
Meredith Coll (NC)
Miami U (OH)
Michigan State U (MI)
Midwestern State U (TX)
Millikin U (IL)
Mississippi Coll (MS)
Missouri Baptist U (MO)
Missouri Southern State U (MO)
Missouri State U (MO)
Moravian Coll (PA)
Mount Allison U (NB, Canada)
Mount Vernon Nazarene U (OH)
Naropa U (CO)
Nebraska Wesleyan U (NE)
New England Conservatory of Music (MA)
The New School for Jazz and Contemporary Music (NY)
New World School of the Arts (FL)
New York U (NY)
North Carolina School of the Arts (NC)
Northern Arizona U (AZ)
Northwestern Coll (MN)
Northwestern State U of Louisiana (LA)
Northwestern U (IL)
Northwest Nazarene U (ID)
Notre Dame de Namur U (CA)
Oakland City U (IN)
Oakland U (MI)
Ohio Northern U (OH)
Ohio U (OH)
Ohio Wesleyan U (OH)
Oklahoma Wesleyan U (OK)
Old Dominion U (VA)
Oral Roberts U (OK)
Otterbein Coll (OH)
Ouachita Baptist U (AR)
Pacific U (OR)
Palm Beach Atlantic U (FL)
Peace Coll (NC)
Penn State U Park (PA)
Piedmont Coll (GA)
Pittsburg State U (KS)
Point Loma Nazarene U (CA)
Presbyterian Coll (SC)
Queens Coll of the City U of New York (NY)
Randolph Coll (VA)
Rhode Island Coll (RI)
Rice U (TX)
Rockford Coll (IL)
Roosevelt U (IL)
Rowan U (NJ)
St. Cloud State U (MN)
Saint Mary-of-the-Woods Coll (IN)
St. Mary's Coll of Maryland (MD)
Saint Mary's U of Minnesota (MN)
St. Olaf Coll (MN)
Saint Vincent Coll (PA)
Saint Xavier U (IL)
Salem Coll (NC)
Salisbury U (MD)
Samford U (AL)
Sam Houston State U (TX)
San Francisco State U (CA)
Sarah Lawrence Coll (NY)
Seton Hill U (PA)
Shenandoah U (VA)
Simpson Coll (IA)
Slippery Rock U of Pennsylvania (PA)
Southeastern Louisiana U (LA)
Southeastern Oklahoma State U (OK)
Southeastern U (FL)
Southern Adventist U (TN)
Southern Methodist U (TX)
Southern U and Ag and Mech Coll (LA)
Southwestern U (TX)
State U of New York at Binghamton (NY)
State U of New York Coll at Potsdam (NY)
Stephen F. Austin State U (TX)
Stetson U (FL)
Syracuse U (NY)
Taylor U (IN)
Temple U (PA)
Texas A&M U–Commerce (TX)
Texas Christian U (TX)
Texas State U-San Marcos (TX)
Texas Tech U (TX)
Toccoa Falls Coll (GA)
Transylvania U (KY)
Trinity Christian Coll (IL)
Trinity U (TX)
Truman State U (MO)
Union Coll (NE)
Union U (TN)
U at Buffalo, the State U of New York (NY)
The U of Akron (OH)
The U of Arizona (AZ)
U of California, Irvine (CA)
U of Central Arkansas (AR)
U of Central Florida (FL)
U of Colorado at Boulder (CO)
U of Denver (CO)
U of Evansville (IN)
U of Georgia (GA)
U of Hartford (CT)
U of Houston (TX)
U of Idaho (ID)
U of Illinois at Urbana–Champaign (IL)
U of Indianapolis (IN)
U of Kansas (KS)
U of Louisiana at Lafayette (LA)
U of Louisiana at Monroe (LA)
U of Mary (ND)
U of Mary Hardin-Baylor (TX)
U of Maryland, Coll Park (MD)
U of Massachusetts Amherst (MA)
U of Massachusetts Lowell (MA)
U of Miami (FL)
U of Michigan–Flint (MI)
U of Missouri–Kansas City (MO)
U of Missouri–St. Louis (MO)
The U of Montana (MT)
U of Nebraska at Omaha (NE)
U of Nevada, Reno (NV)
U of New Hampshire (NH)
U of New Mexico (NM)
The U of North Carolina at Chapel Hill (NC)
The U of North Carolina at Charlotte (NC)
The U of North Carolina at Greensboro (NC)
The U of North Carolina at Pembroke (NC)
The U of North Carolina Wilmington (NC)
U of North Dakota (ND)
U of Northern Iowa (IA)
U of North Florida (FL)
U of North Texas (TX)
U of Oklahoma (OK)
U of Oregon (OR)
U of Puget Sound (WA)
U of Redlands (CA)
U of Regina (SK, Canada)
U of Rhode Island (RI)
U of St. Francis (IL)
U of Southern California (CA)
U of Southern Maine (ME)
U of South Florida (FL)
The U of Tampa (FL)
The U of Tennessee at Martin (TN)
The U of Texas at Austin (TX)
The U of Texas at San Antonio (TX)
U of Tulsa (OK)
U of Vermont (VT)
The U of Western Ontario (ON, Canada)
U of West Florida (FL)
U of West Georgia (GA)
U of Windsor (ON, Canada)
U of Wisconsin–Superior (WI)
U of Wyoming (WY)
Valdosta State U (GA)
Valparaiso U (IN)
Virginia Commonwealth U (VA)
Viterbo U (WI)
Wartburg Coll (IA)
Washburn U (KS)
Washington State U (WA)
Weber State U (UT)
Webster U (MO)
West Chester U of Pennsylvania (PA)
Western Carolina U (NC)
Western Connecticut State U (CT)
Western Illinois U (IL)
Western Michigan U (MI)
West Texas A&M U (TX)
Wheaton Coll (IL)
Whitman Coll (WA)
Willamette U (OR)
William Jewell Coll (MO)
Wright State U (OH)
Xavier U of Louisiana (LA)
York U (ON, Canada)
Youngstown State U (OH)

MUSIC RELATED

Bellarmine U (KY)
Bethel Coll (KS)
Bob Jones U (SC)
Bowling Green State U (OH)
Brigham Young U (UT)
Brown U (RI)
California Inst of the Arts (CA)
California State U, Chico (CA)
Capital U (OH)
Central Michigan U (MI)
Claremont McKenna Coll (CA)
Coker Coll (SC)
Coll of Santa Fe (NM)
Coll of the Ozarks (MO)
Connecticut Coll (CT)
DePaul U (IL)
Dickinson Coll (PA)
Duquesne U (PA)
Greenville Coll (IL)
Hampton U (VA)
Illinois Wesleyan U (IL)
Indiana State U (IN)
Indiana U Bloomington (IN)
Indiana U South Bend (IN)
Keene State Coll (NH)
Marylhurst U (OR)
Mercer U (GA)
Milligan Coll (TN)
Northwestern U (IL)
Ohio Northern U (OH)
Roosevelt U (IL)
St. Mary's Coll of Maryland (MD)
Saint Mary's U of Minnesota (MN)
St. Olaf Coll (MN)
San Diego State U (CA)
School of the Art Inst of Chicago (IL)
Shenandoah U (VA)
Southeastern U (FL)
Transylvania U (KY)
The U of Akron (OH)
The U of Arizona (AZ)
U of California, Riverside (CA)
U of Denver (CO)
U of Hartford (CT)
U of Louisiana at Lafayette (LA)
U of Miami (FL)
The U of North Carolina at Asheville (NC)
U of Saint Francis (IN)
U of Southern California (CA)
U of the Incarnate Word (TX)
U of Tulsa (OK)
The U of Western Ontario (ON, Canada)
Western Illinois U (IL)
Western Kentucky U (KY)
West Virginia U (WV)
Wheaton Coll (IL)

MUSIC TEACHER EDUCATION

Abilene Christian U (TX)
Acadia U (NS, Canada)
Adams State Coll (CO)
Adrian Coll (MI)
Alabama Ag and Mech U (AL)
Alabama State U (AL)
Alderson-Broaddus Coll (WV)
Alma Coll (MI)
Anderson U (IN)
Anderson U (SC)
Andrews U (MI)
Anna Maria Coll (MA)
Appalachian State U (NC)
Aquinas Coll (MI)
Arizona State U (AZ)
Arkansas State U (AR)
Arlington Baptist Coll (TX)
Armstrong Atlantic State U (GA)
Asbury Coll (KY)
Ashford U (IA)
Ashland U (OH)
Atlantic Union Coll (MA)
Auburn U (AL)
Augsburg Coll (MN)
Augustana Coll (IL)
Augustana Coll (SD)
Augusta State U (GA)
Baker U (KS)
Baldwin-Wallace Coll (OH)
Ball State U (IN)
Baptist Bible Coll of Pennsylvania (PA)
The Baptist Coll of Florida (FL)
Baylor U (TX)
Belmont U (TN)
Beloit Coll (WI)
Bemidji State U (MN)
Benedictine Coll (KS)
Benedictine U (IL)
Berklee Coll of Music (MA)
Berry Coll (GA)
Bethany Coll (KS)
Bethany U (CA)
Bethel Coll (TN)
Bethel U (MN)
Bethune-Cookman U (FL)
Bishop's U (QC, Canada)
Bluefield Coll (VA)
Bluffton U (OH)
Bob Jones U (SC)
Boise State U (ID)
The Boston Conservatory (MA)
Boston U (MA)
Bowling Green State U (OH)
Bradley U (IL)
Brenau U (GA)
Brevard Coll (NC)
Brewton-Parker Coll (GA)
Bridgewater Coll (VA)
Bridgewater State Coll (MA)
Brigham Young U (UT)
Brock U (ON, Canada)
Bryan Coll (TN)
Bucknell U (PA)
Buffalo State Coll, State U of New York (NY)
Butler U (IN)
California Lutheran U (CA)
California State U, Chico (CA)
California State U, Dominguez Hills (CA)
California State U, Fresno (CA)
California State U, Fullerton (CA)
Calvin Coll (MI)
Capital U (OH)
Carroll Coll (WI)
Carson-Newman Coll (TN)
Case Western Reserve U (OH)
Castleton State Coll (VT)
Catawba Coll (NC)
The Catholic U of America (DC)
Cedarville U (OH)
Centenary Coll of Louisiana (LA)
Central Coll (IA)
Central Connecticut State U (CT)
Central Michigan U (MI)
Central Washington U (WA)
Chapman U (CA)
Chestnut Hill Coll (PA)
Chicago State U (IL)
City Coll of the City U of New York (NY)
Claflin U (SC)
Clarion U of Pennsylvania (PA)
Clarke Coll (IA)
Clearwater Christian Coll (FL)
Coker Coll (SC)
The Coll of New Jersey (NJ)
The Coll of Saint Rose (NY)
Coll of the Ozarks (MO)
Colorado State U (CO)
Columbia Coll (SC)
Columbus State U (GA)
Concordia Coll (MN)
Concordia U (MI)
Concordia U Chicago (IL)
Concordia U, Nebraska (NE)
Concordia U, St. Paul (MN)
Concordia U Wisconsin (WI)
Concord U (WV)
Connecticut Coll (CT)
Converse Coll (SC)
Cornell Coll (IA)
Cornerstone U (MI)
Crown Coll (MN)
Culver-Stockton Coll (MO)
Dakota Wesleyan U (SD)
Dallas Baptist U (TX)
Dana Coll (NE)
Davis & Elkins Coll (WV)
Delta State U (MS)
DePaul U (IL)
DePauw U (IN)
Dordt Coll (IA)
Dowling Coll (NY)
Drake U (IA)
Drury U (MO)
Duquesne U (PA)
East Carolina U (NC)
East Central U (OK)
Eastern Kentucky U (KY)
Eastern Mennonite U (VA)
Eastern Michigan U (MI)
Eastern New Mexico U (NM)
East Texas Baptist U (TX)
Elizabethtown Coll (PA)
Elon U (NC)
Emmanuel Coll (GA)
Emporia State U (KS)

MAJORS AND MORE

Evangel U (MO)
Fairfield U (CT)
Fairmont State U (WV)
Faith Baptist Bible Coll and Theological Sem (IA)
Fayetteville State U (NC)
Five Towns Coll (NY)
Florida Ag and Mech U (FL)
Florida Atlantic U (FL)
Florida Intl U (FL)
Florida Memorial U (FL)
Florida Southern Coll (FL)
Florida State U (FL)
Fort Lewis Coll (CO)
Freed-Hardeman U (TN)
Free Will Baptist Bible Coll (TN)
Fresno Pacific U (CA)
Furman U (SC)
Gardner-Webb U (NC)
George Fox U (OR)
Georgetown Coll (KY)
Georgia Coll & State U (GA)
Georgia Southern U (GA)
Gettysburg Coll (PA)
Glenville State Coll (WV)
Gonzaga U (WA)
Gordon Coll (MA)
Grace Bible Coll (MI)
Grace Coll (IN)
Grace U (NE)
Grambling State U (LA)
Grand Valley State U (MI)
Greensboro Coll (NC)
Greenville Coll (IL)
Grove City Coll (PA)
Gustavus Adolphus Coll (MN)
Hamline U (MN)
Hampton U (VA)
Hannibal-LaGrange Coll (MO)
Harding U (AR)
Hardin-Simmons U (TX)
Hartwick Coll (NY)
Hastings Coll (NE)
Heidelberg Coll (OH)
Henderson State U (AR)
Hofstra U (NY)
Hope Coll (MI)
Hope Intl U (CA)
Houghton Coll (NY)
Houston Baptist U (TX)
Howard Payne U (TX)
Humboldt State U (CA)
Huntington U (IN)
Idaho State U (ID)
Illinois State U (IL)
Illinois Wesleyan U (IL)
Immaculata U (PA)
Indiana U Bloomington (IN)
Indiana U–Purdue U Fort Wayne (IN)
Indiana U South Bend (IN)
Indiana Wesleyan U (IN)
Inter American U of Puerto Rico, San Germán Campus (PR)
Iowa State U of Science and Technology (IA)
Iowa Wesleyan Coll (IA)
Ithaca Coll (NY)
Jackson State U (MS)
Jacksonville State U (AL)
Jacksonville U (FL)
Jamestown Coll (ND)
Jarvis Christian Coll (TX)
John Brown U (AR)
Johnson State Coll (VT)
Judson Coll (AL)
Judson U (IL)
Kansas State U (KS)
Kean U (NJ)
Keene State Coll (NH)
Kennesaw State U (GA)
Kent State U (OH)
Kentucky Christian U (KY)
Kutztown U of Pennsylvania (PA)
Lambuth U (TN)
La Sierra U (CA)
Lawrence U (WI)
Lebanon Valley Coll (PA)
Lee U (TN)
Lenoir-Rhyne Coll (NC)
Liberty U (VA)
Limestone Coll (SC)
Lincoln U (MO)
Lincoln U (PA)
Lindenwood U (MO)
Lipscomb U (TN)
Livingstone Coll (NC)
Longwood U (VA)
Louisiana Coll (LA)
Louisiana State U and Ag and Mech Coll (LA)
Loyola U New Orleans (LA)
Lubbock Christian U (TX)
Malone Coll (OH)
Manchester Coll (IN)
Manhattanville Coll (NY)
Mansfield U of Pennsylvania (PA)
Maranatha Baptist Bible Coll (WI)
Marian Coll (IN)
Marian Coll of Fond du Lac (WI)
Maryville Coll (TN)
Marywood U (PA)
The Master's Coll and Sem (CA)
McGill U (QC, Canada)
McKendree U (IL)
McNeese State U (LA)
Memorial U of Newfoundland (NL, Canada)
Mercer U (GA)
Mercyhurst Coll (PA)
Meredith Coll (NC)
Messiah Coll (PA)
Methodist U (NC)
Miami U (OH)
Miami U Hamilton (OH)
Michigan State U (MI)
MidAmerica Nazarene U (KS)
Midland Lutheran Coll (NE)
Midwestern State U (TX)
Millersville U of Pennsylvania (PA)
Milligan Coll (TN)
Millikin U (IL)
Minnesota State U Mankato (MN)
Minot State U (ND)
Mississippi Coll (MS)
Mississippi State U (MS)
Mississippi U for Women (MS)
Mississippi Valley State U (MS)
Missouri Baptist U (MO)
Missouri State U (MO)
Montana State U (MT)
Montana State U–Billings (MT)
Moravian Coll (PA)
Morningside Coll (IA)
Mount Marty Coll (SD)
Mount Mary Coll (WI)
Mount Mercy Coll (IA)
Mount Vernon Nazarene U (OH)
Murray State U (KY)
Nazareth Coll of Rochester (NY)
Nebraska Wesleyan U (NE)
New Jersey City U (NJ)
New York U (NY)
Nicholls State U (LA)
North Carolina Ag and Tech State U (NC)
North Carolina Central U (NC)
North Central Coll (IL)
North Dakota State U (ND)
Northeastern State U (OK)
Northern Arizona U (AZ)
Northern Illinois U (IL)
Northern Michigan U (MI)
Northern State U (SD)
North Georgia Coll & State U (GA)
North Greenville U (SC)
Northland Coll (WI)
Northwestern Coll (IA)
Northwestern Coll (MN)
Northwestern Oklahoma State U (OK)
Northwestern State U of Louisiana (LA)
Northwestern U (IL)
Northwest Missouri State U (MO)
Northwest Nazarene U (ID)
Nyack Coll (NY)
Oakland City U (IN)
Oakland U (MI)
Oakwood Coll (AL)
Oberlin Coll (OH)
Ohio Northern U (OH)
Ohio U (OH)
Ohio Wesleyan U (OH)
Oklahoma Christian U (OK)
Oklahoma City U (OK)
Oklahoma State U (OK)
Old Dominion U (VA)
Oral Roberts U (OK)
Otterbein Coll (OH)
Ouachita Baptist U (AR)
Pacific Lutheran U (WA)
Pacific Union Coll (CA)
Pacific U (OR)
Palm Beach Atlantic U (FL)
Peabody Conservatory of Music of The Johns Hopkins U (MD)
Penn State U Park (PA)
Pepperdine U, Malibu (CA)
Peru State Coll (NE)
Pfeiffer U (NC)
Pillsbury Baptist Bible Coll (MN)
Pittsburg State U (KS)
Plymouth State U (NH)
Point Loma Nazarene U (CA)
Presbyterian Coll (SC)
Prescott Coll (AZ)
Providence Coll (RI)
Queens Coll of the City U of New York (NY)
Quincy U (IL)
Rhode Island Coll (RI)
Rider U (NJ)
Ripon Coll (WI)
Roberts Wesleyan Coll (NY)
Roosevelt U (IL)
Rutgers, The State U of New Jersey, New Brunswick (NJ)
Saginaw Valley State U (MI)
St. Ambrose U (IA)
St. Cloud State U (MN)
Saint Mary-of-the-Woods Coll (IN)
Saint Mary's Coll (IN)
Saint Mary's U of Minnesota (MN)
St. Norbert Coll (WI)
St. Olaf Coll (MN)
Saint Vincent Coll (PA)
Saint Xavier U (IL)
Salve Regina U (RI)
Samford U (AL)
Sam Houston State U (TX)
San Diego Christian Coll (CA)
San Diego State U (CA)
Seattle Pacific U (WA)
Seton Hill U (PA)
Shenandoah U (VA)
Shorter Coll (GA)
Simpson Coll (IA)
Simpson U (CA)
Sonoma State U (CA)
South Carolina State U (SC)
South Dakota State U (SD)
Southeastern Louisiana U (LA)
Southeastern Oklahoma State U (OK)
Southeastern U (FL)
Southeast Missouri State U (MO)
Southern Adventist U (TN)
Southern Arkansas U–Magnolia (AR)
Southern Methodist U (TX)
Southern U and Ag and Mech Coll (LA)
Southern Utah U (UT)
Southern Wesleyan U (SC)
Southwest Baptist U (MO)
Southwestern Coll (AZ)
Southwestern Coll (KS)
Southwestern Oklahoma State U (OK)
Southwestern U (TX)
Southwest Minnesota State U (MN)
Spring Arbor U (MI)
State U of New York at Fredonia (NY)
State U of New York Coll at Potsdam (NY)
Stephen F. Austin State U (TX)
Sterling Coll (KS)
Stetson U (FL)
Susquehanna U (PA)
Syracuse U (NY)
Tabor Coll (KS)
Tarleton State U (TX)
Taylor U (IN)
Temple U (PA)
Tennessee Technological U (TN)
Texas A&M U–Commerce (TX)
Texas Christian U (TX)
Texas Lutheran U (TX)
Texas Southern U (TX)
Toccoa Falls Coll (GA)
Towson U (MD)
Transylvania U (KY)
Trevecca Nazarene U (TN)
Trinity Christian Coll (IL)
Trinity Intl U (IL)
Union Coll (NE)
Union U (TN)
The U of Akron (OH)
The U of Alabama (AL)
The U of Arizona (AZ)
U of Arkansas at Fort Smith (AR)
U of Arkansas at Monticello (AR)
U of Arkansas at Pine Bluff (AR)
The U of British Columbia (BC, Canada)
U of Central Florida (FL)
U of Central Missouri (MO)
U of Central Oklahoma (OK)
U of Charleston (WV)
U of Cincinnati (OH)
U of Colorado at Boulder (CO)
U of Connecticut (CT)
U of Dayton (OH)
U of Delaware (DE)
U of Evansville (IN)
U of Florida (FL)
U of Georgia (GA)
U of Guam (GU)
U of Hartford (CT)
U of Idaho (ID)
U of Illinois at Urbana–Champaign (IL)
U of Indianapolis (IN)
The U of Iowa (IA)
U of Kansas (KS)
U of Lethbridge (AB, Canada)
U of Louisiana at Lafayette (LA)
U of Louisiana at Monroe (LA)
U of Louisville (KY)
U of Maine (ME)
U of Mary (ND)
U of Mary Hardin-Baylor (TX)
U of Maryland, Coll Park (MD)
U of Maryland Eastern Shore (MD)
U of Mary Washington (VA)
U of Miami (FL)
U of Michigan (MI)
U of Michigan–Flint (MI)
U of Minnesota, Duluth (MN)
U of Minnesota, Twin Cities Campus (MN)
U of Missouri–Columbia (MO)
U of Missouri–Kansas City (MO)
U of Missouri–St. Louis (MO)
The U of Montana (MT)
The U of Montana–Western (MT)
U of Nebraska at Omaha (NE)
U of Nevada, Reno (NV)
U of New Brunswick Fredericton (NB, Canada)
U of New Hampshire (NH)
U of New Mexico (NM)
The U of North Carolina at Charlotte (NC)
The U of North Carolina at Greensboro (NC)
The U of North Carolina at Pembroke (NC)
The U of North Carolina Wilmington (NC)
U of North Dakota (ND)
U of Northern Colorado (CO)
U of Northern Iowa (IA)
U of North Florida (FL)
U of Oregon (OR)
U of Portland (OR)
U of Prince Edward Island (PE, Canada)
U of Puget Sound (WA)
U of Redlands (CA)
U of Regina (SK, Canada)
U of Rhode Island (RI)
U of Rio Grande (OH)
U of Rochester (NY)
U of St. Francis (IL)
U of St. Thomas (MN)
U of St. Thomas (TX)
U of Sioux Falls (SD)
U of South Carolina (SC)
U of South Carolina Aiken (SC)
The U of South Dakota (SD)
U of Southern California (CA)
U of Southern Maine (ME)
U of Southern Mississippi (MS)
U of South Florida (FL)
The U of Tampa (FL)
The U of Tennessee (TN)
The U of Tennessee at Martin (TN)
U of the District of Columbia (DC)
U of the Pacific (CA)
U of the Virgin Islands (VI)
The U of Toledo (OH)
U of Toronto (ON, Canada)
U of Tulsa (OK)
U of Vermont (VT)
U of Victoria (BC, Canada)
The U of Western Ontario (ON, Canada)
U of West Georgia (GA)
U of Windsor (ON, Canada)
U of Wisconsin–Madison (WI)
U of Wisconsin–Milwaukee (WI)
U of Wisconsin–Oshkosh (WI)
U of Wisconsin–Stevens Point (WI)
U of Wisconsin–Superior (WI)
U of Wisconsin–Whitewater (WI)
U of Wyoming (WY)
Utah State U (UT)
Utah Valley State Coll (UT)
Valdosta State U (GA)
Valley City State U (ND)
Valparaiso U (IN)
VanderCook Coll of Music (IL)
Viterbo U (WI)
Walla Walla U (WA)
Warner Pacific Coll (OR)
Wartburg Coll (IA)
Washburn U (KS)
Washington Bible Coll (MD)
Washington State U (WA)
Wayland Baptist U (TX)
Wayne State Coll (NE)
Weber State U (UT)
Webster U (MO)
West Chester U of Pennsylvania (PA)
Western Carolina U (NC)
Western Connecticut State U (CT)
Western Michigan U (MI)
Western New Mexico U (NM)
Western State Coll of Colorado (CO)
Western Washington U (WA)
Westfield State Coll (MA)
West Liberty State Coll (WV)
West Virginia Wesleyan Coll (WV)
Wheaton Coll (IL)
Whitworth U (WA)
Wichita State U (KS)
Wiley Coll (TX)
William Jewell Coll (MO)
William Paterson U of New Jersey (NJ)
Wilmington Coll (OH)
Wingate U (NC)
Winona State U (MN)
Winthrop U (SC)
Wright State U (OH)
Xavier U (OH)
Xavier U of Louisiana (LA)
York Coll (NE)
York Coll of Pennsylvania (PA)
York U (ON, Canada)
Youngstown State U (OH)

MUSIC THEORY AND COMPOSITION

Arizona State U (AZ)
Baldwin-Wallace Coll (OH)
Bard Coll (NY)
Bard Coll at Simon's Rock (MA)
Baylor U (TX)
Bennington Coll (VT)
Berklee Coll of Music (MA)
The Boston Conservatory (MA)
Boston U (MA)
Bowling Green State U (OH)
Bradley U (IL)
Brigham Young U (UT)
Bucknell U (PA)
Butler U (IN)
California Baptist U (CA)
California Inst of the Arts (CA)
California State U, Chico (CA)
California State U, Long Beach (CA)
Calvin Coll (MI)
Canadian Mennonite U (MB, Canada)
Capital U (OH)
Carnegie Mellon U (PA)
Carson-Newman Coll (TN)
The Catholic U of America (DC)
Cedarville U (OH)
Centenary Coll of Louisiana (LA)
Central Michigan U (MI)
Central Washington U (WA)
Chapman U (CA)
Christopher Newport U (VA)
City Coll of the City U of New York (NY)
Clayton State U (GA)
Coll of Santa Fe (NM)
Concordia Coll (MN)
Concordia U (QC, Canada)
Cornerstone U (MI)
Dallas Baptist U (TX)
DePaul U (IL)
DePauw U (IN)
Drury U (MO)
East Carolina U (NC)
Florida State U (FL)
George Fox U (OR)
Georgia Southern U (GA)
Grace U (NE)
Hardin-Simmons U (TX)
Hofstra U (NY)
Hope Coll (MI)
Houghton Coll (NY)
Houston Baptist U (TX)
Huntington U (IN)
Illinois Wesleyan U (IL)
Indiana Wesleyan U (IN)
Ithaca Coll (NY)
Jacksonville U (FL)
Lawrence U (WI)
Lehigh U (PA)
Linfield Coll (OR)
Lipscomb U (TN)
Loyola Marymount U (CA)
Loyola U New Orleans (LA)
Lynchburg Coll (VA)
Mannes Coll The New School for Music (NY)
Marylhurst U (OR)
McGill U (QC, Canada)
Memorial U of Newfoundland (NL, Canada)
Meredith Coll (NC)
Michigan State U (MI)
Mississippi Coll (MS)
Moravian Coll (PA)
New England Conservatory of Music (MA)
The New School for Jazz and Contemporary Music (NY)
New York U (NY)
Northwestern Coll (MN)
Northwestern U (IL)
Northwest Nazarene U (ID)
Nyack Coll (NY)
Oakland U (MI)
Oberlin Coll (OH)
Ohio U (OH)
Oklahoma City U (OK)
Oral Roberts U (OK)
Ouachita Baptist U (AR)
Palm Beach Atlantic U (FL)
Point Loma Nazarene U (CA)
Randolph Coll (VA)
Rice U (TX)
Rider U (NJ)
Roosevelt U (IL)

MAJORS AND MORE

Rowan U (NJ)
St. Cloud State U (MN)
St. Mary's Coll of Maryland (MD)
St. Olaf Coll (MN)
Samford U (AL)
Sarah Lawrence Coll (NY)
Seton Hill U (PA)
Shenandoah U (VA)
Southern Adventist U (TN)
Southern Methodist U (TX)
Southwestern U (TX)
State U of New York Coll at Potsdam (NY)
Stetson U (FL)
Syracuse U (NY)
Temple U (PA)
Texas Christian U (TX)
Texas Tech U (TX)
Trinity Intl U (IL)
Trinity U (TX)
The U of Akron (OH)
The U of British Columbia (BC, Canada)
U of Central Missouri (MO)
U of Delaware (DE)
U of Georgia (GA)
U of Hartford (CT)
U of Houston (TX)
U of Idaho (ID)
U of Illinois at Urbana–Champaign (IL)
The U of Iowa (IA)
U of Kansas (KS)
U of Louisiana at Lafayette (LA)
U of Mary Hardin-Baylor (TX)
U of Miami (FL)
U of Michigan (MI)
U of Missouri–Kansas City (MO)
U of Nebraska at Omaha (NE)
U of Nevada, Las Vegas (NV)
The U of North Carolina at Greensboro (NC)
U of Northern Iowa (IA)
U of North Texas (TX)
U of Oklahoma (OK)
U of Oregon (OR)
U of Redlands (CA)
U of Regina (SK, Canada)
U of Rhode Island (RI)
U of Rochester (NY)
U of Southern California (CA)
The U of Texas at Austin (TX)
The U of Texas at San Antonio (TX)
U of the Pacific (CA)
U of Tulsa (OK)
U of Victoria (BC, Canada)
The U of Western Ontario (ON, Canada)
U of West Georgia (GA)
U of Windsor (ON, Canada)
U of Wyoming (WY)
Valparaiso U (IN)
Wartburg Coll (IA)
Washington State U (WA)
Washington U in St. Louis (MO)
Webster U (MO)
West Chester U of Pennsylvania (PA)
Western Connecticut State U (CT)
Western Michigan U (MI)
West Texas A&M U (TX)
Wheaton Coll (IL)
Whitman Coll (WA)
Willamette U (OR)
William Jewell Coll (MO)
Wright State U (OH)
York U (ON, Canada)
Youngstown State U (OH)

MUSIC THERAPY

Anna Maria Coll (MA)
Appalachian State U (NC)
Arizona State U (AZ)
Augsburg Coll (MN)
Baldwin-Wallace Coll (OH)
Berklee Coll of Music (MA)
Canadian Mennonite U (MB, Canada)
Chapman U (CA)
Colorado State U (CO)
Converse Coll (SC)
Duquesne U (PA)
East Carolina U (NC)
Eastern Michigan U (MI)
Elizabethtown Coll (PA)
Florida State U (FL)
Georgia Coll & State U (GA)
Immaculata U (PA)
Indiana U–Purdue U Fort Wayne (IN)
Marylhurst U (OR)
Maryville U of Saint Louis (MO)
Marywood U (PA)
Michigan State U (MI)
Molloy Coll (NY)
Montclair State U (NJ)
Nazareth Coll of Rochester (NY)
Queens U of Charlotte (NC)
Saint Mary-of-the-Woods Coll (IN)
Sam Houston State U (TX)
Shenandoah U (VA)
Slippery Rock U of Pennsylvania (PA)
Southern Methodist U (TX)
Southwestern Oklahoma State U (OK)
State U of New York at Fredonia (NY)
State U of New York at New Paltz (NY)
Temple U (PA)
Texas Woman's U (TX)
U of Dayton (OH)
U of Evansville (IN)
U of Georgia (GA)
The U of Iowa (IA)
U of Kansas (KS)
U of Louisville (KY)
U of Miami (FL)
U of Minnesota, Twin Cities Campus (MN)
U of North Dakota (ND)
U of the Incarnate Word (TX)
U of the Pacific (CA)
U of Windsor (ON, Canada)
U of Wisconsin–Eau Claire (WI)
U of Wisconsin–Milwaukee (WI)
U of Wisconsin–Oshkosh (WI)
Utah State U (UT)
Wartburg Coll (IA)
Western Michigan U (MI)
West Texas A&M U (TX)
Wilfrid Laurier U (ON, Canada)

NATURAL RESOURCE ECONOMICS

Cornell U (NY)
Michigan State U (MI)

NATURAL RESOURCES AND CONSERVATION RELATED

Mount Mercy Coll (IA)
Penn State Abington (PA)
Penn State Altoona (PA)
Penn State Berks (PA)
Penn State Erie, The Behrend Coll (PA)
Penn State U Park (PA)
St. Gregory's U, Shawnee (OK)
Stephen F. Austin State U (TX)
Sterling Coll (VT)
U of Alaska Fairbanks (AK)
The U of British Columbia (BC, Canada)
U of California, Davis (CA)
U of Louisiana at Lafayette (LA)
Utah State U (UT)

NATURAL RESOURCES/ CONSERVATION

Carroll Coll (WI)
Central Michigan U (MI)
Clemson U (SC)
Colorado State U (CO)
Cornell U (NY)
The Evergreen State Coll (WA)
Frostburg State U (MD)
Harvard U (MA)
Humboldt State U (CA)
Keene State Coll (NH)
Kent State U (OH)
Marlboro Coll (VT)
McGill U (QC, Canada)
Montana State U (MT)
Mountain State U (WV)
Mount Vernon Nazarene U (OH)
New Jersey Inst of Technology (NJ)
North Carolina State U (NC)
Northern Michigan U (MI)
Northland Coll (WI)
Northwest Missouri State U (MO)
Penn State Abington (PA)
Penn State Altoona (PA)
Penn State Berks (PA)
Penn State Erie, The Behrend Coll (PA)
Penn State U Park (PA)
Peru State Coll (NE)
Prescott Coll (AZ)
Purdue U (IN)
Rutgers, The State U of New Jersey, New Brunswick (NJ)
Slippery Rock U of Pennsylvania (PA)
Southeastern Oklahoma State U (OK)
State U of New York Coll of Environmental Science and Forestry (NY)
Sterling Coll (VT)
Texas A&M U (TX)
Texas A&M U at Galveston (TX)
Texas A&M U–Commerce (TX)
Texas Tech U (TX)
Thompson Rivers U (BC, Canada)
Tusculum Coll (TN)
U of Alaska Southeast (AK)
The U of British Columbia (BC, Canada)
U of California, Berkeley (CA)
U of California, Davis (CA)
U of Connecticut (CT)
U of Illinois at Urbana–Champaign (IL)
U of Louisiana at Lafayette (LA)
U of Maryland, Coll Park (MD)
U of Michigan–Flint (MI)
U of Minnesota, Crookston (MN)
U of Missouri–Columbia (MO)
The U of Montana (MT)
U of Nebraska–Lincoln (NE)
U of Nevada, Reno (NV)
U of New Hampshire (NH)
U of Rhode Island (RI)
U of Vermont (VT)
U of Wisconsin–Milwaukee (WI)
U of Wisconsin–Stevens Point (WI)
Washington State U (WA)
Washington U in St. Louis (MO)
Winona State U (MN)

NATURAL RESOURCES/ CONSERVATION RELATED

Sterling Coll (VT)
U of Illinois at Urbana–Champaign (IL)

NATURAL RESOURCES MANAGEMENT

Central Washington U (WA)
Glenville State Coll (WV)
Green Mountain Coll (VT)
Keystone Coll (PA)
Massachusetts Maritime Acad (MA)
Moravian Coll (PA)
Rutgers, The State U of New Jersey, New Brunswick (NJ)
Sterling Coll (VT)
The U of British Columbia (BC, Canada)
U of Hawaii at Manoa (HI)
U of Illinois at Urbana–Champaign (IL)
The U of Tennessee at Martin (TN)

NATURAL RESOURCES MANAGEMENT AND POLICY

Alaska Pacific U (AK)
Albright Coll (PA)
Ball State U (IN)
Bowling Green State U (OH)
California State U, Chico (CA)
Carnegie Mellon U (PA)
Clark U (MA)
Colorado State U (CO)
Grand Valley State U (MI)
Humboldt State U (CA)
Huntington U (IN)
Iowa State U of Science and Technology (IA)
Johnson State Coll (VT)
Louisiana State U and Ag and Mech Coll (LA)
McGill U (QC, Canada)
New Mexico Highlands U (NM)
North Carolina State U (NC)
North Dakota State U (ND)
Northland Coll (WI)
Oregon State U (OR)
Paul Smith's Coll (NY)
Prescott Coll (AZ)
Roanoke Coll (VA)
Rochester Inst of Technology (NY)
Sewanee: The U of the South (TN)
South Dakota State U (SD)
State U of New York Coll of Environmental Science and Forestry (NY)
Sterling Coll (VT)
Tuskegee U (AL)
The U of British Columbia (BC, Canada)
U of California, Berkeley (CA)
U of California, San Diego (CA)
U of Delaware (DE)
U of Idaho (ID)
U of Illinois at Urbana–Champaign (IL)
U of La Verne (CA)
U of Maine (ME)
U of Massachusetts Amherst (MA)
U of Miami (FL)
U of Michigan (MI)
U of Minnesota, Twin Cities Campus (MN)
The U of Montana (MT)
U of Nebraska–Lincoln (NE)
U of Nevada, Reno (NV)
U of New Hampshire (NH)
U of Rhode Island (RI)
The U of Tennessee at Martin (TN)
The U of Western Ontario (ON, Canada)
U of Windsor (ON, Canada)
U of Wisconsin–Madison (WI)
U of Wisconsin–Stevens Point (WI)
Western Carolina U (NC)
West Virginia U (WV)

NATURAL SCIENCES

Alderson-Broaddus Coll (WV)
Atlantic Union Coll (MA)
Augsburg Coll (MN)
Avila U (MO)
Azusa Pacific U (CA)
Bard Coll at Simon's Rock (MA)
Bemidji State U (MN)
Benedictine Coll (KS)
Bernard M. Baruch Coll of the City U of New York (NY)
Bethel Coll (KS)
Bishop's U (QC, Canada)
California State U, Fresno (CA)
California State U, Los Angeles (CA)
California State U, San Bernardino (CA)
Calvin Coll (MI)
Cameron U (OK)
Case Western Reserve U (OH)
Castleton State Coll (VT)
Central Christian Coll of Kansas (KS)
Central Coll (IA)
Christian Brothers U (TN)
Colgate U (NY)
Coll of Mount St. Joseph (OH)
Coll of Saint Benedict (MN)
Coll of Saint Mary (NE)
The Coll of St. Scholastica (MN)
Coll of the Atlantic (ME)
Concordia U (OR)
Concordia U Chicago (IL)
Concordia U, Nebraska (NE)
Daemen Coll (NY)
Dallas Baptist U (TX)
Defiance Coll (OH)
Doane Coll (NE)
Dordt Coll (IA)
Dowling Coll (NY)
Eastern Kentucky U (KY)
Erskine Coll (SC)
The Evergreen State Coll (WA)
Felician Coll (NJ)
Florida Southern Coll (FL)
Fresno Pacific U (CA)
Georgian Court U (NJ)
Grand Valley State U (MI)
Hofstra U (NY)
Houghton Coll (NY)
Humboldt State U (CA)
Indiana U East (IN)
Inter American U of Puerto Rico, San Germán Campus (PR)
Iowa Wesleyan Coll (IA)
The Johns Hopkins U (MD)
Johnson C. Smith U (NC)
Juniata Coll (PA)
Kenyon Coll (OH)
Lakehead U (ON, Canada)
Lees-McRae Coll (NC)
Lee U (TN)
Lesley U (MA)
LeTourneau U (TX)
Lewis-Clark State Coll (ID)
Lock Haven U of Pennsylvania (PA)
Longwood U (VA)
Loyola Marymount U (CA)
Madonna U (MI)
Marlboro Coll (VT)
The Master's Coll and Sem (CA)
McGill U (QC, Canada)
Midland Lutheran Coll (NE)
Minnesota State U Mankato (MN)
Monmouth Coll (IL)
Mount Allison U (NB, Canada)
Muhlenberg Coll (PA)
New Coll of Florida (FL)
Northland Coll (WI)
Oakwood Coll (AL)
Oklahoma Wesleyan U (OK)
Park U (MO)
Pepperdine U, Malibu (CA)
Peru State Coll (NE)
Redeemer U Coll (ON, Canada)
St. Cloud State U (MN)
Saint John's U (MN)
St. Thomas Aquinas Coll (NY)
Sarah Lawrence Coll (NY)
Shawnee State U (OH)
Shimer Coll (IL)
Shorter Coll (GA)
Siena Heights U (MI)
Spelman Coll (GA)
State U of New York Coll at Geneseo (NY)
Sterling Coll (VT)
Tabor Coll (KS)
Taylor U (IN)
Thomas Edison State Coll (NJ)
Trent U (ON, Canada)
U of Cincinnati (OH)
U of La Verne (CA)
U of Maine (ME)
U of Nebraska at Omaha (NE)
U of New Hampshire (NH)
U of Pennsylvania (PA)
U of Pittsburgh at Johnstown (PA)
U of Puerto Rico at Utuado (PR)
U of Puerto Rico, Cayey U Coll (PR)
U of Puget Sound (WA)
U of Science and Arts of Oklahoma (OK)
The U of Toledo (OH)
U of Wisconsin–Stevens Point (WI)
Virginia Wesleyan Coll (VA)
Viterbo U (WI)
Washington U in St. Louis (MO)
Winona State U (MN)
Xavier U (OH)
York Coll (NE)
York U (ON, Canada)

NAVAL ARCHITECTURE AND MARINE ENGINEERING

Maine Maritime Acad (ME)
Massachusetts Maritime Acad (MA)
Memorial U of Newfoundland (NL, Canada)
Texas A&M U at Galveston (TX)
United States Coast Guard Acad (CT)
United States Merchant Marine Acad (NY)
United States Naval Acad (MD)
U of Michigan (MI)
U of New Orleans (LA)
Webb Inst (NY)

NAVY/MARINE CORPS R.O.T.C./NAVAL SCIENCE

Hampton U (VA)
Rensselaer Polytechnic Inst (NY)
U of Idaho (ID)

NEAR AND MIDDLE EASTERN STUDIES

American Public U System (WV)
American U of Beirut (Lebanon)
Barnard Coll (NY)
Bates Coll (ME)
Brandeis U (MA)
Brown U (RI)
Claremont McKenna Coll (CA)
Cornell U (NY)
Dartmouth Coll (NH)
Emory & Henry Coll (VA)
The George Washington U (DC)
Harvard U (MA)
Indiana U Bloomington (IN)
The Johns Hopkins U (MD)
McGill U (QC, Canada)
New York U (NY)
Oberlin Coll (OH)
Portland State U (OR)
Princeton U (NJ)
Rutgers, The State U of New Jersey, New Brunswick (NJ)
Sarah Lawrence Coll (NY)
Smith Coll (MA)
Texas State U-San Marcos (TX)
The U of Arizona (AZ)
U of California, Berkeley (CA)
U of California, Santa Barbara (CA)
U of Chicago (IL)
U of Massachusetts Amherst (MA)
U of Michigan (MI)
U of Minnesota, Twin Cities Campus (MN)
The U of Texas at Austin (TX)
The U of Toledo (OH)
U of Toronto (ON, Canada)
U of Utah (UT)
Washington U in St. Louis (MO)
Wellesley Coll (MA)

NEUROANATOMY

McGill U (QC, Canada)

NEUROBIOLOGY AND NEUROPHYSIOLOGY

Andrews U (MI)
Florida State U (FL)
New Coll of Florida (FL)
St. Lawrence U (NY)
U of California, Davis (CA)

NEUROSCIENCE

Agnes Scott Coll (GA)
Allegheny Coll (PA)
Amherst Coll (MA)
Baldwin-Wallace Coll (OH)
Barnard Coll (NY)

Bates Coll (ME)
Baylor U (TX)
Bishop's U (QC, Canada)
Boston U (MA)
Bowdoin Coll (ME)
Bowling Green State U (OH)
Brandeis U (MA)
Brigham Young U (UT)
Brock U (ON, Canada)
Brown U (RI)
Canisius Coll (NY)
Cedar Crest Coll (PA)
Centenary Coll of Louisiana (LA)
Central Michigan U (MI)
Clark U (MA)
Colgate U (NY)
The Colorado Coll (CO)
Concordia U (QC, Canada)
Connecticut Coll (CT)
Dickinson Coll (PA)
Drake U (IA)
Drew U (NJ)
Emmanuel Coll (MA)
Emory U (GA)
Franklin & Marshall Coll (PA)
Furman U (SC)
Hamilton Coll (NY)
Harvard U (MA)
Haverford Coll (PA)
Indiana U Bloomington (IN)
John Carroll U (OH)
The Johns Hopkins U (MD)
Kenyon Coll (OH)
King's Coll (PA)
Lawrence U (WI)
Lehigh U (PA)
Macalester Coll (MN)
Massachusetts Inst of Technology (MA)
Memorial U of Newfoundland (NL, Canada)
Middlebury Coll (VT)
Montana State U (MT)
Mount Holyoke Coll (MA)
Muhlenberg Coll (PA)
New York U (NY)
Northwestern U (IL)
Oberlin Coll (OH)
Ohio Wesleyan U (OH)
Pitzer Coll (CA)
Pomona Coll (CA)
Regis U (CO)
Rice U (TX)
St. Lawrence U (NY)
Scripps Coll (CA)
Skidmore Coll (NY)
Smith Coll (MA)
Stonehill Coll (MA)
Texas Christian U (TX)
Trinity Coll (CT)
Trinity U (TX)
Tulane U (LA)
Union Coll (NY)
U of California, *Irvine* (CA)
U of California, Los Angeles (CA)
U of California, Riverside (CA)
U of California, Santa Cruz (CA)
U of Delaware (DE)
U of Evansville (IN)
U of King's Coll (NS, Canada)
U of Lethbridge (AB, Canada)
U of Miami (FL)
U of Minnesota, Twin Cities Campus (MN)
U of Pennsylvania (PA)
U of Pittsburgh (PA)
The U of Scranton (PA)
U of Southern California (CA)
The U of Texas at Dallas (TX)
U of Toronto (ON, Canada)
U of Windsor (ON, Canada)
Ursinus Coll (PA)
Washington and Lee U (VA)
Washington State U (WA)
Washington U in St. Louis (MO)
Wellesley Coll (MA)
Westminster Coll (UT)
Westmont Coll (CA)
Wofford Coll (SC)

NON-PROFIT MANAGEMENT
Austin Peay State U (TN)
Clarkson U (NY)
Duquesne U (PA)
Fresno Pacific U (CA)
Gettysburg Coll (PA)
Hawai'i Pacific U (HI)
Manchester Coll (IN)
Mountain State U (WV)
Pace U (NY)
Salem Coll (NC)
Southern Adventist U (TN)
Southern Vermont Coll (VT)
Southwest Minnesota State U (MN)
Trinity Intl U (IL)
U of Baltimore (MD)
Warren Wilson Coll (NC)
Washburn U (KS)

NORWEGIAN
Brigham Young U (UT)
Pacific Lutheran U (WA)
St. Olaf Coll (MN)

NUCLEAR ENGINEERING
Georgia Inst of Technology (GA)
Idaho State U (ID)
Kansas State U (KS)
Massachusetts Inst of Technology (MA)
Missouri U of Science and Technology (MO)
North Carolina State U (NC)
Oregon State U (OR)
Penn State Abington (PA)
Penn State Altoona (PA)
Penn State Berks (PA)
Penn State Erie, The Behrend Coll (PA)
Penn State U Park (PA)
Purdue U (IN)
Rensselaer Polytechnic Inst (NY)
South Carolina State U (SC)
Texas A&M U (TX)
The U of Arizona (AZ)
U of California, Berkeley (CA)
U of Cincinnati (OH)
U of Florida (FL)
U of Illinois at Urbana–Champaign (IL)
U of Michigan (MI)
U of New Mexico (NM)
The U of Tennessee (TN)
U of Wisconsin–Madison (WI)
Worcester Polytechnic Inst (MA)

NUCLEAR ENGINEERING TECHNOLOGY
Old Dominion U (VA)
Thomas Edison State Coll (NJ)
United States Merchant Marine Acad (NY)

NUCLEAR MEDICAL TECHNOLOGY
Baptist Coll of Health Sciences (TN)
Barry U (FL)
Benedictine U (IL)
California State U, Dominguez Hills (CA)
Cedar Crest Coll (PA)
Ferris State U (MI)
Indiana U of Pennsylvania (PA)
Indiana U–Purdue U Indianapolis (IN)
Indiana U South Bend (IN)
Indiana U Southeast (IN)
Lewis U (IL)
Loras Coll (IA)
Massachusetts Coll of Pharmacy and Health Sciences (MA)
Medical Coll of Georgia (GA)
North Central Coll (IL)
Oakland U (MI)
Old Dominion U (VA)
Peru State Coll (NE)
Robert Morris U (PA)
Roosevelt U (IL)
St. Cloud State U (MN)
Saint Louis U (MO)
Saint Mary's U of Minnesota (MN)
Salem State Coll (MA)
U at Buffalo, the State U of New York (NY)
The U of Alabama at Birmingham (AL)
U of Arkansas for Medical Sciences (AR)
U of Central Arkansas (AR)
U of Cincinnati (OH)
The U of Findlay (OH)
The U of Iowa (IA)
U of Missouri–Columbia (MO)
U of Nebraska Medical Center (NE)
U of Nevada, Las Vegas (NV)
U of Oklahoma Health Sciences Center (OK)
U of St. Francis (IL)
U of the Incarnate Word (TX)
U of Vermont (VT)
U of Wisconsin–La Crosse (WI)
Weber State U (UT)
Wheeling Jesuit U (WV)
York Coll of Pennsylvania (PA)

NUCLEAR/NUCLEAR POWER TECHNOLOGY
U of North Texas (TX)

NUCLEAR PHYSICS
Harvard U (MA)

NURSING ADMINISTRATION
Clarkson Coll (NE)
Emmanuel Coll (MA)
Nebraska Wesleyan U (NE)
The U of Western Ontario (ON, Canada)
U of Windsor (ON, Canada)
Wheeling Jesuit U (WV)

NURSING (LICENSED PRACTICAL/VOCATIONAL NURSE TRAINING)
The U of Akron (OH)
The U of Western Ontario (ON, Canada)

NURSING MIDWIFERY
U of Toronto (ON, Canada)

NURSING (REGISTERED NURSE TRAINING)
Abilene Christian U (TX)
Adams State Coll (CO)
Adelphi U (NY)
Alcorn State U (MS)
Alderson-Broaddus Coll (WV)
Allen Coll (IA)
Alvernia Coll (PA)
American U of Beirut (Lebanon)
Anderson U (IN)
Andrews U (MI)
Anna Maria Coll (MA)
Appalachian State U (NC)
Arkansas State U (AR)
Armstrong Atlantic State U (GA)
Athabasca U (AB, Canada)
Atlantic Union Coll (MA)
Auburn U (AL)
Auburn U Montgomery (AL)
Augsburg Coll (MN)
Augustana Coll (SD)
Austin Peay State U (TN)
Azusa Pacific U (CA)
Baker U (KS)
Ball State U (IN)
Baptist Coll of Health Sciences (TN)
Barnes-Jewish Coll, Goldfarb School of Nursing (MO)
Barry U (FL)
Barton Coll (NC)
Baylor U (TX)
Bellarmine U (KY)
Belmont U (TN)
Bemidji State U (MN)
Berea Coll (KY)
Berry Coll (GA)
Bethel Coll (KS)
Bethel Coll (TN)
Bethel U (MN)
Bethune-Cookman U (FL)
Biola U (CA)
Blessing-Rieman Coll of Nursing (IL)
Bloomfield Coll (NJ)
Bloomsburg U of Pennsylvania (PA)
Bob Jones U (SC)
Boise State U (ID)
Boston Coll (MA)
Bowling Green State U (OH)
Bradley U (IL)
Brenau U (GA)
Brigham Young U (UT)
British Columbia Inst of Technology (BC, Canada)
Cabarrus Coll of Health Sciences (NC)
California Baptist U (CA)
California State U, Chico (CA)
California State U, Dominguez Hills (CA)
California State U, East Bay (CA)
California State U, Fresno (CA)
California State U, Fullerton (CA)
California State U, Long Beach (CA)
California State U, Los Angeles (CA)
California State U, Sacramento (CA)
California State U, San Bernardino (CA)
California State U, Stanislaus (CA)
Calvin Coll (MI)
Capital U (OH)
Carlow U (PA)
Carroll Coll (WI)
Carson-Newman Coll (TN)
Case Western Reserve U (OH)
The Catholic U of America (DC)
Cedarville U (OH)
Central Connecticut State U (CT)
Chatham U (PA)
Chicago State U (IL)
Clarion U of Pennsylvania (PA)
Clarkson Coll (NE)
Clayton State U (GA)
Clemson U (SC)
Cleveland State U (OH)
Colby-Sawyer Coll (NH)
The Coll at Brockport, State U of New York (NY)
Coll of Mount St. Joseph (OH)
Coll of Mount Saint Vincent (NY)
The Coll of New Jersey (NJ)
The Coll of New Rochelle (NY)
Coll of Saint Benedict (MN)
Coll of Saint Mary (NE)
The Coll of St. Scholastica (MN)
Coll of the Ozarks (MO)
Colorado State U-Pueblo (CO)
Columbia Coll of Nursing (WI)
Columbus State U (GA)
Concordia Coll (MN)
Concordia U (OR)
Concordia U Chicago (IL)
Concordia U Wisconsin (WI)
Creighton U (NE)
Crown Coll (MN)
Culver-Stockton Coll (MO)
Curry Coll (MA)
Daemen Coll (NY)
Davenport U, Dearborn (MI)
Davenport U, Grand Rapids (MI)
Delta State U (MS)
DePaul U (IL)
DeSales U (PA)
Dillard U (LA)
Dixie State Coll of Utah (UT)
Dominican Coll (NY)
Dominican U of California (CA)
Dordt Coll (IA)
Duquesne U (PA)
D'Youville Coll (NY)
East Carolina U (NC)
East Central U (OK)
Eastern Illinois U (IL)
Eastern Mennonite U (VA)
Eastern Michigan U (MI)
Eastern New Mexico U (NM)
East Stroudsburg U of Pennsylvania (PA)
East Tennessee State U (TN)
East Texas Baptist U (TX)
Edinboro U of Pennsylvania (PA)
Emory U (GA)
Emporia State U (KS)
Endicott Coll (MA)
Fairfield U (CT)
Fairleigh Dickinson U, Coll at Florham (NJ)
Fairleigh Dickinson U, Metropolitan Campus (NJ)
Fairmont State U (WV)
Fayetteville State U (NC)
Felician Coll (NJ)
Ferris State U (MI)
Finlandia U (MI)
Fitchburg State Coll (MA)
Florida Ag and Mech U (FL)
Florida Atlantic U (FL)
Florida Gulf Coast U (FL)
Florida Intl U (FL)
Florida Southern Coll (FL)
Florida State U (FL)
Framingham State Coll (MA)
Franciscan U of Steubenville (OH)
Francis Marion U (SC)
Gannon U (PA)
Gardner-Webb U (NC)
George Fox U (OR)
George Mason U (VA)
Georgetown U (DC)
Georgia Coll & State U (GA)
Georgia Southern U (GA)
Georgia Southwestern State U (GA)
Georgia State U (GA)
Glenville State Coll (WV)
Gonzaga U (WA)
Grace U (NE)
Grambling State U (LA)
Grand Canyon U (AZ)
Grand Valley State U (MI)
Grand View Coll (IA)
Gustavus Adolphus Coll (MN)
Gwynedd-Mercy Coll (PA)
Hampton U (VA)
Hannibal-LaGrange Coll (MO)
Harding U (AR)
Hardin-Simmons U (TX)
Hartwick Coll (NY)
Hawai'i Pacific U (HI)
Henderson State U (AR)
Holy Names U (CA)
Hope Coll (MI)
Houston Baptist U (TX)
Humboldt State U (CA)
Hunter Coll of the City U of New York (NY)
Husson Coll (ME)
Idaho State U (ID)
Illinois State U (IL)
Illinois Wesleyan U (IL)
Indiana State U (IN)
Indiana U Bloomington (IN)
Indiana U East (IN)
Indiana U Kokomo (IN)
Indiana U Northwest (IN)
Indiana U of Pennsylvania (PA)
Indiana U–Purdue U Fort Wayne (IN)
Indiana U–Purdue U Indianapolis (IN)
Indiana U South Bend (IN)
Indiana U Southeast (IN)
Indiana Wesleyan U (IN)
Inter American U of Puerto Rico, Fajardo Campus (PR)
Inter American U of Puerto Rico, San Germán Campus (PR)
Iowa Wesleyan Coll (IA)
Jacksonville State U (AL)
Jacksonville U (FL)
James Madison U (VA)
Jamestown Coll (ND)
Jefferson Coll of Health Sciences (VA)
The Johns Hopkins U (MD)
Keiser U, Fort Lauderdale (FL)
Kennesaw State U (GA)
Kent State U (OH)
Kentucky Christian U (KY)
Kentucky State U (KY)
Keuka Coll (NY)
King Coll (TN)
Kutztown U of Pennsylvania (PA)
Kuyper Coll (MI)
Kwantlen U Coll (BC, Canada)
LaGrange Coll (GA)
Lakehead U (ON, Canada)
Lake Superior State U (MI)
Lander U (SC)
La Roche Coll (PA)
La Salle U (PA)
Laurentian U (ON, Canada)
Lehman Coll of the City U of New York (NY)
Le Moyne Coll (NY)
Lenoir-Rhyne Coll (NC)
Lewis-Clark State Coll (ID)
Lewis U (IL)
Liberty U (VA)
Lincoln U (MO)
Linfield Coll (OR)
Lipscomb U (TN)
Loma Linda U (CA)
Louisiana Coll (LA)
Lourdes Coll (OH)
Loyola U Chicago (IL)
Loyola U New Orleans (LA)
Luther Coll (IA)
Lynchburg Coll (VA)
Madonna U (MI)
Malone Coll (OH)
Mansfield U of Pennsylvania (PA)
Maranatha Baptist Bible Coll (WI)
Marian Coll (IN)
Marian Coll of Fond du Lac (WI)
Marquette U (WI)
Marshall U (WV)
Marymount U (VA)
Maryville U (TN)
Maryville U of Saint Louis (MO)
Marywood U (PA)
Massachusetts Coll of Pharmacy and Health Sciences (MA)
McGill U (QC, Canada)
McKendree U (IL)
McMurry U (TX)
McNeese State U (LA)
Medcenter One Coll of Nursing (ND)
Medgar Evers Coll of the City U of New York (NY)
Medical Coll of Georgia (GA)
Memorial U of Newfoundland (NL, Canada)
Mercer U (GA)
Mercy Coll (NY)
Mesa State Coll (CO)
Messiah Coll (PA)
Metropolitan State U (MN)
Miami U (OH)
Michigan State U (MI)
MidAmerica Nazarene U (KS)
Middle Tennessee State U (TN)
Midland Lutheran Coll (NE)
Midway Coll (KY)
Midwestern State U (TX)
Millersville U of Pennsylvania (PA)
Milligan Coll (TN)
Millikin U (IL)
Milwaukee School of Eng (WI)
Minnesota State U Mankato (MN)
Minot State U (ND)
Misericordia U (PA)
Mississippi Coll (MS)
Missouri Southern State U (MO)
Missouri State U (MO)
Molloy Coll (NY)
Montana State U (MT)
Moravian Coll (PA)
Morehead State U (KY)

Morningside Coll (IA)
Mountain State U (WV)
Mount Carmel Coll of Nursing (OH)
Mount Marty Coll (SD)
Mount Mary Coll (WI)
Mount Mercy Coll (IA)
Mount Saint Mary Coll (NY)
Mount Vernon Nazarene U (OH)
Murray State U (KY)
Nazareth Coll of Rochester (NY)
Nebraska Methodist Coll (NE)
Neumann Coll (PA)
New Jersey Inst of Technology (NJ)
Newman U (KS)
New Mexico Highlands U (NM)
New York Inst of Technology (NY)
New York U (NY)
Niagara U (NY)
Nicholls State U (LA)
North Carolina Ag and Tech State U (NC)
North Carolina Central U (NC)
North Dakota State U (ND)
Northeastern State U (OK)
Northern Arizona U (AZ)
Northern Illinois U (IL)
Northern Michigan U (MI)
North Georgia Coll & State U (GA)
Northwestern Coll (IA)
Northwestern Oklahoma State U (OK)
Northwestern State U of Louisiana (LA)
Northwest Nazarene U (ID)
Norwich U (VT)
Nova Southeastern U (FL)
Oakland U (MI)
Oakwood Coll (AL)
Oklahoma City U (OK)
Oklahoma Wesleyan U (OK)
Old Dominion U (VA)
Oral Roberts U (OK)
Otterbein Coll (OH)
Our Lady of the Lake Coll (LA)
Pace U (NY)
Pacific Lutheran U (WA)
Pacific Union Coll (CA)
Palm Beach Atlantic U (FL)
Penn State Abington (PA)
Penn State Altoona (PA)
Penn State Berks (PA)
Penn State Erie, The Behrend Coll (PA)
Penn State Harrisburg (PA)
Penn State U Park (PA)
Piedmont Coll (GA)
Pittsburg State U (KS)
Point Loma Nazarene U (CA)
Prairie View A&M U (TX)
Presentation Coll (SD)
Purdue U (IN)
Purdue U Calumet (IN)
Purdue U North Central (IN)
Queen's U at Kingston (ON, Canada)
Quincy U (IL)
Quinnipiac U (CT)
Radford U (VA)
Ramapo Coll of New Jersey (NJ)
Regis Coll (MA)
Regis U (CO)
Research Coll of Nursing (MO)
Rhode Island Coll (RI)
The Richard Stockton Coll of New Jersey (NJ)
Robert Morris U (PA)
Roberts Wesleyan Coll (NY)
Rockford Coll (IL)
Rockhurst U (MO)
Rogers State U (OK)
Rowan U (NJ)
Russell Sage Coll (NY)
Rutgers, The State U of New Jersey, Camden (NJ)
Rutgers, The State U of New Jersey, Newark (NJ)
Rutgers, The State U of New Jersey, New Brunswick (NJ)
Sacred Heart U (CT)
Saginaw Valley State U (MI)
St. Ambrose U (IA)
St. Cloud State U (MN)
Saint Francis U (PA)
St. Francis Xavier U (NS, Canada)
St. John Fisher Coll (NY)
Saint John's U (MN)
Saint Joseph Coll (CT)
Saint Joseph's Coll (IN)
St. Joseph's Coll, New York (NY)
St. Joseph's Coll, Suffolk Campus (NY)
Saint Louis U (MO)
Saint Mary's Coll (IN)
Saint Mary's Coll of California (CA)
St. Olaf Coll (MN)
Saint Xavier U (IL)
Salem State Coll (MA)
Salisbury U (MD)
Salve Regina U (RI)
Samford U (AL)
Samuel Merritt Coll (CA)
San Diego State U (CA)
San Francisco State U (CA)
Seattle Pacific U (WA)
Seattle U (WA)
Seton Hill U (PA)
Shawnee State U (OH)
Shenandoah U (VA)
Shepherd U (WV)
Simmons Coll (MA)
Slippery Rock U of Pennsylvania (PA)
Sonoma State U (CA)
South Carolina State U (SC)
South Dakota State U (SD)
Southeastern Louisiana U (LA)
Southeast Missouri State U (MO)
Southern Connecticut State U (CT)
Southern Illinois U Edwardsville (IL)
Southern Oregon U (OR)
Southern U and Ag and Mech Coll (LA)
Southern Vermont Coll (VT)
South U, West Palm Beach (FL)
Southwest Baptist U (MO)
Southwestern Adventist U (TX)
Southwestern Coll (KS)
Southwestern Oklahoma State U (OK)
Spring Hill Coll (AL)
State U of New York at Binghamton (NY)
State U of New York at New Paltz (NY)
State U of New York at Plattsburgh (NY)
State U of New York Downstate Medical Center (NY)
State U of New York Inst of Technology (NY)
Stephen F. Austin State U (TX)
Stillman Coll (AL)
Stony Brook U, State U of New York (NY)
Tarleton State U (TX)
Temple U (PA)
Tennessee State U (TN)
Tennessee Technological U (TN)
Tennessee Wesleyan Coll (TN)
Texas A&M Intl U (TX)
Texas Christian U (TX)
Texas Southern U (TX)
Texas Woman's U (TX)
Thomas More Coll (KY)
Thomas U (GA)
Thompson Rivers U (BC, Canada)
Towson U (MD)
Trent U (ON, Canada)
Trinity Christian Coll (IL)
Troy U (AL)
Truman State U (MO)
Tuskegee U (AL)
Union Coll (NE)
Union U (TN)
Université de Sherbrooke (QC, Canada)
Université du Québec en Outaouais (QC, Canada)
U at Buffalo, the State U of New York (NY)
The U of Akron (OH)
The U of Alabama (AL)
The U of Alabama at Birmingham (AL)
The U of Alabama in Huntsville (AL)
The U of Arizona (AZ)
U of Arkansas (AR)
U of Arkansas at Fort Smith (AR)
U of Arkansas at Monticello (AR)
U of Arkansas at Pine Bluff (AR)
U of Arkansas for Medical Sciences (AR)
The U of British Columbia (BC, Canada)
The U of British Columbia–Okanagan (BC, Canada)
U of Central Arkansas (AR)
U of Central Florida (FL)
U of Central Missouri (MO)
U of Central Oklahoma (OK)
U of Charleston (WV)
U of Cincinnati (OH)
U of Colorado Denver (CO)
U of Connecticut (CT)
U of Delaware (DE)
U of Evansville (IN)
U of Florida (FL)
U of Guam (GU)
U of Hartford (CT)
U of Hawaii at Manoa (HI)
U of Houston–Victoria (TX)
U of Illinois at Chicago (IL)
The U of Iowa (IA)
U of Lethbridge (AB, Canada)
U of Louisiana at Lafayette (LA)
U of Louisiana at Monroe (LA)
U of Louisville (KY)
U of Maine (ME)
U of Maine at Fort Kent (ME)
U of Mary (ND)
U of Mary Hardin-Baylor (TX)
U of Massachusetts Amherst (MA)
U of Massachusetts Boston (MA)
U of Massachusetts Dartmouth (MA)
U of Massachusetts Lowell (MA)
U of Memphis (TN)
U of Miami (FL)
U of Michigan (MI)
U of Michigan–Flint (MI)
U of Minnesota, Twin Cities Campus (MN)
U of Mississippi Medical Center (MS)
U of Missouri–Columbia (MO)
U of Missouri–Kansas City (MO)
U of Missouri–St. Louis (MO)
U of Nebraska Medical Center (NE)
U of Nevada, Las Vegas (NV)
U of Nevada, Reno (NV)
U of New Brunswick Fredericton (NB, Canada)
U of New England (ME)
U of New Hampshire (NH)
U of New Mexico (NM)
U of North Alabama (AL)
The U of North Carolina at Chapel Hill (NC)
The U of North Carolina at Charlotte (NC)
The U of North Carolina at Greensboro (NC)
The U of North Carolina at Pembroke (NC)
The U of North Carolina Wilmington (NC)
U of North Dakota (ND)
U of Northern Colorado (CO)
U of North Florida (FL)
U of Oklahoma Health Sciences Center (OK)
U of Ottawa (ON, Canada)
U of Pennsylvania (PA)
U of Pittsburgh (PA)
U of Pittsburgh at Bradford (PA)
U of Portland (OR)
U of Prince Edward Island (PE, Canada)
U of Puerto Rico at Utuado (PR)
U of Regina (SK, Canada)
U of Rhode Island (RI)
U of Rochester (NY)
U of St. Francis (IL)
U of Saint Francis (IN)
U of Saint Mary (KS)
U of San Diego (CA)
The U of Scranton (PA)
U of South Alabama (AL)
U of South Carolina (SC)
U of South Carolina Aiken (SC)
U of South Carolina Upstate (SC)
U of Southern Indiana (IN)
U of Southern Maine (ME)
U of Southern Mississippi (MS)
U of South Florida (FL)
The U of Tampa (FL)
The U of Tennessee (TN)
The U of Tennessee at Chattanooga (TN)
The U of Tennessee at Martin (TN)
The U of Texas at Arlington (TX)
The U of Texas at Austin (TX)
The U of Texas at Brownsville (TX)
The U of Texas at El Paso (TX)
The U of Texas at Tyler (TX)
The U of Texas Medical Branch (TX)
The U of Texas–Pan American (TX)
U of the Incarnate Word (TX)
U of the Virgin Islands (VI)
The U of Toledo (OH)
U of Toronto (ON, Canada)
U of Tulsa (OK)
U of Utah (UT)
U of Vermont (VT)
U of Victoria (BC, Canada)
U of Virginia (VA)
U of Washington, Bothell (WA)
U of Washington, Tacoma (WA)
The U of Western Ontario (ON, Canada)
U of West Florida (FL)
U of West Georgia (GA)
U of Windsor (ON, Canada)
U of Wisconsin–Eau Claire (WI)
U of Wisconsin–Green Bay (WI)
U of Wisconsin–Madison (WI)
U of Wisconsin–Milwaukee (WI)
U of Wisconsin–Oshkosh (WI)
U of Wisconsin–Parkside (WI)
U of Wyoming (WY)
Ursuline Coll (OH)
Utah Valley State Coll (UT)
Utica Coll (NY)
Valdosta State U (GA)
Valparaiso U (IN)
Villa Julie Coll (MD)
Villanova U (PA)
Virginia Commonwealth U (VA)
Viterbo U (WI)
Wagner Coll (NY)
Walla Walla U (WA)
Walsh U (OH)
Washburn U (KS)
Washington State U (WA)
Waynesburg U (PA)
Wayne State U (MI)
Webster U (MO)
Wesley Coll (DE)
West Chester U of Pennsylvania (PA)
Western Carolina U (NC)
Western Connecticut State U (CT)
Western Kentucky U (KY)
Western Michigan U (MI)
Western New Mexico U (NM)
West Liberty State Coll (WV)
Westminster Coll (UT)
West Suburban Coll of Nursing (IL)
West Texas A&M U (TX)
West Virginia U (WV)
West Virginia Wesleyan Coll (WV)
Wheeling Jesuit U (WV)
Whitworth U (WA)
Widener U (PA)
Wilkes U (PA)
William Jewell Coll (MO)
William Paterson U of New Jersey (NJ)
Wilmington U (DE)
Winona State U (MN)
Worcester State Coll (MA)
Wright State U (OH)
York Coll of Pennsylvania (PA)
York Coll of the City U of New York (NY)
York U (ON, Canada)
Youngstown State U (OH)

NURSING RELATED

Adelphi U (NY)
Avila U (MO)
British Columbia Inst of Technology (BC, Canada)
Capital U (OH)
Coll of Staten Island of the City U of New York (NY)
Eastern Kentucky U (KY)
Edinboro U of Pennsylvania (PA)
Grand Canyon U (AZ)
Lubbock Christian U (TX)
Madonna U (MI)
Minot State U (ND)
New York Inst of Technology (NY)
Northeastern U (MA)
Roberts Wesleyan Coll (NY)
San Diego State U (CA)
Thomas More Coll (KY)
U at Buffalo, the State U of New York (NY)
The U of Akron (OH)
U of California, Irvine (CA)
U of California, Los Angeles (CA)
U of Massachusetts Dartmouth (MA)
U of Pennsylvania (PA)
U of Saint Francis (IN)
The U of Toledo (OH)
Wheaton Coll (IL)
Wright State U (OH)

NURSING SCIENCE

Bellarmine U (KY)
Benedictine U (IL)
Brock U (ON, Canada)
Bryan Coll (TN)
Cedar Crest Coll (PA)
Clarke Coll (IA)
Clarkson Coll (NE)
Coll of Saint Elizabeth (NJ)
Columbia Coll, Caguas (PR)
Columbia Coll, Yauco (PR)
Fairleigh Dickinson U, Metropolitan Campus (NJ)
Holy Family U (PA)
Holy Names U (CA)
Immaculata U (PA)
Kean U (NJ)
Lander U (SC)
Mercy Coll of Health Sciences (IA)
Midway Coll (KY)
Millersville U of Pennsylvania (PA)
Missouri Baptist U (MO)
Monmouth U (NJ)
Mount Aloysius Coll (PA)
National U (CA)
New Jersey City U (NJ)
New Jersey Inst of Technology (NJ)
Queens U of Charlotte (NC)
St. Francis Xavier U (NS, Canada)
Southern Adventist U (TN)
South U, Tampa (FL)
State U of New York Upstate Medical U (NY)
Thompson Rivers U (BC, Canada)
U of Delaware (DE)
U of Kansas (KS)
U of New Hampshire at Manchester (NH)
U of Victoria (BC, Canada)
Wichita State U (KS)
Xavier U (OH)
York U (ON, Canada)

NUTRITIONAL SCIENCES

California State U, Los Angeles (CA)
Oklahoma State U (OK)

NUTRITION SCIENCE

California Polytechnic State U, San Luis Obispo (CA)
Washington State U (WA)

NUTRITION SCIENCES

American U of Beirut (Lebanon)
Auburn U (AL)
Benedictine U (IL)
Boston U (MA)
Brigham Young U (UT)
Case Western Reserve U (OH)
Coll of Saint Benedict (MN)
Cornell U (NY)
Drexel U (PA)
Florida State U (FL)
Goddard Coll (VT)
Hampshire Coll (MA)
Huntington Coll of Health Sciences (TN)
La Salle U (PA)
McGill U (QC, Canada)
Michigan State U (MI)
Mount Saint Vincent U (NS, Canada)
New York Inst of Technology (NY)
Purdue U (IN)
Russell Sage Coll (NY)
Rutgers, The State U of New Jersey, New Brunswick (NJ)
Saint Joseph Coll (CT)
Texas Woman's U (TX)
U at Buffalo, the State U of New York (NY)
The U of Arizona (AZ)
U of California, Berkeley (CA)
U of California, Davis (CA)
U of Connecticut (CT)
U of Delaware (DE)
U of Georgia (GA)
U of Missouri–Columbia (MO)
U of Nevada, Las Vegas (NV)
The U of North Carolina at Greensboro (NC)
U of the District of Columbia (DC)
U of the Incarnate Word (TX)
U of Vermont (VT)

OCCUPATIONAL AND ENVIRONMENTAL HEALTH NURSING

British Columbia Inst of Technology (BC, Canada)

OCCUPATIONAL HEALTH AND INDUSTRIAL HYGIENE

California State U, Fresno (CA)
Clarkson U (NY)
Montana Tech of The U of Montana (MT)
Mountain State U (WV)
Oakland U (MI)
Purdue U (IN)

OCCUPATIONAL SAFETY AND HEALTH TECHNOLOGY

Ball State U (IN)
California State U, Fresno (CA)
Central Washington U (WA)
Columbia Southern U (AL)
Embry-Riddle Aeronautical U (FL)
Fairmont State U (WV)
Grand Valley State U (MI)
Indiana State U (IN)
Indiana U of Pennsylvania (PA)
Jacksonville State U (AL)
Keene State Coll (NH)
Marshall U (WV)
Millersville U of Pennsylvania (PA)
Montana Tech of The U of Montana (MT)
Murray State U (KY)
National U (CA)
North Carolina Ag and Tech State U (NC)
Oregon State U (OR)
Rochester Inst of Technology (NY)
Slippery Rock U of Pennsylvania (PA)

Southeastern Louisiana U (LA)
Southeastern Oklahoma State U (OK)
Southwest Baptist U (MO)
Texas Southern U (TX)
U of Central Missouri (MO)
U of Central Oklahoma (OK)
U of New Haven (CT)
U of North Dakota (ND)
U of Wisconsin–Whitewater (WI)
Utah State U (UT)

OCCUPATIONAL THERAPIST ASSISTANT
Grand Valley State U (MI)
Southeastern Louisiana U (LA)

OCCUPATIONAL THERAPY
Alabama State U (AL)
Augustana Coll (IL)
Baker Coll of Flint (MI)
Bay Path Coll (MA)
Boston U (MA)
Brenau U (GA)
Calvin Coll (MI)
Cleveland State U (OH)
Coll of Saint Benedict (MN)
Concordia U Wisconsin (WI)
Dominican Coll (NY)
Dominican U of California (CA)
Drury U (MO)
Duquesne U (PA)
D'Youville Coll (NY)
Eastern Kentucky U (KY)
Eastern Michigan U (MI)
Elizabethtown Coll (PA)
Florida Ag and Mech U (FL)
Florida Gulf Coast U (FL)
Florida Intl U (FL)
Hamline U (MN)
Hawai'i Pacific U (HI)
Husson Coll (ME)
Illinois Coll (IL)
Indiana U–Purdue U Indianapolis (IN)
Ithaca Coll (NY)
Keuka Coll (NY)
Lenoir-Rhyne Coll (NC)
McKendree U (IL)
Mount Aloysius Coll (PA)
Mount Mary Coll (WI)
New York Inst of Technology (NY)
Queen's U at Kingston (ON, Canada)
Quinnipiac U (CT)
Russell Sage Coll (NY)
Sacred Heart U (CT)
Saint Francis U (PA)
Saint John's U (MN)
Saint Louis U (MO)
Saint Vincent Coll (PA)
Shawnee State U (OH)
State U of New York Downstate Medical Center (NY)
Stephens Coll (MO)
Towson U (MD)
Tuskegee U (AL)
U at Buffalo, the State U of New York (NY)
The U of British Columbia (BC, Canada)
The U of Findlay (OH)
U of Hartford (CT)
U of Kansas (KS)
U of Louisiana at Monroe (LA)
U of Minnesota, Twin Cities Campus (MN)
U of Missouri–Columbia (MO)
U of New England (ME)
U of New Hampshire (NH)
U of Ottawa (ON, Canada)
U of Pittsburgh (PA)
U of Southern California (CA)
U of Southern Indiana (IN)
U of Utah (UT)
The U of Western Ontario (ON, Canada)
U of Wisconsin–Madison (WI)
U of Wisconsin–Milwaukee (WI)
Wartburg Coll (IA)
Western Michigan U (MI)
Western New Mexico U (NM)
West Virginia U (WV)
Worcester State Coll (MA)
Xavier U (OH)
York Coll of the City U of New York (NY)

OCEAN ENGINEERING
California State U, Long Beach (CA)
Florida Atlantic U (FL)
Florida Inst of Technology (FL)
Massachusetts Inst of Technology (MA)
Memorial U of Newfoundland (NL, Canada)
Texas A&M U (TX)
Texas A&M U at Galveston (TX)
United States Naval Acad (MD)
U of New Hampshire (NH)
U of Rhode Island (RI)
Virginia Polytechnic Inst and State U (VA)

OCEANOGRAPHY
Coll of the Atlantic (ME)
Florida Inst of Technology (FL)
U of South Carolina (SC)

OCEANOGRAPHY (CHEMICAL AND PHYSICAL)
Central Michigan U (MI)
Hawai'i Pacific U (HI)
Humboldt State U (CA)
Kutztown U of Pennsylvania (PA)
Maine Maritime Acad (ME)
Memorial U of Newfoundland (NL, Canada)
Millersville U of Pennsylvania (PA)
North Carolina State U (NC)
Old Dominion U (VA)
Rider U (NJ)
Texas A&M U at Galveston (TX)
United States Coast Guard Acad (CT)
United States Naval Acad (MD)
The U of British Columbia (BC, Canada)
U of Miami (FL)
U of New Hampshire (NH)
U of Victoria (BC, Canada)

OFFICE MANAGEMENT
Babson Coll (MA)
Bob Jones U (SC)
Central Washington U (WA)
Delta State U (MS)
Eastern Kentucky U (KY)
Eastern Michigan U (MI)
Indiana State U (IN)
Indiana U of Pennsylvania (PA)
Maranatha Baptist Bible Coll (WI)
Mayville State U (ND)
Miami U (OH)
Miami U Hamilton (OH)
Middle Tennessee State U (TN)
Mississippi Valley State U (MS)
Mount Vernon Nazarene U (OH)
Murray State U (KY)
Southeastern Oklahoma State U (OK)
Southeast Missouri State U (MO)
Southwest Baptist U (MO)
Stephen F. Austin State U (TX)
Tarleton State U (TX)
Texas Southern U (TX)
U of Central Missouri (MO)
U of Puerto Rico at Utuado (PR)
U of South Carolina (SC)
U of Southern Indiana (IN)
U of the Sacred Heart (PR)
Valley City State U (ND)
Weber State U (UT)
Wright State U (OH)

OPERATIONS MANAGEMENT
Auburn U (AL)
Babson Coll (MA)
Baylor U (TX)
Boise State U (ID)
Boston Coll (MA)
Boston U (MA)
California State U, Chico (CA)
California State U, Long Beach (CA)
Central Michigan U (MI)
Central Washington U (WA)
Clarkson U (NY)
Concordia U (QC, Canada)
Duquesne U (PA)
Edinboro U of Pennsylvania (PA)
Excelsior Coll (NY)
Farmingdale State Coll (NY)
Ferris State U (MI)
Florida Southern Coll (FL)
Georgia State U (GA)
Golden Gate U (CA)
Indiana State U (IN)
Indiana U–Purdue U Fort Wayne (IN)
Indiana U–Purdue U Indianapolis (IN)
Iowa State U of Science and Technology (IA)
Kent State U (OH)
Le Moyne Coll (NY)
Loyola U Chicago (IL)
Marian Coll of Fond du Lac (WI)
McGill U (QC, Canada)
Metropolitan State U (MN)
Miami U (OH)
Michigan State U (MI)
Michigan Technological U (MI)
Missouri Baptist U (MO)
National American U, Rapid City (SD)
National U (CA)
Northeastern State U (OK)
Northern Illinois U (IL)
Oakland U (MI)
Purdue U (IN)
Remington Coll–Honolulu Campus (HI)
Remington Coll–Largo Campus (FL)
Remington Coll–Memphis Campus (TN)
Remington Coll–Mobile Campus (AL)
Remington Coll–San Diego Campus (CA)
Remington Coll–Tampa Campus (FL)
Saginaw Valley State U (MI)
Sam Houston State U (TX)
San Diego State U (CA)
Seattle U (WA)
Tennessee Technological U (TN)
Texas A&M U–Commerce (TX)
Texas Southern U (TX)
Thomas Edison State Coll (NJ)
Tri-State U (IN)
The U of Akron (OH)
The U of Arizona (AZ)
U of Delaware (DE)
U of Houston (TX)
U of Idaho (ID)
U of Illinois at Urbana–Champaign (IL)
U of Indianapolis (IN)
U of Michigan–Flint (MI)
U of Nebraska at Kearney (NE)
The U of North Carolina at Asheville (NC)
The U of North Carolina at Charlotte (NC)
U of North Texas (TX)
U of Pennsylvania (PA)
U of St. Thomas (MN)
The U of Scranton (PA)
The U of Texas at San Antonio (TX)
The U of Toledo (OH)
U of Wisconsin–Whitewater (WI)
Utah State U (UT)
Utah Valley State Coll (UT)
Washington State U (WA)
Washington U in St. Louis (MO)
Western Washington U (WA)
Widener U (PA)
Wright State U (OH)

OPERATIONS RESEARCH
Babson Coll (MA)
Bernard M. Baruch Coll of the City U of New York (NY)
Bob Jones U (SC)
California State U, Fullerton (CA)
Carnegie Mellon U (PA)
Cornell U (NY)
Georgia State U (GA)
Miami U (OH)
New York U (NY)
Princeton U (NJ)
Syracuse U (NY)
United States Air Force Acad (CO)
United States Coast Guard Acad (CT)
U of California, Berkeley (CA)
U of Cincinnati (OH)
U of Illinois at Urbana–Champaign (IL)
U of New Brunswick Fredericton (NB, Canada)
U of Toronto (ON, Canada)
York U (ON, Canada)

OPHTHALMIC AND OPTOMETRIC SUPPORT SERVICES AND ALLIED PROFESSIONS RELATED
Tennessee Wesleyan Coll (TN)

OPHTHALMIC LABORATORY TECHNOLOGY
Abilene Christian U (TX)
U of Ottawa (ON, Canada)

OPHTHALMIC/OPTOMETRIC SERVICES
State U of New York Coll at Oneonta (NY)

OPHTHALMIC TECHNOLOGY
Louisiana State U Health Sciences Center (LA)
Old Dominion U (VA)

OPTICAL SCIENCES
Saginaw Valley State U (MI)
The U of Arizona (AZ)
U of Rochester (NY)

ORGANIC CHEMISTRY
McGill U (QC, Canada)
Sarah Lawrence Coll (NY)
The U of Western Ontario (ON, Canada)

ORGANIZATIONAL BEHAVIOR
Anderson U (IN)
Argosy U, Atlanta (GA)
Argosy U, Chicago (IL)
Argosy U, Denver (CO)
Argosy U, Orange County (CA)
Argosy U, Schaumburg (IL)
Argosy U, Seattle (WA)
Argosy U, Twin Cities (MN)
Argosy U, Washington DC (VA)
Athabasca U (AB, Canada)
Benedictine U (IL)
Bluffton U (OH)
Boston U (MA)
Brown U (RI)
Carroll Coll (WI)
Claflin U (SC)
The Coll of St. Scholastica (MN)
Denison U (OH)
DePaul U (IL)
Eastern Mennonite U (VA)
Florida Inst of Technology (FL)
Greenville Coll (IL)
Loyola U Chicago (IL)
McGill U (QC, Canada)
Memorial U of Newfoundland (NL, Canada)
Miami U (OH)
Mid-Continent U (KY)
Midway Coll (KY)
Mountain State U (WV)
National U (CA)
Northwestern U (IL)
Oakland City U (IN)
Oral Roberts U (OK)
Penn State Abington (PA)
Penn State Altoona (PA)
Penn State Berks (PA)
Penn State Erie, The Behrend Coll (PA)
Penn State Harrisburg (PA)
Penn State U Park (PA)
Pitzer Coll (CA)
Regent U (VA)
Rider U (NJ)
Robert Morris U (PA)
St. Ambrose U (IA)
Saint Louis U (MO)
Santa Clara U (CA)
Scripps Coll (CA)
Simpson U (CA)
U of Houston (TX)
U of Illinois at Urbana–Champaign (IL)
U of Michigan–Flint (MI)
U of North Texas (TX)
U of St. Francis (IL)
U of the Incarnate Word (TX)
The U of Toledo (OH)
U of Tulsa (OK)
The U of Western Ontario (ON, Canada)
Wayne State U (MI)
Woodbury U (CA)
York U (ON, Canada)

ORGANIZATIONAL COMMUNICATION
Aquinas Coll (MI)
Assumption Coll (MA)
Brigham Young U (UT)
California State U, Chico (CA)
Capital U (OH)
Carroll Coll (WI)
Central Michigan U (MI)
The Coll at Brockport, State U of New York (NY)
Dana Coll (NE)
Emmanuel Coll (GA)
Indiana U–Purdue U Fort Wayne (IN)
Iona Coll (NY)
Lipscomb U (TN)
Lynchburg Coll (VA)
Marian Coll of Fond du Lac (WI)
Marist Coll (NY)
Marylhurst U (OR)
McKendree U (IL)
North Central Coll (IL)
Ohio Northern U (OH)
Palm Beach Atlantic U (FL)
Pfeiffer U (NC)
Shorter Coll (GA)
Temple U (PA)
Toccoa Falls Coll (GA)
The U of Akron (OH)
U of Houston (TX)
U of Illinois at Urbana–Champaign (IL)
U of Michigan–Flint (MI)
U of Northern Iowa (IA)
U of Windsor (ON, Canada)
Valparaiso U (IN)
Western Kentucky U (KY)
Western Michigan U (MI)
Wright State U (OH)

ORNAMENTAL HORTICULTURE
Auburn U (AL)
California State Polytechnic U, Pomona (CA)
California State U, Fresno (CA)
Cornell U (NY)
Delaware Valley Coll (PA)
Florida Ag and Mech U (FL)
Florida Southern Coll (FL)
Iowa State U of Science and Technology (IA)
Tarleton State U (TX)
Texas A&M U (TX)
U of Delaware (DE)
U of Florida (FL)
U of Illinois at Urbana–Champaign (IL)
U of Maine (ME)
The U of Tennessee (TN)
U of the District of Columbia (DC)
U of Wisconsin–Platteville (WI)

ORTHOTICS/PROSTHETICS
Florida Intl U (FL)
The U of Texas Southwestern Medical Center at Dallas (TX)

PACIFIC AREA/PACIFIC RIM STUDIES
Claremont McKenna Coll (CA)
Hawai'i Pacific U (HI)
U of Hawaii at Manoa (HI)
U of Victoria (BC, Canada)

PAINTING
Alberta Coll of Art & Design (AB, Canada)
Aquinas Coll (MI)
Art Acad of Cincinnati (OH)
Bard Coll at Simon's Rock (MA)
Bennington Coll (VT)
Bethany Coll (KS)
Boston U (MA)
Brigham Young U (UT)
Buffalo State Coll, State U of New York (NY)
California Coll of the Arts (CA)
California State U, East Bay (CA)
California State U, Long Beach (CA)
The Catholic U of America (DC)
The Cleveland Inst of Art (OH)
The Coll at Brockport, State U of New York (NY)
Coll of Santa Fe (NM)
Colorado State U (CO)
Concordia U (QC, Canada)
Drake U (IA)
Ferris State U (MI)
Grace Coll (IN)
Harding U (AR)
Henderson State U (AR)
Hofstra U (NY)
Indiana U–Purdue U Fort Wayne (IN)
Indiana Wesleyan U (IN)
Kansas City Art Inst (MO)
Laguna Coll of Art & Design (CA)
Lewis U (IL)
Maryland Inst Coll of Art (MD)
Marywood U (PA)
Massachusetts Coll of Art and Design (MA)
Memorial U of Newfoundland (NL, Canada)
Memphis Coll of Art (TN)
Montserrat Coll of Art (MA)
Northwest Nazarene U (ID)
NSCAD U (NS, Canada)
Oakland U (MI)
Ohio Northern U (OH)
Ohio U (OH)
Paier Coll of Art, Inc. (CT)
Pittsburg State U (KS)
Pratt Inst (NY)
Providence Coll (RI)
Rocky Mountain Coll of Art + Design (CO)
Rutgers, The State U of New Jersey, New Brunswick (NJ)
St. Cloud State U (MN)
Salve Regina U (RI)

MAJORS AND MORE

Sam Houston State U (TX)
Sarah Lawrence Coll (NY)
Savannah Coll of Art and Design (GA)
School of the Art Inst of Chicago (IL)
School of the Museum of Fine Arts, Boston (MA)
School of Visual Arts (NY)
Seton Hill U (PA)
Shawnee State U (OH)
State U of New York at New Paltz (NY)
Temple U (PA)
Texas Christian U (TX)
Trinity Christian Coll (IL)
U of Dallas (TX)
U of Georgia (GA)
U of Hartford (CT)
U of Houston (TX)
U of Illinois at Urbana–Champaign (IL)
The U of Iowa (IA)
U of Kansas (KS)
U of Massachusetts Dartmouth (MA)
U of Miami (FL)
U of Michigan (MI)
U of Missouri–St. Louis (MO)
U of Oregon (OR)
U of Regina (SK, Canada)
U of Windsor (ON, Canada)
Virginia Commonwealth U (VA)
Washington U in St. Louis (MO)
Western State Coll of Colorado (CO)
Western Washington U (WA)
West Virginia Wesleyan Coll (WV)
York U (ON, Canada)

PALEONTOLOGY

Mercyhurst Coll (PA)
North Carolina State U (NC)
U of Toronto (ON, Canada)

PARALEGAL/LEGAL ASSISTANT

Patricia Stevens Coll (MO)

PARKS, RECREATION AND LEISURE

Alabama State U (AL)
Alaska Pacific U (AK)
Alcorn State U (MS)
Arizona State U at the West campus (AZ)
Ashland U (OH)
Auburn U (AL)
Belmont U (TN)
Bemidji State U (MN)
Bethany Coll (KS)
Bluffton U (OH)
Boston U (MA)
Bowling Green State U (OH)
Brevard Coll (NC)
Bridgewater State Coll (MA)
Brigham Young U (UT)
Brock U (ON, Canada)
California Polytechnic State U, San Luis Obispo (CA)
California State U, Chico (CA)
California State U, Dominguez Hills (CA)
California State U, East Bay (CA)
California State U, Fresno (CA)
California State U, Long Beach (CA)
California State U, Sacramento (CA)
Calvin Coll (MI)
Carson-Newman Coll (TN)
Catawba Coll (NC)
Central Michigan U (MI)
Central State U (OH)
Central Washington U (WA)
Cheyney U of Pennsylvania (PA)
The Coll at Brockport, State U of New York (NY)
Concordia U (QC, Canada)
Davis & Elkins Coll (WV)
Dordt Coll (IA)
Elon U (NC)
Emporia State U (KS)
Evangel U (MO)
Ferrum Coll (VA)
Fort Lewis Coll (CO)
Frostburg State U (MD)
Georgia Coll & State U (GA)
Georgia Southern U (GA)
Gordon Coll (MA)
Grand Canyon U (AZ)
Green Mountain Coll (VT)
Greenville Coll (IL)
High Point U (NC)
Houghton Coll (NY)
Howard Payne U (TX)
Humboldt State U (CA)
Huntington U (IN)
Indiana U Bloomington (IN)
Ithaca Coll (NY)
Jacksonville State U (AL)
Johnson State Coll (VT)
Kutztown U of Pennsylvania (PA)
Lakehead U (ON, Canada)
Lake Superior State U (MI)
Lindsey Wilson Coll (KY)
Lock Haven U of Pennsylvania (PA)
Lyndon State Coll (VT)
Maryville Coll (TN)
Memorial U of Newfoundland (NL, Canada)
Messiah Coll (PA)
Midland Lutheran Coll (NE)
Minnesota State U Mankato (MN)
Mississippi U for Women (MS)
Missouri State U (MO)
Missouri Valley Coll (MO)
Montclair State U (NJ)
Morgan State U (MD)
Morris Coll (SC)
Mount Olive Coll (NC)
New England Coll (NH)
New Mexico Highlands U (NM)
North Carolina Ag and Tech State U (NC)
North Dakota State U (ND)
Northern Arizona U (AZ)
Northern Michigan U (MI)
Northland Coll (WI)
Northwest Missouri State U (MO)
Northwest Nazarene U (ID)
Ohio U (OH)
Oregon State U (OR)
Pacific Union Coll (CA)
Prescott Coll (AZ)
Presentation Coll (SD)
Radford U (VA)
Redeemer U Coll (ON, Canada)
St. Joseph's Coll, Suffolk Campus (NY)
St. Thomas Aquinas Coll (NY)
Salem State Coll (MA)
San Diego State U (CA)
San Francisco State U (CA)
Shaw U (NC)
Shepherd U (WV)
Shorter Coll (GA)
Southeastern Oklahoma State U (OK)
Southeast Missouri State U (MO)
Southern Connecticut State U (CT)
Southern Illinois U Carbondale (IL)
Southern Wesleyan U (SC)
Southwest Baptist U (MO)
Southwestern Oklahoma State U (OK)
Spring Arbor U (MI)
State U of New York at Plattsburgh (NY)
State U of New York Coll of Environmental Science and Forestry (NY)
Sterling Coll (VT)
Temple U (PA)
Tennessee State U (TN)
Texas A&M U (TX)
Thomas Edison State Coll (NJ)
Troy U (AL)
Tyndale U Coll & Sem (ON, Canada)
U of Arkansas at Pine Bluff (AR)
U of Central Missouri (MO)
U of Hawaii at Manoa (HI)
U of Idaho (ID)
U of Illinois at Urbana–Champaign (IL)
The U of Iowa (IA)
U of Lethbridge (AB, Canada)
U of Maine at Machias (ME)
U of Mary Hardin-Baylor (TX)
U of Minnesota, Duluth (MN)
U of Mississippi (MS)
U of Missouri–Columbia (MO)
The U of Montana (MT)
U of Nebraska at Kearney (NE)
U of Nebraska at Omaha (NE)
U of Nevada, Las Vegas (NV)
U of Nevada, Reno (NV)
U of New Brunswick Fredericton (NB, Canada)
U of New Hampshire (NH)
U of New Mexico (NM)
The U of North Carolina at Greensboro (NC)
U of Northern Iowa (IA)
U of Ottawa (ON, Canada)
U of South Alabama (AL)
The U of South Dakota (SD)
U of Southern Mississippi (MS)
The U of Tennessee at Chattanooga (TN)
The U of Toledo (OH)
U of Utah (UT)
U of Windsor (ON, Canada)
U of Wisconsin–Madison (WI)
U of Wisconsin–Milwaukee (WI)
Utah State U (UT)
Virginia Commonwealth U (VA)
Virginia Wesleyan Coll (VA)
Wesley Coll (DE)
Western Michigan U (MI)
Western State Coll of Colorado (CO)
Western Washington U (WA)
Westfield State Coll (MA)
West Virginia U (WV)
William Jewell Coll (MO)
William Paterson U of New Jersey (NJ)
Wingate U (NC)
Winona State U (MN)
York Coll of Pennsylvania (PA)

PARKS, RECREATION AND LEISURE FACILITIES MANAGEMENT

Alderson-Broaddus Coll (WV)
Appalachian State U (NC)
Ball State U (IN)
California State U, Chico (CA)
California State U, Fresno (CA)
California State U, Sacramento (CA)
Central Michigan U (MI)
Chicago State U (IL)
Clemson U (SC)
Coll of the Ozarks (MO)
Colorado State U (CO)
Concord U (WV)
East Carolina U (NC)
Eastern Illinois U (IL)
Eastern Michigan U (MI)
East Stroudsburg U of Pennsylvania (PA)
Ferris State U (MI)
Florida Ag and Mech U (FL)
Florida Intl U (FL)
Florida State U (FL)
Georgia Southwestern State U (GA)
Grand Valley State U (MI)
Hannibal-LaGrange Coll (MO)
Hastings Coll (NE)
Henderson State U (AR)
High Point U (NC)
Humboldt State U (CA)
Illinois State U (IL)
Indiana Wesleyan U (IN)
Inter American U of Puerto Rico, Aguadilla Campus (PR)
Kansas State U (KS)
Kean U (NJ)
Kent State U (OH)
Keystone Coll (PA)
Lake Superior State U (MI)
Lyndon State Coll (VT)
Marshall U (WV)
Methodist U (NC)
Michigan State U (MI)
Middle Tennessee State U (TN)
Minnesota State U Mankato (MN)
Missouri Valley Coll (MO)
Mount Marty Coll (SD)
Murray State U (KY)
New England Coll (NH)
New Mexico Highlands U (NM)
North Carolina Central U (NC)
North Carolina State U (NC)
Northern Arizona U (AZ)
Northland Coll (WI)
Ohio U (OH)
Old Dominion U (VA)
Oral Roberts U (OK)
Oregon State U (OR)
Paul Smith's Coll (NY)
Penn State Abington (PA)
Penn State Altoona (PA)
Penn State Berks (PA)
Penn State Erie, The Behrend Coll (PA)
Penn State U Park (PA)
Slippery Rock U of Pennsylvania (PA)
South Dakota State U (SD)
Sterling Coll (VT)
Texas A&M U (TX)
Texas State U-San Marcos (TX)
Thomas U (GA)
Tri-State U (IN)
Union Coll (KY)
Union U (TN)
The U of British Columbia (BC, Canada)
U of Connecticut (CT)
U of Florida (FL)
U of Houston–Clear Lake (TX)
U of Maine (ME)
U of Maine at Machias (ME)
U of Miami (FL)
U of Minnesota, Twin Cities Campus (MN)
The U of North Carolina at Chapel Hill (NC)
The U of North Carolina at Greensboro (NC)
The U of North Carolina at Pembroke (NC)
The U of North Carolina Wilmington (NC)
U of North Dakota (ND)
U of Northern Colorado (CO)
U of North Texas (TX)
U of St. Francis (IL)
The U of Tennessee (TN)
U of Vermont (VT)
U of West Georgia (GA)
U of Wisconsin–La Crosse (WI)
Western Carolina U (NC)
Western Illinois U (IL)
Western Kentucky U (KY)
Western State Coll of Colorado (CO)
West Virginia U (WV)
Winona State U (MN)

PARKS, RECREATION, AND LEISURE RELATED

Belhaven Coll (MS)
Brigham Young U (UT)
Coker Coll (SC)
The Coll at Brockport, State U of New York (NY)
Franklin Coll (IN)
Hawai'i Pacific U (HI)
Lambuth U (TN)
Malone Coll (OH)
North Carolina State U (NC)
Plymouth State U (NH)
Sage Coll of Albany (NY)
St. Edward's U (TX)
Southern Wesleyan U (SC)
Trinity Christian Coll (IL)
U of North Alabama (AL)
The U of Toledo (OH)
Utah State U (UT)
Western State Coll of Colorado (CO)

PASTORAL COUNSELING AND SPECIALIZED MINISTRIES RELATED

Cedarville U (OH)
Davis Coll (NY)
Greenville Coll (IL)
Harding U (AR)
Horizon Coll & Sem (SK, Canada)
Lipscomb U (TN)
Madonna U (MI)
Malone Coll (OH)
Multnomah Bible Coll and Biblical Sem (OR)
Northwestern Coll (MN)
Oak Hills Christian Coll (MN)
Ouachita Baptist U (AR)
St. John's U (NY)
Trinity Intl U (IL)
Vennard Coll (IA)

PASTORAL STUDIES/ COUNSELING

Abilene Christian U (TX)
Baptist Bible Coll of Pennsylvania (PA)
The Baptist Coll of Florida (FL)
Barclay Coll (KS)
Belmont U (TN)
Bethany U (CA)
Biola U (CA)
Canadian Mennonite U (MB, Canada)
Cedarville U (OH)
Central Christian Coll of Kansas (KS)
Clearwater Christian Coll (FL)
Collège Dominicain de Philosophie et de Théologie (ON, Canada)
Coll of Mount St. Joseph (OH)
Concordia U Chicago (IL)
Concordia U, Nebraska (NE)
Concordia U Wisconsin (WI)
Cornerstone U (MI)
Crown Coll (MN)
Dallas Baptist U (TX)
Davis Coll (NY)
East Texas Baptist U (TX)
Emmanuel Coll (GA)
Eugene Bible Coll (OR)
Faith Baptist Bible Coll and Theological Sem (IA)
Faulkner U (AL)
Fresno Pacific U (CA)
Gardner-Webb U (NC)
George Fox U (OR)
Grace Bible Coll (MI)
Grace U (NE)
Greenville Coll (IL)
Harding U (AR)
Hillsdale Free Will Baptist Coll (OK)
Horizon Coll & Sem (SK, Canada)
Houghton Coll (NY)
Indiana Wesleyan U (IN)
John Brown U (AR)
John Wesley Coll (NC)
Kuyper Coll (MI)
Lee U (TN)
Lindenwood U (MO)
Maranatha Baptist Bible Coll (WI)
Marian Coll (IN)
The Master's Coll and Sem (CA)
Milligan Coll (TN)
Multnomah Bible Coll and Biblical Sem (OR)
Nazarene Bible Coll (CO)
Nebraska Christian Coll (NE)
Newman U (KS)
North Greenville U (SC)
Northwest Nazarene U (ID)
Nyack Coll (NY)
Oak Hills Christian Coll (MN)
Oral Roberts U (OK)
Ouachita Baptist U (AR)
Pacific Union Coll (CA)
Pillsbury Baptist Bible Coll (MN)
Roberts Wesleyan Coll (NY)
Saint Francis U (PA)
St. Gregory's U, Shawnee (OK)
Saint Joseph's Coll (IN)
St. Thomas U (FL)
San Diego Christian Coll (CA)
Southeastern Bible Coll (AL)
Southeastern U (FL)
Southern Baptist Theological Sem (KY)
Southwest Baptist U (MO)
Southwestern Coll (KS)
Spring Arbor U (MI)
Tabor Coll (KS)
Taylor U Fort Wayne (IN)
Trinity Coll of Florida (FL)
Tyndale U Coll & Sem (ON, Canada)
Union Coll (NE)
U of Mary Hardin-Baylor (TX)
U of Saint Mary (KS)
U of St. Thomas (TX)
Vanguard U of Southern California (CA)
Vennard Coll (IA)
Walsh U (OH)
Warner Pacific Coll (OR)
Washington Bible Coll (MD)

PATHOLOGIST ASSISTANT

St. John's U (NY)
Wayne State U (MI)

PATHOLOGY/ EXPERIMENTAL PATHOLOGY

U of Connecticut (CT)
The U of North Carolina at Chapel Hill (NC)

PEACE STUDIES AND CONFLICT RESOLUTION

American Public U System (WV)
Bennington Coll (VT)
Canadian Mennonite U (MB, Canada)
Chapman U (CA)
Clark U (MA)
Colgate U (NY)
Coll of Saint Benedict (MN)
DePauw U (IN)
Earlham Coll (IN)
Eastern Mennonite U (VA)
Elizabethtown Coll (PA)
George Mason U (VA)
Gettysburg Coll (PA)
Goucher Coll (MD)
Guilford Coll (NC)
Hamline U (MN)
Hampshire Coll (MA)
Haverford Coll (PA)
Juniata Coll (PA)
Kent State U (OH)
Le Moyne Coll (NY)
Manchester Coll (IN)
Molloy Coll (NY)
Mount Saint Vincent U (NS, Canada)
Naropa U (CO)
Nazareth Coll of Rochester (NY)
Northland Coll (WI)
Norwich U (VT)
Ohio Dominican U (OH)
Saint John's U (MN)
Salisbury U (MD)
U of California, Berkeley (CA)
U of Hawaii at Manoa (HI)
U of Missouri–Columbia (MO)
The U of North Carolina at Chapel Hill (NC)
U of Ottawa (ON, Canada)
U of St. Thomas (MN)
U of Toronto (ON, Canada)

MAJORS AND MORE

The U of Western Ontario (ON, Canada)
The U of Winnipeg (MB, Canada)
U of Wisconsin–Milwaukee (WI)
U of Wisconsin–Superior (WI)
Wellesley Coll (MA)
Whitworth U (WA)

PEDIATRIC NURSING
British Columbia Inst of Technology (BC, Canada)
U at Buffalo, the State U of New York (NY)

PERFUSION TECHNOLOGY
State U of New York Upstate Medical U (NY)

PERIOPERATIVE/ OPERATING ROOM AND SURGICAL NURSING
British Columbia Inst of Technology (BC, Canada)
Murray State U (KY)
Texas A&M Intl U (TX)

PETROLEUM ENGINEERING
California State Polytechnic U, Pomona (CA)
Colorado School of Mines (CO)
Louisiana State U and Ag and Mech Coll (LA)
Marietta Coll (OH)
Missouri U of Science and Technology (MO)
Montana Tech of The U of Montana (MT)
New Mexico Inst of Mining and Technology (NM)
Penn State Abington (PA)
Penn State Altoona (PA)
Penn State Berks (PA)
Penn State Erie, The Behrend Coll (PA)
Penn State U Park (PA)
Stanford U (CA)
Texas A&M U (TX)
Texas Tech U (TX)
U of Alaska Fairbanks (AK)
U of Kansas (KS)
U of Louisiana at Lafayette (LA)
U of Oklahoma (OK)
U of Regina (SK, Canada)
U of Southern California (CA)
The U of Texas at Austin (TX)
U of Toronto (ON, Canada)
U of Tulsa (OK)
U of Wyoming (WY)
West Virginia U (WV)

PETROLEUM TECHNOLOGY
American U of Beirut (Lebanon)
Mercyhurst Coll (PA)
Nicholls State U (LA)
U of Pittsburgh at Bradford (PA)

PHARMACOLOGY
Georgia Southern U (GA)
Stony Brook U, State U of New York (NY)
U at Buffalo, the State U of New York (NY)
The U of British Columbia (BC, Canada)
U of California, Santa Barbara (CA)
U of Cincinnati (OH)
U of Toronto (ON, Canada)
The U of Western Ontario (ON, Canada)
U of Wisconsin–Madison (WI)

PHARMACOLOGY AND TOXICOLOGY
U at Buffalo, the State U of New York (NY)
U of the Sciences in Philadelphia (PA)
The U of Western Ontario (ON, Canada)
Washington State U (WA)
Wright State U (OH)

PHARMACOLOGY AND TOXICOLOGY RELATED
The George Washington U (DC)

PHARMACY
Butler U (IN)
Drake U (IA)
Florida Ag and Mech U (FL)
Lipscomb U (TN)
Massachusetts Coll of Pharmacy and Health Sciences (MA)
Memorial U of Newfoundland (NL, Canada)
North Dakota State U (ND)
Northeastern U (MA)
Ohio Northern U (OH)
Purdue U (IN)
Rutgers, The State U of New Jersey, New Brunswick (NJ)
St. John's U (NY)
St. Louis Coll of Pharmacy (MO)
Saint Vincent Coll (PA)
Simmons Coll (MA)
South Dakota State U (SD)
Southwestern Oklahoma State U (OK)
Texas Southern U (TX)
The U of British Columbia (BC, Canada)
U of Cincinnati (OH)
U of Connecticut (CT)
U of Houston (TX)
The U of Iowa (IA)
U of Kansas (KS)
U of Louisiana at Monroe (LA)
U of Mississippi (MS)
U of Missouri–Kansas City (MO)
The U of Montana (MT)
U of New Mexico (NM)
U of Pittsburgh (PA)
U of Rhode Island (RI)
U of the Pacific (CA)
The U of Toledo (OH)
U of Toronto (ON, Canada)
U of Utah (UT)
U of Wisconsin–Madison (WI)
Wilkes U (PA)

PHARMACY ADMINISTRATION/ PHARMACEUTICS
DeSales U (PA)
Drake U (IA)
U at Buffalo, the State U of New York (NY)

PHARMACY, PHARMACEUTICAL SCIENCES, AND ADMINISTRATION RELATED
Albany Coll of Pharmacy of Union U (NY)
Duquesne U (PA)
Massachusetts Coll of Pharmacy and Health Sciences (MA)
Ohio Northern U (OH)
U at Buffalo, the State U of New York (NY)
U of California, Irvine (CA)
U of Connecticut (CT)
The U of North Carolina at Chapel Hill (NC)
U of the Sciences in Philadelphia (PA)
The U of Toledo (OH)
Wilkes U (PA)

PHARMACY TECHNICIAN
The U of Montana (MT)

PHILOSOPHY
Acadia U (NS, Canada)
Adelphi U (NY)
Adrian Coll (MI)
Agnes Scott Coll (GA)
Albertus Magnus Coll (CT)
Albion Coll (MI)
Albright Coll (PA)
Alfred U (NY)
Allegheny Coll (PA)
Alma Coll (MI)
Alvernia Coll (PA)
American U (DC)
The American U of Athens (Greece)
American U of Beirut (Lebanon)
Amherst Coll (MA)
Anderson U (IN)
Appalachian State U (NC)
Aquinas Coll (MI)
Arizona State U (AZ)
Arkansas State U (AR)
Ashland U (OH)
Assumption Coll (MA)
Auburn U (AL)
Augsburg Coll (MN)
Augustana Coll (IL)
Augustana Coll (SD)
Austin Coll (TX)
Austin Peay State U (TN)
Ave Maria U (FL)
Azusa Pacific U (CA)
Baker U (KS)
Baldwin-Wallace Coll (OH)
Ball State U (IN)
Bard Coll (NY)
Bard Coll at Simon's Rock (MA)
Barnard Coll (NY)
Barry U (FL)
Bates Coll (ME)
Baylor U (TX)
Belhaven Coll (MS)
Bellarmine U (KY)
Belmont Abbey Coll (NC)
Belmont U (TN)
Beloit Coll (WI)
Bemidji State U (MN)
Benedictine Coll (KS)
Benedictine U (IL)
Bennington Coll (VT)
Bentley Coll (MA)
Berea Coll (KY)
Bernard M. Baruch Coll of the City U of New York (NY)
Bethany Coll (KS)
Bethel U (MN)
Biola U (CA)
Bishop's U (QC, Canada)
Bloomfield Coll (NJ)
Bloomsburg U of Pennsylvania (PA)
Boise State U (ID)
Boston Coll (MA)
Boston U (MA)
Bowdoin Coll (ME)
Bowling Green State U (OH)
Bradley U (IL)
Brandeis U (MA)
Bridgewater State Coll (MA)
Brigham Young U (UT)
Brock U (ON, Canada)
Brown U (RI)
Bryn Mawr Coll (PA)
Bucknell U (PA)
Buffalo State Coll, State U of New York (NY)
Butler U (IN)
Cabrini Coll (PA)
California Baptist U (CA)
California Inst of Technology (CA)
California Lutheran U (CA)
California Polytechnic State U, San Luis Obispo (CA)
California State Polytechnic U, Pomona (CA)
California State U, Chico (CA)
California State U, Dominguez Hills (CA)
California State U, East Bay (CA)
California State U, Fresno (CA)
California State U, Fullerton (CA)
California State U, Long Beach (CA)
California State U, Los Angeles (CA)
California State U, Sacramento (CA)
California State U, San Bernardino (CA)
California State U, Stanislaus (CA)
Calvin Coll (MI)
Canadian Mennonite U (MB, Canada)
Canisius Coll (NY)
Capital U (OH)
Carlow U (PA)
Carnegie Mellon U (PA)
Carson-Newman Coll (TN)
Case Western Reserve U (OH)
Catawba Coll (NC)
The Catholic U of America (DC)
Cedarville U (OH)
Centenary Coll of Louisiana (LA)
Central Coll (IA)
Central Connecticut State U (CT)
Central Michigan U (MI)
Central Washington U (WA)
Centre Coll (KY)
Chapman U (CA)
Christendom Coll (VA)
Christian Brothers U (TN)
Christopher Newport U (VA)
City Coll of the City U of New York (NY)
Claremont McKenna Coll (CA)
Clarion U of Pennsylvania (PA)
Clark Atlanta U (GA)
Clarke Coll (IA)
Clark U (MA)
Clemson U (SC)
Cleveland State U (OH)
Coastal Carolina U (SC)
Colby Coll (ME)
Colgate U (NY)
The Coll at Brockport, State U of New York (NY)
Collège Dominicain de Philosophie et de Théologie (ON, Canada)
Coll of Charleston (SC)
The Coll of Idaho (ID)
Coll of Mount Saint Vincent (NY)
The Coll of New Jersey (NJ)
The Coll of New Rochelle (NY)
Coll of Saint Benedict (MN)
Coll of Saint Elizabeth (NJ)
Coll of Staten Island of the City U of New York (NY)
Coll of the Atlantic (ME)
Coll of the Holy Cross (MA)
Coll of the Ozarks (MO)
The Coll of William and Mary (VA)
The Colorado Coll (CO)
Colorado State U (CO)
Concordia Coll (MN)
Concordia U (MI)
Concordia U (QC, Canada)
Concordia U Chicago (IL)
Connecticut Coll (CT)
Cornell Coll (IA)
Cornell U (NY)
Cornerstone U (MI)
Covenant Coll (GA)
Creighton U (NE)
Curry Coll (MA)
Dakota Wesleyan U (SD)
Dallas Baptist U (TX)
Dartmouth Coll (NH)
Davidson Coll (NC)
Denison U (OH)
DePaul U (IL)
DePauw U (IN)
DeSales U (PA)
Dickinson Coll (PA)
Doane Coll (NE)
Dominican U (IL)
Dordt Coll (IA)
Dowling Coll (NY)
Drake U (IA)
Drew U (NJ)
Drury U (MO)
Duke U (NC)
Duquesne U (PA)
D'Youville Coll (NY)
Earlham Coll (IN)
East Carolina U (NC)
Eastern Illinois U (IL)
Eastern Kentucky U (KY)
Eastern Michigan U (MI)
East Stroudsburg U of Pennsylvania (PA)
East Tennessee State U (TN)
Eckerd Coll (FL)
Edinboro U of Pennsylvania (PA)
Elizabethtown Coll (PA)
Elon U (NC)
Emory & Henry Coll (VA)
Emory U (GA)
Erskine Coll (SC)
Eugene Lang Coll The New School for Liberal Arts (NY)
Excelsior Coll (NY)
Fairfield U (CT)
Fairleigh Dickinson U, Coll at Florham (NJ)
Fairleigh Dickinson U, Metropolitan Campus (NJ)
Felician Coll (NJ)
Ferrum Coll (VA)
Flagler Coll (FL)
Florida Ag and Mech U (FL)
Florida Atlantic U (FL)
Florida Gulf Coast U (FL)
Florida Intl U (FL)
Florida State U (FL)
Fort Lewis Coll (CO)
Franciscan U of Steubenville (OH)
Franklin & Marshall Coll (PA)
Franklin Coll (IN)
Freed-Hardeman U (TN)
Frostburg State U (MD)
Furman U (SC)
Gannon U (PA)
George Fox U (OR)
George Mason U (VA)
Georgetown Coll (KY)
Georgetown U (DC)
The George Washington U (DC)
Georgia Coll & State U (GA)
Georgia Southern U (GA)
Georgia State U (GA)
Gettysburg Coll (PA)
Gonzaga U (WA)
Gordon Coll (MA)
Goucher Coll (MD)
Grand Valley State U (MI)
Green Mountain Coll (VT)
Greenville Coll (IL)
Grinnell Coll (IA)
Grove City Coll (PA)
Guilford Coll (NC)
Gustavus Adolphus Coll (MN)
Hamilton Coll (NY)
Hamline U (MN)
Hampden-Sydney Coll (VA)
Hampshire Coll (MA)
Hanover Coll (IN)
Hardin-Simmons U (TX)
Hartwick Coll (NY)
Harvard U (MA)
Hastings Coll (NE)
Haverford Coll (PA)
Heidelberg Coll (OH)
Hendrix Coll (AR)
High Point U (NC)
Hillsdale Coll (MI)
Hobart and William Smith Colls (NY)
Hofstra U (NY)
Hollins U (VA)
Holy Apostles Coll and Sem (CT)
Holy Names U (CA)
Hood Coll (MD)
Hope Coll (MI)
Houghton Coll (NY)
Howard Payne U (TX)
Humboldt State U (CA)
Hunter Coll of the City U of New York (NY)
Huntington U (IN)
Idaho State U (ID)
Illinois Coll (IL)
Illinois State U (IL)
Illinois Wesleyan U (IL)
Indiana State U (IN)
Indiana U Bloomington (IN)
Indiana U Northwest (IN)
Indiana U of Pennsylvania (PA)
Indiana U–Purdue U Fort Wayne (IN)
Indiana U–Purdue U Indianapolis (IN)
Indiana U South Bend (IN)
Indiana U Southeast (IN)
Indiana Wesleyan U (IN)
Iona Coll (NY)
Iowa State U of Science and Technology (IA)
Ithaca Coll (NY)
Jacksonville U (FL)
Jamestown Coll (ND)
John Carroll U (OH)
The Johns Hopkins U (MD)
Juniata Coll (PA)
Kalamazoo Coll (MI)
Kansas State U (KS)
Kent State U (OH)
Kentucky Wesleyan Coll (KY)
Kenyon Coll (OH)
King's Coll (PA)
The King's U Coll (AB, Canada)
Knox Coll (IL)
Kutztown U of Pennsylvania (PA)
Lafayette Coll (PA)
Lake Forest Coll (IL)
Lakehead U (ON, Canada)
La Salle U (PA)
Laurentian U (ON, Canada)
Lawrence U (WI)
Lebanon Valley Coll (PA)
Lehigh U (PA)
Lehman Coll of the City U of New York (NY)
Le Moyne Coll (NY)
Lenoir-Rhyne Coll (NC)
Lewis & Clark Coll (OR)
Lewis U (IL)
Liberty U (VA)
Lincoln U (PA)
Linfield Coll (OR)
Lipscomb U (TN)
List Coll, The Jewish Theological Sem (NY)
Lock Haven U of Pennsylvania (PA)
Loras Coll (IA)
Louisiana Coll (LA)
Louisiana State U and Ag and Mech Coll (LA)
Loyola Coll in Maryland (MD)
Loyola Marymount U (CA)
Loyola U Chicago (IL)
Loyola U New Orleans (LA)
Luther Coll (IA)
Lycoming Coll (PA)
Lynchburg Coll (VA)
Macalester Coll (MN)
Madonna U (MI)
Manchester Coll (IN)
Manhattanville Coll (NY)
Mansfield U of Pennsylvania (PA)
Marian Coll (IN)
Marietta Coll (OH)
Marist Coll (NY)
Marlboro Coll (VT)
Marquette U (WI)
Mary Baldwin Coll (VA)
Marymount U (VA)
Massachusetts Coll of Liberal Arts (MA)
Massachusetts Inst of Technology (MA)
McDaniel Coll (MD)
McGill U (QC, Canada)
McKendree U (IL)
Memorial U of Newfoundland (NL, Canada)
Mercer U (GA)
Mercyhurst Coll (PA)
Merrimack Coll (MA)
Messiah Coll (PA)
Metropolitan State U (MN)
Miami U (OH)
Miami U Hamilton (OH)

MAJORS AND MORE

Michigan State U (MI)
Middlebury Coll (VT)
Middle Tennessee State U (TN)
Millersville U of Pennsylvania (PA)
Millikin U (IL)
Millsaps Coll (MS)
Mills Coll (CA)
Minnesota State U Mankato (MN)
Misericordia U (PA)
Mississippi State U (MS)
Missouri State U (MO)
Missouri U of Science and Technology (MO)
Missouri Valley Coll (MO)
Molloy Coll (NY)
Monmouth Coll (IL)
Montana State U (MT)
Montclair State U (NJ)
Moravian Coll (PA)
Morehead State U (KY)
Morehouse Coll (GA)
Morgan State U (MD)
Morningside Coll (IA)
Mount Allison U (NB, Canada)
Mount Holyoke Coll (MA)
Mount Mary Coll (WI)
Mount Mercy Coll (IA)
Mount St. Mary's Coll (CA)
Mount St. Mary's U (MD)
Mount Saint Vincent U (NS, Canada)
Mount Vernon Nazarene U (OH)
Muhlenberg Coll (PA)
Murray State U (KY)
Nazareth Coll of Rochester (NY)
Nebraska Wesleyan U (NE)
New Coll of Florida (FL)
New England Coll (NH)
New Jersey City U (NJ)
New York U (NY)
Niagara U (NY)
North Carolina State U (NC)
North Carolina Wesleyan Coll (NC)
North Central Coll (IL)
North Dakota State U (ND)
Northeastern Illinois U (IL)
Northeastern U (MA)
Northern Arizona U (AZ)
Northern Illinois U (IL)
Northern Michigan U (MI)
Northland Coll (WI)
Northwestern Coll (IA)
Northwestern U (IL)
Northwest Missouri State U (MO)
Northwest Nazarene U (ID)
Notre Dame de Namur U (CA)
Nyack Coll (NY)
Oakland U (MI)
Oberlin Coll (OH)
Occidental Coll (CA)
Oglethorpe U (GA)
Ohio Dominican U (OH)
Ohio Northern U (OH)
Ohio U (OH)
Ohio Wesleyan U (OH)
Oklahoma City U (OK)
Oklahoma State U (OK)
Old Dominion U (VA)
Oregon State U (OR)
Otterbein Coll (OH)
Ouachita Baptist U (AR)
Pacific Lutheran U (WA)
Pacific U (OR)
Paine Coll (GA)
Palm Beach Atlantic U (FL)
Penn State Abington (PA)
Penn State Altoona (PA)
Penn State Berks (PA)
Penn State Erie, The Behrend Coll (PA)
Penn State U Park (PA)
Pepperdine U, Malibu (CA)
Piedmont Coll (GA)
Pitzer Coll (CA)
Plymouth State U (NH)
Point Loma Nazarene U (CA)
Pomona Coll (CA)
Pontifical Coll Josephinum (OH)
Portland State U (OR)
Presbyterian Coll (SC)
Prescott Coll (AZ)
Princeton U (NJ)
Providence Coll (RI)
Purchase Coll, State U of New York (NY)
Purdue U (IN)
Purdue U Calumet (IN)
Queens Coll of the City U of New York (NY)
Queen's U at Kingston (ON, Canada)
Queens U of Charlotte (NC)
Quincy U (IL)
Randolph Coll (VA)
Randolph-Macon Coll (VA)
Redeemer U Coll (ON, Canada)
Reed Coll (OR)
Regis U (CO)
Rensselaer Polytechnic Inst (NY)
Rhode Island Coll (RI)
Rhodes Coll (TN)
Rice U (TX)
The Richard Stockton Coll of New Jersey (NJ)
Rider U (NJ)
Ripon Coll (WI)
Roanoke Coll (VA)
Roberts Wesleyan Coll (NY)
Rockford Coll (IL)
Rockhurst U (MO)
Roger Williams U (RI)
Rollins Coll (FL)
Roosevelt U (IL)
Rosemont Coll (PA)
Rutgers, The State U of New Jersey, Camden (NJ)
Rutgers, The State U of New Jersey, Newark (NJ)
Rutgers, The State U of New Jersey, New Brunswick (NJ)
Sacred Heart Major Sem (MI)
St. Ambrose U (IA)
St. Andrews Presbyterian Coll (NC)
St. Charles Borromeo Sem, Overbrook (PA)
St. Cloud State U (MN)
St. Edward's U (TX)
Saint Francis U (PA)
St. Francis Xavier U (NS, Canada)
St. Gregory's U, Shawnee (OK)
St. John Fisher Coll (NY)
St. John's Coll (NM)
Saint John's U (MN)
St. John's U (NY)
Saint Joseph Coll (CT)
Saint Joseph's Coll (IN)
Saint Joseph's U (PA)
St. Lawrence U (NY)
Saint Louis U (MO)
Saint Mary's Coll (IN)
Saint Mary's Coll of California (CA)
St. Mary's Coll of Maryland (MD)
St. Mary's U (TX)
Saint Mary's U of Minnesota (MN)
Saint Michael's Coll (VT)
St. Norbert Coll (WI)
St. Olaf Coll (MN)
St. Thomas Aquinas Coll (NY)
St. Thomas U (NB, Canada)
Saint Vincent Coll (PA)
Saint Xavier U (IL)
Salem Coll (NC)
Salisbury U (MD)
Salve Regina U (RI)
Samford U (AL)
Sam Houston State U (TX)
San Diego State U (CA)
San Francisco State U (CA)
Santa Clara U (CA)
Sarah Lawrence Coll (NY)
Scripps Coll (CA)
Seattle Pacific U (WA)
Seattle U (WA)
Sewanee: The U of the South (TN)
Shaw U (NC)
Siena Coll (NY)
Siena Heights U (MI)
Simmons Coll (MA)
Simon Fraser U (BC, Canada)
Simpson Coll (IA)
Skidmore Coll (NY)
Slippery Rock U of Pennsylvania (PA)
Smith Coll (MA)
Sonoma State U (CA)
Southeast Missouri State U (MO)
Southern Connecticut State U (CT)
Southern Illinois U Carbondale (IL)
Southern Illinois U Edwardsville (IL)
Southern Methodist U (TX)
Southwestern U (TX)
Southwest Minnesota State U (MN)
Spelman Coll (GA)
Spring Arbor U (MI)
Spring Hill Coll (AL)
Stanford U (CA)
State U of New York at Binghamton (NY)
State U of New York at Fredonia (NY)
State U of New York at New Paltz (NY)
State U of New York at Oswego (NY)
State U of New York at Plattsburgh (NY)
State U of New York Coll at Geneseo (NY)
State U of New York Coll at Old Westbury (NY)
State U of New York Coll at Oneonta (NY)
State U of New York Coll at Potsdam (NY)
Stetson U (FL)
Stillman Coll (AL)
Stonehill Coll (MA)
Stony Brook U, State U of New York (NY)
Suffolk U (MA)
Susquehanna U (PA)
Swarthmore Coll (PA)
Sweet Briar Coll (VA)
Syracuse U (NY)
Tabor Coll (KS)
Taylor U (IN)
Temple U (PA)
Texas A&M U (TX)
Texas Christian U (TX)
Texas Lutheran U (TX)
Texas State U-San Marcos (TX)
Texas Tech U (TX)
Thiel Coll (PA)
Thomas Edison State Coll (NJ)
Thomas More Coll (KY)
Toccoa Falls Coll (GA)
Towson U (MD)
Transylvania U (KY)
Trent U (ON, Canada)
Trinity Christian Coll (IL)
Trinity Coll (CT)
Trinity Intl U (IL)
Trinity U (TX)
Truman State U (MO)
Tufts U (MA)
Tulane U (LA)
Tyndale U Coll & Sem (ON, Canada)
Union Coll (NY)
Union U (TN)
Université de Sherbrooke (QC, Canada)
U at Albany, State U of New York (NY)
U at Buffalo, the State U of New York (NY)
The U of Akron (OH)
The U of Alabama (AL)
The U of Alabama at Birmingham (AL)
The U of Alabama in Huntsville (AL)
U of Alaska Fairbanks (AK)
The U of Arizona (AZ)
U of Arkansas (AR)
The U of British Columbia (BC, Canada)
The U of British Columbia–Okanagan (BC, Canada)
U of California, Berkeley (CA)
U of California, Davis (CA)
U of California, Irvine (CA)
U of California, Los Angeles (CA)
U of California, Riverside (CA)
U of California, San Diego (CA)
U of California, Santa Barbara (CA)
U of California, Santa Cruz (CA)
U of Central Arkansas (AR)
U of Central Florida (FL)
U of Central Oklahoma (OK)
U of Chicago (IL)
U of Cincinnati (OH)
U of Colorado at Boulder (CO)
U of Colorado Denver (CO)
U of Connecticut (CT)
U of Dallas (TX)
U of Dayton (OH)
U of Delaware (DE)
U of Denver (CO)
U of Evansville (IN)
The U of Findlay (OH)
U of Florida (FL)
U of Georgia (GA)
U of Hartford (CT)
U of Hawaii at Manoa (HI)
U of Hawaii–West Oahu (HI)
U of Houston (TX)
U of Houston–Downtown (TX)
U of Idaho (ID)
U of Illinois at Chicago (IL)
U of Illinois at Springfield (IL)
U of Illinois at Urbana–Champaign (IL)
U of Indianapolis (IN)
The U of Iowa (IA)
U of Kansas (KS)
U of King's Coll (NS, Canada)
U of La Verne (CA)
U of Lethbridge (AB, Canada)
U of Louisiana at Lafayette (LA)
U of Louisville (KY)
U of Maine (ME)
U of Maryland, Baltimore County (MD)
U of Maryland, Coll Park (MD)
U of Mary Washington (VA)
U of Massachusetts Amherst (MA)
U of Massachusetts Boston (MA)
U of Massachusetts Dartmouth (MA)
U of Massachusetts Lowell (MA)
U of Memphis (TN)
U of Miami (FL)
U of Michigan (MI)
U of Michigan–Dearborn (MI)
U of Michigan–Flint (MI)
U of Minnesota, Duluth (MN)
U of Minnesota, Twin Cities Campus (MN)
U of Mississippi (MS)
U of Missouri–Columbia (MO)
U of Missouri–Kansas City (MO)
U of Missouri–St. Louis (MO)
The U of Montana (MT)
U of Nebraska at Omaha (NE)
U of Nebraska–Lincoln (NE)
U of Nevada, Las Vegas (NV)
U of Nevada, Reno (NV)
U of New Brunswick Fredericton (NB, Canada)
U of New Hampshire (NH)
U of New Mexico (NM)
U of New Orleans (LA)
The U of North Carolina at Asheville (NC)
The U of North Carolina at Chapel Hill (NC)
The U of North Carolina at Charlotte (NC)
The U of North Carolina at Greensboro (NC)
U of North Dakota (ND)
U of Northern Colorado (CO)
U of Northern Iowa (IA)
U of North Florida (FL)
U of North Texas (TX)
U of Notre Dame (IN)
U of Oklahoma (OK)
U of Oregon (OR)
U of Ottawa (ON, Canada)
U of Pennsylvania (PA)
U of Pittsburgh (PA)
U of Portland (OR)
U of Prince Edward Island (PE, Canada)
U of Puget Sound (WA)
U of Redlands (CA)
U of Regina (SK, Canada)
U of Rhode Island (RI)
U of Richmond (VA)
U of Rochester (NY)
U of Saint Francis (IN)
U of St. Thomas (MN)
U of St. Thomas (TX)
U of San Diego (CA)
The U of Scranton (PA)
U of Sioux Falls (SD)
U of South Alabama (AL)
U of South Carolina (SC)
The U of South Dakota (SD)
U of Southern California (CA)
U of Southern Indiana (IN)
U of Southern Maine (ME)
U of Southern Mississippi (MS)
U of South Florida (FL)
The U of Tennessee (TN)
The U of Tennessee at Martin (TN)
The U of Texas at Arlington (TX)
The U of Texas at Austin (TX)
The U of Texas at El Paso (TX)
The U of Texas at San Antonio (TX)
The U of Texas–Pan American (TX)
U of the Incarnate Word (TX)
U of the Ozarks (AR)
U of the Pacific (CA)
U of the West (CA)
The U of Toledo (OH)
U of Toronto (ON, Canada)
U of Tulsa (OK)
U of Utah (UT)
U of Vermont (VT)
U of Victoria (BC, Canada)
U of Virginia (VA)
The U of Western Ontario (ON, Canada)
U of West Florida (FL)
U of West Georgia (GA)
U of Windsor (ON, Canada)
The U of Winnipeg (MB, Canada)
U of Wisconsin–Eau Claire (WI)
U of Wisconsin–Green Bay (WI)
U of Wisconsin–La Crosse (WI)
U of Wisconsin–Madison (WI)
U of Wisconsin–Milwaukee (WI)
U of Wisconsin–Oshkosh (WI)
U of Wisconsin–Parkside (WI)
U of Wisconsin–Platteville (WI)
U of Wisconsin–Stevens Point (WI)
U of Wyoming (WY)
Ursinus Coll (PA)
Ursuline Coll (OH)
Utah State U (UT)
Utah Valley State Coll (UT)
Utica Coll (NY)
Valdosta State U (GA)
Valparaiso U (IN)
Vanderbilt U (TN)
Vassar Coll (NY)
Villanova U (PA)
Virginia Commonwealth U (VA)
Virginia Polytechnic Inst and State U (VA)
Virginia Wesleyan Coll (VA)
Wabash Coll (IN)
Wake Forest U (NC)
Walla Walla U (WA)
Walsh U (OH)
Warren Wilson Coll (NC)
Wartburg Coll (IA)
Washburn U (KS)
Washington & Jefferson Coll (PA)
Washington and Lee U (VA)
Washington Coll (MD)
Washington State U (WA)
Washington U in St. Louis (MO)
Wayne State U (MI)
Webster U (MO)
Wellesley Coll (MA)
Wells Coll (NY)
Wesleyan Coll (GA)
Wesleyan U (CT)
West Chester U of Pennsylvania (PA)
Western Carolina U (NC)
Western Illinois U (IL)
Western Kentucky U (KY)
Western Michigan U (MI)
Western New England Coll (MA)
Western Washington U (WA)
Westminster Coll (MO)
Westminster Coll (UT)
Westmont Coll (CA)
West Virginia U (WV)
West Virginia Wesleyan Coll (WV)
Wheaton Coll (IL)
Wheaton Coll (MA)
Wheeling Jesuit U (WV)
Whitman Coll (WA)
Whittier Coll (CA)
Whitworth U (WA)
Wichita State U (KS)
Wiley Coll (TX)
Wilfrid Laurier U (ON, Canada)
Wilkes U (PA)
Willamette U (OR)
William Jewell Coll (MO)
William Paterson U of New Jersey (NJ)
Williams Coll (MA)
Wilmington Coll (OH)
Wingate U (NC)
Winthrop U (SC)
Wittenberg U (OH)
Wofford Coll (SC)
Worcester Polytechnic Inst (MA)
Wright State U (OH)
Xavier U (OH)
Xavier U of Louisiana (LA)
Yale U (CT)
York Coll of Pennsylvania (PA)
York Coll of the City U of New York (NY)
York U (ON, Canada)
Youngstown State U (OH)

PHILOSOPHY AND RELIGIOUS STUDIES RELATED

Appalachian State U (NC)
Arizona State U at the West campus (AZ)
Barton Coll (NC)
Berry Coll (GA)
Bethune-Cookman U (FL)
Bridgewater Coll (VA)
Butler U (IN)
Capital U (OH)
Claflin U (SC)
Claremont McKenna Coll (CA)
Coll of the Ozarks (MO)
Covenant Coll (GA)
Eastern Mennonite U (VA)
Hendrix Coll (AR)
Holy Names U (CA)
Iowa Wesleyan Coll (IA)
James Madison U (VA)
Juniata Coll (PA)
Kean U (NJ)
Lambuth U (TN)
Lyon Coll (AR)
Marymount Manhattan Coll (NY)
Millsaps Coll (MS)
Pace U (NY)
Point Loma Nazarene U (CA)
Radford U (VA)
Roberts Wesleyan Coll (NY)
St. John's Coll (NM)
Saint Joseph's Coll (IN)
Samford U (AL)
San Francisco State U (CA)
Sarah Lawrence Coll (NY)
Southwestern Coll (KS)
State U of New York at Oswego (NY)
Sterling Coll (KS)
Syracuse U (NY)
Union U (TN)
U of Maine at Farmington (ME)
The U of North Carolina at Pembroke (NC)
The U of North Carolina Wilmington (NC)

U of Notre Dame (IN)
The U of Tennessee at Chattanooga (TN)
U of the Ozarks (AR)
Viterbo U (WI)
Washington U in St. Louis (MO)
West Virginia Wesleyan Coll (WV)
Wilson Coll (PA)

PHILOSOPHY RELATED
Claremont McKenna Coll (CA)
Ohio Northern U (OH)
St. John's Coll (NM)
State U of New York at Binghamton (NY)
U of California, Riverside (CA)
U of Pennsylvania (PA)

PHOTOGRAPHIC AND FILM/ VIDEO TECHNOLOGY
The Art Inst of Portland (OR)
Kent State U (OH)
New England School of Communications (ME)
Ohio U (OH)
Rochester Inst of Technology (NY)
St. John's U (NY)
Towson U (MD)

PHOTOGRAPHY
Acad of Art U (CA)
Alberta Coll of Art & Design (AB, Canada)
Albertus Magnus Coll (CT)
Aquinas Coll (MI)
Art Acad of Cincinnati (OH)
The Art Inst of Austin (TX)
The Art Inst of Boston at Lesley U (MA)
The Art Inst of Charleston (SC)
The Art Inst of Houston (TX)
The Art Inst of Indianapolis (IN)
The Art Inst of Las Vegas (NV)
The Art Inst of Seattle (WA)
The Art Insts Intl Minnesota (MN)
Ball State U (IN)
Bard Coll (NY)
Bard Coll at Simon's Rock (MA)
Barry U (FL)
Bennington Coll (VT)
Bradley U (IL)
Bridgewater State Coll (MA)
Brigham Young U (UT)
Buffalo State Coll, State U of New York (NY)
Burlington Coll (VT)
California Coll of the Arts (CA)
California Inst of the Arts (CA)
California State U, East Bay (CA)
California State U, Long Beach (CA)
California State U, Sacramento (CA)
Carlow U (PA)
Carroll Coll (WI)
Carson-Newman Coll (TN)
Chatham U (PA)
The Cleveland Inst of Art (OH)
Coker Coll (SC)
Coll of Santa Fe (NM)
Coll of Visual Arts (MN)
Colorado State U (CO)
Columbia Coll Chicago (IL)
Concordia U (QC, Canada)
Dominican U (IL)
Drexel U (PA)
Eastern Mennonite U (VA)
Ferris State U (MI)
Fitchburg State Coll (MA)
Grand Valley State U (MI)
Hampton U (VA)
Hofstra U (NY)
The Illinois Inst of Art–Schaumburg (IL)
Indiana U–Purdue U Fort Wayne (IN)
Indiana Wesleyan U (IN)
Inter American U of Puerto Rico, San Germán Campus (PR)
Ithaca Coll (NY)
Kansas City Art Inst (MO)
Marlboro Coll (VT)
Maryland Inst Coll of Art (MD)
Marymount Manhattan Coll (NY)
Marywood U (PA)
Massachusetts Coll of Art and Design (MA)
McNeese State U (LA)
Memorial U of Newfoundland (NL, Canada)
Memphis Coll of Art (TN)
Montserrat Coll of Art (MA)
Morningside Coll (IA)
Mount Allison U (NB, Canada)
Nazareth Coll of Rochester (NY)
New England Coll (NH)
The New England Inst of Art (MA)
New York U (NY)
Northern Arizona U (AZ)
Northern Michigan U (MI)
NSCAD U (NS, Canada)
Oakland U (MI)
Otis Coll of Art and Design (CA)
Paier Coll of Art, Inc. (CT)
Parsons The New School for Design (NY)
Pennsylvania Coll of Art & Design (PA)
Point Park U (PA)
Pratt Inst (NY)
Prescott Coll (AZ)
Purchase Coll, State U of New York (NY)
Purdue U (IN)
Ringling Coll of Art and Design (FL)
Rutgers, The State U of New Jersey, New Brunswick (NJ)
St. Edward's U (TX)
St. John's U (NY)
Salem State Coll (MA)
Salve Regina U (RI)
Sam Houston State U (TX)
Sarah Lawrence Coll (NY)
Savannah Coll of Art and Design (GA)
School of the Art Inst of Chicago (IL)
School of the Museum of Fine Arts, Boston (MA)
School of Visual Arts (NY)
Seattle U (WA)
Shawnee State U (OH)
Southern Adventist U (TN)
State U of New York at New Paltz (NY)
Syracuse U (NY)
Temple U (PA)
Texas A&M U–Commerce (TX)
Texas Christian U (TX)
Texas Southern U (TX)
Thomas Edison State Coll (NJ)
Trinity Christian Coll (IL)
The U of Akron (OH)
U of Central Florida (FL)
U of Central Missouri (MO)
U of Central Oklahoma (OK)
U of Dayton (OH)
U of Hartford (CT)
U of Houston (TX)
U of Illinois at Chicago (IL)
U of Illinois at Urbana–Champaign (IL)
The U of Iowa (IA)
U of Maryland, Baltimore County (MD)
U of Massachusetts Dartmouth (MA)
U of Miami (FL)
U of Michigan (MI)
U of Missouri–St. Louis (MO)
U of Oklahoma (OK)
U of Oregon (OR)
Virginia Commonwealth U (VA)
Virginia Intermont Coll (VA)
Washington U in St. Louis (MO)
Watkins Coll of Art and Design (TN)
Weber State U (UT)
Webster U (MO)
Western State Coll of Colorado (CO)
Wright State U (OH)
York U (ON, Canada)
Youngstown State U (OH)

PHOTOJOURNALISM
Bradley U (IL)
Central Michigan U (MI)
Harding U (AR)
Hawai'i Pacific U (HI)
Pittsburg State U (KS)
Point Park U (PA)
Rochester Inst of Technology (NY)
Texas Tech U (TX)
U of Miami (FL)
U of Missouri–Columbia (MO)

PHYSICAL AND THEORETICAL CHEMISTRY
Lehigh U (PA)
Michigan State U (MI)
Rice U (TX)
The U of Western Ontario (ON, Canada)

PHYSICAL ANTHROPOLOGY
The U of Western Ontario (ON, Canada)

PHYSICAL EDUCATION TEACHING AND COACHING
Abilene Christian U (TX)
Adelphi U (NY)
Alabama Ag and Mech U (AL)
Alabama State U (AL)
Albion Coll (MI)
Alderson-Broaddus Coll (WV)
Alice Lloyd Coll (KY)
Alma Coll (MI)
Anderson U (IN)
Anderson U (SC)
Appalachian State U (NC)
Aquinas Coll (MI)
Arkansas State U (AR)
Armstrong Atlantic State U (GA)
Asbury Coll (KY)
Ashland U (OH)
Athens State U (AL)
Auburn U (AL)
Augsburg Coll (MN)
Augustana Coll (IL)
Augustana Coll (SD)
Augusta State U (GA)
Averett U (VA)
Azusa Pacific U (CA)
Ball State U (IN)
Baptist Bible Coll of Pennsylvania (PA)
Barry U (FL)
Barton Coll (NC)
Baylor U (TX)
Belmont U (TN)
Bemidji State U (MN)
Benedictine Coll (KS)
Berry Coll (GA)
Bethany Coll (KS)
Bethany Coll (WV)
Bethel U (MN)
Bethune-Cookman U (FL)
Biola U (CA)
Blackburn Coll (IL)
Bluefield Coll (VA)
Boise State U (ID)
Boston U (MA)
Bowling Green State U (OH)
Brewton-Parker Coll (GA)
Bridgewater Coll (VA)
Bridgewater State Coll (MA)
Brigham Young U (UT)
Brock U (ON, Canada)
Bryan Coll (TN)
California Baptist U (CA)
California Lutheran U (CA)
California State Polytechnic U, Pomona (CA)
California State U, Chico (CA)
California State U, Dominguez Hills (CA)
California State U, East Bay (CA)
California State U, Fresno (CA)
California State U, Long Beach (CA)
California State U, San Bernardino (CA)
California State U, Stanislaus (CA)
Calvin Coll (MI)
Canisius Coll (NY)
Capital U (OH)
Carroll Coll (WI)
Carson-Newman Coll (TN)
Castleton State Coll (VT)
Catawba Coll (NC)
Cedarville U (OH)
Centenary Coll of Louisiana (LA)
Central Connecticut State U (CT)
Central Michigan U (MI)
Central Washington U (WA)
Chicago State U (IL)
The Citadel, The Military Coll of South Carolina (SC)
Clarke Coll (IA)
Clearwater Christian Coll (FL)
Cleveland State U (OH)
Coastal Carolina U (SC)
Coker Coll (SC)
The Coll at Brockport, State U of New York (NY)
Coll of Charleston (SC)
The Coll of Idaho (ID)
The Coll of New Jersey (NJ)
Coll of the Ozarks (MO)
Coll of the Southwest (NM)
The Coll of William and Mary (VA)
Columbus State U (GA)
Concordia Coll (MN)
Concordia U (MI)
Concordia U (OR)
Concordia U Chicago (IL)
Concordia U, Nebraska (NE)
Concordia U, St. Paul (MN)
Concordia U Wisconsin (WI)
Concord U (WV)
Cornell Coll (IA)
Cornerstone U (MI)
Crown Coll (MN)
Culver-Stockton Coll (MO)
Dakota State U (SD)
Dakota Wesleyan U (SD)
Dallas Baptist U (TX)
Dana Coll (NE)
Davis & Elkins Coll (WV)
Defiance Coll (OH)
Delta State U (MS)
Denison U (OH)
DePaul U (IL)
DePauw U (IN)
Dillard U (LA)
Doane Coll (NE)
Dordt Coll (IA)
East Carolina U (NC)
East Central U (OK)
Eastern Connecticut State U (CT)
Eastern Illinois U (IL)
Eastern Kentucky U (KY)
Eastern Mennonite U (VA)
Eastern Michigan U (MI)
Eastern New Mexico U (NM)
East Stroudsburg U of Pennsylvania (PA)
East Texas Baptist U (TX)
Elon U (NC)
Endicott Coll (MA)
Erskine Coll (SC)
Evangel U (MO)
Fairmont State U (WV)
Faulkner U (AL)
Fayetteville State U (NC)
Ferrum Coll (VA)
Florida Ag and Mech U (FL)
Florida Intl U (FL)
Florida Memorial U (FL)
Florida Southern Coll (FL)
Florida State U (FL)
Fort Lewis Coll (CO)
Franklin Coll (IN)
Freed-Hardeman U (TN)
Free Will Baptist Bible Coll (TN)
Fresno Pacific U (CA)
Frostburg State U (MD)
Gardner-Webb U (NC)
George Fox U (OR)
George Mason U (VA)
Georgia Coll & State U (GA)
Georgia Southern U (GA)
Georgia Southwestern State U (GA)
Gettysburg Coll (PA)
Glenville State Coll (WV)
Gonzaga U (WA)
Grace Coll (IN)
Grambling State U (LA)
Grand Canyon U (AZ)
Grand Valley State U (MI)
Greensboro Coll (NC)
Greenville Coll (IL)
Gustavus Adolphus Coll (MN)
Hamline U (MN)
Hampton U (VA)
Hannibal-LaGrange Coll (MO)
Hanover Coll (IN)
Hardin-Simmons U (TX)
Hastings Coll (NE)
Heidelberg Coll (OH)
Henderson State U (AR)
High Point U (NC)
Hillsdale Coll (MI)
Hofstra U (NY)
Hope Coll (MI)
Houghton Coll (NY)
Houston Baptist U (TX)
Howard Payne U (TX)
Humboldt State U (CA)
Hunter Coll of the City U of New York (NY)
Huntingdon Coll (AL)
Huntington U (IN)
Husson Coll (ME)
Huston-Tillotson U (TX)
Idaho State U (ID)
Illinois Coll (IL)
Illinois State U (IL)
Indiana State U (IN)
Indiana U Bloomington (IN)
Indiana U of Pennsylvania (PA)
Indiana U–Purdue U Indianapolis (IN)
Indiana Wesleyan U (IN)
Inter American U of Puerto Rico, Fajardo Campus (PR)
Inter American U of Puerto Rico, San Germán Campus (PR)
Iowa Wesleyan Coll (IA)
Ithaca Coll (NY)
Jackson State U (MS)
Jacksonville State U (AL)
Jacksonville U (FL)
Jamestown Coll (ND)
Jarvis Christian Coll (TX)
John Carroll U (OH)
Johnson C. Smith U (NC)
Johnson State Coll (VT)
Judson U (IL)
Kean U (NJ)
Keene State Coll (NH)
Kennesaw State U (GA)
Kent State U (OH)
Kentucky State U (KY)
Kentucky Wesleyan Coll (KY)
Lakehead U (ON, Canada)
Lambuth U (TN)
Lander U (SC)
Laurentian U (ON, Canada)
Lees-McRae Coll (NC)
Lee U (TN)
Lenoir-Rhyne Coll (NC)
LeTourneau U (TX)
Lewis-Clark State Coll (ID)
Liberty U (VA)
Limestone Coll (SC)
Lincoln U (MO)
Lindenwood U (MO)
Lindsey Wilson Coll (KY)
Lipscomb U (TN)
Livingstone Coll (NC)
Lock Haven U of Pennsylvania (PA)
Longwood U (VA)
Loras Coll (IA)
Louisiana Coll (LA)
Louisiana State U and Ag and Mech Coll (LA)
Lubbock Christian U (TX)
Luther Coll (IA)
Lynchburg Coll (VA)
Lyndon State Coll (VT)
Malone Coll (OH)
Manchester Coll (IN)
Maranatha Baptist Bible Coll (WI)
Marian Coll (IN)
Marshall U (WV)
Maryville Coll (TN)
The Master's Coll and Sem (CA)
Mayville State U (ND)
McDaniel Coll (MD)
McGill U (QC, Canada)
McKendree U (IL)
McMurry U (TX)
McNeese State U (LA)
Memorial U of Newfoundland (NL, Canada)
Meredith Coll (NC)
Messiah Coll (PA)
Methodist U (NC)
Miami U (OH)
Miami U Hamilton (OH)
Michigan State U (MI)
MidAmerica Nazarene U (KS)
Midland Lutheran Coll (NE)
Millikin U (IL)
Minnesota State U Mankato (MN)
Minot State U (ND)
Mississippi State U (MS)
Mississippi U for Women (MS)
Mississippi Valley State U (MS)
Missouri Baptist U (MO)
Missouri State U (MO)
Missouri Valley Coll (MO)
Monmouth Coll (IL)
Montana State U–Billings (MT)
Montclair State U (NJ)
Morehead State U (KY)
Morgan State U (MD)
Mount Vernon Nazarene U (OH)
Murray State U (KY)
Nebraska Wesleyan U (NE)
New England Coll (NH)
New Mexico Highlands U (NM)
Nicholls State U (LA)
North Carolina Ag and Tech State U (NC)
North Carolina Central U (NC)
North Carolina Wesleyan Coll (NC)
North Central Coll (IL)
North Dakota State U (ND)
Northeastern Illinois U (IL)
Northeastern State U (OK)
Northern Arizona U (AZ)
Northern Illinois U (IL)
Northern Michigan U (MI)
Northern State U (SD)
North Georgia Coll & State U (GA)
Northwestern Coll (IA)
Northwestern Coll (MN)
Northwestern Oklahoma State U (OK)
Northwestern State U of Louisiana (LA)
Northwest Missouri State U (MO)
Northwest Nazarene U (ID)
Norwich U (VT)
Oakland City U (IN)
Oakwood Coll (AL)
Ohio Northern U (OH)
Ohio U (OH)
Ohio Valley U (WV)
Ohio Wesleyan U (OH)
Oklahoma Christian U (OK)
Oklahoma City U (OK)
Oklahoma State U (OK)
Oklahoma Wesleyan U (OK)
Old Dominion U (VA)
Oral Roberts U (OK)
Oregon State U (OR)
Otterbein Coll (OH)
Ouachita Baptist U (AR)
Pacific Union Coll (CA)
Palm Beach Atlantic U (FL)
Pepperdine U, Malibu (CA)
Peru State Coll (NE)
Pfeiffer U (NC)

MAJORS AND MORE

Philadelphia Biblical U (PA)
Pillsbury Baptist Bible Coll (MN)
Pittsburg State U (KS)
Prescott Coll (AZ)
Purdue U (IN)
Queens Coll of the City U of New York (NY)
Queen's U at Kingston (ON, Canada)
Quincy U (IL)
Radford U (VA)
Rhode Island Coll (RI)
Ripon Coll (WI)
Rockford Coll (IL)
Rowan U (NJ)
Saginaw Valley State U (MI)
St. Ambrose U (IA)
St. Andrews Presbyterian Coll (NC)
St. Cloud State U (MN)
St. Edward's U (TX)
St. Francis Xavier U (NS, Canada)
Saint Joseph's Coll (IN)
Salem Intl U (WV)
Salem State Coll (MA)
Salisbury U (MD)
Samford U (AL)
Sam Houston State U (TX)
San Diego Christian Coll (CA)
San Francisco State U (CA)
Schreiner U (TX)
Seattle Pacific U (WA)
Shenandoah U (VA)
Simpson Coll (IA)
Slippery Rock U of Pennsylvania (PA)
Sonoma State U (CA)
South Carolina State U (SC)
Southeastern Louisiana U (LA)
Southeastern Oklahoma State U (OK)
Southeast Missouri State U (MO)
Southern Adventist U (TN)
Southern Arkansas U–Magnolia (AR)
Southern Oregon U (OR)
Southern U and Ag and Mech Coll (LA)
Southern Utah U (UT)
Southern Wesleyan U (SC)
Southwest Baptist U (MO)
Southwestern Oklahoma State U (OK)
Southwestern U (TX)
Southwest Minnesota State U (MN)
Spring Arbor U (MI)
State U of New York at Plattsburgh (NY)
Sterling Coll (KS)
Stillman Coll (AL)
Syracuse U (NY)
Tabor Coll (KS)
Tarleton State U (TX)
Taylor U (IN)
Temple U (PA)
Tennessee State U (TN)
Tennessee Technological U (TN)
Texas A&M Intl U (TX)
Texas A&M U–Commerce (TX)
Texas Christian U (TX)
Texas Lutheran U (TX)
Texas Southern U (TX)
Towson U (MD)
Transylvania U (KY)
Trevecca Nazarene U (TN)
Trinity Christian Coll (IL)
Trinity Intl U (IL)
Tri-State U (IN)
Troy U (AL)
Tusculum Coll (TN)
Union Coll (KY)
Union Coll (NE)
Union U (TN)
Université de Sherbrooke (QC, Canada)
The U of Akron (OH)
The U of Alabama (AL)
The U of Alabama at Birmingham (AL)
The U of Arizona (AZ)
U of Arkansas at Monticello (AR)
U of Arkansas at Pine Bluff (AR)
U of Central Arkansas (AR)
U of Central Florida (FL)
U of Central Missouri (MO)
U of Central Oklahoma (OK)
U of Cincinnati (OH)
U of Connecticut (CT)
U of Dayton (OH)
U of Delaware (DE)
U of Evansville (IN)
The U of Findlay (OH)
U of Florida (FL)
U of Georgia (GA)
U of Great Falls (MT)
U of Guam (GU)
U of Hawaii at Manoa (HI)
U of Idaho (ID)
U of Illinois at Urbana–Champaign (IL)
U of Indianapolis (IN)
U of Kansas (KS)
U of Lethbridge (AB, Canada)
U of Louisiana at Lafayette (LA)
U of Louisiana at Monroe (LA)
U of Maine (ME)
U of Mary (ND)
U of Mary Hardin-Baylor (TX)
U of Maryland, Coll Park (MD)
U of Maryland Eastern Shore (MD)
U of Massachusetts Boston (MA)
U of Memphis (TN)
U of Michigan (MI)
U of Minnesota, Duluth (MN)
U of Minnesota, Twin Cities Campus (MN)
U of Missouri–St. Louis (MO)
The U of Montana (MT)
The U of Montana–Western (MT)
U of Nebraska at Kearney (NE)
U of Nebraska at Omaha (NE)
U of Nebraska–Lincoln (NE)
U of Nevada, Las Vegas (NV)
U of Nevada, Reno (NV)
U of New Brunswick Fredericton (NB, Canada)
U of New Hampshire (NH)
U of New Mexico (NM)
U of New Orleans (LA)
The U of North Carolina at Greensboro (NC)
The U of North Carolina at Pembroke (NC)
The U of North Carolina Wilmington (NC)
U of North Dakota (ND)
U of Northern Iowa (IA)
U of North Florida (FL)
U of Pittsburgh (PA)
U of Pittsburgh at Bradford (PA)
U of Puerto Rico at Utuado (PR)
U of Puerto Rico, Cayey U Coll (PR)
U of Regina (SK, Canada)
U of Rhode Island (RI)
U of Richmond (VA)
U of Rio Grande (OH)
U of St. Thomas (MN)
U of South Alabama (AL)
U of South Carolina (SC)
U of South Carolina Upstate (SC)
The U of South Dakota (SD)
U of Southern Indiana (IN)
U of Southern Mississippi (MS)
U of South Florida (FL)
The U of Tampa (FL)
U of the District of Columbia (DC)
U of the Ozarks (AR)
The U of Toledo (OH)
U of Vermont (VT)
U of Victoria (BC, Canada)
U of Virginia (VA)
The U of Western Ontario (ON, Canada)
U of West Georgia (GA)
U of Windsor (ON, Canada)
U of Wisconsin–Madison (WI)
U of Wisconsin–Oshkosh (WI)
U of Wisconsin–Stevens Point (WI)
U of Wisconsin–Superior (WI)
U of Wisconsin–Whitewater (WI)
U of Wyoming (WY)
Utah State U (UT)
Utah Valley State Coll (UT)
Valdosta State U (GA)
Valley City State U (ND)
Valparaiso U (IN)
Vanguard U of Southern California (CA)
Virginia Intermont Coll (VA)
Virginia State U (VA)
Voorhees Coll (SC)
Walla Walla U (WA)
Walsh U (OH)
Warner Pacific Coll (OR)
Wartburg Coll (IA)
Washburn U (KS)
Washington State U (WA)
Wayland Baptist U (TX)
Wayne State Coll (NE)
Wayne State U (MI)
Weber State U (UT)
Wesley Coll (DE)
West Chester U of Pennsylvania (PA)
Western Carolina U (NC)
Western Kentucky U (KY)
Western Michigan U (MI)
Western New Mexico U (NM)
Western State Coll of Colorado (CO)
Western Washington U (WA)
Westfield State Coll (MA)
West Liberty State Coll (WV)
Westminster Coll (MO)
Westmont Coll (CA)
West Virginia U (WV)
West Virginia Wesleyan Coll (WV)
Whittier Coll (CA)
Whitworth U (WA)
Wichita State U (KS)
Wiley Coll (TX)
Wilfrid Laurier U (ON, Canada)
William Jewell Coll (MO)
William Paterson U of New Jersey (NJ)
William Woods U (MO)
Wilmington Coll (OH)
Winona State U (MN)
Winthrop U (SC)
Wright State U (OH)
Xavier U of Louisiana (LA)
York Coll (NE)
York Coll of the City U of New York (NY)
York U (ON, Canada)
Youngstown State U (OH)

PHYSICAL SCIENCES

Asbury Coll (KY)
Auburn U Montgomery (AL)
Augusta State U (GA)
Bemidji State U (MN)
Bennington Coll (VT)
Biola U (CA)
Brock U (ON, Canada)
California State U, East Bay (CA)
California State U, Sacramento (CA)
California State U, Stanislaus (CA)
Calvin Coll (MI)
Colgate U (NY)
Colorado State U (CO)
Concordia U (MI)
Concordia U (OR)
Concordia U Chicago (IL)
Concordia U, Nebraska (NE)
Dakota State U (SD)
Defiance Coll (OH)
Doane Coll (NE)
Eastern Kentucky U (KY)
East Stroudsburg U of Pennsylvania (PA)
Emporia State U (KS)
The Evergreen State Coll (WA)
Florida State U (FL)
Freed-Hardeman U (TN)
Georgia Southwestern State U (GA)
Grace Coll (IN)
Grand Valley State U (MI)
Grand View Coll (IA)
Hampton U (VA)
Harvard U (MA)
Humboldt State U (CA)
Indiana U of Pennsylvania (PA)
Juniata Coll (PA)
Kansas State U (KS)
La Sierra U (CA)
Lincoln U (PA)
Linfield Coll (OR)
Lock Haven U of Pennsylvania (PA)
Loras Coll (IA)
Lyndon State Coll (VT)
The Master's Coll and Sem (CA)
Mayville State U (ND)
Mesa State Coll (CO)
Michigan State U (MI)
Michigan Technological U (MI)
Midland Lutheran Coll (NE)
Minnesota State U Mankato (MN)
Minot State U (ND)
Mississippi U for Women (MS)
Mountain State U (WV)
Muhlenberg Coll (PA)
New Mexico Inst of Mining and Technology (NM)
Northern Arizona U (AZ)
Northwest Missouri State U (MO)
Oregon State U (OR)
Otterbein Coll (OH)
Pacific Union Coll (CA)
Penn State Erie, The Behrend Coll (PA)
Purdue U North Central (IN)
Ripon Coll (WI)
Rowan U (NJ)
St. Cloud State U (MN)
St. Francis Xavier U (NS, Canada)
St. John's Coll (NM)
St. John's U (NY)
Saint Michael's Coll (VT)
San Diego State U (CA)
San Francisco State U (CA)
Shawnee State U (OH)
Southern Utah U (UT)
Southwestern U (TX)
Taylor U (IN)
Texas A&M Intl U (TX)
Trent U (ON, Canada)
Tri-State U (IN)
Troy U (AL)
United States Naval Acad (MD)
U of Arkansas at Monticello (AR)
U of California, Berkeley (CA)
U of California, Riverside (CA)
U of Dayton (OH)
U of Guam (GU)
U of Houston–Clear Lake (TX)
U of Maryland, Coll Park (MD)
U of North Alabama (AL)
U of North Dakota (ND)
U of Ottawa (ON, Canada)
U of Pittsburgh (PA)
U of Pittsburgh at Bradford (PA)
U of Rio Grande (OH)
U of Southern California (CA)
U of the Pacific (CA)
The U of Toledo (OH)
U of Utah (UT)
U of Wisconsin–Superior (WI)
U of Wyoming (WY)
Warner Pacific Coll (OR)
Washington State U (WA)
Wayland Baptist U (TX)
Wesleyan Coll (GA)
Western New Mexico U (NM)
Westfield State Coll (MA)
Wiley Coll (TX)
William Paterson U of New Jersey (NJ)
Winona State U (MN)
York U (ON, Canada)

PHYSICAL SCIENCES RELATED

Baldwin-Wallace Coll (OH)
Cedar Crest Coll (PA)
Central Connecticut State U (CT)
The Coll of St. Scholastica (MN)
Covenant Coll (GA)
Eastern Michigan U (MI)
Florida State U (FL)
Frostburg State U (MD)
George Mason U (VA)
New Mexico Inst of Mining and Technology (NM)
Ohio U (OH)
Stony Brook U, State U of New York (NY)
U of California, Davis (CA)
The U of North Carolina at Chapel Hill (NC)
U of Saint Francis (IN)
U of the Ozarks (AR)
U of Toronto (ON, Canada)
Worcester Polytechnic Inst (MA)

PHYSICAL SCIENCE TECHNOLOGIES RELATED

Missouri State U (MO)

PHYSICAL THERAPIST ASSISTANT

Mercyhurst Coll (PA)

PHYSICAL THERAPY

Andrews U (MI)
Armstrong Atlantic State U (GA)
Boston U (MA)
Bradley U (IL)
California State U, Fresno (CA)
Chicago State U (IL)
Clarke Coll (IA)
Cleveland State U (OH)
Coll of Saint Benedict (MN)
Concordia U Wisconsin (WI)
Duquesne U (PA)
Florida Ag and Mech U (FL)
Grand Valley State U (MI)
Gustavus Adolphus Coll (MN)
Hamline U (MN)
Hampton U (VA)
Hawai'i Pacific U (HI)
Hope Intl U (CA)
Husson Coll (ME)
Indiana U Southeast (IN)
Ithaca Coll (NY)
Keystone Coll (PA)
Marquette U (WI)
Merrimack Coll (MA)
Mount Aloysius Coll (PA)
Mount Saint Mary Coll (NY)
Mount Vernon Nazarene U (OH)
Nazareth Coll of Rochester (NY)
New York Inst of Technology (NY)
Northeastern U (MA)
Northern Illinois U (IL)
Northwest Nazarene U (ID)
Oklahoma Wesleyan U (OK)
Queen's U at Kingston (ON, Canada)
Quinnipiac U (CT)
Russell Sage Coll (NY)
Sacred Heart U (CT)
St. Cloud State U (MN)
Saint Francis U (PA)
Saint John's U (MN)
Saint Louis U (MO)
Saint Mary's U of Minnesota (MN)
Saint Vincent Coll (PA)
Simmons Coll (MA)
State U of New York Coll of Environmental Science and Forestry (NY)
State U of New York Downstate Medical Center (NY)
Tarleton State U (TX)
Tennessee State U (TN)
Texas Southern U (TX)
The U of British Columbia (BC, Canada)
U of Connecticut (CT)
The U of Findlay (OH)
U of Hartford (CT)
U of Maryland, Baltimore County (MD)
U of Maryland Eastern Shore (MD)
U of Minnesota, Twin Cities Campus (MN)
The U of Montana (MT)
U of New England (ME)
U of North Dakota (ND)
U of Ottawa (ON, Canada)
The U of Tennessee at Chattanooga (TN)
The U of Toledo (OH)
U of Utah (UT)
The U of Western Ontario (ON, Canada)
U of Wisconsin–La Crosse (WI)
U of Wisconsin–Milwaukee (WI)
Vanguard U of Southern California (CA)
West Virginia U (WV)
Wheeling Jesuit U (WV)
Winona State U (MN)

PHYSICIAN ASSISTANT

Alderson-Broaddus Coll (WV)
Augsburg Coll (MN)
Bethel Coll (TN)
Boise State U (ID)
Butler U (IN)
California State U, Dominguez Hills (CA)
Catawba Coll (NC)
City Coll of the City U of New York (NY)
Duquesne U (PA)
Gannon U (PA)
Gardner-Webb U (NC)
The George Washington U (DC)
Grand Valley State U (MI)
High Point U (NC)
Hofstra U (NY)
Jefferson Coll of Health Sciences (VA)
Kettering Coll of Medical Arts (OH)
Lenoir-Rhyne Coll (NC)
Marquette U (WI)
Medical Coll of Georgia (GA)
Methodist U (NC)
New York Inst of Technology (NY)
Pace U (NY)
Peru State Coll (NE)
Philadelphia U (PA)
Quinnipiac U (CT)
Rochester Inst of Technology (NY)
Saint Francis U (PA)
St. John's U (NY)
Saint Vincent Coll (PA)
Salem Coll (NC)
Sam Houston State U (TX)
Seton Hill U (PA)
Southern Illinois U Carbondale (IL)
South U (GA)
State U of New York Downstate Medical Center (NY)
Union Coll (NE)
The U of Alabama at Birmingham (AL)
The U of Findlay (OH)
U of New England (ME)
U of New Mexico (NM)
U of Saint Francis (IN)
The U of Texas–Pan American (TX)
U of Wisconsin–La Crosse (WI)
U of Wisconsin–Madison (WI)
Wagner Coll (NY)
Wake Forest U (NC)
Wichita State U (KS)

PHYSICS

Abilene Christian U (TX)
Acadia U (NS, Canada)
Adelphi U (NY)
Adrian Coll (MI)
Agnes Scott Coll (GA)
Alabama Ag and Mech U (AL)
Albion Coll (MI)
Albright Coll (PA)
Alfred U (NY)
Allegheny Coll (PA)
Alma Coll (MI)
American U (DC)
The American U of Athens (Greece)
American U of Beirut (Lebanon)
Amherst Coll (MA)

Anderson U (IN)
Andrews U (MI)
Angelo State U (TX)
Appalachian State U (NC)
Aquinas Coll (MI)
Arizona State U (AZ)
Arkansas State U (AR)
Armstrong Atlantic State U (GA)
Ashland U (OH)
Athens State U (AL)
Auburn U (AL)
Augsburg Coll (MN)
Augustana Coll (IL)
Augustana Coll (SD)
Augusta State U (GA)
Austin Coll (TX)
Austin Peay State U (TN)
Azusa Pacific U (CA)
Baker U (KS)
Baldwin-Wallace Coll (OH)
Ball State U (IN)
Bard Coll (NY)
Bard Coll at Simon's Rock (MA)
Barnard Coll (NY)
Bates Coll (ME)
Baylor U (TX)
Belmont U (TN)
Beloit Coll (WI)
Bemidji State U (MN)
Benedictine Coll (KS)
Benedictine U (IL)
Bennington Coll (VT)
Berea Coll (KY)
Berry Coll (GA)
Bethany Coll (WV)
Bethel Coll (KS)
Bethel U (MN)
Bethune-Cookman U (FL)
Bishop's U (QC, Canada)
Bloomsburg U of Pennsylvania (PA)
Bluffton U (OH)
Bob Jones U (SC)
Boise State U (ID)
Boston Coll (MA)
Boston U (MA)
Bowdoin Coll (ME)
Bowling Green State U (OH)
Bradley U (IL)
Brandeis U (MA)
Bridgewater Coll (VA)
Bridgewater State Coll (MA)
Brigham Young U (UT)
Brock U (ON, Canada)
Brown U (RI)
Bryn Mawr Coll (PA)
Bucknell U (PA)
Buffalo State Coll, State U of New York (NY)
Butler U (IN)
California Inst of Technology (CA)
California Lutheran U (CA)
California Polytechnic State U, San Luis Obispo (CA)
California State Polytechnic U, Pomona (CA)
California State U, Chico (CA)
California State U, Dominguez Hills (CA)
California State U, East Bay (CA)
California State U, Fresno (CA)
California State U, Fullerton (CA)
California State U, Long Beach (CA)
California State U, Los Angeles (CA)
California State U, Sacramento (CA)
California State U, San Bernardino (CA)
California State U, Stanislaus (CA)
Calvin Coll (MI)
Cameron U (OK)
Canisius Coll (NY)
Carnegie Mellon U (PA)
Carson-Newman Coll (TN)
The Catholic U of America (DC)
Cedarville U (OH)
Centenary Coll of Louisiana (LA)
Central Coll (IA)
Central Connecticut State U (CT)
Central Michigan U (MI)
Central Washington U (WA)
Centre Coll (KY)
Chatham U (PA)
Chicago State U (IL)
Christian Brothers U (TN)
Christopher Newport U (VA)
The Citadel, The Military Coll of South Carolina (SC)
City Coll of the City U of New York (NY)
Claremont McKenna Coll (CA)
Clarion U of Pennsylvania (PA)
Clark Atlanta U (GA)
Clarkson U (NY)
Clark U (MA)
Clemson U (SC)
Cleveland State U (OH)
Coastal Carolina U (SC)
Colby Coll (ME)
Colgate U (NY)
The Coll at Brockport, State U of New York (NY)
Coll of Charleston (SC)
The Coll of Idaho (ID)
The Coll of New Jersey (NJ)
The Coll of New Rochelle (NY)
Coll of Saint Benedict (MN)
Coll of Staten Island of the City U of New York (NY)
Coll of the Holy Cross (MA)
The Coll of William and Mary (VA)
The Colorado Coll (CO)
Colorado State U (CO)
Colorado State U-Pueblo (CO)
Concordia Coll (MN)
Concordia U (MI)
Concordia U (QC, Canada)
Cornell Coll (IA)
Cornell U (NY)
Covenant Coll (GA)
Creighton U (NE)
Curry Coll (MA)
Dartmouth Coll (NH)
Davidson Coll (NC)
Denison U (OH)
DePaul U (IL)
DePauw U (IN)
Dickinson Coll (PA)
Dillard U (LA)
Doane Coll (NE)
Dordt Coll (IA)
Drake U (IA)
Drew U (NJ)
Drury U (MO)
Duke U (NC)
Duquesne U (PA)
Earlham Coll (IN)
East Carolina U (NC)
East Central U (OK)
Eastern Illinois U (IL)
Eastern Kentucky U (KY)
Eastern Michigan U (MI)
Eastern New Mexico U (NM)
East Stroudsburg U of Pennsylvania (PA)
East Tennessee State U (TN)
Eckerd Coll (FL)
Edinboro U of Pennsylvania (PA)
Elizabethtown Coll (PA)
Elon U (NC)
Emory & Henry Coll (VA)
Emory U (GA)
Emporia State U (KS)
Erskine Coll (SC)
Excelsior Coll (NY)
Fairfield U (CT)
Fairleigh Dickinson U, Metropolitan Campus (NJ)
Florida Ag and Mech U (FL)
Florida Atlantic U (FL)
Florida Inst of Technology (FL)
Florida Intl U (FL)
Florida State U (FL)
Fort Lewis Coll (CO)
Francis Marion U (SC)
Franklin & Marshall Coll (PA)
Frostburg State U (MD)
Furman U (SC)
George Mason U (VA)
Georgetown Coll (KY)
Georgetown U (DC)
The George Washington U (DC)
Georgia Inst of Technology (GA)
Georgian Court U (NJ)
Georgia Southern U (GA)
Georgia State U (GA)
Gettysburg Coll (PA)
Gonzaga U (WA)
Gordon Coll (MA)
Goucher Coll (MD)
Grambling State U (LA)
Grand Valley State U (MI)
Greenville Coll (IL)
Grinnell Coll (IA)
Grove City Coll (PA)
Guilford Coll (NC)
Gustavus Adolphus Coll (MN)
Hamilton Coll (NY)
Hamline U (MN)
Hampden-Sydney Coll (VA)
Hampshire Coll (MA)
Hampton U (VA)
Hanover Coll (IN)
Harding U (AR)
Hardin-Simmons U (TX)
Hartwick Coll (NY)
Harvard U (MA)
Harvey Mudd Coll (CA)
Hastings Coll (NE)
Haverford Coll (PA)
Heidelberg Coll (OH)
Henderson State U (AR)
Hendrix Coll (AR)
Hillsdale Coll (MI)
Hobart and William Smith Colls (NY)
Hofstra U (NY)
Hollins U (VA)
Hope Coll (MI)
Houghton Coll (NY)
Houston Baptist U (TX)
Humboldt State U (CA)
Hunter Coll of the City U of New York (NY)
Idaho State U (ID)
Illinois Coll (IL)
Illinois Inst of Technology (IL)
Illinois State U (IL)
Illinois Wesleyan U (IL)
Indiana State U (IN)
Indiana U Bloomington (IN)
Indiana U of Pennsylvania (PA)
Indiana U–Purdue U Fort Wayne (IN)
Indiana U–Purdue U Indianapolis (IN)
Indiana U South Bend (IN)
Iona Coll (NY)
Iowa State U of Science and Technology (IA)
Ithaca Coll (NY)
Jackson State U (MS)
Jacksonville State U (AL)
Jacksonville U (FL)
James Madison U (VA)
Jarvis Christian Coll (TX)
John Carroll U (OH)
The Johns Hopkins U (MD)
Juniata Coll (PA)
Kalamazoo Coll (MI)
Kansas State U (KS)
Kent State U (OH)
Kentucky Wesleyan Coll (KY)
Kenyon Coll (OH)
Kettering U (MI)
King Coll (TN)
Knox Coll (IL)
Kutztown U of Pennsylvania (PA)
Lafayette Coll (PA)
Lake Forest Coll (IL)
Lakehead U (ON, Canada)
Laurentian U (ON, Canada)
Lawrence Technological U (MI)
Lawrence U (WI)
Lebanon Valley Coll (PA)
Lehigh U (PA)
Lehman Coll of the City U of New York (NY)
Le Moyne Coll (NY)
Lenoir-Rhyne Coll (NC)
Lewis & Clark Coll (OR)
Lewis U (IL)
Lincoln U (MO)
Lincoln U (PA)
Linfield Coll (OR)
Lipscomb U (TN)
Lock Haven U of Pennsylvania (PA)
Longwood U (VA)
Loras Coll (IA)
Louisiana Coll (LA)
Louisiana State U and Ag and Mech Coll (LA)
Loyola Coll in Maryland (MD)
Loyola Marymount U (CA)
Loyola U Chicago (IL)
Loyola U New Orleans (LA)
Luther Coll (IA)
Lycoming Coll (PA)
Lynchburg Coll (VA)
Macalester Coll (MN)
Manchester Coll (IN)
Manhattanville Coll (NY)
Mansfield U of Pennsylvania (PA)
Marietta Coll (OH)
Marlboro Coll (VT)
Marquette U (WI)
Marshall U (WV)
Mary Baldwin Coll (VA)
Massachusetts Coll of Liberal Arts (MA)
Massachusetts Inst of Technology (MA)
McDaniel Coll (MD)
McGill U (QC, Canada)
McMurry U (TX)
McNeese State U (LA)
Memorial U of Newfoundland (NL, Canada)
Mercer U (GA)
Mercyhurst Coll (PA)
Messiah Coll (PA)
Miami U (OH)
Miami U Hamilton (OH)
Michigan State U (MI)
Michigan Technological U (MI)
Middlebury Coll (VT)
Middle Tennessee State U (TN)
Midwestern State U (TX)
Miles Coll (AL)
Millersville U of Pennsylvania (PA)
Millikin U (IL)
Millsaps Coll (MS)
Minnesota State U Mankato (MN)
Minot State U (ND)
Mississippi Coll (MS)
Mississippi State U (MS)
Missouri Southern State U (MO)
Missouri State U (MO)
Missouri U of Science and Technology (MO)
Monmouth Coll (IL)
Montana State U (MT)
Montclair State U (NJ)
Moravian Coll (PA)
Morehead State U (KY)
Morehouse Coll (GA)
Morgan State U (MD)
Morningside Coll (IA)
Mount Allison U (NB, Canada)
Mount Holyoke Coll (MA)
Mount Vernon Nazarene U (OH)
Muhlenberg Coll (PA)
Murray State U (KY)
Nebraska Wesleyan U (NE)
New Coll of Florida (FL)
New Jersey City U (NJ)
New Mexico Highlands U (NM)
New Mexico Inst of Mining and Technology (NM)
New York Inst of Technology (NY)
New York U (NY)
North Carolina Ag and Tech State U (NC)
North Carolina Central U (NC)
North Carolina State U (NC)
North Central Coll (IL)
North Dakota State U (ND)
Northeastern Illinois U (IL)
Northeastern U (MA)
Northern Arizona U (AZ)
Northern Illinois U (IL)
Northern Michigan U (MI)
North Georgia Coll & State U (GA)
Northwestern Oklahoma State U (OK)
Northwestern State U of Louisiana (LA)
Northwestern U (IL)
Northwest Missouri State U (MO)
Northwest Nazarene U (ID)
Norwich U (VT)
Oakland U (MI)
Oberlin Coll (OH)
Occidental Coll (CA)
Oglethorpe U (GA)
Ohio Northern U (OH)
Ohio U (OH)
Ohio Wesleyan U (OH)
Oklahoma City U (OK)
Oklahoma State U (OK)
Old Dominion U (VA)
Oral Roberts U (OK)
Oregon State U (OR)
Otterbein Coll (OH)
Ouachita Baptist U (AR)
Pace U (NY)
Pacific Lutheran U (WA)
Pacific Union Coll (CA)
Pacific U (OR)
Penn State Abington (PA)
Penn State Altoona (PA)
Penn State Berks (PA)
Penn State Erie, The Behrend Coll (PA)
Penn State U Park (PA)
Piedmont Coll (GA)
Pittsburg State U (KS)
Pitzer Coll (CA)
Point Loma Nazarene U (CA)
Polytechnic U, Brooklyn Campus (NY)
Pomona Coll (CA)
Portland State U (OR)
Prairie View A&M U (TX)
Presbyterian Coll (SC)
Princeton U (NJ)
Purchase Coll, State U of New York (NY)
Purdue U (IN)
Purdue U Calumet (IN)
Queens Coll of the City U of New York (NY)
Queen's U at Kingston (ON, Canada)
Radford U (VA)
Ramapo Coll of New Jersey (NJ)
Randolph Coll (VA)
Randolph-Macon Coll (VA)
Reed Coll (OR)
Rhode Island Coll (RI)
Rhodes Coll (TN)
Rice U (TX)
The Richard Stockton Coll of New Jersey (NJ)
Rider U (NJ)
Roanoke Coll (VA)
Roberts Wesleyan Coll (NY)
Rockhurst U (MO)
Rollins Coll (FL)
Rose-Hulman Inst of Technology (IN)
Royal Military Coll of Canada (ON, Canada)
Rutgers, The State U of New Jersey, Camden (NJ)
Rutgers, The State U of New Jersey, Newark (NJ)
Rutgers, The State U of New Jersey, New Brunswick (NJ)
Saginaw Valley State U (MI)
St. Ambrose U (IA)
St. Cloud State U (MN)
St. Francis Xavier U (NS, Canada)
St. John Fisher Coll (NY)
St. John's Coll (NM)
Saint John's U (MN)
St. John's U (NY)
Saint Joseph's U (PA)
St. Lawrence U (NY)
Saint Louis U (MO)
Saint Mary's Coll of California (CA)
St. Mary's Coll of Maryland (MD)
St. Mary's U (TX)
Saint Michael's Coll (VT)
St. Norbert Coll (WI)
St. Olaf Coll (MN)
Saint Vincent Coll (PA)
Salisbury U (MD)
Samford U (AL)
Sam Houston State U (TX)
San Diego State U (CA)
San Francisco State U (CA)
Santa Clara U (CA)
Sarah Lawrence Coll (NY)
Scripps Coll (CA)
Seattle Pacific U (WA)
Seattle U (WA)
Seton Hill U (PA)
Sewanee: The U of the South (TN)
Shaw U (NC)
Shippensburg U of Pennsylvania (PA)
Siena Coll (NY)
Simon Fraser U (BC, Canada)
Skidmore Coll (NY)
Slippery Rock U of Pennsylvania (PA)
Smith Coll (MA)
Sonoma State U (CA)
South Carolina State U (SC)
South Dakota School of Mines and Technology (SD)
South Dakota State U (SD)
Southeastern Louisiana U (LA)
Southeast Missouri State U (MO)
Southern Adventist U (TN)
Southern Connecticut State U (CT)
Southern Illinois U Carbondale (IL)
Southern Illinois U Edwardsville (IL)
Southern Methodist U (TX)
Southern Oregon U (OR)
Southern Polytechnic State U (GA)
Southern U and Ag and Mech Coll (LA)
Southwestern Coll (KS)
Southwestern Oklahoma State U (OK)
Southwestern U (TX)
Spelman Coll (GA)
Spring Arbor U (MI)
Stanford U (CA)
State U of New York at Binghamton (NY)
State U of New York at Fredonia (NY)
State U of New York at New Paltz (NY)
State U of New York at Oswego (NY)
State U of New York at Plattsburgh (NY)
State U of New York Coll at Geneseo (NY)
State U of New York Coll at Oneonta (NY)
State U of New York Coll at Potsdam (NY)
Stephen F. Austin State U (TX)
Stetson U (FL)
Stony Brook U, State U of New York (NY)
Suffolk U (MA)
Susquehanna U (PA)
Swarthmore Coll (PA)
Sweet Briar Coll (VA)
Syracuse U (NY)
Tarleton State U (TX)
Taylor U (IN)
Temple U (PA)
Tennessee State U (TN)
Tennessee Technological U (TN)
Texas A&M U (TX)
Texas A&M U–Commerce (TX)
Texas Christian U (TX)
Texas Lutheran U (TX)
Texas Southern U (TX)
Texas State U-San Marcos (TX)
Texas Tech U (TX)
Thiel Coll (PA)
Thomas More Coll (KY)
Thompson Rivers U (BC, Canada)
Tougaloo Coll (MS)

Towson U (MD)
Transylvania U (KY)
Trent U (ON, Canada)
Trevecca Nazarene U (TN)
Trinity Coll (CT)
Trinity U (TX)
Truman State U (MO)
Tufts U (MA)
Tulane U (LA)
Tuskegee U (AL)
Union Coll (NE)
Union Coll (NY)
Union U (TN)
United States Air Force Acad (CO)
United States Naval Acad (MD)
Université de Sherbrooke (QC, Canada)
U at Albany, State U of New York (NY)
U at Buffalo, the State U of New York (NY)
The U of Akron (OH)
The U of Alabama (AL)
The U of Alabama at Birmingham (AL)
The U of Alabama in Huntsville (AL)
U of Alaska Fairbanks (AK)
The U of Arizona (AZ)
U of Arkansas (AR)
U of Arkansas at Pine Bluff (AR)
The U of British Columbia (BC, Canada)
The U of British Columbia–Okanagan (BC, Canada)
U of California, Berkeley (CA)
U of California, Davis (CA)
U of California, Irvine (CA)
U of California, Los Angeles (CA)
U of California, Riverside (CA)
U of California, San Diego (CA)
U of California, Santa Barbara (CA)
U of California, Santa Cruz (CA)
U of Central Arkansas (AR)
U of Central Florida (FL)
U of Central Missouri (MO)
U of Central Oklahoma (OK)
U of Chicago (IL)
U of Cincinnati (OH)
U of Colorado at Boulder (CO)
U of Colorado Denver (CO)
U of Connecticut (CT)
U of Dallas (TX)
U of Dayton (OH)
U of Delaware (DE)
U of Denver (CO)
U of Evansville (IN)
U of Florida (FL)
U of Georgia (GA)
U of Hartford (CT)
U of Hawaii at Manoa (HI)
U of Houston (TX)
U of Idaho (ID)
U of Illinois at Chicago (IL)
U of Illinois at Urbana–Champaign (IL)
U of Indianapolis (IN)
The U of Iowa (IA)
U of Kansas (KS)
U of King's Coll (NS, Canada)
U of La Verne (CA)
U of Lethbridge (AB, Canada)
U of Louisiana at Lafayette (LA)
U of Louisville (KY)
U of Maine (ME)
U of Maryland, Baltimore County (MD)
U of Maryland, Coll Park (MD)
U of Mary Washington (VA)
U of Massachusetts Amherst (MA)
U of Massachusetts Boston (MA)
U of Massachusetts Dartmouth (MA)
U of Massachusetts Lowell (MA)
U of Memphis (TN)
U of Miami (FL)
U of Michigan–Dearborn (MI)
U of Michigan–Flint (MI)
U of Minnesota, Duluth (MN)
U of Minnesota, Twin Cities Campus (MN)
U of Mississippi (MS)
U of Missouri–Columbia (MO)
U of Missouri–Kansas City (MO)
U of Missouri–St. Louis (MO)
The U of Montana (MT)
U of Nebraska at Kearney (NE)
U of Nebraska at Omaha (NE)
U of Nebraska–Lincoln (NE)
U of Nevada, Las Vegas (NV)
U of Nevada, Reno (NV)
U of New Brunswick Fredericton (NB, Canada)
U of New Hampshire (NH)
U of New Mexico (NM)
U of New Orleans (LA)
U of North Alabama (AL)
The U of North Carolina at Asheville (NC)
The U of North Carolina at Chapel Hill (NC)
The U of North Carolina at Charlotte (NC)
The U of North Carolina at Greensboro (NC)
The U of North Carolina at Pembroke (NC)
The U of North Carolina Wilmington (NC)
U of North Dakota (ND)
U of Northern Colorado (CO)
U of North Florida (FL)
U of North Texas (TX)
U of Notre Dame (IN)
U of Oklahoma (OK)
U of Oregon (OR)
U of Ottawa (ON, Canada)
U of Pennsylvania (PA)
U of Pittsburgh (PA)
U of Portland (OR)
U of Prince Edward Island (PE, Canada)
U of Puerto Rico at Humacao (PR)
U of Puget Sound (WA)
U of Redlands (CA)
U of Regina (SK, Canada)
U of Rhode Island (RI)
U of Richmond (VA)
U of Rochester (NY)
U of St. Thomas (MN)
U of San Diego (CA)
U of Science and Arts of Oklahoma (OK)
The U of Scranton (PA)
U of South Alabama (AL)
U of South Carolina (SC)
The U of South Dakota (SD)
U of Southern California (CA)
U of Southern Maine (ME)
U of Southern Mississippi (MS)
U of South Florida (FL)
The U of Tennessee (TN)
The U of Tennessee at Chattanooga (TN)
The U of Texas at Arlington (TX)
The U of Texas at Austin (TX)
The U of Texas at Brownsville (TX)
The U of Texas at Dallas (TX)
The U of Texas at El Paso (TX)
The U of Texas at San Antonio (TX)
The U of Texas–Pan American (TX)
U of the District of Columbia (DC)
U of the Pacific (CA)
The U of Toledo (OH)
U of Toronto (ON, Canada)
U of Tulsa (OK)
U of Utah (UT)
U of Vermont (VT)
U of Victoria (BC, Canada)
U of Virginia (VA)
The U of Western Ontario (ON, Canada)
U of West Florida (FL)
U of West Georgia (GA)
U of Windsor (ON, Canada)
The U of Winnipeg (MB, Canada)
U of Wisconsin–Eau Claire (WI)
U of Wisconsin–La Crosse (WI)
U of Wisconsin–Milwaukee (WI)
U of Wisconsin–Oshkosh (WI)
U of Wisconsin–Parkside (WI)
U of Wisconsin–Stevens Point (WI)
U of Wisconsin–Whitewater (WI)
U of Wyoming (WY)
Ursinus Coll (PA)
Utah State U (UT)
Utah Valley State Coll (UT)
Utica Coll (NY)
Valdosta State U (GA)
Valparaiso U (IN)
Vanderbilt U (TN)
Vassar Coll (NY)
Villanova U (PA)
Virginia Commonwealth U (VA)
Virginia Military Inst (VA)
Virginia Polytechnic Inst and State U (VA)
Virginia State U (VA)
Wabash Coll (IN)
Wagner Coll (NY)
Wake Forest U (NC)
Walla Walla U (WA)
Wartburg Coll (IA)
Washburn U (KS)
Washington & Jefferson Coll (PA)
Washington and Lee U (VA)
Washington Coll (MD)
Washington State U (WA)
Washington U in St. Louis (MO)
Wayne State U (MI)
Weber State U (UT)
Wellesley Coll (MA)
Wells Coll (NY)
Wesleyan Coll (GA)
Wesleyan U (CT)
West Chester U of Pennsylvania (PA)
Western Illinois U (IL)
Western Kentucky U (KY)
Western Michigan U (MI)
Western State Coll of Colorado (CO)
Western Washington U (WA)
Westminster Coll (MO)
Westminster Coll (UT)
Westmont Coll (CA)
West Texas A&M U (TX)
West Virginia U (WV)
West Virginia Wesleyan Coll (WV)
Wheaton Coll (IL)
Wheaton Coll (MA)
Wheeling Jesuit U (WV)
Whitman Coll (WA)
Whittier Coll (CA)
Whitworth U (WA)
Wichita State U (KS)
Widener U (PA)
Wiley Coll (TX)
Wilfrid Laurier U (ON, Canada)
Willamette U (OR)
William Jewell Coll (MO)
Williams Coll (MA)
Winona State U (MN)
Wittenberg U (OH)
Wofford Coll (SC)
Worcester Polytechnic Inst (MA)
Xavier U (OH)
Xavier U of Louisiana (LA)
Yale U (CT)
York Coll of the City U of New York (NY)
York U (ON, Canada)
Youngstown State U (OH)

PHYSICS RELATED

Angelo State U (TX)
Bridgewater Coll (VA)
Bridgewater State Coll (MA)
Brigham Young U (UT)
California State U, Chico (CA)
Carnegie Mellon U (PA)
Carson-Newman Coll (TN)
The Coll at Brockport, State U of New York (NY)
Drexel U (PA)
Embry-Riddle Aeronautical U (AZ)
Embry-Riddle Aeronautical U (FL)
Hampden-Sydney Coll (VA)
Indiana U of Pennsylvania (PA)
Lawrence Technological U (MI)
Linfield Coll (OR)
New Jersey Inst of Technology (NJ)
North Carolina State U (NC)
Northern Arizona U (AZ)
Ohio Northern U (OH)
Ohio U (OH)
Presbyterian Coll (SC)
Rutgers, The State U of New Jersey, Newark (NJ)
Spring Arbor U (MI)
State U of New York at Binghamton (NY)
U at Buffalo, the State U of New York (NY)
U of Alaska Fairbanks (AK)
U of California, Davis (CA)
U of Nevada, Las Vegas (NV)
U of Northern Iowa (IA)
U of North Texas (TX)
U of Notre Dame (IN)
U of Ottawa (ON, Canada)
U of Puerto Rico at Utuado (PR)
U of Regina (SK, Canada)
U of Rochester (NY)
The U of Western Ontario (ON, Canada)
Whitman Coll (WA)
Wright State U (OH)

PHYSICS TEACHER EDUCATION

Alma Coll (MI)
Appalachian State U (NC)
Arkansas State U (AR)
Auburn U (AL)
Baylor U (TX)
Bethel U (MN)
Bethune-Cookman U (FL)
Bishop's U (QC, Canada)
Bridgewater Coll (VA)
Brigham Young U (UT)
Cedarville U (OH)
Centenary Coll of Louisiana (LA)
Central Michigan U (MI)
Christian Brothers U (TN)
City Coll of the City U of New York (NY)
The Coll at Brockport, State U of New York (NY)
The Coll of New Jersey (NJ)
Colorado State U (CO)
Concordia Coll (MN)
Concordia U (MI)
Concordia U, Nebraska (NE)
Connecticut Coll (CT)
Cornell U (NY)
DePaul U (IL)
East Central U (OK)
Eastern Mennonite U (VA)
Eastern Michigan U (MI)
Florida Inst of Technology (FL)
Grambling State U (LA)
Greenville Coll (IL)
Gustavus Adolphus Coll (MN)
Hastings Coll (NE)
Hofstra U (NY)
Hope Coll (MI)
Husson Coll (ME)
Indiana U Bloomington (IN)
Indiana U–Purdue U Fort Wayne (IN)
Indiana U South Bend (IN)
Ithaca Coll (NY)
Juniata Coll (PA)
King Coll (TN)
Kutztown U of Pennsylvania (PA)
Le Moyne Coll (NY)
Lincoln U (MO)
Lipscomb U (TN)
Mansfield U of Pennsylvania (PA)
Maryville Coll (TN)
Mayville State U (ND)
McGill U (QC, Canada)
Miami U Hamilton (OH)
Minot State U (ND)
Missouri State U (MO)
Moravian Coll (PA)
Mount Vernon Nazarene U (OH)
Murray State U (KY)
New York Inst of Technology (NY)
New York U (NY)
North Carolina Central U (NC)
North Carolina State U (NC)
North Dakota State U (ND)
Northeastern State U (OK)
Northern Arizona U (AZ)
Northern Michigan U (MI)
Northwestern State U of Louisiana (LA)
Ohio Dominican U (OH)
Ohio Northern U (OH)
Ohio Wesleyan U (OH)
Old Dominion U (VA)
Pace U (NY)
Pittsburg State U (KS)
Purdue U (IN)
Queens Coll of the City U of New York (NY)
Rhode Island Coll (RI)
Roberts Wesleyan Coll (NY)
Saginaw Valley State U (MI)
St. Ambrose U (IA)
St. John's U (NY)
Saint Mary's U of Minnesota (MN)
Saint Vincent Coll (PA)
Shawnee State U (OH)
Southern Arkansas U–Magnolia (AR)
Southern U and Ag and Mech Coll (LA)
State U of New York Coll at Oneonta (NY)
State U of New York Coll at Potsdam (NY)
Syracuse U (NY)
Union Coll (NE)
The U of Arizona (AZ)
U of California, San Diego (CA)
U of Central Missouri (MO)
U of Delaware (DE)
U of Evansville (IN)
U of Illinois at Chicago (IL)
U of Illinois at Urbana–Champaign (IL)
The U of Iowa (IA)
U of Louisiana at Lafayette (LA)
U of Louisiana at Monroe (LA)
U of Maryland, Baltimore County (MD)
U of Michigan–Flint (MI)
U of Missouri–Columbia (MO)
U of Missouri–St. Louis (MO)
U of Nebraska–Lincoln (NE)
U of Regina (SK, Canada)
U of Rio Grande (OH)
U of St. Thomas (MN)
The U of South Dakota (SD)
U of West Georgia (GA)
U of Windsor (ON, Canada)
Utah State U (UT)
Utica Coll (NY)
Valparaiso U (IN)
Washington U in St. Louis (MO)
Weber State U (UT)
Western Michigan U (MI)
Wheeling Jesuit U (WV)
William Jewell Coll (MO)
Xavier U (OH)
York U (ON, Canada)

PHYSIOLOGICAL PSYCHOLOGY/ PSYCHOBIOLOGY

Albright Coll (PA)
Averett U (VA)
Centre Coll (KY)
Claremont McKenna Coll (CA)
Earlham Coll (IN)
Florida Atlantic U (FL)
Grand Valley State U (MI)
Hamilton Coll (NY)
Harvard U (MA)
Holy Family U (PA)
Holy Names U (CA)
Hope Intl U (CA)
The Johns Hopkins U (MD)
La Sierra U (CA)
Lebanon Valley Coll (PA)
Lincoln U (PA)
Medaille Coll (NY)
Mills Coll (CA)
Mount Allison U (NB, Canada)
Oberlin Coll (OH)
Occidental Coll (CA)
Quinnipiac U (CT)
Ripon Coll (WI)
Saint Mary's Coll of California (CA)
Scripps Coll (CA)
Simmons Coll (MA)
State U of New York at Binghamton (NY)
Swarthmore Coll (PA)
U of California, Los Angeles (CA)
U of California, Riverside (CA)
U of Colorado Denver (CO)
U of New Brunswick Fredericton (NB, Canada)
U of New England (ME)
The U of Western Ontario (ON, Canada)
Vassar Coll (NY)
Washington Coll (MD)
Wheaton Coll (MA)
Wilson Coll (PA)
York Coll (NE)

PHYSIOLOGY

Brigham Young U (UT)
California State U, Long Beach (CA)
McGill U (QC, Canada)
Michigan State U (MI)
Northern Michigan U (MI)
Oklahoma State U (OK)
Southern Illinois U Carbondale (IL)
The U of Arizona (AZ)
The U of British Columbia (BC, Canada)
U of California, Los Angeles (CA)
U of California, Santa Barbara (CA)
U of Colorado at Boulder (CO)
U of Illinois at Urbana–Champaign (IL)
U of Oregon (OR)
U of Ottawa (ON, Canada)

PIANO AND ORGAN

Abilene Christian U (TX)
Acadia U (NS, Canada)
Andrews U (MI)
Augustana Coll (IL)
Baldwin-Wallace Coll (OH)
Ball State U (IN)
Baptist Bible Coll of Pennsylvania (PA)
Barry U (FL)
Belmont U (TN)
Bennington Coll (VT)
Berklee Coll of Music (MA)
Bob Jones U (SC)
The Boston Conservatory (MA)
Boston U (MA)
Bowling Green State U (OH)
Brigham Young U (UT)
Bryan Coll (TN)
Butler U (IN)
California Inst of the Arts (CA)
California State U, Chico (CA)
Calvin Coll (MI)
Canadian Mennonite U (MB, Canada)
Capital U (OH)
Carnegie Mellon U (PA)
Carson-Newman Coll (TN)
Catawba Coll (NC)
The Catholic U of America (DC)
Cedarville U (OH)
Centenary Coll of Louisiana (LA)
Central Washington U (WA)
Coker Coll (SC)
The Colburn School Conservatory of Music (CA)
Columbia Coll (SC)
Concordia U Chicago (IL)
Concordia U, Nebraska (NE)
Converse Coll (SC)
Dallas Baptist U (TX)
Dordt Coll (IA)

Drake U (IA)
East Central U (OK)
East Texas Baptist U (TX)
Florida State U (FL)
Furman U (SC)
Grace U (NE)
Grand Valley State U (MI)
Hannibal-LaGrange Coll (MO)
Hardin-Simmons U (TX)
Hastings Coll (NE)
Heidelberg Coll (OH)
Hillsdale Free Will Baptist Coll (OK)
Hope Coll (MI)
Houghton Coll (NY)
Howard Payne U (TX)
Huntington U (IN)
Illinois Wesleyan U (IL)
Indiana U–Purdue U Fort Wayne (IN)
Inter American U of Puerto Rico, San Germán Campus (PR)
Ithaca Coll (NY)
Kent State U (OH)
Lawrence U (WI)
Lee U (TN)
Lipscomb U (TN)
Louisiana Coll (LA)
Loyola U New Orleans (LA)
Manhattan School of Music (NY)
Mannes Coll The New School for Music (NY)
Maranatha Baptist Bible Coll (WI)
Maryville Coll (TN)
The Master's Coll and Sem (CA)
McGill U (QC, Canada)
Memorial U of Newfoundland (NL, Canada)
Millikin U (IL)
Minnesota State U Mankato (MN)
Mississippi Coll (MS)
Mount Allison U (NB, Canada)
New England Conservatory of Music (MA)
The New School for Jazz and Contemporary Music (NY)
New York U (NY)
North Carolina School of the Arts (NC)
North Greenville U (SC)
Northwestern Coll (MN)
Northwestern U (IL)
Northwest Missouri State U (MO)
Notre Dame de Namur U (CA)
Nyack Coll (NY)
Oakland U (MI)
Oberlin Coll (OH)
Ohio U (OH)
Oklahoma City U (OK)
Oral Roberts U (OK)
Otterbein Coll (OH)
Ouachita Baptist U (AR)
Pacific Union Coll (CA)
Palm Beach Atlantic U (FL)
Peabody Conservatory of Music of The Johns Hopkins U (MD)
Prairie View A&M U (TX)
Queens U of Charlotte (NC)
Rider U (NJ)
Roberts Wesleyan Coll (NY)
Roosevelt U (IL)
St. Cloud State U (MN)
Samford U (AL)
Sarah Lawrence Coll (NY)
Seton Hill U (PA)
Shenandoah U (VA)
Shorter Coll (GA)
Southeastern U (FL)
Southern Methodist U (TX)
Southwestern Oklahoma State U (OK)
Spring Arbor U (MI)
State U of New York at Fredonia (NY)
Stetson U (FL)
Susquehanna U (PA)
Tabor Coll (KS)
Taylor U (IN)
Texas A&M U–Commerce (TX)
Texas Christian U (TX)
Texas Southern U (TX)
Trinity Christian Coll (IL)
Truman State U (MO)
Union U (TN)
The U of Akron (OH)
The U of British Columbia (BC, Canada)
U of Central Oklahoma (OK)
U of Cincinnati (OH)
U of Delaware (DE)
The U of Iowa (IA)
U of Kansas (KS)
U of Miami (FL)
U of Michigan (MI)
U of New Hampshire (NH)
U of Oklahoma (OK)
U of Redlands (CA)
The U of Tennessee at Martin (TN)
U of the Pacific (CA)
U of Tulsa (OK)
U of Victoria (BC, Canada)
The U of Western Ontario (ON, Canada)
Valparaiso U (IN)
Vanderbilt U (TN)
Walla Walla U (WA)
Weber State U (UT)
West Chester U of Pennsylvania (PA)
Whitworth U (WA)
Willamette U (OR)
Xavier U of Louisiana (LA)
York U (ON, Canada)

PLANETARY ASTRONOMY AND SCIENCE

California Inst of Technology (CA)
McGill U (QC, Canada)
The U of Western Ontario (ON, Canada)

PLANT GENETICS

Brigham Young U (UT)
Purdue U (IN)

PLANT MOLECULAR BIOLOGY

Pittsburg State U (KS)
U of Illinois at Urbana–Champaign (IL)

PLANT PATHOLOGY/ PHYTOPATHOLOGY

Auburn U (AL)
Cornell U (NY)
Michigan State U (MI)
State U of New York Coll of Environmental Science and Forestry (NY)
U of Florida (FL)

PLANT PHYSIOLOGY

Florida State U (FL)
Pittsburg State U (KS)
State U of New York Coll of Environmental Science and Forestry (NY)

PLANT PROTECTION

U of Hawaii at Manoa (HI)

PLANT PROTECTION AND INTEGRATED PEST MANAGEMENT

California State Polytechnic U, Pomona (CA)
Florida Ag and Mech U (FL)
Iowa State U of Science and Technology (IA)
Lubbock Christian U (TX)
Mississippi State U (MS)
North Dakota State U (ND)
State U of New York Coll of Environmental Science and Forestry (NY)
Sterling Coll (VT)
Texas A&M U (TX)
Texas Tech U (TX)
U of Delaware (DE)
U of Georgia (GA)
U of Illinois at Urbana–Champaign (IL)
U of Nebraska–Lincoln (NE)
The U of Tennessee (TN)
Washington State U (WA)
West Texas A&M U (TX)

PLANT SCIENCES

Arkansas State U (AR)
Auburn U (AL)
California State U, Fresno (CA)
Colorado State U (CO)
Cornell U (NY)
Lakehead U (ON, Canada)
Louisiana State U and Ag and Mech Coll (LA)
Lubbock Christian U (TX)
McGill U (QC, Canada)
Middle Tennessee State U (TN)
Montana State U (MT)
Nova Scotia Ag Coll (NS, Canada)
Oklahoma State U (OK)
Rutgers, The State U of New Jersey, New Brunswick (NJ)
Southeast Missouri State U (MO)
Southern Illinois U Carbondale (IL)
State U of New York Coll of Agriculture and Technology at Cobleskill (NY)
State U of New York Coll of Environmental Science and Forestry (NY)
Sterling Coll (VT)
Tuskegee U (AL)
The U of Arizona (AZ)
U of California, Santa Cruz (CA)
U of Florida (FL)
U of Georgia (GA)
U of Louisiana at Lafayette (LA)
U of Maine (ME)
U of Maryland, Coll Park (MD)
U of Massachusetts Amherst (MA)
U of Minnesota, Twin Cities Campus (MN)
U of Missouri–Columbia (MO)
The U of Tennessee (TN)
U of Vermont (VT)
The U of Western Ontario (ON, Canada)
Utah State U (UT)

PLANT SCIENCES RELATED

Auburn U (AL)
Sterling Coll (VT)
U of Florida (FL)
U of Wyoming (WY)
Utah State U (UT)
West Virginia U (WV)

PLASTICS ENGINEERING TECHNOLOGY

Ball State U (IN)
Eastern Michigan U (MI)
Ferris State U (MI)
Pittsburg State U (KS)
Shawnee State U (OH)
Western Michigan U (MI)
Western Washington U (WA)

PLAYWRITING AND SCREENWRITING

Bard Coll (NY)
Bard Coll at Simon's Rock (MA)
Bennington Coll (VT)
Brigham Young U (UT)
Chapman U (CA)
Columbia Coll Chicago (IL)
Concordia U (QC, Canada)
DePaul U (IL)
Drexel U (PA)
Emerson Coll (MA)
Hampshire Coll (MA)
Loyola Marymount U (CA)
Metropolitan State U (MN)
New York U (NY)
Ohio U (OH)
Palm Beach Atlantic U (FL)
Purchase Coll, State U of New York (NY)
Sarah Lawrence Coll (NY)
U of Southern California (CA)
York U (ON, Canada)

POLISH

Madonna U (MI)
U of Illinois at Chicago (IL)

POLITICAL COMMUNICATION

Emerson Coll (MA)
Nebraska Wesleyan U (NE)
Western Kentucky U (KY)

POLITICAL SCIENCE AND GOVERNMENT

Abilene Christian U (TX)
Acadia U (NS, Canada)
Adams State Coll (CO)
Adelphi U (NY)
Agnes Scott Coll (GA)
Alabama Ag and Mech U (AL)
Alabama State U (AL)
Albertus Magnus Coll (CT)
Albion Coll (MI)
Albright Coll (PA)
Alcorn State U (MS)
Alderson-Broaddus Coll (WV)
Alfred U (NY)
Allegheny Coll (PA)
Alma Coll (MI)
Alvernia Coll (PA)
American Jewish U (CA)
American U (DC)
The American U of Athens (Greece)
American U of Beirut (Lebanon)
Amherst Coll (MA)
Anderson U (IN)
Andrews U (MI)
Angelo State U (TX)
Anna Maria Coll (MA)
Appalachian State U (NC)
Aquinas Coll (MI)
Arizona State U (AZ)
Arizona State U at the West campus (AZ)
Arkansas State U (AR)
Armstrong Atlantic State U (GA)
Ashland U (OH)
Assumption Coll (MA)
Athabasca U (AB, Canada)
Athens State U (AL)
Auburn U (AL)
Auburn U Montgomery (AL)
Augsburg Coll (MN)
Augustana Coll (IL)
Augustana Coll (SD)
Augusta State U (GA)
Austin Coll (TX)
Austin Peay State U (TN)
Averett U (VA)
Avila U (MO)
Azusa Pacific U (CA)
Baker U (KS)
Baldwin-Wallace Coll (OH)
Ball State U (IN)
Bard Coll (NY)
Bard Coll at Simon's Rock (MA)
Barnard Coll (NY)
Barry U (FL)
Barton Coll (NC)
Bates Coll (ME)
Baylor U (TX)
Bellarmine U (KY)
Belmont Abbey Coll (NC)
Belmont U (TN)
Beloit Coll (WI)
Bemidji State U (MN)
Benedictine Coll (KS)
Benedictine U (IL)
Bennington Coll (VT)
Berea Coll (KY)
Bernard M. Baruch Coll of the City U of New York (NY)
Berry Coll (GA)
Bethany Coll (KS)
Bethany Coll (WV)
Bethel U (MN)
Bethune-Cookman U (FL)
Bishop's U (QC, Canada)
Blackburn Coll (IL)
Bloomfield Coll (NJ)
Bloomsburg U of Pennsylvania (PA)
Bob Jones U (SC)
Boise State U (ID)
Boston Coll (MA)
Boston U (MA)
Bowdoin Coll (ME)
Bowling Green State U (OH)
Bradley U (IL)
Brenau U (GA)
Brewton-Parker Coll (GA)
Bridgewater Coll (VA)
Bridgewater State Coll (MA)
Brigham Young U (UT)
Brock U (ON, Canada)
Brown U (RI)
Bryan Coll (TN)
Bryn Mawr Coll (PA)
Bucknell U (PA)
Buffalo State Coll, State U of New York (NY)
Butler U (IN)
Cabrini Coll (PA)
California Baptist U (CA)
California Inst of Technology (CA)
California Lutheran U (CA)
California Polytechnic State U, San Luis Obispo (CA)
California State Polytechnic U, Pomona (CA)
California State U, Chico (CA)
California State U, Dominguez Hills (CA)
California State U, East Bay (CA)
California State U, Fresno (CA)
California State U, Fullerton (CA)
California State U, Long Beach (CA)
California State U, Los Angeles (CA)
California State U, Sacramento (CA)
California State U, San Bernardino (CA)
California State U, San Marcos (CA)
California State U, Stanislaus (CA)
Calumet Coll of Saint Joseph (IN)
Calvin Coll (MI)
Cameron U (OK)
Canadian Mennonite U (MB, Canada)
Canisius Coll (NY)
Capital U (OH)
Carlow U (PA)
Carnegie Mellon U (PA)
Carroll Coll (WI)
Carson-Newman Coll (TN)
Case Western Reserve U (OH)
Catawba Coll (NC)
The Catholic U of America (DC)
Cedar Crest Coll (PA)
Cedarville U (OH)
Centenary Coll (NJ)
Centenary Coll of Louisiana (LA)
Central Coll (IA)
Central Connecticut State U (CT)
Central Michigan U (MI)
Central State U (OH)
Central Washington U (WA)
Centre Coll (KY)
Chapman U (CA)
Chatham U (PA)
Chestnut Hill Coll (PA)
Cheyney U of Pennsylvania (PA)
Chicago State U (IL)
Christendom Coll (VA)
Christopher Newport U (VA)
The Citadel, The Military Coll of South Carolina (SC)
City Coll of the City U of New York (NY)
Claremont McKenna Coll (CA)
Clarion U of Pennsylvania (PA)
Clark Atlanta U (GA)
Clarkson U (NY)
Clark U (MA)
Clemson U (SC)
Cleveland State U (OH)
Coastal Carolina U (SC)
Coker Coll (SC)
Colby Coll (ME)
Colgate U (NY)
The Coll at Brockport, State U of New York (NY)
Coll of Charleston (SC)
The Coll of Idaho (ID)
The Coll of New Jersey (NJ)
The Coll of New Rochelle (NY)
Coll of Saint Benedict (MN)
The Coll of Saint Rose (NY)
Coll of Santa Fe (NM)
Coll of Staten Island of the City U of New York (NY)
Coll of the Holy Cross (MA)
Coll of the Ozarks (MO)
The Coll of William and Mary (VA)
The Colorado Coll (CO)
Colorado State U (CO)
Colorado State U-Pueblo (CO)
Columbia Coll (SC)
Columbus State U (GA)
Concordia Coll (MN)
Concordia U (CA)
Concordia U (QC, Canada)
Concordia U Chicago (IL)
Concord U (WV)
Connecticut Coll (CT)
Converse Coll (SC)
Cornell Coll (IA)
Cornell U (NY)
Cornerstone U (MI)
Creighton U (NE)
Curry Coll (MA)
Daemen Coll (NY)
Dallas Baptist U (TX)
Dartmouth Coll (NH)
Davidson Coll (NC)
Davis & Elkins Coll (WV)
Delta State U (MS)
Denison U (OH)
DePaul U (IL)
DePauw U (IN)
DeSales U (PA)
Dickinson Coll (PA)
Dillard U (LA)
Doane Coll (NE)
Dominican U (IL)
Dominican U of California (CA)
Dordt Coll (IA)
Dowling Coll (NY)
Drake U (IA)
Drew U (NJ)
Drury U (MO)
Duke U (NC)
Duquesne U (PA)
Earlham Coll (IN)
East Carolina U (NC)
East Central U (OK)
Eastern Connecticut State U (CT)
Eastern Illinois U (IL)
Eastern Kentucky U (KY)
Eastern Michigan U (MI)
Eastern New Mexico U (NM)
East Stroudsburg U of Pennsylvania (PA)
East Tennessee State U (TN)
Eckerd Coll (FL)
Edinboro U of Pennsylvania (PA)
Elizabethtown Coll (PA)
Elon U (NC)
Emmanuel Coll (MA)
Emory & Henry Coll (VA)
Emory U (GA)
Emporia State U (KS)
Eugene Lang Coll The New School for Liberal Arts (NY)
Evangel U (MO)
The Evergreen State Coll (WA)
Excelsior Coll (NY)
Fairfield U (CT)
Fairleigh Dickinson U, Coll at Florham (NJ)
Fairleigh Dickinson U, Metropolitan Campus (NJ)

Fairmont State U (WV)
Faulkner U (AL)
Fayetteville State U (NC)
Felician Coll (NJ)
Ferrum Coll (VA)
Fitchburg State Coll (MA)
Flagler Coll (FL)
Florida Ag and Mech U (FL)
Florida Atlantic U (FL)
Florida Gulf Coast U (FL)
Florida Intl U (FL)
Florida Memorial U (FL)
Florida Southern Coll (FL)
Florida State U (FL)
Fort Lewis Coll (CO)
Framingham State Coll (MA)
Franciscan U of Steubenville (OH)
Francis Marion U (SC)
Franklin & Marshall Coll (PA)
Franklin Coll (IN)
Fresno Pacific U (CA)
Frostburg State U (MD)
Furman U (SC)
Gannon U (PA)
Gardner-Webb U (NC)
George Mason U (VA)
Georgetown Coll (KY)
Georgetown U (DC)
The George Washington U (DC)
Georgia Coll & State U (GA)
Georgia Southern U (GA)
Georgia Southwestern State U (GA)
Georgia State U (GA)
Gettysburg Coll (PA)
Gonzaga U (WA)
Gordon Coll (MA)
Goucher Coll (MD)
Grambling State U (LA)
Grand Valley State U (MI)
Grand View Coll (IA)
Greensboro Coll (NC)
Greenville Coll (IL)
Grinnell Coll (IA)
Grove City Coll (PA)
Guilford Coll (NC)
Gustavus Adolphus Coll (MN)
Hamilton Coll (NY)
Hamline U (MN)
Hampden-Sydney Coll (VA)
Hampshire Coll (MA)
Hampton U (VA)
Hanover Coll (IN)
Harding U (AR)
Hardin-Simmons U (TX)
Hartwick Coll (NY)
Harvard U (MA)
Hastings Coll (NE)
Haverford Coll (PA)
Hawai'i Pacific U (HI)
Heidelberg Coll (OH)
Henderson State U (AR)
Hendrix Coll (AR)
High Point U (NC)
Hillsdale Coll (MI)
Hobart and William Smith Colls (NY)
Hofstra U (NY)
Hollins U (VA)
Hood Coll (MD)
Hope Coll (MI)
Houghton Coll (NY)
Houston Baptist U (TX)
Howard Payne U (TX)
Humboldt State U (CA)
Hunter Coll of the City U of New York (NY)
Huntingdon Coll (AL)
Huntington U (IN)
Huston-Tillotson U (TX)
Idaho State U (ID)
Illinois Coll (IL)
Illinois Inst of Technology (IL)
Illinois State U (IL)
Illinois Wesleyan U (IL)
Indiana State U (IN)
Indiana U Bloomington (IN)
Indiana U East (IN)
Indiana U Northwest (IN)
Indiana U of Pennsylvania (PA)
Indiana U–Purdue U Fort Wayne (IN)
Indiana U–Purdue U Indianapolis (IN)
Indiana U South Bend (IN)
Indiana U Southeast (IN)
Indiana Wesleyan U (IN)
Inter American U of Puerto Rico, San Germán Campus (PR)
Iona Coll (NY)
Iowa State U of Science and Technology (IA)
Ithaca Coll (NY)
Jackson State U (MS)
Jacksonville State U (AL)
Jacksonville U (FL)
James Madison U (VA)
Jamestown Coll (ND)
John Carroll U (OH)
The Johns Hopkins U (MD)
Johnson C. Smith U (NC)
Johnson State Coll (VT)
Juniata Coll (PA)
Kalamazoo Coll (MI)
Kansas State U (KS)
Kean U (NJ)
Kennesaw State U (GA)
Kent State U (OH)
Kentucky State U (KY)
Kentucky Wesleyan Coll (KY)
Kenyon Coll (OH)
King Coll (TN)
King's Coll (PA)
Knox Coll (IL)
Kutztown U of Pennsylvania (PA)
Lafayette Coll (PA)
LaGrange Coll (GA)
Lake Forest Coll (IL)
Lakehead U (ON, Canada)
Lake Superior State U (MI)
Lambuth U (TN)
Lander U (SC)
La Salle U (PA)
La Sierra U (CA)
Laurentian U (ON, Canada)
Lawrence U (WI)
Lebanon Valley Coll (PA)
Lehigh U (PA)
Lehman Coll of the City U of New York (NY)
Le Moyne Coll (NY)
LeMoyne-Owen Coll (TN)
Lenoir-Rhyne Coll (NC)
Lewis & Clark Coll (OR)
Lewis U (IL)
Liberty U (VA)
Lincoln U (MO)
Lincoln U (PA)
Lindenwood U (MO)
Linfield Coll (OR)
Lipscomb U (TN)
Livingstone Coll (NC)
Lock Haven U of Pennsylvania (PA)
Longwood U (VA)
Loras Coll (IA)
Louisiana State U and Ag and Mech Coll (LA)
Loyola Coll in Maryland (MD)
Loyola Marymount U (CA)
Loyola U Chicago (IL)
Loyola U New Orleans (LA)
Luther Coll (IA)
Lycoming Coll (PA)
Lynchburg Coll (VA)
Lyon Coll (AR)
Macalester Coll (MN)
Malone Coll (OH)
Manchester Coll (IN)
Manhattanville Coll (NY)
Mansfield U of Pennsylvania (PA)
Marian Coll (IN)
Marian Coll of Fond du Lac (WI)
Marietta Coll (OH)
Marist Coll (NY)
Marlboro Coll (VT)
Marquette U (WI)
Marshall U (WV)
Martin U (IN)
Mary Baldwin Coll (VA)
Marymount Manhattan Coll (NY)
Marymount U (VA)
Maryville Coll (TN)
Massachusetts Inst of Technology (MA)
The Master's Coll and Sem (CA)
McDaniel Coll (MD)
McGill U (QC, Canada)
McKendree U (IL)
McMurry U (TX)
McNeese State U (LA)
Memorial U of Newfoundland (NL, Canada)
Mercer U (GA)
Mercyhurst Coll (PA)
Meredith Coll (NC)
Merrimack Coll (MA)
Mesa State Coll (CO)
Messiah Coll (PA)
Methodist U (NC)
Miami U (OH)
Miami U Hamilton (OH)
Michigan State U (MI)
Middlebury Coll (VT)
Middle Tennessee State U (TN)
Midwestern State U (TX)
Miles Coll (AL)
Millersville U of Pennsylvania (PA)
Millikin U (IL)
Millsaps Coll (MS)
Mills Coll (CA)
Minnesota State U Mankato (MN)
Mississippi Coll (MS)
Mississippi State U (MS)
Mississippi U for Women (MS)
Mississippi Valley State U (MS)
Missouri Southern State U (MO)
Missouri State U (MO)
Missouri Valley Coll (MO)
Molloy Coll (NY)
Monmouth Coll (IL)
Monmouth U (NJ)
Montana State U (MT)
Montclair State U (NJ)
Moravian Coll (PA)
Morehead State U (KY)
Morehouse Coll (GA)
Morgan State U (MD)
Morningside Coll (IA)
Morris Coll (SC)
Mount Allison U (NB, Canada)
Mount Aloysius Coll (PA)
Mount Holyoke Coll (MA)
Mount Mercy Coll (IA)
Mount Saint Mary Coll (NY)
Mount St. Mary's Coll (CA)
Mount St. Mary's U (MD)
Mount Saint Vincent U (NS, Canada)
Muhlenberg Coll (PA)
Murray State U (KY)
Nazareth Coll of Rochester (NY)
Nebraska Wesleyan U (NE)
Neumann Coll (PA)
New Coll of Florida (FL)
New England Coll (NH)
New Jersey City U (NJ)
New Mexico Highlands U (NM)
New York Inst of Technology (NY)
New York U (NY)
Niagara U (NY)
Nicholls State U (LA)
North Carolina Ag and Tech State U (NC)
North Carolina Central U (NC)
North Carolina State U (NC)
North Carolina Wesleyan Coll (NC)
North Central Coll (IL)
North Dakota State U (ND)
Northeastern Illinois U (IL)
Northeastern State U (OK)
Northeastern U (MA)
Northern Arizona U (AZ)
Northern Illinois U (IL)
Northern Michigan U (MI)
Northern State U (SD)
North Georgia Coll & State U (GA)
Northwestern Coll (IA)
Northwestern Oklahoma State U (OK)
Northwestern State U of Louisiana (LA)
Northwestern U (IL)
Northwest Missouri State U (MO)
Northwest Nazarene U (ID)
Norwich U (VT)
Notre Dame de Namur U (CA)
Oakland U (MI)
Oberlin Coll (OH)
Occidental Coll (CA)
Oglethorpe U (GA)
Ohio Dominican U (OH)
Ohio Northern U (OH)
Ohio U (OH)
Ohio Wesleyan U (OH)
Oklahoma City U (OK)
Oklahoma State U (OK)
Oklahoma Wesleyan U (OK)
Old Dominion U (VA)
Oral Roberts U (OK)
Oregon State U (OR)
Otterbein Coll (OH)
Ouachita Baptist U (AR)
Pace U (NY)
Pacific Lutheran U (WA)
Pacific Union Coll (CA)
Pacific U (OR)
Palm Beach Atlantic U (FL)
Park U (MO)
Patrick Henry Coll (VA)
Penn State Abington (PA)
Penn State Altoona (PA)
Penn State Berks (PA)
Penn State Erie, The Behrend Coll (PA)
Penn State U Park (PA)
Pepperdine U, Malibu (CA)
Pfeiffer U (NC)
Piedmont Coll (GA)
Pittsburg State U (KS)
Pitzer Coll (CA)
Plymouth State U (NH)
Point Loma Nazarene U (CA)
Point Park U (PA)
Pomona Coll (CA)
Portland State U (OR)
Prairie View A&M U (TX)
Presbyterian Coll (SC)
Prescott Coll (AZ)
Princeton U (NJ)
Providence Coll (RI)
Purchase Coll, State U of New York (NY)
Purdue U (IN)
Purdue U Calumet (IN)
Queens Coll of the City U of New York (NY)
Queen's U at Kingston (ON, Canada)
Queens U of Charlotte (NC)
Quincy U (IL)
Quinnipiac U (CT)
Radford U (VA)
Ramapo Coll of New Jersey (NJ)
Randolph Coll (VA)
Randolph-Macon Coll (VA)
Redeemer U Coll (ON, Canada)
Reed Coll (OR)
Regent U (VA)
Regis Coll (MA)
Regis U (CO)
Rhode Island Coll (RI)
Rhodes Coll (TN)
Rice U (TX)
The Richard Stockton Coll of New Jersey (NJ)
Rider U (NJ)
Ripon Coll (WI)
Roanoke Coll (VA)
Rockford Coll (IL)
Rockhurst U (MO)
Roger Williams U (RI)
Rollins Coll (FL)
Roosevelt U (IL)
Rosemont Coll (PA)
Rowan U (NJ)
Russell Sage Coll (NY)
Rutgers, The State U of New Jersey, Camden (NJ)
Rutgers, The State U of New Jersey, Newark (NJ)
Rutgers, The State U of New Jersey, New Brunswick (NJ)
Saginaw Valley State U (MI)
St. Ambrose U (IA)
St. Andrews Presbyterian Coll (NC)
St. Cloud State U (MN)
St. Edward's U (TX)
Saint Francis U (PA)
St. Francis Xavier U (NS, Canada)
St. Gregory's U, Shawnee (OK)
St. John Fisher Coll (NY)
Saint John's U (MN)
St. John's U (NY)
Saint Joseph's Coll (IN)
St. Joseph's Coll, Suffolk Campus (NY)
Saint Joseph's U (PA)
St. Lawrence U (NY)
Saint Leo U (FL)
Saint Louis U (MO)
Saint Martin's U (WA)
Saint Mary's Coll (IN)
Saint Mary's Coll of California (CA)
St. Mary's Coll of Maryland (MD)
St. Mary's U (TX)
Saint Michael's Coll (VT)
St. Norbert Coll (WI)
St. Olaf Coll (MN)
St. Thomas U (FL)
St. Thomas U (NB, Canada)
Saint Vincent Coll (PA)
Saint Xavier U (IL)
Salem State Coll (MA)
Salisbury U (MD)
Salve Regina U (RI)
Samford U (AL)
Sam Houston State U (TX)
San Diego State U (CA)
San Francisco State U (CA)
Santa Clara U (CA)
Sarah Lawrence Coll (NY)
Schreiner U (TX)
Scripps Coll (CA)
Seattle Pacific U (WA)
Seattle U (WA)
Seton Hill U (PA)
Sewanee: The U of the South (TN)
Shaw U (NC)
Shenandoah U (VA)
Shepherd U (WV)
Shippensburg U of Pennsylvania (PA)
Siena Coll (NY)
Simmons Coll (MA)
Simon Fraser U (BC, Canada)
Simpson Coll (IA)
Skidmore Coll (NY)
Slippery Rock U of Pennsylvania (PA)
Smith Coll (MA)
Sonoma State U (CA)
South Carolina State U (SC)
South Dakota State U (SD)
Southeastern Louisiana U (LA)
Southeastern Oklahoma State U (OK)
Southeast Missouri State U (MO)
Southern Arkansas U–Magnolia (AR)
Southern Connecticut State U (CT)
Southern Illinois U Carbondale (IL)
Southern Illinois U Edwardsville (IL)
Southern Methodist U (TX)
Southern New Hampshire U (NH)
Southern Oregon U (OR)
Southern U and Ag and Mech Coll (LA)
Southern Utah U (UT)
Southwest Baptist U (MO)
Southwestern Oklahoma State U (OK)
Southwestern U (TX)
Southwest Minnesota State U (MN)
Spelman Coll (GA)
Spring Arbor U (MI)
Spring Hill Coll (AL)
Stanford U (CA)
State U of New York at Binghamton (NY)
State U of New York at Fredonia (NY)
State U of New York at New Paltz (NY)
State U of New York at Oswego (NY)
State U of New York at Plattsburgh (NY)
State U of New York Coll at Geneseo (NY)
State U of New York Coll at Oneonta (NY)
State U of New York Coll at Potsdam (NY)
Stephen F. Austin State U (TX)
Stetson U (FL)
Stonehill Coll (MA)
Stony Brook U, State U of New York (NY)
Suffolk U (MA)
Susquehanna U (PA)
Swarthmore Coll (PA)
Sweet Briar Coll (VA)
Syracuse U (NY)
Tarleton State U (TX)
Taylor U (IN)
Temple U (PA)
Tennessee State U (TN)
Tennessee Technological U (TN)
Texas A&M Intl U (TX)
Texas A&M U (TX)
Texas A&M U–Commerce (TX)
Texas Christian U (TX)
Texas Coll (TX)
Texas Lutheran U (TX)
Texas Southern U (TX)
Texas State U-San Marcos (TX)
Texas Tech U (TX)
Texas Woman's U (TX)
Thiel Coll (PA)
Thomas Edison State Coll (NJ)
Thomas U (GA)
Thompson Rivers U (BC, Canada)
Tougaloo Coll (MS)
Towson U (MD)
Transylvania U (KY)
Trent U (ON, Canada)
Trinity Coll (CT)
Trinity U (TX)
Troy U (AL)
Truman State U (MO)
Tufts U (MA)
Tulane U (LA)
Tuskegee U (AL)
Union Coll (NY)
Union U (TN)
United States Air Force Acad (CO)
United States Coast Guard Acad (CT)
United States Naval Acad (MD)
U at Albany, State U of New York (NY)
U at Buffalo, the State U of New York (NY)
The U of Alabama (AL)
The U of Alabama at Birmingham (AL)
The U of Alabama in Huntsville (AL)
U of Alaska Fairbanks (AK)
The U of Arizona (AZ)
U of Arkansas (AR)
U of Arkansas at Monticello (AR)
U of Arkansas at Pine Bluff (AR)
U of Baltimore (MD)
The U of British Columbia (BC, Canada)
The U of British Columbia–Okanagan (BC, Canada)
U of California, Berkeley (CA)
U of California, Davis (CA)
U of California, Irvine (CA)
U of California, Los Angeles (CA)
U of California, Riverside (CA)
U of California, San Diego (CA)
U of California, Santa Barbara (CA)
U of California, Santa Cruz (CA)
U of Central Arkansas (AR)
U of Central Florida (FL)
U of Central Missouri (MO)
U of Central Oklahoma (OK)
U of Chicago (IL)
U of Cincinnati (OH)
U of Colorado at Boulder (CO)
U of Colorado Denver (CO)

MAJORS AND MORE

U of Connecticut (CT)
U of Dallas (TX)
U of Dayton (OH)
U of Delaware (DE)
U of Denver (CO)
U of Evansville (IN)
The U of Findlay (OH)
U of Florida (FL)
U of Georgia (GA)
U of Great Falls (MT)
U of Guam (GU)
U of Hartford (CT)
U of Hawaii at Manoa (HI)
U of Hawaii–West Oahu (HI)
U of Houston (TX)
U of Houston–Clear Lake (TX)
U of Houston–Downtown (TX)
U of Idaho (ID)
U of Illinois at Chicago (IL)
U of Illinois at Springfield (IL)
U of Illinois at Urbana–Champaign (IL)
U of Indianapolis (IN)
The U of Iowa (IA)
U of Kansas (KS)
U of King's Coll (NS, Canada)
U of La Verne (CA)
U of Lethbridge (AB, Canada)
U of Louisiana at Lafayette (LA)
U of Louisiana at Monroe (LA)
U of Louisville (KY)
U of Maine (ME)
U of Maine at Farmington (ME)
U of Mary Hardin-Baylor (TX)
U of Maryland, Baltimore County (MD)
U of Maryland, Coll Park (MD)
U of Mary Washington (VA)
U of Massachusetts Amherst (MA)
U of Massachusetts Boston (MA)
U of Massachusetts Dartmouth (MA)
U of Massachusetts Lowell (MA)
U of Memphis (TN)
U of Miami (FL)
U of Michigan (MI)
U of Michigan–Dearborn (MI)
U of Michigan–Flint (MI)
U of Minnesota, Duluth (MN)
U of Minnesota, Twin Cities Campus (MN)
U of Mississippi (MS)
U of Missouri–Columbia (MO)
U of Missouri–Kansas City (MO)
U of Missouri–St. Louis (MO)
U of Montevallo (AL)
U of Nebraska at Kearney (NE)
U of Nebraska at Omaha (NE)
U of Nebraska–Lincoln (NE)
U of Nevada, Las Vegas (NV)
U of Nevada, Reno (NV)
U of New Brunswick Fredericton (NB, Canada)
U of New England (ME)
U of New Hampshire (NH)
U of New Haven (CT)
U of New Mexico (NM)
U of New Orleans (LA)
U of North Alabama (AL)
The U of North Carolina at Asheville (NC)
The U of North Carolina at Chapel Hill (NC)
The U of North Carolina at Charlotte (NC)
The U of North Carolina at Greensboro (NC)
The U of North Carolina at Pembroke (NC)
The U of North Carolina Wilmington (NC)
U of North Dakota (ND)
U of Northern Colorado (CO)
U of Northern Iowa (IA)
U of North Florida (FL)
U of North Texas (TX)
U of Notre Dame (IN)
U of Oklahoma (OK)
U of Oregon (OR)
U of Ottawa (ON, Canada)
U of Pennsylvania (PA)
U of Pittsburgh (PA)
U of Pittsburgh at Bradford (PA)
U of Pittsburgh at Johnstown (PA)
U of Portland (OR)
U of Prince Edward Island (PE, Canada)
U of Puerto Rico at Utuado (PR)
U of Puget Sound (WA)
U of Redlands (CA)
U of Regina (SK, Canada)
U of Rhode Island (RI)
U of Richmond (VA)
U of Rio Grande (OH)
U of Rochester (NY)
U of St. Francis (IL)
U of Saint Mary (KS)
U of St. Thomas (MN)
U of St. Thomas (TX)
U of San Diego (CA)
U of Science and Arts of Oklahoma (OK)
The U of Scranton (PA)
U of Sioux Falls (SD)
U of South Alabama (AL)
U of South Carolina (SC)
U of South Carolina Aiken (SC)
U of South Carolina Upstate (SC)
The U of South Dakota (SD)
U of Southern California (CA)
U of Southern Indiana (IN)
U of Southern Maine (ME)
U of Southern Mississippi (MS)
U of South Florida (FL)
The U of Tampa (FL)
The U of Tennessee (TN)
The U of Tennessee at Chattanooga (TN)
The U of Tennessee at Martin (TN)
The U of Texas at Arlington (TX)
The U of Texas at Austin (TX)
The U of Texas at Brownsville (TX)
The U of Texas at Dallas (TX)
The U of Texas at El Paso (TX)
The U of Texas at San Antonio (TX)
The U of Texas at Tyler (TX)
The U of Texas of the Permian Basin (TX)
The U of Texas–Pan American (TX)
U of the District of Columbia (DC)
U of the Incarnate Word (TX)
U of the Ozarks (AR)
U of the Pacific (CA)
The U of Toledo (OH)
U of Toronto (ON, Canada)
U of Tulsa (OK)
U of Utah (UT)
U of Vermont (VT)
U of Victoria (BC, Canada)
U of Virginia (VA)
The U of Virginia's Coll at Wise (VA)
The U of Western Ontario (ON, Canada)
U of West Florida (FL)
U of West Georgia (GA)
U of Windsor (ON, Canada)
The U of Winnipeg (MB, Canada)
U of Wisconsin–Eau Claire (WI)
U of Wisconsin–Green Bay (WI)
U of Wisconsin–La Crosse (WI)
U of Wisconsin–Madison (WI)
U of Wisconsin–Milwaukee (WI)
U of Wisconsin–Oshkosh (WI)
U of Wisconsin–Parkside (WI)
U of Wisconsin–Platteville (WI)
U of Wisconsin–Stevens Point (WI)
U of Wisconsin–Superior (WI)
U of Wisconsin–Whitewater (WI)
U of Wyoming (WY)
Ursinus Coll (PA)
Utah State U (UT)
Utah Valley State Coll (UT)
Utica Coll (NY)
Valdosta State U (GA)
Valparaiso U (IN)
Vanderbilt U (TN)
Vanguard U of Southern California (CA)
Vassar Coll (NY)
Villanova U (PA)
Virginia Commonwealth U (VA)
Virginia Intermont Coll (VA)
Virginia Polytechnic Inst and State U (VA)
Virginia State U (VA)
Virginia Wesleyan Coll (VA)
Voorhees Coll (SC)
Wabash Coll (IN)
Wagner Coll (NY)
Wake Forest U (NC)
Walsh U (OH)
Wartburg Coll (IA)
Washburn U (KS)
Washington & Jefferson Coll (PA)
Washington and Lee U (VA)
Washington Coll (MD)
Washington State U (WA)
Washington U in St. Louis (MO)
Wayland Baptist U (TX)
Wayne State Coll (NE)
Wayne State U (MI)
Weber State U (UT)
Webster U (MO)
Wellesley Coll (MA)
Wells Coll (NY)
Wesleyan Coll (GA)
Wesleyan U (CT)
Wesley Coll (DE)
West Chester U of Pennsylvania (PA)
Western Carolina U (NC)
Western Connecticut State U (CT)
Western Illinois U (IL)
Western Kentucky U (KY)
Western Michigan U (MI)
Western New England Coll (MA)
Western State Coll of Colorado (CO)
Western Washington U (WA)
Westfield State Coll (MA)
West Liberty State Coll (WV)
Westminster Coll (MO)
Westminster Coll (UT)
Westmont Coll (CA)
West Texas A&M U (TX)
West Virginia U (WV)
West Virginia Wesleyan Coll (WV)
Wheaton Coll (IL)
Wheaton Coll (MA)
Wheeling Jesuit U (WV)
Whitman Coll (WA)
Whittier Coll (CA)
Whitworth U (WA)
Wichita State U (KS)
Widener U (PA)
Wilfrid Laurier U (ON, Canada)
Wilkes U (PA)
Willamette U (OR)
William Jewell Coll (MO)
William Paterson U of New Jersey (NJ)
Williams Coll (MA)
William Woods U (MO)
Wilmington Coll (OH)
Winona State U (MN)
Winthrop U (SC)
Wittenberg U (OH)
Wofford Coll (SC)
Woodbury U (CA)
Wright State U (OH)
Xavier U (OH)
Xavier U of Louisiana (LA)
Yale U (CT)
York Coll of Pennsylvania (PA)
York Coll of the City U of New York (NY)
York U (ON, Canada)
Youngstown State U (OH)

POLITICAL SCIENCE AND GOVERNMENT RELATED

Brandeis U (MA)
Capital U (OH)
Claremont McKenna Coll (CA)
Monmouth Coll (IL)
Muhlenberg Coll (PA)
North Carolina State U (NC)
Peace Coll (NC)
Regis Coll (MA)
Saint Mary's Coll of California (CA)
Saint Mary's U of Minnesota (MN)
Southern Vermont Coll (VT)
U of California, Davis (CA)
U of California, Riverside (CA)
U of Northern Iowa (IA)
U of Saint Francis (IN)
Whitman Coll (WA)

POLYMER CHEMISTRY

Clemson U (SC)
Harvard U (MA)
Pittsburg State U (KS)
Rochester Inst of Technology (NY)
State U of New York Coll of Environmental Science and Forestry (NY)
The U of Akron (OH)
U of Wisconsin–Stevens Point (WI)
Winona State U (MN)

POLYMER/PLASTICS ENGINEERING

Ball State U (IN)
Case Western Reserve U (OH)
North Dakota State U (ND)
Penn State Erie, The Behrend Coll (PA)
The U of Akron (OH)
U of Illinois at Urbana–Champaign (IL)
U of Massachusetts Lowell (MA)
U of Southern California (CA)
Winona State U (MN)

PORTUGUESE

Brigham Young U (UT)
Florida Intl U (FL)
Georgetown U (DC)
Harvard U (MA)
Indiana U Bloomington (IN)
Marlboro Coll (VT)
New York U (NY)
Rutgers, The State U of New Jersey, New Brunswick (NJ)
Smith Coll (MA)
Stanford U (CA)
Tulane U (LA)
U of California, Los Angeles (CA)
U of California, Santa Barbara (CA)
U of Florida (FL)
U of Illinois at Urbana–Champaign (IL)
The U of Iowa (IA)
U of Massachusetts Amherst (MA)
U of Massachusetts Dartmouth (MA)
U of Minnesota, Twin Cities Campus (MN)
U of New Mexico (NM)
U of Southern California (CA)
The U of Texas at Austin (TX)
U of Toronto (ON, Canada)
U of Wisconsin–Madison (WI)
Vanderbilt U (TN)
Yale U (CT)

POULTRY SCIENCE

Auburn U (AL)
Mississippi State U (MS)
North Carolina State U (NC)
Stephen F. Austin State U (TX)
Texas A&M U (TX)
Tuskegee U (AL)
U of Arkansas (AR)
U of Florida (FL)
U of Georgia (GA)
U of Maryland Eastern Shore (MD)
U of Wisconsin–Madison (WI)
Virginia Polytechnic Inst and State U (VA)

PRE-DENTISTRY STUDIES

Abilene Christian U (TX)
Acadia U (NS, Canada)
Adams State Coll (CO)
Albertus Magnus Coll (CT)
Alderson-Broaddus Coll (WV)
Allegheny Coll (PA)
Alma Coll (MI)
Anderson U (IN)
Ashland U (OH)
Atlantic Union Coll (MA)
Auburn U (AL)
Augsburg Coll (MN)
Augustana Coll (IL)
Augustana Coll (SD)
Ball State U (IN)
Barry U (FL)
Baylor U (TX)
Belmont Abbey Coll (NC)
Beloit Coll (WI)
Benedictine U (IL)
Bethany Coll (WV)
Blackburn Coll (IL)
Boise State U (ID)
Boston U (MA)
Buffalo State Coll, State U of New York (NY)
California State U, Chico (CA)
California State U, Dominguez Hills (CA)
California State U, East Bay (CA)
Calvin Coll (MI)
Capital U (OH)
Carroll Coll (WI)
Catawba Coll (NC)
Cedar Crest Coll (PA)
Cedarville U (OH)
Centenary Coll of Louisiana (LA)
Central Christian Coll of Kansas (KS)
City Coll of the City U of New York (NY)
Claremont McKenna Coll (CA)
Clarkson U (NY)
Clark U (MA)
The Coll at Brockport, State U of New York (NY)
Coll of Charleston (SC)
Coll of Mount Saint Vincent (NY)
Coll of Saint Benedict (MN)
Coll of Saint Mary (NE)
Concordia Coll (MN)
Concordia U Chicago (IL)
Concordia U, Nebraska (NE)
Cornerstone U (MI)
Davis & Elkins Coll (WV)
Defiance Coll (OH)
DeSales U (PA)
Dickinson Coll (PA)
Dominican U (IL)
Dordt Coll (IA)
Drake U (IA)
Drury U (MO)
East Central U (OK)
Eastern Mennonite U (VA)
Elizabethtown Coll (PA)
Elon U (NC)
Emory & Henry Coll (VA)
Evangel U (MO)
Florida Ag and Mech U (FL)
Florida Southern Coll (FL)
Florida State U (FL)
Furman U (SC)
Gardner-Webb U (NC)
The George Washington U (DC)
Georgia Southern U (GA)
Gettysburg Coll (PA)
Grand Valley State U (MI)
Grove City Coll (PA)
Gustavus Adolphus Coll (MN)
Hamline U (MN)
Hampton U (VA)
Harding U (AR)
Hardin-Simmons U (TX)
Harvard U (MA)
Hastings Coll (NE)
Heidelberg Coll (OH)
High Point U (NC)
Hillsdale Coll (MI)
Hobart and William Smith Colls (NY)
Hofstra U (NY)
Holy Family U (PA)
Houghton Coll (NY)
Humboldt State U (CA)
Huntington U (IN)
Illinois Coll (IL)
Immaculata U (PA)
Indiana U–Purdue U Fort Wayne (IN)
Indiana Wesleyan U (IN)
Iowa State U of Science and Technology (IA)
Iowa Wesleyan Coll (IA)
Jacksonville U (FL)
John Carroll U (OH)
Juniata Coll (PA)
Kansas State U (KS)
Kent State U (OH)
Kentucky Wesleyan Coll (KY)
Kenyon Coll (OH)
Keuka Coll (NY)
King's Coll (PA)
LaGrange Coll (GA)
Lake Superior State U (MI)
Lambuth U (TN)
La Salle U (PA)
La Sierra U (CA)
Lawrence U (WI)
Lehigh U (PA)
Le Moyne Coll (NY)
LeTourneau U (TX)
Lewis U (IL)
Limestone Coll (SC)
Lindenwood U (MO)
Lindsey Wilson Coll (KY)
Lipscomb U (TN)
Lock Haven U of Pennsylvania (PA)
Longwood U (VA)
Lycoming Coll (PA)
Lynchburg Coll (VA)
Manchester Coll (IN)
Marian Coll (IN)
Marquette U (WI)
Mayville State U (ND)
McKendree U (IL)
Mercer U (GA)
Mercyhurst Coll (PA)
Methodist U (NC)
Miami U (OH)
Michigan Technological U (MI)
Midland Lutheran Coll (NE)
Midwestern State U (TX)
Millikin U (IL)
Minnesota State U Mankato (MN)
Mississippi Coll (MS)
Missouri U of Science and Technology (MO)
Missouri Valley Coll (MO)
Molloy Coll (NY)
Morgan State U (MD)
Morningside Coll (IA)
Mount Allison U (NB, Canada)
Mount Mary Coll (WI)
Mount Mercy Coll (IA)
Mount Vernon Nazarene U (OH)
Nazareth Coll of Rochester (NY)
Newman U (KS)
New York U (NY)
Niagara U (NY)
North Central Coll (IL)
Northern Michigan U (MI)
Northern State U (SD)
North Georgia Coll & State U (GA)
Northland Coll (WI)
Northwestern Oklahoma State U (OK)
Northwest Missouri State U (MO)
Northwest Nazarene U (ID)
Notre Dame de Namur U (CA)
Oglethorpe U (GA)
Ohio Northern U (OH)
Ohio Wesleyan U (OH)
Oklahoma City U (OK)
Oklahoma Wesleyan U (OK)
Otterbein Coll (OH)
Ouachita Baptist U (AR)
Pacific Union Coll (CA)
Pacific U (OR)
Pepperdine U, Malibu (CA)
Peru State Coll (NE)
Pittsburg State U (KS)
Purdue U (IN)
Purdue U Calumet (IN)
Queens U of Charlotte (NC)
Quincy U (IL)
Quinnipiac U (CT)
Redeemer U Coll (ON, Canada)

MAJORS AND MORE

Regis U (CO)
Ripon Coll (WI)
Roberts Wesleyan Coll (NY)
Rochester Inst of Technology (NY)
Rockford Coll (IL)
Roger Williams U (RI)
Rollins Coll (FL)
Roosevelt U (IL)
Rutgers, The State U of New Jersey, New Brunswick (NJ)
Sacred Heart U (CT)
St. Cloud State U (MN)
Saint Francis U (PA)
St. Francis Xavier U (NS, Canada)
St. Gregory's U, Shawnee (OK)
Saint John's U (MN)
St. Joseph's Coll, Suffolk Campus (NY)
Saint Martin's U (WA)
Saint Mary-of-the-Woods Coll (IN)
St. Mary's U (TX)
Saint Michael's Coll (VT)
St. Thomas U (FL)
Salem State Coll (MA)
Sam Houston State U (TX)
Sarah Lawrence Coll (NY)
Schreiner U (TX)
Seattle Pacific U (WA)
Seton Hill U (PA)
Siena Coll (NY)
Simmons Coll (MA)
Simpson Coll (IA)
Sonoma State U (CA)
Southwestern Oklahoma State U (OK)
Southwest Minnesota State U (MN)
Spring Hill Coll (AL)
State U of New York at Oswego (NY)
State U of New York Coll at Geneseo (NY)
State U of New York Coll at Oneonta (NY)
State U of New York Coll of Environmental Science and Forestry (NY)
Stetson U (FL)
Susquehanna U (PA)
Tabor Coll (KS)
Tarleton State U (TX)
Taylor U (IN)
Tennessee Technological U (TN)
Texas Lutheran U (TX)
Texas Southern U (TX)
Thiel Coll (PA)
Thompson Rivers U (BC, Canada)
Tougaloo Coll (MS)
Trinity Christian Coll (IL)
Trinity U (TX)
Truman State U (MO)
Union U (TN)
U of Arkansas at Monticello (AR)
U of Bridgeport (CT)
The U of British Columbia (BC, Canada)
U of Central Missouri (MO)
U of Dallas (TX)
U of Dayton (OH)
U of Evansville (IN)
U of Hartford (CT)
U of Houston (TX)
U of Illinois at Chicago (IL)
U of Indianapolis (IN)
The U of Iowa (IA)
U of Maryland, Baltimore County (MD)
U of Maryland, Coll Park (MD)
U of Maryland Eastern Shore (MD)
U of Mary Washington (VA)
U of Massachusetts Amherst (MA)
U of Minnesota, Duluth (MN)
U of Minnesota, Twin Cities Campus (MN)
U of Missouri–St. Louis (MO)
The U of Montana–Western (MT)
U of Nebraska–Lincoln (NE)
U of New Brunswick Fredericton (NB, Canada)
U of New England (ME)
U of Pittsburgh at Johnstown (PA)
U of Portland (OR)
U of Prince Edward Island (PE, Canada)
U of Puget Sound (WA)
U of Regina (SK, Canada)
U of Rio Grande (OH)
U of St. Francis (IL)
U of St. Thomas (TX)
U of Sioux Falls (SD)
The U of Tampa (FL)
The U of Tennessee at Martin (TN)
The U of Toledo (OH)
U of Victoria (BC, Canada)
U of Windsor (ON, Canada)
The U of Winnipeg (MB, Canada)
U of Wisconsin–Milwaukee (WI)
U of Wisconsin–Oshkosh (WI)
U of Wisconsin–Parkside (WI)
Utah State U (UT)
Utica Coll (NY)
Valley City State U (ND)
Villa Julie Coll (MD)
Virginia Wesleyan Coll (VA)
Wagner Coll (NY)
Walla Walla U (WA)
Walsh U (OH)
Washburn U (KS)
Washington Coll (MD)
Washington U in St. Louis (MO)
Waynesburg U (PA)
Wells Coll (NY)
West Liberty State Coll (WV)
Westmont Coll (CA)
West Virginia Wesleyan Coll (WV)
Wheeling Jesuit U (WV)
Whitworth U (WA)
Widener U (PA)
Wiley Coll (TX)
William Paterson U of New Jersey (NJ)
Wilmington Coll (OH)
Winona State U (MN)
Wofford Coll (SC)
Wright State U (OH)
Xavier U of Louisiana (LA)
York U (ON, Canada)
Youngstown State U (OH)

PRE-ENGINEERING

Adams State Coll (CO)
Anderson U (SC)
Azusa Pacific U (CA)
Bethel Coll (TN)
Drake U (IA)
Eastern Mennonite U (VA)
Kutztown U of Pennsylvania (PA)
Lewis & Clark Coll (OR)
Lewis U (IL)
Midwestern State U (TX)
Newman U (KS)
Northwest Nazarene U (ID)
Ouachita Baptist U (AR)
Pittsburg State U (KS)
Roberts Wesleyan Coll (NY)
Scripps Coll (CA)
U of Georgia (GA)
The U of Montana (MT)
Valley City State U (ND)
Wagner Coll (NY)
Waynesburg U (PA)

PRE-LAW

Hawai'i Pacific U (HI)
Northwest Nazarene U (ID)
Pacific Lutheran U (WA)
U of California, Santa Cruz (CA)

PRE-LAW STUDIES

Abilene Christian U (TX)
Acadia U (NS, Canada)
Adams State Coll (CO)
Adrian Coll (MI)
Albertus Magnus Coll (CT)
Albion Coll (MI)
Albright Coll (PA)
Alderson-Broaddus Coll (WV)
Allegheny Coll (PA)
Alma Coll (MI)
Alvernia Coll (PA)
Anderson U (IN)
Andrews U (MI)
Aquinas Coll (MI)
Ashford U (IA)
Ashland U (OH)
Atlantic Union Coll (MA)
Auburn U (AL)
Augsburg Coll (MN)
Augustana Coll (IL)
Augustana Coll (SD)
Azusa Pacific U (CA)
Babson Coll (MA)
Ball State U (IN)
Bard Coll at Simon's Rock (MA)
Barnard Coll (NY)
Barry U (FL)
Baylor U (TX)
Bay Path Coll (MA)
Belmont Abbey Coll (NC)
Beloit Coll (WI)
Bemidji State U (MN)
Benedictine U (IL)
Bennington Coll (VT)
Bethany Coll (WV)
Biola U (CA)
Blackburn Coll (IL)
Bob Jones U (SC)
Bowling Green State U (OH)
Brewton-Parker Coll (GA)
Buffalo State Coll, State U of New York (NY)
California State Polytechnic U, Pomona (CA)
California State U, Dominguez Hills (CA)
California State U, Fresno (CA)
Calumet Coll of Saint Joseph (IN)
Calvin Coll (MI)
Catawba Coll (NC)
Cedar Crest Coll (PA)
Cedarville U (OH)
Centenary Coll of Louisiana (LA)
Central Christian Coll of Kansas (KS)
Christopher Newport U (VA)
City Coll of the City U of New York (NY)
Claremont McKenna Coll (CA)
Clarkson U (NY)
Clark U (MA)
Clearwater Christian Coll (FL)
The Coll at Brockport, State U of New York (NY)
Coll of Mount Saint Vincent (NY)
The Coll of New Jersey (NJ)
The Coll of New Rochelle (NY)
Coll of Saint Benedict (MN)
Coll of Saint Mary (NE)
Coll of the Ozarks (MO)
Concordia Coll (MN)
Concordia Coll–New York (NY)
Concordia U (MI)
Concordia U Chicago (IL)
Concordia U, Nebraska (NE)
Concordia U Wisconsin (WI)
Cornerstone U (MI)
Creighton U (NE)
Crown Coll (MN)
Curry Coll (MA)
Davis & Elkins Coll (WV)
Defiance Coll (OH)
Dominican Coll (NY)
Dominican U (IL)
Dordt Coll (IA)
Drake U (IA)
Drury U (MO)
East Central U (OK)
Eastern Mennonite U (VA)
Elizabethtown Coll (PA)
Elon U (NC)
Emmanuel Coll (GA)
Emory & Henry Coll (VA)
Evangel U (MO)
Faulkner U (AL)
Felician Coll (NJ)
Florida State U (FL)
Fontbonne U (MO)
Francis Marion U (SC)
Fresno Pacific U (CA)
Furman U (SC)
Gannon U (PA)
Gardner-Webb U (NC)
The George Washington U (DC)
Gettysburg Coll (PA)
Grambling State U (LA)
Grand Valley State U (MI)
Grand View Coll (IA)
Grove City Coll (PA)
Gustavus Adolphus Coll (MN)
Hamline U (MN)
Hampton U (VA)
Hannibal-LaGrange Coll (MO)
Hardin-Simmons U (TX)
Hartwick Coll (NY)
Harvard U (MA)
Hastings Coll (NE)
Haverford Coll (PA)
Heidelberg Coll (OH)
High Point U (NC)
Hobart and William Smith Colls (NY)
Hofstra U (NY)
Holy Family U (PA)
Houghton Coll (NY)
Houston Baptist U (TX)
Howard Payne U (TX)
Humboldt State U (CA)
Huntington U (IN)
Illinois Coll (IL)
Indiana Wesleyan U (IN)
Iowa State U of Science and Technology (IA)
Iowa Wesleyan Coll (IA)
Ithaca Coll (NY)
Jacksonville U (FL)
John Carroll U (OH)
Juniata Coll (PA)
Kentucky Wesleyan Coll (KY)
Kenyon Coll (OH)
Keuka Coll (NY)
King Coll (TN)
King's Coll (PA)
LaGrange Coll (GA)
Lake Superior State U (MI)
Lambuth U (TN)
La Sierra U (CA)
Lawrence U (WI)
Lees-McRae Coll (NC)
Le Moyne Coll (NY)
Lenoir-Rhyne Coll (NC)
LeTourneau U (TX)
Lewis U (IL)
Limestone Coll (SC)
Lindenwood U (MO)
Lindsey Wilson Coll (KY)
Lipscomb U (TN)
Longwood U (VA)
Louisiana Coll (LA)
Lubbock Christian U (TX)
Lycoming Coll (PA)
Lynchburg Coll (VA)
Manchester Coll (IN)
Mansfield U of Pennsylvania (PA)
Marian Coll (IN)
Marlboro Coll (VT)
Marquette U (WI)
The Master's Coll and Sem (CA)
Mayville State U (ND)
McKendree U (IL)
Medaille Coll (NY)
Mercyhurst Coll (PA)
Methodist U (NC)
Miami U (OH)
Michigan State U (MI)
Michigan Technological U (MI)
Midland Lutheran Coll (NE)
Midwestern State U (TX)
Millikin U (IL)
Minnesota State U Mankato (MN)
Mississippi Coll (MS)
Missouri U of Science and Technology (MO)
Missouri Valley Coll (MO)
Molloy Coll (NY)
Montana State U–Billings (MT)
Morgan State U (MD)
Morningside Coll (IA)
Mount Allison U (NB, Canada)
Mount Aloysius Coll (PA)
Mount Mary Coll (WI)
Mount Mercy Coll (IA)
Mount Saint Mary Coll (NY)
Mount Vernon Nazarene U (OH)
National American U, Rapid City (SD)
National U (CA)
Nazareth Coll of Rochester (NY)
New England Coll (NH)
Newman U (KS)
Niagara U (NY)
North Central Coll (IL)
Northern Arizona U (AZ)
Northern Michigan U (MI)
Northern State U (SD)
Northland Coll (WI)
Northwestern Oklahoma State U (OK)
Northwest Missouri State U (MO)
Northwest Nazarene U (ID)
Notre Dame de Namur U (CA)
Nova Southeastern U (FL)
Oakland City U (IN)
Oglethorpe U (GA)
Ohio Northern U (OH)
Ohio U (OH)
Ohio Wesleyan U (OH)
Oklahoma Christian U (OK)
Oklahoma City U (OK)
Oklahoma Wesleyan U (OK)
Otterbein Coll (OH)
Ouachita Baptist U (AR)
Pacific Union Coll (CA)
Palm Beach Atlantic U (FL)
Pepperdine U, Malibu (CA)
Peru State Coll (NE)
Pfeiffer U (NC)
Pittsburg State U (KS)
Purdue U Calumet (IN)
Queens U of Charlotte (NC)
Quinnipiac U (CT)
Redeemer U Coll (ON, Canada)
Regis U (CO)
Rensselaer Polytechnic Inst (NY)
Ripon Coll (WI)
Roberts Wesleyan Coll (NY)
Rochester Inst of Technology (NY)
Rockford Coll (IL)
Rollins Coll (FL)
Roosevelt U (IL)
Rutgers, The State U of New Jersey, New Brunswick (NJ)
St. Andrews Presbyterian Coll (NC)
St. Cloud State U (MN)
Saint Francis U (PA)
St. Francis Xavier U (NS, Canada)
St. Gregory's U, Shawnee (OK)
Saint John's U (MN)
St. Joseph's Coll, New York (NY)
St. Joseph's Coll, Suffolk Campus (NY)
Saint Martin's U (WA)
Saint Mary-of-the-Woods Coll (IN)
Saint Michael's Coll (VT)
St. Thomas U (FL)
Salem State Coll (MA)
Sam Houston State U (TX)
Sarah Lawrence Coll (NY)
Schreiner U (TX)
Seattle Pacific U (WA)
Seton Hill U (PA)
Shawnee State U (OH)
Siena Coll (NY)
Siena Heights U (MI)
Simmons Coll (MA)
Simpson Coll (IA)
Smith Coll (MA)
Sonoma State U (CA)
South Dakota State U (SD)
Southern Oregon U (OR)
Southern Vermont Coll (VT)
Southwestern Oklahoma State U (OK)
Southwest Minnesota State U (MN)
State U of New York at Binghamton (NY)
State U of New York at Fredonia (NY)
State U of New York at Oswego (NY)
State U of New York Coll at Geneseo (NY)
State U of New York Coll at Oneonta (NY)
State U of New York Coll of Environmental Science and Forestry (NY)
Stephens Coll (MO)
Stetson U (FL)
Suffolk U (MA)
Susquehanna U (PA)
Taylor U (IN)
Tennessee Technological U (TN)
Texas Lutheran U (TX)
Thiel Coll (PA)
Tiffin U (OH)
Toccoa Falls Coll (GA)
Trinity U (TX)
Tri-State U (IN)
Truman State U (MO)
Tusculum Coll (TN)
Union U (TN)
U of Arkansas at Monticello (AR)
U of Bridgeport (CT)
The U of British Columbia (BC, Canada)
U of California, Riverside (CA)
U of California, Santa Barbara (CA)
U of Cincinnati (OH)
U of Dallas (TX)
U of Dayton (OH)
The U of Findlay (OH)
U of Houston (TX)
U of Illinois at Chicago (IL)
U of Illinois at Urbana–Champaign (IL)
U of Indianapolis (IN)
The U of Iowa (IA)
U of Louisiana at Lafayette (LA)
U of Maryland, Coll Park (MD)
U of Maryland Eastern Shore (MD)
U of Mary Washington (VA)
U of Minnesota, Duluth (MN)
U of Minnesota, Twin Cities Campus (MN)
U of Missouri–St. Louis (MO)
The U of Montana (MT)
The U of Montana–Western (MT)
U of New Brunswick Fredericton (NB, Canada)
U of Pittsburgh at Johnstown (PA)
U of Portland (OR)
U of Puget Sound (WA)
U of Regina (SK, Canada)
U of Rio Grande (OH)
U of St. Thomas (TX)
U of Sioux Falls (SD)
The U of Tampa (FL)
The U of Toledo (OH)
U of Victoria (BC, Canada)
U of West Georgia (GA)
U of Windsor (ON, Canada)
The U of Winnipeg (MB, Canada)
U of Wisconsin–Milwaukee (WI)
U of Wisconsin–Oshkosh (WI)
U of Wisconsin–Parkside (WI)
U of Wisconsin–Superior (WI)
Utah State U (UT)
Utica Coll (NY)
Valley City State U (ND)
Vanguard U of Southern California (CA)
Villa Julie Coll (MD)
Virginia Intermont Coll (VA)
Virginia Wesleyan Coll (VA)
Wabash Coll (IN)
Wagner Coll (NY)
Walla Walla U (WA)
Warner Pacific Coll (OR)
Washburn U (KS)
Washington Coll (MD)
Waynesburg U (PA)
Webber Intl U (FL)
Wells Coll (NY)
Western New Mexico U (NM)
Western State Coll of Colorado (CO)
West Liberty State Coll (WV)
Westminster Coll (MO)
Westmont Coll (CA)
West Texas A&M U (TX)
West Virginia Wesleyan Coll (WV)
Wheeling Jesuit U (WV)
Whitworth U (WA)
Wiley Coll (TX)

William Paterson U of New Jersey (NJ)
Wilmington Coll (OH)
Wingate U (NC)
Winona State U (MN)
Wofford Coll (SC)
Wright State U (OH)
Xavier U of Louisiana (LA)
York U (ON, Canada)
Youngstown State U (OH)

PRE-MEDICAL STUDIES

Abilene Christian U (TX)
Acadia U (NS, Canada)
Adams State Coll (CO)
Adrian Coll (MI)
Alabama State U (AL)
Albertus Magnus Coll (CT)
Albion Coll (MI)
Alderson-Broaddus Coll (WV)
Allegheny Coll (PA)
Alma Coll (MI)
Alvernia Coll (PA)
American Jewish U (CA)
Anderson U (IN)
Andrews U (MI)
Ashford U (IA)
Ashland U (OH)
Atlantic Union Coll (MA)
Auburn U (AL)
Augsburg Coll (MN)
Augustana Coll (IL)
Augustana Coll (SD)
Averett U (VA)
Ball State U (IN)
Bard Coll (NY)
Bard Coll at Simon's Rock (MA)
Barnard Coll (NY)
Barry U (FL)
Baylor U (TX)
Belmont Abbey Coll (NC)
Beloit Coll (WI)
Bemidji State U (MN)
Benedictine U (IL)
Bennington Coll (VT)
Bethany Coll (WV)
Blackburn Coll (IL)
Bluffton U (OH)
Bob Jones U (SC)
Boise State U (ID)
Bryan Coll (TN)
Buffalo State Coll, State U of New York (NY)
California State Polytechnic U, Pomona (CA)
California State U, Chico (CA)
California State U, Dominguez Hills (CA)
California State U, East Bay (CA)
Calvin Coll (MI)
Capital U (OH)
Carroll Coll (WI)
Catawba Coll (NC)
Cedar Crest Coll (PA)
Cedarville U (OH)
Centenary Coll of Louisiana (LA)
Central Christian Coll of Kansas (KS)
City Coll of the City U of New York (NY)
Claremont McKenna Coll (CA)
Clarkson U (NY)
Clark U (MA)
Clearwater Christian Coll (FL)
The Coll at Brockport, State U of New York (NY)
Coll of Charleston (SC)
The Coll of Idaho (ID)
Coll of Mount Saint Vincent (NY)
The Coll of New Jersey (NJ)
The Coll of New Rochelle (NY)
Coll of Saint Benedict (MN)
Coll of Saint Mary (NE)
Coll of the Holy Cross (MA)
Coll of the Ozarks (MO)
Concordia Coll (MN)
Concordia U (MI)
Concordia U (OR)
Concordia U Chicago (IL)
Concordia U, Nebraska (NE)
Concord U (WV)
Cornell U (NY)
Cornerstone U (MI)
Davis & Elkins Coll (WV)
Defiance Coll (OH)
DeSales U (PA)
Dickinson Coll (PA)
Dominican U (IL)
Dordt Coll (IA)
Drake U (IA)
Drury U (MO)
Duquesne U (PA)
Earlham Coll (IN)
East Central U (OK)
Eastern Mennonite U (VA)
Elizabethtown Coll (PA)
Elon U (NC)
Emory & Henry Coll (VA)
Evangel U (MO)
Felician Coll (NJ)
Florida Inst of Technology (FL)
Florida Southern Coll (FL)
Florida State U (FL)
Fontbonne U (MO)
Fresno Pacific U (CA)
Furman U (SC)
Gannon U (PA)
Gardner-Webb U (NC)
The George Washington U (DC)
Georgia Southern U (GA)
Gettysburg Coll (PA)
Grand Valley State U (MI)
Grove City Coll (PA)
Gustavus Adolphus Coll (MN)
Hamline U (MN)
Hampton U (VA)
Harding U (AR)
Hardin-Simmons U (TX)
Hartwick Coll (NY)
Harvard U (MA)
Hastings Coll (NE)
Haverford Coll (PA)
Hawai'i Pacific U (HI)
Heidelberg Coll (OH)
High Point U (NC)
Hillsdale Coll (MI)
Hobart and William Smith Colls (NY)
Hofstra U (NY)
Holy Family U (PA)
Houghton Coll (NY)
Howard Payne U (TX)
Humboldt State U (CA)
Huntington U (IN)
Huston-Tillotson U (TX)
Illinois Coll (IL)
Indiana U–Purdue U Fort Wayne (IN)
Indiana Wesleyan U (IN)
Inter American U of Puerto Rico, Bayamón Campus (PR)
Iowa State U of Science and Technology (IA)
Iowa Wesleyan Coll (IA)
Ithaca Coll (NY)
Jacksonville U (FL)
John Carroll U (OH)
Johnson State Coll (VT)
Juniata Coll (PA)
Kansas State U (KS)
Kent State U (OH)
Kentucky Wesleyan Coll (KY)
Kenyon Coll (OH)
Kettering Coll of Medical Arts (OH)
Keuka Coll (NY)
King Coll (TN)
King's Coll (PA)
LaGrange Coll (GA)
Lambuth U (TN)
La Salle U (PA)
La Sierra U (CA)
Lawrence U (WI)
Lees-McRae Coll (NC)
Lehigh U (PA)
Le Moyne Coll (NY)
Lenoir-Rhyne Coll (NC)
LeTourneau U (TX)
Lewis U (IL)
Limestone Coll (SC)
Lindenwood U (MO)
Lindsey Wilson Coll (KY)
Lipscomb U (TN)
Lock Haven U of Pennsylvania (PA)
Longwood U (VA)
Lourdes Coll (OH)
Lycoming Coll (PA)
Lynchburg Coll (VA)
Manchester Coll (IN)
Manhattanville Coll (NY)
Marian Coll (IN)
Marlboro Coll (VT)
Marquette U (WI)
Massachusetts Coll of Pharmacy and Health Sciences (MA)
The Master's Coll and Sem (CA)
Mayville State U (ND)
McKendree U (IL)
Memorial U of Newfoundland (NL, Canada)
Mercer U (GA)
Mercyhurst Coll (PA)
Methodist U (NC)
Miami U (OH)
Michigan State U (MI)
Michigan Technological U (MI)
Midland Lutheran Coll (NE)
Midwestern State U (TX)
Millikin U (IL)
Minnesota State U Mankato (MN)
Mississippi Coll (MS)
Missouri U of Science and Technology (MO)
Missouri Valley Coll (MO)
Molloy Coll (NY)
Montana State U–Billings (MT)
Morgan State U (MD)
Morningside Coll (IA)
Mountain State U (WV)
Mount Allison U (NB, Canada)
Mount Mary Coll (WI)
Mount Mercy Coll (IA)
Mount Vernon Nazarene U (OH)
Nazareth Coll of Rochester (NY)
Newman U (KS)
New York Inst of Technology (NY)
New York U (NY)
Niagara U (NY)
North Carolina Wesleyan Coll (NC)
North Central Coll (IL)
Northern Arizona U (AZ)
Northern Michigan U (MI)
Northern State U (SD)
North Georgia Coll & State U (GA)
Northland Coll (WI)
Northwestern Oklahoma State U (OK)
Northwestern U (IL)
Northwest Missouri State U (MO)
Northwest Nazarene U (ID)
Notre Dame de Namur U (CA)
Nova Southeastern U (FL)
Oakland City U (IN)
Oglethorpe U (GA)
Ohio Northern U (OH)
Ohio Wesleyan U (OH)
Oklahoma City U (OK)
Oklahoma Wesleyan U (OK)
Oregon Inst of Technology (OR)
Otterbein Coll (OH)
Ouachita Baptist U (AR)
Pacific Lutheran U (WA)
Pacific Union Coll (CA)
Pacific U (OR)
Penn State Abington (PA)
Penn State Altoona (PA)
Penn State Berks (PA)
Penn State Erie, The Behrend Coll (PA)
Penn State U Park (PA)
Pepperdine U, Malibu (CA)
Peru State Coll (NE)
Pfeiffer U (NC)
Philadelphia U (PA)
Pittsburg State U (KS)
Pitzer Coll (CA)
Pomona Coll (CA)
Purdue U (IN)
Purdue U Calumet (IN)
Queens U of Charlotte (NC)
Quincy U (IL)
Quinnipiac U (CT)
Redeemer U Coll (ON, Canada)
Regis U (CO)
Rensselaer Polytechnic Inst (NY)
Ripon Coll (WI)
Roberts Wesleyan Coll (NY)
Rochester Inst of Technology (NY)
Rockford Coll (IL)
Roger Williams U (RI)
Rollins Coll (FL)
Roosevelt U (IL)
Rutgers, The State U of New Jersey, New Brunswick (NJ)
Sacred Heart U (CT)
St. Andrews Presbyterian Coll (NC)
St. Cloud State U (MN)
Saint Francis U (PA)
St. Francis Xavier U (NS, Canada)
St. Gregory's U, Shawnee (OK)
St. John's Coll (NM)
Saint John's U (MN)
St. Joseph's Coll, Suffolk Campus (NY)
Saint Martin's U (WA)
Saint Mary-of-the-Woods Coll (IN)
Saint Michael's Coll (VT)
St. Thomas Aquinas Coll (NY)
St. Thomas U (FL)
Salem State Coll (MA)
Samford U (AL)
Sam Houston State U (TX)
Sarah Lawrence Coll (NY)
Schreiner U (TX)
Scripps Coll (CA)
Seattle Pacific U (WA)
Seton Hill U (PA)
Shawnee State U (OH)
Siena Coll (NY)
Simmons Coll (MA)
Simpson Coll (IA)
Smith Coll (MA)
Sonoma State U (CA)
Southeastern U (FL)
Southern Oregon U (OR)
Southern Wesleyan U (SC)
Southwestern Oklahoma State U (OK)
Southwest Minnesota State U (MN)
Spring Hill Coll (AL)
State U of New York at Binghamton (NY)
State U of New York at Fredonia (NY)
State U of New York at Oswego (NY)
State U of New York Coll at Geneseo (NY)
State U of New York Coll at Oneonta (NY)
State U of New York Coll of Environmental Science and Forestry (NY)
Stetson U (FL)
Susquehanna U (PA)
Tabor Coll (KS)
Tarleton State U (TX)
Taylor U (IN)
Tennessee Technological U (TN)
Texas Lutheran U (TX)
Texas Southern U (TX)
Thiel Coll (PA)
Thompson Rivers U (BC, Canada)
Trinity Christian Coll (IL)
Trinity Intl U (IL)
Trinity U (TX)
Tri-State U (IN)
Truman State U (MO)
Tusculum Coll (TN)
Union U (TN)
Université de Sherbrooke (QC, Canada)
U of Arkansas at Monticello (AR)
U of Arkansas at Pine Bluff (AR)
U of Bridgeport (CT)
The U of British Columbia (BC, Canada)
U of California, Santa Cruz (CA)
U of Central Missouri (MO)
U of Cincinnati (OH)
U of Dallas (TX)
U of Dayton (OH)
U of Evansville (IN)
The U of Findlay (OH)
U of Georgia (GA)
U of Hartford (CT)
U of Houston (TX)
U of Idaho (ID)
U of Indianapolis (IN)
The U of Iowa (IA)
U of Maine (ME)
U of Maine at Machias (ME)
U of Maryland, Baltimore County (MD)
U of Maryland Eastern Shore (MD)
U of Mary Washington (VA)
U of Massachusetts Amherst (MA)
U of Minnesota, Duluth (MN)
U of Minnesota, Twin Cities Campus (MN)
U of Missouri–St. Louis (MO)
The U of Montana (MT)
The U of Montana–Western (MT)
U of Nebraska–Lincoln (NE)
U of Nevada, Reno (NV)
U of New Brunswick Fredericton (NB, Canada)
U of New England (ME)
U of New Hampshire (NH)
U of Notre Dame (IN)
U of Pittsburgh at Johnstown (PA)
U of Portland (OR)
U of Prince Edward Island (PE, Canada)
U of Puget Sound (WA)
U of Regina (SK, Canada)
U of Rio Grande (OH)
U of St. Francis (IL)
U of St. Thomas (TX)
U of Sioux Falls (SD)
The U of Tampa (FL)
The U of Tennessee at Martin (TN)
The U of Toledo (OH)
U of Victoria (BC, Canada)
U of West Georgia (GA)
U of Windsor (ON, Canada)
The U of Winnipeg (MB, Canada)
U of Wisconsin–Milwaukee (WI)
U of Wisconsin–Oshkosh (WI)
U of Wisconsin–Parkside (WI)
Utah State U (UT)
Utica Coll (NY)
Valley City State U (ND)
Villa Julie Coll (MD)
Virginia Intermont Coll (VA)
Virginia Wesleyan Coll (VA)
Wabash Coll (IN)
Wagner Coll (NY)
Walla Walla U (WA)
Walsh U (OH)
Warner Pacific Coll (OR)
Washburn U (KS)
Washington Coll (MD)
Washington U in St. Louis (MO)
Waynesburg U (PA)
Wells Coll (NY)
West Chester U of Pennsylvania (PA)
West Liberty State Coll (WV)
Westmont Coll (CA)
West Virginia Wesleyan Coll (WV)
Wheeling Jesuit U (WV)
Whitworth U (WA)
Widener U (PA)
Wiley Coll (TX)
William Paterson U of New Jersey (NJ)
Wilmington Coll (OH)
Wingate U (NC)
Winona State U (MN)
Wofford Coll (SC)
Wright State U (OH)
Xavier U of Louisiana (LA)
York U (ON, Canada)
Youngstown State U (OH)

PRE-NURSING STUDIES

Adams State Coll (CO)
Allegheny Coll (PA)
Baylor U (TX)
Brigham Young U (UT)
California State U, Fullerton (CA)
Canadian Mennonite U (MB, Canada)
Cleveland State U (OH)
Concordia U (MI)
Concordia U, Nebraska (NE)
Dordt Coll (IA)
Eastern Mennonite U (VA)
Gettysburg Coll (PA)
Juniata Coll (PA)
Limestone Coll (SC)
Lindenwood U (MO)
Lipscomb U (TN)
Missouri Valley Coll (MO)
Montana State U–Billings (MT)
Oklahoma City U (OK)
Ouachita Baptist U (AR)
St. Gregory's U, Shawnee (OK)
Sam Houston State U (TX)
Tennessee Wesleyan Coll (TN)
U of Maryland, Baltimore County (MD)
The U of Winnipeg (MB, Canada)

PRE-PHARMACY STUDIES

Abilene Christian U (TX)
Adams State Coll (CO)
Allegheny Coll (PA)
Ashland U (OH)
Auburn U (AL)
Barry U (FL)
Belmont Abbey Coll (NC)
Bethel Coll (TN)
Carroll Coll (WI)
Central Christian Coll of Kansas (KS)
Coll of Saint Benedict (MN)
Coll of the Ozarks (MO)
Concordia U, Nebraska (NE)
Dordt Coll (IA)
Drury U (MO)
East Central U (OK)
Florida State U (FL)
Gardner-Webb U (NC)
Georgia Southern U (GA)
Gettysburg Coll (PA)
Hardin-Simmons U (TX)
Holy Family U (PA)
Iowa Wesleyan Coll (IA)
Juniata Coll (PA)
King Coll (TN)
King's Coll (PA)
Lambuth U (TN)
Le Moyne Coll (NY)
Lewis U (IL)
Limestone Coll (SC)
Lindsey Wilson Coll (KY)
Lipscomb U (TN)
Longwood U (VA)
Mayville State U (ND)
Michigan Technological U (MI)
Midwestern State U (TX)
Millikin U (IL)
Mississippi Coll (MS)
Missouri Valley Coll (MO)
Montana State U–Billings (MT)
Mount Allison U (NB, Canada)
Mount Vernon Nazarene U (OH)
Northern Michigan U (MI)
Northwest Nazarene U (ID)
Oklahoma City U (OK)
Oregon State U (OR)
Ouachita Baptist U (AR)
Pittsburg State U (KS)
Roberts Wesleyan Coll (NY)
Roosevelt U (IL)
St. Cloud State U (MN)
St. Gregory's U, Shawnee (OK)
Saint John's U (MN)
Saint Martin's U (WA)
Saint Mary-of-the-Woods Coll (IN)
Sam Houston State U (TX)
Tarleton State U (TX)
Texas Southern U (TX)
Truman State U (MO)
Tusculum Coll (TN)
Union U (TN)
U of Central Missouri (MO)
U of Charleston (WV)
U of Connecticut (CT)
U of Evansville (IN)
The U of Iowa (IA)

MAJORS AND MORE

U of Maryland, Baltimore County (MD)
U of Minnesota, Duluth (MN)
U of Missouri–St. Louis (MO)
The U of Montana (MT)
U of Nebraska–Lincoln (NE)
U of Regina (SK, Canada)
U of Saint Francis (IN)
U of St. Thomas (TX)
The U of Tennessee at Martin (TN)
U of Utah (UT)
U of Windsor (ON, Canada)
The U of Winnipeg (MB, Canada)
U of Wisconsin–Parkside (WI)
Valley City State U (ND)
Washburn U (KS)
Washington U in St. Louis (MO)
Westmont Coll (CA)
West Virginia Wesleyan Coll (WV)
Wingate U (NC)
Wright State U (OH)
York U (ON, Canada)
Youngstown State U (OH)

PRE-THEOLOGY/PRE-MINISTERIAL STUDIES

Adrian Coll (MI)
Alma Coll (MI)
Ashland U (OH)
Ave Maria U (FL)
Baptist Bible Coll of Pennsylvania (PA)
California Baptist U (CA)
California Christian Coll (CA)
Central Christian Coll of Kansas (KS)
Coll of Saint Benedict (MN)
Concordia Coll (MN)
Concordia U (MI)
Concordia U (OR)
Concordia U Chicago (IL)
Concordia U, Nebraska (NE)
Cornerstone U (MI)
Crossroads Coll (MN)
Grace U (NE)
Juniata Coll (PA)
Kuyper Coll (MI)
Lambuth U (TN)
Loras Coll (IA)
Minnesota State U Mankato (MN)
Mount Allison U (NB, Canada)
Northwestern Coll (MN)
Ohio Northern U (OH)
Ohio Wesleyan U (OH)
Point Loma Nazarene U (CA)
Redeemer U Coll (ON, Canada)
Roberts Wesleyan Coll (NY)
Saint John's U (MN)
Shorter Coll (GA)
Southeastern U (FL)
Tennessee Wesleyan Coll (TN)
Trinity Christian Coll (IL)
Trinity Coll of Florida (FL)
Trinity Intl U (IL)
U of Dallas (TX)
U of Indianapolis (IN)
U of Rio Grande (OH)
Wagner Coll (NY)
Washburn U (KS)
Waynesburg U (PA)
Westmont Coll (CA)
Williamson Christian Coll (TN)

PRE-VETERINARY STUDIES

Abilene Christian U (TX)
Acadia U (NS, Canada)
Adams State Coll (CO)
Adrian Coll (MI)
Albertus Magnus Coll (CT)
Albion Coll (MI)
Alderson-Broaddus Coll (WV)
Allegheny Coll (PA)
Alma Coll (MI)
Anderson U (IN)
Andrews U (MI)
Ashland U (OH)
Atlantic Union Coll (MA)
Auburn U (AL)
Augsburg Coll (MN)
Augustana Coll (IL)
Augustana Coll (SD)
Barry U (FL)
Becker Coll (MA)
Belmont Abbey Coll (NC)
Bemidji State U (MN)
Benedictine U (IL)
Bethany Coll (WV)
Blackburn Coll (IL)
Bob Jones U (SC)
Boise State U (ID)
Buffalo State Coll, State U of New York (NY)
California State Polytechnic U, Pomona (CA)
California State U, Chico (CA)
California State U, Dominguez Hills (CA)
California State U, East Bay (CA)
Calvin Coll (MI)
Capital U (OH)
Carroll Coll (WI)
Catawba Coll (NC)
Cedar Crest Coll (PA)
Cedarville U (OH)
Centenary Coll of Louisiana (LA)
Central Christian Coll of Kansas (KS)
City Coll of the City U of New York (NY)
Clarkson U (NY)
Clark U (MA)
The Coll at Brockport, State U of New York (NY)
Coll of Saint Benedict (MN)
Coll of Saint Mary (NE)
Coll of the Atlantic (ME)
Coll of the Ozarks (MO)
Colorado State U (CO)
Concordia Coll (MN)
Concordia U, Nebraska (NE)
Concord U (WV)
Cornerstone U (MI)
Davis & Elkins Coll (WV)
Defiance Coll (OH)
DeSales U (PA)
Dominican U (IL)
Dordt Coll (IA)
Drake U (IA)
Drury U (MO)
East Central U (OK)
Eastern Mennonite U (VA)
Elizabethtown Coll (PA)
Elon U (NC)
Emory & Henry Coll (VA)
Evangel U (MO)
Florida Southern Coll (FL)
Florida State U (FL)
Furman U (SC)
Gardner-Webb U (NC)
Georgia Southern U (GA)
Gettysburg Coll (PA)
Grand Valley State U (MI)
Grove City Coll (PA)
Gustavus Adolphus Coll (MN)
Hamline U (MN)
Hampton U (VA)
Harding U (AR)
Hartwick Coll (NY)
Harvard U (MA)
Hastings Coll (NE)
Haverford Coll (PA)
Heidelberg Coll (OH)
High Point U (NC)
Hillsdale Coll (MI)
Hobart and William Smith Colls (NY)
Hofstra U (NY)
Holy Family U (PA)
Houghton Coll (NY)
Humboldt State U (CA)
Huntington U (IN)
Illinois Coll (IL)
Immaculata U (PA)
Indiana Wesleyan U (IN)
Iowa State U of Science and Technology (IA)
Iowa Wesleyan Coll (IA)
Jacksonville U (FL)
John Carroll U (OH)
Juniata Coll (PA)
Kansas State U (KS)
Kentucky Wesleyan Coll (KY)
Kenyon Coll (OH)
Keuka Coll (NY)
King Coll (TN)
King's Coll (PA)
LaGrange Coll (GA)
Lambuth U (TN)
La Salle U (PA)
Lawrence U (WI)
Lees-McRae Coll (NC)
Le Moyne Coll (NY)
LeTourneau U (TX)
Lewis U (IL)
Limestone Coll (SC)
Lindenwood U (MO)
Lindsey Wilson Coll (KY)
Lipscomb U (TN)
Lock Haven U of Pennsylvania (PA)
Longwood U (VA)
Lycoming Coll (PA)
Lynchburg Coll (VA)
Manchester Coll (IN)
Marian Coll (IN)
Marlboro Coll (VT)
Mayville State U (ND)
McKendree U (IL)
Mercyhurst Coll (PA)
Methodist U (NC)
Miami U (OH)
Michigan State U (MI)
Michigan Technological U (MI)
Midland Lutheran Coll (NE)
Midwestern State U (TX)
Millikin U (IL)
Minnesota State U Mankato (MN)
Mississippi Coll (MS)
Missouri Valley Coll (MO)
Molloy Coll (NY)
Morningside Coll (IA)
Mount Allison U (NB, Canada)
Mount Mary Coll (WI)
Mount Mercy Coll (IA)
Mount Vernon Nazarene U (OH)
Nazareth Coll of Rochester (NY)
Newman U (KS)
Niagara U (NY)
North Central Col (IL)
Northern Arizona U (AZ)
Northern Michigan U (MI)
North Georgia Coll & State U (GA)
Northland Coll (WI)
Northwest Missouri State U (MO)
Northwest Nazarene U (ID)
Nova Scotia Ag Coll (NS, Canada)
Oakland City U (IN)
Oglethorpe U (GA)
Ohio Northern U (OH)
Ohio Wesleyan U (OH)
Oklahoma City U (OK)
Oklahoma State U (OK)
Oklahoma Wesleyan U (OK)
Otterbein Coll (OH)
Ouachita Baptist U (AR)
Pacific Union Coll (CA)
Pacific U (OR)
Peru State Coll (NE)
Pittsburg State U (KS)
Purdue U Calumet (IN)
Queens U of Charlotte (NC)
Quincy U (IL)
Quinnipiac U (CT)
Redeemer U Coll (ON, Canada)
Regis U (CO)
Ripon Coll (WI)
Roberts Wesleyan Coll (NY)
Rochester Inst of Technology (NY)
Rockford Coll (IL)
Roger Williams U (RI)
Sacred Heart U (CT)
St. Andrews Presbyterian Coll (NC)
St. Cloud State U (MN)
Saint Francis U (PA)
St. Francis Xavier U (NS, Canada)
Saint John's U (MN)
St. Joseph's Coll, Suffolk Campus (NY)
Saint Martin's U (WA)
Saint Mary-of-the-Woods Coll (IN)
Saint Michael's Coll (VT)
Salem State Coll (MA)
Sarah Lawrence Coll (NY)
Seton Hill U (PA)
Simpson Coll (IA)
Sonoma State U (CA)
Southwestern Oklahoma State U (OK)
Southwest Minnesota State U (MN)
Spring Hill Coll (AL)
State U of New York at Fredonia (NY)
State U of New York at Oswego (NY)
State U of New York Coll at Geneseo (NY)
State U of New York Coll at Oneonta (NY)
State U of New York Coll of Environmental Science and Forestry (NY)
Stetson U (FL)
Susquehanna U (PA)
Tarleton State U (TX)
Taylor U (IN)
Tennessee Technological U (TN)
Texas A&M U (TX)
Texas Lutheran U (TX)
Thiel Coll (PA)
Thompson Rivers U (BC, Canada)
Trinity Christian Coll (IL)
Trinity U (TX)
Tri-State U (IN)
Truman State U (MO)
Tusculum Coll (TN)
The U of Arizona (AZ)
U of Arkansas at Monticello (AR)
U of Bridgeport (CT)
The U of British Columbia (BC, Canada)
U of Central Missouri (MO)
U of Cincinnati (OH)
U of Evansville (IN)
The U of Findlay (OH)
U of Georgia (GA)
U of Hartford (CT)
U of Houston (TX)
U of Illinois at Urbana–Champaign (IL)
U of Indianapolis (IN)
The U of Iowa (IA)
U of Maine (ME)
U of Mary Washington (VA)
U of Massachusetts Amherst (MA)
U of Minnesota, Duluth (MN)
U of Minnesota, Twin Cities Campus (MN)
U of Missouri–St. Louis (MO)
The U of Montana–Western (MT)
U of Nebraska–Lincoln (NE)
U of Nevada, Reno (NV)
U of New Brunswick Fredericton (NB, Canada)
U of New Hampshire (NH)
U of Pittsburgh at Johnstown (PA)
U of Prince Edward Island (PE, Canada)
U of Puget Sound (WA)
U of Regina (SK, Canada)
U of Rio Grande (OH)
U of St. Francis (IL)
U of St. Thomas (TX)
U of Sioux Falls (SD)
The U of Tampa (FL)
The U of Tennessee at Martin (TN)
The U of Toledo (OH)
U of Victoria (BC, Canada)
U of West Georgia (GA)
The U of Winnipeg (MB, Canada)
U of Wisconsin–Oshkosh (WI)
U of Wisconsin–Parkside (WI)
Utah State U (UT)
Utica Coll (NY)
Valley City State U (ND)
Villa Julie Coll (MD)
Virginia Intermont Coll (VA)
Virginia Wesleyan Coll (VA)
Wabash Coll (IN)
Walla Walla U (WA)
Walsh U (OH)
Warner Pacific Coll (OR)
Washburn U (KS)
Washington Coll (MD)
Washington U in St. Louis (MO)
Waynesburg U (PA)
Wells Coll (NY)
Western New Mexico U (NM)
Westmont Coll (CA)
West Virginia Wesleyan Coll (WV)
Wheeling Jesuit U (WV)
Whitworth U (WA)
Widener U (PA)
Wilmington Coll (OH)
Wingate U (NC)
Winona State U (MN)
Wofford Coll (SC)
Wright State U (OH)
Xavier U of Louisiana (LA)
York U (ON, Canada)
Youngstown State U (OH)

PRINTING MANAGEMENT

Carroll Coll (WI)
Ferris State U (MI)
Kean U (NJ)
U of Central Missouri (MO)

PRINTMAKING

Alberta Coll of Art & Design (AB, Canada)
Aquinas Coll (MI)
Art Acad of Cincinnati (OH)
Ball State U (IN)
Bard Coll at Simon's Rock (MA)
Bennington Coll (VT)
Bradley U (IL)
Brigham Young U (UT)
Buffalo State Coll, State U of New York (NY)
California Coll of the Arts (CA)
California State U, East Bay (CA)
California State U, Long Beach (CA)
The Cleveland Inst of Art (OH)
Coll of Visual Arts (MN)
Colorado State U (CO)
Concordia U (QC, Canada)
Drake U (IA)
Grand Valley State U (MI)
Indiana U–Purdue U Fort Wayne (IN)
Indiana Wesleyan U (IN)
Kansas City Art Inst (MO)
Kent State U (OH)
Laguna Coll of Art & Design (CA)
Longwood U (VA)
Maryland Inst Coll of Art (MD)
Massachusetts Coll of Art and Design (MA)
McNeese State U (LA)
Memorial U of Newfoundland (NL, Canada)
Memphis Coll of Art (TN)
Mississippi U for Women (MS)
Montserrat Coll of Art (MA)
Mount Allison U (NB, Canada)
Northern Michigan U (MI)
Northwest Nazarene U (ID)
NSCAD U (NS, Canada)
Ohio Northern U (OH)
Ohio U (OH)
Pratt Inst (NY)
Purchase Coll, State U of New York (NY)
Rutgers, The State U of New Jersey, New Brunswick (NJ)
St. Cloud State U (MN)
Sarah Lawrence Coll (NY)
Savannah Coll of Art and Design (GA)
School of the Art Inst of Chicago (IL)
School of the Museum of Fine Arts, Boston (MA)
School of Visual Arts (NY)
Seton Hill U (PA)
Sonoma State U (CA)
State U of New York at New Paltz (NY)
Temple U (PA)
Texas Christian U (TX)
Trinity Christian Coll (IL)
The U of Akron (OH)
U of Dallas (TX)
U of Georgia (GA)
U of Houston (TX)
The U of Iowa (IA)
U of Kansas (KS)
U of Massachusetts Dartmouth (MA)
U of Miami (FL)
U of Michigan (MI)
U of Missouri–St. Louis (MO)
U of Oregon (OR)
U of Regina (SK, Canada)
The U of Texas at El Paso (TX)
U of Windsor (ON, Canada)
Washington U in St. Louis (MO)
Western State Coll of Colorado (CO)
Western Washington U (WA)
York U (ON, Canada)

PROFESSIONAL STUDIES

Bemidji State U (MN)
Coll of St. Joseph (VT)
Kent State U (OH)
Mount Aloysius Coll (PA)
Saint Mary-of-the-Woods Coll (IN)
Southern Vermont Coll (VT)
U of Memphis (TN)
U of Oklahoma (OK)

PSYCHIATRIC/MENTAL HEALTH SERVICES TECHNOLOGY

Franciscan U of Steubenville (OH)

PSYCHOLOGY

Abilene Christian U (TX)
Acadia U (NS, Canada)
Adams State Coll (CO)
Adelphi U (NY)
Adrian Coll (MI)
Agnes Scott Coll (GA)
Alabama Ag and Mech U (AL)
Alabama State U (AL)
Alaska Pacific U (AK)
Albertus Magnus Coll (CT)
Albion Coll (MI)
Albright Coll (PA)
Alcorn State U (MS)
Alderson-Broaddus Coll (WV)
Alfred U (NY)
Allegheny Coll (PA)
Alliant Intl U (CA)
Alliant Intl U–México City (Mexico)
Alma Coll (MI)
Alvernia Coll (PA)
American Jewish U (CA)
American Public U System (WV)
American U (DC)
American U of Beirut (Lebanon)
The American U of Paris (France)
Amherst Coll (MA)
Anderson U (IN)
Anderson U (SC)
Andrews U (MI)
Angelo State U (TX)
Anna Maria Coll (MA)
Appalachian State U (NC)
Aquinas Coll (MI)
Argosy U, Atlanta (GA)
Argosy U, Chicago (IL)
Argosy U, Dallas (TX)
Argosy U, Denver (CO)
Argosy U, Hawai'i (HI)
Argosy U, Inland Empire (CA)
Argosy U, Nashville (TN)
Argosy U, Orange County (CA)
Argosy U, Phoenix (AZ)
Argosy U, San Diego (CA)
Argosy U, San Francisco Bay Area (CA)
Argosy U, Santa Monica (CA)
Argosy U, Sarasota (FL)
Argosy U, Schaumburg (IL)
Argosy U, Seattle (WA)
Argosy U, Tampa (FL)

Argosy U, Twin Cities (MN)
Argosy U, Washington DC (VA)
Arizona State U (AZ)
Arizona State U at the West campus (AZ)
Arkansas State U (AR)
Armstrong Atlantic State U (GA)
Asbury Coll (KY)
Ashford U (IA)
Ashland U (OH)
Assumption Coll (MA)
Athabasca U (AB, Canada)
Athens State U (AL)
Atlantic Union Coll (MA)
Auburn U (AL)
Auburn U Montgomery (AL)
Augsburg Coll (MN)
Augustana Coll (IL)
Augustana Coll (SD)
Augusta State U (GA)
Austin Coll (TX)
Austin Peay State U (TN)
Averett U (VA)
Avila U (MO)
Azusa Pacific U (CA)
Baker U (KS)
Baldwin-Wallace Coll (OH)
Ball State U (IN)
Baptist Bible Coll of Pennsylvania (PA)
Barclay Coll (KS)
Bard Coll (NY)
Bard Coll at Simon's Rock (MA)
Barnard Coll (NY)
Barry U (FL)
Barton Coll (NC)
Bastyr U (WA)
Bates Coll (ME)
Baylor U (TX)
Bay Path Coll (MA)
Becker Coll (MA)
Belhaven Coll (MS)
Bellarmine U (KY)
Belmont Abbey Coll (NC)
Belmont U (TN)
Beloit Coll (WI)
Bemidji State U (MN)
Benedictine Coll (KS)
Benedictine U (IL)
Bennington Coll (VT)
Berea Coll (KY)
Bernard M. Baruch Coll of the City U of New York (NY)
Berry Coll (GA)
Bethany Coll (KS)
Bethany Coll (WV)
Bethany Lutheran Coll (MN)
Bethany U (CA)
Bethel Coll (KS)
Bethel Coll (TN)
Bethel U (MN)
Bethune-Cookman U (FL)
Biola U (CA)
Bishop's U (QC, Canada)
Blackburn Coll (IL)
Bloomfield Coll (NJ)
Bloomsburg U of Pennsylvania (PA)
Bluefield Coll (VA)
Bluffton U (OH)
Boise State U (ID)
Boston Coll (MA)
Boston U (MA)
Bowdoin Coll (ME)
Bowling Green State U (OH)
Bradley U (IL)
Brandeis U (MA)
Brenau U (GA)
Brevard Coll (NC)
Brewton-Parker Coll (GA)
Bridgewater Coll (VA)
Bridgewater State Coll (MA)
Brigham Young U (UT)
Brock U (ON, Canada)
Brown U (RI)
Bryan Coll (TN)
Bryn Mawr Coll (PA)
Bucknell U (PA)
Buffalo State Coll, State U of New York (NY)
Burlington Coll (VT)
Butler U (IN)
Cabrini Coll (PA)
California Baptist U (CA)
California Lutheran U (CA)
California Polytechnic State U, San Luis Obispo (CA)
California State Polytechnic U, Pomona (CA)
California State U, Chico (CA)
California State U, Dominguez Hills (CA)
California State U, East Bay (CA)
California State U, Fresno (CA)
California State U, Fullerton (CA)
California State U, Long Beach (CA)
California State U, Los Angeles (CA)
California State U, Sacramento (CA)
California State U, San Bernardino (CA)
California State U, San Marcos (CA)
California State U, Stanislaus (CA)
Calumet Coll of Saint Joseph (IN)
Calvin Coll (MI)
Cambridge Coll (MA)
Cameron U (OK)
Canadian Mennonite U (MB, Canada)
Canisius Coll (NY)
Capital U (OH)
Carlow U (PA)
Carnegie Mellon U (PA)
Carroll Coll (WI)
Carson-Newman Coll (TN)
Cascade Coll (OR)
Case Western Reserve U (OH)
Castleton State Coll (VT)
Catawba Coll (NC)
The Catholic U of America (DC)
Cedar Crest Coll (PA)
Cedarville U (OH)
Centenary Coll (NJ)
Centenary Coll of Louisiana (LA)
Central Christian Coll of Kansas (KS)
Central Coll (IA)
Central Connecticut State U (CT)
Central Michigan U (MI)
Central State U (OH)
Central Washington U (WA)
Centre Coll (KY)
Chaminade U of Honolulu (HI)
Chapman U (CA)
Chatham U (PA)
Chestnut Hill Coll (PA)
Cheyney U of Pennsylvania (PA)
Chicago State U (IL)
Christian Brothers U (TN)
The Citadel, The Military Coll of South Carolina (SC)
City Coll of the City U of New York (NY)
City U of Seattle (WA)
Claremont McKenna Coll (CA)
Clarion U of Pennsylvania (PA)
Clark Atlanta U (GA)
Clarke Coll (IA)
Clarkson U (NY)
Clark U (MA)
Clayton State U (GA)
Clearwater Christian Coll (FL)
Clemson U (SC)
Cleveland State U (OH)
Coastal Carolina U (SC)
Coker Coll (SC)
Colby Coll (ME)
Colby-Sawyer Coll (NH)
Colgate U (NY)
The Coll at Brockport, State U of New York (NY)
Coll of Charleston (SC)
The Coll of Idaho (ID)
Coll of Mount St. Joseph (OH)
Coll of Mount Saint Vincent (NY)
The Coll of New Jersey (NJ)
The Coll of New Rochelle (NY)
Coll of Saint Benedict (MN)
Coll of Saint Elizabeth (NJ)
Coll of St. Joseph (VT)
Coll of Saint Mary (NE)
The Coll of Saint Rose (NY)
The Coll of St. Scholastica (MN)
Coll of Staten Island of the City U of New York (NY)
Coll of the Atlantic (ME)
Coll of the Holy Cross (MA)
Coll of the Ozarks (MO)
Coll of the Southwest (NM)
The Coll of William and Mary (VA)
The Colorado Coll (CO)
Colorado State U (CO)
Colorado State U-Pueblo (CO)
Columbia Coll (SC)
Columbus State U (GA)
Concordia Coll (MN)
Concordia U (CA)
Concordia U (MI)
Concordia U (OR)
Concordia U (QC, Canada)
Concordia U Chicago (IL)
Concordia U, Nebraska (NE)
Concordia U, St. Paul (MN)
Concordia U Wisconsin (WI)
Concord U (WV)
Connecticut Coll (CT)
Converse Coll (SC)
Cornell Coll (IA)
Cornell U (NY)
Cornerstone U (MI)
Covenant Coll (GA)
Creighton U (NE)
Culver-Stockton Coll (MO)
Curry Coll (MA)
Daemen Coll (NY)
Dakota Wesleyan U (SD)
Dallas Baptist U (TX)
Dana Coll (NE)
Dartmouth Coll (NH)
Davidson Coll (NC)
Davis & Elkins Coll (WV)
Defiance Coll (OH)
Delta State U (MS)
Denison U (OH)
DePaul U (IL)
DePauw U (IN)
DeSales U (PA)
Dickinson Coll (PA)
Dillard U (LA)
Doane Coll (NE)
Dominican Coll (NY)
Dominican U (IL)
Dominican U of California (CA)
Dordt Coll (IA)
Dowling Coll (NY)
Drake U (IA)
Drew U (NJ)
Drexel U (PA)
Drury U (MO)
Duke U (NC)
Duquesne U (PA)
D'Youville Coll (NY)
Earlham Coll (IN)
East Carolina U (NC)
East Central U (OK)
Eastern Connecticut State U (CT)
Eastern Illinois U (IL)
Eastern Kentucky U (KY)
Eastern Mennonite U (VA)
Eastern Michigan U (MI)
East Stroudsburg U of Pennsylvania (PA)
East Tennessee State U (TN)
East Texas Baptist U (TX)
Eckerd Coll (FL)
Edinboro U of Pennsylvania (PA)
Elizabethtown Coll (PA)
Elon U (NC)
Emmanuel Coll (GA)
Emmanuel Coll (MA)
Emory & Henry Coll (VA)
Emory U (GA)
Emporia State U (KS)
Endicott Coll (MA)
Erskine Coll (SC)
Eugene Lang Coll The New School for Liberal Arts (NY)
Evangel U (MO)
Excelsior Coll (NY)
Fairfield U (CT)
Fairleigh Dickinson U, Coll at Florham (NJ)
Fairleigh Dickinson U, Metropolitan Campus (NJ)
Fairmont State U (WV)
Faulkner U (AL)
Fayetteville State U (NC)
Felician Coll (NJ)
Ferris State U (MI)
Ferrum Coll (VA)
Fitchburg State Coll (MA)
Flagler Coll (FL)
Florida Ag and Mech U (FL)
Florida Atlantic U (FL)
Florida Gulf Coast U (FL)
Florida Inst of Technology (FL)
Florida Intl U (FL)
Florida Memorial U (FL)
Florida Southern Coll (FL)
Florida State U (FL)
Fontbonne U (MO)
Fort Lewis Coll (CO)
Framingham State Coll (MA)
Franciscan U of Steubenville (OH)
Francis Marion U (SC)
Franklin & Marshall Coll (PA)
Franklin Coll (IN)
Freed-Hardeman U (TN)
Fresno Pacific U (CA)
Frostburg State U (MD)
Furman U (SC)
Gannon U (PA)
Gardner-Webb U (NC)
George Fox U (OR)
George Mason U (VA)
Georgetown Coll (KY)
Georgetown U (DC)
The George Washington U (DC)
Georgia Coll & State U (GA)
Georgian Court U (NJ)
Georgia Southern U (GA)
Georgia Southwestern State U (GA)
Georgia State U (GA)
Gettysburg Coll (PA)
Gonzaga U (WA)
Gordon Coll (MA)
Goucher Coll (MD)
Grace Coll (IN)
Grace U (NE)
Grambling State U (LA)
Grand Canyon U (AZ)
Grand Valley State U (MI)
Grand View Coll (IA)
Green Mountain Coll (VT)
Greensboro Coll (NC)
Greenville Coll (IL)
Grinnell Coll (IA)
Grove City Coll (PA)
Guilford Coll (NC)
Gustavus Adolphus Coll (MN)
Gwynedd-Mercy Coll (PA)
Hamilton Coll (NY)
Hamline U (MN)
Hampden-Sydney Coll (VA)
Hampshire Coll (MA)
Hampton U (VA)
Hannibal-LaGrange Coll (MO)
Hanover Coll (IN)
Harding U (AR)
Hardin-Simmons U (TX)
Hartwick Coll (NY)
Harvard U (MA)
Hastings Coll (NE)
Haverford Coll (PA)
Hawai'i Pacific U (HI)
Heidelberg Coll (OH)
Henderson State U (AR)
Hendrix Coll (AR)
High Point U (NC)
Hilbert Coll (NY)
Hillsdale Coll (MI)
Hillsdale Free Will Baptist Coll (OK)
Hobart and William Smith Colls (NY)
Hofstra U (NY)
Hollins U (VA)
Holy Family U (PA)
Holy Names U (CA)
Hood Coll (MD)
Hope Coll (MI)
Hope Intl U (CA)
Houghton Coll (NY)
Houston Baptist U (TX)
Howard Payne U (TX)
Humboldt State U (CA)
Hunter Coll of the City U of New York (NY)
Huntingdon Coll (AL)
Huntington U (IN)
Huston-Tillotson U (TX)
Idaho State U (ID)
Illinois Coll (IL)
Illinois Inst of Technology (IL)
Illinois State U (IL)
Illinois Wesleyan U (IL)
Immaculata U (PA)
Indiana State U (IN)
Indiana Tech (IN)
Indiana U Bloomington (IN)
Indiana U East (IN)
Indiana U Kokomo (IN)
Indiana U Northwest (IN)
Indiana U of Pennsylvania (PA)
Indiana U–Purdue U Fort Wayne (IN)
Indiana U–Purdue U Indianapolis (IN)
Indiana U South Bend (IN)
Indiana U Southeast (IN)
Indiana Wesleyan U (IN)
Inter American U of Puerto Rico, San Germán Campus (PR)
Iona Coll (NY)
Iowa State U of Science and Technology (IA)
Iowa Wesleyan Coll (IA)
Ithaca Coll (NY)
Jackson State U (MS)
Jacksonville State U (AL)
Jacksonville U (FL)
James Madison U (VA)
Jamestown Coll (ND)
John Brown U (AR)
John Carroll U (OH)
John F. Kennedy U (CA)
The Johns Hopkins U (MD)
Johnson C. Smith U (NC)
Johnson State Coll (VT)
John Wesley Coll (NC)
Judson Coll (AL)
Judson U (IL)
Juniata Coll (PA)
Kalamazoo Coll (MI)
Kansas State U (KS)
Kean U (NJ)
Keene State Coll (NH)
Kennesaw State U (GA)
Kent State U (OH)
Kentucky State U (KY)
Kentucky Wesleyan Coll (KY)
Kenyon Coll (OH)
Keuka Coll (NY)
King Coll (TN)
King's Coll (PA)
The King's U Coll (AB, Canada)
Knox Coll (IL)
Kutztown U of Pennsylvania (PA)
Lafayette Coll (PA)
LaGrange Coll (GA)
Lake Forest Coll (IL)
Lakehead U (ON, Canada)
Lake Superior State U (MI)
Lambuth U (TN)
Lander U (SC)
La Roche Coll (PA)
La Salle U (PA)
La Sierra U (CA)
Laurentian U (ON, Canada)
Lawrence Technological U (MI)
Lawrence U (WI)
Lebanon Valley Coll (PA)
Lees-McRae Coll (NC)
Lee U (TN)
Lehigh U (PA)
Lehman Coll of the City U of New York (NY)
Le Moyne Coll (NY)
Lenoir-Rhyne Coll (NC)
LeTourneau U (TX)
Lewis & Clark Coll (OR)
Lewis-Clark State Coll (ID)
Lewis U (IL)
Liberty U (VA)
Life U (GA)
Limestone Coll (SC)
Lincoln U (MO)
Lincoln U (PA)
Lindenwood U (MO)
Lindsey Wilson Coll (KY)
Linfield Coll (OR)
Lipscomb U (TN)
Livingstone Coll (NC)
Lock Haven U of Pennsylvania (PA)
Longwood U (VA)
Loras Coll (IA)
Louisiana Coll (LA)
Louisiana State U and Ag and Mech Coll (LA)
Lourdes Coll (OH)
Loyola Coll in Maryland (MD)
Loyola Marymount U (CA)
Loyola U Chicago (IL)
Loyola U New Orleans (LA)
Lubbock Christian U (TX)
Luther Coll (IA)
Lycoming Coll (PA)
Lynchburg Coll (VA)
Lyndon State Coll (VT)
Lyon Coll (AR)
Macalester Coll (MN)
Madonna U (MI)
Malone Coll (OH)
Manchester Coll (IN)
Manhattanville Coll (NY)
Mansfield U of Pennsylvania (PA)
Marian Coll (IN)
Marian Coll of Fond du Lac (WI)
Marietta Coll (OH)
Marist Coll (NY)
Marlboro Coll (VT)
Marquette U (WI)
Marshall U (WV)
Martin U (IN)
Mary Baldwin Coll (VA)
Marylhurst U (OR)
Marymount Manhattan Coll (NY)
Marymount U (VA)
Maryville Coll (TN)
Maryville U of Saint Louis (MO)
Marywood U (PA)
Massachusetts Coll of Liberal Arts (MA)
McDaniel Coll (MD)
McGill U (QC, Canada)
McKendree U (IL)
McMurry U (TX)
McNeese State U (LA)
Medaille Coll (NY)
Medgar Evers Coll of the City U of New York (NY)
Memorial U of Newfoundland (NL, Canada)
Mercer U (GA)
Mercy Coll (NY)
Mercyhurst Coll (PA)
Meredith Coll (NC)
Merrimack Coll (MA)
Mesa State Coll (CO)
Messiah Coll (PA)
Methodist U (NC)
Metropolitan State U (MN)
Miami U (OH)
Miami U Hamilton (OH)
Michigan State U (MI)
Michigan Technological U (MI)
MidAmerica Nazarene U (KS)
Mid-Continent U (KY)
Middlebury Coll (VT)
Middle Tennessee State U (TN)
Midland Lutheran Coll (NE)
Midway Coll (KY)
Midwestern State U (TX)
Millersville U of Pennsylvania (PA)
Milligan Coll (TN)
Millikin U (IL)
Millsaps Coll (MS)
Mills Coll (CA)
Minnesota State U Mankato (MN)
Minot State U (ND)
Misericordia U (PA)

Mississippi Coll (MS)
Mississippi State U (MS)
Mississippi U for Women (MS)
Missouri Baptist U (MO)
Missouri State U (MO)
Missouri U of Science and Technology (MO)
Missouri Valley Coll (MO)
Mitchell Coll (CT)
Molloy Coll (NY)
Monmouth Coll (IL)
Monmouth U (NJ)
Montana State U (MT)
Montana State U–Billings (MT)
Montclair State U (NJ)
Moravian Coll (PA)
Morehead State U (KY)
Morehouse Coll (GA)
Morgan State U (MD)
Morningside Coll (IA)
Mountain State U (WV)
Mount Allison U (NB, Canada)
Mount Aloysius Coll (PA)
Mount Holyoke Coll (MA)
Mount Ida Coll (MA)
Mount Marty Coll (SD)
Mount Mary Coll (WI)
Mount Mercy Coll (IA)
Mount Olive Coll (NC)
Mount Saint Mary Coll (NY)
Mount St. Mary's Coll (CA)
Mount St. Mary's U (MD)
Mount Saint Vincent U (NS, Canada)
Mount Vernon Nazarene U (OH)
Muhlenberg Coll (PA)
Murray State U (KY)
Naropa U (CO)
National-Louis U (IL)
National U (CA)
Nazareth Coll of Rochester (NY)
Nebraska Wesleyan U (NE)
Neumann Coll (PA)
New Coll of Florida (FL)
New England Coll (NH)
New Jersey City U (NJ)
Newman U (KS)
New Mexico Highlands U (NM)
New Mexico Inst of Mining and Technology (NM)
New York Inst of Technology (NY)
New York U (NY)
Niagara U (NY)
Nicholls State U (LA)
Nichols Coll (MA)
North Carolina Ag and Tech State U (NC)
North Carolina Central U (NC)
North Carolina State U (NC)
North Carolina Wesleyan Coll (NC)
North Central Coll (IL)
Northcentral U (AZ)
North Dakota State U (ND)
Northeastern Illinois U (IL)
Northeastern State U (OK)
Northeastern U (MA)
Northern Arizona U (AZ)
Northern Illinois U (IL)
Northern Michigan U (MI)
Northern State U (SD)
North Georgia Coll & State U (GA)
North Greenville U (SC)
Northland Coll (WI)
Northwestern Coll (IA)
Northwestern Coll (MN)
Northwestern Oklahoma State U (OK)
Northwestern State U of Louisiana (LA)
Northwestern U (IL)
Northwest Missouri State U (MO)
Northwest Nazarene U (ID)
Norwich U (VT)
Notre Dame de Namur U (CA)
Nova Southeastern U (FL)
Nyack Coll (NY)
Oakland U (MI)
Oakwood Coll (AL)
Oberlin Coll (OH)
Occidental Coll (CA)
Oglethorpe U (GA)
Ohio Dominican U (OH)
Ohio Northern U (OH)
Ohio U (OH)
Ohio Valley U (WV)
Ohio Wesleyan U (OH)
Oklahoma Christian U (OK)
Oklahoma City U (OK)
Oklahoma Panhandle State U (OK)
Oklahoma State U (OK)
Old Dominion U (VA)
Oral Roberts U (OK)
Oregon State U (OR)
Otterbein Coll (OH)
Ouachita Baptist U (AR)
Pace U (NY)
Pacific Lutheran U (WA)
Pacific Union Coll (CA)
Pacific U (OR)
Paine Coll (GA)
Palm Beach Atlantic U (FL)
Park U (MO)
Peace Coll (NC)
Penn State Abington (PA)
Penn State Altoona (PA)
Penn State Berks (PA)
Penn State Erie, The Behrend Coll (PA)
Penn State Harrisburg (PA)
Penn State U Park (PA)
Pepperdine U, Malibu (CA)
Peru State Coll (NE)
Pfeiffer U (NC)
Philadelphia U (PA)
Piedmont Coll (GA)
Pikeville Coll (KY)
Pittsburg State U (KS)
Pitzer Coll (CA)
Plymouth State U (NH)
Point Loma Nazarene U (CA)
Point Park U (PA)
Pomona Coll (CA)
Portland State U (OR)
Prairie View A&M U (TX)
Presbyterian Coll (SC)
Prescott Coll (AZ)
Princeton U (NJ)
Providence Coll (RI)
Purchase Coll, State U of New York (NY)
Purdue U (IN)
Purdue U Calumet (IN)
Queens Coll of the City U of New York (NY)
Queen's U at Kingston (ON, Canada)
Queens U of Charlotte (NC)
Quincy U (IL)
Quinnipiac U (CT)
Radford U (VA)
Ramapo Coll of New Jersey (NJ)
Randolph Coll (VA)
Randolph-Macon Coll (VA)
Redeemer U Coll (ON, Canada)
Reed Coll (OR)
Regent U (VA)
Regis Coll (MA)
Regis U (CO)
Rensselaer Polytechnic Inst (NY)
Rhode Island Coll (RI)
Rhodes Coll (TN)
Rice U (TX)
The Richard Stockton Coll of New Jersey (NJ)
Rider U (NJ)
Ripon Coll (WI)
Roanoke Coll (VA)
Robert Morris U (PA)
Roberts Wesleyan Coll (NY)
Rochester Coll (MI)
Rochester Inst of Technology (NY)
Rockford Coll (IL)
Rockhurst U (MO)
Roger Williams U (RI)
Rollins Coll (FL)
Roosevelt U (IL)
Rosemont Coll (PA)
Rowan U (NJ)
Royal Military Coll of Canada (ON, Canada)
Russell Sage Coll (NY)
Rutgers, The State U of New Jersey, Camden (NJ)
Rutgers, The State U of New Jersey, Newark (NJ)
Rutgers, The State U of New Jersey, New Brunswick (NJ)
Sage Coll of Albany (NY)
Saginaw Valley State U (MI)
St. Ambrose U (IA)
St. Andrews Presbyterian Coll (NC)
St. Cloud State U (MN)
St. Edward's U (TX)
Saint Francis U (PA)
St. Francis Xavier U (NS, Canada)
St. Gregory's U, Shawnee (OK)
St. John Fisher Coll (NY)
Saint John's U (MN)
St. John's U (NY)
Saint Joseph Coll (CT)
Saint Joseph's Coll (IN)
St. Joseph's Coll, New York (NY)
St. Joseph's Coll, Suffolk Campus (NY)
Saint Joseph's U (PA)
St. Lawrence U (NY)
Saint Leo U (FL)
Saint Louis U (MO)
Saint Martin's U (WA)
Saint Mary-of-the-Woods Coll (IN)
Saint Mary's Coll (IN)
Saint Mary's Coll of California (CA)
St. Mary's Coll of Maryland (MD)
St. Mary's U (TX)
Saint Mary's U of Minnesota (MN)
Saint Michael's Coll (VT)
St. Norbert Coll (WI)
St. Olaf Coll (MN)
St. Thomas Aquinas Coll (NY)
St. Thomas U (FL)
St. Thomas U (NB, Canada)
Saint Vincent Coll (PA)
Saint Xavier U (IL)
Salem Coll (NC)
Salem State Coll (MA)
Salisbury U (MD)
Salve Regina U (RI)
Samford U (AL)
Sam Houston State U (TX)
San Diego Christian Coll (CA)
San Diego State U (CA)
San Francisco State U (CA)
Santa Clara U (CA)
Sarah Lawrence Coll (NY)
Schiller Intl U (United Kingdom)
Schreiner U (TX)
Scripps Coll (CA)
Seattle Pacific U (WA)
Seattle U (WA)
Seton Hill U (PA)
Sewanee: The U of the South (TN)
Shawnee State U (OH)
Shaw U (NC)
Shenandoah U (VA)
Shepherd U (WV)
Shippensburg U of Pennsylvania (PA)
Shorter Coll (GA)
Siena Coll (NY)
Siena Heights U (MI)
Simmons Coll (MA)
Simon Fraser U (BC, Canada)
Simpson Coll (IA)
Simpson U (CA)
Skidmore Coll (NY)
Slippery Rock U of Pennsylvania (PA)
Smith Coll (MA)
Sonoma State U (CA)
South Carolina State U (SC)
South Dakota State U (SD)
Southeastern Louisiana U (LA)
Southeastern Oklahoma State U (OK)
Southeastern U (FL)
Southeast Missouri State U (MO)
Southern Adventist U (TN)
Southern Arkansas U–Magnolia (AR)
Southern Connecticut State U (CT)
Southern Illinois U Carbondale (IL)
Southern Illinois U Edwardsville (IL)
Southern Methodist U (TX)
Southern New Hampshire U (NH)
Southern Oregon U (OR)
Southern Polytechnic State U (GA)
Southern U and Ag and Mech Coll (LA)
Southern Utah U (UT)
Southern Vermont Coll (VT)
Southern Wesleyan U (SC)
South U, Tampa (FL)
Southwest Baptist U (MO)
Southwestern Adventist U (TX)
Southwestern Coll (KS)
Southwestern Oklahoma State U (OK)
Southwestern U (TX)
Southwest Minnesota State U (MN)
Spelman Coll (GA)
Spring Arbor U (MI)
Spring Hill Coll (AL)
Stanford U (CA)
State U of New York at Binghamton (NY)
State U of New York at Fredonia (NY)
State U of New York at New Paltz (NY)
State U of New York at Oswego (NY)
State U of New York at Plattsburgh (NY)
State U of New York Coll at Geneseo (NY)
State U of New York Coll at Old Westbury (NY)
State U of New York Coll at Oneonta (NY)
State U of New York Coll at Potsdam (NY)
State U of New York Inst of Technology (NY)
Stephen F. Austin State U (TX)
Stephens Coll (MO)
Stetson U (FL)
Stonehill Coll (MA)
Stony Brook U, State U of New York (NY)
Suffolk U (MA)
Susquehanna U (PA)
Swarthmore Coll (PA)
Sweet Briar Coll (VA)
Syracuse U (NY)
Tabor Coll (KS)
Tarleton State U (TX)
Taylor U (IN)
Temple U (PA)
Tennessee State U (TN)
Tennessee Technological U (TN)
Tennessee Wesleyan Coll (TN)
Texas A&M Intl U (TX)
Texas A&M U (TX)
Texas A&M U–Commerce (TX)
Texas Christian U (TX)
Texas Lutheran U (TX)
Texas Southern U (TX)
Texas State U-San Marcos (TX)
Texas Tech U (TX)
Texas Woman's U (TX)
Thiel Coll (PA)
Thomas Coll (ME)
Thomas Edison State Coll (NJ)
Thomas More Coll (KY)
Thomas U (GA)
Thompson Rivers U (BC, Canada)
Tiffin U (OH)
Tougaloo Coll (MS)
Towson U (MD)
Transylvania U (KY)
Trent U (ON, Canada)
Trevecca Nazarene U (TN)
Trinity Christian Coll (IL)
Trinity Coll (CT)
Trinity Intl U (IL)
Trinity Lutheran Coll (WA)
Trinity U (TX)
Tri-State U (IN)
Troy U (AL)
Truman State U (MO)
Tufts U (MA)
Tulane U (LA)
Tusculum Coll (TN)
Tuskegee U (AL)
Tyndale U Coll & Sem (ON, Canada)
Union Coll (KY)
Union Coll (NE)
Union Coll (NY)
Union U (TN)
Université de Sherbrooke (QC, Canada)
Université du Québec en Outaouais (QC, Canada)
U at Albany, State U of New York (NY)
U at Buffalo, the State U of New York (NY)
The U of Akron (OH)
The U of Alabama (AL)
The U of Alabama at Birmingham (AL)
The U of Alabama in Huntsville (AL)
U of Alaska Fairbanks (AK)
The U of Arizona (AZ)
U of Arkansas (AR)
U of Arkansas at Fort Smith (AR)
U of Arkansas at Monticello (AR)
U of Arkansas at Pine Bluff (AR)
U of Baltimore (MD)
U of Bridgeport (CT)
The U of British Columbia (BC, Canada)
The U of British Columbia–Okanagan (BC, Canada)
U of California, Berkeley (CA)
U of California, Davis (CA)
U of California, Irvine (CA)
U of California, Los Angeles (CA)
U of California, Riverside (CA)
U of California, San Diego (CA)
U of California, Santa Barbara (CA)
U of California, Santa Cruz (CA)
U of Central Arkansas (AR)
U of Central Florida (FL)
U of Central Missouri (MO)
U of Central Oklahoma (OK)
U of Charleston (WV)
U of Chicago (IL)
U of Cincinnati (OH)
U of Colorado at Boulder (CO)
U of Colorado Denver (CO)
U of Connecticut (CT)
U of Dallas (TX)
U of Dayton (OH)
U of Delaware (DE)
U of Denver (CO)
U of Evansville (IN)
The U of Findlay (OH)
U of Florida (FL)
U of Georgia (GA)
U of Great Falls (MT)
U of Guam (GU)
U of Hartford (CT)
U of Hawaii at Manoa (HI)
U of Hawaii–West Oahu (HI)
U of Houston (TX)
U of Houston–Clear Lake (TX)
U of Houston–Downtown (TX)
U of Houston–Victoria (TX)
U of Idaho (ID)
U of Illinois at Chicago (IL)
U of Illinois at Springfield (IL)
U of Illinois at Urbana–Champaign (IL)
U of Indianapolis (IN)
The U of Iowa (IA)
U of Kansas (KS)
U of King's Coll (NS, Canada)
U of La Verne (CA)
U of Lethbridge (AB, Canada)
U of Louisiana at Lafayette (LA)
U of Louisiana at Monroe (LA)
U of Louisville (KY)
U of Maine (ME)
U of Maine at Farmington (ME)
U of Maine at Machias (ME)
U of Mary (ND)
U of Mary Hardin-Baylor (TX)
U of Maryland, Baltimore County (MD)
U of Maryland, Coll Park (MD)
U of Maryland U Coll (MD)
U of Mary Washington (VA)
U of Massachusetts Amherst (MA)
U of Massachusetts Boston (MA)
U of Massachusetts Dartmouth (MA)
U of Massachusetts Lowell (MA)
U of Memphis (TN)
U of Miami (FL)
U of Michigan (MI)
U of Michigan–Dearborn (MI)
U of Michigan–Flint (MI)
U of Minnesota, Duluth (MN)
U of Minnesota, Twin Cities Campus (MN)
U of Mississippi (MS)
U of Missouri–Columbia (MO)
U of Missouri–Kansas City (MO)
U of Missouri–St. Louis (MO)
The U of Montana (MT)
U of Montevallo (AL)
U of Nebraska at Kearney (NE)
U of Nebraska at Omaha (NE)
U of Nebraska–Lincoln (NE)
U of Nevada, Las Vegas (NV)
U of Nevada, Reno (NV)
U of New Brunswick Fredericton (NB, Canada)
U of New England (ME)
U of New Hampshire (NH)
U of New Hampshire at Manchester (NH)
U of New Haven (CT)
U of New Mexico (NM)
U of New Orleans (LA)
U of North Alabama (AL)
The U of North Carolina at Asheville (NC)
The U of North Carolina at Chapel Hill (NC)
The U of North Carolina at Charlotte (NC)
The U of North Carolina at Greensboro (NC)
The U of North Carolina at Pembroke (NC)
The U of North Carolina Wilmington (NC)
U of North Dakota (ND)
U of Northern Colorado (CO)
U of Northern Iowa (IA)
U of North Florida (FL)
U of North Texas (TX)
U of Notre Dame (IN)
U of Oklahoma (OK)
U of Oregon (OR)
U of Ottawa (ON, Canada)
U of Pennsylvania (PA)
U of Pittsburgh (PA)
U of Pittsburgh at Bradford (PA)
U of Pittsburgh at Johnstown (PA)
U of Portland (OR)
U of Prince Edward Island (PE, Canada)
U of Puerto Rico, Cayey U Coll (PR)
U of Puget Sound (WA)
U of Redlands (CA)
U of Regina (SK, Canada)
U of Rhode Island (RI)
U of Richmond (VA)
U of Rochester (NY)
U of St. Francis (IL)
U of Saint Francis (IN)
U of Saint Mary (KS)
U of St. Thomas (MN)
U of St. Thomas (TX)
U of San Diego (CA)
U of Science and Arts of Oklahoma (OK)
The U of Scranton (PA)
U of Sioux Falls (SD)
U of South Alabama (AL)
U of South Carolina Aiken (SC)
U of South Carolina Beaufort (SC)
U of South Carolina Upstate (SC)
The U of South Dakota (SD)
U of Southern California (CA)
U of Southern Indiana (IN)
U of Southern Maine (ME)
U of Southern Mississippi (MS)
U of South Florida (FL)

The U of Tampa (FL)
The U of Tennessee (TN)
The U of Tennessee at Chattanooga (TN)
The U of Tennessee at Martin (TN)
The U of Texas at Arlington (TX)
The U of Texas at Austin (TX)
The U of Texas at Brownsville (TX)
The U of Texas at Dallas (TX)
The U of Texas at El Paso (TX)
The U of Texas at San Antonio (TX)
The U of Texas at Tyler (TX)
The U of Texas of the Permian Basin (TX)
The U of Texas–Pan American (TX)
U of the District of Columbia (DC)
U of the Incarnate Word (TX)
U of the Ozarks (AR)
U of the Pacific (CA)
U of the Sacred Heart (PR)
U of the Sciences in Philadelphia (PA)
U of the Virgin Islands (VI)
U of the West (CA)
The U of Toledo (OH)
U of Toronto (ON, Canada)
U of Tulsa (OK)
U of Utah (UT)
U of Vermont (VT)
U of Victoria (BC, Canada)
U of Virginia (VA)
The U of Virginia's Coll at Wise (VA)
The U of Western Ontario (ON, Canada)
U of West Florida (FL)
U of West Georgia (GA)
U of Windsor (ON, Canada)
The U of Winnipeg (MB, Canada)
U of Wisconsin–Eau Claire (WI)
U of Wisconsin–Green Bay (WI)
U of Wisconsin–La Crosse (WI)
U of Wisconsin–Madison (WI)
U of Wisconsin–Milwaukee (WI)
U of Wisconsin–Oshkosh (WI)
U of Wisconsin–Parkside (WI)
U of Wisconsin–Platteville (WI)
U of Wisconsin–Stevens Point (WI)
U of Wisconsin–Superior (WI)
U of Wisconsin–Whitewater (WI)
U of Wyoming (WY)
Ursinus Coll (PA)
Ursuline Coll (OH)
Utah State U (UT)
Utah Valley State Coll (UT)
Utica Coll (NY)
Valdosta State U (GA)
Valley City State U (ND)
Valparaiso U (IN)
Vanderbilt U (TN)
Vanguard U of Southern California (CA)
Vassar Coll (NY)
Vennard Coll (IA)
Villa Julie Coll (MD)
Villanova U (PA)
Virginia Commonwealth U (VA)
Virginia Intermont Coll (VA)
Virginia Military Inst (VA)
Virginia Polytechnic Inst and State U (VA)
Virginia State U (VA)
Virginia Wesleyan Coll (VA)
Viterbo U (WI)
Wabash Coll (IN)
Wagner Coll (NY)
Wake Forest U (NC)
Walla Walla U (WA)
Walsh U (OH)
Warner Pacific Coll (OR)
Warren Wilson Coll (NC)
Wartburg Coll (IA)
Washburn U (KS)
Washington & Jefferson Coll (PA)
Washington and Lee U (VA)
Washington Coll (MD)
Washington U in St. Louis (MO)
Wayland Baptist U (TX)
Waynesburg U (PA)
Wayne State Coll (NE)
Wayne State U (MI)
Weber State U (UT)
Webster U (MO)
Wellesley Coll (MA)
Wells Coll (NY)
Wesleyan Coll (GA)
Wesleyan U (CT)
Wesley Coll (DE)
West Chester U of Pennsylvania (PA)
Western Carolina U (NC)
Western Connecticut State U (CT)
Western Illinois U (IL)
Western Kentucky U (KY)
Western Michigan U (MI)
Western New England Coll (MA)
Western New Mexico U (NM)
Western State Coll of Colorado (CO)
Western Washington U (WA)
Westfield State Coll (MA)
West Liberty State Coll (WV)
Westminster Coll (MO)
Westminster Coll (UT)
Westmont Coll (CA)
West Texas A&M U (TX)
West Virginia U (WV)
West Virginia Wesleyan Coll (WV)
Wheaton Coll (IL)
Wheaton Coll (MA)
Wheeling Jesuit U (WV)
Whitman Coll (WA)
Whittier Coll (CA)
Whitworth U (WA)
Wichita State U (KS)
Widener U (PA)
Wilfrid Laurier U (ON, Canada)
Wilkes U (PA)
Willamette U (OR)
William Jessup U (CA)
William Jewell Coll (MO)
William Paterson U of New Jersey (NJ)
Williams Coll (MA)
William Woods U (MO)
Wilmington Coll (OH)
Wilmington U (DE)
Wingate U (NC)
Winona State U (MN)
Winthrop U (SC)
Wittenberg U (OH)
Wofford Coll (SC)
Woodbury U (CA)
Worcester State Coll (MA)
Wright State U (OH)
Xavier U (OH)
Xavier U of Louisiana (LA)
Yale U (CT)
York Coll (NE)
York Coll of Pennsylvania (PA)
York Coll of the City U of New York (NY)
York U (ON, Canada)
Youngstown State U (OH)

PSYCHOLOGY RELATED

Adams State Coll (CO)
Alvernia Coll (PA)
Anderson U (SC)
Asbury Coll (KY)
Burlington Coll (VT)
California State U, Monterey Bay (CA)
Clayton State U (GA)
The Evergreen State Coll (WA)
Kean U (NJ)
Loyola U Chicago (IL)
Madonna U (MI)
Mayville State U (ND)
Mount Holyoke Coll (MA)
North Carolina State U (NC)
Northwest Christian Coll (OR)
Ohio Northern U (OH)
Rhode Island Coll (RI)
Saint Mary's Coll of California (CA)
St. Mary's Coll of Maryland (MD)
State U of New York at Oswego (NY)
Towson U (MD)
U of California, Riverside (CA)
U of Michigan–Flint (MI)
U of New England (ME)
U of Puerto Rico at Utuado (PR)
U of Puerto Rico, Cayey U Coll (PR)
U of St. Thomas (MN)
The U of Toledo (OH)
The U of Western Ontario (ON, Canada)
Western State Coll of Colorado (CO)

PSYCHOLOGY TEACHER EDUCATION

Alma Coll (MI)
Brigham Young U (UT)
California Lutheran U (CA)
Carroll Coll (WI)
Concordia U (MI)
Lenoir-Rhyne Coll (NC)
Ohio Wesleyan U (OH)
Pittsburg State U (KS)
St. Ambrose U (IA)
Shawnee State U (OH)
Tusculum Coll (TN)
U of Michigan–Flint (MI)
U of Missouri–St. Louis (MO)
Valparaiso U (IN)
Wayne State Coll (NE)
Widener U (PA)
York Coll (NE)

PSYCHOMETRICS AND QUANTITATIVE PSYCHOLOGY

North Dakota State U (ND)

PUBLIC ADMINISTRATION

Alfred U (NY)
American U of Beirut (Lebanon)
Athabasca U (AB, Canada)
Auburn U (AL)
Augustana Coll (IL)
Baylor U (TX)
Bernard M. Baruch Coll of the City U of New York (NY)
Blackburn Coll (IL)
Boise State U (ID)
Bowling Green State U (OH)
Brock U (ON, Canada)
California State Polytechnic U, Pomona (CA)
California State U, Chico (CA)
California State U, Dominguez Hills (CA)
California State U, East Bay (CA)
California State U, Fresno (CA)
California State U, Fullerton (CA)
California State U, San Bernardino (CA)
Calvin Coll (MI)
Capital U (OH)
Cedarville U (OH)
Cleveland State U (OH)
Concordia U (QC, Canada)
Doane Coll (NE)
Eastern Michigan U (MI)
Elon U (NC)
Evangel U (MO)
Ferris State U (MI)
Flagler Coll (FL)
Florida Ag and Mech U (FL)
Florida Atlantic U (FL)
Florida Intl U (FL)
Florida Memorial U (FL)
George Mason U (VA)
Grambling State U (LA)
Grand Valley State U (MI)
Hamline U (MN)
Harding U (AR)
Harris-Stowe State U (MO)
Hastings Coll (NE)
Hawai'i Pacific U (HI)
Heidelberg Coll (OH)
Henderson State U (AR)
Indiana U Bloomington (IN)
Indiana U East (IN)
Indiana U Kokomo (IN)
Indiana U Northwest (IN)
Indiana U–Purdue U Fort Wayne (IN)
Indiana U–Purdue U Indianapolis (IN)
Indiana U South Bend (IN)
Inter American U of Puerto Rico, San Germán Campus (PR)
Iowa State U of Science and Technology (IA)
James Madison U (VA)
John Carroll U (OH)
Juniata Coll (PA)
Kean U (NJ)
Kentucky State U (KY)
Kutztown U of Pennsylvania (PA)
La Salle U (PA)
Lewis U (IL)
Lincoln U (MO)
Lincoln U (PA)
Lindenwood U (MO)
Lipscomb U (TN)
Louisiana Coll (LA)
Mesa State Coll (CO)
Metropolitan State U (MN)
Miami U (OH)
Miami U Hamilton (OH)
Michigan State U (MI)
Millsaps Coll (MS)
Minnesota State U Mankato (MN)
Mississippi Valley State U (MS)
Missouri State U (MO)
Missouri Valley Coll (MO)
Murray State U (KY)
Northeastern U (MA)
Northern Michigan U (MI)
Northern State U (SD)
North Georgia Coll & State U (GA)
Northwest Missouri State U (MO)
Oakland U (MI)
Ohio Wesleyan U (OH)
Park U (MO)
Plymouth State U (NH)
Point Park U (PA)
Rhode Island Coll (RI)
Roger Williams U (RI)
Roosevelt U (IL)
Saginaw Valley State U (MI)
St. Ambrose U (IA)
St. Cloud State U (MN)
Saint Francis U (PA)
Saint Joseph's U (PA)
St. Thomas U (FL)
Samford U (AL)
San Diego State U (CA)
Seattle U (WA)
Shaw U (NC)
Shenandoah U (VA)
Shippensburg U of Pennsylvania (PA)
Siena Heights U (MI)
Southern New Hampshire U (NH)
Southwest Minnesota State U (MN)
Stephen F. Austin State U (TX)
Stonehill Coll (MA)
Suffolk U (MA)
Syracuse U (NY)
Tennessee State U (TN)
Texas Southern U (TX)
Texas State U-San Marcos (TX)
Texas Woman's U (TX)
Thomas Edison State Coll (NJ)
U at Albany, State U of New York (NY)
The U of Arizona (AZ)
U of Arkansas (AR)
U of California, Riverside (CA)
U of Central Arkansas (AR)
U of Central Florida (FL)
U of Guam (GU)
U of Hawaii–West Oahu (HI)
U of Kansas (KS)
U of La Verne (CA)
U of Lethbridge (AB, Canada)
U of Maine (ME)
The U of Maine at Augusta (ME)
U of Maine at Fort Kent (ME)
U of Maine at Machias (ME)
U of Michigan–Flint (MI)
U of Missouri–St. Louis (MO)
U of New Haven (CT)
The U of North Carolina at Pembroke (NC)
U of North Dakota (ND)
U of Northern Iowa (IA)
U of North Texas (TX)
U of Oklahoma (OK)
U of Oregon (OR)
U of Ottawa (ON, Canada)
U of Pittsburgh (PA)
U of Regina (SK, Canada)
U of St. Thomas (MN)
U of Southern California (CA)
The U of Tennessee (TN)
The U of Tennessee at Martin (TN)
The U of Texas at Brownsville (TX)
The U of Texas at Dallas (TX)
U of Toronto (ON, Canada)
U of Victoria (BC, Canada)
The U of Western Ontario (ON, Canada)
U of Windsor (ON, Canada)
U of Wisconsin–Green Bay (WI)
U of Wisconsin–Stevens Point (WI)
U of Wisconsin–Whitewater (WI)
Virginia Intermont Coll (VA)
Virginia State U (VA)
Wagner Coll (NY)
Washburn U (KS)
Waynesburg U (PA)
Wayne State U (MI)
Western Carolina U (NC)
Western New Mexico U (NM)
West Texas A&M U (TX)
Winona State U (MN)
Wright State U (OH)
York U (ON, Canada)

PUBLIC ADMINISTRATION AND SOCIAL SERVICE PROFESSIONS RELATED

Columbia Coll (SC)
Eastern Michigan U (MI)
Kentucky Wesleyan Coll (KY)
Mercy Coll (NY)
Milligan Coll (TN)
Northeastern Illinois U (IL)
Northern Arizona U (AZ)
Ohio U (OH)
Quincy U (IL)
Roosevelt U (IL)
Troy U (AL)

PUBLIC/APPLIED HISTORY AND ARCHIVAL ADMINISTRATION

Clayton State U (GA)
East Carolina U (NC)
Meredith Coll (NC)
U of California, Santa Barbara (CA)
Western Michigan U (MI)

PUBLIC HEALTH

Alma Coll (MI)
Boise State U (ID)
Brock U (ON, Canada)
California State U, Dominguez Hills (CA)
California State U, Long Beach (CA)
Dillard U (LA)
East Tennessee State U (TN)
Grand Valley State U (MI)
Hampshire Coll (MA)
Hunter Coll of the City U of New York (NY)
Indiana U Bloomington (IN)
The Johns Hopkins U (MD)
Maryville U of Saint Louis (MO)
Minnesota State U Mankato (MN)
Monroe Coll, Bronx (NY)
Oregon State U (OR)
The Richard Stockton Coll of New Jersey (NJ)
Rutgers, The State U of New Jersey, New Brunswick (NJ)
St. Joseph's Coll, New York (NY)
Slippery Rock U of Pennsylvania (PA)
Southern Connecticut State U (CT)
State U of New York Coll at Old Westbury (NY)
Truman State U (MO)
Tufts U (MA)
TUI U (CA)
U of Cincinnati (OH)
U of Minnesota, Twin Cities Campus (MN)
U of Southern Mississippi (MS)
The U of Tampa (FL)
West Chester U of Pennsylvania (PA)
William Paterson U of New Jersey (NJ)
Winona State U (MN)
York U (ON, Canada)

PUBLIC HEALTH/ COMMUNITY NURSING

Capital U (OH)
Northern Illinois U (IL)
The U of Western Ontario (ON, Canada)
Wright State U (OH)

PUBLIC HEALTH EDUCATION AND PROMOTION

American U (DC)
Appalachian State U (NC)
California State U, Long Beach (CA)
Central Michigan U (MI)
Chicago State U (IL)
Coastal Carolina U (SC)
Dillard U (LA)
East Carolina U (NC)
Georgia Southern U (GA)
Ithaca Coll (NY)
Laurentian U (ON, Canada)
Liberty U (VA)
Malone Coll (OH)
Mountain State U (WV)
North Carolina Central U (NC)
Oklahoma State U (OK)
Plymouth State U (NH)
Southeastern Louisiana U (LA)
Temple U (PA)
U of Michigan–Flint (MI)
The U of North Carolina at Greensboro (NC)
The U of North Carolina at Pembroke (NC)
U of Northern Colorado (CO)
U of St. Thomas (MN)
U of Southern California (CA)
The U of Toledo (OH)
The U of Western Ontario (ON, Canada)
Walla Walla U (WA)

PUBLIC HEALTH RELATED

Indiana U Bloomington (IN)
Indiana U–Purdue U Indianapolis (IN)
Malone Coll (OH)
U of California, Berkeley (CA)
U of California, Irvine (CA)
U of Illinois at Urbana–Champaign (IL)
Utah State U (UT)

PUBLIC POLICY ANALYSIS

Albion Coll (MI)
Anna Maria Coll (MA)
Bernard M. Baruch Coll of the City U of New York (NY)
Brigham Young U (UT)
Carlow U (PA)
Carnegie Mellon U (PA)
Central Washington U (WA)
Chatham U (PA)
Coll of the Atlantic (ME)
The Coll of William and Mary (VA)

Cornell U (NY)
DePaul U (IL)
Dickinson Coll (PA)
Duke U (NC)
The George Washington U (DC)
Georgia Inst of Technology (GA)
Grand Valley State U (MI)
Hamilton Coll (NY)
Harvard U (MA)
Hobart and William Smith Colls (NY)
Houston Baptist U (TX)
Immaculata U (PA)
Indiana U Bloomington (IN)
Indiana U–Purdue U Fort Wayne (IN)
Kenyon Coll (OH)
Mills Coll (CA)
New Coll of Florida (FL)
North Carolina State U (NC)
Northern Arizona U (AZ)
Northwestern U (IL)
Occidental Coll (CA)
Penn State Harrisburg (PA)
Pomona Coll (CA)
Princeton U (NJ)
Rice U (TX)
Rochester Inst of Technology (NY)
St. Cloud State U (MN)
St. Mary's Coll of Maryland (MD)
Saint Vincent Coll (PA)
Sarah Lawrence Coll (NY)
Simmons Coll (MA)
Southern Methodist U (TX)
Stanford U (CA)
Suffolk U (MA)
Trinity Coll (CT)
U at Albany, State U of New York (NY)
U of California, Riverside (CA)
U of Charleston (WV)
U of Chicago (IL)
U of Cincinnati (OH)
U of Denver (CO)
U of Massachusetts Boston (MA)
The U of North Carolina at Chapel Hill (NC)
U of Oregon (OR)
U of Pennsylvania (PA)
U of Rhode Island (RI)
U of Southern California (CA)
The U of Toledo (OH)
U of Wisconsin–Whitewater (WI)
Virginia Polytechnic Inst and State U (VA)
Washington and Lee U (VA)
Wells Coll (NY)
York U (ON, Canada)

PUBLIC RELATIONS

Christian Brothers U (TN)
San Diego State U (CA)
Southern Methodist U (TX)
State U of New York at Plattsburgh (NY)

PUBLIC RELATIONS, ADVERTISING, AND APPLIED COMMUNICATION RELATED

Belmont U (TN)
Brigham Young U (UT)
California Lutheran U (CA)
Carroll Coll (WI)
The Coll at Brockport, State U of New York (NY)
The Coll of St. Scholastica (MN)
Duquesne U (PA)
East Central U (OK)
Eastern Kentucky U (KY)
John Brown U (AR)
Lambuth U (TN)
Madonna U (MI)
Marietta Coll (OH)
Marywood U (PA)
Murray State U (KY)
Pittsburg State U (KS)
Rochester Inst of Technology (NY)
Saint Mary's U of Minnesota (MN)
Shorter Coll (GA)
Slippery Rock U of Pennsylvania (PA)
Southern New Hampshire U (NH)
Spring Arbor U (MI)
Spring Hill Coll (AL)
Texas A&M U (TX)
Thompson Rivers U (BC, Canada)
U of Central Arkansas (AR)
U of Vermont (VT)
Virginia State U (VA)

PUBLIC RELATIONS/IMAGE MANAGEMENT

Alabama State U (AL)
American U (DC)
The American U of Athens (Greece)
Andrews U (MI)
Appalachian State U (NC)
Auburn U (AL)
Baldwin-Wallace Coll (OH)
Ball State U (IN)
Barry U (FL)
Boston U (MA)
Bowling Green State U (OH)
Bradley U (IL)
Buffalo State Coll, State U of New York (NY)
California Lutheran U (CA)
California State Polytechnic U, Pomona (CA)
California State U, Chico (CA)
California State U, Dominguez Hills (CA)
California State U, East Bay (CA)
California State U, Fresno (CA)
California State U, Fullerton (CA)
California State U, Long Beach (CA)
Capital U (OH)
Carroll Coll (WI)
Castleton State Coll (VT)
Central Michigan U (MI)
Central Washington U (WA)
Chapman U (CA)
Clarke Coll (IA)
Cleveland State U (OH)
The Coll at Brockport, State U of New York (NY)
Coll of the Ozarks (MO)
Colorado State U (CO)
Columbia Coll (SC)
Columbia Coll Chicago (IL)
Concordia Coll (MN)
Curry Coll (MA)
Drake U (IA)
Drury U (MO)
Duquesne U (PA)
East Central U (OK)
Eastern Kentucky U (KY)
Eastern Michigan U (MI)
Emerson Coll (MA)
Ferris State U (MI)
Florida Ag and Mech U (FL)
Florida Southern Coll (FL)
Florida State U (FL)
Freed-Hardeman U (TN)
George Fox U (OR)
Georgia Southern U (GA)
Gonzaga U (WA)
Grand Canyon U (AZ)
Grand Valley State U (MI)
Greenville Coll (IL)
Hampton U (VA)
Harding U (AR)
Hastings Coll (NE)
Hawai'i Pacific U (HI)
Heidelberg Coll (OH)
Hofstra U (NY)
Howard Payne U (TX)
Huntington U (IN)
Illinois State U (IL)
Iona Coll (NY)
Ithaca Coll (NY)
John Brown U (AR)
Kent State U (OH)
La Salle U (PA)
Lewis U (IL)
Lindenwood U (MO)
Lipscomb U (TN)
Loras Coll (IA)
Madonna U (MI)
Mansfield U of Pennsylvania (PA)
Marist Coll (NY)
Marquette U (WI)
The Master's Coll and Sem (CA)
McKendree U (IL)
Mercyhurst Coll (PA)
MidAmerica Nazarene U (KS)
Middle Tennessee State U (TN)
Minnesota State U Mankato (MN)
Mississippi Coll (MS)
Monmouth Coll (IL)
Montana State U–Billings (MT)
Mount Mary Coll (WI)
Mount Mercy Coll (IA)
Mount Saint Mary Coll (NY)
Mount Saint Vincent U (NS, Canada)
Murray State U (KY)
New England Coll (NH)
New England School of Communications (ME)
North Carolina State U (NC)
Northeastern State U (OK)
Northern Arizona U (AZ)
Northern Michigan U (MI)
Northwestern Coll (MN)
Northwest Missouri State U (MO)
Northwest Nazarene U (ID)
Ohio Dominican U (OH)
Ohio Northern U (OH)
Ohio U (OH)
Ohio U–Zanesville (OH)
Oklahoma Christian U (OK)
Oklahoma City U (OK)
Otterbein Coll (OH)
Pacific Union Coll (CA)
Paine Coll (GA)
Pepperdine U, Malibu (CA)
Pfeiffer U (NC)
Purdue U (IN)
Purdue U Calumet (IN)
Quincy U (IL)
Quinnipiac U (CT)
Regis Coll (MA)
Rider U (NJ)
Rochester Inst of Technology (NY)
Roosevelt U (IL)
St. Ambrose U (IA)
St. Cloud State U (MN)
Saint Francis U (PA)
St. John's U (NY)
Salem State Coll (MA)
Sam Houston State U (TX)
San Diego State U (CA)
Seattle U (WA)
Simmons Coll (MA)
Southern Adventist U (TN)
Southern Methodist U (TX)
State U of New York at Oswego (NY)
Stephens Coll (MO)
Suffolk U (MA)
Susquehanna U (PA)
Tabor Coll (KS)
Temple U (PA)
Texas State U-San Marcos (TX)
Texas Tech U (TX)
Union Coll (NE)
Union U (TN)
The U of Akron (OH)
The U of Alabama (AL)
U of Central Missouri (MO)
U of Central Oklahoma (OK)
U of Dayton (OH)
U of Delaware (DE)
The U of Findlay (OH)
U of Florida (FL)
U of Georgia (GA)
U of Houston (TX)
U of Idaho (ID)
U of Louisiana at Lafayette (LA)
U of Mary (ND)
U of Miami (FL)
U of Northern Iowa (IA)
U of Oklahoma (OK)
U of Oregon (OR)
U of Pittsburgh at Bradford (PA)
U of Rio Grande (OH)
U of South Carolina (SC)
U of Southern California (CA)
U of Southern Indiana (IN)
The U of Tampa (FL)
The U of Texas at Arlington (TX)
The U of Texas at Austin (TX)
U of Toronto (ON, Canada)
U of Utah (UT)
U of Wisconsin–Madison (WI)
Ursuline Coll (OH)
Utica Coll (NY)
Valparaiso U (IN)
Walla Walla U (WA)
Wartburg Coll (IA)
Wayne State U (MI)
Weber State U (UT)
Webster U (MO)
Western Kentucky U (KY)
West Virginia Wesleyan Coll (WV)
Wheeling Jesuit U (WV)
William Woods U (MO)
Winona State U (MN)
Xavier U (OH)
York Coll of Pennsylvania (PA)

PUBLISHING

Benedictine U (IL)
California State U, Chico (CA)
Emerson Coll (MA)
Rochester Inst of Technology (NY)
Saint Mary's U of Minnesota (MN)
U of Missouri–Columbia (MO)

PURCHASING, PROCUREMENT/ ACQUISITIONS AND CONTRACTS MANAGEMENT

Arizona State U (AZ)
California State U, East Bay (CA)
Central Michigan U (MI)
Miami U (OH)
North Georgia Coll & State U (GA)
Saint Joseph's U (PA)
Saint Louis U (MO)
Southwestern Coll (KS)
U of Houston–Downtown (TX)
U of Illinois at Urbana–Champaign (IL)
U of the District of Columbia (DC)
Wright State U (OH)

QUALITY CONTROL AND SAFETY TECHNOLOGIES RELATED

Madonna U (MI)
Rochester Inst of Technology (NY)

QUALITY CONTROL TECHNOLOGY

Bowling Green State U (OH)
California State U, Long Beach (CA)
Ferris State U (MI)
U of Puerto Rico at Utuado (PR)
Winona State U (MN)

RABBINICAL STUDIES

Ohr Somayach/Joseph Tanenbaum Educational Center (NY)
Talmudic Coll of Florida (FL)

RADIATION BIOLOGY

Grand Valley State U (MI)

RADIATION PROTECTION/ HEALTH PHYSICS TECHNOLOGY

Indiana U East (IN)
Indiana U–Purdue U Indianapolis (IN)
Indiana U South Bend (IN)
Indiana U Southeast (IN)
Oregon State U (OR)

RADIO AND TELEVISION

Alabama State U (AL)
Appalachian State U (NC)
Arizona State U (AZ)
Arkansas State U (AR)
Auburn U (AL)
Barry U (FL)
Baylor U (TX)
Belmont U (TN)
Bemidji State U (MN)
Biola U (CA)
Bob Jones U (SC)
Boston U (MA)
Bradley U (IL)
Buffalo State Coll, State U of New York (NY)
Butler U (IN)
California State U, Fresno (CA)
California State U, Fullerton (CA)
California State U, Long Beach (CA)
California State U, Los Angeles (CA)
Castleton State Coll (VT)
Cedarville U (OH)
Central State U (OH)
Central Washington U (WA)
Chicago State U (IL)
The Coll at Brockport, State U of New York (NY)
Colorado State U (CO)
Columbia Coll Chicago (IL)
Concordia Coll (MN)
Curry Coll (MA)
Drake U (IA)
East Central U (OK)
Eastern Kentucky U (KY)
Emerson Coll (MA)
Evangel U (MO)
Florida State U (FL)
Freed-Hardeman U (TN)
George Fox U (OR)
The George Washington U (DC)
Georgia Southern U (GA)
Grand Valley State U (MI)
Grand View Coll (IA)
Hardin-Simmons U (TX)
Hastings Coll (NE)
Hofstra U (NY)
Iona Coll (NY)
Ithaca Coll (NY)
John Brown U (AR)
Kent State U (OH)
La Salle U (PA)
Lindenwood U (MO)
Lyndon State Coll (VT)
Marietta Coll (OH)
Marist Coll (NY)
The Master's Coll and Sem (CA)
Mercyhurst Coll (PA)
Messiah Coll (PA)
Michigan State U (MI)
Minot State U (ND)
Murray State U (KY)
New England School of Communications (ME)
New York Inst of Technology (NY)
New York U (NY)
North Central Coll (IL)
Northeastern U (MA)
Northern Arizona U (AZ)
Northwestern Coll (MN)
Northwestern U (IL)
Northwest Missouri State U (MO)
Ohio Northern U (OH)
Ohio U (OH)
Oklahoma Christian U (OK)
Oklahoma City U (OK)
Otterbein Coll (OH)
Pacific U (OR)
Palm Beach Atlantic U (FL)
Pittsburg State U (KS)
Point Park U (PA)
Purdue U Calumet (IN)
Quincy U (IL)
Roosevelt U (IL)
Sacred Heart U (CT)
St. Ambrose U (IA)
St. Cloud State U (MN)
Salem Intl U (WV)
Sam Houston State U (TX)
San Diego State U (CA)
San Francisco State U (CA)
Southeastern U (FL)
Southern Illinois U Carbondale (IL)
Southwest Minnesota State U (MN)
State U of New York at Fredonia (NY)
State U of New York at Plattsburgh (NY)
Stephen F. Austin State U (TX)
Stephens Coll (MO)
Susquehanna U (PA)
Syracuse U (NY)
Texas A&M U–Commerce (TX)
Texas Christian U (TX)
Texas Southern U (TX)
Texas State U-San Marcos (TX)
Texas Tech U (TX)
Troy U (AL)
Union U (TN)
The U of Akron (OH)
The U of Alabama (AL)
The U of Arizona (AZ)
U of Central Florida (FL)
U of Central Missouri (MO)
U of Central Oklahoma (OK)
U of Cincinnati (OH)
U of Dayton (OH)
U of Florida (FL)
U of Idaho (ID)
U of Miami (FL)
U of Mississippi (MS)
U of Missouri–Columbia (MO)
The U of Montana (MT)
U of Montevallo (AL)
U of Northern Iowa (IA)
U of North Texas (TX)
U of Pittsburgh at Bradford (PA)
U of Sioux Falls (SD)
U of Southern California (CA)
U of Southern Indiana (IN)
U of Southern Mississippi (MS)
The U of Tennessee (TN)
The U of Texas at Arlington (TX)
The U of Texas at Austin (TX)
U of Utah (UT)
The U of Western Ontario (ON, Canada)
U of Windsor (ON, Canada)
U of Wisconsin–Madison (WI)
U of Wisconsin–Oshkosh (WI)
U of Wisconsin–Superior (WI)
Valparaiso U (IN)
Vanguard U of Southern California (CA)
Walla Walla U (WA)
Waynesburg U (PA)
Wayne State U (MI)
Weber State U (UT)
Webster U (MO)
Western Illinois U (IL)
Western Kentucky U (KY)
William Woods U (MO)
Winona State U (MN)
Xavier U (OH)
Youngstown State U (OH)

RADIO AND TELEVISION BROADCASTING TECHNOLOGY

Alabama Ag and Mech U (AL)
Asbury Coll (KY)
Eastern Michigan U (MI)
Emerson Coll (MA)
Ferris State U (MI)
Gannon U (PA)
Gardner-Webb U (NC)
Iona Coll (NY)
Lewis U (IL)
New England School of Communications (ME)
Northwest Nazarene U (ID)
Ohio U (OH)
Trevecca Nazarene U (TN)
U of Puerto Rico at Utuado (PR)

RADIOLOGICAL SCIENCE

Alderson-Broaddus Coll (WV)
U of Toronto (ON, Canada)

RADIOLOGIC TECHNOLOGY/SCIENCE
Austin Peay State U (TN)
Averett U (VA)
Baptist Coll of Health Sciences (TN)
Clarion U of Pennsylvania (PA)
Coll of St. Joseph (VT)
The George Washington U (DC)
Holy Family U (PA)
Indiana U Northwest (IN)
Indiana U South Bend (IN)
Indiana U Southeast (IN)
Jamestown Coll (ND)
Jefferson Coll of Health Sciences (VA)
Kent State U (OH)
Kettering Coll of Medical Arts (OH)
Marian Coll of Fond du Lac (WI)
Massachusetts Coll of Pharmacy and Health Sciences (MA)
Medical Coll of Georgia (GA)
Midwestern State U (TX)
Missouri State U (MO)
Mount Aloysius Coll (PA)
North Dakota State U (ND)
Northwestern State U of Louisiana (LA)
Oakland U (MI)
Oregon Inst of Technology (OR)
Quinnipiac U (CT)
State U of New York Upstate Medical U (NY)
Suffolk U (MA)
U of Charleston (WV)
The U of Iowa (IA)
U of Mary (ND)
U of Missouri–Columbia (MO)
U of Nebraska Medical Center (NE)
U of Oklahoma Health Sciences Center (OK)
U of Pittsburgh at Bradford (PA)
U of St. Francis (IL)
U of South Alabama (AL)
Virginia Commonwealth U (VA)
Widener U (PA)

RADIO, TELEVISION, AND DIGITAL COMMUNICATION RELATED
Brigham Young U (UT)
California State Polytechnic U, Pomona (CA)
Capital U (OH)
Central Michigan U (MI)
Clark Atlanta U (GA)
The Coll at Brockport, State U of New York (NY)
Drake U (IA)
Emerson Coll (MA)
Florida State U (FL)
Hofstra U (NY)
John Brown U (AR)
Madonna U (MI)
Neumann Coll (PA)
Rogers State U (OK)
Sacred Heart U (CT)
Spring Hill Coll (AL)
Texas Southern U (TX)
The U of Akron (OH)
Western Carolina U (NC)

RADIO/TELEVISION BROADCASTING TECHNOLOGY
Pittsburg State U (KS)

RANGE SCIENCE AND MANAGEMENT
Brigham Young U (UT)
Colorado State U (CO)
Humboldt State U (CA)
Montana State U (MT)
Oregon State U (OR)
South Dakota State U (SD)
Sterling Coll (VT)
Tarleton State U (TX)
Texas A&M U (TX)
Texas Tech U (TX)
U of Idaho (ID)
U of Nebraska–Lincoln (NE)
U of Wyoming (WY)
Utah State U (UT)

READING TEACHER EDUCATION
Abilene Christian U (TX)
Aquinas Coll (MI)
Baylor U (TX)
Boise State U (ID)
Catawba Coll (NC)
Clarion U of Pennsylvania (PA)
Dordt Coll (IA)
Eastern Michigan U (MI)
Edinboro U of Pennsylvania (PA)
Grand Valley State U (MI)
Harding U (AR)
Hardin-Simmons U (TX)
Jarvis Christian Coll (TX)
Longwood U (VA)
Lyndon State Coll (VT)
Millersville U of Pennsylvania (PA)
Mount Saint Vincent U (NS, Canada)
Murray State U (KY)
North Georgia Coll & State U (GA)
Northwest Missouri State U (MO)
Ohio U (OH)
St. Cloud State U (MN)
St. Mary's U (TX)
Sam Houston State U (TX)
State U of New York Coll at Oneonta (NY)
Tennessee State U (TN)
Texas A&M Intl U (TX)
Texas A&M U–Commerce (TX)
Texas Southern U (TX)
The U of British Columbia (BC, Canada)
U of Central Missouri (MO)
U of Central Oklahoma (OK)
U of Georgia (GA)
U of Great Falls (MT)
The U of Montana (MT)
U of Nebraska–Lincoln (NE)
The U of North Carolina at Pembroke (NC)
U of Northern Iowa (IA)
U of Wisconsin–Superior (WI)
West Chester U of Pennsylvania (PA)
Wingate U (NC)
Winona State U (MN)
Wright State U (OH)
York Coll (NE)

REAL ESTATE
Angelo State U (TX)
Arizona State U (AZ)
Ball State U (IN)
Baylor U (TX)
California State Polytechnic U, Pomona (CA)
California State U, Dominguez Hills (CA)
California State U, East Bay (CA)
California State U, Fresno (CA)
Central Michigan U (MI)
Clarion U of Pennsylvania (PA)
Delta State U (MS)
DePaul U (IL)
Eastern Kentucky U (KY)
Florida Atlantic U (FL)
Florida Intl U (FL)
Georgia State U (GA)
Marylhurst U (OR)
Minnesota State U Mankato (MN)
Mississippi State U (MS)
Monmouth U (NJ)
Morehead State U (KY)
New York U (NY)
St. Cloud State U (MN)
San Diego State U (CA)
San Francisco State U (CA)
Temple U (PA)
Texas Christian U (TX)
Thomas Edison State Coll (NJ)
The U of British Columbia (BC, Canada)
U of Central Oklahoma (OK)
U of Cincinnati (OH)
U of Connecticut (CT)
U of Denver (CO)
U of Florida (FL)
U of Georgia (GA)
U of Illinois at Urbana–Champaign (IL)
U of Memphis (TN)
U of Mississippi (MS)
U of Missouri–Columbia (MO)
U of Nebraska at Omaha (NE)
U of Nevada, Las Vegas (NV)
U of Northern Iowa (IA)
U of North Texas (TX)
U of Pennsylvania (PA)
U of St. Thomas (MN)
U of South Carolina (SC)
The U of Texas at Arlington (TX)
The U of Texas at El Paso (TX)
U of West Georgia (GA)
U of Wisconsin–Madison (WI)
U of Wisconsin–Milwaukee (WI)

RECORDING ARTS TECHNOLOGY
The Art Inst of Atlanta (GA)
The Art Inst of Austin (TX)
The Art Inst of California–Los Angeles (CA)
Butler U (IN)
Columbia Coll Chicago (IL)
Indiana U Bloomington (IN)
Intl Acad of Design & Technology (FL)
Ithaca Coll (NY)
Lebanon Valley Coll (PA)
Malone Coll (OH)
Mississippi Valley State U (MS)
New England School of Communications (ME)
Savannah Coll of Art and Design (GA)
Texas Southern U (TX)
Texas State U-San Marcos (TX)
York Coll of Pennsylvania (PA)

RECREATION PRODUCTS/ SERVICES MARKETING OPERATIONS
U of Arkansas (AR)

REGIONAL STUDIES
The Colorado Coll (CO)
McGill U (QC, Canada)
Mercer U (GA)
Pitzer Coll (CA)
Washington U in St. Louis (MO)

REHABILITATION AND THERAPEUTIC PROFESSIONS RELATED
Assumption Coll (MA)
East Stroudsburg U of Pennsylvania (PA)
Hilbert Coll (NY)
Indiana U of Pennsylvania (PA)
Marshall U (WV)
Montana State U–Billings (MT)
Penn State Abington (PA)
Penn State Altoona (PA)
Penn State Berks (PA)
Penn State Erie, The Behrend Coll (PA)
Penn State U Park (PA)
Southern Illinois U Carbondale (IL)
Southern U and Ag and Mech Coll (LA)
Troy U (AL)
U of Maine at Farmington (ME)
U of North Texas (TX)
U of Pittsburgh (PA)
The U of Texas–Pan American (TX)
The U of Western Ontario (ON, Canada)
U of Wisconsin–La Crosse (WI)
Wilson Coll (PA)

REHABILITATION THERAPY
Baker Coll of Muskegon (MI)
Boston U (MA)
California State U, Los Angeles (CA)
East Stroudsburg U of Pennsylvania (PA)
Ithaca Coll (NY)
Montana State U–Billings (MT)
Northeastern U (MA)
Southern U and Ag and Mech Coll (LA)
Stephen F. Austin State U (TX)
Thomas U (GA)
The U of British Columbia (BC, Canada)
U of Maine at Farmington (ME)
U of Maryland Eastern Shore (MD)
U of Ottawa (ON, Canada)
York U (ON, Canada)

RELIGIOUS EDUCATION
Andrews U (MI)
Aquinas Coll (MI)
Asbury Coll (KY)
Ashland U (OH)
Baptist Bible Coll of Pennsylvania (PA)
Barclay Coll (KS)
Bethany Bible Coll (NB, Canada)
Biola U (CA)
Bob Jones U (SC)
Bryan Coll (TN)
Canadian Mennonite U (MB, Canada)
Capital U (OH)
The Catholic U of America (DC)
Cedarville U (OH)
Coll of Mount St. Joseph (OH)
Coll of Saint Benedict (MN)
Columbia Coll (SC)
Concordia U (MI)
Concordia U (OR)
Concordia U Chicago (IL)
Concordia U, Nebraska (NE)
Concordia U, St. Paul (MN)
Concordia U Texas (TX)
Cornerstone U (MI)
Crossroads Coll (MN)
Crown Coll (MN)
Dallas Baptist U (TX)
Davis & Elkins Coll (WV)
Defiance Coll (OH)
East Texas Baptist U (TX)
Erskine Coll (SC)
Eugene Bible Coll (OR)
Faith Baptist Bible Coll and Theological Sem (IA)
Faulkner U (AL)
Florida Southern Coll (FL)
Franciscan U of Steubenville (OH)
Free Will Baptist Bible Coll (TN)
Gardner-Webb U (NC)
George Fox U (OR)
Grace U (NE)
Great Lakes Christian Coll (MI)
Hannibal-LaGrange Coll (MO)
Harding U (AR)
Hebrew Coll (MA)
Heritage Baptist Coll and Heritage Theological Sem (ON, Canada)
Heritage Bible Coll (NC)
Hillsdale Free Will Baptist Coll (OK)
Holy Family U (PA)
Houghton Coll (NY)
Howard Payne U (TX)
Indiana Wesleyan U (IN)
John Brown U (AR)
John Carroll U (OH)
John Wesley Coll (NC)
Kuyper Coll (MI)
LaGrange Coll (GA)
La Roche Coll (PA)
La Salle U (PA)
Lee U (TN)
Lenoir-Rhyne Coll (NC)
List Coll, The Jewish Theological Sem (NY)
Louisiana Coll (LA)
Loyola U Chicago (IL)
Loyola U New Orleans (LA)
Malone Coll (OH)
Maranatha Baptist Bible Coll (WI)
Marian Coll (IN)
The Master's Coll and Sem (CA)
Master's Coll and Sem (ON, Canada)
McGill U (QC, Canada)
Messiah Coll (PA)
MidAmerica Nazarene U (KS)
Mid-Continent U (KY)
Missouri Baptist U (MO)
Morris Coll (SC)
Mount Mary Coll (WI)
Mount Vernon Nazarene U (OH)
Multnomah Bible Coll and Biblical Sem (OR)
Nazarene Bible Coll (CO)
Nebraska Christian Coll (NE)
North Greenville U (SC)
Northwestern Coll (IA)
Northwest Nazarene U (ID)
Nyack Coll (NY)
Oak Hills Christian Coll (MN)
Oakland City U (IN)
Oakwood Coll (AL)
Oklahoma Christian U (OK)
Oklahoma City U (OK)
Oral Roberts U (OK)
Ozark Christian Coll (MO)
Pepperdine U, Malibu (CA)
Pfeiffer U (NC)
Pillsbury Baptist Bible Coll (MN)
St. Edward's U (TX)
Saint John's U (MN)
St. Louis Christian Coll (MO)
Saint Mary's U of Minnesota (MN)
Saint Vincent Coll (PA)
Seattle Pacific U (WA)
Simpson U (CA)
Southeastern Bible Coll (AL)
Southern Adventist U (TN)
Southwest Baptist U (MO)
Sterling Coll (KS)
Talmudic Coll of Florida (FL)
Taylor U (IN)
Taylor U Fort Wayne (IN)
Thiel Coll (PA)
Toccoa Falls Coll (GA)
Trinity Christian Coll (IL)
Tyndale U Coll & Sem (ON, Canada)
Union Coll (NE)
U of Dayton (OH)
U of the Ozarks (AR)
The U of Western Ontario (ON, Canada)
Vanguard U of Southern California (CA)
Vennard Coll (IA)
Wayland Baptist U (TX)
West Virginia Wesleyan Coll (WV)
Wheaton Coll (IL)
York Coll (NE)

RELIGIOUS/SACRED MUSIC
Anderson U (IN)
Anderson U (SC)
Aquinas Coll (MI)
Atlantic Union Coll (MA)
Augustana Coll (IL)
Ave Maria U (FL)
Baptist Bible Coll of Pennsylvania (PA)
Barclay Coll (KS)
Baylor U (TX)
Belmont U (TN)
Bethany Lutheran Coll (MN)
Bethany U (CA)
Bethel Coll (TN)
Bethel U (MN)
Bluefield Coll (VA)
Bryan Coll (TN)
Calvin Coll (MI)
Cedarville U (OH)
Centenary Coll of Louisiana (LA)
Central Christian Coll of Kansas (KS)
Clearwater Christian Coll (FL)
Coll of the Ozarks (MO)
Concordia Coll–New York (NY)
Concordia U (MI)
Concordia U Chicago (IL)
Concordia U, Nebraska (NE)
Concordia U, St. Paul (MN)
Concordia U Texas (TX)
Crossroads Coll (MN)
Dallas Baptist U (TX)
Drake U (IA)
East Texas Baptist U (TX)
Emmanuel Coll (GA)
Erskine Coll (SC)
Eugene Bible Coll (OR)
Evangel U (MO)
Faith Baptist Bible Coll and Theological Sem (IA)
Florida Southern Coll (FL)
Franciscan U of Steubenville (OH)
Free Will Baptist Bible Coll (TN)
Fresno Pacific U (CA)
Furman U (SC)
Gardner-Webb U (NC)
Grace U (NE)
Great Lakes Christian Coll (MI)
Gustavus Adolphus Coll (MN)
Hannibal-LaGrange Coll (MO)
Hardin-Simmons U (TX)
Hebrew Coll (MA)
Heritage Baptist Coll and Heritage Theological Sem (ON, Canada)
Hillsdale Free Will Baptist Coll (OK)
Hope Intl U (CA)
Horizon Coll & Sem (SK, Canada)
Houston Baptist U (TX)
Howard Payne U (TX)
Huntington U (IN)
Indiana Wesleyan U (IN)
Johnson Bible Coll (TN)
Kentucky Christian U (KY)
Kuyper Coll (MI)
Lambuth U (TN)
Lenoir-Rhyne Coll (NC)
Liberty U (VA)
Louisiana Coll (LA)
Loyola U New Orleans (LA)
Malone Coll (OH)
Maranatha Baptist Bible Coll (WI)
The Master's Coll and Sem (CA)
McGill U (QC, Canada)
MidAmerica Nazarene U (KS)
Mississippi Coll (MS)
Missouri Baptist U (MO)
Moravian Coll (PA)
Mount Vernon Nazarene U (OH)
Multnomah Bible Coll and Biblical Sem (OR)
Nazarene Bible Coll (CO)
Nebraska Christian Coll (NE)
North Carolina Central U (NC)
North Greenville U (SC)
Northwest Nazarene U (ID)
Nyack Coll (NY)
Oklahoma City U (OK)
Oral Roberts U (OK)
Ouachita Baptist U (AR)
Ozark Christian Coll (MO)
Palm Beach Atlantic U (FL)
Pfeiffer U (NC)
Pillsbury Baptist Bible Coll (MN)
Point Loma Nazarene U (CA)
Presbyterian Coll (SC)
Rider U (NJ)
St. Louis Christian Coll (MO)
St. Mary's Coll of Maryland (MD)
Samford U (AL)
San Diego Christian Coll (CA)
Seton Hill U (PA)
Shorter Coll (GA)
Southeastern Bible Coll (AL)
Southern Wesleyan U (SC)
Southwestern Oklahoma State U (OK)
Susquehanna U (PA)
Taylor U (IN)
Toccoa Falls Coll (GA)
Trevecca Nazarene U (TN)
Trinity Intl U (IL)
Trinity Lutheran Coll (WA)
Union U (TN)

MAJORS AND MORE

U of Mary Hardin-Baylor (TX)
Valparaiso U (IN)
Wartburg Coll (IA)
Wayland Baptist U (TX)
William Jewell Coll (MO)
Wittenberg U (OH)

RELIGIOUS STUDIES

Adrian Coll (MI)
Agnes Scott Coll (GA)
Albertus Magnus Coll (CT)
Albion Coll (MI)
Albright Coll (PA)
Allegheny Coll (PA)
Alma Coll (MI)
Alvernia Coll (PA)
American Public U System (WV)
Amherst Coll (MA)
Anderson U (IN)
Anderson U (SC)
Andrews U (MI)
Appalachian State U (NC)
Aquinas Coll (MI)
Arizona State U (AZ)
Arlington Baptist Coll (TX)
Ashford U (IA)
Ashland U (OH)
Athens State U (AL)
Atlantic Union Coll (MA)
Augsburg Coll (MN)
Augustana Coll (IL)
Augustana Coll (SD)
Austin Coll (TX)
Averett U (VA)
Avila U (MO)
Azusa Pacific U (CA)
Baker U (KS)
Baldwin-Wallace Coll (OH)
Ball State U (IN)
Bard Coll (NY)
Bard Coll at Simon's Rock (MA)
Barnard Coll (NY)
Bates Coll (ME)
Baylor U (TX)
Beloit Coll (WI)
Bemidji State U (MN)
Benedictine Coll (KS)
Berea Coll (KY)
Bethany Bible Coll (NB, Canada)
Bethany Coll (KS)
Bethany Coll (WV)
Bethany Lutheran Coll (MN)
Bethel Coll (KS)
Biola U (CA)
Bishop's U (QC, Canada)
Bloomfield Coll (NJ)
Bluefield Coll (VA)
Bluffton U (OH)
Boston U (MA)
Bowdoin Coll (ME)
Bradley U (IL)
Brevard Coll (NC)
Brewton-Parker Coll (GA)
Brown U (RI)
Bryn Mawr Coll (PA)
Bucknell U (PA)
Butler U (IN)
Cabrini Coll (PA)
California Lutheran U (CA)
California State U, Dominguez Hills (CA)
California State U, East Bay (CA)
California State U, Fresno (CA)
California State U, Fullerton (CA)
California State U, Long Beach (CA)
California State U, Sacramento (CA)
Calumet Coll of Saint Joseph (IN)
Calvin Coll (MI)
Canadian Mennonite U (MB, Canada)
Canisius Coll (NY)
Capital U (OH)
Carroll Coll (WI)
Carson-Newman Coll (TN)
Case Western Reserve U (OH)
Catawba Coll (NC)
The Catholic U of America (DC)
Cedarville U (OH)
Centenary Coll of Louisiana (LA)
Central Christian Coll of Kansas (KS)
Central Coll (IA)
Central Michigan U (MI)
Central Washington U (WA)
Centre Coll (KY)
Chaminade U of Honolulu (HI)
Chapman U (CA)
Christian Brothers U (TN)
Claremont McKenna Coll (CA)
Clark Atlanta U (GA)
Clarke Coll (IA)
Cleveland State U (OH)
Colby Coll (ME)
Colgate U (NY)
Coll of Charleston (SC)
The Coll of Idaho (ID)
Coll of Mount St. Joseph (OH)
Coll of Mount Saint Vincent (NY)
The Coll of New Rochelle (NY)
The Coll of Saint Rose (NY)
The Coll of St. Scholastica (MN)
Coll of the Holy Cross (MA)
The Coll of William and Mary (VA)
The Colorado Coll (CO)
Columbia Coll (SC)
Concordia Coll (MN)
Concordia Coll–New York (NY)
Concordia U (MI)
Concordia U (OR)
Concordia U (QC, Canada)
Concordia U Texas (TX)
Concordia U Wisconsin (WI)
Connecticut Coll (CT)
Converse Coll (SC)
Cornell Coll (IA)
Cornell U (NY)
Cornerstone U (MI)
Culver-Stockton Coll (MO)
Daemen Coll (NY)
Dakota Wesleyan U (SD)
Dana Coll (NE)
Dartmouth Coll (NH)
Davidson Coll (NC)
Davis & Elkins Coll (WV)
Defiance Coll (OH)
Denison U (OH)
DePaul U (IL)
DePauw U (IN)
Dickinson Coll (PA)
Dillard U (LA)
Doane Coll (NE)
Dominican U (IL)
Dominican U of California (CA)
Dordt Coll (IA)
Drake U (IA)
Drew U (NJ)
Drury U (MO)
Duke U (NC)
Earlham Coll (IN)
Eastern New Mexico U (NM)
East Texas Baptist U (TX)
Eckerd Coll (FL)
Elizabethtown Coll (PA)
Elon U (NC)
Emmanuel Coll (MA)
Emory & Henry Coll (VA)
Emory U (GA)
Erskine Coll (SC)
Eugene Lang Coll The New School for Liberal Arts (NY)
Fairfield U (CT)
Faulkner U (AL)
Felician Coll (NJ)
Ferrum Coll (VA)
Florida Ag and Mech U (FL)
Florida Intl U (FL)
Florida Memorial U (FL)
Florida Southern Coll (FL)
Florida State U (FL)
Fontbonne U (MO)
Franklin & Marshall Coll (PA)
Franklin Coll (IN)
Fresno Pacific U (CA)
Furman U (SC)
Gardner-Webb U (NC)
George Fox U (OR)
George Mason U (VA)
Georgetown Coll (KY)
The George Washington U (DC)
Georgian Court U (NJ)
Georgia State U (GA)
Gettysburg Coll (PA)
Gonzaga U (WA)
Goucher Coll (MD)
Grand Canyon U (AZ)
Grand View Coll (IA)
Greensboro Coll (NC)
Greenville Coll (IL)
Grinnell Coll (IA)
Grove City Coll (PA)
Guilford Coll (NC)
Gustavus Adolphus Coll (MN)
Hamilton Coll (NY)
Hamline U (MN)
Hampden-Sydney Coll (VA)
Hampshire Coll (MA)
Hampton U (VA)
Hartwick Coll (NY)
Harvard U (MA)
Hastings Coll (NE)
Haverford Coll (PA)
Heidelberg Coll (OH)
Hellenic Coll (MA)
Hendrix Coll (AR)
High Point U (NC)
Hillsdale Coll (MI)
Hobart and William Smith Colls (NY)
Hofstra U (NY)
Hollins U (VA)
Holy Apostles Coll and Sem (CT)
Holy Family U (PA)
Holy Names U (CA)
Hood Coll (MD)
Hope Coll (MI)
Houghton Coll (NY)
Houston Baptist U (TX)
Howard Payne U (TX)
Humboldt State U (CA)
Hunter Coll of the City U of New York (NY)
Huntingdon Coll (AL)
Huntington U (IN)
Illinois Coll (IL)
Illinois Wesleyan U (IL)
Indiana U Bloomington (IN)
Indiana U East (IN)
Indiana U of Pennsylvania (PA)
Indiana U–Purdue U Indianapolis (IN)
Iona Coll (NY)
Iowa State U of Science and Technology (IA)
Jamestown Coll (ND)
Jarvis Christian Coll (TX)
John Brown U (AR)
John Carroll U (OH)
John Wesley Coll (NC)
Judson Coll (AL)
Juniata Coll (PA)
Kalamazoo Coll (MI)
Kenyon Coll (OH)
King Coll (TN)
Lafayette Coll (PA)
LaGrange Coll (GA)
Lambuth U (TN)
La Roche Coll (PA)
La Salle U (PA)
La Sierra U (CA)
Laurentian U (ON, Canada)
Lawrence U (WI)
Lebanon Valley Coll (PA)
Lees-McRae Coll (NC)
Lehigh U (PA)
Le Moyne Coll (NY)
Lenoir-Rhyne Coll (NC)
LeTourneau U (TX)
Lewis & Clark Coll (OR)
Lewis U (IL)
Liberty U (VA)
Lincoln U (PA)
Lindenwood U (MO)
Linfield Coll (OR)
List Coll, The Jewish Theological Sem (NY)
Loras Coll (IA)
Louisiana Coll (LA)
Lourdes Coll (OH)
Loyola Coll in Maryland (MD)
Loyola U New Orleans (LA)
Luther Coll (IA)
Lycoming Coll (PA)
Lynchburg Coll (VA)
Macalester Coll (MN)
Madonna U (MI)
Manchester Coll (IN)
Manhattanville Coll (NY)
Maranatha Baptist Bible Coll (WI)
Marlboro Coll (VT)
Marquette U (WI)
Martin U (IN)
Mary Baldwin Coll (VA)
Marylhurst U (OR)
Marymount U (VA)
Maryville Coll (TN)
Marywood U (PA)
The Master's Coll and Sem (CA)
McDaniel Coll (MD)
McGill U (QC, Canada)
McKendree U (IL)
McMurry U (TX)
Memorial U of Newfoundland (NL, Canada)
Mercyhurst Coll (PA)
Meredith Coll (NC)
Merrimack Coll (MA)
Messiah Coll (PA)
Methodist U (NC)
Miami U (OH)
Michigan State U (MI)
MidAmerica Nazarene U (KS)
Middlebury Coll (VT)
Midland Lutheran Coll (NE)
Miles Coll (AL)
Millsaps Coll (MS)
Missouri Baptist U (MO)
Missouri State U (MO)
Missouri Valley Coll (MO)
Molloy Coll (NY)
Monmouth Coll (IL)
Montclair State U (NJ)
Moravian Coll (PA)
Morehouse Coll (GA)
Morgan State U (MD)
Morningside Coll (IA)
Mount Allison U (NB, Canada)
Mount Holyoke Coll (MA)
Mount Marty Coll (SD)
Mount Mary Coll (WI)
Mount Mercy Coll (IA)
Mount Olive Coll (NC)
Mount St. Mary's Coll (CA)
Mount Saint Vincent U (NS, Canada)
Muhlenberg Coll (PA)
Naropa U (CO)
Nazareth Coll of Rochester (NY)
Nebraska Christian Coll (NE)
Nebraska Wesleyan U (NE)
New Coll of Florida (FL)
New York U (NY)
Niagara U (NY)
North Carolina State U (NC)
North Carolina Wesleyan Coll (NC)
North Central Coll (IL)
Northern Arizona U (AZ)
North Greenville U (SC)
Northland Coll (WI)
Northwestern Coll (IA)
Northwestern U (IL)
Northwest Nazarene U (ID)
Notre Dame de Namur U (CA)
Nyack Coll (NY)
Oakland City U (IN)
Oberlin Coll (OH)
Occidental Coll (CA)
Ohio Northern U (OH)
Ohio Valley U (WV)
Ohio Wesleyan U (OH)
Oklahoma Christian U (OK)
Oklahoma City U (OK)
Oklahoma Wesleyan U (OK)
Otterbein Coll (OH)
Pacific Islands Bible Coll (GU)
Pacific Lutheran U (WA)
Pacific Union Coll (CA)
Paine Coll (GA)
Palm Beach Atlantic U (FL)
Penn State Abington (PA)
Penn State Altoona (PA)
Penn State Berks (PA)
Penn State Erie, The Behrend Coll (PA)
Penn State U Park (PA)
Pepperdine U, Malibu (CA)
Pfeiffer U (NC)
Philadelphia Biblical U (PA)
Piedmont Coll (GA)
Pikeville Coll (KY)
Pitzer Coll (CA)
Pomona Coll (CA)
Presbyterian Coll (SC)
Princeton U (NJ)
Purdue U (IN)
Queens Coll of the City U of New York (NY)
Queen's U at Kingston (ON, Canada)
Queens U of Charlotte (NC)
Rabbinical Coll of America (NJ)
Randolph Coll (VA)
Randolph-Macon Coll (VA)
Redeemer U Coll (ON, Canada)
Reed Coll (OR)
Regis U (CO)
Rhodes Coll (TN)
Rice U (TX)
Ripon Coll (WI)
Roanoke Bible Coll (NC)
Roanoke Coll (VA)
Rollins Coll (FL)
Rosemont Coll (PA)
Rutgers, The State U of New Jersey, New Brunswick (NJ)
St. Andrews Presbyterian Coll (NC)
Saint Francis U (PA)
St. Francis Xavier U (NS, Canada)
St. John Fisher Coll (NY)
St. John's Coll (NM)
Saint Joseph Coll (CT)
Saint Joseph's U (PA)
St. Lawrence U (NY)
Saint Martin's U (WA)
Saint Mary-of-the-Woods Coll (IN)
Saint Mary's Coll (IN)
Saint Mary's Coll of California (CA)
St. Mary's Coll of Maryland (MD)
Saint Michael's Coll (VT)
St. Norbert Coll (WI)
St. Olaf Coll (MN)
St. Thomas Aquinas Coll (NY)
St. Thomas U (FL)
St. Thomas U (NB, Canada)
Saint Xavier U (IL)
Salem Coll (NC)
Salve Regina U (RI)
Samford U (AL)
San Diego State U (CA)
San Francisco State U (CA)
Santa Clara U (CA)
Sarah Lawrence Coll (NY)
Schreiner U (TX)
Scripps Coll (CA)
Seattle U (WA)
Seton Hill U (PA)
Sewanee: The U of the South (TN)
Shaw U (NC)
Shenandoah U (VA)
Shorter Coll (GA)
Siena Coll (NY)
Siena Heights U (MI)
Simpson Coll (IA)
Skidmore Coll (NY)
Smith Coll (MA)
Southeastern Bible Coll (AL)
Southern Adventist U (TN)
Southern Methodist U (TX)
Southern Wesleyan U (SC)
Southwest Baptist U (MO)
Southwestern Adventist U (TX)
Southwestern U (TX)
Spelman Coll (GA)
Spring Arbor U (MI)
Stanford U (CA)
State U of New York Coll at Old Westbury (NY)
Steinbach Bible Coll (MB, Canada)
Stetson U (FL)
Stonehill Coll (MA)
Stony Brook U, State U of New York (NY)
Susquehanna U (PA)
Swarthmore Coll (PA)
Sweet Briar Coll (VA)
Syracuse U (NY)
Tabor Coll (KS)
Taylor U (IN)
Taylor U Coll and Sem (AB, Canada)
Temple U (PA)
Tennessee Wesleyan Coll (TN)
Texas Christian U (TX)
Texas Coll (TX)
Thiel Coll (PA)
Thomas Edison State Coll (NJ)
Thomas More Coll (KY)
Toccoa Falls Coll (GA)
Towson U (MD)
Transylvania U (KY)
Trevecca Nazarene U (TN)
Trinity Christian Coll (IL)
Trinity Coll (CT)
Trinity U (TX)
Truman State U (MO)
Tulane U (LA)
Union Coll (KY)
Union Coll (NE)
Union U (TN)
U at Albany, State U of New York (NY)
The U of Alabama (AL)
The U of Arizona (AZ)
U of Bridgeport (CT)
The U of British Columbia (BC, Canada)
U of California, Berkeley (CA)
U of California, Davis (CA)
U of California, Irvine (CA)
U of California, Los Angeles (CA)
U of California, Riverside (CA)
U of California, San Diego (CA)
U of California, Santa Barbara (CA)
U of Central Arkansas (AR)
U of Chicago (IL)
U of Colorado at Boulder (CO)
U of Dayton (OH)
U of Denver (CO)
The U of Findlay (OH)
U of Florida (FL)
U of Georgia (GA)
U of Great Falls (MT)
U of Hawaii at Manoa (HI)
U of Illinois at Urbana–Champaign (IL)
U of Indianapolis (IN)
The U of Iowa (IA)
U of Kansas (KS)
U of King's Coll (NS, Canada)
U of La Verne (CA)
U of Lethbridge (AB, Canada)
U of Mary (ND)
U of Mary Hardin-Baylor (TX)
U of Mary Washington (VA)
U of Miami (FL)
U of Michigan (MI)
U of Minnesota, Twin Cities Campus (MN)
U of Missouri–Columbia (MO)
U of Nebraska at Omaha (NE)
U of New Mexico (NM)
The U of North Carolina at Asheville (NC)
The U of North Carolina at Chapel Hill (NC)
The U of North Carolina at Charlotte (NC)
The U of North Carolina at Greensboro (NC)
U of North Dakota (ND)
U of Northern Iowa (IA)
U of Oklahoma (OK)
U of Oregon (OR)
U of Ottawa (ON, Canada)
U of Pennsylvania (PA)
U of Pittsburgh (PA)
U of Prince Edward Island (PE, Canada)
U of Puget Sound (WA)
U of Redlands (CA)
U of Regina (SK, Canada)
U of Richmond (VA)
U of Rochester (NY)
U of Saint Francis (IN)

U of St. Thomas (MN)
U of San Diego (CA)
The U of Scranton (PA)
U of South Carolina (SC)
U of Southern California (CA)
U of Southern Mississippi (MS)
U of South Florida (FL)
The U of Tennessee (TN)
The U of Texas at Austin (TX)
U of the Incarnate Word (TX)
U of the Ozarks (AR)
U of the Pacific (CA)
The U of Toledo (OH)
U of Toronto (ON, Canada)
U of Tulsa (OK)
U of Vermont (VT)
U of Virginia (VA)
The U of Western Ontario (ON, Canada)
The U of Winnipeg (MB, Canada)
U of Wisconsin–Eau Claire (WI)
U of Wisconsin–Milwaukee (WI)
U of Wisconsin–Oshkosh (WI)
Vanderbilt U (TN)
Vanguard U of Southern California (CA)
Vassar Coll (NY)
Vennard Coll (IA)
Villanova U (PA)
Virginia Commonwealth U (VA)
Virginia Intermont Coll (VA)
Virginia U of Lynchburg (VA)
Virginia Wesleyan Coll (VA)
Viterbo U (WI)
Wabash Coll (IN)
Wake Forest U (NC)
Walla Walla U (WA)
Walsh U (OH)
Warner Pacific Coll (OR)
Wartburg Coll (IA)
Washburn U (KS)
Washington and Lee U (VA)
Washington U in St. Louis (MO)
Webster U (MO)
Wellesley Coll (MA)
Wells Coll (NY)
Wesleyan Coll (GA)
Wesleyan U (CT)
Western Kentucky U (KY)
Western Michigan U (MI)
Westminster Coll (MO)
Westmont Coll (CA)
West Virginia Wesleyan Coll (WV)
Wheaton Coll (IL)
Wheaton Coll (MA)
Wheeling Jesuit U (WV)
Whitman Coll (WA)
Whittier Coll (CA)
Whitworth U (WA)
Wiley Coll (TX)
Wilfrid Laurier U (ON, Canada)
Willamette U (OR)
William Jewell Coll (MO)
Williams Coll (MA)
Wilmington Coll (OH)
Wingate U (NC)
Winthrop U (SC)
Wittenberg U (OH)
Wofford Coll (SC)
Wright State U (OH)
Yale U (CT)
York Coll (NE)
York U (ON, Canada)
Youngstown State U (OH)

RELIGIOUS STUDIES RELATED

Bryn Athyn Coll of the New Church (PA)
Claremont McKenna Coll (CA)
Ohio Northern U (OH)
Point Loma Nazarene U (CA)
Saint Louis U (MO)
Sarah Lawrence Coll (NY)
U of Regina (SK, Canada)
U of the West (CA)
The U of Western Ontario (ON, Canada)
The U of Winnipeg (MB, Canada)
Ursuline Coll (OH)

RESORT MANAGEMENT

California State U, Chico (CA)
Coastal Carolina U (SC)
Florida Gulf Coast U (FL)
Green Mountain Coll (VT)

RESPIRATORY CARE THERAPY

Armstrong Atlantic State U (GA)
Baptist Coll of Health Sciences (TN)
Bellarmine U (KY)
Boise State U (ID)
Florida Ag and Mech U (FL)
Gannon U (PA)
Georgia State U (GA)
Gwynedd-Mercy Coll (PA)
Hannibal-LaGrange Coll (MO)
Indiana U East (IN)
Indiana U of Pennsylvania (PA)
Indiana U–Purdue U Indianapolis (IN)
Indiana U South Bend (IN)
Indiana U Southeast (IN)
Kettering Coll of Medical Arts (OH)
La Roche Coll (PA)
Loma Linda U (CA)
Marshall U (WV)
Medical Coll of Georgia (GA)
Midland Lutheran Coll (NE)
Midwestern State U (TX)
Missouri State U (MO)
Mountain State U (WV)
National-Louis U (IL)
Nebraska Methodist Coll (NE)
North Dakota State U (ND)
Salisbury U (MD)
Sam Houston State U (TX)
Shenandoah U (VA)
State U of New York Upstate Medical U (NY)
Stony Brook U, State U of New York (NY)
Tennessee State U (TN)
Texas Southern U (TX)
Texas State U-San Marcos (TX)
Thompson Rivers U (BC, Canada)
The U of Akron (OH)
The U of Alabama at Birmingham (AL)
U of Central Florida (FL)
U of Hartford (CT)
U of Indianapolis (IN)
U of Kansas (KS)
U of Mary (ND)
U of Missouri–Columbia (MO)
U of South Alabama (AL)
The U of Texas Medical Branch (TX)
U of the Ozarks (AR)
Wheeling Jesuit U (WV)
York Coll of Pennsylvania (PA)
Youngstown State U (OH)

RESTAURANT, CULINARY, AND CATERING MANAGEMENT

The Art Inst of Atlanta (GA)
The Art Inst of California–Inland Empire (CA)
The Art Inst of California–Los Angeles (CA)
The Art Inst of California–Orange County (CA)
The Art Inst of California–Sacramento (CA)
The Art Inst of California–San Diego (CA)
The Art Inst of California–Sunnyvale (CA)
The Art Inst of Charleston (SC)
The Art Inst of Houston (TX)
The Art Inst of Indianapolis (IN)
The Art Inst of Jacksonville (FL)
The Art Inst of Las Vegas (NV)
The Art Inst of Michigan (MI)
The Art Inst of Pittsburgh (PA)
The Art Inst of Salt Lake City (UT)
The Art Insts Intl Minnesota (MN)
The Illinois Inst of Art–Chicago (IL)
Lindenwood U (MO)
U of Illinois at Urbana–Champaign (IL)
Virginia Intermont Coll (VA)

RESTAURANT/FOOD SERVICES MANAGEMENT

The Art Inst of California–San Diego (CA)
The Art Inst of Las Vegas (NV)
Colorado State U (CO)
Cornell U (NY)
Niagara U (NY)
Southwest Minnesota State U (MN)
The U of Alabama (AL)
U of Missouri–Columbia (MO)

RETAILING

Brigham Young U (UT)
Central Michigan U (MI)
Southern New Hampshire U (NH)

RETAIL MANAGEMENT

The Art Inst of Atlanta–Decatur (GA)
The Art Inst of Austin (TX)
The Art Inst of Dallas (TX)
The Art Inst of Indianapolis (IN)
The Art Inst of Las Vegas (NV)

ROBOTICS

Worcester Polytechnic Inst (MA)

ROBOTICS TECHNOLOGY

Alcorn State U (MS)
Indiana State U (IN)
Indiana U–Purdue U Indianapolis (IN)
Lake Superior State U (MI)
Purdue U (IN)
U of Rio Grande (OH)

ROMANCE LANGUAGES

Albertus Magnus Coll (CT)
Bard Coll (NY)
Beloit Coll (WI)
Bernard M. Baruch Coll of the City U of New York (NY)
Bowdoin Coll (ME)
Bryn Mawr Coll (PA)
Cameron U (OK)
The Catholic U of America (DC)
City Coll of the City U of New York (NY)
Colgate U (NY)
Dartmouth Coll (NH)
DePauw U (IN)
Dowling Coll (NY)
Franklin Coll Switzerland (Switzerland)
Gettysburg Coll (PA)
Harvard U (MA)
Haverford Coll (PA)
Hunter Coll of the City U of New York (NY)
Kenyon Coll (OH)
Manhattanville Coll (NY)
Marlboro Coll (VT)
Mount Allison U (NB, Canada)
Mount Holyoke Coll (MA)
New York U (NY)
Northwest Missouri State U (MO)
Oberlin Coll (OH)
Pitzer Coll (CA)
Point Loma Nazarene U (CA)
Pomona Coll (CA)
Ripon Coll (WI)
Rockford Coll (IL)
St. Thomas Aquinas Coll (NY)
Sarah Lawrence Coll (NY)
Truman State U (MO)
Tufts U (MA)
U at Albany, State U of New York (NY)
The U of British Columbia (BC, Canada)
U of Chicago (IL)
U of Cincinnati (OH)
U of Maine (ME)
U of Maryland, Coll Park (MD)
U of Michigan (MI)
U of Nevada, Las Vegas (NV)
U of New Brunswick Fredericton (NB, Canada)
U of New Hampshire (NH)
The U of North Carolina at Chapel Hill (NC)
U of Notre Dame (IN)
U of Oregon (OR)
U of Toronto (ON, Canada)
U of Victoria (BC, Canada)
U of Windsor (ON, Canada)
Washington U in St. Louis (MO)
Wesleyan U (CT)
York U (ON, Canada)

ROMANCE LANGUAGES RELATED

The Colorado Coll (CO)
Hood Coll (MD)
Houston Baptist U (TX)
Merrimack Coll (MA)
U of Georgia (GA)
U of Michigan–Flint (MI)
The U of North Carolina at Chapel Hill (NC)
U of Pennsylvania (PA)

RUSSIAN

American U (DC)
Amherst Coll (MA)
Arizona State U (AZ)
Bard Coll (NY)
Barnard Coll (NY)
Bates Coll (ME)
Baylor U (TX)
Beloit Coll (WI)
Boston Coll (MA)
Boston U (MA)
Bowdoin Coll (ME)
Bowling Green State U (OH)
Brandeis U (MA)
Brigham Young U (UT)
Bryn Mawr Coll (PA)
Bucknell U (PA)
Claremont McKenna Coll (CA)
Colgate U (NY)
Coll of the Holy Cross (MA)
The Colorado Coll (CO)
Cornell Coll (IA)
Cornell U (NY)
Dartmouth Coll (NH)
Dickinson Coll (PA)
Drew U (NJ)
Duke U (NC)
Emory U (GA)
Ferrum Coll (VA)
Florida State U (FL)
Georgetown U (DC)
The George Washington U (DC)
Goucher Coll (MD)
Grinnell Coll (IA)
Gustavus Adolphus Coll (MN)
Harvard U (MA)
Haverford Coll (PA)
Hobart and William Smith Colls (NY)
Hofstra U (NY)
Hunter Coll of the City U of New York (NY)
Juniata Coll (PA)
Kent State U (OH)
Knox Coll (IL)
La Salle U (PA)
Lawrence U (WI)
Lehman Coll of the City U of New York (NY)
Loyola U New Orleans (LA)
McGill U (QC, Canada)
Memorial U of Newfoundland (NL, Canada)
Miami U (OH)
Miami U Hamilton (OH)
Michigan State U (MI)
Middlebury Coll (VT)
New Coll of Florida (FL)
New York U (NY)
Northeastern U (MA)
Northern Illinois U (IL)
Oberlin Coll (OH)
Ohio U (OH)
Oklahoma State U (OK)
Ouachita Baptist U (AR)
Penn State Abington (PA)
Penn State Altoona (PA)
Penn State Berks (PA)
Penn State Erie, The Behrend Coll (PA)
Penn State U Park (PA)
Pitzer Coll (CA)
Pomona Coll (CA)
Portland State U (OR)
Purdue U (IN)
Queens Coll of the City U of New York (NY)
Reed Coll (OR)
Rice U (TX)
Rider U (NJ)
Rutgers, The State U of New Jersey, New Brunswick (NJ)
Saint Louis U (MO)
St. Olaf Coll (MN)
San Diego State U (CA)
Sarah Lawrence Coll (NY)
Scripps Coll (CA)
Seattle Pacific U (WA)
Sewanee: The U of the South (TN)
Smith Coll (MA)
Stony Brook U, State U of New York (NY)
Swarthmore Coll (PA)
Syracuse U (NY)
Temple U (PA)
Texas A&M U (TX)
Trinity Coll (CT)
Trinity U (TX)
Truman State U (MO)
Tufts U (MA)
Tulane U (LA)
U at Albany, State U of New York (NY)
The U of Arizona (AZ)
The U of British Columbia (BC, Canada)
U of California, Davis (CA)
U of California, Irvine (CA)
U of California, Los Angeles (CA)
U of California, Riverside (CA)
U of California, San Diego (CA)
U of Chicago (IL)
U of Denver (CO)
U of Florida (FL)
U of Georgia (GA)
U of Hawaii at Manoa (HI)
U of Illinois at Chicago (IL)
U of Illinois at Urbana–Champaign (IL)
The U of Iowa (IA)
U of King's Coll (NS, Canada)
U of Maryland, Coll Park (MD)
U of Massachusetts Boston (MA)
U of Michigan (MI)
U of Minnesota, Twin Cities Campus (MN)
U of Missouri–Columbia (MO)
The U of Montana (MT)
U of Nebraska–Lincoln (NE)
U of New Brunswick Fredericton (NB, Canada)
U of New Hampshire (NH)
U of New Mexico (NM)
U of Northern Iowa (IA)
U of Notre Dame (IN)
U of Oklahoma (OK)
U of Ottawa (ON, Canada)
U of Pennsylvania (PA)
U of Pittsburgh (PA)
U of Rochester (NY)
U of St. Thomas (MN)
U of Southern California (CA)
U of South Florida (FL)
The U of Tennessee (TN)
The U of Texas at Arlington (TX)
The U of Texas at Austin (TX)
U of Toronto (ON, Canada)
U of Utah (UT)
U of Vermont (VT)
U of Victoria (BC, Canada)
U of Windsor (ON, Canada)
U of Wisconsin–Madison (WI)
U of Wisconsin–Milwaukee (WI)
U of Wyoming (WY)
Vanderbilt U (TN)
Vassar Coll (NY)
Wake Forest U (NC)
Washington U in St. Louis (MO)
Wellesley Coll (MA)
Wesleyan U (CT)
West Chester U of Pennsylvania (PA)
Wheaton Coll (MA)
Williams Coll (MA)
Yale U (CT)
York U (ON, Canada)

RUSSIAN STUDIES

American U (DC)
Bard Coll (NY)
Barnard Coll (NY)
Beloit Coll (WI)
Boston Coll (MA)
Boston U (MA)
Brown U (RI)
California State U, Fullerton (CA)
Claremont McKenna Coll (CA)
Colby Coll (ME)
Colgate U (NY)
Coll of the Holy Cross (MA)
The Coll of William and Mary (VA)
The Colorado Coll (CO)
Concordia Coll (MN)
Cornell U (NY)
Dartmouth Coll (NH)
DePauw U (IN)
Dickinson Coll (PA)
Florida State U (FL)
George Mason U (VA)
The George Washington U (DC)
Grand Valley State U (MI)
Gustavus Adolphus Coll (MN)
Hamilton Coll (NY)
Hamline U (MN)
Harvard U (MA)
Hobart and William Smith Colls (NY)
Iowa State U of Science and Technology (IA)
Kent State U (OH)
Knox Coll (IL)
Lafayette Coll (PA)
La Salle U (PA)
Lawrence U (WI)
Lehigh U (PA)
Macalester Coll (MN)
Marlboro Coll (VT)
McGill U (QC, Canada)
Middlebury Coll (VT)
Mount Holyoke Coll (MA)
Muhlenberg Coll (PA)
Oberlin Coll (OH)
Rhodes Coll (TN)
Rice U (TX)
Rutgers, The State U of New Jersey, New Brunswick (NJ)
St. Olaf Coll (MN)
San Diego State U (CA)
Sewanee: The U of the South (TN)
Smith Coll (MA)
Stetson U (FL)
Syracuse U (NY)
Texas State U-San Marcos (TX)
Texas Tech U (TX)
Tufts U (MA)
Tulane U (LA)
U at Albany, State U of New York (NY)
U of Alaska Fairbanks (AK)
The U of British Columbia (BC, Canada)
U of California, Los Angeles (CA)
U of California, Riverside (CA)
U of California, San Diego (CA)
U of California, Santa Cruz (CA)
U of Chicago (IL)
U of Colorado at Boulder (CO)
U of Houston (TX)
U of Illinois at Urbana–Champaign (IL)

The U of Iowa (IA)
U of Kansas (KS)
U of Maryland, Coll Park (MD)
U of Massachusetts Amherst (MA)
U of Michigan (MI)
U of Minnesota, Twin Cities Campus (MN)
U of Missouri–Columbia (MO)
The U of Montana (MT)
U of New Mexico (NM)
The U of North Carolina at Chapel Hill (NC)
U of Northern Iowa (IA)
U of Oregon (OR)
U of Rochester (NY)
U of St. Thomas (MN)
U of Southern Maine (ME)
The U of Texas at Austin (TX)
U of Toronto (ON, Canada)
U of Tulsa (OK)
U of Vermont (VT)
U of Victoria (BC, Canada)
U of Wisconsin–Milwaukee (WI)
Washington and Lee U (VA)
Washington U in St. Louis (MO)
Wellesley Coll (MA)
Wesleyan U (CT)
Wheaton Coll (MA)
Wittenberg U (OH)
Yale U (CT)
York U (ON, Canada)

SAFETY/SECURITY TECHNOLOGY
Farmingdale State Coll (NY)
Keene State Coll (NH)
Madonna U (MI)
U of Central Oklahoma (OK)

SALES AND MARKETING/ MARKETING AND DISTRIBUTION TEACHER EDUCATION
Bowling Green State U (OH)
Colorado State U (CO)
East Carolina U (NC)
Eastern Michigan U (MI)
Eastern New Mexico U (NM)
Fayetteville State U (NC)
Kent State U (OH)
Middle Tennessee State U (TN)
New York Inst of Technology (NY)
North Carolina State U (NC)
Old Dominion U (VA)
State U of New York at Oswego (NY)
U of Georgia (GA)
U of Nebraska–Lincoln (NE)
U of North Dakota (ND)
Utah State U (UT)
Wright State U (OH)

SALES, DISTRIBUTION AND MARKETING
Babson Coll (MA)
Baylor U (TX)
Brock U (ON, Canada)
Central Michigan U (MI)
Dowling Coll (NY)
Fairleigh Dickinson U, Coll at Florham (NJ)
Hampton U (VA)
Harding U (AR)
HEC Montreal (QC, Canada)
Husson Coll (ME)
Kennesaw State U (GA)
McKendree U (IL)
Metropolitan State U (MN)
Middle Tennessee State U (TN)
Quinnipiac U (CT)
St. Mary's U (TX)
Saint Mary's U of Minnesota (MN)
Seton Hill U (PA)
Syracuse U (NY)
Texas A&M U (TX)
Trinity Christian Coll (IL)
Tuskegee U (AL)
The U of Akron (OH)
U of Baltimore (MD)
The U of Findlay (OH)
U of Georgia (GA)
U of Houston (TX)
U of Illinois at Urbana–Champaign (IL)
U of Memphis (TN)
U of North Texas (TX)
U of Pennsylvania (PA)
U of Wisconsin–Superior (WI)
West Chester U of Pennsylvania (PA)
Wichita State U (KS)
York U (ON, Canada)

SANITATION TECHNOLOGY
Grand Valley State U (MI)

SANSKRIT AND CLASSICAL INDIAN LANGUAGES
U of Chicago (IL)
U of Hawaii at Manoa (HI)

SCANDINAVIAN LANGUAGES
Augsburg Coll (MN)
Augustana Coll (IL)
Concordia Coll (MN)
Gustavus Adolphus Coll (MN)
Harvard U (MA)
U of California, Berkeley (CA)
U of California, Los Angeles (CA)
U of Minnesota, Twin Cities Campus (MN)
U of North Dakota (ND)
The U of Texas at Austin (TX)
U of Wisconsin–Madison (WI)

SCANDINAVIAN STUDIES
Gustavus Adolphus Coll (MN)
Luther Coll (IA)
Pacific Lutheran U (WA)
Sterling Coll (VT)
U of Michigan (MI)

SCHOOL LIBRARIAN/ SCHOOL LIBRARY MEDIA
The Coll of St. Scholastica (MN)
U of Great Falls (MT)

SCHOOL PSYCHOLOGY
Iona Coll (NY)

SCIENCE TEACHER EDUCATION
Abilene Christian U (TX)
Adrian Coll (MI)
Alabama State U (AL)
Alfred U (NY)
Alice Lloyd Coll (KY)
Alma Coll (MI)
Alvernia Coll (PA)
Anderson U (IN)
Andrews U (MI)
Aquinas Coll (MI)
Ashford U (IA)
Ashland U (OH)
Assumption Coll (MA)
Athens State U (AL)
Auburn U (AL)
Augustana Coll (IL)
Ball State U (IN)
Baptist Bible Coll of Pennsylvania (PA)
Baylor U (TX)
Beloit Coll (WI)
Bemidji State U (MN)
Benedictine U (IL)
Bethel U (MN)
Bishop's U (QC, Canada)
Bluefield Coll (VA)
Bob Jones U (SC)
Boise State U (ID)
Boston U (MA)
Bowling Green State U (OH)
Brewton-Parker Coll (GA)
Brigham Young U (UT)
Brock U (ON, Canada)
Bryan Coll (TN)
Buffalo State Coll, State U of New York (NY)
California Lutheran U (CA)
California State U, San Marcos (CA)
Calumet Coll of Saint Joseph (IN)
Calvin Coll (MI)
Canisius Coll (NY)
Capital U (OH)
Carroll Coll (WI)
Castleton State Coll (VT)
Cedarville U (OH)
Central Michigan U (MI)
Central Washington U (WA)
City Coll of the City U of New York (NY)
Clarion U of Pennsylvania (PA)
Clemson U (SC)
The Coll at Brockport, State U of New York (NY)
Coll of Saint Mary (NE)
Coll of the Atlantic (ME)
Coll of the Ozarks (MO)
Coll of the Southwest (NM)
Colorado State U (CO)
Columbus State U (GA)
Concordia Coll (MN)
Concordia Coll–New York (NY)
Concordia U (MI)
Concordia U (OR)
Concordia U Chicago (IL)
Concordia U, Nebraska (NE)
Concordia U Wisconsin (WI)
Cornell U (NY)
Cornerstone U (MI)
Covenant Coll (GA)
Culver-Stockton Coll (MO)
Dakota Wesleyan U (SD)
Dallas Baptist U (TX)
Dana Coll (NE)
Defiance Coll (OH)
Dillard U (LA)
Dordt Coll (IA)
Duquesne U (PA)
East Carolina U (NC)
East Central U (OK)
Eastern Illinois U (IL)
Eastern Kentucky U (KY)
Eastern Michigan U (MI)
Elizabethtown Coll (PA)
Elon U (NC)
Evangel U (MO)
Fairmont State U (WV)
Florida Atlantic U (FL)
Florida Inst of Technology (FL)
Florida Intl U (FL)
Florida State U (FL)
Freed-Hardeman U (TN)
Fresno Pacific U (CA)
Gettysburg Coll (PA)
Glenville State Coll (WV)
Grace Coll (IN)
Grambling State U (LA)
Grand Valley State U (MI)
Greensboro Coll (NC)
Grove City Coll (PA)
Hamline U (MN)
Hannibal-LaGrange Coll (MO)
Harding U (AR)
Hardin-Simmons U (TX)
Hastings Coll (NE)
Heidelberg Coll (OH)
Henderson State U (AR)
Hofstra U (NY)
Hope Coll (MI)
Houston Baptist U (TX)
Howard Payne U (TX)
Hunter Coll of the City U of New York (NY)
Huntington U (IN)
Indiana State U (IN)
Indiana U Bloomington (IN)
Indiana U of Pennsylvania (PA)
Indiana U–Purdue U Fort Wayne (IN)
Indiana U South Bend (IN)
Indiana Wesleyan U (IN)
Inter American U of Puerto Rico, San Germán Campus (PR)
Iona Coll (NY)
Ithaca Coll (NY)
Judson Coll (AL)
Juniata Coll (PA)
Keene State Coll (NH)
Kent State U (OH)
Kutztown U of Pennsylvania (PA)
Lakehead U (ON, Canada)
La Salle U (PA)
Le Moyne Coll (NY)
LeMoyne-Owen Coll (TN)
Lenoir-Rhyne Coll (NC)
Lewis-Clark State Coll (ID)
Lindenwood U (MO)
Longwood U (VA)
Louisiana Coll (LA)
Lyndon State Coll (VT)
Madonna U (MI)
Malone Coll (OH)
Manchester Coll (IN)
Mansfield U of Pennsylvania (PA)
Maranatha Baptist Bible Coll (WI)
Marian Coll of Fond du Lac (WI)
Marquette U (WI)
Marywood U (PA)
The Master's Coll and Sem (CA)
McGill U (QC, Canada)
Memorial U of Newfoundland (NL, Canada)
Mercyhurst Coll (PA)
Methodist U (NC)
Miami U (OH)
Miami U Hamilton (OH)
Michigan Technological U (MI)
Midland Lutheran Coll (NE)
Millersville U of Pennsylvania (PA)
Minnesota State U Mankato (MN)
Minot State U (ND)
Mississippi Coll (MS)
Mississippi U for Women (MS)
Mississippi Valley State U (MS)
Missouri Baptist U (MO)
Missouri State U (MO)
Missouri Valley Coll (MO)
Montana State U–Billings (MT)
Moravian Coll (PA)
Morningside Coll (IA)
Mount Mercy Coll (IA)
Mount Vernon Nazarene U (OH)
Murray State U (KY)
Nazareth Coll of Rochester (NY)
Nebraska Wesleyan U (NE)
New Mexico Highlands U (NM)
Niagara U (NY)
Nicholls State U (LA)
North Carolina State U (NC)
North Dakota State U (ND)
Northeastern State U (OK)
Northern Arizona U (AZ)
Northern Michigan U (MI)
North Georgia Coll & State U (GA)
Northland Coll (WI)
Northwestern Oklahoma State U (OK)
Northwest Missouri State U (MO)
Oakland City U (IN)
Oakwood Coll (AL)
Ohio Dominican U (OH)
Ohio Northern U (OH)
Ohio U (OH)
Oklahoma Christian U (OK)
Oklahoma City U (OK)
Oklahoma Wesleyan U (OK)
Oral Roberts U (OK)
Otterbein Coll (OH)
Ouachita Baptist U (AR)
Pace U (NY)
Peru State Coll (NE)
Pfeiffer U (NC)
Pillsbury Baptist Bible Coll (MN)
Prescott Coll (AZ)
Purdue U (IN)
Purdue U Calumet (IN)
Queen's U at Kingston (ON, Canada)
Rhode Island Coll (RI)
Rider U (NJ)
Roberts Wesleyan Coll (NY)
Rochester Coll (MI)
Sacred Heart U (CT)
Saginaw Valley State U (MI)
St. Ambrose U (IA)
St. Cloud State U (MN)
Saint Francis U (PA)
St. John Fisher Coll (NY)
St. Joseph's Coll, Suffolk Campus (NY)
Saint Joseph's U (PA)
Samford U (AL)
Seattle Pacific U (WA)
Shawnee State U (OH)
Southeastern Louisiana U (LA)
Southeastern Oklahoma State U (OK)
Southeastern U (FL)
Southeast Missouri State U (MO)
Southern Arkansas U–Magnolia (AR)
Southern Illinois U Edwardsville (IL)
Southern U and Ag and Mech Coll (LA)
Southern Wesleyan U (SC)
Southwest Baptist U (MO)
Southwestern Oklahoma State U (OK)
Southwestern U (TX)
State U of New York at Fredonia (NY)
State U of New York at Oswego (NY)
State U of New York Coll at Old Westbury (NY)
State U of New York Coll at Oneonta (NY)
State U of New York Coll at Potsdam (NY)
State U of New York Coll of Environmental Science and Forestry (NY)
Tabor Coll (KS)
Tarleton State U (TX)
Taylor U (IN)
Temple U (PA)
Texas A&M Intl U (TX)
Texas Christian U (TX)
Trinity Christian Coll (IL)
Tri-State U (IN)
Union U (TN)
The U of Akron (OH)
The U of Arizona (AZ)
U of Arkansas at Fort Smith (AR)
The U of British Columbia (BC, Canada)
U of Central Arkansas (AR)
U of Central Florida (FL)
U of Central Oklahoma (OK)
U of Charleston (WV)
U of Dayton (OH)
U of Evansville (IN)
The U of Findlay (OH)
U of Georgia (GA)
U of Great Falls (MT)
U of Illinois at Chicago (IL)
U of Illinois at Urbana–Champaign (IL)
U of Indianapolis (IN)
The U of Iowa (IA)
U of Lethbridge (AB, Canada)
U of Louisiana at Lafayette (LA)
U of Maine (ME)
U of Maine at Farmington (ME)
U of Maine at Machias (ME)
U of Mary Hardin-Baylor (TX)
U of Maryland, Coll Park (MD)
U of Michigan–Dearborn (MI)
U of Michigan–Flint (MI)
U of Minnesota, Duluth (MN)
U of Minnesota, Twin Cities Campus (MN)
U of Mississippi (MS)
U of Missouri–Columbia (MO)
The U of Montana (MT)
The U of Montana–Western (MT)
U of Nebraska–Lincoln (NE)
U of Nevada, Reno (NV)
U of New Brunswick Fredericton (NB, Canada)
U of New Hampshire (NH)
The U of North Carolina at Pembroke (NC)
U of North Dakota (ND)
U of Northern Iowa (IA)
U of North Florida (FL)
U of Notre Dame (IN)
U of Oklahoma (OK)
U of Pittsburgh at Johnstown (PA)
U of Puerto Rico at Utuado (PR)
U of Puerto Rico, Cayey U Coll (PR)
U of Regina (SK, Canada)
U of Rio Grande (OH)
U of St. Francis (IL)
U of Saint Francis (IN)
U of St. Thomas (MN)
U of Sioux Falls (SD)
The U of South Dakota (SD)
U of South Florida (FL)
The U of Tennessee at Chattanooga (TN)
The U of Tennessee at Martin (TN)
The U of Toledo (OH)
U of Toronto (ON, Canada)
U of Vermont (VT)
U of Windsor (ON, Canada)
U of Wisconsin–Eau Claire (WI)
U of Wisconsin–La Crosse (WI)
U of Wisconsin–Madison (WI)
U of Wisconsin–Platteville (WI)
U of Wisconsin–Superior (WI)
U of Wisconsin–Whitewater (WI)
Ursuline Coll (OH)
Utah State U (UT)
Utah Valley State Coll (UT)
Valley City State U (ND)
Valparaiso U (IN)
Viterbo U (WI)
Walsh U (OH)
Warner Pacific Coll (OR)
Washington U in St. Louis (MO)
Waynesburg U (PA)
Wayne State Coll (NE)
Wayne State U (MI)
Weber State U (UT)
Western Carolina U (NC)
Western Michigan U (MI)
Western New Mexico U (NM)
Western State Coll of Colorado (CO)
Western Washington U (WA)
Westfield State Coll (MA)
Wheaton Coll (IL)
Wheeling Jesuit U (WV)
Wichita State U (KS)
Widener U (PA)
William Woods U (MO)
Wilmington Coll (OH)
Wilmington U (DE)
Winona State U (MN)
Wright State U (OH)
Xavier U (OH)
Xavier U of Louisiana (LA)
York Coll (NE)
York Coll of Pennsylvania (PA)
York U (ON, Canada)
Youngstown State U (OH)

SCIENCE TECHNOLOGIES RELATED
Athens State U (AL)
Bridgewater State Coll (MA)
Carlow U (PA)
Clemson U (SC)
Kean U (NJ)
Lehigh U (PA)
Madonna U (MI)
Northern Arizona U (AZ)
The U of Arizona (AZ)
Willamette U (OR)

SCIENCE, TECHNOLOGY AND SOCIETY
Butler U (IN)
Carnegie Mellon U (PA)
Cleveland State U (OH)
Colby Coll (ME)
Coll of the Ozarks (MO)
Cornell U (NY)
Embry-Riddle Aeronautical U (AZ)
Georgetown U (DC)
Georgia Inst of Technology (GA)
James Madison U (VA)

Massachusetts Inst of Technology (MA)
Michigan State U (MI)
New Jersey Inst of Technology (NJ)
North Carolina State U (NC)
Northwestern U (IL)
Pitzer Coll (CA)
Rensselaer Polytechnic Inst (NY)
Rutgers, The State U of New Jersey, Newark (NJ)
Samford U (AL)
Scripps Coll (CA)
Slippery Rock U of Pennsylvania (PA)
Stanford U (CA)
Texas Southern U (TX)
U of King's Coll (NS, Canada)
U of Nevada, Reno (NV)
U of Puget Sound (WA)
U of Windsor (ON, Canada)
Vassar Coll (NY)
Washington U in St. Louis (MO)
Wesleyan U (CT)
Worcester Polytechnic Inst (MA)
York U (ON, Canada)

SCULPTURE

Alberta Coll of Art & Design (AB, Canada)
Aquinas Coll (MI)
Art Acad of Cincinnati (OH)
Ball State U (IN)
Bard Coll at Simon's Rock (MA)
Bennington Coll (VT)
Bethany Coll (KS)
Boston U (MA)
Bradley U (IL)
Brigham Young U (UT)
Buffalo State Coll, State U of New York (NY)
California Coll of the Arts (CA)
California Inst of the Arts (CA)
California State U, East Bay (CA)
California State U, Long Beach (CA)
The Catholic U of America (DC)
The Cleveland Inst of Art (OH)
The Coll at Brockport, State U of New York (NY)
Coll of Santa Fe (NM)
Coll of Visual Arts (MN)
Colorado State U (CO)
Concordia U (QC, Canada)
Drake U (IA)
Ferris State U (MI)
Grand Valley State U (MI)
Indiana U–Purdue U Fort Wayne (IN)
Inter American U of Puerto Rico, San Germán Campus (PR)
Kansas City Art Inst (MO)
Kent State U (OH)
Laguna Coll of Art & Design (CA)
Longwood U (VA)
Marlboro Coll (VT)
Maryland Inst Coll of Art (MD)
Marywood U (PA)
Massachusetts Coll of Art and Design (MA)
Memorial U of Newfoundland (NL, Canada)
Memphis Coll of Art (TN)
Mercyhurst Coll (PA)
Minnesota State U Mankato (MN)
Montserrat Coll of Art (MA)
Mount Allison U (NB, Canada)
Northern Michigan U (MI)
Northwest Missouri State U (MO)
Northwest Nazarene U (ID)
Notre Dame de Namur U (CA)
NSCAD U (NS, Canada)
Ohio Northern U (OH)
Ohio U (OH)
Otis Coll of Art and Design (CA)
Portland State U (OR)
Pratt Inst (NY)
Rochester Inst of Technology (NY)
Rocky Mountain Coll of Art + Design (CO)
Rutgers, The State U of New Jersey, New Brunswick (NJ)
St. Cloud State U (MN)
Sarah Lawrence Coll (NY)
Savannah Coll of Art and Design (GA)
School of the Art Inst of Chicago (IL)
School of the Museum of Fine Arts, Boston (MA)
School of Visual Arts (NY)
Seton Hill U (PA)
Sonoma State U (CA)
State U of New York at Binghamton (NY)
State U of New York at New Paltz (NY)
Temple U (PA)
Texas Christian U (TX)
Trinity Christian Coll (IL)
The U of Akron (OH)
U of Dallas (TX)
U of Georgia (GA)
U of Hartford (CT)
U of Houston (TX)
U of Illinois at Urbana–Champaign (IL)
The U of Iowa (IA)
U of Kansas (KS)
U of Massachusetts Dartmouth (MA)
U of Miami (FL)
U of Michigan (MI)
U of Oregon (OR)
U of Regina (SK, Canada)
The U of Texas at El Paso (TX)
U of Windsor (ON, Canada)
U of Wisconsin–Milwaukee (WI)
Virginia Commonwealth U (VA)
Washington U in St. Louis (MO)
Western Michigan U (MI)
Western State Coll of Colorado (CO)
Western Washington U (WA)
York U (ON, Canada)

SECONDARY EDUCATION

Abilene Christian U (TX)
Acadia U (NS, Canada)
Adams State Coll (CO)
Adrian Coll (MI)
Alabama Ag and Mech U (AL)
Alabama State U (AL)
Albertus Magnus Coll (CT)
Albion Coll (MI)
Albright Coll (PA)
Alderson-Broaddus Coll (WV)
Alfred U (NY)
Alice Lloyd Coll (KY)
Alma Coll (MI)
American U (DC)
Andrews U (MI)
Aquinas Coll (MI)
Arizona State U (AZ)
Arizona State U at the West campus (AZ)
Ashford U (IA)
Ashland U (OH)
Assumption Coll (MA)
Athens State U (AL)
Atlantic Union Coll (MA)
Auburn U (AL)
Auburn U Montgomery (AL)
Augsburg Coll (MN)
Augustana Coll (IL)
Augustana Coll (SD)
Baker U (KS)
Ball State U (IN)
Baptist Bible Coll of Pennsylvania (PA)
Baylor U (TX)
Belmont Abbey Coll (NC)
Beloit Coll (WI)
Bemidji State U (MN)
Benedictine Coll (KS)
Benedictine U (IL)
Bennington Coll (VT)
Biola U (CA)
Bishop's U (QC, Canada)
Blackburn Coll (IL)
Bluefield Coll (VA)
Boise State U (ID)
Boston Coll (MA)
Brewton-Parker Coll (GA)
Brock U (ON, Canada)
Bryan Coll (TN)
Bucknell U (PA)
Buffalo State Coll, State U of New York (NY)
Butler U (IN)
Calumet Coll of Saint Joseph (IN)
Calvin Coll (MI)
Cameron U (OK)
Canisius Coll (NY)
Capital U (OH)
Carson-Newman Coll (TN)
Catawba Coll (NC)
The Catholic U of America (DC)
Cedar Crest Coll (PA)
Cedarville U (OH)
Centenary Coll (NJ)
Centenary Coll of Louisiana (LA)
Central State U (OH)
Centre Coll (KY)
Cheyney U of Pennsylvania (PA)
The Citadel, The Military Coll of South Carolina (SC)
City Coll of the City U of New York (NY)
Clarke Coll (IA)
Clark U (MA)
Clemson U (SC)
The Coll at Brockport, State U of New York (NY)
The Coll of New Jersey (NJ)
Coll of Saint Benedict (MN)
Coll of St. Joseph (VT)
Coll of Saint Mary (NE)
Coll of the Atlantic (ME)
Coll of the Ozarks (MO)
Coll of the Southwest (NM)
Concordia Coll (MN)
Concordia Coll–New York (NY)
Concordia U (MI)
Concordia U (OR)
Concordia U Chicago (IL)
Concordia U, Nebraska (NE)
Concordia U, St. Paul (MN)
Concordia U Texas (TX)
Concordia U Wisconsin (WI)
Concord U (WV)
Connecticut Coll (CT)
Converse Coll (SC)
Cornell Coll (IA)
Cornerstone U (MI)
Dakota Wesleyan U (SD)
Dallas Baptist U (TX)
Dana Coll (NE)
Defiance Coll (OH)
Delaware Valley Coll (PA)
DePaul U (IL)
Dominican Coll (NY)
Dordt Coll (IA)
Dowling Coll (NY)
Drake U (IA)
Drury U (MO)
Duquesne U (PA)
East Central U (OK)
Eastern Connecticut State U (CT)
Eastern Kentucky U (KY)
Eastern Mennonite U (VA)
East Stroudsburg U of Pennsylvania (PA)
Elizabethtown Coll (PA)
Elon U (NC)
Emmanuel Coll (MA)
Emporia State U (KS)
Evangel U (MO)
Fairfield U (CT)
Fairmont State U (WV)
Faulkner U (AL)
Fitchburg State Coll (MA)
Flagler Coll (FL)
Florida Gulf Coast U (FL)
Florida Memorial U (FL)
Florida Southern Coll (FL)
Florida State U (FL)
Fontbonne U (MO)
Fort Lewis Coll (CO)
Freed-Hardeman U (TN)
Free Will Baptist Bible Coll (TN)
Fresno Pacific U (CA)
Frostburg State U (MD)
Furman U (SC)
Gannon U (PA)
Gardner-Webb U (NC)
Gettysburg Coll (PA)
Glenville State Coll (WV)
Gonzaga U (WA)
Grace Bible Coll (MI)
Grace U (NE)
Grambling State U (LA)
Grand Canyon U (AZ)
Grand Valley State U (MI)
Green Mountain Coll (VT)
Greensboro Coll (NC)
Grove City Coll (PA)
Guilford Coll (NC)
Gustavus Adolphus Coll (MN)
Gwynedd-Mercy Coll (PA)
Hamline U (MN)
Hampton U (VA)
Hannibal-LaGrange Coll (MO)
Harding U (AR)
Harris-Stowe State U (MO)
Hastings Coll (NE)
Heidelberg Coll (OH)
High Point U (NC)
Hillsdale Coll (MI)
Hillsdale Free Will Baptist Coll (OK)
Hofstra U (NY)
Holy Family U (PA)
Hope Coll (MI)
Houghton Coll (NY)
Houston Baptist U (TX)
Howard Payne U (TX)
Humboldt State U (CA)
Hunter Coll of the City U of New York (NY)
Huntington U (IN)
Huston-Tillotson U (TX)
Idaho State U (ID)
Illinois Coll (IL)
Indiana U Bloomington (IN)
Indiana U East (IN)
Indiana U Kokomo (IN)
Indiana U Northwest (IN)
Indiana U of Pennsylvania (PA)
Indiana U–Purdue U Fort Wayne (IN)
Indiana U–Purdue U Indianapolis (IN)
Indiana U South Bend (IN)
Indiana U Southeast (IN)
Indiana Wesleyan U (IN)
Inter American U of Puerto Rico, San Germán Campus (PR)
Iona Coll (NY)
Iowa State U of Science and Technology (IA)
Iowa Wesleyan Coll (IA)
Ithaca Coll (NY)
Jacksonville State U (AL)
Jacksonville U (FL)
Jamestown Coll (ND)
Jarvis Christian Coll (TX)
John Brown U (AR)
John Carroll U (OH)
Johnson State Coll (VT)
Judson U (IL)
Juniata Coll (PA)
Kansas State U (KS)
Keene State Coll (NH)
Kentucky Wesleyan Coll (KY)
Keuka Coll (NY)
King's Coll (PA)
Kutztown U of Pennsylvania (PA)
Kuyper Coll (MI)
Lake Forest Coll (IL)
Lakehead U (ON, Canada)
Lake Superior State U (MI)
Lambuth U (TN)
Lander U (SC)
La Salle U (PA)
La Sierra U (CA)
Lawrence U (WI)
Lee U (TN)
Le Moyne Coll (NY)
Lenoir-Rhyne Coll (NC)
Lesley U (MA)
LeTourneau U (TX)
Lincoln U (PA)
Lindenwood U (MO)
Lindsey Wilson Coll (KY)
Lock Haven U of Pennsylvania (PA)
Longwood U (VA)
Loras Coll (IA)
Louisiana Coll (LA)
Louisiana State U and Ag and Mech Coll (LA)
Lourdes Coll (OH)
Loyola U Chicago (IL)
Lubbock Christian U (TX)
Lynchburg Coll (VA)
Madonna U (MI)
Maharishi U of Management (IA)
Manchester Coll (IN)
Manhattanville Coll (NY)
Mansfield U of Pennsylvania (PA)
Maranatha Baptist Bible Coll (WI)
Marian Coll (IN)
Marian Coll of Fond du Lac (WI)
Marietta Coll (OH)
Marist Coll (NY)
Marquette U (WI)
Marshall U (WV)
Martin U (IN)
Maryville U of Saint Louis (MO)
The Master's Coll and Sem (CA)
McGill U (QC, Canada)
McKendree U (IL)
McMurry U (TX)
McNeese State U (LA)
Memorial U of Newfoundland (NL, Canada)
Mercyhurst Coll (PA)
Merrimack Coll (MA)
Methodist U (NC)
Miami U (OH)
Michigan Technological U (MI)
MidAmerica Nazarene U (KS)
Midland Lutheran Coll (NE)
Midway Coll (KY)
Midwestern State U (TX)
Miles Coll (AL)
Millersville U of Pennsylvania (PA)
Minnesota State U Mankato (MN)
Mississippi Coll (MS)
Mississippi State U (MS)
Mississippi U for Women (MS)
Missouri Southern State U (MO)
Missouri U of Science and Technology (MO)
Missouri Valley Coll (MO)
Molloy Coll (NY)
Monmouth Coll (IL)
Monmouth U (NJ)
Montana State U (MT)
Montana State U–Billings (MT)
Moravian Coll (PA)
Morgan State U (MD)
Morningside Coll (IA)
Mount Marty Coll (SD)
Mount Mary Coll (WI)
Mount Mercy Coll (IA)
Mount Saint Mary Coll (NY)
Mount Saint Vincent U (NS, Canada)
Mount Vernon Nazarene U (OH)
Murray State U (KY)
Nazareth Coll of Rochester (NY)
Nebraska Christian Coll (NE)
New England Coll (NH)
Newman U (KS)
New York U (NY)
Niagara U (NY)
Nichols Coll (MA)
North Carolina State U (NC)
North Carolina Wesleyan Coll (NC)
North Central Coll (IL)
Northeastern State U (OK)
Northern Michigan U (MI)
Northern State U (SD)
North Georgia Coll & State U (GA)
Northland Coll (WI)
Northwestern Coll (IA)
Northwestern Oklahoma State U (OK)
Northwestern U (IL)
Northwest Missouri State U (MO)
Northwest Nazarene U (ID)
Nova Southeastern U (FL)
Nyack Coll (NY)
Oakland City U (IN)
Ohio Dominican U (OH)
Ohio Northern U (OH)
Ohio U (OH)
Ohio Valley U (WV)
Ohio Wesleyan U (OH)
Oklahoma Christian U (OK)
Oklahoma City U (OK)
Oklahoma State U (OK)
Oklahoma Wesleyan U (OK)
Otterbein Coll (OH)
Ouachita Baptist U (AR)
Pacific U (OR)
Palm Beach Atlantic U (FL)
Penn State Abington (PA)
Penn State Altoona (PA)
Penn State Berks (PA)
Penn State Erie, The Behrend Coll (PA)
Penn State U Park (PA)
Pepperdine U, Malibu (CA)
Peru State Coll (NE)
Pillsbury Baptist Bible Coll (MN)
Point Park U (PA)
Prescott Coll (AZ)
Providence Coll (RI)
Purdue U (IN)
Purdue U Calumet (IN)
Queens U of Charlotte (NC)
Rhode Island Coll (RI)
Rider U (NJ)
Ripon Coll (WI)
Roberts Wesleyan Coll (NY)
Rochester Coll (MI)
Rockford Coll (IL)
Rockhurst U (MO)
Roger Williams U (RI)
Roosevelt U (IL)
Sacred Heart U (CT)
St. Ambrose U (IA)
St. Cloud State U (MN)
Saint Francis U (PA)
St. Francis Xavier U (NS, Canada)
Saint John's U (MN)
St. John's U (NY)
Saint Joseph Coll (CT)
Saint Joseph's Coll (IN)
St. Joseph's Coll, Suffolk Campus (NY)
Saint Joseph's U (PA)
Saint Martin's U (WA)
Saint Mary-of-the-Woods Coll (IN)
Saint Michael's Coll (VT)
St. Thomas Aquinas Coll (NY)
St. Thomas U (FL)
Salem Intl U (WV)
Salisbury U (MD)
Salve Regina U (RI)
San Diego Christian Coll (CA)
Shawnee State U (OH)
Shepherd U (WV)
Siena Coll (NY)
Siena Heights U (MI)
Simmons Coll (MA)
Simpson Coll (IA)
Slippery Rock U of Pennsylvania (PA)
Southeastern Oklahoma State U (OK)
Southern Connecticut State U (CT)
Southern U and Ag and Mech Coll (LA)
Southern Utah U (UT)
Southwestern Coll (AZ)
Southwestern Oklahoma State U (OK)
Spring Arbor U (MI)
Spring Hill Coll (AL)
State U of New York at Fredonia (NY)
State U of New York at New Paltz (NY)
State U of New York at Oswego (NY)
State U of New York Coll at Old Westbury (NY)
State U of New York Coll at Oneonta (NY)
Stetson U (FL)
Suffolk U (MA)
Susquehanna U (PA)
Tabor Coll (KS)

MAJORS AND MORE

Tarleton State U (TX)
Taylor U (IN)
Tennessee Technological U (TN)
Tennessee Wesleyan Coll (TN)
Texas A&M U–Commerce (TX)
Texas Christian U (TX)
Texas Southern U (TX)
Thiel Coll (PA)
Thomas U (GA)
Tougaloo Coll (MS)
Trent U (ON, Canada)
Trevecca Nazarene U (TN)
Trinity Christian Coll (IL)
Trinity Intl U (IL)
Tri-State U (IN)
Troy U (AL)
Tufts U (MA)
Tusculum Coll (TN)
Union Coll (KY)
Union Coll (NE)
Union U (TN)
Université de Sherbrooke (QC, Canada)
Université du Québec en Outaouais (QC, Canada)
The U of Alabama (AL)
The U of Alabama at Birmingham (AL)
The U of Arizona (AZ)
U of Arkansas at Pine Bluff (AR)
The U of British Columbia (BC, Canada)
U of Central Missouri (MO)
U of Central Oklahoma (OK)
U of Cincinnati (OH)
U of Dallas (TX)
U of Dayton (OH)
The U of Findlay (OH)
U of Great Falls (MT)
U of Guam (GU)
U of Hartford (CT)
U of Hawaii at Manoa (HI)
U of Idaho (ID)
U of Illinois at Chicago (IL)
U of Illinois at Urbana–Champaign (IL)
U of Indianapolis (IN)
The U of Iowa (IA)
U of Kansas (KS)
U of Louisiana at Lafayette (LA)
U of Maine (ME)
U of Maine at Farmington (ME)
U of Maryland, Coll Park (MD)
U of Mary Washington (VA)
U of Miami (FL)
U of Michigan (MI)
U of Michigan–Dearborn (MI)
U of Mississippi (MS)
U of Missouri–Columbia (MO)
U of Missouri–Kansas City (MO)
U of Missouri–St. Louis (MO)
The U of Montana (MT)
The U of Montana–Western (MT)
U of Montevallo (AL)
U of Nebraska at Omaha (NE)
U of Nevada, Las Vegas (NV)
U of New Brunswick Fredericton (NB, Canada)
U of New Hampshire (NH)
U of New Mexico (NM)
U of North Alabama (AL)
U of North Florida (FL)
U of Pittsburgh at Bradford (PA)
U of Pittsburgh at Johnstown (PA)
U of Portland (OR)
U of Prince Edward Island (PE, Canada)
U of Redlands (CA)
U of Regina (SK, Canada)
U of Rhode Island (RI)
U of Richmond (VA)
U of Rio Grande (OH)
U of St. Thomas (TX)
The U of Scranton (PA)
U of Sioux Falls (SD)
U of South Alabama (AL)
U of South Carolina Aiken (SC)
U of South Carolina Upstate (SC)
The U of South Dakota (SD)
The U of Tampa (FL)
The U of Tennessee at Chattanooga (TN)
U of the Sacred Heart (PR)
The U of Toledo (OH)
U of Utah (UT)
U of Vermont (VT)
U of Victoria (BC, Canada)
The U of Western Ontario (ON, Canada)
U of West Georgia (GA)
U of Windsor (ON, Canada)
The U of Winnipeg (MB, Canada)
U of Wisconsin–Madison (WI)
U of Wisconsin–Milwaukee (WI)
U of Wisconsin–Oshkosh (WI)
U of Wisconsin–Platteville (WI)
U of Wisconsin–Stevens Point (WI)
U of Wisconsin–Whitewater (WI)
U of Wyoming (WY)
Utah State U (UT)
Utica Coll (NY)
Valdosta State U (GA)
Valley City State U (ND)
Valparaiso U (IN)
Vanderbilt U (TN)
Vanguard U of Southern California (CA)
Vennard Coll (IA)
Villanova U (PA)
Virginia Intermont Coll (VA)
Virginia Polytechnic Inst and State U (VA)
Virginia Wesleyan Coll (VA)
Wagner Coll (NY)
Walsh U (OH)
Warner Pacific Coll (OR)
Warren Wilson Coll (NC)
Wartburg Coll (IA)
Washburn U (KS)
Washington U in St. Louis (MO)
Waynesburg U (PA)
Weber State U (UT)
Wells Coll (NY)
West Chester U of Pennsylvania (PA)
Western Connecticut State U (CT)
Western Michigan U (MI)
Western New England Coll (MA)
Western New Mexico U (NM)
Western Washington U (WA)
West Liberty State Coll (WV)
Westminster Coll (MO)
Westmont Coll (CA)
West Virginia U (WV)
West Virginia Wesleyan Coll (WV)
Wheaton Coll (IL)
Wheeling Jesuit U (WV)
Whitworth U (WA)
Wichita State U (KS)
William Jewell Coll (MO)
William Paterson U of New Jersey (NJ)
William Woods U (MO)
Wilmington Coll (OH)
Winona State U (MN)
Wright State U (OH)
Xavier U of Louisiana (LA)
York Coll (NE)
York Coll of Pennsylvania (PA)
York U (ON, Canada)
Youngstown State U (OH)

SECONDARY SCHOOL ADMINISTRATION/ PRINCIPALSHIP

Auburn U (AL)
The U of North Carolina at Pembroke (NC)

SECURITIES SERVICES ADMINISTRATION

American Public U System (WV)
Central Pennsylvania Coll (PA)
The Coll at Brockport, State U of New York (NY)
Davenport U, Dearborn (MI)
Davenport U, Grand Rapids (MI)
Duquesne U (PA)
St. John's U (NY)
Southwestern Coll (KS)

SECURITY AND LOSS PREVENTION

Eastern Kentucky U (KY)
Farmingdale State Coll (NY)
Northern Michigan U (MI)

SECURITY AND PROTECTIVE SERVICES RELATED

American Public U System (WV)
Concordia U (MI)
Eastern Michigan U (MI)
Lewis U (IL)
Massachusetts Maritime Acad (MA)
Midway Coll (KY)
North Dakota State U (ND)
Northwestern Oklahoma State U (OK)
Point Park U (PA)
St. Ambrose U (IA)
Thomas Edison State Coll (NJ)
Virginia Commonwealth U (VA)
Washburn U (KS)
Western Illinois U (IL)

SELLING SKILLS AND SALES

Bradley U (IL)

SEMITIC LANGUAGES

U of Pennsylvania (PA)
The U of Texas at Austin (TX)

SIGN LANGUAGE INTERPRETATION AND TRANSLATION

Bloomsburg U of Pennsylvania (PA)
Columbia Coll Chicago (IL)
Converse Coll (SC)
Eastern Kentucky U (KY)
Idaho State U (ID)
Indiana U–Purdue U Indianapolis (IN)
Maryville Coll (TN)
Mount Aloysius Coll (PA)
Northeastern U (MA)
Ozark Christian Coll (MO)
U of Louisville (KY)
U of New Hampshire at Manchester (NH)
U of New Mexico (NM)
U of Northern Colorado (CO)
U of North Florida (FL)
William Woods U (MO)
York U (ON, Canada)

SLAVIC, BALTIC, AND ALBANIAN LANGUAGES RELATED

Rutgers, The State U of New Jersey, Newark (NJ)
The U of North Carolina at Chapel Hill (NC)

SLAVIC LANGUAGES

Boston Coll (MA)
Connecticut Coll (CT)
Duke U (NC)
Harvard U (MA)
Indiana U Bloomington (IN)
Northwestern U (IL)
Princeton U (NJ)
Stanford U (CA)
U at Albany, State U of New York (NY)
The U of British Columbia (BC, Canada)
U of California, Berkeley (CA)
U of California, Los Angeles (CA)
U of California, Santa Barbara (CA)
U of Chicago (IL)
U of Georgia (GA)
U of Illinois at Chicago (IL)
U of Illinois at Urbana–Champaign (IL)
U of Kansas (KS)
U of Pittsburgh (PA)
U of Southern California (CA)
U of Toronto (ON, Canada)
U of Victoria (BC, Canada)
U of Virginia (VA)
U of Windsor (ON, Canada)
U of Wisconsin–Madison (WI)
U of Wisconsin–Milwaukee (WI)
Wayne State U (MI)

SLAVIC STUDIES

Barnard Coll (NY)
Baylor U (TX)
Connecticut Coll (CT)
Lawrence U (WI)
Northwestern U (IL)
Oakland U (MI)

SMALL BUSINESS ADMINISTRATION

American InterContinental U (CA)
American InterContinental U (FL)
American InterContinental U (TX)
American InterContinental U Buckhead Campus (GA)
American InterContinental U Dunwoody Campus (GA)
Babson Coll (MA)
Bradley U (IL)
Carroll Coll (WI)
Carson-Newman Coll (TN)
Husson Coll (ME)
Lewis-Clark State Coll (ID)
Lincoln U (CA)
North Central Coll (IL)
Northern Michigan U (MI)

SOCIAL AND PHILOSOPHICAL FOUNDATIONS OF EDUCATION

Northwestern U (IL)
Texas Southern U (TX)
Washington U in St. Louis (MO)

SOCIAL PSYCHOLOGY

Bennington Coll (VT)
Brigham Young U (UT)
Clarion U of Pennsylvania (PA)
Florida Atlantic U (FL)
Inter American U of Puerto Rico, Aguadilla Campus (PR)
Kwantlen U Coll (BC, Canada)
Lawrence U (WI)
Maryville U of Saint Louis (MO)
Moravian Coll (PA)
Paine Coll (GA)
Penn State Abington (PA)
U of California, Irvine (CA)
U of Nevada, Reno (NV)
U of New England (ME)
U of Wisconsin–Superior (WI)

SOCIAL SCIENCES

Adams State Coll (CO)
Adelphi U (NY)
Adrian Coll (MI)
Alabama State U (AL)
Albertus Magnus Coll (CT)
Alice Lloyd Coll (KY)
Alma Coll (MI)
Alvernia Coll (PA)
American Public U System (WV)
Andrews U (MI)
Angelo State U (TX)
Aquinas Coll (MI)
Arizona State U at the West campus (AZ)
Asbury Coll (KY)
Ashford U (IA)
Ashland U (OH)
Augsburg Coll (MN)
Azusa Pacific U (CA)
Ball State U (IN)
Bemidji State U (MN)
Benedictine Coll (KS)
Benedictine U (IL)
Bennington Coll (VT)
Berry Coll (GA)
Bethany Lutheran Coll (MN)
Bethany U (CA)
Bethel U (MN)
Biola U (CA)
Bishop's U (QC, Canada)
Bloomsburg U of Pennsylvania (PA)
Bluefield Coll (VA)
Bluefield State Coll (WV)
Bluffton U (OH)
Boise State U (ID)
Brewton-Parker Coll (GA)
Brock U (ON, Canada)
California Baptist U (CA)
California Lutheran U (CA)
California Polytechnic State U, San Luis Obispo (CA)
California State Polytechnic U, Pomona (CA)
California State U, Los Angeles (CA)
California State U, Sacramento (CA)
California State U, San Bernardino (CA)
California State U, San Marcos (CA)
California State U, Stanislaus (CA)
Calvin Coll (MI)
Castleton State Coll (VT)
Central Christian Coll of Kansas (KS)
Central Coll (IA)
Central Connecticut State U (CT)
Central Michigan U (MI)
Chaminade U of Honolulu (HI)
Cheyney U of Pennsylvania (PA)
Clarion U of Pennsylvania (PA)
Clarkson U (NY)
Cleveland State U (OH)
Colgate U (NY)
Coll of Mount Saint Vincent (NY)
Coll of Saint Benedict (MN)
Coll of Saint Mary (NE)
The Coll of St. Scholastica (MN)
Coll of the Southwest (NM)
Colorado State U (CO)
Colorado State U-Pueblo (CO)
Columbia Coll (SC)
Concordia Coll–New York (NY)
Concordia U (MI)
Concordia U (OR)
Concordia U, Nebraska (NE)
Cornell U (NY)
Daniel Webster Coll (NH)
Defiance Coll (OH)
Delta State U (MS)
DePaul U (IL)
Doane Coll (NE)
Dominican Coll (NY)
Dominican U (IL)
Dordt Coll (IA)
Dowling Coll (NY)
Drexel U (PA)
Eastern Mennonite U (VA)
Eastern Michigan U (MI)
Eastern New Mexico U (NM)
East Stroudsburg U of Pennsylvania (PA)
East-West U (IL)
Edinboro U of Pennsylvania (PA)
Elizabethtown Coll (PA)
Emporia State U (KS)
Eugene Lang Coll The New School for Liberal Arts (NY)
The Evergreen State Coll (WA)
Faulkner U (AL)
Felician Coll (NJ)
Florida Ag and Mech U (FL)
Florida Atlantic U (FL)
Florida Southern Coll (FL)
Florida State U (FL)
Fontbonne U (MO)
Freed-Hardeman U (TN)
Fresno Pacific U (CA)
Frostburg State U (MD)
Gannon U (PA)
Gardner-Webb U (NC)
Gettysburg Coll (PA)
Grand Valley State U (MI)
Gustavus Adolphus Coll (MN)
Hamline U (MN)
Hampton U (VA)
Harding U (AR)
Harvard U (MA)
Hawai'i Pacific U (HI)
Hofstra U (NY)
Holy Apostles Coll and Sem (CT)
Holy Family U (PA)
Hope Coll (MI)
Hope Intl U (CA)
Howard Payne U (TX)
Humboldt State U (CA)
Indiana State U (IN)
Indiana Wesleyan U (IN)
Inter American U of Puerto Rico, San Germán Campus (PR)
Iona Coll (NY)
Ithaca Coll (NY)
James Madison U (VA)
John Brown U (AR)
The Johns Hopkins U (MD)
Johnson C. Smith U (NC)
Juniata Coll (PA)
Kansas State U (KS)
Keene State Coll (NH)
Kent State U (OH)
Kentucky State U (KY)
Keuka Coll (NY)
The King's U Coll (AB, Canada)
Kutztown U of Pennsylvania (PA)
Lake Superior State U (MI)
La Salle U (PA)
Lees-McRae Coll (NC)
Lehigh U (PA)
LeMoyne-Owen Coll (TN)
Lesley U (MA)
Lewis-Clark State Coll (ID)
Liberty U (VA)
Livingstone Coll (NC)
Lock Haven U of Pennsylvania (PA)
Loyola U New Orleans (LA)
Lycoming Coll (PA)
Lyndon State Coll (VT)
Mansfield U of Pennsylvania (PA)
Marlboro Coll (VT)
Marylhurst U (OR)
Marywood U (PA)
Mayville State U (ND)
McKendree U (IL)
Memorial U of Newfoundland (NL, Canada)
Mercy Coll (NY)
Mercyhurst Coll (PA)
Mesa State Coll (CO)
Metropolitan State U (MN)
Michigan State U (MI)
Michigan Technological U (MI)
Mid-Continent U (KY)
Midland Lutheran Coll (NE)
Miles Coll (AL)
Minnesota State U Mankato (MN)
Minot State U (ND)
Mississippi Coll (MS)
Mississippi U for Women (MS)
Missouri Baptist U (MO)
Moravian Coll (PA)
Morehead State U (KY)
Mount Aloysius Coll (PA)
Mount Saint Mary Coll (NY)
Mount St. Mary's Coll (CA)
Mount St. Mary's U (MD)
Mount Saint Vincent U (NS, Canada)
Mount Vernon Nazarene U (OH)
Muhlenberg Coll (PA)
National-Louis U (IL)
Nazareth Coll of Rochester (NY)
New Coll of Florida (FL)
New York Inst of Technology (NY)
New York U (NY)
Niagara U (NY)
North Carolina Ag and Tech State U (NC)
North Central Coll (IL)
North Dakota State U (ND)
Northern Arizona U (AZ)
North Georgia Coll & State U (GA)

MAJORS AND MORE

Northland Coll (WI)
Northwestern Oklahoma State U (OK)
Northwest Missouri State U (MO)
Northwest Nazarene U (ID)
Notre Dame de Namur U (CA)
Nyack Coll (NY)
Oakland City U (IN)
Oakwood Coll (AL)
Ohio U (OH)
Oklahoma Panhandle State U (OK)
Oklahoma Wesleyan U (OK)
Pace U (NY)
Pacific Union Coll (CA)
Peru State Coll (NE)
Pfeiffer U (NC)
Piedmont Coll (GA)
Pikeville Coll (KY)
Plymouth State U (NH)
Point Loma Nazarene U (CA)
Point Park U (PA)
Portland State U (OR)
Providence Coll (RI)
Purdue U (IN)
Quinnipiac U (CT)
Radford U (VA)
Ramapo Coll of New Jersey (NJ)
Rensselaer Polytechnic Inst (NY)
Robert Morris U (PA)
Rockford Coll (IL)
Rockhurst U (MO)
Rogers State U (OK)
Roger Williams U (RI)
Roosevelt U (IL)
Rosemont Coll (PA)
Royal Military Coll of Canada (ON, Canada)
St. Cloud State U (MN)
St. Gregory's U, Shawnee (OK)
Saint John's U (MN)
St. John's U (NY)
St. Joseph's Coll, New York (NY)
St. Joseph's Coll, Suffolk Campus (NY)
Saint Joseph's U (PA)
Saint Mary-of-the-Woods Coll (IN)
Saint Mary's Coll of California (CA)
Saint Mary's U of Minnesota (MN)
St. Thomas Aquinas Coll (NY)
Saint Xavier U (IL)
Salem State Coll (MA)
Samford U (AL)
San Diego Christian Coll (CA)
San Diego State U (CA)
San Francisco State U (CA)
Sarah Lawrence Coll (NY)
Sewanee: The U of the South (TN)
Shawnee State U (OH)
Shimer Coll (IL)
Shorter Coll (GA)
Siena Heights U (MI)
Simpson Coll (IA)
South Carolina State U (SC)
Southern Illinois U Carbondale (IL)
Southern Methodist U (TX)
Southern New Hampshire U (NH)
Southern Oregon U (OR)
Southern Utah U (UT)
Southern Wesleyan U (SC)
Southwestern Adventist U (TX)
Spring Arbor U (MI)
Spring Hill Coll (AL)
State U of New York at Binghamton (NY)
State U of New York Coll at Old Westbury (NY)
State U of New York Empire State Coll (NY)
Stephen F. Austin State U (TX)
Stetson U (FL)
Stony Brook U, State U of New York (NY)
Suffolk U (MA)
Syracuse U (NY)
Tabor Coll (KS)
Taylor U (IN)
Texas A&M Intl U (TX)
Texas A&M U–Commerce (TX)
Thomas Edison State Coll (NJ)
Thomas U (GA)
Thompson Rivers U (BC, Canada)
Towson U (MD)
Trent U (ON, Canada)
Trevecca Nazarene U (TN)
Trinity Intl U (IL)
Tri-State U (IN)
Troy U (AL)
Union Coll (KY)
Union Coll (NE)
Union Coll (NY)
United States Air Force Acad (CO)
Université du Québec en Outaouais (QC, Canada)
The U of Akron (OH)
U of Alaska Southeast (AK)
U of Arkansas at Monticello (AR)
U of Arkansas at Pine Bluff (AR)
U of Bridgeport (CT)
The U of British Columbia (BC, Canada)
U of California, Irvine (CA)
U of California, Riverside (CA)
U of Central Florida (FL)
U of Chicago (IL)
U of Cincinnati (OH)
U of Denver (CO)
The U of Findlay (OH)
U of Great Falls (MT)
U of Hawaii–West Oahu (HI)
U of Houston–Downtown (TX)
U of Houston–Victoria (TX)
U of La Verne (CA)
U of Lethbridge (AB, Canada)
U of Maine at Fort Kent (ME)
U of Mary (ND)
U of Maryland Eastern Shore (MD)
U of Maryland U Coll (MD)
U of Michigan (MI)
U of Michigan–Dearborn (MI)
U of Michigan–Flint (MI)
The U of Montana (MT)
The U of Montana–Western (MT)
U of Montevallo (AL)
U of Nevada, Las Vegas (NV)
U of North Dakota (ND)
U of Northern Colorado (CO)
U of North Texas (TX)
U of Ottawa (ON, Canada)
U of Pennsylvania (PA)
U of Pittsburgh (PA)
U of Pittsburgh at Bradford (PA)
U of Pittsburgh at Johnstown (PA)
U of Puerto Rico at Utuado (PR)
U of Regina (SK, Canada)
U of Rio Grande (OH)
U of St. Thomas (MN)
U of South Carolina Beaufort (SC)
U of Southern California (CA)
U of Southern Indiana (IN)
U of Southern Maine (ME)
U of South Florida (FL)
The U of Tampa (FL)
The U of Texas–Pan American (TX)
U of the Ozarks (AR)
U of the Pacific (CA)
U of the Sacred Heart (PR)
U of the Virgin Islands (VI)
U of Utah (UT)
U of West Florida (FL)
U of Windsor (ON, Canada)
U of Wisconsin–Madison (WI)
U of Wisconsin–Platteville (WI)
U of Wisconsin–Stevens Point (WI)
U of Wisconsin–Superior (WI)
U of Wisconsin–Whitewater (WI)
U of Wyoming (WY)
Utica Coll (NY)
Valley City State U (ND)
Valparaiso U (IN)
Virginia Wesleyan Coll (VA)
Viterbo U (WI)
Washington U in St. Louis (MO)
Wayland Baptist U (TX)
Waynesburg U (PA)
Wayne State Coll (NE)
Webster U (MO)
Wesleyan Coll (GA)
Wesleyan U (CT)
Western Carolina U (NC)
Western Connecticut State U (CT)
Western Kentucky U (KY)
Western Michigan U (MI)
Western New Mexico U (NM)
West Liberty State Coll (WV)
Westminster Coll (UT)
Westmont Coll (CA)
West Texas A&M U (TX)
Widener U (PA)
Wiley Coll (TX)
William Paterson U of New Jersey (NJ)
Wilmington Coll (OH)
Wilson Coll (PA)
Winona State U (MN)
Worcester Polytechnic Inst (MA)
York Coll of Pennsylvania (PA)
York U (ON, Canada)
Youngstown State U (OH)

SOCIAL SCIENCES RELATED

Abilene Christian U (TX)
Adelphi U (NY)
Anna Maria Coll (MA)
Bloomsburg U of Pennsylvania (PA)
Boston U (MA)
Carnegie Mellon U (PA)
Central Michigan U (MI)
Cleveland State U (OH)
Colby-Sawyer Coll (NH)
The Colorado Coll (CO)
Concordia U (QC, Canada)
Concordia U Texas (TX)
Connecticut Coll (CT)
Cornell U (NY)
Covenant Coll (GA)
Eastern Michigan U (MI)
Georgetown U (DC)
Gettysburg Coll (PA)
Indiana U Bloomington (IN)
Indiana U Kokomo (IN)
Lehigh U (PA)
Marywood U (PA)
Midwestern State U (TX)
Millersville U of Pennsylvania (PA)
Mississippi Coll (MS)
Monmouth U (NJ)
Mount Holyoke Coll (MA)
New Mexico Highlands U (NM)
Northwest Christian Coll (OR)
Northwestern U (IL)
Plymouth State U (NH)
Queens Coll of the City U of New York (NY)
Roosevelt U (IL)
Rutgers, The State U of New Jersey, New Brunswick (NJ)
Saint Mary's Coll of California (CA)
Sarah Lawrence Coll (NY)
Simon Fraser U (BC, Canada)
Skidmore Coll (NY)
Swarthmore Coll (PA)
Towson U (MD)
Transylvania U (KY)
The U of Akron (OH)
The U of Alabama at Birmingham (AL)
U of California, Berkeley (CA)
U of California, Riverside (CA)
U of Denver (CO)
U of Illinois at Springfield (IL)
U of Massachusetts Amherst (MA)
U of New England (ME)
U of Puerto Rico at Utuado (PR)
U of Rochester (NY)
The U of Western Ontario (ON, Canada)
U of West Florida (FL)
U of Wisconsin–Green Bay (WI)
Ursinus Coll (PA)
Washington U in St. Louis (MO)
Wayland Baptist U (TX)
Whitman Coll (WA)

SOCIAL SCIENCE TEACHER EDUCATION

Alma Coll (MI)
Arkansas State U (AR)
Averett U (VA)
Baylor U (TX)
Bridgewater Coll (VA)
Brigham Young U (UT)
California Lutheran U (CA)
Carroll Coll (WI)
Central Washington U (WA)
Concordia U Chicago (IL)
Concordia U, Nebraska (NE)
Cornerstone U (MI)
Dana Coll (NE)
Delta State U (MS)
DePaul U (IL)
Dillard U (LA)
Dominican Coll (NY)
Dordt Coll (IA)
Eastern Illinois U (IL)
Eastern Mennonite U (VA)
Eastern Michigan U (MI)
East Stroudsburg U of Pennsylvania (PA)
Elon U (NC)
Emmanuel Coll (GA)
Emporia State U (KS)
Fayetteville State U (NC)
Ferris State U (MI)
Florida Atlantic U (FL)
Florida Intl U (FL)
Florida State U (FL)
Grace U (NE)
Grambling State U (LA)
Hastings Coll (NE)
Hope Intl U (CA)
Howard Payne U (TX)
Indiana U of Pennsylvania (PA)
Jackson State U (MS)
Johnson State Coll (VT)
Judson Coll (AL)
Keene State Coll (NH)
Kennesaw State U (GA)
Kutztown U of Pennsylvania (PA)
Lenoir-Rhyne Coll (NC)
Lewis-Clark State Coll (ID)
Liberty U (VA)
Lindenwood U (MO)
Lindsey Wilson Coll (KY)
Lyndon State Coll (VT)
Mansfield U of Pennsylvania (PA)
Marquette U (WI)
Marywood U (PA)
Mayville State U (ND)
McGill U (QC, Canada)
McKendree U (IL)
Mercyhurst Coll (PA)
Michigan State U (MI)
Millikin U (IL)
Minot State U (ND)
Mississippi Coll (MS)
Mississippi Valley State U (MS)
Montana State U–Billings (MT)
Murray State U (KY)
Nebraska Wesleyan U (NE)
North Dakota State U (ND)
Northern Arizona U (AZ)
North Georgia Coll & State U (GA)
Northwest Nazarene U (ID)
Oakland City U (IN)
Pace U (NY)
Point Park U (PA)
Prescott Coll (AZ)
Rhode Island Coll (RI)
Sacred Heart U (CT)
St. Ambrose U (IA)
Saint Mary's U of Minnesota (MN)
Samford U (AL)
Seattle Pacific U (WA)
Simpson U (CA)
Southeastern U (FL)
Southwest Baptist U (MO)
Southwestern Oklahoma State U (OK)
State U of New York Coll at Oneonta (NY)
Stetson U (FL)
Taylor U (IN)
Union Coll (NE)
The U of Arizona (AZ)
U of Central Florida (FL)
U of Evansville (IN)
U of Georgia (GA)
U of Great Falls (MT)
U of Illinois at Chicago (IL)
U of Illinois at Urbana–Champaign (IL)
U of Maine at Farmington (ME)
U of Maine at Fort Kent (ME)
U of Maine at Machias (ME)
U of Mary (ND)
U of Minnesota, Twin Cities Campus (MN)
The U of Montana (MT)
The U of Montana–Western (MT)
U of Nebraska–Lincoln (NE)
U of Nevada, Reno (NV)
The U of North Carolina at Greensboro (NC)
U of North Dakota (ND)
U of Northern Iowa (IA)
U of Puerto Rico, Cayey U Coll (PR)
U of Rio Grande (OH)
The U of South Dakota (SD)
U of South Florida (FL)
The U of Tampa (FL)
U of Wisconsin–Superior (WI)
Utica Coll (NY)
Valley City State U (ND)
Valparaiso U (IN)
Wartburg Coll (IA)
Washington U in St. Louis (MO)
Wayne State Coll (NE)
Weber State U (UT)
Western Michigan U (MI)
Western State Coll of Colorado (CO)
Westminster Coll (UT)
Westmont Coll (CA)
York Coll (NE)
York U (ON, Canada)
Youngstown State U (OH)

SOCIAL STUDIES TEACHER EDUCATION

Abilene Christian U (TX)
Alice Lloyd Coll (KY)
Alma Coll (MI)
Anderson U (IN)
Appalachian State U (NC)
Aquinas Coll (MI)
Augustana Coll (SD)
Averett U (VA)
Baptist Bible Coll of Pennsylvania (PA)
Baylor U (TX)
Bethany Coll (KS)
Bethel U (MN)
Bethune-Cookman U (FL)
Bluefield Coll (VA)
Bob Jones U (SC)
Boston U (MA)
Bowling Green State U (OH)
Buffalo State Coll, State U of New York (NY)
Cabrini Coll (PA)
Calumet Coll of Saint Joseph (IN)
Capital U (OH)
Carlow U (PA)
Carroll Coll (WI)
Castleton State Coll (VT)
Cedarville U (OH)
Centenary Coll of Louisiana (LA)
Central Michigan U (MI)
City Coll of the City U of New York (NY)
Clarion U of Pennsylvania (PA)
Clearwater Christian Coll (FL)
Colby-Sawyer Coll (NH)
The Coll at Brockport, State U of New York (NY)
The Coll of Saint Rose (NY)
Colorado State U (CO)
Columbus State U (GA)
Concordia Coll (MN)
Concordia U (MI)
Concordia U (OR)
Concordia U, St. Paul (MN)
Cornerstone U (MI)
Crown Coll (MN)
Daemen Coll (NY)
Dakota Wesleyan U (SD)
Dordt Coll (IA)
Dowling Coll (NY)
Duquesne U (PA)
East Carolina U (NC)
Eastern Michigan U (MI)
East Texas Baptist U (TX)
Elon U (NC)
Erskine Coll (SC)
Ferris State U (MI)
Franklin Coll (IN)
Gannon U (PA)
Glenville State Coll (WV)
Grace Coll (IN)
Grand Valley State U (MI)
Greensboro Coll (NC)
Gustavus Adolphus Coll (MN)
Harding U (AR)
Hardin-Simmons U (TX)
Hastings Coll (NE)
Hofstra U (NY)
Holy Family U (PA)
Hope Coll (MI)
Houston Baptist U (TX)
Howard Payne U (TX)
Huston-Tillotson U (TX)
Illinois State U (IL)
Indiana State U (IN)
Indiana U Bloomington (IN)
Indiana U Northwest (IN)
Indiana U–Purdue U Fort Wayne (IN)
Indiana U–Purdue U Indianapolis (IN)
Indiana U South Bend (IN)
Indiana U Southeast (IN)
Indiana Wesleyan U (IN)
Inter American U of Puerto Rico, San Germán Campus (PR)
Iona Coll (NY)
Ithaca Coll (NY)
John Brown U (AR)
Johnson C. Smith U (NC)
Johnson State Coll (VT)
Juniata Coll (PA)
Keene State Coll (NH)
Kennesaw State U (GA)
Kent State U (OH)
Kentucky Christian U (KY)
Kentucky Wesleyan Coll (KY)
Keuka Coll (NY)
Keystone Coll (PA)
Le Moyne Coll (NY)
LeMoyne-Owen Coll (TN)
Lenoir-Rhyne Coll (NC)
Limestone Coll (SC)
Madonna U (MI)
Malone Coll (OH)
Manhattanville Coll (NY)
Mansfield U of Pennsylvania (PA)
Maranatha Baptist Bible Coll (WI)
Marist Coll (NY)
Marquette U (WI)
Maryville Coll (TN)
McGill U (QC, Canada)
McNeese State U (LA)
Mercy Coll (NY)
Messiah Coll (PA)
Metropolitan State U (MN)
Miami U (OH)
Miami U Hamilton (OH)
MidAmerica Nazarene U (KS)
Millersville U of Pennsylvania (PA)
Minnesota State U Mankato (MN)
Misericordia U (PA)
Mississippi Coll (MS)
Molloy Coll (NY)
Moravian Coll (PA)
Morris Coll (SC)
Mount Vernon Nazarene U (OH)
Murray State U (KY)
Nazareth Coll of Rochester (NY)
New York Inst of Technology (NY)
New York U (NY)
Niagara U (NY)
Nicholls State U (LA)
North Carolina State U (NC)
Northeastern State U (OK)
Northern Michigan U (MI)
Northwestern Coll (MN)
Northwestern State U of Louisiana (LA)
Oakland City U (IN)
Ohio Dominican U (OH)
Ohio Northern U (OH)
Ohio U (OH)

Ohio Wesleyan U (OH)
Oklahoma Christian U (OK)
Oral Roberts U (OK)
Ouachita Baptist U (AR)
Pace U (NY)
Penn State Harrisburg (PA)
Pfeiffer U (NC)
Philadelphia Biblical U (PA)
Pillsbury Baptist Bible Coll (MN)
Pittsburg State U (KS)
Purdue U (IN)
Queens Coll of the City U of New York (NY)
Roberts Wesleyan Coll (NY)
Rochester Coll (MI)
St. Edward's U (TX)
Saint Francis U (PA)
St. Gregory's U, Shawnee (OK)
St. John's U (NY)
Saint Joseph's U (PA)
St. Mary's U (TX)
St. Olaf Coll (MN)
Seton Hill U (PA)
Shawnee State U (OH)
Siena Heights U (MI)
Southeastern Louisiana U (LA)
Southeastern Oklahoma State U (OK)
Southeast Missouri State U (MO)
Southern Arkansas U–Magnolia (AR)
Southern New Hampshire U (NH)
Southern U and Ag and Mech Coll (LA)
Southwestern U (TX)
State U of New York Coll at Old Westbury (NY)
State U of New York Coll at Potsdam (NY)
Syracuse U (NY)
Temple U (PA)
Texas A&M Intl U (TX)
Texas Christian U (TX)
Texas Lutheran U (TX)
Thomas More Coll (KY)
Tri-State U (IN)
The U of Akron (OH)
The U of Arizona (AZ)
U of Arkansas at Fort Smith (AR)
U of Central Arkansas (AR)
U of Central Oklahoma (OK)
U of Charleston (WV)
U of Evansville (IN)
U of Great Falls (MT)
U of Illinois at Urbana–Champaign (IL)
U of Indianapolis (IN)
The U of Iowa (IA)
U of Lethbridge (AB, Canada)
U of Louisiana at Lafayette (LA)
U of Louisiana at Monroe (LA)
U of Maine (ME)
U of Mary Hardin-Baylor (TX)
U of Maryland, Coll Park (MD)
U of Michigan–Dearborn (MI)
U of Michigan–Flint (MI)
U of Minnesota, Duluth (MN)
U of Mississippi (MS)
U of Missouri–Columbia (MO)
U of Missouri–St. Louis (MO)
U of Nevada, Reno (NV)
U of New Orleans (LA)
The U of North Carolina at Greensboro (NC)
The U of North Carolina at Pembroke (NC)
U of Northern Iowa (IA)
U of Oklahoma (OK)
U of Pittsburgh at Johnstown (PA)
U of Puerto Rico, Cayey U Coll (PR)
U of Regina (SK, Canada)
U of St. Francis (IL)
U of Saint Francis (IN)
U of St. Thomas (MN)
The U of Toledo (OH)
U of Vermont (VT)
U of Wisconsin–Eau Claire (WI)
U of Wisconsin–La Crosse (WI)
U of Wisconsin–Superior (WI)
Ursuline Coll (OH)
Utah State U (UT)
Utica Coll (NY)
Virginia Intermont Coll (VA)
Virginia Wesleyan Coll (VA)
Viterbo U (WI)
Washington U in St. Louis (MO)
Waynesburg U (PA)
Wayne State U (MI)
Weber State U (UT)
West Chester U of Pennsylvania (PA)
Western Carolina U (NC)
Wheaton Coll (IL)
Wheeling Jesuit U (WV)
Widener U (PA)
Wingate U (NC)
Wright State U (OH)
Xavier U of Louisiana (LA)
York Coll (NE)
York Coll of Pennsylvania (PA)
York U (ON, Canada)
Youngstown State U (OH)

SOCIAL WORK

Abilene Christian U (TX)
Adelphi U (NY)
Adrian Coll (MI)
Alabama Ag and Mech U (AL)
Alabama State U (AL)
Albertus Magnus Coll (CT)
Alvernia Coll (PA)
Anderson U (IN)
Andrews U (MI)
Anna Maria Coll (MA)
Appalachian State U (NC)
Arizona State U at the West campus (AZ)
Arkansas State U (AR)
Asbury Coll (KY)
Ashland U (OH)
Auburn U (AL)
Augsburg Coll (MN)
Augustana Coll (SD)
Augusta State U (GA)
Austin Peay State U (TN)
Avila U (MO)
Azusa Pacific U (CA)
Ball State U (IN)
Barton Coll (NC)
Baylor U (TX)
Belhaven Coll (MS)
Belmont U (TN)
Bemidji State U (MN)
Bethany Coll (KS)
Bethany Coll (WV)
Bethel Coll (KS)
Bethel U (MN)
Bloomsburg U of Pennsylvania (PA)
Bluffton U (OH)
Boise State U (ID)
Bowling Green State U (OH)
Bradley U (IL)
Bridgewater State Coll (MA)
Brigham Young U (UT)
Buffalo State Coll, State U of New York (NY)
Cabrini Coll (PA)
California State U, East Bay (CA)
California State U, Fresno (CA)
California State U, Long Beach (CA)
California State U, Los Angeles (CA)
California State U, Sacramento (CA)
California State U, San Bernardino (CA)
Calvin Coll (MI)
Capital U (OH)
Carlow U (PA)
Castleton State Coll (VT)
The Catholic U of America (DC)
Cedar Crest Coll (PA)
Cedarville U (OH)
Central Connecticut State U (CT)
Central Michigan U (MI)
Central State U (OH)
Chapman U (CA)
Chatham U (PA)
Christopher Newport U (VA)
Clark Atlanta U (GA)
Clarke Coll (IA)
Cleveland State U (OH)
Coker Coll (SC)
The Coll at Brockport, State U of New York (NY)
Coll of Mount St. Joseph (OH)
The Coll of New Rochelle (NY)
Coll of Saint Benedict (MN)
The Coll of Saint Rose (NY)
The Coll of St. Scholastica (MN)
Coll of Staten Island of the City U of New York (NY)
Coll of the Ozarks (MO)
Colorado State U (CO)
Colorado State U-Pueblo (CO)
Columbia Coll (SC)
Concordia Coll (MN)
Concordia Coll–New York (NY)
Concordia U (OR)
Concordia U Chicago (IL)
Concordia U Wisconsin (WI)
Concord U (WV)
Cornerstone U (MI)
Creighton U (NE)
Daemen Coll (NY)
Dana Coll (NE)
Defiance Coll (OH)
Delta State U (MS)
Dominican Coll (NY)
Dordt Coll (IA)
East Carolina U (NC)
East Central U (OK)
Eastern Connecticut State U (CT)
Eastern Kentucky U (KY)
Eastern Mennonite U (VA)
Eastern Michigan U (MI)
East Tennessee State U (TN)
Edinboro U of Pennsylvania (PA)
Elizabethtown Coll (PA)
Evangel U (MO)
Ferris State U (MI)
Ferrum Coll (VA)
Florida Ag and Mech U (FL)
Florida Atlantic U (FL)
Florida Gulf Coast U (FL)
Florida Intl U (FL)
Florida State U (FL)
Franciscan U of Steubenville (OH)
Freed-Hardeman U (TN)
Fresno Pacific U (CA)
Frostburg State U (MD)
Gannon U (PA)
George Fox U (OR)
George Mason U (VA)
Georgian Court U (NJ)
Georgia State U (GA)
Gordon Coll (MA)
Grace Coll (IN)
Grambling State U (LA)
Grand Valley State U (MI)
Greenville Coll (IL)
Gwynedd-Mercy Coll (PA)
Hampton U (VA)
Harding U (AR)
Hardin-Simmons U (TX)
Hawai'i Pacific U (HI)
Henderson State U (AR)
Holy Family U (PA)
Hood Coll (MD)
Hope Coll (MI)
Hope Intl U (CA)
Howard Payne U (TX)
Humboldt State U (CA)
Huntington U (IN)
Idaho State U (ID)
Illinois State U (IL)
Immaculata U (PA)
Indiana State U (IN)
Indiana U Bloomington (IN)
Indiana U East (IN)
Indiana U–Purdue U Indianapolis (IN)
Indiana Wesleyan U (IN)
Inter American U of Puerto Rico, Fajardo Campus (PR)
Iona Coll (NY)
Jackson State U (MS)
Jacksonville State U (AL)
James Madison U (VA)
Johnson C. Smith U (NC)
Juniata Coll (PA)
Kansas State U (KS)
Kean U (NJ)
Kennesaw State U (GA)
Kent State U (OH)
Kentucky Christian U (KY)
Kentucky State U (KY)
Keuka Coll (NY)
Kutztown U of Pennsylvania (PA)
Kuyper Coll (MI)
Lakehead U (ON, Canada)
La Salle U (PA)
La Sierra U (CA)
Laurentian U (ON, Canada)
Lehman Coll of the City U of New York (NY)
LeMoyne-Owen Coll (TN)
Lewis-Clark State Coll (ID)
Lewis U (IL)
Limestone Coll (SC)
Lindenwood U (MO)
Lipscomb U (TN)
Livingstone Coll (NC)
Lock Haven U of Pennsylvania (PA)
Longwood U (VA)
Loras Coll (IA)
Louisiana Coll (LA)
Lourdes Coll (OH)
Loyola U Chicago (IL)
Lubbock Christian U (TX)
Luther Coll (IA)
Madonna U (MI)
Malone Coll (OH)
Manchester Coll (IN)
Mansfield U of Pennsylvania (PA)
Marian Coll of Fond du Lac (WI)
Marist Coll (NY)
Marquette U (WI)
Marshall U (WV)
Mary Baldwin Coll (VA)
Marywood U (PA)
McDaniel Coll (MD)
McGill U (QC, Canada)
McKendree U (IL)
Memorial U of Newfoundland (NL, Canada)
Mercy Coll (NY)
Mercyhurst Coll (PA)
Meredith Coll (NC)
Messiah Coll (PA)
Methodist U (NC)
Metropolitan State U (MN)
Miami U (OH)
Michigan State U (MI)
Middle Tennessee State U (TN)
Midwestern State U (TX)
Miles Coll (AL)
Millersville U of Pennsylvania (PA)
Millikin U (IL)
Minnesota State U Mankato (MN)
Minot State U (ND)
Misericordia U (PA)
Mississippi Coll (MS)
Mississippi State U (MS)
Mississippi Valley State U (MS)
Missouri State U (MO)
Molloy Coll (NY)
Monmouth U (NJ)
Montclair State U (NJ)
Morehead State U (KY)
Morgan State U (MD)
Mountain State U (WV)
Mount Ida Coll (MA)
Mount Mary Coll (WI)
Mount Mercy Coll (IA)
Mount Saint Mary Coll (NY)
Mount St. Mary's Coll (CA)
Mount Vernon Nazarene U (OH)
Murray State U (KY)
Nazareth Coll of Rochester (NY)
Nebraska Wesleyan U (NE)
New York U (NY)
Niagara U (NY)
North Carolina Ag and Tech State U (NC)
North Carolina Central U (NC)
North Carolina State U (NC)
Northeastern Illinois U (IL)
Northeastern State U (OK)
Northern Arizona U (AZ)
Northern Michigan U (MI)
Northwestern Coll (IA)
Northwestern Oklahoma State U (OK)
Northwestern State U of Louisiana (LA)
Northwest Nazarene U (ID)
Nyack Coll (NY)
Oakland U (MI)
Oakwood Coll (AL)
Oglethorpe U (GA)
Ohio Dominican U (OH)
Ohio U (OH)
Oral Roberts U (OK)
Pacific Lutheran U (WA)
Pacific Union Coll (CA)
Pacific U (OR)
Philadelphia Biblical U (PA)
Pikeville Coll (KY)
Pittsburg State U (KS)
Plymouth State U (NH)
Point Loma Nazarene U (CA)
Prairie View A&M U (TX)
Presentation Coll (SD)
Providence Coll (RI)
Purdue U (IN)
Quincy U (IL)
Radford U (VA)
Ramapo Coll of New Jersey (NJ)
Redeemer U Coll (ON, Canada)
Regis Coll (MA)
Rhode Island Coll (RI)
The Richard Stockton Coll of New Jersey (NJ)
Roberts Wesleyan Coll (NY)
Rockford Coll (IL)
Rutgers, The State U of New Jersey, Camden (NJ)
Rutgers, The State U of New Jersey, Newark (NJ)
Rutgers, The State U of New Jersey, New Brunswick (NJ)
Sacred Heart U (CT)
Saginaw Valley State U (MI)
St. Cloud State U (MN)
St. Edward's U (TX)
Saint Francis U (PA)
Saint John's U (MN)
Saint Joseph Coll (CT)
Saint Joseph's Coll (IN)
Saint Leo U (FL)
Saint Louis U (MO)
Saint Mary's Coll (IN)
St. Olaf Coll (MN)
St. Thomas U (NB, Canada)
Salem State Coll (MA)
Salisbury U (MD)
Salve Regina U (RI)
San Diego State U (CA)
San Francisco State U (CA)
Seattle U (WA)
Seton Hill U (PA)
Shaw U (NC)
Shepherd U (WV)
Shippensburg U of Pennsylvania (PA)
Siena Coll (NY)
Siena Heights U (MI)
Skidmore Coll (NY)
Slippery Rock U of Pennsylvania (PA)
South Carolina State U (SC)
Southeastern Louisiana U (LA)
Southeastern U (FL)
Southeast Missouri State U (MO)
Southern Adventist U (TN)
Southern Arkansas U–Magnolia (AR)
Southern Connecticut State U (CT)
Southern Illinois U Carbondale (IL)
Southern Illinois U Edwardsville (IL)
Southern U and Ag and Mech Coll (LA)
Southwestern Adventist U (TX)
Southwestern Oklahoma State U (OK)
Southwest Minnesota State U (MN)
Spring Arbor U (MI)
State U of New York at Fredonia (NY)
State U of New York at Plattsburgh (NY)
Stephen F. Austin State U (TX)
Stony Brook U, State U of New York (NY)
Suffolk U (MA)
Syracuse U (NY)
Tarleton State U (TX)
Taylor U (IN)
Taylor U Fort Wayne (IN)
Temple U (PA)
Tennessee State U (TN)
Tennessee Technological U (TN)
Texas A&M U–Commerce (TX)
Texas Christian U (TX)
Texas Coll (TX)
Texas Southern U (TX)
Texas State U-San Marcos (TX)
Texas Tech U (TX)
Texas Woman's U (TX)
Thomas U (GA)
Thompson Rivers U (BC, Canada)
Trinity Christian Coll (IL)
Trinity Lutheran Coll (WA)
Troy U (AL)
Tuskegee U (AL)
Union Coll (NE)
Union U (TN)
Université de Sherbrooke (QC, Canada)
Université du Québec en Outaouais (QC, Canada)
U at Albany, State U of New York (NY)
The U of Akron (OH)
The U of Alabama (AL)
The U of Alabama at Birmingham (AL)
U of Alaska Fairbanks (AK)
U of Arkansas (AR)
U of Arkansas at Monticello (AR)
U of Arkansas at Pine Bluff (AR)
The U of British Columbia (BC, Canada)
The U of British Columbia–Okanagan (BC, Canada)
U of California, Berkeley (CA)
U of Central Florida (FL)
U of Central Missouri (MO)
U of Cincinnati (OH)
The U of Findlay (OH)
U of Georgia (GA)
U of Guam (GU)
U of Hawaii at Manoa (HI)
U of Houston–Clear Lake (TX)
U of Illinois at Chicago (IL)
U of Illinois at Springfield (IL)
U of Indianapolis (IN)
The U of Iowa (IA)
U of Kansas (KS)
U of Louisiana at Monroe (LA)
U of Maine (ME)
U of Mary (ND)
U of Mary Hardin-Baylor (TX)
U of Maryland, Baltimore County (MD)
U of Maryland Eastern Shore (MD)
U of Memphis (TN)
U of Michigan–Flint (MI)
U of Mississippi (MS)
U of Missouri–Columbia (MO)
U of Missouri–St. Louis (MO)
The U of Montana (MT)
U of Montevallo (AL)
U of Nebraska at Kearney (NE)
U of Nebraska at Omaha (NE)
U of Nevada, Las Vegas (NV)
U of Nevada, Reno (NV)
U of New Hampshire (NH)
U of North Alabama (AL)
The U of North Carolina at Charlotte (NC)
The U of North Carolina at Greensboro (NC)
The U of North Carolina at Pembroke (NC)
The U of North Carolina Wilmington (NC)
U of North Dakota (ND)
U of Northern Iowa (IA)
U of North Texas (TX)

U of Oklahoma (OK)
U of Ottawa (ON, Canada)
U of Pittsburgh (PA)
U of Portland (OR)
U of Puerto Rico at Humacao (PR)
U of Puerto Rico at Utuado (PR)
U of Regina (SK, Canada)
U of Rio Grande (OH)
U of St. Francis (IL)
U of Saint Francis (IN)
U of St. Thomas (MN)
U of Sioux Falls (SD)
The U of South Dakota (SD)
U of Southern Indiana (IN)
U of Southern Maine (ME)
U of Southern Mississippi (MS)
U of South Florida (FL)
The U of Tennessee (TN)
The U of Tennessee at Chattanooga (TN)
The U of Tennessee at Martin (TN)
The U of Texas at Arlington (TX)
The U of Texas at Austin (TX)
The U of Texas at El Paso (TX)
The U of Texas–Pan American (TX)
U of the District of Columbia (DC)
U of the Sacred Heart (PR)
U of the Virgin Islands (VI)
The U of Toledo (OH)
U of Utah (UT)
U of Vermont (VT)
U of Victoria (BC, Canada)
U of Washington, Tacoma (WA)
The U of Western Ontario (ON, Canada)
U of West Florida (FL)
U of Windsor (ON, Canada)
U of Wisconsin–Eau Claire (WI)
U of Wisconsin–Green Bay (WI)
U of Wisconsin–Madison (WI)
U of Wisconsin–Milwaukee (WI)
U of Wisconsin–Oshkosh (WI)
U of Wisconsin–Superior (WI)
U of Wisconsin–Whitewater (WI)
U of Wyoming (WY)
Ursuline Coll (OH)
Utah State U (UT)
Valparaiso U (IN)
Virginia Commonwealth U (VA)
Virginia Intermont Coll (VA)
Virginia State U (VA)
Viterbo U (WI)
Walla Walla U (WA)
Warner Pacific Coll (OR)
Warren Wilson Coll (NC)
Wartburg Coll (IA)
Washburn U (KS)
Wayne State U (MI)
Weber State U (UT)
West Chester U of Pennsylvania (PA)
Western Carolina U (NC)
Western Connecticut State U (CT)
Western Illinois U (IL)
Western Kentucky U (KY)
Western Michigan U (MI)
Western New England Coll (MA)
Western New Mexico U (NM)
Westfield State Coll (MA)
West Texas A&M U (TX)
West Virginia U (WV)
Wheelock Coll (MA)
Whittier Coll (CA)
Wichita State U (KS)
Widener U (PA)
Wiley Coll (TX)
William Woods U (MO)
Wilmington Coll (OH)
Winona State U (MN)
Winthrop U (SC)
Wright State U (OH)
Xavier U (OH)
York Coll of the City U of New York (NY)
York U (ON, Canada)
Youngstown State U (OH)

SOCIAL WORK RELATED
Miami U Hamilton (OH)
The U of Western Ontario (ON, Canada)

SOCIOBIOLOGY
Beloit Coll (WI)
Harvard U (MA)
Tufts U (MA)

SOCIOLOGY
Abilene Christian U (TX)
Acadia U (NS, Canada)
Adams State Coll (CO)
Adelphi U (NY)
Adrian Coll (MI)
Agnes Scott Coll (GA)
Alabama Ag and Mech U (AL)
Alabama State U (AL)
Albertus Magnus Coll (CT)
Albion Coll (MI)
Albright Coll (PA)
Alcorn State U (MS)
Alfred U (NY)
Alma Coll (MI)
American Public U System (WV)
American U (DC)
The American U of Athens (Greece)
American U of Beirut (Lebanon)
Amherst Coll (MA)
Anderson U (IN)
Andrews U (MI)
Angelo State U (TX)
Anna Maria Coll (MA)
Appalachian State U (NC)
Aquinas Coll (MI)
Arizona State U (AZ)
Arizona State U at the West campus (AZ)
Arkansas State U (AR)
Asbury Coll (KY)
Ashland U (OH)
Assumption Coll (MA)
Athabasca U (AB, Canada)
Athens State U (AL)
Auburn U (AL)
Auburn U Montgomery (AL)
Augsburg Coll (MN)
Augustana Coll (IL)
Augustana Coll (SD)
Augusta State U (GA)
Austin Coll (TX)
Austin Peay State U (TN)
Averett U (VA)
Avila U (MO)
Azusa Pacific U (CA)
Baker U (KS)
Baldwin-Wallace Coll (OH)
Ball State U (IN)
Bard Coll (NY)
Bard Coll at Simon's Rock (MA)
Barnard Coll (NY)
Barry U (FL)
Bates Coll (ME)
Baylor U (TX)
Bellarmine U (KY)
Belmont Abbey Coll (NC)
Belmont U (TN)
Beloit Coll (WI)
Bemidji State U (MN)
Benedictine Coll (KS)
Benedictine U (IL)
Bennington Coll (VT)
Berea Coll (KY)
Bernard M. Baruch Coll of the City U of New York (NY)
Bethany Coll (KS)
Bethany Lutheran Coll (MN)
Bethel Coll (TN)
Bethune-Cookman U (FL)
Biola U (CA)
Bishop's U (QC, Canada)
Bloomfield Coll (NJ)
Bloomsburg U of Pennsylvania (PA)
Bluffton U (OH)
Boise State U (ID)
Boston Coll (MA)
Boston U (MA)
Bowdoin Coll (ME)
Bowling Green State U (OH)
Bradley U (IL)
Brandeis U (MA)
Brewton-Parker Coll (GA)
Bridgewater Coll (VA)
Bridgewater State Coll (MA)
Brigham Young U (UT)
Brock U (ON, Canada)
Brown U (RI)
Bryn Mawr Coll (PA)
Bucknell U (PA)
Buffalo State Coll, State U of New York (NY)
Butler U (IN)
Cabrini Coll (PA)
California Baptist U (CA)
California Lutheran U (CA)
California State Polytechnic U, Pomona (CA)
California State U, Dominguez Hills (CA)
California State U, East Bay (CA)
California State U, Fresno (CA)
California State U, Fullerton (CA)
California State U, Long Beach (CA)
California State U, Los Angeles (CA)
California State U, Sacramento (CA)
California State U, San Bernardino (CA)
California State U, San Marcos (CA)
California State U, Stanislaus (CA)
Calvin Coll (MI)
Cameron U (OK)
Canisius Coll (NY)
Capital U (OH)
Carlow U (PA)
Carroll Coll (WI)
Carson-Newman Coll (TN)
Case Western Reserve U (OH)
Castleton State Coll (VT)
Catawba Coll (NC)
The Catholic U of America (DC)
Cedarville U (OH)
Centenary Coll (NJ)
Centenary Coll of Louisiana (LA)
Central Coll (IA)
Central Connecticut State U (CT)
Central Michigan U (MI)
Central State U (OH)
Central Washington U (WA)
Centre Coll (KY)
Chapman U (CA)
Chestnut Hill Coll (PA)
Cheyney U of Pennsylvania (PA)
Chicago State U (IL)
Christopher Newport U (VA)
City Coll of the City U of New York (NY)
Claflin U (SC)
Claremont McKenna Coll (CA)
Clarion U of Pennsylvania (PA)
Clark Atlanta U (GA)
Clarkson U (NY)
Clark U (MA)
Clemson U (SC)
Cleveland State U (OH)
Coastal Carolina U (SC)
Coker Coll (SC)
Colby Coll (ME)
Colgate U (NY)
The Coll at Brockport, State U of New York (NY)
Coll of Charleston (SC)
The Coll of Idaho (ID)
Coll of Mount St. Joseph (OH)
Coll of Mount Saint Vincent (NY)
The Coll of New Jersey (NJ)
The Coll of New Rochelle (NY)
Coll of Saint Benedict (MN)
Coll of Saint Elizabeth (NJ)
The Coll of Saint Rose (NY)
Coll of Staten Island of the City U of New York (NY)
Coll of the Holy Cross (MA)
Coll of the Ozarks (MO)
The Coll of William and Mary (VA)
The Colorado Coll (CO)
Colorado State U (CO)
Colorado State U-Pueblo (CO)
Columbus State U (GA)
Concordia Coll (MN)
Concordia U (MI)
Concordia U (QC, Canada)
Concordia U Chicago (IL)
Concordia U, Nebraska (NE)
Concordia U, St. Paul (MN)
Concord U (WV)
Connecticut Coll (CT)
Converse Coll (SC)
Cornell Coll (IA)
Cornell U (NY)
Cornerstone U (MI)
Covenant Coll (GA)
Creighton U (NE)
Curry Coll (MA)
Dakota Wesleyan U (SD)
Dallas Baptist U (TX)
Dartmouth Coll (NH)
Davidson Coll (NC)
Davis & Elkins Coll (WV)
Denison U (OH)
DePaul U (IL)
DePauw U (IN)
Dickinson Coll (PA)
Dillard U (LA)
Doane Coll (NE)
Dominican U (IL)
Dordt Coll (IA)
Dowling Coll (NY)
Drake U (IA)
Drew U (NJ)
Drexel U (PA)
Drury U (MO)
Duke U (NC)
Duquesne U (PA)
D'Youville Coll (NY)
Earlham Coll (IN)
East Carolina U (NC)
East Central U (OK)
Eastern Connecticut State U (CT)
Eastern Illinois U (IL)
Eastern Kentucky U (KY)
Eastern Mennonite U (VA)
Eastern Michigan U (MI)
Eastern New Mexico U (NM)
East Stroudsburg U of Pennsylvania (PA)
East Tennessee State U (TN)
East Texas Baptist U (TX)
East-West U (IL)
Eckerd Coll (FL)
Edinboro U of Pennsylvania (PA)
Elizabethtown Coll (PA)
Elon U (NC)
Emmanuel Coll (MA)
Emory & Henry Coll (VA)
Emory U (GA)
Emporia State U (KS)
Eugene Lang Coll The New School for Liberal Arts (NY)
Evangel U (MO)
Excelsior Coll (NY)
Fairfield U (CT)
Fairleigh Dickinson U, Coll at Florham (NJ)
Fairleigh Dickinson U, Metropolitan Campus (NJ)
Fairmont State U (WV)
Fayetteville State U (NC)
Felician Coll (NJ)
Ferris State U (MI)
Ferrum Coll (VA)
Fitchburg State Coll (MA)
Flagler Coll (FL)
Florida Ag and Mech U (FL)
Florida Atlantic U (FL)
Florida Gulf Coast U (FL)
Florida Intl U (FL)
Florida Memorial U (FL)
Florida Southern Coll (FL)
Florida State U (FL)
Fontbonne U (MO)
Fort Lewis Coll (CO)
Framingham State Coll (MA)
Franciscan U of Steubenville (OH)
Francis Marion U (SC)
Franklin & Marshall Coll (PA)
Franklin Coll (IN)
Frostburg State U (MD)
Furman U (SC)
Gardner-Webb U (NC)
George Fox U (OR)
George Mason U (VA)
Georgetown Coll (KY)
Georgetown U (DC)
The George Washington U (DC)
Georgia Coll & State U (GA)
Georgian Court U (NJ)
Georgia Southern U (GA)
Georgia Southwestern State U (GA)
Georgia State U (GA)
Gettysburg Coll (PA)
Gonzaga U (WA)
Gordon Coll (MA)
Goucher Coll (MD)
Grace Coll (IN)
Grambling State U (LA)
Grand Canyon U (AZ)
Grand Valley State U (MI)
Green Mountain Coll (VT)
Greensboro Coll (NC)
Greenville Coll (IL)
Grinnell Coll (IA)
Grove City Coll (PA)
Guilford Coll (NC)
Gustavus Adolphus Coll (MN)
Gwynedd-Mercy Coll (PA)
Hamilton Coll (NY)
Hamline U (MN)
Hampshire Coll (MA)
Hampton U (VA)
Hannibal-LaGrange Coll (MO)
Hanover Coll (IN)
Hardin-Simmons U (TX)
Hartwick Coll (NY)
Harvard U (MA)
Hastings Coll (NE)
Haverford Coll (PA)
Hawai'i Pacific U (HI)
Henderson State U (AR)
Hendrix Coll (AR)
High Point U (NC)
Hillsdale Coll (MI)
Hobart and William Smith Colls (NY)
Hofstra U (NY)
Hollins U (VA)
Holy Family U (PA)
Holy Names U (CA)
Hood Coll (MD)
Hope Coll (MI)
Houghton Coll (NY)
Houston Baptist U (TX)
Howard Payne U (TX)
Humboldt State U (CA)
Hunter Coll of the City U of New York (NY)
Huntington U (IN)
Huston-Tillotson U (TX)
Idaho State U (ID)
Illinois Coll (IL)
Illinois State U (IL)
Illinois Wesleyan U (IL)
Immaculata U (PA)
Indiana State U (IN)
Indiana U Bloomington (IN)
Indiana U East (IN)
Indiana U Kokomo (IN)
Indiana U Northwest (IN)
Indiana U of Pennsylvania (PA)
Indiana U–Purdue U Fort Wayne (IN)
Indiana U–Purdue U Indianapolis (IN)
Indiana U South Bend (IN)
Indiana U Southeast (IN)
Indiana Wesleyan U (IN)
Inter American U of Puerto Rico, Fajardo Campus (PR)
Inter American U of Puerto Rico, San Germán Campus (PR)
Iona Coll (NY)
Iowa State U of Science and Technology (IA)
Ithaca Coll (NY)
Jackson State U (MS)
Jacksonville State U (AL)
Jacksonville U (FL)
James Madison U (VA)
Jarvis Christian Coll (TX)
John Carroll U (OH)
The Johns Hopkins U (MD)
Johnson State Coll (VT)
Judson U (IL)
Juniata Coll (PA)
Kalamazoo Coll (MI)
Kansas State U (KS)
Kean U (NJ)
Keene State Coll (NH)
Kennesaw State U (GA)
Kent State U (OH)
Kentucky Wesleyan Coll (KY)
Kenyon Coll (OH)
Keuka Coll (NY)
King's Coll (PA)
The King's U Coll (AB, Canada)
Knox Coll (IL)
Kutztown U of Pennsylvania (PA)
Lafayette Coll (PA)
LaGrange Coll (GA)
Lake Forest Coll (IL)
Lakehead U (ON, Canada)
Lake Superior State U (MI)
Lambuth U (TN)
Lander U (SC)
La Roche Coll (PA)
La Salle U (PA)
La Sierra U (CA)
Laurentian U (ON, Canada)
Lebanon Valley Coll (PA)
Lees-McRae Coll (NC)
Lee U (TN)
Lehigh U (PA)
Lehman Coll of the City U of New York (NY)
Le Moyne Coll (NY)
LeMoyne-Owen Coll (TN)
Lenoir-Rhyne Coll (NC)
Lewis & Clark Coll (OR)
Lewis U (IL)
Lincoln U (MO)
Lincoln U (PA)
Lindenwood U (MO)
Linfield Coll (OR)
Livingstone Coll (NC)
Lock Haven U of Pennsylvania (PA)
Longwood U (VA)
Loras Coll (IA)
Louisiana Coll (LA)
Louisiana State U and Ag and Mech Coll (LA)
Lourdes Coll (OH)
Loyola Coll in Maryland (MD)
Loyola Marymount U (CA)
Loyola U Chicago (IL)
Loyola U New Orleans (LA)
Luther Coll (IA)
Lycoming Coll (PA)
Lynchburg Coll (VA)
Macalester Coll (MN)
Madonna U (MI)
Manchester Coll (IN)
Manhattanville Coll (NY)
Mansfield U of Pennsylvania (PA)
Marian Coll (IN)
Marian Coll of Fond du Lac (WI)
Marlboro Coll (VT)
Marquette U (WI)
Marshall U (WV)
Martin U (IN)
Mary Baldwin Coll (VA)
Marylhurst U (OR)
Marymount Manhattan Coll (NY)
Marymount U (VA)
Maryville Coll (TN)
Maryville U of Saint Louis (MO)
Massachusetts Coll of Liberal Arts (MA)
McDaniel Coll (MD)
McGill U (QC, Canada)
McKendree U (IL)
McMurry U (TX)
McNeese State U (LA)
Memorial U of Newfoundland (NL, Canada)
Mercer U (GA)
Mercy Coll (NY)
Mercyhurst Coll (PA)
Meredith Coll (NC)
Merrimack Coll (MA)

MAJORS AND MORE

Mesa State Coll (CO)
Messiah Coll (PA)
Methodist U (NC)
Miami U (OH)
Miami U Hamilton (OH)
Michigan State U (MI)
MidAmerica Nazarene U (KS)
Middlebury Coll (VT)
Middle Tennessee State U (TN)
Midland Lutheran Coll (NE)
Midwestern State U (TX)
Millersville U of Pennsylvania (PA)
Milligan Coll (TN)
Millikin U (IL)
Millsaps Coll (MS)
Mills Coll (CA)
Minnesota State U Mankato (MN)
Minot State U (ND)
Mississippi Coll (MS)
Mississippi State U (MS)
Mississippi Valley State U (MS)
Missouri Southern State U (MO)
Missouri State U (MO)
Missouri Valley Coll (MO)
Molloy Coll (NY)
Monmouth Coll (IL)
Montana State U (MT)
Montana State U–Billings (MT)
Montclair State U (NJ)
Moravian Coll (PA)
Morehead State U (KY)
Morehouse Coll (GA)
Morgan State U (MD)
Morris Coll (SC)
Mount Allison U (NB, Canada)
Mount Holyoke Coll (MA)
Mount Mercy Coll (IA)
Mount Saint Mary Coll (NY)
Mount St. Mary's Coll (CA)
Mount St. Mary's U (MD)
Mount Saint Vincent U (NS, Canada)
Mount Vernon Nazarene U (OH)
Muhlenberg Coll (PA)
Murray State U (KY)
National U (CA)
Nazareth Coll of Rochester (NY)
Nebraska Wesleyan U (NE)
New Coll of Florida (FL)
New England Coll (NH)
New Jersey City U (NJ)
Newman U (KS)
New York Inst of Technology (NY)
New York U (NY)
Niagara U (NY)
Nicholls State U (LA)
North Carolina Ag and Tech State U (NC)
North Carolina Central U (NC)
North Carolina State U (NC)
North Carolina Wesleyan Coll (NC)
North Central Coll (IL)
North Dakota State U (ND)
Northeastern Illinois U (IL)
Northeastern State U (OK)
Northeastern U (MA)
Northern Arizona U (AZ)
Northern Illinois U (IL)
Northern Michigan U (MI)
Northern State U (SD)
North Georgia Coll & State U (GA)
Northland Coll (WI)
Northwestern Coll (IA)
Northwestern Oklahoma State U (OK)
Northwestern State U of Louisiana (LA)
Northwestern U (IL)
Northwest Missouri State U (MO)
Notre Dame de Namur U (CA)
Oakland U (MI)
Oberlin Coll (OH)
Occidental Coll (CA)
Oglethorpe U (GA)
Ohio Dominican U (OH)
Ohio Northern U (OH)
Ohio U (OH)
Ohio Wesleyan U (OH)
Oklahoma City U (OK)
Oklahoma State U (OK)
Old Dominion U (VA)
Oregon State U (OR)
Otterbein Coll (OH)
Ouachita Baptist U (AR)
Pacific Lutheran U (WA)
Pacific Union Coll (CA)
Pacific U (OR)
Paine Coll (GA)
Park U (MO)
Penn State Abington (PA)
Penn State Altoona (PA)
Penn State Berks (PA)
Penn State Erie, The Behrend Coll (PA)
Penn State Harrisburg (PA)
Penn State U Park (PA)
Pepperdine U, Malibu (CA)
Pfeiffer U (NC)
Piedmont Coll (GA)
Pikeville Coll (KY)
Pittsburg State U (KS)
Pitzer Coll (CA)
Point Loma Nazarene U (CA)
Pomona Coll (CA)
Portland State U (OR)
Prairie View A&M U (TX)
Presbyterian Coll (SC)
Prescott Coll (AZ)
Princeton U (NJ)
Providence Coll (RI)
Purchase Coll, State U of New York (NY)
Purdue U (IN)
Purdue U Calumet (IN)
Queens Coll of the City U of New York (NY)
Queen's U at Kingston (ON, Canada)
Quinnipiac U (CT)
Radford U (VA)
Ramapo Coll of New Jersey (NJ)
Randolph Coll (VA)
Randolph-Macon Coll (VA)
Redeemer U Coll (ON, Canada)
Reed Coll (OR)
Regis Coll (MA)
Regis U (CO)
Rhode Island Coll (RI)
Rhodes Coll (TN)
Rice U (TX)
The Richard Stockton Coll of New Jersey (NJ)
Rider U (NJ)
Ripon Coll (WI)
Roanoke Coll (VA)
Roberts Wesleyan Coll (NY)
Rockford Coll (IL)
Rockhurst U (MO)
Roger Williams U (RI)
Rollins Coll (FL)
Roosevelt U (IL)
Rosemont Coll (PA)
Rowan U (NJ)
Russell Sage Coll (NY)
Rutgers, The State U of New Jersey, Camden (NJ)
Rutgers, The State U of New Jersey, Newark (NJ)
Rutgers, The State U of New Jersey, New Brunswick (NJ)
Saginaw Valley State U (MI)
St. Ambrose U (IA)
St. Cloud State U (MN)
St. Edward's U (TX)
Saint Francis U (PA)
St. Francis Xavier U (NS, Canada)
St. Gregory's U, Shawnee (OK)
St. John Fisher Coll (NY)
Saint John's U (MN)
St. John's U (NY)
Saint Joseph Coll (CT)
Saint Joseph's Coll (IN)
St. Joseph's Coll, Suffolk Campus (NY)
Saint Joseph's U (PA)
St. Lawrence U (NY)
Saint Leo U (FL)
Saint Louis U (MO)
Saint Mary's Coll (IN)
Saint Mary's Coll of California (CA)
St. Mary's Coll of Maryland (MD)
St. Mary's U (TX)
Saint Mary's U of Minnesota (MN)
Saint Michael's Coll (VT)
St. Norbert Coll (WI)
St. Olaf Coll (MN)
St. Thomas U (FL)
St. Thomas U (NB, Canada)
Saint Vincent Coll (PA)
Saint Xavier U (IL)
Salem Coll (NC)
Salem State Coll (MA)
Salisbury U (MD)
Salve Regina U (RI)
Samford U (AL)
Sam Houston State U (TX)
San Diego State U (CA)
San Francisco State U (CA)
Santa Clara U (CA)
Sarah Lawrence Coll (NY)
Scripps Coll (CA)
Seattle Pacific U (WA)
Seattle U (WA)
Seton Hill U (PA)
Shawnee State U (OH)
Shaw U (NC)
Shenandoah U (VA)
Shepherd U (WV)
Shippensburg U of Pennsylvania (PA)
Shorter Coll (GA)
Siena Coll (NY)
Simmons Coll (MA)
Simon Fraser U (BC, Canada)
Simpson Coll (IA)
Skidmore Coll (NY)
Slippery Rock U of Pennsylvania (PA)
Smith Coll (MA)
Sonoma State U (CA)
South Carolina State U (SC)
South Dakota State U (SD)
Southeastern Louisiana U (LA)
Southeastern Oklahoma State U (OK)
Southern Arkansas U–Magnolia (AR)
Southern Connecticut State U (CT)
Southern Illinois U Carbondale (IL)
Southern Illinois U Edwardsville (IL)
Southern Methodist U (TX)
Southern Oregon U (OR)
Southern U and Ag and Mech Coll (LA)
Southern Utah U (UT)
Southwest Baptist U (MO)
Southwestern U (TX)
Southwest Minnesota State U (MN)
Spelman Coll (GA)
Spring Arbor U (MI)
Spring Hill Coll (AL)
Stanford U (CA)
State U of New York at Binghamton (NY)
State U of New York at Fredonia (NY)
State U of New York at New Paltz (NY)
State U of New York at Oswego (NY)
State U of New York at Plattsburgh (NY)
State U of New York Coll at Geneseo (NY)
State U of New York Coll at Old Westbury (NY)
State U of New York Coll at Oneonta (NY)
State U of New York Coll at Potsdam (NY)
State U of New York Inst of Technology (NY)
Stephen F. Austin State U (TX)
Stetson U (FL)
Stonehill Coll (MA)
Stony Brook U, State U of New York (NY)
Suffolk U (MA)
Susquehanna U (PA)
Swarthmore Coll (PA)
Sweet Briar Coll (VA)
Syracuse U (NY)
Tabor Coll (KS)
Tarleton State U (TX)
Taylor U (IN)
Temple U (PA)
Tennessee State U (TN)
Tennessee Technological U (TN)
Texas A&M Intl U (TX)
Texas A&M U (TX)
Texas A&M U–Commerce (TX)
Texas Christian U (TX)
Texas Coll (TX)
Texas Lutheran U (TX)
Texas Southern U (TX)
Texas State U-San Marcos (TX)
Texas Tech U (TX)
Texas Woman's U (TX)
Thiel Coll (PA)
Thomas Edison State Coll (NJ)
Thomas More Coll (KY)
Thomas U (GA)
Thompson Rivers U (BC, Canada)
Tougaloo Coll (MS)
Transylvania U (KY)
Trent U (ON, Canada)
Trinity Christian Coll (IL)
Trinity Coll (CT)
Trinity U (TX)
Troy U (AL)
Truman State U (MO)
Tufts U (MA)
Tulane U (LA)
Tuskegee U (AL)
Union Coll (NY)
Union U (TN)
Université du Québec en Outaouais (QC, Canada)
U at Albany, State U of New York (NY)
U at Buffalo, the State U of New York (NY)
The U of Akron (OH)
The U of Alabama (AL)
The U of Alabama at Birmingham (AL)
The U of Alabama in Huntsville (AL)
U of Alaska Fairbanks (AK)
The U of Arizona (AZ)
U of Arkansas (AR)
U of Arkansas at Pine Bluff (AR)
The U of British Columbia (BC, Canada)
The U of British Columbia–Okanagan (BC, Canada)
U of California, Berkeley (CA)
U of California, Davis (CA)
U of California, Irvine (CA)
U of California, Los Angeles (CA)
U of California, Riverside (CA)
U of California, San Diego (CA)
U of California, Santa Barbara (CA)
U of California, Santa Cruz (CA)
U of Central Arkansas (AR)
U of Central Florida (FL)
U of Central Missouri (MO)
U of Central Oklahoma (OK)
U of Chicago (IL)
U of Cincinnati (OH)
U of Colorado at Boulder (CO)
U of Colorado Denver (CO)
U of Connecticut (CT)
U of Dayton (OH)
U of Delaware (DE)
U of Denver (CO)
U of Evansville (IN)
The U of Findlay (OH)
U of Florida (FL)
U of Georgia (GA)
U of Great Falls (MT)
U of Guam (GU)
U of Hartford (CT)
U of Hawaii at Manoa (HI)
U of Hawaii–West Oahu (HI)
U of Houston (TX)
U of Houston–Clear Lake (TX)
U of Houston–Downtown (TX)
U of Idaho (ID)
U of Illinois at Chicago (IL)
U of Illinois at Urbana–Champaign (IL)
U of Indianapolis (IN)
The U of Iowa (IA)
U of Kansas (KS)
U of King's Coll (NS, Canada)
U of La Verne (CA)
U of Lethbridge (AB, Canada)
U of Louisiana at Lafayette (LA)
U of Louisiana at Monroe (LA)
U of Louisville (KY)
U of Maine (ME)
U of Maine at Farmington (ME)
U of Mary Hardin-Baylor (TX)
U of Maryland, Baltimore County (MD)
U of Maryland, Coll Park (MD)
U of Maryland Eastern Shore (MD)
U of Mary Washington (VA)
U of Massachusetts Amherst (MA)
U of Massachusetts Boston (MA)
U of Massachusetts Dartmouth (MA)
U of Massachusetts Lowell (MA)
U of Memphis (TN)
U of Miami (FL)
U of Michigan (MI)
U of Michigan–Dearborn (MI)
U of Michigan–Flint (MI)
U of Minnesota, Duluth (MN)
U of Minnesota, Twin Cities Campus (MN)
U of Mississippi (MS)
U of Missouri–Columbia (MO)
U of Missouri–Kansas City (MO)
U of Missouri–St. Louis (MO)
The U of Montana (MT)
U of Montevallo (AL)
U of Nebraska at Kearney (NE)
U of Nebraska at Omaha (NE)
U of Nebraska–Lincoln (NE)
U of Nevada, Las Vegas (NV)
U of Nevada, Reno (NV)
U of New Brunswick Fredericton (NB, Canada)
U of New England (ME)
U of New Hampshire (NH)
U of New Mexico (NM)
U of New Orleans (LA)
U of North Alabama (AL)
The U of North Carolina at Asheville (NC)
The U of North Carolina at Chapel Hill (NC)
The U of North Carolina at Charlotte (NC)
The U of North Carolina at Greensboro (NC)
The U of North Carolina at Pembroke (NC)
The U of North Carolina Wilmington (NC)
U of North Dakota (ND)
U of Northern Colorado (CO)
U of Northern Iowa (IA)
U of North Florida (FL)
U of North Texas (TX)
U of Notre Dame (IN)
U of Oklahoma (OK)
U of Oregon (OR)
U of Ottawa (ON, Canada)
U of Pennsylvania (PA)
U of Pittsburgh (PA)
U of Pittsburgh at Bradford (PA)
U of Pittsburgh at Johnstown (PA)
U of Portland (OR)
U of Prince Edward Island (PE, Canada)
U of Puerto Rico at Utuado (PR)
U of Puerto Rico, Cayey U Coll (PR)
U of Puget Sound (WA)
U of Redlands (CA)
U of Regina (SK, Canada)
U of Rhode Island (RI)
U of Richmond (VA)
U of Rio Grande (OH)
U of Saint Francis (IN)
U of Saint Mary (KS)
U of St. Thomas (MN)
U of San Diego (CA)
U of Science and Arts of Oklahoma (OK)
The U of Scranton (PA)
U of Sioux Falls (SD)
U of South Alabama (AL)
U of South Carolina (SC)
U of South Carolina Aiken (SC)
U of South Carolina Upstate (SC)
The U of South Dakota (SD)
U of Southern California (CA)
U of Southern Indiana (IN)
U of Southern Maine (ME)
U of Southern Mississippi (MS)
U of South Florida (FL)
The U of Tampa (FL)
The U of Tennessee (TN)
The U of Tennessee at Chattanooga (TN)
The U of Tennessee at Martin (TN)
The U of Texas at Arlington (TX)
The U of Texas at Austin (TX)
The U of Texas at Brownsville (TX)
The U of Texas at Dallas (TX)
The U of Texas at El Paso (TX)
The U of Texas at San Antonio (TX)
The U of Texas at Tyler (TX)
The U of Texas of the Permian Basin (TX)
The U of Texas–Pan American (TX)
U of the District of Columbia (DC)
U of the Incarnate Word (TX)
U of the Ozarks (AR)
U of the Pacific (CA)
The U of Toledo (OH)
U of Toronto (ON, Canada)
U of Tulsa (OK)
U of Utah (UT)
U of Vermont (VT)
U of Victoria (BC, Canada)
U of Virginia (VA)
The U of Virginia's Coll at Wise (VA)
The U of Western Ontario (ON, Canada)
U of West Georgia (GA)
U of Windsor (ON, Canada)
The U of Winnipeg (MB, Canada)
U of Wisconsin–Eau Claire (WI)
U of Wisconsin–La Crosse (WI)
U of Wisconsin–Madison (WI)
U of Wisconsin–Milwaukee (WI)
U of Wisconsin–Oshkosh (WI)
U of Wisconsin–Parkside (WI)
U of Wisconsin–Stevens Point (WI)
U of Wisconsin–Superior (WI)
U of Wisconsin–Whitewater (WI)
U of Wyoming (WY)
Ursinus Coll (PA)
Ursuline Coll (OH)
Utah State U (UT)
Utica Coll (NY)
Valdosta State U (GA)
Valparaiso U (IN)
Vanderbilt U (TN)
Vanguard U of Southern California (CA)
Vassar Coll (NY)
Villanova U (PA)
Virginia Commonwealth U (VA)
Virginia Polytechnic Inst and State U (VA)
Virginia State U (VA)
Virginia U of Lynchburg (VA)
Virginia Wesleyan Coll (VA)
Viterbo U (WI)
Voorhees Coll (SC)
Wagner Coll (NY)
Wake Forest U (NC)
Walla Walla U (WA)
Walsh U (OH)
Warren Wilson Coll (NC)
Wartburg Coll (IA)
Washburn U (KS)
Washington & Jefferson Coll (PA)
Washington and Lee U (VA)
Washington Coll (MD)
Washington State U (WA)
Waynesburg U (PA)
Wayne State Coll (NE)
Wayne State U (MI)
Weber State U (UT)
Wellesley Coll (MA)
Wells Coll (NY)

Wesleyan U (CT)
West Chester U of Pennsylvania (PA)
Western Carolina U (NC)
Western Connecticut State U (CT)
Western Illinois U (IL)
Western Kentucky U (KY)
Western Michigan U (MI)
Western New England Coll (MA)
Western New Mexico U (NM)
Western State Coll of Colorado (CO)
Western Washington U (WA)
Westfield State Coll (MA)
West Liberty State Coll (WV)
Westminster Coll (MO)
Westminster Coll (UT)
Westmont Coll (CA)
West Texas A&M U (TX)
West Virginia U (WV)
West Virginia Wesleyan Coll (WV)
Wheaton Coll (IL)
Wheaton Coll (MA)
Whitman Coll (WA)
Whittier Coll (CA)
Whitworth U (WA)
Wichita State U (KS)
Widener U (PA)
Wiley Coll (TX)
Wilfrid Laurier U (ON, Canada)
Wilkes U (PA)
Willamette U (OR)
William Paterson U of New Jersey (NJ)
Williams Coll (MA)
Wingate U (NC)
Winona State U (MN)
Winthrop U (SC)
Wittenberg U (OH)
Wofford Coll (SC)
Worcester State Coll (MA)
Wright State U (OH)
Xavier U (OH)
Xavier U of Louisiana (LA)
Yale U (CT)
York Coll of Pennsylvania (PA)
York Coll of the City U of New York (NY)
York U (ON, Canada)
Youngstown State U (OH)

SOIL CONSERVATION

Ball State U (IN)
California State Polytechnic U, Pomona (CA)
U of Delaware (DE)
U of New Hampshire (NH)
The U of Tennessee at Martin (TN)
U of Wisconsin–Stevens Point (WI)

SOIL SCIENCE AND AGRONOMY

Colorado State U (CO)
McGill U (QC, Canada)
Michigan State U (MI)
North Carolina State U (NC)
North Dakota State U (ND)
Penn State Abington (PA)
Penn State Altoona (PA)
Penn State Berks (PA)
Penn State Erie, The Behrend Coll (PA)
Penn State U Park (PA)
Sterling Coll (VT)
The U of British Columbia (BC, Canada)
U of California, Davis (CA)
U of Delaware (DE)
U of Florida (FL)
U of Idaho (ID)
U of Maine (ME)
U of Minnesota, Twin Cities Campus (MN)
U of Nebraska–Lincoln (NE)
Utah State U (UT)

SOIL SCIENCES

Oregon State U (OR)
The U of Arizona (AZ)

SOIL SCIENCES RELATED

Brigham Young U (UT)
Sterling Coll (VT)

SOLAR ENERGY TECHNOLOGY

Appalachian State U (NC)
Sterling Coll (VT)

SOUTH ASIAN LANGUAGES

Claremont McKenna Coll (CA)
Northwestern U (IL)
The U of British Columbia (BC, Canada)
U of Chicago (IL)
U of Hawaii at Manoa (HI)
Yale U (CT)

SPANISH

Abilene Christian U (TX)
Adams State Coll (CO)
Adelphi U (NY)
Adrian Coll (MI)
Agnes Scott Coll (GA)
Alabama State U (AL)
Albertus Magnus Coll (CT)
Albion Coll (MI)
Albright Coll (PA)
Alfred U (NY)
Allegheny Coll (PA)
Alma Coll (MI)
American U (DC)
Amherst Coll (MA)
Anderson U (IN)
Anderson U (SC)
Andrews U (MI)
Angelo State U (TX)
Anna Maria Coll (MA)
Appalachian State U (NC)
Aquinas Coll (MI)
Arizona State U (AZ)
Arizona State U at the West campus (AZ)
Arkansas State U (AR)
Armstrong Atlantic State U (GA)
Asbury Coll (KY)
Ashland U (OH)
Assumption Coll (MA)
Auburn U (AL)
Augsburg Coll (MN)
Augustana Coll (IL)
Augustana Coll (SD)
Augusta State U (GA)
Austin Coll (TX)
Austin Peay State U (TN)
Azusa Pacific U (CA)
Baker U (KS)
Baldwin-Wallace Coll (OH)
Ball State U (IN)
Bard Coll (NY)
Bard Coll at Simon's Rock (MA)
Barnard Coll (NY)
Barry U (FL)
Barton Coll (NC)
Bates Coll (ME)
Baylor U (TX)
Belmont U (TN)
Beloit Coll (WI)
Bemidji State U (MN)
Benedictine Coll (KS)
Benedictine U (IL)
Bennington Coll (VT)
Berea Coll (KY)
Bernard M. Baruch Coll of the City U of New York (NY)
Berry Coll (GA)
Bethany Coll (WV)
Bethel Coll (KS)
Bethel U (MN)
Biola U (CA)
Bishop's U (QC, Canada)
Blackburn Coll (IL)
Bloomsburg U of Pennsylvania (PA)
Bluffton U (OH)
Bob Jones U (SC)
Boise State U (ID)
Boston Coll (MA)
Boston U (MA)
Bowdoin Coll (ME)
Bowling Green State U (OH)
Bradley U (IL)
Brandeis U (MA)
Bridgewater Coll (VA)
Bridgewater State Coll (MA)
Brigham Young U (UT)
Brock U (ON, Canada)
Brown U (RI)
Bryan Coll (TN)
Bryn Mawr Coll (PA)
Bucknell U (PA)
Buffalo State Coll, State U of New York (NY)
Butler U (IN)
Cabrini Coll (PA)
California Baptist U (CA)
California Lutheran U (CA)
California State Polytechnic U, Pomona (CA)
California State U, Dominguez Hills (CA)
California State U, East Bay (CA)
California State U, Fresno (CA)
California State U, Fullerton (CA)
California State U, Long Beach (CA)
California State U, Los Angeles (CA)
California State U, Sacramento (CA)
California State U, San Bernardino (CA)
California State U, San Marcos (CA)
California State U, Stanislaus (CA)
Calvin Coll (MI)
Canisius Coll (NY)
Capital U (OH)
Carlow U (PA)
Carnegie Mellon U (PA)
Carroll Coll (WI)
Carson-Newman Coll (TN)
Case Western Reserve U (OH)
Castleton State Coll (VT)
Catawba Coll (NC)
The Catholic U of America (DC)
Cedarville U (OH)
Centenary Coll of Louisiana (LA)
Central Coll (IA)
Central Connecticut State U (CT)
Central Michigan U (MI)
Centre Coll (KY)
Chapman U (CA)
Chatham U (PA)
Chestnut Hill Coll (PA)
Cheyney U of Pennsylvania (PA)
Chicago State U (IL)
Christopher Newport U (VA)
City Coll of the City U of New York (NY)
Claremont McKenna Coll (CA)
Clarion U of Pennsylvania (PA)
Clark Atlanta U (GA)
Clarke Coll (IA)
Clark U (MA)
Cleveland State U (OH)
Coastal Carolina U (SC)
Colby Coll (ME)
Colgate U (NY)
The Coll at Brockport, State U of New York (NY)
Coll of Charleston (SC)
The Coll of Idaho (ID)
Coll of Mount Saint Vincent (NY)
The Coll of New Jersey (NJ)
The Coll of New Rochelle (NY)
Coll of Saint Benedict (MN)
Coll of Saint Elizabeth (NJ)
The Coll of Saint Rose (NY)
Coll of Staten Island of the City U of New York (NY)
Coll of the Holy Cross (MA)
Coll of the Ozarks (MO)
The Coll of William and Mary (VA)
The Colorado Coll (CO)
Colorado State U (CO)
Columbia Coll (SC)
Columbus State U (GA)
Concordia Coll (MN)
Concordia U (MI)
Concordia U (QC, Canada)
Concordia U, Nebraska (NE)
Concordia U Wisconsin (WI)
Connecticut Coll (CT)
Converse Coll (SC)
Cornell Coll (IA)
Cornell U (NY)
Cornerstone U (MI)
Creighton U (NE)
Daemen Coll (NY)
Dakota Wesleyan U (SD)
Dana Coll (NE)
Dartmouth Coll (NH)
Davidson Coll (NC)
Davis & Elkins Coll (WV)
Denison U (OH)
DePaul U (IL)
DePauw U (IN)
DeSales U (PA)
Dickinson Coll (PA)
Dillard U (LA)
Doane Coll (NE)
Dominican Coll (NY)
Dominican U (IL)
Dordt Coll (IA)
Drew U (NJ)
Drury U (MO)
Duke U (NC)
Duquesne U (PA)
Earlham Coll (IN)
East Carolina U (NC)
Eastern Connecticut State U (CT)
Eastern Kentucky U (KY)
Eastern Mennonite U (VA)
Eastern Michigan U (MI)
Eastern New Mexico U (NM)
East Stroudsburg U of Pennsylvania (PA)
East Texas Baptist U (TX)
Eckerd Coll (FL)
Edinboro U of Pennsylvania (PA)
Elizabethtown Coll (PA)
Elon U (NC)
Emmanuel Coll (MA)
Emory & Henry Coll (VA)
Emory U (GA)
Endicott Coll (MA)
Erskine Coll (SC)
Evangel U (MO)
Fairfield U (CT)
Fairleigh Dickinson U, Coll at Florham (NJ)
Fairleigh Dickinson U, Metropolitan Campus (NJ)
Fayetteville State U (NC)
Ferrum Coll (VA)
Flagler Coll (FL)
Florida Ag and Mech U (FL)
Florida Atlantic U (FL)
Florida Gulf Coast U (FL)
Florida Intl U (FL)
Florida Southern Coll (FL)
Florida State U (FL)
Fort Lewis Coll (CO)
Franciscan U of Steubenville (OH)
Francis Marion U (SC)
Franklin & Marshall Coll (PA)
Franklin Coll (IN)
Fresno Pacific U (CA)
Furman U (SC)
Gardner-Webb U (NC)
George Fox U (OR)
Georgetown Coll (KY)
Georgetown U (DC)
The George Washington U (DC)
Georgia Coll & State U (GA)
Georgian Court U (NJ)
Georgia Southern U (GA)
Georgia State U (GA)
Gettysburg Coll (PA)
Gonzaga U (WA)
Gordon Coll (MA)
Goucher Coll (MD)
Grace Coll (IN)
Grambling State U (LA)
Grand Valley State U (MI)
Greensboro Coll (NC)
Greenville Coll (IL)
Grinnell Coll (IA)
Grove City Coll (PA)
Guilford Coll (NC)
Gustavus Adolphus Coll (MN)
Hamilton Coll (NY)
Hamline U (MN)
Hampden-Sydney Coll (VA)
Hanover Coll (IN)
Harding U (AR)
Hardin-Simmons U (TX)
Hartwick Coll (NY)
Harvard U (MA)
Hastings Coll (NE)
Haverford Coll (PA)
Heidelberg Coll (OH)
Henderson State U (AR)
Hendrix Coll (AR)
High Point U (NC)
Hillsdale Coll (MI)
Hobart and William Smith Colls (NY)
Hofstra U (NY)
Hollins U (VA)
Holy Family U (PA)
Holy Names U (CA)
Hood Coll (MD)
Hope Coll (MI)
Houghton Coll (NY)
Houston Baptist U (TX)
Howard Payne U (TX)
Humboldt State U (CA)
Hunter Coll of the City U of New York (NY)
Idaho State U (ID)
Illinois Coll (IL)
Illinois State U (IL)
Illinois Wesleyan U (IL)
Immaculata U (PA)
Indiana State U (IN)
Indiana U Bloomington (IN)
Indiana U Northwest (IN)
Indiana U of Pennsylvania (PA)
Indiana U–Purdue U Fort Wayne (IN)
Indiana U–Purdue U Indianapolis (IN)
Indiana U South Bend (IN)
Indiana U Southeast (IN)
Indiana Wesleyan U (IN)
Inter American U of Puerto Rico, San Germán Campus (PR)
Iona Coll (NY)
Iowa State U of Science and Technology (IA)
Ithaca Coll (NY)
Jacksonville State U (AL)
Jacksonville U (FL)
John Brown U (AR)
John Carroll U (OH)
The Johns Hopkins U (MD)
Johnson C. Smith U (NC)
Juniata Coll (PA)
Kalamazoo Coll (MI)
Kean U (NJ)
Keene State Coll (NH)
Kent State U (OH)
Kentucky Wesleyan Coll (KY)
Kenyon Coll (OH)
King Coll (TN)
King's Coll (PA)
Knox Coll (IL)
Kutztown U of Pennsylvania (PA)
Lafayette Coll (PA)
LaGrange Coll (GA)
Lake Forest Coll (IL)
Lambuth U (TN)
Lander U (SC)
La Roche Coll (PA)
La Salle U (PA)
La Sierra U (CA)
Laurentian U (ON, Canada)
Lawrence U (WI)
Lebanon Valley Coll (PA)
Lehigh U (PA)
Lehman Coll of the City U of New York (NY)
Le Moyne Coll (NY)
Lenoir-Rhyne Coll (NC)
Lewis & Clark Coll (OR)
Liberty U (VA)
Lincoln U (MO)
Lincoln U (PA)
Lindenwood U (MO)
Linfield Coll (OR)
Lipscomb U (TN)
Lock Haven U of Pennsylvania (PA)
Longwood U (VA)
Loras Coll (IA)
Louisiana Coll (LA)
Louisiana State U and Ag and Mech Coll (LA)
Loyola Coll in Maryland (MD)
Loyola Marymount U (CA)
Loyola U Chicago (IL)
Loyola U New Orleans (LA)
Luther Coll (IA)
Lynchburg Coll (VA)
Lyon Coll (AR)
Macalester Coll (MN)
Madonna U (MI)
Malone Coll (OH)
Manchester Coll (IN)
Manhattanville Coll (NY)
Mansfield U of Pennsylvania (PA)
Marian Coll (IN)
Marian Coll of Fond du Lac (WI)
Marietta Coll (OH)
Marist Coll (NY)
Marlboro Coll (VT)
Marquette U (WI)
Mary Baldwin Coll (VA)
Maryville Coll (TN)
Marywood U (PA)
McDaniel Coll (MD)
McGill U (QC, Canada)
McMurry U (TX)
McNeese State U (LA)
Memorial U of Newfoundland (NL, Canada)
Mercer U (GA)
Mercy Coll (NY)
Meredith Coll (NC)
Merrimack Coll (MA)
Mesa State Coll (CO)
Messiah Coll (PA)
Methodist U (NC)
Miami U (OH)
Miami U Hamilton (OH)
Michigan State U (MI)
MidAmerica Nazarene U (KS)
Middlebury Coll (VT)
Midwestern State U (TX)
Millersville U of Pennsylvania (PA)
Millikin U (IL)
Millsaps Coll (MS)
Mills Coll (CA)
Minnesota State U Mankato (MN)
Minot State U (ND)
Mississippi Coll (MS)
Mississippi U for Women (MS)
Missouri Southern State U (MO)
Missouri State U (MO)
Molloy Coll (NY)
Monmouth Coll (IL)
Montana State U–Billings (MT)
Montclair State U (NJ)
Moravian Coll (PA)
Morehead State U (KY)
Morehouse Coll (GA)
Morningside Coll (IA)
Mount Allison U (NB, Canada)
Mount Holyoke Coll (MA)
Mount Mary Coll (WI)
Mount St. Mary's Coll (CA)
Mount St. Mary's U (MD)
Mount Saint Vincent U (NS, Canada)
Mount Vernon Nazarene U (OH)
Muhlenberg Coll (PA)
Murray State U (KY)
Nazareth Coll of Rochester (NY)
Nebraska Wesleyan U (NE)
New Coll of Florida (FL)
New Jersey City U (NJ)
New Mexico Highlands U (NM)
New York U (NY)
Niagara U (NY)
North Carolina Central U (NC)
North Carolina State U (NC)
North Central Coll (IL)
North Dakota State U (ND)
Northeastern Illinois U (IL)
Northeastern State U (OK)

MAJORS AND MORE

Northeastern U (MA)
Northern Arizona U (AZ)
Northern Illinois U (IL)
Northern Michigan U (MI)
Northern State U (SD)
North Georgia Coll & State U (GA)
Northwestern Coll (IA)
Northwestern Oklahoma State U (OK)
Northwestern U (IL)
Northwest Missouri State U (MO)
Northwest Nazarene U (ID)
Oakland U (MI)
Oakwood Coll (AL)
Oberlin Coll (OH)
Occidental Coll (CA)
Oglethorpe U (GA)
Ohio Northern U (OH)
Ohio U (OH)
Ohio Wesleyan U (OH)
Oklahoma Christian U (OK)
Oklahoma City U (OK)
Oklahoma Panhandle State U (OK)
Oklahoma State U (OK)
Old Dominion U (VA)
Oral Roberts U (OK)
Oregon State U (OR)
Otterbein Coll (OH)
Ouachita Baptist U (AR)
Pace U (NY)
Pacific Lutheran U (WA)
Pacific Union Coll (CA)
Pacific U (OR)
Park U (MO)
Peace Coll (NC)
Penn State Abington (PA)
Penn State Altoona (PA)
Penn State Berks (PA)
Penn State Erie, The Behrend Coll (PA)
Penn State U Park (PA)
Pepperdine U, Malibu (CA)
Piedmont Coll (GA)
Pittsburg State U (KS)
Pitzer Coll (CA)
Plymouth State U (NH)
Point Loma Nazarene U (CA)
Pomona Coll (CA)
Portland State U (OR)
Prairie View A&M U (TX)
Presbyterian Coll (SC)
Prescott Coll (AZ)
Princeton U (NJ)
Providence Coll (RI)
Purchase Coll, State U of New York (NY)
Purdue U (IN)
Purdue U Calumet (IN)
Queens Coll of the City U of New York (NY)
Queen's U at Kingston (ON, Canada)
Quinnipiac U (CT)
Ramapo Coll of New Jersey (NJ)
Randolph Coll (VA)
Randolph-Macon Coll (VA)
Reed Coll (OR)
Regis Coll (MA)
Regis U (CO)
Rhode Island Coll (RI)
Rhodes Coll (TN)
Rice U (TX)
Rider U (NJ)
Ripon Coll (WI)
Roanoke Coll (VA)
Rockford Coll (IL)
Rockhurst U (MO)
Rollins Coll (FL)
Roosevelt U (IL)
Rosemont Coll (PA)
Rowan U (NJ)
Russell Sage Coll (NY)
Rutgers, The State U of New Jersey, Camden (NJ)
Rutgers, The State U of New Jersey, Newark (NJ)
Rutgers, The State U of New Jersey, New Brunswick (NJ)
Saginaw Valley State U (MI)
St. Ambrose U (IA)
St. Cloud State U (MN)
St. Edward's U (TX)
Saint Francis U (PA)
St. John Fisher Coll (NY)
Saint John's U (MN)
St. John's U (NY)
Saint Joseph Coll (CT)
St. Joseph's Coll, New York (NY)
St. Joseph's Coll, Suffolk Campus (NY)
Saint Joseph's U (PA)
St. Lawrence U (NY)
Saint Louis U (MO)
Saint Mary's Coll (IN)
Saint Mary's Coll of California (CA)
St. Mary's U (TX)
Saint Mary's U of Minnesota (MN)
Saint Michael's Coll (VT)
St. Norbert Coll (WI)
St. Olaf Coll (MN)
St. Thomas Aquinas Coll (NY)
St. Thomas U (NB, Canada)
Saint Vincent Coll (PA)
Saint Xavier U (IL)
Salem Coll (NC)
Salisbury U (MD)
Salve Regina U (RI)
Samford U (AL)
Sam Houston State U (TX)
San Diego State U (CA)
San Francisco State U (CA)
Santa Clara U (CA)
Sarah Lawrence Coll (NY)
Scripps Coll (CA)
Seattle Pacific U (WA)
Seattle U (WA)
Seton Hill U (PA)
Sewanee: The U of the South (TN)
Shaw U (NC)
Shenandoah U (VA)
Shepherd U (WV)
Shippensburg U of Pennsylvania (PA)
Shorter Coll (GA)
Siena Coll (NY)
Siena Heights U (MI)
Simmons Coll (MA)
Simpson Coll (IA)
Skidmore Coll (NY)
Slippery Rock U of Pennsylvania (PA)
Smith Coll (MA)
Sonoma State U (CA)
South Carolina State U (SC)
South Dakota State U (SD)
Southeastern Louisiana U (LA)
Southeastern Oklahoma State U (OK)
Southeast Missouri State U (MO)
Southern Adventist U (TN)
Southern Arkansas U–Magnolia (AR)
Southern Connecticut State U (CT)
Southern Illinois U Carbondale (IL)
Southern Methodist U (TX)
Southern Oregon U (OR)
Southern U and Ag and Mech Coll (LA)
Southern Utah U (UT)
Southwest Baptist U (MO)
Southwestern U (TX)
Southwest Minnesota State U (MN)
Spelman Coll (GA)
Spring Arbor U (MI)
Spring Hill Coll (AL)
Stanford U (CA)
State U of New York at Binghamton (NY)
State U of New York at Fredonia (NY)
State U of New York at New Paltz (NY)
State U of New York at Oswego (NY)
State U of New York at Plattsburgh (NY)
State U of New York Coll at Geneseo (NY)
State U of New York Coll at Old Westbury (NY)
State U of New York Coll at Oneonta (NY)
State U of New York Coll at Potsdam (NY)
Stephen F. Austin State U (TX)
Stetson U (FL)
Stony Brook U, State U of New York (NY)
Suffolk U (MA)
Susquehanna U (PA)
Swarthmore Coll (PA)
Sweet Briar Coll (VA)
Syracuse U (NY)
Tarleton State U (TX)
Taylor U (IN)
Temple U (PA)
Tennessee State U (TN)
Tennessee Technological U (TN)
Tennessee Wesleyan Coll (TN)
Texas A&M Intl U (TX)
Texas A&M U (TX)
Texas A&M U–Commerce (TX)
Texas Christian U (TX)
Texas Lutheran U (TX)
Texas Southern U (TX)
Texas State U-San Marcos (TX)
Texas Tech U (TX)
Towson U (MD)
Transylvania U (KY)
Trinity Christian Coll (IL)
Trinity Coll (CT)
Trinity U (TX)
Truman State U (MO)
Tufts U (MA)
Tulane U (LA)
Union Coll (NE)
Union U (TN)
U at Albany, State U of New York (NY)
U at Buffalo, the State U of New York (NY)
The U of Akron (OH)
The U of Alabama (AL)
The U of Alabama at Birmingham (AL)
The U of Arizona (AZ)
U of Arkansas (AR)
U of Arkansas at Fort Smith (AR)
The U of British Columbia (BC, Canada)
The U of British Columbia–Okanagan (BC, Canada)
U of California, Berkeley (CA)
U of California, Davis (CA)
U of California, Irvine (CA)
U of California, Los Angeles (CA)
U of California, Riverside (CA)
U of California, San Diego (CA)
U of California, Santa Barbara (CA)
U of Central Arkansas (AR)
U of Central Florida (FL)
U of Central Missouri (MO)
U of Central Oklahoma (OK)
U of Chicago (IL)
U of Cincinnati (OH)
U of Colorado at Boulder (CO)
U of Colorado Denver (CO)
U of Connecticut (CT)
U of Dallas (TX)
U of Dayton (OH)
U of Delaware (DE)
U of Denver (CO)
U of Evansville (IN)
The U of Findlay (OH)
U of Florida (FL)
U of Georgia (GA)
U of Hawaii at Manoa (HI)
U of Houston (TX)
U of Houston–Downtown (TX)
U of Idaho (ID)
U of Illinois at Chicago (IL)
U of Illinois at Urbana–Champaign (IL)
U of Indianapolis (IN)
The U of Iowa (IA)
U of Kansas (KS)
U of King's Coll (NS, Canada)
U of La Verne (CA)
U of Louisiana at Lafayette (LA)
U of Louisiana at Monroe (LA)
U of Louisville (KY)
U of Maine (ME)
U of Mary Hardin-Baylor (TX)
U of Maryland, Coll Park (MD)
U of Mary Washington (VA)
U of Massachusetts Amherst (MA)
U of Massachusetts Boston (MA)
U of Massachusetts Dartmouth (MA)
U of Miami (FL)
U of Michigan (MI)
U of Michigan–Dearborn (MI)
U of Michigan–Flint (MI)
U of Minnesota, Duluth (MN)
U of Minnesota, Twin Cities Campus (MN)
U of Mississippi (MS)
U of Missouri–Columbia (MO)
U of Missouri–Kansas City (MO)
U of Missouri–St. Louis (MO)
The U of Montana (MT)
U of Nebraska at Kearney (NE)
U of Nebraska at Omaha (NE)
U of Nebraska–Lincoln (NE)
U of Nevada, Las Vegas (NV)
U of Nevada, Reno (NV)
U of New Brunswick Fredericton (NB, Canada)
U of New Hampshire (NH)
U of New Mexico (NM)
U of New Orleans (LA)
The U of North Carolina at Asheville (NC)
The U of North Carolina at Charlotte (NC)
The U of North Carolina at Greensboro (NC)
The U of North Carolina at Pembroke (NC)
The U of North Carolina Wilmington (NC)
U of North Dakota (ND)
U of Northern Colorado (CO)
U of Northern Iowa (IA)
U of North Florida (FL)
U of North Texas (TX)
U of Notre Dame (IN)
U of Oklahoma (OK)
U of Oregon (OR)
U of Ottawa (ON, Canada)
U of Pennsylvania (PA)
U of Pittsburgh (PA)
U of Portland (OR)
U of Prince Edward Island (PE, Canada)
U of Puerto Rico at Utuado (PR)
U of Puerto Rico, Cayey U Coll (PR)
U of Puget Sound (WA)
U of Redlands (CA)
U of Regina (SK, Canada)
U of Rhode Island (RI)
U of Richmond (VA)
U of Rochester (NY)
U of St. Thomas (MN)
U of St. Thomas (TX)
U of San Diego (CA)
The U of Scranton (PA)
U of South Carolina (SC)
U of South Carolina Upstate (SC)
The U of South Dakota (SD)
U of Southern California (CA)
U of Southern Indiana (IN)
U of South Florida (FL)
The U of Tampa (FL)
The U of Tennessee (TN)
The U of Tennessee at Chattanooga (TN)
The U of Tennessee at Martin (TN)
The U of Texas at Arlington (TX)
The U of Texas at Austin (TX)
The U of Texas at Brownsville (TX)
The U of Texas at El Paso (TX)
The U of Texas at San Antonio (TX)
The U of Texas at Tyler (TX)
The U of Texas of the Permian Basin (TX)
The U of Texas–Pan American (TX)
U of the District of Columbia (DC)
U of the Incarnate Word (TX)
U of the Ozarks (AR)
U of the Pacific (CA)
U of Toledo (OH)
U of Toronto (ON, Canada)
U of Tulsa (OK)
U of Utah (UT)
U of Vermont (VT)
U of Victoria (BC, Canada)
U of Virginia (VA)
The U of Virginia's Coll at Wise (VA)
The U of Western Ontario (ON, Canada)
U of West Georgia (GA)
U of Windsor (ON, Canada)
U of Wisconsin–Eau Claire (WI)
U of Wisconsin–Green Bay (WI)
U of Wisconsin–La Crosse (WI)
U of Wisconsin–Madison (WI)
U of Wisconsin–Milwaukee (WI)
U of Wisconsin–Oshkosh (WI)
U of Wisconsin–Parkside (WI)
U of Wisconsin–Platteville (WI)
U of Wisconsin–Stevens Point (WI)
U of Wisconsin–Whitewater (WI)
U of Wyoming (WY)
Ursinus Coll (PA)
Utah State U (UT)
Utah Valley State Coll (UT)
Valdosta State U (GA)
Valley City State U (ND)
Valparaiso U (IN)
Vanderbilt U (TN)
Vanguard U of Southern California (CA)
Vassar Coll (NY)
Villanova U (PA)
Virginia Polytechnic Inst and State U (VA)
Virginia Wesleyan Coll (VA)
Viterbo U (WI)
Wabash Coll (IN)
Wagner Coll (NY)
Wake Forest U (NC)
Walla Walla U (WA)
Walsh U (OH)
Warren Wilson Coll (NC)
Wartburg Coll (IA)
Washburn U (KS)
Washington & Jefferson Coll (PA)
Washington and Lee U (VA)
Washington Coll (MD)
Washington U in St. Louis (MO)
Wayland Baptist U (TX)
Wayne State Coll (NE)
Weber State U (UT)
Webster U (MO)
Wellesley Coll (MA)
Wells Coll (NY)
Wesleyan Coll (GA)
Wesleyan U (CT)
West Chester U of Pennsylvania (PA)
Western Carolina U (NC)
Western Connecticut State U (CT)
Western Illinois U (IL)
Western Kentucky U (KY)
Western Michigan U (MI)
Western New Mexico U (NM)
Western State Coll of Colorado (CO)
Western Washington U (WA)
Westminster Coll (MO)
Westmont Coll (CA)
West Texas A&M U (TX)
Wheaton Coll (IL)
Wheeling Jesuit U (WV)
Whitman Coll (WA)
Whittier Coll (CA)
Whitworth U (WA)
Wichita State U (KS)
Widener U (PA)
Wilfrid Laurier U (ON, Canada)
Wilkes U (PA)
Willamette U (OR)
William Jewell Coll (MO)
William Paterson U of New Jersey (NJ)
Williams Coll (MA)
William Woods U (MO)
Wilmington Coll (OH)
Wilson Coll (PA)
Wingate U (NC)
Winona State U (MN)
Wittenberg U (OH)
Wofford Coll (SC)
Worcester State Coll (MA)
Wright State U (OH)
Xavier U (OH)
Xavier U of Louisiana (LA)
Yale U (CT)
York Coll of Pennsylvania (PA)
York Coll of the City U of New York (NY)
York U (ON, Canada)
Youngstown State U (OH)

SPANISH AND IBERIAN STUDIES

Bard Coll at Simon's Rock (MA)
Barnard Coll (NY)
McGill U (QC, Canada)
Santa Clara U (CA)
U of Houston (TX)
The U of Winnipeg (MB, Canada)
York U (ON, Canada)

SPANISH LANGUAGE TEACHER EDUCATION

Abilene Christian U (TX)
Alma Coll (MI)
Anderson U (IN)
Anderson U (SC)
Appalachian State U (NC)
Arkansas State U (AR)
Assumption Coll (MA)
Auburn U (AL)
Baylor U (TX)
Bethel U (MN)
Bishop's U (QC, Canada)
Bob Jones U (SC)
Bridgewater Coll (VA)
Brigham Young U (UT)
California Lutheran U (CA)
Carroll Coll (WI)
The Catholic U of America (DC)
Cedarville U (OH)
Centenary Coll of Louisiana (LA)
Central Michigan U (MI)
Central Washington U (WA)
The Coll at Brockport, State U of New York (NY)
The Coll of New Jersey (NJ)
Coll of Saint Mary (NE)
The Coll of Saint Rose (NY)
Colorado State U (CO)
Concordia Coll (MN)
Concordia U (MI)
Concordia U, Nebraska (NE)
Concordia U Wisconsin (WI)
Connecticut Coll (CT)
Daemen Coll (NY)
DePaul U (IL)
Dordt Coll (IA)
Dowling Coll (NY)
Duquesne U (PA)
East Carolina U (NC)
Eastern Mennonite U (VA)
Eastern Michigan U (MI)
East Texas Baptist U (TX)
Evangel U (MO)
Fayetteville State U (NC)
Franklin Coll (IN)
Georgia Southern U (GA)
Grace Coll (IN)
Greensboro Coll (NC)
Greenville Coll (IL)
Harding U (AR)
Hardin-Simmons U (TX)
Hastings Coll (NE)
Hofstra U (NY)
Hope Coll (MI)
Howard Payne U (TX)
Indiana U Bloomington (IN)
Indiana U Northwest (IN)
Indiana U–Purdue U Fort Wayne (IN)
Indiana U–Purdue U Indianapolis (IN)
Indiana U South Bend (IN)
Inter American U of Puerto Rico, Aguadilla Campus (PR)

MAJORS AND MORE

Iona Coll (NY)
Ithaca Coll (NY)
Juniata Coll (PA)
Keene State Coll (NH)
Kent State U (OH)
Kentucky Wesleyan Coll (KY)
King Coll (TN)
Kutztown U of Pennsylvania (PA)
Le Moyne Coll (NY)
Liberty U (VA)
Lindenwood U (MO)
Lipscomb U (TN)
Malone Coll (OH)
Manhattanville Coll (NY)
Mansfield U of Pennsylvania (PA)
Marian Coll of Fond du Lac (WI)
Marist Coll (NY)
Maryville Coll (TN)
Marywood U (PA)
Mercy Coll (NY)
Messiah Coll (PA)
Miami U Hamilton (OH)
MidAmerica Nazarene U (KS)
Minot State U (ND)
Missouri State U (MO)
Molloy Coll (NY)
Montana State U–Billings (MT)
Moravian Coll (PA)
Mount Mary Coll (WI)
Mount Vernon Nazarene U (OH)
Murray State U (KY)
Niagara U (NY)
North Carolina Central U (NC)
North Carolina State U (NC)
North Dakota State U (ND)
Northeastern State U (OK)
Northern Arizona U (AZ)
Northern Michigan U (MI)
Northwest Nazarene U (ID)
Ohio Northern U (OH)
Ohio U (OH)
Ohio Wesleyan U (OH)
Old Dominion U (VA)
Oral Roberts U (OK)
Pace U (NY)
Pittsburg State U (KS)
Purdue U (IN)
Rhode Island Coll (RI)
Saginaw Valley State U (MI)
St. Ambrose U (IA)
St. Edward's U (TX)
St. John's U (NY)
St. Joseph's Coll, Suffolk Campus (NY)
Saint Mary's U of Minnesota (MN)
Saint Xavier U (IL)
Salve Regina U (RI)
Seton Hill U (PA)
Southeastern Louisiana U (LA)
Southeastern Oklahoma State U (OK)
Southern Arkansas U–Magnolia (AR)
Southern U and Ag and Mech Coll (LA)
Southwest Minnesota State U (MN)
State U of New York at Plattsburgh (NY)
State U of New York Coll at Old Westbury (NY)
State U of New York Coll at Oneonta (NY)
State U of New York Coll at Potsdam (NY)
Taylor U (IN)
Texas A&M Intl U (TX)
The U of Akron (OH)
The U of Arizona (AZ)
U of Arkansas at Fort Smith (AR)
U of Evansville (IN)
U of Illinois at Chicago (IL)
U of Illinois at Urbana–Champaign (IL)
U of Indianapolis (IN)
The U of Iowa (IA)
U of Louisiana at Lafayette (LA)
U of Louisiana at Monroe (LA)
U of Maine (ME)
U of Michigan–Flint (MI)
U of Minnesota, Duluth (MN)
U of Missouri–St. Louis (MO)
U of Nebraska–Lincoln (NE)
The U of North Carolina at Charlotte (NC)
The U of North Carolina at Greensboro (NC)
The U of North Carolina Wilmington (NC)
U of Puerto Rico at Utuado (PR)
U of Puerto Rico, Cayey U Coll (PR)
The U of South Dakota (SD)
The U of Tennessee at Martin (TN)
The U of Toledo (OH)
Utah Valley State Coll (UT)
Valley City State U (ND)
Valparaiso U (IN)
Viterbo U (WI)
Washington U in St. Louis (MO)
Weber State U (UT)
Western Carolina U (NC)
Western Michigan U (MI)
Western State Coll of Colorado (CO)
Wheeling Jesuit U (WV)
Widener U (PA)
William Jewell Coll (MO)
Xavier U of Louisiana (LA)
Youngstown State U (OH)

SPECIAL EDUCATION

Abilene Christian U (TX)
Alabama Ag and Mech U (AL)
Alabama State U (AL)
Albright Coll (PA)
Alcorn State U (MS)
Anderson U (SC)
Arizona State U (AZ)
Arizona State U at the West campus (AZ)
Arkansas State U (AR)
Armstrong Atlantic State U (GA)
Ashland U (OH)
Athens State U (AL)
Auburn U (AL)
Augustana Coll (SD)
Augusta State U (GA)
Austin Peay State U (TN)
Avila U (MO)
Ball State U (IN)
Barry U (FL)
Barton Coll (NC)
Baylor U (TX)
Bellarmine U (KY)
Belmont U (TN)
Benedictine Coll (KS)
Benedictine U (IL)
Bethel Coll (TN)
Bloomsburg U of Pennsylvania (PA)
Bob Jones U (SC)
Boise State U (ID)
Boston U (MA)
Bowling Green State U (OH)
Brenau U (GA)
Bridgewater State Coll (MA)
Brigham Young U (UT)
Buffalo State Coll, State U of New York (NY)
Cabrini Coll (PA)
Calvin Coll (MI)
Capital U (OH)
Carlow U (PA)
Carson-Newman Coll (TN)
Cedarville U (OH)
Centenary Coll (NJ)
Central State U (OH)
Central Washington U (WA)
Cheyney U of Pennsylvania (PA)
City U of Seattle (WA)
Clarion U of Pennsylvania (PA)
Clarke Coll (IA)
Clemson U (SC)
Cleveland State U (OH)
Coastal Carolina U (SC)
Coll of Charleston (SC)
Coll of Mount St. Joseph (OH)
The Coll of New Jersey (NJ)
The Coll of New Rochelle (NY)
Coll of Saint Mary (NE)
The Coll of Saint Rose (NY)
Coll of the Southwest (NM)
Columbia Coll (SC)
Concordia U, Nebraska (NE)
Concord U (WV)
Converse Coll (SC)
Culver-Stockton Coll (MO)
Curry Coll (MA)
Dakota State U (SD)
Dakota Wesleyan U (SD)
Dana Coll (NE)
Delta State U (MS)
DePaul U (IL)
Dillard U (LA)
Doane Coll (NE)
Dominican Coll (NY)
Dowling Coll (NY)
Duquesne U (PA)
East Carolina U (NC)
East Central U (OK)
Eastern Illinois U (IL)
Eastern Kentucky U (KY)
Eastern Michigan U (MI)
Eastern New Mexico U (NM)
East Stroudsburg U of Pennsylvania (PA)
East Tennessee State U (TN)
Elon U (NC)
Erskine Coll (SC)
Evangel U (MO)
Fairmont State U (WV)
Felician Coll (NJ)
Fitchburg State Coll (MA)
Florida Atlantic U (FL)
Florida Gulf Coast U (FL)
Fontbonne U (MO)
Freed-Hardeman U (TN)
Furman U (SC)
Gannon U (PA)
Georgia Coll & State U (GA)
Georgia Southern U (GA)
Georgia Southwestern State U (GA)
Glenville State Coll (WV)
Gonzaga U (WA)
Gordon Coll (MA)
Goucher Coll (MD)
Grace Coll (IN)
Grambling State U (LA)
Grand Canyon U (AZ)
Grand Valley State U (MI)
Green Mountain Coll (VT)
Greensboro Coll (NC)
Greenville Coll (IL)
Gwynedd-Mercy Coll (PA)
Hampton U (VA)
Hastings Coll (NE)
Heidelberg Coll (OH)
High Point U (NC)
Holy Family U (PA)
Houghton Coll (NY)
Houston Baptist U (TX)
Huntington U (IN)
Idaho State U (ID)
Illinois State U (IL)
Indiana State U (IN)
Indiana U Bloomington (IN)
Indiana U of Pennsylvania (PA)
Indiana U South Bend (IN)
Indiana U Southeast (IN)
Indiana Wesleyan U (IN)
Inter American U of Puerto Rico, Fajardo Campus (PR)
Iowa Wesleyan Coll (IA)
Jackson State U (MS)
Jacksonville State U (AL)
Jacksonville U (FL)
Jarvis Christian Coll (TX)
John Brown U (AR)
John Carroll U (OH)
Kean U (NJ)
Keene State Coll (NH)
Kent State U (OH)
Keuka Coll (NY)
King's Coll (PA)
Kutztown U of Pennsylvania (PA)
Lambuth U (TN)
Lander U (SC)
La Salle U (PA)
Lee U (TN)
Le Moyne Coll (NY)
LeMoyne-Owen Coll (TN)
Lesley U (MA)
Lewis U (IL)
Liberty U (VA)
Lincoln U (MO)
Lincoln U (PA)
Lindenwood U (MO)
Lock Haven U of Pennsylvania (PA)
Longwood U (VA)
Louisiana Coll (LA)
Loyola Coll in Maryland (MD)
Loyola U Chicago (IL)
Lubbock Christian U (TX)
Lynchburg Coll (VA)
Lyndon State Coll (VT)
Madonna U (MI)
Manchester Coll (IN)
Mansfield U of Pennsylvania (PA)
Marian Coll (IN)
Marist Coll (NY)
Marywood U (PA)
McNeese State U (LA)
Medgar Evers Coll of the City U of New York (NY)
Memorial U of Newfoundland (NL, Canada)
Mercy Coll (NY)
Mercyhurst Coll (PA)
Methodist U (NC)
Miami U (OH)
Miami U Hamilton (OH)
Michigan State U (MI)
Middle Tennessee State U (TN)
Midway Coll (KY)
Millersville U of Pennsylvania (PA)
Misericordia U (PA)
Mississippi Coll (MS)
Mississippi State U (MS)
Mississippi U for Women (MS)
Missouri State U (MO)
Missouri Valley Coll (MO)
Molloy Coll (NY)
Monmouth U (NJ)
Montana State U–Billings (MT)
Morehead State U (KY)
Morningside Coll (IA)
Mount Marty Coll (SD)
Mount Saint Mary Coll (NY)
Mount Vernon Nazarene U (OH)
Murray State U (KY)
Nazareth Coll of Rochester (NY)
Nebraska Wesleyan U (NE)
New England Coll (NH)
New Jersey City U (NJ)
New Mexico Highlands U (NM)
New York U (NY)
Niagara U (NY)
North Carolina Ag and Tech State U (NC)
Northeastern Illinois U (IL)
Northeastern State U (OK)
Northern Arizona U (AZ)
Northern Illinois U (IL)
Northern Michigan U (MI)
Northern State U (SD)
North Georgia Coll & State U (GA)
Northwestern Oklahoma State U (OK)
Northwest Missouri State U (MO)
Ohio Dominican U (OH)
Ohio U (OH)
Oral Roberts U (OK)
Penn State Abington (PA)
Penn State Altoona (PA)
Penn State Berks (PA)
Penn State Erie, The Behrend Coll (PA)
Penn State U Park (PA)
Peru State Coll (NE)
Pfeiffer U (NC)
Piedmont Coll (GA)
Presbyterian Coll (SC)
Prescott Coll (AZ)
Providence Coll (RI)
Purdue U Calumet (IN)
Quincy U (IL)
Rhode Island Coll (RI)
Roberts Wesleyan Coll (NY)
Rockford Coll (IL)
Roosevelt U (IL)
Rowan U (NJ)
Saginaw Valley State U (MI)
St. Cloud State U (MN)
Saint Francis U (PA)
St. John Fisher Coll (NY)
St. John's U (NY)
Saint Joseph Coll (CT)
St. Joseph's Coll, Suffolk Campus (NY)
Saint Joseph's U (PA)
Saint Martin's U (WA)
Saint Mary-of-the-Woods Coll (IN)
St. Thomas Aquinas Coll (NY)
Salve Regina U (RI)
Seattle Pacific U (WA)
Seton Hill U (PA)
Shawnee State U (OH)
Simmons Coll (MA)
Slippery Rock U of Pennsylvania (PA)
South Carolina State U (SC)
Southeastern Louisiana U (LA)
Southeastern U (FL)
Southeast Missouri State U (MO)
Southern Connecticut State U (CT)
Southern Illinois U Carbondale (IL)
Southern Illinois U Edwardsville (IL)
Southern U and Ag and Mech Coll (LA)
Southern Utah U (UT)
Southern Wesleyan U (SC)
Southwestern Oklahoma State U (OK)
Southwest Minnesota State U (MN)
Spring Arbor U (MI)
State U of New York at New Paltz (NY)
State U of New York at Plattsburgh (NY)
State U of New York Coll at Geneseo (NY)
State U of New York Coll at Old Westbury (NY)
Syracuse U (NY)
Tabor Coll (KS)
Tennessee State U (TN)
Tennessee Technological U (TN)
Texas A&M Intl U (TX)
Texas A&M U–Commerce (TX)
Texas Christian U (TX)
Texas Southern U (TX)
Towson U (MD)
Trinity Christian Coll (IL)
Troy U (AL)
Tufts U (MA)
Tusculum Coll (TN)
Union Coll (KY)
Union U (TN)
Université de Sherbrooke (QC, Canada)
Université du Québec en Outaouais (QC, Canada)
The U of Akron (OH)
The U of Alabama (AL)
The U of Alabama at Birmingham (AL)
The U of Arizona (AZ)
U of Arkansas at Monticello (AR)
U of Arkansas at Pine Bluff (AR)
The U of British Columbia (BC, Canada)
U of Central Florida (FL)
U of Central Missouri (MO)
U of Central Oklahoma (OK)
U of Cincinnati (OH)
U of Connecticut (CT)
U of Dayton (OH)
U of Evansville (IN)
The U of Findlay (OH)
U of Florida (FL)
U of Great Falls (MT)
U of Guam (GU)
U of Hartford (CT)
U of Hawaii at Manoa (HI)
U of Idaho (ID)
U of Illinois at Urbana–Champaign (IL)
U of Lethbridge (AB, Canada)
U of Louisiana at Lafayette (LA)
U of Louisiana at Monroe (LA)
U of Maine at Farmington (ME)
U of Mary Hardin-Baylor (TX)
U of Maryland, Coll Park (MD)
U of Maryland Eastern Shore (MD)
U of Memphis (TN)
U of Miami (FL)
U of Minnesota, Duluth (MN)
U of Mississippi (MS)
U of Missouri–St. Louis (MO)
U of Nebraska at Kearney (NE)
U of Nevada, Las Vegas (NV)
U of Nevada, Reno (NV)
U of New Brunswick Fredericton (NB, Canada)
U of New Mexico (NM)
U of North Alabama (AL)
The U of North Carolina at Greensboro (NC)
The U of North Carolina Wilmington (NC)
U of Northern Colorado (CO)
U of Northern Iowa (IA)
U of North Florida (FL)
U of Oklahoma (OK)
U of Puerto Rico, Cayey U Coll (PR)
U of St. Francis (IL)
U of Saint Francis (IN)
The U of Scranton (PA)
U of South Alabama (AL)
U of South Carolina Aiken (SC)
The U of South Dakota (SD)
U of Southern Mississippi (MS)
U of South Florida (FL)
The U of Tennessee (TN)
The U of Tennessee at Chattanooga (TN)
The U of Tennessee at Martin (TN)
U of the District of Columbia (DC)
U of the Pacific (CA)
The U of Toledo (OH)
U of Utah (UT)
U of Victoria (BC, Canada)
The U of Western Ontario (ON, Canada)
U of West Florida (FL)
U of West Georgia (GA)
U of Windsor (ON, Canada)
U of Wisconsin–Eau Claire (WI)
U of Wisconsin–Madison (WI)
U of Wisconsin–Milwaukee (WI)
U of Wisconsin–Oshkosh (WI)
U of Wisconsin–Superior (WI)
U of Wisconsin–Whitewater (WI)
U of Wyoming (WY)
Ursuline Coll (OH)
Utah State U (UT)
Valdosta State U (GA)
Vanderbilt U (TN)
Walsh U (OH)
Waynesburg U (PA)
Wayne State Coll (NE)
Wayne State U (MI)
West Chester U of Pennsylvania (PA)
Western Carolina U (NC)
Western Illinois U (IL)
Western Kentucky U (KY)
Western New Mexico U (NM)
Western Washington U (WA)
Westfield State Coll (MA)
West Virginia Wesleyan Coll (WV)
Wheelock Coll (MA)
Whitworth U (WA)
Widener U (PA)
Wiley Coll (TX)
William Paterson U of New Jersey (NJ)
William Woods U (MO)
Winona State U (MN)
Winthrop U (SC)
Xavier U (OH)
Xavier U of Louisiana (LA)
York Coll (NE)
York Coll of Pennsylvania (PA)
York U (ON, Canada)
Youngstown State U (OH)

SPECIAL EDUCATION (ADMINISTRATION)

Wright State U (OH)

SPECIAL EDUCATION (DEVELOPMENTALLY DELAYED)

St. Joseph's Coll, Suffolk Campus (NY)

SPECIAL EDUCATION (EARLY CHILDHOOD)

Canisius Coll (NY)
Harding U (AR)
Juniata Coll (PA)
Keuka Coll (NY)
Purdue U (IN)
St. Joseph's Coll, Suffolk Campus (NY)
State U of New York Coll at Geneseo (NY)
The U of Akron (OH)
U of Illinois at Urbana–Champaign (IL)
U of Northern Iowa (IA)
U of Vermont (VT)

SPECIAL EDUCATION (EMOTIONALLY DISTURBED)

Augsburg Coll (MN)
Central Michigan U (MI)
East Carolina U (NC)
Eastern Mennonite U (VA)
Eastern Michigan U (MI)
Florida Intl U (FL)
Florida State U (FL)
Greensboro Coll (NC)
Hope Coll (MI)
Loras Coll (IA)
Marywood U (PA)
Southern Wesleyan U (SC)
Trinity Christian Coll (IL)
U of Maine at Farmington (ME)
The U of North Carolina Wilmington (NC)
U of South Florida (FL)
The U of Toledo (OH)
Wright State U (OH)

SPECIAL EDUCATION (GIFTED AND TALENTED)

Flagler Coll (FL)
Texas Christian U (TX)
U of Great Falls (MT)
Wright State U (OH)

SPECIAL EDUCATION (HEARING IMPAIRED)

Augustana Coll (SD)
Barton Coll (NC)
Boston U (MA)
Bowling Green State U (OH)
The Coll of New Jersey (NJ)
Eastern Kentucky U (KY)
Eastern Michigan U (MI)
Flagler Coll (FL)
Indiana U of Pennsylvania (PA)
Lambuth U (TN)
Lenoir-Rhyne Coll (NC)
Michigan State U (MI)
Minot State U (ND)
Syracuse U (NY)
Texas Christian U (TX)
U of Nebraska–Lincoln (NE)
The U of North Carolina at Greensboro (NC)
U of Science and Arts of Oklahoma (OK)
U of Southern Mississippi (MS)
The U of Toledo (OH)
U of Tulsa (OK)
Utah Valley State Coll (UT)

SPECIAL EDUCATION (MENTALLY RETARDED)

Augusta State U (GA)
Bradley U (IL)
Central Michigan U (MI)
Columbus State U (GA)
East Carolina U (NC)
Eastern Mennonite U (VA)
Eastern Michigan U (MI)
Florida Intl U (FL)
Florida State U (FL)
Greensboro Coll (NC)
Loras Coll (IA)
Minot State U (ND)
Northern Michigan U (MI)
Oakland City U (IN)
Shaw U (NC)
Southern Wesleyan U (SC)
Trinity Christian Coll (IL)
U of Maine at Farmington (ME)
U of Mary (ND)
The U of North Carolina at Charlotte (NC)
The U of North Carolina at Pembroke (NC)
The U of North Carolina Wilmington (NC)
U of Northern Iowa (IA)
U of Rio Grande (OH)
U of South Florida (FL)
Western Michigan U (MI)
Wright State U (OH)

SPECIAL EDUCATION (MULTIPLY DISABLED)

Dominican Coll (NY)
Ohio U (OH)
U of Illinois at Urbana–Champaign (IL)
The U of North Carolina Wilmington (NC)
U of Northern Iowa (IA)
The U of Toledo (OH)
Wright State U (OH)

SPECIAL EDUCATION (ORTHOPEDIC AND OTHER PHYSICAL HEALTH IMPAIRMENTS)

Eastern Michigan U (MI)
Wright State U (OH)

SPECIAL EDUCATION RELATED

Auburn U (AL)
East Carolina U (NC)
Harding U (AR)
Juniata Coll (PA)
Kean U (NJ)
Keene State Coll (NH)
Lock Haven U of Pennsylvania (PA)
Minot State U (ND)
Mount Saint Mary Coll (NY)
Southeastern Oklahoma State U (OK)
U of Missouri–Columbia (MO)
U of Nebraska–Lincoln (NE)
U of Southern Indiana (IN)
The U of Toledo (OH)
U of Wyoming (WY)
Wright State U (OH)
Xavier U of Louisiana (LA)

SPECIAL EDUCATION (SPECIFIC LEARNING DISABILITIES)

Appalachian State U (NC)
Aquinas Coll (MI)
Baldwin-Wallace Coll (OH)
Bethune-Cookman U (FL)
Bloomfield Coll (NJ)
Bradley U (IL)
East Carolina U (NC)
Eastern Mennonite U (VA)
Eastern Michigan U (MI)
Flagler Coll (FL)
Florida Intl U (FL)
Florida Southern Coll (FL)
Florida State U (FL)
Greensboro Coll (NC)
Harding U (AR)
Hope Coll (MI)
Madonna U (MI)
Malone Coll (OH)
Michigan State U (MI)
Northeastern State U (OK)
Northwestern U (IL)
Southern Wesleyan U (SC)
State U of New York at New Paltz (NY)
Trinity Christian Coll (IL)
U of Maine at Farmington (ME)
The U of North Carolina at Pembroke (NC)
The U of North Carolina Wilmington (NC)
U of Rio Grande (OH)
U of South Carolina Upstate (SC)
U of South Florida (FL)
The U of Toledo (OH)
West Virginia Wesleyan Coll (WV)
Wheeling Jesuit U (WV)
Wright State U (OH)

SPECIAL EDUCATION (SPEECH OR LANGUAGE IMPAIRED)

Alabama Ag and Mech U (AL)
Baylor U (TX)
Buffalo State Coll, State U of New York (NY)
Eastern Kentucky U (KY)
Eastern Michigan U (MI)
Emerson Coll (MA)
Ithaca Coll (NY)
Kutztown U of Pennsylvania (PA)
Minot State U (ND)
New York U (NY)
Northern Arizona U (AZ)
Pace U (NY)
The U of Toledo (OH)
Wayne State U (MI)
West Chester U of Pennsylvania (PA)
Western Kentucky U (KY)

SPECIAL EDUCATION (VISION IMPAIRED)

Auburn U (AL)
Eastern Michigan U (MI)
Florida State U (FL)
Hood Coll (MD)
Kutztown U of Pennsylvania (PA)
The U of Toledo (OH)
Western Michigan U (MI)

SPECIAL PRODUCTS MARKETING

Ball State U (IN)
Buffalo State Coll, State U of New York (NY)
Concord U (WV)
Dominican U (IL)
Fashion Inst of Technology (NY)
Iowa State U of Science and Technology (IA)
Mount Saint Vincent U (NS, Canada)
North Carolina Wesleyan Coll (NC)
Oregon State U (OR)
Rochester Inst of Technology (NY)
Saint Joseph's U (PA)
San Francisco State U (CA)
Stephen F. Austin State U (TX)
U of Maryland Eastern Shore (MD)
Western New Mexico U (NM)

SPEECH AND RHETORIC

Adams State Coll (CO)
Alabama State U (AL)
Arkansas State U (AR)
Asbury Coll (KY)
Ashland U (OH)
Auburn U (AL)
Augsburg Coll (MN)
Augustana Coll (IL)
Ball State U (IN)
Bates Coll (ME)
Belmont U (TN)
Bemidji State U (MN)
Bethune-Cookman U (FL)
Bloomsburg U of Pennsylvania (PA)
Bob Jones U (SC)
Bowling Green State U (OH)
Brigham Young U (UT)
Butler U (IN)
California State U, East Bay (CA)
California State U, Fresno (CA)
California State U, Fullerton (CA)
California State U, Long Beach (CA)
California State U, Los Angeles (CA)
Calvin Coll (MI)
Capital U (OH)
Carson-Newman Coll (TN)
Cedarville U (OH)
Clarion U of Pennsylvania (PA)
Clark Atlanta U (GA)
Clemson U (SC)
The Coll at Brockport, State U of New York (NY)
The Coll of New Jersey (NJ)
Coll of Saint Benedict (MN)
Coll of the Ozarks (MO)
Colorado State U (CO)
Concordia Coll (MN)
Concordia U, Nebraska (NE)
Cornell Coll (IA)
Cornerstone U (MI)
Creighton U (NE)
Denison U (OH)
Dillard U (LA)
Dowling Coll (NY)
Drake U (IA)
Duquesne U (PA)
East Central U (OK)
Eastern Illinois U (IL)
Eastern Kentucky U (KY)
East Tennessee State U (TN)
East Texas Baptist U (TX)
Emerson Coll (MA)
Evangel U (MO)
Fairmont State U (WV)
Ferris State U (MI)
Frostburg State U (MD)
George Mason U (VA)
The George Washington U (DC)
Georgia Coll & State U (GA)
Georgia Southern U (GA)
Georgia State U (GA)
Gonzaga U (WA)
Grand Canyon U (AZ)
Greenville Coll (IL)
Gustavus Adolphus Coll (MN)
Hannibal-LaGrange Coll (MO)
Hardin-Simmons U (TX)
Hastings Coll (NE)
Houston Baptist U (TX)
Howard Payne U (TX)
Humboldt State U (CA)
Illinois Coll (IL)
Illinois State U (IL)
Indiana U Bloomington (IN)
Indiana U South Bend (IN)
Iowa State U of Science and Technology (IA)
Ithaca Coll (NY)
Jackson State U (MS)
Kent State U (OH)
Kutztown U of Pennsylvania (PA)
Lehman Coll of the City U of New York (NY)
Lewis U (IL)
Lipscomb U (TN)
Lock Haven U of Pennsylvania (PA)
Louisiana Coll (LA)
Louisiana State U and Ag and Mech Coll (LA)
Lynchburg Coll (VA)
Madonna U (MI)
Manchester Coll (IN)
Marietta Coll (OH)
Marquette U (WI)
Marshall U (WV)
The Master's Coll and Sem (CA)
McKendree U (IL)
McNeese State U (LA)
Miami U (OH)
Minnesota State U Mankato (MN)
Minot State U (ND)
Mississippi Valley State U (MS)
Missouri Valley Coll (MO)
Monmouth Coll (IL)
Morehead State U (KY)
Morgan State U (MD)
Mount Mercy Coll (IA)
Murray State U (KY)
Nebraska Wesleyan U (NE)
North Carolina Ag and Tech State U (NC)
North Central Coll (IL)
North Dakota State U (ND)
Northeastern Illinois U (IL)
Northeastern State U (OK)
Northern Arizona U (AZ)
Northern State U (SD)
Northwestern Coll (IA)
Northwestern Oklahoma State U (OK)
Northwestern U (IL)
Northwest Missouri State U (MO)
Ohio U (OH)
Oklahoma Christian U (OK)
Oklahoma City U (OK)
Oklahoma State U (OK)
Old Dominion U (VA)
Oregon State U (OR)
Pace U (NY)
Pepperdine U, Malibu (CA)
Portland State U (OR)
Rider U (NJ)
St. Cloud State U (MN)
Saint John's U (MN)
St. John's U (NY)
St. Joseph's Coll, New York (NY)
St. Joseph's Coll, Suffolk Campus (NY)
St. Mary's U (TX)
Samford U (AL)
Sam Houston State U (TX)
San Diego State U (CA)
San Francisco State U (CA)
Shippensburg U of Pennsylvania (PA)
South Dakota State U (SD)
Southeast Missouri State U (MO)
Southern Illinois U Carbondale (IL)
Southern Illinois U Edwardsville (IL)
Southern U and Ag and Mech Coll (LA)
Southern Utah U (UT)
State U of New York at New Paltz (NY)
State U of New York Coll at Oneonta (NY)
State U of New York Coll at Potsdam (NY)
Stephen F. Austin State U (TX)
Susquehanna U (PA)
Syracuse U (NY)
Tarleton State U (TX)
Temple U (PA)
Texas A&M U (TX)
Texas Southern U (TX)
Texas State U-San Marcos (TX)
Texas Tech U (TX)
Thomas More Coll (KY)
Trinity U (TX)
Troy U (AL)
Truman State U (MO)
Union U (TN)
U at Albany, State U of New York (NY)
The U of Alabama in Huntsville (AL)
U of Arkansas at Monticello (AR)
U of Arkansas at Pine Bluff (AR)
U of California, Berkeley (CA)
U of Central Arkansas (AR)
U of Central Florida (FL)
U of Central Missouri (MO)
U of Georgia (GA)
U of Hawaii at Manoa (HI)
U of Houston (TX)
U of Houston–Downtown (TX)
U of Illinois at Chicago (IL)
U of Illinois at Urbana–Champaign (IL)
The U of Iowa (IA)
U of Kansas (KS)
U of Louisiana at Monroe (LA)
U of Michigan (MI)
The U of Montana (MT)
U of Montevallo (AL)
U of Nebraska at Kearney (NE)
U of Nebraska at Omaha (NE)
U of New Mexico (NM)
U of North Alabama (AL)
The U of North Carolina at Greensboro (NC)
U of Northern Iowa (IA)
U of North Texas (TX)
U of Pittsburgh (PA)
U of Richmond (VA)
U of Sioux Falls (SD)
U of South Florida (FL)
The U of Tennessee (TN)
The U of Texas at Arlington (TX)
The U of Texas at El Paso (TX)
The U of Texas at Tyler (TX)
The U of Texas of the Permian Basin (TX)
U of the Virgin Islands (VI)
U of Utah (UT)
U of Wisconsin–Platteville (WI)
U of Wisconsin–Superior (WI)
U of Wisconsin–Whitewater (WI)
Utah State U (UT)
Vanguard U of Southern California (CA)
Wabash Coll (IN)
Walla Walla U (WA)
West Chester U of Pennsylvania (PA)
Western Kentucky U (KY)
West Texas A&M U (TX)
West Virginia Wesleyan Coll (WV)
Whitworth U (WA)
Willamette U (OR)
William Jewell Coll (MO)
Winona State U (MN)
York Coll of Pennsylvania (PA)
York Coll of the City U of New York (NY)
Youngstown State U (OH)

SPEECH-LANGUAGE PATHOLOGY

Abilene Christian U (TX)
Augustana Coll (IL)
Bob Jones U (SC)
Columbia Coll (SC)
Duquesne U (PA)
Eastern Michigan U (MI)
Emerson Coll (MA)
Grambling State U (LA)
Harding U (AR)
Jackson State U (MS)
James Madison U (VA)
Lehman Coll of the City U of New York (NY)
Loyola Coll in Maryland (MD)
Marshall U (WV)
Marymount Manhattan Coll (NY)
Miami U (OH)
Miami U Hamilton (OH)
Mount Saint Mary Coll (NY)
Northern Michigan U (MI)
Northwestern U (IL)
Pace U (NY)
Purdue U (IN)
Rockhurst U (MO)
St. Cloud State U (MN)
Saint Xavier U (IL)
Texas Christian U (TX)
Towson U (MD)
U of Central Missouri (MO)
U of Maryland, Coll Park (MD)
U of Montevallo (AL)
U of Nebraska–Lincoln (NE)
U of Nevada, Reno (NV)
U of Northern Colorado (CO)
U of Northern Iowa (IA)
U of Oklahoma Health Sciences Center (OK)
U of Science and Arts of Oklahoma (OK)
The U of Tennessee (TN)

MAJORS AND MORE

The U of Toledo (OH)
The U of Western Ontario (ON, Canada)
U of West Georgia (GA)
U of Wisconsin–Whitewater (WI)
Valdosta State U (GA)
Xavier U of Louisiana (LA)

SPEECH TEACHER EDUCATION

Anderson U (IN)
Arkansas State U (AR)
Baylor U (TX)
Brigham Young U (UT)
Capital U (OH)
Central Michigan U (MI)
Concordia U (MI)
Concordia U Chicago (IL)
Concordia U, Nebraska (NE)
Culver-Stockton Coll (MO)
Dordt Coll (IA)
East Central U (OK)
East Texas Baptist U (TX)
Evangel U (MO)
Harding U (AR)
Hardin-Simmons U (TX)
Hastings Coll (NE)
Howard Payne U (TX)
Indiana U Bloomington (IN)
Indiana U–Purdue U Fort Wayne (IN)
Indiana U–Purdue U Indianapolis (IN)
Kean U (NJ)
McNeese State U (LA)
Murray State U (KY)
North Dakota State U (ND)
Northeastern State U (OK)
Northwestern Oklahoma State U (OK)
Northwestern State U of Louisiana (LA)
Pillsbury Baptist Bible Coll (MN)
St. Ambrose U (IA)
Samford U (AL)
Southeastern Louisiana U (LA)
Southeast Missouri State U (MO)
Southwest Baptist U (MO)
Taylor U (IN)
The U of Arizona (AZ)
U of Indianapolis (IN)
The U of Iowa (IA)
U of Louisiana at Lafayette (LA)
U of Louisiana at Monroe (LA)
U of Michigan–Flint (MI)
The U of North Carolina at Greensboro (NC)
U of Northern Iowa (IA)
U of Rio Grande (OH)
The U of South Dakota (SD)
Wayne State Coll (NE)
William Jewell Coll (MO)
York Coll (NE)

SPEECH/THEATER EDUCATION

Augustana Coll (SD)
Baptist Bible Coll of Pennsylvania (PA)
Bemidji State U (MN)
Boston U (MA)
Culver-Stockton Coll (MO)
Delta State U (MS)
Grambling State U (LA)
Hamline U (MN)
King Coll (TN)
McKendree U (IL)
Midland Lutheran Coll (NE)
Northwestern Coll (IA)
Oklahoma City U (OK)
Saginaw Valley State U (MI)
St. Ambrose U (IA)
St. Cloud State U (MN)
Southwest Minnesota State U (MN)
U of St. Thomas (MN)
U of Windsor (ON, Canada)
Viterbo U (WI)
Wartburg Coll (IA)
William Woods U (MO)
York Coll (NE)
York U (ON, Canada)

SPEECH THERAPY

Auburn U (AL)
Augustana Coll (IL)
Eastern Kentucky U (KY)
Emerson Coll (MA)
Fontbonne U (MO)
Hampton U (VA)
Indiana U Bloomington (IN)
Murray State U (KY)
Northwestern U (IL)
St. Cloud State U (MN)
State U of New York at Fredonia (NY)
State U of New York Coll at Geneseo (NY)
Texas Southern U (TX)
The U of British Columbia (BC, Canada)
U of New Hampshire (NH)
U of Oklahoma Health Sciences Center (OK)
U of Redlands (CA)
The U of Toledo (OH)
U of Wisconsin–Madison (WI)
Xavier U of Louisiana (LA)

SPORT AND FITNESS ADMINISTRATION/ MANAGEMENT

Abilene Christian U (TX)
Alice Lloyd Coll (KY)
Alvernia Coll (PA)
American Public U System (WV)
Anna Maria Coll (MA)
Arkansas State U (AR)
Asbury Coll (KY)
Augustana Coll (SD)
Averett U (VA)
Baker U (KS)
Baldwin-Wallace Coll (OH)
Ball State U (IN)
Barry U (FL)
Barton Coll (NC)
Baylor U (TX)
Becker Coll (MA)
Belhaven Coll (MS)
Bemidji State U (MN)
Bethany Coll (KS)
Bethany Coll (WV)
Bluffton U (OH)
Bowling Green State U (OH)
Bridgewater State Coll (MA)
Brock U (ON, Canada)
Calvin Coll (MI)
Cedarville U (OH)
Centenary Coll (NJ)
Central Christian Coll of Kansas (KS)
Central Michigan U (MI)
Central Washington U (WA)
Claflin U (SC)
Clarke Coll (IA)
Cleveland State U (OH)
Coastal Carolina U (SC)
Coker Coll (SC)
Colby-Sawyer Coll (NH)
The Coll at Brockport, State U of New York (NY)
The Coll of Idaho (ID)
Coll of Mount St. Joseph (OH)
Columbia Southern U (AL)
Concordia U (OR)
Concordia U, Nebraska (NE)
Concordia U Wisconsin (WI)
Cornerstone U (MI)
Crown Coll (MN)
Culver-Stockton Coll (MO)
Dana Coll (NE)
Daniel Webster Coll (NH)
Davenport U, Dearborn (MI)
Davenport U, Grand Rapids (MI)
Davis & Elkins Coll (WV)
Defiance Coll (OH)
DeSales U (PA)
Drury U (MO)
Eastern Connecticut State U (CT)
Eastern Mennonite U (VA)
Edinboro U of Pennsylvania (PA)
Elon U (NC)
Emmanuel Coll (GA)
Endicott Coll (MA)
Erskine Coll (SC)
Faulkner U (AL)
Ferrum Coll (VA)
Fitchburg State Coll (MA)
Flagler Coll (FL)
Florida State U (FL)
Fontbonne U (MO)
Fort Lewis Coll (CO)
Fresno Pacific U (CA)
Frostburg State U (MD)
Gannon U (PA)
Gardner-Webb U (NC)
George Fox U (OR)
Georgia Southern U (GA)
Glenville State Coll (WV)
Gonzaga U (WA)
Grace Coll (IN)
Grand Canyon U (AZ)
Greensboro Coll (NC)
Greenville Coll (IL)
Guilford Coll (NC)
Hampton U (VA)
Harding U (AR)
Hastings Coll (NE)
Henderson State U (AR)
High Point U (NC)
Holy Family U (PA)
Howard Payne U (TX)
Husson Coll (ME)
Indiana U Bloomington (IN)
Indiana Wesleyan U (IN)
Iowa Wesleyan Coll (IA)
Ithaca Coll (NY)
Johnson C. Smith U (NC)
Johnson State Coll (VT)
Judson U (IL)
Keene State Coll (NH)
Kennesaw State U (GA)
Kentucky Wesleyan Coll (KY)
Keystone Coll (PA)
Lambuth U (TN)
Laurentian U (ON, Canada)
Lenoir-Rhyne Coll (NC)
LeTourneau U (TX)
Liberty U (VA)
Limestone Coll (SC)
Lindenwood U (MO)
Livingstone Coll (NC)
Longwood U (VA)
Loras Coll (IA)
Lubbock Christian U (TX)
Lynchburg Coll (VA)
Lyndon State Coll (VT)
Malone Coll (OH)
Marian Coll (IN)
Marian Coll of Fond du Lac (WI)
Marymount U (VA)
Maryville U of Saint Louis (MO)
Medaille Coll (NY)
Mercyhurst Coll (PA)
Mesa State Coll (CO)
Messiah Coll (PA)
Methodist U (NC)
Miami U (OH)
MidAmerica Nazarene U (KS)
Midway Coll (KY)
Midwestern State U (TX)
Millikin U (IL)
Minnesota State U Mankato (MN)
Minot State U (ND)
Misericordia U (PA)
Mississippi Coll (MS)
Mississippi U for Women (MS)
Missouri Baptist U (MO)
Missouri Valley Coll (MO)
Mitchell Coll (CT)
Montana State U (MT)
Montana State U–Billings (MT)
Morehead State U (KY)
Morgan State U (MD)
Mount St. Mary's U (MD)
National U (CA)
Nebraska Wesleyan U (NE)
Neumann Coll (PA)
New England Coll (NH)
New York U (NY)
Niagara U (NY)
Nichols Coll (MA)
North Carolina State U (NC)
North Central Coll (IL)
North Dakota State U (ND)
Northern Michigan U (MI)
North Greenville U (SC)
Northwest Missouri State U (MO)
Northwood U (MI)
Northwood U, Florida Campus (FL)
Nova Southeastern U (FL)
Ohio Dominican U (OH)
Ohio Northern U (OH)
Ohio U (OH)
Old Dominion U (VA)
Otterbein Coll (OH)
Pfeiffer U (NC)
Quincy U (IL)
Robert Morris U (PA)
Rochester Coll (MI)
Rogers State U (OK)
Sacred Heart U (CT)
St. Ambrose U (IA)
St. John's U (NY)
Saint Leo U (FL)
Saint Mary's Coll of California (CA)
St. Thomas U (FL)
Salem Intl U (WV)
Salem State Coll (MA)
Shawnee State U (OH)
Siena Heights U (MI)
Simpson Coll (IA)
Slippery Rock U of Pennsylvania (PA)
Southeast Missouri State U (MO)
Southern Adventist U (TN)
Southern New Hampshire U (NH)
Southern Wesleyan U (SC)
Southwest Baptist U (MO)
Southwestern Coll (KS)
Spring Arbor U (MI)
State U of New York at Oswego (NY)
Stetson U (FL)
Taylor U (IN)
Tennessee Wesleyan Coll (TN)
Texas Lutheran U (TX)
Texas State U-San Marcos (TX)
Thomas Coll (ME)
Towson U (MD)
Tri-State U (IN)
Troy U (AL)
Tusculum Coll (TN)
Union Coll (KY)
Union Coll (NE)
Union U (TN)
The U of Akron (OH)
U of Dayton (OH)
U of Delaware (DE)
U of Evansville (IN)
U of Florida (FL)
U of Georgia (GA)
U of Illinois at Urbana–Champaign (IL)
U of Indianapolis (IN)
The U of Iowa (IA)
U of Louisville (KY)
U of Mary (ND)
U of Mary Hardin-Baylor (TX)
U of Massachusetts Amherst (MA)
U of Memphis (TN)
U of Miami (FL)
U of Michigan (MI)
U of Minnesota, Crookston (MN)
U of Nebraska at Kearney (NE)
U of Nevada, Las Vegas (NV)
U of New England (ME)
U of North Florida (FL)
U of Pittsburgh at Bradford (PA)
U of Regina (SK, Canada)
U of Saint Mary (KS)
U of South Carolina (SC)
The U of Tennessee (TN)
The U of Texas at Austin (TX)
U of Tulsa (OK)
U of Victoria (BC, Canada)
U of Windsor (ON, Canada)
U of Wisconsin–Parkside (WI)
Valparaiso U (IN)
Virginia Intermont Coll (VA)
Wartburg Coll (IA)
Washington State U (WA)
Wayne State Coll (NE)
Webber Intl U (FL)
Western Carolina U (NC)
Western Kentucky U (KY)
Western New England Coll (MA)
Western State Coll of Colorado (CO)
West Virginia U (WV)
West Virginia Wesleyan Coll (WV)
Widener U (PA)
Wilmington Coll (OH)
Wilmington U (DE)
Wingate U (NC)
Winona State U (MN)
Winthrop U (SC)
Xavier U (OH)
York Coll (NE)
York Coll of Pennsylvania (PA)
York U (ON, Canada)

STATISTICS

American U (DC)
American U of Beirut (Lebanon)
Appalachian State U (NC)
Barnard Coll (NY)
Baylor U (TX)
Bernard M. Baruch Coll of the City U of New York (NY)
Bowling Green State U (OH)
Brigham Young U (UT)
Brock U (ON, Canada)
California Polytechnic State U, San Luis Obispo (CA)
California State Polytechnic U, Pomona (CA)
California State U, East Bay (CA)
California State U, Fullerton (CA)
California State U, Long Beach (CA)
Carnegie Mellon U (PA)
Case Western Reserve U (OH)
Central Michigan U (MI)
Clarkson U (NY)
The Coll of New Jersey (NJ)
Concordia U (QC, Canada)
DePaul U (IL)
Eastern Kentucky U (KY)
Eastern Michigan U (MI)
Eastern New Mexico U (NM)
Florida Intl U (FL)
Florida State U (FL)
The George Washington U (DC)
Grace Coll (IN)
Grand Valley State U (MI)
Harvard U (MA)
Hunter Coll of the City U of New York (NY)
Indiana U Bloomington (IN)
Indiana U–Purdue U Fort Wayne (IN)
Iowa State U of Science and Technology (IA)
Kansas State U (KS)
Kenyon Coll (OH)
Lehigh U (PA)
Loyola U Chicago (IL)
Luther Coll (IA)
Marquette U (WI)
McGill U (QC, Canada)
Memorial U of Newfoundland (NL, Canada)
Mercyhurst Coll (PA)
Miami U (OH)
Miami U Hamilton (OH)
Michigan State U (MI)
Michigan Technological U (MI)
Mount Holyoke Coll (MA)
Mount Saint Vincent U (NS, Canada)
New York U (NY)
North Carolina State U (NC)
North Dakota State U (ND)
Northwestern U (IL)
Oakland U (MI)
Ohio Northern U (OH)
Ohio Wesleyan U (OH)
Oklahoma State U (OK)
Penn State Abington (PA)
Penn State Altoona (PA)
Penn State Berks (PA)
Penn State Erie, The Behrend Coll (PA)
Penn State U Park (PA)
Purdue U (IN)
Queen's U at Kingston (ON, Canada)
Rice U (TX)
Rochester Inst of Technology (NY)
Roosevelt U (IL)
Rutgers, The State U of New Jersey, New Brunswick (NJ)
St. Cloud State U (MN)
St. Mary's U (TX)
Sam Houston State U (TX)
San Diego State U (CA)
San Francisco State U (CA)
Simon Fraser U (BC, Canada)
Sonoma State U (CA)
Southern Methodist U (TX)
Stanford U (CA)
State U of New York Coll at Oneonta (NY)
The U of Akron (OH)
The U of British Columbia (BC, Canada)
U of California, Berkeley (CA)
U of California, Davis (CA)
U of California, Los Angeles (CA)
U of California, Riverside (CA)
U of California, Santa Barbara (CA)
U of Central Florida (FL)
U of Chicago (IL)
U of Connecticut (CT)
U of Florida (FL)
U of Georgia (GA)
U of Houston (TX)
U of Illinois at Chicago (IL)
U of Illinois at Urbana–Champaign (IL)
The U of Iowa (IA)
U of King's Coll (NS, Canada)
U of Maryland, Baltimore County (MD)
U of Michigan (MI)
U of Minnesota, Duluth (MN)
U of Missouri–Columbia (MO)
U of Missouri–Kansas City (MO)
The U of Montana (MT)
U of Nebraska at Kearney (NE)
U of Nevada, Las Vegas (NV)
U of New Brunswick Fredericton (NB, Canada)
U of New Hampshire (NH)
U of New Mexico (NM)
The U of North Carolina at Greensboro (NC)
The U of North Carolina Wilmington (NC)
U of North Florida (FL)
U of Ottawa (ON, Canada)
U of Pennsylvania (PA)
U of Pittsburgh (PA)
U of Regina (SK, Canada)
U of Rochester (NY)
U of South Carolina (SC)
The U of Tennessee (TN)
The U of Tennessee at Martin (TN)
The U of Texas at Dallas (TX)
The U of Texas at El Paso (TX)
The U of Texas at San Antonio (TX)
U of Toronto (ON, Canada)
U of Vermont (VT)
U of Victoria (BC, Canada)
The U of Western Ontario (ON, Canada)
U of Windsor (ON, Canada)
The U of Winnipeg (MB, Canada)
U of Wisconsin–Madison (WI)
U of Wisconsin–Milwaukee (WI)
U of Wyoming (WY)
Utah State U (UT)
Virginia Polytechnic Inst and State U (VA)
Washington U in St. Louis (MO)
Western Michigan U (MI)
Wilfrid Laurier U (ON, Canada)
Winona State U (MN)
Wright State U (OH)
Xavier U of Louisiana (LA)
York U (ON, Canada)

STATISTICS RELATED
Brigham Young U (UT)
Ohio Northern U (OH)

STRINGED INSTRUMENTS
U of Kansas (KS)

STRUCTURAL BIOLOGY
U of Connecticut (CT)

STRUCTURAL ENGINEERING
The American U of Athens (Greece)
Clarkson U (NY)
Lehigh U (PA)
Penn State Harrisburg (PA)
U at Buffalo, the State U of New York (NY)
U of California, San Diego (CA)
U of Illinois at Urbana–Champaign (IL)
U of Southern California (CA)
The U of Toledo (OH)
Western Michigan U (MI)

SUBSTANCE ABUSE/ ADDICTION COUNSELING
Alvernia Coll (PA)
Argosy U, Chicago (IL)
Argosy U, Dallas (TX)
Argosy U, Denver (CO)
Argosy U, Nashville (TN)
Argosy U, Orange County (CA)
Argosy U, Phoenix (AZ)
Argosy U, Schaumburg (IL)
Argosy U, Seattle (WA)
Argosy U, Twin Cities (MN)
Argosy U, Washington DC (VA)
Bethany U (CA)
Calumet Coll of Saint Joseph (IN)
The Coll at Brockport, State U of New York (NY)
Coll of St. Joseph (VT)
Hawai'i Pacific U (HI)
Indiana U–Purdue U Fort Wayne (IN)
Indiana Wesleyan U (IN)
Martin U (IN)
Metropolitan State U (MN)
Minot State U (ND)
National-Louis U (IL)
Newman U (KS)
Northwestern State U of Louisiana (LA)
St. Cloud State U (MN)
U of Central Arkansas (AR)
U of Great Falls (MT)
U of Lethbridge (AB, Canada)
U of Mary (ND)
The U of South Dakota (SD)
The U of Texas–Pan American (TX)
The U of Western Ontario (ON, Canada)
Washburn U (KS)

SURVEYING ENGINEERING
Florida Atlantic U (FL)
Purdue U (IN)
U of Maine (ME)

SURVEY TECHNOLOGY
British Columbia Inst of Technology (BC, Canada)
California State Polytechnic U, Pomona (CA)
East Tennessee State U (TN)
Ferris State U (MI)
Idaho State U (ID)
Michigan Technological U (MI)
Nicholls State U (LA)
Oregon Inst of Technology (OR)
Polytechnic U of Puerto Rico (PR)
Purdue U (IN)
Southern Polytechnic State U (GA)
Thomas Edison State Coll (NJ)
Troy U (AL)
The U of Akron (OH)
U of Arkansas at Monticello (AR)
U of Florida (FL)
U of Maine (ME)
U of New Brunswick Fredericton (NB, Canada)
U of Wisconsin–Madison (WI)

SWEDISH
Augustana Coll (IL)
Brigham Young U (UT)

SYSTEM ADMINISTRATION
Dordt Coll (IA)
Michigan Technological U (MI)
Rochester Inst of Technology (NY)
U of Great Falls (MT)

SYSTEM, NETWORKING, AND LAN/WAN MANAGEMENT
Alcorn State U (MS)
National American U, Rapid City (SD)
Rochester Inst of Technology (NY)
U of Great Falls (MT)
U of Northern Iowa (IA)

SYSTEMS ENGINEERING
Case Western Reserve U (OH)
Florida Intl U (FL)
George Mason U (VA)
The George Washington U (DC)
Harvard U (MA)
Maine Maritime Acad (ME)
Missouri U of Science and Technology (MO)
Montana Tech of The U of Montana (MT)
Ohio U (OH)
Providence Coll (RI)
Rensselaer Polytechnic Inst (NY)
Rochester Inst of Technology (NY)
Rose-Hulman Inst of Technology (IN)
Southern Polytechnic State U (GA)
State U of New York at Binghamton (NY)
United States Naval Acad (MD)
The U of Arizona (AZ)
U of California, San Diego (CA)
U of Florida (FL)
U of Maine (ME)
U of Memphis (TN)
U of Pennsylvania (PA)
U of Regina (SK, Canada)
U of Southern California (CA)
U of Virginia (VA)
Washington U in St. Louis (MO)
Wright State U (OH)

SYSTEMS SCIENCE AND THEORY
Carnegie Mellon U (PA)
James Madison U (VA)
Marshall U (WV)
Miami U (OH)
Stanford U (CA)
Washington U in St. Louis (MO)
Wright State U (OH)
Yale U (CT)

TALMUDIC STUDIES
List Coll, The Jewish Theological Sem (NY)
Talmudic Coll of Florida (FL)

TAMIL
U of Chicago (IL)

TAXATION
Capital U (OH)
Drexel U (PA)
McGill U (QC, Canada)

TECHNICAL AND BUSINESS WRITING
Allegheny Coll (PA)
Bob Jones U (SC)
Boise State U (ID)
Bowling Green State U (OH)
Carlow U (PA)
Carnegie Mellon U (PA)
Cedarville U (OH)
Clarkson U (NY)
Coker Coll (SC)
Drexel U (PA)
Eastern Michigan U (MI)
Farmingdale State Coll (NY)
Ferris State U (MI)
Grand Valley State U (MI)
Illinois Inst of Technology (IL)
Indiana U–Purdue U Fort Wayne (IN)
Iowa State U of Science and Technology (IA)
James Madison U (VA)
King Coll (TN)
Kutztown U of Pennsylvania (PA)
Maryville Coll (TN)
Metropolitan State U (MN)
Miami U (OH)
Miami U Hamilton (OH)
Michigan State U (MI)
Michigan Technological U (MI)
Missouri State U (MO)
Montana Tech of The U of Montana (MT)
Mount Mary Coll (WI)
New Jersey Inst of Technology (NJ)
New Mexico Inst of Mining and Technology (NM)
New York Inst of Technology (NY)
Northwestern Coll (MN)
Ohio Northern U (OH)
Penn State Berks (PA)
Pennsylvania Coll of Technology (PA)
Pittsburg State U (KS)
San Francisco State U (CA)
Spring Arbor U (MI)
Tarleton State U (TX)
Tennessee Technological U (TN)
U of Arkansas at Fort Smith (AR)
U of Baltimore (MD)
U of Hartford (CT)
U of Houston–Downtown (TX)
The U of Montana (MT)
U of Victoria (BC, Canada)
Valparaiso U (IN)
Weber State U (UT)
Webster U (MO)
Winthrop U (SC)
Worcester Polytechnic Inst (MA)
York Coll of Pennsylvania (PA)
York U (ON, Canada)
Youngstown State U (OH)

TECHNICAL TEACHER EDUCATION
Bowling Green State U (OH)
Eastern Illinois U (IL)
Eastern Kentucky U (KY)
Ferris State U (MI)
Mississippi State U (MS)
New York Inst of Technology (NY)
Oklahoma State U (OK)
Pittsburg State U (KS)
Queen's U at Kingston (ON, Canada)
Rhode Island Coll (RI)
South Dakota State U (SD)
Texas Christian U (TX)
The U of Akron (OH)
U of Idaho (ID)
U of Illinois at Urbana–Champaign (IL)
U of Missouri–Columbia (MO)
U of Nebraska at Kearney (NE)
The U of Tennessee (TN)
Utah State U (UT)
Valley City State U (ND)
Wayne State U (MI)
Wright State U (OH)

TECHNOLOGY/INDUSTRIAL ARTS TEACHER EDUCATION
Appalachian State U (NC)
Bemidji State U (MN)
Brigham Young U (UT)
Buffalo State Coll, State U of New York (NY)
Central Connecticut State U (CT)
Central Michigan U (MI)
Central Washington U (WA)
Chicago State U (IL)
The Coll of New Jersey (NJ)
Coll of the Ozarks (MO)
Concordia U, Nebraska (NE)
Eastern Kentucky U (KY)
Eastern Michigan U (MI)
Fitchburg State Coll (MA)
Georgia Southern U (GA)
Grambling State U (LA)
Illinois State U (IL)
Jackson State U (MS)
Kean U (NJ)
Keene State Coll (NH)
Kent State U (OH)
Lindenwood U (MO)
Michigan Technological U (MI)
Middle Tennessee State U (TN)
Millersville U of Pennsylvania (PA)
Mississippi State U (MS)
Montana State U (MT)
Murray State U (KY)
New Mexico Highlands U (NM)
North Carolina State U (NC)
Northern Arizona U (AZ)
Northern Michigan U (MI)
Purdue U (IN)
Rhode Island Coll (RI)
St. Cloud State U (MN)
St. John Fisher Coll (NY)
Sam Houston State U (TX)
Southeast Missouri State U (MO)
Southwestern Oklahoma State U (OK)
State U of New York at Oswego (NY)
Texas Southern U (TX)
U of Georgia (GA)
U of Idaho (ID)
U of Lethbridge (AB, Canada)
The U of Montana–Western (MT)
U of Nebraska–Lincoln (NE)
U of Nevada, Reno (NV)
U of New Mexico (NM)
U of Northern Iowa (IA)
U of Southern Mississippi (MS)
U of Wyoming (WY)
Utah State U (UT)
Valley City State U (ND)
Viterbo U (WI)
Wayne State Coll (NE)
Western Michigan U (MI)
Westfield State Coll (MA)

TELECOMMUNICATIONS
Ball State U (IN)
California State Polytechnic U, Pomona (CA)
California State U, East Bay (CA)
California State U, Monterey Bay (CA)
Grand Valley State U (MI)
Howard Payne U (TX)
Inter American U of Puerto Rico, Bayamón Campus (PR)
Ithaca Coll (NY)
Kutztown U of Pennsylvania (PA)
Michigan State U (MI)
Morgan State U (MD)
Murray State U (KY)
National U (CA)
New York Inst of Technology (NY)
Ohio U (OH)
Pace U (NY)
Pacific U (OR)
Pepperdine U, Malibu (CA)
Rochester Inst of Technology (NY)
Roosevelt U (IL)
Salem Intl U (WV)
Southern Polytechnic State U (GA)
Texas Southern U (TX)
U of Georgia (GA)
U of the Sacred Heart (PR)
U of Wisconsin–Platteville (WI)
Winona State U (MN)

TELECOMMUNICATIONS TECHNOLOGY
Ferris State U (MI)
Rochester Inst of Technology (NY)
St. John's U (NY)
U of the Sacred Heart (PR)

TEXTILE SCIENCE
Florida State U (FL)
North Carolina State U (NC)

TEXTILE SCIENCES AND ENGINEERING
Auburn U (AL)
Clemson U (SC)
Georgia Inst of Technology (GA)
North Carolina State U (NC)
Philadelphia U (PA)
U of Massachusetts Dartmouth (MA)

THEATER DESIGN AND TECHNOLOGY
Bard Coll at Simon's Rock (MA)
Baylor U (TX)
Bennington Coll (VT)
Boston U (MA)
Bowling Green State U (OH)
Brigham Young U (UT)
California Design Coll (CA)
California Inst of the Arts (CA)
Centenary Coll (NJ)
Central Michigan U (MI)
Coker Coll (SC)
Coll of Santa Fe (NM)
Columbia Coll Chicago (IL)
Cornell U (NY)
Davis & Elkins Coll (WV)
DePaul U (IL)
Doane Coll (NE)
Elizabethtown Coll (PA)
Elon U (NC)
Emerson Coll (MA)
Fitchburg State Coll (MA)
Five Towns Coll (NY)
Florida State U (FL)
George Fox U (OR)
Greensboro Coll (NC)
Huntington U (IN)
Illinois Wesleyan U (IL)
Ithaca Coll (NY)
Kean U (NJ)
Keene State Coll (NH)
Memorial U of Newfoundland (NL, Canada)
Michigan Technological U (MI)
Millikin U (IL)
North Carolina School of the Arts (NC)
Oakland U (MI)
Ohio U (OH)
Oklahoma City U (OK)
Oral Roberts U (OK)
Penn State Abington (PA)
Penn State Altoona (PA)
Penn State Berks (PA)
Penn State Erie, The Behrend Coll (PA)
Penn State U Park (PA)
Purchase Coll, State U of New York (NY)
Seton Hill U (PA)
Shenandoah U (VA)
State U of New York at Binghamton (NY)
State U of New York at New Paltz (NY)
Texas Tech U (TX)
Trinity U (TX)
U of Alaska Fairbanks (AK)
The U of Arizona (AZ)
U of Connecticut (CT)
U of Delaware (DE)
U of Kansas (KS)
U of Lethbridge (AB, Canada)
U of Miami (FL)
U of Michigan (MI)
U of Michigan–Flint (MI)
U of New Mexico (NM)
U of Regina (SK, Canada)
U of Southern California (CA)
Webster U (MO)
Western State Coll of Colorado (CO)
William Woods U (MO)
Wright State U (OH)

THEATER LITERATURE, HISTORY AND CRITICISM
Averett U (VA)
Bard Coll (NY)
Bard Coll at Simon's Rock (MA)
Bennington Coll (VT)
Boston U (MA)
Bowdoin Coll (ME)
Clark Atlanta U (GA)
DePaul U (IL)
Marymount Manhattan Coll (NY)
Memorial U of Newfoundland (NL, Canada)
Moravian Coll (PA)
New York U (NY)
Northwestern U (IL)
Ohio U (OH)
Saint Mary's Coll of California (CA)
Texas Christian U (TX)
U of Connecticut (CT)
U of Illinois at Urbana–Champaign (IL)
Washington & Jefferson Coll (PA)
Washington U in St. Louis (MO)
West Virginia U (WV)

THEATER/THEATER ARTS MANAGEMENT
Berry Coll (GA)
California Inst of the Arts (CA)
Coll of Santa Fe (NM)
East Central U (OK)
Eastern Michigan U (MI)
Elizabethtown Coll (PA)
Juniata Coll (PA)
Miami U Hamilton (OH)
Oglethorpe U (GA)
Ohio Northern U (OH)
Ohio U (OH)
Pittsburg State U (KS)
St. Cloud State U (MN)
Seton Hill U (PA)
The U of British Columbia (BC, Canada)
U of Evansville (IN)
The U of Iowa (IA)
U of Miami (FL)
U of Southern California (CA)

THEOLOGICAL AND MINISTERIAL STUDIES RELATED
Baptist Bible Coll of Pennsylvania (PA)
California Baptist U (CA)
Concordia U (QC, Canada)
Hardin-Simmons U (TX)
Horizon Coll & Sem (SK, Canada)
Huntington U (IN)
Northwest Christian Coll (OR)
Northwestern Coll (MN)
Palm Beach Atlantic U (FL)
Point Loma Nazarene U (CA)
Quincy U (IL)
Trinity Coll of Florida (FL)
U of Saint Francis (IN)
Williamson Christian Coll (TN)

THEOLOGY
American Baptist Coll of American Baptist Theological Sem (TN)
Anderson U (IN)
Andrews U (MI)
Anna Maria Coll (MA)
Appalachian Bible Coll (WV)

Assumption Coll (MA)
Atlantic Union Coll (MA)
Augsburg Coll (MN)
Ave Maria U (FL)
Azusa Pacific U (CA)
Barry U (FL)
Bellarmine U (KY)
Belmont Abbey Coll (NC)
Bethany U (CA)
Biola U (CA)
Bluefield Coll (VA)
Boston Coll (MA)
Brewton-Parker Coll (GA)
California Baptist U (CA)
Calumet Coll of Saint Joseph (IN)
Calvin Coll (MI)
Canadian Mennonite U (MB, Canada)
Carlow U (PA)
Cedarville U (OH)
Christendom Coll (VA)
Collège Dominicain de Philosophie et de Théologie (ON, Canada)
Coll of Emmanuel and St. Chad (SK, Canada)
Coll of Saint Benedict (MN)
Coll of Saint Elizabeth (NJ)
Coll of Saint Mary (NE)
Concordia U (CA)
Concordia U (OR)
Concordia U (QC, Canada)
Concordia U Chicago (IL)
Concordia U, Nebraska (NE)
Concordia U, St. Paul (MN)
Concordia U Wisconsin (WI)
Creighton U (NE)
Crossroads Coll (MN)
Crown Coll (MN)
Dakota Wesleyan U (SD)
DeSales U (PA)
Dordt Coll (IA)
Duquesne U (PA)
Eastern Mennonite U (VA)
Faulkner U (AL)
Franciscan U of Steubenville (OH)
Gannon U (PA)
Georgetown U (DC)
Grace Bible Coll (MI)
Hanover Coll (IN)
Harding U (AR)
Hardin-Simmons U (TX)
Hellenic Coll (MA)
Heritage Baptist Coll and Heritage Theological Sem (ON, Canada)
Hillsdale Free Will Baptist Coll (OK)
Holy Trinity Orthodox Sem (NY)
Horizon Coll & Sem (SK, Canada)
Houghton Coll (NY)
Howard Payne U (TX)
Huntington U (IN)
Immaculata U (PA)
Indiana Wesleyan U (IN)
John Brown U (AR)
John Wesley Coll (NC)
King's Coll (PA)
The King's U Coll (AB, Canada)
Kuyper Coll (MI)
Lake Forest Coll (IL)
Lee U (TN)
Louisiana Coll (LA)
Loyola Marymount U (CA)
Loyola U Chicago (IL)
Madonna U (MI)
Marian Coll (IN)
The Master's Coll and Sem (CA)
Master's Coll and Sem (ON, Canada)
McGill U (QC, Canada)
MidAmerica Nazarene U (KS)
Morris Coll (SC)
Mount St. Mary's U (MD)
Mount Vernon Nazarene U (OH)
Multnomah Bible Coll and Biblical Sem (OR)
Nebraska Christian Coll (NE)
Newman U (KS)
North Greenville U (SC)
Northwest Nazarene U (ID)
Nyack Coll (NY)
Oakland City U (IN)
Oakwood Coll (AL)
Ohio Dominican U (OH)
Oklahoma Wesleyan U (OK)
Oral Roberts U (OK)
Ouachita Baptist U (AR)
Ozark Christian Coll (MO)
Pacific Lutheran U (WA)
Pacific Union Coll (CA)
Providence Coll (RI)
Queen's U at Kingston (ON, Canada)
Quincy U (IL)
Redeemer U Coll (ON, Canada)
Roanoke Bible Coll (NC)
Roanoke Coll (VA)
Rockhurst U (MO)
St. Ambrose U (IA)
St. Gregory's U, Shawnee (OK)
Saint John's U (MN)
St. John's U (NY)
Saint Leo U (FL)
St. Louis Christian Coll (MO)
Saint Louis U (MO)
Saint Mary-of-the-Woods Coll (IN)
Saint Mary's Coll of California (CA)
St. Mary's U (TX)
Saint Mary's U of Minnesota (MN)
Saint Vincent Coll (PA)
San Diego Christian Coll (CA)
Seattle Pacific U (WA)
Southeastern Bible Coll (AL)
Southern Adventist U (TN)
Southern Wesleyan U (SC)
Southwest Baptist U (MO)
Southwestern Adventist U (TX)
Spring Arbor U (MI)
Spring Hill Coll (AL)
Taylor U (IN)
Texas Lutheran U (TX)
Trinity Christian Coll (IL)
Union Coll (NE)
Union U (TN)
U of Dallas (TX)
U of Great Falls (MT)
U of Mary (ND)
U of Mary Hardin-Baylor (TX)
U of Notre Dame (IN)
U of Portland (OR)
U of St. Francis (IL)
U of Saint Francis (IN)
U of Saint Mary (KS)
U of St. Thomas (TX)
U of Toronto (ON, Canada)
The U of Western Ontario (ON, Canada)
The U of Winnipeg (MB, Canada)
Valparaiso U (IN)
Vennard Coll (IA)
Walla Walla U (WA)
Walsh U (OH)
Warner Pacific Coll (OR)
Wheeling Jesuit U (WV)
William Jessup U (CA)
Xavier U (OH)
Xavier U of Louisiana (LA)

THEOLOGY AND RELIGIOUS VOCATIONS RELATED
Abilene Christian U (TX)
Arlington Baptist Coll (TX)
Ave Maria U (FL)
Baptist Bible Coll of Pennsylvania (PA)
Crossroads Coll (MN)
Hope Coll (MI)
Horizon Coll & Sem (SK, Canada)
Lubbock Christian U (TX)
Master's Coll and Sem (ON, Canada)
Missouri Baptist U (MO)
St. Edward's U (TX)
St. Mary's Coll of Maryland (MD)
Simpson U (CA)
Southeastern U (FL)
Union U (TN)
U of St. Thomas (TX)
Wayland Baptist U (TX)
Williamson Christian Coll (TN)

THEORETICAL AND MATHEMATICAL PHYSICS
Sweet Briar Coll (VA)
U at Buffalo, the State U of New York (NY)
The U of Western Ontario (ON, Canada)

THERAPEUTIC RECREATION
Alderson-Broaddus Coll (WV)
Ashland U (OH)
Belmont Abbey Coll (NC)
Brigham Young U (UT)
California State U, Chico (CA)
California State U, East Bay (CA)
Calvin Coll (MI)
Catawba Coll (NC)
Central Michigan U (MI)
Coker Coll (SC)
The Coll at Brockport, State U of New York (NY)
Concordia U (QC, Canada)
East Carolina U (NC)
Eastern Michigan U (MI)
Grand Valley State U (MI)
Hampton U (VA)
Ithaca Coll (NY)
Lincoln U (PA)
Longwood U (VA)
Mercy Coll (NY)
Minnesota State U Mankato (MN)
Northeastern U (MA)
Northland Coll (WI)
Northwest Missouri State U (MO)
Pittsburg State U (KS)
St. Andrews Presbyterian Coll (NC)
St. Cloud State U (MN)
St. Joseph's Coll, Suffolk Campus (NY)
Shaw U (NC)
Shorter Coll (GA)
Southern U and Ag and Mech Coll (LA)
Southwestern Oklahoma State U (OK)
Temple U (PA)
The U of Akron (OH)
The U of Iowa (IA)
U of Nebraska at Kearney (NE)
U of New Hampshire (NH)
The U of North Carolina Wilmington (NC)
U of Southern Maine (ME)
U of Wisconsin–La Crosse (WI)
U of Wisconsin–Milwaukee (WI)
Utica Coll (NY)
Voorhees Coll (SC)
Western Carolina U (NC)
Winona State U (MN)

TIBETAN
U of Chicago (IL)

TOOL AND DIE TECHNOLOGY
Utah State U (UT)

TOURISM AND TRAVEL SERVICES MANAGEMENT
Alliant Intl U (CA)
Alliant Intl U–México City (Mexico)
The American U of Athens (Greece)
Arkansas State U (AR)
Ball State U (IN)
Becker Coll (MA)
Bowling Green State U (OH)
Brock U (ON, Canada)
California State U, Chico (CA)
Concord U (WV)
Dowling Coll (NY)
Ferrum Coll (VA)
Florida Intl U (FL)
Fort Lewis Coll (CO)
Grand Valley State U (MI)
Hawai'i Pacific U (HI)
Indiana U–Purdue U Indianapolis (IN)
Inter American U of Puerto Rico, Fajardo Campus (PR)
Johnson State Coll (VT)
Mansfield U of Pennsylvania (PA)
Mount Saint Vincent U (NS, Canada)
New York U (NY)
Niagara U (NY)
North Carolina State U (NC)
Northeastern State U (OK)
Purdue U (IN)
St. Cloud State U (MN)
St. Thomas U (FL)
Salem State Coll (MA)
Schiller Intl U (FL)
Southern New Hampshire U (NH)
Sullivan U (KY)
Texas A&M U (TX)
U of Hawaii at Manoa (HI)
U of Maine at Machias (ME)
U of Nevada, Las Vegas (NV)
U of New Hampshire (NH)
The U of Texas at San Antonio (TX)
U of the Sacred Heart (PR)
Webber Intl U (FL)
Western Michigan U (MI)

TOURISM AND TRAVEL SERVICES MARKETING
Central Connecticut State U (CT)
Mount Saint Vincent U (NS, Canada)
Rochester Inst of Technology (NY)
Thompson Rivers U (BC, Canada)
U of Central Missouri (MO)
U of Missouri–Columbia (MO)
U of the Sacred Heart (PR)
Western Michigan U (MI)

TOURISM PROMOTION
Bowling Green State U (OH)

TOURISM/TRAVEL MARKETING
Mitchell Coll (CT)

TOXICOLOGY
Ashland U (OH)
Clarkson U (NY)
Eastern Michigan U (MI)
Felician Coll (NJ)
Humboldt State U (CA)
Minnesota State U Mankato (MN)
Penn State U Park (PA)
St. John's U (NY)
U of California, Berkeley (CA)
U of Louisiana at Monroe (LA)
U of Toronto (ON, Canada)
The U of Western Ontario (ON, Canada)
U of Wisconsin–Madison (WI)

TRADE AND INDUSTRIAL TEACHER EDUCATION
Athens State U (AL)
Auburn U (AL)
Ball State U (IN)
Bemidji State U (MN)
Buffalo State Coll, State U of New York (NY)
California State U, Fresno (CA)
California State U, Long Beach (CA)
California State U, San Bernardino (CA)
Carroll Coll (WI)
Central Washington U (WA)
The Coll of Saint Rose (NY)
Concordia U, Nebraska (NE)
Eastern Kentucky U (KY)
Fitchburg State Coll (MA)
Florida Ag and Mech U (FL)
Florida Intl U (FL)
Indiana State U (IN)
Indiana U of Pennsylvania (PA)
Iowa State U of Science and Technology (IA)
Keene State Coll (NH)
Kent State U (OH)
Memorial U of Newfoundland (NL, Canada)
Murray State U (KY)
New York Inst of Technology (NY)
North Carolina Ag and Tech State U (NC)
Prairie View A&M U (TX)
San Diego State U (CA)
San Francisco State U (CA)
South Carolina State U (SC)
Southern Illinois U Carbondale (IL)
State U of New York at Oswego (NY)
Temple U (PA)
Texas A&M U–Commerce (TX)
U of Arkansas at Pine Bluff (AR)
U of Central Florida (FL)
U of Central Oklahoma (OK)
U of Idaho (ID)
U of Louisville (KY)
U of Nebraska–Lincoln (NE)
U of Nevada, Reno (NV)
U of New Hampshire (NH)
U of North Florida (FL)
U of Regina (SK, Canada)
U of Southern Maine (ME)
U of South Florida (FL)
U of the District of Columbia (DC)
U of the Virgin Islands (VI)
The U of Toledo (OH)
U of West Florida (FL)
U of Wyoming (WY)
Valdosta State U (GA)
Virginia State U (VA)
Wayland Baptist U (TX)
Western Kentucky U (KY)
Western New Mexico U (NM)
Wright State U (OH)

TRANSPORTATION AND HIGHWAY ENGINEERING
U of Arkansas (AR)
U of Toronto (ON, Canada)

TRANSPORTATION AND MATERIALS MOVING RELATED
Dowling Coll (NY)
Syracuse U (NY)
United States Merchant Marine Acad (NY)

TRANSPORTATION MANAGEMENT
American Public U System (WV)
Arkansas State U (AR)
Bridgewater State Coll (MA)
McGill U (QC, Canada)
U of North Florida (FL)
U of Pennsylvania (PA)
U of Wisconsin–Superior (WI)

TRANSPORTATION TECHNOLOGY
Dowling Coll (NY)
Eastern Kentucky U (KY)
Maine Maritime Acad (ME)
Niagara U (NY)
North Carolina Ag and Tech State U (NC)
Tennessee State U (TN)
Texas A&M U at Galveston (TX)
The U of British Columbia (BC, Canada)
U of Cincinnati (OH)

TURF AND TURFGRASS MANAGEMENT
Clemson U (SC)
Colorado State U (CO)
Delaware Valley Coll (PA)
North Carolina State U (NC)
North Dakota State U (ND)
Penn State Abington (PA)
Penn State Altoona (PA)
Penn State Berks (PA)
Penn State Erie, The Behrend Coll (PA)
Penn State U Park (PA)
Rutgers, The State U of New Jersey, New Brunswick (NJ)
State U of New York Coll of Agriculture and Technology at Cobleskill (NY)
Tennessee Technological U (TN)
U of Georgia (GA)
U of Minnesota, Crookston (MN)
U of Rhode Island (RI)

TURKIC, URAL-ALTAIC, CAUCASIAN, AND CENTRAL ASIAN LANGUAGES RELATED
U of Michigan (MI)

TURKISH
U of Chicago (IL)
The U of Texas at Austin (TX)

UKRAINE STUDIES
Bard Coll at Simon's Rock (MA)

URBAN EDUCATION AND LEADERSHIP
Harris-Stowe State U (MO)
U of Missouri–Kansas City (MO)

URBAN FORESTRY
Southern U and Ag and Mech Coll (LA)
Texas A&M U (TX)
U of California, Davis (CA)
U of Illinois at Urbana–Champaign (IL)

URBAN STUDIES/AFFAIRS
Albertus Magnus Coll (CT)
Aquinas Coll (MI)
Augsburg Coll (MN)
Barnard Coll (NY)
Baylor U (TX)
Beulah Heights U (GA)
Boston U (MA)
Brown U (RI)
Bryn Mawr Coll (PA)
Buffalo State Coll, State U of New York (NY)
Butler U (IN)
California State Polytechnic U, Pomona (CA)
Canisius Coll (NY)
Cleveland State U (OH)
Coll of Charleston (SC)
Coll of Mount Saint Vincent (NY)
Concordia U (QC, Canada)
Connecticut Coll (CT)
DePaul U (IL)
Dillard U (LA)
Eugene Lang Coll The New School for Liberal Arts (NY)
Florida Intl U (FL)
Florida Memorial U (FL)
Furman U (SC)
Georgia State U (GA)
Hamline U (MN)
Hampshire Coll (MA)
Harris-Stowe State U (MO)
Harvard U (MA)
Haverford Coll (PA)
Hobart and William Smith Colls (NY)
Hunter Coll of the City U of New York (NY)
Jackson State U (MS)
Lehigh U (PA)
Lipscomb U (TN)
Loyola Marymount U (CA)
McGill U (QC, Canada)
Metropolitan Coll of New York (NY)
MidAmerica Nazarene U (KS)
Minnesota State U Mankato (MN)

MAJORS AND MORE

Morehouse Coll (GA)
Mount Mercy Coll (IA)
New Coll of Florida (FL)
New Jersey City U (NJ)
New York U (NY)
Northeastern Illinois U (IL)
Northwestern U (IL)
Oglethorpe U (GA)
Ohio Wesleyan U (OH)
Portland State U (OR)
Queens Coll of the City U of New York (NY)
Rhodes Coll (TN)
Roosevelt U (IL)
Rutgers, The State U of New Jersey, Camden (NJ)
Rutgers, The State U of New Jersey, New Brunswick (NJ)
St. Cloud State U (MN)
Saint Louis U (MO)
San Diego State U (CA)
San Francisco State U (CA)
Sarah Lawrence Coll (NY)
Stanford U (CA)
Towson U (MD)
Trinity U (TX)
Tufts U (MA)
U at Albany, State U of New York (NY)
The U of British Columbia (BC, Canada)
U of California, Berkeley (CA)
U of California, San Diego (CA)
U of Cincinnati (OH)
U of Connecticut (CT)
U of Lethbridge (AB, Canada)
U of Minnesota, Duluth (MN)
U of Minnesota, Twin Cities Campus (MN)
U of Missouri–Kansas City (MO)
U of New Orleans (LA)
U of Pennsylvania (PA)
U of Pittsburgh (PA)
U of Richmond (VA)
U of Southern California (CA)
The U of Tampa (FL)
The U of Texas at Austin (TX)
The U of Toledo (OH)
U of Toronto (ON, Canada)
U of Utah (UT)
U of Washington, Tacoma (WA)
The U of Western Ontario (ON, Canada)
The U of Winnipeg (MB, Canada)
U of Wisconsin–Green Bay (WI)
U of Wisconsin–Madison (WI)
U of Wisconsin–Milwaukee (WI)
U of Wisconsin–Oshkosh (WI)
Vanderbilt U (TN)
Vassar Coll (NY)
Virginia Commonwealth U (VA)
Washington U in St. Louis (MO)
Worcester State Coll (MA)
Wright State U (OH)
York U (ON, Canada)

URDU
U of Chicago (IL)

VEHICLE AND VEHICLE PARTS AND ACCESSORIES MARKETING
Northwood U, Florida Campus (FL)
Northwood U, Texas Campus (TX)

VETERINARY/ANIMAL HEALTH TECHNOLOGY
Brigham Young U (UT)
Medaille Coll (NY)
Michigan State U (MI)
Murray State U (KY)
North Dakota State U (ND)
Purdue U (IN)
Thomas Edison State Coll (NJ)
U of Nebraska–Lincoln (NE)
Wilson Coll (PA)

VETERINARY SCIENCES
American U of Beirut (Lebanon)
Becker Coll (MA)
Northland Coll (WI)
Rutgers, The State U of New Jersey, New Brunswick (NJ)
U of Idaho (ID)

VETERINARY TECHNOLOGY
Michigan State U (MI)
Mount Ida Coll (MA)
Quinnipiac U (CT)

VIOLIN, VIOLA, GUITAR AND OTHER STRINGED INSTRUMENTS
Acadia U (NS, Canada)
Augustana Coll (IL)
Ball State U (IN)
Bennington Coll (VT)
Berklee Coll of Music (MA)
The Boston Conservatory (MA)
Brigham Young U (UT)
Butler U (IN)
California Inst of the Arts (CA)
Capital U (OH)
Carnegie Mellon U (PA)
The Colburn School Conservatory of Music (CA)
Converse Coll (SC)
Five Towns Coll (NY)
Florida State U (FL)
Grand Valley State U (MI)
Hardin-Simmons U (TX)
Hastings Coll (NE)
Heidelberg Coll (OH)
Hope Coll (MI)
Houghton Coll (NY)
Howard Payne U (TX)
Inter American U of Puerto Rico, San Germán Campus (PR)
Lawrence U (WI)
Manhattan School of Music (NY)
Mannes Coll The New School for Music (NY)
McGill U (QC, Canada)
Memorial U of Newfoundland (NL, Canada)
Mount Allison U (NB, Canada)
New England Conservatory of Music (MA)
The New School for Jazz and Contemporary Music (NY)
Northwestern Coll (MN)
Northwestern U (IL)
Northwest Missouri State U (MO)
Oberlin Coll (OH)
Oklahoma City U (OK)
Otterbein Coll (OH)
Peabody Conservatory of Music of The Johns Hopkins U (MD)
Roosevelt U (IL)
St. Cloud State U (MN)
Sarah Lawrence Coll (NY)
Seton Hill U (PA)
State U of New York at Fredonia (NY)
Stetson U (FL)
Susquehanna U (PA)
The U of Akron (OH)
The U of British Columbia (BC, Canada)
U of Central Oklahoma (OK)
U of Cincinnati (OH)
The U of Iowa (IA)
U of Kansas (KS)
U of Michigan (MI)
U of New Hampshire (NH)
U of Oklahoma (OK)
U of Southern California (CA)
The U of Western Ontario (ON, Canada)
U of Wisconsin–Milwaukee (WI)
Vanderbilt U (TN)
Willamette U (OR)
Xavier U of Louisiana (LA)

VISUAL AND PERFORMING ARTS
Alderson-Broaddus Coll (WV)
Angelo State U (TX)
Arizona State U at the West campus (AZ)
Armstrong Atlantic State U (GA)
Ashford U (IA)
Assumption Coll (MA)
Bard Coll at Simon's Rock (MA)
Barnard Coll (NY)
Bennington Coll (VT)
Bethel Coll (KS)
Bloomfield Coll (NJ)
Brown U (RI)
California Baptist U (CA)
California State U, San Marcos (CA)
Cameron U (OK)
Centenary Coll of Louisiana (LA)
Claremont McKenna Coll (CA)
Clemson U (SC)
Concordia U (QC, Canada)
Cooper Union for the Advancement of Science and Art (NY)
Delta State U (MS)
Eastern Connecticut State U (CT)
East Stroudsburg U of Pennsylvania (PA)
Eckerd Coll (FL)
Emerson Coll (MA)
The Evergreen State Coll (WA)
Fairfield U (CT)
Fairleigh Dickinson U, Coll at Florham (NJ)
Fairleigh Dickinson U, Metropolitan Campus (NJ)
Frostburg State U (MD)
Gannon U (PA)
George Mason U (VA)
Gettysburg Coll (PA)
Iowa State U of Science and Technology (IA)
Ithaca Coll (NY)
Jackson State U (MS)
Jacksonville U (FL)
Johnson State Coll (VT)
Kutztown U of Pennsylvania (PA)
LaGrange Coll (GA)
Lambuth U (TN)
Loras Coll (IA)
Loyola U New Orleans (LA)
Maryland Inst Coll of Art (MD)
Massachusetts Coll of Liberal Arts (MA)
Miami Intl U of Art & Design (FL)
Mississippi State U (MS)
Missouri State U (MO)
Naropa U (CO)
New Mexico Highlands U (NM)
North Carolina School of the Arts (NC)
Northwestern U (IL)
Ohio Northern U (OH)
Ohio U (OH)
Penn State Abington (PA)
Penn State Altoona (PA)
Penn State Berks (PA)
Penn State Erie, The Behrend Coll (PA)
Penn State U Park (PA)
Providence Coll (RI)
Purchase Coll, State U of New York (NY)
Purdue U (IN)
Ramapo Coll of New Jersey (NJ)
Regis U (CO)
The Richard Stockton Coll of New Jersey (NJ)
Roger Williams U (RI)
Rutgers, The State U of New Jersey, New Brunswick (NJ)
St. Gregory's U, Shawnee (OK)
Saint Joseph's U (PA)
Sarah Lawrence Coll (NY)
Savannah Coll of Art and Design (GA)
School of the Art Inst of Chicago (IL)
Shenandoah U (VA)
South Dakota State U (SD)
Southeast Missouri State U (MO)
State U of New York at Binghamton (NY)
State U of New York Coll at Old Westbury (NY)
State U of New York Coll at Potsdam (NY)
Texas Southern U (TX)
Thompson Rivers U (BC, Canada)
Truman State U (MO)
Tusculum Coll (TN)
The U of Alabama at Birmingham (AL)
The U of Arizona (AZ)
The U of British Columbia (BC, Canada)
The U of British Columbia–Okanagan (BC, Canada)
U of Louisiana at Lafayette (LA)
U of Maine at Machias (ME)
U of Maryland, Baltimore County (MD)
U of Maryland, Coll Park (MD)
U of Michigan (MI)
U of Pennsylvania (PA)
U of Regina (SK, Canada)
U of Rio Grande (OH)
U of St. Francis (IL)
U of Saint Mary (KS)
U of Southern Mississippi (MS)
The U of Tampa (FL)
The U of Tennessee at Martin (TN)
The U of Texas at Austin (TX)
The U of Texas at Dallas (TX)
U of the Sacred Heart (PR)
U of Toronto (ON, Canada)
U of Utah (UT)
U of Windsor (ON, Canada)
U of Wisconsin–Superior (WI)
Vassar Coll (NY)
Virginia State U (VA)
Viterbo U (WI)
Western Kentucky U (KY)
Western Washington U (WA)
Wichita State U (KS)
William Jessup U (CA)
York U (ON, Canada)

VISUAL AND PERFORMING ARTS RELATED
Adelphi U (NY)
Baldwin-Wallace Coll (OH)
Bard Coll at Simon's Rock (MA)
Brigham Young U (UT)
Claremont McKenna Coll (CA)
Clemson U (SC)
Coll of Visual Arts (MN)
Dana Coll (NE)
Illinois State U (IL)
Indiana U Bloomington (IN)
Kutztown U of Pennsylvania (PA)
Marywood U (PA)
Millikin U (IL)
Ohio Northern U (OH)
Providence Coll (RI)
Purchase Coll, State U of New York (NY)
Queens Coll of the City U of New York (NY)
Rensselaer Polytechnic Inst (NY)
Rice U (TX)
St. Cloud State U (MN)
Saint Mary's Coll of California (CA)
Samford U (AL)
Sarah Lawrence Coll (NY)
School of the Art Inst of Chicago (IL)
School of the Museum of Fine Arts, Boston (MA)
Scripps Coll (CA)
Simon Fraser U (BC, Canada)
Southwestern U (TX)
Spring Arbor U (MI)
State U of New York Coll at Geneseo (NY)
Stetson U (FL)
Syracuse U (NY)
Thompson Rivers U (BC, Canada)
U of California, Davis (CA)
U of New Haven (CT)
U of Oklahoma (OK)
U of Puerto Rico at Utuado (PR)
U of Wisconsin–Green Bay (WI)
Western State Coll of Colorado (CO)

VOCATIONAL REHABILITATION COUNSELING
East Carolina U (NC)
Emporia State U (KS)
Florida State U (FL)
Louisiana State U Health Sciences Center (LA)
Maryville U of Saint Louis (MO)
Southern U and Ag and Mech Coll (LA)
U of Illinois at Urbana–Champaign (IL)
U of North Dakota (ND)
U of Northern Colorado (CO)
Wright State U (OH)

VOICE AND OPERA
Abilene Christian U (TX)
Acadia U (NS, Canada)
Andrews U (MI)
Augustana Coll (IL)
Ball State U (IN)
Bard Coll (NY)
Barry U (FL)
Belmont U (TN)
Bennington Coll (VT)
Berklee Coll of Music (MA)
The Boston Conservatory (MA)
Boston U (MA)
Bowling Green State U (OH)
Brigham Young U (UT)
Bryan Coll (TN)
Butler U (IN)
California Inst of the Arts (CA)
California State U, Long Beach (CA)
Calvin Coll (MI)
Canadian Mennonite U (MB, Canada)
Capital U (OH)
Carnegie Mellon U (PA)
Carson-Newman Coll (TN)
Catawba Coll (NC)
The Catholic U of America (DC)
Cedarville U (OH)
Centenary Coll of Louisiana (LA)
Central Washington U (WA)
Chapman U (CA)
Clarke Coll (IA)
Coker Coll (SC)
Columbia Coll (SC)
Concordia Coll (MN)
Concordia U Chicago (IL)
Concordia U, Nebraska (NE)
Converse Coll (SC)
Dordt Coll (IA)
Drake U (IA)
East Central U (OK)
East Texas Baptist U (TX)
Five Towns Coll (NY)
Florida State U (FL)
Furman U (SC)
Grace U (NE)
Grand Valley State U (MI)
Hannibal-LaGrange Coll (MO)
Hardin-Simmons U (TX)
Hastings Coll (NE)
Heidelberg Coll (OH)
Hope Coll (MI)
Houghton Coll (NY)
Howard Payne U (TX)
Huntington U (IN)
Illinois Wesleyan U (IL)
Inter American U of Puerto Rico, San Germán Campus (PR)
Ithaca Coll (NY)
Jacksonville U (FL)
Lawrence U (WI)
Lee U (TN)
Lipscomb U (TN)
Louisiana Coll (LA)
Loyola Marymount U (CA)
Manhattan School of Music (NY)
Mannes Coll The New School for Music (NY)
Maryville Coll (TN)
The Master's Coll and Sem (CA)
McGill U (QC, Canada)
Memorial U of Newfoundland (NL, Canada)
Mercyhurst Coll (PA)
MidAmerica Nazarene U (KS)
Millikin U (IL)
Minnesota State U Mankato (MN)
Mississippi Coll (MS)
Mount Allison U (NB, Canada)
New England Conservatory of Music (MA)
New York U (NY)
North Carolina School of the Arts (NC)
Northern State U (SD)
North Greenville U (SC)
Northwestern Coll (MN)
Northwestern U (IL)
Northwest Missouri State U (MO)
Notre Dame de Namur U (CA)
Nyack Coll (NY)
Oakland U (MI)
Oberlin Coll (OH)
Ohio U (OH)
Oklahoma Christian U (OK)
Oklahoma City U (OK)
Oral Roberts U (OK)
Otterbein Coll (OH)
Ouachita Baptist U (AR)
Palm Beach Atlantic U (FL)
Peabody Conservatory of Music of The Johns Hopkins U (MD)
Peru State Coll (NE)
Prairie View A&M U (TX)
Queens U of Charlotte (NC)
Rider U (NJ)
Roberts Wesleyan Coll (NY)
Roosevelt U (IL)
St. Cloud State U (MN)
Samford U (AL)
San Diego Christian Coll (CA)
Sarah Lawrence Coll (NY)
Seton Hill U (PA)
Shorter Coll (GA)
Southeastern U (FL)
Southern Methodist U (TX)
Southwestern Oklahoma State U (OK)
State U of New York at Fredonia (NY)
Stetson U (FL)
Susquehanna U (PA)
Tabor Coll (KS)
Taylor U (IN)
Temple U (PA)
Texas Southern U (TX)
Trinity U (TX)
Truman State U (MO)
Union U (TN)
The U of Akron (OH)
The U of British Columbia (BC, Canada)
U of Central Oklahoma (OK)
U of Cincinnati (OH)
U of Idaho (ID)
U of Illinois at Urbana–Champaign (IL)
The U of Iowa (IA)
U of Kansas (KS)
U of Miami (FL)
U of Michigan (MI)
U of Nebraska at Omaha (NE)
U of New Hampshire (NH)
U of Oklahoma (OK)
U of Redlands (CA)
The U of Tennessee at Martin (TN)
U of the Pacific (CA)
U of Tulsa (OK)
U of Victoria (BC, Canada)
The U of Western Ontario (ON, Canada)
U of Wisconsin–Milwaukee (WI)
Valparaiso U (IN)
Vanderbilt U (TN)
Walla Walla U (WA)
Washington U in St. Louis (MO)
West Chester U of Pennsylvania (PA)
Whitworth U (WA)
Willamette U (OR)

William Paterson U of New Jersey (NJ)
Winona State U (MN)
York U (ON, Canada)

WALDORF/STEINER TEACHER EDUCATION
U of Michigan–Flint (MI)

WATER QUALITY AND WASTEWATER TREATMENT MANAGEMENT AND RECYCLING TECHNOLOGY
Mississippi Valley State U (MS)
Murray State U (KY)

WATER RESOURCES ENGINEERING
Central State U (OH)
State U of New York Coll of Environmental Science and Forestry (NY)
The U of Arizona (AZ)
U of Illinois at Urbana–Champaign (IL)
U of Nevada, Reno (NV)
U of Southern California (CA)

WATER, WETLANDS, AND MARINE RESOURCES MANAGEMENT
Colorado State U (CO)
Florida Gulf Coast U (FL)
Sterling Coll (VT)
Texas State U-San Marcos (TX)
U of Georgia (GA)
Western State Coll of Colorado (CO)

WEB/MULTIMEDIA MANAGEMENT AND WEBMASTER
The Art Inst of Austin (TX)
Duquesne U (PA)
Grace U (NE)
Hawai'i Pacific U (HI)
Kentucky State U (KY)
Lewis-Clark State Coll (ID)
Limestone Coll (SC)
The New England Inst of Art (MA)
New England School of Communications (ME)
Rochester Inst of Technology (NY)
U of Great Falls (MT)
U of St. Francis (IL)

WEB PAGE, DIGITAL/MULTIMEDIA AND INFORMATION RESOURCES DESIGN
The Art Inst of Atlanta (GA)
The Art Inst of Atlanta–Decatur (GA)
The Art Inst of California–Inland Empire (CA)
The Art Inst of California–Los Angeles (CA)
The Art Inst of California–Sacramento (CA)
The Art Inst of California–San Francisco (CA)
The Art Inst of California–Sunnyvale (CA)
The Art Inst of Charleston (SC)
The Art Inst of Dallas (TX)
The Art Inst of Houston (TX)
The Art Inst of Indianapolis (IN)
The Art Inst of Jacksonville (FL)
The Art Inst of Las Vegas (NV)
The Art Inst of Michigan (MI)
The Art Inst of Phoenix (AZ)
The Art Inst of Portland (OR)
The Art Inst of Salt Lake City (UT)
The Art Inst of Seattle (WA)
The Art Inst of Tucson (AZ)
The Art Inst of Washington (VA)
The Art Insts Intl Minnesota (MN)
Azusa Pacific U (CA)
Bishop's U (QC, Canada)
California Design Coll (CA)
The Cleveland Inst of Art (OH)
Columbia Coll Chicago (IL)
Dakota State U (SD)
Dana Coll (NE)
DePaul U (IL)
Drexel U (PA)
Duquesne U (PA)
The Illinois Inst of Art–Chicago (IL)
The Illinois Inst of Art–Schaumburg (IL)
Intl Acad of Design & Technology (FL)
Iona Coll (NY)
Liberty U (VA)
Medaille Coll (NY)
National American U–Sioux Falls Branch (SD)
Neumont U (UT)
The New England Inst of Art (MA)
New England School of Communications (ME)
Quinnipiac U (CT)
Rochester Inst of Technology (NY)
School of the Art Inst of Chicago (IL)
Stetson U (FL)
Tennessee Technological U (TN)
Thiel Coll (PA)
U of Great Falls (MT)
The U of North Carolina at Asheville (NC)
U of Wisconsin–Stevens Point (WI)
Utah Valley State Coll (UT)

WELDING TECHNOLOGY
Ferris State U (MI)
LeTourneau U (TX)
Lewis-Clark State Coll (ID)
Montana Tech of The U of Montana (MT)

WESTERN CIVILIZATION
The American U of Athens (Greece)
Belmont U (TN)
Concordia U (QC, Canada)
Gettysburg Coll (PA)
Grand Valley State U (MI)
Harvard U (MA)
St. John's Coll (MD)
St. John's Coll (NM)
Sarah Lawrence Coll (NY)
Thomas Aquinas Coll (CA)
U of King's Coll (NS, Canada)

WILDLIFE AND WILDLANDS SCIENCE AND MANAGEMENT
Arkansas State U (AR)
Auburn U (AL)
Brigham Young U (UT)
Coll of the Ozarks (MO)
Colorado State U (CO)
Dakota Wesleyan U (SD)
Delaware Valley Coll (PA)
Eastern Kentucky U (KY)
Eastern New Mexico U (NM)
Frostburg State U (MD)
Grand Valley State U (MI)
Humboldt State U (CA)
Lake Superior State U (MI)
McGill U (QC, Canada)
McNeese State U (LA)
Michigan Technological U (MI)
Mississippi State U (MS)
Missouri State U (MO)
Murray State U (KY)
North Carolina State U (NC)
Northern Arizona U (AZ)
Northland Coll (WI)
Northwest Missouri State U (MO)
Oregon State U (OR)
Peru State Coll (NE)
Prescott Coll (AZ)
Purdue U (IN)
South Dakota State U (SD)
Southeastern Oklahoma State U (OK)
State U of New York Coll of Agriculture and Technology at Cobleskill (NY)
State U of New York Coll of Environmental Science and Forestry (NY)
Stephen F. Austin State U (TX)
Sterling Coll (VT)
Tarleton State U (TX)
Tennessee Technological U (TN)
Texas A&M U (TX)
Texas Tech U (TX)
U of Alaska Fairbanks (AK)
The U of Arizona (AZ)
U of Arkansas at Monticello (AR)
The U of British Columbia (BC, Canada)
U of Delaware (DE)
U of Florida (FL)
U of Georgia (GA)
U of Idaho (ID)
U of Illinois at Urbana–Champaign (IL)
U of Maine (ME)
U of Massachusetts Amherst (MA)
U of Missouri–Columbia (MO)
The U of Montana (MT)
U of Nevada, Reno (NV)
U of New Brunswick Fredericton (NB, Canada)
U of New Hampshire (NH)
U of Puerto Rico at Humacao (PR)
U of Rhode Island (RI)
The U of Tennessee (TN)
The U of Tennessee at Martin (TN)
U of Wisconsin–Madison (WI)
U of Wisconsin–Stevens Point (WI)
Utah State U (UT)
Western New Mexico U (NM)
West Texas A&M U (TX)
West Virginia U (WV)
Winona State U (MN)

WILDLIFE BIOLOGY
Baker U (KS)
Ball State U (IN)
Clemson U (SC)
Coll of the Atlantic (ME)
Colorado State U (CO)
Grand Valley State U (MI)
Kansas State U (KS)
Lees-McRae Coll (NC)
McGill U (QC, Canada)
Northeastern State U (OK)
Northland Coll (WI)
Northwest Missouri State U (MO)
Ohio U (OH)
St. Cloud State U (MN)
State U of New York Coll of Environmental Science and Forestry (NY)
Sterling Coll (VT)
Texas State U-San Marcos (TX)
U of Michigan (MI)
U of Michigan–Flint (MI)
U of New Brunswick Fredericton (NB, Canada)
U of New Hampshire (NH)
U of North Dakota (ND)
U of Vermont (VT)
U of Wyoming (WY)
Winona State U (MN)

WIND/PERCUSSION INSTRUMENTS
Acadia U (NS, Canada)
Augustana Coll (IL)
Ball State U (IN)
Berklee Coll of Music (MA)
The Boston Conservatory (MA)
Bryan Coll (TN)
Butler U (IN)
Capital U (OH)
Chapman U (CA)
Concordia U Chicago (IL)
Five Towns Coll (NY)
Florida State U (FL)
Grand Valley State U (MI)
Houghton Coll (NY)
Howard Payne U (TX)
Inter American U of Puerto Rico, San Germán Campus (PR)
Lawrence U (WI)
Manhattan School of Music (NY)
Maryville Coll (TN)
Memorial U of Newfoundland (NL, Canada)
Mercyhurst Coll (PA)
Minnesota State U Mankato (MN)
Mount Allison U (NB, Canada)
New England Conservatory of Music (MA)
Northwestern U (IL)
Northwest Missouri State U (MO)
Oberlin Coll (OH)
Oklahoma Christian U (OK)
Oklahoma City U (OK)
Otterbein Coll (OH)
Palm Beach Atlantic U (FL)
Peabody Conservatory of Music of The Johns Hopkins U (MD)
Peru State Coll (NE)
Prairie View A&M U (TX)
Roosevelt U (IL)
Sarah Lawrence Coll (NY)
Seton Hill U (PA)
Southwestern Oklahoma State U (OK)
State U of New York at Fredonia (NY)
Susquehanna U (PA)
Temple U (PA)
Texas Southern U (TX)
U of Central Oklahoma (OK)
U of Cincinnati (OH)
The U of Iowa (IA)
U of Kansas (KS)
U of Michigan (MI)
U of New Hampshire (NH)
U of Oklahoma (OK)
U of Wisconsin–Milwaukee (WI)
Vanderbilt U (TN)
Xavier U of Louisiana (LA)

WOMEN'S STUDIES
Agnes Scott Coll (GA)
Albion Coll (MI)
Albright Coll (PA)
Allegheny Coll (PA)
American Public U System (WV)
American U (DC)
Amherst Coll (MA)
Arizona State U (AZ)
Arizona State U at the West campus (AZ)
Athabasca U (AB, Canada)
Augsburg Coll (MN)
Augustana Coll (IL)
Bard Coll at Simon's Rock (MA)
Barnard Coll (NY)
Bates Coll (ME)
Beloit Coll (WI)
Bennington Coll (VT)
Berea Coll (KY)
Bishop's U (QC, Canada)
Bowdoin Coll (ME)
Bowling Green State U (OH)
Brandeis U (MA)
Brock U (ON, Canada)
Brown U (RI)
Bucknell U (PA)
Burlington Coll (VT)
California State U, Fresno (CA)
California State U, Fullerton (CA)
California State U, Long Beach (CA)
California State U, San Marcos (CA)
Canisius Coll (NY)
Case Western Reserve U (OH)
Central Michigan U (MI)
Chatham U (PA)
City Coll of the City U of New York (NY)
Claremont McKenna Coll (CA)
Clark U (MA)
Colby Coll (ME)
Colgate U (NY)
The Coll at Brockport, State U of New York (NY)
The Coll of New Jersey (NJ)
The Coll of New Rochelle (NY)
Coll of Saint Benedict (MN)
Coll of Staten Island of the City U of New York (NY)
The Coll of William and Mary (VA)
The Colorado Coll (CO)
Concordia U (QC, Canada)
Connecticut Coll (CT)
Cornell Coll (IA)
Cornell U (NY)
Curry Coll (MA)
Dartmouth Coll (NH)
Denison U (OH)
DePaul U (IL)
DePauw U (IN)
Dickinson Coll (PA)
Dominican U of California (CA)
Drew U (NJ)
Duke U (NC)
Earlham Coll (IN)
East Carolina U (NC)
Eastern Michigan U (MI)
Eckerd Coll (FL)
Edinboro U of Pennsylvania (PA)
Emory U (GA)
Eugene Lang Coll The New School for Liberal Arts (NY)
Florida Intl U (FL)
Florida State U (FL)
Fort Lewis Coll (CO)
Georgetown U (DC)
Georgia State U (GA)
Gettysburg Coll (PA)
Goucher Coll (MD)
Grand Valley State U (MI)
Guilford Coll (NC)
Hamilton Coll (NY)
Hamline U (MN)
Hampshire Coll (MA)
Harvard U (MA)
Haverford Coll (PA)
Hobart and William Smith Colls (NY)
Hofstra U (NY)
Hollins U (VA)
Hunter Coll of the City U of New York (NY)
Illinois Wesleyan U (IL)
Indiana U–Purdue U Fort Wayne (IN)
Indiana U South Bend (IN)
Iowa State U of Science and Technology (IA)
Kansas State U (KS)
Kenyon Coll (OH)
Knox Coll (IL)
Lakehead U (ON, Canada)
Laurentian U (ON, Canada)
Lehigh U (PA)
List Coll, The Jewish Theological Sem (NY)
Louisiana State U and Ag and Mech Coll (LA)
Loyola U Chicago (IL)
Luther Coll (IA)
Macalester Coll (MN)
Marlboro Coll (VT)
Marquette U (WI)
McGill U (QC, Canada)
Memorial U of Newfoundland (NL, Canada)
Meredith Coll (NC)
Metropolitan State U (MN)
Miami U (OH)
Middlebury Coll (VT)
Mills Coll (CA)
Minnesota State U Mankato (MN)
Montclair State U (NJ)
Mount Holyoke Coll (MA)
Mount Saint Vincent U (NS, Canada)
Nazareth Coll of Rochester (NY)
Nebraska Wesleyan U (NE)
Northeastern Illinois U (IL)
Northeastern U (MA)
Northern Arizona U (AZ)
Northwestern U (IL)
Oakland U (MI)
Oberlin Coll (OH)
Occidental Coll (CA)
Ohio Wesleyan U (OH)
Old Dominion U (VA)
Pace U (NY)
Pacific Lutheran U (WA)
Penn State Abington (PA)
Penn State Altoona (PA)
Penn State Berks (PA)
Penn State Erie, The Behrend Coll (PA)
Penn State U Park (PA)
Pitzer Coll (CA)
Pomona Coll (CA)
Portland State U (OR)
Purchase Coll, State U of New York (NY)
Purdue U (IN)
Queens Coll of the City U of New York (NY)
Queen's U at Kingston (ON, Canada)
Randolph-Macon Coll (VA)
Rhode Island Coll (RI)
Rice U (TX)
Roosevelt U (IL)
Rosemont Coll (PA)
Rutgers, The State U of New Jersey, Newark (NJ)
Rutgers, The State U of New Jersey, New Brunswick (NJ)
St. Francis Xavier U (NS, Canada)
Saint Joseph Coll (CT)
Saint Louis U (MO)
Saint Mary's Coll of California (CA)
Saint Michael's Coll (VT)
St. Olaf Coll (MN)
San Diego State U (CA)
San Francisco State U (CA)
Sarah Lawrence Coll (NY)
Scripps Coll (CA)
Simmons Coll (MA)
Simon Fraser U (BC, Canada)
Skidmore Coll (NY)
Smith Coll (MA)
Sonoma State U (CA)
Southwestern U (TX)
Spelman Coll (GA)
Stanford U (CA)
State U of New York at Fredonia (NY)
State U of New York at New Paltz (NY)
State U of New York at Oswego (NY)
State U of New York at Plattsburgh (NY)
State U of New York Coll at Potsdam (NY)
Stony Brook U, State U of New York (NY)
Suffolk U (MA)
Syracuse U (NY)
Temple U (PA)
Towson U (MD)
Trent U (ON, Canada)
Trinity Coll (CT)
Tufts U (MA)
Tulane U (LA)
U at Albany, State U of New York (NY)
U at Buffalo, the State U of New York (NY)
The U of Arizona (AZ)
The U of British Columbia (BC, Canada)
U of California, Berkeley (CA)
U of California, Davis (CA)
U of California, Irvine (CA)
U of California, Los Angeles (CA)
U of California, Riverside (CA)
U of California, San Diego (CA)
U of California, Santa Barbara (CA)
U of California, Santa Cruz (CA)
U of Colorado at Boulder (CO)
U of Connecticut (CT)
U of Delaware (DE)
U of Florida (FL)
U of Georgia (GA)

U of Hawaii at Manoa (HI)
U of Houston–Clear Lake (TX)
U of Illinois at Urbana–Champaign (IL)
The U of Iowa (IA)
U of Kansas (KS)
U of King's Coll (NS, Canada)
U of Louisville (KY)
U of Maine (ME)
U of Maine at Farmington (ME)
U of Maryland, Baltimore County (MD)
U of Maryland, Coll Park (MD)
U of Massachusetts Amherst (MA)
U of Massachusetts Boston (MA)
U of Massachusetts Dartmouth (MA)
U of Miami (FL)
U of Michigan (MI)
U of Michigan–Dearborn (MI)
U of Minnesota, Duluth (MN)
U of Minnesota, Twin Cities Campus (MN)
The U of Montana (MT)
U of Nebraska at Omaha (NE)
U of Nebraska–Lincoln (NE)
U of Nevada, Las Vegas (NV)
U of Nevada, Reno (NV)
U of New Hampshire (NH)
U of New Mexico (NM)
U of New Orleans (LA)
The U of North Carolina at Asheville (NC)
The U of North Carolina at Chapel Hill (NC)
The U of North Carolina at Greensboro (NC)
U of Oklahoma (OK)
U of Oregon (OR)
U of Ottawa (ON, Canada)
U of Pennsylvania (PA)
U of Regina (SK, Canada)
U of Rhode Island (RI)
U of Richmond (VA)
U of Rochester (NY)
U of St. Thomas (MN)
U of South Carolina (SC)
U of Southern Maine (ME)
U of South Florida (FL)
The U of Texas at Austin (TX)
The U of Toledo (OH)
U of Toronto (ON, Canada)
U of Utah (UT)
U of Vermont (VT)
U of Victoria (BC, Canada)
The U of Western Ontario (ON, Canada)
U of Windsor (ON, Canada)
The U of Winnipeg (MB, Canada)
U of Wisconsin–Madison (WI)
U of Wisconsin–Milwaukee (WI)
U of Wisconsin–Whitewater (WI)
U of Wyoming (WY)
Vassar Coll (NY)
Virginia Commonwealth U (VA)
Virginia Wesleyan Coll (VA)
Warren Wilson Coll (NC)
Washington State U (WA)
Washington U in St. Louis (MO)
Wellesley Coll (MA)
Wells Coll (NY)
Wesleyan U (CT)
West Chester U of Pennsylvania (PA)
Western Illinois U (IL)
Western Michigan U (MI)
Western Washington U (WA)
Wheaton Coll (MA)
Wichita State U (KS)
Wilfrid Laurier U (ON, Canada)
Willamette U (OR)
Williams Coll (MA)
Wright State U (OH)
Yale U (CT)
York U (ON, Canada)

WOOD SCIENCE AND WOOD PRODUCTS/PULP AND PAPER TECHNOLOGY

Miami U (OH)
Mississippi State U (MS)
North Carolina State U (NC)
Oregon State U (OR)
Pittsburg State U (KS)
State U of New York Coll of Environmental Science and Forestry (NY)
The U of British Columbia (BC, Canada)
U of Maine (ME)
U of Massachusetts Amherst (MA)
U of Minnesota, Twin Cities Campus (MN)
U of Toronto (ON, Canada)
U of Wisconsin–Stevens Point (WI)
West Virginia U (WV)

WORK AND FAMILY STUDIES

Brigham Young U (UT)
Miami U Hamilton (OH)
Texas Tech U (TX)
Ursuline Coll (OH)

YOUTH MINISTRY

Anderson U (IN)
Andrews U (MI)
Asbury Coll (KY)
Baptist Bible Coll of Pennsylvania (PA)
Benedictine Coll (KS)
Bethel U (MN)
Bluffton U (OH)
Bryan Coll (TN)
Canadian Mennonite U (MB, Canada)
Cedarville U (OH)
Central Christian Coll of Kansas (KS)
Concordia U Wisconsin (WI)
Crossroads Coll (MN)
Davis Coll (NY)
Dordt Coll (IA)
Eastern Mennonite U (VA)
East Texas Baptist U (TX)
Eugene Bible Coll (OR)
Gardner-Webb U (NC)
George Fox U (OR)
Gordon Coll (MA)
Grace Bible Coll (MI)
Grace Coll (IN)
Grace U (NE)
Great Lakes Christian Coll (MI)
Greenville Coll (IL)
Harding U (AR)
Hardin-Simmons U (TX)
Hillsdale Free Will Baptist Coll (OK)
Horizon Coll & Sem (SK, Canada)
John Brown U (AR)
Kentucky Christian U (KY)
Kuyper Coll (MI)
Lindenwood U (MO)
Lipscomb U (TN)
Lubbock Christian U (TX)
Malone Coll (OH)
Maranatha Baptist Bible Coll (WI)
Master's Coll and Sem (ON, Canada)
Mount Vernon Nazarene U (OH)
Multnomah Bible Coll and Biblical Sem (OR)
North Greenville U (SC)
Northwestern Coll (MN)
Oak Hills Christian Coll (MN)
Ouachita Baptist U (AR)
Pfeiffer U (NC)
Pillsbury Baptist Bible Coll (MN)
Point Loma Nazarene U (CA)
Rochester Coll (MI)
Saint Mary's U of Minnesota (MN)
Southeastern U (FL)
Southern Baptist Theological Sem (KY)
Southwestern Coll (AZ)
Spring Arbor U (MI)
Taylor U Fort Wayne (IN)
Toccoa Falls Coll (GA)
Trinity Coll of Florida (FL)
Trinity Intl U (IL)
U of Indianapolis (IN)
U of Sioux Falls (SD)
Vanguard U of Southern California (CA)
Vennard Coll (IA)
Washington Bible Coll (MD)

YOUTH SERVICES

The U of Western Ontario (ON, Canada)

ZOOLOGY/ANIMAL BIOLOGY

Andrews U (MI)
Auburn U (AL)
Ball State U (IN)
Bennington Coll (VT)
Brigham Young U (UT)
California State Polytechnic U, Pomona (CA)
California State U, Long Beach (CA)
Coll of the Atlantic (ME)
Colorado State U (CO)
Delaware Valley Coll (PA)
Florida State U (FL)
Humboldt State U (CA)
Idaho State U (ID)
Juniata Coll (PA)
Kent State U (OH)
Malone Coll (OH)
McGill U (QC, Canada)
Memorial U of Newfoundland (NL, Canada)
Miami U (OH)
Miami U Hamilton (OH)
Michigan State U (MI)
North Carolina State U (NC)
North Dakota State U (ND)
Northern Arizona U (AZ)
Northern Michigan U (MI)
Northland Coll (WI)
Northwest Missouri State U (MO)
Ohio U (OH)
Ohio Wesleyan U (OH)
Oklahoma State U (OK)
Oregon State U (OR)
Purdue U (IN)
Rutgers, The State U of New Jersey, Newark (NJ)
San Francisco State U (CA)
Sonoma State U (CA)
Southeastern Oklahoma State U (OK)
Southern Illinois U Carbondale (IL)
Southern Utah U (UT)
State U of New York at Oswego (NY)
State U of New York Coll of Environmental Science and Forestry (NY)
Tarleton State U (TX)
Texas A&M U (TX)
Texas State U-San Marcos (TX)
Texas Tech U (TX)
Texas Woman's U (TX)
The U of Akron (OH)
The U of British Columbia (BC, Canada)
U of California, Davis (CA)
U of California, Santa Barbara (CA)
U of Florida (FL)
U of Hawaii at Manoa (HI)
U of Idaho (ID)
U of Maine (ME)
U of Michigan (MI)
The U of Montana (MT)
U of New Brunswick Fredericton (NB, Canada)
U of New Hampshire (NH)
U of Oklahoma (OK)
U of Rhode Island (RI)
The U of Tennessee (TN)
The U of Texas at El Paso (TX)
U of Toronto (ON, Canada)
U of Vermont (VT)
U of Victoria (BC, Canada)
U of Wisconsin–Madison (WI)
U of Wisconsin–Milwaukee (WI)
U of Wyoming (WY)
Utah State U (UT)
Weber State U (UT)
Western New Mexico U (NM)
Winona State U (MN)

ZOOLOGY/ANIMAL BIOLOGY RELATED

Thompson Rivers U (BC, Canada)

Entrance Difficulty

This listing groups colleges by their own assessment of their entrance difficulty level. The colleges were asked to select the level that most closely corresponds to their entrance difficulty, according to the guidelines below. Institutions for which high school class rank and/or standardized test scores do not apply as admission criteria were asked to select the level that best indicates their entrance difficulty as compared to other institutions.

Most Difficult

More than 75 percent of the freshmen were in the top 10 percent of their high school class and scored over 1310 on the SAT (critical reading and mathematical combined) or over 29 on the ACT (composite); about 30 percent or fewer of the applicants were accepted.

Amherst Coll (MA)
Barnard Coll (NY)
Bates Coll (ME)
Bowdoin Coll (ME)
Brandeis U (MA)
Brown U (RI)
Bryn Mawr Coll (PA)
Bucknell U (PA)
California Inst of Technology (CA)
Carnegie Mellon U (PA)
Claremont McKenna Coll (CA)
The Colburn School Conservatory of Music (CA)
Colby Coll (ME)
Colgate U (NY)
Columbia U (NY)
Cooper Union for the Advancement of Science and Art (NY)
Cornell U (NY)
Dartmouth Coll (NH)
Duke U (NC)
Emory U (GA)
Georgetown U (DC)
Gettysburg Coll (PA)
Grove City Coll (PA)
Harvard U (MA)
Harvey Mudd Coll (CA)
Haverford Coll (PA)
The Johns Hopkins U (MD)
The Juilliard School (NY)
Lafayette Coll (PA)
Lehigh U (PA)
Massachusetts Inst of Technology (MA)
Middlebury Coll (VT)
New York U (NY)
Northwestern U (IL)
Pomona Coll (CA)
Princeton U (NJ)
Queen's U at Kingston (ON, Canada)
Reed Coll (OR)
Rice U (TX)
Royal Military Coll of Canada (ON, Canada)
Stanford U (CA)
Swarthmore Coll (PA)
Trinity Coll (CT)
Tufts U (MA)
United States Air Force Acad (CO)
U of Chicago (IL)
U of Notre Dame (IN)
U of Pennsylvania (PA)
U of Southern California (CA)
Washington and Lee U (VA)
Washington U in St. Louis (MO)
Webb Inst (NY)
Wellesley Coll (MA)
Wesleyan U (CT)
Williams Coll (MA)
Yale U (CT)

Very Difficult

More than 50 percent of the freshmen were in the top 10 percent of their high school class and scored over 1230 on the SAT or over 26 on the ACT; about 60 percent or fewer applicants were accepted.

Agnes Scott Coll (GA)
Allegheny Coll (PA)
American U (DC)
Austin Coll (TX)
Babson Coll (MA)
Bard Coll (NY)
Bard Coll at Simon's Rock (MA)
Beloit Coll (WI)
Bennington Coll (VT)
Bentley Coll (MA)
Berea Coll (KY)
Bernard M. Baruch Coll of the City U of New York (NY)
Boston Coll (MA)
Boston U (MA)
California Inst of the Arts (CA)
Case Western Reserve U (OH)
Centre Coll (KY)
Christendom Coll (VA)
Clarkson U (NY)
The Coll of Idaho (ID)
The Coll of New Jersey (NJ)
Coll of the Atlantic (ME)
Coll of the Holy Cross (MA)
The Coll of William and Mary (VA)
The Colorado Coll (CO)
Colorado School of Mines (CO)
Connecticut Coll (CT)
Davidson Coll (NC)
Denison U (OH)
Dickinson Coll (PA)
Earlham Coll (IN)
Emerson Coll (MA)
Florida State U (FL)
Franklin & Marshall Coll (PA)
Franklin W. Olin Coll of Eng (MA)
Furman U (SC)
The George Washington U (DC)
Georgia Inst of Technology (GA)
Grinnell Coll (IA)
Gustavus Adolphus Coll (MN)
Hamilton Coll (NY)
Hampshire Coll (MA)
Hendrix Coll (AR)
Hillsdale Coll (MI)
Hobart and William Smith Colls (NY)
Illinois Inst of Technology (IL)
Illinois Wesleyan U (IL)
James Madison U (VA)
The Jewish Theological Sem (NY)
Kalamazoo Coll (MI)
Kenyon Coll (OH)
Kettering U (MI)
The King's Coll (NY)
Knox Coll (IL)
Laguna Coll of Art & Design (CA)
Lake Forest Coll (IL)
Lawrence U (WI)
Lewis & Clark Coll (OR)
Loyola Marymount U (CA)
Macalester Coll (MN)
Manhattan School of Music (NY)
Mannes Coll The New School for Music (NY)
Marist Coll (NY)
Maryland Inst Coll of Art (MD)
Massachusetts Coll of Art and Design (MA)
McGill U (QC, Canada)
Missouri U of Science and Technology (MO)
Mount Holyoke Coll (MA)
Muhlenberg Coll (PA)
New Coll of Florida (FL)
New England Conservatory of Music (MA)
The New School for Jazz and Contemporary Music (NY)
North Carolina School of the Arts (NC)
North Carolina State U (NC)
Northeastern U (MA)
NSCAD U (NS, Canada)
Oberlin Coll (OH)
Occidental Coll (CA)
Oglethorpe U (GA)
Ohio Wesleyan U (OH)
Parsons Paris (France)
Parsons The New School for Design (NY)
Patrick Henry Coll (VA)
Peabody Conservatory of Music of The Johns Hopkins U (MD)
Penn State Abington (PA)
Penn State Altoona (PA)
Penn State Berks (PA)
Penn State Erie, The Behrend Coll (PA)
Penn State Harrisburg (PA)
Penn State U Park (PA)
Pepperdine U, Malibu (CA)
Polytechnic U, Brooklyn Campus (NY)
Pratt Inst (NY)
Presbyterian Coll (SC)
Providence Coll (RI)
Queens Coll of the City U of New York (NY)
Rensselaer Polytechnic Inst (NY)
Rhodes Coll (TN)
The Richard Stockton Coll of New Jersey (NJ)
Rollins Coll (FL)
Rose-Hulman Inst of Technology (IN)
St. John's Coll (NM)
St. Lawrence U (NY)
St. Mary's Coll of Maryland (MD)
St. Olaf Coll (MN)
Sarah Lawrence Coll (NY)
Scripps Coll (CA)
Sewanee: The U of the South (TN)
Skidmore Coll (NY)
Smith Coll (MA)
Southwestern U (TX)
Spelman Coll (GA)
State U of New York at Binghamton (NY)
State U of New York at New Paltz (NY)
State U of New York at Plattsburgh (NY)
State U of New York Coll at Geneseo (NY)
State U of New York Coll at Oneonta (NY)
Stonehill Coll (MA)
Stony Brook U, State U of New York (NY)
Syracuse U (NY)
Thomas Aquinas Coll (CA)
Transylvania U (KY)
Trinity U (TX)
Tulane U (LA)
Union Coll (NY)
United States Coast Guard Acad (CT)
United States Merchant Marine Acad (NY)
United States Naval Acad (MD)
The U of British Columbia (BC, Canada)
U of California, Berkeley (CA)
U of California, Los Angeles (CA)
U of California, Riverside (CA)
U of California, San Diego (CA)
U of California, Santa Barbara (CA)
U of California, Santa Cruz (CA)
U of Florida (FL)
U of Illinois at Urbana–Champaign (IL)
U of Mary Washington (VA)
U of Miami (FL)
U of Michigan (MI)
The U of North Carolina at Chapel Hill (NC)
U of North Florida (FL)
U of Richmond (VA)
U of Rochester (NY)
U of San Diego (CA)
The U of Texas at Austin (TX)
The U of Texas at Dallas (TX)
The U of Texas Medical Branch (TX)
U of Toronto (ON, Canada)
U of Tulsa (OK)
U of Virginia (VA)
The U of Western Ontario (ON, Canada)
U of Wisconsin–Madison (WI)
Ursinus Coll (PA)
Vanderbilt U (TN)

Entrance Difficulty

Very Difficult

Vassar Coll (NY)
Villanova U (PA)
Wake Forest U (NC)
Washington & Jefferson Coll (PA)
Wheaton Coll (IL)
Wheaton Coll (MA)
Whitman Coll (WA)
Whitworth U (WA)
Willamette U (OR)
Wofford Coll (SC)
Worcester Polytechnic Inst (MA)

Moderately Difficult

More than 75 percent of the freshmen were in the top half of their high school class and scored over 1010 on the SAT or over 18 on the ACT; about 85 percent or fewer of the applicants were accepted.

Abilene Christian U (TX)
Acadia U (NS, Canada)
Adams State Coll (CO)
Adelphi U (NY)
Adrian Coll (MI)
Alaska Pacific U (AK)
Alberta Coll of Art & Design (AB, Canada)
Albertus Magnus Coll (CT)
Albion Coll (MI)
Albright Coll (PA)
Alderson-Broaddus Coll (WV)
Alfred U (NY)
Alice Lloyd Coll (KY)
Allen Coll (IA)
Alliant Intl U–México City (Mexico)
Alma Coll (MI)
Alvernia Coll (PA)
American Jewish U (CA)
The American U of Athens (Greece)
The American U of Paris (France)
Anderson U (IN)
Andrews U (MI)
Angelo State U (TX)
Appalachian State U (NC)
Aquinas Coll (MI)
Arizona State U (AZ)
Arizona State U at the West campus (AZ)
Art Acad of Cincinnati (OH)
The Art Inst of Atlanta (GA)
The Art Inst of Boston at Lesley U (MA)
The Art Inst of Houston (TX)
The Art Inst of Philadelphia (PA)
The Art Inst of Seattle (WA)
The Art Inst of Tampa (FL)
Asbury Coll (KY)
Ashland U (OH)
Assumption Coll (MA)
Atlantic Union Coll (MA)
Auburn U (AL)
Auburn U Montgomery (AL)
Augsburg Coll (MN)
Augustana Coll (IL)
Augustana Coll (SD)
Austin Peay State U (TN)
Ave Maria U (FL)
Averett U (VA)
Azusa Pacific U (CA)
Baker U (KS)
Baldwin-Wallace Coll (OH)
Ball State U (IN)
Baptist Coll of Health Sciences (TN)
Barry U (FL)
Baylor U (TX)
Bay Path Coll (MA)
Belhaven Coll (MS)
Bellarmine U (KY)
Belmont Abbey Coll (NC)
Belmont U (TN)
Bemidji State U (MN)
Benedictine Coll (KS)
Benedictine U (IL)
Berklee Coll of Music (MA)
Berry Coll (GA)
Bethany Bible Coll (NB, Canada)
Bethany Coll (KS)
Bethany Coll (WV)
Bethany Lutheran Coll (MN)
Bethel Coll (KS)
Bethel U (MN)
Biola U (CA)
Bishop's U (QC, Canada)
Blackburn Coll (IL)
Blessing-Rieman Coll of Nursing (IL)
Bloomfield Coll (NJ)
Bloomsburg U of Pennsylvania (PA)
Bluffton U (OH)
Boricua Coll (NY)
Boston Baptist Coll (MA)
The Boston Conservatory (MA)
Bowling Green State U (OH)
Bradley U (IL)
Brenau U (GA)
Bridgewater Coll (VA)
Bridgewater State Coll (MA)
Brigham Young U (UT)
British Columbia Inst of Technology (BC, Canada)
Brock U (ON, Canada)
Bryan Coll (TN)
Buffalo State Coll, State U of New York (NY)
Burlington Coll (VT)
Butler U (IN)
Cabarrus Coll of Health Sciences (NC)
Cabrini Coll (PA)
California Coll of the Arts (CA)
California Lutheran U (CA)
California Maritime Acad (CA)
California Polytechnic State U, San Luis Obispo (CA)
California State Polytechnic U, Pomona (CA)
California State U, Chico (CA)
California State U, Dominguez Hills (CA)
California State U, East Bay (CA)
California State U, Fullerton (CA)
California State U, Long Beach (CA)
California State U, Los Angeles (CA)
California State U, Sacramento (CA)
California State U, San Bernardino (CA)
California State U, San Marcos (CA)
Calvin Coll (MI)
Canadian Mennonite U (MB, Canada)
Canisius Coll (NY)
Capital U (OH)
Carlow U (PA)
Carroll Coll (WI)
Carson-Newman Coll (TN)
Castleton State Coll (VT)
Catawba Coll (NC)
The Catholic U of America (DC)
Cedar Crest Coll (PA)
Cedarville U (OH)
Centenary Coll (NJ)
Centenary Coll of Louisiana (LA)
Central Coll (IA)
Central Connecticut State U (CT)
Central Michigan U (MI)
Central Washington U (WA)
Chapman U (CA)
Chatham U (PA)
Chestnut Hill Coll (PA)
Christian Brothers U (TN)
The Citadel, The Military Coll of South Carolina (SC)
City Coll of the City U of New York (NY)
Clark Atlanta U (GA)
Clarke Coll (IA)
Clarkson Coll (NE)
Clark U (MA)
Cleary U (MI)
Clemson U (SC)
The Cleveland Inst of Art (OH)
Cleveland State U (OH)
Coastal Carolina U (SC)
Cogswell Polytechnical Coll (CA)
Coker Coll (SC)
Colby-Sawyer Coll (NH)
The Coll at Brockport, State U of New York (NY)
Coll for Creative Studies (MI)
Coll of Charleston (SC)
Coll of Mount St. Joseph (OH)
Coll of Mount Saint Vincent (NY)
The Coll of New Rochelle (NY)
Coll of Saint Benedict (MN)
Coll of Saint Elizabeth (NJ)
The Coll of Saint Rose (NY)
The Coll of St. Scholastica (MN)
Coll of Santa Fe (NM)
Coll of Staten Island of the City U of New York (NY)
Coll of the Ozarks (MO)
Coll of the Southwest (NM)
Coll of Visual Arts (MN)
Colorado State U (CO)
Colorado State U-Pueblo (CO)
Columbia Coll (SC)
Columbia Coll of Nursing (WI)
Columbus Coll of Art & Design (OH)
Concordia Coll (MN)
Concordia Coll–New York (NY)
Concordia U (CA)
Concordia U (MI)
Concordia U (OR)
Concordia U (QC, Canada)
Concordia U Chicago (IL)
Concordia U, Nebraska (NE)
Concordia U Texas (TX)
Concordia U Wisconsin (WI)
Converse Coll (SC)
Cornell Coll (IA)
Covenant Coll (GA)
Creighton U (NE)
Culver-Stockton Coll (MO)
Curry Coll (MA)
Daemen Coll (NY)
Dakota Wesleyan U (SD)
Dallas Baptist U (TX)
Dana Coll (NE)
Daniel Webster Coll (NH)
Davis & Elkins Coll (WV)
Defiance Coll (OH)
Delaware Valley Coll (PA)
DePaul U (IL)
DePauw U (IN)
DeSales U (PA)
DigiPen Inst of Technology (WA)
Dillard U (LA)
Doane Coll (NE)
Dominican U (IL)
Dominican U of California (CA)
Dordt Coll (IA)
Dowling Coll (NY)
Drake U (IA)
Drew U (NJ)
Drexel U (PA)
Drury U (MO)
Duquesne U (PA)
D'Youville Coll (NY)
East Carolina U (NC)
Eastern Connecticut State U (CT)
Eastern Illinois U (IL)
Eastern Mennonite U (VA)
Eastern Michigan U (MI)
East Stroudsburg U of Pennsylvania (PA)
East Tennessee State U (TN)
East Texas Baptist U (TX)
Eckerd Coll (FL)
Ecole Hôtelière de Lausanne (Switzerland)
Edinboro U of Pennsylvania (PA)
Elizabethtown Coll (PA)
Elon U (NC)
Embry-Riddle Aeronautical U (AZ)
Embry-Riddle Aeronautical U (FL)
Emmanuel Coll (MA)
Emory & Henry Coll (VA)
Endicott Coll (MA)
Erskine Coll (SC)
Eugene Lang Coll The New School for Liberal Arts (NY)
Evangel U (MO)
The Evergreen State Coll (WA)
Fairfield U (CT)
Fairleigh Dickinson U, Coll at Florham (NJ)
Fairleigh Dickinson U, Metropolitan Campus (NJ)
Farmingdale State Coll (NY)
Fashion Inst of Technology (NY)
Felician Coll (NJ)
Fitchburg State Coll (MA)
Five Towns Coll (NY)
Flagler Coll (FL)
Florida Ag and Mech U (FL)
Florida Atlantic U (FL)
Florida Coll (FL)
Florida Gulf Coast U (FL)
Florida Inst of Technology (FL)
Florida Intl U (FL)
Florida Southern Coll (FL)
Fontbonne U (MO)
Fort Lewis Coll (CO)
Framingham State Coll (MA)
Franciscan U of Steubenville (OH)
Francis Marion U (SC)
Franklin Coll (IN)
Franklin Coll Switzerland (Switzerland)
Freed-Hardeman U (TN)
Fresno Pacific U (CA)
Frostburg State U (MD)
Gannon U (PA)
Gardner-Webb U (NC)
George Fox U (OR)
George Mason U (VA)
Georgetown Coll (KY)
Georgia Coll & State U (GA)
Georgian Court U (NJ)
Georgia Southern U (GA)
Georgia Southwestern State U (GA)
Georgia State U (GA)
Goddard Coll (VT)
Golden Gate U (CA)
Goldey-Beacom Coll (DE)
Gonzaga U (WA)
Gordon Coll (MA)

Goucher Coll (MD)
Grace Coll (IN)
Grace U (NE)
Grand Canyon U (AZ)
Grand Valley State U (MI)
Great Lakes Christian Coll (MI)
Green Mountain Coll (VT)
Greensboro Coll (NC)
Greenville Coll (IL)
Guilford Coll (NC)
Gutenberg Coll (OR)
Gwynedd-Mercy Coll (PA)
Hamline U (MN)
Hampden-Sydney Coll (VA)
Hampton U (VA)
Hannibal-LaGrange Coll (MO)
Hanover Coll (IN)
Harding U (AR)
Hardin-Simmons U (TX)
Hartwick Coll (NY)
Hastings Coll (NE)
Hawai'i Pacific U (HI)
HEC Montreal (QC, Canada)
Heidelberg Coll (OH)
Henderson State U (AR)
High Point U (NC)
Hofstra U (NY)
Hollins U (VA)
Holy Family U (PA)
Holy Names U (CA)
Hood Coll (MD)
Hope Coll (MI)
Hope Intl U (CA)
Houghton Coll (NY)
Houston Baptist U (TX)
Howard Payne U (TX)
Humboldt State U (CA)
Hunter Coll of the City U of New York (NY)
Huntingdon Coll (AL)
Huntington U (IN)
Husson Coll (ME)
Huston-Tillotson U (TX)
Illinois Coll (IL)
Illinois State U (IL)
Immaculata U (PA)
Indiana State U (IN)
Indiana Tech (IN)
Indiana U Bloomington (IN)
Indiana U East (IN)
Indiana U of Pennsylvania (PA)
Indiana U–Purdue U Indianapolis (IN)
Indiana U South Bend (IN)
Indiana Wesleyan U (IN)
Inter American U of Puerto Rico, Aguadilla Campus (PR)
Inter American U of Puerto Rico, Fajardo Campus (PR)
Inter American U of Puerto Rico, San Germán Campus (PR)
Intl U in Geneva (Switzerland)
Iona Coll (NY)
Iowa State U of Science and Technology (IA)
Iowa Wesleyan Coll (IA)
Ithaca Coll (NY)
Jacksonville U (FL)
Jefferson Coll of Health Sciences (VA)
John Brown U (AR)
John Carroll U (OH)
Johnson Bible Coll (TN)
Johnson C. Smith U (NC)
Johnson State Coll (VT)
Judson Coll (AL)
Judson U (IL)
Juniata Coll (PA)
Kansas City Art Inst (MO)
Kean U (NJ)
Keene State Coll (NH)
Kennesaw State U (GA)
Kent State U (OH)
Kentucky Christian U (KY)
Kentucky Wesleyan Coll (KY)
Kettering Coll of Medical Arts (OH)
Keuka Coll (NY)
King Coll (TN)
King's Coll (PA)
The King's U Coll (AB, Canada)
Kutztown U of Pennsylvania (PA)
Kuyper Coll (MI)
Laboratory Inst of Merchandising (NY)
LaGrange Coll (GA)
Lakehead U (ON, Canada)
Lake Superior State U (MI)
Lambuth U (TN)
Lander U (SC)
La Salle U (PA)
La Sierra U (CA)
Lawrence Technological U (MI)
Lebanon Valley Coll (PA)
Lehman Coll of the City U of New York (NY)
Le Moyne Coll (NY)
Lenoir-Rhyne Coll (NC)
Lesley U (MA)
Lewis U (IL)
Limestone Coll (SC)
Lincoln U (PA)
Lindenwood U (MO)
Linfield Coll (OR)
Lipscomb U (TN)
Lock Haven U of Pennsylvania (PA)
Logan U-Coll of Chiropractic (MO)
Longwood U (VA)
Loras Coll (IA)
Louisiana Coll (LA)
Louisiana State U and Ag and Mech Coll (LA)
Loyola Coll in Maryland (MD)
Loyola U Chicago (IL)
Loyola U New Orleans (LA)
Lubbock Christian U (TX)
Luther Coll (IA)
Lycoming Coll (PA)
Lynchburg Coll (VA)
Lyndon State Coll (VT)
Lyon Coll (AR)
Madonna U (MI)
Maharishi U of Management (IA)
Maine Maritime Acad (ME)
Malone Coll (OH)
Manchester Coll (IN)
Manhattanville Coll (NY)
Mansfield U of Pennsylvania (PA)
Marian Coll (IN)
Marian Coll of Fond du Lac (WI)
Marietta Coll (OH)
Marlboro Coll (VT)
Marquette U (WI)
Marshall U (WV)
Mary Baldwin Coll (VA)
Marymount Manhattan Coll (NY)
Marymount U (VA)
Maryville Coll (TN)
Maryville U of Saint Louis (MO)
Marywood U (PA)
Massachusetts Coll of Liberal Arts (MA)
Massachusetts Coll of Pharmacy and Health Sciences (MA)
Massachusetts Maritime Acad (MA)
The Master's Coll and Sem (CA)
McDaniel Coll (MD)
McKendree U (IL)
McMurry U (TX)
McNeese State U (LA)
Medaille Coll (NY)
Medcenter One Coll of Nursing (ND)
Medical Coll of Georgia (GA)
Memorial U of Newfoundland (NL, Canada)
Memphis Coll of Art (TN)
Mercer U (GA)
Mercyhurst Coll (PA)
Meredith Coll (NC)
Merrimack Coll (MA)
Messiah Coll (PA)
Methodist U (NC)
Metropolitan Coll of New York (NY)
Miami Intl U of Art & Design (FL)
Miami U (OH)
Michigan State U (MI)
Michigan Technological U (MI)
Middle Tennessee State U (TN)
Midland Lutheran Coll (NE)
Millersville U of Pennsylvania (PA)
Milligan Coll (TN)
Millikin U (IL)
Millsaps Coll (MS)
Mills Coll (CA)
Milwaukee School of Eng (WI)
Minnesota State U Mankato (MN)
Misericordia U (PA)
Mississippi Coll (MS)
Mississippi State U (MS)
Mississippi U for Women (MS)
Missouri Baptist U (MO)
Missouri Southern State U (MO)
Missouri State U (MO)
Molloy Coll (NY)
Monmouth Coll (IL)
Monmouth U (NJ)
Monroe Coll, Bronx (NY)
Monroe Coll, New Rochelle (NY)
Montana State U (MT)
Montana State U–Billings (MT)
Montana Tech of The U of Montana (MT)
Montclair State U (NJ)
Montserrat Coll of Art (MA)
Moravian Coll (PA)
Morehouse Coll (GA)
Morgan State U (MD)
Morningside Coll (IA)
Mount Allison U (NB, Canada)
Mount Carmel Coll of Nursing (OH)
Mount Ida Coll (MA)
Mount Mary Coll (WI)
Mount Mercy Coll (IA)
Mount Saint Mary Coll (NY)
Mount St. Mary's Coll (CA)
Mount St. Mary's U (MD)
Mount Saint Vincent U (NS, Canada)
Mount Vernon Nazarene U (OH)
Multnomah Bible Coll and Biblical Sem (OR)
Murray State U (KY)
Naropa U (CO)
Nazareth Coll of Rochester (NY)
Nebraska Methodist Coll (NE)
Nebraska Wesleyan U (NE)
Neumann Coll (PA)
Neumont U (UT)
New England Coll (NH)
New Jersey City U (NJ)
New Jersey Inst of Technology (NJ)
New Mexico Inst of Mining and Technology (NM)
New Saint Andrews Coll (ID)
The New School for General Studies (NY)
New York Inst of Technology (NY)
New York School of Interior Design (NY)
Niagara U (NY)
Nichols Coll (MA)
North Carolina Ag and Tech State U (NC)
North Carolina Wesleyan Coll (NC)
North Central Coll (IL)
North Dakota State U (ND)
Northeastern State U (OK)
Northern Arizona U (AZ)
Northern Illinois U (IL)
North Georgia Coll & State U (GA)
Northland Coll (WI)
Northwest Christian Coll (OR)
Northwestern Coll (IA)
Northwestern Coll (MN)
Northwestern Oklahoma State U (OK)
Northwestern State U of Louisiana (LA)
Northwest Missouri State U (MO)
Northwest Nazarene U (ID)
Northwood U (MI)
Northwood U, Florida Campus (FL)
Northwood U, Texas Campus (TX)
Norwich U (VT)
Nova Southeastern U (FL)
Nyack Coll (NY)
Oakland U (MI)
Ohio Dominican U (OH)
Ohio Northern U (OH)
Ohio U (OH)
Ohr Somayach/Joseph Tanenbaum Educational Center (NY)
Oklahoma City U (OK)
Oklahoma State U (OK)
Oral Roberts U (OK)
Oregon Inst of Technology (OR)
Oregon State U (OR)
Otis Coll of Art and Design (CA)
Otterbein Coll (OH)
Ouachita Baptist U (AR)
Pace U (NY)
Pacific Lutheran U (WA)
Pacific Union Coll (CA)
Pacific U (OR)
Palm Beach Atlantic U (FL)
Palmer Coll of Chiropractic (IA)
Park U (MO)
Patricia Stevens Coll (MO)
Peace Coll (NC)
Pennsylvania Coll of Art & Design (PA)
Pfeiffer U (NC)
Philadelphia Biblical U (PA)
Philadelphia U (PA)
Piedmont Coll (GA)
Pitzer Coll (CA)
Plymouth State U (NH)
Point Loma Nazarene U (CA)
Point Park U (PA)
Portland State U (OR)
Prairie View A&M U (TX)
Prescott Coll (AZ)
Purchase Coll, State U of New York (NY)
Purdue U (IN)
Purdue U Calumet (IN)
Queens U of Charlotte (NC)
Quincy U (IL)
Quinnipiac U (CT)
Radford U (VA)

Entrance Difficulty

Moderately Difficult

Ramapo Coll of New Jersey (NJ)
Randolph Coll (VA)
Randolph-Macon Coll (VA)
Redeemer U Coll (ON, Canada)
Regis Coll (MA)
Regis U (CO)
Research Coll of Nursing (MO)
Rhode Island Coll (RI)
Rider U (NJ)
Ringling Coll of Art and Design (FL)
Ripon Coll (WI)
Roanoke Coll (VA)
Robert Morris U (PA)
Roberts Wesleyan Coll (NY)
Rochester Inst of Technology (NY)
Rockford Coll (IL)
Rockhurst U (MO)
Rocky Mountain Coll of Art + Design (CO)
Roger Williams U (RI)
Roosevelt U (IL)
Rosemont Coll (PA)
Rowan U (NJ)
Russell Sage Coll (NY)
Rutgers, The State U of New Jersey, Camden (NJ)
Rutgers, The State U of New Jersey, Newark (NJ)
Rutgers, The State U of New Jersey, New Brunswick (NJ)
Sacred Heart Major Sem (MI)
Sacred Heart U (CT)
Saginaw Valley State U (MI)
St. Ambrose U (IA)
St. Andrews Presbyterian Coll (NC)
St. Charles Borromeo Sem, Overbrook (PA)
St. Cloud State U (MN)
St. Edward's U (TX)
Saint Francis U (PA)
St. Francis Xavier U (NS, Canada)
St. John Fisher Coll (NY)
St. John's Coll (MD)
Saint John's U (MN)
St. John's U (NY)
Saint Joseph's Coll (IN)
St. Joseph's Coll, New York (NY)
St. Joseph's Coll, Suffolk Campus (NY)
Saint Joseph's U (PA)
Saint Leo U (FL)
St. Louis Coll of Pharmacy (MO)
Saint Louis U (MO)
Saint Martin's U (WA)
Saint Mary-of-the-Woods Coll (IN)
Saint Mary's Coll (IN)
Saint Mary's Coll of California (CA)
St. Mary's U (TX)
Saint Mary's U of Minnesota (MN)
Saint Michael's Coll (VT)
St. Norbert Coll (WI)
St. Thomas Aquinas Coll (NY)
St. Thomas U (FL)
St. Thomas U (NB, Canada)
Saint Vincent Coll (PA)
Saint Xavier U (IL)
Salem Coll (NC)
Salisbury U (MD)
Salve Regina U (RI)
Samford U (AL)
Sam Houston State U (TX)
Samuel Merritt Coll (CA)
San Diego Christian Coll (CA)
San Diego State U (CA)
Santa Clara U (CA)
Savannah Coll of Art and Design (GA)
School of the Art Inst of Chicago (IL)
School of the Museum of Fine Arts, Boston (MA)
School of Visual Arts (NY)
Schreiner U (TX)
Seattle Pacific U (WA)
Seattle U (WA)
Seton Hill U (PA)
Shenandoah U (VA)
Shepherd U (WV)
Shimer Coll (IL)
Shippensburg U of Pennsylvania (PA)
Shorter Coll (GA)
Siena Coll (NY)
Siena Heights U (MI)
Simmons Coll (MA)
Simon Fraser U (BC, Canada)
Simpson Coll (IA)
Simpson U (CA)
Slippery Rock U of Pennsylvania (PA)
Soka U of America (CA)
Sonoma State U (CA)
South Dakota School of Mines and Technology (SD)
Southeastern Bible Coll (AL)
Southeastern Louisiana U (LA)
Southeastern Oklahoma State U (OK)
Southeast Missouri State U (MO)
Southern Adventist U (TN)
Southern Arkansas U–Magnolia (AR)
Southern California Sem (CA)
Southern Connecticut State U (CT)
Southern Illinois U Carbondale (IL)
Southern Illinois U Edwardsville (IL)
Southern Methodist U (TX)
Southern New Hampshire U (NH)
Southern Oregon U (OR)
Southern Polytechnic State U (GA)
Southern U and Ag and Mech Coll (LA)
Southern Utah U (UT)
Southwest Baptist U (MO)
Southwestern Coll (KS)
Spring Arbor U (MI)
Spring Hill Coll (AL)
State U of New York at Fredonia (NY)
State U of New York at Oswego (NY)
State U of New York Coll at Old Westbury (NY)
State U of New York Coll at Potsdam (NY)
State U of New York Coll of Environmental Science and Forestry (NY)
State U of New York Downstate Medical Center (NY)
State U of New York Inst of Technology (NY)
State U of New York Upstate Medical U (NY)
Stephen F. Austin State U (TX)
Stephens Coll (MO)
Sterling Coll (VT)
Stetson U (FL)
Suffolk U (MA)
Susquehanna U (PA)
Sweet Briar Coll (VA)
Tabor Coll (KS)
Talmudic Coll of Florida (FL)
Tarleton State U (TX)
Taylor U (IN)
Taylor U Fort Wayne (IN)
Tennessee Technological U (TN)
Texas A&M Intl U (TX)
Texas A&M U (TX)
Texas A&M U at Galveston (TX)
Texas A&M U–Commerce (TX)
Texas Christian U (TX)
Texas Lutheran U (TX)
Texas State U-San Marcos (TX)
Texas Tech U (TX)
Thiel Coll (PA)
Thomas More Coll (KY)
Toccoa Falls Coll (GA)
Towson U (MD)
Trent U (ON, Canada)
Trevecca Nazarene U (TN)
Trinity Christian Coll (IL)
Trinity Intl U (IL)
Tri-State U (IN)
Troy U (AL)
Truman State U (MO)
Tusculum Coll (TN)
Tuskegee U (AL)
Tyndale U Coll & Sem (ON, Canada)
Union Coll (KY)
Union Coll (NE)
Union U (TN)
Université de Sherbrooke (QC, Canada)
U at Albany, State U of New York (NY)
U at Buffalo, the State U of New York (NY)
The U of Akron (OH)
The U of Alabama (AL)
The U of Alabama at Birmingham (AL)
The U of Alabama in Huntsville (AL)
The U of Arizona (AZ)
U of Arkansas (AR)
U of Bridgeport (CT)
The U of British Columbia–Okanagan (BC, Canada)
U of California, Davis (CA)
U of Central Arkansas (AR)
U of Central Florida (FL)
U of Central Missouri (MO)
U of Charleston (WV)
U of Cincinnati (OH)
U of Colorado at Boulder (CO)
U of Colorado Denver (CO)
U of Connecticut (CT)
U of Dallas (TX)
U of Dayton (OH)
U of Delaware (DE)
U of Denver (CO)
U of Evansville (IN)
The U of Findlay (OH)
U of Georgia (GA)
U of Hartford (CT)
U of Hawaii at Manoa (HI)
U of Hawaii–West Oahu (HI)
U of Houston (TX)
U of Idaho (ID)
U of Illinois at Chicago (IL)
U of Illinois at Springfield (IL)
U of Indianapolis (IN)
The U of Iowa (IA)
U of Kansas (KS)
U of King's Coll (NS, Canada)
U of La Verne (CA)
U of Lethbridge (AB, Canada)
U of Louisiana at Lafayette (LA)
U of Louisville (KY)
U of Maine (ME)
U of Maine at Farmington (ME)
U of Maine at Fort Kent (ME)
U of Maine at Machias (ME)
U of Mary (ND)
U of Mary Hardin-Baylor (TX)
U of Maryland, Baltimore County (MD)
U of Maryland, Coll Park (MD)
U of Maryland Eastern Shore (MD)
U of Massachusetts Amherst (MA)
U of Massachusetts Boston (MA)
U of Massachusetts Dartmouth (MA)
U of Massachusetts Lowell (MA)
U of Memphis (TN)
U of Michigan–Dearborn (MI)
U of Michigan–Flint (MI)
U of Minnesota, Crookston (MN)
U of Minnesota, Duluth (MN)
U of Minnesota, Twin Cities Campus (MN)
U of Mississippi (MS)
U of Missouri–Columbia (MO)
U of Missouri–Kansas City (MO)
U of Missouri–St. Louis (MO)
The U of Montana (MT)
U of Montevallo (AL)
U of Nebraska at Kearney (NE)
U of Nebraska–Lincoln (NE)
U of Nebraska Medical Center (NE)
U of Nevada, Las Vegas (NV)
U of Nevada, Reno (NV)
U of New Brunswick Fredericton (NB, Canada)
U of New England (ME)
U of New Hampshire (NH)
U of New Hampshire at Manchester (NH)
U of New Haven (CT)
U of New Mexico (NM)
U of New Orleans (LA)
The U of North Carolina at Asheville (NC)
The U of North Carolina at Charlotte (NC)
The U of North Carolina at Greensboro (NC)
The U of North Carolina at Pembroke (NC)
The U of North Carolina Wilmington (NC)
U of Northern Colorado (CO)
U of Northern Iowa (IA)
U of North Texas (TX)
U of Oklahoma (OK)
U of Oregon (OR)
U of Ottawa (ON, Canada)
U of Pittsburgh (PA)
U of Pittsburgh at Johnstown (PA)
U of Portland (OR)
U of Prince Edward Island (PE, Canada)
U of Puerto Rico at Humacao (PR)
U of Puerto Rico at Utuado (PR)
U of Puerto Rico, Cayey U Coll (PR)
U of Puget Sound (WA)
U of Redlands (CA)
U of Rhode Island (RI)
U of St. Francis (IL)
U of Saint Francis (IN)
U of Saint Mary (KS)
U of St. Thomas (MN)
U of St. Thomas (TX)
U of Science and Arts of Oklahoma (OK)
The U of Scranton (PA)
U of Sioux Falls (SD)
U of South Alabama (AL)
U of South Carolina (SC)
U of South Carolina Aiken (SC)
U of South Carolina Upstate (SC)
The U of South Dakota (SD)
U of Southern Indiana (IN)
U of Southern Maine (ME)
U of Southern Mississippi (MS)
U of South Florida (FL)
The U of Tennessee (TN)
The U of Tennessee at Chattanooga (TN)
The U of Tennessee at Martin (TN)
The U of Texas at Arlington (TX)
The U of Texas at San Antonio (TX)

MAJORS AND MORE

The U of Texas at Tyler (TX)
The U of Texas of the Permian Basin (TX)
The U of Texas Southwestern Medical Center at Dallas (TX)
U of the Incarnate Word (TX)
U of the Ozarks (AR)
U of the Pacific (CA)
U of the Sacred Heart (PR)
U of the Sciences in Philadelphia (PA)
U of Utah (UT)
U of Vermont (VT)
U of Victoria (BC, Canada)
The U of Virginia's Coll at Wise (VA)
U of Washington, Bothell (WA)
U of West Florida (FL)
U of Windsor (ON, Canada)
The U of Winnipeg (MB, Canada)
U of Wisconsin–Eau Claire (WI)
U of Wisconsin–Green Bay (WI)
U of Wisconsin–La Crosse (WI)
U of Wisconsin–Milwaukee (WI)
U of Wisconsin–Oshkosh (WI)
U of Wisconsin–Parkside (WI)
U of Wisconsin–Platteville (WI)
U of Wisconsin–Stevens Point (WI)
U of Wisconsin–Superior (WI)
U of Wisconsin–Whitewater (WI)
U of Wyoming (WY)
Utah State U (UT)
Utica Coll (NY)
Valdosta State U (GA)
Valparaiso U (IN)
VanderCook Coll of Music (IL)
Vanguard U of Southern California (CA)
Vennard Coll (IA)
Vermont Tech Coll (VT)
Villa Julie Coll (MD)
Virginia Military Inst (VA)
Virginia Polytechnic Inst and State U (VA)
Virginia Wesleyan Coll (VA)
Viterbo U (WI)
Voorhees Coll (SC)
Wabash Coll (IN)
Wagner Coll (NY)
Walla Walla U (WA)
Walsh U (OH)
Warner Pacific Coll (OR)
Warren Wilson Coll (NC)
Wartburg Coll (IA)
Washington Bible Coll (MD)
Washington Coll (MD)
Washington State U (WA)
Watkins Coll of Art and Design (TN)
Waynesburg U (PA)
Wayne State U (MI)
Webber Intl U (FL)
Webster U (MO)
Wells Coll (NY)
Wentworth Inst of Technology (MA)
Wesleyan Coll (GA)
Wesley Coll (DE)
West Chester U of Pennsylvania (PA)
Western Carolina U (NC)
Western Connecticut State U (CT)
Western Illinois U (IL)
Western Intl U (AZ)
Western Kentucky U (KY)
Western Michigan U (MI)
Western New England Coll (MA)
Western State Coll of Colorado (CO)
Western Washington U (WA)
Westfield State Coll (MA)
Westminster Coll (MO)
Westminster Coll (UT)
Westmont Coll (CA)
West Suburban Coll of Nursing (IL)
West Texas A&M U (TX)
West Virginia U (WV)
West Virginia Wesleyan Coll (WV)
Wheeling Jesuit U (WV)
Wheelock Coll (MA)
Whittier Coll (CA)
Widener U (PA)
Wilfrid Laurier U (ON, Canada)
Wilkes U (PA)
William Jewell Coll (MO)
William Paterson U of New Jersey (NJ)
William Woods U (MO)
Wilmington Coll (OH)
Wilson Coll (PA)
Wingate U (NC)
Winona State U (MN)
Winthrop U (SC)
Wittenberg U (OH)
Woodbury U (CA)
Worcester State Coll (MA)
Xavier U (OH)
Xavier U of Louisiana (LA)
York Coll (NE)
York Coll of Pennsylvania (PA)
York Coll of the City U of New York (NY)
York U (ON, Canada)

Minimally Difficult

Most freshmen were not in the top half of their high school class and scored somewhat below 1010 on the SAT or below 19 on the ACT; up to 95 percent of the applicants were accepted.

Alabama Ag and Mech U (AL)
Alabama State U (AL)
Alcorn State U (MS)
Amberton U (TX)
American Coll of Thessaloniki (Greece)
American InterContinental U (CA)
American InterContinental U (FL)
American InterContinental U (TX)
American InterContinental U Buckhead Campus (GA)
American InterContinental U Dunwoody Campus (GA)
American InterContinental U-London (United Kingdom)
American InterContinental U Online (IL)
Anderson U (SC)
Anna Maria Coll (MA)
Arkansas State U (AR)
Armstrong Atlantic State U (GA)
The Art Inst of California–San Diego (CA)
The Art Inst of Fort Lauderdale (FL)
The Art Inst of Pittsburgh (PA)
The Art Insts Intl Minnesota (MN)
Ashford U (IA)
Augusta State U (GA)
Avila U (MO)
Baptist Bible Coll of Pennsylvania (PA)
Barclay Coll (KS)
Barton Coll (NC)
Beacon Coll (FL)
Becker Coll (MA)
Bethany U (CA)
Bethel Coll (TN)
Bethune-Cookman U (FL)
Bluefield Coll (VA)
Bob Jones U (SC)
Boise State U (ID)
Brevard Coll (NC)
Brewton-Parker Coll (GA)
Bryn Athyn Coll of the New Church (PA)
California Baptist U (CA)
California State U, Fresno (CA)
California State U, Monterey Bay (CA)
Cambridge Coll (MA)
Cameron U (OK)
Central Christian Coll of Kansas (KS)
Central Pennsylvania Coll (PA)
Central State U (OH)
Chaminade U of Honolulu (HI)
Cheyney U of Pennsylvania (PA)
Chicago State U (IL)
Claflin U (SC)
Clarion U of Pennsylvania (PA)
Clayton State U (GA)
Clearwater Christian Coll (FL)
Cleveland Chiropractic Coll-Los Angeles Campus (CA)
Coll of St. Joseph (VT)
Coll of Saint Mary (NE)
Colorado Tech U—Colorado Springs (CO)
Colorado Tech U—Denver (CO)
Colorado Tech U—North Kansas City (MO)
Colorado Tech U—Online (CO)
Colorado Tech U—Sioux Falls (SD)
Columbus State U (GA)
Concordia U, St. Paul (MN)
Concord U (WV)
Cornerstone U (MI)
Crown Coll (MN)
Dakota State U (SD)
Dallas Christian Coll (TX)
Davenport U, Dearborn (MI)
Davenport U, Grand Rapids (MI)
Davis Coll (NY)
Delta State U (MS)
DeVry Coll of New York (NY)
DeVry U, Phoenix (AZ)
DeVry U, Fremont (CA)
DeVry U, Long Beach (CA)
DeVry U, Pomona (CA)
DeVry U, Miramar (FL)
DeVry U, Orlando (FL)
DeVry U, Alpharetta (GA)
DeVry U, Decatur (GA)
DeVry U, Addison (IL)
DeVry U, Chicago (IL)
DeVry U, Tinley Park (IL)
DeVry U, Indianapolis (IN)
DeVry U (MD)
DeVry U, Kansas City (MO)
DeVry U (NV)
DeVry U (NJ)
DeVry U, Charlotte (NC)
DeVry U, Columbus (OH)
DeVry U (OR)
DeVry U, Fort Washington (PA)
DeVry U, Irving (TX)
DeVry U, Arlington (VA)
DeVry U, Federal Way (WA)
DeVry U, Milwaukee (WI)
East Central U (OK)
Eastern New Mexico U (NM)
East-West U (IL)
Electronic Data Processing Coll of Puerto Rico (PR)
Embry-Riddle Aeronautical U Worldwide (FL)
Emmanuel Coll (GA)
Eugene Bible Coll (OR)
Everest U, Tampa (FL)
Everest U, Tampa (FL)
Fairmont State U (WV)
Faith Baptist Bible Coll and Theological Sem (IA)
Faulkner U (AL)
Fayetteville State U (NC)
Ferris State U (MI)
Ferrum Coll (VA)
Finlandia U (MI)
Global Coll of Long Island U (NY)
Grace Bible Coll (MI)
Grand View Coll (IA)
Harrisburg U of Science and Technology (PA)
Hebrew Coll (MA)
Hellenic Coll (MA)
Heritage Bible Coll (NC)
Hilbert Coll (NY)
Hodges U (FL)
Horizon Coll & Sem (SK, Canada)
Hussian School of Art (PA)
Idaho State U (ID)
Indiana U Kokomo (IN)
Indiana U Northwest (IN)
Indiana U–Purdue U Fort Wayne (IN)
Indiana U Southeast (IN)
Intl Acad of Design & Technology (IL)
Jackson State U (MS)
Jacksonville State U (AL)
Jamestown Coll (ND)
Jarvis Christian Coll (TX)
John Wesley Coll (NC)
Keiser U, Fort Lauderdale (FL)
Kentucky State U (KY)
Keystone Coll (PA)
La Roche Coll (PA)
Laurentian U (ON, Canada)
Lees-McRae Coll (NC)
Lee U (TN)
LeMoyne-Owen Coll (TN)
Lewis-Clark State Coll (ID)
Liberty U (VA)
Life U (GA)
Lincoln U (CA)
Lindsey Wilson Coll (KY)
Livingstone Coll (NC)
Mercy Coll (NY)
Mesa State Coll (CO)
Metropolitan State U (MN)
Michigan Jewish Inst (MI)
MidAmerica Nazarene U (KS)
Mid-Continent U (KY)
Midway Coll (KY)
Midwestern State U (TX)
Minot State U (ND)
Mississippi Valley State U (MS)
Missouri Valley Coll (MO)
Mitchell Coll (CT)
Morehead State U (KY)
Mount Aloysius Coll (PA)
Mount Marty Coll (SD)
Mount Olive Coll (NC)
National-Louis U (IL)
National U (CA)
Nebraska Christian Coll (NE)
The New England Inst of Art (MA)
New England School of Communications (ME)
Newman U (KS)
New Mexico Highlands U (NM)
North Carolina Central U (NC)
Northcentral U (AZ)
Northeastern Illinois U (IL)

Entrance Difficulty

Minimally Difficult

Northern Michigan U (MI)
Northern State U (SD)
North Greenville U (SC)
Notre Dame de Namur U (CA)
Nova Scotia Ag Coll (NS, Canada)
Oak Hills Christian Coll (MN)
Oakland City U (IN)
Oakwood Coll (AL)
Ohio Valley U (WV)
Oklahoma Wesleyan U (OK)
Our Lady of the Lake Coll (LA)
Pacific States U (CA)
Paier Coll of Art, Inc. (CT)
Paine Coll (GA)
Paul Smith's Coll (NY)
Pittsburg State U (KS)
Polytechnic U of Puerto Rico (PR)
Pontifical Coll Josephinum (OH)
Purdue U North Central (IN)
Rabbinical Coll of America (NJ)
Regent U (VA)
Roanoke Bible Coll (NC)
Robert Morris Coll (IL)
Rochester Coll (MI)
Sage Coll of Albany (NY)
St. Gregory's U, Shawnee (OK)
St. Louis Christian Coll (MO)
Salem Intl U (WV)
Salem State Coll (MA)
Schiller Intl U (FL)
Schiller Intl U (France)
Schiller Intl U (United Kingdom)
Shaw U (NC)
South Carolina State U (SC)
South Dakota State U (SD)
Southeastern U (FL)
Southern Vermont Coll (VT)
Southern Wesleyan U (SC)
Southwestern Adventist U (TX)
Southwestern Coll (AZ)
Southwestern Oklahoma State U (OK)
Southwest Minnesota State U (MN)
State U of New York Coll of Agriculture and Technology at Cobleskill (NY)
State U of New York Empire State Coll (NY)
Steinbach Bible Coll (MB, Canada)
Sterling Coll (KS)
Stillman Coll (AL)
Sullivan U (KY)
Taylor U Coll and Sem (AB, Canada)
Tennessee State U (TN)
Tennessee Wesleyan Coll (TN)
Texas Woman's U (TX)
Thomas Coll (ME)
Tiffin U (OH)
Tougaloo Coll (MS)
Trinity Coll of Florida (FL)
Trinity Lutheran Coll (WA)
Truett-McConnell Coll (GA)
TUI U (CA)
U of Alaska Fairbanks (AK)
U of Arkansas at Fort Smith (AR)
U of Baltimore (MD)
U of Central Oklahoma (OK)
U of Houston–Clear Lake (TX)
U of Houston–Victoria (TX)
The U of Montana–Western (MT)
U of Nebraska at Omaha (NE)
U of North Alabama (AL)
U of North Dakota (ND)
U of Pittsburgh at Bradford (PA)
U of Regina (SK, Canada)
U of South Carolina Beaufort (SC)
The U of Texas at El Paso (TX)
U of the Virgin Islands (VI)
U of Washington, Tacoma (WA)
U of West Georgia (GA)
Ursuline Coll (OH)
Virginia Intermont Coll (VA)
Virginia State U (VA)
Wayland Baptist U (TX)
West Liberty State Coll (WV)
Wiley Coll (TX)
Wright State U (OH)

Noncompetitive

Virtually all applicants were accepted regardless of high school rank or test scores.

Acad of Art U (CA)
American Baptist Coll of American Baptist Theological Sem (TN)
American Public U System (WV)
Antioch U McGregor (OH)
Appalachian Bible Coll (WV)
Arlington Baptist Coll (TX)
The Art Inst of California–Los Angeles (CA)
The Art Inst of Charleston (SC)
The Art Inst of Dallas (TX)
Athabasca U (AB, Canada)
Athens State U (AL)
Baker Coll of Auburn Hills (MI)
Baker Coll of Cadillac (MI)
Baker Coll of Clinton Township (MI)
Baker Coll of Flint (MI)
Baker Coll of Jackson (MI)
Baker Coll of Muskegon (MI)
Baker Coll of Owosso (MI)
Baker Coll of Port Huron (MI)
The Baptist Coll of Florida (FL)
Beulah Heights U (GA)
Bluefield State Coll (WV)
Boston Architectural Coll (MA)
California Christian Coll (CA)
Calumet Coll of Saint Joseph (IN)
Cascade Coll (OR)
Charter Oak State Coll (CT)
City U of Seattle (WA)
Cleveland Chiropractic Coll-Kansas City Campus (KS)
Collège Dominicain de Philosophie et de Théologie (ON, Canada)
Coll of Biblical Studies–Houston (TX)
Coll of Emmanuel and St. Chad (SK, Canada)
Columbia Coll, Caguas (PR)
Columbia Coll Chicago (IL)
Columbia Southern U (AL)
Crossroads Coll (MN)
DeVry U, Westminster (CO)
Dixie State Coll of Utah (UT)
Dominican Coll (NY)
Eastern Kentucky U (KY)
Emporia State U (KS)
Excelsior Coll (NY)
Florida Memorial U (FL)
Free Will Baptist Bible Coll (TN)
Full Sail U (FL)
Glenville State Coll (WV)
Grambling State U (LA)
Granite State Coll (NH)
Grantham U (MO)
Harris-Stowe State U (MO)
Heritage Baptist Coll and Heritage Theological Sem (ON, Canada)
Heritage Christian U (AL)
Hillsdale Free Will Baptist Coll (OK)
Holy Apostles Coll and Sem (CT)
Holy Trinity Orthodox Sem (NY)
Huntington Coll of Health Sciences (TN)
Intl Acad of Design & Technology (FL)
John F. Kennedy U (CA)
Jones Coll, Jacksonville (FL)
Kansas State U (KS)
LA Coll Intl (CA)
Lexington Coll (IL)
Lincoln U (MO)
Magnolia Bible Coll (MS)
Maranatha Baptist Bible Coll (WI)
Martin U (IN)
Marylhurst U (OR)
Master's Coll and Sem (ON, Canada)
Mayville State U (ND)
Medgar Evers Coll of the City U of New York (NY)
Miami U Hamilton (OH)
Midwives Coll of Utah (UT)
Miles Coll (AL)
Morris Coll (SC)
Mountain State U (WV)
National American U, Rapid City (SD)
National American U–Sioux Falls Branch (SD)
Nazarene Bible Coll (CO)
New World School of the Arts (FL)
Nicholls State U (LA)
Ohio U–Zanesville (OH)
Oklahoma Christian U (OK)
Oklahoma Panhandle State U (OK)
Ozark Christian Coll (MO)
Peirce Coll (PA)
Pennsylvania Coll of Technology (PA)
Peru State Coll (NE)
Pikeville Coll (KY)
Pillsbury Baptist Bible Coll (MN)
Presentation Coll (SD)
Remington Coll–Mobile Campus (AL)
Rogers State U (OK)
Shasta Bible Coll (CA)
Shawnee State U (OH)
Texas Coll (TX)
Texas Southern U (TX)
Thomas Edison State Coll (NJ)
Thomas U (GA)
Université du Québec en Outaouais (QC, Canada)
U of Alaska Southeast (AK)
U of Arkansas at Monticello (AR)
U of Great Falls (MT)
U of Guam (GU)
U of Houston–Downtown (TX)
U of Louisiana at Monroe (LA)
The U of Maine at Augusta (ME)
U of Maryland U Coll (MD)
U of Rio Grande (OH)
The U of Texas at Brownsville (TX)
The U of Texas–Pan American (TX)
U of the District of Columbia (DC)
The U of Toledo (OH)
Utah Valley State Coll (UT)
Valley City State U (ND)
Virginia U of Lynchburg (VA)
Washburn U (KS)
Wayne State Coll (NE)
Weber State U (UT)
Western New Mexico U (NM)
Wichita State U (KS)
William Jessup U (CA)
Williamson Christian Coll (TN)
Wilmington U (DE)
Woodbury Coll (VT)
World Coll (VA)
Youngstown State U (OH)

Cost Ranges

Less than $2000

Colleges with No Room and Board or with Room Only
Alice Lloyd Coll (KY)
U of Puerto Rico at Humacao (PR)
U of Puerto Rico, Cayey U Coll (PR)

Colleges with Room and Board
The Colburn School Conservatory of Music (CA)

$2000–$3999

Colleges with No Room and Board or with Room Only
Athens State U (AL)
Bluefield State Coll (WV)
Clayton State U (GA)
Inter American U of Puerto Rico, Aguadilla Campus (PR)
New World School of the Arts (FL)
U of Hawaii–West Oahu (HI)
The U of Texas Medical Branch (TX)
The U of Texas Southwestern Medical Center at Dallas (TX)
U of the District of Columbia (DC)
World Coll (VA)

Colleges with Room and Board
Virginia U of Lynchburg (VA)

$4000–$5999

Colleges with No Room and Board or with Room Only
Bernard M. Baruch Coll of the City U of New York (NY)
Coll of Biblical Studies–Houston (TX)
Coll of Staten Island of the City U of New York (NY)
Columbia Coll, Yauco (PR)
Columbia Southern U (AL)
Concordia U (QC, Canada) **(room only)**
Electronic Data Processing Coll of Puerto Rico (PR)
Embry-Riddle Aeronautical U Worldwide (FL)
Granite State Coll (NH)
Indiana U East (IN)
Indiana U Kokomo (IN)
Indiana U Northwest (IN)
Indiana U South Bend (IN)
Indiana U Southeast (IN)
Inter American U of Puerto Rico, Bayamón Campus (PR)
Inter American U of Puerto Rico, Fajardo Campus (PR)
Lehman Coll of the City U of New York (NY)
Logan U-Coll of Chiropractic (MO)
Metropolitan State U (MN)
Miami U Hamilton (OH)
Queens Coll of the City U of New York (NY)
Southern Utah U (UT) **(room only)**
State U of New York Empire State Coll (NY)
Thomas Edison State Coll (NJ)
U of Guam (GU)
U of Houston–Downtown (TX)
U of Houston–Victoria (TX)
The U of Maine at Augusta (ME)
U of Maine at Machias (ME)
U of Maryland U Coll (MD)
U of Nebraska Medical Center (NE)
U of Oklahoma Health Sciences Center (OK)
York Coll of the City U of New York (NY)

Colleges with Room and Board
Holy Trinity Orthodox Sem (NY)
Medgar Evers Coll of the City U of New York (NY)
New Mexico Highlands U (NM)

$6000–$7999

Colleges with No Room and Board or with Room Only
Amberton U (TX)
American Public U System (WV)
Baker Coll of Allen Park (MI)
Baker Coll of Auburn Hills (MI)
Baker Coll of Cadillac (MI)
Baker Coll of Clinton Township (MI)
Baker Coll of Jackson (MI)
Baker Coll of Port Huron (MI)
Cleveland Chiropractic Coll-Kansas City Campus (KS)
Cleveland Chiropractic Coll-Los Angeles Campus (CA)
Coll of Emmanuel and St. Chad (SK, Canada)
Columbia Coll, Caguas (PR)
Grantham U (MO)
Holy Apostles Coll and Sem (CT)
Indiana State U (IN)
Iowa State U of Science and Technology (IA)
Jones Coll, Jacksonville (FL)
Jones Coll, Miami (FL)
Martin U (IN)
Medical Coll of Georgia (GA) **(room only)**
North Carolina Ag and Tech State U (NC) **(room only)**
Northeastern Illinois U (IL)
Our Lady of the Lake Coll (LA)
Palmer Coll of Chiropractic (IA)
Purdue U North Central (IN)
Southern California Sem (CA)
U of Baltimore (MD)
U of Michigan–Dearborn (MI)
U of Michigan–Flint (MI)
The U of Texas at Brownsville (TX) **(room only)**
U of the Sacred Heart (PR) **(room only)**
U of Washington, Bothell (WA)

Colleges with Room and Board
Berea Coll (KY)
Cameron U (OK)
Dixie State Coll of Utah (UT)
East Central U (OK)
Heritage Bible Coll (NC)
Inter American U of Puerto Rico, San Germán Campus (PR)
McNeese State U (LA)
Northwestern Oklahoma State U (OK)
Oklahoma Panhandle State U (OK)
Southwestern Oklahoma State U (OK)
U of Arkansas at Monticello (AR)
U of Louisiana at Lafayette (LA)
U of Louisiana at Monroe (LA)

$8000–$9999

Colleges with No Room and Board or with Room Only
Armstrong Atlantic State U (GA) **(room only)**
Auburn U (AL) **(room only)**
Baker Coll of Flint (MI) **(room only)**
Baker Coll of Muskegon (MI) **(room only)**
Baker Coll of Owosso (MI) **(room only)**
Boricua Coll (NY)
Cabarrus Coll of Health Sciences (NC)
California State U, San Marcos (CA) **(room only)**
Hunter Coll of the City U of New York (NY) **(room only)**
Kennesaw State U (GA) **(room only)**
Lincoln U (CA)
Magnolia Bible Coll (MS) **(room only)**
National U (CA)
Nazarene Bible Coll (CO)
New Saint Andrews Coll (ID)
Northcentral U (AZ)
Pacific States U (CA)
Shasta Bible Coll (CA) **(room only)**
TUI U (CA)
U of Massachusetts Boston (MA)
U of New Hampshire at Manchester (NH)
U of Wisconsin–Madison (WI)
Williamson Christian Coll (TN)
Wilmington U (DE)

Colleges with Room and Board
Adams State Coll (CO)
Alabama Ag and Mech U (AL)
Alabama State U (AL)
Alcorn State U (MS)
American Baptist Coll of American Baptist Theological Sem (TN)
Angelo State U (TX)
Auburn U Montgomery (AL)
Columbus State U (GA)
Delta State U (MS)
Eastern New Mexico U (NM)
Emporia State U (KS)
Fayetteville State U (NC)
Georgia Southwestern State U (GA)
Glenville State Coll (WV)
Grambling State U (LA)
Henderson State U (AR)
Idaho State U (ID)
Jacksonville State U (AL)
Lewis-Clark State Coll (ID)
Louisiana State U Health Sciences Center (LA)
Mayville State U (ND)
Midwestern State U (TX)
Minot State U (ND)
Mississippi U for Women (MS)
Mississippi Valley State U (MS)
New Mexico Inst of Mining and Technology (NM)
Nicholls State U (LA)
North Carolina Central U (NC)
Northeastern State U (OK)
Northern State U (SD)
North Georgia Coll & State U (GA)
Northwestern State U of Louisiana (LA)
Pittsburg State U (KS)
Southeastern Louisiana U (LA)
Southeastern Oklahoma State U (OK)
Southern Arkansas U–Magnolia (AR)
Southern Baptist Theological Sem (KY)
Southern Polytechnic State U (GA)
Troy U (AL)
The U of Montana–Western (MT)
U of New Orleans (LA)
U of North Alabama (AL)
The U of North Carolina at Pembroke (NC)
U of Science and Arts of Oklahoma (OK)
U of South Alabama (AL)
U of Southern Mississippi (MS)
The U of Tennessee at Martin (TN)
The U of Texas of the Permian Basin (TX)
The U of Texas–Pan American (TX)
U of West Georgia (GA)
Utah State U (UT)
Utah Valley State Coll (UT)
Valley City State U (ND)
Wayne State Coll (NE)
Webb Inst (NY)
Weber State U (UT)
Western New Mexico U (NM)

$10,000–$11,999

Colleges with No Room and Board or with Room Only
Baptist Coll of Health Sciences (TN) **(room only)**
Boston Architectural Coll (MA)
Calumet Coll of Saint Joseph (IN)
Cambridge Coll (MA)
Hussian School of Art (PA)

MAJORS AND MORE

Indiana U–Purdue U Fort Wayne (IN) **(room only)**
Medcenter One Coll of Nursing (ND)
Michigan Jewish Inst (MI)
Salem State Coll (MA) **(room only)**
Southeastern Bible Coll (AL) **(room only)**
U of Management and Technology (VA)
U of South Carolina Beaufort (SC) **(room only)**
The U of Texas at El Paso (TX) **(room only)**
U of Wisconsin–Milwaukee (WI) **(room only)**
Walden U (MN)

Colleges with Room and Board
Appalachian State U (NC)
Arkansas State U (AR)
Arlington Baptist Coll (TX)
Austin Peay State U (TN)
The Baptist Coll of Florida (FL)
Boise State U (ID)
California Christian Coll (CA)
California State Polytechnic U, Pomona (CA)
California State U, Fresno (CA)
California State U, Los Angeles (CA)
California State U, San Bernardino (CA)
California State U, Stanislaus (CA)
Colorado State U-Pueblo (CO)
Concord U (WV)
Dakota State U (SD)
East Carolina U (NC)
Eastern Kentucky U (KY)
East Tennessee State U (TN)
Fairmont State U (WV)
Florida Ag and Mech U (FL)
Florida Atlantic U (FL)
Florida State U (FL)
Georgia Southern U (GA)
Heritage Baptist Coll and Heritage Theological Sem (ON, Canada)
Horizon Coll & Sem (SK, Canada)
Indiana U–Purdue U Indianapolis (IN)
Jackson State U (MS)
Kentucky State U (KY)
Lincoln U (MO)
Louisiana State U and Ag and Mech Coll (LA)
Marshall U (WV)
Mesa State Coll (CO)
Middle Tennessee State U (TN)
Minnesota State U Mankato (MN)
Mississippi State U (MS)
Missouri Southern State U (MO)
Missouri State U (MO)
Montana State U–Billings (MT)
Montana Tech of The U of Montana (MT)
Morehead State U (KY)
Murray State U (KY)
New Coll of Florida (FL)
North Carolina School of the Arts (NC)
North Dakota State U (ND)
Northern Arizona U (AZ)
Oklahoma State U (OK)
Pacific Islands Bible Coll (GU)
Purdue U Calumet (IN)
Rogers State U (OK)
St. Cloud State U (MN)
Sam Houston State U (TX)
Shepherd U (WV)
South Dakota School of Mines and Technology (SD)
South Dakota State U (SD)
Southeast Missouri State U (MO)
Southern U and Ag and Mech Coll (LA)
Steinbach Bible Coll (MB, Canada)
Taylor U Coll and Sem (AB, Canada)
Tennessee State U (TN)
Tennessee Technological U (TN)
Texas A&M Intl U (TX)
Texas A&M U at Galveston (TX)
Texas A&M U–Commerce (TX)
The U of Alabama (AL)
The U of Alabama at Birmingham (AL)
The U of Alabama in Huntsville (AL)
U of Alaska Fairbanks (AK)
U of Alaska Southeast (AK)
U of Arkansas at Pine Bluff (AR)
U of Central Arkansas (AR)
U of Central Florida (FL)
U of Central Oklahoma (OK)
U of Florida (FL)
U of Idaho (ID)
U of Lethbridge (AB, Canada)
U of Memphis (TN)
U of Mississippi (MS)
The U of Montana (MT)
U of Montevallo (AL)
U of Nebraska at Kearney (NE)
U of New Mexico (NM)
The U of North Carolina at Asheville (NC)
The U of North Carolina at Charlotte (NC)
The U of North Carolina at Greensboro (NC)
The U of North Carolina Wilmington (NC)
U of North Dakota (ND)
U of Northern Colorado (CO)
U of North Florida (FL)
U of North Texas (TX)
U of Oklahoma (OK)
The U of South Dakota (SD)
U of Southern Indiana (IN)
U of South Florida (FL)
U of the Virgin Islands (VI)
U of Utah (UT)
U of West Florida (FL)
U of Wisconsin–Eau Claire (WI)
U of Wisconsin–Green Bay (WI)
U of Wisconsin–La Crosse (WI)
U of Wisconsin–Oshkosh (WI)
U of Wisconsin–Parkside (WI)
U of Wisconsin–Platteville (WI)
U of Wisconsin–Stevens Point (WI)
U of Wisconsin–Superior (WI)
U of Wisconsin–Whitewater (WI)
U of Wyoming (WY)
Valdosta State U (GA)
Washburn U (KS)
Western Carolina U (NC)
Western State Coll of Colorado (CO)
West Liberty State Coll (WV)
West Virginia U (WV)
Wichita State U (KS)

$12,000–$13,999

Colleges with No Room and Board or with Room Only
City Coll of the City U of New York (NY) **(room only)**
City U of Seattle (WA)
DeVry U, Phoenix (AZ)
DeVry U, Long Beach (CA)
DeVry U, Pomona (CA)
DeVry U, Sherman Oaks (CA)
DeVry U, Westminster (CO)
DeVry U, Miramar (FL)
DeVry U, Orlando (FL)
DeVry U, Alpharetta (GA)
DeVry U, Decatur (GA)
DeVry U, Addison (IL)
DeVry U, Chicago (IL)
DeVry U, Tinley Park (IL)
DeVry U, Indianapolis (IN)
DeVry U, Edina (MN)
DeVry U, Kansas City (MO)
DeVry U (NV)
DeVry U, Charlotte (NC)
DeVry U, Columbus (OH)
DeVry U (OK)
DeVry U (OR)
DeVry U (TN)
DeVry U, Houston (TX)
DeVry U, Irving (TX)
DeVry U (UT)
DeVry U, Milwaukee (WI)
East-West U (IL)
Golden Gate U (CA)
John F. Kennedy U (CA)
John Wesley Coll (NC) **(room only)**
Mercy Coll of Health Sciences (IA)
Ohr Somayach/Joseph Tanenbaum Educational Center (NY)
Paier Coll of Art, Inc. (CT)
Peirce Coll (PA)
Regent U (VA)
Salem Intl U (WV)
Thomas U (GA) **(room only)**
U of Houston–Clear Lake (TX) **(room only)**

Colleges with Room and Board
Arizona State U at the West campus (AZ)
Augusta State U (GA)
Bemidji State U (MN)
Bloomsburg U of Pennsylvania (PA)
Bridgewater State Coll (MA)
Buffalo State Coll, State U of New York (NY)
California Maritime Acad (CA)
California Polytechnic State U, San Luis Obispo (CA)
California State U, Dominguez Hills (CA)
California State U, Monterey Bay (CA)
California State U, Sacramento (CA)
Central State U (OH)
Central Washington U (WA)
Cheyney U of Pennsylvania (PA)
Clarion U of Pennsylvania (PA)
Colorado State U (CO)
East Stroudsburg U of Pennsylvania (PA)
Edinboro U of Pennsylvania (PA)
The Evergreen State Coll (WA)
Fitchburg State Coll (MA)
Florida Gulf Coast U (FL)
Fort Lewis Coll (CO)
Framingham State Coll (MA)
Francis Marion U (SC)
Frostburg State U (MD)
George Mason U (VA)
Georgia Coll & State U (GA)
Georgia Inst of Technology (GA)
Goddard Coll (VT)
Harris-Stowe State U (MO)
Heritage Christian U (AL)
Hillsdale Free Will Baptist Coll (OK)
Indiana U of Pennsylvania (PA)
James Madison U (VA)
Jarvis Christian Coll (TX)
Johnson Bible Coll (TN)
Kansas State U (KS)
Kettering Coll of Medical Arts (OH)
The King's U Coll (AB, Canada)
Kutztown U of Pennsylvania (PA)
Lakehead U (ON, Canada)
Lock Haven U of Pennsylvania (PA)
Mansfield U of Pennsylvania (PA)
Massachusetts Coll of Liberal Arts (MA)
Miles Coll (AL)
Millersville U of Pennsylvania (PA)
Montana State U (MT)
Morgan State U (MD)
Morris Coll (SC)
Mountain State U (WV)
North Carolina State U (NC)
Northern Michigan U (MI)
Northwest Missouri State U (MO)
Nova Scotia Ag Coll (NS, Canada)
Ohio U–Zanesville (OH)
Oregon State U (OR)
Ozark Christian Coll (MO)
Park U (MO)
Prairie View A&M U (TX)
Radford U (VA)
Rhode Island Coll (RI)
Saginaw Valley State U (MI)
St. Louis Christian Coll (MO)
Shawnee State U (OH)
Shippensburg U of Pennsylvania (PA)
Siena Heights U (MI)
Sonoma State U (CA)
Southern Illinois U Edwardsville (IL)
Southern Oregon U (OR)
Southwest Minnesota State U (MN)
State U of New York at Fredonia (NY)
State U of New York at New Paltz (NY)
State U of New York at Plattsburgh (NY)
State U of New York Coll at Old Westbury (NY)
State U of New York Coll at Oneonta (NY)
State U of New York Coll at Potsdam (NY)
State U of New York Inst of Technology (NY)
Stephen F. Austin State U (TX)
Talmudic Coll of Florida (FL)
Tarleton State U (TX)
Texas Southern U (TX)
Texas State U-San Marcos (TX)
Texas Woman's U (TX)
Truman State U (MO)
The U of Arizona (AZ)
U of Arkansas (AR)
U of Central Missouri (MO)
U of Georgia (GA)
U of Hawaii at Manoa (HI)
U of Kansas (KS)
U of Louisville (KY)
U of Maine at Fort Kent (ME)
U of Maryland Eastern Shore (MD)
U of Nebraska at Omaha (NE)
U of Nebraska–Lincoln (NE)
The U of North Carolina at Chapel Hill (NC)
U of Northern Iowa (IA)
U of Oregon (OR)
U of South Carolina Aiken (SC)
U of South Carolina Upstate (SC)
The U of Tennessee (TN)
The U of Tennessee at Chattanooga (TN)
The U of Texas at Arlington (TX)
The U of Texas at Tyler (TX)
U of the West (CA)
The U of Virginia's Coll at Wise (VA)
The U of Western Ontario (ON, Canada)
U of Windsor (ON, Canada)
Vennard Coll (IA)
Virginia Commonwealth U (VA)
Virginia Polytechnic Inst and State U (VA)
Virginia State U (VA)
West Chester U of Pennsylvania (PA)

Western Kentucky U (KY)
Western Washington U (WA)
Westfield State Coll (MA)
Wiley Coll (TX)
Winona State U (MN)
Worcester State Coll (MA)
Youngstown State U (OH)

$14,000–$15,999

Colleges with No Room and Board or with Room Only
Alliant Intl U (CA)
American U of Beirut (Lebanon) **(room only)**
Antioch U McGregor (OH)
Antioch U Santa Barbara (CA)
Cleary U (MI)
Davenport U, Dearborn (MI) **(room only)**
Davenport U, Grand Rapids (MI) **(room only)**
DeVry Coll of New York (NY)
DeVry U, Fremont (CA)
DeVry U (MD)
DeVry U (NJ)
DeVry U, Fort Washington (PA)
DeVry U, Arlington (VA)
DeVry U, Federal Way (WA)
DeVry U Online (IL)
Everest U, Tampa (FL)
Harrisburg U of Science and Technology (PA)
Hodges U (FL)
The Jewish Theological Sem (NY)
Lourdes Coll (OH)
Marylhurst U (OR)
Mount Carmel Coll of Nursing (OH)
Patricia Stevens Coll (MO)
Pennsylvania Coll of Art & Design (PA)
St. Joseph's Coll, New York (NY)
St. Joseph's Coll, Suffolk Campus (NY)

Colleges with Room and Board
Appalachian Bible Coll (WV)
Arizona State U (AZ)
Ball State U (IN)
Beulah Heights U (GA)
Blackburn Coll (IL)
Boston Baptist Coll (MA)
Bowling Green State U (OH)
Brigham Young U (UT)
Bryn Athyn Coll of the New Church (PA)
Castleton State Coll (VT)
Central Connecticut State U (CT)
Chicago State U (IL)
The Citadel, The Military Coll of South Carolina (SC)
Coastal Carolina U (SC)
The Coll at Brockport, State U of New York (NY)
Cooper Union for the Advancement of Science and Art (NY)
Eastern Connecticut State U (CT)
Eastern Illinois U (IL)
Eastern Michigan U (MI)
Fashion Inst of Technology (NY)
Florida Intl U (FL)
Georgia State U (GA)
Grand Valley State U (MI)
Huston-Tillotson U (TX)
Illinois State U (IL)
Indiana U Bloomington (IN)
Johnson State Coll (VT)
Keene State Coll (NH)
Kent State U (OH)
Lake Superior State U (MI)
Lander U (SC)
LeMoyne-Owen Coll (TN)
Lincoln U (PA)
Longwood U (VA)
Louisiana Coll (LA)
Lyndon State Coll (VT)
Maranatha Baptist Bible Coll (WI)
Massachusetts Maritime Acad (MA)
Missouri U of Science and Technology (MO)
Northern Illinois U (IL)
Oakland U (MI)
Oregon Inst of Technology (OR)
Paine Coll (GA)
Penn State Abington (PA)
Pillsbury Baptist Bible Coll (MN)
Portland State U (OR)
Purchase Coll, State U of New York (NY)
Purdue U (IN)
Roanoke Bible Coll (NC)
Salisbury U (MD)
San Diego State U (CA)
Slippery Rock U of Pennsylvania (PA)
South Carolina State U (SC)
Southern Illinois U Carbondale (IL)
State U of New York at Binghamton (NY)
State U of New York at Oswego (NY)
State U of New York Coll at Geneseo (NY)
State U of New York Coll of Agriculture and Technology at Cobleskill (NY)
Stony Brook U, State U of New York (NY)
Texas A&M U (TX)
Texas Coll (TX)
Texas Tech U (TX)
Towson U (MD)
Tyndale U Coll & Sem (ON, Canada)
U at Albany, State U of New York (NY)
U at Buffalo, the State U of New York (NY)
U of Colorado at Boulder (CO)
U of Colorado Denver (CO)
U of Houston (TX)
The U of Iowa (IA)
U of Maine (ME)
U of Maine at Farmington (ME)
U of Massachusetts Lowell (MA)
U of Minnesota, Crookston (MN)
U of Minnesota, Duluth (MN)
U of Minnesota, Twin Cities Campus (MN)
U of Missouri–Columbia (MO)
U of Missouri–St. Louis (MO)
U of Nevada, Las Vegas (NV)
U of Nevada, Reno (NV)
U of South Carolina (SC)
U of Southern Maine (ME)
The U of Texas at Dallas (TX)
The U of Texas at San Antonio (TX)
U of Virginia (VA)
Virginia Military Inst (VA)
Voorhees Coll (SC)
Washington State U (WA)
Wayland Baptist U (TX)
Wayne State U (MI)
Western Connecticut State U (CT)
Western Illinois U (IL)
Western Michigan U (MI)
Wright State U (OH)

$16,000–$17,999

Colleges with No Room and Board or with Room Only
The American U of Athens (Greece) **(room only)**
California State U, Chico (CA)
Crossroads Coll (MN) **(room only)**
Metropolitan Coll of New York (NY)
South U, Tampa (FL)
Woodbury Coll (VT)

Colleges with Room and Board
Bob Jones U (SC)
Central Michigan U (MI)
Clarkson Coll (NE)
Clemson U (SC)
Cleveland State U (OH)
Coll of Charleston (SC)
The Coll of William and Mary (VA)
Colorado School of Mines (CO)
Dallas Christian Coll (TX)
Davis Coll (NY)
Dillard U (LA)
Emmanuel Coll (GA)
Faith Baptist Bible Coll and Theological Sem (IA)
Farmingdale State Coll (NY)
Ferris State U (MI)
Florida Coll (FL)
Florida Memorial U (FL)
Free Will Baptist Bible Coll (TN)
Grove City Coll (PA)
Gutenberg Coll (OR)
Harding U (AR)
Kean U (NJ)
Kentucky Christian U (KY)
Lee U (TN)
Madonna U (MI)
Maine Maritime Acad (ME)
Michigan State U (MI)
Michigan Technological U (MI)
New England School of Communications (ME)
New Jersey City U (NJ)
Oak Hills Christian Coll (MN)
Ohio U (OH)
Plymouth State U (NH)
Polytechnic U of Puerto Rico (PR)
Queen's U at Kingston (ON, Canada)
Rabbinical Coll of America (NJ)
Shaw U (NC)
Southern Connecticut State U (CT)
State U of New York Coll of Environmental Science and Forestry (NY)
Stillman Coll (AL)
Tougaloo Coll (MS)
Trinity Coll of Florida (FL)
The U of Akron (OH)
U of California, San Diego (CA)
U of Delaware (DE)
U of Illinois at Springfield (IL)
U of Mary (ND)
U of Maryland, Baltimore County (MD)
U of Maryland, Coll Park (MD)
U of Massachusetts Amherst (MA)
U of Massachusetts Dartmouth (MA)
U of Missouri–Kansas City (MO)
U of Pittsburgh at Johnstown (PA)
U of Rhode Island (RI)
The U of Texas at Austin (TX)
The U of Toledo (OH)
Vermont Tech Coll (VT)
Washington Bible Coll (MD)
Winthrop U (SC)

$18,000–$19,999

Colleges with No Room and Board or with Room Only
Barnes-Jewish Coll, Goldfarb School of Nursing (MO)
DigiPen Inst of Technology (WA)
LA Coll Intl (CA)
Molloy Coll (NY)
National-Louis U (IL)
New York School of Interior Design (NY)
Sullivan U (KY) **(room only)**

Colleges with Room and Board
Barclay Coll (KS)
Bethel Coll (TN)
Bethune-Cookman U (FL)
Brewton-Parker Coll (GA)
California State U, East Bay (CA)
Central Pennsylvania Coll (PA)
Christopher Newport U (VA)
Claflin U (SC)
Clearwater Christian Coll (FL)
Coll of the Southwest (NM)
East Texas Baptist U (TX)
Evangel U (MO)
Faulkner U (AL)
Grace Bible Coll (MI)
Great Lakes Christian Coll (MI)
Hannibal-LaGrange Coll (MO)
Husson Coll (ME)
Jamestown Coll (ND)
Judson Coll (AL)
Kuyper Coll (MI)
Life U (GA)
Lindenwood U (MO)
Livingstone Coll (NC)
Lubbock Christian U (TX)
Massachusetts Coll of Art and Design (MA)
Mid-Continent U (KY)
Mississippi Coll (MS)
Monroe Coll, New Rochelle (NY)
Montclair State U (NJ)
Mount Olive Coll (NC)
Multnomah Bible Coll and Biblical Sem (OR)
North Greenville U (SC)
Ohio Valley U (WV)
Penn State Altoona (PA)
Penn State Berks (PA)
Penn State Erie, The Behrend Coll (PA)
Pennsylvania Coll of Technology (PA)
Pikeville Coll (KY)
Presentation Coll (SD)
The Richard Stockton Coll of New Jersey (NJ)
Rowan U (NJ)
Rutgers, The State U of New Jersey, Camden (NJ)
Sacred Heart Major Sem (MI)
Southwestern Coll (AZ)
State U of New York Upstate Medical U (NY)
Temple U (PA)
Toccoa Falls Coll (GA)
Truett-McConnell Coll (GA)
U of California, Irvine (CA)
U of California, Los Angeles (CA)
U of California, Riverside (CA)
U of California, Santa Barbara (CA)
U of Cincinnati (OH)
U of Connecticut (CT)
U of Illinois at Chicago (IL)
U of Illinois at Urbana–Champaign (IL)
U of Michigan (MI)
U of New Hampshire (NH)
U of Pittsburgh at Bradford (PA)
William Paterson U of New Jersey (NJ)

York Coll (NE)

$20,000–$24,999

Colleges with No Room and Board or with Room Only
The Art Insts Intl Minnesota (MN)
Bastyr U (WA) **(room only)**
Cogswell Polytechnical Coll (CA) **(room only)**
Coll of Visual Arts (MN)
Goldey-Beacom Coll (DE) **(room only)**
Intl Acad of Design & Technology (IL)
Laguna Coll of Art & Design (CA)
Lexington Coll (IL)
Nebraska Methodist Coll (NE) **(room only)**
Prescott Coll (AZ) **(room only)**
Robert Morris Coll (IL) **(room only)**
Schiller Intl U (FL) **(room only)**
Watkins Coll of Art and Design (TN) **(room only)**
West Suburban Coll of Nursing (IL)

Colleges with Room and Board
Abilene Christian U (TX)
Allen Coll (IA)
Anderson U (SC)
Ashford U (IA)
Atlantic Union Coll (MA)
Ave Maria U (FL)
Baker U (KS)
Baptist Bible Coll of Pennsylvania (PA)
Belhaven Coll (MS)
Benedictine Coll (KS)
Bethany Coll (KS)
Bethany Lutheran Coll (MN)
Bethel Coll (KS)
Bluefield Coll (VA)
Bryan Coll (TN)
California State U, Long Beach (CA)
Carson-Newman Coll (TN)
Cascade Coll (OR)
Central Christian Coll of Kansas (KS)
Clark Atlanta U (GA)
Coker Coll (SC)
The Coll of New Jersey (NJ)
Coll of St. Joseph (VT)
Columbia Coll of Nursing (WI)
Cornerstone U (MI)
Culver-Stockton Coll (MO)
Dakota Wesleyan U (SD)
Dallas Baptist U (TX)
Dana Coll (NE)
Doane Coll (NE)
Drury U (MO)
Finlandia U (MI)
Flagler Coll (FL)
Franciscan U of Steubenville (OH)
Freed-Hardeman U (TN)
Gardner-Webb U (NC)
Grace U (NE)
Grand Canyon U (AZ)
Grand View Coll (IA)
Hampton U (VA)
Hardin-Simmons U (TX)
Hawai'i Pacific U (HI)
Hilbert Coll (NY)
Houston Baptist U (TX)
Howard Payne U (TX)
Humboldt State U (CA)
Iowa Wesleyan Coll (IA)
Jefferson Coll of Health Sciences (VA)
John Brown U (AR)
Johnson C. Smith U (NC)
Kentucky Wesleyan Coll (KY)
Lambuth U (TN)
LeTourneau U (TX)
Liberty U (VA)
Limestone Coll (SC)
Lindsey Wilson Coll (KY)
Lipscomb U (TN)
Lyon Coll (AR)
Marian Coll of Fond du Lac (WI)
McMurry U (TX)
Mercy Coll (NY)
Miami U (OH)
MidAmerica Nazarene U (KS)
Midway Coll (KY)
Milligan Coll (TN)
Missouri Baptist U (MO)
Missouri Valley Coll (MO)
Monroe Coll, Bronx (NY)
Mount Aloysius Coll (PA)
Mount Marty Coll (SD)
Mount Vernon Nazarene U (OH)
New Jersey Inst of Technology (NJ)
Northwood U (MI)
Northwood U, Florida Campus (FL)
Northwood U, Texas Campus (TX)
Nyack Coll (NY)
Oakland City U (IN)
Oakwood Coll (AL)
Oklahoma Christian U (OK)
Oklahoma Wesleyan U (OK)
Oral Roberts U (OK)
Ouachita Baptist U (AR)
Penn State Harrisburg (PA)
Penn State U Park (PA)
Philadelphia Biblical U (PA)
Piedmont Coll (GA)
Pontifical Coll Josephinum (OH)
Ramapo Coll of New Jersey (NJ)
Rochester Coll (MI)
Rutgers, The State U of New Jersey, Newark (NJ)
Rutgers, The State U of New Jersey, New Brunswick (NJ)
St. Charles Borromeo Sem, Overbrook (PA)
St. Gregory's U, Shawnee (OK)
St. Mary's Coll of Maryland (MD)
Samford U (AL)
San Francisco State U (CA)
Schreiner U (TX)
Shorter Coll (GA)
Southeastern U (FL)
Southern Adventist U (TN)
Southern Vermont Coll (VT)
Southern Wesleyan U (SC)
Southwest Baptist U (MO)
Southwestern Adventist U (TX)
Southwestern Coll (KS)
Spring Arbor U (MI)
State U of New York Downstate Medical Center (NY)
Sterling Coll (KS)
Tennessee Wesleyan Coll (TN)
Tiffin U (OH)
Trevecca Nazarene U (TN)
Trinity Lutheran Coll (WA)
Tusculum Coll (TN)
Tuskegee U (AL)
Union Coll (KY)
Union Coll (NE)
U of Advancing Technology (AZ)
U of California, Berkeley (CA)
U of California, Santa Cruz (CA)
U of Great Falls (MT)
U of Mary Hardin-Baylor (TX)
U of Pittsburgh (PA)
U of Rio Grande (OH)
U of Saint Mary (KS)
U of Sioux Falls (SD)
U of the Ozarks (AR)
U of Vermont (VT)
Waynesburg U (PA)
Webber Intl U (FL)
Wesleyan Coll (GA)
Westminster Coll (MO)
William Woods U (MO)
Xavier U of Louisiana (LA)
York Coll of Pennsylvania (PA)

$25,000–$29,999

Colleges with No Room and Board or with Room Only
Art Acad of Cincinnati (OH) **(room only)**
The Art Inst of Atlanta (GA) **(room only)**
The Art Inst of Fort Lauderdale (FL) **(room only)**
The Art Inst of Washington (VA) **(room only)**
Biola U (CA)
Burlington Coll (VT) **(room only)**
California Design Coll (CA) **(room only)**
Loma Linda U (CA) **(room only)**
Marquette U (WI)
Memphis Coll of Art (TN) **(room only)**
Montserrat Coll of Art (MA) **(room only)**
Otis Coll of Art and Design (CA)
Vanguard U of Southern California (CA) **(room only)**

Colleges with Room and Board
Acad of Art U (CA)
Alaska Pacific U (AK)
Albany Coll of Pharmacy of Union U (NY)
Albertus Magnus Coll (CT)
Alderson-Broaddus Coll (WV)
Anderson U (IN)
Andrews U (MI)
Aquinas Coll (MI)
The Art Inst of Pittsburgh (PA)
Asbury Coll (KY)
Augustana Coll (SD)
Averett U (VA)
Avila U (MO)
Barton Coll (NC)
Belmont Abbey Coll (NC)
Benedictine U (IL)
Berry Coll (GA)
Bethany Coll (WV)
Bethany U (CA)
Blessing-Rieman Coll of Nursing (IL)
Bloomfield Coll (NJ)
Bluffton U (OH)
Bradley U (IL)
Brenau U (GA)
Brevard Coll (NC)
California Baptist U (CA)
California State U, Fullerton (CA)
Calvin Coll (MI)
Carlow U (PA)
Carroll Coll (WI)
Catawba Coll (NC)
Cedarville U (OH)
Centenary Coll of Louisiana (LA)
Chaminade U of Honolulu (HI)
Christendom Coll (VA)
Christian Brothers U (TN)
Clarke Coll (IA)
The Coll of Idaho (ID)
Coll of Mount St. Joseph (OH)
Coll of Saint Mary (NE)
The Coll of Saint Rose (NY)
Columbia Coll (SC)
Columbia Coll Chicago (IL)
Columbus Coll of Art & Design (OH)
Concordia U (CA)
Concordia U (MI)
Concordia U (OR)
Concordia U Chicago (IL)
Concordia U, Nebraska (NE)
Concordia U Texas (TX)
Concordia U Wisconsin (WI)
Covenant Coll (GA)
Crown Coll (MN)
Daemen Coll (NY)
Davis & Elkins Coll (WV)
Defiance Coll (OH)
Dominican Coll (NY)
Dominican U (IL)
Dordt Coll (IA)
Dowling Coll (NY)
D'Youville Coll (NY)
Eastern Mennonite U (VA)
Elon U (NC)
Erskine Coll (SC)
Ferrum Coll (VA)
Five Towns Coll (NY)
Florida Southern Coll (FL)
Fontbonne U (MO)
Franklin Coll (IN)
Fresno Pacific U (CA)
Gannon U (PA)
Georgetown Coll (KY)
Grace Coll (IN)
Greenville Coll (IL)
Hastings Coll (NE)
Heidelberg Coll (OH)
Hellenic Coll (MA)
Hillsdale Coll (MI)
Houghton Coll (NY)
Huntingdon Coll (AL)
Huntington U (IN)
Illinois Coll (IL)
Indiana Tech (IN)
Indiana Wesleyan U (IN)
Judson U (IL)
Keuka Coll (NY)
Keystone Coll (PA)
King Coll (TN)
LaGrange Coll (GA)
La Roche Coll (PA)
La Sierra U (CA)
Lawrence Technological U (MI)
Lees-McRae Coll (NC)
Lewis U (IL)
Loras Coll (IA)
Malone Coll (OH)
Marian Coll (IN)
Mary Baldwin Coll (VA)
Marymount U (VA)
Maryville U of Saint Louis (MO)
McKendree U (IL)
Medaille Coll (NY)
Mercyhurst Coll (PA)
Methodist U (NC)
Midland Lutheran Coll (NE)
Morehouse Coll (GA)
Morningside Coll (IA)
Mount Mary Coll (WI)
Mount Mercy Coll (IA)
Mount Saint Mary Coll (NY)
Naropa U (CO)
Nebraska Wesleyan U (NE)

MAJORS AND MORE

Neumann Coll (PA)
Newman U (KS)
North Carolina Wesleyan Coll (NC)
Northland Coll (WI)
Northwest Christian Coll (OR)
Northwestern Coll (IA)
Northwestern Coll (MN)
Northwest Nazarene U (ID)
Nova Southeastern U (FL)
Ohio Dominican U (OH)
Oklahoma City U (OK)
Pacific Union Coll (CA)
Palm Beach Atlantic U (FL)
Patrick Henry Coll (VA)
Paul Smith's Coll (NY)
Peace Coll (NC)
Pfeiffer U (NC)
Point Park U (PA)
Queens U of Charlotte (NC)
Quincy U (IL)
Research Coll of Nursing (MO)
Ripon Coll (WI)
Robert Morris U (PA)
Rockhurst U (MO)
Rocky Mountain Coll of Art + Design (CO)
Roosevelt U (IL)
Sage Coll of Albany (NY)
St. Ambrose U (IA)
St. Andrews Presbyterian Coll (NC)
Saint Joseph's Coll (IN)
Saint Leo U (FL)
St. Louis Coll of Pharmacy (MO)
Saint Mary-of-the-Woods Coll (IN)
St. Mary's U (TX)
St. Thomas Aquinas Coll (NY)
St. Thomas U (FL)
Saint Xavier U (IL)
Salem Coll (NC)
San Diego Christian Coll (CA)
Simpson U (CA)
Spelman Coll (GA)
Sterling Coll (VT)
Tabor Coll (KS)
Taylor U Fort Wayne (IN)
Texas Lutheran U (TX)
Thiel Coll (PA)
Thomas Aquinas Coll (CA)
Thomas Coll (ME)
Thomas More Coll (KY)
Trinity Christian Coll (IL)
Trinity Intl U (IL)
Union U (TN)
U of Charleston (WV)
U of Indianapolis (IN)
U of St. Francis (IL)
U of Saint Francis (IN)
U of St. Thomas (TX)
The U of Tampa (FL)
U of the Incarnate Word (TX)
U of Tulsa (OK)
Ursuline Coll (OH)
VanderCook Coll of Music (IL)
Villa Julie Coll (MD)
Virginia Intermont Coll (VA)
Viterbo U (WI)
Walla Walla U (WA)
Walsh U (OH)
Warner Pacific Coll (OR)
Warren Wilson Coll (NC)
Webster U (MO)
Wells Coll (NY)
Wentworth Inst of Technology (MA)
Wesley Coll (DE)
Westminster Coll (UT)
West Virginia Wesleyan Coll (WV)
William Jessup U (CA)
William Jewell Coll (MO)
Wilmington Coll (OH)
Wingate U (NC)

$30,000 and over

Colleges with No Room and Board or with Room Only
The Art Inst of California–Los Angeles (CA) **(room only)**
The Art Inst of California–San Diego (CA) **(room only)**
The Art Inst of Dallas (TX) **(room only)**
California Coll of the Arts (CA) **(room only)**
Coll for Creative Studies (MI) **(room only)**
Collins Coll: A School of Design and Technology (AZ) **(room only)**
The King's Coll (NY) **(room only)**
Miami Intl U of Art & Design (FL) **(room only)**
Neumont U (UT)
Samuel Merritt Coll (CA) **(room only)**
School of the Art Inst of Chicago (IL) **(room only)**
School of the Museum of Fine Arts, Boston (MA) **(room only)**
School of Visual Arts (NY) **(room only)**
Swarthmore Coll (PA) **(room only)**

Colleges with Room and Board
Adelphi U (NY)
Adrian Coll (MI)
Agnes Scott Coll (GA)
Albion Coll (MI)
Albright Coll (PA)
Alfred U (NY)
Allegheny Coll (PA)
Alma Coll (MI)
Alvernia Coll (PA)
American Jewish U (CA)
American U (DC)
The American U of Paris (France)
Amherst Coll (MA)
Anna Maria Coll (MA)
The Art Inst of Boston at Lesley U (MA)
The Art Inst of Houston (TX)
The Art Inst of Seattle (WA)
Ashland U (OH)
Assumption Coll (MA)
Augsburg Coll (MN)
Augustana Coll (IL)
Austin Coll (TX)
Azusa Pacific U (CA)
Babson Coll (MA)
Baldwin-Wallace Coll (OH)
Bard Coll (NY)
Bard Coll at Simon's Rock (MA)
Barnard Coll (NY)
Barry U (FL)
Bates Coll (ME)
Baylor U (TX)
Bay Path Coll (MA)
Beacon Coll (FL)
Becker Coll (MA)
Bellarmine U (KY)
Belmont U (TN)
Beloit Coll (WI)
Bennington Coll (VT)
Bentley Coll (MA)
Berklee Coll of Music (MA)
Bethel U (MN)
Boston Coll (MA)
The Boston Conservatory (MA)
Boston U (MA)
Bowdoin Coll (ME)
Brandeis U (MA)
Bridgewater Coll (VA)
Brown U (RI)
Bryn Mawr Coll (PA)
Bucknell U (PA)
Butler U (IN)
Cabrini Coll (PA)
California Inst of Technology (CA)
California Lutheran U (CA)
Canisius Coll (NY)
Capital U (OH)
Carnegie Mellon U (PA)
Case Western Reserve U (OH)
The Catholic U of America (DC)
Cedar Crest Coll (PA)
Centenary Coll (NJ)
Central Coll (IA)
Centre Coll (KY)
Chapman U (CA)
Chatham U (PA)
Chestnut Hill Coll (PA)
Claremont McKenna Coll (CA)
Clarkson U (NY)
Clark U (MA)
The Cleveland Inst of Art (OH)
Colby Coll (ME)
Colby-Sawyer Coll (NH)
Colgate U (NY)
Coll of Mount Saint Vincent (NY)
The Coll of New Rochelle (NY)
Coll of Saint Benedict (MN)
Coll of Saint Elizabeth (NJ)
The Coll of St. Scholastica (MN)
Coll of Santa Fe (NM)
Coll of the Atlantic (ME)
Coll of the Holy Cross (MA)
The Colorado Coll (CO)
Columbia U (NY)
Concordia Coll (MN)
Concordia Coll–New York (NY)
Concordia U, St. Paul (MN)
Connecticut Coll (CT)
Converse Coll (SC)
Cornell Coll (IA)
Cornell U (NY)
Creighton U (NE)
Curry Coll (MA)
Daniel Webster Coll (NH)
Dartmouth Coll (NH)
Davidson Coll (NC)
Delaware Valley Coll (PA)
Denison U (OH)
DePaul U (IL)
DePauw U (IN)
DeSales U (PA)
Dickinson Coll (PA)
Dominican U of California (CA)
Drake U (IA)
Drew U (NJ)
Drexel U (PA)
Duke U (NC)
Duquesne U (PA)
Earlham Coll (IN)
Eckerd Coll (FL)
Elizabethtown Coll (PA)
Embry-Riddle Aeronautical U (AZ)
Embry-Riddle Aeronautical U (FL)
Emerson Coll (MA)
Emmanuel Coll (MA)
Emory & Henry Coll (VA)
Emory U (GA)
Endicott Coll (MA)
Eugene Lang Coll The New School for Liberal Arts (NY)
Fairfield U (CT)
Fairleigh Dickinson U, Coll at Florham (NJ)
Fairleigh Dickinson U, Metropolitan Campus (NJ)
Felician Coll (NJ)
Florida Inst of Technology (FL)
Franklin & Marshall Coll (PA)
Franklin Coll Switzerland (Switzerland)
Franklin W. Olin Coll of Eng (MA)
Furman U (SC)
George Fox U (OR)
Georgetown U (DC)
The George Washington U (DC)
Georgian Court U (NJ)
Gettysburg Coll (PA)
Global Coll of Long Island U (NY)
Gonzaga U (WA)
Gordon Coll (MA)
Goucher Coll (MD)
Green Mountain Coll (VT)
Greensboro Coll (NC)
Grinnell Coll (IA)
Guilford Coll (NC)
Gustavus Adolphus Coll (MN)
Gwynedd-Mercy Coll (PA)
Hamilton Coll (NY)
Hamline U (MN)
Hampden-Sydney Coll (VA)
Hampshire Coll (MA)
Hanover Coll (IN)
Hartwick Coll (NY)
Harvard U (MA)
Harvey Mudd Coll (CA)
Haverford Coll (PA)
Hendrix Coll (AR)
High Point U (NC)
Hobart and William Smith Colls (NY)
Hofstra U (NY)
Hollins U (VA)
Holy Family U (PA)
Holy Names U (CA)
Hood Coll (MD)
Hope Coll (MI)
Hope Intl U (CA)
Illinois Inst of Technology (IL)
Illinois Wesleyan U (IL)
Immaculata U (PA)
Iona Coll (NY)
Ithaca Coll (NY)
Jacksonville U (FL)
John Carroll U (OH)
The Johns Hopkins U (MD)
The Juilliard School (NY)
Juniata Coll (PA)
Kalamazoo Coll (MI)
Kansas City Art Inst (MO)
Kenyon Coll (OH)
Kettering U (MI)
King's Coll (PA)
Knox Coll (IL)
Laboratory Inst of Merchandising (NY)
Lafayette Coll (PA)
Lake Forest Coll (IL)
La Salle U (PA)
Lawrence U (WI)
Lebanon Valley Coll (PA)
Lehigh U (PA)

Cost Ranges

$30,000 and over

Le Moyne Coll (NY)
Lenoir-Rhyne Coll (NC)
Lesley U (MA)
Lewis & Clark Coll (OR)
Linfield Coll (OR)
Loyola Marymount U (CA)
Loyola U Chicago (IL)
Loyola U New Orleans (LA)
Luther Coll (IA)
Lycoming Coll (PA)
Lynchburg Coll (VA)
Macalester Coll (MN)
Maharishi U of Management (IA)
Manchester Coll (IN)
Manhattanville Coll (NY)
Mannes Coll The New School for Music (NY)
Marietta Coll (OH)
Marist Coll (NY)
Marlboro Coll (VT)
Maryland Inst Coll of Art (MD)
Marymount Manhattan Coll (NY)
Maryville Coll (TN)
Marywood U (PA)
Massachusetts Coll of Pharmacy and Health Sciences (MA)
Massachusetts Inst of Technology (MA)
The Master's Coll and Sem (CA)
McDaniel Coll (MD)
Mercer U (GA)
Meredith Coll (NC)
Merrimack Coll (MA)
Messiah Coll (PA)
Middlebury Coll (VT)
Millikin U (IL)
Millsaps Coll (MS)
Mills Coll (CA)
Milwaukee School of Eng (WI)
Misericordia U (PA)
Mitchell Coll (CT)
Monmouth Coll (IL)
Monmouth U (NJ)
Moravian Coll (PA)
Mount Holyoke Coll (MA)
Mount Ida Coll (MA)
Mount St. Mary's Coll (CA)
Mount St. Mary's U (MD)
Muhlenberg Coll (PA)
Nazareth Coll of Rochester (NY)
New England Coll (NH)
New England Conservatory of Music (MA)
The New England Inst of Art (MA)
The New School for General Studies (NY)
The New School for Jazz and Contemporary Music (NY)
New York Inst of Technology (NY)
New York U (NY)
Niagara U (NY)
Nichols Coll (MA)
North Central Coll (IL)
Northeastern U (MA)
Northwestern U (IL)
Norwich U (VT)
Notre Dame de Namur U (CA)
Oberlin Coll (OH)
Occidental Coll (CA)
Oglethorpe U (GA)
Ohio Northern U (OH)
Ohio Wesleyan U (OH)
Otterbein Coll (OH)
Pace U (NY)
Pacific Lutheran U (WA)
Pacific U (OR)
Parsons The New School for Design (NY)
Peabody Conservatory of Music of The Johns Hopkins U (MD)
Pepperdine U, Malibu (CA)
Philadelphia U (PA)
Pitzer Coll (CA)
Point Loma Nazarene U (CA)
Polytechnic U, Brooklyn Campus (NY)
Pomona Coll (CA)
Pratt Inst (NY)
Presbyterian Coll (SC)
Princeton U (NJ)
Providence Coll (RI)
Quinnipiac U (CT)
Randolph Coll (VA)
Randolph-Macon Coll (VA)
Reed Coll (OR)
Regis Coll (MA)
Regis U (CO)
Rensselaer Polytechnic Inst (NY)
Rhodes Coll (TN)
Rice U (TX)
Rider U (NJ)
Ringling Coll of Art and Design (FL)
Roanoke Coll (VA)
Roberts Wesleyan Coll (NY)
Rochester Inst of Technology (NY)
Rockford Coll (IL)
Roger Williams U (RI)
Rollins Coll (FL)
Rose-Hulman Inst of Technology (IN)
Rosemont Coll (PA)
Russell Sage Coll (NY)
Sacred Heart U (CT)
St. Edward's U (TX)
Saint Francis U (PA)
St. John Fisher Coll (NY)
St. John's Coll (MD)
St. John's Coll (NM)
Saint John's U (MN)
St. John's U (NY)
Saint Joseph Coll (CT)
Saint Joseph's U (PA)
St. Lawrence U (NY)
Saint Louis U (MO)
Saint Martin's U (WA)
Saint Mary's Coll (IN)
Saint Mary's Coll of California (CA)
Saint Mary's U of Minnesota (MN)
Saint Michael's Coll (VT)
St. Norbert Coll (WI)
St. Olaf Coll (MN)
Saint Vincent Coll (PA)
Salve Regina U (RI)
Santa Clara U (CA)
Sarah Lawrence Coll (NY)
Savannah Coll of Art and Design (GA)
Scripps Coll (CA)
Seattle Pacific U (WA)
Seattle U (WA)
Seton Hill U (PA)
Sewanee: The U of the South (TN)
Shenandoah U (VA)
Shimer Coll (IL)
Siena Coll (NY)
Simmons Coll (MA)
Simpson Coll (IA)
Skidmore Coll (NY)
Smith Coll (MA)
Soka U of America (CA)
Southern Methodist U (TX)
Southern New Hampshire U (NH)
Southwestern U (TX)
Spring Hill Coll (AL)
Stanford U (CA)
Stephens Coll (MO)
Stetson U (FL)
Stonehill Coll (MA)
Suffolk U (MA)
Susquehanna U (PA)
Sweet Briar Coll (VA)
Syracuse U (NY)
Taylor U (IN)
Texas Christian U (TX)
Transylvania U (KY)
Trinity Coll (CT)
Trinity U (TX)
Tri-State U (IN)
Tufts U (MA)
Tulane U (LA)
Union Coll (NY)
U of Bridgeport (CT)
U of California, Davis (CA)
U of Chicago (IL)
U of Dallas (TX)
U of Dayton (OH)
U of Denver (CO)
U of Evansville (IN)
The U of Findlay (OH)
U of Hartford (CT)
U of La Verne (CA)
U of Miami (FL)
U of New England (ME)
U of New Haven (CT)
U of Notre Dame (IN)
U of Pennsylvania (PA)
U of Portland (OR)
U of Puget Sound (WA)
U of Redlands (CA)
U of Richmond (VA)
U of Rochester (NY)
U of St. Thomas (MN)
U of San Diego (CA)
The U of Scranton (PA)
U of Southern California (CA)
U of the Pacific (CA)
U of the Sciences in Philadelphia (PA)
Ursinus Coll (PA)
Utica Coll (NY)
Valparaiso U (IN)
Vanderbilt U (TN)
Vassar Coll (NY)
Villanova U (PA)
Virginia Wesleyan Coll (VA)
Wabash Coll (IN)
Wagner Coll (NY)
Wake Forest U (NC)
Wartburg Coll (IA)
Washington & Jefferson Coll (PA)
Washington and Lee U (VA)
Washington Coll (MD)
Washington U in St. Louis (MO)
Wellesley Coll (MA)
Wesleyan U (CT)
Western New England Coll (MA)
Westmont Coll (CA)
Wheaton Coll (IL)
Wheaton Coll (MA)
Wheeling Jesuit U (WV)
Wheelock Coll (MA)
Whitman Coll (WA)
Whittier Coll (CA)
Whitworth U (WA)
Widener U (PA)
Wilkes U (PA)
Willamette U (OR)
Williams Coll (MA)
Wilson Coll (PA)
Wittenberg U (OH)
Wofford Coll (SC)
Woodbury U (CA)
Worcester Polytechnic Inst (MA)
Xavier U (OH)
Yale U (CT)

Geographical Listing of College Close-Ups

U.S. AND U.S. TERRITORIES

MAJORS AND MORE

New York

North Carolina

North Dakota

Ohio

Oklahoma

Oregon

Pennsylvania

MAJORS AND MORE

Alphabetical Listing of Colleges and Universities

In this listing, the page locations of the profiles are printed in regular type, **Special Messages** in *italics*, and **College Close-Ups** in **bold type.** When there is more than one number in **bold type,** it indicates that the institution has more than one **College Close-Up.**

MAJORS AND MORE

MAJORS AND MORE

MAJORS AND MORE

College Data Center

ALABAMA

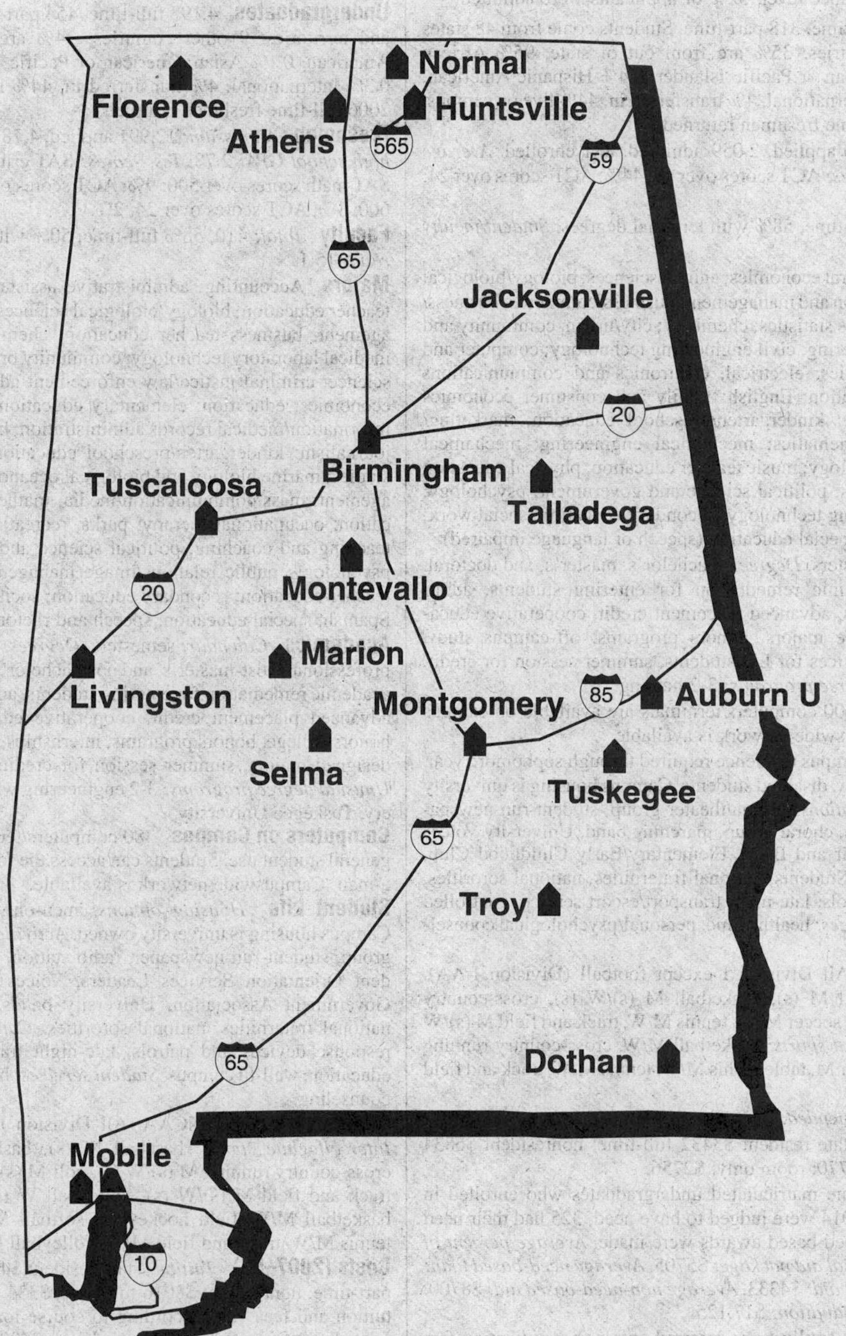

Normal
Florence
Huntsville
Athens
565
59
65
Jacksonville
20
Birmingham
Tuscaloosa
Talladega
Montevallo
20
Marion
Livingston
Auburn U
85
Montgomery
Selma
Tuskegee
65
Troy
65
Dothan
Mobile
10

Alabama Agricultural and Mechanical University

Huntsville, Alabama www.aamu.edu/

- **State-supported** university, founded 1875
- **Suburban** 2001-acre campus
- **Endowment** $29.3 million
- **Coed** 4,716 undergraduate students, 93% full-time, 53% women, 47% men
- **Minimally difficult** entrance level, 32% of applicants were admitted

Undergraduates 4,398 full-time, 318 part-time. Students come from 48 states and territories, 45 other countries, 35% are from out of state, 95% African American, 0.1% Asian American or Pacific Islander, 0.4% Hispanic American, 0.1% Native American, 2% international, 4% transferred in, 44% live on campus. *Retention:* 69% of 2006 full-time freshmen returned.

Freshmen *Admission:* 6,490 applied, 2,059 admitted, 881 enrolled. *Average high school GPA:* 2.8. *Test scores:* ACT scores over 18: 44%; ACT scores over 24: 5%.

Faculty *Total:* 382, 82% full-time, 58% with terminal degrees. *Student/faculty ratio:* 14:1.

Majors Accounting; agricultural economics; animal sciences; biology/biological sciences; business administration and management; business/commerce; business/managerial economics; business statistics; chemistry; city/urban, community and regional planning; civil engineering; civil engineering technology; computer and information sciences; economics; electrical, electronics and communications engineering; elementary education; English; family and consumer economics related; finance; food science; kindergarten/preschool education; marketing/marketing management; mathematics; mechanical engineering; mechanical engineering/mechanical technology; music teacher education; physical education teaching and coaching; physics; political science and government; psychology; radio and television broadcasting technology; secondary education; social work; sociology; special education; special education (speech or language impaired).

Academics *Calendar:* semesters. *Degrees:* bachelor's, master's, and doctoral. *Special study options:* academic remediation for entering students, adult/continuing education programs, advanced placement credit, cooperative education, distance learning, double majors, honors programs, off-campus study, part-time degree program, services for LD students, summer session for credit. *ROTC:* Army (b). *Unusual degree programs:* 3-2 nursing.

Computers on Campus 1,000 computers/terminals are available on campus for general student use. Campuswide network is available.

Student Life *Housing:* on-campus residence required through sophomore year. *Options:* men-only, women-only, disabled students. Campus housing is university owned. *Activities and organizations:* drama/theater group, student-run newspaper, radio and television station, choral group, marching band, University Voices Gospel Choir, University Choir and Band, Elementary/Early Childhood Club, National Alliance of Business Students, national fraternities, national sororities. *Campus security:* 24-hour patrols, late-night transport/escort service, controlled dormitory access. *Student services:* health clinic, personal/psychological counseling.

Athletics Member NCAA. All Division I except football (Division I-AA). *Intercollegiate sports:* baseball M (s), basketball M (s)/W (s), cross-country running M (s)/W (s), golf M (s), soccer M (s), tennis M/W, track and field M (s)/W (s), volleyball W (s). *Intramural sports:* basketball M/W, cross-country running M/W, football M, golf M, soccer M, table tennis M/W, tennis M/W, track and field M/W, volleyball W.

Standardized Tests *Recommended:* ACT (for admission).

Costs (2008–09) *Tuition:* state resident $3432 full-time; nonresident $6834 full-time. *Room and board:* $4770; room only: $2756.

Financial Aid Of all full-time matriculated undergraduates who enrolled in 2005, 7,840 applied for aid, 7,014 were judged to have need, 325 had their need fully met. In 2005, 710 non-need-based awards were made. *Average percent of need met:* 26%. *Average financial aid package:* $5705. *Average need-based loan:* $3006. *Average need-based gift aid:* $4333. *Average non-need-based aid:* $8700. *Average indebtedness upon graduation:* $17,125.

Applying *Options:* electronic application, deferred entrance. *Application fee:* $10. *Required:* high school transcript, minimum 2.0 GPA. *Recommended:* 1 letter of recommendation. *Application deadlines:* 7/15 (freshmen), rolling (transfers). *Notification:* continuous (freshmen), continuous (transfers).

Freshman Application Contact Dr. Evelyn Ellis, Interim Director of Admissions, Alabama Agricultural and Mechanical University, PO Box 908, Normal, AL 35762. *Phone:* 256-372-5245. *Toll-free phone:* 800-553-0816. *Fax:* 256-851-9747.

Alabama State University

Montgomery, Alabama www.alasu.edu/

- **State-supported** comprehensive, founded 1867, part of Alabama Commission on Higher Education
- **Urban** 172-acre campus
- **Endowment** $46.1 million
- **Coed** 4,647 undergraduate students, 90% full-time, 60% women, 40% men
- **Minimally difficult** entrance level, 37% of applicants were admitted

Undergraduates 4,193 full-time, 454 part-time. Students come from 41 states and territories, 9 other countries, 34% are from out of state, 98% African American, 0.1% Asian American or Pacific Islander, 0.3% Hispanic American, 0.3% international, 4% transferred in, 44% live on campus. *Retention:* 55% of 2006 full-time freshmen returned.

Freshmen *Admission:* 12,991 applied, 4,781 admitted, 1,366 enrolled. *Average high school GPA:* 2.78. *Test scores:* SAT critical reading scores over 500: 11%; SAT math scores over 500: 9%; ACT scores over 18: 26%; SAT math scores over 600: 1%; ACT scores over 24: 2%.

Faculty *Total:* 410, 58% full-time, 50% with terminal degrees. *Student/faculty ratio:* 15:1.

Majors Accounting; administrative assistant and secretarial science; art; art teacher education; biology/biological sciences; business administration and management; business teacher education; chemistry; child development; clinical/medical laboratory technology; community organization and advocacy; computer science; criminal justice/law enforcement administration; dramatic/theater arts; economics; education; elementary education; English; finance; French; health information/medical records administration; history; information science/studies; journalism; kindergarten/preschool education; liberal arts and sciences/liberal studies; marine biology and biological oceanography; marketing/marketing management; mass communication/media; mathematics; music; music teacher education; occupational therapy; parks, recreation and leisure; physical education teaching and coaching; political science and government; pre-medical studies; psychology; public relations/image management; radio and television; science teacher education; secondary education; social sciences; social work; sociology; Spanish; special education; speech and rhetoric; teacher assistant/aide.

Academics *Calendar:* semesters. *Degrees:* bachelor's, master's, doctoral, first professional, post-master's, and postbachelor's certificates. *Special study options:* academic remediation for entering students, adult/continuing education programs, advanced placement credit, cooperative education, double majors, freshman honors college, honors programs, internships, part-time degree program, student-designed majors, summer session for credit. *ROTC:* Army (c), Air Force (b). *Unusual degree programs:* 3-2 engineering with Auburn University at Montgomery, Tuskegee University.

Computers on Campus 380 computers/terminals are available on campus for general student use. Students can access the following: online (class) registration, e-mail. Campuswide network is available.

Student Life *Housing options:* men-only, women-only, disabled students. Campus housing is university owned. *Activities and organizations:* drama/theater group, student-run newspaper, radio station, choral group, marching band, Student Orientation Services Leaders, Voices of Praise Gospel Choir, Student Government Association, University bands, Commuter Student Association, national fraternities, national sororities. *Campus security:* 24-hour emergency response devices and patrols, late-night transport/escort service, self-defense education, well-lit campus. *Student services:* health clinic, personal/psychological counseling.

Athletics Member NCAA. All Division I except football (Division I-AA). *Intercollegiate sports:* baseball M (s), basketball M (s)/W (s), bowling W, cross-country running M (s)/W (s), golf M (s), softball W (s), tennis M (s)/W (s), track and field M (s)/W (s), volleyball W (s). *Intramural sports:* baseball M, basketball M/W, field hockey M, softball M/W, swimming and diving M/W, tennis M/W, track and field M/W, volleyball M/W.

Costs (2007–08) *Tuition:* state resident $4008 full-time, $167 per credit hour part-time; nonresident $8016 full-time, $334 per credit hour part-time. Full-time tuition and fees vary according to course load. Part-time tuition and fees vary according to course load. *Required fees:* $500 full-time, $125 per term part-time. *Room and board:* $4150; room only: $1980. Room and board charges vary according to board plan and housing facility. *Payment plan:* deferred payment. *Waivers:* employees or children of employees.

Financial Aid Of all full-time matriculated undergraduates who enrolled in 2007, 4,193 applied for aid, 4,041 were judged to have need, 723 had their need fully met. In 2007, 85 non-need-based awards were made. *Average percent of need met:* 73%. *Average financial aid package:* $9043. *Average need-based loan:* $3986. *Average need-based gift aid:* $4108. *Average non-need-based aid:* $6023. *Average indebtedness upon graduation:* $26,926.

Applying *Options:* electronic application, early admission, deferred entrance. *Application fee:* $25. *Required:* high school transcript, minimum 2.0 GPA. *Recommended:* essay or personal statement, interview. *Application deadlines:* 7/30 (freshmen), 7/30 (transfers). *Notification:* continuous (freshmen), continuous (transfers).

Freshman Application Contact Dr. Martha Pettway, Director of Admissions and Recruitment, Alabama State University, PO Box 271, Montgomery, AL 36101-0271. *Phone:* 334-229-4291. *Toll-free phone:* 800-253-5037. *Fax:* 334-229-4984. *E-mail:* mpettway@alasu.edu.

AMRIDGE UNIVERSITY

Montgomery, Alabama **www.amridgeuniversity.edu/**

- **Independent** university, founded 1967, affiliated with Church of Christ
- **Urban** 9-acre campus
- **Endowment** $750,000
- **Coed**
- **Minimally difficult** entrance level

Faculty *Student/faculty ratio:* 11:1.

Academics *Calendar:* semesters. *Degrees:* bachelor's, master's, doctoral, and first professional.

Costs (2007–08) *Tuition:* $6240 full-time, $260 per semester hour part-time. Full-time tuition and fees vary according to class time. Part-time tuition and fees vary according to class time.

Financial Aid Of all full-time matriculated undergraduates who enrolled in 2003, 330 applied for aid, 300 were judged to have need, 275 had their need fully met. In 2003, 20 non-need-based awards were made. *Average percent of need met:* 85. *Average financial aid package:* $8500. *Average need-based loan:* $5500. *Average need-based gift aid:* $6500. *Average non-need-based aid:* $4000. *Average indebtedness upon graduation:* $18,000.

Applying *Application fee:* $50. *Required:* high school transcript, minimum 2.0 GPA.

Freshman Application Contact Mr. Rick Johnson, Director of Enrollment Management, Amridge University, 1200 Taylor Road, Montgomery, AL 36117. *Phone:* 334-387-3877. *Toll-free phone:* 800-351-4040 Ext. 213. *Fax:* 334-387-3878. *E-mail:* admissions@regions.edu.

See page 270 for the College Close-Up.

ANDREW JACKSON UNIVERSITY

Birmingham, Alabama **www.aju.edu/**

- **Private** comprehensive, founded 1994
- **Coed**
- **Noncompetitive** entrance level

Faculty *Student/faculty ratio:* 11:1.

Academics *Degrees:* certificates, associate, bachelor's, and master's (offers primarily external degree programs).

Applying *Application fee:* $75. *Required:* interview. *Required for some:* high school transcript.

Freshman Application Contact Tammy Kassner, Senior Admissions Representative, Andrew Jackson University, 10 Old Montgomery Highway, Birmingham, AL 35209. *Phone:* 205-871-9288. *Fax:* 800-321-9694. *E-mail:* info@aju.edu.

ATHENS STATE UNIVERSITY

Athens, Alabama **www.athens.edu/**

- **State-supported** upper-level, founded 1822, part of The Alabama College System
- **Small-town** 45-acre campus
- **Endowment** $1.5 million
- **Coed** 3,072 undergraduate students, 44% full-time, 67% women, 33% men
- **Noncompetitive** entrance level

Undergraduates 1,345 full-time, 1,727 part-time. Students come from 7 states and territories, 5% are from out of state, 11% African American, 0.8% Asian American or Pacific Islander, 0.9% Hispanic American, 3% Native American.

Faculty *Total:* 177, 42% full-time, 38% with terminal degrees. *Student/faculty ratio:* 23:1.

Majors Accounting; art; behavioral sciences; biology/biological sciences; business administration and management; business, management, and marketing related; chemistry; computer science; criminal justice/law enforcement administration; elementary education; English; health science; history; humanities; human resources management; information science/studies; kindergarten/preschool education; mathematics; physical education teaching and coaching; physics; political science and government; psychology; religious studies; science teacher education; science technologies related; secondary education; sociology; special education; trade and industrial teacher education.

Academics *Calendar:* semesters. *Degree:* certificates and bachelor's. *Special study options:* adult/continuing education programs, advanced placement credit, cooperative education, distance learning, double majors, independent study, internships, off-campus study, part-time degree program, study abroad, summer session for credit.

Computers on Campus 210 computers/terminals are available on campus for general student use. Students can access the following: online (class) registration, grades, transcripts, schedules, e-mail. Campuswide network is available.

Student Life *Housing:* college housing not available. *Activities and organizations:* drama/theater group, student-run newspaper, national sororities. *Student services:* personal/psychological counseling.

Athletics *Intramural sports:* table tennis M/W, volleyball M/W.

Costs (2007–08) *Tuition:* state resident $2640 full-time, $110 per credit hour part-time; nonresident $5280 full-time, $220 per credit hour part-time. *Required fees:* $600 full-time, $25 per credit hour part-time. *Waivers:* senior citizens and employees or children of employees.

Financial Aid Of all full-time matriculated undergraduates who enrolled in 2004, 2,827 applied for aid, 1,693 were judged to have need. 16 Federal Work-Study jobs (averaging $3769). 25 state and other part-time jobs (averaging $5000). *Average indebtedness upon graduation:* $12,510.

Applying *Options:* electronic application, deferred entrance. *Application fee:* $30. *Application deadline:* rolling (transfers). *Notification:* continuous (transfers).

Application Contact Ms. Necedah Henderson, Coordinator of Admissions, Athens State University, 300 North Beaty Street, Athens, AL 35611. *Phone:* 256-233-8217. *Toll-free phone:* 800-522-0272. *Fax:* 256-233-6565. *E-mail:* necedah.henderson@athens.edu.

AUBURN UNIVERSITY

Auburn University, Alabama **www.auburn.edu/**

- **State-supported** university, founded 1856
- **Small-town** 1875-acre campus with easy access to Atlanta and Birmingham
- **Endowment** $378.6 million
- **Coed** 19,812 undergraduate students, 92% full-time, 49% women, 51% men
- **Moderately difficult** entrance level, 69% of applicants were admitted

Undergraduates 18,148 full-time, 1,664 part-time. Students come from 52 states and territories, 48 other countries, 31% are from out of state, 9% African American, 2% Asian American or Pacific Islander, 2% Hispanic American, 0.7% Native American, 0.6% international, 7% transferred in, 14% live on campus. *Retention:* 86% of 2006 full-time freshmen returned.

Freshmen *Admission:* 17,798 applied, 12,291 admitted, 4,191 enrolled. *Average high school GPA:* 3.6. *Test scores:* SAT critical reading scores over 500: 83%; SAT math scores over 500: 86%; ACT scores over 18: 96%; SAT critical reading scores over 600: 30%; SAT math scores over 600: 40%; ACT scores over 24: 63%; SAT critical reading scores over 700: 5%; SAT math scores over 700: 6%; ACT scores over 30: 20%.

Faculty *Total:* 1,286, 88% full-time. *Student/faculty ratio:* 18:1.

Majors Accounting; adult and continuing education; aerospace, aeronautical and astronautical engineering; agricultural/biological engineering and bioengineering; agricultural economics; agricultural teacher education; agriculture; agronomy and crop science; airline pilot and flight crew; animal sciences; anthropology; apparel and textiles; applied mathematics; aquaculture; architectural engineering; architecture; audiology and speech-language pathology; aviation/airway management; biochemistry; biology/biological sciences; biomedical sciences; botany/plant biology; broadcast journalism; business administration and management; business/managerial economics; business teacher education; chemical engineering; chemistry; child development; civil engineering; clinical laboratory science/medical technology; clinical/medical laboratory technology; commercial and advertising art; communication and journalism related; computer and information sciences; computer engineering; computer engineering related; computer hardware engineering; computer software engineering; criminology; dairy science; design and visual communications; dramatic/theater arts; early childhood education; economics; electrical, electronics and communications engineering; elementary education; engineering; English; English as a second/foreign language (teaching); English/language arts teacher education; environmental design/architecture; environmental science; environmental studies; family and consumer sciences/human sciences; finance; fine/studio arts; food science; foods, nutrition, and wellness; foreign languages and literatures; forest sciences and biology; French; French language teacher education; geography; geological/geophysical engineering; geology/earth science; German; German language teacher education; graphic design; health/health care administration; health teacher education; history; history teacher education; horticultural science; hospitality administration related; hotel/motel administration; human development and family studies; human resources management; industrial design; industrial engineering; interior architecture; international business/trade/commerce; journalism; kindergarten/preschool education; landscape architecture; logistics and materials management; management information systems; marine biology and biological oceanography; marketing/marketing management; mass communication/media; materials engineering; mathematics; mathematics teacher education; mechanical engineering; medical laboratory technology; medical microbiology and bacteriology; microbiology; molecular biology; music teacher education; nursing (registered nurse training); nutrition sciences; operations management; ornamental horticulture; parks, recreation and leisure; philosophy; physical education teaching and coaching; physics; physics teacher education; plant pathology/phytopathology; plant sciences; plant sciences related; political science and government; poultry science; pre-dentistry studies; pre-law studies; pre-medical studies; pre-pharmacy studies; pre-veterinary studies; psychology; public administration; public relations/image management; radio and television; science teacher education; secondary education; secondary school administration/principalship; social work; sociology; Spanish; Spanish language teacher education; special education; special education related; special education (vision impaired); speech and rhetoric; speech therapy; textile sciences and engineering; trade and industrial teacher education; wildlife and wildlands science and management; zoology/animal biology.

Academics *Calendar:* semesters. *Degrees:* bachelor's, master's, doctoral, first professional, and post-master's certificates. *Special study options:* accelerated degree program, adult/continuing education programs, advanced placement credit, cooperative education, distance learning, double majors, English as a second language, honors programs, independent study, internships, part-time degree program, services for LD students, study abroad, summer session for credit. *ROTC:* Army (b), Navy (b), Air Force (b). *Unusual degree programs:* 3-2 engineering.

Computers on Campus 1,722 computers/terminals are available on campus for general student use. Students can access the following: computer help desk, free student e-mail accounts, online (class) grades, online (class) registration, pay Bursar online, course materials available online. Campuswide network is available. 100% of college-owned or -operated housing units are wired for high-speed Internet access. Wireless service is available via entire campus.

Student Life *Housing options:* coed, men-only, women-only, disabled students. Campus housing is university owned. *Activities and organizations:* drama/theater group, student-run newspaper, radio and television station, choral group, marching band, Student Government Association, University Program Council, IMPACT (volunteer opportunities), national fraternities, national sororities. *Campus security:* 24-hour emergency response devices and patrols, late-night transport/escort service, controlled dormitory access. *Student services:* health clinic, personal/psychological counseling.

Athletics Member NCAA. All Division I except football (Division I-A). *Intercollegiate sports:* baseball M (s), basketball M (s)/W (s), cross-country running M (s)/W (s), equestrian sports W (s), golf M (s)/W (s), gymnastics W (s), soccer W (s), softball W (s), swimming and diving M (s)/W (s), tennis M (s)/W (s), track and field M (s)/W (s), volleyball W (s). *Intramural sports:* badminton M/W, basketball M/W, bowling M/W, crew M (c)/W (c), football M/W, golf M/W, lacrosse M (c)/W (c), racquetball M/W, rugby M (c), sailing M (c)/W (c), soccer M (c)/W (c), softball M/W, swimming and diving M/W, table tennis M (c)/W (c), tennis M (c)/W (c), track and field M/W, volleyball M/W, wrestling M (c).

Standardized Tests *Required:* SAT or ACT (for admission).

Costs (2007–08) *Tuition:* state resident $5490 full-time, $217 per credit hour part-time; nonresident $15,990 full-time, $651 per credit hour part-time. Full-time tuition and fees vary according to course load, program, and reciprocity agreements. Part-time tuition and fees vary according to course load, program, and reciprocity agreements. *Required fees:* $344 full-time. *Room only:* $3200. Room and board charges vary according to housing facility. *Payment plan:* tuition prepayment. *Waivers:* employees or children of employees.

Financial Aid Of all full-time matriculated undergraduates who enrolled in 2006, 7,729 applied for aid, 5,857 were judged to have need, 1,788 had their need fully met. 380 Federal Work-Study jobs (averaging $3118). In 2006, 1596 non-need-based awards were made. *Average percent of need met:* 44%. *Average financial aid package:* $7917. *Average need-based loan:* $3990. *Average need-based gift aid:* $4764. *Average non-need-based aid:* $4059. *Average indebtedness upon graduation:* $25,176.

Applying *Options:* electronic application, early admission, deferred entrance. *Application fee:* $25. *Required:* high school transcript, minimum 2.0 GPA. *Required for some:* minimum 3.0 GPA. *Application deadlines:* rolling (freshmen), rolling (transfers). *Notification:* 10/1 (freshmen), continuous (transfers).

Freshman Application Contact Mr. Michael M. Waldrop, Associate Director, Marketing and Recruitment, Auburn University, 202 Mary Martin Hall, Auburn, AL 36849-5145. *Phone:* 334-844-6446. *Toll-free phone:* 800-AUBURN9. *E-mail:* admissions@auburn.edu.

AUBURN UNIVERSITY MONTGOMERY

Montgomery, Alabama **www.aum.edu/**

- **State-supported** comprehensive, founded 1967, part of Auburn University
- **Suburban** 500-acre campus
- **Endowment** $36.2 million
- **Coed** 4,348 undergraduate students, 64% full-time, 64% women, 36% men
- **Moderately difficult** entrance level, 92% of applicants were admitted

Undergraduates 2,788 full-time, 1,560 part-time. 3% are from out of state, 32% African American, 2% Asian American or Pacific Islander, 1% Hispanic American, 0.5% Native American, 15% transferred in, 13% live on campus. *Retention:* 57% of 2006 full-time freshmen returned.

Freshmen *Admission:* 1,210 applied, 1,110 admitted, 642 enrolled. *Test scores:* ACT scores over 18: 79%; ACT scores over 24: 17%; ACT scores over 30: 1%.

Faculty *Total:* 330, 59% full-time. *Student/faculty ratio:* 15:1.

Majors Accounting; art; biology/biological sciences; business administration and management; business/commerce; business/managerial economics; communication/speech communication and rhetoric; criminal justice/safety; elementary education; English; finance; foreign languages and literatures; history; human resources management; liberal arts and sciences/liberal studies; management information systems; marketing/marketing management; mathematics; nursing (registered nurse training); physical sciences; political science and government; psychology; secondary education; sociology.

Academics *Calendar:* semesters. *Degrees:* bachelor's, master's, doctoral, and post-master's certificates. *Special study options:* academic remediation for entering students, accelerated degree program, adult/continuing education programs, advanced placement credit, cooperative education, distance learning, double majors, English as a second language, honors programs, independent study, internships, off-campus study, part-time degree program, services for LD students, study abroad, summer session for credit. *ROTC:* Army (b), Air Force (c).

Computers on Campus 478 computers/terminals are available on campus for general student use. Students can access the following: campus intranet, computer help desk, free student e-mail accounts, online (class) registration. Campuswide network is available. 100% of college-owned or -operated housing units are wired for high-speed Internet access. Wireless service is available via classrooms, computer labs, libraries, student centers.

Student Life *Housing options:* coed, disabled students. Campus housing is university owned. *Activities and organizations:* drama/theater group, student-run newspaper, choral group, Student Government Association, Baptist campus ministries, American Humanics, Campus Activities Board, Student Government Association, national fraternities, national sororities. *Campus security:* 24-hour emergency response devices and patrols, student patrols, late-night transport/escort service, controlled dormitory access. *Student services:* health clinic, personal/psychological counseling.

Athletics Member NAIA. *Intercollegiate sports:* baseball M (s), basketball M (s)/W (s), soccer M (s)/W (s), tennis M (s)/W (s). *Intramural sports:* basketball M/W, bowling M/W, football M/W, soccer M/W, softball M/W, tennis M/W, volleyball M/W.

Standardized Tests *Required:* SAT or ACT (for admission).

Costs (2007–08) *Tuition:* state resident $5010 full-time, $158 per credit hour part-time; nonresident $14,490 full-time, $474 per credit hour part-time. Full-time tuition and fees vary according to course load. *Required fees:* $270 full-time, $6 per semester hour part-time, $45 per term part-time. *Room and board:* $3050; room only: $2890. Room and board charges vary according to housing facility. *Payment plan:* deferred payment. *Waivers:* employees or children of employees.

Financial Aid Of all full-time matriculated undergraduates who enrolled in 2007, 1,639 applied for aid, 1,291 were judged to have need, 1,209 had their need fully met. 46 Federal Work-Study jobs (averaging $2869). *Average financial aid package:* $5746. *Average need-based loan:* $3590. *Average need-based gift aid:* $3367.

Applying *Options:* electronic application, deferred entrance. *Application fee:* $25. *Required:* high school transcript. *Application deadlines:* rolling (freshmen), rolling (transfers). *Notification:* continuous (freshmen), continuous (transfers).

Freshman Application Contact Mr. Ronnie McKinney, Assistant Director of Admissions, Auburn University Montgomery, PO Box 244023, Montgomery, AL 36124-4023. *Phone:* 334-244-3598. *Toll-free phone:* 800-227-2649. *Fax:* 334-244-3795. *E-mail:* rmckinne@aum.edu.

BIRMINGHAM-SOUTHERN COLLEGE

Birmingham, Alabama **www.bsc.edu/**

- **Independent Methodist** comprehensive, founded 1856
- **Urban** 196-acre campus
- **Endowment** $122.4 million
- **Coed**
- **Moderately difficult** entrance level

Birmingham-Southern is a nationally recognized institution noted for high-quality liberal arts academics; service-learning, leadership studies, Interim Term, and study-abroad programs; and an outstanding record of job placement and graduate admission to medical, law, and professional schools. *The Princeton Review, Money* magazine, Loren Pope's *40 Colleges That Change Lives, The Fiske Guide to Colleges,* and *Kiplinger's* magazine have recognized Birmingham-Southern, which has the oldest Phi Beta Kappa chapters in Alabama.

Faculty *Student/faculty ratio:* 11:1.

Academics *Calendar:* 4-1-4. *Degrees:* bachelor's and master's.

Student Life *Campus security:* 24-hour emergency response devices and patrols, late-night transport/escort service, controlled dormitory access, vehicle safety inspection.

Athletics Member NCAA. All Division I.

Standardized Tests *Required:* SAT or ACT (for admission).

Costs (2007–08) *Comprehensive fee:* $32,362 includes full-time tuition ($23,600), mandatory fees ($700), and room and board ($8062). Part-time tuition: $983 per credit hour. *College room only:* $5000.

Financial Aid Of all full-time matriculated undergraduates who enrolled in 2006, 589 applied for aid, 463 were judged to have need, 185 had their need fully met. 154 Federal Work-Study jobs (averaging $1916). 275 state and other part-time jobs (averaging $1456). In 2006, 537 non-need-based awards were made. *Average percent of need met:* 87. *Average financial aid package:* $22,166. *Average need-based loan:* $4370. *Average need-based gift aid:* $7010. *Average non-need-based aid:* $9586.

Applying *Options:* electronic application, early admission, early action, deferred entrance. *Application fee:* $25. *Required:* essay or personal statement, high school transcript, minimum 2.0 GPA, 1 letter of recommendation. *Required for some:* interview. *Recommended:* interview.

Freshman Application Contact Ms. Sheri E. Salmon, Associate Vice President for Admission, Birmingham-Southern College, Box 549008, Birmingham, AL 35254. *Phone:* 205-226-4696. *Toll-free phone:* 800-523-5793. *Fax:* 205-226-3074. *E-mail:* admitme@bsc.edu.

See page 272 for the College Close-Up.

COLUMBIA SOUTHERN UNIVERSITY

Orange Beach, Alabama **www.columbiasouthern.edu/**

- **Proprietary** comprehensive, founded 1993
- **Small-town** campus
- **Coed** 8,392 undergraduate students
- **Noncompetitive** entrance level, 37% of applicants were admitted

Undergraduates Students come from 52 states and territories, 27 other countries, 98% are from out of state.

Freshmen *Admission:* 2,566 applied, 960 admitted.

Faculty *Total:* 106, 15% full-time, 37% with terminal degrees.

Majors Business administration and management; business/commerce; criminal justice/safety; education; environmental studies; fire protection and safety technology; fire services administration; health/health care administration; human resources management and services related; information technology; international business/trade/commerce; management information systems and services related; marketing/marketing management; occupational safety and health technology; psychology; sport and fitness administration/management.

Academics *Calendar:* modular. *Degrees:* certificates, associate, bachelor's, master's, doctoral, first professional, postbachelor's, and first professional certificates (offers only distance learning degree programs). *Special study options:* academic remediation for entering students, adult/continuing education programs, distance learning, external degree program, part-time degree program.

Computers on Campus Students can access the following: computer help desk, online (class) grades, online (class) registration, online (class) schedules.

Student Life *Housing:* college housing not available.

Costs (2008–09) *Tuition:* $4694 full-time, $185 per credit hour part-time. *Required fees:* $20 full-time, $20 per year part-time.

Applying *Options:* electronic application. *Application fee:* $25. *Required for some:* high school transcript. *Application deadlines:* rolling (freshmen), rolling (transfers).

Freshman Application Contact Ms. Kathy Cole, Director of Admissions, Columbia Southern University, PO Box 3110, 25326 Canal Road, Orange Beach, AL 36561. *Phone:* 251-981-3771. *Toll-free phone:* 800-977-8449. *Fax:* 251-981-3815. *E-mail:* kathy@columbiasouthern.edu.

CONCORDIA COLLEGE

Selma, Alabama **www.concordiaselma.edu/**

Freshman Application Contact Ms. Phyllis Richardson, Director, STARS, Concordia College, Kreft, 1804 Green Street, Selma, AL 36700. *Phone:* 334-874-5700 Ext. 102. *Fax:* 334-874-5755. *E-mail:* prichrdson@concordiaselma.edu.

FAULKNER UNIVERSITY

Montgomery, Alabama **www.faulkner.edu/**

- **Independent** comprehensive, founded 1942, affiliated with Church of Christ
- **Urban** 75-acre campus
- **Endowment** $18.4 million
- **Coed** 2,528 undergraduate students, 74% full-time, 60% women, 40% men
- **Minimally difficult** entrance level, 59% of applicants were admitted

Undergraduates 1,864 full-time, 664 part-time. Students come from 31 states and territories, 18 other countries, 12% are from out of state, 45% African American, 0.5% Asian American or Pacific Islander, 0.9% Hispanic American, 0.4% Native American, 0.6% international, 7% transferred in, 23% live on campus. *Retention:* 54% of 2006 full-time freshmen returned.

Freshmen *Admission:* 982 applied, 579 admitted, 285 enrolled. *Average high school GPA:* 3.06. *Test scores:* SAT critical reading scores over 500: 36%; SAT math scores over 500: 38%; ACT scores over 18: 86%; SAT critical reading scores over 600: 6%; SAT math scores over 600: 6%; ACT scores over 24: 15%; ACT scores over 30: 1%.

Faculty *Total:* 155, 68% full-time, 57% with terminal degrees. *Student/faculty ratio:* 19:1.

Majors Accounting; administrative assistant and secretarial science; athletic training; biblical studies; biology/biological sciences; biomedical technology; business administration and management; clinical laboratory science/medical technology; clinical/medical laboratory technology; computer management; computer typography and composition equipment operation; criminal justice/law enforcement administration; criminology; divinity/ministry; dramatic/theater arts; education; elementary education; English; health information/medical records administration; history; humanities; human resources management; information science/studies; kindergarten/preschool education; legal assistant/paralegal; liberal arts and sciences/liberal studies; marketing/marketing management; pastoral studies/counseling; physical education teaching and coaching; physical sciences; political science and government; pre-engineering; pre-law studies; psychology; religious education; religious studies; secondary education; social sciences; sport and fitness administration/management; theology.

Academics *Calendar:* semesters. *Degrees:* associate, bachelor's, master's, and first professional. *Special study options:* academic remediation for entering students, accelerated degree program, adult/continuing education programs, advanced placement credit, distance learning, double majors, freshman honors college, honors programs, independent study, internships, off-campus study, part-time degree program, services for LD students, study abroad, summer session for credit. *ROTC:* Army (c), Air Force (c).

Computers on Campus 228 computers/terminals and 150 ports are available on campus for general student use. Students can access the following: computer help desk, free student e-mail accounts, online (class) grades, student account access. Campuswide network is available. 25% of college-owned or -operated housing units are wired for high-speed Internet access.

Student Life *Housing:* on-campus residence required through junior year. *Options:* men-only, women-only, disabled students. Campus housing is university owned. Freshman applicants given priority for college housing. *Activities and organizations:* drama/theater group, student-run newspaper, choral group, Student government, Senators, Christians in Action, acappella chorus. *Campus security:* 24-hour emergency response devices and patrols, student patrols, late-night transport/escort service. *Student services:* health clinic, personal/psychological counseling.

Athletics Member NAIA, NCCAA. *Intercollegiate sports:* baseball M (s), basketball M (s), football M (s), golf M (s), soccer M (s)/W (s), softball W (s), volleyball W (s). *Intramural sports:* basketball M/W, bowling M/W, football M/W, golf M/W, racquetball M/W, soccer M/W, softball M/W, table tennis M/W, ultimate Frisbee M/W, volleyball M/W.

Standardized Tests *Required:* SAT or ACT (for admission).

Costs (2008–09) *Comprehensive fee:* $19,070 includes full-time tuition ($12,720) and room and board ($6350). Part-time tuition: $445 per semester hour. *College room only:* $3150.

Financial Aid Of all full-time matriculated undergraduates who enrolled in 2007, 1,711 applied for aid, 1,335 were judged to have need, 120 had their need fully met. 131 Federal Work-Study jobs (averaging $1337). 4 state and other part-time jobs (averaging $800). In 2007, 55 non-need-based awards were made. *Average percent of need met:* 59%. *Average financial aid package:* $7350. *Average need-based loan:* $4950. *Average need-based gift aid:* $3900. *Average non-need-based aid:* $2650. *Average indebtedness upon graduation:* $19,300.

Applying *Options:* electronic application, early admission, deferred entrance. *Application fee:* $10. *Required:* high school transcript, minimum 2.0 GPA. *Recommended:* essay or personal statement, 2 letters of recommendation, interview. *Application deadlines:* rolling (freshmen), rolling (transfers).

Freshman Application Contact Mr. Keith Mock, Director of Admissions, Faulkner University, 5345 Atlanta Highway, Montgomery, AL 36109. *Phone:* 334-386-7200. *Toll-free phone:* 800-879-9816. *Fax:* 334-386-7137. *E-mail:* admissions@faulkner.edu.

HERITAGE CHRISTIAN UNIVERSITY

Florence, Alabama **www.hcu.edu/**

- **Independent** comprehensive, founded 1971, affiliated with Church of Christ
- **Small-town** 43-acre campus
- **Endowment** $5.3 million
- **Coed, primarily men** 93 undergraduate students, 45% full-time, 18% women, 82% men
- **Noncompetitive** entrance level, 56% of applicants were admitted

Undergraduates 42 full-time, 51 part-time. Students come from 9 states and territories, 5 other countries, 63% are from out of state, 12% African American, 1% Asian American or Pacific Islander, 10% international, 22% transferred in.

Freshmen *Admission:* 25 applied, 14 admitted, 2 enrolled.

Faculty *Total:* 29, 34% full-time, 31% with terminal degrees. *Student/faculty ratio:* 9:1.

Majors Biblical studies.

Academics *Calendar:* semesters. *Degrees:* associate, bachelor's, and master's. *Special study options:* academic remediation for entering students, accelerated degree program, adult/continuing education programs, distance learning, external degree program, independent study, internships, part-time degree program, summer session for credit.

Computers on Campus 12 computers/terminals are available on campus for general student use. Students can access the following: online (class) grades, online (class) registration, online (class) schedules. Campuswide network is available. 100% of college-owned or -operated housing units are wired for high-speed Internet access. Wireless service is available via entire campus.

Student Life *Housing options:* men-only, women-only, disabled students. Campus housing is university owned. *Activities and organizations:* drama/theater group, Missions Club, Preachers Club, Student Government Association, Christian Ladies Organization, HCU Skit Team. *Student services:* personal/psychological counseling.

Athletics *Intramural sports:* softball M/W.

Costs (2008–09) *Comprehensive fee:* $12,960 includes full-time tuition ($9660) and room and board ($3300). Part-time tuition: $322 per hour. *Required fees:* $20 per hour part-time. *College room only:* $3000.

Financial Aid Of all full-time matriculated undergraduates who enrolled in 2004, 29 applied for aid, 28 were judged to have need. 10 Federal Work-Study jobs (averaging $1234). In 2004, 11 non-need-based awards were made. *Average percent of need met:* 29%. *Average financial aid package:* $2165. *Average non-need-based aid:* $5589. *Average indebtedness upon graduation:* $23,236.

Applying *Options:* early admission, deferred entrance. *Application fee:* $25. *Required:* high school transcript, 3 letters of recommendation. *Required for some:* TOEFL. *Recommended:* interview. *Application deadlines:* rolling (freshmen), rolling (transfers). *Notification:* continuous until 7/1 (freshmen), continuous (transfers).

Freshman Application Contact Mr. Travis Harmon, Dean of Students, Heritage Christian University, PO Box HCU, Florence, AL 35630-0050. *Phone:* 256-766-6610. *Toll-free phone:* 800-367-3565. *Fax:* 256-766-9289. *E-mail:* tharmon@hcu.edu.

HERZING COLLEGE

Birmingham, Alabama **www.herzing.edu/birmingham/**

Director of Admissions Ms. Tess Anderson, Admissions Coordinator, Herzing College, 280 West Valley Avenue, Birmingham, AL 35209. *Phone:* 205-916-2800. *E-mail:* admiss@bhm.herzing.edu.

HUNTINGDON COLLEGE

Montgomery, Alabama **www.huntingdon.edu/**

- **Independent United Methodist** 4-year, founded 1854
- **Suburban** 71-acre campus with easy access to Birmingham
- **Endowment** $48.4 million
- **Coed** 954 undergraduate students, 82% full-time, 49% women, 51% men
- **Moderately difficult** entrance level, 66% of applicants were admitted

Undergraduates 787 full-time, 167 part-time. Students come from 19 states and territories, 4 other countries, 18% are from out of state, 15% African American, 0.7% Asian American or Pacific Islander, 1% Hispanic American, 0.8% Native American, 0.5% international, 10% transferred in, 72% live on campus. *Retention:* 60% of 2006 full-time freshmen returned.

Freshmen *Admission:* 985 applied, 649 admitted, 255 enrolled. *Average high school GPA:* 3.34. *Test scores:* SAT critical reading scores over 500: 53%; SAT math scores over 500: 53%; ACT scores over 18: 92%; SAT critical reading scores over 600: 23%; SAT math scores over 600: 27%; ACT scores over 24: 29%; SAT critical reading scores over 700: 7%; SAT math scores over 700: 3%; ACT scores over 30: 2%.

Faculty *Total:* 64, 69% full-time, 66% with terminal degrees. *Student/faculty ratio:* 15:1.

Majors Accounting; art; athletic training; biology/biological sciences; business/commerce; cell biology and histology; chemistry; communication/speech communication and rhetoric; education; English; history; kinesiology and exercise science; mathematics; music; physical education teaching and coaching; political science and government; psychology; religious studies.

Academics *Calendar:* semesters. *Degrees:* certificates, associate, and bachelor's. *Special study options:* accelerated degree program, adult/continuing education programs, advanced placement credit, cooperative education, double majors, honors programs, independent study, internships, off-campus study, part-time degree program, student-designed majors, study abroad, summer session for credit. *ROTC:* Army (c), Air Force (c). *Unusual degree programs:* 3-2 engineering with Auburn University, The University of Alabama at Birmingham.

Computers on Campus 13 computers/terminals are available on campus for general student use. Students can access the following: campus intranet, computer help desk, free student e-mail accounts, online (class) grades, online (class) schedules. Campuswide network is available. 100% of college-owned or -operated housing units are wired for high-speed Internet access. Wireless service is available via classrooms, learning centers, libraries.

Student Life *Housing:* on-campus residence required through junior year. *Options:* coed, disabled students. Campus housing is university owned. Freshman campus housing is guaranteed. *Activities and organizations:* drama/theater group, student-run newspaper, choral group, marching band, SGA, Accounting Club, Chi Omega, International Student Association, Alpha Omicron Pi, national fraternities, national sororities. *Campus security:* 24-hour emergency response devices and patrols, late-night transport/escort service, controlled dormitory access, electronic video surveillance. *Student services:* health clinic.

Athletics Member NCAA. All Division III. *Intercollegiate sports:* baseball M, basketball M/W, football M, golf M, soccer M/W, softball W, tennis M/W, volleyball W. *Intramural sports:* baseball M/W (c), basketball M/W, cheerleading M (c)/W (c), crew M/W, football M/W, golf M/W, rugby M/W, sailing M/W, soccer M/W, softball M/W, table tennis M/W, tennis M/W, volleyball M/W.

Standardized Tests *Required:* SAT or ACT (for admission).

Costs (2008–09) *Comprehensive fee:* $26,970 includes full-time tuition ($19,320), mandatory fees ($700), and room and board ($6950). Part-time tuition: $800 per semester hour.

Financial Aid Of all full-time matriculated undergraduates who enrolled in 2002, 525 applied for aid, 421 were judged to have need, 218 had their need fully met. 126 Federal Work-Study jobs (averaging $796). In 2002, 119 non-need-based awards were made. *Average percent of need met:* 83%. *Average financial aid package:* $10,686. *Average need-based loan:* $3179. *Average need-based gift aid:* $6569. *Average non-need-based aid:* $5691. *Average indebtedness upon graduation:* $15,621.

Applying *Options:* electronic application, deferred entrance. *Application fee:* $20. *Required:* high school transcript, minimum 2.25 GPA. *Required for some:* 2 letters of recommendation, interview, auditions for music students; portfolios for art students. *Recommended:* essay or personal statement, 3 letters of recommendation. *Application deadlines:* rolling (freshmen), rolling (transfers).

Freshman Application Contact Office of Admission, Huntingdon College, 1500 East Fairview Avenue, Montgomery, AL 36106. *Phone:* 334-833-4497. *Toll-free phone:* 800-763-0313. *Fax:* 334-833-4347. *E-mail:* admiss@huntingdon.edu.

See page 274 for the College Close-Up.

ITT Technical Institute

Birmingham, Alabama **www.itt-tech.edu/**

- **Proprietary** primarily 2-year, founded 1994, part of ITT Educational Services, Inc
- **Suburban** campus
- **Coed**
- **Minimally difficult** entrance level

Academics *Calendar:* quarters. *Degrees:* associate and bachelor's.

Student Life *Campus security:* 24-hour emergency response devices.

Standardized Tests *Required:* Wonderlic aptitude test (for admission).

Applying *Options:* deferred entrance. *Application fee:* $100. *Required:* high school transcript, interview. *Recommended:* letters of recommendation.

Freshman Application Contact Mr. Jesse L. Johnson, Director of Recruitment, ITT Technical Institute, 6270 Park South Drive, Bessemer, AL 35022. *Phone:* 205-497-5700. *Toll-free phone:* 800-488-7033. *Fax:* 205-497-5799.

Jacksonville State University

Jacksonville, Alabama **www.jsu.edu/**

- **State-supported** comprehensive, founded 1883
- **Small-town** 459-acre campus with easy access to Birmingham
- **Coed** 7,485 undergraduate students, 78% full-time, 58% women, 42% men
- **Minimally difficult** entrance level, 86% of applicants were admitted

Undergraduates 5,819 full-time, 1,666 part-time. Students come from 50 states and territories, 64 other countries, 17% are from out of state, 26% African American, 0.8% Asian American or Pacific Islander, 1% Hispanic American, 0.5% Native American, 2% international, 9% transferred in, 16% live on campus. *Retention:* 69% of 2006 full-time freshmen returned.

Freshmen *Admission:* 3,299 applied, 2,853 admitted, 1,302 enrolled. *Average high school GPA:* 3.17. *Test scores:* SAT critical reading scores over 500: 26%; SAT math scores over 500: 26%; ACT scores over 18: 67%; SAT critical reading scores over 600: 4%; SAT math scores over 600: 4%; ACT scores over 24: 14%; ACT scores over 30: 1%.

Faculty *Total:* 456, 70% full-time, 49% with terminal degrees. *Student/faculty ratio:* 20:1.

Majors Accounting; animal genetics; anthropology; Army R.O.T.C./military science; art; biology/biological sciences; business administration and management; chemistry; clothing/textiles; communication/speech communication and rhetoric; computer and information sciences; corrections; criminal justice/law enforcement administration; criminal justice/police science; dietetics; dramatic/theater arts; ecology; economics; education; educational/instructional media design; educational psychology; electrical, electronic and communications engineering technology; elementary education; English; environmental biology; family and consumer sciences/home economics teacher education; family and consumer sciences/human sciences; finance; foods, nutrition, and wellness; forensic science and technology; French; geography; geology/earth science; German; health and physical education; health teacher education; history; industrial technology; kindergarten/preschool education; kinesiology and exercise science; marine biology and biological oceanography; marketing/marketing management; mathematics; middle school education; music; music teacher education; nursing (registered nurse training); occupational safety and health technology; parks, recreation and leisure; physical education teaching and coaching; physics; political science and government; psychology; secondary education; social work; sociology; Spanish; special education.

Academics *Calendar:* semesters. *Degrees:* bachelor's, master's, and post-master's certificates. *Special study options:* academic remediation for entering students, accelerated degree program, adult/continuing education programs, advanced placement credit, cooperative education, distance learning, double majors, honors programs, independent study, internships, part-time degree program, services for LD students, summer session for credit. *ROTC:* Army (b).

Computers on Campus 330 computers/terminals are available on campus for general student use. Campuswide network is available.

Student Life *Housing options:* coed, men-only, women-only, disabled students. Campus housing is university owned. *Activities and organizations:* drama/theater group, student-run newspaper, radio and television station, choral group, marching band, Student Government Association, Archaeology Club, Campus Fellowship Clubs, Computer Science Club, Biology Club, national fraternities, national sororities. *Campus security:* 24-hour emergency response devices and patrols, student patrols, late-night transport/escort service, night security officer in female residence halls. *Student services:* health clinic, personal/psychological counseling.

Athletics Member NCAA. All Division I except football (Division I-AA). *Intercollegiate sports:* baseball M (s), basketball M (s)/W (s), cross-country running M (s)/W (s), golf M (s)/W (s), riflery M (s)/W (s), soccer W (s), softball W (s), tennis M (s)/W (s), volleyball W (s). *Intramural sports:* badminton M (c)/W (c), basketball M (c)/W (c), bowling M (c)/W (c), football M (c), golf M (c)/W (c), racquetball M (c)/W (c), soccer M (c)/W (c), softball M (c)/W (c), table tennis M (c)/W (c), tennis M (c)/W (c), volleyball M (c)/W (c).

Standardized Tests *Required:* SAT or ACT (for admission).

Costs (2007–08) *Tuition:* state resident $5070 full-time, $169 per credit hour part-time; nonresident $10,140 full-time, $338 per credit hour part-time. *Room and board:* $3763. Room and board charges vary according to board plan and housing facility. *Waivers:* employees or children of employees.

Financial Aid Of all full-time matriculated undergraduates who enrolled in 2005, 3,266 had their need fully met. 380 Federal Work-Study jobs (averaging $1164). 517 state and other part-time jobs (averaging $2518). In 2005, 807 non-need-based awards were made. *Average percent of need met:* 40%. *Average financial aid package:* $6675. *Average need-based loan:* $5670. *Average need-based gift aid:* $3745. *Average non-need-based aid:* $1200. *Average indebtedness upon graduation:* $17,125.

Applying *Options:* early admission, deferred entrance. *Application fee:* $20. *Required:* high school transcript. *Application deadlines:* rolling (freshmen), rolling (out-of-state freshmen), rolling (transfers). *Notification:* continuous (freshmen), continuous (out-of-state freshmen), continuous (transfers).

Freshman Application Contact Ms. Martha Mitchell, Director of Admission, Jacksonville State University, 700 Pelham Road North, Jacksonville, AL 36265. *Phone:* 256-782-5363. *Toll-free phone:* 800-231-5291. *Fax:* 256-782-5291. *E-mail:* info@jsu.edu.

Judson College

Marion, Alabama **www.judson.edu/**

- **Independent Baptist** 4-year, founded 1838
- **Rural** 80-acre campus with easy access to Birmingham
- **Endowment** $15.1 million
- **Women only** 311 undergraduate students, 77% full-time
- **Moderately difficult** entrance level, 80% of applicants were admitted

Undergraduates 241 full-time, 70 part-time. Students come from 24 states and territories, 4 other countries, 27% are from out of state, 15% African American, 0.3% Asian American or Pacific Islander, 0.6% Hispanic American, 0.3% Native American, 1% international, 10% transferred in, 62% live on campus. *Retention:* 60% of 2006 full-time freshmen returned.

Freshmen *Admission:* 309 applied, 248 admitted, 79 enrolled. *Average high school GPA:* 3.22. *Test scores:* SAT critical reading scores over 500: 84%; SAT math scores over 500: 100%; ACT scores over 18: 91%; SAT critical reading scores over 600: 34%; SAT math scores over 600: 50%; ACT scores over 24: 37%; SAT critical reading scores over 700: 17%; SAT math scores over 700: 17%; ACT scores over 30: 6%.

Faculty *Total:* 36, 58% full-time, 58% with terminal degrees. *Student/faculty ratio:* 9:1.

Majors Art; biology/biological sciences; business/commerce; chemistry; criminal justice/law enforcement administration; elementary education; English; English/language arts teacher education; history; interdisciplinary studies; mathematics; mathematics teacher education; modern languages; music; music teacher education; psychology; religious studies; science teacher education; social science teacher education.

Academics *Calendar:* semesters plus 2-month term. *Degree:* bachelor's. *Special study options:* academic remediation for entering students, accelerated degree program, adult/continuing education programs, advanced placement credit, distance learning, double majors, independent study, internships, off-campus study, part-time degree program, student-designed majors, study abroad, summer session for credit. *ROTC:* Army (c).

Computers on Campus 75 computers/terminals are available on campus for general student use. Students can access the following: campus intranet, computer help desk, free student e-mail accounts, online (class) grades. Campuswide network is available. 100% of college-owned or -operated housing units are wired for high-speed Internet access. Wireless service is available via dorm rooms.

Student Life *Housing:* on-campus residence required through senior year. *Options:* women-only. Campus housing is university owned. *Activities and organizations:* drama/theater group, student-run newspaper, choral group, marching band, Student Government Association, campus ministries, choir, Ambassadors, Science Club. *Campus security:* 24-hour emergency response devices and patrols, late-night transport/escort service, controlled dormitory access. *Student services:* personal/psychological counseling.

Athletics *Intercollegiate sports:* basketball W (s), equestrian sports W, softball W (s), tennis W (s), volleyball W (s). *Intramural sports:* basketball W, field hockey W, softball W, tennis W, volleyball W.

Standardized Tests *Required:* SAT or ACT (for admission).

Costs (2007–08) *Comprehensive fee:* $18,240 includes full-time tuition ($10,920), mandatory fees ($200), and room and board ($7120). Full-time tuition and fees vary according to course load. Part-time tuition: $360 per semester hour. Part-time tuition and fees vary according to course load. *Payment plan:* installment. *Waivers:* employees or children of employees.

Financial Aid Of all full-time matriculated undergraduates who enrolled in 2006, 201 applied for aid, 180 were judged to have need, 45 had their need fully met. 72 Federal Work-Study jobs (averaging $1800). 32 state and other part-time jobs (averaging $1500). In 2006, 35 non-need-based awards were made. *Average percent of need met:* 85%. *Average financial aid package:* $11,730. *Average need-based loan:* $4126. *Average need-based gift aid:* $8047. *Average non-need-based aid:* $6503. *Average indebtedness upon graduation:* $18,747.

Applying *Options:* electronic application, early admission, deferred entrance. *Application fee:* $32. *Required:* high school transcript, minimum 2.0 GPA, 2 letters of recommendation, interview. *Recommended:* essay or personal statement. *Application deadlines:* rolling (freshmen), rolling (out-of-state freshmen), rolling (transfers). *Notification:* continuous (freshmen), continuous (out-of-state freshmen), continuous (transfers).

Freshman Application Contact Mrs. Charlotte Clements, Vice President for Admissions and Financial Aid, Judson College, PO Box 120, 302 Bibb Street, Marion, AL 36756. *Phone:* 334-683-5110. *Toll-free phone:* 800-447-9472. *Fax:* 334-683-5282. *E-mail:* admissions@judson.edu.

MILES COLLEGE

Fairfield, Alabama — www.miles.edu/

- **Independent Christian Methodist Episcopal** 4-year, founded 1905
- **Suburban** 76-acre campus
- **Endowment** $13.1 million
- **Coed** 1,738 undergraduate students, 91% full-time, 54% women, 46% men
- **Noncompetitive** entrance level, 26% of applicants were admitted

Undergraduates 1,589 full-time, 149 part-time. Students come from 23 states and territories, 21% are from out of state, 95% African American, 23% transferred in, 40% live on campus. *Retention:* 60% of 2006 full-time freshmen returned.

Freshmen *Admission:* 2,905 applied, 768 admitted, 362 enrolled. *Average high school GPA:* 2.5. *Test scores:* ACT scores over 18: 11%; ACT scores over 24: 1%.

Faculty *Total:* 147, 71% full-time, 31% with terminal degrees. *Student/faculty ratio:* 14:1.

Majors Accounting and business/management; African studies; behavioral sciences; biology/biological sciences; business administration and management; chemistry; communication and media related; computer and information sciences; criminal justice/law enforcement administration; early childhood education; education; elementary education; English; English/language arts teacher education; environmental science; history; mass communication/media; mathematics; mathematics teacher education; physics; political science and government; religious studies; secondary education; social sciences; social work.

Academics *Calendar:* semesters. *Degree:* bachelor's. *Special study options:* academic remediation for entering students, accelerated degree program, adult/continuing education programs, cooperative education, double majors, honors programs, internships, off-campus study, part-time degree program, services for LD students, summer session for credit. *ROTC:* Army (c), Air Force (c). *Unusual degree programs:* 3-2 engineering with Tuskegee University, University of Alabama at Birmingham, UAB Walker College, Tennessee State University; social work with Alabama A&M University; physics with Tuskegee University, Alabama Agricultural and Mechanical University.

Computers on Campus 50 computers/terminals are available on campus for general student use.

Student Life *Housing options:* coed, men-only, women-only. Campus housing is university owned. *Activities and organizations:* drama/theater group, student-run newspaper, television station, choral group, marching band, Choir, Education Club, Student Government Association, Phi Beta Lambda Business Club, Communications Club, national fraternities, national sororities. *Campus security:* 24-hour emergency response devices and patrols. *Student services:* health clinic, personal/psychological counseling.

Athletics Member NCAA, NAIA. All NCAA Division III. *Intercollegiate sports:* baseball M (s), basketball M (s)/W (s), cheerleading W (s), cross-country running M (s), football M (s), softball W (s), track and field M (s). *Intramural sports:* basketball M/W, cross-country running M/W, tennis M/W, track and field M/W, volleyball W.

Standardized Tests *Recommended:* ACT (for admission), ACT (for placement).

Costs (2007–08) *Comprehensive fee:* $12,407 includes full-time tuition ($6545), mandatory fees ($506), and room and board ($5356). Full-time tuition and fees vary according to course load. Part-time tuition: $275 per credit. *Required fees:* $253 per term part-time. *College room only:* $3090. Room and board charges vary according to housing facility. *Payment plans:* installment, deferred payment. *Waivers:* employees or children of employees.

Financial Aid Of all full-time matriculated undergraduates who enrolled in 2002, 1,696 applied for aid, 1,673 were judged to have need, 1,254 had their need fully met. 355 Federal Work-Study jobs (averaging $804). In 2002, 23 non-need-based awards were made. *Average percent of need met:* 75%. *Average financial aid package:* $6702. *Average need-based loan:* $1382. *Average need-based gift aid:* $1939. *Average non-need-based aid:* $609. *Average indebtedness upon graduation:* $17,500.

Applying *Required for some:* essay or personal statement, high school transcript. *Application deadlines:* 8/23 (freshmen), rolling (transfers). *Notification:* continuous (freshmen), continuous (transfers).

Freshman Application Contact Mr. Christopher Robertson, Director of Admissions and Recruitment, Miles College, 5500 Myron Massey Boulevard, Bell Building, Fairfield, AL 35064. *Phone:* 205-929-1657. *Toll-free phone:* 800-445-0708. *Fax:* 205-929-1627. *E-mail:* admissions@miles.edu.

OAKWOOD COLLEGE

Huntsville, Alabama — www.oakwood.edu/

- **Independent Seventh-day Adventist** upper-level, founded 1896
- 1200-acre campus
- **Coed** 1,824 undergraduate students, 94% full-time, 58% women, 42% men
- **Minimally difficult** entrance level, 57% of applicants were admitted

Undergraduates 1,712 full-time, 112 part-time. Students come from 43 states and territories, 21 other countries, 81% are from out of state, 89% African American, 0.2% Asian American or Pacific Islander, 0.5% Hispanic American, 0.1% Native American, 7% international, 6% transferred in, 64% live on campus.

Freshmen *Admission:* 1,492 applied, 856 admitted.

Faculty *Total:* 171, 60% full-time, 47% with terminal degrees. *Student/faculty ratio:* 14:1.

Majors Accounting; administrative assistant and secretarial science; applied mathematics; biblical studies; biochemistry; biology/biological sciences; business administration and management; business teacher education; chemistry; clinical laboratory science/medical technology; commercial and advertising art; computer science; dietetics; economics; elementary education; engineering; English; family and consumer sciences/home economics teacher education; family and consumer sciences/human sciences; French; history; information science/studies; interdisciplinary studies; mass communication/media; mathematics; music; music teacher education; natural sciences; nursing (registered nurse training); occupational therapy; pastoral studies/counseling; physical education teaching and coaching; physical therapy; psychology; religious education; religious studies; science teacher education; social sciences; social work; Spanish; theology.

Academics *Calendar:* semesters. *Degrees:* associate, bachelor's, master's, and postbachelor's certificates. *Special study options:* academic remediation for entering students, advanced placement credit, double majors, honors programs, internships, off-campus study, part-time degree program, study abroad. *Unusual degree programs:* 3-2 engineering with Alabama Agricultural and Mechanical University, The University of Alabama in Huntsville.

Computers on Campus 350 computers/terminals are available on campus for general student use. Students can access the following: campus intranet, computer help desk, free student e-mail accounts, online (class) grades, online (class) registration, online (class) schedules. Campuswide network is available. Wireless service is available via classrooms, libraries.

Student Life *Housing options:* men-only, women-only. Campus housing is university owned. Freshman applicants given priority for college housing. *Activities and organizations:* student-run newspaper, radio station, choral group, United Student Movement. *Campus security:* 24-hour patrols, student patrols, late-night transport/escort service. *Student services:* health clinic, personal/psychological counseling.

Athletics *Intercollegiate sports:* basketball M/W. *Intramural sports:* basketball M/W, football M, golf M, gymnastics M/W, racquetball M/W, soccer M, softball M/W, swimming and diving M/W, table tennis M/W, tennis M/W, track and field M/W, volleyball M/W.

Standardized Tests *Required:* SAT or ACT (for admission).

Costs (2008–09) *Comprehensive fee:* $20,632 includes full-time tuition ($12,420), mandatory fees ($754), and room and board ($7458). Part-time tuition: $536 per hour. *College room only:* $3150.

Financial Aid Of all full-time matriculated undergraduates who enrolled in 2001, 1,422 applied for aid, 1,422 were judged to have need, 131 had their need fully met. *Average percent of need met:* 77%. *Average financial aid package:* $6500. *Average need-based loan:* $4500. *Average need-based gift aid:* $2500. *Average non-need-based aid:* $2000. *Average indebtedness upon graduation:* $15,000.

Applying *Options:* early action, deferred entrance. *Application fee:* $25. *Application deadlines:* rolling (transfers), 3/30 (early action). *Notification:* 4/15 (early action).

Application Contact Mr. Jason McCracken, Director of Enrollment Management, Oakwood College, 7000 Adventist Boulevard, NW, Huntsville, AL 35896. *Phone:* 256-726-7354. *Toll-free phone:* 800-358-3978. *Fax:* 256-726-7154. *E-mail:* admission@oakwood.edu.

REMINGTON COLLEGE–MOBILE CAMPUS

Mobile, Alabama **www.remingtoncollege.edu/**

- **Proprietary** primarily 2-year
- **Suburban** 5-acre campus
- **Coed**
- **Noncompetitive** entrance level

Majors Computer systems networking and telecommunications; criminal justice/law enforcement administration; electrical, electronics and communications engineering; operations management.

Academics *Calendar:* quarters. *Degrees:* diplomas, associate, and bachelor's. *Special study options:* adult/continuing education programs, cooperative education, services for LD students.

Financial Aid Of all full-time matriculated undergraduates who enrolled in 2006, 500 applied for aid, 500 were judged to have need. *Average percent of need met:* 45%. *Average financial aid package:* $7043. *Average need-based loan:* $3000. *Average need-based gift aid:* $7043. *Average indebtedness upon graduation:* $14,000.

Freshman Application Contact Remington College–Mobile Campus, 828 Downtowner Loop West, Mobile, AL 36609. *Phone:* 251-343-8200. *Toll-free phone:* 800-866-0850.

SAMFORD UNIVERSITY

Birmingham, Alabama **www.samford.edu/**

- **Independent Baptist** university, founded 1841
- **Suburban** 180-acre campus
- **Endowment** $301.0 million
- **Coed** 2,860 undergraduate students, 94% full-time, 64% women, 36% men
- **Moderately difficult** entrance level, 92% of applicants were admitted

A Samford education is carefully designed to provide personal empowerment, academic and career competency, social and civic responsibility, and ethical and spiritual strength. It is built around broadening international awareness and the development of transferable skills, such as computer familiarity in every academic major, to keep Samford graduates on the leading edge in a constantly changing career environment.

Undergraduates 2,683 full-time, 177 part-time. Students come from 25 states and territories, 10 other countries, 61% are from out of state, 6% African American, 1% Asian American or Pacific Islander, 1% Hispanic American, 0.2% Native American, 4% transferred in, 42% live on campus. *Retention:* 83% of 2006 full-time freshmen returned.

Freshmen *Admission:* 1,810 applied, 1,661 admitted, 713 enrolled. *Average high school GPA:* 3.61. *Test scores:* SAT critical reading scores over 500: 82%; SAT math scores over 500: 73%; ACT scores over 18: 100%; SAT critical reading scores over 600: 34%; SAT math scores over 600: 35%; ACT scores over 24: 58%; SAT critical reading scores over 700: 10%; SAT math scores over 700: 6%; ACT scores over 30: 15%.

Faculty *Total:* 438, 64% full-time, 71% with terminal degrees. *Student/faculty ratio:* 12:1.

Majors Accounting; Asian studies; athletic training; biochemistry; biology/biological sciences; biology teacher education; business administration and management; cartography; chemistry; classical, ancient Mediterranean and Near Eastern studies and archaeology; classics and languages, literatures and linguistics; commercial and advertising art; community organization and advocacy; computer science; counseling psychology; criminal justice/law enforcement administration; dramatic/theater arts; engineering physics; engineering related; English; English/language arts teacher education; environmental science; environmental studies; family and community services; foreign languages and literatures; French; general studies; geography; German; health and physical education; history; history teacher education; human development and family studies; human nutrition; human resources management; interior design; international business/trade/commerce; international relations and affairs; journalism; kinesiology and exercise science; Latin; Latin American studies; marine biology and biological oceanography; mathematics; music performance; music teacher education; music theory and composition; nursing (registered nurse training); philosophy; philosophy and religious studies related; physical education teaching and coaching; physics; piano and organ; political science and government; pre-medical studies; psychology; public administration; religious/sacred music; religious studies; science teacher education; science, technology and society; social sciences; social science teacher education; sociology; Spanish; speech and rhetoric; speech teacher education; visual and performing arts related; voice and opera.

Academics *Calendar:* 4-1-4. *Degrees:* certificates, associate, bachelor's, master's, doctoral, first professional, and post-master's certificates. *Special study options:* accelerated degree program, adult/continuing education programs, advanced placement credit, cooperative education, distance learning, double majors, honors programs, independent study, internships, off-campus study, part-time degree program, services for LD students, study abroad, summer session for credit. *ROTC:* Army (c), Air Force (b). *Unusual degree programs:* 3-2 engineering with The University of Alabama at Birmingham, Auburn University, Washington University in St. Louis, Mercer University.

Computers on Campus 330 computers/terminals are available on campus for general student use. Students can access the following: campus intranet, computer help desk, free student e-mail accounts, online (class) grades, online (class) registration, online (class) schedules. Campuswide network is available. Wireless service is available via computer centers, dorm rooms, learning centers, student centers.

Student Life *Housing:* on-campus residence required for freshman year. *Options:* men-only, women-only, disabled students. Campus housing is university owned. Freshman campus housing is guaranteed. *Activities and organizations:* drama/theater group, student-run newspaper, radio station, choral group, marching band, student ministries, student government, national fraternities, national sororities. *Campus security:* 24-hour emergency response devices and patrols, late-night transport/escort service. *Student services:* health clinic, personal/psychological counseling.

Athletics Member NCAA. All Division I except football (Division I-AA). *Intercollegiate sports:* baseball M (s), basketball M (s)/W (s), cross-country running M (s)/W (s), golf M (s)/W (s), soccer M (c)/W (s), softball W (s), tennis M (s)/W (s), track and field M (s)/W (s), volleyball W (s). *Intramural sports:* basketball M/W, bowling M/W, cheerleading M/W, football M/W, golf M/W, racquetball M/W, rock climbing M/W, soccer M/W, softball M/W, table tennis M/W, tennis M/W, ultimate Frisbee M (c)/W (c), volleyball M/W.

Standardized Tests *Required:* SAT or ACT (for admission).

Costs (2007–08) *Comprehensive fee:* $24,240 includes full-time tuition ($17,920) and room and board ($6320). Full-time tuition and fees vary according to course load. Part-time tuition: $600 per credit. Part-time tuition and fees vary according to course load. *College room only:* $3220. Room and board charges vary according to board plan and housing facility. *Waivers:* employees or children of employees.

Financial Aid Of all full-time matriculated undergraduates who enrolled in 2006, 1,477 applied for aid, 1,064 were judged to have need, 251 had their need fully met. 650 Federal Work-Study jobs (averaging $1800). 550 state and other part-time jobs (averaging $1500). In 2006, 650 non-need-based awards were made. *Average percent of need met:* 68%. *Average financial aid package:*

$12,542. *Average need-based loan:* $3763. *Average need-based gift aid:* $7872. *Average non-need-based aid:* $4875. *Average indebtedness upon graduation:* $18,700.

Applying *Options:* electronic application, early admission, deferred entrance. *Application fee:* $35. *Required:* essay or personal statement, 1 letter of recommendation, leadership resumé. *Required for some:* high school transcript. *Recommended:* interview. *Application deadlines:* 12/15 (freshmen), 8/15 (transfers). *Notification:* continuous (freshmen).

Freshman Application Contact Dr. Phil Kimrey, Dean of Admissions and Financial Aid, Samford University, 800 Lakeshore Drive, Samford Hall, Birmingham, AL 35229-0002. *Phone:* 205-726-3673. *Toll-free phone:* 800-888-7218. *Fax:* 205-726-2171. *E-mail:* admiss@samford.edu.

See page 276 for the College Close-Up.

SOUTHEASTERN BIBLE COLLEGE

Birmingham, Alabama **www.sebc.edu/**

- **Independent nondenominational** 4-year, founded 1935
- **Suburban** 10-acre campus
- **Coed** 220 undergraduate students, 72% full-time, 40% women, 60% men
- **Moderately difficult** entrance level, 96% of applicants were admitted

Undergraduates 159 full-time, 61 part-time. Students come from 2 other countries, 16% are from out of state, 28% African American, 0.5% Native American, 0.9% international, 21% transferred in, 25% live on campus. *Retention:* 67% of 2006 full-time freshmen returned.

Freshmen *Admission:* 79 applied, 76 admitted, 34 enrolled.

Faculty *Total:* 29, 31% full-time, 59% with terminal degrees. *Student/faculty ratio:* 11:1.

Majors Biblical studies; education; music; pastoral studies/counseling; religious education; religious/sacred music; religious studies; theology.

Academics *Calendar:* semesters. *Degrees:* diplomas, associate, and bachelor's (associate). *Special study options:* academic remediation for entering students, adult/continuing education programs, advanced placement credit, double majors, independent study, internships, part-time degree program, summer session for credit.

Computers on Campus 30 computers/terminals are available on campus for general student use. Students can access the following: free student e-mail accounts. Wireless service is available via entire campus.

Student Life *Housing options:* men-only, women-only. Campus housing is university owned. *Activities and organizations:* choral group, Student Council, Student Missions Fellowship, chorale. *Campus security:* 24-hour emergency response devices, student patrols.

Athletics *Intercollegiate sports:* basketball M/W. *Intramural sports:* soccer M/W, table tennis M/W, tennis M/W.

Standardized Tests *Required:* SAT or ACT (for admission).

Costs (2007–08) *Tuition:* $9240 full-time, $330 per semester hour part-time. Full-time tuition and fees vary according to course load and program. Part-time tuition and fees vary according to course load and program. *Required fees:* $250 full-time. *Room only:* $2200. *Payment plan:* installment.

Financial Aid Of all full-time matriculated undergraduates who enrolled in 2005, 188 applied for aid, 183 were judged to have need. 10 Federal Work-Study jobs (averaging $1200). 10 state and other part-time jobs (averaging $2000). *Average percent of need met:* 70%. *Average financial aid package:* $6457. *Average need-based loan:* $4250. *Average need-based gift aid:* $4000. *Average indebtedness upon graduation:* $20,000.

Applying *Options:* electronic application, deferred entrance. *Application fee:* $30. *Required:* essay or personal statement, high school transcript, minimum 1.5 GPA, 2 letters of recommendation. *Required for some:* interview. *Application deadlines:* 8/1 (freshmen), 8/1 (transfers). *Notification:* continuous until 9/1 (freshmen), continuous until 9/1 (transfers).

Freshman Application Contact Mrs. Katy Holmes, Admissions Counselor, Southeastern Bible College, 2545 Valleydale Road, Birmingham, AL 35244. *Phone:* 205-970-9211. *Toll-free phone:* 800-749-8878. *Fax:* 205-970-9207. *E-mail:* kholmes@sebc.edu.

SOUTH UNIVERSITY

Montgomery, Alabama **www.southuniversity.edu/**

- **Proprietary** comprehensive, founded 1887
- **Urban** 4-acre campus
- **Coed**

Majors Business administration and management; criminal justice/law enforcement administration; health/health care administration; information technology; legal studies.

Academics *Calendar:* quarters. *Degrees:* associate, bachelor's, and master's.

Freshman Application Contact South University, 5355 Vaughn Road, Montgomery, AL 36116. *Phone:* 800-688-0932. *Fax:* 334-395-8859.

See page 278 for the College Close-Up.

SPRING HILL COLLEGE

Mobile, Alabama **www.shc.edu/**

- **Independent Roman Catholic (Jesuit)** comprehensive, founded 1830
- **Suburban** 450-acre campus
- **Endowment** $31.4 million
- **Coed** 1,318 undergraduate students, 89% full-time, 67% women, 33% men
- **Moderately difficult** entrance level, 66% of applicants were admitted

Undergraduates 1,168 full-time, 150 part-time. Students come from 37 states and territories, 8 other countries, 52% are from out of state, 16% African American, 1% Asian American or Pacific Islander, 6% Hispanic American, 0.7% Native American, 0.7% international, 2% transferred in, 74% live on campus. *Retention:* 79% of 2006 full-time freshmen returned.

Freshmen *Admission:* 3,042 applied, 2,003 admitted, 383 enrolled. *Average high school GPA:* 3.48. *Test scores:* SAT critical reading scores over 500: 73%; SAT math scores over 500: 70%; SAT writing scores over 500: 71%; ACT scores over 18: 99%; SAT critical reading scores over 600: 28%; SAT math scores over 600: 17%; SAT writing scores over 600: 25%; ACT scores over 24: 50%; SAT critical reading scores over 700: 3%; SAT math scores over 700: 2%; SAT writing scores over 700: 5%; ACT scores over 30: 5%.

Faculty *Total:* 147, 54% full-time, 61% with terminal degrees. *Student/faculty ratio:* 13:1.

Majors Accounting; arts management; art therapy; biochemistry; biology/biological sciences; biopsychology; business administration and management; chemistry; computer and information sciences; dramatic/theater arts; early childhood education; education; elementary education; engineering related; English; English language and literature related; finance; fine/studio arts; general studies; graphic design; history; humanities; interdisciplinary studies; international business/trade/commerce; international relations and affairs; journalism; marine biology and biological oceanography; marketing/marketing management; mathematics; multi-/interdisciplinary studies related; nursing (registered nurse training); philosophy; political science and government; pre-dentistry studies; pre-medical studies; pre-veterinary studies; psychology; public relations, advertising, and applied communication related; radio, television, and digital communication related; secondary education; social sciences; sociology; Spanish; theology.

Academics *Calendar:* semesters. *Degrees:* certificates, associate, bachelor's, master's, and postbachelor's certificates. *Special study options:* academic remediation for entering students, accelerated degree program, adult/continuing education programs, advanced placement credit, distance learning, double majors, honors programs, independent study, internships, off-campus study, part-time degree program, services for LD students, student-designed majors, study abroad, summer session for credit. *ROTC:* Army (c), Air Force (c). *Unusual degree programs:* 3-2 business administration; engineering with Marquette University, University of Alabama at Birmingham, University of Florida, Auburn University, Texas A & M University.

Computers on Campus 194 computers/terminals and 250 ports are available on campus for general student use. Students can access the following: campus intranet, computer help desk, free student e-mail accounts, online (class) grades, online (class) registration, online (class) schedules. Campuswide network is available. 100% of college-owned or -operated housing units are wired for high-speed Internet access.

Student Life *Housing:* on-campus residence required through senior year. *Options:* coed, men-only, women-only. Campus housing is university owned. Freshman campus housing is guaranteed. *Activities and organizations:* drama/theater group, student-run newspaper, choral group, Student Government Association, Multicultural Student Union, Circle K, Campus Programming Board, Habitat for Humanity, national fraternities, national sororities. *Campus security:* 24-hour emergency response devices and patrols, late-night transport/escort service, controlled dormitory access. *Student services:* health clinic, personal/psychological counseling.

Athletics Member NAIA. *Intercollegiate sports:* baseball M (s), basketball M (s)/W (s), cross-country running M (s)/W (s), golf M (s)/W (s), soccer M (s)/W (s), softball W (s), tennis M (s)/W (s), volleyball W (s). *Intramural sports:* basketball M/W, football M/W, racquetball M/W, rugby M (c), soccer M/W, table tennis M/W, volleyball M/W.

Standardized Tests *Required:* SAT or ACT (for admission).

Costs (2007–08) *Comprehensive fee:* $31,800 includes full-time tuition ($21,686), mandatory fees ($1414), and room and board ($8700). Part-time tuition: $810 per semester hour. *Required fees:* $46 per semester hour part-time. *College room only:* $4500. Room and board charges vary according to board plan and housing facility. *Payment plan:* installment. *Waivers:* employees or children of employees.

Financial Aid Of all full-time matriculated undergraduates who enrolled in 2007, 900 applied for aid, 773 were judged to have need, 177 had their need fully met. 203 Federal Work-Study jobs (averaging $1093). 74 state and other part-time jobs (averaging $1023). In 2007, 346 non-need-based awards were made. *Average percent of need met:* 80%. *Average financial aid package:* $21,618. *Average need-based loan:* $4663. *Average need-based gift aid:* $15,786. *Average non-need-based aid:* $12,358. *Average indebtedness upon graduation:* $13,176.

Applying *Options:* electronic application, early admission, deferred entrance. *Application fee:* $25. *Required:* essay or personal statement, high school transcript, 1 letter of recommendation. *Recommended:* minimum 2.5 GPA, interview. *Application deadlines:* 7/15 (freshmen), 7/15 (out-of-state freshmen), rolling (transfers). *Notification:* continuous (freshmen), continuous (out-of-state freshmen), continuous (transfers).

Freshman Application Contact Admissions Office, Spring Hill College, 4000 Dauphin Street, Mobile, AL 36608-1791. *Phone:* 251-380-3030. *Toll-free phone:* 800-SHC-6704. *Fax:* 251-460-2186. *E-mail:* admit@shc.edu.

STILLMAN COLLEGE

Tuscaloosa, Alabama **www.stillman.edu/**

- **Independent** 4-year, founded 1876, affiliated with Presbyterian Church (U.S.A.)
- **Urban** 100-acre campus with easy access to Birmingham
- **Endowment** $25.8 million
- **Coed** 915 undergraduate students, 97% full-time, 54% women, 46% men
- **Minimally difficult** entrance level, 37% of applicants were admitted

Undergraduates 892 full-time, 23 part-time. Students come from 26 states and territories, 1 other country, 34% are from out of state, 91% African American, 0.1% Asian American or Pacific Islander, 0.4% Hispanic American, 0.1% international, 5% transferred in, 75% live on campus. *Retention:* 82% of 2006 full-time freshmen returned.

Freshmen *Admission:* 3,739 applied, 1,391 admitted, 385 enrolled. *Average high school GPA:* 2.6. *Test scores:* SAT critical reading scores over 500: 9%; SAT math scores over 500: 11%; ACT scores over 18: 40%; SAT critical reading scores over 600: 2%; SAT math scores over 600: 4%; ACT scores over 24: 7%; ACT scores over 30: 3%.

Faculty *Total:* 57, 82% full-time, 61% with terminal degrees. *Student/faculty ratio:* 16:1.

Majors Art; biology/biological sciences; business administration and management; computer and information sciences; computer science; education; English; history; mass communication/media; mathematics; music; nursing (registered nurse training); philosophy; physical education teaching and coaching.

Academics *Calendar:* semesters. *Degree:* bachelor's. *Special study options:* academic remediation for entering students, advanced placement credit, cooperative education, distance learning, double majors, honors programs, independent study, internships, summer session for credit. *ROTC:* Army (c). *Unusual degree programs:* 3-2 engineering with Tuskegee University, The University of Alabama; nursing with The University of Alabama, The University of Alabama at Birmingham.

Computers on Campus 130 computers/terminals are available on campus for general student use. Students can access the following: campus intranet, computer help desk, free student e-mail accounts, online (class) grades, online (class) schedules. Campuswide network is available. 100% of college-owned or -operated housing units are wired for high-speed Internet access.

Student Life *Housing:* on-campus residence required for freshman year. *Options:* men-only, women-only. Campus housing is university owned. Freshman campus housing is guaranteed. *Activities and organizations:* drama/theater group, student-run newspaper, choral group, marching band, Stillman Blue Pride Marching Band, Sophisticated Unlimited Modeling Troupe, Christian Student Association, Student Government Association, Student in Free Enterprise, national fraternities, national sororities. *Campus security:* 24-hour patrols. *Student services:* health clinic, personal/psychological counseling.

Athletics Member NCAA. All Division II. *Intercollegiate sports:* baseball M, basketball M/W, cross-country running M/W, football M, softball W, tennis M/W, track and field M/W, volleyball W. *Intramural sports:* badminton M (c)/W (c), baseball M (c), basketball M (c)/W (c), football M (c)/W (c), softball M (c)/W (c), table tennis M (c)/W (c).

Standardized Tests *Required:* SAT or ACT (for admission).

Costs (2007–08) *Comprehensive fee:* $17,960 includes full-time tuition ($11,030), mandatory fees ($1155), and room and board ($5775). Part-time tuition: $456 per credit. *Required fees:* $82 per term part-time. *Room and board:* Room and board charges vary according to housing facility. *Payment plan:* deferred payment. *Waivers:* employees or children of employees.

Financial Aid Of all full-time matriculated undergraduates who enrolled in 2001, 178 Federal Work-Study jobs (averaging $1035). *Average indebtedness upon graduation:* $19,000.

Applying *Options:* electronic application, early admission, deferred entrance. *Application fee:* $50. *Required:* high school transcript, minimum 2.0 GPA. *Required for some:* letters of recommendation. *Recommended:* essay or personal statement, interview. *Application deadlines:* rolling (freshmen), rolling (transfers).

Director of Admissions Monica Finch, Director of Admissions, Stillman College, PO Box 1430, 3600 Stillman Boulevard, Tuscaloosa, AL 35403. *Phone:* 205-366-8837. *Toll-free phone:* 800-841-5722. *Fax:* 205-366-8941. *E-mail:* mfinch@stillman.edu.

TALLADEGA COLLEGE

Talladega, Alabama **www.talladega.edu/**

- **Independent** 4-year, founded 1867
- **Small-town** 130-acre campus with easy access to Birmingham
- **Coed**
- **Minimally difficult** entrance level

Faculty *Student/faculty ratio:* 9:1.

Academics *Calendar:* semesters. *Degree:* bachelor's.

Student Life *Campus security:* 24-hour patrols, late-night transport/escort service, campus police.

Standardized Tests *Recommended:* SAT or ACT (for admission).

Costs (2007–08) *Comprehensive fee:* $11,548. Part-time tuition: $280 per credit hour. *Required fees:* $204 per term part-time. *Payment plans:* tuition prepayment, installment.

Financial Aid Of all full-time matriculated undergraduates who enrolled in 2003, 407 applied for aid, 375 were judged to have need, 100 had their need fully met. 141 Federal Work-Study jobs (averaging $691). *Average percent of need met:* 90. *Average financial aid package:* $5000. *Average need-based loan:* $5335. *Average need-based gift aid:* $3025. *Average non-need-based aid:* $5774. *Average indebtedness upon graduation:* $12,790. *Financial aid deadline:* 6/30.

Applying *Options:* electronic application, early admission, deferred entrance. *Application fee:* $25. *Required:* essay or personal statement, high school transcript, minimum 2.0 GPA, 1 letter of recommendation.

Freshman Application Contact Mr. Monroe Thornton, Director of Admissions, Talladega College, 627 West Battle Street, Talladega, AL 35160. *Phone:* 256-761-6219. *Toll-free phone:* 800-762-2468 (in-state); 800-633-2440 (out-of-state). *Fax:* 205-362-0274. *E-mail:* admissions@talladega.edu.

TROY UNIVERSITY

Troy, Alabama **www.troy.edu/**

- **State-supported** comprehensive, founded 1887, part of Troy University System
- **Small-town** 512-acre campus
- **Endowment** $20.5 million
- **Coed** 21,299 undergraduate students, 47% full-time, 56% women, 44% men
- **Moderately difficult** entrance level, 64% of applicants were admitted

Undergraduates 9,986 full-time, 11,313 part-time. Students come from 54 states and territories, 57 other countries, 48% are from out of state, 37% African American, 1% Asian American or Pacific Islander, 4% Hispanic American, 1% Native American, 2% international, 8% transferred in, 29% live on campus. *Retention:* 68% of 2006 full-time freshmen returned.

Freshmen *Admission:* 5,237 applied, 3,363 admitted, 2,783 enrolled. *Test scores:* ACT scores over 18: 68%; ACT scores over 24: 18%; ACT scores over 30: 2%.

Faculty *Total:* 1,602, 30% full-time. *Student/faculty ratio:* 21:1.

Majors Accounting; art; athletic training; biology/biological sciences; broadcast journalism; business administration and management; business/commerce; business, management, and marketing related; chemistry; computer and information sciences; corrections; criminal justice/safety; dramatic/theater arts; early childhood education; education; education (multiple levels); electrical, electronic and communications engineering technology; elementary education; English; environmental science; finance; fine/studio arts; foreign languages and literatures; history; human resources management; journalism; kindergarten/preschool education; liberal arts and sciences/liberal studies; management information systems; marine biology and biological oceanography; marketing related; mathematics; music; nursing (registered nurse training); parks, recreation and leisure; physical education teaching and coaching; physical sciences; political science and government; psychology; public administration and social service professions related; radio and television; rehabilitation and therapeutic professions related; secondary education; social sciences; social work; sociology; special education; speech and rhetoric; sport and fitness administration/management; survey technology.

Academics *Calendar:* semesters. *Degrees:* associate, bachelor's, master's, and post-master's certificates. *Special study options:* academic remediation for entering students, accelerated degree program, adult/continuing education programs, advanced placement credit, distance learning, double majors, English as a second language, external degree program, honors programs, independent study, internships, part-time degree program, services for LD students, study abroad, summer session for credit. *ROTC:* Army (b), Air Force (b).

Computers on Campus 1,570 computers/terminals are available on campus for general student use. Students can access the following: computer help desk, free student e-mail accounts, online (class) grades, online (class) registration, online (class) schedules. Campuswide network is available.

Student Life *Housing:* on-campus residence required for freshman year. *Options:* coed, men-only, women-only. Campus housing is university owned. Freshman campus housing is guaranteed. *Activities and organizations:* drama/theater group, student-run newspaper, television station, choral group, marching band, band, choir, yearbook, Activities Council, national fraternities, national sororities. *Campus security:* 24-hour emergency response devices and patrols, student patrols, late-night transport/escort service, controlled dormitory access. *Student services:* health clinic, personal/psychological counseling.

Athletics Member NCAA. All Division I except football (Division I-A). *Intercollegiate sports:* baseball M (s), basketball M (s)/W (s), cross-country running M (s)/W (s), soccer W (s), softball W (s), tennis M (s)/W (s), track and field M (s), volleyball W (s). *Intramural sports:* basketball M/W, bowling M/W, cross-country running M/W, football M, soccer W, softball W, tennis M/W, track and field M/W, volleyball W.

Standardized Tests *Required:* SAT or ACT (for admission).

Costs (2007–08) *Tuition:* state resident $4164 full-time, $174 per credit hour part-time; nonresident $8328 full-time, $348 per credit hour part-time. *Required fees:* $100 full-time, $50 per term part-time. *Room and board:* $5718; room only: $3046. Room and board charges vary according to board plan and housing facility. *Payment plan:* installment. *Waivers:* employees or children of employees.

Financial Aid Of all full-time matriculated undergraduates who enrolled in 2007, 6,073 applied for aid, 6,068 were judged to have need. 550 Federal Work-Study jobs (averaging $2000). In 2007, 1492 non-need-based awards were made. *Average financial aid package:* $3905. *Average need-based loan:* $3894. *Average need-based gift aid:* $3846. *Average non-need-based aid:* $2874.

Applying *Options:* electronic application, deferred entrance. *Application fee:* $30. *Required:* high school transcript. *Recommended:* interview. *Application deadlines:* rolling (freshmen), rolling (transfers).

Freshman Application Contact Mr. Buddy Starling, Dean of Enrollment Management, Troy University, 134 Adams Administration Building, Troy, AL 36082. *Phone:* 334-670-3243. *Toll-free phone:* 800-551-9716. *Fax:* 334-670-3733. *E-mail:* bstar@troy.edu.

See page 280 for the College Close-Up.

TUSKEGEE UNIVERSITY

Tuskegee, Alabama **www.tuskegee.edu/**

- **Independent** comprehensive, founded 1881
- **Small-town** 4390-acre campus
- **Coed** 2,514 undergraduate students, 97% full-time, 55% women, 45% men
- **Moderately difficult** entrance level, 58% of applicants were admitted

Undergraduates 2,443 full-time, 71 part-time. Students come from 40 states and territories, 30 other countries, 68% are from out of state, 86% African American, 0.1% Hispanic American, 0.2% Native American, 1% international, 7% transferred in, 63% live on campus. *Retention:* 71% of 2006 full-time freshmen returned.

Freshmen *Admission:* 3,092 applied, 1,800 admitted, 795 enrolled. *Average high school GPA:* 3.2. *Test scores:* SAT critical reading scores over 500: 74%; SAT math scores over 500: 76%; ACT scores over 18: 44%; SAT critical reading scores over 600: 28%; SAT math scores over 600: 34%; SAT critical reading scores over 700: 2%; SAT math scores over 700: 3%.

Faculty *Total:* 280, 93% full-time, 75% with terminal degrees. *Student/faculty ratio:* 11:1.

Majors Accounting; aerospace, aeronautical and astronautical engineering; agricultural business and management; agriculture; agronomy and crop science; animal sciences; architecture; biology/biological sciences; building/home/construction inspection; business administration and management; chemical engineering; chemistry; clinical laboratory science/medical technology; computer science; construction engineering technology; dietetics; economics; electrical, electronics and communications engineering; elementary education; engineering technology; English; environmental studies; finance; food science; foods, nutrition, and wellness; history; hospitality administration; hospitality and recreation marketing; management science; marketing/marketing management; mathematics; mechanical engineering; natural resources management and policy; nursing (registered nurse training); occupational therapy; physics; plant sciences; political science and government; poultry science; psychology; sales, distribution and marketing; social work; sociology.

Academics *Calendar:* semesters. *Degrees:* bachelor's, master's, doctoral, and first professional. *Special study options:* academic remediation for entering students, cooperative education, English as a second language, honors programs, internships, off-campus study, part-time degree program, summer session for credit. *ROTC:* Army (b), Air Force (b). *Unusual degree programs:* 3-2 forestry with Auburn University, Iowa State University of Science and Technology, University of Michigan, Idaho State University.

Computers on Campus 1,000 computers/terminals are available on campus for general student use. Students can access the following: online (class) registration. Campuswide network is available.

Student Life *Housing:* on-campus residence required through sophomore year. *Options:* coed, men-only, women-only. Freshman applicants given priority for college housing. *Activities and organizations:* drama/theater group, student-run newspaper, choral group, marching band, national fraternities, national sororities. *Campus security:* 24-hour emergency response devices and patrols, late-night transport/escort service. *Student services:* health clinic, personal/psychological counseling.

Athletics Member NCAA. All Division II. *Intercollegiate sports:* baseball M (s), basketball M (s)/W (s), cross-country running M/W, football M (s), golf M (s), riflery M/W, soccer M, tennis M (s)/W (s), track and field M (s)/W (s), volleyball W (s). *Intramural sports:* badminton M/W, basketball M/W, football M, golf M, gymnastics M/W, riflery M/W, soccer M, swimming and diving M/W, tennis M/W, track and field M/W, volleyball M/W.

Standardized Tests *Required:* SAT or ACT (for admission).

Costs (2008–09) *Comprehensive fee:* $22,580 includes full-time tuition ($14,740), mandatory fees ($710), and room and board ($7130). Part-time tuition: $605 per credit.

Financial Aid Of all full-time matriculated undergraduates who enrolled in 2006, 2,519 applied for aid, 2,142 were judged to have need, 1,379 had their need fully met. 525 Federal Work-Study jobs (averaging $1879). 425 state and other part-time jobs (averaging $4739). In 2006, 887 non-need-based awards were made. *Average percent of need met:* 85%. *Average financial aid package:* $13,824. *Average need-based loan:* $6006. *Average need-based gift aid:* $8000. *Average non-need-based aid:* $6000. *Average indebtedness upon graduation:* $30,000.

Applying *Options:* electronic application, early admission. *Application fee:* $25. *Required:* high school transcript, minimum 2.0 GPA. *Application deadlines:* 4/15 (freshmen), 4/15 (transfers).

Freshman Application Contact Mr. Robert Laney Jr., Admissions, Tuskegee University, 102 Old Administration Building, Tuskegee, AL 36088. *Phone:* 334-727-8500. *Toll-free phone:* 800-622-6531.

UNITED STATES SPORTS ACADEMY

Daphne, Alabama **www.ussa.edu**

THE UNIVERSITY OF ALABAMA

Tuscaloosa, Alabama **www.ua.edu/**

- **State-supported** university, founded 1831, part of The University of Alabama System
- **Suburban** 1000-acre campus with easy access to Birmingham
- **Endowment** $445.8 million
- **Coed** 21,081 undergraduate students, 92% full-time, 53% women, 47% men

• **Moderately difficult** entrance level, 64% of applicants were admitted

Undergraduates 19,361 full-time, 1,720 part-time. Students come from 50 states and territories, 45 other countries, 23% are from out of state, 11% African American, 0.9% Asian American or Pacific Islander, 2% Hispanic American, 0.6% Native American, 1% international, 7% transferred in, 29% live on campus. *Retention:* 86% of 2006 full-time freshmen returned.

Freshmen *Admission:* 14,313 applied, 9,140 admitted, 4,538 enrolled. *Average high school GPA:* 3.4. *Test scores:* SAT critical reading scores over 500: 73%; SAT math scores over 500: 76%; ACT scores over 18: 99%; SAT critical reading scores over 600: 33%; SAT math scores over 600: 32%; ACT scores over 24: 51%; SAT critical reading scores over 700: 9%; SAT math scores over 700: 8%; ACT scores over 30: 14%.

Faculty *Total:* 1,275, 77% full-time, 83% with terminal degrees. *Student/faculty ratio:* 19:1.

Majors Accounting; advertising; aerospace, aeronautical and astronautical engineering; American studies; anthropology; apparel and textiles; art history, criticism and conservation; Asian studies; athletic training; audiology and speech-language pathology; biology/biological sciences; business administration and management; business/managerial economics; chemical engineering; chemistry; civil engineering; communication/speech communication and rhetoric; computer science; construction engineering; criminal justice/safety; dance; dietetics; dramatic/theater arts; early childhood education; electrical, electronics and communications engineering; elementary education; English; environmental science; family resource management; finance; fine/studio arts; foreign languages and literatures; geography; geology/earth science; health professions related; history; hospital and health care facilities administration; human development and family studies; human development and family studies related; interdisciplinary studies; interior design; international relations and affairs; journalism; Latin American studies; management information systems; management science; marine biology and biological oceanography; marketing/marketing management; mathematics; mechanical engineering; metallurgical engineering; microbiology; music; music teacher education; nursing (registered nurse training); philosophy; physical education teaching and coaching; physics; political science and government; psychology; public relations/image management; radio and television; religious studies; restaurant/food services management; secondary education; social work; sociology; Spanish; special education.

Academics *Calendar:* semesters. *Degrees:* bachelor's, master's, doctoral, first professional, post-master's, and postbachelor's certificates. *Special study options:* academic remediation for entering students, accelerated degree program, adult/continuing education programs, advanced placement credit, cooperative education, distance learning, double majors, English as a second language, external degree program, freshman honors college, honors programs, independent study, internships, off-campus study, part-time degree program, services for LD students, student-designed majors, study abroad, summer session for credit. *ROTC:* Army (b), Air Force (b). *Unusual degree programs:* business administration; engineering; nursing; social work.

Computers on Campus 2,200 computers/terminals are available on campus for general student use. Students can access the following: campus intranet, computer help desk, free student e-mail accounts, online (class) grades, online (class) registration, online (class) schedules. Campuswide network is available. 100% of college-owned or -operated housing units are wired for high-speed Internet access. Wireless service is available via classrooms, computer centers, dorm rooms, libraries, student centers.

Student Life *Housing:* on-campus residence required for freshman year. *Options:* coed, men-only, women-only, cooperative, disabled students. Campus housing is university owned. Freshman campus housing is guaranteed. *Activities and organizations:* drama/theater group, student-run newspaper, radio station, choral group, marching band, Coordinating Council of Student Organizations, Residence Hall Association, International Student Association, Student Government Association, African-American Association, national fraternities, national sororities. *Campus security:* 24-hour emergency response devices and patrols, student patrols, late-night transport/escort service, controlled dormitory access, crime prevention programs, community police protection. *Student services:* health clinic, personal/psychological counseling, women's center, legal services.

Athletics Member NCAA. All Division I except football (Division I-A). *Intercollegiate sports:* baseball M (s), basketball M (s)/W (s), cheerleading M (s)/W (s), crew W (s), cross-country running M (s)/W (s), golf M (s)/W (s), gymnastics W (s), soccer W (s), softball W (s), swimming and diving M (s)/W (s), tennis M (s)/W (s), track and field M (s)/W (s), volleyball W (s). *Intramural sports:* badminton M/W, basketball M/W, bowling M/W, crew M (c)/W (c), football M/W, golf M/W, lacrosse M (c)/W (c), racquetball M (c)/W (c), rugby M (c), soccer M (c)/W (c), softball M/W, squash M/W, table tennis M/W, tennis M (c)/W (c), track and field M/W, ultimate Frisbee M (c)/W (c), volleyball M/W, water polo M (c)/W (c), wrestling M (c)/W.

Standardized Tests *Required:* SAT or ACT (for admission).

Costs (2007–08) *Tuition:* state resident $5700 full-time; nonresident $16,518 full-time. Full-time tuition and fees vary according to course load. Part-time tuition and fees vary according to course load. *Room and board:* $5868; room only: $3750. Room and board charges vary according to board plan and housing facility. *Payment plans:* installment, deferred payment. *Waivers:* employees or children of employees.

Financial Aid Of all full-time matriculated undergraduates who enrolled in 2006, 8,561 applied for aid, 6,840 were judged to have need, 919 had their need fully met. 708 Federal Work-Study jobs (averaging $2105). In 2006, 5030 non-need-based awards were made. *Average percent of need met:* 65%. *Average financial aid package:* $10,589. *Average need-based loan:* $4525. *Average need-based gift aid:* $4285. *Average non-need-based aid:* $6258. *Average indebtedness upon graduation:* $17,146.

Applying *Options:* electronic application, early admission. *Application fee:* $35. *Required:* high school transcript, minimum 3.0 GPA. *Required for some:* essay or personal statement, letters of recommendation, interview. *Application deadline:* 2/1 (freshmen). *Notification:* continuous (freshmen), continuous (transfers).

Freshman Application Contact Ms. Mary K. Spiegel, Executive Director of Undergraduate Admissions, The University of Alabama, Box 870132, 203 Student Services Center, Tuscaloosa, AL 35487-0132. *Phone:* 205-348-5666. *Toll-free phone:* 800-933-BAMA. *Fax:* 205-348-9046. *E-mail:* admissions@ua.edu.

THE UNIVERSITY OF ALABAMA AT BIRMINGHAM

Birmingham, Alabama **main.uab.edu/**

- **State-supported** university, founded 1969, part of University of Alabama System
- **Urban** 265-acre campus
- **Endowment** $304.3 million
- **Coed** 10,796 undergraduate students, 73% full-time, 60% women, 40% men
- **Moderately difficult** entrance level, 77% of applicants were admitted

Undergraduates 7,833 full-time, 2,963 part-time. Students come from 44 states and territories, 90 other countries, 6% are from out of state, 29% African American, 4% Asian American or Pacific Islander, 1% Hispanic American, 0.3% Native American, 2% international, 10% transferred in, 17% live on campus. *Retention:* 75% of 2006 full-time freshmen returned.

Freshmen *Admission:* 4,398 applied, 3,373 admitted, 1,416 enrolled. *Average high school GPA:* 3.43. *Test scores:* ACT scores over 18: 100%; ACT scores over 24: 49%; ACT scores over 30: 8%.

Faculty *Total:* 895, 92% full-time, 86% with terminal degrees. *Student/faculty ratio:* 18:1.

Majors Accounting; African-American/Black studies; anthropology; biological and physical sciences; biology/biological sciences; biomedical/medical engineering; business administration and management; business/managerial economics; chemistry; civil engineering; clinical laboratory science/medical technology; communication/speech communication and rhetoric; computer and information sciences; corrections and criminal justice related; cytotechnology; electrical, electronics and communications engineering; elementary education; English; finance; fine/studio arts; French; health information/medical records administration; health teacher education; history; kindergarten/preschool education; management information systems; marketing/marketing management; materials engineering; mathematics; mechanical engineering; medical radiologic technology; music; nuclear medical technology; nursing (registered nurse training); philosophy; physical education teaching and coaching; physician assistant; physics; political science and government; psychology; respiratory care therapy; secondary education; social sciences related; social work; sociology; Spanish; special education; visual and performing arts.

Academics *Calendar:* semesters. *Degrees:* certificates, bachelor's, master's, doctoral, first professional, post-master's, and postbachelor's certificates. *Special study options:* academic remediation for entering students, adult/continuing education programs, advanced placement credit, cooperative education, double majors, honors programs, independent study, internships, off-campus study, part-time degree program, services for LD students, student-designed majors, study abroad, summer session for credit. *ROTC:* Army (b), Air Force (c). *Unusual degree programs:* 3-2 accounting.

Computers on Campus 400 computers/terminals are available on campus for general student use. Students can access the following: campus intranet, free student e-mail accounts, online (class) grades, online (class) registration, online (class) schedules, transcript requests. Campuswide network is available. Wireless service is available via classrooms, dorm rooms, libraries, student centers.

Student Life *Housing options:* coed, women-only. Campus housing is university owned and is provided by a third party. *Activities and organizations:* drama/theater group, student-run newspaper, radio station, choral group, marching band, campus ministries, service-oriented groups, sports-affiliated groups, national fraternities, national sororities. *Campus security:* 24-hour emergency response devices and patrols, late-night transport/escort service, controlled dormitory access. *Student services:* health clinic, personal/psychological counseling, women's center.

Athletics Member NCAA. All Division I except football (Division I-A). *Intercollegiate sports:* baseball M (s), basketball M (s)/W (s), cross-country running W (s), golf M (s)/W (s), riflery M/W, soccer M (s)/W (s), softball W (s), swimming and diving W (s), tennis M (s)/W (s), track and field W (s), volleyball W (s). *Intramural sports:* badminton M/W, baseball M, basketball M/W, bowling M/W, football M/W, golf M/W, racquetball M/W, soccer M/W, softball M/W, swimming and diving M/W, table tennis M/W, tennis M/W, track and field M/W, ultimate Frisbee M/W, volleyball M/W, wrestling M.

Standardized Tests *Required:* SAT or ACT (for admission).

Costs (2007–08) *Tuition:* state resident $3384 full-time, $141 per credit hour part-time; nonresident $8472 full-time, $353 per credit hour part-time. *Required fees:* $824 full-time. *Room and board:* $7640; room only: $3990.

Financial Aid Of all full-time matriculated undergraduates who enrolled in 2005, 5,081 applied for aid, 4,114 were judged to have need, 548 had their need fully met. In 2005, 1484 non-need-based awards were made. *Average percent of need met:* 40%. *Average financial aid package:* $14,304. *Average need-based loan:* $3876. *Average need-based gift aid:* $3309. *Average non-need-based aid:* $9814. *Average indebtedness upon graduation:* $17,650.

Applying *Options:* electronic application, early admission, deferred entrance. *Application fee:* $35. *Required:* high school transcript, minimum 2.0 GPA. *Application deadlines:* 3/1 (freshmen), 5/1 (transfers). *Notification:* continuous (freshmen), continuous (transfers).

Freshman Application Contact Ms. Chenise Ryan, Director of Undergraduate Admissions, The University of Alabama at Birmingham, Office of Undergraduate Admissions, HUC 260, 1530 3rd Avenue South, Birmingham, AL 35294-1150. *Phone:* 205-934-8221. *Toll-free phone:* 800-421-8743. *Fax:* 205-975-7114. *E-mail:* undergradadmit@uab.edu.

See page 282 for the College Close-Up.

The University of Alabama in Huntsville

Huntsville, Alabama **www.uah.edu/**

- **State-supported** university, founded 1950, part of University of Alabama System
- **Suburban** 400-acre campus
- **Endowment** $45.6 million
- **Coed** 5,751 undergraduate students, 74% full-time, 48% women, 52% men
- **Moderately difficult** entrance level, 88% of applicants were admitted

Undergraduates 4,233 full-time, 1,518 part-time. Students come from 44 states and territories, 61 other countries, 14% are from out of state, 15% African American, 3% Asian American or Pacific Islander, 2% Hispanic American, 2% Native American, 3% international, 11% transferred in, 18% live on campus. *Retention:* 77% of 2006 full-time freshmen returned.

Freshmen *Admission:* 1,850 applied, 1,628 admitted, 800 enrolled. *Average high school GPA:* 3.31. *Test scores:* SAT critical reading scores over 500: 74%; SAT math scores over 500: 75%; ACT scores over 18: 100%; SAT critical reading scores over 600: 27%; SAT math scores over 600: 30%; ACT scores over 24: 58%; SAT critical reading scores over 700: 6%; SAT math scores over 700: 3%; ACT scores over 30: 9%.

Faculty *Total:* 465, 62% full-time, 70% with terminal degrees. *Student/faculty ratio:* 16:1.

Majors Accounting; art; biology/biological sciences; business administration and management; chemical engineering; chemistry; civil engineering; computer and information sciences; computer engineering; electrical, electronics and communications engineering; elementary education; engineering related; English; finance; foreign languages and literatures; history; industrial engineering; management information systems; marketing/marketing management; mathematics; mechanical engineering; music; nursing (registered nurse training); philosophy; physics; political science and government; psychology; sociology; speech and rhetoric.

Academics *Calendar:* semesters. *Degrees:* bachelor's, master's, doctoral, post-master's, and postbachelor's certificates. *Special study options:* academic remediation for entering students, adult/continuing education programs, advanced placement credit, cooperative education, distance learning, double majors, English as a second language, honors programs, independent study, internships, off-campus study, part-time degree program, services for LD students, study abroad, summer session for credit. *ROTC:* Army (c). *Unusual degree programs:* 3-2 engineering with Oakwood College, Morehouse College, Clark Atlanta University, Fisk University.

Computers on Campus 1,153 computers/terminals are available on campus for general student use. Students can access the following: campus intranet, computer help desk, free student e-mail accounts, online (class) grades, online (class) registration, online (class) schedules. Campuswide network is available. 100% of college-owned or -operated housing units are wired for high-speed Internet access. Wireless service is available via classrooms, computer centers, computer labs, learning centers, libraries, student centers.

Student Life *Housing options:* coed, disabled students. Campus housing is university owned. *Activities and organizations:* drama/theater group, student-run newspaper, choral group, Black Student Organization, Student Government Association, Campus Crusade, International Cultural Organization, Institute of Electrical and Electronic Engineers, national fraternities, national sororities. *Campus security:* 24-hour emergency response devices and patrols, late-night transport/escort service, controlled dormitory access. *Student services:* health clinic, personal/psychological counseling.

Athletics Member NCAA. All Division II except ice hockey (Division I). *Intercollegiate sports:* archery M (c)/W (c), badminton M (c)/W (c), baseball M (s), basketball M (s)/W (s), bowling M (c)/W (c), cheerleading M (s)/W (s), crew M (c)/W (c), cross-country running M (s)/W (s), ice hockey M (s), soccer M (s)/W (s), softball W (s), tennis M (s)/W (s), track and field M (s)/W (s), volleyball W (s). *Intramural sports:* badminton M/W, basketball M/W, football M/W, golf M/W, racquetball M/W, soccer M/W, softball M/W, table tennis M/W, ultimate Frisbee M/W, volleyball M/W.

Standardized Tests *Required:* SAT or ACT (for admission).

Costs (2007–08) *Tuition:* state resident $5216 full-time, $166 per credit hour part-time; nonresident $11,024 full-time, $355 per credit hour part-time. Full-time tuition and fees vary according to course load. Part-time tuition and fees vary according to course load. *Room and board:* $6290; room only: $4340. Room and board charges vary according to board plan and housing facility. *Payment plan:* deferred payment. *Waivers:* employees or children of employees.

Financial Aid Of all full-time matriculated undergraduates who enrolled in 2007, 3,292 applied for aid, 1,727 were judged to have need, 296 had their need fully met. 66 Federal Work-Study jobs (averaging $3756). In 2007, 902 non-need-based awards were made. *Average percent of need met:* 64%. *Average financial aid package:* $7137. *Average need-based loan:* $5105. *Average need-based gift aid:* $4371. *Average non-need-based aid:* $2928. *Average indebtedness upon graduation:* $21,544. *Financial aid deadline:* 7/31.

Applying *Options:* electronic application, deferred entrance. *Application fee:* $30. *Required:* high school transcript. *Application deadline:* 8/15 (freshmen). *Notification:* continuous (freshmen), continuous (transfers).

Freshman Application Contact Ms. Sandra Patterson, Director of Admissions, The University of Alabama in Huntsville, 301 Sparkman Drive, Huntsville, AL 35899. *Phone:* 256-824-6070. *Toll-free phone:* 800-UAH-CALL. *Fax:* 256-824-6073. *E-mail:* admitme@email.uah.edu.

See page 284 for the College Close-Up.

University of Mobile

Mobile, Alabama **www.umobile.edu/**

- **Independent Southern Baptist** comprehensive, founded 1961
- **Suburban** 830-acre campus
- **Endowment** $12.4 million
- **Coed**
- **Moderately difficult** entrance level

Faculty *Student/faculty ratio:* 14:1.

Academics *Calendar:* semesters. *Degrees:* associate, bachelor's, and master's.

Student Life *Campus security:* 24-hour emergency response devices and patrols, controlled dormitory access.

Athletics Member NAIA.

Standardized Tests *Required:* SAT or ACT (for admission).

Costs (2007–08) *Comprehensive fee:* $20,530 includes full-time tuition ($12,780), mandatory fees ($610), and room and board ($7140). Full-time tuition and fees vary according to course load. Part-time tuition: $445 per semester hour. Part-time tuition and fees vary according to course load. *Required fees:* $75 per term part-time. *College room only:* $4260. Room and board charges vary according to housing facility.

Financial Aid Of all full-time matriculated undergraduates who enrolled in 2007, 698 applied for aid, 616 were judged to have need. 92 Federal Work-Study jobs (averaging $1755). *Average percent of need met:* 79. *Average financial aid package:* $8628. *Average need-based loan:* $2163. *Average need-based gift aid:* $2072.

Applying *Options:* early admission, deferred entrance. *Application fee:* $30. *Required:* high school transcript, minimum 2.0 GPA. *Required for some:* interview.

Freshman Application Contact Mrs. Kathy Lee, Assistant Director of Admissions, University of Mobile, 5735 College Parkway, Mobile, AL 36613-2842. *Phone:* 251-442-2638. *Toll-free phone:* 800-946-7267. *Fax:* 251-442-2498. *E-mail:* adminfo@umobile.edu.

UNIVERSITY OF MONTEVALLO

Montevallo, Alabama **www.montevallo.edu/**

- **State-supported** comprehensive, founded 1896
- **Small-town** 106-acre campus with easy access to Birmingham
- **Endowment** $11.0 million
- **Coed** 2,513 undergraduate students, 90% full-time, 67% women, 33% men
- **Moderately difficult** entrance level, 78% of applicants were admitted

Undergraduates 2,256 full-time, 257 part-time. Students come from 27 states and territories, 21 other countries, 3% are from out of state, 14% African American, 0.7% Asian American or Pacific Islander, 2% Hispanic American, 0.3% Native American, 2% international, 9% transferred in, 39% live on campus. *Retention:* 73% of 2006 full-time freshmen returned.

Freshmen *Admission:* 1,437 applied, 1,120 admitted, 491 enrolled. *Average high school GPA:* 3.3. *Test scores:* ACT scores over 18: 96%; ACT scores over 24: 31%; ACT scores over 30: 2%.

Faculty *Total:* 215, 64% full-time, 57% with terminal degrees. *Student/faculty ratio:* 16:1.

Majors Accounting; art; audiology and hearing sciences; biology/biological sciences; business administration and management; chemistry; counselor education/school counseling and guidance; dramatic/theater arts; early childhood education; education; educational leadership and administration; elementary education; English; family and consumer sciences/human sciences; finance; foreign languages and literatures; health and physical education; history; management information systems; marketing/marketing management; mathematics; music; political science and government; psychology; radio and television; secondary education; social sciences; social work; sociology; speech and rhetoric; speech-language pathology.

Academics *Calendar:* semesters. *Degrees:* bachelor's, master's, and post-master's certificates. *Special study options:* academic remediation for entering students, accelerated degree program, advanced placement credit, double majors, honors programs, independent study, internships, part-time degree program, services for LD students, study abroad, summer session for credit. *ROTC:* Army (c), Air Force (c). *Unusual degree programs:* 3-2 engineering with Auburn University, University of Alabama at Birmingham.

Computers on Campus 250 computers/terminals are available on campus for general student use. Students can access the following: online (class) registration. Campuswide network is available. 100% of college-owned or -operated housing units are wired for high-speed Internet access. Wireless service is available via classrooms, computer centers, computer labs, dorm rooms, libraries, student centers.

Student Life *Housing:* on-campus residence required for freshman year. *Options:* coed, men-only, women-only. Campus housing is university owned. Freshman campus housing is guaranteed. *Activities and organizations:* drama/theater group, student-run newspaper, television station, choral group, Golden Key, Student Government Association, University Programming Council, campus ministries, African-American Association, national fraternities, national sororities. *Campus security:* 24-hour emergency response devices and patrols, late-night transport/escort service, controlled dormitory access. *Student services:* health clinic, personal/psychological counseling.

Athletics Member NCAA. All Division II. *Intercollegiate sports:* baseball M (s), basketball M (s)/W (s), golf M (s)/W (s), soccer M (s)/W (s), tennis W (s), volleyball W (s). *Intramural sports:* basketball M/W, bowling M, football M, golf M, tennis M/W, volleyball M/W.

Standardized Tests *Required:* SAT or ACT (for admission). *Recommended:* ACT (for admission).

Costs (2007–08) *Tuition:* state resident $5850 full-time, $195 per credit hour part-time; nonresident $11,700 full-time, $390 per credit hour part-time. Full-time tuition and fees vary according to course load. Part-time tuition and fees vary according to course load. *Required fees:* $230 full-time. *Room and board:* $4360.

Financial Aid Of all full-time matriculated undergraduates who enrolled in 2003, 1,871 applied for aid, 1,414 were judged to have need, 526 had their need fully met. 136 Federal Work-Study jobs (averaging $1410). In 2003, 434 non-need-based awards were made. *Average percent of need met:* 79%. *Average financial aid package:* $7150. *Average need-based loan:* $2670. *Average need-based gift aid:* $4178. *Average non-need-based aid:* $3938. *Average indebtedness upon graduation:* $11,550.

Applying *Options:* electronic application, early admission, deferred entrance. *Application fee:* $25. *Required:* high school transcript, minimum 2.0 GPA. *Recommended:* interview. *Application deadlines:* 8/1 (freshmen), rolling (transfers).

Freshman Application Contact Mr. Lynn Gurganus, Director of Admissions, University of Montevallo, Station 6030, Montevallo, AL 35115-6030. *Phone:* 205-665-6030. *Toll-free phone:* 800-292-4349. *Fax:* 205-665-6032. *E-mail:* admissions@montevallo.edu.

UNIVERSITY OF NORTH ALABAMA

Florence, Alabama **www.una.edu/**

- **State-supported** comprehensive, founded 1830
- **Urban** 125-acre campus
- **Coed** 5,768 undergraduate students, 89% full-time, 56% women, 44% men
- **Minimally difficult** entrance level, 85% of applicants were admitted

Undergraduates 5,122 full-time, 646 part-time. Students come from 36 states and territories, 53 other countries, 19% are from out of state, 10% African American, 0.7% Asian American or Pacific Islander, 1% Hispanic American, 1% Native American, 10% international, 10% transferred in, 23% live on campus. *Retention:* 64% of 2006 full-time freshmen returned.

Freshmen *Admission:* 2,302 applied, 1,947 admitted, 1,023 enrolled. *Average high school GPA:* 2.93. *Test scores:* SAT critical reading scores over 500: 30%; SAT math scores over 500: 39%; ACT scores over 18: 84%; SAT math scores over 600: 13%; ACT scores over 24: 25%; ACT scores over 30: 2%.

Faculty *Total:* 360, 64% full-time, 48% with terminal degrees. *Student/faculty ratio:* 21:1.

Majors Accounting; biological and biomedical sciences related; biology/biological sciences; business administration and management; business/managerial economics; chemistry; computer and information sciences; counseling psychology; criminal justice/law enforcement administration; education (multiple levels); elementary education; English; family and consumer sciences/human sciences; finance; fine arts related; fine/studio arts; foreign languages and literatures; general studies; geography; geology/earth science; history; kindergarten/preschool education; management information systems; marine biology and biological oceanography; marketing/marketing management; mathematics; music; nursing (registered nurse training); parks, recreation, and leisure related; physical sciences; physics; political science and government; psychology; secondary education; social work; sociology; special education; speech and rhetoric.

Academics *Calendar:* semesters. *Degrees:* bachelor's, master's, and post-master's certificates. *Special study options:* academic remediation for entering students, accelerated degree program, adult/continuing education programs, advanced placement credit, cooperative education, distance learning, double majors, English as a second language, freshman honors college, honors programs, independent study, internships, part-time degree program, services for LD students, student-designed majors, summer session for credit. *ROTC:* Army (b).

Computers on Campus 850 computers/terminals are available on campus for general student use. Students can access the following: free student e-mail accounts, online (class) registration, online (class) schedules. Campuswide network is available. Wireless service is available via learning centers.

Student Life *Housing options:* coed, men-only, women-only. Campus housing is university owned. *Activities and organizations:* drama/theater group, student-run newspaper, radio station, choral group, marching band, Student Government Association, University Program Council, Baptist campus ministries, Physical Education Majors Club, Residence Hall Association, national fraternities, national sororities. *Campus security:* 24-hour emergency response devices and patrols, student patrols, late-night transport/escort service, controlled dormitory access. *Student services:* health clinic, personal/psychological counseling, women's center.

Athletics Member NCAA. All Division II. *Intercollegiate sports:* baseball M (s), basketball M (s)/W (s), cross-country running M (s)/W (s), football M (s), golf M (s), soccer W (s), softball W (s), tennis M (s)/W (s), volleyball W (s). *Intramural sports:* badminton M/W, baseball M, basketball M/W, bowling M/W, cross-country running M/W, football M/W, golf M, racquetball M/W, softball W, swimming and diving M/W, table tennis M/W, tennis M/W, volleyball M/W, weight lifting M/W.

Standardized Tests *Required:* SAT or ACT (for admission).

Costs (2008–09) *Tuition:* state resident $4410 full-time, $147 per credit hour part-time; nonresident $8820 full-time, $294 per credit hour part-time. *Required fees:* $983 full-time. *Room and board:* $4460.

Financial Aid Of all full-time matriculated undergraduates who enrolled in 2006, 3,174 applied for aid, 2,571 were judged to have need, 909 had their need fully met. 214 Federal Work-Study jobs (averaging $1240). In 2006, 669 non-need-based awards were made. *Average percent of need met:* 60%. *Average financial aid package:* $4483. *Average need-based loan:* $3704. *Average need-based gift aid:* $2918. *Average non-need-based aid:* $1647. *Average indebtedness upon graduation:* $16,488.

Applying *Options:* electronic application, early admission, deferred entrance. *Application fee:* $25. *Required:* high school transcript. *Application deadlines:* rolling (freshmen), rolling (transfers).

Freshman Application Contact Mrs. Kim O. Mauldin, Director of Admissions, University of North Alabama, Office of Admissions, Box 5011, Florence, AL 35632-0001. *Phone:* 256-765-4680. *Toll-free phone:* 800-TALKUNA. *Fax:* 256-765-4329. *E-mail:* admissions@una.edu.

University of South Alabama

Mobile, Alabama **www.usouthal.edu/**

- **State-supported** university, founded 1963
- **Suburban** 1225-acre campus
- **Endowment** $331.7 million
- **Coed** 10,690 undergraduate students, 73% full-time, 60% women, 40% men
- **Moderately difficult** entrance level, 90% of applicants were admitted

Undergraduates 7,790 full-time, 2,900 part-time. Students come from 49 states and territories, 100 other countries, 19% are from out of state, 19% African American, 3% Asian American or Pacific Islander, 2% Hispanic American, 0.8% Native American, 5% international, 11% transferred in, 15% live on campus. *Retention:* 70% of 2006 full-time freshmen returned.

Freshmen *Admission:* 2,966 applied, 2,655 admitted, 1,529 enrolled. *Test scores:* ACT scores over 18: 85%; ACT scores over 24: 33%; ACT scores over 30: 5%.

Faculty *Total:* 1,044, 71% full-time. *Student/faculty ratio:* 16:1.

Majors Accounting; anthropology; art; atmospheric sciences and meteorology; audiology and speech-language pathology; biology/biological sciences; biomedical sciences; business administration and management; business/commerce; chemical engineering; chemistry; civil engineering; clinical laboratory science/medical technology; communication/speech communication and rhetoric; computer and information sciences; computer engineering; criminal justice/law enforcement administration; dramatic/theater arts; early childhood education; e-commerce; electrical, electronics and communications engineering; elementary education; English; finance; foreign languages and literatures; geography; geology/earth science; health/medical preparatory programs related; history; liberal arts and sciences and humanities related; marketing/marketing management; mathematics and statistics related; mechanical engineering; multi-/interdisciplinary studies related; music; nursing (registered nurse training); parks, recreation and leisure; philosophy; physical education teaching and coaching; physics; political science and government; psychology; radiologic technology/science; respiratory care therapy; secondary education; sociology; special education.

Academics *Calendar:* semesters. *Degrees:* certificates, bachelor's, master's, doctoral, first professional, post-master's, and postbachelor's certificates. *Special study options:* academic remediation for entering students, accelerated degree program, adult/continuing education programs, advanced placement credit, cooperative education, distance learning, double majors, English as a second language, external degree program, freshman honors college, independent study, internships, part-time degree program, services for LD students, student-designed majors, study abroad, summer session for credit. *ROTC:* Army (b), Air Force (b).

Computers on Campus 500 computers/terminals are available on campus for general student use. Students can access the following: campus intranet, computer help desk, free student e-mail accounts, online (class) grades, online (class) registration, online (class) schedules. Campuswide network is available. 100% of college-owned or -operated housing units are wired for high-speed Internet access. Wireless service is available via entire campus.

Student Life *Housing options:* coed. Campus housing is university owned and is provided by a third party. *Activities and organizations:* drama/theater group, student-run newspaper, radio and television station, choral group, Student Government Association, African American Student Association, Council of International Student Organizations, Alpha Epsilon Delta Pre-Health Professions, Panhellenic Council, national fraternities, national sororities. *Campus security:* 24-hour emergency response devices and patrols, late-night transport/escort service. *Student services:* health clinic, personal/psychological counseling, legal services.

Athletics Member NCAA. All Division I. *Intercollegiate sports:* baseball M (s), basketball M (s)/W (s), cross-country running M (s)/W (s), fencing M (c)/W (c), football M (c), golf M/W, soccer W (s), tennis M (s)/W (s), track and field M (s)/W (s), volleyball W (s). *Intramural sports:* badminton M/W, basketball M/W, bowling M/W, cheerleading M (c)/W (c), golf M/W, racquetball M/W, sailing M (c)/W (c), soccer M/W, softball M/W, table tennis M/W, tennis M/W, volleyball M/W, water polo M/W.

Standardized Tests *Required:* SAT or ACT (for admission).

Costs (2007–08) *Tuition:* state resident $4020 full-time, $134 per credit hour part-time; nonresident $8040 full-time, $268 per credit hour part-time. *Required fees:* $802 full-time, $280 per term part-time. *Room and board:* $4820; room only: $2590. Room and board charges vary according to board plan, housing facility, and location. *Payment plan:* installment. *Waivers:* employees or children of employees.

Financial Aid Of all full-time matriculated undergraduates who enrolled in 2007, 3,041 applied for aid, 3,035 were judged to have need, 2,596 had their need fully met. *Average percent of need met:* 27%. *Average indebtedness upon graduation:* $21,700.

Applying *Options:* electronic application, early admission. *Application fee:* $35. *Required:* high school transcript. *Recommended:* minimum 2.0 GPA. *Application deadlines:* 7/15 (freshmen), 8/10 (transfers). *Notification:* continuous until 8/18 (freshmen), continuous until 8/18 (transfers).

Freshman Application Contact Mr. Christopher A. Lynch, Director, New Student Recruitment, University of South Alabama, 307 University Boulevard, Mobile, AL 36688-0002. *Phone:* 251-460-6141. *Toll-free phone:* 800-872-5247. *E-mail:* admiss@usouthal.edu.

The University of West Alabama

Livingston, Alabama **www.uwa.edu/**

- **State-supported** comprehensive, founded 1835
- **Small-town** 595-acre campus
- **Endowment** $480,483
- **Coed**
- **Minimally difficult** entrance level

Faculty *Student/faculty ratio:* 28:1.

Academics *Calendar:* semesters. *Degrees:* associate, bachelor's, and master's.

Student Life *Campus security:* 24-hour patrols.

Athletics Member NCAA. All Division II.

Standardized Tests *Required:* SAT or ACT (for admission).

Costs (2007–08) *Tuition:* state resident $4108 full-time, $174 part-time; nonresident $8216 full-time, $348 part-time. Part-time tuition and fees vary according to course level. *Required fees:* $500 full-time. *Room and board:* $3624; room only: $1640. Room and board charges vary according to board plan and housing facility.

Financial Aid Of all full-time matriculated undergraduates who enrolled in 2005, 1,516 applied for aid, 1,280 were judged to have need, 524 had their need fully met. 176 Federal Work-Study jobs (averaging $1221). In 2005, 251 non-need-based awards were made. *Average percent of need met:* 85. *Average financial aid package:* $10,222. *Average need-based loan:* $4239. *Average need-based gift aid:* $3761. *Average non-need-based aid:* $3144. *Average indebtedness upon graduation:* $16,043.

Applying *Options:* electronic application, early admission, deferred entrance. *Application fee:* $20. *Required:* high school transcript, minimum 2.0 GPA.

Freshman Application Contact Mr. Danny Buckalew, The University of West Alabama, Station 4, Livingston, AL 35470. *Phone:* 205-652-3581. *Toll-free phone:* 800-621-7742 (in-state); 800-621-8044 (out-of-state). *Fax:* 205-652-3522. *E-mail:* db@uwa.edu.

Virginia College at Birmingham

Birmingham, Alabama **www.vc.edu/**

Director of Admissions Joe Rogalski, Director of Admissions, Virginia College at Birmingham, 65 Bagby Drive, PO Box 19249, Birmingham, AL 35209. *Phone:* 205-802-1200.

AMRIDGE UNIVERSITY

MONTGOMERY, ALABAMA

The University

Founded in 1967, Amridge University is an independent coeducational institution dedicated to the spirit of its ideals and Christian heritage. All Amridge University programs are taught from a Christian perspective. Amridge University is one of the nation's leading universities offering distance learning programs and services to adults nationally. Adding to the prestige of the University is its selection by the U.S. Department of Education as one of fifteen initial participants in the Distance Education Demonstration Program. Amridge University worked with the U.S. Department of Education to develop a national model to help chart the future of distance learning.

Accredited by the Southern Association of Colleges and Schools, Amridge University grants associate, bachelor's, master's, and doctoral degrees, all available via a distance learning format. Graduate degrees are awarded in counseling, family therapy, organizational leadership, and religious studies. These degrees foster leadership, counseling and family therapy skills, knowledge, and biblical and Christian ministry skills. The counseling degrees are designed to help prepare students for licensure. Doctoral degrees include Doctor of Ministry and Doctor of Philosophy degrees. These are advanced professional degrees for community, organization, and church-related vocations, with a concentration designed to prepare participants to counsel families and individuals.

The policy of Amridge University is to provide reasonable accommodation for persons who are handicapped or disabled as designated in Section 504 of the Rehabilitation Act of 1973 and the Americans with Disabilities Act of 1990. Although the Morgan W. Brown building is not equipped with an elevator, the needs of the physically challenged can be met from the first floor. These include registration, counseling, library facilities, classroom facilities, rest rooms, break room facilities, and others. Ample parking is provided.

Location

Amridge University is located in Montgomery, Alabama, the capital city of the state. Strategically located in the central part of the state between [illegible] and Mobile, and Atlanta, Georgia, Montgomery is one of the fastest-growing cities in the state and the region. The city is clean and modern, with beautiful residential areas, parks and playgrounds, and fine schools and universities. Students and families can also enjoy its museums, zoo, and capital facilities.

Montgomery has two major U.S. Air Force installations: Maxwell Air Force Base and Gunter Annex. Maxwell is where the Air War College is located; it is a strategic center for education.

The metropolitan area has a population of more than 350,000 citizens. There are many churches and educational institutions. The city has an abundance of good housing in addition to other advantages. Employment can be found easily in Montgomery.

Majors and Degrees

Undergraduate degrees are awarded in biblical studies, business, human services, human development, human resource management, liberal studies, management communication, public safety and criminal justice. These degrees emphasize biblical and Christian ministry skills, human development skills, knowledge of the arts, and management/communication skills. Amridge University students are fully matriculated students of Amridge University with full student privileges, rights, and responsibilities.

Academic Programs

Amridge University is primarily a distance learning institution, although there are many classes offered on campus. The academic year consists of three semesters: fall, spring, and summer.

A student must fulfill the required semester hours in general as well as the basic requirements of the core curriculum. All core and major requirements can be completed from the University. Amridge University program has no traditional structure.

Distance education is approved by the Southern Association of Colleges and Schools and the U.S. Department of Education, ensuring that distance education students receive the same high-quality education as on-campus students. Faculty and student services for students on campus are available to distance learners. Amridge University ensures that students have regular contact with faculty and staff members via e-mail and telephone. No residency is required for undergraduates.

In addition to offering distance learning to a diverse range of individuals, Amridge University is participating in the eArmyU of Army Colleges and Universities. eArmyU is the Army's popular e-learning virtual university, offering tens of thousands of enlisted soldiers the opportunity to earn a college degree during their enlistment. With the flexibility of eArmyU, soldiers can continue their education uninterrupted, completing their degrees in a timely manner. Amridge University is a participating member of the eArmyU project. This is a college-level learning program that offers easy access to distance learning for their education.

Academic Facilities

Amridge University offers classes at its campus, including the Turner University Center, in Montgomery and [illegible]. The main building houses the administration offices, classrooms, and the Library Resource Center.

Costs

Undergraduate tuition per semester hour is approximately [illegible].

AMRIDGE UNIVERSITY

MONTGOMERY, ALABAMA

The University

Founded in 1967, Amridge University is an independent, coeducational institution dedicated to the spirit of its ideals and Christian heritage. All Amridge University programs are taught from a Christian perspective. Amridge University is one of the nation's leading universities offering distance learning programs and services to adults nationally. Adding to the prestige of the University is its selection by the U.S. Department of Education as one of fifteen initial participants in the Distance Education Demonstration Program. Amridge University worked with the U.S. Department of Education to develop a national model to help chart the future of distance learning.

Accredited by the Southern Association of Colleges and Schools, Amridge University grants associate, bachelor's, master's, and doctoral degrees, all available via a distance learning format. Graduate degrees are awarded in counseling/family therapy, organizational leadership, and religious studies. These degrees foster leadership, counseling and family therapy skills, knowledge, and biblical and Christian ministry skills. The counseling degrees are designed to help prepare students for licensure. Doctoral degrees include Doctor of Ministry and Doctor of Philosophy degrees. These are advanced professional degrees for community organization and church-related vocations, with a concentration designed to prepare participants to counsel families and individuals.

The policy of Amridge University is to provide reasonable accommodation for persons who are handicapped or disabled as designated in Section 504 of the Rehabilitation Act of 1973 and the Americans with Disabilities Act of 1990. Although the Morgan W. Brown building is not equipped with an elevator, the needs of the physically challenged can be met from the first floor. These include registration, counseling, library facilities, classroom facilities, rest rooms, break room facilities, and others. Ample parking is provided.

Location

Amridge University is located in Montgomery, Alabama, the capital city of the state. Strategically located in the central part of the state between Huntsville and Mobile and Atlanta, Georgia, Montgomery is one of the fastest-growing cities in the state and the region. The city is clean and modern, with beautiful residential areas, parks and playgrounds, and fine schools and universities. Students and families can also enjoy its museums, zoo, and capital facilities.

Montgomery has two major U.S. Air Force installations: Maxwell Air Force Base and Gunter Annex. Maxwell is where the Air War College is located and is a strategic center for education.

The metropolitan area has a population of more than 350,000 citizens. There are many churches and educational institutions. The city has an abundance of good housing in addition to other advantages. Employment can be found easily in Montgomery.

Majors and Degrees

Undergraduate degrees are awarded in Biblical studies, business, homeland security, human development, human resource management, liberal studies, management communication, and public safety and criminal justice. These degrees promote biblical and Christian ministry skills, human development skills, knowledge in the arts, and management communication skills. Amridge University students are fully matriculated students of Amridge University with full student privileges, rights, and responsibilities.

Academic Programs

Amridge University is primarily a distance learning institution, although there are many classes offered on campus. The academic year consists of three semesters: fall, spring, and summer.

A student must fulfill the required semester hours in a major as well as the basic requirements of the core curriculum. All core and major requirements can be received from the University. Amridge University programs have a traditional structure.

Distance education is approved by the Southern Association of Colleges and Schools and the U.S. Department of Education, ensuring that distance education students receive the same high-quality education as on-campus students. Faculty and student services for students on campus are available to distance learners. Amridge University ensures that students have regular contact with faculty and staff members via e-mail and telephone. No residency is required for undergraduates.

In addition to offering distance learning to a diverse array of individuals, Amridge University is participating in the expansion of eArmyU colleges and universities. eArmyU is the army's popular e-learning virtual university, offering tens of thousands of enrolled soldiers the opportunity to earn a college degree during their enlistment. With the flexibility of eArmyU, soldier-students continue their education uninterrupted, completing their degrees in a timely manner while they serve. Amridge University is a participating member of the GoArmyEd project. This is an online, streamlined process giving soldiers easy access to obtaining funding for their educations.

Academic Facilities

Amridge University sits stately on a 9-acre campus, adjoining Auburn University at Montgomery and Interstate 85. A beautiful building houses the administration offices, classrooms, and Library Resource Center.

Costs

Undergraduate tuition per semester hour is approximately $260.

Financial Aid

Aid from institutionally generated funds is provided on the basis of academic merit, financial need, and other criteria. A limited number of scholarships are available. Priority is given to early applicants.

Federal funding available for undergraduates includes Federal Pell Grants, Federal Supplemental Educational Opportunity Grants (FSEOG), Academic Competitiveness Grant (ACG), the SMART Grant, the Federal Work-Study Program, and FFEL subsidized and unsubsidized loans. Eighty percent of students receive financial aid.

Faculty

The instructional faculty members total about 85. Approximately 65 percent of the full-time faculty members hold doctoral degrees, 100 percent hold master's degrees, and 100 percent hold terminal degrees. Faculty members specialize in their areas and have exceptional training in distance learning delivery.

Student Government

Student volunteers serve as members of the Student Advisory Committee. Volunteers are appointed by the Student Services Team, with recommendations from the deans. The committee meets on a regular term basis and is reorganized on a yearly basis. Concerns, recommendations, and requests are presented directly from the committee to the appropriate University area.

Admission Requirements

Amridge University is open to all persons who are of good character and who are academically qualified. The University has developed a streamlined admissions process to help potential students complete the process in a timely manner so they can begin their studies. As new technologies and processes become available, Amridge University makes every effort to adopt and use the latest technologies to help the admissions process. Transfer students in good academic standing are invited to apply to Amridge University. Prospective students must submit a $50 nonrefundable fee along with the completed application for admission.

Application and Information

For further information, students may contact:

Rick Johnson
Amridge University
1200 Taylor Road
Montgomery, Alabama 36117
Phone: 334-387-7513
800-351-4040 Ext. 7513 (toll-free)
Fax: 334-387-3878
E-mail: admissions@amridgeuniversity.edu
Web site: http://www.amridgeuniversity.edu

BIRMINGHAM–SOUTHERN COLLEGE

BIRMINGHAM, ALABAMA

The College

Birmingham-Southern College (BSC) was created through a merger of Southern University (established in 1856) and Birmingham College (established in 1898). Since 1959, when *Harper's Magazine* called it "one of the leading small colleges in the South," Birmingham-Southern continues to be recognized as one of the nation's outstanding liberal arts institutions. Birmingham-Southern is ranked in the top tier of national liberal arts colleges in several publications. *Money* ranked Birmingham-Southern as one of the 100 Best College Buys. The College has also been recognized by the John Templeton Foundation's Honor Roll as one of 100 schools nationwide that emphasize character building as an integral part of the college experience and as one of twenty-six private colleges and universities nationwide named a Best Buy in the *Fiske Guide to Colleges*. Birmingham-Southern also is among the 100 Colleges Worth Considering, as compiled by *Washington Post* staff writer Jay Mathews; one of America's Best Christian Colleges by Institutional Research and Evaluation, Inc.; one of the nation's top thirty colleges by the *Washington Times;* and one of the forty schools in Loren Pope's *Colleges That Change Lives;* and one of *The Best 366 Colleges* by the Princeton Review.

Birmingham-Southern is accredited by AACSB International–The Association to Advance Collegiate Schools of Business and is a Phi Beta Kappa institution.

Each year, Birmingham-Southern ranks first in Alabama and among the nation's best in percentage of all graduates accepted to medical, dental, or health career programs; the College also ranks high nationally in graduates accepted to law school.

Birmingham-Southern competes in NCAA Division III athletics and supports twenty-one varsity sports. New sports include football, men's and women's indoor and outdoor track and field, and men's and women's lacrosse. The College has more than eighty clubs and organizations and intramural sports. Its enrollment averages around 1,350 students per year.

At the graduate level, Birmingham-Southern offers Master of Arts in Public and Private Management and Master of Music degrees.

Location

Located on a 197-acre hilltop campus in western Birmingham, the College is just 3 miles via I-59/20 from the downtown business district. Birmingham, which is Alabama's largest city, has been honored by the U.S. Conference of Mayors as the "Most Livable City in America" and offers fine restaurants, museums, city and state parks, and theater. Its offerings are supplemented by the activities of four other Birmingham colleges. Birmingham's 17,000-seat Civic Center is the setting for many outstanding cultural and athletic events.

Majors and Degrees

Birmingham-Southern offers the undergraduate degrees of Bachelor of Arts, Bachelor of Science, Bachelor of Music, Bachelor of Music Education, and Bachelor of Fine Arts. Departmental majors include accounting, art, art education, biology, business administration, chemistry, computer science, dance, economics, education, engineering (3-2 program), English, environmental studies (3-2 program), French, German, history, international studies, mathematics, music, music education, nursing (3-2 program), philosophy, physics, political science, psychology, religion, sociology, Spanish, theater arts, and urban environmental studies. Individualized and interdisciplinary majors are also available.

Academic Programs

The College operates on a 4-1-4 calendar. Thirty-six units are required for the bachelor's degree; these comprise 32 regular term units and 4 Interim Term units. The minimum residence requirement is two years. In addition to its traditional liberal arts programs, Birmingham-Southern offers a number of individualized learning opportunities to meet students' special needs and career goals. These are the Honors Program, the Mentor Program, independent study, the student internship program, individualized majors, and the Interim Term. The College emphasizes international opportunities for students through course offerings, visitors to the campus, and international travel/study programs. Through the Associated Colleges of the South, the College offers international programs in England, Brazil, and Central Europe.

Credit is available through Advanced Placement tests and also may be earned through a College-approved internship program.

Birmingham-Southern offers several special programs, including a one-week Student Leaders in Service program and a dual-enrollment program that enables high school seniors to take college-credit courses.

Off-Campus Programs

The College sponsors an internship program, through which students may earn credit for actual work experience. Depending on their major, students may be assigned positions in business, government, industry, human services, or other preprofessional areas of interest. In addition, students may take part in a cooperative exchange program that enables them to take courses at the University of Alabama at Birmingham, Miles College, or Samford University. They also may participate in Army ROTC at the University of Alabama at Birmingham or Air Force ROTC at Samford University.

Academic Facilities

Birmingham-Southern College features several new facilities, including the Norton Campus Center, the Striplin Physical Fitness Center, the Stephens Science Center, and the Admission Welcome Center. Under construction are an environmental lake and park area for student use and a football complex. BSC is home to the Meyer Planetarium, the first public planetarium in Alabama. The only split-revolve-lift stage in the country is housed in the College Theatre. Six fraternity houses on fraternity row recently opened, and a major renovation to Daniel Men's Residence Hall resulted in suite-style living. A newly renovated Humanities Center also recently opened.

Costs

Tuition at BSC for 2007–08 was $23,600, and room and board fees averaged $7100. There was a $320 student activity fee. Estimated expenses for books and supplies were $1000. Transportation and personal expenses are additional costs.

Financial Aid

Birmingham-Southern feels strongly that well-qualified students should have an opportunity for a college education regardless of economic circumstances. More than 98 percent of the College's students receive financial aid of some kind. Birmingham-Southern students received more than $22 million in aid last year. Scholarships and grants range from $1000 to full tuition and may be renewed annually. Each student requesting financial assistance must submit the Free Application for Federal Student Aid (FAFSA). With the exception of the College's competitive scholarship programs and the Alabama Student Grant, all financial assistance awarded through the Office of Student Financial Aid Services is based on a demonstrated need determined from the required forms. Preference is given to those students who file by the March 1 priority deadline. In addition to the need-based programs, Birmingham-Southern awards more than $1.5 million in merit-based scholarships through a scholarship competition that is held in the spring.

Faculty

The faculty is composed of 110 full-time and 32 part-time teaching members; approximately 96 percent hold a Ph.D. degree or the terminal degree in their field. In addition to teaching, the faculty's major responsibility is advising students. Faculty members are actively involved in cocurricular activities that are planned primarily for students, and all are assigned a limited number of student advisees. They work closely with these students in planning and developing individual programs to fulfill the students' career interests. The student-faculty ratio is 12:1, and no freshman English class has more than 16 students.

Student Government

The Student Government Association of the College is chartered to operate under a constitution developed by the students, faculty members, and administration. Through a large measure of self-government, this organization helps provide a well-balanced intellectual, educational, and social cocurricular program for all students. The Honor Code makes each student responsible for upholding the social and academic standards of the College. Students serve on numerous College committees, including recruitment, curriculum, fund-raising, and governance task forces.

Admission Requirements

Approximately 375 freshmen are selected for admission on the basis of high school record, ACT or SAT scores, academic courses attempted, an admission essay, an interview, and recommendations of school officials. Applicants are expected to have completed at least 16 units of course work, 12 of which must be in academic subjects. Four units of English and at least 2 units each of mathematics, history, science, and social sciences are required, and 2 units of a foreign language are recommended. Students are encouraged to take more than the minimum units required in academic subjects.

Although an interview is not required except in the case of early admission, each applicant is encouraged to visit the campus and talk with an admission counselor or the Dean of Enrollment Management.

Transfer applicants must have at least a C average (2.0 on a 4.0 scale) on a full schedule of courses that are acceptable to Birmingham-Southern and a status of good standing with a clear academic and social record from the last college attended. If the applicant has attended more than one college, his or her overall average at these schools must meet the minimum academic-year grade point average required at Birmingham-Southern. Transfer students may enroll at the beginning of any term.

Application and Information

The College considers applications on a rolling admission basis. The priority deadline for scholarship applications is a January 1 postmark.

Preview Days are held in September, October, November, and April, and the College offers two Preview Days during the summer.

Inquiries concerning admission should be addressed to:

Sheri S. Salmon
Dean of Enrollment Management
Birmingham-Southern College
900 Arkadelphia Road
Box 549008
Birmingham, Alabama 35254
Phone: 205-226-4696
800-523-5793 (toll-free)
E-mail: admission@bsc.edu
Web site: http://www.bsc.edu

A view of the campus at Birmingham-Southern College.

HUNTINGDON COLLEGE

MONTGOMERY, ALABAMA

The College

Huntingdon College, grounded in the Judeo-Christian tradition of the United Methodist Church, is committed to nurturing growth in faith, wisdom, and service and to graduating individuals prepared to succeed in a rapidly changing world. Founded in 1854, Huntingdon is a coeducational liberal arts college. The College motto is "Enter to grow in wisdom; go forth to apply wisdom in service."

The Huntingdon experience combines liberal arts education with communication and information technology, hands-on learning, and travel/study. Huntingdon students are provided laptop computers upon enrollment, theirs to keep at graduation, and each student is offered the opportunity to participate in a travel/study experience during the junior or senior year. Internships, student-faculty research, independent study, departmental honors, and practicum experiences ensure that students have a real-world understanding of their fields of interest.

Huntingdon's more than 950 students represent twenty states and ten countries. Over the past fifteen years, 96 percent of those graduates who have sought admission to law schools have been accepted, and 88 percent of those who have sought admission to medical schools have been accepted. In most other fields, the graduate or professional school acceptance rate is nearly 100 percent. The mean grade point average of the 2007 freshman class was 3.15, the mean ACT composite average score was 22, and the mean combined SAT score was 1059. Huntingdon is consistently listed among *U.S. News and World Report*'s "America's Best Colleges" and is listed among *Peterson's Competitive Colleges* and the *Princeton Review*'s "Best Colleges: Region by Region" (2007). The campus is listed on the National Register of Historic Places.

Huntingdon's student life program offers more than fifty clubs and organizations, including fraternities and sororities, student government, academic honoraries, spiritual life organizations, intramural sports, and a performing arts program with instrumental offerings in concert band, indoor percussion, concert choir, and theater. NCAA Division III intercollegiate athletics include men's varsity baseball, basketball, cross-country, football, golf, soccer, and tennis, and women's varsity basketball, cross-country, golf, soccer, softball, tennis, and volleyball; in addition, Huntingdon offers cheerleading, dance team, marching band, and intramural sports. Huntingdon is a residential campus, with about 70 percent of full-time students living in campus residence halls.

In addition to myriad opportunities for students to be involved, serve, learn, and lead, Huntingdon's Office of Student Life provides services and individual counseling for career and vocation development, student involvement and leadership, student health services, campus ministries, and residence life.

Location

Huntingdon's 71-acre campus is located in one of Montgomery's oldest and most beautiful residential neighborhoods, historic Old Cloverdale. The campus, originally designed by members of the Olmsted family, famous for Central Park, the Biltmore Estate, and the National Mall, is a naturally picturesque park. Buildings of collegiate Gothic Revival architecture surround a central Green, where many of the College's most memorable events take place. Montgomery enjoys warm summers and mild winters and is only 90 miles from Birmingham, 170 miles from Atlanta, 300 miles from New Orleans, and 160 miles from the spectacular white sand beaches of the Gulf Coast.

Alabama's capital city, Montgomery, has been a crossroads of historic tradition and cultural change. At the center of events from the Civil War to the Civil Rights Movement, Montgomery is home to a breadth of cultural and historic landmarks and performing arts programs, including the world-famous Alabama Shakespeare Festival, the Montgomery Museum of Fine Arts, Blount Cultural Park, the Civil Rights Memorial, the Rosa Parks Museum, Dexter Avenue King Memorial Baptist Church, the first White House of the Confederacy, the Capitol, the Montgomery Symphony, the Montgomery Ballet, the Alabama Dance Theater, and a host of civic, cultural, and performing organizations.

Majors and Degrees

Huntingdon College offers the Bachelor of Arts degree with majors in accounting–five year option, accounting–four year option, art, athletic training, biochemistry, biology, business administration (endorsement in economics and finance), cell biology, chemistry, coaching education, communication studies, elementary education (grades K–6), English (concentrations in creative writing, film studies, and theater), history, human performance (concentrations in exercise science and in sport management), mathematics, music, political science, psychology, religion, and religion (concentration in ministries).

Preprofessional programs offer preparation for the study of dentistry, engineering (dual degree), law, medicine, optometry, pharmacy, physical therapy, theology/ministry, and veterinary medicine.

Teacher certification programs are available in secondary education (grades 6–12) in chemistry, English language arts, history, and mathematics.

Academic Programs

Huntingdon's core curriculum develops the skills and knowledge necessary for professional success: writing, communication, a second language, and a fundamental knowledge of Western culture through historical and biblical study. Freshmen participate in four-year plans of study, which facilitates graduation within four years. Advanced Placement and International Baccalaureate credit are available.

Superb lecture and cultural programs bring current issues, topics of interest, and the arts to life for Huntingdon students via the Stallworth Lecture Series, the Elizabeth Belcher Cheek Piano Concert Series, the Rhoda Ellison Lecture Series, Founders Day Convocation, Martin Luther King Jr. Convocation, and other events during the year. In recent years, Huntingdon lecturers have included Janet Reno, Dee Dee Myers, Dr. Jane Goodall (animal behaviorist), Dr. Jack Horner and Dr. Paul Sereno (dinosaur experts), Dr. Donald Johanson (paleoanthropologist), Dr. Dan Carter (historian/Academy Award–winning documentary producer), Andrew Hudgins '73 (Pulitzer-nominated poet), and Dr. Martin Marty (theologian).

Huntingdon's calendar observes the semester system with an optional May Term and two 5-week summer sessions. Classes begin near the end of August and conclude near the end of April. New student orientation and registration is offered in three summer sessions just prior to the beginning of the fall semester, and one orientation and registration session is offered prior to the beginning of the spring semester.

Off-Campus Programs

Huntingdon students may participate in the Marine Environmental Sciences Consortium on Dauphin Island in Alabama. Participation in Air Force ROTC at Alabama State University or in Army ROTC at Auburn University at Montgomery is also available to students enrolled at Huntingdon. Through the Montgomery Higher Education Consortium, Huntingdon students may take courses at Auburn at Montgomery and at Faulkner University.

The College offers travel/study opportunities as part of each student's educational experience. Students may choose from travel/study programs offered in May of the junior or senior year. Many opportunities are offered with most costs covered within regular tuition and fees. Past study opportunities have included sites in Australia, China, Costa Rica, England, France, Germany, Hawaii, Italy, Kenya, Mexico, Northern Ireland, Peru, and Spain. Study experiences are faculty-directed and are offered for academic credit.

Academic Facilities

The College's Houghton Memorial Library holds nearly 110,000 volumes, periodicals, audiovisual materials, and microforms. Personal laptops are provided for each full-time student and the student-computer ratio is 1:1+. Smith Music Building offers a 120-seat recital hall, music studios, a music library, rehearsal and practice rooms, four pipe organs, eighteen grand pianos, and six upright pianos. The College's main building, Flowers Hall, was built in 1909 and houses the College chapel and Bellingrath Memorial Organ. Ligon Chapel is a 540-seat facility where weekly services are offered, as are lectures and other community-wide events. Athletic facilities for football and volleyball are located at the new Charles Lee Football Field at W. James Samford Jr. Stadium and the James W. Wilson Gymnasium, respectively. The Catherine Dixon Roland Arena is housed in Delchamps Student Center on the main campus, along with the Hawks Nest student lounge and the College bookstore. The College has completed the first phase of an extensive renovation and expansion project in Bellingrath Hall, which houses the science programs, laboratories, and research equipment, with more significant renovations to continue in the future. In 2003, the College completed renovation of the Dr. Laurie Jean Weil Center for Teacher Education and Human Performance to house its education, human performance, and psychology programs, offering extensive space and equipment for these popular programs. Other recent renovations and additions include the new Java City coffee house, renovations to the Seay Twins Art Gallery, the Tomberlin Fitness Center, W. James Samford Jr. Stadium, and the Will and Kelly Wilson Community and Athletic Center.

Costs

Tuition for the 2008–09 academic year (two semesters) is $19,320; room, board, and student fees are approximately $7650. Books and supplies average about $900 per academic year. New freshmen and transfer students assume a Levelized Tuition Plan and pay the same tuition and fees cost each year for all four years of enrollment (no annual increases in tuition are incurred).

Financial Aid

At Huntingdon, financing an education is a cooperative effort. Through a variety of resources, Huntingdon College administers more than $9 million in aid to approximately 99 percent of its students. These resources include institutional scholarships, gifts, and endowments as well as federal grants, loans, and work-study assignments. In addition, the school benefits from the Alabama Student Assistance and the Alabama Student Grant programs. To apply for financial aid, students must apply for admission and complete the Free Application for Federal Student Aid (FAFSA). Although the majority of financial aid is based upon demonstrated financial need, Huntingdon awards scholarships for achievement, circumstance, and academic merit; dependents of Alabama Power, ALFA, and the U.S. Military, Methodist students; and others. Freshmen applying for honors scholarships must be admitted by December 31.

Faculty

The faculty is composed of 43 full-time and 14 part-time teaching members; approximately 85 percent hold terminal degrees in their fields. In addition to teaching, the faculty's major responsibility is advising students. Faculty members work closely with students to plan and develop individual programs to fulfill the student's career interests. The student-faculty ratio is 15:1.

Student Government

The Student Government Association, authorized by the College administration, represents all full-time students in the School of Liberal Arts. Based upon the honor system, it places responsibilities for the enforcement of regulations and the safeguarding of standards upon the individual. The association encourages student leadership and good citizenship through communication, cooperation, and endeavors among students, faculty members, administrators, and other officials. The legislative powers of the association are vested in the Senate, which is composed of representatives from other leading organizations on campus. The Executive Council members are elected by the student body each spring. The Student Government Association and the College Activity Board, funded by the activity fee, present a variety of activities throughout the year. These include dances, festivals, parties, movies, special programs, and many other social events as well as such special events as the Presidential Banquet, Homecoming, pageants, and Family Weekend.

Admission Requirements

Huntingdon College is an equal opportunity educational institution and, as such, does not discriminate in its admission policy on the basis of race, color, sex, age, creed, national origin, or handicap. Huntingdon places primary emphasis on the strength of the student's secondary school record. Required test scores (ACT or SAT), school recommendations, and other personal qualifications as demonstrated by extracurricular activities are also carefully evaluated by the Office of Admission and Financial Aid. High school graduation or a GED certificate is required.

Prospective students and their parents are encouraged to call the Office of Admission and Financial Aid to plan a visit to the campus, take a tour, and meet with an Admission Counselor.

Transfer applicants must meet freshman admission standards and have at least a C average (2.25 on a 4.0 scale) with a minimum of 24 hours of academic work. Applicants must be in good standing from the last college attended. If the applicant has attended more than one college, the overall grade point average obtained at these schools must meet the minimum academic average required at Huntingdon. Transfer students may enroll at the beginning of any semester.

Application and Information

Applications are processed and notification is given on a rolling basis. Huntingdon College does not have an early admission program. Materials to be sent include the completed Application for Admission, a $20 application fee, and an official high school transcript and scores on the ACT or SAT. For more information, students should contact:

Office of Admission and Financial Aid
Huntingdon College
1500 East Fairview Avenue
Montgomery, Alabama 36106-2148
Phone: 334-833-4497
800-763-0313 (toll-free)
Fax: 334-833-4347
E-mail: admiss@huntingdon.edu
Web site: http://www.huntingdon.edu

Huntingdon College's John Jefferson Flowers Memorial Hall (1909) is the central figure of a handsome group of collegiate Gothic buildings.

SAMFORD UNIVERSITY

BIRMINGHAM, ALABAMA

The University

Samford University is a private, comprehensive liberal arts university with high-academic standards. The University's academic reputation is due to well-prepared, accessible faculty members who take time to know and interact with students. Samford, which has some 4,500 students, offers a wide range of extracurricular activities diverse enough to satisfy the social, cultural, physical, and spiritual needs of all of its students. A lively Greek system; an honors program; men's and women's intramural and varsity athletics, including seventeen NCAA Division I sports; music and drama groups; an award-winning debate program; and other interest groups bond the students and faculty members into a community of friends and scholars. Students come from forty-four states and thirty-three countries. A large number of students live on campus, enhancing the sense of school spirit and involvement. Students enjoy modern recreational facilities, including a concert hall, a theater, an indoor pool, racquetball and tennis courts, and an indoor track. Comfortable housing, including modern apartment-style units and fraternity/sorority residence facilities, is available.

Samford University has ranked third among 130 regional universities in the South, as published by *U.S. News & World Report*; marked as "very competitive" by *Barron's Profiles of American Colleges*; and has been selected for *Peterson's Competitive Colleges*. Samford programs are included in *The Templeton Guide: Colleges that Encourage Character Development.*

Special student services include an active and successful Career Development Center, which offers guidance in career exploration as well as ample opportunities for placement interviews. Co-op programs add work experience and business contacts to the rewards of achievement and income for the participants. The co-op program is an excellent source of financial assistance that complements the significant scholarship and federal aid programs available to Samford students.

In addition to its extensive undergraduate program, Samford University grants the following graduate degrees: Doctor of Education in educational leadership, Doctor of Ministry, Doctor of Pharmacy, Educational Specialist, Juris Doctor, Master of Accountancy, Master of Business Administration, Master of Comparative Law, Master of Divinity, Master of Science in Environmental Management, Master of Music, Master of Music Education, Master of Science in Education, Master of Science in Nursing, and Master of Theological Studies.

Location

Samford's wooded 180-acre campus, with its Georgian architecture, is one of the most beautiful in the nation. Located in the picturesque, mountainous area of Shades Valley, the campus is less than 6 miles from the heart of Birmingham, Alabama's largest city and the state's industrial, business, and cultural center. Birmingham annually hosts the Region's Charity Classic Professional Golf Association Champions Tournament and other major sports events. The city attracts national entertainment acts to its civic center, historic Alabama Theater, and Oak Mountain Outdoor Amphitheater. Gulf Coast beaches to the south and ski slopes to the north can be reached within 4½ hours by car. The world's largest space and rocket museum, located in Huntsville, Alabama, is also only a short drive away. Alabama's abundant freshwater lakes and rivers are sites for enjoyable outings. One of the South's largest shopping centers, the Riverchase Galleria, is only 7 miles from the Samford campus. The Samford student enjoys the best of two worlds: a suburban setting for study, contemplation, and social enjoyment and easy access to the varied offerings of a metropolitan area.

Majors and Degrees

Samford University offers an Associate of Science (A.S.) degree in the following concentrations: administrative/community services and natural/environmental sciences.

The Bachelor of Arts (B.A.) degree is attained through the following majors: classics, communication studies, English, English (with a concentration in film studies), family studies, family studies (with a concentration in child life), fine arts, fine arts (with a concentration in graphic design), French, German, Greek, history, interior design, journalism and mass communication, Latin, music, musical theater, philosophy, philosophy and religion, physics, political science, psychology, religion, religion (with a concentration in congregational studies), sociology, Spanish, and theater. The interdisciplinary concentrations offered in the Bachelor of Arts degree are Asian studies, international relations, language and world trade (with a specialty in French, German, Spanish, or world languages), Latin American studies, and public administration.

The Samford University Metro College offers the Bachelor of Science in Interdisciplinary Studies (B.S.I.S.) degree in the following concentrations: administrative/community services, counseling foundations, human resource development, and liberal studies.

The Bachelor of Music (B.M.) degree is offered in the following majors: church music, music, music education (instrumental, vocal, and choral), music theory/composition, musical theater, performance (instrumental, organ, piano, and voice), and performance with a pedagogy emphasis (piano).

Students can earn a Bachelor of Science (B.S.) degree through the following majors: athletic training, biology, biology (with an emphasis in marine science), chemistry, computer science, engineering and mathematics (dual-degree), engineering and physics (dual degree), engineering physics, environmental science, exercise science, fine arts, fine arts (with a concentration in graphic design), fitness and health promotion, fitness and health promotion/nutrition and dietetics (dual major), geography, mathematics, music, nutrition and dietetics, physics, and sports medicine (premedicine). The interdisciplinary concentrations offered in the Bachelor of Science degree are biochemistry and environmental science/geographic information science.

The University offers the Bachelor of Science in Business Administration (B.S.B.A.) in the following majors: accounting, economics, management, management (with a finance concentration), and management (with a marketing concentration).

The Bachelor of Science in Education (B.S.E.) is attained through the following majors: early childhood/special education/elementary/collaborative teacher education, English/language arts education, history/social science education, physical education, physical education (with athletic training option), P–12 education, secondary education, and teacher education.

The University offers the Bachelor of Science in Nursing (B.S.N.) in the nursing major.

Various preprofessional programs are offered, including predental, pre-engineering, prelaw, premedicine, preoptometry, prepharmacy, and pre–veterinary medicine.

The Degree with Honors is available to students whose academic achievement is remarkable.

Academic Programs

In order to graduate, students must complete a minimum of 128 semester credits with an average grade of C or better. The core curriculum consists of the following six courses: Cultural Perspectives I and II, Communication Arts I and II, Biblical Perspectives, and Concepts of Fitness and Health. The curriculum is designed to address ideas and issues that cross the usual disciplinary boundaries and to help students actively engage in learning rather than simply memorizing notes for an exam. The core is also designed to promote a global perspective, recognizing the influence and achievement of many cultures.

In addition, students complete several education courses designed to prepare them for work in a major field and/or to help them experience the sciences, the social sciences, the humanities, and the fine arts.

At least 40 credits must be earned in junior- and senior-level courses. At least 50 percent of credits must be earned at Samford University.

Between the end of the sophomore year and graduation, undergraduate students (including transfer students) must pass a writing proficiency test.

Off-Campus Programs

A semester-abroad program at Samford's Daniel House Study Centre in London, England, or a variety of other locations (Costa Rica, France, Germany, Spain) offers opportunities to develop a broad worldview.

Academic Facilities

The Harwell Goodwin Davis Library furnishes the facilities and materials necessary for reference, research, and independent study. Its reading areas with individual carrels provide ideal working conditions for Samford students. The open-stack system allows students easy access to a collection of more than 1 million volumes of books, periodicals, microfilm and microfiche, records, and tape. The library annually adds 7,000 volumes and 2,600 government documents. The library's Multimedia Collection houses the Religious Education Curriculum Laboratory and provides audiovisual aids and hardware, computers, and computer software. A staff of professional librarians guides students in the use of the fully equipped library. The Alabama Baptist Historical Commission's collection of Baptist church records and other important historical materials are located in the library and maintained by the Special Collection Department. Historical documents are also preserved through an active microfilming program. The Samford library system includes the Lucille Stewart Beeson Law Library, which has more than 232,850 volumes; the Education Curriculum Laboratory; the Global Drug Information Center; the Global Center; and the Music Library, which has more than 8,000 CDs, records, scores, and audiocassettes. University library holdings are accessed through a state-of-the-art library system. Other libraries in the Birmingham area cooperate with Samford on a reciprocal basis.

Costs

The cost of attending Samford is significantly lower than that of many institutions of comparable size and commitment to quality. The basic charge for 2007–08, including tuition ($18,000), room, and board, was $24,290. The typical student spends about $750 per year for books and supplies.

Financial Aid

At Samford University, a student's educational costs are frequently offset by scholarship and other financial assistance programs, which annually total more than $30 million. The application for admission also serves as the application for merit-based scholarships. Students interested in need-based opportunities should complete the Free Application for Federal Student Aid (FAFSA) by the March 1 priority filing date. In addition, non-need-based scholarship awards, usually based on academic merit, range up to full tuition.

Faculty

Samford's faculty consists of 264 full-time and 160 part-time members who have earned academic degrees from universities throughout the world. All classes are taught by members of the faculty; the faculty-student ratio is 1:13. Faculty members serve as academic advisers and also serve on many University committees.

Student Government

The Student Government Association (SGA) provides an excellent opportunity for students to participate in and influence governance. The SGA has autonomy in many programs, activities, and budgetary decisions; through the Student Senate, proposals related to improvement of campus life are sent to the University administration for consideration. The largest SGA organization is the Student Activities Council. Through its committees a variety of activities are provided, including concerts, lectures, dances, and outdoor recreation. The largest student-run activity is Step Sing, an annual variety show involving several hundred students that fills the 2,700-seat concert hall for three consecutive nights. Students are also involved in disciplining students who do not live up to University values. Alcohol is not permitted on campus, and regular visitation by persons of the opposite sex in residence hall rooms is not allowed.

Admission Requirements

Samford University seeks to enroll students capable of success in a challenging academic environment. Every applicant is evaluated individually on the basis of academic preparedness and potential, as well as personal fit with the mission and purpose of the University. The Admission Committee considers factors such as the strength of the high school curriculum, grade point average, standardized test scores, demonstrated leadership skills, and recommendations. The freshman class that entered in 2006 possessed an ACT composite middle 50 percent range of 23 to 28; the SAT middle 50 percent range was 1040 to 1250. The average high school grade point average of the entering class was 3.6. These statistics continue to demonstrate the competitive environment of Samford. International students must also demonstrate proficiency on the Test of English as a Foreign Language (TOEFL). Transfer students should have completed at least 24 semester hours or 36 quarter hours and maintained at least a 2.5 cumulative grade point average. Early admission is available to high school juniors who present an outstanding academic record and the recommendations of their parents and principal. Credit can be earned through IB and Advanced Placement tests. One school recommendation and an essay are required of every applicant, and a campus visit is strongly recommended.

Application and Information

Applications are received and notification is processed on a monthly rolling basis beginning in November. Students may also apply online by visiting the University's Web site. Applications are accepted until the class is filled.

Application inquiries should be addressed to:

Phil Kimrey, Ed.D.
Dean of Admission and Financial Aid
Samford University
Birmingham, Alabama 35229
Phone: 205-726-3673
800-888-7218 (toll-free)
Web site: http://www.samford.edu/admission

The Harwell G. Davis Library on the campus of Samford University.

SOUTH UNIVERSITY

MONTGOMERY, ALABAMA

SouthUniversity℠

The University

Established in 1899, South University is a private academic institution dedicated to providing educational opportunities for the intellectual, social, and professional development of a diverse student population. To achieve this, the University offers focused and balanced curricula at the associate, bachelor's, and master's degree levels in the areas of business, criminal justice, health-care management, health professions, information technology, and legal studies. In addition, the University offers a Master of Arts degree in professional counseling, a Master of Business Administration, and a Master of Business Administration in health-care administration.

South University in Montgomery became part of South University in 1997 and has been part of the postsecondary education community in Alabama since 1887.

South University in Montgomery has a diverse student body enrolled in day, evening, weekend, and online classes. South University is designed to accommodate the range of needs of its student body. Students are primarily commuters who live within 50 miles of the city. They include men and women who have enrolled directly after completing high school, who have transferred from another college or university, or who have experience in the workforce and are pursuing an education that will prepare them to expand their current position or help them take a new professional direction.

South University in Montgomery is located in a modern 26,000-square-foot building on a 3.75-acre campus. The two-story building houses computer and health professions labs, classrooms, a library, a student lounge, a bookstore, and faculty and administrative offices. Since most students live within driving distance of the campus, the campus does not offer or operate student housing. If housing is needed, prospective students should contact the Admissions Office.

South University is accredited by the Commission on Colleges of the Southern Association of Colleges and Schools (SACS, 1866 Southern Lane, Decatur, Georgia 30033-4097; 404-679-4501) to award associate, bachelor's, master's, and doctoral degrees. South University in Montgomery is authorized as an educational institution under Act No. 2004-282, Regular Session, Alabama Legislature, 2004, to conduct programs within the state of Alabama. The institution is also authorized by the State Approving Agency for the training of veterans under chapters 31, 34, and 35.

Certain programs offered at South University in Montgomery have earned programmatic accreditation. The Associate of Science degree program in medical assisting is accredited by the Commission on Accreditation of Allied Health Education Programs (CAAHEP, 1361 Park Street, Clearwater, Florida 33756; 727-210-2350) on recommendation of the Curriculum Review Board of the American Association of Medical Assistants Endowment (AAMAE). The Bachelor of Science in legal studies and Associate of Science in paralegal studies degree programs are approved by the American Bar Association (321 North Clark Street, Chicago, Illinois 60610; 312-988-5617). The Associate of Science in physical therapist assisting degree program is an expansion program accredited by the Commission on Accreditation in Physical Therapy Education of the American Physical Therapy Association (1111 North Fairfax Street, Alexandria, Virginia 22314; 703-684-2782).

Location

The campus is located on the rapidly growing east side of Alabama's capital city. As the state capital, Montgomery is a hub of government, banking, and law as well as a state center for culture and entertainment. Montgomery is situated in the middle of the southeastern U.S. and is less than a 3-hour drive from Atlanta and the Gulf of Mexico.

Majors and Degrees

South University in Montgomery awards the following two-year degrees: Associate of Science in business administration, Associate of Science in information technology, Associate of Science in medical assisting, Associate of Science in paralegal studies, and Associate of Science in physical therapist assisting.

The following four-year bachelor's degrees are awarded: Bachelor of Business Administration, Bachelor of Science in criminal justice, Bachelor of Science in health-care management, Bachelor of Science in information technology, Bachelor of Science in legal studies, and Bachelor of Arts in psychology.

Academic Programs

South University offers degree programs that are designed to meet the needs and objectives of students. Each curriculum combines didactic and practical educational experiences that provide students with the academic background needed to pursue the professions of their choice. In addition, faculty members strive to instill the value not only of education and professionalism but also of contribution and commitment to the advancement of community.

South University operates on a quarter academic calendar, and each University quarter comprises eleven weeks. Associate degree programs require a minimum of eight quarters to complete, and bachelor's degree programs require a minimum of twelve quarters for completion. Programs are offered on a year-round basis, providing students with the ability to work uninterrupted toward their degrees. More importantly, students have the opportunity to take classes on campus, online, or a combination of both through South University's unique Plus+ program. Combining campus and online classes provides students with maximum flexibility, allowing them to organize their college education around their work and/or family commitments.

Academic Facilities

The library has wireless technology throughout, comfortable seating, and quiet study space. The collection includes books, print and online periodicals, CDs, videos, and numerous online proprietary databases. Materials are housed in circulating, reference, and reserve collections and have been selected to support the academic programs. Also for student use, the library has a modern computer lab with ten workstations, each with Internet access, online database services, an office suite, tutorials, and class-support software.

Costs

For information about tuition and fees, prospective students should contact the South University Admissions Office.

Financial Aid

South University's Student Financial Services Office helps qualified students secure financial assistance to complete their studies. The University participates in several student aid programs. Forms of federal financial aid available to qualified students include the Federal Pell Grant Program, Federal Supplemental Educational Opportunity Grant (FSEOG) Program, Federal Work-Study Program, Federal Perkins Loan Program, Federal Stafford Student Loan Program (subsidized and unsubsidized), and Federal PLUS Loan Program. South University employs the Federal Methodology of Need Analysis, approved by the U.S. Department of Education, as a fair and equitable means of determining a family's ability to contribute to the student's educational expenses, as well as eligibility for other financial aid programs. Qualified students may apply for veterans' educational benefits. Students also are encouraged to investigate the availability of grants and scholarships through community resources.

Faculty

The South University in Montgomery faculty includes individuals of high academic distinction. Of the more than 40 instructors, 38 percent hold terminal degrees within their fields of expertise. In addition to teaching, faculty members strive to help students develop the requisites to appreciate knowledge and understand how experiences in the classroom and laboratory relate to professional performance in the workplace. The average student-faculty ratio per class is 13:1. Each student is assigned a faculty adviser, who oversees the student's progress and can answer questions about academic and career concerns. Students are encouraged to discuss program-related issues with and seek academic and career advice from their faculty advisers.

Admission Requirements

To be admitted to South University, prospective undergraduate students must be high school graduates or hold a GED certificate and submit an SAT or ACT score or a satisfactory score on the University-administered admissions examination. Transfer students must meet University-established criteria for acceptance as a transfer student.

All applicants must demonstrate English as a first language through submission of a diploma from a secondary school (or above) in which English is the official language of instruction. Applicants whose first language is not English must submit a Test of English as a Foreign Language (TOEFL) score. Applicants should contact the Admissions Office to determine other examinations/scores that are acceptable as an alternative to the TOEFL.

Applicants not meeting the entrance testing standards for general admission may be accepted under academic support admission.

Application and Information

Applicants must complete and submit an application form along with transcripts from high school and all colleges attended. Applicants must also complete all tests administered by the University or submit their SAT or ACT scores to the Registrar's Office. Applications are accepted on a rolling basis and should be made as far in advance as possible. Admissions officers are available weekdays, Saturdays, and by appointment. An appointment for an admissions interview or tour of the campus should be made in advance.

All international (nonimmigrant) applicants to South University must meet the same admissions standards as all other students. In addition, international applicants must have official educational records prepared in English, verify sufficient funds to cover the cost of the educational program, and meet certain other immigration-mandated criteria. South University in Montgomery is authorized under federal law to admit nonimmigrant students.

For additional information, prospective students should contact:

Director of Admissions
South University
5355 Vaughn Road
Montgomery, Alabama 36116-1120
Phone: 334-395-8800
866-629-2962 (toll-free)
Fax: 334-395-8859
Web site: http://www.southuniversity.edu

South University in Montgomery, Alabama, has a diverse student body enrolled in day, evening, weekend, and online classes.

TROY UNIVERSITY

TROY, ALABAMA

The University

Troy University was founded in 1887 as Troy State Normal School. The name was changed to Troy State Teachers College in 1929, to Troy State College in 1957, and to Troy State University in 1967 when it was granted university status. Founded as a teacher-training institution more than 100 years ago, the University now offers applied science, arts and sciences, business and commerce, education, fine arts, health and human services, journalism and communications, and preprofessional programs. The University operates four campuses in Alabama and more than fifty sites in twelve states and eight other countries. The availability of programs on these branch campuses may vary.

Students come from throughout the United States and several other countries. The total University enrollment is more than 28,000. There are 6,000 students enrolled at the main campus in Troy. Approximately one third live on campus in men's, women's, or coeducational residence halls or in sorority or fraternity housing. Noncommuting students who are under 19 at the time of registration are required to live in University housing for one academic year. All students who live in the residence halls must choose from one of four meal plans. The Trojan Center provides areas for student services, dining, recreation, and quiet study. The offices of Student Activities, Student Government, the Union Board, *The Palladium* (yearbook), and the Interfraternity and Panhellenic Councils are all located in the Trojan Center, and a performing arts theater, expanded food court, fitness center, a full-service Barnes and Noble Bookstore, and a Starbucks café have recently been added.

The Ralph Wyatt Adams Administration Building contains the business office and University College in addition to the offices of enrollment management, financial aid, University records, public affairs, alumni affairs, development, institutional research and planning, student affairs, financial affairs, academic affairs, and the chancellor of the Troy University System. Students may conduct most of their collegiate business within this one building.

Students participate in the Sound of the South Marching Band, Collegiate Singers, weekly newspaper, yearbook, radio and television stations, University Dancers, debate and forensics, musical theater productions, pageants, foreign language clubs, religious organizations, intramural sports, service clubs, honor societies, ethnic and political organizations, Trojan Ambassadors, social fraternities and sororities, and special interest clubs. A championship golf course is located on campus. The natatorium building houses an indoor swimming pool, a sauna, a weight room, and a gymnasium. Lighted tennis and handball courts, a 30,000-seat football stadium, a 3,000-seat gymnasium, a baseball complex, a modern field house, intramural fields, an outdoor pool, sand volleyball courts, a state-of-the-art track, and a press box with VIP seating are among the athletic facilities. Troy University is affiliated with the NCAA and fields fifteen intercollegiate sports. The Trojans play at the Division I-A level in all sports, and there are men's and women's rodeo teams, which are part of the National Intercollegiate Rodeo Association.

Location

The University's beautifully landscaped 577-acre campus is situated in a residential area of Troy. The city offers numerous cultural resources. The State Theater, home of the Alabama Shakespeare Festival, is less than an hour's drive from the campus. Rivers, lakes, streams, and farmland surround Troy. Birmingham, Atlanta, and Mobile are a few hours away, and the Gulf of Mexico is only 2 hours away.

Majors and Degrees

Troy University awards a Bachelor of Arts (B.A.) or a Bachelor of Science (B.S.) degree in accounting, art, art history, athletic training, biology, broadcast journalism, business administration, chemistry, collaborative K–6 education, computer science, criminal justice, dramatic arts, economics, English, environmental science, finance, general science, geomatics, graphic design, health education, history, journalism, management, marine biology, marketing, mathematics, medical technology, music education, nursing, physical education, physical science, political science, psychology, rehabilitation, risk management and insurance, secondary education, social work, sociology, speech communication, and sports and fitness management. Preprofessional concentrations are available in agriculture, dentistry, engineering, forestry, law, medicine, optometry, pharmacy, physical therapy, and veterinary medicine.

Academic Programs

The general studies curriculum, consisting of 60 semester hours, is required of all students pursuing a bachelor's degree. It provides work in English grammar and composition, biology, algebra or general mathematics, music, literature, and visual arts. In addition to this, the student must select one series of courses in U.S. history or history of Western civilization; three courses chosen from anthropology, economics, ethics, geography, mythology, philosophy, political science, psychology, religion, or sociology; one course in earth or physical science; one course in microcomputing; and one course in speech in order to complete the general studies requirements. Ten hours in a foreign language satisfies an elective portion of the general studies requirements.

Most degrees require 120 semester hours, 60 of which consist of major and/or minor courses. Double majors are available in various combinations. Besides meeting the requirements of a specific degree program, the student may choose courses from the general curriculum to satisfy elective requirements. Proficiency in English and mathematics is emphasized. The B.A. is awarded to students who enroll in at least 12 semester hours of a foreign language (French, German, Spanish, or Latin); other students are awarded the B.S. The average course load per term is 15 semester hours, or five classes carrying 3 semester hours of credit each. Students are encouraged to enroll in general studies and major courses simultaneously.

Academic Facilities

The University Library contains 247,761 volumes, more than 500 maps, 500,000 units of microtext, 47,000 government documents, and subscriptions to 1,500 periodicals and more than seventy newspapers. The library is part of an ultramodern Educational Resources Center, designed for comprehensive study and research, and includes a complete audiovisual facility. The Hall School of Journalism within this center features a 100,000-watt FM radio station affiliated with National Public Radio and a cablevision-affiliated television studio. The Office of Communications Services includes a photography laboratory and studios, a printing and quick copy facility, and a graphics design studio.

The Claudia Crosby Theater is a complete theater facility used for plays, pageants, ceremonies, and commencement exercises. It also provides a facility for students enrolled in the Department of Speech and Theatre. John Maloy Long Hall contains an acoustically perfect recording studio for the symphonic and concert bands and the collegiate and madrigal singers. McCartha Hall, housing the School of Education, contains a reading laboratory and an all-purpose lecture hall. A computer center is located in Bibb Graves Hall, along with offices and classrooms for the Sorrell College of Business and the Department of History and Social Sciences. The Center for Business and Economic Services, an office for research and information, is also located in Bibb Graves Hall. McCall and Sorrell halls contain laboratories and classrooms for science and mathematics. Smith Hall houses classrooms, offices, and lecture halls for the Department of English and studios for the Department of Music. *The Alabama Literary Review* operates from offices in Smith Hall. The Writing Center, staffed by permanent faculty members and student tutors, provides free services for students having difficulty with writing assignments. A similar facility, the Mathematics and Natural Science Laboratory, is designed to foster proficiency in those areas. A Fine Arts Center contains classrooms, studios, galleries, and a complete library to meet the needs of art, art history, and foreign language students.

Costs

Approximate annual full-time student expenses for the 2007–08 academic year for fall through spring were as follows: in-state tuition, $4164; out-of-state tuition, $8328; on-campus housing (standard rate), $2400; meal plan, $2884; and books and expenses, $1000.

Financial Aid

The University encourages all students to apply for admission regardless of their financial status. Scholarships, grants, loans, and work-study awards are given on the basis of priority and need analysis. For each academic year, beginning in September, the priority deadline is May 1. Approximately 70 percent of the current students are receiving financial assistance.

The University has an extensive scholarship program, which is based upon academic achievement and demonstration of leadership or particular talents. The following Troy University academic and leadership scholarships are awarded: Scholar's Award, a four-year full-tuition, room, and board award; Chancellor's Award, a four-year full-tuition award; and Leadership Award, for varied amounts. Other scholarships include athletic grants-in-aid and departmental and organizational awards.

Faculty

Individualized instruction and friendly student-teacher rapport are the keynotes of education at Troy University. Even tenured full professors teach introductory-level courses. The number of courses taught by graduate teaching assistants is kept at a minimum. The visiting professor program has featured such dignitaries as Dr. Edward Teller, the nuclear physicist; Patrick Buchanan, syndicated columnist and former Presidential candidate; and Cyril Northcote Parkinson, the author of *Parkinson's Law*.

Student Government

The University's Student Government Association (SGA) consists of the president, vice president, secretary, and clerk, who are elected by the student body to one-year terms. Senators are elected from each residence hall and from commuter seats. Senators may be chosen to serve on committees concerning academic affairs, publications, public relations, the Union Board, the Judicial Board, and curriculum revision. The SGA president is the only student member of the University's Board of Trustees.

Admission Requirements

Admission is based on the grade point average in high school or in previous college work along with acceptable ACT or SAT scores. Students are given placement examinations in mathematics and English before registering for classes in their first term of enrollment. Transfer students with fewer than 20 semester hours of college work are treated as beginning freshmen. Visits to the campus are recommended but are not required. Upon tentative acceptance of the application, the prospective student is required to attend IMPACT, Troy's precollege orientation, which takes place during the summer before the fall term. Similar shorter sessions are presented prior to each term. A student may enroll for any term, fall through summer. Prospective students are encouraged to visit the admissions office and make application well in advance of the term in which they wish to enroll.

Application and Information

There is no application deadline, but high school seniors are encouraged to apply as soon as possible during their senior year; housing assignments are made in the early spring. The application fee is $30.

Admissions Office
Troy University
111 Adams Administration Building
Troy, Alabama 36082
Phone: 334-670-3179
800-551-9716 (toll-free)
Web site: http://www.troy.edu

THE UNIVERSITY OF ALABAMA AT BIRMINGHAM

UAB

BIRMINGHAM, ALABAMA

The University

The University of Alabama at Birmingham (UAB) is a fully accredited research university and academic health center with an annual enrollment of more than 16,000 students. In a short time, UAB has established outstanding programs through six liberal arts and professional schools, six health professional schools, and graduate programs serving all major units. As the University has grown, so have its contributions to the state, the nation, and the world. UAB is committed to education, research, and service programs of excellent quality and far-reaching scope. In terms of federal research and development funding, UAB ranks twenty-sixth nationally and first in the state of Alabama, receiving more funding than all Alabama universities combined. In such an environment, undergraduate students can pursue a wide array of research opportunities and gain valuable experience that pays off later in graduate studies or career development.

Part of the UAB experience is student life, consisting of a rich mix of academic organizations, honor clubs, social fraternities and sororities, volunteer groups, and activities ranging from intramural sports and SGA (Student Government Association) to supporting Blazer sports as a member of the "Gang-Green" spirit group. With more than 150 campus organizations to keep students involved, UAB offers the chance to make lifelong friendships while assisting in the development of skills essential to leadership and teamwork. The South is the place for sports year-round, and UAB is no exception. The athletic program is a Division I member of the NCAA and a founding member of Conference USA. UAB has seventeen intercollegiate teams, including men's and women's basketball, golf, rifle, soccer, and tennis; men's baseball and football; and women's cross-country, track, softball, synchronized swimming, and volleyball. A new Campus Recreation Center offers free weights, court sports, swimming pools/lazy river, fitness classes, nutrition education, fitness areas, a climbing wall, a juice bar, and much more. A brand new freshman residence hall as well as the new state-of-the-art "Commons on the Green" dining facility, which also includes a diner and "C-Store," opened fall 2006.

Location

Birmingham earned the name "The Magic City" during its first boom days. The expression still rings true as the metropolitan area continues to mirror UAB's phenomenal growth and reflects the many cultural opportunities available within the city. Birmingham is easily reached from major national routes (Interstates 20, 59, and 65), and UAB is only minutes away from the Birmingham International Airport.

Majors and Degrees

UAB's degree programs offer strong career preparation. With fifty majors from which to choose, UAB's broad curriculum allows students to explore new interests while receiving specialized training. Students may also integrate different areas of knowledge by choosing a minor in an additional field of study or by exploring the possibilities for developing an individually designed major.

The School of Arts and Humanities offers the Bachelor of Arts degree in African-American studies, art (concentrations in art education, art history, ceramic sculpture, drawing, graphic design, painting, photography, printmaking, and sculpture), communication studies (concentrations in broadcasting, communication arts, journalism, mass communication, and public relations), English (concentration in creative writing), foreign languages (tracks in French and Spanish), music (concentration in music education and music technology), philosophy, and theater.

The School of Business offers the Bachelor of Science degree in accounting (concentrations in forensic accounting and information technology auditing), economics (concentrations in economic analysis and policy and quantitative methods), finance (concentrations in financial investments and institutions and financial management), industrial distribution (concentrations in e-business engineering and medical equipment and supplies marketing), information systems, management (concentrations in general management, human resource management, management information systems, and operations management), and marketing.

The School of Education offers the Bachelor of Science degree in early childhood education, elementary education, health education, high school education, physical education, and special education.

The School of Engineering offers the Bachelor of Science degree in biomedical engineering, civil engineering, electrical engineering, materials engineering, and mechanical engineering.

The School of Health Related Professions offers the Bachelor of Science degree in cytotechnology, health information management, health sciences, medical technology, nuclear medicine technology, radiologic sciences (concentrations in advanced imaging and radiation therapy), and respiratory therapy.

The School of Natural Sciences and Mathematics offers the Bachelor of Science degree in biology, chemistry, computer and information sciences, mathematics (concentrations in applied math and scientific computation), natural science, and physics.

The School of Nursing awards the Bachelor of Science degree. Students interested in pursuing the nursing degree and who meet the University's admission requirements are admitted to UAB as prenursing students. To be eligible for admission in good standing to the School of Nursing, students must successfully complete a prescribed set of courses with an acceptable grade point average.

The School of Social and Behavioral Sciences offers the Bachelor of Arts degree in anthropology, economics, history, international studies, political science, and sociology and the Bachelor of Science degree in criminal justice, psychology, and social work.

Academic Programs

UAB's undergraduate instructional programs are broad based and designed to serve the needs of its diverse student body while providing a strong general education foundation. All programs of study leading to the baccalaureate degree have as an essential component a common core curriculum. The minimum total credit hours required for a baccalaureate degree is 120 semester hours with a cumulative grade point average of at least 2.0 (C) in all credit hours attempted. A student may obtain a certain number of semester hours of academic credit for knowledge acquired independently through Advanced Placement (AP), International Baccalaureate (I.B.), College-Level Examination Program (CLEP), Credit by Examination (CBE), evaluation of noncollegiate-sponsored courses, armed services courses, and prior learning.

The UAB Honors Academy offers rare and valuable opportunities to explore knowledge from new angles, enriching the overall educational experience for future success. The University

Honors Program concentrates on the vast resources of a major research university in a small, liberal arts setting; the Science and Technology Honors Program offers students interested in a science or technology career the opportunity to work closely with world-renowned researchers; the Global and Community Leadership Honors Program draws from a community-based and cross-cultural perspective that prepares students for leadership roles on community and worldwide levels; and qualified students interested in a career in medicine, optometry, or dentistry may be accepted to professional school at UAB before they begin college through the Early Admission to Medical Professional Schools Program.

There are two academic semesters and a summer term during a calendar year. The fall and spring semesters each consist of approximately sixteen weeks of classes. Summer term offers several options, including twelve-week, nine-week, three-week, and 4½-week terms.

Academic Facilities

The UAB campus occupies more than 100 major buildings, more than 11 million gross square feet, and almost 90 square blocks near downtown Birmingham. The undergraduate area of campus is concentrated within an eight-square-block area, however, giving students the convenience and togetherness that is so important to the college experience.

The Mervyn H. Sterne Library houses a collection of more than 1.5 million items selected to support teaching and research at UAB. In addition, the collection consists of microforms and other print and nonprint materials. The Lister Hill Library of the Health Sciences is also available and provides a comprehensive collection of materials for medical study and research. Between the two, there are 26,000 periodicals available either in print or online.

UAB is the home of the Alys Robinson Stephens Performing Arts Center, with state-of-the-art concert halls and practice facilities. This beautiful facility draws national and international performers, enhancing the strong cultural opportunities in Birmingham.

A new 95,000-gross-square-foot academic building is planned to open January 2008. The new facility will house the School of Social and Behavioral Sciences, providing additional classroom space as well as a 200-station computer mathematics laboratory.

Costs

For the 2007–08 academic year, tuition was $141 per semester hour for in-state students and $353 per semester hour for out-of-state students. Based on a full (12 hours per semester) load of course work for the academic year, tuition and fees for Alabama residents are estimated at $4208 and $9296 for nonresidents. A typical amount for books and supplies total approximately $900 per academic year. A shared room in a residence hall ranges from $3460 to $6440 per academic year. Blazer Hall, the freshman dorm, charges $4300 for the academic year.

Financial Aid

UAB's financial aid package consists of loans, employment, and grants and scholarships, enabling students from all economic backgrounds to attend UAB. Financial aid applications are available in early January for the following academic year, with a priority packaging deadline of April 1.

UAB awards over 1,500 scholarships each year. Students admitted by November 1 are automatically considered for all academic scholarships for which they are qualified. Awards are distributed on a first-come, first-served basis, so students are encouraged to apply and be admitted to the University as early as possible. Students admitted after November 1 will be considered for scholarships on a funds-available basis.

Faculty

UAB has 2,049 full-time faculty members, with more than 90 percent holding doctoral degrees. The student-faculty ratio is 18:1, with the vast majority of freshman- and sophomore-level courses taught by full-time faculty members.

Student Government

In addition to eight student government associations, the Office of Student Life offers many student-run committees and programs that are open to all students. These committees provide entertainment through comedy, music, movies, lectures, and multicultural programming. Other opportunities to lead and serve include social fraternities and sororities, a student leadership program, an ambassador program, a volunteer program, a scholarship pageant, and three award-winning student publications.

Admission Requirements

UAB is an equal educational opportunity institution. The requirements for regular admission for entering freshmen include a minimum high school GPA of 2.25 on a 4.0 scale, a minimum ACT score of 20 or SAT score of 950, and completion of a pre-college curriculum (4 years of English, 3 years of math (algebra I and higher), 3 years of social sciences, 3 years of science (2 with lab components), 1 year of foreign language, and 2 additional core courses to total 17). For tentative action, a transcript may be sent during the student's senior year in high school. A final transcript must be sent upon graduation.

Transfer students must have a minimum cumulative GPA of 2.0 on a 4.0 scale after completing 24 semester hours (or 36 quarter hours) of college-level work. Students with previous college work must submit an official transcript from each institution attended and must be eligible to enroll at the last institution attended. UAB also encourages international students who have academic, linguistic, and financial capabilities to apply for admission.

Application and Information

All students who wish to attend UAB must complete an application for admission and submit proof of immunization against measles. An application may be submitted as early as one year prior to admission. A completed application, a nonrefundable $35 application fee ($30 for online applications), and all supporting documentation must be received by the Office of Undergraduate Admission by the priority deadline for the term for which admission is requested. The application priority deadline for fall term is March 1. For an application and further information, students should contact:

UAB Undergraduate Admission
Hill University Center, Room 260
1530 3rd Avenue, South
Birmingham, Alabama 35294-1150
Phone: 205-934-8221
800-421-8473 (toll-free)
E-mail: undergradadmit@uab.edu
Internet: http://www.uab.edu

THE UNIVERSITY OF ALABAMA IN HUNTSVILLE

UAHuntsville
THE UNIVERSITY OF ALABAMA IN HUNTSVILLE

HUNTSVILLE, ALABAMA

The University

The University of Alabama in Huntsville (UA Huntsville) is a public, four-year, coeducational national research university and is a member of the University of Alabama System. UA Huntsville was founded in 1950 as an extension center of the University of Alabama and became an autonomous campus in 1969. UA Huntsville has earned national recognition in engineering and the sciences, and its programs in the humanities, fine arts, social sciences, business, and nursing are outstanding. Students interact with some of the most productive researchers in their respective disciplines. Close ties with business, industry, and government give students real-world opportunities and experience. UA Huntsville partners with more than 100 high-tech industries as well as major federal laboratories such as NASA's Marshall Space Flight Center, the National Space Science and Technology Center, and the U.S. Army's Redstone Arsenal. Its unique location provides many unparalleled co-op opportunities for students to earn a significant portion of their college costs and maximize their employment potential. Students have unusual opportunities to work with some of the top scientists in the country. UA Huntsville is accredited by the Southern Association of Colleges and Schools' Commission on Colleges. UA Huntsville also holds professional accreditation from the American Chemical Society; the Computing Sciences Accreditation Board; the Accreditation Board for Engineering and Technology, Inc.; the Commission on Collegiate Nursing Education; the National Association of Schools of Art and Design; the National Association of Schools of Music; the National Council for Accreditation of Teacher Education; the Accreditation Council for Cooperative Education; and AACSB International–The Association to Advance Collegiate Schools of Business.

The fall 2007 enrollment consisted of 5,751 undergraduate and 1,513 graduate students. Eighty-one percent are from Alabama, 8 percent are from other countries, 54 percent are men, and 46 percent are women. UA Huntsville students represent more than forty states and seventy countries. Of the total undergraduate enrollment, 22 percent are members of ethnic minority groups. Fifty percent of the entering freshman class had ACT scores between 22 and 27; the median GPA was 3.3.

Postbaccalaureate certificates are available in accounting, environmental science, human resource management, nursing education, software engineering, teaching of English to speakers of other languages, and technical communications for individuals. Through the School of Graduate Studies, students may earn the master's degree in accounting, aerospace engineering, atmospheric science, biological science, chemical engineering, chemistry, civil engineering, computer engineering, computer science, electrical engineering, English, history, industrial and systems engineering, management, management information systems, materials science, mathematics, mechanical engineering, nursing, operations research, physics, psychology, public affairs, and software engineering. The Master of Business Administration (M.B.A.) is also offered. The Ph.D. degree is awarded in applied mathematics, atmospheric science, biotechnology, civil engineering, computer engineering, computer science, electrical engineering, industrial and systems engineering, materials science, mechanical engineering, optical science and engineering, and physics.

UA Huntsville has more than 125 active student groups and organizations, including national fraternities and sororities, honor societies, special interest groups, religious organizations, the Student Government Association (SGA), the student-run newspaper, the student-run literary magazine, minority student organizations, international student organizations, the choir, the chorus, a film and lecture series, service organizations, professional interest groups, and intramural athletics. The University is a member of the NCAA Division II and the Gulf South Conference and competes in the following intercollegiate sports: men's baseball, basketball, cross-country, soccer, tennis, and track and field and women's basketball, cross-country, soccer, softball, tennis, track and field, and volleyball. UA Huntsville also competes at the NCAA Division I level in men's ice hockey.

On-campus housing is available for undergraduate and graduate students and consists of three traditional residence halls and one apartment-style complex. The Central Campus Residence Hall, a seven-story residence hall, is the designated freshmen housing facility that offers private bedrooms and semiprivate baths. This hall is located in the center of campus and is connected to the University Center by an enclosed walkway. The University Center offers most student services and houses the Charger Café. The North Campus Residence Hall opened in 2002, and North Campus Residence Hall II opened in 2005. Both offer private bedrooms and semiprivate baths. Student apartments in Southeast Housing are reserved for upperclassmen and graduate students. Private apartments are available for married students and students with children. Handicapped-accessible apartments are available. In addition, five on-campus fraternity and sorority houses with private bedrooms opened in 2006. Meals are available in the University Center cafeteria.

Location

The University of Alabama in Huntsville is located in the Tennessee River Valley of north-central Alabama, 100 miles north of Birmingham and 100 miles south of Nashville, Tennessee. Huntsville is the home of more than fifty Fortune 500 companies that specialize in high technology, including aerospace engineering, rocket propulsion, computer technology, weapons systems, telecommunications, software engineering, information systems design, and engineering services. Most of these companies, as well as the UA Huntsville campus, are located in Cummings Research Park, one of the top ten research parks in the world and the second-largest research park in the U.S.

Majors and Degrees

The Colleges of Business Administration, Engineering, Liberal Arts, Nursing, and Science and the School of Graduate Studies administer the degree programs of the University. The College of Business Administration awards the Bachelor of Science in Business Administration (B.S.B.A.) degree in the fields of accounting, finance, management, management information systems, and marketing. The College of Engineering awards the Bachelor of Science in Engineering (B.S.E.) degree in aerospace (with an option in mechanical), chemical, civil, computer, electrical, industrial and systems, mechanical, and optical engineering. The College of Nursing awards the Bachelor of Science in Nursing (B.S.N.) degree. The Bachelor of Arts (B.A.) degree is awarded by the College of Liberal Arts in the fields of art, communication arts, education, English, foreign languages (French, German, Russian, Spanish), foreign languages/international trade, history, music, philosophy, political science, psychology, and sociology. In the College of Science, the Bachelor of Science (B.S.) degree is available in biological science, chemistry, computer science, mathematics, and physics. A Bachelor of Arts degree is available in biological science and mathematics.

Undergraduate teacher certification programs are offered in collaborative teaching endorsement (K–6 or 6–12), elementary education (K–6), middle school (4–8), music education (P–12), or secondary/high school education (6–12), with majors in biology, chemistry, English, language arts, foreign language (French, German, Russian, and Spanish), general science, history, mathematics, physics, social science, and sociology.

Academic Programs

The general education course work is designed to broaden intellectual awareness and enhance cultural literacy and analytical thinking. All undergraduates are required to complete course work in English composition, humanities and fine arts, history, social and behavioral sciences, natural and physical sciences, and mathematics. B.A., B.S., B.S.B.A., and B.S.N. degrees require the completion of at least 128 total semester hours; B.S.E. degrees in computer, electrical, and optical engineering require 128; B.S.E. degrees in industrial and systems engineering, 130; B.S.E in chemical engineering, 131; and B.S.E. in mechanical, mechanical with aerospace, and civil engineering, 132. A variety of special academic programs and options are available, including cooperative education, cross-registration with other institutions, distance learning, double majors, dual enrollment, intensive English program, honors program, independent study, internships, and learning disabilities services. Credit is awarded for appropriate scores on CLEP and AP examinations. UA Huntsville offers Army ROTC at a participating institution off campus. Special services are available for students with disabilities, including note-taking, readers, tape recorders, tutors, interpreters for the hearing impaired, special transportation, special housing, adaptive equipment, and Braille services. The fall 2008 semester begins August 18 and ends December 5; spring semester 2009 begins January 5 and ends April 29. Two summer sessions are offered beginning May 26 and June 29, 2009.

Academic Facilities

The 400-acre campus is in northwest Huntsville. All academic buildings have been constructed since 1960 and exemplify modern functional design. The UA Huntsville library houses a collection of more than 336,000 print volumes, a selective collection of over 500,000 U.S. government publications, more than 600,000 materials in microform and manuscript collections, approximately 52,000 electronic periodicals, more than 58,000 electronic books, and over 350 databases. The UA Huntsville Art Gallery hosts art exhibits by local, regional, and national artists as well as by students and faculty members. More than 1,100 personal computers are available across the campus for student use. Computer labs, one of which is open 24 hours a day, are located in several buildings and staffed to provide assistance. Access to the University fiber-optic network is available in all buildings, including all residence halls. Internet access and e-mail are available to all students. UA Huntsville has a number of state-of-the-art research labs accessible to undergraduates.

Costs

In 2007–08, tuition for undergraduate Alabama residents was $5216 (15 credits each semester) for the academic year. Out-of-state students paid $11,024 (15 credits each semester) for the academic year. Undergraduates can expect to spend approximately $940 on books and supplies for the academic year. Undergraduate students pay an estimated $4340 for room, from $550 to $1600 for board, $1215 for transportation, and $1730 for personal and miscellaneous expenses per year.

Financial Aid

UA Huntsville awards nearly $25 million annually in need-based and non-need-based financial aid in the form of scholarships, grants, loans, and campus jobs. Financial aid programs available include veterans' educational benefits, Federal Work Study, Federal Stafford Student Loans (subsidized and unsubsidized), Federal PLUS Loans, Consolidation Loans, Federal Pell Grants, Federal SMART Grants, Academic Competitiveness Grants, Federal Supplemental Educational Opportunity Grants (FSEOG), state scholarships and grants, private scholarships, and institutional scholarships. Non-need-based scholarships are available for athletics, ROTC, academic merit, creative and performing arts, special achievement, leadership skills, and minority status. Students should submit the Free Application for Federal Student Aid (FAFSA) before April 1 for priority consideration and no later than the final closing date of July 31. Award notifications are made on a rolling basis. The priority date for scholarship application is December 1.

Faculty

Of the 289 full-time instructional faculty members, 91 percent hold the Ph.D. or other terminal degree in their field. The student-faculty ratio is 16:1. Graduate students teach 5 percent of introductory undergraduate courses. The average introductory lecture class size is 31.

Student Government

The primary purpose of the Student Government Association is to improve the educational environment and promote the welfare of students in all areas of University life. The SGA is responsible for developing and sponsoring programs that enrich the students' cultural, intellectual, and social life. An executive branch, a 15-member legislature, and a 5-member arbitration board are responsible for carrying out the official business of the organization. The SGA sponsors more than 125 clubs and organizations in addition to providing many student services, such as health insurance, special rates for community cultural events, and a student directory.

Admission Requirements

High school graduates may be admitted as regular freshmen based on acceptable high school achievement and standardized test scores (SAT or ACT), which are considered together. A higher result in one area offsets a lower performance in the other. For example, a minimum high school GPA of 2.5 is required if the ACT composite score is 21 or the combined SAT score is 930. A high school GPA of 2.0 requires an ACT composite score of 23 or higher or a combined SAT score of 1050 or higher. Applicants should present a minimum of 20 Carnegie high school units, including 4 of English; 4 of social studies and history; 3 of mathematics, including 1 of algebra, 1 of geometry, and 1 of algebra II/trigonometry (recommended by all Colleges); 3 of science, including 1 of biology (recommended), 1 of chemistry or physics (recommended by all Colleges), and sufficient academic electives to meet the required 20 units. First-time freshmen and transfer students are admitted every academic term. Transfer students with fewer than 18 hours of earned college credit are admitted based on high school transcripts, test scores, and college course work. Transfer students are required to submit transcripts of all university work and have at least a 2.0 average on all work attempted to qualify for regular admission.

Application and Information

Completed applications and a nonrefundable $30 application fee must be received no later than August 1 for admission in the fall semester and by December 15 for admission in the spring semester. Admission notifications are sent on a rolling basis. Online applications are encouraged and can be accessed at http://apply.uah.edu. For a paper application form and more information, students should contact:

Office of Admissions
The University of Alabama in Huntsville
301 Sparkman Drive
Huntsville, Alabama 35899
Phone: 256-824-2773
800-UAH-CALL (toll-free)
Fax: 256-824-6073
E-mail: admitme@uah.edu
Web site: http://www.uah.edu

ALASKA

Barrow
Nome
Fairbanks
Glennallen
Anchorage
Juneau
Sitka

ALASKA BIBLE COLLEGE

Glennallen, Alaska **www.akbible.edu/**

- **Independent nondenominational** 4-year, founded 1966
- **Rural** 80-acre campus
- **Endowment** $46,777
- **Coed**
- **Minimally difficult** entrance level

Faculty *Student/faculty ratio:* 7:1.

Academics *Calendar:* semesters. *Degrees:* certificates, associate, and bachelor's.

Student Life *Campus security:* 24-hour emergency response devices.

Standardized Tests *Required:* SAT or ACT (for admission).

Costs (2007–08) *Comprehensive fee:* $11,590 includes full-time tuition ($6500), mandatory fees ($90), and room and board ($5000). Part-time tuition: $285 per credit hour. *College room only:* $2500. Room and board charges vary according to board plan and housing facility.

Financial Aid Of all full-time matriculated undergraduates who enrolled in 2004, 35 applied for aid, 33 were judged to have need. 27 state and other part-time jobs (averaging $1800). *Average indebtedness upon graduation:* $8500. *Financial aid deadline:* 7/1.

Applying *Options:* deferred entrance. *Application fee:* $35. *Required:* essay or personal statement, high school transcript, minimum 2.0 GPA, 2 letters of recommendation, interview.

Freshman Application Contact Mrs. Carol C. Ridley, Director of Admissions, Alaska Bible College, Box 289, 200 College Road, Glennallen, AK 99588-0289. *Phone:* 907-822-3201. *Toll-free phone:* 800-478-7884. *Fax:* 907-822-5027. *E-mail:* info@akbible.edu.

ALASKA PACIFIC UNIVERSITY

Anchorage, Alaska **www.alaskapacific.edu/**

- **Independent** comprehensive, founded 1959
- **Suburban** 170-acre campus
- **Endowment** $32.5 million
- **Coed** 514 undergraduate students, 59% full-time, 68% women, 32% men
- **Moderately difficult** entrance level, 93% of applicants were admitted

Undergraduates 302 full-time, 212 part-time. Students come from 19 states and territories, 2 other countries, 26% are from out of state, 6% African American, 2% Asian American or Pacific Islander, 5% Hispanic American, 16% Native American, 0.4% international, 8% transferred in, 31% live on campus. *Retention:* 59% of 2006 full-time freshmen returned.

Freshmen *Admission:* 128 applied, 119 admitted, 43 enrolled. *Average high school GPA:* 3.22. *Test scores:* SAT critical reading scores over 500: 79%; SAT math scores over 500: 64%; ACT scores over 18: 89%; SAT critical reading scores over 600: 34%; SAT math scores over 600: 9%; ACT scores over 24: 50%; SAT critical reading scores over 700: 1%.

Faculty *Total:* 114, 42% full-time, 32% with terminal degrees. *Student/faculty ratio:* 7:1.

Majors Accounting and business/management; business administration and management; elementary education; environmental science; health/health care administration; human services; liberal arts and sciences/liberal studies; marine biology and biological oceanography; middle school education; natural resources management and policy; parks, recreation and leisure; psychology; technology/industrial arts teacher education.

Academics *Calendar:* semesters. *Degrees:* certificates, associate, bachelor's, master's, and postbachelor's certificates. *Special study options:* academic remediation for entering students, accelerated degree program, adult/continuing education programs, advanced placement credit, distance learning, double majors, independent study, internships, part-time degree program, services for LD students, student-designed majors, study abroad, summer session for credit. *ROTC:* Air Force (c).

Computers on Campus 50 computers/terminals and 480 ports are available on campus for general student use. Campuswide network is available. 100% of college-owned or -operated housing units are wired for high-speed Internet access. Wireless service is available via entire campus.

Student Life *Housing:* on-campus residence required for freshman year. *Options:* coed. Campus housing is university owned. Freshman campus housing is guaranteed. *Activities and organizations:* drama/theater group, student-run newspaper, choral group, Environmental Club, Student Government Association, Psychology Club, Student Organization of Native Americans, Students for Free Enterprise. *Campus security:* 24-hour emergency response devices, student patrols, late-night transport/escort service, controlled dormitory access. *Student services:* personal/psychological counseling.

Athletics *Intramural sports:* basketball M/W, skiing (cross-country) M/W, soccer M/W.

Standardized Tests *Required:* SAT or ACT (for admission).

Costs (2007–08) *Comprehensive fee:* $28,610 includes full-time tuition ($20,900), mandatory fees ($110), and room and board ($7600). Part-time tuition: $695 per semester hour. *Required fees:* $55 per term part-time.

Financial Aid Of all full-time matriculated undergraduates who enrolled in 2007, 248 applied for aid, 195 were judged to have need, 89 had their need fully met. 58 Federal Work-Study jobs (averaging $1433). In 2007, 42 non-need-based awards were made. *Average percent of need met:* 92%. *Average financial aid package:* $14,788. *Average need-based loan:* $4520. *Average need-based gift aid:* $7904. *Average non-need-based aid:* $9552. *Average indebtedness upon graduation:* $10,197.

Applying *Options:* electronic application, early decision, deferred entrance. *Application fee:* $25. *Required:* essay or personal statement, high school transcript, minimum 2.5 GPA, 2 letters of recommendation. *Required for some:* interview. *Application deadlines:* 8/15 (freshmen), 8/15 (transfers).

Freshman Application Contact Mr. Michael Warner, Director of Admissions, Alaska Pacific University, Anchorage, AK 99508. *Phone:* 907-564-8248. *Toll-free phone:* 800-252-7528. *Fax:* 907-564-8317. *E-mail:* admissions@alaskapacific.edu.

CHARTER COLLEGE

Anchorage, Alaska **www.chartercollege.edu/**

Director of Admissions Ms. Lily Sirianni, Vice President, Charter College, 2221 East Northern Lights Boulevard, Suite 120, Anchorage, AK 99508-4157. *Phone:* 907-277-1000. *Toll-free phone:* 800-279-1008.

UNIVERSITY OF ALASKA ANCHORAGE

Anchorage, Alaska **www.uaa.alaska.edu/**

- **State-supported** comprehensive, founded 1954, part of University of Alaska System
- **Urban** 428-acre campus
- **Endowment** $7.3 million
- **Coed**
- **Noncompetitive** entrance level

Faculty *Student/faculty ratio:* 18:1.

Academics *Calendar:* semesters. *Degrees:* certificates, associate, bachelor's, and master's.

Student Life *Campus security:* 24-hour emergency response devices and patrols, student patrols, late-night transport/escort service, controlled dormitory access.

Athletics Member NCAA. All Division II.

Standardized Tests *Required:* SAT or ACT (for admission).

Costs (2007–08) *Tuition:* state resident $3840 full-time, $158 per credit part-time; nonresident $12,810 full-time, $427 per credit part-time. Full-time tuition and fees vary according to course level. Part-time tuition and fees vary according to course level. *Required fees:* $560 full-time, $35 per term part-time. *Room and board:* $8230; room only: $4630. Room and board charges vary according to board plan and housing facility.

Financial Aid Of all full-time matriculated undergraduates who enrolled in 2007, 3,870 applied for aid, 2,854 were judged to have need, 1,261 had their need fully met. 129 Federal Work-Study jobs (averaging $2557). In 2007, 776 non-need-based awards were made. *Average percent of need met:* 71. *Average financial aid package:* $13,027. *Average need-based loan:* $3508. *Average need-based gift aid:* $1996. *Average non-need-based aid:* $2200.

Applying *Options:* deferred entrance. *Application fee:* $40. *Required:* minimum 2.0 GPA. *Required for some:* high school transcript.

Freshman Application Contact Enrollment Services, University of Alaska Anchorage, 3211 Providence Drive, Anchorage, AK 99508-8046. *Phone:* 907-786-1480. *Fax:* 907-786-4888. *E-mail:* enroll@uaa.alaska.edu.

See page 292 for the College Close-Up.

UNIVERSITY OF ALASKA FAIRBANKS

Fairbanks, Alaska **www.uaf.edu/**

- **State-supported** university, founded 1917, part of University of Alaska System
- **Small-town** 2250-acre campus
- **Coed** 7,568 undergraduate students, 44% full-time, 59% women, 41% men
- **Minimally difficult** entrance level, 78% of applicants were admitted

The University of Alaska Fairbanks (UAF) is America's Arctic university of northern scholarship, discovery, and adventure. Located in interior Alaska, a land of rivers, forests, mountains, wildlife, and the Northern Lights, the University is known for research in Arctic phenomena, including global climate change. The 2,250-acre campus offers state-of-the-art classrooms, laboratories, recreational facilities, and residence halls.

Undergraduates 3,346 full-time, 4,222 part-time. Students come from 13 states and territories, 36 other countries, 13% are from out of state, 3% African American, 4% Asian American or Pacific Islander, 3% Hispanic American, 19% Native American, 2% international, 6% transferred in, 31% live on campus. *Retention:* 72% of 2006 full-time freshmen returned.

Freshmen *Admission:* 1,758 applied, 1,373 admitted, 958 enrolled. *Average high school GPA:* 3.21. *Test scores:* SAT critical reading scores over 500: 53%; SAT math scores over 500: 58%; SAT writing scores over 500: 42%; ACT scores over 18: 81%; SAT critical reading scores over 600: 19%; SAT math scores over 600: 22%; SAT writing scores over 600: 13%; ACT scores over 24: 34%; SAT critical reading scores over 700: 4%; SAT math scores over 700: 3%; SAT writing scores over 700: 1%; ACT scores over 30: 3%.

Faculty *Total:* 1,074, 32% full-time, 39% with terminal degrees. *Student/faculty ratio:* 10:1.

Majors Accounting; accounting technology and bookkeeping; airframe mechanics and aircraft maintenance technology; airline pilot and flight crew; American Indian/Native American studies; American Native/Native American languages; anthropology; applied mathematics; area studies related; art; biological and physical sciences; biology/biological sciences; business administration and management; carpentry; chemistry; child care provision; child development; civil engineering; clinical/medical laboratory assistant; communication/speech communication and rhetoric; community organization and advocacy; computer and information sciences; computer engineering; computer installation and repair technology; computer science; construction management; corrections and criminal justice related; culinary arts; dental assisting; economics; education related; electrical, electronics and communications engineering; elementary education; English; fire science; fishing and fisheries sciences and management; foreign languages and literatures; foreign languages related; geography; geological/geophysical engineering; geology/earth science; history; industrial production technologies related; industrial technology; Japanese; journalism; legal assistant/paralegal; liberal arts and sciences/liberal studies; linguistics; mathematics; mechanical engineering; medical/clinical assistant; mental and social health services and allied professions related; mining and petroleum technologies related; multi-/interdisciplinary studies related; music; natural resources and conservation related; natural resources management and policy; petroleum engineering; philosophy; physics; physics related; political science and government; psychology; public health; Russian studies; science technologies related; social work; sociology; teacher assistant/aide; theater design and technology; wildlife and wildlands science and management.

Academics *Calendar:* semesters. *Degrees:* certificates, associate, bachelor's, master's, and doctoral. *Special study options:* academic remediation for entering students, accelerated degree program, advanced placement credit, cooperative education, distance learning, double majors, external degree program, honors programs, independent study, internships, off-campus study, part-time degree program, services for LD students, student-designed majors, study abroad, summer session for credit. *ROTC:* Army (b). *Unusual degree programs:* 3-2 computer science.

Computers on Campus 125 computers/terminals are available on campus for general student use. Students can access the following: computer help desk, free student e-mail accounts, online (class) grades, online (class) registration, online (class) schedules, university portal; campus wireless access. Campuswide network is available. 100% of college-owned or -operated housing units are wired for high-speed Internet access. Wireless service is available via classrooms, computer centers, computer labs, dorm rooms, learning centers, libraries, student centers.

Student Life *Housing options:* coed, cooperative, disabled students. Campus housing is university owned. Freshman applicants given priority for college housing. *Activities and organizations:* drama/theater group, student-run newspaper, radio and television station, choral group, United Campus Ministry, Northern Star Chinese Student Association, Golden Key National Honor Society, UAF Good Time Swing Dance Club, University Women's Association, national fraternities, national sororities. *Campus security:* 24-hour emergency response devices and patrols, student patrols, late-night transport/escort service, controlled dormitory access, ID check at door of residence halls, crime prevention and safety workshops. *Student services:* health clinic, personal/psychological counseling, women's center, legal services.

Athletics Member NCAA. All Division II except ice hockey (Division I), men's and women's riflery (Division I). *Intercollegiate sports:* basketball M (s)/W (s), cross-country running M (s)/W (s), ice hockey M (s), riflery M (s)/W (s), skiing (cross-country) M (s)/W (s), swimming and diving W (s), volleyball W (s). *Intramural sports:* badminton M/W, basketball M/W, bowling M/W, cheerleading M (c)/W (c), cross-country running M/W, fencing M (c)/W (c), ice hockey M/W, racquetball M/W, riflery M/W, rock climbing M/W, skiing (cross-country) M/W, skiing (downhill) M/W, soccer M/W, softball M/W, swimming and diving M/W, table tennis M/W, tennis M/W, ultimate Frisbee M/W, volleyball M/W, water polo M/W, wrestling M/W.

Standardized Tests *Required:* SAT or ACT (for admission), SAT or ACT (for placement).

Costs (2008–09) *Tuition:* state resident $4020 full-time, $134 per credit part-time; nonresident $13,440 full-time, $448 per credit part-time. *Required fees:* $736 full-time, $8 per credit part-time, $48 per term part-time. *Room and board:* $6030; room only: $3440.

Financial Aid Of all full-time matriculated undergraduates who enrolled in 2007, 2,952 applied for aid, 1,409 were judged to have need, 585 had their need fully met. In 2007, 847 non-need-based awards were made. *Average percent of need met:* 56%. *Average financial aid package:* $9906. *Average need-based loan:* $9091. *Average need-based gift aid:* $4841. *Average non-need-based aid:* $6916. *Average indebtedness upon graduation:* $28,204.

Applying *Options:* electronic application, early admission, deferred entrance. *Application fee:* $40. *Required:* high school transcript, minimum 2.0 GPA. *Application deadlines:* 8/1 (freshmen), 8/1 (transfers). *Notification:* continuous (freshmen), continuous (transfers).

Freshman Application Contact Tim Stickel, Acting Director, Admissions, University of Alaska Fairbanks, PO Box 757480, Fairbanks, AK 99775-7480. *Phone:* 907-474-7500. *Toll-free phone:* 800-478-1823. *Fax:* 907-474-5379. *E-mail:* admissions@uaf.edu.

See page 294 for the College Close-Up.

UNIVERSITY OF ALASKA SOUTHEAST

Juneau, Alaska **www.uas.alaska.edu/**

- **State-supported** comprehensive, founded 1972, part of University of Alaska System
- **Small-town** 198-acre campus
- **Endowment** $3.3 million
- **Coed** 2,699 undergraduate students, 27% full-time, 65% women, 35% men
- **Noncompetitive** entrance level, 50% of applicants were admitted

Undergraduates 742 full-time, 1,957 part-time. Students come from 44 states and territories, 5 other countries, 17% are from out of state, 1% African American, 3% Asian American or Pacific Islander, 2% Hispanic American, 15% Native American, 2% international, 6% transferred in. *Retention:* 55% of 2006 full-time freshmen returned.

Freshmen *Admission:* 298 applied, 150 admitted, 144 enrolled. *Test scores:* SAT critical reading scores over 500: 40%; SAT math scores over 500: 54%; ACT scores over 18: 100%; SAT critical reading scores over 600: 14%; SAT math scores over 600: 41%; ACT scores over 24: 86%; SAT critical reading scores over 700: 4%; SAT math scores over 700: 3%; ACT scores over 30: 16%.

Faculty *Total:* 224, 48% full-time, 22% with terminal degrees. *Student/faculty ratio:* 11:1.

Majors Administrative assistant and secretarial science; biology/biological sciences; business administration and management; construction trades; consumer economics; education; engineering-related technologies; English language and literature related; general studies; health professions related; history; humanities; legal studies; liberal arts and sciences/liberal studies; mathematics; natural resources/conservation; social sciences.

Academics *Calendar:* semesters. *Degrees:* certificates, associate, bachelor's, and master's. *Special study options:* academic remediation for entering students, adult/continuing education programs, advanced placement credit, cooperative education, distance learning, independent study, internships, off-campus study, part-time degree program, services for LD students, student-designed majors, study abroad, summer session for credit.

Computers on Campus 75 computers/terminals are available on campus for general student use. Students can access the following: online (class) registration. Campuswide network is available.

Student Life *Housing options:* coed, disabled students. Freshman applicants given priority for college housing. *Activities and organizations:* student-run newspaper, Native Student Club. *Campus security:* 24-hour emergency response devices and patrols, late-night transport/escort service, controlled dormitory access. *Student services:* health clinic, personal/psychological counseling.

Athletics *Intercollegiate sports:* riflery M (c)/W (c). *Intramural sports:* basketball M/W, racquetball M/W, riflery M/W, skiing (cross-country) M/W, skiing (downhill) M/W, softball M/W, tennis M/W, ultimate Frisbee M/W, volleyball M/W.

Standardized Tests *Required:* SAT or ACT (for admission).

Costs (2007–08) *Tuition:* state resident $3840 full-time, $128 per credit part-time; nonresident $12,810 full-time, $427 per credit part-time. *Required fees:* $796 full-time. *Room and board:* $6714; room only: $4177.

Financial Aid Of all full-time matriculated undergraduates who enrolled in 2007, 36 Federal Work-Study jobs (averaging $2134). *Average indebtedness upon graduation:* $19,979.

Applying *Options:* early admission, deferred entrance. *Application fee:* $40. *Required:* high school transcript, minimum 2.0 GPA. *Required for some:* essay or personal statement. *Application deadlines:* rolling (freshmen), rolling (transfers). *Notification:* continuous (freshmen), continuous (transfers).

Freshman Application Contact Ms. Deema Ferguson, Admissions Clerk, University of Alaska Southeast, 11120 Glacier Highway, Juneau, AK 99801-8625. *Phone:* 907-796-6294. *Toll-free phone:* 877-796-4827. *Fax:* 907-796-6365. *E-mail:* admissions@uas.alaska.edu.

See page 296 for the College Close-Up.

UNIVERSITY OF ALASKA ANCHORAGE

ANCHORAGE, ALASKA

The University

The University of Alaska Anchorage (UAA) is a public institution accredited by the Commission on Colleges of the Northwest Association of Schools and Colleges. Since its creation, UAA has established a record of continuing growth and development in its academic, vocational, and public-service activities. The University of Alaska Anchorage promotes student success by maintaining a strong emphasis on faculty excellence and student services. Programs are focused on student needs and support the development of students by contributing to their cultural, social, intellectual, physical, and emotional growth. UAA also provides support services for students with special needs. UAA offers a broad range of certificate, associate degree, bachelor's degree, and master's degree programs. Programs span the social sciences, English literature, creative writing, and foreign languages as well as the natural sciences, mathematics, engineering, and the fine arts, thus providing students with the opportunity to pursue interests beyond their selected academic fields and explore a variety of subjects. UAA also offers a statewide distance education and independent-learning program with multimedia distribution.

The academic units on the Anchorage campus are the College of Arts and Sciences, the College of Business and Public Policy, the College of Education, the College of Health and Social Welfare, the Community and Technical College, the School of Engineering, and the School of Nursing. Research units include the Alaska Center for Rural Health, the American Russian Center, the Center for Alcohol and Addiction Studies, the Center for Community Engagement and Learning, the Center for Economic Development, the Center for Economic Education, the Center for Human Development, the Environmental and Natural Resources Institute (the Alaska Natural Heritage Program, the Alaska State Climate Center, the Arctic Environmental and Information Data Center, and Resource Solutions), the Institute for Circumpolar Health Studies, the Institute of Social and Economic Research, the Justice Center, the North Pacific Fisheries Observer Training Center, the Small Business Development Center (Procurement Technical Assistance Center, BUY ALASKA, and Technology Research Development Center), and the University of Alaska Center for Economic Development.

The University offers a wide range of programs at the graduate level, including the Master of Arts (M.A.) in anthropology, education, English, and interdisciplinary studies; the Master of Business Administration (M.B.A.) in general management; the Master of Civil Engineering (M.C.E.); the Master of Education (M.Ed.) in adult education, counselor education, early childhood special education, educational leadership, master teacher studies, and special education; the Master of Fine Arts (M.F.A.) in creative writing and literary arts; the Master in Public Administration (M.P.A.); the Master of Public Health (M.P.H.) in public health practice; the Master of Science (M.S.) in Arctic engineering, biological sciences, civil engineering, clinical psychology, computer science, engineering management, environmental quality engineering, environmental quality science, global supply-chain management, interdisciplinary studies, nursing science, project management, and science management; and the Master of Social Work (M.S.W.). There are also graduate certificate options, including family nurse practitioner studies and psychiatric and mental health nurse practitioner studies as well as educational leadership: principal and educational leadership: superintendent studies.

Location

The University of Alaska campus is nestled in a lush greenbelt filled with ponds, lakes, and spruce forests, surrounded by the mountains and glaciers of Chugach State Park and the beautiful Cook Inlet. Student housing and classrooms are within easy walking distance. An extensive system of trails provides opportunities for running, cross-country skiing, in-line skating, and biking. The geographical features in the Anchorage area provide world-class climbing, downhill skiing, and snowboarding. Cook Inlet and nearby Prince William Sound offer an amazingly rich and diverse marine environment supporting a host of marine mammals and legendary salmon runs. These waters contribute to the area's relatively mild weather and are well known among the world's windsurfers and sea kayakers. Summertime temperatures range between 60 and 70 degrees. Winters include snow from October to April but are less severe in Anchorage than in many other U.S. cities. Anchorage, a city of 266,000 people, is the chief business, professional, international, transportation, and entertainment center of the state.

Majors and Degrees

The Bachelor of Arts degree (B.A.) is awarded in anthropology, art, biological sciences, computer science, early childhood education, economics, elementary education, English, history, hospitality and restaurant management, interdisciplinary studies, journalism and public communication, justice, languages, mathematics, music, philosophy, political science, psychology, sociology, and theater. The Bachelor of Business Administration degree (B.B.A.) is awarded in accounting, economics, finance, global logistics management, management, management information systems, and marketing. The Bachelor of Fine Arts degree (B.F.A.) is awarded in art. The Bachelor of Human Services degree (B.H.S.) is awarded in human services. The Bachelor of Liberal Studies degree (B.L.S.) is awarded in liberal studies. The Bachelor of Music degree (B.M.) is awarded in music education emphasis and performance. The Bachelor of Science degree (B.S.) is awarded in anthropology, aviation technology, biological science, chemistry, civil engineering, computer science, geological science, geomatics, health sciences, interdisciplinary studies, mathematics, medical technology, natural science, nursing science, physical education, psychology, sociology, and technology. The Bachelor of Social Work degree (B.S.W.) is offered in social work.

The Associate of Arts degree (A.A.) is awarded with a general studies program. The Associate of Applied Science degree (A.A.S.) is awarded in accounting; air traffic control; apprenticeship technologies; architectural engineering technology; automotive technology; aviation administration; aviation maintenance technology; business computer information systems; computer information and office systems; construction management; culinary arts; dental assisting; dental hygiene; early childhood development; fire service administration; geomatics; heavy-duty transportation and equipment; human services; medical assisting; medical laboratory technology; nursing; occupational safety and health; paramedical technology; professional piloting; radiologic technology; small-business administration; telecommunications, electronics, and computer technology; and welding and nondestructive testing technology.

Certificate programs designed to meet the needs of students who wish to attain a high level of proficiency in specific career areas are offered in applied ethics, architectural drafting, automotive technology, aviation maintenance technology, civil drafting, computer and networking technology, computer information and office systems, dental assisting, early childhood development, geographic information systems, heavy-duty transportation and equipment, industrial welding technology, logistics, massage therapy, mechanical and electrical drafting, nondestructive testing technology, paralegal studies, practical nursing, structural drafting, and telecommunications and electronic systems.

Academic Programs

UAA's fall semester begins in August; the spring semester, in January; and the summer session, in May. An undergraduate student who registers for 12 or more semester credits is considered to be full-time. The minimum number of semester credits that must be earned for a baccalaureate degree, including those accepted by transfer, is 120. A minimum of 60 semester credits is required to complete the Associate of Arts and Associate of Applied Science degree programs. Completion requirements vary from one discipline to another. All degree programs offered by UAA require students to maintain a GPA of at least 2.0; some programs require a higher GPA.

Degree-seeking students with experience acquired outside the conventional college classroom have an opportunity to demonstrate college-level achievement. UAA grants Advanced Placement credit for satisfactory performance (scores of 3 or higher) on the College Board Advanced Placement tests. UAA's credit-by-examination program rewards students who do well on either the College-Level Examination Program (CLEP) or the challenge examinations, the latter of which are locally developed comprehensive exams covering specific subject areas. Credit may be granted for military service. Details on eligibility, restrictions, and procedures are in the course catalog.

Academic Facilities

The Consortium Library, located on the Anchorage campus, serves the academic clientele of the University and that of its nearby neighbor, Alaska Pacific University. The Anchorage campus consists of twenty academic, administrative, and laboratory structures. These include specially equipped buildings for the arts, culinary arts, allied health science, automotive and diesel, business, and engineering programs. A new 120,000-square-foot Integrated Science Building and planetarium to house world-class research and cutting-edge instructional facilities in the natural and physical sciences with emphasis on global warming is scheduled to open in fall 2009. The Merrill Aviation Complex houses the aviation program. In Anchorage, courses are also taught at Elmendorf Air Force Base, Fort Richardson, and Chugiak–Eagle River.

Costs

In 2008–09, Alaska residents pay $134 per semester credit for lower-division undergraduate courses and $151 per semester credit for upper-division courses. Nonresident students pay $448 per semester credit for lower-division undergraduate courses and $465 for upper-division courses. Students enrolled under the Western Undergraduate Exchange pay $201 per semester credit for lower-division courses. On-campus apartments and residence halls with meals range from $2960 to $4400 per semester. Extra funds are needed for student activity fees, textbooks, and miscellaneous expenses.

Financial Aid

The Office of Student Financial Aid assists students and prospective students in securing the funds needed to begin or continue studies at the University. The state and federal government make available financial assistance in the form of grants, loans, and employment opportunities for students who demonstrate the need for such assistance. The amount and type of award may vary, depending upon state and federal guidelines, student need, and availability of funds. Applications for aid should be received by April 1 of the year the student plans to enroll. In addition to government funds, the University and many private organizations offer scholarships, tuition waivers, and veteran benefits.

Faculty

A high percentage of UAA faculty members have doctoral degrees. Students find their introductory classes taught by highly qualified and experienced faculty members. The student-faculty ratio on the Anchorage campus is 20:1, and the average class size is 18. Faculty members in the academic units also serve students as academic advisers.

Student Government

The Union of Students of the University of Alaska Anchorage (USUAA) is the sole official representative for students on campus. This body is duly recognized by the Board of Regents. USUAA administers funds for various student organizations, programs, and activities, such as movie tickets, concerts, dances, special events, lectures, legal services, the Club Council, the student radio station, and the student newspaper.

Admission Requirements

To qualify for admission to a certificate or associate degree program, a student should have earned either a high school diploma, a GED certificate, or at least 60 college-level semester credits; otherwise, the student must be at least 18 years of age and have participated in UAA's Ability to Benefit process. The certificate- or associate degree–seeking freshman (with fewer than 30 college-level semester credits) must submit a final official high school transcript or official GED score. Official transcripts from all accredited colleges and universities are also required. In addition, it is recommended that students take an approved placement test.

To qualify for admission to baccalaureate programs, a student must satisfy at least one of the following criteria: graduation from high school with a GPA of at least 2.5 or successful completion of the GED program and completion of either the SAT, the ACT, or an approved test; completion of at least 30 college-level semester credits with a GPA of at least 2.0 and a high school diploma, a GED certificate, or completion of UAA's Ability to Benefit Process; or completion of at least 60 college-level semester credits with a GPA of at least 2.0. Baccalaureate degree–seeking freshmen (with fewer than 30 college-level semester credits) must submit final official high school transcripts or an official GED score; official copies of ACT, SAT, or approved test scores; and official transcripts from all accredited colleges and universities.

To qualify as a transfer student, a student must graduate from high school and have earned at least 30 college-level semester credits. A student who has not graduated from high school must have at least 60 college-level semester credits or complete the Ability to Benefit process.

International students who intend to reside in the U.S for the purpose of pursuing a certificate or degree as F-1 visa students and need a Form I-20 Certificate of Eligibility for Nonimmigrant F-1 Student Status must meet University and degree program admission requirements. In addition to being admitted to an undergraduate program, international students must submit the following: an official TOEFL score of at least 450 for the paper-based test or 133 for the computer-based test; a statement of financial support for the anticipated period of study and evidence of the funds, such as a bank statement; and English translations of all required documents.

Application and Information

Prospective baccalaureate degree, associate degree, and certificate students must submit the application for admission and a nonrefundable $40 application fee. Deadlines for receipt of the application and all supporting documents are July 1 for the fall semester and November 1 for the spring semester.

For more information concerning admission or the general curriculum, students should contact:

Cecile Mitchell
Director, Enrollment Services
University of Alaska Anchorage
P.O. Box 141629
Anchorage, Alaska 99514-1629
Phone: 907-786-1480
Web site: http://www.uaa.alaska.edu/

UNIVERSITY OF ALASKA FAIRBANKS

FAIRBANKS, ALASKA

The University

Founded in 1917, the University provides education, research, and service in the "last frontier." The Fairbanks campus, one of three in the statewide system of higher education, is the primary administrative and research center, with branches in Bethel, Dillingham, Kotzebue, and Nome, along with rural centers throughout the state.

The total University of Alaska Fairbanks (UAF) enrollment is slightly over 10,000 students. Eighty-five percent of the students have Alaskan residency, although nearly half of the students graduated from high schools in forty-nine states and thirty-eight other countries. The nine residence halls on campus are renovated and are capable of lodging 1,322 students. The Student Apartment Complex has sixty furnished two-bedroom units reserved for sophomore and upperclass students. The Eileen Panigeo MacLean House, housing for rural students, holds 22 students. The University also manages 153 furnished apartments for students with families.

The large campus contains a core of academic buildings and residences, as well as miles of ski trails, two lakes, and an arboretum. Most of the University's research institutes, including the noted Geophysical Institute and the International Arctic Research Center, are clustered on the West Ridge. The University's Agricultural Experiment Station farm is on campus, as are a Cooperative Fish and Wildlife Research Unit and various state and federal agencies and laboratories. The University awards graduate degrees in many of the same areas as the undergraduate studies, often in conjunction with one of its research institutes. A natural science facility that houses chemistry, physics, geology, and earth sciences was completed relatively recently.

Intercollegiate athletics include men's and women's basketball, cross-country running and skiing, and riflery and women's volleyball and swim teams. The University sponsors an outstanding men's intercollegiate ice-hockey team, which plays at the 4,665-seat Carlson Center. The UAF hockey team is a member of the Central Collegiate Hockey Association (CCHA). The Student Recreation Complex houses a variety of sports and physical activities facilities, including multipurpose areas for basketball, volleyball, badminton, tennis, calisthenics, dance, gymnastics, judo, and karate; a rifle and pistol range; courts for handball, racquetball, and squash; an elevated 200-meter, three-lane jogging track; a swimming pool; weight-training and modern fitness equipment areas; an ice arena for recreational skating and hockey; a special aerobics area; and a three-story climbing wall. The cheery and roomy student union, the William Ransom Wood Center, is the focus of various out-of-class activities for students and faculty members. The center houses meeting and exhibit rooms, lounges and television areas, the student government offices, campus information, a pub, a bowling alley, a games room, a cafeteria, a snack bar, an espresso bar, and a photography darkroom.

Location

The campus of the University of Alaska Fairbanks is situated on a ridge overlooking the valley of the Tanana River and the city of Fairbanks. Serving a population of more than 85,000 within the 7,561-square-mile North Star Borough, Fairbanks is a major trade center for outlying villages in Interior Alaska. The city is connected with the rest of the state and the lower forty-eight states by air and highway. Municipal bus service is available between downtown Fairbanks, the surrounding area, and the campus. Shuttle bus service is available around the UAF campus.

Fairbanks offers the sophistication of larger cities through such luxuries as first-run movies and fine restaurants while maintaining the atmosphere of smaller, more personal towns. Denali National Park and other vast wilderness areas are close at hand, and Anchorage is 350 miles south via the Parks Highway. Members of the Fairbanks community and the University join together in the University-Fairbanks Symphony Orchestra and in many other musical and theatrical enterprises.

Majors and Degrees

The University of Alaska Fairbanks awards certificates, A.A. and A.A.S. degrees, and B.A., B.S., B.B.A., B.Ed., B.M., and B.F.A. degrees in accounting, airframe studies, Alaska Native studies, anthropology, applied accounting, applied business, applied physics, apprenticeship technology, art, arts and sciences, aviation maintenance technology, aviation technology, biochemistry, biological sciences, business administration, chemistry, civil engineering, communication, community health, computer science, culinary arts, dental assistant studies, drafting technology, early childhood, earth science, economics, electrical engineering, elementary education, emergency medical services, emergency services, English, Eskimo, fisheries, foreign languages, general science, geography (environmental studies), geological engineering, geology, ground vehicle maintenance technology, health-care reimbursement, health technology, history, human services, Japanese studies, journalism, justice, linguistics, maintenance technology, mathematics, mechanical engineering, medical assistant studies, microcomputer support specialist studies, mining engineering, molecular biology, music, Native language education, natural resources management (including forestry), Northern studies, office management and technology, paralegal studies, petroleum engineering, philosophy, phlebotomy, physics, political science, powerplant studies, process technology, psychology, renewable resources, rural development, rural human services, Russian studies, social work, sociology, statistics, technology, theater, tribal management, and wildlife biology. Preprofessional advising is available in dentistry, law, library science, medicine, physical therapy, and veterinary medicine.

Academic Programs

The academic year is divided into two semesters; registration is in early April for the fall semester and in November for the spring semester. Preregistration is available for returning students. In addition, there are three-week, six-week, and twelve-week summer sessions. UAF offers an early orientation for new students in the fall and spring semesters. The University is organized into four colleges and four professional schools: the College of Liberal Arts, the College of Natural Science and Mathematics, the College of Engineering and Mines, the College of Rural Alaska, and the Schools of Natural Resources and Agricultural Sciences, Education, Fisheries and Ocean Sciences, and Management. A minimum of 120 credits must be completed for the four-year baccalaureate degree programs.

Students who receive scores of 3 or higher on the College Board's Advanced Placement tests may be awarded credit by the University. Currently enrolled students may challenge courses for credit by successfully completing College-Level Examination Program (CLEP) examinations or by completing locally prepared examinations. Requests for advanced-placement credit and credit by examination are coordinated through the Office of Admissions.

The honors program is designed for highly motivated undergraduate students who wish to acquire a superior understanding of the natural and social sciences, the arts, and the humanities. Prospective honors students need a minimum ACT composite score of 29 or a minimum combined SAT score of approximately 1270, with a minimum 3.6 high school GPA.

Off-Campus Programs

The University maintains exchange programs with various universities in Canada; universities in Australia, Austria, Chile, Denmark, England, Finland, France, Germany, Japan, Mexico, Norway, Russia, Scotland, and Taiwan; and multiple other universities through the North 2 North Exchange program. The University also participates in the Northwest Interinstitutional Council for Study Abroad, providing students with an opportunity to enroll in liberal arts programs in Austria, England, France, Greece, Italy, and Spain. UAF is also a member of the National Student Exchange, participating with more than 180 colleges and universities throughout the United States, in U.S. territories, and at nine locations in Canada.

Academic Facilities

The Fine Arts Complex features a 480-seat theater, a 1,072-seat concert hall, FM public radio (KUAC) and educational-television (PBS) studios, an art gallery, and the Elmer E. Rasmuson Library. The library collection contains more than 1.75 million volumes, including the prestigious Alaska and Polar Regions Collection. Electronic catalogs provide access to collections in 11,000 libraries nationwide.

Students have free use of the University's academic computing facilities (Aurora), which are accessible from Windows and Macintosh computer labs and via remote access. Various schools and colleges have their own special-purpose computer labs.

The University Museum attracts more than 100,000 visitors each year to Interior Alaska and is located on the UAF campus. The museum collects, preserves, and exhibits materials from Alaska and the North.

Costs

In 2006–07, tuition and fees were $2135 per semester for full-time (15 credits) students. Nonresident students paid an additional $4185 for 15 credits of tuition each semester. Residents of Alaska, the Yukon Territory, British Columbia, and the Northwest Territories are exempt from the nonresident tuition fee. To qualify as a resident, a student must have been living in Alaska for two years. Students who initially register as nonresidents may apply for resident status after living in state for twelve months, under the University's "bona fide resident" provision. The approximate cost per semester for books and supplies is $500 and for personal items and recreation, $450. A double-occupancy residence hall room on campus costs $1495 per semester. Meals, which all residence hall occupants are required to purchase, cost approximately $1295 per semester. These costs are subject to change. Married student housing on campus is also available.

Financial Aid

A large portion of financial aid is derived from the Alaska Supplemental Education Loan Program, which is available to all students attending UAF, regardless of residency. Three kinds of aid are available: grants and scholarships (which need not be repaid), loans, and part-time employment. Students who seek financial assistance for the fall term should submit applications by February 15. Inquiries should be addressed to the Financial Aid Office, University of Alaska Fairbanks, P.O. Box 756560, Fairbanks, Alaska 99775-6560.

The Chancellor's Scholarship, a one-year tuition waiver, is available to entering freshmen with a minimum 3.0 GPA and 1150 SAT combined score or 25 ACT composite score. To apply, students should submit a scholarship application, an application for admission, a high school transcript, and test scores for review. The deadline for scholarships is February 15. National Merit finalists qualify for a four-year tuition waiver plus a $20,000 scholarship.

Faculty

Sixty-six percent of the 784 faculty members hold doctoral degrees, and many are actively engaged in research. In keeping with University policy, faculty members provide academic counseling for students. The combination of a student-faculty ratio of 15:1 and easy access to instructors for help outside of class produces a maximum educational benefit for students.

Student Government

The Associated Students of the University of Alaska Fairbanks (ASUAF) protects students' rights through its various governmental functions and also offers educational, social, recreational, and service activities. The school newspaper, *Sun Star*, is published weekly with the sponsorship of ASUAF, which also supports KSUA, the campus radio station; the international cinema and weekly movie series; and dances, concerts, and other entertainment. ASUAF publishes the results of its faculty evaluations and sends several student lobbyists to the Alaska state legislature in Juneau each spring. A student member sits on the Board of Regents of the University.

Admission Requirements

For admission to a baccalaureate program, applicants must be high school graduates with a cumulative grade point average of at least 2.0 and have earned a GPA of at least 2.5 in a high school core curriculum of 16 credits. Transfer students must also have a minimum grade point average of 2.0 in all previous college work. Applicants for a major in a scientific or technical field may be required to present a higher grade point average and to have completed specific background courses before being accepted into the major department. All entering freshmen are required to submit scores from the ACT or SAT examination prior to registration for placement in English and math courses.

Application and Information

The application deadlines are July 1 for the fall semester and November 1 for the spring semester. Applications are processed after the deadlines only as long as space is available. Applicants are notified of the admission decision as soon as all application material has been received. Only accepted students are allowed to apply for campus housing. Students who desire campus housing should apply for admission as early as possible.

For further information, applicants should contact:

Office of Admissions
University of Alaska Fairbanks
P.O. Box 757480
Fairbanks, Alaska 99775-7480
Phone: 907-474-7500
800-478-1UAF (toll-free)
Web site: http://www.uaf.edu

The Plaza outside the classroom buildings at the University of Alaska Fairbanks. The flags represent the fifty states of the United States.

UNIVERSITY OF ALASKA SOUTHEAST

JUNEAU, KETCHIKAN, AND SITKA, ALASKA

The University

The University of Alaska Southeast (UAS) combines time-proven methods of learning with an innovative curriculum that relies heavily on the use of technology, fieldwork, and undergraduate research to create a new-century liberal arts approach. UAS graduates are excellent communicators, job-ready professionals, and well-prepared candidates for graduate school. The University does not mold its students to fit into a predictable box but guides individuals to explore and refine their unique talents and interests. UAS students discover their career paths through scientific and literary exploration, business internships, exposure to civic leaders, and artistic expression. The small class sizes and engaging faculty members allow the University to employ a more personal approach that ensures its students are being challenged academically and that the needs of each are being met. It is the mission of UAS to help students turn their passion into meaningful and fulfilling careers.

UAS has a total student population of approximately 4,100 students. The main campus in Juneau comprises 3,000 of those students; 64 percent of students are women and 36 percent are men. About 36 percent of the student body consists of people of Alaska Native, Asian, Pacific Island, African, and Hispanic ancestry.

Banfield Hall is reserved for freshmen, but on-campus housing, including apartment-style housing, is available to all students. Meal plans are required for residents of Banfield Hall.

The new Student Recreation Center houses the basketball court, suspended running track, climbing wall, and weight-training and cardiovascular equipment. The new center also offers a student lounge with a wide-screen TV, pool tables, a dance floor, and a movie screen with a surround-sound system.

Location

Juneau's population is approximately 32,000. It is the third most populous city in the state and the largest city in Southeast Alaska. UAS is surrounded by the Tongass National Forest, which contains the world's last great expanse of ancient temperate rainforest. Juneau averages 56 inches of annual precipitation. The winters are surprisingly warm, with average temperatures in the high 20s, and average summer temperatures are in the high 60s.

Juneau has several daily flights to Anchorage and Seattle. It is accessible by plane and ferry but not by road. The state runs a year-round ferry service between Bellingham, Washington, and Southeast Alaska cities. Those who bring cars must use the barge service or the Alaska Marine Highway System. The ferries provide a spectacular cruise through the beautiful Inside Passage.

The main campus is located 11 miles from downtown Juneau between the shores of Auke Lake and Auke Bay. The campus is often referred to as the most beautiful place in Juneau. One glance across Auke Lake to the Mendenhall Towers, which cradle the Mendenhall Glacier, is all it takes for someone to know they've found the right place.

Majors and Degrees

UAS offers Bachelor of Arts degrees in biology, elementary education, English (with emphases in creative writing, literature, and literature and the environment), and social science (with emphases in anthropology, economics, government, history, psychology, and sociology). UAS also offers a Bachelor of Business Administration degree (with emphases in accounting, entrepreneurship, health-care administration, human resources management, and marketing); a Bachelor of Liberal Arts degree (with emphases in art, general studies, human communication, and language arts and communication); and Bachelor of Science degrees in biology, environmental science, marine biology, and mathematics.

UAS also offers associate degrees in apprenticeship technology, business administration, computer information and office systems, construction technology, early childhood education, environmental technology, fisheries technology, health information management, health sciences, nursing (through University of Alaska Anchorage), paralegal studies, and power technology (automotive, diesel, or USCG Marine Oiler).

In addition, certificate programs are available in accounting technician studies, automotive technology, child development, community wellness advocate, computer information and office systems, drafting technology, early childhood education, environmental technology, fisheries technology, health-care privacy, health information management coding specialist studies, law enforcement, outdoor skills and leadership, prenursing qualifications, pre–radiologic technology qualification, residential building science, and small-business management.

Academic Programs

UAS operates on a semester system, with the fall semester beginning in late August or early September and the spring semester beginning in mid-January.

A minimum of 120 semester credits are required to complete most baccalaureate degree programs, a minimum of 60 semester credits are required to complete an associate degree program, and a minimum of 30 semester credits are required to complete a certificate program. For all programs, students must maintain a minimum 2.0 GPA; in some core program areas, the minimum GPA requirement is higher.

Advanced Placement credit is given to high school students who achieve scores of 3 or higher on the College Board's Advanced Placement tests. Students who are currently enrolled may challenge courses for credit through either the College-Level Examination Program (CLEP) or University challenge examinations. Requests by students for Advanced Placement credit and credit by examination are coordinated through the Office of Admissions and Records.

Academic Facilities

The Technical Education Center is located in downtown Juneau on the waterfront. It serves as the base for the vocational/technical programs, such as auto, construction, and power technology.

The Egan Library contains more than 135,000 volumes. This award-winning facility offers seating for more than 200 users, the most current computer technology for access to information, and extended hours for student study. The Learning Center, which offers tutoring programs and academic assistance, is housed in the Egan Library.

The campus operates on a wireless network, which allows students access to the UAS network, the Internet, and e-mail from virtually anywhere on campus.

Costs

For purposes of tuition, a resident is any person who has been physically present in Alaska for two years and who declares their intention to remain in Alaska indefinitely. Others exempt from nonresident fees are residents of British Columbia, Yukon, Northwest and Nunavut Territories, active military personnel stationed in Alaska and their dependents, and residents of several foreign sister cities. UAS also participates in the Western Undergraduate Exchange (WUE) program for all degree programs. Students from the fourteen-member states are eligible for WUE tuition rates.

For 2007–08, in-state full-time tuition cost $1632 per semester, or $136 per credit hour (average cost based on 12 credits). Full-time nonresident students paid $5220 per semester ($435 per credit hour, based on 12 credits). Tuition for Western Undergraduate Exchange students was $2400 per semester ($200 per credit hour, based on 12 credits).

Campus housing is available in Juneau. Freshman housing at Banfield Hall was $1795 per semester per person. Residents of Banfield Hall are required to have a roommate and purchase the meal plan, which cost an additional $1085 per semester in 2007–08. Apartment-style housing with private rooms is available at a cost of $2095 per person per semester, and family housing is available at a cost of $4500 per semester. (Costs are estimated.)

Financial Aid

Prospective students should submit the Free Application for Federal Student Aid (FAFSA) at http://www.fafsa.ed.gov, using 001065 as the UAS federal school code, and visit the University's financial aid Web site at http://www.uas.alaska.edu/financial_aid.

UAS participates in the Federal Pell Grant, Federal Supplemental Educational Opportunity Grant, Federal Stafford Student Loan, and Federal Work-Study programs in addition to state student loan, family loan, and grant programs. Most aid is awarded on the basis of financial need. Some scholarships, however, are based on academic potential and performance.

The deadline for merit-based UAS scholarships is February 15. To apply for need-based programs, students should log into the secured portion of UAOnline (http://www.UAOnline.alaska.edu) and complete the online scholarship application. New students may access the scholarship application from the signature page portion of the admission application (https://uaonline.alaska.edu/banprod/owa/bwskalog.P_DispLoginNon). Additional scholarship information is also located on the Financial Aid Office's scholarship Web site (http://www.uas.alaska.edu/financial_aid/types/scholarships/apply.html).

Faculty

UAS has an excellent student-faculty ratio of 12:1. The class size for lower-division courses averages between 15 and 20 students. Due to the small, intimate nature of the campus, faculty members play an integral role in their students' success and offer individual attention often unheard of at larger liberal arts institutions.

Student Government

The student government plays an important role in the development of UAS policies and activities. Students serve on a number of important committees and participate in lobbying the state legislature on behalf of students' interests.

Admission Requirements

UAS is an open-enrollment institution. Admission is on a rolling basis, and applications are processed in the order they are received. Applicants applying for the fall semester should aim to have their admissions packet complete by August 1 to allow adequate time for academic advising and financial aid planning. Students are considered for admission when the University has the completed application, the application fee, and official transcripts (high school transcripts showing GPA and graduation date, and/or official postsecondary transcripts from all accredited institutions). Successful completion of the GED test is accepted as an equivalency of high school graduation. High school graduates from Alaska must also pass all sections of the High School Qualifying Exam to be admitted. Students wishing to pursue a bachelor's degree are required to submit SAT or ACT test scores as well. Applicants out of high school for longer than three years are not required to submit SAT or ACT test scores. Applicants generally receive an initial response within two weeks of receipt of the completed application packet.

It is the goal of UAS to help anyone who has a strong desire to pursue higher education. Students whose cumulative GPA is below 2.0 are admitted on probation and must obtain a minimum GPA of 2.0 during their first semester.

Application and Information

To apply, students must complete an application form and send it with the required $40 processing fee to the Office of Admissions and Records on the Juneau campus. Students can mail or fax applications or apply online.

For further information, application forms, or any other materials, prospective applicants can use the inquiry form on the UAS Web site or contact:

Office of Admissions and Records
University of Alaska Southeast
11120 Glacier Highway
Juneau, Alaska 99801
Phone: 907-796-6100
877-465-4827 (toll-free)
Fax: 907-796-6365
E-mail: uas.info@uas.alaska.edu
Web site: http://www.uas.alaska.edu

Environmental science students at UAS have measured the face of the LeConte Glacier near Petersburg.

ARIZONA

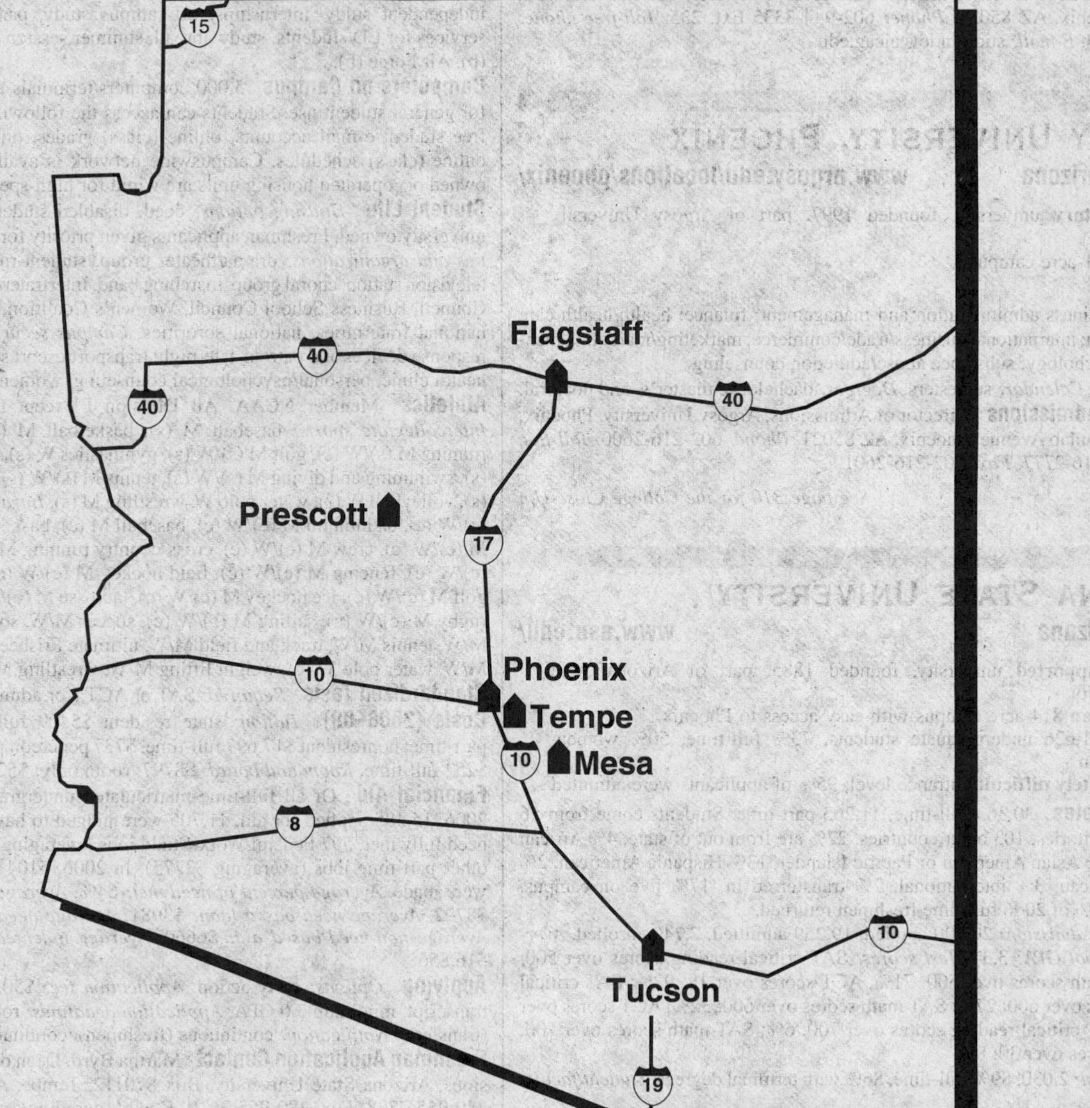

15
40
Flagstaff
40
40
Prescott
17
Phoenix
10
Tempe
10
Mesa
8
10
Tucson
19

AMERICAN INDIAN COLLEGE OF THE ASSEMBLIES OF GOD, INC.

Phoenix, Arizona **www.aicag.edu/**

Director of Admissions Ms. Sandy Ticeahkie, Director of Admissions, American Indian College of the Assemblies of God, Inc., 10020 North 15th Avenue, Phoenix, AZ 85021. *Phone:* 602-944-3335 Ext. 235. *Toll-free phone:* 800-933-3828. *E-mail:* sticeahkie@aicag.edu.

ARGOSY UNIVERSITY, PHOENIX

Phoenix, Arizona **www.argosy.edu/locations/phoenix/**

- **Proprietary** university, founded 1997, part of Argosy University System
- **Urban** 1-acre campus
- **Coed**

Majors Business administration and management; finance; health/health care administration; international business/trade/commerce; marketing/marketing management; psychology; substance abuse/addiction counseling.

Academics *Calendar:* semesters. *Degrees:* bachelor's, master's, and doctoral.

Director of Admissions Director of Admissions, Argosy University, Phoenix, 2233 West Dunlap Avenue, Phoenix, AZ 85021. *Phone:* 602-216-2600. *Toll-free phone:* 866-216-2777. *Fax:* 602-216-2601.

See page 310 for the College Close-Up.

ARIZONA STATE UNIVERSITY

Tempe, Arizona **www.asu.edu/**

- **State-supported** university, founded 1885, part of Arizona State University
- **Suburban** 814-acre campus with easy access to Phoenix
- **Coed** 41,626 undergraduate students, 73% full-time, 50% women, 50% men
- **Moderately difficult** entrance level, 95% of applicants were admitted

Undergraduates 30,363 full-time, 11,263 part-time. Students come from 56 states and territories, 103 other countries, 27% are from out of state, 4% African American, 6% Asian American or Pacific Islander, 13% Hispanic American, 2% Native American, 3% international, 7% transferred in, 17% live on campus. *Retention:* 78% of 2006 full-time freshmen returned.

Freshmen *Admission:* 20,290 applied, 19,259 admitted, 7,740 enrolled. *Average high school GPA:* 3.34. *Test scores:* SAT critical reading scores over 500: 66%; SAT math scores over 500: 71%; ACT scores over 18: 92%; SAT critical reading scores over 600: 27%; SAT math scores over 600: 32%; ACT scores over 24: 46%; SAT critical reading scores over 700: 6%; SAT math scores over 700: 6%; ACT scores over 30: 8%.

Faculty *Total:* 2,030, 89% full-time, 86% with terminal degrees. *Student/faculty ratio:* 22:1.

Majors Accounting; aerospace, aeronautical and astronautical engineering; African-American/Black studies; American Indian/Native American studies; anthropology; architecture; art; biochemistry; biology/biological sciences; biomedical/medical engineering; botany/plant biology; business administration and management; chemical engineering; chemistry; city/urban, community and regional planning; civil engineering; clinical laboratory science/medical technology; communication disorders; communication/speech communication and rhetoric; computational mathematics; computer engineering; computer science; conservation biology; construction management; criminal justice/safety; dance; design and applied arts related; dramatic/theater arts; early childhood education; East Asian languages related; economics; education related; electrical, electronics and communications engineering; elementary education; English; family resource management; film/video and photographic arts related; finance; French; geography; geology/earth science; German; graphic design; Hispanic-American, Puerto Rican, and Mexican-American/Chicano studies; history; industrial design; industrial engineering; interdisciplinary studies; interior architecture; international/global studies; Italian; journalism; journalism related; kinesiology and exercise science; landscape architecture; liberal arts and sciences/liberal studies; management information systems; marketing/marketing management; materials engineering; mathematics; mechanical engineering; microbiology; molecular biology; multi-/interdisciplinary studies related; music; music performance; music teacher education; music theory and composition; music therapy; philosophy; physics; political science and government; psychology; purchasing, procurement/acquisitions and contracts management; radio and television; real estate; religious studies; Russian; secondary education; sociology; Spanish; special education; women's studies.

Academics *Calendar:* semesters. *Degrees:* bachelor's, master's, doctoral, first professional, post-master's, and postbachelor's certificates. *Special study options:* academic remediation for entering students, accelerated degree program, adult/continuing education programs, advanced placement credit, cooperative education, distance learning, double majors, freshman honors college, honors programs, independent study, internships, off-campus study, part-time degree program, services for LD students, study abroad, summer session for credit. *ROTC:* Army (b), Air Force (b).

Computers on Campus 5,000 computers/terminals are available on campus for general student use. Students can access the following: computer help desk, free student e-mail accounts, online (class) grades, online (class) registration, online (class) schedules. Campuswide network is available. 100% of college-owned or -operated housing units are wired for high-speed Internet access.

Student Life *Housing options:* coed, disabled students. Campus housing is university owned. Freshman applicants given priority for college housing. *Activities and organizations:* drama/theater group, student-run newspaper, radio and television station, choral group, marching band, Interfraternity Council, Panhellenic Council, Business School Council, Women's Coalition, International Coalition, national fraternities, national sororities. *Campus security:* 24-hour emergency response devices and patrols, late-night transport/escort service. *Student services:* health clinic, personal/psychological counseling, women's center, legal services.

Athletics Member NCAA. All Division I except football (Division I-A). *Intercollegiate sports:* baseball M (s), basketball M (s)/W (s), cross-country running M (s)/W (s), golf M (s)/W (s), gymnastics W (s), soccer W (s), softball W (s), swimming and diving M (s)/W (s), tennis M (s)/W (s), track and field M (s)/W (s), volleyball W (s), water polo W, wrestling M (s). *Intramural sports:* archery M (c)/W (c), badminton M (c)/W (c), baseball M (c), basketball M/W, cheerleading M (c)/W (c), crew M (c)/W (c), cross-country running M/W, equestrian sports M (c)/W (c), fencing M (c)/W (c), field hockey M (c)/W (c), football M (c)/W (c), golf M (c)/W (c), ice hockey M (c)/W (c), lacrosse M (c)/W (c), racquetball M/W, rugby M (c)/W (c), sailing M (c)/W (c), soccer M/W, softball M/W, table tennis M/W, tennis M/W, track and field M/W, ultimate Frisbee M (c)/W (c), volleyball M/W, water polo W (c), weight lifting M/W, wrestling M.

Standardized Tests *Required:* SAT or ACT (for admission).

Costs (2008–09) *Tuition:* state resident $5409 full-time, $283 per credit part-time; nonresident $17,697 full-time, $737 per credit part-time. *Required fees:* $252 full-time. *Room and board:* $8797; room only: $5247.

Financial Aid Of all full-time matriculated undergraduates who enrolled in 2006, 15,385 applied for aid, 11,705 were judged to have need, 2,414 had their need fully met. 597 Federal Work-Study jobs (averaging $1604). 4,776 state and other part-time jobs (averaging $2775). In 2006, 5104 non-need-based awards were made. *Average percent of need met:* 64%. *Average financial aid package:* $8792. *Average need-based loan:* $3981. *Average need-based gift aid:* $5892. *Average non-need-based aid:* $6660. *Average indebtedness upon graduation:* $16,856.

Applying *Options:* early action. *Application fee:* $50. *Required:* high school transcript, minimum 3.0 GPA. *Application deadlines:* rolling (freshmen), rolling (transfers). *Notification:* continuous (freshmen), continuous (transfers).

Freshman Application Contact Martha Byrd, Dean of Undergraduate Admissions, Arizona State University, Box 870112, Tempe, AZ 85287-0112. *Phone:* 480-965-7788. *Fax:* 480-965-3610. *E-mail:* ugradinq@asu.edu.

ARIZONA STATE UNIVERSITY AT THE DOWNTOWN PHOENIX CAMPUS

Phoenix, Arizona

ARIZONA STATE UNIVERSITY AT THE POLYTECHNIC CAMPUS

Mesa, Arizona **www.poly.asu.edu/**

- **State-supported** comprehensive, founded 1995, part of Arizona State University
- **Suburban** 600-acre campus with easy access to Phoenix
- **Coed**
- **Moderately difficult** entrance level

Academics *Calendar:* semesters. *Degrees:* bachelor's and master's.

Student Life *Campus security:* 24-hour emergency response devices and patrols, late-night transport/escort service.

Standardized Tests *Recommended:* SAT or ACT (for admission).
Costs (2007–08) *Tuition:* state resident $4620 full-time, $290 per credit part-time; nonresident $16,853 full-time, $752 per credit part-time. Full-time tuition and fees vary according to course load, degree level, location, and program. Part-time tuition and fees vary according to course load, degree level, location, and program. *Required fees:* $148 full-time, $37 per term part-time. *Room and board:* $7320; room only: $4620. Room and board charges vary according to board plan, housing facility, location, and student level.
Financial Aid Of all full-time matriculated undergraduates who enrolled in 2005, 796 applied for aid, 582 were judged to have need, 82 had their need fully met. 37 Federal Work-Study jobs (averaging $1833). 207 state and other part-time jobs (averaging $3098). In 2005, 76 non-need-based awards were made. *Average percent of need met:* 60. *Average financial aid package:* $8439. *Average need-based loan:* $4677. *Average need-based gift aid:* $4823. *Average non-need-based aid:* $4327.
Applying *Options:* electronic application, early action. *Application fee:* $50. *Required:* high school transcript. *Required for some:* essay or personal statement, interview. *Recommended:* minimum 3.0 GPA.
Freshman Application Contact Matthew Engel, Arizona State University at the Polytechnic Campus, 7001 East Williams Field Road #350, Mesa, AZ 85212. *Phone:* 480-727-1165. *Fax:* 480-727-1008. *E-mail:* poly@au.edu.

ARIZONA STATE UNIVERSITY AT THE WEST CAMPUS

Phoenix, Arizona **www.west.asu.edu/**

- **State-supported** comprehensive, founded 1984, part of Arizona State University
- **Urban** 300-acre campus
- **Coed** 7,271 undergraduate students, 74% full-time, 64% women, 36% men
- **Moderately difficult** entrance level, 93% of applicants were admitted

Undergraduates 5,375 full-time, 1,896 part-time. Students come from 40 states and territories, 17 other countries, 7% are from out of state, 5% African American, 5% Asian American or Pacific Islander, 20% Hispanic American, 3% Native American, 0.7% international, 14% transferred in, 5% live on campus. *Retention:* 75% of 2006 full-time freshmen returned.
Freshmen *Admission:* 1,549 applied, 1,448 admitted, 607 enrolled. *Average high school GPA:* 3.39. *Test scores:* SAT critical reading scores over 500: 53%; SAT math scores over 500: 55%; ACT scores over 18: 85%; SAT critical reading scores over 600: 17%; SAT math scores over 600: 15%; ACT scores over 24: 33%; SAT critical reading scores over 700: 1%; SAT math scores over 700: 1%; ACT scores over 30: 1%.
Faculty *Total:* 483, 55% full-time. *Student/faculty ratio:* 21:1.
Majors Accounting; American studies; biology/biological sciences; communication/speech communication and rhetoric; computer and information sciences; criminal justice/law enforcement administration; early childhood education; elementary education; English; ethnic, cultural minority, and gender studies related; history; international business/trade/commerce; marketing/marketing management; multi-/interdisciplinary studies related; parks, recreation and leisure; philosophy and religious studies related; political science and government; psychology; secondary education; social sciences; social work; sociology; Spanish; special education; visual and performing arts; women's studies.
Academics *Calendar:* semesters. *Degrees:* bachelor's, master's, doctoral, and postbachelor's certificates. *Special study options:* adult/continuing education programs, advanced placement credit, distance learning, double majors, freshman honors college, honors programs, independent study, internships, part-time degree program, services for LD students, student-designed majors, study abroad, summer session for credit.
Computers on Campus 766 computers/terminals and 4,582 ports are available on campus for general student use. Students can access the following: computer help desk, free student e-mail accounts, online (class) grades, online (class) registration, online (class) schedules. Campuswide network is available. 100% of college-owned or -operated housing units are wired for high-speed Internet access. Wireless service is available via classrooms, computer centers, computer labs, learning centers, libraries, student centers.
Student Life *Housing options:* coed, disabled students. Campus housing is provided by a third party. Freshman applicants given priority for college housing. *Activities and organizations:* student-run newspaper. *Campus security:* 24-hour emergency response devices and patrols, student patrols, late-night transport/escort service. *Student services:* health clinic, personal/psychological counseling, women's center.
Standardized Tests *Required:* SAT or ACT (for admission).
Costs (2007–08) *Tuition:* state resident $4620 full-time, $240 per credit hour part-time; nonresident $16,853 full-time, $702 per credit hour part-time. Part-time tuition and fees vary according to course load. *Required fees:* $146 full-time. *Room and board:* $7320; room only: $4620. *Payment plan:* installment. *Waivers:* employees or children of employees.
Financial Aid Of all full-time matriculated undergraduates who enrolled in 2004, 2,265 applied for aid, 1,916 were judged to have need, 263 had their need fully met. 94 Federal Work-Study jobs (averaging $2793). 201 state and other part-time jobs (averaging $2720). In 2004, 255 non-need-based awards were made. *Average percent of need met:* 61%. *Average financial aid package:* $7926. *Average need-based loan:* $4619. *Average need-based gift aid:* $5160. *Average non-need-based aid:* $3613. *Average indebtedness upon graduation:* $16,438. *Financial aid deadline:* 3/1.
Applying *Options:* electronic application. *Application fee:* $25. *Required:* high school transcript. *Recommended:* minimum 3.0 GPA. *Application deadlines:* rolling (freshmen), rolling (transfers). *Notification:* continuous (freshmen), continuous (transfers).
Freshman Application Contact Mr. Thomas Cabot, Registrar, Arizona State University at the West campus, PO Box 37100, 4701 West Thunderbird Road, Phoenix, AZ 85069-7100. *Phone:* 602-543-8134. *Fax:* 602-543-8312. *E-mail:* cabot@asu.edu.

THE ART CENTER DESIGN COLLEGE

Tucson, Arizona **www.theartcenter.edu/**

Freshman Application Contact Ms. Colleen Gimbel-Froebe, Director of Enrollment Management, The Art Center Design College, 2525 North Country Club Road, Tucson, AZ 85716-2505. *Phone:* 520-325-0123. *Toll-free phone:* 800-825-8753. *Fax:* 520-325-5535. *E-mail:* cgf@theartcenter.edu.

THE ART INSTITUTE OF PHOENIX

Phoenix, Arizona **www.aipx.artinstitutes.edu/**

- **Proprietary** 4-year, founded 1995, part of Education Management Corporation
- **Suburban** 3-acre campus
- **Coed**
- **Minimally difficult** entrance level

Faculty *Student/faculty ratio:* 17:1.
Majors Advertising; animation, interactive technology, video graphics and special effects; cinematography and film/video production; culinary arts; fashion merchandising; graphic design; interior design; Web page, digital/multimedia and information resources design.
Academics *Calendar:* quarters. *Degrees:* diplomas, associate, and bachelor's.
Student Life *Campus security:* 24-hour emergency response devices, late-night transport/escort service, security guard during open hours.
Costs (2007–08) *Tuition:* tuition cost varies by program. Prospective students should contact the school for current tuition costs. Other charges include a starting kit for all first-quarter students. Kits vary in price depending on the program of study.
Financial Aid Of all full-time matriculated undergraduates who enrolled in 2005, 22 Federal Work-Study jobs (averaging $2087).
Applying *Application fee:* $50. *Required:* essay or personal statement, high school transcript, interview. *Recommended:* minimum 2.0 GPA.
Freshman Application Contact The Art Institute of Phoenix, 2233 West Dunlap Avenue, Phoenix, AZ 85021-2859. *Phone:* 602-331-7500. *Toll-free phone:* 800-474-2479. *Fax:* 602-331-5302. *E-mail:* aipxadm@aii.edu.

See page 312 for the College Close-Up.

THE ART INSTITUTE OF TUCSON

Tucson, Arizona **www.artinstitutes.edu/tucson**

- **Proprietary** 4-year

Majors Advertising; animation, interactive technology, video graphics and special effects; cinematography and film/video production; culinary arts; fashion/apparel design; fashion merchandising; graphic design; interior design; Web page, digital/multimedia and information resources design.
Freshman Application Contact Admissions Director, The Art Institute of Tucson, 5099 E. Grant Road, Tucson, AZ 85712. *Phone:* 866-690-8850.

See page 314 for the College Close-Up.

Brown Mackie College–Tucson

Tucson, Arizona **www.brownmackie.edu/tucson/**

Majors Accounting; business administration and management; computer science; criminal justice/safety.

Director of Admissions Admissions Office, 4585 East Speedway, #204, Tucson, AZ 85712. *Phone:* 520-327-6866. *Fax:* 520-325-0108.

See page 316 for the College Close-Up.

College of the Humanities and Sciences, Harrison Middleton University

Tempe, Arizona

Collins College: A School of Design and Technology

Tempe, Arizona **www.collinscollege.edu/**

- **Proprietary** 4-year, founded 1978, part of Career Education Corporation
- **Urban** 3-acre campus with easy access to Phoenix
- **Coed** 1,287 undergraduate students, 100% full-time, 23% women, 77% men

Undergraduates 1,287 full-time. Students come from 50 states and territories, 70% are from out of state, 6% African American, 2% Asian American or Pacific Islander, 9% Hispanic American, 5% Native American.

Faculty *Total:* 102, 54% full-time. *Student/faculty ratio:* 30:1.

Majors Cinematography and film/video production; commercial and advertising art; computer technology/computer systems technology; design and visual communications; graphic design; information technology; interior design.

Academics *Calendar:* trimesters. *Degrees:* associate and bachelor's.

Computers on Campus Students can access the following: computer help desk. Wireless service is available via entire campus.

Student Life *Housing:* college housing not available.

Standardized Tests *Recommended:* SAT and SAT Subject Tests or ACT (for admission).

Costs (2007–08) *Tuition:* $39,146 full-time. Full-time tuition and fees vary according to course load. Part-time tuition and fees vary according to course load. *Room only:* $4860. *Waivers:* employees or children of employees.

Financial Aid Of all full-time matriculated undergraduates who enrolled in 2005, 2,736 applied for aid, 2,576 were judged to have need, 65 had their need fully met. 65 Federal Work-Study jobs (averaging $3000). In 2005, 27 non-need-based awards were made. *Average percent of need met:* 65%. *Average financial aid package:* $11,500. *Average need-based loan:* $4880. *Average need-based gift aid:* $4000. *Average non-need-based aid:* $11,500. *Average indebtedness upon graduation:* $18,000.

Applying *Options:* early admission, deferred entrance. *Application fee:* $50. *Required:* high school transcript, interview. *Recommended:* letters of recommendation. *Application deadlines:* rolling (freshmen), rolling (transfers). *Notification:* continuous (freshmen), continuous (transfers).

Freshman Application Contact Admissions Department, Collins College: A School of Design and Technology, 1140 South Priest, Tempe, AZ 85281. *Phone:* 480-966-3000. *Toll-free phone:* 800-876-7070. *Fax:* 480-966-2599. *E-mail:* contact@collinscollege.edu.

DeVry University

Mesa, Arizona

DeVry University

Phoenix, Arizona **www.devry.edu/**

- **Proprietary** comprehensive, founded 1967, part of DeVry University
- **Urban** 18-acre campus
- **Coed** 1,039 undergraduate students, 71% full-time, 21% women, 79% men
- **Minimally difficult** entrance level

Undergraduates 736 full-time, 303 part-time. 6% are from out of state, 9% African American, 6% Asian American or Pacific Islander, 19% Hispanic American, 7% Native American, 0.8% international, 12% transferred in. *Retention:* 52% of 2006 full-time freshmen returned.

Freshmen *Admission:* 243 enrolled.

Faculty *Total:* 66, 53% full-time. *Student/faculty ratio:* 20:1.

Majors Business administration and management; business administration, management and operations related; computer engineering technology; computer software engineering; computer systems analysis; computer systems networking and telecommunications; electrical, electronic and communications engineering technology.

Academics *Calendar:* semesters. *Degrees:* associate, bachelor's, and master's. *Special study options:* academic remediation for entering students, accelerated degree program, adult/continuing education programs, advanced placement credit, distance learning, part-time degree program, services for LD students, summer session for credit. *ROTC:* Air Force (b).

Computers on Campus 436 computers/terminals are available on campus for general student use. Students can access the following: online (class) registration. Campuswide network is available.

Student Life *Housing:* college housing not available. *Activities and organizations:* Telecommunications Club, Board and Ski Club, Travel Club, SIFE, Institute of Electronic and Electrical Engineers. *Campus security:* 24-hour emergency response devices, student patrols, late-night transport/escort service, trained security personnel on duty, lighted pathways/sidewalks.

Athletics *Intramural sports:* softball M/W.

Costs (2008–09) *Tuition:* $13,810 full-time, $515 per credit part-time.

Financial Aid Of all full-time matriculated undergraduates who enrolled in 2002, 1,911 applied for aid, 1,830 were judged to have need, 42 had their need fully met. In 2002, 97 non-need-based awards were made. *Average percent of need met:* 40%. *Average financial aid package:* $9288. *Average need-based loan:* $6294. *Average need-based gift aid:* $4531. *Average non-need-based aid:* $10,981.

Applying *Options:* electronic application, early admission, deferred entrance. *Application fee:* $50. *Required:* high school transcript, interview. *Application deadlines:* rolling (freshmen), rolling (transfers). *Notification:* continuous (freshmen), continuous (transfers).

Director of Admissions Admissions Office, DeVry University, 2149 West Dunlap Avenue, Phoenix, AZ 85021-2995.

Embry-Riddle Aeronautical University

Prescott, Arizona **www.embryriddle.edu/**

- **Independent** comprehensive, founded 1978
- **Suburban** 547-acre campus
- **Endowment** $60.0 million
- **Coed** 1,676 undergraduate students, 92% full-time, 17% women, 83% men
- **Moderately difficult** entrance level, 85% of applicants were admitted

Undergraduates 1,544 full-time, 132 part-time. Students come from 52 states and territories, 29 other countries, 79% are from out of state, 3% African American, 7% Asian American or Pacific Islander, 8% Hispanic American, 1% Native American, 4% international, 6% transferred in, 48% live on campus. *Retention:* 76% of 2006 full-time freshmen returned.

Freshmen *Admission:* 1,288 applied, 1,096 admitted, 400 enrolled. *Average high school GPA:* 3.47. *Test scores:* SAT critical reading scores over 500: 70%; SAT math scores over 500: 80%; ACT scores over 18: 95%; SAT critical reading scores over 600: 25%; SAT math scores over 600: 33%; ACT scores over 24: 66%; SAT critical reading scores over 700: 3%; SAT math scores over 700: 5%; ACT scores over 30: 14%.

Faculty *Total:* 130, 78% full-time, 58% with terminal degrees. *Student/faculty ratio:* 14:1.

Majors Aeronautics/aviation/aerospace science and technology; aerospace, aeronautical and astronautical engineering; airline pilot and flight crew; atmospheric sciences and meteorology; business administration, management and operations related; computer engineering; computer software engineering; electrical, electronics and communications engineering; international relations and affairs; physics related; science, technology and society.

Academics *Calendar:* semesters. *Degrees:* bachelor's and master's. *Special study options:* academic remediation for entering students, accelerated degree program, adult/continuing education programs, advanced placement credit, cooperative education, distance learning, double majors, English as a second language, honors programs, independent study, internships, part-time degree program, services for LD students, student-designed majors, study abroad, summer session for credit. *ROTC:* Army (b), Air Force (b).

Computers on Campus 450 computers/terminals are available on campus for general student use. Students can access the following: online (class) registration. Campuswide network is available. Wireless service is available via entire campus.

Student Life *Housing:* on-campus residence required for freshman year. *Options:* coed. Freshman campus housing is guaranteed. *Activities and organizations:* student-run newspaper, radio and television station, Hawaii Club, Strike Eagles, Theta XI, American Institute of Aeronautics and Astronautics (AIAA), Arnold Air Society, national fraternities, national sororities. *Campus security:* 24-hour emergency response devices and patrols, student patrols, late-night transport/escort service. *Student services:* health clinic, personal/psychological counseling.

Athletics Member NAIA. *Intercollegiate sports:* volleyball W (s), wrestling M (s). *Intramural sports:* archery M/W, badminton M/W, basketball M/W, bowling M/W, cross-country running M/W, fencing M (c)/W (c), lacrosse M (c)/W (c), racquetball M/W, rugby M (c)/W (c), skiing (cross-country) M (c)/W (c), skiing (downhill) M (c)/W (c), soccer M (c)/W (c), softball M/W, swimming and diving M/W, table tennis M/W, tennis M/W, track and field M/W, volleyball M/W, weight lifting M/W.

Standardized Tests *Required:* SAT and SAT Subject Tests or ACT (for admission).

Costs (2007–08) *Comprehensive fee:* $33,344 includes full-time tuition ($25,400), mandatory fees ($730), and room and board ($7214). Part-time tuition: $1060 per credit hour. *College room only:* $3990. Room and board charges vary according to board plan and housing facility. *Payment plans:* installment, deferred payment. *Waivers:* employees or children of employees.

Financial Aid Of all full-time matriculated undergraduates who enrolled in 2007, 1,161 applied for aid, 1,006 were judged to have need. 48 Federal Work-Study jobs (averaging $787). 410 state and other part-time jobs (averaging $1000). *Average financial aid package:* $16,151. *Average need-based loan:* $5408. *Average need-based gift aid:* $9521. *Average indebtedness upon graduation:* $54,159.

Applying *Options:* electronic application, deferred entrance. *Application fee:* $50. *Required:* high school transcript, minimum 2.0 GPA. *Required for some:* minimum 3.0 GPA, medical examination for flight students. *Recommended:* essay or personal statement, letters of recommendation, interview. *Application deadlines:* rolling (freshmen), rolling (transfers). *Notification:* continuous (freshmen), continuous (transfers).

Freshman Application Contact Mr. Bill Thompson, Director of Admissions, Embry-Riddle Aeronautical University, 3700 Willow Creek Road, Prescott, AZ 86301-3720. *Phone:* 928-777-6600. *Toll-free phone:* 800-888-3728. *Fax:* 928-777-6606. *E-mail:* pradmit@erau.edu.

See page 318 for the College Close-Up.

EVEREST COLLEGE

Phoenix, Arizona **www.everest.edu/**

- **Proprietary** primarily 2-year, founded 1982, part of Corinthian Colleges, Inc
- **Urban** campus
- **Coed**
- **Noncompetitive** entrance level

Faculty *Student/faculty ratio:* 23:1.

Academics *Calendar:* 6 or 12 week terms. *Degrees:* diplomas, associate, and bachelor's.

Student Life *Campus security:* 24-hour emergency response devices and patrols.

Costs (2007–08) *Tuition:* $13,056 full-time, $272 per quarter hour part-time. *Required fees:* $100 full-time, $25 per term part-time.

Applying *Options:* deferred entrance. *Required:* high school transcript, minimum 2.0 GPA, interview. *Required for some:* essay or personal statement.

Freshman Application Contact Mr. Jim Askins, Director of Admissions, Everest College, 10400 North 25th Avenue, Suite 190, Phoenix, AZ 85021. *Phone:* 602-942-4141. *Fax:* 602-943-0960. *E-mail:* jaskins@cci.edu.

GRAND CANYON UNIVERSITY

Phoenix, Arizona **www.gcu.edu/**

- **Independent Southern Baptist** comprehensive, founded 1949
- **Urban** 90-acre campus
- **Coed** 4,822 undergraduate students, 36% full-time, 71% women, 29% men
- **Moderately difficult** entrance level, 73% of applicants were admitted

Undergraduates 1,714 full-time, 3,108 part-time. Students come from 50 states and territories, 12 other countries, 61% are from out of state, 3% African American, 0.6% Asian American or Pacific Islander, 3% Hispanic American, 0.2% Native American, 0.7% international, 14% transferred in, 40% live on campus. *Retention:* 69% of 2006 full-time freshmen returned.

Freshmen *Admission:* 822 applied, 601 admitted, 466 enrolled. *Average high school GPA:* 2.56.

Faculty *Total:* 514, 9% full-time, 29% with terminal degrees. *Student/faculty ratio:* 13:1.

Majors Accounting; athletic training; biblical studies; biology/biological sciences; biology teacher education; business administration and management; chemistry teacher education; communication/speech communication and rhetoric; criminal justice/safety; early childhood education; education; elementary education; English; English as a second/foreign language (teaching); English/language arts teacher education; general studies; health professions related; history; human resources management and services related; marketing/marketing management; mass communication/media; mathematics teacher education; nursing (registered nurse training); nursing related; parks, recreation and leisure; physical education teaching and coaching; psychology; public relations/image management; religious studies; secondary education; sociology; special education; speech and rhetoric; sport and fitness administration/management.

Academics *Calendar:* semesters. *Degrees:* bachelor's, master's, doctoral, and post-master's certificates. *Special study options:* academic remediation for entering students, accelerated degree program, adult/continuing education programs, advanced placement credit, cooperative education, distance learning, double majors, English as a second language, freshman honors college, honors programs, independent study, internships, off-campus study, part-time degree program, study abroad, summer session for credit. *ROTC:* Army (b), Air Force (c).

Computers on Campus 65 computers/terminals are available on campus for general student use. Students can access the following: campus intranet, computer help desk, free student e-mail accounts, online (class) grades, online (class) registration, online (class) schedules. Campuswide network is available. 100% of college-owned or -operated housing units are wired for high-speed Internet access. Wireless service is available via computer centers, computer labs, dorm rooms, learning centers, libraries, student centers.

Student Life *Housing options:* men-only, women-only, disabled students. Campus housing is university owned and leased by the school. *Activities and organizations:* choral group, Associated Students of Grand Canyon University, Fellowship for Christian Athletes, Student Nurses Association, International Student Association, Student Ministries. *Campus security:* 24-hour emergency response devices and patrols, late-night transport/escort service, controlled dormitory access. *Student services:* health clinic.

Athletics Member NCAA. All Division II. *Intercollegiate sports:* baseball M (s), basketball M (s)/W (s), cross-country running M, golf M (s)/W, lacrosse M, soccer M (s)/W (s), softball W, swimming and diving M/W, tennis W (s), volleyball W (s), wrestling M (s). *Intramural sports:* basketball M/W, football M/W, softball M/W, volleyball M/W.

Costs (2008–09) *One-time required fee:* $550. *Comprehensive fee:* $23,926 includes full-time tuition ($15,480), mandatory fees ($550), and room and board ($7896). Part-time tuition: $645 per credit. *Required fees:* $275 per term part-time. *College room only:* $7280.

Financial Aid Of all full-time matriculated undergraduates who enrolled in 2007, 1,102 applied for aid, 942 were judged to have need, 155 had their need fully met. *Average financial aid package:* $3371. *Average need-based loan:* $3701. *Average need-based gift aid:* $3360.

Applying *Options:* early admission, deferred entrance. *Application fee:* $100. *Required:* minimum 2.25 GPA. *Application deadlines:* rolling (freshmen), rolling (transfers). *Notification:* continuous (freshmen), continuous until 9/1 (transfers).

Freshman Application Contact Enrollment, Grand Canyon University, 3300 West Camelback Road, PO Box 11097, Phoenix, AZ 86017-3030. *Phone:* 800-486-7085. *Toll-free phone:* 800-800-9776. *E-mail:* admissionsonline@gcu.edu.

See page 320 for the College Close-Up.

HIGH-TECH INSTITUTE

Phoenix, Arizona **www.high-techinstitute.com/**

Freshman Application Contact Mr. Glen Husband, Vice President of Admissions, High-Tech Institute, 1515 East Indian School Road, Phoenix, AZ 85014-4901. *Phone:* 602-279-9700.

INTERNATIONAL BAPTIST COLLEGE

Tempe, Arizona **www.tri-citybaptist.org/ibc/**

Freshman Application Contact Ms. Rebecca M. Stertzbach, Director of Recruitment, International Baptist College, 2150 East Southern Avenue, Tempe, AZ 85282. *Phone:* 480-838-7070 Ext. 262. *Toll-free phone:* 800-422-4858. *Fax:* 480-505-3299. *E-mail:* jeff.caupp@ibconline.edu.

INTERNATIONAL IMPORT-EXPORT INSTITUTE

Phoenix, Arizona **www.iiei.edu/**

Director of Admissions Dr. Donald N. Burton, International Import-Export Institute, 2432 West Peoria Avenue, Suite 1026, Phoenix, AZ 85029. *Phone:* 602-648-5750. *Toll-free phone:* 800-474-8013. *Fax:* 602-648-5755. *E-mail:* director@expandglobal.com.

INTERNATIONAL INSTITUTE OF THE AMERICAS

Mesa, Arizona **www.iia-online.com/site/**

- **Independent** primarily 2-year, founded 1982
- **Urban** campus
- **Coed**
- **Noncompetitive** entrance level

Faculty *Student/faculty ratio:* 10:1.
Academics *Calendar:* semesters. *Degrees:* diplomas, associate, and bachelor's.
Student Life *Campus security:* 24-hour emergency response devices.
Costs (2007–08) *Tuition:* $10,250 full-time. Full-time tuition and fees vary according to degree level and program. *Required fees:* $200 full-time.
Applying *Application fee:* $200. *Required:* interview.
Freshman Application Contact Mr. Todd Olehausen, Campus Director, International Institute of the Americas, 925 South Gilbert Road, Suite 201, Mesa, AZ 85204-4448. *Phone:* 480-545-8755. *Toll-free phone:* 888-886-2428. *Fax:* 480-926-1371. *E-mail:* wging@iia.edu.

INTERNATIONAL INSTITUTE OF THE AMERICAS

Phoenix, Arizona **www.iia-online.com/site/**

- **Independent** primarily 2-year, founded 1979
- **Urban** campus
- **Coed**
- **Noncompetitive** entrance level

Faculty *Student/faculty ratio:* 12:1.
Academics *Calendar:* semesters. *Degrees:* diplomas, associate, and bachelor's.
Student Life *Campus security:* 24-hour emergency response devices.
Costs (2007–08) *Tuition:* $9850 full-time. *Required fees:* $200 full-time.
Applying *Options:* electronic application, early admission, deferred entrance. *Application fee:* $200. *Required:* interview.
Freshman Application Contact Mr. Lynn McConnell, Campus Director, International Institute of the Americas, 6049 North 43 Avenue, Phoenix, AZ 85019. *Phone:* 602-242-6265. *Toll-free phone:* 800-793-2428. *Fax:* 602-973-2572. *E-mail:* lmcconnell@iia.edu.

INTERNATIONAL INSTITUTE OF THE AMERICAS

Tucson, Arizona **www.iia-online.com/site/**

- **Independent** primarily 2-year, founded 1979
- **Urban** campus
- **Coed**
- **Noncompetitive** entrance level

Faculty *Student/faculty ratio:* 10:1.
Academics *Calendar:* semesters. *Degrees:* diplomas, associate, and bachelor's.
Student Life *Campus security:* 24-hour emergency response devices.
Costs (2007–08) *Tuition:* $10,250 full-time. Full-time tuition and fees vary according to degree level and program. *Required fees:* $200 full-time.
Applying *Application fee:* $200. *Required:* interview.
Freshman Application Contact Ms. Leigh Anne Pechota, Campus Director, International Institute of the Americas, 5441 East 22nd Street, Suite 125, Tucson, AZ 85711-5444. *Phone:* 520-748-9799. *Toll-free phone:* 888-292-2428. *Fax:* 520-748-9355. *E-mail:* lpechota@iia.edu.

ITT TECHNICAL INSTITUTE

Phoenix, Arizona **www.itt-tech.edu/**

Freshman Application Contact Mr. Gene McWhorter, Director of Recruitment, ITT Technical Institute, 4837 East McDowell Road, Phoenix, AZ 85008. *Phone:* 602-252-2331. *Toll-free phone:* 800-879-4881.

ITT TECHNICAL INSTITUTE

Tempe, Arizona **www.itt-tech.edu/**

- **Proprietary** 4-year, founded 1963

Academics *Degrees:* associate and bachelor's.
Standardized Tests *Required:* Wonderlic aptitude test (for admission).
Applying *Application fee:* $100. *Required:* high school transcript, interview. *Recommended:* letters of recommendation.
Freshman Application Contact Ms. Patti Moberly, Director of Recruitment, ITT Technical Institute, 5005 South Wendler Drive, Tempe, AZ 85282. *Phone:* 602-437-7500. *Toll-free phone:* 800-879-4881.

ITT TECHNICAL INSTITUTE

Tucson, Arizona **www.itt-tech.edu/**

- **Proprietary** primarily 2-year, founded 1984, part of ITT Educational Services, Inc
- **Urban** 3-acre campus
- **Coed**
- **Minimally difficult** entrance level

Academics *Calendar:* quarters. *Degrees:* associate and bachelor's.
Standardized Tests *Required:* Wonderlic aptitude test (for admission).
Applying *Options:* deferred entrance. *Application fee:* $100. *Required:* high school transcript, interview. *Recommended:* letters of recommendation.
Freshman Application Contact Ms. Linda Lemken, Director of Recruitment, ITT Technical Institute, 1455 West River Road, Tucson, AZ 85704. *Phone:* 520-408-7488. *Toll-free phone:* 800-870-9730.

MIDWESTERN UNIVERSITY, GLENDALE CAMPUS

Glendale, Arizona **www.midwestern.edu/**

Application Contact Mr. James Walter, Director of Admissions, Midwestern University, Glendale Campus, 19555 North 59th Avenue, Glendale, AZ 85308. *Phone:* 623-572-3340. *Toll-free phone:* 888-247-9277 (in-state); 888-247-9271 (out-of-state). *Fax:* 623-572-3229. *E-mail:* admissionaz@midwestern.edu.

NORTHCENTRAL UNIVERSITY

Prescott Valley, Arizona **www.ncu.edu/**

- **Proprietary** comprehensive
- **Coed** 285 undergraduate students, 100% full-time, 49% women, 51% men
- **Minimally difficult** entrance level

Undergraduates 285 full-time. Students come from 53 states and territories, 4 other countries, 84% are from out of state, 12% African American, 3% Asian American or Pacific Islander, 6% Hispanic American, 1% Native American.

Faculty *Total:* 416, 3% full-time. *Student/faculty ratio:* 16:1.
Majors Business administration and management; general studies; marriage/family counseling; psychology.
Academics *Calendar:* continuous. *Degrees:* bachelor's, master's, doctoral, and post-master's certificates (offers only distance learning programs). *Special study options:* accelerated degree program, advanced placement credit, distance learning, external degree program, part-time degree program, summer session for credit.
Computers on Campus Students can access the following: campus intranet, computer help desk, online (class) grades, online (class) registration, online (class) schedules. Campuswide network is available. Wireless service is available via entire campus.
Student Life *Housing:* college housing not available.
Costs (2008–09) *Tuition:* $8250 full-time, $275 per credit part-time. *Required fees:* $90 full-time.
Applying *Options:* electronic application. *Application fee:* $50. *Required:* essay or personal statement, high school transcript. *Application deadlines:* rolling (freshmen), rolling (transfers). *Notification:* continuous (freshmen), continuous (transfers).
Director of Admissions Mr. Brent Passey, Director of Admissions, Northcentral University, 10000 East University Drive, Prescott Valley, AZ 86314. *Phone:* 866-776-0331 Ext. 8085. *Toll-free phone:* 888-327-2877. *Fax:* 928-541-7817. *E-mail:* info@ncu.edu.

NORTHERN ARIZONA UNIVERSITY

Flagstaff, Arizona **www.nau.edu/**

- **State-supported** university, founded 1899, part of Arizona State University System, under the Arizona Board of Regents
- **Small-town** 730-acre campus
- **Endowment** $16.0 million
- **Coed** 15,569 undergraduate students, 82% full-time, 60% women, 40% men
- **Moderately difficult** entrance level, 75% of applicants were admitted

Undergraduates 12,844 full-time, 2,725 part-time. Students come from 54 states and territories, 64 other countries, 21% are from out of state, 3% African American, 2% Asian American or Pacific Islander, 12% Hispanic American, 6% Native American, 2% international, 12% transferred in, 40% live on campus. *Retention:* 71% of 2006 full-time freshmen returned.
Freshmen *Admission:* 15,486 applied, 11,629 admitted, 3,171 enrolled. *Average high school GPA:* 3.4. *Test scores:* SAT critical reading scores over 500: 62%; SAT math scores over 500: 65%; SAT writing scores over 500: 54%; ACT scores over 18: 88%; SAT critical reading scores over 600: 21%; SAT math scores over 600: 22%; SAT writing scores over 600: 14%; ACT scores over 24: 37%; SAT critical reading scores over 700: 3%; SAT math scores over 700: 2%; SAT writing scores over 700: 1%; ACT scores over 30: 2%.
Faculty *Total:* 1,500, 52% full-time, 57% with terminal degrees. *Student/faculty ratio:* 17:1.
Majors Accounting; advertising; American government and politics; American Indian/Native American studies; anthropology; art; art history, criticism and conservation; arts management; art teacher education; astronomy; biology/biological sciences; biology teacher education; botany/plant biology; business administration and management; business administration, management and operations related; business/commerce; business/managerial economics; cell biology and anatomical sciences related; chemistry; chemistry related; civil engineering; communication and journalism related; communication/speech communication and rhetoric; community health and preventive medicine; computer and information sciences; computer and information sciences related; construction engineering technology; counselor education/school counseling and guidance; criminal justice/law enforcement administration; dental hygiene; drama and dance teacher education; dramatic/theater arts; early childhood education; ecology; economics; education; educational leadership and administration; education (specific subject areas) related; electrical, electronics and communications engineering; elementary education; engineering; engineering physics; English; English as a second/foreign language (teaching); English/language arts teacher education; environmental/environmental health engineering; environmental studies; finance; forest sciences and biology; French; general studies; geochemistry; geography; geology/earth science; German; health science; health teacher education; history; history teacher education; hotel and restaurant management; hotel/motel administration; humanities; interior design; international relations and affairs; journalism; kinesiology and exercise science; liberal arts and sciences and humanities related; liberal arts and sciences/liberal studies; management information systems; marine biology and biological oceanography; marketing/marketing management; mathematics; mathematics teacher education; mechanical engineering; medical microbiology and bacteriology; music; music performance; music teacher education; nursing (registered nurse training); parks, recreation and leisure; parks, recreation and leisure facilities management; philosophy; photography; physical education teaching and coaching; physical sciences; physics; physics related; physics teacher education; political science and government; pre-law studies; pre-medical studies; pre-veterinary studies; psychology; public administration and social service professions related; public policy analysis; public relations/image management; radio and television; religious studies; science teacher education; science technologies related; social sciences; social science teacher education; social work; sociology; Spanish; Spanish language teacher education; special education; special education (speech or language impaired); speech and rhetoric; technology/industrial arts teacher education; wildlife and wildlands science and management; women's studies; zoology/animal biology.
Academics *Calendar:* semesters. *Degrees:* certificates, bachelor's, master's, doctoral, and postbachelor's certificates. *Special study options:* accelerated degree program, advanced placement credit, cooperative education, distance learning, double majors, English as a second language, freshman honors college, honors programs, independent study, internships, off-campus study, part-time degree program, services for LD students, study abroad, summer session for credit. *ROTC:* Army (b), Air Force (b).
Computers on Campus 903 computers/terminals are available on campus for general student use. Students can access the following: computer help desk, free student e-mail accounts, online (class) grades, online (class) registration, online (class) schedules. Campuswide network is available. 100% of college-owned or -operated housing units are wired for high-speed Internet access. Wireless service is available via classrooms, computer centers, computer labs, learning centers, libraries.
Student Life *Housing options:* coed, men-only, women-only, disabled students. Campus housing is university owned and is provided by a third party. Freshman campus housing is guaranteed. *Activities and organizations:* drama/theater group, student-run newspaper, radio and television station, choral group, marching band, ASNAU, Black Student Union, New Student Organization, Cardinal Key Society, Blue Key Society, national fraternities, national sororities. *Campus security:* 24-hour emergency response devices and patrols, late-night transport/escort service, controlled dormitory access. *Student services:* health clinic, personal/psychological counseling, women's center.
Athletics Member NCAA. All Division I. *Intercollegiate sports:* basketball M (s)/W (s), cheerleading M (s)/W (s), cross-country running M (s)/W (s), football M (s), golf W (s), soccer W (s), swimming and diving W (s), tennis M (s)/W (s), track and field M (s)/W (s), volleyball W (s). *Intramural sports:* archery M/W, badminton M/W, baseball M, basketball M/W, bowling M/W, cross-country running M/W, fencing M/W, football M/W, ice hockey M, lacrosse M/W, racquetball M/W, rugby M/W, skiing (cross-country) M/W, skiing (downhill) M/W, soccer M (c), softball M/W, swimming and diving W, table tennis M/W, ultimate Frisbee M/W, volleyball M/W, water polo M/W, weight lifting M/W.
Standardized Tests *Required:* SAT or ACT (for admission).
Costs (2007–08) *Tuition:* state resident $4594 full-time, $308 per credit hour part-time; nonresident $14,428 full-time, $662 per credit hour part-time. Full-time tuition and fees vary according to location and program. Part-time tuition and fees vary according to location and program. *Required fees:* $250 full-time, $68 per credit hour part-time. *Room and board:* $6572; room only: $3624. Room and board charges vary according to board plan and housing facility. *Waivers:* employees or children of employees.
Financial Aid Of all full-time matriculated undergraduates who enrolled in 2007, 8,648 applied for aid, 6,364 were judged to have need, 1,128 had their need fully met. 515 Federal Work-Study jobs (averaging $1847). 3,328 state and other part-time jobs (averaging $2164). In 2007, 1962 non-need-based awards were made. *Average percent of need met:* 68%. *Average financial aid package:* $8769. *Average need-based loan:* $4063. *Average need-based gift aid:* $5332. *Average non-need-based aid:* $3330. *Average indebtedness upon graduation:* $16,170.
Applying *Options:* electronic application, deferred entrance. *Application fee:* $25. *Required:* high school transcript, minimum 3.0 GPA. *Required for some:* letters of recommendation. *Application deadlines:* rolling (freshmen), rolling (transfers). *Notification:* continuous (freshmen), continuous (transfers).
Freshman Application Contact James E. Casebeer, Associate Director, Northern Arizona University, PO Box 4084, Flagstaff, AZ 86011. *Phone:* 928-523-6080. *Toll-free phone:* 888-MORE-NAU. *Fax:* 928-523-1230. *E-mail:* undergraduate.admissions@nau.edu.

See page 322 for the College Close-Up.

PRESCOTT COLLEGE

Prescott, Arizona **www.prescott.edu/**

- **Independent** comprehensive, founded 1966
- **Small-town** 4-acre campus
- **Endowment** $728,726
- **Coed** 694 undergraduate students, 87% full-time, 59% women, 41% men
- **Moderately difficult** entrance level, 83% of applicants were admitted

Undergraduates 602 full-time, 92 part-time. Students come from 48 states and territories, 4 other countries, 62% are from out of state, 1% African American, 1% Asian American or Pacific Islander, 6% Hispanic American, 1% Native American, 0.9% international, 12% transferred in, 2% live on campus. *Retention:* 73% of 2006 full-time freshmen returned.

Freshmen *Admission:* 252 applied, 209 admitted, 71 enrolled. *Average high school GPA:* 3.09. *Test scores:* SAT critical reading scores over 500: 77%; SAT math scores over 500: 70%; SAT writing scores over 500: 66%; ACT scores over 18: 100%; SAT critical reading scores over 600: 44%; SAT math scores over 600: 34%; SAT writing scores over 600: 37%; ACT scores over 24: 26%; SAT critical reading scores over 700: 19%; SAT math scores over 700: 6%; SAT writing scores over 700: 4%; ACT scores over 30: 13%.

Faculty *Total:* 70, 49% full-time, 41% with terminal degrees. *Student/faculty ratio:* 9:1.

Majors Accounting; anthropology; art; art therapy; bilingual and multilingual education; biology/biological sciences; communication/speech communication and rhetoric; computer and information sciences; criminal justice/safety; dance; dramatic/theater arts; ecology; education; elementary education; English/language arts teacher education; environmental design/architecture; environmental education; environmental studies; film/cinema studies; history; human development and family studies; human ecology; humanities; interdisciplinary studies; kindergarten/preschool education; Latin American studies; liberal arts and sciences/liberal studies; literature; management science; marine science/merchant marine officer; mathematics teacher education; mental health/rehabilitation; middle school education; music teacher education; natural resources/conservation; natural resources management and policy; parks, recreation and leisure; philosophy; photography; physical education teaching and coaching; political science and government; psychology; science teacher education; secondary education; social science teacher education; sociology; Spanish; special education; wildlife and wildlands science and management.

Academics *Calendar:* quarters (4-week blocks followed by 10-week terms for each quarter). *Degrees:* bachelor's, master's, doctoral, and postbachelor's certificates. *Special study options:* adult/continuing education programs, advanced placement credit, double majors, external degree program, independent study, internships, off-campus study, services for LD students, student-designed majors, summer session for credit.

Computers on Campus 30 computers/terminals and 20 ports are available on campus for general student use. Students can access the following: campus intranet, computer help desk, free student e-mail accounts. Campuswide network is available. 100% of college-owned or -operated housing units are wired for high-speed Internet access. Wireless service is available via computer centers, computer labs, dorm rooms, libraries.

Student Life *Housing options:* coed. Campus housing is university owned. Freshman applicants given priority for college housing. *Activities and organizations:* drama/theater group, student-run newspaper, Student Advisory Council, Aztlan Center, HUB (Helping Understand Bikes), WEB (Women's Empowerment Breakthrough), Ripple Project. *Campus security:* 24-hour emergency response devices. *Student services:* personal/psychological counseling.

Standardized Tests *Required:* SAT or ACT (for admission).

Costs (2007–08) *One-time required fee:* $1030. *Tuition:* $19,980 full-time, $555 per credit hour part-time. Full-time tuition and fees vary according to course load and degree level. *Required fees:* $200 full-time, $100 per term part-time. *Room only:* $3120. *Payment plans:* installment, deferred payment. *Waivers:* employees or children of employees.

Financial Aid Of all full-time matriculated undergraduates who enrolled in 2004, 486 applied for aid, 474 were judged to have need. 165 Federal Work-Study jobs (averaging $1373). 64 state and other part-time jobs (averaging $1010). *Average percent of need met:* 43%. *Average financial aid package:* $9839. *Average need-based loan:* $3978. *Average need-based gift aid:* $4530. *Average indebtedness upon graduation:* $18,235.

Applying *Options:* electronic application, deferred entrance. *Application fee:* $25. *Required:* high school transcript, 2 letters of recommendation. *Required for some:* essay or personal statement, interview. *Application deadlines:* 8/15 (freshmen), 8/15 (transfers). *Early decision deadline:* 12/1. *Notification:* continuous (freshmen), continuous (transfers), 12/15 (early decision).

Freshman Application Contact Prescott College, 220 Grove Avenue, Prescott, AZ 86301. *Phone:* 800-628-6364. *Toll-free phone:* 800-628-6364.

See page 324 for the College Close-Up.

SOUTHWESTERN COLLEGE

Phoenix, Arizona **www.swcaz.edu/**

- **Independent Conservative Baptist** 4-year, founded 1960
- **Urban** 19-acre campus
- **Coed** 361 undergraduate students
- **Minimally difficult** entrance level, 48% of applicants were admitted

Undergraduates 40% live on campus. *Retention:* 61% of 2006 full-time freshmen returned.

Freshmen *Admission:* 210 applied, 101 admitted. *Average high school GPA:* 3.3.

Faculty *Total:* 33, 27% full-time, 100% with terminal degrees. *Student/faculty ratio:* 17:1.

Majors Biblical studies; business administration and management; counseling psychology; elementary education; music teacher education; secondary education; youth ministry.

Academics *Calendar:* 4-4-1. *Degrees:* associate and bachelor's. *Special study options:* academic remediation for entering students, adult/continuing education programs, advanced placement credit, double majors, internships, summer session for credit. *ROTC:* Air Force (c).

Computers on Campus 44 computers/terminals are available on campus for general student use. Campuswide network is available.

Student Life *Housing options:* men-only, women-only, disabled students. Campus housing is university owned. Freshman campus housing is guaranteed. *Activities and organizations:* drama/theater group, student-run newspaper, choral group, newspaper, drama, choral group, Student Leadership Council. *Campus security:* controlled dormitory access.

Athletics Member NCCAA. *Intercollegiate sports:* basketball M/W, soccer M, volleyball W. *Intramural sports:* basketball M/W, football M/W, softball M/W, table tennis M/W, volleyball M/W.

Standardized Tests *Required:* SAT and SAT Subject Tests or ACT (for admission).

Costs (2008–09) *Comprehensive fee:* $18,768 includes full-time tuition ($13,764) and room and board ($5004). Part-time tuition: $570 per credit hour. *College room only:* $3724.

Financial Aid Of all full-time matriculated undergraduates who enrolled in 2004, 201 applied for aid, 201 were judged to have need. 19 Federal Work-Study jobs (averaging $1480). In 2004, 267 non-need-based awards were made. *Average percent of need met:* 3%. *Average financial aid package:* $5500. *Average need-based loan:* $4500. *Average need-based gift aid:* $1400. *Average non-need-based aid:* $1100. *Average indebtedness upon graduation:* $17,125.

Applying *Options:* electronic application, deferred entrance. *Application fee:* $30. *Required:* essay or personal statement, high school transcript, minimum 2.0 GPA, 1 letter of recommendation. *Application deadlines:* 8/1 (freshmen), 8/1 (transfers). *Notification:* continuous until 8/20 (freshmen), continuous (transfers).

Freshman Application Contact Rebekah Dubina, Admissions Advisor, Southwestern College, 2625 East Cactus Road, Administration Building, Phoenix, AZ 85015. *Phone:* 602-386-4106. *Toll-free phone:* 800-247-2697. *Fax:* 602-404-2159. *E-mail:* rebekah@swcaz.edu.

UNIVERSITY OF ADVANCING TECHNOLOGY

Tempe, Arizona **www.uat.edu/**

- **Proprietary** comprehensive, founded 1983
- **Urban** campus
- **Coed, primarily men** 1,195 undergraduate students, 100% full-time, 8% women, 92% men

Undergraduates 1,195 full-time. Students come from 37 states and territories, 62% are from out of state, 4% African American, 2% Asian American or Pacific Islander, 6% Hispanic American, 0.4% Native American, 1% international, 22% live on campus.

Freshmen *Admission:* 596 enrolled. *Average high school GPA:* 2.5.

Faculty *Total:* 54, 52% full-time. *Student/faculty ratio:* 19:1.

Majors Cinematography and film/video production; commercial and advertising art; computer graphics; computer programming; computer systems analysis; data processing and data processing technology; design and visual communications.

Academics *Calendar:* semesters. *Degrees:* associate, bachelor's, and master's. *Special study options:* cooperative education, distance learning, double majors, independent study, internships, summer session for credit.

Computers on Campus 400 computers/terminals and 300 ports are available on campus for general student use. Students can access the following: campus intranet, free student e-mail accounts, online (class) grades, online (class) registration, online (class) schedules. Campuswide network is available. 100% of college-owned or -operated housing units are wired for high-speed Internet access. Wireless service is available via entire campus.

Student Life *Housing:* on-campus residence required for freshman year. *Options:* coed. Campus housing is university owned, leased by the school and is provided by a third party. *Activities and organizations:* student-run newspaper, television station, Web Club, Gaming Club, Animation Club, Video Club, student government. *Campus security:* 24-hour patrols. *Student services:* personal/psychological counseling.

Athletics *Intramural sports:* fencing M/W, softball M/W.

Standardized Tests *Required for some:* SAT (for admission), ACT (for admission), SAT or ACT (for admission).

Costs (2007–08) *Comprehensive fee:* $24,448 includes full-time tuition ($16,300), mandatory fees ($100), and room and board ($8048). *College room only:* $6360. *Payment plan:* installment. *Waivers:* employees or children of employees.

Applying *Options:* electronic application. *Required:* essay or personal statement, high school transcript, interview. *Required for some:* minimum 2.5 GPA. *Application deadline:* rolling (freshmen).

Freshman Application Contact Admissions Office, University of Advancing Technology, 2625 West Baseline Road, Tempe, AZ 85283-1042. *Phone:* 602-383-8228. *Toll-free phone:* 602-383-8228 (in-state); 800-658-5744 (out-of-state). *Fax:* 602-383-8222. *E-mail:* admissions@uat.edu.

See page 326 for the College Close-Up.

THE UNIVERSITY OF ARIZONA

Tucson, Arizona — www.arizona.edu/

- **State-supported** university, founded 1885, part of Arizona Board of Regents
- **Urban** 362-acre campus
- **Endowment** $214.3 million
- **Coed** 29,070 undergraduate students, 87% full-time, 53% women, 47% men
- **Moderately difficult** entrance level, 80% of applicants were admitted

Undergraduates 25,228 full-time, 3,842 part-time. Students come from 55 states and territories, 124 other countries, 34% are from out of state, 3% African American, 6% Asian American or Pacific Islander, 16% Hispanic American, 2% Native American, 3% international, 9% transferred in, 20% live on campus. *Retention:* 80% of 2006 full-time freshmen returned.

Freshmen *Admission:* 21,103 applied, 16,780 admitted, 6,569 enrolled. *Average high school GPA:* 3.44. *Test scores:* SAT critical reading scores over 500: 71%; SAT math scores over 500: 72%; ACT scores over 18: 94%; SAT critical reading scores over 600: 28%; SAT math scores over 600: 30%; ACT scores over 24: 50%; SAT critical reading scores over 700: 5%; SAT math scores over 700: 7%; ACT scores over 30: 8%.

Faculty *Total:* 1,462, 96% full-time, 98% with terminal degrees. *Student/faculty ratio:* 18:1.

Majors Accounting; aerospace, aeronautical and astronautical engineering; agricultural/biological engineering and bioengineering; agricultural economics; agricultural teacher education; agriculture; animal sciences; anthropology; architecture; art history, criticism and conservation; art teacher education; Asian studies (East); astronomy; atmospheric sciences and meteorology; biochemistry; biology/biological sciences; biology teacher education; business/commerce; business/managerial economics; cell biology and histology; chemical engineering; chemistry; chemistry teacher education; city/urban, community and regional planning; civil engineering; classics; clinical laboratory science/medical technology; communication disorders; communication/speech communication and rhetoric; computer and information sciences; computer engineering; consumer economics; creative writing; criminal justice/law enforcement administration; dance; drama and dance teacher education; dramatic/theater arts; early childhood education; economics; education (specific subject areas) related; electrical, electronics and communications engineering; elementary education; engineering; engineering/industrial management; engineering physics; engineering related; English; English as a second/foreign language (teaching); English/language arts teacher education; entrepreneurship; environmental science; environmental studies; family and consumer sciences/home economics teacher education; finance; fine/studio arts; foreign language teacher education; French; French language teacher education; geography; geological engineering; geology/earth science; German; German language teacher education; health/health care administration; health teacher education; Hispanic-American, Puerto Rican, and Mexican-American/Chicano studies; history; history teacher education; human development and family studies; human resources management; industrial/manufacturing engineering; Italian; Jewish/Judaic studies; journalism; Judaic studies; kindergarten/preschool education; landscape architecture; Latin American studies; liberal arts and sciences/liberal studies; linguistics; management information systems; marketing/marketing management; materials science; mathematics; mathematics teacher education; mechanical engineering; mining and mineral engineering; multi-/interdisciplinary studies related; music; music performance; music related; music teacher education; Near and Middle Eastern studies; nuclear engineering; nursing (registered nurse training); nutrition sciences; operations management; optical sciences; philosophy; physical education teaching and coaching; physics; physics teacher education; physiology; plant sciences; political science and government; pre-veterinary studies; psychology; public administration; radio and television; religious studies; Russian; science teacher education; science technologies related; secondary education; social science teacher education; social studies teacher education; sociology; soil sciences; Spanish; Spanish language teacher education; special education; speech teacher education; systems engineering; theater design and technology; visual and performing arts; water resources engineering; wildlife and wildlands science and management; women's studies.

Academics *Calendar:* semesters. *Degrees:* bachelor's, master's, doctoral, first professional, and postbachelor's certificates. *Special study options:* adult/continuing education programs, advanced placement credit, distance learning, double majors, English as a second language, freshman honors college, honors programs, independent study, internships, part-time degree program, services for LD students, study abroad, summer session for credit. *ROTC:* Army (b), Navy (b), Air Force (b). *Unusual degree programs:* 3-2 business administration with American Graduate School of International Management.

Computers on Campus 2,500 computers/terminals are available on campus for general student use. Students can access the following: campus intranet, computer help desk, free student e-mail accounts, online (class) grades, online (class) registration, online (class) schedules. Campuswide network is available. Wireless service is available via computer centers, computer labs, libraries, student centers.

Student Life *Housing options:* coed, women-only, disabled students. Campus housing is university owned and leased by the school. Freshman applicants given priority for college housing. *Activities and organizations:* drama/theater group, student-run newspaper, radio and television station, choral group, marching band, Student Government Association, national fraternities, national sororities. *Campus security:* 24-hour patrols, student patrols, late-night transport/escort service, emergency telephones. *Student services:* health clinic, personal/psychological counseling, women's center, legal services.

Athletics Member NCAA. All Division I except football (Division I-A). *Intercollegiate sports:* baseball M (s), basketball M (s)/W (s), cross-country running M (s)/W (s), golf M (s)/W (s), gymnastics W (s), ice hockey M (c), lacrosse M (c)/W (c), rock climbing M (c)/W (c), soccer M (c)/W (s), softball W (s), swimming and diving M (s)/W (s), tennis M (s)/W (s), track and field M (s)/W (s), volleyball M (c)/W (s), wrestling M (c). *Intramural sports:* badminton M/W, basketball M/W, bowling M/W, cross-country running M/W, football M/W, golf M/W, racquetball M/W, soccer M/W, softball M/W, swimming and diving M/W, table tennis M/W, tennis M/W, track and field M/W, volleyball M/W, water polo M/W, weight lifting M/W, wrestling M.

Standardized Tests *Recommended:* SAT or ACT (for admission).

Costs (2007–08) *Tuition:* state resident $4824 full-time, $252 per credit hour part-time; nonresident $16,058 full-time, $669 per credit hour part-time. Full-time tuition and fees vary according to course load. Part-time tuition and fees vary according to course load. *Required fees:* $224 full-time, $75 per term part-time. *Room and board:* $7370; room only: $4670. Room and board charges vary according to board plan and housing facility. *Waivers:* employees or children of employees.

Financial Aid Of all full-time matriculated undergraduates who enrolled in 2006, 13,033 applied for aid, 9,638 were judged to have need, 1,071 had their need fully met. In 2006, 5431 non-need-based awards were made. *Average percent of need met:* 65%. *Average financial aid package:* $8629. *Average need-based loan:* $4162. *Average need-based gift aid:* $6510. *Average non-need-based aid:* $5140. *Average indebtedness upon graduation:* $18,241.

Applying *Options:* electronic application, early admission. *Application fee:* $25. *Required:* high school transcript. *Required for some:* minimum 3.0 GPA, letters of recommendation, interview. *Application deadlines:* 4/1 (freshmen), 6/1 (transfers). *Notification:* continuous (freshmen).

Director of Admissions Ms. Kasey Urquidez, Director of Recruitment, Admissions, The University of Arizona, PO Box 210040, Tucson, AZ 85721-0040. *Phone:* 520-621-3237. *Fax:* 520-621-9799. *E-mail:* appinfo@arizona.edu.

UNIVERSITY OF PHOENIX

Phoenix, Arizona **www.uopxonline.com/**

- **Proprietary** comprehensive, founded 1989
- **Coed**
- **Noncompetitive** entrance level

Faculty *Student/faculty ratio:* 16:1.

Academics *Calendar:* continuous. *Degrees:* certificates, associate, bachelor's, master's, doctoral, post-master's, and postbachelor's certificates.

Costs (2007–08) *Tuition:* $10,727 full-time, $358 per credit part-time. Full-time tuition and fees vary according to course level.

Financial Aid *Average financial aid package:* $3846. *Average need-based gift aid:* $1919.

Applying *Options:* deferred entrance. *Application fee:* $45. *Required:* 1 letter of recommendation. *Required for some:* high school transcript.

Freshman Application Contact Ms. Beth Barilla, Associate Vice President, Student Admissions and Services, University of Phoenix, 4615 East Elwood Street, Mail Stop AA-K101, Phoenix, AZ 85040-1958. *Phone:* 480-317-6000. *Toll-free phone:* 800-776-4867 (in-state); 800-228-7240 (out-of-state). *Fax:* 480-894-1758. *E-mail:* beth.barilla@phoenix.edu.

UNIVERSITY OF PHOENIX–PHOENIX CAMPUS

Phoenix, Arizona **www.phoenix.edu/**

- **Proprietary** comprehensive, founded 1976
- **Urban** campus
- **Coed**
- **Noncompetitive** entrance level

Faculty *Student/faculty ratio:* 9:1.

Academics *Calendar:* continuous. *Degrees:* bachelor's, master's, post-master's, and postbachelor's certificates.

Student Life *Campus security:* 24-hour patrols, late-night transport/escort service.

Costs (2007–08) *Tuition:* $10,290 full-time, $343 per credit part-time. Full-time tuition and fees vary according to course level.

Financial Aid *Average financial aid package:* $4921. *Average need-based gift aid:* $2276.

Applying *Options:* deferred entrance. *Application fee:* $45. *Required:* 1 letter of recommendation. *Required for some:* high school transcript.

Freshman Application Contact Ms. Beth Barilla, Associate Vice President, Student Admissions and Services, University of Phoenix–Phoenix Campus, 4615 East Elwood Street, Mail Stop AA-K101, Phoenix, AZ 85040-1958. *Phone:* 480-317-6000. *Toll-free phone:* 800-776-4867 (in-state); 800-228-7240 (out-of-state). *Fax:* 480-894-1758. *E-mail:* beth.barilla@phoenix.edu.

UNIVERSITY OF PHOENIX–SOUTHERN ARIZONA CAMPUS

Tucson, Arizona **www.phoenix.edu/**

- **Proprietary** comprehensive, founded 1979
- **Urban** campus
- **Coed**
- **Noncompetitive** entrance level

Faculty *Student/faculty ratio:* 8:1.

Academics *Calendar:* continuous. *Degrees:* certificates, bachelor's, master's, and post-master's certificates.

Student Life *Campus security:* late-night transport/escort service.

Costs (2007–08) *Tuition:* $10,350 full-time, $345 per credit part-time. Full-time tuition and fees vary according to course level.

Financial Aid *Average financial aid package:* $4838. *Average need-based gift aid:* $2484.

Applying *Options:* deferred entrance. *Application fee:* $45. *Required:* 1 letter of recommendation. *Required for some:* high school transcript.

Freshman Application Contact Ms. Beth Barilla, Associate Vice President, Student Admissions and Services, University of Phoenix–Southern Arizona Campus, 4615 East Elwood Street, Mail Stop AA-K101, Phoenix, AZ 85040-1958. *Phone:* 480-317-6000. *Toll-free phone:* 800-776-4867 (in-state); 800-228-7240 (out-of-state). *Fax:* 480-894-1758. *E-mail:* beth.barilla@phoenix.edu.

WESTERN INTERNATIONAL UNIVERSITY

Phoenix, Arizona **www.wintu.edu/**

- **Proprietary** comprehensive, founded 1978, administratively affiliated with Apollo Group, Inc
- **Urban** 4-acre campus
- **Coed** 1,957 undergraduate students, 100% full-time, 66% women, 34% men
- **Moderately difficult** entrance level, 79% of applicants were admitted

Undergraduates 1,957 full-time. Students come from 50 states and territories, 45 other countries, 18% are from out of state, 8% African American, 2% Asian American or Pacific Islander, 12% Hispanic American, 3% Native American, 2% international, 98% transferred in.

Freshmen *Admission:* 775 applied, 616 admitted, 35 enrolled.

Faculty *Total:* 375, 23% with terminal degrees. *Student/faculty ratio:* 10:1.

Majors Accounting; behavioral sciences; business administration and management; computer management; criminal justice/law enforcement administration; finance; health/health care administration; information science/studies; international business/trade/commerce; international relations and affairs; liberal arts and sciences/liberal studies; marketing/marketing management.

Academics *Calendar:* continuous. *Degrees:* certificates, associate, bachelor's, and master's. *Special study options:* academic remediation for entering students, accelerated degree program, adult/continuing education programs, advanced placement credit, distance learning, double majors, English as a second language, honors programs, independent study, part-time degree program, study abroad, summer session for credit.

Computers on Campus 50 computers/terminals are available on campus for general student use. Campuswide network is available. Wireless service is available via entire campus.

Student Life *Housing:* college housing not available. *Activities and organizations:* Delta Mu Delta Honor Society, Upsilon Pi Epsilon Honor Society, International Student Organization, Golden Key Honor Society. *Campus security:* 24-hour emergency response devices and patrols, late-night transport/escort service.

Costs (2007–08) *Tuition:* $8400 full-time, $350 per credit part-time. Full-time tuition and fees vary according to degree level and location. Part-time tuition and fees vary according to degree level and location. *Payment plan:* deferred payment. *Waivers:* employees or children of employees.

Applying *Options:* deferred entrance. *Application fee:* $85. *Required:* high school transcript, minimum 2.5 GPA. *Recommended:* interview. *Application deadlines:* rolling (freshmen), rolling (transfers).

Freshman Application Contact Ms. Karen Janitell, Executive Director of Enrollment, Western International University, 9215 North Black Canyon Highway, Phoenix, AZ 85021. *Phone:* 602-943-2311 Ext. 1063. *E-mail:* karen.janitell@apollogrp.edu.

The University

Argosy University is a leading institution offering a variety of degree programs that focus on the human side of success alongside professional competence. For students looking for a more personal approach to education, Argosy University may just be the answer. With forty-eight graduate and undergraduate programs across nineteen campuses and two states, Argosy University emphasizes interpersonal skills as well as academic learning. All of its programs are taught by practicing professionals who bring real-world experience into the classroom so students graduate with both a solid foundation of knowledge and the power to put it to work. To accommodate busy working adults, many programs at Argosy University are structured flexibly, with both campus and online learning and evening, weekend, and daytime classes. There is also a wide range of financial aid options for students who qualify.

Argosy University is a private institution of higher education dedicated to providing high-quality professional education programs at the doctoral, master's, bachelor's, and associate degree levels as well as continuing education to individuals who seek to advance their professional and personal lives. The University emphasizes programs in the behavioral sciences (psychology and counseling), business, education, and the health-care professions. A limited number of preprofessional programs and general education offerings are provided to permit students to prepare for entry into these professional fields. The programs of Argosy University are designed to instill the knowledge, skills, and ethical values of professional practice and to foster values of social responsibility, in a supportive, learning-centered environment of mutual respect and professional excellence.

With nineteen campuses nationwide, Argosy University provides students with a network of resources found at larger universities, including a career resources office, an academic resources center, and extensive information access for research. The University's innovative programs feature dynamic, relevant, and practical curricula delivered in flexible class formats, and its unique scheduling options that make it easier to fit school into their busy lives. They can choose from day and evening classes, on campus or online. Many students find a combination of both to be an ideal way of continuing their education while meeting family and professional demands.

Most students are full-time working professionals who live within driving distance of the campus. The University does not offer or operate student housing.

Argosy University is accredited by The Higher Learning Commission of the North Central Association, 30 North LaSalle Street, Suite 2400, Chicago, Illinois 60602; 800-621-7440 (http://www.ncahlc.org).

Location

Argosy University operates nineteen locations across the U.S. and offers a variety of degree programs online (http://www.argosy.edu). Campus locations include the following:

Atlanta, 980 Hammond Drive, Suite 100, Atlanta, Georgia 30328; phone: 770-671-1200 or 888-671-4777 (toll-free)

Chicago, 225 North Michigan Avenue, Suite 1300, Chicago, Illinois 60601; phone: 312-777-7600 or 800-626-4123 (toll-free)

Dallas, 8080 Park Lane, Suite 400A, Dallas, Texas 75231; phone: 214-890-9900 or 866-954-9900 (toll-free)

Denver, 1200 Lincoln Street, Denver, Colorado 80203; phone: 303-248-2700 or 866-431-5981 (toll-free)

Hawaii, 400 ASB Tower, 1001 Bishop Street, Honolulu, Hawaii 96813; phone: 808-536-5555 or 888-323-2777 (toll-free)

Inland Empire, 636 East Brier Drive, Suite 235, San Bernardino, California 92408; phone: 909-915-3800 or 866-217-9075 (toll-free)

Nashville, 100 Centerview Drive, Suite 225, Nashville, Tennessee 37214; phone: 615-525-2800 or 866-833-6598 (toll-free)

Orange County, 3501 West Sunflower Avenue, Suite 110, Santa Ana, California 92704; phone: 714-338-6200 or 800-716-9598 (toll-free)

Phoenix, 2233 West Dunlap Avenue, Phoenix, Arizona 85021; phone: 602-216-2600 or 866-216-2777 (toll-free)

Salt Lake City, 121 West Election Road, Suite 300, Draper, Utah 84020; phone: 888-639-4756 (toll-free)

San Diego, 1615 Murray Canyon Road, San Diego, California 92108; phone: 619-321-3000 or 866-505-0333 (toll-free)

San Francisco Bay Area, 1005 Atlantic Avenue, Alameda, California 94501; phone: 510-217-4700 or 866-215-2777 (toll-free)

Santa Monica, 2200 Colorado Avenue, Santa Monica, California 90404; phone: 310-866-4000 or 866-505-0332 (toll-free)

Sarasota, 5250 17th Street, Sarasota, Florida 34235; phone: 941-379-0404 or 800-331-5995 (toll-free)

Schaumburg, 999 North Plaza Drive, Suite 111, Schaumburg, Illinois 60173-5403; phone: 847-969-4900 or 866-290-2777 (toll-free)

Seattle, 2601-A Elliott Avenue, Seattle, Washington 98121; phone: 206-283-4500 or 888-283-2777 (toll-free)

Tampa, Parkside at Tampa Bay Park, 4401 North Himes Avenue, Suite 150, Tampa, Florida 33614; phone: 813-393-5290 or 800-850-6488 (toll-free)

Twin Cities, 1515 Central Parkway, Eagan, Minnesota 55121; phone: 651-846-2882 or 888-844-2004 (toll-free)

Washington DC, 1550 Wilson Boulevard, Suite 600, Arlington, Virginia 22209; phone: 703-526-5800 or 866-703-2777 (toll-free)

Majors and Degrees

Argosy University's College of Business offers a Bachelor of Science (B.S.) in Business Administration program. Argosy University's College of Psychology and Behavioral Sciences offers the Bachelor of Arts (B.A.) in Psychology degree program.

Academic Programs

The B.S. in Business Administration program prepares students for entry- to mid-level positions within the public or private sector. The curriculum is structured to help students develop competencies in oral and written communication, leadership, team skills, situation-focused learning, and the analysis and execution of solutions in various business situations. Students may choose one of five optional concentrations: customized professional concentration, finance, health-care management, international business, or marketing.

The B.A. in Psychology program is designed to help students begin many service careers in such capacities as entry-level counselor, case manager, or human resources administrator and

ARGOSY UNIVERSITY

ARGOSY UNIVERSITY

The University

Argosy University is a leading institution offering a variety of degree programs that focus on the human side of success alongside professional competence. For students looking for a more personal approach to education, Argosy University may just be the answer. With forty-eight graduate and undergraduate programs, across nineteen campuses and twelve states, Argosy University emphasizes interpersonal skills as well as academic learning. All of its programs are taught by practicing professionals who bring real-world experience into the classroom. So students graduate with both a solid foundation of knowledge and the power to put it to work. To accommodate busy working adults, many programs at Argosy University are structured flexibly—with both campus and online learning and evening, weekend, and daytime classes. There is also a wide range of financial aid options for students who qualify.

Argosy University is a private institution of higher education dedicated to providing high-quality professional education programs at the doctoral, master's, bachelor's, and associate degree levels as well as continuing education to individuals who seek to advance their professional and personal lives. The University emphasizes programs in the behavioral sciences (psychology and counseling), business, education, and the health-care professions. A limited number of preprofessional programs and general education offerings are provided to permit students to prepare for entry into these professional fields. The programs of Argosy University are designed to instill the knowledge, skills, and ethical values of professional practice and to foster values of social responsibility in a supportive, learning-centered environment of mutual respect and professional excellence.

With nineteen campuses nationwide, Argosy University provides students with a network of resources found at larger universities, including a career resources office, an academic resources center, and extensive information access for research. The University's innovative programs feature dynamic, relevant, and practical curricula delivered in flexible class formats. Students enjoy scheduling options that make it easier to fit school into their busy lives. They can choose from day and evening courses, on campus or online. Many students find a combination of both to be an ideal way of continuing their education while meeting family and professional demands.

Most students are full-time working professionals who live within driving distance of the campus. The University does not offer or operate student housing.

Argosy University is accredited by The Higher Learning Commission of the North Central Association (30 North LaSalle Street, Suite 2400, Chicago, Illinois 60602; 800-621-7440; http://ncahlc.org).

Location

Argosy University operates nineteen locations across the U.S. and offers a variety of degree programs online (http://www.argosy.edu). Campus locations include the following:

Atlanta, 980 Hammond Drive, Suite 100, Atlanta, Georgia 30328; phone: 770-671-1200 or 888-671-4777 (toll-free)

Chicago, 225 North Michigan Avenue, Suite 1300, Chicago, Illinois 60601; phone: 312-777-7600 or 800-626-4123 (toll-free)

Dallas, 8080 Park Lane, Suite 400A, Dallas, Texas 75231; phone: 214-890-9900 or 866-954-9900 (toll-free)

Denver, 1200 Lincoln Street, Denver, Colorado 80203; phone: 303-248-2700 or 866-431-5981 (toll-free)

Hawai'i, 400 ASB Tower, 1001 Bishop Street, Honolulu, Hawaii 96813; phone: 808-536-5555 or 888-323-2777 (toll-free)

Inland Empire, 636 East Brier Drive, Suite 235, San Bernardino, California 92408; phone: 909-915-3800 or 866-217-9075 (toll-free)

Nashville, 100 Centerview Drive, Suite 225, Nashville, Tennessee 37214; phone: 615-525-2800 or 866-833-6598 (toll-free)

Orange County, 3501 West Sunflower Avenue, Suite 110, Santa Ana, California 92704; phone: 714-338-6200 or 800-716-9598 (toll-free)

Phoenix, 2233 West Dunlap Avenue, Phoenix, Arizona 85021; phone: 602-216-2600 or 866-216-2777 (toll-free)

Salt Lake City, 121 West Election Road, Suite 300, Draper, Utah 84020; phone: 888-639-4756 (toll-free)

San Diego, 7650 Mission Valley Road, San Diego, California 92108; phone: 858-598-1900 or 866-505-0333 (toll-free)

San Francisco Bay Area, 1005 Atlantic Avenue, Alameda, California 94501; phone: 510-217-4700 or 866-215-2777 (toll-free)

Santa Monica, 2950 31st Street, Santa Monica, California 90405; phone: 310-866-4000 or 866-505-0332 (toll-free)

Sarasota, 5250 17th Street, Sarasota, Florida 34235; phone: 941-379-0404 or 800-331-5995 (toll-free)

Schaumburg, 999 North Plaza Drive, Suite 111, Schaumburg, Illinois 60173-5403; phone: 847-969-4900 or 866-290-2777 (toll-free)

Seattle, 2601-A Elliott Avenue, Seattle, Washington 98121; phone: 206-283-4500 or 888-283-2777 (toll-free)

Tampa, Parkside at Tampa Bay Park, 4401 North Hines Avenue, Suite 150, Tampa, Florida 33614; phone: 813-393-5290 or 800-850-6488 (toll-free)

Twin Cities, 1515 Central Parkway, Eagan, Minnesota 55121; phone: 651-846-2882 or 888-844-2004 (toll-free)

Washington DC, 1550 Wilson Boulevard, Suite 600, Arlington, Virginia 22209; phone: 703-526-5800 or 866-703-2777 (toll-free)

Majors and Degrees

Argosy University's College of Business offers a Bachelor of Science (B.S.) in Business Administration program. Argosy University's College of Psychology and Behavioral Sciences offers the Bachelor of Arts (B.A.) in Psychology degree program.

Academic Programs

The B.S. in Business Administration program prepares students for entry- to mid-level positions within the public or private sector. The curriculum is structured to help students develop competencies in oral and written communication, leadership, team skills, solutions-focused learning, and the analysis and execution of solutions in various business situations. Students may choose one of five optional concentrations: customized professional concentration, finance, health-care management, international business, or marketing.

The B.A. in Psychology program is designed to help students begin human services careers in such capacities as entry-level counselor, case manager, or human resources administrator and

in management and business services roles. The program also lays the foundation for graduate study. Students may choose an optional concentration from the following three options: criminal justice, organizational psychology, or substance abuse. This dynamic program is built around a flexible class approach.

Argosy University's bachelor's degree programs are open to students and working professionals with no college experience, plus those who have already earned college credit at a community college, junior college, or other university.

Academic Facilities

Argosy University libraries provide curriculum support and educational resources including current text materials, diagnostic training documents, reference materials and databases, journals and dissertations, and major and current titles in program areas. There is an online public-access catalog of library resources available throughout the Argosy University system. Students enjoy full remote access to their campus library database, enabling them to study and conduct research at home. Academic databases offer dissertation abstracts, academic journals, and professional periodicals. All library computers are Internet accessible. Software applications include Word, Excel, PowerPoint, SPSS, and various test-scoring programs.

Costs

Tuition varies by program. Students should contact the Argosy University campus of their choice for tuition information.

Financial Aid

A wide range of financial aid options is available to students who qualify. Argosy University offers access to federal and state aid programs, merit-based awards, grants, loans, and a work-study program. As a first step, students should complete the Free Application for Federal Student Aid (FAFSA). Prospective students can apply electronically at http://www.fafsa.ed.gov or at the campus. To receive consideration for financial aid and ensure timely receipt of funds, it is best to submit an application promptly.

Faculty

The Argosy University faculty is composed of working professionals who have a passion to help students succeed. Members bring real-world experience and the latest practice innovations to the academic setting. The diverse faculty is widely recognized for contributions to the field. Most hold doctoral degrees. They provide a substantive education that combines comprehensive knowledge with critical skills and practical workplace relevance. Above all, faculty members are committed to their students' personal and professional development.

Student Government

Argosy University campuses offer unique opportunities for student involvement beyond individual programs of study. Most faculty committees include a student representative. In addition, a student group meets with faculty members and administrators regularly to discuss pertinent campus-related issues.

Admission Requirements

Admission requirements differ depending on the number of college credits completed prior to application.

Students who have earned 12 or fewer semester college credits must provide proof of high school graduation or GED and meet one of the following conditions for admission: ACT composite score of 18 or above, or a combined math and verbal SAT score of 870, or minimum ACCUPLACER scores of 86 in sentence skills and 53 in algebra. Applicants who do not meet any of the above conditions for admission will be admitted with academic support if they provide proof of high school graduation or GED and meet one of the following: ACT composite score of 14 to 17, or a combined math and verbal SAT score of 660 to 869, or minimum ACCUPLACER scores of 54 in sentence skills and 36 in arithmetic.

Applicants who have earned 13 or more semester college credits must provide proof of high school graduation or GED and meet one of the following conditions for admission: cumulative college GPA of 2.0 or above or minimum ACCUPLACER scores of 86 for sentence skills and 53 in algebra. Students who do not meet either of the above criteria will be admitted with academic support if they provide proof of high school graduation or GED and meet the following condition: minimum ACCUPLACER scores of 54 in reading and 36 in arithmetic.

Students admitted with academic support are limited to 12 credit hours of study during their first semester (6 credit hours per session). Students admitted with academic support will be required to complete developmental English and/or math courses unless they meet the following conditions: Writing Review (ENG099)—must meet one of the following: a minimum ACCUPLACER score of 86 in sentence skills, or a minimum ACT verbal score of 18, or a minimum SAT verbal score of 425, or completion of a college-level English composition course with a grade of C or above; Mathematics Review I (MAT096)—must meet one of the following: a minimum ACCUPLACER score of 53 in algebra, or a minimum ACT math score of 18, or a minimum SAT math score of 440, or completion of a college-level English composition course with a grade of C or above.

Other admission requirements may include credit hours of qualified transfer credit with a grade of C- or better from a regionally accredited institution or a nationally accredited institution approved and documented by the faculty and dean of the College of Business, or the College of Professional Psychology, at Argosy University or completion of an Associate of Arts or Associate of Science degree from a regionally accredited institution. A maximum of 78 lower-division or 90 total credit hours may be transferred. A minimum written TOEFL score of 500 (paper-based test), 173 (computer-based test), or 61 (Internet-based test) is required for all applicants whose native language is not English or who have not graduated from an institution in which English is the language of instruction.

Official transcripts from approved postsecondary institutions must include a minimum grade point average of 2.0 (on a scale of 4.0) for all academic work completed. Exceptions may be made for extenuating circumstances. All applications must include a completed application form, proof of high school graduation or successful completion of the GED test, official postsecondary transcripts, and a nonrefundable (except in California) application fee. Additional materials are required prior to matriculation. Some programs have additional application requirements or include exceptions to admission requirements. An admissions representative can provide further information.

Application and Information

Argosy University accepts students on a rolling admissions basis year-round, depending on availability of required courses. Applications for admission are available online at http://www.argosy.edu or by contacting one of the campus locations.

Argosy University
205 North Michigan Avenue, Suite 1300
Chicago, Illinois 60601-2250
Phone: 312-899-9900
800-377-0617 (toll-free)
E-mail: auadmissions@argosy.edu
Web site: http://www.argosy.edu

THE ART INSTITUTE OF PHOENIX

PHOENIX, ARIZONA

The Institute

At The Art Institute of Phoenix, students are trained to utilize program-specific technology to bring their creative goals to life. Graduates are prepared for entry-level positions using the specialized skills and competencies employers seek.

Students come to The Art Institute of Phoenix from across United States and abroad. The student population includes recent high school graduates, transfer students, and those who have left a previous employment situation to study and train for a new career. Students are creative, competitive, and open to new ideas. They place great value on an education that prepares them for an exciting entry-level position in the arts. Assistance is available to help students with resume writing, networking, and keeping abreast of what employers are looking for in job candidates.

The Art Institute of Phoenix provides Internet access for students throughout the school. Students may also utilize multiple computer labs, a Learning Resource Center, a student supply store, a Career Services Center, and a student lounge. Many student organizations and clubs exist to build friendships with like-minded classmates who are also refining their creative talents.

Through a special arrangement with select apartment complexes close to the school, The Art Institute of Phoenix offers students the opportunity to live in nearby furnished apartments.

The Art Institute of Phoenix is accredited by the Accrediting Council for Independent Colleges and Schools (ACICS) to award bachelor's degrees, associate degrees, and diplomas. ACICS is listed as a nationally recognized accrediting agency by the U.S. Department of Education. Its accreditation of degree-granting institutions is recognized by the Council for Higher Education Accreditation. ACICS can be contacted at 750 First Street NE, Suite 980, Washington, D.C. 20002; phone: 202-336-6780. The Associate of Applied Science in Culinary Arts degree program is accredited by the American Culinary Federation (ACF). The Bachelor of Arts in Interior Design degree program is accredited by the Council for Interior Design Accreditation.

Location

Phoenix is one of the fastest-growing metropolitan areas in the country. Located in the heart of the beautiful Sonoran Desert, Phoenix is the gateway to cool pine forests, the red rock towers of Sedona, and the Grand Canyon. The city offers sun-filled days and a nightlife that ranges from top comedy and music clubs to the Phoenix Art Museum and Phoenix Symphony Orchestra. Professional sports teams include the Diamondbacks, Suns, Cardinals, and Coyotes.

Majors and Degrees

The Art Institute of Phoenix offers Bachelor of Arts degree programs (thirty-six months) in advertising, culinary arts, digital filmmaking and video production, fashion marketing, game art and design, graphic design, interior design, media arts and animation, visual and game programming, visual effects and motion graphics, and Web design and interactive media. Associate of Applied Science degree programs (sixteen to twenty-one months) are offered in baking and pastry arts, culinary arts, and graphic design.

Academic Programs

The Art Institute of Phoenix is in session year-round. Depending on the program, students graduate in nine to thirty-six months with a diploma, an Associate of Applied Science degree, or a Bachelor of Arts degree in their chosen field.

Academic Facilities

The Art Institute of Phoenix is located in a four-story building in the northwest corner of Phoenix. Students enjoy scenic mountain views from many of the building's large picture windows. With sun streaming into classrooms and computer laboratories, student creativity flows easily. Classroom and computer laboratory facilities are well maintained, with a full-time technology manager located on-site. The culinary arts kitchens are spacious and filled with commercial equipment similar to that with which students will work in entry-level positions. Digital media production students have access to a full television studio and control room, along with editing suites to complete their work.

Costs

Tuition cost varies by program. Prospective students should contact the school for current tuition costs. Other charges include a starting kit for all first-quarter students. Kits vary in price depending on the program of study.

Financial Aid

Financial aid is available for those who qualify. Students who require financial assistance should first complete and submit a Free Application for Federal Student Aid (FAFSA) and meet with a financial aid officer. The officer determines the student's level of need based on a required federal formula, the cost of education, and other factors. Gift aid is available in the form of Federal Pell Grants, Federal Supplemental Educational Opportunity Grants, and veterans' benefits. Loans include Federal Stafford Student Loans, Federal PLUS loans, and alternative loans. Scholarships are available from the school and private sources. Application deadlines and eligibility requirements vary by program.

Faculty

The Art Institute of Phoenix offers personal attention from knowledgeable, professional instructors. Many of the faculty members are working professionals who bring practical knowledge and professional experience to the classroom. The faculty members at The Art Institute of Phoenix are available for student appointments to discuss academic issues. Faculty members also offer tutoring to students in need of extra help.

Student Government

The President's Club is a school organization that promotes the philosophy of "students helping students." Those students selected to join the club assist new students with adjusting to life in Phoenix, studies at The Art Institute of Phoenix, and school activities. Criteria for selection into this club are a minimum GPA of 3.0 at The Art Institute of Phoenix, good attendance, completion of at least one full quarter of study, a desire to assist other students, and responsible behavior.

Admission Requirements

Many prospective students meet with an assistant director of admissions to discuss future goals and plan the admissions process. For admission to The Art Institute of Phoenix, students are evaluated on the basis of previous education, background, and a demonstrated interest in the selected program. Portfolio submission is encouraged but not required.

As part of the application process, students must write two essays stating how an education at The Art Institute of Phoenix will help them to attain their creative goals. Successful admission into The Art Institute of Phoenix and a satisfactory program start is dependent upon the essay; grade point average, as evidenced in transcript evaluation; an evaluation of General Educational Development (GED) test scores; a review of nationally based exams (preferred but not required), such as the SAT or ACT; and a personal interview with an assistant director of admissions. There is a $50 application fee.

Application and Information

To obtain an application, make arrangements for an interview, or tour the school, prospective students should contact:

The Art Institute of Phoenix
2233 West Dunlap Avenue
Phoenix, Arizona 85021-2859
Phone: 602-331-7500
800-474-2479 (toll-free)
Fax: 602-331-5300
Web site: http://www.artinstitutes.edu/phoenix

The Art Institute of Phoenix.

THE ART INSTITUTE OF TUCSON

TUCSON, ARIZONA

The Institute

The Art Institute of Tucson provides students with an educational environment and dedicated faculty members committed to preparing students for entry-level positions in the creative arts. Under the guidance of industry professionals, students learn by doing the types of tasks they are likely to encounter in the workplace. In addition, assistance is available to help students with resume writing, networking, and keeping aware of what employers are looking for in job candidates. The school offers seven bachelor's degree programs and two associate degree programs.

The school offers assistance in helping students secure housing.

The student population includes recent high school graduates, transfer students, and those who have left a previous employment situation to study and train for a new career. Students are creative, competitive, and open to new ideas. They place great value on an education that prepares them for an exciting entry-level position in the arts.

The Art Institute of Tucson places a high value on the quality of student life—both in and out of the classroom. Students participate in a wide variety of activities, including clubs and organizations, community service, and various committees designed to enhance the quality of student life.

The Art Institute of Tucson is accredited by the Accrediting Council for Independent Colleges and Schools (ACICS). Final approval for the change of ownership and the name change (it is currently operating as Tucson Design College) from the Accrediting Council for Independent Colleges and Schools and the Arizona State Board of Private Postsecondary Education is pending.

Location

Tucson is home to nearly 520,000—the largest city in southern Arizona and the second-largest city in the state. Annual events include the Gem and Mineral Show, Folk Festival, and Fourth Avenue Street Fair. There are also museums, performing arts, and sports venues as well as 120 parks.

Majors and Degrees

Bachelor's degree programs are offered in advertising, culinary arts, digital filmmaking and video production, graphic design, interior design, media arts and animation, and Web design and interactive media.

Associate degrees are offered in graphic design and Web design and interactive media.

Academic Programs

The Art Institute of Tucson operates on a year-round, four-quarter system.

Academic Facilities

The Art Institute of Tucson contains classrooms, Mac and PC computer labs, and a library for student use. There is also a bookstore.

Costs

Tuition cost varies by program. Prospective students should contact the school for current tuition costs. Other charges include a starting kit for all first-quarter students. Kits vary in price depending on the program of study.

Financial Aid

Financial aid is available for those who qualify. Students who require financial assistance should first complete and submit a Free Application for Federal Student Aid (FAFSA) and meet with a financial aid officer. The officer determines the level of need based on a required federal formula, the cost of education, and other factors. Gift aid is available in the form of Federal Pell Grants, Federal Supplemental Educational Opportunity Grants, and veterans' benefits. Loans include Federal Stafford Loans, Federal PLUS Loans, and alternative loans. Other scholarships are available from the school and private sources. Application deadlines and eligibility requirements vary by program.

Faculty

Faculty members at The Art Institute of Tucson have professional knowledge that they bring into the classroom. The school's faculty members provide their students with a real-world, relevant educational experience.

Admission Requirements

Applicants must provide proof of high school graduation or achievement of a General Educational Development (GED) certificate as a prerequisite for admission. In lieu of documenting high school graduation or a GED certificate, applicants may provide proof of attaining an associate degree or higher from an accredited institution. An official transcript indicating date of high school graduation, GED certificate (including test scores), or date of college graduation (including degree granted) is required as proof.

All individuals seeking admission to The Art Institute of Tucson are interviewed in person or by phone by an assistant director of admissions, and each applicant must create an original essay of at least 150 words stating how an education at The Art Institute of Tucson would help the student achieve career goals. There is a $50 application fee.

Application and Information

To obtain an application, make arrangements for an interview, or tour the school, students should contact:

The Art Institute of Tucson
5099 East Grant Road, Suite 100
Tucson, Arizona 85712
Phone: 520-318-2700
866-690-8850 (toll-free)
Fax: 520-881-4234
Web site: http://www.artinstitutes.edu/tucson

The Art Institute of Atlanta®, GA; The Art Institute of Atlanta®–Decatur, GA; The Art Institute of Austin[SM], TX; The Art Institute of California[SM]–Inland Empire; The Art Institute of California[SM]–Los Angeles; The Art Institute of California[SM]–Orange County; The Art Institute of California[SM]–Sacramento; The Art Institute of California[SM]–San Diego; The Art Institute of California[SM]–San Francisco; The Art Institute of California[SM]–Sunnyvale; The Art Institute of Charleston[SM], SC, A branch of The Art Institute of Atlanta, GA; The Art Institute of Charlotte®, NC; The Art Institute of Colorado® (Denver); The Art Institute of Dallas®, TX; The Art Institute of Fort Lauderdale®, FL; The Art Institute of Houston®, TX; The Art Institute of Indianapolis[SM], IN*; The Art Institute of Jacksonville[SM], FL, A branch of Miami International University of Art & Design; The Art Institute of Las Vegas®, NV; The Art Institute of Michigan[SM] (Detroit); The Art Institute of New York City®, NY; The Art Institute of Ohio[SM]–Cincinnati**; The Art Institute of Philadelphia®, PA; The Art Institute of Phoenix®, AZ; The Art Institute of Pittsburgh®, PA; The Art Institute of Pittsburgh®–Online Division; The Art Institute of Portland®, OR; The Art Institute of Salt Lake City[SM], UT; The Art Institute of Seattle®, WA; The Art Institute of Tampa[SM], FL, A branch of Miami International University of Art & Design; The Art Institute of Tennessee[SM]–Nashville, A branch of The Art Institute of Atlanta, GA; The Art Institute of Tucson[SM], AZ; The Art Institute of Washington® (Arlington, VA), A branch of The Art Institute of Atlanta, GA; The Art Institute of York–Pennsylvania[SM]; The Art Institutes International Minnesota[SM] (Minneapolis); California Design College[SM] (Los Angeles–Wilshire Blvd.); The Illinois Institute of Art®–Chicago; The Illinois Institute of Art®–Schaumburg; Miami International University of Art & Design[SM], FL; The New England Institute of Art® (Boston, MA).

*The Art Institute of Indianapolis is licensed by the Indiana Commission on Proprietary Education, 302 W. Washington St., Rm. E201, Indianapolis, IN 46204, AC-0080.

**The Art Institute of Ohio–Cincinnati, 8845 Governors Hill Drive, Suite 100, Cincinnati, OH 45249-3317, OH Reg. #04-01-1698B.

BROWN MACKIE COLLEGE–TUCSON

TUCSON, ARIZONA

The College

Brown Mackie College–Tucson is dedicated to providing educational programs that prepare students for entry-level positions in a competitive, rapidly changing workplace. The College provides bachelor's degrees, associate degrees, and certificate programs in the fields of business, health care, legal assistance, criminal justice, and computer technology to approximately 300 students.

Brown Mackie College–Tucson was founded in 1972 as Chaparral College, when Rockland West Corporation formed a partnership with Lamson Business College. In the beginning, it was a career college that offered associate in business degrees and diploma programs focusing on accounting, business, computer training, and secretarial skills. In 1994, Chaparral College became accredited as a junior college and began offering associate of science and associate of arts degrees. In 1996, it received status as a senior college by the Accrediting Council of Independent Colleges and Schools (ACICS).

Originally located at 5001 East Speedway, with a branch location at Oracle and Fort Lowell Roads, the two campuses were merged in 1986 and moved into a new facility at 4585 East Speedway, where the College remains today. In June 2007, Chaparral College was purchased by Education Management Corporation (EDMC) and named Brown Mackie College–Tucson. Located at 210 Sixth Avenue, 33rd Floor, Pittsburgh, Pennsylvania 15222, EDMC has been in business for more than forty years. One of the largest providers of private postsecondary education in North America, EDMC has seventy-five campus locations in twenty-five states and two Canadian provinces.

Brown Mackie College–Tucson is accredited by the Accrediting Council for Independent Colleges and Schools to award bachelor's degrees, associate degrees, and certificates. The U.S. Department of Education and The Council for Higher Education recognize the ACICS as a national accrediting agency. The ACICS can be contacted at 750 First Street NE, Suite 980, Washington, D.C. 20002.

This institution is licensed by the Arizona State Board for Private Postsecondary Education, 1400 West Washington Street, Room 260, Phoenix, Arizona 85007; phone: 620-543-5709.

Location

Tucson is home to nearly 520,000—the largest city in southern Arizona and the second-largest city in the state. Annual events include the Gem and Mineral Show, Folk Festival, and Fourth Avenue Street Fair. There are also museums, performing arts, and sports venues as well as 120 parks. The campus is nonresidential; public transportation and ample free parking are available.

Majors and Degrees

Brown Mackie College–Tucson provides higher education to traditional and nontraditional students through bachelor's degree, associate degree, and certificate programs that assist in enhancing their career opportunities, broadening their perspectives through appropriate general education courses, thinking independently and critically, and improving problem-solving abilities. The College strives to develop within its students the desire for lifelong and continued education.

The Bachelor of Science degree (184 credits) is awarded in accounting, business administration, criminal justice, and legal studies.

The Associate of Science degree (96 credits) is awarded in accounting technology, business management, computer networking and security, criminal justice, early childhood education, information technology, medical assisting, paralegal studies, and surgical technology.

A postbachelor's certificate is awarded in accounting.

Academic Programs

Each College quarter comprises twelve weeks. Bachelor's degree programs require a minimum of sixteen quarters to complete. Associate degree programs require a minimum of eight quarters to complete. Programs are offered on a year-round basis, providing students with the ability to work uninterrupted toward their degrees.

Academic Facilities

A modern facility, Brown Mackie College–Tucson offers more than 22,000 square feet of tastefully decorated classrooms, laboratories, and office space designed to the specifications of the College for its business, medical, and technical programs. Instructional equipment is comparable to current technology used in business and industry today. Modern classrooms for special instructional needs offer full multimedia capabilities with surround sound and overhead projectors accessible through computer, DVD, or VHS. Internet access and instructional resources are available at the College's library.

Costs

Tuition in the 2007–08 academic year for all bachelor's and associate degrees and certificates was $250 per credit hour; fees were $15 per credit hour. Textbook expenses were estimated at $372 per quarter.

Financial Aid

The College maintains a full-time staff of financial aid professionals to assist qualified students in obtaining the financial assistance they require to meet their educational expenses. Available resources include federal and state aid, student loans from private lenders, and federal work-study opportunities, both on and off college premises. Federal assistance programs are administered through the U.S. Department of Education, Office of Student Financial Assistance. Any U.S. citizen, national, or person in the United States for other than temporary reasons who is enrolled or accepted for enrollment may apply for these programs. Most forms of financial assistance are available for each July 1–June 30 award period. Every student considering application for financial aid should request a copy of the current *Student Guide,* published by the U.S. Department of Education. This important document may be obtained in the Student Financial Services Office and assists students in understanding eligibility requirements, the application process, deadlines, and the various forms of grants and loans available.

Each year, the College makes available scholarships of $1000 each to qualifying seniors from area high schools. No more than one scholarship is awarded per high school. In order to qualify, a senior must be graduating from a participating high school, must be maintaining a cumulative grade point average of at least 2.0, and must submit a brief essay. The student's extracurricular activities and community service are also considered. The President's Scholarship is available only to students enrolling in one of the College's degree programs. Students awarded the scholarship must enroll at Brown Mackie College—Tucson between June and September immediately following their high school graduation. Applications for these scholarships can be obtained from the guidance departments of participating high schools. These applications must be completed and returned to the College by March 31. Those awarded scholarships are notified by April 30.

Faculty

Experienced faculty members provide academic support and are committed to the academic and technical preparation of their students. The College has 18 full-time and 35 part-time instructors, with a student-faculty ratio of 15:1. Each student is assigned a faculty adviser.

Admission Requirements

Each applicant for admission is assigned an Assistant Director of Admissions, who directs the applicant through the steps of the admissions process, providing information on curriculum, policies, procedures, and services and assisting the applicant in setting necessary appointments and interviews. To qualify for admission, each applicant must provide documentation of graduation from an accredited high school or from a state-approved secondary education curriculum or provide official documentation of high school graduation equivalency. All transcripts become the property of the College. Admission to the College is based on the applicant's meeting the stated requirements, a review of the applicant's previous educational records, and a review of the applicant's career interests. If previous academic records indicate the College's education and training programs would not benefit the applicant, the College reserves the right to advise the applicant not to enroll. Special requirements for enrollment into certain programs are discussed in the descriptions of those programs.

As part of the admissions process, students are given an assessment of academic skills. Although the results of this assessment do not determine eligibility for admission, they provide the College with a means of determining the need for academic support as well as a means by which the College can evaluate the effectiveness of its educational programs. All new students are required to complete this assessment, which is readministered at the end of the student's program so results may be compared with those of the initial administration.

Application and Information

Applicants must complete and submit an application form, along with documentation of graduation from an accredited high school or state-approved secondary education curriculum or official documentation of high school graduation equivalency.

For additional information, students should contact:

Director of Admissions
Brown Mackie College–Tucson
4585 East Speedway Boulevard, Suite 204
Tucson, Arizona 85712
Phone: 520-327-6866
Fax: 520-325-0108
E-mail: kcooper@brownmackie.edu
Web site: http://www.brownmackie.edu

EMBRY-RIDDLE AERONAUTICAL UNIVERSITY

EMBRY-RIDDLE
AERONAUTICAL UNIVERSITY

PRESCOTT, ARIZONA

The University

Embry-Riddle Aeronautical University's Prescott, Arizona, campus is recognized and respected worldwide as a center for cutting-edge instruction and training for tomorrow's leaders. For the last thirty years, the Prescott campus has developed a reputation based on its leadership role in aviation and aerospace education as well as its commitment to strong academic preparation and a solid learning environment.

Embry-Riddle is a private, independent, four-year university and is accredited by the Commission on Colleges of the Southern Association of Colleges and Schools.

The campus offers twelve undergraduate degree programs, all with a special emphasis on aviation, aerospace, and related fields of global influence. The coed student population of 1,700 undergraduates comes from all fifty states and thirty different countries. There is a close-knit residential atmosphere; nearly 850 students live in three different on-campus residence hall communities that offer both traditional rooms and apartment-style suites. Freshmen are required to live on campus. Most students take advantage of on-campus dining facilities and a variety of meal plan options.

There are more than seventy-five student clubs and organizations, including professional associations, fraternities and sororities, specialty clubs, and intramural sports. The National Association of Intercollegiate Athletics (NAIA) men's soccer and wrestling teams, and the NAIA women's soccer and volleyball teams compete both regionally and nationally. The Golden Eagles precision flight team has consistently ranked among the top in the country in the Safety and Flight Evaluation Conference (SAFECON) competitions and has captured the national championship title six times.

Guided by its worldwide network of alumni, Embry-Riddle's reputation has grown steadily in the aviation, aerospace, and business communities. Within one year of graduation, 96 percent of Embry-Riddle graduates from all campuses are either employed or have decided to continue their education.

Location

Just like its people, the University's location is warm and friendly. Prescott, a mile-high city on the Colorado Plateau, is home to the world's largest stand of ponderosa pine trees. The campus is about 100 miles northwest of Phoenix, 260 miles southeast of Las Vegas, and 375 miles east of Los Angeles. Prescott's climate reflects seasonable weather that is excellent for flying, with daytime averages of 80°F in the summer and 45°F in the winter. The local mountains exhibit the spirit of the rugged West, with students enjoying snow skiing, hiking, mountain biking, kayaking, rock climbing, and tours of the Grand Canyon. Known as a vacation getaway, Prescott offers shopping, entertainment, health, and recreational options in a friendly small-town atmosphere. For a taste of big-city life, Phoenix is a 1½-hour drive. The campus is situated on 539 acres, but campus life is centered in a 1-mile walking radius. The Flight Training Center is located nearby at the Prescott Municipal Airport.

Majors and Degrees

The undergraduate academic preparation provides a strong foundation for all students, whether or not they choose a career in aviation. Each major is a combination of general education, specialized focus, and applied technology.

The Bachelor of Science in aeronautical science, the professional pilot program, emphasizes hands-on training and prepares students for a career in the aviation industry with airlines, corporate and commercial aviation, or the military. Flight courses lead to certification as an instrument-rated multi-engine commercial pilot. Certified Flight Instructor ratings are also available, although they are not required for the degree program. Students may also take professional-level courses in aircraft systems, flight methodology, and many other flight-related topics.

The Bachelor of Science in aeronautics is specially designed to build upon pre-existing experience or training in aviation or other technical fields. It also allows the flexibility to build, from scratch, a major with an aviation focus and a professional outcome. The program provides an opportunity to acquire a broad-based education in aviation-specific courses and related instruction in business, computer science, economics, humanities, communication, social science, mathematics physical science, and other non-aviation-related fields.

The Bachelor of Science in aerospace engineering allows students to focus on the design of either aircraft or spacecraft. The program's focus is primarily on the engineering of mission-oriented vehicles for atmospheric or space flight. Students study aerodynamics, structures, propulsion, space systems, controls, materials, instrumentation, electrical fundamentals, computer applications, orbital mechanics, and design.

The Bachelor of Science in aerospace studies is a unique interdisciplinary degree with unlimited potential. Aerospace studies allows students to customize their undergraduate curriculum to match their specific career goals and interests by choosing three minor areas of study to create their own major. This program produces students who cross boundaries, make creative connections, and become leaders in or out of the aviation and aerospace field.

The Bachelor of Science in applied meteorology provides a practical understanding of the physics and dynamics of the atmosphere and prepares graduates for a range of meteorologist positions in government or industry. Students use a state-of-the-art weather center and computer-equipped classrooms to understand and forecast complex atmospheric phenomena ranging from severe thunderstorms and tornadoes, cyclones, fronts, and jet streams to the global climate and how it is changing. With a focus on climatology and its applications, this program offers areas of concentration in flight, meteorology for aviation operations, military meteorology, and research.

The Bachelor of Science degree in aviation business administration integrates in-depth study of aviation, transportation, and government interface with a strong business foundation. The program focuses on business and management principals, finance and accounting, information systems, technology, communication and quantitative skills, global marketplace awareness, and teamwork dynamics. Specialized aviation-related studies include management, finance, flight operations, and airport management. This is the only aviation business administration program approved by the Aviation Accreditation Board International (AABI).

The Bachelor of Science in aviation environmental science program is the only undergraduate environmental science program in the country with a focus on the aviation and aerospace industry. The program offers a multidisciplinary education with areas of concentration in applied environmental science and environmental management. Graduates have the knowledge and technical skills needed to tackle the unique environmental and safety problems found in the aviation and aerospace industry, such as noise abatement, wildlife habitat, and hazardous materials.

The Bachelor of Science in computer engineering degree gives a broad background in computer hardware design, including embedded control systems, real-time systems, software engineering, and telecommunication systems. The program's emphasis on real-time embedded control systems and hardware/software interfaces provides program graduates with employment opportunities beyond those of graduates of traditional computer engineering programs.

The Bachelor of Science degree in electrical engineering is a systems-oriented program of study that includes analog and digital circuits, communication systems, computers, control systems, electromagnetic fields, energy sources and systems, and electronic materials and devices related to aerospace and avionics.

The Bachelor of Science in global security and intelligence studies (GSIS) program is designed to prepare security and intelligence professionals to work in the interrelated fields of global politics, economics, social change, science, and technology. GSIS graduates become problem-solvers with expertise in such issues as terrorism and asymmetrical warfare, transportation security (especially aviation and aerospace), threats to manufacturing facilities and corporate offices, and threats to computer systems and telecommunications infrastructure.

The Bachelor of Science in mechanical engineering focuses on the design of propulsion or robotic systems, such as autonomous ground, air, or space vehicles. Courses cover robotics, controls, vibration and acoustics, machine design, and numerical modeling.

The Bachelor of Science in space physics prepares students to excel in a wide range of careers and scientific pursuits, from solving problems associated with prolonged space missions to unraveling the mysteries of the universe. Areas of concentration include astrophysics, particle physics and cosmology, exotic propulsion, and remote sensing.

Academic Programs

Along with their major, students may opt to select a minor from many fields, such as air traffic control, Asian studies, aviation safety, or helicopter flight; or they may work toward an Aircraft Dispatcher Certificate. Army and Air Force Reserve Officer Training Corps (ROTC) courses are also available to all Embry-Riddle students and may lead to a position as a commissioned officer.

Education at Embry-Riddle goes far beyond the classroom. Through participation in internships and cooperative education (co-op) arrangements, students in all fields of study gain valuable work experience with companies such as Continental Airlines, Delta Air Lines, the Federal Aviation Administration (FAA), Honeywell, Gulfstream Aerospace Corporation, Lockheed Martin, NASA, Northwest Airlines, the Naval Air Systems Command, the CIA, and Raytheon. Study-abroad programs provide a variety of international study options. A Foreign Language Institute at the Prescott campus offers summer immersion in either Arabic or Chinese. Opportunities for undergraduate research abound, including FAA-supported research exploring wildlife management at airports and NSF-funded research in both astrophysics and emerging threats to aviation facilities.

Academic Facilities

Tucked into the rolling hillsides, the campus blends nature with the layout of its buildings. The new Hazy Library and Learning Center is under final construction and scheduled to open in 2008. The library is home to the Aviation Safety and Security Archives as well as the Kalusa Collection, the world's largest to-scale collection of miniature airplane models. A brand-new dining hall just opened in January 2008; an interfaith chapel is also under construction and will open in 2008 as well.

The Robertson Aviation Safety Center houses the nation's only university level accident investigation laboratory. This outdoor facility features an in-the-field investigation lab for studying wreckage sites of actual aircraft accidents.

Classroom buildings house specialized labs, including the airway science, particle physics, exotic propulsion, optics, and remote sensing labs. There is also a campus observatory housing a CCD (charged coupled device) debris telescope.

The Academic Complex has two computer design labs for engineering students and a weather center. Rooftop weather instrumentation includes state-of-the-art weather observing equipment, a weather radar, and a weather balloon launching facility.

The Aerospace Experimentation and Fabrication Building (AXFAB) offers leading-edge resources to students. Labs include a fabrication suite with a machine shop, materials science and testing labs, structures lab, structural dynamics lab, and space systems lab. Within its labs, students utilize the two-axis electromagnetic shaker to simulate the vibration environment of a space launch, vacuum chambers to simulate space environment, and two stereo-lithography 3-D printers to bring their own designs to life.

Students are able to test their designs in four wind tunnels, three subsonic and one supersonic, located in the Tracy Doryland Wind Tunnel Building. Additional equipment includes a water tunnel for flow visualization and a micro-turbojet used in a rockets and turbine engines course.

The 22,000-square-foot King Engineering and Technology Center houses a computer science classroom, the Computer-Aided Engineering Lab, and the UNIX Lab, which provide students with the latest in computer technologies. This center also houses the Linear Lab, Electrical Engineering Senior Design Lab, Electronics Power Lab, Honeywell Control, System Integration Lab, and the Machine Vision Lab, which specializes in applied research and development leading to the advancement of robust solutions for machine vision, machine perception, and robotics applications.

College of Engineering labs and equipment at the Prescott Campus are easily accessible and used exclusively by undergraduate students. Numerous hands-on lab and design experiences provide students the opportunity to use their knowledge, test their analyses, and work in a team environment.

Two miles from campus, the Embry-Riddle Flight Training Center occupies several buildings at the Prescott Municipal Airport. Currently, the Prescott fleet includes Cessna 172s, Piper Seminoles, an American Champion Decathlon for extreme attitude recovery, a Cessna 182-RG, and two Cessna 150s for the flight team. New DA42 Diamond Twin Stars are be added to the fleet in summer 2008. All aircraft are ADS-b equipped, and the Cessnas and Diamonds are equipped with Garmin G1000 navigation systems. Also at the flight line are flight-training devices (FTDs), including three Cessna 172 and two Seminole Level 6 FTDs (all with 220-degree visual displays), two Frasca 141 FTDs, one Frasca 142 FTD, and an Airbus A320 simulator.

Athletic facilities on campus include an activities hub with indoor volleyball and basketball courts, a fitness center, a training room with a whirlpool, a multipurpose gym, and a matted room for wrestling, aerobics, and martial arts. Other facilities include a softball field, intercollegiate soccer field, tennis courts, sand volleyball courts, a 25-yard swimming pool, racquetball courts, a running track, and a multisport recreation field.

Costs

The 2008–09 academic year tuition for all programs is $13,210 per semester for full-time students. Flight fees are charged in addition to tuition. On-campus housing accommodations range from $2175 to $2350 per semester, depending on the residence hall; the required meal plan for freshmen is $1675 per semester. Students also need to account for the cost of books, transportation, and personal expenses.

Financial Aid

Students and their families find many sources of aid available to assist with paying the costs of a private university. Embry-Riddle participates in all national and state assistance programs. The completion of the Department of Education's Free Application for Federal Student Aid (FAFSA) form is necessary for students to receive consideration for these funds. In addition, Embry-Riddle provides assistance in the form of academic scholarships, need-based grants, on-campus jobs, veterans' educational benefits, and ROTC incentives.

Faculty

One of Embry-Riddle's greatest strengths is its faculty. Faculty members, not graduate students, teach classes. The average class size is 21 students, with an overall student-faculty ratio of 14:1. Faculty members keep regular office hours and consider it their most important role to enhance the individual learning of each student. Faculty members bring both teaching and industry backgrounds to the classroom; most have extensive practical experience in their field, along with outstanding academic credentials.

Admission Requirements

Each student receives individual consideration for admission, which is based on a variety of factors and circumstances. Completion of the Embry-Riddle application for admission begins this process; students also need to submit official transcripts, score reports for either the SAT or ACT, and two letters of recommendation. Acceptance notification takes place throughout the year.

Application and Information

For additional information, including information on campus visits and application forms, students should contact:

Embry-Riddle Aeronautical University Admissions
3700 Willow Creek Road
Prescott, Arizona 86301
Phone: 928-777-6600
800-888-3728 (toll-free)
E-mail: pradmit@erau.edu
Web site: http://www.erauprescott.com

GRAND CANYON UNIVERSITY

PHOENIX, ARIZONA

The University

Founded in 1949, Grand Canyon University (GCU) is an accredited, private, Christian university located in Phoenix, Arizona. The University offers online and campus-based bachelor's and master's degree programs through the Ken Blanchard College of Business, College of Education, College of Nursing and Health Sciences, and College of Liberal Arts. With an online and campus-based enrollment of more than 14,000 students, GCU emphasizes individual attention for both traditional undergraduate students and working professionals. More than just a four-year education, Grand Canyon University (GCU) is a robust living and learning experience that nurtures students' growth physically, mentally, and spiritually.

While surrounding students with the social, cultural, and recreational opportunities of a lifetime, GCU enables them to build a solid academic foundation for a rich and rewarding life. A degree from Grand Canyon University represents a well-rounded education accomplished through a wide range of educational, artistic, social, and spiritual activities. Students enjoy small class sizes, hands-on learning opportunities, and stimulating courses; serve in student government; participate in "Adopt-a-Block," an outreach to the surrounding neighborhoods; become mentors and student counselors or serve in the on-campus ministry; take part in intercollegiate and intramural sports; and enjoy campuswide social events.

For GCU students, their future starts the day they move onto campus. Hegel Hall is a modern dormitory residence featuring all the amenities college students want. Spacious dorm suites include a furnished living room, a private bathroom, and two bedrooms, each equipped with a vanity sink and mirror, individual closets, beds, study desks, and chairs. Telephone, basic cable, and high-speed wireless Internet are also part of the resident's daily life. Designed to facilitate social interaction and serious study, the comfortably appointed suite becomes home to 4 GCU students.

Surrounding the GCU dorms and student apartments is a beautiful, parklike environment and an exciting campus lifestyle. This includes an active student center, complete with a fitness center, a copy center, an outstanding full-service cafeteria, and a gourmet coffee shop, Latté Dah. Students enjoy kicking back in big cushy chairs and catching up on their favorite shows on large-screen plasma TVs. They also enjoy student movie nights and other events on "The Slab," an outdoor gathering area that invites students to take a break and enjoy Arizona's wonderful weather.

While exploring a major field of study in depth at Grand Canyon University, students are exposed to a wide range of experiences both on and off the campus. This diversity is a key element of the University's vision of educating students for successful careers and lives. Even though fellow GCU students come from a wide variety of backgrounds, they all share the same commitment to academic excellence and intellectual growth; they are all pursuing the goal of a high-quality education. GCU students make friends quickly in the coed community, and they share a wealth of new and exciting experiences. Many of the alumni happily report their GCU college roommates and classmates have continued to be great friends and an integral part of their life after college.

Students who enjoy sports should consider GCU their playing field. From intramural athletics to pickup games of Ultimate Frisbee on Mariposa Lawn, they experience life at its fullest. The GCU Antelopes ("Lopes") compete in a variety of Division II intercollegiate sports as well as intramural sports. GCU offers a complete exercise facility outfitted with the finest equipment as well as tennis courts and two indoor basketball courts.

Beyond the fun, there's faith. GCU students can expect to be part of a student body that comes together to celebrate a mutual faith. Students see the celebration of that faith at the Gathering (a contemporary evening chapel), at the Grand Celebration (a weekly worship assembly), through GCU's campus and community ministries and mission trips. Chapel meetings, which feature music, drama, and speakers from various denominational backgrounds, offer the opportunity to become energized and inspired by a supportive Christian community.

To help prospective and current students achieve career goals, Grand Canyon University provides comprehensive guidance and resources for lifelong career development. GCU workshops provide students with valuable information on topics such as resume writing, interview preparation, developing job leads through networking, and adapting to changes associated with local business conditions.

GCU holds the following accreditations: the Higher Learning Commission of the North Central Association of Colleges and Schools (30 North LaSalle Street, Suite 2400, Chicago, Illinois 60602-2504; telephone: 800-621-7440 (toll-free); Web site: http://www.ncahigherlearningcommission.org/); the Association of Collegiate Business Schools and Programs (ACBSP), through the Ken Blanchard College of Business, for the following business degrees: Bachelor of Science (B.S.) with majors in accounting, business administration, and marketing and Master of Business Administration (M.B.A.); and the Commission on Collegiate Nursing Education (One Dupont Circle NW, Suite 530, Washington, D.C. 20036; telephone: 202-887-6791) and the Arizona State Board of Nursing for the Bachelor of Science in Nursing degree program.

The Arizona State Department of Education has given formal approval of the work done at the University for the certification of elementary and secondary teachers and for the renewal of certificates.

Location

New students quickly discover there is more to the Grand Canyon University experience than classroom learning and campus living. Grand Canyon University is located just minutes from downtown Phoenix, Arizona's state capital and one of the fastest-growing regions in the nation. The greater Phoenix metropolitan area, known as the "Valley of the Sun" for its more than 300 days of sunshine each year, offers numerous educational, social, cultural, and recreational activities that enhance university life. GCU is next door to myriad urban activities and attractions, including cultural and artistic centers, world-class concerts, five major professional sports teams, and expansive shopping malls plus all the outdoor attractions expected from a city famous for its year-round sunshine, including golf, hiking, biking, horseback riding, and water sports.

Within a 2-hour drive of Grand Canyon University's campus is some of the best snow skiing in the Western United States. GCU students flourish in the school's Southwestern environment. Surrounded by rugged mountains, lush valleys, and the arid beauty of the Sonoran Desert, Grand Canyon University students feel a part of the larger human experience.

Majors and Degrees

Grand Canyon University comprises four renowned institutes of education (Ken Blanchard College of Business, College of Liberal Arts, College of Education, and College of Nursing and Health Sciences) and more than 100 esteemed academic programs. Specific study areas include accounting, applied management, art (art education and graphic design), athletic training, biochemistry, biology (environmental, general, human, and secondary teaching), business administration, chemistry (general and secondary teaching), Christian studies (applied ministry: biblical and theological studies, applied ministry: pastoral, applied ministry: worship, and applied ministry: youth), communications (public relations and broadcasting), corporate fitness and wellness, elementary education, English literature, English teaching, history, history education, international studies, justice studies, marketing, mathematics, mathematics engineering, mathematics secondary teaching, music education (choral conducting and instrumental conducting), nursing, organizational sociology, philosophy, physical education, physical science, physics (secondary teaching), political science, psychology, public safety administration, recreation, science for elementary teachers, sociology, special education, and speech teaching.

Academic Programs

The Grand Canyon University curriculum is challenging and radiates from a strong core of liberal arts and sciences. The University provides both traditional and innovative programs that enable students to think critically and creatively, solve problems through open-minded analysis, and communicate effectively. Academic habits acquired at Grand Canyon University stay with Grand Canyon University graduates, enabling them to live flexible lives, to be open to new career opportunities, and to develop confidence in their ability to learn and adapt.

The curriculum at Grand Canyon University is not easy. It requires the highest levels of personal commitment, intellectual honesty, and academic diligence. The course work is rigorous but helps individuals discover their talents and perfect their skills.

Academic Facilities

Grand Canyon University consists of thirty-six buildings on a 90-acre campus. The campus features the Fleming Library, which houses a collection of more than 166,000 volumes, 700 periodicals, newspapers, microfilm, and audiovisual materials. Fleming Library is a member of the CCLC network and as a designated depository receives a variety of government documents. Library holdings are expanded by CD-ROM databases, computerized database searches, and interlibrary loans. Computers housed in the library have Internet access to assist students. Grand Canyon University also offers all students access to the Online Library.

The majority of classes are held in the Fleming Classroom Building, with additional classes held in the Weidenaar Classroom Building, Wallace Building, Williams Building, Tell Science Building, and College of Nursing and Health Sciences. Ethington Memorial Theatre sets the perfect stage for drama and other productions, with more than 300 seats. The C. J. and Thema Smith Arts Complex houses the A. P. Tell Gallery and other tailored creative spaces. The Tell Science Building and College of Nursing are both equipped with state-of-the-art laboratory, computer, multimedia, and clinical learning spaces.

There are two computer labs on campus, both outfitted with new Dell OptiPlex computers and 17-inch monitors. The computer labs offer Internet access and a host of applications for use outside of the classroom. Each student has an individual login ID and secured space on a server to store personal files. In addition to the lab computers, wireless access is available for students with laptops. During 2007, the University planned a $6-million renovation that includes an aquatics center for competitions and student's leisure use; a desert walk; the opening of the promenade; the construction of laboratories (including wet labs) for the purpose of academic programs; updating and expanding the library; the construction of The Rock, a student social center with a rock-climbing wall, cafés, music listening and memorabilia, and other opportunities sponsored by Alice Cooper; and the converting the entire campus to wireless.

Costs

The application fee is $100. In 2007–08, students pursuing undergraduate professional studies paid $375 per credit hour. Traditional undergraduate students taking 1–11 credits paid $580 per credit hour. Students carrying 12–18 credits paid block tuition of $6960 per semester; students carrying 19 or more credits paid block tuition plus $580 for each credit hour above 19. All traditional undergraduate students taking 9 or more credits were charged a $250 facilities fee each semester.

In 2007–08, students living in dorm rooms paid approximately $1200 to $6200 per semester for room and board, depending on individual desires. One-bed, one-bath units in the North Rim Apartments cost about $3400 per semester; two-bed, one-bath units, about $3900; and two-bed, two-bath units about $4700. Although phone service is the responsibility of the student, basic cable service is included in the rent. Grand Canyon University reserves the right to change all fees and charges, without notice, if necessary.

Financial Aid

Grand Canyon University has made a commitment to their students by keeping costs down year after year and focusing its dollars on what benefits students directly. This effort has fostered an educational experience that offers high value and quality for the educational investment made. GCU's Office of Finance and the Business Office are committed to working with the individual and their family to discuss various financial options and ensure every available resource is utilized to meet their personal financial needs.

More than 80 percent of Grand Canyon University students receive some form of financial assistance to help meet the cost of their education. In addition to federal and state financial aid, Grand Canyon University has academic and other specific-criteria scholarships and aid available. Grand Canyon University also offers Federal Work-Study programs, on-campus part-time jobs, connections to providers of off-campus jobs, and federal community service opportunities.

Faculty

Grand Canyon University's professors are highly qualified in their respective fields, having garnered many awards as authors, presenters, and teachers. They give individual attention to students, stress mutual interaction with others, and use cutting-edge, research-based pedagogy to convey the most current information. With a 13:1 student-teacher ratio, classes at GCU are small, so students enjoy the highest level of personal attention from professors who know them by name. Professors at GCU are at their student's side every step of the way, helping them explore their academic gifts. They are also spiritual visionaries who help learners incorporate their faith regardless of the discipline they pursue.

Student Government

The ASGCU is GCU's student-led government. The student-elect President is the direct link between the undergraduate student body and the GCU administration. The President advocates for the needs of the student body and is the person the administration looks to when seeking student opinion on decisions made by the University. The President oversees the cabinet, which includes the Vice President, Intramurals Coordinator, Marketing Director, Community Service Director, Events Coordinator, Communications Director, and the Student Voice Director.

Admission Requirements

For admission to Grand Canyon University, students should submit an application for admission and the application fee to the University's Office of Admission. Freshmen must submit their official high school transcript and/or GED scores and have their ACT or SAT scores submitted to Grand Canyon University. Transfer students must have their transcripts forwarded to Grand Canyon University.

Application and Information

Grand Canyon University operates on a rolling admission system. Applicants generally receive an admission decision within ten days after all required documents are on file in the Office of Admission. It is to the student's advantage to apply as early as possible. Applications for financial aid and housing cannot be completely processed and transcripts are not evaluated until the admission application is complete.

For further information and application materials, students should contact:

Office of Enrollment
Grand Canyon University
3300 West Camelback Road
Phoenix, Arizona 85017
Phone: 800-486-7085 (toll-free)
E-mail: admissionsground@gcu.edu
Web site: http://www.gcu.edu/petersons

NORTHERN ARIZONA UNIVERSITY

FLAGSTAFF, ARIZONA

The University

Northern Arizona University (NAU) is a fully accredited, state-supported, four-year institution with 11,945 full-time undergraduate students on its main campus. Since 1899, the University has made a major commitment to undergraduate education, and its goal is to preserve a friendly campus atmosphere and close student-faculty relationships through classroom teaching of the highest quality and faculty guidance for each student.

The University is composed of the Colleges of Applied Health and Human Services, Arts and Letters, Education, Engineering and Natural Sciences, and Social and Behavioral Sciences; the W. A. Franke College of Business; and the School of Forestry. More than 150 undergraduate, master's, and doctoral degrees are offered in a number of interdisciplinary and preprofessional majors.

The University has a strong commitment to student advising, and regular office hours are maintained by faculty members. The Gateway Student Success Center offers academic advising services and career exploration assistance for all students who are undecided on a degree program. An average class size of 27 is another example of the institution's attention to high-quality education.

As a residential campus, Northern Arizona University provides an atmosphere of friendship and community. Fifty percent of the undergraduate students live in the eighteen residence halls and 226 family housing apartments located on the campus. Of the 11,945 full-time undergraduates enrolled in the 2006 fall semester, 4,853 were men (41 percent) and 7,092 were women (59 percent).

The campus includes three student unions, a student health center, an Olympic-size swimming and diving complex, a 16,230-seat multiuse wooden dome, and a multipurpose recreational facility.

Northern Arizona University is an Equal Opportunity/Affirmative Action institution.

Location

Northern Arizona University's 730-acre mountain campus is located in Flagstaff, a community with 61,000 residents. Flagstaff is located at an elevation of 7,000 feet, just south of the 12,600-foot-high San Francisco Peaks, a major winter-sports center. The University is at the junction of Interstate Highways 40 (U.S. 66) and 17, less than a 3-hour drive from Phoenix and about a 5-hour drive from Tucson, Arizona; Albuquerque, New Mexico; and Las Vegas, Nevada. The city is served by Amtrak, Greyhound buses, and a commercial airline. The campus is surrounded by scenic beauty and natural wonders such as the Grand Canyon and, a student favorite, Oak Creek Canyon. The varied landscape of mountains, gorges, forests, and lakes provides the University with natural classrooms and laboratories for research as well as recreation.

Majors and Degrees

Northern Arizona University offers baccalaureate degrees in ninety-one major areas, embracing most of the recognized fields in the arts and sciences and a number of interdisciplinary majors. The University also offers a number of specialized programs, including criminal justice, dental hygiene, forestry, hotel and restaurant management, and parks and recreation management.

Academic Programs

A four-year baccalaureate degree program at Northern Arizona University requires the successful completion of 120 semester hours of course work, including 35 hours of liberal studies courses. The liberal studies program consists of foundation studies and studies in various disciplines designed to assist students in cultivating their abilities to recognize significant problems and to define, analyze, and defend solutions in a variety of contexts. Major-field requirements vary from 35 to 73 semester hours. Students may combine a major field with one or more 18-hour minors, take two majors or an extended major of 63 to 65 hours in a field of their interest, or select a merged major program.

Northern Arizona University has a long-established honors program, which is designed to challenge the talented student. This leads to graduation with honors, and honors students may elect to take the special degree of Bachelor of Arts: Honors. The program provides special courses and seminars and offers superior students opportunities for independent study and research.

A three-year bachelor's degree program is available, offering intellectual and academic challenges for well-prepared and motivated students and allowing them to take the fast track to graduation and graduate programs.

Off-Campus Programs

The University actively cooperates in the work and research programs of several major scientific institutions that are located close to its campus. These include the Lowell Observatory; the U.S. Naval Observatory's Flagstaff station; various facilities of the U.S. Geological Survey, including its space-oriented Astrogeology Center; the U.S. Forest Service Rocky Mountain and Range Experiment station; and the Museum of Northern Arizona and its multidisciplinary Colton Research Center. The specialized libraries, laboratories, and other facilities of these institutions are available to qualified students at the University. Northern Arizona University also conducts scientific field work in many of the distinctive natural areas of northern Arizona, including the nearby Grand Canyon.

Northern Arizona University offers study-abroad opportunities at more than fifty universities in thirty countries, including Australia, Canada, China, Finland, France, Germany, Great Britain, Guatemala, Ireland, Italy, Japan, Mexico, Netherlands, New Zealand, South Korea, Spain, Sweden, and Switzerland. Opportunities to study abroad in conjunction with the University Studies Abroad Consortium offer another twenty-four locations. Students may study for a semester or a year. Through field trips and classroom study, students explore the history, literature, language, and culture of these regions. All students except freshmen may apply.

Through the National Student Exchange program, students have an opportunity to broaden their educational horizons by attending a college or university in another state for one semester or one year while paying tuition and fees at NAU. There are more than 180 participating institutions nationwide.

Academic Facilities

Northern Arizona University's facilities for education and research are extensive. The University's Cline Library provides both individual student and group research, study, and computing. Its collections include books, movies, audio recordings, and the Colorado Plateau Archives. The library's Web site provides access to electronic books, journals, services, and digital archives 24 hours a day, seven days a week. Within the library, students have access to 180 computers, group study rooms, a coffee shop, and a multimedia production workstation.

State-of-the-art laboratories serve students in the sciences and health professions. Specially designed studios, workrooms, theaters, auditoriums, and an art gallery are available to students in the creative arts. Closed-circuit television hookups, language laboratories, and an observatory are used regularly by students for both learning and research.

The University makes extensive use of the spectacular Colorado Plateau country surrounding its campus as a natural laboratory for anthropology, biology, ecology, environmental sciences, geology, geophysics, paleontology, and other sciences. Prehistoric Indian ruins and the living cultures of the Navajo, Hopi, and many other Native American peoples of the Southwest provide rich resources for students of archaeology, anthropology, ethnology, and linguistics. Students have access to the 50,000-acre Centennial Forest for environmental and forestry research. The area's 7,000-foot elevation and unusually clear, dry air have made it a major center for astronomy and the atmospheric sciences.

Costs

For 2007–08, the charges for an academic year of two semesters for an in-state student were tuition and fees, $4844, and average board and room, $6432. Books and supplies averaged $828. The total estimated cost for Arizona residents was $12,104 per academic year. The out-of-state tuition and fees were $14,678, for an academic-year cost of $21,938. This does not include travel or personal expenses, which vary for each student. All costs are subject to change by the Arizona Board of Regents.

Financial Aid

Northern Arizona University maintains an extensive program of financial assistance to aid students in pursuing their educational goals. The amount of financial aid awarded to a student is based upon the student's need level, as computed from the Free Application for Federal Student Aid (FAFSA). However, some scholarships are awarded on the basis of a student's demonstration of academic excellence and/or participation in various University activities.

In the 2006–07 academic year, more than $110 million was available for loans, scholarships, grants, veterans' benefits, and work-study programs. About 68 percent of the students received some form of financial aid.

Along with grants, loans, and scholarships, on- and off-campus employment is available to help students meet financial obligations. More than 4,500 NAU students are currently employed in a wide variety of jobs on the campus.

Faculty

Northern Arizona University's faculty is made up of outstanding and dedicated professionals. More than 56 percent of the 755 full-time and 737 part-time faculty members hold doctoral degrees. Many are nationally distinguished scientists and scholars. The student-faculty ratio is 16:1, with more than 83 percent of the classes taught by faculty members rather than graduate assistants.

Student Government

Each student who enters the University is a member of the Associated Students of Northern Arizona University (ASNAU), which represents the students' interests in all matters that affect them.

Other student groups include the Associated Students for Women's Issues, Association of University Residence Halls, Pan-Hellenic Council, and Inter-Fraternity Council. Students can belong to one or more of the 120 student groups and organizations.

Admission Requirements

New freshmen are admitted if they have a cumulative GPA of 3.0 or better (on a 4.0 scale) or a minimum ACT composite score of 22 (24 for non-Arizona residents) or a minimum combined SAT score of 1040 (1100 for nonresidents) or a top 25 percent class rank and have no deficiencies in the high school course requirements. High school course requirements include 4 units of English, 4 units of math, 3 units of laboratory science, 2 units of social studies, 2 units of foreign language, and 1 unit of fine art. Students with both a math deficiency and a lab science deficiency are not admissible.

New freshmen are considered for admission if they have a cumulative GPA between 2.5 and 2.99 or a top 50 percent class rank and have no more than one deficiency in any two of the subject areas in the high school course requirements listed above. Transfer students who have earned fewer than 12 transferable academic semester credits must meet the same criteria as new freshmen.

Transfer students are offered admission if they have completed an associate degree, the Arizona General Education Curriculum (AGEC), or the California Inter-segmental General Education Transfer Curriculum (IGETC). Transfer students who have earned more than 12 college credits should visit NAU's Web site for complete admission requirements.

The priority deadlines are March 1 for the fall semester, December 1 for the spring semester, and May 1 for summer sessions. Applications and supporting documents received after these dates are processed on a space-available basis.

Application and Information

For more information, students should consult the University Web site or contact the Office of Admissions.

Office of Undergraduate Admissions
Northern Arizona University
Box 4084
Flagstaff, Arizona 86011-4084
Phone: 928-523-5511
888-628-2968 (toll-free)
E-mail: undergraduate.admissions@nau.edu
Internet: http://home.nau.edu

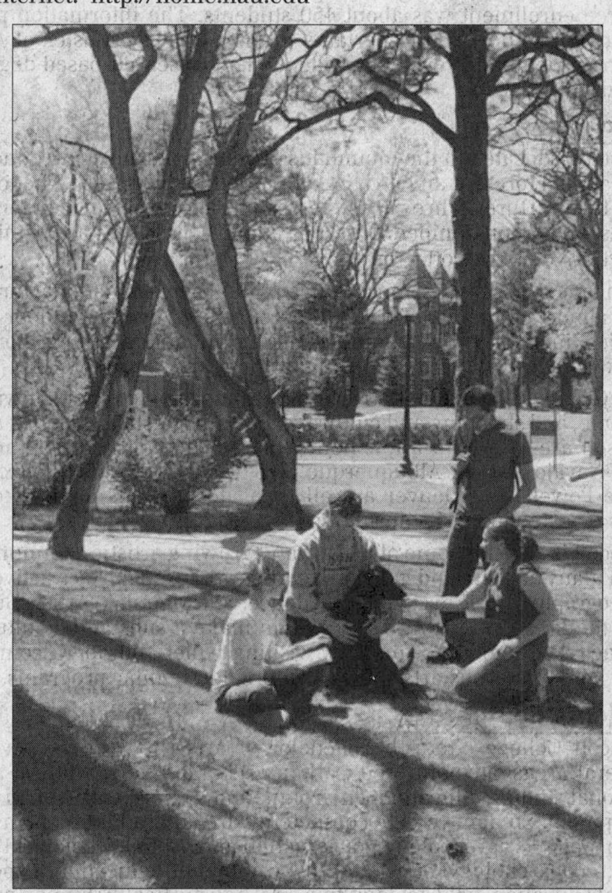

A friendly residential campus and the four-season climate of Flagstaff, Arizona, attract about 14,500 undergraduate students each year to Northern Arizona University.

PRESCOTT COLLEGE
Resident Degree Program
PRESCOTT, ARIZONA

The College

Prescott College is a small, private liberal arts college dedicated to environmental protection; social justice; service learning; experiential education; small, innovative classes; a large field-based curriculum; and the integration of the intellectual, emotional, spiritual, and social development of students. Prescott College, founded in 1966, is a small college trying to make a big difference in the world.

At Prescott College, a student's education is as individual as he or she is. The College believes that education should be personalized—a meaningful activity that goes beyond imparting facts. A Prescott College education instills values, critical-thinking skills, and the ability to adapt to the ever-changing internal landscape of ideas and knowledge as well as the ever-changing external landscape of today's social and physical ecology.

Prescott College offers bachelor's, master's, and Ph.D. degrees. A bachelor's degree can be earned via one of two routes: as a full-time resident student or as an adult student with limited residency. These routes are referred to, respectively, as the Resident Degree Program (RDP) and the Adult Degree Program (ADP). The 2006–07 resident degree enrollment was about 450 students. The information provided in this description pertains to the RDP. The Master of Arts degree is a limited-residency, independent, research-based degree program.

Location

Prescott is located in the mountains of central Arizona, surrounded by national forest at an elevation of more than 5,200 feet. The town is at the juncture of three ecosystems: interior chaparral, Ponderosa pines, and Pinon-Juniper. Desert or alpine ecosystems are within a short drive of Prescott.

With four mild seasons, more than a million acres of national forest, and almost 800 miles of trails, Prescott offers diverse outdoor activities, including rock climbing, hiking, mountain biking, horseback riding, and nearby canoeing, rafting, and snow skiing.

The Grand Canyon, the red rocks of Sedona, the old mining town of Jerome, and shopping and cultural events in Flagstaff, Phoenix, and Tucson are all within a few hours' drive. The Four Corners area, The Navajo Nation, Albuquerque, Las Vegas, San Diego, Mexico, Lake Powell, and Denver are all great destinations for weekend trips or extended visits during breaks.

Prescott is also the home of a lively and growing artistic community, with many art fairs and gallery openings. Many people are active in photography, music, weaving, and dance. The Mountain Artists Guild and the Prescott Fine Arts Association make a substantial cultural impact. The Phoenix Symphony, visiting ballet and opera companies, and numerous arts shows also provide regular programs.

Majors and Degrees

Prescott College offers the Bachelor of Arts (B.A.) degree in six general areas: adventure education, arts and letters, cultural and regional studies, education, environmental studies, and human development. Students create competence-based graduation plans in such topics as agroecology, conservation, counseling, ecological design, ecopsychology, education, environmental education, experiential education, field ecology, fine arts, holistic health, human ecology, literature, natural history, peace studies, philosophy, photography, psychology, religion, social and political studies, wilderness leadership, and writing.

Academic Programs

Prescott College is known for its innovative approach to higher education. It offers small classes (a student-faculty ratio of 10:1 in classrooms), extensive field work (a student-faculty ratio of 5:1 in the field), a close community atmosphere, and the opportunity for students to design their own educational paths. The philosophy of experiential education emphasizes the concept that learning is a lifelong process that helps students gain competence, creativity, and self-direction. In cooperation with an outstanding faculty, students are able to work in such special interdisciplinary fields as cultural and regional studies, ecopsychology, education and interpretation, human ecology, outdoor adventure education, social and political studies, and wilderness leadership.

Academic Facilities

Prescott College does not have a sprawling campus with ivy-covered towers. The campus, located near downtown Prescott, is an eclectic mix of buildings that once served other purposes. "Recycling" buildings is one tangible way in which the College demonstrates sustainability and minimizes its footprint upon the environment.

Prescott College's recently completed building, the Crossroads Center, incorporates various recycled or environmentally friendly elements in its design and construction. For example, the bathrooms feature original murals designed by Prescott students. The granite used in the murals was excess material donated to the project by a local enterprise that manufactures and installs countertops.

Many classes at the College are held in the field. Prescott uses the Southwest for ecological field studies, wilderness pursuits, social observations, artistic endeavors, and therapeutic facilitation. The fragile Southwestern desert can convey to students the vulnerability of the Equatorial rain forest and the destructibility of the Siberian tundra. The proximity to the Mexican border provides access to the crucial interactions between developing world politics, economics, and social and environmental issues. Thus, the Southwest provides a unique microcosm of the rapidly changing globe.

The Prescott College Information Commons (library) has a collection of more than 28,000 volumes, 125 microforms, 1,200 audiocassettes and videocassettes, and 408 periodical titles, all of which relate specifically to the College's program offerings. The Information Commons is computer-networked with all the regional libraries in the area, including two other college libraries and the public libraries. If students have difficulty locating information from any of these sources, the College librarian borrows books through the interlibrary loan system. Because the College places great emphasis on student services, faculty and staff members work diligently to assist each student in finding all information necessary for his or her pursuit of knowledge.

There are three fully equipped computer labs on campus. All labs are staffed full-time by a competent team of computer professionals and College work-study students. Laser printers are available, and students have access to the Internet for research and e-mail. The largest lab houses IBM-compatible computers. The Geographic Information Science Lab has its own computer lab for conducting research in land-use planning and management. The College also offers a Mac lab for fine arts students who are interested in graphic manipulation and digital imaging.

In addition, the College has a campus in Tucson and three off-campus research stations—Kino Bay, Walnut Creek Station, and Wolfberry Farm. The Tucson campus of Prescott College serves students who are enrolled in either the Adult Degree Program, through which working adults earn a bachelor's degree, or the Master of Arts degree program.

The Kino Bay Center for Cultural and Ecological Studies is Prescott's field station on the Sonoran shores of the Gulf of California, one of the most remote and unexplored seas remaining in the world today. The Kino Bay Center provides educational opportunities for hands-on field study in the areas of marine studies, environmental sciences, resource conservation and management, cultural studies, Latin American studies, adventure education, writing, and Spanish language studies.

Wolfberry Farm is Prescott College's experimental farm dedicated to education, demonstration, and research in agroecology. The 36-acre farm is located 20 miles southwest of Prescott in Skull Valley, a town with a rich agricultural history. Students address the question: Can agriculture be more ecologically sustainable and economically viable? They experiment with water-saving irrigation technologies, regional and adapted crops, specialty crops, and fertility-generating rotations.

The Walnut Creek Station for Educational Research is run through a collaborative partnership between Prescott College, Yavapai College, Sharlot Hall Museum, Northern Arizona University, and the Prescott National Forest. During the high season, two or three classes per week use the station for courses, including Ecopsychology, Interpreting Nature Through Art and Photography, Geographical Information Systems, Drawing and Painting the Southwestern Landscape, Aboriginal Living Skills, Wildlife Management, Riparian Restoration, and many independent studies.

In addition, the station hosts research projects such as the Hantavirus Longitudinal Study, which was funded by the Centers for Disease Control; the Arenavirus Distribution Study, funded by the National Institutes of Health; an Arizona Department of Water Resources inventory and monitoring study grant; and the Rattlesnake Radio Telemetry Project.

Costs

Tuition for 2007–08 is $19,980; tuition increases may occur in July of each year.

Financial Aid

The types of financial aid available are Federal Pell Grants, Prescott College grants, Arizona State Student Incentive Grants, Federal Supplemental Educational Opportunity Grants, student employment, Federal Stafford Student Loans, the Arizona Voucher Program, campus employment, and scholarships. More than 67 percent of the students at Prescott College receive financial aid.

Prescott College uses the Free Application for Federal Student Aid (FAFSA) to determine a student's financial need. Students wishing to apply for aid for the fall term should complete the financial aid form by April 15 for priority funding. Aid is awarded on a first-come, first-served basis until all available funds are used. FAFSA forms take four to six weeks to process, so students should submit them early, even if their plans are indefinite. Students who complete forms online may experience a quicker response than those who complete paper applications.

Faculty

Faculty members at Prescott College are devoted solely to the instruction of students. They are not burdened by the traditional "publish or perish" mandate faced by most educators; instead, they direct their energy toward being innovative instructors, positive role models, mentors, advisers, and friends. The College recognizes the importance of individualized attention and small classes. Faculty members are committed to the educational mission of Prescott College and thoroughly enjoy teaching, participating in College social activities, and working with individual students to help them comprehend challenging material. Approximately 60 percent of the 45 full-time RDP faculty members hold doctorates or terminal degrees.

Student Government

Students participate in all levels of governance at Prescott College. Currently, 1 student is a full voting member of the Board of Trustees. Students are also represented on hiring committees. The Student Union is composed of all full-time students, each of whom has a vote.

Admission Requirements

In evaluating an applicant, the Admissions Committee seeks evidence of preparation for college-level academic work, a strong sense of community, and a desire to become a self-directed learner. The Admissions Committee looks for the ability to plan and make decisions and commitments and carry them out effectively. The applicant's essays, letter of recommendation, and transcripts are the strongest determining factors in the admission decision. Visits to the College and personal interviews are strongly recommended; in some cases, they are required. Students who consider applying to Prescott College should first attempt to gain a thorough understanding of the College's educational philosophy and practices.

Prescott College has created a special learning environment that requires motivation, maturity, and a desire to be actively involved in learning.

Application and Information

The Admissions Office strongly encourages applicants to submit all required application materials by the priority filing date. Complete files are then reviewed by the Admissions Committee, and admissions decisions are communicated by the notification date. Files that are received or completed after the priority filing date are still considered on a rolling basis.

Once students are offered admission to an incoming class, they must submit a tuition deposit prior to the reply date to give evidence of intention to enroll and to reserve a space in that class. Tuition deposits are nonrefundable; applicants are advised to submit them only after determining that they are ready to commit to Prescott College. Tuition deposits received after the reply date are accepted on a first-come, first-served basis until the class has filled. Students whose deposits are received after the class is filled are placed on a wait list.

Applications for fall should be received by March 1; for spring, the priority filing date is November 1. The reply dates (deposit due dates) for fall and spring are, respectively, May 1 and December 1. Applications that are received or completed after the priority filing date are still considered. These applications are reviewed after those that were received and completed by the priority filing date.

For more information, students should contact:

Resident Degree Program–Admissions
Prescott College
220 Grove Avenue
Prescott, Arizona 86301
Phone: 928-350-2100
877-350-2100 (toll-free)
E-mail: admissions@prescott.edu
Web site: http://www.prescott.edu

Prescott College students experience active education in a Southwestern classroom.

COLLEGE DATA CENTER • ARIZONA

UNIVERSITY OF ADVANCING TECHNOLOGY

TEMPE, ARIZONA

The University

The University of Advancing Technology (UAT) is a unique, technology-infused private college founded by a techno-geek for techno-geeks. Its mission is to educate students in the fields of advancing technology to become innovators of the future. UAT's campus culture is devoted to continually nurturing a thriving geek community where everyone's personal lives and professional aspirations revolve around technology. UAT offers students a well-rounded education in a nontraditional setting. Students who are seeking a strictly career-oriented technical college experience will not find it here. Because of UAT's dedication to both scholastic excellence and technological innovation, it stands apart in academia as an ideal destination for the geeks of the world who feel disenfranchised by conventional institutions of higher learning. For the student who is looking at the future of technology and wishes to become a vital part of it, UAT beckons.

The beginning of the twenty-first century is an exciting time to be in the technology community, and UAT is serious about technology. As the twenty-first century unfolds, it is becoming more and more apparent how technology in all its manifestations profoundly alters how people work, live, play, and interact with each other. UAT students benefit from their fundamental understanding of both theoretical and applied aspects of technology. As technologists, UAT students see that there will always be newer and newer tools created to address mankind's emergent needs and desires. Changing the world through technology is inherent in UAT's mission. Current subjects of ongoing research and scholarship at UAT include robotics and embedded systems, artificial life programming, network security, game development, and other areas of advanced technology.

UAT has always devoted all of its resources to creating a vital academic environment where students are challenged to achieve, explore new and traditional concepts, and practice what they learn in real-world situations. This combination of research, scholarship, and application creates technically adept graduates who are equally at home in academia and the working world and valued by both. UAT graduates thrive in the digital age and meet and surpass every expectation of their high-technology employers and peers. They enter the professional world with accredited associate and bachelor's degrees, and many return to pursue a master's degree in the Graduate College of Applied Technology.

When the University of Advancing Technology was founded in 1983 (as the CAD Institute), it was conceived as a small school for training engineers and architects in the completely new field of computer-aided engineering. Its original students came to the CAD Institute seeking professional development training and certifications. From this beginning as a technical school, the institution became involved with advances in computer graphics and unique approaches to technology education. In 1998, the school moved to the new campus in Tempe, which was designed in accordance with Feng Shui principles. In 2002, the school changed its name to University of Advancing Technology to reflect its current broad technology focus.

UAT's 1,200 students (from all fifty states and many other countries) still find plenty of time to time to participate in clubs and other activities that enhance UAT's geek-friendly environment, such as ancient games, anime, technology philosophy, Yu-Gi-Oh, game developers, Web development, biking, C++, and photography. Special on-campus events include live-action games, Oktoberfest, LAN parties, Guitar Hero tournaments, and Thanksgiving dinner.

At any time, day or night, there are groups of students pounding coffee while working on course work and projects, looking to create the next big thing. It is not uncommon to see students burning the midnight oil, pulling all-nighters, exchanging ideas, and searching for solutions to perfect their creative innovations. There are students on their own laptops and PDAs, interacting and creating. There are also gatherings of students and instructors engaged in discussions of the latest technology developments and how they can make them better. UAT has an academic and social environment that integrates the contemporary and advancing principles of education and technology with its Year-Round Balanced Learning (YRBL) teaching model to create a unique collaborative educational environment.

Location

Located in sunny Tempe, Arizona, near the heart of downtown Phoenix, a booming urban center in the Sonoran desert, the University of Advancing Technology is 4 hours from Mexico and 2 hours from snowboarding. The campus is accessible from all parts of the Phoenix metropolitan region by public transportation, bicycle, or automobile. Students live on campus in Founder's Hall, the resident student complex, or off campus in nearby neighborhoods. The University is close to major freeways, bus lines, and Sky Harbor Airport, which is a major international airport that serves the entire Phoenix metropolitan area. Other local amenities include shopping, arts districts, and other attractions associated with a dynamic urban center.

Arizona is a land of incredible beauty, contrast, and opportunity. Tempe is located in the "Valley of the Sun", which is surrounded by beautiful mountain ranges. Within a short drive are attractions like the Grand Canyon (4½ hours), a variety of lakes and rivers (30–90 minutes), the red rocks of Sedona (2 hours), and the exquisite Sonoran Desert, just outside of town. UAT is close to every desert sport imaginable—golf, mountain biking, hiking, swimming, rollerblading, and skateboarding.

Majors and Degrees

UAT offers Bachelor of Arts, Bachelor of Science, Associate of Arts, and Associate of Science degrees in twenty advancing technology disciplines, including artificial life programming, computer forensics, digital animation, digital art and design, game art and animation, game design, game programming, network security, and robotics and embedded systems.

Academic Programs

The Bachelor of Arts and Bachelor of Science programs require a minimum of 120 semester credits, including 84 core credits, forty 300/400–level credits, and 36 general education credits. The Associate of Arts and Associate of Science programs require a minimum of 60 semester credits: 45 core credits, and 15 general education credits.

Academic Facilities

The University is open 24/7. In just about every corner of campus, there are hundreds of computers, including Macs and state-of-the-art video game consoles. Students at UAT are immersed in a world of technology. From the miles of cables and walls of servers in the open-viewed server rooms to the vast array of industry technology in the NT lab, students who love technology feel right at home.

As an institution, UAT is dedicated to planning, implementing, and sharing its research with others in technology and academia. The UAT research centers operate within the University to further knowledge creation, foster institutional and community awareness, and improve initiatives in their focal areas. In addition, each research center publishes works to the broader community through a variety of channels (technology journals, online journals, and conference papers. In 1992, the University founded its first research center, the Computer Reality Center. It performed research primarily for the computer graphics industry, with specific emphasis on the field of virtual reality. The center adopted the Hyperlearning model and developed UAT's current teaching model, Year-Round Balanced Learning. YRBL combines lecture, tutorial teaching, group recollection, student teachback, and discovery learning. Year-round classes are available both on the campus and online, and students produce projects for a graduation portfolio to demonstrate an understanding of what they are learning.

Through research of learning and teaching methodologies, the Center for Learning Excellence develops and supports educational models that enable the University to build innovative and balanced learning experiences. Its main goal is to apply its research toward developing the UAT Faculty Certification Program. This program ensures baseline effective teaching preparation within UAT's learning model for all faculty members before they are assigned to the classroom. The center routinely assesses instruction at UAT in relation to student learning outcomes.

The Center for Institutional Research is the center for ongoing institutional research that accumulates, generates, maintains, communicates, and disseminates institutional information to support assessment and general awareness of student learning. The center also evaluates and reviews the efficacy of institutional policies.

The Center for Technology Studies conducts original research and produces works published in the broader community and furthers community understanding of technology disciplines, their applications, and their relevance in the global society. Within the center is the Center for Information Assurance, which produces knowledge solely within the information assurance disciplines at UAT: computer forensics and network security at the undergraduate level and information security at the graduate level.

Whenever and wherever possible, the campus and technology resources are open to allow students and professionals alike to participate collaboratively in this endeavor, whether as team members on a student project, speaking at Technology Forum, or submitting work to the University's *Journal of Advancing Technology.*

Costs

Undergraduate tuition for 2008–09 is $8400 per semester. Tuition for UAT-Online students is $4900 per semester. Housing costs are about $6615 per year.

Financial Aid

Average aid per academic year for first-academic-year freshmen is $11,784. The percentage of freshmen who receive aid is 84 percent. The percentage of freshmen who receive UAT academic scholarships is 26 percent. The average amount of scholarships received per freshman student per academic year is $1200.

Faculty

UAT's faculty comprises members who are thinkers, teachers, technological gurus, industry experts, and student mentors. They garner their skills, knowledge, and expertise from a range of experiences—from the classrooms of academe to the boardrooms of industry, from community meeting halls to international conferences. They are a group governed by their passion for technology, their students, and their own academic and professional growth. Sixty-four faculty members, distinguished by their academic abilities and accomplishments within their respective fields, serve as both instructors and mentors.

Student Government

The University-sanctioned student government was formed to give the student body at UAT a collective voice and set traditions within the University. University Student Government (USG) performs important roles in encouraging self-directed Student Life organizations, coordinating student community service activities, and providing a venue for feedback between students and staff members. Students are encouraged to participate in the Student Government, which holds monthly open meetings.

Admission Requirements

The University of Advancing Technology strives to admit undergraduate students who embody its passion for technology, are a cultural match to the University, demonstrate adequate academic achievement, and have a dedication to lifelong learning. All undergraduate applicants are evaluated based on these criteria: academic history and achievements; personal expression; desire to attend UAT; how they might fit with UAT's geek-friendly culture, passion, and aptitude for technology; and the supportiveness of the applicant's network of family, friends, and peers to achieve their educational goals (for UAT-Online applicants, employer support is also evaluated). All applicants are encouraged to submit high school transcripts, ACT and/or SAT scores, Advanced Placement scores, and college transcripts, so UAT's Admissions Office may thoroughly review the applicant's academic history.

In addition to the standard admission requirements, non-U.S. citizens applying for admission to the University of Advancing Technology must provide proof of English proficiency in one of the following ways: Test of English as a Foreign Language (TOEFL) with a score of 550 or higher on the paper-based test, 79 or higher on the Internet-based test, or 213 or higher on the computer-based test; successful completion of Level 108 from an ELS Center; ASPECT English Language Proficiency Level 5; or attendance for one year at a regionally accredited U.S. college or university and completion of English 101 (or equivalent) with grade C or better. Proof of English proficiency is not required if English is the applicant's native language. Official transcripts must be submitted with an English translation and be evaluated as a U.S. high school equivalent by Educational Credential Evaluators, Inc., P.O. Box 17499, Milwaukee, Wisconsin 53217-0499, U.S.A. (http://www.ece.org).

Application and Information

UAT has an admissions application that helps both the student and the admissions staff determine if the applicant and UAT are a good match. Students should complete and submit the application to the UAT Admissions Office prior to consideration. Students may apply online at http://www.uat.edu/admissions. To request an application, students should either e-mail admissions@uat.edu or call 877-UAT-GEEK (toll-free).

UAT Admissions
University of Advancing Technology
2625 West Baseline Road
Tempe, Arizona 85283-1056
Phone: 602-383-8228
800-658-5744 (toll-free)
E-mail: admission@uat.edu
Web site: http://www.uat.edu

ARKANSAS

Siloam Springs
Fayetteville
Walnut Ridge
Batesville
State University
55
40
Clarksville
Russellville
Searcy
Conway
40
Little Rock
Pine Bluff
Arkadelphia
30
Monticello
Magnolia

ARKANSAS BAPTIST COLLEGE

Little Rock, Arkansas **www.arkansasbaptist.edu/**

Freshman Application Contact Mrs. Jamesetta Ballard, Director of Admissions and Enrollment, Arkansas Baptist College, 1600 Bishop Street, Little Rock, AR 72202. *Phone:* 501-374-7856.

ARKANSAS STATE UNIVERSITY

Jonesboro, Arkansas **www.astate.edu/**

- **State-supported** university, founded 1909, part of Arkansas State University System
- **Small-town** 2008-acre campus with easy access to Memphis
- **Endowment** $43.6 million
- **Coed** 9,385 undergraduate students, 79% full-time, 60% women, 40% men
- **Minimally difficult** entrance level, 80% of applicants were admitted

Arkansas State University (ASU) has been powering minds for almost 100 years. ASU offers more than 200 degree programs from the associate to the doctoral level, more than 300 campus organizations, thirty intramural sports, twenty-one national Greek organizations, and one of only two NCAA Division I-A programs in the state. There is a world of possibilities to power a student's future at http://www.astate.edu.

Undergraduates 7,368 full-time, 2,017 part-time. Students come from 41 states and territories, 33 other countries, 11% are from out of state, 17% African American, 0.7% Asian American or Pacific Islander, 1% Hispanic American, 0.4% Native American, 0.6% international, 9% transferred in, 23% live on campus. *Retention:* 69% of 2006 full-time freshmen returned.

Freshmen *Admission:* 3,298 applied, 2,634 admitted, 1,733 enrolled. *Average high school GPA:* 3.17. *Test scores:* ACT scores over 18: 80%; ACT scores over 24: 33%; ACT scores over 30: 3%.

Faculty *Total:* 632, 73% full-time, 51% with terminal degrees. *Student/faculty ratio:* 17:1.

Majors Accounting; administrative assistant and secretarial science; agribusiness; agricultural teacher education; agriculture; animal sciences; art; art teacher education; athletic training; audiology and speech-language pathology; automobile/automotive mechanics technology; biology/biological sciences; biology teacher education; business administration and management; business/managerial economics; business teacher education; chemistry; chemistry teacher education; clinical laboratory science/medical technology; commercial and advertising art; communication and journalism related; computer and information sciences; computer science; criminal justice/law enforcement administration; criminal justice/police science; criminology; data processing and data processing technology; dramatic/theater arts; early childhood education; economics; electrical, electronic and communications engineering technology; emergency medical technology (EMT paramedic); engineering; engineering technologies related; engineering technology; English; English/language arts teacher education; finance; food technology and processing; forensic science and technology; French; French language teacher education; general studies; geography; graphic communications; health and physical education; history; interdisciplinary studies; international business/trade/commerce; journalism; kinesiology and exercise science; management information systems; marketing/marketing management; mathematics; mathematics teacher education; medical radiologic technology; middle school education; multi-/interdisciplinary studies related; music; music performance; music teacher education; nursing (registered nurse training); philosophy; physical education teaching and coaching; physical therapist assistant; physics; physics teacher education; plant sciences; political science and government; psychology; radio and television; social science teacher education; social work; sociology; Spanish; Spanish language teacher education; special education; speech and rhetoric; speech teacher education; sport and fitness administration/management; technology/industrial arts teacher education; tourism and travel services management; transportation management; wildlife and wildlands science and management.

Academics *Calendar:* semesters. *Degrees:* certificates, associate, bachelor's, master's, doctoral, post-master's, and postbachelor's certificates (specialist). *Special study options:* academic remediation for entering students, accelerated degree program, advanced placement credit, distance learning, double majors, honors programs, independent study, internships, off-campus study, part-time degree program, services for LD students, study abroad, summer session for credit. *ROTC:* Army (b).

Computers on Campus 550 computers/terminals and 4,242 ports are available on campus for general student use. Students can access the following: campus intranet, computer help desk, free student e-mail accounts, online (class) grades, online (class) registration, online (class) schedules. Campuswide network is available. 99% of college-owned or -operated housing units are wired for high-speed Internet access. Wireless service is available via entire campus.

Student Life *Housing:* on-campus residence required for freshman year. *Options:* coed, men-only, women-only. Campus housing is university owned. *Activities and organizations:* drama/theater group, student-run newspaper, radio and television station, choral group, marching band, Student Activities Board, Baptist Collegiate Ministries, Student Government Association, International Student Association, Public Perceptions Style Entourage, national fraternities, national sororities. *Campus security:* 24-hour emergency response devices and patrols, student patrols, late-night transport/escort service, controlled dormitory access, check-in desk. *Student services:* health clinic, personal/psychological counseling.

Athletics Member NCAA. All Division I except football (Division I-A). *Intercollegiate sports:* baseball M (s), basketball M (s)/W (s), bowling W (s), cross-country running M (s)/W (s), golf M (s)/W (s), soccer W (s), tennis W (s), track and field M (s)/W (s), volleyball W (s). *Intramural sports:* archery M/W, badminton M/W, basketball M/W, bowling M/W, equestrian sports M/W, football M/W, golf M/W, racquetball M/W, rugby M/W, soccer M/W, softball M/W, table tennis M/W, tennis M/W, ultimate Frisbee M/W, volleyball M/W.

Standardized Tests *Required:* SAT or ACT (for admission). *Required for some:* ACT ASSET or ACT COMPASS. *Recommended:* ACT (for admission).

Costs (2007–08) *Tuition:* state resident $4620 full-time, $154 per credit hour part-time; nonresident $12,000 full-time, $400 per credit hour part-time. Full-time tuition and fees vary according to course load, location, and program. Part-time tuition and fees vary according to course load, location, and program. *Required fees:* $1390 full-time, $44 per credit hour part-time, $25 per term part-time. *Room and board:* $4710. Room and board charges vary according to board plan and housing facility. *Payment plan:* installment. *Waivers:* senior citizens and employees or children of employees.

Financial Aid Of all full-time matriculated undergraduates who enrolled in 2007, 6,702 applied for aid, 6,450 were judged to have need, 1,570 had their need fully met. 310 Federal Work-Study jobs (averaging $3500). In 2007, 725 non-need-based awards were made. *Average percent of need met:* 57%. *Average financial aid package:* $9300. *Average need-based loan:* $4800. *Average need-based gift aid:* $5500. *Average non-need-based aid:* $6200. *Average indebtedness upon graduation:* $18,500. *Financial aid deadline:* 7/1.

Applying *Options:* electronic application, early admission, deferred entrance. *Application fee:* $15. *Required:* high school transcript, minimum 2.0 GPA, proof of immunization, proof of enrollment in selective service for men over 18. *Application deadlines:* rolling (freshmen), rolling (transfers). *Notification:* continuous (freshmen), continuous (transfers).

Freshman Application Contact Ms. Tammy Fowler, Director of Admissions, Arkansas State University, PO Box 1630, State University, AR 72467. *Phone:* 870-972-3024. *Toll-free phone:* 800-382-3030. *Fax:* 870-910-3406. *E-mail:* admissions@astate.edu.

ARKANSAS TECH UNIVERSITY

Russellville, Arkansas **www.atu.edu/**

- **State-supported** comprehensive, founded 1909
- **Small-town** 516-acre campus
- **Endowment** $19.0 million
- **Coed**
- **Moderately difficult** entrance level

Faculty *Student/faculty ratio:* 18:1.

Academics *Calendar:* semesters. *Degrees:* certificates, associate, bachelor's, master's, and post-master's certificates (Educational Specialist's).

Student Life *Campus security:* 24-hour patrols, late-night transport/escort service, controlled dormitory access.

Athletics Member NCAA. All Division II.

Standardized Tests *Required:* SAT or ACT (for admission).

Costs (2007–08) *Tuition:* state resident $4590 full-time, $153 per credit hour part-time; nonresident $9180 full-time, $306 per credit hour part-time. Full-time tuition and fees vary according to course load and location. Part-time tuition and fees vary according to course load and location. *Required fees:* $530 full-time, $8 per credit hour part-time, $145 per term part-time. *Room and board:* $4640; room only: $2656. Room and board charges vary according to board plan and housing facility. *Payment plans:* installment, deferred payment.

Financial Aid Of all full-time matriculated undergraduates who enrolled in 2005, 3,784 applied for aid, 3,253 were judged to have need, 771 had their need fully met. 250 Federal Work-Study jobs (averaging $1109). 435 state and other part-time jobs (averaging $1077). In 2005, 1042 non-need-based awards were made. *Average percent of need met:* 43. *Average financial aid package:* $4960.

Average need-based loan: $2299. *Average need-based gift aid:* $2547. *Average non-need-based aid:* $5884. *Average indebtedness upon graduation:* $18,155.

Applying *Options:* electronic application, deferred entrance. *Required:* high school transcript, minimum 2.0 GPA.

Freshman Application Contact Ms. Shauna Donnell, Director of Enrollment Management, Arkansas Tech University, L.L. "Doc" Bryan Student Services Building, Suite 141, Russellville, AR 72801-2222. *Phone:* 479-968-0343. *Toll-free phone:* 800-582-6953. *Fax:* 479-964-0522. *E-mail:* tech.enroll@atu.edu.

CENTRAL BAPTIST COLLEGE

Conway, Arkansas **www.cbc.edu/**

- **Independent Baptist** 4-year, founded 1952
- **Small-town** 11-acre campus
- **Endowment** $974,667
- **Coed**
- **Minimally difficult** entrance level

Faculty *Student/faculty ratio:* 15:1.

Academics *Calendar:* semesters. *Degrees:* associate and bachelor's.

Athletics Member NCCAA.

Standardized Tests *Required:* ACT (for admission).

Costs (2007–08) *Comprehensive fee:* $13,900 includes full-time tuition ($8400), mandatory fees ($500), and room and board ($5000). Part-time tuition: $280 per semester hour.

Applying *Options:* electronic application, early admission. *Application fee:* $25. *Required:* essay or personal statement, high school transcript, minimum 2.5 GPA, 2 letters of recommendation.

Freshman Application Contact Ms. Lindsay Watson, Admissions Counselor, Central Baptist College, 1501 College Avenue, Conway, AR 72034. *Phone:* 501-329-6872 Ext. 145. *Toll-free phone:* 800-205-6872. *Fax:* 501-329-2941. *E-mail:* lwatson@cbc.edu.

HARDING UNIVERSITY

Searcy, Arkansas **www.harding.edu/**

- **Independent** comprehensive, founded 1924, affiliated with Church of Christ
- **Small-town** 215-acre campus with easy access to Little Rock
- **Endowment** $101.7 million
- **Coed** 4,125 undergraduate students, 94% full-time, 55% women, 45% men
- **Moderately difficult** entrance level, 80% of applicants were admitted

Located in the beautiful foothills of the Ozark Mountains, Harding is one of America's more highly regarded private universities. At Harding, students build lifetime friendships and, upon graduation, are favorably recruited. Harding's Christian environment and challenging academic programs develop students who can compete and succeed.

Undergraduates 3,891 full-time, 234 part-time. Students come from 49 states and territories, 49 other countries, 70% are from out of state, 4% African American, 0.8% Asian American or Pacific Islander, 2% Hispanic American, 0.8% Native American, 5% international, 5% transferred in, 73% live on campus. *Retention:* 80% of 2006 full-time freshmen returned.

Freshmen *Admission:* 1,768 applied, 1,416 admitted, 965 enrolled. *Average high school GPA:* 3.46. *Test scores:* SAT critical reading scores over 500: 68%; SAT math scores over 500: 69%; ACT scores over 18: 95%; SAT critical reading scores over 600: 34%; SAT math scores over 600: 34%; ACT scores over 24: 56%; SAT critical reading scores over 700: 11%; SAT math scores over 700: 6%; ACT scores over 30: 15%.

Faculty *Total:* 429, 53% full-time, 50% with terminal degrees. *Student/faculty ratio:* 17:1.

Majors Accounting; advertising; art teacher education; art therapy; athletic training; biblical studies; biochemistry; biology/biological sciences; biology teacher education; broadcast journalism; business administration and management; business/corporate communications; chemistry; Christian studies; clinical laboratory science/medical technology; communication disorders; computer and information sciences; computer engineering; computer science; corrections and criminal justice related; counselor education/school counseling and guidance; design and applied arts related; dietetics; digital communication and media/multimedia; divinity/ministry; dramatic/theater arts; early childhood education; economics; educational leadership and administration; education (multiple levels); electrical, electronics and communications engineering; elementary education; English; English/language arts teacher education; family and consumer sciences/home economics teacher education; family and consumer sciences/human sciences; fashion merchandising; fine/studio arts; French; French language teacher education; general studies; graphic design; health/health care administration; health teacher education; history; human development and family studies related; humanities; human resources management; information technology; interior design; international business/trade/commerce; international/global studies; kinesiology and exercise science; legal studies; marketing/marketing management; marriage and family therapy/counseling; mathematics; mathematics teacher education; mechanical engineering; middle school education; missionary studies and missiology; music; music teacher education; nursing (registered nurse training); painting; pastoral counseling and specialized ministries related; pastoral studies/counseling; photojournalism; physics; political science and government; pre-dentistry studies; pre-medical studies; pre-veterinary studies; psychology; public administration; public relations/image management; reading teacher education; religious education; sales, distribution and marketing; science teacher education; secondary education; social sciences; social studies teacher education; social work; Spanish; Spanish language teacher education; special education (early childhood); special education related; special education (specific learning disabilities); speech-language pathology; speech teacher education; sport and fitness administration/management; theology; youth ministry.

Academics *Calendar:* semesters. *Degrees:* certificates, bachelor's, master's, doctoral, first professional, and post-master's certificates. *Special study options:* academic remediation for entering students, accelerated degree program, adult/continuing education programs, advanced placement credit, cooperative education, distance learning, double majors, English as a second language, freshman honors college, honors programs, independent study, internships, part-time degree program, services for LD students, study abroad, summer session for credit. *ROTC:* Army (c).

Computers on Campus 495 computers/terminals are available on campus for general student use. Students can access the following: campus intranet, computer help desk, free student e-mail accounts, online (class) grades, online (class) registration, online (class) schedules. Campuswide network is available. 100% of college-owned or -operated housing units are wired for high-speed Internet access.

Student Life *Housing:* on-campus residence required through senior year. *Options:* men-only, women-only, disabled students. Campus housing is university owned. Freshman campus housing is guaranteed. *Activities and organizations:* drama/theater group, student-run newspaper, radio and television station, choral group, marching band, Bisons for Christ, Harding in Action, JOY, Concert choir, ONE. *Campus security:* 24-hour emergency response devices and patrols, late-night transport/escort service, controlled dormitory access. *Student services:* health clinic, personal/psychological counseling.

Athletics Member NCAA. All Division II. *Intercollegiate sports:* baseball M (s), basketball M (s)/W (s), cheerleading W, cross-country running M (s)/W (s), football M (s), golf M (s)/W (s), lacrosse M (c), soccer M (s)/W (s), tennis M (s)/W (s), track and field M (s)/W (s), ultimate Frisbee M/W, volleyball W (s). *Intramural sports:* basketball M/W, cross-country running M/W, football M/W, golf M/W, racquetball M/W, soccer M/W, softball M/W, swimming and diving M/W, table tennis M/W, tennis M/W, track and field M/W, ultimate Frisbee M/W, volleyball M/W, weight lifting M/W.

Standardized Tests *Required:* SAT or ACT (for admission).

Costs (2007–08) *Comprehensive fee:* $17,938 includes full-time tuition ($11,940), mandatory fees ($420), and room and board ($5578). Full-time tuition and fees vary according to course load. Part-time tuition: $398 per semester hour. Part-time tuition and fees vary according to course load. *Required fees:* $21 per semester hour part-time. *College room only:* $2810. Room and board charges vary according to board plan and housing facility. *Payment plans:* tuition prepayment, installment. *Waivers:* senior citizens and employees or children of employees.

Financial Aid Of all full-time matriculated undergraduates who enrolled in 2006, 2,745 applied for aid, 2,061 were judged to have need, 548 had their need fully met. 505 Federal Work-Study jobs (averaging $951). 989 state and other part-time jobs (averaging $1091). In 2006, 483 non-need-based awards were made. *Average percent of need met:* 70%. *Average financial aid package:* $9959. *Average need-based loan:* $5030. *Average need-based gift aid:* $5282. *Average non-need-based aid:* $3412. *Average indebtedness upon graduation:* $28,386.

Applying *Options:* electronic application, early admission, early action, deferred entrance. *Application fee:* $35. *Required:* high school transcript, 2 letters of recommendation. *Notification:* continuous (freshmen), continuous (transfers).

Freshman Application Contact Mr. Glenn Dillard, Assistant Vice President for Enrollment Management, Harding University, Box 12255, Searcy, AR 72149-0001. *Phone:* 501-279-4407. *Toll-free phone:* 800-477-4407. *Fax:* 501-279-4129. *E-mail:* admissions@harding.edu.

HENDERSON STATE UNIVERSITY

Arkadelphia, Arkansas **www.hsu.edu/**

- **State-supported** comprehensive, founded 1890
- **Small-town** 139-acre campus with easy access to Little Rock
- **Coed** 3,125 undergraduate students, 89% full-time, 54% women, 46% men
- **Moderately difficult** entrance level, 66% of applicants were admitted

Undergraduates 2,773 full-time, 352 part-time. Students come from 31 states and territories, 28 other countries, 14% are from out of state, 20% African American, 0.5% Asian American or Pacific Islander, 2% Hispanic American, 0.6% Native American, 2% international, 8% transferred in. *Retention:* 61% of 2006 full-time freshmen returned.

Freshmen *Admission:* 2,425 applied, 1,595 admitted, 803 enrolled. *Average high school GPA:* 3.14. *Test scores:* SAT math scores over 500: 53%; SAT writing scores over 500: 38%; ACT scores over 18: 84%; SAT math scores over 600: 15%; SAT writing scores over 600: 24%; ACT scores over 24: 38%; SAT math scores over 700: 6%; ACT scores over 30: 4%.

Faculty *Total:* 230, 68% full-time, 52% with terminal degrees. *Student/faculty ratio:* 17:1.

Majors Accounting; aeronautics/aviation/aerospace science and technology; art; art teacher education; athletic training; biology/biological sciences; business/commerce; business teacher education; chemistry; child care and support services management; clinical laboratory science/medical technology; computer and information sciences; dramatic/theater arts; early childhood education; education (specific subject areas) related; English; family and consumer sciences/human sciences; history; journalism; management information systems; mathematics; middle school education; music; music performance; music teacher education; nursing (registered nurse training); painting; parks, recreation and leisure facilities management; physical education teaching and coaching; physics; political science and government; psychology; public administration; science teacher education; social work; sociology; Spanish; sport and fitness administration/management.

Academics *Calendar:* semesters. *Degrees:* associate, bachelor's, and master's. *Special study options:* academic remediation for entering students, advanced placement credit, distance learning, honors programs, internships, off-campus study, part-time degree program, services for LD students, summer session for credit.

Computers on Campus 125 computers/terminals are available on campus for general student use. Campuswide network is available.

Student Life *Housing:* on-campus residence required for freshman year. *Options:* coed, men-only, women-only. Campus housing is university owned and is provided by a third party. Freshman applicants given priority for college housing. *Activities and organizations:* drama/theater group, student-run newspaper, radio and television station, choral group, marching band, Heart and Key, Student Government Association, Residence Hall Association, national fraternities, national sororities. *Campus security:* 24-hour emergency response devices and patrols, controlled dormitory access. *Student services:* health clinic, personal/psychological counseling.

Athletics Member NCAA. All Division II. *Intercollegiate sports:* baseball M (s), basketball M (s)/W (s), cross-country running M/W (s), football M (s), golf M (s)/W (s), softball W (s), swimming and diving M (s)/W (s), tennis M (s)/W (s), volleyball W (s). *Intramural sports:* basketball M/W, football M, golf M/W, soccer M, swimming and diving M/W, tennis M/W, volleyball W.

Standardized Tests *Required:* SAT or ACT (for admission). *Recommended:* ACT (for admission).

Costs (2008–09) *Tuition:* state resident $3936 full-time, $164 per credit hour part-time; nonresident $7872 full-time, $328 per credit hour part-time. *Required fees:* $1003 full-time. *Room and board:* $4860.

Financial Aid Of all full-time matriculated undergraduates who enrolled in 2002, 2,771 applied for aid, 1,690 were judged to have need, 1,041 had their need fully met. 107 state and other part-time jobs (averaging $1648). In 2002, 516 non-need-based awards were made. *Average percent of need met:* 79%. *Average financial aid package:* $5640. *Average need-based loan:* $3820. *Average need-based gift aid:* $4400. *Average non-need-based aid:* $5735. *Average indebtedness upon graduation:* $16,500.

Applying *Options:* electronic application, deferred entrance. *Required:* high school transcript. *Required for some:* essay or personal statement, 3 letters of recommendation. *Recommended:* minimum 2.5 GPA. *Application deadlines:* 7/15 (freshmen), rolling (transfers). *Notification:* continuous (freshmen), continuous (transfers).

Freshman Application Contact Ms. Vikita Hardwrick, Director of University Relations/Admissions, Henderson State University, 1100 Henderson Street, PO Box 7560, Arkadelphia, AR 71999-0001. *Phone:* 870-230-5028. *Toll-free phone:* 800-228-7333. *Fax:* 870-230-5066. *E-mail:* hardwrv@hsu.edu.

HENDRIX COLLEGE

Conway, Arkansas **www.hendrix.edu/**

- **Independent United Methodist** comprehensive, founded 1876
- **Suburban** 158-acre campus with easy access to Little Rock
- **Endowment** $192.2 million
- **Coed** 1,191 undergraduate students, 99% full-time, 55% women, 45% men
- **Very difficult** entrance level, 83% of applicants were admitted

Undergraduates 1,178 full-time, 13 part-time. Students come from 37 states and territories, 9 other countries, 46% are from out of state, 4% African American, 3% Asian American or Pacific Islander, 3% Hispanic American, 0.8% Native American, 1% international, 1% transferred in, 84% live on campus. *Retention:* 86% of 2006 full-time freshmen returned.

Freshmen *Admission:* 1,323 applied, 1,094 admitted, 371 enrolled. *Average high school GPA:* 3.7. *Test scores:* SAT critical reading scores over 500: 94%; SAT math scores over 500: 91%; ACT scores over 18: 100%; SAT critical reading scores over 600: 69%; SAT math scores over 600: 54%; ACT scores over 24: 88%; SAT critical reading scores over 700: 24%; SAT math scores over 700: 12%; ACT scores over 30: 37%.

Faculty *Total:* 132, 70% full-time, 80% with terminal degrees. *Student/faculty ratio:* 11:1.

Majors Accounting; American studies; anthropology; art; biochemistry/biophysics and molecular biology; biology/biological sciences; business/managerial economics; chemical physics; chemistry; computer science; early childhood education; economics; English; environmental studies; French; German; health services/allied health/health sciences; history; interdisciplinary studies; international relations and affairs; kinesiology and exercise science; mathematics; music; philosophy; philosophy and religious studies related; physics; political science and government; psychology; religious studies; sociology; Spanish.

Academics *Calendar:* semesters. *Degrees:* bachelor's and master's. *Special study options:* advanced placement credit, cooperative education, double majors, honors programs, independent study, internships, off-campus study, services for LD students, student-designed majors, study abroad. *ROTC:* Army (c). *Unusual degree programs:* 3-2 engineering with Columbia University, Vanderbilt University, Washington University in St. Louis.

Computers on Campus 75 computers/terminals are available on campus for general student use, Students can access the following: campus intranet, computer help desk, free student e-mail accounts, online (class) grades, online (class) registration, online (class) schedules. Campuswide network is available. 100% of college-owned or -operated housing units are wired for high-speed Internet access. Wireless service is available via entire campus.

Student Life *Housing:* on-campus residence required through senior year. *Options:* coed, men-only, women-only. Campus housing is university owned and leased by the school. Freshman campus housing is guaranteed. *Activities and organizations:* drama/theater group, student-run newspaper, radio station, choral group, Volunteer Action Center, Student Government, Music ensembles, Multicultural Development Committee, Social Committee. *Campus security:* 24-hour emergency response devices and patrols, late-night transport/escort service, controlled dormitory access. *Student services:* health clinic, personal/psychological counseling.

Athletics Member NCAA. All Division III. *Intercollegiate sports:* baseball M, basketball M/W, cross-country running M/W, field hockey W, golf M/W, lacrosse W, soccer M/W, softball W, swimming and diving M/W, tennis M/W, track and field M/W, volleyball W. *Intramural sports:* badminton M/W, basketball M/W, football M/W, racquetball M/W, soccer M/W, softball M/W, tennis M/W, ultimate Frisbee M/W, volleyball M/W.

Standardized Tests *Required:* SAT or ACT (for admission).

Costs (2007–08) *Comprehensive fee:* $31,698 includes full-time tuition ($24,198), mandatory fees ($300), and room and board ($7200). Full-time tuition and fees vary according to course load. Part-time tuition: $3062 per course. Part-time tuition and fees vary according to course load. *College room only:* $3350. Room and board charges vary according to board plan and housing facility. *Payment plan:* installment. *Waivers:* employees or children of employees.

Financial Aid Of all full-time matriculated undergraduates who enrolled in 2007, 901 applied for aid, 692 were judged to have need, 275 had their need fully met. 450 Federal Work-Study jobs (averaging $1357). 209 state and other part-time jobs (averaging $1315). In 2007, 506 non-need-based awards were made. *Average percent of need met:* 83%. *Average financial aid package:* $19,017. *Average need-based loan:* $4647. *Average need-based gift aid:* $14,631. *Average non-need-based aid:* $17,618. *Average indebtedness upon graduation:* $17,490.

Applying *Options:* electronic application, early admission, deferred entrance. *Application fee:* $40. *Required:* essay or personal statement, high school transcript. *Required for some:* interview. *Recommended:* 1 letter of recommendation. *Application deadlines:* 8/1 (freshmen), 8/1 (transfers). *Notification:* continuous (freshmen), continuous (transfers).

Freshman Application Contact Ms. Laura E. Martin, Director of Admission, Hendrix College, 1600 Washington Avenue, Conway, AR 72032. *Phone:* 501-450-1362. *Toll-free phone:* 800-277-9017. *Fax:* 501-450-3843. *E-mail:* martinl@hendrix.edu.

ITT Technical Institute

Little Rock, Arkansas **www.itt-tech.edu/**

- **Proprietary** primarily 2-year, founded 1993, part of ITT Educational Services, Inc
- **Urban** campus
- **Coed**
- **Minimally difficult** entrance level

Academics *Calendar:* quarters. *Degrees:* associate and bachelor's.

Standardized Tests *Required:* Wonderlic aptitude test (for admission).

Applying *Options:* deferred entrance. *Application fee:* $100. *Required:* high school transcript, interview. *Recommended:* letters of recommendation.

Freshman Application Contact Ms. Terri Lowery, Director of Recruitment, ITT Technical Institute, 4520 South University Avenue, Little Rock, AR 72204. *Phone:* 501-565-5550. *Toll-free phone:* 800-359-4429.

John Brown University

Siloam Springs, Arkansas **www.jbu.edu/**

- **Independent interdenominational** comprehensive, founded 1919
- **Small-town** 200-acre campus
- **Endowment** $52.9 million
- **Coed** 1,702 undergraduate students, 95% full-time, 53% women, 47% men
- **Moderately difficult** entrance level, 76% of applicants were admitted

Undergraduates 1,617 full-time, 85 part-time. Students come from 40 states and territories, 45 other countries, 74% are from out of state, 3% African American, 1% Asian American or Pacific Islander, 3% Hispanic American, 2% Native American, 6% international, 4% transferred in, 75% live on campus. *Retention:* 80% of 2006 full-time freshmen returned.

Freshmen *Admission:* 891 applied, 680 admitted, 363 enrolled. *Average high school GPA:* 3.57. *Test scores:* SAT critical reading scores over 500: 76%; SAT math scores over 500: 79%; ACT scores over 18: 97%; SAT critical reading scores over 600: 39%; SAT math scores over 600: 37%; ACT scores over 24: 63%; SAT critical reading scores over 700: 15%; SAT math scores over 700: 8%; ACT scores over 30: 16%.

Faculty *Total:* 152, 52% full-time, 53% with terminal degrees. *Student/faculty ratio:* 13:1.

Majors Accounting; athletic training; biblical studies; biochemistry; biology/biological sciences; biology teacher education; broadcast journalism; business administration and management; business teacher education; chemistry; chemistry teacher education; computer graphics; construction engineering; construction management; divinity/ministry; early childhood education; education; electrical, electronics and communications engineering; elementary education; engineering; engineering/industrial management; engineering technology; English; English as a second/foreign language (teaching); English/language arts teacher education; environmental science; environmental studies; health teacher education; history; interdisciplinary studies; international business/trade/commerce; international relations and affairs; journalism; kindergarten/preschool education; kinesiology and exercise science; liberal arts and sciences/liberal studies; marketing/marketing management; mass communication/media; mathematics; mechanical engineering; middle school education; missionary studies and missiology; music; music teacher education; pastoral studies/counseling; psychology; public relations, advertising, and applied communication related; public relations/image management; radio and television; radio, television, and digital communication related; religious education; religious studies; secondary education; social sciences; social studies teacher education; Spanish; special education; theology; youth ministry.

Academics *Calendar:* semesters. *Degrees:* bachelor's and master's. *Special study options:* academic remediation for entering students, adult/continuing education programs, advanced placement credit, distance learning, double majors, English as a second language, external degree program, freshman honors college, honors programs, independent study, internships, services for LD students, study abroad. *ROTC:* Army (c), Air Force (c).

Computers on Campus 100 computers/terminals are available on campus for general student use. Students can access the following: campus intranet, computer help desk, free student e-mail accounts, online (class) grades, online (class) registration, online (class) schedules. Campuswide network is available. 100% of college-owned or -operated housing units are wired for high-speed Internet access. Wireless service is available via classrooms, dorm rooms, learning centers, libraries, student centers.

Student Life *Housing:* on-campus residence required through junior year. *Options:* coed, men-only, women-only. Campus housing is university owned. *Activities and organizations:* drama/theater group, student-run newspaper, radio and television station, choral group, Student Government Association, Student Ministries Organization, Student Missionary Fellowship, African Heritage Fellowship. *Campus security:* 24-hour emergency response devices and patrols, late-night transport/escort service. *Student services:* health clinic, personal/psychological counseling.

Athletics Member NAIA. *Intercollegiate sports:* basketball M (s)/W (s), soccer M (s)/W (s), tennis M (s)/W (s), volleyball W (s). *Intramural sports:* baseball M, basketball M/W, football M/W, golf M, racquetball M/W, rugby M, soccer M/W, softball M/W, tennis M/W, volleyball M/W.

Standardized Tests *Required:* SAT or ACT (for admission).

Costs (2008–09) *One-time required fee:* $25. *Comprehensive fee:* $24,646 includes full-time tuition ($17,256), mandatory fees ($810), and room and board ($6580).

Financial Aid Of all full-time matriculated undergraduates who enrolled in 2006, 1,088 applied for aid, 33 had their need fully met. 297 Federal Work-Study jobs (averaging $1362). 255 state and other part-time jobs (averaging $1318). In 2006, 220 non-need-based awards were made. *Average percent of need met:* 50%. *Average financial aid package:* $13,310. *Average need-based loan:* $4039. *Average need-based gift aid:* $5550. *Average non-need-based aid:* $5338.

Applying *Options:* deferred entrance. *Application fee:* $25. *Required:* essay or personal statement, high school transcript, minimum 2.5 GPA, 2 letters of recommendation. *Recommended:* interview. *Application deadlines:* rolling (freshmen), rolling (transfers). *Notification:* continuous (freshmen), continuous (transfers).

Freshman Application Contact Mr. Don Crandall, Vice President for Enrollment Management, John Brown University, 200 West University Street, Siloam Springs, AR 72761-2121. *Phone:* 479-524-7150. *Toll-free phone:* 877-JBU-INFO. *Fax:* 479-524-4196. *E-mail:* dcrandal@jbu.edu.

Lyon College

Batesville, Arkansas **www.lyon.edu/**

- **Independent Presbyterian** 4-year, founded 1872
- **Small-town** 136-acre campus
- **Endowment** $49.0 million
- **Coed** 495 undergraduate students, 94% full-time, 54% women, 46% men
- **Moderately difficult** entrance level, 69% of applicants were admitted

Lyon College is a private, residential, coeducational, undergraduate liberal arts college affiliated with the Presbyterian Church (U.S.A.). It is distinguished by its accomplished faculty, student-run honor system, innovative residential house system, and endowed international studies program. Lyon competes in the TranSouth Athletic Conference (NAIA). More information is available at the College Web site (http://www.lyon.edu).

Undergraduates 464 full-time, 31 part-time. Students come from 21 states and territories, 11 other countries, 25% are from out of state, 3% African American, 1% Asian American or Pacific Islander, 2% Hispanic American, 2% Native American, 2% international, 11% transferred in, 82% live on campus. *Retention:* 64% of 2006 full-time freshmen returned.

Freshmen *Admission:* 856 applied, 587 admitted, 142 enrolled. *Average high school GPA:* 3.65. *Test scores:* SAT critical reading scores over 500: 83%; SAT math scores over 500: 78%; ACT scores over 18: 100%; SAT critical reading scores over 600: 22%; SAT math scores over 600: 35%; ACT scores over 24: 57%; SAT critical reading scores over 700: 4%; SAT math scores over 700: 9%; ACT scores over 30: 6%.

Faculty *Total:* 62, 71% full-time, 66% with terminal degrees. *Student/faculty ratio:* 10:1.

Majors Accounting; art; biochemistry; biology/biological sciences; business administration and management; chemistry; computer science; dramatic/theater arts; early childhood education; economics; English; environmental studies; history; mathematics; music; philosophy and religious studies related; political science and government; psychology; Spanish.

Academics *Calendar:* semesters. *Degree:* bachelor's. *Special study options:* academic remediation for entering students, accelerated degree program, advanced placement credit, double majors, independent study, internships, part-time degree program, student-designed majors, study abroad, summer session for credit. *Unusual degree programs:* 3-2 engineering with University of Missouri-Rolla, University of Arkansas.

Computers on Campus 101 computers/terminals are available on campus for general student use. Students can access the following: campus intranet, computer help desk, free student e-mail accounts, online (class) grades, online (class) registration, online (class) schedules. Campuswide network is available. 100% of college-owned or -operated housing units are wired for high-speed Internet access. Wireless service is available via entire campus.

Student Life *Housing:* on-campus residence required through junior year. *Options:* coed, men-only, women-only. Campus housing is university owned. Freshman campus housing is guaranteed. *Activities and organizations:* drama/theater group, student-run newspaper, choral group, Baptist Christian Ministry, Student Activities Council, Pre-Med Club, national fraternities, national sororities. *Campus security:* 24-hour patrols, late-night transport/escort service. *Student services:* health clinic, personal/psychological counseling.

Athletics Member NAIA. *Intercollegiate sports:* baseball M (s), basketball M (s)/W (s), cross-country running M (s)/W (s), golf M (s)/W (s), soccer M (s)/W (s), softball W (s), tennis M (s)/W (s), volleyball W (s). *Intramural sports:* archery M/W, badminton M/W, basketball M/W, football M/W, softball M/W, table tennis M/W, tennis M/W, ultimate Frisbee M/W, volleyball M/W.

Standardized Tests *Required:* SAT or ACT (for admission).

Costs (2007–08) *Comprehensive fee:* $22,604 includes full-time tuition ($15,466), mandatory fees ($494), and room and board ($6644). Part-time tuition: $644 per credit hour. *College room only:* $2734. *Payment plan:* installment. *Waivers:* employees or children of employees.

Financial Aid Of all full-time matriculated undergraduates who enrolled in 2007, 375 applied for aid, 327 were judged to have need, 109 had their need fully met. 121 Federal Work-Study jobs (averaging $1266). In 2007, 130 non-need-based awards were made. *Average percent of need met:* 80%. *Average financial aid package:* $14,548. *Average need-based loan:* $4752. *Average need-based gift aid:* $11,052. *Average non-need-based aid:* $10,940. *Average indebtedness upon graduation:* $16,234.

Applying *Options:* electronic application, early admission, deferred entrance. *Application fee:* $25. *Required:* high school transcript, minimum 2.5 GPA. *Required for some:* essay or personal statement, 2 letters of recommendation. *Application deadlines:* rolling (freshmen), rolling (transfers). *Notification:* continuous (freshmen), continuous (transfers).

Freshman Application Contact Lyon College, PO Box 2317, Batesville, AR 72503-2317. *Phone:* 870-307-7250. *Toll-free phone:* 800-423-2542.

OUACHITA BAPTIST UNIVERSITY

Arkadelphia, Arkansas **www.obu.edu/**

- **Independent Baptist** 4-year, founded 1886
- **Small-town** 84-acre campus with easy access to Little Rock
- **Endowment** $77.3 million
- **Coed** 1,448 undergraduate students, 96% full-time, 55% women, 45% men
- **Moderately difficult** entrance level, 69% of applicants were admitted

Undergraduates 1,389 full-time, 59 part-time. Students come from 32 states and territories, 49 other countries, 48% are from out of state, 7% African American, 0.6% Asian American or Pacific Islander, 2% Hispanic American, 0.6% Native American, 3% international, 4% transferred in, 88% live on campus. *Retention:* 77% of 2006 full-time freshmen returned.

Freshmen *Admission:* 1,283 applied, 884 admitted, 372 enrolled. *Average high school GPA:* 3.49. *Test scores:* SAT critical reading scores over 500: 66%; SAT math scores over 500: 69%; ACT scores over 18: 93%; SAT critical reading scores over 600: 36%; SAT math scores over 600: 33%; ACT scores over 24: 48%; SAT critical reading scores over 700: 9%; SAT math scores over 700: 4%; ACT scores over 30: 10%.

Faculty *Total:* 145, 81% full-time, 60% with terminal degrees. *Student/faculty ratio:* 11:1.

Majors Accounting; art teacher education; athletic training; biblical studies; biology/biological sciences; business administration and management; chemistry; communication disorders sciences and services related; communication/speech communication and rhetoric; computer science; dietetics; dramatic/theater arts; early childhood education; education; English; fine/studio arts; French; graphic design; history; kinesiology and exercise science; mass communication/media; mathematics; middle school education; missionary studies and missiology; music; music history, literature, and theory; music performance; music teacher education; music theory and composition; pastoral counseling and specialized ministries related; pastoral studies/counseling; philosophy; physical education teaching and coaching; physics; piano and organ; political science and government; pre-dentistry studies; pre-engineering; pre-law studies; pre-medical studies; pre-nursing studies; pre-pharmacy studies; pre-veterinary studies; psychology; religious/sacred music; Russian; science teacher education; secondary education; social studies teacher education; sociology; Spanish; theology; voice and opera; youth ministry.

Academics *Calendar:* semesters. *Degrees:* associate and bachelor's. *Special study options:* academic remediation for entering students, accelerated degree program, advanced placement credit, cooperative education, double majors, English as a second language, honors programs, internships, off-campus study, part-time degree program, study abroad, summer session for credit. *ROTC:* Army (b). *Unusual degree programs:* 3-2 engineering with University of Arkansas at Fayetteville.

Computers on Campus 250 computers/terminals and 1,301 ports are available on campus for general student use. Students can access the following: campus intranet, computer help desk, free student e-mail accounts, online (class) grades, online (class) schedules, student Web portal. Campuswide network is available. 100% of college-owned or -operated housing units are wired for high-speed Internet access. Wireless service is available via classrooms, computer centers, computer labs, dorm rooms, learning centers, libraries, student centers.

Student Life *Housing:* on-campus residence required through senior year. *Options:* men-only, women-only, disabled students. Campus housing is university owned and leased by the school. Freshman campus housing is guaranteed. *Activities and organizations:* drama/theater group, student-run newspaper, television station, choral group, marching band, Phi Beta Lambda, Campus Activities Board, Student Education Association, Student Foundation, International Club. *Campus security:* 24-hour emergency response devices and patrols, controlled dormitory access. *Student services:* health clinic, personal/psychological counseling.

Athletics Member NCAA. All Division II. *Intercollegiate sports:* baseball M (s), basketball M (s)/W (s), cheerleading M/W, cross-country running W (s), football M (s), golf M (s), soccer M (s)/W (s), softball W (s), swimming and diving M (s)/W (s), tennis M (s)/W (s), volleyball W (s). *Intramural sports:* basketball M/W, football M/W, soccer M, softball M/W, table tennis M/W.

Standardized Tests *Required:* SAT or ACT (for admission).

Costs (2008–09) *Comprehensive fee:* $23,930 includes full-time tuition ($18,000), mandatory fees ($400), and room and board ($5530). Part-time tuition: $515 per semester hour.

Financial Aid Of all full-time matriculated undergraduates who enrolled in 2007, 899 applied for aid, 699 were judged to have need, 309 had their need fully met. 228 state and other part-time jobs (averaging $1632). In 2007, 686 non-need-based awards were made. *Average percent of need met:* 85%. *Average financial aid package:* $14,043. *Average need-based loan:* $3950. *Average need-based gift aid:* $10,800. *Average non-need-based aid:* $7312. *Average indebtedness upon graduation:* $14,591. *Financial aid deadline:* 6/1.

Applying *Options:* deferred entrance. *Application fee:* $50. *Required:* high school transcript, minimum 2.75 GPA. *Recommended:* interview. *Application deadlines:* 8/15 (freshmen), 8/15 (transfers). *Notification:* continuous (freshmen), continuous (transfers).

Freshman Application Contact Ms. Keisha Pittman, Director of Admissions Counseling, Ouachita Baptist University, OBU Box 3776, Arkadelphia, AR 71998-0001. *Phone:* 870-245-5110. *Toll-free phone:* 800-342-5628. *Fax:* 870-245-5500. *E-mail:* pittmank@obu.edu.

PHILANDER SMITH COLLEGE

Little Rock, Arkansas **www.philander.edu/**

- **Independent United Methodist** 4-year, founded 1877
- **Urban** 25-acre campus
- **Coed**
- **Minimally difficult** entrance level

Faculty *Student/faculty ratio:* 11:1.

Academics *Calendar:* semesters. *Degree:* bachelor's.

Student Life *Campus security:* 24-hour emergency response devices and patrols, student patrols, controlled dormitory access.

Athletics Member NSCAA.

Applying *Options:* electronic application, deferred entrance. *Application fee:* $25. *Required:* high school transcript, minimum 2.0 GPA. *Required for some:* essay or personal statement, interview.

Freshman Application Contact Mr. George Gray, Director of Recruitment and Admissions, Philander Smith College, 812 West 13th Street, Little Rock, AR

72202-3718. *Phone:* 501-370-5310. *Toll-free phone:* 800-446-6772. *Fax:* 501-370-5225. *E-mail:* ggray@philander.edu.

SOUTHERN ARKANSAS UNIVERSITY–MAGNOLIA

Magnolia, Arkansas **www.saumag.edu/**

- **State-supported** comprehensive, founded 1909, part of Southern Arkansas University System
- **Small-town** 781-acre campus
- **Endowment** $21.9 million
- **Coed** 2,806 undergraduate students, 82% full-time, 59% women, 41% men
- **Moderately difficult** entrance level, 73% of applicants were admitted

Undergraduates 2,304 full-time, 502 part-time. Students come from 26 states and territories, 29 other countries, 22% are from out of state, 31% African American, 0.6% Asian American or Pacific Islander, 1% Hispanic American, 0.5% Native American, 5% international, 8% transferred in, 36% live on campus. *Retention:* 62% of 2006 full-time freshmen returned.

Freshmen *Admission:* 1,657 applied, 1,211 admitted, 537 enrolled. *Average high school GPA:* 3.13. *Test scores:* SAT critical reading scores over 500: 28%; SAT math scores over 500: 50%; ACT scores over 18: 70%; SAT critical reading scores over 600: 4%; SAT math scores over 600: 20%; ACT scores over 24: 19%; SAT math scores over 700: 6%; ACT scores over 30: 2%.

Faculty *Total:* 205, 74% full-time. *Student/faculty ratio:* 16:1.

Majors Accounting; administrative assistant and secretarial science; agricultural business and management; agricultural teacher education; agriculture; art; art teacher education; biological and physical sciences; biology/biological sciences; biology teacher education; broadcast journalism; business/commerce; business teacher education; chemistry; chemistry teacher education; clinical laboratory science/medical technology; community organization and advocacy; computer and information sciences; criminal justice/safety; dramatic/theater arts; elementary education; engineering physics; English; English/language arts teacher education; general studies; history; industrial technology; journalism; kindergarten/preschool education; kinesiology and exercise science; mass communication/media; mathematics; mathematics teacher education; music teacher education; nursing (registered nurse training); physical education teaching and coaching; physics teacher education; political science and government; psychology; science teacher education; social studies teacher education; social work; sociology; Spanish; Spanish language teacher education.

Academics *Calendar:* semesters. *Degrees:* certificates, associate, bachelor's, and master's. *Special study options:* academic remediation for entering students, accelerated degree program, adult/continuing education programs, advanced placement credit, distance learning, double majors, freshman honors college, honors programs, independent study, internships, part-time degree program, services for LD students, study abroad, summer session for credit.

Computers on Campus 194 computers/terminals and 194 ports are available on campus for general student use. Students can access the following: campus intranet, computer help desk, free student e-mail accounts, online (class) grades, online (class) registration, online (class) schedules. Campuswide network is available. 100% of college-owned or -operated housing units are wired for high-speed Internet access. Wireless service is available via computer centers, computer labs, dorm rooms, libraries, student centers.

Student Life *Housing:* on-campus residence required through sophomore year. *Options:* coed, men-only, women-only. Campus housing is university owned and is provided by a third party. Freshman campus housing is guaranteed. *Activities and organizations:* drama/theater group, student-run newspaper, radio station, choral group, marching band, Student Government Association, IMPACT, national fraternities, national sororities. *Campus security:* 24-hour emergency response devices, student patrols, late-night transport/escort service, controlled dormitory access. *Student services:* health clinic, personal/psychological counseling.

Athletics Member NCAA. All Division II. *Intercollegiate sports:* baseball M (s), basketball M (s)/W (s), cross-country running M/W (s), football M (s), golf M, softball W (s), tennis W (s), track and field M/W, volleyball W (s). *Intramural sports:* badminton M/W, basketball M/W, football M, golf M, softball M/W, swimming and diving M/W, table tennis M/W, tennis M/W, volleyball M/W.

Standardized Tests *Required:* SAT or ACT (for admission). *Recommended:* ACT (for admission).

Costs (2008–09) *Tuition:* state resident $4800 full-time, $160 per hour part-time; nonresident $7260 full-time, $242 per hour part-time. *Required fees:* $846 full-time, $27 per hour part-time, $13 per term part-time. *Room and board:* $4250; room only: $2130.

Financial Aid Of all full-time matriculated undergraduates who enrolled in 2007, 1,822 applied for aid, 1,640 were judged to have need, 1,305 had their need fully met. 1,022 Federal Work-Study jobs (averaging $2614). 378 state and other part-time jobs (averaging $2862). In 2007, 253 non-need-based awards were made. *Average percent of need met:* 100%. *Average financial aid package:* $4135. *Average need-based loan:* $3221. *Average need-based gift aid:* $3169. *Average non-need-based aid:* $4411. *Average indebtedness upon graduation:* $14,375.

Applying *Options:* electronic application, early admission, deferred entrance. *Required:* high school transcript. *Required for some:* interview. *Application deadlines:* 8/27 (freshmen), 8/27 (transfers).

Director of Admissions Ms. Sarah Jennings, Dean of Enrollment Services, Southern Arkansas University–Magnolia, PO Box 9382, Magnolia, AR 71754-9382. *Phone:* 870-235-4040. *Toll-free phone:* 800-332-7286. *E-mail:* addanna@saumag.edu.

UNIVERSITY OF ARKANSAS

Fayetteville, Arkansas **www.uark.edu/**

- **State-supported** university, founded 1871, part of University of Arkansas System
- **Suburban** 410-acre campus
- **Endowment** $876.8 million
- **Coed** 14,948 undergraduate students, 85% full-time, 49% women, 51% men
- **Moderately difficult** entrance level, 62% of applicants were admitted

Ranked among top public institutions by *U.S. News & World Report*, the University of Arkansas excels as a nationally competitive, student-centered research university. Distinctive features include an Honors College, study-abroad and undergraduate research opportunities, championship NCAA Division I sports, learning centers, and more than 230 registered student organizations.

Undergraduates 12,730 full-time, 2,218 part-time. Students come from 47 states and territories, 102 other countries, 24% are from out of state, 5% African American, 3% Asian American or Pacific Islander, 3% Hispanic American, 2% Native American, 2% international, 8% transferred in, 29% live on campus. *Retention:* 83% of 2006 full-time freshmen returned.

Freshmen *Admission:* 10,132 applied, 6,262 admitted, 2,899 enrolled. *Average high school GPA:* 3.59. *Test scores:* SAT critical reading scores over 500: 79%; SAT math scores over 500: 81%; SAT critical reading scores over 600: 38%; SAT math scores over 600: 44%; SAT critical reading scores over 700: 10%; SAT math scores over 700: 10%.

Faculty *Total:* 930, 92% full-time, 84% with terminal degrees. *Student/faculty ratio:* 17:1.

Majors Accounting; agribusiness; agricultural/biological engineering and bioengineering; agricultural communication/journalism; agricultural teacher education; American studies; animal sciences; anthropology; apparel and textiles; architecture; art; biology/biological sciences; business administration and management; business/commerce; business/managerial economics; cell biology and anatomical sciences related; chemical engineering; chemistry; civil engineering; classics and languages, literatures and linguistics; communication/speech communication and rhetoric; computer and information sciences; computer engineering; criminal justice/safety; crop production; dramatic/theater arts; early childhood education; earth sciences; economics; electrical, electronics and communications engineering; elementary education; English; environmental science; finance; food science; foods, nutrition, and wellness; French; geological and earth sciences/geosciences related; geology/earth science; German; health and physical education; health science; history; horticultural science; hospitality administration; human development and family studies; industrial engineering; information technology; interior design; international business/trade/commerce; international relations and affairs; journalism; kinesiology and exercise science; landscape architecture; logistics and materials management; marketing/marketing management; mathematics; mechanical engineering; middle school education; music; nursing (registered nurse training); philosophy; physics; political science and government; poultry science; psychology; public administration; recreation products/services marketing operations; social work; sociology; Spanish; transportation and highway engineering.

Academics *Calendar:* semesters. *Degrees:* bachelor's, master's, doctoral, first professional, post-master's, and postbachelor's certificates. *Special study options:* accelerated degree program, advanced placement credit, cooperative education, distance learning, double majors, English as a second language, freshman honors college, honors programs, independent study, internships, part-time degree program, services for LD students, study abroad, summer session for credit. *ROTC:* Army (b), Air Force (b). *Unusual degree programs:* 3-2 law.

Computers on Campus 2,270 computers/terminals are available on campus for general student use. Students can access the following: online (class) registration. Campuswide network is available. 100% of college-owned or -operated housing units are wired for high-speed Internet access. Wireless service is available via entire campus.

Student Life *Housing:* on-campus residence required for freshman year. *Options:* coed, men-only, women-only. Campus housing is university owned. Freshman campus housing is guaranteed. *Activities and organizations:* drama/theater group, student-run newspaper, radio and television station, choral group, marching band, Gamma Beta Phi, University Baptist Collegiate Ministry, Associated Student Government, Black Students Association, Hot Pink Ribbon Club, national fraternities, national sororities. *Campus security:* 24-hour emergency response devices and patrols, student patrols, late-night transport/escort service, controlled dormitory access, RAD (Rape Aggression Defense program). *Student services:* health clinic, personal/psychological counseling, women's center, legal services.

Athletics Member NCAA. All Division I except football (Division I-A). *Intercollegiate sports:* baseball M (s), basketball M (s)/W (s), cross-country running M (s)/W (s), golf M (s)/W (s), gymnastics W (s), soccer W (s), softball W (s), swimming and diving W (s), tennis M (s)/W (s), track and field M (s)/W (s), volleyball W (s). *Intramural sports:* badminton M/W, basketball M/W, bowling M/W, cheerleading M (c)/W (c), crew M (c)/W (c), football M, golf M/W, racquetball M/W, rugby M (c)/W (c), soccer M/W, softball M/W, tennis M/W, ultimate Frisbee M/W, volleyball M (c)/W (c), water polo M/W.

Standardized Tests *Required:* SAT or ACT (for admission).

Costs (2007–08) *Tuition:* state resident $4772 full-time, $159 per hour part-time; nonresident $13,226 full-time, $441 per hour part-time. Full-time tuition and fees vary according to program. Part-time tuition and fees vary according to program. *Required fees:* $1266 full-time. *Room and board:* $7017; room only: $4387. Room and board charges vary according to board plan and housing facility. *Payment plan:* installment. *Waivers:* senior citizens and employees or children of employees.

Financial Aid Of all full-time matriculated undergraduates who enrolled in 2006, 6,077 applied for aid, 4,520 were judged to have need, 732 had their need fully met. 1,211 Federal Work-Study jobs (averaging $1853). In 2006, 2177 non-need-based awards were made. *Average percent of need met:* 73%. *Average financial aid package:* $8068. *Average need-based loan:* $4292. *Average need-based gift aid:* $3953. *Average non-need-based aid:* $5845. *Average indebtedness upon graduation:* $18,170.

Applying *Options:* electronic application, early admission, early action. *Application fee:* $40. *Required:* high school transcript. *Recommended:* minimum 3.0 GPA. *Application deadlines:* 8/15 (freshmen), 8/15 (transfers), 11/15 (early action). *Notification:* 10/1 (freshmen), continuous (transfers), 12/15 (early action).

Freshman Application Contact Dawn Medley, Director, University of Arkansas, 232 Silas H. Hunt Hall, Office of Admissions, Fayetteville, AR 72701-1201. *Phone:* 479-575-5346. *Toll-free phone:* 800-377-5346 (in-state); 800-377-8632 (out-of-state). *Fax:* 479-575-7515. *E-mail:* uofa@uark.edu.

UNIVERSITY OF ARKANSAS AT FORT SMITH

Fort Smith, Arkansas **www.uafortsmith.edu/**

- **State and locally supported** 4-year, founded 1928, part of University of Arkansas System
- **Suburban** 120-acre campus
- **Endowment** $42.8 million
- **Coed** 6,641 undergraduate students, 62% full-time, 59% women, 41% men
- **Minimally difficult** entrance level, 67% of applicants were admitted

Undergraduates 4,117 full-time, 2,524 part-time. Students come from 32 states and territories, 9 other countries, 14% are from out of state, 4% African American, 4% Asian American or Pacific Islander, 4% Hispanic American, 5% Native American, 0.1% international, 5% transferred in, 3% live on campus. *Retention:* 68% of 2006 full-time freshmen returned.

Freshmen *Admission:* 2,776 applied, 1,849 admitted, 1,168 enrolled. *Average high school GPA:* 3.21. *Test scores:* ACT scores over 18: 84%; ACT scores over 24: 29%; ACT scores over 30: 2%.

Faculty *Total:* 365, 56% full-time. *Student/faculty ratio:* 18:1.

Majors Accounting; administrative assistant and secretarial science; biology/biological sciences; biology teacher education; business administration and management; chemistry; child development; computer and information sciences; criminal justice/safety; dental hygiene; diagnostic medical sonography and ultrasound technology; drafting/design technology; early childhood education; electrical/electronics equipment installation and repair; English/language arts teacher education; forensic science and technology; general studies; history; history teacher education; legal assistant/paralegal; mathematics; mathematics teacher education; middle school education; multi-/interdisciplinary studies related; music; music teacher education; nursing (registered nurse training); psychology; radiologic technology/science; respiratory care therapy; science teacher education; social studies teacher education; Spanish; Spanish language teacher education; surgical technology; technical and business writing; visual and performing arts.

Academics *Calendar:* semesters. *Degrees:* certificates, associate, and bachelor's. *Special study options:* academic remediation for entering students, accelerated degree program, adult/continuing education programs, advanced placement credit, cooperative education, distance learning, double majors, English as a second language, external degree program, honors programs, internships, off-campus study, part-time degree program, services for LD students, summer session for credit. *ROTC:* Army (c), Air Force (c).

Computers on Campus 590 computers/terminals and 2,000 ports are available on campus for general student use. Students can access the following: computer help desk, free student e-mail accounts, online (class) grades, online (class) registration, online (class) schedules, online subscription databases. Campuswide network is available. 100% of college-owned or -operated housing units are wired for high-speed Internet access. Wireless service is available via classrooms, computer centers, computer labs, dorm rooms, learning centers, libraries, student centers.

Student Life *Housing options:* coed. Campus housing is university owned. *Activities and organizations:* drama/theater group, choral group, Student Activities Council, Phi Beta Lambda, Drama Club, Organization of Adult & Returning Students (OARS), Baptist Collegiate Ministry, national fraternities, national sororities. *Campus security:* 24-hour emergency response devices and patrols, late-night transport/escort service. *Student services:* health clinic, personal/psychological counseling.

Athletics Member NJCAA. *Intercollegiate sports:* baseball M (s), basketball M (s)/W (s), golf M (s)/W (s), tennis M (s)/W (s), volleyball W (s). *Intramural sports:* basketball M/W, cheerleading M/W, football M/W, riflery M (c)/W (c), softball M/W, table tennis M/W, volleyball M/W.

Standardized Tests *Required:* ACT (for admission).

Costs (2008–09) *Tuition:* state resident $109 per credit hour part-time; nonresident $280 per credit hour part-time. *Required fees:* $29 per credit hour part-time, $35 per term part-time.

Financial Aid Of all full-time matriculated undergraduates who enrolled in 2004, 2,564 applied for aid, 2,232 were judged to have need, 215 had their need fully met. 110 Federal Work-Study jobs (averaging $3000). 94 state and other part-time jobs (averaging $3000). In 2004, 350 non-need-based awards were made. *Average percent of need met:* 62%. *Average financial aid package:* $5568. *Average need-based loan:* $3183. *Average need-based gift aid:* $3504. *Average non-need-based aid:* $2643. *Average indebtedness upon graduation:* $7339.

Applying *Options:* electronic application, early admission, deferred entrance. *Required:* high school transcript. *Application deadlines:* rolling (freshmen), rolling (transfers).

Freshman Application Contact Office of Admissions and School Relations, University of Arkansas at Fort Smith, 5210 Grand Avenue, PO Box 3649, Fort Smith, AR 72913-3649. *Phone:* 479-788-7104. *Toll-free phone:* 888-512-5466. *Fax:* 479-788-7016. *E-mail:* information@uafortsmith.edu.

UNIVERSITY OF ARKANSAS AT LITTLE ROCK

Little Rock, Arkansas **www.ualr.edu/**

- **State-supported** university, founded 1927, part of University of Arkansas System
- **Urban** 150-acre campus
- **Endowment** $7.6 million
- **Coed**
- **Minimally difficult** entrance level

Faculty *Student/faculty ratio:* 16:1.

Academics *Calendar:* semesters. *Degrees:* certificates, associate, bachelor's, master's, doctoral, first professional, and post-master's certificates.

Student Life *Campus security:* 24-hour emergency response devices, student patrols, late-night transport/escort service.

Athletics Member NCAA. All Division I.

Standardized Tests *Required:* SAT or ACT (for placement).

Costs (2007–08) *Tuition:* state resident $4613 full-time, $154 per credit hour part-time; nonresident $12,105 full-time, $404 per credit hour part-time. *Required fees:* $1127 full-time, $38 per credit hour part-time. *Room only:* $3100.

Financial Aid *Average financial aid package:* $7190.

Applying *Options:* early admission, deferred entrance. *Required:* high school transcript, minimum 2.5 GPA, proof of immunization.

Freshman Application Contact Ms. Tammy Harrison, Director of Admissions, University of Arkansas at Little Rock, 2801 South University Avenue, Little

Rock, AR 72204-1099. *Phone:* 501-569-3127. *Toll-free phone:* 800-482-8892. *Fax:* 501-569-8956. *E-mail:* twharrison@ualn.edu.

UNIVERSITY OF ARKANSAS AT MONTICELLO

Monticello, Arkansas **www.uamont.edu/**

- **State-supported** comprehensive, founded 1909, part of University of Arkansas System
- **Small-town** 1600-acre campus
- **Endowment** $2.8 million
- **Coed** 3,067 undergraduate students, 73% full-time, 59% women, 41% men
- **Noncompetitive** entrance level, 60% of applicants were admitted

Undergraduates 2,247 full-time, 820 part-time. Students come from 24 states and territories, 4 other countries, 11% are from out of state, 32% African American, 0.3% Asian American or Pacific Islander, 1% Hispanic American, 0.7% Native American, 0.3% international, 9% transferred in, 25% live on campus. *Retention:* 48% of 2006 full-time freshmen returned.

Freshmen *Admission:* 1,636 applied, 987 admitted, 630 enrolled. *Average high school GPA:* 2.9. *Test scores:* ACT scores over 18: 66%; ACT scores over 24: 17%; ACT scores over 30: 1%.

Faculty *Total:* 241, 72% full-time, 35% with terminal degrees. *Student/faculty ratio:* 17:1.

Majors Accounting; agricultural production; agriculture; art; biological and physical sciences; biology/biological sciences; business administration and management; business teacher education; chemistry; criminal justice/law enforcement administration; criminal justice/safety; education; elementary education; English; forensic science and technology; forestry; health and physical education; history; industrial mechanics and maintenance technology; journalism; liberal arts and sciences/liberal studies; management information systems; mathematics; multi-/interdisciplinary studies related; music; music teacher education; nursing (registered nurse training); physical education teaching and coaching; physical sciences; political science and government; pre-dentistry studies; pre-law studies; premedical studies; pre-veterinary studies; psychology; social sciences; social work; special education; speech and rhetoric; survey technology; wildlife and wildlands science and management; wood science and wood products/pulp and paper technology.

Academics *Calendar:* semesters. *Degrees:* certificates, associate, bachelor's, master's, and postbachelor's certificates. *Special study options:* academic remediation for entering students, accelerated degree program, advanced placement credit, distance learning, double majors, independent study, off-campus study, part-time degree program, summer session for credit. *ROTC:* Army (b).

Computers on Campus 400 computers/terminals are available on campus for general student use. Students can access the following: campus intranet, computer help desk, free student e-mail accounts, online (class) grades, online (class) registration, online (class) schedules. Campuswide network is available. Wireless service is available via libraries.

Student Life *Housing options:* coed, men-only, women-only. Campus housing is university owned. *Activities and organizations:* drama/theater group, student-run newspaper, choral group, marching band, national fraternities, national sororities. *Campus security:* 24-hour emergency response devices and patrols. *Student services:* health clinic, personal/psychological counseling.

Athletics Member NCAA. All Division II. *Intercollegiate sports:* baseball M (s), basketball M (s)/W (s), cross-country running W, football M (s), golf M (s), softball W (s), tennis W. *Intramural sports:* baseball M, basketball M/W, cross-country running M/W, football M/W, golf M/W, racquetball M/W, soccer M/W, softball M/W, table tennis M/W, tennis M/W, track and field M/W, volleyball M/W.

Costs (2007–08) *Tuition:* state resident $3240 full-time, $108 per hour part-time; nonresident $7170 full-time, $239 per hour part-time. Full-time tuition and fees vary according to location and program. Part-time tuition and fees vary according to location and program. *Required fees:* $1060 full-time, $40 per hour part-time. *Room and board:* $3690; room only: $1430. Room and board charges vary according to board plan and housing facility. *Payment plan:* installment. *Waivers:* senior citizens and employees or children of employees.

Financial Aid Of all full-time matriculated undergraduates who enrolled in 2006, 166 Federal Work-Study jobs (averaging $1159). 292 state and other part-time jobs (averaging $1388).

Applying *Options:* early admission, deferred entrance. *Required:* high school transcript, proof of immunization. *Application deadlines:* 8/1 (freshmen), 8/1 (transfers).

Freshman Application Contact Ms. Mary Whiting, Director of Admissions, University of Arkansas at Monticello, PO Box 3600, Monticello, AR 71656. *Phone:* 870-460-1026. *Toll-free phone:* 800-844-1826. *E-mail:* admissions@uamont.edu.

UNIVERSITY OF ARKANSAS AT PINE BLUFF

Pine Bluff, Arkansas **www.uapb.edu/**

- **State-supported** comprehensive, founded 1873, part of University of Arkansas System
- **Urban** 327-acre campus
- **Coed** 3,099 undergraduate students, 87% full-time, 58% women, 42% men
- 64% of applicants were admitted

Undergraduates 2,694 full-time, 405 part-time. Students come from 30 states and territories, 17 other countries, 33% are from out of state, 96% African American, 0.2% Asian American or Pacific Islander, 0.3% Hispanic American, 0.5% international, 5% transferred in, 43% live on campus. *Retention:* 57% of 2006 full-time freshmen returned.

Freshmen *Admission:* 2,169 applied, 1,394 admitted, 819 enrolled. *Test scores:* ACT scores over 18: 30%; ACT scores over 24: 2%.

Faculty *Total:* 240, 68% full-time, 52% with terminal degrees. *Student/faculty ratio:* 18:1.

Majors Accounting; agricultural economics; agricultural teacher education; agriculture; agronomy and crop science; animal sciences; art; art teacher education; automobile/automotive mechanics technology; biology/biological sciences; business administration and management; business/managerial economics; business teacher education; chemistry; clothing/textiles; computer science; corrections; criminal justice/law enforcement administration; criminal justice/police science; dietetics; dramatic/theater arts; economics; elementary education; English; environmental biology; family and consumer sciences/home economics teacher education; family and consumer sciences/human sciences; fashion merchandising; fish/game management; gerontology; history; hotel/motel administration; industrial arts; industrial technology; kindergarten/preschool education; mathematics; music; music teacher education; nursing (registered nurse training); parks, recreation and leisure; physical education teaching and coaching; physics; political science and government; pre-medical studies; psychology; secondary education; social sciences; social work; sociology; special education; speech and rhetoric; trade and industrial teacher education.

Academics *Calendar:* semesters. *Degrees:* certificates, associate, bachelor's, and master's. *Special study options:* academic remediation for entering students, accelerated degree program, adult/continuing education programs, advanced placement credit, cooperative education, distance learning, double majors, external degree program, honors programs, independent study, internships, off-campus study, part-time degree program, services for LD students, summer session for credit. *ROTC:* Army (b). *Unusual degree programs:* 3-2 engineering with University of Arkansas (Fayetteville).

Computers on Campus 1,000 computers/terminals are available on campus for general student use. Campuswide network is available.

Student Life *Housing options:* men-only, women-only. Campus housing is university owned. *Activities and organizations:* drama/theater group, student-run newspaper, radio and television station, choral group, marching band, Pre-Alumni Club, Honors College, national fraternities, national sororities. *Campus security:* 24-hour emergency response devices. *Student services:* health clinic, personal/psychological counseling.

Athletics Member NCAA, NAIA. All NCAA Division I except football (Division I-AA), golf (Division I-AA). *Intercollegiate sports:* baseball M, basketball M (s)/W (s), cross-country running M/W, track and field M/W, volleyball W (s). *Intramural sports:* baseball M, basketball M, bowling M/W, cross-country running M, football M/W, golf M/W, gymnastics M/W, racquetball M/W, softball M/W, swimming and diving M/W, table tennis M/W, tennis M/W, track and field M/W, volleyball M/W, weight lifting M/W.

Costs (2007–08) *Tuition:* state resident $3300 full-time, $110 per credit hour part-time; nonresident $7710 full-time, $257 per credit hour part-time. *Required fees:* $1199 full-time, $7 per credit hour part-time, $23 per term part-time. *Room and board:* $6070; room only: $3510. Room and board charges vary according to board plan and housing facility.

Financial Aid Of all full-time matriculated undergraduates who enrolled in 2005, 2,825 applied for aid, 2,825 were judged to have need, 1,200 had their need fully met. 328 Federal Work-Study jobs (averaging $1000). *Average percent of need met:* 70%. *Average financial aid package:* $8121. *Average need-based loan:* $4500. *Average need-based gift aid:* $1000.

Applying *Options:* early admission, deferred entrance. *Required:* high school transcript, minimum 2.0 GPA. *Application deadline:* rolling (freshmen). *Notification:* continuous (freshmen), continuous (transfers).

Director of Admissions Mrs. Erica W. Fulton, Director of Admissions and Academic Records, University of Arkansas at Pine Bluff, Mail Slot 4981, 1200 North University Drive, Pine Bluff, AR 71611. *Phone:* 870-575-8487. *Toll-free phone:* 800-264-6585.

UNIVERSITY OF ARKANSAS FOR MEDICAL SCIENCES

Little Rock, Arkansas **www.uams.edu/**

- **State-supported** upper-level, founded 1879, part of University of Arkansas System
- **Urban** 5-acre campus
- **Endowment** $31.0 million
- **Coed** 834 undergraduate students, 73% full-time, 81% women, 19% men

Undergraduates 611 full-time, 223 part-time. 15% African American, 2% Asian American or Pacific Islander, 2% Hispanic American, 0.6% Native American.

Majors Biomedical technology; clinical laboratory science/medical technology; cytotechnology; emergency medical technology (EMT paramedic); nuclear medical technology; nursing (registered nurse training); respiratory care therapy; surgical technology.

Academics *Calendar:* semesters. *Degrees:* certificates, associate, bachelor's, master's, doctoral, and first professional (bachelor's degree is upper-level). *Special study options:* part-time degree program, services for LD students. *ROTC:* Army (c).

Computers on Campus Students can access the following: campus intranet, computer help desk, free student e-mail accounts. Campuswide network is available. 100% of college-owned or -operated housing units are wired for high-speed Internet access.

Student Life *Housing options:* coed. *Campus security:* 24-hour emergency response devices and patrols, late-night transport/escort service, controlled dormitory access. *Student services:* health clinic, personal/psychological counseling.

Athletics *Intercollegiate sports:* ultimate Frisbee M/W, volleyball M/W. *Intramural sports:* basketball M/W, football M, golf M, ultimate Frisbee M/W, volleyball M/W.

Financial Aid Of all full-time matriculated undergraduates who enrolled in 2005, 734 applied for aid, 686 were judged to have need. 9 Federal Work-Study jobs (averaging $1201). *Average percent of need met:* 62%. *Average financial aid package:* $3000. *Average need-based loan:* $4000. *Average need-based gift aid:* $500. *Average indebtedness upon graduation:* $7000.

Director of Admissions Ms. Mona Stiles, Admissions Officer, University of Arkansas for Medical Sciences, 4301 West Markham-Slot 601, Little Rock, AR 72205-7199. *Phone:* 501-686-5730.

UNIVERSITY OF CENTRAL ARKANSAS

Conway, Arkansas **www.uca.edu/**

- **State-supported** comprehensive, founded 1907
- **Small-town** 365-acre campus
- **Endowment** $1.0 million
- **Coed** 10,675 undergraduate students, 84% full-time, 58% women, 42% men
- **Moderately difficult** entrance level, 49% of applicants were admitted

Undergraduates 9,018 full-time, 1,657 part-time. Students come from 44 states and territories, 61 other countries, 6% are from out of state, 15% African American, 1% Asian American or Pacific Islander, 2% Hispanic American, 0.8% Native American, 4% international, 6% transferred in, 66% live on campus. *Retention:* 71% of 2006 full-time freshmen returned.

Freshmen *Admission:* 5,780 applied, 2,811 admitted, 1,793 enrolled. *Average high school GPA:* 3.3. *Test scores:* ACT scores over 18: 90%; ACT scores over 24: 45%; ACT scores over 30: 11%.

Faculty *Total:* 696, 73% full-time, 55% with terminal degrees. *Student/faculty ratio:* 18:1.

Majors Accounting; African-American/Black studies; art; athletic training; audiology and speech-language pathology; biological and physical sciences; biology/biological sciences; business administration and management; business/commerce; business teacher education; cardiovascular technology; chemistry; cinematography and film/video production; clinical laboratory science/medical technology; community health services counseling; computer and information sciences; dramatic/theater arts; economics; English composition; English/language arts teacher education; environmental studies; family and consumer sciences/home economics teacher education; family and consumer sciences/human sciences; finance; French; general studies; geography; health professions related; history; insurance; international/global studies; journalism; kindergarten/preschool education; kinesiology and exercise science; management information systems; marketing/marketing management; mathematics; mathematics teacher education; middle school education; multi-/interdisciplinary studies related; music; music performance; nuclear medical technology; nursing (registered nurse training); philosophy; physical education teaching and coaching; physics; political science and government; psychology; public administration; public relations, advertising, and applied communication related; religious studies; science teacher education; social studies teacher education; sociology; Spanish; speech and rhetoric; substance abuse/addiction counseling.

Academics *Calendar:* semesters. *Degrees:* certificates, associate, bachelor's, master's, doctoral, post-master's, and postbachelor's certificates. *Special study options:* academic remediation for entering students, accelerated degree program, advanced placement credit, cooperative education, distance learning, double majors, English as a second language, freshman honors college, honors programs, independent study, internships, part-time degree program, study abroad, summer session for credit. *ROTC:* Army (b). *Unusual degree programs:* 3-2 engineering with Arkansas State University.

Computers on Campus 643 computers/terminals are available on campus for general student use. Students can access the following: campus intranet, computer help desk, free student e-mail accounts, online (class) grades, online (class) registration, online (class) schedules. Campuswide network is available. 100% of college-owned or -operated housing units are wired for high-speed Internet access. Wireless service is available via entire campus.

Student Life *Housing:* on-campus residence required for freshman year. *Options:* coed, men-only, women-only, disabled students. Campus housing is university owned and leased by the school. Freshman campus housing is guaranteed. *Activities and organizations:* drama/theater group, student-run newspaper, radio and television station, choral group, marching band, Student Government Association, national fraternities, national sororities. *Campus security:* 24-hour emergency response devices and patrols, student patrols, late-night transport/escort service, controlled dormitory access, security personnel at entrances during evening hours. *Student services:* health clinic, personal/psychological counseling, women's center.

Athletics Member NCAA. All Division I. *Intercollegiate sports:* baseball M (s), basketball M (s)/W (s), cheerleading M (s)/W (s), cross-country running M (s)/W (s), football M (s), golf M (s)/W (s), soccer M (s)/W (s), softball W (s), tennis W (s), track and field M (s)/W (s), volleyball W (s). *Intramural sports:* badminton M/W, basketball M/W, bowling M/W, cross-country running M/W, football M/W, golf M/W, soccer M (c)/W, softball M/W, table tennis M/W, tennis M/W, track and field M/W, volleyball M/W.

Standardized Tests *Required:* SAT or ACT (for admission).

Costs (2007–08) *Tuition:* state resident $4830 full-time, $161 per credit hour part-time; nonresident $9660 full-time, $322 per credit hour part-time. Part-time tuition and fees vary according to course load. *Required fees:* $1375 full-time, $39 per credit hour part-time, $92 per term part-time. *Room and board:* $4600; room only: $2680. Room and board charges vary according to board plan and housing facility. *Payment plan:* installment. *Waivers:* senior citizens and employees or children of employees.

Applying *Options:* electronic application, early admission, deferred entrance. *Required:* high school transcript. *Application deadlines:* rolling (freshmen), rolling (transfers). *Notification:* continuous (freshmen), continuous (transfers).

Freshman Application Contact Ms. Melissa Goff, Director of Institutional Research and Admissions, University of Central Arkansas, 201 Donaghey Avenue, Conway, AR 72035. *Phone:* 501-450-5371. *Toll-free phone:* 800-243-8245. *Fax:* 501-450-5228. *E-mail:* mgoff@uca.edu.

UNIVERSITY OF PHOENIX–LITTLE ROCK CAMPUS

Little Rock, Arkansas **www.phoenix.edu/**

- **Proprietary** comprehensive, founded 2003
- **Urban** campus
- **Coed**
- **Noncompetitive** entrance level

Faculty *Student/faculty ratio:* 6:1.

Academics *Calendar:* continuous. *Degrees:* bachelor's and master's.

Student Life *Campus security:* late-night transport/escort service.

Costs (2007–08) *Tuition:* $10,740 full-time, $358 per credit part-time. Full-time tuition and fees vary according to course level.
Financial Aid *Average financial aid package:* $4311. *Average need-based gift aid:* $2117.
Applying *Options:* deferred entrance. *Application fee:* $45. *Required:* 1 letter of recommendation. *Required for some:* high school transcript.
Freshman Application Contact Ms. Beth Barilla, Associate Vice President, Student Admissions and Services, University of Phoenix–Little Rock Campus, 4615 East Elwood Street, Mail Stop AA-K101, Phoenix, AZ 85040-1958. *Phone:* 480-317-6000. *Toll-free phone:* 800-776-4867 (in-state); 800-228-7240 (out-of-state). *Fax:* 480-894-1758. *E-mail:* beth.barilla@phoenix.edu.

UNIVERSITY OF THE OZARKS

Clarksville, Arkansas **www.ozarks.edu/**

- **Independent Presbyterian** 4-year, founded 1834
- **Small-town** 56-acre campus with easy access to Little Rock
- **Endowment** $95.1 million
- **Coed** 622 undergraduate students, 94% full-time, 54% women, 46% men
- **Moderately difficult** entrance level, 97% of applicants were admitted

Undergraduates 583 full-time, 39 part-time. Students come from 24 states and territories, 20 other countries, 49% are from out of state, 4% African American, 3% Asian American or Pacific Islander, 5% Hispanic American, 4% Native American, 17% international, 5% transferred in, 66% live on campus. *Retention:* 67% of 2006 full-time freshmen returned.
Freshmen *Admission:* 656 applied, 635 admitted, 165 enrolled. *Average high school GPA:* 3.38. *Test scores:* SAT critical reading scores over 500: 55%; SAT math scores over 500: 64%; ACT scores over 18: 96%; SAT critical reading scores over 600: 22%; SAT math scores over 600: 25%; ACT scores over 24: 38%; SAT critical reading scores over 700: 5%; SAT math scores over 700: 4%; ACT scores over 30: 4%.
Faculty *Total:* 62, 73% full-time, 58% with terminal degrees. *Student/faculty ratio:* 11:1.
Majors Accounting; art; art teacher education; biology/biological sciences; broadcast journalism; business administration and management; business teacher education; chemistry; dramatic/theater arts; economics; elementary education; English; English/language arts teacher education; environmental studies; fine/studio arts; general studies; history; humanities; marketing/marketing management; mass communication/media; mathematics; middle school education; music; philosophy; philosophy and religious studies related; physical education teaching and coaching; physical sciences related; political science and government; psychology; religious education; religious studies; respiratory care therapy; social sciences; sociology; Spanish.
Academics *Calendar:* semesters. *Degree:* bachelor's. *Special study options:* academic remediation for entering students, advanced placement credit, cooperative education, double majors, English as a second language, independent study, internships, off-campus study, part-time degree program, services for LD students, study abroad, summer session for credit. *Unusual degree programs:* 3-2 engineering with University of Arkansas; theology with University of Dubuque, marine biology with University of South Mississippi, respiratory therapy with Arkansas Valley Technical Institute.
Computers on Campus 120 computers/terminals are available on campus for general student use. Students can access the following: campus intranet, computer help desk, free student e-mail accounts. Campuswide network is available. 100% of college-owned or -operated housing units are wired for high-speed Internet access.
Student Life *Housing:* on-campus residence required through sophomore year. *Options:* coed, men-only, women-only. Campus housing is university owned. Freshman campus housing is guaranteed. *Activities and organizations:* drama/theater group, student-run radio and television station, choral group, Phi Beta Lambda, Planet Club, SGA, Student Foundation Board, Baptist Campus Ministries. *Campus security:* 24-hour emergency response devices and patrols, late-night transport/escort service. *Student services:* health clinic.
Athletics Member NCAA. All Division III. *Intercollegiate sports:* baseball M, basketball M/W, cheerleading M/W, cross-country running M/W, soccer M/W, softball W, tennis M/W. *Intramural sports:* badminton M/W, basketball M/W, bowling M/W, football M/W, racquetball M/W, soccer M, softball M/W, table tennis M/W, tennis M/W, ultimate Frisbee M/W, volleyball M/W, weight lifting M/W.
Standardized Tests *Required:* SAT or ACT (for admission).
Costs (2007–08) *Comprehensive fee:* $21,585 includes full-time tuition ($15,630), mandatory fees ($480), and room and board ($5475). Part-time tuition: $654 per credit hour. *College room only:* $2500. Room and board charges vary according to board plan and housing facility. *Payment plan:* installment. *Waivers:* employees or children of employees.
Financial Aid Of all full-time matriculated undergraduates who enrolled in 2007, 344 applied for aid, 314 were judged to have need, 123 had their need fully met. 118 Federal Work-Study jobs (averaging $824). 227 state and other part-time jobs (averaging $956). In 2007, 221 non-need-based awards were made. *Average percent of need met:* 84%. *Average financial aid package:* $19,370. *Average need-based loan:* $6470. *Average need-based gift aid:* $12,142. *Average non-need-based aid:* $14,580. *Average indebtedness upon graduation:* $18,817.
Applying *Options:* electronic application, deferred entrance. *Application fee:* $30. *Required:* minimum 2.0 GPA. *Required for some:* essay or personal statement, high school transcript, letters of recommendation, interview. *Application deadlines:* rolling (freshmen), rolling (transfers). *Notification:* continuous (freshmen), continuous (transfers).
Freshman Application Contact Ms. Kimberly Myrick, Dean of Enrollment, University of the Ozarks, 415 North College Avenue, Clarksville, AR 72830-2880. *Phone:* 479-979-1227. *Toll-free phone:* 800-264-8636. *Fax:* 479-979-1417. *E-mail:* admiss@ozarks.edu.

WILLIAMS BAPTIST COLLEGE

Walnut Ridge, Arkansas **www.wbcoll.edu/**

- **Independent Southern Baptist** 4-year, founded 1941
- **Rural** 180-acre campus
- **Endowment** $7.9 million
- **Coed**
- **Minimally difficult** entrance level

Williams Baptist College is a four-year liberal arts college in Walnut Ridge, Arkansas. Known for its caring, Christ-centered atmosphere, Williams makes the college experience a personal journey in higher learning. It features small classes and more than twenty-five academic programs. WBC's Eagles belong to the NAIA and field six varsity teams. Telephone: 800-722-4434 (toll-free); World Wide Web: http://www.wbcoll.edu.

Faculty *Student/faculty ratio:* 13:1.
Academics *Calendar:* semesters. *Degrees:* associate and bachelor's.
Student Life *Campus security:* 24-hour emergency response devices, student patrols.
Athletics Member NAIA, NCCAA.
Standardized Tests *Required:* SAT or ACT (for admission).
Costs (2007–08) *Comprehensive fee:* $15,070 includes full-time tuition ($9700), mandatory fees ($670), and room and board ($4700).
Financial Aid Of all full-time matriculated undergraduates who enrolled in 2006, 476 applied for aid, 376 were judged to have need. 203 Federal Work-Study jobs (averaging $1061). 47 state and other part-time jobs (averaging $822). In 2006, 125 non-need-based awards were made. *Average financial aid package:* $10,041. *Average need-based loan:* $3425. *Average need-based gift aid:* $2196. *Average non-need-based aid:* $3562. *Average indebtedness upon graduation:* $15,990.
Applying *Options:* electronic application. *Application fee:* $20. *Required:* high school transcript, minimum 2.5 GPA. *Required for some:* essay or personal statement. *Recommended:* interview.
Freshman Application Contact Mrs. Angela Flippo, Vice President for Enrollment, Williams Baptist College, PO Box 3665, Walnut Ridge, AR 72476. *Phone:* 870-759-4117. *Toll-free phone:* 800-722-4434. *Fax:* 870-886-3924. *E-mail:* admissions@wbcoll.edu.

CALIFORNIA

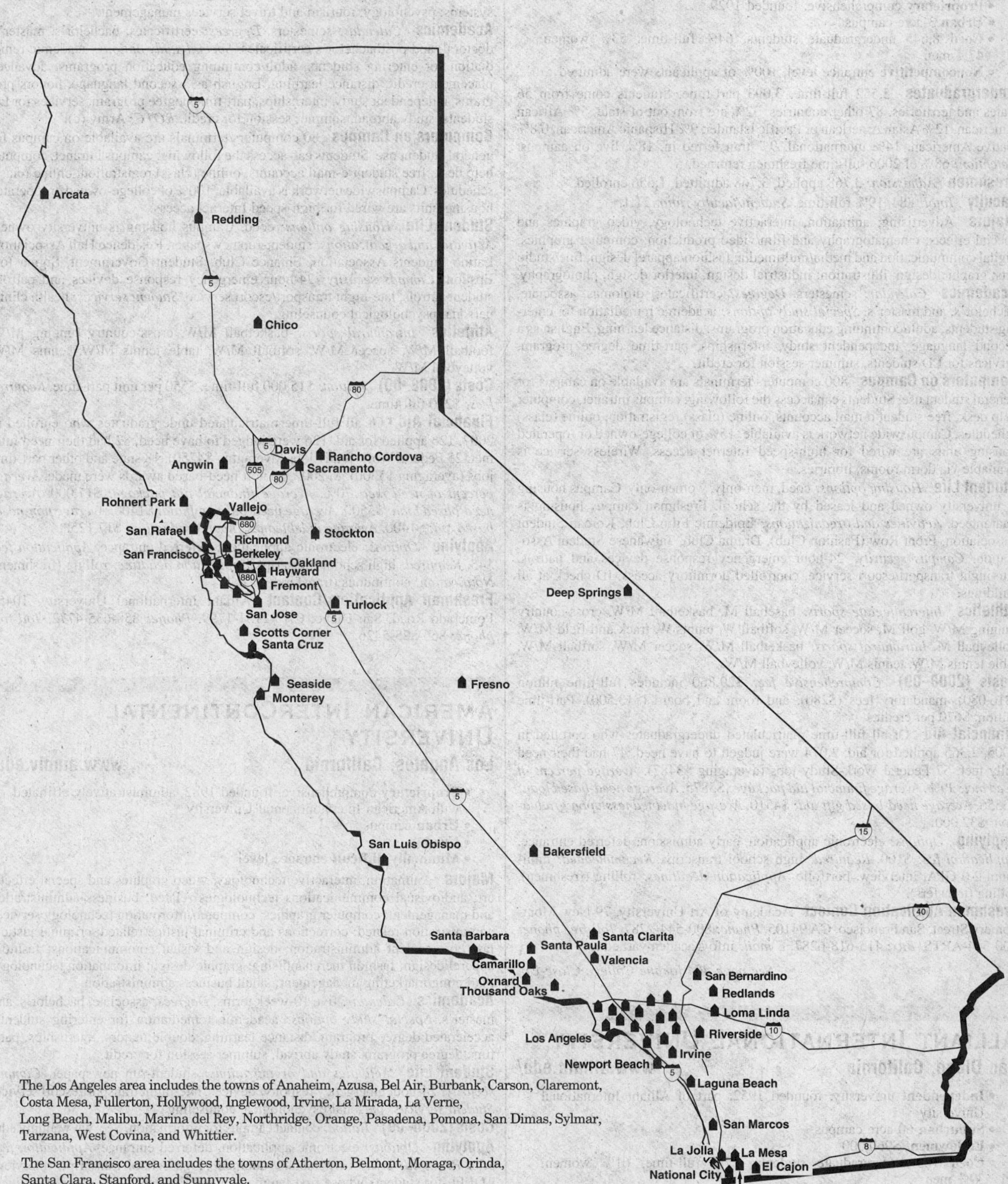

The Los Angeles area includes the towns of Anaheim, Azusa, Bel Air, Burbank, Carson, Claremont, Costa Mesa, Fullerton, Hollywood, Inglewood, Irvine, La Mirada, La Verne, Long Beach, Malibu, Marina del Rey, Northridge, Orange, Pasadena, Pomona, San Dimas, Sylmar, Tarzana, West Covina, and Whittier.

The San Francisco area includes the towns of Atherton, Belmont, Moraga, Orinda, Santa Clara, Stanford, and Sunnyvale.

ACADEMY OF ART UNIVERSITY

San Francisco, California **www.academyart.edu/**

- **Proprietary** comprehensive, founded 1929
- **Urban** 3-acre campus
- **Coed** 8,645 undergraduate students, 64% full-time, 53% women, 47% men
- **Noncompetitive** entrance level, 100% of applicants were admitted

Undergraduates 5,552 full-time, 3,093 part-time. Students come from 56 states and territories, 87 other countries, 32% are from out of state, 5% African American, 12% Asian American or Pacific Islander, 9% Hispanic American, 0.8% Native American, 14% international, 9% transferred in, 18% live on campus. *Retention:* 68% of 2006 full-time freshmen returned.

Freshmen *Admission:* 3,768 applied, 3,768 admitted, 1,656 enrolled.

Faculty *Total:* 884, 19% full-time. *Student/faculty ratio:* 21:1.

Majors Advertising; animation, interactive technology, video graphics and special effects; cinematography and film/video production; computer graphics; digital communication and media/multimedia; fashion/apparel design; fine/studio arts; graphic design; illustration; industrial design; interior design; photography.

Academics *Calendar:* semesters. *Degrees:* certificates, diplomas, associate, bachelor's, and master's. *Special study options:* academic remediation for entering students, adult/continuing education programs, distance learning, English as a second language, independent study, internships, part-time degree program, services for LD students, summer session for credit.

Computers on Campus 800 computers/terminals are available on campus for general student use. Students can access the following: campus intranet, computer help desk, free student e-mail accounts, online (class) registration, online (class) schedules. Campuswide network is available. 15% of college-owned or -operated housing units are wired for high-speed Internet access. Wireless service is available via dorm rooms, libraries.

Student Life *Housing options:* coed, men-only, women-only. Campus housing is university owned and leased by the school. Freshman campus housing is guaranteed. *Activities and organizations:* Epidemic Film Club, Korean Student Association, Front Row (Fashion Club), Drama Club, Taiwanese Student Association. *Campus security:* 24-hour emergency response devices and patrols, late-night transport/escort service, controlled dormitory access, ID check at all buildings.

Athletics *Intercollegiate sports:* baseball M, basketball M/W, cross-country running M/W, golf M, soccer M/W, softball W, tennis W, track and field M/W, volleyball M. *Intramural sports:* basketball M/W, soccer M/W, softball M/W, table tennis M/W, tennis M/W, volleyball M/W.

Costs (2008–09) *Comprehensive fee:* $29,860 includes full-time tuition ($16,080), mandatory fees ($280), and room and board ($13,500). Part-time tuition: $670 per credit.

Financial Aid Of all full-time matriculated undergraduates who enrolled in 2005, 2,365 applied for aid, 2,074 were judged to have need, 47 had their need fully met. 57 Federal Work-Study jobs (averaging $3487). *Average percent of need met:* 29%. *Average financial aid package:* $5875. *Average need-based loan:* $3556. *Average need-based gift aid:* $4510. *Average indebtedness upon graduation:* $32,000.

Applying *Options:* electronic application, early admission, deferred entrance. *Application fee:* $100. *Required:* high school transcript. *Recommended:* minimum 2.0 GPA, interview, portfolio. *Application deadlines:* rolling (freshmen), rolling (transfers).

Freshman Application Contact Academy of Art University, 79 New Montgomery Street, San Francisco, CA 94105. *Phone:* 800-544-2787. *Toll-free phone:* 800-544-ARTS. *Fax:* 415-618-6287. *E-mail:* info@academyart.edu.

See page 404 for the College Close-Up.

ALLIANT INTERNATIONAL UNIVERSITY

San Diego, California **www.alliant.edu/**

- **Independent** university, founded 1952, part of Alliant International University
- **Suburban** 60-acre campus
- **Endowment** $960,000
- **Coed** 183 undergraduate students, 77% full-time, 61% women, 39% men

Undergraduates 140 full-time, 43 part-time. Students come from 15 states and territories, 35 other countries, 10% are from out of state, 8% African American, 5% Asian American or Pacific Islander, 15% Hispanic American, 23% international, 28% transferred in, 35% live on campus.

Faculty *Total:* 288, 45% full-time, 100% with terminal degrees. *Student/faculty ratio:* 15:1.

Majors Business administration and management; education related; hotel/motel administration; international business/trade/commerce; international relations and affairs; journalism; Latin American studies; management information systems; psychology; tourism and travel services management.

Academics *Calendar:* semesters. *Degrees:* certificates, bachelor's, master's, doctoral, and postbachelor's certificates. *Special study options:* academic remediation for entering students, adult/continuing education programs, advanced placement credit, distance learning, English as a second language, honors programs, independent study, internships, part-time degree program, services for LD students, study abroad, summer session for credit. *ROTC:* Army (c).

Computers on Campus 80 computers/terminals are available on campus for general student use. Students can access the following: campus intranet, computer help desk, free student e-mail accounts, online (class) registration, online (class) schedules. Campuswide network is available. 100% of college-owned or -operated housing units are wired for high-speed Internet access.

Student Life *Housing options:* coed. Campus housing is university owned. *Activities and organizations:* student-run newspaper, Residence Hall Association, Latino Students Association, Finance Club, Student Government, Sigma Iota Epsilon. *Campus security:* 24-hour emergency response devices and patrols, student patrols, late-night transport/escort service. *Student services:* health clinic, personal/psychological counseling.

Athletics *Intramural sports:* basketball M/W, cross-country running M/W, football M/W, soccer M/W, softball M/W, table tennis M/W, tennis M/W, volleyball M/W.

Costs (2008–09) *Tuition:* $15,000 full-time, $550 per unit part-time. *Required fees:* $220 full-time.

Financial Aid Of all full-time matriculated undergraduates who enrolled in 2007, 126 applied for aid, 126 were judged to have need, 82 had their need fully met. 25 Federal Work-Study jobs (averaging $4750). 18 state and other part-time jobs (averaging $5300). In 2007, 10 non-need-based awards were made. *Average percent of need met:* 70%. *Average financial aid package:* $17,000. *Average need-based loan:* $5500. *Average need-based gift aid:* $1400. *Average non-need-based aid:* $1400. *Average indebtedness upon graduation:* $17,125.

Applying *Options:* electronic application, deferred entrance. *Application fee:* $45. *Required:* high school transcript. *Application deadline:* rolling (freshmen). *Notification:* continuous (transfers).

Freshman Application Contact Alliant International University, 10455 Pomerado Road, San Diego, CA 92131-1799. *Phone:* 858-635-4772. *Toll-free phone:* 866-825-5426.

AMERICAN INTERCONTINENTAL UNIVERSITY

Los Angeles, California **www.aiuniv.edu/**

- **Proprietary** comprehensive, founded 1982, administratively affiliated with American InterContinental University
- **Urban** campus
- **Coed**
- **Minimally difficult** entrance level

Majors Animation, interactive technology, video graphics and special effects; art; audiovisual communications technologies related; business administration and management; computer graphics; computer/information technology services administration related; corrections and criminal justice related; criminal justice/law enforcement administration; design and visual communications; fashion/apparel design; fashion merchandising; graphic design; information technology; marketing/marketing management; small business administration.

Academics *Calendar:* five 10-week terms. *Degrees:* associate, bachelor's, and master's. *Special study options:* academic remediation for entering students, accelerated degree program, distance learning, double majors, internships, part-time degree program, study abroad, summer session for credit.

Student Life *Activities and organizations:* student-run newspaper. *Campus security:* 24-hour emergency response devices, late-night transport/escort service. *Student services:* personal/psychological counseling.

Costs (2008–09) *Tuition:* contact campus for information. See: www.aiuniv.edu.

Applying *Options:* electronic application, deferred entrance. *Application fee:* $50. *Required:* essay or personal statement, high school transcript, interview, TOEFL for students whose first language is not English. *Application deadlines:* rolling (freshmen), rolling (transfers).

Freshman Application Contact Director of High School Admissions, American InterContinental University, 12655 West Jefferson Boulevard, Los Angeles, CA 90066. *Phone:* 310-302-2000 Ext. 2632. *Toll-free phone:* 888-594-9888.

AMERICAN JEWISH UNIVERSITY

Bel Air, California **www.ajula.edu/**

- **Independent Jewish** comprehensive, founded 1947
- **Suburban** 28-acre campus with easy access to Los Angeles
- **Coed** 115 undergraduate students, 100% full-time, 49% women, 51% men
- **Moderately difficult** entrance level

Undergraduates 115 full-time. Students come from 10 states and territories, 3 other countries, 30% are from out of state, 10% transferred in, 70% live on campus. *Retention:* 68% of 2006 full-time freshmen returned.

Freshmen *Admission:* 18 enrolled. *Average high school GPA:* 3.3.

Faculty *Total:* 91, 21% full-time, 42% with terminal degrees. *Student/faculty ratio:* 7:1.

Majors Business/managerial economics; interdisciplinary studies; Jewish/Judaic studies; liberal arts and sciences/liberal studies; literature; political science and government; pre-medical studies; psychology.

Academics *Calendar:* semesters. *Degrees:* bachelor's and master's. *Special study options:* academic remediation for entering students, advanced placement credit, cooperative education, double majors, independent study, internships, off-campus study, part-time degree program, services for LD students, student-designed majors, study abroad, summer session for credit. *Unusual degree programs:* 3-2 business administration with non-profit management; MAEd.

Computers on Campus 16 computers/terminals are available on campus for general student use. Wireless service is available via entire campus.

Student Life *Housing:* on-campus residence required through junior year. *Options:* coed. Campus housing is university owned. Freshman campus housing is guaranteed. *Activities and organizations:* drama/theater group, student-run newspaper, choral group, ASUJC, Graduate Student Association, Resident Life Council, College Urban Fellows, UJ Chorale. *Campus security:* 24-hour emergency response devices and patrols, controlled dormitory access. *Student services:* health clinic, personal/psychological counseling.

Standardized Tests *Required:* SAT or ACT (for admission).

Costs (2007–08) *Comprehensive fee:* $32,190 includes full-time tuition ($20,400), mandatory fees ($900), and room and board ($10,890). Part-time tuition: $850 per credit. *Room and board:* Room and board charges vary according to board plan. *Payment plan:* installment. *Waivers:* employees or children of employees.

Financial Aid Of all full-time matriculated undergraduates who enrolled in 2007, 88 applied for aid, 88 were judged to have need, 88 had their need fully met. 28 Federal Work-Study jobs (averaging $1904). In 2007, 10 non-need-based awards were made. *Average percent of need met:* 100%. *Average financial aid package:* $20,400. *Average need-based loan:* $4047. *Average need-based gift aid:* $9328. *Average non-need-based aid:* $5865.

Applying *Options:* electronic application, early admission, early decision, deferred entrance. *Application fee:* $35. *Required:* essay or personal statement, high school transcript, 2 letters of recommendation. *Required for some:* interview. *Recommended:* minimum 3.3 GPA, interview. *Application deadlines:* rolling (freshmen), rolling (transfers). *Early decision deadline:* 12/31. *Notification:* continuous (freshmen), continuous (transfers), 1/31 (early decision).

Freshman Application Contact Ms. Julie Brydon, Undergraduate Admissions Administrative Assistant, American Jewish University, 15600 Mulholland Drive, Bel Air, CA 90077. *Phone:* 310-440-1247. *Toll-free phone:* 888-853-6763. *Fax:* 310-471-3657. *E-mail:* admissions@ajula.edu.

ANTIOCH UNIVERSITY LOS ANGELES

Culver City, California **www.antiochla.edu/**

- **Independent** upper-level, founded 1972, part of Antioch University
- **Urban** 1-acre campus with easy access to Los Angeles
- **Coed**
- **Moderately difficult** entrance level

Faculty *Student/faculty ratio:* 14:1.

Academics *Calendar:* quarters. *Degrees:* bachelor's, master's, post-master's, and postbachelor's certificates.

Student Life *Campus security:* 24-hour emergency response devices, late-night transport/escort service.

Costs (2007–08) *Tuition:* $15,498 full-time, $501 per credit part-time.

Applying *Options:* deferred entrance. *Application fee:* $60.

Application Contact Admissions, Antioch University Los Angeles, 400 Corporate Pointe, Culver City, CA 90230. *Phone:* 310-578-1080 Ext. 217. *Toll-free phone:* 800-7ANTIOCH. *Fax:* 310-822-4824. *E-mail:* admissions@antiochla.edu.

ANTIOCH UNIVERSITY SANTA BARBARA

Santa Barbara, California **www.antiochsb.edu/**

- **Independent** upper-level, founded 1977, part of Antioch University
- **Small-town** campus with easy access to Los Angeles
- **Coed** 96 undergraduate students, 29% full-time, 75% women, 25% men

Undergraduates 28 full-time, 68 part-time. Students come from 1 other country, 1% African American, 1% Asian American or Pacific Islander, 33% Hispanic American, 4% Native American, 1% international, 100% transferred in.

Faculty *Total:* 69, 23% full-time. *Student/faculty ratio:* 15:1.

Majors General studies.

Academics *Calendar:* quarters. *Degrees:* bachelor's, master's, and doctoral. *Special study options:* academic remediation for entering students, accelerated degree program, adult/continuing education programs, double majors, independent study, internships, part-time degree program, student-designed majors, summer session for credit.

Computers on Campus 14 computers/terminals are available on campus for general student use. Students can access the following: computer help desk, free student e-mail accounts, online (class) grades, online (class) registration, online (class) schedules. Campuswide network is available.

Student Life *Housing:* college housing not available. *Campus security:* late-night transport/escort service.

Costs (2007–08) *Tuition:* $14,640 full-time, $490 per unit part-time. *Required fees:* $56 full-time. *Payment plan:* installment. *Waivers:* employees or children of employees.

Financial Aid Of all full-time matriculated undergraduates who enrolled in 2003, 23 Federal Work-Study jobs (averaging $2120).

Applying *Options:* electronic application, deferred entrance. *Application fee:* $60. *Application deadline:* rolling (transfers).

Application Contact Director of Admissions, Antioch University Santa Barbara, 801 Garden Street, Santa Barbara, CA 93101-1580. *Phone:* 805-962-8179. *Fax:* 805-962-4786. *E-mail:* admissions@antiochsb.edu.

ARGOSY UNIVERSITY, INLAND EMPIRE

San Bernardino, California
www.argosy.edu/locations/los-angeles-inland-empire/

- **Proprietary** university, founded 2006
- **Coed**

Majors Business administration and management; criminal justice/law enforcement administration; finance; international business/trade/commerce; marketing/marketing management; psychology.

Admissions Office Contact Argosy University, Inland Empire, 636 East Brier Drive, Suite 235, San Bernardino, CA 92408. *Toll-free phone:* 866-217-9075.

See page 406 for the College Close-Up.

ARGOSY UNIVERSITY, ORANGE COUNTY

Santa Ana, California
www.argosy.edu/locations/los-angeles-orange-county/

- **Proprietary** university
- **Urban** campus with easy access to Los Angeles and San Diego
- **Coed**

Majors Business administration and management; criminal justice/law enforcement administration; finance; health/health care administration; international business/trade/commerce; marketing/marketing management; organizational behavior; psychology; substance abuse/addiction counseling.

Academics *Calendar:* semesters. *Degrees:* associate, bachelor's, master's, and doctoral.

Freshman Application Contact Director of Admissions, Argosy University, Orange County, 3501 West Sunflower Avenue, Suite 110, Santa Ana, CA 92704. *Phone:* 714-338-6200. *Toll-free phone:* 800-716-9598.

See page 406 for the College Close-Up.

ARGOSY UNIVERSITY, SAN DIEGO

San Diego, California **www.argosy.edu/locations/san-diego/**

- **Proprietary** university
- **Coed**

Majors Business administration and management; criminal justice/law enforcement administration; finance; health/health care administration; international business/trade/commerce; marketing/marketing management; psychology.

Academics *Degrees:* associate, bachelor's, master's, and doctoral.

Director of Admissions Admissions Director, Argosy University, San Diego, 1615 Murray Canyon Road, Suite 100, San Diego, CA 92108. *Toll-free phone:* 866-505-0333.

See page 406 for the College Close-Up.

ARGOSY UNIVERSITY, SAN FRANCISCO BAY AREA

Alameda, California **www.argosy.edu/locations/san-francisco/**

- **Proprietary** university, founded 1998, administratively affiliated with Education Management Corporation
- **Urban** campus with easy access to Oakland and San Francisco
- **Coed**

Majors Business administration and management; criminal justice/law enforcement administration; finance; health/health care administration; international business/trade/commerce; marketing/marketing management; psychology.

Academics *Calendar:* semesters. *Degrees:* bachelor's, master's, and doctoral.

Director of Admissions Argosy University, San Francisco Bay Area, 1005 Atlantic Avenue, Alameda, CA 94501. *Phone:* 510-217-4700. *Toll-free phone:* 866-215-2777 (in-state); 866-215-2777 (out-of-state). *Fax:* 510-217-4800.

See page 406 for the College Close-Up.

ARGOSY UNIVERSITY, SANTA MONICA

Santa Monica, California
www.argosy.edu/locations/los-angeles-santa-monica/

- **Proprietary** university
- **Coed**

Majors Business administration and management; criminal justice/law enforcement administration; finance; health/health care administration; international business/trade/commerce; marketing/marketing management; psychology.

Academics *Degrees:* associate, bachelor's, master's, and doctoral.

Freshman Application Contact Argosy University, Santa Monica, 2950 31st Street, Santa Monica, CA 90405. *Phone:* 310-866-4000. *Toll-free phone:* 866-505-0332.

See page 406 for the College Close-Up.

ART CENTER COLLEGE OF DESIGN

Pasadena, California **www.artcenter.edu/**

- **Independent** comprehensive, founded 1930
- **Suburban** 175-acre campus with easy access to Los Angeles
- **Endowment** $43.2 million
- **Coed**
- **Very difficult** entrance level

Faculty *Student/faculty ratio:* 12:1.

Academics *Calendar:* trimesters. *Degrees:* bachelor's and master's.

Student Life *Campus security:* 24-hour emergency response devices and patrols.

Standardized Tests *Required for some:* SAT or ACT (for admission).

Costs (2007–08) *Tuition:* $29,344 full-time. *Required fees:* $235 full-time.

Financial Aid Of all full-time matriculated undergraduates who enrolled in 2005, 1,090 applied for aid. 150 Federal Work-Study jobs (averaging $2000). *Average percent of need met:* 60. *Average financial aid package:* $13,708. *Average need-based loan:* $5283. *Average need-based gift aid:* $8227. *Average indebtedness upon graduation:* $70,000.

Applying *Options:* electronic application, deferred entrance. *Application fee:* $50. *Required:* essay or personal statement, high school transcript, portfolio. *Recommended:* minimum 3.0 GPA, interview.

Freshman Application Contact Elias Gonzales, Interim Director, Admissions, Art Center College of Design, 1700 Lida Street, Pasadena, CA 91103-1999. *Phone:* 626-396-2373. *Fax:* 626-795-0578. *E-mail:* admissions@artcenter.edu.

THE ART INSTITUTE OF CALIFORNIA–INLAND EMPIRE

San Bernardino, California
www.artinstitutes.edu/inlandempire/

- **Proprietary** 4-year, administratively affiliated with Education Management Corporation
- **Suburban** campus
- **Coed**
- **Noncompetitive** entrance level

Academics *Degree:* bachelor's.

Majors Animation, interactive technology, video graphics and special effects; fashion merchandising; graphic design; interior design; restaurant, culinary, and catering management; Web page, digital/multimedia and information resources design.

Student Life *Campus security:* 24-hour emergency response devices and patrols, late-night transport/escort service, controlled dormitory access.

Standardized Tests *Recommended:* SAT or ACT (for admission).

Costs (2007–08) *Tuition:* tuition cost varies by program. Prospective students should contact the school for current tuition costs. Other charges include a starting kit for all first-quarter students. Kits vary in price depending on the program of study.

Applying *Application fee:* $150. *Required:* essay or personal statement, high school transcript, interview. *Required for some:* letters of recommendation.

Freshman Application Contact Admissions Office, The Art Institute of California–Inland Empire, 630 East Brier Drive, San Bernardino, CA 92408. *Phone:* 909-915-2100. *Toll-free phone:* 800-353-0812. *Fax:* 909-915-2130. *E-mail:* mjeffs@aii.edu.

See page 408 for the College Close-Up.

THE ART INSTITUTE OF CALIFORNIA–LOS ANGELES

Santa Monica, California **www.aicala.artinstitutes.edu/**

- **Proprietary** 4-year, part of Education Management Corporation
- **Urban** campus
- **Coed** 2,068 undergraduate students, 100% full-time, 34% women, 66% men
- **Noncompetitive** entrance level, 56% of applicants were admitted

Undergraduates 2,068 full-time. Students come from 21 states and territories, 22 other countries, 6% African American, 9% Asian American or Pacific Islander, 19% Hispanic American, 0.6% Native American, 3% international, 15% live on campus.

Freshmen *Admission:* 589 applied, 328 admitted, 328 enrolled. *Average high school GPA:* 2.64.

Faculty *Total:* 120, 48% full-time, 4% with terminal degrees. *Student/faculty ratio:* 19:1.

Majors Animation, interactive technology, video graphics and special effects; cinematography and film/video production; culinary arts; graphic design; interior design; recording arts technology; restaurant, culinary, and catering management; web page, digital/multimedia and information resources design.

Academics *Calendar:* quarters. *Degrees:* associate and bachelor's. *Special study options:* academic remediation for entering students, adult/continuing education programs, advanced placement credit, distance learning, honors programs, independent study, internships, services for LD students, study abroad, summer session for credit.

Computers on Campus 400 computers/terminals are available on campus for general student use. Students can access the following: online (class) registration. Campuswide network is available.

Student Life *Housing options:* men-only, women-only. Campus housing is leased by the school. *Campus security:* 24-hour patrols. *Student services:* personal/psychological counseling.

Costs (2007–08) *Tuition:* $21,840 full-time, $455 per credit part-time. *Room only:* $10,652.

Applying *Options:* electronic application, deferred entrance. *Application fee:* $50. *Required:* essay or personal statement, high school transcript, interview. *Required for some:* minimum 2.5 GPA, letters of recommendation, portfolio. *Application deadlines:* rolling (freshmen), rolling (transfers). *Notification:* continuous (freshmen), continuous (transfers).

Freshman Application Contact Assistant Director of Admissions, The Art Institute of California–Los Angeles, 2900 31st Street, Santa Monica, CA 90405-3035. *Phone:* 310-752-4700. *Toll-free phone:* 888-646-4610. *Fax:* 310-752-4708. *E-mail:* ailaadm@aii.edu.

See page 410 for the College Close-Up.

THE ART INSTITUTE OF CALIFORNIA–ORANGE COUNTY

Santa Ana, California **www.aicaoc.artinstitutes.edu/**

- **Proprietary** 4-year, founded 2000, part of Education Management Corporation
- **Urban** campus with easy access to Orange County, Los Angeles
- **Coed** 1,761 undergraduate students, 79% full-time, 41% women, 59% men

Undergraduates 1,391 full-time, 370 part-time. Students come from 23 states and territories, 9% are from out of state, 1% African American, 5% Asian American or Pacific Islander, 8% Hispanic American, 0.3% Native American, 9% live on campus.

Freshmen *Admission:* 460 enrolled.

Faculty *Total:* 114, 54% full-time. *Student/faculty ratio:* 19:1.

Majors Advertising; animation, interactive technology, video graphics and special effects; cooking and related culinary arts; industrial design; interior design; restaurant, culinary, and catering management.

Academics *Calendar:* quarters. *Degrees:* associate and bachelor's. *Special study options:* academic remediation for entering students, advanced placement credit, cooperative education, distance learning, independent study, internships, services for LD students, study abroad.

Computers on Campus 312 computers/terminals are available on campus for general student use. Students can access the following: campus intranet, free student e-mail accounts, online (class) registration. Campuswide network is available.

Student Life *Housing options:* coed, disabled students. Campus housing is leased by the school. Freshman campus housing is guaranteed. *Activities and organizations:* student-run newspaper, Pastry Club, GDSA (Game Developers Student Association), Women in Animation, Classic Game Club, AIGA (American Institute of Graphic Arts). *Campus security:* late-night transport/escort service. *Student services:* personal/psychological counseling.

Costs (2007–08) *Tuition:* tuition costs may be obtained by contacting the school or by visiting the school's Web site. Additional expenses include a first-quarter starting kit and lab fees for some programs.

Applying *Options:* electronic application, early admission, early decision, deferred entrance. *Required:* essay or personal statement, high school transcript, interview. *Required for some:* minimum 2.5 GPA, letters of recommendation, portfolio. *Recommended:* minimum 2.0 GPA, letters of recommendation. *Application deadlines:* rolling (freshmen), rolling (transfers). *Notification:* continuous (freshmen), continuous (transfers).

Freshman Application Contact Mr. Steve Rickard, The Art Institute of California–Orange County, 3601 West Sunflower Avenue, Santa Ana, CA 92704. *Phone:* 714-830-0200. *Toll-free phone:* 888-549-3055. *Fax:* 714-556-3055. *E-mail:* srickard@aii.edu.

See page 412 for the College Close-Up.

THE ART INSTITUTE OF CALIFORNIA–SACRAMENTO

Sacramento, California **www.artinstitutes.edu/sacramento/**

- **Proprietary** 4-year

Majors Animation, interactive technology, video graphics and special effects; cinematography and film/video production; graphic design; interior design; restaurant, culinary, and catering management; Web page, digital/multimedia and information resources design.

Freshman Application Contact Admissions Director, The Art Institute of California–Sacramento, 2850 Gateway Oaks Drive, Suite 100, Sacramento, CA 95833. *Phone:* 800-477-1957.

See page 414 for the College Close-Up.

THE ART INSTITUTE OF CALIFORNIA–SAN DIEGO

San Diego, California **www.aica.artinstitutes.edu/**

- **Proprietary** 4-year, founded 1981, part of Education Management Corporation
- **Urban** campus
- **Coed** 2,145 undergraduate students
- **Minimally difficult** entrance level

Undergraduates Students come from 30 states and territories, 15% are from out of state, 3% African American, 9% Asian American or Pacific Islander, 17% Hispanic American, 0.7% Native American, 0.3% international, 12% live on campus. *Retention:* 63% of 2005 full-time freshmen returned.

Freshmen *Average high school GPA:* 2.29.

Faculty *Total:* 125, 50% full-time, 100% with terminal degrees. *Student/faculty ratio:* 22:1.

Majors Advertising; animation, interactive technology, video graphics and special effects; design and applied arts related; digital communication and media/multimedia; interior design; intermedia/multimedia; restaurant, culinary, and catering management; restaurant/food services management.

Academics *Calendar:* quarters. *Degrees:* associate and bachelor's. *Special study options:* cooperative education, double majors, internships, services for LD students, summer session for credit.

Computers on Campus 350 computers/terminals are available on campus for general student use. Students can access the following: computer help desk, free student e-mail accounts, online (class) grades, online (class) registration, online (class) schedules. Campuswide network is available. Wireless service is available via entire campus.

Student Life *Housing options:* men-only, women-only. Campus housing is leased by the school and is provided by a third party. Freshman applicants given priority for college housing. *Activities and organizations:* drama/theater group, student-run newspaper, Advertising Club-AAF, Concept Art Club, ASID, Ambassadors, AIGA. *Campus security:* 24-hour emergency response devices. *Student services:* personal/psychological counseling.

Standardized Tests *Required for some:* SAT or ACT (for admission).

Costs (2007–08) *Tuition:* $22,272 full-time, $464 per credit part-time. tuition cost varies by program. Prospective students should contact the school for current tuition costs. Other charges include a starting kit for all first-quarter students. Kits vary in price depending on the program of study. *Room only:* $10,272. *Payment plan:* installment. *Waivers:* employees or children of employees.

Applying *Options:* electronic application, early admission, deferred entrance. *Application fee:* $50. *Required:* essay or personal statement, high school transcript, interview, minimum GPA of 2.5 and portfolio required for GAD students. *Required for some:* minimum 2.5 GPA, letters of recommendation. *Recommended:* minimum 2.0 GPA. *Application deadlines:* rolling (freshmen), rolling (transfers). *Notification:* continuous (freshmen), continuous (transfers).

Freshman Application Contact The Art Institute of California-San Diego, 7650 Mission Valley Road, San Diego, CA 92108. *Phone:* 858-598-1399. *Toll-free phone:* 866-275-2422. *Fax:* 619-291-3206. *E-mail:* info@aii.edu.

See page 416 for the College Close-Up.

THE ART INSTITUTE OF CALIFORNIA–SAN FRANCISCO

San Francisco, California **www.aicasf.artinstitutes.edu/**

- **Proprietary** 4-year, founded 1939, part of Education Management Corporation
- **Urban** campus
- **Coed**
- **Moderately difficult** entrance level

Faculty *Student/faculty ratio:* 16:1.

Majors Advertising; animation, interactive technology, video graphics and special effects; cinematography and film/video production; computer programming (specific applications); fashion/apparel design; fashion merchandising; graphic design; interior design; Web page, digital/multimedia and information resources design.

Academics *Calendar:* quarters. *Degrees:* associate and bachelor's.

Student Life *Campus security:* 24-hour emergency response devices, late-night transport/escort service.

Costs (2007–08) *Tuition:* tuition cost varies by program. Prospective students should contact the school for current tuition costs. Other charges include a starting kit for all first-quarter students. Kits vary in price depending on the program of study.

Applying *Options:* electronic application, deferred entrance. *Application fee:* $50. *Required:* essay or personal statement, high school transcript, interview. *Required for some:* letters of recommendation. *Recommended:* minimum 2.0 GPA.

Freshman Application Contact Mr. Clark Dawood, Dean of Student Affairs, The Art Institute of California–San Francisco, 1170 Market Street, San Francisco, CA 94102-4908. *Phone:* 415-276-1004. *Toll-free phone:* 888-493-3261.

See page 418 for the College Close-Up.

THE ART INSTITUTE OF CALIFORNIA–SUNNYVALE

Sunnyvale, California **www.artinstitutes.edu/sunnyvale/**

- **Proprietary** 4-year

Majors Cinematography and film/video production; fashion merchandising; graphic design; interior design; restaurant, culinary, and catering management; Web page, digital/multimedia and information resources design.

Freshman Application Contact Admissions Director, The Art Institute of California–Sunnyvale, 1120 Kifer Road, Sunnyvale, CA 94086. *Phone:* 866-583-7961.

See page 420 for the College Close-Up.

AZUSA PACIFIC UNIVERSITY

Azusa, California **www.apu.edu/**

- **Independent nondenominational** comprehensive, founded 1899
- **Small-town** 60-acre campus with easy access to Los Angeles
- **Endowment** $33.1 million
- **Coed** 4,615 undergraduate students, 85% full-time, 63% women, 37% men
- **Moderately difficult** entrance level, 73% of applicants were admitted

Undergraduates 3,924 full-time, 691 part-time. Students come from 48 states and territories, 47 other countries, 19% are from out of state, 5% African American, 7% Asian American or Pacific Islander, 14% Hispanic American, 0.5% Native American, 3% international, 8% transferred in, 48% live on campus. *Retention:* 80% of 2006 full-time freshmen returned.

Freshmen *Admission:* 3,229 applied, 2,370 admitted, 855 enrolled. *Average high school GPA:* 3.59. *Test scores:* SAT critical reading scores over 500: 67%; SAT math scores over 500: 67%; ACT scores over 18: 94%; SAT critical reading scores over 600: 25%; SAT math scores over 600: 24%; ACT scores over 24: 45%; SAT critical reading scores over 700: 2%; SAT math scores over 700: 5%; ACT scores over 30: 6%.

Faculty *Total:* 351, 91% full-time, 69% with terminal degrees.

Majors Accounting; applied art; athletic training; biblical studies; biochemistry; biology/biological sciences; business administration and management; chemistry; communication/speech communication and rhetoric; computer science; cultural studies; divinity/ministry; English; health science; history; international relations and affairs; liberal arts and sciences/liberal studies; management information systems; marketing/marketing management; mathematics; music; natural sciences; nursing (registered nurse training); philosophy; physical education teaching and coaching; physics; political science and government; pre-engineering; pre-law studies; psychology; religious studies; social sciences; social work; sociology; Spanish; theology; web page, digital/multimedia and information resources design.

Academics *Calendar:* semesters. *Degrees:* bachelor's, master's, doctoral, and first professional. *Special study options:* academic remediation for entering students, accelerated degree program, adult/continuing education programs, advanced placement credit, cooperative education, distance learning, double majors, English as a second language, freshman honors college, honors programs, independent study, internships, off-campus study, part-time degree program, services for LD students, study abroad, summer session for credit. *ROTC:* Army (c).

Computers on Campus 300 computers/terminals are available on campus for general student use. Students can access the following: campus intranet, computer help desk, free student e-mail accounts, online (class) grades, online (class) registration. Campuswide network is available. Wireless service is available via entire campus.

Student Life *Housing options:* coed, men-only, women-only. Campus housing is university owned and leased by the school. Freshman applicants given priority for college housing. *Activities and organizations:* drama/theater group, student-run newspaper, radio and television station, choral group, marching band, community service groups, choir, outreach ministries groups, Habitat for Humanity, Multi-Ethnic Student Alliance (MESA). *Campus security:* 24-hour emergency response devices and patrols, student patrols, late-night transport/escort service, controlled dormitory access. *Student services:* health clinic, personal/psychological counseling.

Athletics Member NAIA. *Intercollegiate sports:* baseball M (s), basketball M (s)/W (s), cross-country running M (s)/W (s), football M (s), golf M (s), soccer M (s)/W (s), softball W (s), tennis M (s), track and field M (s)/W (s), volleyball M/W (s). *Intramural sports:* basketball M/W, football M/W, golf M/W, skiing (downhill) M/W, soccer W, volleyball M/W.

Standardized Tests *Required:* SAT or ACT (for admission).

Costs (2007–08) *Comprehensive fee:* $32,648 includes full-time tuition ($24,430), mandatory fees ($700), and room and board ($7518). Full-time tuition and fees vary according to course load. Part-time tuition: $1020 per unit. Part-time tuition and fees vary according to course load. *College room only:* $3880. Room and board charges vary according to board plan, housing facility, and student level. *Payment plan:* installment. *Waivers:* employees or children of employees.

Financial Aid Of all full-time matriculated undergraduates who enrolled in 2005, 3,921 applied for aid, 2,433 were judged to have need, 419 had their need fully met. 761 Federal Work-Study jobs (averaging $1479). In 2005, 940 non-need-based awards were made. *Average percent of need met:* 61%. *Average financial aid package:* $19,785. *Average need-based loan:* $7888. *Average need-based gift aid:* $9006. *Average non-need-based aid:* $4741. *Average indebtedness upon graduation:* $18,777. *Financial aid deadline:* 7/1.

Applying *Options:* early admission, early action, deferred entrance. *Application fee:* $45. *Required:* essay or personal statement, high school transcript, minimum 2.8 GPA, 2 letters of recommendation. *Required for some:* interview. *Application deadlines:* 6/1 (freshmen), 6/1 (transfers), 12/1 (early action). *Notification:* continuous (freshmen), continuous (transfers), 1/15 (early action).

Freshman Application Contact Ms. Lynnette Barnes, Processing Coordinator, Azusa Pacific University, 901 East Alosta Avenue, PO Box 7000, Azusa, CA 91702-7000. *Phone:* 626-815-6000 Ext. 3419. *Toll-free phone:* 800-TALK-APU. *E-mail:* admissions@apu.edu.

See page 422 for the College Close-Up.

BETHANY UNIVERSITY

Scotts Valley, California **www.bethany.edu/**

- **Independent Assemblies of God** comprehensive, founded 1919
- **Small-town** 40-acre campus with easy access to San Francisco and San Jose
- **Endowment** $1.5 million
- **Coed** 463 undergraduate students, 83% full-time, 59% women, 41% men
- **Minimally difficult** entrance level, 51% of applicants were admitted

Undergraduates 385 full-time, 78 part-time. Students come from 15 states and territories, 4 other countries, 15% are from out of state, 9% African American, 6% Asian American or Pacific Islander, 15% Hispanic American, 0.6% Native American, 0.9% international, 14% transferred in, 80% live on campus. *Retention:* 65% of 2006 full-time freshmen returned.

Freshmen *Admission:* 284 applied, 144 admitted, 71 enrolled. *Average high school GPA:* 3.00. *Test scores:* SAT critical reading scores over 500: 46%; SAT math scores over 500: 36%; ACT scores over 18: 58%; SAT critical reading scores over 600: 11%; SAT math scores over 600: 9%; ACT scores over 24: 18%; SAT critical reading scores over 700: 1%; SAT math scores over 700: 2%; ACT scores over 30: 2%.

Faculty *Total:* 72, 38% full-time, 26% with terminal degrees. *Student/faculty ratio:* 11:1.

Majors Ancient Near Eastern and biblical languages; biblical studies; divinity/ministry; dramatic/theater arts; education; elementary education; English; interdisciplinary studies; international relations and affairs; kindergarten/preschool education; liberal arts and sciences/liberal studies; music teacher education; pastoral studies/counseling; psychology; religious/sacred music; social sciences; substance abuse/addiction counseling; theology.

Academics *Calendar:* semesters. *Degrees:* certificates, associate, bachelor's, and master's. *Special study options:* academic remediation for entering students, accelerated degree program, adult/continuing education programs, advanced placement credit, distance learning, external degree program, independent study, internships, part-time degree program, services for LD students, summer session for credit.

Computers on Campus 17 computers/terminals are available on campus for general student use. Students can access the following: campus intranet, free student e-mail accounts, online (class) grades, online (class) registration, online (class) schedules. Campuswide network is available. Wireless service is available via dorm rooms, learning centers, libraries, student centers.

Student Life *Housing:* on-campus residence required through junior year. *Options:* men-only, women-only. Campus housing is university owned. Freshman campus housing is guaranteed. *Activities and organizations:* drama/theater group, student-run newspaper, choral group. *Campus security:* 24-hour emergency response devices, student patrols, controlled dormitory access. *Student services:* personal/psychological counseling.

Athletics Member NAIA. *Intercollegiate sports:* baseball M, basketball M (s)/W (s), cross-country running M (s)/W (s), golf M/W, soccer M/W, softball W (s), volleyball M/W (s). *Intramural sports:* basketball M/W, volleyball W.

Standardized Tests *Required:* SAT or ACT (for admission).

Costs (2008–09) *Comprehensive fee:* $25,200 includes full-time tuition ($17,600), mandatory fees ($550), and room and board ($7050). Part-time tuition: $735 per unit. *Required fees:* $275 per term part-time. *College room only:* $3500.

Financial Aid Of all full-time matriculated undergraduates who enrolled in 2003, 370 applied for aid, 331 were judged to have need, 50 had their need fully met. 38 Federal Work-Study jobs (averaging $2011). In 2003, 15 non-need-based awards were made. *Average percent of need met:* 39%. *Average financial aid package:* $10,250. *Average need-based loan:* $4570. *Average need-based gift aid:* $7423. *Average non-need-based aid:* $6000. *Average indebtedness upon graduation:* $21,000.

Applying *Options:* electronic application, early admission, deferred entrance. *Application fee:* $35. *Required:* high school transcript, minimum 2.0 GPA, Christian commitment. *Application deadlines:* 7/31 (freshmen), 7/31 (transfers). *Notification:* continuous until 7/31 (freshmen), continuous until 7/31 (transfers).

Freshman Application Contact Bethany University, 800 Bethany Drive, Scotts Valley, CA 95066-2820. *Phone:* 831-438-3800 Ext. 3900. *Toll-free phone:* 800-843-9410. *Fax:* 831-438-4517. *E-mail:* info@bethany.edu.

BETHESDA CHRISTIAN UNIVERSITY

Anaheim, California **www.bcu.edu/**

Director of Admissions Jacquie Ha, Director of Admission, Bethesda Christian University, 730 North Euclid Street, Anaheim, CA 92801. *Phone:* 714-517-1945. *Fax:* 714-517-1948. *E-mail:* admission@bcu.edu.

BIOLA UNIVERSITY

La Mirada, California **www.biola.edu/**

- **Independent interdenominational** university, founded 1908
- **Suburban** 95-acre campus with easy access to Los Angeles
- **Endowment** $43.7 million
- **Coed** 3,989 undergraduate students
- **Moderately difficult** entrance level, 82% of applicants were admitted

Undergraduates Students come from 49 states and territories, 42 other countries, 25% are from out of state, 4% African American, 10% Asian American or Pacific Islander, 12% Hispanic American, 1% Native American, 4% international, 63% live on campus. *Retention:* 83% of 2006 full-time freshmen returned.

Freshmen *Admission:* 2,315 applied, 1,891 admitted. *Average high school GPA:* 3.51.

Faculty *Total:* 389, 55% full-time. *Student/faculty ratio:* 17:1.

Majors Adult and continuing education; anthropology; biblical studies; bilingual and multilingual education; biochemistry; biology/biological sciences; business administration and management; clinical psychology; commercial and advertising art; communication disorders; computer and information sciences; divinity/ministry; drawing; education; education (K-12); elementary education; English; fine/studio arts; history; humanities; kinesiology and exercise science; mathematics; missionary studies and missiology; music; nursing (registered nurse training); pastoral studies/counseling; philosophy; physical education teaching and coaching; physical sciences; pre-law studies; psychology; radio and television; religious education; religious studies; secondary education; social sciences; sociology; Spanish; theology.

Academics *Calendar:* 4-1-4. *Degrees:* certificates, bachelor's, master's, doctoral, and first professional. *Special study options:* academic remediation for entering students, accelerated degree program, adult/continuing education programs, advanced placement credit, cooperative education, double majors, English as a second language, honors programs, independent study, internships, off-campus study, part-time degree program, services for LD students, study abroad, summer session for credit. *ROTC:* Army (c), Air Force (c). *Unusual degree programs:* 3-2 engineering with University of Southern California; biblical and theological studies.

Computers on Campus 165 computers/terminals are available on campus for general student use. Students can access the following: campus intranet, computer help desk, free student e-mail accounts, online (class) grades, online (class) registration, online (class) schedules. Campuswide network is available. 100% of college-owned or -operated housing units are wired for high-speed Internet access. Wireless service is available via computer centers, computer labs, dorm rooms, libraries, student centers.

Student Life *Housing:* on-campus residence required through sophomore year. *Options:* men-only, women-only. Campus housing is university owned. Freshman campus housing is guaranteed. *Activities and organizations:* drama/theater group, student-run newspaper, radio and television station, choral group, Korean Student Association, Brothers and Sisters in Christ, Accounting Society, Maharlika (Filipino Club), SOUL (Seeking Out Unity and Love). *Campus security:* 24-hour emergency response devices and patrols, student patrols, late-night transport/escort service, controlled dormitory access, access gates to roads through the middle of campus. *Student services:* health clinic, personal/psychological counseling, legal services.

Athletics Member NAIA. *Intercollegiate sports:* baseball M (s), basketball M (s)/W (s), cheerleading W, cross-country running M (s)/W (s), golf M (s)/W (s), soccer M (s)/W (s), softball W (s), swimming and diving M (s)/W (s), tennis M (s)/W (s), track and field M (s)/W (s), volleyball W (s). *Intramural sports:* basketball M/W, football M/W, soccer M/W, softball M/W, ultimate Frisbee M/W, volleyball M/W.

Standardized Tests *Required:* SAT or ACT (for admission).

Costs (2008–09) *Tuition:* $26,424 full-time.

Financial Aid Of all full-time matriculated undergraduates who enrolled in 2004, 2,216 applied for aid, 1,933 were judged to have need, 258 had their need fully met. 85 Federal Work-Study jobs (averaging $3011). In 2004, 315 non-need-based awards were made. *Average percent of need met:* 70%. *Average financial aid package:* $15,200. *Average need-based loan:* $2969. *Average need-based gift aid:* $9514. *Average non-need-based aid:* $11,205. *Average indebtedness upon graduation:* $28,007.

Applying *Options:* electronic application, early admission, early action, deferred entrance. *Application fee:* $45. *Required:* essay or personal statement, high school transcript, 2 letters of recommendation. *Required for some:* interview. *Recommended:* minimum 3.0 GPA, interview. *Application deadlines:* 3/1 (freshmen), 3/1 (transfers), 12/1 (early action). *Notification:* 4/1 (freshmen), 4/1 (transfers), 1/15 (early action).

Freshman Application Contact Mr. Andre Stephens, Director of Enrollment Management, Biola University, 13800 Biola Avenue, La Mirada, CA 90639. *Phone:* 562-903-4752. *Toll-free phone:* 800-652-4652. *Fax:* 562-903-4709. *E-mail:* admissions@biola.edu.

See page 424 for the College Close-Up.

BROOKS INSTITUTE OF PHOTOGRAPHY

Santa Barbara, California **www.brooks.edu/**

Director of Admissions Ms. Inge B. Kautzmann, Director of Admissions, Brooks Institute of Photography, 801 Alston Road, Santa Barbara, CA 93108. *Phone:* 805-966-3888 Ext. 4601. *Toll-free phone:* 888-304-3456. *E-mail:* admissions@brooks.edu.

CALIFORNIA BAPTIST UNIVERSITY

Riverside, California **www.calbaptist.edu/**

- **Independent Southern Baptist** comprehensive, founded 1950
- **Suburban** 110-acre campus with easy access to Los Angeles
- **Endowment** $11.0 million
- **Coed** 2,974 undergraduate students, 86% full-time, 64% women, 36% men
- **Minimally difficult** entrance level, 72% of applicants were admitted

Undergraduates 2,550 full-time, 424 part-time. Students come from 35 states and territories, 30 other countries, 6% are from out of state, 8% African American,

3% Asian American or Pacific Islander, 17% Hispanic American, 1% Native American, 2% international, 10% transferred in, 65% live on campus. *Retention:* 85% of 2006 full-time freshmen returned.

Freshmen *Admission:* 1,354 applied, 981 admitted, 497 enrolled. *Average high school GPA:* 3.34. *Test scores:* SAT critical reading scores over 500: 55%; SAT math scores over 500: 50%; ACT scores over 18: 79%; SAT critical reading scores over 600: 14%; SAT math scores over 600: 14%; ACT scores over 24: 24%; SAT critical reading scores over 700: 2%; SAT math scores over 700: 1%; ACT scores over 30: 1%.

Faculty *Total:* 321, 37% full-time, 40% with terminal degrees. *Student/faculty ratio:* 17:1.

Majors Accounting; acting/directing; adult and continuing education; behavioral sciences; biblical studies; biology/biological sciences; business administration and management; Christian studies; civil engineering; communication and journalism related; communication/speech communication and rhetoric; criminal justice/law enforcement administration; digital communication and media/multimedia; dramatic/theater arts; education; electrical, electronics and communications engineering; engineering; English; health and physical education related; health services/allied health/health sciences; history; information science/studies; intercultural/multicultural and diversity studies; interdisciplinary studies; journalism; kinesiology and exercise science; liberal arts and sciences/liberal studies; marketing/marketing management; mathematics; mechanical engineering; missionary studies and missiology; music; music performance; music theory and composition; nursing (registered nurse training); philosophy; physical education teaching and coaching; political science and government; pre-theology/pre-ministerial studies; psychology; social sciences; sociology; Spanish; theological and ministerial studies related; theology; visual and performing arts.

Academics *Calendar:* 2-4-4-2. *Degrees:* bachelor's and master's. *Special study options:* accelerated degree program, adult/continuing education programs, advanced placement credit, distance learning, double majors, English as a second language, honors programs, independent study, internships, off-campus study, part-time degree program, study abroad, summer session for credit. *ROTC:* Army (c), Air Force (c).

Computers on Campus 279 computers/terminals are available on campus for general student use. Students can access the following: campus intranet, computer help desk, free student e-mail accounts, online (class) grades, online (class) registration, online (class) schedules. Campuswide network is available. Wireless service is available via classrooms, computer labs.

Student Life *Housing:* on-campus residence required for freshman year. *Options:* men-only, women-only. Campus housing is university owned. Freshman applicants given priority for college housing. *Activities and organizations:* drama/theater group, student-run newspaper, choral group, Student Senate, Fellowship of Christian Athletes, Blue Crew, Christian student organizations, Community Life Committees. *Campus security:* 24-hour emergency response devices and patrols, student patrols, late-night transport/escort service, controlled dormitory access. *Student services:* personal/psychological counseling.

Athletics Member NAIA. *Intercollegiate sports:* baseball M (s), basketball M (s)/W (s), cheerleading M (s)/W (s), golf M (s)/W (s), soccer M (s)/W (s), softball W (s), swimming and diving M (s)/W (s), tennis M (s)/W (s), volleyball M (s)/W (s), water polo M (s)/W (s), wrestling M (s). *Intramural sports:* basketball M/W, bowling M/W, football M/W, golf M, softball M/W, table tennis M/W, tennis M/W, volleyball M/W.

Standardized Tests *Required:* SAT or ACT (for admission).

Costs (2007–08) *Comprehensive fee:* $28,150 includes full-time tuition ($19,240), mandatory fees ($1400), and room and board ($7510). Full-time tuition and fees vary according to class time and program. Part-time tuition: $740 per semester hour. Part-time tuition and fees vary according to class time and program. *College room only:* $3300. Room and board charges vary according to board plan and housing facility. *Payment plan:* installment. *Waivers:* employees or children of employees.

Financial Aid Of all full-time matriculated undergraduates who enrolled in 2005, 1,958 applied for aid, 1,892 were judged to have need, 387 had their need fully met. 149 Federal Work-Study jobs (averaging $849). In 2005, 39 non-need-based awards were made. *Average percent of need met:* 67%. *Average financial aid package:* $11,670. *Average need-based loan:* $4360. *Average need-based gift aid:* $8920. *Average non-need-based aid:* $5900. *Average indebtedness upon graduation:* $21,700.

Applying *Options:* early admission, early action, deferred entrance. *Application fee:* $45. *Required:* essay or personal statement, high school transcript, minimum 2.0 GPA, 2 letters of recommendation. *Recommended:* interview. *Application deadlines:* rolling (freshmen), rolling (transfers), 12/1 (early action). *Notification:* continuous until 9/6 (freshmen), continuous until 6/9 (out-of-state freshmen), continuous (transfers), 12/20 (early action).

Freshman Application Contact Mr. Allen Johnson, Director, Undergraduate Admissions, California Baptist University, 8432 Magnolia Avenue, Riverside, CA 92504-3297. *Phone:* 951-343-4212. *Toll-free phone:* 877-228-8866. *Fax:* 951-343-4525. *E-mail:* admissions@calbaptist.edu.

CALIFORNIA CHRISTIAN COLLEGE

Fresno, California **www.calchristiancollege.org/**

- **Independent religious** 4-year
- **Urban** 5-acre campus with easy access to Fresno
- **Endowment** $85,132
- **Coed** 28 undergraduate students, 89% full-time, 36% women, 64% men
- **Noncompetitive** entrance level

Undergraduates 25 full-time, 3 part-time. Students come from 1 other state, 7% African American, 4% Asian American or Pacific Islander, 54% Hispanic American, 4% transferred in, 33% live on campus. *Retention:* 100% of 2006 full-time freshmen returned.

Freshmen *Admission:* 10 enrolled. *Average high school GPA:* 2.50.

Faculty *Total:* 8, 25% full-time, 38% with terminal degrees. *Student/faculty ratio:* 6:1.

Majors Pre-theology/pre-ministerial studies.

Academics *Calendar:* semesters. *Degrees:* associate and bachelor's. *Special study options:* academic remediation for entering students, accelerated degree program, cooperative education, independent study, part-time degree program, summer session for credit.

Computers on Campus 6 computers/terminals are available on campus for general student use. Students can access the following: word processing.

Student Life *Housing:* on-campus residence required through sophomore year. *Options:* coed. Campus housing is university owned. *Activities and organizations:* drama/theater group, student-run newspaper, choral group. *Student services:* personal/psychological counseling.

Athletics *Intramural sports:* basketball M/W.

Standardized Tests *Required:* standardized Bible content tests (for admission). *Recommended:* SAT or ACT (for admission).

Costs (2008–09) *Comprehensive fee:* $10,840 includes full-time tuition ($6600), mandatory fees ($500), and room and board ($3740). Part-time tuition: $275 per unit.

Financial Aid Of all full-time matriculated undergraduates who enrolled in 2007, 25 applied for aid, 25 were judged to have need. 8 Federal Work-Study jobs (averaging $963). *Average percent of need met:* 49%. *Average financial aid package:* $9742. *Average need-based loan:* $4050. *Average need-based gift aid:* $5569. *Average indebtedness upon graduation:* $19,466.

Applying *Options:* electronic application. *Application fee:* $40. *Required:* essay or personal statement, high school transcript, minimum 2.0 GPA, 2 letters of recommendation, statement of faith, moral/ethical statement. *Recommended:* interview. *Application deadlines:* rolling (freshmen), rolling (transfers). *Notification:* continuous (freshmen), continuous (transfers).

Director of Admissions Mrs. Phyllis LoForti, Director of Admissions and Recruitment, California Christian College, 4881 East University Avenue, Fresno, CA 93703. *Phone:* 559-251-4215 Ext. 5571. *E-mail:* cccadmisions@sbcglobal.net.

CALIFORNIA COAST UNIVERSITY

Santa Ana, California **www.calcoast.edu/**

Director of Admissions Dr. William L. Barcroft, Dean of Admissions, California Coast University, 700 North Main Street, Santa Ana, CA 92701. *Toll-free phone:* 888-CCU-UNIV.

CALIFORNIA COLLEGE

San Diego, California **www.cc-sd.edu**

CALIFORNIA COLLEGE OF THE ARTS

San Francisco, California **www.cca.edu/**

- **Independent** comprehensive, founded 1907
- **Urban** 4-acre campus
- **Endowment** $31.4 million

- **Coed** 1,318 undergraduate students, 90% full-time, 61% women, 39% men
- **Moderately difficult** entrance level, 78% of applicants were admitted

California College of the Arts (CCA) is the largest regionally accredited, independent school of art and design in the western United States. CCA offers twenty undergraduate programs in architecture, design, the fine arts, and writing, including a new major in animation. At CCA, students make art that makes a difference.

Undergraduates 1,190 full-time, 128 part-time. Students come from 36 states and territories, 24 other countries, 27% are from out of state, 3% African American, 14% Asian American or Pacific Islander, 10% Hispanic American, 0.8% Native American, 7% international, 14% transferred in, 17% live on campus. *Retention:* 71% of 2006 full-time freshmen returned.

Freshmen *Admission:* 996 applied, 778 admitted, 187 enrolled. *Average high school GPA:* 3.18. *Test scores:* SAT critical reading scores over 500: 71%; SAT math scores over 500: 58%; SAT writing scores over 500: 71%; ACT scores over 18: 87%; SAT critical reading scores over 600: 33%; SAT math scores over 600: 21%; SAT writing scores over 600: 21%; ACT scores over 24: 37%; SAT critical reading scores over 700: 5%; SAT math scores over 700: 1%; SAT writing scores over 700: 1%.

Faculty *Total:* 485, 14% full-time, 62% with terminal degrees. *Student/faculty ratio:* 14:1.

Majors Applied art; architecture; art; ceramic arts and ceramics; commercial and advertising art; drawing; fashion/apparel design; fiber, textile and weaving arts; film/cinema studies; fine/studio arts; industrial design; interior architecture; metal and jewelry arts; painting; photography; printmaking; sculpture.

Academics *Calendar:* semesters. *Degrees:* bachelor's and master's. *Special study options:* academic remediation for entering students, advanced placement credit, cooperative education, double majors, honors programs, independent study, internships, off-campus study, services for LD students, student-designed majors, study abroad, summer session for credit.

Computers on Campus 260 computers/terminals and 33 ports are available on campus for general student use. Students can access the following: computer help desk, free student e-mail accounts, online (class) grades, online (class) schedules. Campuswide network is available. 100% of college-owned or -operated housing units are wired for high-speed Internet access. Wireless service is available via entire campus.

Student Life *Housing options:* coed. Campus housing is university owned. Freshman campus housing is guaranteed. *Activities and organizations:* ALPHA RO CHI (Allied ARB Fraternity), Community for Environmental Arts and Design, Asian Student Association, Glass League, Queer Art. *Campus security:* 24-hour emergency response devices and patrols, late-night transport/escort service. *Student services:* personal/psychological counseling.

Standardized Tests *Required for some:* TOEFL. *Recommended:* SAT or ACT (for admission).

Costs (2008–09) *Tuition:* $31,032 full-time, $1293 per unit part-time. *Required fees:* $350 full-time. *Room only:* $6600.

Financial Aid Of all full-time matriculated undergraduates who enrolled in 2006, 877 applied for aid, 805 were judged to have need, 36 had their need fully met. 756 Federal Work-Study jobs (averaging $2028). 67 state and other part-time jobs (averaging $2474). In 2006, 73 non-need-based awards were made. *Average percent of need met:* 55%. *Average financial aid package:* $19,275. *Average need-based loan:* $4856. *Average need-based gift aid:* $13,126. *Average non-need-based aid:* $5695. *Average indebtedness upon graduation:* $33,188.

Applying *Options:* electronic application, deferred entrance. *Application fee:* $50. *Required:* essay or personal statement, high school transcript, minimum 2.0 GPA, 2 letters of recommendation, portfolio. *Required for some:* interview. *Application deadlines:* 2/1 (freshmen), rolling (transfers). *Notification:* continuous (freshmen), continuous (transfers).

Freshman Application Contact Ms. Robynne Royster, Director of Admissions, California College of the Arts, 1111 Eighth Street at 16th and Wisconsin, San Francisco, CA 94107. *Phone:* 415-703-9523 Ext. 9532. *Toll-free phone:* 800-447-1ART. *Fax:* 415-703-9539. *E-mail:* enroll@cca.edu.

See page 426 for the College Close-Up.

CALIFORNIA DESIGN COLLEGE

Los Angeles, California **www.cdc.edu/**

- **Proprietary** 4-year, founded 1992, part of Education Management Corporation
- **Urban** campus
- **Coed** 882 undergraduate students, 59% full-time, 77% women, 23% men

Undergraduates 523 full-time, 359 part-time. 2% African American, 3% Asian American or Pacific Islander, 6% Hispanic American, 0.8% Native American, 15% live on campus. *Retention:* 80% of 2006 full-time freshmen returned.

Freshmen *Admission:* 500 admitted, 52 enrolled.

Faculty *Total:* 81, 21% full-time, 32% with terminal degrees. *Student/faculty ratio:* 27:1.

Majors Animation, interactive technology, video graphics and special effects; fashion/apparel design; fashion merchandising; graphic design; interior design; theater design and technology; web page, digital/multimedia and information resources design.

Academics *Calendar:* quarters. *Degrees:* associate and bachelor's. *Special study options:* academic remediation for entering students, adult/continuing education programs, advanced placement credit, cooperative education, distance learning, part-time degree program, study abroad.

Computers on Campus 162 computers/terminals are available on campus for general student use. Students can access the following: computer help desk. Campuswide network is available.

Student Life *Housing options:* coed, men-only, women-only, disabled students. Campus housing is leased by the school. *Campus security:* 24-hour emergency response devices and patrols, late-night transport/escort service, controlled dormitory access. *Student services:* personal/psychological counseling.

Costs (2007–08) *Tuition:* $20,880 full-time, $464 per credit part-time. tuition is $21,024 for full-time students. Housing is $9288. Part-time tuition is $438 per credit hour. Other charges include a starting kit for all first-quarter students. Kits vary in price, depending on the program of study. *Required fees:* $150 full-time. *Room only:* $8685.

Financial Aid Of all full-time matriculated undergraduates who enrolled in 2006, 50 Federal Work-Study jobs (averaging $800).

Applying *Options:* electronic application, deferred entrance. *Application fee:* $50. *Required:* essay or personal statement, high school transcript, interview. *Required for some:* letters of recommendation, portfolio. *Application deadlines:* rolling (freshmen), rolling (transfers). *Notification:* continuous (freshmen), continuous (transfers).

Director of Admissions Ms. Melissa Romero, Director of Admissions, California Design College, 3440 Wilshire Boulevard, Tenth Floor, Los Angeles, CA 90010. *Phone:* 213-251-3636 Ext. 153. *Toll-free phone:* 213-251-3636 (in-state); 877-468-6232 (out-of-state). *Fax:* 213-385-3545.

See page 428 for the College Close-Up.

CALIFORNIA INSTITUTE OF INTEGRAL STUDIES

San Francisco, California **www.ciis.edu/**

Application Contact Admissions Department/Student Worker, California Institute of Integral Studies, 1453 Mission Street, San Francisco, CA 94103. *Phone:* 415-575-6156. *Fax:* 415-575-1268. *E-mail:* info@ciis.edu.

CALIFORNIA INSTITUTE OF TECHNOLOGY

Pasadena, California **www.caltech.edu/**

- **Independent** university, founded 1891
- **Suburban** 124-acre campus with easy access to Los Angeles
- **Endowment** $1.2 billion
- **Coed** 913 undergraduate students, 100% full-time, 31% women, 69% men
- **Most difficult** entrance level, 17% of applicants were admitted

Undergraduates 913 full-time. Students come from 49 states and territories, 32 other countries, 69% are from out of state, 0.8% African American, 38% Asian American or Pacific Islander, 5% Hispanic American, 0.3% Native American, 9% international, 1% transferred in, 97% live on campus. *Retention:* 98% of 2006 full-time freshmen returned.

Freshmen *Admission:* 3,597 applied, 607 admitted, 231 enrolled. *Test scores:* SAT critical reading scores over 500: 100%; SAT math scores over 500: 100%; ACT scores over 18: 100%; SAT critical reading scores over 600: 97%; SAT math scores over 600: 100%; ACT scores over 24: 100%; SAT critical reading scores over 700: 80%; SAT math scores over 700: 100%; ACT scores over 30: 99%.

Faculty *Total:* 311, 94% full-time, 95% with terminal degrees. *Student/faculty ratio:* 3:1.

Majors Applied mathematics; astrophysics; biology/biological sciences; business/managerial economics; chemical engineering; chemistry; computational mathematics; computer engineering; computer science; economics; electrical, electronics and communications engineering; English; environmental/environmental health engineering; geochemistry; geology/earth science; geophysics and seismology; history; history of science and technology; materials science; mathematics; mechanical engineering; philosophy; physics; planetary astronomy and science; political science and government.

Academics *Calendar:* 3 ten-week terms. *Degrees:* bachelor's, master's, and doctoral. *Special study options:* cooperative education, double majors, English as a second language, independent study, off-campus study, services for LD students, student-designed majors, study abroad. *ROTC:* Army (c), Air Force (c).

Computers on Campus 600 computers/terminals are available on campus for general student use. Students can access the following: computer help desk, free student e-mail accounts, online (class) grades, online (class) registration, online (class) schedules. Campuswide network is available. 100% of college-owned or -operated housing units are wired for high-speed Internet access. Wireless service is available via entire campus.

Student Life *Housing:* on-campus residence required for freshman year. *Options:* coed. Campus housing is university owned. Freshman campus housing is guaranteed. *Activities and organizations:* drama/theater group, student-run newspaper, choral group, Instrumental music groups, Entrepreneur's Club, Glee Club, Theater Arts, Ultimate Disc Club. *Campus security:* 24-hour emergency response devices and patrols, late-night transport/escort service. *Student services:* health clinic, personal/psychological counseling, women's center.

Athletics Member NCAA. All Division III. *Intercollegiate sports:* baseball M, basketball M/W, cross-country running M/W, fencing M/W, ice hockey M (c), rugby M (c), soccer M/W (c), swimming and diving M/W, tennis M/W, track and field M/W, volleyball M (c)/W, water polo M/W. *Intramural sports:* badminton M/W, baseball M, basketball M/W, cross-country running M/W, fencing M/W, football M/W, golf M, ice hockey M, racquetball M, soccer M/W, softball M/W, squash M/W, swimming and diving M/W, table tennis M/W, tennis M/W, track and field M/W, ultimate Frisbee M/W, volleyball M/W, water polo M/W.

Standardized Tests *Required:* SAT or ACT (for admission), SAT Subject Tests (for admission).

Costs (2008–09) *Comprehensive fee:* $44,661 includes full-time tuition ($31,437), mandatory fees ($3078), and room and board ($10,146). *College room only:* $5733.

Financial Aid Of all full-time matriculated undergraduates who enrolled in 2007, 559 applied for aid, 480 were judged to have need, 480 had their need fully met. 307 Federal Work-Study jobs (averaging $1875). 30 state and other part-time jobs (averaging $2084). In 2007, 80 non-need-based awards were made. *Average percent of need met:* 100%. *Average financial aid package:* $29,533. *Average need-based loan:* $2168. *Average need-based gift aid:* $26,164. *Average non-need-based aid:* $27,098. *Average indebtedness upon graduation:* $6268.

Applying *Options:* electronic application, early admission, early action, deferred entrance. *Application fee:* $60. *Required:* essay or personal statement, high school transcript, 2 letters of recommendation. *Application deadlines:* 1/1 (freshmen), 2/15 (transfers), 11/1 (early action). *Notification:* 4/1 (freshmen), 6/1 (transfers), 12/15 (early action).

Director of Admissions Mr. Rick T. Bischoff, Director of Admissions, California Institute of Technology, 1200 East California Boulevard, Pasadena, CA 91125-0001. *Phone:* 626-395-6341. *E-mail:* rbisch@caltech.edu.

California Institute of the Arts

Valencia, California **www.calarts.edu/**

- **Independent** comprehensive, founded 1961
- **Suburban** 60-acre campus with easy access to Los Angeles
- **Endowment** $108.9 million
- **Coed** 820 undergraduate students, 99% full-time, 46% women, 54% men
- **Very difficult** entrance level, 32% of applicants were admitted

Undergraduates 810 full-time, 10 part-time. Students come from 49 states and territories, 31 other countries, 63% are from out of state, 9% African American, 9% Asian American or Pacific Islander, 12% Hispanic American, 0.6% Native American, 8% international, 14% transferred in, 40% live on campus. *Retention:* 78% of 2006 full-time freshmen returned.

Freshmen *Admission:* 2,914 applied, 940 admitted, 134 enrolled.

Faculty *Total:* 300, 52% full-time. *Student/faculty ratio:* 7:1.

Majors Acting; art; commercial and advertising art; computer graphics; dance; dramatic/theater arts; dramatic/theater arts and stagecraft related; film/cinema studies; film/video and photographic arts related; fine/studio arts; graphic design; jazz/jazz studies; music; music performance; music related; music theory and composition; photography; piano and organ; sculpture; theater design and technology; theater/theater arts management; violin, viola, guitar and other stringed instruments; voice and opera.

Academics *Calendar:* semesters. *Degrees:* certificates, bachelor's, master's, and postbachelor's certificates. *Special study options:* advanced placement credit, cooperative education, independent study, internships, services for LD students, student-designed majors, study abroad.

Computers on Campus 40 computers/terminals are available on campus for general student use. Students can access the following: computer help desk, free student e-mail accounts, online (class) grades. Campuswide network is available. Wireless service is available via libraries.

Student Life *Housing options:* coed, disabled students. Campus housing is university owned. Freshman applicants given priority for college housing. *Activities and organizations:* drama/theater group, student-run radio and television station, choral group. *Campus security:* 24-hour emergency response devices and patrols, late-night transport/escort service, controlled dormitory access. *Student services:* health clinic, personal/psychological counseling.

Costs (2008–09) *Room and board:* $8648; room only: $4985.

Financial Aid Of all full-time matriculated undergraduates who enrolled in 2006, 610 applied for aid, 485 were judged to have need, 43 had their need fully met. 178 Federal Work-Study jobs (averaging $1836). 16 state and other part-time jobs (averaging $1700). In 2006, 83 non-need-based awards were made. *Average percent of need met:* 86%. *Average financial aid package:* $27,631. *Average need-based loan:* $5535. *Average need-based gift aid:* $12,227. *Average non-need-based aid:* $4375. *Average indebtedness upon graduation:* $30,051.

Applying *Options:* electronic application. *Application fee:* $70. *Required:* essay or personal statement, high school transcript, 2 letters of recommendation, portfolio or audition. *Required for some:* interview. *Application deadlines:* 1/5 (freshmen), 1/5 (transfers). *Notification:* continuous (freshmen).

Freshman Application Contact Director of Admissions, California Institute of the Arts, 24700 McBean Parkway, Valencia, CA 91355. *Phone:* 661-255-1050. *Toll-free phone:* 800-545-2787. *Fax:* 661-253-7710. *E-mail:* admiss@calarts.edu.

See page 430 for the College Close-Up.

California Lutheran University

Thousand Oaks, California **www.callutheran.edu/**

- **Independent Lutheran** comprehensive, founded 1959
- **Suburban** 290-acre campus with easy access to Los Angeles
- **Endowment** $56.7 million
- **Coed** 2,129 undergraduate students, 89% full-time, 57% women, 43% men
- **Moderately difficult** entrance level, 68% of applicants were admitted

California Lutheran University (CLU) is a comprehensive, private university that is deeply rooted in matters of both faith and reason. A challenging interdisciplinary core curriculum supports thirty-six majors and twenty-eight minors. CLU is located in the southern California city of Thousand Oaks. For more information, students may visit the Web site at http://www.callutheran.edu.

Undergraduates 1,892 full-time, 237 part-time. Students come from 44 states and territories, 54 other countries, 20% are from out of state, 4% African American, 5% Asian American or Pacific Islander, 17% Hispanic American, 0.5% Native American, 3% international, 8% transferred in, 63% live on campus. *Retention:* 77% of 2006 full-time freshmen returned.

Freshmen *Admission:* 2,445 applied, 1,656 admitted, 424 enrolled. *Average high school GPA:* 3.5. *Test scores:* SAT critical reading scores over 500: 68%; SAT math scores over 500: 76%; SAT writing scores over 500: 70%; ACT scores over 18: 97%; SAT critical reading scores over 600: 26%; SAT math scores over 600: 30%; SAT writing scores over 600: 21%; ACT scores over 24: 56%; SAT critical reading scores over 700: 3%; SAT math scores over 700: 3%; SAT writing scores over 700: 3%; ACT scores over 30: 15%.

Faculty *Total:* 287, 48% full-time, 61% with terminal degrees. *Student/faculty ratio:* 15:1.

Majors Accounting; art; art teacher education; athletic training; biochemistry; biology/biological sciences; biomedical/medical engineering; business administration and management; chemistry; computer and information sciences; computer science; criminal justice/law enforcement administration; digital communication and media/multimedia; dramatic/theater arts; economics; English; French; French language teacher education; geology/earth science; German; German language teacher education; history; information science/studies; interdisciplinary studies; international relations and affairs; journalism; kinesiology and exercise science; liberal arts and sciences/liberal studies; marketing/marketing management; mass communication/media; mathematics; mathematics teacher education; molecular biology; multi-/interdisciplinary studies related; music; music teacher education; philosophy; physical education teaching and coaching; physics; political science and government; psychology; psychology teacher education; public relations, advertising, and applied communication related;

public relations/image management; religious studies; science teacher education; social sciences; social science teacher education; sociology; Spanish; Spanish language teacher education.

Academics *Calendar:* semesters. *Degrees:* certificates, bachelor's, master's, doctoral, post-master's, and postbachelor's certificates. *Special study options:* accelerated degree program, adult/continuing education programs, advanced placement credit, cooperative education, double majors, honors programs, independent study, internships, off-campus study, part-time degree program, student-designed majors, study abroad, summer session for credit. *ROTC:* Army (c), Air Force (c). *Unusual degree programs:* 3-2 computer science.

Computers on Campus 300 computers/terminals are available on campus for general student use. Students can access the following: campus intranet, computer help desk, free student e-mail accounts, online (class) grades, online (class) registration, online (class) schedules. Campuswide network is available. 100% of college-owned or -operated housing units are wired for high-speed Internet access. Wireless service is available via entire campus.

Student Life *Housing:* on-campus residence required through junior year. *Options:* coed, disabled students. Campus housing is university owned. Freshman campus housing is guaranteed. *Activities and organizations:* drama/theater group, student-run newspaper, radio and television station, choral group, student government, music and drama clubs, service organizations, campus ministry organizations, multicultural organizations. *Campus security:* 24-hour emergency response devices and patrols, late-night transport/escort service, controlled dormitory access, escort service; shuttle service. *Student services:* health clinic, personal/psychological counseling, women's center.

Athletics Member NCAA. All Division III. *Intercollegiate sports:* baseball M, basketball M/W, cheerleading M/W, cross-country running M/W, football M, golf M, soccer M/W, softball W, swimming and diving M/W, tennis M/W, track and field M/W, volleyball W, water polo M/W. *Intramural sports:* badminton M (c)/W (c), basketball M (c)/W (c), football M (c)/W (c), lacrosse M (c)/W (c), rugby M (c), soccer M (c)/W (c), softball M (c)/W (c), tennis M (c)/W (c), volleyball M (c)/W (c), water polo M (c)/W (c).

Standardized Tests *Required:* SAT or ACT (for admission).

Costs (2008–09) *Comprehensive fee:* $37,500 includes full-time tuition ($27,600), mandatory fees ($250), and room and board ($9650). Part-time tuition: $890 per unit.

Financial Aid Of all full-time matriculated undergraduates who enrolled in 2006, 1,375 applied for aid, 1,136 were judged to have need, 145 had their need fully met. 370 Federal Work-Study jobs (averaging $2500). 180 state and other part-time jobs (averaging $2500). In 2006, 555 non-need-based awards were made. *Average percent of need met:* 77%. *Average financial aid package:* $16,600. *Average need-based loan:* $4500. *Average need-based gift aid:* $13,600. *Average non-need-based aid:* $9530. *Average indebtedness upon graduation:* $21,000.

Applying *Options:* electronic application, deferred entrance. *Application fee:* $45. *Required:* essay or personal statement, high school transcript, minimum 2.8 GPA, 1 letter of recommendation. *Recommended:* minimum 3.0 GPA, interview. *Application deadline:* 3/15 (freshmen). *Notification:* 12/1 (freshmen), 5/1 (transfers).

Freshman Application Contact Mr. Matthew Ward, Dean of Undergraduate Enrollment, California Lutheran University, Office of Admission, #1350, Thousand Oaks, CA 91360. *Phone:* 805-493-3135. *Toll-free phone:* 877-258-3678. *Fax:* 805-493-3114. *E-mail:* cluadm@clunet.edu.

See page 432 for the College Close-Up.

California Maritime Academy

Vallejo, California **www.csum.edu/**

- **State-supported** 4-year, founded 1929, part of California State University System
- **Suburban** 64-acre campus with easy access to San Francisco
- **Coed** 865 undergraduate students, 100% full-time, 17% women, 83% men
- **Moderately difficult** entrance level, 79% of applicants were admitted

Undergraduates 865 full-time. Students come from 16 states and territories, 12 other countries, 14% are from out of state, 65% live on campus. *Retention:* 89% of 2006 full-time freshmen returned.

Freshmen *Admission:* 945 applied, 744 admitted. *Average high school GPA:* 3.4.

Faculty *Total:* 77. *Student/faculty ratio:* 22:1.

Majors Business administration and management; engineering technologies related; marine technology; mechanical engineering.

Academics *Calendar:* semesters. *Degree:* bachelor's. *Special study options:* academic remediation for entering students, advanced placement credit, distance learning, internships, summer session for credit.

Computers on Campus 75 computers/terminals are available on campus for general student use. Students can access the following: campus intranet, computer help desk, free student e-mail accounts, online (class) grades, online (class) registration, online (class) schedules. Campuswide network is available. 100% of college-owned or -operated housing units are wired for high-speed Internet access. Wireless service is available via entire campus.

Student Life *Housing:* on-campus residence required through junior year. *Options:* coed. Campus housing is university owned. Freshman campus housing is guaranteed. *Activities and organizations:* student-run newspaper, choral group, Sailing Club, Dive Club, drill team. *Campus security:* 24-hour patrols, student patrols. *Student services:* health clinic, personal/psychological counseling.

Athletics Member NAIA. *Intercollegiate sports:* basketball M (s)/W (s), crew M/W, golf M (s)/W, rugby M, sailing M/W, soccer M (s), volleyball W (s), water polo M/W. *Intramural sports:* baseball M, basketball M/W, football M/W, golf M/W, racquetball M/W, rugby M, sailing M/W, softball M/W, tennis M/W, volleyball M/W.

Standardized Tests *Required:* SAT or ACT (for admission).

Costs (2008–09) *Tuition:* state resident $0 full-time; nonresident $10,170 full-time. *Required fees:* $3836 full-time. *Room and board:* $8830; room only: $4200.

Financial Aid *Average percent of need met:* 50%. *Average financial aid package:* $15,329.

Applying *Options:* electronic application. *Application fee:* $55. *Required:* high school transcript, minimum 2.0 GPA, health form. *Notification:* continuous (freshmen), continuous (transfers).

Freshman Application Contact California Maritime Academy, 200 Maritime Academy Drive, Vallejo, CA 94590-0644. *Phone:* 707-654-1330. *Toll-free phone:* 800-561-1945.

California National University for Advanced Studies

Northridge, California **www.cnuas.edu/**

Freshman Application Contact Ms. Stephanie Smith, Registrar, California National University for Advanced Studies, California National University Admissions, 8550 Balboa Boulevard, Suite 210, Northridge, CA 91325. *Phone:* 818-830-2411. *Toll-free phone:* 800-744-2822 (in-state); 800-782-2422 (out-of-state). *Fax:* 818-830-2418. *E-mail:* cnuadms@mail.cnuas.edu.

California Polytechnic State University, San Luis Obispo

San Luis Obispo, California **www.calpoly.edu/**

- **State-supported** comprehensive, founded 1901, part of California State University System
- **Small-town** 6000-acre campus
- **Coed** 18,842 undergraduate students, 95% full-time, 43% women, 57% men
- **Moderately difficult** entrance level, 45% of applicants were admitted

Undergraduates 17,843 full-time, 999 part-time. Students come from 46 states and territories, 39 other countries, 3% are from out of state, 1% African American, 11% Asian American or Pacific Islander, 11% Hispanic American, 0.8% Native American, 0.7% international, 4% transferred in. *Retention:* 90% of 2006 full-time freshmen returned.

Freshmen *Admission:* 30,176 applied, 13,520 admitted, 4,369 enrolled. *Average high school GPA:* 3.7. *Test scores:* SAT critical reading scores over 500: 85%; SAT math scores over 500: 93%; ACT scores over 18: 99%; SAT critical reading scores over 600: 37%; SAT math scores over 600: 60%; ACT scores over 24: 72%; SAT critical reading scores over 700: 5%; SAT math scores over 700: 14%; ACT scores over 30: 12%.

Faculty *Total:* 1,294, 61% full-time, 61% with terminal degrees. *Student/faculty ratio:* 20:1.

Majors Aerospace, aeronautical and astronautical engineering; agricultural/biological engineering and bioengineering; agricultural business and management; agriculture; agronomy and crop science; animal sciences; applied art; architectural engineering; architecture; biochemistry; biology/biological sciences; biomedical/medical engineering; business administration and management; chemistry; child development; city/urban, community and regional planning;

civil engineering; commercial and advertising art; computer engineering; computer science; computer software engineering; construction management; cultural studies; dairy science; developmental and child psychology; economics; electrical, electronics and communications engineering; engineering science; English; environmental biology; environmental/environmental health engineering; food science; foods, nutrition, and wellness; forestry; geology/earth science; graphic communications; history; horticultural science; industrial engineering; industrial technology; interdisciplinary studies; journalism; kinesiology and exercise science; landscape architecture; liberal arts and sciences/liberal studies; manufacturing engineering; materials engineering; mathematics; mechanical engineering; mechanical engineering/mechanical technology; medical microbiology and bacteriology; modern languages; music; nutrition science; parks, recreation and leisure; philosophy; physics; political science and government; psychology; social sciences; statistics.

Academics *Calendar:* quarters. *Degrees:* bachelor's and master's. *Special study options:* academic remediation for entering students, advanced placement credit, cooperative education, distance learning, double majors, English as a second language, external degree program, honors programs, independent study, internships, off-campus study, part-time degree program, services for LD students, study abroad, summer session for credit. *ROTC:* Army (b).

Computers on Campus Students can access the following: campus intranet, free student e-mail accounts, online (class) grades, online (class) registration, online (class) schedules. Campuswide network is available. Wireless service is available via classrooms, computer centers, computer labs, learning centers, libraries, student centers.

Student Life *Housing options:* coed, men-only, women-only. Campus housing is university owned. *Activities and organizations:* drama/theater group, student-run newspaper, radio and television station, choral group, marching band, national fraternities, national sororities. *Campus security:* 24-hour emergency response devices and patrols, student patrols, late-night transport/escort service, controlled dormitory access. *Student services:* health clinic, personal/psychological counseling, women's center, legal services.

Athletics Member NCAA. All Division I except football (Division I-AA). *Intercollegiate sports:* baseball M (s), basketball M (s)/W (s), cross-country running M (s)/W (s), golf M (s)/W (s), soccer M (s)/W (s), softball W (s), swimming and diving M (s)/W (s), tennis M (s)/W (s), track and field M (s)/W (s), volleyball W (s), wrestling M (s). *Intramural sports:* badminton M/W, basketball M, bowling M/W, equestrian sports M/W, fencing M/W, field hockey M/W, football M, lacrosse M/W, rugby M, sailing M/W, soccer M/W, softball W, volleyball M/W, water polo M/W.

Standardized Tests *Required:* SAT or ACT (for admission).

Costs (2007–08) *Tuition:* state resident $0 full-time; nonresident $14,859 full-time, $226 per unit part-time. Full-time tuition and fees vary according to course load, degree level, and program. Part-time tuition and fees vary according to course load, degree level, and program. *Required fees:* $4689 full-time, $1054 per term part-time. *Room and board:* $8817; room only: $4971. Room and board charges vary according to board plan and housing facility. *Payment plan:* installment. *Waivers:* employees or children of employees.

Financial Aid Of all full-time matriculated undergraduates who enrolled in 2005, 8,449 applied for aid, 5,664 were judged to have need, 370 had their need fully met. *Average percent of need met:* 64%. *Average financial aid package:* $7456. *Average need-based loan:* $3952. *Average need-based gift aid:* $1794. *Average indebtedness upon graduation:* $14,032. *Financial aid deadline:* 6/30.

Applying *Options:* electronic application, early admission, early decision. *Application fee:* $55. *Required:* high school transcript. *Application deadlines:* 11/30 (freshmen), 11/30 (transfers). *Early decision deadline:* 10/31. *Notification:* 4/1 (freshmen), 4/1 (transfers), 12/15 (early decision).

Freshman Application Contact Mr. James Maraviglia, Director of Admissions and Evaluations, California Polytechnic State University, San Luis Obispo, San Luis Obispo, CA 93407. *Phone:* 805-756-2311. *Fax:* 805-756-5400. *E-mail:* admissions@calpoly.edu.

CALIFORNIA STATE POLYTECHNIC UNIVERSITY, POMONA

Pomona, California **www.csupomona.edu/**

- **State-supported** comprehensive, founded 1938, part of California State University System
- **Urban** 1400-acre campus with easy access to Los Angeles
- **Endowment** $33.7 million
- **Coed** 19,615 undergraduate students, 83% full-time, 43% women, 57% men
- **Moderately difficult** entrance level, 69% of applicants were admitted

Undergraduates 16,338 full-time, 3,277 part-time. Students come from 34 states and territories, 59 other countries, 2% are from out of state, 4% African American, 29% Asian American or Pacific Islander, 29% Hispanic American, 0.4% Native American, 6% international, 7% transferred in, 9% live on campus. *Retention:* 80% of 2006 full-time freshmen returned.

Freshmen *Admission:* 21,836 applied, 15,021 admitted, 3,620 enrolled. *Average high school GPA:* 3.24. *Test scores:* SAT critical reading scores over 500: 46%; SAT math scores over 500: 65%; ACT scores over 18: 80%; SAT critical reading scores over 600: 11%; SAT math scores over 600: 25%; ACT scores over 24: 27%; SAT critical reading scores over 700: 1%; SAT math scores over 700: 4%; ACT scores over 30: 2%.

Faculty *Total:* 1,177, 51% full-time, 54% with terminal degrees. *Student/faculty ratio:* 23:1.

Majors Accounting; aerospace, aeronautical and astronautical engineering; agricultural/biological engineering and bioengineering; agricultural business and management; agricultural teacher education; agriculture; agronomy and crop science; animal sciences; anthropology; applied mathematics; architecture; art; behavioral sciences; bilingual and multilingual education; biology/biological sciences; biology/biotechnology laboratory technician; botany/plant biology; business administration and management; chemical engineering; chemistry; city/urban, community and regional planning; civil engineering; commercial and advertising art; computer and information sciences; computer engineering; computer science; construction engineering technology; counselor education/school counseling and guidance; cultural studies; dietetics; dramatic/theater arts; economics; electrical, electronic and communications engineering technology; electrical, electronics and communications engineering; engineering technologies related; engineering technology; English; ethnic, cultural minority, and gender studies related; family and consumer sciences/human sciences; farm and ranch management; finance; foods, nutrition, and wellness; geography; geology/earth science; history; horticultural science; hotel/motel administration; humanities; human resources management; industrial engineering; information science/studies; insurance; international business/trade/commerce; journalism; landscape architecture; liberal arts and sciences/liberal studies; marketing/marketing management; mass communication/media; materials engineering; mathematics; mechanical engineering; mechanical engineering/mechanical technology; medical microbiology and bacteriology; music; ornamental horticulture; petroleum engineering; philosophy; physical education teaching and coaching; physics; plant protection and integrated pest management; political science and government; pre-law studies; pre-medical studies; pre-veterinary studies; psychology; public administration; public relations/image management; radio, television, and digital communication related; real estate; social sciences; sociology; soil conservation; Spanish; statistics; survey technology; telecommunications; urban studies/affairs; zoology/animal biology.

Academics *Calendar:* quarters. *Degrees:* bachelor's and master's. *Special study options:* academic remediation for entering students, adult/continuing education programs, advanced placement credit, cooperative education, double majors, English as a second language, honors programs, internships, off-campus study, part-time degree program, services for LD students, study abroad, summer session for credit. *ROTC:* Army (b), Air Force (c).

Computers on Campus 1,850 computers/terminals are available on campus for general student use. Students can access the following: campus intranet, computer help desk, free student e-mail accounts, online (class) grades, online (class) registration, online (class) schedules. Campuswide network is available. 100% of college-owned or -operated housing units are wired for high-speed Internet access. Wireless service is available via entire campus.

Student Life *Housing options:* coed, disabled students. Campus housing is university owned. *Activities and organizations:* drama/theater group, student-run newspaper, choral group, Rose Float Club, Ridge Runners Ski Club, Barkada (Asian club), American Marketing Association, Cal Poly Society of Accountants, national fraternities, national sororities. *Campus security:* 24-hour emergency response devices and patrols, student patrols, late-night transport/escort service, video camera surveillance. *Student services:* health clinic, personal/psychological counseling, women's center.

Athletics Member NCAA. All Division II. *Intercollegiate sports:* baseball M (s), basketball M (s)/W (s), cross-country running M (s)/W (s), soccer M (s)/W (s), tennis M (s)/W (s), track and field M (s)/W (s), volleyball W (s). *Intramural sports:* basketball M/W, bowling M/W, football M/W, softball M/W, tennis M/W, volleyball M/W.

Standardized Tests *Required:* SAT or ACT (for admission).

Costs (2007–08) *Tuition:* state resident $0 full-time; nonresident $10,170 full-time, $226 per term part-time. *Required fees:* $3279 full-time, $2117 per year part-time. *Room and board:* $8493; room only: $5121. Room and board charges vary according to board plan and housing facility. *Payment plans:* installment, deferred payment. *Waivers:* employees or children of employees.

Financial Aid Of all full-time matriculated undergraduates who enrolled in 2007, 9,547 applied for aid, 7,962 were judged to have need, 2,225 had their need fully met. 264 Federal Work-Study jobs (averaging $2773). In 2007, 19 non-need-based awards were made. *Average percent of need met:* 77%. *Average financial aid package:* $8867. *Average need-based loan:* $3887. *Average need-based gift aid:* $6508. *Average non-need-based aid:* $3081. *Average indebtedness upon graduation:* $10,487.

Applying *Options:* electronic application. *Application fee:* $55. *Required:* high school transcript, minimum 2.0 GPA. *Application deadlines:* 11/30 (freshmen), 11/30 (transfers). *Notification:* continuous until 11/1 (freshmen), 5/1 (transfers).

Freshman Application Contact Mr. Scott J. Duncan, Director, Admissions, California State Polytechnic University, Pomona, Pomona, CA 91768. *Phone:* 909-869-3258. *Fax:* 909-869-4529. *E-mail:* admissions@csupomona.edu.

See page 434 for the College Close-Up.

CALIFORNIA STATE UNIVERSITY, BAKERSFIELD

Bakersfield, California **www.csubak.edu/**

Freshman Application Contact Dr. Kendyl Magnuson, Associate Dean of Admissions and Records, California State University, Bakersfield, 9001 Stockdale Highway, Balersfield, CA 93311-1099. *Phone:* 661-664-3036. *Toll-free phone:* 800-788-2782. *E-mail:* admissions@csub.edu.

CALIFORNIA STATE UNIVERSITY CHANNEL ISLANDS

Camarillo, California **www.csuci.edu/**

- **State-supported** comprehensive, founded 2002, part of California State University System
- **Suburban** campus
- **Endowment** $7.9 million
- **Coed**
- **Noncompetitive** entrance level

Faculty *Student/faculty ratio:* 19:1.

Academics *Degrees:* bachelor's, master's, and postbachelor's certificates.

Student Life *Campus security:* 24-hour emergency response devices and patrols, late-night transport/escort service, controlled dormitory access.

Standardized Tests *Required:* SAT or ACT (for admission).

Costs (2007–08) *Tuition:* nonresident $10,170 full-time, $339 per unit part-time. *Required fees:* $3332 full-time, $804 per term part-time. *Room and board:* $9800; room only: $7000.

Applying *Application fee:* $50. *Required:* high school transcript, minimum 2.0 GPA. *Recommended:* minimum 3.0 GPA.

Freshman Application Contact Ms. Ginger Reyes, California State University Channel Islands, One University Drive, Camarillo, CA 93012. *Phone:* 805-437-8520. *Fax:* 805-437-8519. *E-mail:* prospective.student@csuci.edu.

CALIFORNIA STATE UNIVERSITY, CHICO

Chico, California **www.csuchico.edu/**

- **State-supported** comprehensive, founded 1887, part of California State University System
- **Small-town** 119-acre campus
- **Endowment** $32.9 million
- **Coed** 15,645 undergraduate students, 91% full-time, 52% women, 48% men
- **Moderately difficult** entrance level, 95% of applicants were admitted

Undergraduates 14,164 full-time, 1,481 part-time. Students come from 45 states and territories, 45 other countries, 2% are from out of state, 2% African American, 6% Asian American or Pacific Islander, 12% Hispanic American, 1% Native American, 2% international, 10% transferred in, 13% live on campus. *Retention:* 80% of 2006 full-time freshmen returned.

Freshmen *Admission:* 13,857 applied, 13,120 admitted, 2,771 enrolled. *Average high school GPA:* 3.13. *Test scores:* SAT critical reading scores over 500: 51%; SAT math scores over 500: 60%; ACT scores over 18: 84%; SAT critical reading scores over 600: 13%; SAT math scores over 600: 17%; ACT scores over 24: 26%; SAT critical reading scores over 700: 1%; SAT math scores over 700: 1%; ACT scores over 30: 1%.

Faculty *Total:* 1,009, 56% full-time, 57% with terminal degrees. *Student/faculty ratio:* 22:1.

Majors Accounting; accounting and computer science; agricultural business and management; agricultural teacher education; agronomy and crop science; American studies; animal sciences; anthropology; applied mathematics; art; art history, criticism and conservation; art teacher education; Asian studies; biochemistry; biology/biological sciences; biology teacher education; business administration and management; business administration, management and operations related; chemistry; chemistry related; chemistry teacher education; city/urban, community and regional planning; civil engineering; clinical laboratory science/medical technology; communication and journalism related; communication disorders; communication/speech communication and rhetoric; computer and information sciences and support services related; computer engineering; computer graphics; computer science; construction engineering technology; criminal justice/safety; design and visual communications; dietetics; dramatic/theater arts; dramatic/theater arts and stagecraft related; early childhood education; ecology; economics; economics related; educational/instructional media design; electrical, electronics and communications engineering; engineering/industrial management; engineering related; English; English/language arts teacher education; ethnic, cultural minority, and gender studies related; finance; fine/studio arts; French; French language teacher education; geography; geological and earth sciences/geosciences related; geology/earth science; German; German language teacher education; gerontology; graphic design; health and physical education; health services/allied health/health sciences; health teacher education; history; humanities; human resources management; hydrology and water resources science; information technology; interior design; international economics; international relations and affairs; Jewish/Judaic studies; journalism; kinesiology and exercise science; Latin American studies; legal assistant/paralegal; legal studies; liberal arts and sciences/liberal studies; linguistics; management information systems; management information systems and services related; marketing/marketing management; mass communication/media; mathematics; mathematics teacher education; mechanical engineering; microbiology; multi-/interdisciplinary studies related; music; music performance; music related; music teacher education; music theory and composition; natural resources management and policy; nursing (registered nurse training); operations management; organizational communication; parks, recreation and leisure; parks, recreation and leisure facilities management; philosophy; physical education teaching and coaching; physics; physics related; piano and organ; political science and government; pre-dentistry studies; pre-medical studies; pre-veterinary studies; psychology; public administration; public relations/image management; publishing; resort management; therapeutic recreation; tourism and travel services management.

Academics *Calendar:* semesters. *Degrees:* certificates, bachelor's, master's, post-master's, and postbachelor's certificates. *Special study options:* academic remediation for entering students, adult/continuing education programs, advanced placement credit, cooperative education, distance learning, double majors, English as a second language, external degree program, honors programs, independent study, internships, off-campus study, part-time degree program, services for LD students, student-designed majors, study abroad, summer session for credit.

Computers on Campus 962 computers/terminals and 1,205 ports are available on campus for general student use. Students can access the following: online (class) registration, student account information, e-mail, calendar, transcripts. Campuswide network is available. 100% of college-owned or -operated housing units are wired for high-speed Internet access. Wireless service is available via computer centers, learning centers, libraries, student centers.

Student Life *Housing options:* coed, women-only, disabled students. Campus housing is university owned. Freshman applicants given priority for college housing. *Activities and organizations:* drama/theater group, student-run newspaper, radio station, choral group, Scour and Devour, Panhellenic Council, The Edge Campus Christian Fellowship, Golden Key International Honor Society, Music & Entertainment Industry, national fraternities, national sororities. *Campus security:* 24-hour emergency response devices and patrols, student patrols, late-night transport/escort service, controlled dormitory access, crime prevention workshops, RAD self-defense program, Chico Safe Rides, blue light emergency phones, freshmen safety orientation. *Student services:* health clinic, personal/psychological counseling, women's center, legal services.

Athletics Member NCAA. All Division II. *Intercollegiate sports:* badminton M (c)/W (c), baseball M (s), basketball M (s)/W (s), bowling M (c)/W (c), cross-country running M (s)/W (s), field hockey M (c)/W (c), golf M (s)/W (s), lacrosse M (c)/W (c), rock climbing M (c)/W (c), rugby M (c)/W (c), soccer M (s)/W (s), softball W (s), track and field M (s)/W (s), ultimate Frisbee M (c)/W (c), volleyball M (c)/W (c), water polo M (c)/W (c). *Intramural sports:* badminton M/W, basketball M/W, bowling M/W, cheerleading M/W, fencing M (c)/W (c), field hockey M/W, football M/W, golf M/W, racquetball M/W, rock climbing M/W, soccer M/W, softball M/W, swimming and diving M/W, track and field M/W, ultimate Frisbee M/W, volleyball M/W, weight lifting M/W, wrestling M/W.

Standardized Tests *Required:* SAT or ACT (for admission).

Costs (2008–09) *Tuition:* nonresident $13,220 full-time, $339 per unit part-time. *Required fees:* $4144 full-time.

Financial Aid Of all full-time matriculated undergraduates who enrolled in 2007, 7,537 applied for aid, 6,343 were judged to have need, 1,487 had their need fully met. 750 Federal Work-Study jobs (averaging $2500). In 2007, 1838 non-need-based awards were made. *Average percent of need met:* 87%. *Average financial aid package:* $9965. *Average need-based loan:* $4554. *Average need-based gift aid:* $6540. *Average non-need-based aid:* $6020. *Average indebtedness upon graduation:* $8600.

Applying *Options:* electronic application, deferred entrance. *Application fee:* $55. *Required:* high school transcript, GPA of 10th and 11th grade college prep courses only. *Required for some:* minimum 2.0 GPA. *Application deadlines:* 11/30 (freshmen), 11/30 (transfers). *Notification:* 3/1 (freshmen), 3/1 (transfers).

Freshman Application Contact Rocky Raquel, Interim Director of Admissions, California State University, Chico, 400 West First Street, Chico, CA 95929-0722. *Phone:* 530-898-4428. *Toll-free phone:* 800-542-4426. *Fax:* 530-898-6456. *E-mail:* info@csuchico.edu.

CALIFORNIA STATE UNIVERSITY, DOMINGUEZ HILLS

Carson, California **www.csudh.edu/**

- **State-supported** comprehensive, founded 1960, part of California State University System
- **Urban** 350-acre campus with easy access to Los Angeles
- **Endowment** $6.7 million
- **Coed** 8,774 undergraduate students, 61% full-time, 68% women, 32% men
- **Moderately difficult** entrance level, 12% of applicants were admitted

Undergraduates 5,375 full-time, 3,399 part-time. Students come from 19 states and territories, 33 other countries, 28% African American, 8% Asian American or Pacific Islander, 38% Hispanic American, 0.3% Native American, 2% international, 13% transferred in, 6% live on campus. *Retention:* 60% of 2006 full-time freshmen returned.

Freshmen *Admission:* 10,234 applied, 1,236 admitted, 995 enrolled. *Average high school GPA:* 2.92.

Faculty *Total:* 888, 34% full-time, 44% with terminal degrees. *Student/faculty ratio:* 17:1.

Majors Accounting; African-American/Black studies; anthropology; applied art; art; art history, criticism and conservation; behavioral sciences; bilingual and multilingual education; biochemistry; biology/biological sciences; business administration and management; chemistry; child development; clinical laboratory science/medical technology; clinical/medical laboratory technology; commercial and advertising art; computer science; criminal justice/law enforcement administration; cytotechnology; dramatic/theater arts; economics; English; finance; fine/studio arts; French; geography; geology/earth science; gerontology; health/health care administration; health science; Hispaniç-American, Puerto Rican, and Mexican-American/Chicano studies; history; humanities; human resources management; human services; information science/studies; interdisciplinary studies; international business/trade/commerce; labor and industrial relations; liberal arts and sciences/liberal studies; linguistics; literature; management information systems; marketing/marketing management; mass communication/media; mathematics; medical/clinical assistant; medical microbiology and bacteriology; music; music teacher education; nuclear medical technology; nursing (registered nurse training); parks, recreation and leisure; philosophy; physical education teaching and coaching; physician assistant; physics; political science and government; pre-dentistry studies; pre-law studies; pre-medical studies; pre-veterinary studies; psychology; public administration; public health; public relations/image management; real estate; religious studies; sociology; Spanish.

Academics *Calendar:* semesters. *Degrees:* bachelor's, master's, post-master's, and postbachelor's certificates. *Special study options:* academic remediation for entering students, adult/continuing education programs, advanced placement credit, cooperative education, English as a second language, external degree program, honors programs, internships, off-campus study, part-time degree program, student-designed majors, study abroad, summer session for credit. *ROTC:* Army (c), Air Force (c).

Computers on Campus 256 computers/terminals and 200 ports are available on campus for general student use. Students can access the following: free student e-mail accounts, online (class) grades, online (class) registration, online (class) schedules. Campuswide network is available. Wireless service is available via dorm rooms, libraries, student centers.

Student Life *Housing options:* coed. Campus housing is university owned. *Activities and organizations:* drama/theater group, student-run newspaper, radio station, choral group, Latino Business Students Association, Black Business Student Association, Espirito de Nuestro Futuro, Organization of African Studies, Recreation Club, national fraternities, national sororities. *Campus security:* 24-hour emergency response devices, student patrols, late-night transport/escort service, campus police. *Student services:* health clinic, personal/psychological counseling, women's center.

Athletics Member NCAA. All Division II. *Intercollegiate sports:* baseball M (s), basketball M (s)/W (s), cross-country running W (s), golf M, soccer M (s)/W (s), softball W (s), track and field W (s), volleyball W (s). *Intramural sports:* basketball M/W, cross-country running M/W, football M/W, golf M/W, soccer M/W, softball M/W, swimming and diving M/W, tennis M/W, track and field M (c)/W (c), volleyball M/W, water polo M/W, weight lifting M/W.

Standardized Tests *Required:* SAT or ACT (for admission).

Costs (2007–08) *Tuition:* state resident $0 full-time; nonresident $10,170 full-time, $339 per unit part-time. *Required fees:* $3377 full-time, $1109 per term part-time. *Room and board:* $8690; room only: $4500. Room and board charges vary according to housing facility. *Payment plan:* installment. *Waivers:* senior citizens and employees or children of employees.

Financial Aid Of all full-time matriculated undergraduates who enrolled in 2005, 4,730 applied for aid, 4,436 were judged to have need, 210 had their need fully met. 240 Federal Work-Study jobs (averaging $1312). In 2005, 55 non-need-based awards were made. *Average percent of need met:* 67%. *Average financial aid package:* $8239. *Average need-based loan:* $4258. *Average need-based gift aid:* $4975. *Average non-need-based aid:* $2669. *Average indebtedness upon graduation:* $15,232. *Financial aid deadline:* 4/15.

Applying *Options:* electronic application. *Application fee:* $55. *Required:* high school transcript. *Application deadlines:* rolling (freshmen), rolling (transfers). *Notification:* continuous (freshmen), continuous (transfers).

Freshman Application Contact Information Center, California State University, Dominguez Hills, 1000 East Victoria Street, Carson, CA 90747-0001. *Phone:* 310-243-3696.

CALIFORNIA STATE UNIVERSITY, EAST BAY

Hayward, California **www.csueastbay.edu/**

- **State-supported** comprehensive, founded 1957, part of California State University System
- **Suburban** 343-acre campus with easy access to San Francisco
- **Endowment** $6.1 million
- **Coed** 9,838 undergraduate students, 81% full-time, 61% women, 39% men
- **Moderately difficult** entrance level, 70% of applicants were admitted

California State University, East Bay (CSUEB), with scenic hilltop campuses in Hayward and Concord overlooking beautiful San Francisco Bay, is the East Bay's regional university of choice. A strong professional focus, small classes, personalized instruction, and low fees have earned CSUEB a reputation as a top value in public higher education.

Undergraduates 7,981 full-time, 1,857 part-time. 1% are from out of state, 18% transferred in, 3% live on campus. *Retention:* 76% of 2006 full-time freshmen returned.

Freshmen *Admission:* 6,813 applied, 4,766 admitted, 1,047 enrolled. *Average high school GPA:* 3.00. *Test scores:* SAT critical reading scores over 500: 29%; SAT math scores over 500: 36%; ACT scores over 18: 58%; SAT critical reading scores over 600: 6%; SAT math scores over 600: 9%; ACT scores over 24: 16%; SAT critical reading scores over 700: 1%; SAT math scores over 700: 1%; ACT scores over 30: 3%.

Faculty *Total:* 738, 45% full-time. *Student/faculty ratio:* 23:1.

Majors Accounting; advertising; African-American/Black studies; American Indian/Native American studies; anthropology; applied mathematics; art history, criticism and conservation; arts management; Asian-American studies; athletic training; audiology and speech-language pathology; biochemistry; biology/biological sciences; biomedical technology; broadcast journalism; business administration and management; business/managerial economics; ceramic arts and ceramics; chemistry; child development; clinical/medical laboratory technology; commercial and advertising art; computer graphics; computer science; computer systems networking and telecommunications; corrections; creative writing; criminal justice/law enforcement administration; criminal justice/police science; cultural studies; dance; developmental and child psychology; dramatic/theater arts; drawing; ecology; economics; English; environmental studies; finance; fine/studio arts; French; geography; geology/earth science; gerontology; health science; Hispanic-American, Puerto Rican, and Mexican-American/Chicano studies; history; human development and family studies; human ecology; human resources management; industrial and organizational psychology; industrial engineering; information science/studies; interdisciplinary studies; international relations and affairs; journalism; kinesiology and exercise science; Latin American studies;

liberal arts and sciences/liberal studies; management information systems; marketing/marketing management; mass communication/media; mathematics; music; nursing (registered nurse training); painting; parks, recreation and leisure; philosophy; photography; physical education teaching and coaching; physical sciences; physics; political science and government; pre-dentistry studies; pre-medical studies; pre-veterinary studies; printmaking; psychology; public administration; public relations/image management; purchasing, procurement/acquisitions and contracts management; real estate; religious studies; sculpture; social work; sociology; Spanish; speech and rhetoric; statistics; telecommunications; therapeutic recreation.

Academics *Calendar:* quarters. *Degrees:* certificates, bachelor's, master's, and postbachelor's certificates. *Special study options:* academic remediation for entering students, accelerated degree program, adult/continuing education programs, advanced placement credit, cooperative education, distance learning, double majors, English as a second language, honors programs, independent study, internships, off-campus study, part-time degree program, services for LD students, student-designed majors, study abroad, summer session for credit.

Computers on Campus 700 computers/terminals are available on campus for general student use. Students can access the following: campus intranet, computer help desk, free student e-mail accounts, online (class) grades, online (class) registration, online (class) schedules. Campuswide network is available. Wireless service is available via entire campus.

Student Life *Housing options:* coed, disabled students. Campus housing is university owned and leased by the school. Freshman applicants given priority for college housing. *Activities and organizations:* drama/theater group, student-run newspaper, radio and television station, choral group, Vietnamese Student Association, Accounting Association, Filipino-American Students Association, Movimiento Estudiantil Chicano, Hayward Orientation Team, national fraternities, national sororities. *Campus security:* 24-hour emergency response devices and patrols, late-night transport/escort service. *Student services:* health clinic, personal/psychological counseling, legal services.

Athletics Member NCAA, NAIA. All NCAA Division III. *Intercollegiate sports:* baseball M, basketball M/W, cross-country running M/W, soccer M/W, softball W, swimming and diving W, volleyball W, water polo W. *Intramural sports:* badminton M/W, basketball M/W, golf M/W, gymnastics M, racquetball M/W, soccer M/W, softball M/W, swimming and diving M/W, tennis M/W, volleyball M/W, weight lifting M/W.

Standardized Tests *Required for some:* SAT or ACT (for admission).

Costs (2007–08) *Tuition:* nonresident $11,481 full-time, $953 per unit part-time. *Required fees:* $3345 full-time, $191 per term part-time. *Room and board:* $4942.

Financial Aid Of all full-time matriculated undergraduates who enrolled in 2007, 3,542 applied for aid, 3,351 were judged to have need, 490 had their need fully met. *Average percent of need met:* 63%. *Average financial aid package:* $8016. *Average need-based loan:* $8140. *Average need-based gift aid:* $6220. *Average indebtedness upon graduation:* $12,521.

Applying *Options:* electronic application, early admission, deferred entrance. *Application fee:* $55. *Required:* high school transcript, minimum 2.0 GPA, CSU eligibility index. *Application deadlines:* 3/1 (freshmen), 8/31 (transfers). *Notification:* continuous (freshmen), continuous (transfers).

Freshman Application Contact Mr. Dave Vasquez, Director of Admissions, California State University, East Bay, 25800 Carlos Bee Boulevard, Hayward, CA 94542-3035. *Phone:* 510-885-3248. *Fax:* 510-885-4059. *E-mail:* admissions@csueeastbay.edu.

CALIFORNIA STATE UNIVERSITY, FRESNO

Fresno, California — www.csufresno.edu/

- **State-supported** comprehensive, founded 1911, part of California State University System
- **Urban** 1410-acre campus
- **Endowment** $111.0 million
- **Coed** 19,191 undergraduate students, 81% full-time, 58% women, 42% men
- **Minimally difficult** entrance level, 69% of applicants were admitted

Undergraduates 15,513 full-time, 3,678 part-time. Students come from 50 states and territories, 69 other countries, 0.8% are from out of state, 6% African American, 15% Asian American or Pacific Islander, 33% Hispanic American, 0.9% Native American, 2% international, 9% transferred in, 6% live on campus. *Retention:* 81% of 2006 full-time freshmen returned.

Freshmen *Admission:* 13,447 applied, 9,253 admitted, 2,637 enrolled. *Average high school GPA:* 3.25. *Test scores:* SAT critical reading scores over 500: 30%; SAT math scores over 500: 40%; ACT scores over 18: 61%; SAT critical reading scores over 600: 7%; SAT math scores over 600: 10%; ACT scores over 24: 16%; SAT critical reading scores over 700: 1%; SAT math scores over 700: 1%; ACT scores over 30: 1%.

Faculty *Total:* 1,345, 53% full-time, 55% with terminal degrees. *Student/faculty ratio:* 20:1.

Majors Accounting; African-American/Black studies; agricultural business and management; agricultural teacher education; agronomy and crop science; animal physiology; animal sciences; anthropology; art; audiology and speech-language pathology; biological and physical sciences; biology/biological sciences; business administration and management; cell biology and histology; chemistry; child development; civil engineering; cognitive science; commercial and advertising art; communication disorders; communication/speech communication and rhetoric; computer and information sciences; computer engineering; computer science; construction engineering technology; construction management; criminology; dance; dietetics; dramatic/theater arts; ecology; economics; electrical, electronics and communications engineering; English; environmental science; family and consumer economics related; finance; foods, nutrition, and wellness; French; geography; geology/earth science; graphic design; health science; Hispanic-American, Puerto Rican, and Mexican-American/Chicano studies; history; human resources management; industrial arts; industrial technology; interior design; international business/trade/commerce; journalism; liberal arts and sciences/liberal studies; linguistics; management information systems; marketing/marketing management; mass communication/media; mathematics; mechanical engineering; molecular biology; music; music history, literature, and theory; music teacher education; natural sciences; nursing (registered nurse training); occupational health and industrial hygiene; occupational safety and health technology; ornamental horticulture; parks, recreation and leisure; parks, recreation and leisure facilities management; philosophy; physical education teaching and coaching; physical therapy; physics; plant sciences; political science and government; pre-law studies; psychology; public administration; public relations/image management; radio and television; real estate; religious studies; social work; sociology; Spanish; speech and rhetoric; trade and industrial teacher education; women's studies.

Academics *Calendar:* semesters. *Degrees:* certificates, bachelor's, master's, and doctoral. *Special study options:* academic remediation for entering students, accelerated degree program, adult/continuing education programs, advanced placement credit, cooperative education, distance learning, double majors, English as a second language, freshman honors college, honors programs, independent study, internships, off-campus study, part-time degree program, services for LD students, student-designed majors, study abroad, summer session for credit. *ROTC:* Army (b), Air Force (b).

Computers on Campus 859 computers/terminals and 100 ports are available on campus for general student use. Students can access the following: campus intranet, computer help desk, free student e-mail accounts, online (class) grades, online (class) registration, online (class) schedules, common applications. Campuswide network is available. 100% of college-owned or -operated housing units are wired for high-speed Internet access. Wireless service is available via classrooms, computer centers, computer labs, learning centers, libraries, student centers.

Student Life *Housing options:* coed, men-only, women-only. Campus housing is university owned. *Activities and organizations:* drama/theater group, student-run newspaper, radio station, choral group, marching band, national fraternities, national sororities. *Campus security:* 24-hour emergency response devices and patrols, late-night transport/escort service, controlled dormitory access. *Student services:* health clinic, personal/psychological counseling, women's center.

Athletics Member NCAA. All Division I except football (Division I-A). *Intercollegiate sports:* baseball M (s), basketball M (s)/W (s), cross-country running M (s)/W (s), equestrian sports W (s), golf M (s), soccer M (s)/W (s), softball W (s), swimming and diving W (s), tennis M (s)/W (s), track and field M (s)/W (s), volleyball W (s), wrestling M (s). *Intramural sports:* archery M/W, badminton M/W, baseball M, basketball M/W, bowling M/W, cross-country running M/W, equestrian sports W, fencing M/W, golf M/W, gymnastics M/W, racquetball M/W, skiing (cross-country) M/W, softball W, swimming and diving W, tennis M/W, volleyball M/W, water polo M, wrestling M.

Standardized Tests *Required:* SAT or ACT (for admission).

Costs (2007–08) *Tuition:* state resident $0 full-time; nonresident $10,170 full-time, $339 per unit part-time. *Required fees:* $3299 full-time, $1068 per term part-time. *Room and board:* $7053; room only: $3793. Room and board charges vary according to board plan. *Payment plan:* installment. *Waivers:* senior citizens and employees or children of employees.

Financial Aid Of all full-time matriculated undergraduates who enrolled in 2007, 9,858 applied for aid, 8,645 were judged to have need, 2,849 had their need fully met. 382 Federal Work-Study jobs (averaging $3080). In 2007, 240 non-need-based awards were made. *Average percent of need met:* 70%. *Average financial aid package:* $8105. *Average need-based loan:* $4198. *Average need-based gift aid:* $6745. *Average non-need-based aid:* $2576.

Applying *Options:* electronic application. *Application fee:* $55. *Required:* high school transcript, minimum 2.0 GPA. *Application deadline:* 4/1 (freshmen). *Notification:* continuous (freshmen).

Freshman Application Contact Ms. Yolanda Deleon, Admissions Officer, California State University, Fresno, 5150 North Maple Avenue, M/S JA 57, Fresno, CA 93740-8026. *Phone:* 559-278-6115. *Fax:* 559-278-4812. *E-mail:* yolandad@csufresno.edu.

CALIFORNIA STATE UNIVERSITY, FULLERTON

Fullerton, California **www.fullerton.edu/**

- **State-supported** comprehensive, founded 1957, part of California State University System
- **Suburban** 225-acre campus with easy access to Los Angeles
- **Endowment** $13.3 million
- **Coed** 31,750 undergraduate students, 72% full-time, 58% women, 42% men
- **Moderately difficult** entrance level, 61% of applicants were admitted

Undergraduates 22,724 full-time, 9,026 part-time. Students come from 40 states and territories, 61 other countries, 1% are from out of state, 4% African American, 22% Asian American or Pacific Islander, 30% Hispanic American, 0.5% Native American, 4% international, 13% transferred in, 2% live on campus. *Retention:* 79% of 2006 full-time freshmen returned.

Freshmen *Admission:* 29,812 applied, 18,042 admitted, 4,154 enrolled. *Average high school GPA:* 3.18. *Test scores:* SAT critical reading scores over 500: 41%; SAT math scores over 500: 49%; ACT scores over 18: 73%; SAT critical reading scores over 600: 8%; SAT math scores over 600: 13%; ACT scores over 24: 27%; SAT critical reading scores over 700: 1%; SAT math scores over 700: 1%; ACT scores over 30: 1%.

Faculty *Total:* 1,997, 45% full-time. *Student/faculty ratio:* 23:1.

Majors Accounting; advertising; African-American/Black studies; American studies; anthropology; applied mathematics; art; art history, criticism and conservation; Asian-American studies; biochemistry; biology/biological sciences; business administration and management; business/managerial economics; chemistry; civil engineering; communication disorders; communication/speech communication and rhetoric; comparative literature; computer engineering; computer science; criminal justice/safety; dance; dramatic/theater arts; early childhood education; economics; electrical, electronics and communications engineering; engineering; engineering science; English; entrepreneurship; European studies; finance; fine/studio arts; French; geography; geology/earth science; German; health and physical education; health professions related; health services/allied health/health sciences; Hispanic-American, Puerto Rican, and Mexican-American/Chicano studies; history; hospitality administration related; human services; information science/studies; international business/trade/commerce; Japanese; journalism; Latin American studies; liberal arts and sciences/liberal studies; linguistics; marketing/marketing management; mathematics; mechanical engineering; music; music performance; music teacher education; nursing (registered nurse training); operations research; philosophy; physics; political science and government; pre-nursing studies; psychology; public administration; public relations/image management; radio and television; religious studies; Russian studies; sociology; Spanish; speech and rhetoric; statistics; women's studies.

Academics *Calendar:* semesters. *Degrees:* bachelor's, master's, doctoral, post-master's, and postbachelor's certificates. *Special study options:* academic remediation for entering students, adult/continuing education programs, advanced placement credit, cooperative education, distance learning, double majors, English as a second language, freshman honors college, honors programs, independent study, internships, off-campus study, part-time degree program, services for LD students, student-designed majors, study abroad, summer session for credit. *ROTC:* Army (b).

Computers on Campus 2,000 computers/terminals are available on campus for general student use. Students can access the following: campus intranet, computer help desk, free student e-mail accounts, online (class) grades, online (class) registration, online (class) schedules. Campuswide network is available. Wireless service is available via entire campus.

Student Life *Housing options:* coed. Campus housing is university owned. *Activities and organizations:* drama/theater group, student-run newspaper, radio station, choral group, Pan Hellenic Council, American Marketing Association, Lacrosse Club, Samaritans-volunteer service club, Human Services Student Association, national fraternities, national sororities. *Campus security:* 24-hour emergency response devices and patrols, student patrols, late-night transport/escort service, controlled dormitory access. *Student services:* health clinic, personal/psychological counseling, women's center, legal services.

Athletics Member NCAA. All Division I. *Intercollegiate sports:* baseball M (s), basketball M (s)/W (s), cross-country running M (s)/W (s), fencing M (s)/W (s), gymnastics W (s), soccer M (s)/W (s), softball W (s), tennis W (s), track and field M (s)/W (s), volleyball W (s), wrestling M (s). *Intramural sports:* badminton M/W, basketball M/W, bowling M/W, football M/W, gymnastics M/W, racquetball M/W, rugby M, skiing (downhill) M/W, soccer M, softball M/W, swimming and diving M/W, table tennis M/W, tennis M/W, volleyball M/W, wrestling M.

Standardized Tests *Required:* SAT (for admission), SAT or ACT (for admission).

Costs (2007–08) *Tuition:* nonresident $13,512 full-time, $339 per unit part-time. Full-time tuition and fees vary according to course load. Part-time tuition and fees vary according to course load. *Required fees:* $3342 full-time. *Room and board:* $9035. *Payment plans:* installment, deferred payment. *Waivers:* senior citizens and employees or children of employees.

Financial Aid Of all full-time matriculated undergraduates who enrolled in 2007, 13,134 applied for aid, 9,893 were judged to have need, 185 had their need fully met. 768 Federal Work-Study jobs (averaging $2185). In 2007, 1667 non-need-based awards were made. *Average percent of need met:* 61%. *Average financial aid package:* $7293. *Average need-based loan:* $4226. *Average need-based gift aid:* $6454. *Average non-need-based aid:* $5029. *Average indebtedness upon graduation:* $14,556.

Applying *Options:* electronic application. *Application fee:* $55. *Required:* high school transcript, minimum 2.0 GPA. *Application deadlines:* 11/30 (freshmen), rolling (transfers). *Notification:* continuous (freshmen), continuous (transfers).

Freshman Application Contact Ms. Nancy J. Dority, Assistant Vice President of Enrollment Services, California State University, Fullerton, Office of Admissions and Records, PO Box 6900, 800 North State College Boulevard, Fullerton, CA 92834-6900. *Phone:* 714-278-2370. *Fax:* 714-278-2356. *E-mail:* admissions@fullerton.edu.

CALIFORNIA STATE UNIVERSITY, LONG BEACH

Long Beach, California **www.csulb.edu/**

- **State-supported** comprehensive, founded 1949, part of California State University System
- **Suburban** 320-acre campus with easy access to Los Angeles
- **Endowment** $36.1 million
- **Coed** 30,605 undergraduate students, 79% full-time, 60% women, 40% men
- **Moderately difficult** entrance level, 47% of applicants were admitted

Undergraduates 24,305 full-time, 6,300 part-time. Students come from 46 states and territories, 94 other countries, 1% are from out of state, 6% African American, 23% Asian American or Pacific Islander, 27% Hispanic American, 0.6% Native American, 5% international, 11% transferred in, 7% live on campus. *Retention:* 85% of 2006 full-time freshmen returned.

Freshmen *Admission:* 45,189 applied, 21,245 admitted, 4,212 enrolled. *Average high school GPA:* 3.34. *Test scores:* SAT critical reading scores over 500: 49%; SAT math scores over 500: 59%; ACT scores over 18: 74%; SAT critical reading scores over 600: 12%; SAT math scores over 600: 19%; ACT scores over 24: 24%; SAT critical reading scores over 700: 1%; SAT math scores over 700: 1%; ACT scores over 30: 1%.

Faculty *Total:* 2,263, 43% full-time, 55% with terminal degrees. *Student/faculty ratio:* 20:1.

Majors Accounting; acting; aerospace, aeronautical and astronautical engineering; African-American/Black studies; American studies; ancient/classical Greek; anthropology; apparel and textiles; applied mathematics; art; art history, criticism and conservation; art teacher education; Asian-American studies; Asian studies; athletic training; audiology and hearing sciences; audiology and speech-language pathology; biochemistry; biochemistry/biophysics and molecular biology; biology/biological sciences; biology teacher education; biomedical/medical engineering; botany/plant biology; broadcast journalism; business administration and management; business/managerial economics; cell biology and histology; ceramic arts and ceramics; chemical engineering; chemistry; child development; Chinese; cinematography and film/video production; civil engineering; classics and classical languages related; commercial and advertising art; communication disorders; comparative literature; computer engineering; computer engineering technology; computer science; construction engineering; construction engineering technology; construction management; creative writing; criminal justice/law enforcement administration; dance; dance related; dietetics; directing and theatrical production; dramatic/theater arts; drawing; ecology; economics; electrical, electronic and communications engineering technology; electrical, electronics and communications engineering; engineering; engineering/industrial management; engineering related; engineering technology; English; English/language arts teacher education; environmental engineering technology; environmental science; family and consumer sciences/human sciences; family and consumer sciences/human sciences related; fashion merchandising; fiber, textile and weaving arts; film/cinema studies; finance; fine arts related; fine/studio arts; foods and nutrition related; French; geography; geology/earth science; German; graphic design; health and physical education related; health/health care administration; health science; Hispanic-American, Puerto Rican, and Mexican-American/Chicano studies; history; hotel/motel administration; human development and family studies; human resources management; illustration; industrial design; industrial engineering; industrial technology; interdisciplinary studies; interior design; international business/trade/commerce; international relations and affairs; Italian; Japanese; journalism; journalism related; kinesiology and exercise science; kinesiotherapy; liberal arts and sciences/liberal studies; literature; management information systems; manufacturing technology; marine biology and biological oceanography; marketing/marketing management; mass communication/media; materials engineering; mathematics; mathematics teacher education; mechanical engineering; mechanical engineering/mechanical technology; medical radiologic technology; metal and jewelry arts; microbiology; multi-/interdisciplinary studies related; music; music history, literature, and theory; music performance; music theory and composition; nursing (registered nurse training); ocean engineering; operations management; painting; parks, recreation and leisure; philosophy; photography; physical education teaching and coaching; physics; physiology; political science and government; printmaking; psychology; public health; public health education and promotion; public relations/image management; quality control technology; radio and television; religious studies; sculpture; social work; sociology; Spanish; speech and rhetoric; statistics; trade and industrial teacher education; voice and opera; women's studies; zoology/animal biology.

Academics *Calendar:* semesters. *Degrees:* bachelor's, master's, and post-bachelor's certificates. *Special study options:* academic remediation for entering students, accelerated degree program, adult/continuing education programs, advanced placement credit, distance learning, double majors, English as a second language, honors programs, independent study, internships, off-campus study, part-time degree program, services for LD students, student-designed majors, study abroad, summer session for credit. *ROTC:* Army (b).

Computers on Campus 2,000 computers/terminals are available on campus for general student use. Campuswide network is available.

Student Life *Housing options:* coed. *Activities and organizations:* drama/theater group, student-run newspaper, radio and television station, choral group, national fraternities, national sororities. *Campus security:* 24-hour emergency response devices and patrols, student patrols, late-night transport/escort service. *Student services:* health clinic, personal/psychological counseling, women's center, legal services.

Athletics Member NCAA. All Division I. *Intercollegiate sports:* archery M (c)/W (c), badminton M (c)/W (c), basketball M (s)/W (s), bowling M (c)/W (c), crew M (c)/W (c), cross-country running M (s)/W (s), fencing M (c)/W (c), golf M/W, rugby M (c), sailing M (c)/W (c), skiing (downhill) M (c)/W (c), soccer M (c)/W (s), softball W (s), table tennis M (c), tennis W (s), track and field M (s)/W (s), volleyball M (s)/W (s), water polo M (s)/W (s). *Intramural sports:* basketball M/W, gymnastics M/W, racquetball M/W, softball W, swimming and diving M/W, table tennis W (c), tennis W, track and field M (c)/W (c), volleyball M/W.

Standardized Tests *Required:* SAT or ACT (for admission).

Costs (2008–09) *Tuition:* nonresident $10,170 full-time, $339 per unit part-time. *Required fees:* $3394 full-time. *Room and board:* $7940.

Financial Aid Of all full-time matriculated undergraduates who enrolled in 2007, 16,408 applied for aid, 14,816 were judged to have need, 6,046 had their need fully met. In 2007, 1436 non-need-based awards were made. *Average percent of need met:* 86%. *Average financial aid package:* $11,250. *Average need-based loan:* $3190. *Average need-based gift aid:* $5100. *Average non-need-based aid:* $2064. *Average indebtedness upon graduation:* $10,183.

Applying *Options:* electronic application. *Application fee:* $55. *Required:* high school transcript. *Required for some:* minimum 2.0 GPA, minimum GPA of 2.4 for nonresidents. *Application deadlines:* 11/30 (freshmen), 11/30 (transfers). *Notification:* continuous (freshmen), continuous (transfers).

Freshman Application Contact Mr. Thomas Enders, Director of Enrollment Services, California State University, Long Beach, Brotman Hall, 1250 Bellflower Boulevard, Long Beach, CA 90840. *Phone:* 562-985-4641.

CALIFORNIA STATE UNIVERSITY, LOS ANGELES

Los Angeles, California **www.calstatela.edu/**

- **State-supported** comprehensive, founded 1947, part of California State University System
- **Urban** 173-acre campus
- **Endowment** $13.6 million
- **Coed** 15,727 undergraduate students, 74% full-time, 61% women, 39% men
- **Moderately difficult** entrance level, 63% of applicants were admitted

Undergraduates 11,691 full-time, 4,036 part-time. Students come from 49 states and territories, 50 other countries, 4% are from out of state, 8% African American, 19% Asian American or Pacific Islander, 46% Hispanic American, 0.4% Native American, 6% international, 15% transferred in, 6% live on campus. *Retention:* 72% of 2006 full-time freshmen returned.

Freshmen *Admission:* 20,436 applied, 12,805 admitted, 1,931 enrolled. *Average high school GPA:* 3.1. *Test scores:* SAT critical reading scores over 500: 21%; SAT math scores over 500: 24%; SAT writing scores over 500: 20%; ACT scores over 18: 44%; SAT critical reading scores over 600: 4%; SAT math scores over 600: 5%; SAT writing scores over 600: 3%; ACT scores over 24: 7%; SAT critical reading scores over 700: 1%; SAT math scores over 700: 1%; SAT writing scores over 700: 1%; ACT scores over 30: 1%.

Faculty *Total:* 1,226, 47% full-time. *Student/faculty ratio:* 21:1.

Majors African-American/Black studies; anthropology; art; Asian-American studies; Asian studies; aviation/airway management; biochemistry; biology/biological sciences; business administration and management; chemistry; child development; Chinese; civil engineering; communication disorders; communication/speech communication and rhetoric; computer and information sciences; computer and information sciences and support services related; computer science; criminal justice/safety; dance; dietetics; dramatic/theater arts; early childhood education; economics; electrical, electronics and communications engineering; engineering; English; fire services administration; foods, nutrition, and wellness; French; geography; geology/earth science; health professions related; health science; Hispanic-American, Puerto Rican, and Mexican-American/Chicano studies; history; industrial technology; information technology; interdisciplinary studies; Japanese; kinesiology and exercise science; Latin American studies; liberal arts and sciences/liberal studies; mathematics; mechanical engineering; microbiology; multi-/interdisciplinary studies related; music; music performance; natural sciences; nursing (registered nurse training); nutritional sciences; philosophy; physics; political science and government; psychology; radio and television; rehabilitation therapy; social sciences; social work; sociology; Spanish; speech and rhetoric.

Academics *Calendar:* quarters. *Degrees:* bachelor's, master's, and doctoral. *Special study options:* academic remediation for entering students, accelerated degree program, adult/continuing education programs, advanced placement credit, cooperative education, distance learning, double majors, English as a second language, honors programs, independent study, internships, off-campus study, part-time degree program, services for LD students, student-designed majors, study abroad, summer session for credit. *ROTC:* Army (c), Air Force (c). *Unusual degree programs:* 3-2 nursing.

Computers on Campus 1,500 computers/terminals are available on campus for general student use. Campuswide network is available. Wireless service is available via classrooms, computer centers, computer labs, dorm rooms, learning centers, libraries, student centers.

Student Life *Housing options:* coed. Campus housing is university owned. *Activities and organizations:* drama/theater group, student-run newspaper, choral group, Society of Hispanic Engineering and Science Students, Institute of Electrical and Electronics Engineer, Sigma Delta PI, Asian Unified, Society of Automotive Engineers, national fraternities, national sororities. *Campus security:* 24-hour emergency response devices, student patrols, late-night transport/escort service. *Student services:* health clinic, personal/psychological counseling, women's center, legal services.

Athletics Member NCAA. All Division II. *Intercollegiate sports:* baseball M (s), basketball M (s)/W (s), cross-country running W (s), soccer M (s)/W (s), tennis W (s), track and field M (s)/W (s), volleyball W (s). *Intramural sports:* basketball M/W, bowling M/W, gymnastics M/W, racquetball M/W, skiing (cross-country) M/W, soccer M/W, softball M/W, swimming and diving M/W, tennis M/W, track and field M/W, volleyball M/W, water polo M/W, wrestling M.

Standardized Tests *Required for some:* SAT or ACT (for admission).

Costs (2008–09) *Tuition:* state resident $0 full-time; nonresident $11,513 full-time, $226 per unit part-time. *Required fees:* $3377 full-time, $737 per term part-time. *Room and board:* $8406; room only: $5094.

Financial Aid Of all full-time matriculated undergraduates who enrolled in 2006, 7,436 applied for aid, 7,426 were judged to have need, 639 had their need fully met. 272 Federal Work-Study jobs (averaging $4058). *Average percent of need met:* 65%. *Average financial aid package:* $7672. *Average need-based loan:* $3990. *Average need-based gift aid:* $6130.

Applying *Options:* electronic application, early admission. *Application fee:* $55. *Required:* high school transcript. *Application deadlines:* 6/15 (freshmen), 6/15 (transfers).

Freshman Application Contact Mr. Vince Lopez, Director of Outreach and Recruitment, California State University, Los Angeles, 5151 State University Drive, Los Angeles, CA 90032-8530. *Phone:* 323-343-3839. *E-mail:* admission@calstatela.edu.

CALIFORNIA STATE UNIVERSITY, MONTEREY BAY

Seaside, California csumb.edu/

- **State-supported** comprehensive, founded 1994, part of California State University System
- **Small-town** 1500-acre campus with easy access to San Jose
- **Endowment** $4.9 million
- **Coed** 3,619 undergraduate students, 90% full-time, 56% women, 44% men
- **Minimally difficult** entrance level, 69% of applicants were admitted

Undergraduates 3,242 full-time, 377 part-time. Students come from 41 states and territories, 26 other countries, 2% are from out of state, 4% African American, 7% Asian American or Pacific Islander, 28% Hispanic American, 0.8% Native American, 1% international, 13% transferred in, 42% live on campus. *Retention:* 67% of 2006 full-time freshmen returned.

Freshmen *Admission:* 7,254 applied, 4,996 admitted, 745 enrolled. *Average high school GPA:* 3.05. *Test scores:* SAT critical reading scores over 500: 45%; SAT math scores over 500: 46%; SAT writing scores over 500: 46%; ACT scores over 18: 72%; SAT critical reading scores over 600: 11%; SAT math scores over 600: 10%; SAT writing scores over 600: 8%; ACT scores over 24: 21%; SAT math scores over 700: 1%; ACT scores over 30: 1%.

Faculty *Total:* 315, 33% full-time, 43% with terminal degrees. *Student/faculty ratio:* 22:1.

Majors Art; athletic training; behavioral sciences; biology/biological sciences; business administration and management; communication/speech communication and rhetoric; consumer/homemaking education; dramatic/theater arts; environmental biology; environmental studies; foreign languages and literatures; geology/earth science; humanities; human services; interdisciplinary studies; international business/trade/commerce; international/global studies; international relations and affairs; liberal arts and sciences/liberal studies; mathematics related; psychology related; telecommunications.

Academics *Calendar:* semesters. *Degrees:* bachelor's and master's. *Special study options:* academic remediation for entering students, adult/continuing education programs, cooperative education, distance learning, double majors, external degree program, independent study, internships, part-time degree program, services for LD students, student-designed majors, study abroad, summer session for credit.

Computers on Campus 800 computers/terminals are available on campus for general student use. Students can access the following: campus intranet, computer help desk, free student e-mail accounts, online (class) grades, online (class) registration, online (class) schedules. Campuswide network is available. 100% of college-owned or -operated housing units are wired for high-speed Internet access. Wireless service is available via entire campus.

Student Life *Housing:* on-campus residence required through sophomore year. *Options:* coed, disabled students. Campus housing is university owned. Freshman campus housing is guaranteed. *Activities and organizations:* drama/theater group, student-run newspaper, radio station, choral group, MEChA, Black Students United, Business Club, Anime Club, Disc Golf. *Campus security:* 24-hour emergency response devices and patrols, student patrols, late-night transport/escort service, controlled dormitory access. *Student services:* health clinic, personal/psychological counseling.

Athletics Member NCAA, NAIA. *Intercollegiate sports:* baseball M (s), basketball M/W (s), cross-country running M (s)/W (s), golf M (s)/W (s), sailing M/W, soccer M (s)/W (s), softball W (s), volleyball W (s), water polo W (s). *Intramural sports:* rugby M/W, sailing M/W.

Standardized Tests *Required for some:* SAT or ACT (for admission).

Costs (2007–08) *Tuition:* state resident $0 full-time; nonresident $10,170 full-time, $339 per credit hour part-time. *Required fees:* $3000 full-time, $1046 per term part-time. *Room and board:* $9152; room only: $4850.

Financial Aid In 2002, 70 non-need-based awards were made. *Average percent of need met:* 75%. *Average financial aid package:* $7152. *Average indebtedness upon graduation:* $8263.

Applying *Options:* electronic application, deferred entrance. *Application fee:* $55. *Required:* high school transcript, minimum 2.0 GPA. *Application deadlines:* 7/15 (freshmen), 8/4 (transfers).

Freshman Application Contact Admissions and Recruitment, California State University, Monterey Bay, 100 Campus Center, Building 47, Seaside, CA 93955. *Phone:* 831-582-3738. *Fax:* 831-582-3783. *E-mail:* admissions@csumb.edu.

CALIFORNIA STATE UNIVERSITY, NORTHRIDGE

Northridge, California www.csun.edu/

- **State-supported** comprehensive, founded 1958, part of California State University System
- **Urban** 356-acre campus with easy access to Los Angeles
- **Endowment** $2.4 million
- **Coed**
- **Moderately difficult** entrance level

Faculty *Student/faculty ratio:* 23:1.

Academics *Calendar:* semesters. *Degrees:* bachelor's and master's.

Student Life *Campus security:* 24-hour emergency response devices, late-night transport/escort service.

Athletics Member NCAA. All Division I except football (Division II).

Standardized Tests *Required:* SAT or ACT (for admission).

Costs (2007–08) *Tuition:* state resident $0 full-time; nonresident $8136 full-time, $339 per unit part-time. *Required fees:* $3350 full-time, $1675 per term part-time. *Room and board:* $9350; room only: $5413. Room and board charges vary according to board plan and housing facility.

Financial Aid Of all full-time matriculated undergraduates who enrolled in 2006, 13,896 applied for aid, 12,781 were judged to have need. 646 Federal Work-Study jobs (averaging $2592). In 2006, 771 non-need-based awards were made. *Average financial aid package:* $7416. *Average need-based loan:* $4029. *Average need-based gift aid:* $4954. *Average non-need-based aid:* $1461. *Average indebtedness upon graduation:* $13,225.

Applying *Options:* electronic application, early admission, early action. *Application fee:* $55. *Required:* high school transcript.

Freshman Application Contact Ms. Mary Baxton, Associate Director of Admissions and Records, California State University, Northridge, 18111 Nordhoff Street, Northridge, CA 91330-8207. *Phone:* 818-677-3777. *Fax:* 818-677-3766. *E-mail:* admissions.records@csun.edu.

CALIFORNIA STATE UNIVERSITY, SACRAMENTO

Sacramento, California www.csus.edu/

- **State-supported** comprehensive, founded 1947, part of California State University System
- **Urban** 300-acre campus
- **Coed** 23,724 undergraduate students, 76% full-time, 57% women, 43% men
- **Moderately difficult** entrance level, 67% of applicants were admitted

Undergraduates 18,045 full-time, 5,679 part-time. 1% are from out of state, 8% African American, 19% Asian American or Pacific Islander, 14% Hispanic American, 0.9% Native American, 1% international, 10% transferred in, 5% live on campus. *Retention:* 77% of 2006 full-time freshmen returned.

Freshmen *Admission:* 17,491 applied, 11,658 admitted, 2,087 enrolled. *Average high school GPA:* 3.18. *Test scores:* SAT critical reading scores over 500: 37%; SAT math scores over 500: 46%; ACT scores over 18: 78%; SAT critical reading scores over 600: 8%; SAT math scores over 600: 12%; ACT scores over 24: 24%; SAT critical reading scores over 700: 1%; SAT math scores over 700: 1%; ACT scores over 30: 1%.

Faculty *Total:* 1,654, 50% full-time, 52% with terminal degrees. *Student/faculty ratio:* 21:1.

Majors American Sign Language (ASL); anthropology; art; Asian studies; audiology and speech-language pathology; biology/biological sciences; business administration and management; chemistry; child development; civil engineering; communication/speech communication and rhetoric; computer engineering;

computer science; construction engineering technology; criminal justice/law enforcement administration; cultural studies; dance; dramatic/theater arts; economics; electrical, electronics and communications engineering; English; environmental studies; family/consumer studies; film/cinema studies; French; geography; geology/earth science; gerontology; graphic design; health science; history; humanities; interior design; journalism; kinesiology and exercise science; liberal arts and sciences/liberal studies; marketing/marketing management; mass communication/media; mathematics; mechanical engineering; mechanical engineering/mechanical technology; music; nursing (registered nurse training); parks, recreation and leisure; parks, recreation and leisure facilities management; philosophy; photography; physical sciences; physics; political science and government; psychology; religious studies; social sciences; social work; sociology; Spanish.

Academics *Calendar:* semesters. *Degrees:* bachelor's, master's, and doctoral. *Special study options:* academic remediation for entering students, accelerated degree program, advanced placement credit, cooperative education, distance learning, double majors, English as a second language, honors programs, independent study, internships, off-campus study, part-time degree program, services for LD students, student-designed majors, study abroad, summer session for credit. *ROTC:* Army (c), Air Force (b).

Computers on Campus 700 computers/terminals are available on campus for general student use. Students can access the following: computer help desk, free student e-mail accounts, online (class) grades, online (class) registration, online (class) schedules, online transcripts. Campuswide network is available. 100% of college-owned or -operated housing units are wired for high-speed Internet access. Wireless service is available via entire campus.

Student Life *Housing options:* coed. Campus housing is university owned. *Activities and organizations:* drama/theater group, student-run newspaper, radio station, choral group, marching band, Ski Club, California Nursing Student Association, Delta Sigma Pi (Business Fraternity), EOP, Studies Humanitas, national fraternities, national sororities. *Campus security:* 24-hour emergency response devices and patrols, student patrols, late-night transport/escort service, controlled dormitory access. *Student services:* health clinic, personal/psychological counseling, women's center, legal services.

Athletics Member NCAA. All Division I except football (Division I-AA). *Intercollegiate sports:* baseball M (s), basketball M (s)/W (s), bowling M (c)/W (c), cheerleading M/W, crew M (s)/W (s), cross-country running M (s)/W (s), golf M (s)/W, gymnastics W (s), ice hockey M (c), lacrosse M (c)/W (c), racquetball M (c)/W (c), rugby M (c), skiing (downhill) M (c)/W (c), soccer M (s)/W (s), softball W (s), tennis M (s)/W (s), track and field M (s)/W (s), volleyball M (c)/W (s). *Intramural sports:* basketball M/W, crew M/W, football M/W, golf M/W, ice hockey M, skiing (downhill) M/W, soccer M/W, softball M/W, table tennis M/W, tennis M/W, volleyball M/W, water polo M/W, weight lifting M/W.

Standardized Tests *Required for some:* SAT or ACT (for admission).

Costs (2007–08) *Tuition:* state resident $0 full-time; nonresident $12,942 full-time, $339 per unit part-time. *Required fees:* $4752 full-time, $1608 per year part-time. *Room and board:* $8598; room only: $5778. Room and board charges vary according to board plan. *Payment plan:* installment. *Waivers:* senior citizens and employees or children of employees.

Financial Aid Of all full-time matriculated undergraduates who enrolled in 2005, 10,826 applied for aid, 9,325 were judged to have need, 83 had their need fully met. 431 Federal Work-Study jobs (averaging $2412). In 2005, 857 non-need-based awards were made. *Average percent of need met:* 61%. *Average financial aid package:* $8354. *Average need-based loan:* $3803. *Average need-based gift aid:* $2259. *Average non-need-based aid:* $6078. *Average indebtedness upon graduation:* $10,868.

Applying *Options:* electronic application, early action, deferred entrance. *Application fee:* $55. *Required:* minimum 2.0 GPA. *Required for some:* high school transcript. *Application deadlines:* 8/1 (freshmen), 7/1 (transfers), 11/30 (early action). *Notification:* 11/1 (freshmen), 12/1 (transfers), 11/1 (early action).

Freshman Application Contact Mr. Emiliano Diaz, Director of University Outreach Services, California State University, Sacramento, 6000 J Street, Lassen Hall, Sacramento, CA 95819-6048. *Phone:* 916-278-3901. *Fax:* 916-278-5603. *E-mail:* admissions@csus.edu.

CALIFORNIA STATE UNIVERSITY, SAN BERNARDINO

San Bernardino, California **www.csusb.edu/**

- **State-supported** comprehensive, founded 1965, part of California State University System
- **Suburban** 430-acre campus with easy access to Los Angeles
- **Coed** 13,311 undergraduate students, 83% full-time, 65% women, 35% men
- **Moderately difficult** entrance level, 61% of applicants were admitted

Undergraduates 11,067 full-time, 2,244 part-time. Students come from 37 states and territories, 43 other countries, 1% are from out of state, 12% African American, 8% Asian American or Pacific Islander, 37% Hispanic American, 0.7% Native American, 3% international, 12% transferred in, 11% live on campus. *Retention:* 82% of 2006 full-time freshmen returned.

Freshmen *Admission:* 9,987 applied, 6,107 admitted, 1,722 enrolled. *Average high school GPA:* 3.22. *Test scores:* SAT math scores over 500: 33%; SAT writing scores over 500: 28%; ACT scores over 18: 13%; SAT math scores over 600: 7%; SAT writing scores over 600: 5%; ACT scores over 24: 2%.

Faculty *Total:* 633, 71% full-time. *Student/faculty ratio:* 21:1.

Majors Accounting; American studies; anthropology; art; art history, criticism and conservation; biochemistry; biology/biological sciences; business administration and management; business/managerial economics; chemistry; computer and information sciences; computer science; creative writing; criminal justice/law enforcement administration; developmental and child psychology; dietetics; dramatic/theater arts; economics; English; environmental studies; finance; foods, nutrition, and wellness; French; geography; geology/earth science; health/health care administration; health science; health teacher education; history; human development and family studies; humanities; human services; interdisciplinary studies; liberal arts and sciences/liberal studies; management information systems; marketing/marketing management; mathematics; music; natural sciences; nursing (registered nurse training); philosophy; physical education teaching and coaching; physics; political science and government; psychology; public administration; social sciences; social work; sociology; Spanish; trade and industrial teacher education.

Academics *Calendar:* quarters. *Degrees:* bachelor's and master's. *Special study options:* accelerated degree program, adult/continuing education programs, cooperative education, distance learning, double majors, honors programs, independent study, internships, off-campus study, part-time degree program, services for LD students, student-designed majors, study abroad, summer session for credit. *ROTC:* Army (b), Air Force (b).

Computers on Campus 1,300 computers/terminals are available on campus for general student use. Students can access the following: online (class) registration. Campuswide network is available.

Student Life *Housing options:* coed, women-only. Campus housing is university owned and is provided by a third party. Freshman applicants given priority for college housing. *Activities and organizations:* drama/theater group, student-run newspaper, radio station, choral group, national fraternities, national sororities. *Campus security:* 24-hour emergency response devices and patrols, student patrols, late-night transport/escort service, residence staff on call 24 hours. *Student services:* health clinic, personal/psychological counseling, women's center, legal services.

Athletics Member NCAA. All Division II. *Intercollegiate sports:* baseball M (s), basketball M (s)/W (s), golf M (s), soccer M (s)/W (s), softball W (s), swimming and diving M (s)/W (s), volleyball W (s). *Intramural sports:* basketball M/W, field hockey M/W, football M/W, soccer M/W, softball M, volleyball M/W.

Standardized Tests *Required:* SAT or ACT (for admission).

Costs (2007–08) *Tuition:* state resident $0 full-time; nonresident $8136 full-time, $226 per unit part-time. Part-time tuition and fees vary according to course load. *Required fees:* $3398 full-time, $536 per term part-time. *Room and board:* $7517; room only: $6093. Room and board charges vary according to board plan and housing facility. *Waivers:* employees or children of employees.

Financial Aid Of all full-time matriculated undergraduates who enrolled in 2007, 8,620 applied for aid, 7,768 were judged to have need, 1,362 had their need fully met. 312 Federal Work-Study jobs (averaging $5039). In 2007, 30 non-need-based awards were made. *Average percent of need met:* 72%. *Average financial aid package:* $8840. *Average need-based loan:* $3928. *Average need-based gift aid:* $6291. *Average non-need-based aid:* $3655. *Average indebtedness upon graduation:* $17,946.

Applying *Options:* early admission. *Application fee:* $55. *Required:* high school transcript, minimum 2.0 GPA. *Application deadlines:* rolling (freshmen), rolling (transfers). *Notification:* continuous (freshmen), continuous (transfers).

Freshman Application Contact Ms. Cynthia Olivo, Associate Director, California State University, San Bernardino, 5500 University Parkway, University Hall, Room 107, San Bernardino, CA 92407-2397. *Phone:* 909-537-5188. *Fax:* 909-537-7034. *E-mail:* moreinfo@mail.csusb.edu.

CALIFORNIA STATE UNIVERSITY, SAN MARCOS

San Marcos, California **www.csusm.edu/**

- **State-supported** comprehensive, founded 1990, part of California State University System
- **Suburban** 304-acre campus with easy access to San Diego
- **Endowment** $5.9 million
- **Coed** 6,327 undergraduate students, 74% full-time, 61% women, 39% men
- **Moderately difficult** entrance level, 44% of applicants were admitted

Undergraduates 4,658 full-time, 1,669 part-time. Students come from 1 other state, 3% African American, 11% Asian American or Pacific Islander, 21% Hispanic American, 0.9% Native American, 3% international, 17% transferred in, 7% live on campus. *Retention:* 73% of 2006 full-time freshmen returned.

Freshmen *Admission:* 6,586 applied, 2,877 admitted, 804 enrolled. *Average high school GPA:* 3.12. *Test scores:* SAT critical reading scores over 500: 41%; SAT math scores over 500: 47%; SAT critical reading scores over 600: 8%; SAT math scores over 600: 10%; SAT critical reading scores over 700: 1%; SAT math scores over 700: 1%.

Faculty *Total:* 444, 41% full-time, 62% with terminal degrees. *Student/faculty ratio:* 24:1.

Majors Accounting; biochemistry; biology/biological sciences; business administration and management; cell biology and histology; chemistry; communication/speech communication and rhetoric; computer science; ecology; economics; English; history; liberal arts and sciences/liberal studies; mathematics; molecular biology; political science and government; psychology; science teacher education; social sciences; sociology; Spanish; visual and performing arts; women's studies.

Academics *Calendar:* semesters. *Degrees:* bachelor's and master's. *Special study options:* academic remediation for entering students, adult/continuing education programs, advanced placement credit, distance learning, double majors, English as a second language, independent study, internships, off-campus study, part-time degree program, services for LD students, student-designed majors, study abroad, summer session for credit. *ROTC:* Army (c), Navy (c), Air Force (c).

Computers on Campus 1,300 computers/terminals are available on campus for general student use. Students can access the following: online (class) registration. Campuswide network is available.

Student Life *Housing options:* men-only, women-only, disabled students. Campus housing is provided by a third party. *Activities and organizations:* drama/theater group, student-run newspaper, choral group, Accounting Club, Liberal Studies Club, MECHA, Sigma IOTA Epsilon, national fraternities, national sororities. *Campus security:* 24-hour patrols, student patrols, late-night transport/escort service. *Student services:* health clinic, personal/psychological counseling, women's center.

Athletics Member NAIA. *Intercollegiate sports:* cross-country running M/W, golf M (s)/W, track and field M/W. *Intramural sports:* basketball M/W, football M/W, soccer M/W, volleyball M/W.

Standardized Tests *Required for some:* SAT or ACT (for admission).

Costs (2007–08) *Tuition:* state resident $0 full-time; nonresident $8136 full-time, $339 per unit part-time. Part-time tuition and fees vary according to course load. *Required fees:* $3092 full-time, $1105 per term part-time. *Room only:* $5600. Room and board charges vary according to housing facility. *Waivers:* senior citizens and employees or children of employees.

Financial Aid Of all full-time matriculated undergraduates who enrolled in 2004, 2,081 applied for aid, 1,730 were judged to have need. 193 Federal Work-Study jobs (averaging $2035). 18 state and other part-time jobs (averaging $821). *Average financial aid package:* $6946. *Average need-based loan:* $4099. *Average need-based gift aid:* $3831. *Average indebtedness upon graduation:* $13,112.

Applying *Options:* electronic application. *Application fee:* $55. *Required:* high school transcript, minimum 3.0 GPA. *Application deadlines:* 11/30 (freshmen), 11/30 (transfers). *Notification:* continuous (freshmen), continuous (transfers).

Freshman Application Contact Ms. Cherine Heckman, Director of Admissions, California State University, San Marcos, 333 South Twin Oaks Valley Road, San Marcos, CA 92096-0001. *Phone:* 760-750-4848. *Fax:* 760-750-3248. *E-mail:* apply@csusm.edu.

CALIFORNIA STATE UNIVERSITY, STANISLAUS

Turlock, California **www.csustan.edu/**

- **State-supported** comprehensive, founded 1957, part of California State University System
- **Small-town** 228-acre campus
- **Endowment** $7.6 million
- **Coed** 7,088 undergraduate students, 70% full-time, 65% women, 35% men
- 65% of applicants were admitted

Undergraduates 4,927 full-time, 2,161 part-time. Students come from 20 states and territories, 46 other countries, 0.2% are from out of state, 4% African American, 12% Asian American or Pacific Islander, 30% Hispanic American, 1% Native American, 1% international, 14% transferred in, 8% live on campus. *Retention:* 81% of 2006 full-time freshmen returned.

Freshmen *Admission:* 4,689 applied, 3,061 admitted, 987 enrolled. *Average high school GPA:* 3.2. *Test scores:* SAT critical reading scores over 500: 35%; SAT math scores over 500: 42%; ACT scores over 18: 71%; SAT critical reading scores over 600: 8%; SAT math scores over 600: 9%; ACT scores over 24: 18%; SAT critical reading scores over 700: 1%; SAT math scores over 700: 1%; ACT scores over 30: 1%.

Faculty *Total:* 516, 57% full-time, 56% with terminal degrees. *Student/faculty ratio:* 19:1.

Majors Agriculture; anthropology; art; biology/biological sciences; business administration and management; business, management, and marketing related; chemistry; cognitive psychology and psycholinguistics; communication/speech communication and rhetoric; computer and information sciences; criminal justice/law enforcement administration; dramatic/theater arts; economics; English; fine/studio arts; French; geography; geology/earth science; history; information science/studies; liberal arts and sciences/liberal studies; mathematics; multi-/interdisciplinary studies related; music; music performance; nursing (registered nurse training); philosophy; physical education teaching and coaching; physical sciences; physics; political science and government; psychology; social sciences; sociology; Spanish.

Academics *Calendar:* 4-1-4. *Degrees:* bachelor's, master's, and postbachelor's certificates. *Special study options:* academic remediation for entering students, adult/continuing education programs, advanced placement credit, cooperative education, distance learning, double majors, English as a second language, honors programs, independent study, internships, off-campus study, part-time degree program, services for LD students, student-designed majors, study abroad, summer session for credit.

Computers on Campus 150 computers/terminals are available on campus for general student use. Students can access the following: online (class) registration. Campuswide network is available.

Student Life *Housing options:* coed. Campus housing is university owned and leased by the school. *Activities and organizations:* drama/theater group, student-run newspaper, radio station, choral group, MECHA, national fraternities, national sororities. *Campus security:* 24-hour emergency response devices and patrols, student patrols, late-night transport/escort service, controlled dormitory access. *Student services:* health clinic, personal/psychological counseling, women's center.

Athletics Member NCAA. All Division II. *Intercollegiate sports:* baseball M, basketball M/W, cross-country running M/W, golf M, soccer M/W, softball W, track and field M/W, volleyball W.

Standardized Tests *Required for some:* SAT or ACT (for admission).

Costs (2007–08) *Tuition:* state resident $0 full-time; nonresident $10,170 full-time, $339 per unit part-time. *Required fees:* $3307 full-time, $995 per term part-time. *Room and board:* $7707; room only: $6707. Room and board charges vary according to board plan and housing facility. *Payment plans:* installment, deferred payment. *Waivers:* adult students, senior citizens, and employees or children of employees.

Financial Aid Of all full-time matriculated undergraduates who enrolled in 2007, 3,989 applied for aid, 3,398 were judged to have need, 19 had their need fully met. 152 Federal Work-Study jobs (averaging $2431). In 2007, 32 non-need-based awards were made. *Average percent of need met:* 40%. *Average financial aid package:* $8445. *Average need-based loan:* $4262. *Average need-based gift aid:* $8446. *Average non-need-based aid:* $3497. *Average indebtedness upon graduation:* $16,500.

Applying *Options:* electronic application. *Application fee:* $55. *Required:* high school transcript. *Required for some:* interview. *Recommended:* minimum 3.0 GPA. *Application deadlines:* 2/1 (freshmen), rolling (transfers). *Notification:* continuous (freshmen), continuous (transfers).

Freshman Application Contact Student Outreach, California State University, Stanislaus, Enrollment Services, One University Circle, Turlock, CA 95382. *Phone:* 209-667-3122. *Toll-free phone:* 800-300-7420. *Fax:* 209-667-3788. *E-mail:* outreach_help_desk@csustan.edu.

CHAPMAN UNIVERSITY

Orange, California **www.chapman.edu/**

- **Independent** comprehensive, founded 1861, affiliated with Christian Church (Disciples of Christ)
- **Suburban** 76-acre campus with easy access to Los Angeles
- **Endowment** $210.7 million
- **Coed** 4,193 undergraduate students, 95% full-time, 59% women, 41% men
- **Moderately difficult** entrance level, 49% of applicants were admitted

Undergraduates 3,981 full-time, 212 part-time. Students come from 47 states and territories, 32 other countries, 25% are from out of state, 2% African American, 8% Asian American or Pacific Islander, 10% Hispanic American, 0.8% Native American, 2% international, 7% transferred in, 42% live on campus. *Retention:* 87% of 2006 full-time freshmen returned.

Freshmen *Admission:* 4,861 applied, 2,399 admitted, 937 enrolled. *Average high school GPA:* 3.67. *Test scores:* SAT critical reading scores over 500: 98%; SAT math scores over 500: 95%; SAT writing scores over 500: 98%; ACT scores over 18: 99%; SAT critical reading scores over 600: 55%; SAT math scores over 600: 55%; SAT writing scores over 600: 56%; ACT scores over 24: 80%; SAT critical reading scores over 700: 9%; SAT math scores over 700: 11%; SAT writing scores over 700: 9%; ACT scores over 30: 16%.

Faculty *Total:* 607, 51% full-time. *Student/faculty ratio:* 14:1.

Majors Accounting; American history; art; art history, criticism and conservation; athletic training; biology/biological sciences; biopsychology; broadcast journalism; business administration and management; business/managerial economics; chemistry; cinematography and film/video production; communication/speech communication and rhetoric; computer and information sciences; computer science; conducting; creative writing; dance; dramatic/theater arts; English; European history; exercise physiology; film/cinema studies; fine/studio arts; French; graphic design; liberal arts and sciences/liberal studies; mathematics; molecular biology; music; music performance; music teacher education; music theory and composition; music therapy; peace studies and conflict resolution; philosophy; playwriting and screenwriting; political science and government; psychology; public relations/image management; religious studies; social work; sociology; Spanish; voice and opera; wind/percussion instruments.

Academics *Calendar:* 4-1-4. *Degrees:* bachelor's, master's, doctoral, first professional, and postbachelor's certificates. *Special study options:* academic remediation for entering students, adult/continuing education programs, advanced placement credit, distance learning, double majors, English as a second language, honors programs, independent study, internships, part-time degree program, services for LD students, student-designed majors, study abroad, summer session for credit. *ROTC:* Army (c), Air Force (c). *Unusual degree programs:* 3-2 engineering with University of California, Irvine.

Computers on Campus 453 computers/terminals are available on campus for general student use. Students can access the following: campus intranet, computer help desk, free student e-mail accounts, online (class) grades, online (class) registration, online (class) schedules. Campuswide network is available. 100% of college-owned or -operated housing units are wired for high-speed Internet access. Wireless service is available via entire campus.

Student Life *Housing options:* coed, disabled students. Campus housing is university owned. Freshman campus housing is guaranteed. *Activities and organizations:* drama/theater group, student-run newspaper, radio station, choral group, Associated Students, Disciples on Campus, Gamma Beta Phi honor society, national fraternities, national sororities. *Campus security:* 24-hour emergency response devices and patrols, late-night transport/escort service, controlled dormitory access, full safety education program. *Student services:* health clinic, personal/psychological counseling.

Athletics Member NCAA. All Division III. *Intercollegiate sports:* baseball M, basketball M/W, cheerleading M (c)/W (c), crew M (c)/W, cross-country running M/W, football M, golf M, lacrosse M (c), soccer M/W, softball W, swimming and diving M (c)/W, tennis M/W, track and field W, volleyball W, water polo M/W. *Intramural sports:* basketball M/W, soccer M/W, tennis M/W, volleyball M/W.

Standardized Tests *Required:* SAT or ACT (for admission). *Recommended:* SAT Subject Tests (for admission).

Costs (2008–09) *Comprehensive fee:* $46,015 includes full-time tuition ($33,760), mandatory fees ($940), and room and board ($11,315). Part-time tuition: $1050 per credit.

Financial Aid Of all full-time matriculated undergraduates who enrolled in 2005, 3,545 applied for aid, 2,306 were judged to have need, 2,306 had their need fully met. 686 Federal Work-Study jobs (averaging $1510). In 2005, 659 non-need-based awards were made. *Average percent of need met:* 100%. *Average financial aid package:* $21,566. *Average need-based loan:* $4426. *Average need-based gift aid:* $18,118. *Average non-need-based aid:* $15,981. *Average indebtedness upon graduation:* $22,955.

Applying *Options:* electronic application, early action. *Application fee:* $55. *Required:* essay or personal statement, high school transcript, 1 letter of recommendation. *Recommended:* interview. *Application deadlines:* 1/15 (freshmen), 3/15 (transfers), 11/15 (early action). *Notification:* continuous (freshmen), continuous (transfers), 1/15 (early action).

Freshman Application Contact Mr. Michael Drummy, Assistant Vice President of Enrollment Services and Chief Admission Officer, Chapman University, One University Drive, Orange, CA 92866. *Phone:* 714-997-6711. *Toll-free phone:* 888-CUAPPLY. *Fax:* 714-997-6713. *E-mail:* admit@chapman.edu.

See page 436 for the College Close-Up.

CHARLES R. DREW UNIVERSITY OF MEDICINE AND SCIENCE

Los Angeles, California **www.cdrewu.edu/**

Freshman Application Contact Ms. Maranda Montgomery, Director, Student Affairs, Charles R. Drew University of Medicine and Science, 1731 East 120th Street, Keck Building, Los Angeles, CA 90059. *Phone:* 323-357-3638. *Fax:* 323-563-4923. *E-mail:* mmmontgo@cdrewu.edu.

CLAREMONT MCKENNA COLLEGE

Claremont, California **www.claremontmckenna.edu/**

- **Independent** 4-year, founded 1946, part of The Claremont Colleges Consortium
- **Small-town** 50-acre campus with easy access to Los Angeles
- **Endowment** $474.0 million
- **Coed** 1,135 undergraduate students, 100% full-time, 46% women, 54% men
- **Most difficult** entrance level, 18% of applicants were admitted

Undergraduates 1,135 full-time. Students come from 47 states and territories, 23 other countries, 55% are from out of state, 4% African American, 13% Asian American or Pacific Islander, 13% Hispanic American, 0.2% Native American, 5% international, 2% transferred in, 97% live on campus. *Retention:* 97% of 2006 full-time freshmen returned.

Freshmen *Admission:* 3,778 applied, 671 admitted, 268 enrolled. *Test scores:* SAT critical reading scores over 500: 100%; SAT math scores over 500: 100%; SAT critical reading scores over 600: 90%; SAT math scores over 600: 90%; SAT critical reading scores over 700: 52%; SAT math scores over 700: 53%.

Faculty *Total:* 143, 78% full-time, 96% with terminal degrees. *Student/faculty ratio:* 9:1.

Majors Accounting; African-American/Black studies; American government and politics; American studies; anthropology; archeology; area, ethnic, cultural, and gender studies related; area studies related; art; art history, criticism and conservation; Asian-American studies; Asian studies; biochemistry; biology/biological sciences; biophysics; chemistry; Chinese; Chinese studies; classics and languages, literatures and linguistics; computer and information sciences; computer science; dance; dramatic/theater arts; East Asian languages related; economics; economics related; engineering; engineering/industrial management; engineering related; engineering science; English; environmental studies; ethnic, cultural minority, and gender studies related; European studies; European studies (Western); film/cinema studies; fine/studio arts; French; French studies; German; Germanic languages; German studies; Hispanic-American, Puerto Rican, and Mexican-American/Chicano studies; history; international business/trade/commerce; international economics; international relations and affairs; Italian; Japanese; Japanese studies; Korean studies; Latin; Latin American studies; legal studies; literature; mathematics; modern Greek; modern languages; music; music related; Near and Middle Eastern studies; Pacific area/Pacific rim studies; philosophy; philosophy and religious studies related; philosophy related; physics; physiological psychology/psychobiology; political science and government; political science and government related; pre-dentistry studies; pre-law studies; premedical studies; psychology; religious studies; religious studies related; Russian; Russian studies; sociology; South Asian languages; Spanish; visual and performing arts; visual and performing arts related; women's studies.

Academics *Calendar:* semesters. *Degree:* bachelor's. *Special study options:* accelerated degree program, advanced placement credit, double majors, honors programs, independent study, internships, off-campus study, services for LD students, student-designed majors, study abroad. *ROTC:* Army (b), Air Force (c). *Unusual degree programs:* 3-2 business administration with Claremont Graduate School, University of Chicago; engineering with Stanford University, Harvey Mudd College, Columbia University, University of California System schools, University of Southern California; education, management information systems, computer information systems with Claremont Graduate School, applied biology with Keck Graduate Institute.

Computers on Campus 125 computers/terminals are available on campus for general student use. Students can access the following: campus intranet, computer help desk, free student e-mail accounts, online (class) grades, online (class) schedules. Campuswide network is available. 100% of college-owned or -operated housing units are wired for high-speed Internet access.

Student Life *Housing:* on-campus residence required for freshman year. *Options:* coed, disabled students. Campus housing is university owned. Freshman campus housing is guaranteed. *Activities and organizations:* drama/theater group, student-run newspaper, radio station, choral group, student government, Debate/Forensics Club, newspaper, Volunteer Student Admission Committee, Civitas (community service club). *Campus security:* 24-hour emergency response devices and patrols, student patrols, late-night transport/escort service, controlled dormitory access. *Student services:* health clinic, personal/psychological counseling, women's center.

Athletics Member NCAA. All Division III. *Intercollegiate sports:* badminton M (c)/W (c), baseball M, basketball M/W, cheerleading M (c)/W (c), cross-country running M/W, football M, golf M, lacrosse M (c)/W, rugby M (c)/W (c), skiing (downhill) M (c)/W (c), soccer M/W, softball W, swimming and diving M/W, tennis M/W, track and field M/W, volleyball M (c)/W, water polo M/W. *Intramural sports:* archery M/W, badminton M/W, basketball M/W, bowling M/W, crew M/W, equestrian sports M/W, fencing M/W, football M/W, golf W, racquetball M/W, sailing M/W, soccer M/W, softball M/W, squash M/W, swimming and diving M/W, table tennis M/W, tennis M/W, ultimate Frisbee M/W, volleyball M/W, water polo M/W, weight lifting M/W.

Standardized Tests *Required:* SAT or ACT (for admission). *Required for some:* SAT Subject Tests (for admission).

Costs (2007–08) *One-time required fee:* $210. *Comprehensive fee:* $45,516 includes full-time tuition ($34,980) and room and board ($10,536). Full-time tuition and fees vary according to reciprocity agreements. Part-time tuition: $5830 per course. Part-time tuition and fees vary according to reciprocity agreements. *College room only:* $5790. Room and board charges vary according to board plan and housing facility. *Payment plans:* tuition prepayment, installment. *Waivers:* employees or children of employees.

Financial Aid Of all full-time matriculated undergraduates who enrolled in 2006, 555 applied for aid, 530 were judged to have need, 524 had their need fully met. 280 Federal Work-Study jobs (averaging $1000). In 2006, 17 non-need-based awards were made. *Average percent of need met:* 100%. *Average financial aid package:* $28,191. *Average need-based loan:* $3604. *Average need-based gift aid:* $23,674. *Average non-need-based aid:* $8271. *Average indebtedness upon graduation:* $10,518.

Applying *Options:* electronic application, early admission, early decision, deferred entrance. *Application fee:* $60. *Required:* essay or personal statement, high school transcript, minimum 3.0 GPA, 3 letters of recommendation. *Recommended:* interview. *Application deadlines:* 1/2 (freshmen), 4/1 (transfers). *Early decision deadline:* 11/15 (for plan 1), 1/2 (for plan 2). *Notification:* 4/1 (freshmen), 5/15 (transfers), 12/15 (early decision plan 1), 2/15 (early decision plan 2).

Freshman Application Contact Mr. Richard C. Vos, Vice President/Dean of Admission and Financial Aid, Claremont McKenna College, 890 Columbia Avenue, Claremont, CA 91711. *Phone:* 909-621-8088. *Fax:* 909-621-8516. *E-mail:* admission@claremontmckenna.edu.

CLEVELAND CHIROPRACTIC COLLEGE-LOS ANGELES CAMPUS

Los Angeles, California **www.clevelandchiropractic.edu/**

- **Independent** upper-level, founded 1911, administratively affiliated with Cleveland Chiropractic College-Kansas City
- **Urban** campus
- **Coed** 104 undergraduate students, 76% full-time, 38% women, 62% men
- **Minimally difficult** entrance level, 51% of applicants were admitted

Undergraduates 79 full-time, 25 part-time. Students come from 10 states and territories, 2 other countries, 8% are from out of state, 5% African American, 15% Asian American or Pacific Islander, 14% Hispanic American, 2% international, 74% transferred in.

Freshmen *Admission:* 37 applied, 19 admitted.

Faculty *Total:* 38, 66% full-time, 95% with terminal degrees. *Student/faculty ratio:* 7:1.

Majors Biology/biological sciences.

Academics *Calendar:* trimesters. *Degrees:* associate, bachelor's, and first professional. *Special study options:* accelerated degree program, adult/continuing education programs, advanced placement credit, cooperative education, distance learning, double majors, part-time degree program, summer session for credit.

Computers on Campus 30 computers/terminals and 30 ports are available on campus for general student use. Students can access the following: campus intranet, free student e-mail accounts, Internet. Campuswide network is available. 100% of college-owned or -operated housing units are wired for high-speed Internet access. Wireless service is available via classrooms, computer centers, learning centers, student centers.

Student Life *Housing:* college housing not available. *Activities and organizations:* SCCA, SACA, Gonstead Club, Student Council, SICA. *Student services:* health clinic, personal/psychological counseling.

Standardized Tests *Recommended:* SAT or ACT (for admission).

Costs (2008–09) *Tuition:* $6158 full-time, $257 per credit part-time. *Required fees:* $200 full-time, $200 per year part-time.

Applying *Options:* electronic application. *Application fee:* $50. *Application deadline:* 9/29 (transfers). *Notification:* 8/30 (transfers).

Application Contact Ms. Norma Ngiramolan, Cleveland Chiropractic College-Los Angeles Campus, 590 North Vermont Avenue, Los Angeles, CA 90004-2196. *Phone:* 323-906-2162. *Toll-free phone:* 800-446-CCLA. *Fax:* 323-906-2094. *E-mail:* la.admissions@cleveland.edu.

COGSWELL POLYTECHNICAL COLLEGE

Sunnyvale, California **www.cogswell.edu/**

- **Independent** 4-year, founded 1887
- **Suburban** 2-acre campus with easy access to San Francisco and San Jose
- **Endowment** $9.2 million
- **Coed, primarily men** 230 undergraduate students, 48% full-time, 18% women, 82% men
- **Moderately difficult** entrance level, 61% of applicants were admitted

Cogswell College is an accredited four-year college in Silicon Valley. Programs include digital art and animation, digital audio, and engineering. Alumni work in animation, film, gaming, engineering, and other entertainment industries. For long-term success in any of these fast-paced fields, Cogswell is a great start.

Undergraduates 111 full-time, 119 part-time. Students come from 13 states and territories, 16% are from out of state, 3% African American, 11% Asian American or Pacific Islander, 9% Hispanic American, 7% transferred in, 13% live on campus. *Retention:* 90% of 2006 full-time freshmen returned.

Freshmen *Admission:* 41 applied, 25 admitted, 22 enrolled. *Average high school GPA:* 3.07.

Faculty *Total:* 47, 23% full-time, 30% with terminal degrees. *Student/faculty ratio:* 7:1.

Majors Animation, interactive technology, video graphics and special effects; audio engineering; computer graphics; computer software engineering; digital communication and media/multimedia; electrical, electronics and communications engineering; fire science.

Academics *Calendar:* semesters. *Degree:* bachelor's. *Special study options:* adult/continuing education programs, advanced placement credit, distance learning, double majors, external degree program, internships, part-time degree program, summer session for credit.

Computers on Campus 224 computers/terminals are available on campus for general student use. Students can access the following: computer help desk, free student e-mail accounts, online (class) grades, online (class) registration, online (class) schedules. Campuswide network is available. 100% of college-owned or -operated housing units are wired for high-speed Internet access. Wireless service is available via classrooms, computer centers, computer labs, learning centers, libraries, student centers.

Student Life *Housing options:* Campus housing is provided by a third party. *Activities and organizations:* student-run radio station, ASB. *Campus security:* 24-hour emergency response devices. *Student services:* personal/psychological counseling.

Athletics *Intercollegiate sports:* fencing M/W.

Costs (2008–09) *Tuition:* $17,088 full-time, $712 per credit part-time. *Required fees:* $180 full-time, $90 per term part-time. *Room only:* $3500.

Financial Aid Of all full-time matriculated undergraduates who enrolled in 2006, 116 applied for aid, 114 were judged to have need. 15 Federal Work-Study jobs (averaging $3000). In 2006, 12 non-need-based awards were made. *Average*

need-based loan: $4472. *Average need-based gift aid:* $3484. *Average non-need-based aid:* $834. *Average indebtedness upon graduation:* $46,689.
Applying *Options:* deferred entrance. *Application fee:* $55. *Required:* essay or personal statement, high school transcript, minimum 2.7 GPA. *Required for some:* letters of recommendation, interview, portfolio. *Application deadlines:* 3/1 (freshmen), 3/1 (transfers). *Notification:* continuous (freshmen), continuous (transfers).
Freshman Application Contact Mr. Bill Souza, Admissions Coordinator, Cogswell Polytechnical College, 1175 Bordeaux Drive, Sunnyvale, CA 94089. *Phone:* 408-541-0100 Ext. 155. *Toll-free phone:* 800-264-7955. *Fax:* 408-747-0764. *E-mail:* info@cogswell.edu.

THE COLBURN SCHOOL CONSERVATORY OF MUSIC

Los Angeles, California **www.colburnschool.edu/**

- **Independent** 4-year, founded 1980
- **Urban** campus with easy access to Los Angeles
- **Endowment** $16.6 million
- **Coed** 51 undergraduate students, 100% full-time, 57% women, 43% men
- **Most difficult** entrance level, 19% of applicants were admitted

Undergraduates 51 full-time. Students come from 17 states and territories, 7 other countries, 41% international, 100% live on campus. *Retention:* 100% of 2006 full-time freshmen returned.
Freshmen *Admission:* 166 applied, 32 admitted.
Faculty *Total:* 28, 36% full-time, 14% with terminal degrees. *Student/faculty ratio:* 6:1.
Majors Music performance; piano and organ; violin, viola, guitar and other stringed instruments.
Academics *Calendar:* semesters. *Degrees:* certificates, diplomas, bachelor's, and postbachelor's certificates. *Special study options:* English as a second language.
Computers on Campus 12 computers/terminals are available on campus for general student use. Students can access the following: computer help desk, free student e-mail accounts. Campuswide network is available. 100% of college-owned or -operated housing units are wired for high-speed Internet access. Wireless service is available via classrooms, computer centers, computer labs, dorm rooms, libraries.
Student Life *Housing:* on-campus residence required through senior year. *Options:* coed. Campus housing is university owned. Freshman campus housing is guaranteed. *Campus security:* 24-hour patrols, trained security personnel during open building hours. *Student services:* personal/psychological counseling.
Standardized Tests *Recommended:* SAT or ACT (for admission).
Costs (2008–09) *Comprehensive fee:* includes mandatory fees ($1400).
Applying *Options:* electronic application, deferred entrance. *Application fee:* $100. *Required:* essay or personal statement, high school transcript, 2 letters of recommendation, interview, TOEFL score required for all non-native English speakers. *Application deadlines:* 1/15 (freshmen), 1/15 (transfers). *Notification:* 4/1 (freshmen), 4/1 (transfers).
Freshman Application Contact Ms. Agnieszka Laskus, Assistant for Admissions and Records, The Colburn School Conservatory of Music, 200 Grand Avenue, Los Angeles, CA 90012. *Phone:* 213-621-4534. *Fax:* 213-625-0371. *E-mail:* admissions@colburnschool.edu.

COLEMAN COLLEGE

San Diego, California **www.coleman.edu/**

Freshman Application Contact Admissions Department, Coleman College, 7380 Parkway Drive, La Mesa, CA 91942-1500. *Phone:* 619-465-3990. *E-mail:* jschafer@cts.com.

COLUMBIA COLLEGE HOLLYWOOD

Tarzana, California **www.columbiacollege.edu/**

- **Independent** 4-year, founded 1952
- **Urban** 1-acre campus
- **Coed**
- **Minimally difficult** entrance level

Academics *Calendar:* quarters. *Degrees:* associate and bachelor's.
Student Life *Campus security:* late-night transport/escort service.
Costs (2007–08) *Tuition:* $13,758 full-time, $375 per unit part-time.
Financial Aid Of all full-time matriculated undergraduates who enrolled in 2003, 103 applied for aid, 103 were judged to have need. 3 Federal Work-Study jobs (averaging $2023). *Average financial aid package:* $3827. *Average need-based gift aid:* $3745. *Average indebtedness upon graduation:* $35,125.
Applying *Options:* deferred entrance. *Application fee:* $50. *Required:* essay or personal statement, high school transcript, minimum 2.0 GPA, 2 letters of recommendation, interview. *Recommended:* portfolio.
Freshman Application Contact Carmen Munoz, Admissions Director, Columbia College Hollywood, 18618 Oxnard Street, Tarzana, CA 91356. *Phone:* 818-345-8414. *Toll-free phone:* 800-785-0585. *Fax:* 818-345-9053. *E-mail:* admissions@columbiacollege.edu.

See page 438 for the College Close-Up.

CONCORDIA UNIVERSITY

Irvine, California **www.cui.edu/**

- **Independent** comprehensive, founded 1972, affiliated with Lutheran Church–Missouri Synod, part of The Concordia University System
- **Suburban** 70-acre campus with easy access to Los Angeles
- **Coed** 1,256 undergraduate students, 96% full-time, 61% women, 39% men
- **Moderately difficult** entrance level, 67% of applicants were admitted

Undergraduates 1,212 full-time, 44 part-time. Students come from 34 states and territories, 5 other countries, 17% are from out of state, 4% African American, 4% Asian American or Pacific Islander, 13% Hispanic American, 0.9% Native American, 2% international, 11% transferred in, 83% live on campus. *Retention:* 73% of 2006 full-time freshmen returned.
Freshmen *Admission:* 827 applied, 557 admitted, 226 enrolled. *Average high school GPA:* 3.51. *Test scores:* SAT critical reading scores over 500: 55%; SAT math scores over 500: 56%; ACT scores over 18: 93%; SAT critical reading scores over 600: 19%; SAT math scores over 600: 19%; ACT scores over 24: 32%; SAT critical reading scores over 700: 1%; SAT math scores over 700: 1%; ACT scores over 30: 4%.
Faculty *Total:* 282, 32% full-time, 38% with terminal degrees. *Student/faculty ratio:* 14:1.
Majors Art; behavioral sciences; biblical languages/literatures; biology/biological sciences; business administration and management; chemistry; communication/speech communication and rhetoric; dramatic/theater arts; early childhood education; English; film/cinema studies; history; humanities; information technology; international/global studies; kinesiology and exercise science; liberal arts and sciences/liberal studies; mathematics; music; political science and government; psychology; theology.
Academics *Calendar:* semesters. *Degrees:* bachelor's and master's (associate's degree for international students only). *Special study options:* accelerated degree program, adult/continuing education programs, advanced placement credit, cooperative education, distance learning, double majors, English as a second language, external degree program, honors programs, independent study, internships, off-campus study, part-time degree program, student-designed majors, study abroad, summer session for credit.
Computers on Campus 103 computers/terminals are available on campus for general student use. Students can access the following: campus intranet, computer help desk, online (class) grades, online (class) registration, online (class) schedules. Campuswide network is available. 100% of college-owned or -operated housing units are wired for high-speed Internet access. Wireless service is available via classrooms, computer centers, dorm rooms, student centers.
Student Life *Housing:* on-campus residence required through senior year. *Options:* men-only, women-only. Campus housing is university owned. Freshman campus housing is guaranteed. *Activities and organizations:* drama/theater group, student-run newspaper, radio station, choral group, Screaming Eagles, Lacrosse club, Golden Eagles, Ethic Bowl, Cross Cultural Link. *Campus security:* 24-hour patrols, student patrols, late-night transport/escort service, lighted walkways. *Student services:* health clinic, personal/psychological counseling.
Athletics Member NAIA. *Intercollegiate sports:* baseball M (s), basketball M (s)/W (s), cross-country running M (s)/W (s), golf M (s)/W (s), soccer M (s)/W (s), softball M/W (s), track and field M (s)/W (s), volleyball W (s). *Intramural sports:* basketball M/W, bowling M/W, football M/W, soccer M/W, softball M/W, table tennis M/W, track and field M/W, volleyball M/W.
Standardized Tests *Required:* SAT or ACT (for admission).
Costs (2007–08) *One-time required fee:* $300. *Comprehensive fee:* $29,860 includes full-time tuition ($22,080), mandatory fees ($300), and room and board ($7480). Part-time tuition: $625 per unit. Part-time tuition and fees vary according to course load. *College room only:* $4640. Room and board charges vary

according to board plan. *Payment plans:* installment, deferred payment. *Waivers:* employees or children of employees.

Financial Aid Of all full-time matriculated undergraduates who enrolled in 2007, 1,069 applied for aid, 766 were judged to have need, 173 had their need fully met. 49 Federal Work-Study jobs (averaging $1831). 171 state and other part-time jobs (averaging $1700). In 2007, 236 non-need-based awards were made. *Average percent of need met:* 70%. *Average financial aid package:* $22,074. *Average need-based loan:* $4377. *Average need-based gift aid:* $11,713. *Average non-need-based aid:* $6857. *Average indebtedness upon graduation:* $20,254. *Financial aid deadline:* 4/1.

Applying *Options:* electronic application, deferred entrance. *Application fee:* $50. *Required:* high school transcript, 2 letters of recommendation. *Recommended:* minimum 2.8 GPA, interview. *Application deadlines:* rolling (freshmen), rolling (transfers). *Notification:* continuous (freshmen), continuous (transfers).

Freshman Application Contact Ms. Lori McDonald, Executive Director of Enrollment Services, Concordia University, 1530 Concordia West, Irvine, CA 92612-3299. *Phone:* 949-854-8002 Ext. 1170. *Toll-free phone:* 800-229-1200. *Fax:* 949-854-6894. *E-mail:* admission@cui.edu.

DESIGN INSTITUTE OF SAN DIEGO

San Diego, California www.disd.edu/

Director of Admissions Ms. Paula Parrish, Director of Admissions, Design Institute of San Diego, 8555 Commerce Avenue, San Diego, CA 92121. *Phone:* 858-566-1200. *Toll-free phone:* 800-619-4337. *E-mail:* admisssions@disd.edu.

DEVRY UNIVERSITY

Elk Grove, California

DEVRY UNIVERSITY

Fremont, California www.devry.edu/

- **Proprietary** comprehensive, founded 1998, part of DeVry University
- **Suburban** 17-acre campus with easy access to San Francisco
- **Coed** 1,414 undergraduate students, 65% full-time, 30% women, 70% men
- **Minimally difficult** entrance level

Undergraduates 919 full-time, 495 part-time. 2% are from out of state, 10% African American, 26% Asian American or Pacific Islander, 18% Hispanic American, 1% Native American, 0.5% international, 13% transferred in. *Retention:* 56% of 2006 full-time freshmen returned.

Freshmen *Admission:* 291 enrolled.

Faculty *Total:* 114, 34% full-time. *Student/faculty ratio:* 18:1.

Majors Accounting; biomedical technology; business administration and management; business administration, management and operations related; computer engineering technology; computer software engineering; computer systems analysis; computer systems networking and telecommunications; electrical, electronic and communications engineering technology; health information/medical records technology; web page, digital/multimedia and information resources design.

Academics *Calendar:* semesters. *Degrees:* associate, bachelor's, and master's. *Special study options:* academic remediation for entering students, accelerated degree program, adult/continuing education programs, advanced placement credit, distance learning, part-time degree program, services for LD students, summer session for credit.

Computers on Campus 350 computers/terminals are available on campus for general student use. Students can access the following: online (class) registration. Campuswide network is available.

Student Life *Housing:* college housing not available. *Activities and organizations:* Latino-American Student Organization, Telecommunications Club, Chess Club. *Campus security:* 24-hour emergency response devices and patrols, late-night transport/escort service, lighted pathways/sidewalks.

Athletics *Intramural sports:* baseball M/W, basketball M/W, soccer M/W.

Costs (2008–09) *Tuition:* $14,480 full-time, $540 per credit part-time. *Required fees:* $180 full-time.

Financial Aid Of all full-time matriculated undergraduates who enrolled in 2002, 1,580 applied for aid, 1,487 were judged to have need, 27 had their need fully met. In 2002, 125 non-need-based awards were made. *Average percent of need met:* 44%. *Average financial aid package:* $10,351. *Average need-based loan:* $6394. *Average need-based gift aid:* $6863. *Average non-need-based aid:* $12,699.

Applying *Options:* electronic application, early admission, deferred entrance. *Application fee:* $50. *Required:* high school transcript, interview. *Application deadlines:* rolling (freshmen), rolling (transfers). *Notification:* continuous (freshmen), continuous (transfers).

Freshman Application Contact DeVry University, 6600 Dumbarton Circle, Fremont, CA 94555-3615.

DEVRY UNIVERSITY

Irvine, California

DEVRY UNIVERSITY

Long Beach, California www.devry.edu/

- **Proprietary** comprehensive, founded 1984, part of DeVry University
- **Urban** 23-acre campus with easy access to Los Angeles
- **Coed** 828 undergraduate students, 49% full-time, 32% women, 68% men
- **Minimally difficult** entrance level

Undergraduates 407 full-time, 421 part-time. 1% are from out of state, 13% African American, 24% Asian American or Pacific Islander, 38% Hispanic American, 0.4% Native American, 0.2% international, 10% transferred in. *Retention:* 46% of 2006 full-time freshmen returned.

Freshmen *Admission:* 127 enrolled.

Faculty *Total:* 83, 20% full-time. *Student/faculty ratio:* 17:1.

Majors Business administration and management; business administration, management and operations related; computer engineering technology; computer software engineering; computer systems analysis; computer systems networking and telecommunications; electrical, electronic and communications engineering technology; health information/medical records technology.

Academics *Calendar:* semesters. *Degrees:* associate, bachelor's, and master's. *Special study options:* academic remediation for entering students, accelerated degree program, adult/continuing education programs, advanced placement credit, distance learning, part-time degree program, services for LD students, summer session for credit.

Computers on Campus 458 computers/terminals are available on campus for general student use. Students can access the following: online (class) registration. Campuswide network is available.

Student Life *Housing:* college housing not available. *Activities and organizations:* Teamnet, Society of Hispanic Professional Engineers, National Society of Black Engineers, Institute of Electronics and Electrical Engineers, United Islands. *Campus security:* 24-hour emergency response devices and patrols, late-night transport/escort service, motion detectors, closed hours.

Costs (2008–09) *Tuition:* $13,810 full-time, $515 per credit part-time. *Required fees:* $180 full-time.

Financial Aid Of all full-time matriculated undergraduates who enrolled in 2003, 1,572 applied for aid, 1,498 were judged to have need, 46 had their need fully met. In 2003, 106 non-need-based awards were made. *Average percent of need met:* 43%. *Average financial aid package:* $10,063. *Average need-based loan:* $5999. *Average need-based gift aid:* $5911. *Average non-need-based aid:* $13,231.

Applying *Options:* electronic application, early admission, deferred entrance. *Application fee:* $50. *Required:* high school transcript, interview. *Application deadlines:* rolling (freshmen), rolling (transfers). *Notification:* continuous (freshmen), continuous (transfers).

Freshman Application Contact DeVry University, 3880 Kilroy Airport Way, Long Beach, CA 90806-2449.

DEVRY UNIVERSITY

Palmdale, California www.devry.edu/

Director of Admissions Admissions Office, DeVry University, 38256 Sierra Highway, Suite D, Palmdale, CA 93550. *Toll-free phone:* 866-986-9388.

DEVRY UNIVERSITY

Pomona, California www.devry.edu/

- **Proprietary** comprehensive, founded 1983, part of DeVry University
- **Urban** 15-acre campus with easy access to Los Angeles
- **Coed** 1,544 undergraduate students, 49% full-time, 28% women, 72% men

• **Minimally difficult** entrance level

Undergraduates 752 full-time, 792 part-time. 1% are from out of state, 9% African American, 17% Asian American or Pacific Islander, 41% Hispanic American, 0.5% Native American, 0.5% international, 15% transferred in. *Retention:* 49% of 2006 full-time freshmen returned.

Freshmen *Admission:* 281 enrolled.

Faculty *Total:* 84, 30% full-time. *Student/faculty ratio:* 25:1.

Majors Accounting; biomedical technology; business administration and management; business administration, management and operations related; computer engineering technology; computer software engineering; computer systems analysis; computer systems networking and telecommunications; electrical, electronic and communications engineering technology; health information/medical records technology; web page, digital/multimedia and information resources design.

Academics *Calendar:* semesters. *Degrees:* associate, bachelor's, and master's. *Special study options:* academic remediation for entering students, accelerated degree program, adult/continuing education programs, advanced placement credit, distance learning, part-time degree program, services for LD students, summer session for credit.

Computers on Campus 513 computers/terminals are available on campus for general student use. Students can access the following: online (class) registration. Campuswide network is available.

Student Life *Housing:* college housing not available. *Activities and organizations:* Phi Beta Lambda, Society of Hispanic Professional Engineers, National Society of Black Engineers, International Telecommunications Management Association, United Islands Student Association. *Campus security:* 24-hour emergency response devices, late-night transport/escort service.

Athletics *Intramural sports:* basketball M/W, softball M/W.

Costs (2008–09) *Tuition:* $13,810 full-time, $515 per credit part-time. *Required fees:* $180 full-time.

Financial Aid Of all full-time matriculated undergraduates who enrolled in 2002, 1,866 applied for aid, 1,791 were judged to have need, 54 had their need fully met. In 2002, 85 non-need-based awards were made. *Average percent of need met:* 43%. *Average financial aid package:* $9829. *Average need-based loan:* $5977. *Average need-based gift aid:* $5797. *Average non-need-based aid:* $12,336.

Applying *Options:* electronic application, early admission, deferred entrance. *Application fee:* $50. *Required:* high school transcript, interview. *Application deadlines:* rolling (freshmen), rolling (transfers). *Notification:* continuous (freshmen), continuous (transfers).

Freshman Application Contact DeVry University, 901 Corporate Center Drive, University Center, Pomona, CA 91768-2642.

DeVry University
San Diego, California

DeVry University
San Francisco, California

DeVry University
Sherman Oaks, California **www.devry.edu/**

• **Proprietary** comprehensive
• **Coed** 462 undergraduate students, 47% full-time, 29% women, 71% men

Undergraduates 218 full-time, 244 part-time. 1% are from out of state, 7% African American, 20% Asian American or Pacific Islander, 32% Hispanic American, 2% Native American, 0.6% international, 13% transferred in. *Retention:* 46% of 2006 full-time freshmen returned.

Freshmen *Admission:* 77 enrolled.

Faculty *Total:* 88, 11% full-time. *Student/faculty ratio:* 10:1.

Majors Business administration and management; business administration, management and operations related; computer engineering technology; computer systems analysis; computer systems networking and telecommunications; electrical, electronic and communications engineering technology; health information/medical records technology.

Academics *Degrees:* associate, bachelor's, and master's. *Special study options:* accelerated degree program, distance learning.

Costs (2008–09) *Tuition:* $13,810 full-time, $515 per credit part-time. *Required fees:* $180 full-time.

Applying *Options:* electronic application, early admission, deferred entrance. *Application fee:* $50. *Application deadlines:* rolling (freshmen), rolling (transfers).

Director of Admissions Admissions Office, DeVry University, 15301 Ventura Boulevard, D-100, Sherman Oaks, CA 91403. *Toll-free phone:* 888-610-0800.

Dominican School of Philosophy and Theology
Berkeley, California **www.dspt.edu/**

• **Independent Roman Catholic** upper-level, founded 1932
• **Urban** campus with easy access to San Francisco
• **Endowment** $1.1 million
• **Coed**
• **Moderately difficult** entrance level

Faculty *Student/faculty ratio:* 4:1.

Academics *Calendar:* semesters. *Degrees:* bachelor's, master's, and first professional.

Student Life *Campus security:* late-night transport/escort service.

Costs (2007–08) *Tuition:* $11,880 full-time, $495 per credit part-time. *Required fees:* $100 full-time, $50 per term part-time.

Applying *Options:* electronic application, early admission, deferred entrance. *Application fee:* $40.

Application Contact Mr. John D. Knutsen, Director of Admissions, Dominican School of Philosophy and Theology, 2301 Vine Street, Berkeley, CA 94709-1295. *Phone:* 510-883-2073. *Fax:* 510-849-1372. *E-mail:* admissions@dspt.edu.

Dominican University of California
San Rafael, California **www.dominican.edu/**

• **Independent** comprehensive, founded 1890, affiliated with Roman Catholic Church
• **Suburban** 80-acre campus with easy access to San Francisco
• **Endowment** $18.3 million
• **Coed** 1,495 undergraduate students, 78% full-time, 76% women, 24% men
• **Moderately difficult** entrance level, 56% of applicants were admitted

Undergraduates 1,169 full-time, 326 part-time. Students come from 26 states and territories, 14 other countries, 6% are from out of state, 7% African American, 21% Asian American or Pacific Islander, 16% Hispanic American, 0.8% Native American, 2% international, 7% transferred in, 45% live on campus. *Retention:* 74% of 2006 full-time freshmen returned.

Freshmen *Admission:* 2,586 applied, 1,446 admitted, 297 enrolled. *Average high school GPA:* 3.25. *Test scores:* SAT critical reading scores over 500: 51%; SAT math scores over 500: 50%; ACT scores over 18: 76%; SAT critical reading scores over 600: 13%; SAT math scores over 600: 11%; ACT scores over 24: 27%; SAT critical reading scores over 700: 2%; ACT scores over 30: 1%.

Faculty *Total:* 345, 23% full-time, 50% with terminal degrees. *Student/faculty ratio:* 11:1.

Majors Art; art history, criticism and conservation; biology/biological sciences; business administration and management; business administration, management and operations related; communication/speech communication and rhetoric; computer graphics; creative writing; dance; e-commerce; English; history; humanities; human resources management; international business/trade/commerce; international/global studies; liberal arts and sciences and humanities related; liberal arts and sciences/liberal studies; music; nursing (registered nurse training); occupational therapy; political science and government; psychology; religious studies; women's studies.

Academics *Calendar:* semesters. *Degrees:* bachelor's, master's, and post-bachelor's certificates. *Special study options:* academic remediation for entering students, adult/continuing education programs, advanced placement credit, double majors, English as a second language, external degree program, honors programs, independent study, internships, off-campus study, part-time degree program, services for LD students, student-designed majors, study abroad, summer session for credit. *Unusual degree programs:* 3-2 occupational therapy.

Computers on Campus 260 computers/terminals and 700 ports are available on campus for general student use. Students can access the following: computer help desk, free student e-mail accounts, online (class) schedules, Microsoft Office Application (Word, Excel, PowerPoint). Campuswide network is available.

Wireless service is available via classrooms, computer centers, computer labs, dorm rooms, libraries, student centers.

Student Life *Housing options:* coed. Campus housing is university owned. Freshman applicants given priority for college housing. *Activities and organizations:* drama/theater group, student-run newspaper, radio station, choral group, Students Promoting Dominican Islands, Perceptions, Science Club, Filipino Club, Scripture Union. *Campus security:* 24-hour emergency response devices and patrols, late-night transport/escort service, controlled dormitory access. *Student services:* health clinic, personal/psychological counseling.

Athletics Member NAIA. *Intercollegiate sports:* basketball M (s)/W (s), golf M (s)/W (s), lacrosse M (s), soccer M (s)/W (s), softball W (s), tennis W (s), volleyball W (s).

Standardized Tests *Required:* SAT or ACT (for admission). *Recommended:* SAT Subject Tests (for admission).

Costs (2008–09) *Comprehensive fee:* $44,920 includes full-time tuition ($32,160), mandatory fees ($200), and room and board ($12,560). Part-time tuition: $1340 per unit. *Required fees:* $100 per term part-time. *College room only:* $7300.

Financial Aid Of all full-time matriculated undergraduates who enrolled in 2005, 946 applied for aid, 879 were judged to have need, 66 had their need fully met. 284 Federal Work-Study jobs (averaging $2431). 24 state and other part-time jobs (averaging $7751). In 2005, 149 non-need-based awards were made. *Average percent of need met:* 15%. *Average financial aid package:* $20,605. *Average need-based loan:* $4778. *Average need-based gift aid:* $5682. *Average non-need-based aid:* $7474. *Average indebtedness upon graduation:* $17,607.

Applying *Options:* electronic application, early admission, deferred entrance. *Application fee:* $40. *Required:* essay or personal statement, high school transcript, minimum 2.5 GPA, 1 letter of recommendation. *Required for some:* interview. *Application deadlines:* 8/1 (freshmen), rolling (transfers). *Notification:* continuous until 9/1 (freshmen), continuous (transfers).

Freshman Application Contact Ms. Rebecca Finn Kenney, Director of Undergraduate Admissions, Dominican University of California, 50 Acacia Avenue, San Rafael, CA 94901-2298. *Phone:* 415-485-3204. *Toll-free phone:* 888-323-6763. *Fax:* 415-485-3214. *E-mail:* enroll@dominican.edu.

See page 440 for the College Close-Up.

EMMANUEL BIBLE COLLEGE

Pasadena, California **www.emmanuelbiblecollege.edu/**

Director of Admissions Mr. Hovel Babikian, President, Emmanuel Bible College, 225 East Santa Clara Street, Suite 300, Arcadia, CA 91006. *Phone:* 626-791-2575.

FIDM/THE FASHION INSTITUTE OF DESIGN & MERCHANDISING, LOS ANGELES CAMPUS

Los Angeles, California **www.fidm.edu/**

- **Proprietary** primarily 2-year, founded 1969, part of Fashion Institute of Design and Merchandising
- **Urban** campus
- **Coed**
- **Moderately difficult** entrance level

Faculty *Student/faculty ratio:* 14:1.

Academics *Calendar:* quarters. *Degrees:* associate and bachelor's (also includes Orange County Campus).

Student Life *Campus security:* 24-hour emergency response devices and patrols, late-night transport/escort service.

Standardized Tests *Required:* Wonderlic Aptitude Test (for admission).

Costs (2007–08) *Tuition:* $19,200 full-time, $427 per unit part-time. Full-time tuition and fees vary according to program. Part-time tuition and fees vary according to program. No tuition increase for student's term of enrollment. *Required fees:* $500 full-time.

Financial Aid Of all full-time matriculated undergraduates who enrolled in 2006, 88 Federal Work-Study jobs (averaging $2935).

Applying *Options:* electronic application, deferred entrance. *Application fee:* $225. *Required:* essay or personal statement, high school transcript, 3 letters of recommendation, interview, major-determined project. *Required for some:* 3 letters of recommendation, major-determined project.

Freshman Application Contact Ms. Susan Aronson, Director of Admissions, FIDM/The Fashion Institute of Design & Merchandising, Los Angeles Campus, FIDM LA, 919 South Grand Avenue, Los Angeles, CA 90015. *Phone:* 213-624-1200 Ext. 5400. *Toll-free phone:* 800-624-1200. *Fax:* 213-624-4799. *E-mail:* info@fidm.com.

FRESNO PACIFIC UNIVERSITY

Fresno, California **www.fresno.edu/**

- **Independent** comprehensive, founded 1944, affiliated with Mennonite Brethren Church
- **Suburban** 42-acre campus
- **Endowment** $4.6 million
- **Coed** 1,539 undergraduate students, 85% full-time, 69% women, 31% men
- **Moderately difficult** entrance level, 68% of applicants were admitted

Undergraduates 1,311 full-time, 228 part-time. Students come from 18 states and territories, 36 other countries, 5% are from out of state, 4% African American, 4% Asian American or Pacific Islander, 29% Hispanic American, 1% Native American, 3% international, 7% transferred in, 49% live on campus. *Retention:* 75% of 2006 full-time freshmen returned.

Freshmen *Admission:* 608 applied, 414 admitted, 170 enrolled. *Average high school GPA:* 3.44. *Test scores:* SAT critical reading scores over 500: 40%; SAT math scores over 500: 49%; SAT writing scores over 500: 45%; ACT scores over 18: 70%; SAT critical reading scores over 600: 16%; SAT math scores over 600: 18%; SAT writing scores over 600: 10%; ACT scores over 24: 24%; SAT critical reading scores over 700: 2%; SAT math scores over 700: 2%; ACT scores over 30: 2%.

Faculty *Total:* 355, 26% full-time, 16% with terminal degrees. *Student/faculty ratio:* 11:1.

Majors Accounting; applied mathematics; athletic training; biblical studies; bilingual and multilingual education; biology/biological sciences; business administration and management; chemistry; computer and information sciences; developmental and child psychology; divinity/ministry; education; elementary education; English; finance; history; humanities; international business/trade/commerce; liberal arts and sciences/liberal studies; literature; marketing/marketing management; mass communication/media; mathematics; music; music teacher education; natural sciences; non-profit management; pastoral studies/counseling; physical education teaching and coaching; political science and government; pre-law studies; pre-medical studies; psychology; religious/sacred music; religious studies; science teacher education; secondary education; social sciences; social work; sociology; Spanish; sport and fitness administration/management.

Academics *Calendar:* semesters. *Degrees:* associate, bachelor's, and master's. *Special study options:* accelerated degree program, adult/continuing education programs, advanced placement credit, cooperative education, distance learning, double majors, English as a second language, independent study, internships, off-campus study, part-time degree program, services for LD students, student-designed majors, study abroad, summer session for credit.

Computers on Campus 90 computers/terminals and 768 ports are available on campus for general student use. Students can access the following: campus intranet, computer help desk, free student e-mail accounts, online (class) grades, online (class) registration, online (class) schedules. Campuswide network is available. 100% of college-owned or -operated housing units are wired for high-speed Internet access. Wireless service is available via classrooms, dorm rooms, libraries, student centers.

Student Life *Housing:* on-campus residence required for freshman year. *Options:* men-only, women-only, disabled students. Campus housing is university owned. Freshman campus housing is guaranteed. *Activities and organizations:* drama/theater group, student-run newspaper, choral group, International Club, Kid's Klub, Amigos Unidos, Slavic Club, Women's Soccer Club. *Campus security:* 24-hour emergency response devices and patrols, student patrols, late-night transport/escort service, controlled dormitory access, 24-hour monitored closed-circuit security cameras. *Student services:* health clinic, personal/psychological counseling.

Athletics Member NAIA. *Intercollegiate sports:* baseball M (s), basketball M (s)/W (s), cheerleading W (c), cross-country running M (s)/W (s), soccer M (s)/W (s), swimming and diving M (s)/W (s), tennis M (s)/W (s), track and field M (s)/W (s), volleyball M (c)/W (s), water polo M (s)/W (s). *Intramural sports:* basketball M/W, bowling M/W, football M/W, soccer M/W, ultimate Frisbee M/W, volleyball M/W.

Standardized Tests *Required:* SAT and SAT Subject Tests or ACT (for admission).

Costs (2007–08) *Comprehensive fee:* $28,396 includes full-time tuition ($21,550), mandatory fees ($246), and room and board ($6600). Full-time tuition and fees vary according to program. Part-time tuition: $770 per unit. Part-time tuition and fees vary according to program. *College room only:* $3740. Room and board charges vary according to board plan and housing facility. *Payment plan:* installment. *Waivers:* senior citizens and employees or children of employees.

Financial Aid Of all full-time matriculated undergraduates who enrolled in 2005, 1,111 applied for aid, 919 were judged to have need, 150 had their need fully met. 468 Federal Work-Study jobs (averaging $2733). *Average percent of need met:* 64%. *Average financial aid package:* $16,270. *Average need-based loan:* $4248. *Average need-based gift aid:* $10,489. *Average indebtedness upon graduation:* $15,588.

Applying *Options:* electronic application, early admission, deferred entrance. *Application fee:* $40. *Required:* essay or personal statement, high school transcript, 1 letter of recommendation. *Required for some:* interview. *Recommended:* minimum 3.1 GPA. *Application deadlines:* rolling (freshmen), rolling (transfers). *Notification:* continuous until 7/31 (freshmen), continuous until 7/31 (transfers).

Freshman Application Contact Fresno Pacific University, 1717 South Chestnut Avenue, Fresno, CA 93702-4709. *Phone:* 800-600-6089. *Toll-free phone:* 800-660-6089. *Fax:* 559-453-2007. *E-mail:* ugadmis@fresno.edu.

See page 442 for the College Close-Up.

GOLDEN GATE UNIVERSITY

San Francisco, California **www.ggu.edu/**

- **Independent** university, founded 1901
- **Urban** campus
- **Endowment** $16.6 million
- **Coed** 567 undergraduate students, 24% full-time, 53% women, 47% men
- **Moderately difficult** entrance level

Undergraduates 135 full-time, 432 part-time. Students come from 18 states and territories, 50 other countries, 5% are from out of state, 9% African American, 17% Asian American or Pacific Islander, 11% Hispanic American, 0.5% Native American, 8% international. *Retention:* 80% of 2006 full-time freshmen returned.

Faculty *Total:* 489, 6% full-time, 31% with terminal degrees. *Student/faculty ratio:* 16:1.

Majors Accounting; business administration and management; finance; human resources management; information technology; international business/trade/commerce; marketing/marketing management; operations management.

Academics *Calendar:* trimesters. *Degrees:* certificates, bachelor's, master's, doctoral, and first professional. *Special study options:* academic remediation for entering students, accelerated degree program, adult/continuing education programs, advanced placement credit, distance learning, English as a second language, internships, off-campus study, part-time degree program, summer session for credit.

Computers on Campus 52 computers/terminals are available on campus for general student use. Students can access the following: campus intranet, online (class) registration, online (class) schedules. Campuswide network is available. Wireless service is available via entire campus.

Student Life *Housing:* college housing not available. *Activities and organizations:* student-run newspaper, American Marketing Association, Korean Student Association, Japanese Student Association, Thai Student Association, Computing Society. *Campus security:* late-night transport/escort service. *Student services:* personal/psychological counseling.

Athletics *Intramural sports:* cross-country running M (c)/W (c), racquetball M (c)/W (c), tennis M (c)/W (c).

Costs (2007–08) *Tuition:* $12,240 full-time, $1530 per course part-time.

Financial Aid Of all full-time matriculated undergraduates who enrolled in 2003, 136 applied for aid, 98 were judged to have need, 26 had their need fully met. 2 Federal Work-Study jobs (averaging $5000). In 2003, 50 non-need-based awards were made. *Average percent of need met:* 27%. *Average financial aid package:* $2931. *Average need-based loan:* $2931. *Average need-based gift aid:* $1000. *Average non-need-based aid:* $2000. *Average indebtedness upon graduation:* $17,522.

Applying *Options:* electronic application, deferred entrance. *Application fee:* $55. *Required:* high school transcript, minimum 2.0 GPA. *Required for some:* minimum 3.2 GPA, interview. *Recommended:* essay or personal statement, minimum 3.0 GPA. *Application deadlines:* rolling (freshmen), rolling (transfers). *Notification:* continuous (freshmen), continuous (transfers).

Freshman Application Contact Mr. Louis D. Riccardi Jr., Director of Enrollment Services, Golden Gate University, 536 Mission Street, San Francisco, CA 94105-2968. *Phone:* 415-442-7800. *Toll-free phone:* 800-448-3381. *Fax:* 415-442-7807. *E-mail:* info@ggu.edu.

HARVEY MUDD COLLEGE

Claremont, California **www.hmc.edu/**

- **Independent** 4-year, founded 1955, part of The Claremont Colleges Consortium
- **Suburban** 33-acre campus with easy access to Los Angeles
- **Endowment** $260.8 million
- **Coed** 735 undergraduate students, 100% full-time, 33% women, 67% men
- **Most difficult** entrance level, 28% of applicants were admitted

Undergraduates 735 full-time. Students come from 46 states and territories, 16 other countries, 50% are from out of state, 1% African American, 20% Asian American or Pacific Islander, 8% Hispanic American, 0.8% Native American, 4% international, 0.4% transferred in, 96% live on campus. *Retention:* 96% of 2006 full-time freshmen returned.

Freshmen *Admission:* 2,493 applied, 700 admitted, 196 enrolled. *Test scores:* SAT critical reading scores over 500: 100%; SAT math scores over 500: 100%; SAT writing scores over 500: 100%; SAT critical reading scores over 600: 99%; SAT math scores over 600: 100%; SAT writing scores over 600: 98%; SAT critical reading scores over 700: 74%; SAT math scores over 700: 95%; SAT writing scores over 700: 72%.

Faculty *Total:* 85, 87% full-time, 96% with terminal degrees. *Student/faculty ratio:* 9:1.

Majors Biology/biological sciences; chemistry; computer science; engineering; mathematics; physics.

Academics *Calendar:* semesters. *Degree:* bachelor's. *Special study options:* advanced placement credit, double majors, internships, off-campus study, services for LD students, student-designed majors, study abroad. *ROTC:* Army (c), Air Force (b). *Unusual degree programs:* 3-2 management/engineering with Claremont McKenna College.

Computers on Campus 360 computers/terminals and 1,500 ports are available on campus for general student use. Students can access the following: campus intranet, computer help desk, free student e-mail accounts, online (class) grades, online (class) registration, online (class) schedules. Campuswide network is available. 100% of college-owned or -operated housing units are wired for high-speed Internet access. Wireless service is available via entire campus.

Student Life *Housing:* on-campus residence required for freshman year. *Options:* coed. Campus housing is university owned. Freshman campus housing is guaranteed. *Activities and organizations:* drama/theater group, student-run newspaper, radio station, choral group, Delta "H" Outdoor Club, Etc. Players—Drama Club, club sports, Jazz Orchestra, Society of Women Engineers. *Campus security:* 24-hour emergency response devices and patrols, late-night transport/escort service. *Student services:* health clinic, personal/psychological counseling, women's center.

Athletics Member NCAA. All Division III. *Intercollegiate sports:* baseball M, basketball M/W, cross-country running M/W, football M, golf M, lacrosse W, soccer M/W, softball W, swimming and diving M/W, tennis M/W, track and field M/W, volleyball W, water polo M/W. *Intramural sports:* badminton M (c), fencing M (c)/W (c), football M/W, ice hockey M (c), rugby M (c)/W (c), sailing M (c)/W (c), soccer M/W, swimming and diving M/W, table tennis M (c)/W (c), tennis M/W, ultimate Frisbee M (c)/W (c), volleyball M/W, water polo M.

Standardized Tests *Required:* SAT or ACT (for admission), SAT Subject Test in Math 2C and second exam of choice (Math 1C is not accepted) (for admission).

Costs (2007–08) *Comprehensive fee:* $46,306 includes full-time tuition ($34,669), mandatory fees ($222), and room and board ($11,415). *College room only:* $5851. Room and board charges vary according to board plan. *Payment plan:* installment. *Waivers:* employees or children of employees.

Financial Aid Of all full-time matriculated undergraduates who enrolled in 2006, 465 applied for aid, 391 were judged to have need, 391 had their need fully met. 224 Federal Work-Study jobs (averaging $1919). 13 state and other part-time jobs (averaging $1890). In 2006, 151 non-need-based awards were made. *Average percent of need met:* 100%. *Average financial aid package:* $27,752. *Average need-based loan:* $4280. *Average need-based gift aid:* $24,359. *Average non-need-based aid:* $6843. *Average indebtedness upon graduation:* $18,288. *Financial aid deadline:* 2/1.

Applying *Options:* electronic application, early decision, deferred entrance. *Application fee:* $60. *Required:* essay or personal statement, high school transcript, 3 letters of recommendation. *Recommended:* interview. *Application deadlines:* 1/2 (freshmen), 4/1 (transfers). *Early decision deadline:* 11/15. *Notification:* 4/1 (freshmen), 5/1 (transfers), 12/15 (early decision).

Freshman Application Contact Mr. Peter Osgood, Director of Admissions, Harvey Mudd College, 301 Platt Boulevard, Claremont, CA 91711. *Phone:* 909-621-8011. *Fax:* 909-607-7046. *E-mail:* admission@hmc.edu.

See page 444 for the College Close-Up.

HOLY NAMES UNIVERSITY

Oakland, California **www.hnu.edu/**

- **Independent Roman Catholic** comprehensive, founded 1868
- **Urban** 60-acre campus with easy access to San Francisco
- **Endowment** $8.8 million
- **Coed, primarily women** 657 undergraduate students, 77% full-time, 72% women, 28% men
- **Moderately difficult** entrance level, 27% of applicants were admitted

Undergraduates 508 full-time, 149 part-time. Students come from 9 states and territories, 12 other countries, 9% are from out of state, 30% African American, 13% Asian American or Pacific Islander, 16% Hispanic American, 0.6% Native American, 4% international, 8% transferred in, 31% live on campus. *Retention:* 77% of 2006 full-time freshmen returned.

Freshmen *Admission:* 717 applied, 195 admitted, 139 enrolled. *Average high school GPA:* 3.28. *Test scores:* SAT critical reading scores over 500: 42%; SAT math scores over 500: 46%; ACT scores over 18: 85%; SAT critical reading scores over 600: 5%; SAT math scores over 600: 6%; ACT scores over 24: 15%.

Faculty *Total:* 147, 24% full-time, 56% with terminal degrees. *Student/faculty ratio:* 12:1.

Majors Biological and biomedical sciences related; biology/biological sciences; business administration and management; business/corporate communications; computer/information technology services administration related; computer software and media applications related; English; history; humanities; human resources management; human services; international relations and affairs; liberal arts and sciences/liberal studies; marketing/marketing management; music; music pedagogy; music performance; nursing (registered nurse training); nursing science; philosophy; philosophy and religious studies related; physiological psychology/psychobiology; psychology; religious studies; sociology; Spanish.

Academics *Calendar:* semesters. *Degrees:* bachelor's, master's, post-master's, and postbachelor's certificates. *Special study options:* academic remediation for entering students, accelerated degree program, adult/continuing education programs, advanced placement credit, distance learning, double majors, English as a second language, independent study, internships, part-time degree program, services for LD students, student-designed majors, study abroad, summer session for credit. *ROTC:* Army (c), Air Force (c).

Computers on Campus 80 computers/terminals are available on campus for general student use. Students can access the following: campus intranet, computer help desk, free student e-mail accounts, online (class) schedules. Campuswide network is available. Wireless service is available via computer labs, dorm rooms, libraries.

Student Life *Housing options:* coed. Campus housing is university owned. Freshman campus housing is guaranteed. *Activities and organizations:* drama/theater group, choral group, Drama Club, Latinos Unidos, Black Student Union, Biology Club, Hiking Club. *Campus security:* 24-hour emergency response devices, late-night transport/escort service, controlled dormitory access, 24-hour security main gate. *Student services:* personal/psychological counseling.

Athletics Member NAIA. *Intercollegiate sports:* basketball M (s)/W (s), cross-country running M (s)/W (s), golf M (s), soccer M (s)/W (s), softball W (s), volleyball M (s)/W (s).

Standardized Tests *Required:* SAT or ACT (for admission).

Costs (2007–08) *Comprehensive fee:* $33,460 includes full-time tuition ($24,720), mandatory fees ($340), and room and board ($8400). Full-time tuition and fees vary according to course load. Part-time tuition: $825 per unit. Part-time tuition and fees vary according to course load. *Required fees:* $170 per term part-time. *College room only:* $4410. Room and board charges vary according to board plan. *Payment plan:* installment. *Waivers:* employees or children of employees.

Financial Aid Of all full-time matriculated undergraduates who enrolled in 2006, 373 applied for aid, 247 were judged to have need, 58 had their need fully met. 50 Federal Work-Study jobs (averaging $1699). 53 state and other part-time jobs (averaging $1750). In 2006, 77 non-need-based awards were made. *Average percent of need met:* 43%. *Average financial aid package:* $15,554. *Average need-based loan:* $4154. *Average need-based gift aid:* $13,258. *Average non-need-based aid:* $10,557. *Average indebtedness upon graduation:* $10,500. *Financial aid deadline:* 6/30.

Applying *Options:* electronic application, deferred entrance. *Application fee:* $50. *Required:* high school transcript. *Required for some:* essay or personal statement, interview. *Application deadlines:* 8/1 (freshmen), 8/1 (transfers). *Notification:* continuous (freshmen), continuous (transfers).

Freshman Application Contact Marcia Nance, Holy Names University, 3500 Mountain Boulevard, Oakland, CA 94619. *Phone:* 510-436-1351. *Toll-free phone:* 800-430-1321. *Fax:* 510-436-1325. *E-mail:* admissions@hnu.edu.

HOPE INTERNATIONAL UNIVERSITY

Fullerton, California **www.hiu.edu/**

- **Independent** comprehensive, founded 1928, affiliated with Christian Churches and Churches of Christ
- **Suburban** 16-acre campus with easy access to Los Angeles
- **Endowment** $4.5 million
- **Coed** 677 undergraduate students, 83% full-time, 60% women, 40% men
- **Moderately difficult** entrance level, 71% of applicants were admitted

Undergraduates 560 full-time, 117 part-time. Students come from 26 states and territories, 22 other countries, 24% are from out of state, 5% African American, 5% Asian American or Pacific Islander, 15% Hispanic American, 1% Native American, 2% international, 7% transferred in, 84% live on campus. *Retention:* 71% of 2006 full-time freshmen returned.

Freshmen *Admission:* 413 applied, 292 admitted, 130 enrolled. *Average high school GPA:* 3.3. *Test scores:* SAT critical reading scores over 500: 49%; SAT math scores over 500: 40%; ACT scores over 18: 82%; SAT critical reading scores over 600: 12%; SAT math scores over 600: 9%; ACT scores over 24: 20%; ACT scores over 30: 4%.

Faculty *Total:* 174, 18% full-time, 40% with terminal degrees. *Student/faculty ratio:* 8:1.

Majors Athletic training; biblical studies; business administration and management; child development; elementary education; English/language arts teacher education; general studies; human development and family studies; interdisciplinary studies; music teacher education; physical therapy; physiological psychology/psychobiology; psychology; religious/sacred music; social sciences; social science teacher education; social work.

Academics *Calendar:* 4-1-4. *Degrees:* certificates, associate, bachelor's, and master's. *Special study options:* academic remediation for entering students, accelerated degree program, adult/continuing education programs, advanced placement credit, distance learning, double majors, English as a second language, independent study, internships, off-campus study, part-time degree program, study abroad, summer session for credit.

Computers on Campus 53 computers/terminals and 430 ports are available on campus for general student use. Students can access the following: computer help desk, free student e-mail accounts, online (class) grades, online (class) schedules. Campuswide network is available. 100% of college-owned or -operated housing units are wired for high-speed Internet access. Wireless service is available via entire campus.

Student Life *Housing:* on-campus residence required through sophomore year. *Options:* men-only, women-only. Campus housing is university owned. Freshman campus housing is guaranteed. *Activities and organizations:* drama/theater group, student-run newspaper, choral group, Royal Rowdies, Ultimate Frisbee, Opera-tion Erga, Jujitan Club, Korean Club. *Campus security:* 24-hour emergency response devices and patrols, student patrols. *Student services:* personal/psychological counseling.

Athletics Member NAIA, NCCAA. *Intercollegiate sports:* basketball M (s)/W (s), cheerleading M (s)/W (s), soccer M (s)/W (s), softball W (s), tennis M (s)/W (s), ultimate Frisbee M/W, volleyball M/W (s). *Intramural sports:* golf M, ultimate Frisbee M/W, volleyball M/W.

Standardized Tests *Required:* SAT or ACT (for admission). *Recommended:* SAT (for admission).

Costs (2008–09) *Comprehensive fee:* $30,991 includes full-time tuition ($21,560), mandatory fees ($1201), and room and board ($8230). Part-time tuition: $799 per unit. *College room only:* $4980.

Financial Aid Of all full-time matriculated undergraduates who enrolled in 2003, 540 applied for aid, 488 were judged to have need, 73 had their need fully met. 62 Federal Work-Study jobs (averaging $2000). In 2003, 93 non-need-based awards were made. *Average percent of need met:* 60%. *Average financial aid package:* $10,042. *Average need-based loan:* $3925. *Average need-based gift aid:* $7998. *Average non-need-based aid:* $10,583. *Average indebtedness upon graduation:* $18,045.

Applying *Options:* electronic application, early admission, early decision, early action, deferred entrance. *Application fee:* $40. *Required:* essay or personal statement, high school transcript, minimum 2.5 GPA, 2 letters of recommendation, rank in upper 50% of high school class. *Required for some:* interview. *Application deadlines:* 5/1 (freshmen), 6/1 (transfers), 12/1 (early action). *Early decision deadline:* 12/1. *Notification:* continuous until 7/1 (freshmen), continuous until 7/1 (transfers).

Freshman Application Contact Ms. Midge Madden, Office Manager, Hope International University, 2500 East Nutwood Avenue, Fullerton, CA 92831-3138. *Phone:* 714-879-3901. *Toll-free phone:* 800-762-1294. *Fax:* 714-681-7423. *E-mail:* mfmadden@hiu.edu.

HUMBOLDT STATE UNIVERSITY

Arcata, California www.humboldt.edu/

- **State-supported** comprehensive, founded 1913, part of California State University System
- **Rural** 161-acre campus
- **Endowment** $18.8 million
- **Coed** 6,760 undergraduate students, 90% full-time, 53% women, 47% men
- **Moderately difficult** entrance level, 82% of applicants were admitted

Undergraduates 6,057 full-time, 703 part-time. Students come from 46 states and territories, 17 other countries, 15% are from out of state, 4% African American, 5% Asian American or Pacific Islander, 11% Hispanic American, 2% Native American, 0.2% international, 14% transferred in, 20% live on campus. *Retention:* 75% of 2006 full-time freshmen returned.

Freshmen *Admission:* 8,216 applied, 6,768 admitted, 1,051 enrolled. *Average high school GPA:* 3.09. *Test scores:* SAT critical reading scores over 500: 59%; SAT math scores over 500: 58%; SAT writing scores over 500: 54%; ACT scores over 18: 78%; SAT critical reading scores over 600: 24%; SAT math scores over 600: 20%; SAT writing scores over 600: 15%; ACT scores over 24: 38%; SAT critical reading scores over 700: 4%; SAT math scores over 700: 1%; SAT writing scores over 700: 2%; ACT scores over 30: 3%.

Faculty *Total:* 518, 53% full-time. *Student/faculty ratio:* 19:1.

Majors Accounting; American Indian/Native American studies; anthropology; applied mathematics; art; art history, criticism and conservation; art teacher education; biochemistry; biology/biological sciences; botany/plant biology; broadcast journalism; business administration and management; cell biology and histology; chemistry; child development; clinical laboratory science/medical technology; communication/speech communication and rhetoric; computer science; developmental and child psychology; dramatic/theater arts; economics; education; elementary education; English; environmental biology; environmental/environmental health engineering; environmental studies; fine/studio arts; fish/game management; fishing and fisheries sciences and management; forestry; French; geography; geology/earth science; German; history; hydrology and water resources science; industrial arts; information science/studies; journalism; kindergarten/preschool education; kinesiology and exercise science; liberal arts and sciences/liberal studies; marine biology and biological oceanography; marketing/marketing management; mathematics; medical microbiology and bacteriology; molecular biology; music; music teacher education; natural resources/conservation; natural resources management and policy; natural sciences; nursing (registered nurse training); oceanography (chemical and physical); parks, recreation and leisure; parks, recreation and leisure facilities management; philosophy; physical education teaching and coaching; physical sciences; physics; political science and government; pre-dentistry studies; pre-law studies; pre-medical studies; pre-veterinary studies; psychology; range science and management; religious studies; secondary education; social sciences; social work; sociology; Spanish; speech and rhetoric; toxicology; wildlife and wildlands science and management; zoology/animal biology.

Academics *Calendar:* semesters. *Degrees:* bachelor's, master's, and post-bachelor's certificates. *Special study options:* academic remediation for entering students, adult/continuing education programs, advanced placement credit, cooperative education, distance learning, double majors, English as a second language, honors programs, independent study, internships, off-campus study, part-time degree program, services for LD students, student-designed majors, study abroad, summer session for credit.

Computers on Campus 1,191 computers/terminals are available on campus for general student use. Students can access the following: computer help desk, free student e-mail accounts, online (class) grades, online (class) registration, online (class) schedules. Campuswide network is available. 100% of college-owned or -operated housing units are wired for high-speed Internet access. Wireless service is available via entire campus.

Student Life *Housing options:* coed. Campus housing is university owned. *Activities and organizations:* drama/theater group, student-run newspaper, radio station, choral group, marching band, Student Radio Station, Student Environmental Action Coalition, Youth Educational Services, Ballet Folklorico, International Student Union, national fraternities, national sororities. *Campus security:* 24-hour emergency response devices and patrols, late-night transport/escort service, controlled dormitory access. *Student services:* health clinic, personal/psychological counseling, women's center, legal services.

Athletics Member NCAA. All Division II. *Intercollegiate sports:* basketball M (s)/W (s), cheerleading W (c), crew M (c)/W, cross-country running M (s)/W (s), football M (s), lacrosse M (c), rock climbing M (c)/W (c), soccer M (s)/W (s), softball W (s), track and field M (s)/W (s), volleyball W (s). *Intramural sports:* baseball M (c), basketball M/W, fencing M (c)/W (c), soccer M/W, ultimate Frisbee M (c)/W (c).

Standardized Tests *Required for some:* SAT or ACT (for admission).

Costs (2007–08) *Tuition:* nonresident $10,169 full-time, $339 per unit part-time. *Required fees:* $3843 full-time. *Room and board:* $8522; room only: $5174.

Financial Aid Of all full-time matriculated undergraduates who enrolled in 2006, 4,102 applied for aid, 3,382 were judged to have need, 112 had their need fully met. 300 Federal Work-Study jobs (averaging $2000). In 2005, 56 non-need-based awards were made. *Average percent of need met:* 72%. *Average financial aid package:* $8283. *Average need-based loan:* $629. *Average need-based gift aid:* $4324. *Average non-need-based aid:* $1004. *Average indebtedness upon graduation:* $12,777.

Applying *Options:* electronic application. *Application fee:* $55. *Required:* high school transcript, minimum 2.0 GPA. *Application deadlines:* 1/1 (freshmen), 6/1 (transfers). *Notification:* continuous (freshmen), continuous (transfers).

Freshman Application Contact Ms. Rebecca Kalal, Assistant Director of Admissions, Humboldt State University, 1 Harpst Street, Arcata, CA 95521-8299. *Phone:* 707-826-6221. *Fax:* 707-826-6190. *E-mail:* hsuinfo@humboldt.edu.

HUMPHREYS COLLEGE

Stockton, California www.humphreys.edu/

Director of Admissions Ms. Wilma Okamoto Vaughn, Dean of Administration, Humphreys College, 6650 Inglewood Avenue, Stockton, CA 95207-3896. *Phone:* 209-478-0800.

INTERIOR DESIGNERS INSTITUTE

Newport Beach, California

INTERNATIONAL TECHNOLOGICAL UNIVERSITY

Santa Clara, California www.itu.edu/

Director of Admissions Chun Mou Peng, Director of Operations, International Technological University, 1650 Warbunton Avenue, Santa Clara, CA 95050. *Phone:* 408-556-9027.

ITT TECHNICAL INSTITUTE

Anaheim, California www.itt-tech.edu/

- **Proprietary** primarily 2-year, founded 1982, part of ITT Educational Services, Inc
- **Suburban** 5-acre campus with easy access to Los Angeles
- **Coed**
- **Minimally difficult** entrance level

Academics *Calendar:* quarters. *Degrees:* associate and bachelor's.

Standardized Tests *Required:* Wonderlic aptitude test (for admission).

Financial Aid Of all full-time matriculated undergraduates who enrolled in 2006, 20 Federal Work-Study jobs (averaging $5000).

Applying *Options:* deferred entrance. *Application fee:* $100. *Required:* high school transcript, interview. *Recommended:* letters of recommendation.

Freshman Application Contact Ms. Sheryl Schulgen, Director of Recruitment, ITT Technical Institute, 525 North Muller Avenue, Anaheim, CA 92801. *Phone:* 714-535-3700. *Fax:* 714-535-1802.

ITT TECHNICAL INSTITUTE

Clovis, California

www.itt-tech.edu/campus/school.cfm?lloc_num=61

- **Proprietary** 4-year, founded 2005
- **Coed**

Academics *Calendar:* quarters. *Degrees:* associate and bachelor's.

Freshman Application Contact Ms. Linda Stolling, Director of Recruitment, ITT Technical Institute, 362 North Clovis Avenue, Clovis, CA 93612. *Phone:* 559-325-5400. *Fax:* 559-325-5499.

ITT TECHNICAL INSTITUTE

Lathrop, California www.itt-tech.edu/

- **Proprietary** primarily 2-year, founded 1997, part of ITT Educational Services, Inc
- **Coed**
- **Minimally difficult** entrance level

Academics *Calendar:* quarters. *Degrees:* associate and bachelor's.

Standardized Tests *Required:* Wonderlic aptitude test (for admission).

Applying *Options:* deferred entrance. *Application fee:* $100. *Required:* high school transcript, interview. *Recommended:* letters of recommendation.

Freshman Application Contact Ms. Kathy Paradis, Director of Recruitment, ITT Technical Institute, 16916 South Harlan Road, Lathrop, CA 95330. *Phone:* 209-858-0077. *Toll-free phone:* 800-346-1786.

ITT TECHNICAL INSTITUTE

Oxnard, California www.itt-tech.edu/

- **Proprietary** primarily 2-year, founded 1993, part of ITT Educational Services, Inc
- **Urban** campus with easy access to Los Angeles
- **Coed**
- **Minimally difficult** entrance level

Academics *Calendar:* quarters. *Degrees:* associate and bachelor's.

Student Life *Campus security:* 24-hour emergency response devices and patrols.

Standardized Tests *Required:* Wonderlic aptitude test (for admission).

Applying *Options:* deferred entrance. *Application fee:* $100. *Required:* high school transcript, interview. *Recommended:* letters of recommendation.

Freshman Application Contact Milo Hager, Director of Recruitment, ITT Technical Institute, 2051 Solar Drive, Building B, Oxnard, CA 93036. *Phone:* 805-988-0143. *Toll-free phone:* 800-530-1582.

ITT TECHNICAL INSTITUTE

Rancho Cordova, California www.itt-tech.edu/

- **Proprietary** primarily 2-year, founded 1954, part of ITT Educational Services, Inc
- **Urban** 5-acre campus
- **Coed**
- **Minimally difficult** entrance level

Academics *Calendar:* quarters. *Degrees:* associate and bachelor's.

Standardized Tests *Required:* Wonderlic aptitude test (for admission).

Applying *Options:* deferred entrance. *Application fee:* $100. *Required:* high school transcript, interview. *Recommended:* letters of recommendation.

Freshman Application Contact Mr. Vance Klinke, Director of Recruitment, ITT Technical Institute, 10863 Gold Center Drive, Rancho Cordova, CA 95670. *Phone:* 916-851-3900. *Toll-free phone:* 800-488-8466.

ITT TECHNICAL INSTITUTE

San Bernardino, California www.itt-tech.edu/

- **Proprietary** primarily 2-year, founded 1987, part of ITT Educational Services, Inc
- **Urban** campus with easy access to Los Angeles
- **Coed**
- **Minimally difficult** entrance level

Academics *Calendar:* quarters. *Degrees:* associate and bachelor's.

Standardized Tests *Required:* Wonderlic aptitude test (for admission).

Applying *Options:* deferred entrance. *Application fee:* $100. *Required:* high school transcript, interview. *Recommended:* letters of recommendation.

Freshman Application Contact Director of Recruitment, ITT Technical Institute, 670 East Carnegie Drive, San Bernardino, CA 92408. *Phone:* 909-806-4600. *Toll-free phone:* 800-888-3801.

ITT TECHNICAL INSTITUTE

San Diego, California www.itt-tech.edu/

- **Proprietary** primarily 2-year, founded 1981, part of ITT Educational Services, Inc
- **Suburban** campus
- **Coed**
- **Minimally difficult** entrance level

Academics *Calendar:* quarters. *Degrees:* associate and bachelor's.

Standardized Tests *Required:* Wonderlic aptitude test (for admission).

Applying *Options:* deferred entrance. *Application fee:* $100. *Required:* high school transcript, interview. *Recommended:* letters of recommendation.

Freshman Application Contact Ron Begora, Director of Recruitment, ITT Technical Institute, 9680 Granite Ridge Drive, San Diego, CA 92123. *Phone:* 858-571-8500. *Toll-free phone:* 800-883-0380.

ITT TECHNICAL INSTITUTE

San Dimas, California www.itt-tech.edu/

- **Proprietary** primarily 2-year, founded 1982, part of ITT Educational Services, Inc
- **Suburban** 4-acre campus with easy access to Los Angeles
- **Coed**
- **Minimally difficult** entrance level

Academics *Calendar:* quarters. *Degrees:* associate and bachelor's.

Standardized Tests *Required:* Wonderlic aptitude test (for admission).

Financial Aid Of all full-time matriculated undergraduates who enrolled in 2006, 20 Federal Work-Study jobs (averaging $4500).

Applying *Options:* deferred entrance. *Application fee:* $100. *Required:* high school transcript, interview. *Recommended:* letters of recommendation.

Freshman Application Contact Ms. Laura Brozeck, Director of Recruitment, ITT Technical Institute, 650 West Cienega Avenue, San Dimas, CA 91773. *Phone:* 909-971-2300. *Toll-free phone:* 800-414-6522.

ITT TECHNICAL INSTITUTE

Sylmar, California www.itt-tech.edu/

- **Proprietary** primarily 2-year, founded 1982, part of ITT Educational Services, Inc
- **Urban** campus with easy access to Los Angeles
- **Coed**
- **Minimally difficult** entrance level

Academics *Calendar:* quarters. *Degrees:* associate and bachelor's.

Standardized Tests *Required:* Wonderlic aptitude test (for admission).

Applying *Options:* deferred entrance. *Application fee:* $100. *Required:* high school transcript, interview. *Recommended:* letters of recommendation.

Freshman Application Contact Ms. Kelly Christensen, Director of Recruitment, ITT Technical Institute, 12669 Encinitas Avenue, Sylmar, CA 91342. *Phone:* 818-364-5151. *Toll-free phone:* 800-363-2086.

ITT TECHNICAL INSTITUTE

Torrance, California www.itt-tech.edu/

- **Proprietary** primarily 2-year, founded 1987, part of ITT Educational Services, Inc
- **Urban** campus with easy access to Los Angeles
- **Coed**
- **Minimally difficult** entrance level

Academics *Calendar:* quarters. *Degrees:* associate and bachelor's.

Standardized Tests *Required:* Wonderlic aptitude test (for admission).

Financial Aid Of all full-time matriculated undergraduates who enrolled in 2006, 6 Federal Work-Study jobs (averaging $4000).

Applying *Options:* deferred entrance. *Application fee:* $100. *Required:* high school transcript, interview. *Recommended:* letters of recommendation.

Freshman Application Contact Mr. Freddie Polk, Director of Recruitment, ITT Technical Institute, 20050 South Vermont Avenue, Torrance, CA 90502. *Phone:* 310-380-1555.

JOHN F. KENNEDY UNIVERSITY

Pleasant Hill, California **www.jfku.edu/**

- **Independent** upper-level, founded 1964
- **Suburban** 5-acre campus with easy access to San Francisco
- **Endowment** $1.6 million
- **Coed** 308 undergraduate students, 17% full-time, 71% women, 29% men
- **Noncompetitive** entrance level

Undergraduates 51 full-time, 257 part-time. 9% African American, 8% Asian American or Pacific Islander, 9% Hispanic American, 2% Native American, 2% international, 6% transferred in.

Faculty *Total:* 237, 15% full-time. *Student/faculty ratio:* 9:1.

Majors Accounting; business administration and management; consumer merchandising/retailing management; humanities; liberal arts and sciences/liberal studies; psychology.

Academics *Calendar:* quarters semesters for law school. *Degrees:* bachelor's, master's, doctoral, first professional, and postbachelor's certificates. *Special study options:* adult/continuing education programs, advanced placement credit, independent study, off-campus study, part-time degree program, services for LD students, student-designed majors, summer session for credit.

Computers on Campus 50 computers/terminals are available on campus for general student use. Students can access the following: free student e-mail accounts, online (class) registration, online (class) schedules. Wireless service is available via entire campus.

Student Life *Housing:* college housing not available. *Campus security:* late-night transport/escort service. *Student services:* personal/psychological counseling.

Costs (2007–08) *Tuition:* $12,240 full-time, $340 per unit part-time. Full-time tuition and fees vary according to course level, course load, and program. Part-time tuition and fees vary according to course level, course load, and program. *Required fees:* $168 full-time, $56 per term part-time. *Payment plan:* installment. *Waivers:* employees or children of employees.

Financial Aid Of all full-time matriculated undergraduates who enrolled in 2006, 11 applied for aid, 11 were judged to have need, 11 had their need fully met. *Average percent of need met:* 60%. *Average financial aid package:* $7000. *Average need-based loan:* $6000. *Average need-based gift aid:* $1000. *Average indebtedness upon graduation:* $23,000.

Applying *Options:* electronic application, deferred entrance. *Application fee:* $55. *Application deadline:* rolling (transfers). *Notification:* continuous (transfers).

Director of Admissions Ms. Jen Miller-Hogg, Director of Admissions, John F. Kennedy University, Admissions and Records, John F. Kennedy University, 100 Ellinwood Way, Pleasant Hill, CA 94523. *Phone:* 925-969-3584. *Toll-free phone:* 800-696-JFKU. *E-mail:* jmhogg@jfku.edu.

THE KING'S COLLEGE AND SEMINARY

Van Nuys, California **www.kingscollege.edu/**

Freshman Application Contact Mrs. Marilyn J. Chappell, Director of Admissions, The King's College and Seminary, 14800 Sherman Way, Van Nuys, CA 91405-8040. *Phone:* 818-779-8040. *Toll-free phone:* 888-779-8040. *Fax:* 818-779-8429. *E-mail:* mchappell@kingscollege.edu.

LA COLLEGE INTERNATIONAL

Los Angeles, California **www.lac.edu/**

- **Proprietary** 4-year, founded 1981
- **Urban** campus
- **Coed** 85 undergraduate students, 100% full-time, 44% women, 56% men
- **Noncompetitive** entrance level

Undergraduates 85 full-time. Students come from 10 states and territories, 4 other countries, 20% African American, 9% Asian American or Pacific Islander, 61% Hispanic American, 4% transferred in. *Retention:* 68% of 2006 full-time freshmen returned.

Freshmen *Admission:* 70 enrolled.

Faculty *Total:* 25, 4% with terminal degrees. *Student/faculty ratio:* 5:1.

Majors Business administration and management; computer science; health/health care administration.

Academics *Calendar:* quarters. *Degrees:* certificates, diplomas, associate, and bachelor's. *Special study options:* advanced placement credit, independent study, internships.

Computers on Campus 100 computers/terminals are available on campus for general student use. Students can access the following: computer help desk, free student e-mail accounts. Wireless service is available via entire campus.

Student Life *Housing:* college housing not available. *Campus security:* 24-hour patrols.

Standardized Tests *Required for some:* CPAt.

Costs (2007–08) *Tuition:* $19,575 full-time.

Applying *Application fee:* $75. *Required:* high school transcript, interview.

Director of Admissions Shavonne Turner, Director of Admissions, LA College International, 3200 Wilshire Boulevard 4th Floor, Los Angeles, CA 90010. *Phone:* 213-381-3333. *Toll-free phone:* 800-57 GO ICT. *E-mail:* sturner@lac.edu.

LAGUNA COLLEGE OF ART & DESIGN

Laguna Beach, California **www.lagunacollege.edu/**

- **Independent** 4-year, founded 1962
- **Small-town** 9-acre campus with easy access to Los Angeles
- **Endowment** $411,000
- **Coed** 310 undergraduate students, 100% full-time, 47% women, 53% men
- **Very difficult** entrance level, 88% of applicants were admitted

Undergraduates 310 full-time. Students come from 32 states and territories, 42% are from out of state, 2% African American, 15% Asian American or Pacific Islander, 9% Hispanic American, 0.6% Native American, 6% international. *Retention:* 83% of 2006 full-time freshmen returned.

Freshmen *Admission:* 245 applied, 215 admitted, 70 enrolled. *Average high school GPA:* 3.45. *Test scores:* SAT critical reading scores over 500: 88%; SAT math scores over 500: 80%; ACT scores over 18: 100%; SAT critical reading scores over 600: 66%; SAT math scores over 600: 32%; ACT scores over 24: 80%; SAT critical reading scores over 700: 16%; SAT math scores over 700: 10%; ACT scores over 30: 10%.

Faculty *Total:* 72, 14% full-time. *Student/faculty ratio:* 10:1.

Majors Art; commercial and advertising art; design and applied arts related; design and visual communications; drawing; fine/studio arts; graphic design; illustration; intermedia/multimedia; painting; printmaking; sculpture.

Academics *Calendar:* semesters. *Degrees:* certificates, bachelor's, and master's. *Special study options:* academic remediation for entering students, adult/continuing education programs, advanced placement credit, English as a second language, independent study, internships, off-campus study, part-time degree program, summer session for credit.

Computers on Campus 85 computers/terminals are available on campus for general student use. Students can access the following: campus intranet, computer help desk, free student e-mail accounts. Campuswide network is available. Wireless service is available via entire campus.

Student Life *Housing:* college housing not available. *Activities and organizations:* student-run newspaper. *Campus security:* 24-hour emergency response devices. *Student services:* personal/psychological counseling.

Athletics *Intercollegiate sports:* ultimate Frisbee M (s)/W (s), volleyball M (s)/W (s). *Intramural sports:* ultimate Frisbee M/W, volleyball M/W.

Standardized Tests *Required:* SAT or ACT (for admission).

Costs (2008–09) *Tuition:* $20,600 full-time.

Financial Aid Of all full-time matriculated undergraduates who enrolled in 2006, 302 applied for aid, 274 were judged to have need. 12 Federal Work-Study jobs (averaging $1500). In 2006, 31 non-need-based awards were made. *Average percent of need met:* 70%. *Average financial aid package:* $8000. *Average need-based loan:* $3500. *Average need-based gift aid:* $2500. *Average non-need-based aid:* $2500. *Average indebtedness upon graduation:* $35,125.

Applying *Options:* electronic application, deferred entrance. *Application fee:* $45. *Required:* high school transcript, portfolio. *Notification:* 5/1 (freshmen), 5/30 (transfers).

Director of Admissions Mike Rivas, Vice President of Enrollment, Laguna College of Art & Design, 2222 Laguna Canyon Road, Laguna Beach, CA 92651-1136. *Phone:* 949-376-6000 Ext. 232. *Toll-free phone:* 800-255-0762.

See page 446 for the College Close-Up.

La Sierra University

Riverside, California **www.lasierra.edu/**

- **Independent Seventh-day Adventist** comprehensive, founded 1922
- **Suburban** 100-acre campus with easy access to Los Angeles
- **Coed** 1,457 undergraduate students, 88% full-time, 59% women, 41% men
- **Moderately difficult** entrance level, 45% of applicants were admitted

Undergraduates 1,288 full-time, 169 part-time. Students come from 37 states and territories, 33 other countries, 15% are from out of state, 8% African American, 25% Asian American or Pacific Islander, 26% Hispanic American, 0.5% Native American, 11% international, 14% transferred in, 45% live on campus. *Retention:* 61% of 2006 full-time freshmen returned.

Freshmen *Admission:* 1,307 applied, 593 admitted, 337 enrolled. *Average high school GPA:* 3.29. *Test scores:* SAT critical reading scores over 500: 43%; SAT math scores over 500: 48%; ACT scores over 18: 69%; SAT critical reading scores over 600: 14%; SAT math scores over 600: 15%; ACT scores over 24: 26%; SAT critical reading scores over 700: 2%; SAT math scores over 700: 2%; ACT scores over 30: 6%.

Faculty *Total:* 173, 55% full-time, 49% with terminal degrees. *Student/faculty ratio:* 13:1.

Majors Accounting; art; biochemistry; biology/biological sciences; biophysics; business administration and management; chemistry; communication/speech communication and rhetoric; computer science; elementary education; English; fine/studio arts; health and physical education; history; information science/studies; kinesiology and exercise science; liberal arts and sciences/liberal studies; mathematics; music; music teacher education; physical sciences; physiological psychology/psychobiology; political science and government; pre-dentistry studies; pre-law studies; pre-medical studies; psychology; religious studies; secondary education; social work; sociology; Spanish.

Academics *Calendar:* quarters. *Degrees:* bachelor's, master's, doctoral, post-master's, and postbachelor's certificates. *Special study options:* academic remediation for entering students, accelerated degree program, adult/continuing education programs, advanced placement credit, double majors, English as a second language, honors programs, independent study, internships, off-campus study, part-time degree program, services for LD students, student-designed majors, study abroad, summer session for credit.

Computers on Campus 135 computers/terminals are available on campus for general student use. Students can access the following: free student e-mail accounts, online (class) grades, online (class) registration, online (class) schedules. Campuswide network is available. Wireless service is available via classrooms, computer centers, computer labs, libraries.

Student Life *Housing:* on-campus residence required through sophomore year. *Options:* men-only, women-only. Campus housing is university owned. Freshman campus housing is guaranteed. *Activities and organizations:* drama/theater group, student-run newspaper, choral group, Student Association of LSU, Korean Student Association, Students In Free Enterprise (SIFE), Olé Club, Black Student Association. *Campus security:* 24-hour emergency response devices and patrols, student patrols, late-night transport/escort service. *Student services:* health clinic, personal/psychological counseling, women's center.

Athletics Member NCAA. All Division III. *Intercollegiate sports:* baseball M, basketball M/W, golf M, soccer M/W, softball W, tennis M/W, volleyball W. *Intramural sports:* badminton M/W, basketball M/W, football M/W, softball M/W.

Standardized Tests *Required:* SAT or ACT (for admission).

Costs (2008–09) *Comprehensive fee:* $29,865 includes full-time tuition ($22,320), mandatory fees ($834), and room and board ($6711). Part-time tuition: $620 per quarter hour.

Financial Aid Of all full-time matriculated undergraduates who enrolled in 2005, 1,114 applied for aid, 1,019 were judged to have need, 117 had their need fully met. 269 Federal Work-Study jobs (averaging $2314). In 2005, 373 non-need-based awards were made. *Average percent of need met:* 64%. *Average financial aid package:* $15,006. *Average need-based loan:* $4856. *Average need-based gift aid:* $11,281. *Average non-need-based aid:* $5847. *Average indebtedness upon graduation:* $28,876.

Applying *Options:* electronic application, deferred entrance. *Application fee:* $30. *Required:* essay or personal statement, high school transcript, 2 letters of recommendation. *Required for some:* interview. *Application deadlines:* rolling (freshmen), rolling (transfers). *Notification:* continuous (freshmen), continuous (transfers).

Freshman Application Contact Faye Swayze, Director of Admissions and Registrar, La Sierra University, 4500 Riverwalk Parkway, Riverside, CA 92515. *Phone:* 951-785-2176. *Toll-free phone:* 800-874-5587. *Fax:* 951-785-2477. *E-mail:* admissions@lasierra.edu.

Life Pacific College

San Dimas, California **www.lifepacific.edu/**

Freshman Application Contact Ms. Gina Nicodemus, Director of Admissions, Life Pacific College, 1100 Covina Boulevard, San Dimas, CA 91773-3298. *Phone:* 909-599-5433 Ext. 314. *Toll-free phone:* 877-886-5433 Ext. 314. *Fax:* 909-706-3070. *E-mail:* adm@lifepacific.edu.

Lincoln University

Oakland, California **www.lincolnuca.edu/**

- **Independent** comprehensive, founded 1919
- **Urban** 2-acre campus
- **Coed** 114 undergraduate students, 89% full-time, 65% women, 35% men
- **Minimally difficult** entrance level, 93% of applicants were admitted

Undergraduates 102 full-time, 12 part-time. Students come from 18 other countries, 5% transferred in. *Retention:* 60% of 2006 full-time freshmen returned.

Freshmen *Admission:* 336 applied, 312 admitted, 34 enrolled. *Average high school GPA:* 2.5.

Faculty *Total:* 37, 27% full-time. *Student/faculty ratio:* 14:1.

Majors Business administration and management; diagnostic medical sonography and ultrasound technology; economics; international business/trade/commerce; management information systems; small business administration.

Academics *Calendar:* semesters. *Degrees:* certificates, bachelor's, and master's. *Special study options:* advanced placement credit, English as a second language, internships, summer session for credit.

Computers on Campus 20 computers/terminals are available on campus for general student use. Students can access the following: computer help desk. Wireless service is available via entire campus.

Student Life *Housing:* college housing not available. *Campus security:* 24-hour emergency response devices. *Student services:* personal/psychological counseling.

Costs (2007–08) *Tuition:* $7800 full-time, $325 per unit part-time. Full-time tuition and fees vary according to program. *Required fees:* $430 full-time. *Room only:* Room and board charges vary according to housing facility and location. *Payment plan:* installment.

Applying *Options:* electronic application, deferred entrance. *Application fee:* $75. *Required:* high school transcript, minimum 2.5 GPA. *Required for some:* essay or personal statement, letters of recommendation, interview. *Application deadlines:* 8/22 (freshmen), 8/22 (transfers).

Freshman Application Contact Ms. Helen Zhou, Admissions Officer, Lincoln University, 401 15th Street, Oakland, CA 94612-2801. *Phone:* 510-628-8010. *Fax:* 510-628-8012. *E-mail:* adminofficer@lincolnuca.edu.

Loma Linda University

Loma Linda, California **www.llu.edu/**

- **Independent Seventh-day Adventist** upper-level, founded 1905
- **Small-town** campus with easy access to Los Angeles
- **Endowment** $135.9 million
- **Coed** 1,232 undergraduate students, 72% full-time, 72% women, 28% men

Undergraduates 885 full-time, 347 part-time. Students come from 29 states and territories, 30 other countries, 12% are from out of state, 7% African American, 23% Asian American or Pacific Islander, 17% Hispanic American, 1% Native American, 8% international, 18% transferred in, 27% live on campus.

Faculty *Total:* 840, 66% full-time, 68% with terminal degrees. *Student/faculty ratio:* 8:1.

Majors Audiology and speech-language pathology; clinical laboratory science/medical technology; cytotechnology; dental hygiene; emergency medical technology (EMT paramedic); geology/earth science; health information/medical records administration; medical laboratory technology; medical radiologic technology; nursing (registered nurse training); occupational therapist assistant; physical therapist assistant; respiratory care therapy; Spanish and Iberian studies.

Academics *Calendar:* quarters. *Degrees:* certificates, associate, bachelor's, master's, doctoral, first professional, post-master's, postbachelor's, and first professional certificates (associate degree and nursing students may enter at the sophomore level). *Special study options:* distance learning, English as a second language, independent study, internships, off-campus study.

Computers on Campus 160 computers/terminals are available on campus for general student use. Students can access the following: campus intranet, computer help desk, free student e-mail accounts, online (class) grades, online (class) registration, online (class) schedules, online courses. Campuswide network is available. 100% of college-owned or -operated housing units are wired for high-speed Internet access. Wireless service is available via entire campus.

Student Life *Housing options:* men-only, women-only. Campus housing is university owned. *Activities and organizations:* Students for International Mission Services, Black Health Professional Association, Association of Latin American Students. *Campus security:* 24-hour emergency response devices and patrols, late-night transport/escort service. *Student services:* health clinic, personal/psychological counseling.

Athletics *Intramural sports:* basketball M/W, football M, racquetball M/W, soccer M/W, softball M/W, swimming and diving M/W, tennis M/W, volleyball M/W.

Costs (2007–08) *Tuition:* $25,860 full-time, $495 per unit part-time. *Required fees:* $1460 full-time, $430 per term part-time. *Room only:* $2460.

Financial Aid Of all full-time matriculated undergraduates who enrolled in 2002, 542 applied for aid, 492 were judged to have need, 131 had their need fully met. 85 Federal Work-Study jobs (averaging $3029). In 2002, 54 non-need-based awards were made. *Average percent of need met:* 87%. *Average financial aid package:* $16,862. *Average need-based loan:* $4345. *Average need-based gift aid:* $3118. *Average non-need-based aid:* $12,582. *Average indebtedness upon graduation:* $28,245.

Applying *Options:* deferred entrance. *Application fee:* $60.

Application Contact Admissions Office, Loma Linda University, Loma Linda, CA 92350. *Phone:* 909-558-1000.

LOYOLA MARYMOUNT UNIVERSITY

Los Angeles, California **www.lmu.edu/**

- **Independent Roman Catholic** comprehensive, founded 1911
- **Suburban** 128-acre campus
- **Endowment** $379.3 million
- **Coed** 5,766 undergraduate students, 95% full-time, 58% women, 42% men
- **Very difficult** entrance level, 52% of applicants were admitted

Undergraduates 5,453 full-time, 313 part-time. Students come from 51 states and territories, 38 other countries, 25% are from out of state, 8% African American, 13% Asian American or Pacific Islander, 20% Hispanic American, 0.6% Native American, 2% international, 5% transferred in, 50% live on campus. *Retention:* 88% of 2006 full-time freshmen returned.

Freshmen *Admission:* 8,533 applied, 4,456 admitted, 1,268 enrolled. *Average high school GPA:* 3.64. *Test scores:* SAT critical reading scores over 500: 85%; SAT math scores over 500: 89%; ACT scores over 18: 99%; SAT critical reading scores over 600: 41%; SAT math scores over 600: 48%; ACT scores over 24: 72%; SAT critical reading scores over 700: 6%; SAT math scores over 700: 7%; ACT scores over 30: 11%.

Faculty *Total:* 915, 53% full-time. *Student/faculty ratio:* 13:1.

Majors Accounting; African-American/Black studies; art history, criticism and conservation; Asian-American studies; biochemistry; biology/biological sciences; business administration and management; chemistry; cinematography and film/video production; civil engineering; classics and languages, literatures and linguistics; computer engineering; computer science; conducting; dance; dramatic/theater arts; economics; electrical, electronics and communications engineering; engineering physics; English; European studies; fine/studio arts; French; Hispanic-American, Puerto Rican, and Mexican-American/Chicano studies; history; humanities; international economics; Latin; liberal arts and sciences/liberal studies; mass communication/media; mathematics; mechanical engineering; modern Greek; music; music history, literature, and theory; musicology and ethnomusicology; music theory and composition; natural sciences; philosophy; physics; playwriting and screenwriting; political science and government; psychology; sociology; Spanish; theology; urban studies/affairs; voice and opera.

Academics *Calendar:* semesters. *Degrees:* bachelor's, master's, doctoral, first professional, and postbachelor's certificates. *Special study options:* accelerated degree program, adult/continuing education programs, advanced placement credit, cooperative education, double majors, honors programs, independent study, internships, part-time degree program, services for LD students, student-designed majors, study abroad, summer session for credit. *ROTC:* Army (c), Air Force (b).

Computers on Campus 300 computers/terminals are available on campus for general student use. Campuswide network is available.

Student Life *Housing options:* coed, men-only, women-only. Campus housing is university owned. Freshman campus housing is guaranteed. *Activities and organizations:* drama/theater group, student-run newspaper, radio and television station, choral group, service clubs, Student Government and Activity Board, community service opportunities, student media opportunities, clubs and organizations, national fraternities, national sororities. *Campus security:* 24-hour emergency response devices and patrols, late-night transport/escort service, controlled dormitory access. *Student services:* health clinic, personal/psychological counseling.

Athletics Member NCAA. All Division I. *Intercollegiate sports:* baseball M (s), basketball M (s)/W (s), crew M/W (s), cross-country running M (s)/W (s), golf M (s), lacrosse M (c)/W (c), rugby M (c), soccer M (s)/W (s), softball W (s), swimming and diving W (s), tennis M (s)/W (s), volleyball M (c)/W (s), water polo M (s)/W (s). *Intramural sports:* basketball M/W, football M/W, soccer M/W, softball M/W, tennis M/W, volleyball M/W.

Standardized Tests *Required:* SAT or ACT (for admission).

Costs (2007–08) *One-time required fee:* $250. *Comprehensive fee:* $43,059 includes full-time tuition ($31,168), mandatory fees ($746), and room and board ($11,145). Part-time tuition: $1298 per unit. Part-time tuition and fees vary according to course load. *College room only:* $7368. Room and board charges vary according to board plan and housing facility. *Payment plans:* installment, deferred payment. *Waivers:* employees or children of employees.

Financial Aid Of all full-time matriculated undergraduates who enrolled in 2004, 4,129 applied for aid, 3,410 were judged to have need, 503 had their need fully met. 1,600 Federal Work-Study jobs (averaging $2000). 579 state and other part-time jobs (averaging $2800). In 2004, 130 non-need-based awards were made. *Average percent of need met:* 76%. *Average financial aid package:* $17,254. *Average need-based loan:* $5401. *Average need-based gift aid:* $9378. *Average non-need-based aid:* $9577. *Average indebtedness upon graduation:* $21,164. *Financial aid deadline:* 7/30.

Applying *Options:* electronic application, early admission, deferred entrance. *Application fee:* $50. *Required:* essay or personal statement, high school transcript, 2 letters of recommendation. *Recommended:* interview. *Application deadlines:* 1/15 (freshmen), 6/1 (transfers). *Notification:* continuous (freshmen), continuous (transfers).

Director of Admissions Mr. Matthew X. Fissinger, Director of Admissions, Loyola Marymount University, 1 LMU Drive Suite 100, Los Angeles, CA 90045-8350. *Phone:* 310-338-2750. *Toll-free phone:* 800-LMU-INFO. *E-mail:* admissions@lmu.edu.

See page 448 for the College Close-Up.

THE MASTER'S COLLEGE AND SEMINARY

Santa Clarita, California **www.masters.edu/**

- **Independent nondenominational** comprehensive, founded 1927
- **Suburban** 110-acre campus with easy access to Los Angeles
- **Endowment** $7.9 million
- **Coed** 1,114 undergraduate students, 84% full-time, 51% women, 49% men
- **Moderately difficult** entrance level, 84% of applicants were admitted

Undergraduates 935 full-time, 179 part-time. Students come from 41 states and territories, 39 other countries, 36% are from out of state, 2% African American, 5% Asian American or Pacific Islander, 7% Hispanic American, 1% Native American, 4% international, 9% transferred in, 90% live on campus. *Retention:* 80% of 2006 full-time freshmen returned.

Freshmen *Admission:* 485 applied, 406 admitted, 210 enrolled. *Average high school GPA:* 3.6. *Test scores:* SAT critical reading scores over 500: 75%; SAT math scores over 500: 70%; ACT scores over 18: 94%; SAT critical reading scores over 600: 40%; SAT math scores over 600: 34%; ACT scores over 24: 55%; SAT critical reading scores over 700: 8%; SAT math scores over 700: 5%; ACT scores over 30: 19%.

Faculty *Total:* 169, 41% full-time, 47% with terminal degrees. *Student/faculty ratio:* 16:1.

Majors Accounting; actuarial science; American government and politics; ancient Near Eastern and biblical languages; applied mathematics; biblical studies; biological and physical sciences; biology/biological sciences; business administration and management; computer and information sciences; divinity/ministry; education; elementary education; English; environmental biology; family and consumer sciences/human sciences; finance; foods, nutrition, and wellness; health and physical education; history; kinesiology and exercise science; liberal arts and sciences/liberal studies; management information systems; mass communication/media; mathematics; middle school education; music; music management and merchandising; music teacher education; natural sciences; pastoral studies/counseling; physical education teaching and coaching; physical sciences; piano and organ; political science and government; pre-law studies; pre-medical studies; public relations/image management; radio and television;

religious education; religious/sacred music; religious studies; science teacher education; secondary education; speech and rhetoric; theology; voice and opera.

Academics *Calendar:* semesters. *Degrees:* certificates, bachelor's, master's, doctoral, first professional, and first professional certificates. *Special study options:* academic remediation for entering students, accelerated degree program, adult/continuing education programs, advanced placement credit, cooperative education, double majors, external degree program, independent study, internships, part-time degree program, services for LD students, study abroad, summer session for credit.

Computers on Campus 57 computers/terminals are available on campus for general student use. Students can access the following: free student e-mail accounts, online (class) grades, online (class) registration, online (class) schedules. Campuswide network is available. Wireless service is available via entire campus.

Student Life *Housing:* on-campus residence required through sophomore year. *Options:* men-only, women-only. Campus housing is university owned and leased by the school. Freshman campus housing is guaranteed. *Activities and organizations:* drama/theater group, choral group, College Chorale, Summer Missions, Intramurals, Church Ministries, Drama Club. *Campus security:* 24-hour patrols. *Student services:* health clinic, personal/psychological counseling.

Athletics Member NAIA, NCCAA. *Intercollegiate sports:* baseball M (s), basketball M (s)/W (s), cross-country running M (s)/W (s), golf M (s), soccer M (s)/W (s), softball W (s), volleyball W (s). *Intramural sports:* basketball M/W, football M/W, golf M/W, softball M/W, tennis M/W, volleyball M/W.

Standardized Tests *Required:* SAT or ACT (for admission).

Costs (2008–09) *Comprehensive fee:* $30,370 includes full-time tuition ($23,120) and room and board ($7250). Part-time tuition: $965 per credit hour. *College room only:* $4060.

Financial Aid Of all full-time matriculated undergraduates who enrolled in 2005, 838 applied for aid, 735 were judged to have need, 166 had their need fully met. 45 Federal Work-Study jobs (averaging $2666). In 2005, 198 non-need-based awards were made. *Average percent of need met:* 69%. *Average financial aid package:* $15,054. *Average need-based loan:* $4634. *Average need-based gift aid:* $10,405. *Average non-need-based aid:* $9833. *Average indebtedness upon graduation:* $15,383.

Applying *Options:* electronic application, early admission, early action, deferred entrance. *Application fee:* $40. *Required:* essay or personal statement, high school transcript, minimum 2.5 GPA, 2 letters of recommendation, interview. *Application deadlines:* 3/2 (transfers), 11/15 (early action). *Notification:* 3/15 (freshmen), 3/15 (transfers), 12/22 (early action).

Freshman Application Contact Ms. Hollie Gorsh, Director of Admissions, The Master's College and Seminary, Santa Clarita, CA 91321. *Phone:* 661-259-3540 Ext. 3369. *Toll-free phone:* 800-568-6248. *Fax:* 661-288-1037. *E-mail:* admissions@masters.edu.

MENLO COLLEGE

Atherton, California **www.menlo.edu/**

- **Independent** 4-year, founded 1927
- **Small-town** 45-acre campus with easy access to San Francisco
- **Endowment** $8.6 million
- **Coed**
- **Moderately difficult** entrance level

Faculty *Student/faculty ratio:* 18:1.

Academics *Calendar:* semesters. *Degree:* bachelor's.

Student Life *Campus security:* 24-hour emergency response devices and patrols.

Athletics Member NCAA, NAIA. All NCAA Division III.

Standardized Tests *Required:* SAT or ACT (for admission).

Costs (2007–08) *Comprehensive fee:* $37,880 includes full-time tuition ($27,500), mandatory fees ($400), and room and board ($9980). Full-time tuition and fees vary according to program. Part-time tuition: $1148 per unit. Part-time tuition and fees vary according to course load and program. *Room and board:* Room and board charges vary according to housing facility.

Financial Aid Of all full-time matriculated undergraduates who enrolled in 2006, 429 applied for aid, 396 were judged to have need, 35 had their need fully met. 237 Federal Work-Study jobs (averaging $1000). In 2006, 173 non-need-based awards were made. *Average percent of need met:* 70. *Average financial aid package:* $19,677. *Average need-based loan:* $3285. *Average need-based gift aid:* $16,643. *Average non-need-based aid:* $10,355. *Average indebtedness upon graduation:* $26,243.

Applying *Options:* electronic application, early admission, early action, deferred entrance. *Application fee:* $40. *Required:* essay or personal statement, high school transcript, 1 letter of recommendation. *Recommended:* minimum 3.0 GPA, interview.

Freshman Application Contact Mr. Ken Bowman, Director of Admission, Menlo College, 1000 El Camino Real, Atherton, CA 94027. *Phone:* 650-543-3932. *Toll-free phone:* 800-556-3656. *Fax:* 650-543-4496. *E-mail:* admissions@menlo.edu.

See page 450 for the College Close-Up.

MILLS COLLEGE

Oakland, California **www.mills.edu/**

- **Independent** comprehensive, founded 1852
- **Urban** 135-acre campus with easy access to San Francisco
- **Endowment** $233.7 million
- **Undergraduate: women only; graduate: coed** 941 undergraduate students, 94% full-time, 100% women
- **Moderately difficult** entrance level, 64% of applicants were admitted

Mills College offers a creative learning environment that supports intellectual exploration. Students can participate with faculty members in meaningful work and engage with distinguished professors, thinkers, writers, and artists. Set on a lush 135-acre park-like campus, Mills provides convenient access to the cultural, artistic, social, and professional worlds of the metropolitan San Francisco Bay Area.

Undergraduates 887 full-time, 54 part-time. Students come from 45 states and territories, 16 other countries, 20% are from out of state, 10% African American, 8% Asian American or Pacific Islander, 15% Hispanic American, 1% Native American, 2% international, 13% transferred in, 56% live on campus. *Retention:* 74% of 2006 full-time freshmen returned.

Freshmen *Admission:* 1,098 applied, 707 admitted, 197 enrolled. *Average high school GPA:* 3.61. *Test scores:* SAT critical reading scores over 500: 81%; SAT math scores over 500: 71%; SAT writing scores over 500: 80%; ACT scores over 18: 96%; SAT critical reading scores over 600: 47%; SAT math scores over 600: 31%; SAT writing scores over 600: 42%; ACT scores over 24: 60%; SAT critical reading scores over 700: 12%; SAT math scores over 700: 3%; SAT writing scores over 700: 5%; ACT scores over 30: 14%.

Faculty *Total:* 187, 48% full-time, 73% with terminal degrees. *Student/faculty ratio:* 11:1.

Majors American studies; anthropology; art; art history, criticism and conservation; biochemistry; biology/biological sciences; business/managerial economics; chemistry; comparative literature; computer science; creative writing; cultural studies; dance; developmental and child psychology; economics; engineering; English; environmental science; environmental studies; fine/studio arts; French; French studies; Hispanic-American, Puerto Rican, and Mexican-American/Chicano studies; history; interdisciplinary studies; intermedia/multimedia; international relations and affairs; liberal arts and sciences/liberal studies; mathematics; music; philosophy; physiological psychology/psychobiology; political science and government; psychology; public policy analysis; sociology; Spanish; women's studies.

Academics *Calendar:* semesters. *Degrees:* certificates, bachelor's, master's, doctoral, and postbachelor's certificates. *Special study options:* adult/continuing education programs, advanced placement credit, double majors, honors programs, independent study, internships, off-campus study, services for LD students, student-designed majors, study abroad.

Computers on Campus 307 computers/terminals are available on campus for general student use. Students can access the following: campus intranet, computer help desk, free student e-mail accounts, online (class) grades, online (class) registration, online (class) schedules, online degree. Campuswide network is available. 100% of college-owned or -operated housing units are wired for high-speed Internet access. Wireless service is available via entire campus.

Student Life *Housing options:* coed, women-only, cooperative, disabled students. Campus housing is university owned. Freshman campus housing is guaranteed. *Activities and organizations:* drama/theater group, student-run newspaper, choral group, class organizations, MECHA, ASA (Asian Sisterhood Alliance), Mills Environmental Organization, BWC (Black Women's Collective). *Campus security:* 24-hour emergency response devices and patrols, late-night transport/escort service, controlled dormitory access. *Student services:* health clinic, personal/psychological counseling, women's center.

Athletics Member NCAA, NAIA. All NCAA Division III. *Intercollegiate sports:* crew W, cross-country running W, soccer W, swimming and diving W, tennis W, volleyball W. *Intramural sports:* basketball W, fencing W, soccer W, softball W, tennis W, volleyball W.

Standardized Tests *Required:* SAT or ACT (for admission). *Recommended:* SAT Subject Tests (for admission).

Costs (2007–08) *Comprehensive fee:* $46,252 includes full-time tuition ($32,542), mandatory fees ($2890), and room and board ($10,820). Full-time tuition and fees vary according to course load. Part-time tuition: $5424 per course. Part-time tuition and fees vary according to course load. *College room only:* $5790. Room and board charges vary according to board plan and housing facility. *Payment plan:* installment. *Waivers:* employees or children of employees.

Financial Aid Of all full-time matriculated undergraduates who enrolled in 2005, 731 applied for aid, 673 were judged to have need, 117 had their need fully met. In 2005, 77 non-need-based awards were made. *Average percent of need met:* 83%. *Average financial aid package:* $24,002. *Average need-based loan:* $5490. *Average need-based gift aid:* $18,210. *Average non-need-based aid:* $8100. *Average indebtedness upon graduation:* $19,206. *Financial aid deadline:* 2/15.

Applying *Options:* electronic application, early action, deferred entrance. *Application fee:* $50. *Required:* high school transcript, 2 letters of recommendation, essay or graded paper. *Recommended:* interview. *Application deadlines:* 5/1 (freshmen), 3/1 (transfers), 11/15 (early action). *Notification:* 3/30 (freshmen), 4/1 (transfers), 12/15 (early action).

Freshman Application Contact Ms. Giulietta Aquino, Vice President of Enrollment Management, Mills College, 5000 MacArthur Boulevard, Oakland, CA 94613-1301. *Phone:* 510-430-2135. *Toll-free phone:* 800-87-MILLS. *Fax:* 510-430-3314. *E-mail:* admission@mills.edu.

See page 452 for the College Close-Up.

MOUNT ST. MARY'S COLLEGE

Los Angeles, California **www.msmc.la.edu/**

- **Independent Roman Catholic** comprehensive, founded 1925, administratively affiliated with Sister of St. Joseph Carondelet
- **Suburban** 71-acre campus
- **Endowment** $77.5 million
- **Coed, primarily women** 1,910 undergraduate students, 75% full-time, 93% women, 7% men
- **Moderately difficult** entrance level, 86% of applicants were admitted

Undergraduates 1,441 full-time, 469 part-time. Students come from 13 states and territories, 3% are from out of state, 9% African American, 24% Asian American or Pacific Islander, 45% Hispanic American, 0.5% Native American, 0.1% international, 2% transferred in, 59% live on campus. *Retention:* 72% of 2006 full-time freshmen returned.

Freshmen *Admission:* 1,069 applied, 921 admitted, 376 enrolled. *Average high school GPA:* 3.47.

Faculty *Total:* 318, 26% full-time, 60% with terminal degrees. *Student/faculty ratio:* 14:1.

Majors Accounting; American studies; art; biochemistry; biology/biological sciences; chemistry; developmental and child psychology; education; elementary education; English; French; gerontology; health/health care administration; history; international business/trade/commerce; kindergarten/preschool education; liberal arts and sciences/liberal studies; marketing/marketing management; mathematics; music; philosophy; political science and government; psychology; religious studies; social sciences; social work; sociology; Spanish.

Academics *Calendar:* semesters. *Degrees:* associate, bachelor's, master's, and doctoral. *Special study options:* academic remediation for entering students, accelerated degree program, adult/continuing education programs, advanced placement credit, double majors, English as a second language, freshman honors college, honors programs, independent study, internships, off-campus study, part-time degree program, services for LD students, student-designed majors, study abroad, summer session for credit.

Computers on Campus 125 computers/terminals are available on campus for general student use. Students can access the following: campus intranet, computer help desk, free student e-mail accounts, online (class) grades, online (class) registration, online (class) schedules. Campuswide network is available. 100% of college-owned or -operated housing units are wired for high-speed Internet access. Wireless service is available via entire campus.

Student Life *Housing options:* men-only, women-only. Campus housing is university owned. Freshman applicants given priority for college housing. *Activities and organizations:* drama/theater group, student-run newspaper, choral group, Na Pua O Ka Aina, Pangkat Pilipino, Latinas Unidos, Scholar Mentor Clan, Associated Student Body. *Campus security:* 24-hour patrols, controlled dormitory access. *Student services:* health clinic, personal/psychological counseling.

Athletics *Intramural sports:* badminton M/W, basketball M/W, golf M/W, rock climbing M/W, soccer M/W, swimming and diving M/W, tennis M/W, volleyball M/W.

Standardized Tests *Required:* SAT (for admission), ACT (for admission).

Costs (2008–09) *Comprehensive fee:* $34,978 includes full-time tuition ($24,550), mandatory fees ($808), and room and board ($9620). Part-time tuition: $945 per unit.

Financial Aid Of all full-time matriculated undergraduates who enrolled in 2006, 248 Federal Work-Study jobs (averaging $2531). 22 state and other part-time jobs (averaging $3352). *Financial aid deadline:* 5/15.

Applying *Options:* electronic application, early action, deferred entrance. *Application fee:* $40. *Required:* essay or personal statement, high school transcript, minimum 2.0 GPA, 1 letter of recommendation. *Recommended:* minimum 3.0 GPA, interview. *Application deadlines:* 2/15 (freshmen), 3/15 (transfers), 12/1 (early action). *Notification:* continuous (freshmen), continuous (transfers), 1/1 (early action).

Freshman Application Contact Ms. Shannon Shank, Interim Director of Admissions, Mount St. Mary's College, 12001 Chalon Road, Los Angeles, CA 90049-1599. *Phone:* 310-954-4250. *Toll-free phone:* 800-999-9393. *Fax:* 310-954-4259. *E-mail:* admissions@msmc.la.edu.

MT. SIERRA COLLEGE

Monrovia, California **www.mtsierra.edu/**

Freshman Application Contact Kimberly Rodriguez-Delaney, Director of Admissions, Mt. Sierra College, 101 East Huntington Drive, Monrovia, CA 91016. *Phone:* 626-873-2100. *Toll-free phone:* 888-828-8800. *Fax:* 626-359-5528.

MUSICIANS INSTITUTE

Hollywood, California **www.mi.edu/**

Director of Admissions Mr. Steve Lunn, Admissions Representative, Musicians Institute, 1655 North McCadden Place, Hollywood, CA 90028. *Phone:* 323-462-1384 Ext. 156. *Toll-free phone:* 800-255-PLAY. *E-mail:* admissions@mi.edu.

THE NATIONAL HISPANIC UNIVERSITY

San Jose, California **www.nhu.edu/**

Director of Admissions Ms. Pamela Bustillo, Director of Office of Admissions/Registrar, The National Hispanic University, 14271 Story Road, San Jose, CA 95127-3823. *Phone:* 408-254-6900.

NATIONAL UNIVERSITY

La Jolla, California **www.nu.edu/**

- **Independent** comprehensive, founded 1971, part of National University System
- **Urban** campus
- **Endowment** $334.3 million
- **Coed** 7,417 undergraduate students, 31% full-time, 60% women, 40% men
- **Minimally difficult** entrance level, 58% of applicants were admitted

Undergraduates 2,330 full-time, 5,087 part-time. Students come from 48 states and territories, 74 other countries, 8% are from out of state, 11% African American, 9% Asian American or Pacific Islander, 16% Hispanic American, 0.9% Native American, 1% international. *Retention:* 57% of 2006 full-time freshmen returned.

Freshmen *Admission:* 1,638 applied, 957 admitted, 731 enrolled.

Faculty *Total:* 3,277, 7% full-time, 29% with terminal degrees. *Student/faculty ratio:* 17:1.

Majors Accounting; animation, interactive technology, video graphics and special effects; banking and financial support services; behavioral sciences; biology/biological sciences; business administration and management; child development; computer science; computer software engineering; construction engineering; criminal justice/law enforcement administration; data modeling/warehousing and database administration; drafting/design engineering technologies related; e-commerce; economics; education; English; entrepreneurship; environmental science; finance; general studies; geology/earth science; health science; health services/allied health/health sciences; history; hospitality administration; human resources management; information science/studies; information

COLLEGE DATA CENTER • CALIFORNIA

technology; interdisciplinary studies; intermedia/multimedia; international/global studies; legal studies; management information systems; marketing/marketing management; mathematics; nursing science; occupational safety and health technology; operations management; organizational behavior; pre-law studies; psychology; sociology; sport and fitness administration/management; telecommunications.

Academics *Calendar:* quarters. *Degrees:* certificates, associate, bachelor's, master's, and postbachelor's certificates. *Special study options:* accelerated degree program, adult/continuing education programs, advanced placement credit, distance learning, double majors, English as a second language, independent study, internships, off-campus study, part-time degree program, services for LD students, summer session for credit. *ROTC:* Army (c), Air Force (c).

Computers on Campus 3,100 computers/terminals are available on campus for general student use. Students can access the following: computer help desk, online (class) grades, online (class) registration, online (class) schedules. Campuswide network is available. Wireless service is available via libraries.

Student Life *Housing:* college housing not available. *Activities and organizations:* student-run television station. *Campus security:* 24-hour emergency response devices and patrols, late-night transport/escort service.

Costs (2007–08) *Tuition:* $9720 full-time, $1215 per course part-time. Full-time tuition and fees vary according to course load. Part-time tuition and fees vary according to course load. *Required fees:* $60 full-time. *Waivers:* employees or children of employees.

Financial Aid Of all full-time matriculated undergraduates who enrolled in 2007, 869 applied for aid, 865 were judged to have need, 10 had their need fully met. In 2007, 7 non-need-based awards were made. *Average percent of need met:* 84%. *Average financial aid package:* $9631. *Average need-based loan:* $9982. *Average need-based gift aid:* $9679. *Average non-need-based aid:* $7006. *Average indebtedness upon graduation:* $31,057.

Applying *Options:* electronic application, deferred entrance. *Application fee:* $60. *Required:* high school transcript, minimum 2.0 GPA, interview. *Required for some:* essay or personal statement. *Application deadlines:* rolling (freshmen), rolling (out-of-state freshmen), rolling (transfers). *Notification:* continuous (freshmen), continuous (out-of-state freshmen), continuous (transfers).

Freshman Application Contact Mr. Dominick Giovanniello, Associate Regional Dean, San Diego, National University, 11255 North Torrey Pines Road, La Jolla, CA 92037. *Phone:* 800-628-8648 Ext. 7701. *Toll-free phone:* 800-NAT-UNIV. *Fax:* 858-541-7792. *E-mail:* dgiovann@nu.edu.

NEWSCHOOL OF ARCHITECTURE & DESIGN

San Diego, California **www.newschoolarch.edu/**

Freshman Application Contact Ms. Lexi Rogers, Director of Admissions, Newschool of Architecture & Design, 1249 F Street, San Diego, CA 92101-6634. *Phone:* 619-235-4100 Ext. 106.

NORTHWESTERN POLYTECHNIC UNIVERSITY

Fremont, California **www.npu.edu/**

- **Independent** comprehensive, founded 1984
- **Urban** 2-acre campus with easy access to San Francisco and San Jose
- **Coed**
- 100% of applicants were admitted

Faculty *Student/faculty ratio:* 12:1.

Academics *Calendar:* trimesters. *Degrees:* bachelor's, master's, and doctoral.

Student Life *Campus security:* late-night transport/escort service.

Standardized Tests *Recommended:* SAT (for admission).

Costs (2007–08) *Tuition:* $7200 full-time, $300 per unit part-time. Full-time tuition and fees vary according to course load. Part-time tuition and fees vary according to course load. *Required fees:* $140 full-time, $70 per term part-time. *Room only:* $4500. Room and board charges vary according to housing facility.

Applying *Options:* electronic application. *Application fee:* $60. *Required:* high school transcript, minimum 2.0 GPA. *Required for some:* essay or personal statement, interview. *Recommended:* interview.

Freshman Application Contact Ms. Catherine Meng, Admission Officer, Northwestern Polytechnic University, 117 Fourier Avenue, Fremont, CA 94539. *Phone:* 510-657-5913. *Fax:* 510-657-8975. *E-mail:* admission@npu.edu.

NOTRE DAME DE NAMUR UNIVERSITY

Belmont, California **www.ndnu.edu/**

- **Independent Roman Catholic** comprehensive, founded 1851
- **Suburban** 80-acre campus with easy access to San Francisco
- **Endowment** $12.4 million
- **Coed** 749 undergraduate students, 70% full-time, 67% women, 33% men
- **Minimally difficult** entrance level, 99% of applicants were admitted

Undergraduates 521 full-time, 228 part-time. Students come from 26 states and territories, 10 other countries, 15% are from out of state, 5% African American, 15% Asian American or Pacific Islander, 20% Hispanic American, 0.5% Native American, 3% international, 11% transferred in, 50% live on campus. *Retention:* 72% of 2006 full-time freshmen returned.

Freshmen *Admission:* 503 applied, 498 admitted, 96 enrolled. *Average high school GPA:* 2.86. *Test scores:* SAT critical reading scores over 500: 49%; SAT math scores over 500: 38%; SAT writing scores over 500: 47%; ACT scores over 18: 76%; SAT critical reading scores over 600: 6%; SAT math scores over 600: 12%; SAT writing scores over 600: 10%; ACT scores over 24: 15%.

Faculty *Total:* 159, 36% full-time. *Student/faculty ratio:* 11:1.

Majors Art; biochemistry; biology/biological sciences; business administration and management; communication and journalism related; communication/speech communication and rhetoric; computer and information sciences; dramatic/theater arts; education; elementary education; English; fine/studio arts; history; human services; kinesiology and exercise science; liberal arts and sciences/liberal studies; music; music performance; philosophy; piano and organ; political science and government; pre-dentistry studies; pre-law studies; pre-medical studies; psychology; religious studies; sculpture; social sciences; sociology; voice and opera.

Academics *Calendar:* semesters. *Degrees:* bachelor's, master's, and postbachelor's certificates. *Special study options:* academic remediation for entering students, accelerated degree program, adult/continuing education programs, advanced placement credit, cooperative education, double majors, English as a second language, independent study, internships, off-campus study, part-time degree program, services for LD students, student-designed majors, study abroad, summer session for credit.

Computers on Campus 60 computers/terminals and 10 ports are available on campus for general student use. Students can access the following: campus intranet, computer help desk, free student e-mail accounts, online (class) grades, online (class) registration, online (class) schedules. Campuswide network is available. 100% of college-owned or -operated housing units are wired for high-speed Internet access. Wireless service is available via classrooms, computer centers, computer labs, dorm rooms, learning centers, libraries, student centers.

Student Life *Housing:* on-campus residence required through sophomore year. *Options:* coed, women-only. Campus housing is university owned. Freshman applicants given priority for college housing. *Activities and organizations:* drama/theater group, student-run newspaper, choral group, Associated Students of Notre Dame de Namur University, BizCom, Roteract, Argomaniacs, Hawaiian Club. *Campus security:* 24-hour emergency response devices and patrols, student patrols, late-night transport/escort service, controlled dormitory access. *Student services:* health clinic, personal/psychological counseling.

Athletics Member NCAA. All Division II. *Intercollegiate sports:* basketball M (s)/W (s), cross-country running M (s)/W (s), golf M (s)/W (s), lacrosse M/W (s), soccer M (s)/W (s), softball W (s), tennis W (s), volleyball W (s).

Standardized Tests *Required:* SAT or ACT (for admission).

Costs (2008–09) *Comprehensive fee:* $36,250 includes full-time tuition ($25,300), mandatory fees ($270), and room and board ($10,680). Part-time tuition: $545 per unit. *Required fees:* $30 per term part-time. *College room only:* $7000.

Applying *Options:* electronic application, early action, deferred entrance. *Application fee:* $50. *Required:* essay or personal statement, high school transcript, letters of recommendation, audition is required for music programs. *Required for some:* interview. *Application deadlines:* rolling (freshmen), rolling (transfers). *Notification:* continuous (freshmen), continuous (transfers).

Freshman Application Contact Mr. Brian O'Rourke, Associate Director for Undergraduate Admission, Notre Dame de Namur University, 1500 Ralston Avenue, Belmont, CA 94002-1997. *Phone:* 650-508-3589. *Toll-free phone:* 800-263-0545. *Fax:* 650-508-3426. *E-mail:* Borourke@ndnu.edu.

Occidental College

Los Angeles, California www.oxy.edu/

- **Independent** comprehensive, founded 1887
- **Urban** 120-acre campus
- **Endowment** $377.0 million
- **Coed** 1,863 undergraduate students, 99% full-time, 56% women, 44% men
- **Very difficult** entrance level, 44% of applicants were admitted

Undergraduates 1,836 full-time, 27 part-time. Students come from 47 states and territories, 22 other countries, 51% are from out of state, 6% African American, 13% Asian American or Pacific Islander, 15% Hispanic American, 1% Native American, 2% international, 3% transferred in, 70% live on campus. *Retention:* 92% of 2006 full-time freshmen returned.

Freshmen *Admission:* 5,275 applied, 2,328 admitted, 458 enrolled. *Average high school GPA:* 3.57. *Test scores:* SAT critical reading scores over 500: 97%; SAT math scores over 500: 97%; SAT writing scores over 500: 97%; ACT scores over 18: 100%; SAT critical reading scores over 600: 74%; SAT math scores over 600: 77%; SAT writing scores over 600: 71%; ACT scores over 24: 87%; SAT critical reading scores over 700: 26%; SAT math scores over 700: 20%; SAT writing scores over 700: 21%; ACT scores over 30: 51%.

Faculty *Total:* 227, 69% full-time. *Student/faculty ratio:* 10:1.

Majors American studies; anthropology; art history, criticism and conservation; Asian studies; biochemistry; biology/biological sciences; business/managerial economics; chemistry; cognitive psychology and psycholinguistics; cognitive science; comparative literature; dramatic/theater arts; economics; English; fine/studio arts; French; geology/earth science; geophysics and seismology; history; international relations and affairs; kinesiology and exercise science; mathematics; music; philosophy; physics; physiological psychology/psychobiology; political science and government; psychology; public policy analysis; religious studies; sociology; Spanish; women's studies.

Academics *Calendar:* semesters. *Degrees:* bachelor's and master's. *Special study options:* advanced placement credit, double majors, honors programs, independent study, internships, off-campus study, services for LD students, student-designed majors, study abroad, summer session for credit. *ROTC:* Army (c), Air Force (c). *Unusual degree programs:* 3-2 engineering with California Institute of Technology, Columbia University; law, Columbia University.

Computers on Campus 300 computers/terminals are available on campus for general student use. Students can access the following: computer help desk, free student e-mail accounts, online (class) grades, online (class) registration, online (class) schedules. Campuswide network is available. Wireless service is available via classrooms, computer centers, computer labs, dorm rooms, libraries, student centers.

Student Life *Housing:* on-campus residence required for freshman year. *Options:* coed, women-only. Campus housing is university owned. Freshman campus housing is guaranteed. *Activities and organizations:* drama/theater group, student-run newspaper, radio station, choral group, Black Student Alliance, MEChA/ALAS, Asian Pacific Islander Association, Intervarsity Christian Fellowship, Men's Rugby, national fraternities, national sororities. *Campus security:* 24-hour emergency response devices and patrols, late-night transport/escort service, controlled dormitory access, lighted pathways and sidewalks; whistle alert program. *Student services:* health clinic, personal/psychological counseling, women's center, legal services.

Athletics Member NCAA. All Division III. *Intercollegiate sports:* baseball M, basketball M/W, cheerleading W (c), crew W (c), cross-country running M/W, football M, golf M/W, lacrosse M (c)/W (c), rugby M (c)/W (c), soccer M/W, softball W, swimming and diving M/W, tennis M/W, track and field M/W, ultimate Frisbee M (c)/W (c), volleyball M (c)/W, water polo M/W. *Intramural sports:* basketball M/W, football M/W, volleyball M/W.

Standardized Tests *Required:* SAT or ACT (for admission). *Recommended:* SAT Subject Tests (for admission).

Costs (2008–09) *Comprehensive fee:* $47,363 includes full-time tuition ($36,160), mandatory fees ($933), and room and board ($10,270). Part-time tuition: $1510 per credit. *College room only:* $5840.

Financial Aid Of all full-time matriculated undergraduates who enrolled in 2007, 1,066 applied for aid, 933 were judged to have need, 931 had their need fully met. 684 Federal Work-Study jobs (averaging $2568). 70 state and other part-time jobs (averaging $2581). In 2007, 498 non-need-based awards were made. *Average percent of need met:* 100%. *Average financial aid package:* $32,991. *Average need-based loan:* $6012. *Average need-based gift aid:* $26,015. *Average non-need-based aid:* $12,889. *Average indebtedness upon graduation:* $19,695. *Financial aid deadline:* 2/1.

Applying *Options:* electronic application, early admission, early decision, deferred entrance. *Application fee:* $50. *Required:* essay or personal statement, high school transcript, 2 letters of recommendation. *Recommended:* interview. *Application deadlines:* 1/10 (freshmen), 3/15 (transfers). *Early decision deadline:* 11/15. *Notification:* 4/1 (freshmen), 5/1 (transfers), 12/15 (early decision).

Freshman Application Contact Mr. Vince Cuseo, Dean of Admission, Occidental College, 1600 Campus Road, Los Angeles, CA 90041. *Phone:* 323-259-2700. *Toll-free phone:* 800-825-5262. *Fax:* 323-341-4875. *E-mail:* admission@oxy.edu.

Otis College of Art and Design

Los Angeles, California www.otis.edu/

- **Independent** comprehensive, founded 1918
- **Urban** 5-acre campus
- **Coed** 1,121 undergraduate students, 98% full-time, 68% women, 32% men
- **Moderately difficult** entrance level, 42% of applicants were admitted

Undergraduates 1,104 full-time, 17 part-time. Students come from 31 states and territories, 13 other countries, 21% are from out of state, 3% African American, 28% Asian American or Pacific Islander, 14% Hispanic American, 0.5% Native American, 13% international, 15% transferred in, 9% live on campus. *Retention:* 85% of 2006 full-time freshmen returned.

Freshmen *Admission:* 1,113 applied, 473 admitted, 172 enrolled. *Average high school GPA:* 3.17. *Test scores:* SAT critical reading scores over 500: 45%; SAT math scores over 500: 57%; SAT writing scores over 500: 46%; ACT scores over 18: 71%; SAT critical reading scores over 600: 12%; SAT math scores over 600: 15%; SAT writing scores over 600: 11%; ACT scores over 24: 17%; SAT critical reading scores over 700: 1%; SAT math scores over 700: 1%.

Faculty *Total:* 271, 22% full-time, 7% with terminal degrees. *Student/faculty ratio:* 9:1.

Majors Applied art; art; commercial and advertising art; drawing; environmental design/architecture; fashion/apparel design; fine/studio arts; interior design; photography; sculpture.

Academics *Calendar:* semesters. *Degrees:* bachelor's and master's. *Special study options:* academic remediation for entering students, adult/continuing education programs, advanced placement credit, cooperative education, English as a second language, freshman honors college, honors programs, independent study, internships, off-campus study, study abroad, summer session for credit.

Computers on Campus 240 computers/terminals are available on campus for general student use. Students can access the following: campus intranet, computer help desk, free student e-mail accounts, online (class) grades, online (class) registration, online (class) schedules. Campuswide network is available. Wireless service is available via entire campus.

Student Life *Housing options:* coed. Campus housing is provided by a third party. Freshman applicants given priority for college housing. *Activities and organizations:* student-run newspaper, Student Government Association, international students organization, Otis Students in Service (OASIS), Literary Magazine Club, Campus Crusade. *Campus security:* 24-hour patrols. *Student services:* personal/psychological counseling.

Athletics *Intramural sports:* skiing (downhill) W, soccer M.

Standardized Tests *Required:* SAT or ACT (for admission).

Costs (2007–08) *Tuition:* $28,346 full-time, $945 per credit part-time. *Required fees:* $600 full-time. *Payment plan:* deferred payment. *Waivers:* employees or children of employees.

Financial Aid Of all full-time matriculated undergraduates who enrolled in 2007, 854 applied for aid, 766 were judged to have need, 8 had their need fully met. 298 Federal Work-Study jobs (averaging $2182). 16 state and other part-time jobs (averaging $1062). In 2007, 108 non-need-based awards were made. *Average percent of need met:* 49%. *Average financial aid package:* $16,413. *Average need-based loan:* $4256. *Average need-based gift aid:* $8414. *Average non-need-based aid:* $5160. *Average indebtedness upon graduation:* $37,089.

Applying *Options:* electronic application. *Application fee:* $50. *Required:* essay or personal statement, high school transcript, minimum 2.5 GPA, portfolio. *Recommended:* letters of recommendation, interview. *Application deadlines:* rolling (freshmen), rolling (transfers). *Notification:* continuous (freshmen), continuous (transfers).

Director of Admissions Mr. Marc D. Meredith, Dean of Admissions, Otis College of Art and Design, 9045 Lincoln Boulevard, Los Angeles, CA 90045-9785. *Phone:* 310-665-6820. *Toll-free phone:* 800-527-OTIS. *E-mail:* otisinfo@otisart.edu.

See page 454 for the College Close-Up.

PACIFIC OAKS COLLEGE

Pasadena, California **www.pacificoaks.edu/**

- **Independent** upper-level, founded 1945
- **Small-town** 2-acre campus with easy access to Los Angeles
- **Endowment** $7.3 million
- **Coed, primarily women**
- 77% of applicants were admitted

Faculty *Student/faculty ratio:* 22:1.

Academics *Calendar:* semesters summer sessions and 2 intensive sessions. *Degrees:* bachelor's, master's, post-master's, and postbachelor's certificates.

Costs (2007–08) *Tuition:* $19,080 full-time, $795 per unit part-time. *Required fees:* $60 full-time, $30 per term part-time.

Financial Aid Of all full-time matriculated undergraduates who enrolled in 2006, 11 Federal Work-Study jobs (averaging $5000).

Applying *Options:* deferred entrance. *Application fee:* $55.

Application Contact Ms. Augusta Pickens, Office of Admissions, Pacific Oaks College, 5 Westmoreland Place, Pasadena, CA 91103. *Phone:* 626-397-1349. *Toll-free phone:* 800-684-0900. *Fax:* 626-666-1220. *E-mail:* admissions@pacificoaks.edu.

PACIFIC STATES UNIVERSITY

Los Angeles, California **www.psuca.edu/**

- **Independent** comprehensive, founded 1928
- **Urban** 1-acre campus
- **Coed** 44 undergraduate students
- **Minimally difficult** entrance level, 100% of applicants were admitted

Undergraduates 10% are from out of state, 100% Asian American or Pacific Islander. *Retention:* 75% of 2006 full-time freshmen returned.

Freshmen *Admission:* 50 applied, 50 admitted. *Average high school GPA:* 2.2.

Faculty *Total:* 16, 25% full-time, 63% with terminal degrees. *Student/faculty ratio:* 20:1.

Majors Business administration and management; computer science; electrical, electronics and communications engineering.

Academics *Calendar:* quarters. *Degrees:* bachelor's and master's. *Special study options:* accelerated degree program, adult/continuing education programs, English as a second language, independent study, student-designed majors, study abroad, summer session for credit.

Computers on Campus 25 computers/terminals are available on campus for general student use.

Student Life *Housing:* college housing not available. *Campus security:* patrols by trained security personnel during campus hours.

Costs (2007–08) *Tuition:* $8400 full-time, $195 per unit part-time. Full-time tuition and fees vary according to course load. Part-time tuition and fees vary according to course load and program. *Required fees:* $460 full-time. *Payment plans:* tuition prepayment, installment, deferred payment.

Applying *Options:* electronic application, early admission, deferred entrance. *Application fee:* $100. *Required:* essay or personal statement, high school transcript, minimum 2.5 GPA. *Application deadlines:* 9/21 (freshmen), 10/27 (transfers). *Notification:* continuous (freshmen).

Freshman Application Contact Ms. Marina Miller, Assistant Director of Admissions, Pacific States University, 1516 South Western Avenue, Los Angeles, CA 90006. *Phone:* 323-731-2383. *Toll-free phone:* 888-200-0383. *Fax:* 323-731-7276. *E-mail:* admission@psuca.edu.

PACIFIC UNION COLLEGE

Angwin, California **www.puc.edu/**

- **Independent Seventh-day Adventist** 4-year, founded 1882
- **Rural** 200-acre campus with easy access to San Francisco
- **Endowment** $19.3 million
- **Coed** 1,372 undergraduate students, 89% full-time, 54% women, 46% men
- **Moderately difficult** entrance level, 75% of applicants were admitted

Undergraduates 1,227 full-time, 145 part-time. Students come from 41 states and territories, 30 other countries, 19% are from out of state, 3% African American, 26% Asian American or Pacific Islander, 15% Hispanic American, 0.4% Native American, 7% international, 8% transferred in, 69% live on campus. *Retention:* 73% of 2006 full-time freshmen returned.

Freshmen *Admission:* 1,706 applied, 1,282 admitted, 274 enrolled. *Average high school GPA:* 3.19. *Test scores:* SAT critical reading scores over 500: 61%; SAT math scores over 500: 56%; ACT scores over 18: 75%; SAT critical reading scores over 600: 21%; SAT math scores over 600: 19%; ACT scores over 24: 32%; SAT critical reading scores over 700: 4%; SAT math scores over 700: 3%; ACT scores over 30: 2%.

Faculty *Total:* 96, 92% full-time, 51% with terminal degrees. *Student/faculty ratio:* 15:1.

Majors Accounting; applied mathematics; art; art history, criticism and conservation; behavioral sciences; biblical studies; biochemistry; biology/biological sciences; biophysics; business administration and management; business teacher education; chemistry; child care and support services management; child care provision; clinical laboratory science/medical technology; computer and information sciences; computer management; computer programming; computer science; data processing and data processing technology; drafting and design technology; education; education (K-12); electrical, electronic and communications engineering technology; elementary education; engineering; engineering related; engineering technology; English; finance; fine/studio arts; history; information science/studies; interdisciplinary studies; international business/trade/commerce; journalism; kindergarten/preschool education; kinesiology and exercise science; legal administrative assistant/secretary; management information systems; marketing/marketing management; mass communication/media; mathematics; medical administrative assistant and medical secretary; music; music teacher education; nursing (registered nurse training); parks, recreation and leisure; pastoral studies/counseling; photography; physical education teaching and coaching; physical sciences; physics; piano and organ; political science and government; pre-dentistry studies; pre-law studies; pre-medical studies; pre-veterinary studies; psychology; public relations/image management; religious studies; social sciences; social work; sociology; Spanish; theology.

Academics *Calendar:* quarters. *Degrees:* associate, bachelor's, and master's. *Special study options:* academic remediation for entering students, adult/continuing education programs, advanced placement credit, cooperative education, distance learning, double majors, honors programs, independent study, internships, off-campus study, part-time degree program, services for LD students, student-designed majors, study abroad, summer session for credit.

Computers on Campus 150 computers/terminals and 1,200 ports are available on campus for general student use. Students can access the following: campus intranet, computer help desk, free student e-mail accounts, online (class) grades, online (class) registration, online (class) schedules. Campuswide network is available. Wireless service is available via classrooms.

Student Life *Housing options:* men-only, women-only. Campus housing is university owned. *Activities and organizations:* drama/theater group, student-run newspaper, radio station, choral group, Student Association, Business Club, Asian Student Association, Korean Adventist Student Association, Black Student Forum. *Campus security:* 24-hour emergency response devices and patrols, late-night transport/escort service. *Student services:* health clinic, personal/psychological counseling.

Athletics Member NAIA. *Intercollegiate sports:* basketball M/W, cross-country running M/W, volleyball M/W. *Intramural sports:* badminton M/W, baseball M/W, basketball M/W, cross-country running M/W, football M/W, golf M/W, soccer M/W, softball M/W, tennis M/W, volleyball M/W.

Standardized Tests *Required:* SAT or ACT (for admission).

Costs (2007–08) *Comprehensive fee:* $27,390 includes full-time tuition ($21,300), mandatory fees ($135), and room and board ($5955). Full-time tuition and fees vary according to course load. Part-time tuition: $620 per quarter hour. Part-time tuition and fees vary according to course load. No tuition increase for student's term of enrollment. *Required fees:* $45 per term part-time. *College room only:* $3630. *Payment plan:* installment. *Waivers:* senior citizens and employees or children of employees.

Financial Aid Of all full-time matriculated undergraduates who enrolled in 2007, 1,033 applied for aid, 677 were judged to have need, 180 had their need fully met. 171 Federal Work-Study jobs (averaging $800). In 2007, 32 non-need-based awards were made. *Average percent of need met:* 70%. *Average financial aid package:* $12,755. *Average need-based gift aid:* $7155. *Average non-need-based aid:* $8608. *Average indebtedness upon graduation:* $17,500.

Applying *Options:* electronic application, deferred entrance. *Application fee:* $30. *Required:* high school transcript, minimum 2.3 GPA, 3 letters of recommendation. *Application deadlines:* rolling (freshmen), rolling (transfers).

Freshman Application Contact Mr. Darren Hagen, Director of Enrollment Services, Pacific Union College, Enrollment Services, One Angwin Avenue, Angwin, CA 94508. *Phone:* 707-965-6425. *Toll-free phone:* 800-862-7080. *Fax:* 707-965-6432. *E-mail:* enroll@puc.edu.

PATTEN UNIVERSITY

Oakland, California **www.patten.edu/**

- **Independent interdenominational** comprehensive, founded 1944
- **Urban** 5-acre campus with easy access to San Francisco
- **Endowment** $1.3 million
- **Coed**
- **Noncompetitive** entrance level

Faculty *Student/faculty ratio:* 14:1.

Academics *Calendar:* semesters. *Degrees:* certificates, associate, bachelor's, master's, and postbachelor's certificates.

Student Life *Campus security:* 24-hour emergency response devices, student patrols, late-night transport/escort service.

Athletics Member NAIA.

Standardized Tests *Required:* SAT or ACT (for admission).

Costs (2008–09) *Comprehensive fee:* $19,460 includes full-time tuition ($12,480) and room and board ($6980). Part-time tuition: $520 per unit.

Applying *Options:* early admission, deferred entrance. *Application fee:* $30. *Required:* essay or personal statement, high school transcript, minimum 2.5 GPA, 2 letters of recommendation. *Recommended:* interview.

Freshman Application Contact Ms. Kim Guerra, Patten University, 2433 Coolidge Avenue, Oakland, CA 94601. *Phone:* 510-261-8500 Ext. 7763. *Fax:* 510-534-4344.

PEPPERDINE UNIVERSITY

Malibu, California **www.pepperdine.edu/**

- **Independent** university, founded 1937, affiliated with Church of Christ
- **Small-town** 830-acre campus with easy access to Los Angeles
- **Endowment** $625.5 million
- **Coed** 3,398 undergraduate students, 86% full-time, 55% women, 45% men
- **Very difficult** entrance level, 35% of applicants were admitted

Undergraduates 2,934 full-time, 464 part-time. Students come from 50 states and territories, 64 other countries, 50% are from out of state, 7% African American, 10% Asian American or Pacific Islander, 10% Hispanic American, 1% Native American, 7% international, 1% transferred in, 67% live on campus. *Retention:* 91% of 2006 full-time freshmen returned.

Freshmen *Admission:* 6,661 applied, 2,315 admitted, 752 enrolled. *Average high school GPA:* 3.67. *Test scores:* SAT critical reading scores over 500: 91%; SAT math scores over 500: 92%; SAT writing scores over 500: 92%; ACT scores over 18: 99%; SAT critical reading scores over 600: 58%; SAT math scores over 600: 61%; SAT writing scores over 600: 58%; ACT scores over 24: 78%; SAT critical reading scores over 700: 15%; SAT math scores over 700: 19%; SAT writing scores over 700: 14%; ACT scores over 30: 22%.

Faculty *Total:* 678, 57% full-time, 91% with terminal degrees. *Student/faculty ratio:* 13:1.

Majors Accounting; advertising; art; art history, criticism and conservation; athletic training; biology/biological sciences; business administration and management; chemistry; communication/speech communication and rhetoric; computer science; dramatic/theater arts; dramatic/theater arts and stagecraft related; economics; education; elementary education; English; foods, nutrition, and wellness; French; German; history; humanities; interdisciplinary studies; international business/trade/commerce; international relations and affairs; journalism; kinesiology and exercise science; liberal arts and sciences/liberal studies; mathematics; mathematics teacher education; music; music teacher education; natural sciences; philosophy; physical education teaching and coaching; political science and government; pre-dentistry studies; pre-law studies; pre-medical studies; psychology; public relations/image management; religious education; religious studies; secondary education; sociology; Spanish; speech and rhetoric; telecommunications.

Academics *Calendar:* semesters. *Degrees:* certificates, bachelor's, master's, doctoral, first professional, and post-master's certificates. *Special study options:* advanced placement credit, double majors, honors programs, independent study, internships, part-time degree program, student-designed majors, study abroad, summer session for credit. *ROTC:* Army (c), Air Force (c). *Unusual degree programs:* 3-2 engineering with University of Southern California, Washington University in St. Louis, Boston University.

Computers on Campus 292 computers/terminals are available on campus for general student use. Students can access the following: computer help desk, online (class) grades, online (class) registration. Campuswide network is available. 100% of college-owned or -operated housing units are wired for high-speed Internet access. Wireless service is available via entire campus.

Student Life *Housing:* on-campus residence required through sophomore year. *Options:* men-only, women-only, disabled students. Campus housing is university owned. Freshman campus housing is guaranteed. *Activities and organizations:* drama/theater group, student-run newspaper, radio and television station, choral group, Latino Student Association, Black Student Union, Panhellenic Council, Interfraternity Council, International Justice Mission, national fraternities, national sororities. *Campus security:* 24-hour emergency response devices and patrols, student patrols, late-night transport/escort service, front gate security, 24-hour security in residence halls, controlled access, crime prevention programs. *Student services:* health clinic, personal/psychological counseling.

Athletics Member NCAA. All Division I. *Intercollegiate sports:* baseball M (s), basketball M (s)/W (s), cheerleading M/W, crew M (c)/W (c), cross-country running M (s)/W (s), field hockey W (c), golf M (s)/W (s), lacrosse M (c), rugby M (c), sailing M (c)/W (c), soccer M (c)/W (s), swimming and diving W (s), tennis M (s)/W (s), volleyball M (s)/W (s), water polo M (s)/W (c). *Intramural sports:* badminton M/W, basketball M/W, cross-country running M/W, football M/W, golf M/W, lacrosse M, soccer M/W, softball M/W, swimming and diving M/W, tennis M/W, volleyball M/W.

Standardized Tests *Required:* SAT or ACT (for admission).

Costs (2007–08) *Comprehensive fee:* $44,630 includes full-time tuition ($34,580), mandatory fees ($120), and room and board ($9930). Part-time tuition: $1070 per unit. *Room and board:* Room and board charges vary according to board plan and housing facility. *Payment plans:* installment, deferred payment. *Waivers:* employees or children of employees.

Financial Aid Of all full-time matriculated undergraduates who enrolled in 2005, 1,896 applied for aid, 1,350 were judged to have need, 553 had their need fully met. 785 Federal Work-Study jobs (averaging $1809). 284 state and other part-time jobs (averaging $1999). In 2005, 405 non-need-based awards were made. *Average percent of need met:* 89%. *Average financial aid package:* $30,991. *Average need-based loan:* $9684. *Average need-based gift aid:* $20,855. *Average non-need-based aid:* $18,720. *Average indebtedness upon graduation:* $31,848. *Financial aid deadline:* 2/15.

Applying *Options:* electronic application. *Application fee:* $65. *Required:* essay or personal statement, high school transcript, 2 letters of recommendation. *Recommended:* interview. *Application deadlines:* 1/15 (freshmen), 1/15 (transfers). *Notification:* 4/1 (freshmen), 4/1 (transfers).

Freshman Application Contact Mr. Paul A. Long, Dean of Admission and Enrollment Management, Pepperdine University, 24255 Pacific Coast Highway, Malibu, CA 90263-4392. *Phone:* 310-506-4392. *Fax:* 310-506-4861. *E-mail:* admission-seaver@pepperdine.edu.

PITZER COLLEGE

Claremont, California **www.pitzer.edu/**

- **Independent** 4-year, founded 1963, part of The Claremont Colleges Consortium
- **Suburban** 35-acre campus with easy access to Los Angeles
- **Endowment** $106.4 million
- **Coed** 999 undergraduate students, 96% full-time, 59% women, 41% men
- **Moderately difficult** entrance level, 26% of applicants were admitted

Undergraduates 958 full-time, 41 part-time. Students come from 42 states and territories, 13 other countries, 41% are from out of state, 6% African American, 10% Asian American or Pacific Islander, 14% Hispanic American, 0.3% Native American, 3% international, 2% transferred in, 78% live on campus. *Retention:* 94% of 2006 full-time freshmen returned.

Freshmen *Admission:* 3,748 applied, 983 admitted, 243 enrolled. *Average high school GPA:* 3.72.

Faculty *Total:* 97, 66% full-time, 86% with terminal degrees. *Student/faculty ratio:* 12:1.

Majors African-American/Black studies; American studies; anthropology; art; art history, criticism and conservation; Asian-American studies; Asian studies; biochemistry; biology/biological sciences; chemistry; classics; classics and languages, literatures and linguistics; creative writing; dance; dramatic/theater arts; ecology; economics; engineering; English; environmental science; environmental studies; European studies; film/cinema studies; fine/studio arts; foreign languages and literatures; French; German; Hispanic-American, Puerto Rican, and Mexican-American/Chicano studies; history; interdisciplinary studies; international/global studies; international relations and affairs; Latin American studies; linguistics; literature; mathematics; molecular biology; music; neuroscience; organizational behavior; philosophy; physics; political science and government; pre-medical studies; psychology; regional studies; religious studies; Romance languages; Russian; science, technology and society; sociology; Spanish; women's studies.

Academics *Calendar:* semesters. *Degree:* bachelor's. *Special study options:* adult/continuing education programs, advanced placement credit, cooperative education, double majors, English as a second language, honors programs, independent study, internships, off-campus study, part-time degree program, services for LD students, student-designed majors, study abroad, summer session for credit. *ROTC:* Army (c), Air Force (c). *Unusual degree programs:* 3-2 business administration; public administration, mathematics, psychology with Claremont Graduate University.

Computers on Campus 100 computers/terminals are available on campus for general student use. Students can access the following: campus intranet, computer help desk, free student e-mail accounts. Campuswide network is available. 100% of college-owned or -operated housing units are wired for high-speed Internet access. Wireless service is available via entire campus.

Student Life *Housing:* on-campus residence required for freshman year. *Options:* coed, women-only, cooperative, disabled students. Campus housing is university owned. Freshman campus housing is guaranteed. *Activities and organizations:* drama/theater group, student-run radio station, choral group, Student Senate, The Other Side, Without A Box, Residence Hall Association. *Campus security:* 24-hour emergency response devices and patrols, late-night transport/escort service, controlled dormitory access. *Student services:* health clinic, personal/psychological counseling, women's center.

Athletics Member NCAA. All Division III. *Intercollegiate sports:* baseball M, basketball M/W, cross-country running M/W, football M, golf M, lacrosse W, soccer M/W, softball W, swimming and diving M/W, tennis M/W, track and field M/W, volleyball W, water polo M/W. *Intramural sports:* badminton M/W, baseball M, basketball M/W, fencing M (c)/W (c), football M, lacrosse M (c)/W (c), rugby M (c), sailing M (c)/W (c), skiing (downhill) M (c)/W (c), soccer M/W, softball W, tennis M/W, track and field M/W, ultimate Frisbee M/W, volleyball M (c)/W, water polo M (c)/W (c).

Standardized Tests *Required for some:* SAT or ACT (for admission).

Costs (2007–08) *Comprehensive fee:* $46,124 includes full-time tuition ($32,704), mandatory fees ($3208), and room and board ($10,212). Full-time tuition and fees vary according to course load. Part-time tuition: $4088 per course. Part-time tuition and fees vary according to course load. *College room only:* $6456. Room and board charges vary according to board plan. *Payment plans:* installment, deferred payment. *Waivers:* employees or children of employees.

Financial Aid Of all full-time matriculated undergraduates who enrolled in 2007, 400 applied for aid, 349 were judged to have need, 349 had their need fully met. 302 Federal Work-Study jobs (averaging $2402). In 2007, 53 non-need-based awards were made. *Average percent of need met:* 100%. *Average financial aid package:* $31,956. *Average need-based loan:* $4328. *Average need-based gift aid:* $26,747. *Average non-need-based aid:* $5849. *Average indebtedness upon graduation:* $24,790. *Financial aid deadline:* 2/1.

Applying *Options:* electronic application, early decision, deferred entrance. *Application fee:* $50. *Required:* essay or personal statement, high school transcript, minimum 2.0 GPA, 3 letters of recommendation. *Recommended:* interview. *Application deadlines:* 1/1 (freshmen), 4/15 (transfers). *Early decision deadline:* 11/15. *Notification:* 4/1 (freshmen), 5/15 (transfers), 1/1 (early decision).

Freshman Application Contact Angel Perez, Director of Admission, Pitzer College, 1050 North Mills Avenue, Claremont, CA 91711-6101. *Phone:* 909-621-8129. *Toll-free phone:* 800-748-9371. *Fax:* 909-621-8770. *E-mail:* admission@pitzer.edu.

See page 456 for the College Close-Up.

PLATT COLLEGE

Huntington Beach, California **www.plattcollege.edu/**

Director of Admissions Ms. Lisa Rhodes, President, Platt College, 3901 MacArthur Boulevard, Suite 101, Newport Beach, CA 92660. *Phone:* 949-833-2300 Ext. 222. *Toll-free phone:* 888-866-6697 Ext. 230.

PLATT COLLEGE SAN DIEGO

San Diego, California **www.platt.edu/**

- **Proprietary** primarily 2-year, founded 1879
- **Suburban** campus with easy access to San Diego
- **Coed**

Faculty *Student/faculty ratio:* 15:1.

Academics *Calendar:* continuous. *Degrees:* certificates, diplomas, associate, and bachelor's.

Student Life *Campus security:* 24-hour emergency response devices, surveillance cameras.

Costs (2007–08) *Tuition:* $15,180 full-time. Full-time tuition and fees vary according to program. *Required fees:* $110 full-time. *Payment plans:* tuition prepayment, installment.

Applying *Application fee:* $110. *Required:* high school transcript, interview, Wonderlic aptitude test. *Recommended:* essay or personal statement.

Freshman Application Contact Mr. Craig Hinson, Admissions Representative, Platt College San Diego, 6250 El Cajon Boulevard, San Diego, CA 92115-3919. *Phone:* 619-265-0107. *Toll-free phone:* 866-752-8826. *Fax:* 619-265-8655. *E-mail:* chinson@platt.edu.

POINT LOMA NAZARENE UNIVERSITY

San Diego, California **www.pointloma.edu/**

- **Independent Nazarene** comprehensive, founded 1902
- **Suburban** 88-acre campus
- **Endowment** $27.5 million
- **Coed** 2,346 undergraduate students, 97% full-time, 61% women, 39% men
- **Moderately difficult** entrance level, 73% of applicants were admitted

Undergraduates 2,277 full-time, 69 part-time. Students come from 37 states and territories, 10 other countries, 21% are from out of state, 2% African American, 6% Asian American or Pacific Islander, 11% Hispanic American, 0.9% Native American, 0.5% international, 6% transferred in, 69% live on campus. *Retention:* 87% of 2006 full-time freshmen returned.

Freshmen *Admission:* 1,757 applied, 1,291 admitted, 531 enrolled. *Average high school GPA:* 3.72. *Test scores:* SAT critical reading scores over 500: 79%; SAT math scores over 500: 80%; ACT scores over 18: 97%; SAT critical reading scores over 600: 37%; SAT math scores over 600: 37%; ACT scores over 24: 54%; SAT critical reading scores over 700: 6%; SAT math scores over 700: 4%; ACT scores over 30: 7%.

Faculty *Total:* 177. *Student/faculty ratio:* 16:1.

Majors Accounting; art; art teacher education; athletic training; biblical studies; biochemistry; biology/biological sciences; broadcast journalism; business administration and management; business/corporate communications; chemistry; child development; communication/speech communication and rhetoric; computer science; development economics and international development; dietetics; dramatic/theater arts; engineering physics; English language and literature related; family and community services; family and consumer sciences/human sciences; fine arts related; foods, nutrition, and wellness; graphic communications; graphic design; health and physical education; history; industrial and organizational psychology; international/global studies; journalism; kinesiology and exercise science; liberal arts and sciences/liberal studies; management information systems; mass communication/media; mathematics; music; music performance; music teacher education; music theory and composition; nursing (registered nurse training); philosophy; philosophy and religious studies related; physics; political science and government; pre-theology/pre-ministerial studies; psychology; religious/sacred music; religious studies related; Romance languages; social sciences; social work; sociology; Spanish; theological and ministerial studies related; youth ministry.

Academics *Calendar:* semesters. *Degrees:* bachelor's and master's. *Special study options:* academic remediation for entering students, advanced placement credit, double majors, honors programs, independent study, internships, off-campus study, part-time degree program, services for LD students, study abroad, summer session for credit. *ROTC:* Army (c), Navy (c), Air Force (c).

Computers on Campus 196 computers/terminals are available on campus for general student use. Students can access the following: free student e-mail accounts, online (class) grades, online (class) registration, online (class) schedules. Campuswide network is available. 100% of college-owned or -operated housing units are wired for high-speed Internet access. Wireless service is available via entire campus.

Student Life *Housing:* on-campus residence required through junior year. *Options:* men-only, women-only. Campus housing is university owned. Freshman campus housing is guaranteed. *Activities and organizations:* drama/theater group, student-run newspaper, radio station, choral group, Chi Delta Psi, Psi Omega Theta, SNAPL (nurses association), Chi Beta Sigma, national sororities. *Campus security:* 24-hour patrols, student patrols, late-night transport/escort service. *Student services:* health clinic, personal/psychological counseling, women's center.

Athletics Member NAIA. *Intercollegiate sports:* baseball M (s), basketball M (s)/W (s), cross-country running M (s)/W (s), golf M (s), soccer M (s)/W (s), softball W (s), tennis M (s)/W (s), track and field M (s)/W (s), volleyball W (s). *Intramural sports:* basketball M/W, football M/W, soccer M/W, softball M/W, volleyball M/W.

Standardized Tests *Required:* SAT or ACT (for admission). *Recommended:* SAT (for admission).

Costs (2008–09) *Comprehensive fee:* $32,990 includes full-time tuition ($24,580), mandatory fees ($240), and room and board ($8170). Part-time tuition: $1024 per credit hour. *College room only:* $4500.
Financial Aid Of all full-time matriculated undergraduates who enrolled in 2006, 1,587 applied for aid, 1,298 were judged to have need, 239 had their need fully met. In 2006, 586 non-need-based awards were made. *Average percent of need met:* 61%. *Average financial aid package:* $13,943. *Average need-based loan:* $4105. *Average need-based gift aid:* $10,739. *Average non-need-based aid:* $9409. *Average indebtedness upon graduation:* $19,525.
Applying *Options:* electronic application, early action. *Application fee:* $50. *Required:* essay or personal statement, high school transcript, minimum 2.8 GPA, 2 letters of recommendation. *Required for some:* interview. *Application deadlines:* 3/1 (freshmen), 3/1 (transfers), 12/1 (early action). *Notification:* 4/1 (freshmen), continuous (transfers), 1/15 (early action).
Freshman Application Contact Mr. Chip Killingsworth, Director of Admissions, Point Loma Nazarene University, 3900 Lomaland Drive, San Diego, CA 92106. *Phone:* 619-849-2273. *Toll-free phone:* 800-733-7770. *Fax:* 619-849-2601. *E-mail:* admissions@pointloma.edu.

See page 458 for the College Close-Up.

POMONA COLLEGE

Claremont, California **www.pomona.edu/**

- **Independent** 4-year, founded 1887
- **Suburban** 140-acre campus with easy access to Los Angeles
- **Endowment** $1.8 billion
- **Coed** 1,522 undergraduate students, 100% full-time, 50% women, 50% men
- **Most difficult** entrance level, 16% of applicants were admitted

Undergraduates 1,522 full-time. Students come from 49 states and territories, 31 other countries, 67% are from out of state, 8% African American, 14% Asian American or Pacific Islander, 11% Hispanic American, 0.3% Native American, 3% international, 0.7% transferred in, 98% live on campus. *Retention:* 99% of 2006 full-time freshmen returned.
Freshmen *Admission:* 5,907 applied, 964 admitted, 375 enrolled. *Test scores:* SAT critical reading scores over 500: 100%; SAT math scores over 500: 100%; SAT writing scores over 500: 100%; ACT scores over 18: 100%; SAT critical reading scores over 600: 96%; SAT math scores over 600: 93%; SAT writing scores over 600: 94%; ACT scores over 24: 96%; SAT critical reading scores over 700: 74%; SAT math scores over 700: 71%; SAT writing scores over 700: 65%; ACT scores over 30: 73%.
Faculty *Total:* 209, 86% full-time, 89% with terminal degrees. *Student/faculty ratio:* 8:1.
Majors African-American/Black studies; American studies; anthropology; art; art history, criticism and conservation; Asian-American studies; Asian studies; Asian studies (East); astronomy; biochemistry; biology/biological sciences; chemistry; Chinese; classics and languages, literatures and linguistics; cognitive science; computer science; dance; dramatic/theater arts; ecology; economics; English; environmental studies; film/cinema studies; fine/studio arts; French; geology/earth science; German; Hispanic-American, Puerto Rican, and Mexican-American/Chicano studies; history; humanities; interdisciplinary studies; international relations and affairs; Japanese; Latin American studies; liberal arts and sciences/liberal studies; linguistics; mathematics; medical microbiology and bacteriology; modern languages; molecular biology; music; neuroscience; philosophy; physics; political science and government; pre-medical studies; psychology; public policy analysis; religious studies; Romance languages; Russian; sociology; Spanish; women's studies.
Academics *Calendar:* semesters. *Degree:* bachelor's. *Special study options:* advanced placement credit, double majors, independent study, internships, off-campus study, services for LD students, student-designed majors, study abroad. *ROTC:* Army (c), Air Force (c). *Unusual degree programs:* 3-2 engineering with California Institute of Technology, Washington University in St. Louis.
Computers on Campus 180 computers/terminals are available on campus for general student use. Students can access the following: computer help desk, free student e-mail accounts, online (class) grades, online (class) schedules. Campus-wide network is available. 100% of college-owned or -operated housing units are wired for high-speed Internet access. Wireless service is available via classrooms, computer centers, computer labs, learning centers, libraries, student centers.
Student Life *Housing:* on-campus residence required for freshman year. *Options:* coed. Campus housing is university owned. Freshman campus housing is guaranteed. *Activities and organizations:* drama/theater group, student-run newspaper, radio and television station, choral group, student government, music/choral organizations, service organizations, intramural sports, outdoor activities club. *Campus security:* 24-hour emergency response devices and patrols, late-night transport/escort service, controlled dormitory access. *Student services:* health clinic, personal/psychological counseling, women's center.
Athletics Member NCAA. All Division III. *Intercollegiate sports:* baseball M, basketball M/W, cross-country running M/W, football M, golf M/W, lacrosse W, soccer M/W, softball W, swimming and diving M/W, tennis M/W, track and field M/W, ultimate Frisbee M (c)/W (c), volleyball M (c)/W, water polo M/W. *Intramural sports:* badminton M (c)/W (c), basketball M/W, crew W (c), cross-country running M/W, equestrian sports M (c)/W (c), fencing M/W, field hockey M (c)/W (c), football M, golf M/W, lacrosse M (c), racquetball M/W, rock climbing M/W, skiing (cross-country) M (c)/W (c), skiing (downhill) M (c)/W (c), soccer M/W, softball M/W, squash M/W, swimming and diving M/W, tennis M/W, track and field M/W, ultimate Frisbee M, volleyball M/W, water polo M/W.
Standardized Tests *Required:* SAT and SAT Subject Tests or ACT (for admission).
Costs (2007–08) *Comprehensive fee:* $45,680 includes full-time tuition ($33,635), mandatory fees ($297), and room and board ($11,748). *Room and board:* Room and board charges vary according to board plan. *Payment plan:* installment. *Waivers:* employees or children of employees.
Financial Aid Of all full-time matriculated undergraduates who enrolled in 2007, 1,000 applied for aid, 800 were judged to have need, 800 had their need fully met. 203 Federal Work-Study jobs (averaging $1180). 527 state and other part-time jobs (averaging $1650). *Average percent of need met:* 100%. *Average financial aid package:* $34,000. *Average need-based loan:* $2500. *Average need-based gift aid:* $29,600. *Average indebtedness upon graduation:* $11,300. *Financial aid deadline:* 2/1.
Applying *Options:* electronic application, early admission, early decision, deferred entrance. *Application fee:* $65. *Required:* essay or personal statement, high school transcript, 2 letters of recommendation. *Recommended:* minimum 3.0 GPA, interview, portfolio or tapes for art and performing arts programs. *Application deadlines:* 1/2 (freshmen), 3/15 (transfers). *Early decision deadline:* 11/1 (for plan 1), 12/28 (for plan 2). *Notification:* 4/10 (freshmen), 5/15 (transfers), 12/15 (early decision plan 1), 2/15 (early decision plan 2).
Freshman Application Contact Mr. Bruce Poch, Vice President and Dean of Admissions, Pomona College, 333 North College Way, Claremont, CA 91711. *Phone:* 909-621-8134. *Fax:* 909-621-8952. *E-mail:* admissions@pomona.edu.

REDSTONE COLLEGE–LOS ANGELES

Inglewood, California **www.redstone.edu/**

Director of Admissions Mr. Keith Watson, Director of Admissions, Redstone College–Los Angeles, 8911 Aviation Boulevard, Inglewood, CA 90301-2904. *Phone:* 310-337-4444. *Toll-free phone:* 800-597-8690.

REMINGTON COLLEGE–SAN DIEGO CAMPUS

San Diego, California **www.remingtoncollege.edu/**

- **Proprietary** 4-year, founded 1995
- 2-acre campus

Majors Computer systems networking and telecommunications; criminal justice/law enforcement administration; operations management.
Academics *Degrees:* associate and bachelor's.
Director of Admissions April Webb, Director of Recruitment, Remington College–San Diego Campus, 123 Camino de la Reina, North Building, Suite 100, San Diego, CA 92108. *Phone:* 619-686-8600. *Toll-free phone:* 800-214-7001. *Fax:* 619-686-8684. *E-mail:* april.webb@remingtoncollege.edu.

SAINT MARY'S COLLEGE OF CALIFORNIA

Moraga, California **www.stmarys-ca.edu/**

- **Independent Roman Catholic** comprehensive, founded 1863
- **Suburban** 420-acre campus with easy access to San Francisco
- **Endowment** $165.5 million
- **Coed** 2,685 undergraduate students, 89% full-time, 62% women, 38% men
- **Moderately difficult** entrance level, 82% of applicants were admitted

Undergraduates 2,402 full-time, 283 part-time. Students come from 40 states and territories, 33 other countries, 12% are from out of state, 6% African

American, 10% Asian American or Pacific Islander, 20% Hispanic American, 1% Native American, 2% international, 6% transferred in, 58% live on campus. *Retention:* 77% of 2006 full-time freshmen returned.

Freshmen *Admission:* 3,929 applied, 3,231 admitted, 611 enrolled. *Average high school GPA:* 3.33. *Test scores:* SAT critical reading scores over 500: 68%; SAT math scores over 500: 68%; SAT critical reading scores over 600: 24%; SAT math scores over 600: 22%; SAT critical reading scores over 700: 4%; SAT math scores over 700: 3%.

Faculty *Total:* 487, 40% full-time. *Student/faculty ratio:* 12:1.

Majors Accounting; accounting related; American studies; anthropology; archeology; area, ethnic, cultural, and gender studies related; art; art history, criticism and conservation; biochemistry; biological and biomedical sciences related; biology/biological sciences; business administration and management; business/commerce; chemistry; chemistry related; communication and journalism related; communication/speech communication and rhetoric; dance; dramatic/theater arts; economics; engineering; English; English language and literature related; European studies; finance and financial management services related; foreign languages related; French; German; health and physical education; health and physical education related; health professions related; historic preservation and conservation; history; industrial and organizational psychology; interdisciplinary studies; international business/trade/commerce; international relations and affairs; Italian; kinesiology and exercise science; Latin; Latin American studies; liberal arts and sciences and humanities related; liberal arts and sciences/liberal studies; literature; mathematics; mathematics and computer science; mathematics and statistics related; modern Greek; modern languages; multi-/interdisciplinary studies related; music; nursing (registered nurse training); philosophy; physics; physiological psychology/psychobiology; political science and government; political science and government related; psychology; psychology related; religious studies; social sciences; social sciences related; sociology; Spanish; sport and fitness administration/management; theater literature, history and criticism; theology; visual and performing arts related; women's studies.

Academics *Calendar:* 4-1-4. *Degrees:* certificates, bachelor's, master's, and doctoral. *Special study options:* adult/continuing education programs, advanced placement credit, double majors, honors programs, independent study, internships, off-campus study, part-time degree program, student-designed majors, study abroad. *ROTC:* Army (c), Air Force (c). *Unusual degree programs:* 3-2 engineering with Washington University in St. Louis, University of Southern California, Boston University.

Computers on Campus 325 computers/terminals are available on campus for general student use. Students can access the following: campus intranet, computer help desk, free student e-mail accounts, online (class) grades, online (class) registration, online (class) schedules. Campuswide network is available. Wireless service is available via classrooms, computer centers, computer labs, learning centers, libraries, student centers.

Student Life *Housing options:* coed, disabled students. Campus housing is university owned. Freshman campus housing is guaranteed. *Activities and organizations:* drama/theater group, student-run newspaper, radio and television station, choral group, Gael Force, Student Alumni Association, LASA-Latin American Student Association-Black Student Union, Inter-Varsity Christian Fellowship, Asian Pacific America Student Association. *Campus security:* 24-hour emergency response devices and patrols, late-night transport/escort service. *Student services:* health clinic, personal/psychological counseling, women's center.

Athletics Member NCAA. All Division I. *Intercollegiate sports:* baseball M (s), basketball M (s)/W (s), crew M (c)/W, cross-country running M (s)/W (s), golf M (s), lacrosse M (c)/W, rugby M (c)/W (c), soccer M (s)/W (s), softball W (s), tennis M (s)/W (s), volleyball M (c)/W (s), water polo M (c)/W (c). *Intramural sports:* badminton M/W, basketball M/W, bowling M/W, crew M/W, cross-country running M/W, golf M/W, lacrosse M/W, rugby M/W, skiing (cross-country) M/W, skiing (downhill) M/W, soccer M/W, softball M/W, table tennis M/W, tennis M/W, volleyball M/W, water polo M/W.

Standardized Tests *Required:* SAT or ACT (for admission).

Costs (2007–08) *Comprehensive fee:* $42,170 includes full-time tuition ($30,930), mandatory fees ($150), and room and board ($11,090). Full-time tuition and fees vary according to course load. Part-time tuition: $3865 per course. Part-time tuition and fees vary according to course load. *College room only:* $6220. Room and board charges vary according to board plan and housing facility. *Payment plan:* installment. *Waivers:* employees or children of employees.

Financial Aid Of all full-time matriculated undergraduates who enrolled in 2007, 1,634 applied for aid, 1,476 were judged to have need, 92 had their need fully met. 506 Federal Work-Study jobs (averaging $2220). In 2007, 138 non-need-based awards were made. *Average percent of need met:* 50%. *Average financial aid package:* $23,378. *Average need-based loan:* $4727. *Average need-based gift aid:* $16,813. *Average non-need-based aid:* $9542. *Average indebtedness upon graduation:* $26,230.

Applying *Options:* electronic application, early action, deferred entrance. *Application fee:* $55. *Required:* essay or personal statement, high school transcript, minimum 2.0 GPA, 1 letter of recommendation. *Required for some:* minimum 3.0 GPA, interview. *Recommended:* minimum 3.0 GPA. *Application deadlines:* 2/1 (freshmen), 7/1 (transfers), 11/15 (early action). *Notification:* continuous until 3/15 (freshmen), continuous (transfers), 12/24 (early action).

Freshman Application Contact Ms. Dorothy Jones, Dean of Admissions, Saint Mary's College of California, PO Box 4800, Moraga, CA 94556-4800. *Phone:* 925-631-4224. *Toll-free phone:* 800-800-4SMC. *Fax:* 925-376-7193. *E-mail:* smcadmit@stmarys-ca.edu.

SAMUEL MERRITT COLLEGE

Oakland, California **www.samuelmerritt.edu/**

- **Independent** upper-level, founded 1909
- **Urban** 1-acre campus with easy access to San Francisco
- **Endowment** $28.0 million
- **Coed, primarily women** 469 undergraduate students, 87% full-time, 88% women, 12% men
- **Moderately difficult** entrance level

Undergraduates 407 full-time, 62 part-time. Students come from 8 states and territories, 2% are from out of state, 6% African American, 27% Asian American or Pacific Islander, 10% Hispanic American, 0.7% Native American, 23% transferred in, 6% live on campus.

Faculty *Total:* 187, 39% full-time, 35% with terminal degrees. *Student/faculty ratio:* 9:1.

Majors Nursing (registered nurse training).

Academics *Calendar:* 4-1-4. *Degrees:* bachelor's, master's, doctoral, and first professional (bachelor's degree offered jointly with Saint Mary's College of California). *Special study options:* academic remediation for entering students, accelerated degree program, advanced placement credit, cooperative education, distance learning, independent study, internships, off-campus study, part-time degree program, services for LD students, summer session for credit. *ROTC:* Army (c), Air Force (c).

Computers on Campus 78 computers/terminals are available on campus for general student use. Students can access the following: campus intranet, computer help desk, free student e-mail accounts, online (class) grades, online (class) registration, online (class) schedules. Campuswide network is available. Wireless service is available via entire campus.

Student Life *Housing options:* coed. Campus housing is university owned. *Activities and organizations:* student-run newspaper, Student Body Association, "Green Team", International Health Club, Multicultural Group. *Campus security:* 24-hour emergency response devices and patrols, late-night transport/escort service, controlled dormitory access, 24-hour controlled access. *Student services:* health clinic, personal/psychological counseling.

Costs (2007–08) *One-time required fee:* $130. *Tuition:* $30,974 full-time, $1305 per unit part-time. Full-time tuition and fees vary according to degree level and program. Part-time tuition and fees vary according to degree level and program. *Room only:* $6858. *Payment plan:* installment.

Financial Aid Of all full-time matriculated undergraduates who enrolled in 2004, 321 applied for aid, 319 were judged to have need, 33 had their need fully met. 39 Federal Work-Study jobs (averaging $3300). 22 state and other part-time jobs (averaging $4200). *Average percent of need met:* 84%. *Average financial aid package:* $27,500. *Average need-based loan:* $9500. *Average need-based gift aid:* $12,000. *Average indebtedness upon graduation:* $36,250.

Applying *Options:* deferred entrance. *Application fee:* $50. *Application deadline:* 3/1 (transfers). *Notification:* continuous (transfers).

Application Contact Ms. Anne Seed, Director of Admissions, Samuel Merritt College, 570 Hawthorne Avenue, Oakland, CA 94609. *Phone:* 510-869-6610. *Toll-free phone:* 800-607-MERRITT. *Fax:* 510-869-6525. *E-mail:* admission@samuelmerritt.edu.

SAN DIEGO CHRISTIAN COLLEGE

El Cajon, California **www.sdcc.edu/**

- **Independent nondenominational** 4-year, founded 1970
- **Suburban** 55-acre campus with easy access to San Diego
- **Endowment** $362,118
- **Coed** 463 undergraduate students, 89% full-time, 54% women, 46% men
- **Moderately difficult** entrance level, 71% of applicants were admitted

Undergraduates 412 full-time, 51 part-time. Students come from 11 states and territories, 1 other country, 3% are from out of state, 7% African American, 5% Asian American or Pacific Islander, 14% Hispanic American, 2% Native American, 0.4% international, 10% transferred in, 43% live on campus. *Retention:* 63% of 2006 full-time freshmen returned.

Freshmen *Admission:* 416 applied, 295 admitted, 79 enrolled. *Test scores:* SAT critical reading scores over 500: 44%; SAT math scores over 500: 44%; SAT writing scores over 500: 37%; ACT scores over 18: 64%; SAT critical reading scores over 600: 18%; SAT math scores over 600: 6%; SAT writing scores over 600: 17%; ACT scores over 24: 7%; SAT critical reading scores over 700: 3%.

Faculty *Total:* 68, 47% full-time, 12% with terminal degrees. *Student/faculty ratio:* 8:1.

Majors Adult and continuing education; athletic training; biblical studies; biology/biological sciences; business administration and management; communication/speech communication and rhetoric; counseling psychology; divinity/ministry; education; education (K-12); elementary education; English; history; human development and family studies; interdisciplinary studies; kinesiology and exercise science; liberal arts and sciences/liberal studies; mathematics; multi-/interdisciplinary studies related; music; music teacher education; pastoral studies/counseling; physical education teaching and coaching; psychology; religious/sacred music; secondary education; social sciences; theology; voice and opera.

Academics *Calendar:* semesters. *Degrees:* certificates, bachelor's, and post-bachelor's certificates. *Special study options:* academic remediation for entering students, adult/continuing education programs, advanced placement credit, double majors, English as a second language, honors programs, independent study, internships, part-time degree program, student-designed majors, study abroad, summer session for credit. *ROTC:* Army (c), Air Force (c).

Computers on Campus 187 computers/terminals and 69 ports are available on campus for general student use. Students can access the following: campus intranet, computer help desk, free student e-mail accounts. Campuswide network is available. 100% of college-owned or -operated housing units are wired for high-speed Internet access. Wireless service is available via classrooms, libraries.

Student Life *Housing:* on-campus residence required through sophomore year. *Options:* men-only, women-only. Campus housing is leased by the school. *Activities and organizations:* drama/theater group, student-run newspaper, choral group, Senate, Missions Club, Aviators Club, Women of Influence, Hope Ministries. *Campus security:* 24-hour emergency response devices and patrols. *Student services:* health clinic, personal/psychological counseling.

Athletics Member NAIA, NCCAA. *Intercollegiate sports:* baseball M (s), basketball M (s)/W (s), cross-country running M (s)/W (s), soccer M (s)/W (s), tennis W, track and field M, volleyball W (s). *Intramural sports:* basketball M/W, football M, golf M/W (c), soccer M/W, softball M/W, swimming and diving M/W, tennis M/W, volleyball M/W.

Standardized Tests *Required:* SAT or ACT (for admission), SAT and SAT Subject Tests or ACT (for admission), (for admission).

Costs (2008–09) *One-time required fee:* $100. *Comprehensive fee:* $28,020 includes full-time tuition ($19,980), mandatory fees ($500), and room and board ($7540). Part-time tuition: $833 per unit. *Required fees:* $200 per term part-time.

Financial Aid Of all full-time matriculated undergraduates who enrolled in 2007, 383 applied for aid, 326 were judged to have need, 228 had their need fully met. 17 Federal Work-Study jobs (averaging $1623). 25 state and other part-time jobs (averaging $1669). In 2007, 86 non-need-based awards were made. *Average percent of need met:* 80%. *Average financial aid package:* $16,137. *Average need-based loan:* $4750. *Average need-based gift aid:* $5500. *Average non-need-based aid:* $6122. *Average indebtedness upon graduation:* $16,000.

Applying *Options:* electronic application, deferred entrance. *Application fee:* $25. *Required:* essay or personal statement, high school transcript, 2 letters of recommendation. *Recommended:* minimum 2.75 GPA, interview. *Application deadlines:* 7/1 (freshmen), 7/1 (transfers). *Notification:* continuous (freshmen), continuous (transfers).

Freshman Application Contact Candace Del Giudice, San Diego Christian College, 2100 Greenfield Drive, El Cajon, CA 92019-1157. *Phone:* 619-588-7747. *Toll-free phone:* 800-676-2242. *Fax:* 619-590-1739. *E-mail:* cdelgiudice@sdcc.edu.

SAN DIEGO STATE UNIVERSITY

San Diego, California **www.sdsu.edu/**

- **State-supported** university, founded 1897, part of California State University System
- **Urban** 300-acre campus
- **Endowment** $117.3 million
- **Coed** 30,460 undergraduate students, 83% full-time, 57% women, 43% men
- **Moderately difficult** entrance level, 44% of applicants were admitted

Undergraduates 25,167 full-time, 5,293 part-time. Students come from 51 states and territories, 64 other countries, 5% are from out of state, 4% African American, 16% Asian American or Pacific Islander, 23% Hispanic American, 0.7% Native American, 3% international, 13% transferred in, 15% live on campus. *Retention:* 83% of 2006 full-time freshmen returned.

Freshmen *Admission:* 46,718 applied, 20,629 admitted, 5,601 enrolled. *Average high school GPA:* 3.44. *Test scores:* SAT critical reading scores over 500: 62%; SAT math scores over 500: 69%; ACT scores over 18: 87%; SAT critical reading scores over 600: 16%; SAT math scores over 600: 25%; ACT scores over 24: 37%; SAT critical reading scores over 700: 1%; SAT math scores over 700: 2%; ACT scores over 30: 2%.

Faculty *Total:* 1,779, 55% full-time. *Student/faculty ratio:* 20:1.

Majors Accounting; advertising; aerospace, aeronautical and astronautical engineering; African-American/Black studies; agricultural business and management; American Indian/Native American studies; American studies; anthropology; applied mathematics; art history, criticism and conservation; Asian studies; astronomy; atomic/molecular physics; biology/biological sciences; business/commerce; chemistry; child development; civil engineering; classics and classical languages related; classics and languages, literatures and linguistics; communication and journalism related; communication disorders; comparative literature; computer engineering; computer science; construction engineering technology; creative writing; criminal justice/law enforcement administration; dance; design and visual communications; dietetics; dramatic/theater arts; early childhood education; economics; electrical, electronics and communications engineering; engineering; English; environmental/environmental health engineering; environmental science; environmental studies; European studies; European studies (Central and Eastern); finance; fine/studio arts; French; geography; geology/earth science; German; gerontology; graphic design; health and physical education; health professions related; health services/allied health/health sciences; Hispanic-American, Puerto Rican, and Mexican-American/Chicano studies; history; hospitality administration; humanities; human resources management; information science/studies; information technology; interior design; international business/trade/commerce; international relations and affairs; Japanese; Jewish/Judaic studies; journalism; Judaic studies; Latin American studies; liberal arts and sciences/liberal studies; linguistics; marketing/marketing management; mass communication/media; mathematics; mechanical engineering; microbiology; multi-/interdisciplinary studies related; music related; music teacher education; nursing (registered nurse training); nursing related; operations management; parks, recreation and leisure; philosophy; physical sciences; physics; political science and government; psychology; public administration; public relations; public relations/image management; radio and television; real estate; religious studies; Russian; Russian studies; social sciences; social work; sociology; Spanish; speech and rhetoric; statistics; trade and industrial teacher education; urban studies/affairs; women's studies.

Academics *Calendar:* semesters. *Degrees:* bachelor's, master's, doctoral, post-master's, and postbachelor's certificates. *Special study options:* academic remediation for entering students, advanced placement credit, distance learning, double majors, English as a second language, honors programs, independent study, internships, off-campus study, part-time degree program, services for LD students, student-designed majors, study abroad, summer session for credit. *ROTC:* Army (b), Navy (b), Air Force (b).

Computers on Campus 506 computers/terminals are available on campus for general student use. Students can access the following: online (class) registration. Campuswide network is available.

Student Life *Housing options:* coed, cooperative. Campus housing is university owned. Freshman applicants given priority for college housing. *Activities and organizations:* drama/theater group, student-run newspaper, radio and television station, choral group, marching band, AB Samahan, Asian Pacific Student Alliance, Enviro-Business Society, MECHA, national fraternities, national sororities. *Campus security:* 24-hour emergency response devices and patrols, student patrols, late-night transport/escort service. *Student services:* health clinic, personal/psychological counseling, women's center.

Athletics Member NCAA. All Division I except football (Division I-A). *Intercollegiate sports:* baseball M (s), basketball M (s)/W (s), cross-country running W (s), golf M (s)/W (s), soccer M (s)/W (s), softball W (s), swimming and diving W (s), tennis M (s)/W (s), track and field W (s), volleyball M/W (s), water polo W (s). *Intramural sports:* badminton M (c)/W (c), basketball M/W, crew M/W (c), football M/W, golf M/W, ice hockey M (c), lacrosse M (c)/W (c), racquetball M/W, rugby M (c), sailing M (c)/W (c), skiing (downhill) M (c)/W (c), soccer M (c)/W (c), softball M/W, table tennis M/W, tennis M/W, volleyball M (c)/W (c).

Standardized Tests *Required:* SAT or ACT (for admission).

Costs (2007–08) *Tuition:* state resident $0 full-time; nonresident $10,170 full-time, $339 per unit part-time. Full-time tuition and fees vary according to degree level. Part-time tuition and fees vary according to course load and degree

level. *Required fees:* $3428 full-time, $1060 per term part-time. *Room and board:* $10,904. Room and board charges vary according to board plan and housing facility. *Payment plan:* installment. *Waivers:* employees or children of employees.
Financial Aid Of all full-time matriculated undergraduates who enrolled in 2007, 13,400 applied for aid, 9,450 were judged to have need, 640 had their need fully met. In 2007, 690 non-need-based awards were made. *Average percent of need met:* 69%. *Average financial aid package:* $8540. *Average need-based loan:* $3760. *Average need-based gift aid:* $5940. *Average non-need-based aid:* $1880. *Average indebtedness upon graduation:* $14,500. *Financial aid deadline:* 3/2.
Applying *Options:* electronic application. *Application fee:* $55. *Required:* high school transcript, minimum 2.0 GPA, 2.5 GPA for non-California residents. *Application deadlines:* 11/30 (freshmen), 11/30 (transfers). *Notification:* 3/1 (freshmen), 3/1 (transfers).
Freshman Application Contact Ms. Beverly Arata, Director of Admissions, San Diego State University, 5500 Campanile Drive, San Diego, CA 92182-7455. *Phone:* 619-594-6336. *E-mail:* admissions@sdsu.edu.

SAN FRANCISCO ART INSTITUTE

San Francisco, California www.sfai.edu/

- **Independent** comprehensive, founded 1871
- **Urban** 3-acre campus
- **Endowment** $8.5 million
- **Coed**
- **Moderately difficult** entrance level

Faculty *Student/faculty ratio:* 11:1.
Academics *Calendar:* semesters. *Degrees:* bachelor's, master's, and post-bachelor's certificates.
Student Life *Campus security:* 24-hour patrols, security cameras.
Standardized Tests *Required:* SAT or ACT (for admission).
Financial Aid Of all full-time matriculated undergraduates who enrolled in 2006, 205 applied for aid, 189 were judged to have need, 12 had their need fully met. In 2006, 46 non-need-based awards were made. *Average percent of need met:* 72. *Average financial aid package:* $24,880. *Average need-based loan:* $10,694. *Average need-based gift aid:* $11,441. *Average non-need-based aid:* $24,787.
Applying *Options:* early admission, deferred entrance. *Application fee:* $65. *Required:* essay or personal statement, high school transcript, letters of recommendation, portfolio. *Recommended:* interview.
Freshman Application Contact Office of Admissions, San Francisco Art Institute, 800 Chestnut Street, San Francisco, CA 94133. *Phone:* 415-749-4500. *Toll-free phone:* 800-345-SFAI. *E-mail:* admissions@sfai.edu.

SAN FRANCISCO CONSERVATORY OF MUSIC

San Francisco, California www.sfcm.edu/

- **Independent** comprehensive, founded 1917
- **Urban** 2-acre campus
- **Endowment** $31.3 million
- **Coed**
- **Moderately difficult** entrance level

Faculty *Student/faculty ratio:* 7:1.
Academics *Calendar:* semesters. *Degrees:* diplomas, bachelor's, master's, and post-master's certificates.
Student Life *Campus security:* 24-hour patrols.
Standardized Tests *Recommended:* SAT or ACT (for admission).
Costs (2007–08) *One-time required fee:* $174. *Tuition:* $29,700 full-time, $1320 per credit part-time. *Required fees:* $280 full-time, $140 per term part-time.
Financial Aid Of all full-time matriculated undergraduates who enrolled in 2007, 119 applied for aid, 103 were judged to have need, 24 had their need fully met. 34 Federal Work-Study jobs (averaging $1500). 33 state and other part-time jobs (averaging $1500). In 2007, 71 non-need-based awards were made. *Average percent of need met:* 68. *Average financial aid package:* $19,851. *Average need-based loan:* $7351. *Average need-based gift aid:* $14,090. *Average non-need-based aid:* $12,254. *Average indebtedness upon graduation:* $6500.
Applying *Options:* early admission. *Application fee:* $100. *Required:* essay or personal statement, high school transcript, 2 letters of recommendation, audition.
Freshman Application Contact Mr. Alexander Brose, Director of Admissions, San Francisco Conservatory of Music, 1201 Ortega Street, San Francisco, CA 94122-4411. *Phone:* 800-899-7326. *Fax:* 415-503-6299. *E-mail:* admit@sfcm.edu.

SAN FRANCISCO STATE UNIVERSITY

San Francisco, California www.sfsu.edu/

- **State-supported** comprehensive, founded 1899, part of California State University System
- **Urban** 90-acre campus
- **Endowment** $41.2 million
- **Coed** 24,376 undergraduate students, 80% full-time, 58% women, 42% men
- 67% of applicants were admitted

Undergraduates 19,517 full-time, 4,859 part-time. Students come from 50 states and territories, 80 other countries, 0.8% are from out of state, 6% African American, 31% Asian American or Pacific Islander, 16% Hispanic American, 0.6% Native American, 6% international, 13% transferred in, 3% live on campus. *Retention:* 77% of 2006 full-time freshmen returned.
Freshmen *Admission:* 27,440 applied, 18,370 admitted, 3,466 enrolled. *Average high school GPA:* 3.09. *Test scores:* SAT critical reading scores over 500: 50%; SAT math scores over 500: 52%; SAT writing scores over 500: 51%; ACT scores over 18: 80%; SAT critical reading scores over 600: 15%; SAT math scores over 600: 14%; SAT writing scores over 600: 12%; ACT scores over 24: 25%; SAT critical reading scores over 700: 2%; SAT math scores over 700: 1%; SAT writing scores over 700: 1%; ACT scores over 30: 2%.
Faculty *Total:* 1,845, 50% full-time, 52% with terminal degrees. *Student/faculty ratio:* 22:1.
Majors Accounting; African-American/Black studies; American studies; animal physiology; anthropology; applied mathematics; art; Asian-American studies; astronomy; astrophysics; atmospheric sciences and meteorology; audiology and speech-language pathology; biochemistry; biological and physical sciences; biology/biological sciences; botany/plant biology; business administration and management; cell biology and histology; chemistry; Chinese; civil engineering; classics and languages, literatures and linguistics; clinical laboratory science/medical technology; comparative literature; computer science; consumer merchandising/retailing management; creative writing; criminal justice/law enforcement administration; dance; dietetics; dramatic/theater arts; early childhood education; ecology; economics; electrical, electronics and communications engineering; English; environmental studies; family and consumer sciences/human sciences; film/cinema studies; finance; French; geography; geology/earth science; German; health science; health teacher education; Hispanic-American, Puerto Rican, and Mexican-American/Chicano studies; history; hospitality administration; humanities; industrial arts; industrial design; information science/studies; interior design; international business/trade/commerce; international relations and affairs; Italian; Japanese; Jewish/Judaic studies; journalism; labor and industrial relations; liberal arts and sciences/liberal studies; marine biology and biological oceanography; marketing/marketing management; mathematics; mechanical engineering; medical microbiology and bacteriology; molecular biology; multi-/interdisciplinary studies related; music; music performance; nursing (registered nurse training); parks, recreation and leisure; philosophy; philosophy and religious studies related; physical education teaching and coaching; physical sciences; physics; political science and government; psychology; radio and television; real estate; religious studies; social sciences; social work; sociology; Spanish; special products marketing; speech and rhetoric; statistics; technical and business writing; trade and industrial teacher education; urban studies/affairs; women's studies; zoology/animal biology.
Academics *Calendar:* semesters. *Degrees:* certificates, bachelor's, master's, doctoral, and postbachelor's certificates. *Special study options:* academic remediation for entering students, accelerated degree program, adult/continuing education programs, advanced placement credit, cooperative education, distance learning, double majors, English as a second language, honors programs, independent study, internships, off-campus study, part-time degree program, services for LD students, student-designed majors, study abroad, summer session for credit. *ROTC:* Army (c), Navy (c), Air Force (c).
Computers on Campus 2,800 computers/terminals and 500 ports are available on campus for general student use. Students can access the following: campus intranet, computer help desk, free student e-mail accounts, online (class) grades, online (class) registration, online (class) schedules. Campuswide network is available. 100% of college-owned or -operated housing units are wired for high-speed Internet access. Wireless service is available via classrooms, computer centers, computer labs, dorm rooms, learning centers, libraries, student centers.
Student Life *Housing options:* coed, disabled students. Campus housing is university owned. *Activities and organizations:* drama/theater group, student-run newspaper, radio and television station, choral group, Fraternity/Sorority Council, International Education Exchange Council, Laraza Student Organization, Pilipino American Collegial Endeavor, Black Student Union, national fraternities, national sororities. *Campus security:* 24-hour emergency response devices and patrols,

student patrols, late-night transport/escort service, controlled dormitory access. *Student services:* health clinic, personal/psychological counseling, women's center, legal services.

Athletics Member NCAA. All Division II. *Intercollegiate sports:* baseball M (s), basketball M (s)/W (s), cross-country running M (s)/W (s), soccer M (s)/W (s), softball W (s), track and field W (s), volleyball M (c)/W (c), wrestling M (s). *Intramural sports:* badminton M (c)/W (c), basketball M/W, cross-country running M (c)/W (c), equestrian sports W (c), fencing M (c), sailing M (c)/W (c), soccer M/W, swimming and diving M (c)/W (c), ultimate Frisbee M (c)/W (c), volleyball M/W.

Standardized Tests *Required for some:* SAT or ACT (for admission).

Costs (2007–08) *Tuition:* nonresident $10,170 full-time, $339 per unit part-time. Full-time tuition and fees vary according to degree level. Part-time tuition and fees vary according to degree level. *Required fees:* $3456 full-time, $1146 per term part-time. *Room and board:* $9896; room only: $6388. Room and board charges vary according to board plan and housing facility. *Payment plan:* installment. *Waivers:* senior citizens and employees or children of employees.

Financial Aid Of all full-time matriculated undergraduates who enrolled in 2007, 10,979 applied for aid, 9,350 were judged to have need, 721 had their need fully met. In 2007, 107 non-need-based awards were made. *Average percent of need met:* 61%. *Average financial aid package:* $8864. *Average need-based loan:* $3155. *Average need-based gift aid:* $6396. *Average non-need-based aid:* $1996. *Average indebtedness upon graduation:* $15,337.

Applying *Options:* electronic application. *Application fee:* $55. *Required:* high school transcript. *Application deadlines:* 1/15 (freshmen), 3/3 (transfers). *Notification:* continuous (freshmen), continuous (transfers).

Freshman Application Contact Admissions Officer, San Francisco State University, 1600 Holloway Avenue, San Francisco, CA 94132. *Phone:* 415-338-1113. *Fax:* 415-338-7196. *E-mail:* ugadmit@sfsu.edu.

SAN JOSE STATE UNIVERSITY

San Jose, California **www.sjsu.edu/**

- **State-supported** comprehensive, founded 1857, part of California State University System
- **Urban** 104-acre campus
- **Coed**
- 65% of applicants were admitted

Academics *Calendar:* semesters. *Degrees:* bachelor's and master's.

Student Life *Campus security:* 24-hour emergency response devices and patrols, student patrols, late-night transport/escort service.

Athletics Member NCAA. All Division I except football (Division I-A).

Standardized Tests *Required for some:* SAT or ACT (for admission).

Costs (2007–08) *Tuition:* state resident $0 full-time; nonresident $10,170 full-time, $339 per unit part-time. Full-time tuition and fees vary according to course load. Part-time tuition and fees vary according to course load. *Required fees:* $3632 full-time, $1234 per term part-time. *Room and board:* $9326; room only: $5810. Room and board charges vary according to board plan and housing facility.

Financial Aid Of all full-time matriculated undergraduates who enrolled in 2006, 10,118 applied for aid, 8,312 were judged to have need, 420 had their need fully met. 3,951 Federal Work-Study jobs (averaging $4583). In 2006, 496 non-need-based awards were made. *Average percent of need met:* 74. *Average financial aid package:* $10,985. *Average need-based loan:* $3790. *Average need-based gift aid:* $5725. *Average non-need-based aid:* $1561. *Average indebtedness upon graduation:* $10,821.

Applying *Options:* electronic application. *Application fee:* $55. *Required:* high school transcript.

Freshman Application Contact San Jose State University, One Washington Square, San Jose, CA 95192-0001. *Phone:* 408-283-7500. *Fax:* 408-924-2050. *E-mail:* contact@sjsu.edu.

SANTA CLARA UNIVERSITY

Santa Clara, California **www.scu.edu/**

- **Independent Roman Catholic (Jesuit)** university, founded 1851
- **Suburban** 106-acre campus with easy access to San Francisco and San Jose
- **Endowment** $697.9 million
- **Coed** 4,824 undergraduate students, 98% full-time, 53% women, 47% men
- **Moderately difficult** entrance level, 60% of applicants were admitted

Undergraduates 4,730 full-time, 94 part-time. Students come from 39 states and territories, 16 other countries, 35% are from out of state, 3% African American, 17% Asian American or Pacific Islander, 13% Hispanic American, 0.5% Native American, 3% international, 5% transferred in, 49% live on campus. *Retention:* 92% of 2006 full-time freshmen returned.

Freshmen *Admission:* 9,659 applied, 5,802 admitted, 1,204 enrolled. *Average high school GPA:* 3.5. *Test scores:* SAT critical reading scores over 500: 92%; SAT math scores over 500: 93%; ACT scores over 18: 100%; SAT critical reading scores over 600: 52%; SAT math scores over 600: 61%; ACT scores over 24: 82%; SAT critical reading scores over 700: 9%; SAT math scores over 700: 14%; ACT scores over 30: 22%.

Faculty *Total:* 779, 66% full-time, 77% with terminal degrees. *Student/faculty ratio:* 12:1.

Majors Accounting; accounting and business/management; ancient/classical Greek; ancient studies; anthropology; art history, criticism and conservation; biochemistry; biological and physical sciences; biology/biological sciences; business/managerial economics; chemistry; civil engineering; classics and languages, literatures and linguistics; communication/speech communication and rhetoric; computer engineering; computer science; dramatic/theater arts; economics; electrical, electronics and communications engineering; engineering; engineering physics; English; environmental science; finance; fine/studio arts; French; French studies; German studies; history; interdisciplinary studies; Italian; Italian studies; Latin; liberal arts and sciences/liberal studies; management information systems; marketing/marketing management; mathematics; mechanical engineering; music; organizational behavior; philosophy; physics; political science and government; psychology; religious studies; sociology; Spanish; Spanish and Iberian studies.

Academics *Calendar:* quarters. *Degrees:* bachelor's, master's, doctoral, first professional, post-master's, and postbachelor's certificates. *Special study options:* advanced placement credit, cooperative education, double majors, honors programs, independent study, internships, services for LD students, student-designed majors, study abroad, summer session for credit. *ROTC:* Army (b), Air Force (c).

Computers on Campus 800 computers/terminals and 6,000 ports are available on campus for general student use. Students can access the following: campus intranet, computer help desk, free student e-mail accounts, online (class) grades, online (class) registration, online (class) schedules. Campuswide network is available. 100% of college-owned or -operated housing units are wired for high-speed Internet access. Wireless service is available via entire campus.

Student Life *Housing options:* coed. Campus housing is university owned and leased by the school. Freshman applicants given priority for college housing. *Activities and organizations:* drama/theater group, student-run newspaper, radio station, choral group, Community Action Program, Associated Students, Activities Programming Board, Multicultural Programming Board, Residence Hall Association. *Campus security:* 24-hour emergency response devices and patrols, late-night transport/escort service, controlled dormitory access. *Student services:* health clinic, personal/psychological counseling, legal services.

Athletics Member NCAA. All Division I. *Intercollegiate sports:* baseball M (s), basketball M (s)/W (s), crew M/W, cross-country running M (s)/W (s), equestrian sports M (c)/W (c), field hockey W (c), golf M (s)/W (s), ice hockey M (c), lacrosse M (c)/W (c), rugby M (c)/W (c), sailing M (c)/W (c), soccer M (s)/W (s), softball W (s), swimming and diving M (c)/W (c), tennis M (s)/W (s), track and field M (s)/W (s), volleyball M (c)/W (s), water polo M (s)/W (s). *Intramural sports:* badminton M/W, basketball M/W, football M/W, soccer M/W, softball M/W, table tennis M/W, tennis M/W, ultimate Frisbee M/W, volleyball M/W.

Standardized Tests *Required:* SAT or ACT (for admission).

Costs (2007–08) *Comprehensive fee:* $43,644 includes full-time tuition ($33,000) and room and board ($10,644). Part-time tuition: $1100 per unit. Part-time tuition and fees vary according to course load. *Room and board:* Room and board charges vary according to board plan, housing facility, and student level. *Payment plan:* installment. *Waivers:* employees or children of employees.

Financial Aid Of all full-time matriculated undergraduates who enrolled in 2007, 3,225 applied for aid, 2,315 were judged to have need, 1,180 had their need fully met. 526 Federal Work-Study jobs (averaging $3013). In 2007, 1296 non-need-based awards were made. *Average percent of need met:* 70%. *Average financial aid package:* $21,337. *Average need-based loan:* $5901. *Average need-based gift aid:* $14,533. *Average non-need-based aid:* $9545. *Average indebtedness upon graduation:* $23,773.

Applying *Options:* electronic application, early action, deferred entrance. *Application fee:* $55. *Required:* essay or personal statement, high school transcript, 1 letter of recommendation. *Application deadlines:* 1/7 (freshmen), 5/1 (transfers), 11/1 (early action). *Notification:* continuous until 4/5 (freshmen), 6/1 (transfers), 12/31 (early action).

Freshman Application Contact Ms. Sandra Hayes, Dean of Undergraduate Admissions, Santa Clara University, 500 El Camino Real, Santa Clara, CA 95053. *Phone:* 408-554-4700. *Fax:* 408-554-5255. *E-mail:* ugadmissions@scu.edu.

SCRIPPS COLLEGE

Claremont, California **www.scrippscollege.edu/**

- **Independent** 4-year, founded 1926, part of The Claremont Colleges Consortium
- **Suburban** 30-acre campus with easy access to Los Angeles
- **Endowment** $274.4 million
- **Women only** 899 undergraduate students, 99% full-time
- **Very difficult** entrance level, 43% of applicants were admitted

Undergraduates 894 full-time, 5 part-time. Students come from 44 states and territories, 10 other countries, 58% are from out of state, 4% African American, 13% Asian American or Pacific Islander, 8% Hispanic American, 0.7% Native American, 0.6% international, 2% transferred in, 95% live on campus. *Retention:* 95% of 2006 full-time freshmen returned.

Freshmen *Admission:* 1,969 applied, 844 admitted, 227 enrolled. *Average high school GPA:* 4.0. *Test scores:* SAT critical reading scores over 500: 99%; SAT math scores over 500: 99%; SAT writing scores over 500: 98%; ACT scores over 18: 100%; SAT critical reading scores over 600: 92%; SAT math scores over 600: 87%; SAT writing scores over 600: 91%; ACT scores over 24: 97%; SAT critical reading scores over 700: 48%; SAT math scores over 700: 28%; SAT writing scores over 700: 42%; ACT scores over 30: 53%.

Faculty *Total:* 96, 72% full-time, 99% with terminal degrees. *Student/faculty ratio:* 11:1.

Majors African-American/Black studies; American studies; anthropology; art; art history, criticism and conservation; Asian-American studies; Asian studies; Asian studies (East); biochemistry; biology/biological sciences; chemistry; Chinese; classics and languages, literatures and linguistics; computer science; dance; dramatic/theater arts; economics; English; environmental science; environmental studies; European studies; film/video and photographic arts related; fine/studio arts; foreign languages and literatures; French; geology/earth science; German; Hispanic-American, Puerto Rican, and Mexican-American/Chicano studies; history; international relations and affairs; Italian; Japanese; Jewish/Judaic studies; Latin; Latin American studies; legal studies; linguistics; mass communication/media; mathematics; modern languages; molecular biology; multi-/interdisciplinary studies related; music; neuroscience; organizational behavior; philosophy; physics; physiological psychology/psychobiology; political science and government; pre-engineering; pre-medical studies; psychology; religious studies; Russian; science, technology and society; sociology; Spanish; visual and performing arts related; women's studies.

Academics *Calendar:* semesters. *Degrees:* bachelor's and postbachelor's certificates. *Special study options:* accelerated degree program, advanced placement credit, double majors, independent study, internships, off-campus study, part-time degree program, student-designed majors, study abroad. *ROTC:* Army (c), Air Force (c). *Unusual degree programs:* 3-2 business administration with Claremont Graduate University; engineering with Stanford University, University of Southern California, Harvey Mudd College, University of California, Berkeley, Washington University in St. Louis, Columbia University, Boston University; public policy, religion, government, international studies, economics, philosophy with Claremont Graduate University.

Computers on Campus 72 computers/terminals are available on campus for general student use. Students can access the following: campus intranet, computer help desk, free student e-mail accounts, online (class) grades, online (class) schedules, 2 ports per dorm room. Campuswide network is available. 100% of college-owned or -operated housing units are wired for high-speed Internet access. Wireless service is available via classrooms, computer centers, computer labs, dorm rooms, libraries, student centers.

Student Life *Housing:* on-campus residence required for freshman year. *Options:* women-only, disabled students. Campus housing is university owned. Freshman campus housing is guaranteed. *Activities and organizations:* drama/theater group, student-run newspaper, radio station, choral group, College Council, Asian/Black/Latina clubs, National Organization for Women, Sexual Assault Task Force. *Campus security:* 24-hour emergency response devices and patrols, late-night transport/escort service, controlled dormitory access. *Student services:* health clinic, personal/psychological counseling, women's center.

Athletics Member NCAA. All Division III. *Intercollegiate sports:* basketball W, cross-country running W, fencing W (c), golf W, lacrosse W, rugby W (c), skiing (downhill) W (c), soccer W, softball W, swimming and diving W, tennis W, track and field W, volleyball W, water polo W. *Intramural sports:* basketball W, football W, soccer W, softball W, ultimate Frisbee W, volleyball W, water polo W.

Standardized Tests *Required:* SAT or ACT (for admission).

Costs (2007–08) *Comprehensive fee:* $46,650 includes full-time tuition ($35,636), mandatory fees ($214), and room and board ($10,800). Full-time tuition and fees vary according to program. Part-time tuition: $4455 per course. Part-time tuition and fees vary according to program. *College room only:* $5800. Room and board charges vary according to board plan. *Payment plan:* installment. *Waivers:* employees or children of employees.

Financial Aid Of all full-time matriculated undergraduates who enrolled in 2006, 443 applied for aid, 351 were judged to have need, 351 had their need fully met. 299 Federal Work-Study jobs (averaging $1582). In 2006, 78 non-need-based awards were made. *Average percent of need met:* 100%. *Average financial aid package:* $29,642. *Average need-based loan:* $3789. *Average need-based gift aid:* $25,057. *Average non-need-based aid:* $15,854. *Average indebtedness upon graduation:* $12,071.

Applying *Options:* early admission, early decision, deferred entrance. *Application fee:* $50. *Required:* essay or personal statement, high school transcript, 3 letters of recommendation, graded writing sample. *Recommended:* minimum 3.0 GPA, interview. *Application deadlines:* 1/1 (freshmen), 4/1 (transfers). *Early decision deadline:* 11/1 (for plan 1), 1/1 (for plan 2). *Notification:* 4/1 (freshmen), 5/1 (transfers), 12/15 (early decision plan 1), 2/15 (early decision plan 2).

Freshman Application Contact Ms. Patricia F. Goldsmith, Dean of Admission and Financial Aid, Scripps College, 1030 Columbia Avenue, Claremont, CA 91711. *Phone:* 909-621-8149. *Toll-free phone:* 800-770-1333. *Fax:* 909-607-7508. *E-mail:* admission@scrippscollege.edu.

See page 460 for the College Close-Up.

SHASTA BIBLE COLLEGE

Redding, California **www.shasta.edu/**

- **Independent nondenominational** comprehensive, founded 1971
- **Small-town** 25-acre campus
- **Endowment** $1.1 million
- **Coed** 74 undergraduate students
- **Noncompetitive** entrance level, 85% of applicants were admitted

Undergraduates Students come from 5 states and territories, 1 other country, 12% are from out of state, 1% African American, 1% Asian American or Pacific Islander, 3% Hispanic American, 1% international, 43% live on campus. *Retention:* 83% of 2006 full-time freshmen returned.

Freshmen *Admission:* 13 applied, 11 admitted.

Faculty *Total:* 34, 29% full-time, 29% with terminal degrees. *Student/faculty ratio:* 5:1.

Majors Biblical studies; education; educational leadership and administration.

Academics *Calendar:* semesters. *Degrees:* certificates, diplomas, associate, bachelor's, and master's. *Special study options:* academic remediation for entering students, accelerated degree program, adult/continuing education programs, cooperative education, distance learning, double majors, independent study, part-time degree program, summer session for credit.

Computers on Campus 15 computers/terminals are available on campus for general student use. Students can access the following: campus intranet, free student e-mail accounts, online (class) schedules. Campuswide network is available. Wireless service is available via classrooms, computer centers, computer labs, learning centers, libraries, student centers.

Student Life *Housing options:* men-only, women-only. Campus housing is university owned. Freshman applicants given priority for college housing. *Activities and organizations:* student-run newspaper, choral group. *Campus security:* 24-hour emergency response devices, student patrols. *Student services:* personal/psychological counseling.

Costs (2008–09) *Tuition:* $7200 full-time, $225 per unit part-time. *Required fees:* $470 full-time, $235 per semester part-time. *Room only:* $1650.

Financial Aid Of all full-time matriculated undergraduates who enrolled in 2006, 40 applied for aid, 35 were judged to have need, 3 had their need fully met. 12 Federal Work-Study jobs (averaging $1000). 4 state and other part-time jobs (averaging $1000). In 2006, 58 non-need-based awards were made. *Average percent of need met:* 60%. *Average financial aid package:* $2582. *Average need-based gift aid:* $4050. *Average non-need-based aid:* $500.

Applying *Options:* early admission. *Application fee:* $35. *Required:* essay or personal statement, high school transcript, minimum 2.0 GPA, 4 letters of recommendation. *Required for some:* interview. *Application deadlines:* 8/25 (freshmen), 8/25 (out-of-state freshmen), 8/25 (transfers). *Notification:* continuous until 9/10 (freshmen).

Freshman Application Contact Mr. Mark A. Mueller, Registrar, Shasta Bible College, 2951 Goodwater Avenue, Redding, CA 96002. *Phone:* 530-221-4275 Ext. 206. *Toll-free phone:* 800-800-45BC (in-state); 800-800-6929 (out-of-state). *Fax:* 530-221-6929. *E-mail:* admissions@shasta.edu.

SILICON VALLEY UNIVERSITY

San Jose, California

Simpson University

Redding, California **www.simpsonuniversity.edu/**

- **Independent** comprehensive, founded 1921, affiliated with The Christian and Missionary Alliance
- **Suburban** 92-acre campus
- **Endowment** $4.6 million
- **Coed** 892 undergraduate students, 99% full-time, 67% women, 33% men
- **Moderately difficult** entrance level, 61% of applicants were admitted

Undergraduates 880 full-time, 12 part-time. Students come from 23 states and territories, 6 other countries, 20% are from out of state, 3% African American, 6% Asian American or Pacific Islander, 6% Hispanic American, 1% Native American, 0.7% international, 10% transferred in, 71% live on campus. *Retention:* 64% of 2006 full-time freshmen returned.

Freshmen *Admission:* 661 applied, 405 admitted, 162 enrolled. *Average high school GPA:* 3.36. *Test scores:* SAT critical reading scores over 500: 57%; SAT math scores over 500: 52%; SAT writing scores over 500: 51%; ACT scores over 18: 90%; SAT critical reading scores over 600: 19%; SAT math scores over 600: 19%; SAT writing scores over 600: 16%; ACT scores over 24: 52%; SAT critical reading scores over 700: 2%; SAT math scores over 700: 2%; SAT writing scores over 700: 2%; ACT scores over 30: 2%.

Faculty *Total:* 98, 45% full-time, 48% with terminal degrees. *Student/faculty ratio:* 15:1.

Majors Biblical studies; business administration and management; communication/speech communication and rhetoric; English; English/language arts teacher education; general studies; history; human resources management; liberal arts and sciences/liberal studies; management information systems; mathematics; missionary studies and missiology; music; music teacher education; organizational behavior; psychology; religious education; social science teacher education; theology and religious vocations related.

Academics *Calendar:* semesters. *Degrees:* certificates, associate, bachelor's, master's, and first professional. *Special study options:* accelerated degree program, adult/continuing education programs, advanced placement credit, distance learning, double majors, honors programs, independent study, internships, off-campus study, part-time degree program, services for LD students, student-designed majors, study abroad, summer session for credit.

Computers on Campus 23 computers/terminals are available on campus for general student use. Students can access the following: campus intranet, computer help desk, free student e-mail accounts, online (class) grades, online (class) registration, online (class) schedules. Campuswide network is available. 100% of college-owned or -operated housing units are wired for high-speed Internet access. Wireless service is available via entire campus.

Student Life *Housing:* on-campus residence required through junior year. *Options:* men-only, women-only, disabled students. Campus housing is university owned. Freshman campus housing is guaranteed. *Activities and organizations:* drama/theater group, student-run newspaper, choral group, Summer Missions Trips, Worship Team (chapel), Student Senate, Spiritual Action Committee, Psychology Club. *Campus security:* 24-hour emergency response devices and patrols, student patrols, late-night transport/escort service, controlled dormitory access, emergency whistle program and monthly campus safety meetings. *Student services:* health clinic, personal/psychological counseling.

Athletics Member NAIA, NCCAA. *Intercollegiate sports:* baseball M, basketball M/W, cheerleading W (c), cross-country running M/W, soccer M/W, volleyball W. *Intramural sports:* baseball M (c), basketball M/W, football M (c)/W (c), soccer M (c)/W (c), softball W (c), table tennis M (c)/W (c), volleyball M (c)/W (c).

Standardized Tests *Required:* SAT or ACT (for admission). *Recommended:* SAT Subject Tests (for admission).

Costs (2008–09) *Comprehensive fee:* $26,200 includes full-time tuition ($19,500) and room and board ($6700). Part-time tuition: $825 per unit. *College room only:* $5900.

Financial Aid Of all full-time matriculated undergraduates who enrolled in 2005, 814 applied for aid, 799 were judged to have need, 113 had their need fully met. In 2005, 43 non-need-based awards were made. *Average percent of need met:* 45%. *Average financial aid package:* $7750. *Average need-based loan:* $4200. *Average need-based gift aid:* $8514. *Average non-need-based aid:* $2000. *Average indebtedness upon graduation:* $17,940.

Applying *Options:* electronic application, deferred entrance. *Application fee:* $40. *Required:* essay or personal statement, high school transcript, 2 letters of recommendation, Christian commitment. *Required for some:* interview. *Application deadlines:* rolling (freshmen), rolling (transfers). *Notification:* continuous (freshmen), continuous (transfers).

Freshman Application Contact Mr. James Herberger, Director of Enrollment Management, Simpson University, 2211 College View Drive, Redding, CA 96003. *Phone:* 530-226-5600. *Toll-free phone:* 800-598-2493. *Fax:* 530-226-4861. *E-mail:* admissions@simpsonuniversity.edu.

Soka University of America

Aliso Viejo, California **www.soka.edu/**

- **Independent** 4-year, founded 2001
- **Suburban** 103-acre campus
- **Endowment** $563.0 million
- **Coed** 361 undergraduate students, 100% full-time, 63% women, 37% men
- **Moderately difficult** entrance level, 26% of applicants were admitted

Undergraduates 361 full-time. Students come from 26 states and territories, 32 other countries, 45% are from out of state, 99% live on campus. *Retention:* 91% of 2006 full-time freshmen returned.

Freshmen *Admission:* 378 applied, 100 admitted, 100 enrolled. *Average high school GPA:* 3.61. *Test scores:* SAT critical reading scores over 500: 53%; SAT math scores over 500: 95%; ACT scores over 18: 100%; SAT critical reading scores over 600: 27%; SAT math scores over 600: 75%; ACT scores over 24: 56%; SAT critical reading scores over 700: 7%; SAT math scores over 700: 21%.

Faculty *Total:* 55, 69% full-time, 82% with terminal degrees. *Student/faculty ratio:* 9:1.

Majors Liberal arts and sciences/liberal studies.

Academics *Calendar:* semesters. *Degrees:* bachelor's and master's. *Special study options:* academic remediation for entering students, independent study, internships, services for LD students, study abroad.

Computers on Campus Students can access the following: campus intranet, computer help desk, free student e-mail accounts, online (class) grades, online (class) registration, online (class) schedules, Angel courseware/PeopleSoft Portal. Campuswide network is available. 100% of college-owned or -operated housing units are wired for high-speed Internet access. Wireless service is available via classrooms, computer centers, computer labs, learning centers, libraries, student centers.

Student Life *Housing:* on-campus residence required through senior year. *Options:* coed, disabled students. Campus housing is university owned. Freshman campus housing is guaranteed. *Activities and organizations:* student-run newspaper, choral group. *Campus security:* 24-hour emergency response devices and patrols, late-night transport/escort service, controlled dormitory access. *Student services:* health clinic, personal/psychological counseling.

Athletics Member NAIA. *Intercollegiate sports:* cross-country running M (s)/W (s), soccer M (s)/W (s), swimming and diving M (s)/W (s), track and field M (s)/W (s), water polo M/W. *Intramural sports:* badminton M/W, baseball M, basketball M/W, soccer W, table tennis M/W, tennis M/W, volleyball M/W.

Standardized Tests *Required:* SAT or ACT (for admission).

Costs (2008–09) *Comprehensive fee:* $33,180 includes full-time tuition ($23,434), mandatory fees ($746), and room and board ($9000). Part-time tuition: $976 per credit.

Applying *Options:* electronic application, early admission, deferred entrance. *Application fee:* $45. *Required:* essay or personal statement, high school transcript, 2 letters of recommendation. *Application deadlines:* 1/15 (freshmen), 10/15 (early action). *Notification:* 3/15 (freshmen), 12/1 (early action).

Freshman Application Contact Ms. Marilyn Grove, Director of Student Recruitment Programs, Soka University of America, 1 University Drive, Aliso Viejo, CA 92656. *Phone:* 949-480-4131. *Toll-free phone:* 949-480-4150 (in-state); 888-600-SOKA (out-of-state). *Fax:* 949-480-4151. *E-mail:* admission@soka.edu.

Sonoma State University

Rohnert Park, California **www.sonoma.edu/**

- **State-supported** comprehensive, founded 1960, part of California State University System
- **Small-town** 280-acre campus with easy access to San Francisco
- **Endowment** $37.4 million
- **Coed** 7,606 undergraduate students, 96% full-time, 62% women, 38% men
- **Moderately difficult** entrance level, 73% of applicants were admitted

Undergraduates 7,327 full-time, 279 part-time. Students come from 40 states and territories, 29 other countries, 1% are from out of state, 2% African American, 5% Asian American or Pacific Islander, 11% Hispanic American, 0.8% Native

American, 1% international, 13% transferred in, 31% live on campus. *Retention:* 74% of 2006 full-time freshmen returned.

Freshmen *Admission:* 10,382 applied, 7,549 admitted, 1,690 enrolled. *Average high school GPA:* 3.13. *Test scores:* SAT math scores over 500: 52%; SAT writing scores over 500: 50%; SAT math scores over 600: 12%; SAT writing scores over 600: 10%; SAT math scores over 700: 1%; SAT writing scores over 700: 1%.

Faculty *Total:* 697, 45% full-time, 54% with terminal degrees. *Student/faculty ratio:* 23:1.

Majors African-American/Black studies; American Indian/Native American studies; American studies; animal physiology; anthropology; applied mathematics; art; art history, criticism and conservation; biology/biological sciences; botany/plant biology; business administration and management; business/managerial economics; cell biology and histology; chemistry; clinical/medical laboratory technology; communication/speech communication and rhetoric; computer science; criminal justice/law enforcement administration; cultural studies; developmental and child psychology; dramatic/theater arts; drawing; ecology; economics; engineering science; English; environmental education; environmental studies; fine/studio arts; French; geography; geology/earth science; health science; Hispanic-American, Puerto Rican, and Mexican-American/Chicano studies; history; interdisciplinary studies; international relations and affairs; kinesiology and exercise science; liberal arts and sciences/liberal studies; literature; marine biology and biological oceanography; mass communication/media; mathematics; medical microbiology and bacteriology; multi-/interdisciplinary studies related; music; music teacher education; nursing (registered nurse training); philosophy; physical education teaching and coaching; physics; political science and government; pre-dentistry studies; pre-law studies; pre-medical studies; pre-veterinary studies; printmaking; psychology; sculpture; sociology; Spanish; statistics; women's studies; zoology/animal biology.

Academics *Calendar:* semesters. *Degrees:* bachelor's and master's. *Special study options:* academic remediation for entering students, accelerated degree program, adult/continuing education programs, advanced placement credit, cooperative education, distance learning, double majors, English as a second language, honors programs, independent study, internships, off-campus study, part-time degree program, services for LD students, student-designed majors, study abroad, summer session for credit. *ROTC:* Army (c), Air Force (c).

Computers on Campus 400 computers/terminals are available on campus for general student use. Students can access the following: computer help desk, free student e-mail accounts, online (class) grades, online (class) registration, online (class) schedules. Campuswide network is available. 100% of college-owned or -operated housing units are wired for high-speed Internet access. Wireless service is available via entire campus.

Student Life *Housing options:* coed, women-only. Campus housing is university owned. Freshman applicants given priority for college housing. *Activities and organizations:* drama/theater group, student-run newspaper, radio station, choral group, Accounting Forum, Sonoma Earth Action, Re-Entry Student Association, Lacrosse Club, Inter-Varsity Christian Fellowship, national fraternities, national sororities. *Campus security:* 24-hour emergency response devices and patrols, student patrols, late-night transport/escort service. *Student services:* health clinic, personal/psychological counseling, women's center, legal services.

Athletics Member NCAA. All Division II. *Intercollegiate sports:* baseball M (s), basketball M (s)/W (s), cross-country running M (s), golf M/W, soccer M (s)/W (s), softball W (s), tennis M (s)/W (s), volleyball W (s), water polo W. *Intramural sports:* baseball M, basketball M/W, cheerleading M/W, crew M/W, cross-country running M, fencing M/W, lacrosse M/W, rock climbing M/W, soccer M/W, softball M/W, swimming and diving M/W, volleyball M/W.

Standardized Tests *Required:* SAT or ACT (for admission).

Costs (2007–08) *Tuition:* state resident $0 full-time; nonresident $8136 full-time, $339 per unit part-time. Full-time tuition and fees vary according to course load and degree level. Part-time tuition and fees vary according to course load and degree level. *Required fees:* $3946 full-time, $1973 per term part-time. *Room and board:* $8820. Room and board charges vary according to housing facility. *Waivers:* employees or children of employees.

Financial Aid Of all full-time matriculated undergraduates who enrolled in 2006, 3,509 applied for aid, 2,748 were judged to have need, 712 had their need fully met. 175 Federal Work-Study jobs (averaging $3508). 694 state and other part-time jobs (averaging $2305). In 2006, 117 non-need-based awards were made. *Average percent of need met:* 74%. *Average financial aid package:* $11,148. *Average need-based loan:* $4127. *Average need-based gift aid:* $6028. *Average non-need-based aid:* $1783. *Average indebtedness upon graduation:* $15,170.

Applying *Options:* electronic application, early admission. *Application fee:* $55. *Required:* high school transcript. *Application deadlines:* rolling (freshmen), rolling (transfers). *Notification:* continuous (freshmen), continuous (transfers).

Freshman Application Contact Mr. Gustavo Flores, Director of Admissions, Sonoma State University, 1801 East Cotati Avenue, Rohnert Park, CA 94928. *Phone:* 707-664-2778. *E-mail:* gustavo.flores@sonoma.edu.

SOUTHERN CALIFORNIA INSTITUTE OF ARCHITECTURE

Los Angeles, California **www.sciarc.edu/**

- **Independent** comprehensive, founded 1972
- **Urban** campus
- **Coed**
- **Moderately difficult** entrance level

Faculty *Student/faculty ratio:* 15:1.

Academics *Calendar:* semesters. *Degrees:* bachelor's, master's, and first professional.

Student Life *Campus security:* 24-hour emergency response devices and patrols.

Standardized Tests *Required:* SAT or ACT (for admission).

Costs (2007–08) *Tuition:* $10,772 full-time. *Required fees:* $60 full-time.

Financial Aid Of all full-time matriculated undergraduates who enrolled in 2005, 173 applied for aid, 147 were judged to have need. In 2005, 12 non-need-based awards were made. *Average percent of need met:* 19. *Average financial aid package:* $11,946. *Average need-based loan:* $4589. *Average need-based gift aid:* $4271. *Average non-need-based aid:* $2239. *Average indebtedness upon graduation:* $33,000.

Applying *Options:* deferred entrance. *Application fee:* $60. *Required:* essay or personal statement, high school transcript, minimum 2.0 GPA, 3 letters of recommendation, portfolio. *Recommended:* interview.

Freshman Application Contact Mr. J.J. Jackman, Admissions Director, Southern California Institute of Architecture, Freight Yard, 960 East 3rd Street, Los Angeles, CA 90013. *Phone:* 213-613-2200 Ext. 321. *Toll-free phone:* 800-774-7242. *Fax:* 213-613-2260. *E-mail:* jj@sciarc.edu.

See page 462 for the College Close-Up.

SOUTHERN CALIFORNIA INSTITUTE OF TECHNOLOGY

Anaheim, California **www.scitcollege.com/**

Freshman Application Contact Ms. Soheila Saboury, Director of Admissions, Southern California Institute of Technology, 1900 West Crescent Avenue, Building B, Anaheim, CA 92801. *Phone:* 714-520-5552. *Fax:* 714-520-4520. *E-mail:* ssaboury@scit-scu.edu.

SOUTHERN CALIFORNIA SEMINARY

El Cajon, California **www.socalsem.edu/**

- **Independent interdenominational** comprehensive, founded 1946
- **Endowment** $109,000
- **Coed, primarily men** 73 undergraduate students
- **Moderately difficult** entrance level, 88% of applicants were admitted

Undergraduates Students come from 14 states and territories, 7 other countries, 20% are from out of state.

Freshmen *Admission:* 25 applied, 22 admitted.

Faculty *Total:* 55, 20% full-time, 42% with terminal degrees. *Student/faculty ratio:* 10:1.

Majors Biblical studies.

Academics *Degrees:* associate, bachelor's, master's, and doctoral.

Computers on Campus 12 computers/terminals are available on campus for general student use. Students can access the following: computer help desk, free student e-mail accounts, online (class) registration, online (class) schedules. Campuswide network is available.

Costs (2007–08) *Tuition:* $6960 full-time, $290 per unit part-time. *Required fees:* $152 full-time. *Payment plan:* installment.

Applying *Options:* electronic application, early admission, deferred entrance. *Required:* essay or personal statement, high school transcript, minimum 2.5 GPA, 3 letters of recommendation, interview. *Application deadline:* 8/13 (freshmen). *Notification:* 8/28 (freshmen).

Freshman Application Contact Mr. Steve Perdue, Director of Admissions, Southern California Seminary, 2075 East Madison Avenue, El Cajon, CA 92019. *Phone:* 888-389-7244. *E-mail:* sperdue@socalsem.edu.

STANFORD UNIVERSITY

Stanford, California **www.stanford.edu/**

- **Independent** university, founded 1891
- **Suburban** 8180-acre campus with easy access to San Francisco
- **Endowment** $17.2 billion
- **Coed** 6,584 undergraduate students, 99% full-time, 48% women, 52% men
- **Most difficult** entrance level, 10% of applicants were admitted

Undergraduates 6,523 full-time, 61 part-time. Students come from 52 states and territories, 68 other countries, 50% are from out of state, 9% African American, 24% Asian American or Pacific Islander, 12% Hispanic American, 2% Native American, 6% international, 0.3% transferred in, 95% live on campus. *Retention:* 98% of 2006 full-time freshmen returned.

Freshmen *Admission:* 23,958 applied, 2,464 admitted, 1,721 enrolled. *Test scores:* SAT critical reading scores over 500: 99%; SAT math scores over 500: 100%; SAT writing scores over 500: 100%; ACT scores over 18: 100%; SAT critical reading scores over 600: 92%; SAT math scores over 600: 95%; SAT writing scores over 600: 93%; ACT scores over 24: 98%; SAT critical reading scores over 700: 61%; SAT math scores over 700: 67%; SAT writing scores over 700: 60%; ACT scores over 30: 70%.

Faculty *Total:* 1,049, 98% full-time, 98% with terminal degrees. *Student/faculty ratio:* 6:1.

Majors Aerospace, aeronautical and astronautical engineering; African-American/Black studies; African studies; American Indian/Native American studies; American studies; ancient/classical Greek; ancient studies; anthropology; archeology; art; art history, criticism and conservation; Asian studies; Asian studies (East); biology/biological sciences; biomedical/medical engineering; chemical engineering; chemistry; Chinese; civil engineering; classics and languages, literatures and linguistics; communication/speech communication and rhetoric; comparative literature; computer engineering; computer science; cultural studies; dramatic/theater arts; earth sciences; economics; electrical, electronics and communications engineering; engineering; English; environmental design/architecture; environmental/environmental health engineering; environmental studies; film/cinema studies; fine/studio arts; French; geological and earth sciences/geosciences related; geology/earth science; geophysics and seismology; German; German studies; Hispanic-American, Puerto Rican, and Mexican-American/Chicano studies; history; humanities; industrial design; interdisciplinary studies; international relations and affairs; Italian; Japanese; Latin; linguistics; materials science; mathematics; mathematics and computer science; mechanical engineering; medical biomathematics/biometrics; music; petroleum engineering; philosophy; physics; political science and government; Portuguese; psychology; public policy analysis; religious studies; science, technology and society; Slavic languages; sociology; Spanish; statistics; systems science and theory; urban studies/affairs; women's studies.

Academics *Calendar:* quarters. *Degrees:* bachelor's, master's, doctoral, and first professional. *Special study options:* advanced placement credit, double majors, honors programs, independent study, internships, off-campus study, services for LD students, student-designed majors, study abroad, summer session for credit. *ROTC:* Army (c), Navy (c), Air Force (c).

Computers on Campus 1,000 computers/terminals and 22,000 ports are available on campus for general student use. Students can access the following: campus intranet, computer help desk, free student e-mail accounts, online (class) grades, online (class) registration, online (class) schedules. Campuswide network is available. 100% of college-owned or -operated housing units are wired for high-speed Internet access. Wireless service is available via entire campus.

Student Life *Housing:* on-campus residence required for freshman year. *Options:* coed, women-only, cooperative, disabled students. Campus housing is university owned. Freshman campus housing is guaranteed. *Activities and organizations:* drama/theater group, student-run newspaper, radio and television station, choral group, marching band, Ram's Head (theatre club), Axe Committee (athletic support), Business Association of Engineering Students, Asian-American Student Association, Stanford Daily, national fraternities, national sororities. *Campus security:* 24-hour emergency response devices and patrols, late-night transport/escort service, controlled dormitory access. *Student services:* health clinic, personal/psychological counseling, women's center, legal services.

Athletics Member NCAA, NAIA. All NCAA Division I except football (Division I-A). *Intercollegiate sports:* baseball M (s), basketball M (s)/W (s), crew M/W (s), cross-country running M (s)/W (s), equestrian sports M (c)/W (c), fencing M (s)/W (s), field hockey W (s), golf M (s)/W (s), gymnastics M (s)/W (s), ice hockey M (c), lacrosse M (c)/W (s), racquetball M (c)/W (c), rugby M (c)/W (c), sailing M/W, skiing (cross-country) M (c)/W (c), skiing (downhill) M (c)/W (c), soccer M (s)/W (s), softball W (s), squash M (c)/W, swimming and diving M (s)/W (s), tennis M (s)/W (s), track and field M (s)/W (s), ultimate Frisbee M/W, volleyball M (s)/W (s), water polo M (s)/W (s), wrestling M (s). *Intramural sports:* archery M/W, badminton M/W, baseball M. basketball M/W, bowling M/W, cross-country running M/W, field hockey W, football M/W, golf M/W, gymnastics M/W, soccer M/W, softball M/W, swimming and diving M/W, table tennis M/W, tennis M/W, track and field M/W, volleyball M/W, water polo M/W, wrestling M.

Standardized Tests *Required:* SAT or ACT (for admission). *Recommended:* SAT Subject Tests (for admission).

Costs (2007–08) *Comprehensive fee:* $45,608 includes full-time tuition ($34,800) and room and board ($10,808). *College room only:* $5863. Room and board charges vary according to board plan. *Waivers:* employees or children of employees.

Financial Aid Of all full-time matriculated undergraduates who enrolled in 2005, 3,530 applied for aid, 3,020 were judged to have need, 2,314 had their need fully met. 930 Federal Work-Study jobs (averaging $2877). 847 state and other part-time jobs (averaging $1617). In 2005, 773 non-need-based awards were made. *Average percent of need met:* 100%. *Average financial aid package:* $29,234. *Average need-based loan:* $2193. *Average need-basea gift aid:* $25,315. *Average non-need-based aid:* $3639. *Average indebtedness upon graduation:* $15,758.

Applying *Options:* electronic application, early action, deferred entrance. *Application fee:* $75. *Required:* essay or personal statement, high school transcript, 2 letters of recommendation. *Application deadlines:* 1/1 (freshmen), 3/15 (transfers), 11/1 (early action). *Notification:* 4/1 (freshmen), 5/25 (transfers), 12/15 (early action).

Freshman Application Contact Rick Shaw, Dean of Undergraduate Admission and Financial Aid, Stanford University, Bakewell Building, 355 Galvez Street, Stanford, CA 94305-3020. *Phone:* 650-723-2091. *Fax:* 650-725-2846. *E-mail:* admission@stanford.edu.

See page 464 for the College Close-Up.

THOMAS AQUINAS COLLEGE

Santa Paula, California **www.thomasaquinas.edu/**

- **Independent Roman Catholic** 4-year, founded 1971
- **Rural** 170-acre campus with easy access to Los Angeles
- **Endowment** $12.4 million
- **Coed** 360 undergraduate students, 100% full-time, 49% women, 51% men
- **Very difficult** entrance level, 60% of applicants were admitted

Undergraduates 360 full-time. Students come from 42 states and territories, 9 other countries, 60% are from out of state, 0.3% African American, 3% Asian American or Pacific Islander, 6% Hispanic American, 0.3% Native American, 6% international, 99% live on campus. *Retention:* 92% of 2006 full-time freshmen returned.

Freshmen *Admission:* 222 applied, 134 admitted, 102 enrolled. *Average high school GPA:* 3.57. *Test scores:* SAT critical reading scores over 500: 100%; SAT math scores over 500: 99%; SAT writing scores over 500: 98%; ACT scores over 18: 100%; SAT critical reading scores over 600: 82%; SAT math scores over 600: 60%; SAT writing scores over 600: 74%; ACT scores over 24: 80%; SAT critical reading scores over 700: 42%; SAT math scores over 700: 24%; ACT scores over 30: 20%.

Faculty *Total:* 37, 78% full-time, 65% with terminal degrees. *Student/faculty ratio:* 11:1.

Majors Interdisciplinary studies; liberal arts and sciences/liberal studies; multi-/interdisciplinary studies related; western civilization.

Academics *Calendar:* semesters. *Degree:* bachelor's. *Special study options:* cooperative education.

Computers on Campus 19 computers/terminals and 17 ports are available on campus for general student use. Students can access the following: free student e-mail accounts. Campuswide network is available.

Student Life *Housing:* on-campus residence required through senior year. *Options:* men-only, women-only. Campus housing is university owned. Freshman campus housing is guaranteed. *Activities and organizations:* drama/theater group, choral group, Musical Groups (choir, chamber orchestra), Theatre Group, language clubs, Pro-Life Ministry. *Campus security:* 24-hour emergency response devices, daily security daytime patrol. *Student services:* health clinic, personal/psychological counseling.

Athletics *Intramural sports:* basketball M/W, football M, soccer M/W, softball M/W, table tennis M/W, tennis M/W, ultimate Frisbee M/W, volleyball M/W.

Standardized Tests *Required:* SAT or ACT (for admission).

Costs (2008–09) *Comprehensive fee:* $28,350 includes full-time tuition ($21,400) and room and board ($6950). *College room only:* $5930.

Financial Aid Of all full-time matriculated undergraduates who enrolled in 2007, 273 applied for aid, 250 were judged to have need, 250 had their need fully

met. 215 state and other part-time jobs (averaging $3552). *Average percent of need met:* 100%. *Average financial aid package:* $16,793. *Average need-based loan:* $3438. *Average need-based gift aid:* $12,152. *Average indebtedness upon graduation:* $14,000. *Financial aid deadline:* 3/2.

Applying *Options:* electronic application, early admission, deferred entrance. *Required:* essay or personal statement, high school transcript, 3 letters of recommendation. *Required for some:* interview. *Recommended:* minimum 3.0 GPA. *Application deadline:* rolling (freshmen). *Notification:* continuous (freshmen).

Freshman Application Contact Mr. Jonathan P. Daly, Director of Admissions, Thomas Aquinas College, 10000 North Ojai Road, Santa Paula, CA 93060-9621. *Phone:* 805-525-4417 Ext. 5901. *Toll-free phone:* 800-634-9797. *Fax:* 805-525-9342. *E-mail:* admissions@thomasaqinas.edu.

TRINITY LIFE BIBLE COLLEGE

Sacramento, California **www.tlbc.edu/**

Director of Admissions Ms. Kathy Clarke, Registrar, Trinity Life Bible College, 5225 Hillsdale Boulevard, Sacramento, CA 95842. *Phone:* 916-348-4689. *E-mail:* kclarke@tlbc.edu.

TUI UNIVERSITY

Cypress, California **www.tuiu.edu/**

- **Independent** university
- **Coed** 5,300 undergraduate students, 55% full-time, 32% women, 68% men
- **Minimally difficult** entrance level, 71% of applicants were admitted

Undergraduates 2,913 full-time, 2,387 part-time. Students come from 50 states and territories, 14 other countries, 90% are from out of state, 92% transferred in. *Retention:* 95% of 2006 full-time freshmen returned.

Freshmen *Admission:* 1,136 applied, 801 admitted, 407 enrolled.

Faculty *Total:* 213, 24% full-time, 99% with terminal degrees. *Student/faculty ratio:* 18:1.

Majors Business/commerce; health/health care administration; health teacher education; hospitality administration; management information systems; public health.

Academics *Calendar:* four 12 week sessions per year. *Degrees:* certificates, diplomas, bachelor's, master's, doctoral, and postbachelor's certificates (offers only online degree programs). *Special study options:* adult/continuing education programs, distance learning, part-time degree program, summer session for credit.

Computers on Campus Students can access the following: computer help desk, free student e-mail accounts, online (class) grades, online (class) registration, online (class) schedules. Campuswide network is available.

Student Life *Housing:* college housing not available.

Costs (2008–09) *Tuition:* $8000 full-time, $250 per credit part-time.

Applying *Options:* electronic application. *Required:* high school transcript, minimum 3.0 GPA. *Required for some:* essay or personal statement. *Application deadline:* rolling (freshmen). *Notification:* continuous (freshmen).

Freshman Application Contact Wei Ren-Finaly, Registrar, TUI University, 5336 Plaza Drive, 3rd Floor, Cypress, CA 90630. *Phone:* 714-816-0366. *Fax:* 714-827-7407. *E-mail:* registration@tuiu.edu.

UNIVERSITY OF CALIFORNIA, BERKELEY

Berkeley, California **www.berkeley.edu/**

- **State-supported** university, founded 1868, part of University of California System
- **Urban** 1232-acre campus with easy access to San Francisco
- **Endowment** $2.8 billion
- **Coed** 24,636 undergraduate students, 97% full-time, 54% women, 46% men
- **Very difficult** entrance level, 23% of applicants were admitted

Undergraduates 23,863 full-time, 773 part-time. Students come from 50 states and territories, 80 other countries, 10% are from out of state, 3% African American, 42% Asian American or Pacific Islander, 12% Hispanic American, 0.5% Native American, 3% international, 8% transferred in, 35% live on campus. *Retention:* 97% of 2006 full-time freshmen returned.

Freshmen *Admission:* 43,983 applied, 10,271 admitted, 4,225 enrolled. *Average high school GPA:* 3.9. *Test scores:* SAT critical reading scores over 500: 92%; SAT math scores over 500: 96%; SAT writing scores over 500: 94%; SAT critical reading scores over 600: 73%; SAT math scores over 600: 82%; SAT writing scores over 600: 74%; SAT critical reading scores over 700: 32%; SAT math scores over 700: 46%; SAT writing scores over 700: 32%.

Faculty *Student/faculty ratio:* 15:1.

Majors African-American/Black studies; American Indian/Native American studies; American studies; ancient/classical Greek; anthropology; applied mathematics; architecture; art; art history, criticism and conservation; Asian-American studies; Asian studies; Asian studies (Southeast); astrophysics; atmospheric sciences and meteorology; biology/biological sciences; biomedical/medical engineering; botany/plant biology; business administration and management; cell and molecular biology; Celtic languages; chemical engineering; chemistry; chemistry related; Chinese; civil engineering; classical, ancient Mediterranean and Near Eastern studies and archaeology; classics and languages, literatures and linguistics; cognitive science; comparative literature; computer science; dance; dramatic/theater arts; Dutch/Flemish; economics; electrical, electronics and communications engineering; engineering physics; engineering science; English; environmental/environmental health engineering; environmental science; environmental studies; ethnic, cultural minority, and gender studies related; film/cinema studies; foreign languages related; forest/forest resources management; forestry; French; geography; geological/geophysical engineering; geology/earth science; German; Hispanic-American, Puerto Rican, and Mexican-American/Chicano studies; history; Italian; Japanese; landscape architecture; Latin; Latin American studies; legal studies; linguistics; manufacturing engineering; mass communication/media; materials science; mathematics; mechanical engineering; microbiology; multi-/interdisciplinary studies related; music; natural resources/conservation; natural resources management and policy; Near and Middle Eastern studies; nuclear engineering; nutrition sciences; operations research; peace studies and conflict resolution; philosophy; physical sciences; physics; political science and government; psychology; public health related; religious studies; Scandinavian languages; Slavic languages; social sciences related; social work; sociology; Spanish; speech and rhetoric; statistics; toxicology; urban studies/affairs; women's studies.

Academics *Calendar:* semesters. *Degrees:* certificates, bachelor's, master's, doctoral, and first professional. *Special study options:* accelerated degree program, adult/continuing education programs, advanced placement credit, distance learning, double majors, English as a second language, honors programs, independent study, internships, off-campus study, services for LD students, student-designed majors, study abroad, summer session for credit. *ROTC:* Army (b), Navy (b), Air Force (b).

Computers on Campus Students can access the following: online (class) registration. Campuswide network is available.

Student Life *Housing options:* coed, men-only, women-only, cooperative, disabled students. Campus housing is university owned and is provided by a third party. Freshman campus housing is guaranteed. *Activities and organizations:* drama/theater group, student-run newspaper, radio and television station, choral group, marching band, national fraternities, national sororities. *Campus security:* 24-hour emergency response devices and patrols, late-night transport/escort service, controlled dormitory access, Office of Emergency Preparedness. *Student services:* health clinic, personal/psychological counseling, women's center, legal services.

Athletics Member NCAA. All Division I except football (Division I-A). *Intercollegiate sports:* baseball M (s), basketball M (s)/W (s), crew M (s)/W (s), cross-country running M (s)/W (s), field hockey W (s), golf M (s)/W (s), gymnastics M (s)/W (s), lacrosse W (s), rugby M (s), soccer M (s)/W (s), softball W (s), swimming and diving M (s)/W (s), tennis M (s)/W (s), track and field M (s), volleyball W (s), water polo M (s)/W (s). *Intramural sports:* badminton M (c)/W (c), basketball M/W, crew M (c)/W (c), fencing M (c)/W (c), field hockey M (c), football M/W, gymnastics M (c)/W (c), ice hockey M (c)/W (c), lacrosse M (c), racquetball M (c)/W (c), rugby W (c), sailing M (c)/W (c), skiing (downhill) M (c)/W (c), soccer M/W (c), softball M/W, squash M (c)/W (c), tennis M (c)/W (c), ultimate Frisbee M (c)/W (c), volleyball M (c), water polo M/W.

Standardized Tests *Required:* SAT or ACT (for admission), SAT Subject Tests (for admission).

Costs (2007–08) *Tuition:* state resident $0 full-time; nonresident $19,068 full-time. Full-time tuition and fees vary according to program. *Required fees:* $7164 full-time. *Room and board:* $13,848. Room and board charges vary according to board plan and housing facility. *Payment plan:* installment.

Financial Aid Of all full-time matriculated undergraduates who enrolled in 2006, 14,420 applied for aid, 11,410 were judged to have need, 6,735 had their need fully met. In 2006, 1464 non-need-based awards were made. *Average percent of need met:* 89%. *Average financial aid package:* $15,710. *Average need-based loan:* $4761. *Average need-based gift aid:* $11,541. *Average non-need-based aid:* $2991. *Average indebtedness upon graduation:* $14,751. *Financial aid deadline:* 3/2.

Applying *Options:* electronic application. *Application fee:* $60. *Required:* essay or personal statement, high school transcript. *Application deadlines:* 11/30 (freshmen), 11/30 (transfers). *Notification:* 3/31 (freshmen), 5/1 (transfers).

Freshman Application Contact University of California, Berkeley, Berkeley, CA 94720. *Phone:* 510-642-2316.

UNIVERSITY OF CALIFORNIA, DAVIS

Davis, California **www.ucdavis.edu/**

- **State-supported** university, founded 1905, part of University of California System
- **Suburban** 5993-acre campus with easy access to San Francisco
- **Coed** 23,499 undergraduate students, 99% full-time, 56% women, 44% men
- **Moderately difficult** entrance level, 59% of applicants were admitted

Undergraduates 23,168 full-time, 331 part-time. Students come from 48 states and territories, 101 other countries, 2% are from out of state, 3% African American, 41% Asian American or Pacific Islander, 12% Hispanic American, 0.7% Native American, 2% international, 8% transferred in, 25% live on campus. *Retention:* 90% of 2006 full-time freshmen returned.

Freshmen *Admission:* 35,148 applied, 20,598 admitted, 4,971 enrolled. *Average high school GPA:* 3.7. *Test scores:* SAT critical reading scores over 500: 74%; SAT math scores over 500: 86%; SAT writing scores over 500: 77%; ACT scores over 18: 92%; SAT critical reading scores over 600: 38%; SAT math scores over 600: 54%; SAT writing scores over 600: 39%; ACT scores over 24: 57%; SAT critical reading scores over 700: 7%; SAT math scores over 700: 13%; SAT writing scores over 700: 7%; ACT scores over 30: 10%.

Faculty *Total:* 1,888, 84% full-time, 95% with terminal degrees. *Student/faculty ratio:* 19:1.

Majors Aerospace, aeronautical and astronautical engineering; African-American/Black studies; agricultural business and management related; agriculture and agriculture operations related; American Indian/Native American studies; American studies; animal sciences; animal sciences related; anthropology; apparel and textiles; applied mathematics; art history, criticism and conservation; Asian-American studies; Asian studies (East); atmospheric sciences and meteorology; biology/biological sciences; biomedical/medical engineering; biotechnology; botany/plant biology; cell biology and histology; chemical engineering; chemistry; Chinese; city/urban, community and regional planning; civil engineering; classical, ancient Mediterranean and Near Eastern studies and archaeology; communication/speech communication and rhetoric; comparative literature; computational mathematics; ecology, evolution, systematics and population biology related; economics; electrical, electronics and communications engineering; engineering related; English; entomology; environmental studies; environmental toxicology; exercise physiology; film/cinema studies; fine/studio arts; food science; French; genetics; geology/earth science; German; Hispanic-American, Puerto Rican, and Mexican-American/Chicano studies; history; human development and family studies; hydrology and water resources science; international agriculture; international relations and affairs; Italian; Japanese; landscape architecture; linguistics; materials engineering; mathematics; mechanical engineering; microbiology; molecular biochemistry; multi-/interdisciplinary studies related; music; natural resources and conservation related; natural resources/conservation; neurobiology and neurophysiology; nutrition sciences; philosophy; physical sciences related; physics; physics related; political science and government; political science and government related; psychology; religious studies; Russian; sociology; soil science and agronomy; Spanish; statistics; urban forestry; visual and performing arts related; women's studies; zoology/animal biology.

Academics *Calendar:* quarters. *Degrees:* bachelor's, master's, doctoral, first professional, post-master's, and postbachelor's certificates. *Special study options:* academic remediation for entering students, adult/continuing education programs, advanced placement credit, double majors, English as a second language, freshman honors college, honors programs, independent study, internships, part-time degree program, services for LD students, student-designed majors, study abroad, summer session for credit. *ROTC:* Army (b), Navy (c), Air Force (c).

Computers on Campus 600 computers/terminals are available on campus for general student use. Students can access the following: campus intranet, computer help desk, free student e-mail accounts, online (class) grades, online (class) registration, online (class) schedules, software packages. Campuswide network is available.

Student Life *Housing options:* coed, women-only, cooperative, disabled students. Campus housing is university owned, leased by the school and is provided by a third party. Freshman campus housing is guaranteed. *Activities and organizations:* drama/theater group, student-run newspaper, radio and television station, choral group, marching band, Filipino Student Organization, Vietnamese Student Association, Jewish Student Union, Alpha Phi Omega, national fraternities, national sororities. *Campus security:* 24-hour emergency response devices and patrols, student patrols, late-night transport/escort service, controlled dormitory access, rape prevention programs. *Student services:* health clinic, personal/psychological counseling, women's center, legal services.

Athletics Member NCAA. All Division II except football (Division I-AA), gymnastics (Division I), wrestling (Division I). *Intercollegiate sports:* baseball M, basketball M/W, cross-country running M/W, golf M/W, gymnastics W, lacrosse M/W, soccer M/W, softball W, swimming and diving M/W, tennis M/W, track and field M/W, volleyball M/W, water polo M/W, wrestling M. *Intramural sports:* archery M (c)/W (c), badminton M (c)/W (c), basketball M/W, crew M (c)/W (c), equestrian sports M (c)/W (c), fencing M (c)/W (c), football M/W, golf M/W, gymnastics M (c), ice hockey M (c)/W, lacrosse M (c)/W (c), racquetball M (c)/W (c), riflery M (c)/W (c), rugby M (c), sailing M (c)/W (c), skiing (cross-country) M (c)/W (c), skiing (downhill) M (c)/W (c), soccer M/W, softball M/W, swimming and diving W (c), table tennis M/W, tennis M/W, volleyball M (c)/W, water polo W (c).

Standardized Tests *Required:* SAT or ACT (for admission), SAT Subject Tests (for admission).

Costs (2008–09) *Tuition:* nonresident $19,620 full-time. *Required fees:* $8124 full-time. *Room and board:* $11,533.

Financial Aid Of all full-time matriculated undergraduates who enrolled in 2005, 12,601 applied for aid, 10,412 were judged to have need, 1,743 had their need fully met. In 2005, 1254 non-need-based awards were made. *Average percent of need met:* 75%. *Average financial aid package:* $11,697. *Average need-based loan:* $4515. *Average need-based gift aid:* $9072. *Average non-need-based aid:* $4342. *Average indebtedness upon graduation:* $12,701.

Applying *Options:* electronic application. *Application fee:* $60. *Required:* essay or personal statement, high school transcript, minimum 2.8 GPA, high school subject requirements. *Application deadlines:* 11/30 (freshmen), 11/30 (transfers). *Notification:* continuous until 3/15 (freshmen), continuous until 3/15 (transfers).

Freshman Application Contact Pamela Burnett, Director of Undergraduate Admissions, University of California, Davis, Undergraduate Admission and Outreach Services, 178 Mrak Hall, Davis, CA 95616. *Phone:* 530-752-1011. *Fax:* 530-752-1280. *E-mail:* freshmanadmissions@ucdavis.edu.

UNIVERSITY OF CALIFORNIA, IRVINE

Irvine, California **www.uci.edu/**

- **State-supported** university, founded 1965, part of University of California System
- **Suburban** 1477-acre campus with easy access to Los Angeles
- **Endowment** $234.0 million
- **Coed** 21,696 undergraduate students, 98% full-time, 52% women, 48% men
- 56% of applicants were admitted

Undergraduates 21,156 full-time, 540 part-time. 2% are from out of state, 2% African American, 51% Asian American or Pacific Islander, 12% Hispanic American, 0.4% Native American, 3% international, 7% transferred in, 36% live on campus. *Retention:* 94% of 2006 full-time freshmen returned.

Freshmen *Admission:* 39,956 applied, 22,220 admitted, 4,931 enrolled. *Average high school GPA:* 3.79. *Test scores:* SAT critical reading scores over 500: 81%; SAT math scores over 500: 91%; SAT writing scores over 500: 84%; SAT critical reading scores over 600: 38%; SAT math scores over 600: 60%; SAT writing scores over 600: 41%; SAT critical reading scores over 700: 8%; SAT math scores over 700: 17%; SAT writing scores over 700: 6%.

Faculty *Total:* 1,968, 74% full-time, 85% with terminal degrees. *Student/faculty ratio:* 19:1.

Majors Aerospace, aeronautical and astronautical engineering; African-American/Black studies; anthropology; area, ethnic, cultural, and gender studies related; art history, criticism and conservation; Asian-American studies; Asian studies (East); biochemistry/biophysics and molecular biology; biology/biological sciences; biomedical/medical engineering; business/managerial economics; cell biology and histology; chemical engineering; chemistry; Chinese; civil engineering; classical, ancient Mediterranean and Near Eastern studies and archaeology; classics and languages, literatures and linguistics; comparative literature; computer and information sciences; computer and information sciences and support services related; computer engineering; computer science; criminology; dance; dramatic/theater arts; ecology; ecology, evolution, systematics and population biology related; econometrics and quantitative economics; economics; electrical, electronics and communications engineering; English; environmental design/architecture; environmental/environmental health engineering; European studies; film/cinema studies; fine/studio arts; French; geology/earth science; German; German studies; Hispanic-American, Puerto Rican, and Mexican-American/Chicano studies; history; human ecology; humanities; information science/studies; international/global studies; Japanese; journalism; linguistics; literature; materials engineering; mathematics; mechanical engineering; microbiological sciences and immunology related; microbiology; multi-/interdisciplinary studies related; music; music performance; neuroscience; nursing related; pharmacy, pharmaceutical sciences, and administration related; philosophy; physics; political science and government; psychology; public health related; religious studies; Russian; social psychology; social sciences; sociology; Spanish; women's studies.

Academics *Calendar:* quarters. *Degrees:* bachelor's, master's, doctoral, first professional, and postbachelor's certificates. *Special study options:* academic remediation for entering students, accelerated degree program, distance learning, double majors, English as a second language, honors programs, independent study, internships, off-campus study, services for LD students, study abroad, summer session for credit. *ROTC:* Army (c), Air Force (c). *Unusual degree programs:* 3-2 business administration.

Computers on Campus 1,500 computers/terminals are available on campus for general student use. Students can access the following: campus intranet, computer help desk, free student e-mail accounts, online (class) grades, online (class) registration, online (class) schedules. Campuswide network is available. Wireless service is available via entire campus.

Student Life *Housing options:* coed, men-only, women-only, cooperative, disabled students. Campus housing is university owned and is provided by a third party. Freshman campus housing is guaranteed. *Activities and organizations:* drama/theater group, student-run newspaper, radio station, choral group, national fraternities, national sororities. *Student services:* health clinic, personal/psychological counseling, women's center, legal services.

Athletics Member NCAA. All Division I. *Intercollegiate sports:* baseball M (s), basketball M (s)/W (s), crew M (s)/W (s), cross-country running M (s)/W (s), fencing M/W, golf M (s)/W (s), lacrosse M/W, racquetball M/W, rugby M, sailing M/W, soccer M (s)/W (s), softball M/W, swimming and diving M (s)/W (s), table tennis M/W, tennis M (s)/W (s), track and field M (s)/W (s), volleyball M (s)/W (s), water polo M (s)/W, weight lifting M/W. *Intramural sports:* badminton M (c)/W (c), baseball M, basketball M/W, bowling M (c)/W (c), cheerleading M/W, fencing M (c)/W (c), field hockey M (c)/W (c), golf M/W, ice hockey M (c), lacrosse M (c)/W (c), racquetball M/W, rugby M (c)/W (c), soccer M (c)/W (c), softball M/W, swimming and diving M/W, table tennis M/W, tennis M/W, track and field M/W, ultimate Frisbee M (c)/W (c), volleyball M (c)/W (c), water polo M (c)/W (c), wrestling M (c)/W (c).

Standardized Tests *Required:* SAT and SAT Subject Tests or ACT (for admission).

Costs (2007–08) *Tuition:* state resident $0 full-time; nonresident $19,620 full-time. *Required fees:* $8276 full-time. *Room and board:* $10,547. Room and board charges vary according to board plan and housing facility. *Payment plan:* installment.

Financial Aid Of all full-time matriculated undergraduates who enrolled in 2007, 13,125 applied for aid, 10,263 were judged to have need, 4,397 had their need fully met. 1,838 Federal Work-Study jobs (averaging $2061). In 2007, 804 non-need-based awards were made. *Average percent of need met:* 82%. *Average financial aid package:* $14,129. *Average need-based loan:* $6046. *Average need-based gift aid:* $10,733. *Average non-need-based aid:* $8299. *Average indebtedness upon graduation:* $13,383. *Financial aid deadline:* 5/1.

Applying *Options:* electronic application. *Application fee:* $60. *Required:* essay or personal statement, high school transcript, minimum 2.8 GPA. *Application deadlines:* 11/30 (freshmen), 11/30 (transfers). *Notification:* 3/31 (freshmen), 5/1 (transfers).

Freshman Application Contact University of California, Irvine, 204 Administration, Irvine, CA 92697-1075. *Phone:* 949-824-6703.

UNIVERSITY OF CALIFORNIA, LOS ANGELES

Los Angeles, California **www.ucla.edu/**

- **State-supported** university, founded 1919, part of University of California System
- **Urban** 419-acre campus
- **Coed** 25,928 undergraduate students, 96% full-time, 55% women, 45% men
- **Very difficult** entrance level, 24% of applicants were admitted

Undergraduates 24,931 full-time, 997 part-time. Students come from 49 states and territories, 63 other countries, 4% are from out of state, 3% African American, 38% Asian American or Pacific Islander, 15% Hispanic American, 0.4% Native American, 4% international, 13% transferred in, 35% live on campus. *Retention:* 97% of 2006 full-time freshmen returned.

Freshmen *Admission:* 50,755 applied, 11,963 admitted, 4,564 enrolled. *Average high school GPA:* 4.0. *Test scores:* SAT critical reading scores over 500: 91%; SAT math scores over 500: 93%; SAT writing scores over 500: 93%; ACT scores over 18: 98%; SAT critical reading scores over 600: 66%; SAT math scores over 600: 76%; SAT writing scores over 600: 67%; ACT scores over 24: 79%; SAT critical reading scores over 700: 20%; SAT math scores over 700: 39%; SAT writing scores over 700: 23%; ACT scores over 30: 35%.

Faculty *Total:* 2,654, 73% full-time, 98% with terminal degrees. *Student/faculty ratio:* 16:1.

Majors Aerospace, aeronautical and astronautical engineering; African-American/Black studies; African languages; agricultural/biological engineering and bioengineering; American Indian/Native American studies; American literature; ancient/classical Greek; anthropology; applied mathematics; Arabic; architecture; area, ethnic, cultural, and gender studies related; area studies related; art; art history, criticism and conservation; Asian-American studies; Asian studies; Asian studies (East); Asian studies (Southeast); astrophysics; atmospheric sciences and meteorology; atmospheric sciences and meteorology related; biochemistry; biology/biological sciences; biomathematics and bioinformatics related; biophysics; biotechnology; botany/plant biology; business/managerial economics; cell and molecular biology; chemical engineering; chemistry; Chinese; civil engineering; classical, ancient Mediterranean and Near Eastern studies and archaeology; classics and classical languages related; cognitive science; communication/speech communication and rhetoric; comparative literature; computational mathematics; computer and information sciences; computer engineering; design and applied arts related; development economics and international development; dramatic/theater arts; East Asian languages related; ecology; economics; electrical, electronics and communications engineering; English; environmental science; European studies; film/cinema studies; fine arts related; foreign languages related; French; geography; geography related; geological and earth sciences/geosciences related; geological/geophysical engineering; geology/earth science; geophysics and seismology; German; Hebrew; Hispanic-American, Puerto Rican, and Mexican-American/Chicano studies; history; international economics; international/global studies; Italian; Japanese; Korean; Latin; Latin American studies; liberal arts and sciences and humanities related; linguistic and comparative language studies related; linguistics; marine biology and biological oceanography; materials engineering; materials science; mathematics; mathematics related; mechanical engineering; microbiological sciences and immunology related; multi-/interdisciplinary studies related; music; music history, literature, and theory; musicology and ethnomusicology; neuroscience; nursing related; philosophy; physics; physiological psychology/psychobiology; physiology; political science and government; Portuguese; psychology; religious studies; Russian; Russian studies; Scandinavian languages; Slavic languages; sociology; Spanish; statistics; women's studies.

Academics *Calendar:* quarters. *Degrees:* bachelor's, master's, doctoral, and first professional. *Special study options:* adult/continuing education programs, advanced placement credit, distance learning, double majors, English as a second language, freshman honors college, honors programs, independent study, internships, off-campus study, services for LD students, student-designed majors, study abroad, summer session for credit. *ROTC:* Army (b), Navy (b), Air Force (b).

Computers on Campus 4,134 computers/terminals are available on campus for general student use. Students can access the following: campus intranet, computer help desk, free student e-mail accounts, online (class) grades, online (class) registration, online (class) schedules. Campuswide network is available. 100% of college-owned or -operated housing units are wired for high-speed Internet access. Wireless service is available via entire campus.

Student Life *Housing options:* coed. Campus housing is university owned. *Activities and organizations:* drama/theater group, student-run newspaper, radio and television station, choral group, marching band, Student Alumni Association, student government, Rally Committee, national fraternities, national sororities. *Campus security:* 24-hour emergency response devices and patrols, student patrols, late-night transport/escort service, controlled dormitory access. *Student services:* health clinic, personal/psychological counseling, women's center, legal services.

Athletics Member NCAA. All Division I except football (Division I-A). *Intercollegiate sports:* baseball M (s), basketball M (s)/W (s), crew W, cross-country running M (s)/W (s), golf M (s)/W (s), gymnastics W (s), soccer M (s)/W (s), softball W (s), swimming and diving W (s), tennis M (s)/W (s), track and field M (s)/W (s), volleyball M (s)/W (s), water polo M (s)/W (s). *Intramural sports:* archery M/W, badminton M/W, basketball M/W, bowling M/W, crew M/W, cross-country running M/W, fencing M/W, field hockey W, football M/W, golf M/W, gymnastics M/W, ice hockey M/W, lacrosse M/W, racquetball M/W, riflery M/W, rugby M/W, sailing M/W, skiing (cross-country) M/W, skiing (downhill) M/W, soccer M/W, softball M/W, squash M/W, swimming and diving M/W, table tennis M/W, tennis M/W, track and field M/W, ultimate Frisbee M/W, volleyball M/W, water polo M/W.

Standardized Tests *Required:* SAT or ACT (for admission), SAT Subject Tests (for admission).

Costs (2007–08) *Tuition:* state resident $0 full-time; nonresident $19,068 full-time. *Required fees:* $7038 full-time. *Room and board:* $12,420. Room and board charges vary according to board plan and housing facility.

Financial Aid Of all full-time matriculated undergraduates who enrolled in 2006, 13,747 applied for aid, 12,311 were judged to have need, 4,322 had their need fully met. 2,735 Federal Work-Study jobs (averaging $2127). 600 state and other part-time jobs (averaging $1040). In 2006, 993 non-need-based awards were made. *Average percent of need met:* 82%. *Average financial aid package:* $14,329. *Average need-based loan:* $5539. *Average need-based gift aid:* $10,944. *Average non-need-based aid:* $3938. *Average indebtedness upon graduation:* $15,996.

Applying *Options:* electronic application. *Application fee:* $60. *Required:* essay or personal statement. *Application deadlines:* 11/30 (freshmen), 11/30 (transfers). *Notification:* 3/15 (freshmen), 4/30 (transfers).

Freshman Application Contact Dr. Vu T. Tran, Director of Undergraduate Admissions, University of California, Los Angeles, 405 Hilgard Avenue, Box 951436, Los Angeles, CA 90095-1436. *Phone:* 310-825-3101. *E-mail:* ugadm@saonet.ucla.edu.

UNIVERSITY OF CALIFORNIA, RIVERSIDE

Riverside, California **www.ucr.edu/**

- **State-supported** university, founded 1954, part of University of California System
- **Urban** 1200-acre campus with easy access to Los Angeles
- **Endowment** $120.5 million
- **Coed** 14,973 undergraduate students, 97% full-time, 52% women, 48% men
- **Very difficult** entrance level, 82% of applicants were admitted

Undergraduates 14,556 full-time, 417 part-time. Students come from 32 states and territories, 31 other countries, 1% are from out of state, 7% African American, 42% Asian American or Pacific Islander, 26% Hispanic American, 0.4% Native American, 2% international, 6% transferred in, 35% live on campus. *Retention:* 83% of 2006 full-time freshmen returned.

Freshmen *Admission:* 20,126 applied, 16,592 admitted, 3,729 enrolled. *Average high school GPA:* 3.4. *Test scores:* SAT critical reading scores over 500: 54%; SAT math scores over 500: 67%; SAT writing scores over 500: 56%; ACT scores over 18: 80%; SAT critical reading scores over 600: 15%; SAT math scores over 600: 29%; SAT writing scores over 600: 14%; ACT scores over 24: 25%; SAT critical reading scores over 700: 2%; SAT math scores over 700: 5%; SAT writing scores over 700: 1%; ACT scores over 30: 3%.

Faculty *Total:* 915, 83% full-time, 98% with terminal degrees. *Student/faculty ratio:* 19:1.

Majors African-American/Black studies; American Indian/Native American studies; anthropology; anthropology related; art; art history, criticism and conservation; Asian-American studies; Asian studies; biochemistry; biology/biological sciences; biomedical/medical engineering; biomedical sciences; botany/plant biology; business administration and management; business/managerial economics; chemical engineering; chemistry; Chinese; classics and languages, literatures and linguistics; comparative literature; computer engineering; computer science; creative writing; cultural studies; dance; dramatic/theater arts; economics; economics related; electrical, electronics and communications engineering; English; entomology; environmental/environmental health engineering; environmental studies; ethnic, cultural minority, and gender studies related; fine/studio arts; foreign languages and literatures; foreign languages related; French; geology/earth science; geophysics and seismology; German; Hispanic-American, Puerto Rican, and Mexican-American/Chicano studies; history; history related; human development and family studies; humanities; information science/studies; international/global studies; international relations and affairs; Latin American studies; legal studies; liberal arts and sciences/liberal studies; linguistics; materials science; mathematics; mechanical engineering; multi-/interdisciplinary studies related; music; music related; neuroscience; philosophy; philosophy related; physical sciences; physics; physiological psychology/psychobiology; political science and government; political science and government related; pre-law studies; psychology; psychology related; public administration; public policy analysis; religious studies; Russian; Russian studies; social sciences; social sciences related; sociology; Spanish; statistics; women's studies.

Academics *Calendar:* quarters. *Degrees:* bachelor's, master's, doctoral, and postbachelor's certificates. *Special study options:* academic remediation for entering students, accelerated degree program, adult/continuing education programs, advanced placement credit, cooperative education, double majors, English as a second language, honors programs, independent study, internships, off-campus study, services for LD students, student-designed majors, study abroad, summer session for credit. *ROTC:* Army (c), Air Force (c).

Computers on Campus 793 computers/terminals are available on campus for general student use. Students can access the following: campus intranet, computer help desk, free student e-mail accounts, online (class) grades, online (class) registration, online (class) schedules, online viewing of financial information. Campuswide network is available. Wireless service is available via entire campus.

Student Life *Housing options:* coed. Campus housing is university owned and is provided by a third party. Freshman campus housing is guaranteed. *Activities and organizations:* drama/theater group, student-run newspaper, radio station, choral group, Associated Students, Student Alumni Association, Health Careers Organization, national fraternities, national sororities. *Campus security:* 24-hour emergency response devices and patrols, student patrols, late-night transport/escort service, controlled dormitory access. *Student services:* health clinic, personal/psychological counseling, women's center, legal services.

Athletics Member NCAA. All Division I. *Intercollegiate sports:* baseball M (s), basketball M (s)/W (s), cross-country running M (s)/W (s), golf M (s)/W (s), softball W (s), tennis M (s)/W (s), track and field M (s)/W (s), volleyball W (s). *Intramural sports:* badminton M/W, basketball M/W, cheerleading M (c)/W (c), field hockey M (c)/W (c), football M/W, golf M/W, racquetball M/W, rock climbing M (c)/W (c), rugby M (c)/W (c), skiing (cross-country) M (c)/W (c), skiing (downhill) M (c)/W (c), soccer M/W, softball M/W, table tennis M (c)/W (c), tennis M/W, ultimate Frisbee M (c)/W (c), volleyball M/W.

Standardized Tests *Required:* SAT or ACT (for admission), SAT Subject Tests (for admission).

Costs (2007–08) *Tuition:* state resident $0 full-time; nonresident $19,068 full-time. *Required fees:* $7355 full-time. *Room and board:* $10,800. Room and board charges vary according to board plan and housing facility. *Payment plan:* deferred payment.

Financial Aid Of all full-time matriculated undergraduates who enrolled in 2007, 10,733 applied for aid, 9,279 were judged to have need, 3,645 had their need fully met. 1,910 Federal Work-Study jobs (averaging $2184). In 2007, 138 non-need-based awards were made. *Average percent of need met:* 81%. *Average financial aid package:* $14,311. *Average need-based loan:* $6005. *Average need-based gift aid:* $10,306. *Average non-need-based aid:* $6563. *Average indebtedness upon graduation:* $14,992. *Financial aid deadline:* 3/2.

Applying *Options:* electronic application. *Application fee:* $60. *Required:* essay or personal statement, high school transcript, minimum 2.8 GPA. *Application deadlines:* 11/30 (freshmen), 11/30 (transfers). *Notification:* continuous (freshmen), continuous until 3/1 (transfers).

Freshman Application Contact Emily Engelschall, Director, Undergraduate Recruitment, University of California, Riverside, 1101 Hinderaker Hall, 900 University Avenue, Riverside, CA 92521. *Phone:* 951-827-4531. *Fax:* 951-827-6344. *E-mail:* discover@ucr.edu.

UNIVERSITY OF CALIFORNIA, SAN DIEGO

La Jolla, California **www.ucsd.edu/**

- **State-supported** university, founded 1959, part of University of California System
- **Suburban** 1976-acre campus with easy access to San Diego
- **Coed** 22,048 undergraduate students, 100% full-time, 51% women, 49% men
- **Very difficult** entrance level, 40% of applicants were admitted

Undergraduates 22,048 full-time. 3% are from out of state, 1% African American, 44% Asian American or Pacific Islander, 12% Hispanic American, 7% transferred in, 35% live on campus. *Retention:* 93% of 2006 full-time freshmen returned.

Freshmen *Admission:* 45,072 applied, 17,866 admitted, 4,141 enrolled. *Average high school GPA:* 3.93. *Test scores:* SAT critical reading scores over 500: 88%; SAT math scores over 500: 97%; ACT scores over 18: 97%; SAT critical reading scores over 600: 55%; SAT math scores over 600: 76%; ACT scores over 24: 72%; SAT critical reading scores over 700: 13%; SAT math scores over 700: 30%; ACT scores over 30: 19%.

Faculty *Total:* 1,269, 86% full-time, 89% with terminal degrees. *Student/faculty ratio:* 19:1.

Majors Aerospace, aeronautical and astronautical engineering; animal physiology; anthropology; applied mathematics; archeology; art; art history, criticism and conservation; atomic/molecular physics; biochemistry; biology/biological sciences; biomedical/medical engineering; biophysics; biotechnology; cell biology and histology; chemical engineering; chemistry; chemistry teacher education; Chinese; classics and languages, literatures and linguistics; cognitive psychology and psycholinguistics; computer engineering; computer science; creative writing; cultural studies; dance; dramatic/theater arts; ecology; econometrics and quantitative economics; economics; electrical, electronics and communications engineering; engineering; engineering physics; engineering science; English; environmental studies; film/cinema studies; fine/studio arts; foreign languages and literatures; French; geology/earth science; German; history; human ecology; interdisciplinary studies; intermedia/multimedia; Italian; Japanese; Jewish/Judaic studies; Latin American studies; linguistics; literature; management science; mass communication/media; mathematics; mathematics teacher education; mechanical engineering; medical microbiology and bacteriology; medicinal and pharmaceutical chemistry; molecular biology; music; music history, literature, and theory; natural resources management and policy; philosophy; physics; physics teacher education; political science and government; psychology; religious studies; Russian; Russian studies; sociology; Spanish; structural engineering; systems engineering; urban studies/affairs; women's studies.

Academics *Calendar:* quarters. *Degrees:* bachelor's, master's, doctoral, and first professional. *Special study options:* accelerated degree program, advanced placement credit, cooperative education, double majors, English as a second language, freshman honors college, honors programs, independent study, internships, off-campus study, services for LD students, student-designed majors, study abroad, summer session for credit. *ROTC:* Army (c).

Computers on Campus 1,500 computers/terminals are available on campus for general student use. Students can access the following: computer help desk, free student e-mail accounts, online (class) registration, online (class) schedules. Campuswide network is available.

Student Life *Housing options:* coed, men-only, women-only, disabled students. Campus housing is university owned. Freshman campus housing is guaranteed. *Activities and organizations:* drama/theater group, student-run newspaper, radio and television station, choral group, cultural organizations, recreational clubs, service organizations, spiritual/religious organizations, national fraternities, national sororities. *Campus security:* 24-hour emergency response devices and patrols, student patrols, late-night transport/escort service, crime prevention programs. *Student services:* health clinic, personal/psychological counseling, women's center, legal services.

Athletics Member NCAA. All Division II. *Intercollegiate sports:* baseball M, basketball M/W, crew M/W, cross-country running M/W, fencing M/W, golf M, soccer M/W, softball W, swimming and diving M/W, tennis M/W, track and field M/W, volleyball M/W, water polo M/W. *Intramural sports:* basketball M/W, equestrian sports M (c)/W (c), football M (c)/W (c), ice hockey M, lacrosse M (c)/W (c), racquetball M/W, sailing M (c)/W (c), skiing (downhill) M (c)/W (c), soccer M/W, softball M/W, table tennis M/W, tennis M/W, ultimate Frisbee M (c)/W (c), volleyball M/W, water polo M/W.

Standardized Tests *Required:* ACT Assessment with Writing or SAT Reasoning Test, plus two SAT Subject Tests (for admission).

Costs (2008–09) *Tuition:* state resident $0 full-time; nonresident $20,021 full-time. *Required fees:* $7509 full-time. *Room and board:* $10,237.

Financial Aid Of all full-time matriculated undergraduates who enrolled in 2006, 13,009 applied for aid, 10,769 were judged to have need, 2,745 had their need fully met. 5,040 Federal Work-Study jobs (averaging $1934). In 2006, 619 non-need-based awards were made. *Average percent of need met:* 83%. *Average financial aid package:* $13,745. *Average need-based loan:* $5072. *Average need-based gift aid:* $10,034. *Average non-need-based aid:* $6799. *Average indebtedness upon graduation:* $15,170.

Applying *Options:* electronic application. *Application fee:* $60. *Required:* essay or personal statement, high school transcript, minimum 2.8 GPA. *Required for some:* minimum 3.4 GPA. *Application deadlines:* 11/30 (freshmen), 11/30 (transfers). *Notification:* 3/31 (freshmen), 5/1 (transfers).

Freshman Application Contact Ms. Mae Brown, Assistant Vice Chancellor, Admissions and Relations with Schools, University of California, San Diego, 9500 Gilman Drive, 0021, La Jolla, CA 92093-0021. *Phone:* 858-534-4831. *E-mail:* admissionsinfo@ucsd.edu.

UNIVERSITY OF CALIFORNIA, SANTA BARBARA

Santa Barbara, California **www.ucsb.edu/**

- **State-supported** university, founded 1909, part of University of California System
- **Suburban** 989-acre campus
- **Endowment** $80,336
- **Coed** 18,415 undergraduate students, 98% full-time, 55% women, 45% men
- **Very difficult** entrance level, 54% of applicants were admitted

Undergraduates 17,960 full-time, 455 part-time. Students come from 51 states and territories, 72 other countries, 4% are from out of state, 3% African American, 16% Asian American or Pacific Islander, 19% Hispanic American, 0.7% Native American, 1% international, 7% transferred in, 31% live on campus. *Retention:* 91% of 2006 full-time freshmen returned.

Freshmen *Admission:* 40,933 applied, 22,273 admitted, 4,335 enrolled. *Average high school GPA:* 3.76. *Test scores:* SAT critical reading scores over 500: 85%; SAT math scores over 500: 87%; SAT writing scores over 500: 85%; ACT scores over 18: 97%; SAT critical reading scores over 600: 51%; SAT math scores over 600: 56%; SAT writing scores over 600: 48%; ACT scores over 24: 74%; SAT critical reading scores over 700: 11%; SAT math scores over 700: 13%; SAT writing scores over 700: 8%; ACT scores over 30: 18%.

Faculty *Total:* 1,067, 86% full-time, 100% with terminal degrees. *Student/faculty ratio:* 17:1.

Majors African-American/Black studies; anthropology; applied mathematics related; aquatic biology/limnology; area studies related; art history, criticism and conservation; Asian-American studies; Asian studies; biochemistry; biochemistry, biophysics and molecular biology related; biology/biological sciences; biopsychology; business/managerial economics; cell biology and histology; chemical engineering; chemistry; chemistry related; Chinese; classics and languages, literatures and linguistics; communication/speech communication and rhetoric; comparative literature; computer engineering; computer science; dance; dramatic/theater arts; ecology, evolution, systematics and population biology related; econometrics and quantitative economics; economics; electrical, electronics and communications engineering; English; environmental studies; film/cinema studies; fine/studio arts; French; geography; geology/earth science; geophysics and seismology; German; Hispanic-American, Puerto Rican, and Mexican-American/Chicano studies; history; hydrology and water resources science; interdisciplinary studies; international/global studies; Italian; Japanese; legal studies; liberal arts and sciences and humanities related; liberal arts and sciences/liberal studies; linguistics; marine biology and biological oceanography; mathematics; mechanical engineering; medical microbiology and bacteriology; medieval and Renaissance studies; microbiology; molecular biology; multi-/interdisciplinary studies related; music; Near and Middle Eastern studies; pharmacology; philosophy; physics; physiology; political science and government; Portuguese; pre-law studies; psychology; public/applied history and archival administration; religious studies; Slavic languages; sociology; Spanish; statistics; women's studies; zoology/animal biology.

Academics *Calendar:* quarters plus 6-week summer term. *Degrees:* bachelor's, master's, doctoral, and first professional certificates. *Special study options:* accelerated degree program, advanced placement credit, cooperative education, distance learning, double majors, English as a second language, honors programs, independent study, internships, off-campus study, services for LD students, student-designed majors, study abroad, summer session for credit. *ROTC:* Army (b).

Computers on Campus 3,000 computers/terminals are available on campus for general student use. Campuswide network is available.

Student Life *Housing options:* coed, cooperative. Campus housing is university owned and is provided by a third party. Freshman applicants given priority for college housing. *Activities and organizations:* drama/theater group, student-run newspaper, radio and television station, choral group, national fraternities, national sororities. *Campus security:* 24-hour emergency response devices, late-night transport/escort service. *Student services:* health clinic, personal/psychological counseling, women's center, legal services.

Athletics Member NCAA. All Division I. *Intercollegiate sports:* baseball M (s), basketball M (s)/W (s), bowling M (c)/W (c), crew M (c)/W (c), cross-country running M (s)/W (s), equestrian sports M (c)/W (c), fencing M (c)/W (c), field hockey W (c), golf M (s), gymnastics M (s)/W (s), lacrosse M (c)/W (c), rugby M (c), sailing M (c)/W (c), skiing (downhill) M (c)/W (c), soccer M (s)/W (s), softball W (s), swimming and diving M (s)/W (s), tennis M (s)/W (s), track and field M (s)/W (s), ultimate Frisbee M (c)/W (c), volleyball M (s)/W (s), water polo M (s)/W (s). *Intramural sports:* badminton M/W, basketball M/W, bowling M/W, cross-country running M/W, football M/W, golf M/W, gymnastics M/W, racquetball M/W, soccer M/W, softball M/W, squash M/W, tennis M/W, ultimate Frisbee M/W, volleyball M/W, water polo M/W.

Standardized Tests *Required:* SAT or ACT (for admission), SAT Subject Tests (for admission).

Costs (2007–08) *Tuition:* state resident $0 full-time; nonresident $19,620 full-time. *Required fees:* $7896 full-time. *Room and board:* $11,604; room only: $9091. *Waivers:* employees or children of employees.

Financial Aid Of all full-time matriculated undergraduates who enrolled in 2006, 10,721 applied for aid, 8,328 were judged to have need, 2,319 had their need fully met. In 2006, 327 non-need-based awards were made. *Average percent of need met:* 80%. *Average financial aid package:* $14,216. *Average need-based loan:* $5798. *Average need-based gift aid:* $11,104. *Average non-need-based aid:* $6224.

Applying *Options:* electronic application. *Application fee:* $60. *Required:* essay or personal statement, high school transcript. *Required for some:* interview. *Application deadlines:* 11/30 (freshmen), 11/30 (transfers). *Notification:* 3/15 (freshmen), 5/1 (transfers).

Freshman Application Contact Office of Admissions, University of California, Santa Barbara, 1234 Cheadle Hall, Santa Barbara, CA 93106-2014. *Phone:* 805-893-2881. *Fax:* 805-893-2676. *E-mail:* admissions@sa.ucsb.edu.

UNIVERSITY OF CALIFORNIA, SANTA CRUZ

Santa Cruz, California **www.ucsc.edu/**

- **State-supported** university, founded 1965, part of University of California System
- **Small-town** 2000-acre campus with easy access to San Francisco and San Jose
- **Endowment** $115.2 million
- **Coed** 14,403 undergraduate students, 97% full-time, 54% women, 46% men
- **Very difficult** entrance level, 82% of applicants were admitted

Undergraduates 13,909 full-time, 494 part-time. Students come from 43 states and territories, 78 other countries, 2% are from out of state, 3% African American, 21% Asian American or Pacific Islander, 16% Hispanic American, 0.9% Native American, 0.7% international, 5% transferred in, 47% live on campus. *Retention:* 89% of 2006 full-time freshmen returned.

Freshmen *Admission:* 24,453 applied, 20,059 admitted, 3,704 enrolled. *Average high school GPA:* 3.50. *Test scores:* SAT critical reading scores over 500: 77%; SAT math scores over 500: 81%; SAT writing scores over 500: 77%; ACT scores over 18: 93%; SAT critical reading scores over 600: 36%; SAT math scores over 600: 39%; SAT writing scores over 600: 36%; ACT scores over 24: 56%; SAT critical reading scores over 700: 7%; SAT math scores over 700: 6%; SAT writing scores over 700: 4%; ACT scores over 30: 10%.

Faculty *Total:* 791, 70% full-time, 95% with terminal degrees. *Student/faculty ratio:* 19:1.

Majors Agricultural/biological engineering and bioengineering; American studies; anthropology; art; art history, criticism and conservation; biochemistry; bioinformatics; biology/biological sciences; business/managerial economics; cell biology and histology; chemistry; classics and languages, literatures and linguistics; cognitive psychology and psycholinguistics; computer engineering; computer graphics; computer science; creative writing; developmental and child psychology; dramatic/theater arts; ecology; economics; education; electrical, electronics and communications engineering; environmental studies; family and community services; family/community studies; film/cinema studies; foreign languages and literatures; geology/earth science; German; health science; Hispanic-American, Puerto Rican, and Mexican-American/Chicano studies; history; information science/studies; international economics; Italian studies; Latin American studies; legal studies; linguistics; literature; marine biology and biological oceanography; mathematics; molecular biology; music; neuroscience; philosophy; physics; plant sciences; political science and government; pre-law; pre-medical studies; psychology; Russian studies; sociology; women's studies.

Academics *Calendar:* quarters. *Degrees:* certificates, bachelor's, master's, doctoral, and postbachelor's certificates. *Special study options:* academic remediation for entering students, adult/continuing education programs, advanced placement credit, cooperative education, double majors, English as a second language, freshman honors college, independent study, internships, off-campus study, part-time degree program, services for LD students, student-designed majors, study abroad, summer session for credit. *ROTC:* Army (c), Navy (c), Air Force (c). *Unusual degree programs:* 3-2 engineering with University of California, Berkeley.

Computers on Campus 320 computers/terminals are available on campus for general student use. Students can access the following: computer help desk, free student e-mail accounts, online (class) grades, online (class) registration, online (class) schedules. Campuswide network is available. 100% of college-owned or -operated housing units are wired for high-speed Internet access. Wireless service is available via entire campus.

Student Life *Housing options:* coed, men-only, women-only, cooperative. Campus housing is university owned. Freshman campus housing is guaranteed. *Activities and organizations:* drama/theater group, student-run newspaper, radio and television station, choral group, Filipino Student Association, Movimiento Estudiantil Chicano de Aztlan, African/Black Student Alliance, Asian Pacific Islander Student Alliance, Gay, Lesbian, Bisexual, Trans Network, national fraternities, national sororities. *Campus security:* 24-hour emergency response devices and patrols, late-night transport/escort service, controlled dormitory access, evening main gate security, campus police force and fire station. *Student services:* health clinic, personal/psychological counseling, women's center.

Athletics Member NCAA. All Division III. *Intercollegiate sports:* basketball M/W, cross-country running M (c)/W, equestrian sports M (c)/W (c), fencing M (c)/W (c), golf W, lacrosse M (c)/W (c), rugby M (c)/W (c), sailing M (c)/W (c), soccer M/W, softball W (c), swimming and diving M/W, table tennis M (c)/W (c), tennis M/W, track and field M (c)/W (c), ultimate Frisbee M (c)/W (c), volleyball M/W, water polo M/W. *Intramural sports:* badminton M/W, basketball M/W, cross-country running M/W, fencing M/W, racquetball M/W, soccer M/W, softball M/W, tennis M/W, volleyball M/W.

Standardized Tests *Required:* SAT or ACT (for admission), SAT Subject Tests required in two different areas: history/social science, English literature, mathematics, laboratory science, or language other than English (for admission).

Costs (2008–09) *Tuition:* state resident $0 full-time; nonresident $20,610 full-time. *Required fees:* $9534 full-time. *Room and board:* $12,831.

Financial Aid Of all full-time matriculated undergraduates who enrolled in 2006, 8,470 applied for aid, 6,513 were judged to have need, 2,986 had their need fully met. 1,617 Federal Work-Study jobs (averaging $1219). In 2006, 290 non-need-based awards were made. *Average percent of need met:* 87%. *Average financial aid package:* $14,422. *Average need-based loan:* $5168. *Average need-based gift aid:* $10,582. *Average non-need-based aid:* $7603. *Financial aid deadline:* 6/1.

Applying *Options:* electronic application. *Application fee:* $60. *Required:* essay or personal statement, high school transcript. *Application deadlines:* 11/30 (freshmen), 11/30 (transfers). *Notification:* 3/15 (freshmen), 4/30 (transfers).

Freshman Application Contact University of California, Santa Cruz, Admissions Office, Cook House, Santa Cruz, CA 95064. *Phone:* 831-459-5779.

UNIVERSITY OF LA VERNE

La Verne, California **www.ulv.edu/**

- **Independent** university, founded 1891
- **Suburban** 38-acre campus with easy access to Los Angeles
- **Coed** 1,682 undergraduate students, 95% full-time, 64% women, 36% men
- **Moderately difficult** entrance level, 65% of applicants were admitted

Undergraduates 1,593 full-time, 89 part-time. Students come from 13 states and territories, 5 other countries, 2% are from out of state, 7% African American, 4% Asian American or Pacific Islander, 39% Hispanic American, 0.6% Native American, 1% international, 9% transferred in, 32% live on campus. *Retention:* 85% of 2006 full-time freshmen returned.

Freshmen *Admission:* 1,538 applied, 993 admitted, 336 enrolled. *Average high school GPA:* 3.35. *Test scores:* SAT critical reading scores over 500: 45%; SAT math scores over 500: 44%; SAT writing scores over 500: 40%; ACT scores over 18: 75%; SAT critical reading scores over 600: 9%; SAT math scores over 600: 8%; SAT writing scores over 600: 7%; ACT scores over 24: 16%; SAT math scores over 700: 1%.

Faculty *Total:* 392, 48% full-time. *Student/faculty ratio:* 12:1.

Majors Accounting; anthropology; art; art history, criticism and conservation; athletic training; behavioral sciences; biology/biological sciences; broadcast journalism; business administration and management; chemistry; child development; communication/speech communication and rhetoric; comparative literature; computer engineering; computer science; criminology; dramatic/theater arts; e-commerce; economics; English; environmental biology; French; general studies; health/health care administration; history; international business/trade/commerce; international/global studies; international relations and affairs; journalism; kinesiology and exercise science; legal assistant/paralegal; liberal arts and sciences/liberal studies; marketing/marketing management; mathematics; music; natural resources management and policy; natural sciences; philosophy; physics; political science and government; psychology; public administration; religious studies; social sciences; sociology; Spanish.

Academics *Calendar:* 4-1-4. *Degrees:* certificates, associate, bachelor's, master's, doctoral, first professional, post-master's, and postbachelor's certificates (also offers continuing education program with significant enrollment not reflected in profile). *Special study options:* academic remediation for entering students, accelerated degree program, adult/continuing education programs, advanced placement credit, distance learning, double majors, English as a second language, freshman honors college, honors programs, independent study, internships, off-campus study, part-time degree program, services for LD students, student-designed majors, study abroad, summer session for credit. *ROTC:* Army (c).

Computers on Campus 250 computers/terminals and 250 ports are available on campus for general student use. Students can access the following: computer help desk, free student e-mail accounts, online (class) grades, online (class) registration, online (class) schedules, MyULV (online). Campuswide network is available. 100% of college-owned or -operated housing units are wired for high-speed Internet access. Wireless service is available via dorm rooms, libraries.

Student Life *Housing options:* coed, women-only, disabled students. Campus housing is university owned. Freshman campus housing is guaranteed. *Activities and organizations:* drama/theater group, student-run newspaper, radio and television station, choral group, Latino Student Forum, African-American Student Association, Associated Students Federation, Alpha Kappa Psi, national fraternities, national sororities. *Campus security:* 24-hour emergency response devices and patrols, late-night transport/escort service, controlled dormitory access, whistle program. *Student services:* health clinic, personal/psychological counseling.

Athletics Member NCAA. All Division III.

Standardized Tests *Required:* SAT or ACT (for admission).

Costs (2008–09) *Comprehensive fee:* $37,370 includes full-time tuition ($26,910) and room and board ($10,460). Part-time tuition: $760 per unit. *College room only:* $5620.

Financial Aid Of all full-time matriculated undergraduates who enrolled in 2007, 1,367 applied for aid, 1,271 were judged to have need, 147 had their need fully met. In 2007, 217 non-need-based awards were made. *Average percent of need met:* 52%. *Average financial aid package:* $21,629. *Average need-based loan:* $5268. *Average need-based gift aid:* $10,868. *Average non-need-based aid:* $7954. *Average indebtedness upon graduation:* $17,780.

Applying *Options:* electronic application, deferred entrance. *Application fee:* $50. *Required:* essay or personal statement, high school transcript, 2 letters of recommendation. *Recommended:* interview. *Application deadlines:* 2/1 (freshmen), 4/1 (transfers). *Notification:* continuous (freshmen), continuous (transfers).

Freshman Application Contact Ms. Ana Liza V. Zell, Associate Dean of Undergraduate Admissions, University of La Verne, 1950 Third Street, La Verne, CA 91750. *Phone:* 909-593-3511 Ext. 4035. *Toll-free phone:* 800-876-4858. *Fax:* 909-392-2714. *E-mail:* admissions@ulv.edu.

UNIVERSITY OF PHOENIX–BAY AREA CAMPUS

Pleasanton, California **www.phoenix.edu/**

- **Proprietary** comprehensive
- **Urban** campus
- **Coed**
- **Noncompetitive** entrance level

Faculty *Student/faculty ratio:* 7:1.

Academics *Calendar:* continuous. *Degrees:* associate, bachelor's, and master's.

Student Life *Campus security:* late-night transport/escort service.

Costs (2007–08) *Tuition:* $10,680 full-time, $445 per credit part-time. Full-time tuition and fees vary according to course level.

Financial Aid *Average financial aid package:* $3866. *Average need-based gift aid:* $2673.

Applying *Options:* deferred entrance. *Application fee:* $45. *Required:* 1 letter of recommendation. *Required for some:* high school transcript.

Freshman Application Contact Ms. Beth Barilla, Associate Vice President, Student Admissions and Services, University of Phoenix–Bay Area Campus, 4615 East Elwood Street, Mail Stop AA-K101, Phoenix, AZ 85040-1958. *Phone:* 480-317-6000. *Toll-free phone:* 877-4-STUDENT. *Fax:* 480-594-1758. *E-mail:* beth.barilla@phoenix.edu.

UNIVERSITY OF PHOENIX–CENTRAL VALLEY CAMPUS

Fresno, California **www.phoenix.edu/**

- **Proprietary** comprehensive, founded 2004
- **Urban** campus
- **Coed**
- **Noncompetitive** entrance level

Faculty *Student/faculty ratio:* 9:1.

Academics *Degrees:* certificates, bachelor's, master's, and postbachelor's certificates.

Student Life *Campus security:* late-night transport/escort service.

Costs (2007–08) *Tuition:* $12,690 full-time, $423 per credit part-time. Full-time tuition and fees vary according to course level.

Financial Aid *Average financial aid package:* $5626.

Applying *Options:* deferred entrance. *Application fee:* $45. *Required:* 1 letter of recommendation. *Required for some:* high school transcript.

Freshman Application Contact Ms. Beth Barilla, Associate Vice President, Student Admissions and Services, University of Phoenix–Central Valley Campus, 4615 East Elwood Street, Mail Stop AA-K101, Phoenix, AZ 85040-1958. *Phone:* 480-317-6000. *Toll-free phone:* 888-776-4867 (in-state); 888-228-7240 (out-of-state). *E-mail:* beth.barilla@phoenix.edu.

UNIVERSITY OF PHOENIX–SACRAMENTO VALLEY CAMPUS

Sacramento, California **www.phoenix.edu/**

- **Proprietary** comprehensive, founded 1993
- **Urban** campus
- **Coed**
- **Noncompetitive** entrance level

Faculty *Student/faculty ratio:* 7:1.

Academics *Calendar:* continuous. *Degrees:* bachelor's and master's.

Student Life *Campus security:* late-night transport/escort service.

Costs (2007–08) *Tuition:* $12,900 full-time, $430 per credit part-time. Full-time tuition and fees vary according to course level.

Financial Aid *Average financial aid package:* $4481. *Average need-based gift aid:* $2773.

Applying *Options:* deferred entrance. *Application fee:* $45. *Required:* 1 letter of recommendation. *Required for some:* high school transcript.

Freshman Application Contact Ms. Beth Barilla, Associate Vice President, Student Admissions and Services, University of Phoenix–Sacramento Valley Campus, 4615 East Elwood Street, Mail Stop AA-K101, Phoenix, AZ 85040-1958. *Phone:* 480-317-6000. *Toll-free phone:* 800-776-4867 (in-state); 800-228-7240 (out-of-state). *Fax:* 480-894-1758. *E-mail:* beth.barilla@phoenix.edu.

UNIVERSITY OF PHOENIX–SAN DIEGO CAMPUS

San Diego, California **www.phoenix.edu/**

- **Proprietary** comprehensive, founded 1988
- **Urban** campus
- **Coed**
- **Noncompetitive** entrance level

Faculty *Student/faculty ratio:* 9:1.

Academics *Calendar:* continuous. *Degrees:* certificates, bachelor's, and master's.

Student Life *Campus security:* late-night transport/escort service.

Costs (2007–08) *Tuition:* $11,640 full-time, $388 per credit part-time. Full-time tuition and fees vary according to course level.

Financial Aid *Average financial aid package:* $4180. *Average need-based gift aid:* $2527.

Applying *Options:* deferred entrance. *Application fee:* $45. *Required:* 1 letter of recommendation. *Required for some:* high school transcript.

Freshman Application Contact Ms. Beth Barilla, Associate Vice President, Student Admissions and Services, University of Phoenix–San Diego Campus, 4615 East Elwood Street, Mail Stop AA-K101, Phoenix, AZ 85040-1958. *Phone:* 480-317-6000. *Toll-free phone:* 888-776-4867 (in-state); 888-228-7240 (out-of-state). *Fax:* 480-894-1758. *E-mail:* beth.barilla@phoenix.edu.

UNIVERSITY OF PHOENIX–SOUTHERN CALIFORNIA CAMPUS

Costa Mesa, California **www.phoenix.edu/**

- **Proprietary** comprehensive, founded 1980
- **Urban** campus
- **Coed**
- **Noncompetitive** entrance level

Faculty *Student/faculty ratio:* 10:1.

Academics *Calendar:* continuous. *Degrees:* certificates, bachelor's, and master's.

Student Life *Campus security:* late-night transport/escort service.

Costs (2007–08) *Tuition:* $13,350 full-time, $445 per credit part-time. Full-time tuition and fees vary according to course level.

Financial Aid *Average financial aid package:* $4394. *Average need-based gift aid:* $2690.

Applying *Options:* deferred entrance. *Application fee:* $45. *Required:* 1 letter of recommendation. *Required for some:* high school transcript.

Freshman Application Contact Ms. Beth Barilla, Associate Vice President, Student Admissions and Services, University of Phoenix–Southern California Campus, 4615 East Elwood Street, Mail Stop AA-K101, Phoenix, AZ 85040-1958. *Phone:* 480-317-6000. *Toll-free phone:* 800-776-4867 (in-state); 800-228-7240 (out-of-state). *Fax:* 480-894-1758. *E-mail:* beth.barilla@phoenix.edu.

UNIVERSITY OF REDLANDS

Redlands, California **www.redlands.edu/**

- **Independent** comprehensive, founded 1907
- **Small-town** 140-acre campus with easy access to Los Angeles
- **Endowment** $126.0 million
- **Coed** 2,354 undergraduate students, 99% full-time, 57% women, 43% men
- **Moderately difficult** entrance level, 67% of applicants were admitted

Undergraduates 2,329 full-time, 25 part-time. Students come from 44 states and territories, 14 other countries, 33% are from out of state, 3% African American, 6% Asian American or Pacific Islander, 12% Hispanic American, 0.3% Native American, 1% international, 73% live on campus. *Retention:* 86% of 2006 full-time freshmen returned.

Freshmen *Admission:* 3,607 applied, 2,422 admitted. *Average high school GPA:* 3.58. *Test scores:* SAT critical reading scores over 500: 85%; SAT math scores over 500: 84%; ACT scores over 18: 98%; SAT critical reading scores over 600: 35%; SAT math scores over 600: 35%; ACT scores over 24: 56%; SAT critical reading scores over 700: 7%; SAT math scores over 700: 3%; ACT scores over 30: 8%.

Faculty *Total:* 290, 60% full-time, 59% with terminal degrees.

Majors Accounting; anthropology; art history, criticism and conservation; Asian studies; audiology and speech-language pathology; biology/biological sciences; business administration and management; business/commerce; chemistry; computer science; creative writing; economics; education; elementary education; English; environmental studies; fine/studio arts; French; German; history; interdisciplinary studies; international relations and affairs; liberal arts and sciences/liberal studies; literature; management information systems; mathematics; music; music history, literature, and theory; music performance; music teacher education; music theory and composition; philosophy; physics; piano and organ; political science and government; psychology; religious studies; secondary education; sociology; Spanish; speech therapy; voice and opera.

Academics *Calendar:* 4-4-1. *Degrees:* certificates, bachelor's, master's, post-master's, and postbachelor's certificates. *Special study options:* academic remediation for entering students, adult/continuing education programs, advanced placement credit, double majors, freshman honors college, honors programs, independent study, internships, off-campus study, services for LD students, student-designed majors, study abroad. *ROTC:* Army (c), Air Force (c).

Computers on Campus 746 computers/terminals and 835 ports are available on campus for general student use. Students can access the following: campus intranet, computer help desk, free student e-mail accounts, online (class) grades, online (class) registration, online (class) schedules. Campuswide network is available. 100% of college-owned or -operated housing units are wired for high-speed Internet access. Wireless service is available via entire campus.

Student Life *Housing:* on-campus residence required through senior year. *Options:* coed, men-only, women-only, cooperative, disabled students. Campus housing is university owned. Freshman campus housing is guaranteed. *Activities and organizations:* drama/theater group, student-run newspaper, radio station, choral group, Associated Students, service organizations, cultural organizations, social awareness groups. *Campus security:* 24-hour emergency response devices and patrols, student patrols, late-night transport/escort service, controlled dormitory access, safety whistles. *Student services:* health clinic, personal/psychological counseling, women's center.

Athletics Member NCAA. All Division III. *Intercollegiate sports:* baseball M, basketball M/W, cross-country running M/W, football M, golf M/W, lacrosse W, soccer M/W, softball W, swimming and diving M/W, tennis M/W, track and field M/W, volleyball W, water polo M/W. *Intramural sports:* basketball M/W, football M, racquetball M/W, soccer M/W, softball M/W, table tennis M/W, volleyball W, water polo M/W.

Standardized Tests *Required:* SAT or ACT (for admission).

Costs (2007–08) *Comprehensive fee:* $40,408 includes full-time tuition ($30,326), mandatory fees ($300), and room and board ($9782). Part-time tuition: $975 per credit. Part-time tuition and fees vary according to course load. *Required fees:* $150 per term part-time. *College room only:* $5456. Room and board charges vary according to board plan and housing facility. *Payment plan:* installment. *Waivers:* employees or children of employees.

Financial Aid Of all full-time matriculated undergraduates who enrolled in 2007, 1,858 applied for aid, 1,579 were judged to have need, 1,279 had their need fully met. In 2007, 267 non-need-based awards were made. *Average percent of need met:* 83%. *Average financial aid package:* $29,203. *Average need-based loan:* $8274. *Average need-based gift aid:* $22,281. *Average non-need-based aid:* $10,710. *Average indebtedness upon graduation:* $28,656.

Applying *Options:* electronic application, deferred entrance. *Application fee:* $45. *Required:* essay or personal statement, high school transcript, 2 letters of recommendation. *Recommended:* interview. *Application deadlines:* 4/1 (freshmen), 5/1 (transfers). *Notification:* continuous (freshmen), continuous (transfers).

Freshman Application Contact Mr. Paul Driscoll, Dean of Admissions, University of Redlands, PO Box 3080, Redlands, CA 92373-0999. *Phone:* 909-748-8159. *Toll-free phone:* 800-455-5064. *Fax:* 909-335-4089. *E-mail:* admissions@redlands.edu.

See page 466 for the College Close-Up.

UNIVERSITY OF SAN DIEGO

San Diego, California **www.sandiego.edu/**

- **Independent Roman Catholic** university, founded 1949
- **Urban** 180-acre campus
- **Endowment** $256.5 million
- **Coed** 4,932 undergraduate students, 96% full-time, 58% women, 42% men
- **Very difficult** entrance level, 48% of applicants were admitted

Undergraduates 4,754 full-time, 178 part-time. Students come from 50 states and territories, 36% are from out of state, 2% African American, 10% Asian American or Pacific Islander, 14% Hispanic American, 1% Native American, 2% international, 6% transferred in, 46% live on campus. *Retention:* 85% of 2006 full-time freshmen returned.

Freshmen *Admission:* 10,563 applied, 5,085 admitted, 1,094 enrolled. *Average high school GPA:* 3.76. *Test scores:* SAT critical reading scores over 500: 88%; SAT math scores over 500: 90%; SAT writing scores over 500: 89%; ACT scores over 18: 99%; SAT critical reading scores over 600: 44%; SAT math scores over 600: 53%; SAT writing scores over 600: 47%; ACT scores over 24: 80%; SAT critical reading scores over 700: 6%; SAT math scores over 700: 8%; SAT writing scores over 700: 6%; ACT scores over 30: 14%.

Faculty *Total:* 766, 48% full-time, 72% with terminal degrees. *Student/faculty ratio:* 15:1.

Majors Accounting; anthropology; art; art history, criticism and conservation; biochemistry; biology/biological sciences; business administration and management; business/managerial economics; chemistry; communication/speech communication and rhetoric; computer science; dramatic/theater arts; economics; electrical, electronics and communications engineering; English; finance; French; history; humanities; industrial engineering; intercultural/multicultural and diversity studies; international relations and affairs; liberal arts and sciences/liberal studies; marine biology and biological oceanography; marketing/marketing management; mathematics; mechanical engineering; music; nursing (registered nurse training); philosophy; physics; political science and government; psychology; religious studies; sociology; Spanish.

Academics *Calendar:* 4-1-4. *Degrees:* bachelor's, master's, doctoral, first professional, post-master's, postbachelor's, and first professional certificates. *Special study options:* advanced placement credit, double majors, English as a second language, honors programs, independent study, internships, part-time degree program, services for LD students, study abroad, summer session for credit. *ROTC:* Army (c), Navy (b), Air Force (c).

Computers on Campus Students can access the following: campus intranet, computer help desk, free student e-mail accounts, online (class) grades, online (class) registration, online (class) schedules. Campuswide network is available. 100% of college-owned or -operated housing units are wired for high-speed Internet access.

Student Life *Housing:* on-campus residence required for freshman year. *Options:* coed, women-only, disabled students. Campus housing is university owned. Freshman campus housing is guaranteed. *Activities and organizations:* drama/theater group, student-run newspaper, television station, choral group, national fraternities, national sororities. *Campus security:* 24-hour emergency response devices and patrols, student patrols, late-night transport/escort service, controlled dormitory access. *Student services:* health clinic, personal/psychological counseling, women's center, legal services.

Athletics Member NCAA. All Division I except football (Division I-AA). *Intercollegiate sports:* baseball M (s), basketball M (s)/W (s), crew M (s)/W (s), cross-country running M (s)/W (s), equestrian sports W (c), golf M (s), lacrosse M (c)/W (c), rock climbing M (c), rugby M (c), soccer M (s)/W (s), softball W (s), swimming and diving W (s), tennis M (s)/W (s), track and field W (s), ultimate Frisbee M (c)/W (c), volleyball M (c)/W (s). *Intramural sports:* baseball M (c), basketball M/W, football M/W, golf M/W, sailing M (c)/W (c), soccer M (c)/W (c), softball M/W, tennis M/W, ultimate Frisbee M/W, volleyball M/W, water polo M (c)/W (c).

Costs (2008–09) *Comprehensive fee:* $46,134 includes full-time tuition ($34,000), mandatory fees ($264), and room and board ($11,870). Part-time tuition: $1175 per unit. *Required fees:* $79 per term part-time.

Financial Aid Of all full-time matriculated undergraduates who enrolled in 2006, 2,583 applied for aid, 2,147 were judged to have need, 237 had their need fully met. In 2006, 712 non-need-based awards were made. *Average percent of need met:* 68%. *Average financial aid package:* $21,463. *Average need-based loan:* $6002. *Average need-based gift aid:* $15,826. *Average non-need-based aid:* $9185. *Average indebtedness upon graduation:* $26,639.

Applying *Options:* electronic application, early action, deferred entrance. *Application fee:* $55. *Required:* essay or personal statement, high school transcript, 1 letter of recommendation, SAT with Written test or ACT. *Application deadlines:* 1/15 (freshmen), 3/1 (transfers), 11/15 (early action). *Notification:* 4/15 (freshmen), continuous until 7/15 (transfers), 1/31 (early action).

Freshman Application Contact Mr. Stephen Pultz, Director of Admission, University of San Diego, 5998 Alcala Park, San Diego, CA 92110. *Phone:* 619-260-4506. *Toll-free phone:* 800-248-4873. *Fax:* 619-260-6836. *E-mail:* admissions@sandiego.edu.

See page 468 for the College Close-Up.

UNIVERSITY OF SAN FRANCISCO

San Francisco, California **www.usfca.edu/**

- **Independent Roman Catholic (Jesuit)** university, founded 1855
- **Urban** 55-acre campus with easy access to in San Francisco
- **Endowment** $153.0 million
- **Coed**
- **Moderately difficult** entrance level

Faculty *Student/faculty ratio:* 14:1.

Academics *Calendar:* 4-1-4. *Degrees:* certificates, bachelor's, master's, doctoral, first professional, and post-master's certificates.

Student Life *Campus security:* 24-hour emergency response devices and patrols, late-night transport/escort service, controlled dormitory access.

Athletics Member NCAA. All Division I.

Standardized Tests *Required:* SAT or ACT (for admission).

Costs (2007–08) *Comprehensive fee:* $41,910 includes full-time tuition ($30,840), mandatory fees ($340), and room and board ($10,730). Part-time tuition: $1060 per unit. *Required fees:* $340 per year part-time. *College room only:* $7230.

Financial Aid Of all full-time matriculated undergraduates who enrolled in 2006, 2,932 applied for aid, 2,645 were judged to have need, 380 had their need fully met. 856 Federal Work-Study jobs (averaging $3737). 535 state and other part-time jobs (averaging $3512). In 2006, 146 non-need-based awards were made. *Average percent of need met:* 62. *Average financial aid package:* $22,062. *Average need-based loan:* $5510. *Average need-based gift aid:* $16,200. *Average non-need-based aid:* $14,408. *Average indebtedness upon graduation:* $28,000.

Applying *Options:* electronic application, early action, deferred entrance. *Application fee:* $55. *Required:* essay or personal statement, high school transcript, minimum 2.8 GPA, 1 letter of recommendation. *Required for some:* interview. *Recommended:* minimum 3.0 GPA.

Freshman Application Contact Mr. Michael Hughes, Director, University of San Francisco, 2130 Fulton Street, San Francisco, CA 94117-1080. *Phone:* 415-422-6563. *Toll-free phone:* 415-422-6563 (in-state); 800-CALL USF (out-of-state). *Fax:* 415-422-2217. *E-mail:* admissions@usfca.edu.

See page 470 for the College Close-Up.

UNIVERSITY OF SOUTHERN CALIFORNIA

Los Angeles, California **www.usc.edu/**

- **Independent** university, founded 1880
- **Urban** 155-acre campus
- **Endowment** $3.7 billion
- **Coed** 16,384 undergraduate students, 96% full-time, 50% women, 50% men
- **Most difficult** entrance level, 25% of applicants were admitted

Undergraduates 15,684 full-time, 700 part-time. Students come from 58 states and territories, 115 other countries, 35% are from out of state, 6% African American, 22% Asian American or Pacific Islander, 13% Hispanic American, 0.8% Native American, 9% international, 7% transferred in, 41% live on campus. *Retention:* 96% of 2006 full-time freshmen returned.

Freshmen *Admission:* 33,760 applied, 8,553 admitted, 2,963 enrolled. *Average high school GPA:* 3.71. *Test scores:* SAT critical reading scores over 500: 99%; SAT math scores over 500: 99%; SAT writing scores over 500: 100%; ACT scores over 18: 100%; SAT critical reading scores over 600: 86%; SAT math scores over 600: 91%; SAT writing scores over 600: 90%; ACT scores over 24: 97%; SAT critical reading scores over 700: 35%; SAT math scores over 700: 46%; SAT writing scores over 700: 42%; ACT scores over 30: 58%.

Faculty *Total:* 2,713, 60% full-time, 77% with terminal degrees. *Student/faculty ratio:* 9:1.

Majors Accounting; acting; aerospace, aeronautical and astronautical engineering; African-American/Black studies; American literature; American studies; anthropology; anthropology related; architecture; art; art history, criticism and conservation; Asian-American studies; Asian studies (East); astronomy; biochemistry; biology/biological sciences; biomedical/medical engineering; biophysics; broadcast journalism; business administration and management; business administration, management and operations related; business, management, and marketing related; chemical engineering; chemistry; cinematography and film/video production; city/urban, community and regional planning; civil engineering; classics and languages, literatures and linguistics; cognitive psychology and psycholinguistics; communication/speech communication and rhetoric; comparative literature; computer and information sciences; computer engineering; computer engineering related; computer science; construction engineering; creative writing; cultural studies; dental hygiene; directing and theatrical production; dramatic/theater arts; East Asian languages; economics; electrical, electronics and communications engineering; engineering; English; English literature (British and Commonwealth); environmental/environmental health engineering; environmental studies; ethics; film/cinema studies; fine/studio arts; French; general studies; geography; geology/earth science; German; gerontology; health science; Hispanic-American, Puerto Rican, and Mexican-American/Chicano studies; history; interdisciplinary studies; international business/trade/commerce; international relations and affairs; Italian; jazz/jazz studies; Jewish/Judaic studies; journalism; kinesiology and exercise science; landscape architecture; linguistics; mass communication/media; mathematics; mechanical engineering; music; music management and merchandising; music performance; music related; music teacher education; music theory and composition; neuroscience; occupational therapy; petroleum engineering; philosophy; physical sciences; physics; playwriting and screenwriting; political science and government; polymer/plastics engineering; Portuguese; psychology; public administration; public health education and promotion; public policy analysis; public relations/image management; radio and television; religious studies; Russian; Slavic languages; social sciences; sociology; Spanish; structural engineering; systems engineering; theater design and technology; theater/theater arts management; urban studies/affairs; violin, viola, guitar and other stringed instruments; water resources engineering.

Academics *Calendar:* semesters. *Degrees:* bachelor's, master's, doctoral, first professional, post-master's, postbachelor's, and first professional certificates. *Special study options:* accelerated degree program, advanced placement credit, cooperative education, distance learning, double majors, English as a second language, freshman honors college, honors programs, independent study, internships, off-campus study, part-time degree program, services for LD students, student-designed majors, study abroad, summer session for credit. *ROTC:* Army (b), Navy (b), Air Force (b). *Unusual degree programs:* 3-2 engineering.

Computers on Campus 2,700 computers/terminals and 6,000 ports are available on campus for general student use. Students can access the following: campus intranet, computer help desk, free student e-mail accounts, online (class) grades, online (class) registration, online (class) schedules, online degree progress, financial aid applications, document sharing, calendars, personal Web space, customizable Web portal, course management systems (including data and video). Campuswide network is available. 100% of college-owned or -operated housing units are wired for high-speed Internet access. Wireless service is available via entire campus.

Student Life *Housing options:* coed, disabled students. Campus housing is university owned. Freshman campus housing is guaranteed. *Activities and organizations:* drama/theater group, student-run newspaper, radio and television station, choral group, marching band, Troy Camp, USC Helenes, Program Board, Student Senate, Alpha Phi Omega, national fraternities, national sororities. *Campus security:* 24-hour emergency response devices and patrols, student patrols, late-night transport/escort service, controlled dormitory access. *Student services:* health clinic, personal/psychological counseling, women's center.

Athletics Member NCAA. All Division I except football (Division I-A). *Intercollegiate sports:* archery M (c)/W (c), badminton M (c)/W (c), baseball M (s), basketball M (s)/W (s), cheerleading M (c)/W (c), crew M (c)/W (s), cross-country running M (s)/W (s), equestrian sports M (c)/W (c), fencing M (c)/W (c), golf M (s)/W (s), ice hockey M (c)/W (c), lacrosse M (c)/W (c), racquetball M (c)/W (c), skiing (downhill) M (c)/W (c), soccer M (c)/W (s), softball W (c), squash M (c)/W (c), swimming and diving M (s)/W (s), table tennis

M (c)/W (c), tennis M (s)/W (s), track and field M (s)/W (s), ultimate Frisbee M (c)/W (c), volleyball M (s)/W (s), water polo M (s)/W (s), wrestling M (c). *Intramural sports:* baseball M, basketball M/W, cheerleading M (c)/W (c), football M/W, golf M/W, rock climbing M (c)/W (c), sailing M (c)/W (c), soccer M/W, softball M/W, tennis M/W, volleyball M/W, water polo M (c)/W (c).

Standardized Tests *Required:* SAT or ACT (for admission).

Costs (2007–08) *Comprehensive fee:* $46,668 includes full-time tuition ($35,212), mandatory fees ($598), and room and board ($10,858). Full-time tuition and fees vary according to program. Part-time tuition: $1185 per term. Part-time tuition and fees vary according to course load and program. *College room only:* $5992. Room and board charges vary according to board plan and housing facility. *Payment plans:* tuition prepayment, installment, deferred payment. *Waivers:* employees or children of employees.

Financial Aid Of all full-time matriculated undergraduates who enrolled in 2005, 8,775 applied for aid, 6,876 were judged to have need, 6,556 had their need fully met. 4,994 Federal Work-Study jobs (averaging $2745). In 2005, 3082 non-need-based awards were made. *Average percent of need met:* 100%. *Average financial aid package:* $29,641. *Average need-based loan:* $6099. *Average need-based gift aid:* $19,781. *Average non-need-based aid:* $12,659. *Average indebtedness upon graduation:* $27,420.

Applying *Options:* electronic application. *Application fee:* $65. *Required:* essay or personal statement, high school transcript. *Required for some:* letters of recommendation. *Recommended:* letters of recommendation, interview. *Application deadlines:* 1/10 (freshmen), 2/1 (transfers). *Notification:* 4/1 (freshmen), 6/1 (transfers).

Freshman Application Contact Katharine L. Harrington, Dean/Director of Admission, University of Southern California, University Park Campus, Los Angeles, CA 90089. *Phone:* 213-740-1111. *Fax:* 213-740-6364. *E-mail:* admitusc@usc.edu.

UNIVERSITY OF THE PACIFIC

Stockton, California **www.pacific.edu/**

- **Independent** university, founded 1851
- **Suburban** 175-acre campus with easy access to Sacramento
- **Endowment** $220.5 million
- **Coed** 3,470 undergraduate students, 97% full-time, 55% women, 45% men
- **Moderately difficult** entrance level, 69% of applicants were admitted

Comprehensive is the best word to describe the University of the Pacific. The integration of liberal arts and sciences with professional study provides undergraduate students with a wealth of academic opportunities in a personally supportive community. Located halfway between the San Francisco Bay and the Sierra Nevada mountains, Pacific offers its 3,500 undergraduate students a wide variety of educational, cultural, recreational, and social opportunities.

Undergraduates 3,357 full-time, 113 part-time. Students come from 36 states and territories, 18 other countries, 13% are from out of state, 3% African American, 32% Asian American or Pacific Islander, 10% Hispanic American, 0.6% Native American, 3% international, 6% transferred in, 58% live on campus. *Retention:* 82% of 2006 full-time freshmen returned.

Freshmen *Admission:* 4,976 applied, 3,445 admitted, 766 enrolled. *Average high school GPA:* 3.46. *Test scores:* SAT critical reading scores over 500: 78%; SAT math scores over 500: 89%; SAT writing scores over 500: 77%; ACT scores over 18: 98%; SAT critical reading scores over 600: 35%; SAT math scores over 600: 53%; SAT writing scores over 600: 35%; ACT scores over 24: 59%; SAT critical reading scores over 700: 5%; SAT math scores over 700: 16%; SAT writing scores over 700: 6%; ACT scores over 30: 12%.

Faculty *Total:* 724, 59% full-time, 79% with terminal degrees. *Student/faculty ratio:* 13:1.

Majors Art; art history, criticism and conservation; audiology and speech-language pathology; biochemistry; biology/biological sciences; biomedical/medical engineering; business administration and management; chemistry; chemistry related; civil engineering; classics and languages, literatures and linguistics; commercial and advertising art; communication/speech communication and rhetoric; computer engineering; computer science; dramatic/theater arts; economics; education; electrical, electronics and communications engineering; engineering/industrial management; engineering physics; English; environmental studies; fine/studio arts; French; geology/earth science; German; history; information science/studies; interdisciplinary studies; international relations and affairs; Japanese; kinesiology and exercise science; mathematics; mechanical engineering; museum studies; music; music history, literature, and theory; music management and merchandising; music teacher education; music theory and composition; music therapy; pharmacy; philosophy; physical sciences; physics; piano and organ; political science and government; psychology; religious studies; social sciences; sociology; Spanish; special education; voice and opera.

Academics *Calendar:* semesters. *Degrees:* bachelor's, master's, doctoral, and first professional. *Special study options:* academic remediation for entering students, accelerated degree program, adult/continuing education programs, advanced placement credit, cooperative education, double majors, English as a second language, honors programs, independent study, internships, part-time degree program, services for LD students, student-designed majors, study abroad, summer session for credit. *ROTC:* Air Force (c).

Computers on Campus 350 computers/terminals are available on campus for general student use. Students can access the following: computer help desk, free student e-mail accounts, online (class) grades, online (class) registration, online (class) schedules. Campuswide network is available. Wireless service is available via entire campus.

Student Life *Housing:* on-campus residence required through sophomore year. *Options:* coed. Campus housing is university owned. Freshman campus housing is guaranteed. *Activities and organizations:* drama/theater group, student-run newspaper, radio station, choral group, student government, cultural organizations, Marketing Club, Model United Nations, national fraternities, national sororities. *Campus security:* 24-hour emergency response devices and patrols, late-night transport/escort service, controlled dormitory access. *Student services:* health clinic, personal/psychological counseling, legal services.

Athletics Member NCAA. All Division I. *Intercollegiate sports:* baseball M (s), basketball M (s)/W (s), cross-country running W (s), field hockey W (s), golf M (s), soccer W (s), softball W (s), swimming and diving M (s)/W (s), tennis M (s)/W (s), volleyball M (s)/W (s), water polo M (s)/W (s). *Intramural sports:* badminton M (c)/W (c), basketball M/W, bowling M/W, football M/W, golf M, lacrosse M (c)/W (c), rugby M (c), soccer M (c)/W (c), tennis M/W, volleyball M/W.

Standardized Tests *Required:* SAT or ACT (for admission).

Costs (2007–08) *Comprehensive fee:* $38,190 includes full-time tuition ($28,480), mandatory fees ($500), and room and board ($9210). Part-time tuition: $984 per unit. Part-time tuition and fees vary according to course load. *College room only:* $4610. Room and board charges vary according to board plan and housing facility. *Payment plan:* deferred payment. *Waivers:* employees or children of employees.

Financial Aid Of all full-time matriculated undergraduates who enrolled in 2006, 2,605 applied for aid, 2,272 were judged to have need, 590 had their need fully met. 2,315 Federal Work-Study jobs (averaging $192[illegible]). In 2006, 481 non-need-based awards were made. *Average financial aid package:* $24,110. *Average need-based loan:* $4941. *Average need-based gift aid:* $17,482. *Average non-need-based aid:* $8588.

Applying *Options:* electronic application, early action. *Application fee:* $60. *Required:* essay or personal statement, high school transcript, minimum 2.5 GPA, 1 letter of recommendation. *Required for some:* audition for music program. *Recommended:* minimum 3.0 GPA. *Application deadlines:* 1/15 (freshmen), 6/1 (transfers), 11/15 (early action). *Notification:* continuous (freshmen), continuous (transfers), 1/15 (early action).

Freshman Application Contact Mr. Rich Toledo, Director of Admissions, University of the Pacific, 3601 Pacific Avenue, Stockton, CA 95211. *Phone:* 209-946-2211. *Toll-free phone:* 800-959-2867. *Fax:* 209-946-2413. *E-mail:* admissions@pacific.edu.

See page 472 for the College Close-Up.

UNIVERSITY OF THE WEST

Rosemead, California **www.uwest.edu/**

- **Independent** comprehensive, founded 1991
- **Suburban** 10-acre campus
- **Endowment** $5.6 million
- **Coed** 33 undergraduate students, 94% full-time, 52% women, 48% men
- 97% of applicants were admitted

Undergraduates 31 full-time, 2 part-time. Students come from 3 states and territories, 13 other countries, 6% are from out of state, 6% Hispanic American, 90% international, 30% live on campus.

Freshmen *Admission:* 70 applied, 68 admitted, 33 enrolled.

Faculty *Total:* 87, 10% full-time, 13% with terminal degrees.

Majors Asian history; Buddhist studies; business administration and management; Chinese studies; English; history; philosophy; psychology; religious studies related.

Academics *Calendar:* semesters. *Degrees:* certificates, diplomas, bachelor's, master's, doctoral, first professional, and post-master's certificates. *Special study options:* accelerated degree program, adult/continuing education programs, cooperative education, double majors, English as a second language, independent study, internships, part-time degree program, summer session for credit.

Student Life *Housing options:* coed, disabled students. Campus housing is university owned. Freshman campus housing is guaranteed. *Campus security:* 24-hour patrols.

Standardized Tests *Recommended:* TOEFL.

Costs (2008–09) *Comprehensive fee:* $12,900 includes full-time tuition ($7200), mandatory fees ($270), and room and board ($5430). Part-time tuition: $300 per unit. *Required fees:* $135 per semester part-time.

Financial Aid Of all full-time matriculated undergraduates who enrolled in 2003, 30 applied for aid, 18 were judged to have need. 20 state and other part-time jobs.

Applying *Options:* electronic application, deferred entrance. *Application fee:* $50. *Required:* essay or personal statement, high school transcript, minimum 2.0 GPA, 3 letters of recommendation. *Application deadline:* 6/1 (freshmen). *Notification:* 7/1 (freshmen).

Freshman Application Contact University of the West, 1409 North Walnut Grove Avenue, Rosemead, CA 91770. *Phone:* 626-571-8811 Ext. 120.

See page 474 for the College Close-Up.

VANGUARD UNIVERSITY OF SOUTHERN CALIFORNIA

Costa Mesa, California **www.vanguard.edu/**

- **Independent** comprehensive, founded 1920, affiliated with Assemblies of God
- **Suburban** 38-acre campus with easy access to Los Angeles
- **Endowment** $3.0 million
- **Coed** 1,952 undergraduate students, 78% full-time, 65% women, 35% men
- **Moderately difficult** entrance level, 82% of applicants were admitted

Founded in 1920, Vanguard University of Southern California is a private university of liberal arts and professional studies that offers an education marked by excellence and informed by Christian values. Vanguard's mission includes preparing students for a variety of vocations that are matched to the twenty-first-century marketplace.

Undergraduates 1,513 full-time, 439 part-time. 15% are from out of state, 3% African American, 5% Asian American or Pacific Islander, 17% Hispanic American, 2% Native American, 1% international, 69% live on campus. *Retention:* 73% of 2006 full-time freshmen returned.

Freshmen *Admission:* 947 applied, 772 admitted, 370 enrolled. *Average high school GPA:* 3.39. *Test scores:* SAT critical reading scores over 500: 49%; SAT math scores over 500: 46%; ACT scores over 18: 76%; SAT critical reading scores over 600: 12%; SAT math scores over 600: 13%; ACT scores over 24: 31%; SAT critical reading scores over 700: 1%; SAT math scores over 700: 1%; ACT scores over 30: 4%.

Faculty *Total:* 82, 87% full-time, 73% with terminal degrees. *Student/faculty ratio:* 28:1.

Majors Accounting; anthropology; athletic training; biblical studies; biological and physical sciences; biology/biological sciences; business administration and management; chemistry; cinematography and film/video production; communication/speech communication and rhetoric; dramatic/theater arts; education; English; finance; health and physical education; history; interdisciplinary studies; international business/trade/commerce; kinesiology and exercise science; marketing/marketing management; mathematics; missionary studies and missiology; music; pastoral studies/counseling; physical education teaching and coaching; physical therapy; political science and government; pre-law studies; psychology; radio and television; religious education; religious studies; secondary education; sociology; Spanish; speech and rhetoric; youth ministry.

Academics *Calendar:* semesters. *Degrees:* bachelor's and master's. *Special study options:* accelerated degree program, adult/continuing education programs, advanced placement credit, double majors, external degree program, independent study, internships, off-campus study, part-time degree program, services for LD students, study abroad, summer session for credit. *ROTC:* Air Force (c).

Computers on Campus 150 computers/terminals are available on campus for general student use. Students can access the following: online (class) registration. Campuswide network is available.

Student Life *Housing:* on-campus residence required through junior year. *Options:* coed, men-only, women-only. Campus housing is university owned. Freshman applicants given priority for college housing. *Activities and organizations:* drama/theater group, student-run newspaper, radio station, choral group, Student Ministries, Choral Groups, Orchestral Bands. *Campus security:* 24-hour emergency response devices and patrols, late-night transport/escort service. *Student services:* personal/psychological counseling, women's center.

Athletics Member NAIA. *Intercollegiate sports:* baseball M (s), basketball M (s)/W (s), cross-country running M (s)/W (s), soccer M (s)/W (s), softball W (s), tennis M (s)/W (s), track and field M (s)/W (s), volleyball W (s). *Intramural sports:* basketball M/W, football M/W, soccer M/W, softball M/W.

Standardized Tests *Required:* SAT or ACT (for admission).

Costs (2008–09) *Tuition:* $23,790 full-time. *Required fees:* $520 full-time. *Room only:* $3804.

Financial Aid Of all full-time matriculated undergraduates who enrolled in 2007, 1,224 applied for aid, 957 were judged to have need, 244 had their need fully met. 117 Federal Work-Study jobs (averaging $2950). 32 state and other part-time jobs (averaging $3388). In 2007, 339 non-need-based awards were made. *Average percent of need met:* 75%. *Average financial aid package:* $18,428. *Average need-based loan:* $2816. *Average need-based gift aid:* $12,727. *Average non-need-based aid:* $7144. *Average indebtedness upon graduation:* $18,762. *Financial aid deadline:* 3/2.

Applying *Options:* electronic application, early admission, deferred entrance. *Application fee:* $45. *Required:* essay or personal statement, high school transcript, minimum 2.8 GPA, 2 letters of recommendation. *Required for some:* interview. *Application deadlines:* 1/15 (freshmen), 12/1 (transfers), 12/1 (early action). *Notification:* 3/1 (freshmen), continuous until 8/31 (transfers), 1/15 (early action).

Freshman Application Contact Amberley Wolf, Director of Undergraduate Admissions, Vanguard University of Southern California, 55 Fair Drive, Costa Mesa, CA 92626. *Phone:* 714-556-3610 Ext. 4120. *Toll-free phone:* 800-722-6279. *Fax:* 714-966-5471. *E-mail:* admissions@vanguard.edu.

WESTERN CAREER COLLEGE

Emeryville, California **www.westerncollege.edu/**

Director of Admissions Ms. Marianne Dulay, Admissions Representative, Western Career College, 1400 65th Street, Suite 200, Emeryville, CA 94608. *Phone:* 510-601-0133 Ext. 14. *Toll-free phone:* 800-750-5627.

WESTERN CAREER COLLEGE

Fremont, California **www.westerncollege.edu/**

Director of Admissions Mr. Anton Croos, Admissions Director, Western Career College, 41350 Christy Street, Fremont, CA 94538. *Phone:* 510-623-9966 Ext. 212. *Toll-free phone:* 800-750-5627.

WESTERN CAREER COLLEGE

San Jose, California **www.westerncollege.edu/**

Director of Admissions Ms. Patricia Fraser, Admissions Director, Western Career College, 6201 San Ignacio Avenue, San Jose, CA 95119. *Phone:* 408-360-0840 Ext. 247. *Toll-free phone:* 800-750-5627.

WESTERN CAREER COLLEGE

Walnut Creek, California **www.westerncollege.edu/**

Director of Admissions Mr. Mark Millen, Admissions Director, Western Career College, 2800 Mitchell Drive, Walnut Creek, CA 94598. *Phone:* 925-280-0235 Ext. 37. *Toll-free phone:* 888-203-9947.

WESTMONT COLLEGE

Santa Barbara, California **www.westmont.edu/**

- **Independent nondenominational** 4-year, founded 1937
- **Suburban** 133-acre campus with easy access to Los Angeles
- **Endowment** $66.0 million
- **Coed** 1,336 undergraduate students, 98% full-time, 61% women, 39% men
- **Moderately difficult** entrance level, 73% of applicants were admitted

Undergraduates 1,312 full-time, 24 part-time. Students come from 41 states and territories, 8 other countries, 31% are from out of state, 2% African American, 9% Asian American or Pacific Islander, 10% Hispanic American, 2% Native

American, 0.7% international, 4% transferred in, 80% live on campus. *Retention:* 87% of 2006 full-time freshmen returned.

Freshmen *Admission:* 1,651 applied, 1,208 admitted, 389 enrolled. *Average high school GPA:* 3.77. *Test scores:* SAT critical reading scores over 500: 93%; SAT math scores over 500: 88%; SAT writing scores over 500: 89%; ACT scores over 18: 99%; SAT critical reading scores over 600: 51%; SAT math scores over 600: 52%; SAT writing scores over 600: 51%; ACT scores over 24: 78%; SAT critical reading scores over 700: 12%; SAT math scores over 700: 10%; SAT writing scores over 700: 8%; ACT scores over 30: 19%.

Faculty *Total:* 136, 68% full-time. *Student/faculty ratio:* 12:1.

Majors Anthropology; art; art teacher education; biology/biological sciences; business/commerce; business/managerial economics; chemistry; communication/speech communication and rhetoric; computer science; dance; dramatic/theater arts; economics; education; elementary education; engineering physics; English; English/language arts teacher education; French; history; kinesiology and exercise science; liberal arts and sciences/liberal studies; mathematics; mathematics teacher education; modern languages; music; neuroscience; philosophy; physical education teaching and coaching; physics; political science and government; pre-dentistry studies; pre-law studies; pre-medical studies; pre-pharmacy studies; pre-theology/pre-ministerial studies; pre-veterinary studies; psychology; religious studies; secondary education; social sciences; social science teacher education; sociology; Spanish.

Academics *Calendar:* semesters. *Degrees:* bachelor's and postbachelor's certificates. *Special study options:* academic remediation for entering students, accelerated degree program, advanced placement credit, double majors, honors programs, internships, off-campus study, services for LD students, student-designed majors, study abroad, summer session for credit. *ROTC:* Army (c), Air Force (c). *Unusual degree programs:* 3-2 engineering with Washington University in St. Louis; Boston University; University of Southern California; University of California, Berkeley; Los Angeles; Santa Barbara; California Polytechnic State University; Stanford University.

Computers on Campus 100 computers/terminals are available on campus for general student use. Students can access the following: campus intranet, free student e-mail accounts, online (class) schedules. Campuswide network is available.

Student Life *Housing:* on-campus residence required for freshman year. *Options:* men-only, women-only. Campus housing is university owned. Freshman campus housing is guaranteed. *Activities and organizations:* drama/theater group, student-run newspaper, radio station, choral group, student ministries, student government, competitive athletics, music and theater ensembles, intramural athletics. *Campus security:* 24-hour emergency response devices and patrols, late-night transport/escort service, controlled dormitory access. *Student services:* health clinic, personal/psychological counseling, women's center.

Athletics Member NAIA. *Intercollegiate sports:* baseball M (s), basketball M (s)/W (s), cross-country running M (s)/W (s), lacrosse W (c), rugby M (c), soccer M (s)/W (s), tennis M (s)/W (s), track and field M (s)/W (s), volleyball M (c)/W (s). *Intramural sports:* badminton M/W, basketball M/W, bowling M/W, cheerleading M (c)/W (c), cross-country running M/W, football M/W, golf M/W, racquetball M/W, rock climbing M (c)/W (c), soccer M (c)/W, softball M/W, swimming and diving M/W, table tennis M/W, tennis M/W, ultimate Frisbee M (c), volleyball M/W, water polo M/W.

Standardized Tests *Required:* SAT or ACT (for admission). *Required for some:* TOEFL.

Costs (2007–08) *Comprehensive fee:* $40,834 includes full-time tuition ($30,422), mandatory fees ($790), and room and board ($9622). *College room only:* $5956. Room and board charges vary according to board plan. *Payment plan:* installment. *Waivers:* employees or children of employees.

Financial Aid Of all full-time matriculated undergraduates who enrolled in 2007, 860 applied for aid, 736 were judged to have need, 87 had their need fully met. 164 Federal Work-Study jobs (averaging $938). In 2007, 422 non-need-based awards were made. *Average percent of need met:* 71%. *Average financial aid package:* $21,890. *Average need-based loan:* $6007. *Average need-based gift aid:* $16,262. *Average non-need-based aid:* $10,755. *Average indebtedness upon graduation:* $25,008.

Applying *Options:* electronic application, early action. *Application fee:* $50. *Required:* essay or personal statement, high school transcript, 1 letter of recommendation. *Required for some:* interview. *Recommended:* interview. *Application deadlines:* 2/20 (freshmen), 3/1 (transfers), 11/1 (early action). *Notification:* 4/1 (freshmen), 3/15 (transfers), 12/20 (early action).

Freshman Application Contact Mrs. Joyce Luy, Dean of Admission, Westmont College, 955 La Paz Road, Santa Barbara, CA 93108. *Phone:* 805-565-6200. *Toll-free phone:* 800-777-9011. *Fax:* 805-565-6234. *E-mail:* admissions@westmont.edu.

See page 476 for the College Close-Up.

WESTWOOD COLLEGE–ANAHEIM

Anaheim, California **www.westwood.edu/**

Director of Admissions Mr. Paul Sallenbach, Director of Admissions, Westwood College–Anaheim, 1551 South Douglass Road, Anaheim, CA 92806. *Phone:* 714-226-9990. *Toll-free phone:* 877-650-6050.

WESTWOOD COLLEGE–INLAND EMPIRE

Upland, California **www.westwood.edu/**

Director of Admissions Mr. Lyle Seavers, Director of Admissions, Westwood College–Inland Empire, 20 West 7th Street, Upland, CA 91786-7148. *Phone:* 909-931-7550. *Toll-free phone:* 866-288-9488.

WESTWOOD COLLEGE–LOS ANGELES

Los Angeles, California **www.westwood.edu/**

Director of Admissions Mr. Ron Milman, Director of Admissions, Westwood College–Los Angeles, 3250 Wilshire Boulevard, 4th Floor, Los Angeles, CA 90010. *Phone:* 213-739-9999. *Toll-free phone:* 877-377-4600.

WESTWOOD COLLEGE–SOUTH BAY CAMPUS

Torrance, California **www.westwood.edu/**

Director of Admissions Jesse Kamekona, Director of Admissions, Westwood College–South Bay Campus, 19700 South Vermont Avenue, Suite 100, Torrance, CA 90502. *Phone:* 310-965-0888. *Toll-free phone:* 800-281-2978.

WHITTIER COLLEGE

Whittier, California **www.whittier.edu/**

- **Independent** comprehensive, founded 1887
- **Suburban** 95-acre campus with easy access to Los Angeles
- **Endowment** $55.0 million
- **Coed** 1,259 undergraduate students, 98% full-time, 55% women, 45% men
- **Moderately difficult** entrance level, 67% of applicants were admitted

Undergraduates 1,239 full-time, 20 part-time. Students come from 33 states and territories, 20 other countries, 27% are from out of state, 3% African American, 8% Asian American or Pacific Islander, 30% Hispanic American, 1% Native American, 2% international, 4% transferred in, 68% live on campus. *Retention:* 78% of 2006 full-time freshmen returned.

Freshmen *Admission:* 2,196 applied, 1,469 admitted, 310 enrolled. *Average high school GPA:* 3.4. *Test scores:* SAT critical reading scores over 500: 68%; SAT math scores over 500: 67%; ACT scores over 18: 94%; SAT critical reading scores over 600: 26%; SAT math scores over 600: 27%; ACT scores over 24: 46%; SAT critical reading scores over 700: 4%; SAT math scores over 700: 5%; ACT scores over 30: 11%.

Faculty *Total:* 123, 71% full-time, 83% with terminal degrees. *Student/faculty ratio:* 13:1.

Majors Art; biochemistry; biology/biological sciences; business administration and management; chemistry; developmental and child psychology; dramatic/theater arts; economics; English; French; history; international relations and affairs; kindergarten/preschool education; liberal arts and sciences/liberal studies; mathematics; music; philosophy; physical education teaching and coaching; physics; political science and government; psychology; religious studies; social work; sociology; Spanish.

Academics *Calendar:* 4-1-4. *Degrees:* bachelor's, master's, and first professional. *Special study options:* academic remediation for entering students, accelerated degree program, adult/continuing education programs, advanced placement credit, double majors, independent study, internships, off-campus study, services for LD students, student-designed majors, study abroad, summer session for credit. *ROTC:* Army (c), Air Force (c). *Unusual degree programs:* 3-2 engineering with University of Southern California, Dartmouth College, University of Minnesota, Columbia University, Washington University in St. Louis, Case Western Reserve University, Colorado State University.

Computers on Campus 150 computers/terminals are available on campus for general student use. Campuswide network is available.

Student Life *Housing:* on-campus residence required through junior year. *Options:* coed, women-only. Campus housing is university owned. *Activities and organizations:* drama/theater group, student-run newspaper, radio station, choral group, Hispanic Students Association, Hawaiian Islander Club, choir, Asian Students Association, Students Organized for Multicultural Awareness. *Campus security:* 24-hour emergency response devices and patrols, late-night transport/escort service, controlled dormitory access. *Student services:* health clinic, personal/psychological counseling.

Athletics Member NCAA. All Division III. *Intercollegiate sports:* baseball M, basketball M/W, cross-country running M/W, football M, golf M, lacrosse M/W, soccer M/W, softball W, swimming and diving M/W, tennis M/W, track and field M/W, volleyball W, water polo M/W. *Intramural sports:* basketball M/W, bowling M/W, football M/W, racquetball M/W, skiing (downhill) M/W, softball M/W, table tennis M/W, tennis M/W, volleyball M/W, water polo M/W.

Standardized Tests *Required:* SAT or ACT (for admission). *Recommended:* SAT Subject Tests (for admission).

Costs (2008–09) *Comprehensive fee:* $41,520 includes full-time tuition ($31,950), mandatory fees ($520), and room and board ($9050). Part-time tuition: $1162 per unit.

Financial Aid Of all full-time matriculated undergraduates who enrolled in 2007, 1,232 applied for aid, 840 were judged to have need, 245 had their need fully met. In 2007, 276 non-need-based awards were made. *Average percent of need met:* 93%. *Average financial aid package:* $26,813. *Average need-based loan:* $8207. *Average need-based gift aid:* $11,849. *Average non-need-based aid:* $10,337. *Average indebtedness upon graduation:* $31,179. *Financial aid deadline:* 6/30.

Applying *Options:* electronic application, early action, deferred entrance. *Application fee:* $50. *Required:* essay or personal statement, high school transcript, minimum 2.0 GPA, 2 letters of recommendation. *Required for some:* minimum 3.5 GPA. *Recommended:* minimum 2.5 GPA, interview. *Application deadlines:* rolling (freshmen), rolling (transfers), 12/1 (early action). *Notification:* continuous (freshmen), 3/1 (transfers), 12/31 (early action).

Freshman Application Contact Ms. Lisa Meyer, Vice President for Enrollment, Whittier College, PO Box 634, Whittier, CA 90608-0634. *Phone:* 562-907-4238. *Fax:* 562-907-4870. *E-mail:* admission@whittier.edu.

WILLIAM JESSUP UNIVERSITY

Rocklin, California **www.jessup.edu/**

- **Independent nondenominational** 4-year, founded 1939
- **Suburban** 156-acre campus with easy access to Sacramento
- **Endowment** $815,255
- **Coed** 509 undergraduate students, 84% full-time, 59% women, 41% men
- **Noncompetitive** entrance level, 57% of applicants were admitted

Undergraduates 430 full-time, 79 part-time. Students come from 9 states and territories, 2 other countries, 7% are from out of state, 6% African American, 5% Asian American or Pacific Islander, 8% Hispanic American, 2% Native American, 0.6% international, 10% transferred in, 45% live on campus. *Retention:* 71% of 2006 full-time freshmen returned.

Freshmen *Admission:* 146 applied, 83 admitted, 57 enrolled. *Average high school GPA:* 3.49. *Test scores:* SAT critical reading scores over 500: 75%; SAT math scores over 500: 68%; SAT writing scores over 500: 61%; ACT scores over 18: 100%; SAT critical reading scores over 600: 26%; SAT math scores over 600: 19%; SAT writing scores over 600: 21%; ACT scores over 24: 67%; SAT critical reading scores over 700: 2%; SAT math scores over 700: 2%; SAT writing scores over 700: 2%; ACT scores over 30: 13%.

Faculty *Total:* 112, 21% full-time, 36% with terminal degrees. *Student/faculty ratio:* 9:1.

Majors Business administration, management and operations related; education; intercultural/multicultural and diversity studies; psychology; theology; visual and performing arts.

Academics *Calendar:* semesters. *Degrees:* certificates, associate, bachelor's, and postbachelor's certificates. *Special study options:* academic remediation for entering students, accelerated degree program, adult/continuing education programs, advanced placement credit, double majors, independent study, internships, part-time degree program, services for LD students, summer session for credit.

Computers on Campus 26 computers/terminals are available on campus for general student use. Students can access the following: university student e-mail accounts. Campuswide network is available.

Student Life *Housing:* on-campus residence required through sophomore year. *Options:* men-only, women-only. Campus housing is university owned. Freshman campus housing is guaranteed. *Activities and organizations:* choral group, Missions Club, student leadership, drama team, music ensemble. *Campus security:* student patrols, late-night transport/escort service, controlled dormitory access, day and evening patrols by trained security personnel. *Student services:* personal/psychological counseling.

Athletics Member NAIA. *Intercollegiate sports:* basketball M/W, soccer M/W, volleyball W.

Standardized Tests *Required:* SAT or ACT (for admission).

Costs (2007–08) *Comprehensive fee:* $25,908 includes full-time tuition ($18,790) and room and board ($7118). Full-time tuition and fees vary according to course load. Part-time tuition: $796 per semester hour. Part-time tuition and fees vary according to course load. *Payment plan:* deferred payment. *Waivers:* employees or children of employees.

Financial Aid Of all full-time matriculated undergraduates who enrolled in 2000, 226 applied for aid, 226 were judged to have need. 18 Federal Work-Study jobs (averaging $1792). *Average financial aid package:* $6244. *Average need-based loan:* $1737. *Average need-based gift aid:* $1514.

Applying *Options:* electronic application, early action. *Application fee:* $35. *Required:* essay or personal statement, high school transcript, minimum 2.0 GPA, 2 letters of recommendation. *Application deadlines:* 8/1 (freshmen), 8/1 (transfers). *Notification:* continuous (freshmen), continuous (transfers).

Freshman Application Contact Mr. Vance Pascua, Director of Admission, William Jessup University, 333 Sunset Boulevard, Rocklin, CA 95765. *Phone:* 408-577-2222. *Toll-free phone:* 800-355-7522. *Fax:* 916-577-2220. *E-mail:* admissions@jessup.edu.

WOODBURY UNIVERSITY

Burbank, California **www.woodbury.edu/**

- **Independent** comprehensive, founded 1884
- **Suburban** 22-acre campus with easy access to Los Angeles
- **Endowment** $12.4 million
- **Coed** 1,296 undergraduate students, 81% full-time, 56% women, 44% men
- **Moderately difficult** entrance level, 81% of applicants were admitted

Undergraduates 1,046 full-time, 250 part-time. Students come from 41 other countries, 6% African American, 11% Asian American or Pacific Islander, 32% Hispanic American, 0.2% Native American, 6% international, 13% transferred in, 20% live on campus. *Retention:* 82% of 2006 full-time freshmen returned.

Freshmen *Admission:* 486 applied, 393 admitted, 159 enrolled. *Average high school GPA:* 3.12. *Test scores:* SAT critical reading scores over 500: 31%; SAT math scores over 500: 49%; SAT critical reading scores over 600: 3%; SAT math scores over 600: 13%; SAT critical reading scores over 700: 1%; SAT math scores over 700: 1%.

Faculty *Total:* 237, 19% full-time. *Student/faculty ratio:* 12:1.

Majors Accounting; architecture; business administration and management; business administration, management and operations related; commercial and advertising art; communication/speech communication and rhetoric; fashion/apparel design; fashion merchandising; film/video and photographic arts related; history; information science/studies; interdisciplinary studies; interior architecture; marketing/marketing management; organizational behavior; political science and government; psychology.

Academics *Calendar:* semesters. *Degrees:* bachelor's and master's. *Special study options:* academic remediation for entering students, accelerated degree program, adult/continuing education programs, advanced placement credit, double majors, independent study, internships, part-time degree program, services for LD students, study abroad, summer session for credit.

Computers on Campus 135 computers/terminals are available on campus for general student use. Students can access the following: campus intranet, computer help desk, free student e-mail accounts, online (class) grades, online (class) registration, online (class) schedules. Campuswide network is available. Wireless service is available via classrooms, computer centers, computer labs, libraries.

Student Life *Housing options:* coed. Campus housing is university owned and is provided by a third party. Freshman applicants given priority for college housing. *Activities and organizations:* student-run newspaper, Associated Student Government, Common Threads, American Institute of Architecture Students, Collegiate Entrepreneurs' Organization (CEO), American Institute of Graphic Arts (AIGA), national fraternities, national sororities. *Campus security:* 24-hour patrols, late-night transport/escort service, controlled dormitory access. *Student services:* health clinic, personal/psychological counseling.

Athletics *Intramural sports:* basketball M/W, soccer M/W.

Standardized Tests *Required:* SAT or ACT (for admission).

Costs (2007–08) *Comprehensive fee:* $33,708 includes full-time tuition ($24,858), mandatory fees ($340), and room and board ($8510). Full-time tuition and fees vary according to class time and course load. Part-time tuition: $811 per unit. Part-time tuition and fees vary according to class time and course load. *College room only:* $5200. Room and board charges vary according to board plan and housing facility. *Payment plans:* installment, deferred payment. *Waivers:* employees or children of employees.

Financial Aid Of all full-time matriculated undergraduates who enrolled in 2006, 652 applied for aid, 611 were judged to have need, 39 had their need fully met. 98 Federal Work-Study jobs (averaging $1341). *Average percent of need met:* 57%. *Average financial aid package:* $17,559. *Average need-based loan:* $4523. *Average need-based gift aid:* $13,497. *Average non-need-based aid:* $11,932. *Average indebtedness upon graduation:* $25,941.

Applying *Options:* electronic application, deferred entrance. *Application fee:* $35. *Required:* high school transcript, minimum 2.0 GPA. *Required for some:* portfolio. *Recommended:* essay or personal statement, minimum 3.0 GPA, 2 letters of recommendation, interview. *Application deadlines:* rolling (freshmen), rolling (transfers).

Freshman Application Contact Ms. Sabrina Taylor, Woodbury University, 7500 Glenoaks Boulevard, Burbank, CA 91510-7846. *Phone:* 800-784-9663. *Toll-free phone:* 800-784-WOOD. *Fax:* 818-767-0032. *E-mail:* admissions@woodbury.edu.

YESHIVA OHR ELCHONON CHABAD/ WEST COAST TALMUDICAL SEMINARY

Los Angeles, California

Director of Admissions Rabbi Ezra Binyomin Schochet, Dean, Yeshiva Ohr Elchonon Chabad/West Coast Talmudical Seminary, 7215 Waring Avenue, Los Angeles, CA 90046-7660. *Phone:* 323-937-3763.

ACADEMY OF ART UNIVERSITY

SAN FRANCISCO, CALIFORNIA

The University

In 1929, Academy of Art University founder Richard S. Stephens, who was the advertising creative director of *Sunset* magazine, acted on his belief that "aspiring artists and designers, given proper instruction, hard work, and dedication, can learn the skills needed to become successful professionals." His new school of advertising art consisted of 46 students meeting in one room on San Francisco's Kearny Street. The instructors, who were professional artists, brought real-world problems, situations, solutions, and practical experience to the students. Thus was born the school's philosophy by the founder: Hire today's best practicing professionals to teach the art and design professionals of tomorrow. At that time, advertising consisted primarily of illustrations, photos, and copy. Consequently, it became necessary to teach beginning students the fundamentals of drawing, painting, color, light, and photography as well as layout and typography.

When Richard A. Stephens succeeded his father as president in 1951, the Foundations Department was added, ensuring all students comprehended the basic principles of traditional art and design. Illustration soon expanded to include fine arts (drawing, painting, sculpture, and printmaking), and advertising design spawned the Graphic Design Department. Fashion (design, textiles, and merchandising) and Interior Design Departments were also added. In 1966, the Academy officially became a college, and in a decade, the Master of Fine Arts degree was offered. Five more buildings were purchased, and by 1992, there were more than 2,500 students. The leadership of the Academy was then turned over to the third generation, Elisa Stephens, granddaughter of the school's founder. She quickly determined that the school's small Computer Arts Department had enormous potential to prepare students for multimedia careers when allied with such companies as Silicon Graphics, Pixar, Adobe, and Walt Disney Productions. It is now one of the largest departments at the Academy.

Today, Academy of Art University is the largest private accredited art and design school in the nation with an enrollment of more than 11,500 students from nearly every country in the world. More than one third of the student body is made up of international students. The Academy has more than twenty-two facilities that house classrooms, studios, galleries, and dormitories. The students, who are admitted through an open-enrollment policy, aspire to earn either an A.A., a B.F.A., or a certificate in one of twelve design majors. The school maintains a fleet of buses to connect the different points of the campus, all of which are located within the city limits of San Francisco, one of the world's most vibrant and beautiful cities. The faculty, which is 80 percent part-time and made up of working art and design professionals, is recruited from all across the nation and is drawn to the creative and intellectual center that is the Bay Area. Extensive senior-year internship programs allow students to gain valuable experience and develop strong portfolios in their chosen field before graduation.

Academy of Art University offers an M.F.A. and an M.Arch. program in architecture.

Location

The city of San Francisco is one of the great cultural centers of the world; a melting pot of diversity, ethnicity, and creativity that has spawned major museums and galleries, world-class opera and theaters, dance companies, film production and recording studios, technological innovation, performing artists ranging from classical to popular music, and numerous other cultural opportunities. The city's status as a tourist mecca located on the Pacific Rim ensures that one encounters people from all corners of the world. The climate is moderate and offers kaleidoscopic blends of sunshine and fog nine months of the year. The Northpoint campus is located at world-famous Pier 39; one can view Alcatraz Island from classroom windows. Four other buildings are two blocks from historic Union Square in the commercial heart of the city. Three other buildings are located near the Financial District. The city offers myriad locations for field trips and studio visits. World-renowned artists display their creations in the Academy's four nonprofit art galleries, which are open to the public. The University is an urban institution that both draws upon and contributes to the cultural wealth of the community in which it resides.

Majors and Degrees

Academy of Art University offers A.A. and B.F.A. degrees and certificates in the following majors: advertising (account planning, art direction, copywriting, and television commercials), animation/visual effects (background painting/layout design, character development, game design, storyboard art, VFX/compositing, visual development, and 3-D modeling), computer arts/new media (computer graphics, digital imaging, new media, and Web design), digital arts and communications (client and service-side Internet design creative programming, information architecture, interactive information graphics, interactive modeling, prototyping/testing, and usability), fashion (fashion design, fashion illustration, knitwear, merchandising, and textiles), fine art (ceramics, metal arts, painting/drawing, printmaking, and sculpture), graphic design (corporate and brand identity, motion graphics, multimedia, package design, print and collateral, and Web site design), illustration (cartooning, children's books, editorial, feature film animation, and 2-D animation), industrial design (furniture, product, toy, and transportation), interior architecture and design (commercial, furniture, and residential), motion pictures and television (acting, advertising/director–camera, cinematography, directing, editing, producing, production design, screenwriting, and special effects), and photography (advertising, digital photography, documentary, fine art, photo illustration, and photojournalism).

Academic Programs

A total of 132 credit units are required to earn a Bachelor of Fine Arts degree, consisting of 18 units of foundations courses, 60 units in the major, 12 units of art electives, and 42 units of liberal arts/art history courses. First-year students must complete six foundations courses before the end of the year. Fundamental courses are related specifically to students' majors to prepare them to begin intense focus courses in their field by the sophomore year. All major courses of study are structured so the student builds upon skills learned the previous semester and advances to the next level of technical or creative proficiency. Some related major courses may be taken concurrently. Each course is worth 3 credits. Liberal arts courses teach practical applications for forging a professional career in art and design. International students who come from countries where English is not the primary language may take additional ESL classes, as determined by English language proficiency testing. Students are advised to meet with departmental directors at least once during the academic year to have their progress assessed. Portfolios are reviewed before the junior year to determine whether or not a student has progressed sufficiently to continue study at the Academy.

Academic Facilities

The Academy's facilities reflect its commitment to training students for careers in art and design; not only do students have access to some of the most advanced facilities in the nation, but the Academy continually invests in new equipment to ensure that it remains on the cutting edge of technology. By learning on industry-standard equipment, students gain valuable professional skills that make them highly employable.

The Academy's eight-story Digital Arts Center offers students from the Computer Arts/New Media, Digital Arts and Communications, Animation-Visual Effects, Motion Pictures and Television, Advertising, and Fashion Departments access to an incredible array of technology. The center has a multitude of computer workstations, including Silicon Graphics, Adobe Premier, and autoCAD workstations. Students also have the use of Avid digital-editing suites, multitrack sound-editing studios, a dedicated green-screen studio, and various other video equipment, including Bosch Telecine equipment.

The Photography Department occupies its own building, which houses individual studios and a wide range of equipment, including full-length shooting studios; Hasselblad, Mamyia, Canon, and Sinar cameras; Broncolor, Norman, and Speedotron strobe systems; black-and-white darkrooms; a color lab facility with single-print stations; and the latest technology, such as Macintosh G5 computers for digital imaging and output. In addition, the Academy's modern, professional studio is one of the largest of any photography school in the nation and is ideal for shooting automobiles, motorcycles, and large sets.

The Fine Art Department has been relocated to one of the Academy's newest buildings, and is solely dedicated to painting, drawing, and printmaking. There are five floors occupied by studio space and labs fully equipped for silkscreen, lithography, book arts, etching/intaglio, and relief painting.

The Academy's Fine Art/Sculpture Center is a 58,000-square-foot facility that houses state-of-the-art studios for figure, ceramic, neon/illumination, bronze, metal fabrication, and mold-making sculpture. Students also have use of an off-site bronze-casting facility and foundry. When students graduate from the Academy, they have the opportunity to exhibit in one of the three non-profit galleries located in the heart of downtown San Francisco's premier gallery district. These street-level facilities are an excellent way for students to promote and sell their work and to gain networking experience.

The Library houses more than 30,000 books and magazines, as well as 375 CD titles, 150,000 slides, and 2,000 videos. Computers with Internet access are available to students, as well as an online catalog, color scanners, and color and black-and-white copiers. Workshops and electronic study guides are also available. The Academy Resource Center offers all students free learning support services that include study hall, tutoring, mentoring, mid-point review and study-skills workshops, a writing lab, a state-of-the-art multimedia language lab, an English for Art Program, and a Conversation Partner Program.

Costs

Tuition is $670 per credit unit for undergraduates. Full-time students carry either 12 or 15 units per semester. There is a nonrefundable $140 registration fee—$100 is applicable toward tuition. Lab fees run from $25 to $400 per semester, depending on the class. Tuition and fees are subject to change at any time. Art supplies can run from $250 to $500 per semester, depending on the major. The Academy has most of the expensive technical equipment available for students to borrow or use in a lab.

Academy of Art University operates more than thirteen campus housing facilities within the city. Several housing options are offered, and costs vary from $6600 to $10,000 per academic year (fall and spring semesters). For further information, students may contact the Academy Housing Office directly at 415-618-6335 or via e-mail at housing@academyart.edu.

Financial Aid

The Academy offers financial aid packages consisting of grants, loans, and work-study to eligible students with a demonstrated need. Low-interest loans are available to all eligible students, regardless of need. As financial aid programs, procedures, and eligibility requirements change frequently, applicants should contact the Financial Aid Office for current requirements at the University's address or phone number.

Faculty

The Academy averages nearly 500 faculty members each semester, most of whom are full-time art and design professionals and part-time teachers. The student-teacher ratio for undergraduate classes averages 18:1.

Student Government

Although there is no formal student government, each department has between 2 and 3 student representatives who meet with the president as needed throughout the semester to discuss any student issues.

Admission Requirements

Applicants for the B.F.A. program must have a high school diploma or GED equivalent. There is no portfolio requirement for the A.A. and B.F.A. programs. International students take written and speech tests to determine which ESL classes may have to be completed. Most ESL classes can be taken in conjunction with art and design classes. All foundations classes offer specialized ESL sections with instructors trained for language assistance. The application fee is $100 for undergraduates. A $500 tuition deposit applies to international applicants.

Application and Information

Students may apply to enter the Academy at the beginning of the spring, fall, or summer semesters. Information in this profile is subject to change. Students should contact Academy of Art University for current information or visit its Web site.

For further information and a catalog, students may contact:

Prospective Student Services
Academy of Art University
79 New Montgomery Street
San Francisco, California 94105
Phone: 415-274-2222
800-544-2787 (toll-free)
Fax: 415-618-6287
E-mail: info@academyart.edu
Web site: http://academyart.edu

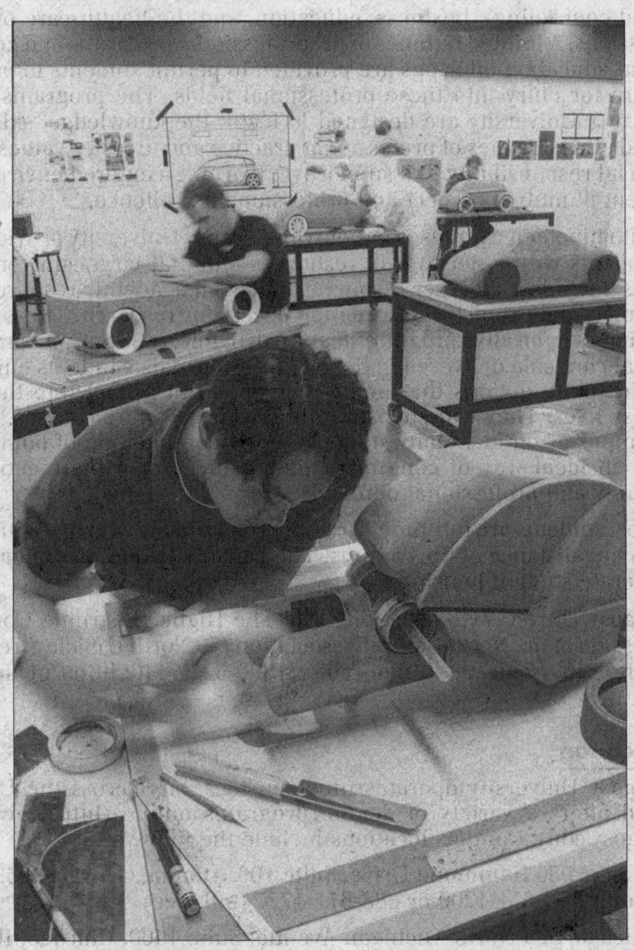

Students working at Academy of Art University.

ARGOSY UNIVERSITY

ARGOSY UNIVERSITY

The University

Argosy University is a leading institution offering a variety of degree programs that focus on the human side of success alongside professional competence. For students looking for a more personal approach to education, Argosy University may just be the answer. With forty-eight graduate and undergraduate programs, across nineteen campuses and twelve states, Argosy University emphasizes interpersonal skills as well as academic learning. All of its programs are taught by practicing professionals who bring real-world experience into the classroom. So students graduate with both a solid foundation of knowledge and the power to put it to work. To accommodate busy working adults, many programs at Argosy University are structured flexibly—with both campus and online learning and evening, weekend, and daytime classes. There is also a wide range of financial aid options for students who qualify.

Argosy University is a private institution of higher education dedicated to providing high-quality professional education programs at the doctoral, master's, bachelor's, and associate degree levels as well as continuing education to individuals who seek to advance their professional and personal lives. The University emphasizes programs in the behavioral sciences (psychology and counseling), business, education, and the health-care professions. A limited number of preprofessional programs and general education offerings are provided to permit students to prepare for entry into these professional fields. The programs of Argosy University are designed to instill the knowledge, skills, and ethical values of professional practice and to foster values of social responsibility in a supportive, learning-centered environment of mutual respect and professional excellence.

With nineteen campuses nationwide, Argosy University provides students with a network of resources found at larger universities, including a career resources office, an academic resources center, and extensive information access for research. The University's innovative programs feature dynamic, relevant, and practical curricula delivered in flexible class formats. Students enjoy scheduling options that make it easier to fit school into their busy lives. They can choose from day and evening courses, on campus or online. Many students find a combination of both to be an ideal way of continuing their education while meeting family and professional demands.

Most students are full-time working professionals who live within driving distance of the campus. The University does not offer or operate student housing.

Argosy University is accredited by The Higher Learning Commission of the North Central Association (30 North LaSalle Street, Suite 2400, Chicago, Illinois 60602; 800-621-7440; http://ncahlc.org).

Location

Argosy University operates nineteen locations across the U.S. and offers a variety of degree programs online (http://www.argosy.edu). Campus locations include the following:

Atlanta, 980 Hammond Drive, Suite 100, Atlanta, Georgia 30328; phone: 770-671-1200 or 888-671-4777 (toll-free)

Chicago, 225 North Michigan Avenue, Suite 1300, Chicago, Illinois 60601; phone: 312-777-7600 or 800-626-4123 (toll-free)

Dallas, 8080 Park Lane, Suite 400A, Dallas, Texas 75231; phone: 214-890-9900 or 866-954-9900 (toll-free)

Denver, 1200 Lincoln Street, Denver, Colorado 80203; phone: 303-248-2700 or 866-431-5981 (toll-free)

Hawai'i, 400 ASB Tower, 1001 Bishop Street, Honolulu, Hawaii 96813; phone: 808-536-5555 or 888-323-2777 (toll-free)

Inland Empire, 636 East Brier Drive, Suite 235, San Bernardino, California 92408; phone: 909-915-3800 or 866-217-9075 (toll-free)

Nashville, 100 Centerview Drive, Suite 225, Nashville, Tennessee 37214; phone: 615-525-2800 or 866-833-6598 (toll-free)

Orange County, 3501 West Sunflower Avenue, Suite 110, Santa Ana, California 92704; phone: 714-338-6200 or 800-716-9598 (toll-free)

Phoenix, 2233 West Dunlap Avenue, Phoenix, Arizona 85021; phone: 602-216-2600 or 866-216-2777 (toll-free)

Salt Lake City, 121 West Election Road, Suite 300, Draper, Utah 84020; phone: 888-639-4756 (toll-free)

San Diego, 7650 Mission Valley Road, San Diego, California 92108; phone: 858-598-1900 or 866-505-0333 (toll-free)

San Francisco Bay Area, 1005 Atlantic Avenue, Alameda, California 94501; phone: 510-217-4700 or 866-215-2777 (toll-free)

Santa Monica, 2950 31st Street, Santa Monica, California 90405; phone: 310-866-4000 or 866-505-0332 (toll-free)

Sarasota, 5250 17th Street, Sarasota, Florida 34235; phone: 941-379-0404 or 800-331-5995 (toll-free)

Schaumburg, 999 North Plaza Drive, Suite 111, Schaumburg, Illinois 60173-5403; phone: 847-969-4900 or 866-290-2777 (toll-free)

Seattle, 2601-A Elliott Avenue, Seattle, Washington 98121; phone: 206-283-4500 or 888-283-2777 (toll-free)

Tampa, Parkside at Tampa Bay Park, 4401 North Hines Avenue, Suite 150, Tampa, Florida 33614; phone: 813-393-5290 or 800-850-6488 (toll-free)

Twin Cities, 1515 Central Parkway, Eagan, Minnesota 55121; phone: 651-846-2882 or 888-844-2004 (toll-free)

Washington DC, 1550 Wilson Boulevard, Suite 600, Arlington, Virginia 22209; phone: 703-526-5800 or 866-703-2777 (toll-free)

Majors and Degrees

Argosy University's College of Business offers a Bachelor of Science (B.S.) in Business Administration program. Argosy University's College of Psychology and Behavioral Sciences offers the Bachelor of Arts (B.A.) in Psychology degree program.

Academic Programs

The B.S. in Business Administration program prepares students for entry- to mid-level positions within the public or private sector. The curriculum is structured to help students develop competencies in oral and written communication, leadership, team skills, solutions-focused learning, and the analysis and execution of solutions in various business situations. Students may choose one of five optional concentrations: customized professional concentration, finance, health-care management, international business, or marketing.

The B.A. in Psychology program is designed to help students begin human services careers in such capacities as entry-level counselor, case manager, or human resources administrator and

in management and business services roles. The program also lays the foundation for graduate study. Students may choose an optional concentration from the following three options: criminal justice, organizational psychology, or substance abuse. This dynamic program is built around a flexible class approach.

Argosy University's bachelor's degree programs are open to students and working professionals with no college experience, plus those who have already earned college credit at a community college, junior college, or other university.

Academic Facilities

Argosy University libraries provide curriculum support and educational resources including current text materials, diagnostic training documents, reference materials and databases, journals and dissertations, and major and current titles in program areas. There is an online public-access catalog of library resources available throughout the Argosy University system. Students enjoy full remote access to their campus library database, enabling them to study and conduct research at home. Academic databases offer dissertation abstracts, academic journals, and professional periodicals. All library computers are Internet accessible. Software applications include Word, Excel, PowerPoint, SPSS, and various test-scoring programs.

Costs

Tuition varies by program. Students should contact the Argosy University campus of their choice for tuition information.

Financial Aid

A wide range of financial aid options is available to students who qualify. Argosy University offers access to federal and state aid programs, merit-based awards, grants, loans, and a work-study program. As a first step, students should complete the Free Application for Federal Student Aid (FAFSA). Prospective students can apply electronically at http://www.fafsa.ed.gov or at the campus. To receive consideration for financial aid and ensure timely receipt of funds, it is best to submit an application promptly.

Faculty

The Argosy University faculty is composed of working professionals who have a passion to help students succeed. Members bring real-world experience and the latest practice innovations to the academic setting. The diverse faculty is widely recognized for contributions to the field. Most hold doctoral degrees. They provide a substantive education that combines comprehensive knowledge with critical skills and practical workplace relevance. Above all, faculty members are committed to their students' personal and professional development.

Student Government

Argosy University campuses offer unique opportunities for student involvement beyond individual programs of study. Most faculty committees include a student representative. In addition, a student group meets with faculty members and administrators regularly to discuss pertinent campus-related issues.

Admission Requirements

Admission requirements differ depending on the number of college credits completed prior to application.

Students who have earned 12 or fewer semester college credits must provide proof of high school graduation or GED and meet one of the following conditions for admission: ACT composite score of 18 or above, or a combined math and verbal SAT score of 870, or minimum ACCUPLACER scores of 86 in sentence skills and 53 in algebra. Applicants who do not meet any of the above conditions for admission will be admitted with academic support if they provide proof of high school graduation or GED and meet one of the following: ACT composite score of 14 to 17, or a combined math and verbal SAT score of 660 to 869, or minimum ACCUPLACER scores of 54 in sentence skills and 36 in arithmetic.

Applicants who have earned 13 or more semester college credits must provide proof of high school graduation or GED and meet one of the following conditions for admission: cumulative college GPA of 2.0 or above or minimum ACCUPLACER scores of 86 for sentence skills and 53 in algebra. Students who do not meet either of the above criteria will be admitted with academic support if they provide proof of high school graduation or GED and meet the following condition: minimum ACCUPLACER scores of 54 in reading and 36 in arithmetic.

Students admitted with academic support are limited to 12 credit hours of study during their first semester (6 credit hours per session). Students admitted with academic support will be required to complete developmental English and/or math courses unless they meet the following conditions: Writing Review (ENG099)—must meet one of the following: a minimum ACCUPLACER score of 86 in sentence skills, or a minimum ACT verbal score of 18, or a minimum SAT verbal score of 425, or completion of a college-level English composition course with a grade of C or above; Mathematics Review I (MAT096)—must meet one of the following: a minimum ACCUPLACER score of 53 in algebra, or a minimum ACT math score of 18, or a minimum SAT math score of 440, or completion of a college-level English composition course with a grade of C or above.

Other admission requirements may include credit hours of qualified transfer credit with a grade of C- or better from a regionally accredited institution or a nationally accredited institution approved and documented by the faculty and dean of the College of Business, or the College of Professional Psychology, at Argosy University or completion of an Associate of Arts or Associate of Science degree from a regionally accredited institution. A maximum of 78 lower-division or 90 total credit hours may be transferred. A minimum written TOEFL score of 500 (paper-based test), 173 (computer-based test), or 61 (Internet-based test) is required for all applicants whose native language is not English or who have not graduated from an institution in which English is the language of instruction.

Official transcripts from approved postsecondary institutions must include a minimum grade point average of 2.0 (on a scale of 4.0) for all academic work completed. Exceptions may be made for extenuating circumstances. All applications must include a completed application form, proof of high school graduation or successful completion of the GED test, official postsecondary transcripts, and a nonrefundable (except in California) application fee. Additional materials are required prior to matriculation. Some programs have additional application requirements or include exceptions to admission requirements. An admissions representative can provide further information.

Application and Information

Argosy University accepts students on a rolling admissions basis year-round, depending on availability of required courses. Applications for admission are available online at http://www.argosy.edu or by contacting one of the campus locations.

Argosy University
205 North Michigan Avenue, Suite 1300
Chicago, Illinois 60601-2250

Phone: 312-899-9900
800-377-0617 (toll-free)
E-mail: auadmissions@argosy.edu
Web site: http://www.argosy.edu

THE ART INSTITUTE OF CALIFORNIA–INLAND EMPIRE

The Art Institute of California™-Inland Empire

SAN BERNARDINO, CALIFORNIA

The Institute

The Art Institute of California–Inland Empire helps students to cultivate and refine the talents and skills that are needed for entry-level positions in the creative arts. Classes are taught in an environment that encourages learning, leadership, and creativity. The school offers six bachelor's degree programs and two associate degree programs.

Faculty and staff members strive to foster development and cultivate artistic growth. Students are given opportunities to develop leadership skills and build relationships. In addition, assistance is available to help students with resume writing, networking, and keeping abreast of what employers are looking for in job candidates.

The Art Institute of California–Inland Empire places a high value on the quality of student life both in and out of the classroom. Students participate in a wide variety of activities, including clubs and organizations, community service opportunities, and various committees designed to enhance the quality of student life.

The Residential Life and Housing Department provides information on independent housing options to all enrolled students requesting such assistance. The Residential Life and Housing staff members coordinate a variety of activities and are available to assist students in arranging suitable living accommodations.

Students come to The Art Institute of California–Inland Empire from throughout the United States. The student population includes recent high school graduates, transfer students, and those who have left a previous employment situation to study and train for a new career. Students are creative, competitive, and open to new ideas.

The Art Institute of California–Inland Empire is accredited by the Accrediting Commission of Career Schools and Colleges of Technology (ACCSCT) as a branch of The Art Institute of California–San Diego. The Art Institute of California–Inland Empire has been granted approval to operate by the California Bureau for Private Postsecondary and Vocational Education (California Department of Consumer Affairs, 1625 North Market Boulevard, Suite S-308, Sacramento, California 95834; phone: 916-574-8200; http://www.bppve.ca.gov).

Location

The Art Institute of California–Inland Empire is located in San Bernardino. Within a short drive from the school, students can enjoy mountains, deserts, Los Angeles, or Mexico. Surfing, water sports, tennis, golf, jogging, mountain biking, and many other outdoor activities are supported by the region's mild climate.

Majors and Degrees

The Art Institute of California–Inland Empire offers bachelor's degrees in culinary management, game art and design, graphic design, interior design, media arts and animation, and Web design and interactive media. Students may also pursue associate degrees in culinary arts and graphic design.

Academic Programs

The academic year is divided into four quarters, beginning in January, April, July, and October. Each program is offered on a year-round basis, allowing students to continue to work uninterrupted toward their degrees.

Academic Facilities

The Art Institute of California–Inland Empire occupies approximately 25,000 square feet. In addition to classrooms, studios, laboratories, offices, a student lounge, a library, and an exhibition gallery, The Art Institute of California–Inland Empire maintains an art supply store for the convenience of students. Equipment provided at The Art Institute of California–Inland Empire is specific to the program of study. This includes, but is not limited to, projectors, editing decks, PC and Macintosh computers, and printers.

Costs

Tuition cost varies by program. Prospective students should contact the school for current tuition costs. Other charges include a starting kit for all first-quarter students. Kits vary in price, depending on the program of study.

Financial Aid

Financial aid is available for those who qualify. Students who require financial assistance should first complete and submit a Free Application for Federal Student Aid (FAFSA) and meet with a financial aid officer. The officer determines the level of need based on a required federal formula, the cost of education, and other factors. Gift aid is available in the form of Federal Pell Grants, Federal Supplemental Educational Opportunity Grants, and veterans' benefits. Loans include Federal Stafford Student Loans, Federal PLUS loans, and alternative loans. Other scholarships are available from the school and private sources. Application deadlines and eligibility requirements vary by program.

Faculty

The Art Institute of California–Inland Empire faculty consists of full-time and part-time instructors, many of whom have advanced degrees and professional experience in their respective fields.

Student Government

The Student Federation is responsible for student government and acts as a liaison between the student body and faculty and staff members.

Admission Requirements

Applicants must provide proof of high school graduation or achievement of a General Educational Development (GED) certificate as a prerequisite for admission. In lieu of documenting high school graduation or a GED certificate, applicants may provide proof of attaining an associate degree or higher from an accredited institution. An official transcript indicating date of high school graduation, GED certificate (including test scores), or date of college graduation (including degree granted), is required as proof.

All individuals seeking admission to The Art Institute of California–Inland Empire are interviewed in person or by phone by an assistant director of admissions, and each applicant must create an original essay of at least 150 words stating how an education at the school would help the student to achieve career goals. There is a $50 application fee.

Application and Information

To obtain an application, make arrangements for an interview, or tour the school, students should contact:

The Art Institute of California–Inland Empire
630 East Brier Drive
San Bernardino, California 92408-2800
Phone: 909-915-2100
800-353-0812 (toll-free)
Fax: 909-915-2130
Web site: http://www.artinstitutes.edu/inlandempire

The Art Institute of Atlanta®, GA; The Art Institute of Atlanta®–Decatur, GA; The Art Institute of Austin℠, TX; The Art Institute of California℠–Inland Empire; The Art Institute of California℠–Los Angeles; The Art Institute of California℠–Orange County; The Art Institute of California℠–Sacramento; The Art Institute of California℠–San Diego; The Art Institute of California℠–San Francisco; The Art Institute of California℠–Sunnyvale; The Art Institute of Charleston℠, SC, A branch of The Art Institute of Atlanta, GA; The Art Institute of Charlotte®, NC; The Art Institute of Colorado® (Denver); The Art Institute of Dallas®, TX; The Art Institute of Fort Lauderdale®, FL; The Art Institute of Houston®, TX; The Art Institute of Indianapolis℠, IN*; The Art Institute of Jacksonville℠, FL, A branch of Miami International University of Art & Design; The Art Institute of Las Vegas®, NV; The Art Institute of Michigan℠ (Detroit); The Art Institute of New York City®, NY; The Art Institute of Ohio℠–Cincinnati**; The Art Institute of Philadelphia®, PA; The Art Institute of Phoenix®, AZ; The Art Institute of Pittsburgh®, PA; The Art Institute of Pittsburgh®–Online Division; The Art Institute of Portland®, OR; The Art Institute of Salt Lake City℠, UT; The Art Institute of Seattle®, WA; The Art Institute of Tampa℠, FL, A branch of Miami International University of Art & Design; The Art Institute of Tennessee℠–Nashville, A branch of The Art Institute of Atlanta, GA; The Art Institute of Tucson℠, AZ; The Art Institute of Washington® (Arlington, VA), A branch of The Art Institute of Atlanta, GA; The Art Institute of York–Pennsylvania℠; The Art Institutes International Minnesota℠ (Minneapolis); California Design College℠ (Los Angeles–Wilshire Blvd.); The Illinois Institute of Art®–Chicago; The Illinois Institute of Art®–Schaumburg; Miami International University of Art & Design℠, FL; The New England Institute of Art® (Boston, MA).

*The Art Institute of Indianapolis is licensed by the Indiana Commission on Proprietary Education, 302 W. Washington St., Rm. E201, Indianapolis, IN 46204, AC-0080.

**The Art Institute of Ohio–Cincinnati, 8845 Governors Hill Drive, Suite 100, Cincinnati, OH 45249-3317, OH Reg. #04-01-1698B.

THE ART INSTITUTE OF CALIFORNIA–LOS ANGELES

SANTA MONICA, CALIFORNIA

The Art Institute of California–Los Angeles

The Institute

The Art Institute of California–Los Angeles prepares students for entry-level positions in creative careers in the arts. The school strives to provide high-quality programs and services that foster the development of student potential. The Art Institute of California–Los Angeles is housed in a 107,000-square-foot building that was designed with the creative student in mind. Bright, spacious classrooms, studios, and labs offer a productive working atmosphere.

The school currently offers ten bachelor's degree programs and five associate degree programs. Each program is offered on a year-round basis, allowing students to continue to work uninterrupted toward their degrees. An impressive faculty of working professionals strives to strengthen students' skills and cultivate their talents. Each student has an academic adviser, who helps to devise career strategies and choose courses consistent with the student's career goals. Programs are carefully defined with support and contributions from the professional community. Curricula are reviewed regularly to keep up with the needs of a changing marketplace. Continuing education is available through the Center for Professional Development of The Art Institute of California–Los Angeles.

The student population includes recent high school graduates, transfer students, and those who have left a previous employment situation to study and train for a new career. Students are creative, competitive, and open to new ideas. They place great value on an education that prepares them for an exciting entry-level position in the arts.

Assistance is available to help students with resume writing, networking, and keeping aware of what employers are looking for in job candidates.

The Office of Residential Life and Housing is committed to providing students with comfortable and convenient housing options. The Art Institute of California–Los Angeles contracts with several local luxury apartment complexes to provide housing to students. Professional residential life staff members live on-site and are available to address student needs. The fully furnished apartment units are located in gated and courtesy-patrolled communities that include on-site parking, fitness centers, swimming pools, and computer rooms. Direct shuttle service is available from school-sponsored housing sites to The Art Institute of California–Los Angeles. The school also provides accommodations to qualified students with disabilities. The Disability Services Office assists qualified students in acquiring reasonable and appropriate accommodations and in supporting their success at the school.

A wide variety of clubs and organizations are available to students, including the Culinary Club, International Student Club, BAMF (comics: writing, drawing, analysis), and Black Ops (PC gaming). The Non-Traditional Student Resource (NTSR) serves as a communication network, fostering a comfortable academic and social atmosphere while providing a support system for nontraditional students.

The Art Institute of California–Los Angeles is accredited by the Accrediting Council for Independent Colleges and Schools (ACICS) to award bachelor's degrees, associate degrees, and diplomas. ACICS is listed as a nationally recognized accrediting agency by the U.S. Department of Education. Its accreditation of degree-granting institutions is recognized by the Council for Higher Education Accreditation. ACICS can be contacted at 750 First Street NE, Suite 980, Washington, D.C. 20002; phone: 202-336-6780. The Art Institute of California–Los Angeles has been granted approval to operate by the California Bureau for Private Post-secondary and Vocational Education (California Department of Consumer Affairs, 1625 North Market Boulevard, Suite S-308, Sacramento, California 95834; phone: 916-574-8200; http://www.bppve.ca.gov).

Location

Located in Los Angeles, the arts and entertainment capital of the world, The Art Institute of California–Los Angeles is within easy driving distance of the Pacific Coast Highway, Century City, and downtown. The city offers a rich diversity of food, fashion, architecture, entertainment, languages, world views, and religions that are showcased in numerous community and ethnic festivals throughout the year. Leisure activities include hiking on Santa Monica Mountain trails or visits to the Getty Museum, Los Angeles County Museum of Art, or Los Angeles Zoo. Students may also enjoy dining and shopping on Santa Monica's Third Street Promenade or in nearby Westwood Village. Music and theater venues include the Hollywood Bowl, the Greek Theatre, the Music Center, and the Dorothy Chandler Pavilion. Other popular destinations are Watts Towers, the La Brea Tar Pits, Hollywood Boulevard's Walk of Fame, and Mann's Chinese Theater.

Majors and Degrees

The Art Institute of California–Los Angeles offers Bachelor of Science degree programs (thirty-six months) in audio production, culinary management, digital filmmaking and video production, game art and design, game programming, graphic design, interior design, media arts and animation, visual effects and motion graphics, and Web design and interactive media.

Associate of Science degree programs (twenty-one months) are available in baking and pastry, culinary arts, graphic design, video production, and Web design and interactive media.

Diplomas are offered in the art of cooking and baking and pastry.

Academic Programs

The academic year is divided into four academic quarters that begin in January, April, July, and October. Associate degree candidates must complete 112 academic credits to graduate, including 28 general education credits. These are generally earned over seven quarters. Bachelor's degree candidates must complete 192 credits, including 56 general education credits. These are generally earned over eleven quarters. All students must complete their programs of study with a minimum 2.0 cumulative GPA.

Academic Facilities

Located at 31st Street in the city of Santa Monica, The Art Institute of California–Los Angeles provides equipment that includes projectors, editing decks, PC and Macintosh computers, printers, and fully equipped kitchens. The library collection includes approximately 15,000 books, 260 periodical subscriptions, and 1,650 items of digital and audiovisual materials. The library is equipped with eight computer stations, has Internet access, and subscribes to online databases. In addition to classrooms, studios, laboratories, offices, a student lounge, a learning resource center, and an exhibition gallery, the school also maintains an art supply store for the convenience of its students.

Costs

Tuition cost varies by program. Prospective students should contact the school for current tuition costs. Other charges include a starting kit for all first-quarter students. Kits vary in price depending on the program of study.

Financial Aid

Financial aid is available for those who qualify. Students who require financial assistance should first complete and submit a Free Application for Federal Student Aid (FAFSA) and meet with a financial aid officer. The officer determines the level of need based on a required federal formula, the cost of education, and other factors. Gift aid is available in the form of Federal Pell Grants, Federal Supplemental Educational Opportunity Grants, and veterans' benefits. Loans include Federal Stafford Student Loans, Federal PLUS loans, and alternative loans. Other scholarships are available from the school and private sources. Application deadlines and eligibility requirements vary by program.

Faculty

The Art Institute of California–Los Angeles faculty comprises full-time and part-time professors, many with advanced degrees and professional experience in their respective fields.

Student Government

The Associated Student Council provides a forum to discuss student issues, facilitates the exchange of ideas and information among students, and acts as a liaison between students and members of the faculty and administration; it also organizes student activities at the school and provides student leadership opportunities. In addition, the Activities and Events Council consists of an elected board, representatives from each student organization, and other interested students.

Admission Requirements

The admission process at The Art Institute of California–Los Angeles includes a student interview with the admissions office (either in person or by phone) and submission of a completed application form, a 150-word essay, high school transcripts or General Educational Development (GED) test scores, and official SAT or ACT scores. Students who are entering the annual scholarship competition must submit a portfolio of their artwork. There is a $50 application fee.

Credit is given for college courses successfully completed with a GPA of 2.0 or better at other accredited institutions where the courses are comparable to those offered by The Art Institute of California–Los Angeles. Students applying for transfer of credit need to present an official transcript of grades and course descriptions, and they may be required to present a portfolio. Credit is also given for a score of 4 or 5 on the Advanced Placement (AP) exam. Official grades must be on file.

Application and Information

To obtain an application, make arrangements for an interview, or tour the school, prospective students should contact:

The Art Institute of California–Los Angeles
2900 31st Street
Santa Monica, California 90405-3035
Phone: 310-752-4700
888-646-4610 (toll-free)
Fax: 310-752-4708
Web site: http://www.artinstitutes.edu/losangeles

The Art Institute of Atlanta®, GA; The Art Institute of Atlanta®–Decatur, GA; The Art Institute of Austin[SM], TX; The Art Institute of California[SM]–Inland Empire; The Art Institute of California[SM]–Los Angeles; The Art Institute of California[SM]–Orange County; The Art Institute of California[SM]–Sacramento; The Art Institute of California[SM]–San Diego; The Art Institute of California[SM]–San Francisco; The Art Institute of California[SM]–Sunnyvale; The Art Institute of Charleston[SM], SC, A branch of The Art Institute of Atlanta, GA; The Art Institute of Charlotte®, NC; The Art Institute of Colorado® (Denver); The Art Institute of Dallas®, TX; The Art Institute of Fort Lauderdale®, FL; The Art Institute of Houston®, TX; The Art Institute of Indianapolis[SM], IN*; The Art Institute of Jacksonville[SM], FL, A branch of Miami International University of Art & Design; The Art Institute of Las Vegas®, NV; The Art Institute of Michigan[SM] (Detroit); The Art Institute of New York City®, NY; The Art Institute of Ohio[SM]–Cincinnati**; The Art Institute of Philadelphia®, PA; The Art Institute of Phoenix®, AZ; The Art Institute of Pittsburgh®, PA; The Art Institute of Pittsburgh®–Online Division; The Art Institute of Portland®, OR; The Art Institute of Salt Lake City[SM], UT; The Art Institute of Seattle®, WA; The Art Institute of Tampa[SM], FL, A branch of Miami International University of Art & Design; The Art Institute of Tennessee[SM]–Nashville, A branch of The Art Institute of Atlanta, GA; The Art Institute of Tucson[SM], AZ; The Art Institute of Washington® (Arlington, VA), A branch of The Art Institute of Atlanta, GA; The Art Institute of York–Pennsylvania[SM]; The Art Institutes International Minnesota[SM] (Minneapolis); California Design College[SM] (Los Angeles–Wilshire Blvd.); The Illinois Institute of Art®–Chicago; The Illinois Institute of Art®–Schaumburg; Miami International University of Art & Design[SM], FL; The New England Institute of Art® (Boston, MA).

*The Art Institute of Indianapolis is licensed by the Indiana Commission on Proprietary Education, 302 W. Washington St., Rm. E201, Indianapolis, IN 46204, AC-0080.

**The Art Institute of Ohio–Cincinnati, 8845 Governors Hill Drive, Suite 100, Cincinnati, OH 45249-3317, OH Reg. #04-01-1698B.

THE ART INSTITUTE OF CALIFORNIA–ORANGE COUNTY

SANTA ANA, CALIFORNIA

The Art Institute of California–Orange County

The Institute

The Art Institute of California–Orange County helps prepare students for entry-level positions in the creative arts through an environment that encourages academic freedom, responsible decision making, and critical thinking. A collaborative environment encourages personal and professional growth while promoting teamwork and communication. The Art Institute of California–Orange County offers eleven bachelor's degree programs and three associate degree programs.

Students are taught professional skills; instructors and staff members assist students in portfolio development and professional resume creation. Many gain on-the-job skills through participation in internships or externships at local companies and nationally recognized corporations. Assistance is available to help students with resume writing, networking, and keeping abreast of what employers are looking for in job candidates.

Students come from across the country and abroad. The student population includes recent high school graduates, transfer students, and those who have left a previous employment situation to study and train for a new career.

The Art Institute of California–Orange County offers school-sponsored housing, featuring furnished apartment units that include laundry facilities, a fitness center, a pool, a spa, and tennis courts. Each unit is within walking distance of a variety of restaurants, grocery stores, and retail establishments. Apartment information and roommate referrals are available to enrolled students who choose to live outside of school-sponsored housing.

The school provides an environment that encourages involvement in a wide variety of academic and nonacademic activities. Student organizations include chapters of the American Institute of Graphic Arts (AIGA), International Game Developers Association (IGDA), and American Society of Interior Designers. Clubs include the Multimedia and Web Design Club, the OC Ad Club, Women in Animation, and the Classic Game Club. Music Madness, Pizza with the Prez, All-School Picnic, Drive-in Movie Night, Stress Relief Events, and Meet the Pros—a professional speaker series—are just a few of the many school-sponsored offerings.

The Art Institute of California–Orange County is accredited by the Accrediting Council for Independent Colleges and Schools (ACICS) to award bachelor's degrees, associate degrees, and diplomas. ACICS is listed as a nationally recognized accrediting agency by the U.S. Department of Education. Its accreditation of degree-granting institutions is recognized by the Council for Higher Education Accreditation. ACICS can be contacted at 750 First Street NE, Suite 980, Washington, D.C. 20002; phone: 202-336-6780. The Art Institute of California–Orange County has been granted approval to operate by the California Bureau for Private Post-secondary and Vocational Education (California Department of Consumer Affairs, 1625 North Market Boulevard, Suite S-308, Sacramento, California 95834; phone: 916-574-8200; http://www.bppve.ca.gov).

Location

The Art Institute of California–Orange County is strategically located in the heart of the booming Southern California region that includes the counties of Orange, Los Angeles, San Diego, and Ventura. Southern California is a central hub of the entertainment, advertising, design, aerospace, and culinary industries. Orange County offers 42 miles of beautiful, sandy Pacific Ocean coastline, and wilderness parks are minutes away for camping, hiking, and biking. The area has more than 250 sunny days a year and is home to Disneyland, Knott's Berry Farm, and world-renowned cultural events, including the annual Laguna Beach Festival of the Arts.

Majors and Degrees

Bachelor of Science degrees are available in advertising, culinary management, fashion design, fashion marketing and management, game art and design, graphic design, industrial design, interior design, media arts and animation, visual and game programming, and Web design and interactive media.

Associate of Science degrees are offered in culinary arts, graphic design, and Web design and interactive media.

Diploma programs are offered in art of cooking and baking and pastry.

Academic Programs

A bachelor's degree requires the completion of 192 credits (thirty-six months), while an associate degree requires the completion of 112 academic credits (twenty-one months). The academic year is divided into four quarters that begin in January, April, July, and October. Each program is offered on a year-round basis, allowing students to continue to work uninterrupted toward their degrees.

The school arranges study trips to local cultural and commercial sites. These visits offer an opportunity for valuable exposure to places and events relating to the student's field of study. In addition, out-of-town seminars and visits may be planned in individual programs.

The Student Tutoring Program is a peer-to-peer tutoring assistance program that is available to all current students. Each tutor has unique qualifications in his or her area of expertise.

Academic Facilities

The Art Institute of California–Orange County was designed with the creative student in mind. Light, spacious classrooms and well-equipped studios, professional-skill kitchens, and computer labs offer a productive working atmosphere to explore and render creativity. On-site equipment includes projectors, editing decks, camcorders, Windows NT and Macintosh computers, printers, and fully equipped kitchens. The Library/Learning Resources Center develops and maintains a readily available collection of books, periodicals, audiovisual materials, and CD-ROMs. Remote access to information sources is available through the Internet. Resources focus on creative art, design, and multimedia production as well as support for general education enhancement in the fine arts, humanities, social sciences, and communication. The school also maintains an art supply store for the convenience of its students. 50 Forks, a dining lab that operates as a full-service restaurant, is overseen by professional chef faculty members and operated by upper-level culinary students as a final passage prior to graduation.

Costs

Tuition costs may be obtained by contacting the school or by visiting the school's Web site. Additional expenses include a first-quarter starting kit and lab fees for some programs.

Financial Aid

Financial aid is available for those who qualify. Students who require financial assistance should first complete and submit a Free Application for Federal Student Aid (FAFSA) and meet with a financial aid officer. The officer determines the level of need based on a required federal formula, the cost of education, and other factors. Gift aid is available in the form of Federal Pell Grants, Federal Supplemental Educational Opportunity Grants, and veterans' benefits. Loans include Federal Stafford Student Loans, Federal PLUS loans, and alternative loans. Other scholarships are available from the school and private sources. Application deadlines and eligibility requirements vary by program.

Faculty

The faculty members at The Art Institute of California–Orange County bring a professional perspective and industry standards into the classroom to better prepare students for entry-level positions upon graduation.

Student Government

The President's Club is a group of students who promote the philosophy of "students helping students." Members act as emissaries for the school and as a liaison between students and faculty and staff members. The club assists new students as well as helping in the organization and promotion of campus activities. Student members must be nominated for the organization by a member of the faculty or staff.

Admission Requirements

Prospective students must hold a high school diploma or General Educational Development (GED) certificate or have earned a bachelor's degree or higher from an accredited institution. High school seniors who have not yet graduated should submit a partial transcript that indicates their expected graduation date. All prospective students are required to submit two essays of approximately one page in length describing what they expect from the school and how an education at The Art Institute of California–Orange County may help them to reach their career goals. Applicants are interviewed either in person or by telephone by an assistant director of admissions. In addition, other standardized exams, such as the SAT or ACT, may be considered. Prospective students may apply at any time prior to the start of the upcoming quarter, and applications may be submitted online or mailed directly to the school. There is a $50 application fee.

Application and Information

To obtain an application, make arrangements for an interview, or tour the school, students should contact:

The Art Institute of California–Orange County
3601 West Sunflower Avenue
Santa Ana, California 92704-7931
Phone: 714-830-0200
888-549-3055 (toll-free)
Fax: 714-556-1923
Web site: http://www.artinstitutes.edu/orangecounty

The Art Institute of Atlanta®, GA; The Art Institute of Atlanta®–Decatur, GA; The Art Institute of Austin[SM], TX; The Art Institute of California[SM]–Inland Empire; The Art Institute of California[SM]–Los Angeles; The Art Institute of California[SM]–Orange County; The Art Institute of California[SM]–Sacramento; The Art Institute of California[SM]–San Diego; The Art Institute of California[SM]–San Francisco; The Art Institute of California[SM]–Sunnyvale; The Art Institute of Charleston[SM], SC, A branch of The Art Institute of Atlanta, GA; The Art Institute of Charlotte®, NC; The Art Institute of Colorado® (Denver); The Art Institute of Dallas®, TX; The Art Institute of Fort Lauderdale®, FL; The Art Institute of Houston®, TX; The Art Institute of Indianapolis[SM], IN*; The Art Institute of Jacksonville[SM], FL, A branch of Miami International University of Art & Design; The Art Institute of Las Vegas®, NV; The Art Institute of Michigan[SM] (Detroit); The Art Institute of New York City®, NY; The Art Institute of Ohio[SM]–Cincinnati**; The Art Institute of Philadelphia®, PA; The Art Institute of Phoenix®, AZ; The Art Institute of Pittsburgh®, PA; The Art Institute of Pittsburgh®–Online Division; The Art Institute of Portland®, OR; The Art Institute of Salt Lake City[SM], UT; The Art Institute of Seattle®, WA; The Art Institute of Tampa[SM], FL, A branch of Miami International University of Art & Design; The Art Institute of Tennessee[SM]–Nashville, A branch of The Art Institute of Atlanta, GA; The Art Institute of Tucson[SM], AZ; The Art Institute of Washington® (Arlington, VA), A branch of The Art Institute of Atlanta, GA; The Art Institute of York–Pennsylvania[SM]; The Art Institutes International Minnesota[SM] (Minneapolis); California Design College[SM] (Los Angeles–Wilshire Blvd.); The Illinois Institute of Art®–Chicago; The Illinois Institute of Art®–Schaumburg; Miami International University of Art & Design[SM], FL; The New England Institute of Art® (Boston, MA).

*The Art Institute of Indianapolis is licensed by the Indiana Commission on Proprietary Education, 302 W. Washington St., Rm. E201, Indianapolis, IN 46204, AC-0080.

**The Art Institute of Ohio–Cincinnati, 8845 Governors Hill Drive, Suite 100, Cincinnati, OH 45249-3317, OH Reg. #04-01-1698B.

THE ART INSTITUTE OF CALIFORNIA–SACRAMENTO

SACRAMENTO, CALIFORNIA

The Art Institute of California™-Sacramento

The Institute

The Art Institute of California–Sacramento provides students with an educational environment and dedicated faculty members committed to preparing students for entry-level positions in the creative arts. Under the guidance of industry professionals, students learn by doing the types of tasks they are likely to encounter in the workplace. In addition, assistance is available to help students with resume writing, networking, and keeping aware of what employers are looking for in job candidates. The school offers seven bachelor's degree programs and three associate degree programs.

The school offers assistance in helping students secure housing.

The student population includes recent high school graduates, transfer students, and those who have left a previous employment situation to study and train for a new career. Students are creative, competitive, and open to new ideas. They place great value on an education that prepares them for an exciting entry-level position in the arts.

The Art Institute of California–Sacramento places a high value on the quality of student life—both in and out of the classroom. Students participate in a wide variety of activities, including clubs and organizations, community service, and various committees designed to enhance the quality of student life.

The Art Institute of California–Sacramento is accredited by the Accrediting Council for Independent Colleges and Schools (ACICS) to award bachelor's and associate degrees. ACICS is listed as a nationally recognized accrediting agency by the U.S. Department of Education. Its accreditation of degree-granting institutions is recognized by the Council for Higher Education Accreditation. ACICS can be contacted at 750 First Street NE, Suite 980, Washington, D.C. 20002; phone: 202-336-6780. The Art Institute of California–Sacramento has been granted approval to operate by the California Bureau for Private Postsecondary and Vocational Education (California Department of Consumer Affairs, 1625 North Market Boulevard, Suite S-308, Sacramento, California 95834; phone: 916-574-8200; http://www.bppve.ca.gov).

Location

Sacramento's metropolitan population of more than 2 million means that students have access to recreation and the arts. A former gold rush town, Sacramento is now the fourth-largest city in California. In addition to state government, the city is a major transportation and commerce hub linking the east with California's coastal cities.

Majors and Degrees

Bachelor's degree programs are offered in culinary management, digital filmmaking and video production, game art and design, graphic design, interior design, media arts and animation, and Web design and interactive media.

Associate degrees are offered in culinary arts, graphic design, and Web design and interactive media.

Academic Programs

The Art Institute of California–Sacramento operates on a year-round, four-quarter system.

Academic Facilities

The Art Institute of California–Sacramento contains classrooms, Mac and PC computer labs, and a library for student use. There is also a bookstore.

Costs

Tuition cost varies by program. Prospective students should contact the school for current tuition costs. Other charges include a starting kit for all first quarter students. Kits vary in price depending on the program of study.

Financial Aid

Financial aid is available for those who qualify. Students who require financial assistance should first complete and submit a Free Application for Federal Student Aid (FAFSA) and meet with a financial aid officer. The officer determines the level of need based on a required federal formula, the cost of education, and other factors. Gift aid is available in the form of Federal Pell Grants, Federal Supplemental Educational Opportunity Grants, and veterans' benefits. Loans include Federal Stafford Loans, Federal PLUS Loans, and alternative loans. Other scholarships are available from the school and private sources. Application deadlines and eligibility requirements vary by program.

Faculty

Faculty members at The Art Institute of California–Sacramento have professional knowledge that they bring into the classroom. The school's faculty members provide their students with a real-world, relevant educational experience.

Admission Requirements

Applicants must provide proof of high school graduation or achievement of a General Educational Development (GED) certificate as a prerequisite for admission. In lieu of documenting high school graduation or a GED certificate, applicants may provide proof of attaining an associate degree or higher from an accredited institution. An official transcript indicating date of high school graduation, GED certificate (including test scores), or date of college graduation (including degree granted) is required as proof.

All individuals seeking admission to The Art Institute of California–Sacramento are interviewed in person or by phone by an assistant director of admissions, and each applicant must create an original essay of at least 150 words stating how an education at The Art Institute of California–Sacramento would help the student achieve career goals. There is a $50 application fee.

Application and Information

To obtain an application, make arrangements for an interview, or tour the school, students should contact:

The Art Institute of California–Sacramento
2850 Gateway Oaks Drive, Suite 100
Sacramento, California 95833
Phone: 916-830-6320
800-477-1957 (toll-free)
Fax: 916-830-6344
Web site: http://www.artinstitutes.edu/sacramento

The Art Institute of Atlanta®, GA; The Art Institute of Atlanta®–Decatur, GA; The Art Institute of Austin℠, TX; The Art Institute of California℠–Inland Empire; The Art Institute of California℠–Los Angeles; The Art Institute of California℠–Orange County; The Art Institute of California℠–Sacramento; The Art Institute of California℠–San Diego; The Art Institute of California℠–San Francisco; The Art Institute of California℠–Sunnyvale; The Art Institute of Charleston℠, SC, A branch of The Art Institute of Atlanta, GA; The Art Institute of Charlotte®, NC; The Art Institute of Colorado® (Denver); The Art Institute of Dallas®, TX; The Art Institute of Fort Lauderdale®, FL; The Art Institute of Houston®, TX; The Art Institute of Indianapolis℠, IN*; The Art Institute of Jacksonville℠, FL, A branch of Miami International University of Art & Design; The Art Institute of Las Vegas®, NV; The Art Institute of Michigan℠ (Detroit); The Art Institute of New York City®, NY; The Art Institute of Ohio℠–Cincinnati**; The Art Institute of Philadelphia®, PA; The Art Institute of Phoenix®, AZ; The Art Institute of Pittsburgh®, PA; The Art Institute of Pittsburgh®–Online Division; The Art Institute of Portland®, OR; The Art Institute of Salt Lake City℠, UT; The Art Institute of Seattle®, WA; The Art Institute of Tampa℠, FL, A branch of Miami International University of Art & Design; The Art Institute of Tennessee℠–Nashville, A branch of The Art Institute of Atlanta, GA; The Art Institute of Tucson℠, AZ; The Art Institute of Washington® (Arlington, VA), A branch of The Art Institute of Atlanta, GA; The Art Institute of York–Pennsylvania℠; The Art Institutes International Minnesota℠ (Minneapolis); California Design College℠ (Los Angeles–Wilshire Blvd.); The Illinois Institute of Art®–Chicago; The Illinois Institute of Art®–Schaumburg; Miami International University of Art & Design℠, FL; The New England Institute of Art® (Boston, MA).

*The Art Institute of Indianapolis is licensed by the Indiana Commission on Proprietary Education, 302 W. Washington St., Rm. E201, Indianapolis, IN 46204, AC-0080.

**The Art Institute of Ohio–Cincinnati, 8845 Governors Hill Drive, Suite 100, Cincinnati, OH 45249-3317, OH Reg. #04-01-1698B.

THE ART INSTITUTE OF CALIFORNIA–SAN DIEGO

The Art Institute of California™•San Diego

SAN DIEGO, CALIFORNIA

The Institute

The Art Institute of California–San Diego helps prepare students for entry-level positions in the creative marketplace by teaching professional skills. Instructors and staff members direct students' portfolio development and resume creation, while partnerships with local and national employers help to deliver relevant education that benefits both students and employers. The school offers nine bachelor's degrees options as well as four associate degree programs.

Academic programs are carefully created with the support and contributions of members of the professional community through Program Advisory Committees. Curricula are further reviewed by faculty members and industry professionals to ensure that they assist students in preparing for the needs of a changing marketplace.

Career Services keeps track of employer satisfaction and industry trends to provide employers with candidates who fulfill their needs while working to assist in graduates' career success. In addition, assistance is available to help students with resume writing, networking, and keeping aware of what employers are looking for in job candidates.

Students come to The Art Institute of California–San Diego from across the United States and abroad. The student population includes recent high school graduates, transfer students, and those who have left a previous employment situation to study and train for a new career. Students are creative, competitive, and open to new ideas. They place great value on an education that prepares them for an exciting entry-level position in the arts.

Students may join the Advertising Club, the American Institute of Graphic Arts (AIGA), the Comic Club, the Level Design Club, the Theatre Club, and the interactive or 3-D clubs. Art Institute of California–San Diego students help the national Ad Club by designing and producing collateral as well as participating in such events as holiday parties, media auctions, and creative shows. Students may also serve on the Student Council, which plans school social and cultural events.

Students may live in school-sponsored housing at The Club at River Run, located 1.5 miles from the school and adjacent to the trolley line. Four students share a two-bedroom, fully furnished apartment. The complex offers many amenities, including a swimming pool, Jacuzzi, tennis courts, fitness center, and a clubhouse. Two resident assistants live in the complex and have organized events such as potlucks, bowling nights, video game tournaments, cookouts, pizza parties, and faculty-student dinners. Security is provided by on-site management during the day and courtesy patrols in the evening hours. Supermarkets, banks, coffee shops, and fast food are conveniently located nearby. The Student Affairs Department provides information on roommate referrals and apartment rentals.

The Art Institute of California–San Diego is accredited by the Accrediting Commission of Career Schools and Colleges of Technology (ACCSCT). The Art Institute of California–San Diego has been granted approval to operate by the California Bureau for Private Post-secondary and Vocational Education (California Department of Consumer Affairs, 1625 North Market Boulevard, Suite S-308, Sacramento, California 95834; phone: 916-574-8200; http://www.bppve.ca.gov).

Location

San Diego was named the "Best Place in America for Business and Careers" by *Forbes* magazine in 2002. Within a 2-hour drive are mountains, deserts, Los Angeles, Mexico, surfing, water sports, tennis, golf, jogging, mountain biking, and beaches. San Diego offers many regional shopping centers as well as picturesque spots, including the San Diego Zoo, Wild Animal Park, Sea World, Seaport Village, Old Town, Horton Plaza, the Gaslamp District, and La Jolla. The opera, symphony, live theater district, professional and collegiate athletic events, and concerts are also nearby. San Diego's average daytime temperature is 70 degrees, and the city averages 267 sunny days each year.

Majors and Degrees

The Art Institute of California–San Diego offers bachelor's degree programs in advertising, culinary management, fashion design, fashion marketing and management, game art and design, graphic design, interior design, media arts and animation, and Web design and interactive media.

Associate degree programs are available in advertising, baking and pastry, culinary arts, and graphic design.

Academic Programs

Transfer students must earn at least 75 of their credits at The Art Institute of California–San Diego in order to complete their programs of study.

The Art Institute of California–San Diego arranges study trips to local cultural and commercial sites. In addition, out-of-town seminars and visits are planned in individual programs. The costs related to optional study trips are not included in regular tuition or fees.

Academic Facilities

The Art Institute of California–San Diego is home to a student book and supply store, student lounge, computer labs with both PC and Macintosh computers, art production studios, life drawing rooms, culinary kitchens and storage, an Interior Design Resource Center, a Learning Resource Center (LRC), administrative offices, and classrooms.

Light, spacious classrooms and well-equipped studios breed creativity. The library and Learning Resource Center provide a readily available collection of books, periodicals, audiovisual materials, and CD-ROMs as well as access to remote sources through the Internet. Resources focus on creative art, design, and multimedia production as well as support for general education enhancement in the fine arts, humanities, social sciences, and communication. The Palette is a restaurant open to the public that is operated by senior-level culinary students and overseen by faculty members who are professional chefs.

Costs

Tuition cost varies by program. Prospective students should contact the school for current tuition costs. Other charges include a starting kit for all first-quarter students. Kits vary in price depending on the program of study.

Financial Aid

Financial aid is available for those who qualify. Students who require financial assistance should first complete and submit a Free Application for Federal Student Aid (FAFSA) and meet with a financial aid officer. The officer determines the level of need based on a required federal formula, the cost of education, and other factors. Gift aid is available in the form of Federal Pell Grants, Federal Supplemental Educational Opportunity Grants, and veterans' benefits. Loans include Federal Stafford Student Loans, Federal PLUS loans, and alternative loans. Other scholarships are available from the school and private sources. Application deadlines and eligibility requirements vary by program.

Faculty

The Art Institute of California–San Diego has part-time and full-time faculty members, many of whom are experienced in their respective fields. By tapping the experience of industry professionals, the school is able to bring a professional perspective into the classroom.

Admission Requirements

Prospective students must be high school graduates or hold a General Educational Development (GED) certificate. High school seniors who have not yet graduated should submit a partial transcript that indicates their expected graduation date. All prospective students are required to write an essay of approximately 150 words describing how an education at The Art Institute of California–San Diego will help them to attain their creative goals. An interview, either in person or by telephone, is required. SAT or ACT scores may also be considered. Applications may be submitted online or mailed to the school. There is a $50 application fee.

Application and Information

To obtain an application or make arrangements for an interview or tour of the school, prospective students should contact:

The Art Institute of California–San Diego
7650 Mission Valley Road
San Diego, California 92108-4423
Phone: 858-598-1200
866-275-2422 (toll-free)
Fax: 619-291-3206
Web site: http://www.artinstitutes.edu/sandiego

The Art Institute of Atlanta®, GA; The Art Institute of Atlanta®–Decatur, GA; The Art Institute of Austin[SM], TX; The Art Institute of California[SM]–Inland Empire; The Art Institute of California[SM]–Los Angeles; The Art Institute of California[SM]–Orange County; The Art Institute of California[SM]–Sacramento; The Art Institute of California[SM]–San Diego; The Art Institute of California[SM]–San Francisco; The Art Institute of California[SM]–Sunnyvale; The Art Institute of Charleston[SM], SC, A branch of The Art Institute of Atlanta, GA; The Art Institute of Charlotte®, NC; The Art Institute of Colorado® (Denver); The Art Institute of Dallas®, TX; The Art Institute of Fort Lauderdale®, FL; The Art Institute of Houston®, TX; The Art Institute of Indianapolis[SM], IN*; The Art Institute of Jacksonville[SM], FL, A branch of Miami International University of Art & Design; The Art Institute of Las Vegas®, NV; The Art Institute of Michigan[SM] (Detroit); The Art Institute of New York City®, NY; The Art Institute of Ohio[SM]–Cincinnati**; The Art Institute of Philadelphia®, PA; The Art Institute of Phoenix®, AZ; The Art Institute of Pittsburgh®, PA; The Art Institute of Pittsburgh®–Online Division; The Art Institute of Portland®, OR; The Art Institute of Salt Lake City[SM], UT; The Art Institute of Seattle®, WA; The Art Institute of Tampa[SM], FL, A branch of Miami International University of Art & Design; The Art Institute of Tennessee[SM]–Nashville, A branch of The Art Institute of Atlanta, GA; The Art Institute of Tucson[SM], AZ; The Art Institute of Washington® (Arlington, VA), A branch of The Art Institute of Atlanta, GA; The Art Institute of York–Pennsylvania[SM]; The Art Institutes International Minnesota[SM] (Minneapolis); California Design College[SM] (Los Angeles–Wilshire Blvd.); The Illinois Institute of Art®–Chicago; The Illinois Institute of Art®–Schaumburg; Miami International University of Art & Design[SM], FL; The New England Institute of Art® (Boston, MA).

*The Art Institute of Indianapolis is licensed by the Indiana Commission on Proprietary Education, 302 W. Washington St., Rm. E201, Indianapolis, IN 46204, AC-0080.

**The Art Institute of Ohio–Cincinnati, 8845 Governors Hill Drive, Suite 100, Cincinnati, OH 45249-3317, OH Reg. #04-01-1698B.

THE ART INSTITUTE OF CALIFORNIA–SAN FRANCISCO

The Art Institute of California™•San Francisco

SAN FRANCISCO, CALIFORNIA

The Institute

The Art Institute of California–San Francisco helps students cultivate and refine the talents and skills that are needed for entry-level positions in the creative arts. Curricula are taught in an environment that encourages free expression, leadership, and responsible decision making. The school offers fourteen bachelor's degree programs to students, as well as five associate degree programs and a master's degree in computer animation.

Faculty and staff members strive to foster development and cultivate artistic growth. Students are given opportunities to develop leadership skills and build relationships. In addition, assistance is available to help students with resume writing, networking, and keeping abreast of what employers are looking for in job candidates.

The Art Institute of California–San Francisco places a high value on the quality of student life both in and out of the classroom. Students participate in a wide variety of activities, including clubs and organizations, community service opportunities, and various committees designed to enhance the quality of student life. Numerous all-school programs and events are planned throughout the year to meet the educational, developmental, and social needs of students. The Art Institute of California–San Francisco also includes a student gallery, a student lounge, staff offices, and an art supply store.

The Art Institute of California–San Francisco helps students to obtain comfortable, affordable housing. The school has two housing locations. Westlake Village Apartments in Daly City offers studio apartments for 2 occupants. Two-bedroom units for 4 occupants are also available. The Fillmore Center in San Francisco offers two- and three-bedroom units for 6 occupants. All apartments are furnished with a full kitchen and one or two bathrooms. Both housing sites are conveniently located within a 20-minute commute of the school, using public transportation. Students may also choose to live in independent housing; those who decide to live off campus are encouraged to begin their housing search early. Roommate referral services are available.

Students come to The Art Institute of California–San Francisco from throughout the United States and abroad. The student population includes recent high school graduates, transfer students, and those who have left a previous employment situation to study and train for a new career. Students are creative, competitive, and open to new ideas. They place great value on an education that prepares them for an exciting entry-level position in the arts. Many clubs and organizations are specific to programs of study, while others are geared toward student interest in photography, the environment, and campus activities. Students also take advantage of San Francisco's clubs, concerts, museums, ethnic restaurants, and Golden Gate Park. Local activities and clubs include the San Francisco Siggraph Chapter, Graphic Design Guild, San Francisco Fashion Group, and Game Developers Local Chapter. In addition, students have attended events such as the International Game Developers Conference, MacWorld, and the HOW Conference.

The Art Institute of California–San Francisco is accredited by the Accrediting Council for Independent Colleges and Schools (ACICS) to award bachelor's and associate degrees. ACICS is listed as a nationally recognized accrediting agency by the U.S. Department of Education. Its accreditation of degree-granting institutions is recognized by the Council for Higher Education Accreditation. ACICS can be contacted at 750 First Street NE, Suite 980, Washington, D.C. 20002; phone: 202-336-6780. The Art Institute of California–San Francisco has been granted approval to operate by the California Bureau for Private Postsecondary and Vocational Education (California Department of Consumer Affairs, 1625 North Market Boulevard, Suite S-308, Sacramento, California 95834; phone: 916-574-8200; http://www.bppve.ca.gov).

Location

The Art Institute of California–San Francisco is located on Market Street, in the center of downtown San Francisco. San Francisco is home to the Golden Gate Bridge, Alcatraz Island, and the Haight-Ashbury district. With a population of more than 700,000, San Francisco has the highest concentration of arts organizations in the world. Students have access to public libraries, including the Center of Performing Arts Library, with its specialized sections on fashion and costuming. Natural attractions include the rolling hills and mountains in nearby wine country and dramatic vistas overlooking the Pacific, which provide options for hiking, biking, and other outdoor activities. Asian, Hispanic, and Italian neighborhoods are within walking distance. Public transportation, including cable cars, is available. The Bay Area and nearby Silicon Valley are home to leading new-media companies.

Majors and Degrees

Bachelor's degrees are offered in advertising, digital filmmaking and video production, fashion design, fashion marketing and management, game art and design, graphic design, interior design, media arts and animation, simulation and virtual environments, visual and game programming, visual effects and motion graphics, and Web design and interactive media.

Associate degrees are available in fashion design, fashion marketing, graphic design, and Web design and interactive media.

Academic Programs

The academic year is divided into four quarters, beginning in January, April, July, and October. A bachelor's degree requires completion of 192 credits (thirty-six months). An associate degree requires completion of 112 academic credits (twenty-one months).

Academic Facilities

The school's 37,000 square feet houses classrooms, studios, offices, an exhibition gallery, a Learning Resource Center with library and research facilities, a student art supply store, and computer labs with Internet T1 connections. The library is constantly updated and supplemented with new acquisitions. At The Art Institute of California–San Francisco, the library offers a collection of books, magazines, newspapers, videos, CDs, and slides that supports program-specific technology. Light, spacious classrooms and equipped studios and computer labs offer a productive working atmosphere in which students can explore and render their creativity.

Costs

Tuition cost varies by program. Prospective students should contact the school for current tuition costs. Other charges include a starting kit for all first-quarter students. Kits vary in price, depending on the program of study.

Financial Aid

Financial aid is available for those who qualify. Students who require financial assistance should first complete and submit a Free Application for Federal Student Aid (FAFSA) and meet with a financial aid officer. The officer determines the level of need based on a required federal formula, the cost of education, and other factors. Gift aid is available in the form of Federal Pell Grants, Federal Supplemental Educational Opportunity Grants, and veterans' benefits. Loans include Federal Stafford Student Loans, Federal PLUS loans, and alternative loans. Other scholarships are available from the school and private sources. Application deadlines and eligibility requirements vary by program.

Faculty

The Art Institute of California–San Francisco faculty consists of full-time instructors and part-time instructors, many of whom have advanced degrees and professional experience in their respective fields.

Student Government

The Student Federation is responsible for student government and acts as a liaison between the student body and faculty and staff members.

Admission Requirements

Prospective students must submit an application for admission, record of proof of high school graduation or a General Educational Development (GED) certificate, high school transcripts, and SAT or ACT scores, if available. High school seniors who have not yet graduated should submit a partial transcript that indicates their expected graduation date. Portfolios are welcomed but are not required. Applicants are evaluated on the basis of their previous education, background, and stated or demonstrated interest in the school's programs. Students must be interviewed either in person or via telephone by an Assistant Director of Admissions. Prospective students may apply at any time prior to the start of the upcoming quarter. There is a $50 application fee.

Application and Information

To obtain an application, make arrangements for an interview, or tour the school, students should contact:

The Art Institute of California–San Francisco
1170 Market Street
San Francisco, California 94102-4928
Phone: 415-865-0198
888-493-3261 (toll-free)
Fax: 415-863-6344
Web site: http://www.artinstitutes.edu/sanfrancisco

The Art Institute of Atlanta®, GA; The Art Institute of Atlanta®–Decatur, GA; The Art Institute of Austin℠, TX; The Art Institute of California℠–Inland Empire; The Art Institute of California℠–Los Angeles; The Art Institute of California℠–Orange County; The Art Institute of California℠–Sacramento; The Art Institute of California℠–San Diego; The Art Institute of California℠–San Francisco; The Art Institute of California℠–Sunnyvale; The Art Institute of Charleston℠, SC, A branch of The Art Institute of Atlanta, GA; The Art Institute of Charlotte®, NC; The Art Institute of Colorado® (Denver); The Art Institute of Dallas®, TX; The Art Institute of Fort Lauderdale®, FL; The Art Institute of Houston®, TX; The Art Institute of Indianapolis℠, IN*; The Art Institute of Jacksonville℠, FL, A branch of Miami International University of Art & Design; The Art Institute of Las Vegas®, NV; The Art Institute of Michigan℠ (Detroit); The Art Institute of New York City®, NY; The Art Institute of Ohio℠–Cincinnati**; The Art Institute of Philadelphia®, PA; The Art Institute of Phoenix®, AZ; The Art Institute of Pittsburgh®, PA; The Art Institute of Pittsburgh®–Online Division; The Art Institute of Portland®, OR; The Art Institute of Salt Lake City℠, UT; The Art Institute of Seattle®, WA; The Art Institute of Tampa℠, FL, A branch of Miami International University of Art & Design; The Art Institute of Tennessee℠–Nashville, A branch of The Art Institute of Atlanta, GA; The Art Institute of Tucson℠, AZ; The Art Institute of Washington® (Arlington, VA), A branch of The Art Institute of Atlanta, GA; The Art Institute of York–Pennsylvania℠; The Art Institutes International Minnesota℠ (Minneapolis); California Design College℠ (Los Angeles–Wilshire Blvd.); The Illinois Institute of Art®–Chicago; The Illinois Institute of Art®–Schaumburg; Miami International University of Art & Design℠, FL; The New England Institute of Art® (Boston, MA).

*The Art Institute of Indianapolis is licensed by the Indiana Commission on Proprietary Education, 302 W. Washington St., Rm. E201, Indianapolis, IN 46204, AC-0080.

**The Art Institute of Ohio–Cincinnati, 8845 Governors Hill Drive, Suite 100, Cincinnati, OH 45249-3317, OH Reg. #04-01-1698B.

THE ART INSTITUTE OF CALIFORNIA–SUNNYVALE

SUNNYVALE, CALIFORNIA

The Institute

The Art Institute of California–Sunnyvale provides students with an educational environment and dedicated faculty members who are committed to preparing students for entry-level positions in the creative arts. Under the guidance of industry professionals, students learn by doing the types of tasks they are likely to encounter in the workplace. In addition, assistance is available to help students with resume writing, networking, and keeping aware of what employers are looking for in job candidates. The school offers six bachelor's degree programs and three associate degree programs.

The school offers assistance in helping students to secure housing.

The student population includes recent high school graduates, transfer students, and those who have left a previous employment situation to study and train for a new career. Students are creative, competitive, and open to new ideas. They place great value on an education that prepares them for an exciting entry-level position in the arts.

The Art Institute of California–Sunnyvale places a high value on the quality of student life—both in and out of the classroom. Students participate in a wide variety of activities, including clubs and organizations, community service, and various committees designed to enhance the quality of student life.

This institution has received temporary approval to operate from the Bureau for Private Postsecondary and Vocational Education (1625 North Market Boulevard, Suite S 202, Sacramento, California 95834; phone: 916-574-7702; http://www.bppve.ca.gov) in order to enable the bureau to conduct a quality inspection of the institution.

Location

Sunnyvale, a town of over 131,000 people, is one of the major cities that make up California's Silicon Valley. It's located between the San Francisco Bay and San Jose, providing easy access to cultural exhibitions, art museums, professional sports, and other entertainment options.

Majors and Degrees

Bachelor's degree programs are offered in culinary management, digital filmmaking and video production, fashion marketing and management, graphic design, interior design, and Web design and interactive media.

Associate degrees are offered in culinary arts, graphic design, and Web design and interactive media.

Academic Programs

The Art Institute of California–Sunnyvale operates on a year-round, four-quarter system.

Academic Facilities

The Art Institute of California–Sunnyvale is a 53,000 square-foot facility that contains classrooms, Mac and PC computer labs, and a library for student use. There is also a bookstore.

Costs

Tuition cost varies by program. Prospective students should contact the school for current tuition costs. Other charges include a starting kit for all first quarter students. Kits vary in price depending on the program of study.

Financial Aid

Financial aid is available for those who qualify. Students who require financial assistance should first complete and submit a Free Application for Federal Student Aid (FAFSA) and meet with a financial aid officer. The officer determines the level of need based on a required federal formula, the cost of education, and other factors. Gift aid is available in the form of Federal Pell Grants, Federal Supplemental Educational Opportunity Grants, and veterans' benefits. Loans include Federal Stafford Loans, Federal PLUS Loans, and alternative loans. Other scholarships are available from the school and private sources. Application deadlines and eligibility requirements vary by program.

Faculty

Faculty members at The Art Institute of California–Sunnyvale have professional knowledge that they bring into the classroom. The school's faculty members provide their students with a real-world, relevant educational experience.

Admission Requirements

Applicants must provide proof of high school graduation or achievement of a General Educational Development (GED) certificate as a prerequisite for admission. In lieu of documenting high school graduation or a GED certificate, applicants may provide proof of attaining an associate degree or higher from an accredited institution. An official transcript indicating date of high school graduation, GED certificate (including test scores), or date of college graduation (including degree granted) is required as proof.

All individuals seeking admission to The Art Institute of California–Sunnyvale are interviewed in person or by phone by an assistant director of admissions, and each applicant must create an original essay of at least 150 words stating how an education at The Art Institute of California–Sunnyvale would help the student to achieve career goals. There is a $50 application fee.

Application and Information

To obtain an application, make arrangements for an interview, or tour the school, students should contact:

The Art Institute of California–Sunnyvale
1120 Kifer Road
Sunnyvale, California 94086
Phone: 408-962-6400
866-583-7961 (toll-free)
Fax: 408-962-6498
Web site: http://www.artinstitutes.edu/sunnyvale

The Art Institute of Atlanta®, GA; The Art Institute of Atlanta®–Decatur, GA; The Art Institute of Austin℠, TX; The Art Institute of California℠–Inland Empire; The Art Institute of California℠–Los Angeles; The Art Institute of California℠–Orange County; The Art Institute of California℠–Sacramento; The Art Institute of California℠–San Diego; The Art Institute of California℠–San Francisco; The Art Institute of California℠–Sunnyvale; The Art Institute of Charleston℠, SC, A branch of The Art Institute of Atlanta, GA; The Art Institute of Charlotte®, NC; The Art Institute of Colorado® (Denver); The Art Institute of Dallas®, TX; The Art Institute of Fort Lauderdale®, FL; The Art Institute of Houston®, TX; The Art Institute of Indianapolis℠, IN*; The Art Institute of Jacksonville℠, FL, A branch of Miami International University of Art & Design; The Art Institute of Las Vegas®, NV; The Art Institute of Michigan℠ (Detroit); The Art Institute of New York City®, NY; The Art Institute of Ohio℠–Cincinnati**; The Art Institute of Philadelphia®, PA; The Art Institute of Phoenix®, AZ; The Art Institute of Pittsburgh®, PA; The Art Institute of Pittsburgh®–Online Division; The Art Institute of Portland®, OR; The Art Institute of Salt Lake City℠, UT; The Art Institute of Seattle®, WA; The Art Institute of Tampa℠, FL, A branch of Miami International University of Art & Design; The Art Institute of Tennessee℠–Nashville, A branch of The Art Institute of Atlanta, GA; The Art Institute of Tucson℠, AZ; The Art Institute of Washington® (Arlington, VA), A branch of The Art Institute of Atlanta, GA; The Art Institute of York–Pennsylvania℠; The Art Institutes International Minnesota℠ (Minneapolis); California Design College℠ (Los Angeles–Wilshire Blvd.); The Illinois Institute of Art®–Chicago; The Illinois Institute of Art®–Schaumburg; Miami International University of Art & Design℠, FL; The New England Institute of Art® (Boston, MA).

*The Art Institute of Indianapolis is licensed by the Indiana Commission on Proprietary Education, 302 West Washington Street, Room E201, Indianapolis, IN 46204, AC-0080.

**The Art Institute of Ohio–Cincinnati, 8845 Governors Hill Drive, Suite 100, Cincinnati, OH 45249-3317, Reg. #04-01-1698B.

AZUSA PACIFIC UNIVERSITY

AZUSA, CALIFORNIA

The University

Celebrating more than 100 years of excellence in Christian higher education, Azusa Pacific University (APU) is a comprehensive university that was founded in 1899. Azusa Pacific earned university status in 1981. Committed to the goal of each student's personal, spiritual, and academic growth, APU provides extensive opportunities for student development with academic emphases in liberal arts and professional studies.

The University is divided into one college and six schools: the College of Liberal Arts and Sciences and the Schools of Music, Nursing, Education, Behavioral and Applied Sciences, Business and Management, and Theology.

On-campus residential living is a distinctive feature of student life at APU, with several areas from which to choose. Each differs in size, location, structure, type, and activities. Each area sponsors individual and large-group events, academic and social activities, spiritual and cultural experiences, indoor and outdoor recreational opportunities, and both highly structured and spontaneous activities.

The University's 8,128 students (4,154 of whom are traditional undergraduates) come from forty-nine states and seventy-two nations and represent fifty Christian denominations. APU students are strong academically, entering with an average GPA of 3.6 and a combined SAT score of 1085. They are often leaders in their high schools, churches, and communities. Azusa Pacific offers excellent leadership development programs that teach students how to be positive contributors to their communities, jobs, and society.

Twenty-three master's degree programs and seven doctorates are offered in addition to the fifty undergraduate programs.

Location

Azusa Pacific University is located in the foothills of the San Gabriel Valley communities of Azusa and Glendora, 26 miles northeast of Los Angeles. APU is only an hour's drive from beaches, amusement parks, mountains, ski resorts, and cultural centers. The climate is moderate, mostly warm and dry throughout the school year.

Majors and Degrees

Azusa Pacific University grants the Bachelor of Arts degree in the fields of art, athletic training, biblical studies, biochemistry, biology, business administration, chemistry, Christian ministries, cinema and broadcast arts, communication studies, English, global studies, graphic design, history, liberal studies, mathematics, mathematics/physics, music, natural science, philosophy, physical education, political science, psychology, social science, social work, sociology, Spanish, theater arts, theology, and youth ministry. The Bachelor of Science degree is awarded in the fields of accounting, applied health, biochemistry, biology, chemistry, computer information systems, computer science, finance, international business, marketing, mathematics, nursing, and physics.

Preprofessional programs are available in allied health and pharmacy, dentistry, law, and medicine. Pre-engineering degree programs (3-2 and 2-2) are also offered.

The Department of Religion and Philosophy offers a ministry credential program that combines academic study with practicum and leads to the Bachelor of Arts degree.

Academic Programs

Azusa Pacific University's undergraduate program operates on the semester system and offers two summer sessions. Many graduate programs are on the quarter system.

The minimum number of credits required for a bachelor's degree is 126. About half of these units must be completed in general studies requirements, as follows: skills and University requirements, 43 units; aesthetics and the creative arts, 3 units; heritage and institutions, 6 units; identity and relationships, 3 units; language and literature, 3 units; nature, 4 units; God's Word and the Christian response, 18 units; and integrative electives, 6 units. Areas of concentration vary in their requirements and many offer several emphases within the major.

The University grants credit for certain scores on Advanced Placement tests and College-Level Examination Program tests, college courses taken while in high school, and the International Baccalaureate.

Academic Facilities

Azusa Pacific's libraries include the William V. Marshburn Memorial Library, the Hugh and Hazel Darling Library, the James L. Stamps Theological Library, and six regional-center libraries. The libraries offer enhanced traditional services as well as state-of-the-art features that facilitate research. Apolis2, the libraries' automated catalog system, is searchable on the World Wide Web, providing increased ease and convenience to aid users in the search process. A unified catalog identifies more than 215,000 books, media, and 1,800 serial titles. More than 630,000 microforms include the Library of American Civilization, Library of American Literature, *New York Times*, and Educational Resources Information Center collections. The University provides access to more than 100 electronic databases, including more than 12,000 full-text serial titles, in addition to an interlibrary loan system that offers access to more than 11 million books and resources to all students.

The holdings of the William V. Marshburn Memorial Library include collections supporting liberal arts and sciences, music, and business. Computer workstations and online services offer electronic access to materials from around the world. Special collections include many rare and valuable items. The Media Center has an extensive collection of scores, videocassettes, and compact discs as well as graphic art materials and equipment. Professional librarians are available for assistance.

The holdings of the Hugh and Hazel Darling Library include collections supporting computer science, education, nursing, and professional psychology and offer students a vast collection of printed books, reference materials, serials, and microfilm. Ninety-seven workstations offer access to more than 100 licensed databases and Web resources globally. There are also five classrooms that are equipped with video projectors, computers, and ISDN lines for distance learning; an auditorium with tiered seating; and a soundstage and TV control room. The design of the building is meant to meet the needs of the twenty-first-century learner.

The newest addition to the APU libraries is the James L. Stamps Theological Library, part of the $12.5-million Duke Academic Complex, which was completed in summer 2003. The library houses a three-story, 50,000-volume book stack dedicated to the APU theology collection; thirty-one workstations; and a number of periodicals. Denominational collections reflecting the rich traditions of the University's Christian heritage are available for research purposes. The rest of the 60,000-square-foot complex houses eighteen technologically advanced classrooms, a lecture hall, forty faculty and staff offices, and two conference rooms. The School of Theology and Department of Art currently reside in the complex.

APU offers a number of technology options on campus, with computer labs in every library and dorm and in the student union. These labs offer PC and Macintosh computers and laser printers.

All Access, the campuswide wireless network, provides Internet access anywhere on campus to all students and faculty and staff members with laptops and wireless connectivity. A wide variety of software is available to fulfill students' needs.

Outstanding features of the Carl E. Wynn Science Center include an electron microscope facility with both scanning and transmission instrumentation for use in cellular and molecular biology, physiology, and ecology courses and practical facilities, such as a greenhouse and a cadaver lab. The Departments of Biology, Chemistry, Mathematics, and Physics offer vigorous programs with the support of the science center.

APU enjoys the state-of-the-art School of Music and chapel complexes. The two-story School of Music contains three large rehearsal rooms, a recording studio, twenty-two instrumental and voice practice rooms, classrooms, and faculty offices. The Munson Chapel seats 300 and is used for intimate group gatherings, vocal and orchestra performances, and special chapel programs.

APU's attractive, landscaped, 103-acre campus houses many contemporary facilities, including Trinity Hall, a 350-bed, 103,000-square-foot residence hall that opened in 2003; the $5-million Wilden Hall of Business and Management; and a modern, lighted athletic complex. All facilities are barrier-free.

The 3,500-seat, $13.5-million Richard and Vivian Felix Event Center, which was designed to meet the University's and community's needs, opened in 2000.

Costs

Expenses per year for 2007–08 are estimated as follows: tuition, $24,430; room, $3880; board, from $2350 (ten meals per week) to $3638 (300-block meal plan); and books and supplies, starting at $1224.

Financial Aid

Azusa Pacific University offers financial aid in the form of employment, loans, grants, and scholarships. Approximately 83 percent of the undergraduate student body receives some form of aid. Each year, approximately $14 million in institutional aid is awarded. Students must reapply for aid yearly. Financial aid for international students may be more limited due to government restrictions and differences in educational systems.

Faculty

The student-faculty ratio is 14:1. There are 352 full-time faculty members, 39 part-time faculty members, and 740 adjunct professors. Seventy-six percent of the faculty members possess terminal degrees. The faculty is primarily a teaching staff. No graduate students serve as undergraduate instructors. Faculty members are highly supportive of and involved in many student activities; they also provide academic advising.

Student Government

The Associated Student Body (ASB) is responsible for representing the students' needs and desires to the administration. Through an annual survey, the ASB can pinpoint major issues that need to be targeted on the APU campus. Elections are held annually in the spring. The student government is made up of a senate and an executive council. ASB also assists student groups requesting funds and participates in student activities on campus.

Students are asked to use personal discretion in activities that may be spiritually or morally destructive. In particular, students are expected to refrain from smoking, drinking, and using or possessing illegal drugs while in residence at the University.

Admission Requirements

Azusa Pacific seeks students who are committed to their own personal, intellectual, and spiritual growth. Consequently, these areas are considered in the admission evaluation. Applicants are required to have earned a minimum GPA of 2.8 in high school or a minimum GPA of 2.2 in previous college work. Minimum SAT and ACT scores are 910 and 19, respectively. Both transfer students and international students who graduated from non-English-speaking schools also need a GPA of at least 2.8. Transfer, international, and older students are encouraged to apply.

Application and Information

Applicants must submit official transcripts of high school and/or previous college work, two references, a signed statement of agreement, and scores on either the ACT or SAT. A nonrefundable $45 application fee must be submitted with the application. International students do not need ACT or SAT scores, but a TOEFL score is required. A $65 application fee applies, and specific application deadlines are enforced. APU follows early action and rolling admission policies, depending on semester and class standing. Students should contact the Office of Undergraduate Admissions for enrollment application deadlines.

For further information, prospective students should contact:

Office of Undergraduate Admissions
Azusa Pacific University
901 East Alosta Avenue
P.O. Box 7000
Azusa, California 91702-7000
Phone: 626-812-3016
800-TALK-APU (information requests, toll-free)
Fax: 626-812-3096
Web site: http://www.apu.edu/start/prospective/undergraduate

For further information, international students should contact:

Office of International Student Services
Azusa Pacific University
901 East Alosta Avenue
P.O. Box 7000
Azusa, California 91702-7000
Phone: 626-812-3055
Fax: 626-815-3801
Web site: http://www.apu.edu/international

The $8-million Hugh and Hazel Darling Library and $12.5-million Duke Academic Complex offer a spectacular array of resources in an environment that is conducive to learning.

BIOLA UNIVERSITY

LA MIRADA, CALIFORNIA

The University

Biola is a private Christian university established in 1908 in Los Angeles with a mission of biblically centered education, scholarship, and service to equip men and women in mind and character to impact the world for the Lord Jesus Christ. More than 5,600 students, who are among the most ethnically diverse body of any Christian college in the U.S., are challenged yearly by faculty and staff members to integrate their faith and learning pursuant to their academic and vocational goals. Biola is a member of the Council for Christian Colleges and Universities (CCCU), an organization consisting of 105 Christian institutions across the U.S.

Location

Biola University's 95-acre campus is located in La Mirada, 22 miles southeast of Los Angeles on the border of Orange County. Centrally located in southern California, Biola is just a short drive to both the beaches and the mountains. Hollywood, the entertainment capital of the world, is just 30 minutes away, and unlimited cultural experiences are available in Orange County and Los Angeles. Los Angeles is the home of the Natural History Museum, Hollywood Bowl, Staples Center, the Great Western Forum, and Dodger Stadium. Disneyland, Anaheim Stadium, and the Arrowhead Pond are a short drive south of Biola. Five major airports, including LAX and John Wayne, are within an hour's drive of the campus. For internships and career opportunities, there are numerous choices.

Majors and Degrees

The Bachelor of Arts and Bachelor of Science degrees are offered with majors in anthropology, art, Bible, biochemistry, biological sciences, business administration, Christian education, cinema and media arts, communication studies, communication disorders, computer science, education/liberal studies, English, history, human biology, humanities, intercultural studies, journalism, kinesiology/health/physical education, mathematics, music, music in worship, nursing, philosophy, physical science, political science, prelaw, psychology, social science, sociology, Spanish, and urban studies. A 3-2 engineering program is offered cooperatively with the University of Southern California.

In all, Biola offers 145 programs ranging from the B.A. to the Ph.D. at seven schools that include the School of Arts and Sciences, Talbot School of Theology, Rosemead School of Psychology, the School of Business, the School of Continuing Studies, the School of Education, and the School of Intercultural Studies. All are regionally and professionally accredited and based on evangelical Christianity.

Academic Programs

The academic year consists of two 15-week semesters. There are also two summer sessions for three and five weeks each plus a three-week interterm each January. As a fully accredited national university, Biola University seeks to instruct Christian men and women in order to produce graduates who are competent in their field of study, knowledgeable in biblical studies, and equipped to serve the Christian community and society at large.

Religious and convocation requirements include 30 hours of biblical studies, attendance at chapel three times a week, and participation in student ministry.

Off-Campus Programs

Biola offers study-abroad programs in China; London, England; Israel; Japan; and Korea. The University also participates in the CCCU programs in Australia; Central America (Costa Rica, Honduras); Egypt; England; the Middle East; Russia; Washington, D.C.; the Au Sable Institute; the Contemporary Music Center at Martha's Vineyard; the Los Angeles Film Institute; and the Colorado Springs Focus on the Family Institute. Each program has unique requirements for admission.

Biola's Organizational Leadership Degree (BOLD) program, in which students can complete their college degree in eighteen months, has extension campuses in La Mirada, Laguna Hills (Orange County), Vista (San Diego County), Palm Desert, Thousand Oaks, Inglewood, and Chino, California. Admission requirements are unique to the program and include completion of a minimum of 40 transferable semester units from an accredited college.

Biola offers courses to teachers in Hong Kong as part of the Biola-RICE (Research Institute for Christian Education) agreement.

Academic Facilities

The Biola University Library currently subscribes to more than 1,100 print periodical titles and has access to more than 13,000 titles online. The library provides access to its holdings through SCROLL, the Web online public access catalog and circulation system, and an increasing number of CD-ROM and online subscription index databases available for patron searching. This 98,000-square-foot, state-of-the-art resource center features 950 study stations, twenty-four group study rooms, twenty multimedia stations, thirty-two online reference stations, a twenty-four workstation instructional lab that seats up to 48 students at a time, and wired and wireless Internet access throughout the building.

Additional facilities include a media center, an on-campus radio station, a TV/film studio, an art studio, an art gallery, and an outdoor pool. Access to the Internet may be found by way of computers in the residence halls as well as throughout the campus. E-mail, Internet research, World Wide Web browsing, word processing, desktop publishing, multimedia presentation, graphic arts design, and application programming may all be accomplished at the computer center and in Biola's computerized classrooms and labs. Resources include two computerized classrooms equipped with Windows NT and Macintosh computers, plus a fully equipped computer lab with more than fifty computers (Mac and PC). Scanners and high-speed black-and-white and color laser printers are also available in the lab. Students can connect to the Internet via Ethernet or AppleTalk in all residence halls or by using the computer lab equipment. Connection to the Internet is via a high-speed T1 line.

Costs

Biola University holds the belief that every student regardless of financial status should have the opportunity to make an investment in his or her tomorrow. Therefore, the University strives to keep the cost of a Biola education within the financial reach of students and their families. For 2007–08, Biola tuition was $24,998, average room was $4092, and board for a twenty-meal plan was $3540.

Financial Aid

Biola offers a generous financial aid program, with $12 million in institutional funds devoted to undergraduates alone. In addition, hundreds of University students receive state and federal grants and scholarships. Seventy-seven percent of Biola students receive some level of financial aid, with the average grant/scholarship award being $9514.

Institutional scholarships include the Academic Scholarship (up to $7500), the Community Service Scholarships ($2700), and Scholarships for Underrepresented Students of Ethnicity (SURGE; up to $6500), all of which are renewable. Other aid options include departmental scholarships (for athletics, music, and communications), international scholarships, dependent scholarships (for families where the primary income is in Christian ministry), and church-matching scholarships. Excellent loan programs and on-campus work opportunities round out the aid packages of most Biola students.

All students are urged to apply for financial aid by March 1, which coincides with the California aid deadline. Applicants should complete the Free Application for Federal Student Aid (FAFSA) and Biola's one-page form, the University Aid Application. In addition, California residents should complete the state GPA verification form.

Faculty

The University's faculty members are mentors and role models in addition to professors. Seventy-two percent of all faculty members have earned doctorates. There are 191 full-time and 204 part-time faculty members. Some have won awards as Fulbright and National Endowment for the Humanities scholars. The student-faculty ratio is 17:1.

Faculty members remain on the cutting edge of their fields by continuing their education as they teach students. Research grants provide professors the time and resources not only to publish in their discipline but also to participate in seminars with topics such as Christianity and science and postmodernism. At these seminars, they consider how to integrate their faith within their fields and broaden their knowledge of other areas. This experience is brought back to their classrooms for their students' benefit.

Student Government

The mission of Biola University's Associated Student Government is to represent the student body on an administrative level, giving ear to the students' voices, providing services, and facilitating events necessary to foster a Christ-centered community.

There are two facets to the Associated Student Government. The Executive Council, comprised of 14 senators, represents residential students and commuters. The Services Council, comprised of nine service boards, provides various services and programming for students. These service boards include Chapel Board, Spirit Board, Multicultural Relations, Intramurals Board, Social Board, International Student Association, the *Chimes* (Biola's student newspaper), the *Biolan* (the yearbook), and the Marketing Board.

With a staff of approximately 60 students and a budget of more than $450,000 annually, the Associated Student Government not only provides high-quality programming but also a multitude of student leadership opportunities each year.

Admission Requirements

Biola seeks students who want to make a difference with their lives and impact the world for Jesus Christ. Candidate selection is based on SAT or ACT scores and high school transcripts. In addition, each applicant must be an evangelical believer in the Christian faith and must submit a reference letter from a pastor. Freshmen who entered Biola in fall 2005 had an average combined SAT score of 1114 and an average GPA of 3.52.

Application and Information

The Office of Admissions is open from 8 to 5 on weekdays. Students are encouraged to apply online at http://www.biola.edu/applynow. To visit the campus or to request information, students can call or write:

Office of Admissions
Biola University
13800 Biola Avenue
La Mirada, California 90639-0001
Phone: 800-OK-BIOLA (toll-free)
E-mail: admissions@biola.edu
Web site: http://www.biola.edu/?asrc=0106

Students on the campus of Biola University.

CALIFORNIA COLLEGE OF THE ARTS

OAKLAND AND SAN FRANCISCO, CALIFORNIA

The College

Founded in 1907, California College of the Arts (CCA) is the largest regionally accredited, independent school of art and design in the western United States. CCA offers twenty undergraduate majors in the areas of art, architecture, design, and writing. The College provides world-class facilities on two dynamic campuses in Oakland and San Francisco. CCA students regularly win major recognition in their fields; in 2005, 12 graphic design students had work in the *Graphis New Talent Design Annual*, and in 2006, products by industrial design students were shown at the Milan Furniture Fair. At CCA, students make art that makes a difference.

CCA is accredited by the Western Association of Schools and Colleges, the National Association of Schools of Art and Design, the National Architectural Accrediting Board, and the Foundation for Interior Design Education Research.

Students and faculty members create a supportive community of friends, colleagues, and mentors in an intimate, private-college environment. CCA has approximately 1,300 undergraduate and 300 graduate students. In the undergraduate population, 59 percent are women, 41 percent are men; 24 percent are from underrepresented populations, and 7 percent are international students. First-time freshmen comprise 50 percent of the entering class; 50 percent are transfer and second-degree students. About 35 percent come from out of state. CCA offers a well-rounded first-year program, with a residence hall housing 75 percent of the first-time freshmen.

CCA offers seven graduate programs: the M.F.A. in design, film (new in 2007), fine arts, and writing; the M.A. in curatorial practice and visual criticism; and the M.Arch. Graduate design disciplines include design for business, graphic design, industrial design, and interaction design. Graduate fine arts media areas include ceramics, drawing/painting, glass, jewelry/metal arts, media arts, photography, printmaking, sculpture, social practices, textiles, wood/furniture, and multidisciplinary work. For more information, students should visit CCA's Web site or e-mail graduateprograms@cca.edu

Campus life includes exhibitions at the CCA Wattis Institute for Contemporary Arts, lectures by visiting artists and scholars, film screenings, literary readings, and more. Through the CCA Center for Art and Public Life, students may teach or create art in the community. CCA's undergraduate exhibition program presents shows throughout the year. The Student Affairs Office sponsors a variety of campus events. Student organizations include preprofessional groups affiliated with local chapters of AIA, AIGA, and other associations.

The Oakland campus offers a traditional college atmosphere and campus housing in a residence hall and CCA-owned apartments. Housing is also available at a residence hall in downtown Oakland. Students are not required to live on campus. CCA offers no meal plan; all residences have kitchens, and each campus has a café. CCA maintains a local housing list to assist students in finding off-campus housing.

Location

The San Francisco Bay Area is known for its thriving art and design community, technological innovation, and environmental leadership. CCA's historical Oakland campus is set on 4 acres in the Rockridge neighborhood, 3 miles from UC Berkeley, and is the home of the fine arts, Bachelor of Arts (B.A.), and first-year programs. In San Francisco, CCA has an urban campus, between the design district and the new UCSF Mission Bay campus, that houses the architecture, design, and graduate programs.

With hundreds of visual arts venues—from major museums to alternative spaces—the Bay Area is a great place to study art. The natural environment is also an inspiration. Beaches and hiking/biking trails are just minutes from urban areas. The Monterey Peninsula, the Sierras (skiing), and Yosemite are within a half-day's drive. Buses and Bay Area Rapid Transit (BART) provide easily accessible public transportation. CCA operates a shuttle between its campuses and residence halls.

Majors and Degrees

CCA offers four-year Bachelor of Fine Arts (B.F.A.) programs in animation (new in 2007), ceramics, community arts, fashion design, glass, graphic design, illustration, industrial design, interior design, jewelry/metal arts, media arts, painting/drawing, photography, printmaking, sculpture, textiles, and wood/furniture and Bachelor of Arts (B.A.) programs in visual studies and writing and literature. The Bachelor of Architecture (B.Arch.) is a five-year program. Students may design an individualized major.

Academic Programs

The B.F.A. requires completion of a minimum of 126 semester units (75 in studio work and 51 in humanities and sciences). The B.A. requires completion of 126 semester units (51 in humanities and sciences, 36 in the major, and 39 in studio work). The B.Arch. requires completion of a minimum of 162 semester units, including the core program and a nine-semester major program.

The core program defines students' first-year experience, emphasizing skill building, experimentation, and critical thinking within a year of cross-disciplinary study, with exposure to a variety of media. The core curriculum includes studio courses and seminars in writing and visual studies.

CCA's humanities and sciences curriculum is based on the belief that visual arts are guided as much by the mind as by the hand. Students acquire oral and written communication skills, tools of critical thinking, and cultural literacy. A precredential teaching concentration, open to students in all majors, satisfies prerequisites for application to postgraduate art teacher credential programs.

CCA operates on the semester system; the fall and spring terms constitute a full academic year. There is a six-week summer session. During the summer, CCA also offers a Pre-College Program and programs for younger students. Extended education courses are offered in fall, spring, and summer.

Off-Campus Programs

CCA students may earn credit for study off campus, through cross-registration at Mills College or Holy Names College in Oakland, or at another art school through the Association of Independent Colleges of Art and Design mobility program.

Through an international exchange program, students may study abroad at schools of art and design in Canada, Denmark, France, Germany, Ireland, Japan, Mexico, the Netherlands, Sweden, and the United Kingdom. Financial aid is available. CCA also offers its own summer study-abroad courses in Europe and Central and South America.

Academic Facilities

Studios and technological resources are usually accessible 16 to 24 hours daily. Campus media centers have equipment available for checkout.

The Oakland campus is the home of fine arts and first-year studios, classrooms, galleries, an auditorium, a library, and administrative offices. Fine arts facilities include studios for ceramics (pot shops, glaze rooms, and fourteen gas and twelve electric kilns, including kilns for large-scale work); drawing/painting; glass (two-bench hot shop with glass furnace and facilities for casting, fusing, and coldworking); jewelry/metal arts (metalsmithing, electroforming, photo fabrication, and enameling); media arts (digital video, Super-8, and 16-mm film production; digital production tools; a sound booth; digital video and sound editing stations; and a hybrid lab for interactive media); photography (two large black-and-white darkrooms, twelve individual darkrooms for color printing, digital workstations, a mural darkroom, an alternative-processes lab, and a lighting studio); printmaking (lithography, etching, and Vandercook presses), silkscreen, and papermaking; sculpture (one of the largest working college foundries; wax, plaster, and clay studios; and an interdisciplinary studio for large-scale work); and textiles (a weaving studio with a variety of looms, a computer lab, print and dye rooms, and a fiber sculpture area).

In San Francisco, CCA's large, light-filled main building contains classrooms, studios, galleries, a lecture hall, and a library. The building houses design, fashion, and wood/furniture studios and individual studio spaces. The campus also includes the newly expanded Graduate Center and a Student Center with administrative offices.

CCA offers a wide range of digital technologies on campus. In addition to departmental labs, there are eight computer labs, which are equipped with the latest hardware and software for fine arts, design, and multimedia production. Labs have Macintosh OSX computers (except the industrial design lab, which has Windows) and a range of software for print and Web graphics, audio/video editing, and 3-D modeling and animation. Hardware includes slide and flatbed scanners, audio/video decks, graphic tablets, CD/DVD burners, color and large-format printers, and more. Library computer labs offer Internet access. A wireless network is accessible in many campus locations.

CCA's libraries hold more than 60,000 books, periodicals, and audiovisual titles and extensive visual resources. On the San Francisco campus, the New Materials Resource Center is a library of samples useful in a range of fields.

San Francisco campus galleries include the CCA Wattis Institute, presenting international exhibitions of contemporary art, and a graduate student gallery. On the Oakland campus, faculty, alumni, and student shows appear at the Oliver Art Center. Other galleries on each campus are reserved for undergraduate shows.

Costs

Tuition and fees for 2007–08 were $29,280 per year for full-time (12–18 units) undergraduate students. For part-time undergraduate students, tuition was $1220 per unit. California and out-of-state residents pay the same tuition. Residence hall fees (for room only) in 2007–08 ranged from $4770 to $6400 by contract for fall through spring. Estimated expenses for one academic year (two semesters) for a student living on campus were approximately $43,000 ($29,280 for tuition, $8935 for room and board, $1400 for books and supplies, and $3300 for miscellaneous expenses).

Financial Aid

Scholarships, grants, loans, and work-study awards are available on the basis of merit and financial need. Students applying for aid should submit the Free Application for Federal Student Aid (FAFSA) to the Federal Student Aid Processing Agency by March 1 for priority consideration. CCA continues to fund students after the priority deadline as long as funds remain available. Applications for Federal Pell Grants and Federal Direct Student Loans may be submitted throughout the school year. CCA is approved for veterans attending under the Veterans Administration Educational Benefits Program. Approximately 75 percent of students attending CCA during 2006–07 received some type of financial aid. CCA offers an extended interest-free payment plan. The Federal Work-Study Program gives eligible students the opportunity for part-time employment to help defray educational costs.

Faculty

In 2007–08, the CCA faculty included 401 artists, architects, designers, writers, and scholars (65 full-time and 336 part-time) who combine teaching with professional work in their fields. Some teach in both the undergraduate and graduate programs. The average class size is 14. Faculty members serve as advisers to first-year students.

Student Government

The Student Council includes students from all areas of CCA and sponsors extracurricular activities, including films, receptions, and shuttles to galleries. Elected officers attend board of trustees meetings. The student handbook is available at CCA's Web site.

Admission Requirements

Students admitted to the undergraduate programs must have a high school diploma or equivalent. CCA takes an individualized approach to the admission process. Applications are reviewed on the basis of a balanced picture that includes academic achievement, creative ability, artistic and professional goals, individual achievements, and supporting documents, such as recommendations and the portfolio of the applicant's work.

Application and Information

CCA has two priority deadlines for fall admission: February 1 for merit scholarship consideration, and March 1 for all other applicants. For spring applicants, the priority deadline is October 1. Students who meet these deadlines are given priority consideration regarding admission, housing, and financial aid. CCA reviews undergraduate applications on a rolling admission basis; applications are reviewed in the order in which they are received, and students are accepted and awarded financial aid after the priority dates. The application fee is $50. Those who want to take one or more individual courses may register as nondegree students on a space-available basis and receive CCA credit for courses completed. CCA encourages students to apply online.

For application forms, a catalog, or general information about CCA, students should visit the College's Web site at http://www.cca.edu/admissions or contact:

Office of Enrollment Services
California College of the Arts
1111 Eighth Street
San Francisco, California 94107-2247
Phone: 800-447-1ART (toll-free)
Fax: 415-703-9539
Web site: http://www.cca.edu

CALIFORNIA DESIGN COLLEGE

LOS ANGELES, CALIFORNIA

The College

California Design College offers hands-on, project-oriented curricula through which students prepare for entry-level employment in the creative arts. The school hosts numerous portfolio shows showcasing student work. California Design College offers seven bachelor's degree programs and four associate degree programs.

The programs are designed with the support and contributions of the professional community in order to reflect industry developments and trends. The experiences of faculty members, many of whom continue to work in their respective career fields, create a dynamic and evolving environment. In addition, the Program Advisory Committee, which is made up of some of the finest design, manufacturing, and technology professionals in the design industry, provides an accurate picture of what is happening in the industry today and what to expect in the future. These elements combine to create an experience with a singular goal that provides meaningful, focused education for the students.

Students come to California Design College from throughout the United States and abroad. The student population includes recent high school graduates, transfer students, and those who have left a previous employment situation to study and train for a new career. Students are creative, competitive, and open to new ideas. They place great value on an education that prepares them for an exciting entry-level position in the arts.

The school's Student Affairs Department sets up a variety of activities to help students experience the world of design. Activities include company tours, alumni visits, internships, field trips, monthly academic seminars, experience with career-planning resources, and a peer-tutor program.

There is no on-campus housing, but the school assists students in locating other housing. In addition, assistance is available to help students with resume writing, networking, and keeping abreast of what employers are looking for in job candidates.

California Design College is accredited by the Accrediting Council for Independent Colleges and Schools (ACICS) and has a Certificate of Institutional Approval from the Bureau for Private Postsecondary and Vocational Education (BPPVE). The school is approved by the Veterans Administration, Bureau for Private Postsecondary and Vocational Education, to train veterans.

Location

Los Angeles offers a rich diversity of food, fashion, architecture, and cultures. It is home to the Los Angeles Museum of Art, Museum of Contemporary Art, J. Paul Getty Museum, and Norton Simon Museum.

California Design College is located on Wilshire Boulevard in a centrally located environment bursting with ideas and energy just a few minutes from many attractions, including Rodeo Drive, Beverly Hills, the Fashion District, and Hollywood. Students may visit the beach, attend the Hollywood Bowl or Greek Theatre, or experience the fame and celebrity of the Hollywood Wax Museum, Hollywood Boulevard's "Walk of Fame," or Mann's Chinese Theater.

Majors and Degrees

California Design College offers bachelor's degree programs (thirty-six months) in fashion design, fashion marketing and management, graphic design, interior design, set and exhibit design, visual effects and motion graphics, and Web design and interactive media. Associate degree programs (eighteen to twenty-seven months) are available in fashion design, fashion marketing, graphic design, and Web design and interactive media.

Academic Programs

The academic year is divided into four quarters. Each program is offered on a year-round basis, allowing students to work uninterrupted toward their degrees. Programs may begin in any quarter.

Online courses are available and can be completed on a flexible schedule.

California Design College arranges study trips to local cultural and commercial sites. Optional out-of-town seminars and visits may be planned in individual programs. The costs related to optional study trips are not included in regular tuition.

Academic Facilities

California Design College's computer design labs are equipped with various software programs and hardware. The Macintosh and PC computer labs house computer workstations, drives for student storage, large-screen monitors, and design software. The facility also includes art classrooms, production classrooms, lecture rooms, student and faculty lounges, and a variety of administrative offices. The Learning Resource Center provides publications, videos, and periodicals. Students also have access to nearby public libraries and the library at The Art Institute of California–Los Angeles.

Costs

Tuition cost varies by program. Prospective students should contact the school for current tuition costs. Other charges include a starting kit for all first-quarter students. Kits vary in price depending on the program of study.

Financial Aid

Financial aid is available for those who qualify. Students who require financial assistance should first complete and submit a Free Application for Federal Student Aid (FAFSA) and meet with a financial aid officer. The officer determines the level of need based on a required federal formula, the cost of education, and other factors. Gift aid is available in the form of Federal Pell Grants, Federal Supplemental Educational Opportunity Grants, and veterans' benefits. Loans include Federal Stafford Student Loans, Federal PLUS loans, and alternative loans. Other scholarships are available from the school and private sources. Application deadlines and eligibility requirements vary by program.

Faculty

The California Design College faculty is composed of individuals from the design world who periodically participate in professional-development seminars to share and enhance their knowledge.

Admission Requirements

Applicants must demonstrate proof of high school graduation or its equivalent through a high school diploma or General Educational Development (GED) transcript. Applicants are interviewed in person or by telephone and are required to write an essay on two of three questions provided in the application for admission. The applicant's academic transcript and essay are evaluated by the Admissions Acceptance Committee, which may request additional records of accomplishments in core academic courses and/or SAT or ACT results. There is a $50 application fee.

Application and Information

To obtain an application, make arrangements for an interview, or tour the school, students should contact:

California Design College
3440 Wilshire Boulevard, 10th Floor
Los Angeles, California 90010-2112
Phone: 213-251-3636
877-468-6232 (toll-free)
Fax: 213-385-3545
Web site: http://www.artinstitutes.edu/cdc

The Art Institute of Atlanta®, GA; The Art Institute of Atlanta®–Decatur, GA; The Art Institute of Austin℠, TX; The Art Institute of California℠–Inland Empire; The Art Institute of California℠–Los Angeles; The Art Institute of California℠–Orange County; The Art Institute of California℠–Sacramento; The Art Institute of California℠–San Diego; The Art Institute of California℠–San Francisco; The Art Institute of California℠–Sunnyvale; The Art Institute of Charleston℠, SC, A branch of The Art Institute of Atlanta, GA; The Art Institute of Charlotte®, NC; The Art Institute of Colorado® (Denver); The Art Institute of Dallas®, TX; The Art Institute of Fort Lauderdale®, FL; The Art Institute of Houston®, TX; The Art Institute of Indianapolis℠, IN*; The Art Institute of Jacksonville℠, FL, A branch of Miami International University of Art & Design; The Art Institute of Las Vegas®, NV; The Art Institute of Michigan℠ (Detroit); The Art Institute of New York City®, NY; The Art Institute of Ohio℠–Cincinnati**; The Art Institute of Philadelphia®, PA; The Art Institute of Phoenix®, AZ; The Art Institute of Pittsburgh®, PA; The Art Institute of Pittsburgh®–Online Division; The Art Institute of Portland®, OR; The Art Institute of Salt Lake City℠, UT; The Art Institute of Seattle®, WA; The Art Institute of Tampa℠, FL, A branch of Miami International University of Art & Design; The Art Institute of Tennessee℠–Nashville, A branch of The Art Institute of Atlanta, GA; The Art Institute of Tucson℠, AZ; The Art Institute of Washington® (Arlington, VA), A branch of The Art Institute of Atlanta, GA; The Art Institute of York–Pennsylvania℠; The Art Institutes International Minnesota℠ (Minneapolis); California Design College℠ (Los Angeles–Wilshire Blvd.); The Illinois Institute of Art®–Chicago; The Illinois Institute of Art®–Schaumburg; Miami International University of Art & Design℠, FL; The New England Institute of Art® (Boston, MA).

*The Art Institute of Indianapolis is licensed by the Indiana Commission on Proprietary Education, 302 W. Washington St., Rm. E201, Indianapolis, IN 46204, AC-0080.

**The Art Institute of Ohio–Cincinnati, 8845 Governors Hill Drive, Suite 100, Cincinnati, OH 45249-3317, OH Reg. #04-01-1698B.

CALIFORNIA INSTITUTE OF THE ARTS

VALENCIA, CALIFORNIA

The Institute

CalArts educates professional artists in a unique learning environment founded on the principles of art-making excellence, experimentation, critical reflection, and independent inquiry. Throughout its history, CalArts has sought to advance the practice of art and promote its understanding in a broad social, cultural, and historical context. CalArts offers students the knowledge and expertise of leading professional artists and scholars and a full complement of art-making tools. In return, it asks for the highest artistic and academic achievement. Reflecting its longstanding commitment to new forms and expressions in art, CalArts invites creative risk-taking and urges active collaboration and exchange among artists, artistic disciplines, and cultural traditions.

CalArts is the first higher educational institution in the United States to offer undergraduate and graduate degrees in both visual and performing arts. It was established in 1961 by Walt and Roy Disney through the merger of two professional schools, the Los Angeles Conservatory of Music and the Chouinard Art Institute.

Since its founding, CalArts has been recognized internationally as a leader in every discipline in which it provides instruction. Its artists and alumni have defined, and continue to extend, the very forefront of creative practice as we know it today.

At the graduate level, the Institute grants the Master of Fine Arts degree in art, dance, film/video, theater, and writing and the Master of Arts degree in aesthetics and politics. Graduate programs take one, two, or three years to complete, depending on the individual program. Certificates and advanced certificates are also offered.

The total enrollment of the Institute is approximately 1,320 men and women, of whom 820 are undergraduates. The student body is gender balanced and geographically diverse, with students hailing from fifty states and thirty-one different countries.

Location

Thirty miles north of downtown Los Angeles, CalArts occupies 60 acres on hills overlooking the incorporated city of Santa Clarita. Rapid development in this peaceful suburban area has resulted in new residential communities and an ever-increasing population of more than 150,000. Los Angeles, the second-largest city in the United States and an important international hub for the arts, offers a vast array of professional and cultural resources.

Majors and Degrees

California Institute of the Arts grants the Bachelor of Fine Arts degree in art, dance, film/video, music, and theater.

Academic Programs

Students must apply to and enroll in a specific program within a particular school. A modified, nontraditional grading system is utilized, with each school's curriculum being determined by the special demands of the discipline. Instruction proceeds according to the student's preparation and need, with the student receiving guidance from a faculty mentor.

Undergraduate programs take four years or eight semesters and a minimum of 120 semester units to complete. All undergraduate students must fulfill the Critical Studies Requirements (40 percent of the total curriculum), which cover the humanities, social sciences, cultural studies, and natural sciences. These courses are intended to inform and influence each student's artistic practice.

Academic Facilities

The Institute has extensive facilities for the visual and performing arts, which consist of studios, workshops, theaters, galleries, editing rooms, sound stages, electronic music and recording studios, computer art and animation labs, and performance spaces. Certain facilities, such as the Walt Disney Modular Theater, are among the most remarkable in the world.

CalArts students also take advantage of a variety of special initiatives designed to respond to the realities of the social and cultural world today. These range from the Community Arts Partnership (CAP), which offers students a chance to teach in community and public school settings to the Cotsen Center for Puppetry and the Arts, which allows students to explore the potential of puppetry in their art-making and from the groundbreaking Center for New Performance, the professional wing of CalArts' Schools of Performance where students and faculty members collaborate on professionally presented performances, to the Institute's contemporary art journal *Afterall*, copublished with London's Central Saint Martins College of Art and Design, and the literary magazine *Black Clock*, published in association with CalArts' M.F.A. Writing Program.

The most momentous of these initiatives is the Roy and Edna Disney/CalArts Theater, or REDCAT, part of the Walt Disney Concert Hall complex in downtown Los Angeles. Designed by Frank Gehry, REDCAT includes a state-of-the-art, flexible performance space, a 3,000-square-foot gallery, and a café. REDCAT plays host to the most interesting new experimental theater, dance, music, art, film and video, and literature from Southern California, the nation, and the world. In the process, CalArts brings new resources to its students' education through performances, master classes, and residencies by visiting artists and helps its students make a seamless transition into the local, national, and international arts communities.

The library contains a collection designed especially for the visual and performing arts. In addition to holding more than 95,000 volumes, the library includes musical scores, sound recordings, films, videotapes, and slides that enable students to progress on their own in obtaining knowledge relevant to their specific studies.

Costs

Tuition for 2008–09 is $32,860 for the academic year. Room charges range from $3575 to $7400 per year, and board costs between $3402 and $3924. The cost of books and supplies varies according to major.

Financial Aid

The Financial Aid Office at CalArts is dedicated to helping students meet the cost of attendance at the Institute. Funds made available through the Financial Aid Office are awarded on a combination of need and artistic merit. Need is determined by completing and submitting the FAFSA (Free Application for Federal Student Aid). CalArts offers a limited number of merit-only awards; however, to be considered for these awards, students must have completed the FAFSA.

CalArts offers the following financial aid programs: Institute scholarships and grants, Federal Pell Grants, Federal Supplemental Educational Opportunity Grants, Federal Work-Study Program awards, Federal Perkins Loans, Federal Stafford Loans, and Cal Grants. Details of these financial aid programs are available from the Financial Aid Office.

Faculty

The faculty numbers approximately 300, including both full- and part-time members. The student-faculty ratio is approximately 7:1. Faculty members maintain active, often prolific, careers in their respective disciplines. Their approach to teaching combines rigorous instruction with careful guidance and individualized attention, a process that empowers students to define their own artistic objectives. Every student works closely with an assigned faculty mentor.

Student Government

Student government is conducted through the Student Council, whose members are elected by the student body. In addition, students are active participants in a variety of Institute-wide standing committees, the composition of which also includes a Board of Trustees, faculty members, and staff members.

Admission Requirements

CalArts welcomes application for admission from any individual engaged in the visual and performing arts. The main criterion for admission is artistic merit, as assessed by the faculty of the individual programs. An artist statement, letters of recommendation, and school transcripts are also required.

Application and Information

For application forms and additional information, prospective students should contact:

Office of Admissions
California Institute of the Arts
24700 McBean Parkway
Valencia, California 91355
Phone: 661-255-1050
E-mail: admiss@calarts.edu
Web site: http://www.calarts.edu

CalArts has extensive facilities for all the visual and performing arts.

CALIFORNIA LUTHERAN UNIVERSITY

THOUSAND OAKS, CALIFORNIA

The University

California Lutheran University (CLU) was founded in 1959, but its history goes back much farther than that. CLU is part of a 500-year-old tradition of Lutheran higher education—a tradition begun on a university campus as a teaching and reforming movement, a tradition of thoughtful investigation and bold discovery.

Following in this tradition, CLU insists on wide-ranging, critical inquiry into matters of both faith and reason. Students are encouraged to investigate personal beliefs that impact their educational and career choices and are asked to reflect on how their intellectual and spiritual convictions come together to define them as a whole person. Ultimately, the goal of CLU is to educate leaders for a global society who are strong in character and judgment, confident in their identity and vocation, and committed to service and justice. The individual exploration of truth is only a starting point for the whole educational experience by which students and professors work together to seek answers to the intellectual and professional questions that face world citizens.

CLU's 225-acre campus is home to 2,000 undergraduate and 1,000 graduate students from across the nation and around the world who represent a diversity of faiths and cultures. CLU provides access to a wide variety of organizations, sports, and other activities, providing ample opportunities for students to develop their leadership skills. KCLU-FM, a National Public Radio affiliate on the CLU campus, provides a valuable service to the community and a learning opportunity for students.

Master's degrees are awarded in business administration, computer science, education, marriage and family counseling, psychology, and public policy and administration. The NCATE-accredited School of Education offers an Ed.D. in educational leadership as well as a number of credential and certificate programs. International M.B.A. and post-M.B.A. programs are offered through the School of Business.

CLU is accredited by the Western Association of Schools and Colleges and is ranked in the top twenty by *U.S. News & World Report.*

Location

Poised at the intersection of the Americas on the Pacific Rim, CLU's location helps prepare students for careers in a global society. Thousand Oaks, which is located in one of America's significant technology corridors, the "101 Corridor," offers the conveniences of an urban area but is situated in an area of scenic natural beauty with open spaces and rolling hills. Because of its location midway between downtown Los Angeles and Santa Barbara and 15 miles inland from the Pacific Ocean, CLU offers students numerous recreational and cultural opportunities as well as internship and career opportunities in government, entertainment, and social services.

Majors and Degrees

CLU offers thirty-five majors within the College of Arts and Science, the School of Business, and the School of Education. In addition, undergraduate preprofessional preparation is available in church vocations, law, and medicine and health-related fields. Undergraduate degrees are offered in accounting, art, biochemistry and molecular biology, bioengineering, biology, business administration, chemistry, communication, computer information systems, computer science, criminal justice, economics, English, environmental science, exercise science and sports medicine, French, geology, German, history, interdisciplinary studies, international studies, liberal studies (education), marketing communication, mathematics, multimedia, music, philosophy, physics, political science, psychology, religion, social science, sociology, Spanish, and theater arts. Minors are offered in art, bioengineering, biology, business administration, chemistry, church music, communication, computer science, economics, English, environmental studies, ethnic studies, French, gender and women's studies, geography, geology, German, Greek, history, international business, international studies, legal studies, mathematics, multimedia, music, philosophy, physics, political science, psychology, religion, religion minor with church vocations, religion minor with youth ministry, sociology, Spanish, and theater arts.

Academic Programs

CLU's integrated curriculum helps students comprehend issues from a variety of perspectives. Students learn to ask the right questions and to think critically in order to analyze, process, transform, and communicate information. With thirty-five majors and thirty-five minors, students are encouraged to sample classes widely to build a broad base of knowledge. CLU feels that while planning for a career is important, the type of education that prepares students for a changing world is one of the greatest gifts a college education can provide.

At the heart of Cal Lutheran's academic program is a general education curriculum called Core 21. Students' views of the world expand as they learn how disciplines connect in this interdisciplinary approach. Core 21 extends through all four years, beginning with Freshman Seminar. CLU realizes that students' interests may not fit neatly into an academic box. Whether a student enters college with a definite major in mind or an awareness of the areas he or she wants to explore, CLU's curriculum offers distinctive ways to combine academic interests and goals with practical career preparation.

Students who wish to delve deeper into the life of the mind in smaller, seminar-style classes may also have access to the Honors Program. Honors courses bring students and faculty members together to contemplate issues of enduring human concern as well as contemporary problems facing society. Students who successfully complete the requisite honors courses over four years are awarded University Honors at graduation. A second honors program, Departmental Honors, is open to junior and senior students who wish to participate in prolonged, mentored scholarship with a faculty member in their chosen major field.

Off-Campus Programs

Students may take courses abroad while maintaining their student status at CLU by enrolling in one of the more than forty study-abroad programs offered. The University offers ongoing study, internship, and exchange programs in Austria, Belgium, Germany, Hong Kong, India, Mexico, Sweden, Tanzania, and Thailand. CLU also offers a Washington, D.C., semester for students in every field of study. This program allows students to live, study, and work in the nation's capital while earning a full semester of academic credit. While completing their professional internship and taking two academic courses, they also participate in orientation sessions, field trips, meetings with experts, and seminars on current events. Students are housed in furnished condominiums across the Potomac River in Arlington, Virginia.

Academic Facilities

The most recent additions to the CLU campus are Grace Hall, a 180-bed residence hall, and the Spies-Bornemann Center for Education Technology, which is designed to promote teaching with technology and houses the School of Education and Communication Department. Several new athletic arenas have just been completed, including the 96,000-square-foot Gilbert Sports and Fitness Center, featuring two gymnasiums, an events center, fitness and strength conditioning centers, dance studios, and a Hall of Fame; the Samuelson Aquatics Center, consisting of a 50-meter by 25-yard pool and diving well, providing the swimming, diving, and water polo teams with an Olympic-quality facility in which to train and compete; the George "Sparky" Anderson baseball field and Ullman Stadium; and new soccer and practice fields.

The campus is distinctive in its combination of mid-century modern and classic-contemporary architecture. The 600-seat Samuelson Chapel, with its towering wall of stained glass, mahogany carvings, and handcrafted Steiner-Reck organ, anchors the campus, which also includes the state-of-the-art Ahmanson Science Center, Pearson Library, and Soiland Humanities Center. The Preus-Brandt Forum is a 250-seat lecture/performance center equipped with modern sound and lighting equipment.

Costs

Tuition for the 2007–08 academic year was $25,790 (12–17 credits per semester). Room and board for the year totaled $9230. Student fees were $200 per year.

Financial Aid

Available assistance includes need-based and non-need-based University scholarships; low-interest, long-term loans from external sources; Federal Supplemental Educational Opportunity Grants; Federal Pell Grants; and Federal Work-Study Program positions. Part-time jobs are available both on and off campus. Applicants for aid should submit the Free Application for Federal Student Aid (FAFSA). The parents' and/or student's most recent IRS 1040 form must also be submitted. The priority application deadline is March 1. CLU scholarships are awarded based on the submission of a completed application.

Faculty

At CLU, professors care passionately about teaching and students. CLU's average class size of 22 students enables faculty members to know their students and enables students to develop relationships with mentors. Students have lively, in-depth discussions with the highly trained faculty members who teach their classes. Eighty-six percent of the full-time faculty members have earned their doctoral or terminal degree. They bring a depth of intellectual expertise and academic curiosity to the classroom. Among the faculty members are a former senior economist of the United Nations Development Programme, as well as master scholars in everything from media law and Mexican narrative to artificial intelligence and classical and quantum chaos. The list of their areas of research and interests—the social psychology of moral development, molecular evolution, economic and business forecasting models, and politics in movies, to name a few—brings a broad and beneficial foundation to students' liberal arts experience.

Student Government

All undergraduate students carrying 9 or more units are automatically members of the Associated Students of California Lutheran University by virtue of their enrollment in the University. Student governance, including allocation of the student activity fee, is conducted by student body–elected officials.

Admission Requirements

Applicants for admission must complete the application form (the CLU application or the Common Application may be used) and submit a high school transcript, SAT or ACT scores, one recommendation, an essay/personal statement, and a $45 non-refundable application fee ($25 for online applications). An interview is not required but is strongly recommended. International students whose native language is not English must also submit TOEFL or IELTS scores. All students are expected to have followed the most competitive college-prep curriculum available to them at their high school. Transfer students must also send a transcript of all completed college work (if more than 28 semester units of college work have been completed, SAT/ACT scores are not required).

Application and Information

The Early Action (EA) deadline is November 15. The Regular Decision Round 1 deadline is January 15, and the Regular Decision Round 2 deadline is March 15. For additional information, interested students should contact:

Office of Admission
California Lutheran University
60 West Olsen Road #1350
Thousand Oaks, California 91360-2700
Phone: 805-493-3135
877-CLU-FOR-U (toll-free)
Fax: 805-493-3114
E-mail: admissions@CalLutheran.edu
Web site: http://www.CalLutheran.edu

At CLU, professors care passionately about teaching and students.

CALIFORNIA STATE POLYTECHNIC UNIVERSITY, POMONA

CAL POLY POMONA

POMONA, CALIFORNIA

The University

California State Polytechnic University, Pomona, commonly referred to as Cal Poly Pomona, has a distinguished history with its origin as a private school. Two national icons, Charles B. Voorhis, a prominent automotive industry figure, and William K. Kellogg, a cereal magnate, contributed to the University becoming one of the nation's top institutions of higher education. Their legacies are evident today in the University's mission statement, vision, and goals. In 1928, retired automotive executive Charles B. Voorhis founded the Voorhis School for Boys in San Dimas, California, a college for homeless young men. Making the welfare of others his primary concern, Voorhis donated over $3 million to religious, educational, and charitable institutions. In 1938, the school was acquired by the state of California and became known as the Voorhis Unit of Cal Poly San Luis Obispo. In 1949, the Voorhis Unit obtained the 377-acre Arabian horse ranch of breakfast-food millionaire, W. K. Kellogg. A stipulation in maintaining the property is that the University continues the tradition of a Sunday Arabian horse show, so Cal Poly Pomona students host public performances on the first Sunday from October through May.

Located on the eastern edge of Southern California's San Gabriel Valley, the 1,400-acre campus features lush rolling hills; flowers, plants, and trees from all seven continents; a rose garden built by W. K. Kellogg; and a beautifully landscaped Japanese garden. The University's aesthetic qualities are one of its best kept secrets. Pasadena architect Myron Hunt (Rose Bowl, Huntington Library) designed W. K. Kellogg's main house. Charles Gibbs Adams (Hearst Castle Gardens) landscaped the grounds, which were later completed by Florence Yoch and Lucile Council, widely recognized as 2 of the finest garden designers and landscape architects in California. Recently, Antoine Predock designed the administration building with a desert theme.

As one of nine polytechnic universities nationwide, Cal Poly Pomona integrates a learn-by-doing approach into its project- and presentation-based course work, making it unique among traditional universities. Its students are among the most sought-after in today's marketplace. A nationally recognized public university, Cal Poly Pomona offers students an excellent environment for academic, personal, and professional success. The U.S. Department of Education, *U.S. News & World Report, Black Issues in Higher Education, Design Intelligence, Hispanic Outlook Magazine, Los Angeles Business Journal,* and Project Connect have ranked Cal Poly Pomona high in numerous categories. Students attending Cal Poly Pomona do not face overloaded classrooms or throngs of teaching assistants. In the belief that education should be a face-to-face interaction between faculty members and students, the University strives to maintain a 23:1 student-teacher ratio, with fewer than 30 students in most classrooms. Quarter-system scheduling allows students to take classes year-round.

A variety of activities and opportunities abound on campus—more than 250 organizations bring students together based on academic and other common interests. Since 1949, student-constructed floats in the annual Tournament of Roses Parade have received over forty-five awards. About 800 students are involved in social Greek organizations, and the forty ethnically based organizations reflect the diverse student body. Students also enrich their educational experience through community service and volunteer opportunities. With twelve intercollegiate sports, Bronco men's and women's teams have won thirteen national championships and compete in the nation's premiere NCAA II conference, the California Collegiate Athletic Association. In addition, intramural/recreational sports involve nearly 2,000 students each year.

Cal Poly Pomona is proud of its recognition as a top university for campus diversity and international students. Cal Poly Pomona's 2,670 faculty and staff members serve just over 20,000 students from forty-nine states and sixty-one countries worldwide. Of the student body, 33 percent are Asian/Pacific Islander; 27 percent, Hispanic; 25.3 percent, Caucasian; 4 percent, African American; and about 0.3 percent are Native American/Alaskan Native.

Cal Poly Pomona has one of the largest on-campus residential populations in the Los Angeles region with 3,000 students. Residence halls accommodate approximately 1,800 students, often in academic major, special interest, or lifestyle theme areas. Adjacent to the campus, the University Village complex accommodates about 1,200 students. Residential Suites houses 400 students and offers suite-style accommodations, an on-site café, and large study areas. Plans call for construction to begin in spring 2008 on residential suites that will provide 600 additional beds; completion is expected by fall 2009.

Location

Located 35 miles east of downtown Los Angeles, Cal Poly Pomona offers the excitement of one of the world's most diverse metropolitan areas and Southern California's magnificent weather, while still retaining the serenity of a foothill community. The University's proximity to business and industry makes it ideal for internships and employment opportunities. In addition, the campus is only a short drive from the beach, mountains, and desert; theaters, museums, and galleries; and such recreational sites as Disneyland, Hollywood Bowl, Kodak Theater, and Knott's Berry Farm.

Majors and Degrees

Bachelor of Arts degrees include art; behavioral science; English; gender, ethnicity, and multicultural studies; history; liberal studies; music; philosophy; political science; psychology; sociology; Spanish; and theater. The Bachelor of Architecture is also offered.

Bachelor of Science degrees include aerospace engineering, agricultural science, animal science, anthropology, apparel merchandising and management, biology, biotechnology, botany, business administration (majors include accounting; computer information systems; e-business; finance, real estate, and law; international business and marketing; management and human resources; and technology and operations management), chemical engineering, chemistry, civil engineering, communication, computer engineering, computer science, economics, electrical engineering, electronics and computer engineering technology, engineering technology, environmental biology, food marketing and agribusiness management, food science and technology, foods and nutrition, geography, geology, graphic design, hotel and restaurant management, industrial engineering, integrated earth studies, kinesiology, landscape architecture, manufacturing engineering, mathematics, mechanical engineering, microbiology, physics, plant science, social sciences, urban and regional planning, and zoology.

Academic Programs

Cal Poly Pomona's motto is *Instrumentum Disciplinae* (Application of Knowledge), and its mission is "to advance learning and knowledge by linking theory and practice in all disciplines and to prepare students for lifelong learning, leadership, and careers in a changing, multicultural world." The University's academic programs emphasize project-based learning. The nationally recognized Interdisciplinary General Education program for first-time freshmen integrates personal experience with the study of literature, the humanities, and social sciences. The Center for Community Service Learning relates academic content and course objectives to issues in the community.

Classes are offered in four 11-week quarters. Candidates for bachelor's degrees must earn at least 180 quarter units and complete the graduation writing requirement. The Four-Year Pledge Program is designed to guarantee graduation within four years for freshmen.

Cal Poly Pomona offers Air Force and Army Reserve Officers' Training Corps, a California Pre-Doctoral Program, an Educational Opportunity Program, the Kellogg Honors College, the Renaissance Scholar Program, University Equity Programs, and other special programs.

Off-Campus Programs

The International Center offers study-abroad programs in China, Costa Rica, Cuba, Germany, Ghana, Greece, London, Mexico, Paris, and Vietnam. These programs are taught by Cal Poly Pomona professors in three-, six- or nine-month periods earning full academic credit. The National Student Exchange is a domestic parallel to study abroad that gives students access to 170 member colleges and universities in forty-eight states as well as Guam, Puerto Rico, and the Virgin Islands. The members range from some of the largest public research universities to some of the best small, specialized colleges in the country, including fifteen Hispanic-serving institutions, fourteen historically black institutions, and a number of ethnically diverse campuses.

Academic Facilities

The library's $63-million addition and renovation is scheduled for completion in spring 2008. As a state-of-the-art regional educational center, the plans include classrooms, technology-research workstations, a two-story reading room, a 24-hour research lab, and a full-service Starbucks. The library received a $2.1-million Title V Hispanic Serving Institution Grant from the U.S. Department of Education. Academic colleges and cultural centers provide specialized collections. The W. K. Kellogg Arabian Horse Library is located in University Plaza, the old horse stables, and features a history of the Kellogg Arabian horse collection. The University supports fifty-four general computer labs and provides a professional staff and help desk.

Indicative of Cal Poly Pomona's hands-on learning are the Collins School for Hospitality Management, AGRIscapes, and the University Farm. The Collins School houses a student-run restaurant, demonstration kitchens, and laboratories and features annual presentations by world-famous chefs. AGRIscapes is a 40-acre research, education, and demonstration center that promotes agricultural and environmental understanding and houses a farm store and nursery. The University Farm has more than 700 acres devoted to pastures and livestock, crops, groves, and ornamental plantings.

The University's special centers and institutes include the American Red Cross' $41.6-million blood-processing center and headquarters, which provides educational and research opportunities; the John T. Lyle Center for Regenerative Studies, an innovative research facility focusing on issues of sustainable living; BioTrek, an unparalleled hands-on learning experience for students to explore the complexities and diversity of plant and animal species; and the Motor Development Clinic, the area's largest program for children with movement problems. Other facilities include the Richard and Dion Neutra VDL Research House; the Apparel Technology and Research Center; the Center for Turf, Irrigation, and Landscape Technology; the Equine Research Center; the Ocean Studies Institute; and the Institute for Cellular and Molecular Biology.

A recent multimillion-dollar building campaign to enhance campus resources resulted in a number of new facilities. Current and future projects include a 2,378-space parking structure, Residential Suites Phase II, and a new College of Business Administration.

Costs

In 2007–08, annual fees for full-time students (6.1 or more units) were $3279. Non-California residents paid an additional $226 per unit. Books and supplies were estimated at $1386 per year. Housing costs varied from $3474 to $9036 for the academic year, depending on choice of accommodation and meal plan.

Financial Aid

The University administers extensive financial aid programs; 66 percent of Cal Poly Pomona students receive more than $72 million in financial aid each year. Applications for academic and merit scholarships must be completed by February 15. Applications for financial aid should be completed after January 1, but no later than March 2, for the following academic year. Students are encouraged to apply for financial aid online on the Federal Student Aid Web site (http://www.fafsa.ed.gov/). Applicants can also contact the Cal Poly Pomona financial aid office (http://www.dsa.csupomona.edu/financial_aid) for additional information.

Many students work on-campus during the academic year, and numerous positions are available off-campus. The Career Center (http://www.career.csupomona.edu) assists all students seeking employment and internships.

Faculty

About two thirds of the faculty members have earned terminal degrees. Faculty members provide direction and guidance to their students, serve as academic advisers, and many advise cocurricular clubs and organizations. Faculty members continue to be honored as Fullbright Scholars, receive state and federal appointments in their respective area of emphasis, author books, and generate millions of dollars in research for the University.

Student Government

The Associated Students, Incorporated (ASI) is the student-government body of Cal Poly Pomona dedicated to enhancing the campus community. ASI represents student concerns through University committees and provides leadership development and involvement opportunities through campus-event planning, student employment, recreational sports, Bronco Student Center programs and services, and the Children's Center.

Admission Requirements

Cal Poly Pomona is ranked as one of the most competitive schools in terms of admissions. For the 2007–08 academic year, 22,000 first-time freshman applications were received for a class of 3,800 students. Architecture, an impacted academic program open only to California residents, received 1,900 applications for an entering class of 225.

First-time freshmen must be high school graduates and must have completed the following college-preparatory courses with a C or better: 4 years of English; 3 years of math; 2 years of social science (including 1 year of U.S. history or U.S. history and government); 2 years of laboratory science (1 biological and 1 physical); 2 years of the same foreign language; 1 year of visual and performing arts (art, dance, music, theater/drama); and 1 year of electives selected from the above areas. For first-time freshmen, qualification for admission is based on a combination of high school grades and ACT or SAT scores. Applicants must take the SAT or ACT. Scores must be received no later than January of the year for which the student is applying.

Upper-division transfer students must have completed at least 60 transferable semester units (90 quarter units), have a grade point average of C or better in all transferable units attempted, must be in good standing at the last college or university attended, and must have completed at least 30 semester units (45 quarter units) of general education courses with a grade of C or better. The 30 semester units must include written communication, oral communication, critical thinking, and college-level math. All 60 transferable semester units must be completed by the end of the previous spring for the fall quarter, the end of the previous summer for the winter quarter, the end of the previous fall for the spring quarter, and the end of the previous fall for the summer quarter.

For international students, Cal Poly Pomona has additional requirements to admit students who hold F-1 and J-1 student visas. Verification of English proficiency, financial resources, and academic performance are all important considerations. Regardless of citizenship, all applicants whose preparatory education was not in English must demonstrate competence in English with a TOEFL score of at least 525 (paper-based test) or 195 (computer-based test).

Admission requirements may be subject to change; students should consult the CSU application or go online to http://www.dsa.csupomona.edu/admissions/.

Application and Information

For fall 2008 admission, applications must be received from October 1 to November 30, 2007. Applications from first-time freshmen are only accepted for each fall quarter. Transfer applications are accepted each quarter (fall, winter, spring, summer). Students are encouraged to apply online at http://www.csumentor.edu. Prospective students should also fill out an online request card at http://dsa.csupomona.edu/admissions/vip.asp. For more information, students should contact:

Office of Admissions and Outreach
California State Polytechnic University, Pomona
3801 West Temple Avenue
Pomona, California 91768
Phone: 909-869-3210
Web site: http://www.csupomona.edu

Cal Poly Pomona's lush 1,400-acre campus offers students an ideal atmosphere for academic enrichment anc social growth.

CHAPMAN UNIVERSITY

ORANGE, CALIFORNIA

The University

During its 146-year history, Chapman has evolved from a small, traditional liberal arts college that was founded in 1861 by members of the First Christian Church (Disciples of Christ) into a mid-sized comprehensive liberal arts and sciences university that is distinguished for its nationally recognized programs in film and television production, business and economics, theater, dance, music, education, and the natural and applied sciences. The mission of Chapman University is to provide personalized education of distinction that leads to inquiring, ethical, and productive lives as global citizens.

Chapman's parklike ivy-covered, tree-lined campus features a blending of fully refurbished historic structures with the newest in state-of-the-art Internet and satellite-connected learning environments. Five residence halls and six on-campus apartment buildings are conveniently located on the edge of the campus. Prominent in the center of the campus is Liberty Plaza, featuring a raised replica of a Lincoln chair that views a 5-ton section of the Berlin Wall.

Chapman University's academic structure includes the Wilkinson College of Letters and Sciences, the CILECT-accredited Dodge College of Film and Media Arts, the AACSB International–accredited Argyros School of Business and Economics, the CTC-approved School of Education, the ABA-accredited School of Law, and the College of Performing Arts, which includes the NASM-accredited School of Music. Other nationally accredited programs include the IFT-accredited program in food sciences and the APTA-accredited program in physical therapy. Chapman has been further recognized by the Templeton Foundation as one of only 100 colleges nationally to be designated as a Templeton Foundation "Character-Building College" for its emphasis on global citizenry and for student involvement in community action and stewardship activities.

In addition to approximately 6,000 undergraduate, graduate, and professional school students enrolled on the campus in Orange, Chapman also enrolls another 8,000 undergraduate and graduate students annually through its Chapman University College and associated network of thirty University College corporate campus centers, serving primarily working adults with evening and weekend program formats, located in California and Washington.

The University environment is electric, involving, and outdoor-oriented. Along with the obvious benefits associated with the southern California climate, Chapman students enjoy a dynamic and involving student activities program. Although predominantly from California, Chapman students come from more than forty states; in addition, approximately 10 percent of its students come from thirty-four other countries. Over the past five years, Chapman students have been named Truman Scholars, Coro Fellows, *USA Today* All-USA College Academic Team members, NCAA All-Americans, and NCAA Academic All-Americans. Chapman's long and distinguished heritage in intercollegiate athletics includes five NCAA national championships in baseball, tennis, and softball. Chapman competes as an independent in the NCAA Division III level and fields teams in baseball, basketball (m/w), crew (m/w), cross-country (m/w), football, golf, lacrosse, soccer (m/w), softball, swimming (w), tennis (m/w), track and field (m/w), volleyball (w), and water polo (m/w). Approximately 20 percent of Chapman's student body participates in intercollegiate athletics. In 2006, 4 student-athletes were named as NCAA All-Americans and 8 as NCAA Academic All-Americans.

More than seventy clubs and organizations are available, many with commitments to a wide range of community service efforts. Chapman's Greek system includes six nationally chartered fraternities for men and five nationally chartered sororities for women. A comprehensive intramural sports program involves myriad sports activities for all campus community members throughout the school year. On-campus intercollegiate athletic events as well as music, art, and theater productions provide students with extensive extracurricular activity options. Chapman's proximity to area recreational and cultural opportunities allows Chapman students to enjoy the essence of what makes Orange County's south coast area an enviable environment in which to live and learn.

Prominent Chapman alumni include the Honorable Loretta Sanchez '88, member of Congress; the Honorable David Bonior '72, member of Congress; CNBC World anchorwoman, Bettina Chua '88; television and film producers John Copeland '73, Jon Garcia '93, and John David Currey '98; cinematographer Gene Jackson '70; television sports analyst Steve Lavin '88; major league baseball executive Gordon Blakely '76; major league baseball Cy Young Award winner Randy Jones '72 ; Tony Award nominee and star of Broadway's *Showboat*, Michel Bell '68; resident tenor at the Staatsoper-Vienna John Nuzzo '91; and former U.S. Ambassador to Spain and philanthropist George L. Argyros '65.

Location

Orange County, California, has been rated by *Places Rated Almanac* as "the #1 place to live in North America," citing superior climate, cultural, recreational, educational, and career-entree opportunities. Los Angeles is 35 miles to the north, and San Diego is 80 miles to the south. Nearby entertainment venues include Disneyland, Knott's Berry Farm, the Orange County Performing Arts Center, major-league baseball, and hockey. Pristine West Coast beaches are less than 10 miles from the campus, and seasonal snow skiing is 90 minutes away. The average year-round temperature on campus is 71°F, and the prevailing sea breeze coming off nearby southwest-facing beaches keeps the air clean and smog free.

Majors and Degrees

Chapman awards the Bachelor of Arts degree in the fields of art, biology, chemistry, communications, dance, economics, English and comparative literature, film and television, French, history, liberal studies (teaching), music, peace studies, philosophy, physical education, political science, psychology, religion, social science, sociology, Spanish, and theater. The Bachelor of Fine Arts degree is offered in creative writing, dance performance, film production, graphic design, studio art, television and broadcast journalism, and theater performance. The Bachelor of Science degree is offered in accounting, applied mathematics, biology, business administration, chemistry, computer information systems, computer science, and natural science. The Bachelor of Music degree is granted in composition, conducting, music education (vocal and instrumental), music performance (vocal and instrumental), and music therapy. Preprofessional or prevocational programs are offered in dentistry, law, medicine, physical therapy, social service, teaching, theology, and veterinary medicine.

Academic Programs

Possibly unique to Chapman is the University's relationship with the professional mentoring program, Inside Track. In addition to traditionally assigned academic advisers from various disciplines and tutoring services provided by the Center for Academic Success, each freshman is also assigned a life coach with whom they meet once weekly to develop critical skills, set goals, and address the many challenges that might interfere with their success. Coaching sessions are focused on personal development, assistance with planning and organization, and, most important, motivation and encouragement. Working in partnership with University administrators and faculty, Inside Track provides an invaluable safety net for students, helping to improve academic preparedness and performance.

The requirements for graduation are commensurate with the liberal arts philosophy of education maintained by Chapman. The program of studies is designed to ensure a breadth of subject matter selection in the liberal arts as well as depth of preparation in the student's major field. The minimum graduation requirements include successful completion (C average) of 124 semester credits, of which 36 must be earned in the upper division. Competence in reading, written communication, oral communication, computation, and library usage is required of all students. Chapman's general education sequence provides a broad introduction to the humanities, social sciences, and natural sciences. Students select general education classes with the guidance of their faculty adviser. A maximum of 32 semester credits may be gained through Advanced Placement (AP), College-Level Examination Program (CLEP), and departmental examinations.

Chapman's academic year operates on a 4-1-4 modified semester system. January is reserved for an optional Interterm. The University College corporate campus locations offer five 10-week terms annually.

Ample opportunities are available for alternative learning experiences. Internships and cooperative education programs are recommended. Students may also undertake in-depth individual study or research in their major field in conjunction with a faculty member.

Academic Facilities

Major facilities additions to the Chapman campus over the past few years include the completion of the 100,000-square-foot Leatherby Libraries complex, housing eight discipline-specific individual libraries, a sculpture garden, a cyber courtyard, and a 24-hour study commons and coffee bar; the Oliphant Hall addition to the School of Music, which includes 24,000 square feet featuring fourteen teaching studios, a sixty-seat lecture hall, music therapy laboratory, and orchestra hall; and the new Interfaith Center, which features the 12,500-square-foot Wallace All-Faiths Chapel. The 90,000-square-foot Argyros Forum includes the primary campus dining area and conference and classroom facilities. The 1,000-seat Memorial Auditorium is listed on the National Register of Historic Places. Athletic facilities include the 4,000-seat Hutton Sports Center arena, four championship tennis courts, and training and fitness facilities for the campus and surrounding community. Currently under construction are a new 5,000-seat outdoor stadium and a 1,000-seat swim stadium/Olympic pool complex. Arnold Beckman Hall is the center for business and information technology, including the Argyros School of Business and Economics, the A. Gary Anderson Center for Economic Research, the Ralph Leatherby Center for Entrepreneurship and Business Ethics, the Walter Schmid Center for International Business, and the Hobbs Institute for Real Estate, Law, and Environmental Studies. The College of Performing Arts facilities include the 250-seat repertory-style Waltmar Theatre and the Guggenheim Art Gallery. The Hashinger Science Center features laboratories for nuclear science, radiation, crystallography, genetics, food science, and physical therapy.

Costs

For the 2007–08 academic year, full-time tuition and fees (including accident and sickness fee, health center fee, and associated student membership fee) are $32,622. Annual room and board costs average $10,616. The estimated cost for books is $700 per year.

Financial Aid

More than 85 percent of Chapman students benefit from some form of financial aid or scholarship assistance. Need-based financial awards include a combination of grants, scholarships, loans, and work-study jobs on campus. Awards are renewable, assuming that students complete the annual application process on time. By using a combination of Chapman's internal resources and federal and state funding, an individual financial aid package can be tailored to meet the student's financial need. Merit and talent scholarship awards, regardless of financial need, round out the types of financial assistance that Chapman offers. Chapman offers an Early Aid Estimator service that gives students an up-front picture of what their prospective aid/scholarship eligibility is, rather than waiting for the postadmission, official aid-awarding period. Students asking for information about Chapman automatically receive the Early Aid Estimator form, along with instructions for completion and submission for analysis.

Faculty

The University's faculty is composed of 256 full-time and 288 part-time members, more than 80 percent of whom hold doctoral or other terminal degrees. Their primary commitment is to undergraduate teaching, although most are also actively involved in scholarly research and publication. Many faculty members teach both undergraduate and graduate courses. Teaching assistants or graduate assistants are not used for the instruction of undergraduate classes. Chapman's favorable student-faculty ratio of 16:1 allows extensive interaction between the faculty members and students.

Student Government

Chapman has an associated student government that actively participates in the administration of the University.

Admission Requirements

Admission to Chapman is selective. In 2007, admission was granted to 47 percent of the applicant pool. The University is interested in admitting students whose prior records indicate that they will be successful in a competitive collegiate environment. Freshman applicants are considered for admission based primarily on the nature and sequence of their high school course work, the grade point average achieved, and their results on either the SAT or ACT examination. Transfer candidates are considered for admission on the basis of their course work and cumulative grade point average earned at other regionally accredited postsecondary institutions.

Application and Information

When applying, candidates are strongly encouraged to visit and tour the campus and participate in an information session led by an admission officer. Arrangements for a group information session and campus tour can be made through the Office of Admission. Freshman applicants can choose either a nonbinding November 15 early action application deadline or the January 15 regular application deadline. Transfer applicants must apply before the March 15 transfer deadline. Freshman candidates who apply after January 15 and transfer candidates who apply after March 15 are considered on a space-available basis.

For further information, students should contact:

Office of Admission
Chapman University
One University Drive
Orange, California 92866
Phone: 714-997-6711
888-CUAPPLY (toll-free)
Fax: 714-997-6713
E-mail: admit@chapman.edu
Web site: http://www.chapman.edu

COLUMBIA COLLEGE HOLLYWOOD

TARZANA, CALIFORNIA

The College

Columbia College Hollywood (CCH) is a leader in preparing students for careers in the film and television/video industry. Known as "the filmmaker's film school," CCH is where industry professionals nurture the talent of their future colleagues by emphasizing hands-on training. The technical and creative advances now being made in the motion picture and television industries make it imperative for aspiring film and video artists to receive cutting-edge training. Since its founding in 1952, CCH has offered that kind of training.

Columbia College Hollywood is a private, nonprofit institution accredited by the Accrediting Commission of Career Schools and Colleges of Technology (ACCSCT). The College is in the final stages of applying for a more expansive dual accreditation with the National Association of Schools of Art and Design. CCH's goal is to turn out artists with technical proficiency and technicians who are also artists. The formula seems to be working: a recent CCH graduate directed the blockbuster film *Flight Plan*, starring Jodie Foster. Another graduate won a 2007 MTV Movie Award for *United 93*. Two CCH graduates recently produced Grand Prize winners at the Sundance Film Festival; others have won awards at the Hollywood and Palm Springs festivals. CCH is proud of its history in finding work for students, and to date, approximately 95 percent of its graduates have been successful in finding work in the entertainment industry.

Columbia College Hollywood's commitment to involving students in the professional film and television/video community is the reason why its campus is located right outside of Los Angeles, one of the world's centers for the motion picture and television industries. It has allowed the school to maintain close relationships with working industry professionals, studios, and production companies and encouraged them to become involved in the educational process at CCH. It also ensures CCH students access to coveted internships and the networking opportunities that drive the entertainment business.

Location

Columbia College Hollywood makes the most of its location in Los Angeles's San Fernando Valley, the heart of the motion picture and television/video industry. CCH students are frequently invited to work on the many films that are produced daily in the L.A. area. The school's Student-Industry Relations Department arranges internships for students with production companies and studios, enabling them to gain invaluable experience and make all-important industry contacts. Apart from the excitement that comes from being at the visual media center of the world, there are the well-known physical attractions of Los Angeles itself: its temperate climate, beaches, mountains, and deserts. Los Angeles is a cultural center as well and is home to museums, galleries, concerts (both classical and popular), major-league sports teams, and live theater.

Majors and Degrees

Columbia College Hollywood offers the Bachelor of Arts (B.A.) degree in cinema and combined cinema/television. Students who wish may pursue an Associate in Arts (A.A.) degree in television/video production. The A.A. and B.A. degree programs can be attended on a full-time or part-time basis.

Academic Programs

The Associate in Arts degree requires 96 units of study, of which 48 units are in general education and 48 units are in television production. The Bachelor of Arts degree requires 192 units of study, 48 of which are in general education and 144 of which are in the program major. In the B.A. programs, cinema and television/video students are enrolled in parallel courses of study for the first five quarters. These courses cover both film and video technology, which gives the student a solid foundation. This is beneficial because the two mediums are merging in the professional world. After the fifth quarter, students continue in their major area of study.

The program in television/video production is designed to provide students with knowledge and skills in the creative, technical, and operational aspects of the medium. Graduates from this course of study are well qualified for a variety of entry-level positions in a television broadcast facility, a non–broadcast video production setting, or an allied industry. Examples of entry-level positions are production assistant, directorial assistant, camera operator, floor director, advertising and sales assistant, copywriter, assistant editor, tape operator, or video engineer.

Through the program in cinema, students learn about the technical and creative aspects of theatrical, documentary, and industrial film production. Graduates from this program are well qualified for entry-level positions such as camera assistant, lighting assistant, grip, dolly grip, budgeting and production assistant, sound recordist, assistant editor, postproduction sound mixer, and assistant director. In order to accommodate working students and the many instructors who hold entertainment industry positions, there are classes held at night and during the afternoon. Some weekend seminars are also offered.

Academic Facilities

Columbia College Hollywood has a nonresidential urban campus that is designed to cater to students' needs in their quest to become great filmmakers. Among its features is an equipment center that contains 16mm cameras, lenses, video cameras, lighting equipment, grip equipment, and sound equipment. Its newly remodeled television studio opened in fall 2004, and a new state-of-the-art soundstage is expected to break ground in 2007. CCH offers both Avid and Macintosh-based Final Cut Pro online-quality digital editing systems and a telecine machine that allows students to shoot in film and finish digitally. The campus also houses a student library of movie and television scripts, industry trade publications, DVD and VHS movies, and traditional literature and research material. There are a computer lab offering budget, planning, and scriptwriting software and an Internet lab for computers with Internet access. Wireless Internet access is available campuswide. Additional features on campus include two projection theaters (twenty-four and seventy-three seats), two permanent shooting sets, study areas, a prop room, computer and screenplay-writing labs, well-equipped classrooms with HD flat-screen televisions, a "shooting gallery" workplace for student filming, and an ADR facility for postproduction sound editing.

Costs

For the 2007–08 academic year, tuition and fees for full-time attendance were approximately $14,000 per academic year. The estimated living costs for an independent student are approximately $8000 per academic year. Campus housing is available on the campus of California State University Northridge (CSUN), and a shuttle provides service back and forth from CSUN to Columbia College. For students who prefer apartment living, ample housing is available in the vicinity of the College.

Financial Aid

Columbia College Hollywood participates in the following federal and state financial aid programs: the Federal Pell Grant, Federal Supplemental Educational Opportunity Grant, Federal Work-Study Program, Federal Family Education Loan (which includes subsidized and unsubsidized Federal Stafford Student Loan), and Cal Grants A, B, and C. The school makes available scholarships for industry internships.

Faculty

The faculty consists of 45 members, the majority of whom hold positions in the television, motion picture, or educational fields, and includes both Emmy and Academy Award winners. The student-faculty ratio is 10:1.

Admission Requirements

Applicants for freshman-level classes must be high school graduates and must have earned a minimum cumulative grade point average of 2.0 or maintained an overall letter grade of C or better during their high school studies. Transcripts must demonstrate high school graduation. Under special circumstances, a passing score on the General Educational Development (GED) test may be accepted by the College in lieu of high school graduation.

Applicants for admission to the College on any other level are required to furnish transcripts of previous course work to establish their academic standing. Applicants to the upper-division programs are required to furnish transcripts verifying completion of an Associate in Arts degree or higher. All transcripts must be sent directly to Columbia College Hollywood by the educational institutions. Two letters of reference from people, other than relatives, who have been acquainted with the applicant for more than one year and are aware of the applicant's interest in the field of cinema, television, or communications media are required; these letters must be mailed directly to Columbia College Hollywood by the writers. A minimum 250-word essay explaining why the applicant wishes to study either film or video and describing his or her career goals is required. SAT scores are not required but may be submitted in support of the student's application.

Students enrolling in Columbia College Hollywood for the first time are encouraged to attend an orientation session. Academic objectives and career goals are discussed, school programs and academic requirements are explained, and registration for classes takes place during the course of orientation. To guarantee enrollment, final registration should be completed at least two weeks prior to the beginning of the quarter.

Advanced standing may be granted to applicants for the programs in television/video production and cinema. Transcripts of the applicants' previous college-level study should be mailed directly to Columbia College by the institution previously attended for evaluation by Columbia College's Admissions Department.

Application and Information

Applications are accepted on a rolling basis throughout the year, and applicants may apply to enroll in the fall, winter, spring, or summer quarters. Late registration can occur up to the close of the first week of the quarter; however, acceptance for enrollment in any particular quarter cannot be guaranteed unless the applicant has been fully matriculated at least one week prior to the beginning of that quarter.

A completed application for admission and an application fee of $50 should be mailed to the College or delivered in person by the applicant. An online application tool is also available, allowing students to apply for admission via the College's Web site.

For more information, students should contact:

Admissions Office
Columbia College Hollywood
18618 Oxnard Street
Tarzana, California 91356
Phone: 818-345-8414
800-785-0585 (toll-free)
Fax: 818-345-9053
E-mail: info@columbiacollege.edu
Web site: http://www.columbiacollege.edu

At Columbia College Hollywood, students use professional equipment on location for a film production workshop class.

COLLEGE DATA CENTER • CALIFORNIA

DOMINICAN UNIVERSITY OF CALIFORNIA

SAN RAFAEL, CALIFORNIA

The University

Dominican University of California is an independent, international, learner-centered university of Dominican heritage. It offers a beautiful setting, a close-knit community of approximately 2,000 students, and an intimate social environment that is an important context for academic goals and personal development.

The University offers many services that support the University's educational programs. It provides tutoring, life-planning, career, and personal counseling without charge to Dominican students; offers housing, health, and job placement services; and helps students make the most of their college experience by its readiness to assist them in resolving problems.

The University and the Associated Students of Dominican University sponsor a number of campus activities each year for both resident and nonresident students. Dominican supports ten intercollegiate teams that compete in the NAIA California Pacific Conference: men's and women's basketball, golf, and soccer; men's lacrosse; and women's softball, tennis, and volleyball. Students can participate in the chorus, drama group, the literary magazine, campus newspaper, campus ministry activities, special interest clubs, dances, and other social events.

Campus Ministry responds to the spiritual needs of Catholic and non-Catholic members of the University community. Catholic liturgies, ecumenical activities for students of all faiths, and community service projects are scheduled throughout the year.

Graduate degrees (M.A., M.S., M.S.N., M.S.O.T., M.F.T., and M.B.A.) are granted in counseling psychology, education, humanities, global strategic management, sustainable enterprise (Green MBA®), nursing, occupational therapy, and strategic leadership.

The University is approved by the California Commission on Teacher Credentialing to prepare and recommend candidates for credentials in elementary, secondary, and special education.

Four residence halls of varied architecture accommodate more than 600 students; there is a dining hall for resident students and others who wish to purchase meals on campus. Forest Meadows, which comprises approximately 25 acres, is the site of the Conlan Recreation Center, a soccer field, tennis courts, and an outdoor amphitheater where commencement exercises are held. The Recreation Center features regulation basketball and volleyball courts, two cross-courts for volleyball and basketball, and 1,285 spectator seats. It also features a weight-training and fitness room, a multipurpose room, lockers, athletic department offices, and conference rooms. Outside is a six-lane, recreational swimming pool and grassy patio area.

Location

The University is located on 80 wooded acres in scenic Marin County, which is 12 miles north of San Francisco and within a half hour's drive of Pacific Ocean beaches.

Majors and Degrees

A broad range of degrees and certificate and credential programs are offered in letters, the arts and sciences, and professional and preprofessional disciplines.

Undergraduate degrees (B.A., B.S., B.S.N., and B.F.A.) are awarded in the academic areas of art, art history, biological sciences (with concentrations in ecology, environmental science, general biology, molecular cell biology, and premedical studies), business administration (with concentrations in accounting, finance, international business, management, management information systems, and marketing), communications (with concentrations in broadcast media, cinema, journalism, and print), dance (LINES ballet), English, English with a writing emphasis, graphic art and design, health science (pre–occupational therapy), history, humanities, interdisciplinary studies, international studies, liberal studies (teacher education), music, music with a performance concentration, nursing, political science, psychology, religion, and women and gender studies.

Minors are offered in chemistry, environmental studies, Latin American studies, philosophy, prelaw, and sports management.

Academic Programs

The General Education Program offers more than a brief exposure to the major areas of knowledge in the humanities, arts, and natural and social sciences. It is designed to provide a sequence of courses with a thematic focus that integrates the wisdom and perspectives of several disciplines. The focus assists students in discovering relationships between areas of knowledge, beliefs, cultures, and peoples that differ globally and historically, as well as in acquiring an awareness of tradition, a love of discovery, a respect for the diversity of the human condition, and a realization of human interdependence. Courses within the General Education Program also expose students to a variety of learning experiences that include discussion, lectures, seminars, simulations, practicums, and quiet reflection.

A strong internship program offers students job experience in areas of their choice.

An evening bachelor's degree-completion program (Pathways) for non-traditional learners is also available.

The ELS Language Centers program provides intensive, high-quality English instruction to prepare international students to enter American colleges and universities. Completion of the ELS Language Centers Program level 112 satisfies Dominican's English requirement for admission.

Off-Campus Programs

Dominican offers exchange programs with Aquinas College, Grand Rapids, Michigan; Barry University, Miami, Florida; the College of New Rochelle, New Rochelle, New York; and St. Thomas Aquinas College, Sparkill, New York. These programs enable students matriculated at any one of the five colleges to spend a semester on a campus in a different part of the country, taking advantage of its location and programs. Students pay tuition on their home campus and room and board on the host campus. Further information about the program, recommended for students in the sophomore or junior year, is available in the campus Service Center.

Individualized programs for study in other countries may be planned in consultation with the Academic Advising Center, the student's academic adviser, and the transcript evaluator. Dominican grants credit for international study only after a student who obtained prior approval of the program of study has returned to the campus and enrolled for the following year.

Academic Facilities

Archbishop Alemany Library houses more than 100,000 volumes in open stacks; 3,200 reels of microfilm; 775 videocassettes, 225 audiocassettes, and compact discs; and subscriptions to 375 periodicals in print and another 19,000 periodical titles in full-text online. Reference services, including access to a variety of computerized databases and indexes, and multimedia facilities are provided to assist students with their studies and assignments. The library also houses the Fletcher Jones Computer Laboratory, an art gallery, a listening room, and a fireplace corner.

Guzman Hall, Albertus Magnus Hall, Bertrand Hall, and the San Marco Art Studios together house faculty offices, science laboratories, lecture halls, a computer center, art galleries and studios, and classrooms. Angelico Hall houses an 850-seat concert auditorium and theater, music studios and practice rooms, and faculty offices.

In 2005, ground was broken on a new $20-million, 35,000-square-foot science and technology facility. The Science Center opened for the fall 2007 classes featuring more than thirty teaching, research, and computer technology labs.

Costs

Undergraduate full-time tuition (12–17 units per semester) was $30,770 per year for 2007–08. Fees were $300; room and board (a fourteen-meal-per-week plan) cost approximately $10,080 for the year.

Financial Aid

Financial aid is awarded on the basis of need and merit. Merit awards are available for both freshmen and transfer students based on academic achievement. Dominican University of California participates in various federal and state need-based financial aid programs and also has its own financial aid funds, donated by generous alumni and friends, available to help meet University costs.

Need-based financial aid comes in the form of scholarships, grants, part-time employment, and loans. The federal and state financial aid programs are the Federal Supplemental Educational Opportunity Grant, Federal Pell Grant, Federal Work-Study Program, Federal Stafford Student Loan, CLAS/PLUS loan, and Cal Grants A and B. Eligibility for need-based aid is determined after the student, who must be a citizen or permanent resident of the United States, files the Free Application for Federal Student Aid (FAFSA) and the Dominican Financial Aid Application. The need-based financial aid deadline for first priority consideration is March 2, although late applications are accepted. Student assistantship positions are also available for graduate students.

Faculty

Students find themselves intellectually challenged by the faculty members, who hold degrees from colleges and universities throughout the world and who are committed to individualized teaching and careful supervision of students' development. Seventy-nine percent of Dominican University's full-time faculty members have terminal degrees (the highest obtainable degree in their field). The student-faculty ratio is 11:1.

Student Government

The primary vehicle through which students plan and provide activities, distribute activity funds, and represent themselves to the University's administration and broader community is ASDU—the Associated Students of Dominican University. ASDU is the student association and the student government body. Through elected and appointed representatives to various Dominican committees and governing groups, students may voice their opinions on institutional matters.

Admission Requirements

Dominican University of California welcomes applications from prospective students of all ages, religions, races, and national origins. The University believes that academic potential is measured by more than grades alone. Each candidate for admission is given individual consideration and is evaluated by the Admissions Office on the basis of the student's past scholastic record, present motivation, and potential intellectual development as indicated by all of the admission materials submitted.

Recommended for undergraduate admission are graduation from an accredited high school with a total of at least 15 units in college-preparatory subjects, to include the following: 4 years of English, 2 years of the same foreign language, 2 years of college-preparatory mathematics (algebra, geometry, algebra 2/trigonometry), 2 years of laboratory sciences to be taken in grades 10–12, and 1 year of U.S. history (1 year of world history or Western civilization is an acceptable alternative for international students). The University encourages students to choose additional courses in at least two of the following areas: English, history, foreign language, social science, advanced mathematics, laboratory science, music, art, and computer science.

Dominican University of California admits highly qualified students after the completion of their junior year in high school if they have fulfilled all admission requirements for freshman standing or passed an equivalency exam and arranged a conference with a member of the admission staff prior to acceptance.

High school seniors wishing to take up to two Dominican courses per semester to meet high school graduation requirements may do so with the written permission of their high school principal or counselor. Arrangements must be made through Academic Advising and Support Services.

Application and Information

The Admissions Office makes its decision on each freshman candidate after receiving his or her completed application form with a $40 nonrefundable fee; an official high school transcript to date; one recommendation from a teacher, administrator, or counselor; scores from either the SAT or the ACT; and a personal essay as described in the application. For information about the SAT, students should write to Educational Testing Service, 1947 Center Street, Berkeley, California 94704 or P.O. Box 592, Princeton, New Jersey 08541. For information about the ACT, students should write to American College Testing Program, Operations Division, P.O. Box 168, Iowa City, Iowa 52243.

Transfer students must also submit the application form, a $40 fee, and their high school transcript if they have fewer than 24 transfer units. In addition, they must send official college transcripts to date, a personal essay as described in the application, proof of high school graduation, and one academic letter of recommendation or one professional letter of reference.

International students should fulfill the admission requirements for native students; however, an SAT or ACT score is not required. Passing scores for the Test of English as a Foreign Language (TOEFL) of at least 550 paper-based or 80 Internet-based or official certification of achieving level 112 in the ELS program may be submitted in lieu of SAT or ACT scores. All transcripts must be translated into English and evaluated by an accredited evaluation agency. In addition, a notarized declaration of finances in U.S. dollars must be submitted.

An interview with a member of the admission staff is strongly recommended to enable the candidate and the University to become acquainted with one another.

Students may apply online at the Web site listed below, or they may obtain application forms and information by contacting:

Office of Admissions
Dominican University of California
50 Acacia Avenue
San Rafael, California 94901-2298
Phone: 415-485-3204
888-323-6763 (toll-free)
Fax: 415-485-3214
E-mail: enroll@dominican.edu
Web site: http://www.dominican.edu

FRESNO PACIFIC UNIVERSITY

FRESNO, CALIFORNIA

The University

Fresno Pacific University (FPU) is an independent university with a main campus in southeast Fresno and academic centers in Visalia, Bakersfield, and North Fresno. It serves about 1,400 undergraduates, 1,000 graduate students, plus thousands more in professional courses.

Academic programs prepare undergraduates for professional careers and graduate study in business, science and health, psychology, social work, teaching, communications, religious studies, and many other fields. Graduate students prepare for professional promotion and certification in business, several areas of education, and conflict resolution in organizations and communities.

The faculty is made up of experts dedicated to teaching. Most hold doctorates and publish regularly in their fields. As a Christian institution, all FPU programs emphasize the importance of values, ethics, and character development for professionals and leaders.

The University's success has been recognized nationally by such publications as *U.S. News & World Report*, which includes FPU in its top tier among Master's Universities—West.

Education at FPU is about equipping motivated students to become leaders; about developing knowledge skills and ethics that serve as tools to build successful futures. FPU does not see its job as filling students' minds with information, but helping them recognize the value of information, where to find it, and how to use it. FPU's reputation for academic excellence attracts both students and faculty members of the highest caliber.

Undergraduate enrollment has grown 60 percent in the last several years, attracting well-prepared students and reflecting the community's ethnic and cultural mosaic. The percentage of students of color in each new class is around 30 percent, while SAT scores and high school grade point averages among the top quarter of each class rival those at several University of California campuses.

On-campus living arrangements include apartments and residence halls as well as University-sponsored houses. Apartment living is available near the University. Host family arrangements can be made for international students. Students are involved in many clubs, organizations and activities. Christian growth opportunities include various settings for worship, prayer, Bible study, and discipleship training. College Hour, a three-times-a-week gathering of the campus community, offers students and faculty members a look at a variety of issues from a Christian perspective as well as the sights and sounds of cultural and artistic presentations and various worship styles.

The Sunbird athletic teams of Fresno Pacific University are members of the National Association of Intercollegiate Athletics (NAIA) and compete at the intercollegiate level in men's basketball, cross-country, soccer, and track, and women's basketball, cross-country, soccer, track, and volleyball. Baseball and tennis programs were added in 2005. Intramural sports programs for both men and women are active throughout the school year. The music department has ensembles ranging from baroque to jazz, several of which tour. A highlight of the year is Unconcert, where students stage an evening of music of their choosing. The theater program produces two full-length productions each year as well as readings and one-act plays. The campus provides convenient access for handicapped people.

The Student Life Office provides personal, job, and career counseling and information on work and service opportunities as well as other support to students.

Location

Fresno Pacific University is the only accredited, private, residential four-year university in California's Central San Joaquin Valley offering bachelor's and master's degrees. The Fresno metropolitan area has an ethnically and culturally diverse population of 500,000. Yosemite, Kings Canyon, and Sequoia National Parks; ski areas; beaches; and cultural and entertainment attractions of San Francisco and Los Angeles are all accessible from Fresno.

Majors and Degrees

Fresno Pacific University offers bachelor's degrees in more than forty areas: applied mathematics, biblical and religious studies, biology, business accounting, business finance, business information systems, business marketing management, business nonprofit administration, chemistry, child development, church music, contemporary Christian ministries, English communication, English drama, English education, English literature, English writing, environmental science, environmental studies, history, intercultural studies, international business, mathematics education, music education, music performance/composition, philosophy, physical education exercise science, physical education health fitness, political science, psychology, social science education, social work, sociology, Spanish language and culture, and teaching/liberal studies. Preprofessional programs are available in law, medicine, and physical therapy.

Academic Programs

An FPU education begins with a broad foundation exposing the student to many areas of study. From this foundation, students learn the intellectual skills necessary to begin study in a major and a minor. Fresno Pacific University operates on a two-semester plus summer academic calendar. The academic year consists of an early fall semester, which ends before the Christmas holiday, and a spring semester, which concludes in May. The minimum number of units for a Bachelor of Arts degree is 124. The General Education Program includes four courses in biblical studies and religion. FPU grants credit for certain scores on Advanced Placement tests and College-Level Examination Program (CLEP) tests.

Off-Campus Programs

The University is part of several consortia that offer international and U.S. settings for off-campus education. Study-abroad programs are available in many countries of the world, including China, Ecuador, England, France, Germany, Greece, India, Japan, Mexico, Russia, and Spain. An American studies program is available in Washington, D.C., as is a film study program in Los Angeles, California. Short-term study-abroad programs led by FPU faculty members are also available to various countries in May of each year.

Academic Facilities

Hiebert Library is owned and operated jointly with the Mennonite Brethren Biblical Seminary. There are currently well over 150,000 volumes, 2,200 journal subscriptions, 250,000 microforms, and an audiovisual collection of 10,000 items. Three computer laboratories are available to all students, where they can access word processing, e-mail, Internet, spreadsheet, database, and other software for their use in class work, research, and writing, using either MS-DOS or Macintosh equipment, including Power Macs.

Recent facilities improvements also enhance learning. A revamped Alumni Hall, dedicated in April 2005, offers a fireplace lounge, coffee bar, and expanded campus bookstore. Steinert Campus Center opened in 2003 as a place to feed the spirit as well as the body. Students and faculty members eat together in the main dining room.

AIMS Hall of Mathematics and Science is more than a great place to learn about biology, physics, chemistry, and mathematics. Its design encourages faculty and students to gather, bringing together people as well as disciplines. The building also features a 41-foot Foucault Pendulum in the lobby—one of four in California and the only one in the Central Valley.

Athletic facilities are also being expanded. The track and soccer fields are among the best in the FPU's conference, and the Harold and Betty Haak Tennis Complex was dedicated in April 2005.

Fine arts facilities are part of the campus master plan, with designs being drawn up for a building for music and drama education and performance.

Costs

The tuition for academic year 2007–08 is $21,550 and room and board are $6600. Other fees are additional.

Financial Aid

Fresno Pacific University offers a variety of federal, state, and private financial aid programs to assist students who would benefit from an education but need financial aid. Such students are encouraged to apply for assistance. More than 97 percent of FPU undergraduate students receive financial assistance in the form of loans, grants, scholarships, and on-campus employment opportunities. Merit scholarships are awarded to students based on academic achievement. Other scholarships include service/leadership, music, drama, and athletics awards. Students wishing to apply for financial aid must be accepted for admission and complete the Free Application for Federal Student Aid (FAFSA) and the FPU Financial Aid Application. California students should complete the FAFSA before the March 2 California Grant deadline and submit the Cal Grant GPA Verification Form in order to be considered for the Cal Grant program. Financial aid for international students is also available on a limited basis. International students should complete the FPU Financial Aid Application only.

Faculty

The faculty members work with students to build relationships that encourage learning. In their first semester, freshmen are matched with a group of peers led by a faculty member to ease their integration into university life. All through their time at FPU, students find most classes have 20 or fewer students.

Two faculty members recently won Fulbright Scholarships. Many other faculty members share their talents in music, art, and drama or consult with businesses and nonprofit agencies. It has been said that the common thread among these dedicated teachers is that they set high goals for students, support their efforts, and celebrate their accomplishments.

Student Government

Fresno Pacific University is committed to helping students develop character and competence in order to become effective leaders who inspire, empower, and serve others. The Undergraduate Students of Fresno Pacific University offers a variety of services, provides student representation to the University, and gives many opportunities for personal, social, spiritual, and political growth for students. Members of the Student Executive Council also serve as members of standing staff and faculty committees within the University governance structure. The Student Executive Council is composed of the following positions: president, vice president, business manager, student ministries, social affairs, commuter representative, secretary, and class senators. Appointment to these leadership roles is conducted through student body elections and personal interviews.

Admission Requirements

Fresno Pacific University welcomes students who qualify academically, who demonstrate the physical and emotional capacity for university work, and who accept the purposes and standards of the University.

Acceptance for admission as a freshman student is based on an eligibility index score determined by a formula using the high school grade point average (excluding physical education, military science, and applied courses) and the total score from either the SAT or the ACT. Applicants must also have a high school diploma or a GED.

Transfer students may bring in a maximum of 70 units of credit from an accredited postsecondary institution. To be granted admission solely on college-level academic work, a minimum of 24 transferable units must have been completed with at least a 2.4 academic GPA.

International students are valuable to Fresno Pacific University. For those seeking improvement in their English language skills, the Intensive English Language Program (IELP) offers various levels of English language instruction. Students may receive university credits for language courses or may enroll in the Language and Culture Studies Program (LCS) to receive a certificate. International students need proficient English skills in order to succeed in undergraduate studies. To study in regular undergraduate courses, students must reach a score of at least 500 (with 50 or higher on each section) on the TOEFL. SAT or ACT scores are useful in considering students for scholarships. An application file can be complete without TOEFL and SAT or ACT scores, although the University strongly recommends that they be submitted.

Application and Information

U.S. students entering directly from high school must submit an application for admission, a $40 nonrefundable application fee, official high school transcripts, SAT or ACT scores, and at least one letter of recommendation.

U.S. transfer students need to submit an application for admission, a $40 nonrefundable application fee, official transcripts from high school verifying graduation, official transcripts from each college attended, and at least one letter of recommendation. Test scores are not required, but they are recommended.

Requirements for international students include the international application form, a $40 nonrefundable application fee, certified and translated transcripts from all secondary schools and postsecondary institutions certifying academically acceptable marks/grades, a completed financial certification form, two letters of recommendation, and a TOEFL score.

For more information, students should contact:

Yammilette Rodriguez, Director of Undergraduate Admissions
Fresno Pacific University
1717 South Chestnut Avenue
Fresno, California 93702
Phone: 559-453-2039
800-660-6089 (toll-free)
E-mail: ugadmis@fresno.edu
Web site: http://www.fresno.edu

For international student information, students should contact:

International Programs and Services Office
Fresno Pacific University
1717 South Chestnut Avenue
Fresno, California 93702
Phone: 559-453-2069
Fax: 559-453-5501
E-mail: ipso@fresno.edu
Web site: http://www.fresno.edu/dept/ipso

Since 1944, Fresno Pacific University has built a reputation for strong academics and character development.

HARVEY MUDD COLLEGE
CLAREMONT, CALIFORNIA

The College

Harvey Mudd College (HMC) was founded in 1955. Its mission is to educate undergraduate men and women in a rigorous academic environment, focusing on mathematics, science, and engineering, and also to provide a rich background in the humanities and social sciences. The faculty members are eminent, experienced professionals—humanists who are aware of technological needs and engineers and scientists who have an abiding faith in liberal learning. Small classes, the excellent faculty, and exceptional students create a setting that is conducive to both teaching and learning. In addition, the style of instruction incorporates both theoretical and hands-on learning. An education at Harvey Mudd College is highly collaborative (students regularly study in groups) and research opportunities abound.

An attitude of mutual trust prevails in all aspects of campus life and is amplified by a spirit of cooperation among students and faculty members and encouraged by the student-directed honor code. Harvey Mudd students deal daily with high standards, demanding course loads, and intense pressure, but in an atmosphere void of intimidation and unreasonable competition.

The undergraduate enrollment is approximately 700 students, of whom about one third are women. In addition to the advantages that all small colleges share, Harvey Mudd has the advantage of being a part of the Claremont Colleges consortium, which has a total undergraduate enrollment of approximately 5,000. Students in the Claremont Colleges share many opportunities in course offerings (about 2,500 course offerings in an academic year), facilities, and extracurricular activities (more than 200 clubs and organizations are open to students). The cluster of adjacent colleges also offers a well-integrated social life and a rich intellectual atmosphere, supported by lectures, concerts, dramatic productions, seminars, colloquia, and festivals. Thus, Harvey Mudd students enjoy the intimate, undergraduate-focused academic experience of a small college but with the diversity of intellectual, social, and cultural opportunities afforded by a larger student body.

Harvey Mudd has a joint program of intercollegiate and intramural sports, with Claremont McKenna and Scripps Colleges (known as CMS Athletics). The varsity athletic teams compete in the Southern California Intercollegiate Athletic Conference. Varsity teams compete in basketball, cross-country, soccer, swimming, tennis, track, and water polo, plus men's baseball, football, and golf and women's volleyball, softball, and lacrosse. Intramural teams are fielded in many sports, the most popular being inner-tube water polo. There are also club sports and recreational activities indigenous to the terrain and climate of the region.

Campus activities include the national champion ballroom dance team; the ETC. Players (a dramatics group); the Forensic Society; departmental organizations; religious activities; the Symphony Orchestra and many other musical groups both instrumental and vocal (all are open-audition); the yearbook; a radio station; clubs for cultural understanding, professional organizations, or for academic competitions; and political clubs. It is very easy for students to join existing clubs or organizations, and it is common for groups of students to form new clubs, often with funding from the College. The eight residence halls tend to be the center of social life on campus. All halls are coed and house students of all class levels. Freshmen are required to live on campus, and more than 95 percent of all students typically reside on campus.

Upon graduation, more than 40 percent of Harvey Mudd's students enter graduate school, often at the nation's most prestigious universities. Virtually all of these students receive fellowships and assistantships. Those choosing to enter into the workforce are recruited heavily, often by many top national and international firms. More than 40 percent of Harvey Mudd alumni hold Ph.D.'s, the highest percentage among undergraduate colleges in the country.

Location

The town of Claremont is located at the base of Mount Baldy. The campus is approximately an hour from the ski slopes, the Pacific Coast beaches, the desert, and the center of Los Angeles, where unlimited social, sports, and cultural activities are available. The town is served by the Ontario International Airport, a 15-minute drive away. With a population of 37,000, Claremont is known throughout southern California for its active support of educational and cultural programs. Adjacent to the Claremont Colleges is Claremont Village, a friendly community featuring sidewalk cafés, specialty shops, tree-lined streets, and Victorian homes. The weather in Claremont is warm and dry, with mild winters.

Majors and Degrees

The Bachelor of Science degree is awarded in biology, chemistry, computer science, engineering (nonspecialized), mathematics, physics, plus three joint majors (biology/chemistry, computer science/mathematics, and mathematical biology). Also available are an off-campus major (at another one of the Claremont Colleges), and IPS (individual program of study). An IPS degree may be built around the College's programs and other interdisciplinary fields.

Academic Programs

The College is an autonomous member of a much larger center of learning, the Claremont Colleges. Cross-registration at the other six Claremont Colleges (Claremont Graduate University, Claremont McKenna, Keck Graduate Institute, Pitzer, Pomona, and Scripps) is encouraged. Thus, students may experience the best that each Claremont College has to offer.

Befitting an undergraduate college, classes are small and interactive. More than 80 percent of the classes have fewer than 30 students and two thirds of the classes hold fewer than 20.

Harvey Mudd students devote approximately one third of their study to a common technical core curriculum in mathematics, physics, chemistry, biology, computing, and engineering design. Approximately a third of the course work is devoted to the humanities and the social sciences, an emphasis that distinguishes HMC from almost all other technical institutions. All students must complete requirements for breadth and a "concentration" that is slightly less than a typical minor. The final third of the work is taken in the student's major, which is not declared until the middle of the sophomore year. The College uses a High Pass/Pass/No Credit grading system in the first semester of the freshman year.

Considered to be one of the best undergraduate research programs in the nation and unique in higher education, the Harvey Mudd Clinic Program provides an exceptional hands-on experience for our students. Clinic teams usually consist of 4 seniors and juniors who work together to resolve real and often interdisciplinary problems proposed by the College's corporate partners, some of the leaders in the fields of science and technology. Team members work under the direction of a student leader, a faculty member, and a liaison from a sponsoring company and are responsible for conducting the work, monitoring the project's progress, managing a budget, and following it through to satisfactory completion (deliverables). This hands-on experience has created numerous summer and full-time employment opportunities for students. More than thirty-five Clinics projects are offered annually. In 2004–05, Mudd Clinic teams filed thirteen patent applications.

A broad range of undergraduate research opportunities is available in theoretical and experimental sciences and mathematics. All students must carry out research or Clinic projects for at least one year. It is not uncommon for undergraduate students at Harvey Mudd to author or coauthor scientific papers that are published in national journals, and the majority of student researchers make presentations at academic conferences.

Academic Facilities

Classroom and laboratory facilities are modern and extensive and are available 24 hours a day. The academic buildings are within a 5-minute walk of all other facilities on campus. A computerized catalog system gives Harvey Mudd students immediate online access to all the holdings of both the Harvey Mudd library, the Seeley Mudd Science Library at Pomona College, and open-stack access to more than 2 million volumes in the library system of the seven Claremont Colleges.

Students have 24-hour access to four public laboratories housing more than seventy-five of the latest Apple Macintosh and Intel based Dell personal computers. In addition, each of the academic departments has computing facilities with the three largest belonging to the computer science, engineering, and mathematics departments. There are numerous other personal computers and workstations in the labs around the College. The campus is fully wireless with all resources attached directly to the campus network. Computer resources are also connected to the central library, the other Claremont campuses, the Internet, and Internet2. From their rooms, students can access any of these resources in addition to databases in the library, software on servers, compute cycles on supercomputers, and archives of public domain software, and they can send electronic mail and surf the Web. They can even create their own resources such as a Web server and attach it to the Net for others to access.

Physics laboratory facilities support student instruction and experimental research in astronomy, electronics, optics, condensed matter, low-temperature physics, atomic physics, nuclear physics, geophysics, and biophysics. Nearby Table Mountain Observatory is available for astronomy observation. Chemistry students conduct research in the areas of synthetic and physical chemistry, organic and inorganic chemistry, biochemistry, crystallography, and liquid crystals and are supported by extensive research instrumentation. Biology has a new confocal microscope, several distributed labs, and a biological field station. Additional facilities include apparatus for molecular biology, neurobiology, artificial intelligence, workshops for engineering design and materials science and a robotics laboratory.

Costs

The total expenses for the 2007–08 academic year are tuition and fees, $34,891, and room and board, $11,415, (sixteen-meal plan plus "flex" meals at campus cafés). The total cost is $48,006, including an estimated $1700 for personal expenses and books. Travel costs are additional.

Financial Aid

The College meets 100 percent of each student's demonstrated financial need. About 80 percent of the students at Harvey Mudd receive some type of financial aid. Scholarships, grants, loans, and work-study positions are available and awarded on the basis of financial need. Harvey Mudd College also has several merit-based scholarships and sponsors National Merit Scholarships. In a typical year, about one quarter of the freshman class includes Merit Scholars or participants in other merit award programs. All aid applicants must file the Free Application for Federal Student Aid (FAFSA) and the College Scholarship Service (CSS) Financial Aid PROFILE. California residents applying for aid must also apply for the Cal Grant.

Faculty

Harvey Mudd's student-faculty ratio is 9:1. With few exceptions, all courses, laboratories, and recitation sessions are taught by full-time faculty members with the terminal degrees in their fields. Faculty members are extremely responsive to their students and set high standards. Professors are accessible well beyond traditional office hours. The easy access to the advice and mentoring of instructors affords Mudd students unusually high levels of success competing for fellowships, graduate school appointments, and as they vie for career placements with leading corporations.

Excellence in teaching is the primary criterion for the reappointment and promotion of faculty members, but most members are also actively involved with students in research.

Student Government

Elected officers participate in the Associated Students of Harvey Mudd College Council. The Student Affairs Committee coordinates most extracurricular and social activities in conjunction with the Dorm Affairs Committee. The student Judicial Board interprets the College's constitution and enforces the honor code. More than 10 percent of the student body is involved in some form of student government.

There are more than 200 leadership positions available to a student body of only 700. This endows students with many opportunities to develop their personal skills, and, because HMC also has a superior academic program, its graduates often gravitate into leadership positions later in life.

Admission Requirements

The quality and number of courses taken and the grades that were earned in secondary school are the most important components of a candidate's application. To be competitive for admission, candidates must excel in a rigorous college-preparatory program, with a heavy emphasis on mathematics and science. Students interested in attending Harvey Mudd must take at least 1 year each of chemistry, physics, and calculus or a college equivalent course. Even though the major thrust of Harvey Mudd's program is in mathematics and science, particular attention is focused on a student's proven talents in English and communication skills. Typical candidates have taken several Advanced Placement (AP) or International Baccalaureate (IB) or even college-level courses; however, candidates who have not had the opportunity to take enriched courses are given every consideration and should not hesitate to apply.

Students must submit scores from either the SAT or the ACT, with writing exams, and must also submit at least two SAT Subject Tests. One of these SAT Subject Tests must be Mathematics Level 2. Because Harvey Mudd desires a multidimensional student body, serious consideration is given to an applicant's extracurricular and leadership activities. Interviews are not required, but a personal interview is strongly recommended and can influence a final decision. Teacher and counselor recommendations are essential to the admission decision.

Admission is highly competitive. For fall 2007, 2493 candidates applied for admission to a freshman class limited to approximately 185 students. Of the typical entering freshman class, 40 percent are from California. Approximately 25 percent are National Merit Scholars, about 25 percent are valedictorians, and about 90 percent rank in the top 10 percent of their graduating high school class. Enrolling students in the middle 50 percent (from the 25th percentile to the 75th percentile) achieved SAT scores ranging from 690 to 760 on the critical reading section, from 680 to 760 on the writing section, and from 740 to 800 on the math section. The middle range on the Mathematics Level 2 SAT Subject test varied from 750 to 800. An average ACT composite score is 32.

Application and Information

Early decision candidates must complete their application by November 15; notification is mailed by December 15. The postmark deadline for regular applications is January 15. Applicants for regular decision are notified April 1.

Thyra Briggs
Vice President and Dean of Admission and Financial Aid
Harvey Mudd College
301 Platt Boulevard
Claremont, California 91711
Phone: 909-621-8011
Fax: 909-607-7046
E-mail: admission@hmc.edu

LAGUNA COLLEGE OF ART & DESIGN

LAGUNA BEACH, CALIFORNIA

The College

Laguna College of Art & Design (LCAD) has redefined the modern college of art and design. Art school is no longer a place to learn just the theories behind what makes art and design work; LCAD also teaches specific skills with tangible outcomes. It is committed to maintaining the highest educational standards while helping artists and designers reach their full creative potential. A balanced and fortified curriculum ensures that graduates are destined to succeed and lead in the many fields of art and design. LCAD is accredited by the National Association of Schools of Art and Design and the Western Association of Schools and Colleges.

What makes the College such an inspirational place is its location. In the early 1900s, artists, intellectuals, and entertainers began making a thriving cultural community of scenic Laguna Beach. Plein air painters like Edgar Payne and Anna Hills founded the Laguna Beach Art Association, and this once-sleepy little town fast gained a reputation as a vibrant hub of visual arts. Today, Laguna Beach still offers the beauty and tranquility that have inspired artists for over a century, making it an idyllic setting for the artists of tomorrow.

LCAD has a number of programs to help students succeed in their studies. The most unique of these is the Laptop Program, which requires all students to own an Apple laptop. Students benefit by having wireless access throughout the campus and community; the ability to work at home or on campus; access to special workshops, which provide additional computer training; reduced prices on peripherals; and on-site, full-time technical support. In addition to the students' laptop computers, there are more than 250 computers on campus, with every lab equipped with G5s.

In addition to its undergraduate programs, Laguna College of Art & Design offers a Master of Fine Arts program with a special emphasis in representational/figurative art.

Location

Laguna Beach is a unique beach community and artist's colony with 7 miles of beaches running along its 9 square miles. Residents enjoy the ambiance provided by sandy beaches, canyons, and coastal hills. Several million visitors arrive every summer to enjoy the picturesque beaches and art festivals and the Pageant of the Masters. Laguna's village-scale shopping district, blufftop walkways, and tram system create a pedestrian environment that is unique in the region. Located an hour south of Los Angeles and an hour north of San Diego, Laguna Beach is in a perfect, centralized location to access the major metropolitan art scenes of Southern California.

Majors and Degrees

Laguna College of Art & Design offers two Bachelor of Fine Arts (B.F.A.) programs. The fine arts program offers a variety of electives in drawing and painting and in sculpture/printmaking in addition to its core courses. The program in visual communications includes majors in animation, graphic design, and illustration.

Academic Programs

The Foundation Program is designed to develop an in-depth understanding of art and life, drawing relevant connections between the social and physical worlds in which the visual artist communicates. Foundation requires six courses and is followed by an introduction to the student's major. For the first two semesters, the student is exposed to painting, drawing, illustration, and graphic design in a unique interdisciplinary curriculum. The final year focuses on assisting students in preparing for a career in the field of their choice.

The liberal arts program (30 units) ensures that each student is a competent communicator, capable of writing and speaking English with clarity, accuracy, and depth. At the core of the course work is a comprehensive curriculum of art history that not only enables students to discover the rich artistic traditions of the world but also to explore the specialized fields of each major.

The fine arts major has nineteen required courses (53 units) and a variety of electives in drawing and painting and in sculpture/printmaking. Majors in visual communications include feature animation (nineteen required courses plus electives), graphic design (seventeen required courses plus electives), and illustration (seventeen required courses plus electives).

The academic year, consisting of two semesters, typically begins in mid- to late August with a new student orientation. Classes start during the last week in August and continue until mid-December, at which time winter holiday begins. The spring semester begins in mid-January and continues until early in May. Students also have a weeklong spring break in mid-March.

Off-Campus Programs

The College keeps history alive through field trips and summer programs that offer opportunities for direct experiences with major world art, from local and regional museums and galleries to the hills of Cezanne and the far-off digs of ancient Greece.

Academic Facilities

The Ruth Salyer Library offers a wealth of visual resources that serve to keep it in the vanguard of documenting the contemporary art scene. The library offers free Internet access and contains approximately 15,000 volumes, exhibition catalogs, museum and gallery publications, CD-ROMs, and a file for local art news and art competitions. It subscribes to more than seventy periodicals.

Costs

In 2006–07, tuition was $9300 per academic semester for full-time students and $775 per unit ($2325 per 3-unit course) for part-time students enrolling in less than 12 units.

The College does not provide campus housing, but the Student Housing Coordinator can assist students in finding affordable housing during their program. Depending on apartment size and location, students can expect to pay at least $500 per month for a shared apartment, $1100 or more for one bedroom, and $1300 and above for two bedrooms.

Financial Aid

To receive financial aid, students must submit a Free Application for Federal Student Aid (FAFSA) and remain in good academic standing. The Cal Grant program awards between

$1000 and $9300 annually to students who maintain a minimum 2.5 GPA and enroll in at least 9 units each semester. The deadline to apply is March 2.

Students may also be eligible to receive a Federal Pell Grant or a Federal Supplemental Educational Opportunity Grant. Educational Assistance awards from the Department of Veterans Affairs are available for veterans and children of deceased or disabled veterans. Private scholarships and grants may be available from the College or other sources.

Several federal loan programs are available to students who cannot otherwise cover the full cost of college. The Stafford Subsidized Loan allows students to borrow up to $23,000 over four years. The Stafford Unsubsidized Loan provides loans of up to $23,000 over four years to independent students and, in special circumstances, dependent undergraduate students. The Parent Loan for Undergraduate Students serves as a supplemental source of money to parents of students. Alternative loans are available for students who have received the maximum award amounts under other loans programs but who require additional funding.

Some students participate in the Federal Work-Study Program, which provides funds in exchange for part-time employment on campus.

Faculty

The College's faculty members are leading figures in their fields, and they strive to create an atmosphere that nurtures the artistic and personal growth of students. Approximately 45 faculty members teach at the College, and many have academic training in their respective fields. The student-faculty ratio is about 10:1.

Admission Requirements

To be admitted to the College, a student must be a high school graduate or equivalent, with demonstrated artistic talent and above-average performance in academic subjects. Prospective students must submit a completed application, official high school transcripts, official SAT or ACT scores, and a portfolio containing twelve images of the student's most recent work. Advanced Placement test scores of 4 or 5 are considered for transfer credit in liberal arts. Campus visits are encouraged but not required.

Application and Information

Although LCAD accepts applications on a rolling basis, students are encouraged to apply early to secure their place in the intended semester. Priority is given to candidates who submit their applications before February 2 (July 1 for admission in the spring). Applicants receive written notification of their admission within three weeks of submitting all application materials. A nonrefundable tuition deposit of $250 is due no later than May 1 for fall semester and January 2 for spring semester.

For more information about the College, students should contact:

Laguna College of Art & Design
2222 Laguna Canyon Road
Laguna Beach, California 92651
Phone: 949-376-6000
800-255-0762 (toll-free)
Fax: 276-944-6935
Web site: http://www.lagunacollege.edu

On the campus of Laguna College of Art & Design.

LOYOLA MARYMOUNT UNIVERSITY

LOS ANGELES, CALIFORNIA

The University

Loyola Marymount University (LMU), situated on a picturesque campus, offers competitive students an education of high quality in a friendly and relaxed atmosphere. As successor to the oldest institution of learning in southern California, St. Vincent's College, the University is steeped in a tradition and history of dedication to academic excellence and the total development of its students. Although the emphasis is within the undergraduate school (full-time enrollment is approximately 5,440 and part-time enrollment is approximately 145), approximately 1,800 students attend the Graduate Division, primarily in the evening hours, working toward master's degrees in the fields of arts, arts in teaching, business administration, education, and science (including engineering). The Ed.D. in educational leadership for social justice is offered by the School of Education. The School of Law, situated at a separate campus, has both day and evening divisions and offers the Juris Doctor degree. Law school enrollment is approximately 1,370.

Sixty-one percent of the undergraduate students live on campus and are able to choose accommodations in one of twelve residential halls or six apartment complexes. Students have access to a sports pavilion, one swimming pool, baseball and soccer fields, tennis and volleyball courts, and four indoor racquetball courts. A new recreation center includes three additional courts and a fitness center. LMU fields teams in eleven intercollegiate sports (baseball, basketball, crew, cross-country, golf, soccer, softball, swimming, tennis, women's volleyball, and water polo) and has club teams in lacrosse, rugby, men's volleyball, and more. More than 2,000 undergraduate students participate in the active intramural program, which includes coed sports. Student organizations include the AM/FM radio station (KXLU), Chemistry Society, Black Students Union, Han Tao Chinese Cultural Club, MEChA, Business Law Society, Student-Athlete Advisory Committee, University choruses, fraternities and sororities, and various honor and service groups. LMU's Debate Team and Air Force ROTC detachment have received national recognition in their respective areas.

Location

LMU is ideally located on a 152-acre mesa that overlooks the southwest section of Los Angeles and the Pacific Ocean from Malibu to Santa Monica. The campus is close to the beach, and the University community enjoys a cool, clean coastal climate. LMU is near the metropolitan complex, but it has the benefits of the slower pace of its residential community, Westchester. Los Angeles International Airport is 10 minutes away, and nearby freeways provide easy access to the city and its cultural and recreational activities.

Majors and Degrees

Loyola Marymount University offers the B.A. in the fields of African American studies, animation, art history, Asian Pacific studies, biology, Chicano studies, classical civilizations, classics, communication studies, dance, economics, English, European studies, film and television production, French, Greek, history, humanities, Latin, liberal studies (elementary education), mathematics, music, philosophy, political science, psychology, recording arts, screenwriting, sociology, Spanish, studio arts, theater arts, theology, urban studies, and women's studies. The College of Business Administration offers the Bachelor of Science degree in accounting and the Bachelor of Business Administration degree with emphases in business law, computer information systems and operations management, finance, international business, management, marketing, and tourism and travel. The College of Science and Engineering offers bachelor's degrees in applied mathematics, athletic training, biochemistry, biology, chemistry, computer science, engineering (civil, electrical, and mechanical), engineering physics, environmental science, mathematics, natural science, and physics. Areas of emphasis can include such fields as computer engineering and marine biology.

Academic Programs

While premajor and major requirements differ with each area of study, a core curriculum is maintained as a degree requirement in the fields of American cultures, college writing, communication skills, creative and critical arts, history, literature, mathematics/science/technology, philosophy, social science, and theology, thus ensuring each student a balanced education. The maximum requirement in each of the core fields is 6 units of academic work. The interdepartmental honors program provides challenges for the exceptional student.

The academic calendar consists of two semesters and a six-week optional summer session. The fall semester begins in late August and ends before Christmas. The spring semester usually begins in mid-January and ends in mid-May. Students may earn credit through Advanced Placement (AP) examinations. In addition, it is possible for students to earn credit by examination for any course offered by LMU.

Off-Campus Programs

Students who are interested in studying abroad have a choice of several University-sponsored programs. LMU offers programs in Africa, Australia, China, England, France, Germany, Greece, Guatemala, Honduras, India, Ireland, Italy, Japan, Mexico, New Zealand, the Philippines, South Korea, and Spain. The University also has numerous affiliated programs, including the Rome Center of Loyola University Chicago and the American Institute for Foreign Study. Choice of programs is made on the basis of the student's interest and ability or skill. Courses may be conducted in English, the language of the country in which the student elects to study, or both. In addition, LMU offers internship programs through which students can earn course credit for independent study that has been approved by the dean of the college in which the student is enrolled. The programs range from student involvement in political campaigns to the counseling of underrepresented youths to professional work at film/TV studios.

Academic Facilities

The Charles Von der Ahe Library contains the undergraduate and graduate research library collections, which total approximately 500,000 books and bound periodicals, 140,000 microforms, 18,000 electronic journals, 130 databases, 36,000 electronic books, and nearly 40,000 audiovisual items. Among the special collections are materials on St. Thomas More, Oliver Goldsmith, Spanish culture and civilization, and German and American philosophy. The library provides carrels for individual study, small group study rooms, and small group showing rooms for video and audio. In summer 2009, LMU will open the new William H. Hannon Library. The Law School Library, located within the School of Law in downtown Los Angeles, contains more than 560,000 volumes and microforms and is a depository for government documents of the state of California and the United States. It also has complete holdings of all publications relating to California law. All students have at their disposal an

IBM 360/30 computer that is equipped to program five languages. The communication arts complex houses the Louis B. Mayer Motion Picture Theatre, a full-size color-television studio, a motion-picture soundstage, and state-of-the-art industry equipment. Strub Theatre offers excellent theatrical facilities for the performing arts of drama and dance.

Costs

Tuition for the 2007–08 academic year was $31,168. The cost of room and board varies with options that students select—for example, a full- or partial-meal plan, an apartment on campus, or a residence hall. However, the average yearly cost is approximately $10,000. Students should expect to spend about $1360 for books and supplies and $1585 for additional miscellaneous expenses.

Financial Aid

Approximately 70 percent of the University's undergraduate students receive some type of financial assistance. The total amount of financial aid awarded to students for the 2007–08 academic year was approximately $98 million. Students applying for aid must file the Free Application for Federal Student Aid (FAFSA) and the CSS Financial Aid PROFILE. All students are expected to apply for the Federal Pell Grant, and California residents must apply for the California grants. Most aid is awarded on the basis of need, but the University does offer merit scholarships (including full-tuition scholarships). The priority date for financial aid is February 15. Aid is awarded after that date on a funds-available basis.

Faculty

LMU's faculty is dedicated to undergraduate teaching and is easily accessible to students. Ninety percent of the faculty members hold a Ph.D. in their area of instruction.

Student Government

The University believes that active student input is an essential part of the undergraduate years. Students sit on every University committee, including the Board of Trustees, with full voting rights. Students operate the campus recreation centers, manage the dormitories as resident advisers, operate a used-book store, and serve as advisers to their academic departments. Student actions have resulted in the development of such things as a campus recreation center, the water polo team, and the complete semester calendar.

Admission Requirements

Admission to LMU is selective, and a candidate is expected to present a better-than-average record in college-preparatory courses. Minimal achievement and limited preparation narrow the candidate's chances for acceptance into the University and into specific programs. In determining an applicant's eligibility, the University gives careful consideration to the student's academic preparation, national test scores, letters of recommendation, extracurricular activities, and family relationships to the University. A personal interview is not required but is recommended if it is convenient. Prospective candidates are always welcome to visit the campus, and personal tours can be arranged on request. Students who, for academic reasons, were not accepted for admission as freshmen may be considered for admission to advanced standing if they have completed at least the equivalent of 30 semester hours of transferable college work with at least a B average.

Application and Information

Applicants must submit official transcripts from the last high school attended and from each college attended, arrange for SAT or ACT scores to be sent to the Office of Admissions, submit a recommendation form from an official of the last school attended, and file an application with the $50 nonrefundable fee. Applications are considered when all necessary documents have been received prior to the deadline of the semester for which application is made. The priority deadline for freshman applicants for the fall semester is November 1 for Early Notification and January 15 for Regular Decision. Early Notification applicants receive a decision by December 20. The deadline for transfer applicants for the fall semester is March 15. For the spring semester for both freshman and transfer students, the priority deadline is October 15.

International students who are not legal residents of the United States must follow the same admission procedure but are also required to submit scores from the Test of English as a Foreign Language (TOEFL) and a statement of financial responsibility for all obligations covering the full period of time for which the student is making application. All records of previous academic training must be original or authentic copies with notarization and have notarized English translations.

For more information about Loyola Marymount University, prospective students should contact:

Matthew X. Fissinger
Director of Admissions
Loyola Marymount University
1 LMU Drive
Los Angeles, California 90045
Phone: 310-338-2750
800-LMU-INFO (toll-free)
Fax: 310-338-2797

Between classes at Loyola Marymount University.

MENLO COLLEGE

ATHERTON, CALIFORNIA

The College

Menlo College, an independent, coeducational, nonsectarian institution, stands out among institutions of higher education in five exciting ways: programs, location, small size, sports, and alumni. Rather than offer a traditional set of majors as many institutions do, Menlo concentrates on providing excellent programs in business management, liberal arts, and mass communication. Menlo's location in the heart of the Silicon Valley allows the College to train tomorrow's leaders in an intimate, student-centered, academically challenging environment. The College is small enough to be a real community but large enough to support a wide array of intercollegiate sports, student organizations, and internship opportunities, giving students the confidence and breadth of experience to flourish after graduation. The College's distinguished alumni provide a strong base of support for graduates, which helps students make the transition from college to career with great success.

A Menlo education is a process that trains and cultivates leaders. This process begins with a broad-based liberal arts foundation in the humanities, mathematics, sciences, and social sciences. At the same time, students are also challenged to enrich and develop their writing, critical-thinking, and decision-making skills. Next, students enter rich major programs staffed with seasoned practitioners who are experts in their respective fields. The advantage is a cutting-edge curriculum that equips students to succeed. Menlo's superior business program is renowned throughout the world and has produced generations of dynamic and successful business, industrial, and civic leaders around the globe.

The learning process does not end in the classroom. Students are encouraged to participate in internships and study programs that bridge the gap between theory and practice. These opportunities range from Fortune 500 companies to innovative start-up enterprises, from San Francisco to South America, Asia, and Europe. Not only do participants gain hands-on experience, but also they grow personally as they encounter diverse peoples, cultures, and values.

As a whole, College-sponsored activities promote self-exploration and often lead to the discovery of hidden talents. Students can participate in a variety of clubs or organizations, ranging from the Alpha Chi National Honor Society and the Poetry, Art, and Music Society to the Menlo Oak Newspaper and the Outdoor Club. Leadership skills are cultivated through an activist student government and student life positions and special workshops that tackle pressing contemporary issues. In addition, Menlo's international exchange programs offer students opportunities to expand their horizons and bring global awareness to their futures.

This commitment to personal and intellectual growth, coupled with Menlo's ideal location in a major metropolitan area, draws students from all across the United States and around the world. The global village is a reality at Menlo, given the broad social, religious, cultural, and national makeup of the student body. The appreciation of different cultures that results becomes a tremendous advantage in the marketplace.

Menlo's warm, friendly atmosphere is enhanced by its residential status. Nearly two thirds of all students live in one of five residence halls. Nearby off-campus apartments (for students who are older than 21 or married) are also an option.

For those who enjoy the exhilaration of intercollegiate competition, Menlo offers men's baseball, basketball, cross-country, football, golf, soccer, and wrestling, and women's sports include basketball, cross-country, soccer, softball, volleyball, and wrestling. The College competes in the NAIA Pacific Conference and the NCAA Division III. Intramural sports are also popular, and altogether almost 40 percent of students participate in sports.

To meet students' health needs, the College provides care via the Menlo Medical Clinic. Counseling services are offered by faculty and resident life staff members.

Whether in the classroom, in the laboratory, or on the playing field, Menlo College nurtures students by creating programs, activities, and services that foster individual success.

Location

Menlo College is located on the San Francisco peninsula in the town of Atherton, a residential community near the cities of Menlo Park and Palo Alto. Major freeways do not pass near the campus, nor is heavy industry nearby. The area ranks among the most attractive and exciting in the world, with numerous cultural resources and a temperate climate. San Francisco lies 30 miles to the north. Many other important educational centers are within an hour's drive of Menlo, making the area an exciting place in which to study and live. To the south is Silicon Valley, where high-tech companies in the electronics, computer, aerospace, biotechnology, and pharmaceutical industries are literally transforming the world in which we live and work. Surrounding the San Francisco Bay Area is the great natural beauty of northern California, extending from the spectacular California coast to the majestic Sierra Nevada Mountains. Favorite spots such as Big Sur, Monterey Bay, Lake Tahoe, Napa Valley, and Yosemite National Park are just a few hours' drive from Menlo.

Majors and Degrees

Menlo College offers a Bachelor of Science degree program in business management, with concentrations in general business management, international management, management information systems, marketing communication, and sports management. The Bachelor of Arts degree is offered in the field of mass communication, with concentrations in marketing communication, media management, and media studies, and in the field of liberal arts, with concentrations in history, humanities, and psychology.

Academic Programs

Menlo College operates on a semester calendar. To earn a bachelor's degree, students must complete 124 units of credit and maintain good academic standing.

The business management major provides a comprehensive management education based on a rigorous core modeled after M.B.A. curricula.

The mass communication major gives students a broad understanding of communication processes through a carefully selected core curriculum. Students are encouraged to pursue their studies with managerial and leadership goals in mind.

The liberal arts major affords an interdisciplinary foundation and the intellectual essence of the management curriculum while integrating the humanities and social sciences.

Menlo's renowned Philler Curtis Program and the Academic Success Center provide dynamic resources for increasing students' academic ability and morale. Included are innovative approaches to individual counseling, tutoring, and developmental courses. The goal is to develop strong self-advocacy and to assist faculty members in meeting the needs of a varied student population using an assortment of individualized, small-group, and computer-based instruction. This method facilitates study and discussion of course material, tutoring, and test preparation.

Off-Campus Programs

The difference between obtaining an exciting professional position with opportunity for advancement and growth and settling for second best often comes down to experience. Internships enable students to apply theory to practice—to take classroom knowledge and test its relevancy. Through the Career Services Office and each academic department, qualified students are urged to participate in local, national, or international internships. Students spend one or more semesters working on or off campus in their fields of study obtaining academic credit and/or financial compensation and valuable insight. Menlo also has exchange agreements with Francisco de Vitoria University in Madrid, Spain; Peking University, in Beijing, China; Anáhuac University, in Mexico City; Universidad Adolfo Ibanez in Chile; Guangdong College of Business in Guangzhou, China; and with Kansai Gaidai University in Japan.

Academic Facilities

Bowman Library maintains a strong collection of books and periodicals, including electronic journals, books, and AV materials. The Bowman Library's Electronic Information Gateway provides access to general and specialized online research databases, including full-text periodicals and reference resources as well as high-speed access to the Internet and World Wide Web. The Bowman Library contains rooms for group study, viewing AV materials, and photocopying. In addition, wireless access to the campus network resources is available through the library's laptop computer checkout program.

The Resource for Online Services and Information Electronically (ROSIE) is Menlo College's electronic information gateway, providing access 24 hours a day, seven days a week through the Web from the library, dorms, and off-campus sites to the online catalog, electronic research databases, and reference assistance. For more information, students should visit http://www.menlo.edu/library. ROSIE also provides access to WOODIE, the online research-skills tutorial required of all students through the Menlo College General Education curriculum.

Menlo College's four computer labs provide students with access to state-of-the-art PC and Macintosh hardware, software, and networking capabilities. All computer-lab equipment is connected to the campus network as well as the Internet and World Wide Web. Classroom labs include both individual workstations and presentation facilities. The Open Access lab is open daily and is staffed by experienced monitors who are familiar with all lab equipment and applications and are able to provide students with the best possible technical and instructional services. With a 5:1 student-computer ratio, Menlo College offers students ample access to a wide range of computing resources for both classroom assignments and personal use.

Costs

Tuition and fees for 2007–08 are $27,950. Residence costs, including room and board, are $9980.

Financial Aid

Menlo is noted for a strong program of merit and need-based aid. Approximately 80 percent of Menlo's students enroll with financial assistance, including Menlo scholarships, achievement awards, and on-campus employment as well as Federal Pell Grants, Federal Stafford Student Loans, State of California Grants, Federal PLUS loans, and others. Students transferring to Menlo are fully eligible to be considered for financial aid. Merit scholarships of up to $12,000 per year are available for both domestic and international students.

Faculty

Menlo's faculty members devote their full attention to teaching. The College faculty is composed of approximately 60 members, both full- and part-time. Guest lecturers from business, industry, and other professions add to the breadth of instruction. Faculty members are readily available to give students personal help and counseling. A student-teacher ratio of 15:1 allows for small classes and individual attention to students' progress.

Student Government

Students elect their own representatives to student government, which is responsible for legislative and executive decisions affecting student activities and the coordination of student affairs. At Menlo, students take the lead in shaping their education and the future of their College.

Admission Requirements

The Admission Committee considers each candidate individually, through the assessment of academic achievement and personal qualities, talents, and interests. There is an early action plan for entering freshmen, and transfer students are welcome. Applicants are evaluated on the basis of their academic record, course of study, personal recommendations, school activities, essay, and scores on either the SAT or ACT. A personal visit is strongly recommended but not required. The College looks for freshmen with both breadth and depth of academic background in college preparatory subjects. Transfer students are evaluated on the strength of their college programs. Applicants are considered without regard to age, race, color, creed, gender, sexual orientation, national origin, marital status, disability, or any other characteristic protected by law.

Application and Information

Students may enter Menlo College at the opening of the fall or spring semester. Application deadlines are: early action deadline, December 1; priority deadline for freshmen, February 1 for fall and November 1 for spring; and priority deadline for transfers, April 1. For further information concerning admission, students should contact:

Office of Admission
Menlo College
1000 El Camino Real
Atherton, California 94027-4301
Phone: 650-543-3753
800-55-MENLO (toll-free)
Fax: 650-543-4496
E-mail: admissions@menlo.edu
Web site: http://www.menlo.edu

MILLS COLLEGE
OAKLAND, CALIFORNIA

The College

For more than 150 years, Mills College has shaped women's lives. Offering a progressive liberal arts curriculum taught by a nationally renowned faculty, Mills gives students the personal attention that leads to extraordinary learning. Through intensive, collaborative study in a community of forward-thinking individuals, students gain the ability to make their voices heard, the strength to risk bold visions, an eagerness to experiment, and a desire to change the world.

Nestled on 135 lush acres in the heart of the San Francisco Bay Area, Mills College is a hidden gem. Its idyllic setting might—at first glance—belie the pulse of activity that beats within its gates. As many have discovered, Mills is home to one of the most dynamic, creative liberal arts educations available to women today.

Historically a college for women only, Mills continues that proud tradition today at the undergraduate level. To provide enhanced professional opportunities for all students, Mills also offers renowned graduate programs that are open to both women and men. Ranked one of the top colleges in the West by *U.S. News & World Report,* Mills is also one of the top 50 colleges for African Americans according to *Black Enterprise* magazine.

Inspired by a teaching philosophy that grows out of a long-standing dedication to women's education, Mills provides a collaborative, interactive learning environment that encourages intellectual exploration and self-discovery. The faculty of nationally and internationally respected scholars and artists is dedicated to developing the strengths of every student, preparing them for lifelong intellectual, personal, and professional growth. With an impressive student-teacher ratio of 11:1, Mills women are assured of access to and support from these inspiring and committed professors. The hallmark of a Mills education is the collaboration between dedicated students and distinguished faculty members that goes beyond the classroom and into meaningful work and innovative research.

In addition to exercising their minds, Mills students also compete in seven intercollegiate sports—cross-country, rowing, soccer, swimming, tennis, track and field, and volleyball—as members of the National Collegiate Athletic Association (NCAA) Division III. Students may also participate in recreational activity courses for credit or take advantage of the on-campus fitness facilities and off-campus activity excursions. Mills offers the Bachelor of Science (B.S.) degree in biochemistry and molecular biology, biology, biopsychology, chemistry, environmental science, and mathematics. Mills also provides the first two years of courses leading to a bachelor of science in nursing degree from Samuel Merritt College.

Location

Located in the foothills of Oakland, California, on the east shore of the San Francisco Bay, Mills offers students access to the diverse metropolitan centers that make up the greater Bay Area. Amid the green rolling hills and the century-old eucalyptus trees of the Mills campus, students find a great place to live and learn, with new friends and new ideas at every turn. The campus is heavily accented with Mediterranean-style buildings, many designed by architectural innovator Julia Morgan. Paths and streams wind their way through tree groves and meadows that pervade the 135-acre wooded campus.

Outside the campus gates, students have access to the dynamic Bay Area, with Berkeley, San Francisco, Napa, and Silicon Valley nearby. Drawing energy from the College's location, Mills students connect with centers of learning, business, and technology; pursue research and internship opportunities; and explore the Bay Area's many sources of cultural, social, and recreational enrichment.

Majors and Degrees

With more than forty different majors at Mills to choose from, students find themselves active, engaged participants in their own learning. Students have the chance to work directly with nationally and internationally renowned faculty members and get involved in their innovative work and research.

Mills offers the Bachelor of Arts (B.A.) degree in American studies; anthropology and sociology; art (history and studio); biochemistry and molecular biology; biology; biopsychology; business economics; chemistry; child development; comparative literature; computer science; dance; economics; English (creative writing and literature); environmental science; environmental studies; ethnic studies; French and Francophone studies; government; history; intermedia arts; international relations; Latin American studies; literary and cultural studies; mathematics; music; philosophy; political, legal, and economic analysis; psychology; public policy; sociology; Spanish and Spanish-American studies; and women's studies. The major in child development meets the requirements for a state child development permit for teaching in preschool and day-care centers and provides a strong basis for graduate school and for many other careers. Special prelaw and premedicine advising is available.

Mills offers the Bachelor of Science (B.S.) degree in biochemistry and molecular biology, biology, biopsychology, chemistry, environmental science, and mathematics. Mills also provides the first two years of courses leading to a Bachelor of Science in nursing degree from Samuel Merritt College.

Students can also choose to create their own major, working with 3 faculty advisers to plan an individual program that draws courses from across the curriculum and creates an integrated and unique educational experience.

Mills offers seven dual-degree programs that enable undergraduates with clear career goals in certain fields to streamline their college and graduate school programs. These include the 4+1 B.A./M.B.A. Business Administration Program, the 4+1 B.A./M.P.P. Public Policy Program, the 4+1 B.A./M.A. Infant Mental Health Program, the 4+1 B.A./M.A. Interdisciplinary Computer Science Program, the 3+2 B.A./B.S. Engineering Program, the integrated 4+1 B.A./M.A. Mathematics Program, and the newest program, the 4+1 B.A./M.A./Credential Program in Teacher Education.

Academic Programs

To earn a Mills bachelor's degree, students complete 34 semester course credits (usually four courses each semester). Grading is traditional, and a pass-fail option is available outside the major.

The innovative general education program is guided by a set of learning outcomes, not a generic list of required courses. Each student designs her own program with the guidance of her faculty adviser, ensuring that a Mills education is tailored to the student's specific needs and interests. The program places the work a student does in her major in a larger context and ensures that she explores and appreciates realms of knowledge beyond her field. The general education requirements fall into three outcome categories: skills (written communication, quantitative and computational reasoning, and information literacy/information technology skills), perspectives (interdisciplinary, women and gender, and multicultural), and disciplinary experiences (creation and criticism in the arts, historical perspectives, natural sciences, and human institutions and behavior).

Career Services offers a four-year counseling program to assist students in clarifying their career and life goals. Workshops, individual counseling sessions, an extensive internship program, a strong alumnae network, and special opportunities to meet Bay Area business leaders and top professional women in every field all help students to focus their interests and plan career goals.

Off-Campus Programs

Mills has exchange or visiting programs with eleven American colleges and universities, including American, Barnard, Manhattanville, Mount Holyoke, Spelman, Swarthmore, Wellesley, and Wheaton.

Adventurous students with a GPA of at least 3.0 may study abroad. With programs in Europe, Africa, South America, Asia, and Australia—in nearly every country in the world—Mills encourages students to study abroad. Students receiving financial aid may continue to do so while studying with an approved program. Mills also has exchange programs with universities in Hong Kong and South Korea.

Sophomores, juniors, and seniors may cross-register for one course per semester at the following schools: Berkeley City College; California College of the Arts; California State University, East Bay; Chabot College; City College of San Francisco; College of Alameda; Contra Costa College; Diablo Valley College; Graduate Theological Union; Holy Names University; Laney College; Merritt College; St. Mary's College of California; Skyline College; Sonoma State University; and University of California, Berkeley.

Academic Facilities

The beautiful, open-stack, computerized F. W. Olin Library attracts students to study as well as research among its 234,972 volumes and 24,370 rare books and manuscripts. A Web-based catalog and more than 60 databases, including Academic Search, LexisNexis, PsycInfo, and ProQuest Research Library, are available 24 hours a day via the library's Web site. The academic computer center, electronic music studio, and excellent laboratory facilities in the physical and life sciences are widely used by students in all majors. The highly regarded Children's School provides a daily laboratory for students preparing for careers in early childhood education. Lisser Hall contains a flexible proscenium stage as well as a small experimental theater. The Mills College Art Museum is a wonderful resource, with its collection of more than 8,000 works of art, the largest permanent collection of any liberal arts college on the West Coast.

Costs

In 2007–08, tuition was $32,542 and room and board were $10,820. Health insurance, a comprehensive fee covering such items as van shuttle service and technology, and associated student fees totaled $2898 for resident and commuting students. Students should calculate the costs of travel, books, and personal expenses on an individual basis.

Financial Aid

Mills College is committed to ensuring that a Mills education is within reach for those who have the desire and the qualifications to attend. Financial aid options at Mills include grants and scholarships, loans, and student employment. Some are funded by Mills directly, and others are state and federal programs.

In fall 2007, more than 80 percent of undergraduates at the College received some type of financial assistance in the form of grants, scholarships, loans, or on-campus employment. Eighty-nine percent of Mills students received some portion of their aid directly from Mills. Awards are based on need and academic merit. Scholarship grants range from $1000 per year to full tuition. Mills makes a special effort to provide financial aid to all students who demonstrate need.

Financial aid applicants are expected to complete the Free Application for Federal Student Aid (FAFSA). The FAFSA is required for non-Mills aid, such as the Federal Pell Grant, FSEOG, Academic Competitiveness Grant, and the Federal SMART Grant. For California residents, the FAFSA is required along with the Cal Grant GPA Verification Form to determine eligibility for a Cal Grant. More than 40 percent of Mills students have some of their determined need offset by such non-Mills awards. Loans may be obtained by most students, and approximately 35 percent of undergraduates are offered campus work opportunities.

All first-year students and transfer candidates must file the Free Application for Federal Student Aid (FAFSA) to be considered for all types of government aid, and California residents must also file the Cal Grant GPA Verification Form. Students who seek Mills need-based scholarship funds must also file the Mills Financial Aid Form. Priority is given to applicants who meet the published deadlines.

Faculty

More than 60 percent of the Mills faculty members are women, enabling students to work with professional women mentors in every academic area. Faculty members are selected for their teaching ability and scholarly achievement; 87 percent of full-time faculty members hold the highest degrees in their fields. Twenty-six percent of the full-time faculty members and 23 percent of the part-time faculty are members of minority groups.

Student Government

An important goal of an education at Mills is to develop leadership skills, and participating in student government can be instrumental in furthering this goal. The Associated Students of Mills College (ASMC) is run by an executive board of fifteen elected or appointed positions. Under the governance of a student-drafted Constitution, the board supports student organizations, student publications, campuswide events, and various student initiatives. From academic issues to social events to honor code concerns, the ASMC is the voice of the student body to the College administration.

Admission Requirements

Most first-year students admitted to Mills have a strong B average and have followed a full college-preparatory course in their secondary school, including 4 years of English, 3 to 4 years of mathematics, 2 to 4 years of foreign languages, 2 to 4 years of social sciences, and 2 to 4 years of a laboratory science. Many students have special talents or have taken course work in the fine arts. Mills is interested in individuals, not statistical averages, so each application is carefully reviewed. Credit for precollege courses is granted under certain conditions for the College Board Advanced Placement tests and the International Baccalaureate program.

Applications from transfers are welcome, as are those from students resuming their education or older women who have delayed their entrance to college or who wish to continue work on their B.A. degrees. The SAT or ACT requirement is waived if 24 or more transferable semester credits are presented. For international applications, both the SAT (or ACT) and the TOEFL are required. Applications should be accompanied by transcripts, letters of recommendation, and SAT/ACT scores. An interview, either on campus or with an alumna representative, is strongly recommended for all applicants. International students are required to interview if English is not their primary language.

Application and Information

The priority scholarship deadline for admission applications is February 1 for first-year students. All students are encouraged to meet this deadline; however, merit scholarship applicants (including international students) must apply by February 1. The regular decision deadline date is March 1 for first-year applicants. The priority scholarship deadline for transfer students is March 1, and the regular decision deadline is April 1. Admission decisions for first-years and transfer students are mailed on a rolling basis.

For admission to the spring term, the deadline for both first-year and transfer applicants is November 1.

For more information, students should contact:

Office of Admission
Mills College
5000 MacArthur Boulevard
Oakland, California 94613
Phone: 510-430-2135
800-87-MILLS (toll-free)
Fax: 510-430-3298
E-mail: admission@mills.edu
Web site: http://www.mills.edu

Mills women discover their best selves—and prepare to change the world.

OTIS COLLEGE OF ART AND DESIGN

LOS ANGELES, CALIFORNIA

The College

Founded in 1918, Otis College of Art and Design prepares diverse students of art and design to enrich the world through their creativity, their skill, and their vision. Its programs embrace new technologies and emerging disciplines, uniting these practices with established strengths in fine arts, design, and fashion. Otis College's reputation attracts students from thirty-nine states and twenty-six countries, making it the most ethnically diverse private art college in the U.S. The College's diversity is its strength; it prepares students to imagine what lies ahead and benefits employers who know the value of creativity. Otis graduates shape the visual world, from museum and exhibition design to the Hollywood screen, from the clothes people wear to the toys children play with. Otis alumni are cultural leaders working around the world in companies like Mattel, Sony Pictures, Nike, Gap, Electronic Arts (SIMS Game), Los Angeles County Museum of Art, Pixar, Hasbro, DKNY, Abercrombie & Fitch, Ben & Jerry's, Warner Bros., and Disney Imagineering (theme park design). Fine arts alumni include Masami Teraoka, Robert Irwin, Billy Al Bengston, Allison Saar, Kerry James Marshall, and Jim Rygiel, who received Academy Awards for special effects work on the *Lord of the Rings* trilogy.

Otis began in 1918 when *Los Angeles Times* founder and editor Harrison Gray Otis bequeathed his property in MacArthur Park to create an art institute. Today, Otis has three campuses and state-of-the-art facilities for its programs in architecture/landscape/interiors, communication arts, digital media, fashion design, fine arts, toy design, and interactive product design. On the graduate level, Otis offers programs in fine arts and writing. Otis' newest building, the Galef Center for Fine Arts, is an "art factory" in which students research painting, sculpture, photography, and new genres in light-filled loft spaces. The building also houses two large museum-quality art galleries.

Otis' approximately 1,050 students earn degrees accredited by both the Western Association of Schools and Colleges and the National Association of Schools of Art and Design. The College also annually enrolls approximately 2,600 weekend and evening students through its continuing education programs.

The College offers two-year M.F.A. programs in writing and fine arts, which allow advanced independent work. In both graduate programs the emphasis is on an interdisciplinary approach to developing artistic vision.

Location

Otis' main 5-acre campus is on Los Angeles' west side in the midst of Southern California's dynamic film, digital imagery, and toy design industries. The proximity of art museums, studios, and galleries allows students to experience some of the most significant fine art in the country. The School of Fashion Design is in the heart of downtown L.A.'s garment district. The third campus, in the beach community of El Segundo, houses individual studios for graduate fine arts majors.

Majors and Degrees

Within the design fields, Otis offers six majors. Communication arts (advertising, graphic design, and illustration) focuses on the connections between applied art and design concepts and current and emerging technologies. Students gain an essential understanding of drawing, painting, typography, narrative sequence, storytelling, visual literacy, and history.

The digital media program endeavors to strike a balance between traditional art and technology, teaching students how to communicate and tell stories through motion, art, and design. The major includes five components: motion graphics, broadcast design, animation, visual effects, and game, which includes two-dimensional (image creation and manipulation, text as image, and typography), three-dimensional (character design and animation, props, vehicles, and virtual sets), motion graphics, interactive design, and Web design.

The architecture/landscape/interiors program offers a synthetic curriculum of the spatial design fields: architecture (buildings), landscape (including parks, gardens, and recreational surfaces), and interiors (spaces within buildings). The focus is on design rather than craft, to train designers for communication and collaboration with builders, craftsmen, and artisans working in any scale, material, or technique.

Toy design combines product design, marketing, and engineering. Each year of the program focuses on a specific category, such as plush, action figures, preschool, vehicles, dolls, or games.

Interactive product design, the newest major at Otis, encourages students to integrate their art-making and creative-thinking skills with engineering and cutting-edge technology to create products with sports, fashion, medical, and lifestyle applications.

In the fashion design program, the year follows the same calendar as the professional seasons, allowing students to work on three collections annually. In the final two years of the program, students interact with professional designers through the Mentor Program.

The fine arts major offers three areas of concentration (painting, photography, and sculpture/new genres) that encourage students to discover their own artistic vision. Faculty members and visiting artists work with students in a cross-disciplinary approach (e.g., painters work with photographers, and video artists interact with sculptors). A new program within fine arts, ACT (Artists, Community and Teaching), gives students a broad introduction to teaching art as a social practice and as a career path.

Academic Programs

The first-year Foundation Program helps new students master a vast array of studio skills, including life drawing, form and space, color and design, and drawing and composition. Liberal studies and art history courses are carefully designed to complement the studio curriculum. At the end of the year, having developed both a creative vocabulary and a grounding in liberal arts, students select a major.

Within each major, the curriculum reinforces creativity through integrated learning. Students take advantage of a coordinated set of offerings and disciplines to gain deep training in each discipline. They graduate with cross-boundary thinking and the ability to formulate transdisciplinary solutions to problems that may not even exist at the time of their matriculation.

Off-Campus Programs

Otis participates in a mobility program with the Association of Independent Colleges of Art and Design (AICAD). Participating colleges include premier AICAD art colleges in the United States as well as selected colleges in Europe (such as London, Paris, and Stockholm) and Canada. The Mobility Program at Otis College of Art and Design allows students to study for one semester at another art college during their junior year. Application procedures and deadlines are available through the Registration Office.

Academic Facilities

Each of the campuses features state-of-the-art tools and equipment. Facilities include a well-equipped wood and plastic shop, which includes a Stratasys Dimension SST 3-D printer; metal shop and foundry; a CNC milling machine; a complete letterpress lab; color and black-and-white photo labs with mural capability; a printmaking studio; and both analog and final cut digital video editing. Students have access to cutting-edge software across several platforms in more than 300 computers, scanners, and output devices, including large-scale output. The library holds an excellent collection of books on the arts, subscribes to more than 150 periodicals, and offers a wide range of electronic resources, such as full-text databases and e-books. The 40,000-square-foot Galef Center for Fine Arts houses painting, sculpture, and photo/video lighting studios as well as dedicated senior studios, work space, classrooms, and galleries for student exhibitions. It also houses the museum-quality Ben Maltz Gallery, which presents a diverse program of group and solo exhibitions in a variety of media.

The Fashion Campus occupies 18,000 square feet of prime space at downtown's California Market Center, the headquarters for the West Coast's fashion design industry. Students design with the latest equipment, study in a dedicated library, and use current computer technology—all in proximity to the professional design studios of Los Angeles' fashion district.

Costs

Tuition and fees for the academic year 2007–08 are $28,346. Housing and cost of living and other incidental personal expenses vary depending upon individual circumstances. These costs are estimated to run from $2400 to $7000 per year.

Financial Aid

Otis awards more than $4 million in scholarships to its students. In addition, aid from other sources, such as the state and federal governments, provides aid monies to more than 78 percent of the student body.

Students must complete the Free Application for Federal Student Aid (FAFSA). California residents should file the Cal Grant GPA Verification Form and FAFSA before February 15. Financial aid is awarded on a first-come, first-served basis according to availability. All aid is based on artistic and academic merit and a student's financial eligibility as determined by the United States Department of Education.

Faculty

The Otis faculty comprises practicing artists and designers who have chosen to enrich their professional experience by sharing their expertise with new generations of artists and designers. Currently, 32 full-time and more than 150 part-time faculty members teach and practice in Los Angeles' thriving art and design community.

Student Government

In the Student Government Association, students from every department of study play an active role in student life and produce a wide variety of student-oriented lectures and events.

Admission Requirements

Admission to Otis is based on artistic and academic preparation. Applicants should have solid academic credentials and basic artistic skills. Required materials for students applying directly from high school (no college experience) are the application and fee, high school transcript, standardized test score (SAT or ACT), essay, and portfolio of original artwork. Required materials for students who have prior college experience are the application and fee, transcripts from all colleges attended, an essay, and a portfolio of original artwork. (In some cases, high school transcripts and/or test scores may also be required for students who have some college work.) Additional requirements for students who are citizens of countries other than the United States are the TOEFL score (or appropriate equivalent), certified and translated copies of transcripts from all work completed outside the U.S., and verification of sufficient funds to pay for tuition and fees and all related expenses.

Application and Information

Students can apply for the B.F.A. program for the fall or spring semester, although sophomore and junior transfer students may only enter in the fall. The priority deadline for the fall semester is the preceding February 15. For the spring semester, it is the preceding December 1. To apply online, students should visit the College's Web site at http://www.otis.edu. For a viewbook, prospective students should call the College's toll-free number at 800-527-OTIS (6847).

Students are encouraged to visit Otis. Tours of the campus, appointments with admission staff members, and opportunities to talk with current students and faculty members are available Monday through Friday throughout the year and on some Saturdays between January and May (holiday weekends are excluded). Saturday appointments should be scheduled at least one month in advance. For more information about Otis or to schedule an appointment, students should contact:

Admissions Office
Otis College of Art and Design
9045 Lincoln Boulevard
Los Angeles, California 90045-9785
Phone: 310-665-6800
800-527-OTIS (6847; toll-free)
Fax: 310-665-6821
E-mail: admissions@otis.edu
Web site: http://www.otis.edu

Otis College of Art and Design is located on the west side of Los Angeles on a 5-acre campus.

PITZER COLLEGE
CLAREMONT, CALIFORNIA

The College

Pitzer is a nationally recognized independent, residential liberal arts college. The College's emphasis on interdisciplinary studies, intercultural understanding, and social responsibility sets it apart from most other colleges in the country. The College believes students should take an active part in formulating their individualized plans of study, bringing a spirit of inquiry and adventure to the planning process. Because there are fewer required general education courses, Pitzer gives its students more freedom to choose the courses they want to take.

Pitzer offers the best of both worlds: membership in a small, close-knit academic community and access to the resources of a midsize university through Pitzer's partnership with The Claremont Colleges. The Claremont Colleges are a consortium of five distinct undergraduate colleges (Pitzer, Claremont McKenna, Harvey Mudd, Pomona, and Scripps) and two graduate institutions (Claremont Graduate University and the Keck Institute for Applied Biological Sciences). Each college has its own personality, but all share major facilities, such as the library, bookstore, campus security, health services, counseling center, ethnic study centers, and chaplains' offices. The total enrollment of all of the colleges is nearly 6,300 students. Students at Pitzer may enroll in courses offered by the other colleges and may consult with professors on all of the adjoining campuses.

The College was founded in 1963. Today, Pitzer offers forty-three majors in the arts, humanities, sciences, and social sciences. Majors currently with the largest enrollments include anthropology, art, biology, economics, English, environmental studies, history, organizational studies, political studies, psychology, and sociology.

In 2007, the first-year class of 244 students represented thirty different states and five other countries. About 50 percent of the first-year students came from outside of California.

Pitzer has a deep commitment to welcoming members of underrepresented groups since its founding. In 2007, members of underrepresented groups made up approximately 30 percent of the entering class: 13 percent Chicano/Latino, 11 percent Asian American and Pacific Islander, 5 percent African American, and 1 percent multiracial.

Residential life plays a significant role in a student's educational experience. Each of Pitzer's residence halls establishes its own Hall Council to serve as a forum for addressing and meeting the needs of the community. Pitzer students have a long tradition of arranging their living communities based on common interests. All rooms are wired for Internet access, television, and phone service. Three new residence halls opened in fall 2007.

Opportunities abound at Pitzer and the other Claremont Colleges. Students may participate in a wide variety of sports, clubs, community service programs, and social activities. Currently, more than 150 student organizations allow students to get involved in a wide variety of activities. Pitzer partners with Pomona College to field NCAA Division III teams in baseball, basketball, cross-country, football, golf, soccer, softball, swimming and diving, tennis, track and field, volleyball, and water polo. Club sports for men include crew, cycling, lacrosse, rugby, Ultimate Frisbee, and volleyball. Club sports for women include crew, cycling, lacrosse, rugby, and Ultimate Frisbee.

Location

Pitzer is located in the city of Claremont (population 35,000) at the base of the San Gabriel Mountains, about 35 miles east of Los Angeles and 78 miles west of Palm Springs. Pitzer is a short drive away from rock climbing at Joshua Tree National Park, ski resorts, the beaches of southern California, and the Getty, Norton Simon, and other Los Angeles County museums.

Majors and Degrees

Pitzer offers the Bachelor of Arts degree in American studies; anthropology; art; art history; Asian American studies; biology; biology-chemistry; black studies; chemistry; Chicano studies; classics; dance; economics; English and world literature; environmental science; environmental studies; gender and feminist studies; history; human biology; international and intercultural studies (Asian Studies, European studies, Latin American and Caribbean studies, Third World studies); linguistics; mathematical economics; mathematics; media studies; molecular biology; music; neuroscience; organismal biology; organizational studies; philosophy; physics; political economy; political studies; psychology; religious studies; science and management; science, technology, and society; sociology; Spanish; and theater.

Minors are available in anthropology, art, art history, Asian American studies, biology, black studies, classics, dance, economics, English and world literature, environmental studies, gender and feminist studies, history, linguistics, mathematics, media studies, music, philosophy, science, technology and society, sociology, Spanish, and theater.

Academic Programs

To earn the Bachelor of Arts degree, students are required to complete thirty-two courses, about one third of which are in the major. Students work with faculty advisers to organize a curriculum that meets the educational objectives of the College: breadth of knowledge, understanding in depth, written expression, interdisciplinary and intercultural exploration, and social responsibility and the ethical implications of knowledge and action. Specific course requirements depend on the student's academic interests. Certain concentrations require a senior thesis.

The system of cross-registration at the Claremont Colleges provides Pitzer students with the opportunity to take advantage of the wide range of courses available at each of the other colleges. Advanced students may also enroll in certain courses at Claremont Graduate University with the instructor's approval.

The College observes a semester calendar; classes begin in early September and end in mid-May. There is a study break near the middle of each semester and another break between semesters from mid-December through mid-January.

Off-Campus Programs

Nearly 70 percent of students participate in study-abroad programs. Pitzer approves thirty-five international study options in Argentina, Australia, Botswana, Bulgaria, Canada, China, Costa Rica, Denmark, Ecuador, England, Finland, France, Germany, Ghana, Hungary, India, Ireland, Japan, Korea, Latvia, Mexico, Morocco, Nepal, South Africa, Spain, Thailand, Turkey, and eleven exchanges with U.S. institutions.

Academic Facilities

The central services of the Claremont Colleges include the Honnold-Mudd Library, which houses more than 2 million volumes and more than 6,000 serial subscriptions. Other shared facilities include theaters, music halls, music and dance studios, the Keck Joint Science Center (shared with Claremont McKenna and Scripps Colleges), and a wellness center that includes counseling and health services.

Specialized facilities at Pitzer include a television studio, film editing suites, art galleries, social science laboratories, an arboretum, a reading library, and several computing facilities, including a 24-hour computer center.

Costs

Expenses for 2007–08 were as follows: tuition and fees, $35,912; room and board, $10,212; and books and personal expenses, $2000. Travel expenses vary. Costs are subject to change for 2008–09.

Financial Aid

One third of Pitzer's students receive aid in the forms of grants, loans, and work-study. To apply for aid, students must complete the Free Application for Federal Student Aid (FAFSA) and the CSS PROFILE. California residents should also apply for California state grants. Students must reapply for aid each spring.

Faculty

Ninety-eight percent of Pitzer's faculty members hold a Ph.D. or the terminal degree in their fields. All courses are taught by the faculty members. The student-faculty ratio is 12:1, and faculty members are readily available for academic advising. Most faculty members are conversant with at least one other field of study in addition to the area of their degrees and may teach in more than one area.

Student Government

Pitzer's governmental structure is distinctive among American colleges. Instead of the traditional student government that restricts student participation to limited areas, students are represented on all standing committees of the College, including those that deal with the most vital and sensitive issues of the College community. Though it demands a serious time commitment from those who choose to participate, it offers interested students an active educational experience and the opportunity to make a genuine impact on the life of the College and its students, faculty, and staff.

Admission Requirements

Pitzer has developed a highly personalized admission process. Each applicant is considered on the basis of his or her own strengths. In general, the College seeks students who have performed well in high school, have shown a significant amount of involvement in activities outside of the classroom, are motivated to learn, and are interested in the opportunity to take an active role in planning their education in a liberal arts framework. The selection process is designed to help achieve a diverse and energetic class. Selection is based on high school transcripts, rigor of curriculum, recommendations, essays, extracurricular activities, and other special talents. Applicants are encouraged to visit the campus and arrange for an interview.

Application and Information

Pitzer College offers both Early Decision and Regular Decision for prospective applicants. Students interested in applying early must submit a completed application by November 15 and are notified January 1. Interviews for Early Decision are required by December 1. Regular Decision candidates must submit their applications for admission by January 1 and are notified by April 1. Applicants must supply an official transcript of grades, two teacher evaluations, one counselor or school official recommendation, and the application fee of $50 by the necessary deadline. Pitzer accepts the Common Application as the only application for admission for first-year students. When submitting the Common Application, students must complete a supplemental form, which is available on the Common Application Web site at http://www.commonapp.org. Pitzer College is test optional in the admission process. Students should contact the College for further details.

For additional information, students should contact:

Office of Admission
Pitzer College
1050 North Mills Avenue
Claremont, California 91711-6101
Phone: 909-621-8129
800-PITZER1 (800-748-9371, toll-free)
Fax: 909-621-8770
E-mail: admission@pitzer.edu
Web site: http://www.pitzer.edu

Students on the campus of Pitzer College.

COLLEGE DATA CENTER • CALIFORNIA

POINT LOMA NAZARENE UNIVERSITY
SAN DIEGO, CALIFORNIA

The University

Point Loma Nazarene University (PLNU) celebrates more than 100 years of pursuing excellence in Christian higher education. Founded as a Bible college in 1901, the University has grown into a leading liberal arts institution. Still, the tradition continues, and the mission remains the same—Point Loma Nazarene University is an academically challenging environment and a community seeking to teach, shape, and send forth compassionate, applied scholars.

Students attending Point Loma can expect Christianity to be incorporated into all aspects of their experience. Academically, three religion courses are integrated into the undergraduate curricula. Professors stimulate students' minds by teaching critical-thinking skills, combining faith into learning by encouraging students to ask tough questions. Within the community, students attend weekly chapel services, gathering together as a family for worship, praise, and teaching. Point Loma offers many exciting opportunities for students to take an active part in ministry. There are more than thirty student-led ministries, including accountability groups, Elderly Outreach, Homeless Outreach, Skaters and Surfers for Christ, Mexico Outreach, and international ministry teams.

Point Loma students can also find a wide variety of extracurricular activities in which to be involved, including student government, yearbook, newspaper, literary magazine, fraternities and sororities, common-interest clubs, professional organizations, forensics, theater, musical choirs and bands, intramural sports, and organized athletics. The University competes in National Association of Intercollegiate Athletics (NAIA) Division I and offers baseball, basketball, cross-country, men's golf, soccer, softball, tennis, track and field, and women's volleyball.

The University offers a personal approach to higher education and enrolls more than 2,300 undergraduate students and 1,000 graduate students. Seventy-five percent of the undergraduate student body lives in technologically advanced on-campus dormitories that range from dorm rooms to apartment-style living spaces. The Church of the Nazarene is the primary supporter of the University financially, yet more than two thirds of the student body represent various other denominations.

Point Loma Nazarene University is accredited by the Western Association of School and Colleges and offers degree programs at the baccalaureate and graduate levels.

Location

Point Loma Nazarene University is located on a stunning 90-acre oceanfront property on the Point Loma peninsula between the San Diego Bay and the shore of the Pacific Ocean. It is 10 minutes from downtown San Diego and the airport, a half hour from Mexico, and 2 hours from Los Angeles. This ideal location in sunny, culturally rich southern California provides students with countless internship and recreational opportunities.

Majors and Degrees

Point Loma Nazarene University offers the Bachelor of Arts, Bachelor of Music, and Bachelor of Science degrees in more than sixty-two majors and concentrations. Point Loma also offers the Bachelor of Science in Nursing degree. Undergraduate majors include accounting, art education, athletic training, biblical studies, biology, biology-chemistry, broadcast journalism, business administration, chemistry, child development, Christian ministry, communication, computer science, consumer and environmental sciences, dietetics, engineering physics, exercise science, family-life services, graphic design, history, industrial-organizational management, information systems, instrumental performance, international development studies, international studies, journalism, liberal studies, literature, managerial and organizational communication, mathematics, media communication, music, music and ministry, music composition, music education, nursing, nutrition and food, philosophy, philosophy and theology, physical education, physics, piano performance, political science, psychology, Romance languages, social science, social work, sociology, Spanish, theater, visual arts, and vocal performance. Optional minors are offered in several departments. Preprofessional and cooperative programs are offered in allied health, engineering, law, medical/dental, and physical therapy and in AFROTC, AROTC, and NROTC programs. Teaching and service credentials offered include Single Subject with CLAD emphasis (secondary and teacher education) and Multiple Subject with CLAD emphasis (elementary and teacher education).

Academic Programs

Point Loma offers a strong Christian liberal arts education that develops character, commitment, reason, and faith. Educationally, Point Loma brings together opportunities for intellectual discourse, leadership development, and spiritual formation within a supportive faith community. The academic program is designed to balance a well-rounded general education program with the depth necessary to concentrate in one of the major programs. The curriculum broadens students' knowledge in the areas of scripture; Christian heritage; analytical, communication, and quantitative skills; natural and social sciences; literature and arts; and historical, cultural, linguistic, and philosophical perspectives. The University offers and encourages travel abroad, semester at sea, and internship programs.

Baccalaureate degrees are conferred upon successful completion of a total of 128 semester units, including a total of 44 upper-division units; satisfactory completion of the general education program; and completion of a major.

Students who have earned a satisfactory score on the Advanced Placement examinations (AP), College-Level Examination Program (CLEP), or International Baccalaureate (I.B.) exams are eligible to receive credit in applicable areas of the curriculum.

The Integrated Semester for Freshmen is a fall-semester program of four classes (14 units) for 48 freshmen. The program provides thematic studies and cross-disciplinary learning in a close-knit learning community, positioning students to achieve academic success in their first semester.

The academic year at Point Loma is divided into fall and spring semesters of sixteen weeks, followed by two 5-week summer sessions and one 3-week session.

Academic Facilities

Point Loma's facilities are technologically developed to provide students with an excellent learning environment. Ryan Library and Learning Center contains more than 450,000 volumes, group study rooms, three computer labs, a language learning center, a media center, and a full television-production studio. In addition to these resources, the library also cooperates with the other universities in San Diego through online sharing of databases and interlibrary loan, giving students access to more than 8 million sources of information. The Bond Academic Center houses the Academic Support Center, Tutorial Center, and additional computer labs. Cooper Music Center provides rehearsal facilities for Point Loma music and instrumental groups and state-of-the-art recording and practice rooms. The Fermanian Business Center offers students professional development services and networking opportunities. All residence halls and classrooms are fully equipped with complete Internet access. Also located on campus are an art center and gallery, science research laboratories, a broadcast radio station, an aerobic fitness center, and a weight room.

Costs

Annual tuition is $23,200 (12–17 units per semester). Room and board cost $7470, and fees are $530. Tuition and related expenses at Point Loma are among the lowest for private colleges and universities in southern California.

Financial Aid

Financial assistance supports students who otherwise would be unable to attend Point Loma. The financial assistance program includes scholarships, grants, loans, part-time employment, and deferred-payment programs. Point Loma understands the financial needs of its students and offers institutional financial aid in the form of Nazarene Church grants, need-based grants (ranging from $500 to $1000), diversity scholarships, multiple-child discounts, and departmental scholarships. Point Loma also awards students who demonstrate strength in music, theater, forensics, and athletics.

Institutional academic scholarships are available to eligible students. For the 2007–08 academic year, Provost's Scholarships ($4000) are guaranteed to first-time freshmen who qualify with a minimum 3.7 weighted GPA and a minimum score of 1200 on the SAT (combined math and critical reading) or 26 on the ACT. Transfer students with 11 or fewer units from another institution are also eligible for this scholarship with a minimum 3.7 high school GPA and a minimum score of 1200 on the SAT (combined math and critical reading) or 26 on the ACT. Transfer students with 12 to 23 units from another institution who have the same high school criteria and a minimum 3.4 unevaluated college transcript GPA are eligible for this scholarship. Transfer students with 24 or more units from another institution are also eligible for this scholarship with a minimum 3.4 unevaluated college transcript GPA. It is renewable with a minimum 3.4 GPA at PLNU.

A total of thirty President's Scholarships ($11,000) were awarded to first-time freshmen for the 2007–08 academic year. Applicants must submit an official seven-semester transcript by February 1 to receive this award. It is renewable with a minimum 3.5 GPA at PLNU. A total of forty-five Trustee's Scholarships ($7000) are scheduled to be awarded to first-time freshmen for the 2007–08 academic year. Applicants must submit an official seven-semester transcript by February 1 to receive this award. This scholarship is renewable with a minimum 3.5 GPA at PLNU.

In addition, first-time freshmen who qualify for the Provost's award were considered for one of two $24,000 awards for the 2007–08 academic year. Applicants must submit an official seven-semester transcript by February 1 to be considered for this selective award.

All students who are residents of California are encouraged to apply for state and federal programs by submitting a completed Free Application for Federal Student Aid (FAFSA).

Faculty

Point Loma prides itself on the outstanding quality of its faculty. Composed of Christian teachers and scholars who are committed to the lives of students, the University's faculty includes 140 full-time members, 80 percent with an earned doctorate or the highest degree in their field. While teaching is their first priority, 60 percent of the faculty members pursue their own research through projects in which students have a vital role. Professors, not teacher's assistants, teach all classes. The average class size is 20 students; 85 percent of undergraduate classes enroll fewer than 50 students. With a student-faculty ratio of 15:1, professors at Point Loma are accessible, holding regular office hours to meet with students, and are dedicated to academic, professional, and Christian mentoring.

Student Government

The Associated Student Body (ASB) of Point Loma Nazarene University is composed of the entire student body and is managed by an elected student board of directors, who sponsor events and organize activities for social, physical, personal, and spiritual growth.

Point Loma Nazarene University seeks to make a meaningful contribution to the religious life of its students. The University is committed, through positive teaching and spiritual guidance, to preserving the vitality of personal and spiritual experience in its campus community. Students joining the community embrace this spirit and contribute to the spiritual liveliness of Point Loma.

Admission Requirements

Point Loma Nazarene University offers admission to qualified applicants who demonstrate academic achievement, extracurricular and community involvement, and the potential to profit from and contribute to the Point Loma community. Transfer and international students and students who are members of underrepresented groups are welcome and encouraged to apply.

Prospective first-time college students are eligible for admission, provided the following conditions are met: a minimum high school GPA of 2.8 with an SAT minimum score of 860 (combined math and critical reading scores) or an ACT composite minimum score of 18. Transfer students may apply, provided they have a minimum GPA of 2.0 (a minimum of 2.8 is recommended). High school transcripts and SAT or ACT scores for transfers must be submitted if the student has fewer than 24 transferable college units at the time of application. For fall 2007, Point Loma accepted 60 percent of the first-time college applicants and 40 percent of transfer applicants. The average GPA of a freshman applicant was 3.7, and the average SAT score was 1170. A limited number of first-year students with a high school GPA or test scores below the University's minimums are considered for provisional standing.

The application for admission includes a formal application for admission, an application fee of $50, two essays, two recommendations, transcripts, and official SAT or ACT score reports. An interview with an admissions counselor, which should be scheduled at least one month before application deadlines, is strongly recommended.

Application and Information

Students may apply as early as the fall semester of their senior year in high school or one year prior to transferring from another college or university. Applicants may apply for early action or regular admission. The deadline to be considered for early action is December 1. Early action is reserved for first-time freshman students who have made Point Loma Nazarene University one of their top choices, and the University provides students with notification of their admission decision by January 15. Early action is not binding; students who are accepted during early action still have until May 1 to make their final college choice. The priority and transfer student deadline for regular admission is March 1. Applicants for regular admission and those not offered admission through early action receive notification after February 1 or as admission files are completed. For more information, to arrange a campus visit, or to request more information or an application, students should contact:

Office of Admissions
Point Loma Nazarene University
3900 Lomaland Drive
San Diego, California 92106
Phone: 619-849-2273
800-733-7770 (toll-free)
Fax: 619-849-2601
Web site: http://www.pointloma.edu

SCRIPPS COLLEGE
CLAREMONT, CALIFORNIA

The College

Since its founding in 1926 as one of the few institutions in the West dedicated to educating women for professional careers as well as personal intellectual growth, Scripps College has championed the qualities of mind and spirit described by its founder, newspaper entrepreneur and philanthropist Ellen Browning Scripps. Scripps remains a women's college because it believes that having women at the core of its concerns provides the very best environment for intellectually ambitious women to learn from a distinguished teaching faculty and from each other. Scripps emphasizes a challenging core curriculum based on interdisciplinary humanistic studies, combined with rigorous training in the disciplines, and sees this as the best possible foundation for any goals a woman may pursue.

Scripps aspires to be a diverse community committed to the principles of free inquiry and free expression based on mutual respect. The College chooses to remain a largely residential college of fewer than 1,000 students, a scale that encourages women to participate actively in their community and to develop a sense of both personal ethics and social responsibility. Scripps cherishes its campus of uncommon beauty, a tribute to the founder's vision that the College's architecture and landscape should reflect and influence taste and judgment.

As full participants in the Claremont Colleges consortium, Scripps students are members of a small university community where they may enjoy academic and other educational opportunities throughout the coordinating colleges and the graduate school. As residents of southern California, Scripps women may explore varied cultural, ethnic, and geographical resources.

Scripps students have the opportunity to participate in a variety of activities on campus, or they may choose to get involved in any of more than 200 five-college clubs, eleven NCAA Division III sports teams, intramural and club sports teams, coffeehouses, and a multitude of five-college and Scripps campus events. In 2000, Scripps dedicated the Elizabeth Hubert Malott Commons, which houses a large centralized dining facility, the student-run Motley Coffeehouse, an expanded Career Planning & Resource Center, a student activities office, the College mailroom, a student store, and a banquet facility that highlights a variety of speakers across many disciplines. Also in 2000, an additional residence hall opened, adding to the beauty of the campus.

Each residence hall has a spacious living room, fast Ethernet connections in each room, a browsing room for quiet study, kitchen and laundry facilities, and a computer room. Wireless connections are available in the residence halls and throughout the campus.

Scripps emphasizes high aspirations, high achievement, and personal integrity in all pursuits, and it expects students, faculty and staff members, and alumnae to contribute to Scripps and to their own communities throughout their professional, social, and civic lives. Scripps believes that this form of challenging and individualized education best prepares women for lives of confidence, courage, and hope.

Location

Listed on the National Register of Historic Places, Scripps is located in Claremont, California, a college town of 39,000 people. It is 35 miles east of Los Angeles and 25 miles east of Pasadena. The mountains, beaches, and deserts of southern California are easily accessible by car. The climate is cool and dry in the winter, warming in the late spring.

Majors and Degrees

Scripps College awards the Bachelor of Arts degree in accounting; American studies; anthropology; art history; Asian-American studies; Asian studies; biology; biology/chemistry; Black studies; chemistry; Chicano studies; Chinese; classics; computer science; dance; economics; English; environmental science; environment, economics, and politics; environmental studies; European studies; foreign languages and literature; French studies; geology; gender and women's studies; German literature/civilization; German studies; Hispanic studies; history; human biology; humanities; Italian literature/civilization; Japanese; Jewish studies; Latin American studies; legal studies; linguistics; mathematical economics; mathematics; media studies; molecular biology; music; neuroscience; organizational studies; philosophy; physics; politics and international relations; psychology; public policy analysis; religious studies; Russian; science and management; science/technology and society; sociology; Spanish literature/civilization; studio arts; theater; and women's studies.

Scripps also cooperates in a dual 3-2 bachelor's degree program in engineering with a large number of institutions, including Boston University, Columbia University, Harvey Mudd College, Rensselaer Polytechnic Institute, USC, and Washington University in St. Louis. Other joint programs offering a bachelor's and a master's degree are available with the Claremont Graduate University in American politics, business administration, economics, international studies, philosophy, public policy studies, and religious studies.

Academic Programs

To graduate with a Bachelor of Arts degree from Scripps, students must successfully complete a minimum of thirty-two courses. Course work is divided into three parts: core curriculum requirements, major concentration course work, and elective or minor concentration course work. Core curriculum requirements provide a solid academic frame, while electives allow students significant flexibility in studying courses from the social sciences, humanities, fine arts, natural sciences, and mathematics. Scripps operates on a semester calendar, beginning in early September and ending in mid-May.

Off-Campus Programs

Local off-campus opportunities include internships with career professionals in a variety of fields: journalism, law, business, communications, medicine, and the arts. Examples of internship sites are the Getty Museum, the Walt Disney Company, Merrill Lynch, Warner Bros., the Minority Advertising Program, and INROADS. Students may also participate in political internships in Washington, D.C., and Sacramento, California, or in other internships in museums, biological field stations, and public policy organizations such as the United Nations.

Approximately 60 percent of Scripps students supplement their education and life experience by studying abroad or participating in domestic off-campus study programs. Students can select from more than fifty international options each year, including France, Germany, Ecuador, Ghana, Greece, Nepal, China, and Japan. Students may also opt for domestic programs—going on exchange to Spelman or combining classes at Drew University or George Washington University with an internship.

Academic Facilities

The Claremont Colleges library system holds more than 2 million volumes. The Denison Library at Scripps houses an impressive humanities and fine art collection and is renowned for its special and rare books. A cross-linked computer system affords access to off-campus libraries, including the University of California system.

The Performing Arts Center is the newest addition to the College's academic facilities. Formerly the Garrison Theater for the Claremont Colleges and newly renovated, the Performing Arts Center provides a new home for the College's Music Department and offers state-of-the-art acoustics and theatrical systems for both instruction and performance.

The Millard Sheets Art Center, a $4-million facility that opened in 1994, provides studio space for painting, drawing, printmaking, and ceramics and contains a state-of-the-art computer art and design laboratory and photography studio. The W. M. Keck Joint Science Center, a national model of undergraduate science facilities that opened in 1992, offers students of biology, chemistry, and physics top-grade facilities, research opportunities, and a biological field station. The Clark Humanities Museum and Ruth Chandler Williamson Art Gallery exhibit the work of professionals and students.

Scripps' computer facilities include a well-equipped microcomputer laboratory that houses both Macintosh- and IBM-platform computers as well as laser printers. There are also thirteen "smart" classrooms at Scripps, each of which is equipped with Dell- or Macintosh-platform computers, projectors, and screens. Scripps has opened a Multimedia Learning Center for faculty use in teaching and a Modern Language Laboratory/Technical Teaching Classroom. Users have access to a six-college network as well as the Internet. The Keck Science Center and the Millard Sheets Art Center each have their own computer labs with discipline-specific software programs. The libraries and music studio also have computer facilities.

Costs

For the 2006–07 academic year, tuition and fees were $33,700, room and board were $10,100, and books and incidentals were approximately $1800.

Financial Aid

It is the goal of Scripps College to attract the best students, regardless of their ability to pay. Approximately 60 percent of Scripps students receive financial aid, usually in a combination of grants and scholarships, loans, and part-time student employment. Awards are based on the financial need of the student. The College also offers a variety of academic scholarships ranging from half tuition to full tuition, room, and board.

Faculty

With a student-faculty ratio of 11.3:1, the College is dedicated to a personalized education. Faculty members remain active in their fields while making teaching Scripps students their first priority. Classes are taught by professors, not by graduate students. Of the full-time ongoing faculty members, 97 percent hold terminal degrees in their field, 58 percent are women, and 100 percent participate in the faculty-student advising program.

Student Government

One of the most important aspects of life at Scripps is the governance system. Students participate in the curricular and policymaking functions of the College. The College council, Scripps Associated Students, is composed of student body officers who are elected each spring and is chaired by the president of the student body. Each of the nine residence halls is self-governing, and students serve on a variety of Board of Trustees committees. The College has a serious commitment to the concept of shared responsibility for governance among students, faculty members, and administrators.

Admission Requirements

Scripps College seeks energetic and intellectually curious students who are interested in pursuing a challenging liberal arts curriculum. In addition to high levels of academic and personal achievement, Scripps values demonstrated leadership, initiative, integrity, and creativity.

The Admission Committee gives careful consideration to every aspect of a student's application. Particular attention is given to the quality of an applicant's academic preparation. A recommended course of study consists of five academic subjects in each year of high school, including 4 years of English, 3 years of mathematics, 3 years of social studies, 3 years of laboratory science (biology, chemistry, or physics), and either 3 years of a foreign language or 2 years each of two different languages. Applicants are encouraged to select honors, Advanced Placement, or International Baccalaureate courses whenever available.

Application and Information

Students applying to Scripps College are expected to submit transcripts of all academic work in high school and college, a counselor recommendation, two academic teacher recommendations from teachers in different academic subject areas, a graded writing assignment, and SAT or ACT results, along with the application and essay. Students are encouraged to take SAT Subject Tests. The deadlines for application are November 1 or January 1 for early decision, November 1 for academic scholarships, and January 1 for regular decision.

Further information is available from:

Office of Admission
Scripps College
1030 Columbia Avenue, P. B. 1265
Claremont, California 91711-3948
Phone: 909-621-8149
800-770-1333 (toll-free)
Fax: 909-607-7508
E-mail: admission@scrippscollege.edu
Web site: http://www.scrippscollege.edu

The Scripps College campus.

SOUTHERN CALIFORNIA INSTITUTE OF ARCHITECTURE

LOS ANGELES, CALIFORNIA

The Institute

Southern California Institute of Architecture (SCI-Arc) is a creative voice for evolving paradigms of culture and building, using Los Angeles as an experimental field, with a constantly renewed community of faculty members and students who continue to "make it new." SCI-Arc's home in downtown Los Angeles allows students to experience firsthand the globalization of business, entertainment, media, and language, combined with the shifting boundaries of disciplines, cultures, and territories. The school stands at an urban pivot point on the east edge of downtown Los Angeles, at a confluence of races, politics, and urban tactics. The extreme social and natural conditions that make Los Angeles a focus of world attention serve as vantage points from which to debate the future of cities, the changing role of the architect, and the nature of architecture itself. As an independent degree-granting institution, the school tests the limits of architecture in order to transform existing conditions into the designs of the future. Its graduates meet the challenges of contemporary design practice by cultivating new visions that respond to the unfurling complexity of the contemporary urban environment. Using emerging technologies and tools, they develop new strategies for practice by uniting the conceptual and the technical. The curriculum tightly weaves the liberal arts and the disciplines of physical sciences, professional practice, and technology into architectural practice. This critical approach is manifested in building and object making, digital media, theoretical research, and creative design.

SCI-Arc began in 1972, when a small group of architects and students proposed a radical alternative to the conventional system of architectural education. United by their commitment to change, they established the school as a mechanism for invention, exploration, and criticism. The students and faculty members felt comfortable with uncertainty and risk and relished independent thinking. Coexistence of diverse approaches and purposeful action generated a community. A passion for developing ideas and constructing them into buildings and cities drove the curriculum. Society and architecture were seen as inseparable.

The Institute holds accreditation by the National Architecture Accrediting Board (NAAB) and the Western Association of Schools and Colleges (WASC) to offer the Bachelor of Architecture degree.

In addition to its undergraduate programs, SCI-Arc offers three Master of Architecture programs, including a three-year program, a two-year program, and an intensive, three-term postgraduate course of research, analysis, and design.

Location

SCI-Arc's location in the heart of the Los Angeles Artist District, southeast of the downtown core, allows students and faculty members to participate fully in a vital urban environment. Adjacent to the toy and garment districts and just south of Little Tokyo, the school is close to museums, theaters, galleries, and many other cultural institutions. Neighbors include Gehry's Concert Hall and Moneo's Cathedral.

Majors and Degrees

The Bachelor of Architecture degree is awarded upon successful completion of a five-year program. Candidates must complete 162 credit units. In addition, students are required to complete seven general studies courses.

Academic Programs

SCI-Arc's undergraduate program educates students to become independent voices in leadership roles within the architectural profession. The program is recognized nationally and internationally for its fluid and experimental curriculum. In design studios and seminar courses, prevailing paradigms of design, production, representation, and technology are challenged.

At SCI-Arc, the undergraduate program consists of three sequential phases: foundation (first and second years), core (third year and first term of fourth year), and advanced studies (second term of fourth year and fifth year). Work in each of these phases in the design studio challenges and reflects course work in associated areas of study. The History, Theory, and Humanities program, the Technology and Professional Practice program, and the Visual Studies program are the underpinning disciplines that extend throughout the five-year course of academic studies. Students examine and develop approaches to the conventions of physical materials, intelligent and sustainable building practices, digital environments, and virtual sites. In the fifth year, prior to graduation, students work with an adviser and a faculty committee to develop an independent and comprehensive thesis project.

Undergraduate students may enter the program from high school into the first-year level or transfer from two-year community college programs with majors in sciences and arts. Others are admitted after working for several years following high school. Previous studies or professional work in architectural design are not required to gain acceptance to the first year of the undergraduate program. Most students complete a portion of core general studies prior to entering SCI-Arc and complete the sequence once enrolled. The diverse population includes students from Asia, Central and South America, Europe, Africa, and North America as well as from various counties in California, including regional Los Angeles communities.

Making + Meaning, an intensive five-week summer foundation program, is open to nonmatriculating students who wish to learn more about the changing nature of the physical environment as well as the history, theory, and practice of architecture. Participants in this 18-year-old program come from the United States, South and Central America, Europe, and Asia and have ranged in age from 16 to 56.

Off-Campus Programs

SCI-Arc encourages educational experiences that expose the student to different cultures and allow direct contact with the great architecture of the past. Its campus in Vico Morcote, a medieval hill town above Lake Lugano in Switzerland, offers a travel/study program that focuses on modern and contemporary architecture. In addition, students participate in traveling studios every year and have recently studied in India, South Korea, Japan, the Netherlands, Mexico, and China. Exchange programs with schools in Mexico, Australia, Denmark, the Netherlands, Japan, Germany, Austria, Israel, and France offer other study options.

Academic Facilities

In SCI-Arc's renovation of the (1907) Freight Depot, a 1,250-foot-long industrial structure in Los Angeles' Artist District, lightweight steel structures were inserted inside a vast corridor of concrete and rebar to create a variety of work spaces. The on-campus community of 485 students and 90 faculty members works together, engaging this rich relationship between old and new and using the building as a laboratory for experimentation.

The Freight Depot, which houses all the school's facilities and is open to students 24 hours a day, includes individual studio spaces for each student; seminar and lecture rooms; the library; a media center; wood, metal, and CNC milling shops; computer labs; and an exhibit gallery. The SCI-Arc Supply Store is located off campus, one block west of the Depot. The computer labs are accessible 24 hours a day, seven days a week, and house both Macs and PCs equipped with the most up-to-date software.

Costs

Tuition and fees for the 2007–08 academic year are $21,544. Living and personal expenses for the academic year are estimated at $10,640.

Financial Aid

Admission to SCI-Arc is determined without regard to a student's ability to pay the full cost of his or her education. The school's financial aid policy is designed to maximize assistance to all admitted students who demonstrate financial need.

U.S. citizens are eligible for Federal Pell Grants, Federal Supplemental Educational Opportunity Grants, Federal Stafford Student Loans, and Federal PLUS loans. The Federal Work-Study Program involves part-time employment for U.S. citizens as well as international students. In addition, scholarships are awarded on the basis of merit and need. A number of scholarships are awarded to entering and continuing students based on merit and/or financial need.

Faculty

Students and faculty members work together in a fluid, nonhierarchical manner, exploring and testing new ideas. The student-faculty ratio is 15:1. The overlap of teaching and practice encourages the sharing of skills and knowledge. The faculty members, who are directed by Eric Owen Moss and the Academic Council, represent a wide range of contemporary approaches to design, history, and urban theory. Among the faculty members are some of the leading practitioners of the discipline of architecture as well as renowned theorists, critics, and historians. These Los Angeles–based practitioners have devoted their careers to investigating how broad aesthetic, social, and cultural concerns can be integrated into an overall understanding of the built and natural environments. Their work has been widely published both nationally and internationally. To complement the richness of local talent and the regional urban experience, SCI-Arc offers studios, workshops, lectures, and seminars by international visiting faculty members.

Faculty members have been awarded numerous Fulbright Fellowships, Graham Foundation Grants, Progressive Architecture awards, AIA awards, Rome prizes, and a MacArthur grant. In addition, books by faculty members have been published by Verso, the University of Michigan Press, Routledge, Princeton Architectural Press, Monacelli Press, MIT Press, Rockport Editions, Rizzoli, Academy Editions, Rotovision, the University of California Press, and Artemis.

Student Government

The student union actively represents the students, who participate in all aspects of the operation of the school, including the lecture series, student journals and other publications, and exhibitions. Student representatives sit on the board of directors, the academic council, the curriculum committee, and other academic committees. Students organize and produce the lecture series and the graduation ceremony and run the lottery for vertical studio placement.

Admission Requirements

The Southern California Institute of Architecture seeks applicants who demonstrate interest, ability, and academic achievement that reveal potential for the study of architecture. Students who have completed high school are eligible for admission to the first professional degree program. One year of college-level work is recommended, and admission preference is given to students who have a balanced education in the arts, sciences, and humanities. Preparation in the visual arts is required; it may include drawing, sculpture, graphics, photography, video, or multimedia experience. International students are encouraged to apply and must submit TOEFL scores of at least 83 on the internet-based exam, 220 on the computer-based exam, or 550 on the paper-based exam.

Application and Information

Completed applications for first-year placement in the fall term are due February 1, transfer applications for fall entrance are due May 1, and transfer applications for spring entrance are accepted on a rolling basis through November. An interview is recommended but not required. Late applications are accepted on a case-by-case basis. Available spaces are limited for students applying for admission beyond the first-year program.

Inquiries and requests for application forms and a course catalog should be addressed to:

Admissions Office
Southern California Institute of Architecture
960 East 3rd Street
Los Angeles, California 90013
Phone: 213-613-2200 Ext. 320
Fax: 213-613-2260
E-mail: admissions@sciarc.edu
Web site: http://www.sciarc.edu

STANFORD UNIVERSITY

STANFORD, CALIFORNIA

The University

The Leland Stanford Junior University, referred to today simply as Stanford University, was founded in 1885 by Leland and Jane Stanford, who devoted their entire fortune and estate to its establishment in memory of their only child, Leland Jr., who died at an age when many young men and women are planning a college education. Leland Stanford was a distinguished businessman, governor of California, and U.S. senator. The Stanfords were widely traveled; they patterned the University's architecture after the great European universities. They wanted students to receive a broad liberal education as well as a practical one. The resulting curriculum was remarkable for its time—one that would cultivate the imagination and develop character.

Although the University has grown and changed in many ways over the years, it is very much a product of its physical setting and of its early educational goals of practicality, humanism, and excellence. In terms of enrollment, Stanford is a medium-sized university, but its campus consists of more than 8,180 acres. Frederick Olmsted, the designer of New York's Central Park and America's foremost landscape architect of his day, was commissioned to locate the original central campus, indicate the layout and general character of the buildings, and plan the grounds. These original buildings with buff sandstone walls, red-tiled roofs, and long sandstone arcades still constitute the center of the campus today. Over the years, newer structures have been built to blend with the original architecture.

There are about 6,800 undergraduates and more than 8,000 graduate students enrolled at the University. Undergraduate students come to Stanford from every state in the Union and about sixty-eight other countries. Although they represent widely differing backgrounds and interests, all have displayed energy, intellectual curiosity, and commitment to their education both in and out of the classroom. First-year students are required to live on campus, although most students choose to live on campus all four years. The undergraduate housing system includes seventy-eight residential facilities, including academic, cross-cultural, Greek, and language theme and academic focus houses; self-managed houses; apartments; suites; and traditional dormitories. Stanford supports a strong program of education in the residential setting to supplement students' classroom programs. Faculty and staff members live in the residences with first-year students; others come for meals and serve as guest speakers.

The scope of extracurricular activities reflects the diversity of backgrounds, interests, abilities, and experiences of the student body, and about 600 organized student groups are available. These include a wide variety of academic, political, religious, social, and ethnic associations. In addition, students actively participate in music, drama, and journalism projects. The University's extensive athletic facilities include a 50,000-seat stadium, a 7,391-seat basketball pavilion, a championship golf course, a fourteen-court tennis complex, and a four-pool swimming complex. Stanford fields thirty-five varsity sports teams, including men's teams in baseball, basketball, crew, cross-country, fencing, football, golf, gymnastics, sailing, soccer, swimming and diving, tennis, track and field, volleyball, water polo, and wrestling and women's teams in basketball, crew, cross-country, fencing, field hockey, golf, gymnastics, lacrosse, sailing, soccer, softball, squash, swimming and diving, synchronized swimming, tennis, track and field, volleyball, and water polo. There is a co-ed varsity sailing team. About twenty additional club sports are available, and extensive intramural programs are also offered.

The University provides many student services, including academic advising, a health center, counseling and psychological services, and career development.

Location

Stanford is adjacent to the suburban communities of Palo Alto and Menlo Park, 30 miles south of San Francisco. Extensive cultural opportunities are available in the area. The famed Monterey Bay is 75 miles to the south; the Sierra Nevada and Yosemite National Park are both 4 hours away.

Majors and Degrees

Stanford awards the Bachelor of Arts (B.A.), Bachelor of Science (B.S.), and Bachelor of Arts and Sciences (B.A.S.) degrees. Students may pursue the following major, minor, and honors areas of study: African and African American studies; American studies; anthropological science; applied physics (minor only); archaeology; art, studio art and art history; Asian American studies; Asian languages (Chinese and Japanese); biological sciences; chemistry; Chicana/o studies; classics; communication; comparative literature; comparative studies in race and ethnicity; cultural and social anthropology; drama; Earth sciences, including Earth systems, Earth resources engineering, geological environmental sciences, and geophysics; East Asian studies; economics; engineering, including aeronautics and astronautics, architectural design, biomechanical, biomedical computation, chemical, civil, computer science, computer systems, electrical, engineering physics, management science and engineering, materials science, mechanical, and product design; English; English literature (minor only); ethics in society (honors only); feminist studies; film and media studies; French; German studies; history; human biology; individually designed majors; interdisciplinary studies in the humanities; international relations; Italian; Jewish studies (minor only); Latin American studies (honors only); linguistics; mathematical and computational science; mathematics; music; Native American studies; philosophy; physics; political science; psychology; public policy; religious studies; science, technology, and society (major and honors); Slavic languages and literature; sociology; Spanish and Portuguese; statistics; symbolic systems; and urban studies.

Academic Programs

Stanford provides the means for undergraduates to acquire a liberal education—one that broadens their knowledge and awareness in each of the major areas of human knowledge, significantly deepens it in one or two, and prepares them for a lifetime of learning. The curriculum allows considerable flexibility. Individually designed majors, double majors that combine bachelor's and master's degrees, tutorials, and honors programs are all available for qualified students. A special emphasis is placed on encouraging close faculty and student interaction in the first two years through Stanford Introductory Studies, which includes freshman seminars. Students may declare a major at any time but must do so by the end of the sophomore year. Freshmen are assigned to general advisers upon entering; when they declare a major, they are assigned to an adviser from the faculty of the major department or program. To earn the B.A., B.S., or B.A.S. degree, students must complete 180 units; fulfill writing, general education, and foreign language requirements; and complete the requirements of at least one major department or program. All students take a three-quarter Introduction to the Humanities sequence as well as five courses in the Disciplinary Breadth category and two courses in the Education for Citizenship category. Stanford's commitment to a broad liberal arts education is expressed through the yearlong course requirement Introduction to the Humanities. The courses build an intellectual foundation in the study of human thought, values, beliefs, creativity, and culture. They also enhance students' skills in analysis, reasoning, argumentation, and oral and written expression. Students may select from a variety of courses that share these common goals. At least 45 units (including the last 18) must be completed at Stanford. With certain limited exceptions, no more than 90 quarter units of credit for work done elsewhere may be counted toward the bachelor's degree at Stanford.

Entering students may be allowed up to 45 units of credit on the basis of successful scores on the College Board's Advanced Placement tests or the International Baccalaureate examinations.

Off-Campus Programs

Stanford has overseas study programs in Australia, Beijing, Berlin, Florence, Kyoto, Moscow, Oxford, Paris, and Santiago. Students may attend these centers for a three-, six-, or nine-month period, obtaining full academic credit. The teaching staff at each center consists of regular Stanford professors and resident academic staff members of the host country. Stanford also provides a special opportunity for students to study classics in Rome, Italy, through a consortium arrangement with other universities. About thirty percent of each graduating class participate in overseas programs.

Stanford students also have the opportunity to study in the nation's capital under the Bing Stanford-in-Washington program. In addition, Stanford offers exchange programs with Dartmouth College, Howard University, Morehouse College, and Spelman College.

Academic Facilities

Stanford's library collection consists of more than 8 million books and journals and thousands of other materials spread among the main Green Library, the Meyer Undergraduate Library, and eighteen branch and department libraries. The undergraduate library serves as the hub of undergraduate resources and contains study carrels, classrooms, listening rooms, and a well-equipped language library with materials for nearly 100 languages. The Green Library houses the library system's central collections and also holds maps, microtexts, newspapers, government documents, rare books, and special collections, including writings of such notables as Sir Isaac Newton, Martin Luther, William Butler Yeats, and John Steinbeck. An added benefit for researchers is the cooperative link between Stanford's libraries and the University of California at Berkeley's library system.

Stanford's facilities are outstanding and include well-equipped classrooms, laboratories, computer facilities, and research centers. Among the University's many distinguished facilities are the Beckman Center for Molecular and Genetic Medicine; the William Gates Computer Science Building; the David Packard Engineering Building; the John C. Blume Earthquake Engineering Center; the Remote Sensing Laboratory; the Stanford Linear Accelerator Center; the Hoover Institution on War, Revolution, and Peace; the Center for Economic Policy Research; the Freeman Spogli Institute for International Studies; and the Clark Center, housing the Bio-X Program for Bioengineering, Biomedicine, and the Biosciences. In addition, the Jasper Ridge Biological Preserve constitutes a natural laboratory for biology and ecology students, and the Hopkins Marine Station in Pacific Grove, California, offers students an excellent opportunity to study marine biology in a natural habitat.

Costs

Tuition for 2007–08 is $34,800. The room rate is $5863, and the board rate is $4945.

Financial Aid

Admission at Stanford is need blind for U.S. citizens and permanent residents. Nearly 77 percent of its undergraduates receive various types of financial assistance from Stanford and/or outside sources, totaling about $113 million annually. Awards range in value depending on need and are renewable for each of the four undergraduate years on the basis of continuing need. Parents with annual income less than $45,000 are not expected to contribute toward educational costs; the expectation for other parents varies based on their financial circumstances. Remaining costs not covered by the parents and student are met with a combination of student loans (usually $2000 per year), job (usually $2000 per year), and scholarship funds. To apply for aid, applicants should complete the Free Application for Federal Student Aid (FAFSA) and the College Scholarship Service PROFILE by February 15 for regular decision applicants.

Many students work on campus during the academic year, and opportunities for off-campus part-time employment are numerous.

Faculty

Stanford has about 1,800 faculty members. A high proportion of the full-time professors are involved in undergraduate teaching and advising. Stanford's current community of scholars includes 17 living Nobel laureates, 4 Pulitzer Prize winners, 1 winner of the Congressional Medal of Honor, 24 MacArthur Fellows, 20 recipients of the National Medal of Science, 3 National Medal of Technology recipients, 228 members of the American Academy of Arts and Sciences, 134 members of the National Academy of Sciences, 83 National Academy of Engineering members, 29 members of the National Academy of Education, 43 American Philosophical Society members, 7 Wolf Foundation Prize for Mathematics winners, 6 winners of the Koret Foundation Prize, and 3 Presidential Medal of Freedom winners. The student-faculty ratio is 7:1. All faculty members keep regular office hours, and students are encouraged to develop contacts with the faculty in and out of the classroom for advice and guidance.

Student Government

The Associated Students of Stanford University (ASSU) represents students and serves as a forum for the expression of student opinion through its executive and legislative branches. The ASSU plans and executes numerous programs and activities. Students have many opportunities to become actively involved on councils, committees, and panels that offer interaction with professors and staff members. Many of the concrete and philosophical changes that have taken place at the University are attributable to student initiative, input, and interaction.

Admission Requirements

Admission is highly competitive, with 22,333 applications received for the 2010 class of 1,648 students. The University seeks an able and diverse student body, and no single criterion determines admission. Students are evaluated individually on the basis of their academic record, test scores, nonacademic achievements, and personal qualities and how well they have used the resources available to them. Every candidate for undergraduate admission must submit SAT, SAT Reasoning Test, or ACT scores. SAT Subject Test scores are strongly recommended in Math Level 2 (formerly IIC) and one additional subject area if submitting the SAT Reasoning Test with Writing, or Math Level 2 and two additional subject tests scores if submitting the ACT or the former SAT without Writing. Transfer students, entering either the sophomore or the junior class, are admitted annually in the fall quarter only. The University does not use any racial, religious, ethnic, geographic, or sex-related quotas in admissions.

Application and Information

Stanford will move to the Common Application in the summer of 2007. Applicants will be required to submit the online version of the Common Application along with the online Stanford Supplement to the Common Application. Detailed course descriptions and University policies can be accessed through the Stanford Bulletin via Stanford's Web pages. Copies can be purchased through the bookstore (phone: 800-333-2670). Applications for the freshman class must be postmarked by January 1. Regular decision applicants are notified around April 1. Stanford also offers a nonbinding, single-choice early action option, with a deadline of November 1. Early action applicants are notified approximately six weeks after the deadline. The deadline for the completion of transfer applications is March 15.

Office of Undergraduate Admission
Montage Hall
Stanford University
355 Galvez Street
Stanford, California 94305-3020
Phone: 650-723-2091
Fax: 650-723-6050
E-mail: admission@stanford.edu
Internet: http://admission.stanford.edu

UNIVERSITY OF REDLANDS

REDLANDS, CALIFORNIA

The University

The University of Redlands has, for more than 100 years, offered its select student body a tradition of superior liberal arts education. While students may select from a variety of programs that prepare them for professional or graduate school, the heart and foundation of Redlands is in liberal studies. Its outstanding faculty, educated in the world's finest colleges and universities, provides students with extraordinary opportunities for learning and growth through excellent teaching and close, informal interaction. Intense intellectual activity is balanced by opportunities for quiet reflection, fun, and recreation.

The University enrolls more than 2,300 students. Sixty percent of the freshman class comes from California and the remainder from forty-two other states and ten countries. In addition to a strong academic program in the liberal arts, the sciences, preprofessional programs, and the arts, many extracurricular programs are available to the student, including debate, music, drama, dance, and athletics. Internships are available for students in many academic programs. The School of Music and the Glenn Wallichs Theatre provide a rich selection of cultural events throughout the year. Prominent speakers are invited to the campus each year to give major addresses and participate in classes and public discussion groups, and many social functions are organized by the Student Life Office and individual residence halls. Additional social opportunities are provided for interested students by local nonresidential fraternities and sororities. A student services center provides assistance in the areas of career and personal counseling and academic support.

Seventy percent of the students live on campus in residence halls that offer a variety of accommodations, including single gender, coed by separate wings, and coed by alternate suites.

The University of Redlands is one of a select number of schools that have a chapter of Phi Beta Kappa, the nation's oldest and most prestigious academic honor society.

The University of Redlands offers master's programs in the fields of business, communicative disorders, education, geographic information systems, and music. The School of Education offers a Doctorate in Leadership for Educational Justice Ed.D. program.

Location

The University is located in the city of Redlands within the San Bernardino Valley. Overlooking the 160-acre campus are the two highest mountains in southern California, Mt. San Gorgonio and Mt. San Bernardino, each more than 10,000 feet high. Redlands has a population of 70,000 and is situated at an elevation of 1,500 feet. Metropolitan Los Angeles to the west and Palm Springs to the east are both about an hour's drive away by freeway.

Majors and Degrees

The B.A. degree is offered in the academic areas of art history, Asian studies, biology, business administration, communicative disorders, creative writing, economics, English literature, environmental studies, French, German, government, history, international relations, music, philosophy, psychology, race and ethnic studies, religion, sociology/anthropology, Spanish, studio art, theater arts, and women's studies. The B.S. degree is offered in accounting, biology, business administration, chemistry, computer science, economics, environmental management, environmental science, mathematics, and physics. The professional degree of Bachelor of Music (B.M.) is offered by the School of Music. Primary and secondary credentials are granted by the School of Education. Strong interdisciplinary programs in Latin American studies, prelaw, and premedicine are also available.

Academic Programs

Academic majors are offered in the spirit of a liberal arts program, with emphasis on developing the whole student. In addition to the standard academic program, international-study programs, independent study, and an honors program are offered to provide greater diversity.

A liberal arts education, by definition, is an exposure to a wide variety of academic disciplines. Typically, such exposure carries no underlying theme but is distributed among broad categories such as the humanities, arts, social sciences, and natural sciences. The University of Redlands has never considered itself typical and, as a result, has developed an unusual approach to the implementation of its liberal arts philosophy by restructuring the general education requirements to provide a contemporary curriculum. This common experience emphasizes competence in writing, computing, problem solving, and creative skills, all of which are fundamental to a lifetime of learning and career development. In addition, the requirements include a first-year seminar that integrates the academic program and close personal relationships between students and faculty members. The overriding emphasis of this innovative curriculum is on a thorough investigation of human values as they affect the individual and society. An examination of the worth of the individual, respect for nature and life, free inquiry, and the understanding of other cultures are a few of the topics covered through various courses. The University hopes that this experience will broaden each student's understanding and better equip them to deal with today's dynamic society.

The Johnston Center for Integrative Studies provides a nontraditional approach for a select group of highly motivated students. Johnston Center students are exempted from most of the academic structure of Redlands and instead negotiate their entire course of study with a faculty/peer committee. Drawing from the Redlands curriculum as well as from courses created each semester by the Johnston community, each student proposes an individually designed general studies program and an area of concentration. Course performance is evaluated in a narrative format rather than with letter grades. These students live in the Johnston Center Complex, a living/learning community that includes student rooms, faculty offices, classrooms, and space for weekly community meetings. Students who are enrolled in the Johnston Center are expected to contribute to the life of the center's community.

The academic calendar divides the school year into a 4-4-1 plan, providing a fall semester, a spring semester, and a May term. The four classes taken in the fall semester are completed prior to the third Friday in December. The spring semester begins in January and runs through April. The four-week May term offers students the chance to pursue one subject in depth. Extensive off-campus opportunities, including internships, international study, and on-campus independent study, are available.

Academic Facilities

The institution has extensive facilities for student use, including a modern library with 400,000 publications, Internet access, and online databases such as Dialog, ABI/Inform, PsychLit, ERIC Wilson Indecis, and Music Index. Additional facilities include the Glenn Wallichs Theatre, the Fletcher Jones Academic Computing Center, the Hunsaker University Center, the Peppers Art Center, and the Stauffer Center for Science and Mathematics. These facilities also provide access to a wireless network. There are forty-two buildings on the 160-acre campus.

Costs

Tuition for 2007–08 is $30,326, and room and board costs are $9702.

Financial Aid

Recognizing that many worthy and capable students find it impossible to obtain a college education without financial assistance, the University has established a program of aid. Most aid is need-based, but no-need scholarships based on academic achievement in high school and/or college are available. Presidential Scholarships are also available, based on grades and test scores, as are Achievement Awards. Talent Awards, ranging from $500 to $8000 each, are available in art, creative writing, debate, and music.

Students seeking financial assistance should inquire through the Office of Admissions when applying for admission. The Free Application for Federal Student Aid (FAFSA) should be submitted by February 15. FAFSA forms received after this date are evaluated subject to the availability of funding. Forms may be obtained most conveniently from high school counselors' offices and college financial aid offices, as well as online at http://www.fafsa.ed.gov.

Faculty

The highly qualified full-time faculty numbers 167 men and women, 90 percent of whom hold doctorates or other terminal degrees in their field. The wide variety of academic backgrounds represented in the faculty provides students with an excellent opportunity to live and work in an atmosphere of intellectual inquiry. Academic advising is handled by faculty members, and all students are assigned an adviser in the area of their major interest.

Student Government

Authority and responsibility for student government is delegated to the Associated Students of the University by the president and the faculty to make possible genuine participation by students in the governance of the University. The organization is composed of all students in the college, and its officers are chosen by the student body. More than sixty positions of representation are open to students on faculty, administrative, trustee, and alumni committees. Among other activities and responsibilities, the student government finances and operates a student-union complex, on-campus shuttle, information center, vending program, convocation series, Internet radio station, and weekly newspaper.

Admission Requirements

Graduation from an accredited high school or the equivalent is necessary for admission. No set pattern of courses in high school is required, but applicants should have had 4 years of work in English and should have completed an academic program strongly emphasizing such studies as foreign language, science, mathematics (including algebra II), and social science. An average grade of at least B should have been maintained in the high school program. Applicants are requested to submit the results of the SAT or the ACT. The writing portion is used for placement in English classes. SAT Subject Tests are not required. Standardized test scores are not required of transfers who bring at least 24 transferable units to the University.

Transfer students should have maintained a minimum 2.8 grade point average and may transfer up to 66 units of credit from a community college. There is a 24-unit residence requirement for transfers from other four-year institutions.

Application and Information

Applications are processed on a rolling basis. Those wishing to be considered for an academic or merit scholarship should apply by December 15. Those applying for need-based financial aid should apply by February 1. Transfer and late applicants should apply by March 1. Applications made after this date are considered on a space-available basis.

Further inquiries should be addressed to:

Dean of Admissions
University of Redlands
P.O. Box 3080
Redlands, California 92373-0999
Phone: 800-455-5064 (toll-free)
Fax: 909-335-4089
E-mail: admissions@redlands.edu
Web site: http://www.redlands.edu

The University of Redlands stands out brilliantly against the majestic San Bernardino Mountains.

UNIVERSITY OF SAN DIEGO

SAN DIEGO, CALIFORNIA

The University

Known for its commitment to Catholic tradition and the liberal arts, the University of San Diego (USD) has created academic programs providing students with the skills necessary to grow and advance personally and professionally. Beyond the traditional arts, sciences, and humanities, USD has developed exceptional programs in business, engineering, marine science, international relations, and the health sciences. With a holistic philosophy, USD seeks to foster competence, international and cultural sensitivity, professional responsibility, and a spirit of compassionate service in each student.

The students who share in the life at USD and contribute to its growth are a diverse group representing all fifty states and more than sixty countries. There are currently 4,962 undergraduates out of a total University enrollment of 7,483 students. Ninety-four percent of USD's freshman students and 46 percent of upperclassmen reside on campus, many in recently constructed facilities. The residence halls consist of traditional dormitories, suites, and apartment-style buildings. Several meal plans are available to accommodate different schedules and tastes in food.

A friendly campus atmosphere, the opportunity for close interaction between faculty members and students, and small classes that facilitate personal attention and faculty accessibility characterize the educational environment at the University of San Diego. Numerous campus activities are available to students, including social and cultural events, special-interest groups and clubs, and intercollegiate and intramural sports. The Office of Campus Recreation complements the academic experience at the University by offering students many opportunities to use their leisure time constructively and enjoyably. The Shiley Theatre is the center of many cultural activities on campus, including concerts, lectures, plays, and recitals. There are also more than seventy student-controlled clubs and organizations, including nationally affiliated fraternities and sororities, national honor societies, and service organizations.

Location

The 180-acre campus sits on a mesa commanding inspiring views of the Pacific Ocean, Mission Bay, and San Diego harbor. Located on the southern tip of California, San Diego offers a wide variety of recreational, business, science, art, and cultural activities. With an average daily temperature of 66 degrees in February and 78 degrees in August, the area is perfect for biking, jogging, tennis, softball, and all aquatic sports. In addition, San Diego is noted for its outstanding zoo, museums, Spanish missions, Sea World, and major sports teams. The proximity to Mexico provides an excellent opportunity for gaining firsthand insights into Mexican culture. The city of San Diego also offers educational advantages to students in the fields of social services, education, environmental and marine science, art, music, and archaeology. The San Diego International Airport, downtown, Mission Bay, and the Aquatic Center are just a few minutes from the campus.

Majors and Degrees

The University confers the Bachelor of Arts, Bachelor of Science, Bachelor of Business Administration, and Bachelor of Accountancy degrees. Undergraduate major programs are offered in accountancy, anthropology, art history, biology, biochemistry, business administration (with minors in finance, information technology management, law and ethics, management, marketing, real estate, and supply chain management), business economics, chemistry, communication studies, computer science, economics, electrical engineering, English, ethnic studies, French, history, interdisciplinary humanities, industrial and systems engineering, international relations, liberal studies, marine science, mathematics, mechanical engineering, music, philosophy, physics, political science, psychology, sociology, Spanish, theater arts, theology and religious studies, and visual arts.

Minors are available in most major areas of study and also in architecture, Asian studies, Catholic studies, environmental studies, gender studies, information science, Italian, leadership studies, and peace and justice studies.

Advanced degree and teaching credential programs are available in bilingual/cross-cultural studies, counselor education, educational administration, elementary and secondary education, pupil personnel services, and special education.

Academic Programs

The Freshman Preceptorial program begins each USD student's academic career with a combination of advising, orientation, and an introduction to college-level scholarship. The preceptor, instructing in a supportive, small-group environment, has frequent contact with each advisee and continues advising throughout the student's general education program. Once students declare a major, the responsibility of advising shifts to a department faculty member, who provides guidance in regard to specialized and professional study. Several programs, such as those in marine science and international relations, combine multiple disciplines, and special advisers are assigned to these areas. All of USD's programs are built solidly on the liberal arts, developing critical thinking skills through an emphasis on fundamental disciplines, written and oral communication, and an understanding of the past. USD gives special attention to the exploration of human and spiritual values, the interrelations of knowledge, and the development of an international perspective.

The University operates on a 4-1-4 academic calendar. Normally, the student is in residence for eight semesters and completes approximately forty-four courses, completing a minimum of 124 units.

The honors program at the University gives promising students the opportunity for both independent academic research and intensive exchange of ideas with other honors students. Selection of students to the program is made primarily on the basis of past academic achievement. The program accepts 100 students per class and offers preceptorial and seminar course work.

College credit may be granted for Advanced Placement courses taken in secondary schools when the classes are completed with scores of 3, 4, or 5 on the appropriate Advanced Placement tests given by the College Board. Certain subjects require a score of 4 or 5 in order to receive college credit.

A number of subject examinations of the College-Level Examination Program (CLEP) have been approved by the University faculty, and in certain specified areas students may qualify for college credit by satisfactory performance on the CLEP tests.

Off-Campus Programs

University of San Diego undergraduate students can live and study in many countries, including Australia, Austria, Costa Rica, England, France, Germany, Ireland, Italy, Japan, Mexico, Scotland, Spain, or the West Indies, while earning credit at USD.

USD conducts a five-week summer session in Guadalajara, Mexico, in cooperation with several other American universities. The summer's experiences include concerts, lectures, and planned tours and excursions.

Academic Facilities

Named Alcalá Park after the Spanish university city of Alcalá de Henares, the campus is built in the style of the sixteenth-century Spanish Renaissance. Several important academic buildings have been constructed in recent years.

Opened in 2004, the 150,000-square-foot Donald Shiley Center for Science and Technology contains seventy-three state-of-the-art laboratory facilities for biology, chemistry, physics, environmental studies, and marine science. In addition, the center features aquariums, an astronomy deck, and a greenhouse.

Through the Joan Kroc Institute for Peace and Justice, the students and faculty members of the University of San Diego have stepped into an active role in the worldwide quest for human dignity and hope. A new School of Peace Studies has been established. The school is a magnet for political leaders and distinguished academics. Students may participate in both undergraduate and graduate programs of study.

Most recently, construction was completed on the School of Leadership and Education Sciences building. The 80,000-square-foot facility is home to several undergraduate and graduate programs. In addition to classrooms and offices, the building offers observation rooms, demonstration classrooms, and labs.

The University Center, a two-story, 78,000-square-foot facility, serves as the hub of student life on campus. It offers students and faculty the use of music and study lounges, student organization offices, and a choice of five dining areas, including a grill, a deli, and a bakery.

Camino Hall is home to Shiley Theatre and also holds offices of the Fine Arts Department, soundproof practice rooms for music students, and foreign language laboratories. Founders Hall includes Founders Chapel and the Founders Art Gallery, which features exhibits by both professional and student artists.

Costs

Tuition for the 2007–08 academic year was $32,300. Estimated residence costs, including room and board, average $11,000 per year, depending on accommodations. Personal expenses, including books, are estimated at $3000.

Financial Aid

In order to be considered for need-based financial assistance, students must complete the Free Application for Federal Student Aid (FAFSA). During the 2006–07 academic year, 70 percent of undergraduate students received some form of financial assistance. Financial assistance can be in the form of loans, grants, scholarships, and student employment. The University offers academic, athletic, and leadership scholarships that are not dependent on financial need.

Faculty

The University of San Diego has a faculty of 367 full-time members and 399 part-time members. More than 97 percent of the faculty members hold earned doctorates or the terminal degree, and all are committed to teaching as their primary responsibility. Only faculty members teach classes, and the members of the undergraduate and graduate faculty are the same. The undergraduate student–faculty ratio of 16:1 fosters small classes, personal instruction, and individual attention, as well as faculty involvement in academic advising and University activities.

Student Government

The officers of USD's Associated Students and the class senators, who together make up the central representative group of the undergraduate students, are responsible for overseeing campus activities and the distribution of student funds.

Admission Requirements

Admission is based upon evidence of the applicant's ability to achieve success—academically, socially, and personally—at the University of San Diego. The admissions process is highly selective. Decisions are based on the following items: the student's high school record, SAT or ACT with writing scores, a letter of academic recommendation, and an essay. The Admission Committee also considers the student's level of commitment to community service, leadership skills, and special talents.

Applicants are expected to present a well-balanced secondary school program comprising at least four academic subjects each year. Both the content of the program and the quality of the student's performance are considered.

Transfer students are considered for admission after the successful completion of 24 semester units of academic course work at an accredited college or university, with a GPA of 3.0 or better.

The University welcomes international students who can demonstrate an ability to undertake college work with success in the United States. TOEFL and SAT scores are required for their admission. Although need-based financial aid is not available to international students, they are considered for merit scholarships.

Arrangements for an admission information session and a campus tour may be made through the Admissions Office. Students are selected without regard to race, religion, handicap, or national or ethnic origin.

Application and Information

Application for admission is made through the Admissions Office. Forms should be completed and filed, together with a transcript of credits, as early as possible and no later than January 15 for freshmen and March 1 for transfers. The application for admission can be found on the University Web site at http://www.sandiego.edu/admissions/undergraduate. USD also accepts the Common Application. Upon receipt of all necessary materials, each application is reviewed. Candidates are notified of acceptance by April 15. USD observes the Candidates Reply Date of May 1 and requires accepted applicants to notify the University of their intentions by that date.

For additional information about the University of San Diego, students should contact:

Director of Admissions
University of San Diego
5998 Alcalá Park
San Diego, California 92110
Phone: 619-260-4506
800-248-4873 (toll-free)
Fax: 619-260-6836
E-mail: admissions@sandiego.edu
Web site: http://www.sandiego.edu

UNIVERSITY OF SAN FRANCISCO

SAN FRANCISCO, CALIFORNIA

The University

From its beginnings as a one-room schoolhouse, founded in 1855 by the Jesuits, the University of San Francisco (USF) has developed into one of the premier Catholic universities on the West Coast. Throughout its history, USF has been committed to preparing students to improve the world in which they live. With more than 5,000 undergraduate students, the University has remained faithful to the Jesuit tradition and has maintained its small class size and low student-faculty ratio. Its programs in the arts, the sciences, business, education, nursing, and the law foster a love of learning grounded by the challenge to serve society.

USF is one of the most diverse university campuses in the United States. Living and learning with a student body that consists of students from all fifty states and eighty countries is a unique opportunity. All new incoming freshman and sophomore students under the age of 21 are required to live on the campus, unless living with their parents. More than 90 percent of the incoming freshmen and 50 percent of all undergraduates live on-campus.

The University offers five on-campus residence halls, two off-campus apartment-style residences, and one off-campus traditional residence hall. Gillson and Hayes-Healey primarily house freshman students, while Phelan and Lone Mountain are for sophomores and upperclass students. Xavier Hall is the only all-women dormitory. Located just twelve blocks from the USF campus, Arrupe Hall is the off-campus traditional residence hall offered to sophomore and upperclass students. Loyola Village is a student residential community that features new apartment-style living for students who are 21 or over or in their junior year. Most rooms in residence halls are doubles, with some single rooms available for upperclass students. Each residence hall has laundry facilities, study/computer rooms, television lounges, and 24-hour front desks.

On the campus, students have access to various University facilities. The Koret Health and Recreation Center is an exciting complex that provides facilities for exercise, racquetball, court games, weight training, and an Olympic-size pool for recreational swimming. Tai Chi, yoga, hip-hop, and spinning are just some of the classes offered at Koret. Outdoor adventures include horseback riding, sailing, and sea kayaking. Intramural and club sports are offered in the fall and spring semesters and include flag football, karate, and volleyball. Division I sports include baseball, basketball, cross-country, golf, soccer, tennis, and women's volleyball.

Dining facilities are located all over campus and are within walking distance of the residence halls and classrooms. Located on the main campus, The Market offers a food court experience with a variety of choices, including ethnic, vegan, and vegetarian options. Other dining options include the Lone Mountain cafeteria, Wolf and Kettle, Jamba Juice, Crossroads coffeehouse, and the Law School Café.

Undergraduates keep busy by participating in more than eighty on-campus, student-run associations, fraternities and sororities, honor societies, and clubs, such as the USF Rugby Club and Los Locos, a club that supports USF athletics. Among these clubs are the oldest continuously performing theater group west of the Mississippi River, an award-winning FM radio station, an award-winning weekly newspaper, and a literary magazine.

For students interested in giving back to the community, the Office of Service-Learning and Community Action forms a partnership between the local community and USF. Students may participate in community service activities that include preparing meals for the homeless, tutoring underprivileged children, habitat restoration, and annual events such as AIDS Walk San Francisco.

Location

The University of San Francisco is located on a stunning 58-acre campus in a residential neighborhood just minutes from downtown San Francisco, the Financial District, Fisherman's Wharf, and the Pacific Ocean. The hilltop campus, renowned for its beautiful landscaping, borders the 1,000-acre Golden Gate Park and offers spectacular panoramic views of the city. The dynamic city of San Francisco keeps students entertained with concerts, the ballet, opera, museum exhibits, theater, and sporting events. Because of the diversity and geographical compactness of San Francisco, students find research facilities, opportunities for community involvement, and employment experiences that can not be matched by most cities.

Majors and Degrees

The College of Arts and Sciences offers both B.A. and B.S. degrees. Majors include architecture and community design, art history/arts management, arts education, biology, chemistry, communication studies, computer science, economics, economics B.A.-M.A. (five-year program), English, environmental science, environmental studies, exercise and sports science, fine arts, French, graphic design, history, international and development economics B.A.-M.A. (five-year program), Latin American studies, mathematics, media studies, performing arts and social justice, philosophy, physics, physics/engineering, politics, psychology, sociology, Spanish, theology/religious studies, undeclared arts, undeclared science, and visual arts. The McLaren College of Business offers Bachelor of Business Administration degrees in accounting, business administration, entrepreneurship, finance, hospitality industry management, international business, management, and marketing. The School of Nursing offers a four-year Bachelor of Science in Nursing for qualified high school graduates and for second-baccalaureate candidates.

USF has more than forty-five minors and offers unique programs that enhance the learning experience at USF. Special programs include Asia Pacific Studies B.A.-M.A. (five-year program); Honors Program in the Humanities; Intensive English Program; 4+3 dual degrees in law, military science, premedical, and other pre-professional health studies; Saint Ignatius Institute Program; and a five-year dual degree Teacher Preparation Program that results in teacher certification at the elementary or secondary level.

Academic Programs

The University of San Francisco is committed to providing students with the essentials of a well-rounded education. A baccalaureate degree is issued upon the successful completion of a 128-unit curriculum. The curriculum consists of 44 units of core courses chosen from six specified categories in addition to 80–85 units that are divided among departmental major requirements and electives. An honors program is available for selected superior students seeking a strong academic challenge. The academic year is based on the two-semester system, with a summer session and a winter intersession also available.

In an effort to encourage high school students to move rapidly into the study of subjects now customarily reserved for colleges, the University of San Francisco honors advanced placement credits, as certified by the College Board's Advanced Placement Program tests. The University also cooperates with the College-Level Examination Program (CLEP). Students intending to earn such credit must take the CLEP examinations prior to registering at the University for their freshman courses.

The USF Pre-Professional Health Committee serves to guide and recommend students to medical and dental professional health schools as well as to schools for pharmacy, optometry, veterinary medicine, and podiatry. A student may complete the premedical or other pre–health science requirements as part of, or in addition to, the requirements of an academic major. The Pre-Professional Health Committee assists students with the application process, develops a professional file for each student, collects and mails recommendations to professional schools, conducts interviews in preparation for application, and endorses approved candidates via a committee letter of recommendation sent to all professional schools selected by the student.

The St. Ignatius Institute has an integrated core curriculum based on the great books of Western civilization and an emphasis upon the great works of Christianity. Any undergraduate student at the University, regardless of major, may take courses through the Institute to meet general education requirements. The University also offers Army ROTC. ROTC scholarships are available for qualified applicants and continuing students.

Off-Campus Programs

The University of San Francisco has numerous study-abroad programs available to students with junior standing and a cumulative minimum GPA of 3.0. Exchanges with Jesuit universities include locations in Japan, Mexico, China, Spain, Philippines, El Salvador, and Chile. USF's St. Ignatius Institute program includes an exchange with Oxford University in England. Affiliations with other Jesuit universities make travel to other countries possible, e.g., Gonzaga University's study-abroad program in Florence, Italy, and Loyola University of Chicago's program in Rome. USF is also an associate member of the Institute of European and Asian Studies, which offers programs in Durham and London, England; Paris, Dijon, and Nantes, France; Berlin and Freiburg, Germany; Vienna, Austria; Madrid and Salamanca, Spain; Milan, Italy; Tokyo and Nagoya, Japan; Moscow, Russia; Adelaide and Canberra, Australia; Beijing, China; and Singapore. Numerous other study-abroad opportunities are also available. USF assists students in selecting a location, applying to programs, making financial arrangements, registering for academic credit, securing a passport and visa, and making travel plans.

A domestic student-exchange program is also available with American University in Washington, D.C.; Jackson State University in Mississippi; and Xavier University in Louisiana.

Academic Facilities

University of San Francisco students have access to Gleeson Library's more than 700,000 volumes and Harney Science Center, which houses the Computer Center, Applied Math Laboratory, the Institute of Chemical Biology, and the Physics Research Laboratories. Cowell Hall, the base for nursing classes and the Nursing Skills Laboratory, also includes the Instructional Media Center. Students also have access to Phelan Hall, the home of KUSF, the University's FM radio station, and *The Foghorn*, the official campus newspaper. Malloy Hall, headquarters for the McLaren College of Business, houses an additional computer laboratory and special seminar rooms.

Costs

Tuition for the 2007–08 school year is $31,180. Room and board are $10,730 for the academic year. Books, fees, travel, and other expenses are about $4200 per year.

Financial Aid

A wide variety of scholarships, grants, loans, and work-study programs are available at the University. Domestic students who wish to be considered for financial aid must submit the Free Application for Federal Student Aid (FAFSA) by February 1. More than two thirds of all USF students receive some type of financial aid. There are also many on- and off-campus jobs available.

The University Scholars Program is available to new domestic freshman applicants who have an exceptional cumulative GPA, SAT combined score, or ACT composite score. Scholars are awarded a non-need-based scholarship that pays a significant percentage of the cost of tuition for four years of undergraduate study. To remain eligible, University Scholars are expected to maintain a minimum GPA of 3.25. Eligible students are identified during the admission process and must apply under early action by the November 15 deadline.

Faculty

The University has a faculty of nearly 240 full-time and 350 part-time members; 91 percent of the full-time faculty members hold doctoral degrees. Approximately 250 faculty members are employed in the undergraduate divisions. The University of San Francisco fosters a close relationship between students and faculty members. This is reflected in the small size of classes, the low student-faculty ratio, and the faculty members' availability for advising. Classes are not taught by student teachers or teachers' assistants.

Student Government

All undergraduates are members of the Associated Students of the University of San Francisco (ASUSF). ASUSF is the official representative body of undergraduate students at USF. The ASUSF government has three functions: to represent the official student viewpoint, to recommend policies, and to fund activities and services. ASUSF consists of three branches: the executive branch, the Student Senate, and the Student Court. The Senate comprises an executive board and student senators.

Admission Requirements

The University seeks students who are sincerely interested in pursuing a well-rounded education. The admission process is selective, and each application is reviewed individually. To enhance the quality and diversity of its student body, the University of San Francisco encourages men and women of all races, nationalities, and religious beliefs to apply. Eligibility is based on high school GPA, the application essay, a personal recommendation, and satisfactory test scores. Domestic applicants are required to submit SAT or ACT test scores. International applicants are required to submit TOEFL test scores; however, if an international applicant submits SAT or ACT test scores, the TOEFL will then be used by academic advisors to place the student in the correct English course upon arrival. It is not used to evaluate admission, but academic advisers use these scores to place students in the correct English course upon arrival.

Application and Information

A completed application includes the application form, a personal essay, all academic transcripts, test scores, and one letter of recommendation. For the fall semester, the application deadlines are November 15 for early action and January 15 for regular action.

Inquiries should be addressed to:

Office of Undergraduate Admission
University of San Francisco
2130 Fulton Street
San Francisco, California 94117-1046
Phone: 415-422-6563
800-CALL-USF (toll-free outside California)
Fax: 415-422-2217
E-mail: admission@usfca.edu
Web site: http://www.usfca.edu

St. Ignatius Church, where all graduation ceremonies are performed by individual college.

UNIVERSITY OF THE PACIFIC

STOCKTON, CALIFORNIA

The University

The University of the Pacific was established in 1851 as California's first chartered institution of higher education. The University's classic college environment combined with modern facilities provides students with the best of both worlds. An independent university known for the diversity of its academic programs and outstanding teaching faculty, Pacific has also acquired a reputation for educational innovation, as demonstrated by the development of its cooperative engineering program, numerous accelerated programs, and its three-year professional programs in pharmacy and dentistry. The University, which draws its 3,500 undergraduate students from more than forty states and fifty countries, is located in a residential area of the city of Stockton. The architecture and landscaping of the 175-acre main campus provide an Ivy League type of setting.

The University of the Pacific is a residential university, offering on-campus housing in fourteen residence halls, eight fraternity and sorority houses, and six apartment complexes (including a married student apartment complex). Approximately 70 percent of the undergraduate students live on campus. Excellent support services are available to Pacific students to enhance their academic and personal development; these are offered through the Career Resource Center, the Office of Services of Students with Disabilities, the Health and Wellness Center, and the Counseling Center. Extracurricular activities include plays, operas, concerts, speakers, and movies in one of four theater/auditoriums on campus; excellent athletic programs at the NCAA Division I intercollegiate, club, intramural, and physical education levels; broadcasting (on KUOP-FM, KPAC, and Tiger TV), journalism (the *Pacifican*), and forensics; professional organizations, a Greek Society, and honor societies; and more than 100 special interest clubs. The McCaffrey Center (student union) houses a grocery store, a bookstore, a movie theater, a games area, two additional dining areas, and the Associated Students of the University of the Pacific (ASUOP) offices. Recreation and athletic facilities include three gyms; playing fields; tennis, volleyball (indoor and outdoor), basketball (indoor and outdoor), and racquetball courts; a 28,000-seat stadium; the 6,000-seat Spanos Center; an Olympic-size swimming pool; an athletic training and fitness center; and a student fitness center.

The University's Arthur A. Dugoni School of Dentistry is located in San Francisco, and Pacific's McGeorge School of Law is in Sacramento. Professional and graduate programs on the Stockton campus include the Doctor of Pharmacy (Pharm.D.) degree; master's and doctoral programs in a variety of areas in education; Master of Arts programs in communication, music therapy, psychology, and sport sciences; Master of Business Administration; Master of Science programs in biological sciences, chemistry, pharmaceutical sciences, and speech-language pathology; and Doctor of Philosophy programs in chemistry and pharmaceutical sciences. Master of Science (M.S.), Doctor of Philosophy (Ph.D.), and Doctor of Physical Therapy (D.P.T.) programs are also available.

Location

Stockton (population 290,000) is California's largest inland port. Situated between San Francisco and the Sierra Nevada, the area provides unlimited cultural and recreational opportunities within a short drive, including entertainment in San Francisco; skiing, camping, and backpacking in the Sierra Nevada; and waterskiing and boating in the California Delta area. Stockton is served by Amtrak, bus lines, and three major freeways. Sacramento and Oakland International Airports are both within an hour drive from campus. The climate during the school year is pleasantly warm, with the rainy season generally restricted to the period between December and March. Summer temperatures are in the 80- and 90-degree ranges. Stockton has a diverse ethnic and economic background, offering opportunities for cultural enrichment and community service. For more information, prospective students should visit http://www.pacific.edu/stockton.

Majors and Degrees

The University of the Pacific offers the undergraduate degrees of Bachelor of Arts, Bachelor of Arts in Liberal Studies, Bachelor of Fine Arts, Bachelor of Music, Bachelor of Science, and Bachelor of Science in Engineering. Major areas are accounting, art, arts and entertainment management, Asian language and studies (emphasis in Japanese and Chinese), athletic training, biochemistry, biological sciences, business administration, business law, chemistry, chemistry-biology, communication, computer science, dental hygiene, economics, education (single and multiple subject teaching credentials), engineering (bio, civil, computer, electrical, management, and mechanical), engineering physics, English, entrepreneurship, finance, French, geology, geophysics, graphic design, history, human resources, international business, international relations and global studies, international studies, Japanese, liberal studies, management informational systems, marketing, mathematics, music (composition, education, history, jazz studies, management, performance, and therapy), philosophy, physical sciences, physics, political science, psychology, real estate management, religious and classic studies, social science, sociology, Spanish, speech-language pathology, sport management, sports medicine, studio art, and theater arts. For a complete listing of majors, prospective students should visit the University's Web site at http://www.pacific.edu/majors.

Special programs include a five-year bachelor's/M.B.A. option; a six-year bachelor's/J.D. option; several predental/D.D.S. accelerated programs; several prepharmacy/Doctor of Pharmacy accelerated programs; a five-year engineering program, which incorporates twelve months of mandatory and paid cooperative education work experience; a three-year accelerated Bachelor of Science degree in dental hygiene; an accelerated three-semester Master of Art program in international relations; an accelerated Bachelor of Science/Master of Science program in speech-language pathology; an accelerated Bachelor of Art/Master of Art or accelerated Bachelor of Art/Doctor of Physical Therapy (D.P.T.) or Doctor of Philosophy in physical therapy degree; an accelerated preliminary or secondary-teaching-credential program (that includes the year of student teaching); an optional cooperative education program in the liberal arts; and preprofessional studies in dentistry, law, medicine, pharmacy, physical therapy, and other fields.

Academic Programs

The University emphasizes a personal approach to education, featuring small classes and close working relationships between students and faculty members. The undergraduate academic programs are arranged through seven schools and colleges, each having its own distinctive features. Students enroll in one division but can take classes in the others and share common facilities. The College of the Pacific is a departmentally arranged liberal arts and sciences college, offering more than sixty different majors, minors, and preprofessional programs. Undergraduate professional divisions include the Conservatory of Music, the Eberhardt School of Business, the Benerd School of Education, the School of Engineering and Computer Science, and the School of International Studies. The Thomas J. Long School of Pharmacy and Health Sciences includes both undergraduate and first professional degree students. The Center for Professional and Continuing Education also offers special academic opportunities.

Each of the University's undergraduate divisions has its own academic requirements. However, the University emphasizes a commitment to the liberal arts and requires all students to have exposure to the humanities, behavioral sciences, natural sciences, and social sciences through a University-wide general education program. Many freshmen enter the University without having decided on a major area of study, and they work extensively with their academic advisers before selecting a major. The liberal arts college allows a considerable amount of flexibility in the academic programs, while the professional schools are more structured in their academic requirements. All divisions on the Stockton campus follow a semester calendar; however, the professional pharmacy, physical therapy, and dental hygiene programs have three terms per year.

Off-Campus Programs

The University of the Pacific currently participates in more than 100 programs in seventy countries in Africa, Asia, Central and South America, the Middle East, North America and the Caribbean, Oceania, and Western and Eastern Europe. Students may pursue interests in virtually any academic discipline and may be allowed independent study, travel, and homestay opportunities. Pacific has arrangements for participation in study abroad direct exchanges with individual universities as well as with the University Studies Abroad Consortium (USAC), the Council on International Education Exchange (CIEE), the Institute for the International Education of Students (IES), and the International Student Exchange Program (ISEP). For more information, students should visit http://www.pacific.edu/studentlife/ips.

Cooperative education and internships play important roles at the University. All engineering students spend two 6-month periods off campus working in full-time paid co-op positions. Students enrolled in all other University divisions have the option of participating in part-time or full-time internships, arranged through the Career Resource Center. For more information, prospective students should visit http://www.pacific.edu/exp.

Academic Facilities

Excellent equipment and facilities are available to assist students in their academic work outside the classroom. The Stockton campus of the University of the Pacific maintains a main library with 375,000 volumes, 1,400 print and more than 19,000 electronically accessible periodicals, 690,000 microform items, and 13,000 video and audio units. Approximately 105 computer workstations and 520 study spaces at tables, carrels, and group study rooms are available for student use. In addition, a science and technology library is maintained by the School of Pharmacy and Health Sciences. Students have access to extensive computer facilities. Also available for students are the Educational Resource Center, language laboratories, the drama studio, music practice rooms, the music laboratory, and the student advising center. For more information, prospective students should visit http://www.pacific.edu/onlinetour.

Costs

For 2007–08, tuition and fees are $28,480, and room and board are $9210.

Financial Aid

The University of the Pacific encourages students to apply for financial aid from all sources, including local clubs and organizations, state and federal programs, and the University. It is the intention of the University, within the limits of its resources, to provide assistance to promising students who would not otherwise be able to attend. To this end, the University has developed a financial aid program that includes scholarships, grants, loans, and job opportunities. Financial aid awards from Pacific are based on a combination of financial need and/or academic achievement. In recent years, Pacific has significantly increased its merit-based scholarship programs and, in 1997, became the first institution to provide matching scholarships to new students who receive a Cal Grant (California state gift aid). More than 75 percent of the student body receive some type of financial aid, and on-campus jobs are available through the Career Resource Center. The priority date to apply for financial aid is February 15 for the fall semester. For more information, prospective students should visit http://www.pacific.edu/financialaid.

Faculty

Of the 400 full-time faculty members on the Stockton campus, 93 percent have earned doctoral degrees or the highest degree in their field. The priority of Pacific's faculty is the education of individual students rather than research. The faculty members are actively engaged in classroom teaching and academic advising and also participate in numerous student social activities on campus. The faculty-student ratio is 1:14. For more information, prospective students should visit http://www.pacific.edu/faculty.

Student Government

The ASUOP, the student government organization, provides many services to the campus. The ASUOP president and Senate express the students' views as they work with the University administration. ASUOP operates a 200-seat movie theater, a grocery store, and a multicultural center. ASUOP Presents brings nationally known speakers and lecturers to the campus, and a very active social commission plans an extensive activities calendar that includes films, festivals, dances, and concerts on campus as well as off-campus events and trips. Each school and college also has its own student association, and all are concerned with both academic and social activities. Students are included on committees reviewing academic affairs and the curriculum structure, evaluating courses and faculty members, and planning future facilities and programs. For more information, prospective students should visit http://www.pacific.edu/asuop.

Admission Requirements

The University of the Pacific seeks freshman applicants who have had strong college-preparatory backgrounds of four academic subjects each semester. A challenging secondary school program of 4 years of English, 4 years of social studies, 3 years of mathematics, 2 years of laboratory sciences, and 2 or more years of foreign language is highly recommended. Science students should have an additional year of math and laboratory science that includes chemistry, physics, and higher mathematics. The University requires an official high school transcript, a counselor or teacher recommendation, SAT or ACT scores, and a personal essay. For more information, prospective students should visit http://www.pacific.edu/admission.

Application and Information

Out-of-state and international students are encouraged to apply, and approximately 240 transfer students and 825 freshmen enroll each year. Early action (nonbinding admission) is available for outstanding students (applying into most programs) who apply by November 15. All students applying for prepharmacy, predentistry, and dental hygiene also use the November 15 deadline. The regular fall application date (for all other programs) is January 15. All interested students are encouraged to arrange with the Office of Admissions to visit the campus. Further information may be obtained by contacting:

Office of Admissions
University of the Pacific
Stockton, California 95211
Phone: 209-946-2211
E-mail: admission@pacific.edu
Web site: http://www.pacific.edu/admission

These students are meeting outside the Holt Memorial Library with the Robert Burns Tower in the background.

UNIVERSITY OF THE WEST

ROSEMEAD, CALIFORNIA

The University

The University of the West (UWest) is a multidisciplinary institution that is committed to providing a comprehensive student-centered educational experience of the highest quality that integrates the finest of liberal arts traditions with a global perspective. It is accredited by the Western Association of Schools and Colleges (WASC). Founded in 1991 by Master Hsing Yun of Fo Guang Shan, the campus features a uniquely multicultural faculty and student body complemented by an equally diverse curriculum that is deeply committed to the interaction of Western and Asian cultures and the comparative teaching of international perspectives. As a physical and intellectual meeting place between East and West, the University welcomes people of all beliefs and world views. Students and faculty members come together as a community of scholars to participate in an ongoing dialogue to advance knowledge, address societal and cultural issues, and promote education and understanding across cultures. At UWest, creativity, adaptability, and leadership are fostered together with tolerance, ethical commitment, and social consciousness.

A range of activities that enhance learning and physical and mental well-being are available to students outside of the classroom. These include lectures, concerts, seminars, noncredit classes, and extracurricular activities.

The Student Recreation Center is equipped with fitness and weight-training equipment, table tennis, billiards, and a student lounge with a kitchen. The two residential halls each have a 24-hour study room, a multipurpose student lounge on each floor, and a laundry facility. Each room is furnished and has its own air-conditioning unit, private bathroom, and telephone and high-speed Internet access. Recreational facilities include a swimming pool, a spa, and exercise and game rooms.

UWest is a member of NAFSA, the Association of International Educators, and the American Association of Collegiate Registrars and Admissions Officers.

Location

UWest is located in the city of Rosemead in Los Angeles County. It occupies 10 acres of beautifully landscaped grounds and has modern, well-equipped facilities.

Majors and Degrees

The University offers Bachelor of Arts (B.A.) degrees in business administration, with majors in accounting, information technologies and management, international business, and marketing; English; history, with tracks in Asian history and Western history; psychology, which integrates Western and Eastern psychology; and religious studies, with majors in Buddhist studies and comparative religious studies. There is also a dual-degree program in religious studies (B.A./M.A.). Several English as a second language (ESL) programs are offered, and there is a Three-in-One education plan that combines English as a second language studies and a B.A./M.A. in religious studies, a B.A./M.A. in business administration, or a B.A./M.A. in psychology.

Academic Programs

The Department of Religious Studies' majors in Buddhist studies and comparative religious studies offer students the unique opportunity to study religion in a setting that is informed by Buddhist wisdom and values and dedicated to furthering religious and cultural understanding between East and West. All Buddhist traditions are covered, and students can choose to study any of the Buddhist canonical languages, i.e., Canonical Chinese, Pali, Sanskrit, or Tibetan. The library contains one of the best American collections of writing from all the major Buddhist traditions.

The business administration majors in accounting, marketing, information technologies and management, and international business address the issues of business and management from the particular perspective of Eastern and Western cultural interaction. Students are educated in small, interactive classes where they can learn, acquire skills, and form attitudes and values that are appropriate for leading and serving in a global society. The campus' Eastern and Western cultural environment furthers students' appreciation and understanding of the intercultural issues that shape business on the Pacific Rim.

The major in English explores the dynamic and reciprocal relationship between language, literature, and culture. Course work is designed to help students develop superior communication skills, understand the nature of language and the way it can be described and analyzed, appreciate the esthetic and intellectual enjoyments of literature, and recognize the cultural values reflected in literature. The major imparts knowledge and skills that are foundational to pursuing a graduate degree in English literature, linguistics, or a related field, such as teaching English as a second language.

The major in history provides students with the unique opportunity to appreciate the interaction between East and West. After a general overview of both Eastern and Western history, students can choose from two tracks: Western history, which covers American, European, African, and Latin American history, and Eastern history, which covers South, East, and Southeast Asian history.

UWest's major in psychology adds the dimension of human interests, values, dignity, and life goals to the traditional study of the human mind and behavior. Course offerings include instruction in the major Eastern and Western psychological theories and applications that have developed in human history. Students are able to focus their study on both of these systems as well as on the integration of the two into a new theory of Buddhist and Western psychology.

All of the bachelor's programs require the completion of a minimum of 120 semester units.

The ESL program provides a variety of instructional formats to improve students' command of the English language and familiarize them with American life and culture, including a residential English program and short-term English Immersion Programs.

Academic Facilities

The library provides access to the University's collection as well as electronic access to the collections of many other public and university libraries. The library also offers Internet access and services and subscribes to several major databases, including LexisNexis and ProQuest. The University's Computer Lab is equipped with Windows-based PCs and provides computer technology for students and faculty members, including Internet access. The Language Lab, which is equipped with the latest audio learning technology, is available for language instruction for both class and self-study uses.

Three research centers are located on campus. The International Academy of Buddhism is designed as an international Buddhist research and publications center. It also serves as a forum for consultation and exchange of information and experience for scholars and students specializing in various aspects of Buddhist studies. The Buddhist Psychology and Counseling Research Center develops a theoretical foundation and practical methodology for integrating Buddhist psychology with modern modalities of counseling so that appropriate therapy can be provided to designated individuals and groups. The Center for the Study of Minority and Small Business helps the Department of Business Administration reach out to minority and small-business sectors for potential resources and support, so that the students at UWest can be exposed to and become familiar with business realities and the existing business environment.

Costs

In 2007, tuition for business administration courses was $300 per unit; all other courses were $250 per unit. Other fees also apply. Room and board are $150 per week (quadruple occupancy), $206 per week (double occupancy), or $304 per week (single occupancy).

Financial Aid

Financial aid is available in the form of federal aid, a work-study program, private scholarships and grants (both need- and merit-based), and a limited number of partial tuition waivers.

Faculty

There are approximately 70 faculty members, and they represent a wide range of ethnic and cultural backgrounds. Many are internationally renowned, and all have excellent qualifications in their subjects.

Student Government

The UWest Student Association acts as a liaison between the University and the students to provide services, programs, and facilities that enhance the quality of education by extending the learning environment beyond the classroom into the extracurricular lives of UWest students. It also provides a forum for student expression and interests. All students who are enrolled at the University are included as members of the Student Association.

Admission Requirements

Applicants are required to supply accurate and complete information on the application for admission form and to submit official transcripts from each school or college attended. Other application requirements and documentation can be found on the University's Web site. Student selection is based on academic achievement and potential, irrespective of ethnicity, gender, disability, or religion.

Application and Information

Application deadlines for domestic applicants are August 15 for fall, December 15 for spring, and May 15 for summer. International applicants (F-1) should apply by July 31 for fall, December 1 for spring, and April 30 for summer. ESL applications are accepted on an ongoing basis. There is a $50 nonrefundable application fee for domestic applicants and a $100 nonrefundable application fee for international applicants ($50 for all ESL applicants).

Ms. Grace Hsiao
Admissions Officer
University of the West
1409 North Walnut Grove Avenue
Rosemead, California 91770
Phone: 626-571-8811 Ext. 120
Fax: 626-571-1413
E-mail: info@uwest.edu
Web site: http://www.uwest.edu

A panoramic view of UWest's campus.

WESTMONT COLLEGE

SANTA BARBARA, CALIFORNIA

The College

Westmont College is a nationally ranked Christian liberal arts college in the evangelical tradition that remains focused on undergraduate education. One of the country's most dynamic interdenominational Christian colleges, Westmont combines a world-class education with an unbeatable coastal Southern California location to prepare students for fulfilling lives of leadership and service.

Residence life, athletics, off-campus programs, and opportunities for local and international outreach contribute to balanced personal and spiritual development. Alumni enter a wide variety of professions and vocations and pursue professional-, master's-, and doctoral-level programs at the world's finest research universities, including UCLA, Stanford, Harvard, Yale, Princeton, the University of Chicago, Cambridge, and many others. Westmont's 1,200 students come to Westmont from the majority of states and many countries throughout the world, the highest percentage come from California. Approximately 65 percent are women, 25 percent are students of color, and 1 percent are international students. Approximately eighty percent of the students live in the five residence halls on campus or the apartment complex off campus.

As a member of the National Association of Intercollegiate Athletics and the Golden State Athletic Conference, Westmont provides intercollegiate sports for men and women in basketball, cross-country, soccer (NAIA champions), tennis, and track and field. Men also compete in intercollegiate baseball, club polo, club rugby, club soccer, and club volleyball, and women also compete in intercollegiate volleyball and club polo. The intramural program offers a wide variety of activities as well.

There are numerous clubs and organizations, including a student newspaper, literary magazine, yearbook, radio station, choral and music ensembles, multicultural club organizations, political organizations, theater productions, community service organizations, and Christian service, mission, and outreach programs. The Ruth Kerr Memorial Student Center (1983) houses the main campus dining facilities. An integral component of the Westmont experience is the Chapel Program, which students are required to attend three days a week. Chapel provides speakers and programs to inspire and challenge students to continue growing in their relationship with Christ.

Location

Ruth Kerr, president of the Kerr Manufacturing Company, was one of the founders of Westmont College. She was instrumental in opening the first campus in Los Angeles in 1937 and in moving the College to Santa Barbara in 1945. Westmont is located on a 111-acre campus, rich with pine, oak, and eucalyptus trees, in Montecito, an estate area of Santa Barbara between the Pacific Ocean and the Santa Ynez Mountains. Students enjoy the beach and mountain trails year-round. Santa Barbara has a wealth of history and culture, and theaters, libraries, community concerts, and other civic offerings are just minutes from the campus.

Majors and Degrees

Westmont awards Bachelor of Arts (B.A.) and Bachelor of Science (B.S.) degrees in twenty-six liberal arts majors. These include alternative major, art, biology, chemistry, communication studies, computer science, economics and business, education, engineering physics, English, English and modern languages, French, history, kinesiology and physical education, mathematics, music, philosophy, physics, political science, psychology, religious studies, social science, sociology and anthropology, Spanish, and theater arts. The College offers a teacher-preparation program, which is approved by the California Commission for Teacher Preparation and Licensing, enabling students to qualify for either the single-subject or the multiple-subject credential. Preprofessional programs include athletic training, dentistry, engineering, law, medicine, ministry and missionary studies, pharmacy, physical therapy, and veterinary studies. A 3-2 program combining liberal arts and engineering is offered in cooperation with Stanford University; the University of Southern California; the University of California, Santa Barbara; Boston University; Washington University (St. Louis); and other institutions having accredited schools of engineering.

Academic Programs

Westmont offers majors, minors, and concentrations in dozens of exciting fields and disciplines, such as dance, European studies, neuroscience, and theater arts. All majors and programs of study feature thought-provoking and inspiring ways to integrate belief, thought, and action and to come to a deeper, more accurate understanding of the world. Westmont's commitment to academic freedom is clear, not only in courses that demand students' best critical thinking, but also through a wide range of opportunities and organizations that explore the world of ideas. Students consider issues of science and religion through the Pascal Society and attend lectures in the humanities sponsored by the Erasmus Society. As an exclusively undergraduate college, Westmont has a deep understanding of the ideas and issues that absorb students. From its faculty and staff members to its alumni, Westmont is committed to helping students grow through their questions toward ever-deeper faith.

Off-Campus Programs

Off-campus programs include the Europe Semester, which is offered each fall and provides the broadest geographical scope, with extended stays in Athens, Florence, Jerusalem, London, Paris, and Rome. The England Semester, offered every other year, combines travel and residential study in the British Isles for students of literature. Semesters in France and Spain offer French and Spanish majors the opportunity to study these languages in their home countries, as does the Latin American Studies Program, which combines the study of Spanish culture and language in Belize, Chile, Costa Rica, and Honduras. Similar programs are offered at Jerusalem University College in Israel; Daystar University in Nairobi, Kenya; the Middle East Studies Program at the American University in Cairo, Egypt; and in the Russian Studies Program in Moscow, Nizhni Novgorod, and St. Petersburg (through Westmont's membership in the Council for Christian Colleges & Universities). Participants in the International Business Institute program visit the major economic and political capitals of Europe and Asia. The Westmont Economics/Business Program in Asia introduces students to the diverse economic growth in the Pacific Rim. The East Asia Program addresses contemporary world issues in China, Japan, and Taiwan. An additional summer program in Asia offers students an opportunity to study life and culture in Sri Lanka. Domestic off-campus programs include the San Francisco Urban Program, which studies modern American urban society and offers internships; the Washington Semester, highlighting national political processes and incorporating internships in national, international, and economic policy, justice, and journalism; a semester at Bethune-Cookman, a historically black college in Florida; the Consortium Visitor Program, enabling students to study at any of the Christian College Consortium's twelve other member colleges; and other programs sponsored by the Council for Christian Colleges and Universities.

Academic Facilities

The trilevel Roger John Voskuyl Library is the academic center of Westmont. The library holds 174,246 catalogued items, 465 print periodical subscriptions, and 2,494 online periodical subscriptions as well as seven classrooms; audiovisual equipment; math, language, and computer laboratories; and three IBM RS-6000 computers, which are used for instructional purposes. Forty-seven lab computers are connected to the mainframe for student use. Westmont has a 100Base-TX Ethernet network with a fiber-optic backbone, operating at 10 MB/second. There are Ethernet connections in every office and dorm room and in many classrooms. The entire network has access to e-mail and the Internet through a T3 line. A total of 100 terminals are available throughout the College for student use. The network accommodates IBM-compatible, Macintosh, and RISC/UNIX microcomputers. The library features an after-hours study room, a rare book archives room, and dozens of individual carrels and lockable study cubicles for faculty members and students. It also houses the Writer's Corner and offices for the Director of First-Year Students and the Career and Life Planning department. Reynolds Art Gallery features art studios and a classroom. Students and professional artists exhibit their work year-round in the gallery. Porter Theatre contains state-of-the-art equipment for dramatic productions and concerts. The George Carroll Observatory contains a 24-inch search-grade reflector telescope, the most powerful telescope between San Francisco and Los Angeles. The Mericos H. Whittier Science Building houses the College's science program and equipment, including an ultracentrifuge, a liquid scintillation counter for measuring radioactivity, physiographic units and other equipment for advanced physiological studies, low-pressure liquid chromatography equipment, sophisticated environmental instrumentation, atomic absorption spectrophotometers, Fourier-transform NMR spectrometers, infrared and ultraviolet-visible spectrophotometers, gas and high-performance liquid chromatographs, and gamma-ray spectrometers.

Costs

Tuition and fees for 2007–08 were $31,212, and room and board for the academic year were $9622. The cost of books, personal expenses, and transportation is estimated at $4320.

Financial Aid

Westmont has a strong financial aid program, so no student should hesitate to apply for lack of financial resources. Eighty-five percent of Westmont's students receive some form of financial assistance; $22 million in total financial aid was awarded to students for 2007–08. Westmont offers Monroe full-tuition scholarships, which are available only to first-year applicants who apply via the early action (nonbinding) process. A select group of these applicants are invited to the campus to participate in a formal competition process. Students should contact the Office of Admission for further details. Other merit awards in the financial aid program are the President's, Provost's, and Dean's Scholarships, which range from $8000 to $12,000. These merit scholarships are awarded to students who have demonstrated impressive academic achievement. Westmont also gives awards to students who demonstrate strength in art, music, theater arts, dance, and athletics. After submitting the Free Application for Federal Student Aid (FAFSA), students may be eligible for generous state grants, aid from federal programs, institutional grants, loans, and work-study programs.

Faculty

One of the highest priorities at Westmont is the attraction and retention of outstanding Christian teachers and scholars. The College's professors are dedicated to the integration of faith and learning, while also being actively involved in the lives of students. There are 90 full-time and 52 part-time faculty members. The student-faculty ratio is 12:1; the average class size is 18. Eighty-nine percent of tenure-track faculty members hold a terminal degree. Westmont's faculty members are committed to teaching at the undergraduate level, and they have additional advising responsibilities with either incoming first-year students or students in their major. A director of first-year programs is responsible for the advising and orientation of new students. Although teaching is their primary scholarly activity, many faculty members engage in research, write books, and publish articles in leading journals and periodicals.

Student Government

The Westmont College Student Association (WCSA) is an entirely self-governing body. Students elect their own WCSA representatives, who are then responsible for organizing social, cultural, and educational activities. They actively participate in and are voting members on almost all faculty committees, while also allocating the student budget to various clubs and organizations. Westmont Student Ministries, another student-managed organization, is responsible for organizing on- and off-campus ministries and mission opportunities.

Admission Requirements

Westmont selects candidates for admission from those prospective students who produce evidence that they are prepared for the academic stimulation and spiritual vitality that are central to the character of Westmont. For example, students should place a high priority on undergraduate education, and living and learning in a classic liberal arts environment should be valued. Applicants must have a clear understanding of the Christian mission of the College as well as an explicit desire to benefit from being in this environment. In addition, applicants should possess the strong moral character, values, personal integrity, and social concern that would be in accord with the Westmont community. All applicants must submit one academic letter of recommendation, official high school or college transcripts, and official SAT or ACT scores. A pastoral/character reference is optional. An interview is strongly encouraged. For transfer students from an accredited two- or four-year college or university or a Bible college or university that is accredited by the American Association of Bible Colleges, the evaluation is based on achievement in solid, transferable course work; an assessment of the personal areas covered by the application (as stated above); and the quality of the written responses. High school records must be submitted if the applicant has completed fewer than 24 college-level credits at the time of application.

Application and Information

Entrance to Westmont is possible at the beginning of either the fall or spring semester. Westmont offers an early action plan. High school seniors interested in applying for early action must submit the application by November 1; notifications are mailed on December 20. The priority deadline for regular decision is February 20 for first-year applicants and March 1 for transfers; notifications are mailed beginning April 1. Applications should be submitted online via Westmont's Web site with an application fee of $35. The fee for Westmont's paper application and all other online versions is $50. The Admissions Office encourages applicants to complete the application process as early as possible. Visitors are welcome at any time. Campus visitors can stay overnight in the residence halls, attend classes and chapel, speak with professors or coaches, have a music audition, share a portfolio with the art department, and have meals with Westmont students. Several Preview Day events are planned each semester. Westmont desires to enroll a well-rounded and balanced first-year class. A goal of Westmont is to create a dynamic as well as culturally and traditionally diverse community of learners who bring with them a variety of attributes, accomplishments, backgrounds, and interests. For further information regarding admissions, students should contact:

Office of Admission
Westmont College
955 La Paz Road
Santa Barbara, California 93108
Phone: 800-777-9011 (toll-free)
Fax: 805-565-6234
E-mail: admissions@westmont.edu
Web site: http://www.westmont.edu/

COLORADO

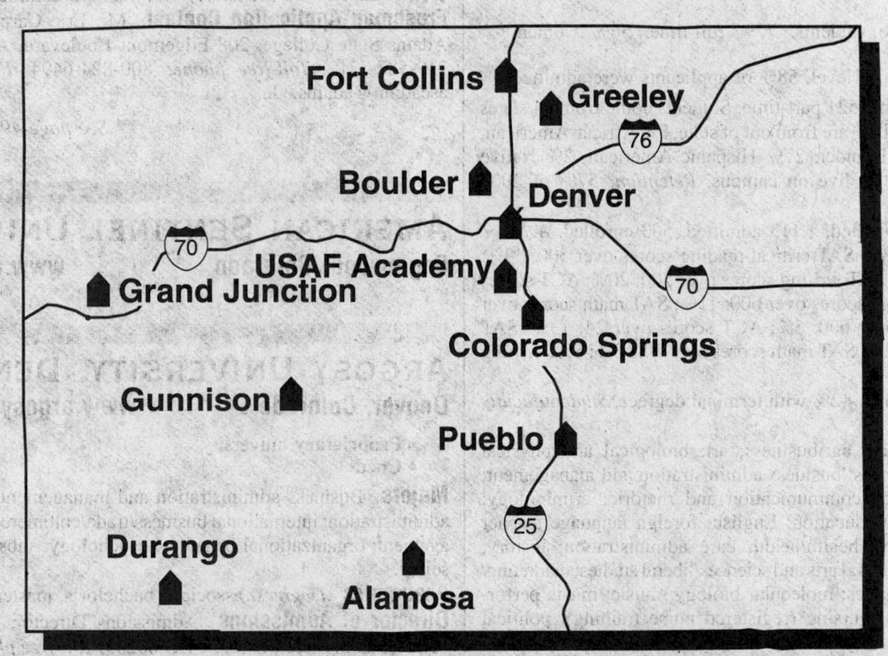

The Denver area includes the towns of Englewood, Greenwood Village, Lakewood, Golden, and Aurora.

ADAMS STATE COLLEGE

Alamosa, Colorado **www.adams.edu/**

- **State-supported** comprehensive, founded 1921
- **Small-town** 90-acre campus
- **Endowment** $65,061
- **Coed** 2,251 undergraduate students, 77% full-time, 56% women, 44% men
- **Moderately difficult** entrance level, 58% of applicants were admitted

Undergraduates 1,730 full-time, 521 part-time. Students come from 44 states and territories, 5 other countries, 15% are from out of state, 8% African American, 2% Asian American or Pacific Islander, 27% Hispanic American, 2% Native American, 8% transferred in, 40% live on campus. *Retention:* 57% of 2006 full-time freshmen returned.

Freshmen *Admission:* 1,928 applied, 1,113 admitted, 503 enrolled. *Average high school GPA:* 2.92. *Test scores:* SAT critical reading scores over 500: 39%; SAT math scores over 500: 39%; SAT writing scores over 500: 20%; ACT scores over 18: 66%; SAT critical reading scores over 600: 11%; SAT math scores over 600: 11%; SAT writing scores over 600: 5%; ACT scores over 24: 13%; SAT critical reading scores over 700: 2%; SAT math scores over 700: 3%; SAT writing scores over 700: 2%.

Faculty *Total:* 184, 60% full-time, 42% with terminal degrees. *Student/faculty ratio:* 14:1.

Majors Accounting and finance; agribusiness; art; biological and physical sciences; biology/biological sciences; business administration and management; chemistry; communication/speech communication and rhetoric; criminology; dramatic/theater arts; elementary education; English; foreign language teacher education; geology/earth science; health/health care administration; history; kinesiology and exercise science; liberal arts and sciences/liberal studies; marketing/marketing management; mathematics; molecular biology; music; music performance; music teacher education; nursing (registered nurse training); political science and government; pre-dentistry studies; pre-engineering; pre-law studies; pre-medical studies; pre-nursing studies; pre-pharmacy studies; pre-veterinary studies; psychology; psychology related; secondary education; social sciences; sociology; Spanish; speech and rhetoric.

Academics *Calendar:* semesters. *Degrees:* associate, bachelor's, and master's. *Special study options:* academic remediation for entering students, accelerated degree program, adult/continuing education programs, advanced placement credit, distance learning, double majors, independent study, internships, off-campus study, part-time degree program, services for LD students, student-designed majors, study abroad, summer session for credit.

Computers on Campus 353 computers/terminals are available on campus for general student use. Students can access the following: campus intranet, computer help desk, free student e-mail accounts, online (class) grades, online (class) registration, online (class) schedules. Campuswide network is available. Wireless service is available via dorm rooms, libraries, student centers.

Student Life *Housing:* on-campus residence required through sophomore year. *Options:* coed, men-only, women-only. Campus housing is university owned. Freshman campus housing is guaranteed. *Activities and organizations:* drama/theater group, student-run newspaper, radio station, choral group, marching band, student government, Student Ambassadors, Program Council, Circle K, Tri Beta. *Campus security:* 24-hour emergency response devices and patrols, student patrols, late-night transport/escort service, controlled dormitory access. *Student services:* health clinic, personal/psychological counseling.

Athletics Member NCAA. All Division II. *Intercollegiate sports:* basketball M (s)/W (s), cross-country running M (s)/W (s), football M (s), golf M (s), softball W (s), track and field M (s)/W (s), volleyball W (s), wrestling M (s). *Intramural sports:* basketball M/W, football M/W, golf M/W, racquetball M/W, soccer M/W, softball M/W, swimming and diving M/W, tennis M/W, volleyball M/W, water polo M/W.

Standardized Tests *Required:* SAT or ACT (for admission).

Costs (2007–08) *Tuition:* state resident $2328 full-time, $97 per credit hour part-time; nonresident $9672 full-time, $403 per credit hour part-time. Full-time tuition and fees vary according to course load and student level. Part-time tuition and fees vary according to course load. *Required fees:* $1136 full-time, $47 per credit hour part-time. *Room and board:* $6410; room only: $3420. Room and board charges vary according to board plan and housing facility. *Payment plans:* installment, deferred payment. *Waivers:* senior citizens and employees or children of employees.

Financial Aid Of all full-time matriculated undergraduates who enrolled in 2006, 1,594 applied for aid, 1,323 were judged to have need, 9 had their need fully met. In 2006, 65 non-need-based awards were made. *Average percent of need met:* 49%. *Average financial aid package:* $6946. *Average need-based loan:* $3332. *Average need-based gift aid:* $3876. *Average non-need-based aid:* $1721. *Average indebtedness upon graduation:* $17,990.

Applying *Options:* electronic application, early admission, deferred entrance. *Application fee:* $20. *Required:* high school transcript, minimum 2.0 GPA. *Required for some:* essay or personal statement, high school transcript, letters of recommendation, interview, audition for music majors. *Application deadlines:* 8/1 (freshmen), 8/1 (transfers). *Notification:* continuous (freshmen).

Freshman Application Contact Mr. Eric Carpio, Director of Admissions, Adams State College, 208 Edgemont Boulevard, Alamosa, CO 81102. *Phone:* 719-587-7712. *Toll-free phone:* 800-824-6494. *Fax:* 719-587-7522. *E-mail:* ascadmit@adams.edu.

See page 494 for the College Close-Up.

AMERICAN SENTINEL UNIVERSITY

Englewood, Colorado **www.americansentinel.edu/**

ARGOSY UNIVERSITY, DENVER

Denver, Colorado **www.argosy.edu/locations/denver/**

- **Proprietary** university
- **Coed**

Majors Business administration and management; finance; health/health care administration; international business/trade/commerce; marketing/marketing management; organizational behavior; psychology; substance abuse/addiction counseling.

Academics *Degrees:* associate, bachelor's, master's, and doctoral.

Director of Admissions Admissions Director, Argosy University, Denver, 1200 Lincoln Street, Denver, CO 80203. *Toll-free phone:* 866-431-5981.

See page 496 for the College Close-Up.

THE ART INSTITUTE OF COLORADO

Denver, Colorado **www.aic.artinstitutes.edu/**

- **Proprietary** 4-year, founded 1952, part of Education Management Corporation
- **Urban** campus
- **Coed**
- **Minimally difficult** entrance level

Faculty *Student/faculty ratio:* 19:1.

Academics *Calendar:* quarters. *Degrees:* diplomas, associate, and bachelor's.

Student Life *Campus security:* 24-hour emergency response devices.

Costs (2007–08) *Tuition:* $20,928 full-time, $436 per credit part-time. Full-time tuition and fees vary according to course load. Part-time tuition and fees vary according to course load. No tuition increase for student's term of enrollment. tuition cost varies by program. Prospective students should contact the school for current tuition costs. Other charges include a starting kit for all first-quarter students. Kits vary in price depending on the program of study. *Room only:* $9000.

Financial Aid Of all full-time matriculated undergraduates who enrolled in 2004, 1,621 applied for aid, 1,621 were judged to have need. 34 state and other part-time jobs. In 2004, 59 non-need-based awards were made. *Average indebtedness upon graduation:* $30,000.

Applying *Options:* early admission, deferred entrance. *Application fee:* $50. *Required:* essay or personal statement, high school transcript, interview.

Freshman Application Contact Mr. Brian Parker, Director of Admissions, The Art Institute of Colorado, 1200 Lincoln Street, Denver, CO 80203. *Phone:* 303-837-0825 Ext. 4729. *Toll-free phone:* 800-275-2420. *Fax:* 303-860-8520. *E-mail:* aicinfo@aii.edu.

See page 498 for the College Close-Up.

ASPEN UNIVERSITY

Denver, Colorado **www.aspen.edu/**

Director of Admissions Admissions, Aspen University, 501 South Cherry Street, Suite 350, Denver, CO 80246. *Phone:* 303-333-4224 Ext. 177. *Toll-free phone:* 800-441-4746 Ext. 177. *Fax:* 303-336-1144. *E-mail:* info@aspen.edu.

CollegeAmerica–Colorado Springs

Colorado Spring, Colorado **www.collegeamerica.com/**

- **Proprietary** primarily 2-year
- **Coed**

Academics *Degrees:* associate and bachelor's.

Freshman Application Contact Admissions Office, CollegeAmerica–Colorado Springs, 3645 Citadel Drive South, Colorado Springs, CO 80909.

CollegeAmerica–Denver

Denver, Colorado **www.collegeamerica.com/**

- **Proprietary** primarily 2-year, founded 1962
- **Urban** campus
- **Coed**
- **Noncompetitive** entrance level

Academics *Degrees:* certificates, associate, and bachelor's.

Freshman Application Contact Admissions Office, CollegeAmerica–Denver, 1385 South Colorado Boulevard, Denver, CO 80222. *Phone:* 303-691-9756. *Toll-free phone:* 800-97-SKILLS.

CollegeAmerica–Fort Collins

Fort Collins, Colorado **www.collegeamerica.edu/**

Director of Admissions Ms. Anna DiTorrice-Mull, Director of Admissions, CollegeAmerica–Fort Collins, 4601 South Mason Street, Fort Collins, CO 80525. *Phone:* 970-223-6060 Ext. 8002. *Toll-free phone:* 800-97-SKILLS.

Colorado Christian University

Lakewood, Colorado **www.ccu.edu/**

- **Independent interdenominational** comprehensive, founded 1914
- **Suburban** 26-acre campus with easy access to Denver
- **Endowment** $17.9 million
- **Coed**
- **Moderately difficult** entrance level

Faculty *Student/faculty ratio:* 21:1.

Academics *Calendar:* semesters. *Degrees:* associate, bachelor's, and master's.

Student Life *Campus security:* 24-hour emergency response devices and patrols, student patrols.

Athletics Member NCAA. All Division II.

Standardized Tests *Required:* SAT or ACT (for admission).

Costs (2007–08) *Comprehensive fee:* $25,975 includes full-time tuition ($18,200), mandatory fees ($150), and room and board ($7625). *College room only:* $4415.

Financial Aid Of all full-time matriculated undergraduates who enrolled in 2004, 750 applied for aid, 615 were judged to have need, 55 had their need fully met. 16 Federal Work-Study jobs (averaging $2000). In 2004, 252 non-need-based awards were made. *Average percent of need met:* 54. *Average financial aid package:* $8931. *Average need-based loan:* $3946. *Average need-based gift aid:* $6056. *Average non-need-based aid:* $12,655. *Average indebtedness upon graduation:* $18,633.

Applying *Options:* electronic application, deferred entrance. *Application fee:* $50. *Required:* essay or personal statement, high school transcript, 2 letters of recommendation, interview. *Required for some:* minimum 2.8 GPA, 3 letters of recommendation, interview.

Freshman Application Contact Mr. Jeff Cazer, Associate, Colorado Christian University, 180 South Garrison Street, Lakewood, CO 80226. *Phone:* 303-963-3200. *Toll-free phone:* 800-44-FAITH. *Fax:* 303-963-3201. *E-mail:* admission@ccu.edu.

See page 500 for the College Close-Up.

The Colorado College

Colorado Springs, Colorado **www.coloradocollege.edu/**

- **Independent** comprehensive, founded 1874
- **Urban** 90-acre campus with easy access to Denver
- **Endowment** $489.1 million
- **Coed** 2,053 undergraduate students, 99% full-time, 54% women, 46% men
- **Very difficult** entrance level, 32% of applicants were admitted

Undergraduates 2,034 full-time, 19 part-time. Students come from 49 states and territories, 25 other countries, 74% are from out of state, 2% African American, 5% Asian American or Pacific Islander, 7% Hispanic American, 0.8% Native American, 3% international, 2% transferred in, 73% live on campus. *Retention:* 96% of 2006 full-time freshmen returned.

Freshmen *Admission:* 4,826 applied, 1,540 admitted, 524 enrolled. *Test scores:* SAT critical reading scores over 500: 97%; SAT math scores over 500: 99%; SAT writing scores over 500: 97%; ACT scores over 18: 100%; SAT critical reading scores over 600: 83%; SAT math scores over 600: 85%; SAT writing scores over 600: 75%; ACT scores over 24: 93%; SAT critical reading scores over 700: 30%; SAT math scores over 700: 22%; SAT writing scores over 700: 25%; ACT scores over 30: 45%.

Faculty *Total:* 186, 86% full-time, 81% with terminal degrees. *Student/faculty ratio:* 11:1.

Majors Anthropology; art history, criticism and conservation; Asian studies; biochemistry; biology/biological sciences; chemistry; classics and languages, literatures and linguistics; comparative literature; computer and information sciences related; creative writing; dance; dramatic/theater arts; econometrics and quantitative economics; economics; economics related; English; environmental science; ethnic, cultural minority, and gender studies related; film/cinema studies; fine/studio arts; French; French studies; geology/earth science; German; health and physical education; Hispanic-American, Puerto Rican, and Mexican-American/Chicano studies; history; international economics; Italian; liberal arts and sciences and humanities related; mathematics; mathematics and computer science; multi-/interdisciplinary studies related; music; neuroscience; philosophy; physics; political science and government; psychology; regional studies; religious studies; Romance languages related; Russian; Russian studies; social sciences related; sociology; Spanish; women's studies.

Academics *Calendar:* modular. *Degrees:* bachelor's and master's (master's degree in education only). *Special study options:* advanced placement credit, double majors, English as a second language, independent study, internships, off-campus study, services for LD students, student-designed majors, study abroad, summer session for credit. *ROTC:* Army (c). *Unusual degree programs:* 3-2 engineering with Rensselaer Polytechnic Institute, Washington University in St. Louis, University of Southern California, Columbia University.

Computers on Campus 208 computers/terminals are available on campus for general student use. Students can access the following: campus intranet, computer help desk, free student e-mail accounts, online (class) grades, online (class) registration, online (class) schedules. Campuswide network is available. 100% of college-owned or -operated housing units are wired for high-speed Internet access. Wireless service is available via entire campus.

Student Life *Housing:* on-campus residence required through junior year. *Options:* coed, men-only, women-only. Campus housing is university owned. Freshman campus housing is guaranteed. *Activities and organizations:* drama/theater group, student-run newspaper, radio station, choral group, Community Service organizations, Outdoor Recreation Committee, Arts and Crafts, Theater workshop, Greek Life, national fraternities, national sororities. *Campus security:* 24-hour emergency response devices and patrols, late-night transport/escort service, controlled dormitory access, whistle program, student escort service, good campus lighting. *Student services:* health clinic, personal/psychological counseling, women's center.

Athletics Member NCAA. All Division III except ice hockey (Division I), soccer (Division I). *Intercollegiate sports:* basketball M/W, cross-country running M/W, equestrian sports M (c)/W (c), field hockey M (c)/W (c), football M, ice hockey M (s)/W (c), lacrosse M/W, rugby M (c)/W (c), skiing (downhill) M (c)/W (c), soccer M/W (s), softball W, swimming and diving M/W, tennis M/W, track and field M/W, ultimate Frisbee M (c)/W (c), volleyball M (c)/W, water polo M (c)/W (c). *Intramural sports:* basketball M/W, football M/W, ice hockey M/W, racquetball M/W, soccer M/W, softball M/W, tennis M (c)/W (c), ultimate Frisbee M/W, volleyball M/W.

Standardized Tests *Required:* SAT or ACT (for admission)

Costs (2007–08) *Comprehensive fee:* $42,470 includes full-time tuition ($33,972) and room and board ($8498). Part-time tuition: $1061 per course. *College room only:* $4630. Room and board charges vary according to board plan and housing facility. *Payment plan:* installment. *Waivers:* employees or children of employees.

Financial Aid Of all full-time matriculated undergraduates who enrolled in 2007, 932 applied for aid, 819 were judged to have need, 512 had their need fully met. 337 Federal Work-Study jobs (averaging $1717). 160 state and other part-time jobs (averaging $1638). In 2007, 115 non-need-based awards were made. *Average percent of need met:* 92%. *Average financial aid package:* $31,635. *Average need-based loan:* $4486. *Average need-based gift aid:* $27,821.

Average non-need-based aid: $12,650. *Average indebtedness upon graduation:* $16,503. *Financial aid deadline:* 2/15.

Applying *Options:* electronic application, early decision, early action, deferred entrance. *Application fee:* $50. *Required:* essay or personal statement, high school transcript, letters of recommendation. *Recommended:* interview. *Application deadlines:* 1/15 (freshmen), 1/15 (out-of-state freshmen), 3/1 (transfers), 11/15 (early action). *Early decision deadline:* 11/15 (for plan 1), 1/1 (for plan 2). *Notification:* 4/1 (freshmen), 4/1 (out-of-state freshmen), 5/1 (transfers), 12/20 (early decision plan 1), 2/10 (early decision plan 2), 1/15 (early action).

Freshman Application Contact Mr. Matt Bonser, Associate Director of Admission, The Colorado College, 900 Block North Cascade, West, Colorado Springs, CO 80903-3294. *Phone:* 719-389-6344. *Toll-free phone:* 800-542-7214. *Fax:* 719-389-6816. *E-mail:* admission@coloradocollege.edu.

COLORADO SCHOOL OF MINES

Golden, Colorado — www.mines.edu/

- **State-supported** university, founded 1874
- **Small-town** 373-acre campus with easy access to Denver
- **Endowment** $175.0 million
- **Coed** 3,310 undergraduate students, 82% full-time, 22% women, 78% men
- **Very difficult** entrance level, 85% of applicants were admitted

Undergraduates 2,713 full-time, 597 part-time. Students come from 44 states and territories, 52 other countries, 20% are from out of state, 2% African American, 5% Asian American or Pacific Islander, 6% Hispanic American, 0.8% Native American, 6% international, 2% transferred in, 25% live on campus. *Retention:* 86% of 2006 full-time freshmen returned.

Freshmen *Admission:* 4,188 applied, 3,557 admitted, 787 enrolled. *Average high school GPA:* 3.7. *Test scores:* SAT critical reading scores over 500: 91%; SAT math scores over 500: 98%; ACT scores over 18: 100%; SAT critical reading scores over 600: 51%; SAT math scores over 600: 76%; ACT scores over 24: 87%; SAT critical reading scores over 700: 11%; SAT math scores over 700: 24%; ACT scores over 30: 23%.

Faculty *Total:* 315, 63% full-time, 84% with terminal degrees. *Student/faculty ratio:* 15:1.

Majors Chemical engineering; chemistry; civil engineering; computer science; economics; electrical, electronics and communications engineering; engineering; engineering physics; engineering science; environmental/environmental health engineering; geological/geophysical engineering; mathematics; mechanical engineering; metallurgical engineering; mining and mineral engineering; petroleum engineering.

Academics *Calendar:* semesters. *Degrees:* bachelor's, master's, doctoral, and first professional. *Special study options:* academic remediation for entering students, accelerated degree program, advanced placement credit, cooperative education, double majors, English as a second language, honors programs, independent study, internships, services for LD students, study abroad, summer session for credit. *ROTC:* Army (b).

Computers on Campus 400 computers/terminals are available on campus for general student use. Students can access the following: campus intranet, computer help desk, free student e-mail accounts, online (class) grades, online (class) registration, online (class) schedules. Campuswide network is available. 100% of college-owned or -operated housing units are wired for high-speed Internet access. Wireless service is available via classrooms, computer labs, student centers.

Student Life *Housing options:* coed, men-only, women-only. Campus housing is university owned. Freshman campus housing is guaranteed. *Activities and organizations:* drama/theater group, student-run newspaper, radio station, choral group, marching band, Residence Hall Association, Society of Women Engineers, American Institute of Chemical Engineers, national fraternities, national sororities. *Campus security:* 24-hour emergency response devices and patrols, late-night transport/escort service, controlled dormitory access. *Student services:* health clinic, personal/psychological counseling.

Athletics Member NCAA. All Division II. *Intercollegiate sports:* baseball M (s), basketball M (s)/W (s), cross-country running M (s)/W (s), football M (s), golf M (s)/W (s), skiing (downhill) M, soccer M (s)/W (s), softball W (s), swimming and diving M (s)/W (s), tennis M (s)/W (s), track and field M (s)/W (s), volleyball W (s), wrestling M (s). *Intramural sports:* badminton M/W, basketball M/W, cross-country running M/W, football M/W, lacrosse M (c), racquetball M/W, rock climbing M (c)/W (c), rugby M (c), soccer M/W, softball M/W, swimming and diving M/W, tennis M/W, track and field M/W, volleyball M/W.

Standardized Tests *Required:* SAT or ACT (for admission).

Costs (2007–08) *Tuition:* state resident $8764 full-time, $325 per semester hour part-time; nonresident $21,750 full-time, $725 per semester hour part-time. Part-time tuition and fees vary according to course load. *Required fees:* $1390 full-time, $80 per semester part-time. *Room and board:* $7350; room only: $3700. Room and board charges vary according to board plan and housing facility. *Payment plan:* installment.

Financial Aid Of all full-time matriculated undergraduates who enrolled in 2007, 2,475 applied for aid, 2,225 were judged to have need, 1,900 had their need fully met. 164 Federal Work-Study jobs (averaging $1200). 560 state and other part-time jobs (averaging $1200). In 2007, 280 non-need-based awards were made. *Average percent of need met:* 93%. *Average financial aid package:* $15,500. *Average need-based loan:* $4200. *Average need-based gift aid:* $8800. *Average non-need-based aid:* $5500. *Average indebtedness upon graduation:* $18,700.

Applying *Options:* electronic application, deferred entrance. *Application fee:* $45. *Required:* high school transcript. *Required for some:* essay or personal statement, letters of recommendation, interview. *Recommended:* rank in upper one-third of high school class. *Application deadlines:* 6/1 (freshmen), 6/1 (transfers). *Notification:* continuous (freshmen), continuous (transfers).

Freshman Application Contact Ms. Heather Boyd, Associate Director of Enrollment Management, Colorado School of Mines, Student Center, 1600 Maple Street, Golden, CO 80401. *Phone:* 303-273-3227. *Toll-free phone:* 800-446-9488 Ext. 3220. *Fax:* 303-273-3509. *E-mail:* admit@mines.edu.

COLORADO STATE UNIVERSITY

Fort Collins, Colorado — www.colostate.edu/

- **State-supported** university, founded 1870, part of Colorado State University System
- **Urban** 579-acre campus with easy access to Denver
- **Endowment** $186.5 million
- **Coed** 21,679 undergraduate students, 88% full-time, 52% women, 48% men
- **Moderately difficult** entrance level, 86% of applicants were admitted

Undergraduates 19,042 full-time, 2,637 part-time. Students come from 53 states and territories, 44 other countries, 17% are from out of state, 2% African American, 3% Asian American or Pacific Islander, 7% Hispanic American, 2% Native American, 2% international, 7% transferred in, 27% live on campus. *Retention:* 81% of 2006 full-time freshmen returned.

Freshmen *Admission:* 11,727 applied, 10,068 admitted, 4,392 enrolled. *Average high school GPA:* 3.5. *Test scores:* SAT critical reading scores over 500: 74%; SAT math scores over 500: 80%; SAT writing scores over 500: 70%; ACT scores over 18: 99%; SAT critical reading scores over 600: 32%; SAT math scores over 600: 36%; SAT writing scores over 600: 25%; ACT scores over 24: 55%; SAT critical reading scores over 700: 6%; SAT math scores over 700: 5%; SAT writing scores over 700: 3%; ACT scores over 30: 7%.

Faculty *Total:* 923, 96% full-time, 99% with terminal degrees. *Student/faculty ratio:* 17:1.

Majors Accounting; agribusiness; agricultural and extension education; agricultural and horticultural plant breeding; agricultural economics; agricultural teacher education; agronomy and crop science; American studies; animal sciences; anthropology; apparel and textile marketing management; apparel and textiles; applied horticulture; applied mathematics; art history, criticism and conservation; art teacher education; Asian-American studies; Asian studies; athletic training; biochemistry; biology/biological sciences; biology teacher education; biomedical sciences; botany/plant biology; business administration and management; business teacher education; ceramic arts and ceramics; chemical engineering; chemistry; chemistry teacher education; civil engineering; commercial and advertising art; communication/speech communication and rhetoric; computer and information sciences; computer engineering; computer science; creative writing; criminal justice/safety; crop production; dance; dietetics; dramatic/theater arts; drawing; economics; electrical, electronics and communications engineering; engineering physics; engineering science; English; English/language arts teacher education; entomology; environmental/environmental health engineering; environmental health; equestrian studies; family and consumer sciences/home economics teacher education; family and consumer sciences/human sciences; fiber, textile and weaving arts; finance; fine/studio arts; fire services administration; fishing and fisheries sciences and management; foods, nutrition, and wellness; foreign languages and literatures; forest sciences and biology; French; French language teacher education; geology/earth science; German; German language teacher education; history; horticultural science; hotel/motel administration; human development and family studies; humanities; human nutrition; information science/studies; interior design; journalism; kinesiology and exercise science; landscape architecture; landscaping and groundskeeping; Latin American studies; liberal arts and sciences/liberal studies; marketing/marketing management; mathematics; mathematics teacher education; mechanical engineering; medical microbiology and bacteriology; metal and jewelry arts; music; music performance; music teacher education; music therapy; natural resources/conservation; natural resources management and policy; painting; parks, recreation and leisure facilities management; philosophy; photography; physical sciences; physics; physics teacher education; plant sciences; political science and government; pre-veterinary studies; printmaking; psychology; public relations/image management; radio and television; range science and management; restaurant/food services management; sales and marketing/marketing and distribution teacher education; science teacher education; sculpture; social sciences; social studies teacher education; social work; sociology; soil science and agronomy; Spanish; Spanish language teacher education; speech and rhetoric; turf and turfgrass management; water, wetlands, and marine resources management; wildlife and wildlands science and management; wildlife biology; zoology/animal biology.

Academics *Calendar:* semesters. *Degrees:* bachelor's, master's, doctoral, and first professional. *Special study options:* accelerated degree program, advanced placement credit, cooperative education, distance learning, double majors, English as a second language, honors programs, independent study, internships, off-campus study, part-time degree program, services for LD students, study abroad, summer session for credit. *ROTC:* Army (b), Air Force (b). *Unusual degree programs:* 3-2 engineering.

Computers on Campus 2,700 computers/terminals and 3,200 ports are available on campus for general student use. Students can access the following: campus intranet, computer help desk, free student e-mail accounts, online (class) grades, online (class) registration, online (class) schedules, online course management, personalized portal services including transcripts and financials (billing, financial aid). Campuswide network is available. 100% of college-owned or -operated housing units are wired for high-speed Internet access. Wireless service is available via classrooms, computer centers, computer labs, libraries, student centers.

Student Life *Housing:* on-campus residence required for freshman year. *Options:* coed, disabled students. Campus housing is university owned. Freshman campus housing is guaranteed. *Activities and organizations:* drama/theater group, student-run newspaper, radio and television station, choral group, marching band, Residence Hall Council, Interfraternity Counsil, Panhellenic Council, Associated Students of CSU (ASCSU Student Government), Snowriders, national fraternities, national sororities. *Campus security:* 24-hour emergency response devices and patrols, student patrols, late-night transport/escort service, controlled dormitory access. *Student services:* health clinic, personal/psychological counseling, women's center, legal services.

Athletics Member NCAA. All Division I except football (Division I-A). *Intercollegiate sports:* baseball M (c), basketball M (s)/W (s), crew M (c)/W (c), cross-country running M (s)/W (s), field hockey M (c)/W (c), golf M (s)/W (s), ice hockey M (c), lacrosse M (c)/W (c), rugby M (c)/W (c), skiing (downhill) M (c)/W (c), soccer M (c)/W (c), softball W (s), swimming and diving W (s), tennis M (c)/W (s), track and field M (s)/W (s), ultimate Frisbee M (c)/W (c), volleyball W (s), water polo M (c)/W (s), wrestling M (c). *Intramural sports:* basketball M/W, bowling M/W, golf M/W, soccer M/W, softball M/W, ultimate Frisbee M/W, volleyball M/W.

Standardized Tests *Required:* SAT or ACT (for admission).

Costs (2007–08) *Tuition:* state resident $4040 full-time, $202 per credit hour part-time; nonresident $17,480 full-time, $874 per credit hour part-time. Full-time tuition and fees vary according to course load. Part-time tuition and fees vary according to course load. *Required fees:* $1379 full-time, $10 per credit hour part-time, $75 per term part-time. *Room and board:* $7382; room only: $3578. Room and board charges vary according to board plan and housing facility. *Payment plan:* installment. *Waivers:* employees or children of employees.

Financial Aid Of all full-time matriculated undergraduates who enrolled in 2006, 11,228 applied for aid, 7,044 were judged to have need, 2,902 had their need fully met. 400 Federal Work-Study jobs (averaging $2031). 1,084 state and other part-time jobs (averaging $1258). In 2006, 1487 non-need-based awards were made. *Average percent of need met:* 76%. *Average financial aid package:* $8685. *Average need-based loan:* $5400. *Average need-based gift aid:* $5908. *Average non-need-based aid:* $3099. *Average indebtedness upon graduation:* $18,912.

Applying *Options:* electronic application, deferred entrance. *Application fee:* $50. *Required:* essay or personal statement, high school transcript, letters of recommendation. *Application deadlines:* 7/1 (freshmen), 7/1 (transfers). *Notification:* continuous (freshmen), continuous (transfers).

Freshman Application Contact Ms. Mary Ontiveros, Associate Vice President for Enrollment and Access and Executive Director of Admissions, Colorado State University, Spruce Hall, Fort Collins, CO 80523-0015. *Phone:* 970-491-6909. *Fax:* 970-491-7799. *E-mail:* admissions@colostate.edu.

See page 502 for the College Close-Up.

COLORADO STATE UNIVERSITY-PUEBLO

Pueblo, Colorado **www.colostate-pueblo.edu/**

- **State-supported** comprehensive, founded 1933, part of Colorado State University System
- **Suburban** 275-acre campus with easy access to Colorado Springs
- **Endowment** $4.1 million
- **Coed** 4,798 undergraduate students, 64% full-time, 58% women, 42% men
- **Moderately difficult** entrance level, 97% of applicants were admitted

Undergraduates 3,076 full-time, 1,722 part-time. Students come from 40 states and territories, 23 other countries, 7% are from out of state, 6% African American, 3% Asian American or Pacific Islander, 25% Hispanic American, 2% Native American, 2% international, 8% transferred in, 10% live on campus. *Retention:* 63% of 2006 full-time freshmen returned.

Freshmen *Admission:* 1,485 applied, 1,441 admitted, 644 enrolled. *Average high school GPA:* 3.1. *Test scores:* SAT critical reading scores over 500: 47%; SAT math scores over 500: 42%; ACT scores over 18: 76%; SAT critical reading scores over 600: 7%; SAT math scores over 600: 11%; ACT scores over 24: 23%; ACT scores over 30: 1%.

Faculty *Total:* 304, 51% full-time. *Student/faculty ratio:* 17:1.

Majors Accounting; automotive engineering technology; biology/biological sciences; business/managerial economics; chemistry; civil engineering technology; engineering; English; fine/studio arts; foreign languages and literatures; history; information science/studies; kinesiology and exercise science; liberal arts and sciences/liberal studies; mass communication/media; music; nursing (registered nurse training); physics; political science and government; psychology; social sciences; social work; sociology.

Academics *Calendar:* semesters. *Degrees:* bachelor's and master's. *Special study options:* academic remediation for entering students, accelerated degree program, adult/continuing education programs, advanced placement credit, cooperative education, distance learning, double majors, English as a second language, external degree program, honors programs, independent study, internships, off-campus study, part-time degree program, services for LD students, study abroad, summer session for credit. *ROTC:* Army (b). *Unusual degree programs:* 3-2 business administration; applied natural science.

Computers on Campus 702 computers/terminals and 650 ports are available on campus for general student use. Students can access the following: computer help desk, free student e-mail accounts, online (class) grades, online (class) registration, online (class) schedules. Campuswide network is available. 100% of college-owned or -operated housing units are wired for high-speed Internet access. Wireless service is available via classrooms, computer centers, computer labs, learning centers, libraries, student centers.

Student Life *Housing:* on-campus residence required for freshman year. *Options:* coed. Campus housing is university owned and is provided by a third party. Freshman campus housing is guaranteed. *Activities and organizations:* student-run newspaper, radio and television station, choral group, Belmont Residence Hall Association, Associated Student Government, Gay/Straight Alliance, Medical Science Society, Bowling Club, national fraternities, national sororities. *Campus security:* 24-hour emergency response devices and patrols, late-night transport/escort service, controlled dormitory access. *Student services:* health clinic, personal/psychological counseling.

Athletics Member NCAA. *Intercollegiate sports:* baseball M, basketball M (s)/W (s), cross-country running W (s), golf M (s)/W (s), soccer M/W, softball W (s), tennis M (s)/W (s), volleyball W (s). *Intramural sports:* basketball M/W, cheerleading W, lacrosse M, racquetball M/W, rock climbing M/W, sailing M/W, skiing (cross-country) M/W, skiing (downhill) M/W, soccer M/W, softball M/W, tennis M/W, ultimate Frisbee M/W, volleyball M/W, weight lifting M/W, wrestling M.

Standardized Tests *Required:* SAT or ACT (for admission), SAT or ACT (for placement).

Costs (2008–09) *Tuition:* state resident $3343 full-time, $139 per credit hour part-time; nonresident $13,543 full-time, $564 per credit hour part-time. *Room and board:* $8092; room only: $5194.

Financial Aid Of all full-time matriculated undergraduates who enrolled in 2007, 1,618 applied for aid, 1,401 were judged to have need, 105 had their need fully met. 229 Federal Work-Study jobs (averaging $1865). 358 state and other part-time jobs (averaging $4157). In 2007, 371 non-need-based awards were made. *Average percent of need met:* 57%. *Average financial aid package:* $7658. *Average need-based loan:* $3723. *Average need-based gift aid:* $5141. *Average non-need-based aid:* $5500. *Average indebtedness upon graduation:* $16,481.

Applying *Options:* electronic application, deferred entrance. *Application fee:* $25. *Required:* minimum 2.0 GPA. *Required for some:* high school transcript, letters of recommendation. *Application deadlines:* 8/1 (freshmen), 8/1 (transfers). *Notification:* continuous (freshmen), continuous (transfers).

Freshman Application Contact Ms. Jennifer Jensen, Associate Director of Admissions and Records, Colorado State University-Pueblo, 2200 Bonforte Boulevard, Pueblo, CO 81001. *Phone:* 719-549-2434. *Fax:* 719-549-2419. *E-mail:* jennifer.jensen@colostate-pueblo.edu.

COLORADO TECHNICAL UNIVERSITY—COLORADO SPRINGS

Colorado Springs, Colorado www.coloradotech.edu/

- **Proprietary** comprehensive, founded 1965, administratively affiliated with Colorado Technical University
- **Suburban** 14-acre campus with easy access to Denver
- **Coed**
- **Minimally difficult** entrance level

Majors Accounting; accounting and finance; business administration and management; computer engineering; computer science; computer software technology; computer systems analysis; computer technology/computer systems technology; criminal justice/law enforcement administration; e-commerce; electrical, electronic and communications engineering technology; electrical, electronics and communications engineering; finance; general studies; graphic design; health/health care administration; health information/medical records technology; human resources management; information science/studies; information technology; management information systems; marketing/marketing management; massage therapy; medical/clinical assistant; medical radiologic technology; surgical technology.

Academics *Calendar:* quarters. *Degrees:* diplomas, associate, bachelor's, master's, and doctoral. *Special study options:* academic remediation for entering students, accelerated degree program, adult/continuing education programs, advanced placement credit, cooperative education, distance learning, double majors, independent study, internships, part-time degree program, services for LD students, summer session for credit. *ROTC:* Army (c).

Computers on Campus Campuswide network is available. Wireless service is available via classrooms, computer centers, computer labs, learning centers, libraries, student centers.

Student Life *Housing:* college housing not available. *Campus security:* 24-hour emergency response devices, late-night transport/escort service.

Costs (2008–09) *Tuition:* Contact campus for cost.

Financial Aid Of all full-time matriculated undergraduates who enrolled in 2006, 70 applied for aid, 55 were judged to have need, 30 had their need fully met. 35 Federal Work-Study jobs (averaging $4619). In 2006, 40 non-need-based awards were made. *Average percent of need met:* 95%. *Average financial aid package:* $9310. *Average need-based loan:* $3500. *Average need-based gift aid:* $5000. *Average indebtedness upon graduation:* $7500.

Applying *Options:* electronic application, deferred entrance. *Application fee:* $50. *Required:* interview. *Application deadlines:* rolling (freshmen), rolling (transfers). *Notification:* continuous (freshmen), continuous (transfers).

Director of Admissions Chief Admission Officer, Colorado Technical University—Colorado Springs, 4435 North Chestnut Street, Colorado Springs, CO 80907-3896. *Phone:* 719-598-0200.

COLORADO TECHNICAL UNIVERSITY—DENVER

Greenwood Village, Colorado www.coloradotech.edu/

- **Proprietary** comprehensive, founded 1965, administratively affiliated with Colorado Technical University
- **Urban** 1-acre campus with easy access to Denver
- **Coed**
- **Minimally difficult** entrance level

Majors Accounting; accounting and finance; business administration and management; computer engineering; computer science; computer software technology; computer systems analysis; computer technology/computer systems technology; criminal justice/law enforcement administration; e-commerce; electrical, electronic and communications engineering technology; electrical, electronics and communications engineering; finance; general studies; graphic design; health/health care administration; health information/medical records technology; human resources management; information science/studies; information technology; management information systems; marketing/marketing management; massage therapy; medical/clinical assistant; medical radiologic technology; surgical technology.

Academics *Calendar:* quarters. *Degrees:* diplomas, associate, bachelor's, and master's. *Special study options:* academic remediation for entering students, adult/continuing education programs, advanced placement credit, cooperative education, distance learning, double majors, independent study, part-time degree program, services for LD students, summer session for credit.

Computers on Campus Campuswide network is available. Wireless service is available via classrooms, computer centers, computer labs, learning centers, libraries, student centers.

Student Life *Housing:* college housing not available. *Campus security:* 24-hour emergency response devices and patrols, late-night transport/escort service.

Costs (2008–09) *Tuition:* Contact campus for cost.

Financial Aid Of all full-time matriculated undergraduates who enrolled in 2001, 2 Federal Work-Study jobs (averaging $3936).

Applying *Options:* electronic application, deferred entrance. *Application fee:* $50. *Application deadlines:* rolling (freshmen), rolling (transfers). *Notification:* continuous (freshmen), continuous (transfers).

Director of Admissions Director of Admissions, Colorado Technical University—Denver, 5775 Denver Tech Center Boulevard, Suite 100, Greenwood Village, CO 80111. *Phone:* 303-694-6600.

COLORADO TECHNICAL UNIVERSITY—ONLINE

Colorado Springs, Colorado www.coloradotech.edu/

- **Proprietary** comprehensive, administratively affiliated with Colorado Technical University
- **Coed**
- **Minimally difficult** entrance level

Majors Accounting; accounting and finance; business administration and management; computer engineering; computer science; computer software technology; computer systems analysis; computer technology/computer systems technology; criminal justice/law enforcement administration; e-commerce; electrical, electronic and communications engineering technology; electrical, electronics and communications engineering; finance; general studies; graphic design; health/health care administration; health information/medical records technology; human resources management; information science/studies; information technology; management information systems; marketing/marketing management.

Academics *Calendar:* quarters. *Degrees:* diplomas, associate, bachelor's, and master's.

Costs (2008–09) *Tuition:* Contact campus for cost.

Applying *Options:* electronic application, deferred entrance. *Application fee:* $50. *Required:* interview. *Application deadlines:* rolling (freshmen), rolling (transfers). *Notification:* continuous (freshmen), continuous (transfers).

Director of Admissions Chief Admission Officer, Colorado Technical University—Online, 4435 West Chestnut Street, Suite E, Colorado Springs, CO 80907. *Phone:* 866-813-1836.

DEVRY UNIVERSITY

Colorado Springs, Colorado www.devry.edu/

Director of Admissions Admissions Office, DeVry University, 1175 Kelly Johnson Boulevard, Colorado Springs, CO 80920. *Toll-free phone:* 866-338-7934.

DEVRY UNIVERSITY

Westminster, Colorado www.devry.edu/

- **Proprietary** comprehensive, founded 1945, administratively affiliated with DeVry, Inc
- **Urban** 3-acre campus with easy access to Denver
- **Coed** 600 undergraduate students, 49% full-time, 36% women, 64% men
- **Noncompetitive** entrance level

Undergraduates 292 full-time, 308 part-time. 4% are from out of state, 7% African American, 4% Asian American or Pacific Islander, 12% Hispanic American, 1% Native American, 0.2% international, 18% transferred in. *Retention:* 44% of 2006 full-time freshmen returned.

Freshmen *Admission:* 94 enrolled.

Faculty *Total:* 35, 49% full-time. *Student/faculty ratio:* 19:1.

Majors Accounting; business administration and management; business administration, management and operations related; computer engineering technology; computer software engineering; computer systems analysis; computer systems networking and telecommunications; electrical, electronic and communications engineering technology; health information/medical records technology; web page, digital/multimedia and information resources design.

Academics *Calendar:* semesters. *Degrees:* associate, bachelor's, and master's. *Special study options:* academic remediation for entering students, accelerated degree program, adult/continuing education programs, distance learning, summer session for credit.

Computers on Campus 83 computers/terminals are available on campus for general student use. Campuswide network is available.

Student Life *Housing:* college housing not available. *Campus security:* 24-hour patrols, late-night transport/escort service. *Student services:* personal/psychological counseling.

Costs (2008–09) *Tuition:* $13,810 full-time, $515 per credit part-time. *Required fees:* $180 full-time.

Financial Aid Of all full-time matriculated undergraduates who enrolled in 2002, 286 applied for aid, 269 were judged to have need, 4 had their need fully met. In 2002, 21 non-need-based awards were made. *Average percent of need met:* 33%. *Average financial aid package:* $7172. *Average need-based loan:* $4815. *Average need-based gift aid:* $4260. *Average non-need-based aid:* $10,657.

Applying *Options:* electronic application, early admission, deferred entrance. *Application fee:* $50. *Required:* high school transcript. *Required for some:* essay or personal statement, interview. *Application deadlines:* rolling (freshmen), rolling (transfers). *Notification:* continuous (freshmen), continuous (transfers).

Freshman Application Contact DeVry University, 1870 West 122nd Avenue, Suite 316, Westminster, CO 80234-2010.

FORT LEWIS COLLEGE

Durango, Colorado **www.fortlewis.edu/**

- **State-supported** 4-year, founded 1911
- **Small-town** 350-acre campus
- **Endowment** $4.8 million
- **Coed** 3,935 undergraduate students, 90% full-time, 48% women, 52% men
- **Moderately difficult** entrance level, 72% of applicants were admitted

Undergraduates 3,542 full-time, 393 part-time. Students come from 48 states and territories, 10 other countries, 29% are from out of state, 1% African American, 1% Asian American or Pacific Islander, 6% Hispanic American, 20% Native American, 0.8% international, 9% transferred in, 34% live on campus. *Retention:* 57% of 2006 full-time freshmen returned.

Freshmen *Admission:* 3,020 applied, 2,181 admitted, 925 enrolled. *Average high school GPA:* 3.03. *Test scores:* SAT critical reading scores over 500: 55%; SAT math scores over 500: 57%; SAT writing scores over 500: 43%; ACT scores over 18: 83%; SAT critical reading scores over 600: 11%; SAT math scores over 600: 13%; SAT writing scores over 600: 8%; ACT scores over 24: 23%; SAT critical reading scores over 700: 1%; SAT writing scores over 700: 1%; ACT scores over 30: 2%.

Faculty *Total:* 239, 74% full-time, 62% with terminal degrees. *Student/faculty ratio:* 17:1.

Majors Accounting; agricultural business and management; American Indian/Native American studies; anthropology; art; arts management; Asian studies; athletic training; biochemistry; biology/biological sciences; biology teacher education; business administration and management; business/managerial economics; cell and molecular biology; chemistry; chemistry teacher education; computer science; cultural studies; dramatic/theater arts; early childhood education; economics; elementary education; engineering/industrial management; engineering physics; English; English language and literature related; English/language arts teacher education; environmental biology; environmental studies; European studies; finance; geology/earth science; history; humanities; information science/studies; international business/trade/commerce; kinesiology and exercise science; Latin American studies; liberal arts and sciences/liberal studies; marketing/marketing management; mathematics; music; music performance; music teacher education; parks, recreation and leisure; philosophy; physical education teaching and coaching; physics; political science and government; psychology; secondary education; sociology; Spanish; sport and fitness administration/management; tourism and travel services management; women's studies.

Academics *Calendar:* modified trimesters. *Degree:* bachelor's. *Special study options:* academic remediation for entering students, accelerated degree program, adult/continuing education programs, advanced placement credit, cooperative education, distance learning, double majors, English as a second language, honors programs, independent study, internships, part-time degree program, services for LD students, student-designed majors, study abroad, summer session for credit. *Unusual degree programs:* 3-2 engineering with Colorado State University, Colorado School of Mines, University of New Mexico, University of Colorado at Boulder, Colorado State University at Pueblo, New Mexico State University; forestry with Colorado State University, Northern Arizona University.

Computers on Campus 672 computers/terminals are available on campus for general student use. Students can access the following: campus intranet, computer help desk, free student e-mail accounts, online (class) grades, online (class) registration, online (class) schedules. Campuswide network is available. 100% of college-owned or -operated housing units are wired for high-speed Internet access. Wireless service is available via computer labs, libraries.

Student Life *Housing:* on-campus residence required for freshman year. *Options:* coed. Campus housing is university owned. Freshman applicants given priority for college housing. *Activities and organizations:* drama/theater group, student-run newspaper, radio station, choral group, Beta Alpha Psi, AISES (American Indian Science and Engineering Club), Master Plan Ministries, Dance Co-Motion, The Independent (Student Newspaper). *Campus security:* 24-hour emergency response devices and patrols, late-night transport/escort service, controlled dormitory access. *Student services:* health clinic, personal/psychological counseling, legal services.

Athletics Member NCAA. All Division II. *Intercollegiate sports:* baseball M (c), basketball M (s)/W (s), cheerleading M (c)/W (c), cross-country running M (s)/W (s), fencing M (c)/W (c), football M (s), golf M (s), ice hockey M (c)/W (c), lacrosse M (c)/W (s), rock climbing M (c)/W (c), rugby M (c)/W (c), skiing (cross-country) M (c)/W (c), skiing (downhill) M (c)/W (c), soccer M (s)/W (s), softball W (s), ultimate Frisbee M (c)/W (c), volleyball W (s), wrestling M (c)/W (c). *Intramural sports:* badminton M/W, basketball M/W, football M/W, golf M/W, racquetball M/W, soccer M/W, softball M/W, ultimate Frisbee M/W, volleyball M/W.

Standardized Tests *Required:* SAT or ACT (for admission).

Costs (2007–08) *One-time required fee:* $135. *Tuition:* state resident $5318 full-time, $222 per credit hour part-time; nonresident $13,848 full-time, $692 per credit hour part-time. Full-time tuition and fees vary according to reciprocity agreements. Part-time tuition and fees vary according to course load and reciprocity agreements. *Required fees:* $1146 full-time, $45 per credit hour part-time. *Room and board:* $6876; room only: $3676. Room and board charges vary according to board plan and housing facility. *Waivers:* minority students and employees or children of employees.

Financial Aid Of all full-time matriculated undergraduates who enrolled in 2006, 2,148 applied for aid, 1,688 were judged to have need, 310 had their need fully met. 155 Federal Work-Study jobs (averaging $2500). 145 state and other part-time jobs (averaging $2400). In 2006, 216 non-need-based awards were made. *Average percent of need met:* 68%. *Average financial aid package:* $7269. *Average need-based loan:* $3687. *Average need-based gift aid:* $4099. *Average non-need-based aid:* $3628. *Average indebtedness upon graduation:* $17,419.

Applying *Options:* electronic application, deferred entrance. *Application fee:* $30. *Required:* high school transcript, minimum 2.0 GPA. *Recommended:* essay or personal statement, letters of recommendation, interview. *Application deadlines:* 8/1 (freshmen), rolling (transfers). *Notification:* continuous (freshmen), continuous (transfers).

Freshman Application Contact Fort Lewis College, 1000 Rim Drive, Durango, CO 81301. *Phone:* 970-247-7184.

ITT TECHNICAL INSTITUTE

Thornton, Colorado **www.itt-tech.edu/**

- **Proprietary** primarily 2-year, founded 1984, part of ITT Educational Services, Inc
- **Suburban** 2-acre campus with easy access to Denver
- **Coed**
- **Minimally difficult** entrance level

Academics *Calendar:* quarters. *Degrees:* associate and bachelor's.

Standardized Tests *Required:* Wonderlic aptitude test (for admission).

Applying *Options:* deferred entrance. *Application fee:* $100. *Required:* high school transcript, interview. *Recommended:* letters of recommendation.

Freshman Application Contact Ms. Tracy Arnett, Director of Recruitment, ITT Technical Institute, 500 East 84th Avenue, Thornton, CO 80229. *Phone:* 303-288-4488. *Toll-free phone:* 800-395-4488.

JOHNSON & WALES UNIVERSITY

Denver, Colorado **www.jwu.edu/**

- **Independent** 4-year, founded 1993, administratively affiliated with Johnson & Wales University (RI)
- **Small-town** campus
- **Endowment** $168.3 million
- **Coed**
- **Minimally difficult** entrance level

Faculty *Student/faculty ratio:* 19:1.

Academics *Calendar:* modular. *Degrees:* associate and bachelor's.

Student Life *Campus security:* 24-hour emergency response devices and patrols, student patrols, late-night transport/escort service.

Athletics Member NAIA.

Standardized Tests *Required for some:* SAT or ACT (for admission). *Recommended:* SAT or ACT (for admission).

Costs (2008–09) *Comprehensive fee:* $30,541 includes full-time tuition ($21,297), mandatory fees ($1288), and room and board ($7956). Part-time tuition: $394 per quarter hour.

Financial Aid Of all full-time matriculated undergraduates who enrolled in 2005, 1,276 applied for aid, 1,119 were judged to have need, 53 had their need fully met. In 2005, 256 non-need-based awards were made. *Average percent of need met:* 65. *Average financial aid package:* $12,710. *Average need-based loan:* $5736. *Average need-based gift aid:* $5184. *Average non-need-based aid:* $5084. *Average indebtedness upon graduation:* $14,798.

Applying *Options:* electronic application, early admission, deferred entrance. *Required:* high school transcript. *Required for some:* essay or personal statement, minimum 2.75 GPA, interview. *Recommended:* minimum 2.0 GPA.

Freshman Application Contact Kim Ostrowski, Director of Admissions, Johnson & Wales University, 7150 Montview Boulevard, Denver, CO 80220. *Phone:* 977-598-3368. *Toll-free phone:* 877-598-3368. *Fax:* 303-256-9333. *E-mail:* den.admissions@jwu.edu.

JONES INTERNATIONAL UNIVERSITY

Centennial, Colorado **www.jonesinternational.edu/**

Freshman Application Contact Ms. Candace Morrissey, Associate Director of Admissions, Jones International University, 9697 East Mineral Avenue, Centennial, CO 80112. *Toll-free phone:* 800-811-5663. *Fax:* 303-799-0966. *E-mail:* admissions@international.edu.

MESA STATE COLLEGE

Grand Junction, Colorado **www.mesastate.edu/**

- **State-supported** comprehensive, founded 1925
- **Small-town** 42-acre campus
- **Coed** 6,035 undergraduate students, 74% full-time, 59% women, 41% men
- **Minimally difficult** entrance level, 82% of applicants were admitted

Undergraduates 4,437 full-time, 1,598 part-time. Students come from 45 states and territories, 14 other countries, 10% are from out of state, 2% African American, 3% Asian American or Pacific Islander, 9% Hispanic American, 2% Native American, 0.2% international, 9% transferred in, 19% live on campus. *Retention:* 54% of 2006 full-time freshmen returned.

Freshmen *Admission:* 3,147 applied, 2,582 admitted, 1,315 enrolled. *Average high school GPA:* 2.95. *Test scores:* SAT critical reading scores over 500: 44%; SAT math scores over 500: 45%; ACT scores over 18: 72%; SAT critical reading scores over 600: 14%; SAT math scores over 600: 7%; ACT scores over 24: 18%; SAT critical reading scores over 700: 1%; ACT scores over 30: 1%.

Faculty *Total:* 438, 51% full-time. *Student/faculty ratio:* 17:1.

Majors Accounting; art; athletic training; automobile/automotive mechanics technology; biology/biological sciences; business administration, management and operations related; business/commerce; communications technology; computer and information sciences; construction trades; cooking and related culinary arts; criminal justice/law enforcement administration; criminal justice/safety; dramatic/theater arts; electrical, electronic and communications engineering technology; emergency medical technology (EMT paramedic); English; environmental science; history; hospitality administration; kinesiology and exercise science; liberal arts and sciences/liberal studies; machine tool technology; management information systems; manufacturing technology; mass communication/media; mathematics; music; nursing (registered nurse training); office management; physical sciences; political science and government; psychology; public administration; radiologic technology/science; social sciences; sociology; Spanish; sport and fitness administration/management.

Academics *Calendar:* semesters. *Degrees:* certificates, associate, bachelor's, and master's. *Special study options:* academic remediation for entering students, accelerated degree program, adult/continuing education programs, advanced placement credit, cooperative education, distance learning, double majors, honors programs, independent study, internships, off-campus study, part-time degree program, services for LD students, student-designed majors, study abroad, summer session for credit. *Unusual degree programs:* 3-2 business administration.

Computers on Campus 350 computers/terminals are available on campus for general student use. Students can access the following: campus intranet, computer help desk, free student e-mail accounts, online (class) grades, online (class) registration, online (class) schedules. Campuswide network is available. 100% of college-owned or -operated housing units are wired for high-speed Internet access. Wireless service is available via computer centers, libraries, student centers.

Student Life *Housing:* on-campus residence required through sophomore year. *Options:* coed, disabled students. Campus housing is university owned. Freshman applicants given priority for college housing. *Activities and organizations:* drama/theater group, student-run newspaper, radio and television station, choral group, Environmental Club, Student Body Association, KMSA radio station, Rodeo Club, Campus Residents Association. *Campus security:* 24-hour emergency response devices and patrols, late-night transport/escort service, controlled dormitory access. *Student services:* health clinic, personal/psychological counseling, legal services.

Athletics Member NCAA. All Division II. *Intercollegiate sports:* baseball M (s), basketball M (s)/W (s), cross-country running W (s), football M (s), golf W (s), ice hockey M, soccer M (s)/W (s), softball W (s), tennis M (s)/W (s), track and field W (s), volleyball W (s), wrestling M (s). *Intramural sports:* badminton M/W, basketball M/W, equestrian sports M/W, football M/W, racquetball M/W, rugby M/W, skiing (cross-country) M/W, skiing (downhill) M/W, soccer M/W, softball M/W, swimming and diving M/W, tennis M/W, track and field W, volleyball M/W, water polo M/W.

Standardized Tests *Required:* SAT or ACT (for admission).

Costs (2007–08) *Tuition:* state resident $3893 full-time, $139 per hour part-time; nonresident $12,054 full-time, $431 per hour part-time. Part-time tuition and fees vary according to course load. *Required fees:* $171 full-time, $11 per hour part-time. *Room and board:* $7077. Room and board charges vary according to board plan and housing facility. *Payment plan:* installment. *Waivers:* employees or children of employees.

Financial Aid Of all full-time matriculated undergraduates who enrolled in 2006, 3,614 applied for aid, 3,237 were judged to have need, 417 had their need fully met. 189 Federal Work-Study jobs (averaging $1428). 394 state and other part-time jobs (averaging $1669). In 2006, 219 non-need-based awards were made. *Average percent of need met:* 49%. *Average financial aid package:* $7081. *Average need-based loan:* $3126. *Average need-based gift aid:* $4104. *Average non-need-based aid:* $2354. *Average indebtedness upon graduation:* $18,353.

Applying *Options:* electronic application, deferred entrance. *Application fee:* $30. *Required:* high school transcript. *Recommended:* essay or personal statement, 2 letters of recommendation. *Application deadlines:* rolling (freshmen), rolling (transfers). *Notification:* continuous (freshmen), continuous (transfers).

Freshman Application Contact Mr. Rance Larsen, Director of Admission, Mesa State College, 1100 North Avenue, Grand Junction, CO 81501. *Phone:* 970-248-1802. *Toll-free phone:* 800-982-MESA. *Fax:* 970-248-1973. *E-mail:* rlarsen@mesastate.edu.

METROPOLITAN STATE COLLEGE OF DENVER

Denver, Colorado **www.mscd.edu/**

Freshman Application Contact Ms. Miriam Tapia, Associate Director, Metropolitan State College of Denver, PO Box 173362, Campus Box 16, Denver, CO 80217-3362. *Phone:* 303-556-2615.

NAROPA UNIVERSITY

Boulder, Colorado **www.naropa.edu/**

- **Independent** comprehensive, founded 1974
- **Urban** 12-acre campus with easy access to Denver
- **Endowment** $5.0 million

- **Coed** 478 undergraduate students, 91% full-time, 63% women, 37% men
- **Moderately difficult** entrance level, 93% of applicants were admitted

Undergraduates 435 full-time, 43 part-time. Students come from 46 states and territories, 8 other countries, 70% are from out of state, 0.7% African American, 2% Asian American or Pacific Islander, 4% Hispanic American, 0.4% Native American, 2% international, 22% transferred in, 17% live on campus. *Retention:* 57% of 2006 full-time freshmen returned.

Freshmen *Admission:* 139 applied, 129 admitted, 69 enrolled. *Average high school GPA:* 3.02.

Faculty *Total:* 194, 26% full-time, 36% with terminal degrees. *Student/faculty ratio:* 9:1.

Majors Dramatic/theater arts; early childhood education; English; environmental studies; fine/studio arts; health and physical education related; multi-/interdisciplinary studies related; music performance; peace studies and conflict resolution; psychology; religious studies; visual and performing arts.

Academics *Calendar:* semesters. *Degrees:* certificates, bachelor's, master's, and first professional. *Special study options:* adult/continuing education programs, advanced placement credit, cooperative education, distance learning, double majors, independent study, internships, part-time degree program, services for LD students, student-designed majors, study abroad, summer session for credit.

Computers on Campus 83 computers/terminals are available on campus for general student use. Students can access the following: computer help desk, free student e-mail accounts, online (class) grades, online (class) registration, online (class) schedules. Campuswide network is available. 100% of college-owned or -operated housing units are wired for high-speed Internet access. Wireless service is available via entire campus.

Student Life *Housing:* on-campus residence required for freshman year. *Options:* coed, cooperative. Campus housing is university owned. Freshman campus housing is guaranteed. *Activities and organizations:* drama/theater group, choral group, UN United Naropa-Student Government, SLP-Student Life Programming, Allies in Action, Root Outdoor Organization, PATH-Peers Assisting with Transformative Health, Peer Education Team. *Campus security:* late-night transport/escort service, controlled dormitory access, foot and vehicle patrol 4:30 p.m.–midnight, 24 hour on-call Safety & Security Manager. *Student services:* personal/psychological counseling.

Costs (2007–08) *Comprehensive fee:* $27,315 includes full-time tuition ($20,738), mandatory fees ($76), and room and board ($6501). Full-time tuition and fees vary according to course load. Part-time tuition: $673 per credit hour. Part-time tuition and fees vary according to course load. *Required fees:* $288 per semester part-time. *College room only:* $4455. Room and board charges vary according to board plan. *Payment plan:* installment. *Waivers:* employees or children of employees.

Financial Aid Of all full-time matriculated undergraduates who enrolled in 2007, 311 applied for aid, 302 were judged to have need, 5 had their need fully met. 216 Federal Work-Study jobs (averaging $3525). 6 state and other part-time jobs (averaging $2817). *Average percent of need met:* 85%. *Average financial aid package:* $19,748. *Average need-based loan:* $4998. *Average need-based gift aid:* $12,969.

Applying *Options:* electronic application, deferred entrance. *Application fee:* $50. *Required:* essay or personal statement, high school transcript, 2 letters of recommendation, interview. *Application deadlines:* 1/15 (freshmen), 1/15 (out-of-state freshmen), rolling (transfers). *Notification:* continuous (freshmen), continuous (out-of-state freshmen).

Freshman Application Contact Ms. Amy Kopkin, Associate Director of Admissions, Naropa University, 2130 Arapahoe Avenue, Boulder, CO 80302. *Phone:* 303-546-5285. *Toll-free phone:* 800-772-0410. *Fax:* 303-546-3583. *E-mail:* admissions@naropa.edu.

See page 504 for the College Close-Up.

NATIONAL AMERICAN UNIVERSITY

Colorado Springs, Colorado **www.national.edu/**

Director of Admissions Ms. Markita McKamie, Director of Admissions, National American University, 5125 North Academy Boulevard, Colorado Springs, CO 80918. *Phone:* 719-277-0588.

NATIONAL AMERICAN UNIVERSITY

Denver, Colorado **www.national.edu/**

- **Proprietary** 4-year, founded 1974
- **Urban** campus
- **Coed**
- **Noncompetitive** entrance level

Faculty *Student/faculty ratio:* 10:1.

Academics *Calendar:* quarters. *Degrees:* certificates, diplomas, associate, bachelor's, and master's.

Student Life *Campus security:* 24-hour emergency response devices and patrols.

Costs (2007–08) *Tuition:* $9720 full-time, $270 per quarter hour part-time.

Applying *Options:* electronic application, early admission, deferred entrance. *Application fee:* $25. *Required:* high school transcript, interview.

Freshman Application Contact National American University, 1325 South Colorado Blvd, Suite 100, Denver, CO 80222. *Phone:* 303-876-7112.

NAZARENE BIBLE COLLEGE

Colorado Springs, Colorado **www.nbc.edu/**

- **Independent** 4-year, founded 1967, affiliated with Church of the Nazarene
- **Urban** 64-acre campus with easy access to Denver
- **Endowment** $2.5 million
- **Coed** 808 undergraduate students, 18% full-time, 37% women, 63% men
- **Noncompetitive** entrance level, 20% of applicants were admitted

Undergraduates 142 full-time, 666 part-time. Students come from 50 states and territories, 1 other country, 55% are from out of state, 3% African American, 0.9% Asian American or Pacific Islander, 3% Hispanic American, 1% Native American, 0.5% international, 9% transferred in. *Retention:* 65% of 2006 full-time freshmen returned.

Freshmen *Admission:* 1,063 applied, 217 admitted, 21 enrolled.

Faculty *Total:* 79, 18% full-time, 68% with terminal degrees. *Student/faculty ratio:* 10:1.

Majors Biblical studies; pastoral studies/counseling; pre-theology/pre-ministerial studies; religious education; religious/sacred music; women's studies.

Academics *Calendar:* quarters. *Degrees:* diplomas, associate, and bachelor's. *Special study options:* academic remediation for entering students, distance learning, double majors, independent study, internships, part-time degree program, summer session for credit.

Computers on Campus 10 computers/terminals are available on campus for general student use. Campuswide network is available.

Student Life *Housing:* college housing not available. *Activities and organizations:* student-run newspaper, choral group. *Campus security:* student patrols. *Student services:* personal/psychological counseling.

Costs (2007–08) *Tuition:* $8100 full-time, $300 per credit hour part-time. *Required fees:* $300 full-time.

Financial Aid Of all full-time matriculated undergraduates who enrolled in 2005, 121 applied for aid, 121 were judged to have need. 5 Federal Work-Study jobs (averaging $3800). *Average indebtedness upon graduation:* $19,908.

Applying *Options:* electronic application, deferred entrance. *Required:* essay or personal statement, high school transcript, 2 letters of recommendation. *Application deadlines:* 7/31 (freshmen), 7/31 (transfers).

Freshman Application Contact Dr. Laurel Matson, Director of Admissions/Public Relations, Nazarene Bible College, 1111 Academy Park Loop, Colorado Springs, CO 80910-3704. *Phone:* 719-884-5061. *Toll-free phone:* 800-873-3873. *Fax:* 719-884-5199.

PLATT COLLEGE

Aurora, Colorado **www.plattcolorado.edu/**

Freshman Application Contact Admissions Office, Platt College, 3100 South Parker Road, Suite 200, Aurora, CO 80014-3141. *Phone:* 303-369-5151.

REGIS UNIVERSITY

Denver, Colorado **www.regis.edu/**

- **Independent Roman Catholic (Jesuit)** comprehensive, founded 1877
- **Suburban** 90-acre campus
- **Endowment** $41.7 million
- **Coed** 7,900 undergraduate students, 34% full-time, 63% women, 37% men
- **Moderately difficult** entrance level, 25% of applicants were admitted

The Regis Guarantee ensures that entering freshmen will graduate in four years—or take the additional course work at no tuition charge. The Learn and Earn Program offers every new freshman the opportunity to work on campus to gain valuable experience and money to help defray expenses. These programs, and the University's most than 130-year history of offering high-quality, value-oriented Jesuit education, make Regis a leader in the Rocky Mountain region.

Undergraduates 2,647 full-time, 5,253 part-time. Students come from 40 states and territories, 29% are from out of state, 5% African American, 4% Asian American or Pacific Islander, 10% Hispanic American, 1% Native American, 0.9% international, 9% transferred in, 45% live on campus. *Retention:* 84% of 2006 full-time freshmen returned.

Freshmen *Admission:* 13,912 applied, 3,435 admitted, 549 enrolled. *Average high school GPA:* 3.5. *Test scores:* SAT critical reading scores over 500: 68%; SAT math scores over 500: 68%; ACT scores over 18: 93%; SAT critical reading scores over 600: 26%; SAT math scores over 600: 28%; ACT scores over 24: 42%; SAT critical reading scores over 700: 4%; SAT math scores over 700: 3%; ACT scores over 30: 6%.

Faculty *Total:* 982, 23% full-time, 32% with terminal degrees. *Student/faculty ratio:* 14:1.

Majors Accounting; biochemistry; biology/biological sciences; business administration and management; chemistry; communication/speech communication and rhetoric; computer science; criminal justice/law enforcement administration; economics; education; elementary education; English; environmental studies; French; health information/medical records administration; history; human ecology; humanities; liberal arts and sciences/liberal studies; mathematics; neuroscience; nursing (registered nurse training); philosophy; political science and government; pre-dentistry studies; pre-law studies; pre-medical studies; pre-veterinary studies; psychology; religious studies; sociology; Spanish; visual and performing arts.

Academics *Calendar:* semesters. *Degrees:* bachelor's, master's, and doctoral. *Special study options:* academic remediation for entering students, accelerated degree program, adult/continuing education programs, advanced placement credit, cooperative education, distance learning, double majors, external degree program, freshman honors college, honors programs, independent study, internships, off-campus study, part-time degree program, services for LD students, student-designed majors, study abroad, summer session for credit. *ROTC:* Army (c), Air Force (c). *Unusual degree programs:* 3-2 engineering with Washington University in St. Louis.

Computers on Campus 300 computers/terminals and 72 ports are available on campus for general student use. Students can access the following: campus intranet, computer help desk, free student e-mail accounts, online (class) grades, online (class) registration, online (class) schedules. Campuswide network is available. 100% of college-owned or -operated housing units are wired for high-speed Internet access. Wireless service is available via entire campus.

Student Life *Housing:* on-campus residence required for freshman year. *Options:* coed. Campus housing is university owned. Freshman campus housing is guaranteed. *Activities and organizations:* drama/theater group, student-run newspaper, radio station, choral group, Programming Activities Council, hall governing boards, Student Executive Board, Outdoor Club, Rugby Club. *Campus security:* 24-hour emergency response devices and patrols, student patrols, late-night transport/escort service, controlled dormitory access. *Student services:* health clinic, personal/psychological counseling.

Athletics Member NCAA. All Division II. *Intercollegiate sports:* baseball M (s), basketball M (s)/W (s), golf M (s)/W (s), lacrosse W (s), soccer M (s)/W (s), softball W (s), volleyball W (s). *Intramural sports:* basketball M/W, bowling M/W, cheerleading M/W, cross-country running M/W, football M/W, ice hockey M, lacrosse M, rugby M, softball W, volleyball M/W.

Standardized Tests *Required:* SAT or ACT (for admission). *Recommended:* SAT Subject Tests (for admission).

Costs (2008–09) *One-time required fee:* $200. *Comprehensive fee:* $37,682 includes full-time tuition ($28,400), mandatory fees ($300), and room and board ($8982). Part-time tuition: $888 per hour. *Required fees:* $240 per year part-time. *College room only:* $5050.

Financial Aid Of all full-time matriculated undergraduates who enrolled in 2005, 1,271 applied for aid, 809 were judged to have need, 278 had their need fully met. 320 Federal Work-Study jobs (averaging $1256). 423 state and other part-time jobs (averaging $2307). In 2005, 136 non-need-based awards were made. *Average percent of need met:* 75%. *Average financial aid package:* $17,572. *Average need-based loan:* $2452. *Average need-based gift aid:* $13,330. *Average non-need-based aid:* $9113.

Applying *Options:* electronic application. *Application fee:* $40. *Required:* essay or personal statement, high school transcript, minimum 2.5 GPA, 1 letter of recommendation. *Required for some:* 2 letters of recommendation, interview. *Application deadlines:* rolling (freshmen), rolling (out-of-state freshmen), rolling (transfers). *Notification:* continuous (freshmen), continuous (transfers).

Freshman Application Contact Mr. Vic Davolt, Director of Admission, Regis University, 3333 Regis Boulevard, Denver, CO 80221-1099. *Phone:* 303-458-4905. *Toll-free phone:* 800-388-2366 Ext. 4900. *Fax:* 303-964-5534. *E-mail:* regisadm@regis.edu.

See page 506 for the College Close-Up.

REMINGTON COLLEGE–COLORADO SPRINGS CAMPUS

Colorado Springs, Colorado **www.remingtoncollege.edu/**

- **Proprietary** 4-year
- **Urban** 3-acre campus

Majors Criminal justice/law enforcement administration.

Academics *Calendar:* quarters. *Degrees:* associate and bachelor's. *Special study options:* cooperative education, distance learning.

Student Life *Housing:* college housing not available. *Campus security:* 24-hour emergency response devices, late-night transport/escort service.

Freshman Application Contact Ms. Shirley McCray, Campus President, Remington College–Colorado Springs Campus, 6050 Erin Park Drive, #250, Colorado Springs, CO 80918. *Phone:* 769-532-1234. *Fax:* 719-264-1234.

ROCKY MOUNTAIN COLLEGE OF ART + DESIGN

Lakewood, Colorado **www.rmcad.edu/**

- **Proprietary** 4-year, founded 1963
- **Suburban** 23-acre campus
- **Coed** 498 undergraduate students, 87% full-time, 58% women, 42% men
- **Moderately difficult** entrance level, 99% of applicants were admitted

Undergraduates 431 full-time, 67 part-time. Students come from 40 states and territories, 3 other countries, 38% are from out of state, 2% African American, 2% Asian American or Pacific Islander, 12% Hispanic American, 0.8% Native American, 2% international, 11% transferred in. *Retention:* 63% of 2006 full-time freshmen returned.

Freshmen *Admission:* 313 applied, 311 admitted, 129 enrolled. *Average high school GPA:* 2.95. *Test scores:* SAT critical reading scores over 500: 48%; SAT math scores over 500: 52%; SAT writing scores over 500: 60%; ACT scores over 18: 70%; SAT critical reading scores over 600: 13%; SAT math scores over 600: 19%; SAT writing scores over 600: 8%; ACT scores over 24: 16%; SAT critical reading scores over 700: 9%; SAT math scores over 700: 4%; ACT scores over 30: 2%.

Faculty *Total:* 65, 38% full-time. *Student/faculty ratio:* 12:1.

Majors Animation, interactive technology, video graphics and special effects; art teacher education; film/video and photographic arts related; graphic design; illustration; interior design; painting; sculpture.

Academics *Calendar:* trimesters. *Degree:* bachelor's. *Special study options:* academic remediation for entering students, accelerated degree program, advanced placement credit, cooperative education, double majors, independent study, internships, part-time degree program, study abroad, summer session for credit.

Computers on Campus 120 computers/terminals are available on campus for general student use. Campuswide network is available.

Student Life *Housing:* college housing not available. *Activities and organizations:* student-run newspaper, Artists Representative Team, The American Society of Interior Designers, The American Institute of Graphic Arts, Art Directors Club of Denver, International Animated Film Association. *Campus security:* 24-hour emergency response devices, late-night transport/escort service. *Student services:* personal/psychological counseling.

Standardized Tests *Required:* SAT or ACT (for admission).
Costs (2007–08) *Comprehensive fee:* $28,192 includes full-time tuition ($19,752) and room and board ($8440). Part-time tuition: $823 per credit.
Financial Aid Of all full-time matriculated undergraduates who enrolled in 2004, 382 applied for aid, 326 were judged to have need, 42 had their need fully met. 22 Federal Work-Study jobs (averaging $1951). 41 state and other part-time jobs (averaging $1978). In 2004, 14 non-need-based awards were made. *Average percent of need met:* 51%. *Average financial aid package:* $7241. *Average need-based loan:* $3610. *Average need-based gift aid:* $1855. *Average non-need-based aid:* $2433. *Average indebtedness upon graduation:* $18,000.
Applying *Options:* electronic application. *Application fee:* $50. *Required:* essay or personal statement, high school transcript, minimum 2.0 GPA, interview, portfolio. *Application deadlines:* rolling (freshmen), rolling (transfers).
Freshman Application Contact Ms. Angela Carlson, Vice President of Admissions and Marketing, Rocky Mountain College of Art + Design, 1600 Pierce Street, Lakewood, CO 80214. *Phone:* 303-753-6046. *Toll-free phone:* 800-888-ARTS. *Fax:* 303-759-4970. *E-mail:* admit@rmcad.edu.

See page 508 for the College Close-Up.

TEIKYO LORETTO HEIGHTS UNIVERSITY
Denver, Colorado

UNITED STATES AIR FORCE ACADEMY
Colorado Springs, Colorado **www.usafa.edu/**

- **Federally supported** 4-year, founded 1954
- **Suburban** 18,000-acre campus with easy access to Denver
- **Coed, primarily men** 4,461 undergraduate students, 100% full-time, 19% women, 81% men
- **Most difficult** entrance level, 14% of applicants were admitted

Undergraduates 4,461 full-time. Students come from 52 states and territories, 14 other countries, 94% are from out of state, 5% African American, 8% Asian American or Pacific Islander, 7% Hispanic American, 2% Native American, 1% international, 100% live on campus. *Retention:* 90% of 2006 full-time freshmen returned.
Freshmen *Admission:* 9,163 applied, 1,287 admitted, 1,214 enrolled. *Average high school GPA:* 3.85. *Test scores:* SAT critical reading scores over 500: 100%; SAT math scores over 500: 91%; SAT writing scores over 500: 97%; ACT scores over 18: 100%; SAT critical reading scores over 600: 73%; SAT math scores over 600: 68%; SAT writing scores over 600: 61%; ACT scores over 24: 100%; SAT critical reading scores over 700: 14%; SAT math scores over 700: 3%; SAT writing scores over 700: 12%; ACT scores over 30: 47%.
Faculty *Total:* 563, 100% full-time, 49% with terminal degrees. *Student/faculty ratio:* 8:1.
Majors Aerospace, aeronautical and astronautical engineering; area studies; atmospheric sciences and meteorology; behavioral sciences; biochemistry; biological and physical sciences; biology/biological sciences; business administration and management; chemistry; civil engineering; computer science; economics; electrical, electronics and communications engineering; engineering; engineering mechanics; engineering science; English; environmental/environmental health engineering; geography; history; humanities; interdisciplinary studies; legal studies; materials science; mathematics; mechanical engineering; military studies; operations research; physics; political science and government; social sciences.
Academics *Calendar:* semesters. *Degree:* bachelor's. *Special study options:* academic remediation for entering students, advanced placement credit, double majors, English as a second language, independent study, internships, off-campus study, student-designed majors, study abroad, summer session for credit.
Computers on Campus 500 computers/terminals are available on campus for general student use. Students can access the following: campus intranet, computer help desk, free student e-mail accounts. Campuswide network is available. Wireless service is available via entire campus.
Student Life *Housing:* on-campus residence required through senior year. *Options:* coed. Campus housing is university owned. Freshman campus housing is guaranteed. *Activities and organizations:* drama/theater group, choral group, marching band, Cadet Ski Club, choir, Scuba Club, Aviation Club, Drum and Bugle Corps. *Campus security:* 24-hour emergency response devices and patrols, late-night transport/escort service, self-defense education, well-lit campus. *Student services:* health clinic, personal/psychological counseling, legal services.
Athletics Member NCAA. All Division I except football (Division I-A). *Intercollegiate sports:* baseball M, basketball M/W, cheerleading M/W, cross-country running M/W, fencing M/W, golf M, gymnastics M/W, ice hockey M, lacrosse M, riflery M/W, rugby W (c), skiing (cross-country) M (c)/W (c), skiing (downhill) M (c)/W (c), soccer M/W, softball W (c), swimming and diving M/W, tennis M/W, track and field M/W, volleyball W, water polo M, weight lifting M (c)/W (c), wrestling M. *Intramural sports:* archery M (c)/W (c), basketball M/W, bowling M (c)/W (c), cross-country running M/W, racquetball M/W, rugby M/W, soccer M/W, softball M/W, swimming and diving M/W, tennis M/W, volleyball M/W, water polo M/W, wrestling M.
Standardized Tests *Required:* SAT or ACT (for admission).
Costs (2007–08) *Tuition:* tuition, room and board, and medical and dental care are provided by the U.S. government. Each cadet receives a salary from which to pay for uniforms, supplies, and personal expenses.
Applying *Options:* electronic application. *Required:* essay or personal statement, high school transcript, minimum 2.0 GPA, interview, authorized nomination. *Application deadlines:* 1/31 (freshmen), 1/31 (transfers). *Notification:* continuous until 5/15 (freshmen), continuous until 5/15 (transfers).
Freshman Application Contact Mr. Rolland Stoneman, Associate Director of Admissions/Selections, United States Air Force Academy, HQ USAFA/RR, 2304 Cadet Drive, Suite 2400, USAF Academy, CO 80840-5025. *Phone:* 719-333-2520. *Toll-free phone:* 800-443-9266. *Fax:* 719-333-3012. *E-mail:* rr_webmail@usafa.af.mil.

See page 510 for the College Close-Up.

UNIVERSITY OF COLORADO AT BOULDER
Boulder, Colorado **www.colorado.edu/**

- **State-supported** university, founded 1876, part of University of Colorado System
- **Suburban** 600-acre campus with easy access to Denver
- **Endowment** $357.3 million
- **Coed** 26,155 undergraduate students, 91% full-time, 47% women, 53% men
- **Moderately difficult** entrance level, 82% of applicants were admitted

Undergraduates 23,860 full-time, 2,295 part-time. Students come from 52 states and territories, 101 other countries, 31% are from out of state, 2% African American, 6% Asian American or Pacific Islander, 6% Hispanic American, 0.8% Native American, 1% international, 0.4% transferred in, 25% live on campus. *Retention:* 83% of 2006 full-time freshmen returned.
Freshmen *Admission:* 19,857 applied, 16,187 admitted, 5,594 enrolled. *Average high school GPA:* 3.56. *Test scores:* SAT critical reading scores over 500: 85%; SAT math scores over 500: 89%; ACT scores over 18: 99%; SAT critical reading scores over 600: 41%; SAT math scores over 600: 49%; ACT scores over 24: 72%; SAT critical reading scores over 700: 7%; SAT math scores over 700: 9%; ACT scores over 30: 15%.
Faculty *Total:* 1,927, 65% full-time, 75% with terminal degrees. *Student/faculty ratio:* 16:1.
Majors Accounting; advertising; aerospace, aeronautical and astronautical engineering; anthropology; applied mathematics; architectural engineering; Asian studies; astronomy; audiology and hearing sciences; biochemistry; broadcast journalism; cell and molecular biology; chemical engineering; chemistry; Chinese; civil engineering; classics and languages, literatures and linguistics; communication and media related; communication/speech communication and rhetoric; computer engineering; computer science; cultural studies; dance; dramatic/theater arts; ecology, evolution, systematics and population biology related; economics; electrical, electronics and communications engineering; engineering physics; English; environmental design/architecture; environmental/environmental health engineering; environmental studies; ethnic, cultural minority, and gender studies related; film/cinema studies; finance; fine/studio arts; French; geography; geology/earth science; Germanic languages; history; humanities; international/global studies; Italian; Japanese; journalism; linguistics; marketing/marketing management; mathematics; mechanical engineering; music; music performance; music teacher education; philosophy; physics; physiology; political science and government; psychology; religious studies; Russian studies; sociology; Spanish; women's studies.
Academics *Calendar:* semesters. *Degrees:* bachelor's, master's, doctoral, and first professional. *Special study options:* accelerated degree program, adult/continuing education programs, advanced placement credit, cooperative education, distance learning, double majors, English as a second language, freshman honors college, honors programs, independent study, internships, off-campus study, part-time degree program, services for LD students, student-designed majors, study abroad, summer session for credit. *ROTC:* Army (b), Navy (b), Air Force (b). *Unusual degree programs:* 3-2 nursing with University of Colorado at

Denver and Health Sciences Center; child health associate, dental hygiene, medical technology, pharmacy at the University of Colorado at Denver and Health Sciences Center.

Computers on Campus 1,581 computers/terminals are available on campus for general student use. Students can access the following: campus intranet, computer help desk, free student e-mail accounts, online (class) grades, online (class) registration, online (class) schedules, standard and academic software, student government voting. Campuswide network is available. 100% of college-owned or -operated housing units are wired for high-speed Internet access.

Student Life *Housing:* on-campus residence required for freshman year. *Options:* coed, disabled students. Freshman campus housing is guaranteed. *Activities and organizations:* drama/theater group, student-run newspaper, radio and television station, choral group, marching band, student government, Ski and Snowboard Club, Environmental Center, AIESEC, Program Council, national fraternities, national sororities. *Campus security:* 24-hour emergency response devices and patrols, student patrols, late-night transport/escort service, controlled dormitory access, University police department. *Student services:* health clinic, personal/psychological counseling, women's center, legal services.

Athletics Member NCAA. All Division I except football (Division I-A). *Intercollegiate sports:* baseball M (c), basketball M (s)/W (s), bowling M (c)/W (c), crew M (c)/W (c), cross-country running M (s)/W (s), equestrian sports M (c)/W (c), fencing M (c)/W (c), field hockey M (c)/W (c), golf M (s)/W (s), ice hockey M (c)/W (c), lacrosse M (c)/W (c), racquetball M (c)/W (c), rugby M (c)/W (c), skiing (cross-country) M (s)/W (s), skiing (downhill) M (s)/W (s), soccer M (c)/W (s), softball W (c), squash M (c)/W (c), swimming and diving M (c)/W (c), tennis W (s), track and field M (s)/W (s), ultimate Frisbee M (c)/W (c), volleyball M (c)/W (s), water polo M (c)/W (c), wrestling M (c). *Intramural sports:* badminton M/W, basketball M/W, cross-country running M (c)/W (c), football M/W (c), ice hockey M/W, racquetball M/W, skiing (cross-country) M (c)/W (c), skiing (downhill) M (c)/W (c), soccer M/W (c), softball M/W, squash M/W, table tennis M/W, tennis M/W, ultimate Frisbee M/W, volleyball M/W (c), water polo M/W.

Standardized Tests *Required:* SAT or ACT (for admission).

Costs (2007–08) *One-time required fee:* $108. *Tuition:* state resident $5418 full-time; nonresident $23,580 full-time. Full-time tuition and fees vary according to program. Part-time tuition and fees vary according to course load and program. *Required fees:* $1217 full-time. *Room and board:* $9088. Room and board charges vary according to board plan, housing facility, and location. *Payment plan:* deferred payment. *Waivers:* senior citizens.

Financial Aid Of all full-time matriculated undergraduates who enrolled in 2007, 19,475 applied for aid, 8,437 were judged to have need, 5,788 had their need fully met. In 2007, 10182 non-need-based awards were made. *Average percent of need met:* 89%. *Average financial aid package:* $11,404. *Average need-based loan:* $5644. *Average need-based gift aid:* $5584. *Average non-need-based aid:* $2505. *Average indebtedness upon graduation:* $18,037.

Applying *Options:* electronic application, deferred entrance. *Application fee:* $50. *Required:* high school transcript, minimum 2.0 GPA. *Required for some:* audition for music program. *Recommended:* essay or personal statement, minimum 3.0 GPA, letters of recommendation. *Application deadlines:* 1/15 (freshmen), 4/1 (transfers). *Notification:* continuous (freshmen), continuous (transfers).

Freshman Application Contact Admissions Office, University of Colorado at Boulder, 552 UCB, Boulder, CO 80309-0030. *Phone:* 303-492-6301. *Fax:* 303-492-7115. *E-mail:* apply@colorado.edu.

See page 512 for the College Close-Up.

UNIVERSITY OF COLORADO AT COLORADO SPRINGS

Colorado Springs, Colorado **www.uccs.edu/**

- **State-supported** comprehensive, founded 1965
- **Suburban** 400-acre campus with easy access to Denver
- **Endowment** $14.7 million
- **Coed**
- **Moderately difficult** entrance level

Faculty *Student/faculty ratio:* 18:1.

Academics *Calendar:* semesters. *Degrees:* certificates, bachelor's, master's, doctoral, and postbachelor's certificates.

Student Life *Campus security:* 24-hour emergency response devices and patrols, student patrols, late-night transport/escort service, controlled dormitory access.

Athletics Member NCAA. All Division II.

Standardized Tests *Required:* SAT or ACT (for admission).

Costs (2007–08) *Tuition:* state resident $6288 full-time, $196 per credit hour part-time; nonresident $15,300 full-time, $765 per credit hour part-time. Full-time tuition and fees vary according to course level, course load, program, and student level. Part-time tuition and fees vary according to course level, course load, program, and student level. *Required fees:* $1038 full-time. *Room and board:* $6898. Room and board charges vary according to board plan and housing facility.

Financial Aid Of all full-time matriculated undergraduates who enrolled in 2007, 3,970 applied for aid, 2,596 were judged to have need, 412 had their need fully met. 80 Federal Work-Study jobs (averaging $3506). 290 state and other part-time jobs (averaging $3774). In 2007, 379 non-need-based awards were made. *Average percent of need met:* 57. *Average financial aid package:* $7399. *Average need-based loan:* $3923. *Average need-based gift aid:* $4414. *Average non-need-based aid:* $1946. *Average indebtedness upon graduation:* $20,561.

Applying *Options:* electronic application, deferred entrance. *Application fee:* $50. *Required:* high school transcript.

Freshman Application Contact Mr. James Tidwell, Assistant Admissions Director, University of Colorado at Colorado Springs, PO Box 7150, Colorado Springs, CO 80933-7150. *Phone:* 719-262-3383. *Toll-free phone:* 800-990-8227 Ext. 3383. *E-mail:* admrec@mail.uccs.edu.

UNIVERSITY OF COLORADO DENVER

Denver, Colorado **www.cudenver.edu/**

- **State-supported** university, founded 1912, part of University of Colorado System
- **Urban** 171-acre campus
- **Endowment** $260.8 million
- **Coed** 11,036 undergraduate students, 56% full-time, 56% women, 44% men
- **Moderately difficult** entrance level, 68% of applicants were admitted

Undergraduates 6,142 full-time, 4,894 part-time. Students come from 51 states and territories, 57 other countries, 4% are from out of state, 4% African American, 9% Asian American or Pacific Islander, 11% Hispanic American, 0.9% Native American, 1% international, 9% transferred in, 4% live on campus. *Retention:* 71% of 2006 full-time freshmen returned.

Freshmen *Admission:* 3,521 applied, 2,380 admitted, 965 enrolled. *Average high school GPA:* 3.32. *Test scores:* SAT critical reading scores over 500: 72%; SAT math scores over 500: 70%; ACT scores over 18: 89%; SAT critical reading scores over 600: 27%; SAT math scores over 600: 24%; ACT scores over 24: 34%; SAT critical reading scores over 700: 4%; SAT math scores over 700: 2%; ACT scores over 30: 2%.

Faculty *Total:* 2,951, 74% full-time, 71% with terminal degrees. *Student/faculty ratio:* 15:1.

Majors Anthropology; biology/biological sciences; biomedical sciences; business administration and management; business/commerce; chemistry; civil engineering; communication/speech communication and rhetoric; computer and information sciences; criminal justice/law enforcement administration; dental hygiene; dramatic/theater arts; economics; electrical, electronics and communications engineering; English; English composition; fine/studio arts; French; geography; history; international/global studies; mathematics; mechanical engineering; multi-/interdisciplinary studies related; music; nursing (registered nurse training); philosophy; physics; physiological psychology/psychobiology; political science and government; psychology; sociology; Spanish.

Academics *Calendar:* semesters. *Degrees:* bachelor's, master's, doctoral, first professional, and post-master's certificates. *Special study options:* accelerated degree program, adult/continuing education programs, advanced placement credit, cooperative education, distance learning, double majors, English as a second language, honors programs, independent study, internships, off-campus study, part-time degree program, services for LD students, student-designed majors, study abroad, summer session for credit. *ROTC:* Army (b), Air Force (c). *Unusual degree programs:* 3-2 business administration; engineering; liberal arts, public affairs.

Computers on Campus 750 computers/terminals are available on campus for general student use. Students can access the following: online (class) registration. Campuswide network is available. 100% of college-owned or -operated housing units are wired for high-speed Internet access.

Student Life *Housing:* on-campus residence required for freshman year. *Options:* coed. Campus housing is provided by a third party. Freshman applicants given priority for college housing. *Activities and organizations:* drama/theater group, student-run newspaper, television station, choral group, Gold Key National Honor Society, Muslim Student Association, Model United Nations (International Forum Club), Psi Chi Honor Society, Associated Engineering Students. *Campus security:* 24-hour emergency response devices and patrols, student patrols, late-night transport/escort service. *Student services:* health clinic, personal/psychological counseling, legal services.

Athletics *Intramural sports:* basketball M/W, football M, lacrosse M (c), rugby M (c), skiing (downhill) M (c)/W (c), tennis M/W, volleyball M/W, water polo M (c)/W (c).

Standardized Tests *Required:* SAT or ACT (for admission).

Costs (2008–09) *Tuition:* state resident $5054 full-time, $216 per semester hour part-time; nonresident $17,010 full-time, $709 per semester hour part-time. *Required fees:* $878 full-time, $15 per semester hour part-time, $397 per year part-time. *Room and board:* $9990; room only: $5940.

Financial Aid Of all full-time matriculated undergraduates who enrolled in 2004, 3,289 applied for aid, 2,698 were judged to have need, 209 had their need fully met. 165 Federal Work-Study jobs (averaging $3613). 176 state and other part-time jobs (averaging $3862). In 2004, 131 non-need-based awards were made. *Average percent of need met:* 71%. *Average financial aid package:* $7837. *Average need-based loan:* $4013. *Average need-based gift aid:* $4421. *Average non-need-based aid:* $1367. *Average indebtedness upon graduation:* $16,933.

Applying *Options:* electronic application, deferred entrance. *Application fee:* $50. *Required:* high school transcript, minimum 2.5 GPA. *Application deadlines:* 7/22 (freshmen), 7/22 (transfers). *Notification:* continuous (freshmen), continuous (transfers).

Freshman Application Contact Ms. Barbara Edwards, Director of Admissions, University of Colorado Denver, PO Box 173364, Campus Box 167, Denver, CO 80217. *Phone:* 303-556-3287. *Fax:* 303-556-4838. *E-mail:* admissions@castle.cudenver.edu.

See page 514 for the College Close-Up.

UNIVERSITY OF DENVER

Denver, Colorado **www.du.edu/**

- **Independent** university, founded 1864
- **Suburban** 125-acre campus
- **Endowment** $277.5 million
- **Coed** 5,285 undergraduate students, 91% full-time, 55% women, 45% men
- **Moderately difficult** entrance level, 74% of applicants were admitted

Undergraduates 4,794 full-time, 491 part-time. Students come from 52 states and territories, 50 other countries, 44% are from out of state, 3% African American, 5% Asian American or Pacific Islander, 7% Hispanic American, 1% Native American, 5% international, 4% transferred in, 41% live on campus. *Retention:* 87% of 2006 full-time freshmen returned.

Freshmen *Admission:* 5,072 applied, 3,755 admitted, 1,138 enrolled. *Average high school GPA:* 3.59. *Test scores:* SAT critical reading scores over 500: 87%; SAT math scores over 500: 90%; ACT scores over 18: 100%; SAT critical reading scores over 600: 44%; SAT math scores over 600: 48%; ACT scores over 24: 74%; SAT critical reading scores over 700: 8%; SAT math scores over 700: 7%; ACT scores over 30: 16%.

Faculty *Total:* 1,149, 50% full-time. *Student/faculty ratio:* 10:1.

Majors Accounting; animal sciences; anthropology; area, ethnic, cultural, and gender studies related; art; art history, criticism and conservation; art teacher education; Asian-American studies; biochemistry; bioinformatics; biological and physical sciences; biology/biological sciences; business administration and management; business/commerce; business/managerial economics; business statistics; chemistry; chemistry related; commercial and advertising art; communication/speech communication and rhetoric; computer engineering; computer science; computer software and media applications related; computer systems analysis; construction management; creative writing; criminology; digital communication and media/multimedia; dramatic/theater arts; ecology; economics; electrical, electronics and communications engineering; engineering; English; environmental science; ethnic, cultural minority, and gender studies related; finance; fine arts related; French; geography; German; graphic design; history; hospitality administration; hotel/motel administration; information technology; international business/trade/commerce; international relations and affairs; Italian; journalism; Latin American studies; management information systems; marketing/marketing management; mathematics; mechanical engineering; molecular biology; multi-/interdisciplinary studies related; music; musicology and ethnomusicology; music performance; music related; philosophy; physics; political science and government; psychology; public policy analysis; real estate; religious studies; Russian; social sciences; social sciences related; sociology; Spanish.

Academics *Calendar:* quarters; semesters for law school. *Degrees:* certificates, bachelor's, master's, doctoral, first professional, post-master's, and postbachelor's certificates. *Special study options:* accelerated degree program, adult/continuing education programs, advanced placement credit, cooperative education, double majors, English as a second language, freshman honors college, honors programs, independent study, internships, part-time degree program, services for LD students, student-designed majors, study abroad, summer session for credit. *ROTC:* Army (c), Air Force (c). *Unusual degree programs:* 3-2 business administration; engineering.

Computers on Campus 300 computers/terminals and 30,000 ports are available on campus for general student use. Students can access the following: campus intranet, computer help desk, free student e-mail accounts, online (class) grades, online (class) registration, online (class) schedules. Campuswide network is available. 95% of college-owned or -operated housing units are wired for high-speed Internet access. Wireless service is available via entire campus.

Student Life *Housing:* on-campus residence required through sophomore year. *Options:* coed, men-only, women-only. Campus housing is university owned. Freshman campus housing is guaranteed. *Activities and organizations:* drama/theater group, student-run newspaper, radio and television station, choral group, student government, Club Sports Council, Programming Board, International Student Organization, Residence Hall Association, national fraternities, national sororities. *Campus security:* 24-hour emergency response devices and patrols, late-night transport/escort service, controlled dormitory access, 24-hour locked residence hall entrances. *Student services:* health clinic, personal/psychological counseling, women's center.

Athletics Member NCAA. All Division I. *Intercollegiate sports:* basketball M (s)/W (s), cheerleading M, golf M (s)/W (s), gymnastics W (s), ice hockey M (s), lacrosse M (s)/W (s), skiing (cross-country) M (s)/W (s), skiing (downhill) M (s)/W (s), soccer M (s)/W (s), swimming and diving M (s)/W (s), tennis M (s)/W (s), volleyball W (s). *Intramural sports:* baseball M (c), basketball M/W, equestrian sports M (c)/W (c), field hockey M (c)/W (c), football M/W, golf M (c)/W (c), ice hockey M (c)/W (c), lacrosse M (c)/W (c), racquetball M (c)/W (c), rugby M (c), skiing (downhill) M (c)/W (c), soccer M (c)/W (c), softball M/W, table tennis M/W, tennis M (c)/W (c), ultimate Frisbee M (c)/W (c), volleyball M (c)/W (c), water polo M (c)/W (c).

Standardized Tests *Required:* SAT or ACT (for admission).

Costs (2007–08) *Comprehensive fee:* $41,910 includes full-time tuition ($31,428), mandatory fees ($804), and room and board ($9678). Full-time tuition and fees vary according to class time, course load, and program. Part-time tuition: $873 per quarter hour. Part-time tuition and fees vary according to class time, course load, and program. *College room only:* $6015. Room and board charges vary according to board plan and housing facility. *Payment plan:* deferred payment. *Waivers:* employees or children of employees.

Financial Aid Of all full-time matriculated undergraduates who enrolled in 2006, 2,322 applied for aid, 1,849 were judged to have need, 252 had their need fully met. 461 Federal Work-Study jobs (averaging $1806). 237 state and other part-time jobs (averaging $1732). In 2006, 1662 non-need-based awards were made. *Average percent of need met:* 72%. *Average financial aid package:* $22,017. *Average need-based loan:* $4259. *Average need-based gift aid:* $17,260. *Average non-need-based aid:* $8908. *Average indebtedness upon graduation:* $26,017.

Applying *Options:* electronic application, early admission, early action, deferred entrance. *Application fee:* $50. *Required:* essay or personal statement, high school transcript, 2 letters of recommendation. *Required for some:* minimum 2.0 GPA. *Recommended:* interview. *Application deadlines:* 1/15 (freshmen), rolling (transfers), 11/1 (early action). *Notification:* 3/15 (freshmen), continuous (transfers), 1/15 (early action).

Freshman Application Contact Mr. Todd Rinehart, Assistant Vice Chancellor for Enrollment, University of Denver, University Park, Denver, CO 80208. *Phone:* 303-871-2036. *Toll-free phone:* 800-525-9495. *Fax:* 303-871-3301. *E-mail:* admission@du.edu.

See page 516 for the College Close-Up.

UNIVERSITY OF NORTHERN COLORADO

Greeley, Colorado **www.unco.edu/**

- **State-supported** university, founded 1890
- **Suburban** 240-acre campus with easy access to Denver
- **Coed** 10,177 undergraduate students, 91% full-time, 61% women, 39% men
- **Moderately difficult** entrance level, 91% of applicants were admitted

Undergraduates 9,229 full-time, 948 part-time. Students come from 48 states and territories, 9% are from out of state, 3% African American, 3% Asian American or Pacific Islander, 8% Hispanic American, 1% Native American, 1% international, 6% transferred in, 28% live on campus. *Retention:* 66% of 2006 full-time freshmen returned.

Freshmen *Admission:* 6,163 applied, 5,600 admitted, 2,272 enrolled. *Average high school GPA:* 3.21. *Test scores:* SAT critical reading scores over 500: 61%; SAT math scores over 500: 62%; SAT writing scores over 500: 65%; ACT scores over 18: 93%; SAT critical reading scores over 600: 21%; SAT math scores over

600: 20%; SAT writing scores over 600: 20%; ACT scores over 24: 33%; SAT critical reading scores over 700: 3%; SAT math scores over 700: 2%; SAT writing scores over 700: 2%; ACT scores over 30: 3%.

Faculty *Total:* 619, 72% full-time. *Student/faculty ratio:* 22:1.

Majors Adult development and aging; African-American/Black studies; audiology and hearing sciences; biology/biological sciences; business administration and management; chemistry; communication/speech communication and rhetoric; criminal justice/safety; dietetics; dramatic/theater arts; dramatic/theater arts and stagecraft related; economics; English; fine/studio arts; foreign languages and literatures; French; geography; geology/earth science; German; Hispanic-American, Puerto Rican, and Mexican-American/Chicano studies; history; human services; interdisciplinary studies; journalism; kinesiology and exercise science; mathematics; multi-/interdisciplinary studies related; music; music teacher education; nursing (registered nurse training); parks, recreation and leisure facilities management; philosophy; physics; political science and government; psychology; public health education and promotion; sign language interpretation and translation; social sciences; sociology; Spanish; special education; speech-language pathology; vocational rehabilitation counseling.

Academics *Calendar:* semesters. *Degrees:* bachelor's, master's, and doctoral (specialist). *Special study options:* academic remediation for entering students, adult/continuing education programs, advanced placement credit, cooperative education, distance learning, double majors, English as a second language, external degree program, honors programs, independent study, internships, off-campus study, part-time degree program, services for LD students, student-designed majors, study abroad, summer session for credit. *ROTC:* Army (b), Air Force (b).

Computers on Campus 1,169 computers/terminals are available on campus for general student use. Students can access the following: computer help desk, free student e-mail accounts, online (class) grades, online (class) registration, online (class) schedules. Campuswide network is available. 100% of college-owned or -operated housing units are wired for high-speed Internet access. Wireless service is available via libraries, student centers.

Student Life *Housing:* on-campus residence required for freshman year. *Options:* coed, women-only, disabled students. Campus housing is university owned. Freshman campus housing is guaranteed. *Activities and organizations:* drama/theater group, student-run newspaper, radio station, choral group, marching band, national fraternities, national sororities. *Campus security:* 24-hour emergency response devices and patrols, student patrols, late-night transport/escort service, controlled dormitory access. *Student services:* health clinic, personal/psychological counseling, women's center, legal services.

Athletics Member NCAA. All Division I. *Intercollegiate sports:* baseball M (s), basketball M (s)/W (s), cross-country running W (s), football M (s), golf M (s)/W (s), lacrosse M (c), rugby M (c)/W (c), soccer M (c)/W (s), softball W (s), swimming and diving W (s), tennis M (s)/W (s), track and field M (s)/W (s), volleyball W (s), wrestling M (s). *Intramural sports:* basketball M/W, football M/W, soccer M/W, softball M/W, volleyball M/W, water polo M/W.

Standardized Tests *Required:* SAT or ACT (for admission).

Costs (2007–08) *Tuition:* state resident $3600 full-time, $150 per credit hour part-time; nonresident $12,180 full-time, $508 per credit hour part-time. Full-time tuition and fees vary according to program. Part-time tuition and fees vary according to program. *Required fees:* $713 full-time, $36 per credit hour part-time. *Room and board:* $7342; room only: $3886. Room and board charges vary according to board plan and housing facility. *Payment plan:* deferred payment.

Financial Aid Of all full-time matriculated undergraduates who enrolled in 2005, 7,245 applied for aid, 4,088 were judged to have need, 2,256 had their need fully met. 249 Federal Work-Study jobs (averaging $1538). 677 state and other part-time jobs (averaging $1568). In 2005, 914 non-need-based awards were made. *Average percent of need met:* 100%. *Average financial aid package:* $10,075. *Average need-based loan:* $3673. *Average need-based gift aid:* $3920. *Average non-need-based aid:* $2786.

Applying *Options:* electronic application, deferred entrance. *Application fee:* $45. *Required:* high school transcript, minimum 2.9 GPA. *Required for some:* interview. *Application deadlines:* 8/1 (freshmen), rolling (transfers). *Notification:* continuous (freshmen), continuous (transfers).

Freshman Application Contact Mr. Chris Dowen, Director of Admissions, University of Northern Colorado, Campus Box 10, Carter Hall 3006, Greeley, CO 80639. *Phone:* 970-351-2881. *Toll-free phone:* 888-700-4UNC. *Fax:* 970-351-2984. *E-mail:* admissions.help@unco.edu.

UNIVERSITY OF PHOENIX–DENVER CAMPUS

Lone Tree, Colorado **www.phoenix.edu/**

- **Proprietary** comprehensive
- **Urban** campus
- **Coed**
- **Noncompetitive** entrance level

Faculty *Student/faculty ratio:* 9:1.

Academics *Calendar:* continuous. *Degrees:* certificates, bachelor's, master's, and post-master's certificates.

Student Life *Campus security:* late-night transport/escort service.

Costs (2007–08) *Tuition:* $10,140 full-time, $338 per credit part-time. Full-time tuition and fees vary according to course level.

Financial Aid *Average financial aid package:* $4347. *Average need-based gift aid:* $2226.

Applying *Options:* deferred entrance. *Application fee:* $45. *Required:* 1 letter of recommendation. *Required for some:* high school transcript.

Freshman Application Contact Ms. Beth Barilla, Associate Vice President, Student Admissions and Services, University of Phoenix–Denver Campus, 4615 East Elwood Street, Mail Stop AA-K101, Phoenix, AZ 85040-1958. *Phone:* 480-317-6000. *Toll-free phone:* 800-776-4867 (in-state); 800-228-7240 (out-of-state). *Fax:* 480-894-1758. *E-mail:* beth.barilla@phoenix.edu.

UNIVERSITY OF PHOENIX–SOUTHERN COLORADO CAMPUS

Colorado Springs, Colorado **www.phoenix.edu/**

- **Proprietary** comprehensive, founded 1999
- **Urban** campus
- **Coed**
- **Noncompetitive** entrance level

Faculty *Student/faculty ratio:* 8:1.

Academics *Calendar:* continuous. *Degrees:* bachelor's and master's.

Student Life *Campus security:* late-night transport/escort service.

Costs (2007–08) *Tuition:* $10,140 full-time, $338 per credit part-time. Full-time tuition and fees vary according to course level.

Financial Aid *Average financial aid package:* $4814. *Average need-based gift aid:* $2134.

Applying *Options:* deferred entrance. *Application fee:* $45. *Required:* 1 letter of recommendation. *Required for some:* high school transcript.

Freshman Application Contact Ms. Beth Barilla, Associate Vice President, Student Admissions and Services, University of Phoenix–Southern Colorado Campus, 4615 East Elwood Street, Mail Stop AA-K101, Phoenix, AZ 85040-1958. *Phone:* 480-317-6000. *Toll-free phone:* 800-776-4867 (in-state); 800-228-7240 (out-of-state). *Fax:* 480-894-1758. *E-mail:* beth.barilla@phoenix.edu.

WESTERN STATE COLLEGE OF COLORADO

Gunnison, Colorado **www.western.edu/**

- **State-supported** 4-year, founded 1901
- **Small-town** 381-acre campus
- **Coed** 2,064 undergraduate students, 90% full-time, 38% women, 62% men
- **Moderately difficult** entrance level, 91% of applicants were admitted

At Western State College of Colorado, in the heart of the Colorado Rocky Mountains, students enjoy a college experience that they simply cannot get anywhere else. Western offers an outstanding combination of location, award-winning bachelor's degree programs, and recreation that students love. Western is now offering a new program in professional land and resource management. The College enrolls 2,500 students from all fifty states of the Union. For more information, students should visit http://www.western.edu or call 800-876-5309 (toll-free).

Undergraduates 1,851 full-time, 213 part-time. Students come from 50 states and territories, 24% are from out of state, 2% African American, 0.8% Asian

American or Pacific Islander, 5% Hispanic American, 1% Native American, 7% transferred in, 40% live on campus. *Retention:* 61% of 2006 full-time freshmen returned.

Freshmen *Admission:* 1,342 applied, 1,217 admitted, 566 enrolled. *Average high school GPA:* 2.99. *Test scores:* SAT critical reading scores over 500: 53%; SAT math scores over 500: 58%; ACT scores over 18: 85%; SAT critical reading scores over 600: 10%; SAT math scores over 600: 14%; ACT scores over 24: 23%; SAT critical reading scores over 700: 1%; ACT scores over 30: 2%.

Faculty *Total:* 146, 75% full-time, 62% with terminal degrees. *Student/faculty ratio:* 16:1.

Majors Accounting; accounting and business/management; accounting and finance; anthropology; art; art teacher education; biochemistry; biological and biomedical sciences related; biology/biological sciences; biology teacher education; business administration and management; business, management, and marketing related; business/managerial economics; cell biology and anatomy; ceramic arts and ceramics; chemistry; chemistry related; chemistry teacher education; clinical psychology; computer science; computer systems networking and telecommunications; creative writing; criminology; dramatic/theater arts; economics; English; English/language arts teacher education; entrepreneurship; environmental biology; environmental studies; fine/studio arts; forensic psychology; geological and earth sciences/geosciences related; geology/earth science; graphic design; history; history teacher education; interdisciplinary studies; kinesiology and exercise science; management information systems; marketing/marketing management; mathematics; mathematics and statistics related; mathematics teacher education; metal and jewelry arts; music; music management and merchandising; music teacher education; painting; parks, recreation and leisure; parks, recreation and leisure facilities management; parks, recreation, and leisure related; photography; physical education teaching and coaching; physics; political science and government; pre-law studies; printmaking; psychology; psychology related; science teacher education; sculpture; social science teacher education; sociology; Spanish; Spanish language teacher education; sport and fitness administration/management; theater design and technology; visual and performing arts related; water, wetlands, and marine resources management.

Academics *Calendar:* semesters. *Degree:* bachelor's. *Special study options:* accelerated degree program, adult/continuing education programs, advanced placement credit, cooperative education, double majors, honors programs, internships, off-campus study, part-time degree program, services for LD students, student-designed majors, study abroad, summer session for credit.

Computers on Campus 175 computers/terminals are available on campus for general student use. Students can access the following: campus intranet, computer help desk, free student e-mail accounts, online (class) grades, online (class) registration, online (class) schedules. Campuswide network is available. Wireless service is available via entire campus.

Student Life *Housing:* on-campus residence required for freshman year. *Options:* coed, men-only, women-only. Campus housing is university owned. Freshman campus housing is guaranteed. *Activities and organizations:* drama/theater group, student-run newspaper, radio and television station, choral group, Mountain Search and Rescue Team, Student Government Association, Rodeo Club, wilderness pursuits, Peak Productions, national fraternities. *Campus security:* 24-hour emergency response devices and patrols, student patrols, late-night transport/escort service, controlled dormitory access. *Student services:* health clinic, personal/psychological counseling.

Athletics Member NCAA. All Division II. *Intercollegiate sports:* baseball M (c), basketball M (s)/W (s), cheerleading M (c)/W (c), cross-country running M (s)/W (s), football M (s), ice hockey M (c), lacrosse M (c)/W (c), rugby M (c)/W (c), skiing (cross-country) M (s)/W (s), skiing (downhill) M (s)/W (s), soccer M (c)/W (c), track and field M (s)/W (s), volleyball M (c)/W (s), wrestling M (s)/W (c). *Intramural sports:* basketball M/W, football M/W, golf M/W, soccer M/W, softball M/W, table tennis M/W, tennis M/W, ultimate Frisbee M/W, volleyball M/W, wrestling M.

Standardized Tests *Required:* SAT or ACT (for admission)

Costs (2007–08) *Tuition:* state resident $2688 full-time, $112 per credit hour part-time; nonresident $11,520 full-time, $480 per credit hour part-time. Full-time tuition and fees vary according to course load. Part-time tuition and fees vary according to course load. *Required fees:* $898 full-time. *Room and board:* $7226; room only: $3930. Room and board charges vary according to board plan and housing facility. *Payment plans:* installment, deferred payment. *Waivers:* senior citizens and employees or children of employees.

Financial Aid Of all full-time matriculated undergraduates who enrolled in 2007, 1,450 applied for aid, 957 were judged to have need, 81 had their need fully met. 121 Federal Work-Study jobs (averaging $953). 120 state and other part-time jobs (averaging $950). In 2007, 483 non-need-based awards were made. *Average percent of need met:* 40%. *Average financial aid package:* $8800. *Average need-based loan:* $5166. *Average need-based gift aid:* $2500. *Average non-need-based aid:* $1600. *Average indebtedness upon graduation:* $17,313.

Applying *Options:* electronic application, deferred entrance. *Application fee:* $30. *Required:* high school transcript. *Required for some:* essay or personal statement, 2 letters of recommendation, interview. *Recommended:* minimum 2.5 GPA. *Application deadline:* 8/1 (freshmen). *Notification:* 11/1 (freshmen), continuous (transfers).

Freshman Application Contact Mr. Timothy Albers, Director of Admissions, Western State College of Colorado, Western State College of Colorado, 6 Admission Office, 600 North Adams, Gunnison, CO 81231. *Phone:* 970-943-2119. *Toll-free phone:* 800-876-5309. *Fax:* 970-943-2212. *E-mail:* discover@western.edu.

See page 518 for the College Close-Up.

WESTWOOD COLLEGE–DENVER NORTH

Denver, Colorado **www.westwood.edu/**

Freshman Application Contact Ms. Dianne Hopkins, New Student Coordinator, Westwood College–Denver North, 7350 North Broadway, Denver, CO 80221-3653. *Phone:* 303-650-5050 Ext. 325. *Toll-free phone:* 800-992-5050. *Fax:* 303-487-0214.

WESTWOOD COLLEGE–DENVER SOUTH

Denver, Colorado **www.westwood.edu/**

Director of Admissions Mr. Ron DeJong, Director of Admissions, Westwood College–Denver South, 3150 South Sheridan Boulevard, Denver, CO 80227-5548. *Phone:* 303-934-2790. *Toll-free phone:* 800-281-2978.

YESHIVA TORAS CHAIM TALMUDICAL SEMINARY

Denver, Colorado

Director of Admissions Rabbi Israel Kagan, Dean, Yeshiva Toras Chaim Talmudical Seminary, 1400 Quitman Street, Denver, CO 80204-1415. *Phone:* 303-629-8200. *Fax:* 303-623-5949.

ADAMS STATE COLLEGE

ALAMOSA, COLORADO

The College

Adams State College is a dynamic place where great stories are written every day. Adams State students experience superior academic programs, outstanding faculty members, a beautiful location, and diversity of thought. Adams State College is committed to providing a high-quality education at an affordable price and offers the lowest tuition among Colorado's four-year colleges and universities. With additional financial aid offerings, such as grants, loans, and work-study opportunities, Adams State is a tremendous value.

The academic and social atmosphere of the campus allows each student to feel at home. The College has excellent physical facilities. Attractive academic buildings are complemented by a complete and comfortable Student Union Building. As a federally designated Hispanic Serving Institution, the student body is composed of individuals from various ethnic and racial backgrounds. The approximate enrollment is 2,500 on-campus students, with 2,000 undergraduates and 500 graduates. The dignity of each person as an individual is paramount, and equal consideration is extended to all. The close working relationship between students and the members of the faculty and administration is indicative of the importance of the individual at Adams State.

At the graduate level, Adams State offers programs leading to the Master of Arts degree in art, elementary education, guidance and counseling, humanities, human performance and physical education, secondary education, and special education/moderate needs (level one).

Adams State College is accredited by the North Central Association of Colleges and Schools, the National Council for Accreditation of Teacher Education, the Council for Accreditation of Counseling and Related Educational Programs, and the National Association of Schools of Music. The College is an institutional member of the American Council on Education and the American Association of Colleges for Teacher Education. It is approved by the American Association of University Women. Adams State is also a member of the North Central Conference on Summer Schools, the Midwestern Association of Graduate Schools, the Association of Collegiate Business Schools and Programs, and the American Assembly of Collegiate Schools of Business.

Location

Adams State College is located in the city of Alamosa, Colorado, with a population of approximately 10,000 residents. Alamosa is located in the beautiful San Luis Valley, the largest alpine basin in North America. Surrounded by the beautiful Sangre de Cristo and San Juan mountain ranges, the San Luis Valley is a great place for access to skiing, hiking, climbing, and other outdoor activities. With year-round sunshine, Adams State College is the perfect place to study, work, and live. Located about 220 miles southwest of Denver, the city is located at the junction of U.S. Highways 160 and 285 on the route of the Old Navajo Trail. Both bus and airline services are available to and from Alamosa. The College is located close to the art centers at Taos and Santa Fe and near excellent recreational opportunities for hiking, mountain climbing, rafting, fishing, and hunting. The Wolf Creek ski area is within an hour's drive of the campus. The San Luis Valley is larger than the state of Connecticut and is surrounded by ranges of mountains that rise more than 14,000 feet above sea level. In the beautiful Sangre de Cristo range to the east, majestic Mount Blanca towers at 14,363 feet. This mountain is nearly equaled in height and is rivaled in beauty by the rugged Crestone Peak and Crestone needles in the same range. The Continental Divide, winding through the San Juan mountain range, is the western boundary of the valley. The floor of the valley is occupied by fertile grain and vegetable farms and extensive grazing lands. Through the center of the valley flows the Rio Grande del Norte.

Majors and Degrees

Bachelor of Arts or Bachelor of Science degrees are awarded in art (emphasis areas in art education, art history, ceramics, design, drawing, metalsmithing, painting, photography, printmaking, or sculpture), biology (emphasis areas in cellular and molecular biology, organismal biology, secondary science education, or wildlife), business administration (emphasis areas in accounting, advertising, agricultural business, business education, economics, finance, general business, health administration, management, management information systems, marketing, pre–international business, or small business), chemistry (emphasis areas in allied health, biochemistry, chemical physics, or secondary science education), earth science (emphasis areas in secondary science education, physical geography: resources planning and management, or geology), elementary education, English (emphasis areas in communications, creative writing, liberal arts, or secondary teacher licensure), history/government (emphasis areas in history, government, or social studies education), human performance and physical education (emphasis areas in K–12 physical education or sports and exercise management), interdisciplinary studies, mathematics (emphasis areas in computer science, math education, or physics), music (emphasis areas in liberal arts, K–12 music education, or performance), nursing (RN–B.S.N.), psychology, sociology (emphasis areas in criminology, general sociology, and social welfare), Spanish (emphasis areas in liberal arts or secondary education), sports psychology, and theater (emphasis areas in liberal arts and secondary education). Associate of Arts degree programs are also available.

Preprofessional studies are offered in dentistry, engineering, law, medicine, optometry, osteopathy, pharmacy, physical therapy, and veterinary medicine.

Academic Programs

The academic year is divided into fall and spring semesters. Normally, the baccalaureate degree is earned in eight semesters, while the Associate of Arts degree is earned in four. The associate degree is conferred upon completion of an approved curriculum with a total of 60 hours of academic credit and, in some A.A. programs, 2 additional hours of credit in physical education activities. The Bachelor of Arts or Bachelor of Science degree is conferred upon completion of an approved curriculum with a total of 120 hours of academic credit plus 2 to 4 semester hours of credit in physical education activities. A minimum cumulative scholastic average of 2.0 must be earned in all courses taken at Adams State College for the A.A., B.S., and B.A. degrees in all areas except teacher education, for which a minimum cumulative grade point average of 2.75 must be earned in all work attempted. All requirements of the general education courses and the major must be satisfied. Students transferring from a two-year college must earn at least 60 additional semester hours to graduate from Adams State College with a bachelor's degree. Opportunities are available for independent study, special-topics courses, and discussion groups on current issues.

Off-Campus Programs

Adams State College participates in the National Student Exchange Program, which allows students to study for up to a year at another college or university throughout the United States, Canada, Puerto Rico, the Virgin Islands, or Guam. Adams State also has a number of study-abroad opportunities at locations overseas through selected departments.

A number of tours to nearby points of historical, archaeological, and ethnological interest are arranged by the College, usually in the spring and summer months.

Academic Facilities

The library, which serves as a government depository, has 142,624 books, 38,226 bound periodicals, 297,484 government documents, 706,547 ERIC microfiche, and 15,250 other nonbook items.

A state-of-the-art science and mathematics building opened in 1998, an art building in 2000, and a theater building in 2001.

Costs

For the 2007–08 academic year, the approximate cost of tuition for Colorado residents was $2330 per year. For nonresident students, the approximate cost of tuition was $9670. Room and board were approximately $6750 per year. Married and family housing is available for approximately $435 per month.

Financial Aid

Opportunities for financial aid are provided through scholarships, grants, loans, and work-study opportunities. Entering freshmen are considered for financial aid by completing the Free Application for Federal Student Aid (FAFSA). Adams State College also offers a wide array of scholarship awards, including a First Generation Scholarship, Good Neighbor Scholarship (for nonresident students), Leadership Scholarship, and more than 200 private Adams State College Foundation awards. Students may apply for scholarships by submitting the Adams State College Scholarship Application prior to March 1. Specific information regarding financial aid and scholarships is available online at http://www.adams.edu as well as through the Office of Admissions.

Faculty

At Adams State College, small classes are the norm. Two thirds of all classes have 20 students or fewer. Faculty members—not student assistants—teach all classes. Adams State prides itself on superior instruction by professors who go out of their way to ensure student success.

Adams State College has 101 full-time faculty members. Of these, 90 hold a doctorate and 11, a master's degree. Faculty members have received degrees from more than 100 colleges and universities. In addition to carrying out their teaching assignments, faculty members serve as counselors and advisers and as members of many committees.

Student Government

Each student at Adams State College becomes a member of the Associated Students and Faculty organization upon registration. The organization was founded to promote cooperation between students and faculty members of the College. The general social life, social programs, and other student activities are directed by this organization. Elected officers and representatives of the student body and elected faculty members form the Associated Students and Faculty Senate, which regulates matters pertaining to student life.

Admission Requirements

Adams State College has been established as a moderately selective institution, requiring a Colorado Commission on Higher Education (CCHE) index requirement of 80 or higher for admission into the bachelor's degree program. A more detailed description of the CCHE index system is described online at http://www.adams.edu. Applicants who do not meet the initial admissions requirements may be considered for admission into the two-year program. Students admitted into the two-year program may pass into the four-year program upon completion of 13 credits and a minimum 2.3 grade point average at Adams State. Prospective transfer students must have completed at least 13 semester hours with a 2.3 average to be unconditionally accepted for admission to Adams State College. Those not meeting these requirements are considered on an individual basis.

Application and Information

First-time students interested in applying for admission to Adams State College may apply for admission anytime after the junior year in high school. Applications are accepted on a rolling basis; however, preference is given to students who apply early in the process. In order to be considered for admission, first-time students must submit the following documents: a completed application for admission (students may apply online at http://www.adams.edu), a nonrefundable $30 application fee, official high school transcripts, and official ACT or SAT scores (Adams State does not consider the writing portion of the ACT or SAT). Nontraditional students, age 23 and older, are not required to submit ACT or SAT scores for admission into the two-year program.

Transfer applicants must submit the application for undergraduate admission, a nonrefundable $30 application fee, and official transcripts from all colleges/universities attended. In addition, students who have completed fewer than 12 semester hours of credit must also submit an official high school transcript and ACT or SAT scores. Application forms, financial aid forms, and other information are mailed upon request. Inquiries should be made to:

Office of Admissions
Adams State College
Alamosa, Colorado 81102
Phone: 719-587-7712
800-824-6494 (toll-free)
Fax: 719-587-7522
E-mail: ascadmit@adams.edu
Web site: http://www.adams.edu

The Rex Activity Center on the campus of Adams State College.

ARGOSY UNIVERSITY

ARGOSY UNIVERSITY

The University

Argosy University is a leading institution offering a variety of degree programs that focus on the human side of success alongside professional competence. For students looking for a more personal approach to education, Argosy University may just be the answer. With forty-eight graduate and undergraduate programs, across nineteen campuses and twelve states, Argosy University emphasizes interpersonal skills as well as academic learning. All of its programs are taught by practicing professionals who bring real-world experience into the classroom. So students graduate with both a solid foundation of knowledge and the power to put it to work. To accommodate busy working adults, many programs at Argosy University are structured flexibly—with both campus and online learning and evening, weekend, and daytime classes. There is also a wide range of financial aid options for students who qualify.

Argosy University is a private institution of higher education dedicated to providing high-quality professional education programs at the doctoral, master's, bachelor's, and associate degree levels as well as continuing education to individuals who seek to advance their professional and personal lives. The University emphasizes programs in the behavioral sciences (psychology and counseling), business, education, and the health-care professions. A limited number of preprofessional programs and general education offerings are provided to permit students to prepare for entry into these professional fields. The programs of Argosy University are designed to instill the knowledge, skills, and ethical values of professional practice and to foster values of social responsibility in a supportive, learning-centered environment of mutual respect and professional excellence.

With nineteen campuses nationwide, Argosy University provides students with a network of resources found at larger universities, including a career resources office, an academic resources center, and extensive information access for research. The University's innovative programs feature dynamic, relevant, and practical curricula delivered in flexible class formats. Students enjoy scheduling options that make it easier to fit school into their busy lives. They can choose from day and evening courses, on campus or online. Many students find a combination of both to be an ideal way of continuing their education while meeting family and professional demands.

Most students are full-time working professionals who live within driving distance of the campus. The University does not offer or operate student housing.

Argosy University is accredited by The Higher Learning Commission of the North Central Association (30 North LaSalle Street, Suite 2400, Chicago, Illinois 60602; 800-621-7440; http://ncahlc.org).

Location

Argosy University operates nineteen locations across the U.S. and offers a variety of degree programs online (http://www.argosy.edu). Campus locations include the following:

Atlanta, 980 Hammond Drive, Suite 100, Atlanta, Georgia 30328; phone: 770-671-1200 or 888-671-4777 (toll-free)

Chicago, 225 North Michigan Avenue, Suite 1300, Chicago, Illinois 60601; phone: 312-777-7600 or 800-626-4123 (toll-free)

Dallas, 8080 Park Lane, Suite 400A, Dallas, Texas 75231; phone: 214-890-9900 or 866-954-9900 (toll-free)

Denver, 1200 Lincoln Street, Denver, Colorado 80203; phone: 303-248-2700 or 866-431-5981 (toll-free)

Hawai'i, 400 ASB Tower, 1001 Bishop Street, Honolulu, Hawaii 96813; phone: 808-536-5555 or 888-323-2777 (toll-free)

Inland Empire, 636 East Brier Drive, Suite 235, San Bernardino, California 92408; phone: 909-915-3800 or 866-217-9075 (toll-free)

Nashville, 100 Centerview Drive, Suite 225, Nashville, Tennessee 37214; phone: 615-525-2800 or 866-833-6598 (toll-free)

Orange County, 3501 West Sunflower Avenue, Suite 110, Santa Ana, California 92704; phone: 714-338-6200 or 800-716-9598 (toll-free)

Phoenix, 2233 West Dunlap Avenue, Phoenix, Arizona 85021; phone: 602-216-2600 or 866-216-2777 (toll-free)

Salt Lake City, 121 West Election Road, Suite 300, Draper, Utah 84020; phone: 888-639-4756 (toll-free)

San Diego, 7650 Mission Valley Road, San Diego, California 92108; phone: 858-598-1900 or 866-505-0333 (toll-free)

San Francisco Bay Area, 1005 Atlantic Avenue, Alameda, California 94501; phone: 510-217-4700 or 866-215-2777 (toll-free)

Santa Monica, 2950 31st Street, Santa Monica, California 90405; phone: 310-866-4000 or 866-505-0332 (toll-free)

Sarasota, 5250 17th Street, Sarasota, Florida 34235; phone: 941-379-0404 or 800-331-5995 (toll-free)

Schaumburg, 999 North Plaza Drive, Suite 111, Schaumburg, Illinois 60173-5403; phone: 847-969-4900 or 866-290-2777 (toll-free)

Seattle, 2601-A Elliott Avenue, Seattle, Washington 98121; phone: 206-283-4500 or 888-283-2777 (toll-free)

Tampa, Parkside at Tampa Bay Park, 4401 North Hines Avenue, Suite 150, Tampa, Florida 33614; phone: 813-393-5290 or 800-850-6488 (toll-free)

Twin Cities, 1515 Central Parkway, Eagan, Minnesota 55121; phone: 651-846-2882 or 888-844-2004 (toll-free)

Washington DC, 1550 Wilson Boulevard, Suite 600, Arlington, Virginia 22209; phone: 703-526-5800 or 866-703-2777 (toll-free)

Majors and Degrees

Argosy University's College of Business offers a Bachelor of Science (B.S.) in Business Administration program. Argosy University's College of Psychology and Behavioral Sciences offers the Bachelor of Arts (B.A.) in Psychology degree program.

Academic Programs

The B.S. in Business Administration program prepares students for entry- to mid-level positions within the public or private sector. The curriculum is structured to help students develop competencies in oral and written communication, leadership, team skills, solutions-focused learning, and the analysis and execution of solutions in various business situations. Students may choose one of five optional concentrations: customized professional concentration, finance, health-care management, international business, or marketing.

The B.A. in Psychology program is designed to help students begin human services careers in such capacities as entry-level counselor, case manager, or human resources administrator and

in management and business services roles. The program also lays the foundation for graduate study. Students may choose an optional concentration from the following three options: criminal justice, organizational psychology, or substance abuse. This dynamic program is built around a flexible class approach.

Argosy University's bachelor's degree programs are open to students and working professionals with no college experience, plus those who have already earned college credit at a community college, junior college, or other university.

Academic Facilities

Argosy University libraries provide curriculum support and educational resources including current text materials, diagnostic training documents, reference materials and databases, journals and dissertations, and major and current titles in program areas. There is an online public-access catalog of library resources available throughout the Argosy University system. Students enjoy full remote access to their campus library database, enabling them to study and conduct research at home. Academic databases offer dissertation abstracts, academic journals, and professional periodicals. All library computers are Internet accessible. Software applications include Word, Excel, PowerPoint, SPSS, and various test-scoring programs.

Costs

Tuition varies by program. Students should contact the Argosy University campus of their choice for tuition information.

Financial Aid

A wide range of financial aid options is available to students who qualify. Argosy University offers access to federal and state aid programs, merit-based awards, grants, loans, and a work-study program. As a first step, students should complete the Free Application for Federal Student Aid (FAFSA). Prospective students can apply electronically at http://www.fafsa.ed.gov or at the campus. To receive consideration for financial aid and ensure timely receipt of funds, it is best to submit an application promptly.

Faculty

The Argosy University faculty is composed of working professionals who have a passion to help students succeed. Members bring real-world experience and the latest practice innovations to the academic setting. The diverse faculty is widely recognized for contributions to the field. Most hold doctoral degrees. They provide a substantive education that combines comprehensive knowledge with critical skills and practical workplace relevance. Above all, faculty members are committed to their students' personal and professional development.

Student Government

Argosy University campuses offer unique opportunities for student involvement beyond individual programs of study. Most faculty committees include a student representative. In addition, a student group meets with faculty members and administrators regularly to discuss pertinent campus-related issues.

Admission Requirements

Admission requirements differ depending on the number of college credits completed prior to application.

Students who have earned 12 or fewer semester college credits must provide proof of high school graduation or GED and meet one of the following conditions for admission: ACT composite score of 18 or above, or a combined math and verbal SAT score of 870, or minimum ACCUPLACER scores of 86 in sentence skills and 53 in algebra. Applicants who do not meet any of the above conditions for admission will be admitted with academic support if they provide proof of high school graduation or GED and meet one of the following: ACT composite score of 14 to 17, or a combined math and verbal SAT score of 660 to 869, or minimum ACCUPLACER scores of 54 in sentence skills and 36 in arithmetic.

Applicants who have earned 13 or more semester college credits must provide proof of high school graduation or GED and meet one of the following conditions for admission: cumulative college GPA of 2.0 or above or minimum ACCUPLACER scores of 86 for sentence skills and 53 in algebra. Students who do not meet either of the above criteria will be admitted with academic support if they provide proof of high school graduation or GED and meet the following condition: minimum ACCUPLACER scores of 54 in reading and 36 in arithmetic.

Students admitted with academic support are limited to 12 credit hours of study during their first semester (6 credit hours per session). Students admitted with academic support will be required to complete developmental English and/or math courses unless they meet the following conditions: Writing Review (ENG099)—must meet one of the following: a minimum ACCUPLACER score of 86 in sentence skills, or a minimum ACT verbal score of 18, or a minimum SAT verbal score of 425, or completion of a college-level English composition course with a grade of C or above; Mathematics Review I (MAT096)—must meet one of the following: a minimum ACCUPLACER score of 53 in algebra, or a minimum ACT math score of 18, or a minimum SAT math score of 440, or completion of a college-level English composition course with a grade of C or above.

Other admission requirements may include credit hours of qualified transfer credit with a grade of C- or better from a regionally accredited institution or a nationally accredited institution approved and documented by the faculty and dean of the College of Business, or the College of Professional Psychology, at Argosy University or completion of an Associate of Arts or Associate of Science degree from a regionally accredited institution. A maximum of 78 lower-division or 90 total credit hours may be transferred. A minimum written TOEFL score of 500 (paper-based test), 173 (computer-based test), or 61 (Internet-based test) is required for all applicants whose native language is not English or who have not graduated from an institution in which English is the language of instruction.

Official transcripts from approved postsecondary institutions must include a minimum grade point average of 2.0 (on a scale of 4.0) for all academic work completed. Exceptions may be made for extenuating circumstances. All applications must include a completed application form, proof of high school graduation or successful completion of the GED test, official postsecondary transcripts, and a nonrefundable (except in California) application fee. Additional materials are required prior to matriculation. Some programs have additional application requirements or include exceptions to admission requirements. An admissions representative can provide further information.

Application and Information

Argosy University accepts students on a rolling admissions basis year-round, depending on availability of required courses. Applications for admission are available online at http://www.argosy.edu or by contacting one of the campus locations.

Argosy University
205 North Michigan Avenue, Suite 1300
Chicago, Illinois 60601-2250
Phone: 312-899-9900
800-377-0617 (toll-free)
E-mail: auadmissions@argosy.edu
Web site: http://www.argosy.edu

THE ART INSTITUTE OF COLORADO

DENVER, COLORADO

The Art Institute of Colorado

The Institute

The Art Institute of Colorado has a mission to provide programs that prepare graduates for entry-level jobs in the creative arts. Programs are developed with and taught by experienced educators, either in traditional classroom settings or through online courses. The school offers eleven bachelor's degree programs, seven associate degree programs, and five diploma programs. Continuing education is available through the Department of Continuing Education at The Art Institute of Colorado.

The student population includes recent high school graduates, transfer students, and those who have left a previous employment situation to study and train for a new career. Students are creative, competitive, and open to new ideas. They place great value on an education that prepares them for an exciting entry-level position in the arts.

The Art Institute of Colorado students come from across the country and around the world. They are dedicated men and women who strive for excellence. International students are provided assistance through the International Student Advisement Office. This office provides a variety of support services and enrichment activities to meet the needs of international students.

The school is committed to helping students throughout their education experience, both in and out of the classroom, with such issues as the transition to academic life and involvement in student activities. In addition, assistance is available to help students with resume writing, networking, and keeping aware of what employers are looking for in job candidates. A variety of support services are available to help qualified students with counseling needs and disability services.

Student Affairs offers a wide variety of student activities to encourage social networking and stress management, including social and athletic events, a quarterly student art show, and creativity-enhancing activities and field trips. In addition, most academic departments sponsor student chapters of professional associations, including the American Culinary Federation, American Institute of Graphic Artists, American Society of Interior Designers, Industrial Designers of America, and Colorado Game Developers Association.

The Art Institute of Colorado's housing facility, the Towers, offers a variety of living accommodations in a fully equipped, partially furnished, apartment-style complex. An on-site professional staff member is available to coordinate activities and to help residents become acquainted with each other and with The Art Institute of Colorado.

The Art Institute of Colorado is accredited by the Accrediting Council for Independent Colleges and Schools (ACICS) to award bachelor's degrees, associate degrees, and diplomas. ACICS is listed as a nationally recognized accrediting agency by the U.S. Department of Education. Its accreditation of degree-granting institutions is recognized by the Council for Higher Education Accreditation. ACICS can be contacted at 750 First Street NE, Suite 980, Washington, D.C. 20002; telephone: 202-336-6780. The Associate of Applied Science in culinary arts program is accredited by the American Culinary Federation (ACF). The Bachelor of Arts in interior design degree program is accredited by the Council for Interior Design Accreditation.

Location

The Art Institute of Colorado is located in Denver, home to many major corporations and high-technology companies. Located near galleries, museums, and theaters, The Art Institute of Colorado provides easy access to music and dance performances at both the Performing Arts Complex and Red Rocks Amphitheater. Denver is a 1-hour drive from world-class skiing and water sports, amid the Rocky Mountains' breathtaking scenery. The city itself offers ample opportunities for biking, hiking, in-line skating, and viewing professional sports.

Majors and Degrees

Bachelor's degrees are offered in culinary management, design management, digital filmmaking and video production, fashion retail management, graphic design, industrial design, interactive media design, interior design, media arts and animation, photography, and visual effects and motion graphics.

Associate degree programs are available in baking and pastry, culinary arts, graphic design, interactive media design, kitchen and bath design, photography, and video production.

Diploma programs are offered in baking and pastry, digital design, photography, the art of cooking, and Web design.

Academic Programs

The Art Institute of Colorado offers Bachelor of Arts degree programs that are thirty-six months in length. Associate degree programs take twenty-one months to complete.

Academic Facilities

The Art Institute of Colorado has twelve computer labs containing more than 250 PC and Macintosh computers. Photography, audiovisual, and technology equipment is available for students to check out through the Media Services Department. Equipment includes analog and digital still cameras as well as audio and lighting equipment.

The library at The Art Institute of Colorado has a collection of 20,000 titles, including books, videotapes, DVDs, and magazines. The library subscribes to more than 200 periodicals and holds up to ten years of back-issue archives supporting major subject areas taught at the school. Tables for group work and Internet terminals for research are available in the library. The Service Bureau is an on-campus facility dedicated to meeting the printing and scanning needs of students.

Costs

Tuition cost varies by program. Prospective students should contact the school for current tuition costs. Other charges include a starting kit for all first-quarter students. Kits vary in price, depending on the program of study.

Financial Aid

Financial aid is available for those who qualify. Students who require financial assistance should first complete and submit a Free Application for Federal Student Aid (FAFSA) and meet with a financial aid officer. The officer determines the level of need based on a required federal formula, the cost of education, and other factors. Gift aid is available in the form of Federal Pell Grants, Federal Supplemental Educational Opportunity Grants, and veterans' benefits. Loans include Federal Stafford Loans, Federal PLUS Loans, and alternative loans. Other scholarships are available from the school and private sources. Application deadlines and eligibility requirements vary by program.

Faculty

The Art Institute of Colorado faculty members are professionals, many of whom have real-world experience in creative arts careers. The school's faculty members encourage students to cultivate conceptual, creative, and problem-solving skills. There are full-time and part-time faculty members.

Admission Requirements

All applicants are evaluated on the basis of previous education, background, and stated or demonstrated interest in a career program. Applicants must provide high school or college transcripts and an essay of approximately 150 words stating how an education at The Art Institute of Colorado will help them attain their creative goals. Portfolios are welcome but not required. Applicants who have taken the SAT or ACT are encouraged to submit scores for evaluation. There is a $50 application fee.

Application and Information

To obtain an application, make arrangements for an interview, or tour the school, prospective students should contact:

The Art Institute of Colorado
1200 Lincoln Street
Denver, Colorado 80203-2172
Phone: 303-837-0825
800-275-2420 (toll-free)
Fax: 303-860-8520
Web site: http://www.artinstitutes.edu/denver

The Art Institute of Atlanta®, GA; The Art Institute of Atlanta®–Decatur, GA; The Art Institute of Austin℠, TX; The Art Institute of California℠–Inland Empire; The Art Institute of California℠–Los Angeles; The Art Institute of California℠–Orange County; The Art Institute of California℠–Sacramento; The Art Institute of California℠–San Diego; The Art Institute of California℠–San Francisco; The Art Institute of California℠–Sunnyvale; The Art Institute of Charleston℠, SC, A branch of The Art Institute of Atlanta, GA; The Art Institute of Charlotte®, NC; The Art Institute of Colorado® (Denver); The Art Institute of Dallas®, TX; The Art Institute of Fort Lauderdale®, FL; The Art Institute of Houston®, TX; The Art Institute of Indianapolis℠, IN*; The Art Institute of Jacksonville℠, FL, A branch of Miami International University of Art & Design; The Art Institute of Las Vegas®, NV; The Art Institute of Michigan℠ (Detroit); The Art Institute of New York City®, NY; The Art Institute of Ohio℠–Cincinnati**; The Art Institute of Philadelphia®, PA; The Art Institute of Phoenix®, AZ; The Art Institute of Pittsburgh®, PA; The Art Institute of Pittsburgh®–Online Division; The Art Institute of Portland®, OR; The Art Institute of Salt Lake City℠, UT; The Art Institute of Seattle®, WA; The Art Institute of Tampa℠, FL, A branch of Miami International University of Art & Design; The Art Institute of Tennessee℠–Nashville, A branch of The Art Institute of Atlanta, GA; The Art Institute of Tucson℠, AZ; The Art Institute of Washington® (Arlington, VA), A branch of The Art Institute of Atlanta, GA; The Art Institute of York–Pennsylvania℠; The Art Institutes International Minnesota℠ (Minneapolis); California Design College℠ (Los Angeles–Wilshire Blvd.); The Illinois Institute of Art®–Chicago; The Illinois Institute of Art®–Schaumburg; Miami International University of Art & Design℠, FL; The New England Institute of Art® (Boston, MA).

*The Art Institute of Indianapolis is licensed by the Indiana Commission on Proprietary Education, 302 W. Washington St., Rm. E201, Indianapolis, IN 46204, AC-0080.

**The Art Institute of Ohio–Cincinnati, 8845 Governors Hill Drive, Suite 100, Cincinnati, OH 45249-3317, OH Reg. #04-01-1698B.

COLORADO CHRISTIAN UNIVERSITY

LAKEWOOD, COLORADO

The University

Located near the foothills of the Rocky Mountains, Colorado Christian University (CCU) is the only member of the Council for Christian Colleges and Universities in the Rocky Mountain region. Founded in 1914, CCU is a private interdenominational institution committed to providing undergraduate and graduate students with a complete education that develops the whole person—academically, professionally, and spiritually. Through offering a variety of programs and activities, CCU challenges students to experience their faith in all aspects of life. As a result, CCU graduates are equipped to be effective leaders in their careers, communities, churches, families, and in the world.

CCU has high academic standards and works with students to help them achieve the highest success. Students are taught by mentors who are experienced practitioners and qualified educators committed to the Christian faith. All students are challenged to incorporate biblical concepts and integrity into the skills and knowledge they're gaining in the classroom, in every major. Through critical thinking and experiential learning opportunities in the classroom, CCU students are prepared to be successful in a wide range of careers.

Community service and personal development are integral parts of the University's educational program. Through service to the community, students discover their gifts, develop skills, learn to lead and to work with others, and experience the joy and personal rewards of community involvement.

Campus housing provides apartment-style living for all students. Each fully furnished apartment unit features a kitchen, living room, bathroom(s), bedrooms, and a balcony. In addition, the dining hall and food service plans are available to all resident students. Various meal plans are available to students to accommodate different schedules.

CCU competes in Division II of the NCAA and is part of the Rocky Mountain Athletic Conference. CCU offers men's and women's basketball, cross-country, golf, soccer, and tennis; men's baseball; and women's volleyball. For students who do not wish to participate in intercollegiate athletics, there are a variety of intramural sports and activities available. Academic and social clubs, discipleship groups, and University retreats provide informal opportunities for students and faculty members to spend time together in recreation, instruction, and fellowship. Both the band and the choir participate in annual tours in Colorado and across the nation.

Colorado Christian University is accredited by the North Central Association of Colleges and Schools. The University is interdenominational and serves individuals and faculty members representing more than thirty Christian denominations. The University enrolls approximately 2,200 undergraduate and graduate students from forty-six states and sixteen countries in its academic programs. The University offers graduate and adult degree programs and has off-campus centers in Denver/Lakewood, Colorado Springs, Loveland, Grand Junction, and other satellite locations throughout Colorado.

Location

Located in the thriving Denver suburb of Lakewood, CCU is about 15 minutes from Denver's popular LoDo area, which is the home of coffeehouses, international-style shopping, and major professional sports teams, including the NFL Denver Broncos, the NBA Denver Nuggets, the MLB Colorado Rockies, and the NHL Colorado Avalanche.

Directly west of CCU and less than 2 hours away are many of the world's best skiing, snowboarding, bicycling, hiking, climbing, white-water rafting, and fly-fishing locations. Denver has more than 300 days of sunshine each year, moderate winters, and mild summer days with comfortably low humidity.

Majors and Degrees

Colorado Christian University offers bachelor's degrees in accounting, biblical studies, biology, business administration, computer information systems, elementary education, English, global studies, history, human communication, liberal arts, mathematics, music, music education, music ministry, psychology, science, secondary education, social science, theology, and youth ministry. Within these programs there are numerous emphases and concentrations. Students may also choose prelaw or premedicine courses of study. Academic minors include accounting, biblical studies, biology, business, chemistry, computer information systems, English, finance, history, human communication, leadership, mathematics, music, music ministry, outdoor leadership, psychology, Spanish, theology, Young Life leadership, and youth ministry.

Academic Programs

Colorado Christian University operates under a semester system offering fall, spring, and summer sessions. To qualify for graduation, students in all majors must complete the required minimum number of credits for their chosen major, including general education and elective courses. Colorado Christian University recognizes the importance of arts and sciences; therefore, the general education requirements include course work in behavioral and social sciences, communication, computers, English, humanities, mathematics, natural science, integrative studies, and biblical studies. The freshman year begins with an integration course that helps new students assimilate into University life. Except for students in teacher licensure and music programs, all students enrolled in Bachelor of Arts majors must complete a two-semester sequence in college-level foreign language courses or the equivalent.

Colorado Christian University may grant college credit for course work taken at another accredited college; through Advanced Placement, International Baccalaureate, College-Level Examination Program, DANTES, or Armed Forces Education; or by examination.

ROTC programs are available to students through cooperation with other colleges in the metropolitan Denver area. Specific ROTC information is available from the Office of Admission.

Off-Campus Programs

As a member of the Council for Christian Colleges and Universities, CCU offers students the opportunity to spend a semester abroad in programs designed to integrate Christian commitment in a world context. The American Studies Program places students in federal, public, and private agencies in Washington, D.C., where students can gain insight into government and public policy. Costa Rica is the setting for the Latin American Studies Program, where students can integrate their faith with knowledge and experience in a Third World country. Students involved in the China Studies Program have the opportunity to explore culture in Beijing, Xiian, and Shanghai and to learn about Chinese history, government, economics, and religion. The Middle East Studies Program in Cairo, Egypt, provides students with the opportunity to study cultures, religions, and conflicts within this diverse region. The Russian Studies Program affords students the opportunity to study Russian language, history, culture, and current events in the cities of Moscow, Nizhni Novgorod, and St. Petersburg. The L.A. Film Institute Program prepares students for the challenges and responsibilities of quality filmmaking, while the Focus on the Family Institute helps equip tomorrow's leaders for family, church, and society. Other off-campus opportunities include the Australia Studies Centre, the Contemporary Music Center, Oxford Programmes at Wycliffe Hall, the Summer Institute of Journalism, the Uganda Studies Program, and opportunities at Jerusalem University College.

Other programs offer majors through cooperation with other state universities or institutes. In such circumstances, students complete general requirements at CCU and professional courses at cooperating institutions.

Academic Facilities

The CCU library includes a computer lab, a curriculum lab, and audiovisual equipment loan as well as book, video, and music collections. Students have access to more than 10,000 full-text journals via the Internet, which augment 400 print journals in the library. Religion, education, psychology, business, and periodical and newspaper indexes are offered through the CCU library with cooperative programs for borrowing materials from other libraries. Computer searching is performed for and by students to obtain the best resources for their assignments. The music facility has a separate music library and also provides multitimbral synthesizers, computer ear-training programs, Finale, Mosaic, Professional Performer, Tap Master rhythm laboratory, and facilities with grand pianos. Athletic facilities, a student center and bookstore, and other facilities all enrich academic life for CCU students.

Costs

The 2007–08 cost for tuition (12–16 credit hours) was $9425 per semester for traditional undergraduate students. Room charges ranged from $1950 to $2250, and meal plans ranged from $1310 to $1650 per semester. All freshmen are required to live on campus and participate in a meal plan unless living at home in the Denver metro area with their parents or a legal guardian.

Financial Aid

Colorado Christian University provides a financial aid program to assist students who need additional resources to meet their educational costs. Students who qualify may be eligible for institutional scholarships and grants based on their talent in the areas of academics, music, or athletics or based on their financial need. Students may also qualify for assistance through federal grant, work, or loan programs. Students applying for financial aid must file the Free Application for Federal Student Aid (FAFSA).

Faculty

CCU faculty members teach primarily undergraduate courses. Small class sizes (most classes have fewer than 25 students), combined with a teaching faculty rather than a research faculty, assure students of personal, high-quality instruction. Faculty members, not teaching assistants, teach all classes. Eighty-five percent of full-time faculty members hold doctoral degrees. An advantage of CCU's faculty is that professors are practitioners in their field—they come with background and experience in the real world, not just from classroom textbooks. This element offers practical, relevant training for students. Faculty members also serve as advisers and mentors to students. They take a sincere and active role in the personal, academic, and spiritual lives of the students.

Student Government

The Associated Students of Colorado Christian University includes all registered students. Officers are chosen annually by election from within the student body and serve through the Student Government Association (SGA). Voicing the concerns and needs of the students to the University administration and providing opportunities for fun and fellowship are at the core of the SGA. SGA serves students through three distinct branches: the Judicial Board, the Senate, and the Committee on Student Activities.

Admission Requirements

Applicants are evaluated on the basis of academic ability, personal and professional goals, character, and Christian commitment. For all programs, those applying are expected to have a high school diploma or the equivalent, with a satisfactory grade point average. Students applying as first-time freshmen or those with fewer than 30 transfer credits should submit the Application for Admission, a high school transcript, SAT or ACT scores, and two character recommendations. Students applying for transfer admission should submit the Application for Admission, all college transcripts, and two character recommendations.

In order to provide a solid foundation for college-level work, it is recommended that the applicant present the equivalent of 16 academic units from an approved high school. Homeschooled students are welcome to apply for admission by following the application procedures listed above. A GED diploma may be required of a homeschooled student, at the discretion of the admission committee, if there is evidence of a discrepancy between the high school transcript and standardized test scores.

Application and Information

For a viewbook and application, students should contact:

Office of Admission
Colorado Christian University
8787 West Alameda Avenue
Lakewood, Colorado 80226
Phone: 303-963-3200
800-44-FAITH (toll-free)
Fax: 303-963-3201
E-mail: admission@ccu.edu
Web site: http://www.ccu.edu

Colorado Christian University students enjoying mountain biking.

COLORADO STATE UNIVERSITY

FORT COLLINS, COLORADO

The University

In 1879, Colorado State University was designated Colorado's land-grant college. The land-grant concept of a balanced program of teaching, research, extension, and public service provides the foundation for the University's teaching and research programs. Today, Colorado State has a commitment to integrating first-rate academic programs with hands-on learning experiences inside and outside the classroom. Education at Colorado State encompasses the major areas of human knowledge—the sciences, the arts, the humanities, and the professions. The mission of the University is to graduate students who possess the knowledge and skills to compete in a global marketplace and live full, rewarding lives. The University historically has had a reputation for excellence in its programs from the baccalaureate to the postgraduate level and has achieved a worldwide reputation in a number of important fields. Colorado State offers graduate degrees in all eight colleges.

The 25,000 students enrolled at Colorado State represent all fifty states and eighty-six countries. The variety of students broadens the educational experience for all and enables students to share their backgrounds and heritages and learn about others in an atmosphere that encourages cultural exchange and an appreciation and respect for diversity.

The University provides a wide range of programs to meet the social, recreational, and academic needs of its diverse student population. There are more than 300 clubs and organizations, including student government, honor societies, sororities and fraternities, athletic clubs, cultural and religious organizations, advocacy offices, and major-oriented or professionally oriented clubs. The Lory Student Center provides a focal point for student life on campus. Many students participate in intramural and club sports. For the more serious-minded athlete, Colorado State offers men's and women's athletics in the Mountain West Conference (MWC) Division I of the National Collegiate Athletic Association (NCAA). All students have access to the sports facilities at the 100,000-square-foot Student Recreation Center, which is open daily for drop-in recreational use. This facility houses a gymnasium with multipurpose courts; an elevated running track; a ten-lane, 25-yard swimming pool and spa pool; and weight, cardio, exercise, and locker rooms; and more.

Colorado State has twelve coed residence halls, each containing recreation and study areas, a laundry room, and vending machines. Residence hall dining centers provide many dining choices for students. The halls offer a wide variety of activities, including educational programs, social gatherings, and recreational events. Several floors within the residence halls are designated for either academic or leisure interests, providing the opportunity for students to live with others with similar interests. These living learning communities include honors, leadership, engineering, natural sciences, and pre–veterinary medicine. All residence halls are nonsmoking.

Location

Fort Collins, a city of 137,000, provides a unique blend of big-city amenities and small-college-town friendliness. It is scenically located at the western edge of the plains at the base of the Rocky Mountain foothills and conveniently located 65 miles north of Denver. The wide-open spaces and majestic Rockies make Fort Collins a very attractive place to live and learn. Areas for camping, hiking, skiing, swimming, boating, rafting, climbing, and fishing are within an easy driving distance of campus.

Majors and Degrees

Colorado State University offers bachelor's degrees through eight colleges. Bachelor of Science degrees are granted through the College of Agricultural Sciences in agricultural business, agricultural economics, agricultural education, animal science, equine science, horticulture, landscape architecture, landscape horticulture, and soil and crop sciences; through the College of Applied Human Sciences in apparel and merchandising, construction management, family and consumer sciences, health and exercise science, human development and family studies, interior design, nutrition and food science, and restaurant and resort management; through the College of Business in business administration, with concentrations in accounting, finance, information systems, marketing, organization and innovation management, and real estate; through the College of Engineering in chemical and biological engineering, civil engineering, computer engineering, electrical engineering, engineering science, environmental engineering, and mechanical engineering; through the Warner College of Natural Resources in fish, wildlife and conservation biology; forestry; geology; natural resources management; natural resource recreation and tourism; rangeland ecology; and watershed science; through the College of Natural Sciences in applied computing technology, biochemistry, biological science, chemistry, computer science, mathematics, natural sciences, physics, psychology, and zoology; and through the College of Veterinary Medicine and Biomedical Sciences in biomedical sciences, environmental health, and microbiology.

Bachelor of Arts degrees are offered through the College of Applied Human Sciences in social work and through the College of Liberal Arts in anthropology; art; economics; English; history; languages, literatures, and cultures; liberal arts; music; performing arts; philosophy; political science; sociology; speech communication; and technical journalism. The Bachelor of Fine Arts and Bachelor of Music degrees are offered through the College of Liberal Arts in art and in music.

Teacher licensure is available in early childhood education; at the secondary level in English, French, German, mathematics, science (biology, chemistry, and geology), social studies, Spanish, and speech; and in grades K–12 in art and music. Vocational secondary education licensure is available in agricultural education, business education, consumer and family studies, marketing education, and trade and industrial education. Preprofessional advising programs are offered in chiropractic, dentistry, law, medicine, nursing, occupational therapy, optometry, pharmacy, physical therapy, physician assistant studies, podiatry, and veterinary medicine.

Academic Programs

More than 150 undergraduate programs of study are offered within the eight colleges, allowing students to shape a course of study that best meets their personal and professional goals. Depending on their degree program, students are required to complete a minimum of 120 credit hours for graduation.

Colorado State provides students with a well-rounded education through the All-University Core Curriculum (AUCC), the centerpiece of Colorado State's integrated learning experience. All students are required to complete the AUCC. Students usually meet the AUCC requirements in their freshman and sophomore years and devote their junior and senior years to specialization in their major field. A concentration—a sequence of at least 12 semester credits of selected courses designed to accommodate the specific interests of a student—may be designated within some majors. Students may also choose to pursue a double major, a minor, or an interdisciplinary studies program.

The Colorado State Honors Program provides academically motivated undergraduates in all majors with intellectual stimulation commensurate with their abilities. It offers small classes and fosters a close intellectual association of students and faculty members.

Off-Campus Programs

The Office of International Programs coordinates many study-abroad programs that allow students to study almost anywhere in the world. Study-abroad programs can range from two-week seminars to semester and yearlong periods of study in any major.

Academic Facilities

Colorado State comprises four campuses covering approximately 4,900 acres. The 579-acre main campus, with nearly 100 academic and administrative buildings, is virtually a city within itself. Classrooms and residence halls are in proximity. South of the main campus is the Veterinary Medical Center (103 acres), one of the nation's top facilities for teaching and research in the clinical sciences. A 1,434-acre agricultural campus supports instruction and research in agronomy and animal science, including the Equine Teaching and Research Center. The Foothills Campus, a 1,705-acre facility located 2 miles west of the main campus, is home to many of the University's renowned research projects. A 1,177-acre mountain campus, Pingree Park, located 55 miles west of the main campus at an elevation of 9,000 feet and bordering Rocky Mountain National Park, is used primarily for summer educational and research programs in forestry and natural resources.

The William E. Morgan Library houses collections totaling 2 million items and provides reading areas for more than 1,500 people. The library collections include books, periodicals, newspapers, journals, manuscripts, microfilms, records, and other reference items. The collection is enriched by a wide selection of electronic resources. The library also offers more than 300 public computers that allow access to specialized indexes and Web-based sources.

Costs

For 2007–08, tuition and fees for full-time (15 credits) undergraduates per semester was $2709 for Colorado residents and $9429 for nonresidents. The average cost of room and board for on-campus housing was $3546. Books were estimated at $450.

Freshman students, unless they are living at home, married, or over 21 years of age, are required to live on campus and are therefore guaranteed a space in the residence halls. Upperclass students may choose to live in the Colorado State residence halls, in the University apartment housing, or in any of the numerous houses or apartments located nearby.

Financial Aid

Colorado State participates in and administers a wide variety of student financial aid programs, including loans, grants, scholarships, work-study, and student employment. Colorado State's Student Financial Services Web site (http://www.sfs.colostate.edu) describes in detail all scholarships and aid offered. Approximately 66 percent of the students at Colorado State received some type of financial assistance. Student Employment Services assists students with locating part-time positions both on and off campus.

Faculty

The Colorado State faculty teaches both graduate and undergraduate students. There are approximately 1,500 faculty members; 99 percent of the tenure-track faculty members hold doctorate, first professional, or other terminal degrees. The student-faculty ratio is 17:1. Faculty members are actively engaged in research, teach undergraduate classes, and serve as advisers.

Student Government

The Associated Students of Colorado State University (ASCSU) comprises all enrolled students. The ASCSU Senate acts as a liaison between the student body and the administration as well as the Board of Governors, the governing body of Colorado State. The ASCSU also offers free legal, consumer, and other services to Colorado State students.

Admission Requirements

Colorado State University selects for admission students who demonstrate the greatest academic potential for successfully attaining a degree and who appear to be the best qualified to benefit from and contribute to the academic and cultural environment of the University. Colorado State is a selective university. In fall 2007, the middle 50 percent of entering freshmen had a GPA range of 3.2 to 3.8, an ACT composite score of 22 to 26, and an SAT (critical reading and math) combined score of 1020 to1220.

Students applying as freshmen must submit a completed application form, a $50 application processing fee, official high school transcripts that include high school class rank, college transcripts for any college course work, scores from either the ACT or SAT, a personal essay, and one recommendation from a teacher, principal, or counselor. Each student's application receives careful, individual, and holistic review that includes assessment of grades, class rank, number of completed academic units, scores on either the ACT or SAT, rigor of high school curriculum, trend in quality of high school performances, involvement in community service, school, and/or family activities, personal or special circumstances, and the ability to contribute to a diverse campus community.

Priority consideration is given to students who have a minimum cumulative 3.25 GPA and satisfactory completion of the following 18 prerequisite high school units: 4 units of English, 4 units of mathematics (must include algebra 1, geometry, and algebra 2), 3 units of social studies (1 unit must be U.S. or world history), 3 units of natural science (2 units must be lab-based), 2 units of the same foreign language, and 2 units of academic electives.

The freshman priority application filing date for fall semester is February 1, and the application deadline for spring semester is December 1. Students are encouraged to apply early, as enrollment limits may be met prior to the deadline.

Undergraduate transfer students who wish to attend Colorado State must submit a completed application form, a $50 application processing fee, official transcripts from all colleges and universities attended, a personal essay (250-word minimum), and one letter of recommendation. To be a strong candidate for admission, applicants should have college-level academic course work and at least a 2.5 cumulative GPA, with a minimum of more than 12 semester credits after high school graduation. These credits must be earned from a college or university accredited by one of the six regional associations of schools and colleges. Transfer applicants must also meet the admission requirement in mathematics. For details on meeting this requirement, students should visit http://www.admissions.colostate.edu/transfer. Other factors considered for admission include academic rigor; trend in grades; involvement in community service, school, work, and/or family activities; ability to contribute to a diverse campus community; and personal or special circumstances. The priority application filing dates for transfer students are May 1 for the fall semester and December 1 for the spring semester.

For current admission information and to apply online, students should visit the Web site at http://www.admissions.colostate.edu. Students may also apply online through the Common Application at http://www.commonapp.org.

Application and Information

The admissions office is open Monday through Friday, from 7:45 to 4:45 during the academic year and from 7:30 to 4:30 during the summer. Student-led campus tours and information sessions are given every weekday. Visit Day programs are offered throughout the year. Students should visit the Office of Admissions Web site at http:www.//admissions.colostate.edu/visit for more information regarding on-campus visits.

Office of Admissions
Colorado State University
1062 Campus Delivery
Fort Collins, Colorado 80523-1062
Phone: 970-491-6909
Internet: http://www.admissions.colostate.edu

NAROPA UNIVERSITY

BOULDER, COLORADO

The College

Naropa University is a private, nonprofit, nonsectarian liberal arts institution with a core mission of contemplative education. This approach to learning integrates the best of Eastern and Western educational traditions, creating a complementary relationship between rigorous academic study and self-exploration at the deepest intuitive level. Naropa graduates are fully formed individuals whose knowledge of themselves elevates their interaction with others.

Contemplative education offers students a highly experiential and transformative learning path that brings a spiritual component to the student's educational experience while sharpening skills crucial to critical thinking: reading, writing, speaking, and listening. This experience lets students be who they are while exploring who they want to be.

The curriculum integrates academic, artistic, and traditional Eastern awareness practices to enhance students' understanding of themselves, their field of study, and the world. As a result, Naropa students are better prepared for the constant challenges and rapid change of modern society. Through disciplines such as sitting mediation, yoga, and t'ai-chi ch'uan, students develop mindfulness and are trained to acknowledge the direct experience of learning, moment by moment. This process brings precision, openness, and kindness to oneself and others; it teaches students how to integrate intellect and intuition; and it amplifies the confidence and desire required to work for the benefit of others. This initiates a lifelong process of creative personal development that goes well beyond the college experience.

Students enjoy an environment of discovery and learning shared between themselves and the faculty. With a dual legacy from both the liberal arts and contemplative practice, a Naropa education offers dynamic, unpredictable, and engaging classes, where real learning and growth take place. Naropa undergraduates are independent thinkers, intellectually curious, civic-minded, adventurous, spiritual, and caring. They come from forty-five states and territories and eight countries, representing a wide range of life experiences, backgrounds, and ages. Of the 1,083 degree-seeking students at Naropa University, 456 are undergraduate students.

Naropa University was founded thirty-three years ago by Chögyam Trungpa Rinpoche, a Tibetan meditation master and scholar, who envisioned a liberal arts institution that would honor and respect the importance of various world wisdom traditions, including his own, and offer an educational experience that integrated knowledge of oneself with knowledge of the external world for a transformative learning path.

Accredited by the Higher Learning Commission of the North Central Association of Colleges and Schools, Naropa University offers B.A. and B.F.A. degrees through its four-year undergraduate program as well as M.A., M.Div., and M.F.A. degrees through its graduate school.

Location

Naropa University is located in Boulder, Colorado, at the base of the Rocky Mountain foothills and 25 miles northwest of Denver. Boulder offers something for everyone and has earned a well-deserved reputation for a great quality of life with a dynamic arts community, excellent music venues, and many cultural events. Hiking, skiing, and snowboarding enthusiasts have ample opportunity to pursue their sport and recreation activities. Boulder has bike paths all over town, and Boulder public transportation provides a frequent and comprehensive bus schedule throughout the day.

Naropa University has three campuses in Boulder, two of which serve undergraduate programs. The Arapahoe campus is home to classrooms for most undergraduate classes, undergraduate advising, University administration, a performing arts center, a meditation hall, the Allen Ginsberg Library, a computer center, an art gallery, student lounges, the bookstore, and the Naropa Café. The Nalanda campus, approximately 3½ miles from the Arapahoe campus, is home to Naropa's performing and visual arts programs.

Majors and Degrees

Naropa University offers a B.F.A. in performance and ten B.A. degree programs: contemplative psychology, early childhood education, environmental studies, interdisciplinary studies, music, peace studies, religious studies, traditional Eastern arts, visual arts, and writing and literature.

The contemplative psychology major integrates Western psychology and Eastern approaches to healing mind and body. Students choose a concentration in psychological science, psychology of health and healing, somatic psychology, or transpersonal and humanistic psychology.

Nurturing the genuine and compassionate nature of teachers, the early childhood education major applies teaching methods drawn from Waldorf, Montessori, and Buddhist traditions. The major offers apprentice-style internships with master teachers from these traditions in a variety of contemplative preschool settings.

The environmental studies major empowers students to develop the knowledge base and skill set needed to address complex environmental issues. Core courses emphasize field science, sacred ecology, sustainability, horticulture, environmental history and justice, and learning community.

Interdisciplinary studies invites students to design a major by selecting courses from two or three disciplines at Naropa. Recent examples of senior work include Documentary Poetics, The Embodied Teacher, and Shambhala Path of Hip-Hop Warriorship.

Naropa's music major gives students fundamental training in musicianship that includes harmonic analysis, ear training, rhythmic acuity, music theory, improvisation, composition, history, and multicultural perspectives.

The peace studies major focuses on the study of peace and explores the causes of violence and war through four related areas of inquiry: history and politics of social change, theory and practice of peacemaking, the arts in peacemaking, and engaged learning.

The major in religious studies emphasizes the role of contemplative practice in the world's great religions, especially Buddhism, and uses present traditions from perspectives sympathetic to the living religious communities themselves.

The traditional Eastern arts major is the only degree program of its kind in the country, combining the practice of sitting meditation with an in-depth study of the philosophy, history, and culture of a body-mind awareness discipline. Concentrations are offered in aikido, t'ai-chi ch'uan, or yoga teacher training.

Visual arts blends traditional and contemporary visual arts study with contemplative practice while offering courses in photography, calligraphy, sculpture, pottery, and several painting media.

Writing and literature offers intensive training in the practice and study of writing through small writing workshops, literary studies courses, and exposure to a range of contemporary writing offered through the Summer Writing Program.

The B.F.A. in performance offers rigorous technical training, an emphasis on student-centered creative process, and a contemplative approach to performance and performance studies.

Academic Programs

Undergraduate students develop competencies in college-level academic studies and are exposed to a breadth of knowledge, practice, and experience necessary for success in their major and minor fields of study. Core course work is designed to help students think and read critically, write effectively, identify and understand multicultural issues, and cultivate awareness and compassion for others. Naropa's core requirements include the humanities, the arts, cultural and historical studies, diversity, world wisdom traditions, contemplative practice, body/mind practice, writing skills, and scientific inquiry. Students explore the meaning of effective citizenship through the integration of classroom learning and community engagement.

Upon completion of 30 semester credits, students may declare a major. Students must complete a total of 120 semester credits to earn an undergraduate degree.

Off-Campus Programs

Students at Naropa University have the opportunity to study abroad during their sophomore and junior years and the fall semester of their senior year. Studying and living overseas with Naropa University fosters intercultural competence and critical thinking and lays the groundwork for compassionate engagement with the world. Currently, Naropa University offers a study-abroad program in Prague, Czech Republic, and will accept applications for spring 2009 beginning August 15, 2008.

Community-based learning is offered through Naropa University's Community Studies Center and provides opportunities for students and faculty members to develop skills for participating in the public life of their communities. Through its emphasis on applied, experiential projects, community-based learning offers Naropa University faculty members and students innovative tools to forward the knowledge of their academic and artistic disciplines, augment student learning, and educate a citizenry to perform the public work of a democracy. The Community Studies Center also provides AmeriCorps scholarship funds for Naropa students involved in community work.

Costs

Undergraduate tuition for the 2007–08 academic year was $20,738. The on-campus room and board costs were $6501.

Financial Aid

Naropa University makes every attempt to assist students who do not have the financial resources to accomplish their educational objectives. Naropa offers institutional grants and scholarships as well as all types of federal student aid. Some financial aid for international students is also available. Approximately 68 percent of Naropa degree-seeking undergraduate students receive financial assistance in the form of loans, student employment, scholarships, and grants.

Faculty

The Naropa University faculty is distinguished by a wealth of experience in the professional, artistic, and scholastic applications of their disciplines. In addition to the outstanding core faculty, an international community of scholars and artists is consistently drawn to Naropa because of its strong vision and leadership in education. The average class size is 14, and Naropa's student-faculty ratio is 10:1.

Student Government

Through the Student Union of Naropa University (SUN), students are able to meet with faculty members and administrators, communicate their concerns, and influence school policy. As a hub for student groups and clubs, SUN also takes active steps to ensure a dignified environment for all Naropa University students.

Admission Requirements

Naropa University seeks students who have a strong appetite for learning and who enjoy experiential education in an academic setting. The Admissions Committee considers academic background, connection to Naropa's unique mission, and ability to engage in contemplative, experiential college work when making admission decisions. A student's transcript, essays, interview, and letters of recommendation play important roles in the admissions process. SAT and ACT scores are optional.

Application and Information

A completed application for admission to Naropa University includes a $50 nonrefundable application fee, three essays, two letters of recommendation, official high school transcripts for freshman applicants (0 to 30 credits), and official transcripts from all previous college-level study. Many departments also require supplemental application materials. An interview, either in person or by telephone, is required for all programs, with the exception of writing and literature.

Prospective students are strongly encouraged to visit the University. The Office of Admissions hosts a preview weekend each semester, and guided campus tours are offered throughout the year.

The suggested deadline for receiving completed applications for the fall semester is January 15 and for the spring semester, October 15. Any applications received after the suggested deadline are reviewed on a space-available basis. For additional information, prospective students should contact:

Admissions Office
Naropa University
2130 Arapahoe Avenue
Boulder, Colorado 80302-6697
Phone: 303-546-3572
800-772-6951 (toll-free)
Fax: 303-546-3583
E-mail: admissions@naropa.edu
Web site: http://www.naropa.edu

The Lincoln Building at Naropa University.

REGIS UNIVERSITY

DENVER, COLORADO

The University

In its 130th year, Regis University is the Rocky Mountain region's only Jesuit university and is well-known for innovation and educational leadership. Continuing a 450-year tradition of academic excellence, Regis is one of twenty-eight Jesuit colleges and universities located in the United States.

U.S. News & World Report named Regis University a "Top School" among colleges and universities in the western United States, marking the thirteenth consecutive year Regis has been in the publication's top tier. The University was also recognized as one of the top 100 universities and colleges for leadership in the field of student character development in *The Templeton Guide: Colleges That Encourage Character Development.* Regis University is ranked by *U.S. News & World Report* as the fifth-best university in the western United States for the highest proportion of classes with 20 or fewer students.

The University has an American Rhodes Scholar, 2 *USA Today* College All-Academic Team selectees (in 1993 and 2000), the top female collegiate athlete in NCAA Division II for 1998–99, 5 Fulbright professors, 2 Fuld Fellows, and a wealth of other national recognition of outstanding academic excellence. More than 90 percent of Regis's full-time faculty members have a Ph.D. or terminal degree in their field.

However, Regis University was not always Regis. The school was started in 1877 in Las Vegas, New Mexico, by a group of exiled Italian Jesuits. It was known as Las Vegas College. In 1884, a second venture, known as Sacred Heart College, was started at Morrison, Colorado.

In 1887, Las Vegas College and Sacred Heart College moved to North Denver, where the joint operation became known as the College of the Sacred Heart. The college was renamed Regis in 1921, in honor of St. John Francis Regis, an eighteenth-century Jesuit missionary and saint who was revered for his exemplary work with poor people in the mountains of France.

On July 1, 1991, Regis College became Regis University, with three constituent schools: Regis College, the School for Professional Studies, and the Rueckert-Hartman School for Health Professions. Regis College is the traditional residential school, with 1,250 students, primarily in the 18- to 23-year-old range. The School for Professional Studies focuses on undergraduate and graduate adult higher education. The Rueckert-Hartman School for Health Professions educates men and women to be leaders who are committed to excellence within the health-care professions.

Regis College primarily serves traditional-aged, mostly residential undergraduate students. The college offers a full range of programs in the liberal arts, sciences, business, and education. Students may choose from twenty-four structured areas of study or design their own programs through the interdisciplinary and flexible major plans. A low student-faculty ratio permits small classes and learning formats that encourage critical thinking, thoughtful discussion, and well-developed communication skills. In the college, students receive highly personalized attention from 93 full-time skilled professors and dedicated scholars.

Four modern residence halls—O'Connell, DeSmet, West, and the townhouse complex—are fully staffed and offer computer labs, free cable TV, local phone service and voice mail, free laundry facilities, lounges, vending machines, and two phone and data lines in each room. More than 80 percent of freshmen live on campus.

Athletic opportunities are offered on all levels: recreational, intramural, and intercollegiate. Regis University is a member of NCAA Division II and the Rocky Mountain Athletic Conference and competes in twelve intercollegiate sports as well as a variety of intramural and club sport programs.

Location

Regis University is located near the base of the Rocky Mountains in a residential suburban neighborhood of northwest Denver, just north of I-70 and 25 minutes from Denver International Airport. Within 15 minutes of the campus is one of the most exciting international downtowns in the world. Thirty minutes west of the campus are the snowcapped peaks of the Rocky Mountains. Denver is one of America's fastest-growing metropolitan regions, with an abundance of cultural and recreational opportunities; it is one of only a few American cities with seven professional sports franchises. Denver has low humidity, and the sun shines about 300 days a year. The metropolitan area averages only 15 inches of precipitation a year, about the same as Los Angeles. Midwinter temperatures of 60 degrees are common. Colorado ski country is nearby; the campus is just 2 hours from Breckenridge, Vail, and Winter Park.

Majors and Degrees

Undergraduate degree offerings include the Bachelor of Arts (B.A.), Bachelor of Science (B.S.), Bachelor of Arts and Science, Classical Bachelor of Arts, and Bachelor of Science in Nursing (B.S.N.) as well as special majors.

Business programs include accounting (major and minor); accounting/M.B.A. (major); business administration, with concentrations in finance, international business, management, management information systems, and marketing (major and minor); economics (major and minor); flexible major; and political economy (major and minor).

Programs in humanities include art history (major), communication (major and minor), English (major and minor), fine arts: visual arts (major and minor), flexible major, French (major and minor), German (course work), Hispanic studies (minor), literature (minor), music (major and minor), Spanish (major and minor), women's studies (major and minor), and writing (minor).

The University offers natural sciences and mathematics programs in biochemistry (major and minor), biology (B.A. and B.S., major and minor), chemistry (major and minor), computer science (major and minor), environmental studies/human ecology (major and minor), exercise science (minor), mathematics (major and minor), neuroscience (major and minor), and physics (minor).

Programs in philosophy and religious studies include Catholic studies (minor), Christian leadership (minor), flexible major, philosophy (major and minor), and religious studies (major and minor).

Social sciences programs include anthropology (minor), criminology (minor), education (licensure), elementary education (licensure), flexible major, history (major and minor), leadership (minor), peace and justice studies (minor), physical education (minor), physical education: coaching/recreation (minor), politics (major and minor), psychology (major and minor), secondary education (licensure), sociology (major and minor), and special education (licensure).

Preprofessional programs are offered in dentistry, law, medicine, and physical therapy. A dual-degree engineering program is also offered.

Academic Programs

Regis is part of a 450-year-old Jesuit tradition that provides a values-centered liberal arts education and is known for service to others. The Core Curriculum, designed to prepare students for life as well as a career, requires students to reflect on the purpose of human existence, to understand the roots of modern culture, to embrace philosophical and religious perspectives, and to think critically. These courses enrich perceptions, challenge assumptions, and broaden visions.

A total of 128 semester hours is required for a bachelor's degree. Regis chooses a select group of students for its honors program each year and offers a schedule of undergraduate courses in the summer session. The University's Center for Service Learning actively involves students in community service projects. Internships and study abroad are offered as well. Other academic programs include the writing program, teacher licensure, the Commitment Program, Air Force Reserve Officer Training Corps, Air Force University Scholarship Program, and the Army Reserve Officer Training Corps (military science).

Academic Facilities

Regis is committed to providing state-of-the-art facilities. The University offers students 24-hour access to personal computers, online service, and research tools in common lab facilities. In addition, labs are located in the three coeducational residence halls, in the town houses, and in specific departments. All students are offered full access to an e-mail account on the Internet.

The University has two libraries, housing more than 280,000 volumes, 2,100 periodical subscriptions, 150,000 microforms, and a 90,000-slide art history collection. Its CARL online catalog is a comprehensive index to the collections and provides 10,000 databases, document delivery options, and full-text online journals. The main library, which includes media services, provides network ports at every place that a student studies for ease of access to the Internet and the Regis database.

The Coors Life Direction Center houses the Office of Career Services and Academic Internships, Personal Counseling, Disabilities Services, the Fitness Program, and the Health Center.

New additions to the campus are the St. John Francis Regis Chapel and the fully renovated Science Building.

Costs

Undergraduate tuition and fees at Regis College for the 2007–08 academic year were $26,900. Room and board for the academic year cost $8870.

Financial Aid

In an effort to keep its high-quality Jesuit education affordable, Regis is committed to helping as many students as possible by continuing to increase scholarships and University grant funds. The student financial aid program invests more than $14 million in undergraduates. More than 90 percent of full-time Regis College students receive some financial assistance. Scholarships and grants are awarded on the basis of need, academic achievement, and leadership. The University participates in all federal and Colorado-supported programs. The Free Application for Federal Student Aid (FAFSA) or Renewal Application must be filed.

Faculty

Regis College has 100 full-time faculty members; 92 percent hold terminal degrees. Ten percent of the faculty members are Jesuit priests, and Regis has no graduate students/teaching assistants on its staff. The college has a 14:1 student-faculty ratio. Some professional staff members and Jesuit priests live and teach on Regis's campus. These committed adults are available for both academic and personal direction for Regis students. In addition, each undergraduate has an individual faculty adviser, who assists students in their academic choices.

Student Government

The Student Government at Regis is led by the Executive Board. The board is supported by the Senate, which comprises class representatives. The student leaders serve on University committees, plan entertainment, help determine student policy, and oversee more than thirty student organizations.

Admission Requirements

Regis College actively recruits students for equal opportunity and nondiscriminatory consideration of eligibility. The average ACT composite score for incoming freshmen is 23, and the average SAT combined score for Math and Critical Reading is 1108 (a new composite score that includes the Writing section has not been calculated yet). Admission is determined by a student's high school record, including grades, test scores, personal ability, and leadership qualities.

Requirements for freshman admission include high school graduation or its equivalent and evidence of college-level competency, as shown in high school courses, grades, ACT or SAT test scores, a personal essay, and recommendations. The new ACT writing component is not required. Freshmen should present a minimum of 15 academic units. Successful candidates must have a satisfactory high school or college record in order to be admitted.

Application and Information

Completed applications for admission should be submitted to the Director of Admissions. Applications may be submitted any time after the beginning of the year. The Office of Admissions usually notifies each applicant regarding the decision within four weeks after the completed application and supporting documents have been received by the Office of Admissions. All requests for information or application forms should be addressed to:

Director of Admissions
Regis College Office of Admissions, A-12
Regis University
3333 Regis Boulevard
Denver, Colorado 80221-1099
Phone: 303-458-4900
800-388-2366 Ext. 4900 (toll-free)
Fax: 303-964-5534
E-mail: regisadm@regis.edu
Web site: http://www.regis.edu

The Regis University campus is located in a pleasant residential neighborhood with beautiful Rocky Mountain views, just a few minutes from downtown Denver.

ROCKY MOUNTAIN COLLEGE OF ART + DESIGN

DENVER, COLORADO

The College

When Philip J. Steele founded Rocky Mountain College of Art + Design (RMCAD) in 1963, his dream was to provide students with an education based on traditional art and design principles in an environment that fostered personal meaning and growth. From years of working as an artist and teacher, he understood that in order to provide a high-quality education, it was essential that students have the opportunity to study with professional artists and designers who could both teach the courses and guide students as they sought to push the boundaries of creativity and innovation. The College continues to reflect this vision today.

As a privately owned institution, RMCAD is regionally accredited by the Higher Learning Commission of the North Central Association of Colleges and Schools and by the National Association of Schools of Art and Design (NASAD). The interior design program is accredited by the Council for Interior Design Accreditation, formerly known as FIDER.

RMCAD's long history of successful alumni is its testimony to an educational philosophy that works. The RMCAD curriculum is specifically designed to facilitate each student's transition from the classroom to employment within their chosen profession. In fact, more than 86 percent of RMCAD graduates report they are working in their field of study.

Location

RMCAD is located on twenty-three wooded acres at the foot of the Rocky Mountains in Lakewood, Colorado, in the west-central part of metropolitan Denver. Looking east from the campus, students can see downtown Denver's skyline; looking west, the beautiful Rocky Mountains. Whether they are into skiing, snowboarding, hiking, or just soaking up Denver's more than 300 days of sunshine each year, students find the Rocky Mountain Front Range is a great place to live. With a population of more than 2 million people, Denver offers students a multitude of ways to spend their free time—from museums to concert halls to shopping centers and entertainment districts.

Majors and Degrees

RMCAD offers a Bachelor of Fine Arts degree in six different areas of study: animation (2-D or 3-D), art education, fine arts, graphic design and interactive media, illustration, and interior design.

Academic Programs

While traditional educational approaches of lecture, demonstration, teaching by example, and presentation of studio technique are utilized, RMCAD is extremely responsive to the contemporary climate of all of the art and design disciplines. Classroom methods incorporate the newest equipment, processes, and ideas to further challenge students in an atmosphere that encourages experimentation with media not yet established as art materials. As a result, graduates are both versatile and qualified to produce complete, professional-quality work.

The strength of all of RMCAD's art and design programs is realized in the development of each student's perceptual, technical, and creative abilities to the highest level. This rigor enables students to realize success in a challenging and competitive marketplace and helps ensure professional opportunities for each student after graduation. Emphasis is placed on skills that include consolidating ideas into visual form, rendering artwork, sharpening communication skills, developing creative concepts, and improving career skills.

The College operates on a traditional semester system. Students who take a full-time course load can complete their program in a minimum of eight semesters.

Academic Facilities

RMCAD's campus includes eighteen historical buildings built in a variety of twentieth-century architectural styles. All of the buildings have been modernized to create a wireless campus with state-of-the-art classrooms. The campus has six Macintosh and Windows NT computer labs that are connected to print centers and are designed for multiuse by all departments. Specific labs are designated for 3-D computer animation, video and sound, multimedia, computer-aided drafting, and advanced special effects. Special learning facilities include a woodshop, ceramics studio, photography lab, professional sound studio, 283-seat theater, 35-seat audiovisual theater, large meeting rooms, and a library/resource center.

The Philip J. Steele Gallery features a rotating schedule of exhibitions that includes a mix of student, faculty, and alumni work as well as displays by community groups and exhibitions by well-known visiting artists. Students can relax or study in the student lounge, take a break between classes on the grassy lawns under 100-year-old trees, shop in the College bookstore, or grab an espresso and a bite to eat at the Underground Café.

Costs

Tuition and fees at Rocky Mountain College of Art + Design for the 2007–08 academic year are $9876 per semester. Housing costs average $5000 per year, depending on accommodations. Books and supplies are approximately $500 per semester. Costs are subject to change.

Financial Aid

A variety of financial aid programs are available to students attending RMCAD. These programs are designed to assist students in meeting their educational expenses. Some financial aid funds are limited, so students are encouraged to apply early. A number of scholarships are awarded annually to RMCAD students who have proven themselves through outstanding work and effort during the academic year. Rocky Mountain College of Art + Design awards artist merit-based scholarships to incoming freshmen and transfer students. Prospective students should contact the Office of Admission or visit RMCAD's Web site for details.

Faculty

Rocky Mountain College of Art + Design employs approximately 25 full-time and 45 part-time or adjunct faculty members. Because RMCAD instructors are working artists, they possess a wide variety of educational and professional backgrounds. A trait they all share, however, is a dedication to the philosophy of integrating real-life experience with academic excellence.

Student Government

All current RMCAD students belong to the Student Government Association (SGA), a group formed to represent the student body to the college and outside community. The SGA coordinates activities, communication, and services of general benefit to RMCAD students. SGA seeks to enhance involvement in curricular, cocurricular, and extracurricular activities. Each spring, representatives are elected to serve as the voting membership of the SGA. The elected students represent their peers on matters that are brought to the attention of the SGA, including proposed programs and policies. The SGA encourages all current RMCAD students to attend meetings and to bring ideas and concerns to the attention of the SGA.

Admission Requirements

Rocky Mountain College of Art + Design admits students who have a desire to explore new possibilities, work hard to realize their personal best, and who are eager to produce original, innovative works. Although a variety of evaluation criteria are necessary for a sound admission decision, evidence of potential in the fine and applied art disciplines is the primary consideration in the admissions process. A degree candidate must either be a graduate of an accredited high school and possess a minimum cumulative grade point average of 2.0 or possess a high school equivalency diploma with satisfactory GED scores. Applicants who do not possess a cumulative grade point average of 2.0 or higher may be admitted with a provisional status. Applicants must also present a portfolio of recent work. Students without a portfolio should ask an admissions counselor about substitute arrangements that may include alternative experiences or examples that illustrate an individual's interest and potential in professional art and design education. An interview with an admissions counselor, either in person or by telephone, is also required. Through the personal interview, applicants gain a better understanding of the visual arts education at Rocky Mountain College of Art + Design.

In addition to the above requirements, transfer students must arrange to have copies of official transcripts from all postsecondary institutions they have attended sent to the Admissions Department for review. Official transcripts for courses completed at colleges outside of the United States must be submitted to the College and to an approved evaluation agency before transfer credit can be evaluated by RMCAD.

Application and Information

Students are accepted to Rocky Mountain College of Art + Design on a rolling basis. Students are encouraged to apply as early as possible, however, in order to be considered for portfolio merit scholarships. Interested students should visit the Rocky Mountain College of Art + Design Web site for more details.

An application and additional information may be obtained by contacting:

Office of Admission
Rocky Mountain College of Art + Design
1600 Pierce Street
Denver, Colorado 80214
Phone: 800-888-2787 (toll-free)
E-mail: admissions@rmcad.edu
Web site: http://www.rmcad.edu

UNITED STATES AIR FORCE ACADEMY

COLORADO SPRINGS, COLORADO

The Academy

Established in 1954, the Air Force Academy prepares and motivates cadets for careers as Air Force officers. The Academy stresses character development, military training, and physical fitness as well as academics, emphasizing leadership in all areas.

The total enrollment is approximately 4,000; nearly 1,300 fourth class (freshman) students enter each year. The composition of the student body mirrors that of the Air Force officer corps: about 21 percent women and 23 percent minorities. Students come from all fifty states and several other countries. Their common bond is the desire to be military officers. All cadets must live in on-campus dormitories and wear uniforms.

The Academy is accredited by the North Central Association of Colleges and Schools. Its engineering programs are approved by the Engineering Accreditation Commission of the Accreditation Board for Engineering and Technology, and its computer courses are approved by the Computing Sciences Accreditation Board. The chemistry and biochemistry majors fulfill the requirements of the Commission on Professional Training of the American Chemical Society.

All cadets must participate in intramural, club, or intercollegiate athletics every semester. The intramural sports include basketball, boxing (men's), cross-country, flag football, flickerball, mountain biking, racquetball, rugby (men's and women's), soccer, softball, team handball, tennis, Ultimate Frisbee, volleyball, and wallyball. The intercollegiate teams compete in Division I of the NCAA regionally and nationally. The men's teams include baseball, basketball, boxing, cheerleading, cross-country, diving, fencing, football, golf, gymnastics, hockey, indoor and outdoor track, lacrosse, rifle, soccer, swimming, tennis, water polo, and wrestling. The women's teams include basketball, cross-country, cheerleading, diving, fencing, gymnastics, indoor and outdoor track, rifle, soccer, swimming, tennis, and volleyball. Cadets may also choose from over 80 extracurricular activities, which include professional organizations, mission support, competitive and recreational clubs, sports groups, and hobby clubs.

Qualified Academy graduates may enter flight training upon graduation, and approximately 75 percent of the students in each graduating class pursue graduate education at other institutions within ten years of their graduation. Each year, numerous Academy graduates receive graduate scholarships and fellowships, such as the Marshall, Rhodes, National Science Foundation, National Collegiate Athletic Association, and Guggenheim awards.

Location

The Academy campus sits in the foothills of the Rampart Range of the Rocky Mountains in a setting of natural beauty. Built on a mesa at 7,000 feet, it is one of Colorado's top tourist attractions. The Cadet Chapel, with its seventeen aluminum spires towering 150 feet into the air, highlights the contemporary architecture of the buildings in the cadet area. The space-age effect reflects the Academy's mission of preparing cadets to become officers and leaders in the Air Force of the future. The Academy borders the northern edge of Colorado Springs, which lies at the foot of the famous 14,100-foot Pikes Peak. Colorado Springs has a metropolitan population of more than 500,000. Denver, the state's capital, has a population of almost 2.5 million in its greater metropolitan area and is located 55 miles north of the Academy. In addition to the social, sports, and cultural activities available in these cities, cadets enjoy skiing, hunting, horseback riding, white-water rafting, and other activities in the Colorado Rocky Mountains and nearby resorts.

Majors and Degrees

Graduates of the four-year service academy receive the Bachelor of Science (B.S.) degree and a commission as second lieutenants in the Air Force. The B.S. is granted in thirty-two majors: aeronautical engineering; astronautical engineering; basic sciences; behavioral sciences; biology; chemistry; civil engineering; computer engineering; computer science; economics; electrical engineering; engineering mechanics; English; environmental engineering; foreign area studies; general engineering; geospatial science; history; humanities; legal studies; management; mathematical sciences; mechanical engineering; meteorology; military strategic studies; operations research; physics; political science; social sciences; space operations; systems engineering; and systems engineering management. The Academy also offers minors in foreign languages and philosophy.

Academic Programs

A class enters the Academy during the last week in June or the first week in July. Incoming cadets undergo a strenuous thirty-eight-day summer training program that tests both their mental and physical abilities. Upperclass cadets conduct basic cadet training; commissioned officers serve as advisers. Basic cadets who complete this program are accepted into the Cadet Wing as fourth-class cadets. The academic year starts in early August and continues through May. During the first two years, cadets concentrate on core courses in engineering, humanities, science, and social science. During the last two years, they specialize in an academic major.

The required core courses prepare cadets for a broad scope of activity as Air Force officers. The core curriculum embraces courses in academic subjects, leadership and military training, and physical education and athletics. In addition, cadets complete the requirements for any of the thirty-two academic majors. To be eligible for graduation, cadets must also demonstrate an aptitude for commissioned service and leadership, demonstrate character consistent with professional military service, maintain a minimum cumulative grade point average and core grade point average of 2.0, and complete a minimum of 141 credit hours. The curriculum includes many elective courses.

All students must begin as freshmen; however, cadets who have taken some of the core course material prior to entry into the Academy may receive transfer or validation credit for this work. They may then substitute other courses for those granted transfer credit. Cadets who maintain the required grade point average may take advanced study classes.

The Academy aviation program familiarizes all cadets with operational activities of the Air Force. Optional courses provide instruction in soaring, parachuting, navigation, and basic flying. Those who take these courses may fulfill the requirements for

Federal Aviation Administration pilot or glider certificates. Cadets who qualify and are selected for pilot or navigator training may enter Air Education and Training Command flight programs following graduation from the Academy. Diversified summer programs in aviation and military training prepare cadets for officer responsibilities in the Air Force. Cadets may select their programs from several optional assignments at the Air Force Academy and other military installations.

Off-Campus Programs

Selected cadets may exchange visits with cadets from the Military Academy, Naval Academy, Coast Guard Academy, or one of fifteen international Air Force academies. The exchange program varies from one to two weeks for most of the international programs to a semester for the other U.S. service academies and the Canadian, Chilean, French, German, and Spanish Air Force academies, to name a few.

Academic Facilities

The Air Force Academy's excellent facilities support the academic, military, and athletics programs. Most classrooms accommodate small class sessions, averaging 17 students. Several classes and assemblies meet in larger lecture halls. Well-equipped laboratories supplement classroom instruction. Cadets conduct experiments using the Aeronautics Laboratory's wind tunnels, shock tubes, and rocket engines. A local network connects every dorm room, faculty and staff office, classroom, and laboratory at the Academy, and all entering cadets purchase notebook computers for academic and personal use. The Academy library, with over 1.5 million volumes, supports all educational programs and maintains a collection of historical materials concerning aeronautics.

Costs

There are no tuition charges; the cost, including room, board, and medical and dental care, is borne entirely by the U.S. government. In addition, cadets receive a monthly salary to pay for supplies, clothing, and personal expenses. Careful management of the money covers obligations, with a small amount remaining for personal use.

Financial Aid

All cadets are on full scholarship at the Air Force Academy, as described above.

Faculty

The Academy's faculty is composed of Air Force officers and civilian professors. A few officers from other branches of the U.S. Armed Forces, those from allied nations, and distinguished civilian visiting professors supplement the faculty. There are no graduate student instructors. Faculty members must have a master's degree, and many have earned doctorates. Their educational backgrounds represent many outstanding colleges and universities in the United States, as well as some international institutions of higher education. Faculty members sponsor, coach, and referee extracurricular activities and athletics; adopt squadrons and attend their special events; and provide academic, career, and personal counseling.

Student Government

The Air Force Academy trains cadets for future leadership by allowing them to hold positions of responsibility in the Cadet Wing, the organization to which all cadets are assigned. The wing is under the operational supervision of first-class cadets (seniors). They hold cadet officer rank and command the wing and the subordinate units of groups, squadrons, flights, and elements. Through this organization, upperclass cadets are responsible for military training of the underclasses, the honor education and honor system, character development, and ethics and human relations programs.

Admission Requirements

Each year, young men and women who are U.S. citizens may be appointed from all states and territories of the nation. Citizens of other countries are admitted in limited numbers. Applicants must be at least 17 and not yet 23 years of age on July 1 of the year in which they desire to be admitted, be unmarried, have no dependents, and be of high moral character. They must be in good physical health.

Applicants must receive an official nomination. Members of Congress make the majority of the nominations for residents of their states and districts. Senators and representatives nominate young men and women who have excelled academically in high school, have demonstrated leadership potential through school activities, are physically fit, are respected by associates, and want to pursue military careers. Applicants need not know their member of Congress personally. Students may be eligible in nomination categories other than congressional. Students should ask high school counselors or Air Force Admissions Liaison Officers about other categories and apply for nominations in all categories for which they are eligible.

To enter the Academy upon graduation from high school, students should apply as soon as possible after January 31 of their junior year. If successful in receiving a nomination, they must take a physical fitness test, a medical exam, and either the SAT or the ACT.

Application and Information

High school juniors may obtain application forms by writing to the address below. Applicants should study the instructions included in the application package and follow the proper application procedures. The package also includes sample letters for requesting nominations. Air Force Admissions Liaison Officers, located in all states, assist students and counselors with the application and testing requirements.

HQ USAFA/RRS
2304 Cadet Drive, Suite 2300
USAF Academy, Colorado 80840-5025
Phone: 719-333-2520
800-443-9266 (toll-free)
Web site: http://www.academyadmissions.com

The Cadet Color Guard is the centerpiece of a Cadet Parade.

UNIVERSITY OF COLORADO AT BOULDER

BOULDER, COLORADO

The University

The University of Colorado at Boulder (CU-Boulder) is a dynamic community of scholars and learners situated on one of the most spectacular college campuses in the country. CU-Boulder is one of thirty-four U.S. public institutions belonging to the prestigious Association of American Universities (AAU) and the only member in the Rocky Mountain region. The university has a proud tradition of academic excellence, with four Nobel laureates and more than fifty members of prestigious academic societies. CU-Boulder was ranked thirty-fourth among the world's universities, both public and private, in a 2006 survey by the Institute for Higher Education at Jiao Tong University in Shanghai, China. CU-Boulder was also included among the best universities in the nation for service learning and civic activism in *Colleges with a Conscience: 81 Great Schools with Outstanding Community Involvement*, published in June 2005.

The campus offers more than 3,400 courses each year in approximately 150 areas of study. There are eighty-five academic majors available at the bachelor's level, forty-eight at the master's level, and forty-four at the doctoral level. Outstanding academic departments and programs include astrophysical and planetary sciences, biochemistry, biology, chemistry, engineering, English, entrepreneurial business, geography, integrative physiology, music, physics, and psychology. Talented undergraduate students may participate in honors programs, the Undergraduate Research Opportunities Program, and ten residential academic programs featuring small-class environments.

Total enrollment for fall 2007 at the Boulder campus was 28,988, including 24,473 undergraduate students. The student population comes from every state in the nation and about 100 countries. Approximately two thirds of the students come from Colorado. Many ethnic, religious, academic, and social backgrounds are represented, fostering the development of a multicultural community that enriches each student's educational experience.

Undergraduate students may apply to the following colleges and schools: Architecture and Planning, Arts and Sciences, Leeds School of Business, Engineering and Applied Science, Music, Journalism and Mass Communication, and Education. Students are admitted to Journalism and Mass Communication only after completing one or two years of study at CU-Boulder, with exceptions for highly qualified new freshmen. The School of Education accepts applications from students after they are enrolled in an approved degree program at CU-Boulder.

CU-Boulder offers a wide variety of campus activities. Students may participate in student government; clubs and organizations; intramural, club, and intercollegiate sports; and fraternities and sororities. An extensive calendar of cultural events is available.

Location

CU-Boulder is located in a scenic valley at the foot of the Rocky Mountains, 1 mile above sea level. With a population of approximately 100,000, Boulder is among the most dynamic, progressive, and attractive cities of its size in the United States. The Colorado state capital, Denver, is a 30-mile drive or bus ride (free for students) from Boulder. Boulder is surrounded by a greenbelt of more than 20,000 acres of open space. Much of the open space and nearby mountains are crisscrossed by an extensive system of hiking, biking, and riding trails. Many CU-Boulder students enjoy skiing, hiking, backpacking, rock climbing, white-water rafting, or mountain biking.

CU-Boulder has been rated as one of the "most artistically successful campuses in the country" in *The Campus as a Work of Art* by Thomas Gaines. The 600-acre main campus, in the heart of the city of Boulder, is distinguished by buildings featuring native sandstone walls and dramatic red-tiled roofs as inspired by the rural Italian architectural style.

Majors and Degrees

CU-Boulder offers the following undergraduate majors: aerospace engineering; anthropology; applied mathematics; architectural engineering; art and art history–art history; art and art history–studio arts; Asian studies; astronomy; biochemistry; business-accounting; business-finance; business-management; business-marketing; business-systems; chemical and biological engineering; chemical engineering; chemistry; Chinese; civil engineering; classics; communication; computer science; dance; ecology and evolutionary biology; economics; electrical and computer engineering; electrical engineering; engineering physics; English; environmental design–architecture; environmental design–design studies; environmental design–planning; environmental engineering; environmental studies; ethnic studies; film studies; French; geography; geology; Germanic studies; history; humanities; integrative physiology; international affairs; Italian; Japanese; journalism-advertising; journalism–broadcast news; journalism–broadcast production management; journalism–media studies; journalism-news/editorial; linguistics; mathematics; mechanical engineering; molecular, cellular, and developmental biology; music; music–arts in music; music education; philosophy; physics; political science; predentistry sequence; premedicine sequence; pre–veterinary medicine sequence; psychology; religious studies; Russian studies; sociology; Spanish; speech, language, and hearing sciences; theater; and women's studies.

The following bachelor's degrees are offered: B.A., B.Envd., B.F.A., B.Mus., B.Mus.Ed., and B.S.

Concurrent bachelor's and master's degree programs are available in the following areas: applied mathematics, business (accounting, finance, systems), classics, cognitive psychology, East Asian languages and literature (Chinese, Japanese), ecology and evolutionary biology, economics, engineering physics, French, Germanic studies, integrative physiology, linguistics, mathematics, physics, religious studies, telecommunications, and in all engineering departments, including aerospace, architectural, chemical, civil, computer science, electrical, electrical and computer, environmental, and mechanical.

Academic Programs

The mission of the University of Colorado at Boulder is to educate undergraduate and graduate students in the accumulated knowledge of humankind, discover new knowledge through research and creative work, and foster critical thought, artistic creativity, professional competence, and responsible citizenship. Depending on their degree program, students may be required to complete 120 or 128 (engineering) semester hours for graduation. CU-Boulder offers a very flexible curriculum. Students may graduate with more than one major and with two different degrees from different colleges. Minors also are offered in arts and sciences, business, and engineering. The College of Arts and Sciences and the College of Engineering and Applied Science offer a four-year graduation guarantee, providing specific requirements are met.

CU-Boulder operates on a two-semester academic calendar. The fall semester begins in late August, and the spring semester begins in early January. Summer Session lasts ten weeks; courses meeting for shorter periods (one to four, five, or eight weeks) are scheduled during the ten-week session.

Off-Campus Programs

CU-Boulder sponsors more than 180 study-abroad programs each year. Programs are offered on six continents in seventy countries, including Australia, Canada, Costa Rica, Cuba, Denmark, Egypt, England, France, Germany, Hungary, Japan, and Mexico. More than twenty-five percent of CU-Bolder students have studied abroad by the time they graduate.

Academic Facilities

The University library system consists of more than 3.6 million volumes, 6.8 million titles on microform, more than 30,000 periodical subscriptions, and more than 450,000 video, graphic, and audio titles. The libraries system includes a main library and five branch libraries: Business, Earth Sciences, Engineering, Math-Physics, and Music. There is also a law library. Other facilities and resources aiding students in their studies include a planetarium and observatory, a natural history museum, extensive computing resources, a state-of-the-art foreign language technology center, a concert hall, and three theaters. The Integrated Teaching and Learning Laboratory and the Discovery Learning Center provide hands-on, real-world experience to engineering undergraduates. Recent additions to the campus include a new humanities building, equipped with smart classrooms, and the new Alliance for Technology, Learning, and Society (ATLAS) Center, which opened in fall 2006. ATLAS was established at CU-Boulder in 1997 with the goal of integrating information technology with all disciplines, people, and communities. A key component of ATLAS is the creation and delivery of technology-centered, multidisciplinary, curricular programs that are available to CU-Boulder undergraduate and graduate students.

Costs

Tuition rates vary by school and college. For 2007–08, annual expenses for Colorado residents who were undergraduate students in the College of Arts and Sciences totaled $17,421 ($6635 for tuition and fees as well as an estimated $1698 for books and supplies and $9088 for room and board). Nonresident tuition and fees were approximately $24,797.

Financial Aid

Approximately half of Boulder undergraduate students receive some type of financial assistance, totaling more than $165 million in awards. Students receive aid in the form of grants, loans, work-study awards, and scholarships. Funding is provided from federal, state, University, and private sources. All students applying for need-based financial aid are required to submit the Free Application for Federal Student Aid (FAFSA). Application forms are available from high school and community college counselors, the CU-Boulder Office of Financial Aid, and online. The priority processing date is April 1. Students may apply for CU-Boulder scholarships online beginning November 1. Students may also obtain loans directly from the Office of Financial Aid rather than from a private lender.

Faculty

Approximately 1,200 full-time instructional faculty members teach undergraduate and graduate courses. The faculty includes nationally and internationally recognized scholars with many academic honors and awards. Tom Cech, former professor of chemistry and biochemistry and now Director of the Howard Hughes Medical Institute, shared the 1989 Nobel Prize in chemistry with Sidney Altman of Yale University. Carl Wieman (also U.S. 2004 Professor of the Year) and Eric Cornell won the 2001 Nobel Prize in physics for their creation of a new state of matter, just above absolute zero. John Hall shared the 2005 Nobel Prize in physics with Theodor W. Hänsch of the Max Planck Institute for Quantum Optics and a professor of physics at Ludwig Maximilians University in Munich, Germany, and Roy J. Glauber, a professor of physics at Harvard University. Kristi Anseth was named among the top 100 young innovators for developing materials that aid in the healing of bones and cartilage. Seven faculty members have received MacArthur Fellowships, known as the "genius grant," the most recent two being in linguistics (2002) and physics (2003).

Student Government

One of the most influential student governments in the nation, the University of Colorado Student Union (UCSU) administers an operating budget of $30 million. UCSU student leaders and volunteers, working with the University staff, make policy decisions concerning the operation of the University Memorial Center, Student Recreation Center, Wardenburg Health Center, cultural events, the campus radio station, and other programs. Student fees and student-generated revenue support all of these activities. The student government also takes an active role in advocating student concerns.

Admission Requirements

Many factors are considered by the University in making admission decisions. Previous academic achievement, the quality of courses taken, GPA, college entrance test scores, the trend in grades, the extent to which the applicant has completed the recommended high school curriculum, the essay, and letters of recommendation are all considered. About 25 percent of the freshman class typically ranks in the top 10 percent of their high school graduating class. In fall 2007, 60 percent of the freshmen were Colorado residents. The University seeks to enroll students from a wide range of ethnic, cultural, economic, geographic, and educational backgrounds. Applications are available online, in Colorado high school guidance offices, in community college counseling centers, and in the CU-Boulder Office of Admissions.

Application and Information

Students are considered for admission for fall, spring, and summer terms. Each year, the Office of Admissions begins notifying applicants of admission decisions in October. Summer and fall application priority dates are January 15 for freshmen and April 1 for transfers. The spring application deadline for freshmen and transfers is October 1. After these dates, applications are considered only if space is available. An online electronic application for admission is available through the University's Web site.

For information and applications, students should contact:

Office of Admissions
University of Colorado at Boulder
552 UCB
Boulder, Colorado 80309-0552
Phone: 303-492-6301
303-492-5998 (TTY)
Web site: http://www.colorado.edu

The University of Colorado at Boulder is a major research and teaching university located in one of the most spectacular environments in the country, at the foot of the Rocky Mountains.

UNIVERSITY OF COLORADO DENVER
Downtown Campus
DENVER, COLORADO

The University

Set against the majestic backdrop of the Rocky Mountains, the University of Colorado Denver (UC Denver) combines a tradition of excellence with a vision for higher education in Colorado. By joining the strengths of a comprehensive campus in downtown Denver with the research and advanced health-care programs of the Anschutz Medical Campus of Aurora, UC Denver serves more than 27,000 students in Denver and Aurora and in online and distance education programs and certificates. The University awards more than 3,400 degrees each year and confers more graduate degrees than any other school in Colorado.

UC Denver consistently ranks among the best in the nation for its academic programs, research, patient care, and community service. It receives more than $368 million in research grants annually. With a solid academic reputation, award-winning faculty members, and renowned researchers, the University offers more than 100 highly rated degree programs through twelve colleges and schools.

The University's twelve schools and colleges provide a breadth of study in more than 100 degree programs. The University has earned such distinctions as having the largest graduate business school and graduate school of education in the state; providing Colorado's only college of architecture and planning and school of medicine; having the first college in Colorado dedicated exclusively to the arts and entertainment; offering an engineering and applied science college and a school for public affairs closely tied to industry trends and standards; having its nursing school consistently ranked in the country's top 15 percent; and being one of the country's top-ranked pharmacy schools and most selective schools of dental medicine. There are seventy-five centers and institutes that extend the reach of teaching and research into benefits for the community. These entities cover a wide range of subject areas, from entrepreneurship and education policy to medical and health concerns.

The 12,200 students on the downtown Denver campus are a diverse mix of ages, ethnicities, and backgrounds, from recent high school graduates to seasoned professionals. One of every 5 students represents an ethnic minority. Students come from throughout Colorado, across the country, and around the world—all seeking a respected educational program, a convenient schedule of offerings, and a lively urban environment. Classes are scheduled days, evenings, weekends, and online to meet their needs and fit their busy lifestyles.

More than sixty student organizations provide a variety of events and activities, from concerts and exhibits to film festivals and nationally renowned speakers. The Career Center offers a full array of services to prepare graduates for professional success.

The downtown campus of UC Denver is just steps away from Denver's historic Lower Downtown (LoDo) district with its myriad entertainment, cultural, and sports venues. Because the University shares the Auraria campus with two other institutions, its students have access to facilities and resources comparable to much larger public universities. They also benefit from a wide array of internship and job opportunities in the vital, growing Denver area.

Student housing is available adjacent to the Auraria Higher Education Center, within easy walking distance of campus and downtown. Campus Village Apartments houses 685 students in apartment-style accommodations and provides students with programs and resources to help foster academic and social success. Through cultural and development programs, Campus Village residents can participate in activities that include nutrition and fitness seminars, community outreach programs, and classes on career planning, time management, and study skills. Features include kitchenettes or full kitchens; lease rates that include heating, cooling, electricity, water, cable, and high-speed Internet service; individual lease agreements for shared units; fully furnished apartments; and various affordable meal plans.

At the downtown Denver campus, more than eighty degree programs at the bachelor's, master's, and doctoral levels span a wide range of fields and disciplines. Programs are available in seven colleges and schools: the College of Architecture and Planning, the College of Arts and Media, the Business School, the School of Education and Human Development, the College of Engineering and Applied Science, the College of Liberal Arts and Sciences, and the School of Public Affairs. The University is fully accredited by the North Central Association of Colleges and Schools.

The University works in partnership with businesses, community organizations, and neighborhoods in the greater Denver area to ensure that the UC Denver education meets the needs of the ever-changing job market. The University is committed to research, technology, and creative scholarship and to providing an academic culture that reflects the diversity, collegiality, and integration of an increasingly global workplace.

Location

The downtown location of UC Denver is ideal for someone who wants the excitement of a dynamic environment in an urban setting. Surrounded by an abundance of recreational, cultural, academic, and professional opportunities, the campus provides a unique urban lifestyle. Just across the street from the revitalized LoDo and within walking distance of the Pepsi Center, Invesco Field, Coors Field, Six Flags Elitch Gardens, and the Denver Performing Arts Complex are a variety of parks, museums, and theaters and an eclectic assortment of restaurants, coffee houses, clubs, and shops. The city offers hundreds of miles of bike trails and even kayaking in Cherry Creek at Confluence Park. At the same time, the campus is less than an hour's drive from some of the world's best skiing, snowboarding, camping, hiking, white-water rafting, and rock climbing.

The Anschutz Medical Campus is a brand new, world-class academic health center with state-of-the-art health-care facilities. Next to the campus is a developing bioscience research park.

Majors and Degrees

A wide variety of undergraduate majors and degrees are offered. In the College of Arts and Media, the Bachelor of Arts (B.A.) is offered in fine arts (art history, drawing, painting, photography, sculpture) and in theater, film, and television. The Bachelor of Fine Arts (B.F.A.) is offered in fine arts (drawing; 3-D graphics and animation; multimedia studies; painting; photography; sculpture; theater, film, and television). The Bachelor of Science (B.S.) can be earned in music (music business, music industry studies, performance, recording arts).

The Business School offers the Bachelor of Science (B.S.) in business administration (accounting, financial management, financial management systems, human resources, information systems, international business, management, marketing).

College of Engineering and Applied Science students can earn a Bachelor of Science (B.S.) in civil engineering, computer science and engineering, electrical engineering, and mechanical engineering.

The College of Liberal Arts and Sciences awards Bachelor of Arts (B.A.) degrees in anthropology, communication, economics, English (creative writing, film studies, literary studies, secondary education), English writing (creative writing, film studies, general studies), French, history, an individually structured major (international affairs or elementary education), philosophy, political science (public policy and administration or secondary education), psychology, sociology, and Spanish. In addition, the Bachelor of Science (B.S.) is granted in biology, chemistry, geography (earth science, environmental science, environmental studies, general geography, urban studies and planning), mathematics (actuarial science, applied mathematics, computer science, probability and statistics, pure mathematics, secondary education), physics (medical physics and pure and applied physics), and psychology.

The School of Public Affairs has just added a highly popular bachelor's degree in criminal justice, and the School of Education and Human Development is now accepting undergraduate students as well.

Academic Programs

While UC Denver's downtown campus is devoted to meeting the needs of Denver and its residents, an increasing number of students come from across the nation and around the world to pursue their studies at the University, which is one of the most selective public universities in the state. A comprehensive core curriculum assures that each student receives a solid educational foundation. Certificate and preprofessional programs increase specialized options available in a wide-ranging curriculum. Programs emphasize practical, hands-on learning as well as research. To graduate, students must complete 120 credit hours and maintain a minimum 2.0 GPA. Courses must include 45 hours of upper-division course work and 30 hours of course work within the chosen major. The academic calendar is separated into fall, spring, and summer semesters, with courses offered days, evenings, weekends, and online.

Off-Campus Programs

The Office of International Education offers study-abroad programs that vary from two weeks to one academic year as well as summer and winter breaks. Although many programs are for language study, a substantial number are taught in English, so knowledge of a second language is not required. Programs are available to students from all disciplines and are presented in a variety of countries worldwide. Students can pay UC Denver tuition and study abroad on an exchange program for an academic semester or year. Either UC Denver or transfer credit may be earned, giving students the opportunity to fulfill degree requirements while experiencing a new culture.

Collaboration between the University and international universities make it possible for students to work toward a University of Colorado degree while living abroad. The advantage of these programs over study abroad is that courses are taught in English and cover the same subject matter as courses taught on the downtown Denver campus.

Academic Facilities

The Auraria Library serves the largest student population in Colorado and contains more than 600,000 books, microforms, and bound periodicals and more than 3,300 current journals and newspaper subscriptions. As a member of the Colorado Alliance of Research Libraries, Auraria Library has access to an additional 6 million volumes through interlibrary loans. Services include an online public-access catalog, computerized literature searches, CD-ROMs, a depository of U.S. and state government publications, and media listening and viewing facilities. The Center for Learning Assistance promotes student success, retention, and graduation through services that include English as a second language training, study-skills courses, academic tutoring, peer advocacy, a test file, and a minority resource library.

Costs

For fall 2007, tuition is $215 per credit hour for Colorado residents and $675 per credit hour for out-of-state residents. Tuition for 12–15 credit hours is $2811 for in-state residents and $8100 for out-of-state residents. Other fees include a student activity fee of $10.50, an information technology fee of $8 per credit hour, and a student services fee of $5 per credit hour. Fees vary according to program and class year; students should consult an admissions adviser to anticipate specific costs.

Financial Aid

The Office of Financial Aid awards more than $60 million in financial aid to qualified students each year. Financial aid is available through scholarships, loans, and work-study opportunities. All students should complete the Free Application for Federal Student Aid (FAFSA) and the University Financial Aid Application (UAPP).

Out-of-state students are eligible for the Denver Bound Scholarship, worth between $8000 and $64,000 over a four-year enrollment period.

Colorado undergraduate students are eligible for direct funding through the College Opportunity Fund (COF), also known as vouchers or stipends. Providing that an undergraduate in-state student applies for and authorizes use of the voucher, COF vouchers will be applied to the student's university bill. Students should visit the University Web site for more details.

Faculty

The downtown campus employs more than 460 faculty members who are renowned educators and experts in their fields. Some have earned the world's most prestigious awards, such as Fulbright Scholarships and Guggenheim Fellowships. Four out of 5 faculty members hold the highest degrees within their fields, many from some of the finest institutions in the world. The downtown campus has a student-faculty ratio of just 14:1, remarkably low for a public university.

Student Government

Downtown campus Executive Board members are elected in the spring to serve the following year. Student government supports cocurricular activities, and funds are set aside for educational and social purposes.

Admission Requirements

Admissions standards define the level of success and achievement necessary to be admitted to the University and include factors that predict academic success, such as ACT or SAT scores, high school course work, and grade point average. Applicants must be high school graduates or have been awarded a high school equivalency certificate by successfully completing the General Education Development (GED) test.

Students transferring to UC Denver must have earned 13–24 collegiate semester credit hours and have a 2.4 minimum GPA, or have earned 30 or more collegiate semester hours with a 2.0 minimum GPA. Details are available on the University's Web site.

Students transferring to UC Denver must have earned 13–24 collegiate semester credit hours and have a 2.4 minimum GPA, or have earned 30 or more collegiate semester hours with a 2.0 minimum GPA. Details are available on the University's Web site.

Students are required to meet the following minimum academic preparation standards: 4 years of English, 3 years of college-preparatory mathematics, 3 years of natural science, 2 years of social science, 2 years of a single foreign language, and 1 year of art.

International students must meet specific program requirements. Those whose first language is not English must have a minimum computer-based TOEFL score of 197 (525 paper-based) or a minimum IELTS score of 6.0. International students must also demonstrate adequate funds or financial support to attend the University.

Application and Information

Each applicant must include a completed application form, a $50 nonrefundable application fee, an official transcript of high school grades (including class rank), and an official copy of SAT or ACT scores. The deadline to apply is July 22 for fall semester, December 1 for spring semester, and May 3 for summer semester.

For more information, prospective students should contact:

Office of Admissions
University of Colorado Denver
Downtown Campus
Campus Box 167, P.O. Box 173364
University of Colorado Denver
Denver, Colorado 80217-3364
Phone: 303-556-2704
Fax: 303-556-4838
E-mail: admissions@cudenver.edu
Web site: http://www.cudenver.edu

The downtown campus of University of Colorado Denver.

UNIVERSITY OF DENVER

DENVER, COLORADO

The University

Since its founding in 1864, the University of Denver (DU) has grown into one of the West's premier private universities, blending the friendliness and personal attention of a small college with the resources and intellectual diversity of an advanced research institution.

As the oldest private university in the Rocky Mountain region, the University is home not only to a top-ranked undergraduate program but also to a number of world-renowned research centers and professional programs, including the Graduate School of International Studies, the Sturm College of Law, and the Graduate School of Professional Psychology.

The 125-acre campus brings together 4,907 traditional undergraduate students and 5,806 graduate students from fifty states and seventy-eight countries. In an environment that prizes academic excellence, integrity, engagement, innovation, and inclusiveness, DU students prepare for lives as committed citizens and trail-blazing professionals.

Whatever their backgrounds and majors, DU students are engaged and active, taking advantage of the region's many recreation and cultural opportunities—everything from world-class skiing and white-water rafting to award-winning professional theater and alternative music. On campus, students attend performances at the three-venue Newman Center for the Performing Arts and cheer for the seventeen varsity teams that compete in NCAA Division I at the Ritchie Center for Sports & Wellness.

The University of Denver is accredited by the North Central Association of Colleges and Schools. The Carnegie Foundation classifies the University of Denver as a Doctoral/Research University–Extensive.

Location

Located just 8 miles from bustling downtown Denver and mere minutes from the Rocky Mountain foothills, the University of Denver's tree-shaded campus is surrounded by pleasant urban neighborhoods offering coffee shops, retail stores, and ethnic restaurants. The institution is located along a light rail line and major bus lines, providing access to the city's arts districts, shopping centers, sports arenas, and an extensive network of parks. DU students can ride all public transportation for free, using their University-supplied Eco-pass.

Majors and Degrees

The University of Denver offers twelve bachelor's degrees in over 100 programs of study, including the arts, business, computer science, engineering, humanities, international studies, mathematics, natural sciences, and social sciences. Students who are interested in preprofessional programs can choose from prelaw, pre-med, predental, and pre-veterinary programs that prepare them for professional study beyond their undergraduate degree.

In addition, the University offers 4+1 and 3+2 dual-degree programs that allow students to complete both a bachelor's and master's degree in five years or less. These dual-degree programs are offered in business, art history, international studies, public policy, and natural sciences, among others. Students in dual-degree programs maintain any financial aid and scholarships through their fifth year.

Academic Programs

Undergraduate programs at the University—which operates on the quarter system—emphasize experiential, active, and cross-disciplinary learning. All first-year undergraduate students are required to have laptop computers, which are used extensively in the classroom. DU students use their laptops as portable libraries and laboratories, extending their educational reach well beyond the classroom walls. The entire campus provides wireless Internet access through a secure connection. This includes classrooms, social areas, and even the campus greens.

First-year students enroll in a first-year seminar. Generally limited to 15 students, these seminars are taught by faculty mentors who advise students on everything from time management to adjusting to college-level work. In addition, all undergraduate students complete foundations courses in English, mathematics and computer science, the arts and humanities, natural sciences, and social sciences. The core curriculum requires that students complete one class from each of three themes: communities and environments, self and identities, and change and continuity.

Students are encouraged to collaborate with faculty members and peers on research projects and creative endeavors. Through the Partners in Scholarship (PinS) program, the University sponsors student work through grants that fund field studies, research trips, and special materials. At year's end, students share their research and findings at a special symposium for their peers.

With its emphasis on hands-on learning, the University's academic programs earn high marks from students. In the 2006 National Survey of Student Engagement, a study of student satisfaction at 557 colleges and universities nationwide, first-year students at DU ranked it significantly higher than other participating doctoral-extensive schools in their appraisal of their level of academic challenge, their involvement in active and collaborative learning, and their interaction with faculty members. This is the fifth consecutive year that DU has achieved this ranking.

Off-Campus Programs

In the interest of preparing its students for the challenges of global citizenship, the University of Denver sponsors Cherrington Global Scholars, a for-credit program that aims to send every eligible junior and senior abroad for at least a quarter of study. The University believes so strongly in this opportunity to make international connections that it ensures that qualifying students pay no more for the experience than they would for a quarter spent on campus. Nearly 70 percent of all students participate in study-abroad programs, and the University budgets more than $9 million each year in support of their study.

Academic Facilities

In the last decade, the University has invested nearly $500 million in new buildings and learning centers to ensure that students can prepare for the challenges awaiting them after graduation. These include the Robert and Judi Newman Center for the Performing Arts, home to the University's celebrated Lamont School of Music and host to a performing arts series known for its eclectic offerings; the Daniels College of Business, which houses eleven case-style meeting rooms, nine seminar classrooms, and an Advanced Technology Center; the School of Hotel, Restaurant and Tourism Management, home to a full-production kitchen, a beverage-management center, a 120-person dining hall, three model hotel rooms, and a student-faculty-staff commons; F. W. Olin Hall, which houses ten teaching labs, a greenhouse, and a full complement of classrooms and group study rooms; and the newly remodeled Sturm Hall, complete with multimedia labs and smart-to-the-seat classrooms, which serves as the headquarters for the humanities and social sciences.

Other new facilities support the University's commitment to community living and wellness and include the Nelson Residence Hall, which features suites, common kitchens on each floor, a central courtyard, a grand dining hall, and an outdoor dining patio and the Ritchie Center for Sports & Wellness, which includes a fitness center, a natatorium, a field house, two ice arenas, a gymnastics venue, and a tennis pavilion.

The University plans to open a new residence hall for fall quarter 2008. The brand-new Nagel Hall will incorporate many features designed to provide a comfortable, welcoming space for students. Nagel Hall is also designed to be build "green" and will be LEED rated.

The University is committing $25 million to construct a new building that will house both the Morgridge College of Education and the Institute for Early Learning and Literacy, which will offer one-on-one literacy tutoring for lower-level first graders.

The University is also home to the full-service Penrose Library whose special collections contain rare books and manuscripts as well as the Beck Archives of the Rocky Mountain Jewish Historical Society and the Carson-Brierly Dance Library.

Costs

For the 2007–08 academic year, tuition was $31,428, fees were estimated at $804, and on-campus room and board costs amounted to $8697—for a total cost of $40,929 Because the University of Denver is a private institution, costs are the same for in-state and out-of-state students.

Financial Aid

The University of Denver offers two types of financial assistance to students: need-based aid, which includes scholarships, grants, loans, and work-study based on financial need, and merit-based awards, which include scholarships based on merit or special talent. Each year, the financial aid office awards $75 million in need- and merit-based assistance to undergraduate students. About 43 percent of full-time DU undergraduates demonstrate financial need and receive some form of need-based assistance.

To recognize achievement in the classroom, the sports arena, leadership, and in music, theater, and art, the University sponsors a number of merit-based scholarships—several of which cover full tuition. Although the requirements vary from scholarship to scholarship, most are renewable each year if the student maintains a specified minimum GPA. A complete listing of scholarships is posted at http://www.du.edu/finaid/.

Need-based financial aid is computed using a number of factors, including family income, assets, size, and the number of family members attending college at the same time. DU utilizes both the CSS Profile and the Free Application for Federal Student Aid (FAFSA) to determine need-based aid. Need-based awards generally combine scholarships, grants, loans, and work-study opportunities from a variety of federal, state, and institutional sources. The financial aid offer may also include any competitive scholarships the student has been awarded at the point of admission.

The priority deadline for applying for financial aid is March 1. Because financial aid funds are limited, students who complete their financial aid applications in a timely manner are more likely to maximize financial aid resources. Funding for certain awards may not be available as time passes. The student's financial aid package cannot be determined until he or she is officially admitted to DU.

For more information on applying for financial aid at DU, students should visit http://www.du.edu/finaid.

Faculty

The University of Denver employs 533 full-time appointed faculty members. DU professors teach 94 percent of undergraduate courses, ensuring that student can work closely with the faculty members. The average class size is 20 students, and 62 percent of fall 2006 classes had fewer than 20 students.

Committed teachers, innovative researchers, and prolific publishers, University of Denver professors often include undergraduate students in their research projects and fieldwork. It is not uncommon for an undergraduate student to share publication credit with a professor.

Student Government

At the University of Denver, the student population is represented by the All Undergraduate Student Association (AUSA) Senate, whose elected representatives participate in the University's legislative process and communicate student issues to the administration. In addition, the AUSA Senate oversees the allocation of the student activities fee and the licensing of DU's 100-plus student organizations.

The AUSA Senate includes senators from each major, each geographic area (on-campus, off-campus), and each class (senior, junior, etc.). The AUSA Executive Board includes an adviser, graduate adviser, president, vice president, and a cabinet of members.

Admission Requirements

Admission to the University of Denver is selective. Students are evaluated individually on the basis of their academic record, test scores, essay, and recommendations.

In making its admission decisions, the University seeks to foster an academic community of geographically, ethnically, and economically diverse learners. The admission committee looks for students who, for all their differences, are committed to integrity, innovation, excellence, and community engagement.

Applicants are required to submit the Common Application, posted on the DU Web site, along with high school transcripts, scores from either the SAT or ACT, an essay, a teacher recommendation, and a high school counselor recommendation. Applicants also are strongly encouraged to participate in the Ammi Hyde Interview, a face-to-face 20-minute conversation with as many as three members of the University community. Interviews are conducted in over 30 major cities across the country in December and February, and on campus throughout the year.

Application and Information

The University of Denver offers two application programs for first-year domestic students seeking fall-quarter admission. Early Action (postmarked by November 1) is a nonbinding program leading to an admission decision in early January. Hyde Interviews for Early Action applicants are conducted in December. Regular Decision (postmarked by January 15) is the final admission deadline for fall-quarter consideration. Admission decisions are mailed in mid-March. Hyde Interviews are conducted in February.

To learn more about the University of Denver, students should contact:

Office of Admission
University of Denver
2197 South University Boulevard
Denver, Colorado 80208
Phone: 303-871-2036
800-525-9495 (toll-free)
E-mail: admission@du.edu
Web site: http://www.du.edu/admission

WESTERN STATE COLLEGE OF COLORADO

WESTERN
STATE COLLEGE OF COLORADO

GUNNISON, COLORADO

The College

Western State College of Colorado (WSC) is more than just a college—it is a destination. WSC students come from all over the United States and from several countries around the world. They are adventurous individuals who have chosen to study in a beautiful mountain setting where the academic experience extends beyond the classroom. The College's professors are well qualified and are accessible to students and committed to teaching. Western is an outstanding college experience because of its small classes, the personalized attention given to each student, and the great activities that are available in and out of the classrooms. Western State College students experience a private-college atmosphere at a public college price.

Western offers twenty-two majors leading to a bachelor's degree as well as teacher licensure programs and several programs leading to minors. The academic programs take advantage of WSC's remarkable mountain setting and rich natural resources and incorporate the environment into the learning experience.

At Western, students have many opportunities to become involved in life outside the classroom. Western's staff and student leaders develop programming each year to support the academic, cultural, and diversity-related interests of the students. Some of the opportunities for students include Wilderness Pursuits, the fitness and health centers, student government, and the WSC Mountain Rescue Team. Students are also welcome to participate in music ensembles, vocal groups, theatrical productions, and the student-run radio station, television station, and newspapers. Western promotes an active and healthy lifestyle and provides many opportunities for athletic participation. Western's intercollegiate athletic teams compete in the Rocky Mountain Athletic Conference (NCAA Division II). Students have organized a number of club sports, with many of the clubs also participating in intercollegiate competition. The intramural sports program provides competitive opportunities in several sports.

Location

Western State College of Colorado is in Gunnison, Colorado. Gunnison and the neighboring town of Crested Butte are special because of the area's unmatched Colorado Rocky Mountain beauty. These authentic, unspoiled towns have many buildings dating back to the 1800s. Beyond its rich history, virtually the entire area is protected by national and state parks and forests, securing a sense of how an unspoiled Colorado must have appeared to brave adventurers centuries ago. Students can immerse themselves in a Colorado that no longer exists elsewhere in the state. They understand why Gunnison and Crested Butte are considered to be the pure and simple Colorado.

Majors and Degrees

Western State College of Colorado offers the Bachelor of Arts degree in accounting, anthropology, art, biology, business administration, chemistry, communication and theater, computer information systems, economics, education, English, environmental studies, geology, history, kinesiology, mathematics, music, outdoor leadership and resort management, political science, psychology, sociology, and Spanish. Minors are offered in all of these disciplines and in computer science, environmental studies, geography, headwaters regional studies, journalism, prelaw, and small business. Other specialties include petroleum geology and professional land and resource management.

Students seeking certification as teachers or school administrators at the elementary or secondary level pursue academic majors in other disciplines while taking the required courses in professional education.

Western State College also awards the Bachelor of Fine Arts degree in art.

Within the academic majors, students may gain preprofessional preparation for dentistry, engineering, law, law enforcement, medicine, nursing, optometry, osteopathy, pharmacy, physical therapy, theology, veterinary medicine, and other professions.

Academic Programs

The faculty of Western is committed to the delivery of a curriculum that requires students to (1) demonstrate mastery of basic skills; (2) engage in breadth of study, integrate knowledge from a variety of fields, and apply what is studied to life; (3) study one discipline or group of disciplines deeply enough to prepare for professional employment and/or future study; and (4) demonstrate leadership and self-discipline. To graduate, students must complete a minimum of 120 semester hours of credit. Successful completion of a core curriculum of interdisciplinary studies and of a concentrated course of study in a selected academic major are also required.

Academic Facilities

Academic facilities at the College include a brand-new building for the Business Administration Department, well-equipped classrooms, four auditoriums (a traditional theater, an experimental theater, a theater-in-the-round, and a recital hall), an art gallery, television and radio studios, laboratories for the natural sciences, botany laboratories, a biofeedback laboratory for psychology, and a darkroom. Western State College is also building a new student union scheduled to open in the spring semester of 2010.

Western State College of Colorado computer laboratory facilities are available in each academic building, the student center, and in every residence hall. Students have high-speed Internet access as part of their computer and e-mail accounts.

The library contains more than 110,000 volumes; more than half a million government documents, microforms, and audiovisual materials; and more than 825 carefully selected periodicals. Computerized access to all local and regional library holdings is available. The library also provides a supervised place for late-evening study and has a staff that is professionally and personally committed to providing the best possible service.

Costs

Tuition for the 2007–08 academic year was $2668 for residents of Colorado, after the $2600 College Opportunity Fund credit available to all Colorado residents. Nonresident tuition was $11,520. Fees totaled $886. Room and board costs were about $7300. The College maintains an excellent accident- and health-insurance plan. The plan covers the expense of illness and injury, subject to certain exclusions. The cost of the insurance for one calendar year was $953. The average cost of books and supplies was $950 per year. (These figures are subject to change.)

Financial Aid

Sufficient financial assistance is available to enable diligent and deserving students to complete their education. At Western, this assistance takes many forms, including state, federal, and institutional scholarships; grants; loans; and opportunities for employment on campus. Interested students should write to the Office of Financial Aid for a booklet that provides essential and up-to-date information. An extraordinary opportunity for qualified students comes through the Foundation Scholarship program funded by the Western State College Foundation.

Faculty

Western State College of Colorado has 110 full-time and 20 part-time teachers. Graduate students do not teach, nor do teaching assistants. While many faculty members do independent research in support of their teaching and some publish the results of their work, the primary basis of their employment is teaching and advising students and assisting with extracurricular student activities. Eighty-five percent of the faculty members hold doctoral degrees.

Student Government

The Student Government Association assumes responsibility through its Student Senate for representing student interests in numerous ways. The Senate assigns student members to important College committees; organizes most extracurricular activities, such as concerts, speakers, movies, club programs, and student media; and participates directly in the processes of budgeting and administering almost half a million dollars in student fees. The students also elect a Student Trustee, who sits as a member of the Board of Trustees for the Consortium of State Colleges.

Admission Requirements

When students apply for admission to Western, each is considered individually for admission. Western looks at their academic records and considers the activities they have participated in and any personal attributes they have chosen to tell about. To be admitted to Western, students should have 4 years of English; 3 years of mathematics, including 2 years of algebra; 3 years of natural and laboratory sciences; 3 years of social studies; and 2 years of academic electives. They should have a GPA of at least 2.5, rank in the upper two thirds of their high school graduating class, and earn a combined score of 950 or higher on the SAT or a composite score of 20 or higher on the ACT. Transfer applicants should have earned a minimum 2.0 GPA in at least 12 academic credit hours, including courses at the collegiate level in mathematics and English. If they do not meet these standards, they should include a personal essay, a list of activities, and two letters of recommendation with their application.

Application and Information

To be considered for admission, students must submit the application form with the $30 application fee; their official transcript (sent by the school), and scores on the SAT or ACT, which may be included on the high school record. Applications may also be made online. Applications are considered as they arrive on the campus, with the first decisions made in October. Students are usually notified of Western's admission decision within two weeks of their application. Transfer students must also submit official college transcripts sent by the college. Transfer applicants with 30 undergraduate credit hours need only submit their college transcripts, the application, and the fee. Transfer students with fewer than 30 credit hours must also submit high school transcripts and ACT or SAT scores.

Application materials and further information may be obtained by contacting:

Office of Admissions
Western State College of Colorado
600 North Adams Street
Gunnison, Colorado 81231
Phone: 800-876-5309 (toll-free)
E-mail: admissions@western.edu
Web site: http://www.western.edu

CONNECTICUT

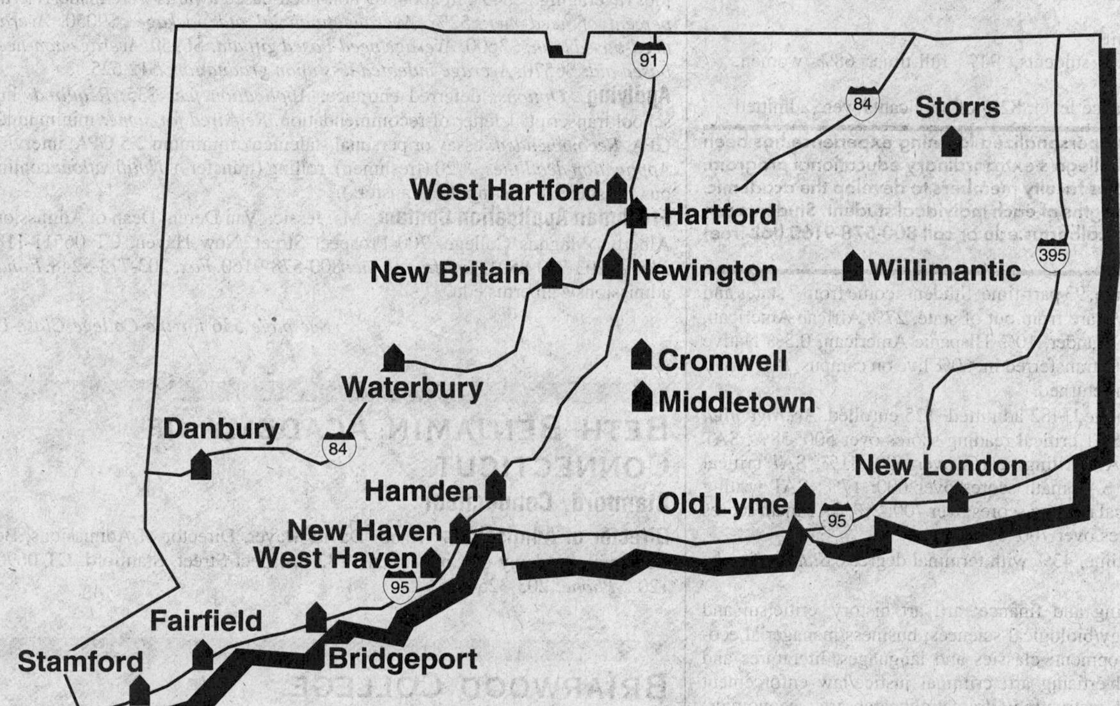

ALBERTUS MAGNUS COLLEGE

New Haven, Connecticut **www.albertus.edu/**

- **Independent Roman Catholic** comprehensive, founded 1925
- **Suburban** 55-acre campus with easy access to New York City and Hartford
- **Endowment** $12.5 million
- **Coed** 1,686 undergraduate students, 94% full-time, 68% women, 32% men
- **Moderately difficult** entrance level, 82% of applicants were admitted

For more than eighty years, the personalized learning experience has been the focus of Albertus Magnus College's extraordinary educational program. This straight-arrow mission allows faculty members to develop the academic, personal, and professional strengths of each individual student. Students can visit the Web site at http://www.albertus.edu or call 800-578-9160 (toll-free) for details.

Undergraduates 1,593 full-time, 93 part-time. Students come from 7 states and territories, 3 other countries, 12% are from out of state, 27% African American, 1% Asian American or Pacific Islander, 10% Hispanic American, 0.3% Native American, 0.2% international, 7% transferred in, 60% live on campus. *Retention:* 78% of 2006 full-time freshmen returned.

Freshmen *Admission:* 587 applied, 482 admitted, 125 enrolled. *Average high school GPA:* 3.00. *Test scores:* SAT critical reading scores over 500: 58%; SAT math scores over 500: 47%; SAT writing scores over 500: 51%; SAT critical reading scores over 600: 16%; SAT math scores over 600: 17%; SAT writing scores over 600: 16%; SAT critical reading scores over 700: 2%; SAT math scores over 700: 2%; SAT writing scores over 700: 1%.

Faculty *Total:* 159, 26% full-time, 43% with terminal degrees. *Student/faculty ratio:* 16:1.

Majors Accounting; accounting and finance; art; art history, criticism and conservation; art therapy; biology/biological sciences; business/managerial economics; chemistry; child development; classics and languages, literatures and linguistics; commercial and advertising art; criminal justice/law enforcement administration; curriculum and instruction; dramatic/theater arts; economics; education; elementary education; English; finance; fine/studio arts; French; general studies; graphic design; health/health care administration; history; humanities; human resources management and services related; human services; information science/studies; interdisciplinary studies; international business/trade/commerce; international economics; Italian; liberal arts and sciences/liberal studies; management information systems; marketing/marketing management; mass communication/media; mathematics; mathematics teacher education; middle school education; philosophy; photography; political science and government; pre-dentistry studies; pre-law studies; pre-medical studies; pre-veterinary studies; psychology; religious studies; Romance languages; secondary education; social sciences; social work; sociology; Spanish; urban studies/affairs.

Academics *Calendar:* semesters. *Degrees:* associate, bachelor's, and master's. *Special study options:* academic remediation for entering students, accelerated degree program, adult/continuing education programs, advanced placement credit, distance learning, double majors, English as a second language, freshman honors college, honors programs, independent study, internships, part-time degree program, services for LD students, student-designed majors, summer session for credit.

Computers on Campus 150 computers/terminals are available on campus for general student use. Students can access the following: campus intranet, computer help desk, free student e-mail accounts, online (class) grades, online (class) registration, online (class) schedules. Campuswide network is available. 100% of college-owned or -operated housing units are wired for high-speed Internet access. Wireless service is available via entire campus.

Student Life *Housing options:* coed, women-only. Campus housing is university owned. Freshman campus housing is guaranteed. *Activities and organizations:* drama/theater group, student-run newspaper, Student Government Association, College Drama, Minority Student Union. *Campus security:* 24-hour emergency response devices and patrols, late-night transport/escort service, controlled dormitory access. *Student services:* health clinic, personal/psychological counseling.

Athletics Member NCAA. All Division III. *Intercollegiate sports:* baseball M, basketball M/W, cross-country running M/W, soccer M/W, softball W, tennis M/W, volleyball M/W. *Intramural sports:* basketball M/W, racquetball M/W, soccer M/W, squash M/W, table tennis M/W.

Standardized Tests *Required:* SAT or ACT (for admission). *Recommended:* SAT Subject Tests (for admission).

Costs (2007–08) *Comprehensive fee:* $29,981 includes full-time tuition ($20,166), mandatory fees ($908), and room and board ($8907). Full-time tuition and fees vary according to class time and program. Part-time tuition: $2017 per course. Part-time tuition and fees vary according to class time and program. *Payment plan:* installment. *Waivers:* senior citizens and employees or children of employees.

Financial Aid Of all full-time matriculated undergraduates who enrolled in 2004, 366 applied for aid, 330 were judged to have need, 77 had their need fully met. 74 Federal Work-Study jobs (averaging $1208). 33 state and other part-time jobs (averaging $2849). In 2004, 69 non-need-based awards were made. *Average percent of need met:* 52%. *Average financial aid package:* $9050. *Average need-based loan:* $3600. *Average need-based gift aid:* $6950. *Average non-need-based aid:* $6570. *Average indebtedness upon graduation:* $12,625.

Applying *Options:* deferred entrance. *Application fee:* $35. *Required:* high school transcript, 1 letter of recommendation. *Required for some:* minimum 2.5 GPA. *Recommended:* essay or personal statement, minimum 2.5 GPA, interview. *Application deadlines:* 8/20 (freshmen), rolling (transfers). *Notification:* continuous (freshmen), continuous (transfers).

Freshman Application Contact Ms. Jessica Van Deren, Dean of Admissions, Albertus Magnus College, 700 Prospect Street, New Haven, CT 06511-1189. *Phone:* 203-773-8501. *Toll-free phone:* 800-578-9160. *Fax:* 203-773-5248. *E-mail:* admissions@albertus.edu.

See page 536 for the College Close-Up.

BETH BENJAMIN ACADEMY OF CONNECTICUT

Stamford, Connecticut

Director of Admissions Rabbi David Mayer, Director of Admissions, Beth Benjamin Academy of Connecticut, 132 Prospect Street, Stamford, CT 06901-1202. *Phone:* 203-325-4351.

BRIARWOOD COLLEGE

Southington, Connecticut **www.briarwood.edu/**

- **Proprietary** primarily 2-year, founded 1966
- **Small-town** 32-acre campus with easy access to Boston and Hartford
- **Endowment** $27,595
- **Coed**
- **Minimally difficult** entrance level

Faculty *Student/faculty ratio:* 10:1.

Academics *Calendar:* semesters. *Degrees:* certificates, diplomas, associate, and bachelor's.

Student Life *Campus security:* 24-hour patrols, late-night transport/escort service.

Costs (2007–08) *Tuition:* $16,400 full-time, $540 per credit part-time. *Required fees:* $220 full-time. *Room only:* $3600.

Financial Aid Of all full-time matriculated undergraduates who enrolled in 2006, 33 Federal Work-Study jobs (averaging $600). 30 state and other part-time jobs.

Applying *Options:* electronic application. *Application fee:* $25. *Required:* high school transcript. *Required for some:* essay or personal statement, letters of recommendation, interview.

Freshman Application Contact Mr. Jack LeConche, Chief Administrative Officer, Briarwood College, 2279 Mount Vernon Road, Southington, CT 06489. *Phone:* 860-628-4751 Ext. 131. *Toll-free phone:* 800-952-2444. *Fax:* 860-628-6444. *E-mail:* leconchej@briarwood.edu.

CENTRAL CONNECTICUT STATE UNIVERSITY

New Britain, Connecticut **www.ccsu.edu/**

- **State-supported** comprehensive, founded 1849, part of Connecticut State University System
- **Suburban** 294-acre campus
- **Endowment** $18.4 million
- **Coed** 9,704 undergraduate students, 79% full-time, 49% women, 51% men
- **Moderately difficult** entrance level, 61% of applicants were admitted

Undergraduates 7,658 full-time, 2,046 part-time. Students come from 27 states and territories, 45 other countries, 5% are from out of state, 8% African

American, 3% Asian American or Pacific Islander, 6% Hispanic American, 0.4% Native American, 1% international, 7% transferred in, 23% live on campus. *Retention:* 79% of 2006 full-time freshmen returned.

Freshmen *Admission:* 5,665 applied, 3,480 admitted, 1,478 enrolled. *Test scores:* SAT critical reading scores over 500: 50%; SAT math scores over 500: 56%; SAT writing scores over 500: 53%; SAT critical reading scores over 600: 10%; SAT math scores over 600: 10%; SAT writing scores over 600: 9%; SAT critical reading scores over 700: 1%.

Faculty *Total:* 885, 49% full-time, 40% with terminal degrees. *Student/faculty ratio:* 16:1.

Majors Accounting; anthropology; art; art teacher education; athletic training; biochemistry; biology/biological sciences; building/construction finishing, management, and inspection related; business administration and management; chemistry; civil engineering technology; communication/speech communication and rhetoric; computer and information sciences; criminology; design and visual communications; dramatic/theater arts; economics; electrical, electronics and communications engineering; elementary education; engineering technology; English; finance; French; geography; geology/earth science; German; history; industrial production technologies related; interdisciplinary studies; international business/trade/commerce; Italian; management information systems; manufacturing technology; marketing/marketing management; mathematics; mechanical engineering/mechanical technology; molecular biology; multi-/interdisciplinary studies related; music; music teacher education; nursing (registered nurse training); philosophy; physical education teaching and coaching; physical sciences related; physics; political science and government; psychology; social sciences; social work; sociology; Spanish; technology/industrial arts teacher education; tourism and travel services marketing.

Academics *Calendar:* semesters. *Degrees:* bachelor's, master's, doctoral, post-master's, and postbachelor's certificates. *Special study options:* academic remediation for entering students, adult/continuing education programs, advanced placement credit, cooperative education, distance learning, English as a second language, honors programs, independent study, internships, off-campus study, part-time degree program, services for LD students, student-designed majors, study abroad, summer session for credit. *ROTC:* Army (c), Air Force (c).

Computers on Campus 880 computers/terminals are available on campus for general student use. Students can access the following: computer help desk, free student e-mail accounts, online (class) grades, online (class) registration, online (class) schedules. Campuswide network is available. Wireless service is available via entire campus.

Student Life *Housing options:* coed, women-only. Campus housing is university owned. *Activities and organizations:* drama/theater group, student-run newspaper, radio and television station, choral group, Inter-Residence Council, Student radio station, Program Council, Outing Club, NAACP, national fraternities, national sororities. *Campus security:* 24-hour emergency response devices and patrols, student patrols, late-night transport/escort service, controlled dormitory access. *Student services:* health clinic, personal/psychological counseling, women's center.

Athletics Member NCAA. All Division I except football (Division I-AA). *Intercollegiate sports:* baseball M (s), basketball M (s)/W (s), cross-country running M (s)/W (s), fencing M (c)/W (c), golf M (s)/W (s), lacrosse M (c)/W (s), soccer M (s)/W (s), softball W (s), swimming and diving W (s), track and field M (s)/W (s), volleyball W (s). *Intramural sports:* badminton M/W, basketball M/W, field hockey W (c), football M, gymnastics W, rugby M (c)/W (c), soccer M/W, softball M/W, volleyball M/W.

Standardized Tests *Required:* SAT (for admission).

Costs (2007–08) *Tuition:* state resident $3346 full-time, $320 per credit part-time; nonresident $10,831 full-time, $320 per credit part-time. Full-time tuition and fees vary according to course level, course load, and reciprocity agreements. Part-time tuition and fees vary according to course level and course load. *Required fees:* $3388 full-time. *Room and board:* $8146; room only: $4748. Room and board charges vary according to board plan. *Payment plan:* installment. *Waivers:* senior citizens and employees or children of employees.

Financial Aid Of all full-time matriculated undergraduates who enrolled in 2006, 5,595 applied for aid, 4,412 were judged to have need, 212 had their need fully met. 289 Federal Work-Study jobs (averaging $1990). 110 state and other part-time jobs (averaging $544). In 2006, 178 non-need-based awards were made. *Average percent of need met:* 71%. *Average financial aid package:* $6835. *Average need-based loan:* $3953. *Average need-based gift aid:* $3990. *Average non-need-based aid:* $2735. *Average indebtedness upon graduation:* $10,500.

Applying *Options:* electronic application. *Application fee:* $50. *Required:* high school transcript, minimum 2.0 GPA. *Required for some:* interview. *Recommended:* minimum 3.0 GPA, 1 letter of recommendation. *Application deadlines:* 6/1 (freshmen), 6/1 (transfers). *Notification:* continuous until 7/1 (freshmen), continuous until 7/1 (transfers).

Freshman Application Contact Mr. Richard Bishop, Interim Director of Admissions, Central Connecticut State University, 1615 Stanley Street, New Britain, CT 06050. *Phone:* 860-832-2285. *Toll-free phone:* 888-733-2278. *Fax:* 860-832-2522. *E-mail:* admissions@ccsu.edu.

See page 538 for the College Close-Up.

CHARTER OAK STATE COLLEGE

New Britain, Connecticut **www.charteroak.edu/**

- **State-supported** 4-year, founded 1973
- **Small-town** campus
- **Endowment** $1.4 million
- **Coed** 1,577 undergraduate students, 5% full-time, 60% women, 40% men
- **Noncompetitive** entrance level

Undergraduates 81 full-time, 1,496 part-time. Students come from 52 states and territories, 3 other countries, 40% are from out of state, 13% African American, 2% Asian American or Pacific Islander, 6% Hispanic American, 1% Native American, 0.1% international, 100% transferred in.

Faculty *Total:* 131. *Student/faculty ratio:* 11:1.

Majors Liberal arts and sciences/liberal studies.

Academics *Calendar:* continuous. *Degrees:* associate and bachelor's (offers only external degree programs). *Special study options:* accelerated degree program, adult/continuing education programs, advanced placement credit, distance learning, external degree program, independent study, part-time degree program, services for LD students, student-designed majors, summer session for credit.

Student Life *Housing:* college housing not available.

Costs (2007–08) *Tuition:* state resident $172 per credit part-time; nonresident $247 per credit part-time.

Financial Aid Of all full-time matriculated undergraduates who enrolled in 2003, 355 applied for aid, 226 were judged to have need, 25 had their need fully met. *Average percent of need met:* 75%. *Average financial aid package:* $4464. *Average need-based loan:* $1800.

Applying *Options:* electronic application, deferred entrance. *Application fee:* $75. *Application deadline:* rolling (transfers). *Notification:* continuous (transfers).

Freshman Application Contact Ms. Lori Pendleton, Director of Admissions, Charter Oak State College, 55 Paul J. Manafort Drive, New Britain, CT 06053-2150. *Phone:* 860-832-3858. *Fax:* 860-832-3999. *E-mail:* info@charteroak.edu.

CONNECTICUT COLLEGE

New London, Connecticut **www.conncoll.edu/**

- **Independent** comprehensive, founded 1911
- **Suburban** 702-acre campus
- **Endowment** $225.0 million
- **Coed** 1,857 undergraduate students, 97% full-time, 60% women, 40% men
- **Very difficult** entrance level, 35% of applicants were admitted

Undergraduates 1,802 full-time, 55 part-time. Students come from 46 states and territories, 74 other countries, 85% are from out of state, 4% African American, 4% Asian American or Pacific Islander, 5% Hispanic American, 0.1% Native American, 5% international, 1% transferred in, 99% live on campus. *Retention:* 90% of 2006 full-time freshmen returned.

Freshmen *Admission:* 4,742 applied, 1,638 admitted, 492 enrolled. *Test scores:* SAT critical reading scores over 500: 100%; SAT math scores over 500: 97%; SAT writing scores over 500: 99%; ACT scores over 18: 99%; SAT critical reading scores over 600: 86%; SAT math scores over 600: 83%; SAT writing scores over 600: 86%; ACT scores over 24: 84%; SAT critical reading scores over 700: 37%; SAT math scores over 700: 23%; SAT writing scores over 700: 41%; ACT scores over 30: 22%.

Faculty *Total:* 245, 70% full-time, 70% with terminal degrees. *Student/faculty ratio:* 9:1.

Majors African studies; American studies; anthropology; architecture; area, ethnic, cultural, and gender studies related; art; art history, criticism and conservation; Asian studies (East); astrophysics; biochemistry; biology/biological sciences; botany/plant biology; cell and molecular biology; chemistry; chemistry related; Chinese; classics and languages, literatures and linguistics; computer science; dance; dramatic/theater arts; ecology; economics; education (multiple levels); elementary education; engineering physics; English; environmental studies; ethnic, cultural minority, and gender studies related; European studies (Central and Eastern); family systems; film/cinema studies; French; German studies; Hispanic-American, Puerto Rican, and Mexican-American/Chicano studies; history; human development and family studies; human ecology; interdisciplinary studies; international relations and affairs; Italian; Italian studies; Japanese; Latin American studies; mathematics; medieval and Renaissance studies; molecular biology; multi-/interdisciplinary studies related; museum studies; music; music related; music teacher education; neuroscience; philosophy; physics teacher education; political science and government; psychology; religious studies; secondary education; Slavic languages; Slavic studies; social sciences related; sociology; Spanish; Spanish language teacher education; urban studies/affairs; women's studies.

Academics *Calendar:* semesters. *Degrees:* bachelor's and master's. *Special study options:* adult/continuing education programs, advanced placement credit, double majors, honors programs, independent study, internships, off-campus study, part-time degree program, student-designed majors, study abroad, summer session for credit. *Unusual degree programs:* 3-2 engineering with Washington University in St. Louis.

Computers on Campus Students can access the following: campus intranet, computer help desk, free student e-mail accounts, online (class) grades, online (class) registration, online (class) schedules. Campuswide network is available. 100% of college-owned or -operated housing units are wired for high-speed Internet access. Wireless service is available via entire campus.

Student Life *Housing:* on-campus residence required through junior year. *Options:* coed, cooperative, disabled students. Campus housing is university owned. Freshman campus housing is guaranteed. *Activities and organizations:* drama/theater group, student-run newspaper, radio station, choral group, Student Government Association, Student Activity Council, Unity House clubs, sports clubs, student radio station. *Campus security:* 24-hour emergency response devices and patrols, late-night transport/escort service, controlled dormitory access. *Student services:* health clinic, personal/psychological counseling, women's center.

Athletics Member NCAA. All Division III. *Intercollegiate sports:* baseball M (c), basketball M/W, crew M/W, cross-country running M/W, equestrian sports M (c)/W (c), field hockey W, ice hockey M/W, lacrosse M/W, rugby W (c), sailing M/W, skiing (cross-country) M (c)/W (c), skiing (downhill) M (c)/W (c), soccer M/W, squash M/W, swimming and diving M/W, tennis M/W, track and field M/W, ultimate Frisbee M (c)/W (c), volleyball M/W, water polo M/W. *Intramural sports:* basketball M/W, football M, golf M/W, ice hockey M/W, lacrosse M, soccer M/W, softball M/W, tennis M/W, volleyball M/W.

Standardized Tests *Required:* ACT or any 2 SAT Subject Tests required (for admission).

Costs (2007–08) *Comprehensive fee:* $46,675. Full-time tuition and fees vary according to program. Part-time tuition: $1084 per credit hour. Part-time tuition and fees vary according to program. *Payment plan:* installment. *Waivers:* senior citizens and employees or children of employees.

Financial Aid Of all full-time matriculated undergraduates who enrolled in 2007, 900 applied for aid, 766 were judged to have need, 766 had their need fully met. 636 Federal Work-Study jobs (averaging $1348). 21 state and other part-time jobs (averaging $903). *Average percent of need met:* 100%. *Average financial aid package:* $29,758. *Average need-based loan:* $4489. *Average need-based gift aid:* $27,515. *Average indebtedness upon graduation:* $21,523. *Financial aid deadline:* 2/1.

Applying *Options:* electronic application, early decision, deferred entrance. *Application fee:* $60. *Required:* essay or personal statement, high school transcript, minimum 2.0 GPA, letters of recommendation. *Recommended:* interview. *Application deadlines:* 1/1 (freshmen), 4/1 (transfers). *Early decision deadline:* 11/15. *Notification:* 3/31 (freshmen), 5/15 (transfers), 12/15 (early decision).

Freshman Application Contact Ms. Martha Merrill, Dean of Admissions and Financial Aid, Connecticut College, 270 Mohegan Avenue, New London, CT 06320-4196. *Phone:* 860-439-2200. *Fax:* 860-439-4301. *E-mail:* admission@conncoll.edu.

EASTERN CONNECTICUT STATE UNIVERSITY

Willimantic, Connecticut **www.easternct.edu/**

- **State-supported** comprehensive, founded 1889, part of Connecticut State University System
- **Small-town** 179-acre campus
- **Endowment** $6.9 million
- **Coed** 4,826 undergraduate students, 82% full-time, 55% women, 45% men
- **Moderately difficult** entrance level, 58% of applicants were admitted

Undergraduates 3,975 full-time, 851 part-time. Students come from 26 states and territories, 34 other countries, 7% are from out of state, 7% African American, 2% Asian American or Pacific Islander, 5% Hispanic American, 0.5% Native American, 0.8% international, 8% transferred in, 52% live on campus. *Retention:* 74% of 2006 full-time freshmen returned.

Freshmen *Admission:* 3,740 applied, 2,167 admitted, 880 enrolled. *Test scores:* SAT critical reading scores over 500: 52%; SAT math scores over 500: 56%; SAT critical reading scores over 600: 11%; SAT math scores over 600: 6%; SAT critical reading scores over 700: 1%; SAT math scores over 700: 1%.

Faculty *Total:* 406, 49% full-time, 51% with terminal degrees. *Student/faculty ratio:* 16:1.

Majors Accounting; art; biochemistry; biology/biological sciences; business administration and management; business/commerce; communication/speech communication and rhetoric; computer and information sciences; developmental and child psychology; early childhood education; economics; elementary education; English; environmental science; general studies; history; industrial and organizational psychology; kindergarten/preschool education; management information systems; mathematics; physical education teaching and coaching; political science and government; psychology; secondary education; social work; sociology; Spanish; sport and fitness administration/management; visual and performing arts.

Academics *Calendar:* semesters. *Degrees:* associate, bachelor's, and master's. *Special study options:* academic remediation for entering students, adult/continuing education programs, advanced placement credit, cooperative education, distance learning, double majors, freshman honors college, honors programs, independent study, internships, off-campus study, part-time degree program, services for LD students, student-designed majors, study abroad, summer session for credit. *ROTC:* Army (c), Air Force (c).

Computers on Campus 637 computers/terminals are available on campus for general student use. Students can access the following: computer help desk, free student e-mail accounts, online (class) grades, online (class) registration, online (class) schedules. Campuswide network is available.

Student Life *Housing options:* coed. Campus housing is university owned. Freshman campus housing is guaranteed. *Activities and organizations:* drama/theater group, student-run newspaper, radio and television station, choral group, M.A.L.E.S, Organization of Latin American Students, 180 Christian Fellowship, A.L.A.Y.A. *Campus security:* 24-hour emergency response devices and patrols, student patrols, late-night transport/escort service, controlled dormitory access. *Student services:* health clinic, personal/psychological counseling, women's center.

Athletics Member NCAA. All Division III. *Intercollegiate sports:* baseball M, basketball M/W, cheerleading W (c), cross-country running M/W, field hockey W, lacrosse M/W, soccer M/W, softball W, swimming and diving W, track and field M/W, volleyball W. *Intramural sports:* badminton M/W, basketball M/W, bowling M (c)/W (c), cross-country running M/W, football M, gymnastics W, racquetball M/W, rugby M/W (c), skiing (cross-country) M/W, skiing (downhill) M/W, soccer M/W, softball M/W, squash M/W, swimming and diving M/W, tennis M/W, track and field M/W, ultimate Frisbee M/W, volleyball M/W, water polo M/W.

Standardized Tests *Required:* SAT or ACT (for admission).

Costs (2007–08) *Tuition:* area resident $3346 full-time, $313 per credit part-time; nonresident $10,831 full-time, $313 per credit part-time. Full-time tuition and fees vary according to course load, degree level, and reciprocity agreements. Part-time tuition and fees vary according to course load and degree level. *Required fees:* $3615 full-time. *Room and board:* $8377; room only: $4677. Room and board charges vary according to board plan and housing facility. *Payment plans:* installment, deferred payment. *Waivers:* senior citizens and employees or children of employees.

Financial Aid Of all full-time matriculated undergraduates who enrolled in 2006, 2,524 applied for aid, 1,935 were judged to have need, 334 had their need fully met. 99 Federal Work-Study jobs (averaging $2530). 36 state and other part-time jobs (averaging $2147). In 2006, 236 non-need-based awards were made. *Average percent of need met:* 73%. *Average financial aid package:* $7337. *Average need-based loan:* $3716. *Average need-based gift aid:* $5141. *Average non-need-based aid:* $2343. *Average indebtedness upon graduation:* $14,101.

Applying *Options:* electronic application, early admission, deferred entrance. *Application fee:* $50. *Required:* high school transcript. *Required for some:* interview. *Recommended:* essay or personal statement, letters of recommendation, rank in upper 50% of high school class. *Application deadlines:* rolling (freshmen), rolling (transfers). *Notification:* continuous (freshmen).

Freshman Application Contact Ms. Kimberly M. Crone, Director of Admissions and Enrollment Management, Eastern Connecticut State University, 83 Windham Street, Willimantic, CT 06336. *Phone:* 860-465-5286. *Toll-free phone:* 877-353-3278. *Fax:* 860-465-5544. *E-mail:* admissions@easternct.edu.

See page 540 for the College Close-Up.

FAIRFIELD UNIVERSITY

Fairfield, Connecticut **www.fairfield.edu/**

- **Independent Roman Catholic (Jesuit)** comprehensive, founded 1942
- **Suburban** 200-acre campus with easy access to New York City
- **Endowment** $268.8 million
- **Coed** 4,030 undergraduate students, 86% full-time, 58% women, 42% men
- **Moderately difficult** entrance level, 55% of applicants were admitted

Undergraduates 3,484 full-time, 546 part-time. Students come from 32 states and territories, 17 other countries, 77% are from out of state, 3% African American, 3% Asian American or Pacific Islander, 6% Hispanic American, 0.2% Native American, 0.7% international, 0.7% transferred in, 97% live on campus. *Retention:* 82% of 2006 full-time freshmen returned.

Freshmen *Admission:* 8,557 applied, 4,686 admitted, 842 enrolled. *Average high school GPA:* 3.4. *Test scores:* SAT critical reading scores over 500: 91%; SAT math scores over 500: 92%; SAT critical reading scores over 600: 41%; SAT math scores over 600: 46%; SAT critical reading scores over 700: 5%; SAT math scores over 700: 6%.

Faculty *Total:* 483, 49% full-time, 66% with terminal degrees. *Student/faculty ratio:* 13:1.

Majors Accounting; American studies; art history, criticism and conservation; biology/biological sciences; business administration and management; chemistry; computer engineering; computer science; computer software engineering; economics; electrical, electronics and communications engineering; English; film/video and photographic arts related; finance; fine/studio arts; French; German; history; information science/studies; international relations and affairs; Italian; management information systems; marketing/marketing management; mass communication/media; mathematics; mechanical engineering; modern languages; music history, literature, and theory; music teacher education; nursing (registered nurse training); philosophy; physics; political science and government; psychology; religious studies; secondary education; sociology; Spanish; visual and performing arts.

Academics *Calendar:* semesters. *Degrees:* associate, bachelor's, master's, and post-master's certificates. *Special study options:* adult/continuing education programs, advanced placement credit, distance learning, double majors, honors programs, independent study, internships, part-time degree program, services for LD students, student-designed majors, study abroad, summer session for credit. *ROTC:* Army (c), Air Force (c). *Unusual degree programs:* 3-2 engineering with University of Connecticut, Rensselaer Polytechnic Institute, Columbia University, Stevens Institute of Technology.

Computers on Campus 200 computers/terminals and 400 ports are available on campus for general student use. Students can access the following: campus intranet, computer help desk, free student e-mail accounts, online (class) grades, online (class) registration, online (class) schedules. Campuswide network is available. 100% of college-owned or -operated housing units are wired for high-speed Internet access. Wireless service is available via classrooms, dorm rooms, libraries, student centers.

Student Life *Housing:* on-campus residence required through senior year. *Options:* coed, disabled students. Campus housing is university owned. Freshman campus housing is guaranteed. *Activities and organizations:* drama/theater group, student-run newspaper, radio and television station, choral group, student government, Glee Club, Residence Hall Council, Theatre Fairfield, Campus Ministry. *Campus security:* 24-hour emergency response devices and patrols, late-night transport/escort service, controlled dormitory access, bicycle patrols. *Student services:* health clinic, personal/psychological counseling, women's center.

Athletics Member NCAA. All Division I. *Intercollegiate sports:* baseball M (s), basketball M (s)/W (s), cheerleading M (c)/W (c), crew M/W, cross-country running M (s)/W (s), equestrian sports M (c)/W (c), field hockey W (s), golf M (s)/W (s), lacrosse M (s)/W (s), soccer M (s)/W (s), softball W (s), swimming and diving M (s)/W (s), tennis M (s)/W (s), volleyball W (s). *Intramural sports:* basketball M/W, field hockey W, football M/W, ice hockey M (c)/W (c), lacrosse M/W, racquetball M/W, rugby M (c)/W (c), sailing M (c)/W (c), skiing (downhill) M (c)/W (c), soccer M (c)/W (c), softball W, table tennis M/W, tennis M (c)/W (c), track and field M/W, volleyball M (c)/W (c).

Standardized Tests *Required:* SAT or ACT (for admission).

Costs (2007–08) *One-time required fee:* $60. *Comprehensive fee:* $44,335 includes full-time tuition ($33,340), mandatory fees ($565), and room and board ($10,430). Part-time tuition: $430 per credit. Part-time tuition and fees vary according to course load and program. *Required fees:* $25 per term part-time. *College room only:* $6230. Room and board charges vary according to board plan and housing facility. *Payment plan:* installment. *Waivers:* employees or children of employees.

Financial Aid Of all full-time matriculated undergraduates who enrolled in 2006, 2,104 applied for aid, 1,693 were judged to have need, 437 had their need fully met. 416 Federal Work-Study jobs (averaging $1316). In 2006, 259 non-need-based awards were made. *Average percent of need met:* 66%. *Average financial aid package:* $19,101. *Average need-based loan:* $4061. *Average need-based gift aid:* $14,078. *Average non-need-based aid:* $11,304. *Average indebtedness upon graduation:* $28,751. *Financial aid deadline:* 2/15.

Applying *Options:* early admission, early action, deferred entrance. *Application fee:* $60. *Required:* essay or personal statement, high school transcript, minimum 3.0 GPA, 1 letter of recommendation, rank in upper 20% of high school class. *Recommended:* interview. *Application deadlines:* 1/15 (freshmen), 6/1 (transfers), 11/15 (early action). *Notification:* 4/1 (freshmen), continuous (transfers), 1/1 (early action).

Freshman Application Contact Ms. Karen Pellegrino, Director of Admission, Fairfield University, 1073 North Benson Road, Fairfield, CT 06824-5195. *Phone:* 203-254-4100. *Fax:* 203-254-4199. *E-mail:* admis@mail.fairfield.edu.

HOLY APOSTLES COLLEGE AND SEMINARY

Cromwell, Connecticut **www.holyapostles.edu/**

- **Independent Roman Catholic** comprehensive, founded 1956
- **Suburban** 17-acre campus with easy access to Hartford, CT New Haven, CT
- **Endowment** $658,000
- **Coed, primarily men** 46 undergraduate students, 37% full-time, 35% women, 65% men
- **Noncompetitive** entrance level, 100% of applicants were admitted

Undergraduates 17 full-time, 29 part-time. Students come from 10 states and territories, 2 other countries, 46% are from out of state, 2% African American, 4% Asian American or Pacific Islander, 9% Hispanic American, 9% international, 11% transferred in. *Retention:* 100% of 2006 full-time freshmen returned.

Freshmen *Admission:* 5 applied, 5 admitted, 5 enrolled.

Faculty *Total:* 26, 38% full-time, 88% with terminal degrees. *Student/faculty ratio:* 11:1.

Majors Humanities; philosophy; religious studies; social sciences.

Academics *Calendar:* semesters. *Degrees:* certificates, associate, bachelor's, master's, first professional, post-master's, postbachelor's, and first professional certificates. *Special study options:* academic remediation for entering students, adult/continuing education programs, distance learning, English as a second language, external degree program, independent study, part-time degree program, services for LD students, summer session for credit.

Computers on Campus 10 computers/terminals are available on campus for general student use. Wireless service is available via libraries.

Student Life *Housing:* college housing not available. *Activities and organizations:* Toastmasters, Pro-Life Organization, Student Council, Schola Choir. *Student services:* personal/psychological counseling.

Standardized Tests *Required:* SAT (for admission).

Costs (2007–08) *Tuition:* $7800 full-time, $325 per credit part-time. *Payment plan:* installment. *Waivers:* employees or children of employees.

Applying *Options:* deferred entrance. *Application fee:* $25. *Required:* high school transcript. *Required for some:* letters of recommendation. *Application deadlines:* rolling (freshmen), rolling (out-of-state freshmen), rolling (transfers).

Freshman Application Contact Mr. Mark Azzara, Holy Apostles College and Seminary, 33 Prospect Hill Road, Cromwell, CT 06416-2005. *Phone:* 860-632-3010. *Toll-free phone:* 800-330-7272. *Fax:* 860-632-3075. *E-mail:* recruitment@holyapostles.edu.

LYME ACADEMY COLLEGE OF FINE ARTS

Old Lyme, Connecticut **www.lymeacademy.edu/**

Director of Admissions Mr. John D. Werenko, Executive Director of Admission, Lyme Academy College of Fine Arts, 84 Lyme Street, Old Lyme, CT 06371. *Phone:* 860-434-5232 Ext. 119.

MITCHELL COLLEGE

New London, Connecticut **www.mitchell.edu/**

- **Independent** 4-year, founded 1938
- **Suburban** 67-acre campus with easy access to Hartford and Providence
- **Coed** 894 undergraduate students, 84% full-time, 51% women, 49% men
- **Minimally difficult** entrance level, 58% of applicants were admitted

Undergraduates 751 full-time, 143 part-time. Students come from 25 states and territories, 5 other countries, 12% African American, 0.8% Asian American or Pacific Islander, 8% Hispanic American, 3% Native American, 0.7% international, 7% transferred in, 75% live on campus.

Freshmen *Admission:* 1,158 applied, 675 admitted, 297 enrolled. *Average high school GPA:* 2.8.

Faculty *Total:* 84, 37% full-time, 32% with terminal degrees. *Student/faculty ratio:* 12:1.

Majors Biological and physical sciences; business administration and management; child development; commercial and advertising art; criminal justice/law enforcement administration; criminal justice/safety; developmental and child psychology; early childhood education; engineering; environmental studies; human development and family studies; human services; liberal arts and sciences/liberal studies; mass communications; parks, recreation and leisure; physical education teaching and coaching; physical sciences; psychology; sport and fitness administration/management; tourism/travel marketing.

Academics *Calendar:* semesters. *Degrees:* associate and bachelor's. *Special study options:* adult/continuing education programs, advanced placement credit, cooperative education, double majors, English as a second language, internships, part-time degree program, services for LD students, summer session for credit.

Computers on Campus 155 computers/terminals are available on campus for general student use. Students can access the following: campus intranet, computer help desk, free student e-mail accounts. Campuswide network is available. Wireless service is available via classrooms, computer centers, computer labs, learning centers, libraries, student centers.

Student Life *Housing:* on-campus residence required for freshman year. *Options:* coed, men-only, women-only. Campus housing is university owned. Freshman campus housing is guaranteed. *Activities and organizations:* drama/theater group, choral group, Multicultural Club, Business Club, student government, student newspaper, Outdoor Adventure Club. *Campus security:* 24-hour emergency response devices and patrols, student patrols, late-night transport/escort service, controlled dormitory access. *Student services:* health clinic, personal/psychological counseling.

Athletics Member NCAA. except baseball (Division III), men's and women's basketball (Division III), men's and women's cheerleading (Division III), men's and women's cross-country running (Division III), men's and women's golf (Division III), lacrosse (Division III), men's and women's soccer (Division III), softball (Division III), volleyball (Division III) *Intercollegiate sports:* baseball M, basketball M/W, cheerleading M/W, cross-country running M/W, golf M/W, lacrosse M, sailing M/W, soccer M/W, softball W, volleyball W. *Intramural sports:* basketball M/W, sailing M/W, soccer M/W, softball M/W, tennis M/W, volleyball M/W.

Costs (2008–09) *Comprehensive fee:* $35,335 includes full-time tuition ($22,846), mandatory fees ($1512), and room and board ($10,977). Part-time tuition: $275 per credit hour. *Required fees:* $35 per term part-time. *College room only:* $5708.

Financial Aid Of all full-time matriculated undergraduates who enrolled in 2004, 491 applied for aid, 414 were judged to have need. 44 Federal Work-Study jobs (averaging $1000). In 2004, 70 non-need-based awards were made. *Average percent of need met:* 89%. *Average financial aid package:* $16,357. *Average need-based loan:* $2904. *Average need-based gift aid:* $8058. *Average non-need-based aid:* $2890.

Applying *Options:* electronic application, early admission, early decision, deferred entrance. *Application fee:* $30. *Required:* essay or personal statement, high school transcript, minimum 2.0 GPA, letters of recommendation. *Recommended:* interview. *Application deadlines:* rolling (freshmen), rolling (transfers). *Early decision deadline:* 11/15. *Notification:* continuous until 8/30 (freshmen), continuous until 8/30 (transfers), 12/15 (early decision).

Freshman Application Contact Ms. Kimberly Hodges, Director of Admissions, Mitchell College, 437 Pequot Avenue, New London, CT 06320. *Phone:* 860-701-5038. *Toll-free phone:* 800-443-2811. *Fax:* 860-444-1209. *E-mail:* admissions@mitchell.edu.

See page 542 for the College Close-Up.

PAIER COLLEGE OF ART, INC.

Hamden, Connecticut **www.paiercollegeofart.edu/**

- **Proprietary** 4-year, founded 1946
- **Suburban** 3-acre campus with easy access to New York City
- **Coed** 249 undergraduate students, 67% full-time, 68% women, 32% men
- **Minimally difficult** entrance level, 78% of applicants were admitted

Undergraduates 168 full-time, 81 part-time. Students come from 1 other state, 4% African American, 2% Asian American or Pacific Islander, 2% Hispanic American, 0.4% Native American, 1% international, 4% transferred in. *Retention:* 81% of 2006 full-time freshmen returned.

Freshmen *Admission:* 73 applied, 57 admitted, 30 enrolled. *Average high school GPA:* 2.6. *Test scores:* SAT critical reading scores over 500: 28%; SAT math scores over 500: 14%; SAT critical reading scores over 600: 3%; SAT math scores over 600: 3%.

Faculty *Total:* 46, 20% full-time, 46% with terminal degrees. *Student/faculty ratio:* 7:1.

Majors Applied art; art; commercial and advertising art; commercial photography; design and applied arts related; design and visual communications; drawing; fine arts related; fine/studio arts; graphic design; illustration; interior design; painting; photography.

Academics *Calendar:* semesters plus 1 summer session. *Degrees:* certificates, diplomas, associate, and bachelor's. *Special study options:* academic remediation for entering students, advanced placement credit, independent study, part-time degree program, services for LD students, study abroad, summer session for credit.

Computers on Campus 40 computers/terminals are available on campus for general student use.

Student Life *Housing:* college housing not available. *Activities and organizations:* Student Council. *Campus security:* evening patrols by security. *Student services:* personal/psychological counseling.

Standardized Tests *Required:* SAT or ACT (for admission).

Costs (2008–09) *Tuition:* $12,000 full-time, $380 per credit part-time. *Required fees:* $385 full-time, $125 per term part-time.

Financial Aid Of all full-time matriculated undergraduates who enrolled in 1999, 102 applied for aid, 92 were judged to have need, 1 had their need fully met. *Average percent of need met:* 62%. *Average financial aid package:* $6717. *Average need-based loan:* $3446. *Average need-based gift aid:* $3460. *Average indebtedness upon graduation:* $13,536.

Applying *Options:* electronic application, deferred entrance. *Application fee:* $25. *Required:* high school transcript, minimum 2.0 GPA, 2 letters of recommendation, interview, portfolio. *Recommended:* essay or personal statement. *Application deadlines:* rolling (freshmen), rolling (transfers). *Notification:* continuous (freshmen), continuous (transfers).

Freshman Application Contact Ms. Lynn Pascale, Secretary to Admissions, Paier College of Art, Inc., 20 Gorham Avenue, Hamden, CT 06514-3902. *Phone:* 203-287-3031. *Fax:* 203-287-3021. *E-mail:* paier.admission@snet.net.

See page 544 for the College Close-Up.

POST UNIVERSITY

Waterbury, Connecticut **www.post.edu/**

Founded in 1890, Post University is a career-oriented and student-focused university located in Waterbury, Connecticut. Post is known for its high-quality academic programs, small classes, national award–winning student activities, and NCAA Division II athletic programs. Its 1,400 full- and part-time students come from throughout the United States and abroad to pursue their personal and professional goals within academic programs that are supported by dedicated faculty members who blend both theory and practice within their classroom experiences. Upon graduation, Post University students are prepared to become the CEOs of their future.

Freshman Application Contact Mr. Jay Murray, Director of Admissions, Post University, PO Box 2540, Waterbury, CT 06723. *Phone:* 203-596-4500. *Toll-free phone:* 800-345-2562. *Fax:* 203-756-5810. *E-mail:* admiss@post.edu.

See page 546 for the College Close-Up.

QUINNIPIAC UNIVERSITY

Hamden, Connecticut **www.quinnipiac.edu/**

- **Independent** comprehensive, founded 1929
- **Suburban** 500-acre campus with easy access to Hartford
- **Endowment** $223.0 million
- **Coed** 5,765 undergraduate students, 95% full-time, 62% women, 38% men
- **Moderately difficult** entrance level, 47% of applicants were admitted

The TD Banknorth Sports Center is the first facility to open on the nearby 200-acre "York Hill" portion of the Quinnipiac campus, with spectacular views of the area and Long Island Sound in the distance. Twin arenas of more than 3,000 seats host exciting basketball and ECAC hockey. Future development (beginning in 2009) includes residence facilities for 1,800 students to provide seniors with Quinnipiac housing as well as a hilltop student center and dining area and additional campus parking.

Undergraduates 5,455 full-time, 310 part-time. Students come from 28 states and territories, 18 other countries, 70% are from out of state, 3% African American, 2% Asian American or Pacific Islander, 5% Hispanic American, 0.2% Native American, 1% international, 3% transferred in, 70% live on campus. *Retention:* 89% of 2006 full-time freshmen returned.

Freshmen *Admission:* 12,060 applied, 5,681 admitted, 1,358 enrolled. *Average high school GPA:* 3.4. *Test scores:* SAT critical reading scores over 500: 82%; SAT math scores over 500: 90%; ACT scores over 18: 100%; SAT critical reading scores over 600: 23%; SAT math scores over 600: 35%; ACT scores over 24: 78%; SAT critical reading scores over 700: 2%; SAT math scores over 700: 3%; ACT scores over 30: 17%.

Faculty *Total:* 778, 36% full-time, 70% with terminal degrees. *Student/faculty ratio:* 15:1.

Majors Accounting; actuarial science; advertising; applied mathematics; athletic training; biochemistry; biological and physical sciences; biology/biological sciences; broadcast journalism; business administration and management; business/managerial economics; chemistry; child development; cinematography and film/video production; communication and journalism related; computer science; criminal justice/safety; developmental and child psychology; dramatic/theater arts; economics; education; English; entrepreneurship; film/cinema studies; finance; gerontology; history; human resources management; human services; information science/studies; international business/trade/commerce; international relations and affairs; journalism; legal assistant/paralegal; legal studies; liberal arts and sciences/liberal studies; literature; marketing/marketing management; mass communication/media; mathematics; medical laboratory technology; medical microbiology and bacteriology; nursing (registered nurse training); occupational therapy; physical therapy; physician assistant; physiological psychology/psychobiology; political science and government; pre-dentistry studies; pre-law studies; pre-medical studies; pre-veterinary studies; psychology; public relations/image management; radiologic technology/science; sales, distribution and marketing; social sciences; sociology; Spanish; veterinary technology; web page, digital/multimedia and information resources design.

Academics *Calendar:* semesters. *Degrees:* bachelor's, master's, doctoral, first professional, and postbachelor's certificates. *Special study options:* adult/continuing education programs, advanced placement credit, distance learning, double majors, honors programs, independent study, internships, part-time degree program, services for LD students, student-designed majors, study abroad, summer session for credit. *ROTC:* Army (c), Air Force (c).

Computers on Campus 600 computers/terminals and 2,500 ports are available on campus for general student use. Students can access the following: campus intranet, computer help desk, free student e-mail accounts, online (class) grades, online (class) registration, online (class) schedules, e-commerce 'Q' card for local merchants, food service, dorm card access. Campuswide network is available. 100% of college-owned or -operated housing units are wired for high-speed Internet access. Wireless service is available via entire campus.

Student Life *Housing options:* coed. Campus housing is university owned. Freshman campus housing is guaranteed. *Activities and organizations:* drama/theater group, student-run newspaper, radio and television station, choral group, student government, Social Programming Board, Drama Club, student newspaper, Chronicle, dance company, national fraternities, national sororities. *Campus security:* 24-hour emergency response devices and patrols, late-night transport/escort service, controlled dormitory access. *Student services:* health clinic, personal/psychological counseling.

Athletics Member NCAA. All Division I. *Intercollegiate sports:* baseball M (s), basketball M (s)/W (s), cross-country running M (s)/W (s), field hockey W (s), golf M (s), ice hockey M (s)/W (s), lacrosse M (s)/W (s), soccer M (s)/W (s), softball W (s), tennis M (s)/W (s), track and field M (s)/W (s), volleyball W (s). *Intramural sports:* baseball M, basketball M/W, bowling M/W, field hockey W, soccer M/W, softball W, tennis M/W, volleyball M/W.

Standardized Tests *Required:* SAT or ACT (for admission).

Costs (2008–09) *Comprehensive fee:* $42,700 includes full-time tuition ($29,700), mandatory fees ($1200), and room and board ($11,800). Part-time tuition: $710 per credit. *Required fees:* $30 per credit part-time.

Financial Aid Of all full-time matriculated undergraduates who enrolled in 2007, 3,783 applied for aid, 3,137 were judged to have need, 447 had their need fully met. 1,362 Federal Work-Study jobs (averaging $2053). 47 state and other part-time jobs (averaging $1744). In 2007, 589 non-need-based awards were made. *Average percent of need met:* 65%. *Average financial aid package:* $16,914. *Average need-based loan:* $4711. *Average need-based gift aid:* $11,504. *Average non-need-based aid:* $8191. *Average indebtedness upon graduation:* $35,086.

Applying *Options:* electronic application, deferred entrance. *Application fee:* $45. *Required:* essay or personal statement, high school transcript, 1 letter of recommendation. *Required for some:* minimum 3.0 GPA. *Recommended:* interview. *Application deadlines:* 2/1 (freshmen), 2/1 (out-of-state freshmen), 4/1 (transfers). *Notification:* continuous (transfers).

Freshman Application Contact Ms. Joan Isaac Mohr, Vice President and Dean of Admissions, Quinnipiac University, 275 Mount Carmel Avenue, Hamden, CT 06518-1940. *Phone:* 203-582-8600. *Toll-free phone:* 800-462-1944. *Fax:* 203-582-8906. *E-mail:* admissions@quinnipiac.edu.

See page 548 for the College Close-Up.

SACRED HEART UNIVERSITY

Fairfield, Connecticut **www.sacredheart.edu/**

- **Independent Roman Catholic** comprehensive, founded 1963
- **Suburban** 65-acre campus with easy access to New York City
- **Endowment** $42.7 million
- **Coed** 4,203 undergraduate students, 81% full-time, 62% women, 38% men
- **Moderately difficult** entrance level, 62% of applicants were admitted

Undergraduates 3,406 full-time, 797 part-time. Students come from 31 states and territories, 41 other countries, 68% are from out of state, 5% African American, 2% Asian American or Pacific Islander, 6% Hispanic American, 0.2% Native American, 1% international, 5% transferred in, 68% live on campus. *Retention:* 80% of 2006 full-time freshmen returned.

Freshmen *Admission:* 6,219 applied, 3,885 admitted, 931 enrolled. *Average high school GPA:* 3.3. *Test scores:* SAT critical reading scores over 500: 68%; SAT math scores over 500: 78%; SAT critical reading scores over 600: 15%; SAT math scores over 600: 19%; SAT critical reading scores over 700: 1%; SAT math scores over 700: 1%.

Faculty *Total:* 497, 38% full-time, 48% with terminal degrees. *Student/faculty ratio:* 13:1.

Majors Athletic training; biochemistry; biological and physical sciences; biology teacher education; business/managerial economics; Celtic languages; chemistry teacher education; cinematography and film/video production; criminal justice/law enforcement administration; data processing and data processing technology; dramatic/theater arts; education; elementary education; English/language arts teacher education; environmental biology; European studies; film/cinema studies; history teacher education; information technology; international business/trade/commerce; international relations and affairs; journalism; kindergarten/preschool education; kinesiology and exercise science; liberal arts and sciences/liberal studies; marketing/marketing management; mathematics and computer science; mathematics teacher education; middle school education; modern languages; molecular biochemistry; music; nursing (registered nurse training); occupational therapy; physical therapy; pre-dentistry studies; pre-medical studies; pre-veterinary studies; radio and television; radio, television, and digital communication related; science teacher education; secondary education; social science teacher education; social work; sport and fitness administration/management.

Academics *Calendar:* semesters. *Degrees:* certificates, associate, bachelor's, master's, doctoral, post-master's, and postbachelor's certificates (also offers part-time program with significant enrollment not reflected in profile). *Special study options:* academic remediation for entering students, accelerated degree program, adult/continuing education programs, advanced placement credit, cooperative education, distance learning, double majors, English as a second language, honors programs, independent study, internships, off-campus study, part-time degree program, services for LD students, student-designed majors, study abroad, summer session for credit. *ROTC:* Army (b). *Unusual degree programs:* 3-2 business administration; physical therapy, occupational therapy.

Computers on Campus 330 computers/terminals are available on campus for general student use. Students can access the following: online (class) registration, intranet. Campuswide network is available.

Student Life *Housing options:* coed, disabled students. Campus housing is university owned and leased by the school. Freshman campus housing is guaranteed. *Activities and organizations:* drama/theater group, student-run newspaper, radio station, choral group, marching band, Student Government Association, marching/pep band, Campus Ministry, Multicultural/International Club. *Campus security:* 24-hour emergency response devices and patrols, late-night transport/escort service, controlled dormitory access, campus housing has sprinklers and fire alarms. *Student services:* health clinic, personal/psychological counseling, women's center.

Athletics Member NCAA. All Division I except football (Division I-AA). *Intercollegiate sports:* baseball M (s), basketball M (s)/W (s), bowling M/W (s), cheerleading W, crew W (s), cross-country running M (s)/W (s), equestrian sports W (s), fencing M/W (s), field hockey W (s), golf M (s)/W (s), ice hockey M (s)/W, lacrosse M (s)/W (s), soccer M (s)/W (s), softball W (s), swimming and diving W (s), tennis M (s)/W (s), track and field M (s)/W (s), volleyball M (s)/W (s), wrestling M (s). *Intramural sports:* basketball M/W, bowling M/W, football M/W, golf M/W, gymnastics W, ice hockey M (c), rock climbing M (c)/W (c), skiing (downhill) M (c)/W (c), soccer M/W, softball M/W, table tennis M/W, tennis M/W, ultimate Frisbee M/W, volleyball M/W, weight lifting M/W.

Standardized Tests *Required:* SAT or ACT (for admission).

Costs (2007–08) *Comprehensive fee:* $38,496 includes full-time tuition ($26,950), mandatory fees ($200), and room and board ($11,346). Full-time tuition and fees vary according to program. Part-time tuition: $425 per credit. Part-time tuition and fees vary according to program. *Required fees:* $76 per term part-time. *College room only:* $8136. Room and board charges vary according to board plan and housing facility. *Payment plan:* installment. *Waivers:* employees or children of employees.

Financial Aid Of all full-time matriculated undergraduates who enrolled in 2007, 2,868 applied for aid, 2,303 were judged to have need, 767 had their need fully met. 514 Federal Work-Study jobs (averaging $1413). 442 state and other part-time jobs (averaging $1248). In 2007, 684 non-need-based awards were made. *Average percent of need met:* 71%. *Average financial aid package:* $16,996. *Average need-based loan:* $7027. *Average need-based gift aid:* $10,731. *Average non-need-based aid:* $10,216. *Average indebtedness upon graduation:* $25,505.

Applying *Options:* electronic application, early admission, early decision, deferred entrance. *Application fee:* $50. *Required:* essay or personal statement, high school transcript, minimum 3.0 GPA, 1 letter of recommendation. *Required for some:* interview. *Recommended:* minimum 3.2 GPA. *Early decision deadline:* 11/15. *Notification:* continuous (freshmen), continuous (transfers), 12/15 (early decision).

Freshman Application Contact Ms. Karen N. Guastelle, Dean of Undergraduate Admissions, Sacred Heart University, 5151 Park Avenue, Fairfield, CT 06825-1000. *Phone:* 203-371-7880. *Fax:* 203-365-7607. *E-mail:* enroll@sacredheart.edu.

See page 550 for the College Close-Up.

SAINT JOSEPH COLLEGE

West Hartford, Connecticut **www.sjc.edu/**

- **Independent Roman Catholic** comprehensive, founded 1932
- **Suburban** 84-acre campus with easy access to Hartford
- **Endowment** $20.1 million
- **Undergraduate: women only; graduate: coed** 995 undergraduate students, 74% full-time, 98% women, 2% men
- 83% of applicants were admitted

Saint Joseph College provides outstanding academic, professional, and leadership opportunities for women. More than thirty programs are accompanied by internships locally and abroad. Success in every program springs from the liberal arts and sciences curriculum and active mentoring by faculty members, advisers, and alumnae. This mentoring guides students directly into postgraduate professional, civic, and academic communities. Students serve on every College committee; like the founding Sisters of Mercy, they perform community service around the world.

Undergraduates 739 full-time, 256 part-time. Students come from 13 states and territories, 8% are from out of state, 12% African American, 3% Asian American or Pacific Islander, 9% Hispanic American, 0.2% Native American, 0.4% international, 10% transferred in. *Retention:* 79% of 2006 full-time freshmen returned.

Freshmen *Admission:* 1,740 applied, 1,446 admitted, 167 enrolled. *Average high school GPA:* 3.1. *Test scores:* SAT critical reading scores over 500: 44%; SAT math scores over 500: 38%; SAT critical reading scores over 600: 8%; SAT math scores over 600: 7%; SAT critical reading scores over 700: 1%; SAT math scores over 700: 1%.

Faculty *Total:* 223, 40% full-time. *Student/faculty ratio:* 10:1.

Majors Accounting; American studies; art history, criticism and conservation; biochemistry; biology/biological sciences; business administration and management; chemistry; child development; early childhood education; economics; elementary education; English; environmental science; family and consumer economics related; family and consumer sciences/human sciences; history; international/global studies; kindergarten/preschool education; liberal arts and sciences/liberal studies; mathematics; nursing (registered nurse training); nutrition sciences; philosophy; psychology; religious studies; secondary education; social work; sociology; Spanish; special education; women's studies.

Academics *Calendar:* semesters. *Degrees:* certificates, bachelor's, master's, post-master's, and postbachelor's certificates. *Special study options:* accelerated degree program, adult/continuing education programs, advanced placement credit, distance learning, double majors, English as a second language, honors programs, independent study, internships, off-campus study, part-time degree program, services for LD students, student-designed majors, study abroad, summer session for credit.

Computers on Campus Students can access the following: campus intranet, computer help desk, free student e-mail accounts, online (class) grades, online (class) registration, online (class) schedules. Campuswide network is available. 100% of college-owned or -operated housing units are wired for high-speed Internet access.

Student Life *Housing options:* women-only, disabled students. Campus housing is university owned. Freshman campus housing is guaranteed. *Activities and organizations:* drama/theater group, choral group, Student Government Association, Student Nurse Association, Psychology Club, SJC choir, Business Society. *Campus security:* 24-hour emergency response devices and patrols, late-night transport/escort service, controlled dormitory access. *Student services:* health clinic, personal/psychological counseling.

Athletics Member NCAA. All Division III. *Intercollegiate sports:* basketball W, cross-country running W, lacrosse W, soccer W, softball W, swimming and diving W, tennis W, volleyball W. *Intramural sports:* badminton W, basketball W, lacrosse W, soccer W, softball W, tennis W, volleyball W, water polo W.

Standardized Tests *Required:* SAT or ACT (for admission). *Recommended:* SAT (for admission).

Costs (2007–08) *Comprehensive fee:* $36,570 includes full-time tuition ($24,040), mandatory fees ($650), and room and board ($11,880). Full-time tuition and fees vary according to program and student level. Part-time tuition: $540 per credit. *Required fees:* $25 per credit part-time. *College room only:* $5474. Room and board charges vary according to board plan. *Payment plan:* installment. *Waivers:* employees or children of employees.

Financial Aid Of all full-time matriculated undergraduates who enrolled in 2006, 714 applied for aid, 686 were judged to have need. In 2006, 50 non-need-based awards were made. *Average percent of need met:* 68%. *Average financial aid package:* $15,936. *Average need-based loan:* $4228. *Average need-based gift aid:* $11,578. *Average non-need-based aid:* $7626. *Average indebtedness upon graduation:* $23,550.

Applying *Options:* electronic application, early admission, early action, deferred entrance. *Application fee:* $50. *Required:* high school transcript. *Recommended:* essay or personal statement, letters of recommendation, interview. *Application deadlines:* rolling (freshmen), rolling (transfers). *Notification:* continuous (freshmen), continuous (transfers).

Freshman Application Contact Office of Admissions, Saint Joseph College, 1678 Asylum Avenue, West Hartford, CT 06117. *Phone:* 866-442-8752. *Toll-free phone:* 866-442-8752. *Fax:* 860-231-5744. *E-mail:* admissions@sjc.edu.

See page 552 for the College Close-Up.

SOUTHERN CONNECTICUT STATE UNIVERSITY

New Haven, Connecticut **www.southernct.edu/**

- **State-supported** comprehensive, founded 1893, part of Connecticut State University System
- **Urban** 168-acre campus with easy access to New York City
- **Endowment** $6.9 million
- **Coed** 8,515 undergraduate students, 84% full-time, 62% women, 38% men
- **Moderately difficult** entrance level, 52% of applicants were admitted

Undergraduates 7,114 full-time, 1,401 part-time. Students come from 32 states and territories, 25 other countries, 6% are from out of state, 12% African American, 2% Asian American or Pacific Islander, 7% Hispanic American, 0.2% Native American, 0.7% international, 10% transferred in, 32% live on campus. *Retention:* 72% of 2006 full-time freshmen returned.

COLLEGE DATA CENTER • CONNECTICUT

Freshmen *Admission:* 6,178 applied, 3,201 admitted, 1,349 enrolled. *Test scores:* SAT critical reading scores over 500: 34%; SAT math scores over 500: 34%; SAT writing scores over 500: 39%; SAT critical reading scores over 600: 6%; SAT math scores over 600: 6%; SAT writing scores over 600: 5%.

Faculty *Total:* 1,053, 42% full-time. *Student/faculty ratio:* 15:1.

Majors Accounting; anthropology; art history, criticism and conservation; art teacher education; biology/biological sciences; business administration and management; business/managerial economics; chemistry; communication/speech communication and rhetoric; computer science; dramatic/theater arts; early childhood education; economics; elementary education; English; finance; fine/studio arts; French; geography; geology/earth science; German; history; Italian; journalism; liberal arts and sciences/liberal studies; library science; marketing/marketing management; mathematics; music; nursing (registered nurse training); parks, recreation and leisure; philosophy; physics; political science and government; psychology; public health; secondary education; social work; sociology; Spanish; special education.

Academics *Calendar:* semesters. *Degrees:* bachelor's, master's, doctoral, and post-master's certificates. *Special study options:* academic remediation for entering students, accelerated degree program, adult/continuing education programs, advanced placement credit, cooperative education, distance learning, double majors, freshman honors college, honors programs, independent study, internships, off-campus study, part-time degree program, services for LD students, student-designed majors, study abroad, summer session for credit. *ROTC:* Army (c), Air Force (c).

Computers on Campus 800 computers/terminals are available on campus for general student use. Students can access the following: computer help desk, free student e-mail accounts, online (class) grades, online (class) registration, online (class) schedules. Campuswide network is available. 100% of college-owned or -operated housing units are wired for high-speed Internet access. Wireless service is available via classrooms, computer centers, computer labs, learning centers, libraries, student centers.

Student Life *Housing options:* coed, disabled students. Campus housing is university owned. Freshman campus housing is guaranteed. *Activities and organizations:* drama/theater group, student-run newspaper, radio and television station, choral group, marching band, People to People, Pre-Law Society, Accounting Society, Crescent Players, Black Student Union, national fraternities, national sororities. *Campus security:* 24-hour emergency response devices and patrols, late-night transport/escort service, controlled dormitory access. *Student services:* health clinic, personal/psychological counseling, women's center.

Athletics Member NCAA. All Division II. *Intercollegiate sports:* baseball M (s), basketball M (s)/W (s), cheerleading M (c)/W (c), cross-country running M (s)/W (s), field hockey W (s), football M (s), gymnastics W (s), lacrosse W (s), rugby M (c)/W (c), soccer M (s)/W (s), softball W (s), swimming and diving M (s)/W (s), track and field M (s)/W (s), ultimate Frisbee M (c)/W (c), volleyball W (s). *Intramural sports:* badminton M/W, basketball M/W, football M/W, ice hockey M (c)/W (c), soccer M/W, softball M/W, tennis M/W, volleyball M/W.

Standardized Tests *Required:* SAT or ACT (for admission).

Costs (2008–09) *Tuition:* state resident $3514 full-time, $357 per credit part-time; nonresident $11,373 full-time, $357 per credit part-time. *Required fees:* $3665 full-time, $55 per term part-time. *Room and board:* $8966; room only: $4976.

Financial Aid Of all full-time matriculated undergraduates who enrolled in 2006, 5,745 applied for aid, 3,490 were judged to have need, 1,339 had their need fully met. 139 Federal Work-Study jobs (averaging $3086). 3 state and other part-time jobs (averaging $2589). In 2006, 291 non-need-based awards were made. *Average percent of need met:* 82%. *Average financial aid package:* $6986. *Average need-based loan:* $3429. *Average need-based gift aid:* $5085. *Average non-need-based aid:* $2903. *Average indebtedness upon graduation:* $15,197. *Financial aid deadline:* 3/9.

Applying *Options:* electronic application, deferred entrance. *Application fee:* $50. *Required:* essay or personal statement, high school transcript. *Recommended:* letters of recommendation. *Application deadlines:* 4/1 (freshmen), 7/15 (transfers). *Notification:* continuous (freshmen), continuous (transfers).

Freshman Application Contact Ms. Paula Kennedy, Associate Director of Admissions, Southern Connecticut State University, Admissions House, 131 Farnham Avenue, New Haven, CT 06515-1202. *Phone:* 203-392-5651. *Fax:* 203-392-5727.

See page 554 for the College Close-Up.

TRINITY COLLEGE

Hartford, Connecticut **www.trincoll.edu/**

- **Independent** comprehensive, founded 1823
- **Urban** 100-acre campus
- **Endowment** $460.3 million
- **Coed** 2,375 undergraduate students, 93% full-time, 50% women, 50% men
- **Most difficult** entrance level, 34% of applicants were admitted

Undergraduates 2,209 full-time, 166 part-time. Students come from 44 states and territories, 31 other countries, 82% are from out of state, 7% African American, 5% Asian American or Pacific Islander, 6% Hispanic American, 0.2% Native American, 4% international, 1% transferred in, 95% live on campus. *Retention:* 90% of 2006 full-time freshmen returned.

Freshmen *Admission:* 5,950 applied, 2,037 admitted, 576 enrolled. *Test scores:* SAT critical reading scores over 500: 98%; SAT math scores over 500: 98%; SAT writing scores over 500: 97%; ACT scores over 18: 100%; SAT critical reading scores over 600: 76%; SAT math scores over 600: 79%; SAT writing scores over 600: 79%; ACT scores over 24: 94%; SAT critical reading scores over 700: 24%; SAT math scores over 700: 19%; SAT writing scores over 700: 33%; ACT scores over 30: 19%.

Faculty *Total:* 255, 68% full-time, 82% with terminal degrees. *Student/faculty ratio:* 10:1.

Majors American studies; anthropology; art; art history, criticism and conservation; biochemistry; biology/biological sciences; biomedical/medical engineering; chemistry; Chinese; classics and languages, literatures and linguistics; comparative literature; computer engineering; computer science; creative writing; dance; dramatic/theater arts; economics; education; electrical, electronics and communications engineering; engineering; English; environmental science; fine/studio arts; French; gay/lesbian studies; German; history; interdisciplinary studies; international relations and affairs; Italian; Japanese; Jewish/Judaic studies; mathematics; mechanical engineering; modern languages; music; neuroscience; philosophy; physics; political science and government; psychology; public policy analysis; religious studies; Russian; sociology; Spanish; women's studies.

Academics *Calendar:* semesters. *Degrees:* bachelor's and master's. *Special study options:* accelerated degree program, adult/continuing education programs, advanced placement credit, double majors, honors programs, independent study, internships, off-campus study, student-designed majors, study abroad, summer session for credit. *ROTC:* Army (c). *Unusual degree programs:* 3-2 engineering with with Rensselaer at Hartford.

Computers on Campus 249 computers/terminals and 3,000 ports are available on campus for general student use. Students can access the following: campus intranet, computer help desk, free student e-mail accounts, online (class) grades, online (class) registration, online (class) schedules, Web pages. Campuswide network is available. 100% of college-owned or -operated housing units are wired for high-speed Internet access. Wireless service is available via classrooms, computer centers, computer labs, learning centers, libraries, student centers.

Student Life *Housing:* on-campus residence required for freshman year. *Options:* coed, disabled students. Campus housing is university owned. Freshman campus housing is guaranteed. *Activities and organizations:* drama/theater group, student-run newspaper, radio station, choral group, Community Outreach, Habitat for Humanity, Activities Council, student government, Multi-Cultural Affairs Committee, national fraternities, national sororities. *Campus security:* 24-hour emergency response devices and patrols, late-night transport/escort service, controlled dormitory access. *Student services:* health clinic, personal/psychological counseling, women's center.

Athletics Member NCAA. All Division III. *Intercollegiate sports:* baseball M, basketball M/W, crew M/W, cross-country running M/W, equestrian sports M (c)/W (c), fencing M (c)/W (c), field hockey W, football M, golf M, ice hockey M/W, lacrosse M/W, riflery M (c)/W (c), rugby M (c)/W (c), sailing M (c)/W (c), skiing (downhill) M (c)/W (c), soccer M/W, softball W, squash M/W, swimming and diving M/W, tennis M/W, track and field M/W, ultimate Frisbee M (c)/W (c), volleyball M (c)/W, water polo M (c)/W (c), wrestling M. *Intramural sports:* badminton M/W, basketball M/W, football M/W, soccer M/W, softball M/W, squash M/W, swimming and diving M/W, tennis M/W, weight lifting M/W.

Standardized Tests *Required:* ACT or SAT and SAT Writing Test or three SAT subject tests (for admission).

Costs (2007–08) *Comprehensive fee:* $46,290 includes full-time tuition ($35,110), mandatory fees ($1760), and room and board ($9420). Full-time tuition and fees vary according to program. Part-time tuition: $1300 per credit hour. Part-time tuition and fees vary according to program. *College room only:* $6090. Room and board charges vary according to board plan. *Payment plan:* installment. *Waivers:* adult students and employees or children of employees.

Financial Aid Of all full-time matriculated undergraduates who enrolled in 2005, 1,068 applied for aid, 912 were judged to have need, 912 had their need fully met. 694 Federal Work-Study jobs (averaging $1520). In 2005, 10 non-need-based awards were made. *Average percent of need met:* 100%. *Average financial aid package:* $25,590. *Average need-based loan:* $4250. *Average need-based gift aid:* $23,183. *Average non-need-based aid:* $27,442. *Average indebtedness upon graduation:* $18,122. *Financial aid deadline:* 3/1.

Applying *Options:* electronic application, early admission, early decision, deferred entrance. *Application fee:* $60. *Required:* essay or personal statement, high school transcript, 3 letters of recommendation. *Recommended:* interview. *Application deadlines:* 1/1 (freshmen), 4/1 (transfers). *Early decision deadline:* 11/15 (for plan 1), 1/1 (for plan 2). *Notification:* 4/1 (freshmen), 6/10 (transfers), 12/15 (early decision plan 1), 2/15 (early decision plan 2).

Director of Admissions Mr. Larry Dow, Dean of Admissions and Financial Aid, Trinity College, 300 Summit Street, Hartford, CT 06106-3100. *Phone:* 860-297-2180. *Fax:* 860-297-2287. *E-mail:* admissions.office@trincoll.edu.

See page 556 for the College Close-Up.

UNITED STATES COAST GUARD ACADEMY

New London, Connecticut **www.uscga.edu/**

- **Federally supported** 4-year, founded 1876
- **Suburban** 110-acre campus with easy access to Providence and Hartford
- **Coed** 963 undergraduate students, 100% full-time, 27% women, 73% men
- **Very difficult** entrance level, 27% of applicants were admitted

Undergraduates 963 full-time. Students come from 51 states and territories, 13 other countries, 94% are from out of state, 3% African American, 4% Asian American or Pacific Islander, 6% Hispanic American, 0.4% Native American, 1% international, 100% live on campus. *Retention:* 88% of 2006 full-time freshmen returned.

Freshmen *Admission:* 1,475 applied, 391 admitted, 252 enrolled. *Average high school GPA:* 3.76. *Test scores:* SAT critical reading scores over 500: 96%; SAT math scores over 500: 100%; ACT scores over 18: 99%; SAT critical reading scores over 600: 58%; SAT math scores over 600: 80%; ACT scores over 24: 92%; SAT critical reading scores over 700: 15%; SAT math scores over 700: 17%; ACT scores over 30: 38%.

Faculty *Total:* 125, 84% full-time, 62% with terminal degrees. *Student/faculty ratio:* 9:1.

Majors Civil engineering; electrical, electronics and communications engineering; management science; mechanical engineering; naval architecture and marine engineering; oceanography (chemical and physical); operations research; political science and government.

Academics *Calendar:* semesters. *Degree:* bachelor's. *Special study options:* academic remediation for entering students, double majors, honors programs, independent study, internships, off-campus study, summer session for credit.

Computers on Campus 325 computers/terminals are available on campus for general student use. Students can access the following: campus intranet, computer help desk, free student e-mail accounts, online (class) grades, online (class) registration, online (class) schedules. Campuswide network is available. 100% of college-owned or -operated housing units are wired for high-speed Internet access.

Student Life *Housing:* on-campus residence required through senior year. *Options:* coed. Campus housing is university owned. Freshman campus housing is guaranteed. *Activities and organizations:* drama/theater group, choral group, marching band. *Campus security:* 24-hour patrols, student patrols. *Student services:* health clinic, personal/psychological counseling, legal services.

Athletics Member NCAA. All Division III. *Intercollegiate sports:* baseball M, basketball M/W, bowling M (c)/W (c), crew M/W, cross-country running M/W, football M, golf M (c)/W (c), ice hockey M (c), lacrosse M (c)/W (c), riflery M/W, rugby M (c)/W (c), sailing M/W, soccer M/W, softball W, swimming and diving M/W, tennis M/W (c), track and field M/W, volleyball W, water polo M (c), wrestling M. *Intramural sports:* basketball M/W, bowling M/W, football M, golf M/W, racquetball M/W, sailing M/W, skiing (downhill) M (c)/W (c), soccer M/W, softball M/W, swimming and diving M/W, table tennis M/W, track and field M/W, ultimate Frisbee M/W, volleyball M/W, water polo M, wrestling M.

Standardized Tests *Required:* SAT or ACT (for admission).

Costs (2008–09) *Tuition:* tuition, room and board, and medical and dental care are provided by the U.S. government. Each cadet receives a salary from which to pay for uniforms, supplies, and personal expenses. Entering freshmen are required to deposit $3000 to defray the initial cost of computer, uniforms, books and other items.

Applying *Options:* electronic application, early action. *Required:* essay or personal statement, high school transcript, 3 letters of recommendation, medical exam, physical fitness exam. *Recommended:* interview. *Application deadlines:* 2/1 (freshmen), 11/1 (early action). *Notification:* continuous until 5/1 (freshmen), 12/15 (early action).

Freshman Application Contact Capt. Susan Bibeau, Director of Admissions, United States Coast Guard Academy, 31 Mohegan Avenue, New London, CT 06320-4195. *Phone:* 860-444-8500. *Toll-free phone:* 800-883-8724. *Fax:* 860-701-6700. *E-mail:* admissions@uscga.edu.

UNIVERSITY OF BRIDGEPORT

Bridgeport, Connecticut **www.bridgeport.edu/**

- **Independent** comprehensive, founded 1927
- **Urban** 86-acre campus with easy access to New York City
- **Endowment** $6.7 million
- **Coed** 1,791 undergraduate students, 68% full-time, 68% women, 32% men
- **Moderately difficult** entrance level, 57% of applicants were admitted

Undergraduates 1,225 full-time, 566 part-time. Students come from 39 states and territories, 58 other countries, 34% are from out of state, 33% African American, 3% Asian American or Pacific Islander, 13% Hispanic American, 0.3% Native American, 14% international, 9% transferred in, 45% live on campus. *Retention:* 51% of 2006 full-time freshmen returned.

Freshmen *Admission:* 4,311 applied, 2,454 admitted, 335 enrolled. *Average high school GPA:* 2.74. *Test scores:* SAT critical reading scores over 500: 23%; SAT math scores over 500: 24%; SAT writing scores over 500: 18%; ACT scores over 18: 72%; SAT critical reading scores over 600: 5%; SAT math scores over 600: 5%; SAT writing scores over 600: 3%; ACT scores over 24: 15%; SAT critical reading scores over 700: 1%; SAT math scores over 700: 1%; SAT writing scores over 700: 1%; ACT scores over 30: 4%.

Faculty *Total:* 436, 26% full-time. *Student/faculty ratio:* 12:1.

Majors Accounting; biology/biological sciences; business administration and management; computer engineering; computer science; dental hygiene; English; fashion merchandising; finance; graphic design; health and physical education related; humanities; human services; illustration; industrial design; information science/studies; interdisciplinary studies; interior design; international business/trade/commerce; international relations and affairs; journalism; liberal arts and sciences/liberal studies; marketing/marketing management; mass communication/media; mathematics; music; pre-dentistry studies; pre-law studies; pre-medical studies; pre-veterinary studies; psychology; religious studies; social sciences.

Academics *Calendar:* semesters. *Degrees:* associate, bachelor's, master's, doctoral, first professional, and post-master's certificates. *Special study options:* academic remediation for entering students, accelerated degree program, adult/continuing education programs, advanced placement credit, cooperative education, distance learning, double majors, English as a second language, honors programs, independent study, internships, off-campus study, part-time degree program, services for LD students, student-designed majors, summer session for credit. *ROTC:* Army (b).

Computers on Campus 500 computers/terminals are available on campus for general student use. Students can access the following: computer help desk, free student e-mail accounts, online (class) grades, online (class) registration, online (class) schedules. Campuswide network is available. 100% of college-owned or -operated housing units are wired for high-speed Internet access. Wireless service is available via classrooms, computer centers, computer labs, dorm rooms, learning centers, libraries, student centers.

Student Life *Housing:* on-campus residence required through sophomore year. *Options:* coed. Campus housing is university owned. Freshman campus housing is guaranteed. *Activities and organizations:* student-run newspaper, radio station, choral group, Student Congress, International Relations Club, Black Students Alliance, Scuba Club, Japanese Student Association, national fraternities, national sororities. *Campus security:* 24-hour emergency response devices and patrols, student patrols, late-night transport/escort service. *Student services:* health clinic, personal/psychological counseling, women's center.

Athletics Member NCAA. All Division II. *Intercollegiate sports:* baseball M (s), basketball M (s)/W (s), cross-country running M/W, gymnastics W (s), soccer M (s)/W (s), softball W (s), swimming and diving W (s), volleyball W (s). *Intramural sports:* basketball M/W, football M/W, golf M/W, racquetball M/W, soccer M/W, softball M/W, tennis M/W.

Standardized Tests *Required:* SAT or ACT (for admission). *Required for some:* SAT Subject Tests (for admission).

Costs (2007–08) *Comprehensive fee:* $32,860 includes full-time tuition ($21,150), mandatory fees ($1710), and room and board ($10,000). Full-time tuition and fees vary according to program. Part-time tuition: $705 per credit.

Part-time tuition and fees vary according to program. *Required fees:* $70 per term part-time. *College room only:* $5200. Room and board charges vary according to board plan and student level. *Payment plans:* installment, deferred payment. *Waivers:* senior citizens and employees or children of employees.

Financial Aid Of all full-time matriculated undergraduates who enrolled in 2006, 913 applied for aid, 901 were judged to have need, 79 had their need fully met. 182 Federal Work-Study jobs (averaging $2000). In 2006, 27 non-need-based awards were made. *Average percent of need met:* 52%. *Average financial aid package:* $19,830. *Average need-based loan:* $5077. *Average need-based gift aid:* $7574. *Average non-need-based aid:* $13,748.

Applying *Options:* electronic application, early admission, early action, deferred entrance. *Application fee:* $25. *Required:* essay or personal statement, high school transcript, minimum 2.0 GPA. *Required for some:* interview, portfolio, audition. *Recommended:* 1 letter of recommendation, interview. *Application deadlines:* rolling (freshmen), rolling (transfers), 1/1 (early action). *Notification:* continuous until 8/1 (freshmen), 1/15 (early action).

Freshman Application Contact University of Bridgeport, 126 Park Avenue, Bridgeport, CT 06604. *Phone:* 203-576-4552. *Toll-free phone:* 800-EXCEL-UB (in-state); 800-243-9496 (out-of-state). *Fax:* 203-576-4941. *E-mail:* admit@bridgeport.edu.

UNIVERSITY OF CONNECTICUT

Storrs, Connecticut **www.uconn.edu/**

- **State-supported** university, founded 1881
- **Rural** 4104-acre campus
- **Endowment** $336.0 million
- **Coed** 16,348 undergraduate students, 96% full-time, 51% women, 49% men
- **Moderately difficult** entrance level, 49% of applicants were admitted

Undergraduates 15,615 full-time, 733 part-time. Students come from 46 states and territories, 62 other countries, 23% are from out of state, 5% African American, 7% Asian American or Pacific Islander, 5% Hispanic American, 0.4% Native American, 1% international, 4% transferred in, 68% live on campus. *Retention:* 93% of 2006 full-time freshmen returned.

Freshmen *Admission:* 21,105 applied, 10,429 admitted, 3,179 enrolled. *Test scores:* SAT critical reading scores over 500: 89%; SAT math scores over 500: 93%; SAT writing scores over 500: 90%; ACT scores over 18: 98%; SAT critical reading scores over 600: 44%; SAT math scores over 600: 56%; SAT writing scores over 600: 47%; ACT scores over 24: 74%; SAT critical reading scores over 700: 7%; SAT math scores over 700: 11%; SAT writing scores over 700: 8%; ACT scores over 30: 13%.

Faculty *Total:* 1,340, 75% full-time, 76% with terminal degrees. *Student/faculty ratio:* 17:1.

Majors Accounting; acting; actuarial science; agricultural economics; agricultural teacher education; agriculture; agronomy and crop science; allied health diagnostic, intervention, and treatment professions related; American studies; animal/livestock husbandry and production; animal physiology; animal sciences; anthropology; applied horticulture; applied mathematics; art history, criticism and conservation; biology/biological sciences; biomedical/medical engineering; biophysics; business/commerce; cell biology and anatomical sciences related; chemical engineering; chemistry; civil engineering; classics and languages, literatures and linguistics; clinical laboratory science/medical technology; cognitive science; communication/speech communication and rhetoric; computer engineering; computer science; cytotechnology; dietetics; dramatic/theater arts; dramatic/theater arts and stagecraft related; ecology; economics; electrical, electronics and communications engineering; elementary education; engineering physics; engineering related; English; environmental/environmental health engineering; environmental studies; finance; fine/studio arts; French; general studies; geography; geology/earth science; German; health/health care administration; history; horticultural science; human development and family studies; industrial engineering; insurance; Italian; journalism; landscape architecture; Latin American studies; linguistics; management information systems; management science; manufacturing engineering; marine biology and biological oceanography; marketing/marketing management; materials engineering; mathematics; mechanical engineering; multi-/interdisciplinary studies related; music; music teacher education; natural resources/conservation; nursing (registered nurse training); nutrition sciences; parks, recreation and leisure facilities management; pathology/experimental pathology; pharmacy; pharmacy, pharmaceutical sciences, and administration related; philosophy; physical education teaching and coaching; physical therapy; physics; political science and government; pre-pharmacy studies; psychology; real estate; sociology; Spanish; special education; statistics; structural biology; theater design and technology; theater literature, history and criticism; urban studies/affairs; women's studies.

Academics *Calendar:* semesters. *Degrees:* associate, bachelor's, master's, doctoral, first professional, post-master's, and postbachelor's certificates. *Special study options:* academic remediation for entering students, accelerated degree program, adult/continuing education programs, advanced placement credit, cooperative education, distance learning, double majors, English as a second language, honors programs, independent study, internships, off-campus study, part-time degree program, services for LD students, student-designed majors, study abroad, summer session for credit. *ROTC:* Army (b), Air Force (b). *Unusual degree programs:* 3-2 education, pharmacy.

Computers on Campus 1,318 computers/terminals are available on campus for general student use. Students can access the following: computer help desk, free student e-mail accounts, online (class) grades, online (class) registration, online (class) schedules. Campuswide network is available. 100% of college-owned or -operated housing units are wired for high-speed Internet access. Wireless service is available via classrooms, computer centers, computer labs, dorm rooms, learning centers, libraries, student centers.

Student Life *Housing options:* coed, men-only, women-only, disabled students. Campus housing is university owned and is provided by a third party. Freshman campus housing is guaranteed. *Activities and organizations:* drama/theater group, student-run newspaper, radio and television station, choral group, marching band, national fraternities, national sororities. *Campus security:* 24-hour emergency response devices, late-night transport/escort service. *Student services:* health clinic, personal/psychological counseling, women's center.

Athletics Member NCAA. All Division I except football (Division I-A). *Intercollegiate sports:* baseball M (s), basketball M (s)/W (s), crew W, cross-country running M (s)/W (s), field hockey W (s), golf M (s), ice hockey M (s)/W (s), lacrosse W, soccer M (s)/W (s), softball W (s), swimming and diving M (s)/W (s), tennis M (s)/W (s), track and field M (s)/W (s), volleyball W (s). *Intramural sports:* badminton M/W, baseball M, basketball M/W, bowling M (c)/W (c), crew M (c), cross-country running M/W, equestrian sports M (c)/W (c), fencing M (c)/W (c), football M, gymnastics W (c), ice hockey M (c)/W (c), lacrosse M (c)/W (c), racquetball M/W, rugby M (c)/W (c), sailing M (c)/W (c), skiing (downhill) M (c)/W (c), soccer M/W, softball M/W, squash M/W, swimming and diving M/W, table tennis M/W, tennis M/W, track and field M/W, volleyball M/W, water polo W, weight lifting M (c), wrestling M (c).

Standardized Tests *Required:* SAT or ACT (for admission).

Costs (2008–09) *Tuition:* state resident $7200 full-time, $300 per credit part-time; nonresident $21,912 full-time, $913 per credit part-time. *Required fees:* $2138 full-time. *Room and board:* $9300; room only: $4210.

Financial Aid Of all full-time matriculated undergraduates who enrolled in 2007, 10,518 applied for aid, 7,654 were judged to have need, 1,258 had their need fully met. 1,937 Federal Work-Study jobs (averaging $2005). 5,502 state and other part-time jobs (averaging $2010). In 2007, 1092 non-need-based awards were made. *Average percent of need met:* 68%. *Average financial aid package:* $10,530. *Average need-based loan:* $4367. *Average need-based gift aid:* $6134. *Average non-need-based aid:* $5664. *Average indebtedness upon graduation:* $20,658.

Applying *Options:* electronic application, early action, deferred entrance. *Application fee:* $70. *Required:* essay or personal statement, high school transcript. *Recommended:* 1 letter of recommendation. *Application deadlines:* 2/1 (freshmen), 4/1 (transfers), 12/1 (early action). *Notification:* continuous until 1/1 (freshmen), continuous until 7/1 (transfers), 2/1 (early action).

Freshman Application Contact Mr. Brian Usher, Associate Director of Admissions, University of Connecticut, 2131 Hillside Road, Unit 3088, Storrs, CT 06269-3088. *Phone:* 860-486-3137. *Fax:* 860-486-1476. *E-mail:* beahusky@uconnvm.uconn.edu.

See page 558 for the College Close-Up.

UNIVERSITY OF HARTFORD

West Hartford, Connecticut **www.hartford.edu/**

- **Independent** comprehensive, founded 1877
- **Suburban** 320-acre campus with easy access to Hartford
- **Endowment** $109.3 million
- **Coed** 5,637 undergraduate students, 85% full-time, 52% women, 48% men
- **Moderately difficult** entrance level, 54% of applicants were admitted

Undergraduates 4,796 full-time, 841 part-time. Students come from 49 states and territories, 47 other countries, 60% are from out of state, 11% African American, 3% Asian American or Pacific Islander, 6% Hispanic American, 0.2% Native American, 4% international, 4% transferred in, 64% live on campus. *Retention:* 69% of 2006 full-time freshmen returned.

Freshmen *Admission:* 11,698 applied, 6,317 admitted, 1,476 enrolled. *Test scores:* SAT critical reading scores over 500: 64%; SAT math scores over 500:

68%; ACT scores over 18: 94%; SAT critical reading scores over 600: 18%; SAT math scores over 600: 21%; ACT scores over 24: 31%; SAT critical reading scores over 700: 1%; SAT math scores over 700: 2%; ACT scores over 30: 2%.

Faculty *Total:* 793, 42% full-time. *Student/faculty ratio:* 14:1.

Majors Accounting; acting; animation, interactive technology, video graphics and special effects; architectural engineering technology; art history, criticism and conservation; arts management; audio engineering; biology/biological sciences; biomedical/medical engineering; business administration and management; business/managerial economics; ceramic arts and ceramics; chemical engineering technology; chemistry; cinematography and film/video production; civil engineering; clinical laboratory science/medical technology; communication/speech communication and rhetoric; computer and information sciences; computer engineering; computer engineering technology; criminal justice/police science; dance; design and visual communications; dramatic/theater arts; drawing; early childhood education; economics; economics related; electrical, electronic and communications engineering technology; electrical, electronics and communications engineering; elementary education; engineering; engineering technologies related; engineering technology; English; entrepreneurship; environmental/environmental health engineering; film/cinema studies; finance; fine arts related; foreign languages and literatures; general studies; health science; history; human services; insurance; interdisciplinary studies; international/global studies; jazz/jazz studies; Jewish/Judaic studies; legal studies; liberal arts and sciences/liberal studies; management information systems; marketing/marketing management; mathematics; mathematics and statistics related; mechanical engineering; mechanical engineering technologies related; medical radiologic technology; multi-/interdisciplinary studies related; music; music history, literature, and theory; music management and merchandising; music performance; music related; music teacher education; music theory and composition; nursing (registered nurse training); occupational therapy; painting; philosophy; photographic and film/video technology; photography; physical therapy; physics; political science and government; pre-dentistry studies; pre-medical studies; pre-veterinary studies; printmaking; psychology; recording arts technology; respiratory care therapy; sculpture; secondary education; sociology; special education; special education related; technical and business writing.

Academics *Calendar:* semesters. *Degrees:* certificates, diplomas, associate, bachelor's, master's, doctoral, post-master's, and postbachelor's certificates. *Special study options:* academic remediation for entering students, adult/continuing education programs, advanced placement credit, cooperative education, distance learning, double majors, English as a second language, honors programs, independent study, internships, off-campus study, part-time degree program, services for LD students, student-designed majors, study abroad, summer session for credit. *ROTC:* Army (c), Air Force (c).

Computers on Campus 400 computers/terminals are available on campus for general student use. Students can access the following: campus intranet, computer help desk, free student e-mail accounts, online (class) grades, online (class) registration, online (class) schedules, student Web pages. Campuswide network is available. 100% of college-owned or -operated housing units are wired for high-speed Internet access. Wireless service is available via classrooms, computer centers, computer labs, libraries, student centers.

Student Life *Housing options:* coed, women-only, disabled students. Campus housing is university owned and leased by the school. Freshman campus housing is guaranteed. *Activities and organizations:* drama/theater group, student-run newspaper, radio and television station, choral group, Program Council, Brothers and Sisters United, Hillel, Student Government Association, Residence Hall Association, national fraternities, national sororities. *Campus security:* 24-hour emergency response devices and patrols, late-night transport/escort service, controlled dormitory access, bicycle patrols. *Student services:* health clinic, personal/psychological counseling, women's center, legal services.

Athletics Member NCAA. All Division I. *Intercollegiate sports:* badminton M (c)/W (c), baseball M (s), basketball M (s)/W (s), cross-country running M (s)/W (s), golf M (s)/W (s), lacrosse M (s), racquetball M (c)/W (c), rugby M (c)/W (c), soccer M (s)/W (s), softball W (s), squash M (c)/W (c), tennis M (s)/W (s), track and field M/W, volleyball M (c)/W (s). *Intramural sports:* basketball M/W, football M/W, racquetball M/W, soccer M/W, softball M/W, tennis M/W, ultimate Frisbee M/W, volleyball M/W, water polo M/W.

Standardized Tests *Required:* SAT or ACT (for admission).

Costs (2008–09) *Comprehensive fee:* $39,048 includes full-time tuition ($26,942), mandatory fees ($1230), and room and board ($10,876). *College room only:* $6706.

Financial Aid Of all full-time matriculated undergraduates who enrolled in 2006, 3,487 applied for aid, 3,129 were judged to have need, 671 had their need fully met. 287 Federal Work-Study jobs (averaging $1436). 108 state and other part-time jobs (averaging $10,667). In 2006, 1290 non-need-based awards were made. *Average percent of need met:* 78%. *Average financial aid package:* $18,826. *Average need-based loan:* $3871. *Average need-based gift aid:* $14,753. *Average non-need-based aid:* $7372. *Average indebtedness upon graduation:* $34,126.

Applying *Options:* electronic application, early admission, deferred entrance. *Application fee:* $35. *Required:* high school transcript. *Recommended:* essay or personal statement, 2 letters of recommendation, interview. *Application deadlines:* rolling (freshmen), rolling (transfers). *Notification:* continuous (freshmen), continuous (transfers).

Freshman Application Contact Mr. Richard Zeiser, Dean of Admissions, University of Hartford, West Hartford, CT 06117. *Phone:* 860-768-4296. *Toll-free phone:* 800-947-4303. *Fax:* 860-768-4961. *E-mail:* admissions@hartford.edu.

See page 560 for the College Close-Up.

UNIVERSITY OF NEW HAVEN

West Haven, Connecticut **www.newhaven.edu/**

- **Independent** comprehensive, founded 1920
- **Suburban** 78-acre campus with easy access to Hartford, New Haven
- **Coed** 3,011 undergraduate students, 86% full-time, 48% women, 52% men
- **Moderately difficult** entrance level, 73% of applicants were admitted

Undergraduates 2,585 full-time, 426 part-time. Students come from 33 states and territories, 33 other countries, 40% are from out of state, 9% African American, 3% Asian American or Pacific Islander, 8% Hispanic American, 0.4% Native American, 2% international, 6% transferred in, 59% live on campus. *Retention:* 79% of 2006 full-time freshmen returned.

Freshmen *Admission:* 3,153 applied, 2,315 admitted, 710 enrolled. *Average high school GPA:* 3.1. *Test scores:* SAT critical reading scores over 500: 52%; SAT math scores over 500: 53%; SAT writing scores over 500: 50%; ACT scores over 18: 82%; SAT critical reading scores over 600: 12%; SAT math scores over 600: 16%; SAT writing scores over 600: 10%; ACT scores over 24: 32%; SAT critical reading scores over 700: 1%; SAT math scores over 700: 1%; SAT writing scores over 700: 1%; ACT scores over 30: 3%.

Faculty *Total:* 499, 36% full-time. *Student/faculty ratio:* 14:1.

Majors Accounting; applied mathematics; biology/biological sciences; biology/biotechnology laboratory technician; business administration and management; business/managerial economics; chemical engineering; chemistry; civil engineering; commercial and advertising art; communication/speech communication and rhetoric; computer and information sciences; computer engineering; computer science; criminal justice/law enforcement administration; criminal justice/police science; dental hygiene; dietetics; ecology; electrical, electronics and communications engineering; engineering; English; finance; fine/studio arts; fire protection and safety technology; fire protection related; foodservice systems administration; forensic science and technology; general studies; history; hospitality administration; hotel/motel administration; information science/studies; interior architecture; international business/trade/commerce; legal studies; liberal arts and sciences/liberal studies; marine biology and biological oceanography; marketing/marketing management; mathematics; mechanical engineering; music; music management and merchandising; occupational safety and health technology; political science and government; psychology; public administration; visual and performing arts related.

Academics *Calendar:* 4-1-4. *Degrees:* certificates, associate, bachelor's, master's, post-master's, and postbachelor's certificates. *Special study options:* academic remediation for entering students, accelerated degree program, adult/continuing education programs, advanced placement credit, cooperative education, double majors, honors programs, independent study, internships, part-time degree program, services for LD students, summer session for credit.

Computers on Campus 300 computers/terminals are available on campus for general student use. Students can access the following: e-mail. Campuswide network is available.

Student Life *Housing options:* coed. Campus housing is university owned. *Activities and organizations:* drama/theater group, student-run newspaper, radio station, choral group, marching band, national fraternities. *Campus security:* 24-hour emergency response devices and patrols, late-night transport/escort service, escort service, vehicle, bicycle and foot patrols, crime prevention programs. *Student services:* health clinic, personal/psychological counseling.

Athletics Member NCAA. All Division II. *Intercollegiate sports:* baseball M (s), basketball M (s)/W (s), cheerleading M/W, cross-country running M (s)/W (s), football M (s), golf M (s), lacrosse W (s), soccer M (s)/W (s), softball W (s), tennis W (s), track and field M (s)/W (s), volleyball M (s)/W (s). *Intramural sports:* basketball M/W, bowling M/W, cross-country running M/W, football M, lacrosse M, racquetball M/W, soccer M/W, softball M/W, table tennis M/W, tennis M/W, ultimate Frisbee M/W, volleyball M/W, weight lifting M/W.

Standardized Tests *Required:* SAT or ACT (for admission). *Recommended:* SAT (for admission).

Costs (2007–08) *Comprehensive fee:* $37,449 includes full-time tuition ($25,380), mandatory fees ($1488), and room and board ($10,581). Full-time tuition and fees vary according to class time, course load, and program. Part-time tuition: $846 per credit hour. Part-time tuition and fees vary according to class time, course load, and program. *College room only:* $6301. Room and board charges vary according to board plan and housing facility. *Payment plan:* installment. *Waivers:* employees or children of employees.

Financial Aid Of all full-time matriculated undergraduates who enrolled in 2007, 2,212 applied for aid, 1,979 were judged to have need, 369 had their need fully met. In 2007, 333 non-need-based awards were made. *Average percent of need met:* 69%. *Average financial aid package:* $17,604. *Average need-based loan:* $4924. *Average need-based gift aid:* $13,378. *Average non-need-based aid:* $15,636. *Average indebtedness upon graduation:* $35,118. *Financial aid deadline:* 3/1.

Applying *Application fee:* $50. *Required:* essay or personal statement, high school transcript, 1 letter of recommendation. *Recommended:* interview. *Application deadlines:* rolling (freshmen), rolling (transfers). *Notification:* continuous (freshmen), continuous (transfers).

Freshman Application Contact Mr. Kevin Phillips, Director of Undergraduate Admissions, University of New Haven, Bayer Hall, 300 Boston Post Road, West Haven, CT 06516. *Phone:* 203-932-7318. *Toll-free phone:* 800-DIAL-UNH. *Fax:* 203-931-6093. *E-mail:* adminfo@newhaven.edu.

See page 562 for the College Close-Up.

WESLEYAN UNIVERSITY

Middletown, Connecticut **www.wesleyan.edu/**

- **Independent** university, founded 1831
- **Small-town** 240-acre campus
- **Endowment** $711.0 million
- **Coed** 2,817 undergraduate students, 99% full-time, 50% women, 50% men
- **Most difficult** entrance level, 27% of applicants were admitted

Undergraduates 2,796 full-time, 21 part-time. Students come from 52 states and territories, 45 other countries, 92% are from out of state, 7% African American, 11% Asian American or Pacific Islander, 8% Hispanic American, 0.5% Native American, 6% international, 2% transferred in, 98% live on campus. *Retention:* 94% of 2006 full-time freshmen returned.

Freshmen *Admission:* 7,750 applied, 2,123 admitted, 733 enrolled. *Average high school GPA:* 3.77. *Test scores:* SAT critical reading scores over 500: 99%; SAT math scores over 500: 100%; SAT writing scores over 500: 100%; ACT scores over 18: 100%; SAT critical reading scores over 600: 89%; SAT math scores over 600: 89%; SAT writing scores over 600: 89%; ACT scores over 24: 98%; SAT critical reading scores over 700: 56%; SAT math scores over 700: 49%; SAT writing scores over 700: 53%; ACT scores over 30: 59%.

Faculty *Total:* 359, 91% full-time, 87% with terminal degrees. *Student/faculty ratio:* 9:1.

Majors African-American/Black studies; American studies; anthropology; archeology; art; art history, criticism and conservation; Asian studies (East); astronomy; biochemistry; biology/biological sciences; chemistry; classics and languages, literatures and linguistics; computer science; dance; dramatic/theater arts; economics; English; environmental studies; European studies (Central and Eastern); film/cinema studies; fine/studio arts; French; geology/earth science; German; health and physical education; history; humanities; interdisciplinary studies; Italian; Latin American studies; mathematics; medieval and Renaissance studies; molecular biology; music; philosophy; physics; political science and government; psychology; religious studies; Romance languages; Russian; Russian studies; science, technology and society; social sciences; sociology; Spanish; women's studies.

Academics *Calendar:* semesters. *Degrees:* bachelor's, master's, doctoral, and post-master's certificates. *Special study options:* accelerated degree program, adult/continuing education programs, advanced placement credit, double majors, English as a second language, honors programs, independent study, internships, off-campus study, services for LD students, student-designed majors, study abroad, summer session for credit. *ROTC:* Air Force (c). *Unusual degree programs:* 3-2 engineering with Columbia University, California Institute of Technology.

Computers on Campus 190 computers/terminals are available on campus for general student use. Students can access the following: campus intranet, computer help desk, free student e-mail accounts, online (class) grades, online (class) registration, online (class) schedules, electronic portfolio, online course drop/add, Blackboard course management system. Campuswide network is available. 100% of college-owned or -operated housing units are wired for high-speed Internet access. Wireless service is available via entire campus.

Student Life *Housing:* on-campus residence required for freshman year. *Options:* coed, disabled students. Campus housing is university owned. Freshman campus housing is guaranteed. *Activities and organizations:* drama/theater group, student-run newspaper, radio station, choral group, community service, Students of Color groups, theater (student and faculty productions), campus publications, intramurals, national fraternities, national sororities. *Campus security:* 24-hour emergency response devices and patrols, student patrols, late-night transport/escort service, controlled dormitory access. *Student services:* health clinic, personal/psychological counseling, women's center.

Athletics Member NCAA. All Division III. *Intercollegiate sports:* baseball M, basketball M/W, crew M/W, cross-country running M/W, equestrian sports M (c)/W (c), field hockey W, football M, golf M, ice hockey M/W, lacrosse M/W, rugby M (c)/W (c), sailing M (c)/W (c), skiing (cross-country) M (c)/W (c), skiing (downhill) M (c)/W (c), soccer M/W, softball W, squash M/W, swimming and diving M/W, tennis M/W, track and field M/W, volleyball M (c)/W, water polo M (c), wrestling M. *Intramural sports:* basketball M/W, ice hockey M, soccer M/W, ultimate Frisbee M/W.

Standardized Tests *Required:* SAT and SAT Subject Tests or ACT (for admission).

Costs (2007–08) *One-time required fee:* $300. *Comprehensive fee:* $46,936 includes full-time tuition ($36,536), mandatory fees ($270), and room and board ($10,130). *Room and board:* Room and board charges vary according to board plan and housing facility. *Payment plan:* installment.

Financial Aid Of all full-time matriculated undergraduates who enrolled in 2006, 1,416 applied for aid, 1,300 were judged to have need, 1,300 had their need fully met. 1,028 Federal Work-Study jobs (averaging $2012). 130 state and other part-time jobs (averaging $1838). *Average percent of need met:* 100%. *Average financial aid package:* $30,543. *Average need-based loan:* $4988. *Average need-based gift aid:* $25,416. *Average indebtedness upon graduation:* $23,375. *Financial aid deadline:* 2/15.

Applying *Options:* electronic application, early admission, early decision, deferred entrance. *Application fee:* $55. *Required:* essay or personal statement, high school transcript, 2 letters of recommendation. *Required for some:* interview. *Recommended:* interview. *Application deadlines:* 1/1 (freshmen), 3/15 (transfers). *Early decision deadline:* 11/15 (for plan 1), 1/1 (for plan 2). *Notification:* 4/1 (freshmen), 5/15 (transfers), 12/15 (early decision plan 1), 2/15 (early decision plan 2).

Freshman Application Contact Ms. Nancy Meislahn, Dean of Admission and Financial Aid, Wesleyan University, Stewart M Reid House, 70 Wyllys Avenue, Middletown, CT 06459-0265. *Phone:* 860-685-3000. *Fax:* 860-685-3001. *E-mail:* admissions@wesleyan.edu.

WESTERN CONNECTICUT STATE UNIVERSITY

Danbury, Connecticut **www.wcsu.edu/**

- **State-supported** comprehensive, founded 1903, part of Connecticut State University System
- **Urban** 340-acre campus with easy access to New York City
- **Endowment** $10.6 million
- **Coed** 5,519 undergraduate students, 79% full-time, 55% women, 45% men
- **Moderately difficult** entrance level, 58% of applicants were admitted

Undergraduates 4,375 full-time, 1,144 part-time. Students come from 18 states and territories, 7 other countries, 9% are from out of state, 7% African American, 4% Asian American or Pacific Islander, 7% Hispanic American, 0.2% Native American, 0.3% international, 9% transferred in, 25% live on campus. *Retention:* 73% of 2006 full-time freshmen returned.

Freshmen *Admission:* 4,345 applied, 2,512 admitted, 934 enrolled. *Average high school GPA:* 2.79. *Test scores:* SAT critical reading scores over 500: 46%; SAT math scores over 500: 45%; SAT writing scores over 500 43%; SAT critical reading scores over 600: 10%; SAT math scores over 600: 9%; SAT writing scores over 600: 6%; SAT critical reading scores over 700: 1%; SAT math scores over 700: 1%.

Faculty *Total:* 528, 40% full-time. *Student/faculty ratio:* 15 1.

Majors Accounting; American studies; anthropology; art; atmospheric sciences and meteorology; biology/biological sciences; business administration and management; chemistry; clinical laboratory science/medical technology; communication/speech communication and rhetoric; community health services counseling; computer science; criminal justice/police science; dramatic/theater arts; economics; elementary education; English; finance; geology/earth science; health teacher education; history; liberal arts and sciences/liberal studies; management information systems; marketing/marketing management; mathematics; music; music performance; music teacher education; music theory and composition; nursing (registered nurse training); political science and government; psychology; secondary education; social sciences; social work; sociology; Spanish.

Academics *Calendar:* semesters. *Degrees:* associate, bachelor's, master's, doctoral, and postbachelor's certificates. *Special study options:* academic remediation for entering students, accelerated degree program, advanced placement credit, cooperative education, distance learning, double majors, English as a second language, honors programs, independent study, internships, off-campus study, part-time degree program, services for LD students, student-designed majors, study abroad, summer session for credit. *ROTC:* Army (c), Air Force (c).

Computers on Campus 928 computers/terminals are available on campus for general student use. Students can access the following: computer help desk, free student e-mail accounts, online (class) grades, online (class) registration, online (class) schedules. Campuswide network is available. 100% of college-owned or -operated housing units are wired for high-speed Internet access. Wireless service is available via classrooms, computer labs, libraries.

Student Life *Housing options:* coed, women-only. Campus housing is university owned. Freshman campus housing is guaranteed. *Activities and organizations:* drama/theater group, student-run newspaper, radio station, choral group, Justice and Law Club, Black Student Alliance, Student Government Association, Music Education National Conference, WXCI, national fraternities, national sororities. *Campus security:* 24-hour emergency response devices and patrols, student patrols, late-night transport/escort service, controlled dormitory access. *Student services:* health clinic, personal/psychological counseling.

Athletics Member NCAA. All Division III. *Intercollegiate sports:* baseball M, basketball M/W, cheerleading W (c), field hockey W, football M, lacrosse M/W, soccer M/W, softball W, swimming and diving W, tennis M/W, volleyball W. *Intramural sports:* basketball M/W, football M, ice hockey M (c), rock climbing M (c)/W (c), softball M/W.

Standardized Tests *Required:* SAT or ACT (for admission).

Costs (2007–08) *Tuition:* $319 per credit hour part-time; state resident $3346 full-time; nonresident $12,066 full-time. Full-time tuition and fees vary according to reciprocity agreements. *Required fees:* $3278 full-time. *Room and board:* $8400; room only: $4900. Room and board charges vary according to housing facility. *Payment plan:* installment. *Waivers:* senior citizens and employees or children of employees.

Financial Aid Of all full-time matriculated undergraduates who enrolled in 2007, 2,781 applied for aid, 2,035 were judged to have need, 504 had their need fully met. 70 Federal Work-Study jobs (averaging $2040). 24 state and other part-time jobs (averaging $2867). In 2007, 85 non-need-based awards were made. *Average percent of need met:* 61%. *Average financial aid package:* $8101. *Average need-based loan:* $2553. *Average need-based gift aid:* $2520. *Average non-need-based aid:* $2120. *Average indebtedness upon graduation:* $12,188. *Financial aid deadline:* 4/1.

Applying *Options:* electronic application, early admission, deferred entrance. *Application fee:* $50. *Required:* high school transcript, standardized test scores. *Required for some:* essay or personal statement, letters of recommendation, interview. *Notification:* continuous (freshmen), continuous (transfers).

Freshman Application Contact Western Connecticut State University, 181 White Street, Danbury, CT 06810. *Phone:* 203-837-9000. *Toll-free phone:* 877-837-9278.

See page 564 for the College Close-Up.

YALE UNIVERSITY

New Haven, Connecticut **www.yale.edu/**

- **Independent** university, founded 1701
- **Urban** 200-acre campus with easy access to New York City
- **Endowment** $22.5 billion
- **Coed** 5,311 undergraduate students, 100% full-time, 49% women, 51% men
- **Most difficult** entrance level, 10% of applicants were admitted

Undergraduates 5,289 full-time, 22 part-time. Students come from 50 states and territories, 74 other countries, 93% are from out of state, 9% African American, 14% Asian American or Pacific Islander, 8% Hispanic American, 1% Native American, 8% international, 0.4% transferred in, 88% live on campus. *Retention:* 99% of 2006 full-time freshmen returned.

Freshmen *Admission:* 19,323 applied, 1,911 admitted, 1,318 enrolled. *Test scores:* SAT critical reading scores over 500: 99%; SAT math scores over 500: 99%; SAT writing scores over 500: 99%; SAT critical reading scores over 600: 97%; SAT math scores over 600: 97%; SAT writing scores over 600: 97%; SAT critical reading scores over 700: 76%; SAT math scores over 700: 76%; SAT writing scores over 700: 75%.

Faculty *Total:* 1,577, 70% full-time, 85% with terminal degrees. *Student/faculty ratio:* 6:1.

Majors African-American/Black studies; African studies; American studies; ancient/classical Greek; anthropology; applied mathematics; archeology; architecture; art; art history, criticism and conservation; Asian studies (East); astronomy; astrophysics; biology/biological sciences; biomedical/medical engineering; cell biology and anatomical sciences related; chemical engineering; chemistry; Chinese; classics and languages, literatures and linguistics; cognitive psychology and psycholinguistics; computer and information sciences; cultural studies; dramatic/theater arts; ecology; economics; electrical, electronics and communications engineering; engineering physics; engineering science; English; environmental/environmental health engineering; environmental studies; ethnic, cultural minority, and gender studies related; evolutionary biology; film/cinema studies; foreign languages related; French; geological and earth sciences/geosciences related; German; history; humanities; Italian; Japanese; Jewish/Judaic studies; Latin; Latin American studies; linguistics; literature; mathematics; mathematics and computer science; mechanical engineering; molecular biology; multi-/interdisciplinary studies related; music; philosophy; physics; political science and government; Portuguese; psychology; religious studies; Russian; Russian studies; sociology; South Asian languages; Spanish; systems science and theory; women's studies.

Academics *Calendar:* semesters. *Degrees:* bachelor's, master's, doctoral, first professional, and post-master's certificates. *Special study options:* accelerated degree program, advanced placement credit, double majors, English as a second language, honors programs, independent study, internships, part-time degree program, student-designed majors, study abroad, summer session for credit. *ROTC:* Army (c), Air Force (c).

Computers on Campus 350 computers/terminals are available on campus for general student use. Students can access the following: online (class) registration. Campuswide network is available. Wireless service is available via entire campus.

Student Life *Housing:* on-campus residence required through sophomore year. *Options:* coed, disabled students. Campus housing is university owned. Freshman campus housing is guaranteed. *Activities and organizations:* drama/theater group, student-run newspaper, radio and television station, choral group, marching band, community service, intramural sports, theater productions, music groups, campus publications, national fraternities, national sororities. *Campus security:* 24-hour emergency response devices and patrols, late-night transport/escort service, controlled dormitory access. *Student services:* health clinic, personal/psychological counseling, women's center.

Athletics Member NCAA. All Division I except football (Division I-AA). *Intercollegiate sports:* baseball M, basketball M/W, crew M/W, cross-country running M/W, fencing M/W, field hockey W, golf M/W, gymnastics W, ice hockey M/W, lacrosse M/W, soccer M/W, softball W, squash M/W, swimming and diving M/W, table tennis M (c), tennis M/W, track and field M/W, volleyball M (c)/W. *Intramural sports:* badminton M (c)/W (c), baseball M, basketball M/W, bowling M/W, crew M/W, cross-country running M/W, equestrian sports M (c)/W (c), field hockey W, football M/W, golf M/W, ice hockey M/W, racquetball M/W, riflery M (c)/W (c), rugby M (c)/W (c), sailing M (c)/W (c), skiing (cross-country) M (c)/W (c), skiing (downhill) M (c)/W (c), soccer M/W, softball M/W, squash M/W, swimming and diving M/W, table tennis M/W, tennis M/W, volleyball M/W, water polo M/W, wrestling M (c).

Standardized Tests *Required:* SAT and SAT Subject Tests or ACT (for admission).

Costs (2007–08) *Comprehensive fee:* $45,000 includes full-time tuition ($34,530) and room and board ($10,470). *College room only:* $5710. *Payment plan:* installment.

Financial Aid Of all full-time matriculated undergraduates who enrolled in 2006, 2,521 applied for aid, 2,292 were judged to have need, 2,292 had their need fully met. 883 Federal Work-Study jobs (averaging $2179). 655 state and other part-time jobs (averaging $3028). *Average percent of need met:* 100%. *Average financial aid package:* $32,533. *Average need-based loan:* $1996. *Average need-based gift aid:* $30,055. *Average indebtedness upon graduation:* $13,344. *Financial aid deadline:* 3/1.

Applying *Options:* electronic application, early admission, early action, deferred entrance. *Application fee:* $75. *Required:* essay or personal statement, high school transcript, 3 letters of recommendation. *Recommended:* interview. *Application deadlines:* 12/31 (freshmen), 3/1 (transfers), 11/1 (early action). *Notification:* 4/1 (freshmen), 5/15 (transfers), 12/15 (early action).

Freshman Application Contact Admissions Director, Yale University, PO Box 208234, New Haven, CT 06520-8234. *Phone:* 203-432-9300. *E-mail:* undergraduate.admissions@yale.edu.

See page 566 for the College Close-Up.

ALBERTUS MAGNUS COLLEGE

NEW HAVEN, CONNECTICUT

The College

Founded in 1925 by the Dominican Sisters of St. Mary of the Springs, Albertus Magnus College educates men and women to become leaders in all walks of life. The College is committed to providing a liberal arts education rooted in the Dominican tradition of scholarship. Professors at Albertus strive to help their students develop in all areas; as much attention is paid to the nurturing of a student's aesthetic, physical, and moral capacities as to his or her intellectual capabilities. In 1992, the College began offering its first graduate-level course of study through the Master of Arts in Liberal Studies program. More recently, the College has expanded its offerings to include graduate-level programs that include the Master of Arts in Liberal Studies program, the Master of Science in Management program, the Master of Arts in Art Therapy program, the Master of Arts in Leadership program, and the Master of Business Administration program.

The traditional undergraduate program has a student body of approximately 500 students, who live and learn on the beautiful 50-acre campus in the Prospect Hill neighborhood of New Haven. Another 1,500 students attend graduate programs or accelerated programs for adults. These students come from various parts of the United States (largely the New England area), Europe, Africa, Asia, and South and Central America. About 60 percent of the students live on campus in student dormitories that are renovated mansions from the early 1900s. The housing program fosters a strong sense of community spirit, and students often plan workshops, parties, and other social and learning events in their residence halls.

The Campus Center is a hub of student activities, such as comedy shows, live music, contests, and other unique functions. The variety of on-campus organizations includes the Student Government Association, the Campus Activities Board, the multicultural student union, a dance team, the Psychology Club, the Art Club, the Business Club, and numerous creative writing options, such as *Breakwater* literary magazine and the English Club. Albertus has recently added a new cyber lounge, The Common Ground, where students can check e-mail, work on homework, and enjoy a cup of coffee.

Students may also share in the excitement of live drama through the College's professionally managed ACT 2 Theatre, providing a number of artistic, academic, and recreational possibilities. In addition, students are encouraged to become part of the New Haven community through extracurricular and volunteer activities. The active Campus Ministry provides opportunities to volunteer, organize campus events, and participate in community service projects.

The Cosgrove, Marcus, Messer Athletic Center houses a 25-yard pool, a Jacuzzi, three racquetball courts, a weight and cardio room, a dance studio, and a gymnasium. In addition to this facility, there are soccer and softball fields, an outdoor track, and several tennis courts. Albertus fields intercollegiate athletic teams in baseball, basketball, cross-country, soccer, tennis, and volleyball for men and basketball, cross-country, soccer, softball, tennis, and volleyball for women. Albertus's teams compete in NCAA Division III/Great Northeast Athletic Conference (GNAC) and the Eastern College Athletic Conference (ECAC). The Athletic Department also offers an intramural program in some sports.

Location

New Haven is a multicultural city with a population of more than 130,000 people. The city hosts approximately 16,000 students attending the seven colleges and universities in the greater New Haven area. This concentration of students creates exciting choices for social, recreational, and cultural activities for Albertus students. The city has some of the finest theaters in the country, including the Long Wharf and Shubert theaters. There are many fantastic art collections, museums, and movie theaters. Large shopping facilities, excellent restaurants, and several recreational areas are only a short distance from the Albertus Magnus College campus.

Majors and Degrees

The Albertus Magnus College traditional undergraduate program confers the Bachelor of Arts, Bachelor of Science, Bachelor of Fine Arts, and Associate of Arts degrees. The areas of study include accounting, art (history and studio), art therapy, biology, business administration, chemistry, child development and mental health, communications, computer information systems, creative writing, criminal justice, drama, education (grades 4–12), English, finance, general studies, graphic design, history, humanities, human services, industrial and organizational psychology, international business, marketing, mathematics, performing communications, philosophy/religion, photography, physical sciences, political science, prelaw, premedicine, psychology, Spanish, sports communications, social science, social work, sociology, urban studies, and visual arts.

Academic Programs

Albertus Magnus College is committed to providing a liberal arts education that promotes the pursuit of truth in all its dimensions. The College recognizes the importance of cultivating core competencies and knowledge if students are to meet the challenges and opportunities they encounter in their communities and workplaces. Albertus has recently developed the Insight Program, which serves as the College's core curriculum. Through this program, students build a thinking framework that supports them throughout their lives as they realize their goals. In addition, the Insight Program helps students improve their capabilities in critical and creative thinking; grasp the methods of scientific, quantitative, mathematical, and philosophical reasoning; and appreciate and assess perspectives different from their own. The B.A. and B.S. degrees require 120 credits for graduation, the B.F.A. requires 127 credits, and the A.A. requires 60 credits. Students may relate academic study to work experience through a system of academically credited internships. The College's Office of Career Services helps graduating students prepare for career direction and job placement. The Academic Development Center and Writing Center provide personal instruction to students who may benefit from additional help with their schoolwork. The centers also provide services to those students with learning disabilities. Students who show strong academic potential may pursue a course of study through the College's honors program. Through the College's system of internships for juniors and seniors, Albertus students have become increasingly involved in the New Haven community and gain valuable, practical, professional training. Often, internships lead to permanent positions with local companies and corporations.

Academic Facilities

Rosary Hall, the College's first building, now houses a library collection of 110,000 volumes, 600 periodicals, 4,400 pieces of microfilm, and full access to the Internet, which includes LexisNexis, EBSCOhost, and PsycINFO. The interlibrary loan program has national access to materials at academic and public libraries across the country. The Media Center has equipment that students may use to produce new materials as well as review older materials. Interlibrary services with other local universities are also available. The New Center for Science, Art and Technology provides the most modern scientific equipment available for students majoring in biological and physical sciences, along with state-of-the-art broadcasting technology for communication students. Aquinas Hall houses the academic computer labs, which are equipped with personal computers, digital scanners, laser printers, and full Internet access. Every classroom in Aquinas Hall is laptop compatible, and the entire campus is engineered for wireless use.

Costs

The costs for the 2007–08 school year were $20,166 for tuition and $8907 for room and board (nineteen meals per week). Expenses for books, travel, and personal supplies vary.

Financial Aid

Albertus Magnus College offers a variety of merit-based scholarships to students who have achieved high academic standing in high school or in their two-year college programs. In addition to scholarships based solely on academics, the College offers scholarships for students who attend Catholic high schools, students who are valedictorians or salutatorians of their high schools, students who live in the New Haven area, and students who have shown a commitment to community service. Interested students should contact the Office of Admission for specific information regarding these and other scholarship opportunities. Scholarships are awarded to eligible students who apply and are accepted to the College prior to March 15.

Approximately 85 percent of the College's students receive financial aid in some form. The College requires that students file the Albertus Magnus College financial aid application form and the Free Application for Federal Student Aid (FAFSA) to be considered for Albertus scholarships and grants, Federal Perkins Loans, Federal Supplemental Educational Opportunity Grants, and Federal Work-Study awards. The College awards financial aid on a rolling basis; however, students who are accepted and submit their FAFSA forms by February 28 are given priority.

Faculty

Faculty members at Albertus come from leading universities of the United States and abroad and are one of the College's greatest assets. Ninety percent of the full- and part-time faculty members hold a Ph.D. or the equivalent. Their primary concern is teaching, although the work of many faculty members has been published. Students find faculty members accessible for academic or personal counseling and for campus sports and activities.

Student Government

Through the Student Government Association (SGA), Albertus students have the primary responsibility for governing their own residential and social life. All full-time matriculated students are members of the SGA and, through its committees and officers, manage student government and social affairs and participate in the campus judicial system. Students serve on faculty committees, the Academic Policy Committee, and the Library Committee.

Admission Requirements

Albertus Magnus College welcomes applications from students of all ages, nationalities, and ethnic, cultural, racial, and religious groups. Applicants may be admitted as freshmen or as transfer, provisional, or special students.

In evaluating freshman candidates, the Office of Admission considers a student's application, counselor recommendation, high school transcript, essay, extracurricular activities, and scores on the SAT or ACT. Emphasis is placed on the student's record of performance rather than on the results of standardized tests.

Transfer students are welcome at the College. They must submit high school records, SAT or ACT scores (if necessary), and college records for evaluation, in addition to the application and the recommendation. Interviews are recommended for freshman and transfer applicants.

More information is available on the College's Web site, http://www.albertus.edu.

Application and Information

The College accepts students for entrance on a rolling admission basis. Students may also apply online at http://www.albertus.edu. As soon as all of a candidate's admission materials have been received, his or her application is considered and notification is made as soon as a decision has been reached.

Application forms, recommendation forms, and information may be obtained by contacting:

Office of Admission
Albertus Magnus College
700 Prospect Street
New Haven, Connecticut 06511-1189
Phone: 203-773-8501
800-578-9160 (toll-free)
Fax: 203-773-5248
E-mail: admissions@albertus.edu
Web site: http://www.albertus.edu

Beautiful Rosary Hall.

CENTRAL CONNECTICUT STATE UNIVERSITY

NEW BRITAIN, CONNECTICUT

The University

Central Connecticut State University (CCSU) is Connecticut's oldest publicly supported institution of higher education. Founded in 1849, CCSU is a regional, comprehensive public university that is dedicated to learning in the liberal arts and sciences and to education for the professions. The Association of American Colleges and Universities selected CCSU as one of sixteen Leadership Institutions in the nation and the only one in Connecticut, honoring CCSU's "visionary innovations in undergraduate education."

CCSU is the largest of the four state universities in the Connecticut State University system, enrolling approximately 7,500 full-time and 2,200 part-time undergraduate students. CCSU's student body represents the spectrum of ethnic and socioeconomic groups. Ninety percent of students are Connecticut residents, with other students coming from more than thirty states and forty other countries. Approximately 2,000 undergraduates live on campus in nine residence halls. Memorial Hall is the main dining facility, where students may choose among five meal plans that cater to different tastes and needs.

CCSU has five schools: the School of Arts and Sciences, School of Business, School of Education and Professional Studies, School of Engineering and Technology, and School of Graduate Studies. CCSU is committed to offering access to its distinctive, high-quality academic programs by offering undergraduate and graduate programs consisting of master's and sixth-year level programs and a doctoral program (Ed.D.) in educational leadership. The University is a responsive and creative intellectual resource of the state.

The Student Center houses the student newspaper, the radio station, dining areas, a game room, TV lounges, computer workstations, and other facilities. Students produce concerts, dances, film series, and other activities. More than 150 campus clubs and organizations are available, covering areas from academic and career groups to honors and professional societies; religious, performing arts, and political clubs; and fraternities and sororities. The Student Government Association funds a yearbook, sports clubs, and cultural and special-interest groups. Extracurricular activities include movies, intramural sports, lectures, musical and dramatic productions, and art exhibits as well as CCSU's eighteen NCAA Division I intercollegiate programs.

Sports for men include baseball, basketball, cross-country, football, golf, indoor and outdoor track, and soccer. Women sports include basketball, cross-country, golf, indoor and outdoor track, lacrosse, soccer, softball, swimming and diving, and volleyball. Students interested in intramural sports enjoy basketball, flag football, floor hockey, softball, and volleyball. The Kaiser Hall Gymnasium offers an Olympic-size swimming pool, modern exercise equipment, a state-of-the-art fitness center, a weight-training room, and an athletic training center. The Kaiser Annex, commonly referred to as the 'Bubble', has a running track and tennis and basketball courts.

The Ruthe Boyea Women's Center is a multipurpose program and service center for students and staff and faculty members. The center offers a variety of services for and about women. Both men and women are welcome to drop in and use the resources, attend activities, or just hang out.

Location

CCSU is located in New Britain, home to a world-renowned art museum, a minor league baseball team, a 1,200-acre municipal park system, and a wide range of cultural activities. The University, located at the edge of the city, is in the heart of Connecticut, 15 minutes from the state capital of Hartford and its many restaurants, theaters, and sports and concert activities. State recreational areas, nature trails, and skiing areas are nearby; there are also convenient shopping areas. New York and Boston are both less than 2 hours away.

Majors and Degrees

CCSU offers four undergraduate degrees: Bachelor of Arts, Bachelor of Fine Arts, Bachelor of Science, and Bachelor of Science in Nursing (B.S.N.).

The Bachelor of Arts is awarded with majors in anthropology, art (art history), communication (broadcast journalism, media studies, organizational communication, promotion/public relations), criminology and criminal justice, design (graphic/information), economics (general, economics–operations research), English, French, geography (environmental, general regional, geographic information science, tourism), German, graphic/information design, history, international studies (interdisciplinary), Italian, mathematics (actuarial science, general, statistics), music (history, jazz studies, performance, theory and composition), philosophy, political science (political science and public administration), psychology, sociology, Spanish, and theater.

The Bachelor of Fine Arts degree is offered in theater, with concentrations in acting, design/technical theater, general, general/directing, general/educational theater, and theater/dance.

Bachelor of Science degree programs include accounting; athletic training; biochemistry; biology (ecology, biodiversity, evolutionary; environmental science); biomolecular sciences (biotechnology, general); chemistry and biochemistry; civil engineering technology; computer engineering technology; computer science; computer science–honors; construction management; earth sciences; education–elementary (interdisciplinary); education–secondary (interdisciplinary); electronics technology; exercise science and health promotion; finance; general science; hospitality and tourism; industrial technology (electromechanical, environmental and occupational safety, graphics, industrial technology, manufacturing, networking technology, technology management); international business management; management (entrepreneurship, human resource); management information systems; manufacturing engineering technology; marketing; mechanical engineering; mechanical engineering technology; nursing (B.S.N.); physics; and technology education.

Certification programs in education for which a Bachelor of Science is awarded include elementary education (1–6), secondary education (7–12), and special subject fields (nursery–12). Single–subject matter majors for the elementary education program are English, geography, history, mathematics, science–biology, and science–earth sciences. Dual subject matter programs include English/geography, history/linguistics, history/writing, mathematics/biology, and mathematics/earth sciences. Majors in secondary education include biology, chemistry, earth sciences, English, French, general science, German, history, Italian, mathematics, physics, social sciences, and Spanish. Special subject field majors are art education, music education, physical education, and technology education.

Preprofessional study is offered in law and health/medical studies.

Academic Programs

The graduation requirement for a bachelor's degree is a minimum of 122 to 130 hours of credit, depending on the student's program of study. Majors consist of a minimum of 30 to 68 prescribed hours of credit in one specific, approved field. A total of 45 credit hours of general education studies must be completed and include writing, foreign language proficiency, and international requirements. Some of the professional B.S. degree programs enable students to develop a minor or a concentration in addition to the major.

CCSU operates on a two-semester system. The fall semester usually starts the first week in September and ends in mid-December. The spring semester runs from the third week of January to mid-May. CCSU offers multiple summer sessions from June to August and two 3-week winter sessions in December and January.

For academically talented students, CCSU offers an honors program. This is a highly competitive program, which emphasizes scholarly activities and offers tuition scholarships.

The Cooperative Education Program (Co-Op) is available for students in good academic standing who have earned at least 30 academic credits at CCSU; students may participate in the program for one or more semesters.

The School of Technology's Pathway programs provide a seamless route between other institutions in the Connecticut State University System and Connecticut's community technical colleges without loss of credit or repeated courses.

Off-Campus Programs

Internships are available through government offices, newspapers, nonprofit agencies, and many businesses. In addition, off-campus internships are possible through study-abroad and consortium arrangements with the University of Connecticut and other institutions in the Connecticut State University System. The study-abroad program offers students a semester-long or yearlong exchange in which they enroll overseas and study via a cultural immersion program.

Academic Facilities

CCSU's 65 developed acres provide students with a full range of learning facilities. The Elihu Burritt Library contains nearly 700,000 volumes, more than 3,000 periodical titles, extensive research materials on microfiche and microfilm, and extensive online services and CD-ROM databases. CCSU's online public catalog provides access to the holdings of all four Connecticut State University libraries. The Marcus White Microcomputer Laboratory, a state-of-the-art facility, offers the latest PCs, Macintoshes, printers, scanners, and online capabilities. Other computer facilities are available in the residence halls. There are more than sixty-five smart classrooms that offer multimedia technology that includes computers, DVD players, satellite teleconferencing capabilities, and high-technology systems. The Samuel S. T. Chen Art Center's gallery area presents changing exhibits, lectures, and programs. The Copernicus Science Computing Laboratory serves the faculty and students in the natural and physical sciences; the lab houses networked PCs and Macintosh computers, printers, scanners, and multimedia projectors. Copernicus Hall houses a planetarium and astronomical observatory, plus well-equipped laboratories for biology, chemistry, engineering, technology, and the physical sciences. Welte Auditorium is a state-of-the-art performance venue for music, dance, theater, and important lectures and conferences.

Costs

Annual tuition and fees for the 2007–08 academic year for Connecticut residents were $6734. Tuition and fees for out-of-state residents were $15,454. On-campus room (double occupancy) and board fees for the year were approximately $7890; costs vary slightly, depending on the meal plan selected and the particular residence hall. Annual costs for books, travel, and personal expenses vary but are estimated at $4000. All costs are subject to change. Students may contact the Bursar's Office for the most current cost information.

Financial Aid

Financial aid includes grants, scholarships, low-interest educational loans, and employment opportunities to students. The University participates in the Federal Pell Grant, Federal Supplemental Educational Opportunity Grant, Federal Perkins Loan, Federal Direct Student Loan, and Federal Work-Study programs. In addition, grants and scholarships are available through University funds and other resources. Approximately two thirds of students attending CCSU receive some type of financial assistance. Financial aid awards are based on demonstrated financial need as determined by the Free Application for Federal Student Aid (FAFSA); the priority filing date for the fall semester is March 1, and November 15 for the spring semester. Prospective students should visit the financial aid Web site at http://www.ccsu.edu/finaid for additional information.

Faculty

CCSU's faculty members are dedicated to teaching; it is their prime concern and the basis of their students' successes. Over 75 percent of CCSU's faculty members hold doctoral degrees, with all other faculty members having advanced degrees. The majority of faculty members are actively involved in research, publishing, and community service. CCSU has a student-faculty ratio of 19:1; this enables students to take advantage of their professors' expertise and to benefit from personal attention.

Student Government

All of CCSU's full-time undergraduate students are members of the Student Government Association (SGA). The SGA Senate is the representative body of the SGA, and the full-time undergraduates democratically elect its members, the Executive Officers and Senators of the SGA. It promotes student participation in various projects, committees, and organizations at the University and at state and national levels that help shape the University and education in Connecticut. The SGA Senate allocates the SGA portion of the student activity fee to promote and fund student clubs, activities, services, and issues that benefit students and their educational opportunities.

Admission Requirements

CCSU is selective in its admission policy. Applicants are considered on an individual basis, with emphasis placed on the applicant's secondary academic school record, competitive SAT or ACT scores, rank in graduating class, and teachers' or guidance counselors' recommendations. CCSU values excellence and achievement in academic scholarship, community and school involvement, and individual achievements. An applicant must be a graduate of an accredited high school or preparatory school or hold an equivalency diploma.

An applicant's secondary school preparation must contain college-preparatory course work, including 4 units of English, 3 units of mathematics (including algebra I and II and geometry), 2 units of science (including 1 unit of a lab science), and 2 units of social sciences (including U.S. history). Completion of 3 consecutive units of the same foreign language through the third level is recommended.

For transfer admissions consideration, an applicant must have earned a minimum of 12 college-level credits (not including remedial work) at regionally accredited postsecondary institutions and have a cumulative college GPA of 2.0 or higher for all course work attempted. Transfer students who have earned a minimum of 12 college-level credits need not submit SAT scores with their application.

The University welcomes applications from students with a broad range of abilities, interests, and backgrounds and evaluates each student on the merits of his or her readiness to succeed, which is based on past demonstrations of academic and personal success. No applicant is denied admission because of race, color, religious belief, national origin, gender, sexual orientation, age, or disability.

Application and Information

Applications can be made after the first quarter of the senior year of high school through May 1 for the fall semester. Applicants should complete the online application, available at http://www.ccsu.edu/menu.htm, and also submit a $50 nonrefundable application fee, a transcript of high school grades and rank in class, and an official copy of SAT or ACT score reports (sent electronically to CCSU). The University adheres to a rolling admission policy. Applicants are usually notified of an admissions decision within one month after the application is complete. Information may be requested from:

Office of Recruitment and Admissions
Central Connecticut State University
1615 Stanley Street
New Britain, Connecticut 06050-4010
Phone: 860-832-CCSU
888-733-2278 (toll-free in Connecticut)
860-832-2289 (tours)
E-mail: admissions@ccsu.edu
tour@ccsu.edu (tours)
Web site: http://www.ccsu.edu

COLLEGE DATA CENTER • CONNECTICUT

EASTERN CONNECTICUT STATE UNIVERSITY

WILLIMANTIC, CONNECTICUT

The University

Eastern Connecticut State University, Connecticut's public liberal arts university, offers thirty-one undergraduate majors and graduate degrees in education and organizational management. Eastern has all the advantages of a private liberal arts college combined with "public-university resources and costs." The University's liberal arts focus and concern for the individual student, along with its small classes, personalized counseling, and independent-study opportunities, encourage intellectual and personal growth and development. The student body (3,900 full-time undergraduates) is heterogeneous, a mixture of various ethnic and socioeconomic groups. Students attending Eastern come from 164 Connecticut towns and more than thirty states and thirty countries. Eastern is a residential liberal arts campus. Most full-time students, including 90 percent of the freshmen, reside on campus. There are seven residence halls and five apartment complexes on campus. Housing is available to students who have been admitted to the University. Hurley Hall, the University's main food court–style dining area, offers unlimited dining during operational hours. On-campus parking is available to all students except freshmen living on campus. There are more than sixty special interest clubs and organizations on campus, as well as a student newspaper, a yearbook, and a literary and arts magazine. Extracurricular events include concerts, dances, films, intramural sports, lectures, musical and dramatic productions, and bus trips to Boston and New York City. Varsity sports for men include baseball, basketball, cross-country, lacrosse, soccer, and track. Women participate in intercollegiate basketball, cross-country, field hockey, lacrosse, soccer, softball, swimming, track, and volleyball. Sports facilities include an athletic center with a 2,800-seat gymnasium for badminton, basketball, tennis, and volleyball; a six-lane swimming pool; handball and squash courts; saunas; a fitness center and rooms for physical conditioning, modern dance, and gymnastics; and an athletic complex that includes a state-of-the-art baseball field with a 1,500-seat grandstand as well as field hockey and multipurpose fields. The University's recently renovated Student Center includes ample meeting space, a theater, multipurpose room, game area, expansive food court, and a glass-enclosed exercise room.

Location

Willimantic, Connecticut, a small city of diversified interests and many styles of living, has a population of 22,000. It has convenient shopping centers and a growing community of ambitious and ecology-minded individuals who are concerned with the city's future. The eastern Connecticut region is famous for its rolling hills, forests, state recreational areas, nature trails, clear lakes and streams, and beaches. Skiing areas are nearby. Hartford is 40 minutes away, and New York City and Boston are both less than 2 hours from Willimantic by car.

Majors and Degrees

Eastern offers four undergraduate degrees: the Bachelor of Arts, the Bachelor of General Studies, the Bachelor of Science, and the Associate in Science. The Bachelor of Arts degree is awarded with majors in economics, English, history, history and social sciences, political science, performing arts (academic tracks in music and theater), psychology, social work, sociology and applied social relations, Spanish, and visual arts (academic tracks in art history, graphic design, painting and drawing, printmaking, and sculpture). The Bachelor of Science degree programs include accounting, biochemistry, biology (academic tracks in premedicine, predentistry, pre–veterinary studies, and ecology), business administration (concentrations in the areas of finance, management, and marketing), business information systems, communication, computer science, early childhood education, elementary education, English, environmental earth science, mathematics, physical education, secondary education, and sport and leisure management. Certification in secondary education is available in biology, English, environmental earth science, history, and mathematics. The associate degree program is available in the arts and sciences. The Bachelor of General Studies is a flexible degree program for adults who are 25 or older. Students may design a program integrating life experience into major or minor concentrations through a learning contract developed with their departmental adviser.

Academic Programs

The graduation requirements for a bachelor's degree embrace the University's liberal arts mission and require a minimum of 120 hours of credit and completion of a major program of study. All degree candidates must take a freshman English composition course and fulfill specified course requirements in a three-tier liberal arts core. The tier system includes study in methods and concepts, synthesis and application, and independent inquiry. The University operates on a two-semester system. The fall semester usually starts the first week in September and ends in mid-December; the spring semester, which includes a one-week break in March, runs from the third week of January to the middle of May. One 6-week and two 3-week sessions are offered during the summer. An Intersession program is offered in January of each year.

Eastern offers an Honors Program for academically talented students. This highly competitive program emphasizes scholarly activity, independent study, and special courses and offers tuition scholarships. The Contract Admissions Program (CAP) is an educational support service that offers counseling, tutoring, developmental courses, and financial assistance to highly motivated students who might otherwise have been denied admission on the basis of traditional criteria. Cooperative Education (Co-op) is an optional work-study program; students may choose to participate in the program for one or more periods.

The University grants credit for Advanced Placement Program examination in all the subject areas tested and accepts up to 60 credit hours earned through the College-Level Examination Program (CLEP). Persons with a minimum of five years of successful work experience in areas of specialization taught by the University may qualify for advanced placement through credit for life experience and learning.

U.S. Army and Air Force ROTC programs, which are offered by the University of Connecticut at Storrs, are available to qualified Eastern students.

Off-Campus Programs

Eastern offers a number of opportunities for off-campus study for college credit. These include off-campus internships, study abroad, and consortium arrangements with the University of Connecticut and other institutions in the Connecticut State University System. Internships are available in the academic areas of applied social relations, biology, business administration, communication, computer science, economics, education, environmental earth science, psychology, public policy and government, and Spanish. Biology majors may study in Belize or Bermuda through the tropical biology program. There are also opportunities to join international study groups for one semester, one academic year, or a summer session. Eastern also participates in the National Student Exchange (NSE) program, which allows students to attend other public colleges and universities across the United States while still paying tuition and fees to Eastern.

Academic Facilities

The J. Eugene Smith Library contains more than 500,000 volumes and 127,000 square feet of educational learning space. The Media Building contains a color television studio, a recording studio, an FM radio station, an electronic auditorium, a computer center, darkrooms, and graphic arts areas and serves as the hub of the audiovisual distribution system. The planetarium contains two electron microscopes and a geology laboratory. The Science Building provides modern, well-equipped laboratories for biology, chemistry, and physics. A new state-of-the-art science building opened in spring 2008. A four-story, 72,000-square-foot classroom building and the library and clock tower serve as the main academic areas of the campus. The Childhood and Family Resource Center, with state-of-the-art classroom and teaching space, meeting facilities, and a full-service day-care center, serves as a model facility for its resources. A new Performing Arts Centers is in the planning stages.

Costs

For 2007–08, tuition and fees for a Connecticut resident were $6961, and nonresident tuition and fees were $15,681 on an annual basis. The fees included a tuition deposit of $200, which is required to secure a place in the University, and a $250 housing deposit. Room was estimated at $4680 and board at $3700 for two semesters. Books and supplies average $900 per year. Tuition and fees are subject to change as warranted and are itemized on the University's Web site.

Financial Aid

Financial aid includes grants and scholarships, low-interest loans, student employment opportunities, and special programs for veterans and their families. The University participates in the Federal Perkins Loan, Federal Pell Grant, Federal Supplemental Educational Opportunity Grant, and Federal Work-Study programs. In addition, it provides aid through alumni funds and other resources of its own. Approximately two thirds of all Eastern students receive financial aid. Awards are based primarily on demonstrated financial need. All students who wish to apply for financial assistance are required to complete the Free Application for Federal Student Aid (FAFSA) and send it to the processing agency by March 15 for the fall semester or by November 15 for the spring semester.

Faculty

The friendliness and approachability of the University's professors are usually noted by the students enrolled at Eastern. While faculty members are focused primarily on quality teaching and the full development of students enrolled, many write and conduct significant research. Faculty members hold advanced degrees from leading American and international colleges and universities; 95 percent hold terminal degrees. Faculty members serve as academic counselors and mentors for students. Full-time advisers and counseling services are available to assist students in matters of personal and academic concern. The student-faculty ratio at Eastern is 16:1. The average class size is 24.

Student Government

An organized plan of student government and student representation on University committees permits students to be actively involved with important issues and develop basic policies for student life. The Student Senate is the governing body; it supervises and coordinates all student activities and serves as a liaison with the faculty, administration, and Board of Trustees.

Admission Requirements

Eastern is considered to be selective in admission. Applicants are considered on an individual basis, with emphasis placed on the applicant's secondary school record, satisfactory SAT or ACT scores, rank in the high school graduating class, personal accomplishments and motivation, and teachers' or guidance counselors' recommendations. Applicants' complete requirements for secondary school graduation or its equivalent should include 16 academic units of college-preparatory work, with the following divisions: English, 4 years; mathematics, 3 years; science, 2 years (including 1 year of laboratory science); social sciences, 2 years (including U.S. history); and foreign language, 2 years (3 years preferred). Students who are admitted without having fulfilled the language requirement must complete one year of a foreign language (6 credits) at Eastern. Deferred admission is also available. A campus visit is strongly suggested, although not required. A limited number of highly motivated students who do not qualify for admission if traditional criteria are used may be admitted to the University by successfully completing the Summer Transition Experience Program/Contract Admission Program or the Summer Proof of Ability Option. Students should contact the Office of Admissions for more information on special admission options.

Application and Information

Applications can be made after the first quarter of the senior year of high school through May 1 for the fall semester. Freshman applicants must submit an admission application; a $50 nonrefundable application fee; a complete transcript of high school grades and rank in class; an essay explaining why Eastern, Connecticut's public liberal arts college, is the right college choice for the applicant; two recommendations from guidance counselors or teachers; and an official copy of the SAT or ACT score report. The University adheres to a rolling admission policy. Applicants are usually notified of the admission decision within one month after the application is complete. Applicants are encouraged to apply online at http://www.easternct.edu. Application forms and information may be requested from:

Kimberly Crone
Director of Admissions and Enrollment Management
Eastern Connecticut State University
83 Windham Street
Willimantic, Connecticut 06226
Phone: 860-465-5286
Fax: 860-465-5544
E-mail: admissions@easternct.edu
Web site: http://www.easternct.edu

Eastern's J. Eugene Smith Library, with more than 500,000 volumes and 127,000 square feet of educational space, serves as the academic hub of the campus.

MITCHELL COLLEGE

NEW LONDON, CONNECTICUT

The College

Mitchell is a private, coeducational four- and two-year residential college. With 850 full-time students and a 12:1 student-faculty ratio, the College provides a supportive student-centered learning environment that addresses the educational needs of all students, including those with learning disabilities. Mitchell is especially proud of its success in working with students who have yet to reach their full academic potential. To that end, the College maintains access for students with varied academic abilities who are highly motivated to succeed.

To help guide students, Mitchell College's mission is connected to five distinctive values: Character, Achievement, Respect, Engagement, and Self-Discovery (CARES). The CARES model provides a learning foundation that emphasizes character development, personal and social responsibility, respect for others, and community service. CARES is a comprehensive hands-on partnership that keeps students on course toward their goal of graduation and beyond.

In fall 2006, the College launched Thames Academy, a postgraduate/precollege program—a year of academic preparation for students between the end of their secondary school/high school education and the start of their college studies. As one of the country's foremost colleges in promoting student academic success, Mitchell provides a challenging education in a caring and supportive environment, focusing on student asset development, rather than deficit management.

Nearly all full-time students are of traditional college age, 18 to 22, and come from throughout the country and around the globe. Most students come from New England states, with about 60 percent from Connecticut, 30 percent from other New England states, and the remaining 10 percent from throughout United States and other countries. International students and representatives of multicultural groups make up approximately 31 percent of the student population. About 150 part-time students, many of whom are adult commuters, enhance the classroom experience.

Nearly 80 percent of full-time students live in three traditional residence halls, each housing 100 students. Each building has three floors with double rooms and common baths. The College also offers four historic Victorian and Colonial waterfront residence halls accommodating between 20 and 35 students each. One waterfront residence is dedicated to Thames Academy, the postgraduate/precollege transitional program. This fall, Mitchell made available themed, apartment-style living, accommodating 16 students. A 126-suite residence hall is planned for fall 2008. Facilities include a fully equipped gymnasium, a fitness center, athletic fields, a sailing dock, and indoor recreation areas.

Clubs for students interested in biking, business, community service, choir, Hillel, music, the newspaper, the yearbook, skiing, multicultural affairs, psychology, and history bring together students with similar interests. Weekends are filled with guest comedians, bands, formal and casual dances, lectures, and organized trips to Boston and New York City.

Mitchell College is a provisional member of the NCAA Division III and fields ten intercollegiate teams. Men play baseball, basketball, cross-country, golf, lacrosse, sailing, soccer, and tennis; women play basketball, cross-country, golf, sailing, soccer, softball, tennis, and volleyball. The College has a history of athletic excellence, winning many national and New England championships. A full schedule of intramural sports is organized for students of all athletic experience and ability.

Location

New London, Connecticut, where Mitchell College makes its home, is a major center of activity in southeastern Connecticut, a region rich in historic significance. This small but sophisticated city, also home to Connecticut College and the U.S. Coast Guard Academy, is a maritime and resort center located midway between Boston and New York City on the main rail line.

The campus is situated in the city's most scenic residential section. Bordered by a long stretch of sandy beach, the campus consists of 68 acres of gently sloping hillside and forest. Places for shopping, banking, dining, and fun are within easy walking distance or can be accessed by buses that pass the College entrance. Major shopping malls, factory outlets, and fine and casual dining are minutes from the campus. The region is also home to major tourist attractions, such as the U.S.S. Nautilus and Submarine Museum, Mystic Marinelife Aquarium, Mystic Seaport, Olde Mystic Village, Ocean Beach Park, Stonington Vineyards, Foxwoods Resort and Casino, the Mohegan Sun Casino, and the Essex Steam Train.

Majors and Degrees

Baccalaureate degrees are offered in business administration, communications, criminal justice, early childhood education, environmental studies, homeland security, hospitality and tourism, human development and family studies, liberal and professional studies, psychology, and sport management. Associate degrees are offered in criminal justice, early childhood education, graphic design, human development and family studies, liberal arts, physical education, and sport management.

Students undecided about their academic majors are enrolled in the Discovery Program, which is specially designed to provide special courses, additional advising, and services to explore their full potential and assistance in choosing a major.

Academic Programs

The academic calendar consists of two full semesters that run from September to December and from January to May. In addition to five summer sessions, Mitchell College also offers STEP, a five-week bridging program for incoming freshmen.

All students must complete the core curriculum, which consists of expository writing, composition and literature, effective speaking, introduction to computer and information systems, an introductory psychology or sociology course, a mathematics course, a lab science, and either U.S. history I and II or Western civilization I and II.

If a student is having difficulty, it is recognized early. Mitchell grades at four, seven, and fifteen-week intervals. If a student is experiencing a problem, faculty members and the student's academic adviser work with the student to get back on course. Mitchell's Tutoring Center provides free, unlimited individualized tutoring by trained professionals (not peer tutors) in every academic discipline. It also offers assistance in improving writing, research, and computer skills as well as test and exam preparation and study skills development. Some of Mitchell's most successful students are regular users of the Tutoring Center, and they attribute much of their success to its programs.

Students with diagnosed learning disabilities may enroll in the College's nationally recognized Learning Resource Center, which provides instruction and support to complement a student's regular academic program. Each student is assigned two learning specialists to work one-on-one with the student and in small-group settings. The program is designed to teach the learning strategies a student needs to gain independence.

Off-Campus Programs

When not in class, Mitchell students gain the skills and experience they need to succeed in their careers and to make a difference in their communities. Nearly all academic programs require or encourage students to participate in volunteer opportunities, internships, or practical experiences as part of their curriculum.

Some of the opportunities include exploring the seacoast with a nationally recognized scientist, teaching at a local elementary school, partnering with a local police officer, helping to negotiate a bill through the state legislature, assisting with advertising campaigns, coaching developmentally challenged athletes and practicing the skills of injury prevention, and sparking the imagination of local school children through storytelling sessions.

Academic Facilities

Mitchell's unique 68-acre waterfront campus includes a 73,590-volume library and two primary classroom buildings. Students have full use of Mitchell's state-of-the-art computing facilities with high-speed, full T1 Internet access. The Mitchell College Library, dining hall, residence hall lounges, and most classrooms are equipped with wireless network and Internet access. Computer access is also available seven days a week in the library and computer labs. Campus computers are fully equipped for e-mail, scanning, network printing, and secure access to each student's individual network server storage. Students have access to extensive online information resources (including journal databases, music databases, and eBooks) via the library Web site. High-speed Internet is also available to each student living in the residence halls. For those who do not own a computer, Mitchell offers a computer purchasing plan through Dell and additional service agreements through a local authorized Dell service provider.

Costs

Tuition, room and board, and fees for the 2006–07 year were $33,499. Additional annual miscellaneous expenses, including books, were estimated at $1500 per year. Students enrolled in the Learning Resource Center paid an additional $6500 per year.

Financial Aid

Mitchell annually awards more than $4 million in financial aid, both in need-based and merit-based scholarships and in grant programs designed to recognize academic and leadership abilities. Accepted students may qualify for grants and scholarships that do not need to be repaid. They include the Connecticut Independent College Student Grant Program, Federal Pell Grants, Federal Supplemental Educational Opportunity Grants, and Mitchell Scholarships. Self-help aid in the form of loans is also available. They include Federal Stafford Student Loans (subsidized and unsubsidized), Federal PLUS Loans, and Federal Perkins Loan programs. On-campus job opportunities are plentiful for students regardless of their financial aid status.

Mitchell Valued Potential (MVP) scholarships are awarded based on an individual student's ability to contribute to the College. They may be given to students who demonstrate potential in leadership, volunteerism, and involvement in school activities. Various payment plans are available.

Faculty

Thirty-one full-time and 53 part-time faculty members teach in Mitchell's classrooms. The student-faculty ratio is 12:1.

Student Government

The Student Government Association (SGA) is made up of officers and senators who represent the residents and commuters. It addresses issues with campus administration, organizes community projects, serves as the active voice for the student body, and sponsors at least one campuswide program each semester. The SGA also works in tandem with the Student Activities Office concerning club funding and overall programming.

Student involvement is not only encouraged but also expected of all Mitchell students. An active student leads to a well-rounded person. Students enhance their life with self-discipline skills, demonstrate selfless service, and become happier members of the College family through involvement in student activities, athletics, campus employment, and community service opportunities.

Admission Requirements

Each student is evaluated individually as soon as the completed application, along with the official transcript, is received. Admission is based on academic preparation, scholastic aptitude, personal character, and potential for academic success. Other important factors taken into consideration include the student's motivation, initiative, maturity, seriousness of purpose, and leadership potential. SAT or ACT test scores are optional. A campus visit and admissions interview are recommended. Open houses are held in October, November, February, March, and April and throughout the summer.

Application and Information

Mitchell uses a rolling admission policy. Students can expect to be notified of decisions within weeks of the College's receipt of completed applications and official transcripts sent directly from the students' high schools.

For more information, students should contact:

Kevin Mayne
Vice President for Enrollment Management and Marketing
Mitchell College
437 Pequot Avenue
New London, Connecticut 06320-4498
Phone: 800-443-2811 (toll-free)
Fax: 860-444-1209
E-mail: admissions@mitchell.edu
Web site: http://www.mitchell.edu

Mitchell College's 68-acre campus is located in New London, Connecticut, where the Thames River meets the Long Island Sound.

PAIER COLLEGE OF ART, INC.

HAMDEN, CONNECTICUT

The College

Paier College of Art, Inc., which was founded in 1946 as Paier School of Applied Arts, has educated artists in advertising, illustration, design, interior design, photography, and graphics as well as in other applied art fields. Upon receiving a charter in 1982, the College expanded its commitment to provide as wide a range of art education as possible while maintaining its focus on preparing its students for professional careers in the arts. At Paier, a professional art education occurs in the context of the education of the individual as a whole. The College maintains close relations with the professional art community as well as with the community at large. Instructors and full-time faculty members are all active professionals in their fields and provide an invaluable resource in terms of professional experience and expertise. The curriculum combines career skills with a background in the liberal arts. This approach to instruction—with its expectations of study in the fine arts through drawing, painting, composition, and computer skills and in the mastery of procedures of the specialized field and development of portfolios geared to the workplace—has attracted students seeking rigorous preparation and has resulted in graduates of Paier College of Art finding rewarding careers in the professional world.

Students participate in semiannual shows and sales that are sponsored by the Student Association. These shows provide the student with exposure and reviews from the community at large, peers, and professionals in the field. Paier College of Art is approved by the Connecticut Board of Governors for Higher Education and accredited by the Accrediting Commission for Career Schools and Colleges of Technology and is a member of the International Council of Design Schools.

The current undergraduate enrollment is 249 men and women. The College provides no on-campus living arrangements. Private houses and apartments near the campus offer accommodations for both men and women. A list of rooms may be obtained from the admission office.

Location

Paier College of Art is located on the edge of New Haven. Public transportation provides students with easy access to other area colleges and universities. New Haven and the surrounding communities contain many centers of art display and activity. The Yale Gallery, the Peabody Museum, and the Mellon Center for British Art are examples of the art collections that are available locally. The greater New Haven area supports many galleries, theaters, and dance and musical organizations. New Haven also supports a variety of shopping facilities, hotels, and restaurants. The rolling, picturesque Connecticut countryside is only a short distance away and is complemented by the fine beaches that dot the length of New England's coastline. All of New England, which is rich in the tradition of early America and alive with the creative energy of a well-educated population, surrounds the Paier student with countless opportunities for cultural experiences. Students are also within easy reach of New York, Hartford, and Boston.

Majors and Degrees

Paier College of Art offers programs of study leading to the Bachelor of Fine Arts (B.F.A.) degree in the following studio majors: fine arts, graphic design, illustration, interior design, and photography. An Associate of Fine Arts (A.F.A.) degree is available in photography. Paier College also offers programs of study leading to a diploma in fine arts, graphic design, illustration, interior design, and photography. Certificate programs are offered in graphic production, interior design, portrait and figure painting, and sharp focus/trompe l'oeil painting. Students completing certificate programs may apply the credits earned toward a Bachelor of Fine Arts degree or diploma in their field.

Academic Programs

Degree and diploma candidates begin with a foundation year of required study. A progressive, contemporary philosophy is shared with a respect for classical tradition and structured discipline. The foundation year of study reflects this philosophy and is and has been directed and staffed by outstanding practitioners since the school's inception a half century ago. Classes are mixed, with candidates for degree, diploma, and certificate programs working together. The same degree of professionalism is demanded of and shown to all students, regardless of their program of study. The B.F.A. requires 130 semester hours of study, of which 88 must be in studio work and 42 must be in the humanities and sciences. The diploma requires 104 semester hours, of which 92 must be in studio work and 12 must be in the humanities and sciences. The A.F.A. in photography requires 43 semester hours of studio work and 21 semester hours in the humanities and sciences. The diploma in photography requires 43 semester hours of studio work and 9 semester hours in the humanities and sciences. Certificate programs require from 28 to 34 semester hours of study, consisting almost entirely of studio work.

Paier College of Art operates on the semester academic calendar. Spring and fall semesters are also supplemented by a summer session.

Academic Facilities

The campus is situated at the corner of Circular and Gorham Avenues. Administration activities, including admissions, personnel matters, consideration and disbursement of financial aid, maintenance of student records, and general administration, are conducted at 20 Gorham Avenue. Instructional activities in classrooms, studios, and laboratories designed for the College's purposes are conducted in four buildings that include the library, the auditorium, the computer lab, and exhibition spaces. The library contains 13,000 volumes, subscribes to 70 periodicals, houses a picture reference file of more than 30,000 images, and has a slide library containing more than 24,000 slides. In addition to extensive holdings in the field of the arts, the library contains a well-balanced collection of volumes in the humanities, social sciences, and physical sciences.

Costs

Tuition for 2008–09 is $12,000 per year for full-time degree students and $10,000 per year for full-time diploma students. Part-time tuition is $380 per semester hour. Fees and supplies vary by program of study.

Financial Aid

Paier College of Art has a program of financial aid for those who are eligible that includes the Federal Pell Grant, Federal Supplemental Educational Opportunity Grant, and Connecticut Independent College Student Grant. Loans may be obtained through the following programs: Federal Perkins Loans, Federal Stafford Student Loans, Universal Education Loans, and Federal PLUS loans. Further information may be obtained from the Office of Financial Aid at Paier College of Art.

Faculty

Faculty members at Paier College of Art are all professionals in their fields. As such, their level of expertise in preparing students to enter their chosen profession is invaluable. There are 39 faculty members, including both full-time and part-time practicing professionals. The student-faculty ratio is 6:1.

Student Government

Every member of the College student body is encouraged to participate in the Student Association, which is a vital and influential force in campus activities. The officers of the Student Association act as a liaison between the students and the College administration. Activities include socials, exhibitions of student and faculty work, field trips to major exhibits in Boston and New York, and cultural presentations.

Admission Requirements

Paier College of Art maintains a rolling admission system in which decisions are made throughout the year. Students may apply for full-time or part-time program status or for full-time or part-time nonmatriculated status. All high school and college transcripts, scores on either the SAT or the ACT (for B.F.A. students only), and two letters of recommendation are required. A nonrefundable application fee of $25 must accompany the completed application materials. An interview is required and is a vital part of the application process. A portfolio of recent artwork should be presented at the interview. Students with earned credit from other colleges may be admitted with advanced standing.

Application and Information

Application forms and additional information are available by contacting:

Office of Admissions
Paier College of Art, Inc.
20 Gorham Avenue
Hamden, Connecticut 06514
Phone: 203-287-3031
Fax: 203-287-3021
E-mail: paier.admission@snet.net
Web site: http://www.paiercollegeofart.edu

Students interact with 3-D sculptures.

POST UNIVERSITY

WATERBURY, CONNECTICUT

The University

Founded in 1890, the mission of Post University is to provide our students with the knowledge, personal skills, and experiences required to become leaders in tomorrow's careers. Post University prepares each student, every day, to be a confident, competent, and competitive participant in a global marketplace. The intimate campus, NCAA division II athletics, a curriculum focus on career and self-awareness, and interdisciplinary leadership core classes provide a lively, challenging, and fun environment to help graduates transition into the world of advanced studies and, eventually, work. At Post, students learn how to think, and they experience how education impacts the world of work.

Approximately two thirds of Post University's students live on campus in one of the six residence halls. International students make up 17 percent of the student body. Over 70 percent of undergraduates participate in activities that include student government, the campus activities team, clubs and organizations, and intramural sports or NCAA Division II athletics. Students also enjoy the nearby cultural and social activities in Waterbury and West Hartford, as well as trips to New York City and Boston.

Post students participate in a year-round schedule of intercollegiate and intramural athletic activities. The Post University Eagles are members of the National Collegiate Athletic Association (NCAA) Division II and the Central Atlantic Collegiate Conference (CACC). Men's intercollegiate sports teams include baseball, basketball, cross-country, golf, soccer, and tennis. Women's athletic teams include basketball, cross-country, soccer, softball, tennis, and volleyball. The University also sponsors an active, coeducational equestrian team. Intramural sports are diverse, ranging from softball and volleyball to basketball and flag football. Students enjoy the facilities of the Drubner Conference and Fitness Center, including a gymnasium, a swimming pool, tennis and racquetball courts, a fitness club, and weight-training rooms. The Drubner Conference and Fitness Center also houses the campus bookstore.

Location

Located midway between New York City and Boston, Post University occupies a 58-acre hilltop residential campus in the suburbs of Waterbury, Connecticut. Post's campus and surrounding community offer a safe, scenic, friendly, and convenient home for students. Its location in the heart of Connecticut provides convenient service from Amtrak's Northeast Corridor as well as airline service to Hartford.

The residence halls range from single rooms to suites consisting of private rooms around a shared living and eating facility. This is in addition to the campus's large dining rooms.

Majors and Degrees

The academic programs at Post University are accredited by the New England Association of Schools and Colleges using the same standards that are applied to other universities, such as Harvard and Yale. Post is licensed by the state of Connecticut to grant associate, baccalaureate, and master's degrees in a number of areas, including business, information technology, health, equine management, and security and social services. In addition, Post has a number of certificate programs that prepare students for the practice of specific specialties and that can be integrated into either an associate or baccalaureate degree.

Academic Programs

For the bachelor's degree, students must complete a minimum of 120 credit hours. To receive an associate degree from Post, students must complete a minimum of 60 credit hours.

All programs offer opportunities for internships and cooperative education. For students seeking additional academic challenges, the Post University Honors Program offers the opportunity to pursue independent research and special projects under the guidance of a faculty member.

The University has a two-semester calendar.

Off-Campus Programs

Post University offers students the opportunity to study abroad through a University-sponsored program and/or an approved study/internship-abroad program at another institution. The equine business management program offers a study-abroad option in England. Through these programs, students have an opportunity to broaden their perspectives and experiences. Courses taken abroad are accepted for degree credit at Post University.

To qualify for study abroad, a student must have a cumulative grade point average of 2.5 or better at the time of attendance.

Academic Facilities

All classroom buildings are equipped with the facilities that are necessary for the applied arts and sciences, business, and liberal arts curricula. The Academic Computer Center houses computers to serve all components of the academic curriculum. The center is open to all students, who use the facility for course assignments, simulations, and special projects. The Harold Leever Learning Center provides learning systems that are structured to meet the needs of individual students. Post's Writing Center is staffed with experienced writing coaches, who work with students at all levels of ability. The Traurig Library and Learning Resource Center has a capacity of more then 84,000 volumes and a growing media collection. As a government document depository, the library houses an extensive government publications collection. University-wide Internet access is available. Students majoring in the equine area use several nearby facilities.

Costs

For 2008–09 full-time resident students pay a comprehensive fee of $31,300, covering tuition, room, and board. For commuting students, the comprehensive fee is $21,750 per year. Equine and laboratory fees, the $40 application fee, and an estimated $500 per year for books and supplies are not included in this basic comprehensive fee.

Financial Aid

Post offers financial assistance through the Federal Work-Study, Federal Supplemental Educational Opportunity Grant, Federal Stafford Student Loan, and Federal Perkins Loan programs. Aid is awarded upon evidence of financial need, as determined by the Free Application for Federal Student Aid (FAFSA). In addition, the University has its own scholarship and grant programs, both academic and athletic, and participates in all state programs that are applicable. In order to apply for financial assistance, a student must apply for admission and be accepted to Post and then submit the FAFSA. An institutional application for financial aid must also be submitted. A student may apply for the Federal Pell Grant by submitting the application directly to the federal government or by submitting the FAFSA.

Faculty

The Post faculty has 32 full-time and 46 part-time members, the majority of whom hold advanced degrees in their respective fields. Faculty members focus on instruction and are involved in all facets of student life. All full-time faculty members serve as academic advisers and maintain weekly office hours for student consultation. The student-faculty ratio is 15:1.

Student Government

Students play active roles in the day-to-day functioning of Post University. The students' official voice at the University is the Student Government Association (SGA), which expresses recommendations pertaining to student life, oversees the operations of each active student group, and decides on funding for each group. The Student Activities Committee participates in the scheduling and programming of campus events. A large percentage of Post University's standing committees include student representatives.

Admission Requirements

Post University welcomes applicants who are motivated to succeed academically and in life. Admission to Post University is based upon an evaluation of the candidate's qualifications and the recommendation of an admissions representative. All decisions are made without regard to race, creed, color, religion, national origin, handicap, or sexual orientation.

Criteria for admission are objective as well as subjective. The applicant's academic experience, standardized test scores, personal qualities, recommendations, and individual characteristics are considered. Post has a rolling admissions policy. The Admissions Committee makes a decision with respect to a candidate's admission to the University as soon as the candidate's file is complete. The minimum requirements to make an admissions decision are official high school transcripts, standardized test scores, and the recommendation of an admissions representative, which is gained through an admissions interview. International students are required to earn a minimum score of 500 on the paper-based version or 173 on the computer-based version of the TOEFL and adhere to the above requirements.

Campus visit appointments may be scheduled Monday through Friday from 10 to 4 and on select Saturdays from 10 to 2. Post periodically offers Group Information Sessions, on-site and off-site Open Houses, and live Internet chats. To schedule a campus visit, students should call the Office of Admission at 800-345-2562 (toll-free) or send an e-mail message to admissions@post.edu.

Transfer candidates must have a minimum GPA of 2.0 and must file transcripts from all other colleges and universities attended. Grades of C or higher may receive transfer credits. The maximum number of transfer credits allowed for bachelor's candidates is 90; the maximum for associate candidates is 30.

Application and Information

To apply, students should submit the application form, the nonrefundable $40 application fee, a recommendation, SAT or ACT scores, and the applicable transcripts. A file must be completed before an admissions decision is made. Post employs a system of rolling admissions. However, each student should attempt to file the application packet as soon as possible. This gives the Admissions Committee the opportunity to carefully review the application and grants the student a chance to begin preparation for life at college. Online applications are available through the University's Web site, at http://www.post.edu.

For additional information, students should contact:

Office of Admission
Post University
800 Country Club Road
P.O. Box 2540
Waterbury, Connecticut 06723-2540
Phone: 203-596-4520
800-345-2562 (toll-free)
Fax: 203-756-5810
E-mail: admissions@post.edu
Web site: http://www.post.edu

The Post University campus is lovely year-round.

QUINNIPIAC UNIVERSITY
HAMDEN, CONNECTICUT

QUINNIPIAC UNIVERSITY

The University

Quinnipiac offers four-year and graduate-level degree programs leading to careers in health sciences, business, communications, natural sciences, education, liberal arts, and law. A curriculum that combines a career focus with a globally oriented liberal arts background prepares graduates for the future, whether they start their careers right after commencement or opt to pursue advanced study.

Quinnipiac is coeducational and nonsectarian and currently enrolls 5,516 full-time undergraduates, 805 full-time graduate and law students, and 921 part-time students in its undergraduate, graduate, professional, and continuing education programs. Twenty-five percent of the students are residents of Connecticut; the rest represent primarily the northeast corridor, in all a total of twenty-four states and several countries. The emphasis at Quinnipiac is on community. Students, faculty members, and staff members interact both in and out of the classroom and office. Quinnipiac is big enough to sustain a wide variety of people and programs but small enough to keep students from getting lost in the shuffle. Life on campus emphasizes students' personal, as well as academic, growth. The approximately seventy-five student organizations and extracurricular activities, including intramural and intercollegiate (NCAA Division I) athletics, give students a chance to exercise their talents, muscles, and leadership skills. The University has a student newspaper, TV station, and an FM radio station (WQAQ) and twenty-one intercollegiate teams in men's baseball, basketball, cross-country, ice hockey, lacrosse, soccer, tennis, and track and in women's basketball, cross-country, field hockey, ice hockey, lacrosse, soccer, softball, tennis, track, and volleyball. Teams compete in the Northeast Conference (NEC); men's and women's ice hockey teams are members in the ECAC.

Quinnipiac's 300-acre Mount Carmel (main) campus has fifty buildings. In addition to its academic facilities, the University has twenty-five residence halls of different styles—traditional three- and four-person rooms, suites, and multilevel suites with kitchens—all with functional furnishings and decor. The residence halls currently house 3,500 men and women, about 95 percent of all freshmen and 70 percent of the total undergraduate population. Construction on the nearby 250 acre York Hill section of the campus will add 1,800 beds plus an additional student center and multilevel parking garage to accommodate seniors in suite-style housing beginning in 2009. The Carl Hansen Student Center, containing recreational facilities, meeting rooms, and offices for student organizations, is adjacent to Alumni Hall, a large multipurpose auditorium used for concerts, lectures, films, and various University and community events.

Facilities for athletic activities are found in and around the gymnasium and recreation center plus the TD Banknorth Sports Center on York Hill, which includes twin 3000-plus-seat arenas for basketball and ice hockey. The Recreation Center includes a 24,000-square-foot recreation/fitness facility with a large free-weight room; an exercise machine center; aerobics studios; basketball, volleyball, and tennis courts; and a suspended indoor track. There are also lighted tennis courts, playing fields, and miles of scenic routes for running and biking.

Career Planning begins in each of the schools with assistance from the deans' offices in health sciences, communications, business, and liberal arts. It begins with faculty advisement, along with career exploration, a focus on internships and clinical placements, exploring various major and job fields, and exposure to prospective employers and job preparation.

Graduate programs lead to the Master of Science degree in accounting, computer information systems, interactive communications, journalism, and molecular and cell biology; the Master of Health Science in medical lab sciences, cardiovascular perfusion, pathologist assistant studies, and physician assistant studies; the Master of Science in Nursing in nurse practitioner studies; the Master of Business Administration; the Master of Business Administration in Health Care Management, the Master of Business Administration–Chartered Financial Analyst, and the Master of Arts in Teaching. A $22-million, on-campus facility houses the Quinnipiac University School of Law and its library. The school offers full-time and part-time programs leading to a J.D. degree or J.D./M.B.A. degree in combination with the School of Business.

Location

Situated at the foot of Sleeping Giant Mountain in Hamden, Connecticut, Quinnipiac provides the best of the suburbs and the city. The University is only 8 miles from New Haven, 30 minutes from Hartford (the state capital), and less than 2 hours from New York City and Boston. Bordering the campus is the 1700-acre Sleeping Giant State Park, for walking and hiking. The campus shuttle takes students to shopping and restaurants in nearby Hamden and North Haven, plus to New Haven, where they can visit the acclaimed Yale Center for British Art, attend a performance at the Schubert or Long Wharf Theater (which hosts productions by Quinnipiac's Theater Department), marvel at the dinosaurs in the Peabody Museum of Natural History, dine in fine restaurants, or find easy access to Metro North and Amtrak at the New Haven train station. Quinnipiac's New England location also makes it convenient to enjoy a day in the surf or on the slopes. The beaches on Long Island Sound are easy to reach, and several ski resorts are only an hour's drive from campus.

Majors and Degrees

The School of Health Sciences grants bachelor's degrees in athletic training/sports medicine, biochemistry, biology, biomedical science, chemistry, diagnostic imaging, microbiology/molecular biology, nursing, occupational therapy (5½-year entry-level master's), physical therapy (6½-year entry-level doctorate), physician assistant studies (6-year freshman entry-level master's), and veterinary technology. Students who wish to prepare for entry into medical, dental, chiropractic, veterinary, or other medical schools work with a premed adviser and take classes that prepare them to sit for the various entrance exams.

The School of Business (accredited by AACSB International) offers bachelor's degree programs in accounting, advertising, biomedical marketing, entrepreneurship, finance, information systems management, international business, management, and marketing. The school also offers a five-year combined-degree program in which students may be awarded the B.S. degree in business and a graduate degree in accounting, business administration, or computer information systems (M.S. or M.B.A.).

The College of Liberal Arts offers bachelor's degree programs in computer science, criminal justice, English, gerontology, history, interactive digital design, legal studies (paralegal), liberal studies, mathematics, political science, psychology, social services, sociology, Spanish, and theater. Students can also design their own majors. Certification for teaching elementary and secondary education is offered through a five-year program, resulting in a Master of Arts in Teaching. A bachelor's degree program in psychobiology is interdisciplinary in nature. Students can also continue their study in graduate programs in business, law, journalism, or interactive communications.

The School of Communications offers undergraduate majors in journalism, media studies, production, and public relations and graduate programs in journalism and interactive communications for writing and design in the journalistic community.

Academic Programs

All degree programs at Quinnipiac University are offered through one of the five academic schools. The academic year consists of two 15-week fall and spring semesters and two summer sessions. All baccalaureate candidates are required to complete the University Curriculum, which consists of up to 46 of the 120 semester hours of credit generally needed for graduation at the bachelor's degree level. The University Curriculum promotes the achievement of college-level competence in English and mathematics and requires study in fine arts, humanities, social sciences, and natural sciences. The foundation of the University Curriculum is three university seminars, which focus on the broad theme of community: individual, national, and global in scope. The Writing Across the Curriculum initiative (WAC) stresses the improvement in writing skills in all subject areas. The University honors program addresses the needs and interests of the most academically talented and committed students. Honors students take a minimum of 21 credits in their existing core curriculum or major courses. Academically talented students are identified during the admission process and are invited to participate in the University honors program. Approximately 60 full-time freshmen enter the honors program each fall.

Advanced placement, credit, or both are given for appropriate scores on Advanced Placement tests and CLEP general and subject examinations as well as for scores of 4 or higher in the International Baccalaureate higher-level subjects.

Off-Campus Programs

Students in any of the four undergraduate schools can get hands-on experience in their field through off-campus internships. The University is affiliated with outstanding health and scientific institutions—such as Children's Hospital (Boston), Yale–New Haven Hospital, Hartford Hospital, Gaylord Rehabilitation Hospital (Wallingford), and the University of Connecticut Health Center—throughout the state and the nation. Opportunities for internships also exist in industry, large and small businesses, media outlets, and social and governmental agencies. Academic credit is available for internships and affiliations, which are often part of degree requirements.

Academic Facilities

Academic life focuses on the Bernhard Library, which opened in the fall of 2000. This attractive facility provides users with 600 seats, arranged as individual carrels and small rooms for group study and is open 24/7 during the fall and spring semesters. A wireless network provides access to automated library systems and extensive Web-based resources. In addition, students use the workstations in the library's Cyber Café for online research and classroom assignments. The library houses an extensive collection of books, periodicals, government documents, films, tapes, and microforms. Members of the Quinnipiac University community may also draw on resources from local and statewide institutions through interlibrary loans and shared electronic resources.

Quinnipiac University was identified as one of the top ten most-wired campuses in the country by *PC Magazine* in January 2007. All incoming students must purchase a University-recommended laptop computer for use in the classroom, residence halls, and library. A 'help desk' offers support to the laptop program. Students can register online, access library resources, course-related materials, complete assignments, and view their grades.

More specialized student-computing facilities are located in classrooms throughout the campus. Tator Hall has five computer classrooms and four teaching laboratories containing approximately 200 computers. The multimedia and video laboratories in the Ed McMahon Mass Communications Center each have fourteen Apple MacIntosh G5 and G4 workstations. The computer cluster in the Financial Technology Center at Quinnipiac University's School of Business is a high-tech, simulated trading floor providing students with the opportunity to access real-time financial data, conduct interactive trading simulations, and develop financial models in preparation for careers in finance.

The Echlin Health Sciences Center houses physical and occupational therapy, nursing, and related fields of study. Buckman Center is where many of the science labs are located, including those for chemistry and veterinary technology. A clinical skills lab, for use by nursing students and the physician assistant program, simulates a critical care hospital center. Also in the Center is the Buckman Theatre, which holds plays, concerts, and lectures. The Lender School of Business has satellite capabilities and the Ed McMahon Mass Communications Center, which contains a state-of-the-art, fully digital, high-definition TV production studio, print journalism and desktop publishing laboratories, and a news technology center.

Costs

The basic 2007–08 cost was $39,920, of which tuition and fees (12–16 credits per semester) were $26,720, and room and board averaged $11,200. Other expenses, estimated at $1200 per year, included books, laboratory and course fees associated with specific courses, and personal travel expenses.

Financial Aid

Quinnipiac designs financial aid packages to include grants and scholarships that do not have to be repaid, self-help financial aid programs such as federal and University-based work study, and loans. Quinnipiac uses the Free Application for Federal Student Aid (FAFSA) to determine need. Transfer students are eligible for the same need-based financial aid consideration as first-time freshmen. Quinnipiac also offers a number of renewable scholarships to new, full-time freshmen and transfer students, awarded on the basis of academic merit.

Faculty

The faculty is characterized by its teaching competence and outstanding academic qualifications. Of the 290 full-time faculty members, 75 percent have earned a Ph.D. or the appropriate terminal degree in their field. The faculty also includes a number of part-time teachers who are practicing professionals and experts in their fields. Classes are taught by these scholars and professionals and not by student instructors, and a low student-faculty ratio promotes close associations among faculty members and students.

Student Government

The Student Government is the student legislative body of Quinnipiac. It represents student opinion, promotes student welfare, supervises student organizations, appropriates funds for student groups, and provides voting student representation on the Board of Trustees.

Admission Requirements

Quinnipiac seeks students from a broad range of backgrounds. Candidates are reviewed for admission once their application is complete. Visits to the campus for either an interview, open house, group information session, or a campus tour are strongly encouraged. Transfer students are welcome to make an appointment to discuss requirements and the transfer of credit from previous institutions. Quinnipiac sponsors four open house programs during the year and several Saturday morning information sessions followed by a campus tour.

Application and Information

Quinnipiac generally receives between 12,000 and 13,000 applications for admission and admits just under 50 percent, to enroll an incoming class of 1,350 freshmen and 200 transfer students. Quinnipiac has a rolling admission policy for its undergraduate programs but recommends that freshman applicants submit their application materials well before the deadline of February 1 and that students applying to the physical therapy, nursing, and physician assistant studies programs submit their applications by November 1. Applications can be filed early in the fall of the senior year of high school. Applications begin to be reviewed as soon as they are complete, and the University begins notifying students of decisions in early January. For most programs, a completed application consists of a Quinnipiac application form; a transcript of completed high school courses, including grades for the first quarter of the senior year; a score report for either the SAT or ACT; a personal statement (250-word minimum essay); letter(s) of recommendation; and the application fee: $45 for paper or $30 online at the University Web site or through the Common Application. Students placed on a waiting list are notified of any openings by June 1. When reviewing applications, the University uses the results of the critical reading and the mathematics sections of the SAT and/or the composite score on the ACT for admission and scholarship purposes. Transfer students must forward a transcript of college course work undertaken. Quinnipiac subscribes to the May 1 Candidates Reply Date Agreement. For information about full-time undergraduate study, students should contact:

Office of Undergraduate Admissions
Quinnipiac University
Hamden, Connecticut 06518-1940
Phone: 203-582-8600
800-462-1944 (toll-free)
Fax: 203-582-8906
E-mail: admissions@quinnipiac.edu
Web site: http://www.quinnipiac.edu

For information regarding transfer and part-time study:

Office of Transfer and Part-time Admissions
Quinnipiac University
Hamden, Connecticut 06518-1940
Phone: 203-582-8612
Fax: 203-582-8906
E-mail: transferadmissions@quinnipiac.edu

SACRED HEART UNIVERSITY

FAIRFIELD, CONNECTICUT

The University

Sacred Heart University, which was established in 1963, is a coeducational independent institution of higher learning in the Catholic intellectual tradition whose primary objective is to prepare men and women to live in and make their contributions to the human community. The University aims to assist in the development of people who are knowledgeable of self, rooted in faith, educated in mind, compassionate in heart, responsive to social and civic obligations, and able to respond to an ever-changing world. Sacred Heart University is committed to combining education for life with preparation for professional excellence.

A Strategic Plan provides a road map for the University as it strives to meet the needs of today's students. The plan calls for the construction of new facilities, such as a new chapel and academic building and updates to the library, as well as the implementation of new academic, athletic, and social programs. Ten residence halls have opened in the last ten years. In addition, the University was one of the first Catholic colleges to introduce a student mobile computing program, providing new students with two wireless notebook computers during their four years.

The current undergraduate enrollment includes approximately 3,200 full-time students. Extracurricular activities include fraternities, sororities, student government, the student newspaper, the student yearbook, a student radio station, academic clubs in almost every area of study, the debate club, the International Club, La Hispanidad, theater, dance, and intramural sports programs. Sacred Heart University offers men's and women's competition in NCAA Division I baseball, basketball, bowling, crew, cross-country, equestrian, fencing, field hockey, football, golf, ice hockey, lacrosse, soccer, softball, swimming and diving, tennis, track and field (indoor and outdoor), volleyball, and wrestling.

In addition to its bachelor's degree programs, the University offers nine graduate degree programs: Master of Arts in Religious Studies (M.A.R.S.), Master of Arts in Teaching (M.A.T.), Master of Business Administration (M.B.A.), Master of Science in Nursing (M.S.N.), Master of Science (M.S.) in chemistry, Master of Science in computer science and information technology, Master of Science in occupational therapy, Master of Science in geriatric rehabilitation and wellness, and Doctor of Physical Therapy (D.P.T.). Many of these programs are five-year combined programs.

Location

Ideally located in Fairfield County in southwestern Connecticut, Sacred Heart University is 1 hour northeast of New York City, 2½ hours southwest of Boston, and 1 hour southwest of Hartford. More than half of the 67-acre campus is surrounded by a thirty-six-hole golf course.

Opportunities for internships and co-op programs are extensive due to the number of corporate headquarters located throughout Fairfield County. Sacred Heart University's neighbors include the world headquarters for General Electric as well as the Discovery Museum of Science and Industry.

Majors and Degrees

Sacred Heart University offers Bachelor of Arts and Bachelor of Science degrees. Programs of study in education and allied health include athletic training, education (elementary and secondary certification), exercise science, nursing, occupational therapy, and physical therapy. In the arts and sciences, the following areas of study are available: art, biology, chemistry, communications/media studies, communications technology, computer science, criminal justice, English, environmental science, French (minor only), history, Italian (minor only), information technology, mathematics, music (minor only), philosophy, political science, psychology, religious studies, social work, sociology, Spanish, and women's studies (minor only). In business, the University offers accounting, business administration, business economics, finance, and sport management.

Preprofessional programs are available in dentistry, law, medicine, optometry, pharmacy, and veterinary medicine.

Special programs include cooperative education, English as a second language, the Honors Program, internships, legislative internships, and study abroad. The University has its own study-abroad programs in Australia, Ireland, and Italy.

Academic Programs

A strong liberal arts core forms the basis for all curricula. Academic course work is divided into four colleges—the College of Arts and Sciences, the John F. Welch College of Business, the College of Education and Health Professions, and the University College. The John F. Welch College of Business received accreditation in March 2007 by AACSB International. The academic year consists of two 15-week semesters.

Candidates for the bachelor's degree must complete at minimum of 120 credits, with a minimum of 30 credits taken at the University. The baccalaureate curriculum is made up of five components: the required core (12 credits), the elective core (33–35 credits), the major field (30–58 credits), and the common core, named The Human Journey (15 credits).

Off-Campus Programs

Through the Internship Program, students combine employment in business, industry, government, or social service agencies with classroom work and receive academic credit for learning derived from the work experience. Cooperative education opportunities are also offered within various departments, such as accounting, communications/media studies, criminal justice, political science, psychology, social work, and sociology. Through a summer internship program, students may be employed in an area related to their major and their career goals. The Career Development Office places 98 percent of University students in a full-time job or graduate school.

Academic Facilities

The University's library contains more than 164,000 volumes, 716 periodical titles, and 110,000 nonprint items. It also provides online database searching services. The Art Department includes studios for graphic design. Science facilities include four biology labs, a climate-controlled greenhouse, a microbiology preparation lab, six chemistry labs, and a neuroscience lab. The modern foreign language laboratory is state-of-the-art. The campus also houses an 850-seat theater, an art gallery, and a professional radio station (National Public Radio).

Sacred Heart University is in the eleventh year of its Student Mobile Computing Program. Full-time students receive two laptop computers during their four years as an undergraduate student. The campus has been transformed into a fully networked environment. Sacred Heart University is one of the first higher educational institutions in the country to deploy a wireless computer network. Sacred Heart University believes that computer literacy is a necessary component of that preparation. Therefore, the University is committed to a system in which students can use their laptop in class, in the library, and in their residence hall.

Costs

Costs for 2006–07 were $23,750 for full-time undergraduate tuition (includes laptop computer and fees) and $9694 for room and board. The cost of books is estimated to be $600 per year.

Financial Aid

Sacred Heart University maintains a strong commitment to provide higher education to as many students as possible by making available scholarships, grants, loans, and part-time employment. Financial aid packages are developed by combining Sacred Heart University's own resources with a variety of federal and state financial aid programs. Eighty-five percent of all students receive some form of financial assistance.

Any undergraduate or graduate student who is enrolled in the University on at least a part-time basis (6 credits per semester) is eligible for consideration. Emphasis is placed on students who are enrolled in a full-time degree program; part-time awards are limited. Applicants for aid must submit the Free Application for Federal Student Aid (FAFSA) and the CSS PROFILE to the College Scholarship Service on or before February 15.

The University offers several sources of financial aid, including academic scholarships, Connecticut Stafford Loans, and Federal Supplemental Educational Opportunity Grants. A Family Allowance is available when 2 or more members of the same family attend the University. Deferred-payment plans and endowed scholarships are also awarded. Employment within the University is awarded under the terms of the Federal Work-Study Program. The Office of Career Development maintains a list of part-time jobs in the local area. Further information can be obtained from the Dean of University Student Financial Assistance.

Faculty

The student-faculty ratio is 13:1. There are 420 faculty members, 200 of whom are full-time. Eighty-two percent have terminal degrees in their field, and 44 percent have tenure. Many faculty members are involved in research, writing, or production, yet their primary focus is on teaching. Close communication between students and faculty members is encouraged. All students are assigned a faculty adviser within their major field and a Student Life Mentor.

Student Government

Students play a major role in planning and decision making. Student Government representatives and class officers are concerned with improving the University and working for the needs of their classmates. In addition to sponsoring many functions, the Student Government serves as a liaison between the administration/staff and the student body.

Admission Requirements

Sacred Heart University is small enough to work with each student individually throughout the admissions process. The University is committed to enrolling a diverse, highly qualified, and well-motivated student body. Candidates for admission must demonstrate their ability to perform academically and contribute significantly to the life of the University. High school seniors should submit an official high school transcript, SAT or ACT scores, one letter of recommendation, an essay, and a completed application. Transfer students should submit an official transcript from all previously attended colleges, a high school transcript, one letter of recommendation, an essay, and a completed application.

Application and Information

Full-time students may enroll in either the fall or the spring semester. All applicants must submit a completed application, all necessary credentials, and an application fee of $50. Applications for the Early Decision Program must be received by November 15. Applications for priority admissions must be received by February 1 for an April 1 notification date. All other applications are considered on a rolling admission basis; candidates are notified of the admission decision as soon as all credentials have been received and reviewed.

Inquiries or application materials should be sent to:

Dean of Undergraduate Admissions
Sacred Heart University
5151 Park Avenue
Fairfield, Connecticut 06825-1000
Phone: 203-371-7880
E-mail: guastellek@sacredheart.edu
Web site: http://www.sacredheart.edu

SAINT JOSEPH COLLEGE
WEST HARTFORD, CONNECTICUT

The College

For seventy-five years, Saint Joseph College has been combining excellence in liberal arts with professional education for women. Founded in 1932 by the Sisters of Mercy, the college for women has expanded to include a coeducational graduate program and a baccalaureate degree program for adults. In partnership with each other, these units of the College offer a diverse student population unmatched opportunities to excel—intellectually, socially, and ethically.

The core values of Catholic identity, commitment to women, compassionate service, academic excellence, respect and integrity, hospitality, and diversity are evident in the College's curriculum and daily life. Students from a multitude of faith traditions and backgrounds are empowered for success.

There are 889 undergraduates in The Women's College, where faculty members and students emphasize leadership in academics, career, and community. Drawing on its Mercy heritage, the College is a community that promotes the growth of the whole person in a caring environment that encourages strong ethical values, personal integrity, and a sense of responsibility to the needs of society. Women lead every organization, from the Business Society and Student Government to Campus Ministry, Multicultural Affairs, and honors societies. They shine in artistic performances, as coordinators of community service projects, and on the athletic fields. Students also serve with faculty members and administrators on College-wide committees. In just thirteen years since The O'Connell Athletic Center was constructed, the College has become competitive in eight NCAA Division III sports: basketball, cross-country, lacrosse, softball, soccer, swimming/diving, tennis, and volleyball. The athletic complex features a six-lane pool, gymnasium, suspended jogging track, dance studio, fitness center, outdoor track, softball field, and tennis courts.

Saint Joseph College has thirteen Georgian brick buildings, including five residence halls, which are arranged around two tree-lined quadrangles on an 84-acre campus. Approximately 70 percent of the first-year students in the Women's College live on campus. Special student services include career planning, alumnae mentoring, internship placement, counseling, health services, academic advisement, and campus ministry. Most recently, the College has announced its plans to build new residence halls allowing for better integration of academic and cocurricular life on campus. New residence halls are scheduled for occupancy in August 2008.

Saint Joseph College alumnae have considerable impact on the welfare of their communities. They are leaders in many fields, including aerospace research, business, medicine, education, social work, environmental science, law, and politics. Recent graduates enjoy successful careers in business, industry, government, nonprofit organizations, education, health care, human services, and the arts.

Saint Joseph College is accredited by the New England Association of Schools and Colleges. The chemistry program is accredited by the American Chemical Society, and the social work program is accredited by the Council on Social Work Education. The Coordinated Undergraduate Program in Dietetics is accredited by the American Dietetic Association. The nursing program is accredited by the Commission on Collegiate Nursing Education.

Location

The College is located in suburban West Hartford, 4 miles from the state capitol and the city of Hartford's arts and entertainment district. Among the nearby attractions are the Hartford Civic Center and Coliseum; Bushnell Memorial Hall, where the latest Broadway musicals are performed; and the Wadsworth Atheneum, the oldest public art gallery in the United States. Hartford is a cosmopolitan city with diverse ethnic flavors. It is also the home of the Tony Award–winning Hartford Stage Company, the Hartford Symphony Orchestra, the Connecticut Opera Company, the Hartford Ballet, and the Dodge Music Center, which features indoor and outdoor concerts. West Hartford Center, just minutes from campus, offers an array of coffee bars, boutiques, movie theaters, and restaurants.

Majors and Degrees

Saint Joseph College has always enjoyed a strong academic reputation based on a combination of liberal arts and professional majors. The College awards the B.A. or B.S. in accounting, American studies, art history, biochemistry, biology, chemistry, child study, dietetics and nutrition, economics, English (literature, writing), environmental science, family studies (family and consumer science, contemporary family issues), history (archives and museum skills), international studies, liberal studies, management, mathematics (math/computer science, math/economics), nursing, philosophy, psychology, religious studies, social work, sociology, Spanish, special education, and women's studies.

Teaching certification is offered in elementary education, secondary education, and special education.

Research, clinical, and work placements are factored into all majors as an important component of each student's program.

Academic Programs

Each student must complete a minimum of 120 credits to obtain a baccalaureate degree, and 47 of those credits must be distributed among the general education/liberal arts courses at the College. Specifically, students must take courses in the humanities, social sciences, natural sciences, philosophy, religious studies, and physical education. An academic counselor assists each student in planning her program of study.

An honors program is available, as are several bachelor's-to-master's degree programs. The Center for Academic Excellence manages the College's award-winning Writing Portfolio Program, which enhances students' writing skills. The center also provides tutoring and other academic support services. Students may design their own major or may develop an interdisciplinary major or minor around a particular theme or problem related to their special talents, personal interests, or career goals. An exciting component of most majors at Saint Joseph College is the internship. Students earn credit for internships at a variety of sites, including the state capitol, the Bushnell Theatre, Aetna, Legislative Office, the Connecticut Department of Economic Development, WVIT-TV, Connecticut Children's Medical Center, the Science Center of Connecticut, and numerous other businesses.

Off-Campus Programs

Students at Saint Joseph College may take courses at cooperating institutions through the Hartford Consortium for Higher Education. This is a special arrangement among seven Hartford-area colleges—Saint Joseph College, Rensselaer at Hartford, Trinity College, Central Connecticut State University, St. Thomas Seminary, Hartford Seminary, and the University of Hartford—through which students are able to cross register for courses. No additional tuition is charged, and all credits are transferable.

Students at Saint Joseph College may study abroad during their junior year, a winter recess, or a summer session. Certain majors have specific international-study recommendations and opportunities, and student are assisted by the Director of International Studies and Programs in planning for an international-study experience.

In addition to programs provided by study-abroad providers, the College has its own program in Guyana. Faculty members also lead occasional trips to Mexico and Europe.

Those students majoring in nursing, social work, and nutrition, and those in the graduate counseling program, may gain practical experience providing community-based, accessible health screenings and referrals; health and nutrition education; counseling services; and social work case management services at The Wellness Center on Church Street in Hartford. The College recently entered into a partnership with the Franciscan Center for Urban Ministry in order to reach out to its neighboring city and enhance the quality of life of its residents in need.

Academic Facilities

The Pope Pius XII Library has a collection of more than 134,000 volumes, including computer databases, periodicals, microforms, audiovisuals, a Sirsi online catalog, and OCLC interlibrary loans. A collection of materials used in elementary and secondary education is featured in the Curriculum Materials Center.

The College uses laboratory schools with several of its academic programs. The renowned School for Young Children, located one block from the campus, and its counterpart, the School for Young Children at Asylum Hill, in Hartford, are operating preschools that provide child study majors with training and experience. The Gengras Center, located on the campus, is a special education school serving children and young adults (ages 3–21) from approximately fifty area cities and towns. It provides for special education needs and also helps to prepare special education teachers.

The College's primary technology centers are located in McDonough Hall; Internet access is available throughout campus. Additional facilities and services include a media center that provides production materials, expertise, and equipment for making and using a number of media instructional aids; science and nursing labs; and the Carol Autorino Center. The center includes Lynch Hall, which houses humanities, faculty offices, and classrooms; the Bruyette Athenaeum, featuring the 365-seat Hoffman Auditorium; the Saint Joseph College Art Gallery; a print study room; large lecture hall; reception room; and music practice rooms. The building also houses the College's archives.

Costs

The tuition and fees for full-time freshmen entering in 2007 are $23,490. Room and board cost $11,500. The cost per credit for part-time students is $530.

Financial Aid

The goal of the Saint Joseph College Financial Aid Program is to place a high-quality, private education within the reach of as many qualified students as possible. This goal is achieved by offering need- and merit-based financial aid that includes a combination of grants, loans, and on-campus employment opportunities. More than 85 percent of full-time undergraduate students receive some form of financial assistance.

Faculty

Saint Joseph College's faculty consists of 85 full-time faculty members and 4 librarians. Of the total faculty, 68.8 percent are women. Of the full-time faculty, 90 percent hold the highest possible degrees in their fields. Small classes benefit both students and professors. The student-faculty ratio is 10:1. The faculty and all members of the College community promote the welfare of students and help them attain the objectives set forth by the College's mission. Faculty members also serve as advisers to many extracurricular activities, including sports, campus ministry, and community service; direct students in independent study; involve students in scholarly research; and act as mentors before and after graduation.

Student Government

The Student Government Association works for effective communication among students, faculty members, and administrators. Students are encouraged to voice their opinions and concerns to the association for consideration and action. In addition, student representatives sit as voting members with faculty members and administrators on major College-wide committees. The Student Government Association encourages the development of leadership skills and provides funds annually for several of its members to attend leadership workshops and conferences.

Admission Requirements

Saint Joseph College seeks women who are willing to accept the challenge of an excellent academic program while pursuing the interests and goals that will shape their future lives. Applications are encouraged from interested students of every race, age, and religious affiliation. In accordance with Section 504 of the Rehabilitation Act of 1973, which prohibits discrimination on the basis of disability, and the Americans with Disabilities Act of 1990, Saint Joseph College is committed to the goal of achieving equal educational opportunities and full participation for people with disabilities in higher education.

Candidates for first-year admission should complete a four-year course of study in a regionally accredited secondary school or have equivalent homeschooling preparation. The program should include 16 academic units in college-preparatory courses distributed among the areas of English, mathematics, natural sciences, social studies, and foreign languages. Applicants are required to submit scores of the SAT or ACT tests. A personal interview is a highly recommended part of the admission procedure, since it offers a mutual opportunity for the student and Admissions Counselors to discuss educational and professional goals.

The Committee on Admissions operates on the principle that a student's ability, motivation, and maturity should be determined by a careful individual review of all the applicant's credentials, including the academic record, standardized test scores, written personal statement, and guidance counselor's evaluation. Special consideration may be given to some applicants whose preparation varies from the recommended pattern but whose record gives evidence of genuine intellectual ability and interest. International students should contact the Office of Admissions for further information.

Saint Joseph College admits qualified students for transfer in both fall and spring semesters.

Application and Information

The Committee on Admissions recommends that application for first-year admission be made in the first semester of the senior year in secondary school. All applications should be completed by April 1. A nonrefundable $50 fee must be sent with paper applications; the application fee is waived for students who apply via http://admissions.sjc.edu. Students are encouraged to complete their FAFSA online at http://www.fafsa.ed.gov as soon as possible after January 1. The priority deadline for completing the FAFSA is February 15. Students should complete the FAFSA using estimated income information if they or their families will not have completed their tax returns prior to February 15.

Transfer applicants for the spring semester should apply by December 1; applicants for the fall semester, by June 1. Students applying to the nursing program should contact the College to learn about special deadlines. Transfer candidates who wish to apply for financial aid should complete or update the FAFSA online by November 15 if applying for the spring semester or by August 15 if applying for the fall semester.

For further information about admission to Saint Joseph College, students should contact:

Nancy D. Wunderly
Director of Admissions
Saint Joseph College
1678 Asylum Avenue
West Hartford, Connecticut 06117
Phone: 860-231-5216
866-44-CTSJC (toll-free)
Fax: 860-231-5744
E-mail: admissions@sjc.edu
Web site: http://admissions.sjc.edu

SOUTHERN CONNECTICUT STATE UNIVERSITY

NEW HAVEN, CONNECTICUT

The University

The rich academic and social environment at Southern Connecticut State University encourages students to discover who they are, who they want to be, and how to realize their dreams. A public coeducational university founded in 1893, Southern offers 117 undergraduate and graduate programs. Fascinating internships, unique research opportunities, a challenging faculty, and a dynamic campus enrich every program. Southern is located in New Haven, the heart of "academic Connecticut."

Southern has six academic schools: Arts and Sciences; Business; Education; Communication, Information, and Library Sciences; Health and Human Services, including nursing, public health, recreation and leisure studies, and social work; and Graduate Studies. Southern offers several honors programs, including the Honors College, for highly motivated students. The Honors College is a four-year alternative program featuring team-taught interdisciplinary courses, symposia, and a written thesis. The Office of Student Supportive Services provides tutorial support for students with special needs.

The student body represents diverse ethnic and socioeconomic groups. Although most students reside in Connecticut, students from thirty-eight states and thirty-nine countries also enroll at Southern. Approximately 13,000 students attend Southern, including about 9,000 undergraduates. Of the 6,700 full-time undergraduates, 2,700 live on campus in eight modern residence halls and town houses. Other students commute or reside in off-campus housing in the Southern neighborhood.

Competitive athletes and eager amateurs enjoy multifaceted intramural and intercollegiate sports programs at Southern. Intramural and club sports include coed three-on-three and five-on-five basketball, cheerleading, flag football, coed floor hockey, a golf tournament, ice hockey (men), karate, rugby (men and women), skiing and snowboarding, coed softball, Ultimate Frisbee, coed soccer, a tennis tournament, Wiffle ball, and coed volleyball. A member of the National Collegiate Athletic Association (NCAA), the Eastern College Athletic Conference, and the Northeast-10 Conference, Southern offers student athletes competitive opportunities in several intercollegiate sports. A university with a long tradition of athletic excellence, Southern ranks among the top ten NCAA Division II colleges and universities, with nine NCAA team championships and sixty-seven individual championships. Southern offers intercollegiate competition in men's baseball, basketball, cross-country, football, soccer, swimming, and track and field. Southern holds six national championships in men's soccer and three in men's gymnastics. Southern offers intercollegiate programs for women in basketball, cross-country, field hockey, gymnastics, lacrosse, soccer, softball, swimming, track and field, and volleyball. Outstanding facilities are available to all athletes in Moore Fieldhouse, Pelz Gymnasium, and the Jess Dow Field outdoor sports complex.

Location

New Haven, Connecticut, is a sophisticated city of 130,000 people on picturesque Long Island Sound. Southern is located in the city's Westville section, near historic West Rock Park. Rich in tradition, New Haven is a classic college town; about 35,000 students attend its half-dozen fine universities and colleges. Only 75 miles from New York City and 3 hours from Boston, New Haven is an integral part of the economic, cultural, and social life of the Northeast. Students enjoy easy access to outstanding cultural opportunities, including movies, restaurants, clubs, concerts, seaside activities, sports, museums, and world-famous theater at the Yale Repertory, the Shubert, and Long Wharf.

Majors and Degrees

Southern offers the Bachelor of Arts (B.A.) and the Bachelor of Science (B.S.) degrees. The Bachelor of Arts degree is awarded in anthropology, art (art history and studio art), biology, chemistry (biochemistry), communication (communication disorders and media studies), earth science, economics, English, French, geography, German, history, Italian, journalism, liberal studies, mathematics, media studies, music, philosophy, physics, political science, psychology, sociology, Spanish, and theater.

The Bachelor of Science degree is awarded in anthropology (archeology, cultural, general, linguistics, and physical), art (ceramics, graphic design, jewelry making, painting, photography, printmaking, and sculpture), biology, business (accounting, business economics, finance, international business, management, managing information systems, and marketing), chemistry and biochemistry, communication (creative message construction, interpersonal/relational, organizational communication, and video production), computer science (information systems), earth science (environmental, geology, and oceanography), exercise science (athletic training, human performance, and teacher education), geography, information and library science, journalism, mathematics, nursing, physics, political science, psychology (research), public health (environmental and health promotion), recreation and leisure (community, outdoor, and therapeutic), social work, and sociology.

The Bachelor of Science degree with teaching certification is offered in art education, early childhood education, and elementary education.

The Bachelor of Science degree with certification for secondary education is offered in biology, chemistry, earth science, English, exercise science, French, geography, German, history and social science, Italian, mathematics, physics, political science, Spanish, sociology, and special education.

Southern also offers preprofessional study in dentistry, engineering, law, medicine, and veterinary medicine.

Academic Programs

The University operates on a two-semester calendar. The fall semester usually begins the first week in September and ends in mid-December. The spring semester, which includes a one-week spring recess in March, begins the third week of January and ends in mid-May. Southern also offers two 5-week summer sessions and a three-week intersession program in January.

Southern maintains a strong commitment to the liberal arts and sciences as fundamental elements of a high-quality education. To ensure all students acquire the best education possible, Southern offers a strong yet flexible program that underscores the basics while encouraging individual choice. All baccalaureate degree candidates must complete a minimum of 122 hours of credit. Majors consist of at least 30 prescribed hours of credit in one specific, approved field. Degree candidates also must fulfill the All-University Requirements, a common core of courses ranging from 41 to 54 credits in liberal studies. In addition, candidates for the B.A. degree must meet a foreign language requirement plus 28 credits of electives from areas of interest. Candidates for the B.S. degree must also satisfy the foreign language requirement and meet certain distribution requirements. Some professional B.S. degree programs enable students to develop a minor or a concentration in addition to the major with 12 credits in electives.

Off-Campus Programs

Southern's location in the heart of a major urban area enables the University to cultivate a growing list of meaningful regional internships. Aspiring social workers enjoy learning opportunities that extend beyond the classroom into New Haven's dynamic urban environment. Students in the B.S. nursing degree program acquire clinical experience at Yale–New Haven Hospital, the Hospital of Saint Raphael, and other sites that are linked by distance learning programs. Internships also are available for journalism students in city newsrooms and local TV stations. The University also offers internships at Long Wharf Theatre; ESPN Broadcasting; the Circle in the Square Theatre in New York City; MTV; Shearson Lehman Brothers, Inc.; and others.

Academic Facilities

A $260-million building program is rapidly transforming Southern campus life. The evolving landscape features a new West Campus Residence Complex and parking garage, a new baseball field, and the expansion of Engleman Hall, the University's main administration and classroom building. Renovations have begun that will double the size of the Hilton C. Buley Library. The new Michael J. Adanti Student Center opened in early 2006. The 125,000-square-foot facility includes a ballroom, a 200-seat movie theater, a fitness center, and an expansive bookstore. A focal point for campus life, the center is also home to Southern's student newspaper, the radio station, a modern cafeteria, a bookstore, a TV lounge, a copy center, and other facilities. Southern supports more than ninety campus clubs and organizations, ranging from academic and career groups, such as the marketing club and the literary magazine, to religious, theatrical, and political clubs. Southern's campus groups sponsor popular extracurricular activities such as film festivals, concerts, and art exhibits.

Southern continues to provide students with a full range of facilities and services throughout the multiphase building project. Operations continue without interruption at the Hilton C. Buley Library, which houses 125,000 electronic databases and academic resources. Seventy Macintosh terminals, laser printers, scanners, and twenty PC compatibles are available in a Macintosh lab in the library's lower level. The library also houses the Learning Resources Center, a well-equipped multimedia education curriculum laboratory. Manson Van B. Jennings Hall contains sixty-six science laboratories, a large amphitheater, classrooms, and the University's Academic Computer Center, with more than 100 workstations for student and faculty research. Additional computer centers are available in residence halls. All on-campus housing includes high-speed Internet service via RESNET. Other campus facilities include a satellite-equipped journalism lab; a modern television studio in Ralph Earl Hall of Fine Arts; the John Lyman Center for the Performing Arts, a 1,650-seat theater for major productions; the Robert Kendall Drama Lab for experimental theater; the Center for the Environment; the Multicultural Center; the Communication Disorders Center; the Adaptive Technology Lab; and the Disability Resources Center.

Costs

Annual tuition and fees for 2007–08 for Connecticut residents are $6624. Tuition and fees for out-of-state residents are $15,344. On-campus room and board fees for the year are $8502. Student books, supplies, and personal expenses average $2000 per year. All costs are subject to change. Prospective students should contact the Office of Financial Aid and Scholarships for current information.

Financial Aid

The Office of Financial Aid and Scholarships coordinates grants, scholarships, long-term low-interest loans, and part-time student employment for students and families who demonstrate financial need. The University offers the Federal Perkins Loan, the Federal Pell Grant, the Federal Supplemental Educational Opportunity Grant, the Federal Stafford Student Loan, the Federal PLUS loan, and the Federal Work-Study Program. Southern also provides alumni scholarships. Southern's Tuition Installment Plan enables matriculated students to make monthly tuition payments throughout the academic year. More than 60 percent of Southern's undergraduates receive financial aid. Students who seek assistance must complete the Free Application for Federal Student Aid (FAFSA) and send it to the central processor for receipt by March 7, 2008. Prospective students can file the FAFSA form on paper or on the Web at http://www.fafsa.ed.gov.

Faculty

Like the University's student body, Southern's faculty members represent a broad spectrum of backgrounds, interests, and scholarly achievements. Southern's more than 700 faculty members share a deep commitment to teaching, writing, and research. More than 90 percent of the 402 full-time faculty members hold Ph.D.'s from major colleges and universities around the world. Many faculty members serve as academic advisers. In addition, the University offers counseling to help students with academic, personal, and career decisions. The student-faculty ratio is 17:1.

Student Government

The Student Government is the voice of the undergraduate student body at Southern. The Student Government's 24 voting members meet regularly to discuss students' interests in several areas, from funding to academic policies. Student Government members also serve with administrators and faculty members on key University committees. Resident students govern themselves through their respective residence hall councils and the Inter-Residence Council.

Admission Requirements

Southern's selective admission policy considers each student as an individual, with particular consideration given to personal accomplishments and motivation. Southern seeks students with diverse cultural values and backgrounds; no applicant is accepted or rejected because of race, color, gender, sexual orientation, age, disability, religion, or national origin. Candidates must be high school graduates or hold an equivalency diploma. Their secondary school program should include at least 13 academic units of college-preparatory work, including 4 years of English, 3 years of mathematics (algebra 1, geometry, and algebra 2), 2 years of foreign language, 2 years of science (including 1 year of laboratory science), and 2 years of social sciences (including U.S. history). Other factors include the student's high school record, class rank (preferably in the upper 50 percent), and competitive SAT or ACT scores.

Application and Information

Candidates for admission should apply by May of their high school senior year. The Admissions Office mails its first acceptance notice December 1. Early applicants have priority for housing and financial aid. Applicants must submit academic records, including a complete transcript of high school grades and class rank; an admission application; a $50 nonrefundable fee; a written recommendation from a high school principal, teacher, or guidance counselor; and a copy of the SAT or ACT report. To request application forms and more information, students should contact the Undergraduate Admission Office, Southern Connecticut State University, 131 Farnham Avenue, New Haven, Connecticut 06515. Students may apply online by visiting the University's Web site and clicking on admissions.

Dr. James L. Williams
Interim Director of Admissions and Enrollment Management
Admissions House
Southern Connecticut State University
131 Farnham Avenue
New Haven, Connecticut 06515-1355
Phone: 203-392-SCSU
888-500-SCSU (toll-free)
Web site: http://www.SouthernCT.edu

Southern's "Serie Metafisica XVIII" (1983), an outdoor sculpture by Herk Van Tongeren, provides the ideal setting for study in the sunshine.

TRINITY COLLEGE

HARTFORD, CONNECTICUT

The College

Since its founding in 1823, Trinity has provided an undergraduate education of uncommon quality. Widely acknowledged as one of the top liberal arts colleges in the country, Trinity has been recognized by a panel of national education editors for its bold and innovative ideas to advance the cause of higher education and ensure greater access.

In its commitment to the rigorous pursuit of the liberal arts and to instruction that is personal and conversational, Trinity is an ideal college. At the same time, Trinity is in close touch with the world beyond its campus. In that respect and in terms of the outstanding opportunities Trinity's capital city location offers students, a Trinity education is indeed a real education.

While remaining faithful to the classic liberal arts tradition, Trinity offers a distinctive educational experience that prepares students for the challenges and opportunities of the twenty-first century. Building on its traditional strengths in arts and humanities and exceptional offerings in science and engineering, Trinity engages students in a conversation with the world through its study-abroad programs, interdisciplinary programs, and innovative, rigorous programs that draw on the rich cultural, educational, and professional assets of Hartford. State-of-the-art electronic facilities support Trinity's pioneering use of information technology in classrooms. The heart of a Trinity education, however, remains the personal encounter between professor and student, the intellectual partnership that discovers a world of ideas and ignites a passion for learning.

Trinity's students come from forty-four states and twenty-four countries. The College believes that a diverse community makes learning flourish. Trinity's undergraduate enrollment of more than 2,100 students is about equally composed of men and women. More than 90 percent of undergraduates live on campus in College housing. Trinity is engaged in continuing campus revitalization programs that preserve its impressive Gothic buildings as it also develops a campus for the twenty-first century.

Trinity offers a rich array of extracurricular activities—films, plays, concerts, musical theater, sports, academic symposia, and visits by nationally and internationally known writers, speakers, and performers. Participation is an important word on campus, and Trinity students have abundant opportunities to lead and to be involved in numerous student clubs; special interest groups; theater, dance, and music groups; debate; academic programs; campus cinema; Trinity's radio station; and many student publications. With 19 acres of playing fields, Trinity also offers an extensive athletic program. More than half of the student body participates on twenty-nine men's and women's varsity teams (Division III) and in twelve intramural sports. The Ferris Athletic Center features a swimming pool, a fully equipped fitness center, crew tanks, eight international-size squash courts, basketball courts, and an indoor track.

Location

Situated on a beautiful 100-acre campus in the center of Hartford, the capital of Connecticut, Trinity offers the best of both worlds—a supportive and active campus community located in a city that provides students with myriad opportunities for internships, community service, and cultural exploration. Hartford's businesses, governmental agencies, cultural organizations, and nonprofit institutions offer Trinity students hundreds of opportunities to explore careers through the College's extensive internship program. Hartford has a number of cultural institutions, including the Wadsworth Atheneum (the oldest public art museum in the nation), Mark Twain House, Harriet Beecher Stowe Center, Connecticut Opera, Hartford Ballet, Hartford Symphony, Hartford Stage, and a number of smaller theaters and clubs that provide a cultural stew of dance, theater, and music. The shopping districts of Hartford and surrounding suburbs are nearby. The impressive Connecticut coast is easily accessible, and Boston and New York are each about 2 hours from campus. Off campus, Trinity has a field station in Ashford, Connecticut, dedicated to research in the natural sciences and a wide range of environmental educational endeavors.

Majors and Degrees

The College offers a Bachelor of Arts degree and a Bachelor of Science degree. Majors offered include American studies; anthropology; art history; biochemistry; biology; chemistry; classical civilization; classics; computer science; economics; educational studies; engineering; English; environmental science; history; international studies; Jewish studies; mathematics; modern languages: Chinese, French, German, Italian, Japanese, Russian, and Spanish; music; neuroscience; philosophy; physics; political science; psychology; public policy and law; religion; sociology; studio arts; theater and dance; and women, gender, and sexuality. Trinity also offers a computer coordinate major, and interdisciplinary majors may be individually constructed. Trinity offers a five-year program in engineering and computer science, which leads to a bachelor's degree from Trinity and a master's degree from Rensselaer Polytechnic Institute through Rensselaer at Hartford.

Academic Programs

Featuring more than 900 courses, Trinity's curriculum provides a framework within which students may explore the many dimensions of an undergraduate education. At the same time, the curriculum offers each student flexibility to experiment, to deepen old interests and develop new ones, and to acquire specialized training in a major field. Students must demonstrate proficiency in writing and mathematics and fulfill a five-part distribution requirement that consists of at least one course in each of the following categories: arts, humanities, natural sciences, numerical and symbolic reasoning, and social sciences.

Off-Campus Programs

More than 50 percent of Trinity students study abroad for a semester or a year at Trinity's Rome Campus, at Trinity in Spain, or in other approved study programs in more than forty countries on six continents. Several Trinity-sponsored global learning sites operate in Austria, Chile, France, Nepal, Russia, South Africa (Cape Town), Trinidad, and Turkey. Through the theater and dance department, Trinity offers the Trinity/La MaMa Performing Arts Program in New York City, an extraordinary program that provides intensive study in theater, dance, and performance.

Academic Facilities

The Raether Library and Information Technology Center is home to the Raether and Watkinson Libraries, as well as the Computing Center. It is a place where students and faculty members come together for the serious work of scholarship, where researchers can pore over a book or conduct investigations through a wide selection of online databases. The Raether Library, one of New England's largest collegiate libraries, houses nearly 1 million print volumes and approximately 700,000 nonprint materials, including slides, microforms, sound recordings, and other materials in audiovisual and electronic formats. In addition, an online catalog linked with Wesleyan University and Connecticut College provides access to more than 2 million titles. The Watkinson Library, with its impressive collection of rare books, manuscripts, and other unique resources, supports a broad range of research interests.

The campus is fully wired, with every student room connected to the College network and the Web. Public access computers are also available 24 hours a day in select facilities.

Costs

Costs for the 2007–08 academic year were $35,110 for tuition, $9420 for room and board, and $1760 for fees.

Financial Aid

The College meets 100 percent of the need of all students who are offered admission and demonstrate financial need. While need status is occasionally a factor, the vast majority of admissions decisions are made on a need-blind basis. Students must file the Free Application for Federal Student Aid (FAFSA) as well as the Financial Aid PROFILE of the College Scholarship Service. Admissions applications are due by January 1; FAFSA and PROFILE applications are due by February 1. Students are notified of admission and aid decisions by the first week of April. Normally, need is met with a financial aid package that includes grant assistance, work-study, and federal student loans. Federal funds for which accepted students are eligible include Pell Grants, Federal Supplemental Educational Opportunity Grants (FSEOG), Perkins Loans, Stafford Loans, and PLUS Loans. Most students who demonstrate need are granted an on-campus job as part of their financial aid package. Approximately 50 percent of all students have a job; about 40 percent of all students have employment based on need. The ratio of grant assistance to loans and work-study aid is sometimes affected by the academic strength of the student's record. Trinity continues to expand its aid budget to keep pace with the College's goal to increase the socioeconomic and ethnic diversity on campus. Forty percent of the students receive financial aid.

Faculty

The distinctive strength of a Trinity education has always been the close interaction between students and a faculty of devoted teacher-scholars. A student-faculty ratio of 11:1 enables supportive yet challenging educational experiences that establish a foundation for lifetime learning and enables students to pursue academic interests with passion. Nearly 30 percent of recent graduating classes collaborated with faculty members in conducting research; many students have made joint presentations at international, national, or local symposia or have published jointly prepared papers. All courses are taught by Trinity faculty members and not by graduate assistants.

Although the first calling of Trinity's professors is teaching, they are also active publishing scholars of national and international distinction. History professor Joan Hedrick, for example, won the Pulitzer Prize for her biography of Harriet Beecher Stowe. Other notable professors include Henry DePhillips, distinguished chemist and researcher on art restoration; Dan Lloyd, acclaimed philosopher and author of *Radiant Cool;* Lesley Farlow, accomplished dancer and choreographer; Samuel Kassow, distinguished historian; and Joseph Bronzino, an authority on biomedical engineering. Trinity professors pride themselves on their accessibility and keen interest in helping students.

Student Government

Trinity fosters the growth of future leaders by providing students with many opportunities to exercise and test their leadership skills. The Student Government Association (SGA), for example, provides students a strong voice in social, cultural, and—through membership on faculty committees—academic matters. Composed of elected class representatives, the SGA constantly seeks the expertise and insights of all interested students, and its committees offer enterprising students many chances to participate and to develop leadership skills.

Admission Requirements

Trinity seeks an ethnically and geographically diverse group of highly motivated students who have completed a rigorous course of study in secondary school and have demonstrated energy, talent, and leadership in a variety of extracurricular activities. Trinity has no specific GPA minimums or test-score cutoffs. The College is highly selective, and its candidates typically have an A– high school average. At least 16 academic units of college-preparatory course work are recommended, including a minimum of 4 years of English, 3 years of foreign language, 2 years of laboratory science, 2 years of algebra, 1 year of geometry, and 2 years of history. Last year, over 6,000 men and women from all over the nation and world applied for admission to the College, which enrolls an entering class of 575 students. Transfer students with a 3.0 GPA in a strong course of study at another accredited college or university are considered for admission to the sophomore or junior classes.

Admissions officers review each application individually; decisions are based on each candidate's academic record (course of study and GPA), recommendations from secondary school teachers and counselors, test scores, personal strengths, talents, activities, and application and supplemental essays.

Application and Information

Students must submit completed applications to the Admissions Office. Application deadlines are November 15 for early decision I applicants (with notification by December 15), January 1 for early decision II applicants (with notification by February 15), and January 1 for regular decision applicants (with notification by April 1). Transfer applicants must submit applications by April 1 for admission in the following fall semester (with notification by early June) and by November 15 for admission in the following spring semester (with notification by early January). Students may submit an electronic Common Application at http://www.commonapp.org.

Inquiries should be made to:

Larry Dow
Dean of Admissions and Financial Aid
Admissions Office
Trinity College
Hartford, Connecticut 06106-3100

Phone: 860-297-2180
Fax: 860-297-2287
E-mail: admissions.office@trincoll.edu
Web site: http://www.trincoll.edu/admissions

The Long Walk at Trinity College.

UNIVERSITY OF CONNECTICUT

STORRS, CONNECTICUT

The University

The University of Connecticut (UConn) is a premier public research university in the United States. Established in 1881 with a class of 12 students, UConn has grown into a nationally ranked university with more than 16,000 undergraduate students, 7,000 graduate and professional students, 1,500 faculty members, and 140,000 alumni. The University has been recognized in numerous college guides for its excellent academic programs, knowledgeable professors, and top-notch athletics. It has also been called a top value and a best buy.

UConn encompasses fifteen schools and colleges that offer eight undergraduate degrees in 100 majors, twelve graduate degrees in eighty fields of study, and graduate professional programs in law, social work, medicine, and dental medicine. The University consistently attracts and accepts some of the nation's most talented students. The University's faculty members are among the most impressive scholars in the U.S. and are recognized throughout the world as leaders in education, research, and scholarship. Ninety-one percent have a Ph.D. or the highest degree in their field.

The University's research activities advance knowledge in a range of academic disciplines. UConn stands among the country's leading institutions in the breadth and contribution of its research. The Carnegie Foundation classifies UConn as a Research I University; it is one of only two public universities in New England to hold this distinction. In terms of research funding, UConn is ranked in the top thirty-five public universities by the National Science Foundation.

UConn's library system maintains the largest publicly supported collection of research materials in Connecticut. The Homer Babbidge Library on the main campus in Storrs contains 2.1 million volumes and is among the top thirty major research libraries nationally in terms of total holdings and funding. The University is home to the Roper Center for Public Opinion Research, the world's most comprehensive library of public opinion and survey data, and the Thomas Dodd Research Center, which maintains an international collection of historical manuscripts and archives, including an agreement between the African National Congress (ANC) and UConn to form a partnership to achieve and share with scholars material from the ANC's struggle for human rights in South Africa.

UConn's flagship campus is located on a beautiful 4,000-acre setting in Storrs, Connecticut. The University also offers the convenience and accessibility of campuses in Stamford, West Hartford, and Waterbury as well as the natural splendor of its Torrington and Avery Point (Groton) facilities. The University's school of law is located in Hartford, while its schools of medicine and dental medicine are located at the University of Connecticut Health Center in Farmington. A graduate school of social work is in West Hartford. Through UCONN 2000 and 21st Century UConn, a landmark twenty-year, $2.3-billion plan to renew, rebuild, and enhance UConn's campuses, the University is building and maintaining superior academic facilities throughout the state and creating state-of-the-art residential and recreational facilities at its main campus in Storrs.

The University of Connecticut maintains a strong tradition of student involvement. More than 250 clubs and organizations offer students access to everything from academic discussion groups to a vast assortment of intramural recreational programs offered in state-of-the-art facilities. UConn's athletic programs perennially rank among the best in the country. UConn offers twenty-four men's and women's varsity sports, most competing at the highest level. The Storrs campus also has student-run media, including radio station WHUS, *The Daily Campus* newspaper, and cable television station UCTV.

Location

The University is located in Storrs, Connecticut, midway between New York and Boston, each of which is about 1½ to 2½ hours away. The most used route to the University is exit 68 off I-84. The University's property to the east of the highway on the knoll where the campus begins includes pastures, hilltop cornfields, and picturesque barns, charming reminders of the area's agricultural origins of more than a century ago. Connecticut's capital city, Hartford, is only a half hour away. UConn is a cultural and recreational focal point in Connecticut.

Majors and Degrees

Undergraduates at the University of Connecticut may major in any of the more than 100 different fields. The College of Liberal Arts and Sciences offers the Bachelor of Arts and Bachelor of Science degrees in approximately thirty-nine academic areas, ranging from anthropology to statistics and including coastal studies, ecology and evolutionary biology, and journalism. The College of Agriculture and Natural Resources offers the Bachelor of Science in ten special areas, including natural resources, environmental science, dietetics, and medical laboratory sciences. The School of Business Administration offers the Bachelor of Science in nine areas, including accounting, finance, and management information systems. The School of Education offers the five-year integrated bachelor's/master's teacher education program as well as the Bachelor of Arts and Bachelor of Science degrees in the Department of Kinesiology including athletic training, fitness management, exercise physiology, sports management, and park and recreational management. The School of Engineering offers the Bachelor of Science in Engineering degree and has programs in biomedical, chemical, civil, computer engineering, computer science, electrical, environmental, materials, mechanical, and metallurgy and materials engineering and management and engineering for manufacturing (in conjunction with the School of Business Administration). The School of Fine Arts offers the Bachelor of Fine Arts and Bachelor of Music degrees with majors in art, dramatic arts, music, and puppetry. The School of Nursing offers the Bachelor of Science in nursing. The School of Pharmacy offers a six-year Doctor of Pharmacy program.

The University offers an individualized major to meet the needs of students whose academic interests encompass two or more of the academic departments. The University also offers a Bachelor of General Studies degree program at the junior-senior level for non-traditional part-time students. A two-year associate degree is available through the Ratcliffe Hicks School of Agriculture.

Academic Programs

Most bachelor's degree programs require the successful completion of 120 semester hours. The exceptions are nursing, which requires 131 semester hours; engineering, which requires 134; pharmacy studies, which requires 125; the integrated bachelor's/Doctor of Pharmacy, which requires 196; and education (an integrated bachelor's and master's degree program), which requires 150 semester hours. All programs require the completion of courses in eight core areas in addition to the work required for the major. UConn follows a two-semester system. Shorter sessions are offered for summer study and during the intersession between the fall and spring semesters.

Entering freshmen at Storrs may be selected for admission to the Honors Scholar Program, a nationally competitive academic program for outstanding students. Admission to the program at a later time, but before the junior year, is open to students who have done exceptional work at the University.

A cooperative education program for students in most majors integrates classroom learning and work experience in business, industry, and public service. The University offers interdisciplinary majors in Latin American, Asian American, Center for European Studies, urban and women's studies, environmental science, and mathematical actuarial science. Individualized majors are available in Judaic, Asian, European, Native American, medieval, and peace studies, as well as in public relations, international studies, and criminology. Intensive study of critical languages such as Arabic, Chinese, or Japanese is also offered. Army and Air Force ROTC programs are available.

UConn also has a Special Program in Medicine that offers students a coordinated curriculum that includes four years of undergraduate preparation and the opportunity to attend UConn's School of Medicine.

Off-Campus Programs

The University grants credit for programs and courses taken abroad through programs sponsored by the University as well as other institutions and agencies in Argentina, Australia, Austria, Brazil, Canada, Chile, China, Costa Rica, Czech Republic, Denmark, Dominican Republic, England, France, Germany, Ghana, Hungary, Ireland, Israel, Italy, Japan, Mexico, the Netherlands, Poland, Portugal, Russia, Spain, Sweden, and Switzerland. The Semester-at-Sea Program is also offered. Since 1968, through the Urban Semester Program, the University has given students a special educational opportunity to live, learn, and work in Hartford, Connecticut. The University also participates in the National Student Exchange Program, which allows students to spend a year of study at another university.

Academic Facilities

The University's facilities are undergoing a huge transformation, thanks to a twenty-year, $2.3-billion commitment from Connecticut's state legislature. Now in its twelfth year, the program already has resulted in a completely renovated Student Recreational Facility, four multilevel buildings that comprise the South Campus residence halls, a 220,000-square-foot chemistry building, a biotechnology building, six additional student residence halls, more than forty classrooms that have been renovated, two parking garages, a new physics/biology building, the Avery Point Marine Sciences Building, a new School of Business Administration, a new Pharmacy and Life Science Complex, a new bookstore, and four new residential complexes. The University's academic core has been transformed into a pedestrian campus.

The Homer Babbidge Library at Storrs houses more than 2 million volumes, more than 3.1 million units of microtext, 603,790 government documents, and 7,867 current periodical subscriptions. It is one of the most technologically sophisticated research libraries in the United States. Specialized libraries in music and pharmacy are housed separately in those schools and raise the library systems total holdings to approximately 2.1 million volumes, including the regional campuses and law school. The art department has spacious, well-lighted studios and galleries, including the new Nafe Katter Theatre for performing arts. Other academic facilities provide specialized classroom and laboratory space for psychology, communication sciences, pathobiology, material sciences, physics, computer science, and human development and family relations, to name but a few. Computer facilities and laboratories are located in libraries, academic buildings, and residential facilities. There are 1,800 computers on campus in approximately ninety computer labs. The University also has an art museum, the William Benton Museum of Art, and the State Museum of Natural History. Theatrical, musical, and speaker programs take place in the Harriet S. Jorgensen Theatre, the Albert N. Jorgensen Auditorium, and the Von der Mehden Recital Hall.

Costs

For students attending the Storrs campus, tuition and University and student fees are $9318 for state residents and $24,030 for out-of-state students in 2008–09. The average residence hall cost is $5090, and the seven-day University meal plan costs $4210. For students attending the University at a regional campus, in-state tuition and University and student fees totaled $7754 in 2007–08.

Financial Aid

Financial assistance in the form of grants, low-interest loans, and part-time employment is administered by the Student Financial Aid Office. All financial aid applications must be submitted by March 1 for both the fall and spring semesters. The assessment of need is based on the ability of the student's family to contribute, the amount of the student's savings for college, and other financial resources that may be available. To be considered for financial aid, applicants must submit the FAFSA. Applicants for the Federal Stafford Student Loan must also file the FAFSA. The University awards a number of renewable merit-based scholarships to students with outstanding academic credentials, as well as to Finalists and Semifinalists in the National Merit Scholarship, National Achievement, and Hispanic Scholars programs.

Faculty

Nearly 91 percent of the University's 1,096 full-time faculty members hold a doctorate or another terminal degree in their field. The student-faculty ratio is 19:1. Faculty members at all levels teach undergraduate courses, including freshman courses. Faculty members engage in a wide variety of research, which in recent years has been sponsored by grants totaling about $110 million for the University and its Health Center schools.

Student Government

All undergraduates are members of the Undergraduate Student Government, the principal and officially recognized organization representing the undergraduate student body. The units of governance and service formed by this body reflect the major areas of interest and need among the students.

Admission Requirements

Applicants must be graduates of an approved secondary school and have completed at least 16 units of work. At least 15 of the secondary school units must consist of college-preparatory work, including 4 years of English, 2 years of a single foreign language (3 years strongly recommended), 3 years of mathematics (2 years of algebra and 1 year of geometry or the equivalent), 2 years of a laboratory science, and 2 years of social science, including at least 1 year of U.S. history. Several of the undergraduate schools and colleges of the University have additional course prerequisites for admission. Applicants should be in the upper range of their high school graduating class and must submit satisfactory scores on the SAT or ACT. SAT Subject Tests are not required for admission. The University is committed to ensuring access to higher education for students from minority groups. Transfer students are also encouraged to apply; their admission depends primarily upon the quality of the college record, the quantity and character of courses completed, and the intended field of study at the University. Advanced standing or course credit may be given to students on the basis of Advanced Placement examinations or through successful completion of regular University courses sponsored by the University at selected Connecticut secondary schools. Campus visits and interviews are encouraged although not required.

Application and Information

Students applying Early Action (deadline December 1) are strongly encouraged to apply online at http://www.admissions.uconn.edu. The application form, also available at the guidance offices of all Connecticut high schools, should be submitted no later than February 1 for Storrs freshmen and July 1 for regional campus freshmen; however, priority is given to applications submitted online. The application deadline for transfer students is April 1. For all students, the financial aid application deadline is March 1.

For more information, students should contact:

Office of Undergraduate Admissions
University of Connecticut
2131 Hillside Road, Box Unit 3088
Storrs, Connecticut 06269-3088

Phone: 860-486-3137 (freshmen and transfers)
860-486-4900 (Lodewick Visitors Center, campus tours)
E-mail: beahusky@uconn.edu
Web site: http://www.uconn.edu/

UNIVERSITY OF HARTFORD

WEST HARTFORD, CONNECTICUT

The University

The University of Hartford is a fully accredited, independent, nonsectarian institution. The University is composed of seven degree-granting schools and colleges: the College of Arts and Sciences; College of Engineering, Technology, and Architecture; College of Education, Nursing, and Health Professions; Hillyer College; the Barney School of Business; the Hartford Art School; and The Hartt School.

The current full-time undergraduate enrollment is more than 4,700 men and women. A wide range of interests, goals, and backgrounds is found among the students, who represent forty-six states and fifty-three countries. There are about 100 organized student groups, including clubs devoted to special interests or to political, professional, religious, or civic activities as well as service learning and community service activities and groups. Intercollegiate (NCAA Division I) and intramural athletics, student publications, and AM and FM radio stations provide further opportunities for extracurricular involvement. In addition, The Hartt School, the Hartford Art School, and the University Players present a variety of concerts, exhibitions, and theatrical productions each year. Recreational and fitness needs of the University community as well as intramural and intercollegiate sports are served by a well-equipped 130,000-square-foot Sports Center and outdoor athletic facilities.

Career Services provides vocational counseling and information on occupations, employers, testing, and graduate schools; serves as a reference and credential source; and provides an on-campus recruiting program for graduating students. University College addresses the needs of the part-time adult learner through courses, programs, and educational counseling. A trained counseling staff is available to assist part-time students in planning their education and resolving their special concerns and needs.

More than 85 percent of all full-time undergraduates reside on campus. The University offers a wide array of types of residence halls, from traditional dormitory-style to fully equipped town house–style apartments.

Location

The University is located in the residential suburb of West Hartford. The area provides an environment conducive to the development of the student's cultural and intellectual pursuits. The many facilities include libraries, museums, theaters, the Hartford Civic Center and Convention Center, a symphony orchestra, several other colleges, modern shopping centers, fine restaurants, an international airport, surface transportation, and intercity highway systems.

Majors and Degrees

The Bachelor of Arts is offered with majors in art history, biology, chemistry, communication, criminal justice, drama, economics, English, foreign languages and literatures, history, international studies, mathematics, multimedia Web design and development, music, philosophy, physics, political economy, politics and government, psychology, rhetoric and professional writing, and sociology. A Bachelor of Arts in secondary education with a major in English or mathematics is offered in the College of Education, Nursing, and Health Professions. The Bachelor of Fine Arts is offered in actor training, ceramics, dance, design, drawing, experimental studio, illustration, music theater, painting, photography, printmaking, sculpture, and video.

The Bachelor of Music is offered at The Hartt School, with majors in applied music (guitar, orchestral instrument, organ, piano, and voice), composition, jazz studies, music education, music history, music management, music production and technology, opera, piano accompanying and ensemble, and theory. A five-year music education program is also offered, as are five-year double-major programs. Two interdisciplinary music programs are available: the Bachelor of Music with an emphasis in management, offered by The Hartt School in conjunction with the Barney School of Business, and the Bachelor of Science in Engineering with an acoustics and music major, offered by the College of Engineering, Technology, and Architecture.

The Bachelor of Science is awarded with majors in biology, chemistry, chemistry-biology, computer science, early childhood education, elementary education, gender studies, health science, human services, legal studies, mathematics, medical technology, nursing (for registered nurses only), physics, radiologic technology, respiratory therapy, and integrated special education/elementary education, offering dual certification and covering emotional disabilities, learning disabilities, and mental retardation. Majors for the Bachelor of Science in Business Administration (B.S.B.A.) degree are accounting, economics and finance, entrepreneurial studies, finance and insurance, insurance, management, and marketing. A combined B.S. in health science and doctorate in physical therapy (B.S./D.P.T.) program is also available.

Additional B.S. programs, offered by the College of Engineering, Technology, and Architecture include ABET-accredited programs in electrical, mechanical, civil, computer, and biomedical engineering as well as interdisciplinary B.S.E. options. The most popular B.S.E. options are acoustics and music, biomedical engineering, and environmental engineering. Technology programs include the Bachelor of Science in architectural engineering technology, audio engineering technology, computer engineering technology, electronic engineering technology, and mechanical engineering technology as well as the Associate in Applied Science in electronic engineering technology (A.S.) and the Associate in Applied Science in computer engineering technology (A.S.).

Hillyer College offers the Associate of Arts and provides the general education course work required to complete most of the University's baccalaureate programs. Particular emphasis is placed on the development of academic skills through small classes and close faculty-student interaction. An Associate of Arts and an Associate of Science in legal assistance are offered through the College of Arts and Sciences.

University Studies offers the Bachelor of University Studies, a B.A. degree program created for the part-time adult student who typically has previous college experience and seeks to complete a baccalaureate degree. Also offered is a B.A. degree program in multimedia Web design and development for full-time undergraduates. Created for students who want to learn how to use and develop multimedia technologies that fit into today's wired world, this program combines courses across several disciplines where students create and use technology with user interaction in mind.

Academic Programs

The University of Hartford enjoys a national reputation for the breadth and depth of its program. More than seventy undergraduate majors are offered through seven schools and colleges.

Students are encouraged to sample a variety of academic areas and can enroll in courses in any of the colleges on campus. Those who have special interests can develop interdisciplinary majors that combine courses from the different schools within the University. Academic advisers are assigned to all students to help guide them in curriculum choices, career exploration, and the transition to University life. In order to help students learn more about how different academic disciplines approach related problems, the All-University Curriculum was developed. Courses are often team taught from different fields of expertise, and topics are examined from the perspective of several academic disciplines. The University also has a special program to assist students who may be undecided about a major. A reading and writing center, where students on an individual basis are helped to increase their proficiency in writing, research, reading comprehension, and speed as well as study and test-taking skills, is available to the entire student body. Further help in math is given through the Math Tutoring Lab, which is staffed by full-time faculty members and math majors. Selected students are encouraged to participate in the Honors Program. Honors students have the opportunity to graduate with an Honors Degree.

Off-Campus Programs

Intercampus registration through the Hartford Consortium for Higher Education permits University of Hartford students to take certain courses at the School of the Hartford Ballet, Saint Joseph College, and Trinity College. Teaching and human services majors in the College of Education, Nursing, and Health Professions have opportunities for field and/or clinical experiences where applicable. A central internship and cooperative education office is available to custom-tailor work experiences within many of the University's programs.

Academic Facilities

Seven schools and colleges are housed on the main campus. The Harry Jack Gray Center houses the William H. Mortensen Library; the Mildred P. Allen Memorial Library; the Museum of American Political Life; the Harry J. Gray Conference Center; the Joseloff Gallery; the University Bookstore; studios for architecture, art, radio, and television; and the Communication Department. The library has approximately 583,000 items, including books, musical scores, recordings, periodicals, journals, and microfilm units as well as the latest in computer technology, including high-speed and wireless Internet access. Extensive resources are also available through the Hartford Consortium for Higher Education, the Hartford Library, and the Inter-Library-Loan systems.

The Asylum Avenue campus is listed on the National Register of Historic Places. The 13-acre wooded campus contains beautiful examples of traditional ivy-covered Georgian architecture.

The University of Hartford Computer Center houses the central computer systems and operates a high-performance campus-wide network, which connects all student residential housing, all academic buildings on campus, and the University's remote locations. The University's network is connected via a high-speed telecommunication link to the Internet and the World Wide Web. The residential network gives each student resident his or her own high-speed Ethernet connection to the campus network and the Internet. The library is connected to the campus network and provides network access through computers in study carrels and study rooms and through wireless access. The online systems of the library include the online catalog for book, audio, and video collections; CD-ROM databases; and easy-to-use Web access for many of the library's online resources and electronic reserves. All of the University network resources may be accessed on campus in any University facility and off campus by using computers with network connectivity.

Public access computing labs, used by all students of the University, are provided at various locations around the campus. In addition, college-specific labs are available to students. All labs are equipped with microcomputers (both PCs and Macs) and are connected to the campus network and the Internet. Typical microcomputer software includes word processing, spreadsheet, database management, and graphics programs; programming languages; and Web browsers for accessing the Internet. Help is available from on-duty lab assistants. In addition to these computer labs, there are specialized computer facilities for instruction and learning. Wireless Internet access is available in all academic buildings, libraries, and dining facilities.

Costs

Tuition for incoming students was $25,806 for the 2007–08 academic year; student service fees, $1190; on-campus room costs, $6424; and board, $3996. A variety of on-campus housing accommodates 3,400 students.

Financial Aid

Financial aid for University of Hartford students totals approximately $98 million annually, including student loans. Scholarships, grants, loans, and work-study opportunities are provided through the federal government, private agencies, interested individuals, and University funds. University funds are disbursed based upon the college or school in which the student is enrolled, availability of funds, applicant pool, and competition for funds. More than 90 percent of all full-time undergraduate students receive some type of University assistance; the average out-of-pocket expense is $18,100 (estimate) per year. Partial-tuition scholarships are awarded to entering students who have demonstrated outstanding academic achievement or talent.

Faculty

There are 700 full-time and adjunct faculty members. The undergraduate and graduate faculties are essentially the same group, and 79 percent of the members hold the terminal degree in their field. Academic and personal advisory service is readily available. Each new student is assigned to a faculty adviser during summer orientation.

Student Government

The student governing body that represents all full-time students is the Student Government Association, through which students and faculty join in developing and coordinating the cocurricular activities of the University. Students are also represented on all major administrative committees, including the Board of Regents.

Admission Requirements

The Office of Admission considers the quality of the secondary school curriculum, academic performance in secondary school, ACT or SAT results, evidence of a desire to succeed, and leadership qualities shown by academic and extracurricular activities. Auditions, portfolios, and other tests are required of music and art applicants.

Application and Information

The University employs a rolling admission policy. For further information, students should visit the University on the Web at http://admission.hartford.edu or contact:

Office of Admission
University of Hartford
West Hartford, Connecticut 06117
Phone: 860-768-4296
800-947-4303 (toll-free)
Fax: 860-768-4961
E-mail: admission@hartford.edu
Internet: http://admission.hartford.edu

COLLEGE DATA CENTER • CONNECTICUT

UNIVERSITY OF NEW HAVEN

WEST HAVEN, CONNECTICUT

The University

The University of New Haven's (UNH) mission is to prepare career-ready graduates for meaningful roles in today's global economy and to nurture pursuit of lifelong learning. Founded in 1920, the University of New Haven is a private, independent institution focused on combining professional education with liberal arts and sciences. UNH is committed to educational innovation, to continuous improvement in career and professional education, and to support of scholarship and professional development. UNH became a four-year college in 1958. Moving to its present location in West Haven in 1960, UNH rapidly expanded its programs, facilities, and faculty, attracting a student body that now stands at more than 4,000—including the current enrollment of 2,424 full-time day students among its undergraduates.

The University is fully accredited by the New England Association of Schools and Colleges (NEASC). Individual programs, departments, and schools hold various forms of national professional accreditation. Four of the University of New Haven's bachelor's degree programs—chemical, civil, electrical, and mechanical engineering—are fully accredited by the Engineering Accreditation Commission of the Accreditation Board for Engineering and Technology, Inc. (EAC/ABET). The computer science program is fully accredited by the Computing Accreditation Commission of the Accreditation Board for Engineering and Technology, Inc. (CAC/ABET).

Despite a broad academic program, UNH is small enough to accommodate individualized educational needs. Programs evolve and adapt to meet changing career interests as well as the requirements of business, industry, and professional fields. Small classes foster close student-faculty relationships. Accelerated weekend and evening programs in business and convenient evening hours provide access for part-time students in engineering, computers, public safety, and the arts and sciences.

The main campus is in West Haven, Connecticut, on a hillside close to Long Island Sound. UNH also operates a satellite branch, the Southeastern Center in New London, Connecticut. Main campus administrative and classroom buildings support the University's four academic colleges: the College of Arts and Sciences, the College of Business, the Tagliatela College of Engineering, and the Henry C. Lee College of Criminal Justice and Forensic Sciences. Following the addition of the Graduate School in 1969, New Haven College was designated a university. Twenty-seven master's degree programs attract full- and part-time graduate students, while more than eighty associate and bachelor's degree programs are available to entering freshmen and transfer students in a great variety of academic disciplines. In 2007, UNH established University College to oversee the graduate school admissions process as well as its evening, accelerated, cohort, and executive degree programs.

Other main campus buildings include the Marvin K. Peterson Library, Echlin Hall, the Bayer Hall admissions building, the Campus Book Store, new residence halls and apartments, and Bartels Hall, the campus center, which houses dining facilities and student activities. The Charger Gymnasium and athletic fields are located on the North Campus, just two short blocks from Maxcy Hall, the main administration building. The David A. Beckerman Recreational Center, a new state-of-the-art athletic facility for the benefit of all students, opened in fall 2007.

UNH is currently an NCAA Division II school and offers seventeen intercollegiate varsity athletic programs as well as an extensive intramural program for both men and women. Varsity teams for men include baseball, basketball, cross-country, golf, indoor track, outdoor track and field, soccer, and volleyball. Women's varsity sports are basketball, cross-country, indoor and outdoor track, lacrosse, soccer, softball, tennis, and volleyball. UNH Charger teams have earned national top-twenty rankings in a variety of sports. The University currently competes in the East Coast Conference (ECC); however, in the fall of 2009, UNH will move from the ECC to the Northeast 10 Conference. Considering a move to NCAA Division I, the University officially entered an exploratory year in June 2007. During this year, UNH will continue to compete as a Division II school.

Approximately two thirds of the full-time undergraduate day students live on campus in the eight residence halls. Approximately fifty clubs and organizations are open to students. Included are student chapters of professional societies, religious organizations, social groups, special-interest clubs, student councils, cultural groups, and fraternities and sororities.

Location

West Haven is contiguous to New Haven. There are theaters that attract star performers from the entertainment world, a deep-water harbor and beaches, fine restaurants, museums, and galleries in the area. Numerous social and cultural programs are presented by the many colleges and universities in the area. New Haven is served by a local airport and major railroads, and its location at the junction of two interstate highways places the University of New Haven within easy driving distance of New York, Boston, Cape Cod, and the ski areas of New England.

Majors and Degrees

The College of Arts and Sciences offers Bachelor of Arts degrees in art, chemistry, communication, English, global studies, graphic design, history, interior design, liberal studies, mathematics, music, music and sound recording, music industry, political science, and psychology; the Bachelor of Science degree in biology, biotechnology, dental hygiene, environmental science, marine biology, mathematics, music and sound recording, and nutrition and dietetics; and the Associate in Science degree in dental hygiene, graphic design, and interior design.

The College of Business offers the Bachelor of Science degree in accounting, business administration, communication, finance, management of sport industries, and marketing and electronic commerce, as well as the Associate in Science degree in business administration and communication. The College of Business also offers the Bachelor of Science degree in hotel and restaurant management and in tourism and hospitality administration.

The Tagliatela College of Engineering offers the Bachelor of Science degree in chemical engineering, chemistry, civil engineering, computer engineering, computer science, electrical engineering, general engineering, information technology, mechanical engineering, and system engineering and the Associate in Science degree in computer science.

The Henry C. Lee College of Criminal Justice and Forensic Sciences offers the Bachelor of Science degree in criminal justice, fire protection engineering, fire science, forensic science, and legal studies and the Associate in Science degree in criminal justice, fire and occupational safety, and legal studies.

Academic Programs

The University of New Haven offers a broad range of programs in both liberal arts and professional areas. Experiential learning is emphasized, and there are diverse and numerous opportunities for career-oriented internships, cooperative education, independent study, and industrial projects. Certain types of professional experience are required in a number of degree programs. The Center for Learning Resources offers a tutoring service that is open to all students.

The undergraduate division operates on a 4-1-4 calendar. Credit is given for successful scores on the CLEP and Advanced Placement examinations. A University honors program provides outstanding study opportunities in most undergraduate disciplines. The residence requirement for all degrees is 30 credit hours.

UNH believes that all students pursuing a bachelor's degree should develop a common set of skills; the University's goal is to prepare all graduates for the complex lives they will lead in a changing world. This can best be done through the University Core Curriculum, which consists of a minimum of 40 credit hours in six basic competencies.

An available option at the University is cooperative education, an academic program that offers students the opportunity to combine career-oriented, compensated, full-time work with their education.

Academic Facilities

The Marvin K. Peterson Library contains more than 400,000 volumes and is a U.S. government documents depository library. Information is accessible through manual as well as electronic retrieval methods. Internet access, online databases, and an online catalog are available. The library subscribes to hundreds of journals and has a CD-ROM collection for accessing materials published in a wide variety of subjects. Through interlibrary loan services, UNH has access to holdings of more than 8,650 libraries.

Communication majors participate in workshops along with studying sound, film, and television production, and radio broadcasting techniques in well-equipped radio/television studios and laboratories. The Tagliatela College of Engineering has modern laboratories and equipment to support its programs. The College of Arts and Sciences maintains art studios, state-of-the-art recording studios, music practice rooms, and science, psychology, and language labs. Hands-on instruction and demonstrations are available in kitchen facilities for students in the hospitality and tourism and nutrition and dietetics programs. Dental hygiene students gain experience in the Dental Hygiene Clinic.

There are more than a dozen computer labs for student use and teaching on campus. One of these is devoted to forensic computing instruction for the Henry C. Lee College of Criminal Justice and Forensic Sciences.

Costs

Full-time undergraduate tuition for the 2006–07 academic year, including the activity and health fees, was $24,645; room and board cost $10,130.

Financial Aid

UNH offers a comprehensive financial aid program that includes University resources as well as state, federal, and private aid programs. Approximately 85 percent of full-time undergraduate students receive some form of assistance. Students receive federal aid through the Federal Pell Grant, Federal Supplemental Educational Opportunity Grant, Federal Work-Study, Federal Perkins Loan, Federal Stafford Student Loan, and Federal PLUS loan programs. The University also administers programs sponsored by the state of Connecticut for Connecticut residents attending the University. Some students also qualify for financial aid from other states and from private companies, organizations, and foundations.

Faculty

It is a long-standing University policy that the faculty members teach a mix of undergraduate and graduate courses in order to preserve academic quality at all levels. Faculty members are selected and promoted primarily on the basis of teaching effectiveness, professional qualifications and performance, and contributions to the academic community. No classes are taught by teaching assistants. Some faculty members hold administrative positions and continue to teach. There are approximately 170 full-time and 200 part-time faculty members, making the student-faculty ratio 15:1. The majority of full-time faculty members (82 percent) hold terminal degrees in their disciplines.

Student Government

The Undergraduate Student Government Association supervises annual expenditures by undergraduate clubs and organizations, directs liaison committees, supports student publications and the student-operated FM radio station, and schedules cultural and social events. Student representatives are elected annually to the University's Board of Governors.

Admission Requirements

To be eligible for admission, one must be a high school graduate or present evidence of equivalent preparation. Scores from the SAT or the ACT are required. The admission decision is based on the student's overall high school record, SAT or ACT results, letters of recommendation, and personal essay.

Prospective students are encouraged to visit the campus for an information session and tour. Out-of-state residents are considered for admission on the same basis as state residents.

Application and Information

To apply to the University of New Haven, a student must submit the completed application form, a nonrefundable $50 fee, official records of all academic work completed, SAT or ACT results, a letter of recommendation, and a personal essay. International students are required to demonstrate proficiency in English as well as provide documentation of financial support. The University of New Haven does not discriminate on the basis of age, color, sex, religion, race, sexual orientation, national origin, or disability in admission or treatment of students, in administration or distribution of financial aid, or in recruitment or treatment of employees. The University is authorized under federal law to enroll nonimmigrant alien students who meet the University's academic and English proficiency standards. The admissions office employs a rolling admissions system.

Undergraduate Admissions
University of New Haven
300 Boston Post Road
West Haven, Connecticut 06516
Phone: 203-932-7319
800-DIAL-UNH (342-5864) Ext. 7319 (toll-free)
E-mail: adminfo@newhaven.edu
Web site: http://www.newhaven.edu

WESTERN CONNECTICUT STATE UNIVERSITY

DANBURY, CONNECTICUT

The University

Founded in 1903, Western Connecticut State University (WestConn) is dedicated to providing both a high-quality university education and a memorable campus experience at an affordable cost. With programs in the arts and sciences, business, and professional studies, WestConn takes pride in providing an outstanding education to more than 4,400 full-time undergraduates and nearly 2,000 graduate or part-time students.

WestConn offers excellent educational programs through five academic units: the Ancell School of Business, the School of Arts and Sciences, the School of Professional Studies, the School of Visual and Performing Arts, and the Division of Graduate Studies and External Programs. The most popular majors include communications, theater arts, education, business, justice and law administration, music, and nursing.

In addition to the University's full menu of undergraduate degrees, the Ancell School of Business offers the Master of Business Administration, Master of Health Administration, and Master of Science in justice administration. The School of Arts and Sciences offers the Master of Arts in biological and environmental sciences, earth and planetary sciences, English, history, and mathematics; the Master of Fine Arts is offered in professional writing. The School of Professional Studies offers the Master of Science in counselor education, elementary education, nursing, and secondary education; also offered are an advanced certificate program in interdisciplinary gerontological studies and WestConn's Doctor of Education (Ed.D.) in instructional leadership. Prelaw and pre–health professions programs also are available. WestConn's newly formed School of Visual and Performing Arts offers the Master of Fine Arts in visual arts and the Master of Music Education.

The University also is rich with a number of learning and social activities beyond the classroom. Students run academic and fraternal organizations, publish an award-winning newspaper and yearbook, and run a radio station. They stage theater and musical productions, participate in cooperative education and internship programs, and administer their own campus government association.

The University provides services for learning-disabled students, study abroad, a University Scholars program, precollegiate and access initiatives, international student services, and community service learning opportunities. A variety of NCAA Division III men's and women's sports are represented on campus, and students enjoy intramural sports and a premier recreation center that includes a swimming pool, an indoor track, and weightlifting machines. The campus also features a child-care center, a counseling center, a health services office, a career development center, and campus ministries.

WestConn is accredited by the New England Association of Schools and Colleges; the Board of Governors for Higher Education, State of Connecticut; the Connecticut State Department of Education; the American Chemical Society; the Commission on Collegiate Nursing Education; the Council on Social Work Education (baccalaureate level); the Council for Accreditation of Counseling and Related Educational Programs; and the National Association of Schools of Music.

Location

WestConn offers two campuses in Danbury, in the heart of western Connecticut, as well as a satellite campus in Waterbury. Danbury is a major city in Fairfield County in the foothills of the Berkshire Mountains, just 65 miles north of Manhattan and 50 miles west of Hartford.

In Danbury, the Midtown campus is a 34-acre, fifteen-building campus with an interesting mix of old and new architecture, and it offers easy access to downtown entertainment, restaurants, and shopping. The 364-acre Westside campus is ideal for hikers and nature buffs who want to discover its woodland wonders while enjoying state-of-the-art facilities. The WestConn-at-Waterbury campus offers a convenient location closer to the center of the state, with the same level of excellent service.

Majors and Degrees

The Ancell School of Business offers the Bachelor of Business Administration in accounting, finance, management, management information systems, and marketing, as well as the Bachelor of Science in justice and law administration.

The School of Arts and Sciences offers the Associate in Science, Bachelor of Arts, and Bachelor of Science degrees. The Associate in Science is offered in liberal arts. The Bachelor of Arts is offered in American studies, anthropology/sociology, biology, chemistry, communication, computer science, earth and planetary sciences–astronomy, economics, English, English–professional writing, history, mathematics, political science, psychology, social sciences, and Spanish. The Bachelor of Science is offered in medical technology and meteorology.

The School of Professional Studies offers the Bachelor of Arts and Bachelor of Science degrees. The Bachelor of Arts is offered in social work. The Bachelor of Science is offered in elementary education, health education, health promotion studies, nursing, and secondary education.

The School of Visual and Performing Arts offers the Bachelor of Arts, Bachelor of Science, and Bachelor of Music degrees. The Bachelor of Arts is offered in art, music, and theater arts. The Bachelor of Science is offered in music education, and the Bachelor of Music is offered with options in classical: voice or instrument or in jazz studies. Auditions are required for entrance into any of the music degree options.

Academic Programs

The University has developed a diverse mix of programs that are designed to inspire students. From the enlightening category of the arts to specialized fields of education, the emphasis is on the individual student's learning experience.

Special offerings at WestConn include the nation's first program in computer information security management and the only licensed meteorology program in Connecticut.

Academic Facilities

A number of facilities contribute to academic life on campus. The newly renovated and expanded library holds more than 200,000 volumes and over 400,000 bound periodicals, microforms, government documents, music scores, electronic resources, and audiovisual items. WestConn's extraordinary Science Building opened in 2005 to great acclaim for its ecology-friendly green design and cutting-edge lab and classroom equipment. Students are also encouraged to make use of WestConn's exceptional computer laboratory facilities and are invited to hone their craft in superior theater and musical facilities. Along with the rest of the greater Danbury community, they benefit from the offerings of the WestConn International Center;

German Studies Center; Institute for Holistic Health Studies; Meteorological Studies and Weather Center; Jane Goodall Center for Excellence in Environmental Studies; Center for Collaboration; Center for Business Research; Center for Excellence in Learning and Teaching; Center for Excellence in the Study of Culture and Values; Center for Galactic Astronomy; Center for Graphics Research; Center for Professional Development; Center for Technology, Research, and Productivity; Westside Nature Preserve; and Westside Observatory and Planetarium.

Costs

As part of the Connecticut State System of Higher Education, WestConn provides a high-quality private university education at an exceptionally reasonable public school cost. It is estimated that a full-time, in-state undergraduate student who lives and has meals on campus pays $15,500 for 2008–09. This estimate of annual costs includes tuition, fees, and room and board. Books, laboratory fees, health insurance, and personal expenses are not included in the estimate.

WestConn participates in the New England Regional Student Program of the New England Board of Higher Education. This program offers residents of other New England states the opportunity to enroll at WestConn at Connecticut resident tuition rates, plus an additional fee, in programs that are not available in their home states. Details about the regional program can be obtained by contacting the Office of University Admissions.

Financial Aid

Any student who is matriculated at WestConn and registering for at least 6 credits per semester may apply for student aid, which includes federal, state, and institutional funding. Students must complete the Free Application for Federal Student Aid (FAFSA) and be sure to list WestConn's school code of 001380 in the college release section. If the student's file is selected for verification, appropriate signed copies of federal income tax returns must be submitted. Academic scholarships are available to students with superior academic credentials. Students with demonstrated financial need also have the opportunity to participate in work-study programs. For more information, students should contact the Financial Aid Office at 203-837-8580 or wcsufinancialaid@wcsu.edu.

Faculty

Nationally respected, WestConn's faculty members and administrators are continually cited for scholarly achievement. The faculty-student ratio is 1:15.4, and nearly 90 percent of the University's full-time faculty members have doctoral, terminal, or first professional degrees.

Admission Requirements

WestConn welcomes applications from all qualified individuals. Admission to the four undergraduate schools is competitive. University admissions criteria include grade point average, types of courses taken, extracurricular activities, and standardized test results. Applications are reviewed by admissions professionals. If an applicant feels that individual circumstances warrant special consideration, a personal letter explaining those circumstances may be submitted with the application.

Academic preparation is the most important factor in determining admission. Freshman candidates for admission must have a high school diploma from an accredited secondary school or an equivalency diploma. General Educational Development (GED) test scores must be converted into a State of Connecticut Equivalency Diploma.

WestConn applicants should present evidence of successful completion of the following academic units in high school with a cumulative grade average of B- (80) or higher: 4 years of English, including writing skills and literature; 3 years of mathematics, including algebra I, geometry, and algebra II; 2 years of social sciences, including U.S. history; 2 years of laboratory sciences; and 2 to 3 years of a single foreign language (3 years are recommended). Academic course work in computer science, visual arts, theater, music, or dance may be substituted for one of the areas above. Those applicants who do not meet these guidelines may be considered under the Educational Achievement and Access Program. For more information about the program, students should contact the Office of University Admissions.

For specific information about transfer student admission, early admission, freshman entrance with advanced standing, special transfer arrangements for associate degree recipients, guest student admission, readmit admission, fresh-start admission, and international student admission, students should contact the Office of University Admissions.

Interviews are not required, but candidates are encouraged to attend an information session before they enroll. These sessions provide information about the University and the admissions process and provide an important opportunity to assess how the University can help students meet their long-term educational goals. They also afford students the opportunity to meet with professors, other potential students, and current students. Student-guided tours are available. While on tour, students are able to visit the library, the residence halls, science and computer laboratories, the student center, and the recreation center. For information about appointments and campus visits, students should call the Office of University Admissions.

Application and Information

WestConn seeks to enroll students who will benefit from and contribute to the University. Rolling admissions for the fall semester begin December 1, with class spaces filled on a first-come basis. Rolling admissions for the spring semester begin October 1, with class spaces filled on a first-come basis. To apply, students should obtain an application from the Office of University Admissions or from a secondary school or community college guidance office. WestConn welcomes transfer and international student applications.

For application forms and more information, students should contact:

Larry Hall
Director of Admissions
Office of University Admissions
Western Connecticut State University
181 White Street
Danbury, Connecticut 06810
Phone: 203-837-9000
877-837-WCSU (toll-free)
E-mail: hallla@wcsu.edu
Web site: http://www.wcsu.edu

A view of the Western Connecticut State University Midtown campus.

YALE UNIVERSITY
NEW HAVEN, CONNECTICUT

The University

Yale University was founded in 1701 as the Collegiate School in Branford, Connecticut, with a gift of books from 10 clergymen. In 1716 it moved to New Haven; it was renamed Yale College in 1718 to honor a generous benefactor, Elihu Yale. Today, the University enrolls more than 11,000 students in the undergraduate college and eleven graduate and professional schools. Diversity is a hallmark of the student population; its more than 5,000 undergraduates come from every state and from almost fifty countries and represent a wide economic, social, and ethnic mix.

Yale's residential college system is the most pervasive influence on undergraduate life and work. The twelve residential colleges are much more than bed, board, and books: they are self-sufficient communities within Yale College. Each college has its own dining hall, library, courtyard, seminar rooms, practice rooms for musicians, and computer cluster and numerous other facilities that range from darkrooms to printing presses to game rooms and saunas. Although students are assigned to a residential college before entrance, most freshmen live on the Old Campus and move into their residential college during the sophomore year. Freshmen participate fully in all aspects of residential college life. The colleges sponsor a wide variety of activities, such as intramural sports, dramatic societies, and newspapers. Most activities, such as the *Yale Daily News*, the Yale Symphony Orchestra, and thirty-five varsity sports, draw students from all of the residential colleges.

Undergraduates are encouraged to enroll in courses that are sufficiently challenging and to pursue an education that covers a wide range of subjects while studying some subjects in great depth. Students may cross-register with most of the graduate and professional schools to take highly advanced courses. In some areas, it is possible to take a combined-degree program. Yale's aim is that the undergraduates use the vast resources of a major research university in every way possible.

The University offers graduate and professional degrees in the Schools of Architecture, Art, Divinity, Drama, Forestry and Environmental Studies, Law, Management, Medicine, Music, and Nursing and in the Graduate School of Arts and Sciences.

Location

Yale University is located in the heart of New Haven, Connecticut, a city of 120,000 on Long Island Sound. Founded in 1658, New Haven was the first planned municipality in the United States. Today, its diversity is manifested in a wide variety of neighborhoods, restaurants, and recreation. Two nationally distinguished theaters, the Yale Repertory and the Long Wharf Theatres, make their homes there. More than 2,000 students each year are involved in the community through volunteer or work-study projects, tutoring in city schools, working in a halfway house or in the local hospitals, or doing an internship in business, journalism, or city government. The University and the city are vitally interdependent.

Majors and Degrees

Yale University confers the Bachelor of Arts (B.A.) and Bachelor of Science (B.S.) degrees. Majors, usually selected at the end of the sophomore or the beginning of the junior year, are available in the following areas: African and African-American studies; American studies; anthropology; applied mathematics; applied physics; archaeological studies; architecture; art; astronomy; astronomy and physics; biology; chemistry; Chinese; classical civilization; classical languages and literatures; cognitive science; computer science; computer science and mathematics; computer science and psychology; East Asian languages and literatures; East Asian studies (China or Japan); economics; economics and mathematics; electrical engineering and computer science; engineering (biomedical engineering, chemical engineering, electrical engineering, engineering sciences (chemical, electrical, mechanical), environmental engineering, mechanical engineering); English; environmental studies; ethics, politics, and economics; ethnicity, race, and migration; film studies; French; geology and geophysics; Germanic languages and literatures; German studies; history; history of art; history of science and medicine; humanities; international studies; Italian; Japanese; Judaic studies; Latin American studies; linguistics; literature; mathematics; mathematics and philosophy; mathematics and physics; molecular biophysics and biochemistry; music; Near Eastern languages and civilizations; philosophy; physics; physics and philosophy; political science; Portuguese; psychology; religious studies; Renaissance studies; Russian; Russian and East European studies; sociology; Spanish; theater studies; and women's and gender studies. In addition, students may create their own programs in a special divisional major. Yale offers a double major, but no minor.

Academic Programs

Yale's academic goal is to provide students with a liberal education by encouraging curiosity, inquiry, and the development of expressive and analytical intellectual skills. In the belief that a liberal education should be neither too focused nor too diffuse, Yale supports the twin principles of depth and breadth in education. To encourage exploration and an interdisciplinary understanding, students are required to take two courses in each of the following areas: humanities and the arts, social sciences, and natural sciences. In addition, students are expected to further develop the skills they bring to college by taking courses in both quantitative reasoning and writing.

As part of the completion of an academic major, each student must fulfill a capstone requirement in their proposed major during the senior year (a senior essay, research project, colloquium, seminar, or the like, varying by discipline). Such an undertaking brings focus and gives occasion for knowledge to build upon knowledge. Thirty-six total term courses or the equivalent are required for graduation. Usually between eleven and fourteen of these courses are taken as part of a student's major, with the exception of certain intensive majors that require more course work. An intermediate proficiency in a foreign language is required for graduation.

All students, except transfers, enter Yale as freshmen, but a student may graduate as much as a year early through the accumulation of acceleration credits. Acceleration credits are given in most subjects for a score of 4 or 5 on the College Board Advanced Placement tests, a score of 6 or 7 on the International Baccalaureate exams, and/or for advanced course work done in the freshman year. Yale also offers special programs such as Directed Studies, a freshman program that surveys the Western cultural tradition, and Perspectives on Science, a lecture and discussion course designed for a limited number of freshmen who have exceptionally strong backgrounds in the natural sciences and mathematics.

Yale operates on a semester calendar. The first semester runs from September through December, and final examinations are held before Winter Break. The second semester begins in mid-January and runs through early May.

Off-Campus Programs

As part of the University's recent goal to encourage every student to take advantage of an international experience before graduation, Yalies participate in an ever-increasing number of summer internships and fellowships around the world. Students may transfer credit to Yale for pre-approved domestic or international study through another university. Yale also offers two programs overseas, open to any student in any discipline beginning in the sophomore year. Students may study British culture at the Mellon Centre for Studies in British Art in London for a semester or an academic year. Yale also offers a joint program with Peking University in Beijing, which allows students to spend a semester at China's top university with no prior knowledge of Chinese required. In addition to these classroom experiences, many students use the Office of International Education and Fellowship Programs as a resource for pursuing overseas opportunities beyond the standard junior term abroad. ROTC programs operated under the auspices of the University of Connecticut are also available.

Academic Facilities

The Yale Library is the second-largest university library and the second-largest research library in the world, containing more than 10 million volumes. Although it is centered in Sterling Memorial Library, the open-stack system provides access to facilities throughout the campus, including the Kline Science Library and the Beinecke Rare Book and Manuscript Library, one of the country's most important and heavily used resources for original scholarship in the humanities.

Science facilities include the Chemical Instrumentation Center in the Sterling Chemistry Laboratory, part of Yale's fifteen-building complex for teaching and research in science. With the commissioning of an ESTU Van de Graaff accelerator, Yale continues its preeminence in nuclear physics. The astronomy department maintains research and teaching facilities in New Haven and nearby Bethany, Connecticut; in Cerro Tololo, Chile; and also at Kitt Peak National Observatory in Arizona.

Yale offers numerous galleries and special collections, among which are the Yale Art Gallery (the oldest college-affiliated gallery in the country), the Peabody Museum of Natural History, and the Yale Center for British Art, which houses the largest collection of British art outside the United Kingdom.

Costs

Tuition for the 2007–08 academic year was $34,530 and room and board were $10,470. Books, supplies and personal expenses were estimated at $2950, bringing the estimated total annual cost to $47,950.

Financial Aid

Admission and financial aid decisions are made independently, and an application for aid in no way affects a student's chances for admission.

Financial need is the only consideration in determining who receives financial aid; there are no athletic or academic scholarships. More than 40 percent of Yale's undergraduates receive aid in the form of gift scholarships, loans, and employment. Yale has eliminated the parental contribution for students whose parents have combined incomes of $45,000 or less and has significantly reduced the expected contribution from parents who together earn less than $60,000. In 2006–07, the average need-based Yale scholarship per student qualifying for aid was $26,100. Furthermore, many students who are not eligible for financial aid participate in the campus employment program or in loan programs to help meet their expenses.

Applicants for financial aid should file the Free Application for Federal Student Aid (FAFSA) and the PROFILE with the College Scholarship Service (CSS) and submit appropriate financial documentation in accordance with Yale application instructions and deadlines. Award notifications are mailed with admission decision letters.

Faculty

The Yale faculty is made up of eminent scholars in every field who usually teach on both the graduate and undergraduate levels. Yale takes pride in the faculty's commitment to undergraduate teaching and in its accessibility to the students. Freshmen frequently have as much access to senior faculty members as upperclass students do; senior faculty members and even department chairs regularly teach introductory-level courses. Eighty-five percent of the courses offered enroll fewer than 25 students. Faculty members hold regular office hours and act as academic advisers to individual students. Most are fellows of the residential colleges and frequently take meals in the college dining halls. A few faculty members live in separate residences within the residential colleges, and many maintain offices there.

Student Government

Each of the twelve residential colleges has its own college council, which has representatives from all four classes. The Yale College Council draws representatives from each residential college and acts as a forum for student opinion and counsel. In addition, students serve on various college and University committees.

Admission Requirements

In selecting a class of 1,300 from more than 20,000 applicants, the Admissions Committee looks for academic ability and achievement combined with such personal strengths as motivation, curiosity, energy, sense of humor, and leadership ability. No two individuals offer these in like proportions; thus, no simple profile of grades, scores, and activities can guarantee admission.

For evidence of academic strength, Yale looks to a student's high school record (quality and breadth of courses selected, as well as grades achieved), test scores on the SAT and two SAT Subject Tests or on the ACT, and recommendations submitted by a counselor and 2 academic teachers. In addition, applicants are asked to supply information about their interests and activities and must write two essays. The personal recommendations and essays are important parts of the application process and should not be underrated by applicants. Interviews are not required; most applicants are interviewed by alumni representatives, although a limited number of appointments are available in New Haven on a first-come, first-served basis. Applicants are urged to visit the campus, preferably during the school year, and are welcome to visit classes, take a tour, and attend an information session in the admissions office.

Application and Information

Students who apply only to Yale under the Single-Choice Early Action must file by November 1. They receive a nonbinding decision in mid-December, meaning that students admitted in the early process are free to apply to other schools in the spring. Students who apply under the regular decision program must file by December 31; decision letters are mailed in early April. Yale University requires the Common Application along with the Yale Common Application Supplement. Students are encouraged to submit their applications online at http://www.yale.edu/admit.

For an application form or additional information, prospective students are encouraged to visit the Web site or to contact:

Office of Undergraduate Admissions
Yale University
P.O. Box 208234
New Haven, Connecticut 06520-8234
Phone: 203-432-9316
E-mail: student.questions@yale.edu
Web site: http://www.yale.edu/admit

DELAWARE

Newark
Wilmington
95
New Castle
Dover

DELAWARE STATE UNIVERSITY

Dover, Delaware www.desu.edu/

- **State-supported** comprehensive, founded 1891, part of Delaware Higher Education Commission
- **Small-town** 400-acre campus
- **Endowment** $20.8 million
- **Coed**
- **Moderately difficult** entrance level

Faculty *Student/faculty ratio:* 14:1.

Academics *Calendar:* semesters. *Degrees:* bachelor's, master's, and doctoral.

Student Life *Campus security:* 24-hour emergency response devices and patrols, student patrols, late-night transport/escort service, controlled dormitory access.

Athletics Member NCAA. All Division I except football (Division I-AA).

Standardized Tests *Required:* SAT or ACT (for admission).

Costs (2007–08) *Tuition:* $224 per credit hour part-time; state resident $6146 full-time, $224 per credit hour part-time; nonresident $13,100 full-time, $513 per credit hour part-time. *Room and board:* $9006; room only: $6010. Room and board charges vary according to board plan and housing facility.

Financial Aid Of all full-time matriculated undergraduates who enrolled in 2004, 2,315 applied for aid, 2,056 were judged to have need, 761 had their need fully met. In 2004, 471 non-need-based awards were made. *Average percent of need met:* 73. *Average financial aid package:* $8026. *Average need-based loan:* $4925. *Average need-based gift aid:* $2443. *Average non-need-based aid:* $5223.

Applying *Options:* electronic application, early admission. *Application fee:* $25. *Required:* high school transcript, minimum 2.0 GPA. *Required for some:* interview.

Freshman Application Contact Mrs. Lawita Cheatham, Executive Director for Admissions, Delaware State University, 1200 North Dupont Highway, Dover, DE 19901. *Phone:* 302-857-6351. *Toll-free phone:* 800-845-2544. *Fax:* 302-857-6908. *E-mail:* gcheatha@desu.edu.

GOLDEY-BEACOM COLLEGE

Wilmington, Delaware goldey.gbc.edu/

- **Independent** comprehensive, founded 1886
- **Suburban** 27-acre campus with easy access to Philadelphia
- **Endowment** $34.8 million
- **Coed** 874 undergraduate students, 69% full-time, 54% women, 46% men
- **Moderately difficult** entrance level

Goldey-Beacom College (GBC) is a small, private, nationally accredited college offering challenging undergraduate degrees in business as well as master's degrees in business administration. The College is known for dedicated faculty members, small class sizes, and individual attention. GBC is recognized regionally as a leader in the business field. Apartment-style housing is available on the safe, suburban campus, which is located 15 minutes from downtown Wilmington.

Undergraduates 606 full-time, 268 part-time. Students come from 22 states and territories, 50 other countries, 40% are from out of state, 8% transferred in, 35% live on campus. *Retention:* 82% of 2006 full-time freshmen returned.

Freshmen *Admission:* 550 applied, 210 enrolled. *Average high school GPA:* 3.1. *Test scores:* SAT critical reading scores over 500: 25%; SAT math scores over 500: 32%; SAT critical reading scores over 600: 4%; SAT math scores over 600: 4%.

Faculty *Total:* 52, 38% full-time, 100% with terminal degrees. *Student/faculty ratio:* 24:1.

Majors Accounting; business administration and management; finance; human resources management; information science/studies; international business/trade/commerce; management information systems; marketing/marketing management.

Academics *Calendar:* semesters. *Degrees:* associate, bachelor's, master's, and postbachelor's certificates. *Special study options:* academic remediation for entering students, accelerated degree program, advanced placement credit, cooperative education, honors programs, internships, part-time degree program, study abroad, summer session for credit. *ROTC:* Air Force (c). *Unusual degree programs:* business administration.

Computers on Campus 150 computers/terminals are available on campus for general student use. Students can access the following: campus intranet, free student e-mail accounts, Blackboard. Campuswide network is available. 100% of college-owned or -operated housing units are wired for high-speed Internet access. Wireless service is available via entire campus.

Student Life *Housing options:* coed. Campus housing is university owned. *Activities and organizations:* student-run newspaper, choral group, Marketing/Management Association, Circle K International, Data Processing Management Association, GBC singers, national fraternities, national sororities. *Campus security:* 24-hour emergency response devices. *Student services:* health clinic.

Athletics Member NCAA. All Division II. *Intercollegiate sports:* basketball M (s)/W (s), field hockey W (c), golf M (s), soccer M (s)/W (s), softball W (s), tennis M/W, track and field M (c)/W (c), volleyball W (s). *Intramural sports:* basketball M/W, football M, golf M/W, soccer M/W, softball M/W, tennis M/W, volleyball M/W.

Standardized Tests *Required:* SAT or ACT (for admission). *Required for some:* DTLS, DTMS.

Costs (2008–09) *Tuition:* $18,500 full-time, $556 per credit part-time. *Required fees:* $340 full-time, $10 per credit part-time. *Room only:* $4982.

Financial Aid Of all full-time matriculated undergraduates who enrolled in 2006, 753 applied for aid, 611 were judged to have need, 28 had their need fully met. In 2006, 178 non-need-based awards were made. *Average percent of need met:* 32%. *Average financial aid package:* $6246. *Average need-based loan:* $3653. *Average need-based gift aid:* $4162. *Average non-need-based aid:* $4170. *Average indebtedness upon graduation:* $11,000.

Applying *Options:* electronic application, early admission, deferred entrance. *Application fee:* $30. *Required:* high school transcript, minimum 2.0 GPA. *Required for some:* 1 letter of recommendation, interview. *Application deadlines:* rolling (freshmen), rolling (transfers). *Notification:* continuous until 8/15 (freshmen), continuous until 8/15 (transfers).

Freshman Application Contact Corinne Clemetsen, Admissions Representative, Goldey-Beacom College, 4701 Limestone Road, Wilmington, DE 19808-1999. *Phone:* 302-225-6237. *Toll-free phone:* 800-833-4877. *Fax:* 302-996-5408. *E-mail:* clemetc@gbc.edu.

UNIVERSITY OF DELAWARE

Newark, Delaware www.udel.edu/

- **State-related** university, founded 1743
- **Small-town** 1000-acre campus with easy access to Philadelphia and Baltimore
- **Endowment** $1.2 billion
- **Coed** 16,272 undergraduate students, 89% full-time, 58% women, 42% men
- **Moderately difficult** entrance level, 56% of applicants were admitted

Undergraduates 14,532 full-time, 1,740 part-time. Students come from 52 states and territories, 100 other countries, 62% are from out of state, 5% African American, 4% Asian American or Pacific Islander, 5% Hispanic American, 0.4% Native American, 1% international, 3% transferred in, 46% live on campus. *Retention:* 90% of 2006 full-time freshmen returned.

Freshmen *Admission:* 20,615 applied, 11,452 admitted, 3,789 enrolled. *Average high school GPA:* 3.6. *Test scores:* SAT critical reading scores over 500: 89%; SAT math scores over 500: 92%; SAT writing scores over 500: 89%; ACT scores over 18: 98%; SAT critical reading scores over 600: 44%; SAT math scores over 600: 56%; SAT writing scores over 600: 48%; ACT scores over 24: 75%; SAT critical reading scores over 700: 9%; SAT math scores over 700: 12%; SAT writing scores over 700: 8%; ACT scores over 30: 12%.

Faculty *Total:* 1,419, 82% full-time, 76% with terminal degrees. *Student/faculty ratio:* 12:1.

Majors Accounting; agribusiness; agricultural/biological engineering and bioengineering; agricultural business and management; agricultural economics; agricultural teacher education; agriculture; agronomy and crop science; animal sciences; anthropology; art; art history, criticism and conservation; Asian studies (East); athletic training; bilingual and multilingual education; biochemistry; biology/biological sciences; biology/biotechnology laboratory technician; biology teacher education; biotechnology; botany/plant biology; business administration and management; business/managerial economics; chemical engineering; chemistry; chemistry teacher education; civil engineering; clinical laboratory science/medical technology; commercial and advertising art; communication/speech communication and rhetoric; community organization and advocacy; comparative literature; computer and information sciences; computer engineering; computer science; consumer economics; criminal justice/law enforcement administration; developmental and child psychology; dietetics; ecology; economics; education; electrical, electronics and communications engineering; elementary education; engineering; English; English as a second/foreign language (teaching); English/language arts teacher education; entomology; environmental engineering technology; environmental/environmental health engineering; environmental studies; family and community services; family and consumer economics related; fashion/apparel design; fashion merchandising; finance; food science; foods, nutrition, and wellness; foreign languages and literatures; foreign language teacher education; French; geography; geology/earth science; geophysics and seismology; German; health and physical education; health teacher education; history; history teacher education; horticultural science; hospitality and recreation marketing; hotel/motel administration; human development and family studies; international relations and affairs; Italian; journalism; kindergarten/preschool education; kinesiology and exercise science; Latin; Latin American studies; liberal arts and sciences/liberal studies; linguistics; management information systems; marketing/marketing management; mass communication/media; mathematics; mathematics teacher education; mechanical engineering; music; music pedagogy; music teacher education; music theory and composition; natural resources management and policy; neuroscience; nursing (registered nurse training); nursing science; nutrition sciences; operations management; ornamental horticulture; philosophy; physical education teaching and coaching; physics; physics teacher education; piano and organ; plant protection and integrated pest management; political science and government; psychology; public relations/image management; sociology; soil conservation; soil science and agronomy; Spanish; sport and fitness administration/management; theater design and technology; wildlife and wildlands science and management; women's studies.

Academics *Calendar:* 4-1-4. *Degrees:* associate, bachelor's, master's, and doctoral. *Special study options:* academic remediation for entering students, accelerated degree program, adult/continuing education programs, advanced placement credit, cooperative education, distance learning, double majors, English as a second language, honors programs, independent study, internships, part-time degree program, services for LD students, student-designed majors, study abroad, summer session for credit. *ROTC:* Army (b), Air Force (b). *Unusual degree programs:* 3-2 engineering; leadership, public administration.

Computers on Campus 908 computers/terminals are available on campus for general student use. Students can access the following: online (class) registration, e-mail, personal Web page. Campuswide network is available.

Student Life *Housing:* on-campus residence required for freshman year. *Options:* coed, women-only, disabled students. Campus housing is university owned. Freshman campus housing is guaranteed. *Activities and organizations:* drama/theater group, student-run newspaper, radio and television station, choral group, marching band, Undergraduate Student Congress, Resident Student Association, Black Student Union, HOLA (Hispanic Student Association), national fraternities, national sororities. *Campus security:* 24-hour emergency response devices and patrols, student patrols, late-night transport/escort service, controlled dormitory access. *Student services:* health clinic, personal/psychological counseling, women's center.

Athletics Member NCAA. All Division I except football (Division I-AA). *Intercollegiate sports:* baseball M (s), basketball M (s)/W (s), bowling M (c)/W (c), cheerleading M (s)/W (s), crew M (c)/W (s), cross-country running M/W, equestrian sports M (c)/W (c), field hockey W (s), golf M, ice hockey M (c), lacrosse M (s)/W (s), rugby W (c), sailing M (c)/W (c), soccer M (s)/W (s), softball W (s), swimming and diving M/W (s), tennis M/W, track and field M/W (s), volleyball W (s), wrestling M (c). *Intramural sports:* badminton M/W, basketball M/W, field hockey W (c), football M/W, golf M/W, lacrosse M (c)/W (c), racquetball M/W, soccer M/W (c), softball M/W, squash M/W, table tennis M/W, tennis M/W, ultimate Frisbee M/W, volleyball M (c)/W (c), water polo M/W.

Standardized Tests *Required:* SAT or ACT (for admission). *Recommended:* SAT Subject Tests (for admission).

Costs (2007–08) *Tuition:* state resident $7340 full-time, $306 per credit part-time; nonresident $18,590 full-time, $775 per credit part-time. *Required fees:* $810 full-time. *Room and board:* $7948; room only: $4748. Room and board charges vary according to housing facility. *Payment plan:* installment. *Waivers:* senior citizens and employees or children of employees.

Financial Aid Of all full-time matriculated undergraduates who enrolled in 2006, 8,257 applied for aid, 5,149 were judged to have need, 2,837 had their need fully met. In 2006, 2551 non-need-based awards were made. *Average percent of need met:* 79%. *Average financial aid package:* $9891. *Average need-based loan:* $5367. *Average need-based gift aid:* $5236. *Average non-need-based aid:* $4204. *Average indebtedness upon graduation:* $17,200. *Financial aid deadline:* 3/15.

Applying *Options:* electronic application, early admission, deferred entrance. *Application fee:* $70. *Required:* essay or personal statement, high school transcript, 1 letter of recommendation. *Application deadlines:* 1/15 (freshmen), 5/1 (transfers). *Notification:* 3/15 (freshmen), continuous (transfers).

Freshman Application Contact Mr. Lou Hirsh, Director of Admissions, University of Delaware, 116 Hullihen Hall, Newark, DE 19716. *Phone:* 302-831-8123. *Fax:* 302-831-6905. *E-mail:* admissions@udel.edu.

WESLEY COLLEGE

Dover, Delaware **www.wesley.edu/**

- **Independent United Methodist** comprehensive, founded 1873
- **Small-town** 40-acre campus
- **Endowment** $5.8 million
- **Coed** 1,767 undergraduate students, 83% full-time, 52% women, 48% men
- **Moderately difficult** entrance level, 67% of applicants were admitted

Undergraduates 1,459 full-time, 308 part-time. Students come from 18 states and territories, 7 other countries, 63% are from out of state, 19% African American, 2% Asian American or Pacific Islander, 2% Hispanic American, 0.2% Native American, 0.8% international, 3% transferred in, 66% live on campus. *Retention:* 53% of 2006 full-time freshmen returned.

Freshmen *Admission:* 2,507 applied, 1,686 admitted, 484 enrolled. *Average high school GPA:* 2.92. *Test scores:* SAT critical reading scores over 500: 27%; SAT math scores over 500: 34%; SAT writing scores over 500: 29%; SAT critical reading scores over 600: 4%; SAT math scores over 600: 6%; SAT writing scores over 600: 4%; SAT critical reading scores over 700: 1%; SAT math scores over 700: 1%; SAT writing scores over 700: 1%.

Faculty *Total:* 157, 44% full-time, 57% with terminal degrees. *Student/faculty ratio:* 17:1.

Majors Accounting; American studies; biology/biological sciences; business administration and management; clinical laboratory science/medical technology; education; English; environmental studies; history; legal assistant/paralegal; liberal arts and sciences/liberal studies; marketing/marketing management; mass communication/media; nursing (registered nurse training); parks, recreation and leisure; physical education teaching and coaching; political science and government; psychology.

Academics *Calendar:* semesters. *Degrees:* certificates, associate, bachelor's, master's, post-master's, and postbachelor's certificates. *Special study options:* academic remediation for entering students, adult/continuing education programs, advanced placement credit, cooperative education, English as a second language, external degree program, freshman honors college, independent study, internships, off-campus study, part-time degree program, services for LD students, study abroad, summer session for credit. *ROTC:* Army (c).

Computers on Campus 225 computers/terminals are available on campus for general student use. Students can access the following: campus intranet, computer help desk, free student e-mail accounts, online (class) grades, online (class) registration, online (class) schedules. Campuswide network is available. 100% of college-owned or -operated housing units are wired for high-speed Internet access. Wireless service is available via entire campus.

Student Life *Housing:* on-campus residence required for freshman year. *Options:* coed, men-only, women-only. Campus housing is university owned. Freshman campus housing is guaranteed. *Activities and organizations:* drama/theater group, student-run newspaper, choral group, Student Activity Board, Student Government Association, National Coeducation Community Service Organization, national fraternities, national sororities. *Campus security:* 24-hour patrols, controlled dormitory access. *Student services:* health clinic, personal/psychological counseling.

Athletics Member NCAA. All Division III. *Intercollegiate sports:* baseball M, basketball M/W, field hockey W, football M, golf M/W, lacrosse M/W, soccer M/W, softball W, tennis M/W. *Intramural sports:* basketball M/W, cross-country running M/W, football M, soccer M/W, track and field M/W, volleyball M/W.

Standardized Tests *Required:* SAT (for admission). *Required for some:* special test for nursing.

Costs (2007–08) *Comprehensive fee:* $25,379 includes full-time tuition ($16,750), mandatory fees ($829), and room and board ($7800). Full-time tuition and fees vary according to class time. Part-time tuition: $610 per credit. *Required fees:* $20 per term part-time. *Room and board:* Room and board charges vary according to board plan and housing facility. *Payment plan:* installment. *Waivers:* senior citizens and employees or children of employees.

Financial Aid Of all full-time matriculated undergraduates who enrolled in 2006, 1,764 applied for aid, 1,601 were judged to have need. 220 Federal Work-Study jobs (averaging $2250). In 2006, 90 non-need-based awards were made. *Average percent of need met:* 80%. *Average financial aid package:* $15,250. *Average need-based loan:* $4250. *Average need-based gift aid:* $6500. *Average non-need-based aid:* $2500. *Average indebtedness upon graduation:* $19,500.

Applying *Options:* electronic application. *Application fee:* $25. *Required:* essay or personal statement, high school transcript, minimum 2.2 GPA, 1 letter of recommendation. *Recommended:* interview. *Application deadlines:* rolling (freshmen), rolling (transfers).

Freshman Application Contact Mr. Arthur Jacobs, Director of Undergraduate Admissions, Wesley College, 120 North State Street, Dover, DE 19901-3875. *Phone:* 302-736-2400. *Toll-free phone:* 800-937-5398 Ext. 2400. *Fax:* 302-736-2382. *E-mail:* admissions@wesley.edu.

See page 574 for the College Close-Up.

WILMINGTON UNIVERSITY

New Castle, Delaware **www.wilmu.edu/**

- **Independent** comprehensive, founded 1967
- **Suburban** 17-acre campus with easy access to Philadelphia
- **Endowment** $12.2 million
- **Coed** 4,638 undergraduate students, 52% full-time, 65% women, 35% men
- **Noncompetitive** entrance level, 100% of applicants were admitted

Undergraduates 2,410 full-time, 2,228 part-time. Students come from 14 states and territories, 28 other countries, 14% are from out of state, 17% African American, 1% Asian American or Pacific Islander, 2% Hispanic American, 0.2% Native American, 12% transferred in. *Retention:* 71% of 2006 full-time freshmen returned.

Freshmen *Admission:* 931 applied, 931 admitted, 526 enrolled.

Faculty *Total:* 894, 9% full-time, 25% with terminal degrees. *Student/faculty ratio:* 17:1.

Majors Accounting; airframe mechanics and aircraft maintenance technology; aviation/airway management; avionics maintenance technology; behavioral sciences; business administration and management; communication and media related; criminal justice/law enforcement administration; early childhood education; finance; human resources management; information technology; kindergarten/preschool education; legal studies; marketing/marketing management; middle school education; nursing (registered nurse training); psychology; science teacher education; sport and fitness administration/management.

Academics *Calendar:* semesters. *Degrees:* certificates, associate, bachelor's, master's, doctoral, post-master's, and postbachelor's certificates. *Special study options:* academic remediation for entering students, accelerated degree program, adult/continuing education programs, cooperative education, distance learning, double majors, external degree program, independent study, internships, part-time degree program, summer session for credit. *ROTC:* Army (c), Air Force (c).

Computers on Campus 600 computers/terminals are available on campus for general student use. Students can access the following: free student e-mail accounts, online (class) grades, online (class) registration, online (class) schedules. Campuswide network is available. Wireless service is available via entire campus.

Student Life *Housing:* college housing not available. *Campus security:* 24-hour emergency response devices and patrols, late-night transport/escort service.

Athletics Member NCAA. All Division II. *Intercollegiate sports:* baseball M (s), basketball M (s)/W (s), cross-country running M (s)/W (s), softball W (s), volleyball W (s).

Costs (2007–08) *Tuition:* $8400 full-time, $280 per credit part-time. Full-time tuition and fees vary according to course load, degree level, and location. Part-time tuition and fees vary according to course load, degree level, and location. *Required fees:* $50 full-time, $25 per term part-time. *Payment plan:* installment. *Waivers:* employees or children of employees.

Financial Aid Of all full-time matriculated undergraduates who enrolled in 2004, 1,217 applied for aid, 900 were judged to have need. 25 Federal Work-Study jobs (averaging $2000). In 2004, 74 non-need-based awards were made. *Average percent of need met:* 48%. *Average financial aid package:* $5770. *Average need-based loan:* $3889. *Average need-based gift aid:* $2464. *Average non-need-based aid:* $1100. *Average indebtedness upon graduation:* $17,486.

Applying *Options:* early admission, deferred entrance. *Application fee:* $25. *Required:* high school transcript. *Recommended:* letters of recommendation, interview. *Application deadlines:* rolling (freshmen), rolling (transfers). *Notification:* continuous (freshmen), continuous (transfers).

Freshman Application Contact Mr. Christopher Ferguson, Director of Admissions, Wilmington University, 320 North DuPont Highway, New Castle, DE 19720-6491. *Phone:* 302-356-6745. *Toll-free phone:* 877-967-5464. *Fax:* 302-328-5902. *E-mail:* inquire@wilmcoll.edu.

WESLEY COLLEGE

DOVER, DELAWARE

The College

Wesley College, the oldest private college in Delaware, is a fully accredited, coeducational, comprehensive liberal arts institution.

Situated on a quiet, historic residential community, Wesley College is affiliated with the United Methodist Church. With an enrollment of more than 2,400 full- and part-time students, mostly representing the mid-Atlantic region. The average class size is 20 students.

The Wesley residence community is made up of seven buildings. Each building has special characteristics that make it unique. The facilities are all air-conditioned, and all rooms offer Internet access. The two newest are apartment style and suite style housing facilities. The purpose of the Residence Program is to enhance the academic mission of Wesley by providing educational and social experiences outside the classroom to help develop contributing members of society.

Each building has a Resident Director and assistant. Student staff members are selected and trained and live on each floor to provide additional resources to their peers. The living arrangement in each hall enables students to get to know one another well and to develop close-knit relationships. Students come from all over the United States and overseas, providing the opportunity to meet and live with people from diverse backgrounds.

Wesley is a member of NCAA Division III intercollegiate athletics and the Capital Athletic Conference. Men have teams in baseball, basketball, cross-country running, football, golf, lacrosse, soccer, tennis, and track and field. Women compete in basketball, cheerleading, cross-country running, field hockey, golf, lacrosse, soccer, softball, tennis, track and field, and volleyball. A well-organized intramural program offers a wide variety of athletics competitions, including, but not limited to, basketball, flag football, soccer, and volleyball.

The mission of the College is to be the premier institution for helping students gain the knowledge, skills, and moral and ethical attitudes necessary to achieve their personal goals and contribute to the welfare of their communities in a global society. The College endeavors to impart a desire for lifelong learning and an enhanced capacity for critical and creative thinking so that students can reap the rewards of intellectual growth and professional effectiveness. As a college in a covenant relationship with the United Methodist Church and founded upon Christian principles, Wesley strives to realize a holistic campus environment of common purpose, caring, tolerance, inclusiveness, responsibility, and service that is the heart of community.

In addition to its undergraduate degrees, Wesley College awards the Master of Science in Nursing (M.S.N.) degree, the Master of Education degree, the Master of Business Administration (M.B.A.) degree, and an M.S. degree in environmental science.

Location

Dover is the capital of the country's first state and has approximately 32,000 residents. New York City, Baltimore, Philadelphia, and Washington, D.C., are within a 3-hour drive of the campus. The College is located within Dover's largest residential community, with stores and banks within easy walking distance and malls and community areas located in a growing area in Dover because of the city's proximity to the Delaware and Chesapeake Bays and to the Atlantic Ocean. Delaware Transit Corporation (DART) provides bus service throughout the city of Dover. Bus service is available to and from the campus. In addition, Delaware's famous beaches are also within easy driving distance of the campus.

Many students become involved in local activities, including volunteer work at private and public agencies. On-campus volunteer activities include a unique three-way partnership between a state-funded elementary and secondary charter school on campus (Campus Community School), the Wesley Boys and Girls Club, and the College. Many students are employed in community businesses through the cooperative education program at Wesley. Others work in part-time jobs to earn extra money. Many local residents also attend Wesley on a part-time basis and enjoy the use of the College's facilities.

Majors and Degrees

Associate of Arts and Bachelor of Science degrees are awarded in accounting, American studies, biology, business administration (international business, management, and marketing), education (elementary K–8 and physical education K–12), English, English education, environmental studies (environmental policy and environmental science), history, international studies, legal studies, liberal studies, mathematics, mathematics education, medical technology, nursing, physical education (exercise science and sports management), political science, and psychology.

Academic Programs

The comprehensive academic calendar year consists of two semesters and a month-long summer session. Winter sessions are available in England and France offering unique opportunities for travel and study.

Bachelor's degree candidates begin with the foundation core curriculum, which emphasizes an overarching theme of the individual in a global community. Interdisciplinary theories and the core requirements and the major programs into a purposeful design. These links are critical thinking, communication across disciplines, technological literacy, multicultural awareness, aesthetic appreciation, and ethical sensibility. The core provides a distinctive undergraduate experience for students, establishes coherent links between the curricular and cocurricular programs, and provides community service options beyond the College campus.

Academic Facilities

The Robert H. Parker Library is the College's library and resource center, with a collection of hardbound volumes, periodicals, journals, and microforms. In addition, Wesley is part of Kent Library, a consortium of Delaware and Kent County libraries. Through the consortium, more than 500,000 volumes are accessible to Wesley students at facilities within a mile of the campus. Computers located in the library are connected to the College's campuswide network and have the capability to access the library's CD-ROM network. Individual and group instruction in the use of information resources, including the

WESLEY COLLEGE
DOVER, DELAWARE

The College

Wesley College, the oldest private college in Delaware, is a fully accredited, coeducational, comprehensive liberal arts institution.

Nestled in a quiet, historic residential community, Wesley College is affiliated with the United Methodist Church, with an enrollment of more than 2,400 full- and part-time students, mostly representing the mid-Atlantic region. The average class size is 20 students.

The Wesley residence community is made up of seven buildings. Each building has special characteristics that make it unique. The facilities are all air conditioned, and all rooms offer Internet access. The two newest are apartment-style and suite-style housing facilities. The purpose of the Residence Program is to enhance the academic mission of Wesley by providing educational and social experiences outside the classroom to help develop contributing members of society.

Each building has a Resident Director and assistant. Student staff members are selected and trained and live on each floor to provide additional resources to their peers. The living arrangement in each hall enables students to get to know one another well and to develop close-knit relationships. Students come from all over the United States and overseas, providing the opportunity to meet and live with people from diverse backgrounds.

Wesley is a member of NCAA Division III intercollegiate athletics and the Capital Athletic Conference. Men have teams in baseball, basketball, cross-country running, football, golf, lacrosse, soccer, tennis, and track and field. Women compete in basketball, cheerleading, cross-country running, field hockey, golf, lacrosse, soccer, softball, tennis, track and field, and volleyball. A well-organized intramural program offers a wide variety of athletics competitions, including, but not limited to, basketball, flag football, soccer, and volleyball.

The mission of the College is to be the premier institution for helping students gain the knowledge, skills, and moral and ethical attitudes necessary to achieve their personal goals and contribute to the welfare of their communities in a global society. The College endeavors to impart a desire for lifelong learning and an enhanced capacity for critical and creative thinking, so that students can reap the rewards of intellectual growth and professional effectiveness. As a college in a covenant relationship with the United Methodist Church and founded upon Christian principles, Wesley strives to realize a holistic campus environment of common purpose, caring, tolerance, inclusiveness, responsibility, and service that is the heart of community.

In addition to its undergraduate degrees, Wesley College awards the Master of Science in Nursing (M.S.N.) degree, two Master of Education degrees, the Master of Business Administration (M.B.A.) degree, and an M.S. degree in environmental sciences.

Location

Dover is the capital of the country's first state and has approximately 35,000 residents. New York City, Baltimore, Philadelphia, and Washington, D.C., are within a 2- to 3-hour drive of the campus. The College is located within Dover's major residential community, with stores and banks within easy walking distance and malls a short commute away. Seafood is a specialty in Dover because of the city's proximity to the Delaware and Chesapeake Bays and to the Atlantic Ocean. Delaware Transit Corporation (DART) provides bus service throughout the city of Dover. Daily bus service is available to and from the campus. In addition, Delaware's famous beaches are also within easy driving distance of the campus.

Many students become involved in local activities, including volunteer work at private and public agencies. On-campus volunteer activities include a unique three-way partnership between a state-funded elementary and secondary charter school (Campus Community Schools), the Wesley Boys and Girls Club, and the College. Many students are employed in community businesses through the cooperative education program at Wesley. Others work in part-time jobs to earn extra money. Many local residents also attend Wesley on a part-time basis and enjoy full use of the College's facilities.

Majors and Degrees

Bachelor of Arts and Bachelor of Science degrees are awarded in accounting, American studies, biology, business administration (international business, management, and marketing), education (elementary K–8 and physical education K–12), English, English education, environmental studies (environmental policy and environmental science), history, international studies, legal studies, liberal studies, mathematics, mathematics education, media arts, medical technology, nursing, physical education (exercise science and sports management), political science, and psychology.

Academic Programs

The comprehensive academic calendar year consists of two semesters and a double summer session. Winter sessions are available in England and France, offering unique opportunities for travel and study.

Bachelor's degree candidates begin with the foundation core curriculum, which emphasizes an overarching theme of the individual in a global community. Interdisciplinary threads bind the core curriculum and the major programs into a purposeful design. These threads are critical thinking, communication across disciplines, technological literacy, multicultural awareness, aesthetic appreciation, and ethical sensibility. The core provides a distinctive undergraduate experience for students, establishes coherent links between the curricular and cocurricular programs, and provides community service options beyond the College campus.

Academic Facilities

The Robert H. Parker Library is the College's library and resources center, with a collection of hardbound volumes, academic journals, and periodicals. In addition, Wesley is part of KentNet, a consortium of Dover-area and Kent County libraries. Through the consortium, more than 500,000 volumes are accessible to Wesley students at facilities within a mile of the campus. Computers located in the library are connected to the College's campuswide network and have the capability to access the library's CD-ROM network. Individual and group instruction on the use of information resources, including the

Internet, is provided by the library staff. The library also carries a collection of videotape titles that are available for individual and group viewing.

Access to new communications technology is provided through facilities equipped for production of on-campus broadcasts or taped distribution. The multimedia lab allows students to create and print electronic messages.

Costs

For 2007–08, Wesley's tuition and fees were $16,750 per year. Room and board costs ranged from $7800 to $11,300 per year. Books and supplies cost about $1000 per year.

Financial Aid

Financial aid is available in the form of endowed scholarships, federal scholarships, grants, work-study programs, and loans. Approximately 85 percent of Wesley students receive financial aid. Wesley uses the Free Application for Federal Student Aid (FAFSA). Students and their families are urged to complete and send their FAFSA as early as possible. Financial aid awards must be confirmed by the student within fifteen days of notification.

Wesley College provides numerous academic scholarships to its top undergraduate students. Applications for these awards are not required. Interested seniors should contact the Office of Admissions.

Faculty

Wesley College emphasizes teaching. More than 80 percent of faculty members hold a doctoral or other terminal degree in their subject area and attend workshops and conferences to keep abreast of current activities in their fields. Most faculty members serve as academic advisers to students. All have regularly scheduled office hours and are available for student conferences on a regular basis.

Student Government

Student leadership develops through various aspects of College governance. Student representatives work in close cooperation with faculty members and administrators.

Admission Requirements

Many factors are considered in the selection of a Wesley student. The most important are the applicant's secondary school courses and grades, along with the required SAT or ACT scores. On-campus interviews are strongly recommended. Secondary school recommendations are also important. International students should submit their applications for admission by February 1 for the following fall semester. Admission decisions are made without regard to race, religion, color, age, gender, handicap, or national origin. Applicants should have 16 secondary school units in English, social studies, laboratory science, mathematics, and electives.

Students, parents, and counselors are welcome to contact the Office of Admissions for information and assistance.

Wesley College reserves the right to change some or all rates, policies, or courses when necessary, without prior notice.

Application and Information

Secondary school records should be attached to the Wesley College application form. Copies of official school records may also be submitted via fax.

To schedule an admissions interview and campus tour, students should call the Office of Admissions. A College prospectus, application form, and financial aid information are available by contacting:

Arthur T. Jacobs Sr.
Director of Undergraduate Admissions
Wesley College
120 North State Street
Dover, Delaware 19901
Phone: 302-736-2400
800-937-5398 Ext. 2400 (toll-free)
Fax: 302-736-2382
E-mail: admissions@wesley.edu
Web site: http://www.wesley.edu

A student relaxes in the beautiful surroundings of Wesley College.

DISTRICT OF COLUMBIA

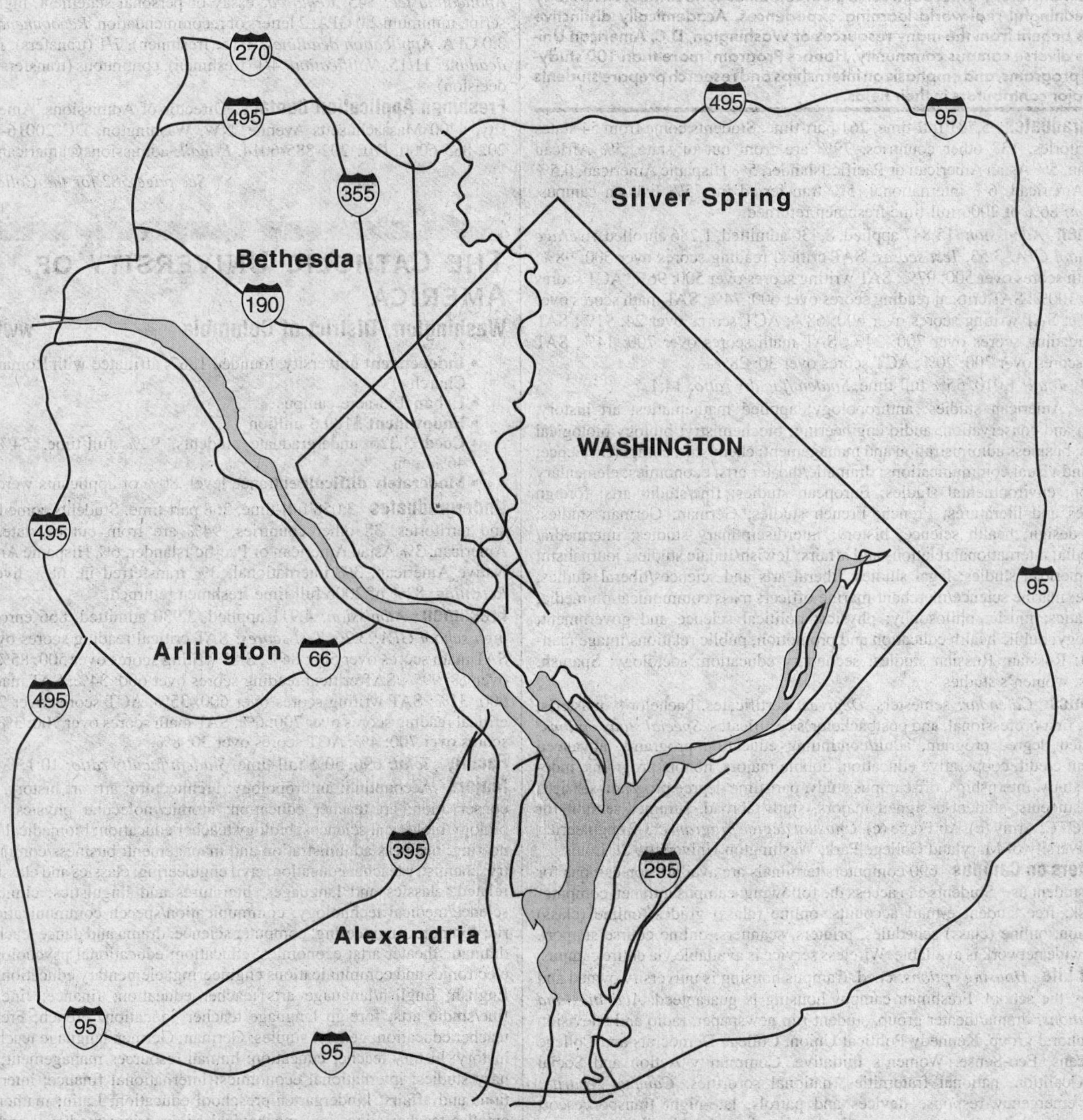

AMERICAN UNIVERSITY

Washington, District of Columbia **www.american.edu/**

- **Independent Methodist** university, founded 1893
- **Suburban** 84-acre campus
- **Endowment** $396.0 million
- **Coed** 6,042 undergraduate students, 96% full-time, 62% women, 38% men
- **Very difficult** entrance level, 53% of applicants were admitted

American University's thorough curriculum combines serious theoretical study with meaningful real-world learning experiences. Academically distinctive students benefit from the many resources of Washington, D.C. American University's diverse campus community, Honors Program, more than 100 study-abroad programs, and emphasis on internships and research prepare students to be major contributors in their fields.

Undergraduates 5,781 full-time, 261 part-time. Students come from 54 states and territories, 137 other countries, 79% are from out of state, 5% African American, 5% Asian American or Pacific Islander, 5% Hispanic American, 0.5% Native American, 6% international, 5% transferred in, 75% live on campus. *Retention:* 86% of 2006 full-time freshmen returned.

Freshmen *Admission:* 15,847 applied, 8,436 admitted, 1,286 enrolled. *Average high school GPA:* 3.53. *Test scores:* SAT critical reading scores over 500: 98%; SAT math scores over 500: 97%; SAT writing scores over 500: 96%; ACT scores over 18: 100%; SAT critical reading scores over 600: 74%; SAT math scores over 600: 63%; SAT writing scores over 600: 68%; ACT scores over 24: 91%; SAT critical reading scores over 700: 24%; SAT math scores over 700: 14%; SAT writing scores over 700: 20%; ACT scores over 30: 28%.

Faculty *Total:* 1,010, 55% full-time. *Student/faculty ratio:* 14:1.

Majors American studies; anthropology; applied mathematics; art history, criticism and conservation; audio engineering; biochemistry; biology/biological sciences; business administration and management; chemistry; computer science; design and visual communications; dramatic/theater arts; economics; elementary education; environmental studies; European studies; fine/studio arts; foreign languages and literatures; French; French studies; German; German studies; graphic design; health science; history; interdisciplinary studies; intermedia/multimedia; international relations and affairs; Jewish/Judaic studies; journalism; Latin American studies; legal studies; liberal arts and sciences/liberal studies; literature; marine science/merchant marine officer; mass communication/media; mathematics; music; philosophy; physics; political science and government; psychology; public health education and promotion; public relations/image management; Russian; Russian studies; secondary education; sociology; Spanish; statistics; women's studies.

Academics *Calendar:* semesters. *Degrees:* certificates, bachelor's, master's, doctoral, first professional, and postbachelor's certificates. *Special study options:* accelerated degree program, adult/continuing education programs, advanced placement credit, cooperative education, double majors, honors programs, independent study, internships, off-campus study, part-time degree program, services for LD students, student-designed majors, study abroad, summer session for credit. *ROTC:* Army (c), Air Force (c). *Unusual degree programs:* 3-2 engineering with University of Maryland College Park; Washington University, St. Louis.

Computers on Campus 690 computers/terminals are available on campus for general student use. Students can access the following: campus intranet, computer help desk, free student e-mail accounts, online (class) grades, online (class) registration, online (class) schedules, printers, scanners, online course support. Campuswide network is available. Wireless service is available via entire campus.

Student Life *Housing options:* coed. Campus housing is university owned and leased by the school. Freshman campus housing is guaranteed. *Activities and organizations:* drama/theater group, student-run newspaper, radio and television station, choral group, Kennedy Political Union, College Democrats and College Republicans, Eco-Sense, Women's Initiative, Community Action and Social Justice Coalition, national fraternities, national sororities. *Campus security:* 24-hour emergency response devices and patrols, late-night transport/escort service, controlled dormitory access. *Student services:* health clinic, personal/psychological counseling.

Athletics Member NCAA. All Division I. *Intercollegiate sports:* basketball M (s)/W (s), cross-country running M (s)/W (s), field hockey W (s), lacrosse W (s), soccer M (s)/W (s), swimming and diving M (s)/W (s), tennis M (s)/W (s), track and field M (s)/W (s), volleyball W (s), wrestling M (s). *Intramural sports:* basketball M/W, cheerleading W, crew M (c)/W (c), equestrian sports M (c)/W (c), field hockey W (c), gymnastics W (c), ice hockey M (c)/W (c), lacrosse M (c)/W (c), rugby M (c)/W (c), sailing M (c)/W (c), skiing (downhill) M (c)/W (c), soccer M/W, softball M/W, ultimate Frisbee M (c)/W (c), volleyball M/W.

Standardized Tests *Required:* SAT or ACT (for admission). *Recommended:* SAT Subject Tests (for admission).

Costs (2008–09) *Comprehensive fee:* $45,701 includes full-time tuition ($32,816), mandatory fees ($467), and room and board ($12,418). Part-time tuition: $1093 per hour.

Financial Aid Of all full-time matriculated undergraduates who enrolled in 2007, 3,562 applied for aid, 2,619 were judged to have need, 1,206 had their need fully met. 2,169 Federal Work-Study jobs (averaging $2016). In 2007, 1141 non-need-based awards were made. *Average percent of need met:* 57%. *Average financial aid package:* $24,294. *Average need-based loan:* $6613. *Average need-based gift aid:* $12,854. *Average non-need-based aid:* $16,994. *Financial aid deadline:* 2/15.

Applying *Options:* electronic application, early decision, deferred entrance. *Application fee:* $45. *Required:* essay or personal statement, high school transcript, minimum 2.0 GPA, 2 letters of recommendation. *Recommended:* minimum 3.0 GPA. *Application deadlines:* 1/15 (freshmen), 7/1 (transfers). *Early decision deadline:* 11/15. *Notification:* 4/1 (freshmen), continuous (transfers), 12/31 (early decision).

Freshman Application Contact Director of Admissions, American University, 4400 Massachusetts Avenue, NW, Washington, DC 20016-8001. *Phone:* 202-885-6000. *Fax:* 202-885-6014. *E-mail:* admissions@american.edu.

See page 582 for the College Close-Up.

THE CATHOLIC UNIVERSITY OF AMERICA

Washington, District of Columbia **www.cua.edu/**

- **Independent** university, founded 1887, affiliated with Roman Catholic Church
- **Urban** 193-acre campus
- **Endowment** $189.6 million
- **Coed** 3,326 undergraduate students, 92% full-time, 54% women, 46% men
- **Moderately difficult** entrance level, 80% of applicants were admitted

Undergraduates 3,058 full-time, 268 part-time. Students come from 52 states and territories, 38 other countries, 94% are from out of state, 5% African American, 3% Asian American or Pacific Islander, 6% Hispanic American, 0.2% Native American, 3% international, 3% transferred in, 68% live on campus. *Retention:* 82% of 2006 full-time freshmen returned.

Freshmen *Admission:* 4,911 applied, 3,930 admitted, 866 enrolled. *Average high school GPA:* 3.26. *Test scores:* SAT critical reading scores over 500: 85%; SAT math scores over 500: 84%; SAT writing scores over 500: 85%; ACT scores over 18: 99%; SAT critical reading scores over 600: 34%; SAT math scores over 600: 31%; SAT writing scores over 600: 35%; ACT scores over 24: 60%; SAT critical reading scores over 700: 6%; SAT math scores over 700: 3%; SAT writing scores over 700: 4%; ACT scores over 30: 8%.

Faculty *Total:* 696, 50% full-time. *Student/faculty ratio:* 10:1.

Majors Accounting; anthropology; architecture; art; art history, criticism and conservation; art teacher education; atomic/molecular physics; biochemistry; biology/biological sciences; biology teacher education; biomedical/medical engineering; business administration and management; business/commerce; chemistry; chemistry teacher education; civil engineering; classics and classical languages related; classics and languages, literatures and linguistics; clinical laboratory science/medical technology; communication/speech communication and rhetoric; computer engineering; computer science; drama and dance teacher education; dramatic/theater arts; economics; education; educational psychology; electrical, electronics and communications engineering; elementary education; engineering; English; English/language arts teacher education; finance; fine arts related; fine/studio arts; foreign language teacher education; French; French language teacher education; general studies; German; German language teacher education; history; history teacher education; human resources management; interdisciplinary studies; international economics; international finance; international relations and affairs; kindergarten/preschool education; Latin; mathematics; mathematics teacher education; mechanical engineering; medieval and Renaissance studies; modern Greek; music; music history, literature, and theory; music performance; music teacher education; music theory and composition; nursing (registered nurse training); painting; philosophy; physics; piano and organ; political science and government; psychology; religious education; religious studies; Romance languages; sculpture; secondary education; social work; sociology; Spanish; Spanish language teacher education; voice and opera.

Academics *Calendar:* semesters. *Degrees:* bachelor's, master's, doctoral, first professional, and post-master's certificates. *Special study options:* accelerated degree program, adult/continuing education programs, advanced placement credit, cooperative education, distance learning, double majors, English as a second language, freshman honors college, honors programs, independent study, internships, off-campus study, part-time degree program, services for LD students, study abroad, summer session for credit. *ROTC:* Army (c), Navy (c), Air Force (c). *Unusual degree programs:* 3-2 engineering; nursing; architecture.

Computers on Campus 450 computers/terminals are available on campus for general student use. Students can access the following: online (class) registration, internet 2, video streaming, online voting, pedagogical software. Campuswide network is available.

Student Life *Housing:* on-campus residence required through sophomore year. *Options:* coed, men-only, women-only, disabled students. Campus housing is university owned. Freshman campus housing is guaranteed. *Activities and organizations:* drama/theater group, student-run newspaper, radio station, choral group, Knights of Columbus, Students for Life, College Republicans, Habitat for Humanity, College Democrats, national fraternities, national sororities. *Campus security:* 24-hour emergency response devices and patrols, late-night transport/escort service, controlled dormitory access, controlled access of academic buildings. *Student services:* health clinic, personal/psychological counseling, women's center, legal services.

Athletics Member NCAA. All Division III. *Intercollegiate sports:* baseball M, basketball M/W, cross-country running M/W, field hockey W, football M, lacrosse M/W, soccer M/W, softball W, swimming and diving M/W, tennis M/W, track and field M/W, volleyball W. *Intramural sports:* basketball M/W, crew M (c)/W (c), equestrian sports M (c)/W (c), football M/W, ice hockey M (c), racquetball M/W, rugby M (c)/W (c), soccer M/W, softball M/W, tennis M/W, track and field M/W, volleyball M/W.

Standardized Tests *Required:* SAT or ACT (for admission). *Recommended:* SAT Subject Tests (for admission).

Costs (2007–08) *One-time required fee:* $400. *Comprehensive fee:* $39,798 includes full-time tuition ($27,700), mandatory fees ($1290), and room and board ($10,808). Full-time tuition and fees vary according to program. Part-time tuition: $1045 per credit. Part-time tuition and fees vary according to course load. *Required fees:* $655 per year part-time. *College room only:* $6224. Room and board charges vary according to board plan and housing facility. *Payment plans:* tuition prepayment, installment. *Waivers:* employees or children of employees.

Financial Aid Of all full-time matriculated undergraduates who enrolled in 2006, 1,948 applied for aid, 1,537 were judged to have need, 824 had their need fully met. In 2006, 1127 non-need-based awards were made. *Average percent of need met:* 84%. *Average financial aid package:* $17,620. *Average need-based loan:* $4674. *Average need-based gift aid:* $12,839. *Average non-need-based aid:* $9263.

Applying *Options:* electronic application, early action, deferred entrance. *Application fee:* $55. *Required:* essay or personal statement, high school transcript, 1 letter of recommendation. *Recommended:* minimum 3.0 GPA, interview. *Application deadlines:* 2/15 (freshmen), 7/15 (transfers), 11/15 (early action). *Notification:* continuous until 3/15 (freshmen), 12/15 (early action).

Freshman Application Contact Ms. Christine Mica, Director of University Admissions, The Catholic University of America, 102 McMahon Hall, 620 Michigan Avenue, NE, Washington, DC 20064. *Phone:* 202-319-5305. *Toll-free phone:* 202-319-5305 (in-state); 800-673-2772 (out-of-state). *Fax:* 202-319-6533. *E-mail:* cua-admissions@cua.edu.

See page 584 for the College Close-Up.

CORCORAN COLLEGE OF ART AND DESIGN

Washington, District of Columbia www.corcoran.edu/

- **Independent** comprehensive, founded 1890
- **Urban** 7-acre campus
- **Endowment** $14.0 million
- **Coed**
- **Moderately difficult** entrance level

Faculty *Student/faculty ratio:* 4:1.

Academics *Calendar:* semesters. *Degrees:* certificates, associate, bachelor's, and master's.

Student Life *Campus security:* 24-hour emergency response devices and patrols, controlled dormitory access, ID check at all entrances.

Standardized Tests *Required:* SAT or ACT (for admission).

Costs (2008–09) *Comprehensive fee:* $39,534 includes full-time tuition ($27,180), mandatory fees ($200), and room and board ($12,154). Part-time tuition: $890 per credit. *College room only:* $9694.

Financial Aid Of all full-time matriculated undergraduates who enrolled in 2006, 200 applied for aid, 200 were judged to have need. 123 Federal Work-Study jobs (averaging $718). In 2006, 60 non-need-based awards were made. *Average percent of need met:* 26. *Average financial aid package:* $13,142. *Average need-based loan:* $4909. *Average need-based gift aid:* $7156. *Average non-need-based aid:* $7621. *Average indebtedness upon graduation:* $30,955.

Applying *Options:* electronic application, early admission, deferred entrance. *Application fee:* $45. *Required:* high school transcript, minimum 2.5 GPA, portfolio. *Required for some:* essay or personal statement, interview. *Recommended:* essay or personal statement, minimum 3.0 GPA, letters of recommendation, interview.

Freshman Application Contact Ms. Elizabeth Smith Paladino, Director of Admissions, Corcoran College of Art and Design, 500 17th Street, NW, Washington, DC 20006-4804. *Phone:* 202-639-1814. *Toll-free phone:* 888-CORCORAN. *Fax:* 202-639-1830. *E-mail:* admissions@corcoran.org.

GALLAUDET UNIVERSITY

Washington, District of Columbia www.gallaudet.edu/

Director of Admissions Ms. Charity Reedy-Hines, Director of Admissions, Gallaudet University, 800 Florida Avenue, NE, Washington, DC 20002-3625. *Phone:* 202-651-5750. *Toll-free phone:* 800-995-0550. *E-mail:* admissions@gallua.gallaudet.edu.

GEORGETOWN UNIVERSITY

Washington, District of Columbia www.georgetown.edu/

- **Independent Roman Catholic (Jesuit)** university, founded 1789
- **Urban** 110-acre campus
- **Endowment** $1.1 billion
- **Coed** 7,038 undergraduate students, 96% full-time, 54% women, 46% men
- **Most difficult** entrance level, 21% of applicants were admitted

Undergraduates 6,789 full-time, 249 part-time. Students come from 53 states and territories, 83 other countries, 98% are from out of state, 7% African American, 9% Asian American or Pacific Islander, 7% Hispanic American, 0.1% Native American, 5% international, 3% transferred in, 71% live on campus. *Retention:* 96% of 2006 full-time freshmen returned.

Freshmen *Admission:* 16,163 applied, 3,363 admitted, 1,582 enrolled. *Test scores:* SAT critical reading scores over 500: 99%; SAT math scores over 500: 99%; SAT critical reading scores over 600: 90%; SAT math scores over 600: 90%; SAT critical reading scores over 700: 50%; SAT math scores over 700: 43%.

Faculty *Total:* 1,439, 57% full-time, 78% with terminal degrees. *Student/faculty ratio:* 11:1.

Majors Accounting; American studies; anthropology; Arabic; art; art history, criticism and conservation; biochemistry; biology/biological sciences; business administration and management; chemistry; Chinese; classics and languages, literatures and linguistics; comparative literature; computer science; economics; English; finance; fine/studio arts; French; German; health science; history; interdisciplinary studies; international business/trade/commerce; international economics; international relations and affairs; Italian; Japanese; liberal arts and sciences/liberal studies; linguistics; marketing/marketing management; mathematics; medieval and Renaissance studies; multi-/interdisciplinary studies related; nursing (registered nurse training); philosophy; physics; political science and government; Portuguese; psychology; Russian; science, technology and society; social sciences related; sociology; Spanish; theology; visual and performing arts; women's studies.

Academics *Calendar:* semesters. *Degrees:* certificates, bachelor's, master's, doctoral, and first professional. *Special study options:* academic remediation for entering students, adult/continuing education programs, advanced placement credit, double majors, English as a second language, honors programs, independent study, internships, off-campus study, services for LD students, student-designed majors, study abroad, summer session for credit. *ROTC:* Army (b), Navy (c), Air Force (c). *Unusual degree programs:* 3-2 foreign service.

Computers on Campus 400 computers/terminals are available on campus for general student use. Students can access the following: online (class) registration, online grade reports. Campuswide network is available.

Student Life *Housing:* on-campus residence required through sophomore year. *Options:* coed, disabled students. Campus housing is university owned. Freshman campus housing is guaranteed. *Activities and organizations:* drama/theater group, student-run newspaper, radio and television station, choral group. *Campus security:* 24-hour emergency response devices and patrols, late-night transport/escort service, controlled dormitory access, student guards at residence halls and academic facilities. *Student services:* health clinic, personal/psychological counseling, women's center.

Athletics Member NCAA. All Division I except football (Division I-AA). *Intercollegiate sports:* baseball M (s), basketball M (s)/W (s), crew M/W, cross-country running M (s)/W (s), field hockey W, golf M (s), ice hockey M (c), lacrosse M (s)/W (s), rugby M (c)/W (c), sailing M/W, soccer M (s)/W (s), softball W (c), swimming and diving M/W, tennis M/W (s), track and field M (s)/W (s), ultimate Frisbee M (c)/W (c), volleyball M (c)/W (s), water polo M (c). *Intramural sports:* basketball M/W, cross-country running M/W, football M/W, golf M/W, racquetball M/W, soccer M/W, softball M/W, squash M/W, table tennis M/W, tennis M/W, track and field M/W, ultimate Frisbee M, volleyball M/W.

Standardized Tests *Required:* SAT or ACT (for admission). *Recommended:* SAT Subject Tests (for admission).

Costs (2007–08) *Comprehensive fee:* $47,714 includes full-time tuition ($35,568) and room and board ($12,146). Part-time tuition: $1482 per credit hour. *College room only:* $8092.

Financial Aid Of all full-time matriculated undergraduates who enrolled in 2007, 3,068 applied for aid, 2,593 were judged to have need, 2,563 had their need fully met. 1,820 Federal Work-Study jobs (averaging $3300). *Average percent of need met:* 100%. *Average financial aid package:* $29,600. *Average need-based loan:* $3576. *Average need-based gift aid:* $23,400. *Average indebtedness upon graduation:* $24,935. *Financial aid deadline:* 2/1.

Applying *Options:* electronic application, early action, deferred entrance. *Application fee:* $65. *Required:* essay or personal statement, high school transcript, 2 letters of recommendation, interview. *Application deadlines:* 1/10 (freshmen), 3/1 (transfers), 11/1 (early action). *Notification:* 4/1 (freshmen), 6/1 (transfers), 12/15 (early action).

Freshman Application Contact Mr. Charles A. Deacon, Dean of Undergraduate Admissions, Georgetown University, 37th and O Street, NW, Washington, DC 20057. *Phone:* 202-687-3600. *Fax:* 202-687-5084.

THE GEORGE WASHINGTON UNIVERSITY

Washington, District of Columbia **www.gwu.edu/**

- **Independent** university, founded 1821
- **Urban** 36-acre campus
- **Endowment** $621.1 million
- **Coed** 10,701 undergraduate students, 90% full-time, 55% women, 45% men
- **Very difficult** entrance level, 37% of applicants were admitted

Undergraduates 9,654 full-time, 1,047 part-time. Students come from 55 states and territories, 101 other countries, 98% are from out of state, 6% African American, 10% Asian American or Pacific Islander, 6% Hispanic American, 0.3% Native American, 4% international, 4% transferred in, 64% live on campus. *Retention:* 90% of 2006 full-time freshmen returned.

Freshmen *Admission:* 19,606 applied, 7,197 admitted, 2,140 enrolled. *Test scores:* SAT critical reading scores over 500: 98%; SAT math scores over 500: 99%; SAT writing scores over 500: 98%; ACT scores over 18: 100%; SAT critical reading scores over 600: 78%; SAT math scores over 600: 76%; SAT writing scores over 600: 78%; ACT scores over 24: 91%; SAT critical reading scores over 700: 24%; SAT math scores over 700: 20%; SAT writing scores over 700: 23%; ACT scores over 30: 23%.

Faculty *Total:* 2,026, 42% full-time, 50% with terminal degrees. *Student/faculty ratio:* 13:1.

Majors Accounting; American studies; anthropology; applied mathematics; archeology; art; art history, criticism and conservation; Asian studies; Asian studies (East); audiology and speech-language pathology; biology/biological sciences; business administration and management; business/managerial economics; chemistry; Chinese; civil engineering; classics and languages, literatures and linguistics; clinical laboratory science/medical technology; clinical/medical laboratory technology; computer and information sciences; computer engineering; computer science; criminal justice/law enforcement administration; dance; diagnostic medical sonography and ultrasound technology; dramatic/theater arts; economics; electrical, electronics and communications engineering; emergency medical technology (EMT paramedic); engineering; English; environmental/environmental health engineering; environmental studies; European studies; finance; fine/studio arts; French; genetics related; geography; geology/earth science; German; history; humanities; human resources management; human services; industrial radiologic technology; interdisciplinary studies; international business/trade/commerce; international relations and affairs; Jewish/Judaic studies; journalism; kinesiology and exercise science; Latin American studies; liberal arts and sciences/liberal studies; marketing/marketing management; mass communication/media; mathematics; mechanical engineering; medical laboratory technology; music; Near and Middle Eastern studies; nuclear medical technology; pharmacology and toxicology related; philosophy; physician assistant; physics; political science and government; pre-dentistry studies; pre-law studies; pre-medical studies; psychology; public policy analysis; radio and television; radiologic technology/science; religious studies; Russian; Russian studies; sociology; Spanish; speech and rhetoric; statistics; systems engineering.

Academics *Calendar:* semesters. *Degrees:* certificates, associate, bachelor's, master's, doctoral, first professional, post-master's, and postbachelor's certificates. *Special study options:* accelerated degree program, adult/continuing education programs, advanced placement credit, cooperative education, distance learning, double majors, English as a second language, honors programs, independent study, internships, off-campus study, part-time degree program, services for LD students, student-designed majors, study abroad, summer session for credit. *ROTC:* Army (c), Navy (b), Air Force (c). *Unusual degree programs:* 3-2 business administration; engineering; chemical toxicology, art therapy, economics, engineering economics, operations research.

Computers on Campus 550 computers/terminals are available on campus for general student use. Campuswide network is available.

Student Life *Housing options:* coed. Campus housing is university owned. Freshman campus housing is guaranteed. *Activities and organizations:* drama/theater group, student-run newspaper, radio and television station, choral group, marching band, Program Board, Student Association, Residence Hall Association, College Democrats, College Republicans, national fraternities, national sororities. *Campus security:* 24-hour emergency response devices and patrols, late-night transport/escort service, controlled dormitory access. *Student services:* health clinic, personal/psychological counseling, legal services.

Athletics Member NCAA. All Division I. *Intercollegiate sports:* baseball M (s), basketball M (s)/W (s), crew M (s)/W (s), cross-country running M (s)/W (s), golf M (s), gymnastics W (s), soccer M (s)/W (s), swimming and diving M (s)/W (s), tennis M (s)/W (s), volleyball W (s), water polo M (s). *Intramural sports:* badminton M (c)/W (c), basketball M/W, bowling M (c)/W (c), equestrian sports M (c)/W (c), fencing M (c)/W (c), football M/W, lacrosse M (c), racquetball M/W, rugby M (c), sailing M (c)/W (c), soccer M/W, softball M/W, squash M (c)/W, swimming and diving M/W, tennis M/W, volleyball M (c)/W, water polo M/W.

Standardized Tests *Required:* SAT or ACT (for admission).

Costs (2008–09) *Comprehensive fee:* $50,357 includes full-time tuition ($40,392), mandatory fees ($45), and room and board ($9920). Part-time tuition: $1123 per credit hour. *College room only:* $6520.

Financial Aid Of all full-time matriculated undergraduates who enrolled in 2005, 4,932 applied for aid, 4,223 were judged to have need, 2,662 had their need fully met. In 2005, 2293 non-need-based awards were made. *Average percent of need met:* 91%. *Average financial aid package:* $33,196. *Average need-based loan:* $6806. *Average need-based gift aid:* $19,828. *Average non-need-based aid:* $19,290. *Average indebtedness upon graduation:* $29,304. *Financial aid deadline:* 2/1.

Applying *Options:* electronic application, early admission, early decision, deferred entrance. *Application fee:* $65. *Required:* essay or personal statement, high school transcript, 2 letters of recommendation. *Recommended:* interview. *Application deadlines:* 1/15 (freshmen), rolling (transfers). *Early decision deadline:* 11/10 (for plan 1), 1/10 (for plan 2). *Notification:* continuous until 3/15 (freshmen), continuous (transfers), 12/15 (early decision plan 1), 2/1 (early decision plan 2).

Director of Admissions Dr. Kathryn M. Napper, Director of Admission, The George Washington University, 2121 I Street, NW, Suite 201, Washington, DC 20052. *Phone:* 202-994-6040. *Fax:* 202-994-0325. *E-mail:* gwadm@gwis2.circ.gwu.edu.

See page 586 for the College Close-Up.

HOWARD UNIVERSITY

Washington, District of Columbia **www.howard.edu/**

Director of Admissions Interim Director of Admissions, Howard University, 2400 Sixth Street, NW, Washington, DC 20059-0002. *Phone:* 202-806-2700. *Toll-free phone:* 800-HOWARD-U.

POTOMAC COLLEGE

Washington, District of Columbia **www.potomac.edu/**

Freshman Application Contact Asha Ellison, Assistant to the President, Potomac College, 4000 Chesapeake Street, NW, Washington, DC 20016. *Phone:* 202-686-0876 Ext. 203. *Toll-free phone:* 888-686-0876. *Fax:* 202-686-0818. *E-mail:* info@potomac.edu.

SOUTHEASTERN UNIVERSITY

Washington, District of Columbia **www.seu.edu/**

- **Independent** 4-year, founded 1879
- **Urban** 1-acre campus
- **Coed, primarily women**
- **Noncompetitive** entrance level

Faculty *Student/faculty ratio:* 7:1.

Academics *Calendar:* quadmester (four 12-week semesters). *Degrees:* certificates, associate, bachelor's, and master's.

Student Life *Campus security:* late-night transport/escort service.

Costs (2008–09) *Tuition:* $9180 full-time, $270 per credit part-time. *Required fees:* $1050 full-time, $350 per term part-time.

Applying *Options:* deferred entrance. *Application fee:* $50. *Required:* high school transcript. *Recommended:* essay or personal statement, interview.

Freshman Application Contact Ms. Halima Griffin, Director of Admission, Southeastern University, 501 I Street, Washington, DC 20024. *Phone:* 202-265-5343. *Fax:* 202-488-8093. *E-mail:* admissions@seu.edu.

STRAYER UNIVERSITY

Washington, District of Columbia **www.strayer.edu/**

Director of Admissions Ms. Deepali Kala, Director of Student Enrollment, Strayer University, 1133 15th Street NW, Washington, DC 20005. *Phone:* 703-339-1850. *Toll-free phone:* 888-4-STRAYER. *Fax:* 703-339-1850. *E-mail:* dk@strayer.edu.

TRINITY (WASHINGTON) UNIVERSITY

Washington, District of Columbia **www.trinitydc.edu/**

Director of Admissions Ms. Marien Noblitt, Vice President for Marketing, Recruiting, and Admissions, Trinity (Washington) University, 125 Michigan Avenue, NE, Washington, DC 20017-1094. *Phone:* 800-492-6882. *Toll-free phone:* 800-IWANTTC. *E-mail:* admissions@trinitydc.edu.

See page 588 for the College Close-Up.

UNIVERSITY OF THE DISTRICT OF COLUMBIA

Washington, District of Columbia **www.udc.edu/**

- **District-supported** comprehensive, founded 1976
- **Urban** 28-acre campus
- **Endowment** $21.8 million
- **Coed** 5,137 undergraduate students, 47% full-time, 60% women, 40% men
- **Noncompetitive** entrance level, 85% of applicants were admitted

Undergraduates 2,436 full-time, 2,701 part-time. Students come from 39 states and territories, 97 other countries, 37% are from out of state, 71% African American, 3% Asian American or Pacific Islander, 6% Hispanic American, 0.1% Native American. *Retention:* 59% of 2006 full-time freshmen returned.

Freshmen *Admission:* 3,801 applied, 3,230 admitted, 1,117 enrolled.

Faculty *Total:* 372, 65% full-time, 33% with terminal degrees. *Student/faculty ratio:* 13:1.

Majors Administrative assistant and secretarial science; advertising; aeronautics/aviation/aerospace science and technology; anthropology; architectural engineering technology; architecture; art; art teacher education; audiology and speech-language pathology; aviation/airway management; avionics maintenance technology; biology/biological sciences; biology/biotechnology laboratory technician; business administration and management; ceramic arts and ceramics; chemical engineering; chemistry; child development; civil engineering; civil engineering technology; clinical laboratory science/medical technology; clinical/medical laboratory technology; clothing/textiles; commercial and advertising art; computer engineering technology; computer science; construction management; corrections; criminal justice/police science; criminology; developmental and child psychology; dramatic/theater arts; economics; electrical, electronic and communications engineering technology; electrical, electronics and communications engineering; elementary education; entrepreneurship; environmental engineering technology; environmental studies; family and consumer sciences/home economics teacher education; family and consumer sciences/human sciences; fashion merchandising; finance; fine/studio arts; food science; food services technology; forestry; French; funeral service and mortuary science; geography; graphic communications related; health teacher education; hospitality administration; hospitality administration related; human resources management and services related; hydrology and water resources science; industrial arts; industrial radiologic technology; information science/studies; kindergarten/preschool education; legal administrative assistant/secretary; marine science/merchant marine officer; mass communication/media; mathematics; mechanical engineering; mechanical engineering/mechanical technology; music teacher education; nursing (licensed practical/vocational nurse training); nutrition sciences; ornamental horticulture; physical education teaching and coaching; physical sciences; physics; political science and government; psychology; purchasing, procurement/acquisitions and contracts management; respiratory care therapy; social work; sociology; Spanish; special education; trade and industrial teacher education; water quality and wastewater treatment management and recycling technology.

Academics *Calendar:* semesters. *Degrees:* associate, bachelor's, and master's. *Special study options:* academic remediation for entering students, accelerated degree program, adult/continuing education programs, cooperative education, English as a second language, external degree program, honors programs, internships, off-campus study, part-time degree program, services for LD students, summer session for credit. *ROTC:* Army (c), Air Force (c).

Computers on Campus 1,500 computers/terminals are available on campus for general student use. Students can access the following: campus intranet, computer help desk, free student e-mail accounts, online (class) grades, online (class) registration, online (class) schedules. Campuswide network is available.

Student Life *Housing:* college housing not available. *Activities and organizations:* drama/theater group, student-run newspaper, choral group, marching band, Caribbean Student Association, Theater Arts Ensemble, National Association for the Advancement of Colored People, national fraternities, national sororities. *Campus security:* 24-hour emergency response devices and patrols. *Student services:* health clinic, personal/psychological counseling.

Athletics Member NCAA. All Division II. *Intercollegiate sports:* golf M (s), soccer M (s), tennis M (s)/W (s), track and field M (s)/W (s), volleyball W (s).

Standardized Tests *Recommended:* SAT (for admission).

Costs (2008–09) *Tuition:* area resident $2520 full-time, $105 per credit part-time; nonresident $5160 full-time, $215 per credit part-time. *Required fees:* $620 full-time, $310 per semester part-time.

Financial Aid Of all full-time matriculated undergraduates who enrolled in 2007, 1,812 applied for aid, 1,617 were judged to have need, 371 had their need fully met. 110 Federal Work-Study jobs (averaging $3000). In 2007, 72 non-need-based awards were made. *Average financial aid package:* $6010. *Average need-based loan:* $4587. *Average need-based gift aid:* $2917. *Average non-need-based aid:* $2252. *Average indebtedness upon graduation:* $16,270.

Applying *Options:* deferred entrance. *Application fee:* $75. *Required:* high school transcript. *Required for some:* GED. *Application deadlines:* 8/1 (freshmen), 8/1 (transfers). *Notification:* continuous until 8/15 (freshmen), continuous until 8/15 (transfers).

Freshman Application Contact Mrs. LaVerne Hill Flannigan, Director of Admission/Recruitment/Registrar, University of the District of Columbia, 4200 Connecticut Avenue NW, Building 39—A-Level, Washington, DC 20008. *Phone:* 202-274-6110. *Fax:* 202-274-5553.

AMERICAN UNIVERSITY

WASHINGTON, D.C.

The University

American University (AU) is for academically distinctive and engaged students who want to turn ideas into action and action into service. AU's thorough curriculum enables students to combine serious theoretical study with meaningful real-world learning experiences.

American's unique core curriculum; Washington, D.C., location; and emphasis on the practical application of knowledge prepares students to be major contributors in their fields. For students in search of a more rigorous academic experience, AU's Honors Program offers exceptional seminars and colloquia. The University College Program is an intensive first-year experience combining class work, residence life, and learning in Washington, D.C. In fall 2007, the University introduced three new programs for undergraduate research funding, giving students the flexibility to pursue their intellectual interests. Many AU students choose to study more than one field or design their own interdisciplinary major to prepare for their professional futures. For example, premed students can major in international studies for a career in international health. The University understands that tomorrow's careers require an understanding of a wide variety of fields, and it encourages students to transcend the traditional boundaries of academic disciplines.

AU's more than 5,000 undergraduates are a microcosm of the world's diversity. From across the United States and more than 140 countries, they share a desire to shape tomorrow's world. AU actively promotes international understanding, and this is reflected in its curriculum offerings, its faculty research, and the regular presence of world leaders on campus.

AU students enjoy the convenience of EagleBuck$, a cashless way to pay on and off campus at the area's most popular businesses. A prepaid, stored-value account that is part of the AU ID card, EagleBuck$ are an easy way for students to obtain food, goods, and services 24 hours a day.

Almost all first-year students and about 65 percent of all students live in on-campus housing. The University's six smoke-free residence halls have been recently renovated and offer a choice of single-sex or coed floors and special interest options, such as the Honors Program floor. Most rooms are for 2 students and have two complete sets of furniture and computer network and telephone access. Laundry and cooking facilities are available on each floor. In conjunction with the installation of new laundry machines throughout the residence halls, AU has implemented a fully computerized laundry service called eSUDS. Students can use a Web application to check if washers and dryers are available in the nearest laundry room. Using the existing EagleBuck$ system, students activate and pay for laundry service by swiping their student ID card through a special laundry room ID reader. When the wash or dry cycle is complete, the student receives notification via e-mail or cell phone. Students have a variety of meal plans from which to choose. AU has a main dining room close to the residence halls and many small cafés. On-campus restaurants include Subway, McDonald's, and Chick-fil-A. Because AU is in a residential neighborhood, students have the option of finding an off-campus apartment within walking distance of the campus.

Nonresidential fraternities and sororities, more than 160 student-run organizations, NCAA Division I athletics, and intramural and club sports offer students a range of opportunities.

Location

At the top of Embassy Row in northwest Washington, D.C., American University's traditional campus (a designated arboretum and public garden) is an 84-acre home base. The incomparable resources of the nation's capital are all just minutes away, as students have easy access to the University shuttle, the subway, city buses, and taxis. AU is convenient to Ronald Reagan Washington National Airport, Dulles International Airport, and Baltimore Washington International Airport and to Union Station and interstate highways.

Majors and Degrees

The College of Arts and Sciences awards B.A., B.F.A., and B.S. degrees in the arts, education, humanities, sciences, and social sciences through its twenty academic units. Prelaw and premedical programs are also available.

The School of International Service offers the B.A. in international studies and in language and area studies.

The School of Public Affairs offers the B.A. degree in justice, law and society, and political science. The school also offers CLEG, a unique interdisciplinary program that combines courses in communication, law, economics, and government.

The School of Communication is a professional school that offers training in broadcast journalism, communication studies, foreign language and communication media, print journalism, public communication, and visual media.

The Kogod School of Business offers the Bachelor of Science in Business Administration (B.S.B.A.), with specializations in accounting, economics, enterprise management, finance, human resource management, international business, international finance, international management, international marketing, management of information technology, marketing, and fields related to international service, including communications, development, economic policy, and regional area studies.

Academic Programs

Students can choose from more than seventy programs in the arts and humanities, business, education, international studies, public affairs, sciences, social sciences, or preprofessional programs in law and medicine. Students may decide to double major and have the option of constructing their own interdisciplinary major. Students may major in one AU school and minor in another school or college. Most majors offer the option of pursuing a combined bachelor's/master's program. Students do not need to formally declare a major until the end of their sophomore year. During the first two years, students choose ten classes from more than 150 specially designed courses in the General Education Program, which is designed for all undergraduate students regardless of major or degree program. Aimed at building a strong intellectual foundation, the courses are drawn from five curricular areas: the creative arts, global and multicultural perspectives, international and intercultural experience, social institutions and behavior, and the natural sciences. Students are required to take two courses in each area, the first of which serves as the foundation course and the second, a more specialized course in an approved sequence. These innovative courses are a vital part of students' intellectual and professional preparation. They improve writing and critical-thinking skills; offer new and balanced scholarship on ethical principles, gender, race, class, and culture; and incorporate quantitative and computing skills as appropriate for their field. In addition, all students are required to complete two courses in English composition and one in college-level mathematics.

The educational goals of the College of Arts and Sciences include teaching students to examine Western and non-Western cultures, appreciate scientific inquiry, master written and oral expression, develop the ability to analyze and synthesize information, and build an understanding of the moral and ethical dimensions that underlie decision making. Working with faculty members and professional academic counselors, students select internships and develop courses of study in more than forty majors in the arts, education, humanities, mathematics, performing arts, sciences, and social sciences. The strong liberal arts curriculum of the college is enhanced by the educational, social, cultural, artistic, and scientific resources of Washington, D.C. The individual strengths of each department are heightened by students' ability to cross the lines between disciplines—expanding their educational horizons while acquiring the skills and knowledge required for success in graduate-level study or in their chosen careers.

American's School of International Service (SIS) is the largest of its kind in the United States and is able to offer serious students a breadth of study in international relations. Among the Association of Professional Schools of International Affairs (APSIA), AU's SIS has the largest number of students who are women and members of minority groups. It ranks sixth among APSIA schools in number of international students. The international studies program begins with foundation courses and core field courses to provide students with the tools to explore specific areas of study in greater depth. Students select an area of specialization from among Africa, the Americas, Asia, Europe, the Middle East, or Russia and Central Eurasia. Students also select a functional field of concentration in business, comparative and international race relations, international politics, U.S. foreign policy, Islamic studies, global environmental politics, international communication, international development, international economic policy, or peace and conflict resolution. The language and area studies major provides a strong foundation in language and culture courses. Students choose one of four areas: French/Western Europe, German/Western Europe, Spanish/Latin America, or Russian area studies.

Students in the School of Public Affairs are engaged in learning about local, national, and international politics, with a focus on public institutions; public policy; crime; justice; and law. These areas frame a comprehensive program that incorporates classroom learning, individualized research projects, relevant field studies, and professional training. Washington's facilities for scholarly research and work opportunities in public affairs are limitless. Students may participate in the school's leadership and summer programs, and they can get involved in the school's Women and Politics, Public Affairs and Advocacy, or Campaign Management Institutes.

The goal of the School of Communication (SOC) is to develop professionally trained communicators who are equipped intellectually and ethically to convey the issues of contemporary society. SOC graduates the third-largest number of communication professionals among U.S. institutions. The curriculum benefits from the environment of Washington, D.C., one of the world's major communications centers. The school emphasizes involving students with Washington's communicators and communication facilities. A strong liberal arts curriculum is required to ensure students' abilities to interpret the world around them.

The Kogod School of Business provides students with a solid foundation in business, including the preparation to be responsible citizens and assume leadership roles in a global business economy. Recognized for academic excellence by *U.S. News & World Report*, Kogod is entrepreneurial, relevant to today's markets, and flexible in its strategies. The school offers a business curriculum derived from a multifunctional view of business that emphasizes critical skills and topics such as communication, e-commerce, teamwork, technology, ethics, and global business. Nearly every major U.S. corporation and many multinational firms have a presence in the Washington, D.C., area, providing Kogod students with limitless opportunities to enhance classroom learning through internship experiences.

Off-Campus Programs

Each year, the University's Career Center provides more than 500 students with internship experience in jobs related to their educational and career goals. Such professional training may be with arts organizations, museums, private business, industry, community and social service organizations, or local, state, and federal governments. Full-time faculty members from nearly all University departments serve as program coordinators.

American University administers its own exciting study-abroad program, called AU Abroad. Students can study at more than 100 locations in thirty-three countries around the world. Built into most of these study programs are opportunities for language immersion and to tour the country, meet and talk with national leaders and academicians, and participate in internships and homestays.

Academic Facilities

The University's facilities include a state-of-the-art language resource center, multimedia design and development labs, and science laboratories; the new Katzen Arts Center, which features more than 130,000 square feet of space for the fine and performing arts; and a sports center with indoor and outdoor tracks, soccer and intramural fields, an Olympic-size pool, and a state-of-the-art fitness center. There are fourteen classroom buildings, a 50,000-watt broadcast center, and an interdenominational religious center. The library is a member of the OCLC network, which gives students online access to 2,000 other member libraries. Computing resources are delivered by a fiber-optic network with connections throughout campus, including all residence hall rooms, as well as through wireless access for laptops, PDAs, and smartphones.

Costs

Undergraduate tuition and fees for the 2007–08 academic year were $30,958. Room and board costs averaged $11,812 for the year. There are several installment payment plans.

Financial Aid

AU recognizes academic achievement and potential and offers merit scholarships to approximately 25 percent of each freshman class. These scholarships are not based on financial need, and no separate application forms are required. The scholarships include awards of up to full tuition. Scholarships are also available for transfer students. The University also supports a multimillion-dollar financial assistance program. Families must apply by February 15 for priority consideration.

Faculty

The faculty represents a rich mix of academic and professional training. Its 504 full-time members are nationally and internationally recognized in their fields, and 96 percent have the highest degree in their field. An important part of American's academic program is the integration of practicing professionals into the faculty. The talent pool available in Washington, D.C., is enormous. Students have the opportunity to learn from professionals from such organizations as the World Bank, Discovery Communications, the Associated Press, the National Endowment for the Arts, the John F. Kennedy Center for the Performing Arts, the National Aeronautics and Space Administration, and other private industries. These faculty members bring a real-world perspective to the classroom experience. The student-faculty ratio is 14:1. The average undergraduate class size is 23 students.

Student Government

The Student Confederation is the representative student government for all full-time undergraduates. There are also school and college councils.

Admission Requirements

Admission to AU is selective and competitive. Each freshman applicant is reviewed individually, with careful consideration given to the high school record, SAT or ACT scores (with writing), the essay, extracurricular activities, and letters of recommendation. Special emphasis is given to leadership qualities, creative endeavors, volunteerism, and entrepreneurship. The middle 50 percent of admitted students have grade point averages between 3.33 and 3.80 (on a 4.0 scale) and combined SAT scores between 1210 and 1360 or ACT scores between 26 and 30. Approximately 20 National Merit Finalists and Semifinalists enroll each year. The University admitted 490 transfer applicants in 2006–07. A minimum GPA of 2.5 (on a 4.0 scale) on all university-level work completed is necessary to be considered competitive for admission. Transfer students should visit the University's Web site for more information.

Application and Information

The deadline for early decision freshmen is November 15, and notification is made by December 31. The regular decision deadline is January 15. While most freshmen are admitted for the fall semester, students may also apply for summer- or spring-semester entry. Transfer applicants may apply for all three terms. Students should call or visit the University's Web site for application requirements. The University participates in the Common Application program and accepts its online and paper application forms. The University also hosts it own online application, for which there is no fee.

Undergraduate Admissions
American University
4400 Massachusetts Avenue, NW
Washington, D.C. 20016-8001
Phone: 202-885-6000
Fax: 202-885-1025
E-mail: admissions@american.edu
Web site: http://admissions.american.edu

THE CATHOLIC UNIVERSITY OF AMERICA

WASHINGTON, D.C.

The University

The Catholic University of America (CUA) in Washington, D.C., offers a strong liberal arts curriculum, small classes, and personal attention from faculty members in a values-based environment.

Founded in 1887 by the U.S. Catholic bishops, CUA is home to more than 3,100 undergraduate and 3,000 graduate students from all fifty states and ninety different countries. Students from all religious traditions are welcome.

While the University maintains a small-college atmosphere, with a student-faculty ratio of 9:1, it is a major research institution. Undergraduates learn from the same professors who conduct research and teach graduate students.

CUA maintains its lush, green grounds through a commitment to ecologically sound practices and is noted for the beautiful architecture found on its 193-acre campus in northeast Washington, D.C. The majority of undergraduates live on campus in eighteen residence halls and twenty-five modular housing units, including an option of honors housing. The University is currently constructing a new student residence, Opus Hall, which will be a seven-story building equipped to house about 400 students.

The University offers many venues for spiritual devotion and growth that enable students of all religious traditions to deepen their faith. Campus Ministry provides many opportunities for community service in the Washington, D.C., area; throughout the United States; and abroad.

A competitive NCAA Division III athletic program enables teams to compete with others who share similar standards of academic and athletic excellence. Intercollegiate teams for women are basketball, cross-country, field hockey, lacrosse, soccer, softball, swimming, tennis, track and field (indoor and outdoor), and volleyball. Men's sports are baseball, basketball, cross-country, football, lacrosse, soccer, swimming, tennis, and track and field (indoor and outdoor). Club sports are extensive, and they include crew, fencing, golf, ice hockey, rugby, and Ultimate Frisbee. A wide range of intramural athletic programs is also offered.

The Raymond A. DuFour Athletic Center houses a main arena and stadium; swimming pool; handball, racquetball, and tennis courts; a dance and aerobics studio; a weight room; indoor and outdoor running tracks; and outdoor playing fields.

Services available to students include individual tutoring and general seminars on research techniques, writing, and study skills; career assessment and placement; disability support; and programs for international students.

A state-of-the-art University center opened in 2003. A variety of food service choices and programs, including concerts, seminars, and lectures, are offered to the campus community.

Location

Located 3 miles north of the Capitol in residential Washington, D.C., CUA is in the same neighborhood as several other educational, medical, and research centers. The University is accessible via D.C.'s public transportation and its subway system, the Metro. CUA has its own stop on the Metro's Red Line.

Majors and Degrees

Undergraduate degrees are offered in eighty-three major programs in six of CUA's ten schools: Architecture and Planning, Arts and Sciences, Engineering, Music, Nursing, and Philosophy.

The School of Arts and Sciences offers the Bachelor of Arts or Bachelor of Science degrees in the following areas: accounting, anthropology, art, art history, biochemistry, biology, chemical physics, chemistry, classical civilization, classics, drama, economics, education (early childhood, elementary, and secondary), education studies (nonteaching), English language and literature, environmental science, finance, French, German, Greek and Latin, history, international business, international economics and finance, Latin and classical humanities, management, management information systems, marketing, mathematics, media studies, medical technology, medieval and Byzantine studies, music, philosophy, physics, politics, psychology, religion and religious education, social work, sociology, Spanish, and Spanish for international service. Predental, prelaw, premedical, and preveterinary programs are available. Students can also select double majors and minors. Accelerated degree programs are available to students who perform at exceptional levels. Possibilities include a three-year Bachelor of Arts program, a five-year bachelor's/master's joint-degree program, and a six-year joint Bachelor of Arts/Juris Doctor program with CUA's Columbus School of Law.

The School of Engineering offers programs leading to a first professional degree in biomedical, civil, computer, construction, electrical, environmental, or mechanical engineering or in computer science.

The School of Architecture and Planning offers a Bachelor of Science in Architecture—a four-year degree program—and the Master of Architecture—an additional 1½-year professional degree program. A dual-degree program is available in architecture and civil engineering as well.

The School of Nursing offers a four-year program leading to a Bachelor of Science in Nursing degree. Also offered is an accelerated B.S.N. program, a twenty-month sequence for students who have a bachelor's degree in another field.

The Benjamin T. Rome School of Music offers four-year programs leading to Bachelor of Music degrees in composition, music education, music history and literature, musical theater, or performance, including orchestral instruments, organ, piano, or voice.

The School of Philosophy offers two programs leading to a Bachelor of Arts degree, including the program of concentration and the prelaw concentration.

Academic Programs

Architecture, engineering, music, and nursing students follow study courses that provide professional training integrated with a broad range of academic disciplines. Students in the School of Arts and Sciences undertake a major course of study within a liberal arts curriculum that encompasses the humanities, languages and literature, philosophy, the social sciences, mathematics and natural sciences, and religion. Most majors require the satisfactory completion of forty courses that are 3 credits each for graduation. Certain majors under the Bachelor of Science degree may require additional credits. In addition to the major, students may complete a minor course sequence by utilizing the elective courses included in the undergraduate program.

CUA maintains small undergraduate classes, even for introductory courses. Faculty members who teach graduate students also teach undergraduates, enabling freshmen to engage in dialogues with teachers and scholars. CUA offers outstanding academic research and library facilities and exposure to graduate and professional-level programs.

Also provided is a University-wide honors program for outstanding undergraduates who seek intense intellectual challenges. The program draws from traditional liberal arts disciplines and professional curricula to offer comprehensive academic experiences.

Off-Campus Programs

CUA belongs to the Consortium of Universities of the Washington Metropolitan Area. Undergraduates, with the approval of their academic advisers, may undertake course work and research at member institutions. Earned credits are applied to the CUA baccalaureate degree.

Washington, D.C.–area internships are available for students in almost every academic area. CUA has a career services center that helps students with internship and career placement. CUA offers students several international internship opportunities as well. These programs include British and Irish politics and society programs in London and Dublin, which incorporate a parliamentary internship. European studies are offered in Leuven, Belgium, with an internship with the European Union.

In addition to numerous internship and study opportunities in the D.C. area, CUA students can take advantage of exciting international education programs. CUAbroad and the University's Center for Global Education offer students numerous opportunities to study and learn in another country and be immersed in a different culture. These experiences help students to become global citizens.

Academic Facilities

More than 1.6 million volumes are available through the CUA library system. This collection is housed in the John K. Mullen of Denver Memorial Library and in six specialized libraries: chemistry; engineering, architecture, and mathematics; library and information science; music; nursing and biology; and physics. Students also have access to the libraries of the Washington, D.C., consortium and institutions such as the Library of Congress, the National Library of Medicine, the Folger Shakespeare Library, and the National Archives.

Catholic University's Center for Planning and Information Technology offers service and support for network, administrative, and academic computing. The center helps members of the University community use information technologies to deliver, access, process, communicate, and disseminate information.

In addition to a central computing cluster for faculty members and students, various labs, networked classrooms, and technology-equipped classrooms are located throughout the campus. VMS is the central operating system. A high-speed fiber network links the entire campus to the Internet, including all academic buildings and residence halls.

The Center for Planning and Information Technology issues a VMS and an NT account to all members of the University community. The VMS account can be used for e-mail and storage of files, and the NT account allows users to log on securely to any machine in an office or computer lab. A campus computing Information Center answers users' computing or information technology questions.

CUA is home to research facilities such as the Vitreous State Laboratory and the Centers of Excellence for Biomedical Engineering, Catholic Education, and other areas.

Costs

Tuition for the 2008–09 academic year is $30,670. Room, board, and fees total approximately $12,650.

Financial Aid

CUA administers two separate and distinct financial assistance programs: academic scholarships and need-based financial aid. A number of scholarships awarded on the basis of academic achievement are available. CUA offers financial aid to students based on need as demonstrated by the Free Application for Federal Student Aid (FAFSA). Loans, work-study, and University grants are available. Candidates who complete the admission application process before February 15 of their senior year are considered for academic scholarships and receive priority for financial aid.

Faculty

CUA has 347 full-time and 349 part-time faculty members. More than 98 percent hold doctoral or appropriate professional degrees. Thirteen percent of full-time faculty members are in religious orders; 87 percent are laypersons.

Student Government

The Undergraduate Student Government (USG) is composed of the legislative, academic, and judicial branches and the treasury and program board. Through this organization, students serve on standing committees and send representatives to the University's Academic Senate and Board of Trustees. USG also governs and allocates student activities fees to student organizations, sponsors functions and social events, and protects students' rights.

Admission Requirements

CUA welcomes applications from men and women of character, intelligence, and motivation, regardless of race, creed, sex, ethnic background, or physical disability. CUA is most interested in students who are best qualified to profit from opportunities offered at the University. For that reason, a selective admission policy is practiced. Successful candidates demonstrate achievement both in a challenging curriculum and on the standardized college entrance examinations. In addition, extracurricular achievements are important, as the admissions committee is interested in both academic and personal achievements.

Application and Information

Early action applicants must apply by November 15 and are notified by December 25. Regular decision applicants must apply by the February 15 deadline and are notified in March. Candidates for freshman admission must submit the secondary school report, high school transcripts, a letter of recommendation, an essay, official SAT or ACT scores, and a $55 application fee.

CUA accepts transfer applicants each semester. Transfer candidates should request applications for transfer admission from the Office of Admissions. In addition to the high school records and SAT or ACT scores, transfer students must submit a transcript from the school the student is attending (a minimum 3.0 GPA is recommended) and a statement of intent. Transfer applicants are notified of their status on a rolling basis.

Office of Admissions
The Catholic University of America
Washington, D.C. 20064
Phone: 202-319-5305
800-673-2772 (toll-free)
Fax: 202-319-6533
E-mail: cua-admissions@cua.edu
Web site: http://www.cua.edu

The Catholic University of America's 193-acre residential campus provides an outstanding atmosphere for learning and living.

THE GEORGE WASHINGTON UNIVERSITY

WASHINGTON, D.C.

THE GEORGE WASHINGTON UNIVERSITY
WASHINGTON DC

The University

Located just four blocks from the White House, The George Washington University (GW) is the largest institution of higher education in the nation's capital. Founded in 1821 by an Act of Congress, GW is a private nonsectarian coeducational institution, accredited by the Middle States Association of Colleges and Universities. GW prides itself in being at the forefront of major research endeavors, while providing a stimulating intellectual environment for its diverse students and faculty members.

The student population at GW consists of approximately 9,700 undergraduates and 10,000 graduates. Undergraduates hail from all fifty states, the District of Columbia, Puerto Rico, the Virgin Islands, and 125 countries. The undergraduate student body is 10.5 percent Asian American, 6 percent African American, 6.5 percent Hispanic American, and 8 percent international.

Both the Foggy Bottom and Mount Vernon campuses are located in historical and prestigious D.C. neighborhoods. The Foggy Bottom campus is situated in the heart of downtown D.C., neighbored by the Kennedy Center, the Watergate complex, the State Department, and the White House. The 26-acre Mount Vernon campus is home to athletic facilities and is surrounded by embassy and diplomatic residences. Both campus communities offer vibrant and distinctive residential options to freshmen and continuing students.

GW guarantees housing for entering freshmen and houses approximately 70 percent of undergraduates in thirty-one residence halls. GW offers a number of living arrangements, including apartment-style living for upperclassmen and residential town houses. GW's community living and learning philosophy guarantees that residence hall life is a valuable extension of the undergraduate experience. With nearly 97 percent of the entering class living in University housing, the atmosphere proves to be academically as well as socially stimulating.

GW hosts a strong intercollegiate varsity athletic program with twenty-two teams participating in the NCAA Division I and Atlantic 10 Conference. They include men's baseball, basketball, crew, cross-country, golf, soccer, swimming and diving, tennis, and water polo, and women's basketball, crew, cross-country, gymnastics, soccer, swimming and diving, tennis, volleyball, and water polo. Students interested in playing sports, but not quite up to the varsity level, may join a number of University-supported intramural sports.

There are more than 400 student-created and student-run organizations at GW. These organizations run the spectrum from academic to cultural, spiritual to recreational, and political to artistic. In addition to these special-interest organizations, GW is home to twenty-five national sororities and fraternities and nineteen honor societies, the Student Association (details in the Student Government section), the Program Board, the *Hatchet* (GW's independent newspaper), and WRGW (the campus radio station). The Student Activities Center plans large-scale events for students on campus, ranging from Welcome Week to Excellence in Student Life Awards to Fall Fest and Spring Fling.

Location

Many students at GW also choose to immerse themselves in the excitement of Washington, which has been called the most livable city on the East Coast. Washington, D.C., offers an infinite array of internships and cooperative education experiences, allowing GW students to explore their career aspirations outside of the four walls of the classroom. GW students have interned at the White House, the World Bank, AOL Time-Warner, the U.S. House of Representatives and Senate, NASA, the National Zoo, CNN, among many other world famous organizations.

The hordes of tourists that flock to Washington, D.C., every year experience the vibrant college town and young professional social scene in the nation's capital. There are more than 400,000 college students at forty-four colleges and universities concentrated in the metropolitan area.

Majors and Degrees

GW offers a wide range of undergraduate programs in six undergraduate schools: the Columbian College of Arts and Sciences, the Elliott School of International Affairs, the School of Business, the School of Engineering and Applied Science, the School of Medicine and Health Sciences, and the School of Public Health and Health Services.

GW offers eighty-seven majors, more than 1,000 courses, and yet, the average class size is only 28. Students may earn an undergraduate degree in a single field of study, or they may choose to double major, major in one field and minor in another, participate in an interdisciplinary program, or create their own individualized field of study.

The University awards an array of bachelor's degrees, including Bachelor of Arts (B.A.), Bachelor of Science (B.S.), Bachelor of Accountancy (B.Accy.), and Bachelor of Business Administration (B.B.A.).

Several joint-degree programs are available to undergraduates. In addition to a six-year B.A./J.D. program and a seven-year B.A/M.D. program, the University offers seventeen 5-year B.A./M.A. programs.

Academic Programs

Most undergraduate students must complete 120 credit hours to be eligible for graduation, which means that the average student carries 15 credit hours (five courses) per semester. All students at GW are required to participate in the University's writing program. In addition, each school has general curriculum requirements, ranging from 17 to 45 credit hours.

GW is home to nineteen honor societies, including Phi Beta Kappa and Golden Key National Honor Society. GW offers a variety of specialized academic programs. The University Honors Program, which does not replace a regular program of study but rather enhances it with intellectually challenging analysis and discussion, consists of approximately 800 undergraduates.

The six-year B.A./J.D. program allows students to accelerate their undergraduate study and complete their bachelor's and J.D. degree programs in six rather than seven years. The seven-year Integrated B.A./M.D. Program is designed for students who wish to obtain a strong foundation in the liberal arts prior to becoming physicians, enabling them to accomplish that goal in a shorter amount of time than a traditional program of study. The Integrated Engineering and Law Program offers highly qualified high school students the opportunity to earn a B.S. degree in engineering or computer science, and a J.D. degree in order to launch successful careers in such fields as patent law, intellectual property rights, and environmental law.

Off-Campus Programs

GW students are encouraged to study abroad in order to expand their world view and their educational opportunities. GW offers study abroad centers in Madrid, Paris, and England, as well as affiliated and exchange programs. Each year, approximately 900 GW undergraduates study abroad in more than forty countries.

Many GW students also take advantage of cooperative education (co-op), which provides students with an opportunity to gain valuable paid work experiences directly related to their major. The Career Center manages the program, in partnership with area employers, to ensure that co-op experiences are substantive and well-supervised. Similarly, many GW students engage in internships, which serve as a means for students to gain practical, professional experience and to augment their academic knowledge. Internships can be paid or unpaid, offered for academic credit, and can last for as long (or short) as the student and employer choose. The Career Center also acts as a clearinghouse for internship positions.

Academic Facilities

The Gelman Library houses more than 2 million volumes and, as a member of the Washington Research Library Consortium (WRLC), offers GW students access to more than 6 million volumes at eight area universities. Gelman Library is open 168 hours per week offering 24-hour study lounges, group discussion rooms, computer labs, walk-up reference consultation, and an interlibrary loan service. GW provides on-site and remote access to ALADIN, the shared online catalogue of WRLC libraries, plus databases indexing periodical articles and some full-text journals. GW is also home to the Eckles Library, the Jacob Burns Law Library, and the Himmelfarb Health Sciences Library.

Most academic buildings, libraries, residence halls, and the Marvin Center house computer labs, many of which are open 24 hours a day. In addition, most students who live on campus in residence halls have individual, high-speed Ethernet connectivity and Internet access.

GW is infused with the latest, state-of-the-art facilities enhancing campus life. Completed and planned projects include a new hospital, the Elliott School of International Affairs classroom and residential complex, the School of Business, the stunning 400-bed Ivory Tower residence hall, and Potomac House, a 700-bed freshman residence hall.

Costs

In response to family concerns about paying for college, GW has instituted a fixed tuition plan. Under this plan, the tuition remains the same each year for students who remain enrolled in full-time status during their undergraduate programs. Therefore, except for marginal increases in housing costs, cost of attendance will not rise. Students entering in fall 2007 paid $39,210 per year for four years. Room and board costs were approximately $11,900.

Financial Aid

The ability to finance a GW education is a priority, so the Office of Student Financial Assistance seeks to assist students and their families in meeting the costs to attend the University. The University budgets more than $85 million for undergraduate financial assistance, which includes scholarships and need-based assistance. In addition, GW offers families the opportunity to participate in a number of payment plans.

By applying for admission, students with outstanding academic credentials are automatically considered for Presidential Academic Scholarships. Approximately 15 percent of freshmen receive merit-based financial assistance. In addition, approximately 60 percent of GW's students receive need-based assistance with an average package of $22,522.

The Presidential Arts Scholarship Program awards scholarships to, and encourages the work of, entering freshmen who have shown promise in the fine arts (ceramics, design, drawing, interior design, painting, photography, and sculpture), music, theater, technical theater, directing, dance, and choreography.

More information about financial aid at GW can be obtained online at http://gwired.gwu.edu/finaid. Both merit scholarships and a portion of need-based financial aid are guaranteed for all four years for students who remain enrolled in full-time status during their undergraduate program.

Faculty

There is 1 faculty member for every 14 students at GW. Ninety-two percent of GW's full-time faculty members hold a doctoral degree. Part-time and adjunct faculty members are often leaders in their fields of expertise. GW professors are engaging, eminently qualified, and well connected, which allows for a robust intellectual community.

Student Government

The Student Association (SA) is an organization chartered by GW's Board of Trustees to represent students and their concerns. Any person registered for any academic credit at GW is a member of the SA. The SA undertakes initiatives related to academics, community service, neighborhood relations, and student activities.

Admission Requirements

GW receives nearly 20,000 applications for freshman admission and aims to recruit a class of 2,200. Admitted students have strong academic records and the demonstrated ability to achieve success in their college endeavors. To be considered for admission, applicants must submit the following credentials: application and fee, high school transcripts, essay, letters of recommendation from a teacher and a guidance counselor, and either SAT or ACT scores. Details can be obtained online at http://www.gwu.edu/. GW also accepts the common application, but requires a supplement to be included. On-campus interviews are not required, but may be helpful.

Application and Information

GW has a number of application options: Regular Decision, Early Decision I, and Early Decision II. Prospective students should consult the Web site (http://www.gwu.edu/) for the application and deadlines.

Office of Admissions
The George Washington University
2121 I Street, NW, Suite 201
Washington, D.C. 20052
Phone: 202-994-6040
E-mail: gwadm@gwu.edu
Web site: http://www.gwu.edu/

Students on campus at The George Washington University.

TRINITY (WASHINGTON) UNIVERSITY

WASHINGTON, D.C.

The College

Trinity in Washington, D.C., educates students who go on to make a difference in the world. With accredited undergraduate and graduate programs for women and men of all ages, Trinity provides a strong liberal arts foundation enhanced by practical experiences and a professional focus.

Trinity's location in the nation's capital offers students unique opportunities, from internships on Capitol Hill and at federal agencies to access to political leaders, journalists, policy experts, and business practitioners. The campus is just minutes from Capitol Hill and downtown Washington and is Metro accessible.

Trinity is affordable, for both students attending college right out of high school and those returning to school while pursuing a full-time career. All Trinity students have full access to the new Trinity Center, a state-of-the-art athletic facility.

Trinity has a demonstrated track record of graduates who secure professional positions after they graduate, are accepted to prestigious graduate programs in a range of fields, and become leaders of innovation, integrity, and influence. Graduates of Trinity include Speaker of the House Nancy Pelosi, the first woman to hold this highest-ranking position in Congress, and Hearst Magazines President Cathie Black.

The College of Arts and Sciences offers women a dynamic undergraduate experience, with leadership development, hands-on internships in Washington, community service opportunities, athletics, student clubs, and campus activities. The College of Arts and Sciences offers a wide choice of academic programs.

The School of Professional Studies is designed for men and women seeking to advance or change their careers. Students benefit from the innovative business, communication, technology, and liberal arts programs at both the undergraduate and graduate levels; flexible evening and weekend classes; and accelerated degree programs.

The School of Education offers graduate degrees in education, counseling, curriculum design, and educational administration. Trinity offers an accelerated certification program for aspiring teachers and a curriculum designed to meet the needs of educators in all stages of their careers.

Trinity has five NCAA Division III athletic programs: basketball, lacrosse, soccer, tennis, and volleyball. The Trinity Center for Women and Girls in Sports—the College's 83,000-square-foot fitness complex—is the nation's largest athletic facility designed especially for women's sports. The Trinity Center houses a competition-size swimming pool, a spa, a basketball and volleyball arena, a weight room, a dance studio, a fitness center, a walking track, and locker rooms. Other new athletic facilities include tennis courts and a field for soccer and lacrosse.

Location

Located on a 26-acre campus just 2½ miles from the U.S. Capitol, Trinity offers all the advantages of living in one of the world's most powerful cities while maintaining the serenity and beauty of a suburban campus. Metro—Washington's bus and subway system—provides easy access to numerous theaters, museums, and historic landmarks in and around the city. Reagan National and Dulles airports as well as the famous Union Station are nearby, and Trinity provides a free shuttle service to and from the nearest Metro station, which is also within walking distance of the campus.

Often referred to as Trinity's extended classroom, Washington offers access to endless political, cultural, and intellectual opportunities. Trinity offers a wide array of internships for academic credit that draw on the abundant resources of the capital area.

Majors and Degrees

Trinity's College of Arts and Sciences and School of Professional Studies offer the Bachelor of Arts (B.A.) and Bachelor of Science (B.S.) degrees in the following areas: biochemistry, biology, business administration, chemistry, economics, education, English, general studies, history, human relations, international affairs, language and cultural studies, mathematics, nursing, political science, psychology, and sociology. Concentrations are available in twenty-nine areas.

Academic Programs

Trinity General Education is an innovative interdisciplinary program designed to provide students with the knowledge, skills, and values to meet the challenges and opportunities of the twenty-first century. Trinity's curriculum and major programs offer a contemporary approach to education by combining the liberal arts with practical experience and a professional focus. Internships and selected career-related courses are available within the curriculum. Advising and career development programs assist in integrating academic success with personal career goals. Academic Services and the Career Services Center provide personal, academic, and career counseling. The on-campus Writing and Math Centers provide students with additional resources for strengthening individual skills in these areas.

Trinity is among the 10 percent of the nation's colleges and universities to be granted a chapter of Phi Beta Kappa, the country's oldest academic honor society.

Off-Campus Programs

Trinity is a member of the Consortium of Universities of the Washington Metropolitan Area, a cooperative arrangement among the major institutions of higher learning in and around the District of Columbia. Member schools share their facilities and give students the opportunity to take courses not offered by their own institution. Other member institutions include American University, Catholic University of America, Gallaudet University, George Mason University, Georgetown University, George Washington University, Howard University, Marymount University, the University of the District of Columbia, and the University of Maryland, College Park.

Academic Facilities

Trinity's Sister Helen Sheehan Library is affiliated with the Washington Research Library Consortium (WRLC), which provides access to a catalog of more than 5 million volumes in the libraries of American, Catholic, Gallaudet, George Mason, George Washington, and Marymount Universities and the University of the District of Columbia. The library also enjoys reciprocity agreements with the libraries at Georgetown University and Howard University. Trinity also has wireless Internet capability across much of the campus, and many of its classrooms are equipped with computers connected to the Internet, digital projectors, and smart boards in order to integrate technology into every aspect of the curriculum.

Costs

In 2007–08, full-time tuition was $18,250. Room and board were $8120.

Financial Aid

Financial assistance is available through grants, campus employment, loans, and scholarships. Trinity offers scholarships to transfer students and has a special scholarship for Phi Theta Kappa members. Nearly 90 percent of Trinity's students receive some form of financial assistance. Trinity's priority deadline for submitting the Free Application for Federal Student Aid (FAFSA) to the Federal Processing Center is March 1. Trinity's FAFSA code is 001460. Students should apply for financial aid as early as possible.

Faculty

There are 91 faculty members, 51 of whom are full-time. Ninety-five percent of the full-time faculty members hold doctoral degrees or the professional equivalent. Trinity's low student-faculty ratio makes it possible for students and faculty members to develop substantive academic relationships.

Student Government

The Student Government Association (SGA) at Trinity carries on a proud tradition of responsible student participation in College governance and academic and social affairs. In addition to representing students and voicing their concerns to the entire Trinity community, the SGA also coordinates student activities and supervises the functions of all committees and organizations that fall under the association. The judicial branch of the Student Government Association is responsible for upholding the College's Honor Agreement.

Admission Requirements

Trinity's College of Arts and Sciences seeks women who have demonstrated academic achievement and potential and who will bring varied interests, talents, and experiences to the community. Applicants are encouraged to complete a four-year secondary school program, including a total of 16 credits (4 in English; 3 each in history, mathematics, science, and social science; and some foreign language). Trinity's College of Arts and Sciences seeks academically well-rounded students, preferably with a 2.5 or higher GPA. School and community activities are important aspects of the application review. SAT or ACT scores, an interview with an admissions counselor, and a campus visit are highly recommended but not required. Although SAT and ACT scores are not required, students who have taken these exams are encouraged to submit their scores. Trinity's SAT code is 5796, and its ACT code is 0696. All international students for whom English is not the first language are required to submit TOEFL scores.

Advanced Placement course work may be considered for credit and advanced standing. Transfer students are encouraged to apply. Credit is given for most course work completed at an appropriately accredited college or university in which a grade of C or higher was earned.

All applicants are invited to arrange a personal interview with an admissions counselor, attend class, and tour the campus. The Office of Admissions is open Monday through Friday from 9 a.m. to 7 p.m. and on Saturday from 8 a.m. to 2 p.m. while school is in session.

Application and Information

Trinity's College of Arts and Sciences offers admission to qualified students in both the fall and the spring. Applications are considered on a rolling basis, and decisions are rendered upon receipt of a completed application and all required supporting credentials. Candidates for financial aid are asked to submit the FAFSA to the Federal Processing Center by March 1 for priority consideration.

For additional information and/or to receive an application, students should contact:

Office of Admissions
Trinity (Washington) University
125 Michigan Avenue, NE
Washington, D.C. 20017-1094
Phone: 202-884-9400
800-492-6882 (toll-free)
Fax: 202-884-9403
E-mail: admissions@trinitydc.edu
Web site: http://www.trinitydc.edu

The Trinity Center for Women and Girls in Sports is the nation's largest athletic facility designed especially for women's sports.

FLORIDA

The Tampa area includes the town of Temple Terrace.

The Miami area includes the towns of Coral Gables, Miami Beach, Miami Shores, and North Miami.

AMERICAN INTERCONTINENTAL UNIVERSITY

Weston, Florida **www.aiuniv.edu/**

- **Proprietary** comprehensive, founded 1998, administratively affiliated with American InterContinental University
- **Suburban** 3-acre campus
- **Coed**
- **Minimally difficult** entrance level

Majors Animation, interactive technology, video graphics and special effects; art; audiovisual communications technologies related; business administration and management; computer graphics; computer/information technology services administration related; corrections and criminal justice related; criminal justice/law enforcement administration; design and visual communications; fashion/apparel design; fashion merchandising; graphic design; information technology; interior design; marketing/marketing management; small business administration.

Academics *Calendar:* five 10-week terms. *Degrees:* associate, bachelor's, and master's. *Special study options:* academic remediation for entering students, adult/continuing education programs, advanced placement credit, distance learning, double majors, independent study, off-campus study, part-time degree program, study abroad, summer session for credit.

Student Life *Activities and organizations:* student-run newspaper. *Student services:* personal/psychological counseling.

Costs (2008–09) *Tuition:* contact campus for information. See: www.aiuniv.edu.

Applying *Options:* electronic application, deferred entrance. *Application fee:* $50. *Required:* essay or personal statement, high school transcript, interview, TOEFL for students whose first language is not English. *Application deadlines:* rolling (freshmen), rolling (transfers). *Notification:* continuous (freshmen), continuous (transfers).

Freshman Application Contact American InterContinental University, Admissions Office, 2250 North Commerce Parkway, Weston, FL 33326. *Phone:* 954-446-6100. *Toll-free phone:* 888-603-4888.

ANGLEY COLLEGE

Deland, Florida **www.angley.edu/**

- **Proprietary** primarily 2-year
- 94 undergraduate students
- 97% of applicants were admitted

Academics *Calendar:* continuous. *Degrees:* diplomas, associate, and bachelor's.

Applying *Application fee:* $25.

Freshman Application Contact Admissions Office, Angley College, 230 North Woodland Boulevard, Suite 310, Deland, FL 32720. *Phone:* 386-740-1215 Ext. 125. *Toll-free phone:* 866-639-1215. *E-mail:* admissions@angley.edu.

ARGOSY UNIVERSITY, SARASOTA

Sarasota, Florida **www.argosy.edu/locations/sarasota/**

- **Proprietary** university, founded 1974, part of Education Management Corporation
- **Coed**

Majors Business administration and management; criminal justice/law enforcement administration; finance; health/health care administration; international business/trade/commerce; marketing/marketing management; psychology.

Academics *Calendar:* semesters. *Degrees:* bachelor's, master's, and doctoral.

Freshman Application Contact Director of Admissions, Argosy University, Sarasota, 5250 17th Street, Sarasota, FL 34235. *Phone:* 800-331-5995. *Toll-free phone:* 800-331-5995.

See page 628 for the College Close-Up.

ARGOSY UNIVERSITY, TAMPA

Tampa, Florida **www.argosy.edu/locations/tampa/**

- **Proprietary** university, administratively affiliated with Education Management Corporation
- **Urban** campus
- **Coed**

Majors Business administration and management; psychology.

Academics *Calendar:* semesters. *Degrees:* bachelor's, master's and doctoral.

Director of Admissions Argosy University, Tampa, 4401 North Himes Avenue Suite 150, Tampa, FL 33614. *Phone:* 813-393-5290. *Toll-free phone:* 800-850-6488.

See page 628 for the College Close-Up.

THE ART INSTITUTE OF FORT LAUDERDALE

Fort Lauderdale, Florida **www.aifl.edu/**

- **Proprietary** 4-year, founded 1968, part of Education Management Corporation, administratively affiliated with The Art Institute of Fort Lauderdale
- **Urban** campus with easy access to Miami
- **Coed** 3,121 undergraduate students, 51% full-time, 55% women, 45% men
- **Minimally difficult** entrance level, 57% of applicants were admitted

Undergraduates 1,599 full-time, 1,522 part-time. Students come from 40 states and territories, 48 other countries, 28% are from out of state, 18% African American, 2% Asian American or Pacific Islander, 36% Hispanic American, 0.2% Native American, 0.1% transferred in, 13% live on campus. *Retention:* 66% of 2006 full-time freshmen returned.

Freshmen *Admission:* 1,362 applied, 778 admitted, 778 enrolled. *Average high school GPA:* 2.5.

Faculty *Total:* 175, 53% full-time, 41% with terminal degrees. *Student/faculty ratio:* 19:1.

Majors Applied art; cinematography and film/video production; clothing/textiles; commercial and advertising art; computer graphics; culinary arts; fashion/apparel design; industrial design; interior design; photography; radio and television.

Academics *Calendar:* quarters. *Degrees:* associate and bachelor's. *Special study options:* academic remediation for entering students, accelerated degree program, adult/continuing education programs, advanced placement credit, cooperative education, English as a second language, honors programs, independent study, internships, off-campus study, services for LD students, study abroad, summer session for credit.

Computers on Campus 700 computers/terminals and 700 ports are available on campus for general student use. Students can access the following: campus intranet, computer help desk, free student e-mail accounts, online (class) grades, online (class) registration, online (class) schedules. Campuswide network is available. 100% of college-owned or -operated housing units are wired for high-speed Internet access.

Student Life *Housing options:* coed. Campus housing is university owned and leased by the school. Freshman campus housing is guaranteed. *Activities and organizations:* student-run radio station, Student Government, International Student Association, Future Video Producers and Broadcasters Club, Fashion Club, American Society of Interior Designers. *Campus security:* 24-hour emergency response devices, late-night transport/escort service, controlled dormitory access. *Student services:* personal/psychological counseling.

Costs (2008–09) *One-time required fee:* $100. *Tuition:* $20,700 full-time, $460 per credit hour part-time. *Room only:* $5880.

Applying *Options:* electronic application. *Application fee:* $50. *Required:* essay or personal statement, high school transcript, interview. *Required for some:* letters of recommendation. *Recommended:* minimum 2.0 GPA. *Application deadlines:* rolling (freshmen), rolling (out-of-state freshmen), rolling (transfers).

Freshman Application Contact Ms. Kim Moss, The Art Institute of Fort Lauderdale, 1799 Southeast 17th Street Causeway, Fort Lauderdale, FL 33316-3000. *Phone:* 954-308-2148. *Toll-free phone:* 800-275-7603. *Fax:* 954-728-8617. *E-mail:* kmoss@aii.edu.

See page 630 for the College Close-Up.

THE ART INSTITUTE OF JACKSONVILLE

Jacksonville, Florida **www.artinstitutes.edu/jacksonville/**

- **Proprietary** 4-year, founded 2006, part of Education Management Corporation
- **Suburban** 1-acre campus
- **Coed**
- **Noncompetitive** entrance level

Majors Cinematography and film/video production; restaurant, culinary, and catering management; Web page, digital/multimedia and information resources design.

Standardized Tests *Recommended:* SAT or ACT (for admission).

Costs (2007–08) *Tuition:* tuition cost varies by program. Prospective students should contact the school for current tuition costs. Other charges include a starting kit for all first-quarter students. Kits vary in price depending on the program of study. *Required fees:* $75 per term part-time.

Applying *Application fee:* $50. *Required:* essay or personal statement, high school transcript, interview. *Recommended:* portfolio.

Director of Admissions Office of Admissions, The Art Institute of Jacksonville, 8775 Baypine Road, Jacksonville, FL 32256. *Phone:* 904-486-3002. *Toll-free phone:* 800-924-1589. *Fax:* 904-732-9423. *E-mail:* scarlstrom@aii.edu.

See page 632 for the College Close-Up.

THE ART INSTITUTE OF TAMPA

Tampa, Florida **www.aita.artinstitutes.edu/**

- **Proprietary** 4-year, part of Education Management Corporation
- **Suburban** campus
- **Coed** 881 undergraduate students, 72% full-time, 46% women, 54% men
- **Moderately difficult** entrance level, 56% of applicants were admitted

Undergraduates 632 full-time, 249 part-time. Students come from 19 states and territories, 4 other countries, 9% are from out of state, 12% African American, 2% Asian American or Pacific Islander, 18% Hispanic American, 0.5% international, 18% transferred in, 18% live on campus.

Freshmen *Admission:* 950 applied, 530 admitted, 249 enrolled.

Faculty *Total:* 89, 25% full-time, 43% with terminal degrees. *Student/faculty ratio:* 12:1.

Majors Advertising; apparel and accessories marketing; cinematography and film/video production; commercial photography; computer graphics; computer programming; culinary arts; graphic design; industrial design; restaurant, culinary, and catering management; web page, digital/multimedia and information resources design.

Academics *Calendar:* quarters. *Degrees:* diplomas, associate, and bachelor's. *Special study options:* adult/continuing education programs, advanced placement credit, cooperative education, internships, part-time degree program, services for LD students, summer session for credit.

Computers on Campus 85 computers/terminals are available on campus for general student use. Students can access the following: campus intranet, computer help desk, free student e-mail accounts, online (class) grades, online (class) registration, online (class) schedules, all hardware and software necessary for degree programs. Campuswide network is available. Wireless service is available via entire campus.

Student Life *Housing options:* coed. Campus housing is provided by a third party. Freshman applicants given priority for college housing. *Activities and organizations:* American Society of Interior Design, The Ink Spots (graphic design club), Fashion Club, Game Art & Design Club. *Campus security:* 24-hour patrols. *Student services:* personal/psychological counseling.

Standardized Tests *Required for some:* ACCUPLACER. *Recommended:* SAT or ACT (for admission).

Costs (2007–08) *Tuition:* tuition cost varies by program. Prospective students should contact the school for current tuition costs. Other charges include a starting kit for all first-quarter students. Kits vary in price depending on the program of study.

Applying *Options:* electronic application. *Application fee:* $50. *Required:* essay or personal statement, high school transcript, minimum 2.0 GPA, interview. *Required for some:* minimum 2.5 GPA, portfolio. *Application deadlines:* 10/9 (freshmen), rolling (transfers). *Notification:* continuous (freshmen), continuous (transfers).

Freshman Application Contact The Art Institute of Tampa, Parkside at Tampa Bay Park, 4401 North Himes Avenue, Suite 150, Tampa, FL 33614-7001. *Phone:* 813-873-2112. *Toll-free phone:* 866-703-3277. *Fax:* 813-873-2171. *E-mail:* aitainformation@aii.edu.

See page 634 for the College Close-Up.

AVE MARIA UNIVERSITY

Ave Maria, Florida **www.avemaria.edu/**

- **Independent Roman Catholic** comprehensive, founded 2002
- **Suburban** campus
- **Coed** 421 undergraduate students, 98% full-time, 54% women, 46% men
- **Moderately difficult** entrance level, 55% of applicants were admitted

Undergraduates 412 full-time, 9 part-time. Students come from 45 states and territories, 13 other countries, 81% are from out of state, 39% transferred in, 97% live on campus. *Retention:* 81% of 2006 full-time freshmen returned.

Freshmen *Admission:* 582 applied, 321 admitted, 187 enrolled. *Average high school GPA:* 3.62. *Test scores:* SAT critical reading scores over 500: 97%; SAT math scores over 500: 86%; SAT writing scores over 500: 98%; ACT scores over 18: 98%; SAT critical reading scores over 600: 73%; SAT math scores over 600: 51%; SAT writing scores over 600: 73%; ACT scores over 24: 54%; SAT critical reading scores over 700: 30%; SAT math scores over 700: 18%; SAT writing scores over 700: 28%; ACT scores over 30: 27%.

Faculty *Total:* 62, 73% full-time, 84% with terminal degrees. *Student/faculty ratio:* 8:1.

Majors American government and politics; biology/biological sciences; classics and languages, literatures and linguistics; economics; English; history; literature; mathematics; philosophy; pre-theology/pre-ministerial studies; religious/sacred music; theology; theology and religious vocations related.

Academics *Calendar:* semesters. *Degrees:* bachelor's, master's, and doctoral. *Special study options:* double majors, study abroad, summer session for credit.

Computers on Campus Students can access the following: campus intranet, computer help desk, free student e-mail accounts, online (class) grades, online (class) registration, online (class) schedules. Campuswide network is available. Wireless service is available via classrooms, computer labs, dorm rooms, libraries, student centers.

Student Life *Housing:* on-campus residence required through senior year. *Options:* men-only, women-only. Campus housing is university owned. Freshman campus housing is guaranteed. *Activities and organizations:* drama/theater group, student-run newspaper, choral group, Students for Life, Chastity Team, Student Government Association, Habitat for Humanity, Faith in Action Ministry. *Campus security:* 24-hour patrols, controlled dormitory access, County Sherriff workstation on campus with deputy patrols. *Student services:* personal/psychological counseling.

Athletics *Intercollegiate sports:* basketball M/W, golf M, soccer M/W, volleyball W. *Intramural sports:* basketball M (c)/W (c), soccer M (c)/W (c), ultimate Frisbee M (c)/W (c), volleyball M (c)/W (c).

Standardized Tests *Required:* SAT or ACT (for admission).

Costs (2008–09) *Comprehensive fee:* $24,500 includes full-time tuition ($16,350), mandatory fees ($550), and room and board ($7600). Part-time tuition: $511 per credit hour. *College room only:* $4150.

Applying *Options:* electronic application, early decision, deferred entrance. *Required:* essay or personal statement, high school transcript, minimum 2.8 GPA, 2 letters of recommendation, activities list. *Application deadlines:* rolling (freshmen), 12/1 (transfers). *Early decision deadline:* 11/1. *Notification:* continuous (freshmen), continuous (transfers).

Freshman Application Contact Ave Maria University, 1025 Commons Circle, Ave Maria, FL 34119. *Phone:* 239-280-2556. *Toll-free phone:* 877-283-8648. *Fax:* 239-280-2559.

See page 636 for the College Close-Up.

THE BAPTIST COLLEGE OF FLORIDA

Graceville, Florida **www.baptistcollege.edu/**

- **Independent Southern Baptist** 4-year, founded 1943
- **Small-town** 165-acre campus
- **Endowment** $4.6 million
- **Coed** 564 undergraduate students, 68% full-time, 36% women, 64% men
- **Noncompetitive** entrance level, 73% of applicants were admitted

Undergraduates 384 full-time, 180 part-time. Students come from 19 states and territories, 6 other countries, 23% are from out of state, 4% African American, 1% Asian American or Pacific Islander, 3% Hispanic American, 0.5% Native American, 0.2% international, 12% transferred in, 31% live on campus. *Retention:* 80% of 2006 full-time freshmen returned.

Freshmen *Admission:* 295 applied, 214 admitted, 39 enrolled.

Faculty *Total:* 63, 41% full-time, 62% with terminal degrees. *Student/faculty ratio:* 12:1.

Majors Biblical studies; child care and support services management; education; elementary education; music teacher education; pastoral studies/counseling.

Academics *Calendar:* 4-4-2. *Degrees:* associate and bachelor's. *Special study options:* academic remediation for entering students, advanced placement credit, distance learning, double majors, independent study, internships, part-time degree program, services for LD students, summer session for credit.

Computers on Campus 25 computers/terminals are available on campus for general student use. Students can access the following: online (class) registration. Campuswide network is available. Wireless service is available via entire campus.

Student Life *Housing:* on-campus residence required through sophomore year. *Options:* men-only, women-only. Campus housing is university owned. Freshman applicants given priority for college housing. *Activities and organizations:* drama/theater group, choral group, Baptist Collegiate Ministry, student government, AACC, Creation Science, WOW/MOW. *Campus security:* student patrols, patrols by police officers 11 p.m. to 7 a.m. *Student services:* personal/psychological counseling.

Athletics *Intramural sports:* basketball M/W, football M/W, soccer M/W, softball M/W, table tennis M/W, tennis M/W, volleyball M/W.

Standardized Tests *Required:* ACT (for admission), SAT or ACT (for admission).

Costs (2007–08) *Comprehensive fee:* $11,586 includes full-time tuition ($7500), mandatory fees ($350), and room and board ($3736). Full-time tuition and fees vary according to course load and location. Part-time tuition: $250 per semester hour. Part-time tuition and fees vary according to course load and location. *Required fees:* $175 per term part-time. *Room and board:* Room and board charges vary according to board plan and housing facility. *Payment plan:* installment. *Waivers:* employees or children of employees.

Financial Aid Of all full-time matriculated undergraduates who enrolled in 2006, 312 applied for aid, 273 were judged to have need, 11 had their need fully met. 27 Federal Work-Study jobs (averaging $1851). In 2006, 59 non-need-based awards were made. *Average percent of need met:* 47%. *Average financial aid package:* $6189. *Average need-based loan:* $3261. *Average need-based gift aid:* $4177. *Average non-need-based aid:* $4141. *Average indebtedness upon graduation:* $5941. *Financial aid deadline:* 4/15.

Applying *Options:* electronic application, early admission, deferred entrance. *Application fee:* $20. *Required:* essay or personal statement, high school transcript, 3 letters of recommendation. *Recommended:* interview. *Application deadlines:* 8/11 (freshmen), 8/11 (transfers). *Notification:* continuous (freshmen), continuous (transfers).

Freshman Application Contact Mrs. Sandra Richards, Director of Marketing, The Baptist College of Florida, 5400 College Drive, Graceville, FL 32440-1898. *Phone:* 850-263-3261. *Toll-free phone:* 800-328-2660 Ext. 460. *Fax:* 850-263-9026. *E-mail:* admissions@baptistcollege.edu.

BARRY UNIVERSITY

Miami Shores, Florida — www.barry.edu/

- **Independent Roman Catholic** university, founded 1940
- **Suburban** 122-acre campus with easy access to Miami
- **Endowment** $23.0 million
- **Coed** 5,088 undergraduate students, 80% full-time, 68% women, 32% men
- **Moderately difficult** entrance level, 57% of applicants were admitted

Undergraduates 4,072 full-time, 1,016 part-time. Students come from 41 states and territories, 24 other countries, 26% are from out of state, 22% African American, 1% Asian American or Pacific Islander, 29% Hispanic American, 0.3% Native American, 4% international, 8% transferred in, 35% live on campus. *Retention:* 64% of 2006 full-time freshmen returned.

Freshmen *Admission:* 3,315 applied, 1,892 admitted, 474 enrolled. *Average high school GPA:* 2.0. *Test scores:* SAT critical reading scores over 500: 37%; SAT math scores over 500: 35%; ACT scores over 18: 77%; SAT critical reading scores over 600: 5%; SAT math scores over 600: 4%; ACT scores over 24: 8%; SAT critical reading scores over 700: 1%; ACT scores over 30: 1%.

Faculty *Total:* 851, 39% full-time. *Student/faculty ratio:* 13:1.

Majors Accounting; acting; advertising; biology/biological sciences; broadcast journalism; business administration and management; chemistry; clinical laboratory science/medical technology; clinical/medical laboratory technology; communication/speech communication and rhetoric; computer science; criminology; cytotechnology; dramatic/theater arts; ecology; economics; education; elementary education; engineering; English; English/language arts teacher education; finance; French; history; information science/studies; international business/trade/commerce; international relations and affairs; journalism; kindergarten/preschool education; kinesiology and exercise science; liberal arts and sciences/liberal studies; literature; management information systems; marine biology and biological oceanography; marketing/marketing management; mass communication/media; mathematics; nuclear medical technology; nursing (registered nurse training); philosophy; photography; physical education teaching and coaching; piano and organ; political science and government; pre-dentistry studies; pre-law studies; pre-medical studies; pre-pharmacy studies; pre-veterinary studies; psychology; public relations/image management; radio and television; sociology; Spanish; special education; sport and fitness administration/management; theology; voice and opera.

Academics *Calendar:* semesters. *Degrees:* certificates, bachelor's, master's, doctoral, first professional, and postbachelor's certificates. *Special study options:* academic remediation for entering students, accelerated degree program, adult/continuing education programs, advanced placement credit, distance learning, double majors, English as a second language, honors programs, independent study, internships, off-campus study, part-time degree program, services for LD students, study abroad, summer session for credit. *ROTC:* Army (c), Air Force (c). *Unusual degree programs:* 3-2 engineering with University of Miami.

Computers on Campus 368 computers/terminals are available on campus for general student use. Campuswide network is available.

Student Life *Housing:* on-campus residence required for freshman year. *Options:* coed, men-only, women-only, disabled students. Campus housing is university owned. *Activities and organizations:* drama/theater group, student-run newspaper, radio and television station, choral group, Student Government Association, Campus Activities Board, SCUBA Society, Caribbean Students Association, Jamaican Association, national fraternities, national sororities. *Campus security:* 24-hour emergency response devices and patrols, late-night transport/escort service. *Student services:* health clinic, personal/psychological counseling.

Athletics Member NCAA. All Division II. *Intercollegiate sports:* baseball M (s), basketball M (s)/W (s), crew W (s), golf M (s)/W (s), soccer M (s)/W (s), softball W (s), tennis M (s)/W (s), volleyball W (s). *Intramural sports:* basketball M/W, football M/W, golf M/W, soccer M/W, softball M/W, volleyball M/W.

Standardized Tests *Required:* SAT or ACT (for admission).

Costs (2007–08) *Comprehensive fee:* $32,700 includes full-time tuition ($24,500) and room and board ($8200). Full-time tuition and fees vary according to program. Part-time tuition: $720 per credit. Part-time tuition and fees vary according to course load. *Room and board:* Room and board charges vary according to board plan. *Payment plans:* tuition prepayment, installment, deferred payment. *Waivers:* employees or children of employees.

Financial Aid Of all full-time matriculated undergraduates who enrolled in 2004, 3,661 applied for aid, 3,401 were judged to have need, 288 had their need fully met. 598 Federal Work-Study jobs (averaging $2432). In 2004, 351 non-need-based awards were made. *Average percent of need met:* 65%. *Average financial aid package:* $14,855. *Average need-based loan:* $4418. *Average need-based gift aid:* $6514. *Average non-need-based aid:* $5623. *Average indebtedness upon graduation:* $23,322.

Applying *Options:* electronic application, early admission, deferred entrance. *Application fee:* $30. *Required:* high school transcript, minimum 2.0 GPA. *Required for some:* essay or personal statement. *Recommended:* interview. *Application deadlines:* rolling (freshmen), rolling (transfers). *Notification:* continuous (freshmen), continuous (transfers).

Freshman Application Contact Barry University, Kelly House, 11300 Northeast Second Avenue, Miami Shores, FL 33161. *Phone:* 305-899-3138. *Toll-free phone:* 800-695-2279.

See page 638 for the College Close-Up.

BEACON COLLEGE

Leesburg, Florida — www.beaconcollege.edu/

- **Independent** 4-year, founded 1989
- **Small-town** 12-acre campus with easy access to Orlando
- **Coed** 116 undergraduate students, 100% full-time, 43% women, 57% men
- **Minimally difficult** entrance level, 71% of applicants were admitted

Undergraduates 116 full-time. Students come from 26 states and territories, 74% are from out of state, 14% African American, 3% Asian American or Pacific Islander, 5% Hispanic American, 12% transferred in, 95% live on campus. *Retention:* 88% of 2006 full-time freshmen returned.

Freshmen *Admission:* 63 applied, 45 admitted, 18 enrolled. *Average high school GPA:* 3.3.

Faculty *Total:* 17, 59% full-time, 47% with terminal degrees. *Student/faculty ratio:* 8:1.

Majors Human services; information science/studies; liberal arts and sciences/liberal studies.

Academics *Calendar:* semesters. *Degrees:* associate and bachelor's. *Special study options:* academic remediation for entering students, advanced placement credit, cooperative education, services for LD students, student-designed majors, study abroad.

Computers on Campus 34 computers/terminals are available on campus for general student use. Students can access the following: campus intranet, free student e-mail accounts. Campuswide network is available.

Student Life *Housing options:* men-only, women-only. Campus housing is university owned. Freshman campus housing is guaranteed. *Activities and organizations:* drama/theater group, student-run newspaper, student government, yearbook, basketball, Book Club, Poets and Writers Association, national fraternities, national sororities. *Campus security:* 24-hour emergency response devices, student patrols, controlled dormitory access. *Student services:* personal/psychological counseling.

Costs (2007–08) *Comprehensive fee:* $32,550 includes full-time tuition ($24,950), mandatory fees ($200), and room and board ($7400). Part-time tuition: $510 per credit. *College room only:* $4600. *Payment plan:* installment.

Applying *Options:* early admission, deferred entrance. *Application fee:* $50. *Required:* essay or personal statement, high school transcript, 3 letters of recommendation, psycho-educational evaluation. *Required for some:* interview. *Notification:* 8/1 (freshmen), 8/1 (transfers).

Freshman Application Contact Dr. Johnny Good, VP—Institutional Effectiveness, Beacon College, 105 East Main Street, Leesburg, FL 34748. *Phone:* 352-352-4081. *Fax:* 352-787-0721. *E-mail:* jgood@beaconcollege.edu.

BELHAVEN COLLEGE

Maitland, Florida

BETHUNE-COOKMAN UNIVERSITY

Daytona Beach, Florida www.bethune.cookman.edu/

- **Independent Methodist** comprehensive, founded 1904
- **Urban** 60-acre campus with easy access to Orlando
- **Endowment** $40.0 million
- **Coed** 3,394 undergraduate students, 94% full-time, 58% women, 42% men
- **Minimally difficult** entrance level, 28% of applicants were admitted

Undergraduates 3,179 full-time, 215 part-time. Students come from 45 states and territories, 32 other countries, 33% are from out of state, 94% African American, 0.2% Asian American or Pacific Islander, 2% Hispanic American, 0.2% Native American, 2% international, 4% transferred in, 54% live on campus. *Retention:* 72% of 2006 full-time freshmen returned.

Freshmen *Admission:* 4,469 applied, 1,240 admitted, 1,109 enrolled. *Average high school GPA:* 2.90. *Test scores:* SAT critical reading scores over 500: 14%; SAT math scores over 500: 11%; ACT scores over 18: 25%; SAT critical reading scores over 600: 1%; SAT math scores over 600: 2%; ACT scores over 24: 1%.

Faculty *Total:* 225, 85% full-time, 52% with terminal degrees. *Student/faculty ratio:* 17:1.

Majors Accounting; biology/biological sciences; biology teacher education; business administration and management; business teacher education; chemistry; chemistry teacher education; clinical laboratory science/medical technology; computer and information sciences; computer engineering; computer science; corrections and criminal justice related; elementary education; English; English/language arts teacher education; gerontology; history; hotel/motel administration; information science/studies; international business/trade/commerce; international relations and affairs; liberal arts and sciences/liberal studies; mass communication/media; mathematics; music performance; music teacher education; nursing (registered nurse training); philosophy and religious studies related; physical education teaching and coaching; physics; physics teacher education; political science and government; psychology; social studies teacher education; sociology; special education (specific learning disabilities); speech and rhetoric.

Academics *Calendar:* semesters. *Degrees:* bachelor's, master's, and first professional. *Special study options:* academic remediation for entering students, accelerated degree program, adult/continuing education programs, advanced placement credit, cooperative education, distance learning, double majors, honors programs, independent study, internships, part-time degree program, study abroad, summer session for credit. *ROTC:* Army (c), Air Force (c). *Unusual degree programs:* 3-2 engineering with Tuskegee University, University of Florida, Florida Atlantic University, Florida Agricultural and Mechanical University, University of Central Florida.

Computers on Campus 451 computers/terminals are available on campus for general student use. Students can access the following: campus intranet, computer help desk, free student e-mail accounts, online (class) grades, online (class) registration, online (class) schedules. Campuswide network is available. 100% of college-owned or -operated housing units are wired for high-speed Internet access. Wireless service is available via entire campus.

Student Life *Housing:* on-campus residence required for freshman year. *Options:* men-only, women-only. Campus housing is university owned. Freshman campus housing is guaranteed. *Activities and organizations:* drama/theater group, student-run newspaper, radio station, choral group, marching band, Concert Chorale, Marching Band, Inspirational Gospel Choir, SGA, national fraternities, national sororities. *Campus security:* 24-hour emergency response devices and patrols, student patrols, late-night transport/escort service. *Student services:* health clinic, personal/psychological counseling.

Athletics Member NCAA. All Division I except football (Division I-AA). *Intercollegiate sports:* baseball M (s), basketball M (s)/W (s), bowling W (s), cross-country running M (s)/W (s), golf M (s)/W (s), softball W (s), tennis M (s)/W (s), track and field M (s)/W (s), volleyball W (s). *Intramural sports:* basketball M/W, football M, racquetball M/W, soccer M, table tennis M/W, volleyball M/W.

Standardized Tests *Required:* SAT or ACT (for admission).

Costs (2007–08) *Comprehensive fee:* $19,760 includes full-time tuition ($12,382) and room and board ($7378). Part-time tuition: $516 per credit hour. *Waivers:* employees or children of employees.

Financial Aid Of all full-time matriculated undergraduates who enrolled in 2006, 2,905 applied for aid, 2,610 were judged to have need, 529 had their need fully met. 300 Federal Work-Study jobs (averaging $2000). 125 state and other part-time jobs (averaging $2000). In 2006, 79 non-need-based awards were made. *Average percent of need met:* 64%. *Average financial aid package:* $14,166. *Average need-based loan:* $3505. *Average need-based gift aid:* $6603. *Average non-need-based aid:* $8035. *Average indebtedness upon graduation:* $32,500.

Applying *Options:* early admission, deferred entrance. *Application fee:* $25. *Required:* high school transcript, minimum 2.25 GPA, 1 letter of recommendation, medical history. *Required for some:* interview. *Recommended:* essay or personal statement. *Application deadlines:* 6/30 (freshmen), 6/30 (transfers). *Notification:* continuous (freshmen), continuous (transfers).

Freshman Application Contact Mr. Les Ferrier, Executive Director of Admissions, Bethune-Cookman University, 640 Dr. Mary McLeod Bethune Boulevard, Daytona Beach, FL 32114-3099. *Phone:* 386-481-2600. *Toll-free phone:* 800-448-0228. *Fax:* 386-481-2601. *E-mail:* admissions@cookman.edu.

See page 640 for the College Close-Up.

CARLOS ALBIZU UNIVERSITY, MIAMI CAMPUS

Miami, Florida www.mia.albizu.edu/

- **Independent** comprehensive, founded 1980, part of Carlos Albizu University
- **Urban** 2-acre campus
- **Coed, primarily women**
- **Minimally difficult** entrance level

Faculty *Student/faculty ratio:* 10:1.

Academics *Calendar:* trimesters. *Degrees:* certificates, diplomas, bachelor's, master's, and doctoral.

Student Life *Campus security:* 24-hour emergency response devices and patrols, late-night transport/escort service.

Costs (2007–08) *Tuition:* $10,980 full-time, $305 per credit part-time. Full-time tuition and fees vary according to course load and program. Part-time tuition and fees vary according to course load and program. *Required fees:* $744 full-time, $248 per term part-time.

Financial Aid Of all full-time matriculated undergraduates who enrolled in 2003, 121 applied for aid, 118 were judged to have need. 27 Federal Work-Study jobs (averaging $3059). *Average percent of need met:* 50. *Average financial aid package:* $7925. *Average need-based loan:* $3549. *Average need-based gift aid:* $5300. *Average indebtedness upon graduation:* $23,000.

Applying *Application fee:* $25. *Required:* high school transcript, minimum 2.0 GPA.

Freshman Application Contact Barbara De la Cruz, Admissions Officer, Carlos Albizu University, Miami Campus, 2173 Northwest 99th Avenue, Miami, FL 33172. *Phone:* 305-593-1223 Ext. 164. *Toll-free phone:* 888-672-3246. *Fax:* 305-593-1854. *E-mail:* bdelacruz@albizu.edu.

CHIPOLA COLLEGE

Marianna, Florida www.chipola.edu/

- **State-supported** primarily 2-year, founded 1947
- **Rural** 105-acre campus
- **Coed**
- **Noncompetitive** entrance level

Faculty *Student/faculty ratio:* 24:1.

Academics *Calendar:* semesters. *Degrees:* certificates, associate, and bachelor's.

Student Life *Campus security:* night security personnel.

Athletics Member NJCAA.

Standardized Tests *Required:* SAT or ACT (for placement).

Costs (2007–08) *Tuition:* state resident $2200 full-time, $68 per hour part-time; nonresident $6000 full-time, $200 per hour part-time.

Applying *Options:* early admission. *Required:* high school transcript.

Freshman Application Contact Dr. Jayne Roberts, Dean of Enrollment Services and Registrar, Chipola College, Marianna, FL 32446. *Phone:* 850-718-2209. *Fax:* 850-718-2287. *E-mail:* robertsj@chipola.edu.

CITY COLLEGE

Fort Lauderdale, Florida www.citycollege.edu/

- **Independent** primarily 2-year, founded 1984
- **Coed**
- 77% of applicants were admitted

Academics *Calendar:* semesters. *Degrees:* certificates, associate, and bachelor's.

Financial Aid Of all full-time matriculated undergraduates who enrolled in 2006, 6 Federal Work-Study jobs.

Applying *Application fee:* $25.

Freshman Application Contact Admissions Office, City College, 2000 West Commercial Boulevard, Suite 200, Fort Lauderdale, FL 33309. *Phone:* 954-492-5353.

CITY COLLEGE

Gainesville, Florida www.citycollege.edu/

- **Independent** primarily 2-year, founded 1986
- **Coed**
- 100% of applicants were admitted

Academics *Calendar:* semesters. *Degrees:* certificates, associate, and bachelor's.

Applying *Application fee:* $25. *Required:* high school transcript.

Freshman Application Contact Admissions Office, City College, 2400 S.W. 13th Street, Gainesville, FL 32608.

CITY COLLEGE

Miami, Florida www.citycollege.edu/

- **Independent** primarily 2-year, founded 1997
- **Coed**
- 79% of applicants were admitted

Academics *Calendar:* semesters. *Degrees:* certificates, associate, and bachelor's.

Applying *Application fee:* $25. *Required:* high school transcript.

Freshman Application Contact Admissions Office, City College, 9300 South Dadeland Boulevard, Suite PH, Miami, FL 33156. *Phone:* 305-666-9242. *Fax:* 305-666-9243.

CLEARWATER CHRISTIAN COLLEGE

Clearwater, Florida www.clearwater.edu/

- **Independent nondenominational** 4-year, founded 1966
- **Suburban** 138-acre campus with easy access to Tampa–St. Petersburg
- **Endowment** $506,399
- **Coed** 594 undergraduate students, 95% full-time, 50% women, 50% men
- **Minimally difficult** entrance level, 93% of applicants were admitted

Undergraduates 565 full-time, 29 part-time. Students come from 38 states and territories, 5 other countries, 48% are from out of state, 3% African American, 2% Asian American or Pacific Islander, 5% Hispanic American, 0.3% Native American, 0.8% international, 7% transferred in, 80% live on campus. *Retention:* 59% of 2006 full-time freshmen returned.

Freshmen *Admission:* 365 applied, 340 admitted, 175 enrolled. *Average high school GPA:* 3.32. *Test scores:* SAT critical reading scores over 500: 63%; SAT math scores over 500: 50%; ACT scores over 18: 90%; SAT critical reading scores over 600: 18%; SAT math scores over 600: 12%; ACT scores over 24: 36%; SAT critical reading scores over 700: 2%; SAT math scores over 700: 3%; ACT scores over 30: 1%.

Faculty *Total:* 51, 63% full-time, 59% with terminal degrees. *Student/faculty ratio:* 15:1.

Majors Accounting; biblical studies; biology/biological sciences; biology teacher education; business administration and management; communication/speech communication and rhetoric; elementary education; English; English/language arts teacher education; general studies; history; humanities; kinesiology and exercise science; mathematics; mathematics teacher education; music; music teacher education; pastoral studies/counseling; physical education teaching and coaching; pre-law studies; pre-medical studies; psychology; religious/sacred music; social studies teacher education.

Academics *Calendar:* semesters. *Degrees:* certificates, associate, bachelor's, and master's. *Special study options:* academic remediation for entering students, advanced placement credit, distance learning, double majors, independent study, internships, part-time degree program, services for LD students, study abroad, summer session for credit. *ROTC:* Army (c), Navy (c), Air Force (c).

Computers on Campus 25 computers/terminals are available on campus for general student use. Students can access the following: campus intranet, computer help desk, free student e-mail accounts, online (class) grades, online (class) schedules. Campuswide network is available. 100% of college-owned or -operated housing units are wired for high-speed Internet access. Wireless service is available via classrooms, computer labs, dorm rooms, libraries.

Student Life *Housing:* on-campus residence required through senior year. *Options:* men-only, women-only. Campus housing is university owned. Freshman campus housing is guaranteed. *Activities and organizations:* drama/theater group, student-run newspaper, choral group, Drama Club, Alpha Chi, College Republicans, Science Club, Student Missionary Fellowship. *Campus security:* 24-hour emergency response devices and patrols. *Student services:* personal/psychological counseling.

Athletics Member NCCAA. *Intercollegiate sports:* baseball M, basketball M/W, golf M/W, soccer M/W, softball W, volleyball W. *Intramural sports:* basketball M/W, football M, table tennis M/W, tennis M/W, volleyball M/W.

Standardized Tests *Required:* SAT or ACT (for admission).

Costs (2007–08) *Comprehensive fee:* $18,770 includes full-time tuition ($12,510), mandatory fees ($650), and room and board ($5610). Part-time tuition: $485 per hour. *College room only:* $3440. *Payment plan:* installment. *Waivers:* employees or children of employees.

Financial Aid Of all full-time matriculated undergraduates who enrolled in 2006, 578 applied for aid, 578 were judged to have need, 14 had their need fully met. 50 Federal Work-Study jobs (averaging $670). 20 state and other part-time jobs (averaging $612). *Average percent of need met:* 45%. *Average financial aid package:* $9270. *Average need-based loan:* $3559. *Average need-based gift aid:* $4269. *Average indebtedness upon graduation:* $16,800.

Applying *Options:* electronic application, early admission, deferred entrance. *Application fee:* $35. *Required:* essay or personal statement, high school transcript, minimum 2.0 GPA, 2 letters of recommendation, Christian testimony. *Recommended:* interview. *Application deadlines:* rolling (freshmen), rolling (transfers). *Notification:* continuous (freshmen), continuous (transfers).

Freshman Application Contact Dr. Keith Hutchison, Director of Admissions, Clearwater Christian College, 3400 Gulf-to-Bay Boulevard, Clearwater, FL 33759-4595. *Phone:* 727-726-1153. *Toll-free phone:* 800-348-4463. *Fax:* 813-726-8597. *E-mail:* admissions@clearwater.edu.

DEVRY UNIVERSITY

Miami, Florida

DeVry University

Miramar, Florida **www.devry.edu/**

- **Proprietary** comprehensive, founded 2002, part of DeVry University
- **Coed** 887 undergraduate students, 50% full-time, 37% women, 63% men
- **Minimally difficult** entrance level

Undergraduates 443 full-time, 444 part-time. 2% are from out of state, 36% African American, 2% Asian American or Pacific Islander, 45% Hispanic American, 0.3% Native American, 5% international, 13% transferred in. *Retention:* 56% of 2006 full-time freshmen returned.

Freshmen *Admission:* 169 enrolled.

Faculty *Total:* 71, 32% full-time. *Student/faculty ratio:* 17:1.

Majors Accounting; biomedical technology; business administration and management; business administration, management and operations related; computer engineering technology; computer systems analysis; computer systems networking and telecommunications; electrical, electronic and communications engineering technology; web page, digital/multimedia and information resources design.

Academics *Calendar:* semesters. *Degrees:* associate, bachelor's, and master's. *Special study options:* academic remediation for entering students, accelerated degree program, advanced placement credit, distance learning, part-time degree program, services for LD students.

Computers on Campus 124 computers/terminals are available on campus for general student use.

Student Life *Housing:* college housing not available.

Costs (2008–09) *Tuition:* $13,810 full-time, $515 per credit part-time. *Required fees:* $180 full-time.

Financial Aid Of all full-time matriculated undergraduates who enrolled in 2003, 164 applied for aid, 161 were judged to have need, 2 had their need fully met. In 2003, 4 non-need-based awards were made. *Average percent of need met:* 41%. *Average financial aid package:* $6248. *Average need-based loan:* $2778. *Average need-based gift aid:* $3847. *Average non-need-based aid:* $7853.

Applying *Options:* electronic application, early admission, deferred entrance. *Application fee:* $50. *Required:* high school transcript, interview. *Application deadlines:* rolling (freshmen), rolling (transfers). *Notification:* continuous (freshmen), continuous (transfers).

Freshman Application Contact DeVry University, 2300 Southwest 145th Avenue, Miramar, FL 33027.

DeVry University

Orlando, Florida **www.devry.edu/**

- **Proprietary** comprehensive, founded 2000, part of DeVry University
- **Urban** 10-acre campus
- **Coed** 1,249 undergraduate students, 52% full-time, 35% women, 65% men
- **Minimally difficult** entrance level

Undergraduates 644 full-time, 605 part-time. 5% are from out of state, 27% African American, 3% Asian American or Pacific Islander, 23% Hispanic American, 0.3% Native American, 2% international, 18% transferred in. *Retention:* 55% of 2006 full-time freshmen returned.

Freshmen *Admission:* 253 enrolled.

Faculty *Total:* 91, 29% full-time. *Student/faculty ratio:* 19:1.

Majors Accounting; biomedical technology; business administration and management; business administration, management and operations related; computer engineering technology; computer software engineering; computer systems analysis; computer systems networking and telecommunications; electrical, electronic and communications engineering technology; web page, digital/multimedia and information resources design.

Academics *Calendar:* semesters. *Degrees:* associate, bachelor's, and master's. *Special study options:* academic remediation for entering students, accelerated degree program, adult/continuing education programs, advanced placement credit, distance learning, part-time degree program, services for LD students, summer session for credit.

Computers on Campus 310 computers/terminals are available on campus for general student use. Students can access the following: online (class) registration. Campuswide network is available.

Student Life *Housing:* college housing not available. *Activities and organizations:* Association for Information Technology Professionals, DeVry Orlando Auto Club, Millenia Engineering Students Association, PBL, The Student Journal. *Campus security:* 24-hour emergency response devices and patrols, late-night transport/escort service, lighted pathways/sidewalks.

Costs (2008–09) *Tuition:* $13,810 full-time, $515 per credit part-time. *Required fees:* $180 full-time.

Financial Aid Of all full-time matriculated undergraduates who enrolled in 2002, 807 applied for aid, 784 were judged to have need, 2 had their need fully met. In 2002, 55 non-need-based awards were made. *Average percent of need met:* 37%. *Average financial aid package:* $7922. *Average need-based loan:* $5178. *Average need-based gift aid:* $4030. *Average non-need-based aid:* $10,566.

Applying *Options:* electronic application, early admission, deferred entrance. *Application fee:* $50. *Required:* high school transcript, interview. *Application deadlines:* rolling (freshmen), rolling (transfers). *Notification:* continuous (freshmen), continuous (transfers).

Freshman Application Contact DeVry University, 4000 Millenia Boulevard, Orlando, FL 32839-2426.

DeVry University

Tampa, Florida

Eckerd College

St. Petersburg, Florida **www.eckerd.edu/**

- **Independent Presbyterian** 4-year, founded 1958
- **Suburban** 188-acre campus with easy access to Tampa
- **Endowment** $26.5 million
- **Coed** 1,835 undergraduate students, 99% full-time, 58% women, 42% men
- **Moderately difficult** entrance level, 67% of applicants were admitted

Undergraduates 1,812 full-time, 23 part-time. Students come from 46 states and territories, 35 other countries, 75% are from out of state, 3% African American, 2% Asian American or Pacific Islander, 4% Hispanic American, 0.3% Native American, 3% international, 3% transferred in, 76% live on campus. *Retention:* 72% of 2006 full-time freshmen returned.

Freshmen *Admission:* 3,118 applied, 2,086 admitted, 539 enrolled. *Average high school GPA:* 3.3. *Test scores:* SAT critical reading scores over 500: 79%; SAT math scores over 500: 76%; SAT writing scores over 500: 76%; ACT scores over 18: 96%; SAT critical reading scores over 600: 35%; SAT math scores over 600: 29%; SAT writing scores over 600: 29%; ACT scores over 24: 59%; SAT critical reading scores over 700: 6%; SAT math scores over 700: 2%; SAT writing scores over 700: 3%; ACT scores over 30: 7%.

Faculty *Total:* 156, 72% full-time, 75% with terminal degrees. *Student/faculty ratio:* 14:1.

Majors American studies; anthropology; biochemistry; biology/biological sciences; business administration and management; chemistry; communication/speech communication and rhetoric; comparative literature; computer science; creative writing; dramatic/theater arts; East Asian languages; economics; environmental studies; foreign languages and literatures; French; history; human development and family studies; humanities; human resources management; interdisciplinary studies; international business/trade/commerce; international relations and affairs; marine biology and biological oceanography; mathematics; modern languages; music; philosophy; physics; political science and government; psychology; religious studies; sociology; Spanish; visual and performing arts; women's studies.

Academics *Calendar:* 4-1-4. *Degree:* bachelor's. *Special study options:* accelerated degree program, adult/continuing education programs, advanced placement credit, cooperative education, double majors, English as a second language, external degree program, honors programs, independent study, internships, off-campus study, part-time degree program, services for LD students, student-designed majors, study abroad, summer session for credit. *ROTC:* Army (c), Air Force (c). *Unusual degree programs:* 3-2 engineering with University of Miami, Columbia University, Washington University in St. Louis, Auburn University.

Computers on Campus 300 computers/terminals and 2,000 ports are available on campus for general student use. Students can access the following: campus intranet, computer help desk, free student e-mail accounts, online (class) grades, online (class) registration, online (class) schedules, free music via Ruckus. Campuswide network is available. 100% of college-owned or -operated housing units are wired for high-speed Internet access. Wireless service is available via entire campus.

Student Life *Housing:* on-campus residence required for freshman year. *Options:* coed, women-only. Campus housing is university owned. Freshman campus housing is guaranteed. *Activities and organizations:* drama/theater group, student-run newspaper, radio and television station, choral group, Earth Society, Water Search and Rescue Team, Triton Tribune, College Choir, Organization of

Students. *Campus security:* 24-hour emergency response devices and patrols, student patrols, late-night transport/escort service, controlled dormitory access. *Student services:* health clinic, personal/psychological counseling, women's center.

Athletics Member NCAA. All Division II. *Intercollegiate sports:* baseball M (s), basketball M (s)/W (s), football W, golf M (s), sailing M/W, soccer M (s)/W (s), softball W (s), tennis M (s)/W (s), volleyball M (c)/W (s). *Intramural sports:* baseball M, basketball M/W, bowling M/W, equestrian sports M (c)/W (c), football M, lacrosse M (c)/W (c), rugby M (c)/W (c), soccer M/W, softball M/W, swimming and diving M (c)/W (c), tennis M (c)/W (c), volleyball M/W.

Standardized Tests *Required:* SAT or ACT (for admission). *Recommended:* SAT Subject Tests (for admission).

Costs (2008–09) *Comprehensive fee:* $39,344 includes full-time tuition ($30,304), mandatory fees ($286), and room and board ($8754). Part-time tuition: $3650 per course. *College room only:* $4264.

Financial Aid Of all full-time matriculated undergraduates who enrolled in 2007, 1,244 applied for aid, 1,037 were judged to have need, 229 had their need fully met. 661 Federal Work-Study jobs (averaging $2000). In 2007, 658 non-need-based awards were made. *Average percent of need met:* 85%. *Average financial aid package:* $24,444. *Average need-based loan:* $3798. *Average need-based gift aid:* $16,942. *Average non-need-based aid:* $9327. *Average indebtedness upon graduation:* $24,749.

Applying *Options:* electronic application, early admission, deferred entrance. *Application fee:* $35. *Required:* essay or personal statement, high school transcript, 1 letter of recommendation. *Recommended:* minimum 3.0 GPA, interview. *Application deadlines:* rolling (freshmen), rolling (transfers). *Notification:* continuous (freshmen), continuous (transfers).

Freshman Application Contact Ms. Donna Grosso, Eckerd College, 4200 54th Avenue South, St. Petersburg, FL 33711. *Phone:* 727-864-8331. *Toll-free phone:* 800-456-9009. *Fax:* 727-866-2304. *E-mail:* admissions@eckerd.edu.

See page 642 for the College Close-Up.

EDWARD WATERS COLLEGE

Jacksonville, Florida **www.ewc.edu/**

- **Independent African Methodist Episcopal** 4-year, founded 1866
- **Urban** 20-acre campus
- **Endowment** $2.0 million
- **Coed**
- **Noncompetitive** entrance level

Academics *Calendar:* semesters. *Degree:* bachelor's.

Student Life *Campus security:* 24-hour emergency response devices and patrols, student patrols, late-night transport/escort service, controlled dormitory access.

Athletics Member NAIA.

Costs (2007–08) *Comprehensive fee:* $15,650 includes full-time tuition ($9176) and room and board ($6474). Part-time tuition: $382 per credit hour. *College room only:* $3124.

Financial Aid Of all full-time matriculated undergraduates who enrolled in 2001, 1,242 applied for aid, 1,242 were judged to have need, 11 had their need fully met. 318 Federal Work-Study jobs (averaging $851). In 2001, 262 non-need-based awards were made. *Average percent of need met:* 61. *Average financial aid package:* $4835. *Average need-based loan:* $2625. *Average need-based gift aid:* $4835. *Average non-need-based aid:* $1488. *Average indebtedness upon graduation:* $9000.

Applying *Application fee:* $25. *Required:* high school transcript, medical forms.

Director of Admissions Mr. Lonnie Morris, Director of Admissions, Edward Waters College, 1658 Kings Road, Jacksonville, FL 32209-6199. *Phone:* 904-470-8202. *Toll-free phone:* 888-898-3191. *E-mail:* Lmorris@ewc.edu.

EMBRY-RIDDLE AERONAUTICAL UNIVERSITY

Daytona Beach, Florida **www.embryriddle.edu/**

- **Independent** comprehensive, founded 1926
- **Suburban** 178-acre campus with easy access to Orlando
- **Endowment** $60.0 million
- **Coed** 4,584 undergraduate students, 90% full-time, 16% women, 84% men
- **Moderately difficult** entrance level, 78% of applicants were admitted

Embry-Riddle teaches science, theory, and business to meet all the demands of employers in the world of aviation and aerospace; the University's impact on the industry through its graduates is significant. Founded just twenty-two years after the Wright brothers first flew, Embry-Riddle teaches its students to solve problems in engineering, business, computer science, technology, maintenance, psychology, communication, and flight. Whatever field students choose, they learn from educators and practitioners who are on the leading edge.

Undergraduates 4,138 full-time, 446 part-time. Students come from 52 states and territories, 85 other countries, 67% are from out of state, 6% African American, 5% Asian American or Pacific Islander, 8% Hispanic American, 0.3% Native American, 9% international, 5% transferred in, 40% live on campus. *Retention:* 79% of 2006 full-time freshmen returned.

Freshmen *Admission:* 3,878 applied, 3,037 admitted, 1,038 enrolled. *Average high school GPA:* 3.26. *Test scores:* SAT critical reading scores over 500: 63%; SAT math scores over 500: 77%; ACT scores over 18: 93%; SAT critical reading scores over 600: 22%; SAT math scores over 600: 37%; ACT scores over 24: 53%; SAT critical reading scores over 700: 3%; SAT math scores over 700: 7%; ACT scores over 30: 8%.

Faculty *Total:* 327, 74% full-time, 51% with terminal degrees. *Student/faculty ratio:* 16:1.

Majors Aeronautics/aviation/aerospace science and technology; aerospace, aeronautical and astronautical engineering; aircraft powerplant technology; airline pilot and flight crew; air traffic control; atmospheric sciences and meteorology; aviation/airway management; business administration, management and operations related; civil engineering related; communication/speech communication and rhetoric; computer engineering; computer software engineering; electrical and electronic engineering technologies related; electrical, electronics and communications engineering; engineering physics; environmental psychology; mechanical engineering; occupational safety and health technology; physics related.

Academics *Calendar:* semesters. *Degrees:* bachelor's and master's. *Special study options:* academic remediation for entering students, adult/continuing education programs, advanced placement credit, cooperative education, distance learning, double majors, English as a second language, independent study, internships, part-time degree program, services for LD students, study abroad, summer session for credit. *ROTC:* Army (b), Navy (b), Air Force (b).

Computers on Campus 996 computers/terminals are available on campus for general student use. Students can access the following: online (class) registration. Campuswide network is available.

Student Life *Housing:* on-campus residence required through sophomore year. *Options:* coed. Campus housing is university owned. Freshman campus housing is guaranteed. *Activities and organizations:* drama/theater group, student-run newspaper, radio station, choral group, Eagle Wing, Future Professional Pilots Association, African Student Association, Caribbean Student Association, Sigma Gamma Tau, national fraternities, national sororities. *Campus security:* 24-hour emergency response devices and patrols, student patrols, late-night transport/escort service, controlled dormitory access. *Student services:* health clinic, personal/psychological counseling.

Athletics Member NAIA. *Intercollegiate sports:* baseball M (s), basketball M (s), cheerleading M/W, cross-country running M/W, golf M (s)/W, soccer M (s)/W (s), tennis M (s)/W, volleyball W (s). *Intramural sports:* badminton M/W, basketball M/W, bowling M (c)/W (c), crew M (c)/W (c), football M/W, golf M/W, ice hockey M (c), lacrosse M (c)/W (c), racquetball M/W, rock climbing M (c)/W (c), sailing M (c)/W (c), skiing (downhill) M/W, soccer M/W, softball M/W, swimming and diving M/W, table tennis M/W, tennis M/W, volleyball M/W, water polo M/W, weight lifting M/W, wrestling M (c).

Standardized Tests *Required:* SAT or ACT (for admission).

Costs (2007–08) *Comprehensive fee:* $35,646 includes full-time tuition ($25,400), mandatory fees ($1096), and room and board ($9150). Part-time tuition: $1060 per credit hour. *College room only:* $4750. Room and board charges vary according to board plan and housing facility. *Payment plans:* installment, deferred payment. *Waivers:* employees or children of employees.

Financial Aid Of all full-time matriculated undergraduates who enrolled in 2007, 2,890 applied for aid, 2,502 were judged to have need. 112 Federal Work-Study jobs (averaging $1364). 1,127 state and other part-time jobs (averaging $1430). *Average financial aid package:* $15,589. *Average need-based loan:* $5298. *Average need-based gift aid:* $8509. *Average indebtedness upon graduation:* $57,502.

Applying *Options:* electronic application, deferred entrance. *Application fee:* $50. *Required:* high school transcript, minimum 2.0 GPA. *Required for some:* minimum 3.0 GPA, medical examination for flight students. *Recommended:* essay or personal statement, letters of recommendation, interview. *Application deadlines:* rolling (freshmen), 5/1 (transfers). *Notification:* continuous (freshmen), continuous (transfers).

Freshman Application Contact Mr. Richard Clarke, Director of Admissions, Embry-Riddle Aeronautical University, 600 South Clyde Morris Boulevard,

Daytona Beach, FL 32114-3900. *Phone:* 386-226-6100. *Toll-free phone:* 800-862-2416. *Fax:* 386-226-7070. *E-mail:* dbadmit@erau.edu.

See page 644 for the College Close-Up.

EMBRY-RIDDLE AERONAUTICAL UNIVERSITY WORLDWIDE

Daytona Beach, Florida **www.embryriddle.edu/**

- **Independent** comprehensive, founded 1970
- **Endowment** $60.0 million
- **Coed** 12,500 undergraduate students, 17% full-time, 12% women, 88% men
- **Minimally difficult** entrance level

Undergraduates 2,094 full-time, 10,406 part-time. 9% African American, 3% Asian American or Pacific Islander, 8% Hispanic American, 0.8% Native American, 0.4% international.

Freshmen *Admission:* 296 enrolled.

Faculty *Total:* 2,340, 6% full-time, 18% with terminal degrees.

Majors Aeronautics/aviation/aerospace science and technology; aircraft powerplant technology; aviation/airway management; business administration, management and operations related.

Academics *Calendar:* 5 9-week terms. *Degrees:* associate, bachelor's, and master's (programs offered at 100 military bases worldwide). *Special study options:* adult/continuing education programs, advanced placement credit, cooperative education, external degree program, independent study, off-campus study, part-time degree program, services for LD students.

Student Life *Housing:* college housing not available.

Costs (2007–08) *Tuition:* $4968 full-time, $207 per credit hour part-time. *Payment plan:* deferred payment. *Waivers:* employees or children of employees.

Financial Aid Of all full-time matriculated undergraduates who enrolled in 2007, 544 applied for aid, 462 were judged to have need. *Average financial aid package:* $5683. *Average need-based loan:* $4154. *Average need-based gift aid:* $3270. *Average indebtedness upon graduation:* $29,305.

Applying *Options:* deferred entrance. *Application fee:* $50. *Required for some:* essay or personal statement, college transcript, statement of good standing from prior institution. *Application deadlines:* rolling (freshmen), rolling (transfers). *Notification:* continuous (freshmen), continuous (transfers).

Freshman Application Contact Mrs. Pam Thomas, Director of Admissions, Records and Registration, Embry-Riddle Aeronautical University Worldwide, 600 South Clyde Morris Boulevard, Daytona Beach, FL 32114-3900. *Phone:* 386-226-6221. *Toll-free phone:* 800-522-6787. *Fax:* 386-226-6984. *E-mail:* ecinfo@erau.edu.

EVEREST UNIVERSITY

Clearwater, Florida **www.everest.edu/**

Freshman Application Contact Mr. Kevin Buskirk, Director of Admissions, Everest University, 2471 McMullen Booth Road, Suite 200, Clearwater, FL 33759. *Phone:* 727-725-2688. *Toll-free phone:* 800-353-FMUS. *Fax:* 727-796-3406. *E-mail:* kbuskirk@cci.edu.

EVEREST UNIVERSITY

Jacksonville, Florida **www.everest.edu/**

Director of Admissions Mr. Robin Manning, Admissions Director, Everest University, 8226 Phillips Highway, Jacksonville, FL 32256. *Phone:* 904-731-4949. *Toll-free phone:* 888-741-4270. *E-mail:* rmanning@cci.edu.

EVEREST UNIVERSITY

Lakeland, Florida **www.everest.edu/**

- **Proprietary** comprehensive, founded 1890, part of Corinthian Colleges, Inc
- **Suburban** 3-acre campus with easy access to Orlando and Tampa–St. Petersburg
- **Coed**
- **Minimally difficult** entrance level

Faculty *Student/faculty ratio:* 18:1.

Academics *Calendar:* quarters. *Degrees:* associate, bachelor's, and master's (bachelor's degree in business administration only).

Student Life *Campus security:* 24-hour patrols.

Standardized Tests *Required:* CPAt (for admission). *Recommended:* SAT or ACT (for admission).

Costs (2007–08) *Tuition:* $299 per credit hour part-time.

Financial Aid Of all full-time matriculated undergraduates who enrolled in 2002, 679 applied for aid, 646 were judged to have need, 10 had their need fully met. 6 Federal Work-Study jobs (averaging $4863). *Average percent of need met:* 76. *Average financial aid package:* $3510. *Average need-based loan:* $3875. *Average need-based gift aid:* $1000. *Average indebtedness upon graduation:* $29,852.

Applying *Options:* early admission. *Application fee:* $25. *Required:* interview. *Recommended:* essay or personal statement, high school transcript, letters of recommendation.

Freshman Application Contact Ms. Patricia Sabol, Director of Student Services, Everest University, Suite 110, 995 East Memorial Boulevard, Lakeland, FL 33801. *Phone:* 863-686-1444. *Toll-free phone:* 877-225-0014. *Fax:* 863-688-9881. *E-mail:* psabol@cci.edu.

EVEREST UNIVERSITY

Melbourne, Florida **www.everest.edu/**

Director of Admissions Mr. Timothy Alexander, Director of Admissions, Everest University, 2401 North Harbor City Boulevard, Melbourne, FL 32935-6657. *Phone:* 321-253-2929 Ext. 121.

EVEREST UNIVERSITY

Orlando, Florida **www.everest.edu/**

Freshman Application Contact Joann Derosa-Weber, Director of Admissions, Everest University, 5421 Diplomat Circle, Orlando, FL 32810-5674. *Phone:* 407-628-5870. *Toll-free phone:* 800-628-5870. *Fax:* 407-628-1344.

EVEREST UNIVERSITY

Orlando, Florida **www.fmu.edu/**

Director of Admissions Ms. Annette Cloin, Director of Admissions, Everest University, 7900 South Park Center Loop, Orlando, FL 32809. *Phone:* 407-851-2525 Ext. 111. *Toll-free phone:* 407-851-2525 (in-state); 888-471-4270 (out-of-state). *Fax:* 407-354-7946.

EVEREST UNIVERSITY

Pompano Beach, Florida **www.fmu.edu/**

- **Proprietary** comprehensive, founded 1940, part of Corinthian Colleges, Inc
- **Urban** campus with easy access to Miami
- **Coed**
- **Minimally difficult** entrance level

Faculty *Student/faculty ratio:* 19:1.

Academics *Calendar:* quarters. *Degrees:* associate, bachelor's, and master's.

Student Life *Campus security:* late-night transport/escort service, building security.

Standardized Tests *Required:* CPAt (for admission). *Recommended:* SAT or ACT (for admission).

Costs (2007–08) *Tuition:* $10,764 full-time, $299 per credit part-time. Full-time tuition and fees vary according to course load and program. Part-time tuition and fees vary according to course load and program. *Required fees:* $180 full-time. *Payment plans:* installment, deferred payment.

Applying *Options:* electronic application, deferred entrance. *Application fee:* $25. *Required:* high school transcript, interview. *Required for some:* essay or personal statement, letters of recommendation.

Freshman Application Contact Ms. Fran Heaston, Director of Admissions, Everest University, Fort Lauderdale, FL 33304. *Phone:* 954-783-7339. *Toll-free phone:* 800-468-0168. *Fax:* 954-783-7964.

EVEREST UNIVERSITY

Tampa, Florida www.fmu.edu/

- **Proprietary** comprehensive, founded 1890, part of Corinthian Colleges, Inc
- **Urban** 4-acre campus
- **Coed** 1,284 undergraduate students
- **Minimally difficult** entrance level

Undergraduates Students come from 15 states and territories, 3 other countries.

Faculty *Total:* 61, 21% full-time. *Student/faculty ratio:* 20:1.

Majors Accounting; business administration and management; commercial and advertising art; computer programming; computer science; criminal justice/law enforcement administration; data processing and data processing technology; legal assistant/paralegal; marketing/marketing management; medical/clinical assistant.

Academics *Calendar:* quarters. *Degrees:* diplomas, associate, bachelor's, and master's. *Special study options:* accelerated degree program, adult/continuing education programs, advanced placement credit, cooperative education, distance learning, double majors, English as a second language, external degree program, independent study, internships, part-time degree program, student-designed majors, summer session for credit.

Computers on Campus 113 computers/terminals are available on campus for general student use.

Student Life *Housing:* college housing not available. *Activities and organizations:* Legal Network, Phi Beta Lambda, Ambassadors Club. *Campus security:* 24-hour emergency response devices, evening and Saturday afternoon patrols by trained security personnel.

Standardized Tests *Required:* CPAt (for admission). *Required for some:* SAT (for admission), ACT (for admission).

Costs (2007–08) *Tuition:* contact institution directly for tuition and expense costs.

Financial Aid Of all full-time matriculated undergraduates who enrolled in 2006, 1,054 applied for aid, 1,054 were judged to have need, 850 had their need fully met. 25 Federal Work-Study jobs (averaging $4000). *Average percent of need met:* 83%. *Average financial aid package:* $6625. *Average need-based loan:* $2625. *Average need-based gift aid:* $1350. *Average indebtedness upon graduation:* $12,000.

Applying *Options:* deferred entrance. *Application fee:* $25. *Required:* high school transcript. *Application deadlines:* rolling (freshmen), rolling (transfers). *Notification:* continuous (freshmen), continuous (transfers).

Director of Admissions Mr. Donnie Broughton, Director of Admissions, Everest University, 3319 West Hillsborough Avenue, Tampa, FL 33614. *Phone:* 813-879-6000 Ext. 129.

EVEREST UNIVERSITY

Tampa, Florida www.fmu.edu/

- **Proprietary** comprehensive, founded 1890, part of Corinthian Colleges, Inc
- **Urban** 5-acre campus
- **Coed** 920 undergraduate students
- **Minimally difficult** entrance level

Undergraduates 29% African American, 1% Asian American or Pacific Islander, 18% Hispanic American, 0.4% Native American.

Faculty *Total:* 53, 45% full-time. *Student/faculty ratio:* 17:1.

Majors Accounting; business administration and management; computer software and media applications related; criminal justice/law enforcement administration; information science/studies; legal assistant/paralegal; medical/clinical assistant; medical insurance/medical billing; nursing (registered nurse training); pharmacy technician; surgical technology.

Academics *Calendar:* quarters. *Degrees:* associate, bachelor's, and master's. *Special study options:* academic remediation for entering students, accelerated degree program, adult/continuing education programs, cooperative education, distance learning, double majors, English as a second language, external degree program, part-time degree program, services for LD students, summer session for credit.

Computers on Campus 125 computers/terminals are available on campus for general student use. Students can access the following: online (class) grades. Campuswide network is available. Wireless service is available via entire campus.

Student Life *Housing:* college housing not available. *Activities and organizations:* Accounting Club, Medical Assistants Club, Paralegal Club, Criminal Justice Club, Surgical Tech. Club. *Campus security:* 24-hour emergency response devices.

Standardized Tests *Required:* CPAt (for admission). *Recommended:* SAT or ACT (for admission).

Costs (2008–09) *Tuition:* $15,120 full-time, $315 per credit part-time. *Required fees:* $240 full-time, $60 per term part-time.

Financial Aid Of all full-time matriculated undergraduates who enrolled in 2001, 1,000 applied for aid, 900 were judged to have need. 41 Federal Work-Study jobs (averaging $2500). In 2001, 200 non-need-based awards were made. *Average percent of need met:* 15%. *Average need-based loan:* $3500. *Average need-based gift aid:* $4000. *Average indebtedness upon graduation:* $15,000.

Applying *Options:* early admission, deferred entrance. *Application fee:* $25. *Required:* high school transcript, interview, minimum CPAt score of 120. *Application deadlines:* rolling (freshmen), rolling (transfers). *Notification:* continuous (freshmen), continuous (transfers).

Freshman Application Contact Ms. Shandretta Pointer, Director of Admissions, Everest University, 3924 Coconut Palm Drive, Tampa, FL 33619. *Phone:* 813-621-0041. *Toll-free phone:* 877-338-0068. *Fax:* 813-628-0919. *E-mail:* spointer@cci.edu.

EVERGLADES UNIVERSITY

Altamonte Springs, Florida www.evergladesuniversity.edu

EVERGLADES UNIVERSITY

Boca Raton, Florida www.evergladesuniversity.edu/

- **Independent** comprehensive, founded 1989
- **Suburban** campus
- **Coed**

Academics *Calendar:* continuous. *Degrees:* bachelor's and master's.

Student Life *Campus security:* 24-hour emergency response devices and patrols, late-night transport/escort service.

Standardized Tests *Required for some:* SAT or ACT (for admission), Otis-Lennon School Ability Test.

Costs (2007–08) *Tuition:* $10,920 full-time. *Required fees:* $800 full-time.

Financial Aid Of all full-time matriculated undergraduates who enrolled in 2002, 408 applied for aid, 408 were judged to have need, 327 had their need fully met. 8 Federal Work-Study jobs (averaging $1481). *Average financial aid package:* $9728. *Average need-based loan:* $9728. *Average indebtedness upon graduation:* $35,125. *Financial aid deadline:* 6/1.

Applying *Options:* electronic application. *Application fee:* $50. *Required:* high school transcript.

Freshman Application Contact Ms. Jean Graham, Everglades University, 5002 T-Rex Avenue, Suite 100, Boca Raton, FL 33431. *Phone:* 561-912-1211. *Toll-free phone:* 888-772-6077. *Fax:* 561-912-1191. *E-mail:* admissions-boca@evergladesuniversity.edu.

EVERGLADES UNIVERSITY

Sarasota, Florida www.evergladesuniversity.edu/

Director of Admissions Mr. Brad Brewer, Campus President, Everglades University, 6151 Lake Osprey Drive, Sarasota, FL 34240. *Phone:* 941-907-2262. *Toll-free phone:* 866-907-2262. *Fax:* 941-907-6634. *E-mail:* bbrewer@evergladesuniversity.edu.

FLAGLER COLLEGE

St. Augustine, Florida www.flagler.edu/

- **Independent** 4-year, founded 1968
- **Small-town** 42-acre campus with easy access to Jacksonville
- **Endowment** $41.9 million
- **Coed** 2,537 undergraduate students, 97% full-time, 61% women, 39% men
- **Moderately difficult** entrance level, 40% of applicants were admitted

Size, cost, location, and excellent academics are the characteristics most often cited by students in their decision to enroll at Flagler. Interested students are encouraged to visit historic St. Augustine and learn how Flagler offers high-quality education in a beautiful setting at a reasonable cost. The cost of tuition, room, and board for the 2007–08 year was just $18,120.

Undergraduates 2,472 full-time, 65 part-time. Students come from 47 states and territories, 25 other countries, 34% are from out of state, 1% African American, 0.9% Asian American or Pacific Islander, 3% Hispanic American, 0.3% Native American, 1% international, 8% transferred in, 34% live on campus. *Retention:* 78% of 2006 full-time freshmen returned.

Freshmen *Admission:* 2,353 applied, 933 admitted, 580 enrolled. *Average high school GPA:* 3.33. *Test scores:* SAT critical reading scores over 500: 88%; SAT math scores over 500: 81%; SAT writing scores over 500: 79%; ACT scores over 18: 100%; SAT critical reading scores over 600: 31%; SAT math scores over 600: 21%; SAT writing scores over 600: 28%; ACT scores over 24: 42%; SAT critical reading scores over 700: 3%; SAT math scores over 700: 1%; SAT writing scores over 700: 3%; ACT scores over 30: 2%.

Faculty *Total:* 180, 48% full-time, 41% with terminal degrees. *Student/faculty ratio:* 21:1.

Majors Accounting; art teacher education; business administration and management; communication and journalism related; dramatic/theater arts; elementary education; English; fine/studio arts; graphic design; history; Latin American studies; liberal arts and sciences/liberal studies; philosophy; political science and government; psychology; public administration; secondary education; sociology; Spanish; special education (gifted and talented); special education (hearing impaired); special education (specific learning disabilities); sport and fitness administration/management.

Academics *Calendar:* semesters. *Degree:* bachelor's. *Special study options:* academic remediation for entering students, advanced placement credit, double majors, independent study, internships, off-campus study, services for LD students, study abroad, summer session for credit.

Computers on Campus 210 computers/terminals are available on campus for general student use. Students can access the following: campus intranet, computer help desk, free student e-mail accounts, online (class) grades, online (class) registration, online (class) schedules. Campuswide network is available. 100% of college-owned or -operated housing units are wired for high-speed Internet access. Wireless service is available via entire campus.

Student Life *Housing:* on-campus residence required for freshman year. *Options:* men-only, women-only. Campus housing is university owned. Freshman campus housing is guaranteed. *Activities and organizations:* drama/theater group, student-run newspaper, radio station, choral group, Inter-Varsity, Mu Epsilon Nu, Sport Management Club, Surf Club, Students in Free Enterprise. *Campus security:* 24-hour emergency response devices and patrols, late-night transport/escort service, controlled dormitory access. *Student services:* health clinic, personal/psychological counseling.

Athletics Member NCAA. All Division II. *Intercollegiate sports:* baseball M (s), basketball M (s)/W (s), cross-country running M (s)/W (s), golf M (s)/W (s), lacrosse M (c), soccer M (s)/W (s), softball W (s), tennis M (s)/W (s), volleyball M (c)/W (s). *Intramural sports:* badminton M/W, basketball M/W, bowling M/W, football M/W, soccer M/W, softball M/W, swimming and diving M/W, table tennis M/W, tennis M/W, volleyball M/W, weight lifting M/W.

Standardized Tests *Required:* SAT or ACT (for admission).

Costs (2007–08) *Comprehensive fee:* $20,500 includes full-time tuition ($13,600) and room and board ($6900). Part-time tuition: $455 per credit. *College room only:* $3400. Room and board charges vary according to board plan and location. *Waivers:* employees or children of employees.

Financial Aid Of all full-time matriculated undergraduates who enrolled in 2007, 1,604 applied for aid, 1,103 were judged to have need, 152 had their need fully met. 193 Federal Work-Study jobs (averaging $1038). 68 state and other part-time jobs (averaging $1126). In 2007, 83 non-need-based awards were made. *Average percent of need met:* 76%. *Average financial aid package:* $12,831. *Average need-based loan:* $4305. *Average need-based gift aid:* $3769. *Average non-need-based aid:* $3130. *Average indebtedness upon graduation:* $15,186.

Applying *Options:* electronic application, early admission, early decision, deferred entrance. *Application fee:* $40. *Required:* essay or personal statement, high school transcript, 1 letter of recommendation. *Recommended:* minimum 2.0 GPA, letters of recommendation, interview, rank in upper 50% of high school class. *Application deadlines:* 3/1 (freshmen), 3/1 (transfers). *Early decision deadline:* 12/1. *Notification:* 3/30 (freshmen), 3/30 (transfers), 12/15 (early decision).

Freshman Application Contact Mr. Marc Williar, Director of Admissions, Flagler College, PO Box 1027, St. Augustine, FL 32085-1027. *Phone:* 904-819-6220. *Toll-free phone:* 800-304-4208. *Fax:* 904-819-6466. *E-mail:* admiss@flagler.edu.

See page 646 for the College Close-Up.

FLORIDA AGRICULTURAL AND MECHANICAL UNIVERSITY

Tallahassee, Florida **www.famu.edu/**

- **State-supported** university, founded 1887, part of State University System of Florida
- **Urban** 419-acre campus
- **Endowment** $74.4 million
- **Coed** 9,591 undergraduate students, 88% full-time, 58% women, 42% men
- **Moderately difficult** entrance level, 63% of applicants were admitted

Undergraduates 8,397 full-time, 1,194 part-time. Students come from 43 states and territories, 44 other countries, 27% are from out of state, 93% African American, 0.7% Asian American or Pacific Islander, 1% Hispanic American, 0.2% Native American, 0.9% international, 2% transferred in. *Retention:* 89% of 2006 full-time freshmen returned.

Freshmen *Admission:* 5,097 applied, 3,233 admitted, 1,890 enrolled. *Average high school GPA:* 3.05. *Test scores:* SAT critical reading scores over 500: 32%; SAT math scores over 500: 28%; ACT scores over 18: 71%; SAT critical reading scores over 600: 8%; SAT math scores over 600: 5%; ACT scores over 24: 11%; SAT critical reading scores over 700: 1%; SAT math scores over 700: 1%; ACT scores over 30: 1%.

Faculty *Total:* 757, 82% full-time, 66% with terminal degrees. *Student/faculty ratio:* 18:1.

Majors Accounting; accounting and business/management; actuarial science; administrative assistant and secretarial science; African-American/Black studies; agricultural business and management; agriculture; animal sciences; architectural engineering technology; architecture; art; art teacher education; biology/biological sciences; business administration and management; business teacher education; chemical engineering; chemistry; civil engineering; civil engineering technology; commercial and advertising art; computer and information sciences; computer engineering; construction engineering technology; criminal justice/law enforcement administration; dramatic/theater arts; economics; education; electrical, electronic and communications engineering technology; electrical, electronics and communications engineering; elementary education; English; entomology; environmental science; finance; finance and financial management services related; French; geography; graphic and printing equipment operation/production; health and physical education; health/health care administration; health information/medical records administration; health teacher education; history; horticultural science; industrial arts; industrial engineering; information science/studies; jazz/jazz studies; journalism; kindergarten/preschool education; landscape architecture; liberal arts and sciences/liberal studies; management information systems; management information systems and services related; mass communication/media; mathematics; mechanical engineering; medical illustration and informatics related; molecular biology; music; music performance; music teacher education; nursing (registered nurse training); occupational therapy; ornamental horticulture; parks, recreation and leisure facilities management; pharmacy; philosophy; physical education teaching and coaching; physical therapy; physics; plant protection and integrated pest management; political science and government; pre-dentistry studies; psychology; public administration; public relations/image management; religious studies; respiratory care therapy; social sciences; social work; sociology; Spanish; trade and industrial teacher education.

Academics *Calendar:* semesters. *Degrees:* associate, bachelor's, master's, doctoral, first professional, and first professional certificates. *Special study options:* academic remediation for entering students, accelerated degree program, adult/continuing education programs, advanced placement credit, cooperative education, honors programs, internships, off-campus study, part-time degree program, services for LD students, summer session for credit. *ROTC:* Army (b), Navy (b), Air Force (c). *Unusual degree programs:* 3-2 business administration; engineering; nursing.

Computers on Campus Campuswide network is available. Wireless service is available via classrooms, computer centers, computer labs, learning centers, libraries, student centers.

Student Life *Housing:* on-campus residence required for freshman year. *Options:* men-only, women-only. Campus housing is university owned and leased by the school. Freshman applicants given priority for college housing. *Activities and organizations:* drama/theater group, student-run newspaper, radio station, choral group, marching band, Gospel Choir, University Marching Band, Alpha Kappa Alpha, Alpha Phi Alpha, SBI, national fraternities, national sororities. *Campus security:* 24-hour emergency response devices and patrols, late-night transport/escort service. *Student services:* health clinic, personal/psychological counseling, women's center.

Athletics Member NCAA. All Division I except football (Division I-AA). *Intercollegiate sports:* baseball M, basketball M (s)/W (s), cross-country running

M (s)/W (s), golf M (s)/W (s), softball W, swimming and diving M (s)/W (s), tennis M (s)/W (s), track and field M (s)/W (s), volleyball W (s). *Intramural sports:* basketball M/W, cross-country running M, football M, soccer M/W, tennis M/W, volleyball M/W.

Standardized Tests *Required:* SAT or ACT (for admission).

Costs (2007–08) *Tuition:* state resident $3157 full-time, $105 per credit hour part-time; nonresident $15,097 full-time, $503 per credit hour part-time. Full-time tuition and fees vary according to course load. Part-time tuition and fees vary according to course load. *Required fees:* $1063 full-time, $5 per term part-time. *Room and board:* $5956; room only: $3208. Room and board charges vary according to board plan and housing facility. *Payment plans:* tuition prepayment, deferred payment. *Waivers:* senior citizens and employees or children of employees.

Financial Aid Of all full-time matriculated undergraduates who enrolled in 2006, 8,195 applied for aid, 8,019 were judged to have need, 2,024 had their need fully met. 265 Federal Work-Study jobs (averaging $1800). In 2006, 447 non-need-based awards were made. *Average percent of need met:* 83%. *Average financial aid package:* $10,478. *Average need-based loan:* $7467. *Average need-based gift aid:* $7498. *Average non-need-based aid:* $8929. *Average indebtedness upon graduation:* $29,742. *Financial aid deadline:* 6/30.

Applying *Options:* electronic application, early admission, deferred entrance. *Application fee:* $20. *Required:* high school transcript, minimum 2.0 GPA. *Required for some:* essay or personal statement, letters of recommendation. *Recommended:* minimum 3.2 GPA. *Application deadlines:* 5/9 (freshmen), 5/1 (transfers). *Notification:* continuous until 8/1 (freshmen), continuous until 8/1 (transfers).

Freshman Application Contact Office of Admissions, Florida Agricultural and Mechanical University, Office of Admissions, Tallahassee, FL 32307. *Phone:* 850-599-3866. *Fax:* 850-599-3069. *E-mail:* admission@famu.edu.

See page 648 for the College Close-Up.

FLORIDA ATLANTIC UNIVERSITY

Boca Raton, Florida **www.fau.edu/**

- **State-supported** university, founded 1961, part of State University System of Florida
- **Suburban** 850-acre campus with easy access to Miami
- **Endowment** $190.2 million
- **Coed** 21,612 undergraduate students, 58% full-time, 59% women, 41% men
- **Moderately difficult** entrance level, 57% of applicants were admitted

Undergraduates 12,555 full-time, 9,057 part-time. Students come from 46 states and territories, 125 other countries, 5% are from out of state, 18% African American, 5% Asian American or Pacific Islander, 19% Hispanic American, 0.4% Native American, 3% international, 14% transferred in, 5% live on campus. *Retention:* 74% of 2006 full-time freshmen returned.

Freshmen *Admission:* 11,822 applied, 6,698 admitted, 2,677 enrolled. *Average high school GPA:* 3.2. *Test scores:* SAT critical reading scores over 500: 24%; SAT math scores over 500: 59%; SAT writing scores over 500: 47%; ACT scores over 18: 90%; SAT critical reading scores over 600: 13%; SAT math scores over 600: 14%; SAT writing scores over 600: 9%; ACT scores over 24: 20%; SAT critical reading scores over 700: 1%; SAT math scores over 700: 1%; SAT writing scores over 700: 1%; ACT scores over 30: 2%.

Faculty *Total:* 1,356, 59% full-time, 51% with terminal degrees. *Student/faculty ratio:* 18:1.

Majors Accounting; anthropology; architecture; art; biology/biological sciences; business administration and management; chemistry; city/urban, community and regional planning; civil engineering; clinical laboratory science/medical technology; communication/speech communication and rhetoric; computer and information sciences; computer engineering; computer technology/computer systems technology; criminal justice/safety; digital communication and media/multimedia; dramatic/theater arts; early childhood education; economics; electrical, electronics and communications engineering; elementary education; English; English/language arts teacher education; finance; French; geography; geology/earth science; German; health/health care administration; health science; health services/allied health/health sciences; history; hospitality administration; human resources management; international business/trade/commerce; Jewish/Judaic studies; kinesiology and exercise science; liberal arts and sciences and humanities related; liberal arts and sciences/liberal studies; linguistics; management information systems; marketing/marketing management; mathematics; mathematics teacher education; mechanical engineering; music; music management and merchandising; music teacher education; nursing (registered nurse training); ocean engineering; philosophy; physics; physiological psychology/psychobiology; political science and government; psychology; public administration; real estate; science teacher education; social psychology; social sciences; social science teacher education; social work; sociology; Spanish; special education; surveying engineering.

Academics *Calendar:* semesters. *Degrees:* certificates, associate, bachelor's, master's, doctoral, and post-master's certificates. *Special study options:* accelerated degree program, adult/continuing education programs, advanced placement credit, cooperative education, distance learning, double majors, English as a second language, freshman honors college, honors programs, independent study, internships, off-campus study, part-time degree program, services for LD students, study abroad, summer session for credit. *ROTC:* Army (c), Air Force (c).

Computers on Campus 1,000 computers/terminals are available on campus for general student use. Students can access the following: campus intranet, computer help desk, free student e-mail accounts, online (class) grades, online (class) registration, online (class) schedules. Campuswide network is available. Wireless service is available via entire campus.

Student Life *Housing:* on-campus residence required for freshman year. *Options:* coed, women-only. Campus housing is university owned. Freshman campus housing is guaranteed. *Activities and organizations:* drama/theater group, student-run newspaper, radio and television station, choral group, marching band, national fraternities, national sororities. *Campus security:* 24-hour emergency response devices and patrols, student patrols, late-night transport/escort service, controlled dormitory access. *Student services:* health clinic, personal/psychological counseling, women's center.

Athletics Member NCAA. All Division I. *Intercollegiate sports:* baseball M (s), basketball M (s)/W (s), cheerleading M/W, cross-country running M/W, football M (s), soccer M/W, softball W (s), tennis M/W, track and field M/W, volleyball W (s). *Intramural sports:* baseball M/W, bowling M/W, football M, ice hockey M (c)/W (c), rock climbing M (c)/W (c), rugby M (c)/W (c), soccer M/W, softball W, table tennis M/W, ultimate Frisbee M/W, volleyball M/W, water polo M (c).

Standardized Tests *Required:* SAT or ACT (for admission).

Costs (2007–08) *Tuition:* state resident $3367 full-time, $112 per credit hour part-time; nonresident $16,431 full-time, $548 per credit hour part-time. Full-time tuition and fees vary according to course load. Part-time tuition and fees vary according to course load. *Room and board:* $8610. Room and board charges vary according to board plan and housing facility. *Payment plans:* tuition prepayment, installment, deferred payment. *Waivers:* senior citizens and employees or children of employees.

Financial Aid Of all full-time matriculated undergraduates who enrolled in 2007, 9,092 applied for aid, 5,680 were judged to have need, 1,115 had their need fully met. 179 Federal Work-Study jobs (averaging $2900). In 2007, 430 non-need-based awards were made. *Average percent of need met:* 81%. *Average financial aid package:* $8028. *Average need-based loan:* $4039. *Average need-based gift aid:* $6137. *Average non-need-based aid:* $2443.

Applying *Options:* electronic application, early admission, deferred entrance. *Application fee:* $30. *Required:* high school transcript. *Application deadline:* 6/1 (freshmen).

Freshman Application Contact Assistant Director, Florida Atlantic University, 777 Glades Road, PO Box 3091, Boca Raton, FL 33431-0991. *Phone:* 561-297-3040. *Toll-free phone:* 800-299-4FAU. *Fax:* 561-297-2758.

See page 650 for the College Close-Up.

FLORIDA CHRISTIAN COLLEGE

Kissimmee, Florida **www.fcc.edu/**

Director of Admissions Mr. Terry Davis, Admissions Director, Florida Christian College, 1011 Bill Beck Boulevard, Kissimmee, FL 34744. *Phone:* 407-847-8966 Ext. 305. *Toll-free phone:* 888-GO-TO-FCC.

FLORIDA COLLEGE

Temple Terrace, Florida **www.floridacollege.edu/**

- **Independent** 4-year, founded 1944
- **Small-town** 95-acre campus with easy access to Tampa
- **Coed** 524 undergraduate students, 95% full-time, 54% women, 46% men
- **Moderately difficult** entrance level, 85% of applicants were admitted

Undergraduates 498 full-time, 26 part-time. 64% are from out of state, 2% African American, 1% Asian American or Pacific Islander, 4% Hispanic American, 0.8% international, 4% transferred in, 73% live on campus.

Freshmen *Admission:* 292 applied, 249 admitted, 223 enrolled.

Faculty *Total:* 41, 76% full-time, 32% with terminal degrees. *Student/faculty ratio:* 15:1.

Majors Biblical studies; business administration and management; elementary education; liberal arts and sciences/liberal studies; music.

Academics *Calendar:* semesters. *Degrees:* associate and bachelor's. *Special study options:* academic remediation for entering students, advanced placement credit, independent study. *ROTC:* Army (c), Air Force (c).

Computers on Campus 76 computers/terminals are available on campus for general student use. Students can access the following: campus intranet, computer help desk, free student e-mail accounts, online (class) grades, online (class) schedules. Campuswide network is available. Wireless service is available via computer centers, computer labs, libraries, student centers.

Student Life *Housing:* on-campus residence required through sophomore year. *Options:* men-only, women-only. Campus housing is university owned. Freshman campus housing is guaranteed. *Activities and organizations:* drama/theater group, choral group, Drama Workshop, concert band, chorus, SBGA, YWTO. *Campus security:* controlled dormitory access, evening patrols by trained security personnel. *Student services:* health clinic, personal/psychological counseling.

Athletics *Intercollegiate sports:* baseball M (s), basketball M (s), volleyball W (s). *Intramural sports:* basketball M/W, football M/W, soccer M/W, softball M/W, volleyball M/W.

Standardized Tests *Required:* SAT or ACT (for admission).

Costs (2007–08) *One-time required fee:* $150. *Comprehensive fee:* $17,340 includes full-time tuition ($11,000), mandatory fees ($700), and room and board ($5640). Part-time tuition: $440 per semester hour. Part-time tuition and fees vary according to course load. *Required fees:* $275 per term part-time. *College room only:* $2440. Room and board charges vary according to board plan and housing facility. *Payment plan:* installment. *Waivers:* employees or children of employees.

Financial Aid Of all full-time matriculated undergraduates who enrolled in 2006, 255 applied for aid, 255 were judged to have need, 44 had their need fully met. In 2006, 89 non-need-based awards were made. *Average percent of need met:* 88%. *Average financial aid package:* $12,517. *Average need-based loan:* $3340. *Average need-based gift aid:* $3418. *Average non-need-based aid:* $2506. *Average indebtedness upon graduation:* $7246. *Financial aid deadline:* 8/1.

Applying *Options:* electronic application. *Application fee:* $25. *Required:* high school transcript, minimum 2.0 GPA, letters of recommendation. *Required for some:* essay or personal statement. *Application deadlines:* 8/1 (freshmen), 8/1 (transfers). *Notification:* continuous (freshmen), continuous (transfers).

Freshman Application Contact Mrs. Shay Angelo, Assistant Director of Admissions, Florida College, 119 North Glen Arven Avenue, Temple Terrace, FL 33617. *Phone:* 813-988-5131 Ext. 6716. *Toll-free phone:* 800-326-7655. *Fax:* 813-899-6772. *E-mail:* admissions@floridacollege.edu.

FLORIDA GULF COAST UNIVERSITY

Fort Myers, Florida **www.fgcu.edu/**

- **State-supported** comprehensive, founded 1991, part of State University System of Florida
- **Suburban** 760-acre campus
- **Endowment** $44.4 million
- **Coed** 8,155 undergraduate students, 77% full-time, 60% women, 40% men
- **Moderately difficult** entrance level, 76% of applicants were admitted

Undergraduates 6,294 full-time, 1,861 part-time. Students come from 46 states and territories, 86 other countries, 9% are from out of state, 4% African American, 2% Asian American or Pacific Islander, 11% Hispanic American, 0.3% Native American, 1% international, 12% transferred in, 15% live on campus. *Retention:* 76% of 2006 full-time freshmen returned.

Freshmen *Admission:* 5,597 applied, 4,273 admitted, 1,902 enrolled. *Average high school GPA:* 3.32. *Test scores:* SAT critical reading scores over 500: 55%; SAT math scores over 500: 58%; ACT scores over 18: 92%; SAT critical reading scores over 600: 10%; SAT math scores over 600: 12%; ACT scores over 24: 19%; SAT critical reading scores over 700: 1%; SAT math scores over 700: 1%; ACT scores over 30: 1%.

Faculty *Total:* 525, 59% full-time, 46% with terminal degrees. *Student/faculty ratio:* 18:1.

Majors Accounting; anthropology; art; athletic training/sports medicine; biology/biological sciences; biomedical/medical engineering; biotechnology; business administration and management; chemistry; civil engineering; clinical laboratory science/medical technology; community health and preventive medicine; computer and information sciences; counselor education/school counseling and guidance; criminalistics and criminal science; criminal justice/safety; dramatic/theater arts; early childhood education; elementary education; English; environmental/environmental health engineering; environmental science; finance; general studies; health services/allied health/health sciences; history; human services; kinesiology and exercise science; legal assistant/paralegal; liberal arts and sciences/liberal studies; management information systems; marketing/marketing management; mass communication/media; mathematics; music performance; nursing (registered nurse training); occupational therapy; philosophy; political science and government; psychology; resort management; secondary education; social work; sociology; Spanish; special education; water, wetlands, and marine resources management.

Academics *Calendar:* semesters. *Degrees:* certificates, associate, bachelor's, and master's. *Special study options:* academic remediation for entering students, accelerated degree program, advanced placement credit, cooperative education, distance learning, double majors, honors programs, independent study, internships, off-campus study, part-time degree program, services for LD students, study abroad, summer session for credit.

Computers on Campus 323 computers/terminals are available on campus for general student use. Students can access the following: online (class) registration, online admissions and advising. Campuswide network is available. 100% of college-owned or -operated housing units are wired for high-speed Internet access.

Student Life *Housing options:* coed. Campus housing is university owned. *Activities and organizations:* drama/theater group, student-run newspaper, Student Government, Ignite (Religious Organization), International Club, Martial Arts Club, Physical Therapy Association, national fraternities, national sororities. *Campus security:* 24-hour emergency response devices and patrols, late-night transport/escort service. *Student services:* health clinic, personal/psychological counseling.

Athletics Member NCAA. All Division I. *Intercollegiate sports:* baseball M (s), basketball M (s)/W (s), cheerleading W, cross-country running M (s)/W (s), golf M (s)/W (s), soccer M (s)/W (s), softball W (s), swimming and diving W (s), tennis M (s)/W (s), volleyball W (s). *Intramural sports:* basketball M/W, cross-country running M (c)/W (c), fencing M (c)/W (c), football M/W, ice hockey M (c), lacrosse M (c)/W (c), sailing M (c)/W (c), skiing (downhill) M (c)/W (c), soccer M/W, softball M/W, swimming and diving M (c)/W (c), table tennis M/W, tennis M (c)/W (c), ultimate Frisbee M/W, volleyball M/W, water polo M/W, weight lifting M (c)/W (c), wrestling M (c)/W (c).

Standardized Tests *Required:* SAT or ACT (for admission).

Costs (2007–08) *Tuition:* state resident $3657 full-time, $74 per credit part-time; nonresident $16,175 full-time, $471 per credit part-time. Full-time tuition and fees vary according to course load. Part-time tuition and fees vary according to course load. *Required fees:* $2042 full-time. *Room and board:* $8267; room only: $5264. Room and board charges vary according to board plan. *Waivers:* senior citizens and employees or children of employees.

Financial Aid Of all full-time matriculated undergraduates who enrolled in 2007, 3,990 applied for aid, 1,936 were judged to have need, 235 had their need fully met. 70 Federal Work-Study jobs (averaging $1316). 425 state and other part-time jobs (averaging $10,968). In 2007, 337 non-need-based awards were made. *Average percent of need met:* 68%. *Average financial aid package:* $6925. *Average need-based loan:* $4833. *Average need-based gift aid:* $3544. *Average non-need-based aid:* $4318. *Average indebtedness upon graduation:* $9449. *Financial aid deadline:* 6/30.

Applying *Options:* electronic application, deferred entrance. *Application fee:* $30. *Required:* high school transcript, minimum 2.0 GPA. *Application deadlines:* 6/1 (freshmen), 6/1 (transfers). *Notification:* continuous (freshmen), continuous (transfers).

Freshman Application Contact Mr. Marc Laviolette, Director of Admissions, Florida Gulf Coast University, 10501 FGCU Boulevard South, Fort Myers, FL 33965-6565. *Phone:* 239-590-7878. *Toll-free phone:* 888-889-1095. *Fax:* 239-590-7894. *E-mail:* admissions@fgcu.edu.

See page 652 for the College Close-Up.

FLORIDA HOSPITAL COLLEGE OF HEALTH SCIENCES

Orlando, Florida **www.fhchs.edu/**

Freshman Application Contact Ms. Katie Shaw, Director of Recruiting, Florida Hospital College of Health Sciences, 800 Lake Estelle Drive, Orlando, FL 32803. *Phone:* 407-303-1878. *Toll-free phone:* 800-500-7747. *Fax:* 407-303-5671. *E-mail:* katie.shaw@fhchs.edu.

FLORIDA INSTITUTE OF TECHNOLOGY

Melbourne, Florida **www.fit.edu/**

- **Independent** university, founded 1958
- **Small-town** 130-acre campus with easy access to Orlando
- **Endowment** $42.9 million

• **Coed** 2,594 undergraduate students, 93% full-time, 30% women, 70% men
• **Moderately difficult** entrance level, 81% of applicants were admitted

Undergraduates 2,410 full-time, 184 part-time. Students come from 50 states and territories, 81 other countries, 46% are from out of state, 3% African American, 2% Asian American or Pacific Islander, 6% Hispanic American, 0.6% Native American, 21% international, 6% transferred in, 49% live on campus. *Retention:* 75% of 2006 full-time freshmen returned.

Freshmen *Admission:* 3,027 applied, 2,451 admitted, 681 enrolled. *Average high school GPA:* 3.41. *Test scores:* SAT critical reading scores over 500: 81%; SAT math scores over 500: 89%; ACT scores over 18: 94%; SAT critical reading scores over 600: 33%; SAT math scores over 600: 45%; ACT scores over 24: 74%; SAT critical reading scores over 700: 5%; SAT math scores over 700: 8%; ACT scores over 30: 17%.

Faculty *Total:* 436, 51% full-time, 74% with terminal degrees. *Student/faculty ratio:* 13:1.

Majors Accounting; aerospace, aeronautical and astronautical engineering; aerospace science; applied mathematics; aquatic biology/limnology; astrophysics; aviation/airway management; biochemistry; biological and physical sciences; biology/biological sciences; biology teacher education; biomedical sciences; business administration and management; chemical engineering; chemistry; chemistry teacher education; civil engineering; clinical psychology; communication/speech communication and rhetoric; computer engineering; computer science; computer software engineering; construction engineering technology; earth sciences; ecology; e-commerce; electrical, electronics and communications engineering; engineering; environmental science; forensic psychology; general studies; history; humanities; information science/studies; interdisciplinary studies; international business/trade/commerce; management information systems; management science; marine biology and biological oceanography; mathematics teacher education; mechanical engineering; meteorology; military studies; molecular biology; multi-/interdisciplinary studies related; ocean engineering; oceanography; organizational behavior; physics; physics teacher education; pre-medical studies; psychology; science teacher education.

Academics *Calendar:* semesters. *Degrees:* bachelor's, master's, doctoral, and post-master's certificates. *Special study options:* academic remediation for entering students, adult/continuing education programs, advanced placement credit, cooperative education, double majors, English as a second language, independent study, internships, part-time degree program, services for LD students, study abroad, summer session for credit. *ROTC:* Army (b).

Computers on Campus 400 computers/terminals and 50 ports are available on campus for general student use. Students can access the following: computer help desk, free student e-mail accounts, online (class) grades, online (class) registration, online (class) schedules. Campuswide network is available. 100% of college-owned or -operated housing units are wired for high-speed Internet access. Wireless service is available via classrooms, computer centers, computer labs, learning centers, libraries, student centers.

Student Life *Housing:* on-campus residence required for freshman year. *Options:* coed. Campus housing is university owned. Freshman campus housing is guaranteed. *Activities and organizations:* drama/theater group, student-run newspaper, radio and television station, choral group, Phi Eta Sigma National Honor Society, Saudi Student House, Newman Club, College Players, Squamish, national fraternities, national sororities. *Campus security:* 24-hour emergency response devices and patrols, late-night transport/escort service, self-defense education. *Student services:* health clinic, personal/psychological counseling.

Athletics Member NCAA. All Division II. *Intercollegiate sports:* baseball M (s), basketball M (s)/W (s), crew M (s)/W (s), cross-country running M (s)/W (s), golf M (s)/W (s), soccer M (s)/W (s), softball W (s), tennis M (s)/W (s), volleyball W (s). *Intramural sports:* badminton M/W, basketball M (c)/W (c), bowling M/W, cheerleading M (c)/W (c), crew M (c), fencing M (c)/W (c), football M/W, ice hockey M (c)/W (c), racquetball M/W, sailing M (c)/W (c), soccer M/W, softball M/W, table tennis M/W, tennis M/W, ultimate Frisbee M/W, volleyball M/W, water polo M/W, wrestling M (c)/W (c).

Standardized Tests *Required:* SAT or ACT (for admission).

Costs (2007–08) *Comprehensive fee:* $36,690 includes full-time tuition ($28,920) and room and board ($7770). Full-time tuition and fees vary according to course load and program. Part-time tuition: $875 per credit hour. Part-time tuition and fees vary according to course load and program. *College room only:* $4370. Room and board charges vary according to board plan and housing facility. *Payment plan:* installment. *Waivers:* senior citizens and employees or children of employees.

Financial Aid Of all full-time matriculated undergraduates who enrolled in 2006, 1,578 applied for aid, 1,396 were judged to have need, 398 had their need fully met. 599 Federal Work-Study jobs (averaging $1445). 5 state and other part-time jobs (averaging $2841). In 2006, 560 non-need-based awards were made. *Average percent of need met:* 82%. *Average financial aid package:* $22,448. *Average need-based loan:* $4810. *Average need-based gift aid:* $14,270. *Average non-need-based aid:* $7991. *Average indebtedness upon graduation:* $25,768.

Applying *Options:* electronic application, early admission, deferred entrance. *Application fee:* $50. *Required:* high school transcript, minimum 2.5 GPA. *Required for some:* minimum 3.0 GPA. *Recommended:* minimum 2.0 GPA. *Application deadlines:* rolling (freshmen), rolling (transfers). *Notification:* continuous (freshmen), continuous (transfers).

Freshman Application Contact Michael J. Perry, Director of Undergraduate Admission, Florida Institute of Technology, 150 West University Boulevard, Melbourne, FL 32901-6975. *Phone:* 321-674-8030. *Toll-free phone:* 800-888-4348. *Fax:* 321-723-9468. *E-mail:* admission@fit.edu.

See page 654 for the College Close-Up.

FLORIDA INTERNATIONAL UNIVERSITY

Miami, Florida **www.fiu.edu/**

• **State-supported** university, founded 1965, part of State University System of Florida
• **Urban** 573-acre campus
• **Endowment** $91.6 million
• **Coed** 31,390 undergraduate students
• **Moderately difficult** entrance level, 47% of applicants were admitted

Undergraduates Students come from 52 states and territories, 175 other countries, 3% are from out of state, 13% African American, 4% Asian American or Pacific Islander, 64% Hispanic American, 0.2% Native American, 4% international, 8% live on campus. *Retention:* 87% of 2006 full-time freshmen returned.

Freshmen *Admission:* 14,917 applied, 6,938 admitted. *Average high school GPA:* 3.66. *Test scores:* SAT critical reading scores over 500: 79%; SAT math scores over 500: 79%; SAT writing scores over 500: 73%; ACT scores over 18: 93%; SAT critical reading scores over 600: 26%; SAT math scores over 600: 24%; SAT writing scores over 600: 19%; ACT scores over 24: 38%; SAT critical reading scores over 700: 2%; SAT math scores over 700: 2%; SAT writing scores over 700: 1%; ACT scores over 30: 2%.

Faculty *Total:* 1,588, 54% full-time, 48% with terminal degrees. *Student/faculty ratio:* 21:1.

Majors Accounting; applied mathematics; architecture related; art history, criticism and conservation; art teacher education; Asian studies; biology/biological sciences; biomedical/medical engineering; broadcast journalism; business administration and management; chemical engineering; chemistry; civil engineering; communication/speech communication and rhetoric; computer and information sciences; computer engineering; computer science; construction engineering technology; criminal justice/safety; dance; dietetics; dramatic/theater arts; economics; electrical, electronics and communications engineering; elementary education; English; English/language arts teacher education; environmental control technologies related; environmental design/architecture; environmental studies; family and consumer sciences/home economics teacher education; finance; fine/studio arts; foreign language teacher education; French; geography; geology/earth science; German; health/health care administration; health information/medical records administration; health science; health services/allied health/health sciences; health teacher education; history; hospitality administration; humanities; human resources management; information technology; insurance; interior design; international business/trade/commerce; international relations and affairs; Italian; kinesiology and exercise science; liberal arts and sciences/liberal studies; logistics and materials management; management information systems; marine biology and biological oceanography; marketing/marketing management; mathematics; mathematics teacher education; mechanical engineering; music; music teacher education; nursing (registered nurse training); occupational therapy; orthotics/prosthetics; parks, recreation and leisure facilities management; philosophy; physical education teaching and coaching; physics; political science and government; Portuguese; psychology; public administration; real estate; religious studies; science teacher education; social science teacher education; social work; sociology; Spanish; special education (emotionally disturbed); special education (mentally retarded); special education (specific learning disabilities); statistics; systems engineering; tourism and travel services management; trade and industrial teacher education; urban studies/affairs; women's studies.

Academics *Calendar:* semesters. *Degrees:* bachelor's, master's, doctoral, and first professional. *Special study options:* accelerated degree program, adult/continuing education programs, advanced placement credit, cooperative education, distance learning, double majors, English as a second language, freshman honors college, honors programs, independent study, internships, off-campus study, part-time degree program, services for LD students, study abroad, summer session for credit. *ROTC:* Army (b), Air Force (b).

Computers on Campus Students can access the following: free student e-mail accounts, online (class) grades, online (class) registration, online (class) schedules, online financial aid and cashier's information. Campuswide network is available. 100% of college-owned or -operated housing units are wired for high-speed Internet access. Wireless service is available via classrooms, computer centers, computer labs, student centers.

Student Life *Housing options:* coed. Campus housing is university owned. *Activities and organizations:* drama/theater group, student-run newspaper, radio station, choral group, marching band, Students for Community Service, Black Student Leadership Council, Hospitality Management Student Club, Hispanic Students Association, Haitian Students Organization, national fraternities, national sororities. *Campus security:* 24-hour emergency response devices and patrols, late-night transport/escort service, controlled dormitory access. *Student services:* health clinic, personal/psychological counseling, women's center, legal services.

Athletics Member NCAA. All Division I. *Intercollegiate sports:* baseball M (s), basketball M (s)/W (s), cross-country running M (s)/W (s), football M (s), golf W (s), soccer M (s)/W (s), softball W (s), tennis W (s), track and field M (s)/W (s), volleyball W (s). *Intramural sports:* basketball M/W, bowling M/W, cross-country running M/W, football M, golf M/W, lacrosse M, racquetball M/W, rugby M, sailing M/W, soccer M/W, softball M/W, swimming and diving M/W, table tennis M/W, tennis M/W, volleyball M/W, weight lifting M/W.

Standardized Tests *Required:* SAT or ACT (for admission).

Costs (2007–08) *Tuition:* state resident $3130 full-time, $104 per credit hour part-time; nonresident $15,529 full-time, $518 per credit hour part-time. Full-time tuition and fees vary according to course load. Part-time tuition and fees vary according to course load. *Required fees:* $284 full-time, $142 per term part-time. *Room and board:* $10,608; room only: $5620. Room and board charges vary according to housing facility. *Waivers:* senior citizens and employees or children of employees.

Financial Aid Of all full-time matriculated undergraduates who enrolled in 2002, 7,190 applied for aid, 5,981 were judged to have need, 317 had their need fully met. 660 Federal Work-Study jobs (averaging $2558). In 2002, 515 non-need-based awards were made. *Average percent of need met:* 53%. *Average financial aid package:* $6140. *Average need-based loan:* $3933. *Average need-based gift aid:* $5067. *Average non-need-based aid:* $1919. *Average indebtedness upon graduation:* $4489.

Applying *Options:* electronic application, early admission, deferred entrance. *Application fee:* $30. *Required:* high school transcript, minimum 3.0 GPA. *Required for some:* 1 letter of recommendation. *Application deadlines:* rolling (freshmen), rolling (transfers). *Notification:* continuous until 7/1 (freshmen), continuous until 7/1 (transfers).

Freshman Application Contact Ms. Carmen Brown, Director of Admissions, Florida International University, University Park, PC 140, 11200 SW 8 Street, PC140, Miami, FL 33199. *Phone:* 305-348-3675. *Fax:* 305-348-3648. *E-mail:* admiss@fiu.edu.

See page 656 for the College Close-Up.

FLORIDA MEMORIAL UNIVERSITY

Miami-Dade, Florida **www.fmuniv.edu/**

- **Independent** 4-year, founded 1879, affiliated with Baptist Church
- **Suburban** 77-acre campus
- **Endowment** $6.7 million
- **Coed** 1,669 undergraduate students, 91% full-time, 62% women, 38% men
- **Noncompetitive** entrance level, 39% of applicants were admitted

Undergraduates 1,516 full-time, 153 part-time. Students come from 37 states and territories, 15 other countries, 12% are from out of state, 84% African American, 3% Hispanic American, 9% international, 8% transferred in. *Retention:* 70% of 2006 full-time freshmen returned.

Freshmen *Admission:* 5,286 applied, 2,061 admitted, 546 enrolled. *Average high school GPA:* 2.7.

Faculty *Total:* 173, 61% full-time. *Student/faculty ratio:* 12:1.

Majors Accounting; air traffic control; aviation/airway management; biology/biological sciences; business administration and management; clinical laboratory science/medical technology; computer science; criminal justice/law enforcement administration; data processing and data processing technology; elementary education; English; mathematics; modern languages; music teacher education; physical education teaching and coaching; political science and government; psychology; public administration; religious studies; secondary education; sociology; urban studies/affairs.

Academics *Calendar:* semesters. *Degrees:* bachelor's and master's. *Special study options:* academic remediation for entering students, cooperative education, English as a second language, external degree program, freshman honors college, honors programs, internships, off-campus study, part-time degree program, summer session for credit. *ROTC:* Army (b), Air Force (c).

Computers on Campus 200 computers/terminals are available on campus for general student use. Students can access the following: campus intranet, computer help desk, free student e-mail accounts, online (class) grades, online (class) registration, online (class) schedules. Campuswide network is available. 100% of college-owned or -operated housing units are wired for high-speed Internet access. Wireless service is available via computer centers, computer labs.

Student Life *Housing options:* coed. Freshman applicants given priority for college housing. *Activities and organizations:* drama/theater group, student-run newspaper, national fraternities, national sororities. *Student services:* health clinic.

Athletics Member NAIA. *Intercollegiate sports:* baseball M, basketball M (s)/W (s), cross-country running M/W, track and field M/W, volleyball M (s)/W (s). *Intramural sports:* basketball M/W, soccer M, swimming and diving M/W, tennis M/W, ultimate Frisbee M/W, volleyball M/W.

Standardized Tests *Recommended:* SAT or ACT (for admission).

Costs (2008–09) *Comprehensive fee:* $17,594 includes full-time tuition ($10,508), mandatory fees ($1746), and room and board ($5340). Part-time tuition: $438 per credit.

Financial Aid Of all full-time matriculated undergraduates who enrolled in 2003, 2,074 applied for aid, 1,763 were judged to have need, 284 had their need fully met. 350 Federal Work-Study jobs (averaging $1600). *Average percent of need met:* 62%. *Average financial aid package:* $10,950. *Average need-based loan:* $3500. *Average need-based gift aid:* $3000. *Average indebtedness upon graduation:* $3500. *Financial aid deadline:* 4/15.

Applying *Options:* electronic application. *Application fee:* $15. *Required:* essay or personal statement, high school transcript, minimum 2.2 GPA, 2 letters of recommendation. *Application deadlines:* 7/1 (freshmen), 7/1 (transfers). *Notification:* continuous (freshmen), continuous (transfers).

Director of Admissions Mrs. Peggy Murray Martin, Director of Admissions and International Student Advisor, Florida Memorial University, 15800 NW 42nd Avenue, Miami Gardens, FL 33054. *Phone:* 305-626-3147. *Toll-free phone:* 800-822-1362.

FLORIDA SOUTHERN COLLEGE

Lakeland, Florida **www.flsouthern.edu/**

- **Independent** comprehensive, founded 1885, affiliated with United Methodist Church
- **Suburban** 100-acre campus with easy access to Tampa and Orlando
- **Endowment** $74.4 million
- **Coed** 1,710 undergraduate students, 96% full-time, 60% women, 40% men
- **Moderately difficult** entrance level, 58% of applicants were admitted

Undergraduates 1,645 full-time, 65 part-time. Students come from 44 states and territories, 31 other countries, 25% are from out of state, 7% African American, 1% Asian American or Pacific Islander, 6% Hispanic American, 0.3% Native American, 4% international, 5% transferred in, 74% live on campus. *Retention:* 71% of 2006 full-time freshmen returned.

Freshmen *Admission:* 2,559 applied, 1,490 admitted, 424 enrolled. *Average high school GPA:* 3.51. *Test scores:* SAT critical reading scores over 500: 66%; SAT math scores over 500: 62%; SAT writing scores over 500: 59%; ACT scores over 18: 94%; SAT critical reading scores over 600: 26%; SAT math scores over 600: 25%; SAT writing scores over 600: 15%; ACT scores over 24: 33%; SAT critical reading scores over 700: 5%; SAT math scores over 700: 1%; SAT writing scores over 700: 2%; ACT scores over 30: 4%.

Faculty *Total:* 181, 59% full-time, 57% with terminal degrees. *Student/faculty ratio:* 13:1.

Majors Accounting; advertising; agricultural business and management; art; art teacher education; athletic training; biology/biological sciences; broadcast journalism; business administration and management; business/commerce; chemistry; commercial and advertising art; communication/speech communication and rhetoric; computer science; criminal justice/safety; dramatic/theater arts; economics; education; elementary education; English; English composition; environmental studies; finance; fine/studio arts; history; horticultural science; hotel/motel administration; humanities; human resources management; international business/trade/commerce; journalism; kindergarten/preschool education; management information systems; marketing/marketing management; mathematics; music; music management and merchandising; music teacher education; natural sciences; nursing (registered nurse training); operations management; ornamental horticulture; physical education teaching and coaching; political science and government; pre-dentistry studies; pre-medical studies; pre-veterinary studies; psychology; public relations/image management; religious education; religious/sacred music;

religious studies; secondary education; social sciences; sociology; Spanish; special education (specific learning disabilities).

Academics *Calendar:* semesters. *Degrees:* bachelor's and master's. *Special study options:* adult/continuing education programs, advanced placement credit, double majors, honors programs, independent study, internships, off-campus study, part-time degree program, study abroad, summer session for credit. *ROTC:* Army (b), Air Force (c). *Unusual degree programs:* 3-2 engineering with Washington University in St. Louis, University of Miami.

Computers on Campus 376 computers/terminals are available on campus for general student use. Students can access the following: campus intranet, computer help desk, free student e-mail accounts, online (class) grades, online (class) registration, online (class) schedules, campus portal. Campuswide network is available. 100% of college-owned or -operated housing units are wired for high-speed Internet access. Wireless service is available via classrooms, computer centers, dorm rooms, libraries, student centers.

Student Life *Housing:* on-campus residence required through junior year. *Options:* coed, men-only, women-only, disabled students. Campus housing is university owned. Freshman campus housing is guaranteed. *Activities and organizations:* drama/theater group, student-run newspaper, radio station, choral group, Student Government Association, Lambda Chi Alpha, Association of Campus Entertainment, Beyond (Campus Ministry), Fellowship of Christian Athletes, national fraternities, national sororities. *Campus security:* 24-hour emergency response devices and patrols, student patrols, late-night transport/escort service, controlled dormitory access. *Student services:* health clinic, personal/psychological counseling.

Athletics Member NCAA. All Division II. *Intercollegiate sports:* baseball M (s), basketball M (s)/W (s), cross-country running M (s)/W (s), golf M (s)/W (s), soccer M (s)/W (s), softball W (s), swimming and diving M (s)/W (s), tennis M (s)/W (s), volleyball M (c)/W (s). *Intramural sports:* basketball M/W, cheerleading W (c), football M/W, golf M/W, soccer W, softball M/W, tennis M/W, ultimate Frisbee M/W, volleyball M/W.

Standardized Tests *Required:* SAT or ACT (for admission).

Costs (2008–09) *Comprehensive fee:* $29,995 includes full-time tuition ($21,620), mandatory fees ($525), and room and board ($7850). Part-time tuition: $650 per credit hour. *Required fees:* $150 per year part-time. *College room only:* $4350.

Financial Aid Of all full-time matriculated undergraduates who enrolled in 2005, 1,507 applied for aid, 1,270 were judged to have need, 434 had their need fully met. 356 Federal Work-Study jobs (averaging $1226). 73 state and other part-time jobs (averaging $1871). In 2005, 229 non-need-based awards were made. *Average percent of need met:* 64%. *Average financial aid package:* $16,993. *Average need-based loan:* $5199. *Average need-based gift aid:* $13,078. *Average non-need-based aid:* $13,443. *Average indebtedness upon graduation:* $16,072. *Financial aid deadline:* 8/1.

Applying *Options:* electronic application, early admission, early decision, deferred entrance. *Application fee:* $30. *Required:* essay or personal statement, high school transcript, 1 letter of recommendation. *Recommended:* minimum 2.0 GPA, interview. *Application deadlines:* 3/1 (freshmen), rolling (transfers). *Early decision deadline:* 12/1. *Notification:* continuous (freshmen), continuous (transfers), 12/15 (early decision).

Freshman Application Contact Florida Southern College, 111 Lake Hollingsworth Drive, Lakeland, FL 33801-5698. *Phone:* 863-680-4131. *Toll-free phone:* 800-274-4131.

See page 658 for the College Close-Up.

FLORIDA STATE UNIVERSITY

Tallahassee, Florida — www.fsu.edu/

- **State-supported** university, founded 1851, part of State University System of Florida
- **Suburban** 451-acre campus
- **Endowment** $549.0 million
- **Coed** 31,595 undergraduate students, 89% full-time, 56% women, 44% men
- **Very difficult** entrance level, 55% of applicants were admitted

Undergraduates 27,976 full-time, 3,619 part-time. Students come from 51 states and territories, 118 other countries, 12% are from out of state, 11% African American, 3% Asian American or Pacific Islander, 11% Hispanic American, 0.6% Native American, 0.4% international, 7% transferred in. *Retention:* 88% of 2006 full-time freshmen returned.

Freshmen *Admission:* 24,343 applied, 13,415 admitted, 6,124 enrolled. *Average high school GPA:* 3.63. *Test scores:* SAT critical reading scores over 500: 97%; SAT math scores over 500: 97%; SAT writing scores over 500: 85%; ACT scores over 18: 100%; SAT critical reading scores over 600: 44%; SAT math scores over 600: 48%; SAT writing scores over 600: 32%; ACT scores over 24: 75%; SAT critical reading scores over 700: 6%; SAT math scores over 700: 6%; SAT writing scores over 700: 4%; ACT scores over 30: 8%.

Faculty *Total:* 1,693, 80% full-time, 92% with terminal degrees. *Student/faculty ratio:* 24:1.

Majors Accounting; acting; advertising; American studies; anthropology; apparel and textile marketing management; apparel and textiles; applied economics; applied mathematics; art history, criticism and conservation; art teacher education; Asian studies; athletic training; atmospheric sciences and meteorology; bilingual and multilingual education; bilingual, multilingual, and multicultural education related; biochemistry; biology/biological sciences; biomathematics and bioinformatics related; biomedical/medical engineering; business administration and management; business/commerce; Caribbean studies; cell and molecular biology; chemical engineering; chemistry; chemistry related; child development; cinematography and film/video production; civil engineering; classics and languages, literatures and linguistics; commercial and advertising art; communication and media related; communication/speech communication and rhetoric; community health services counseling; computer engineering; computer programming; computer science; computer software and media applications related; computer software engineering; creative writing; criminal justice/safety; criminology; dance; dietetics; dramatic/theater arts; early childhood education; ecology; economics; electrical, electronics and communications engineering; elementary education; English; English/language arts teacher education; entrepreneurial and small business related; environmental biology; environmental/environmental health engineering; environmental studies; European studies (Central and Eastern); evolutionary biology; family and consumer economics related; family and consumer sciences/home economics teacher education; family and consumer sciences/human sciences; fashion/apparel design; fashion merchandising; film/cinema studies; finance; fine/studio arts; foods, nutrition, and wellness; foreign language teacher education; French; geography; geology/earth science; German; graphic design; health teacher education; history; hospitality administration; hospitality administration related; housing and human environments; human development and family studies; humanities; human resources management; industrial engineering; information science/studies; interior design; international business/trade/commerce; international relations and affairs; Italian; jazz/jazz studies; kindergarten/preschool education; kinesiology and exercise science; Latin; Latin American studies; liberal arts and sciences/liberal studies; literature; marine biology and biological oceanography; mass communication/media; materials engineering; mathematics; mathematics teacher education; mechanical engineering; meteorology; middle school education; modern Greek; multicultural education; music; music history, literature, and theory; music pedagogy; music performance; music teacher education; music theory and composition; music therapy; neurobiology and neurophysiology; nursing (registered nurse training); nutrition sciences; parks, recreation and leisure facilities management; philosophy; physical education teaching and coaching; physical sciences; physical sciences related; physics; piano and organ; plant physiology; political science and government; pre-dentistry studies; pre-law studies; pre-medical studies; pre-pharmacy studies; pre-veterinary studies; psychology; public relations/image management; radio and television; radio, television, and digital communication related; religious studies; Russian; Russian studies; science teacher education; secondary education; social sciences; social science teacher education; social work; sociology; Spanish; special education (emotionally disturbed); special education (mentally retarded); special education (specific learning disabilities); special education (vision impaired); sport and fitness administration/management; statistics; textile science; theater design and technology; violin, viola, guitar and other stringed instruments; vocational rehabilitation counseling; voice and opera; wind/percussion instruments; women's studies; zoology/animal biology.

Academics *Calendar:* semesters. *Degrees:* certificates, associate, bachelor's, master's, doctoral, first professional, post-master's, and postbachelor's certificates. *Special study options:* accelerated degree program, adult/continuing education programs, advanced placement credit, cooperative education, distance learning, double majors, English as a second language, honors programs, independent study, internships, off-campus study, part-time degree program, services for LD students, study abroad, summer session for credit. *ROTC:* Army (b), Navy (c), Air Force (b). *Unusual degree programs:* 3-2 emotional disturbances/learning disabilities.

Computers on Campus 3,771 computers/terminals are available on campus for general student use. Students can access the following: campus intranet, computer help desk, free student e-mail accounts, online (class) grades, online (class) registration, online (class) schedules, course home pages, course search, online fee payment. Campuswide network is available. Wireless service is available via entire campus.

Student Life *Housing options:* coed, women-only, cooperative, disabled students. Campus housing is university owned. Freshman applicants given priority for college housing. *Activities and organizations:* drama/theater group, student-run newspaper, radio and television station, choral group, marching band, student government, honors program, Gold Key Society, Marching Chiefs, intramural sports, national fraternities, national sororities. *Campus security:* 24-hour emergency response devices and patrols, late-night transport/escort service, controlled dormitory access. *Student services:* health clinic, personal/psychological counseling, women's center, legal services.

Athletics Member NCAA. All Division I except football (Division I-A). *Intercollegiate sports:* baseball M (s), basketball M (s)/W (s), bowling M (c)/W (c), cheerleading M/W, cross-country running M (s)/W (s), golf M (s)/W (s), rugby M (c)/W (c), soccer M (c)/W (s), softball W (s), swimming and diving M (s)/W (s), table tennis M (c)/W (c), tennis M (s)/W (s), track and field M (s)/W (s), volleyball M (c)/W (s), wrestling M (c)/W (c). *Intramural sports:* badminton M (c)/W (c), basketball M/W, bowling M/W, crew M (c)/W (c), equestrian sports M (c)/W (c), fencing M (c)/W (c), football M/W, golf M/W, ice hockey M (c)/W (c), lacrosse M (c)/W (c), racquetball M/W, sailing M (c)/W (c), soccer M/W, softball M/W, squash M (c)/W (c), swimming and diving M/W, table tennis M/W, tennis M/W, track and field M/W, ultimate Frisbee M (c)/W (c), volleyball M/W, water polo M (c)/W (c), weight lifting M/W, wrestling M/W.

Standardized Tests *Required:* SAT or ACT (for admission).

Costs (2007–08) *Tuition:* state resident $3355 full-time, $112 per credit hour part-time; nonresident $16,487 full-time, $550 per credit hour part-time. Full-time tuition and fees vary according to location. Part-time tuition and fees vary according to location. *Room and board:* $8000; room only: $4700. Room and board charges vary according to board plan and housing facility. *Payment plans:* tuition prepayment, installment. *Waivers:* senior citizens and employees or children of employees.

Financial Aid Of all full-time matriculated undergraduates who enrolled in 2007, 14,795 applied for aid, 8,037 were judged to have need, 6,440 had their need fully met. 600 Federal Work-Study jobs (averaging $1200). In 2007, 1108 non-need-based awards were made. *Average percent of need met:* 74%. *Average financial aid package:* $9531. *Average need-based loan:* $3692. *Average need-based gift aid:* $3619. *Average non-need-based aid:* $2090. *Average indebtedness upon graduation:* $13,855.

Applying *Options:* electronic application, early admission. *Application fee:* $30. *Required:* essay or personal statement, high school transcript. *Required for some:* audition. *Recommended:* minimum 3.0 GPA. *Application deadlines:* 2/14 (freshmen), 7/1 (transfers). *Notification:* 3/28 (freshmen), continuous until 7/15 (transfers).

Freshman Application Contact Ms. Janice Finney, Director of Admissions, Florida State University, A2500 University Center, Tallahassee, FL 32306-2400. *Phone:* 850-644-6200. *Fax:* 850-644-0197. *E-mail:* admissions@admin.fsu.edu.

FULL SAIL UNIVERSITY

Winter Park, Florida **www.fullsail.com/**

- **Proprietary** comprehensive, founded 1979
- **Suburban** campus with easy access to Orlando
- **Coed, primarily men** 5,697 undergraduate students, 100% full-time, 12% women, 88% men
- **Noncompetitive** entrance level, 71% of applicants were admitted

Undergraduates 5,697 full-time. Students come from 47 states and territories, 6 other countries, 70% are from out of state.

Freshmen *Admission:* 2,542 applied, 1,813 admitted.

Faculty *Total:* 782. *Student/faculty ratio:* 9:1.

Majors Animation, interactive technology, video graphics and special effects; business, management, and marketing related; computer graphics; design and applied arts related; dramatic/theater arts and stagecraft related; film/video and photographic arts related; recording arts technology.

Academics *Calendar:* modular. *Degrees:* associate, bachelor's, and master's. *Special study options:* academic remediation for entering students, cooperative education, internships, services for LD students, summer session for credit.

Computers on Campus Students can access the following: campus intranet, computer help desk, free student e-mail accounts, online (class) grades, online (class) registration, online (class) schedules. Campuswide network is available. Wireless service is available via entire campus.

Student Life *Housing:* college housing not available. *Options:* Campus housing is provided by a third party. *Activities and organizations:* Student Chapter of Audio Engineering Society. *Campus security:* 24-hour patrols. *Student services:* personal/psychological counseling.

Athletics *Intercollegiate sports:* ultimate Frisbee M (s)/W (s), volleyball M (s)/W (s). *Intramural sports:* ultimate Frisbee M/W, volleyball M/W.

Costs (2008–09) *Tuition:* Please contact school for program costs.

Financial Aid Of all full-time matriculated undergraduates who enrolled in 2006, 212 Federal Work-Study jobs (averaging $561).

Applying *Options:* electronic application. *Application fee:* $150. *Required:* high school transcript. *Required for some:* minimum "A" average in Algebra II. *Application deadline:* rolling (freshmen).

Freshman Application Contact Ms. Mary Beth Plank, Director of Admissions, Full Sail University, 3300 University Boulevard, Winter Park, FL 32792. *Phone:* 407-679-6333 Ext. 2122. *Toll-free phone:* 800-226-7625. *E-mail:* admissions@fullsail.com.

See page 660 for the College Close-Up.

HOBE SOUND BIBLE COLLEGE

Hobe Sound, Florida **www.hsbc.edu/**

Freshman Application Contact Mrs. Ann French, Director of Admissions, Hobe Sound Bible College, PO Box 1065, Hobe Sound, FL 33475-1065. *Phone:* 772-546-5534 Ext. 1015. *Toll-free phone:* 800-881-5534. *Fax:* 772-545-1422. *E-mail:* hsbcuwin@aol.com.

HODGES UNIVERSITY

Naples, Florida **www.hodges.edu/**

- **Independent** comprehensive, founded 1990
- **Suburban** campus with easy access to Miami
- **Endowment** $3.7 million
- **Coed** 1,487 undergraduate students, 76% full-time, 58% women, 32% men
- **Minimally difficult** entrance level, 79% of applicants were admitted

Undergraduates 1,128 full-time, 359 part-time. Students come from 10 states and territories, 3 other countries, 1% are from out of state, 16% African American, 2% Asian American or Pacific Islander, 24% Hispanic American, 0.2% Native American, 0.1% international, 20% transferred in.

Freshmen *Admission:* 210 applied, 166 admitted, 156 enrolled.

Faculty *Total:* 114, 54% full-time, 52% with terminal degrees. *Student/faculty ratio:* 17:1.

Majors Business administration, management and operations related; computer/information technology services administration related; health/health care administration; health information/medical records technology; health/medical preparatory programs related; legal assistant/paralegal; legal professions and studies related; medical/clinical assistant.

Academics *Calendar:* trimesters. *Degrees:* certificates, associate, bachelor's, and master's. *Special study options:* academic remediation for entering students, accelerated degree program, adult/continuing education programs, advanced placement credit, cooperative education, distance learning, double majors, English as a second language, external degree program, internships, part-time degree program, services for LD students, summer session for credit.

Computers on Campus 500 computers/terminals are available on campus for general student use. Students can access the following: free student e-mail accounts. Campuswide network is available. Wireless service is available via classrooms, computer labs, libraries.

Student Life *Housing:* college housing not available. *Activities and organizations:* Ambassadors, Paralegal Club, Institute of Managerial Accountants, Running Club, Entrepreneurial Club. *Campus security:* late-night transport/escort service, building security. *Student services:* personal/psychological counseling.

Standardized Tests *Required for some:* CPAt. *Recommended:* SAT (for admission), ACT (for admission).

Costs (2007–08) *Tuition:* $15,300 full-time, $425 per semester hour part-time. *Required fees:* $380 full-time. *Payment plan:* installment. *Waivers:* employees or children of employees.

Financial Aid Of all full-time matriculated undergraduates who enrolled in 2007, 980 applied for aid, 935 were judged to have need, 175 had their need fully met. 48 Federal Work-Study jobs (averaging $2269). In 2007, 44 non-need-based awards were made. *Average percent of need met:* 1%. *Average financial aid package:* $8950. *Average need-based loan:* $4150. *Average need-based gift aid:* $4400. *Average non-need-based aid:* $205. *Average indebtedness upon graduation:* $18,100.

Applying *Options:* electronic application, deferred entrance. *Application fee:* $20. *Required:* essay or personal statement, high school transcript, interview. *Required for some:* 2 letters of recommendation. *Application deadlines:* rolling (freshmen), rolling (transfers). *Notification:* continuous (freshmen), continuous (transfers).

Freshman Application Contact Hodges University, 2655 Northbrooke Drive, Naples, FL 34119. *Phone:* 239-513-1122 Ext. 104. *Toll-free phone:* 800-466-8017.

INTERNATIONAL ACADEMY OF DESIGN & TECHNOLOGY

Tampa, Florida www.academy.edu/

- **Proprietary** comprehensive, founded 1984, part of Career Education Corporation
- **Urban** 1-acre campus
- **Coed**
- **Noncompetitive** entrance level

Faculty *Total:* 174, 16% full-time. *Student/faculty ratio:* 16:1.

Majors Animation, interactive technology, video graphics and special effects; apparel marketing; cinematography and film/video production; commercial and advertising art; computer graphics; design and visual communications; fashion/apparel design; fashion merchandising; graphic design; interior design; intermedia/multimedia; photography; recording arts technology; web page, digital/multimedia and information resources design.

Academics *Calendar:* quarters. *Degree:* bachelor's. *Special study options:* academic remediation for entering students, accelerated degree program, advanced placement credit, distance learning, internships, study abroad, summer session for credit.

Computers on Campus 310 computers/terminals are available on campus for general student use. Campuswide network is available.

Student Life *Housing options:* Campus housing is provided by a third party. *Activities and organizations:* Student Chapter ASID, Fashion Design International, Computer Animation Club. *Campus security:* 24-hour emergency response devices, late night patrols by trained security personnel.

Costs (2008–09) *Tuition:* $385 per credit hour part-time. *Required fees:* $100 per term part-time.

Financial Aid *Average percent of need met:* 48%.

Applying *Options:* electronic application, early admission, deferred entrance. *Application fee:* $50. *Required:* interview, high school diploma or equivalent. *Recommended:* essay or personal statement. *Application deadlines:* rolling (freshmen), rolling (transfers).

Freshman Application Contact Mr. Jonathan Morris, Vice President of Admissions and Marketing, International Academy of Design & Technology, 5104 Eisenhower Boulevard, Tampa, FL 33634-7350. *Phone:* 813-227-4161. *Toll-free phone:* 800-ACADEMY. *Fax:* 813-881-0008. *E-mail:* admissions@academy.edu.

ITT TECHNICAL INSTITUTE

Fort Lauderdale, Florida www.itt-tech.edu/

- **Proprietary** primarily 2-year, founded 1991, part of ITT Educational Services, Inc
- **Suburban** campus with easy access to Miami
- **Coed**
- **Minimally difficult** entrance level

Academics *Calendar:* quarters. *Degrees:* associate and bachelor's.

Standardized Tests *Required:* Wonderlic aptitude test (for admission).

Applying *Options:* deferred entrance. *Application fee:* $100. *Required:* high school transcript, interview. *Recommended:* letters of recommendation.

Freshman Application Contact Ms. Lori Glaser, Director of Recruitment, ITT Technical Institute, 3401 South University Drive, Fort Lauderdale, FL 33328. *Phone:* 954-476-9300. *Toll-free phone:* 800-488-7797.

ITT TECHNICAL INSTITUTE

Jacksonville, Florida www.itt-tech.edu/

- **Proprietary** primarily 2-year, founded 1991, part of ITT Educational Services, Inc
- **Urban** 1-acre campus
- **Coed**
- **Minimally difficult** entrance level

Academics *Calendar:* quarters. *Degrees:* associate and bachelor's.

Standardized Tests *Required:* Wonderlic aptitude test (for admission).

Financial Aid Of all full-time matriculated undergraduates who enrolled in 2006, 5 Federal Work-Study jobs.

Applying *Options:* deferred entrance. *Application fee:* $100. *Required:* high school transcript, interview. *Recommended:* letters of recommendation.

Freshman Application Contact Mr. Jorge Torres, Director of Recruitment, ITT Technical Institute, 6600-10 Youngerman Circle, Jacksonville, FL 32244. *Phone:* 904-573-9100. *Toll-free phone:* 800-318-1264.

ITT TECHNICAL INSTITUTE

Lake Mary, Florida www.itt-tech.edu/

- **Proprietary** primarily 2-year, founded 1989, part of ITT Educational Services, Inc
- **Suburban** 1-acre campus with easy access to Orlando
- **Coed**
- **Minimally difficult** entrance level

Academics *Calendar:* quarters. *Degrees:* associate and bachelor's.

Standardized Tests *Required:* Wonderlic aptitude test (for admission).

Applying *Options:* deferred entrance. *Application fee:* $100. *Required:* high school transcript, interview. *Recommended:* letters of recommendation.

Freshman Application Contact Gabe Garces, Director of Recruitment, ITT Technical Institute, 1400 International Pkwy South, Lake Mary, FL 32746. *Phone:* 407-660-2900. *Toll-free phone:* 866-489-8441. *Fax:* 407-660-2566.

ITT TECHNICAL INSTITUTE

Miami, Florida www.itt-tech.edu/

- **Proprietary** primarily 2-year, founded 1996, part of ITT Educational Services, Inc
- **Coed**
- **Minimally difficult** entrance level

Academics *Calendar:* quarters. *Degrees:* associate and bachelor's.

Standardized Tests *Required:* Wonderlic aptitude test (for admission).

Applying *Options:* deferred entrance. *Application fee:* $100. *Required:* high school transcript, interview. *Recommended:* letters of recommendation.

Freshman Application Contact Mr. Alan Arellano, Director of Recruitment, ITT Technical Institute, 7955 NW 12th Street, Suite 119, Miami, FL 33126. *Phone:* 305-477-3080.

ITT TECHNICAL INSTITUTE

Tampa, Florida www.itt-tech.edu/

- **Proprietary** primarily 2-year, founded 1981, part of ITT Educational Services, Inc
- **Suburban** campus with easy access to St. Petersburg
- **Coed**
- **Minimally difficult** entrance level

Academics *Calendar:* quarters. *Degrees:* associate and bachelor's.

Standardized Tests *Required:* Wonderlic aptitude test (for admission).

Applying *Options:* deferred entrance. *Application fee:* $100. *Required:* high school transcript, interview. *Recommended:* letters of recommendation.

Freshman Application Contact Mr. Joseph E. Rostkowski, Director of Recruitment, ITT Technical Institute, 4809 Memorial Highway, Tampa, FL 33634. *Phone:* 813-885-2244. *Toll-free phone:* 800-825-2831.

JACKSONVILLE UNIVERSITY

Jacksonville, Florida www.ju.edu/

- **Independent** comprehensive, founded 1934
- **Suburban** 198-acre campus
- **Coed** 2,982 undergraduate students, 72% full-time, 59% women, 41% men
- **Moderately difficult** entrance level, 40% of applicants were admitted

Undergraduates 2,156 full-time, 826 part-time. Students come from 47 states and territories, 50 other countries, 38% are from out of state, 21% African American, 2% Asian American or Pacific Islander, 5% Hispanic American, 0.6% Native American, 2% international, 16% transferred in, 57% live on campus. *Retention:* 65% of 2006 full-time freshmen returned.

Freshmen *Admission:* 6,236 applied, 2,513 admitted, 586 enrolled. *Average high school GPA:* 3.18. *Test scores:* SAT critical reading scores over 500: 49%; SAT math scores over 500: 53%; ACT scores over 18: 86%; SAT critical reading

scores over 600: 16%; SAT math scores over 600: 18%; ACT scores over 24: 20%; SAT critical reading scores over 700: 2%; SAT math scores over 700: 2%; ACT scores over 30: 2%.

Faculty *Total:* 230, 64% full-time, 64% with terminal degrees. *Student/faculty ratio:* 14:1.

Majors Accounting; airline pilot and flight crew; art; art history, criticism and conservation; aviation/airway management; biology/biological sciences; business administration and management; business/commerce; chemistry; communication/speech communication and rhetoric; computer and information sciences; dance; design and visual communications; drama and dance teacher education; dramatic/theater arts; economics; electrical, electronics and communications engineering; elementary education; engineering physics; English; environmental studies; finance; fine/studio arts; French; geography; history; humanities; interdisciplinary studies; international business/trade/commerce; international relations and affairs; kinesiology and exercise science; liberal arts and sciences/liberal studies; management information systems; marine science/merchant marine officer; marketing/marketing management; mathematics; mechanical engineering; music; music management and merchandising; music performance; music teacher education; music theory and composition; nursing (registered nurse training); philosophy; physical education teaching and coaching; physics; political science and government; pre-dentistry studies; pre-law studies; pre-medical studies; pre-veterinary studies; psychology; secondary education; sociology; Spanish; special education; visual and performing arts; voice and opera.

Academics *Calendar:* semesters. *Degrees:* certificates, bachelor's, master's, and first professional certificates. *Special study options:* academic remediation for entering students, accelerated degree program, adult/continuing education programs, advanced placement credit, cooperative education, distance learning, double majors, honors programs, independent study, internships, off-campus study, part-time degree program, services for LD students, student-designed majors, study abroad, summer session for credit. *ROTC:* Navy (b). *Unusual degree programs:* 3-2 engineering with University of Florida, Georgia Institute of Technology, Columbia University, University of Miami, Stevens Institute of Technology, Washington University in St. Louis, Mercer University.

Computers on Campus 450 computers/terminals are available on campus for general student use. Students can access the following: online (class) registration. Campuswide network is available.

Student Life *Housing options:* coed, men-only, women-only, disabled students. Campus housing is university owned. Freshman campus housing is guaranteed. *Activities and organizations:* drama/theater group, student-run newspaper, radio and television station, choral group, Student Government Association, Baptist Campus Ministry, national fraternities, national sororities. *Campus security:* 24-hour emergency response devices and patrols, student patrols, late-night transport/escort service, controlled dormitory access, code lock doors in residence halls, trained security patrols during evening hours. *Student services:* health clinic, personal/psychological counseling.

Athletics Member NCAA. All Division I except football (Division I-AA). *Intercollegiate sports:* baseball M (s), basketball M (s)/W (s), crew M (s)/W (s), cross-country running M/W (s), golf M (s)/W (s), soccer M (s)/W (s), softball W (s), tennis M (s)/W (s), track and field W (s), volleyball W (s). *Intramural sports:* basketball M/W, bowling M/W, cross-country running M/W, football M/W, golf M/W, racquetball M/W, soccer M, softball M/W, swimming and diving M/W, table tennis M/W, tennis M/W, track and field M, volleyball M/W.

Standardized Tests *Required:* SAT or ACT (for admission).

Costs (2008–09) *Comprehensive fee:* $32,660 includes full-time tuition ($23,900) and room and board ($8760). Part-time tuition: $795 per credit hour. *College room only:* $5000.

Financial Aid Of all full-time matriculated undergraduates who enrolled in 2005, 1,511 applied for aid, 1,241 were judged to have need, 340 had their need fully met. 250 Federal Work-Study jobs (averaging $2000). In 2005, 284 non-need-based awards were made. *Average percent of need met:* 82%. *Average financial aid package:* $16,571. *Average need-based loan:* $3963. *Average need-based gift aid:* $5331. *Average non-need-based aid:* $5066. *Average indebtedness upon graduation:* $21,483. *Financial aid deadline:* 3/15.

Applying *Options:* electronic application, early admission, early action, deferred entrance. *Application fee:* $30. *Required:* high school transcript, minimum 2.0 GPA. *Required for some:* essay or personal statement. *Recommended:* letters of recommendation, interview. *Application deadlines:* rolling (freshmen), rolling (transfers), 12/1 (early action). *Notification:* 12/15 (early action).

Freshman Application Contact Ms. Lisa Hannasch, Director of First-Year Student Admission and Enrollment, Jacksonville University, 2800 University Boulevard North, Office of Admissions, Jacksonville, FL 32211. *Phone:* 904-256-7000. *Toll-free phone:* 800-225-2027. *Fax:* 904-256-7012. *E-mail:* admissions@ju.edu.

See page 662 for the College Close-Up.

JOHNSON & WALES UNIVERSITY

North Miami, Florida — www.jwu.edu/

- **Independent** 4-year, founded 1992, administratively affiliated with Johnson & Wales University (RI)
- **Suburban** 8-acre campus with easy access to Miami
- **Coed**
- **Minimally difficult** entrance level

Faculty *Student/faculty ratio:* 28:1.

Academics *Calendar:* quarters. *Degrees:* associate and bachelor's.

Student Life *Campus security:* 24-hour emergency response devices and patrols,,video camera surveillance throughout campus.

Athletics Member NAIA.

Standardized Tests *Required for some:* SAT or ACT (for admission). *Recommended:* SAT or ACT (for admission).

Costs (2008–09) *Comprehensive fee:* $30,541 includes full-time tuition ($21,297), mandatory fees ($1288), and room and board ($7956). Part-time tuition: $394 per quarter hour.

Financial Aid Of all full-time matriculated undergraduates who enrolled in 2005, 1,990 applied for aid, 1,885 were judged to have need, 44 had their need fully met. In 2005, 231 non-need-based awards were made. *Average percent of need met:* 65. *Average financial aid package:* $14,240. *Average need-based loan:* $6249. *Average need-based gift aid:* $6290. *Average non-need-based aid:* $5098. *Average indebtedness upon graduation:* $18,633.

Applying *Options:* early admission, deferred entrance. *Required:* high school transcript. *Required for some:* essay or personal statement, letters of recommendation, interview. *Recommended:* minimum 2.0 GPA.

Freshman Application Contact Mr. Jeff Greenip, Director of Admissions, Johnson & Wales University, 1701 Northeast 127th Street, North Miami, FL 33181. *Phone:* 305-892-7002. *Toll-free phone:* 800-232-2433. *Fax:* 305-892-7020. *E-mail:* admissions.mia@jwu.edu.

JONES COLLEGE

Jacksonville, Florida — www.jones.edu/

- **Independent** 4-year, founded 1918, part of Jones College, Miami Florida
- **Urban** 5-acre campus
- **Coed** 647 undergraduate students, 42% full-time, 79% women, 21% men
- **Noncompetitive** entrance level

Undergraduates 270 full-time, 377 part-time. Students come from 31 states and territories, 3 other countries, 18% are from out of state, 8% transferred in. *Retention:* 55% of 2006 full-time freshmen returned.

Freshmen *Admission:* 21 admitted, 21 enrolled.

Faculty *Total:* 246, 74% full-time, 80% with terminal degrees. *Student/faculty ratio:* 12:1.

Majors Interdisciplinary studies.

Academics *Calendar:* trimesters. *Degrees:* diplomas, associate, and bachelor's. *Special study options:* academic remediation for entering students, accelerated degree program, adult/continuing education programs, advanced placement credit, cooperative education, distance learning, double majors, internships, part-time degree program, student-designed majors, summer session for credit.

Computers on Campus 80 computers/terminals are available on campus for general student use. Students can access the following: campus intranet, computer help desk, free student e-mail accounts, online (class) registration. Campuswide network is available. Wireless service is available via classrooms, computer centers, computer labs, libraries.

Student Life *Housing:* college housing not available. *Campus security:* late-night transport/escort service.

Costs (2008–09) *Tuition:* $6600 full-time, $275 per credit hour part-time. *Required fees:* $90 full-time, $45 per term part-time.

Applying *Required:* interview. *Required for some:* high school transcript. *Application deadline:* rolling (freshmen). *Notification:* continuous (transfers).

Freshman Application Contact Jones College, 5355 Arlington Expressway, Jacksonville, FL 32211-5588. *Phone:* 904-743-1122 Ext. 141.

JONES COLLEGE

Miami, Florida **www.jones.edu/**

- **Independent** 4-year, founded 1987, part of Jones College, Jacksonville, Florida
- **Suburban** campus
- **Coed** 650 undergraduate students, 42% full-time, 79% women, 21% men

Undergraduates 270 full-time, 380 part-time. Students come from 31 states and territories, 3 other countries, 18% are from out of state, 58% African American, 1% Asian American or Pacific Islander, 15% Hispanic American, 0.3% Native American, 0.5% international, 8% transferred in. *Retention:* 55% of 2006 full-time freshmen returned.

Freshmen *Admission:* 21 admitted, 21 enrolled.

Faculty *Total:* 246, 74% full-time, 80% with terminal degrees. *Student/faculty ratio:* 12:1.

Majors Business administration and management; clinical/medical laboratory assistant; computer and information sciences; health services/allied health/health sciences; interdisciplinary studies; legal assistant/paralegal.

Academics *Calendar:* trimesters. *Degrees:* associate and bachelor's.

Computers on Campus Students can access the following: campus intranet, computer help desk, free student e-mail accounts, online (class) schedules. Campuswide network is available. Wireless service is available via classrooms, computer centers, computer labs, libraries.

Student Life *Housing:* college housing not available.

Standardized Tests *Required for some:* CPAt.

Costs (2008–09) *Tuition:* $6600 full-time, $275 per credit hour part-time. *Required fees:* $90 full-time, $45 per term part-time.

Applying *Required:* interview. *Required for some:* high school transcript.

Director of Admissions Frank McCafferty, Director of Admissions, Jones College, 11430 North Kendall Drive, Suite 200, Miami, FL 33176. *Phone:* 904-743-1122 Ext. 141. *E-mail:* lvaughn@jones.edu.

KEISER UNIVERSITY

Fort Lauderdale, Florida **www.keiseruniversity.edu/**

- **Proprietary** comprehensive, founded 1977
- **Urban** campus with easy access to Miami
- **Coed**
- **Minimally difficult** entrance level, 54% of applicants were admitted

Undergraduates 26% African American, 2% Asian American or Pacific Islander, 23% Hispanic American, 0.5% Native American, 1% international.

Freshmen *Admission:* 5,394 applied, 2,895 admitted.

Faculty *Total:* 826, 41% full-time. *Student/faculty ratio:* 11:1.

Majors Accounting; animation, interactive technology, video graphics and special effects; athletic training/sports medicine; baking and pastry arts; biotechnology; business administration and management; CAD/CADD drafting/design technology; clinical/medical laboratory assistant; computer graphics; computer programming; criminalistics and criminal science; criminal justice/law enforcement administration; culinary arts; diagnostic medical sonography and ultrasound technology; elementary education; fashion/apparel design; fashion merchandising; finance; fire science; health science; health services administration; histologic technician; human resources management; information technology; international business/trade/commerce; legal assistant/paralegal; legal studies; management information systems; management science; massage therapy; medical/clinical assistant; medical radiologic technology; nuclear medical technology; nursing (registered nurse training); occupational therapist assistant; physical therapist assistant; surgical technology.

Academics *Calendar:* 3 semesters per year. *Degrees:* associate, bachelor's, and master's (profile includes data from Daytona Beach, Melbourne, Sarasota, Tallahassee, Jacksonville, Orlando, Miami, Tampa, West Palm Beach, St. Petersburg, Port St. Lucie, Miami Lakes, Pembroke Pines, Greenacres and Lakeland campuses; all programs not offered at all locations). *Special study options:* adult/continuing education programs.

Computers on Campus Campuswide network is available.

Student Life *Housing:* college housing not available. *Activities and organizations:* Phi Beta Lambda, national fraternities. *Campus security:* 24-hour emergency response devices. *Student services:* personal/psychological counseling.

Standardized Tests *Required:* SAT, ACT, or Otis-Lennon School Ability Test (for admission).

Costs (2007–08) *Tuition:* tuition varies by program. Contact institution.

Applying *Application fee:* $50. *Required:* high school transcript. *Application deadlines:* rolling (freshmen), rolling (transfers). *Notification:* continuous (freshmen), continuous (transfers).

Freshman Application Contact Keiser University, 1900 West Commercial Boulevard, Fort Lauderdale, FL 33309. *Phone:* 954-776-4476. *Toll-free phone:* 800-749-4456.

See page 664 for the College Close-Up.

LYNN UNIVERSITY

Boca Raton, Florida **www.lynn.edu/**

- **Independent** comprehensive, founded 1962, administratively affiliated with American College Dublin
- **Suburban** 123-acre campus with easy access to Fort Lauderdale
- **Endowment** $13.9 million
- **Coed**
- **Moderately difficult** entrance level

Conveniently located near Miami, Fort Lauderdale, and West Palm Beach, Lynn University stresses individualized learning based on the discovery and development of individual potential and learning styles. Lynn enrolls more than 2,600 students representing forty-six states and ninety-four nations.

Faculty *Student/faculty ratio:* 17:1.

Academics *Calendar:* semesters plus 3 summer sessions. *Degrees:* certificates, bachelor's, master's, doctoral, post-master's, and postbachelor's certificates.

Student Life *Campus security:* 24-hour patrols, late-night transport/escort service, video monitor at residence entrances.

Athletics Member NCAA. All Division II.

Standardized Tests *Required:* SAT or ACT (for admission).

Costs (2007–08) *Comprehensive fee:* $38,500 includes full-time tuition ($27,350), mandatory fees ($1500), and room and board ($9650). Part-time tuition: $760 per credit hour.

Financial Aid Of all full-time matriculated undergraduates who enrolled in 2004, 734 applied for aid, 614 were judged to have need, 71 had their need fully met. 175 Federal Work-Study jobs (averaging $1119). 39 state and other part-time jobs (averaging $5432). In 2004, 482 non-need-based awards were made. *Average percent of need met:* 55. *Average financial aid package:* $16,051. *Average need-based loan:* $4304. *Average need-based gift aid:* $12,320. *Average non-need-based aid:* $12,527. *Average indebtedness upon graduation:* $15,154.

Applying *Options:* electronic application, early admission, deferred entrance. *Application fee:* $35. *Required:* essay or personal statement, high school transcript, minimum 2.5 GPA, letters of recommendation, SAT 850 or ACT 18. *Recommended:* essay or personal statement, minimum 3.0 GPA, interview.

Freshman Application Contact Dr. Brett Ormandy, Director of Admissions, Lynn University, 3601 North Military Trail, Boca Raton, FL 33431-5598. *Phone:* 561-237-7836. *Toll-free phone:* 800-888-LYNN (in-state); 800-888-5966 (out-of-state). *Fax:* 561-237-7100. *E-mail:* bormandy@lynn.edu.

See page 666 for the College Close-Up.

MIAMI DADE COLLEGE

Miami, Florida **www.mdc.edu/**

- **State and locally supported** primarily 2-year, founded 1960, part of Florida Community College System
- **Urban** campus
- **Endowment** $110.0 million
- **Coed**
- **Noncompetitive** entrance level

Faculty *Student/faculty ratio:* 26:1.

Academics *Calendar:* 16-16-6-6. *Degrees:* certificates, associate, and bachelor's.

Student Life *Campus security:* 24-hour patrols.

Athletics Member NJCAA.

Costs (2007–08) *Tuition:* state resident $1934 full-time, $64 per credit part-time; nonresident $9975 full-time, $333 per credit part-time. Full-time tuition and fees vary according to course load and degree level. Part-time tuition and fees vary according to course load and degree level. *Required fees:* $484 full-time, $16 per credit part-time.

Financial Aid Of all full-time matriculated undergraduates who enrolled in 2006, 800 Federal Work-Study jobs (averaging $5000). 125 state and other part-time jobs (averaging $5000).

Applying *Options:* electronic application, early admission. *Application fee:* $20. *Required:* high school transcript.

Freshman Application Contact Dulce Beltran, College Registrar, Miami Dade College, 11011 SW 104th Street, Miami, FL 33176. *Phone:* 305-237-2103. *Fax:* 305-237-2964. *E-mail:* dbeltran@mdc.edu.

MIAMI INTERNATIONAL UNIVERSITY OF ART & DESIGN

Miami, Florida www.artinstitutes.edu/miami

- **Proprietary** comprehensive, founded 1965, part of Education Management Corporation
- **Urban** 4-acre campus
- **Coed** 1,759 undergraduate students, 100% full-time, 63% women, 37% men
- **Moderately difficult** entrance level

Undergraduates 1,759 full-time. Students come from 32 states and territories, 51 other countries, 7% African American, 1% Asian American or Pacific Islander, 38% Hispanic American, 0.3% Native American, 0.2% international, 4% transferred in, 10% live on campus. *Retention:* 87% of 2006 full-time freshmen returned.

Freshmen *Admission:* 912 applied, 511 enrolled. *Average high school GPA:* 2.7.

Faculty *Total:* 110, 41% full-time, 38% with terminal degrees. *Student/faculty ratio:* 20:1.

Majors Advertising; animation, interactive technology, video graphics and special effects; art; cinematography and film/video production; commercial and advertising art; computer graphics; fashion/apparel design; fashion merchandising; graphic design; interior design; metal and jewelry arts; visual and performing arts.

Academics *Calendar:* quarters. *Degrees:* associate, bachelor's, and master's. *Special study options:* academic remediation for entering students, distance learning, English as a second language, internships, services for LD students, summer session for credit.

Computers on Campus 350 computers/terminals are available on campus for general student use. Students can access the following: campus intranet, computer help desk, free student e-mail accounts, online (class) grades, online (class) registration, online (class) schedules.

Student Life *Housing options:* coed. Campus housing is leased by the school. Freshman campus housing is guaranteed. *Campus security:* 24-hour emergency response devices, student patrols, late-night transport/escort service, controlled dormitory access, security service. *Student services:* personal/psychological counseling.

Athletics *Intramural sports:* cross-country running M (c)/W (c), soccer M (c)/W (c), volleyball M (c)/W (c).

Costs (2007–08) *Tuition:* $28,032 full-time, $438 per credit part-time. tuition cost varies by program. Prospective students should contact the school for current tuition costs. Other charges include a starting kit for all first-quarter students. Kits vary in price depending on the program of study. *Room only:* $6150.

Applying *Options:* electronic application, deferred entrance. *Application fee:* $50. *Required:* essay or personal statement, high school transcript, minimum 2.0 GPA, interview, 2 photographs, art portfolio. *Recommended:* 2 letters of recommendation. *Application deadlines:* rolling (freshmen), rolling (transfers). *Notification:* continuous (freshmen), continuous (transfers).

Freshman Application Contact Miami International University of Art & Design, 1501 Biscayne Boulevard, Suite 100, Miami, FL 33132. *Phone:* 305-428-5700. *Toll-free phone:* 800-225-9023.

See page 668 for the College Close-Up.

NEW COLLEGE OF FLORIDA

Sarasota, Florida www.ncf.edu/

- **State-supported** 4-year, founded 1960, part of State University System of Florida
- **Suburban** 144-acre campus with easy access to Tampa–St. Petersburg
- **Coed** 767 undergraduate students, 100% full-time, 61% women, 39% men
- **Very difficult** entrance level, 57% of applicants were admitted

Undergraduates 767 full-time. Students come from 38 states and territories, 21 other countries, 23% are from out of state, 2% African American, 2% Asian American or Pacific Islander, 9% Hispanic American, 0.4% Native American, 0.7% international, 4% transferred in, 72% live on campus. *Retention:* 87% of 2006 full-time freshmen returned.

Freshmen *Admission:* 1,029 applied, 587 admitted, 202 enrolled. *Average high school GPA:* 3.94. *Test scores:* SAT critical reading scores over 500: 100%; SAT math scores over 500: 98%; ACT scores over 18: 100%; SAT critical reading scores over 600: 92%; SAT math scores over 600: 66%; ACT scores over 24: 97%; SAT critical reading scores over 700: 51%; SAT math scores over 700: 15%; ACT scores over 30: 33%.

Faculty *Total:* 85, 81% full-time, 94% with terminal degrees. *Student/faculty ratio:* 10:1.

Majors Anthropology; art history, criticism and conservation; biology/biological sciences; chemistry; classics and classical languages related; comparative literature; economics; English; environmental studies; fine/studio arts; foreign languages and literatures; French; French studies; general studies; German; Germanic languages; history; humanities; international/global studies; liberal arts and sciences/liberal studies; marine biology and biological oceanography; mathematics; medieval and Renaissance studies; music; music history, literature, and theory; natural sciences; neurobiology and neurophysiology; philosophy; physics; political science and government; psychology; public policy analysis; religious studies; Russian; social sciences; sociology; Spanish; urban studies/affairs.

Academics *Calendar:* 4-1-4. *Degree:* bachelor's. *Special study options:* double majors, honors programs, independent study, internships, off-campus study, services for LD students, student-designed majors, study abroad.

Computers on Campus 41 computers/terminals are available on campus for general student use. Students can access the following: campus intranet, computer help desk, free student e-mail accounts, online (class) registration. Campuswide network is available. 100% of college-owned or -operated housing units are wired for high-speed Internet access. Wireless service is available via classrooms, libraries, student centers.

Student Life *Housing:* on-campus residence required through senior year. *Options:* coed, disabled students. Campus housing is university owned. Freshman campus housing is guaranteed. *Activities and organizations:* drama/theater group, student-run newspaper, radio station, choral group, Nice Random Acts of Kindness, Interfaith groups, New College Student Alliance, Feminist Majority Leadership Alliance, Sailing Club. *Campus security:* 24-hour emergency response devices and patrols, late-night transport/escort service. *Student services:* health clinic, personal/psychological counseling, women's center.

Standardized Tests *Required:* SAT or ACT (for admission).

Costs (2007–08) *Tuition:* state resident $3772 full-time; nonresident $21,625 full-time. *Room and board:* $7035; room only: $4586.

Financial Aid Of all full-time matriculated undergraduates who enrolled in 2007, 441 applied for aid, 292 were judged to have need, 225 had their need fully met. 17 Federal Work-Study jobs (averaging $1773). 54 state and other part-time jobs (averaging $2951). In 2007, 415 non-need-based awards were made. *Average percent of need met:* 96%. *Average financial aid package:* $12,116. *Average need-based loan:* $3535. *Average need-based gift aid:* $8169. *Average non-need-based aid:* $3314. *Average indebtedness upon graduation:* $11,720.

Applying *Options:* electronic application, early admission, deferred entrance. *Application fee:* $30. *Required:* essay or personal statement, high school transcript, 1 letter of recommendation. *Recommended:* minimum 3.0 GPA, analytical paper. *Application deadlines:* 4/15 (freshmen), 4/15 (transfers). *Notification:* 4/25 (freshmen), 4/25 (transfers).

Freshman Application Contact Office of Admissions, New College of Florida, 5800 Bay Shore Road, Sarasota, FL 34243-2109. *Phone:* 941-487-5000. *Fax:* 941-487-5010. *E-mail:* admissions@ncf.edu.

See page 670 for the College Close-Up.

NEW WORLD SCHOOL OF THE ARTS

Miami, Florida www.mdc.edu/nwsa

- **State-supported** 4-year, founded 1984, administratively affiliated with Miami Dade College and University of Florida
- **Urban** 5-acre campus
- **Endowment** $5.5 million
- **Coed** 416 undergraduate students, 100% full-time, 58% women, 42% men
- **Noncompetitive** entrance level, 52% of applicants were admitted

Undergraduates 416 full-time. Students come from 13 states and territories, 6% are from out of state, 12% African American, 3% Asian American or Pacific Islander, 53% Hispanic American. *Retention:* 80% of 2006 full-time freshmen returned.

Freshmen *Admission:* 384 applied, 200 admitted, 147 enrolled. *Average high school GPA:* 2.8.

Faculty *Total:* 77, 29% full-time. *Student/faculty ratio:* 5:1.

Majors Acting; dance; dramatic/theater arts; music performance.

Academics *Calendar:* semesters. *Degrees:* associate and bachelor's. *Special study options:* academic remediation for entering students, advanced placement credit, cooperative education, distance learning, double majors, English as a second language, freshman honors college, services for LD students, study abroad, summer session for credit.

Computers on Campus 100 computers/terminals are available on campus for general student use. Students can access the following: campus intranet, computer help desk, free student e-mail accounts, online (class) grades, online (class) registration. Campuswide network is available.

Student Life *Housing:* college housing not available. *Activities and organizations:* student government. *Campus security:* 24-hour patrols. *Student services:* personal/psychological counseling.

Costs (2007–08) *Tuition:* $73 per credit part-time; state resident $3000 full-time, $244 per credit part-time; nonresident $10,000 full-time.

Applying *Required:* essay or personal statement, high school transcript, 2 letters of recommendation, interview, audition. *Application deadline:* rolling (freshmen). *Notification:* continuous until 8/1 (freshmen), continuous until 8/1 (transfers).

Freshman Application Contact Ms. Pamela Neumann, Recruitment and Admissions Coordinator, New World School of the Arts, 300 NE Second Avenue, Miami, FL 33132. *Phone:* 305-237-7007. *Fax:* 305-237-3794. *E-mail:* nwsaadm@mdc.edu.

NORTHWOOD UNIVERSITY, FLORIDA CAMPUS

West Palm Beach, Florida **www.northwood.edu/**

- **Independent** 4-year, founded 1982, administratively affiliated with Northwood University (MI)
- **Suburban** 90-acre campus with easy access to Miami
- **Endowment** $31.1 million
- **Coed** 675 undergraduate students, 97% full-time, 38% women, 62% men
- **Moderately difficult** entrance level, 59% of applicants were admitted

Undergraduates 652 full-time, 23 part-time. Students come from 38 states and territories, 46 other countries, 56% are from out of state, 11% African American, 1% Asian American or Pacific Islander, 10% Hispanic American, 0.1% Native American, 32% international, 18% transferred in, 38% live on campus. *Retention:* 55% of 2006 full-time freshmen returned.

Freshmen *Admission:* 811 applied, 479 admitted, 142 enrolled. *Average high school GPA:* 2.91. *Test scores:* SAT critical reading scores over 500: 22%; SAT math scores over 500: 31%; SAT writing scores over 500: 22%; ACT scores over 18: 75%; SAT critical reading scores over 600: 3%; SAT math scores over 600: 4%; SAT writing scores over 600: 1%; ACT scores over 24: 5%; ACT scores over 30: 1%.

Faculty *Total:* 60, 30% full-time, 15% with terminal degrees. *Student/faculty ratio:* 21:1.

Majors Accounting; advertising; banking and financial support services; business administration and management; computer and information sciences; computer management; hotel/motel administration; international business/trade/commerce; management information systems; marketing/marketing management; sport and fitness administration/management; vehicle and vehicle parts and accessories marketing.

Academics *Calendar:* quarters. *Degree:* bachelor's. *Special study options:* academic remediation for entering students, accelerated degree program, adult/continuing education programs, advanced placement credit, distance learning, double majors, external degree program, honors programs, independent study, internships, off-campus study, part-time degree program, study abroad, summer session for credit.

Computers on Campus 89 computers/terminals are available on campus for general student use. Students can access the following: campus intranet, computer help desk, free student e-mail accounts, online (class) grades, online (class) registration, online (class) schedules. Campuswide network is available. 100% of college-owned or -operated housing units are wired for high-speed Internet access. Wireless service is available via entire campus.

Student Life *Housing:* on-campus residence required for freshman year. *Options:* men-only, women-only, disabled students. Campus housing is university owned. Freshman campus housing is guaranteed. *Activities and organizations:* drama/theater group, student-run newspaper, Student Government Association, International Club, Auto Show. *Campus security:* 24-hour emergency response devices and patrols, student patrols, late-night transport/escort service. *Student services:* health clinic, personal/psychological counseling.

Athletics Member NAIA. *Intercollegiate sports:* baseball M (s), basketball M/W, golf M (s)/W (s), soccer M (s)/W (s), softball W (s), tennis M (s)/W (s), volleyball W (s). *Intramural sports:* basketball M/W, bowling M/W, football M, racquetball M/W, tennis M/W.

Standardized Tests *Required:* SAT or ACT (for admission).

Costs (2007–08) *Comprehensive fee:* $23,904 includes full-time tuition ($15,825), mandatory fees ($885), and room and board ($7194). Part-time tuition: $330 per credit hour. *College room only:* $3720.

Financial Aid Of all full-time matriculated undergraduates who enrolled in 2007, 302 applied for aid, 261 were judged to have need, 50 had their need fully met. 103 Federal Work-Study jobs (averaging $2100). In 2007, 141 non-need-based awards were made. *Average percent of need met:* 58%. *Average financial aid package:* $14,705. *Average need-based loan:* $4054. *Average need-based gift aid:* $6795. *Average non-need-based aid:* $4725. *Average indebtedness upon graduation:* $24,535.

Applying *Options:* electronic application, early admission, deferred entrance. *Application fee:* $25. *Required:* essay or personal statement, high school transcript. *Recommended:* minimum 2.0 GPA, 1 letter of recommendation, interview. *Application deadlines:* rolling (freshmen), rolling (transfers). *Notification:* continuous (freshmen), continuous (transfers).

Freshman Application Contact Mr. John (Jack) M. Letvinchuck, Director of Admissions, Northwood University, Florida Campus, 2600 North Military Trail, West Palm Beach, FL 33409-2911. *Phone:* 561-478-5500. *Toll-free phone:* 800-458-8325. *Fax:* 561-640-3328. *E-mail:* fladmit@northwood.edu.

See page 672 for the College Close-Up.

NOVA SOUTHEASTERN UNIVERSITY

Fort Lauderdale, Florida **www.nova.edu/**

- **Independent** university, founded 1964
- **Suburban** 300-acre campus
- **Endowment** $47.6 million
- **Coed** 5,635 undergraduate students, 64% full-time, 74% women, 26% men
- **Moderately difficult** entrance level, 51% of applicants were admitted

Nova Southeastern University is the nation's sixth-largest independent university, with more than 26,000 students from seventy countries and 110,000 alumni; a sprawling, 300-acre Fort Lauderdale, Florida, campus; and a presence in nine countries around the world.

Undergraduates 3,579 full-time, 2,056 part-time. 25% African American, 6% Asian American or Pacific Islander, 25% Hispanic American, 0.4% Native American, 5% international, 16% transferred in, 15% live on campus. *Retention:* 60% of 2006 full-time freshmen returned.

Freshmen *Admission:* 2,818 applied, 1,433 admitted, 518 enrolled. *Average high school GPA:* 3.44. *Test scores:* SAT critical reading scores over 500: 53%; SAT math scores over 500: 53%; SAT writing scores over 500: 46%; ACT scores over 18: 92%; SAT critical reading scores over 600: 10%; SAT math scores over 600: 9%; SAT writing scores over 600: 9%; ACT scores over 24: 22%.

Faculty *Total:* 1,616, 39% full-time, 82% with terminal degrees. *Student/faculty ratio:* 17:1.

Majors Accounting; American studies; athletic training; biology/biological sciences; business administration and management; communication/speech communication and rhetoric; computer and information sciences; computer science; dramatic/theater arts; economics; educational leadership and administration; elementary education; English; environmental studies; finance; health services/allied health/health sciences; history; humanities; international relations and affairs; legal assistant/paralegal; marine biology and biological oceanography; marketing/marketing management; nursing (registered nurse training); pre-law studies; pre-medical studies; psychology; secondary education; sport and fitness administration/management.

Academics *Calendar:* trimesters. *Degrees:* associate, bachelor's, master's, doctoral, first professional, post-master's, and first professional certificates. *Special study options:* academic remediation for entering students, accelerated degree program, adult/continuing education programs, advanced placement credit, distance learning, double majors, English as a second language, external degree program, honors programs, independent study, internships, off-campus study, part-time degree program, services for LD students, study abroad, summer session for credit. *Unusual degree programs:* 3-2 business administration; marine biology, occupational therapy, criminal justice, psychology, mental health counseling, speech language pathology, computer science, education, physical therapy.

Computers on Campus 2,548 computers/terminals are available on campus for general student use. Students can access the following: computer help desk, free student e-mail accounts, online (class) registration. Campuswide network is

available. 100% of college-owned or -operated housing units are wired for high-speed Internet access. Wireless service is available via entire campus.

Student Life *Housing options:* coed, disabled students. Campus housing is university owned. Freshman campus housing is guaranteed. *Activities and organizations:* drama/theater group, student-run newspaper, radio station, choral group, Pre-Pharmacy Society, Pre-Med Society, Kappa Sigma, Delta Phi Epsilon, PASA, national fraternities, national sororities. *Campus security:* 24-hour emergency response devices and patrols, late-night transport/escort service, controlled dormitory access, shuttle bus service. *Student services:* health clinic, personal/psychological counseling, women's center.

Athletics Member NCAA, NAIA. All NCAA Division II. *Intercollegiate sports:* baseball M (s), basketball M (s)/W (s), cheerleading W, crew W (s), cross-country running M (s)/W (s), golf M (s)/W (s), soccer M (s)/W (s), softball W (s), tennis W (s), volleyball W (s). *Intramural sports:* basketball M, cross-country running M/W, football M, golf M, soccer M/W, softball W, tennis M/W, volleyball W.

Standardized Tests *Required:* SAT or ACT (for admission).

Costs (2007–08) *Comprehensive fee:* $27,192 includes full-time tuition ($18,900), mandatory fees ($550), and room and board ($7742). Full-time tuition and fees vary according to class time and program. Part-time tuition: $630 per credit hour. Part-time tuition and fees vary according to class time, course load, and program. *Room and board:* Room and board charges vary according to board plan and housing facility. *Payment plans:* installment, deferred payment. *Waivers:* employees or children of employees.

Financial Aid Of all full-time matriculated undergraduates who enrolled in 2006, 2,913 applied for aid, 2,703 were judged to have need, 116 had their need fully met. 1,163 Federal Work-Study jobs (averaging $3068). 250 state and other part-time jobs (averaging $2950). In 2006, 390 non-need-based awards were made. *Average percent of need met:* 69%. *Average financial aid package:* $15,100. *Average need-based loan:* $5326. *Average need-based gift aid:* $6334. *Average non-need-based aid:* $3568. *Average indebtedness upon graduation:* $31,368.

Applying *Options:* electronic application, deferred entrance. *Application fee:* $50. *Required:* high school transcript. *Required for some:* essay or personal statement, 3 letters of recommendation, interview. *Recommended:* minimum 2.6 GPA. *Application deadlines:* rolling (freshmen), rolling (out-of-state freshmen), rolling (transfers). *Notification:* continuous (freshmen), continuous (out-of-state freshmen), continuous (transfers).

Freshman Application Contact Ms. Maria Dillard, Director of Enrollment Management, Nova Southeastern University, Enrollment Processing Services, 3301 College Avenue, PO Box 299000, Ft. Lauderdale, FL 33329-9905. *Phone:* 954-262-8000. *Toll-free phone:* 800-541-NOVA. *Fax:* 954-262-3811. *E-mail:* nsuinfo@nova.edu.

See page 674 for the College Close-Up.

OKALOOSA-WALTON COLLEGE

Niceville, Florida **www.owc.edu/**

Freshman Application Contact Ms. Christine Bishop, Registrar/Division Director Enrollment Services, Okaloosa-Walton College, 100 College Boulevard, Niceville, FL 32578. *Phone:* 850-729-5373. *Fax:* 850-729-5323. *E-mail:* registrar@owc.edu.

PALM BEACH ATLANTIC UNIVERSITY

West Palm Beach, Florida **www.pba.edu/**

- **Independent nondenominational** comprehensive, founded 1968
- **Urban** 25-acre campus with easy access to Miami
- **Endowment** $61.5 million
- **Coed** 2,508 undergraduate students, 91% full-time, 62% women, 38% men
- **Moderately difficult** entrance level, 78% of applicants were admitted

The Warren Library is the fifth new structure to be built on Palm Beach Atlantic University's West Palm Beach campus since 2000. The $25.4-million building, which was designed by Leo A. Daly, has seating for 650 library patrons, 120 computers, twenty-eight study rooms, and space for 350,000 books.

Undergraduates 2,272 full-time, 236 part-time. Students come from 51 states and territories, 46 other countries, 22% are from out of state, 15% African American, 2% Asian American or Pacific Islander, 10% Hispanic American, 0.5% Native American, 2% international, 17% transferred in, 53% live on campus. *Retention:* 70% of 2006 full-time freshmen returned.

Freshmen *Admission:* 1,240 applied, 966 admitted, 453 enrolled. *Average high school GPA:* 3.56. *Test scores:* SAT critical reading scores over 500: 75%; SAT math scores over 500: 72%; ACT scores over 18: 99%; SAT critical reading scores over 600: 25%; SAT math scores over 600: 23%; ACT scores over 24: 44%; SAT critical reading scores over 700: 3%; SAT math scores over 700: 1%; ACT scores over 30: 3%.

Faculty *Total:* 347, 48% full-time, 50% with terminal degrees. *Student/faculty ratio:* 15:1.

Majors Accounting and finance; acting; art teacher education; biblical studies; biology/biological sciences; broadcast journalism; business administration and management; business administration, management and operations related; communication/speech communication and rhetoric; computer and information sciences; dance; dramatic/theater arts; education; elementary education; engineering; English; entrepreneurship; fine/studio arts; graphic design; history; human resources management; international business/trade/commerce; journalism; marketing/marketing management; mathematics; music; music performance; music teacher education; music theory and composition; nursing (registered nurse training); organizational communication; philosophy; physical education teaching and coaching; piano and organ; playwriting and screenwriting; political science and government; pre-law studies; psychology; radio and television; religious/sacred music; religious studies; secondary education; theological and ministerial studies related; voice and opera; wind/percussion instruments.

Academics *Calendar:* semesters. *Degrees:* associate, bachelor's, master's, and first professional. *Special study options:* academic remediation for entering students, accelerated degree program, adult/continuing education programs, advanced placement credit, distance learning, double majors, freshman honors college, honors programs, independent study, internships, part-time degree program, student-designed majors, study abroad, summer session for credit.

Computers on Campus 460 computers/terminals and 495 ports are available on campus for general student use. Students can access the following: campus intranet, computer help desk, free student e-mail accounts, online (class) grades, online (class) registration, online (class) schedules. Campuswide network is available. 100% of college-owned or -operated housing units are wired for high-speed Internet access. Wireless service is available via classrooms, computer centers, computer labs, dorm rooms, learning centers, libraries, student centers.

Student Life *Housing:* on-campus residence required through sophomore year. *Options:* coed, men-only, women-only. Campus housing is university owned. Freshman applicants given priority for college housing. *Activities and organizations:* drama/theater group, student-run newspaper, radio and television station, choral group, Christian Pharmacist Fellowship International, Caribbean Fellowship Club, Science Club, Psychology Club, Student Government. *Campus security:* 24-hour emergency response devices and patrols, late-night transport/escort service, controlled dormitory access. *Student services:* health clinic, personal/psychological counseling.

Athletics Member NCAA, NCCAA. All NCAA Division II. *Intercollegiate sports:* baseball M (s), basketball M (s)/W (s), cross-country running M (s)/W (s), soccer M (s)/W (s), softball W (s), tennis M (s)/W (s), volleyball W (s). *Intramural sports:* basketball M/W, bowling M/W, cheerleading M (c)/W (c), golf M/W, lacrosse M (c), racquetball M/W, soccer M/W, table tennis M/W, ultimate Frisbee M/W, volleyball M/W.

Standardized Tests *Required:* SAT or ACT (for admission). *Required for some:* SAT and SAT Subject Tests or ACT (for admission), SAT Subject Tests (for admission).

Costs (2007–08) *Comprehensive fee:* $28,296 includes full-time tuition ($19,950), mandatory fees ($260), and room and board ($8086). Full-time tuition and fees vary according to course load, degree level, location, program, and reciprocity agreements. Part-time tuition: $485 per credit. Part-time tuition and fees vary according to course load, degree level, location, program, and reciprocity agreements. *Required fees:* $95 per term part-time. *College room only:* $4270. Room and board charges vary according to board plan and housing facility. *Payment plan:* installment. *Waivers:* employees or children of employees.

Financial Aid Of all full-time matriculated undergraduates who enrolled in 2005, 1,976 applied for aid, 856 were judged to have need, 528 had their need fully met. 267 Federal Work-Study jobs (averaging $2027). In 2005, 345 non-need-based awards were made. *Average percent of need met:* 32%. *Average financial aid package:* $2448. *Average need-based loan:* $3213. *Average need-based gift aid:* $2145. *Average non-need-based aid:* $1846. *Average indebtedness upon graduation:* $12,883. *Financial aid deadline:* 8/1.

Applying *Options:* electronic application, early admission, early action, deferred entrance. *Application fee:* $30. *Required:* essay or personal statement, high school transcript, minimum 2.0 GPA, 2 letters of recommendation, interview. *Recommended:* minimum 3.0 GPA. *Application deadlines:* rolling (freshmen), 12/1 (early action). *Notification:* continuous (freshmen), 12/15 (early action).

Freshman Application Contact Mr. Rod Sullivan, Vice President of Enrollment Services, Palm Beach Atlantic University, PO Box 24708, West Palm Beach,

FL 33416-4708. *Phone:* 561-803-2102. *Toll-free phone:* 800-238-3998. *Fax:* 561-803-2115. *E-mail:* admit@pba.edu.

See page 676 for the College Close-Up.

POLYTECHNIC UNIVERSITY OF THE AMERICAS–MIAMI CAMPUS

Miami, Florida **www.pupr.edu/miami/**

Director of Admissions Ernesto Castro, Admissions Department, Polytechnic University of the Americas–Miami Campus, 8180 NW 36th Street, Suite 401, Miami, FL 33166. *Phone:* 305-418-4220 Ext. 206. *Toll-free phone:* 888-729-7659. *Fax:* 305-418-4325. *E-mail:* ecastro@pupr.edu.

POLYTECHNIC UNIVERSITY OF THE AMERICAS–ORLANDO CAMPUS

Winter Park, Florida **www.pupr.edu/orlando/**

Director of Admissions Office of Admissions, Polytechnic University of the Americas–Orlando Campus, 4800 Howell Branch Road, Winter Park, FL 32792. *Phone:* 407-677-5661. *Fax:* 407-677-5082.

RASMUSSEN COLLEGE PASCO COUNTY

Holiday, Florida **www.rasmussen.edu/**

Director of Admissions Ms. Claire L. Walker, Senior Admissions Representative, Rasmussen College Pasco County, 2127 Grand Boulevard, Holiday, FL 34690. *Phone:* 727-942-0069. *Toll-free phone:* 888-729-7247.

REMINGTON COLLEGE–LARGO CAMPUS

Largo, Florida **www.remingtoncollege.edu/**

- **Proprietary** primarily 2-year
- **Suburban** campus

Majors Computer systems networking and telecommunications; criminal justice/law enforcement administration; operations management.

Academics *Calendar:* continuous. *Degrees:* diplomas, associate, and bachelor's.

Director of Admissions Kathy McCabe, Director of Recruitment, Remington College–Largo Campus, 8550 Ulmerton Road, Largo, FL 33771. *Phone:* 727-532-1999. *Toll-free phone:* 888-900-2343. *Fax:* 727-530-7710. *E-mail:* kathy.mccabe@remingtoncollege.edu.

REMINGTON COLLEGE–TAMPA CAMPUS

Tampa, Florida **www.remingtoncollege.edu/**

- **Proprietary** primarily 2-year, founded 1948
- **Urban** 10-acre campus

Majors Business administration and management; computer systems networking and telecommunications; criminal justice/law enforcement administration; electrical, electronics and communications engineering; operations management.

Academics *Calendar:* quarters. *Degrees:* diplomas, associate, and bachelor's. *Special study options:* academic remediation for entering students, accelerated degree program, internships.

Student Life *Campus security:* late-night transport/escort service.

Financial Aid Of all full-time matriculated undergraduates who enrolled in 2006, 12 Federal Work-Study jobs (averaging $8000).

Freshman Application Contact Remington College–Tampa Campus, 2410 East Busch Boulevard, Tampa, FL 33612. *Phone:* 813-932-0701. *Toll-free phone:* 800-992-4850.

RINGLING COLLEGE OF ART AND DESIGN

Sarasota, Florida **www.ringling.edu/**

- **Independent** 4-year, founded 1931
- **Small-town** 34-acre campus with easy access to Tampa–St. Petersburg
- **Endowment** $20.2 million
- **Coed** 1,199 undergraduate students, 96% full-time, 54% women, 46% men
- **Moderately difficult** entrance level, 73% of applicants were admitted

Undergraduates 1,149 full-time, 50 part-time. Students come from 44 states and territories, 31 other countries, 51% are from out of state, 3% African American, 6% Asian American or Pacific Islander, 11% Hispanic American, 0.8% Native American, 5% international, 9% transferred in, 53% live on campus. *Retention:* 81% of 2006 full-time freshmen returned.

Freshmen *Admission:* 949 applied, 695 admitted, 292 enrolled. *Average high school GPA:* 3.05.

Faculty *Total:* 136, 52% full-time, 49% with terminal degrees. *Student/faculty ratio:* 13:1.

Majors Animation, interactive technology, video graphics and special effects; film/video and photographic arts related; fine/studio arts; graphic design; illustration; interior design; photography.

Academics *Calendar:* semesters. *Degree:* bachelor's. *Special study options:* academic remediation for entering students, advanced placement credit, independent study, internships, off-campus study, part-time degree program, services for LD students, study abroad.

Computers on Campus 640 computers/terminals are available on campus for general student use. Students can access the following: campus intranet, computer help desk, free student e-mail accounts, online (class) grades, online (class) registration, online (class) schedules, central file storage, high performance computing labs. Campuswide network is available. 100% of college-owned or -operated housing units are wired for high-speed Internet access. Wireless service is available via entire campus.

Student Life *Housing options:* coed, men-only, women-only, disabled students. Campus housing is university owned. Freshman applicants given priority for college housing. *Activities and organizations:* drama/theater group, FEWS, Campus Activities Board, Phi Delta Theta, Sigma Sigma Sigma, Ringling Ambassadors, national fraternities, national sororities. *Campus security:* 24-hour emergency response devices and patrols, late-night transport/escort service, controlled dormitory access, lighted campus. *Student services:* personal/psychological counseling.

Athletics *Intramural sports:* basketball M/W, softball M/W, weight lifting M/W.

Costs (2007–08) *Comprehensive fee:* $34,725 includes full-time tuition ($24,100), mandatory fees ($625), and room and board ($10,000). Full-time tuition and fees vary according to course load, program, and student level. Part-time tuition: $1135 per credit hour. Part-time tuition and fees vary according to course load, program, and student level. *College room only:* $5500. Room and board charges vary according to board plan and housing facility. *Payment plan:* installment. *Waivers:* employees or children of employees.

Financial Aid Of all full-time matriculated undergraduates who enrolled in 2007, 787 applied for aid, 697 were judged to have need, 95 had their need fully met. 207 Federal Work-Study jobs (averaging $1896). In 2007, 125 non-need-based awards were made. *Average percent of need met:* 52%. *Average financial aid package:* $17,477. *Average need-based loan:* $11,896. *Average need-based gift aid:* $7126. *Average non-need-based aid:* $15,183. *Average indebtedness upon graduation:* $48,820.

Applying *Options:* electronic application, deferred entrance. *Application fee:* $40. *Required:* essay or personal statement, high school transcript, minimum 2.0 GPA, 2 letters of recommendation, portfolio, resume. *Recommended:* interview. *Application deadlines:* rolling (freshmen), rolling (transfers). *Notification:* continuous (freshmen), continuous (transfers).

Freshman Application Contact Ms. Amy Fischer, Associate Dean of Admissions, Ringling College of Art and Design, 2700 North Tamiami Trail, Sarasota, FL 34234-5895. *Phone:* 941-309-5034. *Toll-free phone:* 800-255-7695. *Fax:* 941-359-7517. *E-mail:* admissions@ringling.edu.

ROLLINS COLLEGE

Winter Park, Florida www.rollins.edu/

- **Independent** comprehensive, founded 1885
- **Suburban** 70-acre campus with easy access to Orlando
- **Endowment** $372.8 million
- **Coed** 1,778 undergraduate students, 100% full-time, 58% women, 42% men
- **Very difficult** entrance level, 58% of applicants were admitted

Undergraduates 1,778 full-time. Students come from 42 states and territories, 34 other countries, 47% are from out of state, 4% African American, 4% Asian American or Pacific Islander, 10% Hispanic American, 0.4% Native American, 4% international, 3% transferred in, 70% live on campus. *Retention:* 84% of 2006 full-time freshmen returned.

Freshmen *Admission:* 2,900 applied, 1,678 admitted, 525 enrolled. *Average high school GPA:* 3.4. *Test scores:* SAT critical reading scores over 500: 93%; SAT math scores over 500: 91%; ACT scores over 18: 99%; SAT critical reading scores over 600: 49%; SAT math scores over 600: 49%; ACT scores over 24: 68%; SAT critical reading scores over 700: 9%; SAT math scores over 700: 10%; ACT scores over 30: 12%.

Faculty *Total:* 237, 81% full-time, 84% with terminal degrees. *Student/faculty ratio:* 10:1.

Majors Anthropology; art history, criticism and conservation; biochemistry; biology/biological sciences; chemistry; classics and languages, literatures and linguistics; computer science; dramatic/theater arts; economics; education; English; environmental studies; European studies; fine/studio arts; French; history; international business/trade/commerce; international relations and affairs; Latin American studies; marine biology; mathematics; music; philosophy; physics; political science and government; pre-dentistry studies; pre-law studies; pre-medical studies; psychology; religious studies; sociology; Spanish.

Academics *Calendar:* semesters. *Degrees:* bachelor's and master's. *Special study options:* academic remediation for entering students, accelerated degree program, adult/continuing education programs, advanced placement credit, double majors, honors programs, independent study, internships, off-campus study, part-time degree program, services for LD students, student-designed majors, study abroad. *Unusual degree programs:* 3-2 business administration with Crummer Graduate School of Business, Rollins College; engineering with Washington University in St. Louis, Columbia University, Auburn University; forestry with Duke University; medical technology, environmental management with Duke University.

Computers on Campus 240 computers/terminals and 155 ports are available on campus for general student use. Students can access the following: campus intranet, computer help desk, free student e-mail accounts, online (class) grades, online (class) registration, online (class) schedules. Campuswide network is available. 100% of college-owned or -operated housing units are wired for high-speed Internet access. Wireless service is available via entire campus.

Student Life *Housing:* on-campus residence required through sophomore year. *Options:* coed, men-only, women-only, disabled students. Campus housing is university owned. Freshman campus housing is guaranteed. *Activities and organizations:* drama/theater group, student-run newspaper, radio and television station, choral group, IFC (Interfraternity Conference), Panhellenic Conference, Student Government Association, CAC (Cultural Action Committee), ACE (All Campus Events), national fraternities, national sororities. *Campus security:* 24-hour emergency response devices and patrols, late-night transport/escort service, controlled dormitory access. *Student services:* health clinic, personal/psychological counseling.

Athletics Member NCAA. All Division II. *Intercollegiate sports:* baseball M (s), basketball M (s)/W (s), crew M/W, cross-country running M/W, golf M (s)/W (s), lacrosse M/W, sailing M/W, soccer M (s)/W (s), softball W (s), swimming and diving M/W, tennis M (s)/W (s), volleyball W (s). *Intramural sports:* basketball M/W, bowling M/W, cheerleading W (c), football M/W, ice hockey M (c), soccer M/W, softball M/W, table tennis M/W, tennis M/W, ultimate Frisbee M (c)/W (c), volleyball M/W.

Standardized Tests *Required for some:* SAT or ACT (for admission).

Costs (2007–08) *Comprehensive fee:* $42,840 includes full-time tuition ($32,640) and room and board ($10,200). *College room only:* $6000. *Payment plan:* installment. *Waivers:* employees or children of employees.

Financial Aid Of all full-time matriculated undergraduates who enrolled in 2007, 824 applied for aid, 726 were judged to have need, 77 had their need fully met. In 2007, 243 non-need-based awards were made. *Average percent of need met:* 87%. *Average financial aid package:* $30,003. *Average need-based loan:* $4442. *Average need-based gift aid:* $25,439. *Average non-need-based aid:* $13,667. *Average indebtedness upon graduation:* $23,298. *Financial aid deadline:* 3/1.

Applying *Options:* electronic application, early admission, early decision, early action, deferred entrance. *Application fee:* $40. *Required:* essay or personal statement, high school transcript, 1 letter of recommendation. *Recommended:* minimum 2.0 GPA, interview. *Application deadlines:* 2/15 (freshmen), 4/15 (transfers). *Early decision deadline:* 11/15. *Notification:* 4/1 (freshmen), continuous (transfers), 12/15 (early decision).

Freshman Application Contact Mr. David Erdmann, Dean of Admission and Enrollment, Rollins College, 1000 Holt Avenue, Box 2720, Winter Park, FL 32789-4499. *Phone:* 407-646-2161. *Fax:* 407-646-1502. *E-mail:* admission@rollins.edu.

See page 678 for the College Close-Up.

ST. JOHN VIANNEY COLLEGE SEMINARY

Miami, Florida www.sjvcs.edu/

Freshman Application Contact Br. Edward Van Merrienboer, Academic Dean, St. John Vianney College Seminary, 2900 Southwest 87th Avenue, Miami, FL 33165-3244. *Phone:* 305-223-4561 Ext. 13.

SAINT LEO UNIVERSITY

Saint Leo, Florida www.saintleo.edu/

- **Independent Roman Catholic** comprehensive, founded 1889
- **Rural** 186-acre campus with easy access to Tampa and Orlando
- **Endowment** $14.5 million
- **Coed** 1,589 undergraduate students, 95% full-time, 54% women, 46% men
- **Moderately difficult** entrance level, 71% of applicants were admitted

Undergraduates 1,516 full-time, 73 part-time. Students come from 39 states and territories, 37 other countries, 37% are from out of state, 9% African American, 1% Asian American or Pacific Islander, 10% Hispanic American, 0.8% Native American, 10% international, 6% transferred in, 71% live on campus. *Retention:* 69% of 2006 full-time freshmen returned.

Freshmen *Admission:* 2,188 applied, 1,548 admitted, 456 enrolled. *Average high school GPA:* 3.2. *Test scores:* SAT critical reading scores over 500: 47%; SAT math scores over 500: 52%; SAT writing scores over 500: 40%; ACT scores over 18: 93%; SAT critical reading scores over 600: 7%; SAT math scores over 600: 9%; SAT writing scores over 600: 9%; ACT scores over 24: 24%; SAT critical reading scores over 700: 1%; SAT math scores over 700: 1%; SAT writing scores over 700: 1%; ACT scores over 30: 1%.

Faculty *Total:* 139, 63% full-time, 62% with terminal degrees. *Student/faculty ratio:* 15:1.

Majors Accounting; biology/biological sciences; business administration and management; business/commerce; clinical laboratory science/medical technology; communication and media related; community organization and advocacy; criminal justice/safety; elementary education; English; entrepreneurial and small business related; environmental science; history; hospital and health care facilities administration; hospitality administration; human resources management; international relations and affairs; liberal arts and sciences/liberal studies; management information systems; marketing/marketing management; mathematics; middle school education; political science and government; psychology; social work; sociology; sport and fitness administration/management; theology.

Academics *Calendar:* semesters. *Degrees:* associate, bachelor's, master's, and postbachelor's certificates. *Special study options:* academic remediation for entering students, adult/continuing education programs, advanced placement credit, distance learning, double majors, honors programs, independent study, internships, part-time degree program, services for LD students, study abroad, summer session for credit. *ROTC:* Army (c), Air Force (c).

Computers on Campus 1,243 computers/terminals are available on campus for general student use. Students can access the following: campus intranet, computer help desk, free student e-mail accounts, online (class) grades, online (class) registration, online (class) schedules. Campuswide network is available. 100% of college-owned or -operated housing units are wired for high-speed Internet access. Wireless service is available via classrooms, computer centers, computer labs, dorm rooms, learning centers, libraries, student centers.

Student Life *Housing:* on-campus residence required through junior year. *Options:* coed, men-only, women-only, disabled students. Campus housing is university owned. Freshman applicants given priority for college housing. *Activities and organizations:* drama/theater group, student-run newspaper, radio and television station, choral group, Student Government Union, Circle K, Samaritans, American Marketing Association, Campus Activities Board, national fraternities, national sororities. *Campus security:* 24-hour emergency response devices and patrols, late-night transport/escort service, controlled dormitory access. *Student services:* health clinic, personal/psychological counseling.

Athletics Member NCAA. All Division II. *Intercollegiate sports:* baseball M (s), basketball M (s)/W (s), cheerleading M (c)/W (c), cross-country running M (s)/W (s), golf M (s)/W (s), lacrosse M (s), soccer M (s)/W (s), softball W (s), swimming and diving M (s)/W (s), tennis M (s)/W (s), volleyball W (s). *Intramural sports:* basketball M/W, football M/W, golf M/W, racquetball M/W, soccer M/W, softball M/W, table tennis M/W, tennis M/W, ultimate Frisbee M/W, volleyball M/W.

Standardized Tests *Required:* SAT or ACT (for admission).

Costs (2008–09) *Comprehensive fee:* $25,580 includes full-time tuition ($16,500), mandatory fees ($650), and room and board ($8430). *College room only:* $4450.

Financial Aid Of all full-time matriculated undergraduates who enrolled in 2007, 1,260 applied for aid, 1,001 were judged to have need, 469 had their need fully met. 656 Federal Work-Study jobs (averaging $3190). In 2007, 43 non-need-based awards were made. *Average percent of need met:* 87%. *Average financial aid package:* $17,826. *Average need-based loan:* $5027. *Average need-based gift aid:* $10,641. *Average non-need-based aid:* $6375. *Average indebtedness upon graduation:* $20,638.

Applying *Options:* electronic application, early admission, deferred entrance. *Application fee:* $35. *Required:* essay or personal statement, high school transcript, minimum 2.3 GPA, 1 letter of recommendation, minimum SAT score of 900 or ACT score of 19. *Required for some:* interview. *Recommended:* minimum 3.0 GPA, interview. *Application deadlines:* 8/15 (freshmen), 8/1 (transfers). *Notification:* continuous (freshmen), continuous (transfers).

Freshman Application Contact Mr. Martin Smith, Assistant Vice President for Enrollment, Saint Leo University, MC 2008, PO Box 6665, Saint Leo, FL 33574-6665. *Phone:* 352-588-8283. *Toll-free phone:* 800-334-5532. *Fax:* 352-588-8257. *E-mail:* admissions@saintleo.edu.

See page 680 for the College Close-Up.

ST. PETERSBURG COLLEGE

St. Petersburg, Florida **www.spjc.edu/**

Freshman Application Contact Mr. Martyn Clay, Admissions Director/Registrar, St. Petersburg College, PO Box 13489, St. Petersburg, FL 33733-3489. *Phone:* 727-712-5892. *Fax:* 727-712-5872. *E-mail:* information@spcollege.edu.

ST. PETERSBURG THEOLOGICAL SEMINARY

St. Petersburg, Florida **www.sptseminary.edu/**

Application Contact Ms. Carol Cagwin, Director of Admissions, St. Petersburg Theological Seminary, 10830 Navajo Drive, St. Petersburg, FL 33708. *Phone:* 727-399-0276. *Fax:* 727-399-1324. *E-mail:* c.cagwin@sptseminary.edu.

ST. THOMAS UNIVERSITY

Miami Gardens, Florida **www.stu.edu/**

- **Independent Roman Catholic** comprehensive, founded 1961
- **Suburban** 140-acre campus
- **Endowment** $9.1 million
- **Coed** 1,150 undergraduate students, 95% full-time, 57% women, 43% men
- **Moderately difficult** entrance level, 65% of applicants were admitted

Undergraduates 1,087 full-time, 63 part-time. Students come from 25 states and territories, 58 other countries, 11% are from out of state, 27% African American, 1% Asian American or Pacific Islander, 47% Hispanic American, 0.1% Native American, 9% international, 11% transferred in, 19% live on campus. *Retention:* 65% of 2006 full-time freshmen returned.

Freshmen *Admission:* 610 applied, 399 admitted, 226 enrolled. *Average high school GPA:* 2.92. *Test scores:* SAT critical reading scores over 500: 24%; SAT math scores over 500: 20%; SAT writing scores over 500: 20%; ACT scores over 18: 56%; SAT critical reading scores over 600: 2%; SAT math scores over 600: 1%; SAT writing scores over 600: 1%; ACT scores over 24: 7%; SAT critical reading scores over 700: 1%; ACT scores over 30: 1%.

Faculty *Total:* 195, 51% full-time, 59% with terminal degrees.

Majors Accounting; biology/biological sciences; business administration and management; chemistry; computer science; criminal justice/law enforcement administration; elementary education; English; finance; history; hotel/motel administration; information science/studies; international business/trade/commerce; liberal arts and sciences/liberal studies; marketing/marketing management; mass communication/media; pastoral studies/counseling; political science and government; pre-dentistry studies; pre-law studies; pre-medical studies; psychology; public administration; religious studies; secondary education; sociology; sport and fitness administration/management; tourism and travel services management.

Academics *Calendar:* semesters. *Degrees:* bachelor's, master's, doctoral, first professional, post-master's, and postbachelor's certificates. *Special study options:* academic remediation for entering students, adult/continuing education programs, advanced placement credit, distance learning, double majors, freshman honors college, honors programs, independent study, part-time degree program, services for LD students, summer session for credit. *ROTC:* Army (c), Air Force (c).

Computers on Campus 60 computers/terminals are available on campus for general student use. Campuswide network is available.

Student Life *Housing options:* men-only, women-only. *Activities and organizations:* student-run television station, choral group, International Student Organization, Pre-Med Club, Hispanic Heritage Club, Inter-Dorm Council, Communicators Club. *Campus security:* 24-hour emergency response devices and patrols, late-night transport/escort service, controlled dormitory access. *Student services:* health clinic, personal/psychological counseling.

Athletics Member NAIA. *Intercollegiate sports:* baseball M (s), cross-country running M (s)/W (s), golf M (s)/W (s), soccer M (s)/W (s), softball W (s), tennis M (s)/W (s), volleyball W (s). *Intramural sports:* baseball M, basketball M/W, cross-country running M/W, football M, golf M, soccer M/W, softball M/W, table tennis M/W, tennis M/W, volleyball M/W, water polo M/W, weight lifting M/W.

Standardized Tests *Required:* SAT or ACT (for admission).

Costs (2007–08) *Comprehensive fee:* $25,886 includes full-time tuition ($19,680) and room and board ($6206). Full-time tuition and fees vary according to program. Part-time tuition: $395 per credit. *Room and board:* Room and board charges vary according to board plan and housing facility. *Payment plan:* installment. *Waivers:* minority students, children of alumni, and employees or children of employees.

Financial Aid Of all full-time matriculated undergraduates who enrolled in 2006, 930 applied for aid, 757 were judged to have need, 222 had their need fully met. In 2006, 158 non-need-based awards were made. *Average need-based loan:* $3506. *Average need-based gift aid:* $1823. *Average non-need-based aid:* $6292. *Average indebtedness upon graduation:* $17,000.

Applying *Options:* electronic application, deferred entrance. *Application fee:* $40. *Required:* high school transcript, minimum 2.0 GPA. *Recommended:* essay or personal statement, 1 letter of recommendation, interview. *Application deadlines:* rolling (freshmen), rolling (transfers). *Notification:* continuous (freshmen), continuous (transfers).

Freshman Application Contact Mr. Andre Lightbourne, Director of Admissions, St. Thomas University, 1540 Northwest 32nd Avenue, Miami, FL 33054-6459. *Phone:* 305-628-6712. *Toll-free phone:* 800-367-9010. *Fax:* 305-628-6591. *E-mail:* signup@stu.edu.

See page 682 for the College Close-Up.

SCHILLER INTERNATIONAL UNIVERSITY

Largo, Florida **www.schiller.edu/**

- **Independent** comprehensive, founded 1991, part of Schiller International University
- **Suburban** 4-acre campus with easy access to Tampa
- **Coed** 106 undergraduate students
- **Minimally difficult** entrance level, 79% of applicants were admitted

Schiller International University (SIU) is an independent American university with campuses in England, France, Germany, Spain, Switzerland, and the United States. Students can transfer from campus to campus without loss of credit. English is the language of instruction at all campuses. SIU offers undergraduate and graduate students an American education in an international setting.

Undergraduates Students come from 11 states and territories, 50 other countries, 68% are from out of state, 85% live on campus. *Retention:* 75% of 2006 full-time freshmen returned.

Freshmen *Admission:* 127 applied, 100 admitted.

Faculty *Total:* 47, 4% full-time. *Student/faculty ratio:* 10:1.

Majors Hotel/motel administration; interdisciplinary studies; international business/trade/commerce; international relations and affairs; liberal arts and sciences/liberal studies; marketing/marketing management; tourism and travel services management.

Academics *Calendar:* semesters. *Degrees:* diplomas, associate, bachelor's, and master's. *Special study options:* accelerated degree program, adult/continuing education programs, advanced placement credit, distance learning, English as a second language, internships, part-time degree program, student-designed majors, study abroad, summer session for credit. *Unusual degree programs:* international business, international hotel and hospitality management, management of information technology, interdepartmental studies, international relations and diplomacy.

Computers on Campus 42 computers/terminals are available on campus for general student use. Students can access the following: computer help desk, free student e-mail accounts, online (class) schedules. Campuswide network is available. Wireless service is available via entire campus.

Student Life *Housing options:* coed. Campus housing is provided by a third party. Freshman applicants given priority for college housing. *Activities and organizations:* student-run newspaper, student government, student newspaper, Model United Nations, International Food Festival. *Campus security:* night patrols. *Student services:* personal/psychological counseling.

Athletics *Intramural sports:* baseball M, basketball M/W, sailing M/W, soccer M/W, softball M/W, swimming and diving M/W, volleyball M/W.

Costs (2007–08) *Tuition:* $17,530 full-time. Full-time tuition and fees vary according to degree level, location, and reciprocity agreements. Part-time tuition and fees vary according to degree level and location. *Room only:* $3800. Room and board charges vary according to housing facility and location. *Payment plan:* deferred payment.

Applying *Options:* deferred entrance. *Application fee:* $65. *Required:* essay or personal statement, high school transcript. *Recommended:* minimum 2.0 GPA. *Application deadlines:* rolling (freshmen), rolling (transfers).

Freshman Application Contact Ms. Stephanie Givens, Associate Director of Admissions, Schiller International University, 300 East Bay Drive, Largo, FL 33770. *Phone:* 877-748-4338. *Toll-free phone:* 800-336-4133. *Fax:* 727-734-0436. *E-mail:* admissions@schiller.edu.

See page 684 for the College Close-Up.

SOUTHEASTERN UNIVERSITY

Lakeland, Florida **www.seuniversity.edu/**

- **Independent** 4-year, founded 1935, affiliated with Assemblies of God
- **Suburban** 62-acre campus with easy access to Tampa and Orlando
- **Endowment** $4.8 million
- **Coed** 2,931 undergraduate students, 86% full-time, 58% women, 42% men
- **Minimally difficult** entrance level, 78% of applicants were admitted

Undergraduates 2,522 full-time, 409 part-time. Students come from 48 states and territories, 40 other countries, 37% are from out of state, 7% African American, 1% Asian American or Pacific Islander, 11% Hispanic American, 0.2% Native American, 0.1% international, 7% transferred in, 52% live on campus. *Retention:* 64% of 2006 full-time freshmen returned.

Freshmen *Admission:* 1,232 applied, 966 admitted, 567 enrolled. *Average high school GPA:* 3.45. *Test scores:* SAT critical reading scores over 500: 48%; SAT math scores over 500: 57%; SAT writing scores over 500: 54%; ACT scores over 18: 77%; SAT critical reading scores over 600: 16%; SAT math scores over 600: 23%; SAT writing scores over 600: 20%; ACT scores over 24: 25%; SAT critical reading scores over 700: 1%; SAT math scores over 700: 8%; SAT writing scores over 700: 5%; ACT scores over 30: 3%.

Faculty *Total:* 130, 56% full-time, 45% with terminal degrees. *Student/faculty ratio:* 24:1.

Majors Accounting; biblical studies; biology/biological sciences; biology teacher education; broadcast journalism; business administration and management; communication/speech communication and rhetoric; criminal justice/law enforcement administration; dramatic/theater arts; early childhood education; education; elementary education; English; English language and literature related; English/language arts teacher education; finance; history; international business/trade/commerce; journalism; management information systems; marketing/marketing management; mathematics; mathematics teacher education; missionary studies and missiology; music; music performance; music related; music teacher education; pastoral studies/counseling; piano and organ; pre-medical studies; pre-theology/pre-ministerial studies; psychology; radio and television; science teacher education; social science teacher education; social work; special education; theology and religious vocations related; voice and opera; youth ministry.

Academics *Calendar:* semesters. *Degrees:* diplomas, bachelor's, and master's. *Special study options:* accelerated degree program, adult/continuing education programs, advanced placement credit, internships, part-time degree program, summer session for credit. *ROTC:* Army (c), Air Force (c).

Computers on Campus 40 computers/terminals are available on campus for general student use. Students can access the following: campus intranet, computer help desk, free student e-mail accounts, online (class) grades, online (class) registration, online (class) schedules, network programs. Campuswide network is available. 100% of college-owned or -operated housing units are wired for high-speed Internet access. Wireless service is available via classrooms, computer centers, computer labs, learning centers, libraries, student centers.

Student Life *Housing:* on-campus residence required through senior year. *Options:* men-only, women-only. Campus housing is university owned. Freshman campus housing is guaranteed. *Activities and organizations:* drama/theater group, student-run newspaper, radio and television station, choral group, Spanish Club, Traveling Music Groups, Impact (cross-cultural awareness), Psyche, Student Broadcast Organization. *Campus security:* 24-hour emergency response devices and patrols, late-night transport/escort service. *Student services:* health clinic, personal/psychological counseling.

Athletics Member NCCAA. *Intercollegiate sports:* baseball M, basketball M/W, cheerleading M/W, golf M, soccer M/W, tennis W, volleyball W. *Intramural sports:* basketball M/W, football M/W, soccer M/W, softball M/W, ultimate Frisbee M/W, volleyball M/W.

Standardized Tests *Required:* SAT or ACT (for admission).

Costs (2008–09) *Comprehensive fee:* $21,470 includes full-time tuition ($13,960), mandatory fees ($510), and room and board ($7000).

Financial Aid Of all full-time matriculated undergraduates who enrolled in 2005, 1,841 applied for aid, 1,490 were judged to have need, 165 had their need fully met. 85 Federal Work-Study jobs (averaging $1545). In 2005, 548 non-need-based awards were made. *Average percent of need met:* 52%. *Average financial aid package:* $7079. *Average need-based loan:* $2981. *Average need-based gift aid:* $4966. *Average non-need-based aid:* $9333. *Average indebtedness upon graduation:* $21,569.

Applying *Options:* electronic application, early admission, deferred entrance. *Application fee:* $40. *Required:* essay or personal statement, high school transcript, 2 letters of recommendation. *Required for some:* interview. *Application deadlines:* 5/1 (freshmen), 5/1 (transfers). *Notification:* continuous until 8/1 (freshmen), continuous until 8/1 (transfers).

Freshman Application Contact Mr. Omar Rashed, Executive Director, Enrollment Management, Southeastern University, 1000 Longfellow Boulevard, Lakeland, FL 33801. *Phone:* 863-667-5000. *Toll-free phone:* 800-500-8760. *Fax:* 863-667-5200. *E-mail:* admission@seuniversity.edu.

SOUTH UNIVERSITY

Tampa, Florida **www.southuniversity.edu/**

- **Proprietary** 4-year, administratively affiliated with South University
- **Urban** campus
- **Coed**

Majors Business administration and management; health/health care administration; health science; nursing science; psychology.

Academics *Degree:* bachelor's

Freshman Application Contact Admissions, South University, 4401 North Himes Avenue, Suite 175, Tampa, FL 33614. *Toll-free phone:* 800-688-0932. *Fax:* 813-393-3814.

See page 686 for the College Close-Up.

SOUTH UNIVERSITY

West Palm Beach, Florida **www.southuniversity.edu/**

- **Proprietary** comprehensive, founded 1899, part of Education Management Corporation
- **Suburban** 1-acre campus with easy access to Miami
- **Coed**

Majors Business administration and management; criminal justice; graphic design; health/health care administration; health services/allied health/health sciences; information technology; legal studies; nursing (registered nurse training).

Academics *Calendar:* quarters. *Degrees:* associate, bachelor's, and master's.

Freshman Application Contact Admissions, South University, 1760 North Congress Avenue, West Palm Beach, FL 33409. *Toll-free phone:* 866-688-0932. *Fax:* 561-697-9944.

See page 688 for the College Close-Up.

SOUTHWEST FLORIDA COLLEGE

Fort Myers, Florida **www.swfc.edu/**

Freshman Application Contact Ms. Carmen King, Director of Admissions, Southwest Florida College, 1685 Medical Lane, Fort Myers, FL 33907. *Phone:* 239-939-4766. *Toll-free phone:* 866-SWFC-NOW. *Fax:* 239-936-4040.

STETSON UNIVERSITY

DeLand, Florida **www.stetson.edu/**

- **Independent** comprehensive, founded 1883
- **Small-town** 170-acre campus with easy access to Orlando
- **Endowment** $137.6 million
- **Coed** 2,264 undergraduate students, 96% full-time, 59% women, 41% men
- **Moderately difficult** entrance level, 64% of applicants were admitted

Undergraduates 2,176 full-time, 88 part-time. Students come from 43 states and territories, 37 other countries, 19% are from out of state, 5% African American, 2% Asian American or Pacific Islander, 9% Hispanic American, 0.4% Native American, 3% international, 3% transferred in, 72% live on campus. *Retention:* 81% of 2006 full-time freshmen returned.

Freshmen *Admission:* 2,948 applied, 1,897 admitted, 558 enrolled. *Average high school GPA:* 3.70. *Test scores:* SAT critical reading scores over 500: 75%; SAT math scores over 500: 68%; SAT writing scores over 500: 67%; ACT scores over 18: 94%; SAT critical reading scores over 600: 30%; SAT math scores over 600: 22%; SAT writing scores over 600: 22%; ACT scores over 24: 48%; SAT critical reading scores over 700: 7%; SAT math scores over 700: 3%; SAT writing scores over 700: 2%; ACT scores over 30: 6%.

Faculty *Total:* 360, 66% full-time, 82% with terminal degrees. *Student/faculty ratio:* 11:1.

Majors Accounting; American studies; aquatic biology/limnology; art; biochemistry; biology/biological sciences; business administration and management; business/managerial economics; chemistry; clinical laboratory science/medical technology; communication/speech communication and rhetoric; computer science; dramatic/theater arts; e-commerce; economics; education; elementary education; English; entrepreneurial and small business related; environmental science; finance; French; geography; German; health services/allied health/health sciences; history; humanities; international business/trade/commerce; international relations and affairs; kinesiology and exercise science; Latin American studies; management information systems; management science; marketing/marketing management; mathematics; molecular biology; music; music performance; music teacher education; music theory and composition; philosophy; physics; piano and organ; political science and government; pre-dentistry studies; pre-law studies; pre-medical studies; pre-veterinary studies; psychology; religious studies; Russian studies; secondary education; social sciences; social science teacher education; sociology; Spanish; sport and fitness administration/management; violin, viola, guitar and other stringed instruments; visual and performing arts related; voice and opera; web page, digital/multimedia and information resources design.

Academics *Calendar:* semesters. *Degrees:* bachelor's, master's, first professional, post-master's, and first professional certificates. *Special study options:* accelerated degree program, adult/continuing education programs, advanced placement credit, double majors, honors programs, independent study, internships, off-campus study, part-time degree program, student-designed majors, study abroad, summer session for credit. *ROTC:* Army (c). *Unusual degree programs:* 3-2 engineering with University of Florida, University of Miami; forestry with Duke University; American University (Master of Public Administration).

Computers on Campus 450 computers/terminals are available on campus for general student use. Students can access the following: campus intranet, computer help desk, free student e-mail accounts, online (class) grades, online (class) registration, online (class) schedules. Campuswide network is available. 100% of college-owned or -operated housing units are wired for high-speed Internet access. Wireless service is available via entire campus.

Student Life *Housing:* on-campus residence required through junior year. *Options:* coed, men-only, women-only. Campus housing is university owned. Freshman campus housing is guaranteed. *Activities and organizations:* drama/theater group, student-run newspaper, radio station, choral group, Into the Streets, Multi-Cultural Student Council, Black Student Association, Best Buddies, Habitat For Humanity, national fraternities, national sororities. *Campus security:* 24-hour emergency response devices and patrols, late-night transport/escort service. *Student services:* health clinic, personal/psychological counseling, women's center.

Athletics Member NCAA. All Division I. *Intercollegiate sports:* baseball M (s), basketball M (s)/W (s), crew M/W, cross-country running M (s)/W (s), golf M (s)/W (s), soccer M (s)/W (s), softball W (s), tennis M (s)/W (s), volleyball W (s). *Intramural sports:* badminton M/W, basketball M/W, bowling M/W, football M/W, golf M/W, racquetball M/W, soccer M/W, softball M/W, swimming and diving M/W, table tennis M/W, tennis M/W, ultimate Frisbee M/W, volleyball M/W, water polo M/W.

Standardized Tests *Required:* SAT or ACT (for admission).

Costs (2008–09) *Comprehensive fee:* $38,652 includes full-time tuition ($28,456), mandatory fees ($1760), and room and board ($8436). Part-time tuition: $870 per credit hour. *College room only:* $4776.

Financial Aid Of all full-time matriculated undergraduates who enrolled in 2006, 1,345 applied for aid, 1,153 were judged to have need, 357 had their need fully met. 534 Federal Work-Study jobs (averaging $2437). 219 state and other part-time jobs (averaging $3219). In 2006, 814 non-need-based awards were made. *Average percent of need met:* 83%. *Average financial aid package:* $22,727. *Average need-based loan:* $4842. *Average need-based gift aid:* $16,231. *Average non-need-based aid:* $10,809. *Average indebtedness upon graduation:* $22,000.

Applying *Options:* electronic application, early admission, early decision, deferred entrance. *Application fee:* $40. *Required:* essay or personal statement, high school transcript, letters of recommendation. *Recommended:* interview. *Application deadlines:* 3/15 (freshmen), rolling (transfers). *Early decision deadline:* 11/1. *Notification:* 12/1 (freshmen), continuous (transfers), 11/25 (early decision).

Freshman Application Contact Ms. Deborah Thompson, Vice President for Enrollment Management and Campus Life, Stetson University, Unit 8378, Griffith Hall, DeLand, FL 32723. *Phone:* 386-822-7100. *Toll-free phone:* 800-688-0101. *Fax:* 386-822-7112. *E-mail:* admissions@stetson.edu.

TALMUDIC COLLEGE OF FLORIDA

Miami Beach, Florida **www.talmudicu.edu/**

- **Independent Jewish** comprehensive, founded 1974
- **Urban** campus with easy access to Miami
- **Men only** 30 undergraduate students, 100% full-time
- **Moderately difficult** entrance level, 80% of applicants were admitted

Undergraduates 30 full-time. Students come from 5 states and territories, 5 other countries, 95% are from out of state, 17% Hispanic American, 20% international, 83% transferred in, 99% live on campus. *Retention:* 50% of 2006 full-time freshmen returned.

Freshmen *Admission:* 10 applied, 8 admitted, 4 enrolled. *Average high school GPA:* 3.5.

Faculty *Total:* 6, 100% full-time, 100% with terminal degrees. *Student/faculty ratio:* 5:1.

Majors Biblical studies; Jewish/Judaic studies; rabbinical studies; religious education; talmudic studies.

Academics *Calendar:* semesters. *Degrees:* bachelor's, master's, and doctoral. *Special study options:* academic remediation for entering students, adult/continuing education programs, English as a second language, honors programs, independent study, part-time degree program, study abroad, summer session for credit.

Computers on Campus Campuswide network is available.

Student Life *Housing options:* men-only. Campus housing is university owned. Freshman campus housing is guaranteed. *Student services:* personal/psychological counseling.

Costs (2007–08) *Comprehensive fee:* $12,500 includes full-time tuition ($7250), mandatory fees ($250), and room and board ($5000). No tuition increase for student's term of enrollment. *College room only:* $2500. *Payment plans:* installment, deferred payment.

Financial Aid Of all full-time matriculated undergraduates who enrolled in 2002, 55 applied for aid, 49 were judged to have need, 6 had their need fully met. 12 Federal Work-Study jobs (averaging $2200). In 2002, 9 non-need-based awards were made. *Average percent of need met:* 57%. *Average financial aid package:* $7125. *Average need-based loan:* $2780. *Average non-need-based aid:* $4600. *Average indebtedness upon graduation:* $6300.

Applying *Options:* early admission, deferred entrance. *Application fee:* $250. *Required:* high school transcript, interview, placement exam. *Required for some:*

high school transcript. *Recommended:* essay or personal statement, letters of recommendation. *Application deadline:* rolling (freshmen). *Notification:* continuous (transfers).

Freshman Application Contact Peggy Loewy Wellisch, Admissions Director, Talmudic College of Florida, 1910 Alton Road, Miami Beach, FL 33139. *Phone:* 305-534-7050. *Toll-free phone:* 888-825-6834. *Fax:* 305-534-8444. *E-mail:* plw@talmudicu.edu.

TRINITY BAPTIST COLLEGE

Jacksonville, Florida **www.tbc.edu/**

- **Independent Baptist** comprehensive, founded 1974
- **Urban** 148-acre campus
- **Coed**
- **Moderately difficult** entrance level

Faculty *Student/faculty ratio:* 6:1.

Academics *Calendar:* semesters. *Degrees:* diplomas, associate, bachelor's, and master's.

Student Life *Campus security:* 24-hour emergency response devices, student patrols, controlled dormitory access, evening security.

Athletics Member NCCAA.

Standardized Tests *Required:* SAT or ACT (for admission).

Costs (2007–08) *Comprehensive fee:* $11,620 includes full-time tuition ($6410), mandatory fees ($660), and room and board ($4550). Part-time tuition: $270 per semester hour. *College room only:* $2260.

Financial Aid Of all full-time matriculated undergraduates who enrolled in 2001, 264 applied for aid, 168 were judged to have need, 37 had their need fully met. In 2001, 10 non-need-based awards were made. *Average percent of need met:* 55. *Average financial aid package:* $4458. *Average need-based loan:* $2912. *Average need-based gift aid:* $2791. *Average non-need-based aid:* $1279. *Average indebtedness upon graduation:* $6425. *Financial aid deadline:* 4/15.

Applying *Application fee:* $30. *Required:* essay or personal statement, high school transcript, minimum 2.0 GPA, 3 letters of recommendation.

Freshman Application Contact Mr. Larry Appleby, Administrative Dean, Trinity Baptist College, 800 Hammond Boulevard, Jacksonville, FL 32221. *Phone:* 904-596-2538. *Toll-free phone:* 800-786-2206. *Fax:* 904-596-2531. *E-mail:* trinity@tbc.edu.

TRINITY COLLEGE OF FLORIDA

New Port Richey, Florida **www.trinitycollege.edu/**

- **Independent nondenominational** 4-year, founded 1932
- **Small-town** 40-acre campus with easy access to Tampa
- **Endowment** $2.5 million
- **Coed** 180 undergraduate students, 66% full-time, 39% women, 61% men
- **Minimally difficult** entrance level, 69% of applicants were admitted

Undergraduates 119 full-time, 61 part-time. Students come from 8 states and territories, 1 other country, 14% are from out of state, 6% African American, 2% Asian American or Pacific Islander, 7% Hispanic American, 0.6% international, 18% transferred in, 39% live on campus. *Retention:* 58% of 2006 full-time freshmen returned.

Freshmen *Admission:* 102 applied, 70 admitted, 31 enrolled. *Average high school GPA:* 2.90. *Test scores:* SAT critical reading scores over 500: 43%; SAT math scores over 500: 28%; ACT scores over 18: 27%; SAT critical reading scores over 600: 29%; SAT math scores over 600: 14%; SAT critical reading scores over 700: 7%.

Faculty *Total:* 23, 26% full-time, 43% with terminal degrees. *Student/faculty ratio:* 14:1.

Majors Biblical studies; counseling psychology; elementary education; general studies; missionary studies and missiology; pastoral studies/counseling; pre-theology/pre-ministerial studies; theological and ministerial studies related; youth ministry.

Academics *Calendar:* semesters. *Degrees:* certificates, associate, and bachelor's. *Special study options:* academic remediation for entering students, accelerated degree program, adult/continuing education programs, advanced placement credit, cooperative education, double majors, external degree program, honors programs, independent study, internships, part-time degree program, services for LD students, student-designed majors, summer session for credit.

Computers on Campus 12 computers/terminals and 144 ports are available on campus for general student use. Students can access the following: computer help desk, free student e-mail accounts. Campuswide network is available. 100% of college-owned or -operated housing units are wired for high-speed Internet access. Wireless service is available via classrooms, computer labs, libraries, student centers.

Student Life *Housing:* on-campus residence required for freshman year. *Options:* men-only, women-only, disabled students. Campus housing is university owned and leased by the school. Freshman campus housing is guaranteed. *Activities and organizations:* drama/theater group, choral group, Great Commission Missionary Fellowship, Ex Libris CLub, Drama Team, Student Government. *Campus security:* controlled dormitory access, on-campus security personnel. *Student services:* personal/psychological counseling.

Athletics Member NCCAA. *Intercollegiate sports:* basketball M/W, cheerleading W (c), golf M/W, soccer M/W, volleyball W. *Intramural sports:* basketball M, cheerleading W (c), softball W, volleyball M/W.

Standardized Tests *Required:* SAT or ACT (for admission).

Costs (2008–09) *Comprehensive fee:* $16,490 includes full-time tuition ($9760), mandatory fees ($790), and room and board ($5940). Part-time tuition: $405 per credit hour. *Required fees:* $395 per term part-time.

Financial Aid Of all full-time matriculated undergraduates who enrolled in 2007, 117 applied for aid, 117 were judged to have need, 48 had their need fully met. 25 Federal Work-Study jobs (averaging $1800). In 2007, 10 non-need-based awards were made. *Average percent of need met:* 98%. *Average financial aid package:* $8710. *Average need-based loan:* $3659. *Average need-based gift aid:* $2970. *Average non-need-based aid:* $397. *Average indebtedness upon graduation:* $24,197.

Applying *Options:* electronic application, early admission, deferred entrance. *Application fee:* $25. *Required:* essay or personal statement, high school transcript, 3 letters of recommendation, interview. *Recommended:* minimum 2.75 GPA. *Application deadlines:* 8/8 (freshmen), 8/8 (transfers). *Notification:* continuous until 7/31 (freshmen), continuous (transfers).

Freshman Application Contact Mark A. Sawyer, Interim Director of Admissions, Trinity College of Florida, 2430 Welbilt Boulevard, New Port Richey, FL 34655. *Phone:* 727-376-6911 Ext. 309. *Toll-free phone:* 800-388-0869. *Fax:* 727-569-1410. *E-mail:* msawyer@trinitycollege.edu.

UNIVERSIDAD FLET

Miami, Florida **www.flet.edu/**

- **Independent religious** comprehensive, founded 1977
- **Urban** campus
- **Coed**

Faculty *Student/faculty ratio:* 36:1.

Academics *Degrees:* certificates, associate, bachelor's, and master's.

Costs (2008–09) *Tuition:* $1800 full-time, $100 per credit hour part-time. *Required fees:* $20 full-time, $20 per year part-time.

Applying *Options:* electronic application. *Application fee:* $20. *Required:* high school transcript.

Director of Admissions Ms. Lourdes Ramirez, Director of Admissions, Universidad FLET, 14540 SW 136th Street, Suite 202, Miami, FL 33186. *Phone:* 305-378-8700. *Toll-free phone:* 888-376-3538. *Fax:* 305-232-5832. *E-mail:* admissiones@flet.edu.

UNIVERSITY OF CENTRAL FLORIDA

Orlando, Florida **www.ucf.edu/**

- **State-supported** university, founded 1963, part of State University System of Florida
- **Suburban** 1415-acre campus
- **Endowment** $115.3 million
- **Coed** 41,320 undergraduate students, 75% full-time, 54% women, 46% men
- **Moderately difficult** entrance level, 50% of applicants were admitted

Undergraduates 31,050 full-time, 10,270 part-time. Students come from 51 states and territories, 136 other countries, 5% are from out of state, 9% African American, 5% Asian American or Pacific Islander, 13% Hispanic American, 0.4% Native American, 1% international, 11% transferred in, 21% live on campus. *Retention:* 84% of 2006 full-time freshmen returned.

Freshmen *Admission:* 26,312 applied, 13,251 admitted, 6,613 enrolled. *Average high school GPA:* 3.63. *Test scores:* SAT critical reading scores over 500: 89%; SAT math scores over 500: 93%; SAT writing scores over 500: 80%; ACT scores over 18: 100%; SAT critical reading scores over 600: 37%; SAT math scores over 600: 48%; SAT writing scores over 600: 26%; ACT scores over 24:

64%; SAT critical reading scores over 700: 5%; SAT math scores over 700: 7%; SAT writing scores over 700: 3%; ACT scores over 30: 5%.

Faculty *Total:* 1,688, 71% full-time, 67% with terminal degrees. *Student/faculty ratio:* 29:1.

Majors Accounting; actuarial science; advertising; aerospace, aeronautical and astronautical engineering; anthropology; art; art teacher education; audiology and speech-language pathology; biology/biological sciences; business administration and management; business/commerce; business/managerial economics; business teacher education; chemistry; cinematography and film/video production; civil engineering; clinical laboratory science/medical technology; computer and information sciences; computer engineering; computer technology/computer systems technology; criminal justice/safety; dramatic/theater arts; early childhood education; economics; electrical, electronic and communications engineering technology; electrical, electronics and communications engineering; elementary education; engineering technology; English; English/language arts teacher education; environmental/environmental health engineering; finance; fine/studio arts; foreign languages and literatures; foreign language teacher education; forensic science and technology; French; health/health care administration; health information/medical records administration; health science; health services/allied health/health sciences; history; hospitality administration; humanities; industrial engineering; information technology; intermedia/multimedia; journalism; legal assistant/paralegal; liberal arts and sciences/liberal studies; management information systems; marketing/marketing management; mass communication/media; mathematics; mathematics teacher education; mechanical engineering; mechanical engineering technologies related; medical microbiology and bacteriology; medical radiologic technology; music performance; music teacher education; nursing (registered nurse training); philosophy; photography; physical education teaching and coaching; physics; political science and government; psychology; public administration; radio and television; respiratory care therapy; science teacher education; social sciences; social science teacher education; social work; sociology; Spanish; special education; speech and rhetoric; statistics; trade and industrial teacher education.

Academics *Calendar:* semesters. *Degrees:* certificates, associate, bachelor's, master's, doctoral, and postbachelor's certificates. *Special study options:* adult/continuing education programs, advanced placement credit, cooperative education, distance learning, double majors, English as a second language, external degree program, freshman honors college, honors programs, internships, off-campus study, part-time degree program, services for LD students, study abroad, summer session for credit. *ROTC:* Army (b), Air Force (b). *Unusual degree programs:* 3-2 business administration; nursing; history.

Computers on Campus 3,276 computers/terminals and 200 ports are available on campus for general student use. Students can access the following: campus intranet, computer help desk, free student e-mail accounts, online (class) grades, online (class) registration, online (class) schedules. Campuswide network is available. 100% of college-owned or -operated housing units are wired for high-speed Internet access. Wireless service is available via entire campus.

Student Life *Housing options:* coed, men-only, women-only. Campus housing is university owned and is provided by a third party. Freshman applicants given priority for college housing. *Activities and organizations:* drama/theater group, student-run newspaper, radio station, choral group, marching band, student government, Hispanic American Student Association, Volunteer UCF, Pre-Professional Medical Society and Student Nurses Association, African-American Student Union, national fraternities, national sororities. *Campus security:* 24-hour emergency response devices and patrols, late-night transport/escort service, controlled dormitory access. *Student services:* health clinic, personal/psychological counseling, women's center, legal services.

Athletics Member NCAA. All Division I except football (Division I-A). *Intercollegiate sports:* baseball M (s), basketball M (s)/W (s), cheerleading M (s)/W (s), crew W, cross-country running M (s)/W (s), golf M (s)/W (s), soccer M (s)/W (s), tennis M (s)/W (s), track and field W (s), volleyball W (s). *Intramural sports:* baseball M (c), basketball M/W, bowling M (c)/W (c), crew M (c), fencing M (c)/W (c), golf M/W, ice hockey M (c)/W (c), lacrosse M (c)/W (c), racquetball M/W, rock climbing M (c)/W (c), rugby M (c)/W (c), sailing M (c)/W (c), soccer M (c)/W (c), softball M/W, table tennis M (c)/W (c), tennis M (c)/W (c), ultimate Frisbee M (c)/W (c), volleyball M (c)/W (c), water polo M (c)/W (c), weight lifting M/W, wrestling M.

Standardized Tests *Required:* SAT or ACT (for admission).

Costs (2007–08) *Tuition:* state resident $3620 full-time, $119 per credit part-time; nonresident $17,821 full-time, $592 per credit part-time. Full-time tuition and fees vary according to course load. Part-time tuition and fees vary according to course load. *Room and board:* $8164; room only: $4600. Room and board charges vary according to board plan and housing facility. *Payment plans:* tuition prepayment, deferred payment. *Waivers:* senior citizens and employees or children of employees.

Financial Aid Of all full-time matriculated undergraduates who enrolled in 2006, 17,896 applied for aid, 15,541 were judged to have need, 2,181 had their need fully met. In 2006, 857 non-need-based awards were made. *Average percent of need met:* 56%. *Average financial aid package:* $6438. *Average need-based loan:* $4370. *Average need-based gift aid:* $3437. *Average non-need-based aid:* $2075. *Average indebtedness upon graduation:* $13,373. *Financial aid deadline:* 6/30.

Applying *Options:* electronic application, early admission. *Application fee:* $30. *Required:* high school transcript, minimum 2.0 GPA. *Recommended:* essay or personal statement. *Application deadlines:* 3/1 (freshmen), 5/1 (transfers). *Notification:* continuous (freshmen), continuous (transfers).

Freshman Application Contact Dr. Gordon Chavis, Assistant Vice President, University of Central Florida, PO Box 160111, Orlando, FL 32816-0111. *Phone:* 407-823-3000. *Fax:* 407-823-5625. *E-mail:* admission@mail.ucf.edu.

See page 690 for the College Close-Up.

UNIVERSITY OF FLORIDA

Gainesville, Florida **www.ufl.edu/**

- **State-supported** university, founded 1853, part of Board of Trustees
- **Suburban** 2000-acre campus with easy access to Jacksonville
- **Endowment** $996.2 million
- **Coed** 35,189 undergraduate students, 92% full-time, 54% women, 46% men
- **Very difficult** entrance level, 42% of applicants were admitted

Undergraduates 32,470 full-time, 2,719 part-time. Students come from 52 states and territories, 139 other countries, 44% are from out of state, 10% African American, 8% Asian American or Pacific Islander, 14% Hispanic American, 0.3% Native American, 1% international, 5% transferred in, 22% live on campus. *Retention:* 95% of 2006 full-time freshmen returned.

Freshmen *Admission:* 24,126 applied, 10,158 admitted, 6,441 enrolled. *Average high school GPA:* 3.8. *Test scores:* SAT critical reading scores over 500: 92%; SAT math scores over 500: 94%; ACT scores over 18: 97%; SAT critical reading scores over 600: 63%; SAT math scores over 600: 69%; ACT scores over 24: 72%; SAT critical reading scores over 700: 16%; SAT math scores over 700: 21%; ACT scores over 30: 20%.

Faculty *Total:* 2,076, 97% full-time, 85% with terminal degrees. *Student/faculty ratio:* 22:1.

Majors Accounting; advertising; aerospace, aeronautical and astronautical engineering; agricultural and food products processing; agricultural/biological engineering and bioengineering; agricultural economics; agricultural teacher education; agronomy and crop science; American studies; animal sciences; anthropology; architecture; art history, criticism and conservation; art teacher education; Asian studies; astronomy; athletic training; audiology and speech-language pathology; biology/biological sciences; botany/plant biology; business administration and management; chemical engineering; chemistry; civil engineering; classics and languages, literatures and linguistics; community health services counseling; computer and information sciences; computer engineering; construction engineering technology; criminology; dairy science; dance; dramatic/theater arts; East Asian languages related; economics; electrical, electronics and communications engineering; elementary education; engineering science; English; entomology; environmental/environmental health engineering; environmental science; family and community services; finance; fine/studio arts; fire science; food science; forestry; French; geography; geology/earth science; German; graphic design; health services/allied health/health sciences; health teacher education; history; horticultural science; industrial engineering; insurance; interior design; intermedia/multimedia; Jewish/Judaic studies; journalism; kinesiology and exercise science; landscape architecture; linguistics; management science; marketing/marketing management; materials engineering; mathematics; mechanical engineering; medical microbiology and bacteriology; middle school education; multi-/interdisciplinary studies related; music; music teacher education; nuclear engineering; nursing (registered nurse training); ornamental horticulture; parks, recreation and leisure facilities management; philosophy; physical education teaching and coaching; physics; plant pathology/phytopathology; plant sciences; plant sciences related; political science and government; Portuguese; poultry science; psychology; public relations/image management; radio and television; real estate; religious studies; Russian; sociology; soil science and agronomy; Spanish; special education; sport and fitness administration/management; statistics; survey technology; systems engineering; wildlife and wildlands science and management; women's studies; zoology/animal biology.

Academics *Calendar:* semesters. *Degrees:* bachelor's, master's, doctoral, and first professional. *Special study options:* accelerated degree program, adult/continuing education programs, advanced placement credit, cooperative education, distance learning, double majors, English as a second language, external degree program, honors programs, independent study, internships, off-campus study, part-time degree program, services for LD students, student-designed majors, study abroad, summer session for credit. *ROTC:* Army (b), Air Force (b). *Unusual degree programs:* 3-2 business administration.

Computers on Campus 2,200 computers/terminals and 1,000 ports are available on campus for general student use. Students can access the following: campus intranet, computer help desk, free student e-mail accounts, online (class) grades, online (class) registration, online (class) schedules. Campuswide network is available. 100% of college-owned or -operated housing units are wired for high-speed Internet access. Wireless service is available via computer centers, computer labs, learning centers, libraries, student centers.

Student Life *Housing options:* coed, disabled students. Campus housing is university owned. Freshman applicants given priority for college housing. *Activities and organizations:* drama/theater group, student-run newspaper, radio and television station, choral group, marching band, VISA—Volunteers for International Student Affairs, Fellowship of Christian, Black Student Union, Hispanic Student Association, Asian American Student Union, national fraternities, national sororities. *Campus security:* 24-hour emergency response devices and patrols, student patrols, late-night transport/escort service, controlled dormitory access, crime and rape prevention programs. *Student services:* health clinic, personal/psychological counseling, women's center, legal services.

Athletics Member NCAA. All Division I except football (Division I-A). *Intercollegiate sports:* baseball M (s), basketball M (s)/W (s), cross-country running M (s)/W (s), golf M (s)/W (s), gymnastics W (s), soccer W (s), softball W (s), swimming and diving M (s)/W (s), tennis M (s)/W (s), track and field M (s)/W (s), volleyball W (s). *Intramural sports:* badminton M (c)/W (c), baseball M (c), basketball M/W, bowling M/W, cheerleading W (c), crew M (c)/W (c), equestrian sports M (c)/W (c), fencing M (c)/W (c), football M/W, golf M/W, ice hockey M (c), lacrosse M (c)/W (c), racquetball M/W, rugby M (c)/W (c), sailing M (c)/W (c), soccer M/W, softball M/W, swimming and diving M/W, table tennis M (c)/W (c), tennis M/W, track and field M/W, ultimate Frisbee M/W, volleyball M/W, water polo M (c)/W (c), weight lifting M/W, wrestling M/W.

Standardized Tests *Required:* SAT or ACT (for admission).

Costs (2007–08) *Tuition:* state resident $3257 full-time, $74 per credit hour part-time; nonresident $17,841 full-time, $537 per credit hour part-time. *Room and board:* $7020; room only: $4530. Room and board charges vary according to board plan. *Payment plans:* tuition prepayment, deferred payment. *Waivers:* senior citizens and employees or children of employees.

Financial Aid Of all full-time matriculated undergraduates who enrolled in 2006, 16,860 applied for aid, 13,059 were judged to have need, 4,745 had their need fully met. 1,185 Federal Work-Study jobs (averaging $1734). 4,208 state and other part-time jobs (averaging $1688). In 2006, 18104 non-need-based awards were made. *Average percent of need met:* 83%. *Average financial aid package:* $11,105. *Average need-based loan:* $4280. *Average need-based gift aid:* $5402. *Average non-need-based aid:* $4678. *Average indebtedness upon graduation:* $14,988.

Applying *Options:* electronic application. *Application fee:* $30. *Required:* essay or personal statement, high school transcript. *Application deadline:* 11/1 (freshmen). *Notification:* 2/15 (freshmen).

Freshman Application Contact Office of Admissions, University of Florida, 201 Criser Hall, PO Box 114000, Gainesville, FL 32611-4000. *Phone:* 352-392-1365.

UNIVERSITY OF MIAMI

Coral Gables, Florida **www.miami.edu/**

- **Independent** university, founded 1925
- **Suburban** 230-acre campus with easy access to Miami
- **Endowment** $741.3 million
- **Coed** 10,379 undergraduate students, 93% full-time, 54% women, 46% men
- **Very difficult** entrance level, 38% of applicants were admitted

Undergraduates 9,677 full-time, 702 part-time. Students come from 53 states and territories, 114 other countries, 74% are from out of state, 8% African American, 5% Asian American or Pacific Islander, 23% Hispanic American, 0.3% Native American, 6% international, 6% transferred in, 45% live on campus. *Retention:* 90% of 2006 full-time freshmen returned.

Freshmen *Admission:* 19,676 applied, 7,443 admitted, 1,991 enrolled. *Average high school GPA:* 4.0. *Test scores:* SAT critical reading scores over 500: 96%; SAT math scores over 500: 97%; SAT writing scores over 500: 92%; ACT scores over 18: 100%; SAT critical reading scores over 600: 70%; SAT math scores over 600: 78%; SAT writing scores over 600: 57%; ACT scores over 24: 95%; SAT critical reading scores over 700: 17%; SAT math scores over 700: 23%; SAT writing scores over 700: 10%; ACT scores over 30: 45%.

Faculty *Total:* 1,328, 69% full-time, 79% with terminal degrees. *Student/faculty ratio:* 12:1.

Majors Accounting; acting; advertising; aerospace, aeronautical and astronautical engineering; African-American/Black studies; American studies; anthropology; applied mathematics; architectural engineering; architecture; art; art history, criticism and conservation; athletic training; biochemistry; biology/biological sciences; biomedical/medical engineering; biophysics; broadcast journalism; business administration and management; business administration, management and operations related; business/managerial economics; ceramic arts and ceramics; chemistry; chemistry related; cinematography and film/video production; civil engineering; classics and languages, literatures and linguistics; communication/speech communication and rhetoric; computer and information systems security; computer engineering; computer graphics; computer science; conducting; creative writing; criminology; design and visual communications; dramatic/theater arts; dramatic/theater arts and stagecraft related; economics; education; electrical, electronics and communications engineering; elementary education; engineering science; English; entrepreneurship; environmental/environmental health engineering; film/cinema studies; finance; fine/studio arts; French; general studies; geography; geology/earth science; German; graphic design; health and medical administrative services related; health services/allied health/health sciences; history; human resources management; illustration; industrial engineering; information science/studies; international business/trade/commerce; international relations and affairs; jazz/jazz studies; Jewish/Judaic studies; journalism; kinesiology and exercise science; legal studies; marine biology and biological oceanography; marketing/marketing management; mass communication/media; mathematical statistics and probability; mathematics; mathematics and statistics related; mathematics related; mechanical engineering; medical microbiology and bacteriology; meteorology; music; musicology and ethnomusicology; music performance; music related; music teacher education; music theory and composition; music therapy; natural resources management and policy; neuroscience; nursing (registered nurse training); oceanography (chemical and physical); painting; parks, recreation and leisure facilities management; philosophy; photography; photojournalism; physics; piano and organ; political science and government; printmaking; psychology; public relations/image management; radio and television; religious studies; sculpture; secondary education; sociology; Spanish; special education; sport and fitness administration/management; theater design and technology; theater/theater arts management; voice and opera; women's studies.

Academics *Calendar:* semesters. *Degrees:* certificates, bachelor's, master's, doctoral, first professional, post-master's, and postbachelor's certificates. *Special study options:* academic remediation for entering students, accelerated degree program, adult/continuing education programs, advanced placement credit, distance learning, double majors, English as a second language, honors programs, independent study, internships, part-time degree program, services for LD students, student-designed majors, study abroad, summer session for credit. *ROTC:* Army (b), Air Force (b). *Unusual degree programs:* 3-2 business administration; engineering; exercise physiology, Latin American studies, physical therapy, marine geology, medicine.

Computers on Campus 1,800 computers/terminals are available on campus for general student use. Students can access the following: computer help desk, free student e-mail accounts, online (class) grades, online (class) schedules, online student account information. Campuswide network is available. 100% of college-owned or -operated housing units are wired for high-speed Internet access.

Student Life *Housing:* on-campus residence required for freshman year. *Options:* coed, disabled students. Campus housing is university owned. Freshman campus housing is guaranteed. *Activities and organizations:* drama/theater group, student-run newspaper, radio and television station, choral group, marching band, student government, international student organizations, sports and recreation clubs, Association of Commuter Students, United Black Students, national fraternities, national sororities. *Campus security:* 24-hour emergency response devices and patrols, student patrols, late-night transport/escort service, controlled dormitory access, crime prevention and safety workshops, residential college crime watch. *Student services:* health clinic, personal/psychological counseling, women's center.

Athletics Member NCAA. All Division I except football (Division I-A). *Intercollegiate sports:* badminton M (c)/W (c), baseball M (s), basketball M (s)/W (s), cheerleading M/W, crew W (s), cross-country running M (s)/W (s), golf W (s), ice hockey W (c), racquetball M (c)/W (c), soccer W (s), softball W (c), squash M (c)/W (c), swimming and diving W (s), tennis M (s)/W (s), track and field M (s)/W (s), volleyball M (c)/W (s), water polo M (c)/W (c). *Intramural sports:* badminton M/W, baseball M (c), basketball M/W, bowling M (c)/W (c), crew M (c)/W (c), equestrian sports M (c)/W (c), fencing M (c)/W (c), football M, golf M (c)/W (c), lacrosse M (c)/W (c), racquetball M/W, rugby M (c)/W (c), sailing M (c)/W (c), soccer M (c)/W (c), softball M/W, squash M/W, swimming and diving M (c)/W (c), table tennis M (c)/W (c), tennis M (c)/W (c), volleyball W, water polo M/W, weight lifting M/W.

Standardized Tests *Required:* SAT or ACT (for admission). *Required for some:* SAT and SAT Subject Tests or ACT (for admission), SAT Subject Tests (for admission).

Costs (2007–08) *Comprehensive fee:* $42,724 includes full-time tuition ($32,422), mandatory fees ($696), and room and board ($9606). Part-time tuition: $1350 per credit. *College room only:* $5762.

Financial Aid Of all full-time matriculated undergraduates who enrolled in 2007, 5,288 applied for aid, 4,547 were judged to have need, 1,469 had their need fully met. 2,365 Federal Work-Study jobs (averaging $2831). 228 state and other part-time jobs (averaging $5409). In 2007, 2186 non-need-based awards were made. *Average percent of need met:* 81%. *Average financial aid package:* $27,182. *Average need-based loan:* $5923. *Average need-based gift aid:* $19,465. *Average non-need-based aid:* $16,595. *Average indebtedness upon graduation:* $23,576.

Applying *Options:* electronic application, early admission, early decision, early action, deferred entrance. *Application fee:* $65. *Required:* essay or personal statement, high school transcript, letters of recommendation, counselor evaluation. *Required for some:* interview. *Application deadlines:* 1/15 (freshmen), 3/1 (transfers), 11/1 (early action). *Early decision deadline:* 11/1. *Notification:* 4/15 (freshmen), 4/15 (transfers), 12/20 (early decision), 2/1 (early action).

Freshman Application Contact Mr. Edward M. Gillis, Associate Dean of Enrollment and Director of Admission, University of Miami, PO Box 248025, Ashe Building Room 132, 1252 Memorial Drive, Coral Gables, FL 33146-4616. *Phone:* 305-284-4472. *Fax:* 305-284-2507. *E-mail:* admission@miami.edu.

UNIVERSITY OF NORTH FLORIDA

Jacksonville, Florida **www.unf.edu/**

- **State-supported** comprehensive, founded 1965, part of State University System of Florida
- **Urban** 1300-acre campus
- **Endowment** $88.8 million
- **Coed** 14,532 undergraduate students, 72% full-time, 57% women, 43% men
- **Very difficult** entrance level, 66% of applicants were admitted

Undergraduates 10,414 full-time, 4,118 part-time. Students come from 46 states and territories, 68 other countries, 3% are from out of state, 10% African American, 5% Asian American or Pacific Islander, 7% Hispanic American, 0.5% Native American, 1% international, 9% transferred in, 18% live on campus. *Retention:* 77% of 2006 full-time freshmen returned.

Freshmen *Admission:* 9,010 applied, 5,985 admitted, 2,283 enrolled. *Average high school GPA:* 3.46. *Test scores:* SAT critical reading scores over 500: 81%; SAT math scores over 500: 82%; ACT scores over 18: 99%; SAT critical reading scores over 600: 31%; SAT math scores over 600: 33%; ACT scores over 24: 23%; SAT critical reading scores over 700: 4%; SAT math scores over 700: 3%; ACT scores over 30: 1%.

Faculty *Total:* 765, 67% full-time, 63% with terminal degrees. *Student/faculty ratio:* 22:1.

Majors Accounting; anthropology; art; art teacher education; athletic training; banking and financial support services; biology/biological sciences; business administration and management; business/managerial economics; chemistry; civil engineering; computer and information sciences; construction engineering technology; criminal justice/safety; early childhood education; economics; electrical, electronics and communications engineering; elementary education; English; finance; fine/studio arts; general studies; health/health care administration; health services/allied health/health sciences; history; international business/trade/commerce; international/global studies; international relations and affairs; jazz/jazz studies; liberal arts and sciences/liberal studies; marketing/marketing management; mass communication/media; mathematics; mathematics teacher education; mechanical engineering; middle school education; music; music performance; music teacher education; nursing (registered nurse training); philosophy; physical education teaching and coaching; physics; political science and government; psychology; science teacher education; secondary education; sign language interpretation and translation; sociology; Spanish; special education; sport and fitness administration/management; statistics; trade and industrial teacher education; transportation management.

Academics *Calendar:* semesters. *Degrees:* associate, bachelor's, master's, doctoral, post-master's, and postbachelor's certificates (doctoral degree in education only). *Special study options:* accelerated degree program, adult/continuing education programs, advanced placement credit, cooperative education, distance learning, double majors, English as a second language, honors programs, independent study, internships, off-campus study, part-time degree program, services for LD students, student-designed majors, study abroad, summer session for credit. *ROTC:* Navy (c).

Computers on Campus 750 computers/terminals are available on campus for general student use. Students can access the following: campus intranet, computer help desk, free student e-mail accounts, online (class) grades, online (class) registration, online (class) schedules, applications software. Campuswide network is available. 100% of college-owned or -operated housing units are wired for high-speed Internet access. Wireless service is available via entire campus.

Student Life *Housing options:* coed, disabled students. Campus housing is university owned. Freshman applicants given priority for college housing. *Activities and organizations:* drama/theater group, student-run newspaper, radio and television station, choral group, International Student Association, Filipino Student Association, Student Physical Therapy Association, National Education Association, Student Government Association, national fraternities, national sororities. *Campus security:* 24-hour emergency response devices and patrols, student patrols, late-night transport/escort service, controlled dormitory access, electronic parking lot security. *Student services:* health clinic, personal/psychological counseling, women's center.

Athletics Member NCAA. All Division I. *Intercollegiate sports:* baseball M (s), basketball M (s)/W (s), cheerleading M/W, cross-country running M (s)/W (s), golf M (s), soccer M (s)/W (s), softball W (s), swimming and diving W (s), tennis M (s)/W (s), track and field M (s)/W (s), volleyball W (s). *Intramural sports:* badminton M/W, basketball M/W, bowling M/W, football M/W, golf M/W, lacrosse M (c)/W (c), racquetball M (c)/W (c), rugby M, sailing M/W, soccer M/W, softball M/W, squash M/W, swimming and diving M/W, table tennis M/W, tennis M/W, track and field M/W, ultimate Frisbee M (c)/W (c), volleyball M (c)/W (c), water polo M/W, weight lifting M/W, wrestling M/W.

Standardized Tests *Required:* SAT or ACT (for admission).

Costs (2007–08) *Tuition:* state resident $3491 full-time, $116 per credit hour part-time; nonresident $15,133 full-time, $504 per credit hour part-time. *Room and board:* $7071; room only: $4080. Room and board charges vary according to board plan and housing facility. *Payment plan:* deferred payment. *Waivers:* senior citizens and employees or children of employees.

Financial Aid Of all full-time matriculated undergraduates who enrolled in 2007, 5,354 applied for aid, 3,830 were judged to have need, 403 had their need fully met. 85 Federal Work-Study jobs (averaging $3172). In 2007, 1253 non-need-based awards were made. *Average percent of need met:* 89%. *Average financial aid package:* $1443. *Average need-based loan:* $1597. *Average need-based gift aid:* $1085. *Average non-need-based aid:* $1228. *Average indebtedness upon graduation:* $14,189.

Applying *Options:* electronic application, deferred entrance. *Application fee:* $30. *Required:* high school transcript, minimum 2.9 GPA. *Required for some:* essay or personal statement, letters of recommendation, interview. *Recommended:* minimum 3.0 GPA. *Application deadlines:* 7/2 (freshmen), 7/2 (out-of-state freshmen), 7/2 (transfers). *Notification:* continuous (freshmen), continuous (out-of-state freshmen), continuous (transfers).

Freshman Application Contact Mr. John Yancey, Director of Admissions, University of North Florida, 4567 St. Johns Bluff Road South, Jacksonville, FL 32224. *Phone:* 904-620-2624. *Fax:* 904-620-2014. *E-mail:* admissions@unf.edu.

UNIVERSITY OF PHOENIX–CENTRAL FLORIDA CAMPUS

Maitland, Florida **www.phoenix.edu/**

- **Proprietary** comprehensive, founded 1996
- **Urban** campus
- **Coed**
- **Noncompetitive** entrance level

Faculty *Student/faculty ratio:* 9:1.

Academics *Calendar:* continuous. *Degrees:* certificates, bachelor's, and master's.

Student Life *Campus security:* late-night transport/escort service.

Costs (2007–08) *Tuition:* $10,470 full-time, $349 per credit part-time. Full-time tuition and fees vary according to course level.

Financial Aid *Average financial aid package:* $4244. *Average need-based gift aid:* $2236.

Applying *Options:* deferred entrance. *Application fee:* $45. *Required:* 1 letter of recommendation. *Required for some:* high school transcript.

Freshman Application Contact Ms. Beth Barilla, Associate Vice President, Student Admissions and Services, University of Phoenix–Central Florida Campus, 4615 East Elwood Street, Mail Stop AA-K101, Phoenix, AZ 85040-1958. *Phone:* 480-317-6000. *Toll-free phone:* 800-776-4867 (in-state); 800-228-7240 (out-of-state). *Fax:* 480-894-1758. *E-mail:* beth.barilla@phoenix.edu.

UNIVERSITY OF PHOENIX–FORT LAUDERDALE CAMPUS

Fort Lauderdale, Florida www.phoenix.edu/

- **Proprietary** comprehensive
- **Urban** campus
- **Coed**
- **Noncompetitive** entrance level

Faculty *Student/faculty ratio:* 11:1.

Academics *Calendar:* continuous. *Degrees:* certificates, bachelor's, and master's.

Student Life *Campus security:* late-night transport/escort service.

Costs (2007–08) *Tuition:* $10,620 full-time, $354 per credit part-time. Full-time tuition and fees vary according to course level.

Financial Aid *Average financial aid package:* $4226. *Average need-based gift aid:* $2290.

Applying *Options:* deferred entrance. *Application fee:* $45. *Required:* 1 letter of recommendation. *Required for some:* high school transcript.

Freshman Application Contact Ms. Beth Barilla, Associate Vice President, Student Admissions and Services, University of Phoenix–Fort Lauderdale Campus, 4615 East Elwood Street, Mail Stop AA-K101, Phoenix, AZ 85040-1958. *Phone:* 480-317-6000. *Toll-free phone:* 800-228-7240. *Fax:* 480-894-1758. *E-mail:* beth.barilla@phoenix.edu.

UNIVERSITY OF PHOENIX–NORTH FLORIDA CAMPUS

Jacksonville, Florida www.phoenix.edu/

- **Proprietary** comprehensive, founded 1976
- **Urban** campus
- **Coed**
- **Noncompetitive** entrance level

Faculty *Student/faculty ratio:* 9:1.

Academics *Calendar:* continuous. *Degrees:* certificates, bachelor's, and master's.

Student Life *Campus security:* late-night transport/escort service.

Costs (2007–08) *Tuition:* $10,470 full-time, $349 per credit part-time. Full-time tuition and fees vary according to course level.

Financial Aid *Average financial aid package:* $4442.

Applying *Options:* deferred entrance. *Application fee:* $45. *Required:* 1 letter of recommendation. *Required for some:* high school transcript.

Freshman Application Contact Ms. Beth Barilla, Associate Vice President, Student Admissions and Services, University of Phoenix–North Florida Campus, 4615 East Elwood Street, Mail Stop AA-K101, Phoenix, AZ 85040-1958. *Phone:* 480-317-6000. *Toll-free phone:* 800-776-4867 (in-state); 800-894-1758 (out-of-state). *Fax:* 480-894-1758. *E-mail:* beth.barilla@phoenix.edu.

UNIVERSITY OF PHOENIX–WEST FLORIDA CAMPUS

Temple Terrace, Florida www.phoenix.edu/

- **Proprietary** comprehensive
- **Urban** campus
- **Coed**
- **Noncompetitive** entrance level

Faculty *Student/faculty ratio:* 9:1.

Academics *Calendar:* continuous. *Degrees:* certificates, bachelor's, and master's.

Student Life *Campus security:* late-night transport/escort service.

Costs (2007–08) *Tuition:* $10,470 full-time, $349 per credit part-time. Full-time tuition and fees vary according to course level.

Financial Aid *Average financial aid package:* $4157. *Average need-based gift aid:* $2276.

Applying *Options:* deferred entrance. *Application fee:* $45. *Required:* 1 letter of recommendation. *Required for some:* high school transcript.

Freshman Application Contact Ms. Beth Barilla, Associate Vice President, Student Admissions and Services, University of Phoenix–West Florida Campus, 4615 East Elwood Street, Mail Stop AA-K101, Phoenix, AZ 85040-1958. *Phone:* 480-317-6000. *Toll-free phone:* 800-776-4867 (in-state); 800-228-7240 (out-of-state). *Fax:* 480-894-1758. *E-mail:* beth.barilla@phoenix.edu.

UNIVERSITY OF SOUTH FLORIDA

Tampa, Florida www.usf.edu/

- **State-supported** university, founded 1956, part of State University System of Florida
- **Urban** 1913-acre campus
- **Coed** 34,898 undergraduate students, 70% full-time, 59% women, 41% men
- **Moderately difficult** entrance level, 50% of applicants were admitted

Undergraduates 24,600 full-time, 10,298 part-time. Students come from 52 states and territories, 131 other countries, 3% are from out of state, 13% African American, 6% Asian American or Pacific Islander, 13% Hispanic American, 0.5% Native American, 1% international, 14% transferred in, 13% live on campus. *Retention:* 81% of 2006 full-time freshmen returned.

Freshmen *Admission:* 25,216 applied, 12,502 admitted, 4,054 enrolled. *Average high school GPA:* 3.66. *Test scores:* SAT critical reading scores over 500: 79%; SAT math scores over 500: 83%; SAT writing scores over 500: 63%; ACT scores over 18: 100%; SAT critical reading scores over 600: 26%; SAT math scores over 600: 32%; SAT writing scores over 600: 17%; ACT scores over 24: 51%; SAT critical reading scores over 700: 3%; SAT math scores over 700: 4%; SAT writing scores over 700: 2%; ACT scores over 30: 5%.

Majors Accounting; African-American/Black studies; American studies; anthropology; art; art teacher education; athletic training; audiology and speech-language pathology; biological and physical sciences; biology/biological sciences; business administration and management; business/commerce; business/managerial economics; business teacher education; chemical engineering; chemistry; civil engineering; classics and languages, literatures and linguistics; clinical laboratory science/medical technology; communication/speech communication and rhetoric; computer and information sciences; computer engineering; computer/information technology services administration related; criminal justice/safety; dance; drama and dance teacher education; dramatic/theater arts; economics; education; electrical, electronics and communications engineering; elementary education; engineering; English; English/language arts teacher education; environmental studies; finance; foreign language teacher education; French; general studies; geography; geology/earth science; German; gerontology; history; hospitality administration; humanities; industrial engineering; information science/studies; international business/trade/commerce; international relations and affairs; Italian; kindergarten/preschool education; liberal arts and sciences/liberal studies; management information systems; management science; marketing/marketing management; mathematics; mathematics teacher education; mechanical engineering; medical microbiology and bacteriology; modern languages; music performance; music teacher education; nursing (registered nurse training); philosophy; physical education teaching and coaching; physics; political science and government; psychology; religious studies; Russian; science teacher education; social sciences; social science teacher education; social work; sociology; Spanish; special education; special education (emotionally disturbed); special education (mentally retarded); special education (specific learning disabilities); speech and rhetoric; trade and industrial teacher education; women's studies.

Academics *Calendar:* semesters. *Degrees:* associate, bachelor's, master's, doctoral, first professional, and postbachelor's certificates. *Special study options:* academic remediation for entering students, accelerated degree program, adult/continuing education programs, advanced placement credit, cooperative education, distance learning, double majors, external degree program, freshman honors college, honors programs, independent study, internships, off-campus study, part-time degree program, services for LD students, student-designed majors, study abroad, summer session for credit. *ROTC:* Army (b), Navy (b), Air Force (b). *Unusual degree programs:* 3-2 business administration; engineering; nursing.

Computers on Campus 593 computers/terminals are available on campus for general student use. Students can access the following: online (class) registration. Campuswide network is available.

Student Life *Housing options:* coed, men-only, women-only, cooperative, disabled students. Campus housing is university owned. *Activities and organizations:* drama/theater group, student-run newspaper, radio and television station, choral group, marching band, Student Government, Campus Activities Board, USF Ambassadors, Student Admissions Representatives, national fraternities, national sororities. *Campus security:* 24-hour emergency response devices and patrols, student patrols, late-night transport/escort service, controlled dormitory access, residence hall lobby personnel 8 p.m. to 6 a.m. *Student services:* health clinic, personal/psychological counseling, women's center, legal services.

Athletics Member NCAA. All Division I. *Intercollegiate sports:* baseball M (s), basketball M (s)/W (s), cross-country running M (s)/W (s), football M (s), golf M (s)/W (s), soccer M (s)/W (s), softball W (s), tennis M (s)/W (s), track and field M (s)/W (s), volleyball W (s). *Intramural sports:* badminton M/W, basketball M/W, bowling M/W, cross-country running M/W, football M, golf M/W, racquetball M/W, soccer M/W, softball M/W, swimming and diving M/W, table tennis M/W, tennis M/W, track and field M/W, volleyball M/W, wrestling M/W.

Standardized Tests *Required:* SAT or ACT (for admission). *Required for some:* SAT Subject Tests (for admission).

Costs (2007–08) *Tuition:* state resident $3383 full-time, $113 per credit hour part-time; nonresident $16,081 full-time, $536 per credit hour part-time. Full-time tuition and fees vary according to course level, course load, and location. Part-time tuition and fees vary according to course level, course load, and location. *Required fees:* $74 full-time, $37 per term part-time. *Room and board:* $7590; room only: $3760. Room and board charges vary according to board plan, housing facility, and location. *Payment plan:* installment. *Waivers:* senior citizens.

Financial Aid Of all full-time matriculated undergraduates who enrolled in 2007, 14,697 applied for aid, 11,945 were judged to have need, 1,838 had their need fully met. 858 Federal Work-Study jobs (averaging $3600). In 2007, 1890 non-need-based awards were made. *Average percent of need met:* 25%. *Average financial aid package:* $9849. *Average need-based loan:* $4289. *Average need-based gift aid:* $4884. *Average non-need-based aid:* $2473. *Average indebtedness upon graduation:* $18,517.

Applying *Options:* electronic application, early admission. *Application fee:* $30. *Required:* minimum 2.0 GPA. *Required for some:* high school transcript, letters of recommendation. *Application deadlines:* 4/15 (freshmen), 4/15 (transfers). *Notification:* continuous (freshmen), continuous (transfers).

Freshman Application Contact Ms. Alicia Kormowa, Undergraduate Admissions and Recruitment, University of South Florida, 4202 East Fowler Avenue, SVC 1036, Tampa, FL 33620-9951. *Phone:* 813-974-3350. *Toll-free phone:* 877-USF-BULLS. *Fax:* 813-974-9689. *E-mail:* bullseye@admin.usf.edu.

THE UNIVERSITY OF TAMPA

Tampa, Florida **www.ut.edu/**

- **Independent** comprehensive, founded 1931
- **Urban** 90-acre campus
- **Coed** 4,918 undergraduate students, 92% full-time, 59% women, 41% men
- 49% of applicants were admitted

Undergraduates 4,513 full-time, 405 part-time. Students come from 50 states and territories, 100 other countries, 55% are from out of state, 6% African American, 2% Asian American or Pacific Islander, 10% Hispanic American, 0.4% Native American, 8% international, 7% transferred in, 61% live on campus. *Retention:* 72% of 2006 full-time freshmen returned.

Freshmen *Admission:* 7,885 applied, 3,871 admitted, 1,177 enrolled. *Average high school GPA:* 3.29. *Test scores:* SAT critical reading scores over 500: 70%; SAT math scores over 500: 74%; SAT writing scores over 500: 70%; ACT scores over 18: 98%; SAT critical reading scores over 600: 15%; SAT math scores over 600: 18%; SAT writing scores over 600: 16%; ACT scores over 24: 44%; SAT critical reading scores over 700: 1%; SAT math scores over 700: 1%; SAT writing scores over 700: 1%; ACT scores over 30: 3%.

Faculty *Total:* 480, 47% full-time, 57% with terminal degrees. *Student/faculty ratio:* 15:1.

Majors Accounting; advertising; art; athletic training/sports medicine; biochemistry; biology/biological sciences; biology teacher education; business administration and management; chemistry; communication/speech communication and rhetoric; computer graphics; computer programming; creative writing; criminology; cultural studies; dramatic/theater arts; economics; education (K-12); elementary education; English; English/language arts teacher education; entrepreneurship; environmental biology; environmental science; environmental studies; film/cinema studies; finance; finance and financial management services related; forensic science and technology; geography; graphic design; history; information science/studies; international business/trade/commerce; international/global studies; international relations and affairs; kinesiology and exercise science; liberal arts and sciences/liberal studies; management information systems; management science; marine science/merchant marine officer; marketing/marketing management; mass communication/media; mathematics; mathematics teacher education; music; music performance; music teacher education; nursing (registered nurse training); philosophy; physical education teaching and coaching; political science and government; pre-dentistry studies; pre-law studies; pre-medical studies; pre-veterinary studies; psychology; public health; public relations/image management; secondary education; social sciences; social science teacher education; sociology; Spanish; urban studies/affairs; visual and performing arts.

Academics *Calendar:* semesters. *Degrees:* certificates, associate, bachelor's, master's, and post-master's certificates. *Special study options:* academic remediation for entering students, adult/continuing education programs, advanced placement credit, cooperative education, double majors, English as a second language, honors programs, independent study, internships, part-time degree program, services for LD students, study abroad, summer session for credit. *ROTC:* Army (b), Air Force (c). *Unusual degree programs:* 3-2 Bachelor of Science in chemistry/MBA joint program.

Computers on Campus 528 computers/terminals are available on campus for general student use. Students can access the following: campus intranet, computer help desk, free student e-mail accounts, online (class) grades, online (class) registration, online (class) schedules. Campuswide network is available. 100% of college-owned or -operated housing units are wired for high-speed Internet access. Wireless service is available via entire campus.

Student Life *Housing options:* coed. Campus housing is university owned. Freshman applicants given priority for college housing. *Activities and organizations:* drama/theater group, student-run newspaper, radio and television station, choral group, PEACE (volunteer organization), Greek Life, Student Government, Student Productions, Minaret, national fraternities, national sororities. *Campus security:* 24-hour emergency response devices and patrols, late-night transport/escort service, controlled dormitory access. *Student services:* health clinic, personal/psychological counseling.

Athletics Member NCAA. All Division II. *Intercollegiate sports:* baseball M (s), basketball M (s)/W (s), crew M/W (s), cross-country running M (s)/W (s), golf M (s), soccer M (s)/W (s), softball W (s), swimming and diving M (s)/W (s), tennis W (s), volleyball W (s). *Intramural sports:* baseball M/W, basketball M/W, bowling M/W, crew M, equestrian sports W, field hockey W, football M, golf M/W, soccer M/W, softball M/W, swimming and diving M/W, tennis W, volleyball M/W.

Standardized Tests *Required:* SAT or ACT (for admission).

Costs (2007–08) *Comprehensive fee:* $28,298 includes full-time tuition ($19,700), mandatory fees ($982), and room and board ($7616). Full-time tuition and fees vary according to class time. Part-time tuition: $420 per hour. Part-time tuition and fees vary according to class time. *Required fees:* $35 per term part-time. *College room only:* $4076. Room and board charges vary according to board plan and housing facility. *Payment plan:* installment. *Waivers:* employees or children of employees.

Financial Aid Of all full-time matriculated undergraduates who enrolled in 2007, 2,817 applied for aid, 2,279 were judged to have need, 511 had their need fully met. In 2007, 460 non-need-based awards were made. *Average percent of need met:* 75%. *Average financial aid package:* $15,449. *Average need-based loan:* $5328. *Average need-based gift aid:* $7104. *Average non-need-based aid:* $6144. *Average indebtedness upon graduation:* $22,901.

Applying *Options:* electronic application, early admission, deferred entrance. *Application fee:* $40. *Required:* essay or personal statement, high school transcript, minimum 2.0 GPA. *Recommended:* interview. *Application deadlines:* 5/1 (freshmen), rolling (transfers). *Notification:* continuous (transfers).

Freshman Application Contact Mrs. Barbara Strickler, Vice President for Enrollment, The University of Tampa, 401 West Kennedy Boulevard, Tampa, FL 33606-1480. *Phone:* 813-253-6211. *Toll-free phone:* 888-646-2438 (in-state); 888-MINARET (out-of-state). *Fax:* 813-258-7398. *E-mail:* admissions@ut.edu.

See page 692 for the College Close-Up.

UNIVERSITY OF WEST FLORIDA

Pensacola, Florida **uwf.edu/**

- **State-supported** comprehensive, founded 1963, part of State University System of Florida
- **Suburban** 1600-acre campus
- **Endowment** $60.4 million
- **Coed** 8,700 undergraduate students, 71% full-time, 60% women, 40% men
- **Moderately difficult** entrance level, 70% of applicants were admitted

The University of West Florida (UWF)—near historic Pensacola and the world-famous beaches of the Gulf of Mexico—offers an inviting, environmentally friendly setting for study. Small classes, opportunities for individually tailored educational experiences, and scholarships for academic performance help make UWF an extraordinary value in higher education.

Undergraduates 6,170 full-time, 2,530 part-time. Students come from 51 states and territories, 70 other countries, 11% are from out of state, 10% African American, 5% Asian American or Pacific Islander, 5% Hispanic American, 0.9% Native American, 1% international, 10% transferred in, 18% live on campus. *Retention:* 73% of 2006 full-time freshmen returned.

Freshmen *Admission:* 3,371 applied, 2,369 admitted, 1,033 enrolled. *Average high school GPA:* 3.52. *Test scores:* SAT critical reading scores over 500: 66%; SAT math scores over 500: 70%; ACT scores over 18: 99%; SAT critical reading

scores over 600: 27%; SAT math scores over 600: 21%; ACT scores over 24: 38%; SAT critical reading scores over 700: 4%; SAT math scores over 700: 3%; ACT scores over 30: 3%.

Faculty *Total:* 580, 57% full-time, 58% with terminal degrees. *Student/faculty ratio:* 19:1.

Majors Accounting; anthropology; art; biological and physical sciences; biology/biological sciences; business administration and management; business/managerial economics; chemistry; clinical laboratory science/medical technology; communication/speech communication and rhetoric; community health services counseling; computer and information sciences; computer engineering; criminal justice/safety; dramatic/theater arts; early childhood education; economics; electrical, electronics and communications engineering; elementary education; engineering technology; English; environmental studies; finance; fine/studio arts; health and physical education; history; hospitality administration; humanities; international relations and affairs; liberal arts and sciences/liberal studies; management information systems; marine biology and biological oceanography; marketing/marketing management; mathematics; middle school education; music performance; nursing (registered nurse training); philosophy; physics; political science and government; psychology; social sciences; social sciences related; social work; special education; trade and industrial teacher education.

Academics *Calendar:* semesters. *Degrees:* associate, bachelor's, master's, and doctoral (specialists). *Special study options:* advanced placement credit, cooperative education, distance learning, English as a second language, honors programs, independent study, internships, off-campus study, part-time degree program, services for LD students, study abroad, summer session for credit. *ROTC:* Army (b), Air Force (b). *Unusual degree programs:* 3-2 business administration.

Computers on Campus 1,100 computers/terminals and 1,600 ports are available on campus for general student use. Students can access the following: campus intranet, computer help desk, free student e-mail accounts, online (class) grades, online (class) registration, online (class) schedules. Campuswide network is available. 100% of college-owned or -operated housing units are wired for high-speed Internet access. Wireless service is available via entire campus.

Student Life *Housing options:* coed. Campus housing is university owned. *Activities and organizations:* drama/theater group, student-run newspaper, choral group, Marketing Association, Student Council for Exceptional Children, Inter-Varsity Christian Fellowship, Baptist Student Ministry, Golden Key Honor Society, national fraternities, national sororities. *Campus security:* 24-hour emergency response devices and patrols, student patrols, late-night transport/escort service, controlled dormitory access. *Student services:* health clinic, personal/psychological counseling.

Athletics Member NCAA. All Division II. *Intercollegiate sports:* baseball M (s), basketball M (s)/W (s), cross-country running M (s)/W (s), golf M (s), soccer M (s)/W (s), softball W (s), tennis M (s)/W (s), track and field W, volleyball W. *Intramural sports:* basketball M/W, bowling M/W, cheerleading W, fencing M/W, football M/W, sailing M/W, soccer M/W, swimming and diving M/W, tennis M/W, volleyball M/W.

Standardized Tests *Required:* SAT or ACT (for admission).

Costs (2007–08) *Tuition:* state resident $2322 full-time, $112 per semester hour part-time; nonresident $15,093 full-time, $541 per semester hour part-time. Full-time tuition and fees vary according to location and reciprocity agreements. Part-time tuition and fees vary according to location and reciprocity agreements. *Required fees:* $1145 full-time. *Room and board:* $6600. Room and board charges vary according to housing facility. *Payment plans:* tuition prepayment, deferred payment. *Waivers:* senior citizens and employees or children of employees.

Financial Aid Of all full-time matriculated undergraduates who enrolled in 2005, 224 Federal Work-Study jobs (averaging $1434). 1,545 state and other part-time jobs.

Applying *Options:* electronic application, early admission, deferred entrance. *Application fee:* $30. *Required:* high school transcript, minimum 2.0 GPA. *Application deadlines:* 6/30 (freshmen), 6/30 (transfers). *Notification:* continuous (freshmen), continuous (transfers).

Freshman Application Contact Director of Admissions, University of West Florida, Admissions, 11000 University Parkway, Pensacola, FL 32514. *Phone:* 850-474-2230. *Toll-free phone:* 800-263-1074. *Fax:* 850-474-3460. *E-mail:* admissions@uwf.edu.

See page 694 for the College Close-Up.

WARNER SOUTHERN COLLEGE

Lake Wales, Florida **www.warner.edu/**

Freshman Application Contact Mr. Jason Roe, Director of Admissions, Warner Southern College, Warner Southern Center, 13895 Highway 27, Lake Wales, FL 33859. *Phone:* 863-638-7212 Ext. 7213. *Toll-free phone:* 800-949-7248. *Fax:* 863-638-1472. *E-mail:* admissions@warner.edu.

WEBBER INTERNATIONAL UNIVERSITY

Babson Park, Florida **www.webber.edu/**

- **Independent** comprehensive, founded 1927
- **Small-town** 110-acre campus with easy access to Orlando
- **Endowment** $4.7 million
- **Coed** 536 undergraduate students, 89% full-time, 39% women, 61% men
- **Moderately difficult** entrance level, 57% of applicants were admitted

Webber International University celebrated its seventy-fifth anniversary with a name change that reflects the mission of the institution. The University attracts more than 140 international students from every continent except Antarctica. Worldwide business is the focus of the curriculum, and successful employment is a key goal. Students are encouraged to follow careers as executives in established companies, leaders in their home countries, and groundbreaking entrepreneurs in the world of business.

Undergraduates 478 full-time, 58 part-time. Students come from 21 states and territories, 34 other countries, 6% are from out of state, 23% African American, 0.6% Asian American or Pacific Islander, 9% Hispanic American, 0.4% Native American, 15% international, 10% transferred in, 43% live on campus. *Retention:* 59% of 2006 full-time freshmen returned.

Freshmen *Admission:* 407 applied, 230 admitted, 120 enrolled. *Average high school GPA:* 3.16. *Test scores:* SAT critical reading scores over 500: 25%; SAT math scores over 500: 33%; ACT scores over 18: 57%; SAT critical reading scores over 600: 3%; SAT math scores over 600: 3%; ACT scores over 24: 1%; SAT math scores over 700: 1%.

Faculty *Total:* 44, 45% full-time, 39% with terminal degrees. *Student/faculty ratio:* 18:1.

Majors Accounting; business administration and management; business/commerce; computer management; finance; hotel/motel administration; marketing/marketing management; pre-law studies; sport and fitness administration/management; tourism and travel services management.

Academics *Calendar:* semesters. *Degrees:* associate, bachelor's, and master's. *Special study options:* academic remediation for entering students, accelerated degree program, adult/continuing education programs, advanced placement credit, cooperative education, double majors, internships, part-time degree program, services for LD students, study abroad, summer session for credit.

Computers on Campus 92 computers/terminals are available on campus for general student use. Students can access the following: campus intranet, free student e-mail accounts. Campuswide network is available. 100% of college-owned or -operated housing units are wired for high-speed Internet access.

Student Life *Housing:* on-campus residence required for freshman year. *Options:* men-only, women-only. Campus housing is university owned. Freshman campus housing is guaranteed. *Activities and organizations:* student-run newspaper, Fellowship of Christian Athletes, PBL, student government, Society of Hosteleurs, Webber Ambassadors. *Campus security:* 24-hour emergency response devices and patrols, late-night transport/escort service, controlled dormitory access. *Student services:* health clinic.

Athletics Member NAIA. *Intercollegiate sports:* baseball M (s), basketball M (s)/W (s), cross-country running M (s)/W (s), football M (s), golf M (s)/W (s), soccer M (s)/W (s), softball W (s), tennis M (s)/W (s), track and field M (s)/W (s), volleyball M/W. *Intramural sports:* basketball M/W, cheerleading M/W, football M/W, soccer M/W, softball W, table tennis M/W, tennis M/W.

Standardized Tests *Required:* SAT or ACT (for admission).

Costs (2007–08) *Comprehensive fee:* $22,720 includes full-time tuition ($16,760) and room and board ($5960). Full-time tuition and fees vary according to class time and course load. Part-time tuition: $215 per credit hour. Part-time tuition and fees vary according to course load. *College room only:* $3550. Room and board charges vary according to board plan. *Payment plan:* installment. *Waivers:* children of alumni, adult students, senior citizens, and employees or children of employees.

Financial Aid Of all full-time matriculated undergraduates who enrolled in 2007, 337 applied for aid, 269 were judged to have need, 136 had their need fully met. 31 Federal Work-Study jobs (averaging $1370). 29 state and other part-time jobs (averaging $1344). In 2007, 144 non-need-based awards were made. *Average percent of need met:* 63%. *Average financial aid package:* $15,986. *Average need-based loan:* $4235. *Average need-based gift aid:* $11,533. *Average non-need-based aid:* $3772. *Average indebtedness upon graduation:* $20,602. *Financial aid deadline:* 8/1.

Applying *Options:* electronic application, early action. *Application fee:* $35. *Required:* high school transcript, minimum 2.0 GPA. *Required for some:* letters of recommendation, interview. *Recommended:* essay or personal statement. *Application deadlines:* 8/1 (freshmen), 8/1 (transfers), 4/1 (early action).

Freshman Application Contact Ms. Julie Ragans, Director of Admissions, Webber International University, 1201 Scenic Highway, North, PO Box 96, Babson Park, FL 33827. *Phone:* 863-638-2910. *Toll-free phone:* 800-741-1844. *Fax:* 863-638-1591. *E-mail:* admissions@webber.edu.

See page 696 for the College Close-Up.

YESHIVA GEDOLAH RABBINICAL COLLEGE

Miami Beach, Florida

ARGOSY UNIVERSITY

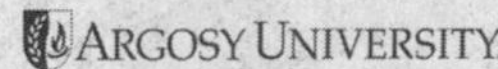

The University

Argosy University is a leading institution offering a variety of degree programs that focus on the human side of success alongside professional competence. For students looking for a more personal approach to education, Argosy University may just be the answer. With forty-eight graduate and undergraduate programs, across nineteen campuses and twelve states, Argosy University emphasizes interpersonal skills as well as academic learning. All of its programs are taught by practicing professionals who bring real-world experience into the classroom. So students graduate with both a solid foundation of knowledge and the power to put it to work. To accommodate busy working adults, many programs at Argosy University are structured flexibly—with both campus and online learning and evening, weekend, and daytime classes. There is also a wide range of financial aid options for students who qualify.

Argosy University is a private institution of higher education dedicated to providing high-quality professional education programs at the doctoral, master's, bachelor's, and associate degree levels as well as continuing education to individuals who seek to advance their professional and personal lives. The University emphasizes programs in the behavioral sciences (psychology and counseling), business, education, and the health-care professions. A limited number of preprofessional programs and general education offerings are provided to permit students to prepare for entry into these professional fields. The programs of Argosy University are designed to instill the knowledge, skills, and ethical values of professional practice and to foster values of social responsibility in a supportive, learning-centered environment of mutual respect and professional excellence.

With nineteen campuses nationwide, Argosy University provides students with a network of resources found at larger universities, including a career resources office, an academic resources center, and extensive information access for research. The University's innovative programs feature dynamic, relevant, and practical curricula delivered in flexible class formats. Students enjoy scheduling options that make it easier to fit school into their busy lives. They can choose from day and evening courses, on campus or online. Many students find a combination of both to be an ideal way of continuing their education while meeting family and professional demands.

Most students are full-time working professionals who live within driving distance of the campus. The University does not offer or operate student housing.

Argosy University is accredited by The Higher Learning Commission of the North Central Association (30 North LaSalle Street, Suite 2400, Chicago, Illinois 60602; 800-621-7440; http://ncahlc.org).

Location

Argosy University operates nineteen locations across the U.S. and offers a variety of degree programs online (http://www.argosy.edu). Campus locations include the following:

Atlanta, 980 Hammond Drive, Suite 100, Atlanta, Georgia 30328; phone: 770-671-1200 or 888-671-4777 (toll-free)

Chicago, 225 North Michigan Avenue, Suite 1300, Chicago, Illinois 60601; phone: 312-777-7600 or 800-626-4123 (toll-free)

Dallas, 8080 Park Lane, Suite 400A, Dallas, Texas 75231; phone: 214-890-9900 or 866-954-9900 (toll-free)

Denver, 1200 Lincoln Street, Denver, Colorado 80203; phone: 303-248-2700 or 866-431-5981 (toll-free)

Hawai'i, 400 ASB Tower, 1001 Bishop Street, Honolulu, Hawaii 96813; phone: 808-536-5555 or 888-323-2777 (toll-free)

Inland Empire, 636 East Brier Drive, Suite 235, San Bernardino, California 92408; phone: 909-915-3800 or 866-217-9075 (toll-free)

Nashville, 100 Centerview Drive, Suite 225, Nashville, Tennessee 37214; phone: 615-525-2800 or 866-833-6598 (toll-free)

Orange County, 3501 West Sunflower Avenue, Suite 110, Santa Ana, California 92704; phone: 714-338-6200 or 800-716-9598 (toll-free)

Phoenix, 2233 West Dunlap Avenue, Phoenix, Arizona 85021; phone: 602-216-2600 or 866-216-2777 (toll-free)

Salt Lake City, 121 West Election Road, Suite 300, Draper, Utah 84020; phone: 888-639-4756 (toll-free)

San Diego, 7650 Mission Valley Road, San Diego, California 92108; phone: 858-598-1900 or 866-505-0333 (toll-free)

San Francisco Bay Area, 1005 Atlantic Avenue, Alameda, California 94501; phone: 510-217-4700 or 866-215-2777 (toll-free)

Santa Monica, 2950 31st Street, Santa Monica, California 90405; phone: 310-866-4000 or 866-505-0332 (toll-free)

Sarasota, 5250 17th Street, Sarasota, Florida 34235; phone: 941-379-0404 or 800-331-5995 (toll-free)

Schaumburg, 999 North Plaza Drive, Suite 111, Schaumburg, Illinois 60173-5403; phone: 847-969-4900 or 866-290-2777 (toll-free)

Seattle, 2601-A Elliott Avenue, Seattle, Washington 98121; phone: 206-283-4500 or 888-283-2777 (toll-free)

Tampa, Parkside at Tampa Bay Park, 4401 North Hines Avenue, Suite 150, Tampa, Florida 33614; phone: 813-393-5290 or 800-850-6488 (toll-free)

Twin Cities, 1515 Central Parkway, Eagan, Minnesota 55121; phone: 651-846-2882 or 888-844-2004 (toll-free)

Washington DC, 1550 Wilson Boulevard, Suite 600, Arlington, Virginia 22209; phone: 703-526-5800 or 866-703-2777 (toll-free)

Majors and Degrees

Argosy University's College of Business offers a Bachelor of Science (B.S.) in Business Administration program. Argosy University's College of Psychology and Behavioral Sciences offers the Bachelor of Arts (B.A.) in Psychology degree program.

Academic Programs

The B.S. in Business Administration program prepares students for entry- to mid-level positions within the public or private sector. The curriculum is structured to help students develop competencies in oral and written communication, leadership, team skills, solutions-focused learning, and the analysis and execution of solutions in various business situations. Students may choose one of five optional concentrations: customized professional concentration, finance, health-care management, international business, or marketing.

The B.A. in Psychology program is designed to help students begin human services careers in such capacities as entry-level counselor, case manager, or human resources administrator and

in management and business services roles. The program also lays the foundation for graduate study. Students may choose an optional concentration from the following three options: criminal justice, organizational psychology, or substance abuse. This dynamic program is built around a flexible class approach.

Argosy University's bachelor's degree programs are open to students and working professionals with no college experience, plus those who have already earned college credit at a community college, junior college, or other university.

Academic Facilities

Argosy University libraries provide curriculum support and educational resources including current text materials, diagnostic training documents, reference materials and databases, journals and dissertations, and major and current titles in program areas. There is an online public-access catalog of library resources available throughout the Argosy University system. Students enjoy full remote access to their campus library database, enabling them to study and conduct research at home. Academic databases offer dissertation abstracts, academic journals, and professional periodicals. All library computers are Internet accessible. Software applications include Word, Excel, PowerPoint, SPSS, and various test-scoring programs.

Costs

Tuition varies by program. Students should contact the Argosy University campus of their choice for tuition information.

Financial Aid

A wide range of financial aid options is available to students who qualify. Argosy University offers access to federal and state aid programs, merit-based awards, grants, loans, and a work-study program. As a first step, students should complete the Free Application for Federal Student Aid (FAFSA). Prospective students can apply electronically at http://www.fafsa.ed.gov or at the campus. To receive consideration for financial aid and ensure timely receipt of funds, it is best to submit an application promptly.

Faculty

The Argosy University faculty is composed of working professionals who have a passion to help students succeed. Members bring real-world experience and the latest practice innovations to the academic setting. The diverse faculty is widely recognized for contributions to the field. Most hold doctoral degrees. They provide a substantive education that combines comprehensive knowledge with critical skills and practical workplace relevance. Above all, faculty members are committed to their students' personal and professional development.

Student Government

Argosy University campuses offer unique opportunities for student involvement beyond individual programs of study. Most faculty committees include a student representative. In addition, a student group meets with faculty members and administrators regularly to discuss pertinent campus-related issues.

Admission Requirements

Admission requirements differ depending on the number of college credits completed prior to application.

Students who have earned 12 or fewer semester college credits must provide proof of high school graduation or GED and meet one of the following conditions for admission: ACT composite score of 18 or above, or a combined math and verbal SAT score of 870, or minimum ACCUPLACER scores of 86 in sentence skills and 53 in algebra. Applicants who do not meet any of the above conditions for admission will be admitted with academic support if they provide proof of high school graduation or GED and meet one of the following: ACT composite score of 14 to 17, or a combined math and verbal SAT score of 660 to 869, or minimum ACCUPLACER scores of 54 in sentence skills and 36 in arithmetic.

Applicants who have earned 13 or more semester college credits must provide proof of high school graduation or GED and meet one of the following conditions for admission: cumulative college GPA of 2.0 or above or minimum ACCUPLACER scores of 86 for sentence skills and 53 in algebra. Students who do not meet either of the above criteria will be admitted with academic support if they provide proof of high school graduation or GED and meet the following condition: minimum ACCUPLACER scores of 54 in reading and 36 in arithmetic.

Students admitted with academic support are limited to 12 credit hours of study during their first semester (6 credit hours per session). Students admitted with academic support will be required to complete developmental English and/or math courses unless they meet the following conditions: Writing Review (ENG099)—must meet one of the following: a minimum ACCUPLACER score of 86 in sentence skills, or a minimum ACT verbal score of 18, or a minimum SAT verbal score of 425, or completion of a college-level English composition course with a grade of C or above; Mathematics Review I (MAT096)—must meet one of the following: a minimum ACCUPLACER score of 53 in algebra, or a minimum ACT math score of 18, or a minimum SAT math score of 440, or completion of a college-level English composition course with a grade of C or above.

Other admission requirements may include credit hours of qualified transfer credit with a grade of C- or better from a regionally accredited institution or a nationally accredited institution approved and documented by the faculty and dean of the College of Business, or the College of Professional Psychology, at Argosy University or completion of an Associate of Arts or Associate of Science degree from a regionally accredited institution. A maximum of 78 lower-division or 90 total credit hours may be transferred. A minimum written TOEFL score of 500 (paper-based test), 173 (computer-based test), or 61 (Internet-based test) is required for all applicants whose native language is not English or who have not graduated from an institution in which English is the language of instruction.

Official transcripts from approved postsecondary institutions must include a minimum grade point average of 2.0 (on a scale of 4.0) for all academic work completed. Exceptions may be made for extenuating circumstances. All applications must include a completed application form, proof of high school graduation or successful completion of the GED test, official postsecondary transcripts, and a nonrefundable (except in California) application fee. Additional materials are required prior to matriculation. Some programs have additional application requirements or include exceptions to admission requirements. An admissions representative can provide further information.

Application and Information

Argosy University accepts students on a rolling admissions basis year-round, depending on availability of required courses. Applications for admission are available online at http://www.argosy.edu or by contacting one of the campus locations.

Argosy University
205 North Michigan Avenue, Suite 1300
Chicago, Illinois 60601-2250
Phone: 312-899-9900
800-377-0617 (toll-free)
E-mail: auadmissions@argosy.edu
Web site: http://www.argosy.edu

THE ART INSTITUTE OF FORT LAUDERDALE

FORT LAUDERDALE, FLORIDA

The Institute

The Art Institute of Fort Lauderdale trains and prepares individuals for entry-level positions in the creative arts. Professional development is encouraged through curricula that emphasize the communication, reasoning, and technical skills potential employers seek.

The Art Institute of Fort Lauderdale offers both bachelor's and associate degree programs. In 2004, the school was named College of the Year by the Florida Association of Postsecondary Schools and Colleges.

The Career Services Office helps students find part-time employment while attending The Art Institute of Fort Lauderdale and entry-level positions in the arts following graduation. Students may also join professional organizations, which put them in contact with professionals from their chosen field.

The student population includes recent high school graduates, transfer students, and those who have left a previous employment situation to study and train for a new career. Students are creative, competitive, and open to new ideas.

Student clubs and organizations have been formed in multimedia, illustration, graphic design, philosophy, fashion design, animation, industrial design, and photography.

School-sponsored housing facilities are close by and are available to those students who prefer a traditional, residential-life environment. Housing facilities allow for easy access to beaches, boating, parks, and shopping. Independent housing information and roommate referrals are also available.

The Art Institute of Fort Lauderdale is accredited by the Accrediting Council for Independent Colleges and Schools (ACICS) to award bachelor's degrees, associate degrees, and diplomas. ACICS is listed as a nationally recognized accrediting agency by the U.S. Department of Education. Its accreditation of degree-granting institutions is recognized by the Council for Higher Education Accreditation. ACICS can be contacted at 750 First Street NE, Suite 980, Washington, D.C. 20002; telephone: 202-336-6780. The Associate of Science in culinary arts program is accredited by the American Culinary Federation (ACF). The Bachelor of Science in interior design degree program is accredited by the Council for Interior Design Accreditation.

Location

Surrounded by waterways, Fort Lauderdale is known as "The Venice of America." The area has an average temperature of 70 degrees in the winter and offers many opportunities for fun in the sun. The Art Institute of Fort Lauderdale is close to 23 miles of beaches, shopping districts, museums, historical sites, restaurants, and nightclubs. Located between Miami and Palm Beach, Fort Lauderdale's many attractions include its world-famous beach, the picturesque Riverwalk, and Las Olas Boulevard—a centerpiece of fashion, fine dining, and entertainment. Tourists and residents alike enjoy the Broward Center for the Performing Arts, Museum of Discovery and Science, Museum of Art, and Old Fort Lauderdale Village and Museum. Fort Lauderdale also supports a diverse range of industries, including marine, manufacturing, finance, insurance, real estate, high technology, avionics/aerospace, and film and television production.

Majors and Degrees

The Art Institute of Fort Lauderdale offers Bachelor of Science degree programs in advertising, culinary management, digital filmmaking and video production, fashion design, fashion merchandising, game art and design, graphic design, illustration, industrial design, interior design, media arts and animation, photography, visual effects and motion graphics, and Web design and interactive media.

Associate of Science degree programs are available in animation art and design, baking and pastry, broadcasting, culinary arts, fashion design, graphic design, photography, video production, and Web design and interactive media.

Diploma programs are offered in applied photography, art of cooking, graphic and desktop design, and residential design.

Academic Programs

The Art Institute of Fort Lauderdale offers Bachelor of Science degree programs (thirty-six months), Associate of Science degree programs (eighteen to twenty-one months), and diploma programs (twelve months).

Academic Facilities

The Art Institute of Fort Lauderdale occupies approximately 140,000 square feet in four separate buildings. The school has fifty different computer and program-specific labs, including those for animation, digital sound, CAD, and fashion design and the Digital Imaging Center. More than 580 PCs and Macintosh computers in a number of labs are available to students. Software programs include Premiere, Dreamweaver, Final Cut Pro, Quark, Illustrator, Photoshop, AutoCAD, Gerber, 3-D Max, Painter, Director, Flash, and Maya. The Nevin C. Meinhardt Memorial Library features a collection of books, periodicals, audiovisual materials, and online databases. The library provides access to remote resources through the Internet and cooperative agreements with other area libraries.

In addition, culinary students receive hands-on training in the bakery and presentation kitchens. The Chef's Palette is an on-site restaurant where students learn firsthand what it takes to operate and manage a restaurant. The Mark K. Wheeler Gallery is located on the first floor of the main building.

Costs

Tuition cost varies by program. Prospective students should contact the school for current tuition costs. Other charges include a starting kit for all first-quarter students. Kits vary in price depending on the program of study.

Financial Aid

Financial aid is available for those who qualify. Students who require financial assistance should first complete and submit a Free Application for Federal Student Aid (FAFSA) and meet with a financial aid officer. The officer determines the level of need based on a required federal formula, the cost of education, and other factors. Gift aid is available in the form of Federal Pell Grants, Federal Supplemental Educational Opportunity Grants, and veterans' benefits. Loans include Federal Stafford Loans, Federal PLUS Loans, and alternative loans. Other scholarships are available from the school and private sources. Application deadlines and eligibility requirements vary by program.

Faculty

The Art Institute of Fort Lauderdale consists of professional faculty members, many of whom have advanced degrees and experience in their chosen fields.

Student Government

All students have the right to participate and vote in Student Government elections and referenda. The Student Government works with faculty and staff members to provide numerous events, including student socials, community outreach programs, volunteer work, and student service events.

Admission Requirements

Admission to The Art Institute of Fort Lauderdale requires a completed application form, evidence of high school graduation or successful completion of the General Education Development (GED) test, and an essay on how the school may assist in achieving the applicant's creative goals. Applicants are also required to schedule an interview with an admissions representative and, if financial aid is needed, to complete the FAFSA and PLUS loan forms found in the application packet. There is a $50 application fee.

Application and Information

To obtain an application, make arrangements for an interview, or tour the school, students should contact:

The Art Institute of Fort Lauderdale
1799 S.E. 17th Street
Fort Lauderdale, Florida 33316-3013

Phone: 954-463-3000
800-275-7603 (toll-free)
Fax: 954-728-8637
Web site: http://www.artinstitutes.edu/fortlauderdale

The Art Institute of Atlanta®, GA; The Art Institute of Atlanta®–Decatur, GA; The Art Institute of Austin℠, TX; The Art Institute of California℠–Inland Empire; The Art Institute of California℠–Los Angeles; The Art Institute of California℠–Orange County; The Art Institute of California℠–Sacramento; The Art Institute of California℠–San Diego; The Art Institute of California℠–San Francisco; The Art Institute of California℠–Sunnyvale; The Art Institute of Charleston℠, SC, A branch of The Art Institute of Atlanta, GA; The Art Institute of Charlotte®, NC; The Art Institute of Colorado® (Denver); The Art Institute of Dallas®, TX; The Art Institute of Fort Lauderdale®, FL; The Art Institute of Houston®, TX; The Art Institute of Indianapolis℠, IN*; The Art Institute of Jacksonville℠, FL, A branch of Miami International University of Art & Design; The Art Institute of Las Vegas®, NV; The Art Institute of Michigan℠ (Detroit); The Art Institute of New York City®, NY; The Art Institute of Ohio℠–Cincinnati**; The Art Institute of Philadelphia®, PA; The Art Institute of Phoenix®, AZ; The Art Institute of Pittsburgh®, PA; The Art Institute of Pittsburgh®–Online Division; The Art Institute of Portland®, OR; The Art Institute of Salt Lake City℠, UT; The Art Institute of Seattle®, WA; The Art Institute of Tampa℠, FL, A branch of Miami International University of Art & Design; The Art Institute of Tennessee℠–Nashville, A branch of The Art Institute of Atlanta, GA; The Art Institute of Tucson℠, AZ; The Art Institute of Washington® (Arlington, VA), A branch of The Art Institute of Atlanta, GA; The Art Institute of York–Pennsylvania℠; The Art Institutes International Minnesota℠ (Minneapolis); California Design College℠ (Los Angeles–Wilshire Blvd.); The Illinois Institute of Art®–Chicago; The Illinois Institute of Art®–Schaumburg; Miami International University of Art & Design℠, FL; The New England Institute of Art® (Boston, MA).

*The Art Institute of Indianapolis is licensed by the Indiana Commission on Proprietary Education, 302 W. Washington St., Rm. E201, Indianapolis, IN 46204, AC-0080.

**The Art Institute of Ohio–Cincinnati, 8845 Governors Hill Drive, Suite 100, Cincinnati, OH 45249-3317, OH Reg. #04-01-1698B.

THE ART INSTITUTE OF JACKSONVILLE

JACKSONVILLE, FLORIDA

The Institute

The Art Institute of Jacksonville helps students cultivate and refine the talents and skills that lead to entry-level positions in the creative arts. Classes are taught in an environment that encourages learning, leadership, and creativity. The school offers five bachelor's degree programs and three associate degree programs.

Faculty and staff members strive to foster development and cultivate artistic growth. Students are given opportunities to develop leadership skills and build relationships. In addition, assistance is available to help students with resume writing, networking, and keeping abreast of what employers are looking for in job candidates.

The Art Institute of Jacksonville places a high value on the quality of student life both in and out of the classroom. Students participate in a wide variety of activities, including clubs and organizations, community service, and various committees designed to enhance the quality of student life.

The school provides information on independent housing options to all enrolled students requesting such assistance.

Students come to The Art Institute of Jacksonville from throughout the United States. The student population includes recent high school graduates, transfer students, and those who have left a previous employment situation to study and train for a new career. Students are creative, competitive, and open to new ideas.

The Art Institute of Jacksonville is a branch of Miami International University of Art & Design, which is accredited to award Associate of Arts, Bachelor of Arts, and Bachelor of Fine Arts degrees by the Commission on Colleges of the Southern Association of Colleges and Schools (SACS; 1866 Southern Lane, Decatur, Georgia 30033-4097; telephone: 404-679-4500; http://www.sacs.org). The Art Institute of Jacksonville is licensed by the Commission for Independent Education, Florida Department of Education. Additional information regarding this institution may be obtained by contacting the Commission for Independent Education (325 West Gaines Street, Suite 1414, Tallahassee, Florida 32399-0400; telephone: 888-224-6684).

Location

The Art Institute of Jacksonville is located in Jacksonville, Florida's largest city. With mild winters and warm summers, Jacksonville is a popular tourist destination. The Jacksonville beaches, Florida Theater, and professional sports teams are exciting entertainment options within the region.

Majors and Degrees

The Art Institute of Jacksonville offers bachelor's and associate degrees. Bachelor's degrees are offered in culinary management, digital filmmaking and video production, graphic design, interior design, and Web design and interactive media. Students may also pursue an Associate of Arts degree in culinary arts, graphic design, or Web design and interactive media design. A diploma program is offered in culinary arts: skills.

Academic Programs

The academic year is divided into four quarters, beginning in January, April, July, and October. Each program is offered on a year-round basis, allowing students to continue to work uninterrupted toward their degrees.

Academic Facilities

The Art Institute of Jacksonville is located on Baypine Road in Jacksonville. The school has a bookstore, Mac and PC computer labs, and classrooms.

Costs

Tuition cost varies by program. Prospective students should contact the school for current tuition costs. Other charges include a starting kit for all first-quarter students. Kits vary in price depending on the program of study.

Financial Aid

Financial aid is available for those who qualify. Students who require financial assistance should first complete and submit a Free Application for Federal Student Aid (FAFSA) and meet with a financial aid officer. The officer determines the student's level of need based on a required federal formula, the cost of education, and other factors. Gift aid is available in the form of Federal Pell Grants, Federal Supplemental Educational Opportunity Grants, and veterans' benefits. Loans include Federal Stafford Loans, Federal PLUS Loans, and alternative loans. Scholarships are available from the school and private sources. Application deadlines and eligibility requirements vary by program.

Faculty

The Art Institute of Jacksonville faculty consists of full-time and part-time instructors, many of whom have advanced degrees and professional experience in their respective fields.

Student Government

The Student Federation is responsible for student government and acts as a liaison between the student body and faculty and staff members.

Admission Requirements

Applicants must provide proof of high school graduation or achievement of a General Educational Development (GED) certificate as a prerequisite for admission. In lieu of documenting high school graduation or a GED certificate, applicants may provide proof of attaining an associate degree or higher from an accredited institution. An official transcript indicating date of high school graduation, GED certificate (including test scores), or date of college graduation (including degree granted) is required as proof.

All individuals seeking admission to The Art Institute of Jacksonville are interviewed in person or by phone by an assistant director of admissions, and each applicant must submit an original essay of at least 150 words stating how an education at the school would help the student to achieve career goals. There is a $50 application fee.

Application and Information

To obtain an application, make arrangements for an interview, or tour the school, students should contact:

The Art Institute of Jacksonville
8775 Baypine Road
Jacksonville, Florida 32256-8528
Phone: 904-486-3000
800-924-1589 (toll-free)
Fax: 904-732-9423
Web site: http://www.artinstitutes.edu/jacksonville

The Art Institute of Atlanta®, GA; The Art Institute of Atlanta®–Decatur, GA; The Art Institute of Austin℠, TX; The Art Institute of California℠–Inland Empire; The Art Institute of California℠–Los Angeles; The Art Institute of California℠–Orange County; The Art Institute of California℠–Sacramento; The Art Institute of California℠–San Diego; The Art Institute of California℠–San Francisco; The Art Institute of California℠–Sunnyvale; The Art Institute of Charleston℠, SC, A branch of The Art Institute of Atlanta, GA; The Art Institute of Charlotte®, NC; The Art Institute of Colorado® (Denver); The Art Institute of Dallas®, TX; The Art Institute of Fort Lauderdale®, FL; The Art Institute of Houston®, TX; The Art Institute of Indianapolis℠, IN*; The Art Institute of Jacksonville℠, FL, A branch of Miami International University of Art & Design; The Art Institute of Las Vegas®, NV; The Art Institute of Michigan℠ (Detroit); The Art Institute of New York City®, NY; The Art Institute of Ohio℠–Cincinnati**; The Art Institute of Philadelphia®, PA; The Art Institute of Phoenix®, AZ; The Art Institute of Pittsburgh®, PA; The Art Institute of Pittsburgh®–Online Division; The Art Institute of Portland®, OR; The Art Institute of Salt Lake City℠, UT; The Art Institute of Seattle®, WA; The Art Institute of Tampa℠, FL, A branch of Miami International University of Art & Design; The Art Institute of Tennessee℠–Nashville, A branch of The Art Institute of Atlanta, GA; The Art Institute of Tucson℠, AZ; The Art Institute of Washington® (Arlington, VA), A branch of The Art Institute of Atlanta, GA; The Art Institute of York–Pennsylvania℠; The Art Institutes International Minnesota℠ (Minneapolis); California Design College℠ (Los Angeles–Wilshire Blvd.); The Illinois Institute of Art®–Chicago; The Illinois Institute of Art®–Schaumburg; Miami International University of Art & Design℠, FL; The New England Institute of Art® (Boston, MA).

*The Art Institute of Indianapolis is licensed by the Indiana Commission on Proprietary Education, 302 W. Washington St., Rm. E201, Indianapolis, IN 46204, AC-0080.

**The Art Institute of Ohio–Cincinnati, 8845 Governors Hill Drive, Suite 100, Cincinnati, OH 45249-3317, OH Reg. #04-01-1698B.

THE ART INSTITUTE OF TAMPA

TAMPA, FLORIDA

The Institute

The Art Institute of Tampa provides programs created to help students to obtain entry-level employment in the creative arts. Students are encouraged to gain an understanding of theoretical and practical knowledge appropriate to their degree objectives, demonstrated through measurable student-learning outcomes specified for each degree program. The Art Institute of Tampa offers twelve bachelor's degree programs and four associate degree programs.

The student population includes recent high school graduates, transfer students, and those who have left a previous employment situation to study and train for a new career. Students are creative, competitive, and open to new ideas. They place great value on an education that prepares them for an exciting entry-level position in the arts.

Classes are sized to allow for individual attention, and course work is developed by industry leaders who are familiar with the professional workplace. Many faculty members work outside of the classroom and bring back practical knowledge that provides students with a relevant, hands-on education. In addition, assistance is available to help students with resume writing, networking, and keeping abreast of what employers are looking for in job candidates.

The active contribution of students to college life supports the creative and intellectual evolution of everyone at The Art Institute of Tampa. Although some students arrive with previous experience in their program fields, others arrive with only their desire to learn. Students come to The Art Institute of Tampa from private schools, public schools, and home-school environments.

Housing placement assistance is available through referrals and other local resources.

The Art Institute of Tampa is a branch of Miami International University of Art & Design, which is accredited by the Commission on Colleges of the Southern Association of Colleges and Schools (SACS) to award Associate of Arts, Bachelor of Arts, and Bachelor of Fine Arts degrees (1866 Southern Lane, Decatur, Georgia 30033-4097; 404-679-4500; http://www.sacs.org). Miami International University of Art & Design and its branch, The Art Institute of Tampa, hold a License by Means of Accreditation from the Florida Commission for Independent Education. Any questions regarding the License by Means of Accreditation should be directed to the Florida Department of Education, Commission for Independent Education, 325 West Gaines Street, Suite 1414, Tallahassee, Florida 32399-0400.

Location

Located in Tampa's bustling business district, The Art Institute of Tampa is situated across from Raymond James Stadium and Al Lopez Park, comprising 126 acres of Florida's fauna and flora. Tampa's balmy climate makes the outdoors enjoyable year-round. Residents enjoy bicycling, jogging, sunbathing, walking, in-line skating, swimming, sport fishing, scuba diving, and snorkeling. Gyms and dance studios offer opportunities for aerobics; weight lifting, ballet, kickboxing, and the martial arts. Local attractions include Busch Gardens, the Florida Aquarium, Lowry Park Zoo, the Tampa Museum of Art, Shakespeare in the Park, the Clearwater Jazz Festival, and the world-renowned Salvador Dalí Museum. Sports fans follow the Tampa Bay Buccaneers, Devil Rays, or Lightning, and popular nightlife spots include Channelside, Bay Street, and Ybor City, the center of the city's bustling music scene. Theater, symphony, and dance performances; museums; and a diverse range of art galleries showcase some of the world's greatest talent. Situated on the west coast of Florida, the Tampa Bay area has grown to become one of the most populous and affluent regions in Florida. With its unique blend of urban excitement and natural beauty, there really is something for everyone who lives in the beautiful, diverse communities connected by green spaces and waterways.

Majors and Degrees

The Art Institute of Tampa offers bachelor's degrees in advertising, culinary management, digital filmmaking and video production, digital photography, fashion and retail management, food and beverage management, game art and design, graphic design, interior design, media arts and animation, visual effects and motion graphics, and Web design and interactive media.

Associate degrees are available in culinary arts, graphic design, Web design and interactive media, and wine, spirits, and beverage management (students must be at least 21 years of age at the time of admission to this program).

Academic Programs

The academic year is divided into four quarters, beginning in January, April, July, and October. Bachelor's degrees require the completion of 192 credits (thirty-six months), and associate degrees require completion of 112 academic credits (twenty-one months).

Academic Facilities

The school's facility features cross-platform computer labs, a resource library, a gallery, and a student lounge. The Art Institute of Tampa offers each student easy access to the technology, tools, and facilities needed to complete projects in all disciplines.

Costs

Tuition cost varies by program. Prospective students should contact the school for current tuition costs. Other charges include a starting kit for all first-quarter students. Kits vary in price, depending on the program of study.

Financial Aid

Financial aid is available for those who qualify. Students who require financial assistance should first complete and submit a Free Application for Federal Student Aid (FAFSA) and meet with a financial aid officer. The officer determines the level of need based on a required federal formula, the cost of education, and other factors. Gift aid is available in the form of Federal Pell Grants, Federal Supplemental Educational Opportunity Grants, and veterans' benefits. Loans include Federal Stafford Student Loans, Federal PLUS loans, and alternative loans. Other scholarships are available from the school and private sources. Application deadlines and eligibility requirements vary by program.

Faculty

The Art Institute of Tampa faculty consists of full-time and part-time instructors. Each instructor brings professional knowledge to their teaching, and many work in their fields of expertise outside of the classroom.

Student Government

Student leadership is fundamental to academic success and is a way to network with and meet other students. Student leaders serve as role models for peers and act as student advocates for the school. Student leadership programs at The Art Institute of Tampa support the mission of the school, help students refine interpersonal skills, implement positive change for the student body, and promote school and community spirit. Students may become active members of The Art Institute of Tampa Student Government, start or join a university club, or attend school-sponsored seminars designed to improve leadership skills.

Admission Requirements

Applicants must demonstrate proof of high school graduation or its equivalent in order to receive final acceptance. An official copy of a high school transcript or General Educational Development (GED) transcript is required. Applicants are also required to interview with the school (either in person or by telephone) and write an essay of approximately 150 words in length describing how an education at The Art Institute of Tampa will help them attain creative goals. The Admissions Acceptance Committee determines the compatibility of the applicant with the school and reserves the right to request the results of the SAT or ACT exam and other additional information. A separate application and enrollment form must be completed and signed by the applicant. Prospective students may apply at any time of the year. Applications may be submitted online or mailed to the school. There is a $50 application fee.

Application and Information

To obtain an application, make arrangements for an interview, or tour the school, students should contact:

The Art Institute of Tampa
Parkside at Tampa Bay Park
4401 North Himes Avenue, Suite 150
Tampa, Florida 36614-7086
Phone: 813-873-2112
866-703-3277 (toll-free)
Fax: 813-873-2171
Web site: http://www.artinstitutes.edu/tampa

The Art Institute of Atlanta®, GA; The Art Institute of Atlanta®–Decatur, GA; The Art Institute of Austin℠, TX; The Art Institute of California℠–Inland Empire; The Art Institute of California℠–Los Angeles; The Art Institute of California℠–Orange County; The Art Institute of California℠–Sacramento; The Art Institute of California℠–San Diego; The Art Institute of California℠–San Francisco; The Art Institute of California℠–Sunnyvale; The Art Institute of Charleston℠, SC, A branch of The Art Institute of Atlanta, GA; The Art Institute of Charlotte®, NC; The Art Institute of Colorado® (Denver); The Art Institute of Dallas®, TX; The Art Institute of Fort Lauderdale®, FL; The Art Institute of Houston®, TX; The Art Institute of Indianapolis℠, IN*; The Art Institute of Jacksonville℠, FL, A branch of Miami International University of Art & Design; The Art Institute of Las Vegas®, NV; The Art Institute of Michigan℠ (Detroit); The Art Institute of New York City®, NY; The Art Institute of Ohio℠–Cincinnati**; The Art Institute of Philadelphia®, PA; The Art Institute of Phoenix®, AZ; The Art Institute of Pittsburgh®, PA; The Art Institute of Pittsburgh®–Online Division; The Art Institute of Portland®, OR; The Art Institute of Salt Lake City℠, UT; The Art Institute of Seattle®, WA; The Art Institute of Tampa℠, FL, A branch of Miami International University of Art & Design; The Art Institute of Tennessee℠–Nashville, A branch of The Art Institute of Atlanta, GA; The Art Institute of Tucson℠, AZ; The Art Institute of Washington® (Arlington, VA), A branch of The Art Institute of Atlanta, GA; The Art Institute of York–Pennsylvania℠; The Art Institutes International Minnesota℠ (Minneapolis); California Design College℠ (Los Angeles–Wilshire Blvd.); The Illinois Institute of Art®–Chicago; The Illinois Institute of Art®–Schaumburg; Miami International University of Art & Design℠, FL; The New England Institute of Art® (Boston, MA).

*The Art Institute of Indianapolis is licensed by the Indiana Commission on Proprietary Education, 302 W. Washington St., Rm. E201, Indianapolis, IN 46204, AC-0080.

**The Art Institute of Ohio–Cincinnati, 8845 Governors Hill Drive, Suite 100, Cincinnati, OH 45249-3317, OH Reg. #04-01-1698B.

AVE MARIA UNIVERSITY

AVE MARIA, FLORIDA

The University

As the first new Catholic university in forty years, Ave Maria University exists to further teaching, research, and learning in the abiding tradition of Catholic thought in both national and international settings. The University sponsors a liberal arts education curriculum dedicated to the advancement of human culture, the promotion of dialogue between faith and reason, and the formation of men and women in the intellectual and moral virtues of the Catholic faith.

The University began as Thomas S. Monaghan's dream to build an institution that would be faithful to the Magisterium and could produce faithful educators, leaders, and mentors. Through his initial financial donation, the University opened its doors in August 2003 with 100 students. In the first semester at its new campus, the University enrollment is over 600 students, demonstrating the growth of which Ave Maria University is capable.

In addition to its undergraduate degree programs, the University's graduate department offers an M.T.S. in pastoral theology and a Master of Arts and Ph.D. in theology.

The Chaplain's Office, in conjunction with Student Life, organizes retreats for students throughout the year. The University also encourages students to find opportunities to serve the poor, the infirm, and the elderly in the local community.

Ave Maria University recognizes the important role that athletics play in forming the whole person. To that end, club and intramural-level sports are offered in men's and women's basketball and soccer as well as golf, tennis, and volleyball. In addition, the University plans to have NAIA division sports beginning in the fall semester of 2008.

Full-time students are required to live on campus, unless they are living at home with their parents. However, students who are 23 or older may only live on campus with permission of the Dean of Students (excepting those discerning a religious vocation). Each residence hall includes a live-in adult residence director and a student resident assistant on each floor. Each hall provides students with common areas, kitchen and laundry facilities, meeting rooms, and a chapel. Choice of housing on campus is granted each year primarily, though not exclusively, on the basis of academic seniority. The University has a private dining area in the Student Union. Breakfast, lunch, and dinner are served Monday through Friday. Brunch and an evening meal are served on Saturdays and Sundays.

Location

Ave Maria University's permanent campus occupies 100 acres of land approximately 20 miles northeast of the city of Naples. The town of Ave Maria, adjoining the University, provides not only residences but a thriving town center, La Piazza, which is home to restaurants, coffee shops, the University Bookstore, and other vendors. Naples, nestled near the beaches of the Gulf of Mexico, is known for world-class shopping, dining, and more than thirty-five golf courses. It is only steps away from the Everglades and boasts one of the nation's best sandboxes and calmest seas. Art lovers can spend an evening at the Philharmonic Center for the Arts or the popular Dinner Theater or visit local art galleries and historic sites around the city. The many nearby parks and nature preserves feature rare species of flora and fauna indigenous to the state.

Majors and Degrees

The University offers a Bachelor of Arts degree in biology, classics and early Christian literature, economics, history, literature, mathematics, music with a concentration in sacred music, philosophy, politics, and theology. Beginning in the fall semester of 2007, a Certificate in Business is also offered, designed for students who wish to have a better understanding of accounting, management, business ethics, and marketing. For men discerning a call to the priesthood, the University offers a Pre-Theologate Program to prepare them for entry into a major seminary. Preprofessional programs in law and medicine are also offered.

Academic Programs

The University's core curriculum requires students to take specific courses in the liberal arts, thus acquiring the indispensable foundation for a lifetime of learning. Of the 128 credits required to earn a bachelor's degree, the core curriculum comprises one half, or 64 credits. The major of study comprises another 32 to 40 credits, and general electives comprise the final 24 to 32 credits. Students are required to take two noncredit practicums in the fine arts, the first in an introduction to Gregorian Chant and the second in chorus, instrumental music, studio art, or theater. Other core courses include three courses each in theology and philosophy; two courses each in history, literature, Latin, and the natural sciences; and one course each in American civilization and mathematics. Some requirements may be met through CLEP, Advanced Placement (with an exam score of 4), and military service.

Off-Campus Programs

The University offers study-abroad programs at Ave Maria University, Latin America, located in San Marcos, Nicaragua, and in Gaming, Austria, at the International Theological Institute. Students may enroll in the program for one semester. Courses are taught in English and correspond to the requirements of the degree programs at the University. The cost for each program is the regular University cost of attendance, although students are expected to cover their travel expenses. Students must have at least sophomore status to enter the programs. Transfer students must have spent at least one full semester at the Ave Maria Florida campus before they are eligible to apply.

Academic Facilities

Ave Maria University's Canizaro Library has 4 librarians and a support staff of 10 members. With more than 190,000 volumes, the Canizaro Library has one of the largest permanent collections in the region. In addition to its impressive open-stack collection, the Canizaro Library has interlibrary loan privileges with university libraries throughout the United States and belongs to the Southwest Florida Library Network consortium. To supplement its print resources, the Canizaro Library provides students and faculty and staff members with access to several electronic databases for research purposes. These can be accessed from any network computer. Computer workstations located throughout the campus are connected to the campus network and include the most up-to-date software. All computer stations are equipped with printers and Internet access. Scanners for photos and graphics are also available. Facilities for viewing audiovisual materials are located throughout the campus. A writing lab program provides students with the opportunity to familiarize themselves with accepted standards for expository writing as well as the institutional style and research conventions.

Costs

For the 2007–08 academic year, undergraduate tuition is $7865 per semester or $15,730 for the year. Other costs per semester include $1935 for housing, $1635 for meals, and additional fees of $265.50. The total cost of attendance is $11,697.50 per semester or $23,395 per academic year.

Financial Aid

Approximately 90 percent of students receive financial assistance. Ave Maria University is Title IV eligible, allowing students to participate in federal student financial aid programs. In addition to federal aid, institutional grants are offered. The Ave Maria University Grant is awarded to students who demonstrate considerable financial need. All financial aid decisions are based on the Free Application for Federal Student Aid (FAFSA). Ave Maria University also offers scholarships to students based on prior academic achievement, ACT or SAT scores, and leadership factors; those interested in a scholarship should apply early (early action deadline is November 15). On-campus employment opportunities are also available. The University offers the option of paying over a five- or ten-month period with no interest.

Faculty

The faculty consists of 54 professors, 95 percent of whom hold the terminal degree (Ph.D. or equivalent) in their fields of study. Faculty members are carefully chosen for a clear and strong commitment to Catholic education, and professors of philosophy and theology annually make the Profession of Faith and renew their Oath of Fidelity to the Magisterium of the Catholic Church.

Student Government

The student body is represented by a president, a vice president, a secretary, a treasurer, and 2 elected representatives from each class. The student representatives are responsible for hosting a number of student activities and programs and for setting the budget for other student organizations.

Admission Requirements

Prospective students are required to have completed at least 15 high school credits with a minimum GPA of 2.8 on a 4.0 scale and have a minimum ACT composite score of 22 or SAT score of 1580 (critical reading, math, and writing). Transfer students must have a college GPA of at least 2.4. In order to be admitted, applicants must submit a completed application form, official SAT or ACT scores, high school and college transcripts, two letters of recommendation, a list of extracurricular activities and other high school achievements, and an essay (prospective students should visit the Web site for essay parameters).

Application and Information

The early action deadline is November 15. Applications are evaluated on a rolling admissions basis. Applications may be submitted online or mailed to:

Office of Admissions
Ave Maria University
5050 Ave Maria Boulevard
Ave Maria, Florida 34142-9505
Phone: 239-280-2556
877-283-8648 (toll-free)
Fax: 239-280-2559
Web site: http://www.avemaria.edu

Students on campus at Ave Maria University.

COLLEGE DATA CENTER • FLORIDA

BARRY UNIVERSITY
MIAMI SHORES, FLORIDA

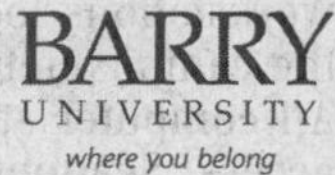

The University

Barry University is an independent Catholic university. Founded in 1940 by the Dominican Sisters of Adrian, Michigan, the University provides a multicultural student body with an affordable, high-quality education; a caring environment; and a religious dimension and encourages a commitment to community service. Classes are small, so students receive personal attention from distinguished faculty members and advisers. The student-faculty ratio is 14:1.

The graceful main campus with Spanish-style architecture is located in Miami Shores. The University also offers programs at forty-eight additional sites from Tallahassee to Key West. Students come from all compass points, age groups, ethnicities, and faiths, representing forty-nine states and eighty countries. Of the more than 9,400 students enrolled, more than 2,800 are full-time undergraduates and nearly 6,500 are graduate and continuing education students.

Barry offers more than fifty undergraduate majors and more than fifty graduate degree programs in the arts and sciences, business, education, graduate medical sciences, human performance and leisure sciences, law, natural and health sciences, nursing, and social work.

Barry holds membership in twenty honor societies and hosts eighty-nine undergraduate and graduate student organizations, including the Barry University Dance Team, the Caribbean Students Association, the Campus Activities Board, and the *Buccaneer* student newspaper, as well as two fraternities and three sororities. Barry also promotes community service organizations, such as Best Buddies and Habitat for Humanity.

The University fields twelve intercollegiate athletic teams that participate in the NCAA Division II and the Sunshine State Conference. Since 1984, the Buccaneers have won eight national championships. Nearly 60 percent of Barry's student-athletes achieve grade point averages above 3.0. Intramural sports include basketball, flag football, golf, sand volleyball, soccer, street hockey, tennis, and volleyball.

Facilities include the David Brinkley Studio television production studio, the Monsignor William Barry Library, an extensive library network, multimedia classrooms, and technologically advanced labs. Students gain hands-on professional experience even before graduation, such as helping to provide basic health care for elementary school children, conducting Alzheimer's research with faculty members, or editing a local news program.

The 78,000-square-foot R. Kirk Landon Student Union houses the offices of student services and student organizations as well as a bookstore, dining room, snack bar, campus game room, and more. A fully equipped fitness center features weight and cardio equipment. Resident students live in eight air-conditioned residence halls where every room is wired for high-speed Internet access. All students may keep cars on campus. The University's Department of Commuter Affairs serves as a resource center for commuters.

The University is accredited by the Southern Association of Colleges and Schools to award bachelor's, master's, specialist, and doctoral degrees. Barry also holds a number of accreditations from professional organizations for specific programs.

Location

Barry University is 5 miles from the ocean in sunny, suburban Miami Shores. The hospitable climate allows for swimming, sailing, waterskiing, scuba diving, and playing golf, tennis, soccer, and other outdoor sports year-round. Nearby, the Florida Keys, the Everglades, and living coral reefs present both recreational and educational opportunities. South Florida is an international business, tourism, and entertainment industry hub with a cosmopolitan multicultural population, offering a wide range of internship and career options as well as a vibrant cultural scene. Highlights include Urban Beach Week, the Calle Ocho Street Festival, the Miami International Book Fair, and the prestigious art fair, Art Basel Miami Beach. The New World Symphony, the Miami International Film Festival, and the Miami City Ballet provide a full season of acclaimed performances. Miami also hosts the Miami Dolphins football team, the Miami Heat basketball team, the Florida Marlins baseball team, and the Florida Panthers hockey team.

Majors and Degrees

Barry University offers the Bachelor of Arts degree in advertising, art (art history, ceramics, drawing, graphic design, and painting), broadcast communication, communication studies, English (literature and professional writing), environmental studies, French, general studies, history, international studies, philosophy, photography (biomedical/forensic, creative, digital imaging, and photo/communication), prelaw, public relations, Spanish (language and literature and translation and interpretation), theater (acting, dance, technical theater, theater production, and theater publicity), and theology.

The Bachelor of Science degree is offered in accounting, athletic training (premedicine and pre–physical therapy specializations and a five-year seamless B.S. to M.S.), biology (biotechnology, ecological studies, histotechnology, marine science, predental, premedical, preoptometry, prepharmacy, pre–physical therapy, pre–physician assistant studies, pre–podiatric medicine, and preveterinary), cardiovascular perfusion, chemistry (biochemistry, environmental chemistry, predental, premedical, prepharmacy, and preveterinary), computer information sciences, computer science, criminology, cytotechnology, diagnostic medical ultrasound technology, economics, education, elementary education, environmental science (biology and chemistry), exceptional student education, exercise science (premedical and pre–physical therapy specializations and a five-year seamless B.S. to M.S.), finance, international business, management, marketing, mathematical sciences (computational mathematics and statistical/actuarial science), medical technology, nuclear medicine technology, physical education, political science, pre-K primary education, psychology (industrial/organizational), sociology, and sport management (diving industry and golf industry).

The University also offers the Bachelor of Science in Nursing, the Bachelor of Fine Arts (art and photography), the Bachelor of Music (music performance, musical theater, and sacred music), and the Bachelor of Social Work.

Minor concentrations are available in specific subject areas as well as in the interdisciplinary areas of Africana studies, film studies, peace studies, and women's studies.

Teaching certification is available for pre-K through primary education, elementary education, exceptional student education, and physical education. A certificate program in the translation and interpretation of Spanish is offered.

Seven accelerated undergraduate degree programs are offered for working adults through Barry's evening and weekend programs.

Academic Programs

The University operates on a semester plan. The first semester extends from the end of August to mid-December, and the second semester extends from mid-January to early May. Two 6-week sessions are offered during the summer. Students must maintain a minimum cumulative grade point average of 2.0 (or C) and earn a minimum of 120 credits for a degree. Of these 120 credits, 9 must be in philosophy and theology, 9 in communication—oral and written, 9 in humanities and arts, 9 in physical or natural sciences and mathematics, and 9 in social and behavioral sciences. The traditional full-time academic load is 12 to 18 credits each semester and 6 credits each summer term. Candidates for degree programs may elect either a major area of specialization or a broad liberal arts program and must satisfy all requirements of the program that they choose to follow, including all professional preparation requirements. Exceptionally well-qualified seniors may earn up to 6 hours of graduate credit with the recommendation of the department chairperson and the dean. Internships are required for many majors.

An ELS Language Centers program is available to international students needing to increase language proficiency. The Clinical Center for Advanced Learning offers a program designed to assist students with learning disabilities who have the intellectual potential and motivation to complete a four-year degree.

The University also offers an active honors program designed to add breadth and depth to the educational experience. The approach is interdisciplinary.

Off-Campus Programs

Barry University offers summer programs abroad. In addition, Barry is a member of the College Consortium for International Studies, enabling students to participate in programs in twenty-five countries offered by member colleges and universities. Barry University students may enroll in Air Force ROTC courses through cross-registration at a nearby university.

Academic Facilities

Students find the high-quality resources they need to support their education at Barry. Campus facilities include the Monsignor William Barry Library, an extensive library network, photography and digital imaging labs, a human performance lab, an athletic training room, a biomechanics lab, a complete television production studio, an academic computing center, multimedia business classrooms, art studios, a performing arts center, a nursing lab, and a cell biology lab as well as several other well-equipped science labs.

Costs

For 2007–08, tuition for full-time undergraduate students for the academic year was $24,500. Student services fees are included in tuition. Room and board costs averaged $7850 (double room). Expenses such as books, supplies, laboratory or other special fees, and transportation are not included in these costs. Barry families can take advantage of a fixed tuition cost in Barry's Tuition Until Graduation program. The program lets families know, upon first-year enrollment, what tuition they will pay until graduation.

Financial Aid

Barry University offers an excellent scholarship and grant program, awarding scholarships each year to students who have demonstrated academic success and promise. These scholarships and grants may be renewed for up to four years as long as the students meet the renewal criteria. Barry need-based grants and athletic scholarships are also available.

Barry also participates in the Federal Pell and Federal Supplemental Educational Opportunity Grant programs, the Federal Perkins Loan Program, the Federal Work-Study Program, the Florida Resident Access Grant Program, the Florida Student Assistance Grant, Florida Bright Futures Scholarships, and the Federal Family Educational Loan Program. Barry awards financial assistance on the basis of financial need and academic excellence. Applicants must submit the Free Application for Federal Student Aid (FAFSA) in order to be considered for aid. Ninety percent of full-time undergraduate students receive assistance from the University. Additional information may be obtained by calling the Office of Financial Aid at 305-899-3673 or 800-495-2279 (toll-free) or by e-mail at finaid@mail.barry.edu.

Faculty

Faculty members are easily accessible to students and are committed to providing individualized attention. The undergraduate faculty members participate in a dynamic academic advisement program. Doctorates are held by 81 percent of the faculty members, and the student-faculty ratio is 14:1.

Student Government

The Student Government Association serves as a liaison between the student body and the administration and faculty. All undergraduate students are members of the association, which is governed by an Executive Board that consists of 4 members and the Senate, which consists of 7 elected representatives. Six members are elected during the spring semester, and the remaining position (Freshman Senator) is filled early in the fall semester. Unless otherwise specified, meetings of the Senate are open, and students are invited and encouraged to attend the weekly sessions.

Admission Requirements

In reviewing the credentials of students seeking admission, Barry University considers an applicant's composite efforts. Candidates must present the following credentials: the completed application form, official high school or college transcripts, and the results of the SAT or ACT.

Application and Information

The University reviews applications as they are completed. Students are advised of their acceptance once the admissions staff has reviewed all required documents. Students may apply any time after completion of the junior year in high school. It is advisable to apply early. The student's completed application form and supporting credentials should be sent to the Assistant Dean for Undergraduate Admission. Students may also apply online at http://www.barry.edu/ugapply.

Ms. Laura Antczak
Director of Undergraduate Admissions
Kelley House
Barry University
11300 Northeast Second Avenue
Miami Shores, Florida 33161-6695
Phone: 305-899-3100
800-695-2279 (toll-free)
Fax: 305-899-2971
E-mail: admissions@mail.barry.edu
Web site: http://www.barry.edu

Barry offers an outstanding environment for quiet reflection and study.

BETHUNE-COOKMAN UNIVERSITY

DAYTONA BEACH, FLORIDA

The University

Bethune-Cookman University is a private, comprehensive, coeducational, residential institution, which operates on a semester calendar and is affiliated with the United Methodist Church. The University is a result of a merger between the Daytona Educational and Industrial Training School for Negro Girls (founded by Mary McLeod Bethune in 1904) and the Darnell Cookman Institute for Men (founded in 1872). It is accredited by the Commission on Colleges of the Southern Association of Colleges and Schools to award the bachelor's degree and master's degree, and by the Florida State Department of Education, the University Senate of the United Methodist Church, the AMA Committee on Allied Health Education and Accreditation, the National Council for Accreditation of Teacher Education, and the National League for Nursing Accrediting Commission. The University is approved by the Florida State Board of Nursing Licensure.

High academic standards, curriculum flexibility, concern for the individual student, and an emphasis on a broad Christian way of life are trademarks of the institution. The 3,400 students at Bethune-Cookman University come from forty-three states and thirty-five international countries. The campus cultural and social activities include choirs, band, drama, student publications, radio broadcasting, clubs, and Greek letter organizations, as well as intramural and NCAA Division I-A and I-AA intercollegiate athletics.

In addition to the undergraduate degree programs offered, the Master of Science in Transformative Leadership Program started August 2006. This online study of leadership advocates value-centered change based on an awareness of the diversity of cultures that effect the global economy. The professional studies program on the campus of Bethune-Cookman University is a program for mature adults. The mission is to provide a high-quality education for adult learners from diverse social economic and educational backgrounds.

Location

Bethune-Cookman University is located in the Atlantic coast city of Daytona Beach, Florida, amid a metropolitan area that has a population of more than 160,000. Its location on Dr. Mary McLeod Bethune Boulevard provides easy access to local business centers, churches, theaters, museums, beaches, recreational facilities, and bus and air terminals. The University is within 100 miles of the Kennedy Space Center, Walt Disney World/EPCOT Center, Sea World, Universal Studios, Marineland, and other such attractions.

Majors and Degrees

The Bachelor of Science degree is awarded in accounting, biology, business administration, business education, chemistry, computer engineering, computer information systems, computer science, criminal justice, elementary education, gerontology, hospitality management, international business, mathematics, medical technology, nursing, physical education, physics, psychology, specific learning disabilities, and varying exceptionalities. The Bachelor of Arts degree is awarded in church music, English, history, international studies, liberal studies, mass communications, modern languages, music, political science, religion and philosophy, social science education, and sociology. The majors in biology, chemistry, English, mathematics, modern languages, music, and physics can carry teacher certification. A dual-degree program in engineering is offered in cooperation with University of Florida, University of Central Florida, Florida Atlantic University, Florida A & M University, and Tuskegee University. Army and Air Force ROTC programs are offered in cooperation with Embry Riddle Aeronautical University in Daytona Beach.

Academic Programs

The academic program follows an educational core-concept approach. Student progress is monitored by the Freshman College. Sequences are required in biology, English, general psychology, mathematics, modern languages, physical education, physical science, religion, and social science. A developmental program seeks to provide courses and growth experiences that develop student competence in communications and mathematics skills for those needing remedial assistance. Academic support and reinforcement activities include individual conferences, periodic academic evaluation, and access to five laboratories for tutoring in reading, writing, speech, mathematics, science, and study skills. The Bethune-Cookman University Honors Program is designed to broaden intellectual horizons and to integrate various areas of knowledge, individualized learning, and independent research. Student Support Service programs are designed to improve student retention as well as academic and personal development. These programs, designed to increase successful matriculation in major fields of study, enrich the curriculum by reinforcing academic skills and course content necessary for success. A cooperative education program and other career-related field experiences are major components in several fields of study.

To receive a degree from Bethune-Cookman University, a student must complete a major in an academic field of study with a minimum of 124 semester hours of work with a minimum cumulative grade point average of 2.0. Upon recommendation of the instructor, a student exhibiting outstanding competence in a given course may receive credit by examination in lieu of taking the course.

Off-Campus Programs

The University operates Continuing Education Program sites in Florida in Fort Pierce, Gainesville, and West Palm Beach. A branch campus is located in Spuds, Florida.

Academic Facilities

Facilities on the 80-acre campus include twelve classroom buildings, a student union building, an infirmary, eleven dormitories, a gymnasium, an athletic weight room, a library resource center, five administrative buildings, a 2,500-seat performing arts center, and a new state-of-the-art President's Banquet and Civic Engagement Center. The library resource center houses an open-stack collection of more than 156,861 volumes, 41,914 microforms, 5,355 films and slides, 1,792 audiocassettes and videocassettes, 800 journals and magazine subscriptions, and a special collection of African-American and Methodist historical materials. The campus Learning Resource Center includes a nonprint media center, a graphics studio, and an ITV studio. The University operates an academic computer center system, with outlets in all classroom buildings. There is also a telecommunications satellite network for mass communications majors. All residence hall rooms are wired for Internet access.

Costs

For the 2007–08 academic year, the basic cost for tuition and fees was $12,382, and room and board were $7378. The approximate cost of books and supplies is $600 per year. Other expenditures for travel, amusement, and incidentals vary according to individual needs.

Financial Aid

The financial aid program includes competitive academic, athletic, band, and choir scholarships; work study awards; and federal and state grants and loans. Applications should be filed by March 1. Notification of awards is generally made in the spring. Applicants for federal and state loans, a grant-in-aid, or a work-study award must file the Free Application for Federal Student Aid (FAFSA).

Faculty

There are 200 full-time teaching faculty members, 65 percent of whom hold the doctoral degree. The student-faculty ratio is 17:1. The faculty members participate actively in all phases of university life.

Student Government

The Student Government Association (SGA) is the representative body for students. The SGA president is the student representative on the University Board of Trustees. There are student representatives on virtually every University committee.

Admission Requirements

Applicants are required to submit the completed B-CU admissions application, their high school transcripts (19 academic credits are required: 4 in English; 3, college-prep math; 3, social science; 3, science; and 6, academic electives), satisfactory SAT or ACT scores, the $25 application fee, a letter of recommendation, and a one-page essay. SAT or ACT scores are required for admission and are also used to determine eligibility for academic merit scholarships. For scholarship evaluation purposes, students intending to take the ACT are required to take the writing section; these scores also assist in evaluation for academic merit scholarships.

Application and Information

The University operates on a two-semester plan with an additional seven-week summer session. Qualified applicants may register at the beginning of any term.

The closing date for students applying for admission for the fall semester is July 30 and November 30 for the spring semester. For more information and application forms, students should contact:

Admissions Office
Bethune-Cookman University
640 Dr. Mary McLeod Bethune Boulevard
Phone: 386-481-2600
800-448-0228 (toll-free)
Fax: 386-481-2601
E-mail: admissions@cookman.edu
Web site: http://www.bethune.cookman.edu

ECKERD COLLEGE
ST. PETERSBURG, FLORIDA

ECKERD COLLEGE

The College

Eckerd College, a liberal arts institution of distinctive quality, was founded in 1958 as Florida Presbyterian College. Its first freshman class entered in 1960. Eckerd College is related by covenant to the Presbyterian Church (U.S.A.), and it is governed by a self-perpetuating Board of Trustees. Dedicated to excellence, Eckerd College has established a national reputation as a leading innovative liberal arts college. Its student body, faculty members, and program attest to the high expectations of its founders and to a remarkable degree of fulfillment in the years that have followed. In addition, the College has been awarded a chapter of Phi Beta Kappa.

Eckerd College currently enrolls 1,835 students (771 men and 1,064 women) from forty-seven states and thirty-five countries. Seventy-five percent of the student body comes from out of state. Campus life includes a multitude of activities that assist students with their intellectual, social, physical, and spiritual growth. Dormitory life is one hub of the College's social environment. More than 79 percent of students live in dorms, and the majority live on campus all four years. The dorms are small and informal; friendships are easily developed in this setting. In 2006, a new 146-bed residence hall opened on campus. Upperclass students may choose to live in the apartment-style town houses located on campus. Through the Eckerd College student government, social and cultural programs are planned for the College community. Four buildings in the center of the campus comprise the Hough Campus Center, which includes a pub, snack bars, lounges, student offices and meeting rooms, and a fitness center. The Campus Center is designed to accommodate meaningful interactions between all members of the College community.

Many special-interest clubs and a range of intramural sports programs are available. In addition, NCAA Division II intercollegiate athletics for men include baseball, basketball, golf, soccer, and tennis. For women, basketball, golf, soccer, softball, tennis, and volleyball are offered. Eckerd College has a varsity sailing team and participates in the South Atlantic Intercollegiate Sailing Association (SAISA) and is a member of the Intercollegiate Sailing Association (ICSA). Club sports include anglers, ballet, cheerleading, dodgeball, fencing, fitness, kite boarding, men's lacrosse, martial arts, outdoor activities, paddling, roller hockey, men's rugby, women's rugby, softball, soccer, surfing, swimming, tennis, Ultimate Frisbee, men's volleyball, and waterskiing. All clubs are coed unless noted. Students also have the opportunity to get involved with the campus television and radio stations, the yearbook, and the weekly newspaper.

Location

The 188-acre campus, bordered in part by a 1¼-mile waterfront, is located in a suburban setting on the southern tip of the peninsula that makes up Pinellas County. This peninsula is bounded on the west by the Gulf of Mexico and on the east by Tampa Bay. St. Petersburg is a city of almost 250,000 people and is a part of the rapidly growing Tampa Bay metropolitan area of approximately 2,600,000. The area has become the national and regional headquarters for many major corporations. Cultural and recreational opportunities are abundant, including art museums, symphony orchestras, professional theater and road-show engagements of Broadway plays, concerts, and year-round professional sports attractions.

Majors and Degrees

The Bachelor of Science is offered in biochemistry, biology, chemistry, computer science, marine sciences, mathematics, physics, and psychology. The Bachelor of Arts is offered in American studies, anthropology, biology, business administration, chemistry, communication, comparative literature, computer science, creative writing, East Asian studies, economics, environmental studies, French, German, history, human development, humanities, interdisciplinary arts, international business, international relations and global affairs, international studies, literature, management, mathematics, modern languages, music, philosophy, physics, political science, psychology, religious studies, sociology, Spanish, theater, visual arts, and women's and gender studies.

If, after undertaking introductory course work in an approved major, students wish to explore more specialized or interdisciplinary subject areas, they may design their own area of concentration with the approval of a 3-member faculty committee. Preprofessional programs include dentistry, engineering and applied science (a 3-2 program), law, medicine, theology, and veterinary medicine.

Academic Programs

The student pursues the study of a major field by joining a Collegium, a group of like-minded scholars who view their subjects, however diverse, in the same way. Each Collegium has its own decision-making group composed of professors and students. Eckerd operates on the 4-1-4 calendar system. Among the programs that illustrate the innovative nature of Eckerd are the mentorship program, a special training program for faculty members to enable them to help students in their academic progress, career planning, and personal growth; Autumn Term, a three-week orientation program for freshmen that includes the first academic course for each student and is designed to provide an intensive foretaste of college living and college academic work; Winter Term, a one-month midyear program especially adaptable to independent study and off-campus projects, first designed and implemented by Eckerd; a series of interdisciplinary seminars to explore issues related to aesthetics, cross-cultural interaction, environmental concerns, and social relations; and a senior capstone experience involving a choice of a thesis, creative project, or comprehensive examination. Eckerd College has pioneered an Academy of Senior Professionals on campus, which prominent retired men and women from around the world are invited to join. These distinguished persons come from professions to which Eckerd students aspire and are available for lectures, advising, career counseling, and mentoring.

Off-Campus Programs

Various kinds of off-campus opportunities are available. Among the many options for international education are the Eckerd College Study Centre in London, yearlong exchange programs in Japan and Korea, and semester-long exchange programs on every continent through Eckerd's affiliation with the International Student Exchange Program. The Sea Semester Program is available for marine science students, and an exchange program with students on other campuses across the country can be arranged for January or for a semester. As part of Career Resources and Applied Liberal Arts programs, many internship and field experience placements are available. These can be taken for credit upon satisfactory completion of an Independent-Study Contract.

Academic Facilities

The new library at Eckerd opened in December 2004. It offers 4.5 linear miles of open shelving; seventeen group-study rooms; five lounges, plus a lanai; fifty-eight computer stations; and wireless access to thousands of online books and periodicals from the terraces and courtyards. Complete laboratory facilities are available for language, marine science, chemistry, physics, biology, and experimental psychology. Two state-of-the-art science buildings include a waterfront marine science laboratory and a marine mammal pathobiology laboratory. The 375-seat Bininger Theatre provides professional facilities for theatrical productions. The Roberts Music Center houses classrooms, practice studios, and acoustically insulated listening rooms. The Griffin Chapel has one of the finest Flentrop organs in the country, and a smaller Flentrop is located in the Music Building. Both instruments are used by students studying the organ. Facilities for physical education include a modern gymnasium and basketball court; a swimming pool; a weight room; tennis and volleyball courts; a soccer complex, with a Sprinturf field and softball and baseball fields; and a fleet of canoes, kayaks, sailboats, sailboards, and waterskiing-equipped power vessels that are used in an extensive waterfront program. The waterfront program also includes the Wallace Boat House, which contains multimedia instruction classrooms, a snack bar, a ship's store, multiple docks and a boat ramp, and a fully equipped and nationally acclaimed Water Search and Rescue Team. The Ransom Center for Visual Arts provides studios for painting, sculpting, silkscreening, weaving, pottery, photography, video graphics, and other media. The Elliot Gallery is a part of the largest building in the art complex and features continuous showings of visiting exhibits as well as exhibits of work by students and faculty members. The Science Auditorium is equipped for films and demonstrations, and films are shown at Miller auditorium both for entertainment and for academic courses. The Information Technology Center houses more than thirty servers that are linked to more than 700 computers for Web site and data services. Students have access to a 24/7 computer lab. Academic computer labs use both Macintosh and IBM-compatible computers throughout the campus. Each residence hall is wired and has wireless access to the Internet and the campus intranet, which includes the library. A Writing Center featuring desktop publishing capabilities is also available to all students.

Costs

For 2007–08, tuition was $28,860 and room and board totaled $8338. Books are nearly $1000 per year. Student fees are $276.

Financial Aid

Academic scholarships ranging from $7500 to $13,000 per year are available to entering freshmen regardless of financial need. A limited number of Artistic Achievement Awards in music, theater, visual art, and creative writing are also available through a separate application process. Specifics on these and other programs are available from the College's admissions office.

Ninety-six percent of all students at Eckerd receive some form of financial aid. Academic performance, personal development, leadership qualities, and potential contribution to the College community are important considerations. Financial need is determined by an evaluation of the Free Application for Federal Student Aid (FAFSA). A student's total financial aid package may consist of a scholarship or grant, work aid, and a loan.

Faculty

The faculty has 155 professors (113 full-time and 42 part-time). Ninety-six percent of full-time faculty members have earned a Ph.D. or other terminal professional degree. The student-faculty ratio is 13:1. No graduate assistants teach courses.

Student Government

Student activities at Eckerd College are administered by the Eckerd College Organization of Students (ECOS). ECOS conducts campus social programs, including dances, concerts, and films; works to create special events and bring speakers to the campus to address issues important to students; and represents student interests in academic policy decisions. Students sit on a variety of standing committees of the faculty, and selected students may attend and speak at faculty meetings.

Admission Requirements

Scores on either the SAT or ACT are required for admission. No specified high school subjects are required, but the following are recommended as minimal: 4 units in English, 3 in mathematics, 2 in a foreign language, 3 in science, and 3 in social studies. Although no minimum high school average or rank is required, students with less than a 2.5 average are seldom admitted. In this year's freshman class, more than 54 percent of the members ranked in the top quarter of their high school graduating class. An interview is recommended but not required. Geographical location and religious preference are not admission factors. Early admission is available to promising high school juniors. In addition, credit and advanced standing are offered through the Advanced Placement Program of the College Board or the International Baccalaureate Program.

Application and Information

Application may be made at any time and should include a $35 application fee. A rolling admission policy is practiced. For more complete information and to make arrangements to visit the campus, students should contact:

Director of Admission
Eckerd College
4200 54th Avenue South
St. Petersburg, Florida 33711
Phone: 727-864-8331
800-456-9009 (toll-free)
Fax: 727-866-2304
E-mail: admissions@eckerd.edu
Web site: http://www.eckerd.edu

Eckerd's waterfront campus on Boca Ciega Bay.

COLLEGE DATA CENTER • FLORIDA

EMBRY-RIDDLE AERONAUTICAL UNIVERSITY

EMBRY-RIDDLE
AERONAUTICAL UNIVERSITY

DAYTONA BEACH, FLORIDA

The University

Embry-Riddle's history, legacy, and reputation date back almost to the time of the Wright brothers. The University prides itself on being the leader in aviation and aerospace education, provided through its residential campuses in Daytona Beach, Florida, and Prescott, Arizona, and its many Worldwide Campus locations, serving the continuing education needs of the aviation industry.

Approximately 4,800 undergraduate students and 400 graduate students are currently enrolled at the Daytona Beach residential campus. Students come from all fifty states and nearly 100 countries, which makes Embry-Riddle truly an international university.

More than twenty bachelor's degree programs and six graduate programs are offered at the Daytona Beach campus. Embry-Riddle's premier aeronautical science (professional pilot) program and award-winning aerospace engineering program are the largest on campus and the largest of their type in the nation.

Students at the Daytona Beach campus enjoy a wide array of activities and clubs, many focused on aviation and aerospace, as well as fraternities, sororities, and recreational opportunities. Forty-three percent of students live on campus.

Embry-Riddle's award-winning precision flight demonstration teams offer students the opportunity to compete nationally in air and ground events. Embry-Riddle also has the largest all-volunteer Air Force ROTC detachment in the country and among the fastest-growing Navy ROTC units and Army ROTC battalions. Embry-Riddle athletes participate in intercollegiate and intramural competitions in many sports, including baseball, basketball, crew, cross-country, golf, soccer, tennis, volleyball, and ice hockey.

The 68,000-square-foot ICI Center contains two full-size NCAA basketball courts, a fitness center, and a weight room. The ICI Center provides a place to host sporting events and assemblies. The University sports complex also includes a soccer field, the Sliwa Stadium ballpark, the Ambassador William Crotty Tennis Center, and the Track and Field Complex. New in 2007, the Tine Davis Fitness Center is adjacent to the Olympic-size pool and features comprehensive fitness services and wellness programs.

The 5,300-square-foot interfaith chapel accommodates the variety of faiths represented by the student body of Embry-Riddle. It consists of a 140-seat nondenominational worship area, four prayer rooms (Catholic, Jewish, Muslim, and Protestant), and administrative spaces for Campus Ministry's 2 chaplains and student assistants.

Location

The year-round clear flying weather and the resort communities surrounding Embry-Riddle's residential campus in Daytona Beach, Florida, offer students an excellent environment in which to study, fly, and enjoy recreational activities. The campus, which is located adjacent to the Daytona Beach International Airport, is only 3 miles from what is called the world's most famous beach. The high-technology industries located in Daytona Beach and nearby Orlando provide the University with an outstanding support base. In addition, the Kennedy Space Center is less than a 2-hour drive away.

Majors and Degrees

The Daytona Beach campus of Embry-Riddle awards undergraduate degrees at the baccalaureate level. Bachelor of Science degrees are offered in a variety of areas, each with a focus on the aviation and aerospace industries. In engineering, students can pursue a Bachelor of Science degree in aerospace engineering, civil engineering, computer engineering, electrical engineering, engineering physics, mechanical engineering, and software engineering. Students who are interested in business administration may elect to major in management or air transportation. For those inclined toward technological pursuits, degrees are offered in aerospace electronics and aviation maintenance science. The College of Aviation awards degrees in aeronautical science (professional piloting), air traffic management, applied meteorology, and safety science. Other aerospace and aviation industry–related majors include aerospace studies, communication, homeland security, human factors psychology, and space physics. Students entering Embry-Riddle with an undecided major have the opportunity to explore a variety of academic pursuits before making a commitment to a specific track.

Academic Programs

Even a field as specialized as aviation requires a broad background. General education courses required of all students who are pursuing a baccalaureate program include communication skills, such as English composition, literature, and technical report writing; humanities; social sciences; mathematics; physical science; economics; and computer science. To ensure academic success, Embry-Riddle provides free tutorial services.

The calendar year is divided into two semesters of fifteen weeks each, with the summer session divided into two terms. The average course load for each fall or spring semester is 15 credit hours.

Academic Facilities

The College of Aviation building at the Daytona Beach campus provides an unsurpassed environment for aviation education and research. The multimillion-dollar simulation laboratories duplicate the components and functions in the national airspace system, including capabilities to replicate actual weather reporting, airports, airways, air traffic control, flow control, and pilot and aircraft performance as found in the national air transportation system. The simulator building, which is located in the greater College of Aviation complex, contains highly sophisticated flight training devices (FTD) that provide realistic training in aircraft used in flight training as well as the major airlines. Flight instruction is provided in the Embry-Riddle fleet of sixty aircraft and a wide array of flight training devices. Aircraft are equipped with Automatic Dependent Surveillance-Broadcast (ADS-B) technology that decreases hazards associated with traffic, weather, and terrain.

The Jack R. Hunt Memorial Library is a 49,000-square-foot facility with a seating capacity of 800. The library houses more than 230,000 volumes and book titles and more than 340,000 items of microfiche, periodicals, documents, newspapers, and media programs. Among the library's resources is a historical aviation collection that includes materials dating from 1909 to the present. The library provides rapid interlibrary loan service and wireless access points as well as computer terminals for research.

The Advanced Flight Simulation Center gives Embry-Riddle students the opportunity to train in world-class simulators. The center, with more than 20,000 square feet of space and four high bays, currently houses the Frasca CRJ 200, several Frasca 141, PA44, and C172 FTDs. These devices exactly duplicate the actual cockpit, adverse weather conditions, a full range of emergency situations, and virtually any flight pattern and complement flight training done in actual aircraft. Flight simulation enables students to learn aircraft performance, experience aerodynamic effects, and perform flight maneuvers immediately and without risk. Qualified to LEVEL 6, the University's devices faithfully reproduce Embry-Riddle's fleet of single-engine and multiengine aircraft. In addition, the General Aviation (GA) fleet is equipped with 220-degree panoramic visual theaters. These theaters display a satellite-based terrain augmented by an extensive airport database. The University's airports include navigation aids, runways, taxiways, towers, hangars, and even lighting systems. Its CRJ-200 FTD includes Collimation technology, which introduces a three-dimensional effect to the visual theater.

The Samuel Goldman Aviation Maintenance Technology Center houses facilities to support instruction in maintenance and repair. Avionics maintains an FAA-certified repair station, which affords avionics students the opportunity to learn the theory and practice of the trouble analysis and repair of airworthy aircraft and equipment. The advanced reciprocating engine lab (FAA Certified Repair Station 708-55) overhauls engines for the Embry-Riddle fleet. Engine test cells allow students to check the effectiveness of their repairs.

The Lehman Engineering and Technology Center houses subsonic and supersonic wind tunnels and a smoke tunnel; structures, materials, and aircraft design and composite materials laboratories; and a computer-aided design/computer-aided manufacturing system. Embry-Riddle is also the country's first university to use its own rapid-prototyping stereolithography for design instruction. Additional facilities to support instruction include the Lindbergh Center, which provides modern classroom facilities and chemistry and physics laboratories; the academic computing center, which provides hands-on experience with both mainframe and personal computers; and the Eagle Works Research Center, which supports both undergraduate and graduate research and other creative activities.

The 18,500-square-foot Capt. Willie Miller Instructional Center, a lecture auditorium and classroom complex, provides space for large audience events, including presentations by distinguished lecturers and speakers.

New in 2008, the College of Business academic building features the Aviation Operations Simulation Lab, which is used to develop and evaluate aviation/airline operational strategies and processes. In addition, the College's Teaching Airport, a partnership between Embry-Riddle and Daytona Beach International Airport, is focused on teaching, research, and public outreach.

Costs

The 2007–08 tuition was $12,700 per semester. Flight fees are charged in addition to tuition. On-campus room and board costs were approximately $4000 per semester. Personal expenses are in addition to the above. (Costs are subject to change.)

Financial Aid

Applicants for financial aid are required to complete the Department of Education's Free Application for Federal Student Aid (FAFSA) and any other documents requested by the University. Students are encouraged to apply early if they wish to be considered for all types of programs. Florida residents may also apply for several additional programs that are available through the state.

Faculty

The faculty members provide an excellent balance of professional experience and academic achievement. There is also a healthy balance between maturity and youth among the faculty. Faculty members who teach in the specialized and major programs have had professional experience in their areas of instruction. The student-faculty ratio is 16:1, and the average class size is 27. The primary concern of each faculty member is personalized teaching in classrooms and laboratories, on the flight line, and in student advising.

Student Government

The University places great emphasis on student self-government. The Student Government Association supports publication of the weekly newspaper and broadcast of the student radio station, Eagles FM.

Admission Requirements

Admission is open to any qualified applicant, regardless of creed, sex, race, national origin, handicap, or geographical location. Admission decisions are based on high school work, college courses attempted, SAT or ACT scores, and letters of recommendation. Embry-Riddle encourages every student to visit the campus before making the decision to attend the University.

Transfer students are required to submit transcripts from all colleges and universities attended. High school transcripts are not required if the student has earned 30 college credits or more.

Application and Information

Embry-Riddle requires each applicant to submit an application form and fee, SAT or ACT scores, two letters of recommendation, and an official high school/college transcript. Flight students must provide an FAA Class I or Class II medical certificate. When a student is accepted for admission, tuition and housing deposits are required by May 1. For further information, interested students should contact:

University Admissions
Embry-Riddle Aeronautical University
P.O. Box 11767
Daytona Beach, Florida 32120-1767
Phone: 386-226-6100
800-862-2416 (toll-free nationwide)
E-mail: univadm@erau.edu
Web site: http://www.embryriddle.edu

Embry-Riddle Aeronautical University's Daytona Beach, Florida, campus.

FLAGLER COLLEGE

ST. AUGUSTINE, FLORIDA

The College

Founded in 1968, Flagler College is an independent nonsectarian college that offers a four-year program leading to the baccalaureate degree in selected preprofessional and liberal studies. The College is coeducational, predominantly residential, and small by intent—enrollment is limited to 2,200 students. Flagler is governed by a Board of Trustees of 17 members and is accredited by the Commission on Colleges of the Southern Association of Colleges and Schools (1866 Southern Lane, Decatur, Georgia 30033-4097; telephone 404-679-4501), one of the six nationally recognized regional accrediting associations.

The campus is situated in the heart of historic St. Augustine, 4 miles from the Atlantic beaches. The focal point of the campus is Ponce de Leon Hall, formerly a famous resort hotel. Described as a masterpiece of American architecture, the Ponce de Leon is listed on the National Register of Historic Places. Ponce de Leon Hall contains a residence hall for 500 students, the dining hall, the infirmary, and some administrative offices. The 19-acre campus includes two men's residence halls, a technologically advanced library, a new multimillion-dollar student union, a newly restored art building, and ten other historic buildings that are used for classrooms, faculty and administrative offices, and recreational and athletic facilities.

The College strives to develop the qualities that smallness fosters. These qualities include, but are not limited to, civility, integrity, loyalty, dependability, and affection. An atmosphere of friendliness and respect prevails throughout the College. Students come from forty-eight states and forty countries or territories; 65 percent of the students are from Florida. The student body is composed of traditional college-age students; most are between the ages of 18 and 22. Students indicate that its size, location, cost, and programs of study are the major reasons for their choosing Flagler.

The College offers a wide range of extracurricular activities that are designed to enrich the student socially, culturally, and physically. There are twenty-three organizations and five honor societies for students to join. The clubs generally fall into the categories of community service, social interest, or those related to a student's major. In addition, some of the favorite pastimes of Flagler students are biking around town, walking through the restoration area, surfing at the beach, competing in a sports event or being a spectator, or just sunning by the pool. Students also make trips to the nearby cities of Jacksonville, Daytona Beach, and Orlando. Athletics play an important role in campus life. Intercollegiate sports for men are baseball, basketball, cross-country, golf, soccer, and tennis. Intercollegiate sports for women are basketball, cross-country, golf, soccer, tennis, and volleyball. A lively intramural sports program is available for both men and women. Athletic and recreational facilities include a gymnasium, tennis courts, and a swimming pool. A 19-acre athletic field for baseball, soccer, softball, and intramurals is located 2 miles from the campus.

Location

St. Augustine is located on the northeast coast of Florida, about midway between Jacksonville and Daytona Beach. Famous as a tourist center, rich in history, and beautifully maintained in all its storied charm, St. Augustine provides an attractive environment for a liberal arts college. Community resources complement the programs offered by the College. Flagler is an important part of the St. Augustine community and seeks to use the educational, cultural, and recreational resources of the community to supplement and enhance the quality of life and the quality of education at the College.

Majors and Degrees

Flagler College awards the Bachelor of Arts degree in the following areas: accounting, art education, business administration, communication, deaf education, elementary education, English, exceptional child education, fine art, graphic design, history, Latin American studies–Spanish, liberal arts, philosophy-religion, political science, psychology, secondary education, sociology, Spanish, sport management, and theater arts. The College also offers a Bachelor of Fine arts in fine arts. In addition, the College offers preprofessional programs in human services, law, and youth ministries.

Academic Programs

The principal focus of the College's academic program is undergraduate education in selected liberal and preprofessional studies. The purposes of the academic program are to provide opportunities for general and specialized learning, to assist students in preparing for careers, and to aid qualified students in pursuing graduate and professional studies.

Flagler operates on a semester calendar with two 14-week semesters. The fall term is completed prior to Christmas, and the spring term ends in late April. All students must complete 33 semester hours in general education requirements, including 6 hours in English composition, 6 hours in mathematics, 3 hours in computer science, 3 hours in speech, and 15 hours in three broad areas: humanities, social sciences, and natural sciences/mathematics. The normal academic load is 15 semester hours, which generally represents five courses per term. The number of credits required for a major varies by department. Education majors are required to complete a highly prescribed course of study leading to certification in two or more areas (e.g., elementary education and specific learning disabilities). A student must complete a minimum of 120 semester hours to satisfy graduation requirements. Business administration and education are the two most popular majors at Flagler.

Advanced placement may be awarded to entering freshmen on the basis of scores earned on the tests of the College-Level Examination Program (CLEP) and/or the Advanced Placement Program (AP Program) of the College Board as well as the International Baccalaureate Higher Level exams.

Off-Campus Programs

Students majoring in deaf education have the benefit of working with faculty members and students at the Florida School for the Deaf and the Blind (FSDB), the largest school of its type in the nation. The FSDB is located in St. Augustine, approximately 2 miles from the College campus. Flagler is certified by the Council on the Education of the Deaf and holds membership in the Northeast Florida Consortium for the Hearing Impaired. In addition, Flagler serves as the Southeast Regional Extension Center for Gallaudet University.

Students may study abroad for a semester, a year, or a summer. The College offers organized trips each summer to Italy and England; however, students may choose their own program and many have traveled to a variety of other places, including Latin America, Spain, Mexico, France, and Australia.

Academic Facilities

The William L. Proctor Library building has three floors. The first two floors are devoted to the library with a capacity for 154,562 holdings. At present the library houses 90,298 print volumes, 83,399 electronic books, 29,468 microform items, 4,358 audiovisual materials, and subscriptions to 473 periodicals. Interlibrary loan service is available for items that the library does not own. Also included on these two floors are study carrels, computer catalog stations, sixty database stations, and an Internet lab. The third floor of building is devoted to computer laboratories for computer science and graphic arts courses. There is also a computer lab for students' word processing needs. Overall, there are 200 computers available for student use. Students receive their own e-mail accounts through the College.

Costs

For 2007–08, costs were $11,810 for tuition and fees and $6310 for room and board. Although other costs vary according to the student's lifestyle, the estimate for books, supplies, and miscellaneous expenses is about $1500 per year.

Financial Aid

Financial aid is awarded primarily on the basis of proven need, as demonstrated by the information given by the applicant on the College application for financial aid and on the Free Application for Federal Student Aid (FAFSA). Awards may consist of grants, loans, campus employment, or some combination of the three. In addition to providing institutional grants, the College participates in all federal programs. Some aid may be awarded solely on the basis of academic achievement, talent, athletic ability, leadership, or character. Approximately 85 percent of the student body receives some form of aid from the College. Only those students who have applied for admission and have been accepted are considered for aid. It is recommended that all the necessary forms be submitted by March 15.

Students who have resided in Florida for at least one year are eligible to receive a tuition offset grant of approximately $3000 per year to attend a private college or university in Florida. Funds for the Florida Resident Access Grant are appropriated by the state legislature, and awards are not based on academic merit or financial need. In addition, Flagler participates in all state-funded programs, including Florida Bright Futures and the Florida Student Assistance Grant; plus, entitlements under the Florida Prepaid College Program may be transferred to Flagler.

Faculty

Teaching is central to Flagler's mission. The College seeks to attract and retain a professionally competent faculty dedicated to the art of teaching and advising. Faculty members at Flagler are committed to high standards of performance and are concerned for the welfare of the College and its students. Faculty members are readily available and meet regularly with students outside the classroom. Many faculty members advise student clubs and organizations and take an active role in student life.

The teaching staff is composed of 75 full-time and 95 part-time faculty members. Half of the full-time faculty members hold earned doctorates. A favorable 20:1 student-faculty ratio ensures small classes, individual attention, and interaction between the faculty and students. The average class size is approximately 22 students; 93 percent of classes have 35 or fewer students.

Student Government

The Student Government Association (SGA) plays an important role in planning and implementing a varied program of campus activities at Flagler. Elected student representatives are responsible for voicing student ideas and opinions in matters of general student concern. The SGA also serves as the coordinating unit for many social, academic, and recreational activities. Members of the SGA serve on several committees of the College and participate in many community services and projects.

Admission Requirements

Flagler seeks students from diverse geographical backgrounds who can benefit from the educational experience offered by the College. Flagler welcomes applications from all qualified men and women without regard to age, sex, race, color, marital status, handicap, religion, or national or ethnic origin. Each applicant is evaluated individually, and admission is determined on the basis of the student's academic preparation, scholastic aptitude, and personal qualities. Other factors taken into consideration are the student's motivation, initiative, maturity, seriousness of purpose, and leadership potential. All admission decisions are made on a "need-blind" basis. The College offers an early decision plan.

For freshman applicants, the high school record remains the most important factor in determining admission to the College. The admission staff takes into consideration the quality of courses selected, grade point average, class rank, test scores, a recommendation from a secondary school counselor, an essay, intended field of study, and participation in extracurricular activities. All freshman applicants are required to submit scores from either the SAT or the ACT. A minimum of 16 high school units is required. The College does not prescribe a particular course of study, but prospective applicants are encouraged to take 4 units of English, 4 units of social studies, 3 units of mathematics, 2 units of science, and 3 units of academic electives.

Students applying for the fine arts, graphic design, and art education programs are required to submit a portfolio of their artwork. Samples of original artwork should be sent as 35 mm slides or prints (not original artwork) and should be addressed to the Director of Admissions at Flagler College.

All transfer students are required to submit an official transcript from each institution attended. In addition, all transfer applicants are required to submit scores from either the SAT or the ACT. Transfer students are expected to have a minimum 2.8 grade point average and may transfer up to 75 semester hours of credit. Those who have earned fewer than 24 semester hours of credit must satisfy requirements for freshman admission. In addition to fulfilling the above requirements, international students must submit scores from the TOEFL or demonstrate proficiency in the English language.

An interview is not required as part of the admission process, but many students regard on-campus interviews as valuable experiences because of the exchange of information. Arrangements for a campus visit should be made with the Admissions Office at least three weeks in advance.

Application and Information

Applications for admission should be submitted in the fall or the winter of the year prior to the desired term of enrollment. Applicants must arrange for transcripts and recommendations to be sent directly to the Admissions Office. The deadline for submitting an application is January 15 for early decision candidates and March 1 for all others.

Application forms and related materials should be sent to:

Director of Admissions
Flagler College
74 King Street
St. Augustine, Florida 32084
Phone: 800-304-4208 (toll-free)
E-mail: admiss@flagler.edu
Web site: http://www.flagler.edu

Flagler students in front of Ponce de Leon Hall.

COLLEGE DATA CENTER • FLORIDA

FLORIDA AGRICULTURAL AND MECHANICAL UNIVERSITY

TALLAHASSEE, FLORIDA

The University

For more than a century, the primary goals of the Florida Agricultural and Mechanical University (FAMU) have been to promote academic excellence and to improve the quality of life for those it serves. Founded in 1887 as the State Normal School for Colored Students, FAMU opened its doors with 2 instructors and 15 students. It was designated a land-grant institution in 1890 and became a university in 1953. It is a full and equal partner in the ten-member State University System.

The FAMU campus, covered by lush shrubbery, flowering plants, and massive oaks, covers 419 acres. Valued at $119 million, the University campus has 111 buildings. Although historically black, the University seeks qualified students from all racial, ethnic, religious, and national backgrounds without regard to age, sex, or physical handicap. The current enrollment is 11,562 (90 percent black, 57 percent women). Graduate degrees in twenty disciplines are coordinated through the School of Graduate Studies, Research and Continuing Education. The FAMU College of Law, located in Orlando, Florida, offers the Juris Doctor (J.D.) degree.

The School of Journalism and Graphic Communication publishes a weekly student newspaper and operates an FM radio station. There are more than 100 student organizations on campus, including nationally affiliated fraternities and sororities, honor societies, religious groups, fashion/modeling clubs, the Literary Guild, Orchesis Contemporary Dance Theatre, the Playmakers Guild, and the FAMU Gospel Choir, which released its first album in 1985. The Marching 100, FAMU's 300-member marching band, has received national television and magazine coverage and, in 1985, became the first band outside the Big 10 Conference to earn the Sousa Foundation's prestigious Sudler Trophy.

The University, a member of the Mid-Eastern Athletic Conference (MEAC), sponsors seventeen NCAA Division I teams for men and women and operates a I-AA football program within that division. Athletic facilities include Bragg Stadium (25,600), with a field house, locker rooms, weight room, and training facility; a track and field complex with an eight-lane, all-weather, 400-meter track; competition-grade tennis courts; two outdoor pools; baseball and softball fields; and a complex that serves as headquarters for the largest women's athletic program at any historically black institution in the country. The intramural sports program is divided into informal free play, competitive sports, and sports clubs.

Location

The University is located on the highest of seven hills in Tallahassee (population 200,000) among the heavily wooded, rolling hills of northwest Florida and only 22 miles from the Gulf of Mexico. There are more than 1,000 acres of public parks and land and numerous lakes nearby. Programs at FAMU, Florida State University, and Tallahassee Community College provide top-name entertainment, much of which is offered free or at reduced prices to students. Students in various disciplines intern or are employed in community businesses and agencies of all three levels of government. The University is located eight blocks from the Capitol Complex, and bus service is available from the campus to shopping malls; state, county, and city offices; and recreational areas. An intercampus shuttle (between FAMU and FSU) and an on-campus shuttle run during class hours daily.

Majors and Degrees

The College of Arts and Sciences offers baccalaureate majors and degrees in Afro-American studies, chemistry, computer information systems, criminal justice, economics, English, fine arts, foreign languages, general biology, history, mathematics, music, philosophy and religion, political science and public management (prelaw and urban studies), physics, predentistry, premedicine, psychology, social work, sociology, and theater.

The College of Education offers baccalaureate degrees in business teacher education; elementary education; health, physical education, and recreation; industrial arts education; office administration; secondary education; and vocational-industrial education.

The FAMU/FSU College of Engineering offers baccalaureate degrees in chemical, civil, electrical, industrial, and mechanical engineering. The College of Engineering Sciences, Technology and Agriculture offers baccalaureate degrees in agribusiness, agricultural science, agricultural engineering, animal science (preveterinary medicine), architectural and construction technology, civil engineering technology, electronic engineering technology, entomology and structural pest control, landscape design, and ornamental horticulture.

The School of Allied Health Sciences offers baccalaureate degrees in health-care management, health information management, occupational therapy, and respiratory therapy and offers a master's degree in physical therapy. The School of Nursing offers a baccalaureate and master's degree program in nursing. The College of Pharmacy and Pharmaceutical Sciences offers three professional degrees.

The School of Architecture offers a four-year, preprofessional baccalaureate degree in architectural studies and a five-year, professional baccalaureate degree in architecture.

The School of Business and Industry offers baccalaureate and five-year M.B.A. degrees in accounting and business administration.

The School of Journalism and Graphic Communication offers baccalaureate degrees in broadcast journalism, graphic design, magazine journalism, newspaper journalism, photography, printing management, printing production, and public relations.

Academic Programs

The School of General Studies facilitates and monitors the general education of all matriculating undecided students. All students take core courses in English, mathematics, humanities, health, American history, natural sciences, and social and behavioral sciences. After completing these core requirements, students select an area of specialization in a major offered in one of the other colleges and schools. A minimum of 120 semester hours is required for the baccalaureate degree.

Students who meet test and grade point average requirements and write an acceptable honors thesis are selected for the Honors Program, which enables them to accelerate completion of the basic requirements, enroll in classes of reduced size, develop leadership skills, have honor courses identified as such on their transcript, and be recognized at the annual All-University Convocation.

FAMU offers Army, Naval, and Air Force ROTC programs.

Off-Campus Programs

The School of Architecture has a center in Washington, D.C., where students may study for one or two semesters. Architecture students have also worked on special projects in Florida and other parts of the continental United States. The College of Pharmacy and Pharmaceutical Sciences has a component in Miami, Florida, through which students receive clinical training in the hospitals of the Miami Medical Center. The College of Pharmacy also operates the Clinical Pharmacology Research Unit in Jackson Towers, Miami, Florida, for human drug studies and other research and research training.

Through the University's Cooperative Education Program, students receive internships and other short-term work-study opportunities in business and industry, education, and government. The Cooperative Education Program has placed students in most of the fifty states. Individual schools and colleges provide undergraduate internships, usually for upper-division students. Students have interned in such places as London, England; San Juan, Puerto Rico; Sydney, Australia; and Geneva, Switzerland. FAMU has three cooperative programs with Florida State University, which is also located in Tallahassee. The general program enables students to take a limited academic load at the other institution.

The Program in Medical Science (PIMS) provides a special route to medical school for students by allowing them to complete the first year of medical study in Tallahassee before transferring to a medical school. The School of Nursing offers the Ph.D. through the University of Florida in Gainesville, Florida. The joint FAMU/FSU College of Engineering program enables students to earn an engineering degree at FAMU while giving them access to course offerings at FSU.

Academic Facilities

The Coleman Memorial Library encompasses Library Service and Instructional Media Services. The library has 400,000 bound volumes, 3,640 periodicals, and 84,500 microfilms; a complete line of audiovisual equipment; a fully equipped television studio; and a photography laboratory. The Florida Black Archives, Research Center and Museum, located on campus, complements academic studies in history and has become a popular tourist attraction. Students have access to the R. A. Gray State Archives, the Leon County Public Library, the Robert Strozier Library at FSU, and the FSU Law Library.

Costs

In 2007–08, basic registration fees for Florida-resident undergraduates were $105.23 per credit hour and for nonresidents, $503.22. The basic cost of University housing was approximately $2030 per semester. Other estimated expenses were board, $1190 per semester for nineteen meals; books, $400; orientation, $30; health fee, $59; Rattler ID Card fee, $5; and transportation fee, $50. For the most current information, students should contact the Office of Admissions and Recruitment.

Financial Aid

Financial aid is awarded according to each student's need in relation to college costs. Awards are available as need-based and non-need-based grants, loans, part-time employment (work-study), and scholarships. These awards may be offered singly or in various combinations. High-achieving high school and transfer students may be eligible for awards under special programs such as Presidential Scholars, Distinguished Scholars Award, and Life Gets Better scholarships. The priority deadline for financial aid application completion is March 1.

Faculty

Approximately 60 percent of the University's 420 faculty members hold doctoral degrees. Faculty members are expected to teach, conduct research, and provide public service. They are heavily involved with student affairs and serve as sponsors and advisers to clubs, student organizations, and professional societies. The overall student-faculty ratio is approximately 29:1; it varies by discipline and course level.

Student Government

Student Government Association officers are elected late in the spring semester and serve for the ensuing academic year. Representatives serve on University committees and advisory groups; each class has elected officers.

Admission Requirements

Florida A&M University encourages applications from qualified students of all national, racial, religious, and ethnic groups. Admission is selective; subject to limitations of curricula, space, and fiscal resources; and based on such factors as grades, test scores, educational objectives, pattern of courses completed, past conduct, recommendations, and personal records.

Although requirements are subject to change without notice, current policy allows students to be considered for admission if they have graduated from a regionally accredited high school or approved GED program and earned at least 18 units of academic credit, of which 4 must be in English (3 with substantial writing requirements), 3 in mathematics (algebra I and higher levels), 3 in natural sciences (2 with substantial lab requirements), 3 in social sciences, and 2 in foreign language. The remaining 4 elective units must come from these subject areas or other courses approved by the State Department of Education and the Florida Board of Governors. Students must submit ACT or SAT (reading and math components) scores.

Applicants with at least a B average (3.0 on a 4.0 scale) in the required high school academic units who submit other evidence of successful academic progress are academically eligible for admission regardless of standardized test scores. Academic eligibility for students with less than a B average is determined on a sliding scale that, as published in the University catalog, relates the GPA to SAT or ACT scores. Students who do not meet these requirements but who bring to the University other important attributes or special talents may be admitted by the University Admissions Committee.

Outstanding students may submit an application for early admission during their junior year in high school (having completed the 18-credit requirement), along with an official high school transcript (a B average or better), SAT (at least 1010 combined reading and math components) or ACT (at least 21 composite) scores, and a recommendation from the principal or designated representative.

Applicants who have attended any accredited institution of higher education and earned 12 or more semester hours are considered transfer students. Undergraduate transfers who enter FAMU with junior-class standing must have passed the College Level Academic Skills Test (CLAST–FAMU exam) to be admitted to upper-level courses and degree programs. Transfer applicants with fewer than 60 semester hours of credit must meet first-time-in-college admission requirements. Undergraduate transfer applicants who have not earned the A.A. degree from a Florida community college or from a state university must be in good standing and eligible to return to the last institution attended, must have earned a minimum of 60 semester hours and maintained at least a C (2.0) average, and must present passing scores on the Florida CLAST before admission to FAMU's upper division. Students who have earned an A.A. degree from an accredited state institution are automatically eligible for admission to non-limited-access programs, under the Florida Community College–State University System Articulation Agreement.

International transfer applicants who are not native English speakers must present a minimum score of 550 (paper-based) or 80 (Internet-based) on the Test of English as a Foreign Language (TOEFL). Credentials of international applicants must be evaluated by a member agency of the National Association of Credential Evaluation Services (NACES). Documents must be submitted directly to the Office of Admissions and Recruitment by the agency.

Admission to certain programs is highly selective. These limited-access programs tend to reach enrollment capacity before the cutoff dates for general admission, so interested students should apply early. Admission to the University does not ensure access to on-campus housing.

Application and Information

Office of Admissions and Recruitment
Florida Agricultural and Mechanical University
Tallahassee, Florida 32307-3200
Phone: 850-599-3796
866-642-1198 (toll-free)
E-mail: admissions@famu.edu
Web site: http://www.famu.edu

FLORIDA ATLANTIC UNIVERSITY

BOCA RATON, FLORIDA

The University

Florida Atlantic University (FAU) is a midsize comprehensive university that serves more than 26,000 students on seven campuses throughout South Florida. FAU was established in 1961, making it the fifth-oldest university in the state system. As an upper-division and graduate state university, FAU admitted its first student in September 1964. In 1984, FAU admitted its first freshman class, instituting a comprehensive four-year undergraduate program. Enrollment has increased from 867 in the first year to more than 26,000 in 2007.

FAU is located in a rapidly expanding metropolitan area encompassing cities and towns from Fort Lauderdale to Port St. Lucie. Since the original Boca Raton campus was founded in 1964, the University has expanded to six other campuses in South Florida: Dania Beach, Davie, Fort Lauderdale, Jupiter, and Port St. Lucie. The residential campus in Boca Raton accommodates 2,408 students in four residence halls and a student apartment complex.

The Boca Raton campus provides an exciting and supportive learning environment for students. The University Center hosts student activities and meetings. In addition, its 2,400-seat auditorium enables students to enjoy performances ranging from rock groups to the Florida Philharmonic Orchestra. The Boca Raton campus is also the home of FAU's Division 1 intercollegiate athletics program and facilities. Its recreation complex includes an aquatic center, gymnasium, tennis courts, track, and a variety of fields for club and intramural sports competition. The five-story S. E. Wimberly Library houses a large collection of monographs, serials, and other academic resources. Computer labs, study lounges, a media center, and tutoring services also provide valuable academic support for students.

One of FAU's newest campuses is located in Dania Beach. The Dania Beach campus, also known as SeaTech, is FAU's Institute for Ocean and Systems Engineering, located on eight acres between the Atlantic Ocean and the Intracoastal Waterway, with valuable access to the ocean and sea water. Established in 1997 as a state-funded Type II research center, the institute is part of FAU's Department of Ocean Engineering.

FAU's Davie campus is located on 38 acres in western Broward County and is FAU's second-largest campus after the Boca Raton campus. The Davie campus has served FAU students since 1990 with 2+2 programs in partnership with Broward Community College.

The Fort Lauderdale campus in downtown Fort Lauderdale (comprising the Reubin O'D. Askew Tower and the new Higher Education Complex) takes advantage of its unique urban setting to serve as a center for FAU programs in creative industries and urban affairs. The campus is part of Fort Lauderdale's evolving, dynamic urban community and provides a laboratory for students in business, computer arts, graphic arts, multimedia communication, architecture, urban and regional planning, and public administration.

The John D. MacArthur Campus is conveniently located off I-95 and Donald Ross Road within Jupiter's Abacoa community. The campus presently enrolls more than 3,600 students and offers a wide range of upper division and graduate programs from six of FAU's colleges, including seventeen bachelor's degrees and seven master's degrees. The MacArthur Campus is also home to FAU's Harriet L. Wilkes Honors College and the Scripps Research Institute.

In 2006, FAU opened the FAU/Harbor Branch Marine Sciences Building—a 40,000-square-foot, joint-use facility housing specially equipped marine science labs, classrooms and video-conferencing equipped meeting rooms—at the Harbor Branch Oceanographic Institution's 600-acre site in Fort Pierce.

The Treasure Coast campus is conveniently situated in St. Lucie West, part of the rapidly developing city of Port St. Lucie. The first-rate facilities are shared with Indian River Community College in a unique 2+2 partnership. Located off I-95 and St. Lucie West Boulevard, the Treasure Coast campus is an easy commute for area students.

The FAU/Harbor Branch Oceanographic Institution Marine Science Partnership Building in Fort Pierce is a new FAU location on the Treasure Coast. This state-of-the-art facility provides an ideal setting for marine science research and teaching.

Through its partnerships with other educational institutions, local businesses, industries, and civic and cultural organizations, FAU enhances the economic, human, and cultural development of the surrounding communities and beyond. Students at Florida Atlantic University may participate in a work-study program that combines their classroom learning with hands-on experience. Many local businesses and government laboratories participate in the program each year.

FAU has developed a new program in medical sciences offered in cooperation with the University of Miami Miller School of Medicine. Students in this program take their first two years of medical school at FAU and complete their clinical studies at the University of Miami.

Florida Atlantic University is accredited by the Commission on Colleges of the Southern Association of Colleges and Schools to award associate, bachelor's, master's, and doctoral degrees. In addition, it is accredited by fourteen professional agencies. FAU is also a member of the National Association of State Universities and Land-Grant Colleges and the Council of Graduate Schools in the United States.

Location

FAU campuses can be found throughout the southeast-Florida region. FAU's main campus in Boca Raton is on an 850-acre site located only 3 miles from the Atlantic Ocean. The campus is conveniently located halfway between Palm Beach and Fort Lauderdale and offers a broad range of academic programs, activities, and services.

Students attending FAU–Boca Raton have some honored guests: burrowing owls. In fact, the Audubon Society has named the site a burrowing owl sanctuary, and FAU varsity athletic teams are known as the "Owls" in their honor.

South Florida's climate is subtropical, with an average year-round temperature of 75 degrees. FAU's campuses are within easy driving distance of some of the most beautiful beaches and recreational facilities to be found anywhere.

Majors and Degrees

FAU offers programs leading to the Bachelor of Arts and Bachelor of Science degrees as well as Associate of Arts and specialized bachelor's degrees. A minimum of 120 credit hours is required for a bachelor's degree.

The College of Architecture, Urban and Public Affairs offers majors in architecture, criminal justice, public management, social work, and urban and regional planning. The Dorothy F. Schmidt College of Arts and Letters offers a general college major and majors in anthropology, art, Caribbean and Latin American studies, English, history, Jewish studies, languages and linguistics (French, German, Italian, Japanese, and Spanish), music, philosophy, political science, social science, sociology, and theater. The Barry Kaye College of Business offers majors in accounting, economics, finance, hospitality and tourism management, industry studies, insurance, international business and trade, management, management information systems, marketing, and real estate. The Harriet L. Wilkes Honors College in Jupiter offers a liberal arts and sciences education in a highly selective environment. Majors include American studies, anthropology, biological sciences/pre-med, chemistry, economics, English literature, environmental studies, history, international studies, Latin American studies, law and society, marine biology, math and science, mathematics, philosophy, physics, political science, psychology, Spanish, and women's studies. The College of Education offers majors in elementary education, exceptional student education, and exercise science and wellness education. Secondary certification is also available. The College of Engineering offers majors in computer science and civil, computer, electrical, mechanical, and ocean engineering. The Christine E. Lynn College of Nursing offers the Bachelor of Science in Nursing degree. The Charles E. Schmidt College of Science has majors in biological science (biotechnology, ecology and organismic biology, marine biology, microbiology, and molecular biology), chemistry, geography, geology, mathematical sciences, physics, psychology, and social psychology.

Academic Programs

Florida Atlantic University prepares its undergraduate students to be productive and thoughtful citizens by offering a broad liberal education coupled with the development of competency in fields of special interest. FAU encourages students to think creatively and critically and provides the intellectual tools needed for lifelong learning.

Off-Campus Programs

FAU has established a work-study program between its colleges and cooperating businesses, industries, and government laboratories. FAU has exchange agreements with international schools in locations ranging from China to Germany. Arrangements must be made through the Office of International Programs (http://www.fau.edu/goabroad).

Academic Facilities

The Boca Raton campus resources feature the S. E. Wimberly Library, with more than 1 million holdings. The Dorothy F. Schmidt College of Arts and Letters features a 75,000-square-foot, three-building complex encompassing a performance arts center, an art gallery, an experimental theater, a visual arts center, lecture halls, classrooms, and offices. The Barry Kaye College of Business occupies a four-story classroom/office building. The College of Education's four-story, 90,000-square-foot facility houses its five academic departments and offers a teaching gymnasium, an early childhood center, and the A. D. Henderson University School, a public elementary, middle, and high school operated by the College of Education. The Science and Engineering and Social Science Buildings were joined by the Physical Science Building and the Charles E. Schmidt Biomedical Center. There is also a marine sciences center, Gumbo Limbo, located between the Intracoastal Waterway and the Atlantic Ocean; it provides teaching and research facilities. The Christine E. Lynn College of Nursing is housed in a state-of-the-art energy and environmentally designed building and is the proud recipient of the Gold Medal for Leadership in Energy and Environmental Design (LEED).

FAU continues to enhance the campus environment with many new facilities in the planning and construction stages. Some future projects on the Boca Raton campus include a gymnasium and arena renovation; a 600-bed residence hall; the College of Business Office Depot Center for Executive Development; a 45,000 square foot Student Recreation Center; the Marleen and Harold Forkas Alumni Center; the Charles E. Schmidt Medical Center, a state-of-the-art teaching hospital; and Innovation Village, FAU's on-campus stadium and arena.

Expansions are underway across all of FAU's seven campuses. On the Davie campus, a new student activity center is under construction. The Treasure Coast campus plans to add additional classroom facilities to accommodate its growing student body.

Costs

For the 2007–08 academic year, in-state tuition was $112.23 per credit hour and out-of-state tuition was $547.69 per credit hour. A full-time course load is 24 to 50 credit hours per academic year. Average room and board costs were $8960. Additional expenses were $766 for books, $1544 for personal items, and $2629 for transportation for off-campus students. Fees are subject to change at any time by action of the Florida legislature.

Financial Aid

Approximately $60 million in financial aid is awarded each year. A comprehensive program of student financial aid includes scholarships, grants, loans, and employment that may provide assistance from initial enrollment through graduate study. Assistance is tailored to fit each student's requirements and may vary during his or her enrollment. As a member of the College Scholarship Service of the College Board, the University is guided by the principles and policies of that organization. Students who are interested in applying for need-based aid must complete the Free Application for Federal Student Aid (FAFSA), which is available online at http://www.fau.edu/finaid and at all U.S. high schools, colleges, and universities. Students are strongly encouraged to complete the FAFSA in January for fall admission. The process of applying for aid normally takes six to eight weeks. The priority deadline is March 1. Students must be notified of their acceptance to the University before award allocations can be made.

There is a variety of scholarships available for academic, athletic, or artistic talent. Students should visit the Admissions Web site at http://www.fau.edu/admissions and click on "Scholarships" for more information.

Faculty

Recognizing that the excellence of its faculty is the true measure of the worth of a university, FAU has brought together a distinguished group of scholars who hold a balanced dedication to both teaching and research. Faculty members come from more than thirty states and several countries. The majority hold a doctorate or professional degree. They all represent a high level of professional experience and academic attainment and are committed to the development of a vigorous educational program of high caliber. The University community has benefited from the presence of 12 Eminent Scholars, distributed over seven colleges. In addition, two Endowed Chairs have been fully funded and five others partially funded. The presence of these distinguished scholars and researchers has greatly enhanced the academic climate of the University and has provided focal points for the development of new programs, particularly at the graduate level.

Student Government

FAU gives students an active role on virtually all University and faculty committees, including the Curriculum Committee. They serve on the Board of Trustees and college advisory councils and operate the Student Government Association and Residence Hall Councils as well as the interclub, interfraternity, and Panhellenic groups. Students also serve on the University Senate along with faculty and staff members.

Admission Requirements

Admission to the University is limited to applicants who have graduated from regionally accredited high schools or who hold a GED certificate. Evaluation is based on the academic course grade point average combined with acceptable results on the SAT or ACT. Candidates for admission should have 18 academic high school units, including 4 units of English, 3 units of mathematics (algebra I and above), 3 units of natural science (2 with labs), 3 units of social science, 2 units of foreign language in sequence, and 3 academic electives. Score reports are accepted directly from the testing agency or from the student's official high school transcript. Applicants who have completed the GED test should request official high school transcripts (if applicable) and an official GED score report from the Department of Education.

Admission for freshman students requires an application for admission, a nonrefundable $30 application fee, official transcripts from an accredited high school, and the official results of the SAT or ACT. Admitted freshmen must confirm their intention to enroll and secure their place with the freshman class by submitting a nonrefundable $200 admissions tuition deposit. The deposit will be applied to the student's tuition and other expenses for the term in which they have been admitted to FAU.

Admission into FAU as an undergraduate transfer requires students to be in good academic standing at their previous college or university and to have a minimum 2.0 GPA. Students with fewer than 60 transferable credits should submit an application for admission, a nonrefundable $30 application fee, official transcripts from high school and previously attended colleges or universities, and acceptable results of the SAT or ACT. Students with 60 or more transferable credits must submit an application for admission, a nonrefundable $30 application fee, and official transcripts from each previously attended college or university.

All freshmen, undergraduate transfer, and second-baccalaureate students who have completed all or part of their education abroad are required to have their foreign credentials evaluated by an independent evaluation service. International students must also furnish evidence of proficiency in English by submitting TOEFL scores. For additional international student requirements, students should visit http://www.fau.edu/admissions and click on "International Freshmen" or "International Transfer".

Application and Information

Office of Undergraduate Admissions
Florida Atlantic University
777 Glades Road
Boca Raton, Florida 33431
Phone: 800-299-4FAU (toll-free)
800-920-8705 (Honors College, toll-free)
E-mail: ugadmissions@fau.edu
hcadmissions@fau.edu (Honors College)
Web site: http://www.fau.edu

FLORIDA GULF COAST UNIVERSITY

FORT MYERS, FLORIDA

The University

Florida Gulf Coast University (FGCU) is located on a scenic 760-acre campus in Fort Myers, Florida, on the southern gulf coast of Florida. Founded in 1997, FGCU is an institution defined by academic quality, student centeredness, and outstanding teaching. Its beautiful campus environment offers exceptional facilities designed and built for a university of the twenty-first century.

A state-supported coed institution, Florida Gulf Coast University is increasingly becoming known as the "university of choice" for high-achieving students. Faculty and staff members are committed to student success, and it is at the center of all University endeavors and one of the University's guiding principles. FGCU's mission focuses on the values of student success, academic freedom, diversity, informed and engaged citizenship, service to the community—particularly Southwest Florida—the use of technology as a fundamental tool toward achieving a high-quality education, collaborative learning, and the constant assessment of all University functions for improvement and continued renewal.

Florida Gulf Coast University offers forty-four undergraduate and twenty-two graduate programs through its five colleges and three schools: the College of Arts and Science, the Lutgert College of Business, the College of Education, the College of Health Professions, the College of Professional Studies, the Bower School of Music, the School of Nursing, and the U. A. Whitaker School of Engineering.

The broad array of undergraduate and graduate programs includes arts and sciences, business, music, engineering, technology, education, environmental science, nursing/allied health, and public and social services. Professional development and continuing education programs are also offered. On-campus courses along with distance education and partnerships with public and private organizations, agencies, and educational institutions enable the University to extend a rich diversity of higher education opportunities to Southwest Florida and beyond.

The Office of Student Affairs offers students a wide variety of clubs and organizations in which to become involved and gain valuable leadership and team-building skills. There are cultural, educational, Greek (fraternities and sororities), honors, media, political, professional, recreational, religious, service, social, and athletic organizations on campus. Extracurricular activities include concerts, dances, lectures, movies, sports, and live performances by comedians and other entertainers. Students not only have the opportunity to participate in these extracurricular activities, they can plan them as well.

Varsity sports teams currently compete in the NCAA Division I and include baseball, basketball, cross-country, golf, soccer, softball, tennis, volleyball, and women's swimming and diving. FGCU is a member of the Atlantic Sun Conference. Students can also participate in intramural sports, such as basketball, cross-country, football, soccer, softball, table tennis, tennis, and volleyball.

The University has a student body of over 9,000 students. The student body comprises 63 percent women and 37 percent men. The average high school GPA was 3.35. FGCU promotes an institutional culture that affirms diversity as a source of renewal and vitality; 5 percent of its students are African American, 2 percent are Asian American, and 10 percent are Hispanic American.

Twenty-three percent of the students at Florida Gulf Coast University live in on-campus housing at North Lake Village, a tranquil setting on the lake, where 4 students share single-bedroom or double-bedroom apartments that are fully furnished and close to the library, student union, fitness center, aquatics center, and all other campus facilities. Planned to open in fall 2008, Everglades Hall is a five-story residence hall that will house first-year students in single-bedroom suites. FGCU's meal plan offers a wide selection of options, and students can eat on campus at various locations, including Einstein's Brothers Bagels, Taco Bell Express, Subway, and Starbucks, as well as The Perch, which features a real-food-on-campus concept.

FGCU has one of the safest campuses in the Florida University System. The University's safety record is due to the dedicated and professional staff members, the University Police, and an involved campus community.

Florida Gulf Coast University is accredited by the Commission on Colleges of the Southern Association of Colleges and Schools (1866 Southern Lane, Decatur, Georgia 30033-4097; telephone: 404-679-4501) to award associate, baccalaureate, and master's degrees.

Location

Located on Florida's gulf coast, the campus is close to the cities of Fort Myers, Cape Coral, and Naples. They offer college students an abundance of recreational activities, including parks, golf courses, tennis courts, swimming pools, shopping, museums, theaters, restaurants, and social outlets.

Majors and Degrees

The Bachelor of Arts degree is awarded in anthropology, art, biology, chemistry, communication, early childhood education, elementary education, English, environmental studies, history, liberal studies, marine science, mathematics, music, philosophy, political science, psychology, secondary education, sociology, Spanish, special education, and theater.

The Bachelor of Science degree is awarded in accounting, athletic training, biology, bioengineering, biotechnology, civil engineering, clinical laboratory science, community health, computer information systems, computer science, criminal forensic studies, criminal justice, environmental engineering, finance, health science, human performance, legal studies, long-term-care administration, management, marketing, mathematics, nursing, resort and hospitality management, and social work.

Academic Programs

Florida Gulf Coast University offers traditional campus and educational experiences along with in-demand degree programs and high-tech instructional tools. The University runs on a semester calendar.

Students at FGCU benefit from smaller class sizes and dedicated teachers who bring to the classrooms the inspiration, insights, and knowledge gained through professional affiliations and research in wide areas of expertise. The University's goal is to provide students with the competencies and skills necessary for success in life and work.

FGCU offers special study options, including academic remediation for incoming students, accelerated degree programs, Advanced Placement (AP) credits, cooperative education, distance learning, double majors, honors programs, independent study, internships, off-campus study, services for learning-disabled (LD) students, study-abroad opportunities, and a summer session.

Off-Campus Programs

The University offers numerous study-abroad opportunities for students who qualify. Students have participated in FGCU study tours and semester programs in locations such as Brazil, China, France, Germany, Guatemala, Honduras, and New Zealand and have earned course credit in a variety of subjects. Through an extensive network of other recognized academic programs offered through provider agencies and other universities, students may participate in accredited programs in cities and countries around the world.

Academic Facilities

As a relatively new institution, Florida Gulf Coast University offers its students the latest in computer science labs, biology labs, and media resources. The FGCU Library has more than 312,000 items in its physical collections as well as a virtual collection of electronic resources that includes more than 17,000 journals. The library offers individual and group study spaces, a large computer lab (105 workstations), group study computer rooms, a 24-hour study space, and a new home for the FGCU Writing Center. The University offers both a television station and an FM radio station. Students gain valuable experience through the Small Business Development Center, Southwest Florida Center for Public and Social Policy, and the John Scott Dailey Institute of Government. Computer labs with full Internet access are located throughout the campus.

Costs

Florida Gulf Coast University offers value-priced, high-quality education and personal attention on par with the finest private universities—with the price tag of Florida's excellent public university system. Tuition per credit hour for undergraduates in 2007–08 was $125.92 for Florida residents and $543.18 for nonresidents. Additional fees apply. The estimated cost of attendance for an undergraduate Florida resident (based on 15 credit hours each semester, a single room, and meals) was tuition and fees, $3738; room and board, $8151; transportation, $1440; books and supplies, $950; and personal expenses, $1400—for an approximate annual cost of $15,679. Nonresident undergraduate costs were tuition and fees, $16,260; room and board, $8151; transportation, $1440; books and supplies, $950; and personal expenses, $1400—for an approximate annual cost of $28,201.

Financial Aid

The Office of Financial Assistance and Scholarships offers a comprehensive financial aid program for students, including scholarships, grants, loans, and work-study employment. During the 2006–07 academic year, FGCU students received over $30 million in federal, state, and institutional financial aid funds, as well as over $1 million in private scholarships. FGCU assists students in financing their educations, advises them of alternative solutions, and counsels them in debt management strategies. FGCU also serves the local community by conducting financial aid workshops in the local high schools, businesses, and various civic organizations.

Faculty

There are 500 faculty members at Florida Gulf Coast University; 335 are employed on a full-time basis. The student-faculty ratio is 17:1.

Student Government

The mission of the Student Government is to provide an intellectual, social, and cultural environment that maximizes student potential and enhances student success. The purpose of the Student Government is to provide equal representation for all students at Florida Gulf Coast University. Student needs rather than institutional preference determine priorities for academic planning, policies, and programs. Student Government serves as an institutional resource to further the development of the student as a contributing member of the community. The Student Government acts as the official voice through which student opinion may be expressed, thus producing students who are engaged in both University activities and community affairs.

Admission Requirements

Students are encouraged to begin the application process at the beginning of their senior year of high school and have all materials sent to the University as soon as possible after the application has been submitted. The average test scores for incoming freshmen are 1026 (critical reading and math) on the SAT and 21.3 on the ACT. Students are strongly encouraged to schedule a visit and tour of the FGCU campus. A nonrefundable $30 application fee is required. Prospective students may apply online or download an application at http://www.fgcu.edu/admissions/prospective/apply.html.

Application and Information

Starting with summer 2008 term, Florida Gulf Coast University has a priority admissions deadline for Freshman/First Time In College Students (FTIC). Students who are admitted by February 15 are given first priority for enrollment under FGCU's Freshman Enrollment CAP. Students who qualify for admission after February 15 will be offered admission to FGCU on a space-available basis. For more information about the priority admissions deadline, students should visit http://www.fgcu.edu/Admissions/Prospective/freshmancriteria.html.

Director of Admissions
Florida Gulf Coast University
10501 FGCU Boulevard South
Fort Myers, Florida 33965-6565
Phone: 239-590-7878
888-889-1095 (toll-free)
E-mail: admissions@fgcu.edu
Web site: http://www.fgcu.edu

FLORIDA INSTITUTE OF TECHNOLOGY

MELBOURNE, FLORIDA

The Institute

Born in the age of space exploration, Florida Institute of Technology was founded in 1958 to offer continuing education to the scientists, engineers, and technicians working at what is now NASA's Kennedy Space Center. As the only independent technological university in the southeastern United States, the university remains dedicated to providing a high-quality education that enhances knowledge through basic and applied research. In support of this mission, Florida Tech is committed to providing students with a world-class faculty, a hands-on and technology-focused curriculum, a high-quality and culturally diverse student body, and personal and career growth opportunities.

Florida Tech is a fully accredited, coeducational, independent, privately supported university that offers more than 145 degree programs in science and engineering, aviation, business, humanities, psychology, education and communication. Doctoral degrees are offered in twenty disciplines, while master's degrees are offered in more than sixty-five areas of study.

Florida Tech has more than 2,300 undergraduate students and more than 2,300 graduate students from fifty states and ninety-eight countries. More than 100 student organizations represent the varied interests of Florida Tech's students, including student government; fraternities and sororities; political and religious groups; college-run radio and television; dance, music, science fiction, choral, and theater performance; and academic and honor organizations.

Florida Tech competes in fifteen intercollegiate sports. Women's sports include basketball, cross-country, golf, rowing, soccer, softball, tennis, and volleyball. Men's sports include baseball, basketball, cross-country, golf, rowing, soccer, and tennis. Panther teams have earned national championships in men's soccer and crew; regional titles in baseball, men's soccer, and women's basketball; and Sunshine State Conference Championships in men's soccer, men's and women's cross-country, men's and women's basketball, and women's rowing. In 2003–04, the women's rowing team won the Sunshine State Conference Championship and advanced to the NCAA Division II Rowing Championships, where they finished third in the nation. In 2002, the women's basketball team won the Sunshine State Conference title and advanced to the NCAA Elite Eight. More than twenty-six intramural sports are offered, and students can take advantage of the subtropical climate to participate in outdoor activities year-round.

Florida Tech is listed as a *Barron's Guide* "Best Buy" in college education. In addition, the university is ranked as a "Best Southeastern College" by *The Princeton Review* in 2006.

According to the last three surveys of Florida Tech graduates, 96 percent are working in their major or in graduate school within six months of graduation, and 53 percent of working grads have a starting salary of more than $45,000 per year.

Florida Tech was the recipient of a $64-million F. W. Olin Foundation grant, resulting in new facilities in engineering, life sciences, physical sciences, and sports and recreation.

Florida Tech's SAT scores are among the highest of any private university in Florida.

Location

Florida Tech is located along the Atlantic coastline of central Florida in Brevard County, better known as the Space Coast. Situated within Florida's High Tech Corridor, it is home to Kennedy Space Center, United Space Alliance, and many other government agencies and technology companies. The area has the nation's fifth-largest high-tech workforce and supports more than 5,000 high-tech companies.

The area's attractive business climate is matched only by its natural resources, many of them ideal for scientific study and research, including the estuarine habitats of the Indian River Lagoon, the Atlantic Ocean marine ecosystem, area beaches and wetlands, thousands of acres of protected wildlife habitats, and a variety of tropical/subtropical Gulf Stream weather phenomena. Research and field projects spearheaded by Florida Tech professors often take students to exotic locations all over the world—from Peru to the Alaskan Arctic and Hungary to Australia.

With the Indian River Lagoon and the Atlantic Ocean less than 5 miles from the campus, water sports such as swimming, sailing, surfing, diving, fishing and boating are popular year-round activities. Central Florida attractions such as Walt Disney World, Sea World, and Universal Orlando are within a 1-hour drive, and Miami is only 3 hours south of the campus.

Majors and Degrees

Florida Tech offers bachelor's degrees in accounting, aeronautical science (flight option available), aerospace engineering, astronomy, astrophysics, aviation computer science, aviation management (flight option available), aviation meteorology (flight option available), aquaculture, biochemistry, biology, biology education, business administration, business and environmental studies, chemical engineering, chemical management, chemistry, chemistry education, civil engineering, communication, computer engineering, computer science, computer science education, earth/space science education, ecology, e-commerce technology, electrical engineering, environmental science, forensic psychology, general science education, humanities, information management, interdisciplinary science, international business, marine biology, mathematics education, mathematical sciences (applied mathematics option available), mechanical engineering, meteorology, military science, molecular biology, ocean engineering, oceanography, physics, physics education, premedical chemistry, preprofessional biology, preprofessional physics, psychology, research chemistry, software engineering, and space sciences.

The university also offers minors in thirteen areas: accounting, biology, business administration, chemistry, communication, computational mathematics, computer science, education, forensic psychology, history, management, management information systems, and psychology.

Academic Programs

The university operates on a semester-based academic year. All majors incorporate some form of scholarly inquiry, such as research, cooperative education, internships, or interdisciplinary design projects. The opportunity for further diversification is provided by minors and course work in education and the liberal arts. Programs in the sciences prepare the student for graduate or professional work. Practical aspects of all engineering disciplines and the computer sciences may be combined with management science for the business minded. A wide variety of programs are available for the environmentalist.

In the College of Aeronautics, the bachelor's programs provide a strong business or science background in the first two years and concentrate on specialized knowledge in the aviation industry during the junior and senior years. For students interested in flight options, training begins immediately within the first week of classes. Flight students earn their FAA commercial, instrument, and multiengine flight certificates and can earn their instructor, air taxi, and airline transport pilot ratings and flight dispatcher certificate.

Students at Florida Tech may qualify for advanced placement through English and mathematics examinations administered by the university. Advanced credit is awarded for Advanced Placement (AP) exams and higher-level International Baccalaureate subjects.

The university offers a four-year Army ROTC program, and it rewards ROTC scholarship winners with a generous supplemental scholarship package. Prospective students should contact an ROTC representative at the university.

Academic Facilities

Florida Tech has more than 125 laboratories and state-of-the-art research facilities, including Aquaculture Laboratory; Center for Airport Management and Development; Center for Applied Business Research; Center for Computational Fluid Dynamics; Center for Distance Learning; Center for Electronic Manufacturability; Center for Environmental Education; Center for Remote Sensing; Center for Software Engineering; Claude Pepper Institute for Aging and Therapeutic Research; Infectious Diseases Laboratory; Joint Center for Advanced Therapeutics and Research; Laser, Optics, and Instrumentation Laboratory; Maglev (magnetic levitation) Laboratory; Microelectronics Laboratory; Research Center for Waste Utilization; Oak Ridge Associated Universities; Robotics and Spatial Systems Laboratory; Southeastern Association for Research in Astronomy; Sportfish Research Institute; Vero Beach Marine Laboratory; and Wind and Hurricane Impacts Research Laboratory.

Computer facilities include three technology-teaching laboratories, a network of Linux workstations, a National Science Foundation–funded computational physics laboratory consisting of twelve Pentium PCs capable of running Linux X Windows and MS Windows, a variety of microcomputers and other types of hardware, and a large number of microcomputer periodicals and current software catalogs. Evans Library houses an additional seventy-microcomputer laboratory with an extensive software library. Additional teaching labs, virtual-reality labs, and online interactive classes with the latest multimedia and information technology are available in the F. W. Olin Engineering Complex. The university also has available a 48-node Beowulf cluster running Linux MPI.

Built into the university's newest academic buildings, the F. W. Olin Engineering Complex, F. W. Olin Physical Sciences Center, and F. W. Olin Life Sciences Building, are some of the latest electronic and communications technology. Also, Florida Tech is constructing the state's largest telescope on top of the recently completed F. W. Olin Physical Sciences Center. Construction of the 32-inch telescope began in 2005 and was expected to take eighteen months to complete.

Flight training is conducted at the Melbourne International Airport, 2 miles from the campus. The Florida Tech fleet has more than thirty modern aircraft and eight sophisticated simulators and includes Piper Cadets and Warriors, new Piper Arrows, twin-engine Piper Seminoles, a Piper Chieftain for multiengine training, and a Cirrus SR20. FIT Aviation recently received certification as a Cirrus Certified Training Center and can offer initial and recurrent training to owners and users of Cirrus aircraft and to university students. Cirrus aircraft are a new breed of technologically advanced planes with composite construction and fully electronic flight instrumentation.

Costs

Tuition for the 2007–08 academic year was $28,920 for science and engineering majors and $26,360 for all other majors. Students pursuing aviation majors with flight training could expect an additional cost of $12,000 per year in flight fees. Room and board costs for the year were approximately $7800.

Financial Aid

There are many different programs available to help cover the cost of higher education. Approximately 80 percent of Florida Tech students qualify for a combination of merit-based scholarships, need-based grants, educational loans, and school-year employment programs. Awards are based on academic promise, need, college costs, and the availability of funds. Monthly installment plans are available for tuition and other expenses. The priority deadline for financial aid is March 1. Students eligible for Veterans Administration benefits may contact the VA representative on the Melbourne campus.

Faculty

The student-faculty ratio is 9:1, and 90 percent of full-time faculty members have a Ph.D. or other terminal degree. The small average class size of 25 provides the opportunity to work one-on-one with some of the finest minds in education. In general, freshman- and sophomore-level instructors carry full-time teaching loads. They are closely involved with student life and serve as advisers and counselors. Upper-level and graduate instructors participate in teaching and research activities. Florida Tech's prime location among a vast array of high-tech corporations and scientific communities provides a wealth of adjunct faculty members who bring skills and expertise from local business and industry.

Student Government

Student government at Florida Tech is the vital link between the administration and the student body and functions as the liaison between the university and the community as well as a catalyst for social change. The organization promotes new ideas and encourages students to participate at all levels of university involvement.

Admission Requirements

Applicants to Florida Tech must demonstrate the readiness to succeed in a challenging academic curriculum. The high school transcript is the most important element of the application. While no minimum grade point average, class rank, or standardized test score is specified, these measures must indicate a readiness for college studies in a chosen academic program.

An applicant who is a U.S. citizen must have earned a high school diploma or high school equivalency credential by the date of first enrollment. Personal recommendations by counselors or faculty members are not required but are taken into consideration in certain circumstances. Transfer students are considered individually on the basis of transcripts and overall performance. Prospective applicants who do not meet the standardized admission requirements but are interested in attending Florida Tech are urged to arrange a personal interview with the admission counselor to receive individual attention.

Application and Information

Florida Tech encourages applicants from every social, ethnic, racial, and religious background. The university practices a rolling admission policy. Fees for applications are $50 when mailed or $40 when submitted online. Completed applications, high school and college transcripts, and standardized test results should be sent to the Office of Admission.

For further information, students may contact:

Office of Admission
Florida Institute of Technology
150 West University Boulevard
Melbourne, Florida 32901-6975
Phone: 321-674-8030
800-888-4348 (toll-free)
E-mail: admission@fit.edu
Web site: http://www.fit.edu

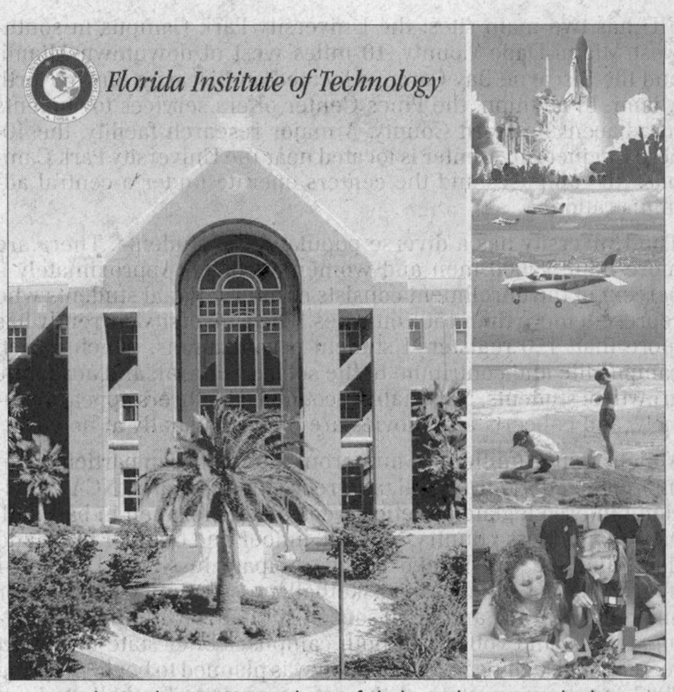

Immersed in a thriving atmosphere of dedicated scientists, high-technology corporations, and natural habitats, Florida Tech responds to the educational and research challenges of the twenty-first century.

FLORIDA INTERNATIONAL UNIVERSITY

MIAMI, FLORIDA

The University

Florida International University (FIU) is Miami's public research university and one of America's most dynamic institutions of higher learning. The University offers more than 200 bachelor's, master's, and doctoral degrees.

Major academic divisions are the Colleges of Architecture and the Arts, Arts and Sciences, Business Administration, Education, Engineering and Computing, Nursing and Health Sciences, and Social Work, Justice, and Public Affairs; the Honors College; and the College of Law. In addition, there are the Schools of Accounting, Hospitality and Tourism Management, Journalism and Mass Communication, Music, and Public Health. The Florida Board of Governors approved the creation of a College of Medicine at FIU. The College expects to admit its first class in the fall of 2009. The University is accredited by the Southern Association of Colleges and Schools. The professional programs of the respective colleges and schools are accredited or approved by the appropriate professional associations. The Carnegie Foundation for the Advancement of Teaching classifies FIU as an RU/H: Research University (high research activity). FIU is a member of Phi Beta Kappa, the country's oldest and most distinguished academic honor society. The University's priorities are to graduate a well-educated, technologically sophisticated, ethnically diverse student body whose members can think critically about a changing world to create greater understanding among the people of the Americas and the world.

FIU has two main sites: the University Park Campus in southwest Miami-Dade County, 10 miles west of downtown Miami, and the Biscayne Bay Campus located on Biscayne Bay in North Miami. In addition, the Pines Center offers services to students in adjacent Broward County. A major research facility, the 40-acre Engineering Center is located near the University Park Campus. All campuses and the centers operate under a central administration.

The University has a diverse population of students. There are more than 38,000 men and women enrolled. Approximately 9 percent of the enrollment consists of international students who represent more than 130 countries. The University currently has more than 150 registered student organizations, which enrich campus life and contribute to the social, cultural, and academic growth of students. Nationally recognized lecturers appear regularly, and concerts and movies are offered, usually at no cost.

Athletic opportunities are numerous. Students can participate in intercollegiate, intramural, and recreational sports. NCAA Division I intercollegiate athletics are available for men in baseball, basketball, cross-country, football, indoor and outdoor track and field, and soccer. Women can participate in NCAA Division I intercollegiate athletics in basketball, cross-country, golf, indoor and outdoor track and field, soccer, softball, swimming and diving, tennis, and volleyball. Both campuses offer state-of-the-art recreational facilities. Construction was planned to begin in spring 2007 for the new, state-of-the-art on-campus football stadium and facility. Completion is scheduled for a September 2008 kick-off.

The University offers apartment-style housing for students at both University Park and Biscayne Bay Campuses. The facilities provide students with the opportunity to live with others in a convenient and supportive residential setting. Most of the residence halls offer a full range of amenities for students, including cable TV, computer connectivity, study rooms, and computer labs as well as a swimming pool and various recreational areas. In addition, the second of three fraternity houses was recently completed, and Lakeview Hall, a new 850-bed residence hall opened in August 2006.

Location

Miami and FIU are comparable in their explosive growth, rich ethnic and cultural diversity, and quest for excellence. FIU is a leading institution in one of the most dynamic, artistically expressive, and cosmopolitan cities in the United States, a gateway to Latin America and the Caribbean. The continued globalization of the world's economic, social, and political systems adds to the importance of FIU's mission and, combined with the subtropical environment and strategic location, strengthens southeast Florida's role as an information and transportation center.

Disney World, the Everglades, marine and state parks, Seaquarium, Metro Zoo, Fairchild Tropical Gardens, world renowned South Beach, and the Parrot Jungle are popular student attractions. Other favorite year-round activities include swimming, waterskiing, scuba diving, sailing, tennis, golf, and horseback riding. Students can also head south for a weekend in the Florida Keys or the Bahamas.

Majors and Degrees

The College of Architecture and the Arts offers a Bachelor of Arts in architecture, a Bachelor of Interior Design, and a Bachelor of Landscape Architecture. A Bachelor of Fine Arts is offered in art, dance, music, and theater. The School of Music offers the Bachelor of Music and a Bachelor of Science in music.

The College of Arts and Sciences offers programs of study that lead to a Bachelor of Arts in art history, Asian studies (second degree), chemistry, dance, earth sciences, economics, English, environmental studies, French, geography, history, humanities, information technology, international relations, liberal studies, philosophy, physics, political science, Portuguese, psychology, religious studies, sociology/anthropology, Spanish, theater, and women's studies. The Bachelor of Science is offered in biology, chemistry, earth sciences, environmental studies, geology, marine biology, mathematical sciences, mathematics, physics, and statistics.

The College of Business Administration offers a Bachelor of Business Administration, with majors in finance, international business, management, management information systems, marketing, personnel management, and real estate. The School of Accounting offers a Bachelor of Accounting. The School of Hospitality and Tourism Management offers programs of study that lead to the Bachelor of Science in hospitality management and travel and tourism management. With the cooperation of industry executives, the school has an internship program that utilizes hotels, motels, restaurants, clubs, airlines, travel agencies, and cruise lines as practice labs for students.

The College of Education offers a Bachelor of Science in art education (1–12), biology education, chemistry education, early childhood education, elementary education with ESOL endorsement, English education, exceptional education with ESOL endorsement, exercise and sports sciences, French education, health occupations education, mathematics education, parks and recreation management, physical education, physics education, social studies education, and Spanish education.

The College of Engineering and Computing offers programs of study that lead to the Bachelor of Science in biomedical engineering, civil engineering, computer engineering, construction management, electrical engineering, environmental and urban systems, industrial and systems engineering, and mechanical engineering. Computer science offers a Bachelor of Science in computer science and information technology.

The College of Nursing and Health Sciences offers a Bachelor of Science in nursing, in addition to bachelor's degrees in dietetics and nutrition, health information management, health sciences, occupational therapy, and physical therapy. The College of Social Work, Justice, and Public Affairs offers Bachelor of Science programs in criminal justice, public administration, and social work. The Stempel School of Public Health offers a Bachelor of Science in dietetics and nutrition.

The School of Journalism and Mass Communication offers a Bachelor of Science in communication, with tracks in advertising, print and broadcast journalism, production, and public relations.

Preprofessional programs are offered in dentistry, law, medicine, pharmacy, and veterinary medicine.

Academic Programs

At the undergraduate level, all students complete 36 semester hours of general education requirements before graduation. These consist of 6 semester hours each in the areas of humanities, mathematics, natural science, social science, and English composition and 6 semester hours in courses that require intensive writing. Students may tailor academic programs to fit their personal goals.

There are three terms in the academic calendar year: fall, spring, and summer. Two terms (or semesters) of full-time attendance constitute an academic year; a normal course load is defined as at least 12 semester hours per term. Mini-terms are also available within the summer semester.

Academic Facilities

At both University Park and Biscayne Bay Campuses, buildings house high-tech media classrooms, lecture halls, computer facilities, and offices. University Park also has laboratories, auditoriums, music and art studios, an international conference theater, and an experimental theater. The state-of-the-art Kovens Conference Center and the Wolfe University Center, located at Biscayne Bay Campus, are multipurpose facilities with ballrooms, theaters, and seminar rooms. The University's libraries contain more than 1.5 million bound volumes, over 3.2 million microforms, and periodical subscriptions in excess of 10,300. FIU continues to expand structurally. New buildings include the marine science facility, the College of Law, a second health sciences building, and a Student Fitness Center. Completion of the Frost Art Museum is expected in 2008.

Costs

Tuition for undergraduate courses during the 2007–08 academic year was $109.40 per credit hour for Florida residents and $522.70 for non–Florida residents. Additional fees assessed per-term include a $134 health fee, a $20 athletic fee, and a $130 parking fee. (These costs are subject to change.)

Financial Aid

The University adheres to the philosophy that a student is entitled to a university education regardless of his or her financial status. The financial aid program at the University includes scholarships, grants, loans, and employment. Awards are based on need, and individual attention is given to each applicant. To apply for aid, students should submit the Free Application for Federal Student Aid (FAFSA). Students are advised to apply before March 1 for priority consideration.

Faculty

The University has more than 1,800 full-time and adjunct faculty members whose backgrounds reflect both quality and diversity. Nearly 90 percent hold terminal degrees in their fields. The faculty members work across disciplinary boundaries with issues central to the environmental, urban, and international missions of the University. The University gives primary consideration to selecting faculty members who have a strong sense of commitment to teaching, research, and counseling students.

Student Government

FIU's Student Government Association (SGA) seeks to include all interested students on University-wide committees and task forces to ensure student representation. The SGA strives to set up programs that entertain, educate, and challenge FIU's community.

Admission Requirements

The University has a preferred application period of July 1 through December 1. Admissions are open on a space-available basis from December 2 through March 1.

Applicants are notified of their admission status (after December 1) once a completed application, appropriate application fee, and all supporting documents have been received and the evaluation process is completed. It is the applicant's responsibility to request official transcripts and test scores, when applicable, from all previously attended institutions. All applicants are considered for admission without regard to race, creed, age, disability, gender, marital status, or national origin.

The University seeks highly motivated students with strong academic backgrounds and exceptional test scores. The quality and number of applicants create competition for a place in the freshman class. Freshman admission requires graduation from an accredited secondary school, 18 academic units in college-preparatory courses, and official SAT or ACT scores. Decisions are based on the student's academic preparation.

Transfer applicants from accredited Florida public community colleges should have an Associate of Arts (A.A.) degree. Applicants who do not hold an A.A. degree must complete 60 semester hours of transferable credit, with a minimum grade point average of 2.0, based on a 4.0 scale. Applicants transferring from a Florida community college or university are required to take the College Level Academic Skills Test (CLAST) prior to admission. For students transferring from out-of-state or private colleges, the test can be taken during the first semester of enrollment. All applicants must meet the criteria published for limited-access programs and should consult the specific college and major for requirements.

International students must submit a Declaration of Finance that shows financial resources sufficient for attending the University and for all living expenses. Students from non-English-speaking countries must also submit a minimum TOEFL score of 500 on the paper-based test, 173 on the computer-based test, or 63 on the Internet-based test (iBT).

Application and Information

Students are invited to visit the beautiful campuses. Tours are available every day of the week (except Wednesday) and the first Saturday of the month (except on national holidays). For a complete schedule and to sign up for a tour, students should visit the Web site at http://admissions.fiu.edu/visitus.

To apply online, students should go to http://admissions.fiu.edu/apply. Additional information about the University can be found on the University's Web site.

Office of Undergraduate Admissions
Florida International University
P.O. Box 659003
Miami, Florida 33265-9003
Phone: 305-348-2363
Fax: 305-348-3648
Web site: http://www.fiu.edu

FLORIDA SOUTHERN COLLEGE

LAKELAND, FLORIDA

The College

Florida Southern College was founded in 1883 by the Methodist Church and has remained an affiliate throughout its 120-year history. The original campus was in Leesburg, but the College moved to Palm Harbor in 1902 and finally settled in Lakeland in 1922. Florida Southern is an intentionally interactive, residential, coeducational, comprehensive college with a strong core in the liberal arts. Although 60 percent of the 1,800 students come from Florida, the remaining 40 percent represent forty-three states and more than thirty other countries. Students come to Florida Southern because they want a liberal arts education and believe a smaller campus is the best place to find it. The atmosphere is relaxed and personal, fostering a very close-knit student body and faculty.

All members of the academic community take pride in the campus, a historic landmark and site of the largest collection of buildings designed by renowned architect Frank Lloyd Wright. Annie Pfeiffer Chapel, the first of the Wright buildings to be completed, hosts regular worship services where students of all denominations are welcome. Specific residence halls are reserved for freshmen. Upperclass students, whether members of fraternities and sororities or independent students, are housed in a variety of on-campus accommodations. Construction has been completed on the Miller Residence Hall, which includes seventy-six rooms, and construction is underway on another new state-of-the-art residential life complex. The George Jenkins Field House, which seats 3,000 people, includes a three-court gymnasium, a weight room, and a sports equipment room. Facilities for tennis, racquetball, dance, swimming, and waterskiing are also available. The Nina B. Hollis Wellness Center features a fully equipped fitness center, an aerobics/dance studio, an intramural gymnasium, and a wide-screen TV/lounge area. There are branches of six national Greek fraternities and five national Greek sororities on campus. Student activities include intercollegiate and intramural sports, drama and music groups, publications, and various clubs and organizations related to academic, political, religious, and social interests. In addition, many students are involved in volunteer programs and internships in the surrounding community.

Location

Florida Southern's campus consists of approximately 100 acres on the shore of Lake Hollingsworth in Lakeland, Florida, a pleasant community of about 120,000 residents in the heart of Florida's high-tech corridor. Lakeland is 45 minutes from Tampa and an hour from Orlando. Within an hour's drive of the state's major recreational attractions, including Walt Disney World and major beaches, the College is ideally situated for internships and job opportunities with leading corporations that tap into one of the largest markets in the U.S. Members of the community come to the College campus to attend Fine Arts Series performances in music, dance, and drama; to hear distinguished speakers; and to participate in College and business symposiums. The Lakeland Center also offers many cultural and entertainment opportunities.

Majors and Degrees

Florida Southern College offers a Bachelor of Arts, Bachelor of Fine Arts, Bachelor of Music, Bachelor of Music Education, or Bachelor of Science degree in the following majors: accounting, art (art education, art history, graphic design, and studio art), athletic training, biology, biochemistry and molecular biology, business administration (concentrations in information technology management, finance, management, international business, and marketing), chemistry, citrus, communication (advertising, public relations, print journalism, and broadcast journalism), criminology, economics, education (elementary education, including specific learning disabilities; prekindergarten/primary; and special education), English (dramatic arts, literature, and writing), history, horticultural science, mathematics, mathematics/computer science, music (music composition, music education, and music performance), nursing, philosophy, physical education, political science, psychology, religion, sociology, Spanish, and theater arts (performance and technical). Divisional majors are available in humanities and social science.

Preprofessional programs are offered in dentistry, engineering, law, medicine, physical therapy, and veterinary medicine. Interdisciplinary professional programs include music management and sport management. Programs in environmental horticulture include recreational turfgrass management as well as two tracks in production and landscape design. Students who wish to teach at the secondary level choose a major in a subject area and complete the requirements for secondary education certification by the state of Florida.

An honors program provides special opportunities for a select group of entering freshmen to explore topics of common interest in an integrated and interdisciplinary fashion. Selection to the honors program is highly competitive; the program is limited to approximately 10 percent of the entering class.

Academic Programs

All degree programs require the satisfactory completion of a minimum of 124 semester hours with a minimum grade point average of 2.0. Grading is traditional, with a pass/fail option available. The College operates on the semester system with two 15-week semesters, and three 4-week summer sessions. The average course load is 15 hours per semester. Students are required to complete a core curriculum of liberal arts and science courses in addition to their major course work. Credit by examination is awarded on the basis of successful scores on Advanced Placement tests, the International Baccalaureate (I.B.), and College-Level Examination Program (CLEP) tests.

Florida Southern has a Career Center that assists students in clarifying their career and life goals and that provides opportunities for them to explore these goals. Approximately 20 percent of Florida Southern graduates go immediately on to graduate work. Internship experiences help to place the vast majority of other graduates in field-related jobs (93 percent of graduates are employed and enrolled in graduate schools within six months of graduation).

Off-Campus Programs

The College sponsors a number of study-abroad opportunities, including May Option experiences Harlaxton Manor (England), Cuernavaca (Mexico), Salamanca and Alicante (Spain), and study-travel on an annually designated itinerary, such as Greece, Italy, and the Cities of Modernism in Europe. Other study-abroad options include Angers (France) and semester or yearlong programs in England, Northern Ireland, and Mexico or a vast array of additional options through one of the College's consortium programs.

Florida Southern participates in the Washington Semester of American University in Washington, D.C., through which selected students spend a semester in Washington studying government and international relations. Selected students may also spend one semester at Drew University in Madison, New Jersey, studying various aspects of the United Nations through Drew University's United Nations Semester.

Academic Facilities

Florida Southern's Roux Library houses a collection of 172,803 volumes; more than 650 periodical subscriptions; access to more than 2,000 full-text electronic periodicals and more than 10,000 electronic books; a 5,700-item media collection that includes videocassettes, CDs, DVDs, and CD-ROMs; a substantial microforms collection; and seating for more than 350 students. The Branscomb Memorial Auditorium seats 1,800 and is nationally known for its nearly perfect acoustical properties. The Ludd M. Spivey Humanities and Fine Arts Center includes the Marjorie M. McKinley Music Building, the Melvin Art Gallery, and the Loca Lee Buckner Theater. The theater seats 350 and is equipped with a hydraulic thrust stage, a computer-controlled lighting system, and laboratories for costume, makeup, and set design. The Polk Science Building houses the College's recently renovated, state-of-the-art science laboratories and one of the few planetariums in central Florida. The Pre-School Laboratory provides an opportunity for students majoring in prekindergarten/primary and elementary education to observe and teach preschoolers.

Costs

The comprehensive cost for 2007–08 was $28,690 ($21,190 for tuition and standard fees and $7500 for room and board). There were additional fees for individual music instruction and the use of practice rooms. Florida Southern estimates that another $1000 is adequate for books and supplies, and $1000 should cover personal expenses, exclusive of travel to and from home. Members of fraternities and sororities have additional expenses related to membership in these organizations.

Financial Aid

The Student Financial Aid Office offers students its counsel and assistance in meeting their educational expenses. Aid is awarded on the basis of an applicant's need, academic performance, and promise. Ninety-three percent of the students at Florida Southern receive financial assistance. To demonstrate need, an applicant is required to file the Free Application for Federal Student Aid (FAFSA). Various forms of aid, such as scholarships, grants, loans, and campus employment, are used to help meet students' needs. Merit scholarships are available, and awards are based on academic promise; performance ability in music, theater, or art; or athletic ability in baseball, basketball, cross-country, golf, soccer, softball, swimming, tennis, or volleyball. Applicants for aid must reapply each year. Florida Southern participates in the Federal Perkins Loan, Federal Supplemental Educational Opportunity Grant, and Federal Work-Study college-based programs. All applicants are expected to apply for any entitlement grant for which they are eligible, such as a Federal Pell Grant and, for Florida residents, a Florida Student Assistance Grant and the Florida Tuition Voucher. The Federal Stafford Loan Program is also available. There are extensive on-campus employment opportunities. The completed FAFSA and the College's financial aid application must be filed with the Student Financial Aid Office by April 1. Early application is encouraged for students seeking academic scholarships.

Faculty

Ninety percent of Florida Southern's faculty members have doctoral or other terminal degrees in their respective fields. The faculty is primarily a teaching faculty; all faculty members have posted office hours and are available for consultation and advising. Faculty members are selected not only for their teaching ability but also for their ability to relate to the needs and concerns of college students. The student-faculty ratio is 13:1.

Student Government

The Student Government Association represents the student body in matters involving the College administration, faculty, and student body and is responsible for coordinating student government. Each full-time student is a member of the association and has a vote in its affairs. The subsidiaries of the association are the Association of Campus Entertainment (ACE), the House of Representatives, the Student Senate, and the four classes: freshman, sophomore, junior, and senior.

Admission Requirements

Florida Southern looks for two things in applicants: performance and promise. The majority of applicants who have been admitted as freshmen have had a grade of B or better in college-preparatory courses (including four courses in English, three in mathematics, and the balance divided among science, foreign language, and social science), have ranked in the upper half of their graduating class, and have earned scores of at least 500 on each of the verbal and math portions of the SAT or a composite score of at least 23 on the ACT. Nevertheless, the Admissions Office is committed to reviewing individual applicants on their own merits, based on the level of challenge attempted, patterns of grades over time, recommendations from appropriate references, and an applicant's own assessment of the learning environment ideally suited to his or her needs. Applicants must graduate from an accredited high school with a minimum of 19 credits, 16 of which must be academic. Qualified high school juniors may apply for early admission if they have the recommendation of their secondary school and have had a personal interview with the Director of Admissions. Applications from transfers are welcome, as are those from students resuming their education and from older students who have delayed their entrance into college. Transfer applicants should have a minimum 2.5 grade point average and be graduates of or eligible to return to their former institutions. Transfer students with fewer than 25 semester hours must submit high school transcripts and standardized test scores. Applicants who hold Associate of Arts degrees from regionally accredited two-year institutions are typically granted junior standing. All applicants are encouraged to interview; an interview may be required for some candidates.

Application and Information

An application is ready for consideration by the Admissions Committee when it has been received with the $30 application fee, required test scores and references, and transcripts from each school attended. Since all students are required to live on campus unless they are seniors, married, or living with their parents, early application is desirable to ensure that housing is available. The freshman application deadline is March 1. The deadline for early decision applicants is December 1.

For more information about Florida Southern College, prospective students should contact:

Office of Admissions
Florida Southern College
111 Lake Hollingsworth Drive
Lakeland, Florida 33801-5698
Phone: 800-274-4131 (toll-free)
E-mail: fscadm@flsouthern.edu
Web site: http://www.flsouthern.edu

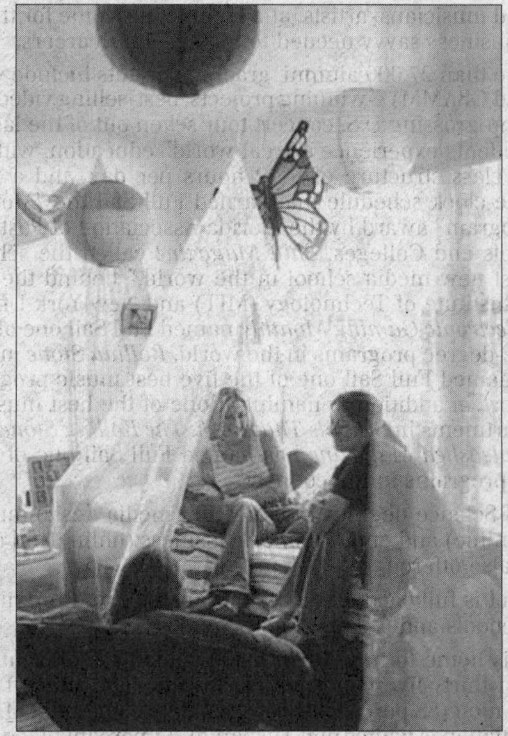

Freshman women's dorm room in Allan Spivey Residence Hall.

FULL SAIL UNIVERSITY

WINTER PARK, FLORIDA

The College

Established in 1979, Full Sail University is a private, coeducational college offering extensive training and education in the entertainment media production industry and entertainment technology. Hands-on experience and solid practical knowledge combine to provide an education where learning meets the real world. Students receive an introduction to many job opportunities in each career field and an overview of what each position requires. Full Sail's campus facilities include recording consoles, Motion Capture Studio, digital video editing workstations, H-D Studio, cameras, concert sound systems, computerized moving lights, and computer/graphic workstations that are used to create Web sites, animation sequences, 3-D graphics, computer generated models, characters, visual effects, and interactive games. Full Sail provides extensive instruction in all of these areas and more, offering a unique style of training that puts students hands-on and right in the middle of the entertainment and media production industry while in school.

Traditional learning techniques have their place at Full Sail, but the technology-intensive field of creative media demands a more rigorous pace than that offered by books, lectures, and seminars. As helpful as those are, their effectiveness is severely limited without practical, hands-on experience inside the school environment. Full Sail takes students' education beyond the confines of the classroom into real-world situations and puts them to work on the same kind of equipment encountered in media production facilities throughout the world.

Instructors and guest lecturers are professionals in their fields, and the low student-faculty ratio in labs allows students to interact with their mentors. Students come to Full Sail from around the world, and musicians, artists, and technicians come for the training and business savvy needed to further their careers.

With more than 27,000 alumni, graduate credits include work on Oscar- and GRAMMY®-winning projects, best-selling video games, and the top-grossing U.S. concert tour seven out of the last seven years. Students experience a "real world" education, with a professional class structure of 8–12 hours per day, and a 24-hour 'round-the-clock schedule that earned Full Sail the "Most Innovative Program" award by the Florida Association of Postsecondary Schools and Colleges. *Shift Magazine* called the school the "third-best new media school in the world," behind the Massachusetts Institute of Technology (MIT) and New York University (NYU). *Electronic Gaming Monthly* named Full Sail one of the top five game-degree programs in the world. *Rolling Stone* magazine recently named Full Sail one of the five best music programs in the country, in addition to naming it one of the best music business departments in *Schools That Rock: The Rolling Stone College Guide*. *Unleashed Magazine* has named Full Sail one of the five best film programs in the country

Master of Science degrees in education media design and technology (online) and entertainment business (online and on campus) are also offered.

The school is fully accredited by the Accrediting Commission of Career Schools and Colleges of Technology (ACCSCT).

Full Sail is home to more than 5,600 students representing fifty states and thirty-five countries worldwide. The student body is primarily men (88 percent). Approximately 68 percent of the student population is white (non-Hispanic), 11 percent black, 12 percent Hispanic, and 4 percent Asian or Pacific Islander.

Full Sail does not feature on-campus living arrangements, but does employ a Housing Manager who is dedicated to providing information about affordable accommodations in the many apartment complexes near the school. The Housing Manager can also help with information about roommates (other incoming Full Sail students), power, phones, furniture, and helpful community programs in the central Florida area.

Location

Full Sail's college campus is situated in a beautiful area of central Florida in Winter Park, a city that plays host to residential communities and light commerce. Thanks to tourism being Central Florida's primary business, entertainment, restaurants, and shopping are plentiful. The school is 20 minutes from downtown Orlando, 35 minutes from Disney and Universal Studios, 1 hour from Cape Canaveral and the Atlantic beaches, and 2 hours from the Gulf of Mexico.

Majors and Degrees

Full Sail currently offers eleven undergraduate degree programs, including Associate of Science degrees in graphic design, recording arts, and show production and touring and Bachelor of Science degrees in computer animation, digital arts and design, entertainment business (online), film, game art, game development, music business, and Web design and development.

Academic Programs

Full Sail's Computer Animation Program features intense, real-world training, getting students ready to make a mark on the growing 3-D animation industry. Students learn how to bring creations to life in the same software package used for major motion pictures and top selling video games. Courses include Animation Production, Character Design and Creation, Art History, and Demo Reel Creation.

Much more than a design school or an art school, Full Sail's Digital Arts and Design Program is carefully created to be a complete digital education. Digital art production, digital publishing, interactive media design, 3-D computer graphics, DVD authoring, Web design, digital video editing, and multimedia production are just a few of the courses that are available to prepare students for a career in digital art and design. Students also are trained on a wide variety of industry-standard software packages by professional instructors with experience in the field.

Full Sail's Entertainment Business Program is a comprehensive business program that combines core courses in subjects like management, marketing, and statistics with more advanced topics like data analysis, international business, and business law, as well as entertainment-specific courses like Artist Management, Entertainment Media Distribution, and Intellectual Property. The program also requires students to develop a business proposal unique to their interests and develop it from start to finish.

Full Sail's Film Program covers the entire filmmaking experience; students work united by their love of movies. Over the course of the program, the experienced, professional staff shows how to execute every position on a film production—from director, cinematographer, and producer to key grip, set dresser, and electrician—and the whole time, students use these newfound skills to actually create films. Full Sail students work in groups that emulate a real-world production crew while creating their projects with digital cameras, 16-mm cameras, and professional 35-mm film cameras, such as the Arricam Studio and Arricam Lite.

The Game Art Program focuses on 3-D art and content creation, with a heavy emphasis on character development, shading and lighting, texturing, and modeling, giving students a solid foundation in the art skills needed for game production. Game art students work together with game development in a real-world production setting, creating a playable game from start to finish.

Full Sail's Game Development Program gets students on the road to a career in developing, designing, and programming games for consoles and computers. Courses go in depth on subjects such as preproduction and creating game documents, programming and implementation, game play and level design, and designing intelligent artificial intelligence. By working in a real-world production environment with a team of programmers, artists, and designers, students develop an entire playable video game from start to finish.

The Music Business Program gives students a practical, real-world music business education where they get training in the core fundamentals of business, such as marketing, advertising, finance, and accounting. Students learn how to develop and run a record label and how to take their creative ideas and turn them into a viable business plan. The Music Business Program was created to complement the Associate of Science degree programs, and completion of both is required for a bachelor's degree. Graduates who have completed an Associate of Science degree in the entertainment field from another school are also invited to apply.

The Web Design and Development Program gives students a well-rounded education in all aspects of Web site creation—front-end design, back-end development, and client-side scripting development and deployment. Students learn coding formats like XHTML, CSS, and XML, as well as Flash and ActionScript 3.0, preparing them for a variety of careers in this growing field.

Full Sail runs on a modular schedule, with new classes beginning every month. Schedules vary depending on the degree programs. Once enrolled, students attend classes and labs five to six days, 35 to 40 hours each week. By doing so, students typically earn a bachelor's degree in less than twenty-one months. Lectures are scheduled during daytime hours, but some labs occur during evening and early morning hours. Full Sail recently won a Florida statewide award for the school with the "Most Innovative Program," due in part to this type of scheduling. It benefits students by ensuring a low student-teacher ratio and by representing the realistic demands of the entertainment and media production industry.

Academic Facilities

The 178-acre Full Sail campus houses more than 100 studios, production suites, soundstages, and computer labs as well as over fifty advanced college classrooms. Full Sail is a production facility that rivals any professional multimedia studio in the world.

Student advisers are available to assist students with questions about academics and referrals, and the Student Services Desk is open 24 hours a day for emergencies. Full Sail students and alumni can also utilize the school's Career Development Center. This center assists students with finding internships and entry-level employment, educates students on how to successfully market themselves, and promotes networking and professional relationships among students, alumni, and industry professionals.

Costs

Tuition costs vary depending on program. Tuition ranges from $33,275 to $69,775 per degree program. At Full Sail, these tuition costs include books, lab fees, course materials, career-development assistance, and lifetime auditing.

Financial Aid

Everyone's financial aid package is unique to them. The type of package that works best is determined by the important decisions made during this process as well as specific needs. Financial advisers work to ensure that students have all the information needed to make financial aid decisions that allow them the opportunity to attend Full Sail. Full Sail wants to assist every financial aid applicant in obtaining the financial aid assistance they are legally entitled to receive. The student's eligibility, the school's packaging criteria, and the amount and types of financial aid available determine this. Since Full Sail is an accredited school, the Financial Aid Department has a number of packages consisting of grants and loans available to those who qualify. These packages are tailored to each student's financial need.

Faculty

Full Sail has 567 full-time instructors, and the student-faculty ratio is 10:1. The typical Full Sail teacher has spent years working in the entertainment and media production industry doing the type of work that he/she now teaches at Full Sail. They have earned hundreds of movie, record, game, television show, and Web credits, including GRAMMY and EMMY awards. These dedicated professionals come to Full Sail because of the school's reputation in the industry as one of the best colleges in entertainment media education. The majority of the instructors continue to be active in their professional fields, which allows them to bring current product knowledge and examples to their students.

Admission Requirements

Admission requirements vary depending on the degree program. Associate and bachelor degree applicants must submit final high school transcripts or GED test scores and two letters of recommendation.

Application and Information

For details concerning applications and deadlines, students should contact a Full Sail Admissions Representative.

Full Sail University
3300 University Boulevard
Winter Park, Florida 39792-7429
Phone: 800-226-7625 (toll-free)
Fax: 407-678-0070
E-mail: admissions@fullsail.com
Web site: http://www.fullsail.com

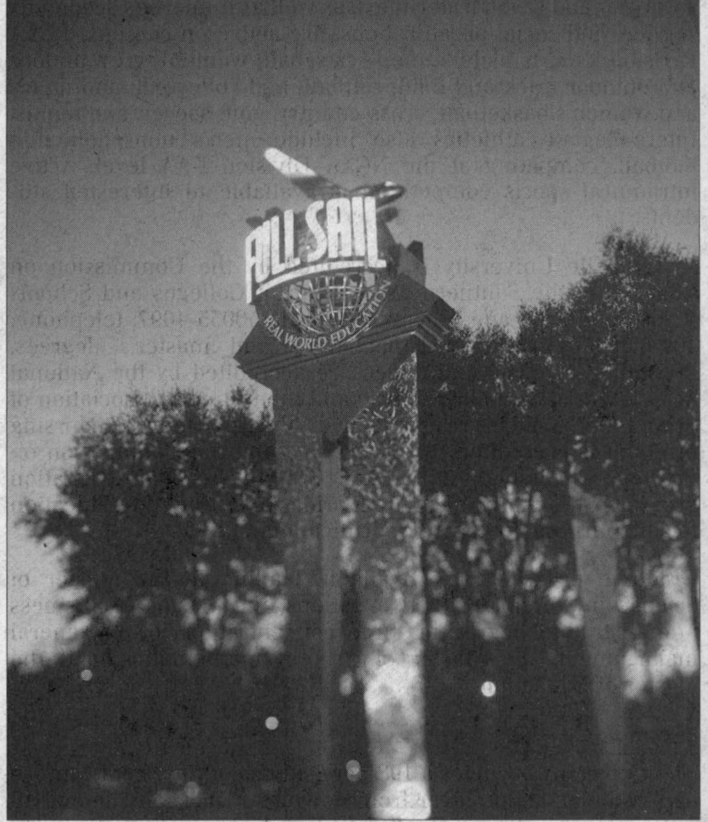

Entrance to Full Sail University.

COLLEGE DATA CENTER • FLORIDA

JACKSONVILLE UNIVERSITY

JACKSONVILLE, FLORIDA

The University

Jacksonville University (JU) is a private, independent, coeducational institution. Originally founded in 1934 as a junior college, the institution served local commuter students for the first twenty-eight years of its existence. In the 1950s, the institution moved to its current location and expanded its courses and degree offerings. With this change, the institution became Jacksonville University. The University's current enrollment is 3,436 undergraduate and graduate students. Some 2,900 students who attend classes on campus come from forty-five states and more than fifty countries. JU accommodates more than 1,000 students in its residence facilities, which include traditional residence halls and apartments with kitchens. The undergraduate population is about evenly split between men and women. The average class size is 18 students, and most classes have fewer than 30 students.

Campus facilities include a student center, a gymnasium, a football stadium, tennis courts, a baseball stadium, intramural fields, a football/soccer/track complex, handball/racquetball courts, and an outdoor pool, all useable throughout most of the year. Ocean beaches are only minutes away by car. Students pursue their creative talents and special interests by participating in cocurricular activities, such as student publications, chorus, orchestra, band, dance, and theatrical productions. Six sororities and seven fraternities, as well as numerous academic, service, and social organizations, are active on campus. NCAA Division I sports include men's baseball; women's crew, indoor and outdoor track and field, softball, and volleyball; and men's and women's basketball, cross-country, golf, soccer, and tennis. Intercollegiate athletics also include men's nonscholarship football, competing at the NCAA Division I-AA level. Active intramural sports competition is available to interested students.

Jacksonville University is accredited by the Commission on Colleges of the Southern Association of Colleges and Schools (1866 Southern Lane, Decatur, Georgia 30033-4097; telephone: 404-679-4501) to award bachelor's and master's degrees. Programs in music and dance are accredited by the National Association of Schools of Music and the National Association of Schools of Dance, respectively. The generic-track nursing program is accredited by the NLNAC and the Commission on Collegiate Nursing Education (CCNE). Teacher education programs are approved by the Florida Department of Education for the purposes of teacher certification.

Graduate programs are available leading to the Master of Science in Nursing with two options, the Master of Business Administration degree in three concentrations or in general management, the Master of Arts in mathematics, and the Master of Education.

Location

The University occupies a 198-acre suburban riverfront campus across the St. Johns River from downtown Jacksonville and 12 miles from the Atlantic Ocean beaches. Jacksonville is the home of a professional symphony orchestra, a performing arts center, theaters, art museums and galleries, the NFL Jacksonville Jaguars, and minor-league baseball, and ice hockey teams. Major airlines serve the Jacksonville International Airport. The region's year-round climate is mild and pleasant, permitting outdoor activity throughout the year.

Majors and Degrees

Jacksonville University offers the following degrees through the Colleges of Arts and Sciences, Business, and Fine Arts: B.A., B.F.A., B.G.S., B.M., B.M.E., B.S., and B.S.N.

Undergraduate academic programs of study include accounting, art, aviation management, aviation management and flight operations, biology, business administration, chemistry, communications, computer art and design, computing sciences, dance, economics, engineering (various disciplines through dual-degree programs), elementary education, English, film, finance, French, geography, glass, history, humanities, international business, jazz studies (music), management, marine science, marketing, mathematics, music, music business, music composition and theory, music education, music performance, music theater, nursing, philosophy, physical education, physics, political science, psychology, sociology, Spanish, and theater arts. Students may also pursue preprofessional programs in dentistry, law, medicine, pharmacy, and veterinary medicine.

Academic Programs

Students enrolled in baccalaureate programs enjoy broad exposure to the liberal arts through a core curriculum. The core provides a foundation for study in the various major fields and is usually completed during the freshman and sophomore years. The core includes courses in English composition and literature, mathematics and computer science, the social sciences, the humanities, history, fine arts, philosophy or religion, the natural sciences, and foreign language.

Generally, students acquire their baccalaureate credits in four years, although year-round enrollment makes it possible to earn a bachelor's degree in three years. All programs require a minimum 2.0 (C) grade point average for graduation. A pass-fail option is also available.

Undergraduate research, internships, study abroad, and an active honors program enhance the educational experience of JU students. Independent study programs enable promising students to pursue individual work in areas of special interest within and outside their major fields of study. In the departmental honors program, advanced study may be concentrated in the major.

JU also awards undergraduate credit through advanced placement and credit by examination. Such credit requires the achievement of satisfactory scores on the College Board's Advanced Placement tests or CLEP examinations.

Jacksonville University has the second largest Naval ROTC unit in the United States. Successful completion of the program leads to an officer's commission in either the U.S. Navy or U.S. Marine Corps.

Off-Campus Programs

Approved study abroad may be integrated as a part of the baccalaureate program. The University coordinates study-abroad programs in countries such as Spain, France, Mexico, Italy, the United Kingdom, Japan, and Australia for students. Summer language programs are popular with many students.

JU faculty members also lead travel-study courses to many countries and regions of the world. With the help of advisers, JU students may also plan individual programs of study abroad.

Academic Facilities

The Carl S. Swisher Library houses a collection numbering more than 700,000 holdings and a computer lab. The Swisher/Merritt-Penticoff/Nelms science complex, along with the Millar Wilson Laboratory, Reid Medical Science Building, and Charter Marine Science Center, house modern laboratories and facilities for biological, chemical, and physics study and research. Marine science facilities include an operational wet lab. The Phillips Fine Arts Building houses the Alexander Brest Museum, two large rehearsal halls, music studios, and practice rooms. Terry Concert Hall is an acoustically balanced facility for orchestra, choral, and band concerts. Studios house painting, ceramics, glassblowing, photography, sculpture, and other art activities. The Alexander Brest Dance Pavilion includes two large dance studios, offices, and dressing rooms. The newly renovated Swisher Theatre is a state-of-the-art teaching and performance theater. Students gain experience with industry-standard lighting and stage controls while presenting University and public performances. The J. Arthur Howard Administration Building centrally locates most administration and student service offices. The J. Henry Gooding Social Science Building contains classrooms, offices, and the Urban Studies Center. Wilma's Little People's School, a child development facility, supports teacher education programs. Two new state-of-the-art buildings house the Davis College of Business, the School of Nursing, and the Dental School of Orthodontics. The new Davis Student Commons is home to Student Life departments and the Billy Nimnicht Fitness Center. The facility also has Nellie's Sports Grill and a game room.

Costs

2007–08, full-time (12–18 credit hours) tuition and fees per year were $22,500; for undergraduate students enrolled in 11 credit hours or less, $750 per credit hour. Residence hall room rental was $4800 per year, and a seven-day meal plan was available at $3760 per year.

Financial Aid

The University offers distinctive merit-based scholarships and grants. These scholarships and grants, which are not based on financial need, range in amounts from $1000 to $18,000 per academic year. Athletic awards are offered based on talent and skill in NCAA Division I sports (except for men's football). JU also participates in a broad range of federal and state programs that include loans, grants, and work-study opportunities. The University requires financial aid applicants to complete the Free Application for Federal Student Aid (FAFSA). The deadline for submission of all forms to ensure the availability of aid for the fall term is March 15.

Faculty

Jacksonville University employs more than 148 full-time faculty members. Faculty members are readily accessible to students and take an active role in the lives of students as teachers, mentors, and friends.

Student Government

Student participation in University governance is a function of the Jacksonville University Student Alliance (JUSA). JUSA is the representative body for all University students. JUSA members represent a variety of different constituencies, such as the academic colleges, residential students, commuter students, and other groups, such as student athletes.

Admission Requirements

Jacksonville University seeks qualified students from diverse social, geographic, cultural, religious, and socioeconomic backgrounds. The Admission Committee evaluates each applicant on an individual basis. Students applying as freshmen should have satisfactorily completed, or be in the process of completing, a standard college-preparatory curriculum. The University requires that applicants complete a minimum of 4 years of English, 3 years of mathematics, 3 years of science, and 3 years of social science. Freshman applicants also must submit scores from either the SAT or ACT. Admission interviews and campus visits are recommended but not required.

The University welcomes applications from transfer and international students; transfers comprise approximately one third of the entering class each year. To be considered for transfer admission, applicants must submit the application form and official copies of transcripts from all colleges attended. Transfers must have a minimum 2.0 college GPA and be in good standing at their previous institution. International applicants should contact the Office of Admission for further information.

Students interested in dance, music, or theater arts are required to audition separately for admission to those programs. Students who plan to major in visual art are required to submit a portfolio of their work. Admission to nursing, teacher education, and fine arts programs occurs after the student is admitted to the University.

New students may enroll for the fall, spring, or summer terms. Students are notified of acceptance beginning in October for the fall term. Applications are reviewed according to date received. Students who apply after March 1 for the fall term are considered on a space-available basis.

Individuals, families, and groups may visit the campus throughout the year, both during the week and on scheduled Saturdays. Campus visits include a meeting with an admission counselor and a campus tour. Open house invitations are extended to prospective students and parents. On-campus overnight visits on weekdays are arranged for interested students given proper notice. Students or parents should call the Office of Admission to make visit arrangements.

Application and Information

Application for freshman admission should be filed as soon as possible after the completion of the junior year in high school. All applications are available from the JU Web site or by contacting the Office of Admission.

Office of Admission
Jacksonville University
2800 University Boulevard North
Jacksonville, Florida 32211-3396
Phone: 904-256-7000
800-225-2027 (toll-free)
E-mail: admissions@ju.edu
Web site: http://www.ju.edu

KEISER UNIVERSITY

FORT LAUDERDALE, FLORIDA

The University

In 1977, Keiser University was founded by the Keiser family in recognition of a need in the community for high-quality career education with a hands-on orientation. This philosophy, combined with solid academics, provides Keiser University graduates with a competitive edge when entering the workforce. With twelve convenient locations throughout Florida, Keiser University offers small class sizes for individualized attention. The University's state-of-the-practice facilities help students gain hands-on experience in career-specific areas. Day, evening, and online classes with course materials that are relevant to current workforce needs ensure that students get the most from their education.

In addition to its associate and bachelor's degrees, Keiser University also offers a Masters of Business Administration (M.B.A.) degree.

The Keiser University environment is a balanced one where students also take part in professional organizations and social activities. On campus, Keiser University students participate in the Student Government Association (SGA), athletic activities, and student parties. Students can also join in sports and social activities with other students from Keiser's affiliate colleges and universities. The University assists all students interested in student housing in finding local apartments and private rooms in proximity to each campus. Adjacent to the campus is a newly renovated student residence that is 4 miles from Fort Lauderdale beach. All University campuses are located along major traffic arteries in order to provide easy commuting for students.

Keiser University is accredited by the Commission on Colleges of the Southern Association of Colleges and Schools (1866 Southern Lane, Decatur, Georgia 30033-4097; telephone: 404-679-4501) to award the associate, bachelor's, and master's degrees.

Location

Keiser University has campus locations throughout sunny Florida, with the main campus in Fort Lauderdale. The other locations are in Daytona Beach, Jacksonville, Kendall, Lakeland, Melbourne, Orlando, Pembroke Pines, Port St. Lucie, Sarasota, Tallahassee, Tampa, and West Palm Beach. Keiser University eCampus is the online division of the Fort Lauderdale campus.

Majors and Degrees

Associate of Arts (A.A.), Associate of Science (A.S.), Bachelor of Arts (B.A.), and Bachelor of Science (B.S.) degrees are offered at Keiser University, both on-campus and online. Not all programs are offered at each campus.

Bachelor's degrees are offered in accounting (B.A., online only), professional accounting (B.A., online only), business administration (B.A., with majors in finance, human resources, international business, management, and marketing), business administration (B.A., online only, in Spanish), criminal justice (B.A.), elementary education (B.S., Sarasota only), health sciences (B.S., online only at most campuses; on campus at Fort Lauderdale), health services administration (B.A.), homeland security (B.A., online only at most campuses; on campus at Fort Lauderdale), information technology management (B.S., online), legal studies (B.A.), management information systems (MIS) (B.A., online only), and nursing (RN to B.S.N., online only).

Associate degrees are offered with majors in accounting (A.A.), baking and pastry arts (A.S.), biotechnology (A.S.), computer-aided drafting (A.S.), computer graphics and design (A.S.), computer programming (A.S.), crime scene technology (A.S.), criminal justice (A.S.), culinary arts (A.S.), diagnostic medical sonography (A.S.), diagnostic vascular sonography (A.S.), fashion design and merchandising (A.S.), fire science (A.S., online only, through Sarasota), health services administration (A.S.), histology technology (A.S.), homeland security (A.S.), information technology (A.S.), massage therapy (A.S.), medical assisting (A.S.), medical laboratory technician studies (A.S.), nuclear medicine technology (A.S.), nursing (A.S.), occupational therapy assistant studies (A.S.), paralegal studies (A.A.), physical therapist assistant studies (A.S.), radiologic technology (A.S.), sports medicine and fitness technology (A.S.), surgical technology (A.S.), video game design (A.S.), and Web site design and development (A.S.).

Academic Programs

Students take one course at a time for 4 to 5 hours a day, which enhances opportunities for practical hands-on learning and helps with the retention of information. Students complete one class at a time before moving to the next class. This promotes focus on each subject while avoiding juggling multiple assignments, projects, and exams at the same time. It also means that students know their complete schedule and date of graduation before beginning their academic program. Students never worry about needing a class that may not be offered in a particular semester.

Academic Facilities

At Keiser University, students gain valuable experience on equipment used in their professions. Computer students have labs that are equipped with the computers, programs, and technology used in some of the most advanced companies in the field. Students majoring in nursing and medical assisting work in the classroom with equipment to familiarize them with real-world medical settings. Keiser University is a member of five regional library cooperatives throughout Florida, which give students unparalleled access to millions of library resources. Keiser University also offers student housing facilities at the Fort Lauderdale campus.

Costs

Tuition varies by program, and students should contact the campus that they wish to attend for specific cost figures.

Financial Aid

For current information about financial aid available to students attending Keiser University, interested students should visit the University's Web site.

Faculty

Qualified instructors with real-world experience compose the Keiser University faculty. Curricula taught by professionals who have faced workplace challenges prepare students to compete and overcome obstacles when they enter their chosen professions. Keiser University faculty members embrace a student-centered approach, which helps students develop the skills and qualifications necessary to succeed in today's competitive job market.

Student Government

The purpose of the Student Government Association is to promote the general welfare of the student body; provide programs of educational, cultural, recreational, and social value to the University community; promote a spirit of harmony among administration, faculty and staff members, and students; meet the responsibilities of self-government; assure students' rights as stated in the statement of students' rights; and provide students with an organization through which their concerns may be registered within a representative and democratic governance. Representatives are elected by students at each campus. Officers are elected from within. SGA schedules periodic meetings as well as special promotions and activities. SGA representatives give a brief presentation at all student orientations. The student government assists in the planning of social, fund-raising, sporting, and community-service activities.

Admission Requirements

For information about the current requirements for admission to the various programs offered by Keiser University, interested students should visit the University's Web site.

Application and Information

Applications are accepted on a rolling basis. For more information on all of the Keiser University campuses, prospective students should visit the University's Web site.

Fort Lauderdale Admissions Office
Keiser University
1500 West Commercial Boulevard
Fort Lauderdale, Florida 33309
Phone: 954-776-4456
888-534-7379 (toll-free)
E-mail: admissions-ftl@keiseruniversity.edu
Web site: http://www.keiseruniversity.edu

COLLEGE DATA CENTER • FLORIDA

LYNN UNIVERSITY

BOCA RATON, FLORIDA

The University

Lynn University in Boca Raton is a private, coeducational, liberal arts university awarding bachelor's, master's, and doctoral degrees in the liberal arts and sciences and professional education. Founded in 1962 and accredited by the Southern Association of Colleges and Schools, Lynn offers a distinctive, innovative, and individualized approach to learning within an international community. The University currently enrolls more than 2,600 students, representing forty-three states and ninety-three nations. Its specialty programs include a Conservatory of Music, a School of Aeronautics, and the Institute for Achievement and Learning, which is an international pioneer in developing successful teaching strategies for students with learning differences.

The University's five colleges and two schools offer twenty-one undergraduate majors and thirty specializations as well as seven master's degrees and a doctoral degree program.

Every major includes opportunities for hands-on learning through projects and internships, giving students the opportunity to acquire the skills and knowledge essential for successful careers in the twenty-first century and for informed and effective citizenship in a global society. More than 60 percent of Lynn's undergraduate students live in one of its five air-conditioned residence halls. Residence halls include study and computer lounges and recreation areas as well as health and fitness facilities with free weights, exercise machines, and cardiovascular equipment.

The Lynn Student Center is a campus hub, housing the dining room, an auditorium, comfortable lounge areas, and the popular Knight's Court snack bar. Right next door is the campus' newest hangout spot, Christine's, which serves a full menu of Starbucks coffee drinks, smoothies, snacks, salads, sandwiches, and desserts. Laundry and mail facilities, the University bookstore, two classroom buildings, the library, a concert hall, international student lounge, a gymnasium, pools, and athletics facilities round out the campus.

University life is designed to create learning opportunities both within and outside the classroom. As a learning-centered community, Lynn University expects students to take responsibility for learning, decision making, and leadership. Students strengthen their leadership talents and develop new ones through Lynn's student involvement program, which consists of more than thirty campus organizations and activities covering a wide variety of special interests, including student government, multicultural organizations, Greek life, and a leadership academy.

The Hannifan Center for Career Development and Internships supports students as they explore their future careers. The center's comprehensive services include workshops, employability skills training, vocational and personality testing, career fairs, and extensive internship placements throughout South Florida, the United States, and the world. After graduation, the center offers alumni lifetime job placement assistance.

Lynn also has a top-ranked NCAA athletic program, which has brought home eighteen national championships and twenty-one Sunshine State Conference championships and has been honored with the selection of two NCAA coaches of the year. The Fighting Knights intercollegiate athletic program includes men's and women's basketball, golf, soccer, and tennis; men's baseball; and women's softball and volleyball.

Location

Located in Boca Raton on Florida's southeastern coast, the Lynn campus is only 50 minutes from Miami, 30 minutes from West Palm Beach, and 30 minutes from Fort Lauderdale. Thanks to its location in the heart of one of the world's leading business, media, and hospitality industry centers, Lynn University students benefit from a wide variety of internship, cultural, and recreational opportunities.

Lynn's safe, beautiful 123-acre campus is three miles from the beaches of the Atlantic Ocean, two miles from the heart of Boca Raton's city center, and only a few minutes' drive from first-class shopping, restaurants, museums, and galleries. Set in a residential area among seven freshwater lakes, palms, and lush tropical foliage, Lynn is easily accessed from three major U.S. airports: West Palm Beach, Fort Lauderdale, and Miami.

Majors and Degrees

The College of Arts and Sciences offers the Bachelor of Arts degree in American studies, English, human services, international relations, and liberal arts and the Bachelor of Science degree in biology, criminal justice, and psychology. Undergraduate students can also pursue a certificate in emergency and disaster management.

Lynn's renowned Conservatory of Music awards the Bachelor of Music (B.M.) in music-performance, with specializations in bass trombone, bassoon, cello, clarinet, double bass, flute, French horn, oboe, percussion, piano, trombone, trumpet, tuba, viola, and violin. The conservatory also offers a Bachelor of Arts in music.

The College of Business and Management offers the Bachelor of Science in business administration, with specializations in aviation management, fashion management, general management, international business, and marketing.

The College of Hospitality Management offers a Bachelor of Science in hospitality management, with specializations in club management, resort and hotel management, spa management, sports and recreation management, and vacation ownership/timeshare management.

The Eugene M. and Christine E. Lynn College of International Communication offers the Bachelor of Arts degree in advertising and public relations; communication, media, and politics; drama; film studies; multimedia journalism; and radio, television, and Internet media. The Bachelor of Science is offered in graphic design, illustration/computer animation, and photography.

The Donald E. and Helen L. Ross College of Education offers the Bachelor of Science in elementary education, with specializations in exceptional student education, grades K–6, and grades K–6 plus pre-K/primary (age 3–grade 3).

Academic Programs

Lynn University is a learning-centered community, with faculty members who love teaching and who challenge students to become active, intentional, and purposeful learners. The University embraces students who have varying levels of academic abilities and learning styles coupled with a strong motivation to excel. Classes are small by design, with an average 15:1 student-faculty ratio.

The entire Lynn University curriculum is innovative, challenging students to build increasing competencies not only in their chosen field of study, but in every area of their life. Students put theory into practice through internships, partnerships with business, and community service projects.

At Lynn, students benefit from an exceptionally strong advising program that pairs each incoming student with a faculty member in the student's chosen major field. Faculty advisers become a mentor throughout each student's academic career and beyond. Many Lynn students establish lifelong relationships with their faculty adviser, whose expert guidance helps students recognize their highest potential.

The Honors Program's innovative curriculum stimulates creative discovery among students with particularly strong academic promise. The innovative curriculum, which is team-taught by faculty members, encompasses the full breadth of the liberal arts and sciences.

Lynn University's Institute for Achievement and Learning is a model for all of higher education. Led by a nationally recognized learning specialist, the institute brings together an array of services and professionals that help support every student, regardless of his or her learning style. For example, the institute's computer software enables students to scan and download textbooks to MP3 players, convert spoken words into text, and record and replay classroom sessions. Under the auspices of the institute, every new student receives a personalized learning inventory that analyzes his or her learning styles and types of intelligences and recommends personalized, proven study strategies.

The Institute for Achievement and Learning's Metamorphosis Program uses a naturalist, experiential coaching model to help students with AD/HD adapt their behavior to transition from seemingly unorganized study skills to patterned, creative living and learning environments. The institute also promotes the professional development of Lynn faculty members and educators in the community.

Lynn University follows a semester calendar and offers a summer session.

Off-Campus Programs

All of Lynn University's international programs are among the best in higher education. For the last two years, *U.S. News & World Report* has ranked Lynn number one for its number of international students among universities its size in the Southeast. Lynn is one of only thirteen U.S. universities to be recognized by NAFSA: The Association of International Educators for the quality of its international programs. At Lynn, every student is encouraged to complete study-abroad academic credits in his or her major. Students can choose from a wide variety of faculty-led international study tours that take place during semester breaks, or they can study abroad for a summer, a semester, or a full academic year.

Academic Facilities

The Ritter Academic Center is the home of the College of Business and Management and houses classrooms, computer labs, and faculty offices. The Assaf Academic Center is the site for most classes offered by the College of Arts and Sciences. The de Hoernle International Center houses the College of Education and the Institute for Achievement and Learning and contains classrooms, computer labs, the Center for International Programs and Services, and the Amarnick-Goldstein Concert Hall. The Eugene M. and Christine E. Lynn Library houses the College of International Communication and also has classrooms, studios, computer labs, a study center, and faculty offices.

Costs

Undergraduate tuition for the 2007–08 academic year was $26,990. Yearly room and board fees totaled $10,100. Student fees vary depending on whether students live on or off campus. Books are purchased separately.

Financial Aid

Lynn is committed to making the University affordable for every student. The University's broad program of student financial aid includes scholarships, grants, work-study, and loans. Academic, athletic, and need-based scholarships are awarded. For complete information on the financial aid process and available programs, interested students should visit http://www.lynn.edu/scholarships.

Faculty

Faculty members are thoroughly committed to teaching and are readily accessible to students. The University has a very favorable student-faculty ratio of 15:1. Seventy percent of full-time faculty members hold doctoral degrees, and the vast majority bring real-world experience in their field—many in some of the world's most prestigious companies and industries—to the classroom.

Student Government

Students annually elect officers of the student body.

Admission Requirements

All candidates for admission must be graduates of an accredited high school or must present formal evidence of having completed high school graduation requirements. Applicants are required to take the SAT or ACT. Greater emphasis is placed on the recommendation of the applicant's guidance counselor than on standardized test scores. A dual-enrollment program is available for exceptionally strong high school students.

High school students who have taken an Advanced Placement test and scored 3 or higher may earn academic credit and be placed in a higher-level course. University credit may also be earned by taking the College-Level Examination Program (CLEP) tests. Lynn also grants International Baccalaureate credit.

International applicants for whom English is not a first language are required to submit results from the TOEFL/IGLTS. All transcripts of previous academic work must be accompanied by certified English translations. Transfer students who have completed a minimum of 12 academic college credits should submit an official transcript from each college attended, along with a recommendation from the Dean of Students at the institution most recently attended. (The form may be downloaded at http://www.lynn.edu/forms.) Those who have accumulated fewer than 12 credits are asked to also submit high school transcripts. Every effort is made to facilitate the transfer of credit from other institutions, and a special transfer adviser is available to ensure proper placement.

Application and Information

There is no formal deadline for admission. Applicants are notified on a rolling basis upon receipt of all credentials. The application fee is $35. For additional information about admission, to obtain an application packet, or to arrange for an interview and tour of the campus, prospective students should contact:

Office of Admissions
Lynn University
3601 North Military Trail
Boca Raton, Florida 33431-5598
Phone: 561-237-7900
800-888-5966 (toll-free)
Fax: 561-237-7100
E-mail: admission@lynn.edu
Web site: http://www.lynn.edu/admission

On the campus of Lynn University.

Lynn University does not discriminate on the basis of race, color, gender, religion, nationality, ethnic origin, disability and/or age in its administration of its educational and admission policies, scholarship and loan programs, and athletic and/or other school administered programs.

MIAMI INTERNATIONAL UNIVERSITY OF ART & DESIGN

Miami International University of Art & Design

MIAMI, FLORIDA

The University

Miami International University of Art & Design prepares graduates for entry-level positions in the creative arts. Students are taught broad foundations in the theory and practice of their course of study. Miami International University of Art & Design offers five master's degree programs, twelve bachelor's degree programs, and three associate degree programs.

The student population includes recent high school graduates, transfer students, and those who have left a previous employment situation to study and train for a new career. Students are creative, competitive, and open to new ideas. They place great value on an education that prepares them for an exciting entry-level position in the arts.

The school works to foster the students' desire to maintain high levels of professionalism in their chosen careers. Special emphasis is placed on helping students identify their personal, academic, and career goals. As part of this objective, the Office of Career Services works with students throughout their education and after graduation, offering career assessment and planning, job search assistance, and networking opportunities.

Services are available to assist students with resume writing, networking, and keeping aware of what employers are looking for in job applicants.

The students' active contributions to campus life support the creative and intellectual evolution of everyone at Miami International University of Art & Design. Through campus clubs and organizations, residence hall activities, and other sponsored events, the school offers numerous opportunities for students to grow and interact outside the classroom. Student clubs and organizations include the American Institute of Graphic Arts (AIGA), American Society of Interior Designers (ASID), International Student Club, and Student Council.

The school offers housing at nearby Edgewater Hall and Vista Hall. Information on independent housing in the area is available through the Office of Student Affairs. Roommate referrals are also available to those students who choose to live off campus.

Miami International University of Art & Design is accredited by the Commission on Colleges of the Southern Association of Colleges and Schools (SACS; 1866 Southern Lane, Decatur, Georgia 30033-4097; phone: 404-679-4500; http://www.sacs.org) to award Associate of Arts, Bachelor of Arts, Bachelor of Fine Arts, and Master of Fine Arts degrees.

Miami International University of Art & Design and its branch, The Art Institute of Tampa, hold a License by Means of Accreditation from the Florida Commission for Independent Education. Any questions regarding the License by Means of Accreditation should be directed to the Florida Department of Education, Commission for Independent Education, 325 West Gaines Street, Suite 1414, Tallahassee, Florida 32399-0400. The Bachelor of Fine Arts in Interior Design degree program is accredited by the Council for Interior Design Accreditation.

Location

Miami is a culturally rich region that celebrates year-round events, including the African-American Heritage Festival, Haitian Heritage Week, Viva Mexico Celebration, Israel Independence Celebration, and Asian Cultural Week. The city is the home of professional sports teams, and residents enjoy the sandy beaches, international cuisine, local clubs, the historic Art Deco District, Coral Gables, and Key Biscayne. The Florida Keys, DisneyWorld, and the Bahamas are all just a short trip away.

Majors and Degrees

Bachelor's degree programs include advertising, audio production, computer animation, fashion design, fashion merchandising, film and digital production, graphic design, interior design, photography, visual and entertainment arts, visual effects and motion graphics, and Web design and interactive media. Associate degrees are offered in accessory design, fashion design, and fashion merchandising.

Academic Programs

Bachelor's degree candidates must complete 192 credits, and associate degree candidates are required to complete 112 academic credits in order to graduate. Advanced Placement and CLEP credit may be earned for up to 25 percent of all required credits.

Academic Facilities

Miami International University of Art & Design is located within a newly renovated 60,000-square-foot academic and administration building. The facility includes thirteen computer labs, including two Master of Fine Arts labs. In addition, industry-related audio and video equipment is available to students.

The school features a 1,000-square-foot painting and sculpture studio, a production facility with studio lighting, and an editing facility with private editing bays. There are also interior design and fashion resource rooms and a dedicated 1,000-square-foot fashion merchandising room.

The Daniel M. Stack Memorial Library contains more than 19,700 volumes and subscribes to more than 200 periodicals specific to the school's academic programs. The library's extensive holdings include a unique collection of *Vogue* (from 1947 through the present), scripts, student theses, multimedia resources, and rare books on the history of fashion.

Costs

Tuition cost varies by program. Prospective students should contact the school for current tuition costs. Other charges include a starting kit for all first-quarter students. Kits vary in price, depending on the program of study.

Financial Aid

Financial aid is available for those who qualify. Students who require financial assistance should first complete and submit a Free Application for Federal Student Aid (FAFSA) and meet with a financial aid officer. The officer determines the level of need based on a required federal formula, the cost of education, and other factors. Gift aid is available in the form of Federal Pell Grants, Federal Supplemental Educational Opportunity Grants, and veterans' benefits. Loans include Federal Stafford Loans, Federal PLUS Loans, and alternative loans. Other scholarships are available from the school and private sources. Application deadlines and eligibility requirements vary by program.

Faculty

Miami International University of Art & Design faculty consists of full-time and part-time professors, many of whom have advanced degrees and professional experience in their respective fields.

Admission Requirements

Prior to receiving final acceptance, applicants to Miami International University of Art & Design must demonstrate proof of high school graduation or its equivalent. An official copy of a high school transcript or General Educational Development (GED) certificate and a 150-word essay must be submitted. Applicants are also interviewed, either in person or by telephone, to explore their background and interest in program offerings. Each applicant's transcript and essay are evaluated by the Admissions Acceptance Committee, which reserves the right to request additional records of accomplishment in core academic courses and/or SAT and ACT results. There is a $50 application fee.

As part of their application, transfer students must submit official transcripts from all previously attended institutions. International students' transcripts must be prepared in English or include a complete and official English translation. Proof of English language proficiency or enrollment in the school's English as a second language (ESL) course is required for all prospective international students.

Application and Information

To obtain an application, make arrangements for an interview, or tour the school, prospective students should contact:

Miami International University of Art & Design
1501 Biscayne Boulevard, Suite 100
Miami, Florida 33132-1418
Phone: 305-428-5700
800-225-9023 (toll-free)
Fax: 305-374-5933
Web site: http://www.artinstitutes.edu/miami

The Art Institute of Atlanta®, GA; The Art Institute of Atlanta®–Decatur, GA; The Art Institute of Austin℠, TX; The Art Institute of California℠–Inland Empire; The Art Institute of California℠–Los Angeles; The Art Institute of California℠–Orange County; The Art Institute of California℠–Sacramento; The Art Institute of California℠–San Diego; The Art Institute of California℠–San Francisco; The Art Institute of California℠–Sunnyvale; The Art Institute of Charleston℠, SC, A branch of The Art Institute of Atlanta, GA; The Art Institute of Charlotte®, NC; The Art Institute of Colorado® (Denver); The Art Institute of Dallas®, TX; The Art Institute of Fort Lauderdale®, FL; The Art Institute of Houston®, TX; The Art Institute of Indianapolis℠, IN*; The Art Institute of Jacksonville℠, FL, A branch of Miami International University of Art & Design; The Art Institute of Las Vegas®, NV; The Art Institute of Michigan℠ (Detroit); The Art Institute of New York City®, NY; The Art Institute of Ohio℠–Cincinnati**; The Art Institute of Philadelphia®, PA; The Art Institute of Phoenix®, AZ; The Art Institute of Pittsburgh®, PA; The Art Institute of Pittsburgh®–Online Division; The Art Institute of Portland®, OR; The Art Institute of Salt Lake City℠, UT; The Art Institute of Seattle®, WA; The Art Institute of Tampa℠, FL, A branch of Miami International University of Art & Design; The Art Institute of Tennessee℠–Nashville, A branch of The Art Institute of Atlanta, GA; The Art Institute of Tucson℠, AZ; The Art Institute of Washington® (Arlington, VA), A branch of The Art Institute of Atlanta, GA; The Art Institute of York–Pennsylvania℠; The Art Institutes International Minnesota℠ (Minneapolis); California Design College℠ (Los Angeles–Wilshire Blvd.); The Illinois Institute of Art®–Chicago; The Illinois Institute of Art®–Schaumburg; Miami International University of Art & Design℠, FL; The New England Institute of Art® (Boston, MA).

*The Art Institute of Indianapolis is licensed by the Indiana Commission on Proprietary Education, 302 West Washington Street, Room E201, Indianapolis, IN 46204, AC-0080.

**The Art Institute of Ohio–Cincinnati, 8845 Governors Hill Drive, Suite 100, Cincinnati, OH 45249-3317, Reg. #04-01-1698B.

NEW COLLEGE OF FLORIDA

SARASOTA, FLORIDA

The College

New College of Florida offers serious students the opportunity to pursue rigorous academic study in an environment designed to promote depth in thinking, free exchange of ideas, and highly individualized interaction with faculty members. Throughout the history of New College, four principles have defined the College's educational philosophy: each student is ultimately responsible for his or her education; the best education demands a joint search for knowledge by exciting teachers and able-minded students; students' progress should be based on demonstrated competence and real mastery rather than on the accumulation of credits and grades; and students should have, from the outset, opportunities to explore, in depth, areas of interest to them.

Study is focused in the arts and sciences and is highly accelerated and independent. Nearly two thirds of the College's graduates pursue graduate or professional study, gaining admission to Harvard, Yale, MIT, Brown, Georgetown, Berkeley, and other leading graduate programs. New College ranks among the top schools in the nation in the percentage of graduates who go on to earn the Ph.D.

New College was founded as a private institution in 1960 with a devotion to the values implicit in a liberal arts education and a dedication to creating an innovative academic program where talented students and outstanding faculty members could come together and pursue learning in a challenging yet nontraditional environment. Entry into Florida's public university system in 1975 served to strengthen and perpetuate the idealistic vision and academic mission of the College's founders. These qualities, as well as the College's national reputation, were enhanced further in 2001 when New College was designated as the "official honors college for the State University System of Florida." A public-private funding arrangement provides students at New College with a private honors college experience at a public college cost. As a result, the College is regularly featured in guidebooks as being among the nation's leading educational values.

New College's student population is 746, of whom approximately 60 percent are women. Currently, 20 percent of students are out-of-state or overseas residents. Through active recruitment of out-of-state students, the College plans to increase this percentage even further in the years ahead. First-year and second-year students must live on campus, but many continuing students choose to live on campus as well. In fact, five new, state-of-the-art residence halls opened at the start of the 2007–08 academic year, thus allowing New College to house 85 percent of students on campus. The new residence halls include a variety of accommodation options to match student lifestyle interests and incorporate the latest in green building technology. Architecture for the new buildings complements existing campus dormitories, such as the College's historic Pei Residence Halls, which were designed by the eminent architect I. M. Pei in the 1960s. The 131-room, three-court Pei complex provides rooms with individual entrances, private baths, central air-conditioning, and various combinations of large picture windows, sliding glass doors, and/or balconies. Two other campus dorms, Dort and Goldstein Residence Halls, provide apartment-style housing with four single rooms, two bathrooms, and a common living room and kitchenette in each unit. Dining facilities on campus include a campus dining hall with full meal plans available for both on- and off-campus students, a snack bar and deli, and the student-owned and -operated Four Winds Café. The College's Counseling and Wellness Center offers basic health care and personal counseling, as well as a variety of related services.

New College student life is informal. Activities are largely student initiated and include academic, artistic, religious, political, and recreational pursuits. The College's 144-acre bayfront location on the Gulf of Mexico includes basketball, racquetball, tennis, and volleyball courts; a multipurpose soccer and athletic field; a running trail; a 25-meter swimming pool; and a comprehensive fitness center. Sailboats, sailboards, and canoes are also available for use by students and faculty members free of charge.

Location

Situated along the coastline of the Gulf of Mexico in southwest Florida, New College serves as the northern gateway to Sarasota, a bustling city with more than 250,000 residents in its environs. Located 50 miles south of Tampa, Sarasota is noted for its recreational, cultural, and artistic attractions, including beautiful white-sand beaches and an abundance of professional theater, art, and music venues. Notably, New College sits adjacent to the world-famous John and Mabel Ringling Museum of Art in Sarasota's historic Indian Beach Sapphire Shores neighborhood. The climate is semitropical, consisting of long, warm springs and autumns plus mild winters. Transportation from throughout the nation and within the city is readily accessible. Many major airlines serve Sarasota Bradenton International Airport, which is proximate to the College. Within the city, buses link the campus to downtown, shopping malls, parks, and beaches. While mass transit is available, bicycling is the favored means of transportation among students.

Majors and Degrees

New College awards the Bachelor of Arts degree in liberal arts and sciences. Each area of concentration (major) at the College is an individualized program of study that students design in consultation with, and with the approval of, faculty members. Areas of concentration include anthropology, art history, biology, British and American literature, chemistry, Chinese language and culture, classics, computer science, economics, environmental studies, foreign language and literature, French language and literature, German language and literature, Hispanic language and culture, Hispanic language and literature, history, humanities, international and area studies, literature, marine biology, mathematics, medieval and Renaissance studies, music, natural sciences, neurobiology, philosophy, physics, political science, psychology, public policy, religion, Russian language and literature, social sciences, sociology, Spanish language and literature, and urban studies. Partial areas of concentration may be pursued in gender studies and in theater. Students may also obtain permission from faculty members for self-designed concentrations. Premed, prelaw, and prebusiness advising and guidelines are provided by faculty members and by the Office of Career Services and Off-Campus Study.

Academic Programs

New College of Florida's academic program aims to encourage academic excellence, creativity, and personal initiative and to provide essential tools for lifelong intellectual and personal growth. The College's distinctive curriculum enables students, in close consultation with faculty members, to develop programs of seminars, tutorials, independent research, and off-campus experiences that meet each student's personal goals.

At the end of each semester, students receive detailed narrative evaluations of their work as well as satisfactory/unsatisfactory assessments. In order to graduate, students must satisfactorily complete seven academic contracts (one per semester), three independent-study projects, a senior thesis or project, and an oral baccalaureate examination. In addition to the requirements for the individual major, students must complete eight courses within the liberal arts curriculum, with at least one course each in the humanities, social sciences, and natural sciences. All students must meet basic mathematics and computer literacy requirements, and pass or be exempted from Florida's College-Level Academic Skills Test.

The College operates on a 4-1-4 calendar year. In January, students undertake independent-study projects, which they design and complete under faculty sponsorship.

Off-Campus Programs

Internships, fieldwork, and independent research away from the campus offer New College students the opportunity to gain new skills and test career interests. Because off-campus study can make a major contribution to an undergraduate education, New College facilitates such study through its flexible, individualized curriculum and special support services. New College is a member of the National Student

Exchange, which provides access to more than 170 universities with programs in the U.S. and abroad (many with comparable tuition costs). Students may also participate in programs offered by independent providers, such as the School for International Training and AustraLearn, as well as international programs available through the State University System of Florida and Center for Cross Cultural Studies. With faculty approval, students may pursue off-campus independent study or participate in programs including Living Routes, which offers nontraditional venues for study abroad.

Academic Facilities

New College's Jane Bancroft Cook Library is befitting of one of the country's leading colleges for the liberal arts and has an "open stack" arrangement that allows free access to most materials. Trustees, faculty members, students, and the New College Library Association have implemented an ambitious acquisition program to expand the current holdings of approximately 267,000 volumes. The library subscribes to more than 800 serial titles, including 700 magazines and journals and many state, national, and international newspapers. In addition, through computer networks and other cooperative programs, New College students and faculty members have access to hundreds of online databases and electronic journals and newspapers, as well as numerous online document delivery services. Through a comprehensive online interlibrary loan system, New College students also have ready access to holdings throughout Florida's public university libraries.

The Sudakoff Conference Center on campus hosts visiting lecturers, meetings of campus and community organizations, and an assortment of diverse special events. The Caples Fine Arts Complex includes the 264-seat Mildred Sainer Music and Arts Pavilion, which features student, local, and national performances; the Lota Mundy Music Building, which houses eight music practice rooms, plus the Benjamin and Barbara Slavin Electronic Music Studio; the Christianne Felsmann Fine Arts Building; the Betty Isermann Fine Arts Gallery and Studio; and a sculpture studio. Science facilities include the R. V. Heiser Natural Sciences Complex, which houses laboratories, classrooms, offices, a computer lab, two electron microscopes, and an auditorium, plus the $2.5-million Rhoda and Jack Pritzker Marine Biology Research Center. The marine center, one of the leading marine research centers in southwest Florida, features state-of-the-art culture rooms, laboratories, and aquariums with water drawn from Sarasota Bay. Saltwater effluent from the tanks is cleaned by means of a wetland constructed in 2001 as part of a New College senior thesis project.

Costs

For the 2006–07 academic year, in-state tuition and fees at New College of Florida were $3734 and out-of-state tuition and fees were $19,964. Room and board costs were $6564.

Financial Aid

The actual cost of providing New College of Florida's highly individualized honors college experience is far greater than the state funding appropriated for support of the College. The New College Foundation secures independent funding designed to provide the difference. Part of the foundation's endowment produces income used for scholarships.

Approximately 94 percent of New College students receive some form of financial assistance, including scholarships from external programs and organizations. To apply for financial aid, students should file the Free Application for Federal Student Aid (FAFSA). March 1 is the priority date for need-based financial aid. All first-time college students who complete applications by February 15 and who are admitted to New College are guaranteed merit scholarship funding. No additional scholarship application is necessary.

Faculty

Of New College's permanent faculty members, 100 percent hold the Ph.D. or terminal degree in their fields. They have come to New College from the finest universities nationally and abroad, drawn by an environment that emphasizes excellence in teaching and fosters a close-knit community of scholars. Faculty members sponsor individual students in the formulation of their academic programs, gradually moving toward a form of mentorship through which joint research is sometimes pursued. An 10:1 student-faculty ratio is a key factor in the College's individualized approach to education.

Student Government

Student input is a decisive factor in campus governance. Student representatives, elected by their peers, serve on most major policymaking committees and are voting participants in divisional and campus-wide faculty meetings. The New College Student Alliance has authority over funding for recreation, social events, and student organizations on campus.

Admission Requirements

New College of Florida seeks highly capable students eager to take responsibility for their own education. The Admissions Committee reviews each candidate individually, assessing his or her potential for success within, and contribution to, the College's unique environment. Writing ability, academic record, and course selection are focal points of the committee's review. The majority of first-year students entering in fall 2006 ranked in the top 10 percent of their high school class. The middle 50 percent of SAT takers scored 1250–1390. The middle 50 percent of ACT takers scored 26–30.

All prospective students may apply for entrance to either the fall or the spring term. Candidates must submit a New College application and fee, official transcript(s), SAT or ACT scores, a letter of recommendation, and one essay. Applicants are encouraged to augment their applications with evidence of maturity, self-discipline, and motivation for rigorous in-depth study. Thorough research into the College and a campus visit are recommended for all those with serious interest in applying.

Application and Information

Admission application materials and descriptive literature are available through the New College Office of Admissions and Financial Aid. The College has four application deadlines for the fall class: December 1, January 15, February 15, and April 15. Notification of the admission decision occurs on January 15, February 15, March 15, and April 25, respectively. A completed application and all supporting documents must be submitted to the Admissions Office before a candidate is considered for admission.

Inquiries and application requests should be directed to:

Kathleen M. Killion
Dean of Admissions and Financial Aid
New College of Florida
5800 Bay Shore Road
Sarasota, Florida 34243-2109
Phone: 941-487-5000
Fax: 941-487-5010
E-mail: admissions@ncf.edu
Web site: http://www.ncf.edu

College Hall, former home of circus magnate Charles Ringling, helps form the picture-perfect setting for New College of Florida.

NORTHWOOD UNIVERSITY, FLORIDA CAMPUS

WEST PALM BEACH, FLORIDA

The University

Northwood University was founded in 1959 by Dr. Arthur E. Turner and Dr. R. Gary Stauffer in order to teach business and management infused with practical experience, based upon the concepts of freedom and free enterprise. Since the early days, the University has grown systemwide to include campuses in Michigan, Texas, and Florida as well as thirty-seven satellite centers throughout the United States, with a system enrollment of more than 7,000 students. Northwood is a private, independent, coeducational institution and is accredited by the North Central Association of Schools and Colleges.

The Florida Campus, which opened in the mid-1980s, has grown to its current enrollment of more than 1,000 students. Attracting students from all over the globe, the campus is host to students who come to Northwood from thirty-seven different states and forty-seven different countries. Approximately 300 of the students reside on campus in attractive apartment-style residence halls.

The campus architecture is quite unique. The buildings are directly influenced by the work of noted architect Alden B. Dow (a student of Frank Lloyd Wright). The low and rounded modern buildings create the feel of a corporate campus surrounded by lakes and dotted with palm trees. It has been described as a corporate campus in paradise.

Outside of the classroom, Northwood offers its students a broad spectrum of activities and clubs in which to participate. Clubs include Delta Epsilon Chi (DECA), Student Government, Campus Crusade for Christ, the CASH Club, the Drama Club, Blue Storm Dance Team, the Cycling Club, Circle K International, and organizations linked to major fields of study. Activities include cultural awareness programs, concerts, Big Brothers/Big Sisters, Northwood's Outstanding Business Leader Forum, intramural sports, and many others.

Athletics play an important role in student life. Northwood's Florida Campus competes in the National Association of Intercollegiate Athletics (NAIA). Men's intercollegiate sports include baseball, basketball, golf, soccer, and tennis. Women's sports include basketball, golf, soccer, softball, tennis, and volleyball. Several of the teams have been nationally ranked and are most competitive within the Florida Sun Conference.

Facilities for tennis, racquetball, swimming, basketball, and fitness are in proximity to the student residence halls. The Countess de Hoernle Student Life Center includes a gym, fitness center, classrooms, bookstore, and snack bar.

Location

The beautiful 90-acre campus is located in West Palm Beach, Florida. West Palm Beach is a 1-hour drive from Ft. Lauderdale, 30 minutes from Boca Raton, and within a 2½-hour drive from Orlando. The Palm Beach International Airport, 10 minutes from the campus, provides easy access to students and visitors.

West Palm Beach offers students a vast array of opportunities for both work and play. Great weather year-round and easy access to outdoor activities ranging from scuba and snorkeling to spring training major-league baseball and concerts at south Florida's premier outdoor concert venue supplement a very active on-campus activity program.

Majors and Degrees

The Florida Campus of Northwood offers Bachelor of Business Administration (B.B.A.) degrees. Degree programs are offered in accounting; advertising/management; aftermarket management; automotive marketing/management; banking and finance/management; entertainment, sport, and promotion management; entrepreneurship; hotel, restaurant, and resort management; international business/management; management; and marketing/management.

Off-Campus Programs

Recognizing that the business world is truly global, the University offers several exciting study-abroad programs for its students. The Term in Europe is a ten-week, traveling study-abroad program that explores the likes of France, Germany, Greece, Hungary, and Italy. The Term in Asia program is a residential study-abroad program in partnership with universities in Southeast Asia. The Term in Australia is a three-week program that includes visits to Sydney, Magnetic Islands, Cairns, Kuranda, and the Great Barrier Reef.

Northwood University's Margaret Chase Smith Library in Skowhegan, Maine, also offers a unique learning experience. The private library is open to serious students who are interested in the compatible, constructive coexistence of government and the private sector. In addition to its invaluable twentieth-century American politics and government collection, the library serves as an arena for free discussion of the economic ideas and ideals upon which the nation was founded.

Academic Facilities

At the heart of Northwood's academic facilities is the DeVos-Cook Academic Center. This facility contains 23,000 square feet of space and houses state-of-the-art classrooms, faculty offices, and computer labs for both instructional and general student use.

Supplementing the DeVos-Cook Center is the Johann M. and Arthur E. Turner Education Center. This modern 38,000-square-foot facility houses the library, an art gallery, administrative offices, conference rooms, classrooms, and an auditorium.

Costs

The annual fee structure for the 2007–08 academic year was $15,825 for tuition, $880 for fees, and $7767 for room and board. Northwood estimates that annual books and supplies cost $1400. Since Northwood is a private university, the tuition and fee charge is the same for both in-state and out-of-state students.

Financial Aid

Approximately 70 percent of students at Northwood's Florida Campus receive some form of financial assistance. The University makes available academic merit scholarships, athletic scholarships, and general need-based aid.

Merit scholarships are based upon academic performance and standardized test results (ACT or SAT). The Freedom Award is $7500 per year for new students who present a grade point average of 3.0 or higher and test scores greater than 1150 on the SAT or 25 on the ACT, or minimum 3.7 GPA and 1050 SAT or 23 ACT. The Free Enterprise award is $5000 per year for new students who present a grade point average of 2.7 or higher with test scores greater than 950 on the SAT or 20 on the ACT, or minimum 3.2 GPA and 890 SAT or 19 ACT. Several other merit-based scholarships are available to those who qualify and are not need-based. Examples include grants for students who have participated in organizations such as DECA, FBLA, BPA, and Junior Achievement. The Presidential Merit Scholarship is a $9000 per year award for new freshmen students with a 3.8 minimum GPA and SAT of 1240 or higher or ACT of 28 or higher.

In order to be considered for all need-based aid programs, students must file the Free Application for Federal Student Aid (FAFSA). Need-based aid is available in the form of federal, state, and Northwood grants, loans, and work-study programs to those who qualify.

Faculty

The student-faculty ratio at Northwood is currently 20:1. This affords the student not only small classes but also the opportunity to work closely with faculty members. The faculty is dedicated to bringing current business practices into the classroom. In addition to the fact that the vast majority of the faculty members hold advanced degrees, more than 90 percent have had prior experience in the business or management world. It is their practical experience in the real world, coupled with small classes, which creates a learning experience that combines both theory and practical skills.

Student Government

The Student Government Association (SGA) assists in the personal, social, and political development of Northwood students, both individually and collectively. The organization consists of 5 major officers, class presidents, and several subcommittees and/or appointed positions. SGA has representatives to confer with Student Services and campus administrative leaders throughout the academic year.

Subcommittees include the Diversity and Cultural Committee, the Peer Education Network, BACCHUS–Alcohol and Drug Education and Awareness, the Food Service Committee, and the Commuter Advisory Board.

Admission Requirements

Northwood University seeks to enroll students who have an interest in pursuing business, management, or entrepreneurship and who have demonstrated that desire through performance in the classroom. When reviewing a candidate for admission, the University takes into consideration the applicant's high school record, the results of the SAT or ACT, and a host of other factors, including extracurricular activity, recommendations, and involvement in business-related activities or clubs.

Northwood strongly encourages students who have followed an approved course of study at another college or university to apply for admission. The University's transfer program is designed to allow each student to transfer the maximum number of credit hours into their program of study. Transfer students with fewer than 40 hours must submit high school transcripts and standardized test scores. All students who apply should be in good academic and social standing at the college from which they are transferring.

All international students are required to take the TOEFL examination, unless they have taken the SAT or ACT. A minimum TOEFL score of 500 on the paper-based exam, 173 computer-based, or 61 Internet-based is required for regular admission. Official transcripts of all secondary (high school) and college work must be provided with the application. All transcripts must be translated into English.

Application and Information

An application is ready for consideration by the Admissions Committee when it has been received with the $25 application fee, required test scores, and transcripts from each school attended. Northwood encourages students to apply via the Web site. For online applications, the application fee is waived.

For more information about Northwood University, prospective students should contact:

Office of Admissions
Northwood University, Florida Campus
2600 North Military Trail
West Palm Beach, Florida 33409
Phone: 561-478-5500
800-458-8325 (toll-free)
E-mail: fladmit@northwood.edu
Web site: http://www.northwood.edu

The Northwood University, Florida Campus, has been described as a corporate campus in paradise.

NOVA SOUTHEASTERN UNIVERSITY

FORT LAUDERDALE, FLORIDA

The University

Years from now, historians will look back and discover that the future officially began in 1964. The Beatles arrived and changed the face of music. The first Ford Mustang rolled out of Detroit. And, in Fort Lauderdale, Florida, a tiny college was born with a handful of students and some revolutionary ideas. That college grew up to become Nova Southeastern University (NSU), and the rest is history.

Today, NSU is the nation's sixth-largest independent university, with more than 26,000 students; 100,000 alumni; a sprawling, 300-acre Fort Lauderdale main campus; and a presence in nine countries around the world. Through five decades of explosive growth, NSU's reputation for academic excellence and innovation continues to flourish.

So what exactly is NSU? NSU does not fit easily within a standardized niche, because neither do its students. For undergraduates, NSU is a small, nurturing, private undergraduate college called Farquhar College of Arts and Sciences. As a small college within a diverse and dynamic University, Farquhar College is an amazing place to begin life's journey. The traditional undergraduate student population is approximately 5,000 students from all fifty states and forty-two other countries. About 1,200 students live on campus in six residential halls. With more than fifty on-campus student organizations, a powerful student government, socially active fraternities and sororities, intramural sports, and NCAA Division II athletics, NSU's Farquhar College has all the elements of a classic, traditional college.

At the same time, NSU is an exciting, multifaceted university. It is young and agile, fearless, and forward thinking. Unusual among institutions of higher education, NSU is truly an institution for all ages. From the University School, for children pre-K through grade 12, to numerous undergraduate and graduate degree programs in a variety of fields and nondegree continuing education programs for retired professionals, all are available at NSU.

Location

Between the undergraduate and graduate programs, NSU offers more than 120 degrees. But for some people, the degrees that matter most are found on a thermometer, and 77°F sounds very good. That is the average temperature in South Florida. So, when students are not in class, they can be outdoors all year round—and they will need that time to experience everything South Florida has to offer.

There is hiking, biking, fishing, boating, and windsurfing and endless open-air festivals and concerts. Fort Lauderdale Beach is 15 minutes to the east and the Everglades are 15 minutes in the other direction. Students can be on South Beach in about half an hour; in 3 hours, they can be screaming their lungs out at one of Orlando's theme parks or chilling in the Florida Keys. For sports fans, there are professional baseball, basketball, hockey, and football. For foodies, there is everything from casual waterfront dives to world-class gourmet cuisine. And for students who view shopping as a competitive sport, South Florida is the Olympics, with everything from funky flea markets to some the world's most exclusive shopping malls and boutiques, all just minutes from campus.

Majors and Degrees

Nova Southeastern University offers bachelor's degrees in accounting, American studies, applied professional studies, athletic training, biology (premedical), business administration, communication studies, computer information systems, computer science, criminal justice, economics, elementary education, English, environmental science/studies, exceptional student education, finance, health science, history, humanities, international studies, legal studies, management, marine biology, marketing, nursing, paralegal studies, prekindergarten/primary education, psychology, secondary biology education, secondary mathematics education, sport and recreation management, and theater.

NSU pioneered the Dual Admission Program for a select group of highly motivated students who have maintained a laser focus on their career goals from an early age. Qualified students in the Dual Admission Program are automatically reserved a seat in one of NSU's graduate or professional schools while they earn their bachelor's degree. In today's competitive world, that is like getting a head start on the rest of their life. Dual-admission programs are offered in accounting, audiology, business administration, computer information systems, computer sciences, conflict analysis and resolution, criminal justice, dental medicine, education, family therapy, human resource management, international business administration, law, leadership, marine biology, mental health counseling, nursing, occupational therapy, optometry, osteopathic medicine, pharmacy, physical therapy, physician assistant studies, psychology, public administration, speech-language pathology, and taxation.

Academic Programs

The undergraduate program at NSU combines a general education curriculum with a set of majors designed to prepare students for their future, whether that is starting a graduate school degree or a professional career. With the incredible personal attention and intimate class sizes of a small, private college and the powerful academic resources of a well-rounded university, students are able to explore an almost limitless range of career paths.

NSU's open-door policy helps build strong connections between faculty members and students. Since classes are taught by professors who are still actively engaged in their professions outside the classroom, students are better prepared for real life.

NSU created the Honors Program for students who have demonstrated a passion for learning and crave more from their college experience. The program is intensely personal, offering broader, richer, and deeper insights into topics that are pleasing to each individual student. The goal is not to make students work harder but to help them get more from the work they do. Carefully selected faculty members and course work ensure that the program is engaging and involving, and emphasis is placed on achieving great understanding of concepts. The program fosters powerful mentoring relationships between students and their professors and provides life-changing learning opportunities through research, social activities, real-world encounters, and study abroad.

Academic Facilities

A tour of the NSU campus is an architectural and intellectual feast, with cutting-edge research and learning facilities at every turn. As a leader in technology and innovation, NSU has been named one of America's "Top 20 Cyber Universities" by *Forbes* magazine. It has also been designated a National Center of Academic Excellence in Information Assistance Education by the National Security Agency and the Department of Homeland Security. Wireless access and computer micro labs throughout the campus make it possible to connect to the world from virtually anywhere. In fact, NSU is so firmly connected to the real world that it may actually be the only college in America with a professional football team. The Miami Dolphins' headquarters and training camp are located right on campus; the Bubble, a 2-acre, inflatable dome, houses one of the team's three practice fields.

The tour would not be complete without mention of three other NSU showcases: The Oceanographic Center, which sits on 10 acres of Atlantic oceanfront and serves as home to the National Coral Reef Institute; the 325,000-square-foot Alvin Sherman Library, Research, and Information Technology Center, the largest library in the state of Florida; and the University Center (UC), which houses a 4,500-seat arena designed to host everything from NSU's NCAA Division II Shark athletics to concerts, a two-story rock-climbing wall, three multipurpose studios for group exercise, a state-of-the-art recreation complex, and a performing arts center with a theater, dressing rooms, costume and scenery shops, and art gallery. A spectacular outdoor pool area, where students can worship the Florida sun, and the Flight Deck, NSU's popular student lounge, are also at the UC.

Costs

Tuition for undergraduate students at Nova Southeastern University varies according to the academic program. For the 2008–09 academic year, tuition for the full-time day program is $19,800, mandatory fees are $325, and the double-occupancy room rate is $2628 per semester. The declining meal plan is $1200 per semester, and textbooks cost $75–$100 per course.

Financial Aid

Nova Southeastern University offers a comprehensive program of financial aid to assist students in meeting their educational expenses. Financial aid packages are available that include scholarships, grants, and loans.

Applicants for financial aid are required to submit the Free Application for Federal Student Aid (FAFSA) to be considered for all campus-based aid programs. Students who apply before April 1 are given priority consideration for funds; however, applications are accepted all year.

Faculty

The undergraduate faculty at Nova Southeastern University is full-time and resident. In addition, faculty members are drawn from qualified professionals in the community as well as from other centers and programs within the University. Most of the faculty members have backgrounds in professional, industrial, managerial, civic, educational, or other private and public sectors of the community. For example, lawyers and judges teach criminal justice courses; accountants, personnel managers, and others teach in their respective fields; and principals and curriculum specialists teach education courses. All faculty members are dedicated to the philosophy that contemporary higher education combines theory and practice and that the education of working professionals and adult students requires the active participation of both the student and the instructor.

Admission Requirements

Admission requirements vary according to the program. A counseling session is recommended. Freshman applicants must submit official high school transcripts and SAT or ACT scores.

Transfer applicants must submit official college transcripts. Each student's record is evaluated individually to determine the number of transferable credits. There is a maximum of 90 transferable credits, and students must complete 30 semester hours at Nova Southeastern University.

Application and Information

The application should be submitted with a nonrefundable $50 application fee. There is no closing date for applications for the fall term. Applicants are notified of the admission decision on a rolling basis.

For further information, prospective applicants are invited to contact:

Office of Undergraduate Admissions
Nova Southeastern University
3301 College Avenue
Fort Lauderdale, Florida 33314
Phone: 954-262-8000
800-338-4723 Ext. 8000 (toll-free)
E-mail: admissions@nova.edu
Web site: http://www.nova.edu/undergrad

Nova Southeastern University's Library, Research, and Information Technology Center is Florida's largest library.

PALM BEACH ATLANTIC UNIVERSITY

WEST PALM BEACH, FLORIDA

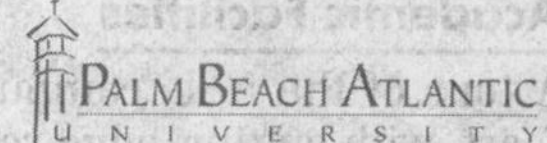

The University

Palm Beach Atlantic University (PBA) was founded in 1968 by concerned Palm Beach County residents who felt the need for a distinctive institution of higher learning that would stress not only academic quality but character development and spiritual maturity. Chartered as a Christian liberal arts college, Palm Beach Atlantic offers a high-quality education for students of all faiths. In 1972, the University was accredited by the Southern Association of Colleges and Schools to award bachelor's degrees.

PBA has grown to serve more than 3,200 students in a variety of traditional and nontraditional programs. Three master's degree programs also are offered: Master of Business Administration, Master of Science in Organizational Leadership, and Master of Science in Counseling Psychology. In 2005, PBA graduated its first class of pharmacy students in its Pharm.D. program.

For both undergraduate and graduate students, Palm Beach Atlantic seeks to promote intellectual, moral, and spiritual growth. The undergraduate may opt for a variety of ways to get involved in college life, including service and leadership organizations, intercollegiate and intramural sports, fine arts, religious groups, and professionally oriented organizations such as Kappa Delta Epsilon and Phi Beta Lambda. Since 2002, the University dedicated an additional 500,000 square feet of campus facilities as part of its comprehensive campus growth plan. The DeSantis Family Chapel provides exciting opportunities for multiple weekly chapels on the PBA campus. Oceanview Residence Hall and Dixie Garage add additional housing and offer convenient access to the University's educational and cultural programs. Vera Lea Rinker Hall houses PBA's School of Music, accredited by the National Association of Schools of Music (NASM). The Gregory building serves nearly 300 pharmacy students, and the Warren Library opened in February 2007.

Location

Palm Beach Atlantic University occupies more than 750,000 square feet in the heart of West Palm Beach on the Intracoastal Waterway across from Palm Beach, approximately 1 mile from the Atlantic Ocean. Palm Beach County provides a broad spectrum of cultural activities in music, theater, fine arts, and sports. The cosmopolitan area of the Palm Beaches, with its shopping, recreation, and service opportunities, is at the University's doorstep.

Majors and Degrees

The Bachelor of Arts is offered in acting for stage and screen; art; art education (K–12); biblical studies; Christian leadership; Christian social ministry; communication studies; cross-cultural and urban studies; dance; English; film production; graphic arts; history; ministry; music; musical theater; organizational communication; philosophy; political science; popular music; prelaw; print journalism; radio and television news; screenwriting; secondary education, with specializations in drama (6–12), English (6–12), social science/history (6–12), and social science/political science (6–12); speech communication; technical theater; television production; and theater arts. A Bachelor of General Studies is also available.

The Bachelor of Music degree is offered in church music, instrument performance, keyboard performance, music composition, music education, and voice performance.

The Bachelor of Science is offered in applied finance and accounting; athletic training; biology (with concentrations in botany, environmental science, field biology, grad school preparation, marine biology, molecular biology and biotechnology, pre-health professional preparation, and zoology); elementary education, with specializations in pre-K primary, middle grades English, middle grades general sciences, middle grades mathematics, middle grades social science, and exceptional students; entrepreneurship and small business; international business; management; marketing; mathematics; nursing; organizational management; physical education (nonteaching); physical education with exercise science; psychology; secondary education, with specializations in biology (6–12), mathematics (6–12), and physical education (6–12); and sport management.

Minors are offered in accounting, art, biblical studies, biology, business administration, chemistry, Christian education, Christian leadership, Christian social ministry, communication, computer science, cross-cultural and urban studies, dance, English, exercise science, film production, graphic arts, history, marketing, mathematics, music, musical theater, oceanography, philosophy, physical education, political science, psychology, public relations, screenwriting, sociology, Spanish, sport management, technical theater, theater arts, TV production, and youth ministry.

Preprofessional programs are offered in engineering (a 2-2 program with the University of Florida), health, and legal studies.

Academic Programs

A minimum of 120 semester hours of academic work with a minimum overall grade point average of 2.0 is required for graduation. The student must complete a major of 30 or more semester hours and a minor of 15 or more hours. Double majors are possible. The major and minor are usually declared by the midpoint of the sophomore year, although changes after this time may be allowed.

Unified Studies is the Palm Beach Atlantic University general education program. It is the graduation requirement that is normative for all undergraduate degrees awarded by the University. Members of the Unified Studies Program faculty seek to employ their collective expertise and intellectual interests within an educational program characterized by innovation and integrated study. Each component of the Unified Studies Program seeks to engage student interest and enthusiasm. Students become active learners with faculty members who model both the life of the mind and the work of the hands.

College-Level Examination Program (CLEP), International Baccalaureate (I.B.), and Advanced Placement (AP) test credits are accepted, and advanced standing is granted to qualified students. Opportunities are available for independent and directed study.

The academic year is divided into two semesters, one running from September through December, the second from January through April. A six-week summer term is offered as well.

Off-Campus Programs

Several courses during the May and summer terms include opportunities for study abroad that carry academic credit. Semester-abroad programs are also available in Australia, China, Costa Rica, Egypt, Great Britain, Russia, and Uganda. Students may also pursue additional studies in selected disciplines such as the American Studies program in Washington, D.C., the Contemporary Music Center at Martha's Vineyard, the Los Angeles Film Studies Institute, or the Washington Journalism Center.

Academic Facilities

PBA is committed to state-of-the-art academic facilities. Every classroom is designated a smart classroom with wireless network access and a projection screen, and every residence hall room has a high-speed Internet connection via PalmNET, the campuswide fiber-optic network.

In February 2007, PBA dedicated the new Warren Library, a state-of-the-art, 80,000-square-foot building. The library contains more than 215,000 volumes, over 2,000 active subscriptions, and access to more than 2 million volumes in the South Florida Library Information Network (SEFLIN).

Costs

The tuition, room, and board costs make PBA an affordable institution in comparison with other colleges across the country. The cost for a full-time student attending Palm Beach Atlantic University during the 2007–08 school year was $19,700 per year (12–18 hours). Room and board costs were approximately $7200 per year. Expenses for books, personal items, and travel should be considered when estimating the total cost of attending the University.

Financial Aid

More than 90 percent of the undergraduate students at PBA receive some type of financial aid. Each student should submit the Free Application for Federal Student Aid (FAFSA). Students may be eligible for federal and state grants, federal loans, and work-study programs as well as institutional grants and scholarships.

Faculty

The University has an outstanding faculty of 164 full- and 78 part-time members who are dedicated to the integration of Christian faith with each discipline. Approximately 75 percent hold earned doctorates, and individualized attention results from the favorable student-faculty ratio of 16:1. The University's family atmosphere allows for a great deal of student-faculty interaction in and out of the classroom. No graduate assistants teach at PBA.

Student Government

An active Student Government Association represents student opinion and plans student activities at the University. Students are represented on most faculty and board committees and are active in setting the direction of the University.

Admission Requirements

High school graduates are required to submit an application with a personal essay, official transcripts indicating at least a 3.0 grade point average in college-preparatory studies, and a minimum score of 960 on the SAT (combined) or 20 on the ACT (composite). An interview with an admission counselor is required. International students must also demonstrate English proficiency on the Test of English as a Foreign Language (TOEFL).

Transfer students must be eligible to return to their previous college or must have been out of school for at least one semester. One academic and one character recommendation are required in addition to official transcripts indicating a grade point average of 2.5 or better in previous college work.

Application and Information

Both freshmen and transfer students are admitted in either semester.

Applications are accepted throughout the year, but students who wish to live in residence halls on campus are encouraged to apply early because of housing capacity limitations. Candidates must submit an official University application to the Admissions Office along with a $30 nonrefundable application fee and the required materials (transcript, test scores, and recommendations).

For materials and additional information, students should contact:

Admissions Office
Palm Beach Atlantic University
P.O. Box 24708
West Palm Beach, Florida 33416-4708
Phone: 561-803-2000
888-GO-TO-PBA (toll-free)
E-mail: admit@pba.edu
Web site: http://www.pba.edu

Palm Beach Atlantic University offers the best of both worlds: the diversity of an urban setting coupled with the recreational activities and stunning vistas of Florida's waterways.

ROLLINS COLLEGE

WINTER PARK, FLORIDA

The College

Founded in 1885, Rollins College is Florida's oldest institution of higher learning. It is coeducational, nondenominational, and independently supported by income from tuition, gifts, and endowment. While most traditional-age undergraduate students pursue their studies in the four-year, residential College of Arts & Sciences, Rollins also offers the Master of Business Administration (M.B.A.) degree in the Crummer Graduate School of Business and undergraduate and graduate degrees in the Hamilton Holt School. The College of Arts & Sciences enrolls approximately 1,750 students from most states and more than forty other countries; the total undergraduate enrollment is 2,900, and the total graduate enrollment is 800.

The 70-acre campus is noted for its beautiful grounds and traditional Spanish-Mediterranean architecture. A recent College campaign raised more than $160 million for financial aid, endowed faculty chairs, programming, and facilities, including the Harold & Ted Alfond Sports Center, the Cornell Campus Center, the Olin Electronic Research and Information Center, and the Marshall and Vera Lea Rinker Building. A $108-million bequest from alumnus George Cornell, the largest gift in Rollins' history, has provided additional resources for scholarships, faculty development, and innovative initiatives.

Location

Winter Park is considered one of the nation's most beautiful residential communities. The town is adjacent to Orlando, one of the nation's fastest-growing and most popular metropolitan areas and an important center of business, science, and technology. Located 50 miles from the Atlantic Ocean and 90 miles from the Gulf of Mexico, the Rollins campus is bounded by Lake Virginia to the east and south.

Majors and Degrees

Rollins College confers the Bachelor of Arts (B.A.) degree in the following major areas: anthropology, art (studio and history), biochemistry/molecular biology, biology, chemistry, classical studies, computer science, critical media and cultural studies, economics, elementary education, English, environmental studies, French, history, international business,. international relations, Latin American and Caribbean studies, marine biology, mathematics, music, philosophy, physics, political science, psychology, religious studies, sociology, Spanish, and theater. Minors are also offered in African and African-American studies, archaeology, Asian studies, Australian studies, business, communications, dance, film studies, German, Jewish studies, Russian, sustainable development and the environment, women's studies, and writing. Preprofessional programs include predentistry, prelaw, premedicine, and pre-veterinary studies. Dual-degree (3-2) programs are available in pre-engineering in cooperation with Auburn University, Case Western Reserve University, Columbia University, and Washington University in St. Louis; in pre–environmental management and preforestry with Duke University; and in business management with the Crummer Graduate School of Business.

Academic Programs

The Rollins faculty has adopted a curriculum based upon a liberal arts foundation from the first year to graduation; it is designed to ensure that broadly educated graduates are well prepared in a field of concentration. In addition to completing approximately one third of their courses in one of the College's twenty-nine majors, students also complete general education requirements, which provide exposure to the ways various areas of knowledge may reinforce and enrich each other. General education requirements fulfill approximately one third of graduation requirements, leaving room for the selection of a minor or second major. In addition, self-designed majors are available to students who desire concentrations in more than one major field. The Honors Degree Program allows selected academically superior students to enter Rollins with full sophomore status and graduate with a special Honors B.A. degree in as few as three years by satisfying stringent criteria. All first-year students participate in the Rollins College Conference (RCC), a fall-semester seminar and cocurricular program taught by faculty members who also serve as the students' academic advisers.

The academic calendar consists of a fifteen-week fall semester and a fifteen-week spring semester.

Credit is awarded for appropriate Advanced Placement examination and CLEP scores, dual-enrollment programs, and achievement in the International Baccalaureate Program.

Off-Campus Programs

For approximately the same tuition and fees that they pay at Rollins, students may study abroad for a semester at Rollins-sponsored programs in Sydney, Australia; Shanghai, China; London, England; Trier, Germany; and Asturias, Spain, as well as a six-week summer program in Madrid. In addition to the traditional semester-long programs, Rollins offers dozens of study-abroad opportunities at various times of the year, in places such as Bali, China, Costa Rica, Dominican Republic, France, Greece, Israel, Italy, Mexico, Namibia, Scotland, Tanzania, and Turkey.

Academic Facilities

The College's academic facilities include the Bush Science Center, the Cornell Fine Arts Center, Cornell Hall for the Social Sciences, the Johnson Center for Psychology, and the newly expanded Keene Hall, which houses the music department. The Olin Library features reader stations, computer terminals, and a 24-hour study area. Through the years, the Annie Russell Theatre/Knowles Memorial Chapel complex has become the traditional landmark of the College.

Costs

The basic academic-year expenses for 2007–08 were $32,640 for tuition and fees and $10,200 for room and board, for a total of $42,840.

Financial Aid

Rollins seeks to help qualified students attend college regardless of their ability to meet the expenses. Funds are provided by Rollins College as well as by federal and state sources. Student aid consists of scholarships, grants, loans, and employment opportunities. Most students receiving aid are given a package consisting of two or three of these forms of aid. Aid is awarded on the basis of proven financial need and academic achievement. To apply for aid, a student must file the Free Application for Federal Student Aid and the Rollins College Undergraduate Financial Aid Application.

A number of renewable academic merit scholarships are available to entering first-year students, including the highly competitive Cornell Scholarships (full tuition, fees, and room and board annually), Deans' Scholarships (up to $10,000 annually in addition to previously awarded scholarships), Alonzo Rollins and Presidential Scholarships for overall academic excellence (up to $15,000 annually), and Donald Cram Scholarships for majors in mathematics and the sciences. All applicants are considered for these scholarships, and financial need is not a criterion. Scholarships are also awarded for artistic and athletic talent. More information may be obtained from the Offices of Admission and Financial Aid.

Due to the high number of student aid applicants and limited funds, it is important that application for admission to the College be made no later than February 1 (January 15 for Cornell and Deans' consideration) and preferably in the fall of the senior year of secondary school. Details and regulations regarding student aid are found in the College's *General Catalogue.*

Faculty

Ninety-four percent of the members of Rollins' teaching faculty hold doctoral degrees or the highest degree available in their fields from distinguished universities in this country and abroad. The student-faculty ratio is 10:1. Students receive instruction from full-time faculty members, who also serve as academic advisers.

Student Government

The Student Government Association (SGA) consists of a student senate elected from across the campus and an executive committee. The SGA is composed of executive, legislative, and judicial branches, each designed to provide a series of checks and balances in the administrative process. The SGA affords students participation in the decision-making process of college life and represents student opinion to the trustees, administration, alumni, faculty, and staff. It provides an avenue for student expression, social interaction, cultural awareness, and student services and publications.

Admission Requirements

Admission is competitive; approximately 3,250 applications are received annually for a first-year class of 515 and a transfer class of 55. More than 80 percent of the members of each entering first-year class rank in the top two fifths of their high school graduating class. The middle 50 percent of College Board SAT combined critical reading and math scores ranged from 1130 to 1290, and the middle 50 percent of ACT composite scores ranged from 24 to 28. A number of factors are considered in the selection process, including the applicant's high school record (including rigor of academic program, grades earned, and class standing), contributions to school and/or community, quality and content of the applicant's essay, counselor's recommendation, results of either the SAT or ACT, and extracurricular involvement.

As of fall 2007, Rollins offered admission applicants either a Test Score Option or a Test Score Waived Option. The Test Score Option is appropriate for applicants seeking academic merit scholarship consideration or for applicants who do not select the Test Score Waived Option; SAT and/or ACT scores are required for Test Score Option applicants. The Test Score Waived Option is not appropriate for applicants wishing to be considered for academic merit scholarships. Candidates selecting the Test Score Waived Option must submit supplemental materials: a graded paper from a core academic course in the junior or senior year (examples include essays or research papers, lab reports, or work in mathematics or related fields) and a "portfolio" reflecting the candidate's strengths, talents, or interests. (This requirement is intentionally left open-ended to provide each candidate creative opportunity. Examples include written work, such as poetry, slides of original art work, multimedia presentations, scrapbooks, videos, or DVDs, of athletic or artistic performances—anything that helps Rollins understand the applicant's talents and interests and their potential to contribute to the Rollins community.)

Application and Information

Candidates are encouraged to apply in the fall of their senior year. Applications should be submitted no later than February 15 of the senior year. Students are notified of a decision by April 1. The Candidates' Reply Date is May 1. An early decision (binding) process is available for 2007–08: applications must be received by November 15. Candidates for early decision are notified by December 15. A deposit of $500 is required to hold a space in the entering class.

Early action (non-binding) applications must be received by December 1. Early action candidates are notified of a decision by February 1. The Candidates' Reply Date is May 1.

Early admission candidates may be considered for entrance prior to secondary school graduation, usually for entrance following their junior year.

Application forms and additional information may be obtained online or by writing or calling:

Office of Admission
Rollins College
1000 Holt Avenue–2720
Winter Park, Florida 32789-4499
Phone: 407-646-2161
Fax: 407-646-1502
E-mail: admission@rollins.edu
Web site: http://www.rollins.edu

The Harold & Ted Alfond Sports Center, a 76,000-square-foot state-of-the-art facility, features a performance court, a recreation gym, and comprehensive aerobics and weight-training areas.

SAINT LEO UNIVERSITY

SAINT LEO, FLORIDA

The University

Founded in 1889, Saint Leo University is now recognized as one of the nation's leading Catholic teaching universities and a school of international consequence. The main campus in Saint Leo, Florida, is home to the vibrant University College, serving the education needs of more than 1,500 traditional-age undergraduate students. The University also offers a variety of dynamic graduate programs, a weekend and evening program for working adults, and both undergraduate and graduate degree programs through sixteen education centers in six states and through the Center for Online Learning, which houses the University's cutting-edge online degree programs.

The University College student body represents thirty-nine states and territories as well as thirty-seven countries. International students make up 10 percent of the student population. Minority students represent 34 percent of the University College enrollment. Approximately 71 percent of traditional full-time students live in one of eleven residence halls.

Students can participate in the nationally recognized honors program and the more than fifty different clubs and organizations on campus, including national fraternities and sororities. The Student Government Union and various campus organizations also sponsor movies, concerts, art exhibits, lectures, dances, and other special events throughout the academic year.

Saint Leo is a member of the Sunshine State Conference and competes in NCAA Division II intercollegiate athletics for men and women. Men's sports include baseball, basketball, cross-country, golf, lacrosse, soccer, swimming, and tennis. Women compete in basketball, cross-country, golf, soccer, softball, swimming, tennis, and volleyball. Cheerleading is offered as a club sport. Students can also participate in a wide variety of intramurals. Campus recreational facilities include lighted racquetball and tennis courts; soccer, baseball, and softball fields; a weight room/fitness center; and a heated outdoor Olympic-size swimming pool. The campus is bordered by a 154-acre lake and an eighteen-hole golf course.

Saint Leo is committed to giving its students an education that prepares them for the future. The goal of the University is to develop the whole person, both academically and personally, by providing a values-based education in the Benedictine tradition. In a recent satisfaction survey, 97 percent of respondents said they would recommend Saint Leo to a friend.

Saint Leo University is accredited by the Commission on Colleges of the Southern Association of Colleges and Schools to award the associate, bachelor's, and master's degrees. Saint Leo University's degree program in social work is accredited by the Commission on Accreditation of the Council on Social Work Education (B.S.W. level). The School of Business is accredited by the International Assembly for Collegiate Business Education (IACBE).The University's undergraduate sport business program is nationally approved by the Sport Management Program Review Council (SMPRC). Saint Leo University also has Teacher Education Programs approval by the State of Florida Department of Education.

In addition to associate and bachelor's degrees, Saint Leo University offers a Master of Business Administration (M.B.A.) degree, a Master of Education (M.Ed.) degree, a Master of Science (M.S.) degree in criminal justice, and Master of Arts (M.A.) degrees in both theology and teaching.

Location

Saint Leo is located 35 minutes north of Tampa and 90 minutes west of Orlando. The lakeside campus occupies 186 acres of rolling hills and wooded grounds. The rural setting is conducive to academic success, but the University is located near enough to metropolitan areas to give the students the advantage of a wide variety of social and professional opportunities.

Majors and Degrees

Saint Leo University offers over forty traditional majors, preprofessional studies, specializations, endorsements, and programs. Degrees offered are the Bachelor of Arts, Bachelor of Science, and Bachelor of Social Work.

The School of Business offers degrees in accounting, business administration (specialization in international business), communication management, computer information systems, entrepreneurship and family business, human resources administration, international hospitality and tourism management, management, marketing, and sport business. The School of Arts and Sciences offers majors in biology, English, environmental science, history, international studies, mathematics, medical technology, political science, psychology, religion, and sociology. The School of Education and Social Services offers majors in criminal justice, elementary education, human services management, middle grades education, and social work.

Preprofessional studies programs in dentistry, law, medicine, and veterinary science are also offered, including 4+4 medical school and 3+4 dental school programs.

Academic Programs

Saint Leo's LINK (Learning Interdisciplinary Knowledge) general education program ensures that all graduates have a solid grounding in theories, issues, and knowledge to prepare them for successful careers and graduate work. The program develops the skills that are the foundation of a liberal arts education and that today's employers demand. Students learn to communicate effectively; function at a high level, both alone and as a part of a team; develop a general knowledge base in many different areas; and analyze and solve problems effectively.

Students complete foundation courses of core requirements (writing, computer literacy, math, and wellness), Perspectives courses (liberal arts, fine arts, humanities, and physical, social, and behavioral sciences), and a senior capstone course that connects all prior course work in the major and leads to research and independent projects demonstrating mastery of the field.

Saint Leo has an academic skills program to assist first-year students in their adjustment to university life. Included in this program are freshman studies, tutoring, and advising. All first-year students at Saint Leo are assigned faculty advisers, who act as mentors from the first day that the student arrives on campus through the time when the student selects a major.

Students who demonstrate course mastery for any course listed in the catalog have the opportunity to receive up to 40 hours of credit through examination. Detailed information about credit by examination is available through the Registrar's Office.

Most students at Saint Leo earn the credits needed for their bachelor's degree through a four-year program of study. All major programs require a 2.0 minimum grade point average for graduation.

Off-Campus Programs

Saint Leo University is committed to helping students expand their horizons through study-abroad programs. Saint Leo currently has partnerships with schools in Australia (Sydney), Ecuador (Quito), England (Bristol, Kent, Sunderland, and York), France (Paris), Ireland (Limerick), Italy (Rome), Scotland (Dundee), Spain (Madrid), and Switzerland (Leysin). Articulation agreements also afford study opportunities throughout Asia and the Pacific Rim. The University continues to add new programs and partnerships in order to provide students with a wide variety of educational and cultural experiences.

Students are also able to work with their professors and academic advisers to identify and pursue a wide variety of internship options, further enhancing the real-world experience component of their education.

Academic Facilities

The Cannon Memorial Library contains more than 140,000 volumes, including access to 57,000 e-books, 38,758 current periodical subscriptions (694 print and 38,064 electronic), and 70 online databases. Also located in the library are the Hugh Culverhouse Computer Instruction Center classrooms, a student computer lab, and two VTT-equipped instruction/conference rooms.

Campus laboratories have all been renovated and feature state-of-the-art equipment. Lab facilities include three teaching labs and one research lab for biology; two teaching labs, one research lab, and an instrumentation room for chemistry; and one physics lab. The bulk of general classroom space is contained in Crawford Hall and Lewis Hall. Additional classrooms are located in Saint Edward and Saint Francis Halls as well as in the Bowman Activity Center.

All students are encouraged to utilize the University's Learning Resource Center (LRC). The LRC features study and meeting space for small groups as well as such technology as high-speed laser printers. Tutoring services are available to students and may be scheduled through the LRC.

The University's exciting new Student Community Center opened in late fall 2007; it includes substantial meeting space for groups of various sizes.

The University's campus is a wireless environment. All students who reside in campus housing receive complimentary use of an IBM ThinkPad laptop computer. For students living off campus, laptops are available for use through the library. Participants in the honors program are eligible to keep their laptops after successful completion of 60 credit hours as honors students.

Costs

For the 2008–09 school year, tuition is $16,500; freshman room and board costs are $8430, and mandatory fees are $600. Miscellaneous indirect costs for the year (such as books, personal living expenses, insurance, and travel) are estimated at $4162.

Financial Aid

Financial aid, both federally funded and awarded by the University, is available in the form of scholarships, grants, and loans. Financial aid is allocated on the basis of academic performance and need, as determined by the federal government from the financial information provided on the Free Application for Federal Student Aid (FAFSA). On-campus jobs are available for students, with priority given to students with demonstrated financial need.

Faculty

At Saint Leo University, outstanding teaching and active learning go hand in hand. Caring and capable faculty members provide students with knowledge, guidance, academic support, and a broad range of learning opportunities both in and outside the classroom. Students enjoy small classes (average class size is 19) and develop close relationships with experienced, well-qualified professors. At Saint Leo, 80 percent of full-time instructional faculty members hold the terminal degree in their field.

Student Government

A significant contribution to the University comes from the activities initiated by the Student Government Union (SGU). The SGU is an annually elected body organized and conducted in accordance with democratic procedures. This organization strives to foster leadership and loyalty among the students, to formulate recommendations for student life, and to recognize all extracurricular activities.

Admission Requirements

All candidates for admission should be, or expect to be, graduates of secondary schools accredited by a regional or state accrediting agency. Applicants should show successful progress toward graduation with a minimum of 16 academic units of course work: 4 units of English, 3 units of mathematics (algebra I and II and geometry), 3 units of social studies, 2 units of science, and 4 units of electives, preferably to include 2 units of a foreign language. All domestic applicants are required to take the SAT or the ACT examination. A letter of recommendation from the student's guidance counselor is also required. Preferred candidates are students with a GPA of B or better and an average SAT combined score (critical reading and math) of 1030 or an average ACT score of 22. The records of students who do not meet these criteria are also reviewed by the Admission Committee and considered for the Learning Enhancement for Academic Progress (LEAP) program, a preparatory program that has a summer attendance component.

Once the applicant has submitted the application with the $35 application fee, high school transcripts, test scores, and letter of recommendation, the file is reviewed and a decision is rendered. Notification is on a rolling basis. The priority application deadline is March 1, but all applicants are encouraged to apply early.

Transfer and international students are also encouraged to apply. The same general admission procedures are required, along with at least a C average for all college work (for transfer students) and a score of at least 550 (paper-based test), 213 (computer-based test), or 75 (Internet-based test) on the TOEFL (for international students for whom English is not the primary language of instruction).

Campus visits and interviews are recommended but not required. The Office of Admission is open from Monday through Friday from 8 a.m. to 5 p.m. and on select Saturdays during the academic year from 9:00 a.m. to noon. Appointments are preferred. Campus tours are available Monday through Friday at 10 a.m., 11 a.m., 2 p.m., and 3 p.m., as well as at 10 a.m. on select Saturdays during the academic year. Summer tours are available Monday through Friday at 10 a.m. and 2 p.m. only. The Office of Admission is closed on Sunday.

Application and Information

Additional information and application forms can be obtained by contacting the Office of Admission.

Martin Smith
Assistant Vice President for Undergraduate Admission
Office of Admission—MC2008
Saint Leo University
P.O. Box 6665
Saint Leo, Florida 33574-6665
Phone: 352-588-8283
800-334-5532 (toll-free)
Fax: 352-588-8257
E-mail: admission@saintleo.edu
Web site: http://www.saintleo.edu

The Saint Leo University campus.

ST. THOMAS UNIVERSITY

MIAMI, FLORIDA

The University

Founded in 1961 by the Augustinian Order of Villanova, Pennsylvania, at the invitation of the late Most Reverend Coleman F. Carroll, the Archbishop of Miami, St. Thomas University has grown from an institution with an initial enrollment of 45 students to become one of Florida's most comprehensive Catholic coeducational universities, with more than 2,600 students in all programs of study. Founded originally as Biscayne College, the institution achieved university status in 1984 and changed its name to St. Thomas University. The University is sponsored by the Archdiocese of Miami and is accredited by the Southern Association of Colleges and Schools. At present, the undergraduate student population represents thirty-five states, the District of Columbia, Puerto Rico, the Virgin Islands, and sixty-five countries. Fifty-nine percent of the undergraduates are women; 20 percent of the undergraduates reside on campus.

The University is located in northwest Miami on a 140-acre campus with fifteen major buildings. The Student Center contains a student lounge, a bookstore, the rathskeller, and other facilities. Adjacent to the University's two dormitories are the dining hall and the University Inn.

Sports facilities include six tennis courts, a recreational swimming pool, two basketball courts, four baseball fields, a soccer field, and two football fields. As a member of the NAIA, St. Thomas supports men's varsity teams in baseball, golf, soccer, and tennis and women's varsity teams in fast-pitch softball, golf, soccer, tennis, and volleyball and men's and women's cross-country. In fall 2008, St. Thomas University will move to NCAA Division II, and it has recently added both men's and women's basketball.

The University offers a full range of cultural, governmental, and social activities, including publications and clubs. The Office of Campus Ministry provides liturgical celebrations in the University chapel and sponsors social justice and community service activities.

The Office of Graduate Studies at St. Thomas University offers the Master of Business Administration (M.B.A.); Master of International Business; Master of Science (M.S.) in educational administration, guidance and counseling, management, marriage and family therapy, mental health counseling, special education, and sports administration; Master of Accounting (M.Acc.); and Master of Arts (M.A.) degrees in communication arts and pastoral ministry. In addition, St. Thomas offers a Ph.D. in practical theology and an Ed.D. in educational leadership. The Ambassador Nicholas H. Morley Law Center was established in 1984 with a charter class of 160 students. St. Thomas University School of Law offers the Juris Doctor degree (J.D.) and is the only accredited Catholic law school south of Georgetown University's law school in Washington, D.C. The School of Law and the Graduate Studies Office offer four joint degree programs, including an M.B.A./J.D. in accounting and international business and an M.S./J.D. in marriage and family counseling and sports administration.

Location

Located midway between Fort Lauderdale and downtown Miami, the University is near numerous cultural and recreational facilities. In fact, St. Thomas is located approximately 1½ miles south of Pro Player Stadium, which is home to the Miami Dolphins. The area's subtropical climate allows students to enjoy the nearby Atlantic Ocean beaches and many other natural attractions, such as the Florida Keys, Everglades National Park, and state and county parks, throughout the year. A short drive from campus are Key Biscayne, Bal Harbour, Miami Beach, Fort Lauderdale, and other cities of Florida's Gold Coast. The city of Miami and surrounding Dade County, known as the "Gateway to South America," house an international banking and trade center and offer a truly cosmopolitan atmosphere.

Majors and Degrees

St. Thomas University awards the Bachelor of Arts (B.A.) or Bachelor of Business Administration (B.B.A.) degree through day and evening programs in twenty-five major fields of study: accounting, biology, business management, communication arts, computer information systems, computer science, criminal justice, elementary education, English, environmental justice, finance, forensic science, global leadership, history, human services, international business, liberal studies, marketing, nursing (a 2+2 program with the University of Miami), pre-engineering (a 2+2 program with the Florida International University), political science, psychology, religious studies, secondary education (social studies), sports administration, and tourism and hospitality management. St. Thomas also offers a minor in environmental studies; preprofessional programs, which include dentistry, law, medicine, and veterinary studies; a joint B.A./J.D. program with the School of Law; and courses in French, humanities, Italian, philosophy, and South Florida regional studies.

Academic Programs

The University's academic calendar consists of two 15-week semesters, beginning in early September and in mid-January, along with two 6-week summer sessions.

To receive a bachelor's degree, students must complete at least 120 semester credits with a minimum grade point average of 2.0 overall and an average of at least 2.25 in their academic major; 30 of the last 36 semester credit hours must be earned and at least half of a student's academic major courses must be taken at St. Thomas University. All students must fulfill the general core education requirements of 42 semester credits, which include courses in English, humanities/foreign language, history, social science, mathematics/physical science, philosophy, and religious studies. An honors program is offered to qualified students to provide them with an interesting, stimulating, alternative way of fulfilling some or all of the University's general education requirements. The normal full-time academic load is 15 semester credit hours, but the load may range between 12 and 18 credit hours per semester. To graduate, all students must take an area of concentration or an academic major. A student may enter as an exploratory or undecided student but, with the assistance of a faculty adviser or a division chairperson, must declare his or her academic major by the second semester of the sophomore year.

Special academic features at the University include the Academic Support Center, Institute for Pastoral Ministries, summer school, and study abroad.

Off-Campus Programs

Internships are offered in nearly every academic major. A cooperative education program is also available. In addition, qualified students may participate in the Semester Abroad Program in Spain.

Academic Facilities

The 50,000-square-foot library houses a 145,000-volume book collection, 850 periodicals, a reference room, a technical processing area, a convocation hall that seats 600 people, four seminar rooms for small classes and group study, and a Media Center with two screening rooms, a video studio, and an audiovisual laboratory with individually wired carrels. Kennedy Hall, the University's main academic center, includes administrative offices, classrooms, science laboratories, the Academic Support Center, the chapel, and a computer lab.

Costs

Tuition for the 2007–08 academic year was $19,680 ($656 per undergraduate semester credit hour), and room and board costs were $6206 for a double room and $9670 for a single room. Insurance, which is mandatory for all resident students, is estimated at $1100 for the year. These costs do not include books, supplies, travel, and personal expenses and are subject to change.

Financial Aid

The University has established a financial aid program to assist as many students as possible. University scholarships and grants, along with federally funded scholarships, grants, loans, and work-study awards, are allocated in a financial aid package according to a student's financial need. Currently, about 92 percent of the University's students receive financial aid. Of all financial aid recipients, 90 percent receive University scholarships and grants. To be eligible for any scholarship or financial aid program, an applicant should complete a Free Application for Federal Student Aid (FAFSA) with the Department of Education. The filing deadline for University financial aid funds is April 1. Applicants should indicate affirmatively on the FAFSA that their information may be forwarded from the U.S. Department of Education in order to be considered for any state grants for which they may be eligible. The application deadline for need-based state financial aid programs is April 1.

Florida applicants who have resided in Florida for the prior twelve consecutive months are eligible to be awarded a Florida Resident Access Grant to attend a private four-year college or university in Florida. The funds for the Florida Resident Grant Program are dependent upon yearly appropriations from the Florida legislature. These funds are outright grants and are not based on financial need.

Faculty

The St. Thomas University faculty is a teaching faculty that is dedicated to furthering the academic and personal growth of students. The undergraduate student-faculty ratio is 14:1. Faculty-student interaction is a hallmark of the University because classes are small and because members of the faculty are available outside the classroom. Faculty members also participate in the academic advisement program to give students individual academic guidance, and they serve as advisers to student clubs and organizations.

Student Government

The Undergraduate Student Government Association, of which all full-time undergraduates are members, provides students with the opportunity to become involved in representative government. This democratic body is governed by elected student officers who serve on the Administrative Council and by representatives from each class who compose the Student Assembly. The association also assists in planning a varied program of social and cultural activities. In addition, students are represented on key committees throughout the University community. The Resident Council, consisting of representatives from each of the four dormitories, voices the concerns of residential students and is involved in the planning and implementation of University policies regarding residential life.

Admission Requirements

St. Thomas University seeks academically prepared students who are eager to improve themselves intellectually, socially, and spiritually within the University community. The Admissions Committee evaluates applicants individually in light of personal accomplishments, motivation, and the academic major selected. The committee places primary emphasis on the secondary school record, SAT or ACT scores, class rank, a personal interview, a recommended 250- to 300-word personal essay, and a teacher's or guidance counselor's recommendation. The committee does not discriminate against applicants on the basis of race, sex, religion, or national origin; in fact, the University welcomes diversity. Applicants for most divisions must have earned 16 units from an accredited high school in a college-preparatory program that included 4 years of English, 2 years of mathematics, 2 years of social studies, 1 year of science, 1 year of a foreign language or computer elective, and six electives; applicants for the Division of Science must have earned 17 units, including 3 years of mathematics (including trigonometry) and 3 years of science, but they need have only four electives. All international applicants for either freshman or transfer entrance must also submit letters of financial guarantee.

The University offers early acceptance, deferred admission, dual enrollment, and early decision. It also gives credit and advanced placement for scores of 3 or better on the Advanced Placement examinations of the College Board. Credit is also awarded for successful scores on both the general and subject tests of the College Board's College-Level Examination Program.

Transfer applicants should be in good academic standing with a GPA of at least 2.25 and not be on disciplinary or academic probation at their former college. The University grants junior-year status to any admitted transfer student graduating from a Florida community college with an Associate of Arts degree. Transfer applicants must submit official transcripts from each of their previous colleges.

Application and Information

To facilitate the admission and financial aid processes, students should submit applications during the fall or winter of their senior year in high school and have all supporting material forwarded directly to the University's Undergraduate Admissions Office. Application for entrance as a resident student for the fall semester should be filed by May 15; for entrance as a commuting student, by August 1. Application for the spring semester should be made by December 15. The University operates with a policy of rolling admissions; beginning December 15, applicants for the fall semester are notified of the admission decision within a three-week period provided that all appropriate information has been received. The University adheres to the College Board's Candidates Reply Date of May 1 and does not require a tuition deposit or a room reservation deposit until May 1 in order to allow students ample opportunity to select the college or university of their choice. Dormitory space, however, is limited and is assigned in the order that room reservation deposits are received.

For further information, students should contact:

St. Thomas University
Office of Admissions
Kennedy Hall
16401 Northwest 37th Avenue
Miami Gardens, Florida 33054
Phone: 305-628-6546
800-367-9010 (toll-free outside Florida)
800-367-9006 (toll-free in Florida)
Fax: 305-628-6591
E-mail: signup@stu.edu
Web site: http://www.stu.edu

SCHILLER INTERNATIONAL UNIVERSITY

LARGO, FLORIDA

The University

Schiller International University (SIU) was founded in 1964. Although originally intended for American students, the University soon attracted men and women from other nations and is now an international, coeducational, four-year institution with seven locations in six countries and alumni from more than 150 countries. SIU prepares students for careers in business and management, multinational organizations, government agencies, academic institutions, and the social services as well as for further study. Through enrollment in both practical and theoretical courses and through discussions with instructors and classmates with multicultural backgrounds, students gain firsthand knowledge of business and cultural relations among the peoples of the world. In addition, SIU students have the unique opportunity to transfer between SIU campuses, without losing any credits, while continuing their chosen program of study. The language of instruction at all campuses is English. The current enrollment is 1,400 students.

SIU students are housed in University residence halls, with selected host families, or in private rooms or apartments. Residence hall accommodations are available at the London and Florida campuses and in Heidelberg, Strasbourg, and Leysin. At all campuses not requiring on-campus residence, or in the event that all residence halls are full, trained staff members assist students in securing housing in the private market or with families. Many Schiller academic programs are also available by distance learning.

SIU offers the Master of Arts degree in international hotel and tourism management and the Master of Arts degree in international relations and diplomacy with an optional specialization in international business or European studies; the Master of Arts degree in communication; the Master of Business Administration degree; the Master of Business Administration degree in financial planning, hotel and tourism management, international business, international hotel and tourism management, and IT management; and the Master of International Management in international business. SIU also offers the Master of Science degree in computer engineering on the Florida campus.

Schiller International University is an accredited member of the Accrediting Council for Independent Colleges and Schools, which is recognized by the United States Department of Education as a national institutional accrediting agency. SIU degrees correspond to the American system of university education.

Location

Schiller International University has campuses in Largo (Tampa area), Florida; central London, England; Paris and Strasbourg, France; Heidelberg, Germany; Madrid, Spain; and Leysin, Switzerland.

SIU Florida (residential), the main campus, is in the city of Largo near the Gulf of Mexico in one of America's most beautiful coastal regions, near the Tampa–St. Petersburg metropolitan area. The campus facilities, two modern buildings, face directly across the street from beautiful Largo Central Park and within eyesight of a new $22-million public library and the renowned Largo Cultural Center. World-famous entertainment centers, amusement parks, and movie production centers are within easy driving distance.

SIU London—Waterloo (central London–residential) is in the magnificent Royal Waterloo House, centrally located near the Waterloo Bridge and the South Bank cultural center.

SIU Paris (nonresidential) is centrally located in a modern building on the left bank of the Seine in the exciting Montparnasse area, with easy access to all of Paris.

SIU Strasbourg (residential) occupies the Château de Pourtalès in Robertsau at the northern edge of the city. The Château offers classroom, dormitory, and dining facilities (two restaurants and a Salon de Thé) and access to the European Community's Parliament Building and Court of Justice in Strasbourg.

SIU Heidelberg (residential) is located next to the Law School of the University of Heidelberg in the center of town. The Graduate Center and student residence are located just across the Neckar River in the beautiful Palais Friedrich.

SIU Madrid (nonresidential) is located in a modern building in the Arguelles, one of the city's most attractive districts.

SIU Leysin, American College of Switzerland (residential), is a campus of SIU located above the eastern end of Lake Geneva in the French-speaking portion of Switzerland, near Geneva and the French and Italian borders.

Majors and Degrees

Schiller International University offers the Bachelor of International Business Administration (B.B.A. in international business) degree, with concentrations in banking, financial management, management, management of information technology, and marketing. Schiller also offers the Bachelor of Business Administration degree in resort/club management and in international hotel and tourism management, with concentrations in hotel management and tourism management, and the B.B.A. in club/resort management.

The Bachelor of Arts (B.A.) degree is offered in interdepartmental studies, international economics, international relations and diplomacy, and psychology. Psychology is offered in conjunction with the New School of Psychotherapy and Counseling, located on the SIU London campus.

The Bachelor of Business Administration (B.B.A.) degree is offered in economics, IT management, and international business administration.

The associate degree in business administration (A.S.) is offered in club management and with an optional concentration in computer system management.

Schiller also offers the associate degree in business administration (A.S.) in international hotel and tourism management, with concentrations in hotel management and tourism management.

Associate of Arts (A.A.) degrees are offered in general studies, with a concentration in art and design.

Diplomas are available in hotel operational management and Swiss hotel management. The hotel operational management diploma requires two semesters of on-campus study and a six-month internship.

Academic Programs

The academic emphasis at Schiller International University is on international business, international relations and diplomacy, international hotel and tourism management, information technology, and languages.

An associate degree program requires 62 credits; a bachelor's degree program requires 124 credits. An average grade of C (2.0) or higher is required for all programs. Each credit reflects 15 academic hours of classroom work; typical courses earn 3–4 credits.

Classes run during two 15-week semesters and a seven-week summer session in a manner similar to that at most universities in the United States.

Academic Facilities

Each campus includes classrooms, computer facilities, a library, and a student lounge. The University library holdings are about 92,000 volumes. In addition, students have access to millions of publications via extensive external libraries for original research.

Costs

For 2008–09, tuition and required fees at the Florida campus are $9082 per semester. Costs at the European campuses vary by campus, but are approximately $10,190 per semester for tuition and required fees. Some campuses offer room and board. Students should contact 866-748-4338 (toll-free) for details about each campus.

Financial Aid

SIU grants two kinds of financial aid: academic tuition awards and University service (work-study) grants for those who qualify. Total aid does not exceed one half of the tuition. Students are encouraged to seek assistance through private or government loan and scholarship programs before applying to the University. Eligible students may apply for a Pell Grant, Supplemental Educational Opportunity Grant, Federal Work-Study, the Federal Family Educational Loan Program, U.S. veterans' training programs (U.S. citizens or eligible noncitizens), or a Canada Student Loan (Canadian citizens only). Applications for financial aid must be received by March 31 for the following academic year.

Faculty

The faculty consists of more than 280 men and women who are academically qualified and experienced in their fields. Extensive student-faculty interaction is encouraged; the student-faculty ratio is about 16:1.

Student Government

Each campus has an elected Student Council that acts as a liaison between the students and the administration and is involved in many areas of academic and social life.

Admission Requirements

Applicants must have completed the secondary level of education in a government-recognized educational system, generally of twelve years' duration, or have the equivalent of five GCE-O-level examinations (British school system). Students who have not completed the equivalent of high school studies or five GCE-O-level examinations may be eligible to apply for special University-preparatory programs.

All nonnative English speakers must take the SIU–English Placement Test when first enrolling. Those whose English language proficiency is not adequate for University-level studies are required to take additional English language courses.

Application and Information

Applications are handled individually and without regard to race, sex, religion, national or ethnic origin, or country of citizenship. Because SIU operates on a rolling admissions system, applicants are advised of their admission status soon after all application materials (a completed application form and official transcripts of all secondary-level education and, for transfer applicants, all college-level study) and the $60 application fee have been received. For application forms or further information, students should contact the University.

Schiller International University
300 East Bay Drive
Largo, Florida 33770
Phone: 866-748-4338 (toll-free)
Fax: 727-734-0359
E-mail: admissions@schiller.edu
Web site: http://www.schiller.edu/

On the campus at Schiller International University.

SOUTH UNIVERSITY

TAMPA, FLORIDA

SouthUniversity℠

The University

Established in 1899, South University is a private academic institution dedicated to providing educational opportunities for the intellectual, social, and professional development of a diverse student population. To achieve this, South University in Tampa offers focused and balanced education at the bachelor's degree level in the areas of health sciences and nursing.

The Tampa location of South University was established in 2006. The University strives to maintain small class sizes that permit students to receive more individualized instruction and interaction with faculty and staff members. In addition, students who have work or family commitments benefit from being able to take classes on campus, online or a combination of both through South University's unique Plus+ program. This program combines both classroom and online learning to provide maximum flexibility, which allows students to organize their college education around their other commitments.

South University in Tampa has a diverse student body enrolled in both day and evening classes. Students are primarily commuters who live within 50 miles of Hillsborough County. They include men and women who have enrolled directly after completing high school, who have transferred from another college or university, or who have experience in the workforce and are pursuing an education that will prepare them to grow in their current position or will take them in a new professional direction.

In addition to classrooms and administrative offices, the campus includes a bookstore, a student lounge, a career services center, and ample parking. Students can relax and gather at a spacious atrium situated in the center of the campus building complex.

Since most students live within driving distance of the campus, the campus does not offer or operate student housing. If housing is needed, students should contact the Admissions Department.

South University is accredited by the Commission on Colleges of the Southern Association of Colleges and Schools (SACS, 1866 Southern Lane, Decatur, Georgia 30033-4097; 404-679-4501) to award associate, bachelor's, master's, and doctoral degrees. The Tampa campus specifically is licensed by the Commission for Independent Education, Florida Department of Education (325 West Gaines Street, Suite 1414, Tallahassee, Florida 32399-0400; 850-245-3200 or 888-224-6684 (toll-free)) to confer Bachelor of Science and master's degrees. In addition, the campus is approved for training military veterans and other individuals by the State of Florida Department of Veterans' Affairs, Division of Veterans' Benefits and Assistance, Bureau of State Approving for Veterans' Training.

Reserve Officer Training Leadership Programs (ROTC) are available through a cooperative agreement for Army, Navy/Marines, and Air Force ROTC candidates.

Location

South University is located in Tampa's bustling business district, near Raymond James Stadium and Al Lopez Park, comprising 126 acres of Florida's fauna and flora. The campus itself is situated in recently renovated space in the Parkside Center at Tampa Bay Park.

Majors and Degrees

The Tampa campus of South University currently awards the following four-year degrees: Bachelor of Science in health science, Bachelor of Science in Nursing, RN to B.S.N. Completion Program, and Bachelor in Business Administration. The campus is adding additional programs in 2008, and students are encouraged to check the University's Web site or contact the Admissions Office for more information.

Academic Programs

The Tampa campus of South University offers education that is designed to meet the needs and objectives of students. The curriculum combines classroom and practical educational experiences that provide students with the academic background needed to pursue the professions of their choice. In addition, faculty members strive to instill the value not only of education and professionalism but also of contribution and commitment to the advancement of community.

Each University quarter comprises eleven weeks. The bachelor's degree programs require a minimum of twelve quarters for completion. The program is offered on a year-round basis, providing students with the ability to work uninterrupted toward their degree.

Academic Facilities

In addition to classrooms and staff offices, facilities at the campus include clinical laboratories for nursing and other students, a science lab, multiple computer labs, student lounges, a library, and an atrium where students can gather or study. Clinical-skills laboratories mimic hospital and outpatient settings and are fully equipped with the latest in patient-care technology.

Costs

For information on South University's tuition and fees, prospective students should contact the campus Admissions Office.

Financial Aid

South University's Office of Student Financial Services helps qualified students secure financial assistance to complete their studies. The University participates in several student aid programs. Forms of financial aid available to qualified students through federal resources include the Federal Pell Grant Program, Federal Supplemental Educational Opportunity Grant (FSEOG) Program, Federal Work-Study Program, Federal Perkins Loan Program, Federal Stafford Student Loan Program (subsidized and unsubsidized), and Federal PLUS Loan Program. Qualified students may also apply for the Florida State Assistance Grant (FSAG), Florida Bright Futures Scholarship Program, and veterans' educational benefits. Students also are encouraged to investigate the availability of grants and scholarships through community resources.

Faculty

Faculty members at the University strive to help students develop the requisites to appreciate knowledge and understand how experiences in the classroom and laboratory relate to professional performance in the workplace. Each student is assigned a faculty adviser, who oversees the student's progress and can answer questions about academic and career concerns. Students are encouraged to discuss program-related issues with and seek academic and career advice from their faculty advisers.

Admission Requirements

To be admitted to South University, prospective students must be high school graduates or hold a GED certificate and submit an SAT or ACT score or a satisfactory score on the University-administered admissions examination. Students who wish to transfer must meet the criteria established for acceptance as a transfer student.

All applicants to South University must demonstrate English as a first language through submission of a diploma from a secondary school (or above) in which English is the official language of instruction. Applicants whose first language is not English must submit a Test of English as a Foreign Language (TOEFL) score. Applicants should contact the Admissions Office to determine other examinations/scores that are acceptable as an alternative to the TOEFL.

Applicants not meeting the testing standards for general admission may be accepted under academic support admission.

Application and Information

Applicants must complete and submit an application form, along with the general application fee, and official transcripts from all high schools and colleges attended. Faxed documents are not considered official. Applicants must also complete all tests administered by the University or submit their SAT or ACT scores to the Registrar's Office. Applications are accepted on a rolling basis and should be made as far in advance as possible.

All international (nonimmigrant) applicants to South University in Tampa must meet the same admissions standards as all other students. In addition, international applicants must have official education records prepared in English, verify sufficient funds to cover the cost of the educational program, and meet certain other immigration-mandated criteria. South University in Tampa is authorized under federal law to admit nonimmigrant students.

Admissions officers are available weekdays, Saturdays, and by appointment. An appointment for an admissions interview or tour of the campus should be made in advance. For additional information, all prospective students should contact:

Director of Admissions
South University
4401 North Himes Avenue
Tampa, Florida 33614
Phone: 813-393-3800
800-846-1472 (toll-free)
Fax: 813-393-3814
E-mail: tampa@southuniversity.edu
Web site: http://www.southuniversity.edu

South University's Tampa campus, located near Raymond James Stadium in the Parkside Center.

SOUTH UNIVERSITY

WEST PALM BEACH, FLORIDA

SouthUniversity℠

The University

Established in 1899, South University is a private academic institution dedicated to providing educational opportunities for the intellectual, social, and professional development of a diverse student population. To achieve this, South University in West Palm Beach offers focused and balanced curricula at the associate and bachelor's degree levels in the areas of business, criminal justice, graphic design, health sciences, information technology, nursing, and legal studies. The University also offers a Master of Arts degree in professional counseling, a Master of Business Administration (M.B.A.), and a Master of Business Administration in health-care administration.

The West Palm Beach location of South University was established in 1974. The University strives to maintain small class sizes that permit students to receive more individualized instruction and interaction with faculty and staff members.

South University in West Palm Beach has a diverse student body enrolled in both day and evening classes. Students are primarily commuters who live within 50 miles of Palm Beach County. They include men and women who have enrolled directly after completing high school, who have transferred from another college or university, or who have experience in the workforce and are pursuing an education that will prepare them to grow in their current role or take a new professional direction.

In addition to classrooms and administrative offices, the campus includes a bookstore, student lounge, career services center, and ample parking. Since most students live within driving distance of the campus, the campus does not offer or operate student housing. If housing is needed, students should contact the Admissions Department.

South University is accredited by the Commission on Colleges of the Southern Association of Colleges and Schools (SACS, 1866 Southern Lane, Decatur, Georgia 30033-4097; 404-679-4501) to award associate, bachelor's, master's, and doctoral degrees. The West Palm Beach campus specifically is licensed by the Commission for Independent Education, Florida Department of Education (325 West Gaines Street, Suite 1514, Tallahassee, Florida 32399-0400; 850-245-3200 or 888-224-6684 (toll-free)) to confer Bachelor of Science and master's degrees. In addition, the campus is approved for training military veterans and other individuals by the State of Florida Department of Veterans' Affairs, Division of Veterans' Benefits and Assistance, Bureau of State Approving for Veterans' Training.

Certain programs offered at the campus have earned programmatic accreditation. The Associate of Science in medical assisting degree program is accredited by the Commission on Accreditation of Allied Health Education Programs (CAAHEP, 1361 Park Street, Clearwater, Florida 33756; 727-210-2350) on recommendation of the Committee on Accreditation for Medical Assisting Education. The Associate of Science in physical therapist assisting degree program is accredited by the Commission on Accreditation in Physical Therapy Education of the American Physical Therapy Association (1111 North Fairfax Street, Alexandria, Virginia 22314; 703-684-2782). The Bachelor of Science in legal studies and Associate of Science in paralegal studies degree programs are approved by the American Bar Association (321 North Clark Street Court, Chicago, Illinois 60610; 312-988-5617). The Florida Board of Nursing has granted South University approval to accept a limited number of qualified applicants per year for admission into the nursing program.

Location

South University in West Palm Beach is centrally located near the heart of Palm Beach County. Midway between Palm Beach International Airport and heavily traveled Okeechobee Boulevard, the campus is just minutes west of both Interstate 95 and downtown West Palm Beach.

Majors and Degrees

The West Palm Beach campus of South University awards the following two-year degrees: Associate of Science in business administration, Associate of Science in graphic design, Associate of Science in information technology, Associate of Science in medical assisting, Associate of Science in paralegal studies, and Associate of Science in physical therapist assisting.

The following four-year bachelor's degrees are awarded: Bachelor of Business Administration, Bachelor of Science in criminal justice, Bachelor of Science in graphic design, Bachelor of Science in health-care management, Bachelor of Science in health science, Bachelor of Science in information technology, Bachelor of Science in legal studies, Bachelor of Science in nursing, and Bachelor of Science in psychology. A Bachelor of Science in Nursing completion program (RN to B.S.N.) for current registered nurses is also available.

Academic Programs

The West Palm Beach campus of South University offers degree programs that are designed to meet the needs and objectives of students. Each curriculum combines didactic and practical educational experiences that provide students with the academic background needed to pursue the professions of their choice. In addition, faculty members strive to instill the value not only of education and professionalism but also of contribution and commitment to the advancement of community.

Each University quarter comprises eleven weeks. Associate degree programs require a minimum of eight quarters to complete, and bachelor's degree programs require a minimum of twelve quarters for completion. Programs at the West Palm Beach campus are offered on a year-round basis, providing students with the ability to work uninterrupted toward their degrees.

Academic Facilities

The West Palm Beach campus is centrally located in three buildings on Florida's affluent Gold Coast and is convenient to downtown, shopping, and local beaches. The campus is equipped with modern computer labs and field-related medical laboratories for use by students pursuing degrees in the allied health science, medical assisting, nursing, and physical therapist assisting programs.

The West Palm Beach campus library houses a large collection that includes extensive law resources. Students may retrieve periodicals in paper or electronic form. Library-based computers provide access to several commercial online services, including Westlaw, the computerized legal research service, and the Southeastern Library Network (SOLINET). CD-ROM resources include the Grolier's Multimedia Encyclopedia and the EBSCO magazine full-text database. Internet access is available in the library.

Costs

For information on South University's tuition and fees, prospective students should contact the campus Admissions Office.

Financial Aid

South University's Office of Student Financial Services helps qualified students secure financial assistance to complete their studies. The University participates in several student aid programs. Forms of financial aid available to qualified students through federal resources include the Federal Pell Grant Program, Federal Supplemental Educational Opportunity Grant (FSEOG) Program, Federal Work-Study Program, Federal Perkins Loan Program, Federal Stafford Loan Program (subsidized and unsubsidized), and Federal PLUS Loan Program. Qualified students may also apply for the Florida State Assistance Grant (FSAG), Florida Bright Futures Scholarship Program, and veterans' educational benefits. Students also are encouraged to investigate the availability of grants and scholarships through community resources.

Faculty

The South University faculty includes individuals of high academic distinction. Of the more than 60 instructors on the West Palm Beach campus, 32 percent hold terminal degrees in their fields of expertise. In addition to teaching, faculty members strive to help students develop the requisites to appreciate knowledge and understand how experiences in the classroom and laboratory relate to professional performance in the workplace. The average student-faculty ratio is 16:1. Each student is assigned a faculty adviser, who oversees the student's progress and can answer questions about academic and career concerns. Students are encouraged to discuss program-related issues with and seek academic and career advice from their faculty advisers.

Admission Requirements

To be admitted to South University, prospective students must be high school graduates or hold a GED certificate and submit an SAT or ACT score or a satisfactory score on the University-administered admissions examination. Students who wish to transfer must meet the criteria established for acceptance as a transfer student.

All applicants to South University must demonstrate English as a first language through submission of a diploma from a secondary school (or above) in which English is the official language of instruction. Applicants whose first language is not English must submit a Test of English as a Foreign Language (TOEFL) score. Applicants should contact the Admissions Office to determine other examinations/scores that are acceptable as an alternative to the TOEFL.

Applicants not meeting the testing standards for general admission may be accepted under academic support admission. General admission to the University does not guarantee admission to the nursing program. To obtain specific entrance requirements for the nursing program, prospective students should contact the campus Admissions Office or visit the South University Web site.

Application and Information

Applicants must complete and submit an application form, along with the general application fee, and official transcripts from all high schools and colleges attended. Faxed documents are not considered official. Applicants must also complete all tests administered by the University or submit their SAT or ACT scores to the Registrar's Office. Applications are accepted on a rolling basis and should be made as far in advance as possible.

All international (nonimmigrant) applicants to South University's West Palm Beach campus must meet the same admissions standards as all other students. In addition, international applicants must have official education records prepared in English, verify sufficient funds to cover the cost of the educational program, and meet certain other immigration-mandated criteria. South University in West Palm Beach is authorized under federal law to admit nonimmigrant students.

Admissions officers are available weekdays, Saturdays, and weekends. An appointment for an admissions interview or tour of the campus should be made in advance. For additional information, all prospective students should contact:

Lisa Sgherza
Director of Admissions
South University
1760 North Congress Avenue
West Palm Beach, Florida 33409-5178
Phone: 561-697-9200
866-629-2902 (toll-free)
Fax: 516-697-9944
Web site: http://www.southuniversity.edu

South University serves the educational needs of students within and beyond Florida's West Palm Beach County.

UNIVERSITY OF CENTRAL FLORIDA

ORLANDO, FLORIDA

The University

The University of Central Florida (UCF) is a comprehensive research university with approximately 48,000 students. As one of the nation's fastest-growing universities in the Southeast and the sixth largest in the nation, UCF enrolls an academically talented and diverse student body representing all fifty states and more than 120 countries. The University offers educational and research programs that complement the regional economy, with strong components in aerospace engineering, business, education, film, health, hospitality management, nursing, and social sciences. UCF's programs in communication and the fine arts help to meet the cultural and recreational needs of a growing metropolitan area. The University also offers many graduate programs leading to master's and doctoral degrees, including a physical therapy master's program. The UCF College of Medicine is scheduled to open in the fall of 2009 and will offer the M.D. degree.

UCF is accredited by the Commission on Colleges of the Southern Association of Colleges and Schools. In addition, a number of scientific, professional, and academic bodies confer accreditation in specific disciplines and groups of disciplines. In the College of Arts and Humanities, accreditation is conferred in music by the National Association of Schools of Music. In the College of Sciences, accreditation is conferred in chemistry by the American Chemical Society. The programs of the International Association for Management Education and the College of Business Administration are accredited at the undergraduate and graduate levels by AACSB International–The Association to Advance Collegiate Schools of Business. In the College of Engineering and Computer Science, programs are accredited by the Engineering Accreditation Commission of the Accreditation Board for Engineering and Technology (ABET), Inc. Also, engineering technology programs in design, electronics, and operations engineering technology are accredited by the Technology Accreditation Commission of ABET. In the College of Health and Public Affairs, programs have been approved by the following agencies: health information management by the American Medical Record Association; cardiopulmonary sciences by the American Registry of Respiratory Therapists; speech pathology and audiology by the American Speech-Language and Hearing Association; and social work by the Council of Social Work Education. The medical records administration, medical technology, and radiologic technology programs have been accredited by the Committee on Allied Health Education and Accreditation and the National Accrediting Agency for Clinical Laboratory Services. All teacher education programs are fully accredited by the Florida State Department of Education and by the National Council for Accreditation of Teacher Education. In the College of Nursing, the program has been approved by the National League for Nursing Accrediting Commission and the Florida Board of Nursing.

UCF has established extensive partnerships with businesses and industries in the central Florida area that provide students with exceptional research and learning experiences. These partnerships bring practical learning environments to UCF students through co-op and internship programs. Joint curriculum development strategies include BE2010, which is a widely modeled business curriculum incorporating classes taught by local business and industry executives.

The on-campus and campus-affiliated housing facilities include traditional residence halls, apartment-style options, and Greek housing that accommodate approximately 10,000 students. Several thousand students live in apartments located within walking distance of the campus. Approximately 400 students live in on-campus Greek housing.

Students participate in more than 350 organizations, including special-interest clubs, multicultural associations, fraternities and sororities, honor societies, and academic and preprofessional organizations. The Offices of Student Life and Student Activities schedule a wide array of extracurricular programs, including concerts, movies, and guest speakers.

The University of Central Florida is a member of the NCAA and Conference USA. All teams compete on the NCAA Division I level. UCF's men's teams compete in intercollegiate baseball, basketball, cross-country, football, golf, soccer, and tennis. Women's teams compete in basketball, cross-country, golf, rowing, soccer, softball, tennis, track, and volleyball. Intercollegiate coed club activities include championship cheerleading, crew, and waterskiing teams. The University intramural sports program offers disc golf, flag football, floor hockey, racquetball, soccer, softball, tennis, and volleyball.

Location

The University of Central Florida is located on 1,415 acres approximately 13 miles east of downtown Orlando. Regional campuses are located in Daytona Beach, Cocoa, and South Lake.

Majors and Degrees

The University offers the degrees of Bachelor of Arts, Bachelor of Engineering Technology, Bachelor of Fine Arts, Bachelor of Science in Business Administration, Bachelor of Science in Education, Bachelor of Science Engineering, Bachelor of Science in Nursing, and Bachelor of Science in Social Sciences. These degrees are available in the colleges listed below, with majors or areas of specialization as indicated.

The College of Arts and Humanities offers degrees in art, digital media, English, film, French, history, humanities, modern language combination, music, music education, philosophy, photography, religious studies, Spanish, and theater.

The College of Business Administration offers degrees in accounting, economics, finance, general business administration, management, management information systems, marketing, and real estate. The College also offers a minor in international business.

The College of Education offers degrees in art education, early childhood education, elementary education, English language arts education, exceptional student education, foreign language education, mathematics education, physical education, science education, social science education, sports and fitness, and technical education and industry training.

The College of Engineering and Computer Science offers degrees in aerospace engineering, civil engineering, computer engineering, computer science, construction engineering, electrical engineering, electrical engineering technology, engineering technology, environmental engineering, industrial engineering, information systems technology, information technology, and mechanical engineering.

The College of Health and Public Affairs offers degrees in cardiopulmonary sciences, communication sciences and disorders, criminal justice, health information management, health sciences–athletic training, health sciences–preclinical allied health track, health services administration, legal studies, public administration, radiologic sciences, and social work.

The College of Nursing offers degrees in nursing.

The College of Sciences offers degrees in actuarial science, advertising/public relations, anthropology, biology, chemistry, forensic science, interpersonal and organizational communications, journalism, mathematics, physics, political science, psychology, radio/television, sociology, social sciences, and statistics.

The Rosen College of Hospitality Management offers degrees in event management, hospitality management, and restaurant and foodservice management.

The Burnett School of Biomedical Sciences offers degrees in biotechnology, medical laboratory sciences, and molecular biology and microbiology. Preprofessional programs are offered in chiropractic, dentistry, medicine, optometry, osteopathy, pharmacy, physical assistant studies, physical therapy, podiatry, and veterinary medicine.

A degree in interdisciplinary studies is available through the Office of Undergraduate Studies.

Academic Programs

UCF provides a total education through a core curriculum of 36 hours of general education courses. In addition to fulfilling the general education requirement, each student must complete the necessary major and/or minor requirements to reach the minimum of 120 semester hours necessary for graduation.

Several special programs help students reach their academic and leadership potential. The Burnett Honors College at UCF encourages students to achieve academic excellence through small classes and interactive symposia. The innovative Leadership Enrichment and Academic Development (LEAD) Scholars Program fosters leadership and service commitment through a comprehensive student development program for freshmen. The Academic Exploration Program (AEP) helps entering freshmen define their career goals and develop an academic strategy to reach those goals. The University also offers an increasing number of Web-based courses and degree programs.

UCF offers Air Force and Army ROTC programs.

Off-Campus Programs

Career Services and Experiential Learning offers programs in which students alternate semesters of classroom study with equal periods of paid employment in government, industry, or business. The Department of Modern Languages offers summer study-abroad programs in Canada, Eastern Europe, France, Germany, Italy, Japan, Poland, Spain, Sweden, and Russia. Courses are available in the subject areas of language (all levels), art, and civilization. UCF is also a participant in the National Student Exchange Consortium.

Academic Facilities

In addition to the academic programs offered on the Orlando campus, students can work toward a degree at campuses located in Cocoa, Daytona Beach, and South Lake. These regional campuses work cooperatively with local community colleges to provide all four years of course work in many academic areas. The library houses nearly 1.4 million volumes and subscribes to more than 10,000 periodicals and journals. In addition, students have access to an online computer catalog that provides information on the collections of the State University System libraries. An extensive online network of more than 500 computer terminals and a network of nearly 1,000 IBM PCs cover the campus. The Institute for Simulation and Training gives students the opportunity to pursue undergraduate research. The College of Optics and Photonics allows faculty members and students to work directly with industry personnel in conducting basic and applied research at the regional and national levels. The Central Florida Research Park, located adjacent to the UCF campus, houses more than ninety important high-technology firms and agencies. This proximity fosters relationships between industry and the University, which strengthens the academic programs at UCF.

Costs

For Florida residents, the cost of tuition and fees in 2007–08, based on a full-time course load, was $3677 for the year; for out-of-state residents, the cost was $17,878. Room and board were approximately $8100 per year, and costs for books and supplies were approximately $800.

Financial Aid

Financial aid is awarded according to each student's demonstrated financial need in relation to college costs and may include grants, loans, scholarships, and part-time employment. Programs based upon need include the Federal Perkins Loan, Federal Pell Grant, Florida Student Assistance Grant, Federal Work-Study, Florida College Career Work-Study Program, and Federal Stafford Student Loan. To qualify for these programs, students must complete the Free Application for Federal Student Aid (FAFSA). The priority application deadline is March 1. Approximately 70 percent of UCF students receive some form of financial assistance.

Faculty

The University's faculty consists of more than 1,200 full-time members and 462 adjunct members. More than 70 percent of the full-time faculty members hold a doctoral degree. Undergraduate instruction is given primarily by the full-time and adjunct faculty members; graduate students play a very minor role in undergraduate instruction. Students are assigned to a faculty adviser in their area of specialization for assistance in academic matters. The student-faculty ratio is 23:1.

Student Government

UCF's Student Government Association, voted the best in Florida for three out of the last four years by *Florida Leader* magazine, provides an opportunity for students to become involved at UCF. Every UCF student is encouraged to voice his or her opinion through senate representatives. Student Government is divided into three branches—the student-elected executive branch, the student-elected legislative branch, and the appointed judicial branch. Student Government is responsible for the allocation of all activity and service fees paid by students as a part of their tuition. This money goes toward student services, including the online Macintosh lab, homecoming activities, campus activities board, legal services, and funding for clubs and organizations. Admission is free to all events directly sponsored by the Student Government.

Admission Requirements

A freshman applicant is a student with fewer than 12 hours of college course work after high school graduation. The most important criteria in the admission decision for these applicants are the high school academic record, quality and level of difficulty of courses, grade point average, grade trends, and SAT or ACT test scores. UCF operates on a rolling admission basis. Students are generally notified of their admission decision within two to three weeks after receipt of the application and all supporting documents. If the number of qualified applicants exceeds the number that the University is permitted to enroll, a waiting list is established.

All applicants must have earned a minimum of 18 high school academic units (yearlong courses that are not remedial in nature). These include 4 units of English (3 must include substantial writing), 3 units of mathematics at or above algebra I, 3 units of natural science (2 must include a laboratory), 3 units of social science, 2 units of one foreign language, and 3 units of academic electives. Grades in honors, International Baccalaureate, Advanced Placement, AICE, and dual-enrollment courses are given additional weight in the GPA computation. Students must meet the Department of Education minimum eligibility to be considered for admission. Applicants should understand that the satisfaction of minimum requirements does not automatically guarantee admission to UCF.

Transfer applicants with fewer than 60 semester hours of college course work must submit official high school transcripts, SAT or ACT test scores, and all official college transcripts. Transfer students with more than 60 semester hours or who have earned an Associate in Arts degree or a statewide articulated Associate in Science degree from a Florida public community college need only to submit all official college transcripts. A transfer credit summary evaluation is provided to students once they are offered admission to UCF.

Application and Information

Students are encouraged to apply several months in advance and can apply online at http://www.admissions.ucf.edu. It is recommended that freshman students apply early during the fall semester of their senior year. Applications are accepted up to one year prior to the start of the term for which enrollment is desired. Priority application deadlines are May 1 for the fall term (July 1 for transfers), November 1 for the spring term, and March 1 for the summer term.

The Campus Visit Experience, which includes an information session and a campus tour, is offered Monday through Friday at 10 and 2 (except holidays). Students can sign up for a campus visit online at http://www.admissions.ucf.edu.

Office of Undergraduate Admissions
University of Central Florida
P.O. Box 160111
Orlando, Florida 32816-0111
Phone: 407-823-3000
E-mail: admission@mail.ucf.edu
Web site: http://www.ucf.edu

THE UNIVERSITY OF TAMPA

TAMPA, FLORIDA

The University

The University of Tampa (UT) is a private comprehensive university that offers challenging learning experiences in four colleges and the John H. Sykes College of Business. Together, they offer hundreds of courses in more than 100 fields of study. In all colleges, students work with experts in their fields, and there is a shared belief in the value of a liberal arts–centered education, practical work experience, and the ability to communicate effectively, all of which are trademarks of a University of Tampa education.

Situated on a beautiful, parklike campus on the Hillsborough River, the University is just two blocks from downtown Tampa. At the center of campus is Plant Hall, once a luxurious 511-room hotel for the rich and famous. Its ornate Victorian gingerbread and Moorish minarets, domes, and cupolas still remain a symbol of the city and one of the finest examples of Moorish architecture in the Western Hemisphere. Although Plant Hall receives most of the attention, the campus has forty-eight other buildings, including a student center, a library, modern art galleries and studios, state-of-the-art science labs, a computer resource center, a television studio, a theater, ten residence halls, and complete athletic facilities. Eighty percent of all residence hall space is new and built since 1998. Representing fifty states and more than eighty countries, 5,400 students, including 4,400 full-time undergraduates, are enrolled. All students may have cars on campus.

The environment outside the classroom is supportive, stimulating, and fun. Students choose from more than 120 student organizations, including honor societies, social clubs, fraternities, and sororities. The University of Tampa has one of the best NCAA Division II sports programs in the nation. Spartan athletes have won ten national championships, including four in baseball, three in men's soccer, and one in women's volleyball. Intercollegiate sports for men and women include basketball, cross-country, soccer, and swimming, and track. Men's baseball and golf and women's crew, softball, tennis, and volleyball are also offered.

The University is accredited by the Southern Association of Colleges and Schools (SACS). The John H. Sykes College of Business is accredited by AACSB International–The Association to Advance Collegiate Schools of Business. The music program is accredited by the National Association of Schools of Music, and all nursing programs are accredited by the National League for Nursing Accrediting Commission. In addition, the University is accredited for teacher education by the Florida State Board of Education and the athletic training program is accredited by the Joint Review Committee on Educational Programs in Athletic Training of the Commission on Accreditation of Allied Health Education Programs (CAAHEP).

On the graduate level, the University offers the Master of Arts in Teaching (M.A.T.), Master of Education (M.Ed.), Master of Business Administration (M.B.A.), Master of Science (M.S.) in accounting, Master of Science in Finance (M.S.F.), Master of Science in Innovation Management (M.S.I.M.), Master of Science in Marketing (M.S.M.), and Master of Science in Nursing (M.S.N.).

Location

There is much more to Tampa's location than beautiful beaches and pleasant year-round temperatures. Home to 2.3 million people, Tampa Bay is one of the fastest-growing areas in the United States. The city is the commercial and cultural center of Florida's west coast. Students attend concerts, art exhibitions, theater productions, dance performances, and special lectures on campus and nearby. Just across the river are the Museum of Art, the St. Pete Times Forum, the Performing Arts Center, the Convention Center, the Aquarium, and a public library. Busch Gardens is just a few miles from campus. Within 1 hour are Disney World and Universal Studios in Orlando. Tampa International Airport, which is just 15 minutes from campus, conveniently connects students with every major city in the United States and around the globe.

Majors and Degrees

The University of Tampa offers bachelor's degrees in accounting, advertising and public relations, art, athletic training, biochemistry, biology, chemistry, communication, criminology, digital arts, economics, education, electronic media and arts technology, English, entrepreneurship, environmental science, exercise science and sport studies, film and media arts, finance, financial services and operations, forensic science, government and world affairs, graphic design, history, international business, international and cultural studies, liberal studies, management, management information systems, marine science (biology and chemistry), marketing, mathematical programming, mathematics, music, nursing, performing arts, philosophy, psychology, social sciences, sociology, Spanish, sport management, theater, and writing.

Certificate programs include early childhood education, European studies, French, German, gerontology, Italian, Latin American studies, and Spanish.

Preprofessional programs include allied health, art therapy, dentistry, law, medicine, and veterinary science.

Minors and concentrations are offered in accounting, advertising, adult fitness, aerospace studies, applied dance, arts administration and management, art history, business administration, chemistry, criminology, dance/theater, economics, English, entrepreneurship, environmental science, exercise science and sports studies, finance, French, government and world affairs, history, humanities, international studies, law and justice, management information systems, marketing, military science, molecular biology, music, philosophy, physical education, psychology, recreation, sociology, theater and speech, Spanish, urban studies, women's studies, and writing.

Academic Programs

The curriculum is designed to give students a broad academic and cultural background as well as concentrated study in a major. Hundreds of internships are available in many areas of study. The baccalaureate experience begins with a special freshman seminar program designed to help students assess their skills and research their interests. Students participate in a special Gateways orientation program during the freshman year. During the first two years, students pursue an integrated core program of thirteen courses consisting of two in English, one in math, one in computer science, two in natural sciences, three in social science, and three in humanities. Prior to graduation, students are also required to take three writing-intensive courses, one course that deals with non-Western/Third World concerns, an international/global awareness course, and an aesthetics course.

Transfer students who have an associate degree may be given full junior status. Students receive advanced placement by earning acceptable scores on Advanced Placement exams, the College-

Level Examination Program (CLEP) tests, or by completing the International Baccalaureate Diploma. As much as one year's credit may be awarded.

For qualifying students, the University offers an honors program of expanded instruction and student research. The program features honors classes, honors floors in residence halls, a senior thesis, and study in London or at Oxford University.

From basic tutoring to graduate school placement test practice, the Academic Center for Excellence helps students stay on track academically. The center is one of the few facilities internationally certified by the College Reading and Learning Association. The Saunders Writing Center also offers free tutorial assistance to students working on writing projects. Other academic support offices include the Academic Advising and Career Services Offices.

Army, Navy, and Air Force ROTC programs are offered.

Off-Campus Programs

One-year study-abroad programs are available during the sophomore and junior years. Programs of shorter duration are also offered such as the Oxford Program in England; the Washington Center in Washington, D.C.; and the Model United Nations Program in Cambridge, Massachusetts.

Academic Facilities

The University has recently undertaken $200 million in construction and technology improvements. These include six new residence halls, a new student center, and the John H. Sykes College of Business building. A high-speed computer network connects the entire campus, and many areas are wireless. Every student has free access to the Internet and e-mail, either from their residence hall room or from one of the convenient computer labs located on campus.

The library is computerized and well equipped to meet the diversified needs of the students. It is also a depository for United States and state government publications.

The University has a fully equipped marine science research center and three boats located on Tampa Bay, which is near the Gulf of Mexico and numerous freshwater lakes, rivers, and cypress swamps. Other facilities include the Ferman Music Center, the Jaeb Computer Center, the R. K. Bailey art studios, and Falk Theatre. There are also a public-access cable television station and a radio station on campus.

Costs

The total estimated cost for the 2007–08 academic year, excluding summer sessions, is $28,298. This figure includes tuition, fees, and average room and board costs of $7616.

Financial Aid

A high-quality, private education at the University of Tampa is not as difficult to finance as students may think. Each family's situation is evaluated individually for need-based assistance. Academic achievements, leadership potential, athletic skills, and other special talents are recognized, regardless of need. ROTC scholarships are also available. The Free Application for Federal Student Aid (FAFSA) is required to determine eligibility for need-based funds. Early estimates of aid are available October through January.

Faculty

UT faculty members hold degrees from the most prestigious universities. Ninety-four percent have Ph.D.'s, and many are Fulbright Scholars and recipients of teaching awards. All classes are taught by professors, not by graduate assistants. Faculty members prize the relationships they are able to cultivate with students in classes where enrollment averages 21. The student-faculty ratio is 17:1. Faculty members also pursue scores of research projects each year, often with students as assistants. The College of Business provides cutting-edge opportunities for practical experience through its Strategic Analysis Program.

Student Government

Student Government is the principal avenue for student participation in campus governance. It also provides leadership and serves as the major coordinating body for more than 120 recognized student organizations, interest groups, fraternities and sororities, residence halls, and student productions.

Admission Requirements

Eighteen high school units are required from the following areas: 4 units in English, 3 units in college-preparatory mathematics, 3 units in science (at least two lab courses), 3 units in social studies, 2 units in foreign language, and 4 units of academic electives. The results of the SAT or the ACT are required. A personal essay and at least one recommendation from a high school counselor are requested.

Early admission may be granted to students who have completed 16 academic units by the end of their junior year and who have a minimum 3.2 average (on a 4.0 scale), good SAT or ACT scores, and their counselor's or principal's recommendation. Transfer students should have an overall 2.8 average or better (on a 4.0 scale) for college or university work attempted.

All international students for whom English is not a native or first language should take the Test of English as a Foreign Language (TOEFL). A minimum score of 550 (PBT) is required (213 CBT or 79–80 iBT).

Application and Information

The University requires a $40 application fee. For more information or to apply online, students may contact:

Office of Admissions
The University of Tampa
401 West Kennedy Boulevard
Tampa, Florida 33606-1490
Phone: 813-253-6211
888-MINARET (toll-free)
Fax: 813-254-4955
E-mail: admissions@ut.edu
Web site: http://www.ut.edu

The University of Tampa's Plant Hall was once a luxury hotel.

COLLEGE DATA CENTER • FLORIDA

UNIVERSITY OF WEST FLORIDA

PENSACOLA, FLORIDA

The University

One of the eleven state universities of Florida, the University of West Florida (UWF) enrolls approximately 10,360 students in its Colleges of Arts and Sciences, Business, and Professional Studies. The University of West Florida, which opened in fall 1967, is located on a 1,600-acre nature preserve 10 miles north of downtown Pensacola. The University's facilities, which are valued at more than $81 million, have been designed to complement the natural beauty of the site.

The University currently enrolls students from forty-nine states and ninety-one countries. Students and professors enjoy a relationship that is more common at a small, private college. Approximately 1,035 freshmen began their studies at UWF last year. The middle 50 percent statistics for the class are as follows: high school grade point average ranged from 3.1 to 4.0; SAT total score ranged from 980 to 1150; and ACT composite ranged from 21 to 25.

In addition to its undergraduate programs, UWF also offers the master's degree in twenty-five areas of study and specialist and Ed.D. degrees in education.

UWF operates centers in downtown Pensacola and at Eglin Air Force Base and a branch campus in Fort Walton Beach (in conjunction with a local community college). In addition, UWF owns 152 acres of beachfront property on nearby Santa Rosa Island, adjacent to the Gulf Islands National Seashore. Available for both recreation and research, this property provides special opportunities for students pursuing degrees in marine biology, maritime studies, and coastal zone studies.

The University of West Florida is a member of the NCAA Division II. Men's sports include baseball, basketball, cross-country, golf, soccer, tennis, and track. Women's sports include basketball, cross-country, golf, soccer, softball, tennis, track, and volleyball. Students also participate in more than nineteen intramural sports and twenty club sports. The Program Council and the Residence Hall Advisory Council provide activities and events that are open to the entire campus community. UWF hosts fifteen national sororities and fraternities; 136 professional, academic, and religious organizations are open to UWF students.

A natatorium housing an Olympic-size pool adjoins the Health, Leisure, Exercise, and Sports Facility, which is the center for indoor sports and large-group activities and events. Soccer fields, tennis courts, handball and racquetball courts, jogging trails, picnic areas, and sites for canoeing are available on campus. Baseball and softball fields and a lighted track complete the UWF sports complex. Sailing and waterskiing facilities are nearby, and campus nature trails attract thousands of visitors annually.

Students may choose to live on or off campus. The Office of Housing oversees 1,450 total residence hall spaces that include low-rise residence halls, two- or four-bedroom residence hall apartments that are equipped with modern conveniences, and three new residence halls, one with 300 spaces and the other two with 200 spaces.

There are also various apartment complexes conveniently located just beyond the campus.

Location

Students and visitors alike delight in the beauty of the campus, which is nestled in the rolling hills outside Pensacola, Florida. Wide verandas, massive moss-draped oaks, and spacious lawns capture the traditional charm and grace of the South, while modern architecture and state-of-the-art facilities blend in naturally among loblolly pines and meandering walkways.

Only minutes from the campus gate are the emerald waters and white beaches of the Gulf of Mexico and the Gulf Islands National Seashore, one of the nation's most beautiful beaches. The Pensacola area attracts vacationers from all around the country to its historic Seville Square, golf tournaments, sailing regattas, restaurants on the bay, and a variety of art and music festivals. WUWF, the University's public radio station, produces a monthly live program, Gulf Coast RadioLive. UWF is 3 hours from New Orleans, 1 hour from Mobile, 3 hours from Tallahassee, and 5 hours from Atlanta.

Majors and Degrees

The University of West Florida awards the bachelor's degree in forty-nine undergraduate programs with many areas of specialization. Undergraduate majors are available in the College of Arts and Sciences in anthropology, art, biology, chemistry, clinical laboratory sciences, communication arts, computer engineering, computer science, electrical engineering, English, environmental studies, fine arts, health sciences, history, interdisciplinary humanities, interdisciplinary information technology, interdisciplinary science, interdisciplinary social sciences, international studies, marine biology, maritime studies, mathematics, music, nursing, oceanography, philosophy, physics, preprofessional studies (dental, medical, pharmacy, veterinarian), political science, psychology, religious studies, studio art, and theater.

Undergraduate majors in the College of Business include accounting, economics, finance, management, management information systems, and marketing. The College of Business is accredited by AACSB International—The Association to Advance Collegiate Schools of Business.

The College of Professional Studies, which includes education programs that are accredited by the National Council for Accreditation of Teacher Education (NCATE), offers professional training and majors leading to bachelor's degrees in the following areas: career and technical studies; community health education; criminal justice; elementary education; engineering technology; exceptional student education; health, leisure, and exercise science; hospitality, recreation, and resort management; legal studies; middle school education; prekindergarten/primary education; prelaw; and social work. There are specialist programs in educational leadership and in curriculum and instruction and a doctoral program in curriculum and instruction.

Academic Programs

A general curriculum is required for entering freshmen and for transfer students without an Associate in Arts degree from a Florida public community college. General studies provide students with a broad foundation in the liberal arts, science, and career and life planning. The academic skills of reading, writing, discourse, critical inquiry, logical thinking, and mathematical reasoning are central elements of the general studies curriculum.

Students of high ability may enter an honors program offering intensive instruction in a more individualized setting. Cooperative education programs are available in nearly every field, allowing UWF students to get a head start on their careers while paying for their education. Army and Air Force ROTC programs and scholarships are also available.

Off-Campus Programs

The Office of International Education and Programs arranges more than twenty study-abroad and student exchange programs on every continent except Antarctica. Participants may study in Australia, Austria, Belgium, Canada, China, Costa Rica, England, Finland, France, Germany, Japan, Mexico, the Netherlands, Portugal, Spain, Switzerland, and Taiwan.

Academic Facilities

The main campus consists of more than 100 buildings. One of the most prominent of these is the five-floor John C. Pace Library, which houses a collection of more than 2.3 million bound volumes and micropieces. Interconnected through computer linkages with state and national libraries for research purposes, the UWF library contains one of the finest special collections about the Gulf Coast area. Some of the items in this collection date back to the fourteenth century, and there are also a manuscript letter signed by Thomas Jefferson, books autographed by Albert Einstein, and materials carried aboard the space shuttle by UWF alumni.

Excellent science and technology laboratories for preprofessional majors, extensive video and film equipment, desktop publishing labs, an AP wire service, and computer science facility also support students' scholarly endeavors. Microcomputers, minicomputers, a diverse inventory of software, a real-time laboratory, modem linkages to residence halls, and 24-hour-a-day access to the computer center all are available to students in every field of study. Other major facilities include a Center for Fine and Performing Arts; a College of Professional Studies Complex; a Student Services Complex; a Health, Leisure, Exercise, and Sports Facility; and a Commons.

Expansion and renovation continue to enhance the main campus. The Commons feature a bookstore, post office, and snack bar. An archaeology building and museum opened in 1999.

Costs

For fall 2007, tuition was $111.71 per credit for Florida residents and $541.10 per credit for out-of-state students. Legal residents of Alabama can qualify for the Alabama Tuition Differential Program, which has a tuition rate that is only slightly higher than the in-state rate. Room and board total $6600, and the cost of books and supplies is estimated at $1000. Transportation and personal expenses vary according to students' individual needs.

Financial Aid

About 65 percent of UWF students receive some form of financial aid and scholarships. UWF is committed to meeting a student's financial need. Aid is awarded on a first-come, first-served basis.

The Scholarship Program for outstanding freshmen allows students to receive early scholarship commitments as soon as they have decided to enroll in UWF. The John C. Pace Jr. scholarships are awarded to meritorious freshmen and transfers with A.A. degrees from Florida's community colleges. Awards are between $1000 and $5000 per year. Special scholarships for students with talent in the arts are awarded. Non-Florida tuition grants that reduce the amount of out-of-state fees are awarded to outstanding freshman and transfer students.

Faculty

Faculty members at the University of West Florida include published authors, scientists engaged in a wide range of research projects, and journalists who are skilled in advertising and filmmaking. Eighty-five percent of the faculty members hold doctoral degrees from major institutions throughout the United States.

Student Government

The Student Government Association is authorized to represent the student body in all matters concerning student life. The basic purposes of the student government are to provide students with an opportunity to participate in the decision-making process of the University; to review, evaluate, and allocate all student activity and service fee monies as allowed by state law (annually, some $1 million is allocated by students); to consider and make recommendations on all phases of student life; and to serve as the principal forum for discussion of matters of broad concern to the students.

Admission Requirements

The University of West Florida admits freshman applicants based on high school GPA, completion of college-preparatory courses, and test scores (either the ACT or the SAT is accepted). Special consideration is given to applicants with special talents. College-preparatory courses should include 4 years of English; 3 each of math (algebra 1 and higher), social science, and natural science; 2 of the same foreign language; and 4 academic electives.

Transfer applicants with fewer than 60 hours are required to submit SAT or ACT test scores and official transcripts from both the college(s) and the high school attended. Students transferring with 60 hours or more must submit their college transcript(s) only.

Application and Information

Students are encouraged to apply early in order to allow time for receipt of transcripts and to receive full consideration for financial aid, scholarships, and housing. Admissions decisions are made on a rolling basis. The University encourages visits to its beautiful campus and offers riding tours Monday through Friday at 10 a.m. and 1 p.m. Central Standard Time. Among the available features on the University's Web site (http://www.uwf.edu) are the catalog, Saturday Open House dates, applications for admission, and the course guide for the current term. The Lighthouse Information System allows applicants to view their admission and financial aid status via the Internet.

Additional information and application materials may be obtained by writing or calling:

Office of Admissions
University of West Florida
11000 University Parkway
Pensacola, Florida 32514-5750
Phone: 850-474-2230
800-263-1074 (toll-free)
E-mail: admissions@uwf.edu
Web site: http://uwf.edu

The UWF Sailing Club goes out for a day of sun and recreation on Pensacola Bay.

COLLEGE DATA CENTER • FLORIDA

WEBBER INTERNATIONAL UNIVERSITY

BABSON PARK, FLORIDA

The University

Webber International University was founded in 1927 by Roger Babson, who was an internationally known economist in the early 1900s. The four-year independent coeducational university is located on a beautiful 110-acre campus along the shoreline of Lake Caloosa, 45 minutes from Disney World, Cypress Gardens, and many other attractions. Webber is accredited by the Southern Association of Colleges and Schools. Built on a strong tradition that sets it apart, the University exemplifies integrity, high standards, and achievement. Webber International University provides an environment that encourages success through academic excellence and hard work. About 319 men and 200 women are enrolled as undergraduates at Webber. Seventy-nine percent are from Florida; the other 21 percent represent nineteen states and thirty-three different countries.

Webber International University's off-campus internship programs provide a real-world business environment for Webber students. Field trips also supplement students' business education.

Webber International University also offers a Master of Business Administration (M.B.A.) program with options in management, accounting, and sport management.

The University offers intercollegiate sports in baseball, basketball, cross-country, football, golf, soccer, tennis, and track and field for men and in basketball, cheerleading, cross-country, golf, soccer, softball, tennis, track and field, and volleyball for women. Intramural athletics are also available for all students. The University's physical education complex includes two gymnasiums, a fitness room, racquetball courts, a soccer field, a junior Olympic-size swimming pool, beach volleyball court, and tennis courts. Webber students also enjoy lakeside activities such as beach volleyball, canoeing, fishing, and kayaking. Among the wide variety of social organizations and clubs are Phi Beta Lambda, a student government association, an international club, Webber ambassadors, Eta Sigma Delta and the Society of Hosteurs, a marketing club, a tourism society, FCA, a sport management club, SIFE, and athletic boosters. These groups and others help to sponsor the various social functions at Webber. The University also offers a Bachelor of Science degree in general business studies.

Location

The town of Babson Park, a very small rural residential community, is located in the heart of Florida's citrus country near a chain of freshwater lakes. The area has a relaxed and friendly atmosphere. Babson Park is conveniently near many major recreational facilities and national tourist attractions in central Florida.

Majors and Degrees

Webber International University offers bachelor's and associate degrees in business administration, with nine different majors: accounting, computer information systems management, finance, hospitality and tourism management, management, marketing, pre-law, and sport management. The University also offers a Bachelor of Science degree in general business studies.

Academic Programs

The school operates on the semester system with two 15-week semesters, a six-week Summer Term A, and a six-week Summer Term B. The University requires the completion of 60 credit hours for the Associate of Science degree and 120 credit hours for the Bachelor of Science degree with a minimum grade point average of 2.0. The average course load is 15 hours per semester. Students in the Bachelor of Science degree program are required to complete approximately 30 hours in the major, 36 hours in the business core, 36 hours in the general education core, and 18 hours of tailored electives. Students in the Associate of Science degree program are required to complete 27 hours in the business core, 18 hours in the general education core, and 15 hours in the major and tailored elective.

The Bachelor of Science degree in general business studies requires the completion of 45 hours in the general business studies core, 39 hours in the general education core, and 36 hours of tailored electives.

All students must complete 30 of the last 33 hours at Webber International University to receive a degree. Credit is awarded for successful scores on Advanced Placement (AP) and College-Level Examination Program (CLEP) general tests.

Off-Campus Programs

The hospitality and marketing departments have arrangements for internship programs with major hotels and restaurants in the Orlando area and major retail stores, both in-state and out-of-state.

The finance department places student interns in various financial institutions and financial departments of local corporations.

Other off-campus experiences include elective courses in which students observe and analyze business operations and functions of local companies and present their findings in a project format comparable to a professional business consultant's.

The departmental field trip is an opportunity for students in all ten majors to travel abroad during a summer semester and to discover business techniques in an international environment.

Academic Facilities

The Roger Babson Learning Center, located in the central part of the campus, is a modern and comprehensive business library facility. The collection currently contains about 33,500 volumes, an assortment of audiovisual materials, and a CD-ROM computer program for reference materials. The library houses computers for student use. Several research databases are available for student access.

The computer resources centers are data processing centers and teaching facilities whose microcomputers offer the latest modern technology for developing student excellence in business, communication, and creativity.

Costs

In 2007–08, the annual fee, which includes tuition, room and board, and the student activities fee, was $24,050. For commuting students, the annual fee was $16,760. These figures were subject to change. The University estimates that $1400 is adequate for books and supplies. Laboratory fees are additional.

Financial Aid

The Student Financial Aid Department offers students its counsel and assistance in meeting their educational expenses. Aid is awarded on the basis of an applicant's need, academic performance, and promise. Approximately 80 percent of the students at Webber International University receive financial assistance. To demonstrate need, applicants are required to file the Free Application for Federal Student Aid (FAFSA). Various types of aid, such as scholarships, grants, loans, and Federal Work-Study awards, are used to meet student needs. A limited number of no-need scholarships are available; these awards are based on academic performance, on community and college service, or on athletic ability in basketball, tennis, volleyball, golf, soccer, softball, cross-country, and track and field. Applicants for aid must reapply each year. Webber participates in the Federal Perkins Loan, Federal Supplemental Educational Opportunity Grant, and Federal Work-Study programs. All applicants are expected to apply for any entitlement grant for which they are eligible, such as the Federal Pell Grant; Florida residents must apply for a Florida Student Assistance Grant and the Florida Tuition Voucher Program. Federal Stafford Student Loans are also available. Financial aid applicants should submit their requests and forms before April 1 in order to be eligible for certain financial aid programs.

Faculty

More than 70 percent of Webber's full-time faculty members hold doctoral degrees. The faculty-student ratio is 1:22, and all students are assigned a faculty adviser. All faculty members have posted office hours and are available for consultation and advising. Many of Webber's faculty members have a minimum of five years' actual professional work experience in their area of specialization in addition to their years of classroom teaching. This combination of applied and classroom work experience gives them an unusual ability to relate to the needs and concerns of their students.

Student Government

The Student Government Association, the chief governing body on Webber's campus, is composed of elected student representatives and a faculty adviser and deals with nonacademic areas of student life. The association serves as an advisory and coordinating body for student organizations and involves students in campus policy and actions. Representatives from various student organizations serve on the Student Government Association, as do members elected from the University community.

Admission Requirements

Applicants must have graduated from high school with a recommended minimum of 4 years of English and 2 to 3 years of mathematics and preparation in seven other academic subjects. Most accepted candidates rank in the top 50 percent of their high school class. Scores on the SAT or ACT are required for admission. International applicants must submit scores on the Test of English as a Foreign Language (TOEFL).

Early admission is possible for promising high school juniors who have test scores near the top 15th percentile statewide or nationally, a minimum 3.0 grade point average (on a 4.0 scale), a strong recommendation from their counselor or principal, and a letter of permission from their parents or guardian. A campus interview with the Dean of Student Development is required.

Applications from transfer students are welcome, as are those from students resuming their education or adult students who have delayed their entrance to college. Transfer students must be in good standing at their former institution.

Applicants who fail to meet regular admission requirements may be considered on an individual basis for the Fresh Start program by the Fresh Start admissions committee. An interview is required for all Fresh Start applicants.

Application and Information

An application is ready for consideration by the Admissions Committee when it has been received with a $35 application fee for domestic students and $75 for international students, the required test scores and references, and transcripts from each school attended. The University uses a system of rolling admissions. It is recommended that applications be submitted as early as possible, since on-campus housing is limited. Freshmen are required to live in the dormitory unless they reside with a parent, guardian, or spouse.

For application forms, catalogs, and additional information, students should contact:

Webber International University
1201 North Scenic Highway
P.O. Box 96
Babson Park, Florida 33827-9990
Phone: 863-638-2910
E-mail: admissions@webber.edu
Web site: http://www.webber.edu

Webber's private beach and pier.

GEORGIA

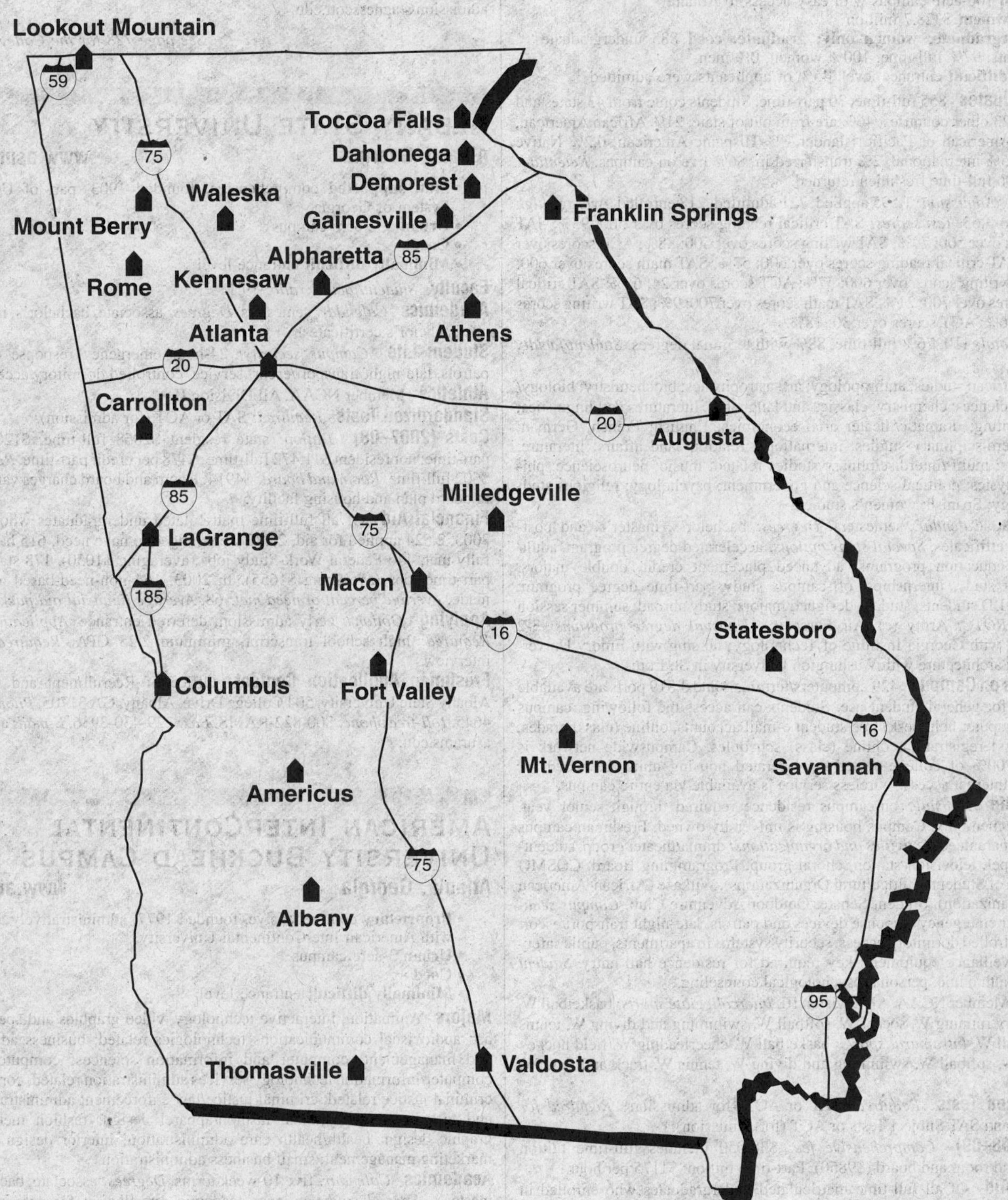

The Atlanta area includes the towns of Decatur, East Point, Lithonia, Marietta, and Morrow.

AGNES SCOTT COLLEGE

Decatur, Georgia **www.agnesscott.edu/**

- **Independent** comprehensive, founded 1889, affiliated with Presbyterian Church (U.S.A.)
- **Urban** 100-acre campus with easy access to Atlanta
- **Endowment** $328.7 million
- **Undergraduate: women only; graduate: coed** 885 undergraduate students, 97% full-time, 100% women, 0% men
- **Very difficult** entrance level, 45% of applicants were admitted

Undergraduates 855 full-time, 30 part-time. Students come from 43 states and territories, 23 other countries, 46% are from out of state, 21% African American, 5% Asian American or Pacific Islander, 4% Hispanic American, 0.2% Native American, 5% international, 2% transferred in, 86% live on campus. *Retention:* 80% of 2006 full-time freshmen returned.

Freshmen *Admission:* 1,595 applied, 721 admitted, 218 enrolled. *Average high school GPA:* 3.65. *Test scores:* SAT critical reading scores over 500: 93%; SAT math scores over 500: 79%; SAT writing scores over 500: 88%; ACT scores over 18: 98%; SAT critical reading scores over 600: 57%; SAT math scores over 600: 33%; SAT writing scores over 600: 57%; ACT scores over 24: 66%; SAT critical reading scores over 700: 21%; SAT math scores over 700: 9%; SAT writing scores over 700: 16%; ACT scores over 30: 18%.

Faculty *Total:* 110, 76% full-time, 88% with terminal degrees. *Student/faculty ratio:* 9:1.

Majors African studies; anthropology; art; astrophysics; biochemistry; biology/biological sciences; chemistry; classics and languages, literatures and linguistics; creative writing; dramatic/theater arts; economics; English; French; German; history; interdisciplinary studies; international relations and affairs; literature; mathematics; multi-/interdisciplinary studies related; music; neuroscience; philosophy; physics; political science and government; psychology; religious studies; sociology; Spanish; women's studies.

Academics *Calendar:* semesters. *Degrees:* bachelor's, master's, and postbachelor's certificates. *Special study options:* accelerated degree program, adult/continuing education programs, advanced placement credit, double majors, independent study, internships, off-campus study, part-time degree program, services for LD students, student-designed majors, study abroad, summer session for credit. *ROTC:* Army (c), Air Force (c). *Unusual degree programs:* 3-2 engineering with Georgia Institute of Technology; nursing with Emory University; art and architecture with Washington University in St. Louis.

Computers on Campus 429 computers/terminals and 3,819 ports are available on campus for general student use. Students can access the following: campus intranet, computer help desk, free student e-mail accounts, online (class) grades, online (class) registration, online (class) schedules. Campuswide network is available. 100% of college-owned or -operated housing units are wired for high-speed Internet access. Wireless service is available via entire campus.

Student Life *Housing:* on-campus residence required through senior year. *Options:* women-only. Campus housing is university owned. Freshman campus housing is guaranteed. *Activities and organizations:* drama/theater group, student-run newspaper, television station, choral group, Programming Board, COSMO (Committee of Student Multicultural Organizations), Witkaze (African-American Student organization), Student Senate, Outdoor Adventure Club. *Campus security:* 24-hour emergency response devices and patrols, late-night transport/escort service, controlled dormitory access, security systems in apartments, public safety facility, surveillance equipment, key required for residence hall entry. *Student services:* health clinic, personal/psychological counseling.

Athletics Member NCAA. All Division III. *Intercollegiate sports:* basketball W, cross-country running W, soccer W, softball W, swimming and diving W, tennis W, volleyball W. *Intramural sports:* basketball W, cheerleading W, field hockey W, soccer W, softball W, swimming and diving W, tennis W, track and field W, volleyball W.

Standardized Tests *Required:* SAT or ACT (for admission). *Required for some:* SAT and SAT Subject Tests or ACT (for admission).

Costs (2008–09) *Comprehensive fee:* $38,050 includes full-time tuition ($28,200) and room and board ($9850). Part-time tuition: $1175 per hour.

Financial Aid Of all full-time matriculated undergraduates who enrolled in 2007, 639 applied for aid, 573 were judged to have need, 446 had their need fully met. 370 Federal Work-Study jobs (averaging $1965). 140 state and other part-time jobs (averaging $1907). In 2007, 229 non-need-based awards were made. *Average percent of need met:* 97%. *Average financial aid package:* $28,138. *Average need-based loan:* $4277. *Average need-based gift aid:* $20,970. *Average non-need-based aid:* $14,352. *Average indebtedness upon graduation:* $24,070. *Financial aid deadline:* 5/1.

Applying *Options:* electronic application, early admission, early decision, deferred entrance. *Application fee:* $35. *Required:* essay or personal statement, high school transcript, 2 letters of recommendation. *Recommended:* minimum 3.0 GPA, interview. *Application deadlines:* 3/1 (freshmen), 3/1 (transfers). *Early decision deadline:* 11/15. *Notification:* continuous until 5/1 (freshmen), continuous (transfers), 12/15 (early decision).

Freshman Application Contact Ms. Stephanie Balmer, Dean of Admission, Agnes Scott College, 141 East College Avenue, Decatur, GA 30030-3797. *Phone:* 404-471-6285. *Toll-free phone:* 800-868-8602. *Fax:* 404-471-6414. *E-mail:* admission@agnesscott.edu.

See page 728 for the College Close-Up.

ALBANY STATE UNIVERSITY

Albany, Georgia **www.asurams.edu/**

- **State-supported** comprehensive, founded 1903, part of University System of Georgia
- **Urban** 232-acre campus
- **Coed**
- **Minimally difficult** entrance level

Faculty *Student/faculty ratio:* 19:1.

Academics *Calendar:* semesters. *Degrees:* associate, bachelor's, master's, and postbachelor's certificates.

Student Life *Campus security:* 24-hour emergency response devices and patrols, late-night transport/escort service, controlled dormitory access.

Athletics Member NCAA. All Division II.

Standardized Tests *Required:* SAT or ACT (for admission).

Costs (2007–08) *Tuition:* state resident $2868 full-time, $120 per credit part-time; nonresident $11,472 full-time, $478 per credit part-time. *Required fees:* $602 full-time. *Room and board:* $4914. Room and board charges vary according to board plan and housing facility.

Financial Aid Of all full-time matriculated undergraduates who enrolled in 2003, 2,524 applied for aid, 2,182 were judged to have need, 615 had their need fully met. 440 Federal Work-Study jobs (averaging $1050). 178 state and other part-time jobs (averaging $1655). In 2003, 164 non-need-based awards were made. *Average percent of need met:* 68. *Average financial aid package:* $7057.

Applying *Options:* early admission, deferred entrance. *Application fee:* $20. *Required:* high school transcript, minimum 2.25 GPA. *Required for some:* interview.

Freshman Application Contact Office of Recruitment and Admissions, Albany State University, 504 College Drive, Albany, GA 31705. *Phone:* 229-430-4645. *Toll-free phone:* 800-822-RAMS. *Fax:* 229-430-3936. *E-mail:* admissions@asurams.edu.

AMERICAN INTERCONTINENTAL UNIVERSITY BUCKHEAD CAMPUS

Atlanta, Georgia **www.aiuniv.edu/**

- **Proprietary** comprehensive, founded 1977, administratively affiliated with American InterContinental University
- **Urban** 3-acre campus
- **Coed**
- **Minimally difficult** entrance level

Majors Animation, interactive technology, video graphics and special effects; art; audiovisual communications technologies related; business administration and management; computer and information sciences; computer graphics; computer/information technology services administration related; corrections and criminal justice related; criminal justice/law enforcement administration; design and visual communications; fashion/apparel design; fashion merchandising; graphic design; health/health care administration; interior design; marketing/marketing management; small business administration.

Academics *Calendar:* five 10-week terms. *Degrees:* associate, bachelor's, and master's. *Special study options:* academic remediation for entering students, accelerated degree program, adult/continuing education programs, advanced placement credit, cooperative education, distance learning, double majors, independent study, internships, part-time degree program, study abroad, summer session for credit.

Student Life *Campus security:* 24-hour patrols.

Costs (2008–09) *Tuition:* contact campus for information. See: www.aiuniv.edu.

Financial Aid *Average financial aid package:* $6850.

Applying *Options:* electronic application, deferred entrance. *Application fee:* $50. *Required:* essay or personal statement, high school transcript, interview.

Application deadlines: rolling (freshmen), rolling (transfers). *Notification:* continuous (freshmen), continuous (transfers).

Freshman Application Contact John Payton, Senior Director of Admissions, American InterContinental University Buckhead Campus, 3330 Peachtree Road, NE, Atlanta, GA 30326. *Phone:* 404-965-5953. *Toll-free phone:* 888-591-7888. *E-mail:* john.payton@buckhead.aiuniv.edu.

AMERICAN INTERCONTINENTAL UNIVERSITY DUNWOODY CAMPUS

Atlanta, Georgia **www.aiuniv.edu/**

- **Proprietary** comprehensive, founded 1970, administratively affiliated with American InterContinental University
- **Urban** 2-acre campus
- **Coed**
- **Minimally difficult** entrance level, 80% of applicants were admitted

Freshmen *Admission:* 367 applied, 294 admitted.

Majors Animation, interactive technology, video graphics and special effects; art; audiovisual communications technologies related; business administration and management; computer and information sciences; computer graphics; computer/information technology services administration related; corrections and criminal justice related; criminal justice/law enforcement administration; design and visual communications; graphic design; information technology; marketing/marketing management; small business administration.

Academics *Calendar:* five 10-week terms. *Degrees:* associate, bachelor's, and master's.

Student Life *Activities and organizations:* student-run newspaper. *Student services:* personal/psychological counseling.

Costs (2008–09) *Tuition:* contact campus for information. See: www.aiuniv.edu.

Applying *Options:* electronic application, deferred entrance. *Application fee:* $50. *Required:* essay or personal statement, high school transcript, interview. *Required for some:* TOEFL for students whose first language is not English. *Application deadlines:* rolling (freshmen), rolling (transfers). *Notification:* continuous (freshmen), continuous (transfers).

Director of Admissions Director of Admissions, American InterContinental University Dunwoody Campus, 6600 Peachtree-Dunwoody Road, 500 Embassy Row, Atlanta, GA 30328. *Phone:* 404-965-6500. *Toll-free phone:* 800-353-1744.

ARGOSY UNIVERSITY, ATLANTA

Atlanta, Georgia **www.argosy.edu/locations/atlanta/**

- **Proprietary** university, founded 1990, administratively affiliated with Education Management Corporation
- **Suburban** campus
- **Coed**

Majors Business administration and management; criminal justice/law enforcement administration; finance; health/health care administration; international business/trade/commerce; marketing/marketing management; organizational behavior; psychology.

Academics *Calendar:* semesters. *Degrees:* bachelor's, master's, and doctoral.

Director of Admissions Argosy University, Atlanta, 980 Hammond Drive, Suite 100, Atlanta, GA 30328. *Phone:* 770-671-1200. *Toll-free phone:* 888-671-4777.

See page 730 for the College Close-Up.

ARMSTRONG ATLANTIC STATE UNIVERSITY

Savannah, Georgia **www.armstrong.edu/**

- **State-supported** comprehensive, founded 1935, part of University System of Georgia
- **Suburban** 250-acre campus
- **Endowment** $2.4 million
- **Coed** 6,054 undergraduate students, 65% full-time, 67% women, 33% men
- **Minimally difficult** entrance level, 60% of applicants were admitted

Undergraduates 3,941 full-time, 2,113 part-time. Students come from 48 states and territories, 75 other countries, 12% are from out of state, 23% African American, 3% Asian American or Pacific Islander, 4% Hispanic American, 0.5% Native American, 2% international, 10% transferred in, 12% live on campus. *Retention:* 70% of 2006 full-time freshmen returned.

Freshmen *Admission:* 2,186 applied, 1,306 admitted, 846 enrolled. *Average high school GPA:* 3.05. *Test scores:* SAT critical reading scores over 500: 50%; ACT scores over 18: 79%; SAT critical reading scores over 600: 11%; ACT scores over 24: 12%; SAT critical reading scores over 700: 1%; ACT scores over 30: 1%.

Faculty *Total:* 491, 59% full-time. *Student/faculty ratio:* 17:1.

Majors Art; art teacher education; biology/biological sciences; business teacher education; chemistry; clinical laboratory science/medical technology; computer science; criminal justice/police science; dental hygiene; dramatic/theater arts; economics; English; health professions related; health science; health teacher education; history; information science/studies; information technology; kindergarten/preschool education; liberal arts and sciences/liberal studies; mathematics; middle school education; music; music teacher education; nursing (registered nurse training); physical education teaching and coaching; physical therapy; physics; political science and government; psychology; respiratory care therapy; Spanish; special education; visual and performing arts.

Academics *Calendar:* semesters. *Degrees:* certificates, associate, bachelor's, master's, post-master's, and postbachelor's certificates. *Special study options:* academic remediation for entering students, adult/continuing education programs, advanced placement credit, cooperative education, distance learning, double majors, honors programs, independent study, internships, off-campus study, part-time degree program, services for LD students, study abroad, summer session for credit. *ROTC:* Army (b), Navy (c). *Unusual degree programs:* 3-2 engineering with Georgia Institute of Technology.

Computers on Campus 230 computers/terminals are available on campus for general student use. Students can access the following: campus intranet, computer help desk, free student e-mail accounts, online (class) grades, online (class) registration, online (class) schedules. Campuswide network is available. 100% of college-owned or -operated housing units are wired for high-speed Internet access. Wireless service is available via entire campus.

Student Life *Housing options:* coed. Campus housing is provided by a third party. *Activities and organizations:* drama/theater group, student-run newspaper, choral group, Wesley Fellowship, Hispanic Student Society, Ebony Coalition, American Chemical Society, Phi Alpha Theta, national fraternities, national sororities. *Campus security:* 24-hour emergency response devices and patrols, student patrols, late-night transport/escort service. *Student services:* health clinic, personal/psychological counseling.

Athletics Member NCAA. All Division II. *Intercollegiate sports:* baseball M (s), basketball M (s)/W (s), golf M (s), softball W (s), tennis M (s)/W (s), volleyball W (s). *Intramural sports:* badminton M/W, basketball M/W, bowling M/W, cheerleading M/W, football M/W, golf M/W, soccer M/W, softball M/W, table tennis M/W, tennis M/W, volleyball M/W, water polo M/W.

Standardized Tests *Required:* SAT or ACT (for admission). *Required for some:* SAT Subject Tests (for admission).

Costs (2007–08) *Tuition:* state resident $2868 full-time, $120 per credit hour part-time; nonresident $11,472 full-time, $478 per credit hour part-time. Full-time tuition and fees vary according to program and student level. Part-time tuition and fees vary according to course load and program. No tuition increase for student's term of enrollment. *Required fees:* $556 full-time, $278 per term part-time. *Room only:* $5000. Room and board charges vary according to board plan and housing facility. *Waivers:* senior citizens.

Financial Aid Of all full-time matriculated undergraduates who enrolled in 2006, 5,718 applied for aid, 3,716 were judged to have need, 663 had their need fully met. 75 Federal Work-Study jobs (averaging $5000). In 2006, 865 non-need-based awards were made. *Average percent of need met:* 85%. *Average financial aid package:* $5750. *Average need-based loan:* $3932. *Average need-based gift aid:* $3000. *Average non-need-based aid:* $3724. *Average indebtedness upon graduation:* $12,500.

Applying *Options:* early admission, deferred entrance. *Application fee:* $25. *Required:* high school transcript, proof of immunization. *Application deadlines:* 6/30 (freshmen), 6/30 (transfers). *Notification:* continuous (freshmen), continuous (transfers).

Freshman Application Contact Mr. Craig Morrison, Assistant Registrar, Armstrong Atlantic State University, Savannah, GA 31419. *Phone:* 912-921-5425. *Toll-free phone:* 800-633-2349. *Fax:* 912-921-5462. *E-mail:* craig.morrison@armstrong.edu.

THE ART INSTITUTE OF ATLANTA

Atlanta, Georgia www.aia.artinstitutes.edu/

- **Proprietary** 4-year, founded 1949, part of Education Management Corporation
- **Suburban** 7-acre campus
- **Coed** 3,187 undergraduate students, 84% full-time, 46% women, 54% men
- **Moderately difficult** entrance level, 46% of applicants were admitted

Undergraduates 2,678 full-time, 509 part-time. Students come from 43 states and territories, 30 other countries, 24% are from out of state, 39% African American, 2% Asian American or Pacific Islander, 4% Hispanic American, 0.5% Native American, 2% international, 21% live on campus.

Freshmen *Admission:* 1,142 applied, 528 admitted, 365 enrolled.

Faculty *Total:* 182, 57% full-time, 42% with terminal degrees. *Student/faculty ratio:* 22:1.

Majors Advertising; animation, interactive technology, video graphics and special effects; apparel and accessories marketing; cinematography and film/video production; commercial and advertising art; commercial photography; computer graphics; culinary arts; graphic design; illustration; interior design; intermedia/multimedia; recording arts technology; restaurant, culinary, and catering management; web page, digital/multimedia and information resources design.

Academics *Calendar:* quarters. *Degrees:* diplomas, associate, and bachelor's. *Special study options:* academic remediation for entering students, adult/continuing education programs, advanced placement credit, distance learning, honors programs, independent study, internships, part-time degree program, services for LD students, study abroad, summer session for credit.

Computers on Campus 467 computers/terminals and 467 ports are available on campus for general student use. Students can access the following: campus intranet, computer help desk, free student e-mail accounts, online (class) grades, online (class) registration, online (class) schedules. Campuswide network is available. 80% of college-owned or -operated housing units are wired for high-speed Internet access. Wireless service is available via libraries, student centers.

Student Life *Housing options:* coed, disabled students. Campus housing is leased by the school. Freshman campus housing is guaranteed. *Activities and organizations:* drama/theater group, AIGA (American Institute of Graphic Artists) Student Chapter, ASID (American Society of Interior Designers) Student Chapter, Student Leadership Council, Aspiring Sound Engineers, AiA Media. *Campus security:* 24-hour emergency response devices and patrols, late-night transport/escort service, controlled dormitory access. *Student services:* personal/psychological counseling.

Standardized Tests *Required for some:* SAT or ACT (for admission), ACT COMPASS.

Costs (2007–08) *Tuition:* $20,880 full-time, $435 per credit hour part-time. tuition cost varies by program. Prospective students should contact the school for current tuition costs. Other charges include a starting kit for all first-quarter students. Kits vary in price depending on the program of study. *Room only:* $9075.

Financial Aid Of all full-time matriculated undergraduates who enrolled in 2003, 2,233 applied for aid, 2,048 were judged to have need. *Average percent of need met:* 65%. *Average financial aid package:* $10,854. *Average need-based loan:* $3500. *Average need-based gift aid:* $2551.

Applying *Options:* electronic application, early admission. *Application fee:* $50. *Required:* essay or personal statement, high school transcript, minimum 2.0 GPA, interview. *Required for some:* minimum 2.5 GPA. *Application deadlines:* rolling (freshmen), rolling (transfers). *Notification:* continuous (freshmen), continuous (transfers).

Freshman Application Contact Mr. Newton Myvett, Vice President/Director of Admissions, The Art Institute of Atlanta, 6600 Peachtree Dunwoody Road, 100 Embassy Row, Atlanta, GA 30328. *Phone:* 800-275-4242. *Toll-free phone:* 800-275-4242. *Fax:* 770-394-0008. *E-mail:* aidadm@aii.edu.

See page 732 for the College Close-Up.

THE ART INSTITUTE OF ATLANTA–DECATUR

Decatur, Georgia www.artinstitutes.edu/decatur/

- **Proprietary** 4-year

Majors Advertising; animation, interactive technology, video graphics and special effects; fashion merchandising, graphic design; interior design; retail management; Web page, digital/multimedia and information resources design.

Freshman Application Contact Admissions Director, The Art Institute of Atlanta–Decatur, One West Court Square, Suite 110, Decatur, GA 30030. *Phone:* 866-856-6203.

See page 734 for the College Close-Up.

ATLANTA CHRISTIAN COLLEGE

East Point, Georgia www.acc.edu/

Freshman Application Contact Ms. Sarah Huxford, Director of Admissions, Atlanta Christian College, 2605 Ben Hill Road, East Point, GA 30344-1999. *Phone:* 404-761-8861. *Toll-free phone:* 800-776-1ACC. *Fax:* 404-669-2024. *E-mail:* admissions@acc.edu.

AUGUSTA STATE UNIVERSITY

Augusta, Georgia www.aug.edu/

- **State-supported** comprehensive, founded 1925, part of University System of Georgia
- **Urban** 72-acre campus
- **Endowment** $333,462
- **Coed** 5,628 undergraduate students, 70% full-time, 64% women, 36% men
- **Minimally difficult** entrance level, 53% of applicants were admitted

Undergraduates 3,936 full-time, 1,692 part-time. Students come from 40 states and territories, 53 other countries, 9% are from out of state, 27% African American, 3% Asian American or Pacific Islander, 3% Hispanic American, 0.3% Native American, 1% international, 7% transferred in, 10% live on campus. *Retention:* 64% of 2006 full-time freshmen returned.

Freshmen *Admission:* 2,363 applied, 1,243 admitted, 971 enrolled. *Average high school GPA:* 2.96. *Test scores:* SAT critical reading scores over 500: 44%; SAT math scores over 500: 48%; SAT critical reading scores over 600: 10%; SAT math scores over 600: 10%; SAT critical reading scores over 700: 1%; SAT math scores over 700: 1%.

Faculty *Total:* 402, 58% full-time, 47% with terminal degrees. *Student/faculty ratio:* 18:1.

Majors Accounting; biology/biological sciences; business administration and management; chemistry; clinical laboratory science/medical technology; communication/speech communication and rhetoric; computer and information sciences; criminal justice/safety; elementary education; English; finance; French; history; intermedia/multimedia; liberal arts and sciences/liberal studies; marketing/marketing management; mathematics; middle school education; music; music performance; music teacher education; nursing (registered nurse training); physical education teaching and coaching; physical sciences; physics; political science and government; psychology; social work; sociology; Spanish; special education; special education (mentally retarded).

Academics *Calendar:* semesters. *Degrees:* associate, bachelor's, master's, and post-master's certificates. *Special study options:* academic remediation for entering students, adult/continuing education programs, advanced placement credit, cooperative education, double majors, English as a second language, honors programs, independent study, internships, off-campus study, part-time degree program, services for LD students, study abroad, summer session for credit. *ROTC:* Army (b).

Computers on Campus 325 computers/terminals are available on campus for general student use. Students can access the following: online (class) registration. Campuswide network is available.

Student Life *Housing options:* coed. Campus housing is university owned. *Activities and organizations:* drama/theater group, student-run newspaper, choral group, Jazz Ensemble, Baptist Student Union, ASU Orchestra, Student Art Association, Black Student Union, national fraternities, national sororities. *Campus security:* 24-hour patrols, late-night transport/escort service. *Student services:* personal/psychological counseling.

Athletics Member NCAA, NAIA. All NCAA Division II. *Intercollegiate sports:* baseball M, basketball M (s)/W (s), cross-country running M (s)/W (s), softball W, tennis M (s)/W (s), volleyball W. *Intramural sports:* softball W, volleyball M/W, weight lifting M/W.

Standardized Tests *Required:* SAT or ACT (for admission).

Costs (2007–08) *Tuition:* state resident $3192 full-time, $133 per credit hour part-time; nonresident $12,792 full-time, $533 per credit hour part-time. No tuition increase for student's term of enrollment. *Required fees:* $536 full-time. *Room and board:* $9600; room only: $4920. *Waivers:* senior citizens and employees or children of employees.

Financial Aid Of all full-time matriculated undergraduates who enrolled in 2006, 2,571 applied for aid, 2,056 were judged to have need, 35 had their need fully met. 84 Federal Work-Study jobs (averaging $2637). 260 state and other part-time jobs (averaging $1681). In 2006, 731 non-need-based awards were made. *Average percent of need met:* 70%. *Average financial aid package:* $12,338. *Average need-based loan:* $7744. *Average need-based gift aid:* $7298. *Average non-need-based aid:* $520. *Average indebtedness upon graduation:* $3191. *Financial aid deadline:* 5/1.

Applying *Options:* electronic application, deferred entrance. *Application fee:* $30. *Required:* high school transcript, minimum 2.0 GPA. *Application deadlines:* 7/21 (freshmen), rolling (transfers). *Notification:* continuous (freshmen), continuous (transfers).

Freshman Application Contact Ms. Jody Wilson, Coordinator of Publications and Marketing, Augusta State University, 2500 Walton Way, Augusta, GA 30904-2200. *Phone:* 706-737-1632. *Toll-free phone:* 800-341-4373. *Fax:* 706-667-4355. *E-mail:* admissions@aug.edu.

BEACON UNIVERSITY

Columbus, Georgia **www.beacon.edu/**

- **Independent religious** comprehensive, founded 1993
- **Urban** 15-acre campus
- **Coed**
- 88% of applicants were admitted

Faculty *Student/faculty ratio:* 5:1.

Academics *Calendar:* semesters. *Degrees:* associate, bachelor's, master's, and doctoral.

Standardized Tests *Required for some:* ACT COMPASS. *Recommended:* SAT or ACT (for admission).

Costs (2007–08) *Tuition:* $5400 full-time, $675 per course part-time. Full-time tuition and fees vary according to course load. Part-time tuition and fees vary according to course load. *Required fees:* $210 full-time, $105 per term part-time.

Financial Aid Of all full-time matriculated undergraduates who enrolled in 2006, 47 applied for aid, 46 were judged to have need, 29 had their need fully met. In 2006, 4 non-need-based awards were made. *Average percent of need met:* 100. *Average financial aid package:* $6008. *Average need-based loan:* $3007. *Average need-based gift aid:* $3705. *Average non-need-based aid:* $1148. *Average indebtedness upon graduation:* $17,341.

Applying *Options:* early admission. *Application fee:* $75. *Required:* high school transcript, minimum 2.0 GPA, 3 letters of recommendation, interview.

Freshman Application Contact Dr. James Cornett, Dean of Student Services, Beacon University, 6003 Veterans Parkway, Columbus, GA 31909. *Phone:* 706-323-5364 Ext. 259. *Fax:* 706-323-5891. *E-mail:* james.cornett@beacon.edu.

BERRY COLLEGE

Mount Berry, Georgia **www.berry.edu/**

- **Independent interdenominational** comprehensive, founded 1902
- **Suburban** 28,000-acre campus with easy access to Atlanta
- **Endowment** $683.3 million
- **Coed** 1,737 undergraduate students, 98% full-time, 66% women, 34% men
- **Moderately difficult** entrance level, 70% of applicants were admitted

Undergraduates 1,701 full-time, 36 part-time. Students come from 39 states and territories, 20 other countries, 17% are from out of state, 3% African American, 2% Asian American or Pacific Islander, 2% Hispanic American, 0.2% Native American, 2% international, 3% transferred in, 77% live on campus. *Retention:* 76% of 2006 full-time freshmen returned.

Freshmen *Admission:* 1,813 applied, 1,278 admitted, 537 enrolled. *Average high school GPA:* 3.61. *Test scores:* SAT critical reading scores over 500: 85%; SAT math scores over 500: 83%; ACT scores over 18: 100%; SAT critical reading scores over 600: 35%; SAT math scores over 600: 30%; ACT scores over 24: 75%; SAT critical reading scores over 700: 7%; SAT math scores over 700: 2%; ACT scores over 30: 16%.

Faculty *Total:* 195, 74% full-time, 71% with terminal degrees. *Student/faculty ratio:* 12:1.

Majors Accounting; animal sciences; art; biology/biological sciences; chemistry; communication and journalism related; computer science; early childhood education; economics; engineering technology; English; environmental science; exercise physiology; finance; French; German; history; international relations and affairs; marketing/marketing management; mathematics; mathematics teacher education; middle school education; multi-/interdisciplinary studies related; music; music management and merchandising; music teacher education; nursing (registered nurse training); philosophy and religious studies related; physical education teaching and coaching; physics; political science and government; psychology; social sciences; Spanish; theater/theater arts management.

Academics *Calendar:* semesters. *Degrees:* bachelor's, master's, and post-master's certificates. *Special study options:* accelerated degree program, adult/continuing education programs, advanced placement credit, cooperative education, double majors, honors programs, independent study, internships, part-time degree program, student-designed majors, study abroad, summer session for credit. *Unusual degree programs:* 3-2 engineering with Georgia Institute of Technology, Mercer University; nursing with Emory University.

Computers on Campus 140 computers/terminals and 80 ports are available on campus for general student use. Students can access the following: campus intranet, computer help desk, free student e-mail accounts, online (class) grades, online (class) registration, online (class) schedules. Campuswide network is available. 100% of college-owned or -operated housing units are wired for high-speed Internet access. Wireless service is available via classrooms, computer centers, computer labs, learning centers, libraries, student centers.

Student Life *Housing:* on-campus residence required through sophomore year. *Options:* coed, men-only, women-only, disabled students. Campus housing is university owned. Freshman campus housing is guaranteed. *Activities and organizations:* drama/theater group, student-run newspaper, television station, choral group, Student Government Association, Baptist College Ministries, Campus Outreach, Athletes Bettering the Community, Viking Crew. *Campus security:* 24-hour emergency response devices and patrols, controlled dormitory access, lighted pathways. *Student services:* health clinic, personal/psychological counseling.

Athletics Member NAIA. *Intercollegiate sports:* baseball M (s), basketball M (s)/W (s), cheerleading M/W, crew M (c)/W (c), cross-country running M (s)/W (s), equestrian sports M (c)/W (s) (c), golf M (s)/W (s), lacrosse M (c)/W (c), soccer M (s)/W (s), tennis M (s)/W (s), track and field M (s)/W (s). *Intramural sports:* badminton M/W, baseball M, basketball M/W, bowling M/W, cross-country running M/W, equestrian sports W, football M/W, golf M/W, racquetball M/W, rock climbing M/W, soccer M/W, softball M/W, swimming and diving M/W, table tennis M/W, tennis M/W, ultimate Frisbee M/W, volleyball M/W, weight lifting M/W.

Standardized Tests *Required:* SAT or ACT (for admission).

Costs (2007–08) *Comprehensive fee:* $28,196 includes full-time tuition ($20,570) and room and board ($7626). Part-time tuition: $679 per credit hour. *College room only:* $4226. Room and board charges vary according to board plan and housing facility. *Payment plan:* installment. *Waivers:* senior citizens and employees or children of employees.

Financial Aid Of all full-time matriculated undergraduates who enrolled in 2007, 1,293 applied for aid, 987 were judged to have need, 265 had their need fully met. 545 Federal Work-Study jobs (averaging $3040). 1,295 state and other part-time jobs (averaging $3221). In 2007, 690 non-need-based awards were made. *Average percent of need met:* 85%. *Average financial aid package:* $16,563. *Average need-based loan:* $3818. *Average need-based gift aid:* $12,682. *Average non-need-based aid:* $17,380. *Average indebtedness upon graduation:* $14,349.

Applying *Options:* electronic application, early admission, deferred entrance. *Application fee:* $50. *Required:* high school transcript, letters of recommendation. *Application deadlines:* 7/25 (freshmen), 7/25 (transfers). *Notification:* continuous (freshmen), continuous (transfers).

Freshman Application Contact Mr. Timothy Tarpley, Associate Director of Admissions and Financial Aid, Berry College, PO Box 490159, 2277 Martha Berry Highway, NW, Mount Berry, GA 30149-0159. *Phone:* 706-236-2215. *Toll-free phone:* 800-237-7942. *Fax:* 706-290-2178. *E-mail:* admissions@berry.edu.

BEULAH HEIGHTS UNIVERSITY

Atlanta, Georgia **www.beulah.org/**

- **Independent Pentecostal** 4-year, founded 1918
- **Urban** 10-acre campus
- **Endowment** $19,881
- **Coed** 620 undergraduate students, 41% full-time, 57% women, 43% men
- **Noncompetitive** entrance level

Undergraduates 256 full-time, 364 part-time. Students come from 22 states and territories, 12 other countries, 30% are from out of state, 77% African American, 0.6% Asian American or Pacific Islander, 1% Hispanic American, 14% international, 8% transferred in, 10% live on campus. *Retention:* 42% of 2006 full-time freshmen returned.

Freshmen *Admission:* 168 applied, 155 enrolled. *Average high school GPA:* 3.0.

Faculty *Total:* 39, 46% full-time, 31% with terminal degrees. *Student/faculty ratio:* 17:1.

Majors Biblical studies; urban studies/affairs.

Academics *Calendar:* semesters. *Degrees:* certificates, associate, and bachelor's. *Special study options:* academic remediation for entering students, accelerated degree program, adult/continuing education programs, advanced placement credit, cooperative education, distance learning, double majors, internships, part-time degree program, summer session for credit.

Computers on Campus 28 computers/terminals are available on campus for general student use. Students can access the following: campus intranet, free student e-mail accounts, online (class) registration, online (class) schedules. Campuswide network is available. 100% of college-owned or -operated housing units are wired for high-speed Internet access. Wireless service is available via entire campus.

Student Life *Housing options:* men-only, women-only. *Activities and organizations:* choral group. *Campus security:* 24-hour emergency response devices, student patrols. *Student services:* personal/psychological counseling.

Athletics *Intercollegiate sports:* ultimate Frisbee M (s)/W (s), volleyball M (s)/W (s). *Intramural sports:* ultimate Frisbee M/W, volleyball M/W.

Standardized Tests *Recommended:* SAT or ACT (for admission).

Costs (2008–09) *One-time required fee:* $35. *Comprehensive fee:* $14,600 includes full-time tuition ($5120), mandatory fees ($480), and room and board ($9000).

Financial Aid Of all full-time matriculated undergraduates who enrolled in 2006, 207 applied for aid, 207 were judged to have need. 14 Federal Work-Study jobs (averaging $2897). *Average percent of need met:* 85%. *Average financial aid package:* $7732. *Average need-based loan:* $4642. *Average need-based gift aid:* $3209. *Average indebtedness upon graduation:* $30,742.

Applying *Options:* electronic application, early admission. *Application fee:* $20. *Required:* high school transcript, minimum 2.0 GPA, 2 letters of recommendation. *Recommended:* interview. *Application deadlines:* rolling (freshmen), rolling (transfers). *Notification:* continuous (freshmen), continuous (transfers).

Director of Admissions Ms. Jacquelyn B. Armstrong, Registrar/Director of Admissions, Beulah Heights University, 892 Berne Street, SE, PO Box 18145, Atlanta, GA 30316. *Phone:* 404-627-2681 Ext. 104. *Toll-free phone:* 888-777-BHBC.

BRENAU UNIVERSITY

Gainesville, Georgia **www.brenau.edu/**

- **Independent** comprehensive, founded 1878
- **Small-town** 57-acre campus with easy access to Atlanta
- **Endowment** $49.8 million
- **Women only** 867 undergraduate students, 92% full-time
- **Moderately difficult** entrance level, 40% of applicants were admitted

Undergraduates 798 full-time, 69 part-time. Students come from 19 states and territories, 24 other countries, 12% are from out of state, 19% African American, 2% Asian American or Pacific Islander, 3% Hispanic American, 0.2% Native American, 6% international, 15% transferred in, 52% live on campus. *Retention:* 62% of 2006 full-time freshmen returned.

Freshmen *Admission:* 2,687 applied, 1,071 admitted, 216 enrolled. *Test scores:* SAT critical reading scores over 500: 61%; SAT math scores over 500: 41%; SAT writing scores over 500: 56%; ACT scores over 18: 88%; SAT critical reading scores over 600: 15%; SAT math scores over 600: 10%; SAT writing scores over 600: 15%; ACT scores over 24: 25%; SAT critical reading scores over 700: 1%; SAT writing scores over 700: 1%.

Faculty *Total:* 114, 61% full-time, 55% with terminal degrees. *Student/faculty ratio:* 10:1.

Majors Accounting; arts management; art teacher education; biology/biological sciences; business administration and management; dance; drama and dance teacher education; dramatic/theater arts; early childhood education; English; fashion merchandising; fine/studio arts; general studies; graphic design; history; interior design; international relations and affairs; law and legal studies related; marketing/marketing management; mass communication/media; middle school education; music; music performance; music teacher education; nursing (registered nurse training); occupational therapy; political science and government; psychology; special education.

Academics *Calendar:* semesters. *Degrees:* bachelor's and master's (also offers coed evening and weekend programs with significant enrollment not reflected in profile). *Special study options:* academic remediation for entering students, accelerated degree program, advanced placement credit, distance learning, double majors, honors programs, independent study, internships, off-campus study, part-time degree program, services for LD students, student-designed majors, study abroad.

Computers on Campus 200 computers/terminals and 5 ports are available on campus for general student use. Students can access the following: campus intranet, computer help desk, free student e-mail accounts, online (class) grades, online (class) registration, online (class) schedules. Campuswide network is available. 100% of college-owned or -operated housing units are wired for high-speed Internet access. Wireless service is available via classrooms, computer centers, computer labs, learning centers, libraries, student centers.

Student Life *Housing:* on-campus residence required through junior year. *Options:* women-only, disabled students. Campus housing is university owned. Freshman campus housing is guaranteed. *Activities and organizations:* drama/theater group, student-run newspaper, radio and television station, choral group, Student Government/Campus Activities Board, Silhouettes (diversity awareness), Recreation Association, DIVAS Peer Education, International Club, national sororities. *Campus security:* 24-hour emergency response devices and patrols, late-night transport/escort service. *Student services:* health clinic, personal/psychological counseling, women's center.

Athletics Member NAIA. *Intercollegiate sports:* basketball W (s), crew W, cross-country running W (s), soccer W (s), softball W (s), swimming and diving W (s), tennis W (s), volleyball W (s).

Standardized Tests *Required:* SAT or ACT (for admission).

Costs (2008–09) *Comprehensive fee:* $28,287 includes full-time tuition ($18,550), mandatory fees ($250), and room and board ($9487). Part-time tuition: $618 per hour. *Required fees:* $125 per term part-time.

Financial Aid Of all full-time matriculated undergraduates who enrolled in 2006, 600 applied for aid, 529 were judged to have need, 168 had their need fully met. 151 Federal Work-Study jobs (averaging $1990). 2 state and other part-time jobs (averaging $1500). In 2006, 191 non-need-based awards were made. *Average percent of need met:* 79%. *Average financial aid package:* $15,574. *Average need-based loan:* $3682. *Average need-based gift aid:* $12,514. *Average non-need-based aid:* $10,634. *Average indebtedness upon graduation:* $16,426.

Applying *Options:* electronic application, deferred entrance. *Application fee:* $35. *Required:* high school transcript, minimum 2.5 GPA, minimum SAT score of 900 or ACT score of 18. *Required for some:* interview. *Recommended:* letters of recommendation. *Application deadlines:* rolling (freshmen), rolling (transfers). *Notification:* continuous (freshmen), continuous (transfers).

Freshman Application Contact Ms. Christina White, Assistant Vice President of Enrollment Management and Dean of Admissions, Brenau University, Admissions, 500 Washington Street, SE, Gainesville, GA 30501. *Phone:* 770-531-6100. *Toll-free phone:* 800-252-5119. *Fax:* 770-538-4701. *E-mail:* wcadmissions@brenau.edu.

BREWTON-PARKER COLLEGE

Mt. Vernon, Georgia **www.bpc.edu/**

- **Independent Southern Baptist** 4-year, founded 1904
- **Rural** 280-acre campus
- **Endowment** $13.9 million
- **Coed** 1,034 undergraduate students, 70% full-time, 62% women, 38% men
- **Minimally difficult** entrance level, 97% of applicants were admitted

Undergraduates 727 full-time, 307 part-time. Students come from 12 states and territories, 5 other countries, 5% are from out of state, 25% African American, 0.7% Asian American or Pacific Islander, 2% Hispanic American, 0.3% Native American, 1% international, 8% transferred in, 35% live on campus. *Retention:* 49% of 2006 full-time freshmen returned.

Freshmen *Admission:* 387 applied, 377 admitted, 338 enrolled. *Test scores:* SAT critical reading scores over 500: 50%; SAT math scores over 500: 47%; ACT scores over 18: 61%; SAT critical reading scores over 600: 14%; SAT math scores over 600: 11%; ACT scores over 24: 12%; SAT critical reading scores over 700: 1%; ACT scores over 30: 1%.

Faculty *Total:* 246, 23% full-time. *Student/faculty ratio:* 7:1.

Majors Accounting; biology/biological sciences; biology teacher education; business administration and management; communication/speech communication and rhetoric; computer and information sciences; early childhood education; education; English; English/language arts teacher education; general studies; health and physical education related; history; history teacher education; information science/studies; mathematics; mathematics teacher education; middle school education; music; music performance; music teacher education; physical education teaching and coaching; political science and government; pre-law studies; psychology; religious studies; science teacher education; secondary education; social sciences; sociology; theology.

Academics *Calendar:* semesters. *Degrees:* associate and bachelor's. *Special study options:* academic remediation for entering students, accelerated degree program, adult/continuing education programs, advanced placement credit, cooperative education, honors programs, independent study, internships, part-time degree program, services for LD students, summer session for credit.

Computers on Campus 104 computers/terminals are available on campus for general student use. Students can access the following: computer help desk, free student e-mail accounts, online (class) grades, online (class) registration, online (class) schedules. Campuswide network is available. 100% of college-owned or -operated housing units are wired for high-speed Internet access. Wireless service is available via classrooms, computer centers, computer labs, libraries, student centers.

Student Life *Housing:* on-campus residence required through junior year. *Options:* men-only, women-only. Campus housing is university owned. Freshman campus housing is guaranteed. *Activities and organizations:* drama/theater group, student-run newspaper, choral group, Council of Intramural Activities, Student Activities Council, Rotaract, Circle K, Baptist Student Union. *Campus security:* 24-hour emergency response devices and patrols, controlled dormitory access. *Student services:* health clinic, personal/psychological counseling.

Athletics Member NAIA. *Intercollegiate sports:* baseball M (s), basketball M (s)/W (s), cheerleading M (s)/W (s), soccer M (s)/W (s), softball W (s), volleyball W (s). *Intramural sports:* basketball M/W, football M/W, softball M/W, table tennis M/W, tennis M/W, ultimate Frisbee M/W, volleyball M/W.

Standardized Tests *Required:* SAT or ACT (for admission).

Costs (2007–08) *Comprehensive fee:* $19,520 includes full-time tuition ($12,800), mandatory fees ($1250), and room and board ($5470). Part-time tuition: $400 per credit hour. *College room only:* $2470. Room and board charges vary according to board plan and housing facility. *Payment plan:* installment. *Waivers:* senior citizens and employees or children of employees.

Financial Aid Of all full-time matriculated undergraduates who enrolled in 2004, 791 applied for aid, 734 were judged to have need, 77 had their need fully met. 237 Federal Work-Study jobs (averaging $856). 57 state and other part-time jobs (averaging $1067). In 2004, 76 non-need-based awards were made. *Average percent of need met:* 59%. *Average financial aid package:* $10,062. *Average need-based loan:* $3245. *Average need-based gift aid:* $7206. *Average non-need-based aid:* $6773. *Average indebtedness upon graduation:* $23,445.

Applying *Options:* early admission. *Application fee:* $25. *Required:* high school transcript, minimum 2.0 GPA. *Application deadlines:* rolling (freshmen), rolling (transfers). *Notification:* continuous (freshmen), continuous (transfers).

Freshman Application Contact Mr. Ken Wuerzberger, Director of Admissions, Brewton-Parker College, PO Box 197, Mt. Vernon, GA 30445. *Phone:* 912-583-3245. *Toll-free phone:* 800-342-1087 Ext. 245. *Fax:* 912-583-3598. *E-mail:* kwuerzberger@bpc.edu.

CARVER BIBLE COLLEGE

Atlanta, Georgia **www.carver.edu/**

Director of Admissions Ms. Patsy S. Singh, Director of Admissions, Carver Bible College, 437 Nelson Street, Atlanta, GA 30313. *Phone:* 404-527-4520.

CLARK ATLANTA UNIVERSITY

Atlanta, Georgia **www.cau.edu/**

- **Independent United Methodist** university, founded 1865
- **Urban** 126-acre campus with easy access to Atlanta
- **Endowment** $47.4 million
- **Coed** 3,533 undergraduate students, 96% full-time, 73% women, 27% men
- **Moderately difficult** entrance level, 66% of applicants were admitted

Undergraduates 3,375 full-time, 158 part-time. Students come from 43 states and territories, 9 other countries, 68% are from out of state, 87% African American, 0.1% Asian American or Pacific Islander, 0.4% Hispanic American, 0.1% Native American, 1% international, 4% transferred in, 25% live on campus. *Retention:* 69% of 2006 full-time freshmen returned.

Freshmen *Admission:* 6,829 applied, 4,517 admitted, 1,061 enrolled. *Average high school GPA:* 2.94. *Test scores:* SAT critical reading scores over 500: 20%; SAT math scores over 500: 18%; ACT scores over 18: 72%; SAT critical reading scores over 600: 2%; SAT math scores over 600: 1%; ACT scores over 24: 7%.

Faculty *Total:* 334, 69% full-time, 57% with terminal degrees. *Student/faculty ratio:* 15:1.

Majors Accounting; art; biology/biological sciences; business administration and management; business/managerial economics; chemistry; computer and information sciences; computer science; criminal justice/safety; education; English; fashion/apparel design; French; history; information science/studies; mathematics; music; philosophy; physics; political science and government; psychology; radio, television, and digital communication related; religious studies; social work; sociology; Spanish; speech and rhetoric; theater literature, history and criticism.

Academics *Calendar:* semesters. *Degrees:* bachelor's, master's, doctoral, and post-master's certificates. *Special study options:* academic remediation for entering students, accelerated degree program, adult/continuing education programs, advanced placement credit, cooperative education, double majors, English as a second language, freshman honors college, honors programs, independent study, internships, off-campus study, part-time degree program, services for LD students, study abroad, summer session for credit. *ROTC:* Navy (c), Air Force (b). *Unusual degree programs:* 3-2 engineering with Georgia Institute of Technology, Boston University, North Carolina Agricultural and Technical State University.

Computers on Campus 650 computers/terminals and 2,000 ports are available on campus for general student use. Students can access the following: computer help desk, free student e-mail accounts, online (class) grades, online (class) registration, online (class) schedules. Campuswide network is available. 100% of college-owned or -operated housing units are wired for high-speed Internet access. Wireless service is available via classrooms, computer centers, computer labs, learning centers, libraries, student centers.

Student Life *Housing:* on-campus residence required through sophomore year. *Options:* coed, men-only, women-only. Campus housing is university owned and is provided by a third party. Freshman applicants given priority for college housing. *Activities and organizations:* drama/theater group, student-run newspaper, radio and television station, choral group, marching band, Spirit Boosters, Pre-Alumni Council, Campus Activities Board, Orientation Guides, National Association for the Advancement of Colored People, national fraternities, national sororities. *Campus security:* 24-hour emergency response devices and patrols, late-night transport/escort service, controlled dormitory access. *Student services:* health clinic, personal/psychological counseling.

Athletics Member NCAA. All Division II. *Intercollegiate sports:* baseball M (s), basketball M (s)/W (s), cheerleading W (s), cross-country running M (s)/W (s), football M (s), golf M (s), softball W (s), tennis W (s), track and field M (s)/W (s), volleyball W (s). *Intramural sports:* cheerleading W, football M/W, swimming and diving M/W, tennis W, track and field M/W, volleyball M/W.

Standardized Tests *Required:* SAT or ACT (for admission).

Costs (2008–09) *Comprehensive fee:* $24,082 includes full-time tuition ($16,328), mandatory fees ($710), and room and board ($7044). Part-time tuition: $680 per credit hour.

Financial Aid Of all full-time matriculated undergraduates who enrolled in 2005, 3,883 applied for aid, 3,712 were judged to have need, 1,567 had their need fully met. 229 Federal Work-Study jobs (averaging $1335). *Average percent of need met:* 8%. *Average financial aid package:* $10,935. *Average need-based loan:* $4526. *Average need-based gift aid:* $3818. *Average indebtedness upon graduation:* $17,751.

Applying *Options:* electronic application, early admission, deferred entrance. *Application fee:* $35. *Required:* essay or personal statement, high school transcript, minimum 2.5 GPA, 2 letters of recommendation. *Required for some:* interview. *Application deadlines:* 6/1 (freshmen), 6/1 (transfers). *Notification:* continuous (freshmen), continuous (transfers).

Freshman Application Contact Office of Admissions, Clark Atlanta University, 223 James P. Brawley Drive, SW, 101 Trevor Arnett Hall, Atlanta, GA 30314-4391. *Phone:* 404-880-8000 Ext. 8021. *Toll-free phone:* 800-688-3228. *Fax:* 404-880-6174. *E-mail:* cauadmissions@cau.edu.

CLAYTON STATE UNIVERSITY

Morrow, Georgia **www.clayton.edu/**

- **State-supported** comprehensive, founded 1969, part of University System of Georgia
- **Suburban** 163-acre campus with easy access to Atlanta
- **Coed** 5,974 undergraduate students, 56% full-time, 7_% women, 29% men
- **Minimally difficult** entrance level, 55% of applicants were admitted

Undergraduates 3,328 full-time, 2,646 part-time. Students come from 45 states and territories, 44 other countries, 12% are from out of state, 56% African American, 5% Asian American or Pacific Islander, 3% Hispanic American, 0.2% Native American, 2% international, 12% transferred in. *Retention:* 61% of 2006 full-time freshmen returned.

Freshmen *Admission:* 5,076 applied, 2,787 admitted, 617 enrolled. *Average high school GPA:* 3.06. *Test scores:* SAT critical reading scores over 500: 40%; SAT math scores over 500: 39%; ACT scores over 18: 84%; SAT critical reading scores over 600: 8%; SAT math scores over 600: 7%; ACT scores over 24: 10%.

Faculty *Total:* 197. *Student/faculty ratio:* 21:1.

Majors Accounting; administrative assistant and secretarial science; agricultural business and management; agricultural mechanization; agriculture; airframe mechanics and aircraft maintenance technology; apparel and accessories marketing; architectural engineering technology; art; artificial intelligence and robotics; art teacher education; aviation/airway management; avionics maintenance technology; biological and physical sciences; biology/biological sciences; business administration and management; business teacher education; chemistry; clinical laboratory science/medical technology; clinical/medical laboratory technology; communication and media related; computer engineering technology; computer/information technology services administration related; computer science; criminal justice/law enforcement administration; data processing and data processing technology; dental hygiene; drafting and design technology; dramatic/theater arts; economics; education; electrical, electronic and communications engineering technology; electromechanical technology; elementary education; emergency medical technology (EMT paramedic); engineering; engineering technology; English; family and consumer sciences/human sciences; fashion merchandising; finance; forestry; French; geology/earth science; health/health care administration; health information/medical records administration; health teacher education; history; human services; information science/studies; instrumentation technology; journalism; kindergarten/preschool education; legal administrative assistant/secretary; legal assistant/paralegal; legal studies; management information systems; marketing/marketing management; marketing related; mass communication/media; mathematics; mechanical design technology; medical/clinical assistant; medical illustration; merchandising; merchandising, sales, and marketing operations related (general); merchandising, sales, and marketing operations related (specialized); middle school education; multi-/interdisciplinary studies related; music; music performance; music theory and composition; nursing (registered nurse training); occupational therapy; parks, recreation and leisure; pharmacy; philosophy; physical education teaching and coaching; physical therapy; physics; political science and government; pre-engineering; psychology; psychology related; public/applied history and archival administration; radiologic technology/science; social sciences; sociology; Spanish; speech and rhetoric; telecommunications; urban studies/affairs; veterinary sciences.

Academics *Calendar:* semesters. *Degrees:* certificates, associate, bachelor's, and master's. *Special study options:* academic remediation for entering students, adult/continuing education programs, advanced placement credit, cooperative education, distance learning, double majors, English as a second language, freshman honors college, honors programs, independent study, internships, off-campus study, part-time degree program, services for LD students, student-designed majors, study abroad, summer session for credit. *ROTC:* Army (c), Navy (c), Air Force (c).

Computers on Campus 3,500 computers/terminals are available on campus for general student use. Students can access the following: online (class) registration. Campuswide network is available.

Student Life *Housing:* college housing not available. *Activities and organizations:* drama/theater group, student-run newspaper, choral group, Accounting Club, International Awareness Club, Black Cultural Awareness Association, Student Government Association, Music Club, national fraternities, national sororities. *Campus security:* 24-hour emergency response devices and patrols, late-night transport/escort service, lighted pathways. *Student services:* health clinic, personal/psychological counseling.

Athletics Member NCAA. All Division II. *Intercollegiate sports:* basketball M (s)/W (s), cheerleading W (s) (c), cross-country running M (s)/W (s), golf M (s), soccer M (s)/W (s), tennis W (s), track and field M (s)/W (s). *Intramural sports:* bowling M/W, softball M/W, table tennis M/W, volleyball M/W.

Standardized Tests *Required:* SAT or ACT (for admission). *Required for some:* SAT Subject Tests (for admission).

Costs (2007–08) *Tuition:* state resident $2640 full-time, $120 per credit hour part-time; nonresident $10,516 full-time, $478 per credit hour part-time. Full-time tuition and fees vary according to course load. Part-time tuition and fees vary according to course load. No tuition increase for student's term of enrollment. *Required fees:* $714 full-time, $357 per term part-time. *Waivers:* senior citizens and employees or children of employees.

Financial Aid Of all full-time matriculated undergraduates who enrolled in 2004, 2,211 applied for aid, 1,903 were judged to have need, 173 had their need fully met. In 2004, 128 non-need-based awards were made. *Average percent of need met:* 59%. *Average financial aid package:* $3347. *Average need-based loan:* $1816. *Average need-based gift aid:* $1569. *Average non-need-based aid:* $743. *Average indebtedness upon graduation:* $16,156.

Applying *Options:* electronic application, early admission, deferred entrance. *Application fee:* $40. *Required:* high school transcript, proof of immunization. *Application deadline:* 7/17 (freshmen). *Notification:* continuous (freshmen), continuous (transfers).

Freshman Application Contact Ms. Carol S. Montgomery, Admissions, Clayton State University, 5900 North Lee Street, Morrow, GA 30260-0285. *Phone:* 678-466-4115. *Fax:* 678-466-4149. *E-mail:* csc-info@clayton.edu.

See page 736 for the College Close-Up.

COLUMBUS STATE UNIVERSITY

Columbus, Georgia **www.colstate.edu/**

- **State-supported** comprehensive, founded 1958, part of University System of Georgia
- **Suburban** 132-acre campus with easy access to Atlanta
- **Coed** 6,548 undergraduate students, 69% full-time, 61% women, 39% men
- **Minimally difficult** entrance level, 56% of applicants were admitted

Undergraduates 4,543 full-time, 2,005 part-time. Students come from 36 states and territories, 36 other countries, 13% are from out of state, 32% African American, 2% Asian American or Pacific Islander, 3% Hispanic American, 0.3% Native American, 1% international, 8% transferred in, 16% live on campus. *Retention:* 72% of 2006 full-time freshmen returned.

Freshmen *Admission:* 3,094 applied, 1,727 admitted, 1,035 enrolled. *Average high school GPA:* 3.01. *Test scores:* SAT critical reading scores over 500: 50%; SAT math scores over 500: 45%; ACT scores over 18: 72%; SAT critical reading scores over 600: 14%; SAT math scores over 600: 10%; ACT scores over 24: 14%; SAT critical reading scores over 700: 1%; SAT math scores over 700: 1%; ACT scores over 30: 1%.

Faculty *Total:* 432, 57% full-time, 54% with terminal degrees. *Student/faculty ratio:* 19:1.

Majors Accounting; art teacher education; biology/biological sciences; business administration and management; business/commerce; chemistry; computer and information sciences; criminal justice/safety; drama and dance teacher education; dramatic/theater arts; drawing; early childhood education; English; English/language arts teacher education; finance; French; geology/earth science; health services/allied health/health sciences; history; kinesiology and exercise science; liberal arts and sciences/liberal studies; management information systems; marketing/marketing management; mathematics; mathematics teacher education; middle school education; music; music performance; music teacher education; nursing (registered nurse training); physical education teaching and coaching; political science and government; psychology; science teacher education; social studies teacher education; sociology; Spanish; special education (mentally retarded).

Academics *Calendar:* semesters. *Degrees:* certificates, associate, bachelor's, master's, post-master's, and postbachelor's certificates. *Special study options:* academic remediation for entering students, adult/continuing education programs, advanced placement credit, cooperative education, distance learning, double majors, English as a second language, freshman honors college, honors programs, independent study, internships, off-campus study, part-time degree program, services for LD students, study abroad, summer session for credit. *ROTC:* Army (b). *Unusual degree programs:* 3-2 engineering with Georgia Institute of Technology.

Computers on Campus 311 computers/terminals are available on campus for general student use. Students can access the following: campus intranet, computer help desk, free student e-mail accounts, online (class) grades, online (class) registration, online (class) schedules. Campuswide network is available. Wireless service is available via computer centers, computer labs, dorm rooms, libraries.

Student Life *Housing options:* coed, men-only, women-only, disabled students. Campus housing is university owned. *Activities and organizations:* drama/theater group, student-run newspaper, choral group, Student Government Association, Student Programming Council, Baptist Student Union, national fraternities, national sororities. *Campus security:* 24-hour emergency response devices and patrols, late-night transport/escort service, controlled dormitory access. *Student services:* health clinic, personal/psychological counseling.

Athletics Member NCAA. All Division II. *Intercollegiate sports:* baseball M (s), basketball M (s)/W (s), cross-country running M (s)/W (s), golf M (s), soccer W (s), softball W (s), tennis M (s)/W (s). *Intramural sports:* badminton M/W, basketball M/W, bowling M/W, cross-country running M/W, football M/W, golf M/W, racquetball M/W, skiing (downhill) M/W, soccer M/W, softball M/W, table tennis M/W, tennis M/W, volleyball M/W.

Standardized Tests *Required:* SAT or ACT (for admission).

Costs (2007–08) *Tuition:* state resident $2868 full-time, $120 per semester hour part-time; nonresident $11,472 full-time, $478 per semester hour part-time. No tuition increase for student's term of enrollment. *Required fees:* $646 full-time. *Room and board:* $6220; room only: $2420. Room and board charges vary according to board plan and location. *Waivers:* senior citizens and employees or children of employees.

Financial Aid Of all full-time matriculated undergraduates who enrolled in 2006, 3,252 applied for aid, 2,375 were judged to have need, 1,294 had their need fully met. 80 Federal Work-Study jobs (averaging $3000). In 2006, 1810 non-need-based awards were made. *Average percent of need met:* 71%. *Average financial aid package:* $3920. *Average need-based loan:* $3718. *Average need-based gift aid:* $3915. *Average non-need-based aid:* $1705. *Average indebtedness upon graduation:* $26,591.

Applying *Options:* electronic application, early admission, deferred entrance. *Application fee:* $25. *Required:* high school transcript, minimum 2.5 GPA, proof of immunization. *Application deadlines:* 7/1 (freshmen), 7/1 (transfers). *Notification:* continuous (freshmen), continuous (transfers).

Freshman Application Contact Ms. Susan Lovell, Director of Admissions, Columbus State University, 4225 University Avenue, Columbus, GA 31907-5645. *Phone:* 706-507-8806. *Toll-free phone:* 866-264-2035. *Fax:* 706-568-5091. *E-mail:* admissions@colstate.edu.

COVENANT COLLEGE

Lookout Mountain, Georgia — www.covenant.edu/

- **Independent** comprehensive, founded 1955, affiliated with Presbyterian Church in America
- **Suburban** 250-acre campus
- **Endowment** $27.6 million
- **Coed** 1,007 undergraduate students, 96% full-time, 56% women, 44% men
- **Moderately difficult** entrance level, 65% of applicants were admitted

Undergraduates 968 full-time, 39 part-time. Students come from 49 states and territories, 18 other countries, 75% are from out of state, 3% African American, 2% Asian American or Pacific Islander, 1% Hispanic American, 0.2% Native American, 1% international, 5% transferred in, 89% live on campus. *Retention:* 80% of 2006 full-time freshmen returned.

Freshmen *Admission:* 939 applied, 610 admitted, 291 enrolled. *Average high school GPA:* 3.6. *Test scores:* SAT critical reading scores over 500: 78%; SAT math scores over 500: 72%; SAT writing scores over 500: 78%; ACT scores over 18: 92%; SAT critical reading scores over 600: 52%; SAT math scores over 600: 37%; SAT writing scores over 600: 36%; ACT scores over 24: 57%; SAT critical reading scores over 700: 15%; SAT math scores over 700: 5%; SAT writing scores over 700: 9%; ACT scores over 30: 16%.

Faculty *Total:* 87, 75% full-time, 77% with terminal degrees. *Student/faculty ratio:* 14:1.

Majors Biblical studies; biological and physical sciences; biology/biological sciences; business/commerce; chemistry; computer science; dramatic/theater arts; economics; elementary education; English; English/language arts teacher education; fine arts related; foreign languages and literatures; history; history teacher education; interdisciplinary studies; mathematics; mathematics teacher education; music; music history, literature, and theory; music performance; philosophy; philosophy and religious studies related; physical sciences related; physics; psychology; science teacher education; social sciences related; sociology.

Academics *Calendar:* semesters. *Degrees:* associate, bachelor's, and master's (master's degree in education only). *Special study options:* academic remediation for entering students, adult/continuing education programs, advanced placement credit, double majors, independent study, internships, off-campus study, part-time degree program, student-designed majors, study abroad, summer session for credit. *Unusual degree programs:* 3-2 engineering with Georgia Institute of Technology; nursing with Vanderbilt University.

Computers on Campus 137 computers/terminals are available on campus for general student use. Students can access the following: free student e-mail accounts, online (class) registration, online student information system. Campus-wide network is available. 100% of college-owned or -operated housing units are wired for high-speed Internet access. Wireless service is available via classrooms, computer labs, dorm rooms, libraries.

Student Life *Housing:* on-campus residence required through junior year. *Options:* men-only, women-only. Campus housing is university owned. Freshman campus housing is guaranteed. *Activities and organizations:* drama/theater group, student-run newspaper, radio station, choral group, Psychology Club, Interpretive Dance Group, Drama Club, Backpacking Club, Various Ministries. *Campus security:* night security guards. *Student services:* health clinic, personal/psychological counseling, women's center.

Athletics Member NAIA. *Intercollegiate sports:* baseball M (s), basketball M (s)/W (s), cross-country running M (s)/W (s), golf M (s), soccer M (s)/W (s), softball W (s), tennis W (s), volleyball W (s). *Intramural sports:* badminton M/W, basketball M/W, football M/W, soccer M/W, volleyball M/W.

Standardized Tests *Required:* SAT or ACT (for admission).

Costs (2007–08) *Comprehensive fee:* $29,330 includes full-time tuition ($22,160), mandatory fees ($680), and room and board ($6490). Full-time tuition and fees vary according to course load. Part-time tuition: $925 per credit hour. Part-time tuition and fees vary according to course load. *Payment plan:* installment. *Waivers:* senior citizens and employees or children of employees.

Financial Aid Of all full-time matriculated undergraduates who enrolled in 2006, 737 applied for aid, 631 were judged to have need, 152 had their need fully met. 313 Federal Work-Study jobs (averaging $1931). 69 state and other part-time jobs (averaging $1681). In 2006, 232 non-need-based awards were made. *Average percent of need met:* 80%. *Average financial aid package:* $17,104. *Average need-based loan:* $4715. *Average need-based gift aid:* $12,094. *Average non-need-based aid:* $6955. *Average indebtedness upon graduation:* $16,385.

Applying *Options:* electronic application, early admission, deferred entrance. *Application fee:* $45. *Required:* essay or personal statement, high school transcript, minimum 2.5 GPA, 2 letters of recommendation, interview. *Application deadlines:* rolling (freshmen), rolling (transfers). *Notification:* continuous (freshmen).

Freshman Application Contact Mrs. Jan Weaver, Assistant Director of Admissions, Covenant College, 14049 Scenic Highway, Lookout Mountain, GA 30750. *Phone:* 706-419-1148. *Toll-free phone:* 888-451-2683. *Fax:* 706-419-2255. *E-mail:* admissions@covenant.edu.

DALTON STATE COLLEGE

Dalton, Georgia — www.daltonstate.edu/

- **State-supported** 4-year, founded 1963, part of University System of Georgia
- **Small-town** 141-acre campus
- **Endowment** $15.2 million
- **Coed**
- **Noncompetitive** entrance level

Faculty *Student/faculty ratio:* 24:1.

Academics *Calendar:* semesters. *Degrees:* certificates, associate, and bachelor's.

Student Life *Campus security:* 24-hour emergency response devices and patrols.

Costs (2007–08) *Tuition:* state resident $1872 full-time, $78 per credit hour part-time; nonresident $7056 full-time, $319 per credit hour part-time. Full-time tuition and fees vary according to student level. Part-time tuition and fees vary according to student level.

Financial Aid Of all full-time matriculated undergraduates who enrolled in 2007, 1,591 applied for aid, 1,173 were judged to have need, 134 had their need fully met. 91 Federal Work-Study jobs (averaging $1433). 98 state and other part-time jobs (averaging $3665). In 2007, 104 non-need-based awards were made. *Average percent of need met:* 70. *Average financial aid package:* $2215. *Average need-based loan:* $1753. *Average need-based gift aid:* $2247. *Average non-need-based aid:* $672. *Average indebtedness upon graduation:* $4049.

Applying *Options:* early admission. *Application fee:* $25. *Required:* high school transcript.

Freshman Application Contact Dr. Angela Harris, Director of Admissions, Dalton State College, 213 North College Drive, Dalton, GA 30720-3797. *Phone:* 706-272-4476. *Toll-free phone:* 800-829-4436. *Fax:* 706-272-2530. *E-mail:* aharris@daltonstate.edu.

DEVRY UNIVERSITY

Alpharetta, Georgia — www.devry.edu/

- **Proprietary** comprehensive, founded 1997, part of DeVry University
- **Suburban** 9-acre campus with easy access to Atlanta
- **Coed** 674 undergraduate students, 44% full-time, 45% women, 55% men
- **Minimally difficult** entrance level

Undergraduates 298 full-time, 376 part-time. 5% are from out of state, 44% African American, 3% Asian American or Pacific Islander, 4% Hispanic American, 0.3% Native American, 1% international, 24% transferred in. *Retention:* 60% of 2006 full-time freshmen returned.

Freshmen *Admission:* 92 enrolled.

Faculty *Total:* 82, 35% full-time. *Student/faculty ratio:* 10:1.

Majors Business administration and management; business administration, management and operations related; computer engineering technology; computer software engineering; computer systems analysis; computer systems networking and telecommunications; electrical, electronic and communications engineering technology; health information/medical records technology; web page, digital/multimedia and information resources design.

Academics *Calendar:* semesters. *Degrees:* associate, bachelor's, and master's. *Special study options:* academic remediation for entering students, accelerated degree program, adult/continuing education programs, advanced placement credit, distance learning, part-time degree program, summer session for credit.
Computers on Campus 218 computers/terminals are available on campus for general student use. Students can access the following: online (class) registration. Campuswide network is available.
Student Life *Housing:* college housing not available. *Activities and organizations:* Epsilon Delta Pi, International Student Organization, Programming Club, Alpha Sigma Lambda, National Society of Black Engineers. *Campus security:* 24-hour emergency response devices, late-night transport/escort service, lighted pathways, video recorder (CCTV).
Costs (2008–09) *Tuition:* $13,810 full-time, $515 per credit part-time. *Required fees:* $180 full-time.
Financial Aid Of all full-time matriculated undergraduates who enrolled in 2002, 1,047 applied for aid, 957 were judged to have need, 41 had their need fully met. In 2002, 133 non-need-based awards were made. *Average percent of need met:* 46%. *Average financial aid package:* $8858. *Average need-based loan:* $5520. *Average need-based gift aid:* $3799. *Average non-need-based aid:* $8453.
Applying *Options:* electronic application, early admission, deferred entrance. *Application fee:* $50. *Required:* high school transcript, interview. *Application deadlines:* rolling (freshmen), rolling (transfers). *Notification:* continuous (freshmen), continuous (transfers).
Freshman Application Contact DeVry University, 2555 Northwinds Parkway, Alpharetta, GA 30004. *Toll-free phone:* 800-346-5420.

DeVry University
Atlanta, Georgia

DeVry University
Decatur, Georgia www.devry.edu/

- **Proprietary** comprehensive, founded 1969, part of DeVry University
- **Suburban** 21-acre campus with easy access to Atlanta
- **Coed** 2,090 undergraduate students, 54% full-time, 50% women, 50% men
- **Minimally difficult** entrance level

Undergraduates 1,137 full-time, 953 part-time. 5% are from out of state, 71% African American, 2% Asian American or Pacific Islander, 2% Hispanic American, 0.2% Native American, 0.8% international, 18% transferred in. *Retention:* 54% of 2006 full-time freshmen returned.
Freshmen *Admission:* 325 enrolled.
Faculty *Total:* 151, 28% full-time. *Student/faculty ratio:* 21:1.
Majors Accounting; biomedical technology; business administration and management; business administration, management and operations related; computer engineering technology; computer software engineering; computer systems analysis; computer systems networking and telecommunications; electrical, electronic and communications engineering technology; health information/medical records technology; web page, digital/multimedia and information resources design.
Academics *Calendar:* semesters. *Degrees:* associate, bachelor's, master's, and postbachelor's certificates. *Special study options:* academic remediation for entering students, accelerated degree program, adult/continuing education programs, advanced placement credit, distance learning, part-time degree program, services for LD students, summer session for credit.
Computers on Campus Students can access the following: online (class) registration. Campuswide network is available.
Student Life *Housing:* college housing not available. *Activities and organizations:* Programming Club, Epsilon Delta Pi, Tau Alpha Pi, National Society of Black Engineers, International Student Organization. *Campus security:* 24-hour emergency response devices and patrols, late-night transport/escort service, lighted pathways/sidewalks.
Athletics *Intramural sports:* basketball M/W, football M/W, softball M/W, volleyball M/W.
Costs (2008–09) *Tuition:* $13,810 full-time, $515 per credit part-time. *Required fees:* $180 full-time.
Financial Aid Of all full-time matriculated undergraduates who enrolled in 2002, 2,255 applied for aid, 2,195 were judged to have need, 49 had their need fully met. In 2002, 137 non-need-based awards were made. *Average percent of need met:* 47%. *Average financial aid package:* $9862. *Average need-based loan:* $5600. *Average need-based gift aid:* $4432. *Average non-need-based aid:* $8842.
Applying *Options:* electronic application, early admission, deferred entrance. *Application fee:* $50. *Required:* high school transcript, interview. *Application deadlines:* rolling (freshmen), rolling (transfers). *Notification:* continuous (freshmen), continuous (transfers).
Freshman Application Contact DeVry University, 250 North Arcadia Avenue, Decatur, GA 30030-2198.

DeVry University
Duluth, Georgia

Emmanuel College
Franklin Springs, Georgia www.ec.edu/

- **Independent** 4-year, founded 1919, affiliated with Pentecostal Holiness Church
- **Rural** 90-acre campus with easy access to Atlanta
- **Endowment** $3.7 million
- **Coed** 658 undergraduate students, 88% full-time, 54% women, 46% men
- **Minimally difficult** entrance level, 41% of applicants were admitted

Undergraduates 581 full-time, 77 part-time. Students come from 22 states and territories, 4 other countries, 23% are from out of state, 15% African American, 0.9% Asian American or Pacific Islander, 3% Hispanic American, 0.5% Native American, 1% international, 10% transferred in, 44% live on campus. *Retention:* 65% of 2006 full-time freshmen returned.
Freshmen *Admission:* 1,341 applied, 544 admitted, 140 enrolled. *Average high school GPA:* 3.17.
Faculty *Total:* 71, 49% full-time, 38% with terminal degrees. *Student/faculty ratio:* 11:1.
Majors Biology/biological sciences; business teacher education; computer and information sciences; elementary education; English; English/language arts teacher education; kinesiology and exercise science; liberal arts and sciences/liberal studies; mass communication/media; mathematics; mathematics teacher education; middle school education; music; music teacher education; office management; organizational communication; pastoral studies/counseling; pre-law studies; pre-pharmacy studies; psychology; religious/sacred music; social science teacher education; sport and fitness administration/management.
Academics *Calendar:* semesters. *Degrees:* associate and bachelor's. *Special study options:* academic remediation for entering students, accelerated degree program, advanced placement credit, distance learning, honors programs, independent study, internships, part-time degree program, summer session for credit.
Computers on Campus 50 computers/terminals are available on campus for general student use. Students can access the following: online (class) registration. Campuswide network is available. 100% of college-owned or -operated housing units are wired for high-speed Internet access. Wireless service is available via entire campus.
Student Life *Housing:* on-campus residence required through sophomore year. *Options:* men-only, women-only. Campus housing is university owned. Freshman campus housing is guaranteed. *Activities and organizations:* drama/theater group, student-run newspaper, choral group, SIFE, FCA, SOS, BSU, International Students Club. *Campus security:* student patrols, controlled dormitory access. *Student services:* personal/psychological counseling.
Athletics Member NAIA, NCCAA. *Intercollegiate sports:* baseball M (s), basketball M (s)/W (s), soccer M (s)/W (s), softball W (s), tennis M (s)/W (s). *Intramural sports:* basketball M/W, football M/W, golf M/W, soccer M/W, tennis M/W, track and field M/W, volleyball M/W, weight lifting M/W.
Standardized Tests *Required:* SAT or ACT (for admission).
Costs (2008–09) *Comprehensive fee:* $17,844 includes full-time tuition ($12,260) and room and board ($5584). Part-time tuition: $504 per hour. *College room only:* $2550.
Financial Aid Of all full-time matriculated undergraduates who enrolled in 2001, 636 applied for aid, 493 were judged to have need, 136 had their need fully met. 209 Federal Work-Study jobs (averaging $2474). 105 state and other part-time jobs (averaging $1408). In 2001, 133 non-need-based awards were made. *Average percent of need met:* 53%. *Average financial aid package:* $8948. *Average need-based loan:* $3319. *Average need-based gift aid:* $3080. *Average non-need-based aid:* $3368. *Average indebtedness upon graduation:* $16,575.
Applying *Options:* electronic application, early admission, deferred entrance. *Application fee:* $25. *Required:* high school transcript. *Application deadlines:* 8/1 (freshmen), 8/1 (transfers). *Notification:* 8/1 (freshmen), continuous until 8/1 (transfers).

Freshman Application Contact Ms. Jessica Dunning, Admissions Assistant, Emmanuel College, PO Box 129, 181 Spring Street, Franklin Springs, GA 30639-0129. *Phone:* 706-245-7226. *Toll-free phone:* 800-860-8800. *E-mail:* admissions@ec.edu.

EMORY UNIVERSITY

Atlanta, Georgia www.emory.edu/

- **Independent Methodist** university, founded 1836
- **Suburban** 634-acre campus
- **Endowment** $5.3 billion
- **Coed** 5,134 undergraduate students, 99% full-time, 56% women, 44% men
- **Most difficult** entrance level, 27% of applicants were admitted

Undergraduates 5,085 full-time, 49 part-time. Students come from 52 states and territories, 60 other countries, 79% are from out of state, 9% African American, 18% Asian American or Pacific Islander, 3% Hispanic American, 0.2% Native American, 7% international, 2% transferred in, 70% live on campus. *Retention:* 94% of 2006 full-time freshmen returned.

Freshmen *Admission:* 15,366 applied, 4,175 admitted, 1,235 enrolled. *Average high school GPA:* 3.72. *Test scores:* SAT critical reading scores over 500: 100%; SAT math scores over 500: 100%; SAT writing scores over 500: 99%; ACT scores over 18: 100%; SAT critical reading scores over 600: 91%; SAT math scores over 600: 95%; SAT writing scores over 600: 89%; ACT scores over 24: 96%; SAT critical reading scores over 700: 48%; SAT math scores over 700: 56%; SAT writing scores over 700: 47%; ACT scores over 30: 70%.

Faculty *Total:* 1,455, 85% full-time, 99% with terminal degrees. *Student/faculty ratio:* 7:1.

Majors Accounting; African-American/Black studies; African studies; American studies; anthropology; art history, criticism and conservation; Asian-American studies; Asian studies; banking and financial support services; biology/biological sciences; biomedical sciences; business administration and management; business/managerial economics; chemistry; Chinese; classics; classics and languages, literatures and linguistics; comparative literature; computer science; creative writing; dance; dramatic/theater arts; economics; education; English; film/cinema studies; finance; fine/studio arts; French; German; history; interdisciplinary studies; international relations and affairs; Italian; Japanese; Jewish/Judaic studies; journalism; Latin; Latin American studies; liberal arts and sciences/liberal studies; literature; marketing/marketing management; mathematics; medieval and Renaissance studies; modern Greek; music; neuroscience; nursing (registered nurse training); philosophy; physics; political science and government; psychology; religious studies; Russian; sociology; Spanish; women's studies.

Academics *Calendar:* semesters. *Degrees:* associate, bachelor's, master's, doctoral, and first professional (enrollment figures include Emory University, Oxford College; application data for main campus only). *Special study options:* accelerated degree program, advanced placement credit, cooperative education, double majors, English as a second language, honors programs, independent study, internships, off-campus study, services for LD students, study abroad, summer session for credit. *ROTC:* Army (c), Navy (c), Air Force (c). *Unusual degree programs:* 3-2 engineering with Georgia Institute of Technology.

Computers on Campus 600 computers/terminals are available on campus for general student use. Students can access the following: campus intranet, computer help desk, free student e-mail accounts, online (class) grades, online (class) registration, online (class) schedules. Campuswide network is available. Wireless service is available via entire campus.

Student Life *Housing:* on-campus residence required through sophomore year. *Options:* coed, men-only, women-only, disabled students. Campus housing is university owned. Freshman campus housing is guaranteed. *Activities and organizations:* drama/theater group, student-run newspaper, radio and television station, choral group, Volunteer Emory, music/theater, student government, Outdoor Emory, athletics, national fraternities, national sororities. *Campus security:* 24-hour emergency response devices and patrols, student patrols, late-night transport/escort service. *Student services:* health clinic, personal/psychological counseling, women's center, legal services.

Athletics Member NCAA. All Division III. *Intercollegiate sports:* badminton M (c)/W (c), baseball M, basketball M/W, bowling M (c)/W (c), crew M (c)/W (c), cross-country running M/W, equestrian sports M (c)/W (c), fencing M (c)/W (c), field hockey W (c), golf M, gymnastics M (c)/W (c), lacrosse M (c)/W (c), racquetball M (c)/W (c), rugby M (c), sailing M (c)/W (c), soccer M/W, softball W, swimming and diving M/W, table tennis M (c)/W (c), tennis M/W, track and field M/W, ultimate Frisbee M (c)/W (c), volleyball M (c)/W, water polo M (c)/W (c), wrestling M (c). *Intramural sports:* badminton M/W, baseball M, basketball M/W, bowling M/W, cheerleading M/W, crew M/W, cross-country running M/W, fencing M/W, field hockey W, football M/W, golf M/W, ice hockey M, lacrosse M, racquetball M/W, rugby M, sailing M/W, soccer M/W, softball M/W, swimming and diving M/W, tennis M/W, track and field M/W, volleyball M/W, water polo M/W, weight lifting M/W, wrestling M.

Standardized Tests *Required:* SAT or ACT (for admission). *Recommended:* SAT Subject Tests (for admission).

Costs (2008–09) *Comprehensive fee:* $47,858 includes full-time tuition ($35,800), mandatory fees ($486), and room and board ($11,572).

Financial Aid Of all full-time matriculated undergraduates who enrolled in 2006, 3,004 applied for aid, 2,520 were judged to have need, 2,520 had their need fully met. 1,802 Federal Work-Study jobs (averaging $1880). 98 state and other part-time jobs (averaging $6020). In 2006, 1092 non-need-based awards were made. *Average percent of need met:* 100%. *Average financial aid package:* $27,971. *Average need-based loan:* $3291. *Average need-based gift aid:* $27,011. *Average non-need-based aid:* $17,013. *Average indebtedness upon graduation:* $24,272. *Financial aid deadline:* 3/1.

Applying *Options:* electronic application, early admission, early decision, deferred entrance. *Application fee:* $50. *Required:* essay or personal statement, high school transcript, 1 letter of recommendation. *Recommended:* minimum 3.0 GPA. *Application deadlines:* 1/15 (freshmen), 6/1 (transfers). *Early decision deadline:* 11/1 (for plan 1), 1/1 (for plan 2). *Notification:* 4/1 (freshmen), continuous (transfers), 12/15 (early decision plan 1), 2/1 (early decision plan 2).

Freshman Application Contact Ms. Jean Jordan, Interim Dean of Admission, Emory University, 200 Boisfeuillet Jones Center, Atlanta, GA 30322-1100. *Phone:* 404-727-6036. *Toll-free phone:* 800-727-6036. *E-mail:* admiss@learnlink.emory.edu.

See page 738 for the College Close-Up.

FORT VALLEY STATE UNIVERSITY

Fort Valley, Georgia www.fvsu.edu/

Freshman Application Contact Mr. Donald Moore, Director of Admissions and Recruitment, Fort Valley State University, 1005 State University Drive, Fort Valley, GA 31030. *Phone:* 478-825-6307. *Toll-free phone:* 800-248-7343. *Fax:* 478-825-6169. *E-mail:* admissap@fvsu.edu.

GAINESVILLE STATE COLLEGE

Oakwood, Georgia www.gc.peachnet.edu/

- **State-supported** primarily 2-year, founded 1964, part of University System of Georgia
- **Small-town** 220-acre campus with easy access to Atlanta
- **Endowment** $9.2 million
- **Coed**
- **Noncompetitive** entrance level

Faculty *Student/faculty ratio:* 24:1.

Academics *Calendar:* semesters. *Degrees:* associate and bachelor's.

Student Life *Campus security:* 24-hour patrols.

Standardized Tests *Recommended:* SAT or ACT (for admission).

Costs (2007–08) *Tuition:* state resident $1872 full-time, $78 per credit hour part-time; nonresident $7488 full-time, $312 per credit hour part-time. No tuition increase for student's term of enrollment. *Required fees:* $180 full-time, $80 per term part-time.

Financial Aid Of all full-time matriculated undergraduates who enrolled in 2006, 40 Federal Work-Study jobs (averaging $2000).

Applying *Options:* early admission. *Application fee:* $35. *Required:* high school transcript.

Freshman Application Contact Mr. W. Mack Palmour, Director of Admissions, Gainesville State College, PO Box 1358, Gainesville, GA 30503. *Phone:* 678-717-3641. *Fax:* 678-717-3751. *E-mail:* mpalmour@gsc.edu.

GEORGIA COLLEGE & STATE UNIVERSITY

Milledgeville, Georgia www.gcsu.edu/

- **State-supported** comprehensive, founded 1889, part of University System of Georgia
- **Small-town** 590-acre campus
- **Endowment** $18.6 million

- **Coed** 5,319 undergraduate students, 91% full-time, 60% women, 40% men
- **Moderately difficult** entrance level, 59% of applicants were admitted

Undergraduates 4,826 full-time, 493 part-time. Students come from 33 states and territories, 47 other countries, 2% are from out of state, 6% African American, 1% Asian American or Pacific Islander, 2% Hispanic American, 0.3% Native American, 2% international, 7% transferred in, 39% live on campus. *Retention:* 81% of 2006 full-time freshmen returned.

Freshmen *Admission:* 3,442 applied, 2,038 admitted, 1,204 enrolled. *Average high school GPA:* 3.31. *Test scores:* SAT critical reading scores over 500: 90%; SAT math scores over 500: 87%; ACT scores over 18: 98%; SAT critical reading scores over 600: 27%; SAT math scores over 600: 29%; ACT scores over 24: 44%; SAT critical reading scores over 700: 3%; SAT math scores over 700: 1%; ACT scores over 30: 2%.

Faculty *Total:* 403, 70% full-time, 58% with terminal degrees. *Student/faculty ratio:* 17:1.

Majors Accounting; art; biology/biological sciences; business administration and management; business/commerce; business/managerial economics; chemistry; computer and information sciences; criminal justice/law enforcement administration; dramatic/theater arts; early childhood education; education related; English; environmental science; French; health teacher education; history; international business/trade/commerce; journalism; liberal arts and sciences and humanities related; management sciences and quantitative methods related; marketing/marketing management; mathematics; middle school education; music; music teacher education; music therapy; nursing (registered nurse training); parks, recreation and leisure; philosophy; physical education teaching and coaching; political science and government; psychology; sociology; Spanish; special education; speech and rhetoric.

Academics *Calendar:* semesters. *Degrees:* bachelor's, master's, and post-master's certificates. *Special study options:* accelerated degree program, advanced placement credit, distance learning, double majors, English as a second language, freshman honors college, honors programs, independent study, internships, part-time degree program, services for LD students, student-designed majors, study abroad, summer session for credit. *ROTC:* Army (c). *Unusual degree programs:* 3-2 engineering with Georgia Institute of Technology.

Computers on Campus 450 computers/terminals are available on campus for general student use. Students can access the following: online (class) registration. Campuswide network is available. 100% of college-owned or -operated housing units are wired for high-speed Internet access. Wireless service is available via entire campus.

Student Life *Housing:* on-campus residence required for freshman year. *Options:* coed. Campus housing is university owned and leased by the school. Freshman applicants given priority for college housing. *Activities and organizations:* drama/theater group, student-run newspaper, radio and television station, choral group, Baptist Collegiate Ministries, Wesley Foundation, Greek Letter School Sororities, Campus Outreach, Greek Letter School Fraternities, national fraternities, national sororities. *Campus security:* 24-hour emergency response devices and patrols, student patrols, late-night transport/escort service, controlled dormitory access. *Student services:* health clinic, personal/psychological counseling, women's center.

Athletics Member NCAA. All Division II. *Intercollegiate sports:* baseball M (s), basketball M (s)/W (s), cheerleading M/W, cross-country running M (s)/W (s), golf M (s), soccer W (s), softball W (s), tennis M (s)/W (s). *Intramural sports:* archery M/W, basketball M/W, bowling M/W, fencing M (c)/W (c), football M/W, golf M, lacrosse M (c)/W (c), racquetball M/W, rugby M (c), soccer M/W, softball M/W, swimming and diving M (c)/W (c), table tennis M/W, tennis M/W, ultimate Frisbee M/W, volleyball M/W, wrestling M.

Standardized Tests *Required:* SAT or ACT (for admission). *Required for some:* SAT Subject Tests (for admission).

Costs (2007–08) *Tuition:* state resident $4208 full-time, $176 per semester hour part-time; nonresident $16,830 full-time, $702 per semester hour part-time. Full-time tuition and fees vary according to student level. No tuition increase for student's term of enrollment. *Required fees:* $858 full-time, $429 per term part-time. *Room and board:* $7380; room only: $3990. Room and board charges vary according to board plan and housing facility. *Waivers:* senior citizens and employees or children of employees.

Financial Aid Of all full-time matriculated undergraduates who enrolled in 2006, 4,252 applied for aid, 1,653 were judged to have need, 21 had their need fully met. In 2006, 121 non-need-based awards were made. *Average percent of need met:* 40%. *Average financial aid package:* $5598. *Average need-based loan:* $2142. *Average need-based gift aid:* $2752. *Average non-need-based aid:* $1869. *Average indebtedness upon graduation:* $14,340.

Applying *Options:* electronic application, early admission, early action, deferred entrance. *Application fee:* $40. *Required:* essay or personal statement, high school transcript, proof of immunization. *Recommended:* interview. *Application deadlines:* 4/1 (freshmen), 7/1 (transfers), 11/1 (early action). *Notification:* continuous (freshmen), continuous (transfers), 12/1 (early action).

Freshman Application Contact Mr. Mike Augustine, Director of Admissions, Georgia College & State University, CPO Box 023, Milledgeville, GA 31061. *Phone:* 478-445-1284. *Toll-free phone:* 800-342-0471. *Fax:* 478-445-3653. *E-mail:* info@gcsu.edu.

GEORGIA INSTITUTE OF TECHNOLOGY

Atlanta, Georgia **www.gatech.edu/**

- **State-supported** university, founded 1885, part of University System of Georgia
- **Urban** 400-acre campus
- **Endowment** $1.6 billion
- **Coed, primarily men** 12,565 undergraduate students, 93% full-time, 30% women, 70% men
- **Very difficult** entrance level, 63% of applicants were admitted

Undergraduates 11,729 full-time, 836 part-time. Students come from 53 states and territories, 74 other countries, 29% are from out of state, 7% African American, 16% Asian American or Pacific Islander, 5% Hispanic American, 0.3% Native American, 5% international, 3% transferred in, 59% live on campus. *Retention:* 92% of 2006 full-time freshmen returned.

Freshmen *Admission:* 9,664 applied, 6,122 admitted, 2,654 enrolled. *Average high school GPA:* 3.73. *Test scores:* SAT critical reading scores over 500: 97%; SAT math scores over 500: 99%; SAT writing scores over 500: 97%; ACT scores over 18: 99%; SAT critical reading scores over 600: 73%; SAT math scores over 600: 93%; SAT writing scores over 600: 67%; ACT scores over 24: 96%; SAT critical reading scores over 700: 21%; SAT math scores over 700: 45%; SAT writing scores over 700: 16%; ACT scores over 30: 37%.

Faculty *Total:* 871, 99% full-time, 98% with terminal degrees. *Student/faculty ratio:* 14:1.

Majors Aerospace, aeronautical and astronautical engineering; applied mathematics; applied mathematics related; architecture; architecture related; biochemistry; biology/biological sciences; biomedical/medical engineering; business administration and management; business/managerial economics; chemical engineering; chemistry; civil engineering; computer and information sciences; computer engineering; digital communication and media/multimedia; electrical, electronics and communications engineering; environmental/environmental health engineering; geological and earth sciences/geosciences related; history and philosophy of science and technology; industrial and organizational psychology; industrial design; industrial engineering; international/global studies; international relations and affairs; materials engineering; mechanical engineering; multi-/interdisciplinary studies related; nuclear engineering; physics; public policy analysis; science, technology and society; textile sciences and engineering.

Academics *Calendar:* semesters. *Degrees:* bachelor's, master's, and doctoral. *Special study options:* academic remediation for entering students, accelerated degree program, advanced placement credit, cooperative education, distance learning, double majors, English as a second language, honors programs, independent study, internships, off-campus study, part-time degree program, services for LD students, student-designed majors, study abroad, summer session for credit. *ROTC:* Army (b), Navy (b), Air Force (b). *Unusual degree programs:* 3-2 engineering with several units of the University System of Georgia, and approximately 28 other colleges and universities throughout the nation.

Computers on Campus 1,996 computers/terminals are available on campus for general student use. Students can access the following: campus intranet, computer help desk, free student e-mail accounts, online (class) grades, online (class) registration, online (class) schedules. Campuswide network is available. 100% of college-owned or -operated housing units are wired for high-speed Internet access. Wireless service is available via classrooms, computer centers, computer labs, dorm rooms, learning centers, libraries, student centers.

Student Life *Housing options:* coed, men-only, women-only, disabled students. Campus housing is university owned. Freshman campus housing is guaranteed. *Activities and organizations:* drama/theater group, student-run newspaper, radio and television station, choral group, marching band, Christian Campus Fellowship, IEEE, Mechanical Engineering Graduate Student Association, Gamma Beta Phi Society, national fraternities, national sororities. *Campus security:* 24-hour emergency response devices and patrols, late-night transport/escort service, controlled dormitory access, self defense education, lighted pathways and walks, video cameras. *Student services:* health clinic, personal/psychological counseling, women's center, legal services.

Athletics Member NCAA. All Division I except football (Division I-A). *Intercollegiate sports:* baseball M (s), basketball M (s)/W (s), cheerleading M (s)/W (s), cross-country running M (s)/W (s), equestrian sports M (c)/W (c), golf M (s), ice hockey M (c), lacrosse M (c)/W (c), rugby M (c), soccer M (c)/W (c), softball W (s), swimming and diving M (s)/W (s), tennis M (s)/W (s), track and field M (s)/W (s), volleyball W (s), wrestling M (c). *Intramural sports:* badminton M/W, baseball M (c), basketball M/W, bowling M (c)/W (c), cheerleading M (c)/W (c), crew M (c)/W (c), equestrian sports M/W, fencing M (c)/W (c), field hockey M (c)/W (c), football M, golf M (c)/W (c), gymnastics M (c)/W (c), ice hockey M (c), lacrosse M (c)/W (c), racquetball M (c)/W (c), sailing M (c)/W (c), soccer M (c)/W (c), softball W, swimming and diving M/W, table tennis M (c)/W (c), tennis M (c)/W (c), track and field M/W, ultimate Frisbee M/W, volleyball M (c)/W (c), water polo M (c)/W (c).

Standardized Tests *Required:* SAT or ACT (for admission).

Costs (2007–08) *Tuition:* state resident $4496 full-time, $188 per hour part-time; nonresident $22,220 full-time, $926 per hour part-time. Full-time tuition and fees vary according to course load, reciprocity agreements, and student level. Part-time tuition and fees vary according to course load, reciprocity agreements, and student level. No tuition increase for student's term of enrollment. *Required fees:* $1146 full-time, $573 per term part-time. *Room and board:* $7328; room only: $4358. Room and board charges vary according to board plan and housing facility.

Financial Aid Of all full-time matriculated undergraduates who enrolled in 2007, 5,014 applied for aid, 2,886 were judged to have need, 1,280 had their need fully met. 434 Federal Work-Study jobs (averaging $1964). In 2007, 779 non-need-based awards were made. *Average percent of need met:* 67%. *Average financial aid package:* $10,475. *Average need-based loan:* $3938. *Average need-based gift aid:* $5191. *Average non-need-based aid:* $3514. *Average indebtedness upon graduation:* $21,436. *Financial aid deadline:* 3/1.

Applying *Options:* electronic application, early admission. *Application fee:* $50. *Required:* essay or personal statement, high school transcript. *Application deadlines:* 1/15 (freshmen), 2/1 (transfers). *Notification:* 3/15 (freshmen), continuous (transfers).

Freshman Application Contact Ms. Ingrid Hayes, Director of Admissions (Undergraduate), Georgia Institute of Technology, 225 North Avenue, NW, Atlanta, GA 30332-0320. *Phone:* 404-894-4154. *Fax:* 404-894-9511. *E-mail:* admission@gatech.edu.

GEORGIA SOUTHERN UNIVERSITY

Statesboro, Georgia **www.georgiasouthern.edu/**

- **State-supported** university, founded 1906, part of University System of Georgia
- **Small-town** 634-acre campus
- **Endowment** $39.4 million
- **Coed** 14,854 undergraduate students, 89% full-time, 49% women, 51% men
- **Moderately difficult** entrance level, 45% of applicants were admitted

Undergraduates 13,272 full-time, 1,582 part-time. Students come from 46 states and territories, 80 other countries, 5% are from out of state, 22% African American, 1% Asian American or Pacific Islander, 2% Hispanic American, 0.3% Native American, 0.9% international, 6% transferred in, 26% live on campus. *Retention:* 79% of 2006 full-time freshmen returned.

Freshmen *Admission:* 8,090 applied, 3,669 admitted, 3,058 enrolled. *Average high school GPA:* 3.16. *Test scores:* SAT critical reading scores over 500: 83%; SAT math scores over 500: 86%; ACT scores over 18: 99%; SAT critical reading scores over 600: 23%; SAT math scores over 600: 25%; ACT scores over 24: 35%; SAT critical reading scores over 700: 2%; SAT math scores over 700: 2%; ACT scores over 30: 2%.

Faculty *Total:* 780, 91% full-time, 77% with terminal degrees. *Student/faculty ratio:* 19:1.

Majors Accounting; anthropology; apparel and textiles; art; athletic training; biology/biological sciences; business administration and management; business/managerial economics; chemistry; civil engineering; civil engineering technology; clinical laboratory science/medical technology; communication/speech communication and rhetoric; computer and information sciences; computer engineering; construction engineering technology; criminal justice/safety; development economics and international development; dramatic/theater arts; economics; education; electrical, electronic and communications engineering technology; electrical, electronics and communications engineering; elementary education; English; English composition; family and consumer sciences/home economics teacher education; finance; foods, nutrition, and wellness; forestry; French; general studies; geography; geology/earth science; German; graphic and printing equipment operation/production; health and physical education; history; hotel/motel administration; human development and family studies; industrial production technologies related; information science/studies; interior design; international business/trade/commerce; international relations and affairs; journalism; kinesiology and exercise science; logistics and materials management; management information systems; marketing/marketing management; mathematics; mechanical engineering; mechanical engineering/mechanical technology; middle school education; music; music performance; music teacher education, music theory and composition; nursing (registered nurse training); parks, recreation and leisure; pharmacology; philosophy; physical education teaching and coaching; physics; political science and government; pre-dentistry studies; pre-medical studies; pre-pharmacy studies; pre-veterinary studies; psychology; public health education and promotion; public relations/image management; radio and television; sociology; Spanish; Spanish language teacher education; special education; speech and rhetoric; sport and fitness administration/management; technology/industrial arts teacher education.

Academics *Calendar:* semesters. *Degrees:* bachelor's, master's, doctoral, and post-master's certificates. *Special study options:* academic remediation for entering students, adult/continuing education programs, advanced placement credit, cooperative education, distance learning, double majors, English as a second language, external degree program, honors programs, independent study, internships, off-campus study, part-time degree program, services for LD students, study abroad, summer session for credit. *ROTC:* Army (b). *Unusual degree programs:* 3-2 engineering with Georgia Institute of Technology; forestry with University of Georgia; physics with Georgia Institute of Technology.

Computers on Campus 2,385 computers/terminals and 5,200 ports are available on campus for general student use. Students can access the following: computer help desk, free student e-mail accounts, online (class) grades, online (class) registration, online (class) schedules. Campuswide network is available. 100% of college-owned or -operated housing units are wired for high-speed Internet access. Wireless service is available via classrooms, computer labs, dorm rooms, libraries, student centers.

Student Life *Housing options:* coed, disabled students. Campus housing is university owned. *Activities and organizations:* drama/theater group, student-run newspaper, radio station, choral group, marching band, Residence Hall Association, Campus Religious Ministries, Student Government Association, Black Student Association, Greek Life, national fraternities, national sororities. *Campus security:* 24-hour emergency response devices and patrols, student patrols, late-night transport/escort service, residence hall security, locked residence hall entrances. *Student services:* health clinic, personal/psychological counseling, women's center, legal services.

Athletics Member NCAA. All Division I except football (Division I-AA). *Intercollegiate sports:* baseball M (s), basketball M (s)/W (s), bowling M (c)/W (c), cheerleading M/W, cross-country running W (s), equestrian sports M (c)/W (c), fencing M (c)/W (c), golf M (s), lacrosse M (c), rugby M (c)/W (c), soccer M (s)/W (s), softball W (s), swimming and diving W (s), tennis M (s)/W (s), track and field W (s), ultimate Frisbee M (c)/W (c), volleyball W (s), wrestling M (c)/W (c). *Intramural sports:* baseball M (c), basketball M/W, bowling M/W, football M/W, golf M/W, soccer M/W, softball M/W, tennis M/W, track and field M (c)/W (c), volleyball M/W.

Standardized Tests *Required:* SAT or ACT (for admission).

Costs (2007–08) *Tuition:* state resident $2958 full-time, $124 per semester hour part-time; nonresident $11,830 full-time, $493 per semester hour part-time. Full-time tuition and fees vary according to degree level and location. Part-time tuition and fees vary according to course load, degree level, and location. No tuition increase for student's term of enrollment. *Required fees:* $1124 full-time, $562 per term part-time. *Room and board:* $6860; room only: $4340. Room and board charges vary according to board plan and housing facility. *Waivers:* senior citizens and employees or children of employees.

Financial Aid Of all full-time matriculated undergraduates who enrolled in 2006, 11,082 applied for aid, 6,545 were judged to have need, 971 had their need fully met. 361 Federal Work-Study jobs (averaging $1172). In 2006, 331 non-need-based awards were made. *Average percent of need met:* 60%. *Average financial aid package:* $6851. *Average need-based loan:* $3825. *Average need-based gift aid:* $4663. *Average non-need-based aid:* $1404. *Average indebtedness upon graduation:* $18,618.

Applying *Options:* electronic application, early admission, deferred entrance. *Application fee:* $30. *Required:* high school transcript, minimum 2.0 GPA, proof of immunization prior to enrollment. *Required for some:* high school transcript. *Application deadlines:* 5/1 (freshmen), 8/1 (transfers). *Notification:* continuous (freshmen), continuous (transfers).

Freshman Application Contact Mrs. Susan Davies, Director, Georgia Southern University, GSU PO Box 8024, Statesboro, GA 30460. *Phone:* 912-681-5391. *Fax:* 912-486-7240. *E-mail:* admissions@georgiasouthern.edu.

GEORGIA SOUTHWESTERN STATE UNIVERSITY

Americus, Georgia **www.gsw.edu/**

- **State-supported** comprehensive, founded 1906, part of University System of Georgia
- **Small-town** 255-acre campus
- **Endowment** $25.0 million
- **Coed** 2,221 undergraduate students, 76% full-time, 65% women, 35% men
- **Moderately difficult** entrance level, 79% of applicants were admitted

Undergraduates 1,680 full-time, 541 part-time. Students come from 31 states and territories, 29 other countries, 4% are from out of state, 31% African American, 1% Asian American or Pacific Islander, 1% Hispanic American, 0.4% Native American, 2% international, 10% transferred in, 34% live on campus. *Retention:* 64% of 2006 full-time freshmen returned.

Freshmen *Admission:* 1,040 applied, 817 admitted, 426 enrolled. *Average high school GPA:* 3.14. *Test scores:* SAT critical reading scores over 500: 44%; SAT math scores over 500: 42%; ACT scores over 18: 78%; SAT critical reading scores over 600: 12%; SAT math scores over 600: 9%; ACT scores over 24: 12%.

Faculty *Total:* 143, 64% full-time, 57% with terminal degrees. *Student/faculty ratio:* 18:1.

Majors Accounting; art; biology/biological sciences; business administration and management; chemistry; computer and information sciences; computer engineering technology; computer programming (specific applications); computer science; dramatic/theater arts; education; elementary education; English; geology/earth science; history; human resources management; management information systems; marketing/marketing management; mathematics; middle school education; music; nursing (registered nurse training); parks, recreation and leisure facilities management; physical education teaching and coaching; physical sciences; political science and government; psychology; sociology; special education.

Academics *Calendar:* semesters. *Degrees:* bachelor's, master's, post-master's, and postbachelor's certificates. *Special study options:* academic remediation for entering students, advanced placement credit, distance learning, double majors, English as a second language, honors programs, internships, off-campus study, part-time degree program, services for LD students, study abroad, summer session for credit. *Unusual degree programs:* 3-2 engineering with Georgia Institute of Technology; math, physics with Georgia Institute of Technology.

Computers on Campus 550 computers/terminals are available on campus for general student use. Students can access the following: free student e-mail accounts, online (class) grades, online (class) registration, online (class) schedules. Campuswide network is available.

Student Life *Housing:* on-campus residence required through sophomore year. *Options:* coed. Campus housing is university owned. Freshman campus housing is guaranteed. *Activities and organizations:* drama/theater group, student-run newspaper, television station, choral group, SUAVE—Strong United Assertive Virtuous Educated, BOLD—Beautiful Outstanding Ladies of Distinction, Residence Hall Association, Baptist Collegiate Ministries, national fraternities, national sororities. *Campus security:* 24-hour emergency response devices and patrols, late-night transport/escort service, controlled dormitory access. *Student services:* health clinic, personal/psychological counseling.

Athletics Member NCAA. All Division II. *Intercollegiate sports:* baseball M (s), basketball M (s)/W (s), golf M, soccer M (s)/W (s), softball W (s), tennis M (s)/W (s), volleyball W (s). *Intramural sports:* badminton M/W, baseball M/W, basketball M/W, football M/W, golf M/W, softball M/W, table tennis M/W, tennis M/W, ultimate Frisbee M/W, volleyball M/W, weight lifting M/W, wrestling M.

Standardized Tests *Required:* SAT or ACT (for admission).

Costs (2007–08) *Tuition:* state resident $2868 full-time, $120 per semester hour part-time; nonresident $11,472 full-time, $478 per semester hour part-time. *Required fees:* $658 full-time. *Room and board:* $5274.

Financial Aid Of all full-time matriculated undergraduates who enrolled in 2007, 1,246 applied for aid, 1,052 were judged to have need, 159 had their need fully met. 67 Federal Work-Study jobs (averaging $1713). In 2007, 115 non-need-based awards were made. *Average percent of need met:* 60%. *Average financial aid package:* $7347. *Average need-based loan:* $3818. *Average need-based gift aid:* $3458. *Average non-need-based aid:* $1852. *Average indebtedness upon graduation:* $17,871.

Applying *Options:* electronic application, early admission, early decision. *Application fee:* $25. *Required:* high school transcript, minimum 2.0 GPA, proof of immunization. *Recommended:* interview. *Application deadlines:* 7/21 (freshmen), 7/21 (transfers). *Early decision deadline:* 12/15. *Notification:* continuous (freshmen), continuous (transfers), 1/15 (early decision).

Freshman Application Contact Mr. David Jenkins, Assistant Director of Admissions, Georgia Southwestern State University, 800 Wheatley Street, Americus, GA 31709. *Phone:* 229-928-1273. *Toll-free phone:* 800-338-0082. *Fax:* 229-931-2983. *E-mail:* gswapps@canes.gsw.edu.

GEORGIA STATE UNIVERSITY

Atlanta, Georgia **www.gsu.edu/**

- **State-supported** university, founded 1913, part of University System of Georgia
- **Urban** 48-acre campus
- **Endowment** $104.7 million
- **Coed** 19,904 undergraduate students, 73% full-time, 61% women, 39% men
- **Moderately difficult** entrance level, 53% of applicants were admitted

Undergraduates 14,587 full-time, 5,317 part-time. Students come from 49 states and territories, 144 other countries, 6% are from out of state, 29% African American, 11% Asian American or Pacific Islander, 5% Hispanic American, 0.3% Native American, 3% international, 10% transferred in, 16% live on campus. *Retention:* 80% of 2006 full-time freshmen returned.

Freshmen *Admission:* 9,775 applied, 5,198 admitted, 2,552 enrolled. *Average high school GPA:* 3.30. *Test scores:* SAT critical reading scores over 500: 73%; SAT math scores over 500: 74%; ACT scores over 18: 90%; SAT critical reading scores over 600: 23%; SAT math scores over 600: 24%; ACT scores over 24: 39%; SAT critical reading scores over 700: 3%; SAT math scores over 700: 2%; ACT scores over 30: 2%.

Faculty *Total:* 1,502, 72% full-time. *Student/faculty ratio:* 17:1.

Majors Accounting; actuarial science; African-American/Black studies; anthropology; art; art teacher education; biology/biological sciences; business administration and management; business/managerial economics; chemistry; computer and information sciences; criminal justice/safety; early childhood education; economics; elementary education; English; facilities planning and management; film/cinema studies; finance; fine/studio arts; foods, nutrition, and wellness; French; geography; geology/earth science; German; health and physical education; history; hotel/motel administration; human resources development; insurance; international business/trade/commerce; journalism; kinesiology and exercise science; marketing/marketing management; mathematics; multi-/interdisciplinary studies related; music management and merchandising; music performance; nursing (registered nurse training); operations management; operations research; philosophy; physics; political science and government; psychology; real estate; religious studies; respiratory care therapy; social work; sociology; Spanish; speech and rhetoric; urban studies/affairs; women's studies.

Academics *Calendar:* semesters. *Degrees:* certificates, bachelor's, master's, doctoral, first professional, post-master's, postbachelor's, and first professional certificates. *Special study options:* academic remediation for entering students, accelerated degree program, advanced placement credit, cooperative education, distance learning, double majors, English as a second language, honors programs, independent study, internships, off-campus study, part-time degree program, services for LD students, study abroad, summer session for credit. *ROTC:* Army (b), Navy (c), Air Force (c). *Unusual degree programs:* 3-2 business administration with bachelor of arts/Master of International Business in French, German or Spanish.

Computers on Campus 1,000 computers/terminals are available on campus for general student use. Students can access the following: computer help desk, free student e-mail accounts, online (class) registration, online (class) schedules. Campuswide network is available. 100% of college-owned or -operated housing units are wired for high-speed Internet access. Wireless service is available via classrooms, computer labs, learning centers, libraries, student centers.

Student Life *Housing options:* coed, disabled students. Campus housing is leased by the school. Freshman applicants given priority for college housing. *Activities and organizations:* drama/theater group, student-run newspaper, radio and television station, choral group, Spotlight Programs Board, Sports Club Council, Greek Organizations, International Student Associations, WRAS (radio station), national fraternities, national sororities. *Campus security:* 24-hour emergency response devices and patrols, late-night transport/escort service, controlled dormitory access. *Student services:* health clinic, personal/psychological counseling.

Athletics Member NCAA. All Division I. *Intercollegiate sports:* baseball M (s), basketball M (s)/W (s), cross-country running M (s)/W (s), golf M (s)/W (s), soccer M (s)/W (s), softball W (s), tennis M (s)/W (s), track and field M (s)/W (s), volleyball W (s). *Intramural sports:* badminton M/W, basketball M/W, bowling M/W, cross-country running M/W, football M/W, soccer M/W (c), softball M/W, table tennis M/W, tennis M/W, track and field M/W, volleyball M/W.

Standardized Tests *Required:* SAT or ACT (for admission). *Required for some:* SAT Subject Tests (for admission).

Costs (2008–09) *Tuition:* state resident $4497 full-time, $188 per semester hour part-time; nonresident $17,985 full-time, $750 per semester hour part-time. *Required fees:* $988 full-time, $494 per term part-time. *Room and board:* $9230; room only: $6746.

Financial Aid Of all full-time matriculated undergraduates who enrolled in 2003, 9,142 applied for aid, 7,360 were judged to have need, 1,311 had their need fully met. 292 Federal Work-Study jobs (averaging $2154). In 2003, 1498 non-need-based awards were made. *Average percent of need met:* 70%. *Average financial aid package:* $7780. *Average need-based loan:* $5457. *Average need-based gift aid:* $4538. *Average non-need-based aid:* $4024. *Average indebtedness upon graduation:* $15,419. *Financial aid deadline:* 11/1.

Applying *Options:* electronic application, deferred entrance. *Application fee:* $50. *Required:* high school transcript, minimum 2.8 GPA, college prep high school curriculum. *Required for some:* interview. *Recommended:* essay or personal statement. *Application deadlines:* 3/1 (freshmen), 6/1 (transfers). *Notification:* continuous (freshmen), continuous (transfers).

Freshman Application Contact Daniel Niccum, Associate Director of Admissions, Georgia State University, PO Box 4009, Atlanta, GA 30302-4009. *Phone:* 404-651-4110. *Fax:* 404-651-4811. *E-mail:* dniccum@gsu.edu.

HERZING COLLEGE

Atlanta, Georgia **www.herzing.edu/atlanta/**

Freshman Application Contact Mrs. Rose White, Director of Admissions, Herzing College, 3355 Lenox Road, Suite 100, Atlanta, GA 30326. *Phone:* 404-816-4533. *Toll-free phone:* 800-573-4533. *Fax:* 404-816-5576. *E-mail:* info@ath.herzing.edu.

ITT TECHNICAL INSTITUTE

Duluth, Georgia **www.itt-tech.edu/**

- **Proprietary** primarily 2-year, founded 2003, part of ITT Educational Services, Inc
- **Coed**
- **Minimally difficult** entrance level

Academics *Calendar:* quarters. *Degrees:* associate and bachelor's.

Standardized Tests *Required:* Wonderlic aptitude test (for admission).

Applying *Options:* deferred entrance. *Application fee:* $100. *Required:* high school transcript, interview. *Recommended:* letters of recommendation.

Freshman Application Contact Mr. Paul Curry, Director of Recruitment, ITT Technical Institute, 10700 Abbotts Bridge Road, Suite 190, Duluth, GA 30097. *Phone:* 678-957-8510. *Toll-free phone:* 866-489-8818.

ITT TECHNICAL INSTITUTE

Kennesaw, Georgia **www.itt-tech.edu/**

- **Proprietary** primarily 2-year, founded 2004, part of ITT Educational Services, Inc
- **Coed**

Academics *Calendar:* quarters. *Degrees:* associate and bachelor's.

Standardized Tests *Required:* Wonderlic aptitude test (for admission).

Applying *Application fee:* $100. *Required:* high school transcript, interview. *Recommended:* letters of recommendation.

Freshman Application Contact Mr. Carmichael James, Director of Recruitment, ITT Technical Institute, 1000 Cobb Place Boulevard NW, Kennesaw, GA 30144. *Phone:* 770-426-2300.

KENNESAW STATE UNIVERSITY

Kennesaw, Georgia **www.kennesaw.edu/**

- **State-supported** comprehensive, founded 1963, part of University System of Georgia
- **Suburban** 240-acre campus with easy access to Atlanta
- **Endowment** $15.7 million
- **Coed** 18,269 undergraduate students, 73% full-time, 61% women, 39% men
- **Moderately difficult** entrance level, 59% of applicants were admitted

Undergraduates 13,301 full-time, 4,968 part-time. Students come from 42 states and territories, 142 other countries, 2% are from out of state, 9% African American, 3% Asian American or Pacific Islander, 3% Hispanic American, 0.4% Native American, 3% international, 9% transferred in, 12% live on campus. *Retention:* 76% of 2006 full-time freshmen returned.

Freshmen *Admission:* 7,265 applied, 4,290 admitted, 2,380 enrolled. *Average high school GPA:* 3.16. *Test scores:* SAT critical reading scores over 500: 72%; SAT math scores over 500: 71%; SAT writing scores over 500: 62%; ACT scores over 18: 97%; SAT critical reading scores over 600: 17%; SAT math scores over 600: 16%; SAT writing scores over 600: 13%; ACT scores over 24: 29%; SAT critical reading scores over 700: 2%; SAT math scores over 700: 1%; SAT writing scores over 700: 1%; ACT scores over 30: 1%.

Faculty *Total:* 1,065, 62% full-time, 59% with terminal degrees. *Student/faculty ratio:* 23:1.

Majors Accounting; African studies; anthropology; art; art teacher education; biochemistry; biology/biological sciences; biology teacher education; biotechnology research; business administration and management; cartography; chemistry; communication/speech communication and rhetoric; computer and information sciences; computer and information systems security; computer science; criminal justice/safety; dramatic/theater arts; economics; elementary education; English; English/language arts teacher education; finance; foreign languages related; geography; history; human services; information science/studies; international business/trade/commerce; international relations and affairs; kinesiology and exercise science; marketing/marketing management; mathematics; mathematics teacher education; middle school education; modern languages; multi-/interdisciplinary studies related; music; music performance; music teacher education; nursing (registered nurse training); physical education teaching and coaching; political science and government; psychology; sales, distribution and marketing; social science teacher education; social studies teacher education; social work; sociology; sport and fitness administration/management.

Academics *Calendar:* semesters. *Degrees:* bachelor's, master's, and doctoral. *Special study options:* adult/continuing education programs, advanced placement credit, cooperative education, distance learning, double majors, English as a second language, honors programs, internships, off-campus study, part-time degree program, services for LD students, study abroad, summer session for credit. *ROTC:* Army (b), Air Force (b).

Computers on Campus 1,087 computers/terminals and 12,000 ports are available on campus for general student use. Students can access the following: campus intranet, computer help desk, free student e-mail accounts, online (class) grades, online (class) registration, online (class) schedules. Campuswide network is available. 100% of college-owned or -operated housing units are wired for high-speed Internet access. Wireless service is available via classrooms, computer centers, computer labs, learning centers, libraries, student centers.

Student Life *Housing options:* coed, disabled students. Campus housing is provided by a third party. Freshman applicants given priority for college housing. *Activities and organizations:* drama/theater group, student-run newspaper, radio station, choral group, Golden Key National Honor Society, Student Government Association, Campus Activities Board, African-American Student Alliance, International Student Association, national fraternities, national sororities. *Campus security:* 24-hour emergency response devices and patrols, student patrols, late-night transport/escort service, controlled dormitory access. *Student services:* health clinic, personal/psychological counseling.

Athletics Member NCAA. All Division II. *Intercollegiate sports:* baseball M (s), basketball M (s)/W (s), cheerleading W, cross-country running M (s)/W (s), golf M (s), softball W (s), tennis M/W (s). *Intramural sports:* basketball M/W, bowling M/W, football M/W, soccer M/W, softball M/W, swimming and diving M/W, tennis M/W, volleyball M/W, weight lifting M/W.

Standardized Tests *Required:* SAT or ACT (for admission).

Costs (2007–08) *Tuition:* state resident $2958 full-time, $124 per credit hour part-time; nonresident $11,830 full-time, $493 per credit hour part-time. Part-time tuition and fees vary according to course load. *Required fees:* $848 full-time. *Room only:* $4599. Room and board charges vary according to housing facility. *Payment plan:* deferred payment. *Waivers:* senior citizens and employees or children of employees.

Financial Aid Of all full-time matriculated undergraduates who enrolled in 2005, 8,568 applied for aid, 4,107 were judged to have need, 673 had their need fully met. 325 Federal Work-Study jobs (averaging $1112). In 2005, 3147 non-need-based awards were made. *Average percent of need met:* 22%. *Average financial aid package:* $9524. *Average need-based loan:* $3402. *Average need-based gift aid:* $2690. *Average non-need-based aid:* $1672. *Average indebtedness upon graduation:* $15,346.

Applying *Options:* electronic application, early admission, deferred entrance. *Application fee:* $40. *Required:* high school transcript, minimum 2.5 GPA, proof of immunization. *Application deadlines:* 5/16 (freshmen), 6/30 (transfers). *Notification:* continuous (freshmen), continuous (transfers).

Freshman Application Contact Admissions Office, Kennesaw State University, 1000 Chastain Road, Campus Box 0115, Kennesaw, GA 30144. *Phone:* 770-423-6300. *Fax:* 770-420-4435. *E-mail:* ksuadmit@ksumail.kennesaw.edu.

LAGRANGE COLLEGE

LaGrange, Georgia — www.lagrange.edu/

- **Independent United Methodist** comprehensive, founded 1831
- **Small-town** 120-acre campus with easy access to Atlanta
- **Endowment** $67.9 million
- **Coed** 998 undergraduate students, 91% full-time, 55% women, 45% men
- **Moderately difficult** entrance level, 57% of applicants were admitted

Undergraduates 913 full-time, 85 part-time. Students come from 20 states and territories, 10 other countries, 11% are from out of state, 21% African American, 2% Asian American or Pacific Islander, 2% Hispanic American, 0.7% Native American, 2% international, 8% transferred in, 62% live on campus. *Retention:* 65% of 2006 full-time freshmen returned.

Freshmen *Admission:* 1,338 applied, 766 admitted, 223 enrolled. *Average high school GPA:* 3.42. *Test scores:* SAT critical reading scores over 500: 50%; ACT scores over 18: 89%; SAT critical reading scores over 600: 12%; ACT scores over 24: 28%; SAT critical reading scores over 700: 2%; ACT scores over 30: 2%.

Faculty *Total:* 122, 56% full-time, 63% with terminal degrees. *Student/faculty ratio:* 12:1.

Majors Accounting; biochemistry; biology/biological sciences; business administration and management; chemistry; computer and information sciences; computer science; dramatic/theater arts; early childhood education; elementary education; English; general studies; history; human services; liberal arts and sciences/liberal studies; mathematics; middle school education; music; nursing (registered nurse training); political science and government; pre-dentistry studies; pre-law studies; pre-medical studies; pre-veterinary studies; psychology; religious education; religious studies; sociology; Spanish; visual and performing arts.

Academics *Calendar:* 4-1-4. *Degrees:* associate, bachelor's, and master's. *Special study options:* adult/continuing education programs, advanced placement credit, double majors, independent study, internships, part-time degree program, services for LD students, study abroad, summer session for credit. *Unusual degree programs:* 3-2 engineering with Georgia Institute of Technology, Auburn University.

Computers on Campus 175 computers/terminals are available on campus for general student use. Students can access the following: campus intranet, computer help desk, free student e-mail accounts, online (class) grades, online (class) registration, online (class) schedules. Campuswide network is available. 100% of college-owned or -operated housing units are wired for high-speed Internet access.

Student Life *Housing:* on-campus residence required through senior year. *Options:* coed, men-only, women-only. Campus housing is university owned. Freshman campus housing is guaranteed. *Activities and organizations:* drama/theater group, student-run newspaper, choral group, Student Government Association, drama/theater groups, Habitat for Humanity, BSU/Wesley Fellowship, national fraternities, national sororities. *Campus security:* 24-hour patrols, controlled dormitory access. *Student services:* health clinic, personal/psychological counseling.

Athletics Member NCAA. All Division III. *Intercollegiate sports:* baseball M, basketball M/W, cheerleading M/W, cross-country running M/W, football M, golf M, soccer M/W, softball W, swimming and diving M/W, tennis M/W, volleyball W. *Intramural sports:* badminton M/W, basketball M/W, football M, soccer M/W, softball M/W, swimming and diving M/W, tennis M/W, ultimate Frisbee M/W, volleyball M/W.

Standardized Tests *Required:* SAT or ACT (for admission).

Costs (2008–09) *Comprehensive fee:* $26,173 includes full-time tuition ($18,500), mandatory fees ($75), and room and board ($7598). Part-time tuition: $762 per hour.

Financial Aid Of all full-time matriculated undergraduates who enrolled in 2006, 845 applied for aid, 696 were judged to have need, 167 had their need fully met. In 2006, 184 non-need-based awards were made. *Average percent of need met:* 85%. *Average financial aid package:* $15,336. *Average need-based loan:* $3795. *Average need-based gift aid:* $9876. *Average non-need-based aid:* $7808. *Average indebtedness upon graduation:* $19,596.

Applying *Options:* electronic application, early admission. *Application fee:* $30. *Required:* essay or personal statement, high school transcript, minimum 2.0 GPA. *Required for some:* 1 letter of recommendation, interview. *Application deadlines:* rolling (freshmen), rolling (transfers). *Notification:* continuous (freshmen), continuous (transfers).

Freshman Application Contact Mr. Dana Paul, Vice President of Enrollment Management, LaGrange College, 601 Broad Street, LaGrange, GA 30240-2999. *Phone:* 706-880-8253. *Toll-free phone:* 800-593-2885. *Fax:* 706-880-8010. *E-mail:* lgcadmis@lagrange.edu.

See page 740 for the College Close-Up.

LIFE UNIVERSITY

Marietta, Georgia — www.life.edu/

- **Independent** comprehensive, founded 1974
- **Suburban** 96-acre campus
- **Coed** 536 undergraduate students, 73% full-time, 49% women, 51% men
- **Minimally difficult** entrance level, 30% of applicants were admitted

Undergraduates 392 full-time, 144 part-time. Students come from 52 states and territories, 23 other countries, 50% are from out of state, 21% African American, 5% Asian American or Pacific Islander, 5% Hispanic American, 0.6% Native American. *Retention:* 59% of 2006 full-time freshmen returned.

Freshmen *Admission:* 194 applied, 59 admitted. *Average high school GPA:* 3.02.

Faculty *Total:* 149, 77% full-time, 83% with terminal degrees. *Student/faculty ratio:* 15:1.

Majors Biology/biological sciences; business administration and management; dietetics; human nutrition; psychology.

Academics *Calendar:* quarters. *Degrees:* associate, bachelor's, master's, and first professional. *Special study options:* academic remediation for entering students, accelerated degree program, advanced placement credit, cooperative education, double majors, English as a second language, independent study, internships, off-campus study, services for LD students, summer session for credit.

Computers on Campus 118 computers/terminals are available on campus for general student use. Students can access the following: online (class) registration. Campuswide network is available. Wireless service is available via classrooms, computer centers, computer labs, learning centers, libraries.

Student Life *Housing options:* Campus housing is university owned. *Campus security:* 24-hour emergency response devices and patrols. *Student services:* health clinic.

Athletics *Intramural sports:* basketball M/W, football M, rugby M, softball M/W, volleyball M/W.

Standardized Tests *Required:* SAT or ACT (for admission).

Costs (2007–08) *Comprehensive fee:* $19,605 includes full-time tuition ($7110), mandatory fees ($495), and room and board ($12,000). Full-time tuition and fees vary according to course load and degree level. Part-time tuition: $158 per credit hour. Part-time tuition and fees vary according to course load and degree level. *Required fees:* $105 per term part-time. *Waivers:* employees or children of employees.

Financial Aid Of all full-time matriculated undergraduates who enrolled in 2007, 407 applied for aid, 354 were judged to have need, 10 had their need fully met. 100 Federal Work-Study jobs (averaging $1900). In 2007, 6 non-need-based awards were made. *Average percent of need met:* 3%. *Average financial aid package:* $5650. *Average need-based loan:* $3000. *Average need-based gift aid:* $3750. *Average non-need-based aid:* $7300. *Average indebtedness upon graduation:* $16,000.

Applying *Options:* electronic application. *Application fee:* $50. *Required:* high school transcript, minimum 2.0 GPA. *Required for some:* minimum SAT score of 860 or ACT score of 18. *Application deadline:* 9/1 (freshmen). *Notification:* continuous (freshmen), continuous (transfers).

Freshman Application Contact Dr. Deb Heairlston, Office of New Student Development, Life University, 1269 Barclay Circle, Marietta, GA 30060. *Phone:* 800-543-3202. *Toll-free phone:* 800-543-3202. *Fax:* 770-426-2895. *E-mail:* admissions@life.edu.

LUTHER RICE UNIVERSITY

Lithonia, Georgia — www.lru.edu/

Freshman Application Contact Mr. Steve Pray, Admissions Counselor, Luther Rice University, 3038 Evans Mill Road, Lithonia, GA 30038-2454. *Phone:* 770-484-1204. *Toll-free phone:* 800-442-1577. *E-mail:* admissions@lru.edu.

MACON STATE COLLEGE

Macon, Georgia www.maconstate.edu/

- **State-supported** 4-year, founded 1968, part of University System of Georgia
- **Urban** 167-acre campus
- **Endowment** $6.2 million
- **Coed**
- **Minimally difficult** entrance level

Faculty *Student/faculty ratio:* 21:1.

Academics *Calendar:* semesters. *Degrees:* certificates, associate, and bachelor's.

Student Life *Campus security:* 24-hour emergency response devices and patrols, late-night transport/escort service.

Standardized Tests *Required:* SAT or ACT (for admission). *Required for some:* SAT Subject Tests (for admission).

Costs (2007–08) *Tuition:* state resident $1604 full-time, $68 per credit hour part-time; nonresident $6412 full-time, $268 per credit hour part-time. *Required fees:* $188 full-time, $94 per term part-time.

Financial Aid Of all full-time matriculated undergraduates who enrolled in 2005, 1,352 were judged to have need, 39 had their need fully met. 106 Federal Work-Study jobs. In 2005, 507 non-need-based awards were made. *Average percent of need met:* 46. *Average financial aid package:* $5984. *Average need-based loan:* $2749. *Average need-based gift aid:* $3031. *Average non-need-based aid:* $1826.

Applying *Options:* electronic application, early admission. *Application fee:* $20. *Required:* high school transcript, minimum 2.0 GPA.

Freshman Application Contact Mr. Ryan Tucker, Admissions Representative, Macon State College, Macon, GA 31206. *Phone:* 478-471-2800. *Toll-free phone:* 800-272-7619 Ext. 2800. *Fax:* 478-471-5343. *E-mail:* mscinfo@mail.maconstate.edu.

MEDICAL COLLEGE OF GEORGIA

Augusta, Georgia www.mcg.edu/

- **State-supported** upper-level, founded 1828, part of University System of Georgia
- **Urban** 100-acre campus
- **Endowment** $7.7 million
- **Coed** 595 undergraduate students, 86% full-time, 88% women, 12% men
- **Moderately difficult** entrance level, 50% of applicants were admitted

Undergraduates 511 full-time, 84 part-time. Students come from 18 states and territories, 19 other countries, 10% are from out of state, 17% African American, 4% Asian American or Pacific Islander, 2% Hispanic American, 1% international, 25% transferred in, 10% live on campus.

Freshmen *Admission:* 890 applied, 444 admitted.

Faculty *Total:* 794, 84% full-time, 75% with terminal degrees. *Student/faculty ratio:* 6:1.

Majors Dental hygiene; diagnostic medical sonography and ultrasound technology; health information/medical records administration; nuclear medical technology; nursing (registered nurse training); physician assistant; radiologic technology/science; respiratory care therapy.

Academics *Calendar:* semesters. *Degrees:* certificates, bachelor's, master's, doctoral, first professional, and postbachelor's certificates. *Special study options:* distance learning, off-campus study, summer session for credit.

Computers on Campus 323 computers/terminals and 323 ports are available on campus for general student use. Students can access the following: computer help desk, free student e-mail accounts. Campuswide network is available. 100% of college-owned or -operated housing units are wired for high-speed Internet access. Wireless service is available via classrooms, computer centers, computer labs, learning centers, libraries, student centers.

Student Life *Housing options:* coed. Campus housing is university owned. *Activities and organizations:* student-run newspaper, choral group, Healthstat, Medical Campus Outreach, International Student Association, Students for International Medicine, MCG Ambassadors. *Campus security:* 24-hour emergency response devices and patrols, late-night transport/escort service. *Student services:* health clinic, personal/psychological counseling.

Athletics *Intramural sports:* basketball M/W, football M/W, golf M, racquetball M, soccer M/W, softball M/W, table tennis M/W, volleyball M/W.

Costs (2007–08) *Tuition:* state resident $4088 full-time, $171 per credit hour part-time; nonresident $16,350 full-time, $682 per credit hour part-time. Full-time tuition and fees vary according to location. Part-time tuition and fees vary according to course load and location. *Required fees:* $687 full-time. *Room only:* $2734. Room and board charges vary according to housing facility.

Financial Aid Of all full-time matriculated undergraduates who enrolled in 2006, 372 applied for aid, 366 were judged to have need, 26 had their need fully met. 23 Federal Work-Study jobs (averaging $861). In 2006, 3 non-need-based awards were made. *Average percent of need met:* 67%. *Average financial aid package:* $7077. *Average need-based loan:* $5423. *Average need-based gift aid:* $3224. *Average non-need-based aid:* $8000. *Average indebtedness upon graduation:* $43,169.

Applying *Application fee:* $30.

Application Contact Ms. Carol S. Nobles, Director of Student Recruitment and Admissions, Medical College of Georgia, AA-170 Administration-Kelly Building, Augusta, GA 30912. *Phone:* 706-721-2725. *Toll-free phone:* 800-519-3388. *Fax:* 706-721-7279. *E-mail:* underadm@mail.mcg.edu.

MERCER UNIVERSITY

Macon, Georgia www.mercer.edu/

- **Independent Baptist** comprehensive, founded 1833
- **Suburban** 150-acre campus with easy access to Atlanta
- **Coed** 2,267 undergraduate students, 97% full-time, 53% women, 47% men
- **Moderately difficult** entrance level, 60% of applicants were admitted

Undergraduates 2,201 full-time, 66 part-time. 23% are from out of state, 17% African American, 7% Asian American or Pacific Islander, 3% Hispanic American, 0.2% Native American, 2% international, 4% transferred in, 69% live on campus. *Retention:* 81% of 2006 full-time freshmen returned.

Freshmen *Admission:* 4,588 applied, 2,748 admitted, 583 enrolled. *Average high school GPA:* 3.6. *Test scores:* SAT critical reading scores over 500: 88%; SAT math scores over 500: 92%; SAT writing scores over 500: 82%; ACT scores over 18: 100%; SAT critical reading scores over 600: 40%; SAT math scores over 600: 42%; SAT writing scores over 600: 34%; ACT scores over 24: 70%; SAT critical reading scores over 700: 7%; SAT math scores over 700: 7%; SAT writing scores over 700: 6%; ACT scores over 30: 15%.

Faculty *Total:* 572, 62% full-time, 70% with terminal degrees. *Student/faculty ratio:* 13:1.

Majors African-American/Black studies; art; biochemistry; biology/biological sciences; business administration, management and operations related; business/commerce; chemistry; Christian studies; classics and languages, literatures and linguistics; communication and journalism related; community organization and advocacy; computer science; criminal justice/safety; dramatic/theater arts; economics; education related; elementary education; engineering; English; environmental science; environmental studies; French; German; health/medical preparatory programs related; history; human services; information science/studies; international relations and affairs; journalism; Latin; liberal arts and sciences/liberal studies; mass communication/media; mathematics; middle school education; multi-/interdisciplinary studies related; music; music performance; music related; music teacher education; nursing (registered nurse training); philosophy; physics; political science and government; pre-dentistry studies; pre-medical studies; psychology; regional studies; sociology; Spanish.

Academics *Calendar:* semesters. *Degrees:* bachelor's, master's, doctoral, first professional, post-master's, and postbachelor's certificates. *Special study options:* accelerated degree program, adult/continuing education programs, advanced placement credit, cooperative education, double majors, English as a second language, honors programs, independent study, internships, off-campus study, part-time degree program, services for LD students, student-designed majors, study abroad, summer session for credit. *ROTC:* Army (b).

Computers on Campus 500 computers/terminals and 2,500 ports are available on campus for general student use. Students can access the following: campus intranet, computer help desk, free student e-mail accounts, online (class) grades, online (class) registration, online (class) schedules. Campuswide network is available. 100% of college-owned or -operated housing units are wired for high-speed Internet access. Wireless service is available via classrooms, computer centers, computer labs, learning centers, libraries, student centers.

Student Life *Housing:* on-campus residence required through sophomore year. *Options:* coed, men-only, women-only, disabled students. Campus housing is university owned. Freshman campus housing is guaranteed. *Activities and organizations:* drama/theater group, student-run newspaper, radio and television station, choral group, Mercer Democrats, Sports Officials Club, MERPmed, Mercer International Student Association, Baptist Collegiate Ministries, national fraternities, national sororities. *Campus security:* 24-hour emergency response devices and patrols, student patrols, late-night transport/escort service, controlled dormitory access, patrols by police officers. *Student services:* health clinic, personal/psychological counseling.

Athletics Member NCAA. All Division I. *Intercollegiate sports:* baseball M (s), basketball M (s)/W (s), cross-country running M (s)/W (s), golf M (s)/W (s), riflery M (s), soccer M (s)/W (s), softball W (s), tennis M (s)/W (s), volleyball W (s). *Intramural sports:* basketball M/W, bowling M/W, equestrian sports W (c), football M/W, golf M/W, soccer M/W, softball M/W, tennis M/W, ultimate Frisbee M/W, volleyball M/W, water polo M/W, wrestling M (c).

Standardized Tests *Required:* SAT or ACT (for admission).

Costs (2007–08) *Comprehensive fee:* $34,975 includes full-time tuition ($26,760), mandatory fees ($200), and room and board ($8015). Full-time tuition and fees vary according to class time, course load, and location. Part-time tuition: $892 per credit hour. Part-time tuition and fees vary according to class time, course load, and location. *Required fees:* $7 per credit hour part-time. *College room only:* $3980. Room and board charges vary according to board plan, housing facility, and location. *Payment plan:* installment. *Waivers:* employees or children of employees.

Financial Aid Of all full-time matriculated undergraduates who enrolled in 2007, 1,698 applied for aid, 1,426 were judged to have need, 704 had their need fully met. 393 Federal Work-Study jobs (averaging $2219). In 2007, 721 non-need-based awards were made. *Average percent of need met:* 88%. *Average financial aid package:* $26,214. *Average need-based loan:* $7257. *Average need-based gift aid:* $16,997. *Average non-need-based aid:* $17,251. *Average indebtedness upon graduation:* $24,251.

Applying *Options:* electronic application, early admission, early action, deferred entrance. *Application fee:* $50. *Required:* high school transcript, minimum 3.0 GPA. *Required for some:* 2 letters of recommendation, interview. *Recommended:* interview, counselor's evaluation. *Application deadlines:* 7/1 (freshmen), rolling (transfers), 11/1 (early action). *Notification:* continuous (freshmen), continuous (transfers), 11/15 (early action).

Freshman Application Contact Mr. Terry Whittum, Senior Vice President, Enrollment Management, Mercer University, 1400 Coleman Avenue, Macon, GA 31207-0003. *Phone:* 478-301-2650. *Toll-free phone:* 800-840-8577. *E-mail:* admissions@mercer.edu.

MOREHOUSE COLLEGE

Atlanta, Georgia **www.morehouse.edu/**

- **Independent** 4-year, founded 1867
- **Urban** 61-acre campus
- **Men only** 2,810 undergraduate students, 95% full-time
- **Moderately difficult** entrance level, 59% of applicants were admitted

Undergraduates 2,659 full-time, 151 part-time. Students come from 41 states and territories, 15 other countries, 69% are from out of state, 95% African American, 0.3% Hispanic American, 3% international, 3% transferred in, 55% live on campus. *Retention:* 83% of 2006 full-time freshmen returned.

Freshmen *Admission:* 2,369 applied, 1,399 admitted, 677 enrolled. *Average high school GPA:* 3.2. *Test scores:* SAT critical reading scores over 500: 59%; SAT math scores over 500: 57%; ACT scores over 18: 90%; SAT critical reading scores over 600: 16%; SAT math scores over 600: 14%; ACT scores over 24: 30%; SAT critical reading scores over 700: 1%; SAT math scores over 700: 1%; ACT scores over 30: 2%.

Faculty *Total:* 236, 68% full-time. *Student/faculty ratio:* 15:1.

Majors African-American/Black studies; art; biology/biological sciences; business administration and management; chemistry; computer and information sciences; dramatic/theater arts; economics; education; engineering; English; French; general studies; health and physical education; history; international relations and affairs; mathematics; music; philosophy; physics; political science and government; psychology; religious studies; sociology; Spanish; urban studies/affairs.

Academics *Calendar:* semesters. *Degree:* bachelor's. *Special study options:* academic remediation for entering students, advanced placement credit, cooperative education, double majors, honors programs, internships, off-campus study, part-time degree program, services for LD students, study abroad, summer session for credit. *ROTC:* Army (b), Navy (b), Air Force (b). *Unusual degree programs:* 3-2 engineering with Georgia Institute of Technology, Boston University, Auburn University, Rensselaer Polytechnic University, Rochester Institute of Technology, Columbia University, Dartmouth College-Thayer School, NC A&T State Univ., Univ. of Florida at Gainesville.

Computers on Campus 355 computers/terminals are available on campus for general student use. Students can access the following: online (class) registration, online (class) schedules. Campuswide network is available.

Student Life *Housing:* on-campus residence required for freshman year. *Options:* men-only. Campus housing is university owned. Freshman campus housing is guaranteed. *Activities and organizations:* drama/theater group, student-run newspaper, choral group, marching band, Glee Club, Political Science Club, STRIPES, national fraternities. *Campus security:* 24-hour emergency response devices and patrols, late-night transport/escort service, controlled dormitory access. *Student services:* health clinic, personal/psychological counseling.

Athletics Member NCAA. All Division II. *Intercollegiate sports:* basketball M (s), cross-country running M (s), football M (s), tennis M (s), track and field M (s). *Intramural sports:* baseball M, basketball M, football M, golf M, soccer M, softball M, swimming and diving M, table tennis M, tennis M, weight lifting M.

Standardized Tests *Required:* SAT or ACT (for admission), SAT Subject Tests (for admission).

Costs (2007–08) *Comprehensive fee:* $27,910 includes full-time tuition ($16,276), mandatory fees ($1706), and room and board ($9928). Part-time tuition: $707 per credit hour. *College room only:* $5658.

Financial Aid Of all full-time matriculated undergraduates who enrolled in 2003, 2,519 applied for aid, 2,508 were judged to have need, 42 had their need fully met. In 2003, 1033 non-need-based awards were made. *Average percent of need met:* 25%. *Average financial aid package:* $11,079. *Average need-based loan:* $3864. *Average need-based gift aid:* $3561. *Average non-need-based aid:* $10,593. *Average indebtedness upon graduation:* $18,000.

Applying *Options:* electronic application, early admission, early action, deferred entrance. *Application fee:* $45. *Required:* essay or personal statement, high school transcript, minimum 2.8 GPA, letters of recommendation. *Recommended:* minimum 3.0 GPA, interview. *Application deadlines:* 2/15 (freshmen), 2/15 (transfers), 11/1 (early action). *Early decision deadline:* 10/15. *Notification:* continuous until 4/1 (freshmen), 4/1 (transfers), 12/15 (early decision), 12/15 (early action).

Freshman Application Contact Mr. Terrance Dixon, Associate Dean for Admissions and Recruitment, Morehouse College, 830 Westview Drive, SW, Atlanta, GA 30314. *Phone:* 404-215-2632. *Toll-free phone:* 800-851-1254. *Fax:* 404-524-5635. *E-mail:* janderso@morehouse.edu.

NORTH GEORGIA COLLEGE & STATE UNIVERSITY

Dahlonega, Georgia **www.ngcsu.edu/**

- **State-supported** comprehensive, founded 1873, part of University System of Georgia
- **Small-town** 140-acre campus with easy access to Atlanta
- **Endowment** $258.3 million
- **Coed** 4,532 undergraduate students, 82% full-time, 60% women, 40% men
- **Moderately difficult** entrance level, 62% of applicants were admitted

Undergraduates 3,728 full-time, 804 part-time. Students come from 40 states and territories, 46 other countries, 23% are from out of state, 3% African American, 1% Asian American or Pacific Islander, 3% Hispanic American, 0.4% Native American, 1% international, 10% transferred in, 32% live on campus. *Retention:* 75% of 2006 full-time freshmen returned.

Freshmen *Admission:* 2,461 applied, 1,519 admitted, 786 enrolled. *Average high school GPA:* 3.3. *Test scores:* SAT critical reading scores over 500: 77%; SAT math scores over 500: 72%; SAT writing scores over 500: 63%; ACT scores over 18: 95%; SAT critical reading scores over 600: 19%; SAT math scores over 600: 17%; SAT writing scores over 600: 15%; ACT scores over 24: 32%; SAT critical reading scores over 700: 1%; SAT writing scores over 700: 1%; ACT scores over 30: 3%.

Faculty *Total:* 367, 55% full-time, 50% with terminal degrees. *Student/faculty ratio:* 16:1.

Majors Accounting; art; art teacher education; biology/biological sciences; business administration and management; business/managerial economics; chemistry; computer and information sciences; computer science; crafts, folk art and artisanry; criminal justice/law enforcement administration; criminal justice/safety; drawing; education; educational leadership and administration; elementary education; English; English/language arts teacher education; family practice nursing/nurse practitioner; finance; French; history; information science/studies; kindergarten/preschool education; marketing/marketing management; mathematics; mathematics teacher education; middle school education; music; music teacher education; nursing (registered nurse training); physical education teaching and coaching; physics; political science and government; pre-dentistry studies; pre-medical studies; pre-veterinary studies; psychology; public administration; purchasing, procurement/acquisitions and contracts management; reading teacher education; science teacher education; secondary education; social sciences; social science teacher education; sociology; Spanish; special education.

Academics *Calendar:* semesters. *Degrees:* certificates, associate, bachelor's, master's, post-master's, and postbachelor's certificates. *Special study options:* academic remediation for entering students, adult/continuing education programs, advanced placement credit, cooperative education, distance learning, double majors, external degree program, freshman honors college, honors programs, independent study, internships, part-time degree program, services for LD students, study abroad, summer session for credit. *ROTC:* Army (b). *Unusual degree programs:* 3-2 engineering with Georgia Institute of Technology, Clemson University; industrial management, computer science with Georgia Institute of Technology.

Computers on Campus 470 computers/terminals are available on campus for general student use. Students can access the following: online (class) registration. Campuswide network is available.

Student Life *Housing:* on-campus residence required through sophomore year. *Options:* coed, men-only, women-only. Campus housing is university owned. *Activities and organizations:* drama/theater group, choral group, Student Government Association, College Union Board, Resident Student Affairs Board, Baptist Student Union, national fraternities, national sororities. *Campus security:* 24-hour emergency response devices and patrols, late-night transport/escort service, controlled dormitory access. *Student services:* health clinic, personal/psychological counseling.

Athletics Member NAIA. *Intercollegiate sports:* baseball M, basketball M (s)/W (s), cheerleading W, cross-country running M (c)/W (c), equestrian sports M/W, riflery M (s)/W (s), soccer M (s) (c)/W (s) (c), softball W, tennis M (s)/W (s), track and field M/W. *Intramural sports:* basketball M/W, football M (c)/W (c), golf M (c)/W (c), soccer M/W, softball M (c), table tennis M/W, volleyball M (c)/W (c), water polo M/W.

Standardized Tests *Required:* SAT or ACT (for admission).

Costs (2007–08) *Tuition:* state resident $2868 full-time, $120 per semester hour part-time; nonresident $11,476 full-time, $478 per semester hour part-time. Part-time tuition and fees vary according to course load. No tuition increase for student's term of enrollment. *Required fees:* $942 full-time, $471 per term part-time. *Room and board:* $5142; room only: $2650. Room and board charges vary according to board plan and housing facility. *Waivers:* senior citizens and employees or children of employees.

Financial Aid Of all full-time matriculated undergraduates who enrolled in 2005, 3,622 applied for aid, 1,802 were judged to have need, 1,400 had their need fully met. In 2005, 3102 non-need-based awards were made. *Average percent of need met:* 90%. *Average financial aid package:* $5782. *Average need-based loan:* $3500. *Average need-based gift aid:* $1100. *Average indebtedness upon graduation:* $9852.

Applying *Options:* electronic application, early admission. *Application fee:* $25. *Required:* high school transcript, minimum 2.0 GPA, proof of immunization. *Application deadlines:* 7/1 (freshmen), rolling (transfers). *Notification:* continuous (freshmen), continuous (transfers).

Freshman Application Contact Jennifer Collins, Director of Admissions, North Georgia College & State University, 82 College Circle, Dahlonega, GA 30533. *Phone:* 706-864-1800. *Toll-free phone:* 800-498-9581. *Fax:* 706-864-1478. *E-mail:* admissions@ngcsu.edu.

OGLETHORPE UNIVERSITY

Atlanta, Georgia **www.oglethorpe.edu/**

- **Independent** comprehensive, founded 1835
- **Suburban** 102-acre campus
- **Endowment** $22.4 million
- **Coed** 958 undergraduate students, 87% full-time, 61% women, 39% men
- **Very difficult** entrance level, 48% of applicants were admitted

Undergraduates 833 full-time, 125 part-time. Students come from 35 states and territories, 20 other countries, 30% are from out of state, 23% African American, 5% Asian American or Pacific Islander, 3% Hispanic American, 0.5% Native American, 5% international, 5% transferred in, 55% live on campus. *Retention:* 81% of 2006 full-time freshmen returned.

Freshmen *Admission:* 1,155 applied, 557 admitted, 179 enrolled. *Average high school GPA:* 3.43. *Test scores:* SAT critical reading scores over 500: 80%; SAT math scores over 500: 77%; SAT writing scores over 500: 76%; ACT scores over 18: 99%; SAT critical reading scores over 600: 37%; SAT math scores over 600: 30%; SAT writing scores over 600: 33%; ACT scores over 24: 57%; SAT critical reading scores over 700: 7%; SAT math scores over 700: 3%; SAT writing scores over 700: 4%; ACT scores over 30: 9%.

Faculty *Total:* 97, 59% full-time, 77% with terminal degrees. *Student/faculty ratio:* 13:1.

Majors Accounting; American studies; art; art history, criticism and conservation; biology/biological sciences; biopsychology; business administration and management; business/managerial economics; chemistry; communication/speech communication and rhetoric; economics; engineering; English; French; history; interdisciplinary studies; international relations and affairs; mass communication/media; mathematics; philosophy; physics; political science and government; pre-dentistry studies; pre-law studies; pre-medical studies; pre-veterinary studies; psychology; social work; sociology; Spanish; theater/theater arts management; urban studies/affairs.

Academics *Calendar:* semesters. *Degrees:* bachelor's and master's. *Special study options:* accelerated degree program, adult/continuing education programs, advanced placement credit, cooperative education, double majors, honors programs, independent study, internships, off-campus study, part-time degree program, services for LD students, student-designed majors, study abroad, summer session for credit. *Unusual degree programs:* 3-2 engineering with Auburn University, Georgia Institute of Technology, University of Florida, University of Southern California.

Computers on Campus 100 computers/terminals are available on campus for general student use. Students can access the following: campus intranet, computer help desk, free student e-mail accounts, online (class) grades, online (class) registration, online (class) schedules. Campuswide network is available. 100% of college-owned or -operated housing units are wired for high-speed Internet access. Wireless service is available via classrooms, computer centers, computer labs, learning centers, libraries, student centers.

Student Life *Housing:* on-campus residence required through sophomore year. *Options:* coed, disabled students. Campus housing is university owned. Freshman campus housing is guaranteed. *Activities and organizations:* drama/theater group, student-run newspaper, radio station, choral group, Alpha Phi Omega, Christian Fellowship, International Club, Playmakers, national fraternities, national sororities. *Campus security:* 24-hour emergency response devices and patrols, late-night transport/escort service, controlled dormitory access. *Student services:* health clinic, personal/psychological counseling.

Athletics Member NCAA. All Division III. *Intercollegiate sports:* baseball M, basketball M/W, cross-country running M/W, golf M/W, soccer M/W, tennis M/W, track and field M/W, volleyball W. *Intramural sports:* badminton M/W, basketball M/W, football M/W, softball M/W, table tennis M/W, ultimate Frisbee M/W, volleyball M/W.

Standardized Tests *Required:* SAT or ACT (for admission).

Costs (2008–09) *Comprehensive fee:* $35,080 includes full-time tuition ($25,380), mandatory fees ($200), and room and board ($9500). Part-time tuition: $1030 per credit hour.

Financial Aid Of all full-time matriculated undergraduates who enrolled in 2007, 606 applied for aid, 522 were judged to have need, 122 had their need fully met. In 2007, 240 non-need-based awards were made. *Average percent of need met:* 76%. *Average financial aid package:* $20,578. *Average need-based loan:* $4657. *Average need-based gift aid:* $16,440. *Average non-need-based aid:* $11,567. *Average indebtedness upon graduation:* $26,299.

Applying *Options:* electronic application, early action, deferred entrance. *Application fee:* $35. *Required:* essay or personal statement, high school transcript, 1 letter of recommendation. *Required for some:* interview. *Recommended:* minimum 2.5 GPA, interview. *Application deadlines:* rolling (freshmen), rolling (transfers), 12/1 (early action). *Notification:* continuous (freshmen), continuous (transfers), 1/1 (early action).

Freshman Application Contact Ms. Lucy Leusch, Vice President for Enrollment and Financial Aid, Oglethorpe University, 4484 Peachtree Road, NE, Atlanta, GA 30319. *Phone:* 404-364-8307. *Toll-free phone:* 800-428-4484. *Fax:* 404-364-8491. *E-mail:* admission@oglethorpe.edu.

See page 742 for the College Close-Up.

PAINE COLLEGE

Augusta, Georgia **www.paine.edu/**

- **Independent Methodist** 4-year, founded 1882
- **Urban** 55-acre campus with easy access to Atlanta
- **Endowment** $10.5 million
- **Coed** 917 undergraduate students, 93% full-time, 67% women, 33% men
- **Minimally difficult** entrance level, 37% of applicants were admitted

Undergraduates 850 full-time, 67 part-time. Students come from 29 states and territories, 6 other countries, 21% are from out of state, 97% African American, 0.2% Asian American or Pacific Islander, 0.2% Hispanic American, 0.3% international, 3% transferred in, 67% live on campus. *Retention:* 60% of 2006 full-time freshmen returned.

Freshmen *Admission:* 2,961 applied, 1,089 admitted, 259 enrolled. *Average high school GPA:* 2.77. *Test scores:* SAT critical reading scores over 500: 11%; SAT math scores over 500: 11%; ACT scores over 18: 28%; SAT critical reading scores over 600: 1%; SAT math scores over 600: 1%; ACT scores over 24: 2%.

Faculty *Total:* 95, 81% full-time, 44% with terminal degrees. *Student/faculty ratio:* 11:1.

Majors Accounting; biology/biological sciences; biology teacher education; broadcast journalism; business administration and management; chemistry; counseling psychology; criminology; dramatic/theater arts; elementary education; English; English/language arts teacher education; environmental science; experimental psychology; history; history teacher education; international business/trade/commerce; journalism; management information systems; marketing/marketing management; mathematics; mathematics and computer science; mathematics teacher education; middle school education; philosophy; psychology; public relations/image management; religious studies; social psychology; sociology.

Academics *Calendar:* semesters. *Degree:* certificates and bachelor's. *Special study options:* academic remediation for entering students, accelerated degree program, advanced placement credit, cooperative education, distance learning, double majors, honors programs, independent study, internships, off-campus study, part-time degree program, study abroad, summer session for credit. *ROTC:* Army (c). *Unusual degree programs:* 3-2 engineering with Tennessee State University, Tuskegee University.

Computers on Campus 130 computers/terminals are available on campus for general student use. Students can access the following: campus intranet, computer help desk, free student e-mail accounts, online (class) grades, online (class) registration, online (class) schedules, Webmail accounts. Campuswide network is available. 100% of college-owned or -operated housing units are wired for high-speed Internet access. Wireless service is available via learning centers, libraries.

Student Life *Housing options:* men-only, women-only. Campus housing is university owned. Freshman applicants given priority for college housing. *Activities and organizations:* drama/theater group, student-run newspaper, choral group, marching band, national fraternities, national sororities. *Campus security:* 24-hour emergency response devices and patrols, late-night transport/escort service. *Student services:* health clinic, personal/psychological counseling.

Athletics Member NCAA. All Division II. *Intercollegiate sports:* baseball M (s), basketball M (s)/W (s), cross-country running M (s)/W (s), golf M (s), softball W (s), track and field M (s)/W (s), volleyball W (s). *Intramural sports:* baseball M, basketball M/W, cheerleading M/W, football M, softball M/W, table tennis M/W, tennis M/W, track and field M/W, volleyball M/W, weight lifting M/W.

Standardized Tests *Required:* SAT or ACT (for admission).

Costs (2007–08) *Comprehensive fee:* $15,910 includes full-time tuition ($9878), mandatory fees ($816), and room and board ($5216). Full-time tuition and fees vary according to course load and reciprocity agreements. Part-time tuition: $412 per credit hour. Part-time tuition and fees vary according to course load, location, and reciprocity agreements. *Room and board:* Room and board charges vary according to housing facility. *Payment plans:* installment, deferred payment. *Waivers:* children of alumni and employees or children of employees.

Financial Aid *Average indebtedness upon graduation:* $2304.

Applying *Options:* electronic application, early admission, deferred entrance. *Application fee:* $25. *Required:* essay or personal statement, high school transcript, minimum 2.0 GPA, 3 letters of recommendation, medical history. *Application deadlines:* 8/1 (freshmen), 8/1 (out-of-state freshmen), 8/1 (transfers). *Notification:* continuous (freshmen), continuous (out-of-state freshmen), continuous (transfers).

Freshman Application Contact Mr. Joseph Tinsley, Director of Admissions, Paine College, 1235 15th Street, Augusta, GA 30901-3182. *Phone:* 706-821-8320. *Toll-free phone:* 800-476-7703. *Fax:* 706-821-8691. *E-mail:* tinsleyj@mail.paine.edu.

PIEDMONT COLLEGE

Demorest, Georgia — www.piedmont.edu/

- **Independent** comprehensive, founded 1897, affiliated with United Church of Christ
- **Rural** 115-acre campus with easy access to Atlanta
- **Endowment** $56.3 million
- **Coed** 1,056 undergraduate students, 85% full-time, 67% women, 33% men
- **Moderately difficult** entrance level, 44% of applicants were admitted

Undergraduates 894 full-time, 162 part-time. Students come from 4 states and territories, 12 other countries, 1% are from out of state, 8% African American, 0.9% Asian American or Pacific Islander, 2% Hispanic American, 0.3% Native American, 0.2% international, 13% transferred in, 39% live on campus. *Retention:* 70% of 2006 full-time freshmen returned.

Freshmen *Admission:* 1,293 applied, 575 admitted, 211 enrolled. *Average high school GPA:* 3.41. *Test scores:* SAT critical reading scores over 500: 52%; SAT math scores over 500: 60%; ACT scores over 18: 100%; SAT critical reading scores over 600: 18%; SAT math scores over 600: 15%; ACT scores over 24: 32%; SAT math scores over 700: 1%; ACT scores over 30: 2%.

Faculty *Total:* 227, 47% full-time, 57% with terminal degrees. *Student/faculty ratio:* 13:1.

Majors Art; biology/biological sciences; business administration and management; chemistry; computer science; criminal justice/law enforcement administration; dramatic/theater arts; elementary and middle school administration/principalship; English; environmental science; environmental studies; fine/studio arts; geology/earth science; history; interdisciplinary studies; kindergarten/preschool education; mass communication/media; mathematics; mathematics and computer science; middle school education; music; music performance; nursing (registered nurse training); philosophy; physics; political science and government; psychology; religious studies; social sciences; sociology; Spanish; special education.

Academics *Calendar:* semesters. *Degrees:* bachelor's, master's, and post-master's certificates. *Special study options:* accelerated degree program, adult/continuing education programs, advanced placement credit, cooperative education, distance learning, double majors, honors programs, independent study, internships, off-campus study, part-time degree program, services for LD students, student-designed majors, study abroad, summer session for credit.

Computers on Campus 150 computers/terminals are available on campus for general student use. Students can access the following: free student e-mail accounts, online (class) grades, online (class) schedules. Campuswide network is available.

Student Life *Housing:* on-campus residence required through sophomore year. *Options:* coed, men-only, women-only, disabled students. Campus housing is university owned. Freshman campus housing is guaranteed. *Activities and organizations:* drama/theater group, student-run newspaper, radio and television station, choral group, Campus Activity Board, Residence Hall Council, Outdoor Club, Team Piedmont, Alpha Phi Omega. *Campus security:* 24-hour emergency response devices and patrols, late-night transport/escort service. *Student services:* personal/psychological counseling.

Athletics Member NCAA. All Division III. *Intercollegiate sports:* baseball M, basketball M/W, cross-country running M/W, golf M/W, soccer M/W, softball W, tennis M/W, volleyball W.

Standardized Tests *Required:* SAT or ACT (for admission).

Costs (2008–09) *Comprehensive fee:* $24,000 includes full-time tuition ($18,000) and room and board ($6000). Part-time tuition: $750 per semester hour.

Financial Aid Of all full-time matriculated undergraduates who enrolled in 2006, 706 applied for aid, 551 were judged to have need, 121 had their need fully met. 84 Federal Work-Study jobs (averaging $1495). 185 state and other part-time jobs (averaging $1640). In 2006, 76 non-need-based awards were made. *Average percent of need met:* 62%. *Average financial aid package:* $14,080. *Average need-based loan:* $3790. *Average need-based gift aid:* $3460. *Average non-need-based aid:* $8375. *Average indebtedness upon graduation:* $15,548.

Applying *Options:* electronic application, early admission, deferred entrance. *Required:* high school transcript. *Required for some:* interview. *Recommended:* essay or personal statement, letters of recommendation. *Application deadlines:* 7/1 (freshmen), 7/1 (transfers).

Freshman Application Contact Ms. Cynthia L. Peterson, Director of Undergraduate Admissions, Piedmont College, PO Box 10, 165 Central Avenue, Demorest, GA 30535. *Phone:* 706-776-0103 Ext. 1188. *Toll-free phone:* 800-277-7020. *Fax:* 706-776-6635. *E-mail:* cpeterson@piedmont.edu.

See page 744 for the College Close-Up.

REINHARDT COLLEGE

Waleska, Georgia — www.reinhardt.edu/

- **Independent** 4-year, founded 1883, affiliated with United Methodist Church
- **Rural** 600-acre campus with easy access to Atlanta
- **Endowment** $4.1 million
- **Coed**
- **Moderately difficult** entrance level

Faculty *Student/faculty ratio:* 12:1.

Academics *Calendar:* semesters. *Degrees:* associate and bachelor's.

Student Life *Campus security:* 24-hour patrols, student patrols, late-night transport/escort service.

Athletics Member NAIA.

Standardized Tests *Required:* SAT or ACT (for admission).

Costs (2007–08) *Comprehensive fee:* $20,988 includes full-time tuition ($14,800), mandatory fees ($170), and room and board ($6018). Part-time tuition: $495 per hour. *Required fees:* $85 per term part-time.

Financial Aid Of all full-time matriculated undergraduates who enrolled in 2006, 670 applied for aid, 339 were judged to have need, 128 had their need fully

met. 68 Federal Work-Study jobs (averaging $1138). 156 state and other part-time jobs (averaging $909). In 2006, 416 non-need-based awards were made. *Average percent of need met:* 49. *Average financial aid package:* $2642. *Average need-based loan:* $3370. *Average need-based gift aid:* $1915. *Average non-need-based aid:* $2902.

Applying *Options:* electronic application, early admission, deferred entrance. *Application fee:* $25. *Required:* high school transcript, minimum 2.0 GPA.

Freshman Application Contact Ms. Julie Fleming, Director of Admissions, Reinhardt College, 7300 Reinhardt College Circle, Waleska, GA 30183-0128. *Phone:* 770-720-5526. *Toll-free phone:* 87-REINHARDT. *Fax:* 770-720-5602. *E-mail:* admissions@mail.reinhardt.edu.

SAVANNAH COLLEGE OF ART AND DESIGN

Savannah, Georgia **www.scad.edu/**

- **Independent** comprehensive, founded 1978
- **Urban** campus
- **Coed** 7,519 undergraduate students, 90% full-time, 55% women, 45% men
- **Moderately difficult** entrance level, 54% of applicants were admitted

An international university for the arts with locations in Atlanta and Savannah, Georgia, and Lacoste, France, Savannah College of Art and Design (SCAD) exists to prepare students for careers in the visual and performing arts, design, and the history of art and architecture. Students may pursue B.A., B.F.A., M.Arch., M.A., M.A.T., M.F.A., and M.U.D. degrees and certificates. Online programs and intercollegiate athletics are also available at SCAD.

Undergraduates 6,752 full-time, 767 part-time. Students come from 55 states and territories, 99 other countries, 80% are from out of state, 5% African American, 2% Asian American or Pacific Islander, 3% Hispanic American, 0.3% Native American, 7% international, 8% transferred in, 30% live on campus. *Retention:* 80% of 2006 full-time freshmen returned.

Freshmen *Admission:* 6,426 applied, 3,460 admitted, 1,603 enrolled. *Average high school GPA:* 3.32. *Test scores:* SAT critical reading scores over 500: 75%; SAT math scores over 500: 70%; SAT writing scores over 500: 68%; ACT scores over 18: 98%; SAT critical reading scores over 600: 34%; SAT math scores over 600: 28%; SAT writing scores over 600: 26%; ACT scores over 24: 53%; SAT critical reading scores over 700: 6%; SAT math scores over 700: 3%; SAT writing scores over 700: 3%; ACT scores over 30: 10%.

Faculty *Total:* 523, 81% full-time, 74% with terminal degrees. *Student/faculty ratio:* 17:1.

Majors Animation, interactive technology, video graphics and special effects; architectural history and criticism; architecture; art history, criticism and conservation; arts management; cinematography and film/video production; city/urban, community and regional planning; commercial and advertising art; commercial photography; computer graphics; creative writing; design and applied arts related; design and visual communications; digital communication and media/multimedia; dramatic/theater arts; drawing; fashion/apparel design; fiber, textile and weaving arts; film/cinema studies; graphic design; historic preservation and conservation; illustration; industrial design; interior design; metal and jewelry arts; painting; photography; printmaking; recording arts technology; sculpture; visual and performing arts.

Academics *Calendar:* quarters. *Degrees:* certificates, bachelor's, master's, and postbachelor's certificates. *Special study options:* advanced placement credit, distance learning, double majors, English as a second language, independent study, internships, off-campus study, part-time degree program, services for LD students, study abroad, summer session for credit.

Computers on Campus 3,338 computers/terminals are available on campus for general student use. Students can access the following: campus intranet, computer help desk, free student e-mail accounts, online (class) grades, online (class) registration, online (class) schedules. Campuswide network is available. 100% of college-owned or -operated housing units are wired for high-speed Internet access. Wireless service is available via computer centers, computer labs, dorm rooms, libraries, student centers.

Student Life *Housing options:* coed, women-only. Campus housing is university owned and leased by the school. Freshman applicants given priority for college housing. *Activities and organizations:* drama/theater group, student-run newspaper, radio station, choral group, Fashion House, Contemporary Animation Society, Christian Student Fellowship, SCAD Swing Club, Digital Media Club. *Campus security:* 24-hour emergency response devices and patrols, student patrols, late-night transport/escort service, controlled dormitory access, video camera surveillance. *Student services:* health clinic, personal/psychological counseling.

Athletics Member NAIA. *Intercollegiate sports:* baseball M (s), basketball M (s)/W (s), cheerleading M/W, cross-country running M (s)/W (s), equestrian sports M (s)/W (s), fencing M (c)/W (c), golf M (s)/W (s), lacrosse W (s), soccer M (s)/W (s), softball W (s), swimming and diving M (s)/W (s), tennis M (s)/W (s), volleyball W (s). *Intramural sports:* basketball M/W, equestrian sports M (c)/W (c), lacrosse M (c), softball M/W, tennis M/W, ultimate Frisbee M/W, volleyball M/W.

Standardized Tests *Required:* SAT or ACT (for admission).

Costs (2008–09) *Comprehensive fee:* $36,480 includes full-time tuition ($25,965), mandatory fees ($500), and room and board ($10,015). Part-time tuition: $2885 per course. *College room only:* $6460.

Financial Aid Of all full-time matriculated undergraduates who enrolled in 2007, 4,263 applied for aid, 3,461 were judged to have need, 1,398 had their need fully met. In 2007, 1917 non-need-based awards were made. *Average percent of need met:* 13%. *Average financial aid package:* $15,500. *Average need-based loan:* $4400. *Average need-based gift aid:* $4600. *Average non-need-based aid:* $11,100.

Applying *Options:* electronic application, early admission. *Application fee:* $50. *Required:* essay or personal statement, high school transcript, 3 letters of recommendation. *Required for some:* portfolio/audition. *Recommended:* interview. *Application deadlines:* rolling (freshmen), rolling (transfers). *Notification:* continuous (freshmen), continuous (transfers).

Freshman Application Contact Ms. Ginger Hansen, Executive Director of Recruitment, Savannah College of Art and Design, 342 Bull Street, PO Box 3146, Savannah, GA 31402-3146. *Phone:* 912-525-5100. *Toll-free phone:* 800-869-7223. *Fax:* 912-525-5983. *E-mail:* admission@scad.edu.

See page 746 for the College Close-Up.

SAVANNAH STATE UNIVERSITY

Savannah, Georgia **www.savstate.edu/**

- **State-supported** comprehensive, founded 1890, part of University System of Georgia
- **Suburban** 165-acre campus
- **Endowment** $2.4 million
- **Coed**
- **Minimally difficult** entrance level

Faculty *Student/faculty ratio:* 19:1.

Academics *Calendar:* semesters. *Degrees:* bachelor's and master's.

Student Life *Campus security:* 24-hour emergency response devices and patrols, late-night transport/escort service, controlled dormitory access.

Athletics Member NCAA. All Division II.

Standardized Tests *Required:* SAT or ACT (for admission). *Required for some:* SAT Subject Tests (for admission). *Recommended:* SAT (for admission).

Costs (2007–08) *Tuition:* state resident $2868 full-time, $120 per hour part-time; nonresident $11,472 full-time, $478 per hour part-time. *Required fees:* $618 full-time, $309 per term part-time. *Room and board:* $5348; room only: $2476.

Financial Aid *Average percent of need met:* 75. *Average financial aid package:* $3200. *Average indebtedness upon graduation:* $11,000. *Financial aid deadline:* 8/1.

Applying *Options:* electronic application, early admission, deferred entrance. *Application fee:* $20. *Required:* high school transcript, minimum 2.0 GPA.

Freshman Application Contact Mrs. Gwendolyn J. Moore, Associate Director of Admissions, Savannah State University, PO Box 20209, Savannah, GA 31404. *Phone:* 912-356-2181. *Toll-free phone:* 800-788-0478. *Fax:* 912-356-2256. *E-mail:* mooreg@savstate.edu.

See page 748 for the College Close-Up.

SHORTER COLLEGE

Rome, Georgia **www.shorter.edu/**

- **Independent Baptist** comprehensive, founded 1873
- **Small-town** 155-acre campus with easy access to Atlanta
- **Endowment** $24.1 million
- **Coed** 1,035 undergraduate students, 96% full-time, 49% women, 51% men
- **Moderately difficult** entrance level, 65% of applicants were admitted

Undergraduates 997 full-time, 38 part-time. Students come from 10 states and territories, 26 other countries, 8% are from out of state, 12% African American,

1% Asian American or Pacific Islander, 3% Hispanic American, 0.7% Native American, 6% international, 7% transferred in, 59% live on campus. *Retention:* 64% of 2006 full-time freshmen returned.

Freshmen *Admission:* 1,131 applied, 731 admitted, 276 enrolled. *Average high school GPA:* 3.19. *Test scores:* SAT critical reading scores over 500: 45%; SAT math scores over 500: 46%; SAT writing scores over 500: 41%; ACT scores over 18: 75%; SAT critical reading scores over 600: 16%; SAT math scores over 600: 13%; SAT writing scores over 600: 11%; ACT scores over 24: 16%; SAT critical reading scores over 700: 3%; SAT math scores over 700: 1%; SAT writing scores over 700: 2%.

Faculty *Total:* 125, 57% full-time, 45% with terminal degrees. *Student/faculty ratio:* 11:1.

Majors Accounting; art; art teacher education; biology/biological sciences; business administration and management; business/managerial economics; chemistry; computer and information sciences; divinity/ministry; dramatic/theater arts; economics; elementary education; English; environmental studies; fine/studio arts; French; general studies; history; liberal arts and sciences/liberal studies; mathematics; mathematics teacher education; middle school education; music; music teacher education; natural sciences; organizational communication; parks, recreation and leisure; piano and organ; pre-theology/pre-ministerial studies; psychology; public relations, advertising, and applied communication related; religious/sacred music; religious studies; social sciences; sociology; Spanish; therapeutic recreation; voice and opera.

Academics *Calendar:* semesters. *Degree:* bachelor's. *Special study options:* academic remediation for entering students, adult/continuing education programs, advanced placement credit, double majors, honors programs, independent study, internships, off-campus study, part-time degree program, services for LD students, student-designed majors, study abroad, summer session for credit.

Computers on Campus 100 computers/terminals are available on campus for general student use. Students can access the following: campus intranet, computer help desk, free student e-mail accounts, online (class) grades, online (class) registration, online (class) schedules. Campuswide network is available. 100% of college-owned or -operated housing units are wired for high-speed Internet access. Wireless service is available via classrooms, computer centers, computer labs, learning centers, libraries, student centers.

Student Life *Housing:* on-campus residence required through senior year. *Options:* men-only, women-only. Campus housing is university owned. Freshman applicants given priority for college housing. *Activities and organizations:* drama/theater group, student-run newspaper, radio and television station, choral group, marching band, Baptist Collegiate Ministries, Student Government Association, Fellowship of Christian Athletes, Habitat for Humanity, SAVE (Students Advocating Volunteer Efforts), national fraternities, national sororities. *Campus security:* 24-hour emergency response devices and patrols. *Student services:* health clinic, personal/psychological counseling.

Athletics Member NAIA. *Intercollegiate sports:* baseball M (s), basketball M (s)/W (s), cheerleading M/W, cross-country running M (s)/W (s), golf M (s)/W (s), soccer M (s)/W (s), softball W (s), tennis M (s)/W (s), track and field M (s)/W (s), volleyball W (s). *Intramural sports:* basketball M/W, bowling M/W, soccer M/W, table tennis M/W, tennis M/W, ultimate Frisbee M/W, volleyball W.

Standardized Tests *Required:* SAT or ACT (for admission).

Costs (2007–08) *Comprehensive fee:* $22,160 includes full-time tuition ($14,850), mandatory fees ($310), and room and board ($7000). Full-time tuition and fees vary according to course load. Part-time tuition: $400 per hour. *College room only:* $3800. Room and board charges vary according to board plan and housing facility. *Payment plan:* installment. *Waivers:* senior citizens and employees or children of employees.

Financial Aid Of all full-time matriculated undergraduates who enrolled in 2007, 707 applied for aid, 609 were judged to have need, 138 had their need fully met. 100 Federal Work-Study jobs (averaging $1965). 69 state and other part-time jobs (averaging $1758). In 2007, 440 non-need-based awards were made. *Average percent of need met:* 70%. *Average financial aid package:* $14,491. *Average need-based loan:* $4224. *Average need-based gift aid:* $11,109. *Average non-need-based aid:* $7166. *Average indebtedness upon graduation:* $18,078.

Applying *Options:* electronic application, early admission, deferred entrance. *Application fee:* $25. *Required:* essay or personal statement, high school transcript. *Required for some:* interview, audition for music and theater programs. *Recommended:* minimum 2.0 GPA, 1 letter of recommendation, interview. *Application deadlines:* 8/25 (freshmen), 8/25 (transfers). *Notification:* continuous (freshmen), continuous (transfers).

Freshman Application Contact Mr. John Head, Vice President for Enrollment Management, Shorter College, 315 Shorter Avenue, Rome, GA 30165. *Phone:* 706-233-7342. *Toll-free phone:* 800-868-6980. *Fax:* 706-233-7224. *E-mail:* admissions@shorter.edu.

See page 750 for the College Close-Up.

SOUTHERN POLYTECHNIC STATE UNIVERSITY

Marietta, Georgia **www.spsu.edu/**

- **State-supported** comprehensive, founded 1948, part of University System of Georgia
- **Suburban** 200-acre campus with easy access to Atlanta
- **Endowment** $5.1 million
- **Coed** 3,937 undergraduate students, 69% full-time, 18% women, 82% men
- **Moderately difficult** entrance level, 61% of applicants were admitted

Undergraduates 2,730 full-time, 1,207 part-time. Students come from 28 states and territories, 102 other countries, 3% are from out of state, 20% African American, 5% Asian American or Pacific Islander, 4% Hispanic American, 0.4% Native American, 5% international, 12% transferred in, 25% live on campus. *Retention:* 76% of 2006 full-time freshmen returned.

Freshmen *Admission:* 1,331 applied, 812 admitted, 517 enrolled. *Average high school GPA:* 3.23. *Test scores:* SAT critical reading scores over 500: 74%; SAT math scores over 500: 86%; ACT scores over 18: 100%; SAT critical reading scores over 600: 19%; SAT math scores over 600: 34%; ACT scores over 24: 26%; SAT critical reading scores over 700: 2%; SAT math scores over 700: 4%; ACT scores over 30: 1%.

Faculty *Total:* 262, 60% full-time, 50% with terminal degrees. *Student/faculty ratio:* 18:1.

Majors Architectural engineering technology; architecture; biology/biological sciences; chemistry; civil engineering technology; communication and media related; computer and information sciences; computer and information sciences and support services related; computer engineering technology; computer software engineering; construction engineering; construction management; electrical, electronic and communications engineering technology; engineering technology; entrepreneurship; industrial production technologies related; information science/studies; information technology; international relations and affairs; liberal arts and sciences/liberal studies; mathematics; mechanical engineering; mechanical engineering/mechanical technology; physics; psychology; survey technology; systems engineering; telecommunications.

Academics *Calendar:* semesters. *Degrees:* certificates, associate, bachelor's, master's, and postbachelor's certificates. *Special study options:* adult/continuing education programs, advanced placement credit, cooperative education, distance learning, double majors, honors programs, independent study, internships, part-time degree program, services for LD students, student-designed majors, study abroad, summer session for credit. *ROTC:* Army (c), Navy (c), Air Force (c).

Computers on Campus 1,500 computers/terminals and 100 ports are available on campus for general student use. Students can access the following: computer help desk, free student e-mail accounts, online (class) grades, online (class) registration, online (class) schedules. Campuswide network is available. 100% of college-owned or -operated housing units are wired for high-speed Internet access. Wireless service is available via classrooms, computer centers, computer labs, learning centers, libraries, student centers.

Student Life *Housing options:* coed. Campus housing is provided by a third party. Freshman applicants given priority for college housing. *Activities and organizations:* student-run newspaper, radio station, International Student Association, Campus Activities Board, National Society of Black Engineers, Aerial Robotics Team, American Society of Civil Engineers, national fraternities, national sororities. *Campus security:* 24-hour emergency response devices and patrols, late-night transport/escort service, controlled dormitory access. *Student services:* health clinic, personal/psychological counseling.

Athletics Member NAIA. *Intercollegiate sports:* baseball M (s), basketball M (s)/W (s), soccer M (s). *Intramural sports:* badminton M/W, basketball M/W, cheerleading W, football M/W, golf M/W, racquetball M/W, rock climbing M/W, softball M/W, table tennis M/W, ultimate Frisbee M/W, volleyball M/W.

Standardized Tests *Required:* SAT or ACT (for admission).

Costs (2007–08) *Tuition:* state resident $3242 full-time, $136 per credit hour part-time; nonresident $12,960 full-time, $540 per credit hour part-time. Full-time tuition and fees vary according to course load. Part-time tuition and fees vary according to course load. No tuition increase for student's term of enrollment. *Required fees:* $630 full-time, $315 per term part-time. *Room and board:* $5780; room only: $3310. Room and board charges vary according to board plan. *Waivers:* senior citizens.

Financial Aid Of all full-time matriculated undergraduates who enrolled in 2005, 1,885 applied for aid, 1,427 were judged to have need, 753 had their need fully met. 17 Federal Work-Study jobs (averaging $3239). In 2005, 26 non-need-based awards were made. *Average percent of need met:* 71%. *Average financial* *aid package:* $2710. *Average need-based loan:* $3306. *Average need-based gift aid:* $2437. *Average non-need-based aid:* $3445. *Average indebtedness upon graduation:* $28,364.

Applying *Options:* electronic application, early admission. *Application fee:* $20. *Required:* high school transcript, minimum 2.5 GPA, proof of immunization. *Application deadlines:* 8/1 (freshmen), 8/1 (out-of-state freshmen), 8/1 (transfers). *Notification:* continuous (freshmen), continuous (out-of-state freshmen), continuous (transfers).

Freshman Application Contact Southern Polytechnic State University, 1100 South Marietta Parkway, Marietta, GA 30060-2896. *Phone:* 678-915-4188. *Toll-free phone:* 800-635-3204.

SOUTH UNIVERSITY

Savannah, Georgia **www.southuniversity.edu/**

- **Proprietary** comprehensive, founded 1899
- **Urban** 9-acre campus
- **Coed**

Majors Business administration and management; criminal justice/law enforcement administration; health/health care administration; information technology; legal studies; nursing science.

Academics *Calendar:* quarters. *Degrees:* associate, bachelor's, master's, and doctoral.

Director of Admissions South University, 709 Mall Boulevard, Savannah, GA 31406. *Phone:* 912-201-8000. *Toll-free phone:* 800-688-0932. *Fax:* 912-201-8070.

See page 752 for the College Close-Up.

SPELMAN COLLEGE

Atlanta, Georgia **www.spelman.edu/**

- **Independent** 4-year, founded 1881
- **Urban** 32-acre campus
- **Endowment** $258.1 million
- **Women only** 2,343 undergraduate students, 95% full-time
- **Very difficult** entrance level, 33% of applicants were admitted

Spelman College is a historically black, privately endowed, four-year liberal arts college for women. Founded in 1881 as the Atlanta Baptist Female Seminary, Spelman today is one of America's top liberal arts colleges, providing academic excellence for women as well as an environment that encourages leadership development and community service experience. Spelman's commitment to excellence is demonstrated by its dedicated, accessible faculty members and low student-faculty ratio as well as by the outstanding success of students and alumnae.

Undergraduates 2,236 full-time, 107 part-time. Students come from 42 states and territories, 18 other countries, 69% are from out of state, 96% African American, 0.1% Hispanic American, 2% international, 2% transferred in, 48% live on campus. *Retention:* 88% of 2006 full-time freshmen returned.

Freshmen *Admission:* 5,656 applied, 1,866 admitted, 557 enrolled. *Average high school GPA:* 3.59. *Test scores:* SAT critical reading scores over 500: 76%; SAT math scores over 500: 69%; ACT scores over 18: 95%; SAT critical reading scores over 600: 23%; SAT math scores over 600: 14%; ACT scores over 24: 39%; SAT critical reading scores over 700: 3%; SAT math scores over 700: 1%; ACT scores over 30: 3%.

Faculty *Total:* 246, 70% full-time. *Student/faculty ratio:* 12:1.

Majors Anthropology; art; biochemistry; biology/biological sciences; chemistry; computer science; developmental and child psychology; dramatic/theater arts; economics; engineering; English; environmental studies; French; history; mathematics; music; natural sciences; philosophy; physics; political science and government; psychology; religious studies; sociology; Spanish; women's studies.

Academics *Calendar:* semesters. *Degree:* bachelor's. *Special study options:* academic remediation for entering students, adult/continuing education programs, advanced placement credit, double majors, honors programs, independent study, internships, off-campus study, part-time degree program, services for LD students, student-designed majors, study abroad. *ROTC:* Army (b), Navy (b), Air Force (c). *Unusual degree programs:* 3-2 engineering with North Carolina Agricultural and Technical State University, Rensselaer Polytechnic Institute, Georgia Institute of Technology, Boston University, The University of Alabama in Huntsville, Auburn University.

Computers on Campus 105 computers/terminals are available on campus for general student use. Students can access the following: online (class) registration. Campuswide network is available.

Student Life *Housing options:* women-only. Campus housing is university owned and leased by the school. Freshman applicants given priority for college housing. *Activities and organizations:* drama/theater group, student-run newspaper, choral group, Student Government Association, Spotlight (newspaper), Health Careers Club, NAACP (campus organization), SHAPE (health organization), national sororities. *Campus security:* 24-hour emergency response devices and patrols, late-night transport/escort service, controlled dormitory access. *Student services:* health clinic, personal/psychological counseling, women's center.

Athletics Member NCAA. *Intercollegiate sports:* basketball W, cross-country running W, golf W, soccer W, tennis W, track and field W, volleyball W. *Intramural sports:* softball W, swimming and diving W.

Standardized Tests *Required:* SAT or ACT (for admission).

Costs (2007–08) *Comprehensive fee:* $25,755 includes full-time tuition ($14,470), mandatory fees ($2535), and room and board ($8750). Part-time tuition: $603 per credit hour.

Financial Aid Of all full-time matriculated undergraduates who enrolled in 2006, 2,107 applied for aid, 1,896 were judged to have need, 112 had their need fully met. In 2006, 175 non-need-based awards were made. *Average percent of need met:* 87%. *Average financial aid package:* $7000. *Average need-based loan:* $4000. *Average need-based gift aid:* $3500.

Applying *Options:* electronic application, early decision, early action. *Application fee:* $35. *Required:* essay or personal statement, high school transcript, minimum 2.0 GPA, 2 letters of recommendation. *Required for some:* interview. *Application deadlines:* 2/1 (freshmen), 4/1 (transfers), 11/15 (early action). *Early decision deadline:* 11/1. *Notification:* 4/1 (freshmen), 5/1 (transfers), 12/5 (early decision), 12/31 (early action).

Freshman Application Contact Ms. Arlene Cash, Vice President for Admissions and Orientation, Spelman College, 350 Spelman Lane, SW, Atlanta, GA 30314-4399. *Phone:* 404-681-3643. *Toll-free phone:* 800-982-2411. *Fax:* 404-270-5201. *E-mail:* admiss@spelman.edu.

See page 754 for the College Close-Up.

THOMAS UNIVERSITY

Thomasville, Georgia **www.thomasu.edu/**

- **Independent** comprehensive, founded 1950
- **Small-town** 24-acre campus
- **Endowment** $4.0 million
- **Coed** 594 undergraduate students, 66% full-time, 74% women, 26% men
- **Noncompetitive** entrance level, 63% of applicants were admitted

Undergraduates 390 full-time, 204 part-time. Students come from 8 states and territories, 13 other countries, 4% are from out of state, 36% African American, 0.5% Asian American or Pacific Islander, 2% Hispanic American, 0.8% Native American, 4% international, 17% transferred in, 9% live on campus. *Retention:* 47% of 2006 full-time freshmen returned.

Freshmen *Admission:* 91 applied, 57 admitted, 36 enrolled.

Faculty *Total:* 82, 50% full-time, 40% with terminal degrees. *Student/faculty ratio:* 12:1.

Majors Accounting; biology/biological sciences; business administration and management; business/commerce; communication/speech communication and rhetoric; criminal justice/law enforcement administration; criminology; early childhood education; English; humanities; kindergarten/preschool education; liberal arts and sciences/liberal studies; mathematics; middle school education; nursing (registered nurse training); parks, recreation and leisure facilities management; political science and government; psychology; rehabilitation therapy; secondary education; social sciences; social work; sociology.

Academics *Calendar:* semesters. *Degrees:* associate, bachelor's, master's, and postbachelor's certificates. *Special study options:* academic remediation for entering students, accelerated degree program, adult/continuing education programs, advanced placement credit, cooperative education, distance learning, double majors, independent study, internships, part-time degree program, services for LD students, study abroad, summer session for credit.

Computers on Campus 50 computers/terminals are available on campus for general student use. Students can access the following: free student e-mail accounts, online (class) schedules. Campuswide network is available.

Student Life *Housing options:* coed. Campus housing is university owned. Freshman applicants given priority for college housing. *Activities and organizations:* drama/theater group, student-run newspaper, choral group, Student Government Association, Professional Management Association, National Society for Leadership and Success. *Campus security:* late-night transport/escort service, controlled dormitory access, evening security guards. *Student services:* personal/psychological counseling.

Athletics Member NAIA. *Intercollegiate sports:* baseball M (s), golf M (s)/W, soccer M (s)/W (s), softball W (s). *Intramural sports:* football M/W, table tennis M/W, tennis M/W, volleyball M/W.

Standardized Tests *Recommended:* SAT (for admission), SAT and SAT Subject Tests or ACT (for admission).

Costs (2007–08) *Tuition:* $10,500 full-time, $415 per semester hour part-time. Full-time tuition and fees vary according to program. Part-time tuition and fees vary according to course load and program. *Required fees:* $540 full-time, $135 per term part-time. *Room only:* $2626. *Payment plan:* installment. *Waivers:* employees or children of employees.

Financial Aid Of all full-time matriculated undergraduates who enrolled in 2006, 634 applied for aid, 634 were judged to have need, 279 had their need fully met. 29 Federal Work-Study jobs (averaging $2181). *Average percent of need met:* 48%. *Average financial aid package:* $5119. *Average need-based loan:* $3475. *Average need-based gift aid:* $2652. *Average indebtedness upon graduation:* $12,000.

Applying *Options:* electronic application, early admission, deferred entrance. *Application fee:* $25. *Required:* high school transcript. *Application deadlines:* rolling (freshmen), rolling (transfers). *Notification:* continuous (freshmen), continuous (transfers).

Freshman Application Contact Thomas University Office of Admission, Thomas University, 1501 Millpond Road, Thomasville, GA 31792. *Phone:* 229-226-1621 Ext. 214. *Toll-free phone:* 800-538-9784. *Fax:* 229-227-6919. *E-mail:* hmueller@thomasu.edu.

TOCCOA FALLS COLLEGE

Toccoa Falls, Georgia **www.tfc.edu/**

- **Independent interdenominational** 4-year, founded 1907
- **Small-town** 500-acre campus
- **Endowment** $2.8 million
- **Coed** 923 undergraduate students, 95% full-time, 56% women, 44% men
- **Moderately difficult** entrance level, 51% of applicants were admitted

Undergraduates 873 full-time, 50 part-time. Students come from 43 states and territories, 31 other countries, 45% are from out of state, 3% African American, 7% Asian American or Pacific Islander, 2% Hispanic American, 2% international, 6% transferred in, 63% live on campus. *Retention:* 66% of 2006 full-time freshmen returned.

Freshmen *Admission:* 1,100 applied, 564 admitted, 215 enrolled. *Average high school GPA:* 3.4. *Test scores:* SAT critical reading scores over 500: 60%; SAT math scores over 500: 53%; ACT scores over 18: 82%; SAT critical reading scores over 600: 22%; SAT math scores over 600: 15%; ACT scores over 24: 39%; SAT critical reading scores over 700: 4%; ACT scores over 30: 2%.

Faculty *Total:* 86, 65% full-time, 40% with terminal degrees. *Student/faculty ratio:* 7:1.

Majors Biblical studies; biology/biological sciences; business administration and management; counseling psychology; early childhood education; English; English/language arts teacher education; general studies; history teacher education; mass communication/media; middle school education; missionary studies and missiology; music; music performance; music teacher education; organizational communication; philosophy; pre-law studies; religious education; religious/sacred music; religious studies; youth ministry.

Academics *Calendar:* semesters. *Degrees:* certificates, associate, and bachelor's. *Special study options:* accelerated degree program, advanced placement credit, double majors, independent study, internships, part-time degree program, services for LD students, study abroad, summer session for credit.

Computers on Campus 60 computers/terminals are available on campus for general student use. Students can access the following: campus intranet, computer help desk, free student e-mail accounts, online (class) grades, online (class) registration, online (class) schedules. Campuswide network is available. 90% of college-owned or -operated housing units are wired for high-speed Internet access. Wireless service is available via computer centers, computer labs, dorm rooms, libraries, student centers.

Student Life *Housing:* on-campus residence required through junior year. *Options:* men-only, women-only. Campus housing is university owned. Freshman campus housing is guaranteed. *Activities and organizations:* drama/theater group, student-run newspaper, radio station, choral group, Outdoor Club, Hmong Student Fellowship, Impact, Student Missionary Fellowship, Fellowship of Christian Athletes. *Campus security:* student patrols. *Student services:* health clinic, personal/psychological counseling.

Athletics Member NCCAA. *Intercollegiate sports:* baseball M, basketball M/W, cross-country running M/W, racquetball M/W, soccer M/W, volleyball W. *Intramural sports:* basketball M/W, soccer M/W.

Standardized Tests *Required:* SAT or ACT (for admission).

Costs (2008–09) *One-time required fee:* $25. *Comprehensive fee:* $19,975 includes full-time tuition ($14,500), mandatory fees ($125), and room and board ($5350). Part-time tuition: $604 per credit hour.

Financial Aid Of all full-time matriculated undergraduates who enrolled in 2005, 765 applied for aid, 675 were judged to have need, 83 had their need fully met. 369 Federal Work-Study jobs (averaging $1336). 154 state and other part-time jobs (averaging $1351). In 2005, 173 non-need-based awards were made. *Average percent of need met:* 60%. *Average financial aid package:* $9653. *Average need-based loan:* $3110. *Average need-based gift aid:* $6486. *Average non-need-based aid:* $7595. *Average indebtedness upon graduation:* $17,273.

Applying *Options:* electronic application, early admission, deferred entrance. *Application fee:* $25. *Required:* essay or personal statement, high school transcript, minimum 2.0 GPA, 1 letter of recommendation. *Required for some:* interview. *Application deadlines:* rolling (freshmen), rolling (transfers). *Notification:* continuous (freshmen), continuous (transfers).

Freshman Application Contact John Gailer, Director of Admissions, Toccoa Falls College, Office of Admissions, PO Box 800899, Toccoa Falls, GA 30598-1000. *Phone:* 888-785-5624. *Fax:* 706-282-6012. *E-mail:* admissions@tfc.edu.

See page 756 for the College Close-Up.

TRUETT-MCCONNELL COLLEGE

Cleveland, Georgia **www.truett.edu/**

- **Independent Baptist** 4-year, founded 1946
- **Rural** 310-acre campus with easy access to Atlanta
- **Coed** 468 undergraduate students, 81% full-time, 50% women, 50% men
- **Minimally difficult** entrance level

Undergraduates 379 full-time, 89 part-time. Students come from 9 states and territories, 5 other countries, 2% are from out of state, 3% transferred in, 66% live on campus. *Retention:* 41% of 2006 full-time freshmen returned.

Freshmen *Admission:* 171 enrolled. *Average high school GPA:* 2.89.

Faculty *Total:* 22, 59% with terminal degrees. *Student/faculty ratio:* 15:1.

Majors Christian studies; early childhood education; education; general studies; history; humanities; liberal arts and sciences/liberal studies; multi-/interdisciplinary studies related; music.

Academics *Calendar:* semesters. *Degrees:* associate and bachelor's. *Special study options:* academic remediation for entering students, accelerated degree program, advanced placement credit, double majors, honors programs, part-time degree program, services for LD students, study abroad, summer session for credit.

Computers on Campus 45 computers/terminals are available on campus for general student use. Students can access the following: computer help desk, free student e-mail accounts, online (class) grades, online (class) registration, online (class) schedules. Campuswide network is available. 100% of college-owned or -operated housing units are wired for high-speed Internet access. Wireless service is available via classrooms, dorm rooms, libraries, student centers.

Student Life *Housing:* on-campus residence required through senior year. *Options:* men-only, women-only. Campus housing is university owned. *Activities and organizations:* choral group, intramurals, Baptist Student Union, College Choir, Student Government Association, Fellowship of Christian Athletes (FCA). *Campus security:* 24-hour weekday patrols, 10-hour weekend patrols by trained security personnel.

Athletics Member NJCAA. *Intercollegiate sports:* baseball M (s), basketball M (s)/W (s), cross-country running M (s)/W (s), golf M (s)/W (s), soccer M (s)/W (s), softball W (s). *Intramural sports:* basketball M/W, football M/W, ultimate Frisbee M/W, volleyball M/W.

Standardized Tests *Required:* SAT or ACT (for admission).

Costs (2008–09) *Comprehensive fee:* $19,100 includes full-time tuition ($13,500), mandatory fees ($500), and room and board ($5100). Part-time tuition: $450 per semester hour. *Required fees:* $250 per semester part-time.

Applying *Options:* electronic application, early admission, deferred entrance. *Application fee:* $25. *Required:* high school transcript, minimum 2.0 GPA, minimum SAT score of 720 or ACT score of 15. *Required for some:* essay or personal statement, letters of recommendation, interview. *Application deadlines:* 8/1 (freshmen), 8/1 (transfers). *Notification:* continuous (freshmen), continuous (transfers).

Freshman Application Contact Mr. Mike W. Davis, Dean of Enrollment Services, Truett-McConnell College, 100 Alumni Drive, Cleveland, GA 30528-9799. *Phone:* 706-865-2134 Ext. 210. *Toll-free phone:* 800-226-8621. *Fax:* 706-865-7615. *E-mail:* admissions@truett.edu.

UNIVERSITY OF GEORGIA

Athens, Georgia **www.uga.edu/**

- **State-supported** university, founded 1785, part of University System of Georgia
- **Suburban** 1289-acre campus with easy access to Atlanta
- **Endowment** $705.3 million
- **Coed** 25,335 undergraduate students, 92% full-time, 58% women, 42% men
- **Moderately difficult** entrance level, 55% of applicants were admitted

Undergraduates 23,418 full-time, 1,917 part-time. Students come from 54 states and territories, 130 other countries, 16% are from out of state, 6% African American, 6% Asian American or Pacific Islander, 2% Hispanic American, 0.3% Native American, 0.7% international, 4% transferred in, 27% live on campus. *Retention:* 93% of 2006 full-time freshmen returned.

Freshmen *Admission:* 16,871 applied, 9,242 admitted, 4,675 enrolled. *Average high school GPA:* 3.79. *Test scores:* SAT critical reading scores over 500: 95%; SAT math scores over 500: 96%; SAT writing scores over 500: 93%; ACT scores over 18: 100%; SAT critical reading scores over 600: 60%; SAT math scores over 600: 62%; SAT writing scores over 600: 57%; ACT scores over 24: 87%; SAT critical reading scores over 700: 15%; SAT math scores over 700: 14%; SAT writing scores over 700: 11%; ACT scores over 30: 22%.

Faculty *Total:* 2,174, 80% full-time, 88% with terminal degrees. *Student/faculty ratio:* 18:1.

Majors Accounting; advertising; African-American/Black studies; agricultural/biological engineering and bioengineering; agricultural business and management; agricultural communication/journalism; agricultural economics; agricultural sciences; agricultural sciences related; agricultural teacher education; ancient/classical Greek; animal health; animal sciences; anthropology; apparel and textiles; applied horticulture; art; art history, criticism and conservation; art teacher education; athletic training/sports medicine; biochemistry; biological and physical sciences; biology/biological sciences; botany/plant biology; broadcast journalism; business, management, and marketing related; cell biology and histology; ceramic sciences and engineering; chemistry; child development; classics and languages, literatures and linguistics; cognitive psychology and psycholinguistics; communication disorders; comparative literature; computer and information sciences; consumer economics; criminal justice/safety; dairy science; dance; dietetics; digital communication and media/multimedia; drama and dance teacher education; dramatic/theater arts; drawing; early childhood education; ecology; economics; English; English/language arts teacher education; entomology; environmental health; environmental science; family and consumer sciences/home economics teacher education; fashion and fabric consulting; fashion merchandising; film/cinema studies; finance; fishing and fisheries sciences and management; food science; foreign languages and literatures; foreign language teacher education; forestry; forest sciences and biology; French; genetics; geography; geology/earth science; German; Germanic languages related; graphic design; health and physical education; health and physical education related; health occupations teacher education; health teacher education; history; horticulture science; housing and human environments; human development and family studies; insurance/risk management; interdisciplinary studies; interior design; interior environments; international business/trade/commerce; international relations and affairs; Italian; Japanese; journalism; landscape architecture; landscaping and groundskeeping; Latin; linguistics; management information systems; marketing/marketing management; mass communication/media; mathematics; mathematics teacher education; medical microbiology and bacteriology; metal and jewelry arts; microbiology; middle school education; modern Greek; music; music performance; music teacher education; music theory and composition; music therapy; nutrition sciences; painting; philosophy; physical education teaching and coaching; physics; plant protection and integrated pest management; plant sciences; political science and government; poultry science; pre-engineering; pre-medical studies; pre-veterinary studies; printmaking; psychology; public relations/image management; reading teacher education; real estate; religious studies; Romance languages related; Russian; sales and marketing/marketing and distribution teacher education; sales, distribution and marketing; science teacher education; sculpture; Slavic languages; social science teacher education; social work; sociology; Spanish; speech and rhetoric; sport and fitness administration/management; statistics; technology/industrial arts teacher education; telecommunications; turf and turfgrass management; water, wetlands, and marine resources management; wildlife and wildlands science and management; women's studies.

Academics *Calendar:* semesters. *Degrees:* certificates, bachelor's, master's, doctoral, first professional, post-master's, postbachelor's, and first professional certificates. *Special study options:* academic remediation for entering students, accelerated degree program, adult/continuing education programs, advanced placement credit, cooperative education, distance learning, double majors, honors programs, independent study, internships, off-campus study, part-time degree program, services for LD students, student-designed majors, study abroad, summer session for credit. *ROTC:* Army (b), Air Force (b).

Computers on Campus 3,100 computers/terminals are available on campus for general student use. Students can access the following: campus intranet, computer help desk, free student e-mail accounts, online (class) grades, online (class) registration, online (class) schedules. Campuswide network is available. 100% of college-owned or -operated housing units are wired for high-speed Internet access. Wireless service is available via classrooms, computer centers, computer labs, dorm rooms, learning centers, libraries, student centers.

Student Life *Housing:* on-campus residence required for freshman year. *Options:* coed, women-only, disabled students. Campus housing is university owned. Freshman campus housing is guaranteed. *Activities and organizations:* drama/theater group, student-run newspaper, radio and television station, choral group, marching band, intramurals, recreational sports program. Communiversity, University Union, Red Coat Band, national fraternities, national sororities. *Campus security:* 24-hour emergency response devices and patrols, late-night transport/escort service, controlled dormitory access. *Student services:* health clinic, personal/psychological counseling, women's center, legal services.

Athletics Member NCAA. All Division I except football (Division I-A). *Intercollegiate sports:* baseball M (s), basketball M (s)/W (s), cheerleading M/W, cross-country running M (s)/W (s), equestrian sports W (s), golf M (s)/W (s), gymnastics W (s), soccer M (c)/W (s), softball W (s), swimming and diving M (s)/W (s), tennis M (s)/W (s), track and field M (s)/W (s), volleyball M (c)/W (s). *Intramural sports:* badminton M (c)/W (c), baseball M (c), basketball M/W, crew M (c)/W (c), cross-country running M/W, equestrian sports M (c)/W (c), fencing M (c), football M, golf M/W, ice hockey M (c), lacrosse M (c)/W (c), racquetball M/W, rugby M (c)/W (c), sailing M (c)/W (c), soccer M/W, softball M/W, swimming and diving M/W, tennis M/W, ultimate Frisbee M (c)/W (c), volleyball M/W, water polo M (c)/W (c), weight lifting M/W, wrestling M (c).

Standardized Tests *Required:* SAT or ACT (for admission). *Recommended:* SAT Subject Tests (for admission).

Costs (2007–08) *Tuition:* state resident $4496 full-time, $187 per credit part-time; nonresident $19,600 full-time, $817 per credit part-time. Full-time tuition and fees vary according to course load, location, program, and student level. Part-time tuition and fees vary according to course load, location, program, and student level. *Required fees:* $1126 full-time, $563 per term part-time. *Room and board:* $7292; room only: $4010. Room and board charges vary according to board plan and housing facility. *Waivers:* senior citizens.

Financial Aid Of all full-time matriculated undergraduates who enrolled in 2007, 10,720 applied for aid, 6,310 were judged to have need, 2,170 had their need fully met. 396 Federal Work-Study jobs (averaging $2553). In 2007, 1462 non-need-based awards were made. *Average percent of need met:* 75%. *Average financial aid package:* $8170. *Average need-based loan:* $3825. *Average need-based gift aid:* $6540. *Average non-need-based aid:* $1955. *Average indebtedness upon graduation:* $14,420.

Applying *Options:* electronic application, early admission, early action, deferred entrance. *Application fee:* $50. *Required:* high school transcript, counselor evaluation. *Recommended:* essay or personal statement, minimum 2.0 GPA. *Application deadlines:* 1/15 (freshmen), 4/1 (transfers), 10/15 (early action). *Notification:* 12/15 (freshmen), continuous (transfers), 12/15 (early action).

Freshman Application Contact Mr. Patrick Winter, Associate Director of Admissions, University of Georgia, Athens, GA 30602. *Phone:* 706-542-8776. *Fax:* 706-542-1466. *E-mail:* undergrad@admissions.uga.edu.

UNIVERSITY OF PHOENIX–ATLANTA CAMPUS

Sandy Springs, Georgia **www.phoenix.edu/**

- **Proprietary** comprehensive
- **Urban** campus
- **Coed**
- **Noncompetitive** entrance level

Faculty *Student/faculty ratio:* 8:1.

Academics *Calendar:* continuous. *Degrees:* bachelor's and master's.

Student Life *Campus security:* late-night transport/escort service.

Costs (2007–08) *Tuition:* $11,430 full-time, $381 per credit part-time. Full-time tuition and fees vary according to course level.

Financial Aid *Average financial aid package:* $4348. *Average need-based loan:* $6122. *Average need-based gift aid:* $2249.

Applying *Options:* deferred entrance. *Application fee:* $45. *Required:* 1 letter of recommendation. *Required for some:* high school transcript.

Freshman Application Contact Ms. Beth Barilla, Associate Vice President, Student Admissions and Services, University of Phoenix–Atlanta Campus, 4615

East Elwood Street, Mail Stop AA-K101, Phoenix, AZ 85040-1958. *Phone:* 480-317-6000. *Toll-free phone:* 800-776-4867 (in-state); 800-228-7240 (out-of-state). *Fax:* 480-894-1758. *E-mail:* beth.barilla@phoenix.edu.

UNIVERSITY OF PHOENIX–COLUMBUS GEORGIA CAMPUS

Columbus, Georgia www.phoenix.edu/

- **Proprietary** comprehensive, founded 2003
- **Urban** campus
- **Coed**
- **Noncompetitive** entrance level

Faculty *Student/faculty ratio:* 9:1.

Academics *Calendar:* continuous. *Degrees:* bachelor's and master's.

Student Life *Campus security:* late-night transport/escort service.

Costs (2007–08) *Tuition:* $10,830 full-time, $361 per credit part-time. Full-time tuition and fees vary according to course level.

Financial Aid *Average financial aid package:* $4527. *Average need-based gift aid:* $2501.

Applying *Options:* deferred entrance. *Application fee:* $45. *Required:* 1 letter of recommendation. *Required for some:* high school transcript.

Freshman Application Contact Ms. Beth Barilla, Associate Vice President, Student Admissions and Services, University of Phoenix–Columbus Georgia Campus, 4747 Hamilton Road, Suite E, Columbus, GA 31904-6321. *Phone:* 480-317-6000. *Toll-free phone:* 800-776-4867 (in-state); 800-228-7240 (out-of-state). *Fax:* 480-894-1758. *E-mail:* beth.barilla@phoenix.edu.

UNIVERSITY OF WEST GEORGIA

Carrollton, Georgia www.westga.edu/

- **State-supported** comprehensive, founded 1933, part of University System of Georgia
- **Small-town** 395-acre campus with easy access to Atlanta
- **Endowment** $17.3 million
- **Coed** 8,842 undergraduate students, 84% full-time, 60% women, 40% men
- **Minimally difficult** entrance level, 53% of applicants were admitted

Undergraduates 7,415 full-time, 1,427 part-time. Students come from 36 states and territories, 76 other countries, 1% are from out of state, 25% African American, 2% Asian American or Pacific Islander, 2% Hispanic American, 0.3% Native American, 1% international, 7% transferred in, 28% live on campus. *Retention:* 73% of 2006 full-time freshmen returned.

Freshmen *Admission:* 5,803 applied, 3,089 admitted, 1,964 enrolled. *Average high school GPA:* 3.04. *Test scores:* SAT critical reading scores over 500: 49%; SAT math scores over 500: 48%; SAT writing scores over 500: 40%; ACT scores over 18: 85%; SAT critical reading scores over 600: 12%; SAT math scores over 600: 10%; SAT writing scores over 600: 7%; ACT scores over 24: 14%; SAT critical reading scores over 700: 1%; SAT math scores over 700: 1%; SAT writing scores over 700: 1%; ACT scores over 30: 1%.

Faculty *Total:* 520, 80% full-time, 70% with terminal degrees. *Student/faculty ratio:* 18:1.

Majors Accounting; anthropology; art; biology/biological sciences; biology teacher education; business administration and management; business/managerial economics; business teacher education; chemistry; chemistry teacher education; computer and information sciences; criminology; dramatic/theater arts; economics; economics related; elementary education; English; environmental science; environmental studies; finance; French; geography; geological and earth sciences/geosciences related; geology/earth science; German; history; international economics; international relations and affairs; journalism; management information systems; marketing/marketing management; mathematics; middle school education; music performance; music teacher education; music theory and composition; nursing (registered nurse training); parks, recreation and leisure facilities management; philosophy; physical education teaching and coaching; physics; physics teacher education; political science and government; pre-law studies; pre-medical studies; pre-veterinary studies; psychology; real estate; secondary education; sociology; Spanish; special education; speech-language pathology.

Academics *Calendar:* semesters. *Degrees:* bachelor's, master's, doctoral, post-master's, and postbachelor's certificates. *Special study options:* academic remediation for entering students, accelerated degree program, adult/continuing education programs, advanced placement credit, cooperative education, distance learning, double majors, external degree program, honors programs, independent study, internships, off-campus study, part-time degree program, services for LD students, study abroad, summer session for credit. *ROTC:* Army (b). *Unusual degree programs:* 3-2 engineering with Georgia Institute of Technology, Auburn University, Mercer University, University of Georgia.

Computers on Campus 1,000 computers/terminals are available on campus for general student use. Students can access the following: campus intranet, computer help desk, free student e-mail accounts, online (class) grades, online (class) registration, online (class) schedules. Campuswide network is available.

Student Life *Housing:* on-campus residence required for freshman year. *Options:* coed, men-only, women-only, cooperative, disabled students. Campus housing is university owned. Freshman campus housing is guaranteed. *Activities and organizations:* drama/theater group, student-run newspaper, radio and television station, choral group, marching band, Black Student Alliance, Student Activities Council, Baptist Student Union, Campus Outreach, United Voices Gospel Choir, national fraternities, national sororities. *Campus security:* 24-hour emergency response devices and patrols, late-night transport/escort service, controlled dormitory access. *Student services:* health clinic, personal/psychological counseling.

Athletics Member NCAA. All Division II. *Intercollegiate sports:* baseball M (s), basketball M (s)/W (s), cheerleading M (s)/W (s), cross-country running M (s)/W (s), football M (s), golf M (s)/W (s), soccer W (s), softball W (s), volleyball W (s). *Intramural sports:* basketball M/W, football M/W, golf M/W, soccer M/W, softball M/W, table tennis M/W, tennis M/W, track and field M/W, ultimate Frisbee M/W, volleyball M/W, water polo M/W, weight lifting M/W.

Standardized Tests *Required:* SAT or ACT (for admission).

Costs (2007–08) *Tuition:* state resident $2958 full-time, $124 per semester hour part-time; nonresident $11,830 full-time, $493 per semester hour part-time. Full-time tuition and fees vary according to course load. Part-time tuition and fees vary according to course load. No tuition increase for student's term of enrollment. *Required fees:* $960 full-time, $26 per semester hour part-time, $173 per term part-time. *Room and board:* $5406; room only: $2620. Room and board charges vary according to board plan and housing facility. *Waivers:* senior citizens.

Financial Aid Of all full-time matriculated undergraduates who enrolled in 2006, 5,092 applied for aid, 3,488 were judged to have need, 644 had their need fully met. 704 Federal Work-Study jobs (averaging $1605). In 2006, 150 non-need-based awards were made. *Average percent of need met:* 61%. *Average financial aid package:* $6590. *Average need-based loan:* $3401. *Average need-based gift aid:* $3341. *Average non-need-based aid:* $2019. *Average indebtedness upon graduation:* $14,781.

Applying *Options:* electronic application, early admission. *Application fee:* $30. *Required:* high school transcript, proof of immunization. *Required for some:* 2 letters of recommendation, interview. *Application deadlines:* 6/1 (freshmen), 6/1 (transfers). *Notification:* continuous until 9/1 (freshmen), continuous (transfers).

Freshman Application Contact Dr. Robert Johnson, Director of Admissions, University of West Georgia, 1601 Maple Street, Carrollton, GA 30118. *Phone:* 770-836-6416. *Fax:* 678-839-4747. *E-mail:* admiss@westga.edu.

See page 758 for the College Close-Up.

VALDOSTA STATE UNIVERSITY

Valdosta, Georgia www.valdosta.edu/

- **State-supported** university, founded 1906, part of University System of Georgia
- **Small-town** 178-acre campus with easy access to Jacksonville
- **Endowment** $23.3 million
- **Coed** 9,728 undergraduate students, 85% full-time, 59% women, 41% men
- **Moderately difficult** entrance level, 63% of applicants were admitted

Undergraduates 8,256 full-time, 1,472 part-time. Students come from 44 states and territories, 58 other countries, 4% are from out of state, 25% African American, 1% Asian American or Pacific Islander, 2% Hispanic American, 0.3% Native American, 1% international, 7% transferred in, 20% live on campus. *Retention:* 71% of 2006 full-time freshmen returned.

Freshmen *Admission:* 5,978 applied, 3,796 admitted, 2,070 enrolled. *Average high school GPA:* 3.06. *Test scores:* SAT critical reading scores over 500: 52%; SAT math scores over 500: 48%; ACT scores over 18: 91%; SAT critical reading scores over 600: 10%; SAT math scores over 600: 7%; ACT scores over 24: 12%; SAT critical reading scores over 700: 1%; SAT math scores over 700: 1%.

Faculty *Total:* 585, 75% full-time. *Student/faculty ratio:* 20:1.

Majors Accounting; administrative assistant and secretarial science; applied mathematics; art; art teacher education; astronomy; athletic training/sports medicine; biology/biological sciences; business administration and management;

business/managerial economics; business teacher education; chemistry; communication/speech communication and rhetoric; computer and information sciences; computer science; criminal justice/safety; dance; dramatic/theater arts; early childhood education; English; environmental studies; finance; French; general studies; history; information science/studies; interior design; kinesiology and exercise science; legal assistant/paralegal; liberal arts and sciences/liberal studies; marketing/marketing management; mass communication/media; mathematics; middle school education; music; music performance; music teacher education; nursing (registered nurse training); philosophy; physical education teaching and coaching; physics; political science and government; psychology; secondary education; sociology; Spanish; special education; speech-language pathology; trade and industrial teacher education.

Academics *Calendar:* semesters. *Degrees:* associate, bachelor's, master's, doctoral, and post-master's certificates. *Special study options:* academic remediation for entering students, accelerated degree program, advanced placement credit, cooperative education, distance learning, double majors, English as a second language, honors programs, independent study, internships, off-campus study, part-time degree program, services for LD students, study abroad, summer session for credit. *ROTC:* Air Force (b).

Computers on Campus 1,400 computers/terminals are available on campus for general student use. Students can access the following: campus intranet, computer help desk, free student e-mail accounts, online (class) grades, online (class) registration, online (class) schedules. Campuswide network is available. 100% of college-owned or -operated housing units are wired for high-speed Internet access. Wireless service is available via entire campus.

Student Life *Housing:* on-campus residence required for freshman year. *Options:* coed, men-only, women-only, disabled students. Campus housing is university owned. Freshman applicants given priority for college housing. *Activities and organizations:* drama/theater group, student-run newspaper, radio and television station, choral group, marching band, national fraternities, national sororities. *Campus security:* 24-hour emergency response devices and patrols, late-night transport/escort service, controlled dormitory access, bicycle patrols, security cameras. *Student services:* health clinic, personal/psychological counseling.

Athletics Member NCAA. All Division II. *Intercollegiate sports:* baseball M (s), basketball M (s)/W (s), cross-country running M (s)/W (s), football M (s), golf M (s), softball W (s), tennis M (s)/W (s), volleyball W (s). *Intramural sports:* basketball M/W, bowling M/W, field hockey M/W, football M/W, golf M/W, racquetball M/W, soccer M/W, softball M/W, tennis M/W, ultimate Frisbee M/W, volleyball M/W.

Standardized Tests *Required:* SAT or ACT (for admission).

Costs (2008–09) *Tuition:* state resident $2958 full-time, $124 per hour part-time; nonresident $11,830 full-time, $493 per hour part-time. *Required fees:* $1080 full-time. *Room and board:* $5990; room only: $3050.

Financial Aid Of all full-time matriculated undergraduates who enrolled in 2007, 6,208 applied for aid, 4,681 were judged to have need, 2,953 had their need fully met. 265 Federal Work-Study jobs (averaging $2225). In 2007, 25 non-need-based awards were made. *Average percent of need met:* 88%. *Average financial aid package:* $11,239. *Average need-based loan:* $5419. *Average need-based gift aid:* $5055. *Average non-need-based aid:* $1593. *Average indebtedness upon graduation:* $16,220.

Applying *Options:* electronic application, early admission, deferred entrance. *Application fee:* $40. *Required:* high school transcript, minimum 2.0 GPA, proof of immunization. *Application deadlines:* 7/1 (freshmen), 7/1 (transfers). *Notification:* continuous (freshmen), continuous (transfers).

Freshman Application Contact Mr. Walter Peacock, Director of Admissions, Valdosta State University, 1500 North Patterson Street, Valdosta, GA 31698. *Phone:* 229-333-5791. *Toll-free phone:* 800-618-1878 Ext. 1. *Fax:* 229-333-5482. *E-mail:* admissions@valdosta.edu.

WESLEYAN COLLEGE

Macon, Georgia **www.wesleyancollege.edu/**

- **Independent United Methodist** comprehensive, founded 1836
- **Suburban** 200-acre campus with easy access to Atlanta
- **Endowment** $50.9 million
- **Undergraduate: women only; graduate: coed** 592 undergraduate students, 64% full-time, 99% women, 1% men
- **Moderately difficult** entrance level, 49% of applicants were admitted

Undergraduates 379 full-time, 213 part-time. Students come from 25 states and territories, 16 other countries, 10% are from out of state, 22% African American, 0.9% Asian American or Pacific Islander, 4% Hispanic American, 0.9% Native American, 30% international, 0.8% transferred in, 76% live on campus. *Retention:* 72% of 2006 full-time freshmen returned.

Freshmen *Admission:* 617 applied, 302 admitted, 110 enrolled. *Average high school GPA:* 3.5. *Test scores:* SAT critical reading scores over 500: 77%; SAT math scores over 500: 89%; ACT scores over 18: 100%; SAT critical reading scores over 600: 37%; SAT math scores over 600: 46%; ACT scores over 24: 36%; SAT critical reading scores over 700: 6%; SAT math scores over 700: 8%; ACT scores over 30: 7%.

Faculty *Total:* 83, 60% full-time, 71% with terminal degrees. *Student/faculty ratio:* 7:1.

Majors Advertising; American studies; art history, criticism and conservation; biology/biological sciences; business administration and management; chemistry; communication/speech communication and rhetoric; computer and information sciences; early childhood education; economics; education; English; environmental science; fine/studio arts; French; history; humanities; interdisciplinary studies; international business/trade/commerce; international relations and affairs; mathematics; middle school education; music; philosophy; physical sciences; physics; political science and government; psychology; religious studies; social sciences; Spanish.

Academics *Calendar:* semesters. *Degrees:* bachelor's and master's. *Special study options:* adult/continuing education programs, advanced placement credit, cooperative education, double majors, honors programs, independent study, internships, off-campus study, part-time degree program, services for LD students, student-designed majors, study abroad, summer session for credit. *Unusual degree programs:* 3-2 engineering with Georgia Institute of Technology, Mercer University, Auburn University.

Computers on Campus 24 computers/terminals are available on campus for general student use. Students can access the following: online (class) registration. Campuswide network is available. 100% of college-owned or -operated housing units are wired for high-speed Internet access. Wireless service is available via classrooms, libraries.

Student Life *Housing:* on-campus residence required through senior year. *Options:* women-only. Campus housing is university owned. Freshman campus housing is guaranteed. *Activities and organizations:* drama/theater group, student-run newspaper, choral group, Student Recreation Council, Campus Activities Board, Student Government Association, Council on Religious Concerns, Christian Fellowship. *Campus security:* 24-hour emergency response devices and patrols, late-night transport/escort service, controlled dormitory access. *Student services:* health clinic, personal/psychological counseling, women's center.

Athletics Member NCAA. All Division III. *Intercollegiate sports:* basketball W, equestrian sports W, soccer W, softball W, tennis W, volleyball W. *Intramural sports:* basketball W, soccer W, softball W, tennis W, volleyball W.

Standardized Tests *Required:* SAT or ACT (for admission).

Costs (2007–08) *Comprehensive fee:* $24,100 includes full-time tuition ($16,500) and room and board ($7600). Part-time tuition: $395 per semester hour.

Financial Aid Of all full-time matriculated undergraduates who enrolled in 2006, 296 applied for aid, 245 were judged to have need, 67 had their need fully met. 48 Federal Work-Study jobs (averaging $1200). 147 state and other part-time jobs (averaging $1200). In 2006, 148 non-need-based awards were made. *Average percent of need met:* 79%. *Average financial aid package:* $10,758. *Average need-based loan:* $3799. *Average need-based gift aid:* $7913. *Average non-need-based aid:* $13,943. *Average indebtedness upon graduation:* $20,988.

Applying *Options:* early admission, early decision, early action, deferred entrance. *Application fee:* $30. *Required:* essay or personal statement, high school transcript, minimum 2.0 GPA. *Recommended:* 2 letters of recommendation, interview. *Application deadlines:* 4/1 (freshmen), rolling (transfers), 2/1 (early action). *Early decision deadline:* 11/15. *Notification:* continuous until 8/1 (freshmen), continuous until 8/1 (transfers), 12/15 (early decision), 3/1 (early action).

Freshman Application Contact Ms. Patricia Gibbs, Vice President for Enrollment Services and Student Affairs, Wesleyan College, 4760 Forsyth Road, Macon, GA 31210-4462. *Phone:* 478-757-5206. *Toll-free phone:* 800-447-6610. *Fax:* 478-757-4030. *E-mail:* admission@wesleyancollege.edu.

See page 760 for the College Close-Up.

WESTWOOD COLLEGE–ATLANTA MIDTOWN

Atlanta, Georgia **www.westwood.edu/**

Director of Admissions Rory Laney, Director of Admissions, Westwood College–Atlanta Midtown, 1100 Spring Street, Ste. 101A, Atlanta, GA 30309. *Phone:* 404-870-8982.

WESTWOOD COLLEGE–ATLANTA NORTHLAKE

Atlanta, Georgia www.westwood.edu/

- **Proprietary** 4-year, part of Alta College, Inc.
- **Coed** 336 undergraduate students

Undergraduates 1% are from out of state, 80% African American, 2% Asian American or Pacific Islander, 2% Hispanic American.

Freshmen *Average high school GPA:* 2.0.

Majors Animation, interactive technology, video graphics and special effects; architectural drafting and CAD/CADD; design and visual communications; e-commerce; graphic design; interior design.

Academics *Degrees:* diplomas, associate, and bachelor's.

Athletics *Intercollegiate sports:* ultimate Frisbee M (s)/W (s), volleyball M (s)/W (s). *Intramural sports:* ultimate Frisbee M/W, volleyball M/W.

Applying *Required:* high school transcript, entrance assessment.

Director of Admissions Westwood College–Atlanta Northlake, 2220 Parklake Drive, Suite 175, Atlanta, GA 30345.

AGNES SCOTT COLLEGE

ATLANTA, GEORGIA

The College

For more than a century, minds have sparked minds at Agnes Scott College, a highly selective, independent, national liberal arts college for women, located in metropolitan Atlanta. Agnes Scott College educates women to think deeply, live honorably, and engage the intellectual and social challenges of their times. Founded in 1889 by Presbyterians, Agnes Scott College is a diverse and growing residential community of scholars with a curriculum that encourages students to become fluent across disciplines, continents, and centuries.

Agnes Scott was the first accredited college or university in Georgia, and the College's Phi Beta Kappa chapter is the second oldest in the state. Agnes Scott's tradition of academic excellence continues today with a student body numbering 1,000. Students come from forty-three states and twenty-three countries, and 92 percent of traditional-age students live on campus in residence halls and apartments. More than 33 percent represent diverse ethnic or cultural backgrounds.

Students may pursue special interests in the arts (music, dance, and theater); with clubs for international cultures, politics, cultural awareness, religious affiliations, and foreign languages; and through student publications, sports, and volunteer community service. Social Council plans dances, mixers, and parties with neighboring colleges. Traditional annual highlights are Black Cat (the culmination of first-year student orientation), Senior Investiture, and Sophomore Family Weekend. The College sponsors a variety of events, from lectures by noted authorities to concerts by world-famous artists; each spring, the Writers' Festival brings well-known authors and poets to the campus for readings and informal meetings with students.

The College is a member of the NCAA Division III and sponsors seven varsity sports: basketball, cross-country, soccer, softball, swimming, tennis, and volleyball. In 2006, three coaches were named conference coach of the year. In cross-country, Agnes Scott College was the 2005 and 2006 Great South Athletic Conference champion. Club and intramural sports are also available. The Woodruff Physical Activities Building features an eight-lane swimming pool, a large weight and aerobic exercise room, a gymnasium, and an athletic training room. The Gellerstedt track is an all-weather, six-lane running track circling the varsity soccer field.

Location

The 100-acre wooded campus is located in metropolitan Atlanta and the vibrant residential community of Decatur. Six miles away is downtown Atlanta, which is accessible by a rapid-transit rail station two blocks from the campus. An international city, Atlanta offers a multitude of opportunities for personal contact with most of the world's cultures and for study, through internships and volunteer work, with art, business, educational, and political organizations. Atlanta is the cultural center of the South, with entertainment and cultural events and facilities ranging from rock concerts to performances by the Atlanta Symphony Orchestra, from local theater to touring Broadway shows, and from recreational parks to major-league sports and the world's largest aquarium.

Majors and Degrees

Agnes Scott College confers the Bachelor of Arts degree, with majors in Africana studies, art history, astrophysics, biochemistry and molecular biology, biology, chemistry, classical languages and literatures, classical civilization, dance, economics, economics and organizational management, English, English literature–creative writing, French, German studies, history, international relations, mathematics, mathematics-economics, mathematics-physics, music, neuroscience, philosophy, physics, political science, psychology, religion and social justice, religious studies, sociology and anthropology, Spanish, studio art, theater, and women's studies. Students may design interdisciplinary majors. Through a dual-degree program, a student may combine three years of liberal arts studies at Agnes Scott with two years of specialized engineering studies at Georgia Institute of Technology or nursing studies at Emory University, receiving a bachelor's degree from each institution. Also available is a 3-4 Master of Architecture program offered with Washington University in St. Louis.

Academic Programs

Agnes Scott's curriculum is designed to help students gain an understanding of the humanities and fine arts, natural sciences and mathematics, and social sciences, with particular competence in one or two disciplines. The graduation requirement of 128 semester hours includes specific standards in English composition and foreign language. The Language Across the Curriculum Program links foreign languages with other disciplines. Students prepare for world citizenship through a curriculum with international perspectives. In the last ten years, Agnes Scott has had 5 Goldwater Scholars, 1 Gates Millennium Scholar, 5 Gillman International Scholars, several Fulbright Scholars, and 1 Pickering Fellow.

The economics and organizational management major is designed to facilitate a student's entry into the business world. The state-approved teacher education program leads to the Georgia professional certificate, which is recognized and accepted by most states. The Irene K. Woodruff Scholars Program provides women beyond traditional college age with the opportunity to complete the Bachelor of Arts degree.

Off-Campus Programs

Study abroad enriches classroom learning experiences and expands world views. Agnes Scott offers two faculty-led programs—the Coca-Cola Global Awareness Program and Global Connections. Recent destinations have included China, Cuba, the Czech Republic, France, Ghana, Greece, India, Ireland, Japan, Jordan, and Mexico. Agnes Scott has a scholarly exchange agreement with Japan's Kinjo Gakuin University and is the only domestic women's college admitted to the International Student Exchange Program (ISEP), which provides study-abroad opportunities with more than 147 institutions in fifty countries.

With opportunities to cross-register at member institutions of the Atlanta Regional Council for Higher Education (ARCHE), Agnes Scott students enjoy the advantages of a small-college environment while benefiting from a variety of programs at neighboring schools, including Emory University, Spelman College, and Georgia Institute of Technology. ARCHE shares courses of instruction, library services, and visiting scholars. Air Force and Army ROTC programs are available through cross-registration at Georgia Tech. An exchange program with Mills College in Oakland, California, enables students to study for a semester or year in the San Francisco Bay Area. Students may participate in the Washington Semester program, which is coordinated by American University, or the PLEN Public Policy Semester, both in Washington, D.C.

Academic Facilities

A $120-million building program to enhance academic and student life facilities is complete. The $36.5-million Bullock Science Center opened in 2003. The Alston Campus Center, which includes meeting rooms, a 24-hour-access Cyber Café, and a computer lab, opened during the 2001 academic year. Other enhancements include a renovated and expanded Evans Hall with a marketplace servery and a 500-car parking and public safety facility.

The Bullock Science Center has laboratories and computer facilities for experimentation and research in biology, chemistry, physics, and psychology. These include a nuclear magnetic resonance (NMR) machine lab; high-end computers for scientific computing, teaching, and research; walk-in controlled-environment rooms; a neurophysiology laboratory; and animal physiology workstations. Bradley Observatory has undergone extensive renovation and addition. The Delafield Planetarium has a computer-controlled Zeiss projector, one of only ten in the United States, as well as its 30-inch Beck telescope, one of the largest in the Southeast.

McCain Library has been completely renovated and doubled in size, with access to the Internet available at every seat. The library contains 221,991 volumes, 18,867 audiovisual items, and 33,125 microforms and receives 15,049 print and electronic periodicals. It also provides a home for the Center for Writing and Speaking. The library holds several noteworthy collections of rare books and manuscripts, including one of the leading Robert Frost collections and the papers of alumna Catherine Marshall LeSourd. Agnes Scott's reciprocal library service gives students direct access to the libraries of eighteen other institutions in the Atlanta-Athens area. Extensive electronic resources are available through the GALILEO project of the University System of Georgia.

Personal computers are available to students in the technology commons, Cyber Café, Academic Computing Center, Center for Writing and Speaking, Science Resource Center, Macintosh lab, and residence halls. Wireless connectivity is available throughout the campus. An interactive learning center, multimedia classrooms, and a computer network with one port per student in residence hall rooms are part of Agnes Scott's commitment to keep pace with current technologies.

Dana Fine Arts Building houses the departments of theater and art; its facilities include a thrust-stage theater, two floors of balcony art studios, pottery and sculpture studios with kilns, and a darkroom. Dalton Gallery exhibits the College's permanent and traveling collections and student and faculty exhibitions. Presser Hall contains soundproof recording studios and practice rooms for music students. Gaines Chapel, with a 3,000-pipe Austin organ, has a large stage for dance, music, and theatrical performances. Maclean Auditorium, which houses a Schlicker organ, is used for chamber music concerts and student recitals.

Costs

Tuition for 2008–09 is $28,200. Room and board are $9850, the student and technology fees are $410, and student health insurance is $450. Personal expenses, including books and supplies, are estimated at $2000.

Financial Aid

Agnes Scott admits most students without regard to financial need, and the College makes every effort to meet the need of qualified students whose resources are insufficient to meet expenses. More than 50 percent of students receive need-based financial assistance through grants, loans, and campus employment. Outstanding first-year students are offered renewable merit-based Honor Scholarships, and music scholarships are available for new students intending to major in music.

Faculty

A 10:1 student-faculty ratio allows for small classes with lively participation and individual attention. One hundred percent of Agnes Scott's tenure-track faculty members hold the highest degree in their field. Senior faculty members teach first-year students as well as upperclass students. Every student is assigned a faculty adviser to assist in course selection and academic counseling.

Student Government

Agnes Scott is a self-governing community, and each student is a member of the Student Government Association. A strong honor system places responsibility for integrity, honesty, and judgment in self-government on the individual and allows unproctored tests and self-scheduled final examinations. Regulations governing student life are made by the students with approval of the Judicial Review Committee, on which the Student Government Association, Student Senate, Honor Court, and Judicial Board presidents serve as voting members. Policies are formulated with the goal of maintaining an individual's maximum freedom within the framework of community responsibility.

Admission Requirements

Agnes Scott admits, without regard to race, color, creed, national or ethnic origin, or physical handicap, students whose academic and personal qualities give promise of success. Transfer and international students are welcome. Each applicant's academic record, SAT or ACT scores, recommendations, and essay are reviewed carefully, and interviews are recommended but not required. Arrangements for an interview at the College, a campus tour with a student guide, and visits to classes may be made by contacting the Office of Admission.

Application and Information

For traditional applicants, an application for admission and supporting credentials should be filed with the Office of Admission by the following dates: November 15 for early action, with notification beginning in mid December; January 15 for scholarship candidates; March 1 for regular decision; and November 1 for the spring semester.

Dean of Admission
Agnes Scott College
141 East College Avenue
Decatur, Georgia 30030-3770
Phone: 404-471-6285
800-868-8602 (toll-free)
Fax: 404-471-6414
E-mail: admission@agnesscott.edu
Web site: http://www.agnesscott.edu

COLLEGE DATA CENTER • GEORGIA

ARGOSY UNIVERSITY

ARGOSY UNIVERSITY

The University

Argosy University is a leading institution offering a variety of degree programs that focus on the human side of success alongside professional competence. For students looking for a more personal approach to education, Argosy University may just be the answer. With forty-eight graduate and undergraduate programs, across nineteen campuses and twelve states, Argosy University emphasizes interpersonal skills as well as academic learning. All of its programs are taught by practicing professionals who bring real-world experience into the classroom. So students graduate with both a solid foundation of knowledge and the power to put it to work. To accommodate busy working adults, many programs at Argosy University are structured flexibly—with both campus and online learning and evening, weekend, and daytime classes. There is also a wide range of financial aid options for students who qualify.

Argosy University is a private institution of higher education dedicated to providing high-quality professional education programs at the doctoral, master's, bachelor's, and associate degree levels as well as continuing education to individuals who seek to advance their professional and personal lives. The University emphasizes programs in the behavioral sciences (psychology and counseling), business, education, and the health-care professions. A limited number of preprofessional programs and general education offerings are provided to permit students to prepare for entry into these professional fields. The programs of Argosy University are designed to instill the knowledge, skills, and ethical values of professional practice and to foster values of social responsibility in a supportive, learning-centered environment of mutual respect and professional excellence.

With nineteen campuses nationwide, Argosy University provides students with a network of resources found at larger universities, including a career resources office, an academic resources center, and extensive information access for research. The University's innovative programs feature dynamic, relevant, and practical curricula delivered in flexible class formats. Students enjoy scheduling options that make it easier to fit school into their busy lives. They can choose from day and evening courses, on campus or online. Many students find a combination of both to be an ideal way of continuing their education while meeting family and professional demands.

Most students are full-time working professionals who live within driving distance of the campus. The University does not offer or operate student housing.

Argosy University is accredited by The Higher Learning Commission of the North Central Association (30 North LaSalle Street, Suite 2400, Chicago, Illinois 60602; 800-621-7440; http://ncahlc.org).

Location

Argosy University operates nineteen locations across the U.S. and offers a variety of degree programs online (http://www.argosy.edu). Campus locations include the following:

Atlanta, 980 Hammond Drive, Suite 100, Atlanta, Georgia 30328; phone: 770-671-1200 or 888-671-4777 (toll-free)

Chicago, 225 North Michigan Avenue, Suite 1300, Chicago, Illinois 60601; phone: 312-777-7600 or 800-626-4123 (toll-free)

Dallas, 8080 Park Lane, Suite 400A, Dallas, Texas 75231; phone: 214-890-9900 or 866-954-9900 (toll-free)

Denver, 1200 Lincoln Street, Denver, Colorado 80203; phone: 303-248-2700 or 866-431-5981 (toll-free)

Hawai'i, 400 ASB Tower, 1001 Bishop Street, Honolulu, Hawaii 96813; phone: 808-536-5555 or 888-323-2777 (toll-free)

Inland Empire, 636 East Brier Drive, Suite 235, San Bernardino, California 92408; phone: 909-915-3800 or 866-217-9075 (toll-free)

Nashville, 100 Centerview Drive, Suite 225, Nashville, Tennessee 37214; phone: 615-525-2800 or 866-833-6598 (toll-free)

Orange County, 3501 West Sunflower Avenue, Suite 110, Santa Ana, California 92704; phone: 714-338-6200 or 800-716-9598 (toll-free)

Phoenix, 2233 West Dunlap Avenue, Phoenix, Arizona 85021; phone: 602-216-2600 or 866-216-2777 (toll-free)

Salt Lake City, 121 West Election Road, Suite 300, Draper, Utah 84020; phone: 888-639-4756 (toll-free)

San Diego, 7650 Mission Valley Road, San Diego, California 92108; phone: 858-598-1900 or 866-505-0333 (toll-free)

San Francisco Bay Area, 1005 Atlantic Avenue, Alameda, California 94501; phone: 510-217-4700 or 866-215-2777 (toll-free)

Santa Monica, 2950 31st Street, Santa Monica, California 90405; phone: 310-866-4000 or 866-505-0332 (toll-free)

Sarasota, 5250 17th Street, Sarasota, Florida 34235; phone: 941-379-0404 or 800-331-5995 (toll-free)

Schaumburg, 999 North Plaza Drive, Suite 111, Schaumburg, Illinois 60173-5403; phone: 847-969-4900 or 866-290-2777 (toll-free)

Seattle, 2601-A Elliott Avenue, Seattle, Washington 98121; phone: 206-283-4500 or 888-283-2777 (toll-free)

Tampa, Parkside at Tampa Bay Park, 4401 North Hines Avenue, Suite 150, Tampa, Florida 33614; phone: 813-393-5290 or 800-850-6488 (toll-free)

Twin Cities, 1515 Central Parkway, Eagan, Minnesota 55121; phone: 651-846-2882 or 888-844-2004 (toll-free)

Washington DC, 1550 Wilson Boulevard, Suite 600, Arlington, Virginia 22209; phone: 703-526-5800 or 866-703-2777 (toll-free)

Majors and Degrees

Argosy University's College of Business offers a Bachelor of Science (B.S.) in Business Administration program. Argosy University's College of Psychology and Behavioral Sciences offers the Bachelor of Arts (B.A.) in Psychology degree program.

Academic Programs

The B.S. in Business Administration program prepares students for entry- to mid-level positions within the public or private sector. The curriculum is structured to help students develop competencies in oral and written communication, leadership, team skills, solutions-focused learning, and the analysis and execution of solutions in various business situations. Students may choose one of five optional concentrations: customized professional concentration, finance, health-care management, international business, or marketing.

The B.A. in Psychology program is designed to help students begin human services careers in such capacities as entry-level counselor, case manager, or human resources administrator and

in management and business services roles. The program also lays the foundation for graduate study. Students may choose an optional concentration from the following three options: criminal justice, organizational psychology, or substance abuse. This dynamic program is built around a flexible class approach.

Argosy University's bachelor's degree programs are open to students and working professionals with no college experience, plus those who have already earned college credit at a community college, junior college, or other university.

Academic Facilities

Argosy University libraries provide curriculum support and educational resources including current text materials, diagnostic training documents, reference materials and databases, journals and dissertations, and major and current titles in program areas. There is an online public-access catalog of library resources available throughout the Argosy University system. Students enjoy full remote access to their campus library database, enabling them to study and conduct research at home. Academic databases offer dissertation abstracts, academic journals, and professional periodicals. All library computers are Internet accessible. Software applications include Word, Excel, PowerPoint, SPSS, and various test-scoring programs.

Costs

Tuition varies by program. Students should contact the Argosy University campus of their choice for tuition information.

Financial Aid

A wide range of financial aid options is available to students who qualify. Argosy University offers access to federal and state aid programs, merit-based awards, grants, loans, and a work-study program. As a first step, students should complete the Free Application for Federal Student Aid (FAFSA). Prospective students can apply electronically at http://www.fafsa.ed.gov or at the campus. To receive consideration for financial aid and ensure timely receipt of funds, it is best to submit an application promptly.

Faculty

The Argosy University faculty is composed of working professionals who have a passion to help students succeed. Members bring real-world experience and the latest practice innovations to the academic setting. The diverse faculty is widely recognized for contributions to the field. Most hold doctoral degrees. They provide a substantive education that combines comprehensive knowledge with critical skills and practical workplace relevance. Above all, faculty members are committed to their students' personal and professional development.

Student Government

Argosy University campuses offer unique opportunities for student involvement beyond individual programs of study. Most faculty committees include a student representative. In addition, a student group meets with faculty members and administrators regularly to discuss pertinent campus-related issues.

Admission Requirements

Admission requirements differ depending on the number of college credits completed prior to application.

Students who have earned 12 or fewer semester college credits must provide proof of high school graduation or GED and meet one of the following conditions for admission: ACT composite score of 18 or above, or a combined math and verbal SAT score of 870, or minimum ACCUPLACER scores of 86 in sentence skills and 53 in algebra. Applicants who do not meet any of the above conditions for admission will be admitted with academic support if they provide proof of high school graduation or GED and meet one of the following: ACT composite score of 14 to 17, or a combined math and verbal SAT score of 660 to 869, or minimum ACCUPLACER scores of 54 in sentence skills and 36 in arithmetic.

Applicants who have earned 13 or more semester college credits must provide proof of high school graduation or GED and meet one of the following conditions for admission: cumulative college GPA of 2.0 or above or minimum ACCUPLACER scores of 86 for sentence skills and 53 in algebra. Students who do not meet either of the above criteria will be admitted with academic support if they provide proof of high school graduation or GED and meet the following condition: minimum ACCUPLACER scores of 54 in reading and 36 in arithmetic.

Students admitted with academic support are limited to 12 credit hours of study during their first semester (6 credit hours per session). Students admitted with academic support will be required to complete developmental English and/or math courses unless they meet the following conditions: Writing Review (ENG099)—must meet one of the following: a minimum ACCUPLACER score of 86 in sentence skills, or a minimum ACT verbal score of 18, or a minimum SAT verbal score of 425, or completion of a college-level English composition course with a grade of C or above; Mathematics Review I (MAT096)—must meet one of the following: a minimum ACCUPLACER score of 53 in algebra, or a minimum ACT math score of 18, or a minimum SAT math score of 440, or completion of a college-level English composition course with a grade of C or above.

Other admission requirements may include credit hours of qualified transfer credit with a grade of C- or better from a regionally accredited institution or a nationally accredited institution approved and documented by the faculty and dean of the College of Business, or the College of Professional Psychology, at Argosy University or completion of an Associate of Arts or Associate of Science degree from a regionally accredited institution. A maximum of 78 lower-division or 90 total credit hours may be transferred. A minimum written TOEFL score of 500 (paper-based test), 173 (computer-based test), or 61 (Internet-based test) is required for all applicants whose native language is not English or who have not graduated from an institution in which English is the language of instruction.

Official transcripts from approved postsecondary institutions must include a minimum grade point average of 2.0 (on a scale of 4.0) for all academic work completed. Exceptions may be made for extenuating circumstances. All applications must include a completed application form, proof of high school graduation or successful completion of the GED test, official postsecondary transcripts, and a nonrefundable (except in California) application fee. Additional materials are required prior to matriculation. Some programs have additional application requirements or include exceptions to admission requirements. An admissions representative can provide further information.

Application and Information

Argosy University accepts students on a rolling admissions basis year-round, depending on availability of required courses. Applications for admission are available online at http://www.argosy.edu or by contacting one of the campus locations.

Argosy University
205 North Michigan Avenue, Suite 1300
Chicago, Illinois 60601-2250

Phone: 312-899-9900
800-377-0617 (toll-free)
E-mail: auadmissions@argosy.edu
Web site: http://www.argosy.edu

THE ART INSTITUTE OF ATLANTA

ATLANTA, GEORGIA

The Institute

At The Art Institute of Atlanta, students are given the opportunity to learn new ways to apply talent, energy, and skill in the creative arts. The school provides an educational environment with a particular focus on changing technologies and other requirements of the global marketplace.

The Art Institute of Atlanta offers fifteen bachelor's degree programs and seven associate degree options to students. The school seeks to provide a curriculum that integrates conceptual and analytical skills with education to prepare students for entry-level employment in the creative arts. Assistance is available to help students with resume writing, networking, and keeping abreast of what employers are looking for in job candidates.

Students come to The Art Institute of Atlanta from across the United States and abroad. The student population includes recent high school graduates, transfer students, and those who have left a previous employment situation to study and train for a new career. Students are creative, competitive, and open to new ideas. They place great value on an education that prepares them for an exciting, entry-level position in the arts.

The Art Institute of Atlanta is accredited by the Commission on Colleges of the Southern Association of Colleges and Schools (SACS; 1866 Southern Lane, Decatur, Georgia 30033-4097; phone: 404-679-4500; http://www.sacs.org) to award the Associate in Arts, the Bachelor of Arts, the Bachelor of Fine Arts, and the Bachelor of Science degrees. The Associate in Arts in Culinary Arts degree program is accredited by the American Culinary Federation (ACF). The Bachelor of Fine Arts in Interior Design degree program is accredited by the Council for Interior Design Accreditation. The Bachelor of Science in Culinary Arts Management program is accredited by the Accrediting Commission of the American Culinary Federation Foundation.

Location

Located in bustling suburban Atlanta, the school is close to public transportation and within walking distance of a shopping center with movie theaters, several restaurants, and stores. One of the city's largest malls is less than a 10-minute drive—or one subway stop from The Art Institute of Atlanta. There are at least thirty restaurants within a 15-minute drive. Students enjoy clubs and concerts, galleries and museums, baseball games, and Rollerblading in Piedmont Park. The High Museum of Art, Michael C. Carlos Museum, Atlanta Contemporary Art Center, and dozens of art galleries throughout the city are wonderful resources for creative-minded students.

Majors and Degrees

The Art Institute of Atlanta offers bachelor's degree programs in advertising, audio production, culinary arts management, digital filmmaking and video production, fashion and retail management, food and beverage management, game art and design, graphic design, illustration and design, interior design, media arts and animation, photographic imaging, visual and game programming, visual effects and motion graphics, and Web design and interactive media.

Associate in Arts degree programs are offered in audio production, culinary arts, graphic design, photographic imaging, video production, Web design and interactive media, and wine, spirits, and beverage management.

Diploma programs are offered in advertising design, commercial photography, culinary arts–baking and pastry, culinary arts–culinary skills, digital design, residential interiors, video skills, and Web design.

Academic Programs

The academic year is divided into four academic quarters that begin in January, April, July, and October. Full-time students typically take 16 academic credits per quarter. An associate degree can be earned in six to seven quarters (approximately two years), and a bachelor's degree can be earned in twelve quarters (three to four years). Students may take online classes in order to earn a degree on a flexible schedule, or they may take online classes as a supplement to traditional classroom learning.

Academic Facilities

Facilities at The Art Institute of Atlanta are concentrated into two buildings for easy access. There are Mac and PC computer labs for student use. Specialty labs and studios include a digital editing lab, digital imaging lab, wet photo lab, audio lab, photography studio, video studio, and control room. The school offers art labs, figure and still-life drawing studios, drafting labs, classrooms wired for Internet access, a conference room, and meeting rooms. The Art Institute of Atlanta library holds more than 40,000 items, including books, videotapes, DVDs, CD-ROMs, more than 40 online full-text databases, and access to libraries at other local colleges and universities. The Interior Design Department has a special resource library.

Culinary arts students learn in professional teaching kitchens. Creations Dining Lab, the teaching dining room of the culinary arts program, allows students to gain hands-on experience similar to what they'll experience in the real world. Students work under the skilled direction of chef instructors to create lunch and dinner for restaurant patrons.

The Gallery, located on the first floor, is a noncommercial exhibition space that reflects and exemplifies the artwork of professionals, faculty members, students, and graduates in their professional fields. The gallery's goals are to inspire and challenge students through examples of accomplished artists, to provide opportunities to increase public awareness of The Art Institute of Atlanta and its importance in the art community, and to enrich the learning community at the school through exhibitions that demonstrate high levels of excellence.

Costs

Tuition cost varies by program. Prospective students should contact the school for current tuition costs. Other charges include a starting kit for all first-quarter students. Kits vary in price depending on the program of study.

Financial Aid

Financial aid is available for those who qualify. Students who require financial assistance should first complete and submit a Free Application for Federal Student Aid (FAFSA) and meet with a financial aid officer. The officer determines the level of need based on a required federal formula, the cost of education, and other factors. Gift aid is available in the form of Federal Pell Grants, Federal Supplemental Educational Opportunity Grants, federal Academic Competitiveness Grants, federal SMART Grants, state grants, and veterans' benefits. Loans include Federal Stafford Loans, Federal PLUS Loans, and alternative loans. Other scholarships are available from the school and private sources. Application deadlines and eligibility requirements vary by program.

Faculty

The Art Institute of Atlanta faculty includes full-time and part-time professors with professional experience in their respective fields. Faculty members pride themselves on building close personal relationships with students. They maintain an informal open-door policy and are available to meet with students and student organizations.

Student Government

The Student Advisory Assembly, the representative body of students, meets regularly to discuss policy matters and to plan programs to enhance student life. The assembly offers a valuable opportunity for students to learn the principles of leadership as well as communication and human relations skills. Other organizations dedicated to student life include the Housing Council, International Student Association, Student Activities Board, and Student Ambassadors. Students may take part in several student organizations, such as professional organizations for creative artists, which provide networking and other career opportunities.

Admission Requirements

To apply to The Art Institute of Atlanta, students must submit an application for admission, a 150-word essay, a signed notice regarding transferability for credit earned, and high school transcripts or General Educational Development (GED) test scores. Official reports of SAT, ACT, ASSET, or COMPASS scores must also be given to the school. Finally, students are required to complete an interview with an assistant director of admissions and to present a portfolio of their work. There is a $50 application fee.

Admissions decisions are made by the Admissions Committee, which consists of school faculty and staff members. The committee determines whether an applicant has a reasonable chance to be successful at The Art Institute of Atlanta, based upon the applicant's academic record, essay, and the appropriateness of stated career goals as they relate to the chosen program of study.

Application and Information

To obtain an application, make arrangements for an interview, or tour the school, students should contact:

The Art Institute of Atlanta
6600 Peachtree Dunwoody Road, N.E.
100 Embassy Row
Atlanta, Georgia 30328-1635
Phone: 770-394-8300
800-275-4242 (toll-free)
Fax: 770-394-0008
Web site: http://www.artinstitutes.edu/atlanta

The Art Institute of Atlanta®, GA; The Art Institute of Atlanta®–Decatur, GA; The Art Institute of Austin℠, TX; The Art Institute of California℠–Inland Empire; The Art Institute of California℠–Los Angeles; The Art Institute of California℠–Orange County; The Art Institute of California℠–Sacramento; The Art Institute of California℠–San Diego; The Art Institute of California℠–San Francisco; The Art Institute of California℠–Sunnyvale; The Art Institute of Charleston℠, SC, A branch of The Art Institute of Atlanta, GA; The Art Institute of Charlotte®, NC; The Art Institute of Colorado® (Denver); The Art Institute of Dallas®, TX; The Art Institute of Fort Lauderdale®, FL; The Art Institute of Houston®, TX; The Art Institute of Indianapolis℠, IN*; The Art Institute of Jacksonville℠, FL, A branch of Miami International University of Art & Design; The Art Institute of Las Vegas®, NV; The Art Institute of Michigan℠ (Detroit); The Art Institute of New York City®, NY; The Art Institute of Ohio℠–Cincinnati**; The Art Institute of Philadelphia®, PA; The Art Institute of Phoenix®, AZ; The Art Institute of Pittsburgh®, PA; The Art Institute of Pittsburgh®–Online Division; The Art Institute of Portland®, OR; The Art Institute of Salt Lake City℠, UT; The Art Institute of Seattle®, WA; The Art Institute of Tampa℠, FL, A branch of Miami International University of Art & Design; The Art Institute of Tennessee℠–Nashville, A branch of The Art Institute of Atlanta, GA; The Art Institute of Tucson℠, AZ; The Art Institute of Washington® (Arlington, VA), A branch of The Art Institute of Atlanta, GA; The Art Institute of York–Pennsylvania℠; The Art Institutes International Minnesota℠ (Minneapolis); California Design College℠ (Los Angeles–Wilshire Blvd.); The Illinois Institute of Art®–Chicago; The Illinois Institute of Art®–Schaumburg; Miami International University of Art & Design℠, FL; The New England Institute of Art® (Boston, MA).

*The Art Institute of Indianapolis is licensed by the Indiana Commission on Proprietary Education, 302 West Washington Street, Room E201, Indianapolis, IN 46204, AC-0080.

**The Art Institute of Ohio–Cincinnati, 8845 Governors Hill Drive, Suite 100, Cincinnati, OH 45249-3317, Reg. #04-01-1698B.

THE ART INSTITUTE OF ATLANTA–DECATUR

DECATUR, GEORGIA

The Institute

The Art Institute of Atlanta–Decatur provides students with an educational environment and dedicated faculty members committed to preparing students for entry-level positions in the creative arts. Under the guidance of industry professionals, students learn by doing the types of tasks they are likely to encounter in the workplace. In addition, assistance is available to help students with resume writing, networking, and keeping aware of what employers are looking for in job candidates. The school offers six bachelor's degree programs and two associate degree programs.

The school offers assistance in helping students to secure housing.

The student population includes recent high school graduates, transfer students, and those who have left a previous employment situation to study and train for a new career. Students are creative, competitive, and open to new ideas. They place great value on an education that prepares them for an exciting entry-level position in the arts.

The Art Institute of Atlanta–Decatur places a high value on the quality of student life—both in and out of the classroom. Students participate in a wide variety of activities, including clubs and organizations, community service, and various committees designed to enhance the quality of student life.

The Art Institute of Atlanta–Decatur is accredited as a satellite of The Art Institute of Atlanta by the Commission on Colleges of the Southern Association of Colleges and Schools (SACS; 1866 Southern Lane, Decatur, Georgia 30033-4097; phone: 404-679-4500; http://www.sacs.org) to award Associate of Applied Arts, Bachelor of Arts, and Bachelor of Fine Arts degrees.

Location

The Art Institute of Atlanta–Decatur offers the advantages of The Art Institute of Atlanta main campus but in a small-town atmosphere in a convenient location on the eastern edge of the metro area.

Majors and Degrees

The Art Institute of Atlanta–Decatur offers bachelor's degree programs in advertising, fashion and retail management, graphic design, interior design, media arts and animation, and Web design and interactive media.

Associate degrees are offered in graphic design and Web design and interactive media.

Diploma programs are available in advertising design, digital design, residential interiors, and Web design.

Academic Programs

The Art Institute of Atlanta–Decatur operates on a year-round, four-quarter system.

Academic Facilities

The Art Institute of Atlanta–Decatur contains classrooms, Mac and PC computer labs, and a library for student use. There is also a bookstore.

Costs

Tuition cost varies by program. Prospective students should contact the school for current tuition costs. Other charges include a starting kit for all first quarter students. Kits vary in price depending on the program of study.

Financial Aid

Financial aid is available for those who qualify. Students who require financial assistance should first complete and submit a Free Application for Federal Student Aid (FAFSA) and meet with a financial aid officer. The officer determines the level of need based on a required federal formula, the cost of education, and other factors. Gift aid is available in the form of Federal Pell Grants, Federal Supplemental Educational Opportunity Grants, and veterans' benefits. Loans include Federal Stafford Loans, Federal PLUS Loans, and alternative loans. Other scholarships are available from the school and private sources. Application deadlines and eligibility requirements vary by program.

Faculty

Faculty members at The Art Institute of Atlanta–Decatur have professional knowledge that they bring into the classroom. The school's faculty members provide their students with a real-world, relevant educational experience.

Admission Requirements

Applicants must provide proof of high school graduation or achievement of a General Educational Development (GED) certificate as a prerequisite for admission. In lieu of documenting high school graduation or a GED certificate, applicants may provide proof of attaining an associate degree or higher from an accredited institution. An official transcript indicating date of high school graduation, GED certificate (including test scores), or date of college graduation (including degree granted) is required as proof.

All individuals seeking admission to The Art Institute of Atlanta–Decatur are interviewed in person or by phone by an assistant director of admissions, and each applicant must submit an original essay of at least 150 words stating how an education at The Art Institute of Atlanta–Decatur would help the student to achieve career goals. There is a $50 application fee.

Application and Information

To obtain an application, make arrangements for an interview, or tour the school, students should contact:

The Art Institute of Atlanta–Decatur
One West Court Square, Suite 110
Decatur, Georgia 30030
Phone: 866-856-6203 (toll-free)
Web site: http://www.artinstitutes.edu/decatur

The Art Institute of Atlanta®, GA; The Art Institute of Atlanta®–Decatur, GA; The Art Institute of Austin℠, TX; The Art Institute of California℠–Inland Empire; The Art Institute of California℠–Los Angeles; The Art Institute of California℠–Orange County; The Art Institute of California℠–Sacramento; The Art Institute of California℠–San Diego; The Art Institute of California℠–San Francisco; The Art Institute of California℠–Sunnyvale; The Art Institute of Charleston℠, SC, A branch of The Art Institute of Atlanta, GA; The Art Institute of Charlotte®, NC; The Art Institute of Colorado® (Denver); The Art Institute of Dallas®, TX; The Art Institute of Fort Lauderdale®, FL; The Art Institute of Houston®, TX; The Art Institute of Indianapolis℠, IN*; The Art Institute of Jacksonville℠, FL, A branch of Miami International University of Art & Design; The Art Institute of Las Vegas®, NV; The Art Institute of Michigan℠ (Detroit); The Art Institute of New York City®, NY; The Art Institute of Ohio℠–Cincinnati**; The Art Institute of Philadelphia®, PA; The Art Institute of Phoenix®, AZ; The Art Institute of Pittsburgh®, PA; The Art Institute of Pittsburgh®–Online Division; The Art Institute of Portland®, OR; The Art Institute of Salt Lake City℠, UT; The Art Institute of Seattle®, WA; The Art Institute of Tampa℠, FL, A branch of Miami International University of Art & Design; The Art Institute of Tennessee℠–Nashville, A branch of The Art Institute of Atlanta, GA; The Art Institute of Tucson℠, AZ; The Art Institute of Washington® (Arlington, VA), A branch of The Art Institute of Atlanta, GA; The Art Institute of York–Pennsylvania℠; The Art Institutes International Minnesota℠ (Minneapolis); California Design College℠ (Los Angeles–Wilshire Blvd.); The Illinois Institute of Art®–Chicago; The Illinois Institute of Art®–Schaumburg; Miami International University of Art & Design℠, FL; The New England Institute of Art® (Boston, MA).

*The Art Institute of Indianapolis is licensed by the Indiana Commission on Proprietary Education, 302 W. Washington St., Rm. E201, Indianapolis, IN 46204, AC-0080.

**The Art Institute of Ohio–Cincinnati, 8845 Governors Hill Drive, Suite 100, Cincinnati, OH 45249-3317, OH Reg. #04-01-1698B.

CLAYTON STATE UNIVERSITY
MORROW, GEORGIA

The University

Clayton State University (CSU) is an outstanding metropolitan institution located 15 miles southeast of downtown Atlanta. The school was established in 1969 in Morrow, Georgia. Today, Clayton State University offers associate, bachelor's, and master's degrees to approximately 6,000 students and further serves the needs of the community through certificate and continuing education programs. Clayton State combines the resources and opportunities of the University System and the cosmopolitan city of Atlanta with the advantages of a small university with close faculty-student relations. Clayton State students can cross-register in courses at nineteen public and private universities in the Atlanta region through the Atlanta Regional Consortium of Higher Education (ARCHE).

Situated just outside downtown Atlanta on a gorgeous lakeside campus, Clayton State's convenient location provides easy access to Metro Atlanta, enabling students to take advantage of internship and career opportunities. The Atlanta region is an international center for business, transportation, communications, information technology, science, health care, and numerous other industries, and it offers vast educational, entertaitment, and cultural opportunities as well as a low cost of living and a sunny, mild climate.

Clayton State is a 100-percent laptop university on a wireless campus with innovative smart classrooms. It was the third public university in the nation to require notebook computers of all students and faculty members. Every Clayton State student must own or have daily access to a notebook computer to use for academic assignments and communications.

Clayton State University is accredited by the Commission on Colleges of the Southern Association of Colleges and Schools (SACS) to award associate and bachelor's degrees. The Nursing program is accredited by the Commission on Collegiate Nursing Education (CCNE). The Dental Hygiene program is accredited by the Commission on Dental Accreditation of the American Dental Association. The Middle-Level Education program is accredited by the National Council for Accreditation of Teacher Education (NCATE). The music degree programs are accredited by the National Association of Schools of Music (NASM). The business degree is accredited by AACSB International–The Association to Advance Collegiate Schools of Business. The Paralegal program is in candidacy for accreditation by the American Bar Association (ABA). The Health-Care Management program is certified by the Association of University Programs in Health Administration (AUPHA).

Clayton State offers a variety of programs to meet students' needs, including career counseling and job placement services. The Center for Academic Assistance helps students strengthen their learning skills.

According to the 2007 *U.S. News & World Report* ranking of colleges, Clayton State has the most diverse student population among comprehensive baccalaureate-level colleges and universities in the southern United States. Students at CSU represent every region of the U.S. and some twenty-five countries.

Student activities at Clayton State include dances, concerts, films, festivals, lectures, recitals, drama presentations, and visual artists-in-residence. Students participate in more than fifty campus clubs and organizations. *Cygnet,* CSU's literary and art journal, publishes selected works of students' poetry, prose, and art. Clayton State is also opening a state-of-the-art Student Activities Center. The 62,000-square-foot building will house a two-court gymnasium, fitness areas (cardiovascular equipment and free weights), and an aerobics studio. In addition, the facility will have meeting rooms for student organizations and clubs, a ballroom, and a game room.

Competing in one of the nation's most competitive NCAA Division II conferences, the Peach Belt, Clayton State has won eleven league championships and has had fourteen teams advance to their respective national tournaments since 2000. CSU teams are consistently chosen among the country's best in the national rankings. Clayton State student-athletes excel individually; since 2002, 18 Laker athletes have received NCAA Division II All-America honors, and many student-athletes have been named Academic All-America. In one season, CSU had the NCAA women's soccer national scoring leader, the women's cross-country individual national runner-up, and the national women's tennis Rookie of the Year. CSU fields teams in twelve NCAA Division II intercollegiate sports.

Clayton State is building its first residence hall, scheduled to open for the fall 2008 semester. The residence hall will house approximately 430 new first-time, full-time freshmen. All new freshmen will be required to live on-campus their first year. This state-of-the-art building will feature four-bedroom, two-bath units with kitchenettes. In addition, residents will have on-site access to study lounges, wireless high-speed Internet, cable television, laundry facilities, and a game room.

Off-campus housing for upperclassmen is available at Clayton Place Apartments, conveniently located across from the main campus entrance. The complex features private bedrooms and baths, high-speed Internet access, washers and dryers, a pool, fitness room, and a clubhouse. Shops, supermarkets, and shopping centers are within walking distance of the campus.

Location

Nestled on a wooded 163-acre campus with five lakes in suburban Atlanta, Clayton State's setting is peaceful, safe, and conducive to learning. The University is near the crossroads of three major interstate highways and is 15 minutes from Hartsfield-Jackson Atlanta International Airport. The campus is accessible by public transportation, with easy access to Atlanta's museums and cultural and entertainment attractions. Atlanta has a large college-student population, with more than forty postsecondary institutions in the region. With a population of over 4.7 million, Atlanta offers *Fortune 500* internships, a wide range of affordable housing, and jobs after graduation.

Majors and Degrees

Clayton State offers associate and bachelor's degree programs and certificates. Four-year programs offered are the Bachelor of Arts (B.A.) in communication and media studies, English, history, integrative studies, middle-level education, and music; the Bachelor of Business Administration (B.B.A.) in accounting, business (general), management, or marketing; the Bachelor of Information Technology (B.I.T.); the Bachelor of Music (B.M.) in composition, music education, and performance; the Bachelor of Science (B.S.) in biology, criminal justice, government, health and fitness management, health-care management, integrative studies, mathematics, political science, psychology and human services, and sociology; the Bachelor of Science in Dental Hygiene (B.S.D.H.); the Bachelor of Science in Information Technology (B.S.I.T.); the Bachelor of Science in Nursing (B.S.N.) in basic licensure or for existing RNs; and the Bachelor of Applied Science (B.A.S.) degree in administrative management and technology management. The interdisciplinary bachelor's degree in the Communication and Media Studies program provides an integrated multimedia program for students who enjoy writing, drawing, photography, Web design, film, and writing for digital media. Clayton State is developing a Bachelor of Theatre degree program.

The Associate of Arts (A.A.) and the Associate of Science (A.S.) are available in the core curriculum (integrative studies). The A.S. Integrative Studies–Pre-Engineering program is designed for students who intend to transfer into engineering at Georgia Tech or other engineering programs. The Prepharmacy program prepares students to transfer into the pharmacy program at the University of Georgia and other universities.

Concentrations in the Associate of Applied Science (A.A.S.) degree are computer network technology, marketing and merchandising technology, medical office administration, office administration, and paralegal studies. The Associate of Applied Science in Information Technology (A.A.S.I.T.) is also offered.

Academic Programs

The academic year consists of two semesters, a special two-week summer session for study-abroad programs, two short summer terms, and one long summer term. Clayton State students benefit from a faculty-student ratio of 1:19 in challenging, small classes that offer close, personal attention from experienced faculty members who are committed to helping students succeed and reach their goals. CSU students engage in opportunities to expand their horizons through faculty research collaborations where they may present or publish their findings together. Many students design their own degree program; others complete internships in Atlanta and other regions. Clayton State students also gain global-learning experiences through study-abroad opportunities.

Each year, outstanding new freshmen enter the Clayton State Honors Program that enriches the already excellent education that Clayton State provides. Honors students receive recognition for their superior academic, leadership development, and campus and community achievements.

Off-Campus Programs

The University currently participates in study-abroad programs sponsored by the European, African, Asian, and Americas Councils of the University System of Georgia. These summer programs, which can be funded by financial aid or HOPE scholarships, offer students up to five weeks of residence in a college environment abroad while earning academic course credit. Clayton State also participates in a student-exchange program with the University of Northumbria in Newcastle, England, in which students can study for a semester or academic year abroad, with the credit earned counting toward their academic program at CSU. Other programs may be available in countries such as England, France, Italy, Spain, and Russia.

The University System of Georgia also participates in the Academic Common Market, which allows students from fourteen states in the Southeast to major in specialized areas not offered in their home state while paying the tuition rate for Georgia students.

Academic Facilities

Clayton State's striking new James Baker University Center provides an exciting center for learning that encompasses classrooms; meeting rooms; faculty, administrative, and student organization offices; the University's College of Information and Mathematical Sciences; dining services; the bookstore; campus computer help desk; and more than 2,000 data drops. Its high-vaulted ceilings, three-story atrium, and soaring window walls make it a bright and cheerful place for the campus community.

Connected to the elegant Baker University Center, the Clayton State library houses a substantial collection of books, microfilms, periodicals, and more than 16,000 pieces of audiovisual software, including slides, videotapes, audiotapes, CDs, and filmstrips. Through the OCLC/SOLINET network, the library has access to the book and periodical holdings of nearly 14,000 academic, public, and special libraries. Clayton State participates in GALILEO, the statewide library initiative, which provides access to numerous periodical and information databases and more than 2,000 full-text periodicals. In addition, the library subscribes to several other electronic and CD-ROM databases. The library seats 450 at tables and study carrels, and specially adapted carrels have been designed for audiovisual playback. Sixty carrels are equipped with Internet connections.

The campus offers the world-famous, acoustically-perfect concert hall, Spivey Hall, the most frequently recorded concert venue on National Public Radio's *Performance Today*. Spivey Hall has developed one of the nation's premier classical, jazz, and world-music series, and its performing artists often teach master classes, giving CSU musicians a rare opportunity for critiques from established music professionals.

Adjacent to Spivey Hall, the Music Education Building houses two large choral and instrumental rehearsal rooms, several ensemble rooms, and eighteen practice rooms. Students have access to state-of-the-art technology in the recording studio and in the electronic music, keyboard, and vocal pedagogy labs.

Clayton Theatre offers several theater productions each year. Recent performances include *Supernatural Shakespeare* and Synge's *Riders to the Sea*.

Clayton State's history program offers specialized course work in archival studies at the Georgia Archives and the National Archives for the Southeast, which border the campus. Both provide exceptional primary-source research materials for CSU's history and political science students. Clayton State is the only university in the U.S. with national and state archives adjacent to its campus.

Costs

For the 2007–08 academic year, tuition and fees were $3582 for in-state residents and $12,186 for out-of-state residents. Room and board were $7550. More information about tuition and fees can be found at http://adminservices.clayton.edu/registrar/fees.htm.

Financial Aid

Clayton State offers assistance to students who need financial support to continue their education. Students can participate in federally funded and state-supported grant and loan programs, including HOPE, the lottery-funded scholarship program for Georgia residents. The University also offers academic and talent scholarships. For more information, students should contact the Financial Aid Office at 678-466-4185 or financialaid@clayton.edu.

Faculty

Clayton State has 210 faculty members; 75 percent hold the highest degrees in their field.

Student Government

The Student Government Association (SGA) works as an advisory body to the University administration and Student and Enrollment Services Committee. SGA maintains the general welfare of the student body by providing students with necessary information that may be of concern and by providing a means for student input and opinion in the organization and operation of student affairs. SGA selects students to serve on campus advisory committees.

Admission Requirements

Clayton State encourages all students to apply and complete their application for fall admission by the February 15 priority deadline to maximize their opportunities for scholarships and financial aid. Applicants for fall entry who have been admitted by February 15 and who also filed their FAFSA application for financial aid by that date are considered in the first review for scholarships and financial aid.

Clayton State seeks to attract academically talented students who are likely to succeed. Admission to CSU is a selective process. Admissions decisions are based on a total view of the student's potential for academic success at the University. Successful freshman applicants can show their potential to succeed in college through their excellent academic achievement in college-preparatory courses in high school and their promising SAT or ACT test scores.

For freshman admission to Clayton State, applicants must graduate from an accredited high school, having completed their college-prep curriculum. Georgia high school graduates must receive the college-prep diploma. For transfer admissions, students must have already completed a minimum of 30 transferable semester credits with a minimum 2.0 GPA.

Application and Information

Applicants must submit the completed application for admission, immunization form, application fee, official transcripts, and test scores. Students who apply online by the priority deadline pay a $15 application fee; students who apply after that date (or those who submit a paper application anytime) pay a $40 application fee. High school and/or college transcripts must be official copies in sealed envelopes provided by the high school and/or college. Test scores (SAT and SAT Subject Tests, ACT, and AP) must be submitted directly from the testing service or on the official high school transcript. In cases requiring the SAT Subject Tests, the University provides information about which tests are needed and what scores are acceptable. The TOEFL is required for international students who are not native speakers of English and who have not completed their education in an English-speaking country. The priority deadlines are February 15 for fall semester; September 1 for spring, and February 1 for summer, respectively. The final deadlines are July 1, December 1, and April 1 for the fall, spring, and summer semesters, respectively.

Office of Admissions
Clayton State University
2000 Clayton State Boulevard
Morrow, Georgia 30260
Phone: 678-466-4115
866-339-2800 (toll-free)
Fax: 678-466-4149
E-mail: csu-info@clayton.edu
Web site: http://www.clayton.edu

EMORY UNIVERSITY
Emory College
ATLANTA, GEORGIA

The University

Founded by the Methodist Church in 1836 as a college in Oxford, Georgia, Emory University received its university charter in 1915 and in the same year moved to its present location in northeast Atlanta. The original campus is now Oxford College of Emory University, a two-year liberal arts division. The main campus occupies 634 acres. The original structures are of Italian Renaissance design and have red-tiled roofs and marble facades. In recent years, Emory has engaged in an extensive building and renovation campaign.

The University continues its commitment to providing students with state-of-the-art facilities, including the completion of a $14.8-million expansion/renovation of the Cox Dining Hall and a $20-million Sorority Housing Complex that opened in 2006 on Fraternity Row. In addition, ground has been broken on a new freshmen residence hall that is scheduled to open in August 2007. This facility will eventually be part of a ten-building freshman residential complex with a focus on new housing initiatives and learning communities.

Emory offers a stimulating intellectual environment in one of America's most exciting cities. The undergraduate college provides the advantages of a small college and the resources of a major university. Selective and innovative, with an emphasis on excellent teaching, Emory offers a rewarding environment for the student with serious intellectual and professional interests. Of the more than 12,000 men and women enrolled at Emory University, approximately 5,500 are undergraduates. Geographic distribution of students is diverse; approximately 60 percent are residents of states outside the Southeast. Sixty-five percent of the students go on to graduate or professional school, and academic competition is rigorous. At the same time, the campus is a friendly one where students and faculty members may interact in a casual and collaborative atmosphere. Nearly 70 percent of the students live on campus in residence halls, fraternity houses, or sorority housing. Extracurricular activities are plentiful and include lectures, concerts, movies, musical groups, theater, journalism, debate, volunteer groups, intramural sports, club sport teams, and intercollegiate athletics. There are more than 220 student organizations that encourage widespread involvement.

Emory athletes compete in ten varsity sports for men and women in the Division III University Athletic Association. This year, Emory finished ninth in the Sears Director's Cup standings. Emory has held a top 10 place in these standing since 2000 and is one of only six schools in the nation to place in the top 20 in both the Sears Directors' Cup standings and the *U.S. News & World Report* ranking of best national universities. Varsity sports include baseball (men's), basketball (men's and women's), cross-country (men's and women's), golf (men's), soccer (men's and women's), softball (women's), swimming and diving (men's and women's), tennis (men's and women's), track and field (men's and women's), and volleyball (women's). Seventy percent of the students participate in intramural, club, and recreational sports.

Emory ResNet provides Ethernet connections in each residence hall room, giving students access to the Internet via the campus computer network. Emory has wireless Internet capabilities in common areas (such as the quadrangle, library, and Cox Hall) and all residence hall rooms. Cable television and local phone service are also available in each student's room. All first- and second-year students are required to live on campus. Housing is guaranteed for four years. Approximately 70 percent of undergraduates live on campus.

Other than Emory and Oxford colleges, major University divisions include the Graduate School of Arts and Sciences; the Schools of Business, Law, Medicine, Nursing, Public Health, and Theology; and the Division of Allied Health Professions.

Location

Emory University's wooded campus is located in the rolling hills of Atlanta in an attractive residential neighborhood called Druid Hills. Adjacent to the campus is Emory Village, a small neighborhood complex of shops and restaurants. Downtown Atlanta, easily accessible by rapid transit from Emory, provides an exciting, eclectic atmosphere in which students can enjoy many recreational and cultural activities. In addition, Atlanta is just a few hours from the mountains of North Georgia and the Carolinas and from the beaches of Georgia and Florida.

Majors and Degrees

Emory College, the undergraduate arts and sciences school of Emory University, offers the B.A. degree in forty-eight areas of study, the B.S. degree in eleven, and the B.B.A. degree in seven.

B.A. programs are offered in African American studies, African studies, American studies, anthropology, art history, Asian and Asian American studies, biology, chemistry, Chinese language and literature, classical civilization, classical studies, classics, comparative literature, computer science, creative writing, dance and movement studies, economics, educational studies, English, environmental studies, film studies, French studies, German studies, Greek, history, interdisciplinary studies in culture and society, international studies, Italian studies, Japanese studies, journalism, Judaic studies, Latin, Latin American and Caribbean studies, mathematics, medieval and Renaissance studies, Middle Eastern studies, music, philosophy, physics, political science, psychology, religion, Russian studies, Russian language and culture, sociology, Spanish, theater studies, and women's studies.

The B.S. degree is offered in anthropology and human biology, applied physics, biology, chemistry, computer science, environmental studies, mathematics, neuroscience and behavioral biology, nursing, physics, and physics and astronomy.

The B.B.A. degree is offered in accounting, communications, decision and information science, finance, international business, marketing, and organization and management.

Joint concentrations are available in anthropology and religion, art history and history, art history and visual arts, classical civilizations and religion, classics and English, classics and history, classics and philosophy, economics and history, economics and mathematics, English and history, history and religion, Judaic studies and religion, linguistics and psychology, linguistics and Russian language, mathematics and computer science, philosophy and religion, and religion and sociology.

Four-year combined bachelor's/master's degree programs are offered in chemistry, computer science, English, history, mathematics, mathematics/computer science, philosophy, political science, and sociology.

Emory offers minors in applied mathematics, Arabic, architectural studies, astronomy, Chinese studies, community building and social change, ethics studies, Hebrew, Hindi, Irish studies, Japanese studies, linguistics, Mediterranean archaeology, Persian, Portuguese, and visual arts. Minors are also available in almost all of the departments that offer a B.A. or B.S.

Emory offers undergraduate degrees in business and nursing through its Goizueta School of Business and Nell Hodgson Woodruff School of Nursing.

Combined-degree programs in engineering are offered in cooperation with the Georgia Institute of Technology.

Academic Programs

The Bachelor of Arts and Bachelor of Science degree programs combine general education in six broadly defined areas with advanced study in a subject of special interest to the individual student. The six areas of general education are seminars and writing, including instruction in English composition and seminars representing a wide range of fields and topics designed to engage students in various aspects of inquiry and research; natural and mathematical science (three courses); social sciences (two courses); humanities (two courses); historical, cultural, and international perspectives, including courses covering Western and non-Western cultures, history, and a year of foreign language study; and health and physical education (4 semester hours). To fulfill these area requirements, a student may choose from a wide variety of courses. In addition to the area requirements, a student must complete a concentration in at least one major field. To graduate, a student must complete satisfactorily a total of 132 semester hours.

The academic calendar is divided into two semesters from September to May, and there is a limited third semester during the summer. Several special programs are available, including honors programs, independent study, internships, combined-degree programs, and the opportunity to take courses in the graduate divisions of the University.

Off-Campus Programs

Emory participates in cross-registration with twenty colleges and universities in the Atlanta area. A semester in Washington, D.C., is available for economics and political science students. Internship programs are available for most majors, and nearly 90 percent of students complete at least one internship while at Emory. Study abroad is highly encouraged, with nearly half of last year's graduating class having had some international exposure during their time at Emory. There are currently 102 study-abroad programs in more than forty-seven countries available to Emory students.

Academic Facilities

Emory's five libraries hold more than 3.1 million volumes plus access to thousands of electronic information resources. Woodruff Library, the central library, which supports the social sciences and humanities, provides an integrated service environment, joining technology and media specialists with librarians. The facility includes an information commons, electronic classrooms, group-study rooms, and data-wired seating and is open 24 hours a day, Sunday through Friday. Emory's $40-million Math and Science Center is the new home for the departments of physics, mathematics and computer science, and environmental studies. From the pristine physics laboratories in the basement to a rooftop environmental classroom and observatory, the building gives faculty members and students unprecedented opportunities for learning, teaching, and research. Among the Whitehead Biomedical Research Building's eight floors of office and state-of-the-art laboratory space are the departments of cell biology, human genetics, and physiology; the Neurodegenerative Disease Center and the Center for Medical Genomics; and major research efforts in pulmonary and critical-care medicine, pathology and laboratory medicine, and digestive diseases. The 90,000-square-foot Donna and Marvin Schwartz Center for Performing Arts provides a central space for Emory's music, theater, and dance programs. The facility includes a world-class concert hall, a theater lab for the development of new works, and a dance studio. Equipped with an orchestra pit and choral balcony, the 825-seat Cherry Logan Emerson Concert Hall is the home stage for Emory ensembles, while the 135-seat theater lab is the home for the Emory Playwriting Center. The dance studio houses Emory's progressive and highly respected dance program.

Costs

For the 2007–08 academic year, tuition is about $33,900, and room and board are approximately $11,000.

Financial Aid

Emory makes every effort to help students who need financial aid. Grants, loans, employment, and deferred payment plans are available. The amount of each grant is determined by financial need, and financial aid decisions are made independently of admission decisions. Merit scholarships are also available through the Emory Scholars Program; interested students must be nominated by their high school. Merit scholarships range from two-thirds tuition to tuition, room, and board. Nomination forms are mailed to high schools in late September, and the application deadline (application, nomination forms, additional requirements) for the Emory Scholars Program is November 1. In addition, Emory offers non-need institutional loans. The state of Georgia provides Tuition Equalization Grants to legal residents of Georgia who enroll at Emory; approximately 50 percent of the students in the College receive aid. More than 2,000 students have part-time employment at the University, including federally funded work-study. To be considered for financial aid, high school seniors should submit the CSS Profile and the Free Application for Federal Student Aid (FAFSA) by February 15.

Faculty

Emory College has more than 900 faculty members and a student-faculty ratio of 7:1. Senior faculty members teach courses at all levels, including first-year courses. Every student is assigned a faculty adviser for assistance in course selection and academic counseling. Faculty members are encouraged to work closely with students, as well as conduct research.

Student Government

Students are involved at various levels of government in the University. Governing organizations with student representation include the Student Government Association (for the entire University), the College Council (primarily undergraduate), and the University Senate (predominantly faculty). Students also serve on all standing committees of the Emory College faculty. Students have a strong voice in residence life governments, social activities, and publications.

Admission Requirements

Admission to Emory is highly selective. The Admission Committee evaluates applicants on the basis of secondary school records, SAT or ACT scores with the writing section, and recommendations from teachers and counselors. The College requires 4 years of high school English, 2 years of algebra and 1 of geometry, and at least 2 years of a foreign language. It strongly recommends that the remaining units include 2 or more years of history or social science, 3 years of laboratory science, and an additional year of mathematics. Students who wish to enter college before high school graduation are considered as early admission candidates. The middle 50 percent of freshmen entering in 2007 scored in the 640–730 range on the verbal portion of the SAT and in the 660–740 range in the math section and completed high school programs with an unweighted B+ average. The middle 50 percent for ACT scores ranged from 29 to 33. Emory seeks students who have not only academic ability but also talent and diversity. The Admission Office encourages visits to the campus and arranges tours and focus sessions with staff members.

Application and Information

Applicants may apply as either early decision or regular decision candidates. Emory offers two rounds of early decision, both of which are binding. The early decision I postmarked deadline is November 1, and decisions are mailed by December 15. The early decision II postmarked deadline is January 1, and decisions are mailed by February 1. Regular decision applicants are encouraged to apply in the fall of the senior year of secondary school, but no later than the postmarked deadline of January 15. Applicants for regular decision are notified by April 1. Materials required for application include the completed application form, a $50 application fee, an official secondary school transcript, a letter of recommendation, and standardized test scores (SAT or ACT with the writing section). SAT Subject Tests are recommended but not required. Test scores should be sent by the applicant's school or the testing center. Emory videos are available on a complimentary loan. Students may call 800-255-0384 (toll-free) or go to the Web site (http://www.videc.com) to order the video/DVD.

Jean Jordan
Interim Dean of Admission
Boisfeuillet Jones Center
Emory University
Atlanta, Georgia 30322
Phone: 404-727-6036
800-727-6036 (toll-free)
E-mail: admiss@learnlink.emory.edu
Web site: http://www.emory.edu

Emory's Italian Renaissance campus is just 5 minutes north of downtown Atlanta.

LAGRANGE COLLEGE
LAGRANGE, GEORGIA

The College

Founded in 1831, LaGrange College is the oldest private college in Georgia. A four-year liberal arts and sciences institution affiliated with the United Methodist Church, LaGrange holds fast to its longstanding mission of challenging students' minds, inspiring their souls—and changing their lives. The College is ranked in the top five and as a "best value" among ninety-three Southern baccalaureate schools by *U.S. News & World Report* and has an enrollment of about 1,100 men and women. LaGrange College students come from twenty-one states and twelve countries, and they enjoy a student-faculty ratio of 12:1. Fully accredited, LaGrange provides a challenging and supportive academic environment. The Bachelor of Arts (B.A.), Bachelor of Science (B.S.), Bachelor of Science in Nursing (B.S.N.), and Bachelor of Music (B.M.) degrees are offered in addition to the Master of Education (M.Ed.) degree and the Master of Arts in Teaching (M.A.T.) degree

LaGrange College students can start their own special-interest group or join one of more than forty clubs and organizations, including student government, honor societies, service clubs, sororities and fraternities, performance groups, religious organizations, and student publications. Students also can get involved in service efforts, such as building homes through Habitat for Humanity, or traveling to Costa Rica or the Czech Republic on a mission trip. On-campus activities include intramural sports tournaments, theater performances, karaoke and open mike competitions, art exhibitions, "Vegas on the Hill," and Greek Week. Off-campus excursions are planned each semester, such as snow-skiing trips to North Carolina or visits to Atlanta Braves games.

LaGrange College's athletic facilities include an indoor competition swimming pool, an outdoor recreational swimming pool, a fully equipped fitness center, a $2-million baseball facility, two gymnasiums, two lighted softball fields, a lighted soccer field, and a training facility. Intercollegiate athletic teams for men include baseball, basketball, cross-country, football, golf, soccer, swimming, and tennis. Women's teams include basketball, cross-country, fast-pitch softball, soccer, swimming, tennis, and volleyball.

More than 60 percent of students live on campus in residence halls that include apartment-style facilities. Meal plan options are offered for the College's dining hall and student grill.

Location

The College is located in a residential section of LaGrange, Georgia, which has a population of 30,000 and was named Intelligent City of the Year by the World Teleport Association for its telecommunication infrastructure and Internet initiatives. LaGrange is home to Fortune 500 companies, unique shops and restaurants, and historic landmarks. Nearby are the world-famous Callaway Gardens, the Warm Springs Foundation, and Franklin D. Roosevelt's Little White House. The West Point Dam on the Chattahoochee River provides one of the largest lakes in the region; waterfronts and a marina are within the city limits of LaGrange. The city is located 65 miles southwest of Atlanta and 55 miles southwest of Hartsfield–Jackson Atlanta International Airport.

Majors and Degrees

LaGrange College offers the Bachelor of Arts (B.A.) degree in art and design, art history/museum studies, biochemistry, biology, business, chemistry, computer science, early childhood education, English, history, human development, interdisciplinary studies, mathematics, music, political science, psychology, religion, sociology, Spanish, and theater arts, with minors available in church leadership, French, Japanese studies, Latin American studies, oikos, philosophy, physical education/coaching, physics, and women's studies. Students interested in middle-grades and secondary education careers first pursue a bachelor's degree in their preferred subject area and then enroll in the College's one-year Master of Arts in Teaching program.

The Bachelor of Science (B.S.) degree is available in accountancy, business management, chemistry, computer science, and mathematics.

The Bachelor of Music degree is available, with concentrations in creative music technologies, performance, and church music.

The Bachelor of Science in Nursing (B.S.N.) degree also is offered.

Preprofessional programs of study, as preparation for graduate and professional study, are available in dentistry, engineering, law, medicine and allied fields, optometry, pharmacy, physical therapy, theology/seminary, and veterinary medicine.

Academic Programs

Each program of study contains a substantial interdisciplinary core component. Providing a background in the natural and social sciences, arts, and humanities, the core helps students see how subjects interrelate, while developing the research and problem-solving skills employers and graduate schools seek most. A minimum of 120 semester hours is required to earn a bachelor's degree; 46 semester hours of liberal studies core courses are required for all bachelor's degrees. Most majors require an additional 36 to 56 semester hours of credit beyond the liberal studies curriculum. Students may be eligible for credit and/or exemption in certain areas through Advanced Placement (AP) tests or the College-Level Examination Program (CLEP).

The College operates on the 4-1-4 academic calendar, a schedule which allows for a one-month January interim term between fall and spring semesters. During January term, students focus on unique subject areas or participate in classes incorporating domestic and international travel.

Academic Facilities

The LaGrange College Library contains more than 135,000 volumes of books and other media. Print sources for 500 journal titles are provided through current subscriptions. GALILEO provides access to more than 75 databases, including several in full text (e.g., LexisNexis). JSTOR supplies access to more than 100 scholarly journals in electronic format. In addition, the library subscribes to subject-specific databases for education, religion, and music.

The campuswide fiber-optic network provides computer access in every dorm room, in all eleven computer labs on campus, and in designated classrooms where network connections are available by every seat. Students are able to access the College library's online catalog, the Internet and World Wide Web, e-mail, and other resources from any of these locations. Students majoring in biochemistry conduct research in the College's DNA fingerprinting lab, which was established with a National Science Foundation grant.

The Lamar Dodd Art Center is a premier facility for the study of art and design and includes a gallery for the College's permanent collection, which includes works by Picasso, Andy Warhol,

Ansel Adams, and other famous artists. Price Theater provides a state-of-the-art proscenium theater with seating for 280, thirty-six fly lines, electronic sound and lighting systems, computer-design capabilities, a full costume and scenery shop, and an actors' lounge. The College's music facilities, which are home to the creative music technologies program, include a fully-equipped MIDI recording studio, MIDI workstations, isolation rooms, and an electroacoustic multimedia recital hall, while the entertainment/music library is home to many original Hollywood music scores.

The College's Callaway Auditorium received a $5.5-million renovation in 2005 that upgraded the venue into a state-of-the-art concert hall with 700 new armchair seats, new curved walls and ceilings, and a 20-foot stage extension.

Costs

Tuition and fees for 2007–08 were $18,500, and room and board were $7598 for the year, bringing the total cost to $26,098. Books and supplies averaged $1000 for the year.

Financial Aid

As a private college, LaGrange is committed to helping meet the difference between the funds any student has available and the cost of attending LaGrange College. Approximately 90 percent of LaGrange students receive some combination of financial awards. These awards may include grants, loans, scholarships, and employment opportunities. Federal financial aid and institutional funds are available to all students who qualify. The state of Georgia provides additional funding for Georgia residents. All Georgia residents who enroll as full-time students receive the Georgia Tuition Equalization Grant in the amount of $1000 per year. The HOPE Scholarship, which totals $3000 per year, is awarded to all Georgia residents who have graduated from high school with a B average and who enter as freshmen. Georgia residents who do not qualify for the HOPE Scholarship as freshmen may be able to obtain the HOPE Scholarship by earning a 3.0 cumulative grade point average. Academic scholarships that range from $1000 to full scholarships are also awarded. All accepted students are considered for scholarships; a separate application is not required.

Faculty

All courses at LaGrange College are taught by professors. Full-time faculty members number 69, 84 percent of whom hold the highest degrees in their fields; 58 are part-time. Faculty members are rewarded for teaching and are not required to conduct research, although many are involved in research efforts. All faculty members teach undergraduates and serve as academic advisers. The student-faculty ratio is 12:1.

Student Government

The LaGrange College Student Government Association (SGA) exists to serve as a medium for student expression, to coordinate campus activities, and to govern within the parameters granted by the president. Student publications are supported by the SGA, including the newspaper and literary magazine. The SGA oversees more than forty clubs and organizations in all, including three national fraternities and three national sororities, as well as service clubs, religious organizations, honorary organizations, and departmental/special-interest groups.

Admission Requirements

LaGrange College seeks to admit any qualified student who desires to study on the LaGrange campus. Preference is given to applicants who have had strong preparation in high school. A typical matriculant should have completed a minimum of 14 units of college-preparatory courses at an approved high school, including 4 units of English, 4 units of college-preparatory mathematics, 3 units of social science, and 3 units of laboratory science.

Freshman applicants should submit a completed application for admission, a $30 nonrefundable application fee, official high school transcripts, and official SAT or ACT scores. Transfer students should submit an application, the application fee, and official transcripts of all college work attempted. Transfer students who have earned fewer than 30 semester hours of credit must also submit official high school transcripts. International and transfer students are encouraged to apply.

Application and Information

Applications for admission are evaluated on a rolling basis and should be submitted at least one month prior to the beginning of the semester in which entrance is desired. Applicants can expect to receive notification within two to three weeks of the date that all documents are submitted. Weekday campus visits are encouraged, and appointments can be arranged by contacting the Admission Office. For additional information, students should contact:

Office of Admission
LaGrange College
601 Broad Street
LaGrange, Georgia 30240
Phone: 706-880-8005
800-593-2885 (toll-free)
Fax: 706-880-8010
E-mail: admission@lagrange.edu
Web site: http://www.lagrange.edu

The William and Evelyn Banks Library overlooks the College's main entrance.

OGLETHORPE UNIVERSITY

ATLANTA, GEORGIA

The University

Standing as a landmark in north Atlanta, Oglethorpe University is located on 105 acres of unquestionable beauty. Only 10 miles from the heart of downtown Atlanta, the campus, with its classic collegiate Gothic architecture, maintains an Old World charm. The current undergraduate enrollment is approximately 900, with nearly 60 percent women and 40 percent men. More than 60 percent of the full-time students live on campus in the seven residence halls. The ethnic and religious backgrounds of the student body are diverse; students come to Oglethorpe from almost forty states and over thirty countries. Oglethorpe students learn to make a life, make a living, and make a difference. Its graduates become community leaders who are distinctive in their ability to think, communicate, and contribute.

Oglethorpe fulfills its promise to make a difference through the Center for Civic Engagement, launched in 2006. The center coordinates volunteer projects for students throughout Atlanta, works with faculty members to develop service-learning components for courses, works with students for civic-oriented internships, and plans cultural excursions.

Numerous activities are offered on campus, such as concerts, exhibitions, and social affairs. The University has a student center, six tennis courts, a Reslite track, an intramural field, a recreational sports facility, and a basketball arena with seating for 2,000. There is an extensive intramural program. Intercollegiate sports are offered for men in baseball, basketball, cross-country, golf, soccer, tennis, and track and field and for women in basketball, cross-country, golf, soccer, tennis, track and field, and volleyball.

There are many avenues for development of leadership potential, including the Rich Foundation Urban Leadership Certificate Program. Omicron Delta Kappa, a national leadership organization, recognizes outstanding leadership on campus. Alpha Phi Omega, a national coeducational service fraternity, is one of Oglethorpe's largest organizations; its purpose is to serve the school, the community, and the nation. Alpha Phi Omega emphasizes service, friendship, and leadership as qualifications for membership. Students also have excellent opportunities to develop their extracurricular interests. More than sixty clubs and organizations are open to students, including fraternities and sororities, honor societies, academic societies, and special-interest groups. One of the distinctive features of Oglethorpe is the interest and support the University gives to such activities. This is in keeping with the goals of the institution, which are to build a community of leaders and to stimulate personal and intellectual growth and development.

In addition to its undergraduate programs, Oglethorpe offers a Master of Arts in Teaching degree.

Location

Students enjoy the many benefits of being on a small urban campus near a large metropolitan cultural center. Metropolitan Atlanta's population is more than 4 million, and the community offers all the entertainment advantages of a large city, including professional athletics, world-renowned museums, concerts by well-known artists, theaters, and restaurants. Cultural centers and recreational facilities are easily accessible, and good transportation is available. Home to one of the busiest airports in the world, Hartsfield-Jackson Atlanta International Airport, the city is a major international transportation hub. Transportation within the city is connected by four major interstates and the Metropolitan Atlanta Rapid Transit Authority (MARTA), which provides bus and rapid rail service to and from Oglethorpe.

Majors and Degrees

Oglethorpe University confers the Bachelor of Arts (B.A.) and Bachelor of Science (B.S.) degrees. Majors leading to the B.A. are offered in American studies, art history, behavioral science and human resource management, communication and rhetoric studies, economics, English, French, history, individually planned major, international studies with or without an Asia concentration, philosophy, politics, psychology, sociology, sociology–social work, Spanish, studio art, and theater. Majors leading to the B.S. are accounting, biology, biopsychology, business administration, chemistry, economics, mathematics, and physics. Preprofessional programs are offered in dentistry, law, medicine, optometry, and pharmacy. Dual-degree programs are offered in engineering in cooperation with Georgia Institute of Technology, Auburn University, the University of Southern California, and the University of Florida and in environmental studies with Duke University's Nicholas School of the Environment. There are also more than twenty minors that students may add to their majors.

Academic Programs

Each new student is assigned a faculty adviser, who is responsible for assisting the student with academic and other matters. Close relationships between students and teachers are the heart of Oglethorpe's educational approach. Fresh Focus, a seminar for freshmen, provides a way for new students to get to know each other and to explore academic programs, career interests, and academic resources.

The program for undergraduates is viewed as a process of personal and intellectual development. The liberal arts and sciences provide the forum for increasing competence in reading, writing, speaking, reasoning, and the fundamental fields of knowledge, the arts and sciences. The unique Core Curriculum constitutes about 25 percent of each student's requirements. The core encourages students to reflect upon and discuss matters that are fundamental to understanding who they are and what they ought to be, forging a community of learners. This includes how they understand themselves as individuals and as members of society, how the study of the past informs a sense of who they are as human beings, and the ways in which the practice of science informs them on the physical and biological processes influencing human nature. Readings are based on primary sources rather than textbooks. The product of the core is a well-rounded student who is able to make a life, make a living, and make a difference.

Off-Campus Programs

Oglethorpe offers a variety of off-campus opportunities for students. The Center for Civic Engagement coordinates service projects and cultural outings on a regular basis. The Career Services office offers excellent internship programs with various scientific, government, and business organizations; recent sites include CNN, the Centers for Disease Control and Prevention, major accounting firms, corporations, and government offices, including placements at the Georgia Capitol.

The University also offers students extensive study-abroad opportunities through Oglethorpe University Students Abroad (OUSA). OUSA offers international exchange partnerships in China, France, Germany, Japan, Latin America, the Netherlands, and Russia. OUSA also coordinates short-term, for-credit trips abroad during winter, spring, and summer breaks.

Academic Facilities

The Philip Weltner Library was dedicated in 1992. The 56,000-square-foot facility houses an art museum, a 24-hour study area, and a viewing room with state-of-the-art equipment. Current library holdings include more than 150,000 books, an extensive collection of movies on DVD, the *New York Times* on microfilm, and more than 800 periodicals. Oglethorpe participates in a library sharing program with eighteen other colleges and universities in the Atlanta area. Several computer laboratories are available for student use. Students have online access to any college library in Georgia through GALILEO.

Costs

The comprehensive fee for 2008–09 is $37,659. This fee includes $25,380 for tuition and fees, $9500 for room and board, and a student activity fee of $100. An additional $2679 should be sufficient for books, supplies, and personal expenses.

Financial Aid

The University offers aid from various federal programs, including the Federal Perkins Loan, Federal PLUS loan, Federal Pell Grant, Federal Supplemental Educational Opportunity Grant, and Federal Work-Study programs. Applications for these funds should be received by March 1. The James Edward Oglethorpe Scholarship Competition for freshmen awards the winners full tuition, as does the Center for Civic Engagement Scholarship. Other scholarships range from $6500 to $14,500 per year. The University also offers academic scholarships for outstanding students. These scholarships are based on scholastic performance. Institutional need-based awards and campus employment are other possibilities. Approximately 95 percent of the University's students receive some type of assistance.

Faculty

Oglethorpe has an outstanding faculty. The *Princeton Review* recently ranked it fifteenth in the nation, and 96 percent of the members hold doctoral or other terminal degrees, many from the finest graduate schools in the country. The student-faculty ratio is 13:1, and no graduate assistants serve as undergraduate instructors. Although Oglethorpe is primarily a teaching institution, faculty members are engaged in various research projects and scholarly pursuits. Professors are available for student counseling and generally take an active role in campus activities.

Student Government

Undergraduate life at Oglethorpe University is, in a large sense, that of a democratic community; student government is mainly self-government. The Oglethorpe Student Association is the organization that guides and governs student life. The Executive Council is made up of a president, a vice president, a secretary, a treasurer, a parliamentarian, and the presidents of the four classes. They work in conjunction with a student senate. The Oglethorpe Honor Code contains the responsibilities that students and faculty members accept by becoming members of the community, which is committed to high standards of academic honesty.

Admission Requirements

Throughout its history, Oglethorpe has welcomed students from all sections of the country as well as from abroad. Admission to the University is selective. It is the policy of the Admission Committee to accept those students who present the strongest evidence of purpose, maturity, scholastic ability, and potential for success. In making these judgments, the committee considers the applicant's high school program and grades, high school rank if available, SAT and/or ACT scores, personal essay, and recommendations of counselors and/or teachers. Students entering Oglethorpe should have completed 4 units of English, 4 of mathematics, 3 of science, and 3 of social studies; 2 units of the same foreign language are recommended.

Candidates for regular decision admission may apply at any time. Applications are reviewed on a rolling basis, beginning immediately after early action reviews (late December) and continuing as long as space in class is available. Early action applicants must apply by December 5. Notification letters are mailed no later than December 20. Transfer applicants and students applying for joint enrollment are welcome.

Application and Information

For additional information, students may contact:

Office of Admission
Oglethorpe University
4484 Peachtree Road, NE
Atlanta, Georgia 30319
Phone: 404-364-8307
800-428-4484 (toll-free)
E-mail: admission@oglethorpe.edu
Web site: http://www.oglethorpe.edu

Oglethorpe's history, dating back to 1835, is reflected in its architecture.

PIEDMONT COLLEGE

DEMOREST, GEORGIA

The College

Founded in 1897, Piedmont is an independent, comprehensive, coeducational liberal arts college with campuses in Demorest and Athens, Georgia. The College enrolls more than 2,000 men and women representing approximately twenty states and ten countries. Piedmont is affiliated with the National Association of Congregational Christian Churches (NACCC) and the historically related United Church of Christ (UCC). Inspired by the liberal arts tradition and a historical association with the Congregational Christian churches, Piedmont College cultivates a diverse, challenging, and caring intellectual environment to encourage academic success and spiritual development. To fulfill its mission, the College offers a number of major fields of study, including specialized professional programs and selected graduate programs. Instructional opportunities are also provided at distant locations to meet the needs of students.

The regular academic year is divided into fall and spring semesters, each approximately sixteen weeks in length. The College offers both day and evening classes, with limited weekend offerings. During the fall and spring semesters, evening and weekend classes are offered in two 8-week sessions, as are all classes at the Athens campus. A schedule of classes is also available for those wishing to attend the College during the summer.

Campus life programs offer numerous opportunities for resident and commuter students to participate in a wide variety of activities that are both planned and spontaneous. The Campus Activity Board (CAB) is responsible for planning events for orientation, homecoming, special dinners, and a variety of other entertainment venues.

A series of lectures, concerts, and plays is presented to develop the student's appreciation of literature, music, and the other art forms. Programming has included performances of masterworks by Bach, Haydn, Mozart, and Mendelssohn; various theater productions; and lectures by artists and writers from across the United States.

Piedmont College is accredited by the Commission on Colleges of the Southern Association of Colleges and Schools to award bachelor's, master's, and education specialist degrees. All teacher education programs offered by Piedmont College, as they appear in its published catalog, have the approval of the Professional Standards Commission of the State of Georgia. The baccalaureate degree program in nursing is approved by the Georgia Board of Nursing and the National League of Nursing Accreditation Commission.

At the graduate level, the Demorest campus offers Master of Arts (M.A.) and Master of Arts in Teaching (M.A.T.) degrees in art education, early childhood education, music education, secondary education (dual degree in broadfield science, history, English, and mathematics), and middle grades education (M.A. only). The College also offers the Education Specialist (Ed.S.) degree in instruction. The Piedmont School of Business offers Master of Business Administration (M.B.A.) degrees in financial services and managerial leadership.

Athens graduate programs include the Master of Business Administration (M.B.A.), with tracks for financial services, health-care management, and managerial leadership. The School of Education offers Master of Arts (M.A.) and Master of Arts in Teaching (M.A.T.) in early childhood education, secondary education (broadfield science, English, history, and mathematics), and special education. The Athens campus also offers the Education Specialist (Ed.S.) degree in instruction.

Location

Piedmont has campuses in Demorest, Georgia, and Athens, Georgia. The Demorest campus is located in Habersham County in northeast Georgia in the foothills of the Appalachian Mountains. Demorest is about 70 miles north of Atlanta. The Athens campus is located at 595 Prince Avenue in Athens.

Piedmont's main campus in Demorest provides ample opportunity for outdoor activities that include hiking, white-water rafting, fishing, and rappelling. For students interested in city life, Piedmont College in Athens offers an abundance of museums, botanical gardens, concert venues, and sporting events as well as outstanding shopping and dining experiences.

Majors and Degrees

At the undergraduate level, Piedmont College offers course work leading to a Bachelor of Arts, Bachelor of Fine Arts, Bachelor of Science, or Bachelor of Science in Nursing degree.

At the Demorest campus, the Bachelor of Arts degree is offered in art, business administration (accounting, computer information systems, general business, human resource management, marketing, management, sports marketing), biology education, criminal justice, drama education, early childhood education, English, English education, history, history education, interdisciplinary studies: environmental studies, mass communications, middle grades education, music (church music, music performance), philosophy/religion, political science, psychology, secondary education (dual degree), social science (broadfield), sociology (criminal justice, legal studies), Spanish, and theater arts.

The Bachelor of Fine Arts degree is offered in two-dimensional and three-dimensional art.

The Bachelor of Science degree is offered in biology, chemistry, chemistry education, environmental geology, environmental science, interdisciplinary studies, mathematics, mathematics education, mathematics/computer information systems, and physics.

At the Athens campus, undergraduate programs include Bachelor of Art (B.A.) degrees in business administration (accounting, general business, technology management), criminal justice (emergency management), education (early childhood, middle grades), graphic design, political science (emergency management), psychology, and sociology.

Academic Programs

The normal study load is five courses or 15 semester hours per semester (fall, spring) for students attending day classes and four courses or 12 semester hours for those taking accelerated evening classes. Students taking a minimum of 12 semester hours are considered full time. Students who wish to take more than 19 semester hours must have a minimum cumulative grade point average of 3.0 and receive permission from the dean of the appropriate school. A student may take no more than 22 hours during any semester.

Summer classes are offered in an accelerated format. Thus, the selection of courses and the total number of credit hours taken must be chosen judiciously by the student with the help of his or her adviser. As during the regular academic year, full-time status is based on 12 semester hours of course work.

Off-Campus Programs

Consistent with its goal to attract top students, Piedmont actively promotes travel opportunities for academic credit within a variety of study areas. Recent programs have included study-abroad trips to Egypt, England, Ireland, Mexico, Russia, and the Czech Republic. Piedmont also offers a long-term study-abroad program whereby students may attend the University of Nottingham, England.

Academic Facilities

The Demorest campus is situated on 100 acres and includes eighteen academic buildings and five residence halls. The campus includes the Arrendale Library, which houses a collection of more than 100,000 volumes, a computer lab, study rooms and carrels, conference facilities, and the College archives. The library's electronic catalog is a state-of-the-art, Web-accessible library system. The library provides access to multiple electronic databases; participates in GALILEO, a statewide electronic research resource; and also provides access to its collections and services via its Web page (http://www.library.piedmont.edu). The College recently opened Stewart Hall, a mathematics, science, and technology center, and in 2007 opened the Swanson Center for performing arts and mass communications.

The Athens campus includes seven academic buildings The Athens Resource Center provides references resources, reserve services, access to electronic resources, and a specialized circulating collection.

Costs

For full-time students (12 to 19 credit hours) at the Demorest campus, tuition for the 2007–08 academic year was $16,500, or $8250 per semester. An additional $687 per credit hour was charged for each credit hour over 19. For students taking 11 credit hours or less, the tuition was $687 per credit hour. (For students taking only one course per semester the tuition was $475 per credit hour.) Room and board, offered only at the Demorest campus, was $3000 per semester, or $6000 per academic year.

For full-time students (12 to 19 credit hours) at the Athens Campus, tuition for the 2007–08 academic year is $10,000, or $5000 per semester. Students who are eligible to take more than 17 hours pay the part-time rate of $417 per additional credit hour.

Financial Aid

The Piedmont College Office of Financial Aid is committed to assisting students and parents to obtain sufficient resources to meet the educational expenses for attendance at this institution. Further, it is the policy of the College to meet 100 percent of demonstrated, unmet financial need, through grants, loans, work-study, and/or scholarship programs for those students who apply for aid by May 1 for the following fall semester. Students applying for the spring or summer semesters should contact the Office of Financial Aid for application deadlines. The four primary sources of student financial assistance—federal, state, institutional, and third-party sources—each require different application procedures. Students receiving financial aid must maintain satisfactory academic progress as outlined in the *Student Handbook* in order to continue to receive financial assistance.

Faculty

There are 95 full-time faculty members and 80 part-time faculty members at Piedmont. There is a low 14:1 student-faculty ratio, which provides students with the opportunity to work one-on-one with faculty members in research settings and in a variety of academic work.

Admission Requirements

A traditional student is defined as a student who has been out of high school for less than five years and has not taken any college courses with the exception of joint-enrollment courses. Traditional freshmen should submit the following items in order to be considered for admission: a completed application form for admission, the required essay, and either an official transcript of all high-school-diploma course work, a certificate from the General Educational Development (GED) test, or an official home-school transcript. Applicants should have completed 21 high school units. Suggested units include 4 English units, 2 algebra units, 1 plane geometry unit, 2 units of the same foreign language, 2 history units, 3 science units, and 1 social studies unit. Applicants must also submit an official score report of the results of the SAT or ACT and an official transcript of all joint-enrollment credits from each college or university attended, if applicable.

Students may be admitted at the beginning of any semester. However, for the best orientation to college life and to take advantage of the planned sequence of courses, fall admission is recommended.

The application deadline for full-time students is thirty days before the semester begins. To ensure a space, however, early application is strongly encouraged. Applicants are informed of their status within four weeks after the application file is completed. Accepted students should confirm their acceptance by submitting an advance deposit of $250. The deposit is refundable if a written request is received by the College sixty days prior to the start of the new semester. Although campus visits are not required for admission, it is recommended that applicants visit the campus to experience it firsthand. Applicants should plan to spend a number of hours attending classes, meeting faculty members and students, and taking a campus and area tour.

Application and Information

For additional information, students should contact:

Office of Admissions
Demorest Campus
Piedmont College
165 Central Avenue
P.O. Box 10
Demorest, Georgia 30535
Phone: 800-277-7020 (toll-free)
Fax: 706-776-6635
E-mail: ugrad@piedmont.edu
Web site: http://www.piedmont.edu

SAVANNAH COLLEGE OF ART AND DESIGN

SAVANNAH, GEORGIA

Savannah College *of* Art *and* Design®

The College

The Savannah College of Art and Design (SCAD) was founded in Savannah, Georgia, in 1978 with a curriculum designed to provide an excellent arts education and effective career preparation for students. Today, with two locations as well as online programs, the College continues to adhere to this mission, attracting students from all fifty states and from more than ninety countries.

The College exists to prepare talented students for professional careers, emphasizing learning through individual attention in a positively oriented university environment. The goal of the College is to nurture and cultivate the unique qualities of each student through an interesting curriculum in an inspiring environment under the leadership of involved professors.

SCAD is a private, nonprofit institution accredited by the Commission on Colleges of the Southern Association of Colleges and Schools (1866 Southern Lane, Decatur, Georgia 30033-4097; telephone: 404-679-4501) to award bachelor's and master's degrees. The College offers Bachelor of Arts, Bachelor of Fine Arts, Master of Architecture, Master of Arts, Master of Arts in Teaching, Master of Fine Arts, and Master of Urban Design degrees, as well as undergraduate and graduate certificates. The five-year professional M.Arch. degree is accredited by the National Architectural Accrediting Board.

Online degree programs are offered through SCAD-eLearning (http://www.scad.edu/elearning).

The Savannah College of Art and Design offers intercollegiate and intramural athletic programs to students in Savannah. The College competes in the Florida Sun Conference of the National Association of Intercollegiate Athletics. SCAD offers men's and women's basketball, cross-country, equestrian, golf, soccer, swimming, and tennis; women's softball and volleyball; and men's baseball and men's and women's lacrosse.

Location

SCAD has locations in Atlanta and Savannah, Georgia. The Savannah campus offers a full university experience in one of the largest National Historic Landmark districts in the United States. The College has been recognized by the National Trust for Historic Preservation, the American Institute of Architects, and the International Downtown Association, among others, for adaptive reuse of historic buildings. The state-of-the-art Atlanta facility is situated in a major metropolitan hub for business, arts, and transportation.

Majors and Degrees

Degrees are offered in advertising design, animation, architectural history, architecture (professional and postprofessional), art history, arts administration, broadcast design and motion graphics, cinema studies, design management, fashion, fibers, film and television, furniture design, graphic design, historic preservation, illustration (and illustration design), industrial design, interactive design and game development, interior design, metals and jewelry, painting, performing arts (and dramatic writing), photography (and commercial, digital, documentary), printmaking, production design, professional writing, sculpture, sequential art, sound design, teaching (art or design), urban design, and visual effects.

Minors are offered in most undergraduate degree programs as well as in accessory design, British-American studies, business management and entrepreneurship, ceramic arts, creative writing, cultural landscape, dance, decorative arts, drawing, electronic design, exhibition design, interaction design, marine design, museum studies, music performance, new media art, portrait arts, storyboarding, and technical direction.

Academic Programs

The College operates on the quarter system. Fall, winter, and spring sessions extend from mid-September through May. Summer sessions run from late June through August. Students may earn credits during all sessions.

A balanced curriculum offers a well-rounded liberal arts education, the traditional components of a fine arts education, the opportunity to acquire contemporary high-tech skills through the use of state-of-the-art facilities, and the option of pursuing double majors and multidisciplinary explorations. Total course of study for the B.F.A. degree consists of 180 quarter credit hours (36 courses). Of these, students take 30 to 50 hours in the foundation studies program, 55 to 65 hours in the liberal arts program (with a concentration on art history classes), 60 to 70 hours in the major area of study, and 10 to 15 hours in electives.

Off-Campus Programs

SCAD offers off-campus programs in Europe, Asia, and throughout the United States, emphasizing artistic, historical, and cultural experiences. Off-campus programs may combine independent study or internships with traditional course work. Some programs focus on specific academic and studio disciplines, while others feature a variety of study options.

Academic Facilities

Architecture, interior design, and historic preservation facilities include an intranet of PCs configured with electronic-design software, including AutoCAD, Bentley Microstation V8, Adobe Photoshop, 3D Studio VIZ, SURFCAM, and Autodesk Maya and Revit. A video microscope, as well as architectural conservation, metals conservation, and paint-analysis labs also are available in the School of Building Arts.

Animation, broadcast design, interactive design and game development, and visual effects facilities offer ready access to high-end industry-standard equipment and software, including an intranet of Macintosh G4, Pentium IV, and SGI workstations configured with a diverse range of graphics software; high-end 2-D, 3-D, interactive, and compositing tools, including the Adobe product line; Flipbook, Autodesk Maya, Anime Studio, Side Effects' Houdini products; Pixar's Renderman; Discreet's 3ds max; the Unreal game engine; and ZBrush and Shake. Other tools include Lightwave and Macromedia products. SCAD's cutting-edge computer systems are combined with two green-screen stages, HD cameras, and a VICON motion capture studio to provide visual effects students with a complete digital production facility.

Fashion and fibers students use computer-aided design workstations and scanners; Juki industrial sewing machines and sergers; a heat transfer press; customized dress forms; weaving facilities, including a variety of four- and eight-shaft floor looms, two AVL CompuDobby looms, and an AVL electronic Jacquard loom; a digital fabric printer; a dye lab; and a screenprinting studio. Fibers students use NedGraphics, an industry standard software program.

The Gulfstream Center for Furniture and Industrial Design in Savannah is a 43,000-square-foot facility with a woodworking and metals and plastics fabrication lab; bench rooms and design studios; a plastic working area; a welding facility; a three-axis computer numeric controlled vertical milling machine; spray booths and a finishing room; and state-of-the-art electronic design studios configured with the latest versions of design and visualization software, such as Auto CAD, Autodesk Studio, Rhino 3-D, SolidWorks, and Maya. The computer lab has two 3-D printers with capabilities to print polycarbonate or ABS 3-D models of computer-generated designs.

Advertising design, graphic design, and illustration facilities include Macintosh computers with CD and DVD burners, scanners, black and white laser printers, light tables, and digital cameras. The Adobe product line; Macromedia Director, Dreamweaver, Flash, and FreeHand; Quark XPress; and other graphics packages are available.

Photography students have access to Macintosh digital imaging labs with extensive peripherals, wide format inkjet printers, a Durst Theta printer, Imacon scanners, professional RA-4 color print processing machines for both negative and reversal papers, E-6 and C-41 color film processing machines, an alternative processes lab, studios, lighting equipment, view camera systems, medium-format camera systems, and digital SLR systems. Some labs are graduate-only.

Metals and jewelry studios include an FDM Prodigy Plus rapid prototyping 3-D printer with capabilities for ABS or wax models of CAD prototypes and four-axis CNC milling machines.

Film and television facilities include the Steadicam EFP and Super Panther Dolly, a chroma key/green screen studio, and a sound stage. The department houses Avid Adrenaline, Symphony, and Xpress DV workstations; MiniDV and DVC Pro cameras; Sony digital high definition selevision cameras; 16mm, Super 16mm, and 35mm cameras; and an all-digital studio. Sound design equipment and software includes 10 DH Pro Tools labs, two dedicated surround sound mix/mastering rooms, a MIDI lab, a recording studio for music production and Foley, two suites for dialog recording and editing, and a professionally equipped location sound cart for film production.

Located next to the High Museum of Art in Midtown Atlanta, the sculpture facility is one of the finest in the Southeast. Designed by architect Renzo Piano, the facility contains a comprehensive wood and metal shop, a foundry for bronze and stainless steel, studios and support equipment, and exhibition space.

Performing Arts facilities include the 1,200-seat historic Lucas Theatre for the Arts, the 1,100-seet Trustees Theater, the 90-seat Afifi Amphitheater at the Pei Ling Chan Garden for the Arts, and the 150-seat black box Mondanaro Theater.

Costs

Undergraduate tuition for 2008–09 is $25,965. All first-time degree-seeking students pay a one-time nonrefundable matriculation fee of $500. The housing fee for the academic year ranges from $6555 for dormitory-style to $7900 for apartment-style housing and requires a $250 nonrefundable deposit. A variety of dining plans offer a designated number of meals per week or quarter; the basic rate per quarter is $1260.

Financial Aid

Approximately 50 percent of undergraduates and 53 percent of freshmen receive financial assistance. The Savannah College of Art and Design has a number of financial aid programs, which may consist of scholarships, grants, loans, or any combination of these, from federal (including the Federal Direct Loan Program), state, and college sources. Students also help finance educational expenses by jobs secured through the Federal Work-Study Program and the College's Student Placement Service. A detailed listing of financial aid programs may be obtained from the admission office.

Faculty

The College maintains a low student-faculty ratio, with small classes taught by professors who hold terminal degrees and/or other outstanding credentials in their fields. Faculty members provide regularly scheduled conferences and extra help sessions.

Student Government

The United Student Forum is the student government of the Savannah College of Art and Design. It meets often to promote productive communication among students and members of the faculty, staff, and administration. It strives to increase student involvement in the SCAD policy decision-making process and to further enhance the mission of the College.

Admission Requirements

Students may apply online at the College's Web site (http://www.scad.edu). Undergraduate application requirements include SAT or ACT scores, official transcripts from the last high school or college attended, a minimum of three recommendations, a statement of purpose, a completed application form, and a nonrefundable application fee of $25 for online applicants and $50 for applications submitted via mail. Portfolio/auditions and interviews are encouraged but are not required for undergraduate admission. Homeschooled, transient, and non-degree-seeking applicants are welcome. A minimum SAT math score of 540 or ACT math score of 23 is required for regular acceptance into the professional architecture program.

A student may be admitted full-time at the end of the junior year in high school (omitting the senior year) or on a part-time basis during the senior year if he or she has a GPA of 3.5 (B+) or higher through the eleventh grade, if the SAT or ACT scores are above the national average, and if the student's counselor and art teacher recommend early admission. The Rising Star program gives rising high school seniors the chance to experience college during a five-week summer program for college credit. Savannah Summer Seminars are one-week workshops open to high school students.

Transfer students may receive a maximum of 90 quarter hours toward a B.F.A. degree. All students must complete in residence the final 45 hours of any degree earned at the College.

International students are encouraged to apply and must submit scores from the Test of English as a Foreign Language (TOEFL), and they must present proof of having adequate funds for their studies. SAT or ACT scores are not required for international students. Scholarships are available.

Exceptions to the general admission criteria may be made for applicants of unusual motivation and ability. The Savannah College of Art and Design admits students of any race, color, and national and ethnic origin to all the rights, privileges, programs, and activities generally accorded or made available to students at the College.

Application and Information

As a general rule, applications for fall quarter should be completed no later than March 1 in order for admission decisions to be rendered by April 1. Scholarships for fall quarter are awarded by May 1 and students are requested to indicate their acceptance of admission and of institutional scholarship offers by June 1 through payment of a one-time matriculation fee. This same time frame applies with corresponding dates for students entering winter, spring, or summer quarters. Applications received less than one month prior to the intended entry date are considered only on a space available basis.

Files are reviewed as soon as they are complete, and applicants are notified immediately of their admission status. Only accepted students are eligible for scholarship consideration and federal/state aid.

For more information about the Savannah College of Art and Design, students should contact:

Savannah and eLearning Admissions:

Admission Department
Savannah College of Art and Design
P.O. Box 2072
Savannah, Georgia 31402-2072
Phone: 912-525-5100
800-869-7223 (toll-free)
Fax: 912-525-5986
E-mail: admission@scad.edu
Web site: http://www.scad.edu

Atlanta Admissions:

Admission Department
Savannah College of Art and Design–Atlanta
P.O. Box 77300
Atlanta, Georgia 30357-77300
Phone: 404-253-2700
877-722-3285 (toll-free)
Fax: 404-253-3466
E-mail: scadatl@scad.edu
Web site: http://www.scad.edu

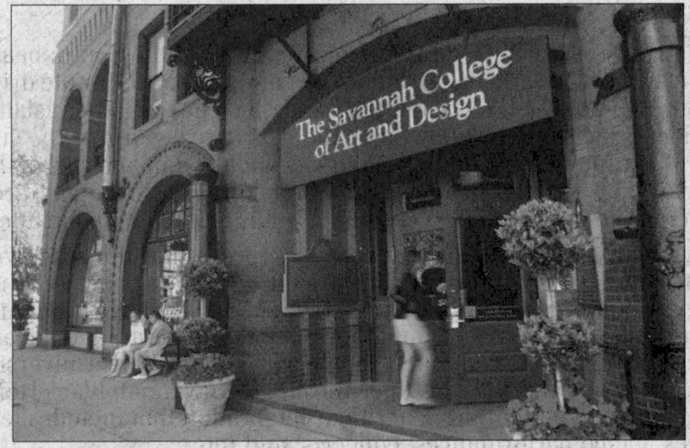

Poetter Hall, Savannah College of Art and Design, Savannah, Georgia.

SAVANNAH STATE UNIVERSITY

SAVANNAH, GEORGIA

The University

Savannah State University has been transforming the lives of generations of students in a nurturing learning environment since its founding in 1890. As a senior institution of the University System of Georgia, Savannah State continues that tradition in classrooms where cutting-edge instruction is complemented by one of the smallest student-faculty ratios in the region. The University is committed to serving students who are well prepared academically. Its programs are designed to provide opportunities for students to improve themselves, attain career objectives, and compete effectively in the job market. Savannah State offers undergraduate and graduate degrees in three colleges: the College of Business Administration, the College of Liberal Arts and Social Sciences, and the College of Sciences and Technology. Master's degrees are available in business administration, marine sciences, public administration, social work, and urban studies. All degree programs at Savannah State University are accredited by the Southern Association of Colleges and Schools. The programs in civil engineering technology and electronics technology are accredited by the Accreditation Board for Engineering and Technology, Inc. (ABET), and the electronics engineering technology program is also accredited by the National Association of Radio and Telecommunications Engineers, Inc. (NARTE). The social work programs are accredited by the Council on Social Work Education (CSWE). The public administration program is accredited by the National Association of Schools of Public Affairs and Administration. The College of Business Administration is accredited by AACSB International–The Association to Advance Collegiate Schools of Business. The mass communications program is accredited by the Accrediting Council on Education in Journalism and Mass Communications (ACEJMC). The chemistry curriculum is certified by the American Chemical Society (ACS).

Most of the 3,000 undergraduate students enrolled at Savannah State University are Georgia residents, although thirty-eight states and thirty other countries are represented. Students can participate in numerous social and academic organizations as well as in intercollegiate and intramural sports. Savannah State athletes compete in baseball, basketball, cross-country, football, tennis, track, volleyball, and more. Campus housing options range from traditional residence halls to fully-furnished one-, two-, and four-bedroom apartments.

Location

The University is located in the Hostess City of the South: beautiful, historic Savannah, Georgia. The campus is a 10-minute drive from the Atlantic Ocean and the sandy beaches of Tybee Island. Students at Savannah State enjoy the best of two worlds—the cultural advantages of a metropolitan city and the sun and surf of the ocean and boating, fishing, and waterskiing on the many area rivers. The city also offers excellent golfing and tennis facilities.

Savannah offers exciting scientific resources like the Skidaway Marine Science Complex. Culturally, the city offers ballet and theater groups, art galleries, African American heritage sites and museums, and a range of outdoor celebrations that take advantage of the city's moderate climate. Savannah State University partners with the city to produce the annual Savannah Black Heritage Festival, a monthlong heritage celebration that includes lectures, dance performances, concerts, and more.

Greater Savannah has a population of approximately 350,000 and is famous for its Low Country cuisine, scenic boat tours, specialty shops, and riverfront activities. The international airport and extensive railway system make Savannah easily accessible to all of the Southeast and the nation.

Majors and Degrees

Savannah State University provides innovative instruction of high quality through the College of Business Administration, the College of Liberal Arts and Social Sciences, and the College of Sciences and Technology.

The College of Business Administration offers programs that lead to the Bachelor of Business Administration in accounting, computer information systems, management, and marketing.

The College of Liberal Arts and Social Sciences grants the Bachelor of Arts degree in Africana studies, English language and literature, history, and mass communication and the Bachelor of Science degree in behavioral analysis, criminal justice, homeland security and emergency management, political science, and sociology. The College offers a Bachelor of Social Work degree and a Bachelor of Fine Arts degree in visual and performing arts with concentrations in music, visual arts, theater, and dance. Minor areas include Africana studies, art, criminal justice, English language and literature, French, gerontology, history, mass communication, political science, psychology, religious and philosophical studies, sociology, Spanish, and theater.

The College of Sciences and Technology offers the Bachelor of Science degree in biology (premedicine or preprofessional), chemistry, civil engineering technology, computer science technology, electronics engineering technology, environmental studies, marine sciences, and mathematics.

Academic Programs

The core curriculum of the University System of Georgia is the foundation upon which all degree programs are built. All candidates for a baccalaureate degree must complete a minimum of 125 semester hours, including health, physical education, and orientation; maintain a scholastic average of C or better; and satisfactorily complete the minimum requirements of the core curriculum and of the specific degree programs. Students must also satisfactorily complete the University System of Georgia Regents' Exam and the major comprehensive examinations as prescribed by their specific schools.

The University offers four-year Naval ROTC programs and two-year and three-year Army ROTC programs through either a scholarship or a regular University program. Graduates receive a commission as a second lieutenant in the U.S. Marine Corps, as an ensign in the U.S. Navy, or as a second lieutenant in the U.S. Army. The Army and Naval ROTC programs constitute academic minors in military science and naval science, respectively.

The University operates on the semester system, with each semester extending over a period of fifteen weeks. Normally, the baccalaureate degree is earned in eight semesters. A full course load is considered to be 12 hours, with the maximum load being 19 hours.

Savannah State may grant credit for satisfactory scores on selected tests of the College-Level Examination Program (CLEP), for satisfactory completion of appropriate courses and tests offered through DANTES (formerly the United States Armed Forces Institute), for work completed at military service schools, and for military experience as recommended by the Commission on Accreditation of Service Experiences of the American Council on Education. Such credits may not exceed more than one fourth of the work counted toward a degree. Advanced Placement scores are accepted from the College Board. College credit is granted for satisfactory scores from the Advanced Placement exam series and for the International Baccalaureate test series.

Off-Campus Programs

The cooperative education program provides an off-campus option that enables students to receive on-the-job training while earning money for their tuition. The University arranges and approves assignments with cooperating companies and agencies, and supervision is provided by representatives of the University as well as the employers.

Savannah State University students travel across the globe. The International Education Program takes students and faculty members to six international locales—Egypt, India, Brazil, the Caribbean, China, and Ghana—as part of a vibrant exchange program.

Academic Facilities

Gordon Library, a modern library with excellent facilities and a well-prepared staff, serves the University and the community. It houses more than 182,000 cataloged volumes, approximately 900 periodicals, more than 558,000 microfilms, and 25,000 bound periodicals. Approximately 8,000 volumes are added yearly to keep the collection up-to-date. There is an extensive collection of materials about African Americans. The library, which is the cultural and intellectual center of the University, can house 290,000 volumes. The building has many conference and individual study areas, an audiovisual department, two Distance Learning Centers, a Curriculum Materials Center, open stacks, classrooms, and computer stations. The library is easily distinguishable from the other buildings on campus because of its distinctive circular shape.

Located next to a salt-marsh estuary, the campus includes a marine wet laboratory, dock, and several boating vessels used for marine science education.

Costs

In 2006–07, tuition and fees were $1589 per semester for Georgia residents and $5381 per semester for non–Georgia residents. These costs include the matriculation fee, health fee, student activity fee, and athletics fee. Books cost approximately $300 per semester. The costs for housing range from $1150 to $2455 per semester, depending on the type of residence hall.

Financial Aid

Almost 90 percent of all Savannah State University students receive financial aid through federal and state grants, including Pell Grants, Supplemental Educational Opportunity Grants, Georgia Incentive Grants, Perkins Loans, College Work-Study Program awards, and work opportunities provided by the University. Students requesting financial aid are required to submit the Free Application for Federal Student Aid (FAFSA).

Faculty

Savannah State University has approximately 160 full-time faculty members, with nearly 70 percent of them holding an earned doctorate. The full-time student-faculty ratio is 22:1.

Student Government

The Student Government Association serves the needs of the students; its members are elected by the student body. This organization is set up with executive, legislative, and judicial branches, and it is influential in campus affairs. The Student Government Association is the chief student organization on campus. It helps to govern the student body as well as to plan social events for the academic year. Students also serve on all major University committees.

Admission Requirements

Factors considered in assessing a student's readiness for admission to Savannah State University include the high school grade point average and curriculum, test scores, previous college work, and other qualifications. Each applicant for admission to the freshman class is required to take the SAT or the ACT. Minimum scores on the SAT are 430 critical reading, and 400 math. The minimum composite score on the ACT is 17; the minimum English and math scores are also 17. Completion of the College Preparatory Curriculum (CPC) is required. Transfers must have maintained a minimum 2.0 grade point average and have completed at least 30 semester credit hours or 45 quarter hours from a regionally accredited institution with two college-level English courses and one college-level math course.

Application and Information

Application can be made anytime following completion of the junior year of high school. Students are notified of the admission decision soon after receipt of the completed application and supporting documents. Students are encouraged to apply online by going to http://www.savstate.edu/em/admissions/.

Office of Admissions
Savannah State University
P.O. Box 20209
Savannah, Georgia 31404
Phone: 912-356-2181
800-788-0478 (toll-free)
Fax: 912-356-2256
Web site: http://www.savstate.edu/em/admissions/

Students studying on the campus of Savannah State University.

SHORTER COLLEGE

ROME, GEORGIA

The College

Since 1873, Shorter College has been combining academic excellence with caring Christian commitment. The College was established through the generosity of a Baptist layman, Alfred Shorter, and the vision of his pastor. They led a group of northwestern Georgia Baptists in founding the school, which was originally named Cherokee Baptist Female College. The name was changed to Shorter Female College in 1878 and to Shorter College in 1923. The College became coeducational in 1951. Shorter's enrollment of 2,763 includes students in both traditional semester programs and innovative continuous programs for working adults. Approximately 1,050 of these students are located on the main campus in Rome, Georgia. Students come from all parts of the United States and from other countries around the world. Shorter College has an overall graduate school acceptance rate of 80 percent and an impressive 82 percent acceptance rate to medical colleges over the past twenty-one years. Shorter College is very committed to providing a high-quality education in an intentionally Christian atmosphere. Each year, the campus is visited by noted Christian leaders, scholars, and outstanding musical performers. The campus minister works with the director of religious activities to provide a wide range of opportunities for spiritual growth. The largest religious organization on campus is the Baptist Student Union (BSU), which includes Christians of many denominations. Student publications include a newspaper, a yearbook, and a literary magazine. Highly skilled music and drama groups include the Shorter Chorale, the Shorter Mixed Chorus, the Shorter Players, the Opera Workshop, and the Wind Ensemble. The Shorter Chorale was selected to represent the United States in choral festivals held in Yugoslavia, France, and Austria and represented the College in St. Petersburg, Russia. Shorter has also been the home of numerous National Metropolitan Opera Audition winners and finalists. The College has two fraternities and three sororities as well as chapters of two national music fraternities and honor societies for majors in biology, communication, English, music, religion, and social sciences. Shorter College is a member of the Southern States Athletic Conference of the NAIA. Varsity teams compete in men's baseball, basketball, cross-country, golf, soccer, tennis, and track and field and in women's basketball, cheerleading, cross-country, fast-pitch softball, golf, soccer, tennis, track and field, and volleyball. The College is a football-only member of the NAIA Division I Mid-South Conference.

Location

The College is situated on 150 acres atop Shorter Hill, in Rome, Georgia (area population 93,000). Rome is located just 65 miles northwest of Atlanta and 65 miles south of Chattanooga, Tennessee, and cultural opportunities abound. In the city of Rome there are the Symphony Orchestra, Rome Little Theatre, Rome Area Council for the Arts events, popular concerts and attractions at the Roman Forum, and the 334,859-volume modern city library. The College sponsors numerous events, including faculty, alumni, student, and guest musical recitals; four guest lecture series; speech festivals and recitals; drama and opera productions; art exhibits; and athletic events.

Majors and Degrees

Shorter College offers six degrees: the Bachelor of Arts, the Bachelor of Science, the Bachelor of Business Administration, the Bachelor of Science in Education, the Bachelor of Fine Arts, and the Bachelor of Music. The Bachelor of Arts is offered in art, communication arts (with concentrations in electronic media and journalism), English, French, health science and counseling, history and political science, international studies, liberal arts, mathematics, music, psychology, public relations, religion and philosophy, sociology, and Spanish. The Bachelor of Science is offered in biology, chemistry, Christian ministries, computer information systems, communication leadership, economics, ecology and field biology, general studies, history and political science, mathematics, mathematics education, ministry studies, psychology, religious studies, sociology, and sports studies. The Bachelor of Business Administration is offered in accounting, accounting–CPA track, and business administration. The Bachelor of Science in Education is offered in early childhood education (K–4) and middle grades (4–8). Programs leading to certification in secondary school teaching are available in English, general science, history, mathematics, and social science. Certification is also offered in music for grades K–12. The Bachelor of Fine Arts is offered in art, musical theater, and theater. The Bachelor of Music is offered in church music, music education, organ performance, piano pedagogy, piano performance, and voice performance. Preprofessional programs are available in allied health, dentistry, law, medicine, pharmacy, physical therapy, physician's assistant studies, and veterinary medicine. Courses are also available in German, health and physical education, and interdisciplinary studies.

Academic Programs

Shorter is accredited by the Southern Association of Colleges and Schools and the National Association of Schools of Music and strives to provide an academic environment of high quality. Teacher programs are approved by the Georgia Professional Standards Commission. Small classes (freshman lecture courses average 22 students) taught by dedicated and highly qualified professors (71 percent of freshman lecture courses are taught by full-time faculty members, 26 percent by full professors) ensure that each student receives an education that is both challenging and personally rewarding. For any degree, a candidate must have earned a minimum of 126 semester hours; some degrees require a greater number of hours. As part of the orientation program at the beginning of the fall semester, each new student is assigned to one of several small orientation groups that assist the student in adjusting to College life; the student is also assigned to an academic adviser, who assists in the selection and scheduling of courses. Early registration sessions are available in the summer. Freshman advisers are specially trained faculty and staff members. The academic calendar is divided into two semesters from September to May, with two "mini" sessions offered during the summer. On-campus evening classes are available in selected disciplines. Shorter offers an honors program that spans all four years and provides students with learning opportunities that are not generally available to undergraduates.

Off-Campus Programs

Shorter's School of Business and School of Education and Social Sciences offer the Professional Studies Programs, which are specifically designed for working adults, on campus and in Lawrenceville, Riverdale, and Marietta, Georgia. Majors are business and human resources. Classes meet one evening or weekend per week, year-round, with a required weekly study group.

Shorter College offers several monthlong study-abroad programs immediately following the end of the second semester in May, including MAYTERM (in Europe), the Asia Program, and the Americas Program. Students earn 12 semester hours of credit through travel, study, and classroom experiences. Students are housed in student residences or college dormitories, and the cost of most meals is usually included. Shorter College faculty members accompany the students and teach the courses that are offered. MAYTERM is usually based at British American College London and includes visits to England and to one other European country. The Asia Program is generally based at Zhengzhou University in China or at Mahidol University in Thailand. The Americas Program includes two weeks in Ecuador and the Galapagos Islands and two weeks in another Central or South American country. Studies in other countries can be arranged on an individual basis through the Office of International Programs.

Academic Facilities

Livingston Library, which was dedicated in 1976 as a memorial to Ray Livingston, houses more than 135,806 books, 582 periodical subscriptions, 7,592 microform materials, 5,227 audio/video items, 38,312 e-books, and 7,000 e-journals. The library also contains conference rooms (for both individual and group study), projection rooms, a graphics preparation room, computer terminals, typewriters, and music listening facilities for student use. The Alice Allgood Cooper Fine Arts Building and the Randall H. Minor Fine Arts Building are connected to form an outstanding fine arts complex, providing up-to-date facilities for the departments of music, communication arts, and art. The Cooper Building contains classrooms, music faculty offices, the art department's drawing and painting studio, and Brookes Chapel, the meeting place for convocations, concerts, recitals, and lectures. A renovated home adjacent to the campus houses expanded art facilities. The Minor Building contains classrooms, twenty-five music practice rooms (with a baby grand piano in each), a choral rehearsal room, faculty offices, photography facilities, a theater, a desktop publishing lab, a radio studio, and an art gallery. Rome Hall was named in honor of the citizens of Rome in appreciation of their generous support of the College. It contains classrooms, science laboratories (including the Stergus Collection of Internal Organs, one of the most complete pathology collections in the United States), faculty offices, lounges, and the Robert T. Connor exhibit of some 150 African and North American animals and skins. Alumni Hall houses the educational materials center and faculty offices. The Winthrop-King Centre houses classrooms, offices for coaches, a basketball gym, a dance and aerobic studio, two racquetball courts, a fitness center, and an indoor jogging track. The Fitton Student Union contains the campus bookstore, a 24-hour study room, a 24-hour game room, and an indoor swimming pool. Two computer labs are available for general student use. Computer labs for business and communication arts are also available. Smaller computer labs are available for art, music, and recreation. All residence halls have computer and Internet access.

Costs

Tuition for 2007–08 was $14,850. Room and board costs were $7000 and fees were $310.

Financial Aid

Shorter College offers aid through each of the five federal programs: the Federal Pell Grant, Federal Supplemental Educational Opportunity Grant, Federal Work-Study Program, Federal Perkins Loan, and Federal Stafford Student Loan. Full-time students who are Georgia residents are eligible to receive the Georgia Tuition Equalization Grant and may be eligible to receive the HOPE Scholarship. Scholarships are offered for achievement in academics, music, art, theater, humanities, and athletics. Awards range from $500 to full tuition. Academic scholarships are renewable each year, provided the student maintains at least the required grade point average. Special grants and scholarships are available to students who plan to enter church-related vocations or who are dependents of full-time employees of a Southern Baptist church, institution, or agency. Small grants are also awarded to students recommended directly by alumni and when 2 or more students from the same family are enrolled at Shorter. One hundred percent of all full-time Shorter students receive some financial aid.

Faculty

The Shorter College faculty is composed of 66 full-time, highly qualified professors, of whom 83 percent hold doctoral degrees. The College also employs 53 part-time faculty members. A favorable student-teacher ratio of 13:1 in traditional programs ensures that each student receives individual attention.

Student Government

One of Shorter's truly distinctive features is that students may participate in a wide variety of significant extracurricular activities, each of which affords a chance to develop social and leadership skills that prepare a student to win in a competitive world. The Student Government Association (SGA) is the official voice of the students. Through SGA's Executive Council, Senate, judicial boards, and special committees, students are directly involved in the life of the College.

Admission Requirements

Students are admitted into the freshman class based on their academic grade point average, SAT or ACT scores, and required essay. A review of the student's goals and their compatibility with the purpose of the College are also determining factors. The College requires 4 years of English, 4 years of mathematics (including 2 years of algebra), 3 years of history/social science, 3 years of science, and 2 units of foreign language. In addition to the general requirements for admission to the College, students majoring in music must meet the following requirements: each student must perform in an audition of approximately 10 minutes in his or her major medium, and each student must take a series of music placement tests. Students must successfully fulfill these requirements prior to the beginning of classes in August of their freshman year, since the music curriculum requires at least four years for completion. An audition is also required for students majoring in theater, and an art portfolio review is required for students majoring in art. High school students who have completed their junior year, have an outstanding academic record, and have completed the units outlined above may be considered for early admission. High school seniors entering their senior year may be admitted on a joint-enrollment basis. Such students should have above-average grades and SAT or ACT scores. Transfer and international students are also welcome to apply. A minimum paper-based TOEFL score of 500 or computer-based score of 173 is required for international students. Credit for college work below a C cannot be transferred. Homeschooled students should contact the Office of Admissions directly for requirements.

Application and Information

Shorter accepts students on a rolling basis. Campus visits are highly recommended through a personal campus tour or one of three Open Houses.

Director of Admissions
Shorter College
315 Shorter Avenue
Rome, Georgia 30165-4298
Phone: 706-233-7319
800-868-6980 Ext. 7319 (toll-free)
Fax: 706-233-7224
E-mail: admissions@shorter.edu
Web site: http://www.shorter.edu

SOUTH UNIVERSITY

SouthUniversity℠

SAVANNAH, GEORGIA

The University

South University is a private academic institution dedicated to providing educational opportunities for the intellectual, social, and professional development of a diverse student population. To achieve this, the Savannah campus offers focused and balanced curricula at the associate and bachelor's degree levels in the areas of business, health sciences, information technology, and legal studies. The University also offers master's degree programs in anesthesiology assistant studies and physician assistant studies. In addition, the campus offers a Master of Arts in Professional Counseling, a Master of Business Administration (M.B.A.), and a Doctor of Pharmacy degree through its School of Pharmacy—one of only three programs in the state of Georgia and the only one in the state that is currently available in an accelerated three-year format. South University is the first university or college in Savannah to offer a health professions doctoral degree program.

South University traces its heritage back to 1899 and today has grown into a multicampus system with locations in Savannah, Georgia; West Palm Beach, Florida; Montgomery, Alabama; Columbia, South Carolina; and, most recently, Tampa, Florida.

The University now offers a wide range of online degree programs. Students can also pursue degrees through a combination of on-campus and online classes as part of the University's unique Plus+ program, which provides maximum scheduling flexibility. This flexibility allows students to organize their college education around work and family commitments. For those who choose to take on-site courses, Savannah campus facilities and amenities include a bookstore, student lounges, a career services center, wireless Internet access, and ample parking in addition to classrooms and offices.

The cornerstone of the Savannah campus is the School of Pharmacy building, which represents the newest construction on campus. The pharmacy building joins the School of Business and School of Health Professions buildings. The University strives to maintain small class sizes that permit students to receive individualized instruction and interaction with faculty and staff members.

The Savannah campus of South University has a diverse student body enrolled in day, evening, and weekend classes. Undergraduate students are primarily commuters who live within 60 miles of the city. Graduate students come from all of the United States and as far away as California and Alaska. They include men and women who have enrolled directly after completing high school, who have transferred from another college or university, or who have experience in the workforce and are pursing an education that will prepare them to grow in their current position or enable them to take a new professional direction. The University offers a school-sponsored housing option in conjunction with local apartment communities for students who are relocating to Savannah to pursue their degrees.

South University is accredited by the Commission on Colleges of the Southern Association of Colleges and Schools (SACS, 1866 Southern Lane, Decatur, Georgia 30033-4097; phone: 404-679-4501) to award associate, bachelor's, master's, and doctoral degrees. The Savannah campus is also authorized under the Georgia Non-public Postsecondary Educational Institutions Act of 1990 to confer those degrees. In addition, the campus is approved for training military veterans and other individuals by the State of Georgia Department of Veterans' Services, State Approving Agency, in Atlanta, Georgia.

Certain programs offered at the Savannah campus have earned programmatic accreditation. The Associate of Science in Medical Assisting degree program is accredited by the Commission on Accreditation of Allied Health Education Programs (CAAHEP, 1361 Park Street, Clearwater, Florida 33756; 727-210-2350) on recommendation of the Committee on Accreditation for Medical Assisting Education. The Associate of Science in Physical Therapist Assisting degree program is an expansion program approved by the Commission on Accreditation in Physical Therapy Education of the American Physical Therapy Association (1111 North Fairfax Street, Alexandria, Virginia 22314; 703-684-2782).

The Physician Assistant Studies program is accredited by the Accreditation Review Commission on Education for the Physician Assistant (ARC-PA), an accreditation status that qualifies graduating students to take the national certifying examination administered by the National Commission on Certification of Physician Assistants (NCCPA). In addition, the South University Physician Assistant Studies program is a member of the Association of Physician Assistant Programs, the national organization representing physician assistant education programs. The Bachelor of Science in Legal Studies and Associate of Science in Paralegal Studies programs are approved by the American Bar Association (321 North Clark Street, Chicago, Illinois 60610; 312-988-5617).

Location

This campus, the largest among South University's locations, is located in the midtown section of historic Savannah, minutes from downtown, cultural activities, and the beach. The buildings are situated on 9 acres of land and are easily accessible from any section of Savannah, the surrounding region, and coastal South Carolina.

Majors and Degrees

The Savannah campus of South University awards the following two-year degrees: Associate of Science in accounting, Associate of Science in business administration, Associate of Science in information technology, Associate of Science in medical assisting, Associate of Science in paralegal studies, and Associate of Science in physical therapist assisting.

Four-year degree programs include a Bachelor of Business Administration, Bachelor of Science in criminal justice, Bachelor of Science in health-care management, Bachelor of Science in information technology, Bachelor of Science in legal studies, and Bachelor of Arts in psychology.

Academic Programs

The Savannah campus of South University offers degree programs that are designed to meet the needs and objectives of students. Each curriculum combines classroom and practical educational experiences that provide students with the academic background needed to pursue the professions of their choice. In addition, faculty members strive to instill the value not only of education and professionalism but also of contribution and commitment to the advancement of community.

South University operates on a quarter system, with each quarter comprising eleven weeks. Associate degree programs require a minimum of eight quarters to complete, and bachelor's degree programs require a minimum of twelve quarters for completion. Undergraduate programs are offered on a year-round basis, providing students with the ability to work uninterrupted toward their degrees.

Academic Facilities

The Savannah campus library has a large collection that includes an extensive law and health professions library. Students may retrieve periodicals in paper or electronic form. Library-based computers provide access to several commercial online services, including Westlaw, the computerized legal research service; GALILEO, the Georgia network of databases; and MEDLINE, for health sciences students. CD-ROM resources include the Encyclopedia Britannica, the Official Code of Georgia Annotated, ADAM, and the EBSCO magazine full-text database. Internet access is available on all computers throughout the campus, and the University offers wireless Internet access through an on-campus Wi-Fi network.

Costs

Tuition information is available by contacting the South University Admissions Department.

Financial Aid

South University's Student Financial Services Office helps qualified students secure financial assistance to complete their studies. The University participates in several student aid programs. Forms of financial aid available to qualified students through federal resources include the Federal Pell Grant Program, Federal Supplemental Educational Opportunity Grant (FSEOG) Program, Federal Work-Study Program, Federal Perkins Loan Program, Federal Stafford Loan Program (subsidized and unsubsidized), and Federal PLUS Loan Program. Qualified students may apply for the Georgia HOPE Scholarship, Georgia Tuition Equalization Grant, Georgia LEAP Grant Program, and veterans' educational benefits. Students are also encouraged to investigate the availability of grants and scholarships through community resources.

Faculty

The South University faculty includes individuals of high academic distinction. Of the more than 80 instructors on the Savannah campus, 40 percent hold terminal degrees. In addition to teaching, faculty members strive to help students develop the requisites to appreciate knowledge and understand how experiences in the classroom and laboratory relate to professional performance in the workplace. The average student-faculty ratio is 14:1. Each student is assigned a faculty adviser who oversees the student's progress and can answer questions about academic and career concerns. Students are encouraged to discuss program-related issues with and seek academic and career advice from their faculty advisers.

Admission Requirements

To be admitted to South University, prospective students must be high school graduates or hold a GED certificate and submit an appropriate SAT or ACT score (students should contact the Admissions Office) or a satisfactory score on the University-administered placement examination. Students who wish to transfer must meet the criteria established for acceptance as a transfer student.

All applicants to South University must demonstrate English proficiency. Students may furnish proof of English as a first language competency through submission of a diploma from a secondary school (or higher level) in which English is the official language of instruction. Applicants whose first language is not English must submit Test of English as a Foreign Language (TOEFL) scores. Applicants should contact the Admissions Office to determine other examinations/scores that are acceptable as an alternative to the TOEFL.

Applicants not meeting the testing standards for general admission may be accepted under academic support admission.

Application and Information

Applicants must complete an application form and submit it along with the general application fee as well as official transcripts from all high schools and colleges attended. Faxed documents are not considered official. Applicants must also complete all tests administered by the University or submit their SAT or ACT scores to the Registrar's Office. Applications are accepted on a rolling basis and should be made as far in advance as possible.

All international (nonimmigrant) applicants to South University must meet the same admissions standards as all other students. In addition, international applicants must have official educational records prepared in English, verify sufficient funds to cover the cost of the educational program, and meet certain other immigration-mandated criteria. South University in Savannah is authorized under federal law to admit nonimmigrant students.

Admissions officers are available weekdays, Saturdays, and by appointment. An appointment for an admissions interview or tour of the campus should be made in advance. For additional information, all prospective students should contact:

Director of Admissions
South University
709 Mall Boulevard
Savannah, Georgia 31406-4805
Phone: 912-201-8000
866-629-2901 (toll-free)
Fax: 912-201-8070
Web site: http://www.southuniversity.edu

South University is located on the south side of historic Savannah, Georgia.

COLLEGE DATA CENTER • GEORGIA

SPELMAN COLLEGE

ATLANTA, GEORGIA

The College

Spelman, a private, independent, historically black, four-year liberal arts college for women, was founded in 1881. The campus has grown from 9 acres of drill ground and five frame barracks used for federal troops after the Civil War to 39 acres and twenty-eight buildings. As an integral part of the Atlanta University Center, Spelman benefits from proximity to and cooperation with the other member institutions, but it maintains its own identity nonetheless, thus offering outstanding opportunities for the education of women for leadership roles.

A focal point of campus activity for the 2,100 women enrolled is the Manley College Center, which houses the dining hall, a food court, faculty and student lounges, student government offices, and some administrative offices. There is a varied program of student and professional cultural activities on the campus. Many of the extracurricular activities are planned and sponsored by the Student Government Association. Others are presented by departmental honor societies and clubs, excellent dance groups, and both jazz and classical instrumental ensembles. The strong tradition in fine arts at Spelman gives students maximum cultural exposure through the renowned Spelman Glee Club, the Spelman-Morehouse Chorus, and the Spelman-Morehouse Players. Health and physical education facilities include a gymnasium, tennis courts, a swimming pool, bowling lanes, dance studios, and a weight room.

Student thought is expressed through several publications: *Reflections*, the yearbook; *Spotlight*, the newspaper; and *Focus*, the literary magazine. Religious life and services form an important part of campus life. Opportunities to experience fellowship in a meaningful fashion, special convocations, and counseling are provided through Sisters Chapel and the Wisdom Center.

Location

Spelman College is located in Atlanta, "The Gateway to the South," a city that is rapidly becoming one of the most dynamic and vital urban areas in the country. Proximity to other colleges and universities in the area provides additional educational, social, and cultural opportunities. Spelman College is one of five institutions that constitute the Atlanta University Center (AUC) consortium.

The city is one of the most exciting learning laboratories imaginable. Here, women can observe politics at work and can meet some of the world's leaders. As an urban center with crucial social problems, Atlanta challenges students to become involved in community programs. The Bonner Office of Community Service coordinates the placement of students in community agencies.

Majors and Degrees

Spelman offers the Bachelor of Arts and the Bachelor of Science degrees. Majors are offered in art, biochemistry, biology, chemistry, child development, comparative women's studies, computer and information sciences, drama, economics, engineering (through participating schools), English, environmental science, French, history, human services, international studies, mathematics, music, philosophy, physics, political science, psychology, religious studies, sociology, sociology/anthropology, and Spanish. An independent major is also available. Special minors are available in dance, film studies and visual culture, Japanese studies, management and organization, teacher certification, women's studies, and writing. Premedical, predentistry, and prelaw sequences are also offered.

Spelman participates in a dual-degree engineering program through which students may combine three years of liberal arts courses at Spelman with two years of engineering studies at Auburn University, Clarkson University, Columbia University, Dartmouth College, Georgia Institute of Technology, North Carolina A&T State University, Rensselaer Polytechnic Institute, Rochester Institute of Technology, University of Alabama in Huntsville , University of Florida, University of Michigan, and University of Missouri–Rolla. Students receive a bachelor's degree from each institution upon completing the program.

Academic Programs

Spelman operates on a two-semester academic calendar. Through its core curriculum, the College introduces students to the principal branches of learning—languages and literature, natural sciences, mathematics, social sciences, fine arts, and humanities. All students are enrolled in courses designed to develop effective writing and reading skills and critical, analytical, and problem-solving skills. An honors program is offered to academically outstanding students.

Credit-hour requirements vary with the major area. The core curriculum requirement includes a two-semester interdisciplinary survey course, African Diaspora and the World, computer literacy, English composition, foreign language, health and physical education, mathematics, and international or women's studies. A minimum of 4 credits is also required in each of the following areas: fine arts, humanities, natural sciences, and social sciences.

Off-Campus Programs

Under the AUC consortium, two undergraduate colleges, one graduate and professional university, and one graduate theological seminary share facilities, resources, and activities. Through cross-registration, Spelman students may elect to take such courses as business administration, mass communication, and social welfare at the other undergraduate institutions.

Academic Facilities

The College's newest building, the state-of-the-art Albro-Falconer-Manley Science Center, was completed in 2000. It is a site for intellectual exchange and scientific creativity, accommodates current research and teaching practices, and supports the use of technology in teaching. The Camille O. Hanks Cosby, Ed.D., Academic Center provides classrooms and laboratories for students studying in the humanities. It houses several interdisciplinary programs and departments and offices for faculty members in English, history, philosophy, religion, and modern foreign languages. The center also features an auditorium, an art museum, the Spelman College archives, the Ennis Cosby Reading Room, educational media, a writing center, and the Women's Research and Resource Center. The Fine Arts Building houses a small, up-to-date proscenium theater, music and art studios, and practice rooms. Spelman students are entitled to use the facilities of the Robert W. Woodruff Library of the Atlanta University Center, which contains approximately 1.5 million volumes. This facility also houses media, curriculum materials, and academic and administrative data processing.

Costs

Tuition costs in 2007–08 were $15,840 per year, room and board were $9200 per year, and fees were $2775. Total costs for students living on campus were $27,815; for students living off campus, costs were $18,615. Additional costs included transportation, $1273; books, $1658; and personal expenses, $2107. These costs are subject to change.

Financial Aid

The College makes every effort to assist students with financial need through scholarships, grants, loans, and work-study programs. The amount of aid is determined by need as indicated by the Free Application for Federal Student Aid (FAFSA). Financial aid funds are limited and are awarded on a first-come, first-served basis. Spelman cannot meet the full documented need of every student who applies for financial aid. Students who submit their FAFSA by February 15 receive priority processing and consideration.

The Spelman scholarship program is meant to encourage academic excellence and to recognize outstanding achievement. Scholarships are awarded to first-year and continuing students on a competitive basis. Consideration is given to academic and personal achievement as evidenced by academic records, standardized test scores, leadership, special talent, character, community service, and, in some cases, financial need. All incoming students are considered for scholarships at the time of application. Additional forms are not required unless students are applying for the Women in Science and Engineering (WISE) Program Scholarship and the Bonner Scholar Program.

Faculty

Spelman's full-time faculty numbers 172 members. More than 83 percent hold doctoral or other terminal degrees. The low student-faculty ratio (11:1) permits individualized instruction and small classes.

Student Government

The Spelman Student Government Association (SSGA) is composed of student representatives who meet regularly to discuss educational and social issues confronting students. The assembly acts as a liaison between the student body and the members of the faculty, staff, and administration. Representatives present proposals, programs, activities, and resolutions that reflect the tenor of student opinion. Meetings of the association are announced and held regularly, and all students are urged to attend.

Admission Requirements

Applicants for first-year admission are selected on the basis of their high school records, SAT or ACT scores, recommendations, and personal information submitted in the application for admission.

A limited number of spaces are available each term for transfer students. Students admitted as transfers are selected based upon their complete academic records, recommendations, personal information submitted in the application for admission, and whether space is available in requested academic majors. In some instances, applicants who have achieved the equivalent of senior status are not considered.

The College selects qualified women candidates without regard to race, religion, color, sexual orientation, national or ethnic origin, or physical challenge. The College seeks to admit students whose credentials give evidence of potential for academic success at Spelman and who demonstrate personal characteristics of high motivation, purpose, and integrity. Interviews are not required. Prospective applicants may request individual information sessions and tours through the Office of Admission.

Application and Information

Completed first-year applications for admission under the early decision plan must be postmarked and mailed by November 1 of the senior year. Notification of the admission decision is made by December 15. Completed first-year applications for admission under the early notification plan must be postmarked and mailed by November 15 of the senior year. Notification of the admission decision is made by December 31. Completed regular first-year applications must be postmarked and mailed by February 1 of the senior year. Notification of the admission decision is April 1.

Transfer applications for the fall term must be postmarked and mailed by April 1. Notification of the admission decision for transfer applicants is May 1. Completed transfer applications for the spring term must be postmarked and mailed by November 1. Notification of the admission decision is made by December 1. For application forms and additional information, students should visit http://www.spelman.edu.

Office of Admission
350 Spelman Lane
Box 277
Spelman College
Atlanta, Georgia 30314
Phone: 404-681-3643
800-982-2411 (toll-free)
E-mail: admiss@spelman.edu
Web site: http://www.spelman.edu

Sisters Chapel at Spelman College.

TOCCOA FALLS COLLEGE

TOCCOA FALLS, GEORGIA

The College

Toccoa Falls College (TFC) provides both the strengths of a Bible college and the strengths of a Christian liberal arts college in a nourishing evangelical Christian environment. TFC was founded in 1907 and moved to its current main campus location in 1911 for the uneducated young people of the South who had no access to a Christian education to prepare them for Christian service. Despite seemingly impossible obstacles, God has led and sustained the College through severe testing—including fire and flood. Throughout its history, the College has consistently transmitted to its students, along with their other studies, a practical knowledge of the Word of God. TFC is now a four-year, independent, interdenominational Christian college that is affiliated with the Christian and Missionary Alliance. TFC offers a wide array of four-year ministry-related, liberal arts, and professional majors at its main campus in Toccoa Falls, Georgia. TFC also offers a two-year Associate of Arts (A.A.) program at both its main campus and its branch campus in Epworth, Georgia.

TFC remains committed to the challenge of preparing men and women to proclaim the gospel of Jesus Christ around the world. Along with their studies, students attend chapel four days per week, participate in student ministry assignments, and enjoy other spiritual formation opportunities as part of the extracurricular program.

TFC is committed to maintaining the highest standards of Christian scholarship. The College is accredited to award associate and bachelor's degrees by the Commission on Colleges of the Southern Association of Colleges and Schools (1866 Southern Lane, Decatur, Georgia 30033-4097; 404-679-4501) and by the Accrediting Association of Bible Colleges (5575 South Semoran Boulevard, Suite 26, Orlando, Florida 32822-1781; 407-207-0808). TFC holds teacher education approval by the Professional Standards Commission of the state of Georgia (1452 Twin Towers East, Atlanta, Georgia 30334; 404-657-9000) and membership in the National Association of Schools of Music (11250 Roger Bacon Drive, Suite 21, Reston, Virginia 22090; 703-437-0700).

Toccoa Falls College enrolls about 850 students each year who are serious about impacting the world with the love and message of Jesus Christ. The majority of the student body consists of traditional residential students. Students at the College come from thirty-eight states and twelve countries and represent twenty-eight evangelical denominations. On-campus housing is required for single students through their junior year. TFC does not offer mixed-gender housing options. Single-gender housing options include residence halls, cottages, mobile housing, and apartments. Married students (13 percent of the TFC student population) can rent apartments from TFC or in the community. Forty percent of the student body lives off campus. Campus dining facilities include a cafeteria, a casual restaurant, a coffee shop, and a formal restaurant. A virtual tour of the campus is available on the College Web site.

Information about student activities can also be found online. Each weekend, the social calendar has something enjoyable to offer, including formal and informal dinners, social events, musical performances, and athletic events. Varsity sports include men's baseball, basketball, and soccer and women's basketball, cross-country, golf, soccer, and volleyball. Intramural sports offer TFC students and staff members the chance to enjoy additional sports, such as coed soccer, volleyball, flag football, Ultimate Frisbee, men's and women's basketball, indoor soccer, and coed softball.

Location

The Toccoa Falls College campus is located on a 1,000-acre tract holding natural forest, mountain streams, and a breathtaking 186-foot waterfall. The thirty-six major campus buildings currently utilize only about 100 acres, leaving the other 900 acres for outdoor recreation and future development.

In northeast Georgia, students have immediate access to lakes, rivers, caving, hiking, fishing, waterskiing, boating, river rafting, rappelling, golf, and camping. The city of Toccoa offers a variety of choices for dining, entertainment, and employment for TFC students. The cities of Athens and Gainesville, Georgia, and Seneca, South Carolina, are within an hour's drive of the campus. The Atlanta metropolitan area is 90 miles from TFC, and the Atlanta airport is about 105 miles away. Atlanta offers a full range of cultural opportunities, including entertainment of all kinds, restaurants, parks, professional athletics (Atlanta Braves, Atlanta Falcons, Atlanta Hawks, and Atlanta Thrashers), shopping, and various other historic charms of the state capital. Students at Toccoa Falls College enjoy big-city advantages and small-town hospitality.

Majors and Degrees

Toccoa Falls College offers students the Bachelor of Science and Bachelor of Arts degrees in the following majors: biblical studies, biology, business administration, Christian education, church music, counseling psychology, cross-cultural business administration, cross-cultural studies, early childhood education, English, family and children's ministries, interpersonal and public communication, mass communication, middle grades education, music, music education, music performance, outdoor leadership and education, pastoral ministries, philosophy and religion, prelaw, premedicine, secondary education (English), secondary education (history), and youth ministries. Toccoa Falls College offers an Associate of Arts degree in general studies.

Academic Programs

Toccoa Falls College operates under a semester calendar with two summer sessions and a winterim session. A minimum of 126 credit hours is required for the bachelor's degree. Core courses in humanities, social sciences, computers/mathematics, and general education are required, as are 42 major-specific credit hours. Students are encouraged to take advantage of CLEP tests and AP courses. Toccoa Falls College recognizes that complete academic preparation for the Christian comes through advanced knowledge of a specific field of study and the integration of faith in learning. Every major includes a minimum of 30 hours of Bible credit to provide a biblical understanding and stimulate spiritual growth along with academic and professional development. Also required is the satisfactory completion of four semesters of student ministry, which gives students the opportunity for a practical ministry outlet.

Academic Facilities

Academic life centers on the Seby Jones Library, which currently houses a total of more than 139,790 holdings, including books, bound volumes, scores, vertical files, audiovisuals, and microfiche, with 300 periodical subscriptions in print and thousands of full-text journals available online. The Seby Jones Library also contains a full-service media center and curriculum labs for the School of Teacher Education. Other resources include the Interlibrary Loan Service, GALILEO (Georgia's statewide resource-sharing project), and direct access to the Internet. Other academic facilities include the computer lab, the Clary Science Building (including chemistry and biology labs), McCarthy Hall (home of the School of Teacher Education), the Woerner World

Missions Building, and the White Memorial Photo Lab, complete with photo labs and curriculum labs for the School of Christian Education. The Grace Chapel and Performing Arts Center is used for artists' series and concerts, while also providing classroom space and practice rooms for the School of Music.

Costs

Tuition for 2007–08 full-time students (12 or more semester hours) was $13,700. Students are charged $5050 for room, meals, and health fees. A student fee of $125 is charged to the student annually. Students should estimate $800 per year for books.

Financial Aid

Toccoa Falls College seeks to assist every qualified student who demonstrates financial need with one or more of the following types of aid: grants, loans, scholarships, work-study programs, and on- or off-campus employment. Funds come from federal, state, private, and school resources. Currently, 93 percent of Toccoa Falls College students receive some type of aid. All students must submit the Free Application for Federal Student Aid (FAFSA) to apply for specific programs. To receive priority consideration for maximum financial aid, students must submit all paperwork by May 1 for the fall semester and November 1 for the spring semester.

Faculty

Students at Toccoa Falls College benefit from professors who are academically qualified and experienced in their field and take a personal interest in their students. While their main responsibility is teaching students, many faculty members are recognized nationally and also publish books, write for major magazines, serve in national organizations, or are featured guest speakers and lecturers. Their primary role on campus is active involvement in the interests of the students and as faculty advisers to assist in the course selection and academic counseling needs of the students. All courses at TFC are taught by degree-holding faculty members, not student-aide teachers. Fifty-eight percent of full-time teaching faculty members hold earned doctoral degrees or the highest degree in their field. There are 68 faculty members; 45 are full-time and 23 are part-time. The student-faculty ratio is 15:1.

Student Government

The Student Government Association (SGA) acts as the umbrella organization over all student groups at Toccoa Falls College. SGA is the legislative and governing organization of the student body and the official representative of the student body to the TFC administration. The purpose of the SGA is to serve the student body, promote unity and spiritual growth, and control the student activity budget. SGA plays a vital role in organizing social events, activities, and spiritual meetings. SGA also stimulates communication between faculty and staff members and students and represents the needs of students to various official administrative committees.

Admission Requirements

TFC encourages applications from students who are interested in studying in an evangelical Christian environment. In selecting students for admission, Toccoa Falls College seeks evidence of Christian commitment and character, as well as the capacity and desire to learn. The Office of Admissions considers applications for admission after the applicant file is complete. A completed admissions file includes a completed and signed application, a $25 nonrefundable application fee, an official high school or GED transcript, official transcripts from all colleges attended, an official SAT or ACT score report, a 250-word testimony, and a pastoral reference. In addition, Toccoa Falls College has the following spiritual requirements: students must have accepted the Lord Jesus Christ as Savior at least six months prior to enrollment; have evidence of good Christian character; have abstained from the use of tobacco, alcohol, and illegal drugs for at least six months prior to enrollment; have regular attendance in an evangelical church; and be in agreement with the College's doctrinal statement and policies, as printed in the current catalog and student handbook. All new freshman, transfer, international, former, joint-enrolled, transient, and audit-only students from both in and out of state are considered on an equal basis. Campus visits and personal interviews with admissions counselors are highly encouraged. Toccoa Falls College reserves the right to examine further an applicant via psychological, achievement, and aptitude tests or personal interview. Toccoa Falls College admits qualified students without regard to race, age, creed, color, gender, physical handicap, or national or ethnic origin.

Application and Information

Qualified students are encouraged to apply as early as possible after the final semester of their junior year in high school. Toccoa Falls College makes admissions decisions on a rolling basis and notifies applicants of their admission status via e-mail, mail, and phone within one week after all materials are received.

For more information, students should contact:

Office of Admissions
Toccoa Falls College
P.O. Box 800–899
Toccoa Falls, Georgia 30598
Phone: 706-886-7299 Ext. 5380
888-785-5624 (toll-free)
Fax: 706-282-6012
E-mail: admissions@tfc.edu
Web site: http://www.tfc.edu

The Toccoa Falls College campus has a beautiful 186-foot waterfall.

UNIVERSITY OF WEST GEORGIA

CARROLLTON, GEORGIA

The University

A coeducational, residential institution, the University of West Georgia (UWG) is a charter member of the University System of Georgia. From its beginnings in 1906 as the Fourth District Agricultural and Mechanical School, West Georgia has grown into a leading comprehensive university that enrolled 10,677 students in fall 2007 from Georgia, forty other states, and eighty-one other countries. About 63 percent of enrolled students are women, and 33 percent belong to minority groups. Today, UWG offers 109 programs of study through three colleges—the College of Arts and Sciences, the Richards College of Business, and the College of Education. Fifty-six programs are available at the bachelor's level, forty at the master's and specialist levels, two at the doctoral level, eight at the postbaccalaureate certificate level, and two at the post-master's certificate level; one certificate is offered that can be earned in less than a year. In addition, the Honors College, the only college of its kind in Georgia, offers an honors curriculum, and the University's Advanced Academy of Georgia is one of approximately fifteen residential early-entrance programs in the nation that allows gifted high school–aged students to live and study full-time at a university while completing high school graduation requirements in absentia. The Graduate School has one of the highest percentages of students enrolled in graduate classes in the University System of Georgia.

UWG takes its mission of Educational Excellence in a Personal Environment seriously. Faculty members teach their own courses and take a personal interest in students. Undergraduates receive access to technology and research opportunities that are not usually available at other schools. In 2003, the Southern Association of Colleges and Schools (SACS) gave UWG a rare commendation for technology resources, equipment, and support, which a SACS visiting team called "far above that of similar institutions." Freshmen live on campus in one of nine residence halls, and every residence hall has an Internet port for each occupant. If they wish, freshmen can join a learning community of students who live in the same hall, share classes, and often earn higher grades as a result of this arrangement. Extracurricular activities are sponsored through approximately 100 student organizations, which cover academics, professional and honor groups, politics, religion, service, recreation and sports, social fraternities and sororities, and a national champion debate team. The UWG Department of Athletics offers a varied and comprehensive intercollegiate program. The University fields teams in eleven sports and competes in the Gulf South Conference of NCAA Division II. Women's teams compete in basketball, cross-country, golf, soccer, softball, and volleyball; men's teams compete in baseball, basketball, cross-country, football, and golf. UWG also has a national champion cheerleading program. The coed squad has captured seven consecutive national Universal Cheerleading Association Division II titles since 2002, and the all-girls' team won the honor in 2004, 2006, 2007, and 2008.

The University of West Georgia is accredited by the Commission on Colleges of the Southern Association of Colleges and Schools to award bachelor's, master's, education specialist, and doctoral degrees. All programs preparing teachers through the master's level are accredited by the National Council for Accreditation of Teacher Education, and the Georgia Professional Standards Commission approves UWG to recommend candidates for education certificates. The College of Education and community counseling programs are accredited by the Council for Accreditation of Counseling and Related Educational Programs. The speech-language pathology program is accredited by the American Speech-Language-Hearing Association. The undergraduate Bachelor of Business Administration and graduate Master of Business Administration and Master of Professional Accounting degrees in the Richards College of Business are accredited by AACSB International–The Association to Advance Collegiate Schools of Business. Only seventeen institutions in Georgia hold this accreditation. Both the Bachelor and Master of Professional Accounting programs are accredited separately by AACSB International. The University's Department of Chemistry is accredited by the American Chemical Society, the Department of Psychology by the Council for Humanistic Transpersonal Psychology, and the computer science program by the Computing Accreditation Commission of the Accreditation Board for Engineering and Technology. The Master of Public Administration degree is accredited by the National Association of Schools of Public Affairs and Administration. Other programs are accredited by the Commission on Collegiate Nursing Education, the National Association of Schools of Theatre, and the National Association of Schools of Music. All art programs are accredited by the National Association of Schools of Art and Design.

Location

Fifty miles west of Atlanta, the campus extends over more than 375 wooded acres, and its picturesque blend of pre–Civil War and late-twentieth-century architecture complements the similar Southern style of surrounding Carrollton, Georgia. Named a City of Excellence in Georgia and listed in *The Best Small Southern Towns* (Peachtree Publishers, 2001), Carrollton is the cultural, educational, health-care, and commercial center for the west Georgia region. A progressive city of about 22,000 with a diverse economic base, Carrollton offers a wide range of opportunities for professional work experiences as well as cultural activities and entertainment. Shops, galleries, and restaurants line the revitalized downtown square, and the city offers movies, dancing, theatrical productions, and dining that ranges from Southern to gourmet and international cuisine. A $6-million Cultural Arts Center showcases the arts, and recreational activities abound through an award-winning parks and recreation program and the county's 34,000 acres of state, public, and private recreational parks and facilities.

Majors and Degrees

UWG offers eleven baccalaureate degrees as follows: Bachelor of Arts in anthropology, art, biology, chemistry, chemistry/secondary education, English, French, geography, German, global studies, history, international economic affairs, mass communications, mathematics, philosophy, political science, psychology, Spanish, and theater; Bachelor of Business Administration in accounting, economics, finance, management, management information systems, marketing, and real estate; Bachelor of Fine Arts in art and art education; Bachelor of Music in music education and in music with studies in business, performance, performance with emphasis in jazz studies, performance with emphasis in piano pedagogy, and theory and composition; Bachelor of Science in biology, biology/secondary education, computer science, criminology, earth science/secondary education, economics, economics/secondary education, geography, geology, mathematics, physics, physics/secondary education, political science, and sociology; Bachelor of Science in Chemistry; Bachelor of Science in Education in business education, early childhood education, middle grades education, physical education, special education, and speech-language pathology; Bachelor of Science in Environmental Science; Bachelor of Science in Environmental Studies; Bachelor of Science in Nursing; and Bachelor of Science in Recreation. Preprofessional programs are available in allied health, dental hygiene, dentistry, forestry, law, medicine, occupational therapy, pharmacy, physical therapy, physician assistant studies, and veterinary studies medicine. A dual-degree program in engineering is offered with Auburn University, Georgia Institute of Technology, Mercer University, and the University of Georgia.

Academic Programs

The academic year consists of two 15-week semesters that begin in August and January, and a summer semester that includes a May minisession and sessions in June and July. During the freshman and sophomore years, students complete the core curriculum, 60 semester hours of general education courses designed by the faculty to provide a foundation for all degree programs. Included in the core are courses in written and oral communication, mathematics, natural science, technology, social science, and the humanities and fine arts as well as courses designed to lead to one's chosen major. Undergraduates have nationally acclaimed access to research opportunities, and instruction is enhanced by faculty member research that is supported by more than $2.4 million in grants.

Off-Campus Programs

The UWG Bachelor of Science in Nursing program is offered in Rome, Georgia, at Georgia Highlands College; in Dalton, Georgia, at Hamilton Medical Center; and also at the University's Newnan Center in Newnan, Georgia. Other off-campus classes are also offered at the University's Newnan Center. Online courses are offered to students through the Distance and Distributed Education Center. Some degrees may be earned by attending only evening and weekend classes. The University of West Georgia has study-abroad opportunities for students at any academic level and in any major. Study-abroad programs for credit are offered in art (Bayeux and Paris); economics and finance (Carrollton, New York, and London); French language and civilization (Tours and Paris); geography (Canada); German language, history, and English (Germany); Japanese language and culture (Kagoshima); management and marketing (Carrollton and London); and Spanish language and culture (Cuernavaca). UWG students may also participate in University System of Georgia summer study-abroad programs, offering core courses in Athens, Berlin, Italy, London, Madrid, Paris, and St. Petersburg. Juniors and seniors may participate in semester- and year-long exchanges available with 141 institutions in forty countries.

Academic Facilities

The $19.5-million Technology-enhanced Learning Center (TLC) is a three-building complex that occupies more than 1 acre and features pioneering classroom and laboratory technology. TLC laboratories offer access to computers and tabletop labs for conducting hands-on experiments while receiving instruction, and about 2,600 computer network connections provide Internet access from virtually anywhere in the complex.

The new $22-million Campus Center houses a 13,000-square-foot fitness center with more than 200 pieces of exercise equipment, two fully equipped aerobics rooms, two indoor basketball courts, an ⅛-mile indoor track, and a 50-foot climbing wall. Personal trainers, fitness classes, and a wide range of intramural sports are available to all students, and recreation equipment can be checked out for such activities as canoeing, kayaking, backpacking, tennis, or baseball. Student organization offices and a 9,000-square-foot ballroom offer expansive areas for group activities, and a game room with pool tables, wide-screen TV, Xboxes, and other games is a great hangout after classes. Wireless service and Internet connections are available throughout the building.

The Townsend Center for the Performing Arts presents a number of special performances and concerts annually by local, regional, and national entertainers and personalities and is available for performances of theatrical and musical events by both student and community groups. The center features a 455-seat proscenium theater, a 155-seat experimental theater, a rehearsal room, dressing rooms, a costume shop, and a set design center.

Costs

Based on a 12-hour or more on-campus semester, tuition and fees for the 2007–08 school year were $1959 per semester for Georgia residents and $6395 per semester for nonresidents. Room charges were $1310 per semester, and board cost $1393 per semester. Books totaled approximately $1000 per semester, and other expenses varied by major. Part-time students are charged tuition and fees per semester credit hour.

Financial Aid

All applicants interested in federal and state financial aid programs must submit a Free Application for Federal Student Aid (FAFSA) and any required documents regarding their own and their family's financial resources. In order to receive financial aid at the University of West Georgia, students must be in good academic standing and they must be accepted for admission. The state of Georgia provides the HOPE Scholarship to eligible students who are Georgia residents. In addition, UWG offers outstanding students a variety of academic and performing arts scholarships. Some academic scholarships are available to students regardless of their major, and others are for students majoring in particular fields. Still others are designed to encourage students from a specific county or minority group to attend the University. Work programs that are open to students include the Federal Work-Study Program, student assistantships, internships, and cooperative work situations.

Faculty

UWG has 415 full-time faculty members, 79 percent of whom hold the terminal degree in their associated field. The student-faculty ratio is approximately 18:1.

Student Government

The Student Government Association deals with matters of student affairs, sets forth general principles of governance of the student body, and approves mandatory student fees. Any enrolled undergraduate or graduate student is eligible to participate in student government.

Admission Requirements

To ensure admission as a freshman, it is desirable for applicants to have a combined SAT score in the range of 950 or higher or an ACT composite score of 19 or higher as well as a high school grade point average in academic courses of 2.4 or higher. In fall 2007, entering freshmen had a mean SAT score of 1011 (509 critical reading, 502 math) and a mean GPA of 3.05. In addition, all freshman/freshman transfer applicants must complete 16 high school college preparatory units (including a math course higher than algebra II/geometry), according to standards approved by the University System of Georgia for admission to a four-year state university. Transfer students are considered for admission on the basis of their previous college records and such additional information as is pertinent to their academic abilities. A minimum college cumulative GPA of 2.0 is required for transfer admission.

Application and Information

Every undergraduate applicant must submit a formal application to the Admissions Office along with a $30 nonrefundable application processing fee. June 1 is the deadline for application and document submissions for fall semester, including final high school/college transcripts. Spring and summer semester deadlines are approximately November 15 for spring and May 15 for summer. Prospective students should visit the University's Web site for additional admissions requirement information. Beginning freshmen are encouraged to complete the application procedures during the first half of their senior year in high school. For further information, students should contact:

Director of Admissions
University of West Georgia
Carrollton, Georgia 30118
Phone: 678-839-4000
E-mail: admiss@westga.edu
Web site: http://www.westga.edu/~admiss

The Southern Association of Colleges and Schools (SACS) has given UWG a rare commendation for technology resources, equipment, and support "far above that of similar institutions."

WESLEYAN COLLEGE

MACON, GEORGIA

The College

Wesleyan College, chartered in 1836, has the distinction of being the world's first college chartered to grant degrees to women. Today, Wesleyan is still dedicated to the education of women and is regarded as one of the nation's finest liberal arts colleges. According to the seventh annual report of the National Survey of Student Engagement (NSSE), Wesleyan outperformed the top 10 percent of colleges and universities in all five categories studied: active and collaborative learning, enriching educational experiences, level of academic challenge, student-faculty interaction, and supportive campus environment.

Wesleyan is a four-year liberal arts college affiliated with the United Methodist Church. Enrollment is limited to fewer than 1,000 students, primarily to support a learner-based curriculum that limits classes to no more than 20 students and to provide opportunities for meaningful participation in the life of the College community. Wesleyan's student body has been cited as among the nation's most diverse. Students from across the U.S. and almost twenty other countries value a rigorous academic program renowned for its high quality. A student-faculty ratio of 10:1 ensures that each student is more than just a grade or a number. The acceptance rate of Wesleyan students into medical, law, business, and other graduate programs is exemplary.

Beyond the academic, Wesleyan offers a thriving residence life program, NCAA Division III athletics, a championship IHSA equestrian program, and meaningful opportunities for community involvement and leadership. The College's beautiful 200-acre wooded campus, along with thirty historically significant buildings, is listed in the National Register of Historic Places as the Wesleyan College Historic District. Beautiful, white-columned Georgian-style buildings surround a classic quadrangle that plays host to many College events. All residence halls have been recently renovated and offer single rooms and suites. On-campus apartment-style living is available. Approximately 90 percent of the students reside on campus.

A fine equestrian center and athletic complex (with fitness center, tennis courts, track, and lighted softball and soccer fields) complete the campus offerings. Other recreational facilities include a gymnasium with a heated pool and a lake with a jogging trail.

Most of the extracurricular activities of Wesleyan's students are coordinated through Activity Councils. The Campus Activities Board plans concert-dance weekends, events with nearby colleges, international fashion shows, holiday trips, and special dinners. The Student Recreation Council coordinates competitive activities in basketball, fencing, golf, soccer, softball, swimming, among others. Wesleyan is a member of the National Collegiate Athletic Association (NCAA) Division III. There are intercollegiate basketball, cross-country, soccer, softball, tennis, volleyball, and IHSA equestrian teams. The Council on Religious Concerns encourages religious life on campus and sponsors activities that involve students with community life. Students volunteer at local institutions such as the Georgia Industrial Children's Home, Macon Outreach, the Methodist Children's Home, and neighborhood schools and churches. They also participate in interest clubs, student publications, performing arts groups, honor societies, and professional fraternities. A number of College traditions are perpetuated by spirited but friendly competition among the four classes.

Location

Wesleyan is located in a suburb of the beautiful, historic city of Macon, Georgia, the third-largest city in the state. Macon is the cultural, educational, medical, and economic leader of middle Georgia and is located about an hour's drive south of Atlanta. The city of Macon offers varied entertainment and many cultural opportunities, including the Georgia Music and Sports Halls of Fame. Visits by nationally and internationally acclaimed speakers and a series of popular and classical concerts are held on the Wesleyan campus each year, as are special events associated with Macon's renowned Cherry Blossom Festival.

Majors and Degrees

Wesleyan College offers undergraduate degrees in thirty-five majors and twenty-nine minors, including self-designed majors and interdisciplinary programs as well as eight preprofessional programs, including dental, engineering, health sciences, law, medicine, pharmacy, seminary, and veterinary medicine. Master of Arts degrees in education and an accelerated Executive Master of Business Administration program enroll both men and women. Wesleyan also offers a dual-degree program in engineering with the Georgia Institute of Technology in Atlanta; Auburn University in Auburn, Alabama; and Mercer University in Macon.

The Bachelor of Arts (A.B.) is offered in advertising and marketing communication, art history, biology, business administration (concentration in accounting or management), chemistry, computer information systems, communication, economics, education (early childhood and middle grades), English, environmental science, French, history, humanities, international business, international relations, mathematics, music (performance emphasis—piano, organ, and voice), philosophy, physics, political science, psychology, religious studies, Spanish, studio art, and theater. In addition to these majors, the following academic concentrations are offered as minors: African American studies, African studies, art history, biology, business management, chemistry, communication, computer science, economics, environmental studies, English, finance, French, history, mathematics, music, neuroscience, philosophy, photography, physics, political science, psychology, religious studies, socio-cultural studies, Spanish, studio art, technology in business administration, theater, and women's studies. Self-designed interdisciplinary majors are also available.

Students may elect to pursue their academic or professional interests through a double major, a major in combination with a minor program of studies, an interdisciplinary major, or an independently developed program of studies.

Wesleyan's dual-degree program in engineering is offered in cooperation with Georgia Institute of Technology, Auburn University, and Mercer University. Three years of study at Wesleyan and two years of study at Georgia Tech, Auburn, or Mercer lead to an A.B. degree from Wesleyan and a B.S. degree from the other institution. Wesleyan's traditional undergraduate programs for women are complemented by a growing number of day, evening, and weekend degree and certificate programs for nontraditional students seeking a flexible schedule.

Academic Programs

The College's goal is to prepare students for a lifetime of learning and change. Each major program contains general education requirements for breadth of learning and major field requirements for career and/or graduate school preparation. All degree programs require the completion of 120 semester hours with a cumulative average of C (2.0) or better.

Wesleyan provides a challenging academic environment coupled with individualized attention. Each student is assisted by a faculty adviser, a preprofessional or career adviser, and a peer counselor in the selection of academic and internship experiences that lead to intellectual and career fulfillment. All classes are offered in a seminar style, with an emphasis on interactive or participatory learning. Each student has a research or internship experience.

Each entering full-time student has the option to purchase a personal computer, for which the College offers special financing options. The ability to utilize information technology toward the enhancement of learning and career preparation is central to the academic program. The networked campus is connected to the Internet, which gives each student access to a world of information from her residence hall. Many common academic areas offer wireless Internet access.

Credit by examination and exemption from required courses are possible with acceptable scores on the Advanced Placement (AP), International Baccalaureate (I.B.), Cambridge International Examinations (CIE), and College-Level Examination Program (CLEP) tests or acceptable grades in high school–college joint enrollment courses. Students may also exempt courses by taking departmental examinations. Thirty semester hours of credit is the maximum a student can receive by exemption through AP, I.B., CIE, CLEP, or departmental exams.

The College operates on an early semester plan. First-semester classes begin in late August and end in early December. The second semester begins in the beginning of January and ends with graduation in early May. Wesleyan College offers an optional May term as well as two summer school sessions.

Off-Campus Programs

Through Wesleyan's International Study Abroad and Exchange Program, students can study abroad for one full year, one semester, a May term, or a summer session. Through cooperative agreements with the Institute for the International Education of Students (IES), National Student Exchange (NSE), and Business Education Initiative (BEI) students may study abroad in Argentina, Australia, Austria, China, France, Germany, Great Britain, Japan, Russia, Spain, and other countries. In addition, Wesleyan has direct exchange agreements with Sookmyung Women's University (South Korea), Osaka University (Japan), Ewha Women's University (South Lorea), Ulyanovsk State University (Russia), and various schools in Northern Ireland.

Off-campus opportunities in Macon are available through the Internship Program, which places students with area businesses, community agencies, health organizations, arts groups, and the media. Summer internships can be arranged through the Governor's Intern Program, in a student's hometown, and in other locations. Academic credit given for off-campus experiences varies.

Academic Facilities

Willet Memorial Library offers a variety of print and electronic resources to support student research and the College's curriculum. The core collection includes more than 143,000 volumes plus subscriptions to 615 periodicals. There are 33,438 items in microform and 4,267 tapes and records. Through the library's participation in GALILEO, students have access to more than 150 bibliographic and full-text databases. The library has informal study areas, individual carrels, seminar rooms, and two smart classrooms. The Georgia Room houses 4,500 rare volumes and treasures of Americana.

The Porter Fine Arts Building serves as a cultural center for the campus and community. It houses the music and theater departments, and, in addition to classrooms, offices, and studios, it contains two art galleries and a studio theater. Its Porter Auditorium has a seating capacity of 1,200 and contains one of the largest pipe organs in the Southeast. Tate Hall contains classrooms for the Humanities, Social Science, and Education divisions. Taylor Hall is currently under renovation but will soon house the Education division and offer new classroom spaces. The art department is located in a 10,000-square-foot building designed exclusively for teaching the studio arts.

The new Munroe Science Center (2007) is a state-of-the-art science facility that serves the increasing number of Wesleyan students enrolled and majoring in biology, chemistry, psychology, and computer science. It also addresses the great need throughout the nation for women skilled in medicine, scientific research, computer technology, and mathematics. Through its eleven teaching laboratories and nine research laboratories, the new facility encourages faculty/student collaboration on research projects, contains interactive laboratories for specific experimentation, and offers individualized instruction in an environmentally efficient and safe setting. State-of-the-art laboratories include cell biology, ecology, physiology, immunology, and instrumental analysis labs as well as general biology, physics, and chemistry labs. Although teaching laboratories serve as classrooms, a small seminar room and two technologically advanced classrooms also are used for instruction. Specialty science spaces include an astronomy observation deck, a greenhouse, a vivarium, an environmental room, and a community learning center.

Costs

Tuition for 2007–08 was $16,500. Room and board cost $7600. Students should also keep in mind the additional cost of books, supplies, travel, and personal expenses.

Financial Aid

Students seeking financial assistance are required to submit the Free Application for Federal Student Aid (FAFSA). Any student who demonstrates financial need is qualified for some type of assistance.

Wesleyan offers scholarships to incoming first-year students on the basis of academic ability, leadership, or special talents. Transfer scholarships are available based on cumulative grade point average and hours earned. Minimum requirements are a 3.0 GPA and 30 semester hours or 45 quarter hours.

Wesleyan participates in the Federal Perkins Loan, Federal Pell Grant, Federal Supplemental Educational Opportunity Grant, Federal Work-Study, and Federal Family Education Loan programs. Any resident of Georgia who wishes to attend a private college in the state and has at least a B average may apply for the Georgia Tuition Equalization Grant and HOPE Grant. Georgia Student Incentive Grants are also available, as are certain loans, other scholarships, and part-time employment. Approximately 85 percent of Wesleyan's students receive financial assistance.

Faculty

The academic program at Wesleyan is guided by an exceptionally able, dedicated, and caring faculty. There are 52 full-time faculty members; 49 have earned doctoral or terminal degrees. The student-faculty ratio is 10:1. No courses are ever taught by graduate assistants. Faculty members serve as academic advisers and help students plan their academic program. Many professors participate in extracurricular activities with students on campus.

Student Government

Wesleyan's Student Government Association (SGA) represents the Wesleyan student body. Students elect representatives to serve on Senate, which is the legislative body. SGA emphasizes responsibility and order, and supports an active liberal arts environment. SGA contributes to cocurricular life at the College, development of leadership and responsible citizenship, in conjunction with Student Affairs.

Admission Requirements

Applicants to Wesleyan must submit a completed application with a $30 application fee, official academic transcripts, official SAT or ACT scores, an evaluation written by a teacher, a recommendation from a guidance counselor or principal, and an essay. The completion of a minimum of 16 academic course units in a secondary school is required. Wesleyan feels that a campus visit is extremely beneficial, and visitors can be full participants in campus activities. An interview is strongly recommended. Applications from transfer and international students are welcome. Credit for work below a grade of C cannot be transferred, and a minimum score of 550 paper-based and 213 computer-based on the Test of English as Foreign Language (TOEFL) is required of international students. Wesleyan accepts qualified students without regard to race, religion, national or ethnic origin, age, sexual orientation, or disability.

Application and Information

Admission to Wesleyan is selective. For additional information or to request an application form, students should contact:

Vice President for Enrollment Services and Student Affairs
Wesleyan College
4760 Forsyth Road
Macon, Georgia 31210-4462
Phone: 478-757-5206
800-447-6610 (toll-free)
E-mail: admission@wesleyancollege.edu
Web site: http://www.wesleyancollege.edu

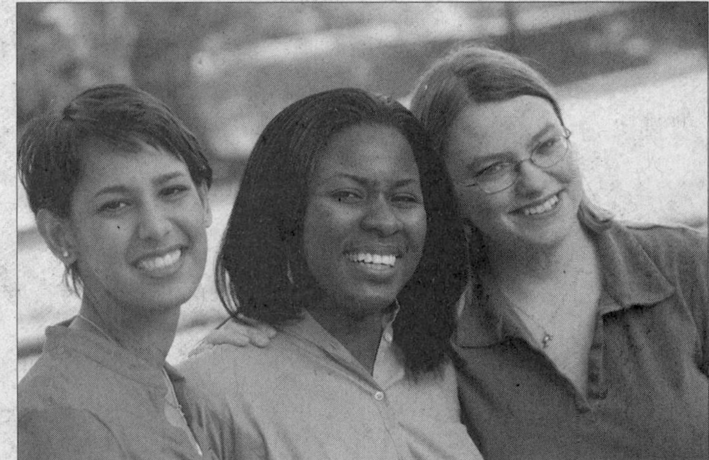

Wesleyan has the distinction of being the world's first college chartered to grant degrees to women.

GUAM

Agana

Mangilao

North Pacific Ocean

PACIFIC ISLANDS BIBLE COLLEGE

Mangilao, Guam **www.pibc.edu**

- **Independent interdenominational** 4-year, founded 1976
- **Coed** 188 undergraduate students, 70% full-time, 57% women, 43% men

Undergraduates 132 full-time, 56 part-time. 97% Asian American or Pacific Islander, 1% international.

Freshmen *Admission:* 30 enrolled.

Faculty *Total:* 22, 55% full-time, 68% with terminal degrees. *Student/faculty ratio:* 7:1.

Majors Religious studies.

Academics *Calendar:* semesters.

Costs (2007–08) *Comprehensive fee:* $11,030 includes full-time tuition ($7650), mandatory fees ($520), and room and board ($2860). Full-time tuition and fees vary according to course load and location. Part-time tuition: $765 per course. Part-time tuition and fees vary according to course load and location. *Required fees:* $185 per term part-time. *Room and board:* Room and board charges vary according to housing facility and location. *Payment plan:* installment. *Waivers:* minority students and employees or children of employees.

Applying *Application fee:* $25. *Required:* essay or personal statement, high school transcript, 2 letters of recommendation, interview. *Required for some:* TOEFL score. *Application deadline:* 8/25 (freshmen).

Freshman Application Contact Ethel Laco, Admissions Office, Pacific Islands Bible College, PO Box 22619, Guam Main Facility, GU 96921-2619. *Phone:* 671-734-1812. *Fax:* 671-734-1813. *E-mail:* guamcampus@pibc.edu.

UNIVERSITY OF GUAM

Mangilao, Guam **www.uog.edu/**

- **Territory-supported** comprehensive, founded 1952
- **Suburban** 100-acre campus
- **Endowment** $6.0 million
- **Coed** 3,020 undergraduate students, 72% full-time, 62% women, 38% men
- **Noncompetitive** entrance level

Undergraduates 2,180 full-time, 840 part-time. Students come from 15 states and territories, 7 other countries, 1% are from out of state, 0.7% African American, 91% Asian American or Pacific Islander, 0.7% Hispanic American, 0.3% Native American, 0.9% international, 0.5% transferred in. *Retention:* 63% of 2006 full-time freshmen returned.

Freshmen *Admission:* 572 enrolled.

Faculty *Total:* 249, 71% full-time. *Student/faculty ratio:* 13:1.

Majors Accounting; agriculture; anthropology; art; art teacher education; Asian studies (East); biological and physical sciences; biology/biological sciences; business administration and management; chemistry; computer science; criminal justice/law enforcement administration; criminal justice/police science; economics; education; elementary education; English; family and consumer sciences/home economics teacher education; finance; history; international business/trade/commerce; kindergarten/preschool education; marketing/marketing management; mass communication/media; mathematics; music teacher education; nursing (registered nurse training); physical education teaching and coaching; physical sciences; political science and government; psychology; public administration; secondary education; social work; sociology; special education.

Academics *Calendar:* semesters. *Degrees:* bachelor's and master's. *Special study options:* academic remediation for entering students, accelerated degree program, advanced placement credit, double majors, English as a second language, honors programs, internships, services for LD students, summer session for credit. *ROTC:* Army (b).

Computers on Campus 150 computers/terminals are available on campus for general student use.

Student Life *Housing options:* coed. Campus housing is university owned. *Activities and organizations:* drama/theater group, student-run newspaper, choral group. *Campus security:* 24-hour emergency response devices and patrols, late-night transport/escort service, controlled dormitory access. *Student services:* health clinic, personal/psychological counseling.

Athletics *Intercollegiate sports:* basketball M (s)/W (s), football M, golf M, soccer M (s), volleyball M (s)/W (s). *Intramural sports:* basketball M/W, bowling M/W, football M, golf M, soccer M, swimming and diving M/W, tennis M/W, volleyball M/W.

Costs (2008–09) *Tuition:* territory resident $4835 full-time, $173 per credit part-time; nonresident $14,414 full-time, $515 per credit part-time. *Required fees:* $450 full-time, $225 per term part-time.

Applying *Options:* early admission, deferred entrance. *Application fee:* $49. *Required:* high school transcript. *Application deadlines:* 6/1 (freshmen), 6/1 (transfers). *Notification:* continuous (freshmen), continuous (transfers).

Freshman Application Contact Dr. Julie Ulloa-Heath, Dean of Enrollment Management and Student Services, University of Guam, UOG Station, Mangilao, GU 96923. *Phone:* 671-735-2290. *E-mail:* julieuh@guam.uog.edu.

HAWAII

Kauai

Oahu
Pearl City
Laie
Honolulu

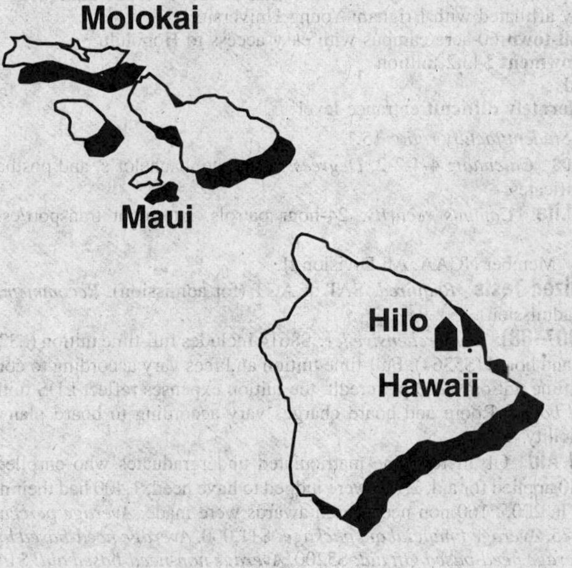
Molokai
Maui
Hilo
Hawaii

ARGOSY UNIVERSITY, HAWAI'I

Honolulu, Hawaii **www.argosy.edu/locations/hawaii/**

- **Proprietary** university, founded 1994
- **Coed**

Majors Business administration and management; finance; international business/trade/commerce; marketing/marketing management; psychology.

Academics *Calendar:* semesters.

Admissions Office Contact Argosy University, Hawai'i, 400 ASB Tower, 1001 Bishop Street, Honolulu, HI 96813. *Toll-free phone:* 888-323-2777

See page 770 for the College Close-Up.

BRIGHAM YOUNG UNIVERSITY–HAWAII

Laie, Hawaii **www.byuh.edu/**

- **Independent Latter-day Saints** 4-year, founded 1955, administratively affiliated with Brigham Young University
- **Small-town** 60-acre campus with easy access to Honolulu
- **Endowment** $43.2 million
- **Coed**
- **Moderately difficult** entrance level

Faculty *Student/faculty ratio:* 15:1.

Academics *Calendar:* 4-4-2-2. *Degrees:* associate, bachelor's, and postbachelor's certificates.

Student Life *Campus security:* 24-hour patrols, late-night transport/escort service.

Athletics Member NCAA. All Division II.

Standardized Tests *Required:* SAT or ACT (for admission). *Recommended:* ACT (for admission).

Costs (2007–08) *Comprehensive fee:* $8614 includes full-time tuition ($3250) and room and board ($5364). Full-time tuition and fees vary according to course load. Part-time tuition: $203 per credit. the tuition expenses reflect LDS tuition. *Room and board:* Room and board charges vary according to board plan and housing facility.

Financial Aid Of all full-time matriculated undergraduates who enrolled in 2006, 2,230 applied for aid, 2,185 were judged to have need, 1,400 had their need fully met. In 2006, 160 non-need-based awards were made. *Average percent of need met:* 75. *Average financial aid package:* $11,000. *Average need-based loan:* $3700. *Average need-based gift aid:* $5200. *Average non-need-based aid:* $1400. *Average indebtedness upon graduation:* $12,418. *Financial aid deadline:* 3/31.

Applying *Options:* electronic application, early admission, deferred entrance. *Application fee:* $30. *Required:* essay or personal statement, high school transcript, minimum 3.0 GPA, resume of activities, ecclesiastical endorsement. *Required for some:* letters of recommendation.

Freshman Application Contact Mr. Arapata P. Meha, Brigham Young University–Hawaii, 55-220 Kulanui Street, BYUH 1973, Laie, Oahu, HI 96762. *Phone:* 808-293-3731. *Fax:* 808-293-3741. *E-mail:* admissions@byuh.edu.

CHAMINADE UNIVERSITY OF HONOLULU

Honolulu, Hawaii **www.chaminade.edu/**

- **Independent Roman Catholic** comprehensive, founded 1955
- **Urban** 62-acre campus
- **Endowment** $8.4 million
- **Coed** 2,004 undergraduate students, 66% full-time, 64% women, 36% men
- **Minimally difficult** entrance level, 94% of applicants were admitted

Undergraduates 1,321 full-time, 683 part-time. Students come from 40 states and territories, 10 other countries, 50% are from out of state, 7% African American, 48% Asian American or Pacific Islander, 9% Hispanic American, 0.8% Native American, 1% international, 6% transferred in, 32% live on campus. *Retention:* 64% of 2006 full-time freshmen returned.

Freshmen *Admission:* 784 applied, 735 admitted, 337 enrolled. *Average high school GPA:* 3.08. *Test scores:* SAT critical reading scores over 500: 42%; SAT math scores over 500: 42%; ACT scores over 18: 85%; SAT critical reading scores over 600: 10%; SAT math scores over 600: 10%; ACT scores over 24: 24%; SAT critical reading scores over 700: 1%; SAT math scores over 700: 1%; ACT scores over 30: 2%.

Faculty *Total:* 131, 63% full-time, 44% with terminal degrees. *Student/faculty ratio:* 12:1.

Majors Accounting; behavioral sciences; biology/biological sciences; business administration and management; computer and information sciences; computer science; criminology; early childhood education; elementary education; English; environmental studies; forensic science and technology; general studies; history; humanities; interior design; international relations and affairs; marketing/marketing management; mass communication/media; psychology; religious studies; social sciences.

Academics *Calendar:* semesters. *Degrees:* associate, bachelor's, master's, and postbachelor's certificates. *Special study options:* academic remediation for entering students, accelerated degree program, adult/continuing education programs, advanced placement credit, distance learning, double majors, independent study, internships, off-campus study, part-time degree program, student-designed majors, summer session for credit. *ROTC:* Army (c), Air Force (c). *Unusual degree programs:* 3-2 engineering with University of Dayton, St. Mary's University of San Antonio; mathematics with St. Mary's University of San Antonio.

Computers on Campus 90 computers/terminals are available on campus for general student use. Students can access the following: computer help desk, free student e-mail accounts, online (class) grades, online (class) registration, online (class) schedules. Campuswide network is available. Wireless service is available via computer centers, computer labs, dorm rooms, learning centers, libraries, student centers.

Student Life *Housing options:* coed, women-only. Campus housing is university owned and leased by the school. *Activities and organizations:* drama/theater group, student-run newspaper, choral group, Lumana O Samoa (Samoan Club), Kaimi Lalakea (Hawaiian Club), Rotaract Club, Residence Hall Association, Chaminade Student Government Association. *Campus security:* 24-hour emergency response devices and patrols, late-night transport/escort service, controlled dormitory access. *Student services:* personal/psychological counseling.

Athletics Member NCAA. All Division II. *Intercollegiate sports:* basketball M (s), cross-country running M (s)/W (s), golf M/W, softball W (s), tennis M (s)/W (s), volleyball W (s), water polo M (s).

Standardized Tests *Required:* SAT or ACT (for admission).

Costs (2008–09) *Comprehensive fee:* $26,560 includes full-time tuition ($16,000), mandatory fees ($140), and room and board ($10,420). Part-time tuition: $533 per credit. *College room only:* $5300.

Financial Aid Of all full-time matriculated undergraduates who enrolled in 2004, 852 applied for aid, 762 were judged to have need, 106 had their need fully met. 120 Federal Work-Study jobs (averaging $1500). In 2004, 176 non-need-based awards were made. *Average percent of need met:* 65%. *Average financial aid package:* $12,846. *Average need-based loan:* $4156. *Average need-based gift aid:* $8257. *Average non-need-based aid:* $4565. *Average indebtedness upon graduation:* $22,263.

Applying *Options:* electronic application, deferred entrance. *Application fee:* $50. *Required:* essay or personal statement, high school transcript. *Required for some:* interview. *Recommended:* minimum 2.25 GPA. *Application deadlines:* rolling (freshmen), rolling (transfers). *Notification:* continuous (freshmen), continuous (transfers).

Freshman Application Contact Martin Motooka, Assistant Director, Chaminade University of Honolulu, 3140 Waialae Avenue, Honolulu, HI 96816-1578. *Phone:* 808-735-4735. *Toll-free phone:* 800-735-3733. *Fax:* 808-739-4647. *E-mail:* admissions@chaminade.edu.

HAWAI'I PACIFIC UNIVERSITY

Honolulu, Hawaii **www.hpu.edu/**

- **Independent** comprehensive, founded 1965
- **Urban** 140-acre campus
- **Endowment** $79.0 million
- **Coed** 6,675 undergraduate students, 61% full-time, 61% women, 39% men
- **Moderately difficult** entrance level, 82% of applicants were admitted

Strategically situated at the crossroads of East and West, Hawai'i Pacific University (HPU) is the ideal location for anyone interested in living and learning in an international setting. More than 8,000 students from all fifty states and more than 100 countries make HPU one of the most diverse universities in the United States.

Undergraduates 4,041 full-time, 2,634 part-time. Students come from 53 states and territories, 105 other countries, 30% are from out of state, 6% African American, 39% Asian American or Pacific Islander, 7% Hispanic American, 1% Native American, 9% international, 12% transferred in, 10% live on campus. *Retention:* 69% of 2006 full-time freshmen returned.

Freshmen *Admission:* 2,948 applied, 2,415 admitted, 616 enrolled. *Average high school GPA:* 3.21. *Test scores:* SAT critical reading scores over 500: 46%; SAT math scores over 500: 42%; SAT writing scores over 500: 39%; ACT scores over 18: 79%; SAT critical reading scores over 600: 11%; SAT math scores over 600: 10%; SAT writing scores over 600: 9%; ACT scores over 24: 21%; SAT critical reading scores over 700: 2%; SAT math scores over 700: 2%; SAT writing scores over 700: 1%; ACT scores over 30: 2%.

Faculty *Total:* 592, 43% full-time, 45% with terminal degrees. *Student/faculty ratio:* 16:1.

Majors Accounting; advertising; American studies; anthropology; applied mathematics; Asian studies; biology/biological sciences; broadcast journalism; business administration and management; business/commerce; business/corporate communications; chiropractic assistant; cinematography and film/video production; communication and journalism related; communication/speech communication and rhetoric; computer and information sciences; computer science; criminal justice/law enforcement administration; economics; engineering related; English; English as a second/foreign language (teaching); entrepreneurship; environmental science; environmental studies; ethnic, cultural minority, and gender studies related; European studies (Central and Eastern); finance; history; human resources development; human resources management; human services; intermedia/multimedia; international business/trade/commerce; international/global studies; international relations and affairs; journalism; management science; marine biology and biological oceanography; marketing/marketing management; mass communication/media; mathematics; mathematics teacher education; military studies; non-profit management; nursing (registered nurse training); occupational therapy; oceanography (chemical and physical); organizational behavior; Pacific area/Pacific rim studies; parks, recreation, and leisure related; photojournalism; physical therapy; political science and government; pre-law; pre-medical studies; psychology; public administration; public relations/image management; social sciences; social work; sociology; substance abuse/addiction counseling; tourism and travel services management; web/multimedia management and webmaster.

Academics *Calendar:* semesters. *Degrees:* certificates, associate, bachelor's, master's, post-master's, and postbachelor's certificates. *Special study options:* academic remediation for entering students, accelerated degree program, adult/continuing education programs, advanced placement credit, cooperative education, distance learning, double majors, English as a second language, freshman honors college, honors programs, independent study, internships, off-campus study, part-time degree program, services for LD students, student-designed majors, study abroad, summer session for credit. *ROTC:* Army (c), Air Force (c). *Unusual degree programs:* 3-2 engineering with Washington University in St. Louis, University of Southern California; S+1 Education Program Teacher Licensing and M.Ed in secondary education.

Computers on Campus 590 computers/terminals are available on campus for general student use. Students can access the following: online (class) registration. Campuswide network is available.

Student Life *Housing options:* coed. Campus housing is university owned and is provided by a third party. Freshman applicants given priority for college housing. *Activities and organizations:* drama/theater group, student-run newspaper, choral group, Association of Students of HPU, Swedish Student Association, President's Hosts, Akamai Advertising, Christian Fellowship. *Campus security:* 24-hour emergency response devices and patrols, student patrols, late-night transport/escort service, controlled dormitory access. *Student services:* health clinic, personal/psychological counseling.

Athletics Member NCAA. All Division II.

Standardized Tests *Required:* SAT or ACT (for admission).

Costs (2008–09) *Comprehensive fee:* $23,640 includes full-time tuition ($13,000), mandatory fees ($80), and room and board ($10,560). Part-time tuition: $542 per credit.

Financial Aid Of all full-time matriculated undergraduates who enrolled in 2007, 2,765 applied for aid, 1,699 were judged to have need, 407 had their need fully met. 206 Federal Work-Study jobs (averaging $3191). In 2007, 273 non-need-based awards were made. *Average percent of need met:* 77%. *Average financial aid package:* $12,890. *Average need-based loan:* $7251. *Average need-based gift aid:* $4240. *Average non-need-based aid:* $3458. *Average indebtedness upon graduation:* $19,000.

Applying *Options:* electronic application, early admission, deferred entrance. *Application fee:* $50. *Required:* high school transcript, minimum 2.5 GPA. *Required for some:* interview. *Recommended:* essay or personal statement, 2 letters of recommendation. *Application deadlines:* rolling (freshmen), rolling (transfers). *Notification:* continuous (transfers).

Freshman Application Contact Mr. Scott Stensrud, Vice President Enrollment Management, Hawai'i Pacific University, 1164 Bishop Street, Honolulu, HI 96813-2785. *Phone:* 808-544-0238. *Toll-free phone:* 866-225-5478. *Fax:* 808-544-1136. *E-mail:* admissions@hpu.edu.

See page 772 for the College Close-Up.

REMINGTON COLLEGE–HONOLULU CAMPUS

Honolulu, Hawaii **www.remingtoncollege.edu/**

- **Proprietary** 4-year
- **Coed**

Majors Computer systems networking and telecommunications; criminal justice/law enforcement administration; international business/trade/commerce; medical office assistant; operations management.

Academics *Degrees:* associate and bachelor's.

Director of Admissions Louis LaMair, Director of Recruitment, Remington College–Honolulu Campus, 1111 Bishop Street, Suite 400, Honolulu, HI 96813. *Phone:* 808-942-1000. *Fax:* 808-533-3064. *E-mail:* louis.lamair@remingtoncollege.edu.

UNIVERSITY OF HAWAII AT HILO

Hilo, Hawaii **www.uhh.hawaii.edu/**

- **State-supported** comprehensive, founded 1970, part of University of Hawaii System
- **Small-town** 115-acre campus
- **Endowment** $2.8 million
- **Coed**
- **Moderately difficult** entrance level

Faculty *Student/faculty ratio:* 11:1.

Academics *Calendar:* semesters. *Degrees:* certificates, bachelor's, master's, and postbachelor's certificates.

Student Life *Campus security:* 24-hour emergency response devices and patrols, controlled dormitory access.

Athletics Member NCAA. All Division II except baseball (Division I).

Standardized Tests *Required:* SAT or ACT (for admission).

Costs (2007–08) *Tuition:* state resident $3528 full-time, $147 per credit hour part-time; nonresident $11,064 full-time, $544 per credit hour part-time. Full-time tuition and fees vary according to reciprocity agreements. Part-time tuition and fees vary according to course load. *Required fees:* $148 full-time, $41 per term part-time. *Room and board:* $6850; room only: $3890. Room and board charges vary according to board plan and housing facility.

Financial Aid Of all full-time matriculated undergraduates who enrolled in 2007, 1,236 applied for aid, 1,223 were judged to have need, 176 had their need fully met. 188 Federal Work-Study jobs (averaging $1219). 434 state and other part-time jobs (averaging $2450). In 2007, 9 non-need-based awards were made. *Average percent of need met:* 68. *Average financial aid package:* $7233. *Average need-based loan:* $4375. *Average need-based gift aid:* $3855. *Average non-need-based aid:* $1370. *Average indebtedness upon graduation:* $13,952.

Applying *Options:* electronic application, deferred entrance. *Application fee:* $50. *Required:* high school transcript. *Required for some:* letters of recommendation. *Recommended:* minimum 3.0 GPA.

Freshman Application Contact Mr. James Cromwell, Student Services Specialist/Director of Admissions, University of Hawaii at Hilo, 200 West Kawili Street, Hilo, HI 96720-4091. *Phone:* 808-974-7414. *Toll-free phone:* 808-974-7414 (in-state); 800-897-4456 (out-of-state). *Fax:* 808-933-0861. *E-mail:* uhhao@hawaii.edu.

See page 774 for the College Close-Up.

UNIVERSITY OF HAWAII AT MANOA

Honolulu, Hawaii **www.uhm.hawaii.edu/**

- **State-supported** university, founded 1907
- **Urban** 300-acre campus
- **Endowment** $207.3 million
- **Coed** 14,037 undergraduate students, 82% full-time, 55% women, 45% men
- **Moderately difficult** entrance level, 68% of applicants were admitted

Undergraduates 11,473 full-time, 2,564 part-time. Students come from 86 other countries, 26% are from out of state, 1% African American, 63% Asian American or Pacific Islander, 2% Hispanic American, 0.5% Native American, 6% international, 13% transferred in, 13% live on campus. *Retention:* 76% of 2006 full-time freshmen returned.

Freshmen *Admission:* 6,167 applied, 4,208 admitted, 1,775 enrolled. *Average high school GPA:* 3.41. *Test scores:* SAT critical reading scores over 500: 66%; SAT math scores over 500: 81%; SAT writing scores over 500: 63%; ACT scores over 18: 95%; SAT critical reading scores over 600: 20%; SAT math scores over 600: 33%; SAT writing scores over 600: 14%; ACT scores over 24: 45%; SAT critical reading scores over 700: 2%; SAT math scores over 700: 6%; SAT writing scores over 700: 1%; ACT scores over 30: 4%.

Faculty *Total:* 1,272, 93% full-time, 87% with terminal degrees. *Student/faculty ratio:* 11:1.

Majors Accounting; agricultural economics; agricultural production; American studies; animal sciences; anthropology; architecture; art; Asian studies; biology/biological sciences; botany/plant biology; business/commerce; business/managerial economics; chemistry; Chinese; civil engineering; classics; communication/speech communication and rhetoric; computer and information sciences; computer science; counselor education/school counseling and guidance; dance; dental hygiene; dietetics; dramatic/theater arts; economics; education; electrical, electronics and communications engineering; elementary education; English; English as a second/foreign language (teaching); entomology; environmental science; environmental studies; ethnic, cultural minority, and gender studies related; family and consumer sciences/human sciences; fashion/apparel design; Filipino/Tagalog; finance; French; geography; geology/earth science; German; health and physical education; history; human development and family studies; human resources management; interdisciplinary studies; international business/trade/commerce; Japanese; journalism; kinesiology and exercise science; Korean; landscape architecture; linguistics; management information systems; marine biology; marketing/marketing management; mathematics; mechanical engineering; meteorology; microbiology; music; natural resources management; nursing (registered nurse training); Pacific area/Pacific rim studies; parks, recreation and leisure; peace studies and conflict resolution; philosophy; physical education teaching and coaching; physics; plant protection; political science and government; psychology; religious studies; Russian; Sanskrit and classical Indian languages; secondary education; social work; sociology; South Asian languages; Spanish; special education; speech and rhetoric; tourism and travel services management; women's studies; zoology/animal biology.

Academics *Calendar:* semesters. *Degrees:* bachelor's, master's, doctoral, first professional, and postbachelor's certificates. *Special study options:* accelerated degree program, advanced placement credit, cooperative education, distance learning, double majors, English as a second language, honors programs, independent study, internships, off-campus study, part-time degree program, services for LD students, student-designed majors, study abroad, summer session for credit. *ROTC:* Army (b), Air Force (b).

Computers on Campus 1,400 computers/terminals are available on campus for general student use. Students can access the following: online (class) registration. Campuswide network is available.

Student Life *Housing options:* coed, disabled students. Campus housing is university owned. *Activities and organizations:* drama/theater group, student-run newspaper, radio station, choral group, marching band, Associated Students of University of Hawaii, Campus Center Board, Broadcast Communication Authority, Board of Publications, Student Activities and Program Fee Board, national fraternities, national sororities. *Campus security:* 24-hour emergency response devices and patrols, student patrols, late-night transport/escort service, controlled dormitory access. *Student services:* health clinic, personal/psychological counseling, women's center.

Athletics Member NCAA. All Division I except football (Division I-A). *Intercollegiate sports:* baseball M (s), basketball M (s)/W (s), cross-country running W (s), golf M (s)/W (s), rugby M (c), sailing M/W, soccer W (s), softball W (s), swimming and diving M (s)/W (s), tennis M (s)/W (s), track and field W (s), volleyball M (s)/W (s), water polo W (s). *Intramural sports:* badminton M/W, basketball M/W, cross-country running M/W, golf M/W, table tennis M/W, tennis M/W, track and field M/W, volleyball M/W, weight lifting M/W.

Standardized Tests *Required:* SAT or ACT (for admission).

Costs (2007–08) *Tuition:* state resident $5136 full-time, $214 per credit hour part-time; nonresident $14,400 full-time, $600 per credit hour part-time. *Required fees:* $254 full-time. *Room and board:* $7185; room only: $4527.

Financial Aid Of all full-time matriculated undergraduates who enrolled in 2006, 6,365 applied for aid, 3,919 were judged to have need, 1,065 had their need fully met. 292 Federal Work-Study jobs (averaging $2192). In 2006, 2419 non-need-based awards were made. *Average percent of need met:* 68%. *Average financial aid package:* $7573. *Average need-based loan:* $3760. *Average need-based gift aid:* $4744. *Average non-need-based aid:* $4464. *Average indebtedness upon graduation:* $11,748.

Applying *Options:* electronic application. *Application fee:* $50. *Required:* high school transcript, minimum 2.8 GPA, minimum SAT score of 510 for verbal, math and writing sections. *Application deadlines:* 5/1 (freshmen), 5/1 (transfers). *Notification:* continuous (freshmen), continuous (transfers).

Freshman Application Contact Ms. Janice Heu, Interim Director of Admissions and Records, University of Hawaii at Manoa, 2600 Campus Road, Room 001, Honolulu, HI 96822. *Phone:* 808-956-8975. *Toll-free phone:* 800-823-9771. *Fax:* 808-956-4148. *E-mail:* ar-info@hawaii.edu.

UNIVERSITY OF HAWAII–WEST OAHU

Pearl City, Hawaii **www.uhwo.hawaii.edu/**

- **State-supported** upper-level, founded 1976, part of University of Hawaii System
- **Small-town** campus with easy access to Honolulu
- **Coed** 940 undergraduate students, 35% full-time, 69% women, 31% men
- **Moderately difficult** entrance level, 89% of applicants were admitted

Undergraduates 332 full-time, 608 part-time. Students come from 1 other country, 8% are from out of state, 2% African American, 62% Asian American or Pacific Islander, 2% Hispanic American, 0.5% Native American, 0.3% international, 31% transferred in.

Freshmen *Admission:* 622 applied, 551 admitted.

Faculty *Total:* 60, 65% full-time. *Student/faculty ratio:* 12:1.

Majors Anthropology; business administration and management; criminal justice/law enforcement administration; economics; elementary education; English; history; humanities; philosophy; political science and government; psychology; public administration; social sciences; sociology.

Academics *Calendar:* semesters. *Degree:* certificates and bachelor's. *Special study options:* advanced placement credit, distance learning, double majors, off-campus study, part-time degree program, services for LD students, study abroad, summer session for credit. *ROTC:* Army (c), Air Force (c).

Computers on Campus 18 computers/terminals are available on campus for general student use. Students can access the following: computer help desk, free student e-mail accounts, online (class) grades, online (class) registration, online (class) schedules. Campuswide network is available. Wireless service is available via classrooms.

Student Life *Housing:* college housing not available. *Campus security:* 24-hour emergency response devices and patrols, late-night transport/escort service. *Student services:* personal/psychological counseling.

Standardized Tests *Required for some:* SAT or ACT (for admission). *Recommended:* SAT or ACT (for admission).

Costs (2008–09) *Tuition:* state resident $3696 full-time, $154 per credit part-time; nonresident $11,568 full-time, $482 per credit part-time. *Required fees:* $10 full-time, $5 per term part-time.

Financial Aid Of all full-time matriculated undergraduates who enrolled in 2006, 125 applied for aid, 114 were judged to have need, 27 had their need fully met. 2 Federal Work-Study jobs (averaging $985). 52 state and other part-time jobs (averaging $2346). In 2006, 6 non-need-based awards were made. *Average financial aid package:* $5386. *Average need-based loan:* $3776. *Average need-based gift aid:* $3731. *Average non-need-based aid:* $2427.

Applying *Application fee:* $50. *Application deadline:* 8/1 (transfers). *Notification:* continuous (transfers).

Application Contact Robyn Oshiro, University of Hawaii–West Oahu, 96-129 Ala Ike, Pearl City, HI 96782. *Phone:* 808-454-4700. *Toll-free phone:* 808-454 Ext. 4700. *Fax:* 808-453-6075. *E-mail:* robyno@hawaii.edu.

UNIVERSITY OF PHOENIX–HAWAII CAMPUS

Honolulu, Hawaii **www.phoenix.edu/**

- **Proprietary** comprehensive
- **Urban** campus
- **Coed**
- **Noncompetitive** entrance level

Faculty *Student/faculty ratio:* 6:1.

Academics *Calendar:* continuous. *Degrees:* bachelor's and master's (courses conducted at 121 campuses and learning centers in 25 states).

Student Life *Campus security:* late-night transport/escort service.

Costs (2007–08) *Tuition:* $12,180 full-time, $406 per credit part-time. Full-time tuition and fees vary according to course level.

Financial Aid *Average financial aid package:* $4557. *Average need-based gift aid:* $2242.

Applying *Options:* deferred entrance. *Application fee:* $45. *Required:* 1 letter of recommendation. *Required for some:* high school transcript.

Freshman Application Contact Ms. Beth Barilla, Associate Vice President, Student Admissions and Services, University of Phoenix–Hawaii Campus, 4615 East Elwood Street, Mail Stop AA-K101, Phoenix, AZ 85040-1958. *Phone:* 480-317-6000. *Toll-free phone:* 800-776-4867 (in-state); 800-228-7240 (out-of-state). *Fax:* 480-894-1758. *E-mail:* beth.barilla@phoenix.edu.

ARGOSY UNIVERSITY

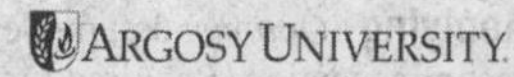

The University

Argosy University is a leading institution offering a variety of degree programs that focus on the human side of success alongside professional competence. For students looking for a more personal approach to education, Argosy University may just be the answer. With forty-eight graduate and undergraduate programs, across nineteen campuses and twelve states, Argosy University emphasizes interpersonal skills as well as academic learning. All of its programs are taught by practicing professionals who bring real-world experience into the classroom. So students graduate with both a solid foundation of knowledge and the power to put it to work. To accommodate busy working adults, many programs at Argosy University are structured flexibly—with both campus and online learning and evening, weekend, and daytime classes. There is also a wide range of financial aid options for students who qualify.

Argosy University is a private institution of higher education dedicated to providing high-quality professional education programs at the doctoral, master's, bachelor's, and associate degree levels as well as continuing education to individuals who seek to advance their professional and personal lives. The University emphasizes programs in the behavioral sciences (psychology and counseling), business, education, and the health-care professions. A limited number of preprofessional programs and general education offerings are provided to permit students to prepare for entry into these professional fields. The programs of Argosy University are designed to instill the knowledge, skills, and ethical values of professional practice and to foster values of social responsibility in a supportive, learning-centered environment of mutual respect and professional excellence.

With nineteen campuses nationwide, Argosy University provides students with a network of resources found at larger universities, including a career resources office, an academic resources center, and extensive information access for research. The University's innovative programs feature dynamic, relevant, and practical curricula delivered in flexible class formats. Students enjoy scheduling options that make it easier to fit school into their busy lives. They can choose from day and evening courses, on campus or online. Many students find a combination of both to be an ideal way of continuing their education while meeting family and professional demands.

Most students are full-time working professionals who live within driving distance of the campus. The University does not offer or operate student housing.

Argosy University is accredited by The Higher Learning Commission of the North Central Association (30 North LaSalle Street, Suite 2400, Chicago, Illinois 60602; 800-621-7440; http://ncahlc.org).

Location

Argosy University operates nineteen locations across the U.S. and offers a variety of degree programs online (http://www.argosy.edu). Campus locations include the following:

Atlanta, 980 Hammond Drive, Suite 100, Atlanta, Georgia 30328; phone: 770-671-1200 or 888-671-4777 (toll-free)

Chicago, 225 North Michigan Avenue, Suite 1300, Chicago, Illinois 60601; phone: 312-777-7600 or 800-626-4123 (toll-free)

Dallas, 8080 Park Lane, Suite 400A, Dallas, Texas 75231; phone: 214-890-9900 or 866-954-9900 (toll-free)

Denver, 1200 Lincoln Street, Denver, Colorado 80203; phone: 303-248-2700 or 866-431-5981 (toll-free)

Hawai'i, 400 ASB Tower, 1001 Bishop Street, Honolulu, Hawaii 96813; phone: 808-536-5555 or 888-323-2777 (toll-free)

Inland Empire, 636 East Brier Drive, Suite 235, San Bernardino, California 92408; phone: 909-915-3800 or 866-217-9075 (toll-free)

Nashville, 100 Centerview Drive, Suite 225, Nashville, Tennessee 37214; phone: 615-525-2800 or 866-833-6598 (toll-free)

Orange County, 3501 West Sunflower Avenue, Suite 110, Santa Ana, California 92704; phone: 714-338-6200 or 800-716-9598 (toll-free)

Phoenix, 2233 West Dunlap Avenue, Phoenix, Arizona 85021; phone: 602-216-2600 or 866-216-2777 (toll-free)

Salt Lake City, 121 West Election Road, Suite 300, Draper, Utah 84020; phone: 888-639-4756 (toll-free)

San Diego, 7650 Mission Valley Road, San Diego, California 92108; phone: 858-598-1900 or 866-505-0333 (toll-free)

San Francisco Bay Area, 1005 Atlantic Avenue, Alameda, California 94501; phone: 510-217-4700 or 866-215-2777 (toll-free)

Santa Monica, 2950 31st Street, Santa Monica, California 90405; phone: 310-866-4000 or 866-505-0332 (toll-free)

Sarasota, 5250 17th Street, Sarasota, Florida 34235; phone: 941-379-0404 or 800-331-5995 (toll-free)

Schaumburg, 999 North Plaza Drive, Suite 111, Schaumburg, Illinois 60173-5403; phone: 847-969-4900 or 866-290-2777 (toll-free)

Seattle, 2601-A Elliott Avenue, Seattle, Washington 98121; phone: 206-283-4500 or 888-283-2777 (toll-free)

Tampa, Parkside at Tampa Bay Park, 4401 North Hines Avenue, Suite 150, Tampa, Florida 33614; phone: 813-393-5290 or 800-850-6488 (toll-free)

Twin Cities, 1515 Central Parkway, Eagan, Minnesota 55121; phone: 651-846-2882 or 888-844-2004 (toll-free)

Washington DC, 1550 Wilson Boulevard, Suite 600, Arlington, Virginia 22209; phone: 703-526-5800 or 866-703-2777 (toll-free)

Majors and Degrees

Argosy University's College of Business offers a Bachelor of Science (B.S.) in Business Administration program. Argosy University's College of Psychology and Behavioral Sciences offers the Bachelor of Arts (B.A.) in Psychology degree program.

Academic Programs

The B.S. in Business Administration program prepares students for entry- to mid-level positions within the public or private sector. The curriculum is structured to help students develop competencies in oral and written communication, leadership, team skills, solutions-focused learning, and the analysis and execution of solutions in various business situations. Students may choose one of five optional concentrations: customized professional concentration, finance, health-care management, international business, or marketing.

The B.A. in Psychology program is designed to help students begin human services careers in such capacities as entry-level counselor, case manager, or human resources administrator and

in management and business services roles. The program also lays the foundation for graduate study. Students may choose an optional concentration from the following three options: criminal justice, organizational psychology, or substance abuse. This dynamic program is built around a flexible class approach.

Argosy University's bachelor's degree programs are open to students and working professionals with no college experience, plus those who have already earned college credit at a community college, junior college, or other university.

Academic Facilities

Argosy University libraries provide curriculum support and educational resources including current text materials, diagnostic training documents, reference materials and databases, journals and dissertations, and major and current titles in program areas. There is an online public-access catalog of library resources available throughout the Argosy University system. Students enjoy full remote access to their campus library database, enabling them to study and conduct research at home. Academic databases offer dissertation abstracts, academic journals, and professional periodicals. All library computers are Internet accessible. Software applications include Word, Excel, PowerPoint, SPSS, and various test-scoring programs.

Costs

Tuition varies by program. Students should contact the Argosy University campus of their choice for tuition information.

Financial Aid

A wide range of financial aid options is available to students who qualify. Argosy University offers access to federal and state aid programs, merit-based awards, grants, loans, and a work-study program. As a first step, students should complete the Free Application for Federal Student Aid (FAFSA). Prospective students can apply electronically at http://www.fafsa.ed.gov or at the campus. To receive consideration for financial aid and ensure timely receipt of funds, it is best to submit an application promptly.

Faculty

The Argosy University faculty is composed of working professionals who have a passion to help students succeed. Members bring real-world experience and the latest practice innovations to the academic setting. The diverse faculty is widely recognized for contributions to the field. Most hold doctoral degrees. They provide a substantive education that combines comprehensive knowledge with critical skills and practical workplace relevance. Above all, faculty members are committed to their students' personal and professional development.

Student Government

Argosy University campuses offer unique opportunities for student involvement beyond individual programs of study. Most faculty committees include a student representative. In addition, a student group meets with faculty members and administrators regularly to discuss pertinent campus-related issues.

Admission Requirements

Admission requirements differ depending on the number of college credits completed prior to application.

Students who have earned 12 or fewer semester college credits must provide proof of high school graduation or GED and meet one of the following conditions for admission: ACT composite score of 18 or above, or a combined math and verbal SAT score of 870, or minimum ACCUPLACER scores of 86 in sentence skills and 53 in algebra. Applicants who do not meet any of the above conditions for admission will be admitted with academic support if they provide proof of high school graduation or GED and meet one of the following: ACT composite score of 14 to 17, or a combined math and verbal SAT score of 660 to 869, or minimum ACCUPLACER scores of 54 in sentence skills and 36 in arithmetic.

Applicants who have earned 13 or more semester college credits must provide proof of high school graduation or GED and meet one of the following conditions for admission: cumulative college GPA of 2.0 or above or minimum ACCUPLACER scores of 86 for sentence skills and 53 in algebra. Students who do not meet either of the above criteria will be admitted with academic support if they provide proof of high school graduation or GED and meet the following condition: minimum ACCUPLACER scores of 54 in reading and 36 in arithmetic.

Students admitted with academic support are limited to 12 credit hours of study during their first semester (6 credit hours per session). Students admitted with academic support will be required to complete developmental English and/or math courses unless they meet the following conditions: Writing Review (ENG099)—must meet one of the following: a minimum ACCUPLACER score of 86 in sentence skills, or a minimum ACT verbal score of 18, or a minimum SAT verbal score of 425, or completion of a college-level English composition course with a grade of C or above; Mathematics Review I (MAT096)—must meet one of the following: a minimum ACCUPLACER score of 53 in algebra, or a minimum ACT math score of 18, or a minimum SAT math score of 440, or completion of a college-level English composition course with a grade of C or above.

Other admission requirements may include credit hours of qualified transfer credit with a grade of C- or better from a regionally accredited institution or a nationally accredited institution approved and documented by the faculty and dean of the College of Business, or the College of Professional Psychology, at Argosy University or completion of an Associate of Arts or Associate of Science degree from a regionally accredited institution. A maximum of 78 lower-division or 90 total credit hours may be transferred. A minimum written TOEFL score of 500 (paper-based test), 173 (computer-based test), or 61 (Internet-based test) is required for all applicants whose native language is not English or who have not graduated from an institution in which English is the language of instruction.

Official transcripts from approved postsecondary institutions must include a minimum grade point average of 2.0 (on a scale of 4.0) for all academic work completed. Exceptions may be made for extenuating circumstances. All applications must include a completed application form, proof of high school graduation or successful completion of the GED test, official postsecondary transcripts, and a nonrefundable (except in California) application fee. Additional materials are required prior to matriculation. Some programs have additional application requirements or include exceptions to admission requirements. An admissions representative can provide further information.

Application and Information

Argosy University accepts students on a rolling admissions basis year-round, depending on availability of required courses. Applications for admission are available online at http://www.argosy.edu or by contacting one of the campus locations.

Argosy University
205 North Michigan Avenue, Suite 1300
Chicago, Illinois 60601-2250
Phone: 312-899-9900
800-377-0617 (toll-free)
E-mail: auadmissions@argosy.edu
Web site: http://www.argosy.edu

HAWAI'I PACIFIC UNIVERSITY

HONOLULU, HAWAI'I

The University

Hawai'i Pacific University (HPU) is a private, nonprofit, nonsectarian university founded in 1965. HPU offers more than fifty undergraduate programs as well as twelve graduate programs. HUP prides itself on maintaining strong academic programs, small class sizes, individual attention to students, and a diverse faculty and student population. HPU is accredited by the Western Association of Schools and Colleges, the National League for Nursing Accrediting Commission, and the Council on Social Work Education to name a few.

HPU is the largest private university in Hawai'i, with 8,200 students from every state in the United States and more than 100 countries. The diversity of the student body stimulates learning about other cultures firsthand, both inside and outside of the classroom. There is no majority population at HPU. Students are encouraged to examine the values, customs, traditions, and principles of others to gain a clearer understanding of their own perspectives. HPU students develop friendships with students from throughout the United States and the world and form important connections for success in the global economy of the twenty-first century.

In addition to the undergraduate programs, HPU offers twelve graduate programs. The Master of Arts (M.A.) is offered in communications, diplomacy and military studies, global leadership and sustainable development, human resource management, organizational change, and teaching English as a second language. The Master of Business Administration (M.B.A.) is available in accounting, e-business, economics, finance, human resource management, information systems, international business, management, marketing, and travel industry management. The Master of Education in secondary education (M.Ed.), the Master of Science in Information Systems (M.S.I.S.), the Master of Science in Marine Science (M.S.M.S.), the Master of Science in Nursing (M.S.N.), as well as the Master of Social Work (M.S.W.) are also offered.

HPU has NCAA Division II intercollegiate sports. Men's athletic programs include baseball, basketball, cross-country, golf, soccer, and tennis. Women's athletics include basketball, cross-country, soccer, softball, tennis, and volleyball.

The housing office at HPU offers many services and living options for students. Residence halls with cafeteria service are available on the windward Hawai'i Loa campus, while off-campus apartments are available in the Honolulu and Waikiki areas for those seeking more independent living arrangements.

Location

HPU combines the best of all possible worlds, operating three campuses as one. Each of the campuses has its own distinct qualities and all the campuses are linked by a free shuttle. The main campus, located in downtown Honolulu, provides a fast-paced, exciting urban environment in the heart of the business community. The location makes it easy for students to find and maintain internship opportunities at neighboring businesses.

Eight miles away, the 135-acre windward Hawai'i Loa campus, which is set in the lush foothills of the Ko'olau mountains, is home to the School of Nursing, the marine science program, and a variety of course offerings. The Hawai'i Loa compus has residence halls, dining commons, the Educational Technology Center, a student center, an art gallery, a theater, and outdoor recreational facilities, including a soccer field, tennis courts, a softball field, and an exercise room.

The third campus, Oceanic Institute, is an applied aquaculture research facility located on a 56-acre site at Makapu'u Point on the windward coast of O'ahu, Hawai'i. At the facility, undergraduate and graduate students are able to get hands-on experience in marine science.

There are also six military campuses located on the island of O'ahu on the following military bases: Pearl Harbor Naval Base, Hickam Air Force Base, Schofield Army Barracks, Tripler Army Medical Center, Marine Corps Base Hawai'i in Kaneohe, and Marine Corps Base Hawai'i at Camp H. M. Smith. These locations provide U.S. service members with educational opportunities. Students may take classes on whichever campus is most convenient.

The beautiful weather, for which Hawai'i is famous, allows for unlimited recreational opportunities year-round. The emphasis on a career-related curriculum keeps students focused on their academic goals. HPU's Career Services Center coordinates cooperative education and internship opportunities that are especially attractive in Hawai'i'scompetitive job market. Students desiring to expand their horizons in preparation for the changing global economy find Hawai'i an exciting learning laboratory where East meets West. The many opportunities available at HPU provide for a healthy combination of school, work, and fun.

Majors and Degrees

Hawai'i Pacific University offers programs that lead to the undergraduate degrees of Bachelor of Arts (B.A.), Bachelor of Science in Business Administration (B.S.B.A.), Bachelor of Science in Nursing (B.S.N.), and Bachelor of Social Work (B.S.W.).

Undergraduate B.A. majors include anthropology, applied sociology (concentrations in business, criminal justice, family and gender studies, and government service), communication, East-West classical studies, economics, English, environmental studies, history, human resource development, human services (general and concentrations in nonprofit management, recreation management, and substance abuse counseling), international relations, international studies (concentrations in American, Asian, comparative, European, and Pacific studies), journalism (general and concentrations in broadcast, design, photojournalism, and print), justice administration, multimedia (concentrations in media studies, video production, and Web design), political science, psychology, social science, and teaching English as a second language.

The B.S. is available in advertising/public relations, biochemistry, biology, computer science, diplomacy and military studies, environmental science, marine biology, mathematics (concentrations in 3-2 engineering, applied math, math education, and pure math), nursing, oceanography, prechiropractic, premedical studies, preoccupational therapy, and pre-physical therapy. The B.S.B.A. is available in accounting, business economics, computer information systems, entrepreneurial studies, finance, general business, human resource management, international business, management, marketing, public administration, and travel industry management.

The Bachelor of Science in Nursing (B.S.N.) and Bachelor of Social Work (B.S.W.) are also available. Dual degrees, double majors, and minors are also offered.

Academic Programs

The baccalaureate student must complete at least 124 semester hours of credit. Forty-five of these credits provide the student with a strong foundation in the liberal arts, with the remaining credits composed of appropriate upper-division classes in the student's major and related areas. The academic year operates on a semester system, with regular fall and spring semesters as well as shorter sessions, including one winter and four summer sessions. A student can earn up to 15 semester hours of credit during these summer sessions. By attending the supplemental summer and winter sessions, a student may complete the baccalaureate degree program in three years. A five-year B.S.B.A./M.B.A. program is also available.

Off-Campus Programs

As part of its emphasis on international education and global citizenship, Hawai'i Pacific University offers study-abroad opportunities that complement and enhance students' academic experience. Study-abroad opportunities are available in Australia, Austria, Brazil, France, Germany, Great Britain, Japan, Korea, Mexico, Norway, Spain, Sweden, Taiwan, and Thailand. HPU undergraduates and graduates who have completed at least one semester of studies at HPU and intend to complete a degree at HPU are eligible to apply.

HPU's academic and cocurricular programs are intertwined with the world of work. The University's Career Services Center offers a comprehensive cooperative education/internship program in which a student may enroll throughout his or her course of study. This program enables students to gain significant experience in a career-related position as well as earn academic credit and a salary. HPU students have done co-ops and internships at some of the world's best-known companies and organizations, including American Express Financial Advisors; Deloitte & Touche, LLP; FBI; Hilton Hotels; Microsoft; Oceanic Institute; Polo Ralph Lauren; and Walt Disney World. The staff at the Career Services Center continues to work with students after graduation, assisting with everything from resume writing to job interview preparation.

Academic Facilities

The downtown campus comprises six buildings in the center of Honolulu's business district. HPU's newest facility is the Frear Center, which houses state-of-the-art classrooms, a communication lab, a robotics lab, and a high-tech information systems classroom. HPU's Meader Library provides a multitude of general and specialized resources, including a business reference collection, a National Endowment for the Humanities (NEH) collection, and many online databases and journals. The circulating book collections support communications, computer studies, education, literature, social sciences, and other curriculum areas. Ample study areas, group study rooms, computer work stations, and wireless Internet are also available. The Tutoring and Testing Center provides free tutoring in all core subjects. The Learning Assistance Center is the home of language labs and an audiotape and audiovisual library as well as the multimedia lab with the latest in interactive computer and CD-ROM technology. The recently expanded computer lab has more than 420 IBM-compatible PCs.

On the suburban and residential windward Hawai'i Loa campus, academic life revolves around the Amos N. Starr and Juliette Montague Cooke Academic Center (AC). The AC houses classrooms; organic chemistry, nuclear magnetic resonance, and regular laboratories; faculty and staff offices; a theater; an art gallery; and the Atherton Library, which includes circulating and reference book collections in the areas of art, history, marine science, nursing, and Hawai'i and the Pacific. In addition, the library provides access to electronic books (e-books), databases, study rooms, and wireless Internet. Computers are also available for library research, e-mail, and word processing. The Academic Computer Center provides access to IBM computers.

Located on the windward shores of O'ahu, just steps from the Pacific Ocean, the Oceanic Institute is a major research center specializing in marine biology, marine aquaculture, biotechnology, and ocean resource management. Learning, internship, and research opportunities abound for undergraduates and graduates in this hands-on learning environment.

Costs

For the 2008–09 academic year, tuition is $13,900 for most majors, while books, supplies, and health insurance cost approximately $2300. Tuition for marine science majors is $15,192, and tuition for junior- or senior-year nursing majors is $18,500. The cost to live in on-campus residence halls or off-campus apartments is comparable; room and board are $10,560 for a double occupancy room. There is an additional $500 refundable security deposit required for residence halls and off-campus apartments.

Financial Aid

HPU participates in most forms of federal financial aid, including student grant and loan programs as well as loans for parents of dependent students. Over 60 percent of the University's students benefit from federal financial aid programs or a wide range of institutional scholarships. Students should complete the Free Application for Federal Student Aid (FAFSA) to be considered for federal aid programs. While aid can be awarded throughout the academic year, students should submit the application prior to the March 1 priority deadline to be considered for all available funding. Students should visit http://www.hpu.edu/financialaid for current financial aid and scholarship information.

Faculty

HPU faculty members are renowned for the personal interest they take in each of their students. HPU is proud to offer more than 500 full-time and part-time faculty members with outstanding academic and business credentials from around the world, ensuring that HPU students can easily access a world's worth of knowledge and experiences. A vast majority of HPU faculty members hold the highest degrees in their fields. The student-faculty ratio is 18:1, and the average class size is less than 25.

Student Government

A variety of on-campus activities and events are organized for students by the Student Life Office, including Movie on the Mall, Music on the Mall, intramural sports tournaments, and recreational activities. Annual events include Club Carnival, Welcome Week, Da Freakshow, Halloween Hoopla, and Pacific Bowl. HPU students can join one of the more than seventy student clubs; run for office in the Associated Students of Hawai'i Pacific University (ASHPU), the University's governing body; participate in Army or Air Force ROTC; write for the student newspaper, *Kalamalama*; edit the school's literary journal, *Hawai'i Pacific Review*; or join HPU's stage and pep band or international choral program.

Admission Requirements

Hawai'i Pacific University seeks students who are motivated and show academic promise. The Admissions Office requires that applicants complete and forward the admission application and their high school transcripts. Transfer students should also submit college transcripts. SAT and/or ACT scores should be submitted if these scores are not posted in their transcripts. First-time freshmen are expected to have a minimum GPA of 2.5 (on a 4.0 scale) in college-preparatory courses. HPU recommends that students complete 4 years of English, 4 years of history or social science, 3 years of math, and 2 years of science. Transfer students with 24 or more postsecondary credits are required to have a GPA of 2.0 or above. For students with less than 24 credits, a combination of college and high school GPA is used.

The marine science and environmental science programs require a GPA of 3.0 or above and 3 years of science, including biology and chemistry (physics is recommended), as well as mathematics through trigonometry (calculus is recommended). Transfer students must demonstrate ability in science and math at the college level. Students not meeting the above criteria are encouraged to enroll at HPU without declaring a major to demonstrate the ability to do college-level work in science and math.

Application and Information

Candidates are notified of admission decisions on a rolling basis, usually within two weeks of receipt of application materials. Early entrance and deferred entrance are available.

For further information and for application materials, students should contact:

Office of Admissions
Hawai'i Pacific University
1164 Bishop Street, Suite 200
Honolulu, Hawai'i 96813

Phone: 808-544-0238
866-CALL-HPU (toll-free in the U.S. and Canada)
Fax: 808-544-1136
E-mail: admissions@hpu.edu
Web site: http://www.hpu.edu

UNIVERSITY OF HAWAII AT HILO

HILO, HAWAII

University
Of Hawai'i
HILO

The University

One of the world's best-kept secrets for a high-quality college education is found at the University of Hawaii at Hilo (UH Hilo). The main ingredients for a successful and enjoyable college life are waiting for students: the Spirit of Aloha within the University and surrounding community, a friendly and caring environment, one-on-one interaction with faculty and staff members, small class size, natural island laboratories, valuable hands-on learning and leadership opportunities, collaborative work with faculty members, and the many exciting outdoor activities. These are the very qualities that have made UH Hilo an increasingly attractive campus for college-seeking students.

UH Hilo is a comprehensive regional institution offering a residential campus experience. As a state university, UH Hilo functions within the University of Hawaii system, serving students from the state of Hawaii, the U.S. mainland, and many countries in Europe, Asia, and Pacific regions.

The University's student population, which stands at more than 3,000, has enjoyed steady increases over the past ten years and currently includes more than 400 international students from thirty-four countries. Recently, *U.S. News & World Report* ranked UH Hilo in the top five for its diversity among both private and public universities in the United States.

UH Hilo is accredited by the Accrediting Commission for Senior Colleges and Universities of the Western Association of Schools and Colleges (WASC). Education program majors are accredited by the National Association of State Directors of Teacher Education Certification. The nursing program is accredited by the National League for Nursing Accrediting Commission (NLNAC). AACSB International recently granted accreditation to the College of Business and Economics.

With the pristine blue waters of the Pacific Ocean, the majestic mountains of Mauna Kea and Mauna Loa, the captivating volcanoes, and the various distinctive types of climatic zones and ecosystems, UH Hilo is fully equipped with natural, living laboratories to command some of the world's best programs in marine science, vulcanology, astronomy, and conservation biology. The rich heritage of the Hawaiian culture paved the way for strong programs in Hawaiian studies at the undergraduate, master's, and doctoral levels. Other graduate degree programs include education, tropical conservation biology and environmental science, counseling psychology, and China-U.S. relations.

The University offers a wide range of activities and services to meet its students' social, cultural, and recreational needs. From the canoe club and international student association to mountain biking and surfing, there are numerous on-campus and off-campus activities for students to participate in, come rain or shine. The athletic department offers various intercollegiate and intramural sports. The Vulcans are members of the National Collegiate Athletic Association (NCAA) Division II in men's basketball, cross-country, golf, soccer, and tennis as well as women's basketball, cross-country, golf, soccer, softball, tennis, and volleyball. The men's baseball team competes on the NCAA Division I level as an independent.

Students can choose to live on or off campus. Currently, more than 600 students are housed in four coeducational residence halls on the campus—two are traditional, one is suite-style, and one is apartment-style. Residents in the traditional and suite-style halls must participate in a board program, with meals served at the residence hall dining room. Off-campus housing includes privately owned apartments, homes, or rooms in the Hilo community. The housing office provides assistance in finding off-campus accommodations.

The newly approved College of Pharmacy enrolled its first class of 90 students pursuing the pharmaceutical doctorate (Pharm.D.) in fall 2007. All Pharm.D. students are required to undergo clinical experiences throughout the program's four-year curriculum.

Location

Located in the city of Hilo, on the east side of the Big Island of Hawaii, UH Hilo is only a 45-minute interisland flight (about 200 air miles) from Honolulu. The peaceful city of Hilo offers a moderate cost of living, clean air, and a low-density population of about 70,000. Within 10 minutes of the campus are shopping malls, theaters, restaurants, grocery stores, and a post office as well as a major harbor and international airport. Some of the world's best beaches and golf courses are only a few hours' drive away. Throughout the winter months, the island of Hawaii is also a popular destination for whales that come to indulge themselves in the lavishness of the warm Hawaiian waters.

Majors and Degrees

More than thirty-five majors are offered through six main colleges. The College of Arts and Science, the largest of the colleges, offers undergraduate degrees in administration of justice, anthropology, art, astronomy, biology (with a premed option), chemistry, communication, computer science, drama, English, geography, geology, health and physical education, history, Japanese studies, linguistics, marine science, mathematics, music, natural sciences, nursing, performing arts, philosophy, physics, political science, psychology, and sociology. Certificates offered within this college include environmental studies, international studies with emphasis in international relations and tourism, marine science option, Pacific Island studies, planning (under the geography program), systems modeling (under the mathematics program), and women's studies.

The College of Business and Economics, accredited by AACSB International, now has a major in accounting and offers a range of courses for students interested in the fields of economics, finance, marketing, management, or tourism.

The College of Agriculture, Forestry, and Natural Resource Management offers the Bachelor of Science degree in seven areas of specialization: agribusiness, agroecology and environmental quality, animal science (options in production and pre–veterinary studies), aquaculture, crop protection, general agriculture, and tropical horticulture.

The College of Hawaiian Language offers undergraduate, graduate, and doctoral programs in Hawaiian language and culture.

The College of Continuing Education and Community Service offers an exciting array of credit, noncredit, professional, and personal-development courses and a customized English as a second language program designed for international students who seek to increase their command of English prior to starting undergraduate studies.

Of particular interest to many students is UH Hilo's Marine Science Summer Program (MSSP). It has received the Excellence of Program Award from the Western Association of Summer Session Administrators, which represents some eighty colleges and universities in the western United States, Canada, and Mexico. The MSSP provides several introductory-level courses, including oceanography, marine biology, and the Hawaii marine field experience.

Quantitative Underwater Ecological Surveying Techniques (QUEST) is a popular one-of-a-kind, two-week-long, full-time course in which students can learn underwater ecological surveying methodologies.

Academic Programs

UH Hilo stresses rigorous education in a caring, personalized atmosphere; encourages student-faculty interaction and collaboration on research projects; and offers hands-on learning and leadership opportunities by utilizing the natural settings of the location as well as by partnering with the business community and various state agencies.

The honors program is designed to motivate, challenge, and enrich students' intellectual curiosity; nurture their intellectual independence; and deepen their sense of scholarship.

Baccalaureate degrees are granted only to students who have satisfactorily completed the program of courses prescribed for their majors, have earned at least a 2.0 cumulative GPA as well as a 2.0 GPA in courses required for the major and minor (if any), have earned a minimum of 30 semester hours in the college from which a degree is sought, were registered and in attendance at the University during the semester or summer session in which the degree is granted, and have met all requirements of their respective colleges and departments.

Off-Campus Programs

At UH Hilo, students can participate in the increasingly popular National Student Exchange Program (NSE). Students can select from more than 170 colleges and universities in the United States to study at for six months to a year. Students who want to live and study in another country have a choice of thirteen other countries to choose from in the Study-Abroad Program. Through exchange agreements, students pay UH Hilo's tuition and enjoy firsthand experiences in other cultures and acquire valuable skills and expertise for an increasingly internationalized and interdependent world.

Academic Facilities

Most of the learning facilities are located on the main campus, which spreads across 115 acres. To serve the needs of the University, there are more than eighty classrooms, a library and media center, faculty and staff buildings, a student services building, a fully equipped theater complex, a campus center for student activities, an athletic complex, tennis courts, and a playing field.

Adjoining the main campus is a 163-acre University Park, which is home to an impressive array of world-class multinational tenants representing science, technology, and agricultural biotechnology. This research park has allowed faculty and staff members to interact with a distinguished community of scientists and technicians from around the world.

Within a 15-minute drive of the main campus is a 110-acre University Agricultural Farm Laboratory, which provides valuable hands-on learning opportunities.

Costs

For 2008–09, tuition per year for full-time undergraduate students is $4056 for Hawaii residents, $12,576 for international students and U.S. students from non-WUE (Western Undergraduate Exchange) states, and $6084 for students from WUE states (Alaska, Arizona, California, Colorado, Hawaii, Idaho, Montana, Nevada, New Mexico, North Dakota, South Dakota, Oregon, Utah, Washington, and Wyoming).

Room and board costs per year are estimated to be $6792; books and supplies, approximately $1058; and fees, about $148. These costs are for the 2007–08 academic year; for current costs, students should visit the Web site at http://www.uhh.hawaii.edu.

Financial Aid

The financial aid program at UH Hilo is designed to provide financial assistance to students who would not be able to attend college without such assistance. Need-based and non-need-based financial assistance is available to students in numerous forms: federal student aid; Hawaii State Tuition Waivers; loans, grants, and scholarships from state and federal agencies; and a range of scholarships from private sponsors/donors.

Federal (Federal Work-Study Program) and state (general) funds are provided for the employment of students under the Student Employment Program. The priority processing deadline is March 1.

Faculty

The faculty members are highly qualified and recognized in their fields of expertise. They hold advanced degrees and are committed to high-quality teaching by incorporating the surrounding natural environment as a leading-edge learning laboratory. Hands-on experience as part of the learning process in the personal settings of UH Hilo's campus invariably broadens students' horizons, thus preparing them to better handle graduate school or the working world.

Student Government

Major student organizations include the UH Hilo Student Association, the Student Activities Council, and the Board of Student Publications. These organizations provide opportunities for students to acquire leadership and social skills.

Admission Requirements

Interested students need to submit their completed application forms, including a $50 application fee, to the Admissions Office. They must also have official high school transcripts sent directly from their high school and have their SAT or ACT (and GED, if applicable) scores sent directly from the testing agencies to the Admissions Office. International students need to complete and submit all required documents as outlined in the application form.

Application and Information

Applications and all supporting documents noted in the application form, including the $50 application fee, should be received by June 1 for U.S. applicants and by May 1 for international (F-1) applicants for the fall semester. The spring-semester application deadline is November 1 for U.S. applicants and October 1 for international (F-1) applicants. For application materials or for more information, students should contact:

Admissions Office
Student Services Building
University of Hawaii at Hilo
200 West Kawili Street
Hilo, Hawaii 96720-4091
Phone: 808-974-7414
800-897-4456 (toll-free, United States only)
Fax: 808-933-0861
E-mail: uhhadm@hawaii.edu
Web site: http://www.uhh.hawaii.edu

A view of the campus of the University of Hawaii at Hilo.

IDAHO

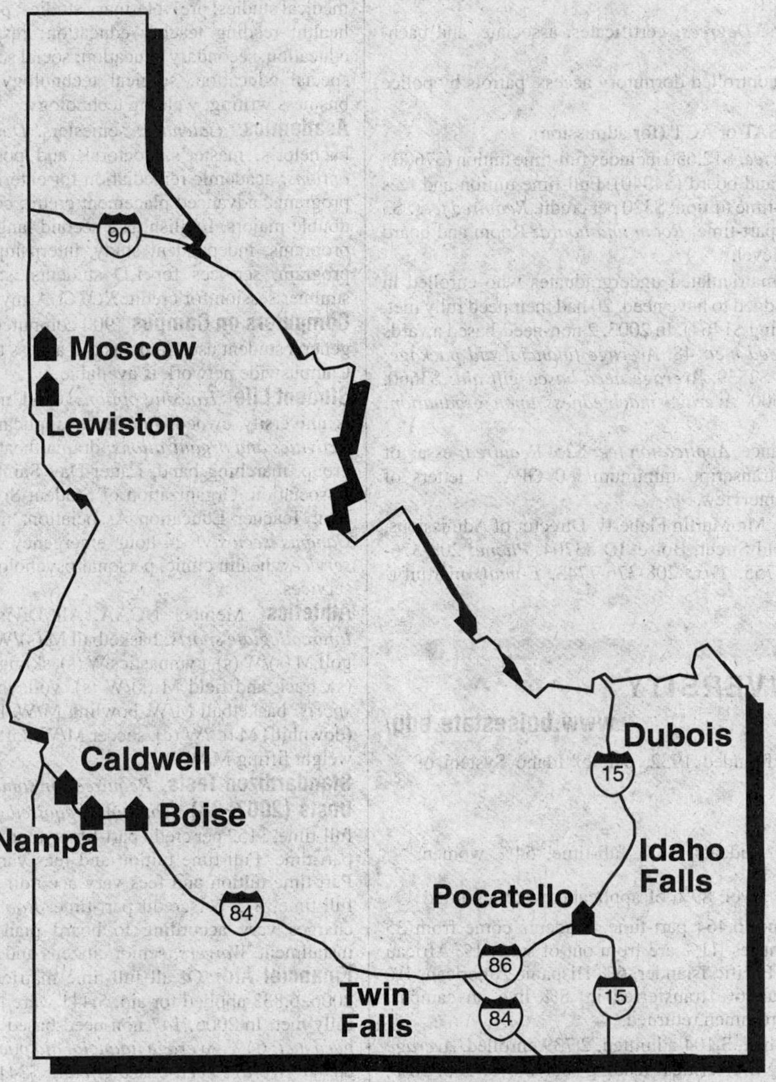
90
Moscow
Lewiston
Caldwell
Nampa
Boise
84
Dubois
15
Idaho Falls
Pocatello
86
15
84
Twin Falls

BOISE BIBLE COLLEGE

Boise, Idaho **www.boisebible.edu/**

- **Independent nondenominational** 4-year, founded 1945
- **Suburban** 17-acre campus
- **Endowment** $507,870
- **Coed**
- **Minimally difficult** entrance level

Faculty *Student/faculty ratio:* 16:1.

Academics *Calendar:* semesters. *Degrees:* certificates, associate, and bachelor's.

Student Life *Campus security:* controlled dormitory access, patrols by police officers.

Standardized Tests *Required:* SAT or ACT (for admission).

Costs (2007–08) *Comprehensive fee:* $12,650 includes full-time tuition ($7600), mandatory fees ($110), and room and board ($4940). Full-time tuition and fees vary according to course load. Part-time tuition: $320 per credit. *Required fees:* $3 per credit part-time, $10 per term part-time. *Room and board:* Room and board charges vary according to student level.

Financial Aid Of all full-time matriculated undergraduates who enrolled in 2003, 84 applied for aid, 80 were judged to have need, 20 had their need fully met. 7 Federal Work-Study jobs (averaging $1464). In 2003, 2 non-need-based awards were made. *Average percent of need met:* 48. *Average financial aid package:* $4380. *Average need-based loan:* $2539. *Average need-based gift aid:* $3660. *Average non-need-based aid:* $3500. *Average indebtedness upon graduation:* $8648.

Applying *Options:* deferred entrance. *Application fee:* $25. *Required:* essay or personal statement, high school transcript, minimum 2.0 GPA, 3 letters of recommendation. *Recommended:* interview.

Freshman Application Contact Mr. Martin Flaherty, Director of Admissions, Boise Bible College, 8695 Marigold Street, Boise, ID 83704. *Phone:* 208-376-7731. *Toll-free phone:* 800-893-7755. *Fax:* 208-376-7743. *E-mail:* martinf@boisebible.edu.

BOISE STATE UNIVERSITY

Boise, Idaho **www.boisestate.edu/**

- **State-supported** university, founded 1932, part of Idaho System of Higher Education
- **Urban** 175-acre campus
- **Endowment** $76.8 million
- **Coed** 17,690 undergraduate students, 63% full-time, 54% women, 46% men
- **Minimally difficult** entrance level, 89% of applicants were admitted

Undergraduates 11,226 full-time, 6,464 part-time. Students come from 35 states and territories, 45 other countries, 11% are from out of state, 1% African American, 3% Asian American or Pacific Islander, 6% Hispanic American, 1% Native American, 1% international, 6% transferred in, 8% live on campus. *Retention:* 64% of 2006 full-time freshmen returned.

Freshmen *Admission:* 3,487 applied, 3,104 admitted, 2,739 enrolled. *Average high school GPA:* 3.28. *Test scores:* SAT critical reading scores over 500: 58%; SAT math scores over 500: 62%; ACT scores over 18: 88%; SAT critical reading scores over 600: 20%; SAT math scores over 600: 20%; ACT scores over 24: 29%; SAT critical reading scores over 700: 3%; SAT math scores over 700: 2%; ACT scores over 30: 4%.

Faculty *Total:* 1,119, 55% full-time, 52% with terminal degrees. *Student/faculty ratio:* 18:1.

Majors Accounting; advertising; anthropology; art; art history, criticism and conservation; art teacher education; athletic training; automobile/automotive mechanics technology; bilingual and multilingual education; biology/biological sciences; business administration and management; business machine repair; business/managerial economics; business teacher education; chemistry; child development; civil engineering; clinical laboratory science/medical technology; commercial and advertising art; computer and information sciences; computer science; computer systems networking and telecommunications; construction management; culinary arts; cultural studies; drafting and design technology; dramatic/theater arts; drawing; economics; education; electrical and electronic engineering technologies related; electrical, electronic and communications engineering technology; electrical, electronics and communications engineering; elementary education; English; environmental health; environmental studies; finance; French; geology/earth science; geophysics and seismology; German; health information/medical records administration; health science; heating, air conditioning, ventilation and refrigeration maintenance technology; history; horticultural science; human resources management; industrial technology; information science/studies; interdisciplinary studies; international business/trade/commerce; kindergarten/preschool education; kinesiology and exercise science; legal assistant/paralegal; liberal arts and sciences/liberal studies; literature; machine tool technology; mass communication/media; mathematics; mechanical engineering/mechanical technology; medical administrative assistant and medical secretary; music; music management and merchandising; music teacher education; nursing (registered nurse training); operations management; perfusion technology; philosophy; physical education teaching and coaching; physician assistant; physics; political science and government; pre-dentistry studies; pre-engineering; premedical studies; pre-veterinary studies; psychology; public administration; public health; reading teacher education; respiratory care therapy; science teacher education; secondary education; social sciences; social work; sociology; Spanish; special education; surgical technology; teacher assistant/aide; technical and business writing; welding technology.

Academics *Calendar:* semesters. *Degrees:* certificates, diplomas, associate, bachelor's, master's, doctoral, and postbachelor's certificates. *Special study options:* academic remediation for entering students, adult/continuing education programs, advanced placement credit, cooperative education, distance learning, double majors, English as a second language, freshman honors college, honors programs, independent study, internships, off-campus study, part-time degree program, services for LD students, student-designed majors, study abroad, summer session for credit. *ROTC:* Army (b).

Computers on Campus 900 computers/terminals are available on campus for general student use. Students can access the following: online (class) registration. Campuswide network is available.

Student Life *Housing options:* coed, men-only, women-only. Campus housing is university owned. Freshman applicants given priority for college housing. *Activities and organizations:* drama/theater group, student-run newspaper, choral group, marching band, Latter-Day Saints Student Association, Residence Hall Association, Organization of Student Social Workers, Marching Band Association, Teacher Education Association, national fraternities, national sororities. *Campus security:* 24-hour emergency response devices and patrols. *Student services:* health clinic, personal/psychological counseling, women's center, legal services.

Athletics Member NCAA. All Division I except football (Division I-A). *Intercollegiate sports:* basketball M (s)/W (s), cross-country running M (s)/W (s), golf M (s)/W (s), gymnastics W (s), skiing (downhill) W, soccer W, tennis M (s)/W (s), track and field M (s)/W (s), volleyball W (s), wrestling M (s). *Intramural sports:* basketball M/W, bowling M/W, lacrosse W (c), racquetball M/W, skiing (downhill) M (c)/W (c), soccer M/W, softball M/W, tennis M/W, volleyball M/W, weight lifting M/W.

Standardized Tests *Required for some:* SAT or ACT (for admission).

Costs (2007–08) *One-time required fee:* $75. *Tuition:* state resident $2775 full-time, $152 per credit part-time; nonresident $10,943 full-time, $152 per credit part-time. Full-time tuition and fees vary according to reciprocity agreements. Part-time tuition and fees vary according to course load. *Required fees:* $1635 full-time, $75 per credit part-time. *Room and board:* $5938. Room and board charges vary according to board plan and housing facility. *Payment plan:* installment. *Waivers:* senior citizens and employees or children of employees.

Financial Aid Of all full-time matriculated undergraduates who enrolled in 2006, 6,833 applied for aid, 5,441 were judged to have need, 840 had their need fully met. In 2006, 147 non-need-based awards were made. *Average percent of need met:* 64%. *Average financial aid package:* $8003. *Average need-based loan:* $4147. *Average need-based gift aid:* $3414. *Average non-need-based aid:* $2492. *Average indebtedness upon graduation:* $20,004. *Financial aid deadline:* 6/1.

Applying *Options:* electronic application. *Application fee:* $40. *Required for some:* high school transcript, minimum 2.0 GPA. *Recommended:* high school transcript. *Application deadlines:* 7/12 (freshmen), 7/12 (transfers). *Notification:* continuous (freshmen), continuous (transfers).

Freshman Application Contact Ms. Jenny Cardenas, Dean of Admissions, Boise State University, Enrollment Services, 1910 University Drive, Boise, ID 83725. *Phone:* 208-426-1177. *Toll-free phone:* 800-632-6586 (in-state); 800-824-7017 (out-of-state). *E-mail:* bsuinfo@boisestate.edu.

THE COLLEGE OF IDAHO

Caldwell, Idaho **www.collegeofidaho.edu/**

- **Independent** comprehensive, founded 1891
- **Suburban** 50-acre campus
- **Endowment** $48.1 million
- **Coed** 826 undergraduate students, 94% full-time, 61% women, 39% men
- **Very difficult** entrance level, 81% of applicants were admitted

Undergraduates 778 full-time, 48 part-time. Students come from 17 states and territories, 11 other countries, 31% are from out of state, 0.7% African American, 3% Asian American or Pacific Islander, 7% Hispanic American, 0.4% Native American, 3% international, 6% transferred in, 57% live on campus. *Retention:* 82% of 2006 full-time freshmen returned.

Freshmen *Admission:* 911 applied, 738 admitted, 242 enrolled. *Average high school GPA:* 3.62. *Test scores:* SAT critical reading scores over 500: 71%; SAT writing scores over 500: 65%; ACT scores over 18: 96%; SAT critical reading scores over 600: 41%; SAT writing scores over 600: 34%; ACT scores over 24: 61%; SAT critical reading scores over 700: 5%; SAT writing scores over 700: 3%; ACT scores over 30: 10%.

Faculty *Total:* 106, 71% full-time, 55% with terminal degrees. *Student/faculty ratio:* 9:1.

Majors Accounting; anthropology; art; biology/biological sciences; business administration and management; chemistry; creative writing; dramatic/theater arts; economics; English; history; international business/trade/commerce; international economics; kinesiology and exercise science; mathematics; music; philosophy; physical education teaching and coaching; physics; political science and government; pre-medical studies; psychology; religious studies; sociology; Spanish; sport and fitness administration/management.

Academics *Calendar:* semesters plus 6-week Winter term. *Degrees:* bachelor's and master's. *Special study options:* advanced placement credit, cooperative education, double majors, honors programs, independent study, internships, off-campus study, part-time degree program, services for LD students, student-designed majors, study abroad. *ROTC:* Army (c). *Unusual degree programs:* 3-2 engineering with University of Idaho, Columbia University, Washington University in St. Louis; nursing with University of Idaho.

Computers on Campus 242 computers/terminals are available on campus for general student use. Students can access the following: campus intranet, computer help desk, free student e-mail accounts, online (class) grades, online (class) registration, online (class) schedules, online course syllabi, course assignments, course discussion, online yearly catalog, College You_Tube. Campuswide network is available. 100% of college-owned or -operated housing units are wired for high-speed Internet access. Wireless service is available via entire campus.

Student Life *Housing:* on-campus residence required through sophomore year. *Options:* coed, disabled students. Campus housing is university owned. Freshman campus housing is guaranteed. *Activities and organizations:* drama/theater group, student-run newspaper, radio station, choral group, Scarlet Masque Drama Group, Association of Latino American Students (ALAS), International Studies Association, Philo-Tech Society, The Environmental Resource or Recreation Association (TERRA), national fraternities, national sororities. *Campus security:* 24-hour emergency response devices and patrols, student patrols, late-night transport/escort service, controlled dormitory access. *Student services:* health clinic, personal/psychological counseling.

Athletics Member NAIA. *Intercollegiate sports:* baseball M (s), basketball M (s)/W (s), cross-country running M (s)/W (s), golf M (s)/W (s), skiing (cross-country) M (s)/W (s), skiing (downhill) M (s)/W (s), soccer M (s)/W (s), softball W (s), swimming and diving M (s)/W (s), tennis W (s), track and field M (s)/W (s), volleyball W (s). *Intramural sports:* badminton M/W, basketball M/W, bowling M/W, cheerleading W, equestrian sports M/W, football M/W, lacrosse M/W, rock climbing M/W, soccer M/W, softball M/W, swimming and diving M/W, table tennis M/W, tennis M/W, ultimate Frisbee M/W, volleyball M/W.

Standardized Tests *Required:* SAT and SAT Subject Tests or ACT (for admission).

Costs (2008–09) *Comprehensive fee:* $25,557 includes full-time tuition ($18,300), mandatory fees ($690), and room and board ($6567). Part-time tuition: $760 per semester hour. *College room only:* $3050.

Financial Aid Of all full-time matriculated undergraduates who enrolled in 2007, 480 applied for aid, 476 were judged to have need, 92 had their need fully met. 155 Federal Work-Study jobs (averaging $866). 34 state and other part-time jobs (averaging $815). In 2007, 270 non-need-based awards were made. *Average percent of need met:* 89%. *Average financial aid package:* $15,382. *Average need-based loan:* $5095. *Average need-based gift aid:* $4326. *Average non-need-based aid:* $10,009. *Average indebtedness upon graduation:* $26,170.

Applying *Options:* electronic application, early admission, early action, deferred entrance. *Required:* essay or personal statement, high school transcript, 1 letter of recommendation. *Recommended:* interview, extracurricular activities. *Application deadlines:* 6/1 (freshmen), rolling (transfers), 12/15 (early action). *Notification:* continuous (freshmen), continuous (transfers).

Freshman Application Contact Ms. Charlene Brown, Director of Admissions, The College of Idaho, 2112 Cleveland Boulevard, Caldwell, ID 83605-4494. *Phone:* 208-459-5689. *Toll-free phone:* 800-244-3246. *Fax:* 208-459-5151. *E-mail:* admission@collegeofidaho.edu.

IDAHO STATE UNIVERSITY

Pocatello, Idaho **www.isu.edu/**

- **State-supported** university, founded 1901
- **Small-town** 972-acre campus
- **Endowment** $37.1 million
- **Coed** 11,024 undergraduate students, 63% full-time, 57% women, 43% men
- **Minimally difficult** entrance level, 80% of applicants were admitted

Undergraduates 6,916 full-time, 4,108 part-time. Students come from 46 states and territories, 71 other countries, 4% are from out of state, 1% African American, 2% Asian American or Pacific Islander, 5% Hispanic American, 2% Native American, 2% international, 6% transferred in, 6% live on campus. *Retention:* 57% of 2006 full-time freshmen returned.

Freshmen *Admission:* 3,713 applied, 2,978 admitted, 1,575 enrolled. *Average high school GPA:* 3.33. *Test scores:* SAT critical reading scores over 500: 59%; SAT math scores over 500: 63%; ACT scores over 18: 81%; SAT critical reading scores over 600: 25%; SAT math scores over 600: 25%; ACT scores over 24: 31%; SAT critical reading scores over 700: 4%; SAT math scores over 700: 6%; ACT scores over 30: 3%.

Faculty *Total:* 789, 78% full-time, 47% with terminal degrees. *Student/faculty ratio:* 14:1.

Majors Accounting; administrative assistant and secretarial science; aircraft powerplant technology; American Native/Native American languages; American Sign Language (ASL); American studies; anthropology; art; autobody/collision and repair technology; automobile/automotive mechanics technology; biochemistry; biology/biological sciences; botany/plant biology; business administration and management; business/commerce; business machine repair; CAD/CADD drafting/design technology; carpentry; chemistry; child care and support services management; civil engineering; civil engineering technology; clinical laboratory science/medical technology; communication/speech communication and rhetoric; communications systems installation and repair technology; computer and information sciences; computer programming (specific applications); criminal justice/police science; criminal justice/safety; culinary arts; dental hygiene; dental laboratory technology; diesel mechanics technology; dietetics; drafting and design technology; drafting/design engineering technologies related; dramatic/theater arts; early childhood education; ecology; economics; electrical, electronic and communications engineering technology; electrical, electronics and communications engineering; electrical/electronics equipment installation and repair; electromechanical technology; elementary education; emergency medical technology (EMT paramedic); energy management and systems technology; English; environmental science; family and consumer sciences/human sciences; finance; fire science; French; general studies; geology/earth science; German; graphic and printing equipment operation/production; health/health care administration; health information/medical records technology; health services/allied health/health sciences; health teacher education; history; human resources management; information science/studies; instrumentation technology; international relations and affairs; laser and optical technology; Latin; machine tool technology; marketing/marketing management; mass communication/media; mathematics; mechanical engineering; mechanics and repair; medical/clinical assistant; medical radiologic technology; microbiology; music; music performance; music teacher education; nuclear engineering; nursing (registered nurse training); occupational therapist assistant; pharmacy technician; philosophy; physical education teaching and coaching; physical therapist assistant; physics; political science and government; psychology; Russian; secondary education; sign language interpretation and translation; social work; sociology; Spanish; special education; survey technology; welding technology; zoology/animal biology.

Academics *Calendar:* semesters. *Degrees:* certificates, associate, bachelor's, master's, doctoral, first professional, post-master's, postbachelor's, and first professional certificates. *Special study options:* academic remediation for entering students, adult/continuing education programs, advanced placement credit, distance learning, double majors, English as a second language, external degree program, honors programs, independent study, internships, off-campus study, part-time degree program, services for LD students, student-designed majors, study abroad, summer session for credit. *ROTC:* Army (c).

Computers on Campus 519 computers/terminals are available on campus for general student use. Students can access the following: computer help desk, online (class) grades, online (class) registration, online (class) schedules. Campuswide network is available. 100% of college-owned or -operated housing units are wired for high-speed Internet access. Wireless service is available via classrooms, computer centers, computer labs, dorm rooms, learning centers, libraries, student centers.

Student Life *Housing options:* coed, men-only, women-only, disabled students. Campus housing is university owned. Freshman campus housing is guaranteed. *Activities and organizations:* drama/theater group, student-run newspaper, radio and television station, choral group, marching band, International Students Association, Vocational Industrial Clubs of America, Latter Day Saints Student Association, Student American Dental Hygienists Association, Academy of Students of Pharmacy, national fraternities, national sororities. *Campus security:* 24-hour emergency response devices and patrols, student patrols, late-night transport/escort service, controlled dormitory access. *Student services:* health clinic, personal/psychological counseling, women's center.

Athletics Member NCAA. All Division I except football (Division I-AA). *Intercollegiate sports:* basketball M (s)/W (s), cross-country running M (s)/W (s), golf M (s)/W (s), sailing W, skiing (downhill) M/W, soccer W (s), softball W, tennis M (s)/W (s), track and field M (s)/W (s), volleyball W (s). *Intramural sports:* badminton M/W, basketball M/W, bowling M/W, cross-country running M/W, fencing M (c)/W (c), field hockey M/W, football M, racquetball M/W, rock climbing M/W, rugby M (c), skiing (cross-country) M/W, skiing (downhill) M/W, soccer M/W, softball M/W, swimming and diving M (c)/W (c), table tennis M/W, tennis M/W, track and field M/W, ultimate Frisbee M/W, volleyball M/W, water polo M/W, weight lifting M (c)/W (c), wrestling M.

Standardized Tests *Required:* SAT or ACT (for admission). *Recommended:* ACT (for admission).

Costs (2007–08) *Tuition:* state resident $2882 full-time, $221 per credit hour part-time; nonresident $11,566 full-time, $341 per credit hour part-time. Full-time tuition and fees vary according to program and reciprocity agreements. Part-time tuition and fees vary according to reciprocity agreements. *Required fees:* $1518 full-time. *Room and board:* $4950; room only: $2250. Room and board charges vary according to board plan and housing facility. *Payment plan:* deferred payment. *Waivers:* senior citizens and employees or children of employees.

Financial Aid Of all full-time matriculated undergraduates who enrolled in 2006, 5,391 applied for aid, 4,752 were judged to have need, 274 had their need fully met. 901 Federal Work-Study jobs (averaging $2370). 817 state and other part-time jobs (averaging $1150). In 2006, 887 non-need-based awards were made. *Average percent of need met:* 53%. *Average financial aid package:* $5987. *Average need-based loan:* $3785. *Average need-based gift aid:* $3277. *Average non-need-based aid:* $2456. *Average indebtedness upon graduation:* $21,862.

Applying *Options:* electronic application, early admission, deferred entrance. *Application fee:* $40. *Required:* high school transcript, minimum 2.0 GPA. *Application deadlines:* 8/1 (freshmen), 8/1 (transfers). *Notification:* continuous (freshmen), continuous (transfers).

Freshman Application Contact Idaho State University, Campus Box 8270, 741 South 7th, Pocatello, ID 83209. *Phone:* 208-282-2475.

ITT TECHNICAL INSTITUTE

Boise, Idaho **www.itt-tech.edu/**

- **Proprietary** primarily 2-year, founded 1906, part of ITT Educational Services, Inc
- **Urban** 1-acre campus
- **Coed**
- **Minimally difficult** entrance level

Academics *Calendar:* quarters. *Degrees:* associate and bachelor's.

Standardized Tests *Required:* Wonderlic aptitude test (for admission).

Financial Aid Of all full-time matriculated undergraduates who enrolled in 2006, 9 Federal Work-Study jobs (averaging $5500).

Applying *Options:* deferred entrance. *Application fee:* $100. *Required:* high school transcript, interview. *Recommended:* letters of recommendation.

Freshman Application Contact Ms. Jennifer Kandler, Director of Recruitment, ITT Technical Institute, 12302 West Explorer Drive, Boise, ID 83713. *Phone:* 208-322-8844. *Toll-free phone:* 800-666-4888. *Fax:* 208-322-0173.

LEWIS-CLARK STATE COLLEGE

Lewiston, Idaho **www.lcsc.edu/**

- **State-supported** 4-year, founded 1893
- **Small-town** 44-acre campus
- **Coed** 3,612 undergraduate students, 63% full-time, 60% women, 40% men
- **Minimally difficult** entrance level, 59% of applicants were admitted

Undergraduates 2,272 full-time, 1,340 part-time. Students come from 37 states and territories, 31 other countries, 14% are from out of state, 1% African American, 1% Asian American or Pacific Islander, 6% Hispanic American, 4% Native American, 4% international, 9% transferred in. *Retention:* 55% of 2006 full-time freshmen returned.

Freshmen *Admission:* 1,179 applied, 697 admitted, 540 enrolled. *Average high school GPA:* 3.03. *Test scores:* SAT critical reading scores over 500: 33%; SAT math scores over 500: 43%; ACT scores over 18: 69%; SAT critical reading scores over 600: 5%; SAT math scores over 600: 12%; ACT scores over 24: 16%; SAT math scores over 700: 1%; ACT scores over 30: 1%.

Faculty *Total:* 158, 94% full-time, 66% with terminal degrees. *Student/faculty ratio:* 14:1.

Majors Accounting technology and bookkeeping; administrative assistant and secretarial science; autobody/collision and repair technology; automobile/automotive mechanics technology; behavioral sciences; biology/biological sciences; business administration and management; chemistry; child development; communication/speech communication and rhetoric; computer and information sciences; computer science; corrections; creative writing; diesel mechanics technology; drafting and design technology; electrical/electronics equipment installation and repair; elementary education; English; English/language arts teacher education; fire science; graphic and printing equipment operation/production; heating, air conditioning, ventilation and refrigeration maintenance technology; hospitality administration; industrial electronics technology; interdisciplinary studies; kinesiology and exercise science; legal administrative assistant/secretary; legal assistant/paralegal; liberal arts and sciences/liberal studies; manufacturing technology; mathematics; mathematics teacher education; mechanics and repair; medical/health management and clinical assistant; medical office assistant; multi-/interdisciplinary studies related; natural sciences; nursing (licensed practical/vocational nurse training); nursing (registered nurse training); physical education teaching and coaching; psychology; radiologic technology/science; science teacher education; small business administration; social sciences; social science teacher education; social work; web/multimedia management and webmaster; welding technology.

Academics *Calendar:* semesters. *Degrees:* certificates, diplomas, associate, and bachelor's. *Special study options:* academic remediation for entering students, accelerated degree program, adult/continuing education programs, advanced placement credit, cooperative education, distance learning, double majors, English as a second language, external degree program, honors programs, independent study, internships, off-campus study, part-time degree program, services for LD students, student-designed majors, study abroad, summer session for credit. *ROTC:* Army (b), Air Force (c).

Computers on Campus 88 computers/terminals are available on campus for general student use. Students can access the following: online (class) registration. Campuswide network is available.

Student Life *Housing options:* coed. Campus housing is university owned, leased by the school and is provided by a third party. *Activities and organizations:* drama/theater group, student-run newspaper, radio station, choral group, Business Students Organization, Ambassadors Club, International Club, honors society, Explorers. *Campus security:* 24-hour emergency response devices and patrols, student patrols, late-night transport/escort service. *Student services:* health clinic, personal/psychological counseling.

Athletics Member NAIA. *Intercollegiate sports:* baseball M (s), basketball M (s)/W (s), cross-country running M (s)/W (s), golf M (s)/W (s), tennis M (s)/W (s), volleyball W (s). *Intramural sports:* badminton M/W, baseball M/W, basketball M/W, bowling M/W, field hockey M/W, football M/W, golf M/W, lacrosse M/W, rock climbing M/W, rugby M/W, skiing (cross-country) M/W, skiing (downhill) M/W, soccer M/W, softball M/W, table tennis M/W, tennis M/W, track and field M/W, volleyball M/W, weight lifting M/W.

Standardized Tests *Required for some:* SAT or ACT (for admission), ACT COMPASS.

Costs (2007–08) *Tuition:* state resident $4092 full-time, $204 per credit part-time; nonresident $11,382 full-time, $204 per credit part-time. Full-time tuition and fees vary according to course load and reciprocity agreements. *Room and board:* $5100. Room and board charges vary according to board plan and housing facility. *Payment plan:* deferred payment. *Waivers:* senior citizens and employees or children of employees.

Financial Aid Of all full-time matriculated undergraduates who enrolled in 2006, 1,690 applied for aid, 1,492 were judged to have need, 84 had their need fully met. 87 Federal Work-Study jobs (averaging $1277). 97 state and other part-time jobs (averaging $1152). In 2006, 185 non-need-based awards were made. *Average percent of need met:* 6%. *Average financial aid package:* $7121. *Average need-based loan:* $3558. *Average need-based gift aid:* $3180. *Average non-need-based aid:* $2142.

Applying *Options:* electronic application, deferred entrance. *Application fee:* $35. *Required:* high school transcript, minimum 2.0 GPA. *Required for some:* interview. *Application deadlines:* rolling (freshmen), rolling (transfers). *Notification:* continuous (freshmen), continuous (transfers).

Freshman Application Contact Soo Lee Bruce-Smith, Coordinator of New Student Recruitment, Lewis-Clark State College, 500 8th Avenue, Lewiston, ID 83501. *Phone:* 208-792-2210. *Toll-free phone:* 800-933-5272. *Fax:* 208-792-2876. *E-mail:* admissions@lcsc.edu.

NEW SAINT ANDREWS COLLEGE

Moscow, Idaho **www.nsa.edu/**

- **Proprietary** 4-year, founded 1993
- **Small-town** campus
- **Coed** 160 undergraduate students, 90% full-time, 56% women, 44% men
- **Moderately difficult** entrance level, 75% of applicants were admitted

Undergraduates 144 full-time, 16 part-time. Students come from 32 states and territories, 7 other countries, 84% are from out of state, 3% Asian American or Pacific Islander, 3% Hispanic American, 1% Native American, 8% international, 3% transferred in. *Retention:* 89% of 2006 full-time freshmen returned.

Freshmen *Admission:* 83 applied, 62 admitted, 48 enrolled. *Test scores:* SAT critical reading scores over 500: 100%; SAT math scores over 500: 63%; ACT scores over 18: 100%; SAT critical reading scores over 600: 63%; SAT math scores over 600: 34%; ACT scores over 24: 65%; SAT critical reading scores over 700: 34%; SAT math scores over 700: 6%; ACT scores over 30: 24%.

Faculty *Total:* 15, 53% full-time, 27% with terminal degrees. *Student/faculty ratio:* 10:1.

Majors Liberal arts and sciences/liberal studies.

Academics *Calendar:* 4 8-week terms. *Degrees:* associate, bachelor's, master's, and postbachelor's certificates. *Special study options:* advanced placement credit, independent study, part-time degree program, summer session for credit.

Computers on Campus 5 computers/terminals are available on campus for general student use. Wireless service is available via entire campus.

Student Life *Housing:* college housing not available. *Activities and organizations:* drama/theater group, choral group, Rugby, theater. *Campus security:* 24-hour emergency response devices.

Standardized Tests *Required:* SAT or ACT (for admission), TOEFL (for admission).

Costs (2008–09) *Tuition:* $8500 full-time, $725 per course part-time.

Applying *Options:* electronic application. *Application fee:* $25. *Required:* essay or personal statement, high school transcript, letters of recommendation. *Required for some:* interview. *Application deadlines:* 2/15 (freshmen), 2/15 (transfers), 12/1 (early action). *Notification:* 3/15 (freshmen), 3/15 (transfers), 1/15 (early action).

Freshman Application Contact Mr. Aaron Rench, Director of Admissions, New Saint Andrews College, PO Box 9025, Moscow, ID 83843. *Phone:* 208-882-1566. *Fax:* 208-882-4293. *E-mail:* info@nsa.edu.

NORTHWEST NAZARENE UNIVERSITY

Nampa, Idaho **www.nnu.edu/**

- **Independent** comprehensive, founded 1913, affiliated with Church of the Nazarene
- **Rural** 85-acre campus
- **Endowment** $21.8 million
- **Coed** 1,266 undergraduate students, 91% full-time, 60% women, 40% men
- **Moderately difficult** entrance level, 70% of applicants were admitted

A Christian university located in southern Idaho, Northwest Nazarene University (NNU) is consistently ranked by *U.S. News & World Report* as a top university and best value choice in the West. New facilities, nearby outdoor recreational areas, and opportunities for international study and service make NNU a place to challenge a student's mind and spirit.

Undergraduates 1,154 full-time, 112 part-time. Students come from 32 states and territories, 7 other countries, 60% are from out of state, 0.7% African American, 1% Asian American or Pacific Islander, 2% Hispanic American, 0.9% Native American, 0.6% international, 6% transferred in, 84% live on campus.

Freshmen *Admission:* 1,088 applied, 758 admitted, 252 enrolled. *Average high school GPA:* 3.46. *Test scores:* SAT critical reading scores over 500: 67%; SAT math scores over 500: 64%; SAT writing scores over 500: 54%; ACT scores over 18: 87%; SAT critical reading scores over 600: 30%; SAT math scores over 600: 22%; SAT writing scores over 600: 20%; ACT scores over 24: 36%; SAT critical reading scores over 700: 3%; SAT math scores over 700: 5%; SAT writing scores over 700: 2%; ACT scores over 30: 7%.

Faculty *Total:* 101, 97% full-time, 68% with terminal degrees. *Student/faculty ratio:* 12:1.

Majors Accounting; ancient Near Eastern and biblical languages; art; art teacher education; athletic training; biblical studies; biochemistry; biology/biological sciences; biology teacher education; business administration and management; cell and molecular biology; ceramic arts and ceramics; chemistry; chemistry teacher education; commercial and advertising art; communication/speech communication and rhetoric; computer science; divinity/ministry; elementary education; engineering physics; English; English/language arts teacher education; finance; forensic science and technology; graphic design; health and physical education; history; history teacher education; humanities; international business/trade/commerce; international relations and affairs; journalism; kinesiology and exercise science; liberal arts and sciences/liberal studies; marketing/marketing management; mass communication/media; mathematics; mathematics teacher education; missionary studies and missiology; music; music performance; music teacher education; music theory and composition; nursing (registered nurse training); painting; parks, recreation and leisure; pastoral studies/counseling; philosophy; physical education teaching and coaching; physical therapy; physics; political science and government; pre-dentistry studies; pre-engineering; pre-law; pre-law studies; pre-medical studies; pre-pharmacy studies; pre-veterinary studies; printmaking; psychology; public relations/image management; radio and television broadcasting technology; religious education; religious/sacred music; religious studies; sculpture; secondary education; social sciences; social science teacher education; social work; Spanish; Spanish language teacher education; theology.

Academics *Calendar:* semesters. *Degrees:* bachelor's and master's. *Special study options:* academic remediation for entering students, accelerated degree program, adult/continuing education programs, advanced placement credit, cooperative education, freshman honors college, honors programs, independent study, internships, off-campus study, part-time degree program, services for LD students, student-designed majors, study abroad, summer session for credit. *ROTC:* Army (b). *Unusual degree programs:* 3-2 engineering with University of Idaho, Boise State University, Walla Walla College.

Computers on Campus 400 computers/terminals are available on campus for general student use. Students can access the following: campus intranet, computer help desk, free student e-mail accounts, online (class) grades, online (class) registration, online (class) schedules, various software packages. Campuswide network is available. 95% of college-owned or -operated housing units are wired for high-speed Internet access. Wireless service is available via entire campus.

Student Life *Housing:* on-campus residence required through sophomore year. *Options:* men-only, women-only, disabled students. Campus housing is university owned. Freshman campus housing is guaranteed. *Activities and organizations:* drama/theater group, student-run newspaper, choral group, student government, Society for a Change, Ground Floor (Graphic Design Club), Fellowship of Christian Athletes, Students in Free Enterprise (SIFE). *Campus security:* 24-hour patrols, student patrols, late-night transport/escort service, controlled dormitory access, residence hall check-in system, on-campus police hub. *Student services:* health clinic, personal/psychological counseling.

Athletics Member NCAA. All Division II. *Intercollegiate sports:* baseball M (s), basketball M (s)/W (s), cheerleading W (c), cross-country running M (s)/W (s), golf M (s), soccer M (c)/W (s), softball W (s), track and field M (s)/W (s), volleyball W (s). *Intramural sports:* basketball M/W, cross-country running M/W, football M/W, softball M/W, table tennis M/W, tennis M/W, ultimate Frisbee M/W, volleyball M/W.

Standardized Tests *Required:* SAT or ACT (for admission).

Costs (2008–09) *Comprehensive fee:* $26,690 includes full-time tuition ($20,900), mandatory fees ($270), and room and board ($5520). Part-time tuition: $905 per credit.

Financial Aid Of all full-time matriculated undergraduates who enrolled in 2006, 863 applied for aid, 726 were judged to have need, 147 had their need fully met. 160 Federal Work-Study jobs (averaging $1419). In 2006, 297 non-need-based awards were made. *Average percent of need met:* 75%. *Average financial aid package:* $13,180. *Average need-based loan:* $4101. *Average need-based gift aid:* $5331. *Average non-need-based aid:* $3837. *Average indebtedness upon graduation:* $25,301.

Applying *Options:* electronic application, early action, deferred entrance. *Application fee:* $25. *Required:* essay or personal statement, high school transcript, minimum 2.5 GPA, 2 letters of recommendation, minimum ACT score of 18 or SAT of 870. *Required for some:* interview. *Application deadlines:* 8/15 (freshmen), 8/15 (transfers), 12/15 (early action). *Notification:* continuous (freshmen), continuous (transfers), 1/15 (early action).

Director of Admissions Stacey Berggren, Director of Admissions, Northwest Nazarene University, 623 Holly Street, Admissions Welcome Center, Nampa, ID 83686. *Phone:* 208-467-8648. *Toll-free phone:* 877-668-4968. *Fax:* 208-467-8645. *E-mail:* slberggren@nnu.edu.

STEVENS-HENAGER COLLEGE

Boise, Idaho

UNIVERSITY OF IDAHO

Moscow, Idaho **www.uidaho.edu/**

- **State-supported** university, founded 1889
- **Small-town** 1450-acre campus
- **Endowment** $186.9 million
- **Coed** 9,018 undergraduate students, 89% full-time, 46% women, 54% men
- **Moderately difficult** entrance level, 77% of applicants were admitted

Undergraduates 7,992 full-time, 1,026 part-time. Students come from 52 states and territories, 35 other countries, 38% are from out of state, 1% African American, 2% Asian American or Pacific Islander, 5% Hispanic American, 1% Native American, 2% international, 7% transferred in, 55% live on campus. *Retention:* 79% of 2006 full-time freshmen returned.

Freshmen *Admission:* 4,577 applied, 3,505 admitted, 1,664 enrolled. *Average high school GPA:* 3.33. *Test scores:* SAT critical reading scores over 500: 68%; SAT math scores over 500: 69%; SAT writing scores over 500: 58%; ACT scores over 18: 91%; SAT critical reading scores over 600: 27%; SAT math scores over 600: 27%; SAT writing scores over 600: 18%; ACT scores over 24: 41%; SAT critical reading scores over 700: 5%; SAT math scores over 700: 6%; SAT writing scores over 700: 3%; ACT scores over 30: 7%.

Faculty *Total:* 687, 87% full-time, 69% with terminal degrees. *Student/faculty ratio:* 16:1.

Majors Accounting; advertising; agricultural/biological engineering and bioengineering; agricultural business and management; agricultural economics; agricultural mechanization; agricultural teacher education; agriculture; agronomy and crop science; American studies; animal sciences; anthropology; applied mathematics; architectural technology; architecture; art; art teacher education; athletic training; biochemistry; biology/biological sciences; business/managerial economics; business teacher education; chemical engineering; chemistry; child development; civil engineering; classics and languages, literatures and linguistics; clothing/textiles; communication/speech communication and rhetoric; computer engineering; computer science; conservation biology; criminal justice/safety; dance; early childhood education; ecology; economics; electrical, electronics and communications engineering; elementary education; engineering; English; entomology; environmental science; family and consumer sciences/human sciences; finance; fine/studio arts; fishing and fisheries sciences and management; food science; foods, nutrition, and wellness; foreign languages and literatures; forest/forest resources management; forestry; forest sciences and biology; French; general studies; geography; geology/earth science; German; history; horticultural science; human resources management; industrial technology; interdisciplinary studies; interior architecture; interior design; international relations and affairs; journalism; kinesiology and exercise science; landscape architecture; Latin; Latin American studies; management information systems; marketing/marketing management; materials engineering; mathematics; mechanical engineering; medical microbiology and bacteriology; metallurgical engineering; microbiology; modern Greek; molecular biology; multi-/interdisciplinary studies related; music; music history, literature, and theory; music management and merchandising; music performance; music teacher education; music theory and composition; natural resources management and policy; Navy/Marine Corps R.O.T.C./naval science; operations management; parks, recreation and leisure; philosophy; physical education teaching and coaching; physics; political science and government; pre-medical studies; psychology; public relations/image management; radio and television; range science and management; secondary education; sociology; soil science and agronomy; Spanish; special education; technical teacher education; technology/industrial arts teacher education; trade and industrial teacher education; veterinary sciences; voice and opera; wildlife and wildlands science and management; zoology/animal biology.

Academics *Calendar:* semesters. *Degrees:* certificates, bachelor's, master's, doctoral, first professional, and post-master's certificates. *Special study options:* academic remediation for entering students, accelerated degree program, adult/continuing education programs, advanced placement credit, cooperative education, distance learning, double majors, honors programs, independent study, internships, off-campus study, part-time degree program, services for LD students, student-designed majors, study abroad, summer session for credit. *ROTC:* Army (b), Navy (b), Air Force (c).

Computers on Campus 670 computers/terminals are available on campus for general student use. Students can access the following: computer help desk, free student e-mail accounts, online (class) grades, online (class) registration, online (class) schedules, student evaluations of teaching. Campuswide network is available. 100% of college-owned or -operated housing units are wired for high-speed Internet access. Wireless service is available via classrooms, computer centers, computer labs, dorm rooms, learning centers, libraries, student centers.

Student Life *Housing options:* coed, men-only, women-only, disabled students. Campus housing is university owned. Freshman campus housing is guaranteed. *Activities and organizations:* drama/theater group, student-run newspaper, radio and television station, choral group, marching band, Greek Life Organizations, Campus Crusade for Christ, Student International Association, Student Recreation Center, Professional/Career, national fraternities, national sororities. *Campus security:* late-night transport/escort service, controlled dormitory access. *Student services:* health clinic, personal/psychological counseling, women's center, legal services.

Athletics Member NCAA. All Division I except football (Division I-A). *Intercollegiate sports:* badminton M (c)/W (c), baseball M (c), basketball M (s)/W (s), cross-country running M (s)/W (s), golf M (s)/W (s), gymnastics M (c)/W (c), ice hockey M (c), riflery M (c)/W (c), rugby M (c)/W (c), skiing (cross-country) M (c)/W (c), skiing (downhill) M (c)/W (c), soccer M (c)/W (s), table tennis M (c)/W (c), tennis M (s)/W (s), track and field M (s)/W (s), ultimate Frisbee M (c)/W (c), volleyball W (s). *Intramural sports:* badminton M/W, baseball M, basketball M/W, equestrian sports M/W, fencing M, football M/W, golf M/W, ice hockey M, racquetball M/W, riflery M/W, rugby M/W, skiing (cross-country) M/W, skiing (downhill) M/W, soccer M/W, softball M/W, squash M/W, swimming and diving M/W, table tennis M/W, tennis M/W, track and field M/W, ultimate Frisbee M/W, volleyball M/W, water polo M, weight lifting M/W, wrestling M.

Standardized Tests *Required:* SAT or ACT (for admission).

Costs (2007–08) *Tuition:* area resident $0 full-time; state resident $0 full-time; nonresident $10,080 full-time, $148 per credit part-time. Full-time tuition and fees vary according to degree level and program. Part-time tuition and fees vary according to course load, degree level, and program. *Required fees:* $4410 full-time, $212 per credit part-time. *Room and board:* $6424. Room and board charges vary according to board plan and housing facility. *Payment plans:* installment, deferred payment. *Waivers:* minority students, children of alumni, senior citizens, and employees or children of employees.

Financial Aid Of all full-time matriculated undergraduates who enrolled in 2006, 6,136 applied for aid, 4,950 were judged to have need, 1,121 had their need fully met. 544 Federal Work-Study jobs (averaging $1500). 238 state and other part-time jobs (averaging $1500). In 2006, 1934 non-need-based awards were made. *Average percent of need met:* 74%. *Average financial aid package:* $9805. *Average need-based loan:* $5851. *Average need-based gift aid:* $3102. *Average non-need-based aid:* $3724. *Average indebtedness upon graduation:* $21,609.

Applying *Options:* electronic application, deferred entrance. *Application fee:* $40. *Required:* high school transcript, minimum 2.2 GPA. *Required for some:* essay or personal statement. *Application deadlines:* 8/1 (freshmen), rolling (transfers). *Notification:* continuous (freshmen), continuous (transfers).

Freshman Application Contact Mr. Dan Davenport, Director of Admissions, University of Idaho, PO Box 444264, Moscow, ID 83844-4264. *Phone:* 208-885-6326. *Toll-free phone:* 888-884-3246. *Fax:* 208-885-9119. *E-mail:* admissions@uidaho.edu.

UNIVERSITY OF PHOENIX–IDAHO CAMPUS

Meridian, Idaho **www.phoenix.edu/**

- **Proprietary** comprehensive
- **Urban** campus
- **Coed**
- **Noncompetitive** entrance level

Faculty *Student/faculty ratio:* 6:1.

Academics *Calendar:* continuous. *Degrees:* bachelor's and master's.

Student Life *Campus security:* late-night transport/escort service.

Costs (2007–08) *Tuition:* $10,410 full-time, $347 per credit part-time. Full-time tuition and fees vary according to course level.

Financial Aid *Average financial aid package:* $4067. *Average need-based gift aid:* $2146.

Applying *Options:* deferred entrance. *Application fee:* $45. *Required:* 1 letter of recommendation. *Required for some:* high school transcript.

Freshman Application Contact Ms. Beth Barilla, Associate Vice President, Student Admissions and Services, University of Phoenix–Idaho Campus, 4615 East Elwood Street, Mail Stop AA-K101, Phoenix, AZ 85040-1958. *Phone:* 480-317-6000. *Toll-free phone:* 800-776-4867 (in-state); 800-228-7240 (out-of-state). *Fax:* 480-894-1758. *E-mail:* beth.barilla@phoenix.edu.

ILLINOIS

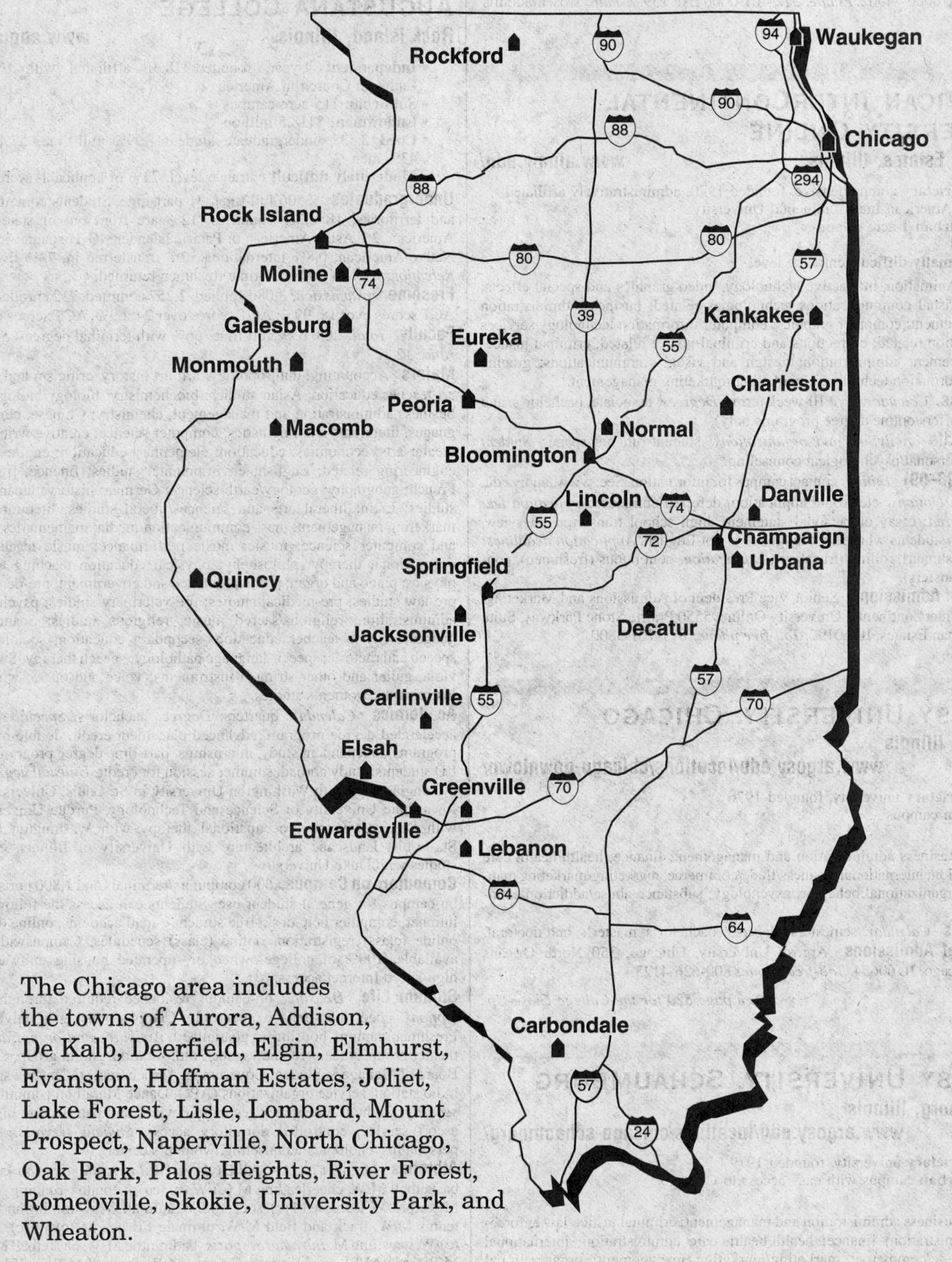

The Chicago area includes the towns of Aurora, Addison, De Kalb, Deerfield, Elgin, Elmhurst, Evanston, Hoffman Estates, Joliet, Lake Forest, Lisle, Lombard, Mount Prospect, Naperville, North Chicago, Oak Park, Palos Heights, River Forest, Romeoville, Skokie, University Park, and Wheaton.

AMERICAN ACADEMY OF ART

Chicago, Illinois **www.aaart.edu/**

Freshman Application Contact Mr. Stuart Rosenbloom, Director of Admissions, American Academy of Art, 332 South Michigan Avenue, Suite 300, Chicago, IL 60604-4302. *Phone:* 312-461-0600 Ext. 159. *E-mail:* srosenbloom@aaart.edu.

AMERICAN INTERCONTINENTAL UNIVERSITY ONLINE

Hoffman Estates, Illinois **www.aiuniv.edu/**

- **Proprietary** comprehensive, founded 1970, administratively affiliated with American InterContinental University
- **Suburban** 1-acre campus
- **Coed**
- **Minimally difficult** entrance level

Majors Animation, interactive technology, video graphics and special effects; art; audiovisual communications technologies related; business administration and management; computer graphics; computer/information technology services administration related; corrections and criminal justice related; criminal justice/law enforcement administration; design and visual communications; graphic design; information technology; marketing/marketing management.

Academics *Calendar:* five 10-week terms. *Degrees:* associate, bachelor's, and master's (offers online degree programs only).

Student Life *Activities and organizations:* student-run newspaper. *Student services:* personal/psychological counseling.

Costs (2008–09) *Tuition:* contact campus for information. See: www.aiuniv.edu.

Applying *Options:* electronic application, deferred entrance. *Application fee:* $50. *Required:* essay or personal statement, high school transcript, interview, TOEFL for students whose first language is not English. *Application deadlines:* rolling (freshmen), rolling (transfers). *Notification:* continuous (freshmen), continuous (transfers).

Director of Admissions Senior Vice President of Admissions and Marketing, American InterContinental University Online, 5550 Prairie Stone Parkway, Suite 400, Hoffman Estates, IL 60192. *Toll-free phone:* 877-701-3800.

ARGOSY UNIVERSITY, CHICAGO

Chicago, Illinois

www.argosy.edu/locations/chicago-downtown/

- **Proprietary** university, founded 1976
- **Urban** campus
- **Coed**

Majors Business administration and management; finance; health/health care administration; international business/trade/commerce; marketing/marketing management; organizational behavior; psychology; substance abuse/addiction counseling.

Academics *Calendar:* semesters. *Degrees:* bachelor's, master's, and doctoral.

Director of Admissions Argosy University, Chicago, 350 North Orleans Street, Chicago, IL 60654. *Toll-free phone:* 800-626-4123.

See page 820 for the College Close-Up.

ARGOSY UNIVERSITY, SCHAUMBURG

Schaumburg, Illinois

www.argosy.edu/locations/chicago-schaumburg/

- **Proprietary** university, founded 1979
- **Suburban** campus with easy access to Chicago
- **Coed**

Majors Business administration and management; criminal justice/law enforcement administration; finance; health/health care administration; international business/trade/commerce; marketing/marketing management; organizational behavior; psychology; substance abuse/addiction counseling.

Academics *Calendar:* semesters. *Degrees:* bachelor's, master's, doctoral, and post-master's certificates.

Director of Admissions Argosy University, Schaumburg, 999 North Plaza Drive, Suite 111, Schaumburg, IL 60173. *Phone:* 847-969-4900. *Toll-free phone:* 866-290-2777. *Fax:* 847-969-4998.

See page 820 for the College Close-Up.

AUGUSTANA COLLEGE

Rock Island, Illinois **www.augustana.edu/**

- **Independent** 4-year, founded 1860, affiliated with Evangelical Lutheran Church in America
- **Suburban** 115-acre campus
- **Endowment** $118.5 million
- **Coed** 2,537 undergraduate students, 99% full-time, 57% women, 43% men
- **Moderately difficult** entrance level, 73% of applicants were admitted

Undergraduates 2,506 full-time, 31 part-time. Students come from 26 states and territories, 18 other countries, 12% are from out of state, 2% African American, 2% Asian American or Pacific Islander, 4% Hispanic American, 0.5% Native American, 0.8% international, 2% transferred in, 73% live on campus. *Retention:* 87% of 2006 full-time freshmen returned.

Freshmen *Admission:* 3,080 applied, 2,257 admitted, 712 enrolled. *Test scores:* ACT scores over 18: 99%; ACT scores over 24: 69%; ACT scores over 30: 13%.

Faculty *Total:* 268, 65% full-time, 66% with terminal degrees. *Student/faculty ratio:* 12:1.

Majors Accounting; anthropology; art; art history, criticism and conservation; art teacher education; Asian studies; biochemistry; biology/biological sciences; business administration and management; chemistry; Chinese; classics and languages, literatures and linguistics; computer science; creative writing; dramatic/theater arts; economics; education; elementary education; engineering physics; engineering related; English; environmental studies; finance; fine/studio arts; French; geography; geology/earth science; German; history; Japanese; jazz/jazz studies; Latin; liberal arts and sciences/liberal studies; literature; marketing/marketing management; mass communication/media; mathematics; mathematics and computer science; music; music performance; music teacher education; occupational therapy; philosophy; physical education teaching and coaching; physics; piano and organ; political science and government; pre-dentistry studies; pre-law studies; pre-medical studies; pre-veterinary studies; psychology; public administration; religious/sacred music; religious studies; Scandinavian languages; science teacher education; secondary education; sociology; Spanish; speech and rhetoric; speech-language pathology; speech therapy; Swedish; violin, viola, guitar and other stringed instruments; voice and opera; wind/percussion instruments; women's studies.

Academics *Calendar:* quarters. *Degree:* bachelor's. *Special study options:* accelerated degree program, advanced placement credit, double majors, honors programs, independent study, internships, part-time degree program, services for LD students, study abroad, summer session for credit. *Unusual degree programs:* 3-2 engineering with Washington University in St. Louis, University of Illinois, Iowa State University of Science and Technology, Purdue University; forestry with Duke University; occupational therapy with Washington University in St. Louis, landscape architecture with University of Illinois, environmental studies with Duke University.

Computers on Campus 600 computers/terminals and 1,800 ports are available on campus for general student use. Students can access the following: campus intranet, computer help desk, free student e-mail accounts, online (class) grades, online (class) registration, online (class) schedules. Campuswide network is available. 100% of college-owned or -operated housing units are wired for high-speed Internet access.

Student Life *Housing:* on-campus residence required through junior year. *Options:* coed, men-only, women-only. Campus housing is university owned. Freshman campus housing is guaranteed. *Activities and organizations:* drama/theater group, student-run newspaper, radio station, choral group, College Union Board of Managers, Student Government Association, student newspaper, student radio station, service organizations (APO, Dance Marathon committee). *Campus security:* 24-hour emergency response devices and patrols, late-night transport/escort service, controlled dormitory access. *Student services:* health clinic, personal/psychological counseling, women's center.

Athletics Member NCAA. All Division III. *Intercollegiate sports:* baseball M, basketball M/W, cheerleading M (c)/W (c), cross-country running M/W, football M, golf M/W, lacrosse M (c), soccer M/W, softball W, swimming and diving M/W, tennis M/W, track and field M/W, ultimate Frisbee M (c)/W (c), volleyball M (c)/W, wrestling M. *Intramural sports:* badminton M/W, basketball M/W, bowling M/W, crew M/W, cross-country running M/W, football M/W, golf M/W, racquetball M/W, rugby M, skiing (cross-country) M/W, skiing (downhill) M/W, soccer M/W, softball M/W, swimming and diving M/W, table tennis M/W, tennis M/W, track and field M/W, ultimate Frisbee M/W, volleyball M/W, wrestling M.

Standardized Tests *Recommended:* SAT or ACT (for admission).
Costs (2007–08) *Comprehensive fee:* $33,717 includes full-time tuition ($25,935), mandatory fees ($549), and room and board ($7233). Full-time tuition and fees vary according to course load. Part-time tuition: $1100 per credit hour. *College room only:* $3660. Room and board charges vary according to board plan and housing facility. *Payment plans:* tuition prepayment, installment. *Waivers:* employees or children of employees.
Financial Aid Of all full-time matriculated undergraduates who enrolled in 2006, 1,938 applied for aid, 1,620 were judged to have need, 463 had their need fully met. 1,008 Federal Work-Study jobs (averaging $1567). In 2006, 309 non-need-based awards were made. *Average percent of need met:* 83%. *Average financial aid package:* $17,681. *Average need-based loan:* $4269. *Average need-based gift aid:* $12,653. *Average non-need-based aid:* $8684. *Average indebtedness upon graduation:* $16,794.
Applying *Options:* electronic application, deferred entrance. *Application fee:* $35. *Required:* high school transcript. *Required for some:* essay or personal statement, interview. *Application deadlines:* rolling (freshmen), rolling (transfers). *Notification:* continuous (freshmen), continuous (transfers).
Freshman Application Contact Megan Cooley, Director of Admissions, Augustana College, 639 38th Street, Rock Island, IL 61201-2296. *Phone:* 309-794-7341. *Toll-free phone:* 800-798-8100. *Fax:* 309-794-7422. *E-mail:* admissions@augustana.edu.

AURORA UNIVERSITY

Aurora, Illinois **www.aurora.edu/**

- **Independent** comprehensive, founded 1893
- **Suburban** 30-acre campus with easy access to Chicago
- **Endowment** $31.2 million
- **Coed**
- **Moderately difficult** entrance level

Aurora University combines a residential and commuter population. The curriculum emphasizes preprofessional programs offered through the College of Education and the College of Professional Studies (social work, health and physical education, nursing, and business), as well as traditional majors offered through the College of Arts and Sciences. The Honors Program offers qualified, highly motivated students an opportunity for advanced course work, innovative seminars, and travel/study experiences.

Faculty *Student/faculty ratio:* 16:1.
Academics *Calendar:* trimesters. *Degrees:* bachelor's, master's, doctoral, post-master's, and postbachelor's certificates.
Student Life *Campus security:* 24-hour emergency response devices and patrols, late-night transport/escort service, controlled dormitory access.
Athletics Member NCAA. All Division III.
Standardized Tests *Required:* SAT or ACT (for admission).
Costs (2007–08) *Comprehensive fee:* $23,884 includes full-time tuition ($16,750), mandatory fees ($100), and room and board ($7034). Full-time tuition and fees vary according to course load, location, and program. Part-time tuition: $510 per semester hour. Part-time tuition and fees vary according to course load, location, and program. *College room only:* $3080. Room and board charges vary according to board plan and housing facility. *Payment plans:* installment, deferred payment.
Financial Aid Of all full-time matriculated undergraduates who enrolled in 2007, 1,485 applied for aid, 1,297 were judged to have need, 488 had their need fully met. 576 Federal Work-Study jobs (averaging $1761). In 2007, 418 non-need-based awards were made. *Average percent of need met:* 89. *Average financial aid package:* $18,658. *Average need-based loan:* $4343. *Average need-based gift aid:* $6037. *Average non-need-based aid:* $9369. *Average indebtedness upon graduation:* $18,078.
Applying *Options:* electronic application, deferred entrance. *Application fee:* $25. *Required:* high school transcript, minimum 2.0 GPA. *Required for some:* 2 letters of recommendation, interview. *Recommended:* essay or personal statement, interview.
Freshman Application Contact Mr. James Lancaster, Director, Freshman Admission, Aurora University, 347 South Gladstone Avenue, Aurora, IL 60506-4892. *Phone:* 630-844-5533. *Toll-free phone:* 800-742-5281. *Fax:* 630-844-5535. *E-mail:* admission@aurora.edu.

See page 822 for the College Close-Up.

BENEDICTINE UNIVERSITY

Lisle, Illinois **www.ben.edu/**

- **Independent Roman Catholic** comprehensive, founded 1887
- **Suburban** 108-acre campus with easy access to Chicago
- **Endowment** $26.9 million
- **Coed** 2,993 undergraduate students, 65% full-time, 57% women, 43% men
- **Moderately difficult** entrance level, 79% of applicants were admitted

Undergraduates 1,958 full-time, 1,035 part-time. Students come from 44 states and territories, 16 other countries, 0.6% are from out of state, 10% African American, 12% Asian American or Pacific Islander, 6% Hispanic American, 0.2% Native American, 0.8% international, 8% transferred in, 21% live on campus. *Retention:* 71% of 2006 full-time freshmen returned.
Freshmen *Admission:* 1,449 applied, 1,150 admitted, 388 enrolled. *Average high school GPA:* 3.35. *Test scores:* ACT scores over 18: 96%; ACT scores over 24: 40%; ACT scores over 30: 5%.
Faculty *Total:* 390, 24% full-time, 28% with terminal degrees. *Student/faculty ratio:* 13:1.
Majors Accounting; arts management; biochemistry; biology/biological sciences; business administration and management; business/commerce; business, management, and marketing related; business/managerial economics; chemistry; clinical laboratory science/medical technology; communication/speech communication and rhetoric; comparative literature; computer science; economics; education; elementary education; engineering science; English; environmental studies; finance; fine/studio arts; health/health care administration; health science; history; information science/studies; international business/trade/commerce; international relations and affairs; marketing/marketing management; mathematics; molecular biology; music; music teacher education; nuclear medical technology; nursing science; nutrition sciences; organizational behavior; philosophy; physics; political science and government; pre-dentistry studies; pre-law studies; premedical studies; pre-veterinary studies; psychology; publishing; science teacher education; secondary education; social sciences; sociology; Spanish; special education.
Academics *Calendar:* semesters. *Degrees:* certificates, associate, bachelor's, master's, doctoral, and postbachelor's certificates. *Special study options:* academic remediation for entering students, accelerated degree program, adult/continuing education programs, advanced placement credit, distance learning, double majors, honors programs, independent study, internships, off-campus study, part-time degree program, services for LD students, study abroad, summer session for credit. *ROTC:* Army (c). *Unusual degree programs:* 3-2 engineering with University of Illinois at Urbana–Champaign, Illinois Institute of Technology, Purdue University; nursing with Rush University.
Computers on Campus 200 computers/terminals are available on campus for general student use. Students can access the following: computer help desk, free student e-mail accounts, online (class) grades, online (class) registration, online (class) schedules. Campuswide network is available. 100% of college-owned or -operated housing units are wired for high-speed Internet access.
Student Life *Housing options:* coed, men-only, women-only. Campus housing is university owned. Freshman campus housing is guaranteed. *Activities and organizations:* student-run newspaper, television station, choral group, Student Government Association, campus ministry, choir/gospel choir. *Campus security:* 24-hour emergency response devices and patrols, late-night transport/escort service, controlled dormitory access. *Student services:* health clinic, personal/psychological counseling.
Athletics Member NCAA. All Division III. *Intercollegiate sports:* baseball M, basketball M/W, cross-country running M/W, football M, golf M, soccer M/W, softball W, swimming and diving M/W, track and field M/W, volleyball W.
Standardized Tests *Required:* ACT (for admission).
Costs (2007–08) *Comprehensive fee:* $28,265 includes full-time tuition ($20,800), mandatory fees ($510), and room and board ($6955). Full-time tuition and fees vary according to class time, degree level, and location. Part-time tuition: $695 per credit hour. Part-time tuition and fees vary according to class time and degree level. *Required fees:* $15 per credit hour part-time. *Room and board:* Room and board charges vary according to board plan and housing facility. *Payment plans:* installment, deferred payment. *Waivers:* employees or children of employees.
Financial Aid Of all full-time matriculated undergraduates who enrolled in 2005, 1,135 applied for aid, 1,130 were judged to have need, 447 had their need fully met. In 2005, 270 non-need-based awards were made. *Average percent of need met:* 85%. *Average financial aid package:* $11,980. *Average need-based loan:* $4170. *Average need-based gift aid:* $6350. *Average non-need-based aid:* $6720.

Applying *Options:* electronic application, deferred entrance. *Application fee:* $40. *Required:* essay or personal statement, high school transcript, letters of recommendation. *Required for some:* interview. *Recommended:* rank in upper 50% of high school class, minimum ACT score of 21. *Application deadlines:* rolling (freshmen), rolling (transfers). *Notification:* continuous (freshmen), continuous (transfers).

Freshman Application Contact Ms. Kari Gibbons, Dean of Enrollment, Benedictine University, 5700 College Road, Lisle, IL 60532-0900. *Phone:* 630-829-6300. *Toll-free phone:* 888-829-6363. *Fax:* 630-829-6301. *E-mail:* admissions@ben.edu.

See page 824 for the College Close-Up.

BLACKBURN COLLEGE

Carlinville, Illinois **www.blackburn.edu/**

- **Independent Presbyterian** 4-year, founded 1837
- **Small-town** 80-acre campus with easy access to St. Louis
- **Endowment** $10.4 million
- **Coed** 617 undergraduate students, 98% full-time, 55% women, 45% men
- **Moderately difficult** entrance level, 61% of applicants were admitted

Undergraduates 604 full-time, 13 part-time. Students come from 10 states and territories, 1 other country, 11% are from out of state, 8% African American, 1% Asian American or Pacific Islander, 1% Hispanic American, 0.3% Native American, 0.3% international, 6% transferred in, 67% live on campus. *Retention:* 61% of 2006 full-time freshmen returned.

Freshmen *Admission:* 969 applied, 595 admitted, 175 enrolled. *Average high school GPA:* 3.2. *Test scores:* ACT scores over 18: 83%; ACT scores over 24: 30%; ACT scores over 30: 2%.

Faculty *Total:* 68, 51% full-time, 62% with terminal degrees. *Student/faculty ratio:* 13:1.

Majors Accounting; art; biology/biological sciences; business administration and management; chemistry; clinical laboratory science/medical technology; communication/speech communication and rhetoric; computer science; criminal justice/law enforcement administration; elementary education; English; environmental science; history; interdisciplinary studies; literature; marketing/marketing management; mathematics; molecular biology; music; physical education teaching and coaching; political science and government; pre-dentistry studies; pre-law studies; pre-medical studies; pre-veterinary studies; psychology; public administration; secondary education; Spanish.

Academics *Calendar:* semesters. *Degree:* bachelor's. *Special study options:* advanced placement credit, cooperative education, double majors, honors programs, independent study, internships, off-campus study, student-designed majors, study abroad, summer session for credit. *Unusual degree programs:* 3-2 engineering with Washington University in St. Louis; nursing with St. John's College.

Computers on Campus 202 computers/terminals are available on campus for general student use. Students can access the following: computer help desk, free student e-mail accounts, online (class) schedules. Campuswide network is available. 100% of college-owned or -operated housing units are wired for high-speed Internet access. Wireless service is available via libraries, student centers.

Student Life *Housing:* on-campus residence required through junior year. *Options:* coed, men-only, women-only. Campus housing is university owned. Freshman campus housing is guaranteed. *Activities and organizations:* drama/theater group, student-run newspaper, choral group, Cultural Expressions, Residence Hall Association, New Student Orientation Committee, Choral groups, Student government. *Campus security:* student patrols, late-night transport/escort service. *Student services:* personal/psychological counseling.

Athletics Member NCAA. All Division III. *Intercollegiate sports:* baseball M, basketball M/W, cheerleading M/W, cross-country running M/W, football M, golf M, soccer M/W, softball W, tennis W, volleyball W. *Intramural sports:* badminton M/W, basketball M/W, racquetball M/W, soccer M/W, tennis W, volleyball M/W.

Standardized Tests *Required:* SAT or ACT (for admission).

Costs (2008–09) *Comprehensive fee:* $15,493 includes full-time tuition ($11,020), mandatory fees ($110), and room and board ($4363). Part-time tuition: $450 per semester hour. *College room only:* $2205.

Financial Aid Of all full-time matriculated undergraduates who enrolled in 2003, 574 applied for aid, 511 were judged to have need, 269 had their need fully met. In 2003, 50 non-need-based awards were made. *Average percent of need met:* 89%. *Average financial aid package:* $9652. *Average need-based loan:* $2677. *Average need-based gift aid:* $7199. *Average non-need-based aid:* $4449. *Average indebtedness upon graduation:* $11,000.

Applying *Options:* electronic application, deferred entrance. *Required:* essay or personal statement, high school transcript, minimum 2.0 GPA. *Required for some:* interview. *Application deadlines:* rolling (freshmen), rolling (transfers). *Notification:* continuous (transfers).

Freshman Application Contact Ron Bryan, Director of Admission, Blackburn College, 700 College Avenue, Carlinville, IL 62626-1498. *Phone:* 217-854-3231 Ext. 4293. *Toll-free phone:* 800-233-3550. *E-mail:* admit@mail.blackburn.edu.

BLESSING-RIEMAN COLLEGE OF NURSING

Quincy, Illinois **www.brcn.edu/**

- **Independent** 4-year, founded 1985
- **Small-town** 1-acre campus
- **Endowment** $7.0 million
- **Coed, primarily women** 211 undergraduate students, 94% full-time, 92% women, 8% men
- **Moderately difficult** entrance level, 77% of applicants were admitted

Undergraduates 198 full-time, 13 part-time. Students come from 8 states and territories, 47% are from out of state, 4% African American, 3% Asian American or Pacific Islander, 0.9% Hispanic American, 0.5% Native American, 12% transferred in, 82% live on campus. *Retention:* 64% of 2006 full-time freshmen returned.

Freshmen *Admission:* 39 applied, 30 admitted, 20 enrolled. *Average high school GPA:* 3.6. *Test scores:* ACT scores over 18: 100%; ACT scores over 24: 67%.

Faculty *Total:* 18, 100% full-time, 28% with terminal degrees. *Student/faculty ratio:* 12:1.

Majors Nursing (registered nurse training).

Academics *Calendar:* semesters. *Degrees:* bachelor's and master's. *Special study options:* academic remediation for entering students, adult/continuing education programs, advanced placement credit, distance learning, double majors, honors programs, internships, part-time degree program, summer session for credit.

Computers on Campus 28 computers/terminals are available on campus for general student use. Students can access the following: campus intranet, computer help desk, free student e-mail accounts. Campuswide network is available. 100% of college-owned or -operated housing units are wired for high-speed Internet access.

Student Life *Housing:* on-campus residence required through sophomore year. *Options:* coed. Campus housing is university owned. Freshman campus housing is guaranteed. *Activities and organizations:* drama/theater group, student-run newspaper, radio station, choral group, Student Nurses Organization, national fraternities, national sororities. *Campus security:* 24-hour patrols, late-night transport/escort service, controlled dormitory access. *Student services:* health clinic, personal/psychological counseling.

Athletics *Intercollegiate sports:* baseball M (s)/W (s), basketball M (s)/W (s), football M (s), soccer M (s)/W (s), volleyball M (s)/W (s). *Intramural sports:* baseball M/W, basketball M/W, football M, soccer M/W, volleyball M/W.

Standardized Tests *Required:* SAT or ACT (for admission).

Costs (2008–09) *Comprehensive fee:* $26,616 includes full-time tuition ($18,664), mandatory fees ($450), and room and board ($7502). Part-time tuition: $488 per credit hour. *College room only:* $3722.

Financial Aid Of all full-time matriculated undergraduates who enrolled in 2006, 91 applied for aid, 91 were judged to have need. *Average percent of need met:* 75%. *Average indebtedness upon graduation:* $11,000.

Applying *Options:* electronic application, deferred entrance. *Required:* high school transcript, minimum 3.0 GPA. *Recommended:* essay or personal statement, interview. *Application deadlines:* rolling (freshmen), rolling (transfers).

Freshman Application Contact Ms. Heather Mutter or Ms. Kate Boster, Admissions Counselors, Blessing-Rieman College of Nursing, PO Box 7005, Quincy, IL 62305-7005. *Phone:* 217-228-5520 Ext. 6984. *Toll-free phone:* 800-877-9140 Ext. 6964. *Fax:* 217-223-4661. *E-mail:* admissions@brcn.edu.

BRADLEY UNIVERSITY

Peoria, Illinois **www.bradley.edu/**

- **Independent** comprehensive, founded 1897
- **Suburban** 85-acre campus with easy access to Chicago and St. Louis
- **Endowment** $252.4 million
- **Coed** 5,215 undergraduate students, 94% full-time, 55% women, 45% men

• **Moderately difficult** entrance level, 83% of applicants were admitted

Undergraduates 4,919 full-time, 296 part-time. Students come from 40 states and territories, 21 other countries, 11% are from out of state, 6% African American, 4% Asian American or Pacific Islander, 3% Hispanic American, 0.4% Native American, 0.7% international, 6% transferred in, 70% live on campus. *Retention:* 89% of 2006 full-time freshmen returned.

Freshmen *Admission:* 4,612 applied, 3,844 admitted, 1,080 enrolled. *Average high school GPA:* 3.6. *Test scores:* SAT critical reading scores over 500: 83%; SAT math scores over 500: 82%; ACT scores over 18: 99%; SAT critical reading scores over 600: 32%; SAT math scores over 600: 45%; ACT scores over 24: 67%; SAT critical reading scores over 700: 5%; SAT math scores over 700: 7%; ACT scores over 30: 10%.

Faculty *Total:* 552, 61% full-time, 50% with terminal degrees. *Student/faculty ratio:* 14:1.

Majors Accounting; acting; acting/directing; actuarial science; advertising; animation, interactive technology, video graphics and special effects; art; art history, criticism and conservation; biochemistry; biology/biological sciences; broadcast journalism; business administration and management; business/managerial economics; cell and molecular biology; ceramic arts and ceramics; chemistry; civil engineering; clinical laboratory science/medical technology; communication/speech communication and rhetoric; computer engineering; computer science; construction engineering; consumer merchandising/retailing management; creative writing; criminal justice/law enforcement administration; dietetics; dramatic/theater arts; drawing; early childhood education; ecology; economics; education (specific subject areas) related; electrical, electronic and communications engineering technology; electrical, electronics and communications engineering; elementary education; engineering physics; English; entrepreneurship; environmental/environmental health engineering; environmental science; family and consumer sciences/human sciences; family resource management; finance; fine/studio arts; French; German; graphic design; health professions related; health science; history; humanities; human resources management; industrial engineering; information science/studies; insurance; international business/trade/commerce; international relations and affairs; journalism; law and legal studies related; liberal arts and sciences/liberal studies; management information systems; manufacturing engineering; manufacturing technology; marketing/marketing management; mathematics; mechanical engineering; music; music performance; music teacher education; music theory and composition; nursing (registered nurse training); philosophy; photography; photojournalism; physical therapy; physics; political science and government; printmaking; psychology; public relations/image management; radio and television; religious studies; sculpture; selling skills and sales; small business administration; social work; sociology; Spanish; special education (mentally retarded); special education (specific learning disabilities).

Academics *Calendar:* semesters. *Degrees:* bachelor's, master's, and first professional. *Special study options:* academic remediation for entering students, accelerated degree program, adult/continuing education programs, advanced placement credit, cooperative education, distance learning, double majors, honors programs, independent study, internships, off-campus study, part-time degree program, student-designed majors, study abroad, summer session for credit. *ROTC:* Army (c). *Unusual degree programs:* 3-2 business administration with accounting.

Computers on Campus 2,000 computers/terminals are available on campus for general student use. Students can access the following: computer help desk, free student e-mail accounts, online (class) grades, online (class) registration, online (class) schedules. Campuswide network is available. 100% of college-owned or -operated housing units are wired for high-speed Internet access. Wireless service is available via entire campus.

Student Life *Housing:* on-campus residence required through sophomore year. *Options:* coed. Campus housing is university owned and is provided by a third party. Freshman campus housing is guaranteed. *Activities and organizations:* drama/theater group, student-run newspaper, radio and television station, choral group, Alpha Phi Omega, Student Activities Council, Habitat for Humanity, BU Dance Marathon, Student Senate, national fraternities, national sororities. *Campus security:* 24-hour emergency response devices and patrols, late-night transport/escort service, controlled dormitory access, bicycle patrol. *Student services:* health clinic, personal/psychological counseling.

Athletics Member NCAA. All Division I. *Intercollegiate sports:* baseball M (s), basketball M (s)/W (s), cheerleading M/W, cross-country running M (s)/W (s), fencing M (c)/W (c), golf M (s)/W (s), ice hockey M (c), soccer M (s)/W (c), softball W (s), table tennis M (c)/W (c), tennis M (s)/W (s), track and field W (s), volleyball W (s). *Intramural sports:* badminton M/W, basketball M/W, bowling M/W, football M/W, golf M/W, lacrosse M (c), racquetball M/W, soccer M/W, softball M/W, swimming and diving M/W, table tennis M/W, tennis M/W, volleyball M/W, water polo M/W, wrestling M.

Standardized Tests *Required:* SAT or ACT (for admission).

Costs (2007–08) *Comprehensive fee:* $28,410 includes full-time tuition ($21,200), mandatory fees ($160), and room and board ($7050). Full-time tuition and fees vary according to student level. Part-time tuition: $580 per credit. Part-time tuition and fees vary according to course load. *College room only:* $4100. Room and board charges vary according to board plan. *Payment plan:* installment. *Waivers:* senior citizens and employees or children of employees.

Financial Aid Of all full-time matriculated undergraduates who enrolled in 2006, 4,229 applied for aid, 3,544 were judged to have need, 1,356 had their need fully met. 386 Federal Work-Study jobs (averaging $1019). In 2006, 1176 non-need-based awards were made. *Average percent of need met:* 71%. *Average financial aid package:* $14,018. *Average need-based loan:* $6201. *Average need-based gift aid:* $9881. *Average non-need-based aid:* $10,609. *Average indebtedness upon graduation:* $15,209.

Applying *Options:* electronic application, early admission, deferred entrance. *Application fee:* $35. *Required:* essay or personal statement, high school transcript, letters of recommendation. *Recommended:* minimum 3.0 GPA, interview. *Application deadline:* rolling (freshmen). *Notification:* continuous (freshmen), continuous (transfers).

Freshman Application Contact Mr. Rodney San Jose, Director of Admissions, Bradley University, 1501 West Bradley Avenue, 100 Swords Hall, Peoria, IL 61625-0002. *Phone:* 309-677-1000. *Toll-free phone:* 800-447-6460. *Fax:* 309-677-2797. *E-mail:* admissions@bradley.edu.

See page 826 for the College Close-Up.

CHICAGO STATE UNIVERSITY

Chicago, Illinois **www.csu.edu/**

• **State-supported** comprehensive, founded 1867
• **Urban** 161-acre campus
• **Endowment** $2.0 million
• **Coed** 5,217 undergraduate students, 63% full-time, 72% women, 28% men
• **Minimally difficult** entrance level, 57% of applicants were admitted

Undergraduates 3,308 full-time, 1,909 part-time. Students come from 29 states and territories, 10 other countries, 2% are from out of state, 85% African American, 0.8% Asian American or Pacific Islander, 7% Hispanic American, 0.2% Native American, 0.4% international, 12% transferred in, 6% live on campus.

Freshmen *Admission:* 2,303 applied, 1,313 admitted, 448 enrolled. *Average high school GPA:* 2.83. *Test scores:* ACT scores over 18: 82%; ACT scores over 24: 4%.

Faculty *Total:* 433, 72% full-time, 62% with terminal degrees. *Student/faculty ratio:* 13:1.

Majors African-American/Black studies; art; bilingual and multilingual education; biology/biological sciences; business administration and management; business teacher education; chemistry; computer science; criminal justice/safety; early childhood education; economics; elementary education; general studies; geography; health information/medical records administration; health services/allied health/health sciences; history; industrial arts; liberal arts and sciences/liberal studies; mathematics; music; music teacher education; nursing (registered nurse training); parks, recreation and leisure facilities management; physical education teaching and coaching; physical therapy; physics; political science and government; psychology; public health education and promotion; radio and television; sociology; Spanish; technology/industrial arts teacher education.

Academics *Calendar:* semesters. *Degrees:* bachelor's, master's, doctoral, and postbachelor's certificates. *Special study options:* academic remediation for entering students, accelerated degree program, adult/continuing education programs, advanced placement credit, cooperative education, distance learning, double majors, external degree program, freshman honors college, honors programs, independent study, internships, off-campus study, part-time degree program, services for LD students, student-designed majors, study abroad, summer session for credit. *ROTC:* Army (b), Navy (c), Air Force (c).

Computers on Campus 75 computers/terminals and 250 ports are available on campus for general student use. Students can access the following: free student e-mail accounts, online (class) grades, online (class) registration, online (class) schedules. Campuswide network is available. 100% of college-owned or -operated housing units are wired for high-speed Internet access. Wireless service is available via libraries.

Student Life *Housing options:* coed. Campus housing is university owned. *Activities and organizations:* drama/theater group, student-run newspaper, radio station, choral group, Math/Computer Science Club, Geographic Society Club, Gospel Choir, Movie Club, national fraternities, national sororities. *Campus security:* 24-hour emergency response devices and patrols, student patrols, late-night transport/escort service, controlled dormitory access. *Student services:* health clinic, personal/psychological counseling, women's center.

Athletics Member NCAA. All Division I. *Intercollegiate sports:* baseball M (s), basketball M (s)/W (s), cross-country running M (s)/W (s), golf M (s)/W (s), tennis M (s)/W (s), track and field M (s)/W (s), volleyball W (s).

Standardized Tests *Required:* SAT or ACT (for admission).

Costs (2008–09) *Tuition:* state resident $6870 full-time, $229 per credit hour part-time; nonresident $13,650 full-time, $455 per credit hour part-time. *Required fees:* $1950 full-time, $375 per term part-time. *Room and board:* $7022.

Applying *Options:* electronic application. *Application fee:* $25. *Required:* high school transcript, minimum 2.5 GPA. *Required for some:* essay or personal statement, interview. *Notification:* continuous (freshmen), continuous (transfers).

Freshman Application Contact Ms. Addie Epps, Director of Admissions, Chicago State University, 95th Street at King Drive, ADM 200, Chicago, IL 60628. *Phone:* 773-995-2513. *Fax:* 773-995-3820. *E-mail:* ug-admissions@csu.edu.

CHRISTIAN LIFE COLLEGE

Mount Prospect, Illinois **www.christianlifecollege.edu/**

Director of Admissions Mr. Jim Spenner, Director of Admissions, Christian Life College, 400 East Gregory Street, Mount Prospect, IL 60056. *Phone:* 847-259-1840 Ext. 17. *E-mail:* jspenner@christianlifecollege.edu.

COLUMBIA COLLEGE CHICAGO

Chicago, Illinois **www.colum.edu/**

- **Independent** comprehensive, founded 1890
- **Urban** campus
- **Endowment** $100.9 million
- **Coed** 11,366 undergraduate students
- **Noncompetitive** entrance level, 95% of applicants were admitted

Undergraduates Students come from 52 states and territories, 36 other countries, 30% are from out of state, 21% live on campus. *Retention:* 66% of 2006 full-time freshmen returned.

Freshmen *Admission:* 4,043 applied, 3,837 admitted. *Average high school GPA:* 2.9. *Test scores:* ACT scores over 18: 79%; ACT scores over 24: 30%; ACT scores over 30: 3%.

Faculty *Total:* 1,477, 22% full-time. *Student/faculty ratio:* 14:1.

Majors Acting; advertising; area, ethnic, cultural, and gender studies related; art; arts management; broadcast journalism; business administration and management; cinematography and film/video production; commercial and advertising art; computer and information sciences and support services related; creative writing; dance; dance therapy; design and visual communications; dramatic/theater arts; early childhood education; education (specific levels and methods) related; education (specific subject areas) related; fashion/apparel design; film/cinema studies; fine/studio arts; industrial design; interdisciplinary studies; interior design; intermedia/multimedia; journalism; kindergarten/preschool education; liberal arts and sciences/liberal studies; marketing/marketing management; multi-/interdisciplinary studies related; music; music management and merchandising; music performance; photography; playwriting and screenwriting; public relations/image management; radio and television; recording arts technology; sign language interpretation and translation; theater design and technology; Web page, digital/multimedia and information resources design; web page, digital/multimedia and information resources design.

Academics *Calendar:* semesters. *Degrees:* certificates, bachelor's, master's, and postbachelor's certificates. *Special study options:* academic remediation for entering students, advanced placement credit, cooperative education, English as a second language, independent study, internships, off-campus study, part-time degree program, services for LD students, student-designed majors, study abroad, summer session for credit.

Computers on Campus 730 computers/terminals are available on campus for general student use. Campuswide network is available.

Student Life *Housing:* on-campus residence required for freshman year. *Options:* coed. Campus housing is university owned and leased by the school. Freshman applicants given priority for college housing. *Activities and organizations:* drama/theater group, student-run newspaper, radio and television station, choral group, Columbia Urban Music Association, International Student Organization, Acianza Latina, Marketing Club. *Campus security:* 24-hour emergency response devices and patrols, late-night transport/escort service, controlled dormitory access, escort upon request. *Student services:* health clinic, personal/psychological counseling.

Athletics *Intramural sports:* basketball M/W, soccer M/W.

Standardized Tests *Recommended:* SAT or ACT (for admission).

Costs (2007–08) *Comprehensive fee:* $29,652 includes full-time tuition ($17,104), mandatory fees ($530), and room and board ($12,018). Part-time tuition: $592 per hour. *College room only:* $9048.

Financial Aid Of all full-time matriculated undergraduates who enrolled in 2006, 8,748 applied for aid, 7,976 were judged to have need, 7,763 had their need fully met. 821 Federal Work-Study jobs (averaging $2250). In 2006, 8 non-need-based awards were made. *Average percent of need met:* 54%. *Average financial aid package:* $3438. *Average need-based loan:* $3971. *Average need-based gift aid:* $4176. *Average non-need-based aid:* $3143.

Applying *Options:* deferred entrance. *Application fee:* $35. *Required:* essay or personal statement, high school transcript, letters of recommendation. *Recommended:* minimum 2.0 GPA, interview. *Application deadlines:* rolling (freshmen), rolling (transfers). *Notification:* continuous (freshmen), continuous (transfers).

Freshman Application Contact Mr. Murphy Monroe, Executive Director of Admissions, Columbia College Chicago, 600 South Michigan Avenue, Chicago, IL 60605-1996. *Phone:* 312-663-1600 Ext. 7131. *Toll-free phone:* 312-663-1600 Ext. 7130. *Fax:* 312-344-8024. *E-mail:* admissions@colum.edu.

See page 828 for the College Close-Up.

CONCORDIA UNIVERSITY CHICAGO

River Forest, Illinois **www.cuchicago.edu/**

- **Independent** comprehensive, founded 1864, affiliated with Lutheran Church–Missouri Synod, part of Concordia University System
- **Suburban** 40-acre campus with easy access to Chicago
- **Endowment** $13.4 million
- **Coed** 1,121 undergraduate students, 87% full-time, 62% women, 38% men
- **Moderately difficult** entrance level, 84% of applicants were admitted

Undergraduates 976 full-time, 145 part-time. Students come from 22 states and territories, 1 other country, 38% are from out of state, 12% African American, 1% Asian American or Pacific Islander, 10% Hispanic American, 8% transferred in, 60% live on campus. *Retention:* 70% of 2006 full-time freshmen returned.

Freshmen *Admission:* 818 applied, 691 admitted, 230 enrolled. *Average high school GPA:* 3.16. *Test scores:* ACT scores over 18: 89%; ACT scores over 24: 41%; ACT scores over 30: 7%.

Faculty *Total:* 354, 29% full-time. *Student/faculty ratio:* 17:1.

Majors Accounting; ancient Near Eastern and biblical languages; art; art teacher education; biological and physical sciences; biology/biological sciences; biology teacher education; business administration and management; chemistry; commercial and advertising art; communication/speech communication and rhetoric; computer science; computer teacher education; dramatic/theater arts; education; elementary education; English; English/language arts teacher education; environmental studies; geography; history; history teacher education; information science/studies; kindergarten/preschool education; kinesiology and exercise science; legal studies; mathematics; mathematics teacher education; music; music teacher education; natural sciences; nursing (registered nurse training); pastoral studies/counseling; philosophy; physical education teaching and coaching; physical sciences; piano and organ; political science and government; pre-dentistry studies; pre-law studies; pre-medical studies; pre-theology/pre-ministerial studies; psychology; religious education; religious/sacred music; science teacher education; secondary education; social science teacher education; social work; sociology; speech teacher education; theology; voice and opera; wind/percussion instruments.

Academics *Calendar:* semesters. *Degrees:* bachelor's, master's, doctoral, post-master's, and postbachelor's certificates. *Special study options:* academic remediation for entering students, accelerated degree program, adult/continuing education programs, advanced placement credit, distance learning, double majors, honors programs, independent study, internships, off-campus study, part-time degree program, services for LD students, study abroad, summer session for credit.

Computers on Campus 85 computers/terminals are available on campus for general student use. Campuswide network is available. Wireless service is available via libraries, student centers.

Student Life *Housing options:* coed, women-only. Campus housing is university owned. *Activities and organizations:* drama/theater group, student-run newspaper, radio station, choral group, Concordia Youth Ministries, Kappelle Choir, Wind Symphony, student government, intramural sports. *Campus security:* 24-hour emergency response devices and patrols, student patrols, late-night transport/escort service, controlled dormitory access, emergency call boxes. *Student services:* personal/psychological counseling, legal services.

Athletics Member NCAA. All Division III. *Intercollegiate sports:* baseball M, basketball M/W, cheerleading M/W, cross-country running M/W, football M, golf M, soccer M/W, softball W, tennis M/W, track and field M/W, volleyball W. *Intramural sports:* badminton M/W, basketball M/W, bowling M/W, football W, swimming and diving M/W, table tennis M/W, tennis M/W, volleyball M/W.

Standardized Tests *Required:* SAT or ACT (for admission).

Costs (2008–09) *Comprehensive fee:* $29,740 includes full-time tuition ($21,950), mandatory fees ($440), and room and board ($7350). Part-time tuition: $685 per semester hour.

Financial Aid Of all full-time matriculated undergraduates who enrolled in 2006, 888 applied for aid, 750 were judged to have need, 289 had their need fully met. In 2006, 178 non-need-based awards were made. *Average percent of need met:* 80%. *Average financial aid package:* $18,926. *Average need-based loan:* $6821. *Average need-based gift aid:* $9409. *Average non-need-based aid:* $7701. *Average indebtedness upon graduation:* $16,393. *Financial aid deadline:* 8/15.

Applying *Options:* electronic application, deferred entrance. *Required:* high school transcript, minimum 2.0 GPA, 1 letter of recommendation, minimum ACT score of 20 or SAT score of 930. *Required for some:* essay or personal statement, interview. *Application deadlines:* rolling (freshmen), rolling (transfers).

Freshman Application Contact Dr. Evelyn Burdick, Vice President for Enrollment Services, Concordia University Chicago, 7400 Augusta Street, River Forest, IL 60305. *Phone:* 708-209-3100. *Toll-free phone:* 800-285-2668. *Fax:* 708-209-3473. *E-mail:* crfadmis@cuchicago.edu.

DePaul University

Chicago, Illinois — www.depaul.edu/

- **Independent Roman Catholic** university, founded 1898
- **Urban** 36-acre campus
- **Endowment** $344.7 million
- **Coed** 15,024 undergraduate students, 80% full-time, 56% women, 44% men
- **Moderately difficult** entrance level, 63% of applicants were admitted

Undergraduates 12,045 full-time, 2,979 part-time. Students come from 50 states and territories, 66 other countries, 19% are from out of state, 9% African American, 9% Asian American or Pacific Islander, 12% Hispanic American, 0.3% Native American, 1% international, 9% transferred in, 13% live on campus. *Retention:* 84% of 2006 full-time freshmen returned.

Freshmen *Admission:* 12,468 applied, 7,896 admitted, 2,522 enrolled. *Average high school GPA:* 3.4. *Test scores:* SAT critical reading scores over 500: 85%; SAT math scores over 500: 82%; SAT writing scores over 500: 86%; ACT scores over 18: 99%; SAT critical reading scores over 600: 42%; SAT math scores over 600: 34%; SAT writing scores over 600: 37%; ACT scores over 24: 60%; SAT critical reading scores over 700: 8%; SAT math scores over 700: 6%; SAT writing scores over 700: 6%; ACT scores over 30: 8%.

Faculty *Total:* 1,794, 48% full-time, 51% with terminal degrees. *Student/faculty ratio:* 17:1.

Majors Accounting; acting; African-American/Black studies; American studies; anthropology; applied mathematics; applied mathematics related; art; art history, criticism and conservation; arts management; art teacher education; art therapy; Asian studies (East); biological and physical sciences; biology/biological sciences; biology teacher education; business administration and management; business administration, management and operations related; business/managerial economics; chemistry; chemistry teacher education; clinical laboratory science/medical technology; communication/speech communication and rhetoric; community organization and advocacy; computer and information sciences and support services related; computer and information systems security; computer graphics; computer programming; computer programming (specific applications); computer science; computer systems networking and telecommunications; computer teacher education; dramatic/theater arts; dramatic/theater arts and stagecraft related; early childhood education; e-commerce; economics; educational psychology; education related; education (specific subject areas) related; elementary education; English; English/language arts teacher education; environmental science; finance; French; French language teacher education; general studies; geography; geography teacher education; German; German language teacher education; health and physical education; health teacher education; history; history teacher education; humanities; human resources management; information science/studies; information technology; international relations and affairs; Islamic studies; Italian; jazz/jazz studies; Jewish/Judaic studies; Latin American studies; management information systems; management science; marketing/marketing management; mathematics; mathematics and computer science; mathematics teacher education; music management and merchandising; music performance; music related; music teacher education; music theory and composition; nursing (registered nurse training); organizational behavior; philosophy; physical education teaching and coaching; physics; physics teacher education; playwriting and screenwriting; political science and government; psychology; public policy analysis; real estate; religious studies; secondary education; social sciences; social science teacher education; sociology; Spanish; Spanish language teacher education; special education; statistics; theater design and technology; theater literature, history and criticism; urban studies/affairs; web page, digital/multimedia and information resources design; women's studies.

Academics *Calendar:* quarters; semesters for law school. *Degrees:* certificates, bachelor's, master's, doctoral, first professional, post-master's, postbachelor's, and first professional certificates. *Special study options:* academic remediation for entering students, accelerated degree program, adult/continuing education programs, advanced placement credit, cooperative education, distance learning, double majors, English as a second language, freshman honors college, honors programs, independent study, internships, part-time degree program, services for LD students, student-designed majors, study abroad, summer session for credit. *ROTC:* Army (c).

Computers on Campus 1,500 computers/terminals and 200 ports are available on campus for general student use. Students can access the following: campus intranet, computer help desk, free student e-mail accounts, online (class) grades, online (class) registration. Campuswide network is available. 100% of college-owned or -operated housing units are wired for high-speed Internet access. Wireless service is available via classrooms, dorm rooms, libraries, student centers.

Student Life *Housing options:* coed. Campus housing is university owned, leased by the school and is provided by a third party. Freshman applicants given priority for college housing. *Activities and organizations:* drama/theater group, student-run newspaper, radio station, choral group, marching band, DePaul Activities Board, Black Student Union, South Asian Student Association, Panhellenic Association, Student Ambassadors, national fraternities, national sororities. *Campus security:* 24-hour emergency response devices and patrols, late-night transport/escort service, controlled dormitory access, security lighting, prevention/awareness programs, on-campus police officers, video cameras, smoke detectors in residence halls. *Student services:* health clinic, personal/psychological counseling, women's center, legal services.

Athletics Member NCAA. All Division I. *Intercollegiate sports:* basketball M (s)/W (s), cross-country running M (s)/W (s), golf M (s), soccer M (s)/W (s), softball W (s), tennis M (s)/W (s), track and field M (s)/W (s), volleyball W (s). *Intramural sports:* badminton M/W, basketball M/W, football M/W, racquetball M/W, soccer M/W, softball W, table tennis M/W, tennis M/W, track and field M/W, ultimate Frisbee M/W, volleyball W, weight lifting M/W.

Standardized Tests *Required:* SAT or ACT (for admission).

Costs (2008–09) *Comprehensive fee:* $34,349 includes full-time tuition ($23,820), mandatory fees ($574), and room and board ($9955). Part-time tuition: $422 per quarter hour. *College room only:* $7390.

Financial Aid Of all full-time matriculated undergraduates who enrolled in 2005, 8,121 applied for aid, 7,075 were judged to have need, 943 had their need fully met. 890 Federal Work-Study jobs (averaging $2472). In 2005, 846 non-need-based awards were made. *Average percent of need met:* 68%. *Average financial aid package:* $16,309. *Average need-based loan:* $4581. *Average need-based gift aid:* $10,461. *Average non-need-based aid:* $8144. *Average indebtedness upon graduation:* $21,061. *Financial aid deadline:* 4/1.

Applying *Options:* electronic application, early action, deferred entrance. *Application fee:* $40. *Required:* high school transcript, minimum 2.0 GPA, 1 letter of recommendation. *Required for some:* minimum 3.0 GPA, interview, audition. *Recommended:* minimum 2.75 GPA. *Application deadlines:* rolling (freshmen), rolling (transfers), 11/15 (early action). *Notification:* 5/1 (freshmen), 1/1 (early action).

Freshman Application Contact Carlene Klaas, Undergraduate Admissions, DePaul University, 1 East Jackson Boulevard, Suite 9100, Chicago, IL 60604. *Phone:* 312-362-8300. *E-mail:* admitdpu@depaul.edu.

See page 830 for the College Close-Up.

DeVry University

Addison, Illinois — www.devry.edu/

- **Proprietary** 4-year, founded 1982, part of DeVry University
- **Suburban** 14-acre campus with easy access to Chicago
- **Coed** 1,321 undergraduate students, 60% full-time, 27% women, 73% men
- **Minimally difficult** entrance level

Undergraduates 788 full-time, 533 part-time. 2% are from out of state, 10% African American, 12% Asian American or Pacific Islander, 14% Hispanic American, 0.1% Native American, 5% international, 15% transferred in. *Retention:* 48% of 2006 full-time freshmen returned.

Freshmen *Admission:* 173 enrolled.

Faculty *Total:* 101, 46% full-time. *Student/faculty ratio:* 15:1.
Majors Biomedical technology; business administration and management; business administration, management and operations related; computer engineering technology; computer software engineering; computer systems analysis; computer systems networking and telecommunications; electrical, electronic and communications engineering technology; web page, digital/multimedia and information resources design.
Academics *Calendar:* semesters. *Degrees:* associate and bachelor's. *Special study options:* academic remediation for entering students, accelerated degree program, adult/continuing education programs, advanced placement credit, distance learning, part-time degree program, summer session for credit.
Computers on Campus 574 computers/terminals are available on campus for general student use. Students can access the following: online (class) registration. Campuswide network is available.
Student Life *Housing:* college housing not available. *Activities and organizations:* Epsilon Delta Phi (EDP), International Student Organizations (ISO), Muslim Student Association (MSA), Institute for Electric and Electronic Engineers. *Campus security:* 24-hour emergency response devices, lighted pathways/sidewalks.
Athletics *Intramural sports:* basketball M/W, soccer M/W, softball M/W, table tennis M/W.
Costs (2008–09) *Tuition:* $13,810 full-time, $515 per credit part-time. *Required fees:* $180 full-time.
Financial Aid Of all full-time matriculated undergraduates who enrolled in 2002, 1,955 applied for aid, 1,769 were judged to have need, 78 had their need fully met. In 2002, 308 non-need-based awards were made. *Average percent of need met:* 52%. *Average financial aid package:* $8431. *Average need-based loan:* $3451. *Average need-based gift aid:* $5239. *Average non-need-based aid:* $7973.
Applying *Options:* electronic application, early admission, deferred entrance. *Application fee:* $50. *Required:* high school transcript, interview. *Application deadlines:* rolling (freshmen), rolling (transfers). *Notification:* continuous (freshmen), continuous (transfers).
Freshman Application Contact DeVry University, 1221 North Swift Road, Addison, IL 60101. *Toll-free phone:* 800-346-5420.

DeVry University
Chicago, Illinois **www.devry.edu/**

- **Proprietary** 4-year, founded 1931, part of DeVry University
- **Urban** 17-acre campus
- **Coed** 1,896 undergraduate students, 52% full-time, 41% women, 59% men
- **Minimally difficult** entrance level

Undergraduates 979 full-time, 917 part-time. 1% are from out of state, 37% African American, 6% Asian American or Pacific Islander, 32% Hispanic American, 0.6% Native American, 5% international, 10% transferred in. *Retention:* 57% of 2006 full-time freshmen returned.
Freshmen *Admission:* 266 enrolled.
Faculty *Total:* 93, 43% full-time. *Student/faculty ratio:* 22:1.
Majors Biomedical technology; business administration and management; business administration, management and operations related; computer engineering technology; computer systems analysis; computer systems networking and telecommunications; electrical, electronic and communications engineering technology; health information/medical records technology; web page, digital/multimedia and information resources design.
Academics *Calendar:* semesters. *Degrees:* associate and bachelor's. *Special study options:* academic remediation for entering students, accelerated degree program, adult/continuing education programs, advanced placement credit, distance learning, part-time degree program, services for LD students, summer session for credit.
Computers on Campus 326 computers/terminals are available on campus for general student use. Students can access the following: online (class) registration. Campuswide network is available.
Student Life *Housing:* college housing not available. *Activities and organizations:* DeVry Student Government Association (DSGA), DeVry Telecommunications Society, Filipinos of a Culturally-Unified Society (FOCUS), Institute of Electrical and Electronics Engineering (IEEE), Society of Mexican-American Engineers and Scientists (MAES). *Campus security:* 24-hour emergency response devices and patrols, late-night transport/escort service, lighted pathways/sidewalks.
Costs (2008–09) *Tuition:* $13,810 full-time, $515 per credit part-time. *Required fees:* $180 full-time.
Financial Aid Of all full-time matriculated undergraduates who enrolled in 2002, 1,927 applied for aid, 1,886 were judged to have need, 27 had their need fully met. In 2002, 71 non-need-based awards were made. *Average percent of need met:* 53%. *Average financial aid package:* $11,079. *Average need-based loan:* $5487. *Average need-based gift aid:* $6731. *Average non-need-based aid:* $8082.
Applying *Options:* electronic application, early admission, deferred entrance. *Application fee:* $50. *Required:* high school transcript, interview. *Application deadlines:* rolling (freshmen), rolling (transfers). *Notification:* continuous (freshmen), continuous (transfers).
Director of Admissions Admissions Office, DeVry University, 3300 North Campbell Avenue, Chicago, IL 60618-5994.

DeVry University
Elgin, Illinois

DeVry University
Gurnee, Illinois

DeVry University
Naperville, Illinois **www.devry.edu/**

- **Proprietary** comprehensive
- **Coed**

Faculty *Student/faculty ratio:* 6:1.
Academics *Calendar:* semesters. *Degrees:* associate, bachelor's, master's, and postbachelor's certificates.
Costs (2007–08) *Tuition:* $14,320 full-time, $525 per credit part-time. *Required fees:* $120 full-time.
Applying *Application fee:* $50.
Director of Admissions Admissions Office, DeVry University, 1200 East Diehl Road, Naperville, IL 60563. *Toll-free phone:* 877-496-9050.

DeVry University
Oakbrook Terrace, Illinois

DeVry University
Tinley Park, Illinois **www.devry.edu/**

- **Proprietary** comprehensive, founded 2000, part of DeVry University
- **Suburban** 12-acre campus
- **Coed** 1,059 undergraduate students, 60% full-time, 29% women, 71% men
- **Minimally difficult** entrance level

Undergraduates 638 full-time, 421 part-time. 8% are from out of state, 34% African American, 2% Asian American or Pacific Islander, 8% Hispanic American, 0.5% Native American, 0.2% international, 16% transferred in. *Retention:* 57% of 2006 full-time freshmen returned.
Freshmen *Admission:* 232 enrolled.
Faculty *Total:* 120, 29% full-time. *Student/faculty ratio:* 14:1.
Majors Biomedical technology; business administration and management; business administration, management and operations related; computer engineering technology; computer software engineering; computer systems analysis; computer systems networking and telecommunications; electrical, electronic and communications engineering technology; web page, digital/multimedia and information resources design.
Academics *Calendar:* semesters. *Degrees:* associate, bachelor's, and master's. *Special study options:* academic remediation for entering students, accelerated degree program, adult/continuing education programs, advanced placement credit, distance learning, part-time degree program, services for LD students, summer session for credit.
Computers on Campus 504 computers/terminals are available on campus for general student use. Students can access the following: online (class) registration. Campuswide network is available.
Student Life *Housing:* college housing not available. *Activities and organizations:* Institute of Electrical and Electronic Engineers (IEEE), Student Leadership,

Hash Bang Slash, OGRE. *Campus security:* 24-hour emergency response devices, late-night transport/escort service, lighted pathways/sidewalks, security patrols.
Costs (2008–09) *Tuition:* $13,810 full-time, $515 per credit part-time. *Required fees:* $180 full-time.
Financial Aid Of all full-time matriculated undergraduates who enrolled in 2002, 1,574 applied for aid, 1,023 were judged to have need, 3 had their need fully met. In 2002, 94 non-need-based awards were made. *Average percent of need met:* 52%. *Average financial aid package:* $9695. *Average need-based loan:* $5510. *Average need-based gift aid:* $6226. *Average non-need-based aid:* $9996.
Applying *Options:* electronic application, early admission, deferred entrance. *Application fee:* $50. *Required:* high school transcript, interview. *Application deadlines:* rolling (freshmen), rolling (transfers). *Notification:* continuous (freshmen), continuous (transfers).
Freshman Application Contact DeVry University, 18624 West Creek Drive, Tinley Park, IL 60477-6243.

DEVRY UNIVERSITY ONLINE

Oakbrook Terrace, Illinois online.devry.edu/

- **Proprietary** comprehensive, founded 2000
- **Coed** 8,729 undergraduate students, 31% full-time, 49% women, 51% men

Undergraduates 2,744 full-time, 5,985 part-time. 24% African American, 2% Asian American or Pacific Islander, 7% Hispanic American, 1% Native American, 26% transferred in. *Retention:* 35% of 2006 full-time freshmen returned.
Freshmen *Admission:* 1,419 enrolled.
Faculty *Total:* 3,111. *Student/faculty ratio:* 6:1.
Majors Accounting; business administration and management; business administration, management and operations related; computer software engineering; computer systems analysis; computer systems networking and telecommunications; health information/medical records technology; web page, digital/multimedia and information resources design.
Academics *Calendar:* semesters. *Degrees:* associate, bachelor's, and master's.
Costs (2008–09) *Tuition:* $14,480 full-time, $540 per credit hour part-time. *Required fees:* $80 full-time.
Applying *Options:* electronic application, early admission, deferred entrance. *Application fee:* $50. *Required:* high school transcript, interview. *Application deadlines:* rolling (freshmen), rolling (transfers). *Notification:* continuous (freshmen), continuous (transfers).
Director of Admissions Admissions Office, DeVry University Online, One Tower Lane, Suite 1000, Oakbrook Terrace, IL 60181. *Toll-free phone:* 866-338-7934.

DOMINICAN UNIVERSITY

River Forest, Illinois www.dom.edu/

- **Independent Roman Catholic** comprehensive, founded 1901
- **Suburban** 30-acre campus with easy access to Chicago
- **Endowment** $20.0 million
- **Coed** 1,598 undergraduate students, 87% full-time, 70% women, 30% men
- **Moderately difficult** entrance level, 85% of applicants were admitted

Undergraduates 1,396 full-time, 202 part-time. Students come from 33 states and territories, 18 other countries, 9% are from out of state, 7% African American, 3% Asian American or Pacific Islander, 22% Hispanic American, 2% international, 11% transferred in, 40% live on campus. *Retention:* 77% of 2006 full-time freshmen returned.
Freshmen *Admission:* 1,265 applied, 1,077 admitted, 367 enrolled. *Average high school GPA:* 3.37. *Test scores:* ACT scores over 18: 95%; ACT scores over 24: 33%; ACT scores over 30: 3%.
Faculty *Total:* 350, 35% full-time, 46% with terminal degrees. *Student/faculty ratio:* 12:1.
Majors Accounting; American studies; art history, criticism and conservation; biochemistry; biology/biological sciences; business administration and management; chemistry; clinical laboratory science/medical technology; commercial and advertising art; computer engineering; computer science; criminology; dietetics; dramatic/theater arts; economics; education (K-12); electrical, electronics and communications engineering; elementary education; English; environmental studies; fashion/apparel design; fashion merchandising; food science; foodservice systems administration; foods, nutrition, and wellness; French; gerontology; history; information science/studies; international business/trade/commerce; Italian; mass communication/media; mathematics; philosophy; photography; political science and government; pre-dentistry studies; pre-law studies; pre-medical studies; pre-veterinary studies; psychology; religious studies; social sciences; sociology; Spanish; special products marketing.
Academics *Calendar:* semesters. *Degrees:* certificates, bachelor's, master's, post-master's, and postbachelor's certificates. *Special study options:* accelerated degree program, adult/continuing education programs, advanced placement credit, distance learning, double majors, English as a second language, honors programs, independent study, internships, off-campus study, part-time degree program, services for LD students, student-designed majors, study abroad, summer session for credit. *Unusual degree programs:* 3-2 engineering with Illinois Institute of Technology; nursing with Rush University; social work; library science, occupational therapy with Rush University, pharmacy with Midwestern University.
Computers on Campus 625 computers/terminals are available on campus for general student use. Students can access the following: campus intranet, computer help desk, free student e-mail accounts, online (class) grades, online (class) registration, online (class) schedules, online student account information, online financial aid information. Campuswide network is available. 100% of college-owned or -operated housing units are wired for high-speed Internet access. Wireless service is available via computer centers, learning centers, libraries, student centers.
Student Life *Housing options:* coed, men-only, women-only. Campus housing is university owned. Freshman applicants given priority for college housing. *Activities and organizations:* drama/theater group, student-run newspaper, choral group, student government, theater, Commuter Student Association, Resident Student Association, International Club. *Campus security:* 24-hour emergency response devices and patrols, student patrols, late-night transport/escort service, controlled dormitory access, door alarms. *Student services:* health clinic, personal/psychological counseling.
Athletics Member NCAA. All Division III. *Intercollegiate sports:* baseball M, basketball M/W, cross-country running M/W, golf M, soccer M/W, softball W, tennis M/W, volleyball M (c)/W. *Intramural sports:* basketball M/W, bowling M/W, football M/W, racquetball M/W, soccer M/W, softball W, tennis M/W, volleyball W, water polo M/W.
Standardized Tests *Required:* SAT or ACT (for admission).
Costs (2007–08) *One-time required fee:* $150. *Comprehensive fee:* $29,450 includes full-time tuition ($22,350), mandatory fees ($100), and room and board ($7000). Full-time tuition and fees vary according to program. Part-time tuition: $745 per semester hour. Part-time tuition and fees vary according to location and program. *Required fees:* $10 per course part-time. *Room and board:* Room and board charges vary according to board plan and housing facility. *Payment plan:* installment. *Waivers:* children of alumni and employees or children of employees.
Financial Aid Of all full-time matriculated undergraduates who enrolled in 2007, 1,098 applied for aid, 980 were judged to have need, 166 had their need fully met. 211 Federal Work-Study jobs (averaging $2001). 181 state and other part-time jobs (averaging $1930). In 2007, 228 non-need-based awards were made. *Average percent of need met:* 79%. *Average financial aid package:* $17,570. *Average need-based loan:* $4163. *Average need-based gift aid:* $13,325. *Average non-need-based aid:* $10,587. *Average indebtedness upon graduation:* $15,036.
Applying *Options:* electronic application, deferred entrance. *Application fee:* $25. *Required:* essay or personal statement, high school transcript, minimum 2.75 GPA. *Required for some:* 2 letters of recommendation, interview. *Recommended:* letters of recommendation, interview. *Application deadlines:* rolling (freshmen), rolling (transfers). *Notification:* continuous (freshmen), continuous (transfers).
Freshman Application Contact Mr. Glenn Hamilton, Director of Freshman Admission, Dominican University, 7900 West Division Street, River Forest, IL 60305. *Phone:* 708-524-6800. *Toll-free phone:* 800-828-8475. *Fax:* 708-524-6864. *E-mail:* domadmis@dom.edu.

See page 832 for the College Close-Up.

EASTERN ILLINOIS UNIVERSITY

Charleston, Illinois www.eiu.edu/

- **State-supported** comprehensive, founded 1895
- **Small-town** 320-acre campus
- **Endowment** $44.3 million
- **Coed** 10,410 undergraduate students, 90% full-time, 58% women, 42% men
- **Moderately difficult** entrance level, 71% of applicants were admitted

Undergraduates 9,362 full-time, 1,048 part-time. Students come from 32 states and territories, 25 other countries, 2% are from out of state, 9% African American, 1% Asian American or Pacific Islander, 3% Hispanic American, 0.4% Native American, 0.5% international, 11% transferred in, 42% live on campus. *Retention:* 82% of 2006 full-time freshmen returned.

Freshmen *Admission:* 7,149 applied, 5,071 admitted, 1,647 enrolled. *Average high school GPA:* 3.43. *Test scores:* ACT scores over 18: 89%; ACT scores over 24: 24%; ACT scores over 30: 2%.

Faculty *Total:* 766, 86% full-time, 58% with terminal degrees. *Student/faculty ratio:* 15:1.

Majors Accounting; African-American/Black studies; art; biology/biological sciences; business administration and management; chemistry; clinical laboratory science/medical technology; communication disorders; computer and information sciences related; computer/information technology services administration related; dramatic/theater arts; economics; elementary education; engineering related; English; family and consumer sciences/human sciences; finance; foreign languages and literatures; geography; geology/earth science; health teacher education; history; industrial technology; journalism; kindergarten/preschool education; liberal arts and sciences/liberal studies; management science; marketing/marketing management; mathematics; mathematics and computer science; middle school education; multi-/interdisciplinary studies related; music; nursing (registered nurse training); parks, recreation and leisure facilities management; philosophy; physical education teaching and coaching; physics; political science and government; psychology; science teacher education; social science teacher education; sociology; special education; speech and rhetoric; technical teacher education.

Academics *Calendar:* semesters. *Degrees:* bachelor's, master's, post-master's, and postbachelor's certificates. *Special study options:* academic remediation for entering students, adult/continuing education programs, advanced placement credit, distance learning, double majors, external degree program, honors programs, independent study, internships, off-campus study, part-time degree program, services for LD students, study abroad, summer session for credit. *ROTC:* Army (b). *Unusual degree programs:* 3-2 engineering with University of Illinois.

Computers on Campus 909 computers/terminals are available on campus for general student use. Students can access the following: computer help desk, free student e-mail accounts, online (class) grades, online (class) registration, online (class) schedules. Campuswide network is available. Wireless service is available via classrooms, computer centers, computer labs, libraries, student centers.

Student Life *Housing:* on-campus residence required for freshman year. *Options:* coed, men-only, women-only, disabled students. Campus housing is university owned. Freshman campus housing is guaranteed. *Activities and organizations:* drama/theater group, student-run newspaper, radio and television station, choral group, marching band, Delta Zeta, Alpha Phi, Kappa Delta, Sigma Kappa, Lambda Chi Alpha, national fraternities, national sororities. *Campus security:* 24-hour emergency response devices and patrols, student patrols. *Student services:* health clinic, personal/psychological counseling, women's center, legal services.

Athletics Member NCAA. All Division I except football (Division I-AA). *Intercollegiate sports:* baseball M (s), basketball M (s)/W (s), cross-country running M (s)/W (s), golf M (s)/W (s), rugby M (c)/W (s), soccer M (s)/W (s), softball W (s), swimming and diving M (s)/W (s), tennis M (s)/W (s), track and field M (s)/W (s), volleyball W (s). *Intramural sports:* badminton M/W, basketball M/W, bowling M/W, football M/W, golf M/W, lacrosse M (c)/W (c), racquetball M/W, soccer M/W, softball M/W, table tennis M/W, tennis M/W, ultimate Frisbee M/W, volleyball M/W, weight lifting M/W.

Standardized Tests *Required:* SAT or ACT (for admission).

Costs (2007–08) *Tuition:* state resident $5832 full-time, $194 per credit hour part-time; nonresident $17,496 full-time, $583 per credit hour part-time. Full-time tuition and fees vary according to course load. Part-time tuition and fees vary according to course load. *Required fees:* $2158 full-time, $78 per credit hour part-time. *Room and board:* $7124. Room and board charges vary according to board plan and housing facility. *Payment plan:* installment. *Waivers:* employees or children of employees.

Financial Aid Of all full-time matriculated undergraduates who enrolled in 2007, 7,682 applied for aid, 4,593 were judged to have need, 557 had their need fully met. In 2007, 431 non-need-based awards were made. *Average percent of need met:* 78%. *Average financial aid package:* $8625. *Average need-based loan:* $3950. *Average need-based gift aid:* $3085. *Average non-need-based aid:* $3594. *Average indebtedness upon graduation:* $15,555.

Applying *Options:* electronic application. *Application fee:* $30. *Required:* high school transcript, minimum 2.25 GPA, audition for music program. *Recommended:* essay or personal statement, letters of recommendation. *Application deadlines:* rolling (freshmen), rolling (transfers). *Notification:* continuous (freshmen), continuous (transfers).

Freshman Application Contact Brenda Major, Director of Admissions, Eastern Illinois University, 600 Lincoln Avenue, Charleston, IL 61920-3099. *Phone:* 217-581-2223. *Toll-free phone:* 800-252-5711. *Fax:* 217-581-7060. *E-mail:* admissions@eiu.edu.

EAST-WEST UNIVERSITY

Chicago, Illinois **www.eastwest.edu/**

- **Independent** 4-year, founded 1978
- **Urban** campus
- **Endowment** $39.6 million
- **Coed** 1,150 undergraduate students, 99% full-time, 65% women, 35% men
- **Minimally difficult** entrance level, 91% of applicants were admitted

Undergraduates 1,139 full-time, 11 part-time. Students come from 5 states and territories, 12 other countries, 8% are from out of state, 70% African American, 2% Asian American or Pacific Islander, 12% Hispanic American, 0.2% Native American, 11% international. *Retention:* 71% of 2006 full-time freshmen returned.

Freshmen *Admission:* 947 applied, 860 admitted. *Average high school GPA:* 2.6. *Test scores:* ACT scores over 18: 30%; ACT scores over 24: 4%; ACT scores over 30: 1%.

Faculty *Total:* 73, 23% full-time, 26% with terminal degrees. *Student/faculty ratio:* 15:1.

Majors Accounting; administrative assistant and secretarial science; behavioral sciences; biology/biological sciences; business administration and management; computer engineering technology; computer programming; computer science; electrical, electronic and communications engineering technology; electrical, electronics and communications engineering; English; finance; Islamic studies; liberal arts and sciences/liberal studies; mathematics; social sciences; sociology.

Academics *Calendar:* quarters. *Degrees:* certificates, associate, and bachelor's. *Special study options:* academic remediation for entering students, double majors, independent study, internships, part-time degree program, summer session for credit.

Computers on Campus 130 computers/terminals are available on campus for general student use. Students can access the following: computer help desk, free student e-mail accounts, online (class) grades, online (class) registration, online (class) schedules. Campuswide network is available.

Student Life *Housing:* college housing not available. *Activities and organizations:* drama/theater group, student-run newspaper, choral group. *Student services:* personal/psychological counseling.

Athletics *Intercollegiate sports:* basketball M.

Standardized Tests *Required:* ACT (for admission).

Costs (2007–08) *Tuition:* $12,825 full-time, $405 per credit hour part-time. Full-time tuition and fees vary according to degree level and program. *Required fees:* $655 full-time. *Payment plan:* installment. *Waivers:* employees or children of employees.

Financial Aid Of all full-time matriculated undergraduates who enrolled in 2006, 1,339 applied for aid, 1,339 were judged to have need. 39 Federal Work-Study jobs (averaging $3200). *Average percent of need met:* 90%. *Average financial aid package:* $9020. *Average indebtedness upon graduation:* $2625.

Applying *Options:* electronic application, early decision. *Application fee:* $40. *Required:* essay or personal statement, high school transcript, minimum 2.0 GPA, interview. *Required for some:* 1 letter of recommendation. *Application deadlines:* rolling (freshmen), rolling (transfers). *Early decision deadline:* 7/1.

Freshman Application Contact Mr. William Link, Director of Admissions, East-West University, 819 South Wabash Avenue, Chicago, IL 60605-2103. *Phone:* 312-939-0111 Ext. 1830. *Fax:* 312-939-0083. *E-mail:* williaml@eastwest.edu.

ELMHURST COLLEGE

Elmhurst, Illinois **www.elmhurst.edu/**

- **Independent** comprehensive, founded 1871, affiliated with United Church of Christ
- **Suburban** 38-acre campus with easy access to Chicago
- **Endowment** $87.0 million
- **Coed**
- **Moderately difficult** entrance level

Faculty *Student/faculty ratio:* 14:1.

Academics *Calendar:* 4-1-4. *Degrees:* bachelor's and master's.

Student Life *Campus security:* 24-hour emergency response devices and patrols, late-night transport/escort service, controlled dormitory access.

Athletics Member NCAA. All Division III.

Standardized Tests *Required:* SAT or ACT (for admission).

Costs (2007–08) *Comprehensive fee:* $31,824 includes full-time tuition ($24,600), mandatory fees ($60), and room and board ($7164). Part-time tuition: $700 per semester hour. *Required fees:* $30 per term part-time. *College room only:* $4200.

Financial Aid Of all full-time matriculated undergraduates who enrolled in 2006, 2,138 applied for aid, 1,611 were judged to have need, 575 had their need fully met. 334 Federal Work-Study jobs (averaging $823). 299 state and other part-time jobs (averaging $1492). In 2006, 520 non-need-based awards were made. *Average percent of need met:* 88. *Average financial aid package:* $15,692. *Average need-based loan:* $3937. *Average need-based gift aid:* $7870. *Average non-need-based aid:* $8662. *Average indebtedness upon graduation:* $17,244.

Applying *Options:* electronic application, deferred entrance. *Required:* high school transcript. *Required for some:* essay or personal statement, letters of recommendation, interview. *Recommended:* essay or personal statement, interview.

Freshman Application Contact Mrs. Stephanie Levenson, Director of Admission, Elmhurst College, 190 Prospect Avenue, Elmhurst, IL 60126. *Phone:* 630-617-3400. *Toll-free phone:* 800-697-1871. *Fax:* 630-617-5501. *E-mail:* admit@elmhurst.edu.

See page 834 for the College Close-Up.

EUREKA COLLEGE

Eureka, Illinois **www.eureka.edu/**

Freshman Application Contact Dr. Brian Sajko, Dean of Admissions and Financial Aid, Eureka College, 300 East College Avenue, Eureka, IL 61530-0128. *Phone:* 309-467-6350. *Toll-free phone:* 888-4-EUREKA. *Fax:* 309-467-6576. *E-mail:* admissions@eureka.edu.

GOVERNORS STATE UNIVERSITY

University Park, Illinois **www.govst.edu/**

Application Contact Mr. Randall Tumblin, Director of Admissions, Governors State University, One University Parkway, University Park, IL 60466. *Phone:* 708-534-4490. *Fax:* 708-534-1640. *E-mail:* gsunow@govst.edu.

GREENVILLE COLLEGE

Greenville, Illinois **www.greenville.edu/**

- **Independent Free Methodist** comprehensive, founded 1892
- **Small-town** 12-acre campus with easy access to St. Louis
- **Endowment** $11.0 million
- **Coed** 1,374 undergraduate students, 97% full-time, 54% women, 46% men
- **Moderately difficult** entrance level, 81% of applicants were admitted

Undergraduates 1,330 full-time, 44 part-time. Students come from 40 states and territories, 16 other countries, 31% are from out of state, 7% African American, 0.9% Asian American or Pacific Islander, 2% Hispanic American, 0.6% Native American, 1% international, 12% transferred in, 56% live on campus. *Retention:* 73% of 2006 full-time freshmen returned.

Freshmen *Admission:* 942 applied, 760 admitted, 307 enrolled. *Average high school GPA:* 3.27. *Test scores:* SAT critical reading scores over 500: 58%; SAT math scores over 500: 52%; ACT scores over 18: 89%; SAT critical reading scores over 600: 21%; SAT math scores over 600: 23%; ACT scores over 24: 40%; SAT critical reading scores over 700: 2%; SAT math scores over 700: 2%; ACT scores over 30: 4%.

Faculty *Total:* 142, 42% full-time, 30% with terminal degrees. *Student/faculty ratio:* 16:1.

Majors Accounting; art; audiovisual communications technologies related; biology/biological sciences; biology teacher education; business administration and management; business, management, and marketing related; chemistry; chemistry teacher education; communication and media related; computer and information sciences; criminal justice/law enforcement administration; dramatic/theater arts; early childhood education; elementary education; English; English/language arts teacher education; environmental biology; history; history teacher education; international/global studies; kinesiology and exercise science; liberal arts and sciences/liberal studies; management information systems; marketing/marketing management; mass communication/media; mathematics; mathematics teacher education; multi-/interdisciplinary studies related; music; music management and merchandising; music related; music teacher education; organizational behavior; parks, recreation and leisure; pastoral counseling and specialized ministries related; pastoral studies/counseling; philosophy; physical education teaching and coaching; physics; physics teacher education; political science and government; psychology; public relations/image management; religious studies; social work; sociology; Spanish; Spanish language teacher education; special education; speech and rhetoric; sport and fitness administration/management; youth ministry.

Academics *Calendar:* 4-1-4. *Degrees:* bachelor's and master's. *Special study options:* academic remediation for entering students, accelerated degree program, adult/continuing education programs, advanced placement credit, cooperative education, double majors, honors programs, independent study, internships, off-campus study, part-time degree program, student-designed majors, study abroad, summer session for credit. *Unusual degree programs.* 3-2 engineering with University of Illinois at Urbana–Champaign; Washington University in St. Louis; nursing with St. John's College of Nursing; chiropractic at Logan College of Chriopractic.

Computers on Campus 65 computers/terminals are available on campus for general student use. Students can access the following: campus intranet, computer help desk, free student e-mail accounts, online (class) grades, online (class) schedules. Campuswide network is available. 100% of college-owned or -operated housing units are wired for high-speed Internet access. Wireless service is available via entire campus.

Student Life *Housing:* on-campus residence required through senior year. *Options:* men-only, women-only. Campus housing is university owned. Freshman campus housing is guaranteed. *Activities and organizations:* drama/theater group, student-run newspaper, radio station, choral group, Campus Activity Board, Intramurals, Greenville Student Outreach, Habitat for Humanity, Student Senate. *Campus security:* 24-hour emergency response devices, student patrols, late-night transport/escort service, controlled dormitory access. *Student services:* personal/psychological counseling.

Athletics Member NCAA, NCCAA. All NCAA Division III. *Intercollegiate sports:* baseball M, basketball M/W, cross-country running M/W, football M, soccer M/W, softball W, tennis M/W, track and field M/W, volleyball W. *Intramural sports:* badminton M/W, basketball M/W, cheerleading W, football M/W, soccer M/W, softball M/W, table tennis M/W, tennis M/W, track and field M/W, volleyball W.

Standardized Tests *Required:* SAT or ACT (for admission).

Costs (2007–08) *Comprehensive fee:* $25,020 includes full-time tuition ($18,532), mandatory fees ($140), and room and board ($6348) Part-time tuition: $390 per credit hour. Part-time tuition and fees vary according to course load. *College room only:* $3018. Room and board charges vary according to housing facility. *Waivers:* senior citizens and employees or children of employees.

Financial Aid Of all full-time matriculated undergraduates who enrolled in 2005, 829 applied for aid, 761 were judged to have need, 112 had their need fully met. 212 Federal Work-Study jobs (averaging $1390). 26 state and other part-time jobs (averaging $827). In 2005, 137 non-need-based awards were made. *Average percent of need met:* 78%. *Average financial aid package:* $14,307. *Average need-based loan:* $4000. *Average need-based gift aid:* $9913. *Average non-need-based aid:* $8104. *Average indebtedness upon graduation:* $19,820.

Applying *Options:* electronic application, early admission, deferred entrance. *Application fee:* $25. *Required:* essay or personal statement, high school transcript, minimum 2.5 GPA, 2 letters of recommendation, agreement to code of conduct. *Required for some:* interview. *Application deadlines:* 8/1 (freshmen), 8/1 (transfers). *Notification:* continuous (freshmen), continuous (transfers).

Freshman Application Contact Mr. Michael Ritter, Director of Admissions, Greenville College, 315 East College Avenue, Greenville, IL 62246. *Phone:* 618-664-7100. *Toll-free phone:* 800-345-4440. *Fax:* 618-664-9841. *E-mail:* admissions@greenville.edu.

HARRINGTON COLLEGE OF DESIGN

Chicago, Illinois **www.interiordesign.edu/**

- **Proprietary** 4-year, founded 1931, part of Career Education Corporation
- **Urban** campus
- **Coed, primarily women**
- **Noncompetitive** entrance level

Faculty *Student/faculty ratio:* 12:1.

Academics *Calendar:* semesters. *Degrees:* certificates, diplomas, associate, and bachelor's.

Student Life *Campus security:* 24-hour emergency response devices and patrols.

Costs (2007–08) *Tuition:* $18,000 full-time, $600 per credit part-time. *Required fees:* $2520 full-time, $1260 per term part-time. *Room only:* $2600.

Financial Aid *Average percent of need met:* 30. *Average financial aid package:* $3500.

Applying *Options:* electronic application, deferred entrance. *Application fee:* $60. *Required:* high school transcript, interview. *Recommended:* essay or personal statement, 1 letter of recommendation.

Freshman Application Contact Ms. Melissa Laurentius, Director of Admissions, Harrington College of Design, 200 West Madison, Chicago, IL 60606. *Toll-free phone:* 877-939-4975. *Fax:* 312-939-8032. *E-mail:* barrington@interiordesign.edu.

HEBREW THEOLOGICAL COLLEGE

Skokie, Illinois **www.htc.edu/**

Freshman Application Contact Rabbi Berish Cardash, Hebrew Theological College, 7135 North Carpenter Road, Skokie, IL 60077-3263. *Phone:* 847-982-2500.

ILLINOIS COLLEGE

Jacksonville, Illinois **www.ic.edu/**

- **Independent interdenominational** 4-year, founded 1829
- **Small-town** 62-acre campus with easy access to St. Louis
- **Endowment** $135.6 million
- **Coed** 1,014 undergraduate students, 97% full-time, 52% women, 48% men
- **Moderately difficult** entrance level, 91% of applicants were admitted

Undergraduates 986 full-time, 28 part-time. Students come from 22 states and territories, 15 other countries, 11% are from out of state, 3% African American, 0.7% Asian American or Pacific Islander, 2% Hispanic American, 0.7% Native American, 2% international, 5% transferred in, 67% live on campus. *Retention:* 80% of 2006 full-time freshmen returned.

Freshmen *Admission:* 917 applied, 838 admitted, 260 enrolled. *Average high school GPA:* 3.29. *Test scores:* SAT critical reading scores over 500: 77%; SAT math scores over 500: 55%; SAT writing scores over 500: 63%; ACT scores over 18: 97%; SAT critical reading scores over 600: 11%; SAT math scores over 600: 44%; SAT writing scores over 600: 50%; ACT scores over 24: 47%; SAT critical reading scores over 700: 11%; ACT scores over 30: 7%.

Faculty *Total:* 89, 81% full-time, 76% with terminal degrees. *Student/faculty ratio:* 13:1.

Majors Accounting; art; biology/biological sciences; business administration and management; business/managerial economics; chemistry; clinical laboratory science/medical technology; computer science; cytotechnology; dramatic/theater arts; early childhood education; economics; education; education (K-12); elementary education; English; environmental studies; finance; French; German; history; information science/studies; interdisciplinary studies; international relations and affairs; liberal arts and sciences/liberal studies; management information systems; mass communication/media; mathematics; music; occupational therapy; philosophy; physical education teaching and coaching; physics; political science and government; pre-dentistry studies; pre-law studies; pre-medical studies; pre-veterinary studies; psychology; religious studies; secondary education; sociology; Spanish; speech and rhetoric.

Academics *Calendar:* semesters. *Degree:* bachelor's. *Special study options:* accelerated degree program, advanced placement credit, double majors, independent study, internships, study abroad, summer session for credit. *Unusual degree programs:* 3-2 engineering with University of Illinois at Urbana-Champaign, Washington University in St. Louis; occupational therapy with Washington University in St. Louis.

Computers on Campus 110 computers/terminals are available on campus for general student use. Students can access the following: computer help desk, free student e-mail accounts, online (class) grades, online (class) registration, online (class) schedules. Campuswide network is available. 30% of college-owned or -operated housing units are wired for high-speed Internet access. Wireless service is available via entire campus.

Student Life *Housing:* on-campus residence required through sophomore year. *Options:* coed, men-only, women-only. Campus housing is university owned. Freshman campus housing is guaranteed. *Activities and organizations:* drama/theater group, student-run newspaper, television station, choral group, Student Activity Board, Forum, Homecoming Committee, literary societies, B.A.S.I.C. (Brothers and Sisters in Christ). *Campus security:* 24-hour emergency response devices and patrols, late-night transport/escort service, controlled dormitory access. *Student services:* health clinic, personal/psychological counseling.

Athletics Member NCAA. All Division III. *Intercollegiate sports:* baseball M, cheerleading W, cross-country running M/W, football M, golf M/W, soccer M/W, softball W, swimming and diving M/W, tennis M/W, track and field M/W, volleyball W. *Intramural sports:* badminton M/W, basketball M/W, fencing M/W, football M, racquetball M/W, softball M/W, swimming and diving M/W, volleyball M/W, water polo M/W, weight lifting M/W.

Standardized Tests *Required:* SAT or ACT (for admission).

Costs (2007–08) *Comprehensive fee:* $25,770 includes full-time tuition ($18,600), mandatory fees ($200), and room and board ($6970). Part-time tuition: $775 per credit hour. *College room only:* $3400. Room and board charges vary according to board plan and housing facility. *Payment plans:* installment, deferred payment. *Waivers:* employees or children of employees.

Financial Aid Of all full-time matriculated undergraduates who enrolled in 2006, 887 applied for aid, 765 were judged to have need, 371 had their need fully met. 479 Federal Work-Study jobs (averaging $1491). 308 state and other part-time jobs (averaging $719). In 2006, 198 non-need-based awards were made. *Average percent of need met:* 91%. *Average financial aid package:* $13,907. *Average need-based loan:* $4640. *Average need-based gift aid:* $7560. *Average non-need-based aid:* $6740. *Average indebtedness upon graduation:* $18,870.

Applying *Options:* electronic application. *Required:* high school transcript, 1 letter of recommendation. *Required for some:* essay or personal statement. *Recommended:* essay or personal statement, minimum 2.5 GPA, interview. *Application deadlines:* 7/1 (freshmen), 7/1 (transfers). *Notification:* continuous until 8/15 (freshmen), continuous until 8/15 (transfers).

Freshman Application Contact Mr. Rick Bystry, Associate Director of Admission, Illinois College, 1101 West College, Jacksonville, IL 62650. *Phone:* 217-245-3030. *Toll-free phone:* 866-464-5265. *Fax:* 217-245-3034. *E-mail:* admissions@ic.edu.

THE ILLINOIS INSTITUTE OF ART–CHICAGO

Chicago, Illinois **www.ilic.artinstitutes.edu/**

- **Proprietary** 4-year, founded 1916, part of Education Management Corporation
- **Urban** 2-acre campus
- **Coed**
- **Minimally difficult** entrance level

Faculty *Student/faculty ratio:* 24:1.

Majors Advertising; animation, interactive technology, video graphics and special effects; cinematography and film/video production; fashion/apparel design; fashion merchandising; interior design; restaurant, culinary, and catering management; Web page, digital/multimedia and information resources design.

Academics *Calendar:* quarters. *Degrees:* associate and bachelor's.

Student Life *Campus security:* 24-hour emergency response devices and patrols.

Standardized Tests *Required for some:* ACT ASSET. *Recommended:* ACT (for admission).

Costs (2007–08) *Tuition:* full-time tuition for 2007–08 is $19,968. Housing costs an additional $11,512. Other charges include a starting kit for all first-quarter students. Kits vary in price, depending on the program of study. Part-time tuition is $416 per credit.

Applying *Options:* electronic application, early admission, deferred entrance. *Application fee:* $50. *Required:* essay or personal statement, high school transcript, interview. *Required for some:* letters of recommendation, portfolio. *Recommended:* minimum 2.0 GPA.

Freshman Application Contact Office of Admissions, The Illinois Institute of Art–Chicago, 350 North Orleans Street, Chicago, IL 60654-1510. *Phone:* 312-280-3500. *Toll-free phone:* 800-351-3450. *Fax:* 312-280-8562.

See page 836 for the College Close-Up.

THE ILLINOIS INSTITUTE OF ART–SCHAUMBURG

Schaumburg, Illinois **www.ilis.artinstitutes.edu/**

- **Proprietary** 4-year, part of Education Management Corporation
- **Suburban** campus
- **Coed**
- **Minimally difficult** entrance level

Faculty *Student/faculty ratio:* 19:1.

Majors Advertising; animation, interactive technology, video graphics and special effects; cinematography and film/video production; fashion merchandising;

graphic design; interior design; photography; Web page, digital/multimedia and information resources design.

Academics *Calendar:* quarters. *Degrees:* certificates, associate, and bachelor's.

Student Life *Campus security:* 24-hour emergency response devices and patrols, student patrols.

Costs (2007–08) *Tuition:* tuition cost varies by program. Prospective students should contact the school for current tuition costs. Other charges include a starting kit for all first-quarter students. Kits vary in price depending on the program of study.

Financial Aid *Average percent of need met:* 61. *Average financial aid package:* $10,122. *Average indebtedness upon graduation:* $21,550.

Applying *Options:* electronic application. *Required:* essay or personal statement, high school transcript, minimum 2.0 GPA. *Required for some:* letters of recommendation, interview.

Freshman Application Contact The Illinois Institute of Art–Schaumburg, 1000 Plaza Drive, Suite 100, Schaumburg, IL 60173. *Phone:* 847-619-3450. *Toll-free phone:* 800-314-3450. *Fax:* 847-619-3064.

See page 838 for the College Close-Up.

ILLINOIS INSTITUTE OF TECHNOLOGY

Chicago, Illinois **www.iit.edu/**

- **Independent** university, founded 1890
- **Urban** 120-acre campus
- **Endowment** $338.1 million
- **Coed** 2,576 undergraduate students, 90% full-time, 27% women, 73% men
- **Very difficult** entrance level, 56% of applicants were admitted

A private, independent, Ph.D.-granting coeducational research university founded in 1890, Illinois Institute of Technology offers students a superb education in engineering, business, architecture, the sciences, psychology, and the humanities in an environment geared toward the undergraduate student. Located 10 minutes from downtown Chicago, IIT provides small class sizes, hands-on projects, undergraduate research, co-op and internship opportunities, and distinguished faculty members. IIT offers substantial need-based and merit scholarships.

Undergraduates 2,326 full-time, 250 part-time. Students come from 47 states and territories, 83 other countries, 34% are from out of state, 4% African American, 14% Asian American or Pacific Islander, 7% Hispanic American, 0.4% Native American, 16% international, 7% transferred in, 53% live on campus. *Retention:* 86% of 2006 full-time freshmen returned.

Freshmen *Admission:* 4,383 applied, 2,474 admitted, 521 enrolled. *Average high school GPA:* 3.77. *Test scores:* SAT critical reading scores over 500: 87%; SAT math scores over 500: 99%; SAT writing scores over 500: 85%; ACT scores over 18: 100%; SAT critical reading scores over 600: 55%; SAT math scores over 600: 82%; SAT writing scores over 600: 45%; ACT scores over 24: 88%; SAT critical reading scores over 700: 14%; SAT math scores over 700: 33%; SAT writing scores over 700: 10%; ACT scores over 30: 32%.

Faculty *Total:* 659, 54% full-time. *Student/faculty ratio:* 8:1.

Majors Aerospace, aeronautical and astronautical engineering; applied mathematics; architectural engineering; architecture; biochemistry/biophysics and molecular biology; biology/biological sciences; biomedical/medical engineering; biophysics; business/commerce; chemical engineering; chemistry; civil engineering; communication and journalism related; computer engineering; computer science; design and visual communications; electrical, electronics and communications engineering; engineering/industrial management; environmental/environmental health engineering; industrial technology; information science/studies; information technology; manufacturing technology; materials engineering; mechanical engineering; metallurgical engineering; multi-/interdisciplinary studies related; physics; political science and government; psychology; technical and business writing.

Academics *Calendar:* semesters. *Degrees:* bachelor's, master's, doctoral, and first professional. *Special study options:* advanced placement credit, cooperative education, distance learning, double majors, English as a second language, independent study, internships, part-time degree program, services for LD students, study abroad, summer session for credit. *ROTC:* Army (b), Navy (b), Air Force (b). *Unusual degree programs:* 3-2 engineering.

Computers on Campus 500 computers/terminals are available on campus for general student use. Students can access the following: campus intranet, computer help desk, free student e-mail accounts, online (class) grades, online (class) registration, online (class) schedules. Campuswide network is available. 75% of college-owned or -operated housing units are wired for high-speed Internet access. Wireless service is available via classrooms, computer centers, computer labs, dorm rooms, learning centers, libraries, student centers.

Student Life *Housing:* on-campus residence required for freshman year. *Options:* coed, men-only, women-only, disabled students. Campus housing is university owned and is provided by a third party. Freshman applicants given priority for college housing. *Activities and organizations:* drama/theater group, student-run newspaper, radio station, choral group, Union Board, Strike Force Bowling, Student Government Association, 33rd Street Production, Commuter Student Associate, national fraternities, national sororities. *Campus security:* 24-hour emergency response devices and patrols, late-night transport/escort service, controlled dormitory access. *Student services:* health clinic, personal/psychological counseling, women's center, legal services.

Athletics Member NAIA. *Intercollegiate sports:* baseball M (s), basketball M (s)/W (s), cross-country running M (s)/W (s), soccer M (s)/W (s), swimming and diving M (s)/W (s), volleyball W (s). *Intramural sports:* badminton M/W, basketball M/W, bowling M (c)/W (c), fencing M (c)/W (c), football M/W, ice hockey M (c)/W (c), lacrosse M (c)/W (c), racquetball M/W, table tennis M/W, tennis M (c)/W (c), track and field M (c)/W (c), ultimate Frisbee M/W, volleyball M/W.

Costs (2007–08) *Comprehensive fee:* $34,364 includes full-time tuition ($24,962), mandatory fees ($784), and room and board ($8618). Part-time tuition: $778 per credit hour. Part-time tuition and fees vary according to course load. *Required fees:* $7 per credit hour part-time, $250 per term part-time. *College room only:* $4550. Room and board charges vary according to board plan and housing facility. *Payment plans:* installment, deferred payment. *Waivers:* employees or children of employees.

Financial Aid Of all full-time matriculated undergraduates who enrolled in 2006, 1,448 applied for aid, 1,304 were judged to have need, 261 had their need fully met. In 2006, 784 non-need-based awards were made. *Average percent of need met:* 85%. *Average financial aid package:* $22,542. *Average need-based loan:* $4410. *Average need-based gift aid:* $13,378. *Average non-need-based aid:* $9901. *Average indebtedness upon graduation:* $21,326.

Applying *Options:* electronic application, deferred entrance. *Required:* essay or personal statement, high school transcript, 1 letter of recommendation, ACT or SAT scores, except for international students coming from countries where the tests are not widely administered. *Recommended:* interview. *Application deadlines:* 8/1 (freshmen), 8/1 (out-of-state freshmen), rolling (transfers). *Notification:* continuous until 11/1 (freshmen), continuous until 11/1 (out-of-state freshmen), continuous (transfers).

Freshman Application Contact Mr. Gerald Doyle, Associate Vice President, Undergraduate Admissions, Illinois Institute of Technology, 10 West 33rd Street, Perlestein Hall Room 101, Chicago, IL 60616-3793. *Phone:* 312-567-3025. *Toll-free phone:* 800-448-2329. *Fax:* 312-567-6939. *E-mail:* admission@iit.edu.

See page 840 for the College Close-Up.

ILLINOIS STATE UNIVERSITY

Normal, Illinois **www.ilstu.edu/**

- **State-supported** university, founded 1857
- **Urban** 850-acre campus
- **Endowment** $78,966
- **Coed** 17,703 undergraduate students, 94% full-time, 57% women, 43% men
- **Moderately difficult** entrance level, 67% of applicants were admitted

Undergraduates 16,630 full-time, 1,073 part-time. Students come from 43 states and territories, 33 other countries, 1% are from out of state, 6% African American, 2% Asian American or Pacific Islander, 4% Hispanic American, 0.3% Native American, 0.6% international, 10% transferred in, 35% live on campus. *Retention:* 83% of 2006 full-time freshmen returned.

Freshmen *Admission:* 12,550 applied, 8,461 admitted, 3,145 enrolled. *Average high school GPA:* 3.38. *Test scores:* ACT scores over 18: 100%; ACT scores over 24: 57%; ACT scores over 30: 4%.

Faculty *Total:* 1,136, 74% full-time, 69% with terminal degrees. *Student/faculty ratio:* 19:1.

Majors Accounting; accounting and business/management; agribusiness; agriculture; anthropology; art; athletic training; audiology and speech-language pathology; biochemistry; biology/biological sciences; business administration and management; business teacher education; chemistry; clinical laboratory science/medical technology; criminal justice/safety; dramatic/theater arts; early childhood education; economics; elementary education; English; environmental health; family and consumer sciences/human sciences; finance; fine/studio arts; French; geography; geology/earth science; German; health information/medical records administration; health teacher education; history; industrial technology; information science/studies; information technology; insurance; interdisciplinary studies; international business/trade/commerce; journalism; kinesiology and exercise science; marketing/marketing management; mass communication/media; mathematics; music; music performance; music teacher education; nursing (registered nurse training); parks, recreation and leisure facilities management; philosophy; physical education teaching and coaching; physics; political science and government; psychology; public relations/image management; social studies teacher education; social work; sociology; Spanish; special education; speech and rhetoric; technology/industrial arts teacher education; visual and performing arts related.

Academics *Calendar:* semesters. *Degrees:* bachelor's, master's, doctoral, post-master's, and postbachelor's certificates. *Special study options:* academic remediation for entering students, accelerated degree program, adult/continuing education programs, advanced placement credit, cooperative education, distance learning, double majors, English as a second language, honors programs, independent study, internships, off-campus study, part-time degree program, services for LD students, student-designed majors, study abroad, summer session for credit. *ROTC:* Army (b). *Unusual degree programs:* 3-2 engineering with University of Illinois.

Computers on Campus 2,530 computers/terminals are available on campus for general student use. Campuswide network is available.

Student Life *Housing:* on-campus residence required through sophomore year. *Options:* coed, women-only, disabled students. Campus housing is university owned. Freshman campus housing is guaranteed. *Activities and organizations:* drama/theater group, student-run newspaper, radio and television station, choral group, marching band, national fraternities, national sororities. *Campus security:* 24-hour emergency response devices and patrols, late-night transport/escort service, controlled dormitory access. *Student services:* health clinic, personal/psychological counseling, women's center, legal services.

Athletics Member NCAA. All Division I except football (Division I-AA). *Intercollegiate sports:* baseball M (s), basketball M (s)/W (s), cross-country running M (s)/W (s), golf M (s)/W (s), gymnastics W (s), soccer W (s), softball W (s), swimming and diving W (s), tennis M (s)/W (s), track and field M (s)/W (s), volleyball W (s). *Intramural sports:* badminton M/W, baseball M, basketball M/W, bowling M (c)/W (c), field hockey M/W, football M, golf M/W, gymnastics M (c), ice hockey M (c), lacrosse M (c), racquetball M/W, rugby M (c)/W (c), soccer M/W, softball M/W, tennis M/W, ultimate Frisbee M/W, volleyball M (c)/W.

Standardized Tests *Required:* SAT or ACT (for admission).

Costs (2007–08) *Tuition:* state resident $6990 full-time, $233 per hour part-time; nonresident $14,310 full-time, $477 per hour part-time. Full-time tuition and fees vary according to course load. Part-time tuition and fees vary according to course load. No tuition increase for student's term of enrollment. *Required fees:* $2029 full-time, $57 per hour part-time, $854 per term part-time. *Room and board:* $6848; room only: $3560. Room and board charges vary according to board plan, housing facility, and location. *Payment plan:* installment. *Waivers:* minority students, senior citizens, and employees or children of employees.

Financial Aid Of all full-time matriculated undergraduates who enrolled in 2007, 11,079 applied for aid, 8,222 were judged to have need, 3,188 had their need fully met. 658 Federal Work-Study jobs (averaging $1937). 43 state and other part-time jobs (averaging $2299). In 2007, 326 non-need-based awards were made. *Average percent of need met:* 81%. *Average financial aid package:* $10,126. *Average need-based loan:* $5754. *Average need-based gift aid:* $8212. *Average non-need-based aid:* $3531. *Average indebtedness upon graduation:* $18,053.

Applying *Options:* electronic application. *Application fee:* $40. *Required:* essay or personal statement, high school transcript. *Application deadlines:* 3/1 (freshmen), rolling (transfers). *Notification:* continuous (freshmen), continuous (transfers).

Freshman Application Contact Ms. Molly Arnold, Director of Admissions, Illinois State University, Campus Box 2200, Normal, IL 61790-2200. *Phone:* 309-438-2181. *Toll-free phone:* 800-366-2478. *Fax:* 309-438-3932. *E-mail:* admissions@ilstu.edu.

ILLINOIS WESLEYAN UNIVERSITY

Bloomington, Illinois **www.iwu.edu/**

- **Independent** 4-year, founded 1850
- **Suburban** 79-acre campus
- **Endowment** $190.5 million
- **Coed** 2,094 undergraduate students, 100% full-time, 58% women, 42% men
- **Very difficult** entrance level, 57% of applicants were admitted

Undergraduates 2,087 full-time, 7 part-time. Students come from 39 states and territories, 22 other countries, 13% are from out of state, 5% African American, 4% Asian American or Pacific Islander, 3% Hispanic American, 0.4% Native American, 2% international, 1% transferred in, 77% live on campus. *Retention:* 92% of 2006 full-time freshmen returned.

Freshmen *Admission:* 2,963 applied, 1,696 admitted, 538 enrolled. *Test scores:* SAT critical reading scores over 500: 90%; SAT math scores over 500: 96%; ACT scores over 18: 100%; SAT critical reading scores over 600: 58%; SAT math scores over 600: 72%; ACT scores over 24: 93%; SAT critical reading scores over 700: 18%; SAT math scores over 700: 22%; ACT scores over 30: 31%.

Faculty *Total:* 231, 70% full-time, 78% with terminal degrees. *Student/faculty ratio:* 11:1.

Majors Accounting; acting; African studies; American studies; anthropology; area studies related; art; Asian studies; biology/biological sciences; business administration and management; chemistry; classics and languages, literatures and linguistics; computer science; dramatic/theater arts; economics; education; elementary education; environmental studies; European studies (Western); French; German; history; insurance; insurance/risk management; international business/trade/commerce; international relations and affairs; Latin American studies; liberal arts and sciences/liberal studies; mathematics; music; music performance; music related; music teacher education; music theory and composition; nursing (registered nurse training); philosophy; physics; piano and organ; political science and government; psychology; religious studies; sociology; Spanish; theater design and technology; voice and opera; women's studies.

Academics *Calendar:* 4-4-1. *Degree:* bachelor's. *Special study options:* advanced placement credit, double majors, honors programs, independent study, internships, off-campus study, services for LD students, student-designed majors, study abroad. *ROTC:* Army (c). *Unusual degree programs:* 3-2 engineering with Case Western Reserve University, Northwestern University, Washington University in St. Louis, Dartmouth College, University of Illinois; forestry with Duke University; occupational therapy.

Computers on Campus 400 computers/terminals are available on campus for general student use. Students can access the following: campus intranet, computer help desk, free student e-mail accounts, online (class) registration. Campuswide network is available. Wireless service is available via classrooms, libraries, student centers.

Student Life *Housing:* on-campus residence required through sophomore year. *Options:* coed, disabled students. Campus housing is university owned. Freshman campus housing is guaranteed. *Activities and organizations:* drama/theater group, student-run newspaper, radio and television station, choral group, Alpha Phi Omega, Christian Fellowship, Students for a Just Society, Black Student Union, Habitat for Humanity, national fraternities, national sororities. *Campus security:* 24-hour emergency response devices and patrols, late-night transport/escort service, controlled dormitory access, emergency response team. *Student services:* health clinic, personal/psychological counseling.

Athletics Member NCAA. All Division III. *Intercollegiate sports:* baseball M, basketball M/W, cheerleading M (c)/W (c), cross-country running M/W, football M, golf M/W, lacrosse M (c), soccer M/W, softball W, swimming and diving M/W, tennis M/W, track and field M/W, ultimate Frisbee M (c)/W (c), volleyball M (c)/W, water polo M (c). *Intramural sports:* badminton M/W, basketball M/W, football M/W, golf M/W, racquetball M/W, soccer M/W, softball M/W, tennis M/W, volleyball M/W.

Standardized Tests *Required:* SAT or ACT (for admission).

Costs (2007–08) *Comprehensive fee:* $37,780 includes full-time tuition ($30,580), mandatory fees ($170), and room and board ($7030). Part-time tuition: $3823 per course. *College room only:* $4330. Room and board charges vary according to board plan and housing facility. *Payment plan:* installment. *Waivers:* employees or children of employees.

Financial Aid Of all full-time matriculated undergraduates who enrolled in 2007, 1,458 applied for aid, 1,210 were judged to have need, 425 had their need fully met. In 2007, 697 non-need-based awards were made. *Average percent of need met:* 90%. *Average financial aid package:* $22,351. *Average need-based loan:* $4520. *Average need-based gift aid:* $17,070. *Average non-need-based aid:* $9939. *Average indebtedness upon graduation:* $24,234. *Financial aid deadline:* 3/1.

Applying *Options:* electronic application, early admission, deferred entrance. *Required:* essay or personal statement, high school transcript, minimum 2.0 GPA, 1 letter of recommendation. *Recommended:* minimum 3.0 GPA, 2 letters of recommendation, interview. *Application deadlines:* rolling (freshmen), 8/15 (transfers). *Notification:* continuous (freshmen), continuous (transfers).

Freshman Application Contact Mr. Tony Bankston, Dean of Admissions, Illinois Wesleyan University, PO Box 2900, Bloomington, IL 61702-2900. *Phone:* 309-556-3031. *Toll-free phone:* 800-332-2498. *Fax:* 309-556-3820. *E-mail:* iwuadmit@iwu.edu.

INTERNATIONAL ACADEMY OF DESIGN & TECHNOLOGY

Chicago, Illinois **www.iadtchicago.edu/**

- **Proprietary** 4-year, founded 1977, part of Career Education Corporation
- **Urban** 1-acre campus
- **Coed, primarily women** 2,335 undergraduate students, 87% full-time, 66% women, 34% men
- **Minimally difficult** entrance level, 27% of applicants were admitted

Undergraduates 2,020 full-time, 315 part-time. Students come from 27 states and territories, 3 other countries, 6% are from out of state, 36% African American, 4% Asian American or Pacific Islander, 20% Hispanic American, 0.5% Native American, 2% international, 8% transferred in. *Retention:* 54% of 2006 full-time freshmen returned.

Freshmen *Admission:* 1,869 applied, 511 admitted, 511 enrolled. *Average high school GPA:* 2.1.

Faculty *Total:* 132, 9% full-time, 13% with terminal degrees. *Student/faculty ratio:* 15:1.

Majors Commercial and advertising art; computer and information sciences and support services related; computer graphics; design and visual communications; fashion/apparel design; fashion merchandising; information technology; interior design; intermedia/multimedia.

Academics *Calendar:* quarters. *Degrees:* associate and bachelor's. *Special study options:* academic remediation for entering students, adult/continuing education programs, advanced placement credit, independent study, internships, part-time degree program, services for LD students, study abroad, summer session for credit.

Computers on Campus 425 computers/terminals are available on campus for general student use. Students can access the following: campus intranet, computer help desk, free student e-mail accounts, online (class) grades, student Website. Campuswide network is available. Wireless service is available via classrooms, computer labs, learning centers, libraries, student centers.

Student Life *Housing:* college housing not available. *Activities and organizations:* student-run newspaper, ASID/IDSA (Interior Design Student Organization), ASA (Anime Student Alliance), Fashion Council, Behind the Scenes, Playback. *Campus security:* 24-hour emergency response devices, building security during hours of operation. *Student services:* personal/psychological counseling.

Costs (2008–09) *Tuition:* $23,040 full-time, $360 per credit part-time. *Required fees:* $600 full-time.

Financial Aid Of all full-time matriculated undergraduates who enrolled in 2002, 30 Federal Work-Study jobs.

Applying *Options:* electronic application, early admission. *Application fee:* $50. *Required:* high school transcript, interview. *Required for some:* GED. *Recommended:* essay or personal statement, minimum 2.0 GPA. *Application deadlines:* rolling (freshmen), rolling (transfers).

Freshman Application Contact Suzanne Reichart, Director of Student Management, International Academy of Design & Technology, One North State Street, Suite 400, Chicago, IL 60602. *Phone:* 312-980-9200. *Toll-free phone:* 877-ACADEMY. *Fax:* 312-541-3929. *E-mail:* sreichart@iadtchicago.edu.

See page 842 for the College Close-Up.

ITT TECHNICAL INSTITUTE

Burr Ridge, Illinois **www.itt-tech.edu/**

- **Proprietary** primarily 2-year, founded 1998, part of ITT Educational Services, Inc
- **Coed**
- **Minimally difficult** entrance level

Academics *Calendar:* quarters. *Degrees:* associate and bachelor's.

Standardized Tests *Required:* Wonderlic aptitude test (for admission).

Applying *Options:* deferred entrance. *Application fee:* $100. *Required:* high school transcript, interview. *Recommended:* letters of recommendation.

Freshman Application Contact Mr. Andrew Mical, Director of Recruitment, ITT Technical Institute, 7040 High Grove Boulevard, Burr Ridge, IL 60527. *Phone:* 630-455-6470. *Toll-free phone:* 877-488-0001. *Fax:* 630-455-6476.

ITT TECHNICAL INSTITUTE

Mount Prospect, Illinois **www.itt-tech.edu/**

- **Proprietary** primarily 2-year, founded 1986, part of ITT Educational Services, Inc
- **Suburban** 1-acre campus with easy access to Chicago
- **Coed**
- **Minimally difficult** entrance level

Academics *Calendar:* quarters. *Degrees:* associate, bachelor's, and master's.

Standardized Tests *Required:* Wonderlic aptitude test (for admission).

Applying *Options:* deferred entrance. *Application fee:* $100. *Required:* high school transcript, interview. *Recommended:* letters of recommendation.

Freshman Application Contact Mr. Cesar Rodriguez Jr., Director of Recruitment, ITT Technical Institute, 1401 Feehanville Drive, Mount Prospect, IL 60056. *Phone:* 847-375-8800.

ITT TECHNICAL INSTITUTE

Orland Park, Illinois **www.itt-tech.edu/**

- **Proprietary** primarily 2-year, founded 1993, part of ITT Educational Services, Inc
- **Suburban** campus with easy access to Chicago
- **Coed**
- **Minimally difficult** entrance level

Academics *Calendar:* quarters. *Degrees:* associate and bachelor's.

Standardized Tests *Required:* Wonderlic aptitude test (for admission).

Financial Aid Of all full-time matriculated undergraduates who enrolled in 2006, 6 Federal Work-Study jobs (averaging $4000).

Applying *Options:* deferred entrance. *Application fee:* $100. *Required:* high school transcript, interview. *Recommended:* letters of recommendation.

Freshman Application Contact Mr. James Tannheimer, ITT Technical Institute, 11551 184th Place, Orland Park, IL 60467. *Phone:* 708-326-3200.

JUDSON UNIVERSITY

Elgin, Illinois **www.judsonu.edu/**

- **Independent Baptist** comprehensive, founded 1963
- **Suburban** 80-acre campus with easy access to Chicago
- **Endowment** $7.0 million
- **Coed** 1,140 undergraduate students, 81% full-time, 61% women, 39% men
- **Moderately difficult** entrance level, 73% of applicants were admitted

Undergraduates 921 full-time, 219 part-time. Students come from 36 states and territories, 23 other countries, 24% are from out of state, 4% African American, 0.8% Asian American or Pacific Islander, 6% Hispanic American, 0.1% Native American, 4% international, 80% transferred in, 66% live on campus. *Retention:* 68% of 2006 full-time freshmen returned.

Freshmen *Admission:* 475 applied, 348 admitted, 154 enrolled. *Average high school GPA:* 3.34. *Test scores:* SAT critical reading scores over 500: 67%; SAT math scores over 500: 63%; ACT scores over 18: 90%; SAT critical reading scores over 600: 32%; SAT math scores over 600: 29%; ACT scores over 24: 47%; SAT critical reading scores over 700: 5%; SAT math scores over 700: 6%; ACT scores over 30: 8%.

Faculty *Total:* 133, 43% full-time, 32% with terminal degrees. *Student/faculty ratio:* 14:1.

Majors Accounting; architecture; art; biblical studies; biology/biological sciences; business administration and management; chemistry; criminal justice/safety; elementary education; English; fine/studio arts; history; human resources management; management information systems; mathematics; music teacher education; physical education teaching and coaching; psychology; secondary education; sociology; sport and fitness administration/management.

Academics *Calendar:* semesters. *Degrees:* bachelor's and master's. *Special study options:* academic remediation for entering students, accelerated degree program, adult/continuing education programs, advanced placement credit, distance learning, double majors, external degree program, honors programs, independent study, internships, off-campus study, part-time degree program, study abroad. *ROTC:* Army (c).

Computers on Campus 90 computers/terminals are available on campus for general student use. Campuswide network is available.

Student Life *Housing:* on-campus residence required through junior year. *Options:* men-only, women-only, disabled students. Campus housing is university owned. Freshman campus housing is guaranteed. *Activities and organizations:* drama/theater group, student-run newspaper, choral group, Judson Choir, Judson Student Organization, Intramurals, Phi Beta Lambda. *Campus security:* 24-hour emergency response devices and patrols, controlled dormitory access. *Student services:* health clinic, personal/psychological counseling.

Athletics Member NAIA, NCCAA. *Intercollegiate sports:* baseball M (s), basketball M (s)/W (s), cross-country running M (s)/W (s), soccer M (s)/W (s), softball W (s), volleyball W (s). *Intramural sports:* badminton M/W, basketball M/W, football M, golf M, racquetball M/W, soccer M/W, softball W, volleyball M/W.

Standardized Tests *Required:* SAT and SAT Subject Tests or ACT (for admission).

Costs (2007–08) *Comprehensive fee:* $27,620 includes full-time tuition ($20,100), mandatory fees ($320), and room and board ($7200). Part-time tuition: $670 per credit hour. Part-time tuition and fees vary according to course load. *Room and board:* Room and board charges vary according to board plan. *Payment plan:* installment. *Waivers:* senior citizens and employees or children of employees.

Financial Aid Of all full-time matriculated undergraduates who enrolled in 2005, 689 applied for aid, 594 were judged to have need, 9 had their need fully met. In 2005, 55 non-need-based awards were made. *Average percent of need met:* 36%. *Average financial aid package:* $12,036. *Average need-based loan:* $3777. *Average need-based gift aid:* $5954. *Average non-need-based aid:* $4405. *Average indebtedness upon graduation:* $21,960.

Applying *Options:* electronic application, early admission, deferred entrance. *Application fee:* $35. *Required:* high school transcript, minimum 2.0 GPA, lifestyle statement. *Required for some:* essay or personal statement, 3 letters of recommendation, interview. *Application deadlines:* rolling (freshmen), rolling (transfers). *Notification:* continuous (freshmen), continuous (transfers).

Freshman Application Contact Mr. William W. Dean, Director of Enrollment Management, Judson University, 1151 North State Street, Elgin, IL 60123-1498. *Phone:* 847-695-2522. *Toll-free phone:* 800-879-5376. *Fax:* 847-628-2526. *E-mail:* bdean@judsoncollege.edu.

KENDALL COLLEGE

Chicago, Illinois **www.kendall.edu/**

- **Independent United Methodist** 4-year, founded 1934
- **Urban** 4-acre campus
- **Coed**
- **Moderately difficult** entrance level

Faculty *Student/faculty ratio:* 19:1.

Academics *Calendar:* quarters. *Degrees:* certificates, associate, and bachelor's.

Student Life *Campus security:* 24-hour emergency response devices and patrols, student patrols, controlled dormitory access, late night security in dorms.

Standardized Tests *Required:* SAT or ACT (for admission).

Financial Aid Of all full-time matriculated undergraduates who enrolled in 2003, 360 were judged to have need. 50 Federal Work-Study jobs (averaging $1162). *Average percent of need met:* 26. *Average indebtedness upon graduation:* $14,125.

Applying *Options:* deferred entrance. *Application fee:* $50. *Required:* essay or personal statement, high school transcript, minimum ACT score of 18. *Required for some:* letters of recommendation, interview. *Recommended:* minimum 2.0 GPA.

Freshman Application Contact Susanne Noel, Vice President of Admissions, Kendall College, 900 North Branch Street, Chicago, IL 60622. *Phone:* 312-752-2020. *Toll-free phone:* 866-667-3344 (in-state); 877-588-8860 (out-of-state). *Fax:* 312-752-2021. *E-mail:* admissions@kendall.edu.

See page 844 for the College Close-Up.

KNOX COLLEGE

Galesburg, Illinois **www.knox.edu/**

- **Independent** 4-year, founded 1837
- **Small-town** 82-acre campus with easy access to Peoria
- **Endowment** $79.5 million
- **Coed** 1,371 undergraduate students, 99% full-time, 58% women, 42% men
- **Very difficult** entrance level, 61% of applicants were admitted

Undergraduates 1,354 full-time, 17 part-time. Students come from 46 states and territories, 36 other countries, 48% are from out of state, 4% African American, 7% Asian American or Pacific Islander, 5% Hispanic American, 0.6% Native American, 6% international, 3% transferred in, 94% live on campus. *Retention:* 91% of 2006 full-time freshmen returned.

Freshmen *Admission:* 2,419 applied, 1,479 admitted, 307 enrolled. *Test scores:* SAT critical reading scores over 500: 99%; SAT math scores over 500: 96%; SAT writing scores over 500: 99%; ACT scores over 18: 100%; SAT critical reading scores over 600: 84%; SAT math scores over 600: 66%; SAT writing scores over 600: 72%; ACT scores over 24: 95%; SAT critical reading scores over 700: 31%; SAT math scores over 700: 18%; SAT writing scores over 700: 19%; ACT scores over 30: 43%.

Faculty *Total:* 138, 71% full-time, 78% with terminal degrees. *Student/faculty ratio:* 12:1.

Majors African-American/Black studies; American studies; anthropology; art; art history, criticism and conservation; Asian studies; biochemistry; biology/biological sciences; chemistry; classics and languages, literatures and linguistics; computer and information sciences; creative writing; dramatic/theater arts; economics; education; English; environmental studies; foreign languages and literatures; French; German; history; international relations and affairs; mathematics; multi-/interdisciplinary studies related; music; philosophy; physics; political science and government; psychology; Russian; Russian studies; sociology; Spanish; women's studies.

Academics *Calendar:* three courses for each of three terms. *Degree:* bachelor's. *Special study options:* academic remediation for entering students, advanced placement credit, double majors, honors programs, independent study, internships, off-campus study, part-time degree program, services for LD students, student-designed majors, study abroad. *Unusual degree programs:* 3-2 engineering with Columbia University, Washington University in St. Louis, Rensselaer Polytechnic Institute, University of Illinois at Urbana-Champaign; forestry with Duke University; nursing with Rush University; occupational therapy, medical technology with Columbia University, Rush University; optometry with Illinois College of Optometry.

Computers on Campus 338 computers/terminals are available on campus for general student use. Students can access the following: campus intranet, computer help desk, free student e-mail accounts, online (class) registration, online (class) schedules, software applications. Campuswide network is available.

Student Life *Housing:* on-campus residence required for freshman year. *Options:* coed, men-only, women-only. Campus housing is university owned. Freshman campus housing is guaranteed. *Activities and organizations:* drama/theater group, student-run newspaper, radio station, choral group, International Club, Allied Blacks for Liberty and Equality, Sexual Equality Awareness Coalition, Union Board, campus radio station, national fraternities, national sororities. *Campus security:* 24-hour emergency response devices and patrols, late-night transport/escort service. *Student services:* health clinic, personal/psychological counseling.

Athletics Member NCAA. except baseball (Division III), men's and women's basketball (Division III), men's and women's cross-country running (Division III), football (Division III), men's and women's golf (Division III), men's and women's soccer (Division III), softball (Division III), men's and women's swimming and diving (Division III), men's and women's tennis (Division III), men's and women's track and field (Division III), volleyball (Division III), wrestling (Division III) *Intercollegiate sports:* baseball M, basketball M/W, cross-country running M/W, football M, golf M/W, soccer M/W, softball W, swimming and diving M/W, tennis M/W, track and field M/W, volleyball W, wrestling M. *Intramural sports:* baseball M, basketball M/W, cross-country running M/W, fencing M/W, lacrosse M/W, soccer M/W, softball M/W, swimming and diving M/W, tennis M/W, track and field M/W, ultimate Frisbee M/W, volleyball M/W, water polo M/W, weight lifting M/W.

Standardized Tests *Recommended:* SAT or ACT (for admission).

Costs (2008–09) *Comprehensive fee:* $37,233 includes full-time tuition ($30,180), mandatory fees ($327), and room and board ($6726). *College room only:* $3336.

Financial Aid Of all full-time matriculated undergraduates who enrolled in 2006, 1,016 applied for aid, 897 were judged to have need, 332 had their need fully met. 665 Federal Work-Study jobs (averaging $1928). 74 state and other part-time jobs (averaging $1915). In 2006, 391 non-need-based awards were made. *Average percent of need met:* 94%. *Average financial aid package:* $23,820. *Average need-based loan:* $5630. *Average need-based gift aid:* $17,710. *Average non-need-based aid:* $10,172. *Average indebtedness upon graduation:* $21,951.

Applying *Options:* electronic application, early admission, early action, deferred entrance. *Application fee:* $40. *Required:* essay or personal statement, high school transcript, 2 letters of recommendation. *Recommended:* interview. *Application deadlines:* 2/1 (freshmen), 4/1 (transfers), 12/1 (early action). *Notification:* 3/31 (freshmen), 5/15 (transfers), 12/31 (early action).

Freshman Application Contact Mr. Paul Steenis, Director of Admissions, Knox College, Box K-148, Galesburg, IL 61401. *Phone:* 309-341-7100. *Toll-free phone:* 800-678-KNOX. *Fax:* 309-341-7070. *E-mail:* admission@knox.edu.

LAKE FOREST COLLEGE

Lake Forest, Illinois **www.lakeforest.edu/**

- **Independent** comprehensive, founded 1857
- **Suburban** 110-acre campus with easy access to Chicago
- **Endowment** $73.3 million
- **Coed** 1,436 undergraduate students, 99% full-time, 59% women, 41% men
- **Very difficult** entrance level, 61% of applicants were admitted

Undergraduates 1,416 full-time, 20 part-time. Students come from 47 states and territories, 67 other countries, 52% are from out of state, 4% African American, 5% Asian American or Pacific Islander, 6% Hispanic American, 0.3% Native American, 8% international, 3% transferred in, 77% live on campus. *Retention:* 82% of 2006 full-time freshmen returned.

Freshmen *Admission:* 2,203 applied, 1,346 admitted, 356 enrolled. *Average high school GPA:* 3.5. *Test scores:* SAT critical reading scores over 500: 88%; SAT math scores over 500: 94%; SAT writing scores over 500: 94%; ACT scores over 18: 100%; SAT critical reading scores over 600: 54%; SAT math scores over 600: 58%; SAT writing scores over 600: 48%; ACT scores over 24: 82%; SAT critical reading scores over 700: 13%; SAT math scores over 700: 13%; SAT writing scores over 700: 6%; ACT scores over 30: 18%.

Faculty *Total:* 154, 58% full-time, 78% with terminal degrees. *Student/faculty ratio:* 13:1.

Majors American studies; anthropology; art history, criticism and conservation; Asian studies; biology/biological sciences; business/managerial economics; chemistry; communication/speech communication and rhetoric; computer science; dramatic/theater arts; economics; education; elementary education; English; environmental studies; fine/studio arts; French; history; international relations and affairs; Latin American studies; mathematics; music; philosophy; physics; political science and government; psychology; secondary education; sociology; Spanish; theology.

Academics *Calendar:* semesters. *Degrees:* bachelor's and master's. *Special study options:* accelerated degree program, adult/continuing education programs, advanced placement credit, double majors, freshman honors college, honors programs, independent study, internships, off-campus study, part-time degree program, services for LD students, student-designed majors, study abroad, summer session for credit. *Unusual degree programs:* 3-2 engineering with Washington University in St. Louis.

Computers on Campus 190 computers/terminals and 1,200 ports are available on campus for general student use. Students can access the following: campus intranet, computer help desk, free student e-mail accounts, online (class) grades, online (class) schedules, file storage. Campuswide network is available. 100% of college-owned or -operated housing units are wired for high-speed Internet access. Wireless service is available via classrooms, computer centers, computer labs, dorm rooms, learning centers, libraries, student centers.

Student Life *Housing options:* coed, women-only, disabled students. Campus housing is university owned. Freshman campus housing is guaranteed. *Activities and organizations:* drama/theater group, student-run newspaper, radio station, choral group, Garrick Players Drama Group, WMXM Radio Station, Intervarsity Christian Fellowship, Athletic Council, Student Affiliates of the American Chemical Society, national fraternities, national sororities. *Campus security:* 24-hour emergency response devices and patrols, student patrols, late-night transport/escort service, controlled dormitory access. *Student services:* health clinic, personal/psychological counseling, women's center.

Athletics Member NCAA. All Division III. *Intercollegiate sports:* basketball M/W, cheerleading M (c)/W (c), cross-country running M/W, football M, golf M (c)/W (c), ice hockey M/W, lacrosse M (c)/W (c), rugby M (c)/W (c), sailing M (c)/W (c), soccer M/W, softball W, swimming and diving M/W, tennis M/W, track and field M (c)/W (c), ultimate Frisbee M (c)/W (c), volleyball M (c)/W, water polo M (c)/W (c). *Intramural sports:* basketball M/W, football M, racquetball M/W, soccer M/W, softball M/W, tennis M/W, volleyball M/W.

Standardized Tests *Required for some:* SAT or ACT (for admission).

Costs (2007–08) *One-time required fee:* $100. *Comprehensive fee:* $38,290 includes full-time tuition ($30,600), mandatory fees ($364), and room and board ($7326). Full-time tuition and fees vary according to course load. Part-time tuition: $3825 per course. Part-time tuition and fees vary according to course load. *College room only:* $3700. Room and board charges vary according to board plan and housing facility. *Payment plan:* installment. *Waivers:* employees or children of employees.

Financial Aid Of all full-time matriculated undergraduates who enrolled in 2006, 1,278 applied for aid, 1,057 were judged to have need, 1,057 had their need fully met. 549 Federal Work-Study jobs (averaging $1707). In 2006, 202 non-need-based awards were made. *Average percent of need met:* 100%. *Average financial aid package:* $23,024. *Average need-based loan:* $5181. *Average need-based gift aid:* $18,769. *Average non-need-based aid:* $11,319. *Average indebtedness upon graduation:* $19,976.

Applying *Options:* electronic application, early admission, early decision, early action, deferred entrance. *Application fee:* $40. *Required:* essay or personal statement, high school transcript, 2 letters of recommendation, graded paper. *Recommended:* interview. *Application deadlines:* 2/15 (freshmen), rolling (transfers), 12/1 (early action). *Early decision deadline:* 12/1. *Notification:* 3/20 (freshmen), continuous (transfers), 12/20 (early decision), 1/20 (early action).

Freshman Application Contact Mr. William Motzer, Vice President for Admissions and Career Services, Lake Forest College, 555 North Sheridan Road, Lake Forest, IL 60045-2399. *Phone:* 847-735-5000. *Toll-free phone:* 800-828-4751. *Fax:* 847-735-6271. *E-mail:* admissions@lakeforest.edu.

See page 846 for the College Close-Up.

LAKEVIEW COLLEGE OF NURSING

Danville, Illinois **www.lakeviewcol.edu/**

Application Contact Amy McFadden, Recruiter, Lakeview College of Nursing, 903 North Logan Avenue, Danville, IL 61832. *Phone:* 217-554-6845. *Toll-free phone:* 217-443-5238 Ext. 5454. *Fax:* 217-442-2279. *E-mail:* amcfadden@lakeviewcol.edu.

LEWIS UNIVERSITY

Romeoville, Illinois **www.lewisu.edu/**

- **Independent** comprehensive, founded 1932, affiliated with Roman Catholic Church
- **Suburban** 375-acre campus with easy access to Chicago
- **Endowment** $47.1 million
- **Coed** 3,848 undergraduate students, 77% full-time, 61% women, 39% men
- **Moderately difficult** entrance level, 68% of applicants were admitted

Lewis University offers more than seventy undergraduate majors and programs of study, accelerated degree-completion programs for adults, and twenty-one graduate programs. Premier programs include aviation, business, criminal/social justice, education, and nursing. In 2007, Lewis received approval from the FAA to offer the air traffic control–CTI program. Lewis is located 30 minutes from Chicago.

Undergraduates 2,963 full-time, 885 part-time. Students come from 32 states and territories, 21 other countries, 4% are from out of state, 11% African American, 4% Asian American or Pacific Islander, 11% Hispanic American, 0.1% Native American, 3% international, 10% transferred in, 30% live on campus. *Retention:* 77% of 2006 full-time freshmen returned.

Freshmen *Admission:* 2,654 applied, 1,795 admitted, 636 enrolled. *Average high school GPA:* 3.18. *Test scores:* SAT critical reading scores over 500: 69%; SAT math scores over 500: 56%; ACT scores over 18: 92%; SAT critical reading scores over 600: 13%; SAT math scores over 600: 19%; ACT scores over 24: 33%; SAT critical reading scores over 700: 6%; SAT math scores over 700: 6%; ACT scores over 30: 4%.

Faculty *Total:* 539, 33% full-time, 28% with terminal degrees. *Student/faculty ratio:* 13:1.

Majors Accounting; airframe mechanics and aircraft maintenance technology; air traffic control; American studies; area studies related; athletic training; aviation/airway management; biochemistry; biology/biological sciences; broadcast journalism; business administration and management; business/managerial economics; chemistry; communications technology; computer and information sciences; computer graphics; computer science; criminal justice/law enforcement administration; criminal justice/safety; diagnostic medical sonography and ultrasound technology; dramatic/theater arts; drawing; economics; elementary education; English; environmental studies; finance; fine/studio arts; fire services administration; history; human resources management; illustration; intermedia/multimedia; international business/trade/commerce; international/global studies; journalism; liberal arts and sciences/liberal studies; marketing/marketing management; mass communication/media; mathematics; music; music management and merchandising; nuclear medical technology; nursing (registered nurse training); painting; philosophy; physics; political science and government; pre-dentistry studies; pre-engineering; pre-law studies; pre-medical studies; pre-pharmacy studies; pre-veterinary studies; psychology; public administration; public relations/image management; radio and television broadcasting technology; religious studies; security and protective services related; social work; sociology; special education; speech and rhetoric.

Academics *Calendar:* semesters. *Degrees:* certificates, associate, bachelor's, master's, doctoral, and post-master's certificates. *Special study options:* academic remediation for entering students, accelerated degree program, adult/continuing education programs, advanced placement credit, distance learning, double majors, English as a second language, honors programs, independent study, internships, off-campus study, part-time degree program, services for LD students, student-designed majors, study abroad, summer session for credit. *ROTC:* Army (c), Air Force (c). *Unusual degree programs:* 3-2 Pharmacy with Chicago College of Pharmacy, Chiropractic Medicine with Logan College.

Computers on Campus 310 computers/terminals and 40 ports are available on campus for general student use. Students can access the following: campus intranet, computer help desk, free student e-mail accounts, online (class) grades, online (class) registration, online (class) schedules, online help, online billing, online financial aid, online application, online housing application. Campuswide network is available. 100% of college-owned or -operated housing units are wired for high-speed Internet access. Wireless service is available via entire campus.

Student Life *Housing options:* coed. Campus housing is university owned. Freshman campus housing is guaranteed. *Activities and organizations:* drama/theater group, student-run newspaper, radio and television station, choral group, Theta Kappa Pi, Scholars Academy, Black Student Union, Fellowship of Justice, Latin American Student Organization, national fraternities, national sororities. *Campus security:* 24-hour emergency response devices and patrols, student patrols, late-night transport/escort service, controlled dormitory access. *Student services:* health clinic, personal/psychological counseling.

Athletics Member NCAA. All Division II. *Intercollegiate sports:* baseball M (s), basketball M (s)/W (s), cheerleading M (s) (c)/W (s) (c), cross-country running M (s)/W (s), golf M (s)/W (s), soccer M (s)/W (s), softball W (s), swimming and diving M (s)/W (s), tennis M (s)/W (s), track and field M (s)/W (s), volleyball M (s)/W (s). *Intramural sports:* basketball M/W, bowling M/W, cheerleading M/W, cross-country running M/W, football M/W, golf M/W, racquetball M/W, soccer M/W, softball W, swimming and diving M/W, tennis M/W, track and field M/W, volleyball M/W.

Standardized Tests *Required:* SAT or ACT (for admission).

Costs (2007–08) *Comprehensive fee:* $28,250 includes full-time tuition ($20,450) and room and board ($7800). Full-time tuition and fees vary according to course load and program. Part-time tuition: $660 per credit hour. Part-time tuition and fees vary according to course load and program. *College room only:* $5200. Room and board charges vary according to board plan and housing facility. *Payment plan:* installment. *Waivers:* children of alumni and employees or children of employees.

Financial Aid Of all full-time matriculated undergraduates who enrolled in 2007, 2,344 applied for aid, 1,930 were judged to have need, 752 had their need fully met. 370 Federal Work-Study jobs (averaging $3000). 170 state and other part-time jobs (averaging $3000). In 2007, 246 non-need-based awards were made. *Average percent of need met:* 77%. *Average financial aid package:* $15,095. *Average need-based loan:* $4126. *Average need-based gift aid:* $6584. *Average non-need-based aid:* $6675. *Average indebtedness upon graduation:* $19,976.

Applying *Options:* electronic application, deferred entrance. *Application fee:* $40. *Required:* high school transcript, minimum 2.0 GPA. *Required for some:* interview. *Application deadlines:* 8/1 (freshmen), rolling (transfers).

Freshman Application Contact Mr. Ryan Cockerill, Director of Freshman Admission, Lewis University, Box 297, One University Parkway, Romeoville, IL 60446. *Phone:* 815-838-0500. *Toll-free phone:* 800-897-9000. *Fax:* 815-836-5002. *E-mail:* admissions@lewisu.edu.

See page 848 for the College Close-Up.

LEXINGTON COLLEGE

Chicago, Illinois **lexingtoncollege.edu/general-education.htm**

- **Independent** 4-year, founded 1977
- **Urban** campus
- **Endowment** $29,600
- **Women only** 57 undergraduate students, 86% full-time
- **Noncompetitive** entrance level, 47% of applicants were admitted

Undergraduates 49 full-time, 8 part-time. Students come from 7 states and territories, 3 other countries, 20% are from out of state, 25% African American, 4% Asian American or Pacific Islander, 18% Hispanic American, 2% Native American, 5% international, 18% transferred in. *Retention:* 79% of 2006 full-time freshmen returned.

Freshmen *Admission:* 64 applied, 30 admitted, 8 enrolled. *Average high school GPA:* 3.39. *Test scores:* ACT scores over 18: 75%; ACT scores over 24: 38%; ACT scores over 30: 13%.

Faculty *Total:* 17, 24% full-time, 100% with terminal degrees. *Student/faculty ratio:* 6:1.

Majors Hospitality administration.

Academics *Calendar:* semesters. *Degrees:* associate and bachelor's. *Special study options:* academic remediation for entering students, adult/continuing education programs, advanced placement credit, cooperative education, independent study, internships, part-time degree program, study abroad.

Computers on Campus 30 computers/terminals are available on campus for general student use. Students can access the following: free student e-mail accounts, academic, coursework-supporting software. Campuswide network is available. Wireless service is available via entire campus.

Student Life *Housing:* college housing not available. *Campus security:* 24-hour emergency response devices and patrols, patrols by municipal security personnel.

Standardized Tests *Required for some:* SAT or ACT (for admission).

Costs (2007–08) *Tuition:* $19,550 full-time, $665 per semester hour part-time. No tuition increase for student's term of enrollment. *Required fees:* $1000 full-time. *Payment plan:* installment. *Waivers:* employees or children of employees.

Financial Aid Of all full-time matriculated undergraduates who enrolled in 2006, 55 applied for aid, 55 were judged to have need. 7 Federal Work-Study jobs (averaging $5721). *Average percent of need met:* 69%. *Average financial aid package:* $10,639. *Average need-based loan:* $7500. *Average need-based gift aid:* $2065. *Average indebtedness upon graduation:* $26,500. *Financial aid deadline:* 10/1.

Applying *Options:* electronic application. *Application fee:* $30. *Required:* essay or personal statement, high school transcript, minimum 2.0 GPA, minimum ACT score of 18 or minimum SAT score of 1000. *Required for some:* 2 letters of recommendation. *Recommended:* interview. *Application deadlines:* rolling (freshmen), rolling (transfers). *Notification:* continuous (freshmen), continuous (transfers).

Freshman Application Contact Ms. Nina Pelligrino, Freshman Admissions Representative, Lexington College, 310 South Peoria Street, Chicago, IL 60607-3534. *Phone:* 312-226-6294 Ext. 228. *Fax:* 312-226-6405. *E-mail:* admissions@lexingtoncollege.edu.

LINCOLN CHRISTIAN COLLEGE

Lincoln, Illinois **www.lccs.edu/**

Freshman Application Contact Mrs. Mary K. Davis, Assistant Director of Admissions, Lincoln Christian College, 100 Campus View Drive, Lincoln, IL 62656. *Phone:* 217-732-3168. *Toll-free phone:* 888-522-5228. *Fax:* 217-732-4199. *E-mail:* coladmis@lccs.edu.

LINCOLN COLLEGE–NORMAL

Normal, Illinois **www.lincolncollege.edu/normal/**

Freshman Application Contact Mr. Joe Hendrix, Dean of Student Affairs, Lincoln College–Normal, 715 West Raab Road, Normal, IL 61761. *Phone:* 309-454-0500. *Toll-free phone:* 800-569-0558. *Fax:* 309-454-5652. *E-mail:* ncadmissionsinfo@lincolncollege.edu.

See page 850 for the College Close-Up.

LOYOLA UNIVERSITY CHICAGO

Chicago, Illinois **www.luc.edu/**

- **Independent Roman Catholic (Jesuit)** university, founded 1870
- **Urban** 105-acre campus
- **Endowment** $373.7 million
- **Coed, primarily women** 9,950 undergraduate students, 92% full-time, 65% women, 35% men
- **Moderately difficult** entrance level, 73% of applicants were admitted

Undergraduates 9,167 full-time, 783 part-time. Students come from 50 states and territories, 82 other countries, 34% are from out of state, 5% African American, 12% Asian American or Pacific Islander, 10% Hispanic American, 0.3% Native American, 1% international, 7% transferred in, 39% live on campus. *Retention:* 84% of 2006 full-time freshmen returned.

Freshmen *Admission:* 17,357 applied, 12,723 admitted, 2,035 enrolled. *Average high school GPA:* 3.54. *Test scores:* SAT critical reading scores over 500: 90%; SAT math scores over 500: 84%; SAT writing scores over 500: 83%; ACT scores over 18: 100%; SAT critical reading scores over 600: 47%; SAT math scores over 600: 40%; SAT writing scores over 600: 36%; ACT scores over 24: 73%; SAT critical reading scores over 700: 8%; SAT math scores over 700: 7%; SAT writing scores over 700: 4%; ACT scores over 30: 16%.

Faculty *Total:* 1,331, 44% full-time. *Student/faculty ratio:* 14:1.

Majors Accounting; advertising; ancient/classical Greek; anthropology; bilingual and multilingual education; bioinformatics; biology/biological sciences; business administration and management; business, management, and marketing related; business/managerial economics; chemistry; classics and languages, literatures and linguistics; clinical nutrition; communication and media related; communication/speech communication and rhetoric; computer and information sciences; computer and information systems security; computer science; criminal justice/safety; dramatic/theater arts; elementary education; English; environmental studies; finance; fine/studio arts; forensic science and technology; French; general studies; German; health/health care administration; history; human resources management; human services; international business/trade/commerce; international relations and affairs; Italian; journalism; Latin; management information systems; marketing/marketing management; mass communication/media; mathematics; mathematics and computer science; mathematics teacher education; music; nursing (registered nurse training); operations management; organizational behavior; philosophy; physics; political science and government; psychology; psychology related; religious education; secondary education; social work; sociology; Spanish; special education; statistics; theology; women's studies.

Academics *Calendar:* semesters. *Degrees:* certificates, bachelor's, master's, doctoral, first professional, post-master's, and postbachelor's certificates (also offers adult part-time program with significant enrollment not reflected in profile). *Special study options:* academic remediation for entering students, accelerated degree program, adult/continuing education programs, advanced placement credit, double majors, English as a second language, honors programs, independent study, internships, off-campus study, part-time degree program, services for LD students, study abroad, summer session for credit. *ROTC:* Army (c), Navy (c), Air Force (c). *Unusual degree programs:* 3-2 engineering with University of Illinois at Urbana-Champaign, Washington University in St. Louis.

Computers on Campus 696 computers/terminals are available on campus for general student use. Students can access the following: campus intranet, computer help desk, free student e-mail accounts, online (class) grades, online (class) registration, online (class) schedules. Campuswide network is available. 40% of college-owned or -operated housing units are wired for high-speed Internet access. Wireless service is available via entire campus.

Student Life *Housing:* on-campus residence required through sophomore year. *Options:* coed, disabled students. Campus housing is university owned. Freshman campus housing is guaranteed. *Activities and organizations:* drama/theater group, student-run newspaper, radio station, Unified Student Government Association, Hillel, College Democrats, Campus Life Union Board, Sororities, national fraternities, national sororities. *Campus security:* 24-hour emergency response devices and patrols, late-night transport/escort service, controlled dormitory access. *Student services:* health clinic, personal/psychological counseling, women's center.

Athletics Member NCAA. All Division I. *Intercollegiate sports:* basketball M (s)/W (s), cross-country running M (s)/W (s), golf M (s)/W (s), soccer M (s)/W (s), softball W, track and field M (s)/W (s), volleyball M (s)/W (s). *Intramural sports:* badminton M/W, baseball M (c), basketball M/W, cross-country running M/W, football M/W, golf M/W, ice hockey M (c), lacrosse M (c)/W (c), racquetball M/W, rugby M (c)/W (c), sailing M/W, soccer M/W, swimming and diving M (c)/W (c), table tennis M/W, tennis M/W, volleyball M/W.

Standardized Tests *Required:* SAT or ACT (for admission).

Costs (2008–09) *Comprehensive fee:* $39,976 includes full-time tuition ($28,700), mandatory fees ($786), and room and board ($10,490). Part-time tuition: $580 per semester hour. *College room only:* $6950.

Financial Aid Of all full-time matriculated undergraduates who enrolled in 2006, 7,138 applied for aid, 6,313 were judged to have need, 767 had their need fully met. 5,233 Federal Work-Study jobs (averaging $2174). In 2006, 1589 non-need-based awards were made. *Average percent of need met:* 83%. *Average financial aid package:* $24,221. *Average need-based loan:* $5378. *Average need-based gift aid:* $14,569. *Average non-need-based aid:* $7557. *Average indebtedness upon graduation:* $26,874.

Applying *Options:* electronic application. *Application fee:* $25. *Required:* essay or personal statement, high school transcript. *Recommended:* interview. *Application deadlines:* 4/1 (freshmen), 7/1 (transfers). *Notification:* continuous (freshmen), continuous (transfers).

Freshman Application Contact Ms. April Hansen, Director of Admission, Loyola University Chicago, 820 North Michigan Avenue, Suite 613, Chicago, IL 60611-9810. *Phone:* 773-508-3079. *Toll-free phone:* 800-262-2373. *Fax:* 312-508-8926. *E-mail:* admission@luc.edu.

See page 852 for the College Close-Up.

MacMurray College

Jacksonville, Illinois **www.mac.edu/**

- **Independent United Methodist** 4-year, founded 1846
- **Small-town** 60-acre campus
- **Endowment** $12.1 million
- **Coed**
- **Moderately difficult** entrance level

Faculty *Student/faculty ratio:* 12:1.

Academics *Calendar:* 4-1-4. *Degrees:* associate and bachelor's.

Student Life *Campus security:* 24-hour emergency response devices, student patrols, late-night transport/escort service, controlled dormitory access.

Athletics Member NCAA. All Division III.

Standardized Tests *Required:* SAT or ACT (for admission).

Costs (2007–08) *Comprehensive fee:* $22,896 includes full-time tuition ($16,400), mandatory fees ($330), and room and board ($6166). Part-time tuition: $400 per credit. *Required fees:* $111 per term part-time. *College room only:* $2900.

Financial Aid Of all full-time matriculated undergraduates who enrolled in 2005, 629 applied for aid, 571 were judged to have need, 134 had their need fully met. 91 Federal Work-Study jobs (averaging $671). 115 state and other part-time jobs (averaging $797). In 2005, 58 non-need-based awards were made. *Average percent of need met:* 77. *Average financial aid package:* $12,981. *Average need-based loan:* $4778. *Average need-based gift aid:* $8856. *Average non-need-based aid:* $12,062. *Average indebtedness upon graduation:* $22,487.

Applying *Options:* electronic application, early admission. *Required:* high school transcript. *Required for some:* essay or personal statement, minimum 2.5 GPA, letters of recommendation, interview.

Freshman Application Contact Ms. Rhonda Cors, Vice President for Enrollment, MacMurray College, 447 East College Avenue, Jacksonville, IL 62650. *Phone:* 217-479-7056. *Toll-free phone:* 800-252-7485. *Fax:* 217-291-0702. *E-mail:* admiss@mac.edu.

McKendree University

Lebanon, Illinois **www.mckendree.edu/**

- **Independent** comprehensive, founded 1828, affiliated with United Methodist Church
- **Small-town** 80-acre campus with easy access to St. Louis
- **Endowment** $20.8 million
- **Coed** 2,456 undergraduate students, 69% full-time, 56% women, 44% men
- **Moderately difficult** entrance level, 71% of applicants were admitted

Undergraduates 1,702 full-time, 754 part-time. Students come from 24 states and territories, 24 other countries, 32% are from out of state, 13% African American, 1% Asian American or Pacific Islander, 2% Hispanic American, 0.3% Native American, 2% international, 13% transferred in, 51% live on campus. *Retention:* 77% of 2006 full-time freshmen returned.

Freshmen *Admission:* 1,097 applied, 778 admitted, 339 enrolled. *Average high school GPA:* 3.5. *Test scores:* SAT critical reading scores over 500: 88%; SAT math scores over 500: 91%; SAT writing scores over 500: 25%; ACT scores over 18: 95%; SAT critical reading scores over 600: 13%; SAT math scores over 600: 27%; SAT writing scores over 600: 13%; ACT scores over 24: 39%; SAT math scores over 700: 18%; ACT scores over 30: 7%.

Faculty *Total:* 144, 65% full-time, 63% with terminal degrees. *Student/faculty ratio:* 13:1.

Majors Accounting; art; art teacher education; athletic training; biology/biological sciences; biology teacher education; business administration and management; business teacher education; chemistry; clinical laboratory science/medical technology; computer science; criminal justice/law enforcement administration; economics; education (K-12); elementary education; English; English/language arts teacher education; finance; history; history teacher education; information science/studies; international relations and affairs; marketing/marketing management; mass communication/media; mathematics; mathematics teacher education; middle school education; music; music teacher education; nursing (registered nurse training); occupational therapy; organizational communication; philosophy; physical education teaching and coaching; political science and government; pre-dentistry studies; pre-law studies; pre-medical studies; pre-veterinary studies; psychology; public relations/image management; religious studies; sales, distribution and marketing; secondary education; social sciences; social science teacher education; social work; sociology; speech and rhetoric; speech/theater education.

Academics *Calendar:* semesters. *Degrees:* bachelor's and master's. *Special study options:* academic remediation for entering students, accelerated degree program, advanced placement credit, double majors, honors programs, independent study, internships, off-campus study, part-time degree program, services for LD students, student-designed majors, study abroad, summer session for credit. *ROTC:* Army (c), Air Force (c). *Unusual degree programs:* 3-2 occupational therapy with Washington University in St. Louis.

Computers on Campus 140 computers/terminals are available on campus for general student use. Students can access the following: campus intranet, computer help desk, free student e-mail accounts, online (class) grades, online (class) registration, online (class) schedules. Campuswide network is available. 100% of college-owned or -operated housing units are wired for high-speed Internet access. Wireless service is available via entire campus.

Student Life *Housing:* on-campus residence required through junior year. *Options:* coed. Campus housing is university owned and leased by the school. Freshman campus housing is guaranteed. *Activities and organizations:* drama/theater group, student-run newspaper, radio station, choral group, marching band, Model United Nations, Campus Christian Fellowship, Team Bogey, Student Government Association, Students Against Social Injustice, national fraternities. *Campus security:* 24-hour emergency response devices and patrols, student patrols, late-night transport/escort service, controlled dormitory access. *Student services:* health clinic, personal/psychological counseling.

Athletics Member NAIA. *Intercollegiate sports:* baseball M (s), basketball M (s)/W (s), bowling M (s)/W (s), cheerleading M (s)/W (s), cross-country running M (s)/W (s), football M (s), golf M (s)/W (s), ice hockey M, soccer M (s)/W (s), softball W (s), tennis M (s)/W (s), track and field M (s)/W (s), volleyball W (s), wrestling M (s). *Intramural sports:* basketball M/W, football M/W, softball M/W, table tennis M/W, ultimate Frisbee M/W, volleyball M/W.

Standardized Tests *Required:* SAT or ACT (for admission).

Costs (2007–08) *Comprehensive fee:* $27,810 includes full-time tuition ($19,500), mandatory fees ($650), and room and board ($7660). Full-time tuition and fees vary according to course load. Part-time tuition: $655 per hour. Part-time tuition and fees vary according to course load. *College room only:* $4060. Room and board charges vary according to board plan and housing facility. *Payment plan:* installment. *Waivers:* employees or children of employees.

Financial Aid Of all full-time matriculated undergraduates who enrolled in 2007, 1,347 applied for aid, 1,195 were judged to have need, 369 had their need fully met. 459 Federal Work-Study jobs (averaging $1655). 175 state and other part-time jobs (averaging $1278). In 2007, 299 non-need-based awards were made. *Average percent of need met:* 82%. *Average financial aid package:* $15,561. *Average need-based loan:* $3654. *Average need-based gift aid:* $12,490. *Average non-need-based aid:* $11,732. *Average indebtedness upon graduation:* $17,648.

Applying *Options:* electronic application, deferred entrance. *Application fee:* $40. *Required:* essay or personal statement, high school transcript, minimum 2.5 GPA, 1 letter of recommendation, rank in upper 50% of high school class, minimum ACT score of 20. *Required for some:* interview. *Application deadlines:* rolling (freshmen), rolling (transfers). *Notification:* continuous (freshmen), continuous (transfers).

Freshman Application Contact Chris Hall, Vice President for Admissions and Financial Aid, McKendree University, 701 College Road, Lebanon, IL 62254. *Phone:* 618-537-6833. *Toll-free phone:* 800-232-7228 Ext. 6831. *Fax:* 618-537-6496. *E-mail:* inquiry@mckendree.edu.

MIDSTATE COLLEGE

Peoria, Illinois **www.midstate.edu/**

Freshman Application Contact Ms. Jessica Hancock, Director of Admissions, Midstate College, 411 West Northmoor Road, Peoria, IL 61614. *Phone:* 309-692-4092. *Fax:* 309-692-3893. *E-mail:* jhancock2@midstate.edu.

MILLIKIN UNIVERSITY

Decatur, Illinois **www.millikin.edu/**

- **Independent** comprehensive, founded 1901, affiliated with Presbyterian Church (U.S.A.)
- **Suburban** 70-acre campus
- **Endowment** $91.8 million
- **Coed** 2,335 undergraduate students, 94% full-time, 61% women, 39% men
- **Moderately difficult** entrance level, 68% of applicants were admitted

Undergraduates 2,205 full-time, 130 part-time. Students come from 35 states and territories, 10 other countries, 12% are from out of state, 9% African American, 1% Asian American or Pacific Islander, 3% Hispanic American, 0.3% Native American, 0.9% international, 5% transferred in, 66% live on campus. *Retention:* 75% of 2006 full-time freshmen returned.

Freshmen *Admission:* 2,656 applied, 1,798 admitted, 477 enrolled. *Test scores:* SAT critical reading scores over 500: 72%; SAT math scores over 500: 76%; SAT writing scores over 500: 68%; ACT scores over 18: 95%; SAT critical reading scores over 600: 39%; SAT math scores over 600: 43%; SAT writing scores over 600: 36%; ACT scores over 24: 44%; SAT critical reading scores over 700: 8%; SAT math scores over 700: 8%; SAT writing scores over 700: 4%; ACT scores over 30: 7%.

Faculty *Total:* 284, 55% full-time, 53% with terminal degrees. *Student/faculty ratio:* 12:1.

Majors Accounting; applied mathematics; arts management; art teacher education; art therapy; athletic training; biology/biological sciences; biology teacher education; business administration, management and operations related; chemistry; chemistry teacher education; commercial and advertising art; communication/speech communication and rhetoric; computer science; criminal justice/law enforcement administration; dramatic/theater arts; early childhood education; elementary education; English; English/language arts teacher education; entrepreneurship; finance; fine/studio arts; history; international business/trade/commerce; international relations and affairs; management information systems; marketing/marketing management; mathematics teacher education; molecular biology; multi-/interdisciplinary studies related; music; music performance; music teacher education; nursing (registered nurse training); philosophy; physical education teaching and coaching; physics; piano and organ; political science and government; pre-dentistry studies; pre-law studies; pre-medical studies; pre-pharmacy studies; pre-veterinary studies; psychology; social science teacher education; social work; sociology; Spanish; sport and fitness administration/management; theater design and technology; visual and performing arts related; voice and opera.

Academics *Calendar:* semesters. *Degrees:* bachelor's and master's. *Special study options:* accelerated degree program, adult/continuing education programs, advanced placement credit, double majors, honors programs, independent study, internships, off-campus study, part-time degree program, services for LD students, student-designed majors, study abroad, summer session for credit. *Unusual degree programs:* 3-2 engineering with Washington University in St. Louis; physical therapy, occupational therapy, medical technology, pharmacy with Midwestern University.

Computers on Campus 198 computers/terminals and 300 ports are available on campus for general student use. Students can access the following: computer help desk, free student e-mail accounts, online (class) grades, online (class) registration, online (class) schedules, online degree audit; online financials (view and pay bills; view financial aid). Campuswide network is available. 100% of college-owned or -operated housing units are wired for high-speed Internet access. Wireless service is available via classrooms, computer centers, computer labs, dorm rooms, learning centers, libraries, student centers.

Student Life *Housing:* on-campus residence required through junior year. *Options:* coed, men-only, women-only, disabled students. Campus housing is university owned, leased by the school and is provided by a third party. Freshman campus housing is guaranteed. *Activities and organizations:* drama/theater group, student-run newspaper, radio station, choral group, University Center Board, Multicultural Student Council, Student Housing Council, Panhellenic Council, Interfraternity Council, national fraternities, national sororities. *Campus security:* 24-hour emergency response devices and patrols, late-night transport/escort service, controlled dormitory access. *Student services:* health clinic, personal/psychological counseling.

Athletics Member NCAA. All Division III. *Intercollegiate sports:* baseball M, basketball M/W, cheerleading M/W, cross-country running M/W, football M, golf M/W, soccer M/W, softball W, swimming and diving M/W, tennis W, track and field M/W, volleyball W, wrestling M. *Intramural sports:* basketball M/W, bowling M/W, soccer M/W, softball M/W, table tennis M/W, volleyball M/W.

Standardized Tests *Required:* SAT or ACT (for admission).

Costs (2007–08) *Comprehensive fee:* $31,055 includes full-time tuition ($23,250), mandatory fees ($595), and room and board ($7210). Full-time tuition and fees vary according to course load. Part-time tuition: $775 per credit hour. *College room only:* $4010. Room and board charges vary according to board plan and housing facility. *Payment plan:* installment. *Waivers:* employees or children of employees.

Financial Aid Of all full-time matriculated undergraduates who enrolled in 2006, 2,055 applied for aid, 1,726 were judged to have need, 1,002 had their need fully met. 452 Federal Work-Study jobs (averaging $971). In 2006, 254 non-need-based awards were made. *Average percent of need met:* 92%. *Average financial aid package:* $16,307. *Average need-based loan:* $4104. *Average need-based gift aid:* $6733. *Average non-need-based aid:* $7641. *Average indebtedness upon graduation:* $21,177.

Applying *Options:* electronic application, deferred entrance. *Required:* high school transcript, minimum 2.0 GPA, 2 letters of recommendation. *Required for some:* audition for school of music; portfolio review for art program; audition for theatre and musical/theatre program. *Recommended:* interview. *Application deadlines:* rolling (freshmen), rolling (transfers). *Notification:* continuous (freshmen), continuous (transfers).

Freshman Application Contact Mr. Joe Havis, Assistant Director of Admission, Millikin University, 1184 West Main Street, Decatur, IL 62522-2084. *Phone:* 217-424-6210. *Toll-free phone:* 800-373-7733. *Fax:* 217-425-4669. *E-mail:* admis@millikin.edu.

MONMOUTH COLLEGE

Monmouth, Illinois **www.monm.edu/**

- **Independent** 4-year, founded 1853, affiliated with Presbyterian Church
- **Small-town** 80-acre campus with easy access to Peoria
- **Endowment** $73.7 million
- **Coed** 1,343 undergraduate students, 99% full-time, 55% women, 45% men
- **Moderately difficult** entrance level, 78% of applicants were admitted

Undergraduates 1,333 full-time, 10 part-time. Students come from 22 states and territories, 13 other countries, 6% are from out of state, 5% African American, 1% Asian American or Pacific Islander, 3% Hispanic American, 0.6% Native American, 2% international, 4% transferred in, 97% live on campus.

Freshmen *Admission:* 1,660 applied, 1,293 admitted, 393 enrolled. *Average high school GPA:* 3.2. *Test scores:* SAT critical reading scores over 500: 80%; SAT math scores over 500: 80%; ACT scores over 18: 93%; SAT critical reading scores over 600: 40%; SAT math scores over 600: 40%; ACT scores over 24: 33%; SAT critical reading scores over 700: 20%; SAT math scores over 700: 20%; ACT scores over 30: 3%.

Faculty *Total:* 132, 69% full-time, 57% with terminal degrees. *Student/faculty ratio:* 13:1.

Majors Accounting; art; biochemistry; biochemistry/biophysics and molecular biology; biological and biomedical sciences related; biology/biological sciences; business administration and management; chemistry; classics and languages, literatures and linguistics; dramatic/theater arts; economics; education; elementary education; English; environmental science; French; history; humanities; Latin; liberal arts and sciences/liberal studies; mathematics; modern Greek; modern languages; music; natural sciences; philosophy; physical education teaching and coaching; physics; political science and government; political science and government related; psychology; public relations/image management; religious studies; secondary education; sociology; Spanish; speech and rhetoric.

Academics *Calendar:* semesters. *Degree:* bachelor's. *Special study options:* advanced placement credit, double majors, honors programs, independent study, internships, off-campus study, part-time degree program, student-designed majors, study abroad. *ROTC:* Army (c). *Unusual degree programs:* 3-2 engineering with Case Western Reserve University, Washington University in St. Louis; nursing with Rush University.

Computers on Campus 300 computers/terminals and 1,350 ports are available on campus for general student use. Students can access the following: campus intranet, computer help desk, free student e-mail accounts, online (class) grades, online (class) registration, online (class) schedules. Campuswide network is available. Wireless service is available via entire campus.

Student Life *Housing:* on-campus residence required through senior year. *Options:* coed, men-only, women-only, disabled students. Campus housing is university owned. Freshman campus housing is guaranteed. *Activities and organizations:* drama/theater group, student-run newspaper, radio and television station, choral group, marching band, M Club, Associated Students of Monmouth College (student government), Crimson Masque (theatre), Blue Key, Relay for Life, national fraternities, national sororities. *Campus security:* 24-hour emergency response devices, late-night transport/escort service, night security. *Student services:* personal/psychological counseling.

Athletics Member NCAA. All Division III. *Intercollegiate sports:* baseball M, basketball M/W, cheerleading M/W, cross-country running M/W, football M, golf M/W, soccer M/W, softball W, swimming and diving M/W, tennis M/W, track and field M/W, volleyball W, water polo M (c)/W (c). *Intramural sports:* badminton M/W, basketball M/W, bowling M/W, golf M/W, soccer M/W, softball M/W, swimming and diving M/W, table tennis M/W, tennis M/W, track and field M/W, ultimate Frisbee M/W, volleyball M/W.

Standardized Tests *Required:* SAT or ACT (for admission).

Costs (2008–09) *Comprehensive fee:* $31,000 includes full-time tuition ($24,000) and room and board ($7000). Part-time tuition: $800 per semester hour. *College room only:* $4100.

Financial Aid Of all full-time matriculated undergraduates who enrolled in 2007, 1,210 applied for aid, 1,046 were judged to have need, 281 had their need fully met. In 2007, 280 non-need-based awards were made. *Average percent of need met:* 87%. *Average financial aid package:* $18,657. *Average need-based loan:* $3315. *Average need-based gift aid:* $14,205. *Average non-need-based aid:* $9656. *Average indebtedness upon graduation:* $22,781.

Applying *Options:* electronic application, deferred entrance. *Required:* high school transcript. *Required for some:* essay or personal statement, 2 letters of recommendation, interview. *Recommended:* interview. *Application deadlines:* rolling (freshmen), rolling (transfers). *Notification:* continuous (freshmen), continuous (transfers).

Freshman Application Contact Ms. Christine Johnston, Dean of Admission, Monmouth College, 700 East Broadway, Monmouth, IL 61462-1998. *Phone:* 309-457-2136. *Toll-free phone:* 800-747-2687. *Fax:* 309-457-2141. *E-mail:* admit@monm.edu.

MOODY BIBLE INSTITUTE

Chicago, Illinois **www.moody.edu/**

Freshman Application Contact Mrs. Marthe Campa, Application Coordinator, Moody Bible Institute, 820 North LaSalle Boulevard, Chicago, IL 60610. *Phone:* 312-329-4266. *Toll-free phone:* 800-967-4MBI. *Fax:* 312-329-8987. *E-mail:* admissions@moody.edu.

NATIONAL-LOUIS UNIVERSITY

Chicago, Illinois **www.nl.edu/**

- **Independent** university, founded 1886
- **Urban** 12-acre campus
- **Endowment** $26.1 million
- **Coed** 1,886 undergraduate students, 70% full-time, 76% women, 24% men
- **Minimally difficult** entrance level

Undergraduates 1,319 full-time, 567 part-time. Students come from 10 states and territories, 1% are from out of state, 32% African American, 3% Asian American or Pacific Islander, 12% Hispanic American, 0.4% Native American, 0.1% international, 24% transferred in. *Retention:* 100% of 2006 full-time freshmen returned.

Freshmen *Admission:* 9 enrolled.

Majors Accounting; anthropology; art; behavioral sciences; biological and physical sciences; biology/biological sciences; business administration and management; clinical laboratory science/medical technology; computer management; dramatic/theater arts; elementary education; English; gerontology; health/health care administration; human development and family studies; human services; industrial radiologic technology; information science/studies; international business/trade/commerce; kindergarten/preschool education; liberal arts and sciences/liberal studies; mathematics; psychology; respiratory care therapy; social sciences; substance abuse/addiction counseling.

Academics *Calendar:* quarters. *Degrees:* bachelor's, master's, doctoral, post-master's, and postbachelor's certificates. *Special study options:* academic remediation for entering students, accelerated degree program, adult/continuing education programs, advanced placement credit, English as a second language, external degree program, honors programs, independent study, internships, part-time degree program, services for LD students, summer session for credit.

Computers on Campus Campuswide network is available.

Student Life *Housing:* college housing not available. *Activities and organizations:* Student Council, Nosotros Unidos, Accounting Club, African-American Club. *Campus security:* 24-hour emergency response devices and patrols. *Student services:* personal/psychological counseling.

Standardized Tests *Required for some:* SAT or ACT (for admission).

Costs (2008–09) *Tuition:* $17,955 full-time, $399 per quarter hour part-time. *Required fees:* $120 full-time, $20 per term part-time.

Financial Aid Of all full-time matriculated undergraduates who enrolled in 2007, 993 applied for aid, 922 were judged to have need, 56 had their need fully met, 45 Federal Work-Study jobs (averaging $2569). In 2007, 73 non-need-based awards were made. *Average percent of need met:* 42%. *Average financial aid package:* $8921. *Average need-based loan:* $3976. *Average need-based gift aid:* $5178. *Average non-need-based aid:* $1310. *Average indebtedness upon graduation:* $21,250.

Applying *Options:* deferred entrance. *Application fee:* $25. *Required:* high school transcript, minimum 2.0 GPA. *Required for some:* 2 letters of recommendation. *Recommended:* interview. *Application deadlines:* rolling (freshmen), rolling (transfers). *Notification:* continuous (freshmen), continuous (transfers).

Freshman Application Contact National-Louis University, 122 South Michigan Avenue, Chicago, IL 60603. *Phone:* 888-NLU-TODAY. *Toll-free phone:* 888-NLU-TODAY (in-state); 800-443-5522 (out-of-state).

NORTH CENTRAL COLLEGE

Naperville, Illinois **www.noctrl.edu/**

- **Independent United Methodist** comprehensive, founded 1861
- **Suburban** 56-acre campus with easy access to Chicago
- **Endowment** $79.7 million
- **Coed** 2,232 undergraduate students, 91% full-time, 57% women, 43% men
- **Moderately difficult** entrance level, 69% of applicants were admitted

Undergraduates 2,039 full-time, 193 part-time. Students come from 27 states and territories, 31 other countries, 8% are from out of state, 3% African American, 3% Asian American or Pacific Islander, 4% Hispanic American, 0.4% Native American, 1% international, 11% transferred in, 52% live on campus. *Retention:* 80% of 2006 full-time freshmen returned.

Freshmen *Admission:* 2,234 applied, 1,552 admitted, 422 enrolled. *Average high school GPA:* 3.56. *Test scores:* ACT scores over 18: 100%; ACT scores over 24: 58%; ACT scores over 30: 11%.

Faculty *Total:* 226, 50% full-time, 60% with terminal degrees. *Student/faculty ratio:* 15:1.

Majors Accounting; actuarial science; applied mathematics; art; art teacher education; Asian studies (East); athletic training; biochemistry; biological and physical sciences; biology/biological sciences; business administration and management; chemistry; classics and languages, literatures and linguistics; creative writing; dramatic/theater arts; dramatic/theater arts and stagecraft related; economics; education; elementary education; English; finance; French; German; graphic design; history; humanities; human resources management; international business/trade/commerce; Japanese; jazz/jazz studies; journalism; kinesiology and exercise science; liberal arts and sciences/liberal studies; management information systems; marketing/marketing management; mathematics; medical radiologic technology; multi-/interdisciplinary studies related; music; music teacher education; nuclear medical technology; organizational communication; philosophy; physical education teaching and coaching; physics; political science and government; pre-dentistry studies; pre-law studies; pre-medical studies; pre-veterinary studies; psychology; radio and television; religious studies; secondary education; small business administration; social sciences; sociology; Spanish; speech and rhetoric; sport and fitness administration/management.

Academics *Calendar:* quarters. *Degrees:* bachelor's, master's, and postbachelor's certificates. *Special study options:* academic remediation for entering students, accelerated degree program, adult/continuing education programs, advanced placement credit, double majors, English as a second language, honors programs, independent study, internships, off-campus study, part-time degree program, services for LD students, student-designed majors, study abroad, summer session for credit. *ROTC:* Army (c), Air Force (c). *Unusual degree programs:* 3-2 engineering with Washington University in St. Louis; University of Illinois at Urbana-Champaign; Marquette University; University of Minnesota, Twin Cities Campus; nursing; medical technology with Rush University.

Computers on Campus 255 computers/terminals and 12 ports are available on campus for general student use. Students can access the following: campus intranet, computer help desk, free student e-mail accounts, online (class) grades, online (class) registration, online (class) schedules, software packages. Campuswide network is available. 100% of college-owned or -operated housing units are wired for high-speed Internet access. Wireless service is available via computer centers, dorm rooms, learning centers, libraries, student centers.

Student Life *Housing options:* coed, men-only, women-only, disabled students. Campus housing is university owned. Freshman applicants given priority for college housing. *Activities and organizations:* drama/theater group, student-run newspaper, radio station, choral group, College Union Activities Board, WONC (student radio station), Cardinals in Action (service group), Students in Free Enterprise (SIFE), Residence Hall Association. *Campus security:* 24-hour emergency response devices and patrols, late-night transport/escort service. *Student services:* health clinic, personal/psychological counseling.

Athletics Member NCAA. All Division III. *Intercollegiate sports:* baseball M, basketball M/W, cheerleading W, cross-country running M/W, football M, golf M/W, lacrosse W, soccer M/W, softball W, swimming and diving M/W, tennis M/W, track and field M/W, volleyball W, wrestling M. *Intramural sports:* badminton M/W, basketball M/W, football M/W, golf M/W, racquetball M/W, soccer M/W, softball M/W, ultimate Frisbee M/W, volleyball M/W.

Standardized Tests *Required:* SAT or ACT (for admission). *Recommended:* ACT (for admission).

Costs (2007–08) *Comprehensive fee:* $32,241 includes full-time tuition ($24,159), mandatory fees ($405), and room and board ($7677). Part-time tuition: $606 per semester hour. Part-time tuition and fees vary according to course load. *Required fees:* $20 per term part-time. *Room and board:* Room and board charges vary according to housing facility. *Payment plan:* installment. *Waivers:* senior citizens and employees or children of employees.

Financial Aid Of all full-time matriculated undergraduates who enrolled in 2007, 1,577 applied for aid, 1,333 were judged to have need, 299 had their need fully met. 280 Federal Work-Study jobs (averaging $746). In 2007, 490 non-need-based awards were made. *Average percent of need met:* 77%. *Average financial aid package:* $18,164. *Average need-based loan:* $4755. *Average need-based gift aid:* $13,506. *Average non-need-based aid:* $9331. *Average indebtedness upon graduation:* $23,575.

Applying *Options:* deferred entrance. *Application fee:* $25. *Required:* high school transcript, minimum 2.5 GPA. *Required for some:* interview. *Recommended:* essay or personal statement, 1 letter of recommendation. *Application deadlines:* rolling (freshmen), rolling (transfers). *Notification:* continuous (freshmen), continuous (transfers).

Freshman Application Contact Ms. Martha Stolze, Director of Freshman Admission, North Central College, 30 North Brainard Street, PO Box 3063, Naperville, IL 60566-7063. *Phone:* 630-637-5800. *Toll-free phone:* 800-411-1861. *Fax:* 630-637-5819. *E-mail:* admissions@noctrl.edu.

See page 854 for the College Close-Up.

NORTHEASTERN ILLINOIS UNIVERSITY

Chicago, Illinois **www.neiu.edu/**

- **State-supported** comprehensive, founded 1961
- **Urban** 67-acre campus
- **Endowment** $2.7 million
- **Coed** 9,115 undergraduate students, 56% full-time, 60% women, 40% men
- **Minimally difficult** entrance level, 68% of applicants were admitted

Undergraduates 5,070 full-time, 4,045 part-time. Students come from 18 states and territories, 45 other countries, 1% are from out of state, 10% African American, 11% Asian American or Pacific Islander, 29% Hispanic American, 0.4% Native American, 2% international, 13% transferred in. *Retention:* 66% of 2006 full-time freshmen returned.

Freshmen *Admission:* 3,601 applied, 2,465 admitted, 957 enrolled. *Average high school GPA:* 2.9. *Test scores:* ACT scores over 18: 66%; ACT scores over 24: 12%; ACT scores over 30: 1%.

Faculty *Total:* 702, 59% full-time, 51% with terminal degrees. *Student/faculty ratio:* 16:1.

Majors Accounting; anthropology; art; bilingual and multilingual education; biology/biological sciences; business administration and management; business/commerce; chemistry; community health services counseling; computer and information sciences; computer science; criminal justice/safety; early childhood education; economics; elementary education; English; environmental studies; finance; French; geography; geology/earth science; history; human resources management; kindergarten/preschool education; liberal arts and sciences/liberal studies; linguistics; marketing/marketing management; mathematics; music; philosophy; physical education teaching and coaching; physics; political science and government; psychology; public administration and social service professions related; social work; sociology; Spanish; special education; speech and rhetoric; urban studies/affairs; women's studies.

Academics *Calendar:* semesters. *Degrees:* bachelor's and master's. *Special study options:* academic remediation for entering students, adult/continuing education programs, advanced placement credit, cooperative education, distance learning, double majors, English as a second language, external degree program, honors programs, independent study, internships, off-campus study, part-time degree program, services for LD students, study abroad, summer session for credit. *ROTC:* Army (c), Air Force (c).

Computers on Campus 360 computers/terminals are available on campus for general student use. Students can access the following: computer help desk, free student e-mail accounts, online (class) grades, online (class) registration, online (class) schedules, productivity software. Campuswide network is available.

Student Life *Housing:* college housing not available. *Activities and organizations:* drama/theater group, student-run newspaper, radio station, student government, Chimexla, WZRD Radio Club, Business and Management Club, Black Heritage Gospel Choir, national sororities. *Campus security:* 24-hour emergency response devices and patrols, late-night transport/escort service. *Student services:* health clinic, personal/psychological counseling, women's center.

Athletics *Intramural sports:* badminton M/W, baseball M, basketball M/W, cross-country running M/W, ice hockey M (c), racquetball M/W, soccer M/W, softball M/W, swimming and diving M/W, table tennis M/W, tennis M/W, volleyball M/W, water polo M/W, weight lifting M/W.

Standardized Tests *Required:* ACT (for admission).

Costs (2007–08) *Tuition:* state resident $5850 full-time, $195 per credit hour part-time; nonresident $11,700 full-time, $390 per credit hour part-time. Full-time tuition and fees vary according to student level. No tuition increase for student's term of enrollment. *Required fees:* $1200 full-time, $43 per credit hour part-time. *Payment plan:* deferred payment. *Waivers:* senior citizens and employees or children of employees.

Financial Aid Of all full-time matriculated undergraduates who enrolled in 2007, 3,214 applied for aid, 2,648 were judged to have need, 310 had their need fully met. 174 Federal Work-Study jobs (averaging $2221). 458 state and other part-time jobs (averaging $1886). In 2007, 121 non-need-based awards were made. *Average percent of need met:* 60%. *Average financial aid package:* $7542. *Average need-based loan:* $4205. *Average need-based gift aid:* $5926. *Average non-need-based aid:* $1462. *Average indebtedness upon graduation:* $10,379.

Applying *Options:* deferred entrance. *Application fee:* $25. *Required:* high school transcript. *Application deadlines:* 7/1 (freshmen), 7/1 (transfers). *Notification:* 9/1 (freshmen), continuous (transfers).

Freshman Application Contact Ms. Zarrin Kerwell, Admissions Counselor, Northeastern Illinois University, 5500 North St. Louis Avenue, Chicago, IL 60625. *Phone:* 773-442-4026. *Fax:* 773-794-6243. *E-mail:* admrec@neiu.edu.

NORTHERN ILLINOIS UNIVERSITY

De Kalb, Illinois **www.niu.edu/**

- **State-supported** university, founded 1895
- **Small-town** 589-acre campus with easy access to Chicago
- **Endowment** $3.2 million
- **Coed** 18,917 undergraduate students, 90% full-time, 52% women, 48% men
- **Moderately difficult** entrance level, 61% of applicants were admitted

Undergraduates 16,940 full-time, 1,977 part-time. Students come from 50 states and territories, 105 other countries, 3% are from out of state, 12% African American, 5% Asian American or Pacific Islander, 7% Hispanic American, 0.2% Native American, 0.7% international, 11% transferred in, 33% live on campus. *Retention:* 76% of 2006 full-time freshmen returned.

Freshmen *Admission:* 16,769 applied, 10,274 admitted, 3,013 enrolled. *Test scores:* ACT scores over 18: 88%; ACT scores over 24: 31%; ACT scores over 30: 2%.

Faculty *Total:* 1,180, 77% full-time, 72% with terminal degrees. *Student/faculty ratio:* 17:1.

Majors Accounting; anthropology; apparel and textiles; applied mathematics; art; art history, criticism and conservation; art teacher education; atmospheric sciences and meteorology; biology/biological sciences; business administration and management; business/commerce; chemistry; clinical laboratory science/ medical technology; communication disorders; communication/speech communication and rhetoric; computational mathematics; computer science; dramatic/ theater arts; economics; education; electrical, electronics and communications engineering; elementary education; engineering technology; English; family and consumer sciences/home economics teacher education; finance; fine/studio arts; foods, nutrition, and wellness; French; geography; geology/earth science; German; health science; health teacher education; history; human development and family studies; industrial engineering; industrial technology; journalism; kindergarten/ preschool education; liberal arts and sciences/liberal studies; management information systems; marketing/marketing management; mathematical statistics and probability; mathematics; mechanical engineering; music; music teacher education; nursing (registered nurse training); operations management; philosophy; physical education teaching and coaching; physical therapy; physics; political science and government; psychology; public health/community nursing; Russian; sociology; Spanish; special education.

Academics *Calendar:* semesters. *Degrees:* bachelor's, master's, doctoral, and first professional. *Special study options:* accelerated degree program, adult/ continuing education programs, advanced placement credit, cooperative education, double majors, honors programs, independent study, internships, off-campus study, part-time degree program, services for LD students, student-designed majors, study abroad, summer session for credit. *ROTC:* Army (b), Air Force (c). *Unusual degree programs:* 3-2 engineering with University of Illinois.

Computers on Campus 1,500 computers/terminals are available on campus for general student use. Students can access the following: computer help desk, free student e-mail accounts, online (class) registration. Campuswide network is available.

Student Life *Housing:* on-campus residence required for freshman year. *Options:* coed. Campus housing is university owned. Freshman applicants given priority for college housing. *Activities and organizations:* drama/theater group, student-run newspaper, radio station, choral group, marching band, American Marketing Association, Delta Sigma Pi, Pi Sigma Epsilon, Black Choir, Student Volunteer Choir, national fraternities, national sororities. *Campus security:* 24-hour emergency response devices and patrols, student patrols, late-night transport/ escort service, controlled dormitory access. *Student services:* health clinic, personal/psychological counseling, women's center, legal services.

Athletics Member NCAA. All Division I except football (Division I-A). *Intercollegiate sports:* baseball M (s), basketball M (s)/W (s), cross-country running W, golf M (s)/W (s), gymnastics W (s), soccer M (s)/W (s), softball W (s), swimming and diving M (s)/W (s), tennis M (s)/W (s), volleyball W (s), wrestling M (s). *Intramural sports:* archery M (c)/W (c), badminton M/W, basketball M/W, bowling M (c)/W (c), cross-country running W, football M/W, golf M/W, ice hockey M (c)/W (c), lacrosse M (c)/W (c), racquetball M/W, rugby M (c)/W (c), skiing (downhill) M (c)/W (c), soccer M/W, softball M/W, table tennis M/W, tennis M/W, track and field M (c)/W (c), volleyball M/W, water polo M (c)/W (c), weight lifting M (c)/W (c).

Standardized Tests *Required:* SAT or ACT (for admission).

Costs (2007–08) *Tuition:* state resident $5940 full-time, $227 per credit hour part-time; nonresident $12,500 full-time, $454 per credit hour part-time. Part-time tuition and fees vary according to course load. No tuition increase for student's term of enrollment. *Required fees:* $1515 full-time, $64 per credit hour part-time. *Room and board:* $7568. Room and board charges vary according to board plan and housing facility. *Payment plan:* installment. *Waivers:* minority students, senior citizens, and employees or children of employees.

Financial Aid Of all full-time matriculated undergraduates who enrolled in 2005, 12,720 applied for aid, 9,091 were judged to have need, 1,596 had their need fully met. 545 Federal Work-Study jobs (averaging $1543). In 2005, 445 non-need-based awards were made. *Average percent of need met:* 68%. *Average financial aid package:* $10,337. *Average need-based loan:* $4027. *Average need-based gift aid:* $4332. *Average non-need-based aid:* $1096. *Average indebtedness upon graduation:* $19,764.

Applying *Options:* electronic application. *Required:* high school transcript, high school rank. *Application deadlines:* 8/1 (freshmen), 8/1 (transfers). *Notification:* continuous (freshmen), continuous (transfers).

Freshman Application Contact Dr. Robert Burk, Director of Admissions, Northern Illinois University, Office of Admissions, DeKalb, IL 60445-2857. *Phone:* 815-753-0446. *Toll-free phone:* 800-892-3050. *E-mail:* admission-info@niu.edu.

NORTH PARK UNIVERSITY

Chicago, Illinois **www.northpark.edu/**

The mission of North Park University, as an intentionally and distinctively Christian university, is to prepare students for lives of significance and service. North Park students learn to interact comfortably and respectfully with people from a wide variety of Christian traditions, other religions and philosophical backgrounds, and the broader culture, while exploring from a Christian perspective the deep questions and issues of life. North Park offers liberal arts as well as professional education. Faculty members are superbly credentialed, devoted to teaching and to preparing students for graduate school and careers. North Park's Chicago location provides outstanding educational, cultural, recreational, spiritual, and artistic opportunities. Hundreds of internships are available, and North Park's Urban Outreach program involves students in community service opportunities.

Freshman Application Contact Office of Admissions, North Park University, 3225 West Foster Avenue, Chicago, IL 60625-4895. *Phone:* 773-244-5500. *Toll-free phone:* 800-888-NPC8. *Fax:* 773-583-0858. *E-mail:* afao@northpark.edu.

See page 856 for the College Close-Up.

NORTHWESTERN UNIVERSITY

Evanston, Illinois **www.northwestern.edu/**

- **Independent** university, founded 1851
- **Suburban** 250-acre campus with easy access to Chicago
- **Endowment** $6.5 billion
- **Coed** 8,284 undergraduate students, 98% full-time, 53% women, 47% men
- **Most difficult** entrance level, 27% of applicants were admitted

Undergraduates 8,111 full-time, 173 part-time. Students come from 51 states and territories, 42 other countries, 75% are from out of state, 6% African American, 17% Asian American or Pacific Islander, 7% Hispanic American, 0.1% Native American, 5% international, 2% transferred in, 65% live on campus. *Retention:* 96% of 2006 full-time freshmen returned.

Freshmen *Admission:* 21,930 applied, 5,872 admitted, 1,981 enrolled. *Test scores:* SAT critical reading scores over 500: 100%; SAT math scores over 500: 99%; SAT writing scores over 500: 100%; ACT scores over 18: 100%; SAT critical reading scores over 600: 94%; SAT math scores over 600: 95%; SAT writing scores over 600: 93%; ACT scores over 24: 96%; SAT critical reading scores over 700: 61%; SAT math scores over 700: 66%; SAT writing scores over 700: 57%; ACT scores over 30: 76%.

Faculty *Total:* 1,142, 88% full-time, 100% with terminal degrees. *Student/faculty ratio:* 7:1.

Majors African-American/Black studies; African studies; American studies; anthropology; applied mathematics; area studies related; art; art history, criticism and conservation; Asian studies; astronomy; audiology and hearing sciences; audiology and speech-language pathology; biochemistry; biological and physical sciences; biology/biological sciences; biomedical/medical engineering; Caribbean studies; cell biology and histology; chemical engineering; chemistry; civil engineering; classics and languages, literatures and linguistics; cognitive psychology and psycholinguistics; communication and media related; communication disorders; communication/speech communication and rhetoric; community organization and advocacy; community psychology; comparative literature; computer and information sciences; computer engineering; computer science; counseling psychology; dance; dramatic/theater arts; East Asian languages related; ecology; economics; education; electrical, electronics and communications engineering; engineering; engineering related; engineering science; English; environmental/environmental health engineering; environmental science; environmental studies; film/cinema studies; French; general studies; geography; geology/earth science; German; history; humanities; industrial engineering; information science/studies; interdisciplinary studies; international relations and affairs; Italian; jazz/jazz studies; journalism; legal studies; liberal arts and sciences/liberal studies; linguistics; manufacturing engineering; materials engineering; materials science; mathematics; mathematics teacher education; mechanical engineering; molecular biology; multi-/interdisciplinary studies related; music; music history, literature, and theory; musicology and ethnomusicology; music performance; music related; music teacher education; music theory and composition; neuroscience; organizational behavior; philosophy; physics; piano and organ; political science and government; pre-medical studies; psychology; public policy analysis; radio and television; religious studies; science, technology and society; secondary education; Slavic languages; Slavic studies; social and philosophical foundations of education; social sciences related; sociology; South Asian languages; Spanish; special education (specific learning disabilities); speech and rhetoric; speech-language pathology; speech therapy; statistics; theater literature, history and criticism; urban studies/affairs; violin, viola, guitar and other stringed instruments; visual and performing arts; voice and opera; wind/percussion instruments; women's studies.

Academics *Calendar:* quarters. *Degrees:* certificates, bachelor's, master's, doctoral, first professional, and post-master's certificates. *Special study options:* accelerated degree program, adult/continuing education programs, advanced placement credit, cooperative education, double majors, honors programs, independent study, internships, part-time degree program, services for LD students, student-designed majors, study abroad, summer session for credit. *ROTC:* Army (c), Navy (b), Air Force (c).

Computers on Campus 678 computers/terminals are available on campus for general student use. Students can access the following: campus intranet, computer help desk, free student e-mail accounts, online (class) grades, online (class) registration, online (class) schedules. Campuswide network is available. 100% of college-owned or -operated housing units are wired for high-speed Internet access.

Student Life *Housing options:* coed, men-only, women-only. Campus housing is university owned. Freshman campus housing is guaranteed. *Activities and organizations:* drama/theater group, student-run newspaper, radio and television station, choral group, marching band, Associated Student Government, Northwestern Community Development Corp., Activities and Organization Board, Dance Marathon, Arts Alliance, national fraternities, national sororities. *Campus security:* 24-hour emergency response devices and patrols, late-night transport/escort service, controlled dormitory access. *Student services:* health clinic, personal/psychological counseling, women's center.

Athletics Member NCAA. All Division I except football (Division I-A). *Intercollegiate sports:* baseball M (s), basketball M (s)/W (s), cheerleading M/W, cross-country running W (s), fencing W (s), field hockey W (s), golf M (s)/W (s), lacrosse W (s), soccer M (s)/W (s), softball W (s), swimming and diving M (s)/W (s), tennis M (s)/W (s), volleyball W (s), wrestling M (s). *Intramural sports:* baseball M (c), basketball M (c)/W (c), crew M (c)/W (c), cross-country running M (c)/W (c), equestrian sports M (c)/W (c), fencing M (c), football M/W, ice hockey M (c)/W (c), lacrosse M (c)/W (c), rugby M (c)/W (c), sailing M (c)/W (c), skiing (downhill) M (c)/W (c), soccer M (c)/W (c), softball M/W, squash M (c)/W (c), swimming and diving M (c)/W (c), table tennis M/W, tennis M/W, ultimate Frisbee M (c)/W (c), volleyball M (c)/W (c), water polo M (c)/W (c).

Standardized Tests *Required:* SAT or ACT (for admission). *Required for some:* SAT Subject Tests (for admission). *Recommended:* SAT Subject Tests (for admission).

Costs (2008–09) *Comprehensive fee:* $48,420 includes full-time tuition ($36,756), mandatory fees ($369), and room and board ($11,295).

Financial Aid Of all full-time matriculated undergraduates who enrolled in 2006, 3,930 applied for aid, 3,345 were judged to have need, 3,345 had their need fully met. 1,126 Federal Work-Study jobs (averaging $2041). 1,046 state and other part-time jobs (averaging $2041). In 2006, 255 non-need-based awards were made. *Average percent of need met:* 100%. *Average financial aid package:* $26,573. *Average need-based loan:* $4540. *Average need-based gift aid:* $22,517. *Average non-need-based aid:* $2347. *Average indebtedness upon graduation:* $18,860. *Financial aid deadline:* 2/1.

Applying *Options:* electronic application, early admission, early decision, deferred entrance. *Application fee:* $65. *Required:* essay or personal statement, high school transcript, 1 letter of recommendation. *Required for some:* audition for music program. *Application deadlines:* 1/1 (freshmen), 5/1 (transfers). *Early decision deadline:* 11/1. *Notification:* 4/15 (freshmen), continuous until 7/1 (transfers), 12/15 (early decision).

Freshman Application Contact Mr. Christopher Watson, Dean of Undergraduate Admission, Northwestern University, PO Box 3060, Evanston, IL 60204-3060. *Phone:* 847-491-7271. *E-mail:* ug-admission@northwestern.edu.

OLIVET NAZARENE UNIVERSITY

Bourbonnais, Illinois **www.olivet.edu/**

Freshman Application Contact Ms. Mary Cary, Applicant Coordinator, Olivet Nazarene University, One University Avenue, Bourbonnais, IL 60914. *Phone:* 815-939-5203. *Toll-free phone:* 800-648-1463.

See page 858 for the College Close-Up.

PRINCIPIA COLLEGE

Elsah, Illinois **www.prin.edu/college/**

Freshman Application Contact Mrs. Martha Quirk, Dean of Admissions, Principia College, One Maybeck Place, Elsah, IL 62028. *Phone:* 618-374-5180. *Toll-free phone:* 800-277-4648 Ext. 2802. *Fax:* 618-374-4000. *E-mail:* collegeadmissions@prin.edu.

QUINCY UNIVERSITY

Quincy, Illinois **www.quincy.edu/**

- **Independent Roman Catholic** comprehensive, founded 1860
- **Small-town** 75-acre campus
- **Coed** 1,078 undergraduate students, 85% full-time, 57% women, 43% men
- **Moderately difficult** entrance level, 96% of applicants were admitted

Undergraduates 912 full-time, 166 part-time. Students come from 30 states and territories, 6 other countries, 28% are from out of state, 7% African American, 0.8% Asian American or Pacific Islander, 3% Hispanic American, 0.6% international, 11% transferred in, 66% live on campus. *Retention:* 72% of 2006 full-time freshmen returned.

Freshmen *Admission:* 726 applied, 695 admitted, 234 enrolled. *Average high school GPA:* 3.2. *Test scores:* SAT critical reading scores over 500: 36%; SAT math scores over 500: 43%; ACT scores over 18: 87%; SAT critical reading scores over 600: 14%; SAT math scores over 600: 14%; ACT scores over 24: 28%; SAT critical reading scores over 700: 7%; ACT scores over 30: 2%.

Faculty *Total:* 135, 38% full-time, 43% with terminal degrees. *Student/faculty ratio:* 13:1.

Majors Accounting; airline pilot and flight crew; arts management; aviation/airway management; biology/biological sciences; business administration and management; chemistry; clinical laboratory science/medical technology; communication/speech communication and rhetoric; computer and information sciences; computer science; criminal justice/safety; elementary education; English; finance; graphic design; history; humanities; human services; information science/studies; journalism; language interpretation and translation; marketing/marketing management; mathematics; music; music teacher education; nursing (registered nurse training); philosophy; physical education teaching and coaching; political science and government; pre-dentistry studies; pre-medical studies; pre-veterinary studies; psychology; public administration and social service professions related;

public relations/image management; radio and television; social work; special education; sport and fitness administration/management; theological and ministerial studies related; theology.

Academics *Calendar:* semesters. *Degrees:* associate, bachelor's, and master's. *Special study options:* academic remediation for entering students, accelerated degree program, adult/continuing education programs, advanced placement credit, distance learning, double majors, English as a second language, honors programs, independent study, internships, part-time degree program, student-designed majors, study abroad, summer session for credit. *Unusual degree programs:* 3-2 engineering with Washington University in St. Louis.

Computers on Campus 190 computers/terminals are available on campus for general student use. Students can access the following: campus intranet, computer help desk, free student e-mail accounts, online (class) grades, online (class) registration, online (class) schedules. Campuswide network is available. 100% of college-owned or -operated housing units are wired for high-speed Internet access. Wireless service is available via classrooms, computer centers, computer labs, dorm rooms, learning centers, libraries, student centers.

Student Life *Housing:* on-campus residence required through sophomore year. *Options:* coed, men-only, women-only. Campus housing is university owned. Freshman campus housing is guaranteed. *Activities and organizations:* drama/theater group, student-run newspaper, radio station, choral group, Student Senate, Campus ministry, Student Programming Board, BACCHUS, Students in Free Enterprise, national fraternities, national sororities. *Campus security:* 24-hour emergency response devices and patrols, student patrols, late-night transport/escort service, controlled dormitory access. *Student services:* health clinic, personal/psychological counseling.

Athletics Member NCAA. All Division II. *Intercollegiate sports:* baseball M (s), basketball M (s)/W (s), football M (s), golf M (s)/W (s), soccer M (s)/W (s), softball W (s), tennis M (s)/W (s), volleyball M (s)/W (s). *Intramural sports:* badminton M/W, baseball M, basketball M/W, bowling M/W, football M/W, golf M, soccer M/W, softball M/W, tennis M/W, volleyball M/W.

Standardized Tests *Required:* SAT or ACT (for admission).

Costs (2008–09) *One-time required fee:* $150. *Comprehensive fee:* $28,690 includes full-time tuition ($20,100), mandatory fees ($690), and room and board ($7900). Part-time tuition: $480 per credit hour. *Required fees:* $15 per credit hour part-time. *College room only:* $4240.

Financial Aid Of all full-time matriculated undergraduates who enrolled in 2007, 815 applied for aid, 694 were judged to have need, 137 had their need fully met. 398 Federal Work-Study jobs (averaging $2000). 35 state and other part-time jobs (averaging $3000). In 2007, 50 non-need-based awards were made. *Average percent of need met:* 78%. *Average financial aid package:* $18,744. *Average need-based loan:* $5015. *Average need-based gift aid:* $14,343. *Average non-need-based aid:* $6878. *Average indebtedness upon graduation:* $19,612.

Applying *Options:* electronic application, early admission, deferred entrance. *Application fee:* $25. *Required:* essay or personal statement, high school transcript, minimum 2.0 GPA. *Required for some:* letters of recommendation. *Recommended:* interview. *Application deadlines:* rolling (freshmen), rolling (transfers). *Notification:* continuous (freshmen), continuous (transfers).

Freshman Application Contact Mrs. Syndi Peck, Director of Admissions, Quincy University, Quincy University, Admissions Office, Quincy, IL 62301. *Phone:* 217-228-5210. *Toll-free phone:* 800-688-4295. *E-mail:* admissions@quincy.edu.

ROBERT MORRIS COLLEGE

Chicago, Illinois www.robertmorris.edu/

- **Independent** comprehensive, founded 1913
- **Urban** campus
- **Endowment** $48.7 million
- **Coed** 4,563 undergraduate students, 95% full-time, 62% women, 38% men
- **Minimally difficult** entrance level, 81% of applicants were admitted

Undergraduates 4,323 full-time, 240 part-time. Students come from 22 states and territories, 20 other countries, 3% are from out of state, 34% African American, 3% Asian American or Pacific Islander, 23% Hispanic American, 0.3% Native American, 0.7% international, 29% transferred in, 5% live on campus. *Retention:* 59% of 2006 full-time freshmen returned.

Freshmen *Admission:* 3,075 applied, 2,493 admitted, 1,035 enrolled. *Average high school GPA:* 2.56.

Faculty *Total:* 326, 38% full-time, 18% with terminal degrees. *Student/faculty ratio:* 23:1.

Majors Accounting technology and bookkeeping; business administration and management; commercial and advertising art; computer programming (specific applications); computer systems networking and telecommunications; culinary arts; design and applied arts related; drafting and design technology; health and physical education; information technology; interior design; legal assistant/paralegal; medical/clinical assistant; surgical technology.

Academics *Calendar:* 5 ten-week academic sessions per year. *Degrees:* diplomas, associate, bachelor's, and master's. *Special study options:* academic remediation for entering students, accelerated degree program, adult/continuing education programs, advanced placement credit, cooperative education, distance learning, freshman honors college, honors programs, internships, part-time degree program, services for LD students, study abroad, summer session for credit. *ROTC:* Army (c).

Computers on Campus 1,792 computers/terminals are available on campus for general student use. Students can access the following: campus intranet, free student e-mail accounts, online (class) grades. Campuswide network is available. Wireless service is available via libraries, student centers.

Student Life *Housing options:* coed. Campus housing is leased by the school. *Activities and organizations:* student-run newspaper, SIFE, Honors Club, Eagle Scholars, Business Professionals of America, Culinary Competition Team. *Campus security:* 24-hour emergency response devices and patrols. *Student services:* personal/psychological counseling.

Athletics Member NAIA. *Intercollegiate sports:* baseball M (s), basketball M (s)/W (s), bowling M (s)/W (s), cross-country running M (s)/W (s), golf M (s)/W (s), ice hockey M (c)/W (c), lacrosse W (s) (c), soccer M (s)/W (s), softball W (s), swimming and diving W (s), tennis W (s), track and field W (s), volleyball W (s). *Intramural sports:* cheerleading W (c).

Costs (2007–08) *Tuition:* $16,800 full-time, $1867 per term part-time. Full-time tuition and fees vary according to course load and program. Part-time tuition and fees vary according to course load and program. *Room only:* $7500. Room and board charges vary according to board plan and housing facility. *Payment plan:* installment. *Waivers:* employees or children of employees.

Financial Aid Of all full-time matriculated undergraduates who enrolled in 2005, 4,534 applied for aid, 4,378 were judged to have need, 175 had their need fully met. 177 Federal Work-Study jobs (averaging $792). In 2005, 136 non-need-based awards were made. *Average percent of need met:* 47%. *Average financial aid package:* $11,059. *Average need-based loan:* $3620. *Average need-based gift aid:* $8262. *Average non-need-based aid:* $9897. *Average indebtedness upon graduation:* $18,479.

Applying *Options:* electronic application, deferred entrance. *Application fee:* $30. *Required:* high school transcript. *Recommended:* minimum 2.0 GPA, interview. *Application deadlines:* rolling (freshmen), rolling (transfers). *Notification:* continuous (freshmen), continuous (transfers).

Freshman Application Contact Ms. Connie Esparza, Vice President for Marketing, Robert Morris College, 401 South State Street, Chicago, IL 60605. *Phone:* 312-935-4141. *Toll-free phone:* 800-RMC-5960. *Fax:* 312-935-4440. *E-mail:* cesparza@robertmorris.edu.

See page 860 for the College Close-Up.

ROCKFORD COLLEGE

Rockford, Illinois www.rockford.edu/

- **Independent** comprehensive, founded 1847
- **Suburban** 130-acre campus with easy access to Chicago
- **Endowment** $9.0 million
- **Coed** 882 undergraduate students, 85% full-time, 63% women, 37% men
- **Moderately difficult** entrance level, 51% of applicants were admitted

Undergraduates 752 full-time, 130 part-time. Students come from 21 states and territories, 4 other countries, 8% are from out of state, 7% African American, 2% Asian American or Pacific Islander, 6% Hispanic American, 0.2% Native American, 0.5% international, 16% transferred in, 35% live on campus. *Retention:* 57% of 2006 full-time freshmen returned.

Freshmen *Admission:* 710 applied, 363 admitted, 116 enrolled. *Average high school GPA:* 3.10. *Test scores:* SAT math scores over 500: 20%; SAT writing scores over 500: 50%; ACT scores over 18: 85%; ACT scores over 24: 25%.

Faculty *Total:* 149, 44% full-time. *Student/faculty ratio:* 11:1.

Majors Accounting; ancient/classical Greek; ancient studies; anthropology; art history, criticism and conservation; biochemistry; biological and physical sciences; biology/biological sciences; business administration and management; chemistry; classics; classics and languages, literatures and linguistics; computer science; dramatic/theater arts; economics; education; elementary education; English; finance; French; history; humanities; international economics; international/global studies; Latin; literature; management information systems; marketing/marketing management; mathematics; music; music performance; nursing (registered nurse training); philosophy; physical education teaching and coaching; political science and government; pre-dentistry studies; pre-law studies; pre-

COLLEGE DATA CENTER • ILLINOIS

medical studies; pre-veterinary studies; psychology; Romance languages; secondary education; social sciences; social work; sociology; Spanish; special education.

Academics *Calendar:* semesters. *Degrees:* bachelor's and master's. *Special study options:* academic remediation for entering students, accelerated degree program, adult/continuing education programs, advanced placement credit, double majors, English as a second language, honors programs, independent study, internships, off-campus study, part-time degree program, services for LD students, study abroad, summer session for credit. *ROTC:* Army (c).

Computers on Campus 75 computers/terminals are available on campus for general student use. Students can access the following: campus intranet, computer help desk, free student e-mail accounts, online (class) grades, online (class) schedules. Campuswide network is available. 100% of college-owned or -operated housing units are wired for high-speed Internet access. Wireless service is available via entire campus.

Student Life *Housing options:* coed, disabled students. Campus housing is university owned. *Activities and organizations:* drama/theater group, student-run radio station, choral group, student government, Intercultural Club, TEACH, Psychology Society, Nursing Student Organization. *Campus security:* 24-hour emergency response devices and patrols, late-night transport/escort service, controlled dormitory access. *Student services:* health clinic, personal/psychological counseling.

Athletics Member NCAA. All Division III. *Intercollegiate sports:* baseball M, basketball M/W, football M, golf M/W, soccer M/W, softball W, tennis M/W, volleyball M (c)/W. *Intramural sports:* basketball M/W, bowling M/W, cheerleading M (c)/W (c), football M/W, table tennis M/W, tennis M/W, volleyball M/W.

Standardized Tests *Required:* SAT or ACT (for admission).

Costs (2008–09) *Comprehensive fee:* $30,250 includes full-time tuition ($23,500) and room and board ($6750). Part-time tuition: $625 per credit. *College room only:* $3850.

Financial Aid Of all full-time matriculated undergraduates who enrolled in 2006, 775 applied for aid, 716 were judged to have need, 97 had their need fully met. 136 Federal Work-Study jobs (averaging $1945). 244 state and other part-time jobs (averaging $1988). In 2006, 68 non-need-based awards were made. *Average percent of need met:* 66%. *Average financial aid package:* $15,407. *Average need-based loan:* $4093. *Average need-based gift aid:* $10,644. *Average non-need-based aid:* $7985. *Average indebtedness upon graduation:* $16,135.

Applying *Options:* electronic application, early admission, deferred entrance. *Application fee:* $35. *Required:* high school transcript. *Required for some:* essay or personal statement, minimum 2.65 GPA, 2 letters of recommendation. *Recommended:* minimum 2.65 GPA, interview, campus visit. *Application deadlines:* 8/15 (freshmen), 8/15 (transfers).

Freshman Application Contact Ms. Kerry Fink, Director of Recruiting, Rockford College, Nelson Hall, Rockford, IL 61108-2393. *Phone:* 815-226-4050. *Toll-free phone:* 800-892-2984. *Fax:* 815-226-2822. *E-mail:* rcadmissions@rockford.edu.

ROOSEVELT UNIVERSITY

Chicago, Illinois **www.roosevelt.edu/**

- **Independent** comprehensive, founded 1945
- **Urban** campus
- **Endowment** $69.0 million
- **Coed** 3,973 undergraduate students, 56% full-time, 66% women, 34% men
- **Moderately difficult** entrance level, 43% of applicants were admitted

Undergraduates 2,221 full-time, 1,752 part-time. Students come from 41 states and territories, 44 other countries, 11% are from out of state, 22% African American, 5% Asian American or Pacific Islander, 11% Hispanic American, 0.2% Native American, 3% international, 20% transferred in, 13% live on campus.

Freshmen *Admission:* 2,100 applied, 902 admitted, 292 enrolled. *Average high school GPA:* 3.14. *Test scores:* SAT critical reading scores over 500: 85%; SAT math scores over 500: 60%; ACT scores over 18: 94%; SAT critical reading scores over 600: 38%; SAT math scores over 600: 30%; ACT scores over 24: 36%; SAT critical reading scores over 700: 6%; SAT math scores over 700: 2%; ACT scores over 30: 6%.

Faculty *Total:* 631, 34% full-time. *Student/faculty ratio:* 13:1.

Majors Accounting; actuarial science; African-American/Black studies; art; art history, criticism and conservation; biology/biological sciences; biotechnology; business administration and management; business/commerce; business/managerial economics; chemistry; clinical laboratory science/medical technology; clinical/medical laboratory science and allied professions related; communication/speech communication and rhetoric; community organization and advocacy; comparative literature; computer science; computer systems networking and telecommunications; dramatic/theater arts; economics; education; education related; electrical, electronic and communications engineering technology; elementary education; English; finance; foreign languages and literatures; geography; gerontology; health/health care administration; health/medical preparatory programs related; health science; history; hospitality administration; human resources management; human services; insurance; international business/trade/commerce; international relations and affairs; jazz/jazz studies; journalism; journalism related; kindergarten/preschool education; labor and industrial relations; legal assistant/paralegal; legal studies; liberal arts and sciences/liberal studies; literature; management science; marketing/marketing management; mathematics; medical laboratory technology; medical radiologic technology; music; music history, literature, and theory; music pedagogy; music performance; music related; music teacher education; music theory and composition; nuclear medical technology; philosophy; piano and organ; political science and government; pre-dentistry studies; pre-law studies; pre-medical studies; pre-pharmacy studies; psychology; public administration; public administration and social service professions related; public relations/image management; radio and television; secondary education; social sciences; social sciences related; sociology; Spanish; special education; statistics; telecommunications; urban studies/affairs; violin, viola, guitar and other stringed instruments; voice and opera; wind/percussion instruments; women's studies.

Academics *Calendar:* semesters. *Degrees:* bachelor's, master's, doctoral, and post-master's certificates. *Special study options:* academic remediation for entering students, accelerated degree program, adult/continuing education programs, advanced placement credit, distance learning, double majors, English as a second language, external degree program, honors programs, independent study, internships, off-campus study, part-time degree program, services for LD students, student-designed majors, study abroad, summer session for credit.

Computers on Campus 250 computers/terminals are available on campus for general student use. Students can access the following: online (class) registration. Campuswide network is available.

Student Life *Housing:* on-campus residence required through sophomore year. *Options:* coed. Campus housing is university owned. Freshman campus housing is guaranteed. *Activities and organizations:* drama/theater group, student-run newspaper, radio station, choral group, International Student Union, RU Proud, RU Latinos, Student Government, Residence Hall Council. *Campus security:* 24-hour emergency response devices and patrols, controlled dormitory access. *Student services:* personal/psychological counseling.

Standardized Tests *Required:* SAT or ACT (for admission).

Costs (2007–08) *Comprehensive fee:* $26,828 includes full-time tuition ($16,680), mandatory fees ($300), and room and board ($9848). Full-time tuition and fees vary according to course load and program. Part-time tuition: $600 per semester hour. Part-time tuition and fees vary according to course load and program. *Required fees:* $125 per term part-time. *College room only:* $6824. Room and board charges vary according to board plan and housing facility. *Payment plans:* installment, deferred payment. *Waivers:* senior citizens and employees or children of employees.

Financial Aid Of all full-time matriculated undergraduates who enrolled in 2004, 1,471 applied for aid, 1,275 were judged to have need, 196 had their need fully met. In 2004, 119 non-need-based awards were made. *Average percent of need met:* 75%. *Average financial aid package:* $13,173. *Average need-based gift aid:* $5579. *Average non-need-based aid:* $5115.

Applying *Options:* electronic application, deferred entrance. *Application fee:* $25. *Required:* essay or personal statement, high school transcript, minimum 2.5 GPA, audition for music and theater programs. *Required for some:* letters of recommendation, interview. *Application deadlines:* 9/1 (freshmen), rolling (transfers). *Notification:* continuous (freshmen), continuous (transfers).

Freshman Application Contact Ms. Gwen Kanelos, Assistant Vice President for Enrollment Services, Roosevelt University, 430 South Michigan Avenue, Room 104, Chicago, IL 60605-1394. *Phone:* 847-619-8620. *Toll-free phone:* 877-APPLYRU. *Fax:* 847-619-8636. *E-mail:* applyru@roosevelt.edu.

See page 862 for the College Close-Up.

RUSH UNIVERSITY

Chicago, Illinois **www.rushu.rush.edu/**

Application Contact Ms. Hicela Castruita Woods, Director of College Admission Services, Rush University, 600 South Paulina, Suite 440, College Admissions Services, Chicago, IL 60612-3878. *Phone:* 312-942-7100. *Fax:* 312-942-2219. *E-mail:* rush_admissions@rush.edu.

SAINT ANTHONY COLLEGE OF NURSING

Rockford, Illinois **www.sacn.edu/**

- **Independent Roman Catholic** upper-level, founded 1915
- **Urban** 17-acre campus with easy access to Chicago
- **Endowment** $600,000
- **Coed, primarily women**
- **Moderately difficult** entrance level

Faculty *Student/faculty ratio:* 9:1.
Academics *Calendar:* semesters. *Degree:* bachelor's.
Student Life *Campus security:* 24-hour emergency response devices and patrols, late-night transport/escort service.
Costs (2007–08) *Tuition:* $17,220 full-time, $539 per credit part-time. *Required fees:* $116 full-time.
Financial Aid Of all full-time matriculated undergraduates who enrolled in 2006, 146 applied for aid, 146 were judged to have need. *Average financial aid package:* $14,778. *Average need-based loan:* $7718. *Average need-based gift aid:* $5030. *Average indebtedness upon graduation:* $21,000.
Applying *Options:* electronic application, deferred entrance. *Application fee:* $50.
Application Contact Ms. Nancy Sanders, Assistant Dean for Admissions and Student Affairs, Saint Anthony College of Nursing, 5658 East State Street, Rockford, IL 61108-2468. *Phone:* 815-395-5100. *Fax:* 815-395-2275. *E-mail:* info@sacn.edu.

ST. AUGUSTINE COLLEGE

Chicago, Illinois **www.staugustinecollege.edu/**

- **Independent** 4-year, founded 1980
- **Urban** 4-acre campus
- **Endowment** $582,787
- **Coed**
- **Noncompetitive** entrance level

Faculty *Student/faculty ratio:* 13:1.
Academics *Calendar:* semesters. *Degrees:* certificates, associate, and bachelor's (offers bilingual Spanish/English degree programs).
Student Life *Campus security:* 24-hour patrols, late-night transport/escort service.
Standardized Tests *Required:* Ability-To-Benefit Admissions Test (for admission).
Costs (2007–08) *Tuition:* $7272 full-time, $303 per credit hour part-time.
Financial Aid Of all full-time matriculated undergraduates who enrolled in 2003, 2,025 applied for aid, 1,699 were judged to have need. 57 Federal Work-Study jobs (averaging $3080). In 2003, 83 non-need-based awards were made. *Average percent of need met:* 75. *Average need-based gift aid:* $5762. *Average non-need-based aid:* $2233.
Applying *Options:* deferred entrance.
Freshman Application Contact Ms. Gloria Quiroz, Director of Recruitment, St. Augustine College, 1345 West Argyle Street, Chicago, IL 60604-3501. *Phone:* 773-878-3256. *Fax:* 773-728-7067. *E-mail:* info@staugustine.edu.

SAINT FRANCIS MEDICAL CENTER COLLEGE OF NURSING

Peoria, Illinois **www.sfmccon.edu/**

- **Independent Roman Catholic** upper-level, founded 1986
- **Urban** campus
- **Coed, primarily women**
- 63% of applicants were admitted

Faculty *Student/faculty ratio:* 8:1.
Academics *Calendar:* semesters. *Degrees:* bachelor's and master's.
Student Life *Campus security:* 24-hour emergency response devices, controlled dormitory access.
Costs (2007–08) *Tuition:* $13,200 full-time, $440 per semester hour part-time. Full-time tuition and fees vary according to course load. Part-time tuition and fees vary according to course load. *Required fees:* $560 full-time, $210 per term part-time. *Room only:* $2000.
Financial Aid Of all full-time matriculated undergraduates who enrolled in 2006, 231 applied for aid, 159 were judged to have need, 23 had their need fully met. In 2006, 67 non-need-based awards were made. *Average percent of need met:* 79. *Average financial aid package:* $13,909. *Average need-based loan:* $7260. *Average need-based gift aid:* $7116. *Average non-need-based aid:* $5224.
Applying *Options:* deferred entrance. *Application fee:* $50.
Director of Admissions Mrs. Janice Farquharson, Director of Admissions and Registrar, Saint Francis Medical Center College of Nursing, 511 Greenleaf Street, Peoria, IL 61603-3783. *Phone:* 309-624-8980.

ST. JOHN'S COLLEGE

Springfield, Illinois
www.st-johns.org/education/schools/nursing/

Application Contact Ms. Beth Beasley, Student Development Officer, St. John's College, 421 North Ninth Street, Springfield, IL 62702-5317. *Phone:* 217-525-5628. *Fax:* 217-757-6870. *E-mail:* college@st-johns.org.

SAINT XAVIER UNIVERSITY

Chicago, Illinois **www.sxu.edu/**

- **Independent Roman Catholic** comprehensive, founded 1847
- **Urban** 70-acre campus
- **Endowment** $12.1 million
- **Coed** 3,288 undergraduate students, 78% full-time, 71% women, 29% men
- **Moderately difficult** entrance level, 77% of applicants were admitted

Undergraduates 2,566 full-time, 722 part-time. Students come from 21 states and territories, 2 other countries, 5% are from out of state, 18% African American, 3% Asian American or Pacific Islander, 14% Hispanic American, 0.4% Native American, 0.5% international, 21% live on campus. *Retention:* 75% of 2006 full-time freshmen returned.
Freshmen *Admission:* 2,289 applied, 1,754 admitted, 514 enrolled.
Faculty *Total:* 402, 46% full-time. *Student/faculty ratio:* 15:1.
Majors Accounting; art; art teacher education; biological and physical sciences; biology/biological sciences; biology teacher education; botany/plant biology; business/commerce; chemistry; communication/speech communication and rhetoric; computer and information sciences; computer science; counseling psychology; criminal justice/safety; elementary education; English; English/language arts teacher education; history; history teacher education; industrial and organizational psychology; international business/trade/commerce; international relations and affairs; kindergarten/preschool education; liberal arts and sciences/liberal studies; mathematics; mathematics teacher education; music; music performance; music teacher education; nursing (registered nurse training); philosophy; political science and government; psychology; religious studies; social sciences; sociology; Spanish; Spanish language teacher education; speech-language pathology.
Academics *Calendar:* semesters. *Degrees:* certificates, bachelor's, master's, post-master's, and postbachelor's certificates. *Special study options:* academic remediation for entering students, accelerated degree program, adult/continuing education programs, advanced placement credit, cooperative education, double majors, English as a second language, honors programs, independent study, internships, part-time degree program, services for LD students, student-designed majors, study abroad, summer session for credit. *ROTC:* Air Force (c).
Computers on Campus 306 computers/terminals are available on campus for general student use. Campuswide network is available.
Student Life *Housing options:* coed. Campus housing is university owned. *Activities and organizations:* drama/theater group, student-run newspaper, radio station, choral group, marching band, Student Activities Board, Black Student Union, UNIDOS (Hispanic Organization), Student Nurses Association, Business Students Association. *Campus security:* 24-hour emergency response devices and patrols, late-night transport/escort service. *Student services:* health clinic, personal/psychological counseling, women's center.
Athletics Member NAIA. *Intercollegiate sports:* baseball M (s), basketball M (s), cross-country running W (s), football M (s), golf M (s), soccer M (s)/W (s), softball W (s), volleyball W (s). *Intramural sports:* basketball M, bowling M/W, volleyball M/W, weight lifting M.
Standardized Tests *Required:* SAT or ACT (for admission).
Costs (2007–08) *Comprehensive fee:* $28,862 includes full-time tuition ($21,016), mandatory fees ($220), and room and board ($7626). Full-time tuition and fees vary according to course load. Part-time tuition: $704 per credit hour. Part-time tuition and fees vary according to course load. *College room only:* $4442. Room and board charges vary according to board plan and housing facility. *Payment plan:* installment. *Waivers:* senior citizens and employees or children of employees.

Financial Aid Of all full-time matriculated undergraduates who enrolled in 2007, 2,322 applied for aid, 2,100 were judged to have need, 497 had their need fully met. 1,373 Federal Work-Study jobs (averaging $2768). 38 state and other part-time jobs (averaging $6030). In 2007, 344 non-need-based awards were made. *Average percent of need met:* 83%. *Average financial aid package:* $8892. *Average need-based loan:* $2310. *Average need-based gift aid:* $5763. *Average non-need-based aid:* $3163. *Average indebtedness upon graduation:* $22,621.

Applying *Options:* electronic application, deferred entrance. *Application fee:* $25. *Required:* high school transcript. *Required for some:* interview. *Recommended:* essay or personal statement, minimum 2.5 GPA, interview. *Application deadlines:* rolling (freshmen), rolling (transfers). *Notification:* continuous (freshmen), continuous (transfers).

Freshman Application Contact Ms. Elizabeth A. Gierach, Assistant Vice President, Saint Xavier University, 3700 West 103rd Street, Chicago, IL 60655-3105. *Phone:* 773-298-3063. *Toll-free phone:* 800-462-9288. *Fax:* 773-298-3076. *E-mail:* admissions@sxu.edu.

See page 864 for the College Close-Up.

SCHOOL OF THE ART INSTITUTE OF CHICAGO

Chicago, Illinois **www.artic.edu/saic/**

- **Independent** comprehensive, founded 1866
- **Urban** 1-acre campus
- **Endowment** $810.6 million
- **Coed** 2,404 undergraduate students, 91% full-time, 64% women, 36% men
- **Moderately difficult** entrance level, 80% of applicants were admitted

Undergraduates 2,187 full-time, 217 part-time. Students come from 48 states and territories, 25 other countries, 76% are from out of state, 3% African American, 11% Asian American or Pacific Islander, 8% Hispanic American, 0.9% Native American, 18% international, 13% transferred in, 31% live on campus. *Retention:* 74% of 2006 full-time freshmen returned.

Freshmen *Admission:* 1,739 applied, 1,392 admitted, 452 enrolled.

Faculty *Total:* 627, 21% full-time. *Student/faculty ratio:* 11:1.

Majors Animation, interactive technology, video graphics and special effects; architecture related; art; art history, criticism and conservation; art teacher education; ceramic arts and ceramics; cinematography and film/video production; computer graphics; creative writing; design and applied arts related; design and visual communications; digital communication and media/multimedia; drawing; fashion/apparel design; fiber, textile and weaving arts; film/cinema studies; film/video and photographic arts related; fine arts related; fine/studio arts; graphic communications; graphic design; illustration; interior architecture; intermedia/multimedia; metal and jewelry arts; music related; painting; photography; printmaking; sculpture; visual and performing arts; visual and performing arts related; web page, digital/multimedia and information resources design.

Academics *Calendar:* semesters. *Degrees:* certificates, bachelor's, and master's. *Special study options:* academic remediation for entering students, advanced placement credit, cooperative education, double majors, English as a second language, independent study, internships, off-campus study, part-time degree program, services for LD students, student-designed majors, study abroad, summer session for credit.

Computers on Campus 280 computers/terminals are available on campus for general student use. Students can access the following: campus intranet, computer help desk, free student e-mail accounts, online (class) grades, online (class) registration, online (class) schedules. Campuswide network is available. 100% of college-owned or -operated housing units are wired for high-speed Internet access. Wireless service is available via entire campus.

Student Life *Housing options:* coed. Campus housing is university owned. *Activities and organizations:* drama/theater group, student-run newspaper, radio and television station, Student Government/Student Union Galleries, Korean Student Association, Agape, Art on Track, Ultimate Frisbee. *Campus security:* 24-hour emergency response devices and patrols, late-night transport/escort service, controlled dormitory access. *Student services:* health clinic, personal/psychological counseling.

Standardized Tests *Required:* SAT or ACT (for admission).

Costs (2007–08) *Tuition:* $30,750 full-time, $1025 per semester hour part-time. *Required fees:* $270 full-time. *Room only:* $8900.

Financial Aid Of all full-time matriculated undergraduates who enrolled in 2006, 1,437 applied for aid, 1,120 were judged to have need. In 2006, 303 non-need-based awards were made. *Average percent of need met:* 70%. *Average financial aid package:* $19,566. *Average need-based loan:* $4840. *Average need-based gift aid:* $10,816. *Average non-need-based aid:* $4557. *Average indebtedness upon graduation:* $26,011.

Applying *Options:* electronic application, early action, deferred entrance. *Application fee:* $65. *Required:* essay or personal statement, high school transcript, 1 letter of recommendation, portfolio. *Recommended:* interview. *Application deadlines:* 6/1 (freshmen), 8/15 (transfers), 1/2 (early action). *Notification:* continuous (freshmen), continuous (transfers), 2/15 (early action).

Freshman Application Contact Mr. Scott Ramon, Director, Undergraduate Admissions, School of the Art Institute of Chicago, 37 South Wabash, Chicago, IL 60603. *Phone:* 312-629-6100. *Toll-free phone:* 800-232-SAIC. *Fax:* 312-629-6101. *E-mail:* admiss@saic.edu.

See page 866 for the College Close-Up.

SHIMER COLLEGE

Chicago, Illinois **www.shimer.edu/**

- **Independent** 4-year, founded 1853
- **Urban** 3-acre campus with easy access to Chicago and Milwaukee
- **Coed** 76 undergraduate students, 64% full-time, 41% women, 59% men
- **Moderately difficult** entrance level, 69% of applicants were admitted

Undergraduates 49 full-time, 27 part-time. Students come from 20 states and territories, 28% are from out of state, 12% African American, 4% Asian American or Pacific Islander, 4% Hispanic American, 3% international, 4% transferred in, 20% live on campus. *Retention:* 66% of 2006 full-time freshmen returned.

Freshmen *Admission:* 45 applied, 31 admitted, 13 enrolled. *Average high school GPA:* 3.29. *Test scores:* SAT critical reading scores over 500: 100%; SAT math scores over 500: 83%; SAT writing scores over 500: 100%; ACT scores over 18: 100%; SAT critical reading scores over 600: 67%; SAT math scores over 600: 33%; SAT writing scores over 600: 50%; ACT scores over 24: 85%; SAT critical reading scores over 700: 50%; SAT writing scores over 700: 17%; ACT scores over 30: 28%.

Faculty *Total:* 16, 75% full-time, 6% with terminal degrees.

Majors General studies; humanities; liberal arts and sciences and humanities related; liberal arts and sciences/liberal studies; literature; natural sciences; social sciences.

Academics *Calendar:* semesters. *Degrees:* bachelor's and postbachelor's certificates. *Special study options:* adult/continuing education programs, cooperative education, distance learning, double majors, independent study, internships, off-campus study, part-time degree program, student-designed majors, study abroad, summer session for credit.

Computers on Campus 9 computers/terminals are available on campus for general student use. Campuswide network is available.

Student Life *Housing options:* coed. Campus housing is university owned and leased by the school. Freshman campus housing is guaranteed. *Activities and organizations:* drama/theater group, student-run newspaper, radio station, choral group, student government, Drama Group, Quality of Life Committee. *Campus security:* 24-hour emergency response devices, late-night transport/escort service. *Student services:* personal/psychological counseling.

Costs (2007–08) *Comprehensive fee:* $33,463 includes full-time tuition ($22,600), mandatory fees ($2245), and room and board ($8618). Part-time tuition: $800 per credit hour.

Financial Aid Of all full-time matriculated undergraduates who enrolled in 2006, 62 applied for aid, 62 were judged to have need. 49 Federal Work-Study jobs (averaging $1900). 12 state and other part-time jobs (averaging $625). In 2006, 5 non-need-based awards were made. *Average percent of need met:* 30%. *Average financial aid package:* $10,954. *Average need-based loan:* $6200. *Average need-based gift aid:* $4010. *Average non-need-based aid:* $6000. *Average indebtedness upon graduation:* $26,000.

Applying *Options:* electronic application, early admission, deferred entrance. *Application fee:* $25. *Required:* essay or personal statement, high school transcript, 1 letter of recommendation, interview. *Application deadlines:* 7/31 (freshmen), rolling (transfers). *Notification:* continuous (freshmen), continuous (transfers).

Freshman Application Contact Ms. Elaine Vincent, Director of Admission, Shimer College, PO Box 500, Waukegan, IL 60079. *Phone:* 312-235-3504. *Toll-free phone:* 800-215-7173. *E-mail:* e.vincent@shimer.edu.

SOUTHERN ILLINOIS UNIVERSITY CARBONDALE

Carbondale, Illinois www.siu.edu/siuc/

- **State-supported** university, founded 1869, part of Southern Illinois University
- **Rural** 1133-acre campus with easy access to St. Louis
- **Endowment** $88.1 million
- **Coed** 16,193 undergraduate students, 89% full-time, 43% women, 57% men
- **Moderately difficult** entrance level, 71% of applicants were admitted

Undergraduates 14,489 full-time, 1,704 part-time. Students come from 50 states and territories, 98 other countries, 14% are from out of state, 18% African American, 2% Asian American or Pacific Islander, 4% Hispanic American, 0.5% Native American, 1% international, 14% transferred in, 30% live on campus. *Retention:* 70% of 2006 full-time freshmen returned.

Freshmen *Admission:* 9,807 applied, 6,941 admitted, 2,636 enrolled. *Test scores:* SAT critical reading scores over 500: 43%; SAT math scores over 500: 47%; SAT writing scores over 500: 36%; ACT scores over 18: 87%; SAT critical reading scores over 600: 11%; SAT math scores over 600: 13%; SAT writing scores over 600: 9%; ACT scores over 24: 28%; SAT critical reading scores over 700: 2%; ACT scores over 30: 3%.

Faculty *Total:* 1,062, 86% full-time, 80% with terminal degrees. *Student/faculty ratio:* 17:1.

Majors Accounting; agricultural economics; agriculture; airline pilot and flight crew; animal sciences; anthropology; apparel and textiles; architecture; art; automotive engineering technology; aviation/airway management; avionics maintenance technology; biology/biological sciences; botany/plant biology; business administration and management; business/managerial economics; chemistry; cinematography and film/video production; civil engineering; classics and languages, literatures and linguistics; communication disorders; computer engineering; computer science; criminal justice/law enforcement administration; dental hygiene; design and visual communications; dramatic/theater arts; early childhood education; economics; electrical and electronic engineering technologies related; electrical, electronics and communications engineering; elementary education; engineering technology; English; finance; fine/studio arts; fire services administration; foods, nutrition, and wellness; foreign languages related; forestry; French; funeral service and mortuary science; geography; geology/earth science; German; health/health care administration; health teacher education; history; hospitality administration related; industrial technology; information science/studies; interior design; journalism; kinesiology and exercise science; legal assistant/paralegal; liberal arts and sciences/liberal studies; linguistics; management science; marketing/marketing management; mathematics; mechanical engineering; medical radiologic technology; microbiology; mining and mineral engineering; multi-/interdisciplinary studies related; music; parks, recreation and leisure; philosophy; physical therapist assistant; physician assistant; physics; physiology; plant sciences; political science and government; psychology; radio and television; rehabilitation and therapeutic professions related; social sciences; social work; sociology; Spanish; special education; speech and rhetoric; trade and industrial teacher education; zoology/animal biology.

Academics *Calendar:* semesters plus 8-week summer session. *Degrees:* associate, bachelor's, master's, doctoral, first professional, postbachelor's, and first professional certificates. *Special study options:* academic remediation for entering students, adult/continuing education programs, advanced placement credit, cooperative education, distance learning, double majors, English as a second language, honors programs, independent study, internships, off-campus study, part-time degree program, services for LD students, study abroad, summer session for credit. *ROTC:* Army (b), Air Force (b).

Computers on Campus 1,776 computers/terminals are available on campus for general student use. Students can access the following: campus intranet, computer help desk, free student e-mail accounts, online (class) grades, online (class) registration, online (class) schedules. Campuswide network is available. 80% of college-owned or -operated housing units are wired for high-speed Internet access. Wireless service is available via classrooms, computer centers, computer labs, learning centers, libraries, student centers.

Student Life *Housing:* on-campus residence required for freshman year. *Options:* coed, men-only, women-only, disabled students. Campus housing is university owned. Freshman campus housing is guaranteed. *Activities and organizations:* drama/theater group, student-run newspaper, radio and television station, choral group, marching band, Greek Life, Black Affairs Council, Hispanic Student Council, Student Programming Council, Residence Hall Association, national fraternities, national sororities. *Campus security:* 24-hour emergency response devices and patrols, student patrols, late-night transport/escort service, well-lit pathways, night safety vans, student transit system. *Student services:* health clinic, personal/psychological counseling, women's center, legal services.

Athletics Member NCAA. All Division I except football (Division I-AA). *Intercollegiate sports:* baseball M (s), basketball M (s)/W (s), cheerleading W (s), cross-country running M (s)/W (s), golf M (s)/W (s), softball W (s), swimming and diving M (s)/W (s), tennis M (s)/W (s), track and field M (s)/W (s), volleyball W (s). *Intramural sports:* archery M (c)/W (c), badminton M (c)/W (c), baseball M (c), basketball M/W, bowling M (c)/W, cross-country running M/W, equestrian sports M (c)/W (c), fencing M (c)/W (c), football M/W, golf M/W, lacrosse M (c), racquetball M (c)/W (c), riflery M (c)/W (c), rock climbing M (c)/W (c), rugby M (c)/W (c), sailing M (c)/W (c), soccer M (c)/W (c), softball M/W, squash M (c)/W, table tennis M (c)/W, tennis M/W, track and field M (c)/W (c), ultimate Frisbee M (c)/W (c), volleyball M (c)/W (c), water polo M (c)/W, weight lifting M (c)/W (c), wrestling M (c).

Standardized Tests *Required:* SAT or ACT (for admission).

Costs (2007–08) *Tuition:* state resident $6348 full-time, $212 per semester hour part-time; nonresident $15,870 full-time, $529 per semester hour part-time. Full-time tuition and fees vary according to course load. Part-time tuition and fees vary according to course load. No tuition increase for student's term of enrollment. *Required fees:* $2551 full-time, $118 per semester hour part-time. *Room and board:* $6666; room only: $3650. Room and board charges vary according to board plan and housing facility. *Payment plan:* installment. *Waivers:* senior citizens and employees or children of employees.

Financial Aid Of all full-time matriculated undergraduates who enrolled in 2006, 10,288 applied for aid, 8,562 were judged to have need, 7,491 had their need fully met. 2,010 Federal Work-Study jobs (averaging $1306). 5,346 state and other part-time jobs (averaging $1772). In 2006, 1283 non-need-based awards were made. *Average percent of need met:* 97%. *Average financial aid package:* $11,613. *Average need-based loan:* $4245. *Average need-based gift aid:* $6713. *Average non-need-based aid:* $4545. *Average indebtedness upon graduation:* $17,295.

Applying *Options:* electronic application, deferred entrance. *Application fee:* $30. *Required:* high school transcript. *Application deadlines:* rolling (freshmen), rolling (transfers). *Notification:* continuous (freshmen), continuous (transfers).

Freshman Application Contact Katharine Suski, Associate Director, Undergraduate Admissions, Southern Illinois University Carbondale, Mail Code 4710, Southern Illinois University Carbondale, Carbondale, IL 62901-4710. *Phone:* 618-536-4405. *Fax:* 618-453-4609. *E-mail:* joinsiuc@siu.edu.

See page 868 for the College Close-Up.

SOUTHERN ILLINOIS UNIVERSITY EDWARDSVILLE

Edwardsville, Illinois www.siue.edu/

- **State-supported** comprehensive, founded 1957, part of Southern Illinois University
- **Suburban** 2660-acre campus with easy access to St. Louis
- **Endowment** $11.3 million
- **Coed** 10,920 undergraduate students, 85% full-time, 54% women, 46% men
- **Moderately difficult** entrance level, 84% of applicants were admitted

Undergraduates 9,246 full-time, 1,674 part-time. Students come from 46 states and territories, 48 other countries, 8% are from out of state, 10% African American, 2% Asian American or Pacific Islander, 2% Hispanic American, 0.2% Native American, 0.6% international, 12% transferred in, 27% live on campus. *Retention:* 72% of 2006 full-time freshmen returned.

Freshmen *Admission:* 5,658 applied, 4,752 admitted, 1,860 enrolled. *Test scores:* ACT scores over 18: 97%; ACT scores over 24: 40%; ACT scores over 30: 4%.

Faculty *Total:* 873, 68% full-time. *Student/faculty ratio:* 17:1.

Majors Accounting; anthropology; art; audiology and speech-language pathology; biology/biological sciences; business administration and management; business/managerial economics; chemistry; civil engineering; computer engineering; computer science; construction engineering technology; criminal justice/safety; dramatic/theater arts; early childhood education; economics; electrical, electronics and communications engineering; elementary education; English; fine/studio arts; foreign languages and literatures; geography; health and physical education; health teacher education; history; industrial engineering; liberal arts and sciences/liberal studies; management information systems; manufacturing engineering; mass communication/media; mathematics; mechanical engineering; music; nursing (registered nurse training); philosophy; physics; political science and government; psychology; science teacher education; social work; sociology; special education; speech and rhetoric.

Academics *Calendar:* semesters. *Degrees:* bachelor's, master's, first professional, post-master's, postbachelor's, and first professional certificates. *Special study options:* academic remediation for entering students, accelerated degree program, adult/continuing education programs, advanced placement credit, cooperative education, distance learning, double majors, English as a second language, honors programs, independent study, internships, off-campus study, part-time degree program, services for LD students, student-designed majors, study abroad, summer session for credit. *ROTC:* Army (b), Air Force (b). *Unusual degree programs:* 3-2 engineering; biological sciences; chemistry; computer science.

Computers on Campus 600 computers/terminals are available on campus for general student use. Students can access the following: computer help desk, free student e-mail accounts, online (class) grades, online (class) registration, online (class) schedules, online job finder. Campuswide network is available.

Student Life *Housing options:* coed, disabled students. Campus housing is university owned. Freshman applicants given priority for college housing. *Activities and organizations:* drama/theater group, student-run newspaper, radio station, choral group, student government, campus newspaper, University Center Board, International Student Council, national fraternities, national sororities. *Campus security:* 24-hour emergency response devices and patrols, student patrols, late-night transport/escort service, controlled dormitory access, 24-hour ID check at residence hall entrances, emergency call boxes located throughout campus. *Student services:* health clinic, personal/psychological counseling, legal services.

Athletics Member NCAA. All Division II. *Intercollegiate sports:* baseball M (s), basketball M (s)/W (s), cross-country running M (s)/W (s), golf M (s)/W (s), soccer M (s)/W (s), softball W (s), tennis M (s)/W (s), track and field M (s)/W (s), volleyball W (s), wrestling M (s). *Intramural sports:* badminton M/W, basketball M/W, bowling M/W, cheerleading M/W, fencing M/W, football M/W, golf M/W, ice hockey M/W, racquetball M/W, rock climbing M/W, soccer M/W, softball M/W, table tennis M/W, tennis M/W, ultimate Frisbee M/W, volleyball M/W, water polo M/W, weight lifting M/W.

Standardized Tests *Required:* SAT or ACT (for admission).

Costs (2007–08) *Tuition:* area resident $5228 full-time; state resident $5938 full-time; nonresident $13,069 full-time. *Required fees:* $1180 full-time. *Room and board:* $6750; room only: $3970.

Financial Aid Of all full-time matriculated undergraduates who enrolled in 2005, 6,414 applied for aid, 4,806 were judged to have need, 1,187 had their need fully met. 507 Federal Work-Study jobs (averaging $1713). 1,544 state and other part-time jobs (averaging $880). In 2005, 961 non-need-based awards were made. *Average percent of need met:* 76%. *Average financial aid package:* $9077. *Average need-based loan:* $3702. *Average need-based gift aid:* $5557. *Average non-need-based aid:* $3923. *Average indebtedness upon graduation:* $17,491.

Applying *Options:* electronic application, early admission, deferred entrance. *Application fee:* $30. *Required:* high school transcript. *Recommended:* minimum 2.5 GPA. *Application deadlines:* 5/1 (freshmen), 7/21 (transfers). *Notification:* continuous (freshmen), continuous (transfers).

Freshman Application Contact Mr. Todd Burrell, Director of Admissions, Southern Illinois University Edwardsville, Campus Box 1600, Randleman Hall, Edwardsville, IL 62026-1600. *Phone:* 618-650-3705. *Toll-free phone:* 800-447-SIUE. *Fax:* 618-650-5013. *E-mail:* admissions@siue.edu.

TELSHE YESHIVA–CHICAGO

Chicago, Illinois

Freshman Application Contact Rosh Hayeshiva, Telshe Yeshiva–Chicago, 3535 West Foster Avenue, Chicago, IL 60625-5598. *Phone:* 773-463-7738.

TRINITY CHRISTIAN COLLEGE

Palos Heights, Illinois — www.trnty.edu/

- **Independent Christian Reformed** 4-year, founded 1959
- **Suburban** 53-acre campus with easy access to Chicago
- **Endowment** $6.2 million
- **Coed** 1,367 undergraduate students, 80% full-time, 69% women, 31% men
- **Moderately difficult** entrance level, 89% of applicants were admitted

Undergraduates 1,092 full-time, 275 part-time. Students come from 35 states and territories, 13 other countries, 34% are from out of state, 8% African American, 1% Asian American or Pacific Islander, 6% Hispanic American, 0.1% Native American, 2% international, 7% transferred in, 53% live on campus. *Retention:* 71% of 2006 full-time freshmen returned.

Freshmen *Admission:* 574 applied, 510 admitted, 240 enrolled. *Average high school GPA:* 3.3. *Test scores:* SAT critical reading scores over 500: 62%; SAT math scores over 500: 57%; ACT scores over 18: 90%; SAT critical reading scores over 600: 29%; SAT math scores over 600: 38%; ACT scores over 24: 45%; SAT critical reading scores over 700: 10%; SAT math scores over 700: 5%; ACT scores over 30: 8%.

Faculty *Total:* 153, 48% full-time, 35% with terminal degrees. *Student/faculty ratio:* 12:1.

Majors Accounting; art; art teacher education; biology/biological sciences; biology teacher education; business administration and management; business administration, management and operations related; business/commerce; business teacher education; ceramic arts and ceramics; chemistry; chemistry teacher education; commercial and advertising art; communication/speech communication and rhetoric; computer science; drawing; education; elementary education; English; English/language arts teacher education; financial planning and services; history; history teacher education; human resources management; kinesiology and exercise science; marketing/marketing management; mathematics; mathematics teacher education; middle school education; music; music performance; music teacher education; nursing (registered nurse training); painting; parks, recreation, and leisure related; philosophy; photography; physical education teaching and coaching; piano and organ; pre-dentistry studies; pre-medical studies; pre-theology/pre-ministerial studies; pre-veterinary studies; printmaking; psychology; religious education; religious studies; sales, distribution and marketing; science teacher education; sculpture; secondary education; social work; sociology; Spanish; special education; special education (emotionally disturbed); special education (mentally retarded); special education (specific learning disabilities); theology.

Academics *Calendar:* semesters plus 2 week interim term. *Degrees:* bachelor's and postbachelor's certificates. *Special study options:* academic remediation for entering students, adult/continuing education programs, advanced placement credit, cooperative education, double majors, honors programs, independent study, internships, off-campus study, part-time degree program, services for LD students, study abroad.

Computers on Campus 140 computers/terminals are available on campus for general student use. Students can access the following: campus intranet, computer help desk, free student e-mail accounts, online (class) grades, online (class) registration, online (class) schedules. Campuswide network is available. 100% of college-owned or -operated housing units are wired for high-speed Internet access. Wireless service is available via entire campus.

Student Life *Housing:* on-campus residence required through senior year. *Options:* coed. Campus housing is university owned. Freshman campus housing is guaranteed. *Activities and organizations:* drama/theater group, student-run newspaper, choral group, Student Association, student ministries, student-run campus newspaper, Pro-Life Task Force, PACE (prison tutoring program). *Campus security:* 24-hour emergency response devices, student patrols, late-night transport/escort service. *Student services:* personal/psychological counseling.

Athletics Member NAIA, NCCAA. *Intercollegiate sports:* baseball M (s), basketball M (s)/W (s), cross-country running M (s)/W (s), soccer M (s)/W (s), softball W (s), track and field M (s)/W (s), volleyball W (s). *Intramural sports:* badminton M/W, basketball M/W, soccer M/W, volleyball W.

Standardized Tests *Required:* SAT or ACT (for admission). *Recommended:* ACT (for admission).

Costs (2007–08) *Comprehensive fee:* $26,166 includes full-time tuition ($18,896), mandatory fees ($150), and room and board ($7120). Part-time tuition: $630 per semester hour. Part-time tuition and fees vary according to course load. *College room only:* $3800. Room and board charges vary according to board plan. *Payment plan:* installment. *Waivers:* senior citizens and employees or children of employees.

Financial Aid Of all full-time matriculated undergraduates who enrolled in 2002, 659 applied for aid, 582 were judged to have need, 126 had their need fully met. 91 Federal Work-Study jobs (averaging $1400). In 2002, 120 non-need-based awards were made. *Average percent of need met:* 67%. *Average financial aid package:* $9875. *Average need-based loan:* $3920. *Average need-based gift aid:* $2572. *Average non-need-based aid:* $1908. *Average indebtedness upon graduation:* $15,728.

Applying *Options:* electronic application, deferred entrance. *Application fee:* $20. *Required:* essay or personal statement, high school transcript, minimum 2.0 GPA, interview. *Required for some:* 1 letter of recommendation. *Application deadlines:* rolling (freshmen), rolling (out-of-state freshmen). *Notification:* continuous (freshmen), continuous (transfers).

Freshman Application Contact Mr. Jeremy Klyn, Director of Admissions, Trinity Christian College, 6601 West College Drive, Palos Heights, IL 60463. *Phone:* 708-239-4708. *Toll-free phone:* 800-748-0085. *Fax:* 708-239-4826. *E-mail:* admissions@trnty.edu.

TRINITY COLLEGE OF NURSING AND HEALTH SCIENCES

Rock Island, Illinois www.trinitycollegeqc.edu/

- **Independent** 4-year, founded 1994, administratively affiliated with Trinity Medical Center
- **Urban** 2-acre campus
- **Endowment** $1.5 million
- **Coed**
- **Moderately difficult** entrance level

Faculty *Student/faculty ratio:* 10:1.

Academics *Calendar:* semesters. *Degrees:* certificates, diplomas, associate, and bachelor's (general education requirements are taken off campus, usually at Black Hawk College, Eastern Iowa Community College District and Western Illinois University).

Student Life *Campus security:* 24-hour emergency response devices, controlled dormitory access.

Standardized Tests *Required:* SAT or ACT (for admission).

Costs (2007–08) *Tuition:* $7848 full-time, $426 per semester hour part-time. *Required fees:* $714 full-time.

Financial Aid Of all full-time matriculated undergraduates who enrolled in 2006, 87 applied for aid, 65 were judged to have need, 2 had their need fully met. In 2006, 3 non-need-based awards were made. *Average non-need-based aid:* $500. *Average indebtedness upon graduation:* $5500.

Applying *Application fee:* $50. *Required:* high school transcript, minimum 2.5 GPA. *Required for some:* minimum 2.75 GPA, minimum ACT score of 21.

Director of Admissions Ms. Barbara Kimpe, Admissions Representative, Trinity College of Nursing and Health Sciences, 2122 25th Avenue, Rock Island, IL 61201. *Phone:* 309-779-7812. *E-mail:* kimpeb@trintyqc.com.

TRINITY INTERNATIONAL UNIVERSITY

Deerfield, Illinois www.tiu.edu/

- **Independent** university, founded 1897, affiliated with Evangelical Free Church of America, administratively affiliated with Evangelical Free Church of America
- **Suburban** 108-acre campus with easy access to Chicago
- **Endowment** $12.0 million
- **Coed** 1,317 undergraduate students, 79% full-time, 59% women, 41% men
- **Moderately difficult** entrance level, 48% of applicants were admitted

Undergraduates 1,035 full-time, 282 part-time. Students come from 33 states and territories, 6 other countries, 58% are from out of state, 13% African American, 3% Asian American or Pacific Islander, 3% Hispanic American, 0.5% Native American, 1% international, 7% transferred in, 55% live on campus. *Retention:* 78% of 2006 full-time freshmen returned.

Freshmen *Admission:* 754 applied, 360 admitted, 166 enrolled. *Average high school GPA:* 3.22. *Test scores:* SAT critical reading scores over 500: 67%; SAT math scores over 500: 60%; ACT scores over 18: 90%; SAT critical reading scores over 600: 27%; SAT math scores over 600: 13%; ACT scores over 24: 40%; SAT critical reading scores over 700: 7%; SAT math scores over 700: 3%; ACT scores over 30: 9%.

Faculty *Total:* 385, 24% full-time, 62% with terminal degrees. *Student/faculty ratio:* 12:1.

Majors Accounting; athletic training; biblical studies; biology/biological sciences; business administration and management; chemistry; communication and media related; computer science; education; education (K-12); elementary education; English; history; humanities; human resources development; human resources management; international business/trade/commerce; liberal arts and sciences/liberal studies; management science; marketing/marketing management; mathematics; music; music history, literature, and theory; music pedagogy; music related; music teacher education; music theory and composition; non-profit management; pastoral counseling and specialized ministries related; philosophy; physical education teaching and coaching; pre-medical studies; pre-nursing studies; pre-theology/pre-ministerial studies; psychology; religious/sacred music; secondary education; social sciences; youth ministry.

Academics *Calendar:* semesters. *Degrees:* bachelor's, master's, doctoral, first professional, and postbachelor's certificates. *Special study options:* academic remediation for entering students, adult/continuing education programs, advanced placement credit, double majors, honors programs, independent study, internships, off-campus study, part-time degree program, study abroad.

Computers on Campus 130 computers/terminals and 1,200 ports are available on campus for general student use. Students can access the following: campus intranet, computer help desk, free student e-mail accounts, online (class) grades, online (class) registration, online (class) schedules. Campuswide network is available. 100% of college-owned or -operated housing units are wired for high-speed Internet access. Wireless service is available via classrooms, computer labs, dorm rooms, libraries, student centers.

Student Life *Housing:* on-campus residence required for freshman year. *Options:* men-only, women-only. Campus housing is university owned. Freshman campus housing is guaranteed. *Activities and organizations:* drama/theater group, student-run newspaper, choral group, Student Government, College Union, Trinity Summer Mission, student newspaper, yearbook. *Campus security:* 24-hour patrols, controlled dormitory access. *Student services:* health clinic, personal/psychological counseling.

Athletics Member NAIA, NCCAA. *Intercollegiate sports:* baseball M (s), basketball M (s)/W (s), football M (s), soccer M (s)/W (s), softball W (s), track and field M/W, volleyball W (s). *Intramural sports:* baseball M, basketball M/W, football M, racquetball M/W, soccer M/W, volleyball W.

Standardized Tests *Required:* SAT or ACT (for admission).

Costs (2007–08) *Comprehensive fee:* $27,820 includes full-time tuition ($20,690), mandatory fees ($330), and room and board ($6800). Full-time tuition and fees vary according to location. Part-time tuition: $860 per hour. Part-time tuition and fees vary according to location. *Required fees:* $165 per year part-time. *College room only:* $3820. Room and board charges vary according to board plan and housing facility. *Payment plan:* installment. *Waivers:* employees or children of employees.

Financial Aid Of all full-time matriculated undergraduates who enrolled in 2007, 885 applied for aid, 810 were judged to have need, 253 had their need fully met. 337 Federal Work-Study jobs (averaging $1895). In 2007, 41 non-need-based awards were made. *Average percent of need met:* 85%. *Average financial aid package:* $16,547. *Average need-based loan:* $5050. *Average need-based gift aid:* $8216. *Average non-need-based aid:* $4535. *Average indebtedness upon graduation:* $20,621.

Applying *Options:* electronic application, early admission, deferred entrance. *Application fee:* $25. *Required:* essay or personal statement, high school transcript, minimum 2.5 GPA, 1 letter of recommendation. *Required for some:* interview. *Recommended:* minimum 3.0 GPA. *Application deadlines:* rolling (freshmen), rolling (transfers). *Notification:* continuous until 9/1 (freshmen).

Freshman Application Contact Mr. Aaron Mahl, Director of Undergraduate Admissions, Trinity International University, 2065 Half Day Road, Deerfield, IL 60015-1284. *Phone:* 847-317-7000. *Toll-free phone:* 800-822-3225. *Fax:* 847-317-8097. *E-mail:* tcadmissions@tiu.edu.

UNIVERSITY OF CHICAGO

Chicago, Illinois www.uchicago.edu/

- **Independent** university, founded 1891
- **Urban** 211-acre campus
- **Endowment** $5.8 billion
- **Coed** 4,926 undergraduate students, 99% full-time, 50% women, 50% men
- **Most difficult** entrance level, 35% of applicants were admitted

The Undergraduate College of the University of Chicago is at the heart of one of the world's great intellectual communities and centers of learning, where 81 Nobel laureates have researched, studied, or taught. The College offers fifty majors and the first established and most extensive general education curriculum.

Undergraduates 4,857 full-time, 69 part-time. 78% are from out of state, 5% African American, 13% Asian American or Pacific Islander, 8% Hispanic American, 0.3% Native American, 8% international, 0.8% transferred in. *Retention:* 98% of 2006 full-time freshmen returned.

Freshmen *Admission:* 10,362 applied, 3,597 admitted, 1,300 enrolled. *Test scores:* SAT critical reading scores over 500: 99%; SAT math scores over 500: 99%; SAT writing scores over 500: 99%; ACT scores over 18: 97%; SAT critical reading scores over 600: 92%; SAT math scores over 600: 92%; SAT writing scores over 600: 91%; ACT scores over 24: 87%; SAT critical reading scores over 700: 64%; SAT math scores over 700: 59%; SAT writing scores over 700: 57%; ACT scores over 30: 74%.

Faculty *Total:* 1,675, 65% full-time, 88% with terminal degrees. *Student/faculty ratio:* 6:1.

Majors African-American/Black studies; African studies; American studies; ancient/classical Greek; ancient Near Eastern and biblical languages; anthropology; applied mathematics; Arabic; area, ethnic, cultural, and gender studies related; art; art history, criticism and conservation; Asian studies; Asian studies

(East); Asian studies (South); Asian studies (Southeast); behavioral sciences; Bengali; biochemistry; biology/biological sciences; chemistry; Chinese; classics and languages, literatures and linguistics; comparative literature; computer science; creative writing; economics; English; English language and literature related; environmental studies; European studies (Central and Eastern); film/cinema studies; fine/studio arts; French; geography; geophysics and seismology; German; Hindi; history; human development and family studies; humanities; interdisciplinary studies; international/global studies; Italian; Japanese; Jewish/Judaic studies; Latin; Latin American studies; liberal arts and sciences/liberal studies; linguistics; mathematics; medieval and Renaissance studies; modern languages; music; music history, literature, and theory; Near and Middle Eastern studies; philosophy; physics; political science and government; psychology; public policy analysis; religious studies; Romance languages; Russian; Russian studies; Sanskrit and classical Indian languages; Slavic languages; social sciences; sociology; South Asian languages; Spanish; statistics; Tamil; Tibetan; Turkish; Urdu.

Academics *Calendar:* quarters. *Degrees:* bachelor's, master's, doctoral, and first professional. *Special study options:* accelerated degree program, adult/continuing education programs, advanced placement credit, double majors, independent study, internships, off-campus study, student-designed majors, study abroad, summer session for credit. *ROTC:* Army (c), Air Force (c). *Unusual degree programs:* 3-2 business administration; social work; public policy, social sciences (MAPSS), international relations.

Computers on Campus 1,000 computers/terminals are available on campus for general student use. Students can access the following: online (class) registration. Campuswide network is available. Wireless service is available via entire campus.

Student Life *Housing:* on-campus residence required for freshman year. *Options:* coed, cooperative, disabled students. Freshman campus housing is guaranteed. *Activities and organizations:* drama/theater group, student-run newspaper, radio station, choral group, national fraternities, national sororities. *Campus security:* 24-hour emergency response devices and patrols, student patrols, late-night transport/escort service, controlled dormitory access. *Student services:* health clinic, personal/psychological counseling, women's center.

Athletics Member NCAA. All Division III. *Intercollegiate sports:* baseball M, basketball M/W, cross-country running M/W, football M, soccer M/W, softball W, swimming and diving M/W, tennis M/W, track and field M/W, volleyball W, wrestling M. *Intramural sports:* archery M/W, badminton M/W, basketball M/W, crew M (c)/W (c), cross-country running M/W, fencing M (c)/W (c), football M/W, gymnastics M (c)/W (c), ice hockey M (c), lacrosse M (c)/W (c), racquetball M/W, rugby M (c)/W (c), sailing M (c)/W (c), softball M/W, squash M (c)/W (c), swimming and diving M/W, table tennis M/W, tennis M/W, track and field M/W, volleyball M (c).

Standardized Tests *Required:* SAT or ACT (for admission).

Costs (2007–08) *Comprehensive fee:* $47,007 includes full-time tuition ($35,169), mandatory fees ($699), and room and board ($11,139). Part-time tuition and fees vary according to course load. *College room only:* $6270. Room and board charges vary according to board plan and housing facility. *Payment plans:* tuition prepayment, installment. *Waivers:* employees or children of employees.

Applying *Options:* electronic application, early admission, early action, deferred entrance. *Application fee:* $60. *Required:* essay or personal statement, high school transcript, 3 letters of recommendation. *Recommended:* interview. *Application deadlines:* 1/2 (freshmen), 4/1 (transfers), 11/1 (early action). *Notification:* 4/1 (freshmen), 5/15 (transfers), 12/15 (early action).

Freshman Application Contact Mr. Theodore O'Neill, Dean of Admissions, University of Chicago, Rosenwald Hall, 1101 East 58th Street, Suite 105, Chicago, IL 60637-1513. *Phone:* 773-702-8650. *Fax:* 773-702-4199. *E-mail:* questions@phoenix.uchicago.edu.

See page 870 for the College Close-Up.

UNIVERSITY OF ILLINOIS AT CHICAGO

Chicago, Illinois **www.uic.edu/**

- **State-supported** university, founded 1946, part of University of Illinois System
- **Urban** 240-acre campus
- **Endowment** $194.7 million
- **Coed** 15,672 undergraduate students, 92% full-time, 53% women, 47% men
- **Moderately difficult** entrance level, 64% of applicants were admitted

Undergraduates 14,438 full-time, 1,234 part-time. Students come from 42 states and territories, 43 other countries, 2% are from out of state, 9% African American, 23% Asian American or Pacific Islander, 16% Hispanic American, 0.2% Native American, 2% international, 11% transferred in, 22% live on campus. *Retention:* 79% of 2006 full-time freshmen returned.

Freshmen *Admission:* 13,595 applied, 8,686 admitted, 3,291 enrolled. *Test scores:* ACT scores over 18: 95%; ACT scores over 24: 50%; ACT scores over 30: 7%.

Faculty *Total:* 1,526, 76% full-time, 73% with terminal degrees. *Student/faculty ratio:* 15:1.

Majors Accounting; African-American/Black studies; anthropology; architecture; art history, criticism and conservation; art teacher education; biochemistry; biology/biological sciences; biology teacher education; biomedical/medical engineering; business administration and management; chemical engineering; chemistry; chemistry teacher education; cinematography and film/video production; civil engineering; classics and languages, literatures and linguistics; commercial and advertising art; computer and information sciences; computer engineering; criminal justice/safety; dietetics; dramatic/theater arts; economics; electrical, electronics and communications engineering; elementary education; engineering/industrial management; engineering physics; English; English/language arts teacher education; entrepreneurship; finance; fine/studio arts; foreign language teacher education; French; French language teacher education; geology/earth science; German; German language teacher education; graphic design; health information/medical records administration; history; history teacher education; industrial design; industrial engineering; Italian; kinesiology and exercise science; Latin American studies; management information systems; marketing/marketing management; mathematics; mathematics and computer science; mathematics teacher education; mechanical engineering; music; nursing (registered nurse training); philosophy; photography; physics; physics teacher education; Polish; political science and government; pre-dentistry studies; pre-law studies; psychology; Russian; science teacher education; secondary education; Slavic languages; social science teacher education; social work; sociology; Spanish; Spanish language teacher education; speech and rhetoric; statistics.

Academics *Calendar:* semesters. *Degrees:* bachelor's, master's, doctoral, first professional, and first professional certificates. *Special study options:* academic remediation for entering students, accelerated degree program, advanced placement credit, cooperative education, distance learning, double majors, English as a second language, honors programs, independent study, internships, off-campus study, part-time degree program, services for LD students, student-designed majors, study abroad, summer session for credit. *ROTC:* Army (b), Navy (c), Air Force (c).

Computers on Campus 800 computers/terminals and 36 ports are available on campus for general student use. Students can access the following: campus intranet, computer help desk, free student e-mail accounts, online (class) grades, online (class) registration, online (class) schedules. Campuswide network is available. 100% of college-owned or -operated housing units are wired for high-speed Internet access. Wireless service is available via entire campus.

Student Life *Housing options:* coed. Campus housing is university owned. *Activities and organizations:* drama/theater group, student-run newspaper, radio and television station, choral group, Golden Key National Honor Society, Chinese Students and Scholars Friendship Association, Muslim Student Association, MBA Association, Alternative Spring Break, national fraternities, national sororities. *Campus security:* 24-hour emergency response devices and patrols, student patrols, late-night transport/escort service, controlled dormitory access, housing ID stickers, guest escort policy, 24-hour closed circuit videos for exits and entrances, security screen for first floor. *Student services:* health clinic, personal/psychological counseling, women's center, legal services.

Athletics Member NCAA. All Division I. *Intercollegiate sports:* baseball M (s), basketball M (s)/W (s), cross-country running M (s)/W (s), gymnastics M (s)/W (s), soccer M (s), softball W (s), swimming and diving M (s)/W (s), tennis M (s)/W (s), track and field M (s)/W (s), volleyball W (s). *Intramural sports:* badminton M/W, basketball M/W, bowling M/W, cross-country running M/W, fencing M (c)/W (c), field hockey M/W, football M/W, golf M/W, lacrosse M (c)/W (c), racquetball M/W, rugby M (c)/W (c), soccer M/W, softball M/W, squash M/W, table tennis M/W, tennis M/W, volleyball M (c)/W, water polo M (c)/W (c), wrestling M.

Standardized Tests *Required:* SAT or ACT (for admission).

Costs (2007–08) *Tuition:* state resident $7424 full-time; nonresident $19,814 full-time. Full-time tuition and fees vary according to program. Part-time tuition and fees vary according to program. No tuition increase for student's term of enrollment. *Required fees:* $3122 full-time. *Room and board:* $7818. Room and board charges vary according to board plan and housing facility. *Payment plan:* installment. *Waivers:* senior citizens and employees or children of employees.

Financial Aid Of all full-time matriculated undergraduates who enrolled in 2006, 9,685 applied for aid, 7,682 were judged to have need, 4,733 had their need fully met. 835 Federal Work-Study jobs (averaging $1604). 2,736 state and other part-time jobs (averaging $1540). In 2006, 1054 non-need-based awards were made. *Average percent of need met:* 92%. *Average financial aid package:*

$11,482. *Average need-based loan:* $4258. *Average need-based gift aid:* $9319. *Average non-need-based aid:* $3787. *Average indebtedness upon graduation:* $15,897.

Applying *Options:* electronic application. *Application fee:* $40. *Required:* high school transcript. *Required for some:* interview. *Recommended:* essay or personal statement. *Application deadlines:* 1/15 (freshmen), 3/1 (transfers). *Notification:* continuous (freshmen), continuous (transfers).

Freshman Application Contact Mr. Thomas E. Glenn, Executive Director of Admissions, University of Illinois at Chicago, Box 5220, Chicago, IL 60680-5220. *Phone:* 312-996-4350. *Fax:* 312-413-7628. *E-mail:* uic.admit@uic.edu.

UNIVERSITY OF ILLINOIS AT SPRINGFIELD

Springfield, Illinois **www.uis.edu/**

- **State-supported** comprehensive, founded 1969, part of University of Illinois System
- **Suburban** 746-acre campus
- **Endowment** $9.6 million
- **Coed** 2,863 undergraduate students, 59% full-time, 56% women, 44% men
- **Moderately difficult** entrance level, 62% of applicants were admitted

Undergraduates 1,692 full-time, 1,171 part-time. Students come from 44 states and territories, 13 other countries, 9% are from out of state, 11% African American, 3% Asian American or Pacific Islander, 3% Hispanic American, 0.6% Native American, 1% international, 21% transferred in, 22% live on campus. *Retention:* 72% of 2006 full-time freshmen returned.

Freshmen *Admission:* 1,112 applied, 685 admitted, 261 enrolled. *Average high school GPA:* 3.24. *Test scores:* ACT scores over 18: 90%; ACT scores over 24: 37%; ACT scores over 30: 5%.

Faculty *Total:* 342, 60% full-time, 65% with terminal degrees. *Student/faculty ratio:* 12:1.

Majors Accounting; biology/biological sciences; business administration and management; business administration, management and operations related; chemistry; clinical laboratory science/medical technology; communication and media related; computer science; criminal justice/safety; economics; educational leadership and administration; English; fine/studio arts; history; legal professions and studies related; liberal arts and sciences/liberal studies; mathematics; philosophy; political science and government; psychology; social sciences related; social work.

Academics *Calendar:* semesters. *Degrees:* bachelor's, master's, doctoral, post-master's, and postbachelor's certificates. *Special study options:* advanced placement credit, cooperative education, distance learning, honors programs, independent study, internships, part-time degree program, services for LD students, student-designed majors, study abroad, summer session for credit.

Computers on Campus 420 computers/terminals and 24 ports are available on campus for general student use. Students can access the following: campus intranet, computer help desk, free student e-mail accounts, online (class) grades, online (class) registration, online (class) schedules. Campuswide network is available. 100% of college-owned or -operated housing units are wired for high-speed Internet access. Wireless service is available via entire campus.

Student Life *Housing:* on-campus residence required for freshman year. *Options:* coed, disabled students. Campus housing is university owned. Freshman campus housing is guaranteed. *Activities and organizations:* drama/theater group, student-run newspaper, choral group, Christian Student Fellowship, Indian Student Organization, Blue Crew, Black Student Union, Student Activities Committee. *Campus security:* 24-hour emergency response devices and patrols, late-night transport/escort service, controlled dormitory access. *Student services:* health clinic, personal/psychological counseling, women's center.

Athletics Member NAIA. *Intercollegiate sports:* basketball M (s)/W (s), cheerleading W, golf M (s)/W (s), soccer M (s), softball W (s), tennis M (s)/W (s), volleyball W (s). *Intramural sports:* badminton M/W, baseball M (c), basketball M/W, bowling M/W, fencing M/W, football M/W, golf M/W, racquetball M/W, skiing (downhill) M/W, soccer M/W, softball M/W, tennis M/W, volleyball M/W.

Standardized Tests *Required:* SAT or ACT (for admission).

Costs (2007–08) *Tuition:* state resident $6360 full-time, $212 per credit hour part-time; nonresident $15,510 full-time, $517 per credit hour part-time. No tuition increase for student's term of enrollment. *Required fees:* $1740 full-time, $626 per term part-time. *Room and board:* $8446; room only: $3800. Room and board charges vary according to board plan and housing facility. *Payment plan:* installment. *Waivers:* senior citizens and employees or children of employees.

Financial Aid Of all full-time matriculated undergraduates who enrolled in 2005, 1,180 applied for aid, 926 were judged to have need, 306 had their need fully met. 74 Federal Work-Study jobs (averaging $1951). 320 state and other part-time jobs (averaging $2358). In 2005, 223 non-need-based awards were made. *Average percent of need met:* 82%. *Average financial aid package:* $8233. *Average need-based loan:* $4018. *Average need-based gift aid:* $5221. *Average non-need-based aid:* $3444. *Average indebtedness upon graduation:* $12,696. *Financial aid deadline:* 11/15.

Applying *Options:* electronic application, deferred entrance. *Application fee:* $40. *Required:* high school transcript. *Required for some:* essay or personal statement, talent/ability. *Application deadlines:* rolling (freshmen), rolling (transfers). *Notification:* 9/15 (freshmen), continuous (transfers).

Freshman Application Contact Dr. Marya Leatherwood, Associate Vice Chancellor and Director of Enrollment Management, University of Illinois at Springfield, One University Plaza, UHB 1080, Springfield, IL 62703. *Phone:* 217-206-6581. *Toll-free phone:* 888-977-4847. *Fax:* 217-206-6048. *E-mail:* admissions@uis.edu.

UNIVERSITY OF ILLINOIS AT URBANA–CHAMPAIGN

Champaign, Illinois **www.uiuc.edu/**

- **State-supported** university, founded 1867, part of University of Illinois System
- **Urban** 1470-acre campus
- **Endowment** $1.1 billion
- **Coed** 30,895 undergraduate students, 98% full-time, 47% women, 53% men
- **Very difficult** entrance level, 71% of applicants were admitted

Undergraduates 30,205 full-time, 690 part-time. Students come from 52 states and territories, 69 other countries, 7% are from out of state, 7% African American, 13% Asian American or Pacific Islander, 7% Hispanic American, 0.3% Native American, 6% international, 3% transferred in, 50% live on campus. *Retention:* 93% of 2006 full-time freshmen returned.

Freshmen *Admission:* 21,645 applied, 15,361 admitted, 6,940 enrolled. *Test scores:* SAT critical reading scores over 500: 88%; SAT math scores over 500: 97%; ACT scores over 18: 99%; SAT critical reading scores over 600: 58%; SAT math scores over 600: 85%; ACT scores over 24: 89%; SAT critical reading scores over 700: 16%; SAT math scores over 700: 47%; ACT scores over 30: 36%.

Faculty *Total:* 2,040, 97% full-time, 92% with terminal degrees. *Student/faculty ratio:* 17:1.

Majors Accounting; accounting and business/management; actuarial science; advertising; aerospace, aeronautical and astronautical engineering; agricultural and extension education; agricultural/biological engineering and bioengineering; agricultural business and management; agricultural communication/journalism; agricultural economics; agricultural mechanization; agricultural public services related; agricultural teacher education; agronomy and crop science; airline pilot and flight crew; animal/livestock husbandry and production; animal sciences; animal sciences related; anthropology; applied horticulture; architecture; architecture related; area studies related; art history, criticism and conservation; art teacher education; Asian studies (East); astronomy; athletic training; atmospheric sciences and meteorology; audiology and hearing sciences; audiology and speech-language pathology; auditing; aviation/airway management; banking and financial support services; biochemistry; biological and biomedical sciences related; biology/biological sciences; biomedical/medical engineering; biophysics; biotechnology; botany/plant biology; broadcast journalism; business administration and management; business/commerce; business teacher education; cell and molecular biology; cell biology and histology; ceramic sciences and engineering; chemical engineering; chemistry; chemistry teacher education; child development; city/urban, community and regional planning; civil engineering; classics and languages, literatures and linguistics; communication and journalism related; communication/speech communication and rhetoric; community health and preventive medicine; comparative literature; computational mathematics; computer and information sciences; computer and information systems security; computer engineering; computer programming; computer science; computer software engineering; construction engineering; consumer economics; crafts, folk art and artisanry; dance; dietetics; directing and theatrical production; dramatic/theater arts; early childhood education; East Asian languages; ecology; economics; economics related; education (multiple levels); electrical, electronics and communications engineering; elementary education; engineering; engineering mechanics; engineering physics; English; English composition; English/language arts teacher education; entomology; entrepreneurship; environmental/environmental health engineering; environmental health; environmental science; family and consumer sciences/human sciences business services related; farm and ranch management; fashion merchandising; film/cinema studies; finance; financial planning and services; food science; food science and technology related; food technology and processing; foreign language teacher education; forestry; forest sciences and biology; French; French language teacher education; general studies;

geography; geological and earth sciences/geosciences related; geology/earth science; geotechnical engineering; German; German language teacher education; graphic design; health services administration; Hebrew; history; history teacher education; horticultural science; hospitality administration; human development and family studies; humanities; human nutrition; human resources management; industrial and organizational psychology; industrial design; industrial engineering; insurance; international agriculture; international/global studies; Italian; jazz/jazz studies; journalism; kindergarten/preschool education; kinesiology and exercise science; landscape architecture; Latin American studies; Latin teacher education; liberal arts and sciences and humanities related; liberal arts and sciences/liberal studies; linguistics; logistics and materials management; management information systems; management science; manufacturing engineering; marketing/marketing management; marketing research; mass communication/media; materials engineering; materials science; mathematics; mathematics and computer science; mathematics teacher education; mechanical engineering; metallurgical engineering; microbiology; music; music history, literature, and theory; music performance; music teacher education; music theory and composition; natural resources/conservation; natural resources/conservation related; natural resources management; natural resources management and policy; nuclear engineering; operations management; operations research; organizational behavior; organizational communication; ornamental horticulture; painting; parks, recreation and leisure; philosophy; photography; physical education teaching and coaching; physics; physics teacher education; physiology; plant molecular biology; plant protection and integrated pest management; political science and government; polymer/plastics engineering; Portuguese; pre-law studies; preveterinary studies; psychology; public health related; purchasing, procurement/acquisitions and contracts management; real estate; religious studies; restaurant, culinary, and catering management; Russian; Russian studies; sales, distribution and marketing; science teacher education; sculpture; secondary education; Slavic languages; social science teacher education; social studies teacher education; sociology; Spanish; Spanish language teacher education; special education; special education (early childhood); special education (multiply disabled); speech and rhetoric; sport and fitness administration/management; statistics; structural engineering; technical teacher education; theater literature, history and criticism; urban forestry; vocational rehabilitation counseling; voice and opera; water resources engineering; wildlife and wildlands science and management; women's studies.

Academics *Calendar:* semesters. *Degrees:* certificates, bachelor's, master's, doctoral, first professional, and post-master's certificates. *Special study options:* academic remediation for entering students, accelerated degree program, advanced placement credit, cooperative education, distance learning, double majors, English as a second language, honors programs, independent study, internships, off-campus study, services for LD students, student-designed majors, study abroad, summer session for credit. *ROTC:* Army (b), Navy (b), Air Force (b). *Unusual degree programs:* 3-2 business administration; engineering; accounting.

Computers on Campus 3,400 computers/terminals and 70,000 ports are available on campus for general student use. Students can access the following: computer help desk, free student e-mail accounts, online (class) grades, online (class) registration, online (class) schedules. Campuswide network is available. 100% of college-owned or -operated housing units are wired for high-speed Internet access. Wireless service is available via classrooms, computer centers, computer labs, dorm rooms, learning centers, libraries, student centers.

Student Life *Housing:* on-campus residence required for freshman year. *Options:* coed, men-only, women-only, cooperative, disabled students. Campus housing is university owned and is provided by a third party. Freshman campus housing is guaranteed. *Activities and organizations:* drama/theater group, student-run newspaper, radio and television station, choral group, marching band, Volunteer Illini Project, October Lovers, Illini Pride Student Board, National Society of Collegiate Scholars, Phi Eta Sigma Freshman Honor Society, national fraternities, national sororities. *Campus security:* 24-hour emergency response devices and patrols, student patrols, late-night transport/escort service, controlled dormitory access, safety training classes, ID cards with safety numbers. *Student services:* health clinic, personal/psychological counseling, women's center, legal services.

Athletics Member NCAA. All Division I except football (Division I-A). *Intercollegiate sports:* baseball M (s), basketball M (s)/W (s), cheerleading M/W, cross-country running M (s)/W (s), golf M (s)/W (s), gymnastics M (s)/W (s), soccer W (s), softball W (s), swimming and diving W (s), tennis M (s)/W (s), track and field M (s)/W (s), volleyball W (s), wrestling M (s). *Intramural sports:* archery M (c)/W (c), badminton M/W, baseball M (c), basketball M/W, bowling M (c)/W (c), cheerleading M (c)/W (c), crew M (c)/W (c), cross-country running M/W, equestrian sports M (c)/W (c), fencing M (c)/W (c), field hockey M (c)/W (c), football M/W (c), golf M/W, gymnastics M (c)/W (c), ice hockey M (c)/W (c), lacrosse M (c)/W (c), racquetball M/W, riflery M (c)/W (c), rock climbing M (c)/W (c), rugby M (c)/W (c), sailing M (c)/W (c), skiing (cross-country) M (c)/W (c), skiing (downhill) M (c)/W (c), soccer M/W, softball M/W, squash M (c)/W (c), swimming and diving W (c), table tennis M (c)/W (c), tennis M/W, ultimate Frisbee M (c)/W (c), volleyball M/W, water polo M (c)/W (c), weight lifting M (c)/W (c), wrestling M.

Standardized Tests *Required:* SAT or ACT (for admission), ACT Writing Component (for admission).

Costs (2007–08) *Tuition:* state resident $8440 full-time; nonresident $22,526 full-time. Full-time tuition and fees vary according to course load, program, and student level. No tuition increase for student's term of enrollment. entering degree-seeking students are guaranteed the same tuition rates for 4 years. *Required fees:* $2690 full-time. *Room and board:* $8196. Room and board charges vary according to board plan and housing facility. *Waivers:* senior citizens and employees or children of employees.

Financial Aid Of all full-time matriculated undergraduates who enrolled in 2005, 16,969 applied for aid, 12,101 were judged to have need, 5,225 had their need fully met. 1,456 Federal Work-Study jobs (averaging $1276). 8,462 state and other part-time jobs (averaging $1732). In 2005, 4589 non-need-based awards were made. *Average percent of need met:* 87%. *Average financial aid package:* $10,180. *Average need-based loan:* $4196. *Average need-based gift aid:* $6531. *Average non-need-based aid:* $3773. *Average indebtedness upon graduation:* $15,413.

Applying *Options:* early action, deferred entrance. *Application fee:* $40. *Required:* essay or personal statement, high school transcript. *Required for some:* letters of recommendation, interview, audition, statement of professional interest. *Application deadlines:* 1/2 (freshmen), 3/1 (transfers), 11/15 (early action). *Notification:* continuous (freshmen), continuous (transfers), 12/14 (early action).

Freshman Application Contact Mrs. Stacey Kostell, Director of Admissions, University of Illinois at Urbana–Champaign, 901 West Illinois, Urbana, IL 61801. *Phone:* 217-333-0302. *Fax:* 217-244-4614. *E-mail:* ugradadmissions@uiuc.edu.

UNIVERSITY OF PHOENIX–CHICAGO CAMPUS

Schaumburg, Illinois **www.phoenix.edu/**

- **Proprietary** comprehensive, founded 2002
- **Urban** campus
- **Coed**
- **Noncompetitive** entrance level

Faculty *Student/faculty ratio:* 8:1.

Academics *Calendar:* continuous. *Degrees:* bachelor's and master's.

Student Life *Campus security:* late-night transport/escort service.

Costs (2007–08) *Tuition:* $11,520 full-time, $384 per credit part-time. Full-time tuition and fees vary according to course level.

Financial Aid *Average financial aid package:* $3787. *Average need-based gift aid:* $2112.

Applying *Options:* deferred entrance. *Application fee:* $45. *Required:* 1 letter of recommendation. *Required for some:* high school transcript.

Freshman Application Contact Ms. Beth Barilla, Associate Vice President, Student Admissions and Services, University of Phoenix–Chicago Campus, 4615 East Elwood Street, Mail Stop AA-K101, Phoenix, AZ 85040-1958. *Phone:* 480-317-6000. *Toll-free phone:* 800-776-4867 (in-state); 800-228-7240 (out-of-state). *Fax:* 480-894-1758. *E-mail:* beth.barilla@phoenix.edu.

UNIVERSITY OF ST. FRANCIS

Joliet, Illinois **www.stfrancis.edu/**

- **Independent Roman Catholic** comprehensive, founded 1920
- **Suburban** 22-acre campus with easy access to Chicago
- **Endowment** $20.7 million
- **Coed** 1,298 undergraduate students, 94% full-time, 69% women, 31% men
- **Moderately difficult** entrance level, 67% of applicants were admitted

Undergraduates 1,215 full-time, 83 part-time. Students come from 19 states and territories, 3% are from out of state, 10% African American, 5% Asian American or Pacific Islander, 8% Hispanic American, 0.1% Native American, 0.6% international, 14% transferred in, 27% live on campus. *Retention:* 74% of 2006 full-time freshmen returned.

Freshmen *Admission:* 766 applied, 510 admitted, 198 enrolled. *Average high school GPA:* 3.19. *Test scores:* ACT scores over 18: 95%; ACT scores over 24: 36%; ACT scores over 30: 5%.

Faculty *Total:* 227, 34% full-time, 39% with terminal degrees. *Student/faculty ratio:* 13:1.

Majors Accounting; biology/biological sciences; business administration and management; clinical laboratory science/medical technology; computer science; elementary education; English; English/language arts teacher education; environmental science; finance; health/health care administration; history; human resources management; information technology; liberal arts and sciences/liberal studies; marketing/marketing management; mass communication/media; mathematics; mathematics and computer science; mathematics teacher education; medical radiologic technology; multi-/interdisciplinary studies related; music; music performance; music teacher education; nuclear medical technology; nursing (registered nurse training); organizational behavior; parks, recreation and leisure facilities management; political science and government; pre-dentistry studies; pre-medical studies; pre-veterinary studies; psychology; radiologic technology/science; science teacher education; social studies teacher education; social work; special education; theology; visual and performing arts; web/multimedia management and webmaster.

Academics *Calendar:* semesters. *Degrees:* bachelor's, master's, and post-master's certificates. *Special study options:* academic remediation for entering students, accelerated degree program, adult/continuing education programs, advanced placement credit, distance learning, double majors, external degree program, honors programs, independent study, internships, off-campus study, part-time degree program, services for LD students, student-designed majors, study abroad, summer session for credit.

Computers on Campus 250 computers/terminals and 1,500 ports are available on campus for general student use. Students can access the following: campus intranet, computer help desk, free student e-mail accounts, online (class) grades, online (class) registration, online (class) schedules. Campuswide network is available. 100% of college-owned or -operated housing units are wired for high-speed Internet access. Wireless service is available via classrooms, computer centers, computer labs, dorm rooms, learning centers, libraries, student centers.

Student Life *Housing options:* coed. Campus housing is university owned. Freshman campus housing is guaranteed. *Activities and organizations:* drama/theater group, student-run newspaper, radio and television station, choral group, Student Activities Board, Black Student Association, Student Business Association, Unidos Vamos a Aleanzar, Student Nurses Organization. *Campus security:* 24-hour emergency response devices and patrols, student patrols, late-night transport/escort service, controlled dormitory access, First Response trained security personnel. *Student services:* personal/psychological counseling.

Athletics Member NAIA. *Intercollegiate sports:* baseball M (s), basketball M (s)/W (s), cheerleading W, cross-country running M (s)/W (s), football M (s), golf M (s)/W (s), soccer M (s)/W (s), softball W (s), tennis M (s)/W (s), track and field M (s)/W (s), volleyball W (s). *Intramural sports:* basketball M/W, bowling M/W, racquetball M/W, volleyball M/W.

Standardized Tests *Required:* SAT or ACT (for admission).

Costs (2007–08) *Comprehensive fee:* $28,440 includes full-time tuition ($20,440), mandatory fees ($390), and room and board ($7610). Part-time tuition: $680 per credit hour. *Room and board:* Room and board charges vary according to board plan and housing facility. *Payment plans:* installment, deferred payment. *Waivers:* children of alumni and employees or children of employees.

Financial Aid Of all full-time matriculated undergraduates who enrolled in 2006, 1,048 applied for aid, 890 were judged to have need, 673 had their need fully met. 282 Federal Work-Study jobs (averaging $1828). 237 state and other part-time jobs (averaging $1791). In 2006, 146 non-need-based awards were made. *Average percent of need met:* 80%. *Average financial aid package:* $16,063. *Average need-based loan:* $4366. *Average need-based gift aid:* $7575. *Average non-need-based aid:* $5806. *Average indebtedness upon graduation:* $18,547.

Applying *Options:* electronic application, deferred entrance. *Application fee:* $30. *Required:* high school transcript, minimum 2.0 GPA. *Required for some:* essay or personal statement, 2 letters of recommendation, interview. *Application deadline:* 8/1 (freshmen). *Notification:* continuous (freshmen), continuous (transfers).

Freshman Application Contact Ms. Meghan Connolly, Director of Undergraduate Admissions, University of St. Francis, 500 North Wilcox Street, Joliet, IL 60435-6188. *Phone:* 800-735-7500. *Toll-free phone:* 800-735-3500 (in-state); 800-735-7500 (out-of-state). *Fax:* 815-740-5032. *E-mail:* mconnolly1@stfrancis.edu.

VANDERCOOK COLLEGE OF MUSIC

Chicago, Illinois **www.vandercook.edu/**

- **Independent** comprehensive, founded 1909
- **Urban** 1-acre campus
- **Endowment** $432,276
- **Coed** 174 undergraduate students, 66% full-time, 47% women, 53% men
- **Moderately difficult** entrance level, 98% of applicants were admitted

Undergraduates 115 full-time, 59 part-time. Students come from 12 states and territories, 17% are from out of state, 16% African American, 7% Asian American or Pacific Islander, 14% Hispanic American, 0.9% international, 2% transferred in, 17% live on campus. *Retention:* 89% of 2006 full-time freshmen returned.

Freshmen *Admission:* 44 applied, 43 admitted, 26 enrolled. *Average high school GPA:* 3.26.

Faculty *Total:* 30, 43% full-time, 30% with terminal degrees. *Student/faculty ratio:* 8:1.

Majors Music teacher education.

Academics *Calendar:* semesters. *Degrees:* bachelor's and master's. *Special study options:* advanced placement credit, independent study, internships.

Computers on Campus 20 computers/terminals are available on campus for general student use. Campuswide network is available.

Student Life *Housing options:* coed. Campus housing is provided by a third party. *Activities and organizations:* choral group, MENC (Music Educators Natural Conference), ACDA (American Choral Directors Association), national fraternities, national sororities. *Campus security:* 24-hour emergency response devices and patrols, late-night transport/escort service, controlled dormitory access.

Standardized Tests *Required for some:* SAT or ACT (for admission).

Costs (2007–08) *Comprehensive fee:* $27,630 includes full-time tuition ($17,980), mandatory fees ($820), and room and board ($8830). Part-time tuition: $620 per credit hour. *College room only:* $4550.

Financial Aid Of all full-time matriculated undergraduates who enrolled in 2006, 7 Federal Work-Study jobs (averaging $500). 37 state and other part-time jobs (averaging $959).

Applying *Options:* deferred entrance. *Application fee:* $35. *Required:* essay or personal statement, high school transcript, 3 letters of recommendation, interview, audition. *Required for some:* minimum 3.0 GPA. *Recommended:* minimum 3.0 GPA. *Application deadlines:* rolling (freshmen), rolling (transfers).

Director of Admissions Ms. Tamara V. Trutwin, Student Recruiter, VanderCook College of Music, 3140 South Federal Street, Chicago, IL 60616. *Toll-free phone:* 800-448-2655. *E-mail:* vcmusic@mcs.com.

WESTERN ILLINOIS UNIVERSITY

Macomb, Illinois **www.wiu.edu/**

- **State-supported** comprehensive, founded 1899
- **Small-town** 1050-acre campus
- **Endowment** $24.8 million
- **Coed** 11,147 undergraduate students, 91% full-time, 47% women, 53% men
- **Moderately difficult** entrance level, 70% of applicants were admitted

Undergraduates 10,158 full-time, 989 part-time. Students come from 43 states and territories, 57 other countries, 5% are from out of state, 7% African American, 1% Asian American or Pacific Islander, 5% Hispanic American, 0.5% Native American, 1% international, 11% transferred in, 51% live on campus. *Retention:* 72% of 2006 full-time freshmen returned.

Freshmen *Admission:* 7,833 applied, 5,490 admitted, 1,955 enrolled. *Average high school GPA:* 3.03. *Test scores:* ACT scores over 18: 90%; ACT scores over 24: 23%; ACT scores over 30: 1%.

Faculty *Total:* 750, 89% full-time, 66% with terminal degrees. *Student/faculty ratio:* 15:1.

Majors Accounting; African-American/Black studies; agriculture; art; bilingual and multilingual education; biology/biological sciences; business administration and management; business/managerial economics; chemistry; chemistry related; clinical laboratory science/medical technology; communication disorders; communication/speech communication and rhetoric; computer and information sciences; computer systems networking and telecommunications; construction management; criminal justice/law enforcement administration; dramatic/theater arts; economics; educational/instructional media design; elementary education; English; family and consumer sciences/human sciences; finance; fine/studio arts; French; geography; geology/earth science; graphic and printing equipment operation/production; health/health care administration; health teacher education; history; human resources management; industrial technology; interdisciplinary studies; journalism; kinesiology and exercise science; liberal arts and sciences/liberal studies; logistics and materials management; management information systems; manufacturing technology; marketing/marketing management; mathematics; meteorology; music; music performance; music related; parks, recreation and leisure facilities management; philosophy; physics; political science and government; psychology; radio and television; security and protective services related; social work; sociology; Spanish; special education; women's studies.

Academics *Calendar:* semesters. *Degrees:* bachelor's, master's, doctoral, post-master's, and postbachelor's certificates. *Special study options:* academic remediation for entering students, adult/continuing education programs, advanced placement credit, distance learning, double majors, English as a second language, external degree program, freshman honors college, honors programs, independent study, internships, off-campus study, part-time degree program, services for LD students, student-designed majors, study abroad, summer session for credit. *ROTC:* Army (b). *Unusual degree programs:* 3-2 engineering with University of Illinois at Urbana–Champaign, Case Western Reserve University.

Computers on Campus 1,000 computers/terminals are available on campus for general student use. Students can access the following: online (class) registration. Campuswide network is available. 100% of college-owned or -operated housing units are wired for high-speed Internet access. Wireless service is available via classrooms, computer labs, dorm rooms, libraries, student centers.

Student Life *Housing:* on-campus residence required through sophomore year. *Options:* coed, men-only, women-only. Campus housing is university owned. Freshman campus housing is guaranteed. *Activities and organizations:* drama/theater group, student-run newspaper, radio and television station, choral group, marching band, Student Government Association, Black Student Association, University Union Board, International Friendship Club, Bureau of Cultural Affairs, national fraternities, national sororities. *Campus security:* 24-hour emergency response devices and patrols, student patrols, late-night transport/escort service, controlled dormitory access. *Student services:* health clinic, personal/psychological counseling, women's center, legal services.

Athletics Member NCAA. All Division I except football (Division I-AA). *Intercollegiate sports:* baseball M (s), basketball M (s)/W (s), cross-country running M (s)/W (s), golf M (s)/W, soccer M (s)/W (s), softball W (s), swimming and diving M (s)/W (s), tennis M (s)/W (s), track and field M (s)/W (s), volleyball W (s). *Intramural sports:* badminton M/W, basketball M/W, bowling M/W, cheerleading M/W, cross-country running M/W, football M/W, golf M/W, lacrosse M, racquetball M/W, rugby M/W, soccer M/W, softball M/W, swimming and diving M/W, table tennis M/W, tennis M/W, volleyball M/W, water polo M/W.

Standardized Tests *Required:* SAT or ACT (for admission).

Costs (2008–09) *Tuition:* state resident $6456 full-time, $215 per semester hour part-time; nonresident $9684 full-time, $323 per semester hour part-time. *Required fees:* $1816 full-time, $61 per semester hour part-time. *Room and board:* $7210; room only: $4350.

Financial Aid Of all full-time matriculated undergraduates who enrolled in 2007, 7,087 applied for aid, 5,523 were judged to have need, 2,174 had their need fully met. 208 Federal Work-Study jobs (averaging $2008). 1,577 state and other part-time jobs (averaging $1016). In 2007, 503 non-need-based awards were made. *Average percent of need met:* 70%. *Average financial aid package:* $8981. *Average need-based loan:* $4232. *Average need-based gift aid:* $7361. *Average non-need-based aid:* $2595. *Average indebtedness upon graduation:* $17,272.

Applying *Options:* electronic application, deferred entrance. *Application fee:* $30. *Required:* high school transcript, GPA greater than or equal to 2.5 on a 4.0 scale and ACT/SAT composite score of greater than or equal to 20/920. *Application deadlines:* 5/15 (freshmen), rolling (transfers). *Notification:* continuous until 8/3 (freshmen), continuous (transfers).

Freshman Application Contact Mr. Eric Campbell, Director of Admissions, Western Illinois University, 1 University Circle, 115 Sherman Hall, Macomb, IL 61455-1390. *Phone:* 309-298-3157. *Toll-free phone:* 877-742-5948. *Fax:* 309-298-3111. *E-mail:* admissions@wiu.edu.

West Suburban College of Nursing

Oak Park, Illinois **www.wscn.edu/**

- **Independent** upper-level, founded 1982
- **Suburban** 10-acre campus with easy access to Chicago
- **Coed** 197 undergraduate students, 81% full-time, 85% women, 15% men
- **Moderately difficult** entrance level, 35% of applicants were admitted

Undergraduates 159 full-time, 38 part-time. Students come from 2 states and territories, 0.5% are from out of state, 16% African American, 30% Asian American or Pacific Islander, 13% Hispanic American, 32% transferred in.

Freshmen *Admission:* 40 applied, 14 admitted.

Faculty *Total:* 24, 71% full-time, 17% with terminal degrees.

Majors Nursing (registered nurse training).

Academics *Calendar:* semesters. *Degrees:* bachelor's and master's. *Special study options:* accelerated degree program, adult/continuing education programs, advanced placement credit, independent study, part-time degree program, summer session for credit.

Computers on Campus 27 computers/terminals are available on campus for general student use. Students can access the following: campus intranet, computer help desk, free student e-mail accounts, online (class) grades, online (class) registration, online (class) schedules. Campuswide network is available. Wireless service is available via entire campus.

Student Life *Housing:* college housing not available. *Campus security:* 24-hour emergency response devices and patrols, late-night transport/escort service, controlled dormitory access.

Costs (2007–08) *Tuition:* $19,780 full-time, $670 per credit hour part-time. *Required fees:* $490 full-time, $120 per term part-time. *Payment plan:* installment. *Waivers:* employees or children of employees.

Applying *Options:* deferred entrance. *Application fee:* $30. *Application deadline:* rolling (transfers). *Notification:* continuous until 8/21 (transfers).

Director of Admissions Ms. Cynthia Valdez, Director of Enrollment Management, West Suburban College of Nursing, 3 Erie Court, Oak Park, IL 60302. *Phone:* 708-763-6530. *Fax:* 708-763-1531.

Westwood College–Chicago Du Page

Woodridge, Illinois **www.westwood.edu/**

Director of Admissions Mr. Scott Kawall, Director of Admissions, Westwood College–Chicago Du Page, 7155 James Avenue, Woodridge, IL 60517-2321. *Phone:* 630-434-8244. *Toll-free phone:* 888-721-7646.

Westwood College–Chicago Loop Campus

Chicago, Illinois **www.westwood.edu/**

Director of Admissions Gus Pyrolis, Acting Director of Admissions, Westwood College–Chicago Loop Campus, 17 North State Street, Suite 1500, Chicago, IL 60602. *Phone:* 312-739-0850.

Westwood College–Chicago O'Hare Airport

Schiller Park, Illinois **www.westwood.edu/**

Director of Admissions Mr. David Traub, Director of Admissions, Westwood College–Chicago O'Hare Airport, 4825 North Scott Street, Suite 100, Schiller Park, IL 60176-1209. *Phone:* 847-928-0200 Ext. 100. *Toll-free phone:* 877-877-8857.

Westwood College–Chicago River Oaks

Calumet City, Illinois **www.westwood.edu/**

Director of Admissions Tash Uray, Director of Admissions, Westwood College–Chicago River Oaks, 80 River Oaks Drive, Suite D-49, Calumet City, IL 60409-5820. *Phone:* 708-832-1988. *Toll-free phone:* 888-549-6873.

Wheaton College

Wheaton, Illinois **www.wheaton.edu/**

- **Independent nondenominational** comprehensive, founded 1860
- **Suburban** 80-acre campus with easy access to Chicago
- **Endowment** $313.1 million
- **Coed** 2,381 undergraduate students, 96% full-time, 51% women, 49% men
- **Very difficult** entrance level, 55% of applicants were admitted

Undergraduates 2,293 full-time, 88 part-time. Students come from 52 states and territories, 18 other countries, 77% are from out of state, 3% African American, 7% Asian American or Pacific Islander, 4% Hispanic American, 0.3% Native American, 1% international, 3% transferred in, 90% live on campus. *Retention:* 96% of 2006 full-time freshmen returned.

Freshmen *Admission:* 2,160 applied, 1,192 admitted, 582 enrolled. *Average high school GPA:* 3.73. *Test scores:* SAT critical reading scores over 500: 99%; SAT math scores over 500: 98%; SAT writing scores over 500: 97%; ACT scores over 18: 100%; SAT critical reading scores over 600: 84%; SAT math scores over 600: 80%; SAT writing scores over 600: 81%; ACT scores over 24: 95%; SAT critical reading scores over 700: 39%; SAT math scores over 700: 26%; SAT writing scores over 700: 31%; ACT scores over 30: 43%.

Faculty *Total:* 299, 65% full-time, 72% with terminal degrees. *Student/faculty ratio:* 12:1.

Majors Anthropology; archeology; art; biblical studies; biology/biological sciences; business/managerial economics; chemistry; classics and classical languages related; communication/speech communication and rhetoric; computer science; economics; elementary education; engineering related; English; environmental studies; French; geology/earth science; German; health services/allied health/health sciences; history; international relations and affairs; mathematics; multi-/interdisciplinary studies related; music; music history, literature, and theory; music performance; music related; music teacher education; music theory and composition; nursing related; philosophy; physics; political science and government; psychology; religious education; religious studies; science teacher education; secondary education; social studies teacher education; sociology; Spanish.

Academics *Calendar:* semesters. *Degrees:* bachelor's, master's, doctoral, and postbachelor's certificates. *Special study options:* advanced placement credit, double majors, independent study, internships, off-campus study, services for LD students, student-designed majors, study abroad, summer session for credit. *ROTC:* Army (b). *Unusual degree programs:* 3-2 engineering with University of Illinois, Case Western Reserve University, Washington University in St. Louis, Illinois Institute of Technology; nursing with Emory University, Johns Hopkins University, Rush University, Vanderbilt University.

Computers on Campus 125 computers/terminals and 4,200 ports are available on campus for general student use. Students can access the following: campus intranet, computer help desk, free student e-mail accounts, online (class) grades, online (class) registration, online (class) schedules, financial information, degree requirements evaluation. Campuswide network is available. 100% of college-owned or -operated housing units are wired for high-speed Internet access. Wireless service is available via computer centers, computer labs, dorm rooms, learning centers, libraries, student centers.

Student Life *Housing:* on-campus residence required through senior year. *Options:* men-only, women-only, cooperative, disabled students. Campus housing is university owned. Freshman campus housing is guaranteed. *Activities and organizations:* drama/theater group, student-run newspaper, radio and television station, choral group, intramurals, Discipleship small groups, Christian Service Council, Orientation Committee, Resident Assistant Staff. *Campus security:* 24-hour emergency response devices and patrols, student patrols, late-night transport/escort service, controlled dormitory access. *Student services:* health clinic, personal/psychological counseling.

Athletics Member NCAA. All Division III. *Intercollegiate sports:* baseball M, basketball M/W, cheerleading M (c)/W (c), crew M (c)/W (c), cross-country running M/W, football M, golf M/W, ice hockey M (c), lacrosse M (c)/W (c), soccer M/W, softball W, swimming and diving M/W, tennis M/W, track and field M/W, volleyball M (c)/W, water polo W, wrestling M. *Intramural sports:* badminton M/W, basketball M/W, bowling M/W, football M/W, soccer M/W, softball M/W, tennis M/W, ultimate Frisbee M/W, volleyball M/W, water polo M/W.

Standardized Tests *Required:* SAT or ACT (for admission).

Costs (2007–08) *Comprehensive fee:* $30,982 includes full-time tuition ($23,730) and room and board ($7252). Part-time tuition: $989 per credit hour. Part-time tuition and fees vary according to course load. *College room only:* $4288. Room and board charges vary according to board plan and housing facility. *Payment plans:* installment, deferred payment. *Waivers:* employees or children of employees.

Financial Aid Of all full-time matriculated undergraduates who enrolled in 2007, 1,658 applied for aid, 1,117 were judged to have need, 341 had their need fully met. In 2007, 435 non-need-based awards were made. *Average percent of need met:* 84%. *Average financial aid package:* $20,591. *Average need-based loan:* $5611. *Average need-based gift aid:* $14,081. *Average non-need-based aid:* $4577. *Average indebtedness upon graduation:* $20,087.

Applying *Options:* electronic application, early action. *Application fee:* $50. *Required:* essay or personal statement, high school transcript, 2 letters of recommendation. *Recommended:* interview. *Application deadlines:* 1/10 (freshmen), 3/1 (transfers), 11/1 (early action). *Notification:* 4/1 (freshmen), 4/1 (transfers), 12/31 (early action).

Freshman Application Contact Ms. Shawn Leftwich, Director of Admissions, Wheaton College, 501 College Avenue, Wheaton, IL 60187. *Phone:* 630-752-5011. *Toll-free phone:* 800-222-2419. *Fax:* 630-752-5285. *E-mail:* admissions@wheaton.edu.

See page 872 for the College Close-Up.

ARGOSY UNIVERSITY

ARGOSY UNIVERSITY

The University

Argosy University is a leading institution offering a variety of degree programs that focus on the human side of success alongside professional competence. For students looking for a more personal approach to education, Argosy University may just be the answer. With forty-eight graduate and undergraduate programs, across nineteen campuses and twelve states, Argosy University emphasizes interpersonal skills as well as academic learning. All of its programs are taught by practicing professionals who bring real-world experience into the classroom. So students graduate with both a solid foundation of knowledge and the power to put it to work. To accommodate busy working adults, many programs at Argosy University are structured flexibly—with both campus and online learning and evening, weekend, and daytime classes. There is also a wide range of financial aid options for students who qualify.

Argosy University is a private institution of higher education dedicated to providing high-quality professional education programs at the doctoral, master's, bachelor's, and associate degree levels as well as continuing education to individuals who seek to advance their professional and personal lives. The University emphasizes programs in the behavioral sciences (psychology and counseling), business, education, and the health-care professions. A limited number of preprofessional programs and general education offerings are provided to permit students to prepare for entry into these professional fields. The programs of Argosy University are designed to instill the knowledge, skills, and ethical values of professional practice and to foster values of social responsibility in a supportive, learning-centered environment of mutual respect and professional excellence.

With nineteen campuses nationwide, Argosy University provides students with a network of resources found at larger universities, including a career resources office, an academic resources center, and extensive information access for research. The University's innovative programs feature dynamic, relevant, and practical curricula delivered in flexible class formats. Students enjoy scheduling options that make it easier to fit school into their busy lives. They can choose from day and evening courses, on campus or online. Many students find a combination of both to be an ideal way of continuing their education while meeting family and professional demands.

Most students are full-time working professionals who live within driving distance of the campus. The University does not offer or operate student housing.

Argosy University is accredited by The Higher Learning Commission of the North Central Association (30 North LaSalle Street, Suite 2400, Chicago, Illinois 60602; 800-621-7440; http://ncahlc.org).

Location

Argosy University operates nineteen locations across the U.S. and offers a variety of degree programs online (http://www.argosy.edu). Campus locations include the following:

Atlanta, 980 Hammond Drive, Suite 100, Atlanta, Georgia 30328; phone: 770-671-1200 or 888-671-4777 (toll-free)

Chicago, 225 North Michigan Avenue, Suite 1300, Chicago, Illinois 60601; phone: 312-777-7600 or 800-626-4123 (toll-free)

Dallas, 8080 Park Lane, Suite 400A, Dallas, Texas 75231; phone: 214-890-9900 or 866-954-9900 (toll-free)

Denver, 1200 Lincoln Street, Denver, Colorado 80203; phone: 303-248-2700 or 866-431-5981 (toll-free)

Hawai'i, 400 ASB Tower, 1001 Bishop Street, Honolulu, Hawaii 96813; phone: 808-536-5555 or 888-323-2777 (toll-free)

Inland Empire, 636 East Brier Drive, Suite 235, San Bernardino, California 92408; phone: 909-915-3800 or 866-217-9075 (toll-free)

Nashville, 100 Centerview Drive, Suite 225, Nashville, Tennessee 37214; phone: 615-525-2800 or 866-833-6598 (toll-free)

Orange County, 3501 West Sunflower Avenue, Suite 110, Santa Ana, California 92704; phone: 714-338-6200 or 800-716-9598 (toll-free)

Phoenix, 2233 West Dunlap Avenue, Phoenix, Arizona 85021; phone: 602-216-2600 or 866-216-2777 (toll-free)

Salt Lake City, 121 West Election Road, Suite 300, Draper, Utah 84020; phone: 888-639-4756 (toll-free)

San Diego, 7650 Mission Valley Road, San Diego, California 92108; phone: 858-598-1900 or 866-505-0333 (toll-free)

San Francisco Bay Area, 1005 Atlantic Avenue, Alameda, California 94501; phone: 510-217-4700 or 866-215-2777 (toll-free)

Santa Monica, 2950 31st Street, Santa Monica, California 90405; phone: 310-866-4000 or 866-505-0332 (toll-free)

Sarasota, 5250 17th Street, Sarasota, Florida 34235; phone: 941-379-0404 or 800-331-5995 (toll-free)

Schaumburg, 999 North Plaza Drive, Suite 111, Schaumburg, Illinois 60173-5403; phone: 847-969-4900 or 866-290-2777 (toll-free)

Seattle, 2601-A Elliott Avenue, Seattle, Washington 98121; phone: 206-283-4500 or 888-283-2777 (toll-free)

Tampa, Parkside at Tampa Bay Park, 4401 North Hines Avenue, Suite 150, Tampa, Florida 33614; phone: 813-393-5290 or 800-850-6488 (toll-free)

Twin Cities, 1515 Central Parkway, Eagan, Minnesota 55121; phone: 651-846-2882 or 888-844-2004 (toll-free)

Washington DC, 1550 Wilson Boulevard, Suite 600, Arlington, Virginia 22209; phone: 703-526-5800 or 866-703-2777 (toll-free)

Majors and Degrees

Argosy University's College of Business offers a Bachelor of Science (B.S.) in Business Administration program. Argosy University's College of Psychology and Behavioral Sciences offers the Bachelor of Arts (B.A.) in Psychology degree program.

Academic Programs

The B.S. in Business Administration program prepares students for entry- to mid-level positions within the public or private sector. The curriculum is structured to help students develop competencies in oral and written communication, leadership, team skills, solutions-focused learning, and the analysis and execution of solutions in various business situations. Students may choose one of five optional concentrations: customized professional concentration, finance, health-care management, international business, or marketing.

The B.A. in Psychology program is designed to help students begin human services careers in such capacities as entry-level counselor, case manager, or human resources administrator and

in management and business services roles. The program also lays the foundation for graduate study. Students may choose an optional concentration from the following three options: criminal justice, organizational psychology, or substance abuse. This dynamic program is built around a flexible class approach.

Argosy University's bachelor's degree programs are open to students and working professionals with no college experience, plus those who have already earned college credit at a community college, junior college, or other university.

Academic Facilities

Argosy University libraries provide curriculum support and educational resources including current text materials, diagnostic training documents, reference materials and databases, journals and dissertations, and major and current titles in program areas. There is an online public-access catalog of library resources available throughout the Argosy University system. Students enjoy full remote access to their campus library database, enabling them to study and conduct research at home. Academic databases offer dissertation abstracts, academic journals, and professional periodicals. All library computers are Internet accessible. Software applications include Word, Excel, PowerPoint, SPSS, and various test-scoring programs.

Costs

Tuition varies by program. Students should contact the Argosy University campus of their choice for tuition information.

Financial Aid

A wide range of financial aid options is available to students who qualify. Argosy University offers access to federal and state aid programs, merit-based awards, grants, loans, and a work-study program. As a first step, students should complete the Free Application for Federal Student Aid (FAFSA). Prospective students can apply electronically at http://www.fafsa.ed.gov or at the campus. To receive consideration for financial aid and ensure timely receipt of funds, it is best to submit an application promptly.

Faculty

The Argosy University faculty is composed of working professionals who have a passion to help students succeed. Members bring real-world experience and the latest practice innovations to the academic setting. The diverse faculty is widely recognized for contributions to the field. Most hold doctoral degrees. They provide a substantive education that combines comprehensive knowledge with critical skills and practical workplace relevance. Above all, faculty members are committed to their students' personal and professional development.

Student Government

Argosy University campuses offer unique opportunities for student involvement beyond individual programs of study. Most faculty committees include a student representative. In addition, a student group meets with faculty members and administrators regularly to discuss pertinent campus-related issues.

Admission Requirements

Admission requirements differ depending on the number of college credits completed prior to application.

Students who have earned 12 or fewer semester college credits must provide proof of high school graduation or GED and meet one of the following conditions for admission: ACT composite score of 18 or above, or a combined math and verbal SAT score of 870, or minimum ACCUPLACER scores of 86 in sentence skills and 53 in algebra. Applicants who do not meet any of the above conditions for admission will be admitted with academic support if they provide proof of high school graduation or GED and meet one of the following: ACT composite score of 14 to 17, or a combined math and verbal SAT score of 660 to 869, or minimum ACCUPLACER scores of 54 in sentence skills and 36 in arithmetic.

Applicants who have earned 13 or more semester college credits must provide proof of high school graduation or GED and meet one of the following conditions for admission: cumulative college GPA of 2.0 or above or minimum ACCUPLACER scores of 86 for sentence skills and 53 in algebra. Students who do not meet either of the above criteria will be admitted with academic support if they provide proof of high school graduation or GED and meet the following condition: minimum ACCUPLACER scores of 54 in reading and 36 in arithmetic.

Students admitted with academic support are limited to 12 credit hours of study during their first semester (6 credit hours per session). Students admitted with academic support will be required to complete developmental English and/or math courses unless they meet the following conditions: Writing Review (ENG099)—must meet one of the following: a minimum ACCUPLACER score of 86 in sentence skills, or a minimum ACT verbal score of 18, or a minimum SAT verbal score of 425, or completion of a college-level English composition course with a grade of C or above; Mathematics Review I (MAT096)—must meet one of the following: a minimum ACCUPLACER score of 53 in algebra, or a minimum ACT math score of 18, or a minimum SAT math score of 440, or completion of a college-level English composition course with a grade of C or above.

Other admission requirements may include credit hours of qualified transfer credit with a grade of C- or better from a regionally accredited institution or a nationally accredited institution approved and documented by the faculty and dean of the College of Business, or the College of Professional Psychology, at Argosy University or completion of an Associate of Arts or Associate of Science degree from a regionally accredited institution. A maximum of 78 lower-division or 90 total credit hours may be transferred. A minimum written TOEFL score of 500 (paper-based test), 173 (computer-based test), or 61 (Internet-based test) is required for all applicants whose native language is not English or who have not graduated from an institution in which English is the language of instruction.

Official transcripts from approved postsecondary institutions must include a minimum grade point average of 2.0 (on a scale of 4.0) for all academic work completed. Exceptions may be made for extenuating circumstances. All applications must include a completed application form, proof of high school graduation or successful completion of the GED test, official postsecondary transcripts, and a nonrefundable (except in California) application fee. Additional materials are required prior to matriculation. Some programs have additional application requirements or include exceptions to admission requirements. An admissions representative can provide further information.

Application and Information

Argosy University accepts students on a rolling admissions basis year-round, depending on availability of required courses. Applications for admission are available online at http://www.argosy.edu or by contacting one of the campus locations.

Argosy University
205 North Michigan Avenue, Suite 1300
Chicago, Illinois 60601-2250

Phone: 312-899-9900
800-377-0617 (toll-free)
E-mail: auadmissions@argosy.edu
Web site: http://www.argosy.edu

AURORA UNIVERSITY
AURORA, ILLINOIS

The University

Aurora University was founded in 1893. The school has grown substantially over the years and has taken on many new challenges. In 1938, it was one of the first small colleges to achieve regional accreditation. In 1947, the college's evening program was instituted—one of the nation's first adult education programs at a liberal arts college. In 1985, Aurora College was reorganized as Aurora University, reflecting both the increased size of the institution and the needs associated with its many new programs. In addition to the College of Arts and Sciences, the University comprises the College of Education and the College of Professional Studies (social work, health and physical education, nursing, and business). Today, the University enrolls 4,000 students in more than forty undergraduate programs and eleven graduate degree programs in business, social work, and education. An Ed.D. degree is offered in educational leadership. Degree programs are also offered on the shores of Geneva Lake in Williams Bay, Wisconsin. Degree programs include the B.S. in communication, marketing, business leadership, and recreation administration; the RN to B.S.N.; the Master of Arts in Teaching; the M.A. in reading instruction; the M.S. in recreation administration; the M.B.A.; a weekend M.S.W. program; and the Ed.D degree.

The University's student body includes 600 on-campus, traditional-age students; 1,400 undergraduate commuters; 1,800 graduate students; and more than 300 students at the George Williams College campus. The majority of Aurora's students come from the upper-Midwest region, but twenty states are also represented.

Social life is based on campus, and most activities are campus-wide. Aurora has more than sixty musical, literary, religious, social, and service clubs and organizations. There are also opportunities to be involved in theater and the highly regarded University Chorale. Aurora University has a long history of excellence in both intercollegiate and intramural athletics. A member of the NCAA Division III, Aurora fields intercollegiate teams in baseball, basketball, cross-country, football, golf, indoor track, soccer, softball, tennis, track, and volleyball, often with championship results.

Aurora University is accredited at the bachelor's, master's, and doctoral degree levels by the Higher Learning Commission of the North Central Association of Colleges and Schools, and its programs are accredited by the Commission on Collegiate Nursing Education, National League for Nursing Accrediting Commission, Illinois Department of Professional Regulation, Council on Social Work Education, National Recreation and Park Association/American Association of Leisure and Recreation, and Association of Collegiate Business Schools and Programs.

Location

Aurora University is located in an attractive residential neighborhood on the southwest side of Aurora, Illinois, which has a population of more than 162,000 and is the state's second-largest city. The 30-acre main campus is located only minutes from the Illinois Research and Development Corridor, the site of dozens of nationally and internationally based businesses and industries. Located within an hour's drive or train ride is Chicago, one of the most vibrant cities in the world.

Majors and Degrees

The Bachelor of Arts degree is awarded in accounting, art, biology, business administration, communication (media studies and professional practice), computer science, criminal justice, elementary education, English, history, management and innovation, management information technology, marketing, physical education (K–12 teacher certification), political science, professional selling and sales management, psychology, religion, sociology, special education, Spanish, and theater. The Bachelor of Science degree is awarded in accounting, biology, business administration, computer science, health science (allied health, predentistry, premedicine, pre–physical therapy, and pre-veterinary studies), management and innovation, management information technology, marketing, mathematics, and physical education (athletic training and fitness and health promotion). The Bachelor of Science in Nursing and the Bachelor of Science in social work are also offered. The University offers supplemental majors in prelaw and secondary education as well as the YMCA Senior Director Certificate Program.

Academic Programs

Aurora University prides itself on its first-year program, which ensures that entering students make a successful transition to college. The only private college in Illinois selected to be part of a national project to create a model of excellence for the first college year, Aurora University recognizes the unique needs of freshmen.

Aurora University offers academic programs combining a liberal arts foundation with majors emphasizing career preparation and selected concentrations. Graduates are educated to be purposeful, ethical, and proficient—equipped for worthwhile careers and productive lives and for venturing forth into a changing world.

To earn a bachelor's degree, students are required to fulfill the general degree requirements of the University and the major requirements for an approved major; complete at least 120 semester hours with a GPA of at least 2.0 on a 4.0 scale, including at least 52 semester hours at a senior college; and complete at least 30 semester hours, including the last 24 for the degree and at least 18 semester hours in the major, at Aurora University.

Entering freshmen who qualify and are highly motivated are invited to join the Honors Program. Students with an ACT of 25 and above and a high school GPA of 3.5 on a 4.0 scale are invited to join. Those in the program participate in innovative seminars, service learning, advanced course work, and other special and cultural events.

Aurora University accepts credits earned through the CLEP, DANTES, Excelsior College Examinations, and NLN Mobility testing programs. In addition, credit based on portfolio assessment is available to students who have significant prior learning from career experience or individual study.

The University observes a semester calendar (two 16-week semesters), with classes beginning in late August and concluding in early May. A three-week May Term offers exciting course work, including international study /travel and unique intensive courses.

Off-Campus Programs

Aurora University offers travel-study programs abroad and within the United States. Recent travel/study destinations included Paris, London, Italy, South Africa, Mexico, and Hungary. The University also has off-campus classes in various locations in Illinois and Wisconsin and several degree programs at the University's George Williams campus near Lake Geneva, Wisconsin.

Academic Facilities

The major buildings at Aurora are marked by the distinctive, red-tiled roofs specified by Charles Eckhart in his donation for the original campus. Dunham Hall houses state-of-the-art computer facilities as well as the Schingoethe Center for Native American Cultures. The newest classroom building houses the Institute for Collaboration, which brings together education, health and human services, business, and government to facilitate the development of collaborative leadership. Other facilities include the fully equipped Perry Theatre, the Parolini Fine Arts Center, science labs, a flora-fauna complex, and the College Commons. Music practice rooms, piano labs, and a spacious art studio are housed in the Parolini Center. The Charles B. Phillips Library has more than 99,000 volumes, 7,000 multimedia materials, and approximately 518 current periodical subscriptions. In addition, the library provides access to approximately 3,700 journals in electronic full text and interfaces with sixty-four other universities.

Costs

Tuition for the 2007–08 school year is $16,750 for full-time students (24–34 semester hours per year), and yearly room and board costs average $6920.

Financial Aid

Aurora University's financial aid program has been designed to make it possible for any academically qualified student to afford the benefits of a private education. The University works with students to determine the amount of their costs and to identify all available resources so students can meet these expenses. Financial aid is awarded based on financial need as reported on the FAFSA. In addition to need-based financial aid, Aurora University offers academic scholarships, including the Board of Trustees Scholarship, Crimi Scholarship, Deans' Scholarship, Solon B. Cousins Scholarship, Aurora University Opportunity Grant, and transfer scholarships.

Faculty

The favorable student-faculty ratio of 16:1 ensures that students receive plenty of individual attention in class. Instructors also make time for students outside of class, acting as mentors and advisers, and they are eager to answer questions and join students in campus activities.

Student Government

The student body is represented by the AUSA (Aurora University Student Association), which provides funding for sixty-three student groups on campus. Students are also active members of committees ranging from faculty searches to ad hoc task forces and are provided with certain voting privileges.

Admission Requirements

The Aurora University Committee on Admission considers the complete record of a candidate for admission. The University seeks qualified students from varied geographical, cultural, economic, racial, and religious backgrounds. Admission requirements include an ACT of 20 or above, a high school GPA of 2.5 or above, and a college-preparatory curriculum. Two general qualities are considered in each candidate: academic ability, enabling the student to benefit from a high-quality academic program, and a diversity of talents and interests that can contribute to making the campus community a better and more interesting place for learning. An application for admission to Aurora University is considered on the basis of the academic ability, achievements, activities, and motivation of the student. Candidates for the Honors Program must have an ACT of 25 or higher and a high school GPA of at least 3.5 on a 4.0 scale. Transfer students with fewer than 30 semester hours of credit should apply in the same manner as freshman applicants. Transfer students with more than 15 semester hours may be admitted to Aurora University if they have a transferable overall GPA of 2.5 or higher. Aurora accepts a maximum of 90 semester hours of transfer credits from a combination of two- and four-year schools. A maximum of 68 semester hours may be transferred from two-year schools. For further information, students should contact a transfer counselor in the Office of Admission and Financial Aid.

Application and Information

To apply for admission to Aurora University, the following items should be sent to the Office of Admission and Financial Aid: a completed application form, an official transcript from the guidance counselor, and official ACT or SAT scores. Transfer students should submit official transcripts from each college or university attended, along with the completed application.

For applications and further information, students may contact:

Office of Admission and Financial Aid
Aurora University
347 South Gladstone Avenue
Aurora, Illinois 60506
Phone: 630-844-5533
800-742-5281 (toll-free)
E-mail: admission@aurora.edu
Web site: http://www.aurora.edu

A view of Eckhart Hall at Aurora University in Aurora, Illinois.

BENEDICTINE UNIVERSITY

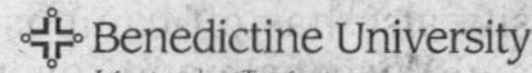

LISLE, ILLINOIS

The University

Benedictine University was founded in 1887 as St. Procopius College. One hundred twenty-one years later, the University remains committed to providing a high-quality, Catholic, liberal education for men and women. The undergraduate enrollment is nearly 3,000 students. The student body comprises students of diverse ages, religions, races, and national origins. Twenty-five percent of the full-time students reside on campus.

Benedictine University is situated on a rolling, tree-covered 108-acre campus of twenty major buildings with air-conditioned classrooms and modern, well-equipped laboratories. A student athletic center features three full-size basketball courts, a competition-size swimming pool, three tennis courts, and training facilities. All of the residence halls are comfortable and spacious and have access to the Internet. On-campus apartments offer one-, two-, and four-bedroom residences. Other features include a scenic lake; a student center with dining halls, lounges, a chapel, a bookstore, and meeting rooms; and the Village of Lisle–Benedictine University Sports Complex, featuring a lighted multipurpose football/soccer stadium with a nine-lane track and lighted baseball and softball fields.

Benedictine University is highly competitive in varsity sports with a total of nineteen sports. Men's varsity sports are baseball, basketball, cross-country, football, golf, soccer, swimming and diving, and track and field (indoor and outdoor). Women's varsity sports are basketball, cross-country, golf, soccer, softball, swimming and diving, tennis, track and field (indoor and outdoor), and volleyball. Aside from varsity and intramural athletic programs, forty organizations and clubs exist on campus, including student government, a student newspaper, an orchestra, a jazz group, an African-American Student Union, a Muslim Student Association, the Association of Latin American Students, campus ministry, and various other extracurricular and academic organizations.

Partnerships support the University's growth in the twenty-first century. In 2003, Benedictine and Springfield College in Illinois partnered to bring Benedictine programs and services to the Springfield area, Illinois' state capital. Benedictine partnered in 2004 with Shenyang University of Technology and Shenyang Jianzhu University in China to bring Master of Business Administration and Master of Science in management information systems programs overseas, as demands are high for American business programs. Also in 2004, the University partnered with the Village of Lisle in the construction of the Village of Lisle-Benedictine University Sports Complex, a multipurpose facility featuring lighted athletic fields with a nine-lane track. Benedictine opened the Moser Center in Naperville in 2006 to meet the needs of adult students and area businesses.

Benedictine University and Springfield College in Illinois became permanent partners in 2003 to bring Benedictine programs and services to the Springfield area, Illinois' state capital. Benedictine recently opened the Moser Center in nearby Naperville to meet the needs of adult students and area businesses.

At Benedictine University, the environment is strengthened by success, not size. Renowned faculty members know students by name and care as much about each student's progress as they do about their own research. Those personal relationships have produced superb results. Benedictine graduates are accepted into some of the most prestigious graduate programs in the country. Approximately two thirds of Benedictine graduates who apply to medical school are accepted, in addition to similar ratios for other health-related professional schools (optometry, pharmacy, physical therapy, and podiatry). The liberal arts curriculum has helped place the University among some of the finest small private schools in the nation.

U.S. News & World Report's 2008 rankings listed Benedictine University as a Top School in the Midwest and sixth in Illinois for campus diversity.

The graduate division offers the following graduate degrees in the business, education, and health areas: the Doctor of Philosophy (Ph.D.) in organization development; the Doctor of Education (Ed.D.) in higher education and organizational change; the Master of Business Administration (M.B.A.); the Master of Arts in Education (M.A.Ed.); the Master of Education (M.Ed.); the Master of Science (M.S.) in accountancy, clinical psychology, clinical exercise physiology, management and organizational behavior, management information systems, nutrition and wellness, and science content and process; and the Master of Public Health (M.P.H.).

Adult undergraduate accelerated programs, taught by distinguished faculty members, are available in the following areas: accounting (B.B.A.), business and economics (B.A.), computer information systems (B.S.), computer science (B.S.), finance (B.A.), health administration (B.B.A.), management (B.A.M.), management and organizational behavior (B.B.A.), marketing (B.A.), nursing and health (B.S.), organizational leadership (B.A.), and psychology (B.A.). The University also offers an Associate of Arts in business administration in an accelerated format.

Location

Benedictine University is 25 miles west of Chicago, in suburban Lisle near Naperville, and is easily accessible from the city and suburbs via the interstate highway system. Metra trains stop in Lisle, and O'Hare International Airport is only a 30-minute drive. In addition to the many social and cultural offerings of the Chicago metropolitan area, the University enjoys the proximity and use of Argonne National Laboratory, Fermi National Accelerator Laboratory, the Morton Arboretum, a ski hill, a riding stable, and several golf courses. The University's location in the high-tech East-West Tollway corridor gives students opportunities for internships and employment.

Majors and Degrees

Benedictine University offers programs leading to the Bachelor of Arts, Bachelor of Business Administration, Bachelor of Science, and Bachelor of Fine Arts. Programs are offered in accounting, bilingual journalism, biochemistry/molecular biology, biology, business and economics (concentration in sports management), chemistry, clinical laboratory science, communication arts (concentration in sports communication), computer information systems, computer science, diagnostic medical sonography, economics, elementary education, engineering science, English language and literature, environmental science, finance, fine arts, global studies, health science, history, international business and economics, international studies (concentration in business and political science), management and organizational behavior, marketing, mathematics (concentration in actuarial science), music (concentration in chamber music), nuclear medicine technology, nutrition (concentration in dietetics), philosophy, physics (concentration in biological physics, engineering physics and physics), political science (concentration in prelaw), prepharmacy, preprofessional health programs (concentration in chiropractic, dentistry, medicine, occupational therapy, optometry, physical therapy, podiatry, and veterinary medicine), psychology, radiation therapy, secondary education, social science, sociology (concentration in criminal justice), Spanish, special education, studio art, and writing and publishing.

In many areas of study, students may opt for a double major. Preprofessional health programs include chiropractic, dentistry, medicine, occupational therapy, optometry, physical therapy, podiatry, and veterinary medicine. Combined professional programs are available with cooperating institutions in clinical laboratory science, nuclear medicine technology, and engineering. A joint engineering program is offered with the Illinois Institute of Technology. A registered nurse may earn a Bachelor of Science degree in nursing. Teacher certification is available in the following majors: biology, business and economics, chemistry, English language and literature, mathematics, physics, social science, and Spanish.

Academic Programs

For graduation, a student must earn at least 120 semester hours, 55 of which must be completed at a four-year regionally accredited college. At least the final 45 semester hours must be completed at Benedictine University. The University makes selective exceptions to the normal academic residency requirement of 45 semester hours for adults who are eligible for the Degree Completion Program. Eligibility is limited to those who have nearly completed their undergraduate studies but, for reasons of employment, career change, or family situation, found it necessary to interrupt their studies.

The Second Major Program is designed for people who already have a degree in one area and would like to gain expertise in another. This program allows the student to concentrate on courses that fulfill the requirements of a second major. The student receives a certificate upon completion.

Each year, a select number of talented and motivated prospective students are invited to participate in the Scholars Program. The program is designed to enhance the college experience by developing students' international awareness and strengthening their leadership ability.

Off-Campus Programs

Benedictine University is a member of a three-school consortium in the west suburban Chicago area through which students are able to take classes at the other member colleges. Study abroad and internships abroad are encouraged to complement a liberal education.

Academic Facilities

The Kindlon Hall of Learning and the Birck Hall of Science bring science and technology to new levels. The Birck Hall of Science houses state-of-the art computer labs, specialized science labs, a research center, and the Jurica Nature Museum.

The Kindlon Hall of Learning houses computer labs, classrooms, multimedia labs, offices, and student lounges. It is also home to the Benedictine Library, which houses more than 120,000 volumes and can be found in the building's impressive four-story tower. The library is also equipped with eleven group study rooms, a computer lab, and an instruction room.

Benedictine University has distance education classrooms that provide students with the capability to interact globally with other colleges and universities in a classroom setting. Scholl Hall houses classrooms and faculty and administrative offices.

Costs

The cost of tuition for the 2007–08 academic year was $20,800. The average cost of room and board was $6953. Mandatory fees totaled $510 and included health, technology, and student activity fees.

Financial Aid

In 2006–07, Benedictine University freshmen received approximately $4.5 million from financial aid sources that included loans, scholarship and grants, tuition remission, and employment opportunities. Ninety-two percent of the freshman class received financial aid. The average package was $14,762. Benedictine University has dedicated more than $8.2 million of the annual budget to providing grants and scholarships to its students. Students who wish to apply for aid must complete the Free Application for Federal Student Aid (FAFSA), the Benedictine University application for financial aid, and the Benedictine University application for admission.

Faculty

The 13:1 student-faculty ratio allows for close interaction between students and faculty members. Of the 94 full-time faculty members, 86 percent hold a Ph.D. or the terminal professional degree in their respective fields. All students are assigned a faculty member as an adviser to help plan programs of study.

Student Government

All full-time enrolled students are automatically members of the student government. The Student Government Association (SGA) is a representative body elected annually by the students to represent their interests. The SGA is responsible for the annual allocation of the student activity fee.

Admission Requirements

The Benedictine University admission philosophy is to select students who are expected to perform successfully in the University's academic programs and become active members of the University community. Typically, Benedictine University's freshman students are in the top third of their high school graduating class, with about 50 percent in the top quarter, and report better-than-average ACT or SAT scores. A minimum of 16 units in academic subjects is required, including 4 units of English, 1 unit of algebra, 1 unit of geometry, 1 unit of history, 1 unit of laboratory science, and 2 units of foreign language. Benedictine University does admit some students who fall below these standards. These applicants receive individual consideration by the Academic Admissions Committee. When appropriate, the committee will place conditions and/or restrictions upon students to help them reach their academic potential.

Students interested in transferring to Benedictine University must have a minimum cumulative average of C (2.0 on a 4.0 scale) or better from all colleges previously attended. Official transcripts from high school and all colleges attended must be submitted directly to the Enrollment Center for evaluation. If fewer than 20 semester hours of transfer credit are submitted, an official high school transcript and SAT or ACT scores are required, and the general admission high school curriculum requirements must also be satisfied. High school information is not required with A.A. or A.S. degrees. Credits transferred from other institutions are evaluated on the basis of their equivalent at Benedictine University. Grades of D are accepted as transfer credit but do not satisfy Benedictine University requirements, which demand a minimum grade of C.

Requests for admission are considered without regard to the applicant's race, religion, gender, age, or disability.

Application and Information

Applications are reviewed on a rolling basis. Students are encouraged to apply for admission at any time after completing their junior year of high school. Transfer students may apply for admission during their last semester or quarter before anticipated transfer to Benedictine University. Earlier applications are encouraged for scholarship and financial aid opportunities.

For further information, students should contact:

Enrollment Center
Benedictine University
5700 College Road
Lisle, Illinois 60532
Phone: 630-829-6300
888-829-6363 (toll-free outside Illinois)
Fax: 630-829-6301
E-mail: admissions@ben.edu
Web site: http://www.ben.edu

The Birck Hall of Science houses science labs, classrooms, offices, a lecture hall, and the Jurica Nature Museum.

BRADLEY UNIVERSITY

PEORIA, ILLINOIS

The University

Bradley University is a four-year, private, independent university in Peoria, Illinois, offering more than 100 academic programs to 6,000 students. Students enjoy extensive resources not available at most small colleges and personal attention not commonly found at large universities. In addition to the traditional liberal arts and sciences, academic programs include business, communications, education, engineering, fine and performing arts, and health sciences. Unique programs include entrepreneurship, multimedia, and a doctoral program in physical therapy.

Located on a 75-acre campus in the heart of Peoria's historic West Bluff neighborhoods, Bradley offers a traditional, residential environment just 1 mile from downtown and 8 miles from the Greater Peoria Regional Airport.

Founded in 1897 by Lydia Moss Bradley, the University has a long and distinguished tradition of academic excellence, a focus on practical skill development through internships and practicums, and a dynamic student life. For her part in establishing this reputation, along with her many other philanthropic and humanitarian achievements, Mrs. Bradley was inducted into the National Women's Hall of Fame.

Bradley's five academic colleges and graduate school are fully accredited by the North Central Association of Colleges and Universities. Students may pursue more than 100 undergraduate academic programs. In addition, the Graduate School offers master's degrees in more than thirty areas of study. Bradley students are encouraged to take advantage of a wealth of internships, co-ops, practicums, and other "real-world" experiences. Bradley's retention, graduation, and placement rates are among the highest in the nation.

In addition to modern academic facilities, there are ten residence halls, which house first-year students as well as upperclassmen; a residential apartment complex for students with junior standing through graduate school; a student center that includes a food court, a cafeteria, and a movie theater; two student cafeterias; and two performing arts facilities.

A 2009 opening is planned for the new student recreation center. The center will include four basketball courts for intramural and recreational games, a championship basketball court, a 1/8-mile running/walking track open to the entire campus population, climbing wall, indoor pool, weight room, and exercise rooms.

Bradley's active cocurricular environment includes more than 220 student organizations, Greek life, a comprehensive student government system, and NCAA Division I athletic programs offering baseball, basketball, cross-country, golf, soccer, and tennis for men and basketball, cross-country, golf, softball, tennis, track, and volleyball for women.

Location

Bradley University is located in Peoria, Illinois, a diverse, metropolitan community of approximately 360,000 residents located along the Illinois River. Peoria is home to several multinational corporations, businesses, and research centers, which offer numerous internships and chances for practicums and cooperative education. The greater Peoria area is the largest metropolitan area in downstate Illinois. In addition, Peoria offers an abundance of fine and performing arts, cultural attractions, shopping, entertainment, and professional sports teams. Both Chicago and St. Louis are less than a 3-hour drive.

Majors and Degrees

The College of Education and Health Sciences awards bachelor's degrees in dietetics, early childhood education, elementary education, family and consumer sciences education, foods and nutrition, general family and consumer sciences, health science (leads to Bradley's doctoral degree in physical therapy), learning behavior specialist studies, learning behavior specialist studies with elementary education, nursing, retail merchandising, secondary education, and special education.

The College of Engineering and Technology awards the Bachelor of Science degree in civil engineering, civil engineering with environmental option, construction, electrical engineering, electrical engineering with computer option, engineering physics, industrial engineering, manufacturing engineering, manufacturing engineering technology (design and systems options are available), mechanical engineering, and mechanical engineering with biomedical option.

The Foster College of Business Administration awards bachelor's degrees in accounting (includes a 3-2 B.S./M.S. option), actuarial science–business, economics, entrepreneurship, finance, international business, management and administration (concentrations in human resource management or legal studies in business), management information systems, and marketing (a concentration in professional selling is available).

Bradley University's College of Liberal Arts and Sciences offers programs in actuarial science–mathematics, administration of criminal justice, biochemistry, biology, cell and molecular biology, chemistry, computer information systems, computer science, economics, English, environmental science, French, German, history, international studies, mathematics, medical technology, philosophy, physics, political science, prelaw, premed, psychology, religious studies, social work, sociology, and Spanish.

The Slane College of Communications and Fine Arts awards bachelor's degrees in art (concentrations in ceramics, drawing, graphic design, painting, photography, printmaking, and sculpture), art education, art history, communication [concentrations in advertising, electronic media (radio/TV), journalism, organizational communication, and public relations], multimedia, music, music business, music composition, music education, music performance, theater performance, and theater production.

Students may select minor areas of study from throughout the five colleges in African American studies, applied ergonomics, art history, Asian studies, biology, business administration, business studies, chemistry, computer science and information systems, decision analysis, economics, English (literature, creative writing, and professional writing), family and consumer sciences, fine arts, French, German, health, history, journalism, Latin American studies, leadership studies, management, management information systems, manufacturing, marketing, mathematics, multimedia, music, philosophy, physics, political science, professional selling, psychology, quality engineering, religious studies, Russian and East European studies, social informatics, sociology, Spanish, studio art, theater arts, Western European studies, and women's studies.

Academic Programs

Although Bradley is in session year-round, the traditional academic year consists of two semesters. All students complete a set of basic general education requirements that blend course work from throughout the University in order to provide each student with a well-rounded education. General education courses include English composition, speech, mathematics, Western and non-Western civilization, literature, art, philosophy, the social sciences, and physical sciences. Considerable freedom is permitted in the selection of this course work. All undergraduate programs are designed so that students can complete their degree in just four years.

Bradley also offers a dynamic honors program for selected recipients of Bradley's prestigious Presidential Scholarship.

The Academic Exploration Program (AEP) allows students who are undecided about a major to receive academic advisement to assist them in declaring a major during their first year of enrollment. There are also special programs for new students who are undecided about which area of study to choose in engineering, business, or communications.

Off-Campus Programs

More than 15 percent of Bradley students take advantage of a study-abroad experience. Bradley has established formal relationships with universities around the world, and students regularly study in Austria, Denmark, Egypt, Germany, Ireland, Mexico, and Spain as well as a variety of other countries. Most academic programs encourage international travel and assist students in scheduling foreign study.

Bradley students also enjoy collaborative learning opportunities in the city of Peoria, including laboratory research at Caterpillar, Inc.; the Downstate Medical Center of Illinois; and the USDA National Center for Agricultural Utilization Research. In addition, the Bradley men's basketball and baseball teams play in professional facilities located in downtown Peoria.

Academic Facilities

The Cullom-Davis Library supports all of the University's programs and offers extensive opportunities for print and computerized research, including online and wireless resources and a Learning Assistance Center. The Michel Student Center hosts conferences, camps, and a variety of entertainers throughout the year. Inside the Caterpillar Global Communications Center, students have access to multimedia classrooms and labs, television and radio studios, video and audio editing suites, and a world-class telecommunication facility. Olin Hall of Science is home to some of the finest undergraduate laboratory facilities in the nation, while Jobst Hall includes robotic and automotive labs and a wind tunnel for engineering students. Several advanced labs throughout the campus provide access to Internet2. Bradley is one of only three private, nondoctoral universities in the nation that is a member of the Internet2 research community. Historic facilities include Westlake Hall, Constance Hall, the Hartmann Center for the Performing Arts, Dingeldine Recital Hall, and the newly renovated Bradley Hall.

Costs

Tuition for the 2007–08 academic year was $21,200. Room and board for the year were $7050. Students also paid a $178 health and activity fee. Books and supplies vary by major and year in school, but they averaged approximately $800.

Financial Aid

The Office of Financial Assistance provides many resources to assist families in managing the cost of a Bradley education. Academic scholarships, which are competitive and renewable, are divided into three categories: the Presidential Scholarship, the Deans Scholarship, and the University Scholarship. Each of these awards is based on a comprehensive review of the student's high school academic record, standardized test scores, cocurricular involvement, letters of recommendation, and personal statement. Bradley also offers scholarships to encourage diversity, talent in the fine and performing arts, and athletic achievement. The University also participates in federally sponsored aid programs, such as the Pell Grant, Work-Study, and Stafford Student Loans. In order to be considered for these sources of financial assistance, students must submit the Free Application for Federal Student Aid (FAFSA).

Faculty

Bradley University is home to more than 375 teaching faculty members. The student-faculty ratio is 14:1, and the average class size is 23 students. Academic, career, and personal counseling is readily available to all students. Bradley University is nationally recognized for the excellence of its faculty members who not only teach undergraduates but also are active researchers and consultants in the academic disciplines.

Student Government

Bradley's Student Senate is the principle body of student participation in University governance and is a visible contributor to the quality of student life on campus. Members of the senate are elected from the general student body and can serve as early as their first year. The Student Senate is an active influence on University policy, and members of the Senate have frequent interaction with University administrators and faculty members.

Admission Requirements

Bradley University encourages applications from qualified students of all backgrounds who feel that they can contribute to the University's diverse intellectual and social environment. Students who have demonstrated past academic achievement and show promise and aptitude for successful performance at Bradley are encouraged to apply for admission. First-time college students are considered for admission based on a review of their high school transcript, standardized test scores (ACT or SAT), cocurricular involvement, letters of recommendation, and a personal statement or essay.

Transfer students in good academic standing are encouraged to apply for admission to Bradley. Transfer students must submit a completed application and official transcripts from all colleges or universities attended. Several majors include additional requirements unique to transfer students.

Application and Information

To be considered for admission, students must submit the Application for Undergraduate Admission during one of three application periods. All freshman applicants must provide an official high school transcript. First-time college students must provide official standardized test scores (ACT or SAT), a personal statement or essay, and at least one letter of recommendation. Bradley strongly encourages students to apply as early as possible during fall of their senior year. The application-review process begins each September. Applications received prior to February 1 are given priority consideration.

An application and additional information may be submitted online or by contacting:

Office of Admissions
Bradley University
1501 West Bradley Avenue
Peoria, Illinois 61625
Phone: 309-677-1000
800-447-6460 (toll-free)
Internet: http://admissions.bradley.edu

COLUMBIA COLLEGE CHICAGO

CHICAGO, ILLINOIS

The College

Columbia College Chicago is the nation's largest and most diverse visual, performing, media, and communication arts college. The foundation of a Columbia education features small class sizes that ensure close interaction with a faculty of working professionals, abundant internship opportunities with major employers in the Chicago and national marketplaces, and outstanding professional facilities that foster learning by doing. All students are encouraged to begin course work in their chosen fields during their freshman year, allowing them four full years in which to master their craft and build professional portfolios, audition tapes, resumes, and clip books. The College provides a strong liberal arts background for the developing artist or communicator and supports student employment goals through a full range of career services.

Columbia's enrollment of more than 12,000 students is drawn from Chicago and its suburbs, the Midwest, across the United States, and more than forty-six other countries. The student body is almost equally divided between men and women. Creative students who enjoy a supportive but challenging environment thrive at Columbia.

Columbia College Chicago's six residence halls extend the supportive philosophy of the College. There are a variety of available housing options with a variety of amenities that may include: computer and study rooms, drawing and painting studio space, music practice space, fitness rooms, an indoor heated pool, lake views, and a laundry room. Apartments, suites, and rooms are fully furnished. All facilities are conveniently located steps from the main campus buildings and close to public transportation, all in the heart of downtown Chicago. Students have access to services such as a student health center, counseling, and a broad host of artistic and academic events. Columbia College students are immersed in a creative environment both in and out of the classroom.

Outside the classroom, students participate in activities that include the College's award-winning student newspaper, radio station, electronic newsletter, two student magazines, cable television soap opera, three theaters, dance center, photography and art museums, and film and video festival. Many of the more than 75 student clubs on campus are linked to an academic discipline and offer opportunities to expand social and professional networking experiences. Several gallery/café environments allow students to relax or study between classes. These centers feature a variety of activities, including art exhibits, film screenings, lectures, and live performances of music, comedy, readings, or dance.

At the graduate level, Columbia awards the Master of Arts (M.A.) in creative writing and writing instruction, dance/movement therapy and counseling (as well as the Graduate Laban Certificate in Movement Analysis, GLCMA), interdisciplinary arts, and journalism. The College awards the Master of Fine Arts (M.F.A.) in architectural studies, creative writing-fiction, creative writing-poetry, creative writing and writing instruction, film and video, interdisciplinary arts and media, interdisciplinary book and paper arts, interior architecture, music composition for the screen, and photography. The Master of Arts in Teaching (M.A.T.) is offered in art education and elementary education (K–9). The Master of Art Management (M.A.M.) is offered in arts entrepreneurship and small business management, arts in youth and community development (AYCD), media management, music business, performing arts management, and visual arts management.

Location

Columbia's campus is set in Chicago's dynamic South Loop neighborhood, across from Grant Park and Lake Michigan. Close to the Art Institute, Navy Pier, the Adler Planetarium, the Field Museum, the Chicago Symphony, and several other colleges and universities. Columbia's faculty members and students utilize the city of Chicago as a social, educational, and professional resource. Convenient public transportation makes all cultural and educational opportunities easily accessible.

Majors and Degrees

Columbia College grants the Bachelor of Arts (B.A.) and the Bachelor of Fine Arts (B.F.A.) degrees and the Bachelor of Music (B.M.) degree in composition.

The School of Fine and Performing Arts offers majors in art and design (advertising art direction, art history, fashion design, fine arts, graphic design, illustration, interior architecture, and product design); arts, entertainment, and media management (small business/arts entrepreneurship, fashion/retail merchandising, media management, music business, performing arts management, sports management, and visual arts management); dance; fiction writing; music (composition; contemporary, urban, and popular music; instrumental jazz; instrumental performance; music composition; vocal jazz; and vocal performance); photography; and theater (acting, directing, musical theater performance, technical theater, and theater design).

The School of Media Arts offers majors in audio arts and acoustics (acoustics, audio for visual media, sound contracting, and sound reinforcement), film and video (alternative forms, audio for visual media, cinematography, computer animation, critical studies, directing, documentary, editing, producing, screenwriting, and traditional animation), game design, interactive arts and media, interdisciplinary (self-designed major), journalism (broadcast, magazine writing and editing, news reporting and writing, and reporting on health, science, and the environment), marketing communication (advertising, creative sports marketing, marketing, and public relations), radio (business, broadcast journalism, and talent/production), and television (broadcast journalism, directing/production, effects/postproduction, interactive television, and writing/producing).

The School of Liberal Arts and Sciences offers majors in American Sign Language–English interpretation, cultural studies, early childhood education, nonfiction, and poetry.

Academic Programs

Columbia supports creative and integrated approaches to education and encourages interdisciplinary study. The B.A. degree is awarded to students who successfully complete 120 semester hours, and the B.F.A. degree is awarded to students who successfully complete 128 semester hours of study in designated programs. Of the required 120 hours toward the completion of the B.A., 48 (36 for B.F.A. candidates) are distributed among courses in the humanities and literature, science and mathematics, English composition, oral communications, social sciences, and computer applications.

The College continues to expand its extensive internship program. Columbia's location allows students to intern with major employers in Chicago. Chicago provides professional settings, classrooms, and internship opportunities for Columbia students.

Columbia College Chicago's Portfolio Center is uniquely geared to provide students with professional-grade portfolio development. The Portfolio Center links industry professionals and alumni with current students through workshops, portfolio development sessions, and networking events. The center also maintains an online Portfolio Archive that serves as an invaluable resource and inspiration for students.

Off-Campus Programs

Columbia has an affiliation agreement with the American Institute for Foreign Study, which enables students to participate in study-abroad programs in numerous countries. Columbia also sponsors and participates in a variety of its own study-abroad programs through individual academic departments. These programs include semesters spent through the Cultural Studies department at the University of East London, a semester exchange with students of the University of East London and Newham Sixth Form College through the Theater Department, and a semester's trip of study to Florence through the Art and Design department—just to name a few. Columbia also offers a number of professional training programs off campus but still within the United States. Comedy studies is a full semester's worth of immersive study in comedic literature, history, writing, and performance under the direction of the experts in comedy at Chicago's

Second City. Open to all Columbia students, the Semester in Los Angeles program is a five-week immersion program in which the student maintains full-time status while gaining invaluable real-world experience. Located in Bungalow 25 on the CBS Studio Lot in Culver City, Columbia is the only institution of higher learning to be permanently located on a studio lot. Students are given lot ID badges and enter the gates of the lot every day, just like working producers, directors, stars, and craft personnel.

Academic Facilities

Columbia College consists of nineteen campus buildings that are located primarily in the historic South Loop neighborhood of downtown Chicago. Advanced facilities for radio, television, art, computer graphics, photography, interactive arts and media, fashion design, and film are state-of-the-industry and include professionally equipped color and black-and-white darkrooms, digital imaging computer facilities, photography and film stages, film and video editing suites, and studios for painting, drawing, and 3-D design. The campus also includes the Museum of Contemporary Photography, one of only a few such facilities in the United States, and the Audio Technology Center, a recording production and research facility. In addition, Columbia has extensive computer facilities that are used by basic computer classes as well as dedicated computer facilities that are utilized by the departments. The centers for dance, music, and theater are separate but conveniently located and are designed for their specific performance needs, including individual and group rehearsal and specialized performance spaces.

The College's 200,000-volume library and instructional service center provides comprehensive information and study facilities. Reading/study rooms and special audiovisual equipment are available for use in individual projects and research. As a member of a statewide online computer catalog and resource-sharing network, Columbia's library provides students with access to the resources of forty-five academic institutions in Illinois, effectively creating an information base of several million volumes. The library also houses special collections, such as the George S. Lurie Memorial Collection of books and resource materials on art, photography, and film; the Black Music Resource Center of books and sound recordings; the Screenwriters' Collection of film and television manuscripts; the History of Photography microfilm collection of books and periodicals; and a nonprint collection of 100,000 slides and more than 7,300 videotapes and films. The latest addition to the library is the Albert P. Weisman Center for the Study of Contemporary Issues in Chicago Journalism. The center includes a print and audiovisual collection and a learning center that explores the development of Chicago's political and social history.

Costs

For the 2008–09 academic year, full tuition (12 to 16 credit hours) is $8975 for each fifteen-week semester, or $17,950 per year. Part-time tuition (up to 11 credit hours) is $621 per credit hour. Summer school tuition is $484 per credit hour. Some courses require additional service or laboratory fees.

To enroll at Columbia College Chicago, applicants are required to confirm their decision by submitting a $250 tuition deposit (nonrefundable after May 1, 2008). Required nonrefundable fees that are charged each semester include the registration fee, $50; the student activity fee, $75 ($40 for part-time students); the U-Pass, $90 (for unlimited access to the public transportation system); and a health center fee, $35 ($20 for part-time students). There is also a one-time $30 library deposit that is refunded when the student leaves the College.

Financial Aid

Columbia College makes every effort to help students obtain financial assistance, including grants, on-campus work, and loans. The Office of Student Financial Services administers federal and state grant and loan programs. The College also provides information for students seeking part-time employment both on and off campus. On-campus jobs are available in technical, clerical, secretarial, and food service areas. Columbia offers institution-based scholarships, such as Presidential Scholarships for freshmen, scholarships for transfer students, academic excellence awards, leadership awards, and housing grants. The Fischetti Scholarships support the efforts of outstanding Columbia journalism students, and the Weisman Scholarships support special communication-related projects. Appropriate scholarship and applications forms for financial aid are available through the Office of Undergraduate Admissions.

Faculty

Many of Columbia's 1,540 full- and part-time faculty members are working professionals (artists, writers, filmmakers, dancers, etc.) with national reputations. The College is constantly seeking individuals who are both gifted teachers and talented professionals. Many faculty members work nearby in the disciplines in which they teach and share practical expertise with students in informal workshop settings and in the classroom. Interaction with faculty members who are practicing professionals provides students with invaluable access to the latest information in their fields. Students also begin developing their own professional network as faculty members share contacts and information on how to break into the market.

Student Government

Through the Student Government Association (SGA) and the Student Organization Council (SOC), students are able to address College-wide and departmental issues and sponsor services and activities. SGA and SOC work closely with the Office of Student Affairs and serve as liaisons to the administration and academic departments. The ninety campus clubs and organizations reflect the interests and the diversity of Columbia's student body. Film screenings, student-produced television shows, dance recitals, poetry readings, plays, campus radio, music concerts, and a national award–winning newspaper are just some of the campus events and activities that are available to students.

Admission Requirements

Columbia College invites applications from all students with creative ability in or inclination to study the arts, media, and communication disciplines in which the College specializes. To apply for admission, students must submit high school transcripts, college transcripts (if applicable), a letter of recommendation, a personal essay, and a $35 application fee. ACT or SAT scores are not required but are strongly encouraged. Graduation from high school or an earned GED certificate is required prior to enrollment. Freshman applicants whose application materials suggest they are likely to be underprepared to meet the College's standards are required to successfully complete the Bridge Program to be admitted to the College. Columbia has a liberal transfer policy.

Application and Information

Students are strongly advised to apply early. The priority date is May 1 for the fall semester, November 15 for the spring semester, and April 15 for the summer term. Applicants are notified of their acceptance within two to four weeks after the College receives all the required information and documents. Students who want to live in campus housing are strongly advised to apply early. Housing assignments are offered on a first-come, first-served basis until full occupancy is achieved.

All students are invited to tour the College. To arrange for a tour or an appointment with an admissions counselor, students should call the Office of Undergraduate Admissions.

For more information, students should contact:

Office of Undergraduate Admissions
Columbia College Chicago
600 South Michigan Avenue
Chicago, Illinois 60605
Phone: 312-344-7130
Fax: 312-344-8024
E-mail: admissions@colum.edu
Web site: http://www.colum.edu

DEPAUL UNIVERSITY

CHICAGO, ILLINOIS

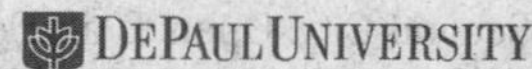

The University

DePaul University is nationally recognized for providing students with a widely respected, immediately applicable education through small classes, highly interactive course work, and an integrated service-learning approach. More than 150 undergraduate degree programs combine practical expertise with classic, broad-based liberal studies, preparing students for both immediate and long-term success. Located in the heart of Chicago, DePaul University offers students unparalleled access to internships and learning opportunities with many of the nation's top corporations and organizations as well as a rich array of cultural events and institutions. The only one of the nation's ten largest private universities to make teaching its primary focus, DePaul provides an interactive learning environment through expert instruction and small class sizes. More than 99 percent of classes are taught by faculty members, not teaching assistants, while 97 percent of classes have fewer than 40 students.

In fall 2007, DePaul enrolled 23,401 students, retaining its place as the nation's largest Catholic university. Of the 3,863 new undergraduates, 2,522 were first-time freshmen. The student body is diverse—about one third of all undergraduates are students of color, including 27 percent of new freshmen. The incoming freshmen are also high caliber, with an average high school GPA of 3.5 and more than 20 percent graduating in the top 10 percent of their class.

In addition to its baccalaureate programs, DePaul offers more than 130 graduate programs, including master's degrees in accountancy, business, computer science, education, liberal arts and sciences, and music; the Master of Fine Arts (M.F.A.) in theater; the Juris Doctor (J.D.); the Master of Law in health law, intellectual property, and taxation; and doctoral programs in computer science, education, philosophy, and psychology.

Recognized by *U.S. News & World Report* as one of twenty-three universities nationwide whose service-learning programs lead to student success, DePaul takes full advantage of its Chicago location. Professors have long-lasting professional relationships with corporations, government agencies, cultural and civic organizations, and a wide array of nonprofits. Students tap into these connections for internships, mentors, class projects, professional contacts, and more. Of DePaul's 125,000 alumni, more than 80,000 reside in the metropolitan area, providing students with a network locally and around the world.

DePaul sponsors nearly 200 student organizations that provide opportunities for leadership, service, professional development, socializing, sports, recreation, and special interests.

Students enjoy the excitement and pride of collegiate sports through the DePaul Blue Demons, who participate in NCAA Division I sports as part of the Big East Conference. Women's sports include basketball, cross-country, soccer, softball, tennis, track and field, and volleyball. Men's sports include basketball, cross-country, golf, soccer, tennis, and track and field. Intramural sports programs, as well as club athletics, also are available throughout the year.

Notable new facilities include the Ray Meyer Athletic and Recreation Center and the student center, the hub of student life on the Lincoln Park Campus. DePaul broke ground in June 2007 on a $40-million environmental science building. Scheduled for completion in November 2008, McGowan South is the second science facility at DePaul named after Msgr. Andrew J. McGowan.

Location

DePaul has six campuses in the Chicago metropolitan area and takes full advantage of its culturally and academically rich environment. The Loop Campus is just blocks from Chicago's business district, the Art Institute, Orchestra Hall, Millennium Park, and Lake Michigan. The 32-acre Lincoln Park Campus provides a classic residential-college experience surrounded by an urban assortment of stores, theaters, restaurants, and music clubs. From either campus, a short walk or ride on public transit enables students to browse unique shops or visit museums, the zoo, ethnic neighborhoods, and professional sports arenas, such as Wrigley Field.

DePaul's four suburban campuses (Naperville, Oak Forest, Rolling Meadows, and O'Hare/Des Plaines) provide convenient locations for adult and graduate students to pursue degree programs.

Majors and Degrees

Bachelor of Arts, Bachelor of Fine Arts, Bachelor of Music, Bachelor of Science, Bachelor of Science in Commerce, and Bachelor of Science in Education degrees are offered through seven undergraduate colleges. More than 130 undergraduate majors and another ninety-seven minors are available. Double majors and minors may be taken in many areas of study.

The College of Liberal Arts and Sciences offers programs in African and black diaspora studies, American studies, anthropology, art and art history, biological sciences, Catholic studies, chemistry, Chinese studies, clinical laboratory science, economics, English, environmental science, French, geography, German, history, international studies, Islamic world studies, Italian, Japanese studies, Latin American and Latino studies, mathematical sciences, mathematics and computer science, nursing (B.S.N. completion only), philosophy, physics, political science, preprofessional studies (dentistry, engineering, law, medicine, osteopathy, veterinary medicine), psychology, public policy (environmental studies, urban studies), religious studies, scientific data analysis and visualization, sociology, Spanish, and women's and gender studies.

The School of Computer Science, Telecommunications, and Information Systems offers programs in computer games development, computer graphics and motion technology, computer science, digital cinema, e-commerce technology, interactive media, information assurance and security engineering, information systems, information technology, math/computer science, and network technology.

The School of Education offers programs in early childhood education, elementary education, music education (joint program with the School of Music), physical education (sport and fitness management and teaching), and secondary education (biology, chemistry, Chinese, English, environmental science, French, German, history, Italian, Japanese, mathematics, physics, social science, Spanish, and visual art).

The College of Commerce offers programs in accountancy, business administration, e-business, economics, finance, management, management information systems, marketing, and real estate.

The College of Communication, DePaul's newest academic college, offers programs in communication, communication and media, communication studies, public relations/advertising, media and cinema studies, and journalism.

The School of Music offers programs in composition, jazz studies, music education, music performance, performing arts management, and sound recording technology.

The Theatre School offers programs in acting, costume design, costume technology, dramaturgy/criticism, lighting design, playwriting, scenic design, stage management, theater arts, theater management, and theater technology.

The School for New Learning (SNL) offers customized degree programs for adults 24 years or older. Students are responsible for designing their own programs and may receive credit for work experience. SNL's Chronic Illness Initiative Inside Track is offered to students ages 18–23 who have chronic illnesses, enabling them to earn a bachelor's degree while managing their symptoms and special needs.

Also available are a five-year joint program with the Illinois Institute of Technology (IIT); a five-year dual-degree program that includes three years of study at DePaul and two years at an accredited school of engineering.

Academic Programs

To be eligible for a degree, undergraduate students must complete at least 192 quarter hours of college academic work with a grade point average of at least 2.0. Typically, thirteen courses are required for a major. Each college follows the liberal studies program, which has two components. The first, called the common core, emphasizes communication, quantitative skills, and intellectual abilities and introduces the University's small-group, highly interactive educational approach. The second part, learning domains, focuses mainly on the subjects that make up the classic liberal arts and sciences curriculum. Breadth of learning is assured by requiring students to do course work in six learning domains: arts and literature; philosophical inquiry; religious dimensions; scientific inquiry; self, society, and the modern world; and understanding the past.

The general education program is integrated throughout the student's educational career through additional common experiences, including the sophomore multiculturalism requirement, junior experiential learning requirement, and senior capstone requirement.

The academic year comprises three quarters. Incoming freshmen may enter with credit earned through credit by exam. Up to 99 quarter hours (equivalent to 66 semester hours) of Advanced Placement, CLEP, or International Baccalaureate credits may be counted toward graduation requirements. Incoming transfer students may combine earned credit through credit by exam and transferable credit hours from two-year institutions (up to 99 quarter hours/66 semester hours) and from four-year institutions (up to 132 quarter hours/88 semester hours). In some cases, degree requirements can be completed in three years. Advanced undergraduates may take graduate courses. Most undergraduates in any college may apply to the Honors Program, which emphasizes cross-cultural and interdisciplinary perspectives with a challenging curriculum that satisfies the required liberal studies core. (Program participation is noted on the students' transcripts.) College-specific honors programs also are offered in accountancy, computer science, finance, and marketing.

Off-Campus Programs

DePaul University has study-abroad programs in numerous locations throughout the world. Students study in Australia, Austria, Belgium, China, England, France, Germany, Greece, Hungary, Ireland, Italy, Japan, Mexico, Poland, Spain, Turkey, and other countries. DePaul sponsors full-year and short-term study tours in order to accommodate students' interests and academic program requirements.

Academic Facilities

The DePaul Center, a $70-million teaching, learning, research, and student services complex, is the cornerstone of the six-building Loop Campus. The computer science building offers more than a dozen specialized labs as well as the new digital animation studio. The Merle Reskin Theatre provides a 1,400-seat performance space for the theater and music schools. Wireless networks and other technological upgrades have been implemented at most other academic facilities at all campuses.

All academic and residential facilities on the 32-acre Lincoln Park Campus are either new or recently rehabbed. Notable buildings include the student center, recreation center, Richardson Library, NCAA athletic center, and the McGowan Center for Biological and Environmental Sciences, a three-story, state-of-the-art facility.

The library system, which includes the Loop library in the DePaul Center, the Richardson Library at the Lincoln Park Campus, and the suburban campus libraries, contain 787,141 volumes and 8,688 print journal subscriptions. The Rinn Law Library has 375,431 volumes and 11,055 print journal subscriptions. The digital collections include more than 14,300 full-text electronic journals, 13,800 electronic books, and 29,000 digital images.

DePaul offers students cutting-edge technology resources, including computer labs, with more than 800 computers for student use, free e-mail and Internet access, online registration and tuition payment services, and in-class technology resources designed to enrich course offerings. In addition, many courses use the University's innovative Course OnLine technology, enabling students to study or make up missed classes by seeing and hearing everything that happened in the classroom.

Costs

For the 2007–08 academic year, full-time tuition for the College of Liberal Arts and Sciences, the College of Commerce, the College of Communication, the School of Education, the School for New Learning, and the School of Computer Science, Telecommunication, and Information Systems was $23,820. Tuition was $27,038 for the School of Music and $27,260 for the Theatre School—tuition for both schools is guaranteed for four years. Average room and board costs for 2007–08 were $9900.

Financial Aid

Scholarships, grants, loans, and work-study opportunities are awarded singly or combined in a financial aid package to meet the demonstrated financial need of about 70 percent of students. Merit scholarships for freshmen and transfer students are based on academic and extracurricular accomplishments. Institutional competitive scholarships for freshmen, with values ranging from $4000 to $14,000 for four years, are based on consideration of class rank, grade point average, and SAT or ACT scores, without regard to need. Institutional scholarships for transfer students range from $2000 to $7000 and may be awarded to students who have a cumulative GPA of 3.5 or above and a minimum of 30 semester (44 quarter) hours of transferable credit before enrolling at DePaul. All other financial aid programs except art, athletic, music, and theater talent awards are based primarily on need.

Students who wish to apply for aid must complete the Free Application for Federal Student Aid (FAFSA) and the DePaul application for admission. Application and notification of aid decisions are on a rolling basis. Students are encouraged to apply before March 1 to receive maximum consideration.

Faculty

In the fall of 2007, about 88 percent of the full-time faculty members held a doctoral degree or terminal degree in their field. Faculty members are selected for their teaching ability and conduct nearly all university classes. DePaul's faculty members also consult with organizations throughout the metropolitan area and world, engage in research, publish in their fields of expertise, and participate in service. Graduate assistants teach less than 1 percent of the classes at DePaul.

Student Government

The Student Government Association offers students the opportunity to become involved in representative government.

Admission Requirements

Current high school students may be considered for admission on the basis of six or more semesters of high school work. However, by the time of enrollment the students must have graduated from an approved secondary school with a minimum of 16 high school units, including 14 of an academic nature. These should include 4 units in English, 3 in mathematics, 2 in laboratory science plus 1 additional science, 2 in social sciences, and 4 additional units of college preparatory subjects. Applicants should rank in the upper half of their class, have a solid GPA, and present strong ACT or SAT scores. Applicants must submit a high school counselor's recommendation. The School of Music and the Theatre School require auditions or interviews for admission. Early action, advanced placement, and dual enrollment while still in high school are available.

To be considered for admission, transfer students must be in good academic standing at the last college/university attended and must have earned a minimum cumulative GPA of 2.0 (C) based on transferable credit. College of Commerce, School of Education, and School of Music applicants must have a cumulative GPA of 2.5 or better; registered nurses interested in the B.S.N. completion program must have at least a 2.5 cumulative GPA. Students who have completed fewer than 30 semester hours (44 quarter hours) of transferable credit need to submit an official high school transcript and ACT/SAT scores.

Rolling admission is on a space-available basis. Early action (for freshman applicants only) deadline is November 15. It is strongly recommended that freshman applicants apply by February 1.

Application and Information

Applicants who are admitted under the early action program receive their decision by January 1. All other applicants are notified on a rolling basis. Campus visits and overnight stays are available for prospective students. Interested students and their families are encouraged to call the admission office to arrange a visit.

For further information, prospective students should contact:

Office of Admission
DePaul University
1 East Jackson Boulevard
Chicago, Illinois 60604-2287
Phone: 312-362-8300
800-4DEPAUL (toll-free outside Illinois)
E-mail: admission@depaul.edu
Web site: http://www.depaul.edu

DOMINICAN UNIVERSITY

RIVER FOREST, ILLINOIS

The University

Dominican University is a distinctively relationship-centered educational community, rooted in the liberal arts and sciences and comprehensive in scope. The University is known for its rigorous and engaging academic programs, for the care and respect with which it mentors students, for its enduring commitment to social justice, and for the enriching diversity of its students and faculty and staff members. Integral to Dominican's success and distinction is the ongoing exploration, clear expression, and shared experience of its Catholic Dominican identity.

At Dominican University, students can do anything and everything—get an education; find a career that's interesting, challenging, and satisfying; make lifelong friends; and become the person they want to be. The University helps students by offering a faculty that guides and supports them, internships that allow them to test-drive their careers, small classes, leadership opportunities, and a campus filled with people who will make them feel cared for and welcome.

The impressive ivy-covered Gothic buildings include Parmer Hall, a state-of-the-art facility for science that also offers numerous high-tech classrooms. There are also a recently redesigned 300,000-volume library with cyber café, a Fine Arts Building with a recital hall and auditorium, four fully networked residence halls, and the Student Center, home to the men's and women's basketball and women's volleyball teams. The center has an elevated running track and a student commons area that overlooks the glass-enclosed racquetball courts. Other varsity sports include men's baseball, cross-country, soccer, and tennis and women's cross-country, soccer, softball, and tennis. There are new intercollegiate and recreational soccer fields.

Rosary College of Arts and Sciences offers more than fifty major fields of study. The University also has four graduate schools: Business, Education, Library and Information Science, and Social Work, as well as a School for Leadership and Continuing Studies. Approximately 50 percent of the corporate librarians or information specialists in the Chicago area are graduates of Dominican University.

With Spring Fling, the Founder's Day Celebration, and the inspiring Candle and Rose ceremony, Dominican University's traditions make college life rewarding and memorable for students. A variety of clubs and honor societies also offer the opportunity for students to get involved. Students often travel off campus, perhaps to a Cubs baseball game at Wrigley Field or to a Chicago soup kitchen as a Campus Ministry volunteer. The University also sponsors a wide range of cultural programs on campus, ranging from lectures, plays, and concert performances by the Vienna Boys Choir and the Chicago Sinfonietta, the orchestra-in-residence, to a popular "roots" music series. Recent theater productions include *Othello, Little Shop of Horrors,* and *Tartuffe.*

Location

Dominican University is located in River Forest, a residential suburb just 10 miles west of Chicago's Loop. Students can take advantage of city offerings by using nearby public transportation, or they can enjoy the surrounding Oak Park–River Forest residential community, which, among other attractions, is home to the largest number of Frank Lloyd Wright houses in the country, including Wright's first home and studio. The nearby communities offer a wide array of ethnic restaurants, pubs with live music, shopping, and movie theaters.

Majors and Degrees

Dominican University awards both the Bachelor of Arts (B.A.) and the Bachelor of Science (B.S.) degrees. Programs include accounting, addiction counseling, African/African-American studies, American studies, art, art history, biology, biology-chemistry, business administration, chemistry, communication arts and sciences, computer information systems, computer science, corporate communication, criminology, economics, education (early childhood, elementary, and secondary), engineering, English, environmental science, fashion design, fashion merchandising, food industry management, food science and nutrition, French, graphic design, health sciences, history, information technology, international business, international relations and diplomacy, Italian, journalism, mathematics, mathematics and computer science, nutrition and dietetics, occupational therapy, pastoral ministry, pharmacy, philosophy, photography, political science, psychology, social science, sociology, Spanish, theater arts, and theology.

The Bachelor of Arts Honors Degree is awarded to students who complete the interdisciplinary Honors Program. There is a popular five-year B.A./M.B.A. program. Preprofessional programs are available in dentistry, law, library and information science, and medicine. In cooperation with Rush University, Dominican University offers an occupational therapy program. Engineering students complete a five-year degree program, earning a Bachelor of Arts degree from Dominican University and a Bachelor of Science degree from Illinois Institute of Technology.

Academic Programs

The curriculum of Rosary College of Arts and Sciences is built around a core of interdisciplinary seminars and liberal arts requirements. One interdisciplinary seminar is taken at each academic level. The liberal arts core requirements include history, philosophy, social sciences, natural sciences, literature and fine arts, and theology. In addition, students must demonstrate proficiency in writing, mathematics, computer applications, research, and a foreign language. Service learning and experiential learning opportunities are available to all students. Students must complete 124 credit hours to graduate.

The Honors Program is designed to adapt the strengths of a small institution to the special needs of superior students. In their senior year, honors program students complete special projects in their major fields.

Off-Campus Programs

Students have a variety of opportunities to study off campus, including more than thirty service learning courses and a growing array of study-abroad programs. Students in the sciences and mathematics have the opportunity to do research at Argonne National Laboratory, one of the outstanding research centers in the country. Juniors and seniors may earn credit through internships arranged by a full-time internship coordinator. The internships provide on-the-job experience that allows students to test-drive their career choice.

Students are encouraged to deepen their understanding of other peoples and cultures through study-abroad programs in China, El Salvador, Florence, Ghana, London, Milan, Oxford, Rome, Salamanca, and South Africa. In addition, Dominican University faculty members assist students who wish to study in other countries.

Academic Facilities

Parmer Hall opened in fall 2007 and showcases the sciences with state-of-the-art laboratories and classrooms. Student commons areas are designed to promote student-faculty interaction. At the heart of academic life is the redesigned Rebecca Crown Library, with more than 300,000 volumes, 1,200 periodicals, and nearly 70,000 federal government documents as well as a popular cyber café. The library's membership in LCS (an online network of more than thirty academic libraries in Illinois) and ILLINET Online (a network of 600 public and academic libraries) provides access to more than 10 million volumes and nearly 10,000 current periodicals. The University also provides computer laboratories and classrooms where students may do class work or personal projects. In the Fine Arts Building, students attend lectures, plays, and musical performances in the auditorium and recital halls or view exhibitions in the art gallery. Lewis Hall provides general classroom space, language labs, and a busy Tech Center.

Costs

Tuition for 2007–08 was $22,350 for full-time students. Room and board charges were approximately $7000; costs may vary, depending on the type of room and meal plan selected. Part-time students were charged $745 per credit hour. The cost of books averages $1000 per academic year.

Financial Aid

Dominican University supports both merit-based and need-based financial aid programs. Academic scholarships that range from $6000 to $14,000 per year are offered to qualified full-time incoming freshmen based on class rank, grades, and ACT or SAT scores. Full-time transfer students with a minimum cumulative GPA of 3.3 at previous institutions also qualify for scholarships. Brechtel Scholarships are offered to outstanding chemistry and biology-chemistry students. Star Scholarships recognize leadership achievements such as Eagle Scout rank or notable community service.

Need-based financial aid programs include grants, loans, and campus employment. Students may apply for financial aid by submitting the Free Application for Federal Student Aid (FAFSA). Aid awards are made on a rolling basis, but early application is encouraged.

Approximately 75 percent of undergraduate students receive some form of financial assistance.

Faculty

Excellent teachers ensure the excellence of education. At Dominican University, more than 90 percent of the faculty members hold doctoral or terminal degrees. With a student-faculty ratio of 12:1, individualized attention is the norm. All classes at Rosary College of Arts and Sciences are taught by faculty members of the University; there are no teaching assistants. The highest priority of the University is teaching. In addition, faculty members conduct research and publish works in their academic disciplines.

All advising is done by members of the faculty, who guide students in choosing their courses, selecting majors, and developing career interests. Close interaction between faculty members and students is the hallmark of the undergraduate program.

Admission Requirements

Graduation from an accredited secondary school is required for admission. Most entering freshmen rank in the upper 25 percent of their graduating class and have an average GPA of 3.4 on a 4.0 scale. Transfer students generally must have a GPA of at least 2.5 from their previous institution. A transfer credit evaluation is made before a deposit is required.

Application and Information

Rosary College of Arts and Sciences operates on a rolling admissions program. However, early application is recommended to ensure that financial aid and housing are available. Students are encouraged to apply online. There is no fee for the online application, but there is a $25 application fee for the paper application. A $100 tuition deposit is required after acceptance. A $100 housing deposit is required for students who plan to live on campus.

For more information, students may contact:

Office of Undergraduate Admissions
Dominican University
7900 West Division
River Forest, Illinois 60305
Phone: 708-524-6800
Fax: 708-524-5990
E-mail: domadmis@dom.edu
Web site: http://www.dom.edu

Dominican University's Parmer Hall.

ELMHURST COLLEGE

ELMHURST, ILLINOIS

The College

Elmhurst is a four-year comprehensive college in the liberal arts tradition. Founded in 1871, the College has a long history of preparing students for lifetimes of professional and personal achievement. Elmhurst is affiliated with the United Church of Christ.

The College offers more than fifty majors, four accelerated majors for adults, fifteen preprofessional programs, and nine graduate programs. The honors program provides extra opportunities for students who are especially talented, curious, and motivated.

Elmhurst ranks in the top tier of Midwest colleges and universities with master's programs, according to *U.S. News & World Report*'s "America's Best Colleges" issue. *The Princeton Review* also lists Elmhurst among the region's premier institutions of higher learning. Students come to Elmhurst from many states and countries and from nearly every religious, racial, and ethnic background.

The student body comprises about 2,500 traditional undergraduate students, 415 adults pursuing an undergraduate degree, and nearly 300 graduate students. Students participate in more than 100 activities, including theater, intramurals, and student government. More than half play intramurals or participate in one of eighteen NCAA Division III varsity teams. Five residence halls and a variety of apartment-style housing options are available for students who want to live on campus.

Location

Elmhurst, Illinois, a quiet suburb of Chicago, is filled with family-owned stores and restaurants, as well as theater, music, art museums, and other recreational activities. In *Chicago* magazine's 2003 study of the "best places to live" among 192 Chicago suburbs, the city of Elmhurst ranked number 1.

The beautiful 38-acre campus looks like a college should look: big trees, broad lawns, and twenty-four stately redbrick buildings. With more than 600 varieties of trees and shrubs, the Elmhurst campus is an arboretum; with modern facilities, top-notch faculty members, and a great geographical location, it's an excellent place to get an education.

Just 16 miles away (30 minutes by train), Chicago has something for everyone. Sports fans can enjoy watching the Bears, Bulls, Cubs, or White Sox in action, or play sports in Millennium Park or along the waterfront. Students who are interested in art or culture can visit the Museum of Contemporary Art, the Art Institute of Chicago, or the 57-acre Museum Campus, featuring the Adler Planetarium and Astronomy Museum. Chicago also features lots of shopping, dining, and nightlife.

Majors and Degrees

The College offers bachelor's degrees in accounting, American studies, art, art business, art education, biology, business administration, chemistry, communication studies, computer game and entertainment technology, computer science, criminal justice, early childhood education, economics, elementary education, English, environmental geosciences, exercise science, finance, French, geography, German, history, information systems, interdisciplinary communication studies, international business, jazz studies, logistics and supply chain management, management, marketing, mathematics, music, music business, music education, musical theater, nursing, organizational communication, philosophy, physical education, physics, political science, psychology, religion and service, religious studies, secondary education, sociology, Spanish, special education, speech-language pathology, theater, theater arts education, theological studies and Christian ministry, and urban studies. Students also may design their own interdepartmental major.

Preprofessional programs are available in actuarial science, allied health sciences, dentistry, engineering, law, library science, medicine, seminary studies, and veterinary medicine.

Academic Programs

Elmhurst College confers four undergraduate degrees: Bachelor of Arts, Bachelor of Science, Bachelor of Music, and Bachelor of Liberal Studies. While requirements for each degree vary, all require a minimum of 128 semester hours of credit. The academic program consists of three interrelated parts: courses that meet the general education requirements, courses that fulfill requirements of the major (24 semester hours), and elective courses that students select to satisfy intellectual curiosity or to enhance the breadth of their academic programs.

The General Education Program includes course work drawn from eleven categories of knowledge: fine arts; global society; human behavior; inquiry and issues in science and technology; Judeo-Christian heritage and religious faith; literature; the natural world; people, power, and politics; the search for humane values; Western culture; and writing and reasoning. An undergraduate student graduating from Elmhurst College completes at least one course, taken for a letter grade, in each of the eleven categories.

Beyond the general education requirements, major-course requirements, and courses taken to fulfill elective requirements, students earning the Bachelor of Science must complete an additional 8 semester hours in mathematics; students earning the Bachelor of Music must complete at least 64 semester hours in music (specific courses are determined by the Department of Music); and students earning the Bachelor of Liberal Studies must complete 32 to 48 semester hours in two areas of concentration (rather than a traditional major). Students are expected to declare their major field of study prior to completion of the sophomore year. Students may also select a maximum of two minors.

Off-Campus Programs

Elmhurst encourages first-, second-, and third-year students to pursue international education programs by going global for a month, a term, or a year. Through a wide range of opportunities to study and work abroad, students refine their language skills, challenge their cultural assumptions, grow as individuals, better understand themselves and their countries, and gain a greater respect for other cultures.

During the January and summer terms, Elmhurst faculty members teach in such places as Costa Rica, England, Germany, Jamaica, and Morocco through the Elmhurst College Abroad program.

In addition to sponsoring its own courses abroad, the College offers programs through a consortium of colleges and through two partnership programs. For example, students can combine classes with internships in Australia, Belgium, France (Paris), Germany, and Spain; students can earn academic credit for participating in service-learning and academic courses in the Czech Republic, Ecuador, India, Mexico, the Philippines, and Scotland; and other programs take students to Austria, China, England, Italy, Ireland, and New Zealand. Elmhurst College also runs official exchange programs with institutions in Ecuador and Morocco.

Academic Facilities

The A. C. Buehler Library provides a wide variety of services for Elmhurst students. Books, periodicals, and audiovisual materials are available, along with interlibrary loan services, databases, electronic journals, and other electronic resources.

The Elmhurst College Learning Center helps students succeed as independent learners. Students can receive one-on-one tutoring in math, reading, writing, and study-skills areas or attend test preparation workshops.

The Computer Science and Technology Center has computer rooms for student use and features forty-two PCs, two Macs, two scanners, and two laser printers. The Center for Professional Excellence offers opportunities for self-assessment, career guidance, graduate school preparation, internships, mentoring, and shadowing.

Costs

Full-time tuition for 2007–08 was $24,600. Part-time tuition was $2800 per full course ($700 per credit hour). Other costs included a matriculation fee of $125 ($50 for transfer students), an academic technology fee of $30 per term, and a residential network fee of $50 per term. Students living on campus can expect to pay $4200 for a double-occupancy room and $3298 for a standard meal plan.

Financial Aid

Financial aid is awarded to approximately 85 percent of entering students. Entering freshmen are eligible for renewable scholarships based on grade point average and composite ACT scores or combined SAT scores. Students should apply for admission by January 15 for scholarship consideration. Other Elmhurst scholarships are awarded based on grade point average, program of study, financial need, and other criteria. Awards range from $1000 to $18,000 per academic year. Elmhurst grants of $1000 to 14,000 per year are available for full-time students.

The Illinois Student Assistance Commission administers grants of $350 to $4968 per year to dependents of Illinois residents. The Department of Education awards Federal Pell Grants of $400 to $4310 per year. Pell recipients may also be eligible for Supplemental Educational Opportunity Grants of $100 to $4000 a year. Student loans include the Federal Direct Loan, Federal Perkins Loan, and Federal PLUS Program. Alternative loans may be available from private lenders.

Faculty

Elmhurst provides superior teaching on a personal scale. All classes are taught by professors, not teaching assistants. About 85 percent of the College's 127 full-time faculty members hold a Ph.D. or other terminal degree in their field. The student-faculty ratio of 13:1 is among the best in higher education. The average class has 19 students.

Student Government

The Student Government Association (SGA) consists of 18 students elected by the student body, 3 members of the faculty elected by the faculty, and 3 administrators selected by the student members. The SGA serves as the major policy-recommending body to the President and Trustees on issues of student and campus life. The Elmhurst College Union Board and its committees serve as the primary student programming organization on campus.

Admission Requirements

Elmhurst seeks students who show evidence of their ability to complete college-level work based on high school performance. Preference is given to students who have completed 16 academic units, including 3 units of English; 2 units each of mathematics, laboratory science, and social studies; and 7 units in additional college-preparatory subjects.

Application and Information

In order to apply, prospective students are required to submit an application for admission. Applications may be completed online, or paper copies can be downloaded or requested from the Office of Admission and Financial Aid. Students must also submit official high school transcripts or GED results, official SAT or ACT scores, and a teacher recommendation. Elmhurst College's ACT code is 1020. An interview and essay are recommended but not required. Applications are accepted on a rolling basis. Freshmen may apply beginning October 1, and transfer students may apply beginning November 1.

Prospective students can arrange an individual visit, which might include an overnight stay and meetings with faculty members, or come for a Preview Day.

Further information about the College, the application process, and campus visits can be obtained from:

Office of Admission
Elmhurst College
190 Prospect Avenue
Elmhurst, Illinois 60126-3296
Phone: 630-617-3400
800-697-1871 (toll-free)
E-mail: admit@elmhurst.edu
Web site: http://www.elmhurst.edu/

THE ILLINOIS INSTITUTE OF ART–CHICAGO

CHICAGO, ILLINOIS

The Illinois Institute of Art Chicago

The Institute

The Illinois Institute of Art–Chicago offers a stimulating learning environment where committed and talented students, led by dedicated and professional faculty members, may develop their creativity and acquire the skills and knowledge needed to pursue an entry-level job in the creative arts. The Illinois Institute of Art–Chicago offers eleven bachelor's degree and five associate degree programs.

Students at The Illinois Institute of Art–Chicago come from throughout the United States and abroad. The student population includes recent high school graduates, transfer students, and those who have left a previous employment situation to study and train for a new career. Students are creative, competitive, and open to new ideas. They place great value on an education that prepares them for an exciting entry-level position in the arts.

Orientation events provide students with an introduction to the school's academic environment, extracurricular life, residence life, and campus surroundings. Student organizations include the American Marketing Association (AMA), Textile Surface Design Club, American Society of Interior Designers (ASID), International Student Association (ISA), and American Institute of Graphic Arts (AIGA).

The school provides opportunities outside of the classroom that enhance students' personal development, including a wide variety of social and educational activities. On-campus activities include student organizations, leadership workshops, special guest presentations, heritage celebrations, holiday events, and unique contests.

Dedicated Career Services staff members offer a range of services to support students' efforts in career planning. With employer contacts and resources across the country, Career Services provides students with proven tips and techniques to start a job search.

The school maintains apartments in downtown Chicago that offer convenient and comfortable living. School-sponsored housing offers studio apartments that house 2 students. Basic utilities, Internet, basic cable, local phone service, and furnishings are included in the rent price.

The Illinois Institute of Art–Chicago is accredited by the Accrediting Commission of Career Schools and Colleges of Technology (ACCSCT) and by the Higher Learning Commission and is a member of the North Central Association (30 North LaSalle Street, Suite 2400, Chicago, Illinois 60602; phone: 800-621-7440 (toll-free); http://www.ncahlc.org). The Associate of Applied Science in Culinary Arts degree program is accredited by the American Culinary Federation (ACF). The Bachelor of Fine Arts in Interior Design degree program is accredited by the Council for Interior Design Accreditation.

Location

Chicago is one of the five most visited cities in the country, with the Museum of Contemporary Art, the Mexican Fine Arts Center Museum, and the Terra Museum of American Art. Neighborhood street fairs and festivals throughout the year celebrate art, food, and creativity. Other attractions include the Sears Tower, Navy Pier, Shedd Aquarium, Field Museum, Adler Planetarium, Lincoln Park Zoo, and a lakefront with beautiful beaches. Music lovers enjoy the Lyric Opera and Chicago Symphony, while sports fans watch the Cubs, White Sox, Bulls, Blackhawks, and Bears.

Majors and Degrees

The Illinois Institute of Art–Chicago offers bachelor's degree programs in advertising, culinary management, digital filmmaking and video production, fashion design, fashion marketing and management, game art and design, interior design, media arts and animation, visual communications, visual effects and motion graphics, and Web design and interactive media. Associate degree programs include accessory design, culinary arts, fashion merchandising, graphic design, and Web design and interactive media. A certificate program is offered in professional cooking.

Academic Programs

The Illinois Institute of Art–Chicago offers bachelor's degree programs (180 academic credits), associate degree programs (96 credits), and certificate programs.

Academic Facilities

The Illinois Institute of Art–Chicago library includes computer workstations; online databases; nearly 11,000 volumes; subscriptions; slides of art history, interior architecture, furniture, and fashion; and a CD sound library. There are computer labs with high-speed Internet access. Studios include editing stations, an audio production studio, and a video production studio.

Culinary facilities include professional kitchens, two storage rooms, and a forty-five-seat restaurant. The Fashion Department contains power sewing machines, large cutting tables, steamers, and computer labs. Fashion marketing classes utilize a walk-in window, props, mannequins, and other display materials. The Interior Design Resource Center contains a variety of contemporary fabrics, wall- and floor-covering samples, manufacturers' furniture catalogs, a new lighting lab, and other design tools.

The 180 North Wabash facility is a satellite location of The Illinois Institute of Art–Chicago.

Costs

Tuition cost varies by program. Prospective students should contact the school for current tuition costs. Other charges include a starting kit for all first-quarter students. Kits vary in price depending on the program of study.

Financial Aid

Financial aid is available for those who qualify. Students who require financial assistance should first complete and submit a Free Application for Federal Student Aid (FAFSA) and meet with a financial aid officer. The officer determines the level of need based on a required federal formula, the cost of education, and other factors. Gift aid is available in the form of Federal Pell Grants, Federal Supplemental Educational Opportunity Grants, and veterans' benefits. Loans include Federal Stafford Student Loans, Federal PLUS loans, and alternative loans. Other scholarships are available from the school and private sources. Application deadlines and eligibility requirements vary by program.

Faculty

The Illinois Institute of Art–Chicago faculty includes full-time and part-time instructors, many of whom have advanced degrees and experience in their respective fields.

Admission Requirements

An assistant director of admissions personally interviews prospective students to assess their potential for success at The Illinois Institute of Art–Chicago. Applicants are required to submit an essay of 150 words (associate degree programs) or 300 words (bachelor's degree programs) describing how they may benefit from an education at The Illinois Institute of Art–Chicago. Proof of high school graduation or equivalency is required for final admission to the school. Applicants must also provide current immunization records. Scores on the SAT or ACT may be considered for admission but are not required. The school reserves the right to request any additional information necessary to evaluate an applicant's potential for academic success. The application for admission and enrollment agreement must be completed and signed by the applicant and parent or guardian (if applicable). There is a $50 application fee.

Application and Information

To obtain an application, make arrangements for an interview, or tour the school, students should contact:

The Illinois Institute of Art–Chicago
350 North Orleans Street
Chicago, Illinois 60654-1593
Phone: 312-280-3500
800-351-3450 (toll-free)
Fax: 312-280-8562
Web site: http://www.artinstitutes.edu/chicago

The Art Institute of Atlanta®, GA; The Art Institute of Atlanta®–Decatur, GA; The Art Institute of Austin[SM], TX; The Art Institute of California[SM]–Inland Empire; The Art Institute of California[SM]–Los Angeles; The Art Institute of California[SM]–Orange County; The Art Institute of California[SM]–Sacramento; The Art Institute of California[SM]–San Diego; The Art Institute of California[SM]–San Francisco; The Art Institute of California[SM]–Sunnyvale; The Art Institute of Charleston[SM], SC, A branch of The Art Institute of Atlanta, GA; The Art Institute of Charlotte®, NC; The Art Institute of Colorado® (Denver); The Art Institute of Dallas®, TX; The Art Institute of Fort Lauderdale®, FL; The Art Institute of Houston®, TX; The Art Institute of Indianapolis[SM], IN*; The Art Institute of Jacksonville[SM], FL, A branch of Miami International University of Art & Design; The Art Institute of Las Vegas®, NV; The Art Institute of Michigan[SM] (Detroit); The Art Institute of New York City®, NY; The Art Institute of Ohio[SM]–Cincinnati**; The Art Institute of Philadelphia®, PA; The Art Institute of Phoenix®, AZ; The Art Institute of Pittsburgh®, PA; The Art Institute of Pittsburgh®–Online Division; The Art Institute of Portland®, OR; The Art Institute of Salt Lake City[SM], UT; The Art Institute of Seattle®, WA; The Art Institute of Tampa[SM], FL, A branch of Miami International University of Art & Design; The Art Institute of Tennessee[SM]–Nashville, A branch of The Art Institute of Atlanta, GA; The Art Institute of Tucson[SM], AZ; The Art Institute of Washington® (Arlington, VA), A branch of The Art Institute of Atlanta, GA; The Art Institute of York–Pennsylvania[SM]; The Art Institutes International Minnesota[SM] (Minneapolis); California Design College[SM] (Los Angeles–Wilshire Blvd.); The Illinois Institute of Art®–Chicago; The Illinois Institute of Art®–Schaumburg; Miami International University of Art & Design[SM], FL; The New England Institute of Art® (Boston, MA).

*The Art Institute of Indianapolis is licensed by the Indiana Commission on Proprietary Education, 302 W. Washington St., Rm. E201, Indianapolis, IN 46204, AC-0080.

**The Art Institute of Ohio–Cincinnati, 8845 Governors Hill Drive, Suite 100, Cincinnati, OH 45249-3317, OH Reg. #04-01-1698B.

THE ILLINOIS INSTITUTE OF ART–SCHAUMBURG

The Illinois Institute of Art · Schaumburg

SCHAUMBURG, ILLINOIS

The Institute

The Illinois Institute of Art–Schaumburg offers a stimulating learning environment where students develop their creativity and learn skills to help them to obtain entry-level positions in the creative arts.

The school offers ten bachelor's degree programs and one associate degree program. Each program is offered on a year-round basis, allowing students to work uninterrupted toward graduation. The curriculum reflects cognitive and creative elements of the arts, complemented by a general education component. Programs are carefully defined with the support and contributions of the community. Continuing education is available through the Center for Professional Development at The Illinois Institute of Art–Schaumburg.

Students at The Illinois Institute of Art–Schaumburg come from throughout the United States and abroad. The student population includes recent high school graduates, transfer students, and those who have left a previous employment situation to study and train for a new career. Students are creative, competitive, and open to new ideas. They place great value on an education that prepares them for an exciting entry-level position in the arts.

Students participate in clubs and organizations that match their personal and professional interests, including the American Institute of Graphic Arts (AIGA), American Society of Interior Designers (ASID), MultiMedia Club, Northern Illinois Macromedia Flash Users Group, Sonic Arts Club, and the student newspaper. In addition, assistance is available to help students with resume writing, networking, and keeping aware of what employers are looking for in job candidates.

Social opportunities include open mike nights, socials in the student lounge, trips to area attractions, and a yearly Leadership Retreat, where numerous speakers discuss various art forms and community issues. The Student Affairs Department encourages student involvement in campus life and promotes each student's personal and professional growth. The school has a Residence Life and Housing Program to provide individuals with the opportunity to live with other students.

The Illinois Institute of Art–Schaumburg is accredited by the Higher Learning Commission and is a member of the North Central Association, 30 North LaSalle Street, Suite 2400, Chicago, Illinois, 60602; 800-621-7440; http://www.ncahlc.org. The Illinois Institute of Art–Schaumburg is also accredited by the Accrediting Commission of Career Schools and Colleges of Technology (ACCSCT) as a branch of The Illinois Institute of Art–Chicago. ACCSCT may be contacted at 2101 Wilson Boulevard, Suite 302, Arlington, Virginia 22201; 703-247-4212. The interior design bachelor's degree program is accredited by the Council for Interior Design Accreditation.

Location

The school is located in the village of Schaumburg, 26 miles northwest of Chicago. Three local forest preserves are home to lakes for canoeing and sailing as well as miles of paved trails for biking, in-line skating, cross-country skiing, and jogging. Schaumburg has movie theaters, restaurants, and Woodfield Mall, a large retail center. Sports fans may follow the Bears, Bulls, Blackhawks, Cubs, or White Sox.

Majors and Degrees

Bachelor's degrees are available in advertising, digital filmmaking and video production, digital photography, fashion marketing and management, game art and design, graphic design, interior design, media arts and animation, visual effects and motion graphics, and Web design and interactive media. Students may also earn an associate degree in graphic design. Diploma programs are offered in digital design, residential planning, and Web design.

Academic Programs

The academic year is divided into quarters. Bachelor's degree candidates must complete a total of 180 academic credits (thirty-six months). Advanced Placement (AP) credit is awarded when the student earns a score of 3 or higher on the AP exam. Transfer students must complete at least 25 percent of their course work at the school.

Academic Facilities

The Illinois Institute of Art–Schaumburg is located in two buildings. Classrooms and computer labs have been custom designed to accommodate program-specific equipment in the media and design fields. The Interior Design Resource Center contains a variety of samples, manufacturers' furniture catalogs, and other design tools. The Learning Resource Center houses program-related books and other media formats as well as a broad spectrum of curriculum-related periodicals, general interest publications, and course syllabi. The Equipment Checkout Facility provides access to a variety of equipment, rooms, and studios, including digital still cameras, digital video cameras, lighting equipment, DAT recorders, a green-screen room, audio recording and mixing suites, a video production studio, and a motion-capture studio that features both cameras and software.

Costs

Tuition cost varies by program. Students should contact the school for current tuition costs. Other charges include a starting kit for all first-quarter students. Kits vary in price depending on the program of study.

Financial Aid

Financial aid is available for those who qualify. Students who require financial assistance should first complete and submit a Free Application for Federal Student Aid (FAFSA) and meet with a financial aid officer. The officer determines the level of need based on a required federal formula, the cost of education, and other factors. Gift aid is available in the form of Federal Pell Grants, Federal Supplemental Educational Opportunity Grants, and veterans' benefits. Loans include Federal Stafford Student Loans, Federal PLUS loans, and alternative loans. Other scholarships are available from the school and private sources. Application deadlines and eligibility requirements vary by program.

Faculty

The Illinois Institute of Art–Schaumburg faculty consists of full-time and part-time instructors, many of whom have advanced degrees and professional experience in their respective fields of study.

Admission Requirements

Prospective students must demonstrate evidence of high school graduation or its equivalent, such as a General Educational Development (GED) certificate, before applying to The Illinois Institute of Art–Schaumburg. All applicants must interview (either in person or over the telephone) with an admissions officer and submit a 300-word essay explaining how an education at The Art Institute of Illinois–Schaumburg will help the student achieve his or her creative goals. Each academic transcript and essay is evaluated by the Admissions Acceptance Committee. The committee reserves the right to request additional information. A separate application and enrollment form must be completed and signed by the applicant and submitted to the school. There is a $50 application fee.

Application and Information

To obtain an application or make arrangements for an interview or tour of the school, students should contact:

The Illinois Institute of Art–Schaumburg
1000 North Plaza Drive, Suite 100
Schaumburg, Illinois 60173-4990
Phone: 847-619-3450
800-314-3450 (toll-free)
Fax: 847-619-3064
Web site: http://www.artinstitutes.edu/schaumburg

The Art Institute of Atlanta®, GA; The Art Institute of Atlanta®–Decatur, GA; The Art Institute of Austin℠, TX; The Art Institute of California℠–Inland Empire; The Art Institute of California℠–Los Angeles; The Art Institute of California℠–Orange County; The Art Institute of California℠–Sacramento; The Art Institute of California℠–San Diego; The Art Institute of California℠–San Francisco; The Art Institute of California℠–Sunnyvale; The Art Institute of Charleston℠, SC, A branch of The Art Institute of Atlanta, GA; The Art Institute of Charlotte®, NC; The Art Institute of Colorado® (Denver); The Art Institute of Dallas®, TX; The Art Institute of Fort Lauderdale®, FL; The Art Institute of Houston®, TX; The Art Institute of Indianapolis℠, IN*; The Art Institute of Jacksonville℠, FL, A branch of Miami International University of Art & Design; The Art Institute of Las Vegas®, NV; The Art Institute of Michigan℠ (Detroit); The Art Institute of New York City®, NY; The Art Institute of Ohio℠–Cincinnati**; The Art Institute of Philadelphia®, PA; The Art Institute of Phoenix®, AZ; The Art Institute of Pittsburgh®, PA; The Art Institute of Pittsburgh®–Online Division; The Art Institute of Portland®, OR; The Art Institute of Salt Lake City℠, UT; The Art Institute of Seattle®, WA; The Art Institute of Tampa℠, FL, A branch of Miami International University of Art & Design; The Art Institute of Tennessee℠–Nashville, A branch of The Art Institute of Atlanta, GA; The Art Institute of Tucson℠, AZ; The Art Institute of Washington® (Arlington, VA), A branch of The Art Institute of Atlanta, GA; The Art Institute of York–Pennsylvania℠; The Art Institutes International Minnesota℠ (Minneapolis); California Design College℠ (Los Angeles–Wilshire Blvd.); The Illinois Institute of Art®–Chicago; The Illinois Institute of Art®–Schaumburg; Miami International University of Art & Design℠, FL; The New England Institute of Art® (Boston, MA).

*The Art Institute of Indianapolis is licensed by the Indiana Commission on Proprietary Education, 302 W. Washington St., Rm. E201, Indianapolis, IN 46204, AC-0080.

**The Art Institute of Ohio–Cincinnati, 8845 Governors Hill Drive, Suite 100, Cincinnati, OH 45249-3317, OH Reg. #04-01-1698B.

ILLINOIS INSTITUTE OF TECHNOLOGY

CHICAGO, ILLINOIS

The Institute

Illinois Institute of Technology (IIT) is a private, Ph.D.-granting research university with undergraduate programs in architecture, business, engineering, humanities, psychology, and science. One of the select institutions in the Association of Independent Technological Universities (AITU), IIT offers exceptional preparation for professions that require technological sophistication. Through a committed faculty and close personal attention, IIT provides a challenging academic program focused on the rigor of the real world. The internationally famous main campus is based on a master plan developed by the late Ludwig Mies van der Rohe, one of the most influential architects of the century, who served for twenty years as director of IIT's College of Architecture. An independent university, the Institute includes the College of Architecture, the Armour College of Engineering, the College of Science and Letters, the Stuart School of Business, the Institute of Psychology, the Institute of Design, and the Chicago-Kent College of Law.

The more than 6,000 students at IIT (more than 2,000 of whom are undergraduates) are encouraged to participate in the many social, cultural, and athletic opportunities available. Student activities include the campus newspaper *(TechNews),* the radio station (WIIT), special interest clubs, theater groups, intramural and varsity athletics, fraternities and sororities, honor societies, professional societies, student government, residence hall organizations, and the student-run Union Board. The VanderCook College of Music is also located on the IIT campus for students interested in studying music or participating in musical performances. Campus facilities include the McCormick Tribune Campus Center, a convenience store and campus book store, a coffee shop, a gymnasium, outdoor tennis and volleyball courts, thirteen residence halls, two resident sorority houses, and six resident fraternity houses. Counseling, job placement, and student health services are included in the various campus services.

Location

IIT stands in the midst of a developing urban area. It is 1 mile west of Lake Michigan and one block from the recent world-champion White Sox ballpark. The campus is located approximately 3 miles south of the Chicago Loop, offering students unlimited opportunities to enjoy art, music, theater, movies, museums, shopping, and other entertainment. Also convenient to the campus are a number of recreational areas, including McCormick Place exhibition hall, Soldier Field, Grant Park, Millennium Park, Lincoln Park Zoo, various bicycle paths, and lakefront beaches. IIT is easily accessible to the rest of Chicago via two major expressways. Bus and elevated train lines have stops on the campus, and the IIT shuttle bus provides free transportation between the campus and the university's Downtown Campus in Chicago's West Loop area.

Majors and Degrees

The Armour College of Engineering offers the Bachelor of Science in aerospace, architectural, biomedical, chemical, civil, computer, electrical, mechanical, and materials science engineering. The College of Science and Letters offers the Bachelor of Science in applied mathematics; biochemistry; biology; chemistry; computer information systems; computer science; humanities; journalism of science, technology, and business; molecular biochemistry and biophysics; physics; political science; and professional and technical communication.

The College of Architecture awards the Bachelor of Architecture degree through its five-year professional degree program.

There are various options and minors available within each curriculum, such as artificial intelligence, bioengineering, business, computer-aided drafting, energy/environment/economics, law, management, manufacturing technology, military science, organizational psychology, polymer science and engineering, and technical communications. Other individualized specializations may be arranged with approval of the dean. Combined undergraduate/graduate degrees include those offered in conjunction with business administration (B.S./M.B.A.), law (B.S./J.D.), and public administration (B.S./M.P.A.).

IIT has also established combined-degree programs in medicine (B.S./D.O.), law (B.S./J.D.), pharmacy (B.S./Pharm.D.), and optometry (B.S./O.D.). Students interested in a combined-degree program must submit an undergraduate application and a supplemental application for the graduate portion of the program.

Academic Programs

While requirements vary according to the major, all IIT students complete a general education core, which includes a minimum of 7 semester hours in mathematics and computer science, 11 semester hours in natural science or engineering, 12 semester hours in the humanities, and 12 semester hours in the social sciences. Students pursuing a Bachelor of Science in an engineering field or in the physical sciences take, in addition, a program that includes further study in mathematics and computer science, chemistry, and physics.

IIT's mission is to advance knowledge through research and scholarship, to cultivate invention improving the human condition, and to educate students from throughout the world for a life of professional achievement, service to society, and individual fulfillment. The Institute is committed to the educational ideal of small undergraduate classes and individual mentoring. IIT's signature Introduction to the Professions (IPRO) program brings students and senior faculty members together each week in small groups, where students interact with their advisers as both teachers and mentors. Throughout the curricula, the IIT interprofessional projects provide a learning environment in which interdisciplinary teams of students apply theoretical knowledge gained in the classroom and laboratory to real-world projects sponsored by industry and government. Many IIT students further enhance their education through a wide variety of research and entrepreneurial projects.

Cooperative education is encouraged. This career development program begins with a freshman year of full-time study and then alternates semesters of study and employment in industry for approximately four additional years. Placement services are provided by the university. More than 90 percent of recent graduates were placed in jobs in the fields of their majors or went on to graduate or professional schools.

Study abroad is available in several academic disciplines through the International Center at IIT.

Academic Facilities

As the central library, the Paul V. Galvin Library provides a broad range of services, including information on engineering, business, science, mathematics, the humanities, architecture, and design via the Internet; numerous electronic and paper-based databases; a document delivery service; interlibrary loan; and special collections. The main campus operates DEC minicomputers, a Silicon Graphics Challenge UNIX multiprocessor, and local UNIX servers. Terminals and microcomputers are located in most academic buildings across the campus, in residence halls, and in Galvin Library. Seminars, tutorials, and computer lab work are conducted in microcomputer classrooms. Among IIT's thirty-two research centers are the Center for Synchrotron Radiation Research, the Fluid Dynamics Research Center, and the Research Laboratory in Human Biomechanics. Most research centers offer undergraduates opportunities to participate on their projects.

Costs

Annual tuition for 2007–08 was $24,962. Other expenses were $8618 for room and board and $794 for fees. The estimated annual total for freshmen was $34,374. Annual tuition covers the fall and spring semesters.

Financial Aid

Most full-time undergraduates at IIT receive financial aid from a variety of sources. IIT participates in the Federal Perkins Loan, Federal Work-Study, Federal Pell Grant, Federal Supplemental Educational Opportunity Grant, federally insured student loan, Illinois State Scholarship Commission Monetary Award, Illinois Guaranteed Loan, and Federal PLUS Loan programs and similar programs. In addition, IIT provides generous merit-based and need-based scholarships and loans from its own funds and from those supported by a number of companies and other organizations. The Camras Scholarships award up to full tuition for the study of any major. All admitted students are automatically reviewed for tuition scholarships. Athletic scholarships are also available for qualified students. Two other programs may be utilized by students working to supplement their financial aid: on-campus employment and the cooperative education program. IIT requires the Free Application for Federal Student Aid (FAFSA). No additional applications or forms are required.

Army, Naval, and Air Force ROTC programs are offered. ROTC scholarship winners receive supplemental scholarships from IIT.

Faculty

There are 359 full-time faculty members and 300 industry professionals as part-time faculty members. The student-faculty ratio is approximately 8:1. All members of the senior teaching faculty instruct in both upper- and lower-division courses. Ninety percent hold doctoral degrees or the highest professional degree in their area.

Student Government

The Student Government Association (SGA) is a vital force in the IIT community. It acts as the students' official voice in communications with faculty and administration, and it plans, develops, and supervises most of the activities pertaining to campus life. In addition to having its own standing committees, SGA is represented on seven of the ten institutional committees pertaining to undergraduates.

Admission Requirements

Admission evaluation is a thorough, personal process. Of paramount consideration is the student's academic performance in high school, specifically in areas that are vital to the student's major at IIT. Minimum high school preparation includes 16 units of credit, including at least 4 units in English, 4 units in mathematics through precalculus, and 3 units of science with 2 lab sciences. Calculus is encouraged but not required. Chemistry and physics are strongly recommended.

A completed application, recommendations, test scores (either SAT or ACT), and an official high school transcript are required for admission.

Application and Information

IIT admits the majority of its students on a rolling basis. Special application deadlines do apply for the College of Architecture, special programs, and some scholarships. Students should visit the Web site for details. Students should apply as early as possible, starting in the senior year of high school; an online application is available at http://apply.iit.edu. In general, applicants can expect notification within two weeks after their completed applications are received.

For further information, students should contact:

Office of Undergraduate Admission
Perlstein Hall 101
Illinois Institute of Technology
10 West 33rd Street
Chicago, Illinois 60616-3793
Phone: 312-567-3025 (in Chicago)
800-448-2329 (toll-free outside Chicago)
Fax: 312-567-6939
E-mail: admission@iit.edu
Web site: http://www.iit.edu

INTERNATIONAL ACADEMY OF DESIGN & TECHNOLOGY

CHICAGO, ILLINOIS

The Academy

The International Academy of Design & Technology in Chicago and Schaumburg offers educational programs in a variety of unique, diverse, energetic, and professional environments. Here students find the real-world guidance they want with the hands-on experience they need. They gain support from outstanding faculty members and fellow students and have the opportunity to cultivate career-building connections that may last a lifetime. The institution is filled with inspiration in the heart of Chicagoland's fashion, interior design, and advertising industries.

The Academy is a postsecondary degree-granting institution with career-based curricula and professional staff members who contribute to students' development in their chosen fields. The Academy provides a high-quality education, prepares students for positions in fields related to their area of study, and provides students with a professional environment that fosters cultural enrichment and personal development. The Academic Department at the Academy maintains high-quality curricula that are sensitive to industry needs, as defined by the Academy's Advisory Boards. The Career Services department offers career-planning services leading to employment opportunities for graduates to allow them to utilize their knowledge, skills, and talents.

The International Academy of Design & Technology in Chicago was founded in 1977 by Clem Stein Jr. as a private institution located in the Merchandise Mart of Chicago. In 1983, the Academy opened a campus in Toronto, Canada. The Tampa, Florida, campus was opened in 1984, and today there are ten campuses nationwide, including the Schaumburg campus, which opened in 2004. In 1997, Career Education Corporation acquired the Academy. Career Education Corporation operates postsecondary institutions throughout the U.S. and abroad. In 2001, the Academy changed its name from the International Academy of Merchandising & Design to the International Academy of Design & Technology, which better reflects the infusion of technology into all of the program curricula.

There are various associations and clubs for Academy students. These clubs include the Fashion Council (fashion design), Behind the Scene (merchandising management), S7UDIO (graphic design), the Information Technology Organization (IT), Playback (multimedia and Web design), the Interior Design Student Association (interior design), Game On (game design), the Movie Club, Resident's Life (international student club), and 360dpi (AIGA student chapter). These clubs are organized by and for students. GLBT@IADT Community is the Academy's outreach to gay, lesbian, bisexual, and transgender students. The Academy also has a student-produced magazine, **Asterisk.*

The Academy is incorporated under the laws of the state of Illinois and accredited by the Accrediting Council for Independent Colleges and Schools (ACICS). The interior design program is accredited by the Council for Interior Design Accreditation.

Location

The Academy is located in Chicago's Loop at historic One North State Street. The campus is close to some of Chicago's famous and world-renowned landmarks. Within walking distance of the campus are the Merchandise Mart and the Apparel Center complex in historic River North and the retail shops of North Michigan Avenue. Along the revitalized State Street are Macy's, Sears, and a multitude of nationally advertised retail outlets. More importantly, the Academy in Chicago is conveniently located in a region known for its internationally prominent advertising, graphic design, and interior design firms.

Nearby cultural and educational resources include the Art Institute of Chicago, the Harold Washington Library, the Chicago Cultural Center, the Athenaeum Museum of Architecture and Design, the Chicago Architecture Foundation, and the Goodman Theatre.

The natural beauty of Grant Park, Millennium Park, and the numerous public art works located throughout the Loop are the ideal complement to IADT Chicago's exciting urban location.

Majors and Degrees

The Academy is authorized by the Illinois Board of Higher Education to grant a Bachelor of Arts degree in merchandising management (tracks in fashion merchandising and retail operations management), a Bachelor of Applied Science degree in information technology, a Bachelor of Science degree in computer forensics, and a Bachelor of Fine Arts degree in fashion design, interior design, and visual communications (tracks in advertising communication, advertising design, game design, graphic design, multimedia and Web design, and video and animation production). The Academy is also authorized to grant Associate of Applied Science degrees in fashion design, merchandising management (tracks in fashion merchandising and retail operations management), information technology, and visual communication (tracks in advertising communication, advertising design, graphic design, multimedia and Web design, and video and animation production).

All degree programs provide students with the opportunity for in-depth career preparation and a firm foundation in general education studies. In the bachelor's degree programs, students benefit from advanced career courses and have the option of choosing elective courses to complete their general education requirements.

Academic Programs

The programs of the Academy involve both classroom education and supervised activities off campus that are designed to prepare students for entry-level positions in their chosen field. Students must take a minimum of 180 quarter hours of study to earn the baccalaureate degree. Transfer credits are acceptable in all programs. Students must take a minimum of 96 quarter hours to earn the Associate of Applied Science degree and must complete all prescribed courses satisfactorily with a minimum grade point average of 2.0.

The curriculum for each program is reviewed periodically by faculty members, program chairs, and members of the program Advisory Boards. Members of the Advisory Boards are experienced professionals in their fields. The Advisory Boards provide the Academy with input on a variety of subjects related to their specific industry. These successful practitioners form an essential link between the academic world and the world that students enter upon graduation.

The Academy's programs are arranged into four quarters of eleven weeks each in a calendar year. A normal full-time load is 12 credit hours per quarter. As a result of the career-oriented emphasis of the Academy, course work is highly specialized and prepares students for entry into a career field. From the point at which they begin their studies at the Academy and continue through to graduation, students are given personal one-on-one academic guidance. Students are regularly advised by the Academy's academic advisers regarding their progress in classes.

Academic Facilities

Classrooms are designed to facilitate learning and consist of lecture rooms, textile labs, drafting labs, design studios, and sewing and pattern-making rooms. Computer labs equipped with Macintosh and IBM-compatible personal computers are used for instruction and practice.

The library houses a growing collection of approximately 6,500 book volumes and 90 periodical subscriptions to support the major programs of study as well as general education courses. The library's multimedia resources consist of more than 600 videos, DVDs, and CDs with image and sound files. Other components of the collection are electronic resources with access to e-books, full-text journals, magazines, and newspaper articles. A professional librarian manages the site and assists students in the use of the library's print collection and online databases. The librarian also facilitates student access to local libraries that participate in the INFOPASS program.

The bookstore sells books and supplies used in the courses taught at the Academy. The bookstore attempts to keep a balance of inventory between new and used books whenever possible. School-specific merchandise and clothing are also available for purchase. The bookstore coordinates book buyback periods at the end of each quarter.

Costs

Tuition for the 2007–08 academic year for all programs was $410 per credit hour for students enrolled in up to 12 credit hours and $360 per credit hour for students enrolled in 13 or more credit hours per term. Books and supplies are additional.

Financial Aid

The Academy helps students find the financial resources they need to achieve their educational goals. The Academy participates in the Federal Pell Grant, Federal Supplemental Educational Opportunity Grant (FSEOG), Federal Stafford Student Loan, and Federal PLUS programs. In addition to state and federal aid, the Academy has its own scholarship programs.

Faculty

Faculty members of the Academy possess extensive academic and professional credentials. Their experience enables them to teach theoretical principles while emphasizing current practices in the field. Faculty members are sought and retained because they are committed to teaching at the undergraduate level. In and out of the classroom, the faculty is an integral part of the students' career preparation.

Admission Requirements

Pursuant to the mission of the institution, the Academy desires to admit students who possess appropriate credentials and have demonstrated the capacity or potential for successfully completing the educational programs offered by the institution. To that end, the institution evaluates all students and makes admission decisions on an individual basis. To assist the admissions personnel in making informed decisions, an admissions interview is required.

Transfer students meeting admission requirements are accepted. Students must have an official transcript from postsecondary institutions previously attended forwarded to the Academy. Credit may be given for a course taken at the previous institution if it is comparable in scope and length to an International Academy course, as stated in the Academy's Transfer Credit Guidelines.

Application and Information

Prospective students should apply for admission as soon as possible in order to be officially accepted for a specific program and its starting date. Prospective students must have an admissions interview, during which they are given an opportunity to tour the Academy with their families to see its equipment and facilities. At this time, there is also an opportunity to ask questions relating to the Academy's curricula and a student's possible career goals.

At the time of application, the student must complete an enrollment agreement, pay a $50 application fee, and complete an attestation of high school graduation or its equivalency or provide proof of high school graduation or its equivalency. Once an applicant has completed and submitted the enrollment agreement, the school reviews the information and informs the applicant of its decision.

For further information, students should contact:

Cecily Arroyo, Vice President of Admissions
International Academy of Design & Technology
One North State Street, Suite 500
Chicago, Illinois 60602-3300
Phone: 888-704-2111 (toll-free)
Fax: 312-541-3929
E-mail: info@iadtchicago.com
Web site: http://www.iadtchicago.edu

KENDALL COLLEGE

CHICAGO, ILLINOIS

The College

The nationally acclaimed School of Culinary Arts at Kendall College has been cultivating exceptional culinary professionals since 1985. Kendall College's bachelor's and associate degree programs are intensive, hands-on, and cutting-edge. The programs are designed to successfully launch students' careers in foodservice, equipped with superb culinary skills and the equally critical business management and communication skills. Kendall College fully prepares its students with the well-rounded education, business acumen, intellectual agility, and professional attitude needed for an enduring career in the culinary arts.

Kendall College's rigorous culinary degree programs are organized sequentially, requiring a minimum of seven quarters of structured study (excluding the Accelerated A.A.S. program), each with hands-on time in the kitchen. Kendall College's faculty members believe that Kendall's seven-quarter regimen of classes is the minimum needed to develop the culinary skills, techniques, and professionalism needed for long-term success. Drawing on their extensive industry experience, Kendall's faculty has designed its programs to prepare students to meet and overcome the real-world challenges they are likely to face as pivotal people in the foodservice industry.

Culinary students in Kendall College's Bachelor of Arts (B.A.) program are immersed in the cuisines and cultures of Latin and South America, the Mediterranean, and Asia, with exciting courses taught by chefs who are natives of those regions. Beyond the culinary arts essentials, Kendall students learn how to plan, build, promote, run, and sustain a flourishing food-related business. Kendall College graduates have the professional skills, attitude, and knowledge needed to succeed in today's fast-paced culinary business world.

Outside of class, Kendall is also committed to providing an active social and cultural life for its students. Kendall College is located in its new $60-million Riverworks Campus in Chicago, Illinois, and students are able to take advantage of the rich resources the city has to offer. Kendall College's residence hall, located at 320 North Michigan Avenue, is steps away from world-class museums, shopping, and entertainment.

Kendall College is accredited by the Commission on Institutions of Higher Education of the North Central Association of Colleges and Schools (NCACS) and the University Senate of the United Methodist Church. The School of Culinary Arts is accredited by the American Culinary Federation (ACF) Accrediting Commission.

Location

Kendall College offers classes at its new Chicago Riverworks campus. Kendall's state-of-the-art facilities prepare its graduates for the newest leading-edge opportunities in the culinary, hospitality, and business industries. The campus is minutes from some of the country's best restaurants, hotels, and companies, providing students prime access to internships and work experiences. The facility offers sweeping views of the Chicago skyline, access to newly developed areas on the Chicago River, and all the cultural and social benefits of the third-largest city in the United States.

Majors and Degrees

Kendall College awards Bachelor of Arts (B.A.) degrees in business management, culinary arts, early childhood education, and hospitality management. The College also awards the Associate of Applied Science (A.A.S.) degree in baking and pastry arts and culinary arts.

The culinary arts program offers certificates in baking and pastry arts, professional catering, professional personal chef, and professional cookery. The hospitality management program offers several concentrations: convention and meeting planning, culinary management, food and beverage operations, hotel management, and international hospitality management.

Academic Programs

Kendall College operates on a quarter system. The first quarter term extends from September to early December, the second term extends from January to March, and the third term extends from April to June. Summer sessions are offered from July to September. Students must fulfill a minimum of 96 quarter hours for an associate degree and a minimum of 192 quarter hours for a bachelor's degree and maintain at least a 2.0 GPA.

Academic Facilities

The Chicago Riverworks campus provides wireless Internet access, labs with the latest computer equipment, and two distance learning videoconference facilities. Classrooms and study environments are high-tech and flexible, designed to give students a first-class, state-of-the-art setting in which to learn. There are student lounges, sixteen kitchens, secure parking spaces, and a number of nearby health clubs.

Costs

In 2007–08, full-time tuition and fees for the School of Hospitality Management were $16,950 for three quarters (12–19 credit hours).

Full-time tuition and fees in the School of Business were $12,000 for three quarters.

Full-time tuition and fees in the School of Culinary Arts were $21,450 for three quarters, including culinary facilities usage.

Full-time tuition and fees in the School of Education were $250 per credit hour for in-classroom courses and $200 per credit hour for online courses.

Housing is located at 320 North Michigan Avenue and at the Presidential Towers, located at 555 West Madison Avenue. Students may lease double- or triple-occupancy apartments for $11,400 per twelve-month lease. Single-occupancy apartments are leased to students for $22,800 per twelve-month lease.

Financial Aid

The College works with each student and develops a needs analysis to determine student eligibility, which then culminates in a financial aid package. It is the goal of Kendall College to seek funding and to package aid to fully meet the needs of all applicants. The financial aid packaging process ensures effective use of available funds, providing fair and equitable treatment of all applicants. Priority is given to applicants who meet the April 1 preferential filing date.

The College administers aid for undergraduates, including need-based, merit-based, and curriculum-specific scholarships; state and federal awards; Federal Supplemental Educational Opportunity Grants (FSEOG); Federal Work-Study Program awards; and opportunities for campus employment.

Faculty

The student-faculty ratio is approximately 19:1. Faculty members at Kendall College believe students work best when they are actively involved in making choices about their own learning. As Kendall students develop clear ideas of what they wish to study, they are provided with the opportunities to use tutorials to continue their education.

Student Government

Kendall College's Student Government Federation is designed to give students a leadership role and voice in building and improving their campus community. The Student Government Federation is elected annually in the fall term and is composed of a president, vice-president, and a group of senators. This group serves in an advisory capacity to the Board of Trustees, the Faculty Senate and various other faculty committees.

Admission Requirements

Kendall assesses its entrance difficulty level as moderate. Admission to Kendall College is open to men and women of all races and religious affiliations. Each applicant is considered on the basis of probable success at Kendall, as indicated primarily by high school grades, class rank, and ACT or SAT test scores. A minimum GPA of 2.0 and an ACT composite score of at least 18 or an SAT score (combined math and verbal) of at least 850 are required for acceptance. If a student falls below either the minimum GPA or the standardized test requirements, the student must complete an entrance examination and submit two letters of recommendation. An essay accompanying the application is required. Qualities of character are also important at Kendall. Therefore, personal interviews and campus visits are encouraged, though not required, to help determine admission.

Application and Information

Prospective students may obtain applications from the Office of Admissions or via the College's Web site. Students may submit the admission application at any time. The Office of Admissions must be sent an official transcript.

For further information, students should contact:

Office of Admissions
Kendall College
900 N. North Branch Street
Chicago, Illinois 60622
Phone: 312-752-2020
877-588-8860 (toll-free)
Fax: 312-752-2021
E-mail: admissions@kendall.edu
Web site: http://www.kendall.edu

A view of Kendall College's new Riverworks campus in Chicago.

COLLEGE DATA CENTER • ILLINOIS

LAKE FOREST COLLEGE

LAKE FOREST, ILLINOIS

The College

Lake Forest College is a coeducational undergraduate community of 1,400 students that celebrates the personal growth accompanying the quest for excellence. Founded in 1857, Lake Forest provides a secure residential campus of great beauty and enriches its curriculum with the vibrant resources of Chicago.

A national liberal arts college, Lake Forest prides itself on diversity, with students representing forty-five states and sixty-five other countries. International students and members of minority groups comprise more than 25 percent of the Lake Forest student body. With a vast majority of its students living in residence halls, Lake Forest fosters interaction and shared experiences among its diverse population. Through its innovative Gates Center for Leadership and Personal Growth, students are provided with many opportunities to develop essential life skills and enhance their college experience.

More than ninety student organizations, groups, and clubs provide students with a wide range of extracurricular opportunities. These enriching experiences work in unison with Lake Forest's high standards of academic excellence and integrity. Lake Forest College helps individuals develop lives of leadership, service, and personal fulfillment.

Lake Forest is a member of NCAA Division III Midwest Conference and competes in the Northern Collegiate Hockey Association. There are seventeen varsity sports teams. The eight men's teams are basketball, cross-country, football, handball, hockey, soccer, swimming and diving, and wrestling. Nine women's teams compete in basketball, cross-country, handball, ice hockey, soccer, softball, swimming and diving, tennis, and volleyball. Intramural and club sports are popular, providing opportunities for all students to be physically active and competitive.

Location

Thirty miles north of Chicago on the western shore of Lake Michigan, Lake Forest College is situated on 107 scenic wooded acres in a residential community. The town of Lake Forest is 25 miles from O'Hare International Airport. Students are within an easy commute by train to Chicago, a world-class city of nearly 3 million people and a treasure of cultural resources. Chicago has become an extension of the campus and many courses are designed to take advantage of the rich resources of the city. Internships, independent study, research projects, and cultural opportunities are readily available. The College's Center for Chicago Programs organizes trips, helps students plan visits to the city, facilitates student internships, brings Chicago-area speakers and performers to campus, and helps professors incorporate Chicago into their classrooms.

Majors and Degrees

Lake Forest College awards the Bachelor of Arts (B.A.) degree in both traditional academic departments and interdisciplinary programs. Departmental majors are art, biology, business, chemistry, communications, computer science, economics, education (in conjunction with another major), English, French, history, mathematics, music, philosophy, physics, politics, psychology, religion, sociology and anthropology, Spanish, and theater. The interdisciplinary majors are American studies, area studies, Asian studies, environmental studies, international relations, and Latin American studies. Language courses are also available in Arabic, Chinese, and Japanese.

Students may create their own majors through the Independent Scholar Program, which enables qualified and motivated students to design and pursue individual degree programs that focus on particular topics or themes rather than on a single academic discipline.

In addition, students can declare a minor in those departmental and nondepartmental programs that have a major, as well as in African American studies, German, metropolitan studies, and women's and gender studies.

Lake Forest offers a cooperative degree (3-2) program with the Sever School of Engineering of Washington University (St. Louis). Students may receive a Bachelor of Arts degree from Lake Forest and a Bachelor of Science degree from Washington University.

Academic Programs

Lake Forest College bases its academic calendar on two 15-week semesters, from late August through mid-December and from mid-January through early May. The curriculum establishes an integrated framework for the general education of undergraduate students across four years of study. The curriculum includes general education requirements, which ensure that students receive educational breadth as well as depth while allowing considerable latitude in designing individual programs of study. Also included are requirements for writing and cultural diversity. To obtain a degree, students are expected to pass thirty-two courses, fulfill the general education requirements, and complete the requirements of a major.

Off-Campus Programs

In addition to a well-established internship program, Lake Forest College provides students with a wide variety of opportunities for off-campus study, both domestic and international. Semester-long options in the United States include the Chicago Arts Program, the Oak Ridge Science Semester, the Chicago Urban Studies Program, the Chicago Program in Business and Society, the Newberry Library Program in the Humanities, and the Washington Semester Program at American University.

There are many options for international study, such as Lake Forest's own international internship programs in Paris, France, and Santiago, Chile; the Ancient Civilizations Program in Greece, which uses historical and archaeological sites and museums to study the ancient Aegean world; and Lake Forest's Beijing program of Asian studies. As a member of the Associated Colleges of the Midwest, Lake Forest also offers programs in such countries as Botswana, Costa Rica, England, India, Italy, Japan, Russia, and Tanzania.

Academic Facilities

Since 2000, Lake Forest College has invested nearly $50 million in campuswide capital improvements, including the Donnelley and Lee Library, Farwell Athletic Field, Deerpath and Nollen residence halls, the Mohr Student Center and Stuart Commons, and technology enhancements in classrooms and dormitories.

The Donnelley and Lee Library is a twenty-first century library and information technology center having recently undergone an $18-million expansion and renovation. The new facility incorporates the latest concepts, ideas, and technological innovations pertaining to teaching and learning while providing a comfortable environment for collaboration, including a 24-hour computer lab, a café, a production and rhetoric room, smart classrooms, and a technology resource center.

Currently, the library contains approximately 300,000 books and government documents and over 1,000 current periodical subscriptions. In addition, the library provides online access to articles from several thousand electronic periodical titles. The library features a strong literacy program, through which students can gain proficiency with a wide variety of information resources. Lake Forest students and faculty members have online access to the holdings of 123 academic and research libraries statewide and can borrow books online from any of those libraries. The library's Special Collections Unit includes the College Archives and houses rare books, manuscripts, and government documents.

Information technology services works closely with library staff members to support the information and technology needs of the campus. There are more than 180 public-access computers available for student use in computing labs on campus. The Brown Technology Resource Center, which is equipped with advanced high-end computing hardware and software, is available for students and faculty members, and technology specialists are on hand for assistance. The library, student center, some classrooms, and all residence hall rooms have wireless access; faculty offices, laboratories, and other classrooms are connected to the College's fiber-optic network.

Among the fifty-five buildings on campus is the Dixon Science Research Center, which is designed for student-faculty research. The modern three-story, 7,500-square-foot facility contains thirteen laboratories and two animal holding facilities. State-of-the-art equipment includes a nuclear magnetic resonance spectrometer with a 400-megahertz superconductivity magnet, a solid-state gamma-ray spectrometer, a multi-imaging phosphorimager, digital-storage oscilloscopes, and fluorescence microscopes.

Costs

Comprehensive fees for 2007–08 were $38,290: tuition and fees, $30,964, and room and board, $7326.

Financial Aid

Lake Forest College provides an affordable, high-quality education while maintaining a strong commitment to supporting each student's demonstrated financial need. More than $18 million is awarded annually in Lake Forest College grant and scholarship assistance.

Lake Forest awards scholarships ranging from $1000 to full tuition in recognition of academic achievement or recognized dedication in the fine arts, foreign languages, leadership, math and computer science, music, natural science, theater, or writing.

Faculty

At the core of the College stands its distinguished faculty of excellent teachers and accomplished scholars. The College seeks and retains faculty members principally because they enjoy and excel at teaching undergraduates. Faculty members, not graduate assistants, teach courses and advise students. A student-faculty ratio of 12:1 gives students easy access to their teachers while providing opportunities for informed counsel about individual programs of study.

The faculty's tradition of teaching excellence is matched and supported by its achievement in scholarly research. More than 98 percent hold a Ph.D. or its equivalent. Faculty members have won national teaching awards and have spoken and consulted throughout the United States and abroad. More than 30 percent have published books in their disciplines. Lake Forest faculty members continually receive fellowships and grants from prestigious institutions and foundations in the U.S. and abroad.

Student Government

The first Lake Forest College student body self-governing organization was the Student Council, which was established in 1917. Today, Student Government is composed of the General Assembly and its subcommittees, the Executive Committee, and the four Student Government officers. Student members of other College governing committees also play an active and important role in the Student Government.

Ultimate responsibility for guiding Lake Forest College rests with the Board of Trustees. The Student Government president and vice-president report to the full board at quarterly meetings. Students at Lake Forest College advise the administration through representation on a variety of governance committees that deal with the hiring of faculty members, institutional priorities such as allocation of the budget, department course offerings, and administering a judicial system. Students also take a prominent role in enhancing the educational growth and social life of the campus community.

Admission Requirements

Lake Forest College has a test-optional admission practice, permitting students to choose whether or not to submit their ACT or SAT scores as part of their application for admission. As a highly selective college that values well-rounded students, Lake Forest evaluates each student based on qualities that determine success in college, including strong academic performance in a challenging high school curriculum, leadership experience and commitment to community, and extracurricular involvement and individual talent. Lake Forest College unequivocally selects its students without regard to social background, religious affiliation, race, national origin, gender, handicap, or financial position. This admission policy is manifest in the diverse nature of the student community.

Students are urged to begin the application procedure early in their final year of secondary school. The Early Action deadline is December 1. This option is nonbinding but allows the student to receive an admission decision as early as mid-January. The Early Decision (binding) deadline is December 1. The Regular Decision deadline is February 15.

Lake Forest recommends a precollege program that includes a minimum of 4 years of English; 3 or more years of mathematics, including algebra II; in-depth study in one or more foreign languages; and 3 or more years of work in both the social and natural sciences. Personal interviews are required for those choosing not to submit standardized test scores and are strongly encouraged for all candidates. The admission staff encourages visits to the campus by prospective students and their families.

Candidates for undergraduate admission may obtain the required application forms by contacting the Admission Office. Lake Forest College also accepts the Common Application in lieu of its own form and gives equal consideration to both. Students may obtain copies of the Common Application from their high school. Students who wish to defer enrollment should complete the application procedure during the final year of secondary school.

Transfer students are admitted at the beginning of each semester. Transfer applicants should have achieved an overall college average of at least a C or its equivalent and be eligible to return to their previous institutions. When a transfer student is admitted to the College, the maximum credit accepted in transfer is 59 semester hours. All transfer students are required to submit the following credentials: an application for admission, a secondary school transcript, transcripts of all college work completed through the most recent term, a three–five page graded essay paper, and a letter of recommendation from the academic dean or a professor at the current college (for students with more than 30 semester hours).

Application and Information

The Admission Office is open from 8:30 a.m. to 5 p.m. on weekdays and 9 a.m. to 1 p.m. on Saturdays throughout the year. For further information, including a campus tour, an interview, or an application form, prospective students should contact:

Admission Office
Lake Forest College
555 North Sheridan Road
Lake Forest, Illinois 60045
Phone: 847-735-5000
800-828-4751 (toll-free)
Fax: 847-735-6271
E-mail: admissions@lakeforest.edu
Web site: http://www.lakeforest.edu

LEWIS UNIVERSITY

ROMEOVILLE, ILLINOIS

The University

Lewis University is a coeducational, comprehensive, Catholic and Lasallian university located in the Midwest, with an enrollment of more than 5,300 students. Lewis demonstrates its commitment to providing a high-quality, mission-based education by providing more than 85 percent of its new incoming students with some form of financial aid. The main campus is a picturesque 376-acre setting with eleven residence halls that house 1,000 students within easy walking distance of all campus buildings.

Lewis has been strengthened by the educational mission of the De La Salle Christian Brothers and their colleagues. Since they arrived on the campus in 1960, the Christian Brothers have been the providers of a high-quality education and personal attention based on the heritage of their founder, Saint John Baptist de La Salle. The student-faculty ratio of 14:1 ensures that students interact with their instructors. Lewis is large enough to provide the resources of a university while maintaining personal contact with each student.

The Lewis education includes small classes, service-learning opportunities, a beautiful and safe campus environment, an ideal location, and an active campus life. These elements combine to provide an educational experience that focuses on career preparation, academic choices, community service, and lifelong learning. Lewis has positioned itself as an academic leader and is recognized for its commitment to mission effectiveness.

The majority of Lewis students are Illinois residents, but students represent more than thirty-six states and twenty-five countries. Campus residence halls allow for various living styles, including apartment and suite arrangements. More than thirty clubs and organizations offer students opportunities for a variety of social, athletic, academic, career, or hobby-related interests. Eighteen intercollegiate sports include men's and women's basketball, cross-country, golf, soccer, swimming, track, tennis, and volleyball plus men's baseball and women's softball. All teams compete in NCAA Division II. Lewis teams have captured the Great Lakes Valley Conference (GLVC) All-Sports Trophy twelve times, more than any other conference member. Lewis student-athletes also excel in the classroom; the University produced 2 Academic All-Americans last year, giving it 8 recipients of that prestigious award in the past six years, and led the GLVC in the number of Academic All-GLVC honorees (103).

On the graduate level, the University offers programs leading to the Master of Business Administration (M.B.A.); the Master of Arts (M.A.) in counseling psychology, education, organizational leadership, and school counseling and guidance; the Master of Education (M.Ed.); the Master of Science (M.S.) in aviation and transportation, criminal/social justice, information security, management, and public safety administration; and the Master of Science in Nursing (M.S.N.). An M.S.N./M.B.A. option is also available. A Certificate of Advanced Study (C.A.S.) leading to a superintendent endorsement or a general administrative endorsement is available as is a Doctor of Education (Ed.D.) in educational leadership for teaching and learning.

Location

Located in Romeoville, Illinois, Lewis is only 30 minutes southwest of Chicago. This allows students to take advantage of the resources of one of the nation's largest cities while enjoying the beautiful suburban campus. Shopping and recreational facilities are located nearby.

Majors and Degrees

Lewis University offers programs leading to the Bachelor of Arts (B.A.) degree in American studies, art studio, athletic training, biochemistry, biology, broadcast journalism, business studies, chemistry, communication studies, communication technology, computer graphic design, computer science, contemporary global studies, criminal/social justice, drawing, education, English, environmental science, fire service administration, fitness management, forensic criminal investigation, health-care leadership, history, human resource management, illustration, international business, liberal arts, mathematics, multimedia journalism, multimedia production, music, music merchandising, painting, philosophy, philosophy of law, physics, print journalism, private security/loss prevention management, psychology, public relations, radio and television broadcasting, social work and human services, sociology, special education, sport management, theater, and theology.

Programs leading to a Bachelor of Science (B.S.) degree include accountancy, biochemistry, business administration, chemistry, computer science, diagnostic medical sonography, economics, environmental science, finance, management information systems, marketing, mathematics, nuclear medicine technology, physics, political science, public administration, and radiation therapy. Preprofessional programs are offered in chiropractic medicine, dentistry, engineering, law, medicine, optometry, pharmacy, physical therapy, physician assistant studies, and veterinary medicine.

To prepare students for careers in aviation, the University offers Bachelor of Science degree programs in aviation administration, aviation flight management, aviation maintenance management, and aviation security and a new program in air traffic control as well as Associate of Science (A.S.) degree programs in air traffic control, aviation flight management, and aviation maintenance technology. Certificate programs are offered in aircraft dispatch and aviation maintenance technology.

The Bachelor of Science in Nursing (B.S.N.) degree is offered in the College of Nursing and Health Professions.

The Bachelor of Elected Studies (B.E.S.) degree and a liberal arts degree may be pursued by students whose educational and career goals lead them to combine course work from several areas. The B.E.S. degree allows students to develop their own major by choosing a concentration from any area of the University. The liberal arts degree permits them to combine two minors into a major.

In addition to its more than seventy undergraduate majors and programs of study, Lewis offers interdisciplinary courses in women's studies and ethnic and cultural studies. Accelerated programs for working adults are available in applied sociology and political science, business administration, health-care leadership, information technology management, management, and RN/B.S.N. completion.

Lewis University's Scholars Academy allows eligible students in every major to enhance their educational opportunities through intensive projects that are arranged by contract with faculty members. Open to all undergraduates, membership in the Scholars Academy requires an ACT score of 24 or higher or a grade point average of 3.25 (B) or better. Members of the Scholars Academy who successfully complete Scholars Activities are awarded a Scholars Diploma upon graduation.

Academic Programs

The undergraduate curriculum has three parts: general education, major required courses, and elective courses. The general education requirements include courses in the humanities and the social or natural sciences that are designed to introduce the student to liberal culture. Requirements for the student's chosen major provide the opportunity for a greater depth of study in one academic field. Electives allow the student to select additional courses that are suited to his or her educational needs. The emphasis on humanities and communication arts in the undergraduate curriculum provides students with the knowledge of history and of the human experience necessary to develop an awareness of and responsiveness to contemporary social issues. Qualified students may receive academic credit through Advanced Placement and CLEP testing and for prior learning.

Students selecting majors in the College of Arts and Sciences discover that course work has been developed to foster critical thinking, open inquiry, precision in thought and expression, and familiarity with a broad range of knowledge. The College of Business seeks to educate individuals who are competent in the functional areas of business and who can recognize the responsibilities of business to the political, social, and economic segments of society. Many of the courses taken by business students are selected from the liberal arts area.

Similarly, the College of Nursing and Health Professions and the College of Education build on a foundation of liberal education. Nursing students take a concentration of natural and behavioral sciences, humanities, and electives during the first two years of the program. The nursing major course work is taken primarily at the upper-division level, with clinical experience acquired in hospitals and other health-care facilities. The nursing program prepares professional nursing practitioners who are competent to deliver health-care services in many situations.

The College of Education prepares future and current teachers and administrators to meet the diverse needs of all students. The college offers teacher education programs for certification in elementary education, English/language arts, mathematics, science (designation in biology, chemistry, or physics), social studies (designation in history or psychology), and special education. A combined certification in elementary education and special education also is offered.

The University operates on a semester system. The fall semester begins the Monday before Labor Day, and the spring semester starts in early January. Summer school sessions are six, eight, or ten weeks in length, depending on the program. A May term offers students the option of taking a four-week class at the end of the spring semester. Accelerated programs offer nine sessions per year in five-week and eight-week formats.

Academic Facilities

Lewis is committed to providing learners with access to modern educational technology. Technologies include computer labs, networks, Internet access, e-mail, classroom media, and distributed learning resources. Lewis University is connected to the Illinois Century Network (ICN), which provides reliable Internet access to schools and other educational entities throughout the state. The campus network includes a high-speed, fiber-optic backbone to all buildings. Many of the buildings have wireless access.

All students receive a campus e-mail address. Staffed computer labs are available during generous hours in all major classroom buildings and provide access to a host of campus resources, including software applications, Web support for classes, library materials, and Internet searching. Lewis also provides specialized computer labs, which are supported for digital music, journalism, writing, graphic arts, nursing, aviation, computer science, and tutoring.

The University Library houses nearly 150,000 volumes and an extensive microfiche and microfilm collection and is a depository for U.S. government documents. Besides housing a specialized music collection and an art-print collection, the library is home to the Archives of the Illinois and Michigan Canal Heritage Corridor. Online public-access terminals are available for use in the Lewis library. Patrons may access the University's card catalog as well as the holdings of more than sixty other academic libraries in Illinois through this computerized system. More than 80 different periodical databases are also available through computer access; many of these full-text and more specialized databases are added each semester. Most of these databases are available online.

The Department of Aviation is housed in the $2.5-million Harold E. White Aviation Center, which is located next to the Lewis University Airport. The airport, which houses more than 300 aircraft, is the site of flight-training and management programs.

Costs

Tuition for 2007–08 for full-time students (24 to 36 credits) was $20,450, while yearly room and board costs averaged $7600, depending on room size and the meal plan chosen. General service fees and student activity fees are included in the tuition.

Financial Aid

Lewis University is committed to helping all students who need financial assistance. Besides assisting students in obtaining federal and state grants, Federal Work-Study Program jobs, or loans (repayable after graduation), the University offers academic and athletic scholarships as well as additional Lewis grants to students with demonstrated financial needs. To be considered for any financial assistance, a student must apply for federal, state, and Lewis aid, using the appropriate forms. Additional information is available from the University's Office of Admission or the Office of Financial Aid Services.

Faculty

The Lewis University faculty places a strong emphasis on scholarship and personal contact. The greater majority of the general faculty members hold doctoral degrees, and 100 percent of the members of the aviation faculty hold FAA-approved licenses. In addition, because the student-faculty ratio is 14:1, classes tend to be close-knit, enhancing the opportunities for extensive interaction between faculty members and students, both in class and through office hours.

Student Government

The Student Governing Board (SGB), which has 11 student members, consists of the Presidents of each of the seven councils: the Commuter Council, the Cultural Awareness Council, the Honorary Organization Council, the Interfratority Council, the Interorganizational Council, the Pan Hellenic Council, and the Residence Hall Council. Four at-large members are appointed by the Office of Student Services. The SGB works to develop an effective activity program, reviews the quality of student life, oversees the effective functioning and financing of student organizations, represents student needs and concerns to the University's administration, and serves as the judicial body in overseeing organizational conduct.

Admission Requirements

Lewis University welcomes candidates for admission who present a strong record of academic success and high motivation. Freshman candidates are required to present ACT or SAT results as well as a record of high school work. Students whose main language is not English also must present a score of at least 500 on the Test of English as a Foreign Language (TOEFL). Applicants for the nursing program also must have taken one year of chemistry, one year of biology, and at least one year of algebra.

Transfer students with fewer than 12 credits should apply in the same manner as freshman applicants. Transfer students who have completed 12 or more college credits may be admitted to the College of Arts and Sciences if they have maintained an overall GPA of 2.0 or higher. (The College of Education, the College of Nursing and Health Professions, and the College of Business have additional transfer requirements. For more information, students should contact the transfer coordinator in the Office of Admission.) Most transfer students have all college credits accepted. However, for the Lewis degree, a maximum of 72 credit hours may be transferred from community colleges.

Application and Information

Application forms for admission and financial aid may be obtained from the Office of Admission. Freshman applicants should submit the application for admission, ACT or SAT scores, and high school transcripts. Transfer applicants who have earned 12 or more credit hours should submit transcripts from each college or university attended and the completed admission application.

Dean of Admission
Lewis University
One University Parkway
Romeoville, Illinois 60446-2200
Phone: 800-897-9000 (toll-free)
E-mail: admissions@lewisu.edu
Web site: http://www.lewisu.edu

Lewis University offers a sprawling campus of more than 376 acres, including eleven residence halls. All campus buildings are within easy walking distance. Pictured is the Brother Paul French, FSC, Learning Resource Center, which houses the Lewis University Library, classrooms, and administrative and faculty offices.

LINCOLN COLLEGE–NORMAL

NORMAL, ILLINOIS

The College

Lincoln College–Normal, a private four-year residential college, offers students the opportunity to study and succeed in a highly supportive environment. The institution is accredited by the North Central Association of Colleges and Schools.

Lincoln College was established in 1979 as an extension of Lincoln College in Lincoln, Illinois, to serve the needs of the area's residents. Since then, Lincoln College–Normal has developed a reputation for not only preparing students to attend a four-year college or university, but for readying its students for the workplace. In 2001, Lincoln College–Normal began offering bachelor's degrees, and students can now receive degrees in liberal arts, business management, criminal justice, or tourism, sport, and hospitality management.

One of the attractions of Lincoln College–Normal is its rich campus life. Of the 550 students who come to the College from throughout the United States and the world, 45 percent live on campus, so there are plenty of opportunities to network, socialize, and study together, or to participate in drama, student government, intramural sports, and other activities. Each fully furnished residential unit includes air conditioning, four private bedrooms, two full baths, living room, kitchen, and laundry facilities, along with cable TV and Internet access. Although all kitchens are fully equipped, students may dine at nearby restaurants using a prepaid off-campus meal plan card. On average, students are 21 years old and have ACT scores of 15 to 21, with an average score of 17.

Location

Normal, Illinois, is one of the fastest growing cities in the Midwest, with a diverse population that has grown 16 percent over the past decade. It has activities for everyone's interests. Arts lovers can enjoy a variety of music and theater. Outdoor enthusiasts can hike and boat at one of two beautiful lakes or walk and rollerblade along Constitution Trail or in the local parks. Historic sites and attractions include the McLean County Courthouse Museum, Funk's Grove, the Children's Discovery Museum, and the Miller Park Zoo. Normal was ranked the fifth-best American city for golf by *Golf Digest*, while *Forbes* has ranked it the fifteenth-best small town for business. Its well-developed transportation network makes it accessible to and from Chicago and Saint Louis; Springfield, Peoria, and Champaign-Urbana are only an hour's drive away.

Majors and Degrees

The College offers the Associate of Art (A.A.), Associate of Science (A.S.), and Associate of Applied Science (A.A.S.) degrees. A Bachelor of Arts (B.A.) program in liberal arts and Bachelor of Science (B.S.) programs in business management, criminal justice studies, and tourism, sport, and hospitality management are also offered. The business and liberal arts bachelor's degrees are now offered in an accelerated format in addition to the traditional format. Affiliated with Lincoln College–Normal is the Midwest College of Cosmetology, which allows students to earn professional certificates in cosmetology, esthetics, nail technology, and massage therapy.

Academic Programs

To earn the Associate of Art degree, students must complete at least 63 credit hours distributed across 18 hours of language and humanities, 3 hours of mathematics, 9 hours of social sciences, 3 hours of computer sciences, 2 hours of physical education, 7 hours of science, and 21 hours of electives.

For an Associate of Science degree, students must complete at least 61 credits made up of 15 hours of language and humanities, 8 hours of science, 6 hours of mathematics, 9 hours of social science, 3 hours of computer science, and 20 hours of electives.

The Associate of Applied Science degree requires either 60 or 66 credit hours. All students must earn 15 credit hours of language and humanities, 3 hours of mathematics, and 6 hours of social science. The cosmetology concentration requires 36 additional hours.

The Bachelor of Arts in Liberal Arts Program consists of 123 credit hours, which are earned in courses including communications; social sciences; humanities; critical reasoning and analytical methods; science, technology, and environment; mathematics; a senior internship or a research project and capstone seminar; and 21 hours of electives.

The Bachelor of Science in Business Management Program requires 123 credit hours in business foundation courses, business management core, mathematics, and 3 in a senior internship or research project.

The Bachelor of Science in Criminal Justice Studies Program requires a total of 122 credit hours including foundation courses in criminal justice, introductory criminology, upper-level core courses in criminology, electives, and 9 credit hours of a senior seminar and internship.

The Bachelor of Science in Tourism, Sport, and Hospitality Management Program requires a total of 120 credit hours. Of these, courses include business foundation course work; core courses in travel, hospitality, and sport; math; electives; course work in the student's concentration in either travel and tourism management, sports management, hospitality management, or meeting and event management; and a senior internship and project.

Students must complete the last 32 hours of the bachelor's degree program at Lincoln College.

The accelerated bridge to education (ABE) program was designed to meet the needs of the working adult. Classes meet only one night during the week and students can complete the remaining coursework from home. Courses are offered every five weeks allowing students to potentially earn 27 credit hours in a calendar year.

Academic Facilities

Milner Library contains 1.5 million catalogued books, 400,000 government publications, nearly 2 million pieces of microform, almost 500,000 maps, and more than 25,000 audio and video recordings. Computer terminals located on each floor allow patrons to search Milner's collection and conduct online research via the Internet and Milner's databases. Lincoln College–Normal also offers free professional tutoring in their Learning Resource Center, helping to make the student's experience as productive as possible. Other services include testing, research assistance, and reserved materials, such as

COLLEGE DATA CENTER • ILLINOIS

books and CDs. Computer labs are available in the Student Commons and the Learning Resource Center, with jacks available for laptops as well. Each student apartment is also furnished with high-speed Internet in every bedroom for students who wish to bring a computer.

Costs

In the 2007–08 academic year, full-time tuition (12–18 credit hours) was $18,000 per year with no additional fees, including books. Students carrying more than 18 credit hours were assessed $200 per additional credit. Full-time students living on the campus paid $1600 per semester for room (including utilities) and board, and a $200 security damage deposit.

Financial Aid

Every year, approximately 82 percent of the students receive financial aid; students may receive $2000 to $7500 in Lincoln College scholarships or grants. All scholarships are renewable with a minimum cumulative GPA of 2.0. Students may also be eligible for one or more grants, including Federal Pell Grants, Federal Supplemental Educational Opportunity Grants, and Illinois State Monetary Awards. The Federal Family Education Loan Program includes both subsidized and unsubsidized low interest loans. The borrower is notified when payments are to begin and is allowed at least five years, but no more than 10 years, to repay the loan. Students who are enrolled in no more than 6 credit hours may receive grants and scholarships that reduce tuition costs.

Faculty

Approximately 40 faculty members teach at the College. Half of these instructors hold a Ph.D. or equivalent terminal degree in their fields, and the others hold a master's degree. Many faculty members also work as tutors at the Learning Resource Center and as academic advisers for the students. The student-faculty ratio is 14:1, and the average class size is 16.

Admission Requirements

Prospective students are required to submit an application for admission, high school transcripts, college transcripts (if applicable), and a $25 application fee. Students may be admitted without restriction with an ACT composite score of 17 or better, or provisionally with a score of 16 or less. Nontraditional students (21 years and over) are exempt from submitting ACT scores.

Application and Information

Prospective students may apply for admission at any time prior to the start of the academic semester. Application materials may be downloaded from the Web site or requested from:

Admissions Office
Lincoln College–Normal
715 West Raab Road
Normal, Illinois 61761
Phone: 309-452-0500
800-569-0558 (toll-free)
E-mail: ncadmissionsinfo@lincolncollege.edu
Web site: http://www.lincolncollege.edu/normal

LOYOLA UNIVERSITY CHICAGO

CHICAGO, ILLINOIS

The University

Consistently ranked a top national university and a best value by *U.S. News & World Report*, Loyola University Chicago is the largest of the twenty-eight Jesuit Catholic universities in the United States, with a total enrollment of 15,545 students from fifty states and eighty-two countries. Loyola offers a total of 188 programs of study—seventy-two undergraduate, seventy-seven graduate, thirty-six doctoral, and three professional programs. Loyola prepares people to lead extraordinary lives by building upon its Jesuit tradition with an innovative Core Curriculum, which equips students with lifelong skills for success, and a strong commitment to develop the whole person—intellectually, socially, physically, and spiritually.

Loyola gives students the best of campus and city life with diverse living and learning opportunities in world-class Chicago. Located off North Michigan Avenue, Chicago's Magnificent Mile, Loyola's dynamic Water Tower Campus is home to the Schools of Business Administration, Communication, Continuing and Professional Studies, Education, Law, and Social Work and connects students to the heart of the city for myriad internship, job, and service opportunities. Loyola's Lake Shore Campus, home to the College of Arts and Sciences, the Graduate School, and the Marcella Niehoff School of Nursing, is located on the picturesque shores of Lake Michigan and offers students a traditional residential campus.

Loyola's student-faculty ratio of 13:1, well below the national average, ensures personal attention. Nearly all of Loyola's 940 full-time faculty members hold Ph.D.'s, and they are routinely called upon as experts in their fields.

Loyola students annually receive more than $180 million in financial assistance from numerous sources, including more than $45 million in Loyola-funded scholarships. Students gain practical experience and leadership, organizational, and life skills by participating in internships, engaging in service opportunities, and joining any of the school's more than 130 academic, social, cultural, and professional student organizations.

For information about admission, academics, housing, financial assistance, student life and more, students should visit http://www.LUC.edu/undergrad.

Location

Loyola's tranquil, residential Lake Shore Campus sits on the shores of Lake Michigan, just 8 miles north of downtown Chicago. The dynamic Water Tower Campus is located just off North Michigan Avenue, Chicago's Magnificent Mile in the heart of the city near theaters, museums, major corporate and financial institutions, and Chicago's most elegant shops and boutiques. A University-operated shuttle bus and convenient public transportation help students easily get back and forth between the two campuses.

Majors and Degrees

Loyola students may choose from seventy-two undergraduate majors and seventy-two minors. Undergraduate degrees offered include the Bachelor of Arts (B.A.), B.A. Classics, Bachelor of Science (B.S.), Bachelor of Business Administration (B.B.A.), Bachelor of Science in Education (B.S.Ed.), Bachelor of Science in Nursing (B.S.N.), and Bachelor of Social Work (B.S.W.) degrees.

The College of Arts and Sciences offers undergraduate majors in anthropology, biochemistry, bioinformatics, biology, black world studies, chemistry, classical civilization, communications networks and security, computer science, criminal justice, ecology, economics, English, environmental sciences (chemistry), environmental studies, fine arts, forensic science, French, Greek (ancient), history, human services, information technology, international film and media studies, international studies, Italian, Latin, mathematics, mathematics and computer science, molecular biology, music, philosophy, philosophy–social justice, physics, physics and computer science, physics and engineering, political science, psychology, religious studies, sociology, sociology and anthropology, software development, Spanish, statistical science, theater, theology, theoretical physics and applied mathematics, and women's and gender studies (as a second major only).

The School of Business Administration offers majors in accounting, economics, entrepreneurship, finance, human resource management, information systems, international business, management, marketing, operations management, and sport management.

The School of Communication offers majors in advertising/public relations, communication studies, and journalism.

The School of Education offers majors in bilingual/bicultural education, elementary education, mathematics education, science education, and special education, along with an expanded secondary education dual-degree program.

The Marcella Niehoff School of Nursing offers the Bachelor of Science in Nursing, a health systems management major, and an accelerated B.S.N. program, which is available to students who have already completed a baccalaureate degree.

The School of Social Work offers an undergraduate major in social work and a combined bachelor's and master's degree in social work, which may be completed in five years.

Other special academic opportunities include preprofessional programs for law and health professions, more than fifteen 5-year (bachelor's/master's) degree programs, interdisciplinary programs, six-year early admission to Loyola's School of Law, early assurance to Loyola's Stritch School of Medicine, and the Loyola/Midwestern University Dual-Acceptance Pharmacy Program.

Academic Programs

Loyola's Core Curriculum sets goals for undergraduate education that focus on skills, values, and knowledge that prepare students for the realities of living and working in today's world. The Core Curriculum gives students who have not yet selected an academic major the opportunity to explore many courses before deciding on a field of study.

Most degrees require 128 credit hours for graduation. Exceptionally well-qualified students may apply to the Interdisciplinary Honors Program. Students may receive credit through the Advanced Placement Program (AP) tests and the International Baccalaureate (I.B.). Certain College-Level Examination Program (CLEP) tests are accepted. Loyola students may participate in Army and Navy ROTC programs through neighboring universities.

Off-Campus Programs

Loyola's John Felice Rome Center in Italy is both one of the largest American university programs in Western Europe and the most popular study-abroad destination for Loyola students.

Students may attend The Beijing Center for Chinese Studies or one of sixty other study-abroad programs in twenty-nine countries.

Academic Facilities

Loyola's state-of-the-art Michael R. and Marilyn C. Quinlan Life Sciences Education and Research Center houses laboratories used for biology, bioinformatics, chemistry, ecology, and other life science courses. It also provides numerous opportunities for undergraduates to engage in scientific research alongside their professors. The Sullivan Center for Student Services, which opened in 2006, consolidates a dozen student services offices into one convenient location.

Loyola's Department of Fine and Performing Arts recently moved into a renovated building that offers state-of-the-art studios for ceramics, metalworking/jewelry, and sculpture. The facility also features a dance studio and art gallery. The newly renovated Mundelein Center for the Fine and Performing Arts, which opened in fall 2007, contains a theater resource center and reading room, music resource center and listening lab, art history resource center, music classrooms, offices, and an auditorium theater. The tenth floor is home to eight fully equipped private practice rooms plus a deluxe music lab.

The University's library system, including the Cudahy Library at the Lake Shore Campus and the Lewis Library at the Water Tower Campus, contains more than 1 million books, 1,400 periodical subscriptions, and access to 30,000 online periodicals. The Loyola University Museum of Art, which recently opened at the Water Tower Campus, displays the University's Medieval and Renaissance collection, along with other permanent collections and rotating exhibitions of professional and student work. The Information Commons, which opened in spring 2008, is a new four-story lakeside research facility that provides individual study space for students, state-of-the-art technology with more than 220 computers, wireless Internet connections, and a lakefront café.

The Medical Center Campus in Maywood, a suburb of Chicago, consists of the Foster G. McGaw Hospital and the Stritch School of Medicine as well as the Mulcahy Outpatient Center, the Russo Surgical Pavilion, and the Cardinal Bernardin Cancer Center.

Costs

Undergraduate tuition in 2008–09 is $28,700. Room and board costs are dependent on a student's selection of residence hall and meal plan.

Financial Aid

Loyola attempts to meet the financial need of as many students as possible. Ninety-four percent of Loyola freshmen receive some form of aid, including University-funded scholarships and grants, federal and state grants, work-study, and loans. Students are encouraged to file the Free Application for Federal Student Aid (FAFSA) before Loyola's March 1 priority date to be considered for as many sources of aid as possible.

Merit scholarships are awarded to entering freshmen who have outstanding academic records. Presidential, Damen, Loyola, and Trustee Scholarships are awarded to students who rank at the top of their high school graduating class and score well on the ACT or SAT. Scholarship amounts for these programs range from $6000 to half-tuition per year. Transfer students who have completed 30 hours of college credit with an outstanding record of academic achievement may receive a Transfer Academic Scholarship. These awards are all renewable for up to three years. Students must be admitted to Loyola prior to February 1 to be considered for scholarships that are automatically awarded with admission.

Students may also look for additional scholarships, which require separate applications. A great place to start is Loyola's list of more than seventy-five types of additional scholarships, twenty of which are awarded without considering financial need. For more information, students should visit http://www.LUC.edu/finaid/scholarships.

Faculty

Nearly all of Loyola's full-time faculty members hold the Ph.D. or the highest degree in their field. Faculty members teach both graduate and undergraduate students, and senior faculty members often teach Core Curriculum courses. With a student-faculty ratio of 13:1, far below the national average, Loyola students have access to faculty members both as teachers and as advisers.

Student Government

Student government at Loyola provides a liaison between students and the administration, emphasizes concerns for student rights, and provides a forum for debate, recommendation, and action on issues that pertain to students. Students also take an active role in University policy and advisory committees and as elected representatives in the residence halls.

Admission Requirements

Students seeking admission to Loyola University Chicago are evaluated on their overall academic record, including ACT or SAT scores. For the freshman class entering in fall 2007, the middle 50 percent of ACT scores ranged between 23 and 28, the middle 50 percent of SAT verbal scores ranged between 530 and 640, the middle 50 percent of SAT math scores ranged between 520 and 640, and the average GPA was 3.68. Most Loyola students rank in the upper quarter of their graduating class, but consideration is given to students in the upper half. Candidates should be graduating from an accredited secondary school with a college-preparatory curriculum, including courses in English, math, social studies, and science. Study of a foreign language is strongly recommended. Students must submit the application for admission along with high school transcripts, test scores, a writing sample, and a secondary school counselor recommendation. Admission counselors are available to meet and talk with students individually either before or after the application is submitted.

Transfer students with 20 semester hours or more of acceptable credit are evaluated on the basis of their college work only.

Application and Information

Applicants are notified of the admission decision three to four weeks after the application, supporting credentials, secondary school counselor recommendation, and $25 application fee are received. The application fee is waived for students who apply online.

Prospective students are encouraged to visit the campus. Undergraduate Admission encourages students to schedule individual appointments and campus tours up to two weeks in advance or to participate in one of the many campus programs offered throughout the year.

To obtain an application and further information and to arrange a visit, students should contact:

Undergraduate Admission Office
Loyola University Chicago
820 North Michigan Avenue
Chicago, Illinois 60611
Phone: 312-915-6500
800-262-2373 (toll-free)
E-mail: admission@luc.edu
Web site: http://www.LUC.edu/undergrad

NORTH CENTRAL COLLEGE

NAPERVILLE, ILLINOIS

The College

Founded in 1861, North Central College has a distinctive heritage as a comprehensive college that educates students in both the liberal arts and sciences and in preprofessional fields.

A private, United Methodist–affiliated institution, the College has long been recognized for academic excellence, with its educational philosophy of incorporating leadership, ethics, and values into academic and cocurricular activities. North Central's 2,550 students include traditional-age undergraduate, part-time, and graduate students. Master's degree programs are offered in business administration, computer science, education, leadership studies, liberal studies, and management information systems. Graduate certificates are available in business foundations, change management, dispute resolution, finance, gender studies, history and nature of science, human resource management, investments and financial planning, leadership studies, management, marketing, multicultural studies, organizational ethics, teacher leadership, and technology in education.

North Central's 59-acre campus has more than twenty major buildings. Facilities include the historic Old Main, built in 1870 and renovated in 1998; the state-of-the-art Cardinal Stadium, which seats 5,500 and is the home to football, soccer, and track; and Pfeiffer Hall, a 1,050-seat auditorium. Kaufman Dining Hall serves the entire campus.

Thirty-five states and twenty-four other countries are represented, and 13 percent of the members of the 2007 freshman class are members of minority groups.

Cocurricular programs parallel many academic majors and include the nationally acclaimed Students in Free Enterprise, Cardinals in Action (a community service organization), campus radio station WONC-89.1 FM, Mock Trial, Model United Nations, and forensics. North Central student athletes compete in nineteen NCAA Division III intercollegiate varsity sports within the College Conference of Illinois and Wisconsin. The varsity sports include baseball, basketball, cross-country, football, golf, soccer, swimming, tennis, track and field, and wrestling for men. Women participate in basketball, cross-country, golf, soccer, softball, swimming, tennis, track and field, and volleyball. Students have many options for social activities: programmed events through the College Union Activities Board, residence life activities, an active intramural program, and travel to both downtown Naperville and Chicago. Student services include centers for academic advising, counseling, writing, foreign language, and career development.

Location

North Central is located in a charming historic district in the heart of Naperville, Illinois, a fast growing community of more than 140,000 residents in the west-suburban area of metropolitan Chicago. The city is a residential community with excellent community services and has become the Midwest center of scientific research and development. It is in the "Silicon Prairie" center of the high-technology Illinois Research and Development Corridor, where some of the nation's largest companies (e.g., BP Amoco, Metropolitan Life, and Nalco Chemical Company) are located. Nearby are Argonne National Laboratory, Fermi National Accelerator Laboratory, and Morton Arboretum. All of these facilities and industries represent unique resources for North Central students—for internships, jobs, and joint research opportunities.

Chicago is just 29 miles away, and the cultural, artistic, and entertainment venues in this great city make it a rich resource for a North Central education. Students can catch the Burlington Northern Railroad just two blocks from the campus for an easy commute.

Majors and Degrees

North Central College awards the Bachelor of Arts (B.A.) degree in accounting, anthropology, art, art education, athletic training, biochemistry, biology, broadcast communication, chemistry, classical civilization, computer science, East Asian studies, economics, education (elementary and secondary), English, entrepreneurship and small business management, exercise science, finance, French, German, global studies, history, human resource management, humanities, interactive media studies, international business, Japanese, management, management information systems, marketing, mathematics, music, musical theater, music education, nuclear medicine technology, organizational communication, philosophy, physical education, physics, political science, print journalism, psychology, radiation therapy, religious studies, science, social science, sociology, sociology and anthropology, Spanish, speech communication, sport management, and theater.

The Bachelor of Science (B.S.) degree is awarded in accounting, actuarial science, applied mathematics, biochemistry, biology, chemistry, computer science, mathematics, nuclear medicine technology, psychology, radiation therapy, and in all economics and business areas.

Preprofessional-professional programs are offered in engineering, health sciences, law, medical technology, and nursing. A 3-2 engineering program is offered in cooperation with the University of Illinois at Urbana-Champaign and the University of Minnesota. Students may also design other majors that bridge two or more areas of study.

Academic Programs

North Central provides a comprehensive education with the goal of preparing students to live free, ethically responsible, and intellectually rewarding lives. Each student must complete a minimum of 120 credit hours, including all general education requirements and an approved major. CLEP, AP, and IB exams are considered for college credit and/or advanced course placement.

The academic year comprises three 10½-week terms and a six-week Interim Term between Thanksgiving and the beginning of the new calendar year. Students usually take three courses during each term, while the Interim Term is used for independent study, taking courses, travel, research, work, or simply relaxation. The College actively supports internships as part of career preparation, and the College Scholars Honors Program is open to select students.

Off-Campus Programs

North Central College provides many opportunities for students to study abroad. Students interested in engaging in intensive Spanish study may travel to Costa Rica each fall term for thirteen weeks. The fifteen-week London term allows students to explore European history and understand the changing contemporary English and continental cultures. The fifteen-week China/Japan term begins in Beijing and then moves to Kyoto, allowing students to live and study in both countries. Other study-abroad possibilities include exchange programs to China, England, France, Japan, Korea, Northern Ireland, and Sweden.

North Central is also one of only twelve colleges and universities in the nation to offer the distinctive Richter Independent Study Fellowship Program, which provides funds of up to $5000 for a single specialized project. Richter Independent Study projects have included travel and research on every continent.

Academic Facilities

WONC (89.1 FM), the College's 1,500-watt radio station, is one of the most powerful student-staffed stations in the Midwest. The station, with three state-of-the-art studios for on-air and audio production work, has won twenty Marconi Awards—more than any other college radio station in the country.

All students and faculty and staff members have access to a voice, video, and data network, including full Internet access from their residence halls, classrooms, computer laboratories, and offices.

Science equipment available for student research projects includes a fourteen-CPU LINUX parallel processor, computer networking and multimedia labs, a 300-MHz magnetic resonance spectrometer, a gas chromatograph/mass spectrometer, a liquid chromatograph, a pulsed nitrogen laser, a phase-contract video microscope, PCR thermal cyclers, and environmental chambers. North Central also has state-of-the-art language and market research laboratories.

Costs

For 2007–08, tuition at North Central College was $24,159. Room and board were $7677. Resident students paid a $225 technology fee. The student activity fee was $180, and estimated additional expenses were $425 for books and supplies. Students should also budget personal expenses and transportation costs.

Financial Aid

The Offices of Administration and Financial Aid are committed to assisting students throughout the process of applying for financial aid. Scholarships, loans, grants, and work-study assistance are awarded on the basis of demonstrated financial need and the academic record. Students are required to submit the Free Application for Federal Student Aid (FAFSA). Funds are also available through the Illinois State Monetary Award Program (for Illinois residents only) and the Federal Pell Grant, Federal Supplemental Educational Opportunity Grant, and the Federal Stafford Student Loan Programs. The College awarded more than $12 million from institutional sources for 2006–07. Merit scholarships range from $6000 to full tuition, renewable annually. Students may also interview and/or audition for scholarships in international business/global studies, science, theater, forensics, and vocal and instrumental music, as well as submit art portfolios.

Faculty

Members of the North Central faculty, 87 percent of whom hold the Ph.D. or another terminal degree, are first—and foremost—teachers. A student-faculty ratio of 15:1 and an average class size of 19 students ensure opportunities for a stimulating exchange of ideas. All faculty members also serve as academic advisers to provide guidance and counseling for students. Students get to know their professors on a personal basis, and the list of independent study projects is extensive. Faculty members teach both undergraduate and graduate courses.

Student Government

The Student Governing Association takes an active role in the development and implementation of policies concerning student life on campus. Representatives of the student body have a voice on faculty, trustee, and administrative committees, while the College Union Activities Board plans social and service events.

Admission Requirements

New students are accepted individually on the basis of their overall academic preparation, character, and potential for success at North Central College. Graduation from an accredited secondary school is a basic requirement for admission. Other criteria used in the selection of prospective students are the high school academic record, personal recommendations of high school counselors, ACT or SAT scores, and involvement in extracurricular activities. Members of the North Central freshman class of 2006–07 scored an average of 25 on the ACT. North Central does not discriminate on the basis of sex, race, ethnic background, age, or physical handicap.

Application and Information

North Central College operates on a rolling admission basis, which allows students to apply at any time during or after their senior year in high school. Students can complete and submit an application for admission on the College's Web site. Applicants receive notification within three weeks after the College receives all documentation. Early application is recommended to ensure availability of campus housing. The application must be accompanied by a $25 fee, an official high school transcript, and official reports of ACT or SAT scores from the testing agency. For additional information or application forms, students should contact:

Office of Admission
North Central College
30 North Brainard Street
Naperville, Illinois 60540
Phone: 630-637-5800
800-411-1861 (toll-free)
Fax: 630-637-5819
E-mail: ncadm@noctrl.edu
Web site: http://www.northcentralcollege.edu

Historic Old Main, built in 1870 and renovated in 1998, houses the Offices of Admission, Financial Aid, and the Registrar.

NORTH PARK UNIVERSITY

CHICAGO, ILLINOIS

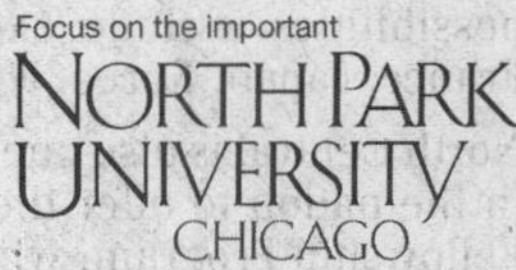

Focus on the important
NORTH PARK
UNIVERSITY
CHICAGO

The University

The mission of North Park, as an intentionally Christian university of the Evangelical Covenant Church, is to prepare students for lives of significance and service through liberal arts, professional, and theological education. The University's vision, building on its core institutional identity—Christian, urban, multicultural—is to fashion a university of uncommon character and enduring excellence where faith and learning meet. In order to fulfill this mission and vision, the University commits itself to operating on the following core values: learning as a gift, joy, and sacred obligation; cultivation of the University, including both internal and external constituencies, as an interrelated learning community; personal concern for students and devotion to their development as whole persons, fidelity to the Christian faith and to the school's particular heritage in the Evangelical Covenant Church; affirmation of racial and ethnic diversity as reflective of the vision of the Kingdom of God; engagement of Chicago as the University's dynamic context for education and service.

North Park students are involved in and committed to a wealth of cocurricular activities that develop them personally, spiritually, and socially. North Park's Outreach Ministries program attracts students from around the country; hundreds of North Park students volunteer in one of more than twenty programs on a weekly basis. Music, theater, and student government as well as athletics and Christian activities, such as chapel, small groups, and service, play an important role in the daily lives of students, who are challenged to examine their values, define their potential, and maximize their personal growth. North Park University is a member of the NCAA Division III and the College Conference of Illinois and Wisconsin (CCIW); men and women participate in national and regional competition in Division III. Competition in intramural sports is open to the entire campus community.

At the graduate level, the University offers a Master of Arts in Community Development (M.A.C.D.), a Master of Business Administration (M.B.A.), a Master of Management (M.M.), a Master of Management (M.M.) in nonprofit administration, a Master of Music in vocal performance, and a Master of Science (M.S.) with a major in nursing with various concentrations; joint graduate degree programs between the seminary and the School of Business and Nonprofit Management; and seminary degrees, including Christian formation, Christian ministry, divinity, and theological studies.

Location

Located in a pleasant residential neighborhood on the northwest side of Chicago, North Park's beautiful park-like 30-acre campus has small-town flavor and warmth, yet its intimate environment is within one of the largest and most exciting metropolitan areas of the world. Chicago offers a multitude of cultural, recreational, and service opportunities—everything from the Art Institute of Chicago and the Chicago Symphony Orchestra to the Chicago Cubs and Bulls to homeless shelters. The North Park campus hosts regular appearances by professional musicians and guest speakers. The impact of the city on the University's education program is significant. Several hundred student internship sites have been identified in the city. Easily accessed by public transportation, city life is available on demand.

Majors and Degrees

North Park University offers the Bachelor of Arts with major concentrations in advertising, Africana studies, art, biblical and theological studies, biology, business and economics (with several concentrations), chemistry, communication arts, constructed majors, education (early childhood, elementary, secondary (certification only) and endorsements in Middle School, English as a Second Language, and Learning Behavior Specialist I), English, exercise science, French, French studies, global studies, history, information studies, mathematics, music, philosophy, physical education, physics, politics and government, psychology, Scandinavian studies, sociology, Spanish, Swedish, and youth ministry.

The Bachelor of Science is offered with major concentrations in advertising, athletic training, biology, business and economics, chemistry, clinical laboratory science, computer science, constructed majors, exercise science, information systems, mathematics, nursing, physical education, and physics.

A student may earn the Bachelor of Music (performance), a Bachelor of Music in worship, or the Bachelor of Music Education.

Preprofessional programs are offered in dentistry, law, medicine, ministry, occupational therapy, optometry, pharmaceutical science, physical therapy, and veterinary medicine. North Park participates in a 3-2 engineering program whereby a student receives a baccalaureate degree from North Park and an engineering degree from another university.

GOAL, a degree completion program for adults, offers accelerated B.A. degrees in human development, management of information technology, and organizational management. Classes meet in the evenings and on weekends.

Academic Programs

The general education program is the core of the curriculum and is foundational for all students and all areas of study and vocation. In its concern with ultimate questions, the development of the person, responsibility to society, and the integration of understanding across disciplinary lines, the program reflects the distinctive values of the Christian liberal arts university. In its concern with basic skills of thinking and communication, the program is directed toward practical success in the wide variety of occupations and roles that graduates enter. The general education curriculum is made up of interdisciplinary courses during the first two years as well as courses in biblical and theological studies, fine arts, languages, mathematics, and science. Students are required to take two courses in the area of biblical and theological studies.

North Park operates on a calendar year consisting of two 16-week semesters and a ten-day interim between the winter and spring terms. Students are considered full-time if they are enrolled in a minimum of 12 semester hours, and the block tuition rate covers 12–17 hours. To graduate, a student must complete 120 semester hours with an overall grade point average of 2.0 or better. There are also requirements for the major and minor.

North Park recognizes high school graduates who have completed college-level courses in high school and have taken the Advanced Placement tests of the College Board. Home-schooled students are encouraged to apply.

North Park seeks and attracts students with superior high school backgrounds and academic aptitude. An honors program that focuses on preparation for graduate school is offered. The North Park Honors Program provides students with enriching supplements to their undergraduate experiences as well as faculty coaching and mentoring. Student research is encouraged and supported in a number of disciplines, and students have opportunity at the conclusion of the academic year to present their research to peers and faculty members.

Off-Campus Programs

North Park students may participate in a number of off-campus programs, including several Best Semester programs of the Council for Christian Colleges and Universities. North Park provides study-abroad programs in France, Scandinavia, Mexico, and Italy. Students also participate in direct exchange programs with about 200 universities throughout the world.

Academic Facilities

Library services at North Park support and extend the academic instruction of the University. Students have immediate access to more than 225,000 bound volumes, 1,500 titles on microform, 1,000 periodical subscriptions, and 5,000 records and tapes. In addition, North Park students have access to the resources of Northeastern Illinois University and all sixteen of the LIBRAS Colleges in the Chicago area. In addition to computer classrooms, North Park offers a full computer center and two student labs. The Center for Africana Studies, Center for Korean Studies, Center for Latino Studies, Center for Middle Eastern Studies, Center for Scandinavian Studies, and Archives for the Swedish American Historical Society are research centers located on the campus that can be used by students.

Costs

Tuition and fees for the 2008–09 academic year are $17,600. Room and board are $7580 for full-time students. Books and supplies are estimated at $1000 but vary according to each student. In 2004, North Park restructured the tuition, scholarship, and financial aid programs into a straightforward and clear presentation of the costs of attendance. The result is a total cost approximately $6000 less than the national average for a private school.

Financial Aid

At North Park, it is desired that no qualified student be prevented from obtaining a college education because of financial inability. A no-haggle approach to financial aid has been greatly appreciated by students and families. Close to 90 percent of North Park students receive some form of financial assistance. The University offers comprehensive academic merit scholarships for those students who demonstrate high academic performance.

Upon submission of the Free Application for Federal Student Aid (FAFSA), North Park awards financial assistance to eligible applicants through a combination of scholarships, grants, loans, and work-study. A student must be admitted to the University before financial aid is awarded.

In addition, competitive scholarships are offered for high-achieving students (Trustee Award), students who intend to teach history at the high school or college level (Virginia E. Hahn History Scholarship), and students who plan to study vocal and instrumental music performance (by audition).

Faculty

North Park faculty members are committed to relating the values and understandings of Christian faith to academic life. Eighty-seven percent of North Park's 130 full-time faculty members have earned doctorates or terminal degrees for their profession in the arts, sciences, and professional disciplines. Coming from a wide variety of Christian denominational and educational backgrounds, faculty members are committed Christians who share a passion for North Park's mission as a Christian liberal arts university and are highly regarded in their scholarly fields.

Student Government

The North Park University Student Association represents the undergraduate student body in all areas of University life. Its elected and appointed members work in cooperation with the administration and the faculty in shaping both academic and other areas of student life.

The association operates through three main branches: the Student Senate, a legislative body of elected representatives; the Executive, whose function is to recommend and execute policy as well as to coordinate the activities of the association; and the Judiciary, which renders interpretations of the Student Association constitution. The association encourages campus dialogue via four student publications and sponsors cultural and social events via the Student Senate, a late-night café, various departments (including Academic Affairs, Social Awareness, and Social Events), and eight special-interest student organizations (including associations for African American, Asian, Catholic, Latin American, Middle Eastern, and Scandinavian students).

Admission Requirements

North Park gives consideration to students who have demonstrated their readiness for college by presenting superior or above-average high school records and satisfactory SAT or ACT scores. The University also considers evidence of serious purpose, the character of the applicant, and participation in extracurricular activities as demonstrated through the application, essay, and personal references. An interview is recommended but not required. North Park University admits students regardless of race, creed, sex, national or ethnic origin, or disability.

North Park welcomes applications from transfer students. The student seeking transfer admission must have a cumulative grade point average of at least 2.5 from an accredited institution in order to be considered.

Application and Information

Admission decisions are made on a rolling basis, with a first priority deadline of January 15 and a second priority deadline of April 1.

To be considered for admission, students need to submit the following: a North Park University application, high school or college transcripts, ACT or SAT test scores, a personal essay, and two references, one from a teacher and a personal reference.

Students are strongly encouraged to visit the campus. Those interested in more detailed information are invited to contact:

Shari Clemens, Director of Undergraduate Enrollment
North Park University
3225 West Foster Avenue
Chicago, Illinois 60625-4895
Phone: 773-244-5500
800-888-6728 (toll-free)
Internet: http://www.northpark.edu/focus

OLIVET NAZARENE UNIVERSITY

BOURBONNAIS, ILLINOIS

The University

Olivet Nazarene University (ONU) is a private, Christian, liberal arts university with a strong emphasis on both academic excellence and Christ-centered living. ONU offers one of the finest liberal arts educations in the Midwest, world-class facilities for learning and entertainment, and an atmosphere that promotes fun, relationship building, and spiritual growth.

Olivet's high retention, graduation, and employment/placement rates demonstrate the University's commitment to students' success. The members of the faculty, staff, and administration are dedicated to teaching, encouraging, and mentoring each student as a whole person—academically, socially, and spiritually.

With 4,600 students (2,600 undergraduates), Olivet offers an ideal student population for a private institution, maintaining diversity without sacrificing personalized attention. Nearly half of the student body comes from the Nazarene denomination, and the rest come from some thirty other denominations. Most U.S. states are represented, as are more than twenty countries.

The campus offers a championship-caliber athletics department (seventeen intercollegiate men's and women's sports in all) and a large intramural sports program. Music and drama groups involve hundreds of students, and many clubs are organized for a wide variety of interests. Olivet students are also heavily involved in dozens of ministry groups and volunteer efforts, small-group Bible studies, and weekly student-led services.

The University recently completed a number of campus improvements, including the renovation of the lower level of Ludwig Center, the student union, to include a glass-enclosed gaming room featuring plasma TV screens, a convenience store, and new student leadership offices. In addition, the first floor of Nesbitt Hall, a residence hall, was converted into a fourth dining option for students, and the Department of Communication moved to a new, technologically advanced facility in Benner Library, which also houses some of the University's art programs, representing a partnership between the departments of communication and art. Future plans call for a new chapel/performing arts center.

The University is home to the Chicago Bears' summer training camp and Shine.fm, a 35,000-watt station ranked among the top stations in the nation and staffed by Olivet's broadcasting students.

In addition to its traditional undergraduate programs, Olivet offers six degree-completion and continuing-studies programs, nearly twenty master's degrees, and a Doctor of Education in ethical leadership. The School of Graduate and Continuing Studies strives to meet the needs of the ever-expanding number of adults returning to school. Adult degree-completion programs are designed to assist working adults so they can complete their degree requirements without an interruption to their employment. The school serves as a resource for adults striving to enhance their personal and professional lives in a constantly changing world.

In addition to the classes held on the main campus, the School of Graduate and Continuing Studies offers courses for students throughout the Chicago area. Numerous students gather with other working adults for classes in churches, schools, hospitals, and other convenient locations near their home or workplace.

Location

The main University campus is located just 50 minutes south of Chicago's Loop in the historic village of Bourbonnais. The area includes malls, restaurants, entertainment, and natural recreation centered on the Kankakee River State Park system. Olivet students enjoy many activities nearby and often make the quick trip north for the limitless offerings of Chicago and its surroundings.

In addition to recreation, students find numerous opportunities for employment and internships in the area, which is ranked as one of the top locations in the nation for small businesses and the vast professional resources of Chicago. Students, faculty members, and staff members also find themselves working side by side in local and regional ministry projects. Olivet students are recognized professionally and ministerially as a valuable commodity by area businesses, churches, and parachurch organizations.

Majors and Degrees

Olivet confers Bachelor of Arts (B.A.) and/or Bachelor of Science (B.S.) degrees in the following fields of study (includes all majors, minors, and concentrations): accounting, art, art (education), athletic coaching, athletic training, Biblical languages, Biblical studies, biochemistry, biology, biology (education), business administration, chemistry, chemistry (education), child development, children's ministry, Christian education, church music, communication studies, computer science, corporate communication, criminal justice, dietetics, digital media (graphics), digital media (photography), digital production, drawing/illustration, early childhood education, economics/finance, electrical engineering, elementary education, engineering, English, English (education), environmental science, exercise science, family and consumer sciences, family and consumer sciences (education), fashion merchandising, film studies, finance, French, general science, general science (education), general studies, geological sciences, Greek, health education, history, history (education), hospitality, housing and environmental design, information systems, intercultural studies, international business, journalism, literature, management, marketing, mass communication, mathematics, mathematics (education), mechanical engineering, military science, missions, music, music composition, music education, music performance, nursing, painting, philosophy, physical education/health, physical science, physical science (education), political science, practical ministries, predentistry, prelaw, premedicine, preoptometry, prepharmacy, pre–physical therapy, pre–physician's assistant studies, pre–veterinarian studies, psychology, psychology (education), public policy, radio, religion, religion and philosophy, science (education), secondary education, social science, social science (education), social work, sociology, Spanish, Spanish (education), sports management, television/video production, theater, writing, youth ministry, and zoology.

Academic Programs

Olivet seeks to offer an "Education with a Christian Purpose." The University believes this commitment to Christ mandates nothing less than the highest-quality academic programs. Olivet's liberal arts curriculum requires that students complete 45 to 58 hours of general education courses. With the addition of major and minor programs of study, students must complete a minimum of 128 credit hours to obtain a bachelor's degree. Credit may be earned through AP and CLEP tests. Students may also participate in ROTC.

Olivet operates on a two-semester schedule, from August to May. Two summer sessions are also available.

Off-Campus Programs

Olivet students are encouraged to participate in the various off-campus study programs offered each semester. International locations include Xiamen, China; San José, Costa Rica; Cairo, Egypt; Drummoyne, Australia; Oxford, England; Nizhni Novgorod and St. Petersburg, Russia; Mukono, Uganda; Sighisoara, Transylvania (Romania); and Quito, Ecuador. Domestic opportunities include the American Studies Program in Washington, D.C.; the Los Angeles Film Studies Program in Los Angeles, California; Focus on the Family Institute in Colorado Springs, Colorado; Contemporary Music Center on Martha's Vineyard; and the AuSable Institute (environmental science) in northern Michigan. Costs are usually comparable to a semester at Olivet, and credit is given for these programs. In addition, some sources of financial aid are applicable.

Many Olivet students participate in numerous educational and missions-oriented short-term trips that are available during the Christmas, spring, and summer breaks.

Academic Facilities

Olivet's 250-acre campus offers leading-edge academic facilities. These include high-quality performance halls and athletic venues; excellent natural science, engineering, and nursing laboratories; smart classrooms; and an observatory. It is one of only a handful of small college campuses in the nation to have a planetarium, which was completely renovated in 2008 with the same technology used in Chicago's Adler Planetarium. Each department uses the top software in its field. More than a dozen campus computer labs are available for student use, and two network ports in each dorm room and the campuswide wireless network give students access to e-mail, the Internet, and classroom applications 24 hours a day.

Benner Library and Resource Center provides unlimited access to any material a student needs, either on site or through the interlibrary loan system. Benner Library offers more than 170,000 books, 350,000 other items in various formats, 700 periodicals, over 15,000 full-text electronic journals, and over 30,412 electronic books.

Costs

Tuition, based on 12 to 18 credit hours, was $10,375 per semester in 2007–08. Room and board, based on double occupancy and the fourteen-meals-per-week plan, cost $3200 per semester.

Financial Aid

Approximately 96 percent of traditional undergraduates receive a total of $24.9 million in scholarships and grants, of which $15.5 million comes from Olivet scholarships and grants.

Olivet's cost is below average for private colleges nationwide. The University also participates in all federal and state financial aid programs. The priority deadline for filing the Free Application for Federal Student Aid (FAFSA) is March 1. To apply for aid, students must fill out the FAFSA as well as Olivet's application for financial aid. The student must be an accepted applicant before a financial aid package can be created. Olivet offers a monthly installment plan in addition to the traditional three-payment plan. Olivet believes funding a student's education is a partnership between each family, Olivet, and the state and federal governments. The friendly staff is committed to making an Olivet education affordable to every young person.

Faculty

Olivet's more than 100 full-time faculty members are the key to excellence in and out of the classroom. Teaching is a ministry for these dedicated Christian individuals, and Olivet's student-faculty ratio gives them an opportunity to teach, mentor, and encourage students on a personal level. To that end, the faculty is heavily involved in campus life, whether sponsoring social organizations or participating in talent shows.

Within the traditional liberal arts curriculum, more than 75 percent of Olivet's faculty members have earned a Ph.D. or other terminal degree in their fields.

Student Government

The Associated Student Council is the student government organization on campus. Its Executive Council consists of a president, vice president of finance, vice president of spiritual life, vice president of social affairs, vice president of women's residential life, vice president of men's residential life, vice president of office management, the *GlimmerGlass* (student newspaper) editor, and the *Aurora* (yearbook) editor. They work alongside the University's administrative team to ensure the health and promotion of campus activities and organizations.

Admission Requirements

Admission to the University is moderately difficult. Students are considered for admission on the basis of their high school GPA and ACT or SAT scores. An ACT score is required for placement in courses. For international students, TOEFL results are an additional factor in the admission decision. Students with low test scores and GPAs may be admitted on a provisional basis. A campus visit and interview are strongly recommended for all prospective students.

Application and Information

Admission is on a rolling basis until the application deadline of May 1. An early decision is required for some scholarships. Students may apply via Olivet's home page online or in print. The application process includes the written (or electronic) application, high school transcripts, ACT or SAT scores, and a health form. There is a $25 application fee, and an Enrollment Deposit is collected to prioritize both student housing and class registration.

For more information or to arrange a campus visit, students should contact:

Office of Admissions
Olivet Nazarene University
One University Avenue
Bourbonnais, Illinois 60914
Phone: 800-648-1463 (toll-free)
E-mail: admissions@olivet.edu
Web site: http://www.olivet.edu

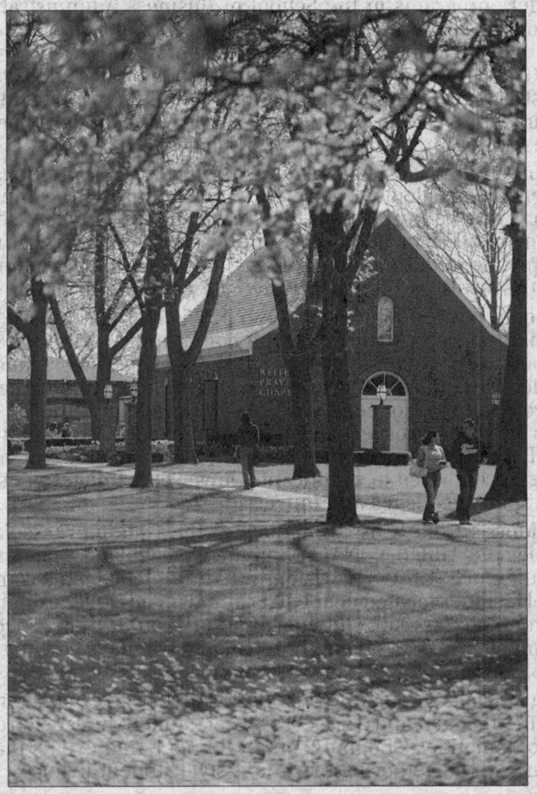

Students on the campus of Olivet Nazarene University.

ROBERT MORRIS COLLEGE

CHICAGO, BENSENVILLE, DUPAGE, ORLAND PARK, LAKE COUNTY, PEORIA, SCHAUMBURG, AND SPRINGFIELD, ILLINOIS

The College

As an accredited, private, not-for-profit institution, Robert Morris College (RMC) grants associate, bachelor's, and master's degrees to more than 3,000 students each year. Its mission is to offer professional, career-focused education in a collegiate setting to diverse communities. Associate degrees in twelve different fields of study; the Bachelor of Business Administration degree, with concentrations in accounting, health/fitness management, hospitality management, and management; the Bachelor of Applied Science degree in graphic design; the Bachelor of Applied Science degree in computer studies; the Bachelor of Professional Studies degree, with concentrations in architectural technology and law office administration; the Master of Business Administration degree; and the Master of Information degree are awarded. RMC is accredited by the Higher Learning Commission and is a member of the North Central Association of Colleges and Schools (30 North LaSalle Street, Suite 2400, Chicago, Illinois 60602; 312-263-0456; http://www.ncahigherlearningcommission.org).

The history of Robert Morris College dates back to the founding of the Moser School, one of the outstanding independent business schools in Chicago, in 1913. Robert Morris College also has origins in Illinois at the site of the former Carthage College. Here, Robert Morris College was chartered and offered associate degrees in both liberal and vocational arts from 1965 to 1974. With the acquisition of the Moser School in 1975, RMC expanded to include business and allied health. The College now provides students with a choice of eight locations: Chicago, Bensenville, DuPage, Orland Park, Lake County, Peoria, Schaumburg, and Springfield, Illinois.

RMC offers programs in the School of Business Administration, the School of Nursing & Health Studies, the School of Computer Studies, the Institute of Culinary Arts, the Institute of Art and Design, and the Morris Graduate School of Management. Each of these divisions uses the most modern computer technology. Acquisition of such technology is imperative to providing real-world educational experiences that are relevant to the evolving workplace.

RMC's unique five-quarter system is designed for continuous learning. It enables students to accelerate their education, completing a bachelor's degree in less than four years and an associate degree in eighteen months. In addition, Robert Morris College is the fifth-largest private undergraduate college in Illinois, and its tuition rate is among the lowest of Illinois' private colleges and universities.

The student body of approximately 7,120 is a cross-cultural, ethnic, and racial mix representative of the communities served. Each student works with a team of program directors, instructors, and placement specialists in an effort to achieve educational and career goals. The records of the College's students and graduates are the best indicators of what a prospective student can expect. More than 90 percent of RMC students graduate from the bachelor's degree program they begin, compared to significantly lower percentages at other private and public colleges and universities.

Robert Morris College is a member of the National Association of Intercollegiate Athletics (NAIA) and the Chicagoland Collegiate Athletic Conference (CCAC), Division II. RMC athletic teams compete in top-level facilities located near each campus. The College offers men's and women's basketball, club hockey, cross-country, golf, soccer, and swimming. It also offers men's baseball and women's bowling, dance, lacrosse, softball, tennis, and volleyball.

Housing is available within walking distance of the main campus at 320 North Michigan and 2 East 8th Street. Student housing provides a wealth of amenities, shopping, entertainment, and events that bring the community together in apartment-style student living.

Location

Located in the heart of Chicago's bustling cultural and financial districts, the College's main campus is minutes from all that Chicago offers, including the Chicago Board of Trade, Art Institute, Field Museum, Merchandise Mart, lakefront, sports arenas, theaters, and all forms of public transportation. The Chicago campus is readily accessible from all parts of the city and suburbs by bus lines and trains. Parking is available in the immediate vicinity. Robert Morris College is across the street from the renowned Harold Washington Public Library.

The Bensenville campus opened to better serve the residents of western Cook and DuPage Counties and to meet the demands of employers in the area. The recently expanded Orland Park campus now includes a technology center with the latest computer facilities available to industry and education. The campus is adjacent to the Orland Square Mall, approximately 30 miles southwest of Chicago. It is accessible via public transportation and I-80 and I-55, which run parallel on the south and north ends of the campus, respectively. Orland Park is becoming a corporate center of the southwest Chicago suburbs, offering students opportunity for professional growth through internships and employment.

The DuPage campus opened on the border between Naperville and Aurora and serves students as well as employers along the East-West High Tech Corridor—the heart of rapid technological development and close to a wide range of employers. The RMC Institute of Culinary Arts started at the DuPage campus and grew so significantly so quickly, the program expanded to the main campus in downtown Chicago and Orland Park.

The Springfield campus—initiated as the first step of the College's commitment to serve central Illinois—is located just east of White Oaks Mall and is accessible by bus; ample parking is also available. This campus has also expanded to a second building at the same location due to expansion of programs and increases in enrollment. The RMC presence in Illinois has further extended to a campus in Peoria, with a busy downtown location. The next location of Robert Morris College, with graduate program offerings, will open in fall 2008.

All RMC campuses provide students with access to the unlimited variety of business services and enhance the students' understanding of the world of work, the employment process, and an appreciation for the attributes of each community.

Majors and Degrees

The Bachelor of Business Administration degree at Robert Morris College offers concentrations in accounting, health/fitness management, hospitality management, and management. The Bachelor of Applied Science degree in graphic design offers a concentration in graphic arts, the Bachelor of Professional Studies degree offers concentrations in architectural technology and law office management, and the Bachelor of Applied Science degree in computer studies offers concentrations in systems integration and networking. The Associate of Applied Science degree is also awarded in accounting, business administration, CADD (architectural/mechanical), computer networking, culinary arts, fitness and exercise, graphic design, interior design, medical assisting, nursing, paralegal studies, pharmacy technology, and surgical technology.

More than twenty-six transfer agreements have been established between RMC and community colleges, allowing students who have earned associate degrees at community colleges in the state of Illinois to complete their bachelor's degrees at RMC by transferring in as a junior.

Academic Programs

The College's academic calendar consists of five quarters, each of which is ten weeks long. The program of study is designed so that students can complete their course work and enter their careers in the shortest time possible.

By concentrating on the specialized subjects related to the student's chosen career field, the College's curricula provide students with the skills and knowledge necessary to enter the job market. Each major consists of courses prescribed by the College to lead to this objective. An associate degree requires at least 92 quarter hours of credit, with a minimum of 36 hours of credit in general education in the areas of communications, humanities, math and science, and social and behavioral science. A minimum of 52 quarter hours of credit are required in career courses, and the remaining hours are electives split between general education and career courses. A bachelor's degree requires a minimum of 188 quarter hours of credit.

Robert Morris College offers students the opportunity to gain experience in their majors and improve their skills through internships and externships. Career services personnel work closely with students to secure positions related to their field of study. Internships offer many educational and professional benefits and provide students with the opportunity to earn academic credit for participating in a career-specific work experience.

Off-Campus Programs

Robert Morris College offers students the opportunity to study abroad in Vienna, Austria; London, England; Florence, Italy; Hamburg, Germany; and Madrid, Spain.

Academic Facilities

General-purpose classrooms are Internet and multimedia ready. Students have ample study, practice, and leisure space on campus. The Student Center at RMC's Chicago Campus has been recognized by *American School & University* as an outstanding design. Specialized laboratories are available for the systems integration, surgical technology, interior space planning and design, and culinary arts programs. The technology-based library has online capabilities that connect the College's various campuses. Students have access via the Internet to advanced research tools, sizable collections of reference and resource volumes, and periodical subscriptions.

Costs

Robert Morris College has one of the lowest tuition rates of any baccalaureate degree–granting private college in the state. Tuition for 2007–08 was $5600 per quarter. Book and supply costs vary by major from $400 to $600 per quarter. Housing and program fees are also applicable.

Financial Aid

Robert Morris College participates in the following federal and state financial aid programs: the Federal Pell Grant, Illinois Monetary Award (SSIG/IMA), Federal Supplemental Educational Opportunity Grant (FSEOG), Federal Stafford Student Loan, Federal Perkins Loan, Federal PLUS loan, and Federal Work-Study (FWS) Program. In addition, the College awards institutional grants on the basis of need, scholarship, residence, academic major, or a combination of these factors. All students must complete a financial planning interview with their admissions counselor, and all are urged to complete the Free Application for Federal Student Aid (FAFSA). Approximately 92 percent of the student body receives some financial assistance. In the 2006–07 academic year, the College awarded more than $17 million in institutional aid.

Faculty

The faculty members at Robert Morris College are selected on the basis of their academic credentials, career experiences in their field, and dedication to giving individual attention to every student. All faculty members possess a master's degree in their chosen field, and many possess a Ph.D. in their area of specialization. In addition to teaching courses, faculty members promote the progress of their students through the individualized academic, employment, and personal development counseling they provide.

Student Government

Robert Morris College has no formal student government. Student representatives serve on committees that make recommendations about campus issues. Student organizations and activities are available.

Admission Requirements

All graduates of accredited high schools or the equivalent (GED) are eligible for admission to the College. All candidates are encouraged to have a personal interview with an admissions representative and take a tour of the campus.

A variety of materials are considered for various applicants. Freshman applicants just graduating from high school must submit their high school record or GED score and test results from the ACT, SAT, Applied Education Skills Assessment (AESA), Advanced Placement, and SAT Subject Area tests.

Those enrolling as an adult must submit their high school record or GED score; test results from the ACT, SAT, AESA, College-Level Examination Program (CLEP), and DANTES; and evidence of a successful employment experience.

Transfer students must present a minimum of 12 transferable credit hours from an accredited institution and their academic records from any high schools and colleges previously attended.

International students must forward their official education records, the results from either the TOEFL or AESA, and an affidavit of financial support.

Home-schooled students must submit a complete transcript of all classes they have taken, curriculum documentation and its state certification, and results from any standardized exams they have taken.

Application and Information

Applications can be obtained by contacting the Admissions Office at any of the College's campuses. The completed application and the $30 nonrefundable application fee ($100 nonrefundable application fee for international students) should be sent to the Admissions Office. The College operates on a rolling admissions basis, and students can enroll during any of the five times offered during the year. For further information, prospective students should visit the Web site or contact:

Robert Morris College
Chicago–Main Campus
401 South State Street
Chicago, Illinois 60605
Phone: 800-RMC-5960 (toll-free)
Web site: http://www.robertmorris.edu

Robert Morris College
Bensenville Campus
1000 Tower Lane
Bensenville, Illinois 60106

Robert Morris College
DuPage Campus
905 Meridian Lake Drive
Aurora, Illinois 60504

Robert Morris College
Orland Park Campus
82 Orland Square
Orland Park, Illinois 60462

Robert Morris College
Lake County Campus
1507 South Waukegan Road
Waukegan, Illinois 60085

Robert Morris College
Peoria Campus
211 Fulton Street
Peoria, Illinois 61602

Robert Morris College
Schaumburg Campus
1000 East Woodfield Road
Schaumburg, Illinois 60173

Robert Morris College
Springfield Campus
3101 Montvale Drive
Springfield, Illinois 62704

ROOSEVELT UNIVERSITY

CHICAGO AND SCHAUMBURG, ILLINOIS

The University

Roosevelt University (RU) was founded in 1945 as an independent, nonsectarian, coeducational institution to provide higher education to all academically qualified students, regardless of social or economic class, racial or ethnic origin, gender, or age. Since 1947, the home of Roosevelt's Chicago Campus has been the famous Auditorium Building, overlooking Buckingham Fountain, Grant Park, and Lake Michigan. The University has restored to their original splendor various areas of this National Historic Landmark building. More recently, RU has expanded its Chicago Campus to include the Gage Building, a few blocks north on Michigan Avenue, across from Millennium Park. Several department offices for RU's professional programs and numerous classrooms are located there. In addition, since 1978, Roosevelt University has offered educational opportunities to the suburban student population. The current Schaumburg Campus was established in 1996 to serve the growing student demand for Roosevelt programs and is the largest, full-service university facility in the northwest suburbs. Students based at both campuses can choose to take some of their courses through RU Online, the University's distance learning program.

Roosevelt University is a national leader in educating socially conscious citizens for active and dedicated lives as leaders in their professions and communities. Deeply rooted in practical scholarship and principles of social justice, RU encourages community partnerships and prepares its diverse graduates for responsible citizenship in a global society. Involvement in the metropolitan experience is an integral part of the academic curriculum. The University is committed to serving the developing needs of Chicago as well as suburban communities.

Roosevelt has an enrollment of approximately 7,200 undergraduate and graduate students among its College of Arts and Sciences, Walter E. Heller College of Business Administration, College of Education, Evelyn T. Stone College of Professional Studies, and Chicago College of Performing Arts (CCPA).

Roosevelt class schedules are flexible, offering day, evening, weekend, and online courses so that students may work while attending school. Approximately 75 percent of Roosevelt students are residents of the greater Chicago metropolitan area; the other students represent other parts of Illinois and more than twenty states and sixty-three countries. The Chicago Campus provides housing for more than 600 students in the University Center and Roosevelt on Washington (ROW) residence halls.

All degree programs at Roosevelt University are accredited by the Higher Learning Commission of the North Central Association of Colleges and Schools. Some individual programs have additional accreditation by organizations, which include the American Bar Association, American Chemical Society, American Psychological Association, Association of Collegiate Business Schools and Programs, Council for Accreditation of Counseling and Related Educational Programs, National Association of Schools of Music, and National Council for Accreditation of Teacher Education.

Location

Roosevelt University's Chicago Campus is conveniently located on Michigan Avenue in the heart of Chicago's cultural, commercial, and political center, within easy commuting distance by car or public transportation. The Schaumburg Campus is located 30 miles northwest of downtown Chicago in Schaumburg, Illinois, near O'Hare International Airport and numerous corporate headquarters.

Majors and Degrees

The Bachelor of Arts (B.A.) degree is awarded in African American studies, art history, biology, chemistry, communications, economics, English, history, information technology, integrated communications, international studies, journalism, legal studies, mathematics, philosophy, political science, psychology, social justice, sociology, and Spanish.

The Bachelor of Arts (B.A.) degree in education is awarded in early childhood, elementary, and special education. A sequence for secondary education teacher certification is available in biology, business education, chemistry, English, mathematics, and social science (economics, history, political science, psychology, sociology).

The Bachelor of Science (B.S.) degree is awarded in actuarial science; allied health (medical technology, nuclear medicine technology, and radiation therapy technology); biology; chemistry; computer science; electronics engineering technology; hospitality and tourism management; mathematics; network computing; nursing; predental, premedical, prepharmacy, and preveterinary studies; and psychology.

The Bachelor of Science in Business Administration (B.S.B.A.) is awarded in accounting, finance, human resource management, management, and marketing.

The Bachelor of Fine Arts (B.F.A.) is awarded in acting and musical theater. The Bachelor of Music (B.M.) degree is awarded in composition, jazz studies, music education, orchestral studies, performance (instrumental, orchestral/band, and voice).

The Bachelor of General Studies (B.G.S.) degree, for students ages 24 and older, is awarded with concentrations in communications, English literature, history, individualized programs, international studies, journalism, languages, liberal arts, political science, psychology, sociology, and women's studies. The Bachelor of Professional Studies (B.P.S.) degree, for students ages 24 and older, is awarded with concentrations in administrative studies, business, computer science, financial services, hospitality and tourism management, organizational communication, organizational leadership, paralegal studies, pre–biotechnology and chemical sciences, professional administration, risk management and financial services, and systems management.

Academic Programs

The requirements for the B.A. and B.S. degrees are completion of a minimum of 120 semester hours with at least a 2.0 average (2.5 in education), a major of no fewer than 24 semester hours, and at least 60 semester hours of work at the advanced level. The requirements for the B.S. degree in business mandates the completion of a minimum of 120 semester hours, a major of no fewer than 18 semester hours, at least 54 semester hours in business administration, and at least 57 semester hours in arts and sciences. The requirements for the B.M. in performance degree are completion of at least 120 semester hours with an average of 2.0 or better (2.3 in music education); participation in orchestra, band, chorus, or other related ensembles; completion of at least 27 semester hours of liberal arts courses; and a senior recital, thesis, or public performance of one original composition. The B.G.S. and B.P.S. are nontraditional degree programs for adults (at least age 24). Degree requirements vary according to the individual student's program.

The University awards credit for successful completion of many CLEP exams and for satisfactory scores on Advanced Placement tests and International Baccalaureate course work.

The Roosevelt Scholars Program is an honors experience that blends academic rigor with opportunities for developing leadership abilities in a metropolitan setting. Generous merit scholarship support is available, along with the opportunity to build valuable mentor relationships with prominent CEOs, scientists, musicians, educators, lawyers, or other top professional leaders in the Chicago area.

Roosevelt University has a special cooperative arrangement with the School of the Art Institute of Chicago (SAIC), in which qualified Roosevelt students can apply courses taken at SAIC to their Roosevelt degree in art history.

Learning and Support Services, a special support program within the Academic Success Center, is available for students with learning challenges. In addition, the Academic Success Center offers tutoring services to all students in all subjects.

Academic Facilities

The collections of RU's main library exceed 400,000 volumes, including 63,000 microforms. The Performing Arts Library houses an additional 40,000 books, 12,000 sound recordings, and 10,000 pieces of sheet music and is furnished with audio equipment for individual listening. Roosevelt students also have access to more than 25 million additional volumes through the University's membership in the Chicago Academic Library Council and the Illinois Library Network. Materials in libraries all over the country can be located quickly by means of the library page on the University's Web site.

Roosevelt's Chicago Campus has numerous computer laboratories, science laboratories, "smart" classrooms, and seminar rooms. Other University academic facilities include numerous practice rooms and lounges. Each year, music students and faculty members present more than 100 recitals and concerts in the renowned Rudolph Ganz Memorial Recital Hall in the Auditorium Building. Operatic and theatrical productions are staged in the O'Malley Theatre and the Miller Studio Theatre, both also in the Auditorium Building. Several art exhibitions each year are on view at the Gage Gallery.

Situated on 30 beautiful acres and housed in a 135,000-square-foot facility, the Schaumburg Campus provides more than sixty classrooms, a library serving research needs, computer classrooms, the Early Childhood Education Center, the Licht Student Center, and state-of-the-art biology, chemistry, and computer labs as well as a digital newsroom convergence lab for journalism classes.

Costs

Undergraduate tuition for the 2007–08 academic year was $16,680 for full-time students in four of RU's five colleges. Full-time undergraduate admission for CCPA students was $23,750. Room and board costs for the school year averaged $9000.

Financial Aid

Scholarships are awarded to entering freshmen and transfer students on the basis of academic merit. The award applies to tuition and may be renewed up to the completion of the bachelor's degree. The University also has a limited number of Music Performance Awards and talent awards for theater majors through the Chicago College of Performing Arts.

Roosevelt's policy is to provide maximum financial assistance for students who demonstrate financial need. Students must submit the Free Application for Federal Student Aid (FAFSA). The priority deadline for applying for University financial aid is April 1 prior to the academic year for which aid is requested.

Faculty

RU has nearly 650 faculty members, more than 200 of whom teach full-time. Although many faculty members conduct serious research and have numerous publications to their credit, they are primarily dedicated to classroom instruction. The student-faculty ratio is 13:1. Most faculty members serve as academic advisers and participate in University affairs through the Faculty Senate, the Board of Trustees, and major RU committees.

Student Government

The student body has its own Student Senate (Student Government Association and Student Alliance), composed of students from the various colleges. Students also serve as voting members of the Faculty Senate and most major University committees and departmental groups.

Admission Requirements

Admission to Roosevelt University is determined on an individual basis. The student's academic ability, as demonstrated by grade point average, standardized test scores, class rank, essays, interview, and recommendations, are all given consideration. Freshman applicants may submit either ACT or SAT scores. Preference is given to applicants in the upper half of their class, with at least 16 units of high school work, a cumulative grade point average of 2.0 or higher, and a minimum ACT composite score of 20 or SAT score of at least 1410.

High school juniors and seniors who are age 16 and older may also attend Roosevelt University while still enrolled in high school through the Early Start Program. A discounted tuition rate is charged for University enrollment concurrent with high school attendance. Regular freshman admission requirements must be met in order for students to enroll. Course work earned in Early Start may be applied toward a Roosevelt degree.

Transfer students must have at least a 2.0 cumulative average (on a 4.0 scale) in all transferable course work. Upon admission, all degree-seeking undergraduate students, including transfer and adult students, are required to take the Roosevelt University Assessment (RUA), a computerized assessment used to determine course placement.

Students applying to the Chicago College of Performing Arts should contact that college directly for further information on admission requirements.

Application and Information

To complete the admission process, students must submit an application; an official high school transcript (or GED test scores); ACT, SAT, or other standardized test scores; official college transcript(s); and the nonrefundable $25 application fee.

For additional information, students should contact the Office of Admission at:

Chicago Campus
Room 104
Roosevelt University
430 South Michigan Avenue
Chicago, Illinois 60605-1395
Phone: 877-APPLY-RU (toll-free)
Fax: 312-341-4316
E-mail: applyRU@roosevelt.edu
Web site: http://www.roosevelt.edu

Schaumburg Campus
Room 110
Roosevelt University
1400 North Roosevelt Boulevard
Schaumburg, Illinois 60173
Phone: 877-APPLY-RU (toll-free)
Fax: 312-341-4316
E-mail: applyRU@roosevelt.edu
Web site: http://www.roosevelt.edu

SAINT XAVIER UNIVERSITY

CHICAGO, ILLINOIS

The University

Saint Xavier University (SXU) is one of the oldest institutions of higher learning in Illinois. Founded in 1846 and chartered in 1847 by the Sisters of Mercy, Saint Xavier continues its commitment to the pursuit of academic excellence within the context of respect, caring, and justice. The members of the University community affirm the rich tradition of Catholic higher education in America—one marked by spiritual development and intellectual vigor.

As a coeducational private Catholic university, Saint Xavier offers a solid liberal arts core and outstanding professional programs. The University serves a diverse student population of more than 5,700. Saint Xavier's students come from throughout the United States and the world, but the majority come from the Midwest region. The University offers a variety of housing options, including residence halls and on-campus apartment living. All campus housing has Internet access and cable television. Students enjoy easy access to Chicago by car and public transportation. Many college activities and a career program take advantage of the city of Chicago.

At Saint Xavier University, students are challenged to critically examine values that recognize individual dignity and worth and promote personal growth, professional integrity, and multicultural experiences. More than forty clubs and organizations sponsor projects, dances, picnics, and lectures, so there are always activities going on outside of class. These clubs and organizations offer students social, cultural, professional, and athletic opportunities beyond the curriculum. As a member of the National Association of Intercollegiate Athletics, SXU's varsity athletic programs include intercollegiate baseball, basketball, cross-country/track, football, and soccer for men and intercollegiate basketball, cross-country/track, soccer, softball, and volleyball for women. A variety of intramural programs are available to all students.

At the graduate level, master's degrees are offered in applied computer science, business administration, nursing, public health, school counseling and community counseling, and speech-language pathology. Also available are graduate certificate programs in pastoral ministry and a variety of business options; a post-master's family nurse practitioner certificate is also available.

Location

Saint Xavier University is located in a residential neighborhood on the city's southwest side, on 103rd Street and Central Park, between Pulaski Road and Kedzie Avenue. The campus is easily accessible by public transportation, major expressways, and through streets, including I-94, I-294, I-57, and Cicero Avenue. SXU is adjacent to the suburbs of Evergreen Park, and Oak Lawn and is 15 miles from the heart of Chicago's Loop, only 8 miles from Midway Airport and 35 miles from O'Hare International Airport.

Majors and Degrees

Saint Xavier University shares in the rich tradition of Catholic liberal arts higher education while offering flexibility in course scheduling and diversity of the degrees available. Saint Xavier University offers programs leading to a bachelor's degree in accounting, art and design, biology, business administration, chemistry, communication, communication sciences and disorders, computer science, computer studies, criminal justice, education, English, history, international business, international studies, liberal studies, mathematics, mathematics education, music, natural science, nursing, philosophy, political science, psychology, religious studies, social science, sociology, and Spanish. Preprofessional programs include dentistry, law, medicine, optometry, pharmacy, podiatry, and veterinary medicine.

Minors are offered in most of the fields listed above as well as in African American studies, anthropology, Catholic studies, Latino/Latin American studies, pastoral ministry, physical education, public administration, and women and gender studies.

The School for Continuing and Professional Studies is a specialized program offering majors in accounting, business administration, computer studies, criminal justice, English, liberal studies, nursing, psychology, clinical/counseling psychology, industrial/organizational psychology, religious studies, RN completion, LPN completion, and sociology.

Academic Programs

Saint Xavier University's core curriculum expresses the University's commitment to the values of a liberal education designed to be both foundational and exploratory. The curriculum develops the student's critical skills of writing, speaking, reading, and thinking as well as an understanding of the methods, approaches, and thought processes of the liberal arts disciplines. The core includes courses in natural science, mathematics, social sciences, history, literature, religious studies, philosophy, writing, and speech.

For graduation, a student must earn at least 120 semester hours, including completion of the University's specified curricular components. Transfer students must complete at least 30 semester hours and one third of the requirement in their major area at the University, including clinical or practicum experience in programs requiring such a component.

Academic Facilities

The academic facilities of the University's Chicago campus include classrooms, labs, a library, Shannon Athletics and Convocation, an auditorium, conference center, residence halls, clinical facilities, and the McDonough Chapel and Mercy Ministry Center.

The University's computer equipment consists of thirteen computer labs. The University is connected to the Internet. Incoming students have the option of attending a workshop on computer literacy and word processing. Tutoring can be scheduled for assistance on several software packages. Advanced career planning software is utilized.

The Byrne Memorial Library at Saint Xavier University houses more than 170,000 volumes and an extensive microfiche and microfilm collection. With membership in three consortia, ILCSO, LIBRAS, and SMRHEC, students have access to the collections of more than 800 academic, public, and special libraries.

Saint Xavier University's interactive learning program uses the technology of live color compressed-video television, which has two-way full-motion video and audio capabilities to link SXU students with any of the nine other colleges and universities involved in this alternative learning program. Participants have the opportunity to speak with their instructor without ever leaving their designated sites.

Costs

Basic tuition for the 2008–09 academic year is $22,486. Basic room and board charges are $8007.

Financial Aid

Saint Xavier University's extensive financial aid program assists more than 90 percent of the student body. The Financial Aid Office participates in and coordinates aid from federal, state, University, and private sources. These funds help eligible students meet the cost of higher education. The University also offers academic and athletic scholarships to eligible students. Transfer students, new freshmen, and continuing studies students may be eligible for a no-need scholarship based on proven academic excellence. The scholarships and awards range is from $750 to $15,000 for full- or part-time students. Any student interested in applying for aid must complete a Free Application for Federal Student Aid, which is used for federal, state, and Saint Xavier University aid programs. Students must file their financial aid application by March 1 to receive maximum consideration.

Faculty

Saint Xavier's 16:1 student-faculty ratio allows students accessibility to faculty members, who offer personal attention and act as both teacher and adviser. The University has 177 full-time faculty members, 85 percent of whom have terminal degrees. Nearly 80 percent of all classes are taught by full-time faculty members.

Student Government

Members of the Student Activities Board (SAB) apply and interview for paid positions in the following areas: finance, interclub council, intramurals, programming, and public relations. SAB offers students a wide variety of programs, such as dances, entertainment events, films, lectures, intramural sports, and parties. The University holds an election to choose the 8-member board who will serve as advisers on student life issues.

Admission Requirements

During the admission process, consideration is given to previous academic work, recommendations from counselors and teachers, and scores on the ACT or SAT as well as the student's ability and desire to do college work. The Admission Committee is interested in the quality of a student's work and the kinds of courses taken in high school. Candidates should have a minimum of 16 units in English, math, natural and social sciences, foreign language, and academic electives. Applicants must submit an application for admission along with high school transcripts, test scores, and a personal statement. Admission counselors are available to guide students through the application process.

Transfer students may be admitted to SXU if they present evidence of at least a 2.5 GPA in all college-level course work. A cumulative grade point average of 2.75 as a minimum is required for nursing applicants. November 1 is the priority application deadline for transfer students who intend to major in nursing. For further information, students should contact the Office of Admission. All transfer credit is subject to validation by the academic departments. SXU will accept a maximum of 70 semester hours from a community college and 90 semester hours from a four-year college/university. Saint Xavier also has a number of transfer articulation agreements with area community colleges and is a participant in the Illinois Articulation Initiative.

Application and Information

Application forms for admission are available from the Office of Admission and online at http://www.sxu.edu. Freshman applicants should submit an application for admission, ACT or SAT scores, high school transcripts, and a personal statement, or they can apply online at the Web site listed. Transfer applicants are required to submit an admission application, personal statement, and a transcript from each institution where college-level work has been completed.

Office of Admission—Chicago Campus
Saint Xavier University
3700 West 103rd Street
Chicago, Illinois 60655
Phone: 773-298-3050
800-462-9288 (toll-free)
Fax: 773-298-3076
E-mail: admission@sxu.edu
Web site: http://www.sxu.edu

Office of Admission—Orland Park Campus
Saint Xavier University
18230 Orland Parkway
Orland Park, Illinois 60467
Phone: 708-802-6200
E-mail: opcadmission@sxu.edu
Web site: http://www.sxu.edu/orland_park/

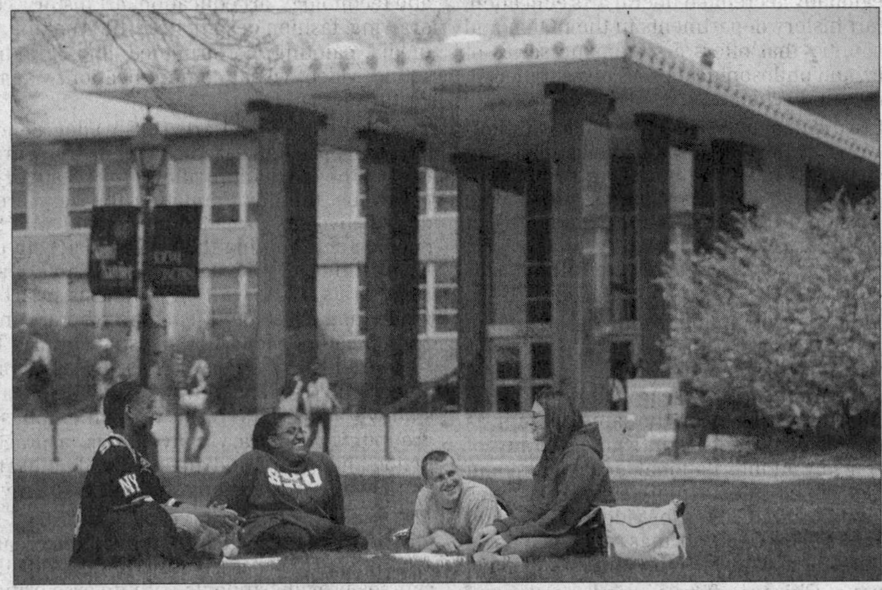

On the campus at Saint Xavier University.

COLLEGE DATA CENTER • ILLINOIS

SCHOOL OF THE ART INSTITUTE OF CHICAGO

CHICAGO, ILLINOIS

The School

Since its founding in 1866, the School of the Art Institute of Chicago (SAIC) has been providing a leading global vision for the education of artists, designers, and others who shape contemporary art practice. The School of the Art Institute of Chicago's primary purpose is to foster the conceptual and technical education of artists, designers, and scholars in a highly professional, studio-oriented, and academically rigorous environment, encouraging excellence, critical inquiry, and experimentation. In 2002, SAIC was recognized as "the most influential art school in the nation" by a poll conducted by Columbia University and a panel of national art critics. *U.S. News & World Report* has consistently ranked SAIC's Master of Fine Arts program as number 1 in the nation.

SAIC's 2,300 undergraduate and more than 600 graduate students and a faculty of artists, designers, and scholars work in an environment that facilitates the exchange of ideas, the sharing of resources, and the critiquing and refining of technical abilities and conceptual concerns.

The School of the Art Institute of Chicago is distinguished from other art and design schools in the breadth and depth of its curriculum in both studio and academic areas, with more than 900 courses offered each semester. SAIC is committed to interdisciplinary exploration and the awareness that the boundaries between artistic fields are not always easily defined. Students are encouraged to experience the full range of studio practices and academic approaches; they do not declare a major but are free to design a path of study that best suits their creative development. A student may choose to do all their course work in one area of study or amongst multiple department areas. SAIC's credit/no-credit grading system encourages students to investigate, develop, or resolve a creative problem by exploring new approaches and to develop the self-motivation and discipline necessary for life as a practicing artist, designer, and scholar in the twenty-first century.

The Departments of Liberal Arts and Art History are central to the life of the School of the Art Institute of Chicago and underscore one of SAIC's primary commitments: to enrich a strong studio program with a first-rate, nationally and regionally accredited liberal arts education. SAIC has one of the largest art history departments in the nation and is the only college in the country that offers a systematic series of courses on the history, theory, and philosophical bases of art criticism, taught by contemporary critics and scholars.

Students may live in one of two distinctive residence halls with loft-style rooms, each with their own bathroom, kitchen, voice mail, and Internet access. The residence halls have 24-hour security and controlled access as well as spacious, well-lit studios, lounge rooms with big screen TVs, computer labs, and laundry facilities. Students can immerse themselves in a community of fellow artists, live in the heart of Chicago's loop, and enjoy conveniences unavailable in most student apartments.

Students have access to a wide variety of unique resources, beginning with the premiere collection of SAIC's sister institution, the Art Institute of Chicago, and its Ryerson Library and Burnham Library of Architecture, the largest art and architecture research libraries in the country. The Gene Siskel Film Center, located in the same building as the 162 North State Street residence, presents significant programs of world cinema and presentations by an international array of film and video artists. SAIC's Video Data Bank houses more than 1,600 titles and is the leading resource in the United States for videotapes by and about contemporary artists. The Poetry Center brings renowned poets and writers to Chicago to share their work with the public.

The School of the Art Institute of Chicago offers a broad spectrum of services to accommodate its diverse population, including an international student office, multicultural affairs office, health and counseling services, a learning center (offering one-on-one tutoring as well as support services for students with learning disabilities), an extensive program for academic advising, and a Career Development Center.

The School of the Art Institute of Chicago is accredited by the Higher Learning Commission of the North Central Association of Colleges and Schools and by the National Association of Schools of Art and Design.

Location

The School of the Art Institute of Chicago is located in the heart of downtown Chicago, home to the nation's second-largest art scene that includes world-class museums, 150 galleries, alternative spaces, and organizations that support the arts. Chicago is a city of diverse neighborhoods, each with its own atmosphere, customs, and cuisine. Students have a wide variety of cultural and recreational resources from which to choose: ballet, opera, theater, orchestra halls, cinemas, libraries, architecture, blues and jazz clubs, parks, ethnic restaurants, a variety of world-class sports venues, and street festivals.

Chicago itself is a vital part of the campus, as a source of social and cultural activities and the stimulus for ideas and attitudes ultimately expressed through art. Peter Frank, art critic and curator says, "Of all American cities, Chicago has contributed the most solid and distinctive artwork and art thinking. The School of the Art Institute of Chicago is at the nucleus of this longstanding distinction."

The School of the Art Institute of Chicago is located across the street from an extraordinary space that rivals the quads of any other big-city college or university. Millennium Park is a twenty-first-century marvel, and SAIC, its faculty members, and students played a key role in its realization. One of the signature pieces of public art at the park, the Crown Fountain by Spanish artist Jaume Plensa, was created with the assistance of both SAIC students and faculty members, who collaborated with Plensa in producing the 1,000 video portraits that are screened continuously on the fountain's twin video towers. The park, with its unique mix of art, architecture, and nature, has become an urban oasis for SAIC students.

Majors and Degrees

Students do not declare majors but are free to concentrate in one or any combination of the following areas: animation, architecture, art and technology, art education, art history, ceramics, designed objects, drawing, fashion design, fiber, filmmaking, interior architecture, new media, painting, performance, photography, print media, sculpture, sound, video, visual communication, visual and critical studies, and writing.

The Bachelor of Fine Arts (B.F.A.) degree in studio allows students to develop a particularized course of study in the visual arts. The openness of the curriculum allows for creative, idiosyncratic, and tailored programs, thereby emulating the very process of art making. Academic advising, provided by the Office of Student Affairs, helps students in determining their particular path of study. The School of the Art Institute of Chicago offers Illinois teacher certification (K–12) through its B.F.A. with an emphasis in art education, with a goal of graduating artists and teachers who are informed and engaged citizens, creators and critics of visual culture. The B.F.A. with an emphasis in art history, theory, and criticism emphasizes art history, theory, and criticism, while allowing students the ability to develop their own studio practice. The B.F.A. with an emphasis in writing offers a solid grounding in literary conventions, a practical exposure to form in fiction and poetry, and an enhanced ability to read and critique peers' work, while encouraging students to openly explore what "writing" is.

The Bachelor of Arts in visual and critical studies allows students to pursue in-depth academic study in the creative environment of an art school, sharing classes with students in the B.F.A. programs. Core courses provide students with diverse critical methods for exploring the cultural meanings of visual phenomena as they relate to social, economic, and material circumstances.

The Bachelor of Interior Architecture (B.I.A.) is intended for students interested in interdisciplinary study and a focus in contemporary, professional design practices, such as sustainability, embedded and emerging technologies, and designed objects.

Academic Programs

Completion of 132 hours is required for the B.F.A. and B.A. degrees; approximately two thirds is in studio areas and one third is in academic course work. All entering students who have completed fewer than 15 credit hours of college-level studio art must enroll in the First Year Experience. Students take liberal arts courses in the humanities, natural sciences, mathematics, and social sciences and are required to complete an art history requirement.

Off-Campus Arrangements

The off-campus study requirement is an opportunity for students to gain practical experience at the same time as they gain a broader sense of society and the world.

Students can choose from a wide variety of off-campus programs. The Mobility program allows students to attend partner schools within the United States and Canada and includes the New York Studio semester. SAIC also maintains semester exchange agreements with more than twenty schools in Europe, Asia, and South America. The Off-Campus Programs Office works closely with students to help them develop their individual programs. SAIC faculty members lead study trips during each summer and winter interim session to such destinations as Cuba, New York, Puerto Rico, Venice, and Vietnam.

SAIC is home to the largest and most successful arts-related cooperative education program in the country, providing employment opportunities throughout Chicago and worldwide with individual artists; museums; galleries; multimedia firms; film, video, and animation production houses; interior architecture firms; fashion designers; and community service organizations.

Academic Facilities

SAIC's campus encompasses seven buildings in downtown Chicago. There are fully equipped studios for each area of concentration, and the School's policy allows 24-hour access to facilities.

The School of the Art Institute of Chicago is committed to new technologies and the integration of computer-based resources throughout the curriculum. Currently, more than sixty digital technology courses are taught each semester in nearly all departmental areas. An aggressive laptop program coupled with state-of-the-art facilities and accessible resources provides cutting-edge capability in every corner of the School. Facilities available to all students include general-access computer labs equipped with the latest-model Apple computers and high-end peripherals; a Service Bureau, providing professional digital output, including laser cutting and 3-D printing; a Media Center, offering a wide variety of equipment for student loan; wood and metal shops; and fabrication studios.

The John M. Flaxman Library collections include approximately 60,000 volumes on art and the liberal arts and sciences, 360 periodical subscriptions, films, videos, audiotapes, CDs, microforms, and picture files. The Joan Flasch Artists' Book Collection contains more than 3,000 artists' books along with a research collection of exhibition catalogs and other related material. The MacLean Visual Resource Center maintains a noncirculating collection of more than 500,000 slides.

Exhibition spaces include the Betty Rymer Gallery, which highlights work from departments and presents special exhibitions, and Gallery 2, with exhibition space, a performance space, and a space designed for site-specific installations. In addition, Gallery X and the Lounge Gallery, sponsored by the Student Union Galleries, provide exhibition space for currently enrolled students.

Costs

Tuition for the 2007–08 academic year was $30,750 for full-time undergraduate students or $1025 per credit hour. For 2007–08, student housing cost $8900 per academic year for a double room.

Financial Aid

The School of the Art Institute of Chicago makes every effort to assist students who need help in financing their education. Through an extensive financial aid program, $13.2 million in gift aid funding from private, institutional, state, and federal sources is distributed annually. In addition to scholarships and grants, the School grants merit scholarships and offers an extensive college work-study program. To apply for financial aid, students should complete the FAFSA. To receive priority consideration, students should submit completed forms to the Financial Aid Office no later than March 1. All awards are made on a first-come, first-served basis to students in good standing who demonstrate need.

Faculty

Faculty members are selected for their skills, insight, and dedication as teachers and for their professional accomplishments as artists, designers, and scholars. There are currently more than 600 full- and part-time faculty members, among them NEA grant recipients, Louis Comfort Tiffany Foundation Fellowship recipients, and Rockefeller Foundation grant recipients. SAIC's faculty members have their work exhibited in museums, galleries, and festivals nationally and internationally. They publish books, plays, poetry, and criticism; organize and curate exhibitions; and design, build, and preserve buildings throughout the world. Each year, 100 or more well-known visiting artists, including poets, political activists, and visual artists, present workshops and provide individual student critiques through the Visiting Artists Program. Notable alumni include Claes Oldenburg, Ivan Albright, Georgia O'Keefe, David Sedaris, Cynthia Rowley, and Vincente Minnelli.

Student Government

Student Government officers are elected each spring, and their mission is to promote student interests and concerns to the broader School community by serving on a variety of faculty and administrative staff committees. Student Government also provides funds for the more than forty student groups on campus. All students are encouraged to attend the weekly open Student Government meetings.

Admission Requirements

To be considered for the undergraduate program, applicants are required to submit an electronic application; a nonrefundable application fee of $65 for domestic students ($85 for international students); a portfolio consisting of ten to fifteen examples of recent work, a minimum of 5 minutes of time-based work, or an "alternative" portfolio submission that demonstrates the applicant's creative intent; a statement of purpose; transcript(s) from high school(s) or an official copy of the high school equivalency certificate; transcripts from any college previously attended; and one letter of recommendation. Domestic applicants must submit either scores from the SAT or the ACT. Any transfer applicant who has successfully completed the School of the Art Institute of Chicago's English requirements and/or other liberal arts course work at another accredited college may be exempt from standardized test requirements for admission. All international undergraduate students who are not U.S. citizens or permanent residents or are nonnative English speakers are required to take either the TOEFL or the IELTS.

Application and Information

Prospective students may apply to the School of the Art Institute of Chicago through the Immediate Decision Option (IDO) or the traditional admission procedure. IDO Days allows prospective students who have submitted all their application materials an opportunity to receive an admissions decision by the end of the day while on the SAIC campus.

Those students applying through the traditional admission procedure are required to submit their applications electronically at http://www.artic.edu/saic/ugapp. The applicant's portfolio and academic credentials are reviewed and evaluated by the Admissions Office. Students are admitted on a rolling basis and are informed of the committee's decision by mail. Students who anticipate a need for financial assistance are urged to complete their applications for admission and financial aid by February 15 for the fall semester and November 15 for the spring semester in order to receive priority consideration. These dates are also the final deadlines for applicants who wish to be considered for the School of the Art Institute of Chicago's Merit Scholarship Program.

Admissions Office
School of the Art Institute of Chicago
36 South Wabash
Chicago, Illinois 60603
Phone: 312-629-6100
800-232-7242 (toll-free)
Fax: 312-629-6101
E-mail: admiss@saic.edu
Web site: http://www.saic.edu

SOUTHERN ILLINOIS UNIVERSITY CARBONDALE

CARBONDALE, ILLINOIS

The University

Southern Illinois University Carbondale (SIUC), chartered in 1869, is a comprehensive state-supported institution with nationally and internationally recognized instructional, research, and service programs. SIUC is fully accredited by the North Central Association of Colleges and Schools.

SIUC offers more than 150 undergraduate majors, specializations, and minors; two associate degree programs; ninety baccalaureate degree programs; sixty master's degree programs; thirty-two doctoral programs; and professional degrees in law and medicine. SIUC is a multicampus university and includes the Carbondale campus as well as the SIUC School of Medicine at Springfield.

During the 2007 academic year, SIUC's enrollment reached 21,003, which included 16,294 undergraduate students, 4,060 graduate students, and 649 professional students. The average age of undergraduates is 24. Five and one half percent of SIUC's enrolled students are international students. Of U.S. students, 15 percent are African American, .5 percent are American Indian/Alaskan, 2 percent are Asian or Pacific Islander, and 3 percent are Hispanic.

Students who are ready to start college but not ready to commit to a specific major can enroll in SIUC's Pre-Major Program. Premajor advisers and career counselors help premajor students plan their education and careers. SIUC faculty members, staff members, and alumni help students arrange internships, cooperative education programs, and work-study programs.

All single freshmen under the age of 21 are required to live on campus unless they are living at home. SIUC University Housing offers four on-campus residential areas for single students. Each area includes a dining hall, post office, and laundry facilities. Learning Resource Centers are available on both sides of campus and offer writing centers, computer labs, and student lounges. University Housing Residence Hall Dining provides a variety of meal plans, with all-you-care-to-eat meals and late night dining. Residence Hall Dining offers a variety of menus, vegetarian and light entrees, display cooking, and a full-time dietitian to help students who have special dietary needs.

Apartment housing is available for upperclass undergraduates, graduate students, and students with families.

SIUC intercollegiate sports teams compete at the NCAA Division I level (football is Division I-AA). Conference affiliations include the Missouri Valley and Gateway Conferences. Intercollegiate sports teams include men's and women's basketball, cross-country, diving, golf, swimming, tennis, and track and field; men's baseball and football; and women's softball and volleyball. The campus holds various playfields, several tennis courts, and a campus lake with a beach and a boat dock. SIUC's Student Recreation Center houses an Olympic-size pool; indoor tracks; handball/racquetball and squash courts; a climbing wall; weight rooms; and basketball, volleyball, and tennis courts. It also offers outdoor equipment rental, an aerobic area, walleyball, martial arts, and dance and cardio studios.

The Student Center is one of the largest student centers in the U.S. without a hotel. It contains a bookstore, several restaurants, a craft shop, a bakery, and facilities for bowling and billiards. It is headquarters for 400 active student organizations and the student government office. It holds four ballrooms and an auditorium. On-campus events throughout the year include concerts, plays, festivals, guest speakers, and musicals.

Location

Carbondale is 6 hours south of Chicago, 2 hours southeast of St. Louis, and 3 hours north of Nashville. Four large recreational lakes, the two great rivers (the Mississippi and the Ohio), and the spectacular 270,000-acre Shawnee National Forest are within minutes of the campus. The mid-South climate is ideal for year-round outdoor activities.

Carbondale is a small city of 26,000 people that supports one large enclosed mall, several mini-malls, theaters, and restaurants. Students frequent the shops and restaurants that line Illinois and Grand Avenues.

Majors and Degrees

The University offers associate in applied science degree programs at the College of Applied Sciences and Arts in aviation flight and physical therapist assistant studies.

The College of Applied Sciences and Arts offers bachelor's degree programs in architectural studies, automotive technology, aviation management, aviation technologies, dental hygiene, electronics systems technologies, fashion design and merchandising, fire service management (off campus only), health-care management, information systems technologies, interior design, mortuary science and funeral service, radiologic sciences, and technical resources management.

The College of Agriculture offers bachelor's degree programs in agribusiness economics, agricultural systems, animal science, forestry, hospitality and tourism administration, human nutrition and dietetics, and plant and soil science.

The College of Business and Administration offers bachelor's degree programs in accounting, business and administration, business economics, finance, management, and marketing.

The College of Education and Human Services offers bachelor's degree programs in athletic training, communication disorders and sciences, early childhood education, elementary education, exercise science, health education, physical education teacher education, recreation, rehabilitation services, social work, special education, and workforce education and development. Teacher preparation is available in art, biological sciences, English, French, German, health education, mathematics, music, physical education, secondary education, social sciences with designations in history and social studies, Spanish, and special education.

The College of Engineering offers bachelor's degree programs in civil engineering, computer engineering, electrical engineering, engineering technology, industrial technology, mechanical engineering, and mining engineering.

The College of Liberal Arts offers bachelor's degrees in administration of justice, anthropology, art, classics, design, economics, English, foreign language and international trade, French, geography and environmental resources, German, history, linguistics, mathematics, music, paralegal studies, philosophy, political science, psychology, sociology, Spanish, speech communication, theater, and university studies.

The College of Mass Communication and Media Arts offers bachelor's degrees in cinema and photography, journalism, and radio-television.

The College of Science offers bachelor's degree programs in biological sciences, chemistry and biochemistry, computer science, environmental studies, geology, mathematics, microbiology, physics, physiology, plant biology, zoology, and preprofessional programs in dentistry, medicine, nursing, optometry, pharmacy, physical therapy, physician assistant studies, podiatry, and veterinary medicine.

In addition to many majors offered at SIUC, specializations are offered in all colleges in many areas.

Academic Programs

Each bachelor's degree candidate must earn a minimum of 120 semester hours of credit, including at least 60 at a senior-level institution and the last 30 at SIUC. Each student must maintain at least a C average in all course work at SIUC. Each student must fulfill the University core curriculum and the specific requirements of their degree programs. SIUC awards credit through qualifying extension and correspondence programs, military experience, the High School Advanced Placement Program, the College-Level Examination Program (CLEP), SIUC's proficiency examination program, and work experience.

SIUC offers honors course work and special recognition for students who demonstrate exceptional academic achievement. The Air Force and Army offer ROTC programs at SIUC. SIUC offers three semesters: fall, spring, and summer.

Off-Campus Programs

At Southern Illinois University Carbondale, distance education courses are offered in interactive, print-based and Web-based formats. Print-based (correspondence) and Web-based courses are offered by the Individualized Learning Program (ILP). Web-based courses and Two-Way Interactive Video courses are offered through the Office of Distance Education. Many of the courses offered through the ILP and other distance education courses can be taken to complete the University Studies Degree (B.A.) in the College of Liberal Arts.

Off-campus credit programs are designed to meet the educational needs of adults wishing to pursue a degree but who are unable to travel to the Carbondale campus. Faculty members who teach off-campus courses travel to distant sites to teach SIUC courses.

Contractual services are provided and include specialized educational services to groups, organizations, governmental agencies, and businesses on a cost-recovery basis. These services are provided regionally, nationally, and internationally.

All credit courses offered through these programs carry full SIUC academic credit and are taught by faculty members appointed by the academic departments of the University. Additional information can be found on the Web (http://www.dce.siu.edu/siuconnected).

Academic Facilities

In addition to the 2.5 million volumes, 3.6 million microfilms, and more than 12,500 periodicals currently available in Morris Library, students and faculty members have access to more than 27,000 full-text electronic journals. SIUC students have access to several computer learning centers that are equipped, in all, with more than 1,600 microcomputers. Additional information can be found on the Web (http://www.lib.siu.edu).

Students learn and practice in the Southern Illinois Airport, outdoor laboratories, the student-run *Daily Egyptian* newspaper, WSIU-TV, WSIU-FM, art and natural history museums, a literary magazine, McCleod Theater, Memorial Hospital, a vivarium, the plant biology greenhouses, the University Farms, and the Touch of Nature Environmental Center.

Costs

Tuition and fee charges for the 2007–08 academic year (fall and spring) for students enrolled in 15 or more semester hours were $8899 for Illinois residents and $18,421 for out-of-state residents, including international students. Room and board were $6666. All costs are subject to change. The cost of books and school supplies varies among programs. The average cost is $900 per academic year. Some courses require that students purchase special materials.

Financial Aid

More than $208 million in financial aid was distributed to more than 79 percent of SIUC students in fiscal year 2008 through federal, state, and institutionally funded financial aid programs.

To apply for financial aid at SIUC, students should complete a Free Application for Federal Student Aid (FAFSA). Applications that are filed before April 1 receive priority consideration for campus-based aid. The FAFSA can be completed electronically at the U.S. Department of Education's Web site (http://www.fafsa.ed.gov). When completing the FAFSA, students should list Southern Illinois University Carbondale (Federal School Code 001758) as a school of choice.

SIUC has one of the largest student employment programs in the country, with approximately 5,400 students employed each year in a wide variety of job classifications. SIUC offers competitive scholarships based on talent and academic achievement.

Faculty

Faculty members are dedicated to excellence in teaching and to their advancement of knowledge in a wide variety of disciplines and professions. Many faculty members are well-known both nationally and internationally for their varied research contributions. The undergraduate student-faculty ratio is 17:1. There are 1,333 full-time and 220 part-time instructional faculty members.

Teaching assistants at SIUC are graduate students who assist faculty members in teaching. While some teach introductory undergraduate classes, others provide support to faculty members by assisting in laboratories, monitoring tests, and helping students.

Student Government

The undergraduate student government consists of a president, vice president, executive assistant, and chief of staff. Under the vice president, there are 43 senators: 1 senator per 388 students. Each student has at least 2 representatives: 1–6 for their residential area, and 1–6 for the college in which they are enrolled. Under the 6 commissioners are a list of committees on which a varying number of students sit to represent the student body. The student government writes and passes legislation on University policies, funding, student organizations, and other matters that affect the students and the University.

Admission Requirements

Freshman applicants whose ACT or SAT scores are at or above the 66th percentile and class rank is in the upper three quarters are admitted. Applicants can also be admitted with an ACT or SAT score at or above the 50th percentile and class rank in the upper half. Finally, applicants can be admitted with an ACT or SAT score at or above the 33rd percentile and class rank in the top quarter. Admission standards are subject to change. Freshman applicants must meet course pattern requirements: 4 years of English, 3 years of mathematics, 3 years of laboratory science, 3 years of social science, and 2 years of electives.

Transfer applicants must have an overall grade point average of at least 2.0 on a 4.0 scale, based on work attempted at all institutions and calculated by SIUC grading policies. Transfer applicants must also be eligible to continue at the last institution attended.

Some programs have higher admission requirements or require additional screening for admission. Undergraduates can apply online (http://salukinet.siu.edu/admit/).

Application and Information

Admission is granted on a rolling basis. Application priority deadlines for freshmen are: June 1 for the summer 2008 term; May 1 for the fall 2008 term; and December 1, 2008, for the spring 2009 term. Application priority deadlines for transfer students are: June 1 for the summer 2008 term; July 1 for the fall 2008 term; and December 1, 2008, for the spring 2009 term. The application fee is $30.

Undergraduate Admissions MC 4710
425 Clocktower Drive
Southern Illinois University Carbondale
Carbondale, Illinois 62901
Phone: 618-536-4405
Fax: 618-453-3250
E-mail: joinsiuc@siu.edu
Web site: http://www.siuc.edu

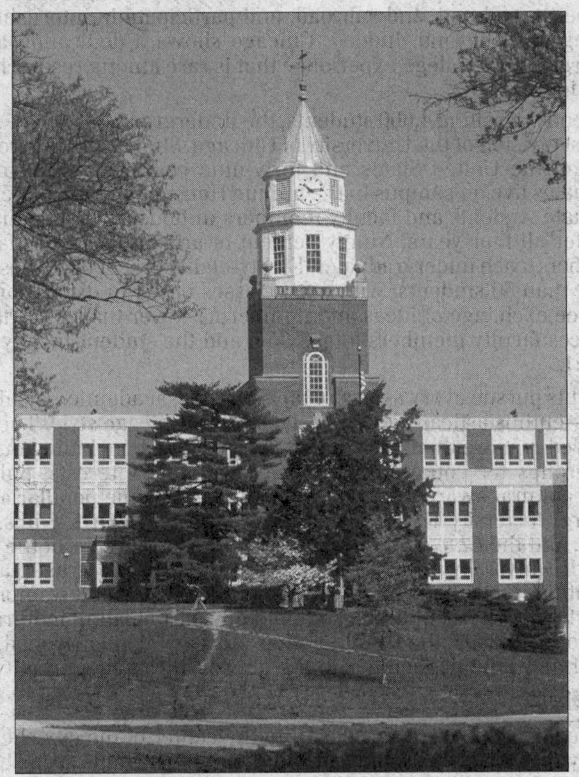

SIUC's Pulliam Hall.

COLLEGE DATA CENTER • ILLINOIS

UNIVERSITY OF CHICAGO
CHICAGO, ILLINOIS

The University

With its Gothic quadrangles, dynamic faculty and student body, exciting research, and seminar-style classes that emphasize critical thinking and interdisciplinary scholarship, the University of Chicago stands as one of the world's great intellectual communities and centers of learning. Founded in 1890 by John D. Rockefeller, who called it "the best investment I ever made," the University is private, nondenominational, and coeducational. Through the years, it has played a leading role in providing equal opportunity for women and minorities in higher education. The strength and distinction of its faculty is reflected in the 81 Nobel laureates who have been associated with Chicago, including 8 current faculty members. In addition to the undergraduate liberal arts college, the University of Chicago is composed of four graduate divisions, six professional schools, an extensive library system, the Graham School of General Studies, the Laboratory Schools, and the University of Chicago Press. In more than a century of challenging existing educational traditions, Chicago has established new ones, such as a coherent program of general education for undergraduates, the four-quarter system, and the "Chicago School" of thought in economics, sociology, and literary criticism.

The University of Chicago stands at the forefront of academic discovery. Some of the innovations and groundbreaking studies of Chicago scholars include carbon-14 dating, REM sleep, urban sociology, classical literary criticism, the first controlled nuclear chain reaction, the F-scale for measuring tornado severity, pioneering scientific archaeology of the ancient Near East, the nation's first living-donor liver transplant, and discovery in the last three years of three new prehistoric creatures from the dinosaur era. Chicago undergraduates are often involved in academic exploration with graduate students and faculty members. In addition, they take graduate-level courses, travel and study abroad, and participate in internships in Chicago and beyond. Indeed, Chicago shows a dedication to the undergraduate college experience that is rare among research universities.

Currently enrolling 4,600 students, the undergraduate college is the largest division of the University of Chicago. Students come from all parts of the United States and forty-nine countries. Most undergraduates live on campus in the unique House System that includes graduate students and faculty members in housing that is guaranteed for all four years. Ninety percent of arts and sciences faculty members teach undergraduates. Eighty-eight percent of classes have fewer than 30 students, with most classes based in discussion and the free exchange of ideas and numbering fewer than 15. Arts and sciences faculty members total 1,055, and the student-faculty ratio is 5.6:1.

Students pursue every aspect of life—athletic, academic, social, cultural—enthusiastically and with a distinctly Chicago style. They are involved in more than 500 student organizations, including numerous groups for community service, academic interests, publications, cultural awareness, music, and theater. Some popular activities are University Theater, Model UN, Quiz Bowl, DOC Films, Jazz X-Tet, and the *Chicago Maroon* newspaper. A member of the Division III University Athletic Association, Chicago is a great place to play athletics, with nineteen varsity sports for men and women and more than 70 percent of the student body participating in intramural sports. In 2003, the Gerald Ratner Athletics Center opened, providing new athletic facilities to the entire Chicago community.

Location

Located approximately 7 miles from the center of the city, the University of Chicago's dramatic Gothic buildings frame tree-shaded quadrangles and occupy a 204-acre campus. Recently, the campus was designated a botanic garden, and, with such architectural landmarks as Rockefeller Chapel and Frank Lloyd Wright's Robie House, it is listed on the National Register of Historic Places. The University's neighborhood, Hyde Park, is a residential community of 43,000 situated on the banks of Lake Michigan. Home to more than 60 percent of the faculty who walk or bike to campus, the neighborhood is often cited as a model of cosmopolitan and multiethnic city living. Other Chicago neighborhoods are accessible by commuter trains, University-operated express buses, and elevated trains. As the largest city in the Midwest and the third-largest in the nation, Chicago offers abundant cultural and entertainment opportunities, including the Lyric Opera, the Chicago Symphony Orchestra, the Art Institute of Chicago, Sox Park and Wrigley Field, the Field Museum of Natural History, Steppenwolf Theatre, and the city's myriad ethnic neighborhoods.

Majors and Degrees

The College of the University of Chicago grants Bachelor of Arts and Bachelor of Science degrees in more than fifty majors in the biological, physical, and social sciences, as well as in the humanities and interdisciplinary areas. A major may provide a comprehensive understanding of a well-defined field, such as anthropology or mathematics, or it may be an interdisciplinary program such as African and African American studies, environmental studies, biological chemistry, or cinema and media studies. Joint B.A./M.A. and B.S./M.S. programs are offered in a number of disciplines.

Degrees are awarded in the following majors: African and African American studies; ancient studies; anthropology; art history; astronomy and astrophysics; biological chemistry; biological sciences; chemistry; cinema and media studies; classical studies; comparative literature; computer science; early Christian literature; East Asian languages and civilizations; economics; English language and literature; environmental studies; fundamentals: issues and texts; gender studies; general studies in the humanities; geography; geophysical sciences; Germanic studies; history; history, philosophy, and social studies of science and medicine (HiPSS); human development; international studies; Jewish studies; Latin American studies; law, letters, and society; linguistics; mathematics; medieval studies; music; Near Eastern languages and civilizations; philosophy; physics; political science; psychology; public policy studies; religion and the humanities; religious studies; Romance languages and literatures; Russian civilization; Slavic languages and literatures; sociology; South Asian languages and civilizations; South Asian studies; statistics; tutorial studies; and visual arts.

Academic Programs

Chicago's undergraduate curriculum is designed to give students the opportunity to fully participate in the intellectual life of a world-renowned research university. The curriculum became famous in American higher education during the 1930s when it challenged the prevailing model of elective-based programs by introducing a coherent core of general education courses. These courses made it possible, then and now, for college students to share certain kinds of crucial intellectual experiences, to create a community of young scholars who can talk across disciplines, and to form habits of mind necessary for advanced study, successful careers, and a productive life.

One third of the courses taken for graduation are modern descendants of that first revolutionary general education core. They include courses in social and natural sciences, humanities, mathematics, Western or non-Western civilization, and art or music. These small, faculty-taught courses, taken in the first two years, lead naturally to the next stages of the curriculum, which is equally divided between courses in the concentration and elective courses. The total program may also include research projects, honors projects, foreign travel and study, and internships. The eventual shape of the individual Chicago experience is determined by the student, in consultations with an academic adviser, departmental adviser, and faculty mentors.

Off-Campus Programs

Students in the College of the University of Chicago are encouraged to study abroad and can take part in programs in many countries. Programs range in length from a summer or a single academic quarter to a full academic year and include course work and other experiences that can be tailored to fit degree programs in any discipline, whether humanities, social sciences, or natural sciences. Most important, all programs provide the opportunity to live among people whose ways of living and thinking challenge students to look at their own lives with a fresh perspective.

These programs are sponsored by the University of Chicago, either alone or in cooperation with other universities and with two groups to which the University belongs: the Associated Colleges of the Midwest (ACM) and the Committee on Institutional Cooperation (CIC). For most programs, participants receive full credit for courses and are eligible for University of Chicago financial aid.

Academic Facilities

One of the strengths of the University of Chicago is that the campus maintains excellent academic facilities that serve the community as a whole. The University library system holds more than 6 million volumes and 7 million manuscripts and archival materials. The Joseph Regenstein Library for humanities and social sciences is one of the nation's largest academic libraries, and John Crerar Library is recognized as one of the best libraries in the country for research and teaching in the sciences, medicine, and technology. Joining Crerar Library to form a science quadrangle is the Kersten Physics Teaching Center, the most advanced facility in the U.S. for the teaching of undergraduate physics. Students in the college have access to all the University's special libraries, including the D'Angelo Law Library, Yerkes Observatory Library for astronomy and astrophysics (home of the world's largest refracting telescope), the Social Service Administration Library, and the Eckhart Library for mathematics and computer science.

Other facilities providing Chicago students with research and internship opportunities are the recently renovated Oriental Institute Museum, a showcase of the history, art, and archaeology of the ancient Near East; the Smart Museum, which houses a collection of more than 7,000 works of art, spanning five centuries of both Western and Eastern civilizations; the Enrico Fermi Institute, which has played a central role in nuclear physics and nuclear chemistry research, elementary particle physics, and astrophysics; Midway Studios, where art students enjoy studio space; and the University of Chicago Medical Center, which includes five major hospitals and 125 specialty outpatient clinics that work to advance biomedical innovation, serve the health needs of the community, and further the knowledge of medical students, physicians, and others dedicated to medicine.

Costs

Tuition for the 2007–08 school year was $35,169, and room and board charges were $11,139. Fees for other services, including books, health insurance, orientation, and activities, totaled $4492.

Financial Aid

Chicago is committed to helping students from all economic backgrounds attend the University and makes admissions decisions on a need-blind basis. Furthermore, the University meets 100 percent of students' demonstrated financial need. More than 65 percent of Chicago students receive some form of financial assistance. Students wishing to apply for financial aid should submit the University of Chicago financial aid application along with the Free Application for Federal Student Aid and the Financial Aid PROFILE of the College Scholarship Service. Merit scholarships also are available.

Faculty

The instructional faculty of the University of Chicago is composed of distinguished scholars and teachers. Faculty members typically teach both undergraduate and graduate courses, and senior professors often teach undergraduate general education courses. Because classes are small and discussion is the preferred mode of instruction, faculty members often become mentors and partners in inquiry with students.

Student Government

Student Government is composed of students in the college and other graduate and professional schools. Student government assists student organizations, sponsors events, and deals with the academic, social, and economic issues of University life. The Student Assembly, the legislative branch, is the only organization on campus that represents all students. Members of the Assembly are elected in the autumn quarter. Student Government also supports a number of committees that focus on issues ranging from student affairs to community relations to student services. The Inter-House Council serves as an advisory body for the House System and allocates money for Inter-House activities.

Admission Requirements

The Office of College Admissions does not have a rigid formula for the successful applicant and considers a candidate's entire application: academic and extracurricular records, essays, letters of recommendation, and SAT or ACT scores. A personal interview is optional and can provide prospective students with a chance to learn more about the college. The essay is an opportunity to show individuality, in addition to clear and effective writing ability.

Though no specific secondary school courses are prescribed, a standard college-preparatory program is recommended: 4 years of English, 3 to 4 years of math and laboratory sciences, 3 or more years of social sciences, and a foreign language. The University of Chicago does not use numerical cut-offs when evaluating applications for admission. Of the 1,284 students in the class of 2011, 80 percent graduated in the top 10 percent of their high school classes. The middle 50 percent of admitted students scored between 1330 and 1540 on the SAT or between 28 and 33 on the ACT.

Application and Information

The University of Chicago offers students two application plans. Early action is for candidates who seek an admission decision in mid-December and a provisional financial aid assessment by early January. Candidates must complete their applications by November 1 and may apply to other schools if they wish. Chicago's early action program is nonbinding; admitted students need not reply to the Office of Admissions until May 1. Regular notification is for candidates who prefer an admission and financial aid decision by early April. Candidates must complete their application by January 1 and must reply to the offer by May 1. Students who have completed one or two years of course work at another college are welcome to apply for transfer admission.

For further information students should contact:

Office of College Admissions
University of Chicago
1101 East 58th Street
Chicago, Illinois 60637
Phone: 773-702-8650
Fax: 773-702-4199
Internet: http://collegeadmissions.uchicago.edu

WHEATON COLLEGE

WHEATON, ILLINOIS

The College

Wheaton College's nearly 150-year history demonstrates the benefits of stable leadership in private Christian higher education—it has had only 7 presidents since it was founded in 1860. Interdenominational and international in constituency, the student body of approximately 2,400 undergraduates (including 200 students in the Conservatory of Music) and approximately 500 graduate students represents all fifty states, some forty countries, and more than thirty Christian denominations. Seventy-nine percent of the undergraduate students come from outside Illinois.

In addition to its undergraduate programs, Wheaton offers master's and doctoral degrees in clinical psychology (M.A., Psy.D.), biblical and theological studies (M.A., Ph.D.), Christian formation and ministry (M.A.), evangelism (M.A.), intercultural studies (M.A.), TESOL (M.A.), and education (M.A.T.).

The student activity calendar includes concerts of all kinds: Chicago outings, on-campus dances, films, theater productions, athletic contests, and banquets. The Office of Christian Outreach provides opportunities for student ministry through student-run missions trips and ministries in urban and suburban Chicago. The Men's Glee Club, Women's Chorale, Concert Choir, Symphonic Band, Symphony Orchestra, Jazz Ensemble, and Gospel Choir, open by audition to all Wheaton students, give concerts throughout the Chicago area and tour other sections of the United States and abroad. Radio broadcasting experience is provided by WETN, the campus FM radio station.

Wheaton is a member of NCAA Division III. Intercollegiate sports include baseball, basketball, cross-country, football, golf, soccer, softball, swimming, tennis, track, volleyball, wrestling, and women's water polo. In addition, the College has a well-developed club sports program, including crew, cheerleading, ice hockey, lacrosse, tae kwon do, and men's volleyball, as well as fifteen intramural sports. The Sports and Recreation Complex, which opened in 2000, comprises the Eckert Recreation Center, a renovated King Arena, and the Chrouser Fitness Center. In addition to housing academic offices and classrooms, the complex's amenities include multiple basketball courts, an 8,000-square-foot weight and fitness area, an elevated running track, an indoor climbing wall, and a glassed-in upper walkway above the fitness center's 35-meter pool.

Through efforts of the student body, the College publishes *The Record*, a weekly newspaper; *Kodon*, the College literary magazine; and *The Tower* yearbook. An additional forty clubs and organizations round out the cocurricular offerings.

Location

Wheaton's 80-acre campus is located in a residential suburb (population 50,000) 25 miles west of Chicago. The educational and cultural features of the Chicago metropolitan area are easily accessible by train and regularly visited by students. The Wheaton area is the home of more than forty Christian organizations.

Majors and Degrees

Wheaton grants the Bachelor of Arts and Bachelor of Science degrees and, through the Wheaton Conservatory of Music, the Bachelor of Music and Bachelor of Music Education degrees.

The following majors are available in the arts and sciences: ancient languages, anthropology, applied health science, archaeology, art, biblical and theological studies, biology, business/economics, chemistry, Christian education and ministry, communication, computer science, economics, education, English, environmental science, geology, history, interdisciplinary studies, international relations, mathematics, modern languages (French, German, and Spanish), music, philosophy, physics, political science, psychology, and sociology. Also, 3-2 programs are available in engineering and nursing, as is a five-year cooperative engineering program with Illinois Institute of Technology.

The Wheaton Conservatory of Music offers a full range of professional music majors, including composition, education, history/literature, performance, music with elective studies in an outside field, and music with an emphasis in a music-related field (such as media/film music, pedagogy, conducting, and collaborative piano). Students seeking these professional music degrees are accepted directly into the program by audition.

An on-campus program in military science leads to a commission in the U.S. Army at graduation. In addition to the majors offered, Wheaton has programs leading to teacher certification and to athletic training certification as well as programs preparing students for careers in business, health professions, law, and ministry.

Academic Programs

Wheaton is a distinctively Christian college where faculty members and students work together, both inside and outside the classroom, to apply Christian principles and values to the needs and problems of the individual and society. The vigorous search for knowledge and wisdom in any area of human activity is based on the belief that all truth is God's truth. The academic curriculum combines with the extensive cocurriculum of artistic, athletic, religious, service, and social activities to achieve a lively interaction of Christian faith, learning, and living. Because of the College's strong commitment to developing effective servant/leaders for the church and society worldwide, there is a particularly strong integration of faith and learning in all degree programs.

To meet the requirements of all baccalaureate degrees, students must complete a minimum of 124 semester hours, 36 of which must be in the upper division, and have at least a C (2.0) average overall.

The major field is selected during the second semester of general education courses taken to meet competency and area requirements. Students must demonstrate competence (either by examination or by taking prescribed courses) in foreign language, mathematics, speech, and writing. All students must complete area requirements in applied health science, art, biblical studies, history, literature, music, natural science, philosophy, and social science. A student may be granted advanced placement or college credit on the basis of examination (SAT Subject Tests or AP). The number of credits granted and the level of placement are determined by the registrar and the chair of the department in which the course is taught.

The College operates on a semester academic calendar, beginning in late August and ending in early May. An eight-week summer term is also offered.

Wheaton offers ten natural science majors—applied health science, biology, chemistry, computer science, environmental studies, geology, liberal arts engineering, liberal arts nursing, mathematics, and physics—in six academic departments. The Wheaton faculty members engage the study of science authoritatively, enthusiastically, and creatively in the classrooms and laboratories and beyond the campus. They are creative and offer more than two dozen general education courses in the natural sciences as well as the majors listed above. The programming includes the use of state-of-the-art technologies and techniques on the main Wheaton campus, cutting edge geological and biological studies in a large science station in the scientifically rich area of the Black Hills of South Dakota, and marine biology studies in Belize.

Off-Campus Programs

Wheaton College offers a variety of off-campus opportunities to enhance students' programs of study. The Wheaton Passage program is a wilderness education experience available to new students at the College's Honey Rock Camp in northern Wisconsin. The Human Needs and Global Resources (HNGR) Program focuses on responses to human needs from a multidisciplinary perspective. It offers a concentration of courses leading to a six-month internship overseas, followed by a seminar on campus. By participating in this program, students can earn up to 24 hours of credit. A similar program in urban studies, Wheaton in Chicago, focuses on urban issues in U.S. cities.

Other special summer programs for credit include field study at the Wheaton College Science Station in the Black Hills of South Dakota; working with youth at Honey Rock Camp; interdisciplinary study in East Asia; the study of English literature in England; language study in France, Germany, and Spain; the Wheaton in the Holy Lands program, involving biblical and archaeological studies; the Arts in London program, which includes course work in music, theater, and art; and an international study program based in England and the Netherlands, offering courses in economics, political science, and psychology.

Wheaton is a member of the Council of Christian Colleges and Universities, based in Washington, D.C. The council's activities increase students' learning opportunities by bringing special programs to campus and by providing off-campus study. Off-campus programs include American Studies in Washington, D.C.; the Washington Journalism Center in Washington, D.C.; the Los Angeles Film Studies Center; the Contemporary Music Center in Martha's Vineyard; Latin American Studies in Costa Rica; Middle East Studies in Cairo; the Australia Studies Center; China Studies Program; the Scholar's Semester in Oxford; Russia Studies Program; and Uganda Studies Program. Wheaton has also recently affiliated with the International Sustainable Development Studies Institute in Thailand. In addition, Wheaton's membership in the Christian College Consortium allows students a semester of study at one of the other twelve consortium colleges.

Cooperative programs in social science are available at American and Drew universities, and students may participate in a European seminar conducted by Gordon College.

Academic Facilities

Recent additions to campus facilities include the Sports and Recreation Complex (2000); the Wade Center (2001), which houses the books and papers of seven British authors, including C. S. Lewis and J. R. R. Tolkien; the Beamer Student Center (2004); and a jumbotron at McCully stadium (2007). In 2008, Wheaton's Memorial Student Center will reopen after an extensive renovation to house the J. Dennis Hastert Center for Economics, Government, and Public Policy, with classroom, research, and public discussion space geared toward the study of economics, politics, and values in business, government, and ministry.

Wheaton's current capital campaign aims to, among other things, strengthen the sciences, stimulate the arts, and enliven the library. For the sciences, a new $80-million science and mathematics facility with expanded teaching labs and research equipment is planned to open in 2011. For the arts, an $11-million renovation of Adams Hall will add art gallery and studio space, and a $9-million renovation of Edman Chapel will further enhance this venue that is often home to concerts from world-class musicians. In addition, the library will be renovated to adequately house its expansive collections.

Costs

Tuition for the 2007–08 year was $23,730; room and board for the year were $7252.

Financial Aid

Most Wheaton College financial aid is allocated on the basis of need as demonstrated by information supplied on the Free Application for Federal Student Aid (FAFSA) and the CSS Profile. Students from Alaska, Illinois, Pennsylvania, Rhode Island, and Vermont are expected to apply for state grants or scholarships along with their application for Wheaton College aid.

Substantial student aid is available in the form of grants, loans, and work-study opportunities provided by government and College resources. The average need-based aid package for freshmen is about $16,297. The Career Development Center provides free service to help students secure part-time jobs and to help prepare for future employment.

Faculty

The 193 Wheaton faculty members, of whom nearly 93 percent hold earned doctorates, come from a variety of colleges and universities in the United States and abroad. As active Christians, they are interested in the spiritual and intellectual development of their students. The faculty members' primary commitment as educators and advisers is enriched by their considerable research, publishing, and artistic performance activities. All undergraduate courses are taught by faculty members.

To ensure a rich range of perspectives and expertise, every department at Wheaton has at least 3 full-time professors, and most have 5 to 10. The student-faculty ratio is 12:1.

Student Government

Student Government ensures a student voice in institutional affairs and provides a wide range of opportunities to develop leadership abilities. Student Leadership Workshops, the apportionment of student fees, and the official representation of the student body are some of the activities under the direction of the Student Government. The College Union, an all-student organization, plans and directs cultural, social, and recreational activities.

Admission Requirements

Wheaton is a selective college that seeks to enroll students who evidence a vital Christian experience, high moral character, personal integrity, social concern, strong academic ability and motivation, and the desire to pursue Christian higher education as defined in the aims and objectives of the College. These qualities are evaluated by consideration of each applicant's academic record, autobiographical essays, test scores, recommendations, optional interview, and participation in extracurricular activities. For students applying to the Conservatory of Music, strong consideration is given to the evaluation of the required audition.

Applicants must have a high school diploma or the equivalent and, at the time of graduation, should have completed a college-preparatory curriculum with a minimum of 18 acceptable units. Of the 18 units, 15 must be in English, foreign language, mathematics, science, and social studies. No units are granted for health, band, choir, driver's education, or physical education, but a maximum of 3 units for vocational subjects is allowed.

Satisfactory scores on the SAT or on the ACT examination are required of all applicants to the freshman class. The middle 50 percent range of scores for those admitted is 27–31 (ACT) and 1240–1420 (SAT composite math and verbal scores).

Application and Information

An application packet, complete with detailed instructions and requirements, can be obtained from the Admissions Office or online. For early action (nonbinding), students seeking admission in the fall term should apply to either the College of Arts and Sciences or the Conservatory of Music by November 1. The regular action deadline is January 10; the transfer application deadline is March 1.

Further information is available from:

Admissions Office
Wheaton College
Wheaton, Illinois 60187
Phone: 630-752-5005
800-222-2419 (toll-free)
E-mail: admissions@wheaton.edu
Web site: http://www.wheaton.edu

INDIANA

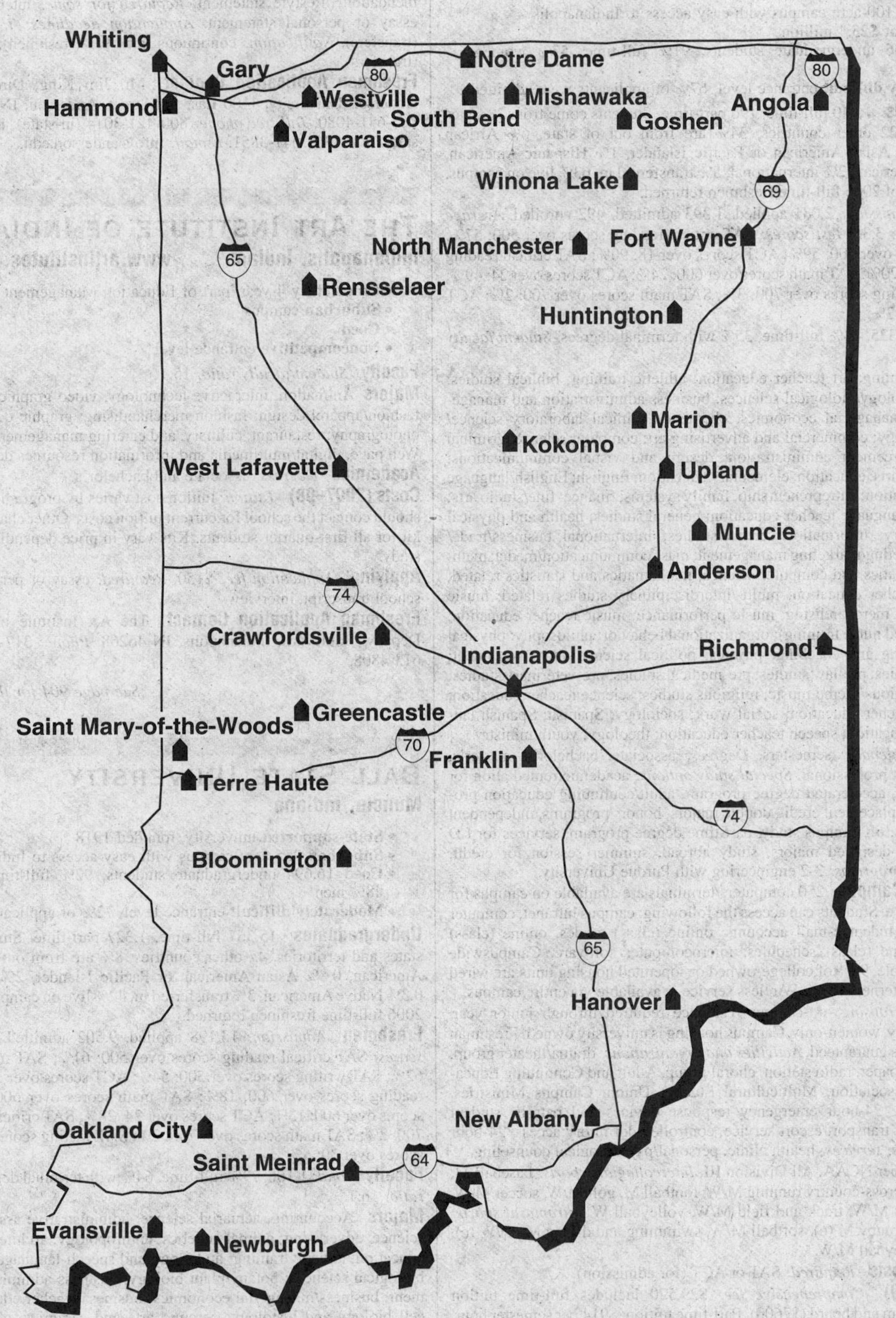

Whiting
Gary
Hammond
80
Westville
Valparaiso
Notre Dame
Mishawaka
South Bend
Goshen
Angola
80
Winona Lake
69
North Manchester
Fort Wayne
65
Rensselaer
Huntington
Marion
Kokomo
Upland
West Lafayette
Muncie
Anderson
74
Crawfordsville
Indianapolis
Richmond
Greencastle
Saint Mary-of-the-Woods
70
Franklin
Terre Haute
74
Bloomington
65
Hanover
New Albany
Oakland City
Saint Meinrad
64
Evansville
Newburgh

ANDERSON UNIVERSITY

Anderson, Indiana **www.anderson.edu/**

- **Independent** comprehensive, founded 1917, affiliated with Church of God
- **Suburban** 100-acre campus with easy access to Indianapolis
- **Endowment** $25.4 million
- **Coed** 2,136 undergraduate students, 91% full-time, 57% women, 43% men
- **Moderately difficult** entrance level, 67% of applicants were admitted

Undergraduates 1,940 full-time, 196 part-time. Students come from 38 states and territories, 22 other countries, 34% are from out of state, 6% African American, 0.6% Asian American or Pacific Islander, 1% Hispanic American, 0.4% Native American, 2% international, 5% transferred in, 63% live on campus. *Retention:* 73% of 2006 full-time freshmen returned.

Freshmen *Admission:* 2,081 applied, 1,393 admitted, 492 enrolled. *Average high school GPA:* 3.36. *Test scores:* SAT critical reading scores over 500: 57%; SAT math scores over 500: 59%; ACT scores over 18: 90%; SAT critical reading scores over 600: 20%; SAT math scores over 600: 24%; ACT scores over 24: 49%; SAT critical reading scores over 700: 3%; SAT math scores over 700: 2%; ACT scores over 30: 12%.

Faculty *Total:* 325, 44% full-time, 35% with terminal degrees. *Student/faculty ratio:* 14:1.

Majors Accounting; art teacher education; athletic training; biblical studies; biochemistry; biology/biological sciences; business administration and management; business/managerial economics; chemistry; clinical laboratory science/medical technology; commercial and advertising art; computer science; criminal justice/law enforcement administration; design and visual communications; dramatic/theater arts; education; elementary education; English; English/language arts teacher education; entrepreneurship; family systems; finance; fine/studio arts; French; French language teacher education; general studies; health and physical education; history; information science/studies; international business/trade/commerce; marketing/marketing management; mass communication/media; mathematics; mathematics and computer science; mathematics and statistics related; mathematics teacher education; multi-/interdisciplinary studies related; music management and merchandising; music performance; music teacher education; nursing (registered nurse training); organizational behavior; philosophy; physical education teaching and coaching; physics; political science and government; pre-dentistry studies; pre-law studies; pre-medical studies; pre-veterinary studies; psychology; religious/sacred music; religious studies; science teacher education; social studies teacher education; social work; sociology; Spanish; Spanish language teacher education; speech teacher education; theology; youth ministry.

Academics *Calendar:* semesters. *Degrees:* associate, bachelor's, master's, doctoral, and first professional. *Special study options:* academic remediation for entering students, accelerated degree program, adult/continuing education programs, advanced placement credit, double majors, honors programs, independent study, internships, off-campus study, part-time degree program, services for LD students, student-designed majors, study abroad, summer session for credit. *Unusual degree programs:* 3-2 engineering with Purdue University.

Computers on Campus 250 computers/terminals are available on campus for general student use. Students can access the following: campus intranet, computer help desk, free student e-mail accounts, online (class) grades, online (class) registration, online (class) schedules, microcomputer software. Campuswide network is available. 98% of college-owned or -operated housing units are wired for high-speed Internet access. Wireless service is available via entire campus.

Student Life *Housing:* on-campus residence required through junior year. *Options:* men-only, women-only. Campus housing is university owned. Freshman campus housing is guaranteed. *Activities and organizations:* drama/theater group, student-run newspaper, radio station, choral group, Adult and Continuing Education Students Association, Multicultural Student Union, Campus Ministries. *Campus security:* 24-hour emergency response devices and patrols, student patrols, late-night transport/escort service, controlled dormitory access, 24-hour crime line. *Student services:* health clinic, personal/psychological counseling.

Athletics Member NCAA. All Division III. *Intercollegiate sports:* baseball M, basketball M/W, cross-country running M/W, football M, golf M/W, soccer M/W, softball W, tennis M/W, track and field M/W, volleyball W. *Intramural sports:* basketball M/W, rugby M (c), softball M/W, swimming and diving M (c)/W (c), tennis M/W, volleyball M/W.

Standardized Tests *Required:* SAT or ACT (for admission).

Costs (2008–09) *Comprehensive fee:* $29,520 includes full-time tuition ($21,920) and room and board ($7600). Part-time tuition: $914 per semester hour. *College room only:* $4860.

Financial Aid Of all full-time matriculated undergraduates who enrolled in 2006, 1,642 applied for aid, 1,472 were judged to have need, 662 had their need fully met. 1,480 Federal Work-Study jobs (averaging $2160). In 2006, 429 non-need-based awards were made. *Average percent of need met:* 76%. *Average financial aid package:* $16,181. *Average need-based loan:* $4586. *Average need-based gift aid:* $11,960. *Average non-need-based aid:* $8792. *Average indebtedness upon graduation:* $25,777.

Applying *Options:* electronic application, deferred entrance. *Application fee:* $25. *Required:* high school transcript, minimum 2.0 GPA, 2 letters of recommendation, lifestyle statement. *Required for some:* interview. *Recommended:* essay or personal statement. *Application deadlines:* 7/1 (freshmen), rolling (transfers). *Notification:* continuous until 9/1 (freshmen), continuous until 9/1 (transfers).

Freshman Application Contact Mr. Jim King, Director of Admissions, Anderson University, 1100 East 5th Street, Anderson, IN 46012-3495. *Phone:* 765-641-4080. *Toll-free phone:* 800-421-3014 (in-state); 800-428-6414 (out-of-state). *Fax:* 765-641-3851. *E-mail:* info@anderson.edu.

THE ART INSTITUTE OF INDIANAPOLIS

Indianapolis, Indiana **www.artinstitutes.edu/indianapolis/**

- **Proprietary** 4-year, part of Education Management Corporation
- **Suburban** campus
- **Coed**
- **Noncompetitive** entrance level

Faculty *Student/faculty ratio:* 15:1.

Majors Animation, interactive technology, video graphics and special effects; fashion/apparel design; fashion merchandising; graphic design; interior design; photography; restaurant, culinary, and catering management, retail management; Web page, digital/multimedia and information resources design.

Academics *Degrees:* associate and bachelor's.

Costs (2007–08) *Tuition:* tuition cost varies by program. Prospective students should contact the school for current tuition costs. Other charges include a starting kit for all first-quarter students. Kits vary in price depending on the program of study.

Applying *Application fee:* $150. *Required:* essay or personal statement, high school transcript, interview.

Freshman Application Contact The Art Institute of Indianapolis, 3500 Depauw Boulevard, Indianapolis, IN 46268. *Phone:* 317-613-4800. *Fax:* 317-613-4808.

See page 904 for the College Close-Up.

BALL STATE UNIVERSITY

Muncie, Indiana **www.bsu.edu/**

- **State-supported** university, founded 1918
- **Suburban** 955-acre campus with easy access to Indianapolis
- **Coed** 16,694 undergraduate students, 92% full-time, 52% women, 48% men
- **Moderately difficult** entrance level, 72% of applicants were admitted

Undergraduates 15,367 full-time, 1,327 part-time. Students come from 49 states and territories, 47 other countries, 8% are from out of state, 7% African American, 0.8% Asian American or Pacific Islander, 2% Hispanic American, 0.3% Native American, 3% transferred in, 42% live on campus. *Retention:* 77% of 2006 full-time freshmen returned.

Freshmen *Admission:* 13,198 applied, 9,502 admitted, 3,773 enrolled. *Test scores:* SAT critical reading scores over 500: 61%; SAT math scores over 500: 62%; SAT writing scores over 500: 54%; ACT scores over 18: 96%; SAT critical reading scores over 600: 18%; SAT math scores over 600: 18%; SAT writing scores over 600: 13%; ACT scores over 24: 28%; SAT critical reading scores over 700: 2%; SAT math scores over 700: 2%; SAT writing scores over 700: 1%; ACT scores over 30: 5%.

Faculty *Total:* 1,166, 79% full-time, 64% with terminal degrees. *Student/faculty ratio:* 16:1.

Majors Accounting; actuarial science; administrative assistant and secretarial science; advertising; animal genetics; anthropology; architecture; art; art teacher education; athletic training; audiology and speech-language pathology; biology/biological sciences; botany/plant biology; business administration and management; business/managerial economics; business teacher education; cartography; cell biology and histology; ceramic arts and ceramics; chemical engineering; chemistry; city/urban, community and regional planning; classics and languages, literatures and linguistics; clinical laboratory science/medical technology; commercial and advertising art; computer science; criminal justice/law enforcement administration; criminology; dance; dietetics; dramatic/theater arts; drawing;

ecology; economics; education; educational/instructional media design; elementary education; emergency medical technology (EMT paramedic); English; environmental design/architecture; environmental studies; family and consumer economics related; family and consumer sciences/home economics teacher education; family and consumer sciences/human sciences; fashion merchandising; finance; fine/studio arts; French; geography; geology/earth science; German; graphic and printing equipment operation/production; health science; health teacher education; history; human resources management; industrial arts; industrial radiologic technology; industrial technology; information science/studies; insurance; Japanese; journalism; kindergarten/preschool education; kinesiology and exercise science; landscape architecture; Latin; Latin American studies; legal administrative assistant/secretary; legal assistant/paralegal; liberal arts and sciences/liberal studies; management information systems; marine biology and biological oceanography; marketing/marketing management; mathematics; medical microbiology and bacteriology; modern Greek; modern languages; molecular biology; music; musical instrument fabrication and repair; music teacher education; natural resources management and policy; nuclear medical technology; nursing (registered nurse training); occupational safety and health technology; parks, recreation and leisure facilities management; philosophy; photography; physical education teaching and coaching; physics; piano and organ; plastics engineering technology; political science and government; polymer/plastics engineering; pre-dentistry studies; pre-law studies; pre-medical studies; printmaking; psychology; public relations/image management; real estate; religious studies; respiratory care therapy; science teacher education; sculpture; secondary education; social sciences; social work; sociology; soil conservation; Spanish; special education; special products marketing; speech and rhetoric; sport and fitness administration/management; telecommunications; tourism and travel services management; trade and industrial teacher education; violin, viola, guitar and other stringed instruments; voice and opera; wildlife biology; wind/percussion instruments; zoology/animal biology.

Academics *Calendar:* semesters. *Degrees:* associate, bachelor's, master's, doctoral, post-master's, and postbachelor's certificates. *Special study options:* academic remediation for entering students, accelerated degree program, adult/continuing education programs, advanced placement credit, cooperative education, distance learning, double majors, English as a second language, freshman honors college, honors programs, independent study, internships, part-time degree program, study abroad, summer session for credit. *ROTC:* Army (b). *Unusual degree programs:* 3-2 engineering with Purdue University, Tri-State University.

Computers on Campus 1,500 computers/terminals are available on campus for general student use. Campuswide network is available.

Student Life *Housing:* on-campus residence required for freshman year. *Options:* coed, men-only, women-only, disabled students. Campus housing is university owned and is provided by a third party. *Activities and organizations:* drama/theater group, student-run newspaper, radio and television station, choral group, marching band, Student Association, Excellence in Leadership, Black Student Association, student voluntary services, national fraternities, national sororities. *Campus security:* 24-hour emergency response devices and patrols, late-night transport/escort service, controlled dormitory access. *Student services:* health clinic, personal/psychological counseling, women's center, legal services.

Athletics Member NCAA. All Division I except football (Division I-A). *Intercollegiate sports:* baseball M (s), basketball M (s)/W (s), cross-country running M (s)/W (s), equestrian sports M (c)/W (c), field hockey W (s), golf M (s), gymnastics W (s), ice hockey M (c), rugby M (c)/W (c), sailing M (c)/W (c), soccer M (c)/W, softball W (s), swimming and diving M (s)/W (s), tennis M (s)/W (s), track and field M (s)/W (s), volleyball M (s)/W (s), water polo M (c), wrestling M (c). *Intramural sports:* archery M/W, badminton M (c)/W (c), basketball M/W, bowling M (c)/W (c), cross-country running M/W, fencing M (c)/W (c), football M, golf M, lacrosse M (c), racquetball M/W, soccer M, softball M/W, squash M/W, swimming and diving M/W, table tennis M (c)/W (c), tennis M/W, track and field M/W, volleyball M/W, weight lifting M (c)/W (c).

Standardized Tests *Required for some:* SAT or ACT (for admission).

Costs (2007–08) *Tuition:* state resident $6672 full-time, $208 per credit hour part-time; nonresident $17,740 full-time, $650 per credit hour part-time. Part-time tuition and fees vary according to course load. *Required fees:* $476 full-time. *Room and board:* $7240. Room and board charges vary according to board plan and housing facility. *Payment plan:* installment. *Waivers:* employees or children of employees.

Financial Aid Of all full-time matriculated undergraduates who enrolled in 2007, 11,867 applied for aid, 9,015 were judged to have need, 2,702 had their need fully met. In 2007, 1305 non-need-based awards were made. *Average percent of need met:* 69%. *Average financial aid package:* $9137. *Average need-based loan:* $4163. *Average need-based gift aid:* $5552. *Average non-need-based aid:* $6930. *Average indebtedness upon graduation:* $19,827.

Applying *Options:* deferred entrance. *Application fee:* $25. *Required:* high school transcript. *Required for some:* essay or personal statement, letters of recommendation, interview. *Application deadlines:* 8/15 (freshmen), rolling (transfers). *Notification:* continuous (freshmen), continuous (transfers).

Freshman Application Contact Ball State University, 2000 University Avenue, Muncie, IN 47306. *Phone:* 765-285-8300. *Toll-free phone:* 800-482-4BSU.

BETHEL COLLEGE

Mishawaka, Indiana **www.bethelcollege.edu**

Freshman Application Contact Randy Beachy, Assistant Vice President for Enrollment/Marketing, Bethel College, 1001 West McKinley Avenue, Mishawaka, IN 46545-5591. *Phone:* 574-257-3339. *Toll-free phone:* 800-422-4101. *Fax:* 574-257-3335. *E-mail:* admissions@bethelcollege.edu.

BROWN MACKIE COLLEGE–FORT WAYNE

Fort Wayne, Indiana **www.brownmackie.edu/FortWayne**

- **Proprietary** 4-year
- **Coed**
- **Noncompetitive** entrance level

Faculty *Student/faculty ratio:* 16:1.

Majors Business administration and management; criminal justice/law enforcement administration; legal studies.

Academics *Calendar:* quarters. *Degrees:* certificates, diplomas, and associate.

Applying *Required:* high school transcript, interview, verify high school graduate or equivalent.

Freshman Application Contact Director of Admissions, 3000 East Coliseum Boulevard, Fort Wayne, IN 46805. *Phone:* 260-484-4400. *Toll-free phone:* 866-433-2289. *Fax:* 260-484-2678. *E-mail:* ktaboh@brownmackie.edu.

See page 906 for the College Close-Up.

BROWN MACKIE COLLEGE–INDIANAPOLIS

Indianapolis, Indiana

Majors Business administration and management; criminal justice/law enforcement administration; legal studies.

Freshman Application Contact Director of Admissions, 1200 N. Meridian street, Suite 100, Indianapolis, IN 46204. *Toll-free phone:* 866-255-0279. *Fax:* 317-632-4557.

See page 908 for the College Close-Up.

BROWN MACKIE COLLEGE–MERRILLVILLE

Merrillville, Indiana

www.brownmackie.edu/locations.asp?locid=19

- **Proprietary** primarily 2-year, founded 1890, part of American Education Centers, Inc
- **Small-town** 2-acre campus with easy access to Chicago
- **Coed**
- **Noncompetitive** entrance level

Faculty *Student/faculty ratio:* 17:1.

Majors Business administration and management; criminal justice/law enforcement administration; legal studies.

Academics *Calendar:* quarters. *Degrees:* certificates, associate, and bachelor's.

Student Life *Campus security:* 24-hour emergency response devices.

Financial Aid Of all full-time matriculated undergraduates who enrolled in 2006, 2 Federal Work-Study jobs.

Applying *Options:* early admission, deferred entrance. *Required:* high school transcript, interview.

Freshman Application Contact Director of Admissions, Brown Mackie College–Merrillville, 1000 East 80th Place, Suite 101N, Merrillville, IN 46410. *Phone:* 800-258-3321. *Fax:* 219-738-1076.

See page 910 for the College Close-Up.

Brown Mackie College–Michigan City

Michigan City, Indiana

www.brownmackie.edu/locations.asp?locid=20

Majors Business administration and management; criminal justice/law enforcement administration; legal studies.

Director of Admissions Director of Admissions, Brown Mackie College–Michigan City, 325 East US Highway 20, Michigan City, IN 46360. *Phone:* 219-877-3100. *Toll-free phone:* 800-519-2416. *Fax:* 219-877-3110.

See page 912 for the College Close-Up.

Brown Mackie College–South Bend

South Bend, Indiana

www.brownmackie.edu/locations.asp?locid=2

- **Proprietary** primarily 2-year, founded 1882, part of American Education Centers, Inc
- **Urban** 5-acre campus with easy access to Chicago
- **Coed** primarily women
- **Minimally difficult** entrance level

Faculty *Student/faculty ratio:* 12:1.

Majors Business administration and management; criminal justice/law enforcement administration; legal studies.

Academics *Calendar:* quarters. *Degrees:* certificates, associate, and bachelor's.

Student Life *Campus security:* 24-hour emergency response devices.

Applying *Options:* deferred entrance. *Required:* essay or personal statement, high school transcript, interview. *Required for some:* minimum 2.0 GPA, 2 letters of recommendation.

Freshman Application Contact Director of Admissions, Brown Mackie College–South Bend, 1030 East Jefferson Boulevard, South Bend, IN 46617-3123. *Phone:* 574-237-0774. *Toll-free phone:* 800-743-2447. *Fax:* 574-237-3585.

See page 914 for the College Close-Up.

Butler University

Indianapolis, Indiana

www.butler.edu/

- **Independent** comprehensive, founded 1855
- **Urban** 290-acre campus
- **Endowment** $163.5 million
- **Coed** 3,617 undergraduate students, 98% full-time, 61% women, 39% men
- **Moderately difficult** entrance level, 76% of applicants were admitted

Butler offers the Engineering Dual Degree Program with the Purdue School of Engineering and Technology at Indianapolis. The program allows students to receive a Butler Bachelor of Science degree in a selected liberal arts and sciences major and a Purdue Bachelor of Science degree in computer, electrical, or mechanical engineering.

Undergraduates 3,562 full-time, 55 part-time. Students come from 47 states and territories, 51 other countries, 40% are from out of state, 3% African American, 2% Asian American or Pacific Islander, 2% Hispanic American, 0.3% Native American, 3% international, 3% transferred in, 67% live on campus. *Retention:* 86% of 2006 full-time freshmen returned.

Freshmen *Admission:* 5,265 applied, 3,987 admitted, 988 enrolled. *Average high school GPA:* 3.7. *Test scores:* SAT critical reading scores over 500: 87%; SAT math scores over 500: 90%; SAT writing scores over 500: 82%; ACT scores over 18: 100%; SAT critical reading scores over 600: 41%; SAT math scores over 600: 49%; SAT writing scores over 600: 35%; ACT scores over 24: 82%; SAT critical reading scores over 700: 7%; SAT math scores over 700: 7%; SAT writing scores over 700: 4%; ACT scores over 30: 23%.

Faculty *Total:* 465, 65% full-time, 60% with terminal degrees. *Student/faculty ratio:* 11:1.

Majors Accounting; actuarial science; anthropology; arts management; audiology and speech-language pathology; biology/biological sciences; chemistry; communication disorders; computer and information sciences; criminology; dance; dramatic/theater arts; economics; elementary education; engineering physics; English; finance; French; German; history; international business/trade/commerce; international relations and affairs; journalism; kindergarten/preschool education; Latin; liberal arts and sciences/liberal studies; management information systems; marketing/marketing management; mathematics; middle school education; modern Greek; music; music history, literature, and theory; music management and merchandising; music performance; music teacher education; music theory and composition; pharmacy; philosophy; philosophy and religious studies related; physician assistant; physics; piano and organ; political science and government; psychology; radio and television; recording arts technology; religious studies; science, technology and society; secondary education; sociology; Spanish; speech and rhetoric; urban studies/affairs; violin, viola, guitar and other stringed instruments; voice and opera; wind/percussion instruments.

Academics *Calendar:* semesters. *Degrees:* associate, bachelor's, master's, and first professional. *Special study options:* adult/continuing education programs, advanced placement credit, cooperative education, double majors, honors programs, independent study, internships, off-campus study, part-time degree program, services for LD students, student-designed majors, study abroad, summer session for credit. *ROTC:* Army (b), Air Force (c). *Unusual degree programs:* 3-2 engineering with Indiana University-Purdue University Indianapolis.

Computers on Campus 430 computers/terminals are available on campus for general student use. Students can access the following: campus intranet, computer help desk, free student e-mail accounts, online (class) grades, online (class) registration, online (class) schedules. Campuswide network is available. 100% of college-owned or -operated housing units are wired for high-speed Internet access. Wireless service is available via entire campus.

Student Life *Housing:* on-campus residence required through junior year. *Options:* coed, women-only. Campus housing is university owned. Freshman campus housing is guaranteed. *Activities and organizations:* drama/theater group, student-run newspaper, television station, choral group, marching band, University YMCA, Student Government Association, Academic Service Honoraries, Alpha Phi Omega, Mortar Board, national fraternities, national sororities. *Campus security:* 24-hour emergency response devices and patrols, late-night transport/escort service, controlled dormitory access. *Student services:* health clinic, personal/psychological counseling.

Athletics Member NCAA. All Division I except football (Division III). *Intercollegiate sports:* baseball M (s), basketball M (s)/W (s), crew M (c)/W (c), cross-country running M (s)/W (s), football M, golf M (s)/W (s), ice hockey M (c), rugby M (c), soccer M (s)/W (s), softball W (s), swimming and diving W, tennis M (s)/W (s), track and field M/W, volleyball W (s). *Intramural sports:* badminton M/W, baseball M, basketball M/W, bowling M/W, football M, soccer M/W, softball M/W, swimming and diving M/W, table tennis M/W, tennis M/W, track and field M/W, volleyball M/W, weight lifting M/W.

Standardized Tests *Required:* SAT or ACT (for admission).

Costs (2007–08) *Comprehensive fee:* $35,766 includes full-time tuition ($26,070), mandatory fees ($736), and room and board ($8960). Full-time tuition and fees vary according to program. Part-time tuition: $1090 per credit. Part-time tuition and fees vary according to program. *Room and board:* Room and board charges vary according to housing facility. *Payment plan:* installment. *Waivers:* employees or children of employees.

Financial Aid Of all full-time matriculated undergraduates who enrolled in 2007, 3,518 applied for aid, 2,461 were judged to have need, 460 had their need fully met. In 2007, 947 non-need-based awards were made. *Average financial aid package:* $18,987. *Average need-based loan:* $5019. *Average need-based gift aid:* $14,499. *Average non-need-based aid:* $10,565.

Applying *Options:* electronic application, early action, deferred entrance. *Application fee:* $35. *Required:* essay or personal statement, high school transcript. *Required for some:* interview, audition. *Application deadlines:* rolling (freshmen), 8/15 (transfers), 12/1 (early action). *Notification:* continuous (freshmen), continuous (transfers), 12/20 (early action).

Freshman Application Contact Mr. Scott McIntyre, Director of Admissions, Butler University, 4600 Sunset Avenue, Indianapolis, IN 46208-3485. *Phone:* 317-940-8100. *Toll-free phone:* 888-940-8100. *Fax:* 317-940-8150. *E-mail:* admission@butler.edu.

See page 916 for the College Close-Up.

Calumet College of Saint Joseph

Whiting, Indiana

www.ccsj.edu/

- **Independent Roman Catholic** comprehensive, founded 1951
- **Urban** 25-acre campus with easy access to Chicago
- **Endowment** $6.0 million
- **Coed** 1,060 undergraduate students, 41% full-time, 55% women, 45% men

• **Noncompetitive** entrance level, 47% of applicants were admitted

Undergraduates 437 full-time, 623 part-time. Students come from 2 states and territories, 27% African American, 0.6% Asian American or Pacific Islander, 23% Hispanic American, 0.8% Native American, 0.2% international, 20% transferred in. *Retention:* 89% of 2006 full-time freshmen returned.

Freshmen *Admission:* 291 applied, 138 admitted, 76 enrolled. *Average high school GPA:* 2.51. *Test scores:* SAT critical reading scores over 500: 17%; SAT math scores over 500: 23%; ACT scores over 18: 53%; SAT critical reading scores over 600: 6%; SAT math scores over 600: 3%; ACT scores over 24: 17%.

Faculty *Total:* 116, 25% full-time, 36% with terminal degrees. *Student/faculty ratio:* 13:1.

Majors Accounting; art teacher education; business administration and management; business teacher education; communication and media related; communication/speech communication and rhetoric; computer science; computer typography and composition equipment operation; criminal justice/law enforcement administration; elementary education; English; English/language arts teacher education; general studies; health/health care administration; human services; information science/studies; intermedia/multimedia; legal assistant/paralegal; liberal arts and sciences/liberal studies; political science and government; pre-law studies; psychology; religious studies; science teacher education; secondary education; social studies teacher education; substance abuse/addiction counseling; theology.

Academics *Calendar:* semesters. *Degrees:* certificates, associate, bachelor's, master's, and postbachelor's certificates. *Special study options:* academic remediation for entering students, accelerated degree program, adult/continuing education programs, advanced placement credit, cooperative education, double majors, external degree program, independent study, internships, part-time degree program, summer session for credit.

Computers on Campus 104 computers/terminals are available on campus for general student use. Students can access the following: computer help desk, free student e-mail accounts, online (class) registration, online (class) schedules. Campuswide network is available. Wireless service is available via student centers.

Student Life *Housing:* college housing not available. *Activities and organizations:* drama/theater group, student-run newspaper, choral group, student government, Los Amigos Hispanic Club, Criminal Justice Club, Drama Club, Black Student Union. *Campus security:* day and night security. *Student services:* personal/psychological counseling.

Athletics Member NAIA. *Intercollegiate sports:* baseball M, basketball M/W, bowling M/W, cross-country running M/W, golf M/W, soccer M/W, softball W, tennis M/W, track and field M/W, volleyball W.

Standardized Tests *Required for some:* ACT COMPASS. *Recommended:* SAT or ACT (for admission).

Costs (2007–08) *Tuition:* $11,500 full-time, $365 per credit hour part-time. *Required fees:* $150 full-time, $150 per year part-time. *Payment plan:* installment. *Waivers:* senior citizens and employees or children of employees.

Financial Aid Of all full-time matriculated undergraduates who enrolled in 2006, 537 applied for aid, 443 were judged to have need, 79 had their need fully met. 43 Federal Work-Study jobs (averaging $1635). 2 state and other part-time jobs (averaging $1848). In 2006, 56 non-need-based awards were made. *Average percent of need met:* 71%. *Average financial aid package:* $9132. *Average need-based loan:* $3664. *Average need-based gift aid:* $10,748. *Average non-need-based aid:* $4225. *Average indebtedness upon graduation:* $22,800.

Applying *Options:* electronic application, deferred entrance. *Required:* high school transcript. *Required for some:* essay or personal statement, interview. *Recommended:* minimum 2.0 GPA, interview. *Application deadlines:* rolling (freshmen), rolling (transfers). *Notification:* continuous (transfers).

Freshman Application Contact Mr. Chuck Walz, Director of Admissions, Calumet College of Saint Joseph, 2400 New York Avenue, Whiting, IN 46394. *Phone:* 219-473-4215 Ext. 379. *Toll-free phone:* 877-700-9100. *Fax:* 219-473-4259. *E-mail:* admissions@ccsj.edu.

CROSSROADS BIBLE COLLEGE

Indianapolis, Indiana **www.crossroads.edu/**

Director of Admissions Nathan McGuire, Director of Admissions, Crossroads Bible College, 601 North Shortridge Road, Indianapolis, IN 46219. *Phone:* 317-352-8736 Ext. 230. *Toll-free phone:* 800-273-2224 Ext. 230. *Fax:* 317-352-9145. *E-mail:* nmcguire@crossroads.edu.

DAVENPORT UNIVERSITY

Granger, Indiana **www.davenport.edu/**

Freshman Application Contact Admissions Office, Davenport University, 415 East Fulton Street, Grand Rapids, MI 49503. *Phone:* 616-698-7111. *Toll-free phone:* 800-632-9569. *Fax:* 616-698-0333. *E-mail:* gradmiss@davenport.edu.

DAVENPORT UNIVERSITY

Merrillville, Indiana **www.davenport.edu/**

Freshman Application Contact Admissions, Davenport University, 415 East Fulton Street, Grand Rapids, MI 49503. *Phone:* 616-698-7111. *Toll-free phone:* 800-632-9569. *Fax:* 616-698-0333. *E-mail:* gradmisss@davenport.edu.

DEPAUW UNIVERSITY

Greencastle, Indiana **www.depauw.edu/**

• **Independent** 4-year, founded 1837, affiliated with United Methodist Church
• **Small-town** 655-acre campus with easy access to Indianapolis
• **Endowment** $490.5 million
• **Coed** 2,398 undergraduate students, 98% full-time, 56% women, 44% men
• **Moderately difficult** entrance level, 69% of applicants were admitted

Undergraduates 2,362 full-time, 36 part-time. Students come from 43 states and territories, 32 other countries, 54% are from out of state, 6% African American, 3% Asian American or Pacific Islander, 3% Hispanic American, 0.3% Native American, 2% international, 0.8% transferred in, 99% live on campus. *Retention:* 87% of 2006 full-time freshmen returned.

Freshmen *Admission:* 3,624 applied, 2,505 admitted, 664 enrolled. *Average high school GPA:* 3.6. *Test scores:* SAT critical reading scores over 500: 95%; SAT math scores over 500: 93%; SAT writing scores over 500: 89%; ACT scores over 18: 99%; SAT critical reading scores over 600: 57%; SAT math scores over 600: 63%; SAT writing scores over 600: 52%; ACT scores over 24: 87%; SAT critical reading scores over 700: 11%; SAT math scores over 700: 16%; SAT writing scores over 700: 12%; ACT scores over 30: 25%.

Faculty *Total:* 288, 80% full-time, 80% with terminal degrees. *Student/faculty ratio:* 10:1.

Majors African-American/Black studies; ancient/classical Greek; anthropology; art history, criticism and conservation; Asian studies (East); athletic training; biochemistry; biology/biological sciences; chemistry; classics and languages, literatures and linguistics; computer science; dramatic/theater arts; economics; elementary education; English; English composition; environmental studies; fine/studio arts; French; geology/earth science; German; history; interdisciplinary studies; kinesiology and exercise science; Latin; mass communication/media; mathematics; multi-/interdisciplinary studies related; music; music management and merchandising; music performance; music teacher education; music theory and composition; peace studies and conflict resolution; philosophy; physical education teaching and coaching; physics; political science and government; psychology; religious studies; Romance languages; Russian studies; sociology; Spanish; women's studies.

Academics *Calendar:* 4-1-4. *Degree:* bachelor's. *Special study options:* advanced placement credit, double majors, honors programs, independent study, internships, off-campus study, part-time degree program, services for LD students, student-designed majors, study abroad. *ROTC:* Army (c), Air Force (c). *Unusual degree programs:* 3-2 engineering with Columbia University, Washington University in St. Louis.

Computers on Campus 424 computers/terminals are available on campus for general student use. Students can access the following: online (class) registration. Campuswide network is available.

Student Life *Housing:* on-campus residence required through senior year. *Options:* coed. Campus housing is university owned. Freshman campus housing is guaranteed. *Activities and organizations:* drama/theater group, student-run newspaper, radio and television station, choral group, marching band, Community Service Program, Union Board, Student Congress, Resident Students Association, Independent Council, national fraternities, national sororities. *Campus security:* 24-hour emergency response devices and patrols, student patrols, late-night transport/escort service, controlled dormitory access. *Student services:* health clinic, personal/psychological counseling, women's center.

Athletics Member NCAA. All Division III. *Intercollegiate sports:* baseball M, basketball M/W, cheerleading M (c)/W (c), crew M (c)/W (c), cross-country running M/W, field hockey W, football M, golf M/W, rugby M (c), soccer M/W, softball W, swimming and diving M/W, tennis M/W, track and field M/W, volleyball W. *Intramural sports:* badminton M/W, basketball M/W, bowling M/W, football M/W, golf M, racquetball M/W, soccer M/W, softball M/W, table tennis M/W, tennis M/W, ultimate Frisbee M/W, volleyball M/W.

Standardized Tests *Required:* SAT or ACT (for admission).

Costs (2007–08) *Comprehensive fee:* $37,800 includes full-time tuition ($29,300), mandatory fees ($400), and room and board ($8100). Part-time tuition: $916 per semester hour. *College room only:* $4250. Room and board charges vary according to board plan. *Payment plans:* tuition prepayment, installment, deferred payment. *Waivers:* employees or children of employees.

Financial Aid Of all full-time matriculated undergraduates who enrolled in 2007, 1,343 applied for aid, 1,143 were judged to have need, 456 had their need fully met. In 2007, 1090 non-need-based awards were made. *Average percent of need met:* 92%. *Average financial aid package:* $24,579. *Average need-based loan:* $3645. *Average need-based gift aid:* $21,238. *Average non-need-based aid:* $16,088. *Average indebtedness upon graduation:* $3500. *Financial aid deadline:* 2/15.

Applying *Options:* electronic application, early admission, early decision, early action, deferred entrance. *Application fee:* $40. *Required:* essay or personal statement, high school transcript, 1 letter of recommendation. *Recommended:* interview. *Application deadlines:* 2/1 (freshmen), 3/1 (transfers), 12/1 (early action). *Early decision deadline:* 11/1. *Notification:* 4/1 (freshmen), 4/1 (transfers), 1/1 (early decision), 2/15 (early action).

Freshman Application Contact Brett Kennedy, Senior Associate Director of Admission, DePauw University, 101 East Seminary Street, Greencastle, IN 46135-0037. *Phone:* 765-658-4006. *Toll-free phone:* 800-447-2495. *Fax:* 765-658-4007. *E-mail:* admission@depauw.edu.

See page 918 for the College Close-Up.

DeVry University

Indianapolis, Indiana

www.devry.edu/

- **Proprietary** comprehensive, part of DeVry University
- **Coed** 185 undergraduate students, 26% full-time, 56% women, 44% men
- **Minimally difficult** entrance level

Undergraduates 48 full-time, 137 part-time. 2% are from out of state, 39% African American, 2% Asian American or Pacific Islander, 2% Hispanic American, 0.5% Native American, 0.5% international, 17% transferred in. *Retention:* 75% of 2006 full-time freshmen returned.

Freshmen *Admission:* 27 enrolled.

Faculty *Total:* 11. *Student/faculty ratio:* 38:1.

Majors Business administration and management; business administration, management and operations related; computer systems analysis; computer systems networking and telecommunications; electrical, electronic and communications engineering technology.

Academics *Calendar:* semesters. *Degrees:* associate, bachelor's, and master's. *Special study options:* academic remediation for entering students, accelerated degree program, adult/continuing education programs, advanced placement credit, distance learning, English as a second language, part-time degree program, services for LD students, summer session for credit.

Student Life *Housing:* college housing not available.

Costs (2008–09) *Tuition:* $13,810 full-time, $515 per credit part-time. *Required fees:* $80 full-time.

Applying *Options:* electronic application, early admission, deferred entrance. *Application fee:* $50. *Required:* high school transcript, interview. *Application deadlines:* rolling (freshmen), rolling (transfers). *Notification:* continuous (freshmen), continuous (transfers).

Director of Admissions Admissions Office, DeVry University, 9100 Keystone Crossing, Suite 350, Indianapolis, IN 46240-2158.

DeVry University

Merrillville, Indiana

Earlham College

Richmond, Indiana

www.earlham.edu/

- **Independent** comprehensive, founded 1847, affiliated with Society of Friends
- **Small-town** 800-acre campus with easy access to Cincinnati, Indianapolis, and Dayton
- **Endowment** $360.4 million
- **Coed** 1,194 undergraduate students, 98% full-time, 55% women, 45% men
- **Very difficult** entrance level, 69% of applicants were admitted

Undergraduates 1,176 full-time, 18 part-time. Students come from 45 states and territories, 62 other countries, 78% are from out of state, 6% African American, 2% Asian American or Pacific Islander, 3% Hispanic American, 0.3% Native American, 11% international, 1% transferred in, 87% live on campus. *Retention:* 84% of 2006 full-time freshmen returned.

Freshmen *Admission:* 1,748 applied, 1,204 admitted, 300 enrolled. *Average high school GPA:* 3.5. *Test scores:* SAT critical reading scores over 500: 85%; SAT math scores over 500: 88%; SAT writing scores over 500: 89%; ACT scores over 18: 98%; SAT critical reading scores over 600: 58%; SAT math scores over 600: 43%; SAT writing scores over 600: 52%; ACT scores over 24: 75%; SAT critical reading scores over 700: 16%; SAT math scores over 700: 8%; SAT writing scores over 700: 14%; ACT scores over 30: 14%.

Faculty *Total:* 104, 93% full-time, 92% with terminal degrees. *Student/faculty ratio:* 12:1.

Majors African-American/Black studies; anthropology; art; biochemistry; biology/biological sciences; business administration and management; business/commerce; chemistry; classics and languages, literatures and linguistics; comparative literature; computer science; dramatic/theater arts; economics; English; environmental studies; French; geological and earth sciences/geosciences related; geology/earth science; German; history; interdisciplinary studies; international relations and affairs; Japanese studies; Latin American studies; mathematics; multi-/interdisciplinary studies related; music; peace studies and conflict resolution; philosophy; physics; physiological psychology/psychobiology; political science and government; pre-medical studies; psychology; religious studies; sociology; Spanish; women's studies.

Academics *Calendar:* semesters. *Degrees:* bachelor's, master's, and first professional. *Special study options:* accelerated degree program, advanced placement credit, double majors, independent study, internships, off-campus study, services for LD students, student-designed majors, study abroad. *Unusual degree programs:* 3-2 engineering with Columbia University, University of Michigan, Rensselaer Polytechnic Institute; forestry with Duke University; nursing with Case Western Reserve University, Washington University in St. Louis, Emory University, Columbia University; architecture with Washington University in St. Louis.

Computers on Campus 164 computers/terminals and 30 ports are available on campus for general student use. Students can access the following: campus intranet, computer help desk, free student e-mail accounts, online (class) grades, online (class) schedules. Campuswide network is available. 95% of college-owned or -operated housing units are wired for high-speed Internet access. Wireless service is available via classrooms, computer centers, computer labs, learning centers, libraries, student centers.

Student Life *Housing:* on-campus residence required through senior year. *Options:* coed, men-only, women-only, disabled students. Campus housing is university owned. Freshman campus housing is guaranteed. *Activities and organizations:* drama/theater group, student-run newspaper, radio station, choral group, Gospel Revelations Chorus, Dance Alloy, club sports, student government, Black Leadership Action Coalition. *Campus security:* 24-hour emergency response devices and patrols, student patrols, late-night transport/escort service, controlled dormitory access. *Student services:* health clinic, personal/psychological counseling, women's center.

Athletics Member NCAA. All Division III. *Intercollegiate sports:* baseball M, basketball M/W, cheerleading W (c), cross-country running M/W, equestrian sports W (c), field hockey W, football M, lacrosse M (c)/W (c), rugby W (c), soccer M/W, tennis M/W, track and field M/W, ultimate Frisbee M (c)/W (c), volleyball M (c)/W. *Intramural sports:* basketball M/W, football M, racquetball M/W, soccer M/W.

Standardized Tests *Required:* SAT or ACT (for admission).

Costs (2007–08) *Comprehensive fee:* $38,018 includes full-time tuition ($30,774), mandatory fees ($740), and room and board ($6504). Part-time tuition: $1026 per credit. *College room only:* $3260. Room and board charges vary according to board plan. *Payment plans:* tuition prepayment, installment, deferred payment. *Waivers:* employees or children of employees.

Financial Aid Of all full-time matriculated undergraduates who enrolled in 2003, 830 applied for aid, 739 were judged to have need, 160 had their need fully

met. In 2003, 182 non-need-based awards were made. *Average percent of need met:* 95%. *Average financial aid package:* $21,215. *Average need-based loan:* $4300. *Average need-based gift aid:* $12,829. *Average non-need-based aid:* $6153. *Average indebtedness upon graduation:* $15,088.

Applying *Options:* electronic application, early admission, early decision, early action, deferred entrance. *Application fee:* $30. *Required:* essay or personal statement, high school transcript, minimum 3.0 GPA, 2 letters of recommendation. *Recommended:* interview. *Application deadlines:* 2/15 (freshmen), 4/1 (transfers), 1/1 (early action). *Early decision deadline:* 12/1. *Notification:* 3/15 (freshmen), 4/15 (transfers), 12/15 (early decision), 2/1 (early action).

Freshman Application Contact Mr. Jeff Rickey, Dean of Admissions and Financial Aid, Earlham College, 801 National Road West, Richmond, IN 47374. *Phone:* 765-983-1600. *Toll-free phone:* 800-327-5426. *Fax:* 765-983-1560. *E-mail:* admission@earlham.edu.

See page 920 for the College Close-Up.

FRANKLIN COLLEGE

Franklin, Indiana www.franklincollege.edu/

- **Independent** 4-year, founded 1834, affiliated with American Baptist Churches in the U.S.A.
- **Small-town** 74-acre campus with easy access to Indianapolis
- **Endowment** $89.6 million
- **Coed** 1,130 undergraduate students, 90% full-time, 49% women, 51% men
- **Moderately difficult** entrance level, 66% of applicants were admitted

A Franklin College education combines traditional liberal arts learning with career-oriented preparation in order to create a solid foundation for lifelong leadership skills and professional success. The College's nationally recognized Leadership and Professional Development Programs are distinguishing features of the Franklin curriculum and serve as proof of their commitment to developing students' broad-based communication, professional, and problem-solving skills. Students are offered a wide variety of diverse opportunities for creative learning and benefit from the small class sizes and personalized relationships with the faculty.

Undergraduates 1,014 full-time, 116 part-time. Students come from 17 states and territories, 3 other countries, 3% are from out of state, 3% African American, 0.7% Asian American or Pacific Islander, 1% Hispanic American, 0.2% Native American, 0.4% international, 2% transferred in, 77% live on campus. *Retention:* 71% of 2006 full-time freshmen returned.

Freshmen *Admission:* 1,517 applied, 1,008 admitted, 389 enrolled. *Average high school GPA:* 3.31. *Test scores:* SAT critical reading scores over 500: 51%; SAT math scores over 500: 59%; SAT writing scores over 500: 51%; ACT scores over 18: 91%; SAT critical reading scores over 600: 16%; SAT math scores over 600: 16%; SAT writing scores over 600: 10%; ACT scores over 24: 24%; SAT critical reading scores over 700: 3%; ACT scores over 30: 2%.

Faculty *Total:* 113, 58% full-time, 58% with terminal degrees. *Student/faculty ratio:* 12:1.

Majors Accounting; American studies; athletic training; biology/biological sciences; biology teacher education; business/commerce; Canadian studies; chemistry; chemistry teacher education; computer and information sciences; computer science; dramatic/theater arts; economics; elementary education; English; English/language arts teacher education; French; French language teacher education; history; journalism; mathematics; mathematics teacher education; parks, recreation, and leisure related; philosophy; physical education teaching and coaching; political science and government; psychology; religious studies; social studies teacher education; sociology; Spanish; Spanish language teacher education.

Academics *Calendar:* 4-1-4. *Degree:* bachelor's. *Special study options:* academic remediation for entering students, advanced placement credit, cooperative education, double majors, independent study, internships, off-campus study, part-time degree program, services for LD students, study abroad, summer session for credit. *ROTC:* Army (c). *Unusual degree programs:* 3-2 engineering with Washington University in St. Louis; forestry with Duke University; nursing with Rush University; public health with University of South Florida.

Computers on Campus 150 computers/terminals are available on campus for general student use. Students can access the following: online (class) registration. Campuswide network is available.

Student Life *Housing:* on-campus residence required through junior year. *Options:* coed. Campus housing is university owned. Freshman campus housing is guaranteed. *Activities and organizations:* drama/theater group, student-run newspaper, radio and television station, choral group, FLOW, FC Volunteers, Student Entertainment Board, Student Congress, national fraternities, national sororities. *Campus security:* 24-hour emergency response devices and patrols, late-night transport/escort service. *Student services:* health clinic, personal/psychological counseling.

Athletics Member NCAA. All Division III. *Intercollegiate sports:* baseball M, basketball M/W, cross-country running M/W, football M, golf M/W, soccer M/W, softball W, tennis M/W, track and field M/W, volleyball W. *Intramural sports:* basketball M/W, softball W, volleyball W.

Standardized Tests *Required:* SAT or ACT (for admission).

Costs (2007–08) *Comprehensive fee:* $27,715 includes full-time tuition ($21,150), mandatory fees ($175), and room and board ($6390). Part-time tuition: $295 per credit hour. Part-time tuition and fees vary according to course load. *College room only:* $3790. Room and board charges vary according to board plan and housing facility. *Payment plan:* installment. *Waivers:* senior citizens and employees or children of employees.

Financial Aid Of all full-time matriculated undergraduates who enrolled in 2007, 952 applied for aid, 854 were judged to have need, 173 had their need fully met. In 2007, 185 non-need-based awards were made. *Average percent of need met:* 84%. *Average financial aid package:* $17,048. *Average need-based loan:* $4113. *Average need-based gift aid:* $13,082. *Average non-need-based aid:* $11,871. *Average indebtedness upon graduation:* $32,778. *Financial aid deadline:* 3/1.

Applying *Options:* electronic application, deferred entrance. *Application fee:* $30. *Required:* essay or personal statement, high school transcript, TOEFL for international students. *Required for some:* interview. *Recommended:* letters of recommendation. *Application deadline:* rolling (freshmen). *Notification:* continuous (freshmen), continuous (transfers).

Freshman Application Contact Ms. Jacqueline Acosta, Director of Admissions, Franklin College, 101 Branigin Boulevard, Franklin, IN 46131-2623. *Phone:* 317-738-8062. *Toll-free phone:* 800-852-0232. *Fax:* 317-738-8274. *E-mail:* jacosta@franklincollege.edu.

See page 922 for the College Close-Up.

GOSHEN COLLEGE

Goshen, Indiana www.goshen.edu/

- **Independent Mennonite** 4-year, founded 1894
- **Small-town** 135-acre campus
- **Endowment** $105.8 million
- **Coed**
- **Moderately difficult** entrance level

Faculty *Student/faculty ratio:* 10:1.

Academics *Calendar:* semesters. *Degrees:* certificates, bachelor's, and master's.

Student Life *Campus security:* 24-hour emergency response devices and patrols, late-night transport/escort service.

Athletics Member NAIA.

Standardized Tests *Required:* SAT or ACT (for admission).

Costs (2008–09) *Comprehensive fee:* $29,750 includes full-time tuition ($22,300) and room and board ($7450). Part-time tuition: $850 per credit hour. *College room only:* $3950.

Financial Aid Of all full-time matriculated undergraduates who enrolled in 2005, 786 applied for aid, 617 were judged to have need, 184 had their need fully met. 614 Federal Work-Study jobs (averaging $775). 16 state and other part-time jobs (averaging $1320). In 2005, 58 non-need-based awards were made. *Average percent of need met:* 87. *Average financial aid package:* $16,555. *Average need-based loan:* $4887. *Average need-based gift aid:* $11,680. *Average non-need-based aid:* $8031. *Average indebtedness upon graduation:* $18,680.

Applying *Options:* electronic application, deferred entrance. *Application fee:* $25. *Required:* essay or personal statement, high school transcript, minimum 2.0 GPA, 2 letters of recommendation. *Recommended:* minimum 2.6 GPA, interview, rank in upper 50% of high school class, minimum SAT score math and verbal of 1000 or ACT score of 22.

Freshman Application Contact Lynn Jackson, Director of Enrollment, Goshen College, 1700 South Main Street, Goshen, IN 46526-4794. *Phone:* 574-535-7535. *Toll-free phone:* 800-348-7422. *Fax:* 574-535-7609. *E-mail:* lynnj@goshen.edu.

See page 924 for the College Close-Up.

GRACE COLLEGE

Winona Lake, Indiana **www.grace.edu/**

- **Independent** comprehensive, founded 1948, affiliated with Fellowship of Grace Brethren Churches, administratively affiliated with Grace Theological Seminary
- **Small-town** 160-acre campus
- **Endowment** $8.4 million
- **Coed** 1,226 undergraduate students, 91% full-time, 49% women, 51% men
- **Moderately difficult** entrance level, 56% of applicants were admitted

Undergraduates 1,118 full-time, 108 part-time. Students come from 36 states and territories, 5 other countries, 39% are from out of state, 11% African American, 1% Asian American or Pacific Islander, 2% Hispanic American, 0.8% Native American, 0.5% international, 4% transferred in, 61% live on campus. *Retention:* 79% of 2006 full-time freshmen returned.

Freshmen *Admission:* 1,536 applied, 865 admitted, 250 enrolled. *Average high school GPA:* 3.53. *Test scores:* SAT critical reading scores over 500: 62%; SAT math scores over 500: 60%; ACT scores over 18: 94%; SAT critical reading scores over 600: 26%; SAT math scores over 600: 25%; ACT scores over 24: 62%; SAT critical reading scores over 700: 8%; SAT math scores over 700: 3%; ACT scores over 30: 12%.

Faculty *Total:* 139, 35% full-time, 34% with terminal degrees. *Student/faculty ratio:* 17:1.

Majors Accounting; administrative assistant and secretarial science; art teacher education; biblical studies; biology/biological sciences; business administration and management; business/commerce; business teacher education; communication/speech communication and rhetoric; counseling psychology; criminal justice/law enforcement administration; criminal justice/safety; drawing; education related; elementary education; English; English/language arts teacher education; finance; foreign languages and literatures; French; French language teacher education; German; German language teacher education; graphic design; health and physical education; history; history related; illustration; information technology; international business/trade/commerce; journalism; management information systems; marketing/marketing management; mathematics; mathematics teacher education; music performance; music teacher education; painting; physical education teaching and coaching; physical sciences; psychology; science teacher education; social studies teacher education; social work; sociology; Spanish; Spanish language teacher education; special education; sport and fitness administration/management; statistics; youth ministry.

Academics *Calendar:* semesters. *Degrees:* certificates, diplomas, associate, bachelor's, master's, doctoral, and first professional. *Special study options:* academic remediation for entering students, accelerated degree program, adult/continuing education programs, advanced placement credit, cooperative education, distance learning, double majors, honors programs, independent study, internships, off-campus study, part-time degree program, services for LD students, study abroad, summer session for credit.

Computers on Campus 100 computers/terminals are available on campus for general student use. Students can access the following: computer help desk, free student e-mail accounts, online (class) grades, online (class) registration, online (class) schedules. Campuswide network is available. 98% of college-owned or -operated housing units are wired for high-speed Internet access. Wireless service is available via entire campus.

Student Life *Housing:* on-campus residence required through senior year. *Options:* men-only, women-only. Campus housing is university owned. Freshman campus housing is guaranteed. *Activities and organizations:* drama/theater group, student-run newspaper, choral group, Grace Ministries in Action, Student Activities Board, Funfest, women's ministries, Breakout. *Campus security:* student patrols, late-night transport/escort service, controlled dormitory access, evening patrols by trained security personnel. *Student services:* health clinic, personal/psychological counseling.

Athletics Member NAIA, NCCAA. *Intercollegiate sports:* baseball M (s), basketball M (s)/W (s), cheerleading M (s)/W (s), cross-country running M (s)/W (s), golf M (s), soccer M (s)/W (s), softball W (s), tennis M (s)/W (s), track and field M (s)/W (s), volleyball W (s). *Intramural sports:* basketball M/W, football M, soccer M/W, softball M/W, table tennis M/W, tennis M/W, volleyball M/W.

Standardized Tests *Required:* SAT or ACT (for admission).

Costs (2007–08) *Comprehensive fee:* $25,584 includes full-time tuition ($18,824), mandatory fees ($400), and room and board ($6360). Part-time tuition: $360 per credit. Part-time tuition and fees vary according to course load. *Required fees:* $280 per year part-time. *College room only:* $3280. Room and board charges vary according to board plan and housing facility. *Payment plan:* installment. *Waivers:* senior citizens and employees or children of employees.

Financial Aid Of all full-time matriculated undergraduates who enrolled in 2006, 719 applied for aid, 622 were judged to have need, 205 had their need fully met. In 2006, 164 non-need-based awards were made. *Average percent of need met:* 85%. *Average financial aid package:* $14,540. *Average need-based loan:* $5890. *Average need-based gift aid:* $9121. *Average non-need-based aid:* $15,009. *Average indebtedness upon graduation:* $18,017.

Applying *Options:* electronic application, early admission, deferred entrance. *Application fee:* $30. *Required:* essay or personal statement, high school transcript, minimum 2.3 GPA, 2 letters of recommendation, personal statement of faith. *Required for some:* interview. *Application deadlines:* 8/1 (freshmen), 8/1 (transfers), 12/1 (early action). *Notification:* continuous until 8/15 (freshmen), continuous until 8/15 (transfers).

Freshman Application Contact Grace College, Admissions Office, 200 Seminary Drive, Winona Lake, IN 46590. *Phone:* 574-372-5100 Ext. 6008. *Toll-free phone:* 800-54-GRACE Ext. 6412 (in-state); 800-54 GRACE Ext. 6412 (out-of-state). *Fax:* 574-372-5120. *E-mail:* enroll@grace.edu.

HANOVER COLLEGE

Hanover, Indiana **www.hanover.edu/**

- **Independent Presbyterian** 4-year, founded 1827
- **Rural** 630-acre campus with easy access to Louisville
- **Endowment** $141.9 million
- **Coed** 929 undergraduate students, 99% full-time, 54% women, 46% men
- **Moderately difficult** entrance level, 66% of applicants were admitted

Hanover College has been offering a classic liberal arts education since 1827. The oldest private college in Indiana, Hanover is nestled among 650 acres overlooking the Ohio River. The College is home to approximately 1,000 students from across the country and abroad who want tradition and innovation. Hanover is consistently ranked by *U.S. News & World Report* and *The Princeton Review* as one of the best colleges in the nation.

Undergraduates 919 full-time, 10 part-time. Students come from 26 states and territories, 13 other countries, 36% are from out of state, 1% African American, 2% Asian American or Pacific Islander, 0.7% Hispanic American, 0.7% Native American, 3% international, 0.9% transferred in, 97% live on campus. *Retention:* 77% of 2006 full-time freshmen returned.

Freshmen *Admission:* 1,894 applied, 1,247 admitted, 231 enrolled. *Average high school GPA:* 3.72. *Test scores:* SAT critical reading scores over 500: 85%; SAT math scores over 500: 84%; SAT writing scores over 500: 75%; ACT scores over 18: 100%; SAT critical reading scores over 600: 40%; SAT math scores over 600: 40%; SAT writing scores over 600: 31%; ACT scores over 24: 67%; SAT critical reading scores over 700: 10%; SAT math scores over 700: 5%; SAT writing scores over 700: 3%; ACT scores over 30: 11%.

Faculty *Total:* 105, 92% full-time, 97% with terminal degrees. *Student/faculty ratio:* 10:1.

Majors Anthropology; art; art history, criticism and conservation; biology/biological sciences; business administration and management; chemistry; classics and languages, literatures and linguistics; computer science; dramatic/theater arts; economics; English; French; geology/earth science; German; history; international/global studies; Latin American studies; mass communication/media; mathematics; medieval and Renaissance studies; music; philosophy; physical education teaching and coaching; physics; political science and government; psychology; sociology; Spanish; theology.

Academics *Calendar:* 4-4-1. *Degree:* bachelor's. *Special study options:* advanced placement credit, double majors, independent study, internships, off-campus study, student-designed majors, study abroad.

Computers on Campus 112 computers/terminals are available on campus for general student use. Students can access the following: campus intranet, computer help desk, free student e-mail accounts, online (class) grades, online (class) registration, online (class) schedules. Campuswide network is available. 75% of college-owned or -operated housing units are wired for high-speed Internet access. Wireless service is available via entire campus.

Student Life *Housing:* on-campus residence required through senior year. *Options:* coed, men-only, women-only. Campus housing is university owned and leased by the school. Freshman campus housing is guaranteed. *Activities and organizations:* drama/theater group, student-run newspaper, radio and television station, choral group, marching band, Christian Life, Baptist Collegiate Ministries, Student Programming Board, Link, American Chemical Society, national fraternities, national sororities. *Campus security:* 24-hour emergency response devices and patrols, late-night transport/escort service, controlled dormitory access. *Student services:* health clinic, personal/psychological counseling.

Athletics Member NCAA. All Division III. *Intercollegiate sports:* baseball M, basketball M/W, cross-country running M/W, football M, golf M/W, soccer M/W, softball W, tennis M/W, track and field M/W, volleyball W. *Intramural sports:* basketball M/W, football M/W, soccer M/W, volleyball M/W.

Standardized Tests *Required:* SAT or ACT (for admission).
Costs (2007–08) *One-time required fee:* $250. *Comprehensive fee:* $31,370 includes full-time tuition ($23,700), mandatory fees ($520), and room and board ($7150). Full-time tuition and fees vary according to reciprocity agreements. Part-time tuition: $2632 per unit. Part-time tuition and fees vary according to course load and reciprocity agreements. *College room only:* $3450. Room and board charges vary according to housing facility and location. *Payment plan:* installment. *Waivers:* senior citizens and employees or children of employees.
Financial Aid Of all full-time matriculated undergraduates who enrolled in 2006, 725 applied for aid, 614 were judged to have need, 274 had their need fully met. In 2006, 325 non-need-based awards were made. *Average percent of need met:* 87%. *Average financial aid package:* $18,447. *Average need-based loan:* $3746. *Average need-based gift aid:* $15,121. *Average non-need-based aid:* $15,588. *Average indebtedness upon graduation:* $17,448.
Applying *Options:* electronic application, early admission, early action, deferred entrance. *Application fee:* $35. *Required:* essay or personal statement, high school transcript, 1 letter of recommendation. *Recommended:* interview. *Application deadlines:* 3/1 (freshmen), rolling (transfers), 12/1 (early action). *Notification:* continuous (freshmen), continuous (transfers), 12/20 (early action).
Freshman Application Contact Mr. Bill Preble, Dean of Admission and Financial Assistance, Hanover College, PO Box 108, Hanover, IN 47243-0108. *Phone:* 812-866-7021. *Toll-free phone:* 800-213-2178. *Fax:* 812-866-7098. *E-mail:* admission@hanover.edu.

See page 926 for the College Close-Up.

HOLY CROSS COLLEGE

Notre Dame, Indiana — www.hcc-nd.edu/

- **Independent Roman Catholic** primarily 2-year, founded 1966
- **Urban** 150-acre campus
- **Coed**
- **Moderately difficult** entrance level

Faculty *Student/faculty ratio:* 12:1.
Academics *Calendar:* semesters. *Degrees:* associate and bachelor's.
Student Life *Campus security:* 24-hour emergency response devices and patrols, 24-hour patrols by trained personnel on certain days.
Standardized Tests *Required:* SAT or ACT (for admission).
Costs (2007–08) *Comprehensive fee:* $23,910 includes full-time tuition ($15,660), mandatory fees ($800), and room and board ($7450). Part-time tuition: $520 per credit hour.
Financial Aid Of all full-time matriculated undergraduates who enrolled in 2006, 54 Federal Work-Study jobs (averaging $857).
Applying *Options:* electronic application, deferred entrance. *Application fee:* $50. *Required:* essay or personal statement, high school transcript, minimum 2.5 GPA, College Success Program (2.0). *Required for some:* letters of recommendation. *Recommended:* interview.
Freshman Application Contact Office of Admissions, Holy Cross College, PO Box 308, Notre Dame, IN 46556. *Phone:* 574-239-8400. *Fax:* 574-239-8323. *E-mail:* vduke@hcc-nd.edu.

See page 928 for the College Close-Up.

HUNTINGTON UNIVERSITY

Huntington, Indiana — www.huntington.edu/

- **Independent** comprehensive, founded 1897, affiliated with Church of the United Brethren in Christ, administratively affiliated with Church of the United Brethren in Christ
- **Small-town** 170-acre campus with easy access to Fort Wayne
- **Endowment** $24.4 million
- **Coed** 923 undergraduate students, 92% full-time, 55% women, 45% men
- **Moderately difficult** entrance level, 86% of applicants were admitted

Huntington University is consistently ranked as one of the top twenty Midwest comprehensive colleges by *U.S. News & World Report*. Since 1897, Huntington has been educating men and women to impact the world for Christ. Huntington offers more than seventy areas of study, including new programs in digital media arts, nursing, and worship leadership. Prospective students can find out more about Huntington and build their own personalized brochure at http://www.huntington.edu/brochure.

Undergraduates 845 full-time, 78 part-time. Students come from 30 states and territories, 17 other countries, 40% are from out of state, 0.5% African American, 0.7% Asian American or Pacific Islander, 0.9% Hispanic American, 0.1% Native American, 4% international, 5% transferred in, 80% live on campus. *Retention:* 72% of 2006 full-time freshmen returned.
Freshmen *Admission:* 797 applied, 685 admitted, 246 enrolled. *Average high school GPA:* 3.4. *Test scores:* SAT critical reading scores over 500: 68%; SAT math scores over 500: 68%; ACT scores over 18: 98%; SAT critical reading scores over 600: 27%; SAT math scores over 600: 29%; ACT scores over 24: 52%; SAT critical reading scores over 700: 7%; SAT math scores over 700: 8%; ACT scores over 30: 13%.
Faculty *Total:* 93, 62% full-time, 55% with terminal degrees. *Student/faculty ratio:* 12:1.
Majors Accounting; art; art teacher education; biblical studies; biological and physical sciences; biology/biological sciences; broadcast journalism; business administration and management; business/managerial economics; business teacher education; chemistry; commercial and advertising art; communication/speech communication and rhetoric; computer science; digital communication and media/multimedia; divinity/ministry; drama and dance teacher education; dramatic/theater arts; economics; education; elementary education; English; film/cinema studies; graphic design; history; journalism; kinesiology and exercise science; mass communication/media; mathematics; middle school education; missionary studies and missiology; music; music management and merchandising; music teacher education; music theory and composition; natural resources management and policy; parks, recreation and leisure; philosophy; physical education teaching and coaching; piano and organ; political science and government; pre-dentistry studies; pre-law studies; pre-medical studies; pre-veterinary studies; psychology; public relations/image management; religious/sacred music; religious studies; science teacher education; secondary education; social work; sociology; special education; theater design and technology; theological and ministerial studies related; theology; voice and opera.
Academics *Calendar:* 4-1-4. *Degrees:* associate, bachelor's, and master's. *Special study options:* academic remediation for entering students, adult/continuing education programs, advanced placement credit, double majors, independent study, internships, off-campus study, part-time degree program, services for LD students, study abroad, summer session for credit.
Computers on Campus 261 computers/terminals are available on campus for general student use. Students can access the following: campus intranet, computer help desk, free student e-mail accounts, online (class) grades, online (class) registration, online (class) schedules. Campuswide network is available. 90% of college-owned or -operated housing units are wired for high-speed Internet access. Wireless service is available via classrooms, computer centers, dorm rooms, learning centers, libraries, student centers.
Student Life *Housing:* on-campus residence required through junior year. *Options:* men-only, women-only. Campus housing is university owned. Freshman campus housing is guaranteed. *Activities and organizations:* drama/theater group, student-run newspaper, radio and television station, choral group, Joe Mertz Volunteer Center for Volunteer Service, Musical Ensembles (Concert Choir, Women's Choral, Handbells, Jazz Band, etc.), Ministry groups, student publications and media, Honor Societies. *Campus security:* 24-hour emergency response devices, late-night transport/escort service, night patrols by trained security personnel. *Student services:* health clinic, personal/psychological counseling.
Athletics Member NAIA, NCCAA. *Intercollegiate sports:* baseball M (s), basketball M (s)/W (s), cross-country running M (s)/W (s), golf M (s), soccer M (s)/W (s), softball W (s), tennis M (s)/W (s), track and field M (s)/W (s), volleyball W (s). *Intramural sports:* basketball M/W, cheerleading M (c)/W (c), football M, racquetball M/W, soccer M/W, softball M/W, ultimate Frisbee M/W, volleyball M/W.
Standardized Tests *Required:* SAT or ACT (for admission).
Costs (2007–08) *Comprehensive fee:* $26,160 includes full-time tuition ($18,980), mandatory fees ($450), and room and board ($6730). Part-time tuition: $570 per semester hour. *Required fees:* $22 per semester hour part-time. *College room only:* $3130. Room and board charges vary according to board plan. *Payment plan:* installment. *Waivers:* senior citizens and employees or children of employees.
Financial Aid Of all full-time matriculated undergraduates who enrolled in 2007, 767 applied for aid, 664 were judged to have need, 85 had their need fully met. 238 Federal Work-Study jobs (averaging $1795). In 2007, 113 non-need-based awards were made. *Average percent of need met:* 73%. *Average financial aid package:* $14,323. *Average need-based loan:* $4803. *Average need-based gift aid:* $11,205. *Average non-need-based aid:* $7140. *Average indebtedness upon graduation:* $24,267.
Applying *Options:* electronic application, deferred entrance. *Application fee:* $20. *Required:* essay or personal statement, high school transcript, minimum 2.3 GPA. *Recommended:* interview. *Application deadlines:* 8/1 (freshmen), rolling (transfers). *Notification:* continuous until 7/1 (freshmen), continuous (transfers).
Freshman Application Contact Mr. Jeff Berggren, Vice President of Enrollment Management and Marketing, Huntington University, 2303 College Avenue,

Huntington, IN 46750-1299. *Phone:* 260-356-6000 Ext. 4016. *Toll-free phone:* 800-642-6493. *Fax:* 260-356-9448. *E-mail:* admissions@huntington.edu.

INDIANA STATE UNIVERSITY

Terre Haute, Indiana **web.indstate.edu/**

- **State-supported** university, founded 1865
- **Small-town** 91-acre campus with easy access to Indianapolis
- **Endowment** $55.3 million
- **Coed** 8,493 undergraduate students, 86% full-time, 51% women, 49% men
- **Moderately difficult** entrance level, 70% of applicants were admitted

Undergraduates 7,266 full-time, 1,227 part-time. Students come from 47 states and territories, 43 other countries, 12% are from out of state, 13% African American, 1% Asian American or Pacific Islander, 1% Hispanic American, 0.4% Native American, 1% international, 7% transferred in, 34% live on campus. *Retention:* 69% of 2006 full-time freshmen returned.

Freshmen *Admission:* 6,428 applied, 4,520 admitted, 1,852 enrolled. *Average high school GPA:* 3.01. *Test scores:* SAT critical reading scores over 500: 34%; SAT math scores over 500: 38%; SAT writing scores over 500: 28%; ACT scores over 18: 73%; SAT critical reading scores over 600: 7%; SAT math scores over 600: 7%; SAT writing scores over 600: 5%; ACT scores over 24: 16%; SAT critical reading scores over 700: 1%; SAT math scores over 700: 1%; ACT scores over 30: 2%.

Faculty *Total:* 640, 70% full-time, 61% with terminal degrees. *Student/faculty ratio:* 17:1.

Majors Accounting; aeronautics/aviation/aerospace science and technology; African-American/Black studies; airline pilot and flight crew; anthropology; apparel and textiles; architectural engineering technology; art; art teacher education; athletic training; audiology and speech-language pathology; automotive engineering technology; aviation/airway management; biology/biological sciences; business administration and management; business teacher education; chemistry; clinical laboratory science/medical technology; communication/speech communication and rhetoric; community health services counseling; computer and information sciences; computer engineering technology; criminology; dramatic/theater arts; early childhood education; economics; education; electrical, electronic and communications engineering technology; elementary education; English; environmental health; family and consumer sciences/human sciences; finance; fine/studio arts; foods, nutrition, and wellness; foreign languages and literatures; French; geography; geology/earth science; German; history; human development and family studies; human resources management; industrial technology; information technology; insurance; interior architecture; liberal arts and sciences/liberal studies; management information systems; management sciences and quantitative methods related; manufacturing technology; marketing/marketing management; mathematics; mechanical engineering technologies related; music; music related; nursing (registered nurse training); occupational safety and health technology; office management; operations management; philosophy; physical education teaching and coaching; physics; political science and government; psychology; robotics technology; science teacher education; social sciences; social studies teacher education; social work; sociology; Spanish; special education; trade and industrial teacher education.

Academics *Calendar:* semesters. *Degrees:* certificates, associate, bachelor's, master's, doctoral, post-master's, and postbachelor's certificates. *Special study options:* academic remediation for entering students, accelerated degree program, adult/continuing education programs, advanced placement credit, cooperative education, distance learning, double majors, English as a second language, honors programs, independent study, internships, off-campus study, part-time degree program, services for LD students, study abroad, summer session for credit. *ROTC:* Army (b), Air Force (b).

Computers on Campus 600 computers/terminals are available on campus for general student use. Students can access the following: campus intranet, computer help desk, free student e-mail accounts, online (class) grades, online (class) registration, online (class) schedules. Campuswide network is available. 100% of college-owned or -operated housing units are wired for high-speed Internet access. Wireless service is available via classrooms, learning centers, libraries, student centers.

Student Life *Housing:* on-campus residence required for freshman year. *Options:* coed, men-only, women-only, disabled students. Campus housing is university owned. Freshman campus housing is guaranteed. *Activities and organizations:* drama/theater group, student-run newspaper, radio station, choral group, marching band, Union Boards, Student Government Association, Panhellenic Council (sororities), Interfraternity Council (fraternities), Pan-Hellenic Council (African American fraternities/sororities), national fraternities, national sororities. *Campus security:* 24-hour emergency response devices and patrols, student patrols, late-night transport/escort service. *Student services:* health clinic, personal/psychological counseling, women's center.

Athletics Member NCAA. All Division I except football (Division I-AA). *Intercollegiate sports:* baseball M (s), basketball M (s)/W (s), cross-country running M (s)/W (s), soccer W (s), softball W (s), tennis M (s)/W (s), track and field M (s)/W (s), volleyball W (s). *Intramural sports:* badminton M/W, basketball M/W, bowling M/W, soccer M/W, softball M/W, swimming and diving M/W, table tennis M/W, tennis M/W, track and field M/W, ultimate Frisbee M/W, volleyball M/W.

Standardized Tests *Required:* SAT or ACT (for admission).

Costs (2008–09) *Tuition:* state resident $6792 full-time, $245 per credit hour part-time; nonresident $15,046 full-time, $530 per credit hour part-time. *Required fees:* $356 full-time, $178 per term part-time.

Financial Aid Of all full-time matriculated undergraduates who enrolled in 2006, 5,816 applied for aid, 4,736 were judged to have need, 495 had their need fully met. 614 Federal Work-Study jobs (averaging $930). In 2006, 735 non-need-based awards were made. *Average percent of need met:* 77%. *Average financial aid package:* $8137. *Average need-based loan:* $3762. *Average need-based gift aid:* $5221. *Average non-need-based aid:* $3637. *Average indebtedness upon graduation:* $20,868. *Financial aid deadline:* 3/1.

Applying *Options:* electronic application, deferred entrance. *Application fee:* $25. *Required:* high school transcript. *Required for some:* letters of recommendation, interview. *Application deadline:* 8/15 (freshmen). *Notification:* continuous (freshmen), continuous (transfers).

Freshman Application Contact Mr. Richard Toomey, Director of Admissions, Indiana State University, Tirey Hall 134, 210 North 7th Street, Terre Haute, IN 47809. *Phone:* 812-237-2121. *Toll-free phone:* 800-742-0891. *Fax:* 812-237-8023. *E-mail:* ADMISU@isugw.indstate.edu.

See page 930 for the College Close-Up.

INDIANA TECH

Fort Wayne, Indiana **www.indianatech.edu**

- **Independent** comprehensive, founded 1930
- **Urban** 25-acre campus
- **Endowment** $36.4 million
- **Coed** 3,064 undergraduate students, 59% full-time, 53% women, 47% men
- **Moderately difficult** entrance level, 65% of applicants were admitted

Undergraduates 1,819 full-time, 1,245 part-time. Students come from 34 states and territories, 6 other countries, 20% African American, 1% Asian American or Pacific Islander, 2% Hispanic American, 0.3% Native American, 0.5% international, 2% transferred in, 45% live on campus. *Retention:* 60% of 2006 full-time freshmen returned.

Freshmen *Admission:* 1,743 applied, 1,129 admitted, 378 enrolled. *Average high school GPA:* 2.80. *Test scores:* SAT critical reading scores over 500: 31%; SAT math scores over 500: 42%; ACT scores over 18: 72%; SAT critical reading scores over 600: 5%; SAT math scores over 600: 10%; ACT scores over 24: 20%; ACT scores over 30: 1%.

Faculty *Total:* 275, 12% full-time, 7% with terminal degrees. *Student/faculty ratio:* 21:1.

Majors Computer engineering; computer science; electrical, electronics and communications engineering; graphic communications; human resources management; human services; industrial/manufacturing engineering; information technology; marketing/marketing management; mechanical engineering; psychology; web page, digital/multimedia and information resources design.

Academics *Calendar:* semesters. *Degrees:* associate, bachelor's, and master's. *Special study options:* academic remediation for entering students, accelerated degree program, adult/continuing education programs, advanced placement credit, distance learning, double majors, external degree program, independent study, internships, part-time degree program, services for LD students, student-designed majors, summer session for credit.

Computers on Campus 330 computers/terminals are available on campus for general student use. Students can access the following: computer help desk, free student e-mail accounts, online (class) grades, online (class) registration, online (class) schedules. Campuswide network is available. 100% of college-owned or -operated housing units are wired for high-speed Internet access. Wireless service is available via entire campus.

Student Life *Housing:* on-campus residence required through sophomore year. *Options:* coed, men-only. Campus housing is university owned. Freshman applicants given priority for college housing. *Activities and organizations:* student-run newspaper, choral group, Student Board, Student Ambassadors, NSBE, SHRM, Sport Recreation and Leisure Society, national fraternities. *Campus security:*

24-hour emergency response devices and patrols, controlled dormitory access. *Student services:* health clinic, personal/psychological counseling.

Athletics Member NAIA. *Intercollegiate sports:* baseball M (s), basketball M (s)/W (s), cheerleading M (s)/W (s), cross-country running M (s)/W (s), golf M (s)/W (s), soccer M (s)/W (s), softball W (s), track and field M (s)/W (s), volleyball W (s). *Intramural sports:* badminton M/W, basketball M/W, bowling M/W, soccer M/W, softball M/W, volleyball M/W.

Standardized Tests *Required:* SAT or ACT (for admission).

Costs (2007–08) *Comprehensive fee:* $26,780 includes full-time tuition ($19,200), mandatory fees ($280), and room and board ($7300). Part-time tuition: $640 per credit hour.

Financial Aid *Average financial aid package:* $9125. *Average indebtedness upon graduation:* $16,500.

Applying *Options:* electronic application, early admission, deferred entrance. *Application fee:* $50. *Required:* high school transcript. *Recommended:* minimum 3.0 GPA, interview, 2 references. *Notification:* continuous until 10/15 (freshmen), continuous until 2/1 (transfers).

Freshman Application Contact Ms. Monica Ladig, Director of Admissions for Day Division, Indiana Tech, 1600 East Washington Boulevard, Fort Wayne, IN 46803. *Phone:* 260-422-5561. *Toll-free phone:* 800-937-2448 (in-state); 888-666-TECH (out-of-state). *Fax:* 260-422-7696. *E-mail:* admissions@indianatech.edu.

See page 932 for the College Close-Up.

INDIANA UNIVERSITY BLOOMINGTON

Bloomington, Indiana **www.iub.edu/**

- **State-supported** university, founded 1820, part of Indiana University System
- **Small-town** 1933-acre campus with easy access to Indianapolis
- **Endowment** $898.5 million
- **Coed** 30,394 undergraduate students, 95% full-time, 51% women, 49% men
- **Moderately difficult** entrance level, 70% of applicants were admitted

Undergraduates 28,790 full-time, 1,604 part-time. Students come from 50 states and territories, 109 other countries, 33% are from out of state, 4% African American, 4% Asian American or Pacific Islander, 2% Hispanic American, 0.3% Native American, 5% international, 3% transferred in, 31% live on campus. *Retention:* 89% of 2006 full-time freshmen returned.

Freshmen *Admission:* 29,059 applied, 20,282 admitted, 7,096 enrolled. *Average high school GPA:* 3.56. *Test scores:* SAT critical reading scores over 500: 80%; SAT math scores over 500: 85%; ACT scores over 18: 98%; SAT critical reading scores over 600: 34%; SAT math scores over 600: 43%; ACT scores over 24: 74%; SAT critical reading scores over 700: 7%; SAT math scores over 700: 9%; ACT scores over 30: 15%.

Faculty *Total:* 2,309, 84% full-time, 69% with terminal degrees. *Student/faculty ratio:* 18:1.

Majors African-American/Black studies; African studies; American studies; anthropology; art; art history, criticism and conservation; arts management; art teacher education; Asian studies; Asian studies (East); Asian studies (South); audiology and speech-language pathology; ballet; bilingual and multilingual education; biochemistry; biological and biomedical sciences related; biology/biological sciences; biology teacher education; biotechnology; business administration and management; business/commerce; chemistry; chemistry teacher education; classics and languages, literatures and linguistics; cognitive science; commercial and advertising art; communication and journalism related; communication/speech communication and rhetoric; comparative literature; computer and information sciences; criminal justice/safety; design and applied arts related; dramatic/theater arts; East Asian languages; economics; education (multiple levels); education (specific subject areas) related; elementary education; English; English/language arts teacher education; environmental science; ethnic, cultural minority, and gender studies related; European studies (Central and Eastern); finance; fine/studio arts; foreign language teacher education; French; French language teacher education; general studies; geography; geology/earth science; German; German language teacher education; health teacher education; history; information technology; interior design; international relations and affairs; Italian; Jewish/Judaic studies; journalism; labor and industrial relations; labor studies; Latin American studies; liberal arts and sciences/liberal studies; linguistics; mathematics; mathematics teacher education; music; musical instrument fabrication and repair; music history, literature, and theory; music performance; music related; music teacher education; Near and Middle Eastern studies; neuroscience; nursing (registered nurse training); occupational safety and health technology; ophthalmic laboratory technology; optometric technician; parks, recreation and leisure; philosophy; physical education teaching and coaching; physics; physics teacher education; political science and government; Portuguese; psychology; public administration; public health; public health related; public policy analysis; recording arts technology; religious studies; science teacher education; secondary education; Slavic languages; social sciences related; social studies teacher education; social work; sociology; Spanish; Spanish language teacher education; special education; speech and rhetoric; speech teacher education; speech therapy; sport and fitness administration/management; statistics; theater design and technology; visual and performing arts related.

Academics *Calendar:* semesters plus 2 summer sessions. *Degrees:* certificates, diplomas, associate, bachelor's, master's, doctoral, first professional, post-master's, and postbachelor's certificates. *Special study options:* academic remediation for entering students, accelerated degree program, adult/continuing education programs, advanced placement credit, cooperative education, distance learning, double majors, English as a second language, external degree program, freshman honors college, honors programs, independent study, internships, off-campus study, part-time degree program, services for LD students, student-designed majors, study abroad, summer session for credit. *ROTC:* Army (b), Air Force (b). *Unusual degree programs:* 3-2 accounting.

Computers on Campus Students can access the following: campus intranet, computer help desk, free student e-mail accounts, online (class) grades, online (class) registration, online (class) schedules, various software packages. Campus-wide network is available. 100% of college-owned or -operated housing units are wired for high-speed Internet access. Wireless service is available via entire campus.

Student Life *Housing:* on-campus residence required for freshman year. *Options:* coed, men-only, women-only, cooperative, disabled students. Campus housing is university owned. Freshman applicants given priority for college housing. *Activities and organizations:* drama/theater group, student-run newspaper, radio and television station, choral group, marching band, Union Board, Student Association, Student Foundation, Habitat for Humanity, Student Athletic Board, national fraternities, national sororities. *Campus security:* 24-hour emergency response devices and patrols, late-night transport/escort service, safety seminars, lighted pathways, escort service, shuttle bus service, emergency telephones. *Student services:* health clinic, personal/psychological counseling, women's center, legal services.

Athletics Member NCAA. All Division I except football (Division I-A). *Intercollegiate sports:* baseball M (s), basketball M (s)/W (s), crew W (s), cross-country running M (s)/W (s), field hockey W, golf M (s)/W (s), soccer M (s)/W (s), softball W (s), swimming and diving M (s)/W (s), tennis M (s)/W (s), track and field M (s)/W (s), volleyball W (s), water polo W (s), wrestling M (s). *Intramural sports:* archery M/W, badminton M (c)/W (c), baseball M/W, basketball M/W, bowling M (c)/W (c), crew M (c)/W (c), cross-country running M/W, equestrian sports M (c)/W (c), fencing M (c)/W (c), field hockey W (c), golf M/W, gymnastics M/W, ice hockey M/W, lacrosse M (c)/W, racquetball M (c)/W (c), riflery M (c)/W (c), sailing M (c)/W (c), skiing (downhill) M (c)/W (c), soccer M/W (c), softball M/W, squash M/W, swimming and diving M/W, table tennis M/W, tennis M (c)/W, track and field M/W, volleyball M/W, water polo M (c)/W, weight lifting M (c)/W (c), wrestling M (c).

Standardized Tests *Required:* SAT or ACT (for admission). *Recommended:* SAT Subject Tests (for admission).

Costs (2007–08) *Tuition:* state resident $7000 full-time, $219 per credit hour part-time; nonresident $21,479 full-time, $671 per credit hour part-time. Full-time tuition and fees vary according to location and program. Part-time tuition and fees vary according to course load, location, and program. *Required fees:* $837 full-time. *Room and board:* $6676; room only: $4172. Room and board charges vary according to board plan and housing facility. *Payment plan:* deferred payment. *Waivers:* employees or children of employees.

Financial Aid Of all full-time matriculated undergraduates who enrolled in 2006, 15,647 applied for aid, 10,777 were judged to have need, 1,860 had their need fully met. In 2006, 5604 non-need-based awards were made. *Average percent of need met:* 68%. *Average financial aid package:* $8761. *Average need-based loan:* $3989. *Average need-based gift aid:* $6716. *Average non-need-based aid:* $4412. *Average indebtedness upon graduation:* $19,763.

Applying *Options:* electronic application, deferred entrance. *Application fee:* $50. *Required:* high school transcript. *Recommended:* interview. *Application deadlines:* rolling (freshmen), rolling (transfers). *Notification:* continuous (freshmen), continuous (transfers).

Freshman Application Contact Ms. Mary Ellen Anderson, Director of Admissions, Indiana University Bloomington, 300 North Jordan Avenue, Bloomington, IN 47405-1106. *Phone:* 812-855-0661. *Fax:* 812-855-5102. *E-mail:* iuadmit@indiana.edu.

INDIANA UNIVERSITY EAST

Richmond, Indiana **www.iu.edu/**

- **State-supported** 4-year, founded 1971, part of Indiana University System
- **Small-town** 174-acre campus with easy access to Indianapolis
- **Endowment** $5.5 million
- **Coed** 2,224 undergraduate students, 56% full-time, 67% women, 33% men
- **Moderately difficult** entrance level, 82% of applicants were admitted

Undergraduates 1,256 full-time, 968 part-time. 14% are from out of state, 4% African American, 0.5% Asian American or Pacific Islander, 2% Hispanic American, 0.3% Native American, 0.3% international, 8% transferred in. *Retention:* 60% of 2006 full-time freshmen returned.

Freshmen *Admission:* 547 applied, 449 admitted, 328 enrolled. *Average high school GPA:* 2.96. *Test scores:* SAT critical reading scores over 500: 27%; SAT math scores over 500: 32%; ACT scores over 18: 82%; SAT critical reading scores over 600: 5%; SAT math scores over 600: 6%; ACT scores over 24: 12%; SAT critical reading scores over 700: 1%.

Faculty *Total:* 191, 42% full-time, 31% with terminal degrees. *Student/faculty ratio:* 14:1.

Majors Art; biology/biological sciences; biotechnology; business/commerce; communication/speech communication and rhetoric; computer and information sciences and support services related; computer programming (specific applications); criminal justice/safety; elementary education; English; general studies; health information/medical records administration; humanities; human services; liberal arts and sciences/liberal studies; medical radiologic technology; natural sciences; nursing (registered nurse training); political science and government; psychology; public administration; radiation protection/health physics technology; radiologic technology/science; religious studies; respiratory care therapy; secondary education; social work; sociology.

Academics *Calendar:* semesters. *Degrees:* associate, bachelor's, and postbachelor's certificates. *Special study options:* academic remediation for entering students, adult/continuing education programs, advanced placement credit, cooperative education, distance learning, double majors, external degree program, independent study, internships, off-campus study, part-time degree program, services for LD students, summer session for credit.

Computers on Campus Students can access the following: campus intranet, computer help desk, free student e-mail accounts, online (class) grades, online (class) registration, online (class) schedules. Campuswide network is available. Wireless service is available via entire campus.

Student Life *Housing:* college housing not available. *Activities and organizations:* drama/theater group, student-run newspaper, television station, Student Government Association, Phi Beta Lambda, Multicultural Awareness Association, Psychology Club, Sociology Club. *Campus security:* 24-hour emergency response devices, late-night transport/escort service, safety awareness, lighted pathways, 14-hour foot and vehicle patrol. *Student services:* personal/psychological counseling.

Athletics Member NAIA. *Intercollegiate sports:* basketball M, cheerleading W, golf M, volleyball W. *Intramural sports:* basketball M (c)/W (c), softball M/W, volleyball M/W.

Standardized Tests *Recommended:* SAT or ACT (for admission).

Costs (2007–08) *Tuition:* state resident $4932 full-time, $164 per credit hour part-time; nonresident $12,471 full-time, $416 per credit hour part-time. Full-time tuition and fees vary according to course load, program, and reciprocity agreements. Part-time tuition and fees vary according to course load, program, and reciprocity agreements. *Required fees:* $360 full-time. *Payment plan:* deferred payment. *Waivers:* employees or children of employees.

Financial Aid Of all full-time matriculated undergraduates who enrolled in 2006, 1,027 applied for aid, 870 were judged to have need, 66 had their need fully met. In 2006, 41 non-need-based awards were made. *Average percent of need met:* 60%. *Average financial aid package:* $6794. *Average need-based loan:* $3274. *Average need-based gift aid:* $4757. *Average non-need-based aid:* $995. *Average indebtedness upon graduation:* $20,182.

Applying *Options:* early admission, deferred entrance. *Application fee:* $25. *Required:* high school transcript. *Recommended:* minimum 2.0 GPA. *Application deadlines:* rolling (freshmen), rolling (transfers). *Notification:* continuous (freshmen), continuous (transfers).

Freshman Application Contact Ms. Molly Vanderpool, Admissions Counselor, Indiana University East, 2325 Chester Boulevard, WZ 116, Richmond, IN 47374-1289. *Phone:* 765-973-8415. *Toll-free phone:* 800-959-EAST. *Fax:* 765-973-8288.

INDIANA UNIVERSITY KOKOMO

Kokomo, Indiana **www.iuk.edu/**

- **State-supported** comprehensive, founded 1945, part of Indiana University System
- **Small-town** 51-acre campus with easy access to Indianapolis
- **Endowment** $6.2 million
- **Coed** 2,696 undergraduate students, 51% full-time, 70% women, 30% men
- **Minimally difficult** entrance level, 83% of applicants were admitted

Undergraduates 1,383 full-time, 1,313 part-time. 1% are from out of state, 4% African American, 1% Asian American or Pacific Islander, 2% Hispanic American, 0.8% Native American, 0.3% international, 7% transferred in. *Retention:* 53% of 2006 full-time freshmen returned.

Freshmen *Admission:* 725 applied, 605 admitted, 435 enrolled. *Average high school GPA:* 2.85. *Test scores:* SAT critical reading scores over 500: 34%; SAT math scores over 500: 43%; ACT scores over 18: 65%; SAT critical reading scores over 600: 8%; SAT math scores over 600: 8%; ACT scores over 24: 16%; SAT critical reading scores over 700: 1%; ACT scores over 30: 1%.

Faculty *Total:* 162, 58% full-time, 39% with terminal degrees. *Student/faculty ratio:* 16:1.

Majors Behavioral sciences; biological and physical sciences; biology/biological sciences; business/commerce; chemistry; clinical laboratory science/medical technology; communication and journalism related; communication/speech communication and rhetoric; computer and information sciences; criminal justice/safety; early childhood education; elementary education; English; general studies; gerontology; humanities; information technology; labor studies; mathematics; medical radiologic technology; nursing (registered nurse training); psychology; public administration; secondary education; social sciences related; sociology.

Academics *Calendar:* semesters. *Degrees:* certificates, associate, bachelor's, master's, and postbachelor's certificates. *Special study options:* academic remediation for entering students, accelerated degree program, adult/continuing education programs, advanced placement credit, distance learning, double majors, external degree program, freshman honors college, honors programs, independent study, internships, part-time degree program, services for LD students, study abroad, summer session for credit. *ROTC:* Army (c).

Computers on Campus Students can access the following: campus intranet, computer help desk, free student e-mail accounts, online (class) grades, online (class) registration, online (class) schedules. Campuswide network is available. Wireless service is available via entire campus.

Student Life *Housing:* college housing not available. *Activities and organizations:* drama/theater group, student-run newspaper, choral group. *Campus security:* 24-hour patrols, late-night transport/escort service, campus police, lighted pathways. *Student services:* personal/psychological counseling.

Athletics *Intramural sports:* basketball M, soccer M/W, softball M/W, volleyball M/W.

Standardized Tests *Required:* SAT or ACT (for admission).

Costs (2007–08) *Tuition:* state resident $4928 full-time, $164 per credit hour part-time; nonresident $12,464 full-time, $415 per credit hour part-time. Full-time tuition and fees vary according to course load and program. Part-time tuition and fees vary according to course load and program. *Required fees:* $397 full-time. *Payment plan:* deferred payment. *Waivers:* employees or children of employees.

Financial Aid Of all full-time matriculated undergraduates who enrolled in 2006, 1,026 applied for aid, 792 were judged to have need, 74 had their need fully met. In 2006, 87 non-need-based awards were made. *Average percent of need met:* 63%. *Average financial aid package:* $6326. *Average need-based loan:* $3328. *Average need-based gift aid:* $4641. *Average non-need-based aid:* $1282. *Average indebtedness upon graduation:* $19,443. *Financial aid deadline:* 3/1.

Applying *Options:* early admission, deferred entrance. *Application fee:* $30. *Required:* high school transcript. *Application deadline:* rolling (freshmen). *Notification:* continuous (freshmen), continuous (transfers).

Freshman Application Contact Mr. David Campbell, Admissions Director, Indiana University Kokomo, PO Box 9003, Kelley Student Center 230A, Kokomo, IN 46904-9003. *Phone:* 765-455-9217. *Toll-free phone:* 888-875-4485. *Fax:* 765-455-9537. *E-mail:* iuadmis@iuk.edu.

INDIANA UNIVERSITY NORTHWEST

Gary, Indiana **www.iun.edu/**

- **State-supported** comprehensive, founded 1959, part of Indiana University System
- **Urban** 38-acre campus with easy access to Chicago
- **Endowment** $9.2 million

- **Coed** 4,150 undergraduate students, 59% full-time, 69% women, 31% men
- **Minimally difficult** entrance level, 78% of applicants were admitted

Undergraduates 2,432 full-time, 1,718 part-time. 1% are from out of state, 22% African American, 2% Asian American or Pacific Islander, 12% Hispanic American, 0.4% Native American, 0.2% international, 8% transferred in. *Retention:* 62% of 2006 full-time freshmen returned.

Freshmen *Admission:* 1,379 applied, 1,077 admitted, 714 enrolled. *Average high school GPA:* 2.67. *Test scores:* SAT critical reading scores over 500: 32%; SAT math scores over 500: 29%; ACT scores over 18: 54%; SAT critical reading scores over 600: 7%; SAT math scores over 600: 8%; ACT scores over 24: 10%; SAT math scores over 700: 1%.

Faculty *Total:* 353, 53% full-time, 48% with terminal degrees. *Student/faculty ratio:* 14:1.

Majors Actuarial science; African-American/Black studies; art; biology/biological sciences; business/commerce; chemistry; clinical/medical laboratory technology; communication/speech communication and rhetoric; computer and information sciences; criminal justice/safety; dental hygiene; dramatic/theater arts; economics; elementary education; English; English/language arts teacher education; French; general studies; geology/earth science; health information/medical records technology; health services administration; history; labor studies; liberal arts and sciences/liberal studies; mathematics; mathematics teacher education; nursing (registered nurse training); philosophy; political science and government; psychology; public administration; radiation protection/health physics technology; radiologic technology/science; respiratory care therapy; secondary education; social studies teacher education; sociology; Spanish; Spanish language teacher education.

Academics *Calendar:* semesters. *Degrees:* certificates, associate, bachelor's, master's, and postbachelor's certificates. *Special study options:* academic remediation for entering students, accelerated degree program, adult/continuing education programs, advanced placement credit, cooperative education, distance learning, double majors, external degree program, honors programs, independent study, internships, off-campus study, part-time degree program, services for LD students, student-designed majors, study abroad, summer session for credit. *ROTC:* Army (b).

Computers on Campus Students can access the following: campus intranet, computer help desk, free student e-mail accounts, online (class) grades, online (class) registration, online (class) schedules. Campuswide network is available. Wireless service is available via entire campus.

Student Life *Housing:* college housing not available. *Activities and organizations:* drama/theater group, student-run newspaper, choral group, Student Government Association, Student Guides Organization, Nursing Association, Dental Association, International Affairs Club, national fraternities, national sororities. *Campus security:* 24-hour emergency response devices and patrols, late-night transport/escort service, lighted pathways. *Student services:* personal/psychological counseling.

Athletics Member NAIA. *Intercollegiate sports:* baseball M, basketball M/W, golf M/W, volleyball W. *Intramural sports:* basketball M (c), bowling M (c)/W (c), fencing M (c)/W (c), soccer M (c), softball M (c)/W (c), table tennis M (c)/W (c), tennis M (c)/W (c), volleyball M (c)/W (c).

Standardized Tests *Required:* SAT or ACT (for admission).

Costs (2007–08) *Tuition:* state resident $4962 full-time, $165 per credit hour part-time; nonresident $12,470 full-time, $416 per credit hour part-time. Full-time tuition and fees vary according to course load and program. Part-time tuition and fees vary according to course load and program. *Required fees:* $436 full-time. *Payment plans:* installment, deferred payment. *Waivers:* senior citizens and employees or children of employees.

Financial Aid Of all full-time matriculated undergraduates who enrolled in 2006, 1,906 applied for aid, 1,587 were judged to have need, 125 had their need fully met. In 2006, 109 non-need-based awards were made. *Average percent of need met:* 56%. *Average financial aid package:* $6694. *Average need-based loan:* $3231. *Average need-based gift aid:* $5111. *Average non-need-based aid:* $3720. *Average indebtedness upon graduation:* $23,024.

Applying *Options:* early admission, deferred entrance. *Application fee:* $25. *Required:* high school transcript, minimum 2.0 GPA. *Application deadlines:* rolling (freshmen), rolling (transfers). *Notification:* continuous (freshmen), continuous (transfers).

Freshman Application Contact Dr. Linda B. Templeton, Director of Admissions, Indiana University Northwest, Hawthorne 100, 3400 Broadway, Gary, IN 46408-1197. *Phone:* 219-980-6767. *Toll-free phone:* 800-968-7486. *Fax:* 219-981-4219. *E-mail:* admit@iun.edu.

INDIANA UNIVERSITY–PURDUE UNIVERSITY FORT WAYNE

Fort Wayne, Indiana **www.ipfw.edu/**

- **State-supported** comprehensive, founded 1917, part of Indiana University System and Purdue University System
- **Urban** 643-acre campus
- **Endowment** $30.2 million
- **Coed** 11,110 undergraduate students, 66% full-time, 56% women, 44% men
- **Minimally difficult** entrance level, 97% of applicants were admitted

Undergraduates 7,323 full-time, 3,787 part-time. Students come from 44 states and territories, 66 other countries, 4% are from out of state, 5% African American, 2% Asian American or Pacific Islander, 3% Hispanic American, 0.4% Native American, 1% international, 7% transferred in, 6% live on campus. *Retention:* 60% of 2006 full-time freshmen returned.

Freshmen *Admission:* 3,103 applied, 3,012 admitted, 2,044 enrolled. *Average high school GPA:* 3.04. *Test scores:* SAT critical reading scores over 500: 39%; SAT math scores over 500: 47%; SAT writing scores over 500: 34%; ACT scores over 18: 79%; SAT critical reading scores over 600: 10%; SAT math scores over 600: 12%; SAT writing scores over 600: 6%; ACT scores over 24: 23%; SAT critical reading scores over 700: 1%; SAT math scores over 700: 1%; ACT scores over 30: 2%.

Faculty *Total:* 775, 49% full-time, 49% with terminal degrees. *Student/faculty ratio:* 17:1.

Majors Accounting; anthropology; architectural engineering technology; art teacher education; audiology and hearing sciences; biology/biological sciences; biology teacher education; business administration and management; business/managerial economics; chemical technology; chemistry; chemistry teacher education; civil engineering; civil engineering technology; clinical laboratory science/medical technology; commercial and advertising art; communication and media related; communication/speech communication and rhetoric; community health services counseling; computational mathematics; computer engineering; computer engineering technology; computer science; computer software and media applications related; construction engineering technology; crafts, folk art and artisanry; criminal justice/law enforcement administration; criminal justice/safety; dental hygiene; dental laboratory technology; dramatic/theater arts; drawing; early childhood education; economics; education; electrical, electronic and communications engineering technology; electrical, electronics and communications engineering; elementary education; English; English composition; English/language arts teacher education; English literature (British and Commonwealth); finance; fine/studio arts; French; French language teacher education; general studies; geology/earth science; German; German language teacher education; graphic design; health/health care administration; health services administration; history; history teacher education; hospitality administration; human services; industrial technology; information science/studies; interior design; labor studies; mass communication/media; mathematics; mathematics and computer science; mathematics teacher education; mechanical engineering; mechanical engineering/mechanical technology; music; music teacher education; music therapy; nursing (registered nurse training); operations management; organizational communication; painting; philosophy; photography; physics; physics teacher education; piano and organ; political science and government; pre-dentistry studies; premedical studies; printmaking; psychology; public administration; public administration and social service professions related; public policy analysis; science teacher education; sculpture; secondary education; social studies teacher education; sociology; Spanish; Spanish language teacher education; speech teacher education; statistics; substance abuse/addiction counseling; technical and business writing; women's studies.

Academics *Calendar:* semesters. *Degrees:* certificates, associate, bachelor's, master's, and postbachelor's certificates. *Special study options:* academic remediation for entering students, accelerated degree program, adult/continuing education programs, advanced placement credit, cooperative education, distance learning, double majors, English as a second language, honors programs, independent study, internships, off-campus study, part-time degree program, services for LD students, student-designed majors, study abroad, summer session for credit.

Computers on Campus 472 computers/terminals are available on campus for general student use. Students can access the following: computer help desk, free student e-mail accounts, online (class) grades, online (class) registration, online (class) schedules, student academic records. Campuswide network is available. 100% of college-owned or -operated housing units are wired for high-speed Internet access. Wireless service is available via entire campus.

Student Life *Housing options:* coed. Campus housing is provided by a third party. *Activities and organizations:* drama/theater group, student-run newspaper, television station, choral group, Campus Ministry, Hispanos Unidos, Sigma Gamma Epsilon, Psi Chi, Upsilon Pi Epsilon. *Campus security:* 24-hour emergency response devices and patrols, late-night transport/escort service, controlled dormitory access. *Student services:* health clinic, personal/psychological counseling, women's center.

Athletics Member NCAA. All Division I. *Intercollegiate sports:* baseball M (s), basketball M (s)/W (s), cross-country running M (s)/W (s), golf M (s)/W (s), soccer M (s)/W (s), softball W (s), tennis M (s)/W (s), track and field W (s), volleyball M (s)/W (s). *Intramural sports:* basketball M/W, football M, golf M/W, racquetball M/W, soccer M/W, softball W, table tennis M/W, tennis M/W, volleyball M/W.

Standardized Tests *Required:* SAT or ACT (for admission).

Costs (2007–08) *Tuition:* state resident $4982 full-time, $185 per credit hour part-time; nonresident $12,500 full-time, $463 per credit hour part-time. Full-time tuition and fees vary according to course load and student level. Part-time tuition and fees vary according to course load and student level. *Required fees:* $699 full-time, $26 per credit hour part-time. *Room only:* $5140. Room and board charges vary according to housing facility. *Payment plans:* installment, deferred payment. *Waivers:* senior citizens and employees or children of employees.

Financial Aid Of all full-time matriculated undergraduates who enrolled in 2004, 5,029 applied for aid, 4,022 were judged to have need, 352 had their need fully met. 171 Federal Work-Study jobs (averaging $1584). In 2004, 1180 non-need-based awards were made. *Average percent of need met:* 78%. *Average financial aid package:* $5976. *Average need-based loan:* $3028. *Average need-based gift aid:* $4049. *Average non-need-based aid:* $1806. *Average indebtedness upon graduation:* $16,880.

Applying *Options:* electronic application, early admission, deferred entrance. *Application fee:* $30. *Required:* high school transcript. *Recommended:* rank in upper 50% of high school class. *Application deadlines:* 8/1 (freshmen), 8/1 (transfers). *Notification:* continuous (freshmen), continuous (transfers).

Freshman Application Contact Ms. Carol Isaacs, Director of Admissions, Indiana University–Purdue University Fort Wayne, 2101 East Coliseum Boulevard, Fort Wayne, IN 46805-1499. *Phone:* 260-481-6812. *Toll-free phone:* 800-324-4739. *Fax:* 260-481-6880. *E-mail:* Ask@ipfw.edu.

INDIANA UNIVERSITY–PURDUE UNIVERSITY INDIANAPOLIS

Indianapolis, Indiana **www.iupui.edu/**

- **State-supported** university, founded 1969, part of Indiana University System
- **Urban** 509-acre campus
- **Endowment** $538.7 million
- **Coed** 21,202 undergraduate students, 68% full-time, 59% women, 41% men
- **Moderately difficult** entrance level, 71% of applicants were admitted

Undergraduates 14,408 full-time, 6,794 part-time. 2% are from out of state, 10% African American, 3% Asian American or Pacific Islander, 3% Hispanic American, 0.3% Native American, 2% international, 8% transferred in, 1% live on campus. *Retention:* 66% of 2006 full-time freshmen returned.

Freshmen *Admission:* 7,958 applied, 5,616 admitted, 2,931 enrolled. *Average high school GPA:* 3.14. *Test scores:* SAT critical reading scores over 500: 44%; SAT math scores over 500: 51%; ACT scores over 18: 81%; SAT critical reading scores over 600: 11%; SAT math scores over 600: 14%; ACT scores over 24: 25%; SAT critical reading scores over 700: 1%; SAT math scores over 700: 1%; ACT scores over 30: 3%.

Faculty *Total:* 3,161, 70% full-time, 65% with terminal degrees. *Student/faculty ratio:* 17:1.

Majors Anthropology; architectural drafting and CAD/CADD; architectural engineering technology; art history, criticism and conservation; art teacher education; biological and physical sciences; biology/biological sciences; biomedical/medical engineering; biomedical technology; biotechnology; business/commerce; chemistry; civil engineering technology; clinical laboratory science/medical technology; communication/speech communication and rhetoric; computer and information sciences; computer and information sciences and support services related; computer engineering; computer engineering technology; criminal justice/safety; cytotechnology; dental hygiene; dental services and allied professions related; digital communication and media/multimedia; early childhood education; economics; education; electrical, electronic and communications engineering technology; electrical, electronics and communications engineering; elementary education; emergency medical technology (EMT paramedic); engineering; English; English/language arts teacher education; environmental science; fine/studio arts; forensic science and technology; French; French language teacher education; general studies; geography; geology/earth science; German; German language teacher education; health/health care administration; health information/medical records administration; health services administration; health teacher education; histologic technician; history; hospitality administration related; information technology; interior design; international relations and affairs; journalism; labor and industrial relations; labor studies; liberal arts and sciences/liberal studies; management information systems and services related; mathematics; mechanical drafting and CAD/CADD; mechanical engineering; mechanical engineering/mechanical technology; medical radiologic technology; multi-/interdisciplinary studies related; nuclear medical technology; nursing (registered nurse training); occupational therapy; operations management; philosophy; physical education teaching and coaching; physics; political science and government; psychology; public administration; public health related; radiation protection/health physics technology; radiologic technology/science; religious studies; respiratory care therapy; robotics technology; secondary education; sign language interpretation and translation; social studies teacher education; social work; sociology; Spanish; Spanish language teacher education; speech teacher education; tourism and travel services management.

Academics *Calendar:* semesters. *Degrees:* certificates, associate, bachelor's, master's, doctoral, first professional, and postbachelor's certificates. *Special study options:* academic remediation for entering students, accelerated degree program, adult/continuing education programs, advanced placement credit, cooperative education, distance learning, double majors, English as a second language, external degree program, honors programs, independent study, internships, off-campus study, part-time degree program, services for LD students, study abroad, summer session for credit. *ROTC:* Army (b), Navy (c), Air Force (c).

Computers on Campus Students can access the following: campus intranet, computer help desk, free student e-mail accounts, online (class) grades, online (class) registration, online (class) schedules. Campuswide network is available. Wireless service is available via entire campus.

Student Life *Housing options:* coed. Campus housing is university owned. *Activities and organizations:* drama/theater group, student-run newspaper, choral group, Undergraduate Student Assembly, Black Student Union, Student Activities Programming Board, national fraternities, national sororities. *Campus security:* 24-hour emergency response devices and patrols, late-night transport/escort service, controlled dormitory access, lighted pathways, self-defense education. *Student services:* health clinic, personal/psychological counseling, women's center.

Athletics Member NCAA. All Division I. *Intercollegiate sports:* basketball M (s)/W (s), cross-country running M (s)/W (s), golf M (s)/W, soccer M (s)/W (s), softball W (s), swimming and diving M (s)/W (s), tennis M (s)/W (s), volleyball W (s). *Intramural sports:* badminton M/W, baseball M, basketball M/W, cross-country running M/W, football M, golf M/W, racquetball M/W, soccer M/W, softball M/W, swimming and diving M/W, table tennis M/W, tennis M/W, track and field M/W, volleyball M/W, water polo M/W.

Standardized Tests *Required:* SAT or ACT (for admission).

Costs (2007–08) *Tuition:* state resident $6221 full-time, $207 per credit hour part-time; nonresident $18,275 full-time, $609 per credit hour part-time. Full-time tuition and fees vary according to course load and program. Part-time tuition and fees vary according to course load and program. *Required fees:* $630 full-time. *Room and board:* $5100; room only: $2700. Room and board charges vary according to board plan and housing facility. *Payment plans:* installment, deferred payment. *Waivers:* employees or children of employees.

Financial Aid Of all full-time matriculated undergraduates who enrolled in 2006, 10,167 applied for aid, 8,542 were judged to have need, 516 had their need fully met. In 2006, 921 non-need-based awards were made. *Average percent of need met:* 54%. *Average financial aid package:* $7664. *Average need-based loan:* $3807. *Average need-based gift aid:* $5623. *Average non-need-based aid:* $2711. *Average indebtedness upon graduation:* $25,007.

Applying *Options:* electronic application, early admission, deferred entrance. *Application fee:* $50. *Required:* high school transcript. *Required for some:* interview. *Recommended:* portfolio for art program. *Application deadlines:* 6/1 (freshmen), rolling (transfers). *Notification:* continuous (freshmen), continuous (transfers).

Freshman Application Contact Mr. Chris J. Foley, Director of Admissions, Indiana University–Purdue University Indianapolis, 425 North University Boulevard, Cavanaugh Hall Room 129, Indianapolis, IN 46202-5143. *Phone:* 317-274-4591. *Fax:* 317-278-1862. *E-mail:* apply@iupui.edu.

INDIANA UNIVERSITY SOUTH BEND

South Bend, Indiana **www.iusb.edu/**

- **State-supported** comprehensive, founded 1922, part of Indiana University System
- **Suburban** 80-acre campus with easy access to Chicago
- **Endowment** $10.7 million

- **Coed** 6,440 undergraduate students, 57% full-time, 62% women, 38% men
- **Moderately difficult** entrance level, 83% of applicants were admitted

Undergraduates 3,686 full-time, 2,754 part-time. 4% are from out of state, 7% African American, 1% Asian American or Pacific Islander, 4% Hispanic American, 0.5% Native American, 2% international, 8% transferred in. *Retention:* 63% of 2006 full-time freshmen returned.

Freshmen *Admission:* 1,905 applied, 1,588 admitted, 1,065 enrolled. *Average high school GPA:* 2.86. *Test scores:* SAT critical reading scores over 500: 38%; SAT math scores over 500: 38%; ACT scores over 18: 73%; SAT critical reading scores over 600: 7%; SAT math scores over 600: 7%; ACT scores over 24: 16%; SAT critical reading scores over 700: 1%; ACT scores over 30: 1%.

Faculty *Total:* 551, 50% full-time, 44% with terminal degrees. *Student/faculty ratio:* 14:1.

Majors Actuarial science; applied mathematics; art; biochemistry; biology/biological sciences; biology teacher education; business/commerce; chemistry; chemistry teacher education; clinical laboratory science/medical technology; clinical/medical laboratory technology; computer and information sciences; computer programming (specific applications); criminal justice/safety; cytotechnology; dental hygiene; dramatic/theater arts; dramatic/theater arts and stagecraft related; early childhood education; economics; education; elementary education; emergency medical technology (EMT paramedic); English; English/language arts teacher education; fine/studio arts; French; general studies; German; health information/medical records administration; health information/medical records technology; health services administration; histologic technician; history; labor studies; liberal arts and sciences/liberal studies; mass communication/media; mathematics; mathematics teacher education; medical radiologic technology; music performance; music related; music teacher education; nuclear medical technology; nursing (registered nurse training); philosophy; physics; physics teacher education; political science and government; psychology; public administration; radiation protection/health physics technology; radiologic technology/science; respiratory care therapy; science teacher education; secondary education; social studies teacher education; sociology; Spanish; Spanish language teacher education; special education; speech and rhetoric; women's studies.

Academics *Calendar:* semesters. *Degrees:* certificates, diplomas, associate, bachelor's, master's, and postbachelor's certificates. *Special study options:* accelerated degree program, adult/continuing education programs, distance learning, double majors, English as a second language, external degree program, honors programs, internships, off-campus study, part-time degree program, study abroad, summer session for credit. *ROTC:* Army (c), Navy (c), Air Force (c).

Computers on Campus Students can access the following: campus intranet, computer help desk, free student e-mail accounts, online (class) grades, online (class) registration, online (class) schedules. Campuswide network is available. Wireless service is available via entire campus.

Student Life *Housing:* college housing not available. *Activities and organizations:* drama/theater group, student-run newspaper, choral group, national fraternities. *Campus security:* 24-hour emergency response devices and patrols, late-night transport/escort service, safety seminars, lighted pathways. *Student services:* personal/psychological counseling, women's center.

Athletics Member NAIA. *Intercollegiate sports:* basketball M (s)/W (s). *Intramural sports:* badminton M/W, baseball M, basketball M/W, cross-country running M/W, golf M/W, racquetball M/W, soccer M/W, volleyball M/W.

Standardized Tests *Required:* SAT or ACT (for admission).

Costs (2007–08) *Tuition:* state resident $5069 full-time, $169 per credit hour part-time; nonresident $13,496 full-time, $450 per credit hour part-time. Full-time tuition and fees vary according to course load and program. Part-time tuition and fees vary according to course load and program. *Required fees:* $422 full-time. *Payment plan:* deferred payment. *Waivers:* employees or children of employees.

Financial Aid Of all full-time matriculated undergraduates who enrolled in 2006, 2,708 applied for aid, 2,156 were judged to have need, 207 had their need fully met. In 2006, 97 non-need-based awards were made. *Average percent of need met:* 60%. *Average financial aid package:* $6507. *Average need-based loan:* $3304. *Average need-based gift aid:* $4864. *Average non-need-based aid:* $3002. *Average indebtedness upon graduation:* $20,540. *Financial aid deadline:* 3/1.

Applying *Options:* deferred entrance. *Application fee:* $47. *Required:* high school transcript, minimum 2.0 GPA. *Required for some:* interview. *Application deadlines:* rolling (freshmen), rolling (transfers). *Notification:* continuous (freshmen), continuous (transfers).

Freshman Application Contact Mr. Jeff Johnston, Director of Recruitment/Admissions, Indiana University South Bend, 1700 Mishawaka Avenue, Administration Building, Room 169, PO Box 7111, South Bend, IN 46634-7111. *Phone:* 574-237-4480. *Toll-free phone:* 877-GO-2-IUSB. *Fax:* 574-237-4834. *E-mail:* admissio@iusb.edu.

INDIANA UNIVERSITY SOUTHEAST

New Albany, Indiana **www.ius.edu/**

- **State-supported** comprehensive, founded 1941, part of Indiana University System
- **Suburban** 177-acre campus with easy access to Louisville
- **Endowment** $14.2 million
- **Coed** 5,434 undergraduate students, 61% full-time, 62% women, 38% men
- **Minimally difficult** entrance level, 89% of applicants were admitted

Undergraduates 3,303 full-time, 2,131 part-time. 25% are from out of state, 5% African American, 1% Asian American or Pacific Islander, 2% Hispanic American, 0.5% Native American, 0.3% international, 8% transferred in. *Retention:* 62% of 2006 full-time freshmen returned.

Freshmen *Admission:* 1,431 applied, 1,273 admitted, 878 enrolled. *Average high school GPA:* 2.9. *Test scores:* SAT critical reading scores over 500: 40%; SAT math scores over 500: 38%; ACT scores over 18: 78%; SAT critical reading scores over 600: 10%; SAT math scores over 600: 7%; ACT scores over 24: 16%; SAT critical reading scores over 700: 2%; SAT math scores over 700: 1%; ACT scores over 30: 2%.

Faculty *Total:* 435, 44% full-time, 43% with terminal degrees. *Student/faculty ratio:* 16:1.

Majors Art; biology/biological sciences; business/commerce; chemistry; chemistry teacher education; clinical laboratory science/medical technology; communication/speech communication and rhetoric; computer and information sciences; computer programming (specific applications); criminal justice/safety; cytotechnology; economics; elementary education; emergency medical technology (EMT paramedic); English; English/language arts teacher education; fine/studio arts; French; general studies; geography; German; health information/medical records administration; health teacher education; history; information technology; international relations and affairs; journalism; liberal arts and sciences/liberal studies; mathematics; mathematics teacher education; medical radiologic technology; multi-/interdisciplinary studies related; music; nuclear medical technology; nursing (registered nurse training); occupational safety and health technology; parks, recreation, and leisure related; philosophy; physical therapy; political science and government; psychology; radiation protection/health physics technology; radiologic technology/science; respiratory care therapy; secondary education; social studies teacher education; sociology; Spanish; special education.

Academics *Calendar:* semesters. *Degrees:* certificates, associate, bachelor's, master's, and postbachelor's certificates. *Special study options:* academic remediation for entering students, accelerated degree program, adult/continuing education programs, advanced placement credit, double majors, external degree program, independent study, internships, off-campus study, part-time degree program, services for LD students, student-designed majors, study abroad, summer session for credit. *ROTC:* Army (b), Navy (b).

Computers on Campus Students can access the following: campus intranet, computer help desk, free student e-mail accounts, online (class) grades, online (class) registration, online (class) schedules. Campuswide network is available. Wireless service is available via entire campus.

Student Life *Housing:* college housing not available. *Activities and organizations:* drama/theater group, student-run newspaper, choral group, national fraternities, national sororities. *Campus security:* 24-hour emergency response devices and patrols, self-defense education, lighted pathways, police department on campus. *Student services:* personal/psychological counseling.

Athletics Member NAIA. *Intercollegiate sports:* baseball M, basketball M (s)/W (s), softball W, tennis M/W, volleyball W (s). *Intramural sports:* basketball M/W, bowling M/W, cross-country running M/W, softball M/W, tennis M/W, volleyball W.

Standardized Tests *Required:* SAT or ACT (for admission).

Costs (2007–08) *Tuition:* state resident $4934 full-time, $164 per credit hour part-time; nonresident $12,471 full-time, $416 per credit hour part-time. Full-time tuition and fees vary according to course load, program, and reciprocity agreements. Part-time tuition and fees vary according to course load, program, and reciprocity agreements. *Required fees:* $442 full-time. *Payment plan:* deferred payment. *Waivers:* employees or children of employees.

Financial Aid Of all full-time matriculated undergraduates who enrolled in 2006, 2,246 applied for aid, 1,784 were judged to have need, 160 had their need fully met. In 2006, 167 non-need-based awards were made. *Average percent of need met:* 61%. *Average financial aid package:* $6266. *Average need-based loan:* $3588. *Average need-based gift aid:* $4564. *Average non-need-based aid:* $1627. *Average indebtedness upon graduation:* $19,526.

Applying *Options:* early admission, deferred entrance. *Application fee:* $30. *Required:* high school transcript. *Required for some:* interview. *Application* *deadlines:* rolling (freshmen), rolling (transfers). *Notification:* continuous (freshmen), continuous (transfers).

Freshman Application Contact Ms. Anne Skuce, Director of Admissions, Indiana University Southeast, University Center Building, Room 100, 4201 Grant Line Road, New Albany, IN 47150. *Phone:* 812-941-2212. *Toll-free phone:* 800-852-8835. *Fax:* 812-941-2595. *E-mail:* admissions@ius.edu.

INDIANA WESLEYAN UNIVERSITY

Marion, Indiana **www.indwes.edu/**

- **Independent Wesleyan** comprehensive, founded 1920
- **Small-town** 132-acre campus with easy access to Indianapolis
- **Endowment** $48.0 million
- **Coed** 3,050 undergraduate students, 92% full-time, 63% women, 37% men
- **Moderately difficult** entrance level, 81% of applicants were admitted

Undergraduates 2,795 full-time, 255 part-time. Students come from 48 states and territories, 14 other countries, 45% are from out of state, 1% African American, 0.6% Asian American or Pacific Islander, 1% Hispanic American, 0.2% Native American, 0.4% international, 4% transferred in, 80% live on campus. *Retention:* 82% of 2006 full-time freshmen returned.

Freshmen *Admission:* 2,261 applied, 1,838 admitted, 747 enrolled. *Average high school GPA:* 3.63. *Test scores:* SAT critical reading scores over 500: 66%; SAT math scores over 500: 67%; ACT scores over 18: 95%; SAT critical reading scores over 600: 26%; SAT math scores over 600: 26%; ACT scores over 24: 56%; SAT critical reading scores over 700: 4%; SAT math scores over 700: 3%; ACT scores over 30: 8%.

Faculty *Total:* 249, 61% full-time, 39% with terminal degrees. *Student/faculty ratio:* 15:1.

Majors Accounting; ancient Near Eastern and biblical languages; art; art teacher education; athletic training; biblical studies; biology/biological sciences; business administration and management; ceramic arts and ceramics; chemistry; clinical laboratory science/medical technology; communication/speech communication and rhetoric; computer and information sciences; computer graphics; creative writing; criminal justice/safety; cultural studies; economics; education; education (K-12); elementary education; English; English/language arts teacher education; finance; general studies; history; kinesiology and exercise science; marketing/marketing management; mathematics; mathematics teacher education; middle school education; music; music teacher education; music theory and composition; nursing (registered nurse training); painting; parks, recreation and leisure facilities management; pastoral studies/counseling; philosophy; photography; physical education teaching and coaching; political science and government; pre-dentistry studies; pre-law studies; pre-medical studies; pre-veterinary studies; printmaking; psychology; religious education; religious/sacred music; science teacher education; secondary education; social sciences; social studies teacher education; social work; sociology; Spanish; special education; sport and fitness administration/management; substance abuse/addiction counseling; theology.

Academics *Calendar:* 4-4-1. *Degrees:* associate, bachelor's, master's, doctoral, post-master's, and postbachelor's certificates (also offers adult program with significant enrollment not reflected in profile). *Special study options:* academic remediation for entering students, accelerated degree program, adult/continuing education programs, advanced placement credit, distance learning, double majors, freshman honors college, honors programs, independent study, internships, off-campus study, part-time degree program, services for LD students, student-designed majors, study abroad, summer session for credit. *ROTC:* Army (c).

Computers on Campus Students can access the following: campus intranet, computer help desk, free student e-mail accounts, online (class) grades, online (class) schedules. Campuswide network is available. 100% of college-owned or -operated housing units are wired for high-speed Internet access. Wireless service is available via classrooms, computer centers, computer labs, learning centers, libraries, student centers.

Student Life *Housing:* on-campus residence required through junior year. *Options:* men-only, women-only. Campus housing is university owned. Freshman campus housing is guaranteed. *Activities and organizations:* drama/theater group, student-run newspaper, radio and television station, choral group, Student Government Organization, Student Activities Council, University Players, World Christian Fellowship, International Student Association. *Campus security:* 24-hour emergency response devices and patrols, late-night transport/escort service, controlled dormitory access. *Student services:* health clinic, personal/psychological counseling.

Athletics Member NAIA, NCCAA. *Intercollegiate sports:* baseball M (s), basketball M (s)/W (s), cheerleading M (s)/W (s), cross-country running M (s)/W (s), golf M (s), soccer M (s)/W (s), softball W (s), tennis M (s)/W (s), track and field M (s)/W (s), volleyball W (s). *Intramural sports:* badminton M/W, basketball M/W, bowling M/W, football M/W, golf M/W, racquetball M/W, soccer M/W, softball M, table tennis M/W, tennis M/W, ultimate Frisbee M/W, volleyball M/W, weight lifting M/W.

Standardized Tests *Required:* SAT or ACT (for admission).

Costs (2008–09) *Comprehensive fee:* $25,940 includes full-time tuition ($19,376) and room and board ($6564). Part-time tuition: $692 per credit hour.

Applying *Options:* electronic application, deferred entrance. *Application fee:* $25. *Required:* essay or personal statement, high school transcript, minimum 2.0 GPA, 1 letter of recommendation. *Required for some:* interview. *Application deadlines:* rolling (freshmen), rolling (transfers). *Notification:* continuous (freshmen), continuous (transfers).

Freshman Application Contact Mr. Daniel Solms, Director of Admissions, Indiana Wesleyan University, 4201 South Washington Street, Marion, IN 46953. *Phone:* 866-GO TO IWU Ext. 2138. *Toll-free phone:* 800-332-6901. *Fax:* 765-677-2333. *E-mail:* admissions@indwes.edu.

INTERNATIONAL BUSINESS COLLEGE

Fort Wayne, Indiana **www.ibcfortwayne.edu/**

- **Proprietary** primarily 2-year, founded 1889, part of Bradford Schools, Inc
- **Suburban** campus
- **Coed**
- 86% of applicants were admitted

Academics *Calendar:* semesters. *Degrees:* diplomas, associate, and bachelor's.

Freshman Application Contact Admissions Office, International Business College, 5699 Coventry Lane, Fort Wayne, IN 46804. *Phone:* 260-459-4500. *Toll-free phone:* 800-589-6363. *Fax:* 260-436-1896.

ITT TECHNICAL INSTITUTE

Fort Wayne, Indiana **www.itt-tech.edu/**

- **Proprietary** primarily 2-year, founded 1967, part of ITT Educational Services, Inc
- **Coed**
- **Minimally difficult** entrance level

Academics *Calendar:* quarters. *Degrees:* associate and bachelor's.

Standardized Tests *Required:* Wonderlic aptitude test (for admission).

Applying *Options:* deferred entrance. *Application fee:* $100. *Required:* high school transcript, interview. *Recommended:* letters of recommendation.

Freshman Application Contact Mr. Mike Cavins, Director of Recruitment, ITT Technical Institute, 2810 Dupont Commerce Court, Fort Wayne, IN 46825. *Phone:* 260-497-6200. *Toll-free phone:* 800-866-4488. *Fax:* 260-497-6299.

ITT TECHNICAL INSTITUTE

Indianapolis, Indiana **www.itt-tech.edu/**

- **Proprietary** founded 1966, part of ITT Educational Services, Inc
- **Suburban** 10-acre campus
- **Coed**
- **Minimally difficult** entrance level

Academics *Calendar:* quarters. *Degrees:* diplomas, associate, and bachelor's.

Standardized Tests *Required:* Wonderlic aptitude test (for admission).

Applying *Options:* deferred entrance. *Application fee:* $100. *Required:* high school transcript, interview. *Recommended:* letters of recommendation.

Freshman Application Contact Mr. James Mills, Director of Recruitment, ITT Technical Institute, 9511 Angola Court, Indianapolis, IN 46268. *Phone:* 317-875-8640. *Toll-free phone:* 800-937-4488.

ITT TECHNICAL INSTITUTE

Newburgh, Indiana **www.itt-tech.edu/**

- **Proprietary** primarily 2-year, founded 1966, part of ITT Educational Services, Inc
- **Coed**
- **Minimally difficult** entrance level

Academics *Calendar:* quarters. *Degrees:* associate and bachelor's.

Standardized Tests *Required:* Wonderlic aptitude test (for admission).
Applying *Options:* deferred entrance. *Application fee:* $100. *Required:* high school transcript, interview. *Recommended:* letters of recommendation.
Freshman Application Contact Mr. Thomas Montgomery, Director of Recruitment, ITT Technical Institute, 10999 Stahl Road, Newburgh, IN 47630. *Phone:* 812-858-1600. *Toll-free phone:* 800-832-4488.

IVY TECH COMMUNITY COLLEGE–NORTHWEST

Gary, Indiana **www.ivytech.edu/**

Freshman Application Contact Ms. Twilla Lewis, Associate Dean of Student Affairs, Ivy Tech Community College–Northwest, 1440 East 35th Avenue, Gary, IN 46409-1499. *Phone:* 219-981-1111 Ext. 2273. *Toll-free phone:* 800-843-4882. *Fax:* 219-981-4415. *E-mail:* tlewis@ivytech.edu.

MANCHESTER COLLEGE

North Manchester, Indiana **www.manchester.edu/**

- **Independent** 4-year, founded 1889, affiliated with Church of the Brethren
- **Small-town** 125-acre campus
- **Endowment** $36.8 million
- **Coed** 1,035 undergraduate students, 97% full-time, 50% women, 50% men
- **Moderately difficult** entrance level, 73% of applicants were admitted

Undergraduates 1,008 full-time, 27 part-time. Students come from 28 states and territories, 26 other countries, 10% are from out of state, 4% African American, 0.8% Asian American or Pacific Islander, 2% Hispanic American, 0.6% Native American, 4% international, 1% transferred in, 75% live on campus.
Freshmen *Admission:* 1,636 applied, 1,202 admitted, 317 enrolled. *Test scores:* SAT critical reading scores over 500: 46%; SAT math scores over 500: 57%; SAT writing scores over 500: 43%; ACT scores over 18: 84%; SAT critical reading scores over 600: 11%; SAT math scores over 600: 18%; SAT writing scores over 600: 10%; ACT scores over 24: 32%; SAT critical reading scores over 700: 3%; SAT math scores over 700: 3%; SAT writing scores over 700: 1%; ACT scores over 30: 4%.
Faculty *Total:* 87, 79% full-time, 80% with terminal degrees. *Student/faculty ratio:* 13:1.
Majors Accounting; art; art teacher education; athletic training; biology/biological sciences; broadcast journalism; business administration and management; business/commerce; chemistry; clinical laboratory science/medical technology; computer science; creative writing; criminal justice/safety; dramatic/theater arts; ecology; economics; education; elementary education; engineering science; English; environmental studies; finance; fine/studio arts; French; German; gerontology; health science; health teacher education; history; interdisciplinary studies; journalism; kindergarten/preschool education; kinesiology and exercise science; literature; marketing/marketing management; mass communication/media; mathematics; music; music teacher education; non-profit management; peace studies and conflict resolution; philosophy; physical education teaching and coaching; physics; political science and government; pre-dentistry studies; pre-law studies; pre-medical studies; pre-theology/pre-ministerial studies; pre-veterinary studies; psychology; religious studies; science teacher education; secondary education; social work; sociology; Spanish; special education; speech and rhetoric.
Academics *Calendar:* 4-1-4. *Degrees:* associate, bachelor's, and master's. *Special study options:* adult/continuing education programs, advanced placement credit, double majors, honors programs, independent study, internships, off-campus study, part-time degree program, services for LD students, student-designed majors, study abroad, summer session for credit. *Unusual degree programs:* 3-2 engineering with Washington University in St. Louis; nursing with Goshen College; physical therapy, occupational therapy.
Computers on Campus 168 computers/terminals are available on campus for general student use. Campuswide network is available.
Student Life *Housing:* on-campus residence required through junior year. *Options:* coed, women-only, disabled students. Campus housing is university owned. Freshman campus housing is guaranteed. *Activities and organizations:* drama/theater group, student-run newspaper, radio station, choral group, volunteer services, Campus Ministry Board, Accounting Club, Manchester Admissions Recruiting Corps, Student Alumni Council. *Campus security:* 24-hour emergency response devices and patrols, student patrols, late-night transport/escort service, alarm system, locked residence hall entrances. *Student services:* health clinic, personal/psychological counseling.
Athletics Member NCAA. All Division III. *Intercollegiate sports:* baseball M, basketball M/W, cheerleading M/W, cross-country running M/W, football M, golf M/W, soccer M/W, softball W, tennis M/W, track and field M/W, volleyball W, wrestling M. *Intramural sports:* badminton M/W, basketball M/W, bowling M/W, football M/W, racquetball M/W, soccer M/W, table tennis M/W, tennis M/W, track and field M/W, ultimate Frisbee M/W, volleyball M/W.
Standardized Tests *Required:* SAT or ACT (for admission).
Costs (2007–08) *One-time required fee:* $225. *Comprehensive fee:* $30,225 includes full-time tuition ($21,000), mandatory fees ($1025), and room and board ($8200). Part-time tuition: $670 per credit hour. Part-time tuition and fees vary according to course load. *Required fees:* $350 per year part-time. *College room only:* $5250. Room and board charges vary according to board plan and housing facility. *Payment plan:* installment. *Waivers:* employees or children of employees.
Financial Aid Of all full-time matriculated undergraduates who enrolled in 2007, 920 applied for aid, 726 were judged to have need, 267 had their need fully met. 495 Federal Work-Study jobs (averaging $1500). In 2007, 108 non-need-based awards were made. *Average percent of need met:* 93%. *Average financial aid package:* $20,866. *Average need-based loan:* $5528. *Average need-based gift aid:* $14,476. *Average non-need-based aid:* $9221. *Average indebtedness upon graduation:* $14,591.
Applying *Options:* electronic application, deferred entrance. *Application fee:* $25. *Required:* high school transcript, 1 letter of recommendation, rank in upper 50% of high school class. *Required for some:* essay or personal statement, minimum 3.0 GPA, interview. *Recommended:* minimum 2.3 GPA, interview. *Application deadlines:* rolling (freshmen), rolling (transfers). *Notification:* continuous (freshmen), continuous (transfers).
Freshman Application Contact Mr. Adam Hohman, Assistant Director of Admissions, Manchester College, 604 East College Avenue, North Manchester, IN 46962. *Phone:* 260-982-5055. *Toll-free phone:* 800-852-3648. *Fax:* 260-982-5239. *E-mail:* admitinfo@manchester.edu.

See page 934 for the College Close-Up.

MARIAN COLLEGE

Indianapolis, Indiana **www.marian.edu/**

- **Independent Roman Catholic** comprehensive, founded 1851
- **Suburban** 114-acre campus
- **Endowment** $14.6 million
- **Coed** 1,982 undergraduate students, 71% full-time, 68% women, 32% men
- **Moderately difficult** entrance level, 62% of applicants were admitted

Undergraduates 1,415 full-time, 567 part-time. Students come from 21 states and territories, 6 other countries, 7% are from out of state, 18% transferred in, 35% live on campus. *Retention:* 76% of 2006 full-time freshmen returned.
Freshmen *Admission:* 1,376 applied, 851 admitted, 286 enrolled. *Average high school GPA:* 3.23. *Test scores:* SAT critical reading scores over 500: 51%; SAT math scores over 500: 56%; SAT critical reading scores over 600: 15%; SAT math scores over 600: 16%; SAT critical reading scores over 700: 1%; SAT math scores over 700: 1%.
Faculty *Total:* 156, 51% full-time, 32% with terminal degrees. *Student/faculty ratio:* 15:1.
Majors Accounting; art history, criticism and conservation; arts management; art teacher education; biology/biological sciences; business administration and management; chemistry; Christian studies; commercial and advertising art; communication/speech communication and rhetoric; economics; education; elementary education; English; finance; fine/studio arts; French; history; human resources management; interior design; liberal arts and sciences/liberal studies; marketing/marketing management; mass communication/media; mathematics; music; music teacher education; nursing (registered nurse training); pastoral studies/counseling; philosophy; physical education teaching and coaching; political science and government; pre-dentistry studies; pre-engineering; pre-law studies; pre-medical studies; pre-veterinary studies; psychology; religious education; secondary education; sociology; Spanish; special education; sport and fitness administration/management; theology.
Academics *Calendar:* semesters. *Degrees:* associate, bachelor's, and master's. *Special study options:* academic remediation for entering students, accelerated degree program, adult/continuing education programs, advanced placement credit, cooperative education, double majors, English as a second language, honors programs, independent study, internships, off-campus study, part-time degree program, services for LD students, study abroad, summer session for credit. *ROTC:* Army (c).

Computers on Campus 225 computers/terminals and 8 ports are available on campus for general student use. Students can access the following: computer help desk, free student e-mail accounts, online (class) grades, online (class) registration, online (class) schedules. Campuswide network is available. 100% of college-owned or -operated housing units are wired for high-speed Internet access. Wireless service is available via entire campus.

Student Life *Housing:* on-campus residence required through junior year. *Options:* coed, cooperative, disabled students. Campus housing is university owned. Freshman campus housing is guaranteed. *Activities and organizations:* drama/theater group, student-run newspaper, choral group, Marian College Student Association (student government), Booster Club, Best Buddies, College Mentors for Kids, Sophia Club. *Campus security:* 24-hour patrols, late-night transport/escort service, controlled dormitory access. *Student services:* health clinic, personal/psychological counseling.

Athletics Member NAIA. *Intercollegiate sports:* baseball M (s), basketball M (s)/W (s), cheerleading M (s)/W (s), cross-country running M (s)/W (s), football M (s), golf M (s)/W (s), soccer M (s)/W (s), softball W (s), tennis M (s)/W (s), track and field M (s)/W (s), volleyball W (s). *Intramural sports:* basketball M/W, fencing M/W, football M/W, racquetball M/W, table tennis M/W, tennis M/W, ultimate Frisbee M/W, volleyball M/W.

Standardized Tests *Required:* SAT or ACT (for admission).

Costs (2007–08) *Comprehensive fee:* $28,200 includes full-time tuition ($20,800) and room and board ($7400). Full-time tuition and fees vary according to course load. Part-time tuition: $870 per credit hour. Part-time tuition and fees vary according to course load. *Room and board:* Room and board charges vary according to board plan and housing facility. *Payment plan:* installment. *Waivers:* children of alumni, senior citizens, and employees or children of employees.

Financial Aid Of all full-time matriculated undergraduates who enrolled in 2005, 959 applied for aid, 861 were judged to have need, 287 had their need fully met. 200 Federal Work-Study jobs (averaging $1500). In 2005, 128 non-need-based awards were made. *Average percent of need met:* 72%. *Average financial aid package:* $15,345. *Average need-based loan:* $3302. *Average need-based gift aid:* $5044. *Average non-need-based aid:* $6901. *Average indebtedness upon graduation:* $14,815.

Applying *Options:* electronic application, early admission, deferred entrance. *Application fee:* $20. *Required:* high school transcript, minimum 2.3 GPA. *Required for some:* essay or personal statement, letters of recommendation, interview. *Application deadlines:* 8/1 (freshmen), 8/1 (transfers). *Notification:* continuous until 8/24 (freshmen), continuous until 8/24 (transfers).

Freshman Application Contact Ms. Luann Brames, Marian College, 3200 Cold Spring Road, Indianapolis, IN 46222-1997. *Phone:* 317-955-6300. *Toll-free phone:* 800-772-7264. *Fax:* 317-955-6401. *E-mail:* admissions@marian.edu.

MARTIN UNIVERSITY

Indianapolis, Indiana **www.martin.edu/**

- **Independent** comprehensive, founded 1977
- **Urban** 5-acre campus
- **Coed** 465 undergraduate students, 47% full-time, 76% women, 24% men
- **Noncompetitive** entrance level

Undergraduates 219 full-time, 246 part-time. Students come from 1 other state, 6 other countries, 92% African American, 0.2% Hispanic American, 0.2% Native American, 1% international. *Retention:* 90% of 2006 full-time freshmen returned.

Freshmen *Admission:* 156 admitted, 49 enrolled.

Faculty *Total:* 38, 84% full-time. *Student/faculty ratio:* 20:1.

Majors Accounting; adult and continuing education; African-American/Black studies; biology/biological sciences; business administration and management; chemistry; communication/speech communication and rhetoric; computer engineering technology; counselor education/school counseling and guidance; criminal justice/law enforcement administration; education; elementary education; English; fine/studio arts; history; humanities; human resources management; insurance; kindergarten/preschool education; marketing/marketing management; mathematics; music; political science and government; psychology; religious studies; secondary education; sociology; substance abuse/addiction counseling.

Academics *Calendar:* semesters. *Degrees:* bachelor's and master's. *Special study options:* academic remediation for entering students, accelerated degree program, adult/continuing education programs, advanced placement credit, double majors, honors programs, independent study, internships, off-campus study, part-time degree program, student-designed majors, summer session for credit.

Computers on Campus 20 computers/terminals are available on campus for general student use.

Student Life *Housing:* college housing not available. *Activities and organizations:* drama/theater group, choral group. *Campus security:* building security, security personnel from 7 a.m. to 9:30 p.m. *Student services:* health clinic, personal/psychological counseling.

Athletics *Intercollegiate sports:* ultimate Frisbee M (s)/W (s), volleyball M (s)/W (s). *Intramural sports:* ultimate Frisbee M/W, volleyball M/W.

Costs (2008–09) *One-time required fee:* $25. *Tuition:* $6760 full-time, $440 per credit part-time. *Required fees:* $320 full-time, $160 per semester hour part-time.

Financial Aid Of all full-time matriculated undergraduates who enrolled in 2005, 351 applied for aid, 340 were judged to have need, 21 had their need fully met. *Average percent of need met:* 78%. *Average financial aid package:* $8779. *Average need-based loan:* $3192. *Average need-based gift aid:* $6705. *Average indebtedness upon graduation:* $27,193.

Applying *Options:* early admission, deferred entrance. *Application fee:* $25. *Required:* essay or personal statement, high school transcript, interview, writing sample. *Application deadlines:* rolling (freshmen), rolling (transfers). *Notification:* continuous (freshmen), continuous (transfers).

Freshman Application Contact Ms. Brenda Shaheed, Director of Enrollment Management, Martin University, PO Box 18567, 2171 Avondale Place, Indianapolis, IN 46218-3867. *Phone:* 317-543-3237. *Fax:* 317-543-4790.

MID-AMERICA COLLEGE OF FUNERAL SERVICE

Jeffersonville, Indiana **www.mid-america.edu/**

- **Independent** primarily 2-year, founded 1905
- **Small-town** 3-acre campus with easy access to Louisville
- **Coed, primarily men**
- **Minimally difficult** entrance level

Faculty *Student/faculty ratio:* 13:1.

Academics *Calendar:* quarters. *Degrees:* associate and bachelor's.

Applying *Options:* deferred entrance. *Application fee:* $25. *Required:* high school transcript.

Freshman Application Contact Mr. Richard Nelson, Dean of Students, Mid-America College of Funeral Service, 3111 Hamburg Pike, Jeffersonville, IN 47130-9630. *Phone:* 812-288-8878. *Toll-free phone:* 800-221-6158. *Fax:* 812-288-5942. *E-mail:* macfs@mindspring.com.

OAKLAND CITY UNIVERSITY

Oakland City, Indiana **www.oak.edu/**

- **Independent General Baptist** comprehensive, founded 1885
- **Rural** 20-acre campus
- **Endowment** $3.1 million
- **Coed** 1,744 undergraduate students, 76% full-time, 55% women, 45% men
- **Minimally difficult** entrance level, 56% of applicants were admitted

Undergraduates 1,322 full-time, 422 part-time. Students come from 11 states and territories, 12 other countries, 17% are from out of state, 11% African American, 0.7% Asian American or Pacific Islander, 0.2% Hispanic American, 0.5% Native American, 0.8% international, 7% transferred in, 49% live on campus. *Retention:* 70% of 2006 full-time freshmen returned.

Freshmen *Admission:* 620 applied, 349 admitted, 349 enrolled. *Average high school GPA:* 3.15. *Test scores:* SAT critical reading scores over 500: 32%; SAT math scores over 500: 38%; SAT writing scores over 500: 34%; ACT scores over 18: 72%; SAT critical reading scores over 600: 7%; SAT math scores over 600: 7%; SAT writing scores over 600: 5%; ACT scores over 24: 19%; SAT math scores over 700: 1%; SAT writing scores over 700: 1%; ACT scores over 30: 2%.

Faculty *Total:* 178, 31% full-time, 16% with terminal degrees. *Student/faculty ratio:* 14:1.

Majors Administrative assistant and secretarial science; applied horticulture; applied mathematics; art; art teacher education; automobile/automotive mechanics technology; biblical studies; biological and physical sciences; biology/biological sciences; biology teacher education; business administration and management; business administration, management and operations related; business teacher education; chemistry; computer engineering technology; computer graphics; computer programming; computer science; criminal justice/law enforcement administration; culinary arts; divinity/ministry; early childhood education; education; elementary education; heating, air conditioning and refrigeration technology; heating, air conditioning, ventilation and refrigeration maintenance technology; humanities; human resources management; industrial design; information science/studies; interdisciplinary studies; liberal arts and sciences/liberal studies; management science; mathematics; mathematics teacher education; middle school education; music; music performance; music teacher education; organizational behavior; physical education teaching and coaching; pre-law studies; pre-medical studies; pre-veterinary studies; religious education; religious studies; science teacher education; secondary education; social sciences; social science teacher education; social studies teacher education; special education (mentally retarded); theology; welding technology.

Academics *Calendar:* semesters. *Degrees:* certificates, diplomas, associate, bachelor's, master's, doctoral, and first professional. *Special study options:* academic remediation for entering students, accelerated degree program, adult/continuing education programs, advanced placement credit, external degree program, part-time degree program, services for LD students, summer session for credit.

Computers on Campus 92 computers/terminals are available on campus for general student use. Students can access the following: campus intranet, free student e-mail accounts, online (class) grades, online (class) schedules. Campuswide network is available. 100% of college-owned or -operated housing units are wired for high-speed Internet access. Wireless service is available via entire campus.

Student Life *Housing:* on-campus residence required for freshman year. *Options:* men-only, women-only. Campus housing is university owned. Freshman campus housing is guaranteed. *Activities and organizations:* drama/theater group, student-run newspaper, choral group, Student Government Association, Good News Players, Art Guild. *Campus security:* 24-hour patrols, student patrols. *Student services:* personal/psychological counseling.

Athletics Member NCAA, NCCAA, NSCAA. All NCAA Division II. *Intercollegiate sports:* baseball M (s), basketball M (s)/W (s), cheerleading W (s), cross-country running M (s)/W (s), golf M (s)/W (s), soccer M (s)/W (s), softball W (s), tennis M (s)/W (s), volleyball W (s). *Intramural sports:* archery M/W, badminton M/W, basketball M/W, bowling M/W, football M, golf M/W, soccer M/W, softball M/W, table tennis M/W, tennis M/W, volleyball M/W.

Standardized Tests *Required:* SAT or ACT (for admission).

Costs (2007–08) *Comprehensive fee:* $20,620 includes full-time tuition ($14,460), mandatory fees ($360), and room and board ($5800). Part-time tuition: $482 per hour. *Required fees:* $15 per hour part-time. *College room only:* $1900. Room and board charges vary according to housing facility. *Waivers:* senior citizens and employees or children of employees.

Financial Aid Of all full-time matriculated undergraduates who enrolled in 2006, 150 Federal Work-Study jobs (averaging $1600). 4 state and other part-time jobs (averaging $1500). *Average percent of need met:* 90%.

Applying *Options:* early admission, deferred entrance. *Application fee:* $35. *Required:* essay or personal statement, high school transcript, minimum 2.0 GPA. *Recommended:* letters of recommendation, interview. *Application deadlines:* rolling (freshmen), rolling (transfers). *Notification:* continuous (freshmen), continuous (transfers).

Freshman Application Contact Mr. Brian Baker, Director of Admissions, Oakland City University, 138 North Lucretia Street, Oakland City, IN 47660. *Phone:* 812-749-1222. *Toll-free phone:* 800-737-5125.

PURDUE UNIVERSITY

West Lafayette, Indiana www.purdue.edu/

- **State-supported** university, founded 1869, part of Purdue University System
- **Suburban** 2307-acre campus with easy access to Indianapolis
- **Endowment** $1.5 billion
- **Coed** 31,186 undergraduate students, 95% full-time, 42% women, 58% men
- **Moderately difficult** entrance level, 79% of applicants were admitted

Undergraduates 29,688 full-time, 1,498 part-time. 26% are from out of state, 4% African American, 6% Asian American or Pacific Islander, 3% Hispanic American, 0.5% Native American, 7% international, 3% transferred in, 40% live on campus. *Retention:* 85% of 2006 full-time freshmen returned.

Freshmen *Admission:* 25,929 applied, 20,429 admitted, 6,755 enrolled. *Average high school GPA:* 3.5. *Test scores:* SAT critical reading scores over 500: 74%; SAT math scores over 500: 85%; ACT scores over 18: 98%; SAT critical reading scores over 600: 30%; SAT math scores over 600: 48%; ACT scores over 24: 67%; SAT critical reading scores over 700: 6%; SAT math scores over 700: 13%; ACT scores over 30: 18%.

Faculty *Total:* 2,387, 88% full-time, 74% with terminal degrees. *Student/faculty ratio:* 14:1.

Majors Accounting; accounting and business/management; accounting and finance; acting; actuarial science; advertising; aeronautical/aerospace engineering technology; aeronautics/aviation/aerospace science and technology; aerospace, aeronautical and astronautical engineering; African-American/Black studies; agricultural and food products processing; agricultural/biological engineering and bioengineering; agricultural communication/journalism; agricultural economics; agricultural mechanization; agricultural production; agricultural teacher education; agriculture; agronomy and crop science; airline pilot and flight crew; air traffic control; animal sciences; anthropology; apparel and textiles; applied horticulture; applied mathematics; architectural engineering technology; art; art history, criticism and conservation; art teacher education; Asian studies; athletic training; atmospheric sciences and meteorology; audiology and hearing sciences; audiology and speech-language pathology; aviation/airway management; biochemistry; biochemistry/biophysics and molecular biology; biological and physical sciences; biology/biological sciences; biology teacher education; biomedical/medical engineering; botany/plant biology; broadcast journalism; business administration and management; business/commerce; cell and molecular biology; chemical engineering; chemistry; chemistry teacher education; civil engineering; classics and languages, literatures and linguistics; clinical laboratory science/medical technology; communication/speech communication and rhetoric; computer and information sciences; computer and information sciences and support services related; computer engineering; computer engineering technology; computer graphics; computer science; computer systems networking and telecommunications; construction engineering; construction engineering technology; creative writing; criminal justice/law enforcement administration; design and visual communications; dietetic technician; dramatic/theater arts; early childhood education; education; electrical, electronic and communications engineering technology; electrical, electronics and communications engineering; elementary education; engineering/industrial management; engineering related; English; entomology; environmental science; family and community services; family and consumer sciences/home economics teacher education; family and consumer sciences/human sciences; farm and ranch management; fashion/apparel design; fashion merchandising; film/cinema studies; financial planning and services; fine/studio arts; fishing and fisheries sciences and management; food science; foods, nutrition, and wellness; foreign languages and literatures; foreign language teacher education; forestry; French language teacher education; French studies; geology/earth science; German language teacher education; German studies; health and physical education; health professions related; health services/allied health/health sciences; health teacher education; history; horticultural science; hospitality administration related; hotel/motel administration; human development and family studies; humanities; human resources management; industrial engineering; industrial technology; interdisciplinary studies; interior design; Japanese; Japanese studies; journalism; kindergarten/preschool education; kinesiology and exercise science; landscape architecture; liberal arts and sciences/liberal studies; management information systems and services related; manufacturing technology; marketing/marketing management; materials engineering; mathematics; mathematics teacher education; mechanical drafting and CAD/CADD; mechanical engineering; mechanical engineering/mechanical technology; mechanical engineering technologies related; meteorology; microbiology; molecular biology; music; natural resources/conservation; nuclear engineering; nursing (registered nurse training); nutrition sciences; occupational health and industrial hygiene; operations management; pharmacy; philosophy; photography; physical education teaching and coaching; physics; physics teacher education; plant genetics; political science and government; pre-dentistry studies; pre-medical studies; psychology; public relations/image management; religious studies; robotics technology; Russian; science teacher education; secondary education; social sciences; social studies teacher education; social work; sociology; Spanish; Spanish language teacher education; special education (early childhood); speech-language pathology; statistics; surveying engineering; survey technology; technology/industrial arts teacher education; tourism and travel services management; trade and industrial teacher education; veterinary/animal health technology; visual and performing arts; wildlife and wildlands science and management; women's studies; zoology/animal biology.

Academics *Calendar:* semesters. *Degrees:* certificates, associate, bachelor's, master's, doctoral, and first professional. *Special study options:* accelerated degree program, adult/continuing education programs, advanced placement credit, cooperative education, distance learning, double majors, English as a second language, freshman honors college, honors programs, independent study, internships, part-time degree program, services for LD students, study abroad, summer session for credit. *ROTC:* Army (b), Navy (b), Air Force (b). *Unusual degree programs:* business administration; engineering; forestry; nursing; social work; pharmacy.

Computers on Campus 1,986 computers/terminals are available on campus for general student use. Students can access the following: free student e-mail accounts, online (class) grades, online (class) schedules. Campuswide network is available. 97% of college-owned or -operated housing units are wired for high-speed Internet access. Wireless service is available via entire campus.

Student Life *Housing options:* coed, men-only, women-only, cooperative, disabled students. Campus housing is university owned. Freshman applicants given priority for college housing. *Activities and organizations:* drama/theater group, student-run newspaper, radio and television station, choral group, marching band, student government, Golden Key National Honor Society, Society of Women Engineers, Purdue student union board, Krannert Graduate Student Association, national fraternities, national sororities. *Campus security:* 24-hour emergency response devices and patrols, student patrols, late-night transport/escort service, controlled dormitory access. *Student services:* health clinic, personal/psychological counseling, women's center.

Athletics Member NCAA. All Division I except football (Division I-A). *Intercollegiate sports:* baseball M (s), basketball M (s)/W (s), cross-country running M (s)/W (s), golf M (s)/W (s), soccer W (s), softball W (s), swimming and diving M (s)/W (s), tennis M (s)/W (s), track and field M (s)/W (s), volleyball W (s), wrestling M (s). *Intramural sports:* archery M (c)/W (c), badminton M/W, basketball M/W, crew M (c)/W (c), cross-country running M/W, equestrian sports M (c)/W (c), fencing M (c)/W (c), football M/W, golf M/W, gymnastics M (c)/W (c), ice hockey M (c), lacrosse M (c)/W (c), racquetball M (c)/W (c), riflery M (c)/W (c), rock climbing M (c)/W (c), rugby M (c), sailing M (c)/W (c), skiing (downhill) M (c)/W (c), soccer M/W, softball M/W, swimming and diving M/W, table tennis M/W, tennis M/W, track and field M/W, ultimate Frisbee M (c)/W (c), volleyball M/W, water polo M (c)/W (c).

Standardized Tests *Required:* SAT or ACT (for admission).

Costs (2008–09) *Tuition:* $262 per credit hour part-time; state resident $7317 full-time; nonresident $22,791 full-time, $771 per credit hour part-time. *Required fees:* $433 full-time. *Room and board:* $7530.

Financial Aid Of all full-time matriculated undergraduates who enrolled in 2007, 18,080 applied for aid, 12,510 were judged to have need, 4,217 had their need fully met. 856 Federal Work-Study jobs (averaging $1811). In 2007, 3509 non-need-based awards were made. *Average percent of need met:* 93%. *Average financial aid package:* $12,807. *Average need-based loan:* $4457. *Average need-based gift aid:* $7030. *Average non-need-based aid:* $5211. *Average indebtedness upon graduation:* $21,636.

Applying *Options:* electronic application, early admission, deferred entrance. *Application fee:* $30. *Required:* high school transcript. *Application deadlines:* 3/1 (freshmen), rolling (transfers). *Notification:* continuous (freshmen).

Freshman Application Contact Ms. Pamela T. Home, Assistant Vice President for Enrollment Management and Dean of Admissions, Purdue University, 475 Stadium Mall Drive, Schleman Mall, West Lafayette, IN 47907-2050. *Phone:* 765-494-1776. *Fax:* 765-494-0544. *E-mail:* admissions@purdue.edu.

PURDUE UNIVERSITY CALUMET

Hammond, Indiana **www.calumet.purdue.edu/**

- **State-supported** comprehensive, founded 1951, part of Purdue University System
- **Urban** 167-acre campus with easy access to Chicago
- **Endowment** $9.9 million
- **Coed** 8,586 undergraduate students, 63% full-time, 56% women, 44% men
- **Moderately difficult** entrance level, 79% of applicants were admitted

Undergraduates 5,422 full-time, 3,164 part-time. Students come from 27 states and territories, 30 other countries, 10% are from out of state, 18% African American, 1% Asian American or Pacific Islander, 14% Hispanic American, 0.4% Native American, 3% international, 7% transferred in. *Retention:* 62% of 2006 full-time freshmen returned.

Freshmen *Admission:* 3,007 applied, 2,367 admitted, 1,452 enrolled. *Test scores:* SAT critical reading scores over 500: 33%; SAT math scores over 500: 35%; SAT critical reading scores over 600: 6%; SAT math scores over 600: 9%; SAT critical reading scores over 700: 1%; SAT math scores over 700: 1%.

Faculty *Total:* 526, 57% full-time, 41% with terminal degrees. *Student/faculty ratio:* 17:1.

Majors Accounting; architectural engineering technology; behavioral sciences; biological and physical sciences; biology/biological sciences; biology/biotechnology laboratory technician; business administration and management; chemistry; child development; civil engineering technology; clinical laboratory science/medical technology; clinical/medical laboratory technology; computer and information sciences; computer engineering; computer engineering technology; computer programming; computer science; construction engineering technology; criminal justice/law enforcement administration; criminal justice/police science; culinary arts; economics; education; electrical, electronic and communications engineering technology; electrical, electronics and communications engineering; elementary education; engineering; engineering technology; English; food services technology; French; German; history; hotel/motel administration; human resources management; industrial technology; information science/studies; journalism; kindergarten/preschool education; literature; marketing/marketing management; mass communication/media; mathematics; mechanical engineering; mechanical engineering/mechanical technology; metallurgical technology; nursing (registered nurse training); philosophy; physics; political science and government; pre-dentistry studies; pre-law studies; pre-medical studies; pre-veterinary studies; psychology; public relations/image management; radio and television; science teacher education; secondary education; sociology; Spanish; special education.

Academics *Calendar:* semesters. *Degrees:* certificates, associate, bachelor's, master's, and postbachelor's certificates. *Special study options:* academic remediation for entering students, accelerated degree program, adult/continuing education programs, advanced placement credit, cooperative education, distance learning, double majors, English as a second language, freshman honors college, honors programs, independent study, internships, part-time degree program, services for LD students, summer session for credit.

Computers on Campus 1,500 computers/terminals are available on campus for general student use. Students can access the following: online (class) registration. Campuswide network is available.

Student Life *Housing options:* Campus housing is university owned and is provided by a third party. *Activities and organizations:* drama/theater group, student-run newspaper, radio and television station, choral group, Los Latinos, student government, Theater Club, Black Student Union, Song Company, national fraternities, national sororities. *Campus security:* 24-hour emergency response devices and patrols, student patrols, late-night transport/escort service. *Student services:* health clinic, personal/psychological counseling.

Athletics Member NAIA. *Intercollegiate sports:* basketball M (s)/W (s). *Intramural sports:* bowling M/W, football M/W, golf M/W, racquetball M/W, sailing M/W, softball M/W, ultimate Frisbee M/W, volleyball M/W.

Standardized Tests *Required:* SAT or ACT (for admission).

Costs (2008–09) *Tuition:* state resident $5757 full-time, $192 per credit hour part-time; nonresident $12,285 full-time, $425 per credit hour part-time. *Room and board:* $6155; room only: $4270.

Financial Aid Of all full-time matriculated undergraduates who enrolled in 2006, 4,354 applied for aid, 3,483 were judged to have need, 307 had their need fully met. 65 Federal Work-Study jobs (averaging $2527). In 2006, 241 non-need-based awards were made. *Average percent of need met:* 20%. *Average financial aid package:* $5720. *Average need-based loan:* $2798. *Average need-based gift aid:* $4490. *Average non-need-based aid:* $2362. *Average indebtedness upon graduation:* $17,661.

Applying *Options:* electronic application, deferred entrance. *Required:* high school transcript, minimum 2.0 GPA. *Application deadlines:* rolling (freshmen), rolling (transfers). *Notification:* continuous (freshmen), continuous (transfers).

Freshman Application Contact Mr. Paul McGuinness, Director of Admissions, Purdue University Calumet, 2200-169th Street, Hammond, IN 46323-2094. *Phone:* 219-989-2213. *Toll-free phone:* 800-447-8738. *E-mail:* adms@calumet.purdue.edu.

PURDUE UNIVERSITY NORTH CENTRAL

Westville, Indiana **www.pnc.edu/**

- **State-supported** comprehensive, founded 1967, part of Purdue University System
- **Rural** 305-acre campus with easy access to Chicago
- **Endowment** $2.1 million
- **Coed** 3,814 undergraduate students, 61% full-time, 59% women, 41% men
- **Minimally difficult** entrance level, 87% of applicants were admitted

Undergraduates 2,314 full-time, 1,500 part-time. Students come from 16 states and territories, 8 other countries, 2% are from out of state, 5% African American, 0.8% Asian American or Pacific Islander, 5% Hispanic American, 0.7% Native American, 0.2% international, 5% transferred in. *Retention:* 53% of 2006 full-time freshmen returned.

Freshmen *Admission:* 1,330 applied, 1,152 admitted, 800 enrolled. *Average high school GPA:* 2.8. *Test scores:* SAT critical reading scores over 500: 31%; SAT math scores over 500: 36%; SAT writing scores over 500: 26%; ACT scores over 18: 81%; SAT critical reading scores over 600: 6%; SAT math scores over 600: 8%; SAT writing scores over 600: 4%; ACT scores over 24: 10%; SAT critical reading scores over 700: 1%; SAT math scores over 700: 1%; ACT scores over 30: 2%.

Faculty *Total:* 285, 39% full-time, 31% with terminal degrees. *Student/faculty ratio:* 17:1.

Majors Architectural engineering technology; behavioral sciences; biology/biological sciences; business administration, management and operations related; business/commerce; civil engineering technology; communication/speech communication and rhetoric; computer engineering technology; construction engineering technology; early childhood education; electrical, electronic and com-

COLLEGE DATA CENTER • INDIANA

munications engineering technology; elementary education; engineering technology; English; industrial technology; information technology; liberal arts and sciences/ liberal studies; mechanical engineering/mechanical technology; nursing (registered nurse training); physical sciences.

Academics *Calendar:* semesters. *Degrees:* certificates, associate, bachelor's, master's, and postbachelor's certificates. *Special study options:* academic remediation for entering students, adult/continuing education programs, advanced placement credit, cooperative education, distance learning, double majors, honors programs, internships, part-time degree program, services for LD students, student-designed majors, study abroad, summer session for credit.

Computers on Campus 450 computers/terminals are available on campus for general student use. Students can access the following: campus intranet, computer help desk, free student e-mail accounts, online (class) grades, online (class) registration, online (class) schedules. Campuswide network is available. Wireless service is available via entire campus.

Student Life *Housing:* college housing not available. *Activities and organizations:* drama/theater group, student-run newspaper, Student Cultural Society, Student Education Association, Construction Club, American Sign Language, F.A.C.E. *Campus security:* 24-hour emergency response devices, late-night transport/escort service. *Student services:* personal/psychological counseling.

Athletics Member NAIA. *Intercollegiate sports:* baseball M, basketball M, cheerleading M/W, softball W, volleyball M.

Standardized Tests *Recommended:* SAT (for admission), ACT (for admission), SAT or ACT (for admission).

Costs (2008–09) *Tuition:* state resident $5447 full-time, $182 per credit hour part-time; nonresident $8125 full-time, $452 per credit hour part-time. *Required fees:* $633 full-time.

Financial Aid Of all full-time matriculated undergraduates who enrolled in 2007, 1,757 applied for aid, 1,378 were judged to have need, 100 had their need fully met. 79 Federal Work-Study jobs (averaging $836). In 2007, 49 non-need-based awards were made. *Average percent of need met:* 62%. *Average financial aid package:* $1668. *Average need-based loan:* $3671. *Average need-based gift aid:* $5013. *Average non-need-based aid:* $1589. *Average indebtedness upon graduation:* $18,937.

Applying *Options:* electronic application, deferred entrance. *Required:* high school transcript. *Required for some:* essay or personal statement, minimum 2.0 GPA, interview. *Application deadlines:* 8/15 (freshmen), 8/15 (transfers). *Notification:* continuous (freshmen), continuous (transfers).

Freshman Application Contact Mr. Anthony Cardenas, Director of Admissions, Purdue University North Central, 1401 South U.S. Highway 421, Westville, IN 46391. *Phone:* 219-785-5283. *Toll-free phone:* 800-872-1231. *Fax:* 219-785-5538. *E-mail:* acardenas@pnc.edu.

ROSE-HULMAN INSTITUTE OF TECHNOLOGY

Terre Haute, Indiana **www.rose-hulman.edu/**

- **Independent** comprehensive, founded 1874
- **Suburban** 200-acre campus with easy access to Indianapolis
- **Endowment** $207.1 million
- **Coed, primarily men** 1,829 undergraduate students, 99% full-time, 21% women, 79% men
- **Very difficult** entrance level, 70% of applicants were admitted

Undergraduates 1,816 full-time, 13 part-time. Students come from 51 states and territories, 21 other countries, 58% are from out of state, 2% African American, 5% Asian American or Pacific Islander, 2% Hispanic American, 0.2% Native American, 2% international, 0.7% transferred in, 74% live on campus. *Retention:* 91% of 2006 full-time freshmen returned.

Freshmen *Admission:* 3,088 applied, 2,152 admitted, 474 enrolled. *Test scores:* SAT critical reading scores over 500: 96%; SAT math scores over 500: 99%; SAT writing scores over 500: 92%; ACT scores over 18: 100%; SAT critical reading scores over 600: 62%; SAT math scores over 600: 86%; SAT writing scores over 600: 52%; ACT scores over 24: 96%; SAT critical reading scores over 700: 16%; SAT math scores over 700: 34%; SAT writing scores over 700: 10%; ACT scores over 30: 46%.

Faculty *Total:* 166, 95% full-time, 98% with terminal degrees. *Student/faculty ratio:* 12:1.

Majors Biology/biological sciences; biomedical/medical engineering; chemical engineering; chemistry; civil engineering; computer engineering; computer science; computer software engineering; economics; electrical, electronics and communications engineering; engineering physics; engineering related; mathematics; mechanical engineering; physics; systems engineering.

Academics *Calendar:* quarters. *Degrees:* bachelor's and master's. *Special study options:* accelerated degree program, adult/continuing education programs, advanced placement credit, cooperative education, double majors, independent study, off-campus study, services for LD students, study abroad, summer session for credit. *ROTC:* Army (b), Air Force (b).

Computers on Campus 45 computers/terminals and 8,000 ports are available on campus for general student use. Students can access the following: campus intranet, computer help desk, free student e-mail accounts, online (class) grades, online (class) registration, online (class) schedules. Campuswide network is available. 100% of college-owned or -operated housing units are wired for high-speed Internet access. Wireless service is available via classrooms, computer centers, computer labs, learning centers, libraries, student centers.

Student Life *Housing:* on-campus residence required for freshman year. *Options:* coed, men-only. Campus housing is university owned. Freshman campus housing is guaranteed. *Activities and organizations:* drama/theater group, student-run newspaper, radio station, choral group, Drama Club, American Society of Civil Engineers, Bowling Club, Residence Hall Association, Gun Club, national fraternities, national sororities. *Campus security:* 24-hour emergency response devices and patrols, late-night transport/escort service, controlled dormitory access. *Student services:* health clinic, personal/psychological counseling.

Athletics Member NCAA. All Division III. *Intercollegiate sports:* baseball M, basketball M/W, cheerleading M/W, cross-country running M/W, football M, golf M/W, riflery M/W, soccer M/W, softball W, swimming and diving M/W, tennis M/W, track and field M/W, volleyball W, wrestling M. *Intramural sports:* basketball M/W, bowling M (c)/W (c), cross-country running M/W, fencing M (c)/W (c), football M/W, golf M/W, lacrosse W (c), racquetball M (c)/W, riflery M (c)/W (c), soccer M/W, softball M/W, table tennis M (c)/W (c), tennis M/W, track and field M/W, ultimate Frisbee M/W, volleyball M/W, water polo M (c)/W (c).

Standardized Tests *Required:* SAT or ACT (for admission).

Costs (2007–08) *Comprehensive fee:* $39,111 includes full-time tuition ($30,243), mandatory fees ($525), and room and board ($8343). Full-time tuition and fees vary according to course load. Part-time tuition: $879 per credit. Part-time tuition and fees vary according to course load. *College room only:* $4761. Room and board charges vary according to board plan. *Payment plans:* tuition prepayment, installment. *Waivers:* employees or children of employees.

Financial Aid Of all full-time matriculated undergraduates who enrolled in 2006, 1,496 applied for aid, 1,242 were judged to have need, 136 had their need fully met. 470 Federal Work-Study jobs (averaging $1579). 612 state and other part-time jobs (averaging $1569). In 2006, 559 non-need-based awards were made. *Average percent of need met:* 79%. *Average financial aid package:* $22,011. *Average need-based loan:* $6945. *Average need-based gift aid:* $15,387. *Average non-need-based aid:* $8343. *Average indebtedness upon graduation:* $29,491.

Applying *Options:* electronic application, deferred entrance. *Application fee:* $40. *Required:* high school transcript, 1 letter of recommendation, curricular. *Recommended:* essay or personal statement, interview. *Application deadline:* 3/1 (freshmen). *Notification:* continuous (freshmen), continuous (transfers).

Freshman Application Contact Mr. James Goecker, Dean of Admissions and Financial Aid, Rose-Hulman Institute of Technology, 5500 Wabash Avenue, CM 1, Terre Haute, IN 47803-3920. *Phone:* 812-877-8894. *Toll-free phone:* 800-248-7448. *Fax:* 812-877-8941. *E-mail:* admissions@rose-hulman.edu.

SAINT JOSEPH'S COLLEGE

Rensselaer, Indiana **www.saintjoe.edu/**

- **Independent Roman Catholic** comprehensive, founded 1889
- **Small-town** 180-acre campus with easy access to Chicago
- **Endowment** $16.8 million
- **Coed** 1,070 undergraduate students, 95% full-time, 60% women, 40% men
- **Moderately difficult** entrance level, 75% of applicants were admitted

Undergraduates 1,018 full-time, 52 part-time. Students come from 20 states and territories, 4 other countries, 26% are from out of state, 8% African American, 0.5% Asian American or Pacific Islander, 4% Hispanic American, 0.9% international, 2% transferred in, 67% live on campus. *Retention:* 67% of 2006 full-time freshmen returned.

Freshmen *Admission:* 1,321 applied, 991 admitted, 286 enrolled. *Average high school GPA:* 3.04. *Test scores:* SAT critical reading scores over 500: 41%; SAT math scores over 500: 52%; ACT scores over 18: 85%; SAT critical reading scores over 600: 10%; SAT math scores over 600: 13%; ACT scores over 24: 26%; SAT critical reading scores over 700: 1%; SAT math scores over 700: 1%; ACT scores over 30: 3%.

Faculty *Total:* 89, 66% full-time, 70% with terminal degrees. *Student/faculty ratio:* 15:1.

Majors Accounting; art teacher education; biochemistry; biology/biological sciences; business/commerce; chemistry; clinical laboratory science/medical technology; computer and information sciences; creative writing; criminal justice/safety; dramatic/theater arts; economics; elementary education; English; fine/studio arts; health and physical education; history; international relations and affairs; management information systems; mass communication/media; mathematics; music history, literature, and theory; music management and merchandising; nursing (registered nurse training); pastoral studies/counseling; philosophy; philosophy and religious studies related; physical education teaching and coaching; political science and government; psychology; secondary education; social work; sociology.

Academics *Calendar:* semesters. *Degrees:* certificates, diplomas, associate, bachelor's, and master's. *Special study options:* academic remediation for entering students, accelerated degree program, advanced placement credit, double majors, honors programs, independent study, internships, part-time degree program, services for LD students, student-designed majors, study abroad, summer session for credit.

Computers on Campus 69 computers/terminals and 47 ports are available on campus for general student use. Students can access the following: campus intranet, computer help desk, free student e-mail accounts. Campuswide network is available. 100% of college-owned or -operated housing units are wired for high-speed Internet access. Wireless service is available via entire campus.

Student Life *Housing:* on-campus residence required through senior year. *Options:* coed, men-only, women-only, disabled students. Campus housing is university owned. Freshman campus housing is guaranteed. *Activities and organizations:* drama/theater group, student-run newspaper, radio and television station, choral group, marching band, Gallagher Charitable Society, Cup O' Joe, Habitat for Humanity, Science Club, Alpha Lambda Delta. *Campus security:* 24-hour emergency response devices and patrols, student patrols, late-night transport/escort service. *Student services:* health clinic, personal/psychological counseling.

Athletics Member NCAA. All Division II. *Intercollegiate sports:* baseball M (s), basketball M (s)/W (s), cheerleading M (s) (c)/W (s) (c), cross-country running M (s)/W (s), football M (s), golf M (s)/W (s), soccer M (s)/W (s), softball W (s), tennis M (s)/W (s), track and field M (s)/W (s), volleyball W (s). *Intramural sports:* basketball M/W, lacrosse M (c)/W (c), softball M/W, ultimate Frisbee M/W, volleyball M/W.

Standardized Tests *Required:* SAT or ACT (for admission).

Costs (2007–08) *Comprehensive fee:* $28,820 includes full-time tuition ($21,710), mandatory fees ($170), and room and board ($6940). Full-time tuition and fees vary according to reciprocity agreements. Part-time tuition: $730 per credit. Part-time tuition and fees vary according to course load and reciprocity agreements. *Room and board:* Room and board charges vary according to housing facility. *Payment plan:* installment. *Waivers:* minority students, children of alumni, and employees or children of employees.

Financial Aid Of all full-time matriculated undergraduates who enrolled in 2006, 763 applied for aid, 634 were judged to have need, 226 had their need fully met. 111 Federal Work-Study jobs (averaging $742). In 2006, 99 non-need-based awards were made. *Average percent of need met:* 84%. *Average financial aid package:* $18,643. *Average need-based loan:* $4144. *Average need-based gift aid:* $12,717. *Average non-need-based aid:* $11,543. *Average indebtedness upon graduation:* $26,406.

Applying *Options:* electronic application, deferred entrance. *Application fee:* $25. *Required:* high school transcript, minimum 2.0 GPA. *Required for some:* essay or personal statement, interview. *Application deadlines:* rolling (freshmen), rolling (transfers). *Notification:* continuous (freshmen), continuous (transfers).

Freshman Application Contact Ms. Karen Raftus, Director of Admissions, Saint Joseph's College, PO Box 815, Rensselaer, IN 47978-0850. *Phone:* 219-866-6170. *Toll-free phone:* 800-447-8781. *Fax:* 219-866-6122. *E-mail:* admissions@saintjoe.edu.

SAINT MARY-OF-THE-WOODS COLLEGE

Saint Mary-of-the-Woods, Indiana **www.smwc.edu/**

- **Independent Roman Catholic** comprehensive, founded 1840
- **Rural** 67-acre campus with easy access to Indianapolis
- **Endowment** $12.7 million
- **Coed, primarily women** 1,519 undergraduate students, 30% full-time, 96% women, 4% men
- **Moderately difficult** entrance level

Undergraduates 460 full-time, 1,059 part-time. Students come from 28 states and territories, 4 other countries, 19% are from out of state, 2% African American, 0.1% Asian American or Pacific Islander, 1% Hispanic American, 0.5% Native American, 1% international, 16% transferred in, 74% live on campus. *Retention:* 82% of 2006 full-time freshmen returned.

Freshmen *Admission:* 218 applied, 113 enrolled. *Average high school GPA:* 3.3. *Test scores:* ACT scores over 18: 83%; ACT scores over 24: 59%; ACT scores over 30: 12%.

Faculty *Total:* 66, 97% full-time, 58% with terminal degrees. *Student/faculty ratio:* 11:1.

Majors Accounting; accounting related; art; art teacher education; biology/biological sciences; business administration and management; business administration, management and operations related; business/commerce; child care and support services management; child care provision; clinical laboratory science/medical technology; communications technologies and support services related; communications technology; computer and information sciences; design and visual communications; dramatic/theater arts; education; education (K-12); elementary education; English; English language and literature related; equestrian studies; fine/studio arts; humanities; human resources management; human services; information science/studies; journalism; kindergarten/preschool education; legal assistant/paralegal; liberal arts and sciences/liberal studies; marketing/marketing management; mass communication/media; mathematics; music; music performance; music teacher education; music therapy; pre-dentistry studies; pre-law studies; pre-medical studies; pre-pharmacy studies; pre-veterinary studies; professional studies; psychology; religious studies; secondary education; social sciences; special education; theology.

Academics *Calendar:* semesters. *Degrees:* certificates, associate, bachelor's, master's, post-master's, and postbachelor's certificates (also offers external degree program with significant enrollment not reflected in profile). *Special study options:* academic remediation for entering students, accelerated degree program, adult/continuing education programs, advanced placement credit, distance learning, double majors, external degree program, independent study, internships, off-campus study, part-time degree program, student-designed majors, study abroad, summer session for credit. *ROTC:* Army (c), Air Force (c).

Computers on Campus 65 computers/terminals and 150 ports are available on campus for general student use. Students can access the following: campus intranet, computer help desk, free student e-mail accounts, online (class) grades, online (class) registration, online (class) schedules. Campuswide network is available. 100% of college-owned or -operated housing units are wired for high-speed Internet access. Wireless service is available via entire campus.

Student Life *Housing:* on-campus residence required through senior year. *Options:* women-only. Campus housing is university owned. Freshman campus housing is guaranteed. *Activities and organizations:* drama/theater group, student-run newspaper, choral group, Student Senate, In-Law, student newspaper, chorale, Diversity "Worldwide Woodsies". *Campus security:* 24-hour patrols. *Student services:* health clinic, personal/psychological counseling.

Athletics *Intercollegiate sports:* basketball W (s), equestrian sports W (s), soccer W (s), softball W (s). *Intramural sports:* soccer W, softball W.

Standardized Tests *Required:* SAT or ACT (for admission).

Costs (2007–08) *Comprehensive fee:* $27,560 includes full-time tuition ($19,530), mandatory fees ($650), and room and board ($7380). Full-time tuition and fees vary according to program. Part-time tuition: $370 per hour. Part-time tuition and fees vary according to program. *Required fees:* $120 per year part-time. *College room only:* $2880. *Payment plan:* installment. *Waivers:* employees or children of employees.

Financial Aid Of all full-time matriculated undergraduates who enrolled in 2005, 83 applied for aid, 83 were judged to have need. 93 Federal Work-Study jobs (averaging $1334). *Average percent of need met:* 80%. *Average financial aid package:* $17,140. *Average need-based loan:* $2939. *Average need-based gift aid:* $5420. *Average indebtedness upon graduation:* $20,180.

Applying *Options:* electronic application, early admission, deferred entrance. *Application fee:* $30. *Required:* essay or personal statement, high school transcript, minimum 2.5 GPA, 1 letter of recommendation. *Recommended:* interview. *Application deadlines:* 8/1 (freshmen), 8/1 (transfers). *Notification:* continuous until 8/20 (freshmen), continuous until 8/20 (transfers).

Freshman Application Contact Mr. Bryan Michel, Associate Director of Admission, Saint Mary-of-the-Woods College, Guerin Hall, Saint Mary-of-the-Woods, IN 47876. *Phone:* 812-535-5106. *Toll-free phone:* 800-926-SMWC. *Fax:* 812-535-5010. *E-mail:* smwcadms@smwc.edu.

SAINT MARY'S COLLEGE

Notre Dame, Indiana **www.saintmarys.edu/**

- **Independent Roman Catholic** 4-year, founded 1844
- **Suburban** 75-acre campus
- **Endowment** $134.9 million
- **Women only** 1,604 undergraduate students, 98% full-time
- **Moderately difficult** entrance level, 81% of applicants were admitted

Undergraduates 1,570 full-time, 34 part-time. Students come from 42 states and territories, 5 other countries, 78% are from out of state, 1% African American,

2% Asian American or Pacific Islander, 6% Hispanic American, 0.4% Native American, 0.4% international, 2% transferred in, 83% live on campus. *Retention:* 86% of 2006 full-time freshmen returned.

Freshmen *Admission:* 1,281 applied, 1,041 admitted, 479 enrolled. *Average high school GPA:* 3.72. *Test scores:* SAT critical reading scores over 500: 84%; SAT math scores over 500: 82%; SAT writing scores over 500: 83%; ACT scores over 18: 98%; SAT critical reading scores over 600: 34%; SAT math scores over 600: 34%; SAT writing scores over 600: 38%; ACT scores over 24: 60%; SAT critical reading scores over 700: 5%; SAT math scores over 700: 4%; SAT writing scores over 700: 5%; ACT scores over 30: 8%.

Faculty *Total:* 218, 63% full-time. *Student/faculty ratio:* 10:1.

Majors Accounting; applied mathematics related; art; art teacher education; biology/biological sciences; business administration and management; business teacher education; chemistry; clinical laboratory science/medical technology; communication/speech communication and rhetoric; creative writing; cytotechnology; dramatic/theater arts; economics; education; elementary education; English literature (British and Commonwealth); finance; French; history; humanities; interdisciplinary studies; international business/trade/commerce; Italian; management information systems; marketing/marketing management; mathematics; mathematics and computer science; music; music teacher education; nursing (registered nurse training); philosophy; political science and government; psychology; religious studies; social work; sociology; Spanish.

Academics *Calendar:* semesters. *Degree:* bachelor's. *Special study options:* academic remediation for entering students, accelerated degree program, advanced placement credit, cooperative education, double majors, independent study, internships, off-campus study, part-time degree program, services for LD students, student-designed majors, study abroad, summer session for credit. *ROTC:* Army (c), Navy (c), Air Force (c). *Unusual degree programs:* 3-2 engineering with University of Notre Dame.

Computers on Campus 209 computers/terminals are available on campus for general student use. Students can access the following: computer help desk, free student e-mail accounts, online (class) registration. Campuswide network is available. 100% of college-owned or -operated housing units are wired for high-speed Internet access. Wireless service is available via classrooms, computer centers, computer labs, dorm rooms, learning centers, libraries, student centers.

Student Life *Housing:* on-campus residence required through junior year. *Options:* women-only. Campus housing is university owned. Freshman campus housing is guaranteed. *Activities and organizations:* drama/theater group, student-run newspaper, television station, choral group, marching band, Student Government Association, Dance Marathon, Class Boards, Residence Hall Association, Student Diversity Board. *Campus security:* 24-hour emergency response devices and patrols, late-night transport/escort service, controlled dormitory access. *Student services:* health clinic, personal/psychological counseling, women's center.

Athletics Member NCAA. All Division III. *Intercollegiate sports:* basketball W, cross-country running W, equestrian sports W (c), field hockey W (c), golf W, gymnastics W (c), skiing (downhill) W (c), soccer W, softball W, swimming and diving W, tennis W, ultimate Frisbee W (c), volleyball W, water polo W (c). *Intramural sports:* cheerleading W (c), lacrosse W (c).

Standardized Tests *Required:* SAT or ACT (for admission).

Costs (2007–08) *Comprehensive fee:* $35,550 includes full-time tuition ($26,285), mandatory fees ($590), and room and board ($8675). Part-time tuition: $1039 per semester hour. *College room only:* $5343.

Financial Aid Of all full-time matriculated undergraduates who enrolled in 2005, 1,119 applied for aid, 913 were judged to have need, 373 had their need fully met. 344 Federal Work-Study jobs (averaging $1451). 923 state and other part-time jobs (averaging $3854). In 2005, 374 non-need-based awards were made. *Average percent of need met:* 81%. *Average financial aid package:* $20,191. *Average need-based loan:* $4544. *Average need-based gift aid:* $10,010. *Average non-need-based aid:* $7237. *Average indebtedness upon graduation:* $35,143.

Applying *Options:* electronic application, early admission, early decision, deferred entrance. *Application fee:* $30. *Required:* essay or personal statement, high school transcript, 1 letter of recommendation. *Recommended:* interview. *Application deadlines:* 2/15 (freshmen), rolling (transfers). *Early decision deadline:* 11/15. *Notification:* continuous (freshmen), continuous (transfers), 12/15 (early decision).

Freshman Application Contact Mona Bowe, Director of Admission, Saint Mary's College, Notre Dame, IN 46556. *Phone:* 574-284-4587. *Toll-free phone:* 800-551-7621. *Fax:* 574-284-4841. *E-mail:* admission@saintmarys.edu.

See page 936 for the College Close-Up.

TAYLOR UNIVERSITY

Upland, Indiana **www.taylor.edu/**

- **Independent interdenominational** comprehensive, founded 1846
- **Rural** 950-acre campus with easy access to Indianapolis
- **Endowment** $72.7 million
- **Coed** 1,879 undergraduate students, 97% full-time, 55% women, 45% men
- **Moderately difficult** entrance level, 91% of applicants were admitted

Since 1846, the mark of a Taylor education has been to enlighten the mind and ignite the soul. Within the context of Taylor's vibrant covenant-based community, students and faculty members pursue learning through a relentless commitment to scholarship, research, and service.

Undergraduates 1,827 full-time, 52 part-time. Students come from 46 states and territories, 24 other countries, 68% are from out of state, 2% African American, 2% Asian American or Pacific Islander, 2% Hispanic American, 2% international, 2% transferred in, 81% live on campus. *Retention:* 87% of 2006 full-time freshmen returned.

Freshmen *Admission:* 1,393 applied, 1,269 admitted, 472 enrolled. *Average high school GPA:* 3.53. *Test scores:* SAT critical reading scores over 500: 81%; SAT math scores over 500: 81%; ACT scores over 18: 96%; SAT critical reading scores over 600: 49%; SAT math scores over 600: 47%; ACT scores over 24: 71%; SAT critical reading scores over 700: 18%; SAT math scores over 700: 11%; ACT scores over 30: 26%.

Faculty *Total:* 187, 65% full-time, 60% with terminal degrees. *Student/faculty ratio:* 13:1.

Majors Accounting; ancient Near Eastern and biblical languages; art; art teacher education; athletic training; biblical studies; biology/biological sciences; biology teacher education; business administration and management; chemistry; chemistry teacher education; clinical laboratory science/medical technology; commercial and advertising art; communication/speech communication and rhetoric; computer engineering; computer graphics; computer programming; computer science; creative writing; dramatic/theater arts; economics; education; elementary education; engineering physics; English; environmental biology; environmental studies; finance; French; history; history teacher education; human resources management; information science/studies; international business/trade/commerce; international economics; international relations and affairs; kindergarten/preschool education; literature; management information systems; marketing/marketing management; mass communication/media; mathematics; middle school education; music; music management and merchandising; music performance; music teacher education; natural sciences; philosophy; physical education teaching and coaching; physical sciences; physics; piano and organ; political science and government; pre-dentistry studies; pre-law studies; pre-medical studies; pre-veterinary studies; psychology; religious education; religious/sacred music; religious studies; science teacher education; secondary education; social sciences; social science teacher education; social work; sociology; Spanish; Spanish language teacher education; speech teacher education; sport and fitness administration/management; theology; voice and opera.

Academics *Calendar:* 4-1-4. *Degrees:* certificates, diplomas, associate, bachelor's, and master's. *Special study options:* academic remediation for entering students, advanced placement credit, cooperative education, distance learning, double majors, English as a second language, honors programs, independent study, internships, off-campus study, part-time degree program, services for LD students, student-designed majors, study abroad, summer session for credit. *Unusual degree programs:* 3-2 engineering with Washington University in St. Louis.

Computers on Campus 387 computers/terminals are available on campus for general student use. Students can access the following: campus intranet, computer help desk, free student e-mail accounts, online (class) grades, online (class) registration, online (class) schedules. Campuswide network is available. 100% of college-owned or -operated housing units are wired for high-speed Internet access. Wireless service is available via entire campus.

Student Life *Housing:* on-campus residence required through junior year. *Options:* men-only, women-only. Campus housing is university owned and is provided by a third party. Freshman campus housing is guaranteed. *Activities and organizations:* drama/theater group, student-run newspaper, radio and television station, choral group, TWO- Taylor World Outreach, IFC- Integration of Faith and Culture, Spring Break Mission Trips, Community Outreach. *Campus security:* 24-hour patrols, student patrols, late-night transport/escort service. *Student services:* health clinic, personal/psychological counseling.

Athletics Member NAIA. *Intercollegiate sports:* baseball M (s), basketball M (s)/W (s), cross-country running M (s)/W (s), equestrian sports M (c)/W (c), football M (s), golf M (s), lacrosse M (c)/W (c), soccer M (s)/W (s), softball W (s), tennis M (s)/W (s), track and field M (s)/W (s), volleyball W (s). *Intramural* *sports:* basketball M/W, football M/W, soccer M/W, softball M/W, table tennis M/W, tennis M/W, ultimate Frisbee M/W, volleyball M/W.

Standardized Tests *Required:* SAT or ACT (for admission).

Costs (2008–09) *Comprehensive fee:* $30,898 includes full-time tuition ($24,314), mandatory fees ($232), and room and board ($6352). Part-time tuition: $868 per credit. *College room only:* $3144.

Financial Aid Of all full-time matriculated undergraduates who enrolled in 2007, 1,272 applied for aid, 1,092 were judged to have need, 276 had their need fully met. 799 Federal Work-Study jobs (averaging $457). In 2007, 396 non-need-based awards were made. *Average percent of need met:* 76%. *Average financial aid package:* $16,085. *Average need-based loan:* $4619. *Average need-based gift aid:* $12,460. *Average non-need-based aid:* $5024. *Average indebtedness upon graduation:* $18,681. *Financial aid deadline:* 3/10.

Applying *Options:* electronic application, early action, deferred entrance. *Application fee:* $25. *Required:* essay or personal statement, high school transcript, 2 letters of recommendation, interview. *Recommended:* minimum 2.8 GPA. *Application deadlines:* rolling (freshmen), rolling (transfers), 12/1 (early action). *Notification:* continuous (freshmen), continuous (transfers), 12/20 (early action).

Freshman Application Contact Mrs. Kathy Thornburgh, Visit Coordinator, Taylor University, 236 West Reade Avenue, Upland, IN 46989-1001. *Phone:* 765-998-5134. *Toll-free phone:* 800-882-3456. *Fax:* 765-998-4925. *E-mail:* admissions@taylor.edu.

See page 938 for the College Close-Up.

TAYLOR UNIVERSITY FORT WAYNE

Fort Wayne, Indiana **www.tayloru.edu/**

- **Independent interdenominational** comprehensive, founded 1992, administratively affiliated with Taylor University
- **Urban** 32-acre campus
- **Endowment** $12.2 million
- **Coed** 964 undergraduate students, 32% full-time, 62% women, 38% men
- **Moderately difficult** entrance level, 68% of applicants were admitted

Undergraduates 306 full-time, 658 part-time. Students come from 22 states and territories, 5 other countries, 24% are from out of state, 4% African American, 0.1% Asian American or Pacific Islander, 1% Hispanic American, 0.3% international, 2% transferred in, 45% live on campus. *Retention:* 59% of 2006 full-time freshmen returned.

Freshmen *Admission:* 321 applied, 219 admitted, 80 enrolled. *Average high school GPA:* 3.17. *Test scores:* SAT critical reading scores over 500: 56%; SAT math scores over 500: 52%; ACT scores over 18: 95%; SAT critical reading scores over 600: 21%; SAT math scores over 600: 19%; ACT scores over 24: 58%; SAT critical reading scores over 700: 10%; SAT math scores over 700: 4%; ACT scores over 30: 17%.

Faculty *Total:* 40, 48% full-time, 40% with terminal degrees. *Student/faculty ratio:* 13:1.

Majors Biblical studies; business administration and management; counseling psychology; creative writing; criminal justice/law enforcement administration; criminal justice/safety; early childhood education; education; English; health/health care administration; intercultural/multicultural and diversity studies; liberal arts and sciences and humanities related; liberal arts and sciences/liberal studies; logistics and materials management; marketing/marketing management; multi-/interdisciplinary studies related; pastoral studies/counseling; religious education; social work; youth ministry.

Academics *Calendar:* 4-1-4. *Degrees:* certificates, associate, and bachelor's. *Special study options:* academic remediation for entering students, accelerated degree program, adult/continuing education programs, advanced placement credit, cooperative education, distance learning, double majors, external degree program, independent study, internships, off-campus study, part-time degree program, services for LD students, student-designed majors, study abroad, summer session for credit.

Computers on Campus 72 computers/terminals are available on campus for general student use. Students can access the following: campus intranet, computer help desk, free student e-mail accounts, online (class) grades, online (class) registration, online (class) schedules. Campuswide network is available.

Student Life *Housing:* on-campus residence required through junior year. *Options:* coed, men-only, women-only. Campus housing is university owned. Freshman applicants given priority for college housing. *Activities and organizations:* drama/theater group, student-run newspaper, choral group, Taylor Student Organization, Lighthouse Mission Trips, Multicultural Activities Council, Taylor World Outreach, Student Activities Council. *Campus security:* student patrols, late-night transport/escort service, controlled dormitory access, 12-hour night patrols by trained personnel. *Student services:* health clinic, personal/psychological counseling.

Athletics *Intercollegiate sports:* basketball M (s)/W (s), soccer M (s)/W (s), softball W (c), volleyball W (s). *Intramural sports:* basketball M/W, football M/W, soccer M/W, table tennis M/W, volleyball M/W.

Standardized Tests *Required:* SAT or ACT (for admission).

Costs (2008–09) *Comprehensive fee:* $26,774 includes full-time tuition ($21,030), mandatory fees ($134), and room and board ($5610). Part-time tuition: $350 per credit hour. *Required fees:* $70 per year part-time. *College room only:* $2520.

Financial Aid Of all full-time matriculated undergraduates who enrolled in 2006, 260 applied for aid, 236 were judged to have need, 56 had their need fully met. 157 Federal Work-Study jobs (averaging $1582). In 2006, 42 non-need-based awards were made. *Average percent of need met:* 84%. *Average financial aid package:* $18,093. *Average need-based loan:* $4790. *Average need-based gift aid:* $13,385. *Average non-need-based aid:* $5918. *Average indebtedness upon graduation:* $21,077.

Applying *Options:* electronic application. *Application fee:* $20. *Required:* essay or personal statement, high school transcript, 2 letters of recommendation. *Recommended:* minimum 3.0 GPA, interview. *Application deadlines:* rolling (freshmen), rolling (out-of-state freshmen), rolling (transfers).

Freshman Application Contact Mr. Leo Gonot, Associate Vice President for Enrollment Management, Taylor University Fort Wayne, 1025 West Rudisill Boulevard, Fort Wayne, IN 46807-2197. *Phone:* 260-744-8689. *Toll-free phone:* 800-233-3922. *Fax:* 260-744-8850. *E-mail:* admissions@fw.taylor.edu.

TRI-STATE UNIVERSITY

Angola, Indiana **www.tristate.edu/**

- **Independent** comprehensive, founded 1884
- **Small-town** 400-acre campus
- **Endowment** $17.8 million
- **Coed** 1,328 undergraduate students, 90% full-time, 32% women, 68% men
- **Moderately difficult** entrance level, 74% of applicants were admitted

Tri-State University (TSU) prepares students for their future. The University's 1,250 students receive a private, career-oriented education and personal attention within a hands-on learning environment. The teaching-focused faculty members are experts in engineering, technology, business, education, mathematics, science, communication, criminal justice, psychology, sport management, and golf management. Students come to TSU to focus on their future.

Undergraduates 1,195 full-time, 133 part-time. Students come from 24 states and territories, 6 other countries, 42% are from out of state, 3% African American, 0.9% Asian American or Pacific Islander, 2% Hispanic American, 0.9% international, 4% transferred in, 70% live on campus. *Retention:* 66% of 2006 full-time freshmen returned.

Freshmen *Admission:* 2,250 applied, 1,657 admitted, 417 enrolled. *Average high school GPA:* 3.33. *Test scores:* SAT critical reading scores over 500: 45%; SAT math scores over 500: 72%; ACT scores over 18: 92%; SAT critical reading scores over 600: 12%; SAT math scores over 600: 33%; ACT scores over 24: 39%; SAT critical reading scores over 700: 1%; SAT math scores over 700: 7%; ACT scores over 30: 5%.

Faculty *Total:* 99, 70% full-time, 51% with terminal degrees. *Student/faculty ratio:* 13:1.

Majors Accounting; biological and physical sciences; biology/biological sciences; business administration and management; chemical engineering; chemistry; civil engineering; communication/speech communication and rhetoric; computer and information sciences; computer engineering; computer science; criminal justice/law enforcement administration; drafting and design technology; education; electrical, electronics and communications engineering; elementary education; engineering/industrial management; engineering technology; English; entrepreneurship; environmental studies; forensic science and technology; hospitality administration; industrial technology; liberal arts and sciences/liberal studies; management information systems; marketing/marketing management; mathematics; mathematics teacher education; mechanical engineering; operations management; parks, recreation and leisure facilities management; physical education teaching and coaching; physical sciences; pre-law studies; pre-medical studies; pre-veterinary studies; psychology; science teacher education; secondary education; social sciences; social studies teacher education; sport and fitness administration/management.

Academics *Calendar:* semesters. *Degrees:* associate, bachelor's, and master's. *Special study options:* academic remediation for entering students, adult/continuing education programs, advanced placement credit, cooperative education, distance learning, double majors, honors programs, internships, part-time degree program, study abroad, summer session for credit. *Unusual degree programs:* 3-2 engineering.

Computers on Campus 150 computers/terminals are available on campus for general student use. Students can access the following: computer help desk, free student e-mail accounts, online (class) grades, online (class) registration, online (class) schedules. Campuswide network is available. 100% of college-owned or -operated housing units are wired for high-speed Internet access. Wireless service is available via entire campus.

Student Life *Housing:* on-campus residence required through sophomore year. *Options:* coed, men-only, women-only. Campus housing is university owned and is provided by a third party. Freshman campus housing is guaranteed. *Activities and organizations:* drama/theater group, student-run newspaper, radio station, choral group, Campus Christian House, Drama Club, Habitat for Humanity, student newspaper, student radio station, national fraternities, national sororities. *Campus security:* 24-hour emergency response devices and patrols, late-night transport/escort service, controlled dormitory access. *Student services:* personal/psychological counseling.

Athletics Member NCAA. All Division III. *Intercollegiate sports:* baseball M, basketball M/W, cross-country running M/W, football M, golf M/W, lacrosse M/W, soccer M/W, softball W, tennis M/W, track and field M/W, volleyball W, wrestling M. *Intramural sports:* badminton M/W, basketball M/W, football M, golf M/W, racquetball M/W, softball M/W, table tennis M/W, volleyball M/W.

Standardized Tests *Required:* SAT or ACT (for admission).

Costs (2008–09) *Comprehensive fee:* $30,150 includes full-time tuition ($23,350), mandatory fees ($100), and room and board ($6700). Part-time tuition: $730 per credit hour.

Financial Aid Of all full-time matriculated undergraduates who enrolled in 2007, 1,169 applied for aid, 817 were judged to have need, 817 had their need fully met. 629 Federal Work-Study jobs (averaging $1794). In 2007, 352 non-need-based awards were made. *Average financial aid package:* $15,496. *Average need-based loan:* $4084. *Average need-based gift aid:* $4157. *Average non-need-based aid:* $6750. *Average indebtedness upon graduation:* $16,950.

Applying *Options:* electronic application. *Required:* high school transcript, minimum 2.5 GPA. *Recommended:* essay or personal statement, letters of recommendation, interview. *Application deadlines:* 8/1 (freshmen), 8/1 (transfers). *Notification:* continuous until 8/15 (freshmen), continuous until 8/15 (transfers).

Freshman Application Contact Mr. Scott Goplin, Dean of Admission, Tri-State University, 1 University Avenue, Angola, IN 46703. *Phone:* 260-665-4365. *Toll-free phone:* 800-347-4TSU. *Fax:* 260-665-4578. *E-mail:* admit@tristate.edu.

See page 940 for the College Close-Up.

UNIVERSITY OF EVANSVILLE

Evansville, Indiana **www.evansville.edu/**

- **Independent** comprehensive, founded 1854, affiliated with United Methodist Church
- **Urban** 75-acre campus
- **Endowment** $84.8 million
- **Coed** 2,784 undergraduate students, 87% full-time, 60% women, 40% men
- **Moderately difficult** entrance level, 89% of applicants were admitted

For more than ten consecutive years, the University of Evansville has been ranked by *U.S. News & World Report* as one of the top 10 outstanding Midwest regional universities and as one of the best values in the Midwest. The University of Evansville is a comprehensive university offering NCAA Division I sports.

Undergraduates 2,422 full-time, 362 part-time. Students come from 41 states and territories, 47 other countries, 40% are from out of state, 3% African American, 0.8% Asian American or Pacific Islander, 2% Hispanic American, 0.2% Native American, 6% international, 2% transferred in, 69% live on campus. *Retention:* 84% of 2006 full-time freshmen returned.

Freshmen *Admission:* 2,863 applied, 2,537 admitted, 652 enrolled. *Average high school GPA:* 3.69. *Test scores:* SAT critical reading scores over 500: 78%; SAT math scores over 500: 83%; SAT writing scores over 500: 75%; ACT scores over 18: 97%; SAT critical reading scores over 600: 34%; SAT math scores over 600: 40%; SAT writing scores over 600: 29%; ACT scores over 24: 63%; SAT critical reading scores over 700: 7%; SAT math scores over 700: 6%; SAT writing scores over 700: 3%; ACT scores over 30: 12%.

Faculty *Total:* 229, 77% full-time, 75% with terminal degrees. *Student/faculty ratio:* 13:1.

Majors Accounting; archeology; art; art history, criticism and conservation; art teacher education; athletic training; biblical studies; biochemistry; biology/biological sciences; biology teacher education; business administration and management; business/managerial economics; chemistry; chemistry teacher education; civil engineering; classics and languages, literatures and linguistics; clinical laboratory science/medical technology; cognitive science; communication and journalism related; communication and media related; computer and information sciences; computer and information sciences and support services related; computer engineering; creative writing; design and visual communications; drama and dance teacher education; dramatic/theater arts; economics; education; electrical, electronics and communications engineering; elementary education; English; English composition; English/language arts teacher education; environmental science; environmental studies; finance; French; French language teacher education; German; German language teacher education; graphic design; health/health care administration; health/medical preparatory programs related; history; international business/trade/commerce; international relations and affairs; kinesiology and exercise science; legal professions and studies related; liberal arts and sciences/liberal studies; management information systems; marketing/marketing management; mathematics; mathematics teacher education; mechanical engineering; multi-/interdisciplinary studies related; music; music management and merchandising; music performance; music teacher education; music therapy; neuroscience; nursing (registered nurse training); philosophy; physical education teaching and coaching; physical therapist assistant; physics; physics teacher education; political science and government; pre-dentistry studies; pre-medical studies; pre-pharmacy studies; pre-veterinary studies; psychology; science teacher education; social science teacher education; social studies teacher education; sociology; Spanish; Spanish language teacher education; special education; sport and fitness administration/management; theater/theater arts management.

Academics *Calendar:* semesters. *Degrees:* associate, bachelor's, master's, doctoral, and postbachelor's certificates. *Special study options:* accelerated degree program, adult/continuing education programs, advanced placement credit, cooperative education, double majors, English as a second language, external degree program, honors programs, independent study, internships, part-time degree program, student-designed majors, study abroad, summer session for credit.

Computers on Campus 300 computers/terminals and 3,000 ports are available on campus for general student use. Students can access the following: campus intranet, computer help desk, free student e-mail accounts, online (class) grades, online (class) schedules. Campuswide network is available. 100% of college-owned or -operated housing units are wired for high-speed Internet access. Wireless service is available via entire campus.

Student Life *Housing:* on-campus residence required for freshman year. *Options:* coed, men-only, women-only. Campus housing is university owned. Freshman campus housing is guaranteed. *Activities and organizations:* student-run newspaper, radio station, choral group, Student Christian Fellowship, Womens Awareness, Quidditch Club, Colleges Against Cancer, Admissions Ambassadors, national fraternities, national sororities. *Campus security:* 24-hour emergency response devices and patrols, student patrols, late-night transport/escort service, controlled dormitory access. *Student services:* health clinic, personal/psychological counseling.

Athletics Member NCAA. All Division I. *Intercollegiate sports:* baseball M (s), basketball M (s)/W (s), cross-country running M (s)/W (s), golf M (s)/W (s), soccer M (s)/W (s), softball W (s), swimming and diving M (s)/W (s), tennis W (s), volleyball W (s). *Intramural sports:* badminton M/W, basketball M/W, bowling M/W, cheerleading M (c)/W (c), cross-country running M/W, football M/W, golf M/W, racquetball M/W, soccer M/W, softball M/W, swimming and diving M/W, table tennis M/W, tennis M/W, ultimate Frisbee M/W, volleyball M/W.

Standardized Tests *Required:* SAT or ACT (for admission).

Costs (2007–08) *Comprehensive fee:* $31,990 includes full-time tuition ($23,710), mandatory fees ($630), and room and board ($7650). Part-time tuition: $650 per hour. Part-time tuition and fees vary according to course load. *Required fees:* $40 per term part-time. *College room only:* $3890. Room and board charges vary according to board plan and housing facility. *Payment plan:* installment. *Waivers:* minority students, children of alumni, senior citizens, and employees or children of employees.

Financial Aid Of all full-time matriculated undergraduates who enrolled in 2007, 1,926 applied for aid, 1,648 were judged to have need, 513 had their need fully met. 421 Federal Work-Study jobs (averaging $1200). 75 state and other part-time jobs (averaging $1131). In 2007, 556 non-need-based awards were made. *Average percent of need met:* 86%. *Average financial aid package:* $20,659. *Average need-based loan:* $5057. *Average need-based gift aid:* $17,132. *Average non-need-based aid:* $11,572. *Average indebtedness upon graduation:* $22,960.

Applying *Options:* electronic application, early action, deferred entrance. *Application fee:* $35. *Required:* high school transcript, 1 letter of recommendation. *Required for some:* essay or personal statement, interview. *Recommended:* minimum 3.0 GPA, interview. *Application deadlines:* 2/1 (freshmen), rolling (transfers), 12/1 (early action). *Notification:* continuous until 3/1 (freshmen), continuous (transfers), 12/15 (early action).

Freshman Application Contact Don Vos, Dean of Admission, University of Evansville, 1800 Lincoln Avenue, Evansville, IN 47722-0002. *Phone:* 812-488-2468. *Toll-free phone:* 800-423-8633 Ext. 2468. *Fax:* 812-488-4076. *E-mail:* admission@evansville.edu.

UNIVERSITY OF INDIANAPOLIS

Indianapolis, Indiana **www.uindy.edu/**

- **Independent** comprehensive, founded 1902, affiliated with United Methodist Church
- **Urban** 65-acre campus
- **Endowment** $77.2 million
- **Coed** 3,511 undergraduate students, 75% full-time, 67% women, 33% men
- **Moderately difficult** entrance level, 82% of applicants were admitted

Undergraduates 2,629 full-time, 882 part-time. 19% are from out of state, 10% African American, 1% Asian American or Pacific Islander, 2% Hispanic American, 0.2% Native American, 5% international, 35% live on campus. *Retention:* 74% of 2006 full-time freshmen returned.

Freshmen *Admission:* 3,192 applied, 2,611 admitted, 743 enrolled. *Average high school GPA:* 3.35. *Test scores:* SAT critical reading scores over 500: 52%; SAT math scores over 500: 57%; SAT writing scores over 500: 47%; ACT scores over 18: 87%; SAT critical reading scores over 600: 16%; SAT math scores over 600: 19%; SAT writing scores over 600: 12%; ACT scores over 24: 32%; SAT critical reading scores over 700: 2%; SAT math scores over 700: 3%; SAT writing scores over 700: 1%; ACT scores over 30: 3%.

Faculty *Total:* 194. *Student/faculty ratio:* 12:1.

Majors Accounting; anthropology; archeology; art; art teacher education; art therapy; athletic training; biology/biological sciences; business/managerial economics; business teacher education; clinical laboratory science/medical technology; commercial and advertising art; communication/speech communication and rhetoric; computer engineering; computer science; dramatic/theater arts; education; elementary education; English; English/language arts teacher education; entrepreneurship; environmental studies; fine/studio arts; French; French language teacher education; geology/earth science; German; history; international business/trade/commerce; international relations and affairs; kinesiology and exercise science; marketing/marketing management; mathematics; mathematics teacher education; mechanical engineering; music; music performance; music teacher education; operations management; philosophy; physical education teaching and coaching; physical therapist assistant; physics; political science and government; pre-dentistry studies; pre-law studies; pre-medical studies; pre-theology/pre-ministerial studies; pre-veterinary studies; psychology; religious studies; respiratory care therapy; science teacher education; secondary education; social studies teacher education; social work; sociology; Spanish; Spanish language teacher education; speech teacher education; sport and fitness administration/management; youth ministry.

Academics *Calendar:* 4-4-1. *Degrees:* associate, bachelor's, master's, and doctoral. *Special study options:* academic remediation for entering students, accelerated degree program, adult/continuing education programs, advanced placement credit, cooperative education, double majors, English as a second language, freshman honors college, honors programs, independent study, internships, off-campus study, part-time degree program, services for LD students, student-designed majors, study abroad, summer session for credit. *ROTC:* Army (c). *Unusual degree programs:* 3-2 engineering with Indiana University & Purdue University Indianapolis; physical therapy, occupational therapy.

Computers on Campus 218 computers/terminals are available on campus for general student use. Students can access the following: campus intranet, computer help desk, free student e-mail accounts, online (class) grades, online (class) schedules. Campuswide network is available. Wireless service is available via entire campus.

Student Life *Housing options:* coed, women-only. Campus housing is university owned. *Activities and organizations:* drama/theater group, student-run newspaper, radio and television station, choral group, Fellowship of Christian Athletes, Intercultural Association, Circle K, Indianapolis Student Government, Residence Hall Association. *Campus security:* 24-hour emergency response devices and patrols, student patrols, late-night transport/escort service, emergency call boxes. *Student services:* health clinic, personal/psychological counseling.

Athletics Member NCAA. All Division II. *Intercollegiate sports:* baseball M (s), basketball M (s)/W (s), cross-country running M (s)/W (s), football M (s), golf M (s)/W (s), soccer M (s)/W (s), softball W (s), swimming and diving M (s)/W (s), tennis M (s)/W (s), track and field M (s)/W (s), volleyball W (s), wrestling M (s). *Intramural sports:* badminton M/W, basketball M/W, cheerleading M/W, football M/W, racquetball M/W, softball M/W, table tennis M/W, tennis M/W, volleyball M/W.

Standardized Tests *Required:* SAT or ACT (for admission).

Costs (2007–08) *Comprehensive fee:* $27,290 includes full-time tuition ($19,540), mandatory fees ($190), and room and board ($7560). Part-time tuition: $814 per hour. Part-time tuition and fees vary according to course load. *College room only:* $3590. Room and board charges vary according to board plan and housing facility. *Waivers:* employees or children of employees.

Financial Aid Of all full-time matriculated undergraduates who enrolled in 2003, 1,288 applied for aid, 1,171 were judged to have need, 402 had their need fully met. 281 Federal Work-Study jobs (averaging $1193). In 2003, 170 non-need-based awards were made. *Average percent of need met:* 85%. *Average financial aid package:* $15,547. *Average need-based loan:* $4451. *Average need-based gift aid:* $8497. *Average non-need-based aid:* $7725. *Average indebtedness upon graduation:* $21,200.

Applying *Options:* electronic application, deferred entrance. *Application fee:* $25. *Required:* high school transcript, minimum 2.0 GPA. *Required for some:* interview. *Application deadlines:* rolling (freshmen), rolling (transfers). *Notification:* continuous (freshmen), continuous (transfers).

Freshman Application Contact Mr. Ronald Wilks, Director of Admissions, University of Indianapolis, 1400 East Hanna Avenue, Indianapolis, IN 46227-3697. *Phone:* 317-788-3216. *Toll-free phone:* 800-232-8634 Ext. 3216. *Fax:* 317-788-3300. *E-mail:* admissions@uindy.edu.

See page 942 for the College Close-Up.

UNIVERSITY OF NOTRE DAME

Notre Dame, Indiana **www.nd.edu/**

- **Independent Roman Catholic** university, founded 1842
- **Suburban** 1250-acre campus
- **Endowment** $6.1 billion
- **Coed** 8,371 undergraduate students, 100% full-time, 47% women, 53% men
- **Most difficult** entrance level, 24% of applicants were admitted

Undergraduates 8,359 full-time, 12 part-time. Students come from 53 states and territories, 43 other countries, 92% are from out of state, 4% African American, 7% Asian American or Pacific Islander, 9% Hispanic American, 0.7% Native American, 3% international, 2% transferred in, 76% live on campus. *Retention:* 97% of 2006 full-time freshmen returned.

Freshmen *Admission:* 14,503 applied, 3,549 admitted, 1,991 enrolled. *Test scores:* SAT critical reading scores over 500: 98%; SAT math scores over 500: 99%; SAT writing scores over 500: 98%; ACT scores over 18: 100%; SAT critical reading scores over 600: 88%; SAT math scores over 600: 92%; SAT writing scores over 600: 85%; ACT scores over 24: 98%; SAT critical reading scores over 700: 51%; SAT math scores over 700: 58%; SAT writing scores over 700: 43%; ACT scores over 30: 83%.

Faculty *Total:* 890. *Student/faculty ratio:* 11:1.

Majors Accounting; aerospace, aeronautical and astronautical engineering; African-American/Black studies; American studies; ancient/classical Greek; anthropology; Arabic; architecture; art history, criticism and conservation; biochemistry; biological and physical sciences; biology/biological sciences; business administration, management and operations related; business/commerce; chemical engineering; chemistry; chemistry related; Chinese; civil engineering; classics and languages, literatures and linguistics; computer and information sciences; computer and information sciences and support services related; computer engineering; design and visual communications; dramatic/theater arts; economics; electrical, electronics and communications engineering; English; environmental/environmental health engineering; environmental science; finance; fine/studio arts; French; German; history; Italian; Japanese; liberal arts and sciences/liberal studies; management information systems; marketing/marketing management; mathematics; mechanical engineering; medieval and Renaissance studies; music; philosophy; philosophy and religious studies related; physics; physics related; political science and government; pre-medical studies; psychology; Romance languages; Russian; science teacher education; sociology; Spanish; theology.

Academics *Calendar:* semesters. *Degrees:* bachelor's, master's, doctoral, and first professional. *Special study options:* accelerated degree program, advanced placement credit, distance learning, double majors, honors programs, independent study, internships, off-campus study, services for LD students, student-designed majors, study abroad, summer session for credit. *ROTC:* Army (b), Navy (b), Air Force (b). *Unusual degree programs:* 3-2 business administration; engineering.

Computers on Campus 221 computers/terminals are available on campus for general student use. Students can access the following: computer help desk, free student e-mail accounts, online (class) grades, online (class) registration, online (class) schedules. Campuswide network is available. Wireless service is available via entire campus.

Student Life *Housing:* on-campus residence required for freshman year. *Options:* men-only, women-only. Campus housing is university owned. Freshman campus housing is guaranteed. *Activities and organizations:* drama/theater group, student-run newspaper, radio station, choral group, marching band, marching band, Circle K, Finance Club, Notre Dame/St. Mary's Right to Life. *Campus security:* 24-hour emergency response devices and patrols, student patrols, late-night transport/escort service, controlled dormitory access, crime prevention and personal safety workshops, full-time trained police investigators, fire sprinklers in all residence halls. *Student services:* health clinic, personal/psychological counseling, women's center, legal services.

Athletics Member NCAA. All Division I except football (Division I-A). *Intercollegiate sports:* baseball M (s), basketball M (s)/W (s), crew W (s), cross-country running M (s)/W (s), fencing M (s)/W (s), golf M (s)/W (s), ice hockey M (s), lacrosse M (s)/W (s), soccer M (s)/W (s), softball W (s), swimming and diving M (s)/W (s), tennis M (s)/W (s), track and field M (s)/W (s), volleyball W (s). *Intramural sports:* badminton M/W, baseball M, basketball M/W, bowling M (c)/W (c), crew M (c), cross-country running M/W, equestrian sports M (c)/W (c), field hockey M (c)/W (c), football M/W, golf M/W, gymnastics M (c)/W (c), ice hockey M/W (c), lacrosse M/W, racquetball M/W, sailing M (c)/W (c), skiing (cross-country) M (c)/W (c), skiing (downhill) M (c)/W (c), soccer M/W, softball M/W, squash M (c)/W (c), table tennis M/W, tennis M/W, ultimate Frisbee M/W, volleyball M (c)/W (c), water polo M (c)/W (c).

Standardized Tests *Required:* SAT or ACT (for admission). *Required for some:* SAT Subject Tests (for admission).

Costs (2007–08) *Comprehensive fee:* $44,477 includes full-time tuition ($34,680), mandatory fees ($507), and room and board ($9290). Part-time tuition: $1445 per credit. *Payment plan:* installment. *Waivers:* employees or children of employees.

Financial Aid Of all full-time matriculated undergraduates who enrolled in 2007, 4,923 applied for aid, 3,902 were judged to have need, 3,765 had their need fully met. 1,743 Federal Work-Study jobs (averaging $2168). 3,863 state and other part-time jobs (averaging $2650). In 2007, 272 non-need-based awards were made. *Average percent of need met:* 99%. *Average financial aid package:* $30,285. *Average need-based loan:* $5170. *Average need-based gift aid:* $22,291. *Average non-need-based aid:* $6328. *Average indebtedness upon graduation:* $27,569. *Financial aid deadline:* 2/15.

Applying *Options:* electronic application, early action, deferred entrance. *Application fee:* $65. *Required:* essay or personal statement, high school transcript, 1 letter of recommendation. *Application deadlines:* 12/31 (freshmen), 4/15 (transfers), 11/1 (early action). *Notification:* 4/10 (freshmen), 12/20 (early action).

Freshman Application Contact Office of Undergraduate Admissions, University of Notre Dame, 220 Main Building, Notre Dame, IN 46556-5612. *Phone:* 574-631-7505. *Fax:* 574-631-8865. *E-mail:* admissions@nd.edu.

UNIVERSITY OF PHOENIX–INDIANAPOLIS CAMPUS

Indianapolis, Indiana **www.phoenix.edu/**

- **Proprietary** comprehensive, founded 2003
- **Urban** campus
- **Coed**
- **Noncompetitive** entrance level

Faculty *Student/faculty ratio:* 7:1.

Academics *Calendar:* continuous. *Degrees:* bachelor's and master's.

Student Life *Campus security:* late-night transport/escort service.

Costs (2007–08) *Tuition:* $10,440 full-time, $348 per credit part-time. Full-time tuition and fees vary according to course level.

Financial Aid *Average financial aid package:* $4196. *Average need-based gift aid:* $2235.

Applying *Options:* deferred entrance. *Application fee:* $45. *Required:* 1 letter of recommendation. *Required for some:* high school transcript.

Freshman Application Contact Ms. Beth Barilla, Associate Vice President, Student Admissions and Services, University of Phoenix–Indianapolis Campus, 4615 East Elwood Street, Mail Stop AA-K101, Phoenix, AZ 85040-1958. *Phone:* 480-317-6000. *Toll-free phone:* 800-776-4867 (in-state); 800-228-7240 (out-of-state). *Fax:* 480-894-1758. *E-mail:* beth.barilla@phoenix.edu.

UNIVERSITY OF SAINT FRANCIS

Fort Wayne, Indiana **www.sf.edu/**

- **Independent Roman Catholic** comprehensive, founded 1890
- **Suburban** 74-acre campus
- **Endowment** $8.5 million
- **Coed** 1,840 undergraduate students, 80% full-time, 69% women, 31% men
- **Moderately difficult** entrance level, 55% of applicants were admitted

Undergraduates 1,470 full-time, 370 part-time. Students come from 15 states and territories, 1 other country, 9% are from out of state, 5% African American, 0.7% Asian American or Pacific Islander, 2% Hispanic American, 0.4% Native American, 13% transferred in, 22% live on campus. *Retention:* 70% of 2006 full-time freshmen returned.

Freshmen *Admission:* 1,125 applied, 623 admitted, 354 enrolled. *Average high school GPA:* 3.16. *Test scores:* SAT critical reading scores over 500: 41%; SAT math scores over 500: 51%; SAT writing scores over 500: 36%; ACT scores over 18: 81%; SAT critical reading scores over 600: 12%; SAT math scores over 600: 13%; SAT writing scores over 600: 7%; ACT scores over 24: 31%; SAT critical reading scores over 700: 1%; SAT math scores over 700: 2%; ACT scores over 30: 3%.

Faculty *Total:* 223, 45% full-time, 29% with terminal degrees. *Student/faculty ratio:* 12:1.

Majors Accounting; American studies; art; art teacher education; biological and physical sciences; biology teacher education; business administration and management; business teacher education; chemistry; chemistry teacher education; clinical laboratory science/medical technology; commercial and advertising art; communication/speech communication and rhetoric; design and applied arts related; education; elementary education; English; English/language arts teacher education; environmental studies; health/health care administration; health professions related; health teacher education; history; human resources management; human services; liberal arts and sciences/liberal studies; mathematics; mathematics teacher education; medical radiologic technology; music related; nursing (registered nurse training); nursing related; philosophy; physical sciences related; physical therapist assistant; physician assistant; political science and government related; pre-pharmacy studies; psychology; religious studies; science teacher education; social studies teacher education; social work; sociology; special education; surgical technology; theological and ministerial studies related; theology.

Academics *Calendar:* semesters. *Degrees:* certificates, associate, bachelor's, master's, and postbachelor's certificates. *Special study options:* academic remediation for entering students, adult/continuing education programs, advanced placement credit, cooperative education, distance learning, double majors, freshman honors college, honors programs, independent study, internships, off-campus study, part-time degree program, services for LD students, study abroad, summer session for credit.

Computers on Campus 297 computers/terminals are available on campus for general student use. Students can access the following: computer help desk, free student e-mail accounts, online (class) grades, online (class) registration, online (class) schedules. Campuswide network is available. 100% of college-owned or -operated housing units are wired for high-speed Internet access. Wireless service is available via entire campus.

Student Life *Housing:* on-campus residence required through sophomore year. *Options:* coed. Campus housing is university owned. Freshman applicants given priority for college housing. *Activities and organizations:* drama/theater group, student-run newspaper, choral group, Student Activities Council, Art Club, Student Government Organization, Student Nursing Association, Residence Hall Council. *Campus security:* 24-hour emergency response devices and patrols, late-night transport/escort service, controlled dormitory access. *Student services:* personal/psychological counseling.

Athletics Member NAIA. *Intercollegiate sports:* baseball M (s), basketball M (s)/W (s), cheerleading M (s)/W (s), cross-country running M (s)/W (s), football M (s), golf M (s)/W, soccer M (s)/W (s), softball W (s), tennis W (s), track and field M (s)/W (s), volleyball W (s). *Intramural sports:* basketball M/W, bowling M/W, soccer M/W, ultimate Frisbee M/W, volleyball W.

Standardized Tests *Required:* SAT or ACT (for admission).

Costs (2007–08) *Comprehensive fee:* $25,576 includes full-time tuition ($18,820), mandatory fees ($750), and room and board ($6006). Full-time tuition and fees vary according to course load. Part-time tuition: $590 per hour. Part-time tuition and fees vary according to course load. *Required fees:* $40 per hour part-time. *Room and board:* Room and board charges vary according to board plan and housing facility. *Payment plans:* installment, deferred payment. *Waivers:* children of alumni, senior citizens, and employees or children of employees.

Financial Aid Of all full-time matriculated undergraduates who enrolled in 2005, 1,181 applied for aid, 1,028 were judged to have need, 280 had their need fully met. 891 Federal Work-Study jobs (averaging $1521). In 2005, 157 non-need-based awards were made. *Average percent of need met:* 77%. *Average financial aid package:* $13,008. *Average need-based loan:* $3209. *Average need-based gift aid:* $9487. *Average non-need-based aid:* $11,062. *Average indebtedness upon graduation:* $21,352. *Financial aid deadline:* 6/30.

Applying *Options:* electronic application, deferred entrance. *Application fee:* $20. *Required:* high school transcript, minimum 2.3 GPA. *Required for some:*

letters of recommendation, interview. *Recommended:* essay or personal statement. *Application deadlines:* rolling (freshmen), rolling (transfers). *Notification:* continuous until 8/15 (freshmen), continuous until 8/15 (transfers).

Freshman Application Contact Mr. Ron Schumacher, Vice President for Enrollment Management, University of Saint Francis, 2701 Spring Street, Fort Wayne, IN 46808. *Phone:* 260-434-3279. *Toll-free phone:* 800-729-4732. *E-mail:* admis@sf.edu.

UNIVERSITY OF SOUTHERN INDIANA

Evansville, Indiana **www.usi.edu/**

- **State-supported** comprehensive, founded 1965, part of Indiana Commission for Higher Education
- **Suburban** 330-acre campus
- **Coed** 9,225 undergraduate students, 83% full-time, 59% women, 41% men
- **Moderately difficult** entrance level, 90% of applicants were admitted

Undergraduates 7,637 full-time, 1,588 part-time. Students come from 31 states and territories, 42 other countries, 9% are from out of state, 5% African American, 0.8% Asian American or Pacific Islander, 0.9% Hispanic American, 0.4% Native American, 2% international, 6% transferred in, 28% live on campus. *Retention:* 63% of 2006 full-time freshmen returned.

Freshmen *Admission:* 4,934 applied, 4,457 admitted, 2,136 enrolled. *Average high school GPA:* 2.96. *Test scores:* SAT critical reading scores over 500: 35%; SAT math scores over 500: 41%; SAT writing scores over 500: 31%; ACT scores over 18: 74%; SAT critical reading scores over 600: 8%; SAT math scores over 600: 8%; SAT writing scores over 600: 5%; ACT scores over 24: 21%; SAT critical reading scores over 700: 1%; SAT math scores over 700: 1%; ACT scores over 30: 2%.

Faculty *Total:* 608, 53% full-time, 40% with terminal degrees. *Student/faculty ratio:* 18:1.

Majors Accounting; advertising; art; biological and physical sciences; biology/biological sciences; biophysics; business administration and management; business/commerce; business, management, and marketing related; business teacher education; chemistry; communication/speech communication and rhetoric; computer and information sciences; data processing and data processing technology; dental assisting; dental hygiene; dramatic/theater arts; e-commerce; economics; education; elementary education; engineering; engineering technologies related; English; entrepreneurship; finance; French; geology/earth science; German; health professions related; history; international relations and affairs; journalism; kinesiology and exercise science; liberal arts and sciences/liberal studies; management information systems and services related; marketing/marketing management; mathematics; medical radiologic technology; nursing (registered nurse training); occupational therapist assistant; occupational therapy; office management; philosophy; physical education teaching and coaching; political science and government; psychology; public relations/image management; radio and television; respiratory care therapy; social sciences; social work; sociology; Spanish; special education related.

Academics *Calendar:* semesters. *Degrees:* certificates, associate, bachelor's, master's, and postbachelor's certificates. *Special study options:* academic remediation for entering students, adult/continuing education programs, advanced placement credit, cooperative education, distance learning, double majors, English as a second language, honors programs, independent study, internships, part-time degree program, services for LD students, study abroad, summer session for credit. *ROTC:* Army (b).

Computers on Campus 306 computers/terminals are available on campus for general student use. Students can access the following: computer help desk, free student e-mail accounts, online (class) grades, online (class) registration, online (class) schedules. Campuswide network is available. 100% of college-owned or -operated housing units are wired for high-speed Internet access. Wireless service is available via entire campus.

Student Life *Housing options:* coed. Campus housing is university owned. *Activities and organizations:* drama/theater group, student-run newspaper, radio station, choral group, student government, national fraternities, national sororities. *Campus security:* 24-hour emergency response devices and patrols, student patrols, late-night transport/escort service, controlled dormitory access. *Student services:* health clinic, personal/psychological counseling.

Athletics Member NCAA. All Division II. *Intercollegiate sports:* baseball M (s), basketball M (s)/W (s), cheerleading M/W, cross-country running M (s)/W (s), golf M (s)/W (s), rugby M (c), soccer M (s)/W (s), softball W (s), tennis M (s)/W (s), ultimate Frisbee M (c)/W (c), volleyball W (s). *Intramural sports:* badminton M/W, basketball M/W, bowling M/W, football M/W, golf M/W, rock climbing M/W, skiing (downhill) M/W, soccer M/W, softball M/W, table tennis M/W, tennis M/W, volleyball M/W.

Standardized Tests *Required:* SAT or ACT (for admission).

Costs (2008–09) *Tuition:* state resident $5019 full-time, $167 per credit hour part-time; nonresident $11,954 full-time, $398 per credit hour part-time. *Required fees:* $200 full-time, $23 per term part-time. *Room and board:* $6542; room only: $3284.

Financial Aid Of all full-time matriculated undergraduates who enrolled in 2006, 5,802 applied for aid, 3,902 were judged to have need, 477 had their need fully met. 114 Federal Work-Study jobs (averaging $2424). In 2006, 557 non-need-based awards were made. *Average percent of need met:* 46%. *Average financial aid package:* $8561. *Average need-based loan:* $4863. *Average need-based gift aid:* $5028. *Average non-need-based aid:* $2082. *Average indebtedness upon graduation:* $15,623. *Financial aid deadline:* 3/1.

Applying *Options:* electronic application. *Application fee:* $25. *Required:* high school transcript. *Required for some:* interview. *Recommended:* essay or personal statement, minimum 2.0 GPA. *Application deadline:* 8/15 (freshmen). *Notification:* continuous until 8/27 (freshmen), continuous (transfers).

Freshman Application Contact Mr. Eric Otto, Director of Admission, University of Southern Indiana, 8600 University Boulevard, Evansville, IN 47712-3590. *Phone:* 812-464-1765. *Toll-free phone:* 800-467-1965. *Fax:* 812-465-7154. *E-mail:* enroll@usi.edu.

VALPARAISO UNIVERSITY

Valparaiso, Indiana **www.valpo.edu/**

- **Independent** comprehensive, founded 1859, affiliated with Lutheran Church
- **Small-town** 310-acre campus with easy access to Chicago
- **Endowment** $193.0 million
- **Coed** 2,915 undergraduate students, 94% full-time, 52% women, 48% men
- **Moderately difficult** entrance level, 90% of applicants were admitted

Undergraduates 2,749 full-time, 166 part-time. Students come from 45 states and territories, 41 other countries, 63% are from out of state, 4% African American, 1% Asian American or Pacific Islander, 4% Hispanic American, 0.3% Native American, 3% international, 3% transferred in, 70% live on campus. *Retention:* 85% of 2006 full-time freshmen returned.

Freshmen *Admission:* 3,475 applied, 3,134 admitted, 715 enrolled. *Average high school GPA:* 3.36. *Test scores:* SAT critical reading scores over 500: 75%; SAT math scores over 500: 78%; SAT writing scores over 500: 70%; ACT scores over 18: 99%; SAT critical reading scores over 600: 34%; SAT math scores over 600: 39%; SAT writing scores over 600: 28%; ACT scores over 24: 66%; SAT critical reading scores over 700: 6%; SAT math scores over 700: 7%; SAT writing scores over 700: 3%; ACT scores over 30: 16%.

Faculty *Total:* 377, 67% full-time, 80% with terminal degrees. *Student/faculty ratio:* 12:1.

Majors Accounting; actuarial science; American studies; art; art teacher education; Asian studies (East); atmospheric sciences and meteorology; biochemistry; biological and physical sciences; biology/biological sciences; biology teacher education; chemistry; chemistry teacher education; civil engineering; classics and languages, literatures and linguistics; communication and journalism related; computer engineering; computer science; criminology; drama and dance teacher education; dramatic/theater arts; economics; economics related; electrical, electronics and communications engineering; elementary education; English; English/language arts teacher education; environmental science; finance; fine/studio arts; foreign language teacher education; French; French language teacher education; geography; geography teacher education; geology/earth science; German; German language teacher education; health and physical education; history; history teacher education; humanities; international business/trade/commerce; international economics; international relations and affairs; journalism; kinesiology and exercise science; management science; management sciences and quantitative methods related; marketing/marketing management; mass communication/media; mathematics; mathematics teacher education; mechanical engineering; middle school education; multi-/interdisciplinary studies related; music; music management and merchandising; music performance; music teacher education; music theory and composition; nursing (registered nurse training); organizational communication; philosophy; physical education teaching and coaching; physics; physics teacher education; piano and organ; political science and government; psychology; psychology teacher education; public relations/image management; radio and television; religious/sacred music; science teacher education; secondary education; social sciences; social science teacher education; social work; sociology; Spanish; Spanish language teacher education; sport and fitness administration/management; teacher assistant/aide; technical and business writing; theology; voice and opera.

Academics *Calendar:* semesters. *Degrees:* certificates, associate, bachelor's, master's, first professional, post-master's, and postbachelor's certificates. *Special study options:* accelerated degree program, adult/continuing education programs, advanced placement credit, cooperative education, distance learning, double majors, English as a second language, freshman honors college, honors programs, independent study, internships, off-campus study, part-time degree program, services for LD students, student-designed majors, study abroad, summer session for credit. *ROTC:* Air Force (c).

Computers on Campus 901 computers/terminals and 5,100 ports are available on campus for general student use. Students can access the following: campus intranet, computer help desk, free student e-mail accounts, online (class) grades, online (class) registration, online (class) schedules, Web academic information, degree audit. Campuswide network is available. 100% of college-owned or -operated housing units are wired for high-speed Internet access. Wireless service is available via classrooms, computer centers, computer labs, dorm rooms, learning centers, libraries, student centers.

Student Life *Housing:* on-campus residence required through junior year. *Options:* coed, women-only. Campus housing is university owned and leased by the school. Freshman campus housing is guaranteed. *Activities and organizations:* drama/theater group, student-run newspaper, radio station, choral group, Union Board, student government, student volunteer organization, chapel programs, national fraternities. *Campus security:* 24-hour emergency response devices and patrols, late-night transport/escort service, controlled dormitory access. *Student services:* health clinic, personal/psychological counseling.

Athletics Member NCAA. All Division I. *Intercollegiate sports:* baseball M (s), basketball M (s)/W (s), cross-country running M (s)/W (s), football M, soccer M (s)/W (s), softball W (s), swimming and diving M (s)/W (s), tennis M (s)/W (s), track and field M (s)/W (s), volleyball W (s). *Intramural sports:* badminton M/W, baseball M, basketball M/W, bowling M/W, cheerleading M/W, football M/W, golf M/W, ice hockey M (c), racquetball M/W, soccer M/W, softball M/W, swimming and diving M/W, table tennis M/W, tennis M/W, ultimate Frisbee M (c)/W (c), volleyball M/W.

Standardized Tests *Required:* SAT or ACT (for admission).

Costs (2007–08) *Comprehensive fee:* $32,350 includes full-time tuition ($24,360), mandatory fees ($840), and room and board ($7150). Part-time tuition: $1125 per credit hour. Part-time tuition and fees vary according to course load. *Required fees:* $20 per credit hour part-time. *College room only:* $4430. Room and board charges vary according to housing facility and student level. *Payment plans:* installment, deferred payment. *Waivers:* employees or children of employees.

Financial Aid Of all full-time matriculated undergraduates who enrolled in 2007, 2,261 applied for aid, 1,930 were judged to have need, 575 had their need fully met. 550 Federal Work-Study jobs (averaging $2000). 650 state and other part-time jobs (averaging $2000). In 2007, 636 non-need-based awards were made. *Average percent of need met:* 83%. *Average financial aid package:* $19,382. *Average need-based loan:* $5607. *Average need-based gift aid:* $15,080. *Average non-need-based aid:* $8745. *Average indebtedness upon graduation:* $26,259.

Applying *Options:* electronic application, early action, deferred entrance. *Application fee:* $30. *Required:* essay or personal statement, high school transcript. *Required for some:* interview. *Recommended:* 2 letters of recommendation, interview. *Application deadlines:* 8/15 (freshmen), 11/1 (early action). *Notification:* continuous (transfers), 12/1 (early action).

Freshman Application Contact Office of Admission, Valparaiso University, Kretzmann Hall, 1700 Chapel Drive, Valparaiso, IN 46383-6493. *Phone:* 219-464-5011. *Toll-free phone:* 888-GO-VALPO. *Fax:* 219-464-6898. *E-mail:* undergrad.admissions@valpo.edu.

See page 944 for the College Close-Up.

WABASH COLLEGE

Crawfordsville, Indiana **www.wabash.edu/**

- **Independent** 4-year, founded 1832
- **Small-town** 50-acre campus with easy access to Indianapolis
- **Endowment** $413.2 million
- **Men only** 917 undergraduate students, 100% full-time
- **Moderately difficult** entrance level, 47% of applicants were admitted

Undergraduates 913 full-time, 4 part-time. Students come from 30 states and territories, 19 other countries, 27% are from out of state, 6% African American, 2% Asian American or Pacific Islander, 5% Hispanic American, 0.1% Native American, 5% international, 0.3% transferred in, 91% live on campus. *Retention:* 88% of 2006 full-time freshmen returned.

Freshmen *Admission:* 1,419 applied, 670 admitted, 250 enrolled. *Average high school GPA:* 3.6. *Test scores:* SAT critical reading scores over 500: 83%; SAT math scores over 500: 90%; SAT writing scores over 500: 75%; ACT scores over 18: 96%; SAT critical reading scores over 600: 38%; SAT math scores over 600: 49%; SAT writing scores over 600: 33%; ACT scores over 24: 57%; SAT critical reading scores over 700: 12%; SAT math scores over 700: 13%; SAT writing scores over 700: 6%; ACT scores over 30: 13%.

Faculty *Total:* 91, 95% full-time, 97% with terminal degrees. *Student/faculty ratio:* 10:1.

Majors Art; biology/biological sciences; chemistry; classics and languages, literatures and linguistics; dramatic/theater arts; economics; English; French; German; history; Latin; mathematics; modern Greek; music; philosophy; physics; political science and government; pre-law studies; pre-medical studies; pre-veterinary studies; psychology; religious studies; Spanish; speech and rhetoric.

Academics *Calendar:* semesters. *Degree:* bachelor's. *Special study options:* advanced placement credit, double majors, independent study, internships, off-campus study, services for LD students, study abroad. *Unusual degree programs:* 3-2 engineering with Columbia University, Washington University in St. Louis; law with Columbia University.

Computers on Campus 350 computers/terminals are available on campus for general student use. Students can access the following: campus intranet, computer help desk, free student e-mail accounts, online (class) grades, online (class) schedules, online course management; degree audit; expenses. Campuswide network is available. 100% of college-owned or -operated housing units are wired for high-speed Internet access. Wireless service is available via entire campus.

Student Life *Housing:* on-campus residence required through sophomore year. *Options:* men-only. Campus housing is university owned. Freshman campus housing is guaranteed. *Activities and organizations:* drama/theater group, student-run newspaper, radio station, choral group, Sphinx Club, Alpha Phi Omega, The Bachelor, Malcolm X Institute, Christian Fellowship, national fraternities. *Campus security:* 24-hour emergency response devices and patrols, late-night transport/escort service. *Student services:* health clinic, personal/psychological counseling.

Athletics Member NCAA. All Division III. *Intercollegiate sports:* baseball M, basketball M, crew M (c), cross-country running M, football M, golf M, lacrosse M (c), rugby M (c), sailing M (c), soccer M, swimming and diving M, tennis M, track and field M, water polo M (c), wrestling M. *Intramural sports:* badminton M, basketball M, bowling M, cross-country running M, football M, golf M, racquetball M, soccer M, softball M, swimming and diving M, table tennis M, tennis M, track and field M, volleyball M, weight lifting M, wrestling M.

Standardized Tests *Required:* SAT or ACT (for admission).

Costs (2007–08) *Comprehensive fee:* $34,050 includes full-time tuition ($25,900), mandatory fees ($450), and room and board ($7700). Part-time tuition: $4317 per course. Part-time tuition and fees vary according to course load. *College room only:* $3100. Room and board charges vary according to board plan and housing facility. *Payment plans:* tuition prepayment, installment. *Waivers:* employees or children of employees.

Financial Aid Of all full-time matriculated undergraduates who enrolled in 2007, 737 applied for aid, 648 were judged to have need, 648 had their need fully met. 862 state and other part-time jobs (averaging $2318). In 2007, 224 non-need-based awards were made. *Average percent of need met:* 100%. *Average financial aid package:* $24,261. *Average need-based loan:* $4998. *Average need-based gift aid:* $16,726. *Average non-need-based aid:* $13,586. *Average indebtedness upon graduation:* $21,497. *Financial aid deadline:* 3/1.

Applying *Options:* electronic application, early admission, early decision, early action, deferred entrance. *Application fee:* $40. *Required:* high school transcript. *Recommended:* essay or personal statement, letters of recommendation, interview. *Application deadlines:* rolling (freshmen), 3/15 (transfers), 12/15 (early action). *Early decision deadline:* 11/15. *Notification:* continuous (freshmen), continuous until 4/1 (transfers), 12/15 (early decision), 1/31 (early action).

Freshman Application Contact Mr. Steve Klein, Dean of Admissions, Wabash College, PO Box 362, Crawfordsville, IN 47933-0352. *Phone:* 765-361-6225. *Toll-free phone:* 800-345-5385. *Fax:* 765-361-6437. *E-mail:* admissions@wabash.edu.

See page 946 for the College Close-Up.

THE ART INSTITUTE OF INDIANAPOLIS

INDIANAPOLIS, INDIANA

The Institute

The Art Institute of Indianapolis provides students with an educational environment and dedicated faculty members committed to preparing students for entry-level positions in the creative arts. The school offers eight bachelor's degree programs and three associate degree programs.

Under the guidance of industry professionals, students learn by doing the types of tasks they are likely to encounter in the workplace. In addition, assistance is available to help students with resume writing, networking, and keeping aware of what employers are looking for in job candidates.

The Student Affairs Office helps students who need assistance in locating housing.

The student population includes recent high school graduates, transfer students, and those who have left a previous employment situation to study and train for a new career. Students are creative, competitive, and open to new ideas. They place great value on an education that prepares them for an exciting entry-level position in the arts.

The Art Institute of Indianapolis places a high value on the quality of student life—both in and out of the classroom. Students participate in a wide variety of activities, including clubs and organizations, community service opportunities, and various committees designed to enhance the quality of student life.

The school's Learning Resource Center helps to meet students' needs for the programs taught at The Art Institute of Indianapolis. It is constantly updated and supplemented with new acquisitions. Instructors are encouraged to look for upcoming books and to advise the administration of any books that may prove useful to their students. Students also have access to the public libraries.

The Art Institute of Indianapolis is accredited by the Accrediting Commission of Career Schools and Colleges of Technology (ACCSCT) as a branch of The Art Institute of Las Vegas. The Art Institute of Indianapolis is licensed by the Indiana Commission on Proprietary Education, 302 West Washington Street, Room E201, Indianapolis, Indiana 46204.

Location

Located in the northwest part of Indianapolis, at the Pyramids, the school is within minutes of a thriving metropolis. The Pyramids are situated on 45 acres, with a 25-acre lake. The Pyramids are adjacent to I-465 for convenient travel to all major thoroughfares.

Majors and Degrees

Bachelor's degree programs are offered in culinary management, digital photography, fashion and retail management, fashion design, graphic design, interior design, media arts and animation, and Web design and interactive media.

Associate degree programs are offered in culinary arts, digital photography, and graphic design, and certificates are available in baking and pastry, culinary arts, digital design, and residential design.

Academic Programs

The Art Institute of Indianapolis operates on a year-round, four-quarter system.

Academic Facilities

The Art Institute of Indianapolis occupies approximately 15,000 square feet, including classrooms, studios, offices, a student lounge, a supply store, and a learning resource center. Equipment provided at The Art Institute of Indianapolis is specific to the program of study and may include projectors, editing decks, camcorders, PC and Macintosh computers, printers, drafting tables, and kitchen appliances.

Costs

Tuition cost varies by program. Prospective students should contact the school for current tuition costs. Other charges include a starting kit for all first quarter students. Kits vary in price depending on the program of study.

Financial Aid

Financial aid is available for those who qualify. Students who require financial assistance should first complete and submit a Free Application for Federal Student Aid (FAFSA) and meet with a financial aid officer. The officer determines the level of need based on a required federal formula, the cost of education, and other factors. Gift aid is available in the form of Federal Pell Grants, Federal Supplemental Educational Opportunity Grants, and veterans' benefits. Loans include Federal Stafford Loans, Federal PLUS Loans, and alternative loans. Other scholarships are available from the school and private sources. Application deadlines and eligibility requirements vary by program.

Faculty

Faculty members at The Art Institute of Indianapolis have professional knowledge that they bring into the classroom. The school's faculty members provide their students with a unique, relevant educational experience.

Admission Requirements

Applicants must provide proof of high school graduation or achievement of a General Educational Development (GED) certificate as a prerequisite for admission. In lieu of documenting high school graduation or a GED certificate, applicants may provide proof of attaining an associate degree or higher from an accredited institution. An official transcript indicating date of high school graduation, GED certificate (including test scores), or date of college graduation (including degree granted) is required as proof.

All individuals seeking admission to The Art Institute of Indianapolis are interviewed in person or by phone by an assistant director of admissions, and each applicant must create an original essay of at least 150 words stating how an education at The Art Institute of Indianapolis would help the student to achieve career goals. There is a $50 application fee.

Application and Information

To obtain an application, make arrangements for an interview, or tour the school, students should contact:

The Art Institute of Indianapolis
3500 Depauw Boulevard, Suite 1010
Indianapolis, Indiana 46268-6124
Phone: 317-613-4800
866-441-9031 (toll-free)
Fax: 317-613-4808
Web site: http://www.artinstitutes.edu/indianapolis

The Art Institute of Atlanta®, GA; The Art Institute of Atlanta®–Decatur, GA; The Art Institute of Austin℠, TX; The Art Institute of California℠–Inland Empire; The Art Institute of California℠–Los Angeles; The Art Institute of California℠–Orange County; The Art Institute of California℠–Sacramento; The Art Institute of California℠–San Diego; The Art Institute of California℠–San Francisco; The Art Institute of California℠–Sunnyvale; The Art Institute of Charleston℠, SC, A branch of The Art Institute of Atlanta, GA; The Art Institute of Charlotte®, NC; The Art Institute of Colorado® (Denver); The Art Institute of Dallas®, TX; The Art Institute of Fort Lauderdale®, FL; The Art Institute of Houston®, TX; The Art Institute of Indianapolis℠, IN*; The Art Institute of Jacksonville℠, FL, A branch of Miami International University of Art & Design; The Art Institute of Las Vegas®, NV; The Art Institute of Michigan℠ (Detroit); The Art Institute of New York City®, NY; The Art Institute of Ohio℠–Cincinnati**; The Art Institute of Philadelphia®, PA; The Art Institute of Phoenix®, AZ; The Art Institute of Pittsburgh®, PA; The Art Institute of Pittsburgh®–Online Division; The Art Institute of Portland®, OR; The Art Institute of Salt Lake City℠, UT; The Art Institute of Seattle®, WA; The Art Institute of Tampa℠, FL, A branch of Miami International University of Art & Design; The Art Institute of Tennessee℠–Nashville, A branch of The Art Institute of Atlanta, GA; The Art Institute of Tucson℠, AZ; The Art Institute of Washington® (Arlington, VA), A branch of The Art Institute of Atlanta, GA; The Art Institute of York–Pennsylvania℠; The Art Institutes International Minnesota℠ (Minneapolis); California Design College℠ (Los Angeles–Wilshire Blvd.); The Illinois Institute of Art®–Chicago; The Illinois Institute of Art®–Schaumburg; Miami International University of Art & Design℠, FL; The New England Institute of Art® (Boston, MA).

*The Art Institute of Indianapolis is licensed by the Indiana Commission on Proprietary Education, 302 W. Washington St., Rm. E201, Indianapolis, IN 46204, AC-0080.

**The Art Institute of Ohio–Cincinnati, 8845 Governors Hill Drive, Suite 100, Cincinnati, OH 45249-3317, OH Reg. #04-01-1698B.

BROWN MACKIE COLLEGE–FORT WAYNE

FORT WAYNE, INDIANA

The College

Brown Mackie College–Fort Wayne is dedicated to providing educational programs that prepare students for entry-level positions in a competitive, rapidly changing workplace. The College provides bachelor's degrees, associate degrees, diploma, and certificate programs in the areas of business and accounting, allied health sciences, legal studies, and computer technology to approximately 870 students.

Brown Mackie College–Fort Wayne is one of the oldest institutions of its kind in the country and the oldest in the state of Indiana. Established in 1882 as the South Bend Commercial College, the school later changed its name to Michiana College. In 1930, the College was incorporated under the laws of the state of Indiana and was authorized to confer associate degrees and certificates in business. In 1992, the College in South Bend added a branch location in Fort Wayne, Indiana. In 2004, Michiana College changed its name to Brown Mackie College–Fort Wayne.

Brown Mackie College–Fort Wayne is accredited by the Accrediting Council for Independent Colleges and Schools(ACICS) to award bachelor's degrees, associate degrees, diplomas, and certificates. The Accrediting Council for Independent Colleges and Schools is listed as a nationally recognized accrediting agency by the United States Department of Education. Its accreditation of degree-granting institutions also is recognized by the Council for Higher Education Accreditation. ACICS can be contacted at 750 First Street, NE, Suite 980, Washington, D.C. 20002-4241; phone: 202-336-6780.

Brown Mackie College–Fort Wayne is owned and operated by Education Management Corporation, 210 Sixth Avenue, 33rd Floor, Pittsburgh, Pennsylvania 15222-2603; http://www.edmc.edu. (AC 0109)

The College's medical assisting degree program is accredited by the Commission on Accreditation of Allied.Health Education Programs (CAAHEP), on recommendation of the Curriculum Review Board of the American Association of Medical Assistants Endowment (AAMAE). The commission's address is 1361 Park Street, Clearwater, Florida 33756; 727-210-2350. The College is licensed and regulated by the Indiana Commission on Proprietary Education, 302 West Washington Street, Indianapolis, Indiana 46204; 317-232-1320 or 800-227-5695 (toll-free). The College's occupational therapy assistant studies program is accredited by the Accreditation Council for Occupational Therapy Education (ACOTE) of the American Occupational Therapy Association (AOTA), 4720 Montgomery Lane, P.O. Box 31220, Bethesda, Maryland 20824-1220; 301-652-2682. The College's practical nursing program is accredited by the Indiana State Board of Nursing, 402 West Washington Street, Room W066, Indianapolis, Indiana 46204; 317-234-2043.

Brown Mackie College–Fort Wayne is a smoke-free institution.

Location

Brown Mackie College–Fort Wayne is located at 3000 East Coliseum Boulevard in Fort Wayne, Indiana. The College facility is accessible by public transportation. Ample parking is provided at no additional charge.

Majors and Degrees

Brown Mackie College–Fort Wayne provides higher education to traditional and nontraditional students through bachelor's degree, associate degree, diploma, and certificate programs that assist them in enhancing their career opportunities, broadening their perspectives through appropriate general education courses, thinking independently and critically, and improving problem-solving abilities. The College strives to develop within its students the desire for lifelong and continued education.

The Bachelor of Science degree (184 credits) is awarded in business administration, criminal justice, and legal studies.

The Associate of Science degree (96 credits) is awarded in accounting technology, business management, computer software technology, criminal justice, health-care administration, medical assisting, paralegal studies, and surgical technology. The Associate of Applied Science degree (96 credits) is awarded in occupational therapy assistant studies.

A diploma (76 credits) is awarded in practical nursing.

The College offers certificate programs (48 credits) in accounting, business, computer software applications, criminal justice, medical assistant studies, medical coding and billing, and paralegal assistant studies.

Academic Programs

Each College quarter comprises twelve weeks. Bachelor's degree programs require a minimum of sixteen quarters to complete. Associate degree programs require a minimum of eight quarters to complete. Programs are offered on a year-round basis, providing students with the ability to work uninterrupted toward their degrees.

Academic Facilities

Brown Mackie College–Fort Wayne consists of 32,000 square feet of classrooms; medical, nursing, computer, and occupational therapy labs; a library; a bookstore; and office space.

Costs

Tuition in the 2007–08 academic year for all programs except practical nursing and occupational therapy assistant studies was $208 per credit hour; fees were $15 per credit hour. Textbook expenses were estimated at $370 per quarter. For the practical nursing program, tuition was $260 per credit hour; fees were $20 per credit hour. Textbook expenses were estimated at $400 for the first term, $600 for the second term, and $100 for the third, fourth, and fifth terms. For the occupational therapy assistant studies program, tuition was $208 per credit hour for general education courses and $310 per credit hour for occupational therapy courses; fees were $15 per credit hour. Textbook expenses were estimated at $370 per quarter for the first six terms and $460 for the seventh term.

Financial Aid

The College maintains a full-time staff of financial aid professionals to assist qualified students in obtaining financial assistance. The College participates in several student aid programs. Forms of financial aid available through federal resources include the Federal Pell Grant Program, Federal

Supplemental Educational Opportunity Grant (FSEOG) Program, Federal Work-Study Program, Federal Perkins Loan Program, Federal Stafford Student Loan Program (subsidized and unsubsidized), and the Federal PLUS Loan Program. Eligible students may apply for Indiana state awards, such as the Frank O'Bannon Grant Program (formerly the Indiana State Grant Program), the Higher Education Award, and Twenty-First Century Scholarships for high school students; for the Core 40 awards; and for veterans' educational benefits. Students with physical or mental disabilities that are a handicap to employment may be eligible for training services through the state Agency for Vocational Rehabilitation. For further information, students should contact the College Student Financial Services Office.

Each year, the College makes available President's Scholarships of $1000 each to qualifying seniors from area high schools. No more than one scholarship is awarded per high school. In order to qualify, a senior must be graduating from a participating high school, must be maintaining a cumulative grade point average of at least 2.0, and must submit a brief essay. The student's extracurricular activities and community service are also considered. The President's Scholarship is available only to students enrolling in one of the College's degree programs. Students awarded the scholarship must enroll at Brown Mackie College–Fort Wayne between June and September immediately following their high school graduation. Applications for these scholarships can be obtained from the guidance departments of participating high schools. These applications must be completed and returned to the College by March 31. Those awarded scholarships are notified by April 30.

Faculty

The College has 23 full-time and 37 part-time instructors, with a student-faculty ratio of 14:1. Each student is assigned a faculty adviser.

Admission Requirements

Each applicant for admission is assigned an Assistant Director of Admissions, who directs the applicant through the steps of the admissions process, providing information on curriculum, policies, procedures, and services and assisting the applicant in setting necessary appointments and interviews. To qualify for admission, each applicant must provide documentation of graduation from an accredited high school or from a state-approved secondary education curriculum or provide official documentation of high school graduation equivalency. All transcripts become the property of the College. Admission to the College is based on the applicant's meeting the stated requirements, a review of the applicant's previous educational records, and a review of the applicant's career interests. If previous academic records indicate the College's education and training programs would not benefit the applicant, the College reserves the right to advise the applicant not to enroll. Special requirements for enrollment into certain programs are discussed in the descriptions of those programs.

As part of the admission process, students are given an assessment of academic skills. Although the results of this assessment do not determine eligibility for admission, they provide the College with a means of determining the need for academic support as well as a means by which the College can evaluate the effectiveness of its educational programs. All new students are required to complete this assessment, which is readministered at the end of the student's program so results may be compared with those of the initial administration.

In addition to the College's general admission requirements, applicants enrolling in the practical nursing program must document the following, which must be completed and a record of proof must appear in the student's file prior to the start of the Nursing Fundamentals course. No student will be admitted to a clinical agency unless all paperwork is completed. The paperwork is a requirement of all contracted agencies. This paperwork includes records of (1) a complete physical, current to within six months of admission; (2) a two-step Mantoux test that is kept current throughout schooling; (3) a hepatitis B vaccination or signed refusal; (4) up-to-date immunizations, including tetanus and rubella; (5) a record of current CPR certification that is maintained throughout the student's clinical experience; and (6) hospitalization insurance or a signed waiver.

Application and Information

Applicants must complete and submit an application form, along with documentation of graduation from an accredited high school or state-approved secondary education curriculum or official documentation of high school graduation equivalency.

For additional information, students should contact:

Director of Admissions
Brown Mackie College–Fort Wayne
3000 East Coliseum Boulevard
Fort Wayne, Indiana 46805
Phone: 260-484-4400
Phone: 866-433-2289 (toll-free)
Fax: 260-484-2678
E-mail: phooks@brownmackie.edu
Web site: http://www.brownmackie.edu

BROWN MACKIE COLLEGE–INDIANAPOLIS

INDIANAPOLIS, INDIANA

The College

Brown Mackie College–Indianapolis is dedicated to providing educational programs that prepare students for entry-level positions in a competitive, rapidly changing workplace. The College provides bachelor's degrees, associate degrees, and certificate programs in the areas of business, allied health sciences, and legal studies to approximately 150 students.

Brown Mackie College–Indianapolis is one of eighteen locations in the Brown Mackie College system of schools (http://www.brownmackie.edu), which is dedicated to providing educational programs that prepare students for entry-level positions in a competitive, rapidly changing workplace. Brown Mackie College system of schools offers bachelor's degree, associate degree, certificate, and diploma programs in health sciences, business, information technology, legal studies, and design to more than 10,000 students in the Midwest and the southeastern and southwestern United States.

Brown Mackie College–Indianapolis was founded in 2007 as a branch of Brown Mackie College–Findlay, Ohio. Both colleges are owned by Stautzenberger College Education Corporation, which, through three intermediary companies, is a subsidiary of Education Management Corporation, located at 210 Sixth Avenue, 33rd Floor, Pittsburgh, Pennsylvania 15222.

Brown Mackie College–Indianapolis is accredited by the Accrediting Council for Independent Colleges and Schools (ACICS) to award bachelor's degrees, associate degrees, and certificates. The U.S. Department of Education and The Council for Higher Education recognize the ACICS as a national accrediting agency. The ACICS can be contacted at 750 First Street NE, Suite 980, Washington, D.C. 20002; phone 202-336-6780.

The College is licensed and regulated by the Indiana Commission on Proprietary Education, 302 West Washington Street, Indianapolis, Indiana 46204; phone: 317-232-1320 or 800-227-5695 (toll-free).

Location

Indianapolis is known as the Crossroads of America because of the many interstates bisecting the city. The school is located on the best-known street in Indianapolis; North Meridian Street forms the east-west boundary of the city and passes through a variety of Indianapolis' colorful neighborhoods. The campus is nonresidential; public transportation and ample free parking are available.

Indianapolis is the thirteenth-largest city in the country and offers students everything that a major metropolitan area has to offer, including major league sports, historic sites, zoos and parks, museums, dining, and a thriving nightlife. Of course, car racing is a popular event in Indianapolis for residents and visitors alike, with the two largest single-day sporting events in the world: the Indianapolis 500 and the Allstate 400 at the Brickyard.

The region helps to stimulate continued economic development by offering incentives and assistance to businesses based in Indianapolis and those moving here. The unemployment rate in the area is lower and the average pay is higher than both the state and national averages. In May 2006, *Forbes* magazine ranked Indianapolis as the tenth best place for businesses and careers. Top employers include Eli Lilly, FedEx, and Rolls-Royce.

Majors and Degrees

Brown Mackie College–Indianapolis provides higher education to traditional and nontraditional students through bachelor's degree, associate degree, and certificate programs that assist them in enhancing their career opportunities, broadening their perspectives through appropriate general education courses, thinking independently and critically, and improving problem-solving abilities. The College strives to develop within its students the desire for lifelong and continued education.

The Bachelor of Science degree (184 credits) is awarded in business administration, criminal justice, and legal studies.

The Associate of Science degree (96 credits) is awarded in business management, criminal justice, health-care administration, medical assisting, and paralegal studies. The Associate of Applied Science degree (96 credits) is awarded in occupational therapy assistant studies.

The College offers certificate programs (48 credits) in business and medical assistant studies.

Academic Programs

Each College quarter comprises twelve weeks. Bachelor's degree programs require a minimum of sixteen quarters to complete. Associate degree programs require a minimum of eight quarters to complete. Programs are offered on a year-round basis, providing students with the ability to work uninterrupted toward their degrees.

Academic Facilities

Opened in January 2008, this modern facility offers more than 22,000 square feet of tastefully decorated classrooms, laboratories, and office space designed to the specifications of the College for its business, medical, and technical programs. Instructional equipment is comparable to current technology used in business and industry today. Modern classrooms for special instructional needs offer full multimedia capabilities with surround sound and overhead projectors accessible through computer, DVD, or VHS. Internet access and instructional resources are available at the College's library. Experienced faculty members provide academic support and are committed to the academic and technical preparation of their students.

Costs

Tuition for programs in the 2007–08 academic year was $225 per credit hour with the exception of the occupational therapy assistant program, which was $225 per credit hour for general courses and $310 per credit hour for program-specific courses. General fees were $15 per credit hour.

Financial Aid

The College maintains a full-time staff of financial aid professionals to assist qualified students in obtaining the financial assistance they require to meet their educational expenses. Available resources include federal and state aid, student loans from private lenders, and federal work-study opportunities, both on and off college premises. Federal assistance programs are administered through the U.S. Department of Education, Office of Student Financial Assistance. Any U.S. citizen, national, or person in the United States for other than temporary reasons who is enrolled or accepted for enrollment may apply for these programs. Most forms of financial assistance are available for each July 1–June 30 award period. Every student considering application for financial aid should request a copy of the current *Student Guide*, published by the U.S. Department of Education. This important document may be obtained in the Student Financial Services Office and assists students in understanding eligibility requirements, the application process, deadlines, and the various forms of grants and loans available.

Each year, the College makes available scholarships of $1000 each to qualifying seniors from area high schools. No more than one scholarship is awarded per high school. In order to qualify, a senior must be graduating from a participating high school, must be maintaining a cumulative grade point average of at least 2.0, and must submit a brief essay. The student's extracurricular activities and community service are also considered. The President's Scholarship is available only to students enrolling in one of the College's degree programs. Students awarded the scholarship must enroll at Brown Mackie College—Indianapolis between June and September immediately following their high school graduation. Applications for these scholarships can be obtained from the guidance departments of participating high schools. These applications must be completed and returned to the College by March 31. Those awarded scholarships are notified by April 30.

Faculty

The College has 2 full-time and 6 part-time instructors, with a student-faculty ratio of 21:1. Faculty members provide tutoring and additional academic services to students as needed.

Admission Requirements

Each applicant for admission is assigned an Assistant Director of Admissions, who directs the applicant through the steps of the admissions process, providing information on curriculum, policies, procedures, and services and assisting the applicant in setting necessary appointments and interviews. To qualify for admission, each applicant must provide documentation of graduation from an accredited high school or from a state-approved secondary education curriculum or provide official documentation of high school graduation equivalency. All transcripts become the property of the College. Admission to the College is based on the applicant's meeting the stated requirements, a review of the applicant's previous educational records, and a review of the applicant's career interests. If previous academic records indicate the College's education and training programs would not benefit the applicant, the College reserves the right to advise the applicant not to enroll. Special requirements for enrollment into certain programs are discussed in the descriptions of those programs.

Students are given an assessment of academic skills during the first month of classes. Although the results of this assessment do not determine eligibility for admission, they provide the College with a means of determining the need for academic support as well as a means by which the College can evaluate the effectiveness of its educational programs. All new students are required to complete this assessment, which is readministered at the end of the student's program so results may be compared with those of the initial administration.

Application and Information

Applicants must complete and submit an application form, along with documentation of graduation from an accredited high school or state-approved secondary education curriculum or official documentation of high school graduation equivalency.

For additional information, students should contact:

Director of Admissions
Brown Mackie College–Indianapolis
1200 North Meridian Street, Suite 100
Indianapolis, Indiana 46204
Phone: 866-255-0279 (toll-free)
Fax: 317-632-4557
E-mail: tmatthews@brownmackie.edu
Web site: http://www.brownmackie.edu

BROWN MACKIE COLLEGE–MERRILLVILLE

MERRILLVILLE, INDIANA

The College

Brown Mackie College–Merrillville is dedicated to providing educational programs that prepare students for entry-level positions in a competitive, rapidly changing workplace. The College provides bachelor's and associate degree, diploma, and certificate programs in business and accounting, allied health sciences, legal studies, and computer technology to approximately 700 students.

Founded in 1890 by A. N. Hirons as LaPorte Business College in LaPorte, Indiana, the institution later became known as Commonwealth Business College. In 1919, ownership was transferred to Grace and J. J. Moore, who successfully operated the College under the name of Reese School of Business for several decades. In 1975, the College came under the ownership of Steven C. Smith as Commonwealth Business College. A second location, now known as Brown Mackie College–Merrillville, was opened in 1984, in Merrillville, Indiana. The College changed ownership again in September 2003 when it was acquired by Education Management Corporation, and the College name was changed to Brown Mackie College–Merrillville in November 2004.

Brown Mackie College–Merrillville is accredited by the Accrediting Council for Independent Colleges and Schools (ACICS) to award associate degrees and certificates. ACICS is listed as a nationally recognized accrediting agency by the U.S. Department of Education. Its accreditation of degree-granting institutions also is recognized by the Council for Higher Education Accreditation. ACICS can be contacted at 750 First Street, NE, Suite 980, Washington, D.C. 20002-4241; 202-336-6780. Brown Mackie College–Merrillville has two branches: Brown Mackie College–Michigan City and Brown Mackie College–Moline.

The College's Medical Assisting degree program is accredited by the Accrediting Bureau of Health Education Schools (ABHES), 7777 Leesburg Pike, Suite 314N, Falls Church, Virginia 22403; 703-917-9503. The College's diploma program in practical nursing is accredited by the Health Professions Bureau (Attn: Indiana State Board of Nursing) 402 West Washington Street, Room W066, Indianapolis, Indiana 46204; 317-234-2043.

The College is a nonresidential, smoke-free institution and a subsidiary of Education Management Corporation, 210 Sixth Avenue, 33rd floor, Pittsburgh, Pennsylvania 15222-2603; http://www.edmc.edu.

Location

Brown Mackie College–Merrillville is located in northwest Indiana, in the Twin Towers business complex of Merrillville just west of the intersection of U.S. Route 30 and Interstate 65. A spacious parking lot provides ample parking at no additional charge.

Majors and Degrees

Brown Mackie College–Merrillville provides higher education to traditional and nontraditional students through bachelor's degree, associate degree, diploma, and certificate programs that assist in enhancing their career opportunities, broadening their perspectives through appropriate general education courses, thinking independently and critically, and improving problem-solving abilities. The College strives to develop within its students the desire for lifelong and continued education.

The Bachelor of Science degree (184 credits) is awarded in business administration, criminal justice, and legal studies.

The Associate of Science degree (96 credits) is awarded in accounting technology, administration in gerontology, business management, computer software technology, criminal justice, medical assisting, medical office management, occupational therapy assistant studies, paralegal studies, and surgical technology.

A diploma program (76 credits) in practical nursing is offered.

The College offers certificate programs (48 credits) in accounting, business, computer software applications, criminal justice, medical assistant studies, and paralegal assistant studies.

Academic Programs

Each College quarter comprises ten to twelve weeks. Bachelor's degree programs require a minimum of sixteen quarters to complete. Associate degree programs require a minimum of eight quarters to complete. Programs are offered on a year-round basis, providing students with the ability to work uninterrupted toward completion of their programs.

Academic Facilities

Occupying 18,000 square feet, Brown Mackie College–Merrillville was opened to students in October 1998 in the Twin Towers complex of Merrillville and comprises several instructional rooms, including five computer labs with networked computers and four medical laboratories. The administrative offices, college library, and student lounge are all easily accessible to students. The College bookstore stocks texts, courseware, and other educational supplies required for courses at the College. Students also find a variety of personal, recreational, and gift items, including apparel, supplies, and general merchandise incorporating the College logo. Hours are posted at the bookstore entrance.

Costs

Tuition for programs in the 2007–08 academic year was $208 per credit hour with the exception of the practical nursing diploma program, which was $260 per credit hour. The length of the program determines total cost. Textbook fees vary according to program.

Financial Aid

The College maintains a full-time staff of financial aid professionals to assist qualified students in obtaining financial assistance. The College participates in several student aid programs. Forms of financial aid available through federal resources include the Federal Pell Grant Program, Federal Supplemental Educational Opportunity Grant (FSEOG) Program, Federal Work-Study Program, Federal Perkins Loan Program, Federal Stafford Student Loan Program (subsidized and unsubsidized), and the Federal PLUS Loan Program. Eligible students may apply for Indiana state awards, such as the Higher Education Award and Twenty-First Century Scholarships for high school students, the Core 40 awards, and veterans' educational benefits. Students with physical or mental disabilities that are a handicap to employment may be eligible for training services through the state's Bureau of Vocational Rehabilitation. For further information, students should contact the College's Student Financial Services Office.

Each year, the College makes available scholarships of $1000 each to qualifying seniors from area high schools. No more than one scholarship is awarded per high school. In order to qualify, a senior must be graduating from a participating high school, must be maintaining a cumulative grade point average of at least 2.0, and must submit a brief essay. The student's extracurricular activities and community service are also considered. The President's Scholarship is available only to students enrolling in one of the College's degree programs. Students awarded the scholarship must enroll at Brown Mackie College–Merrillville between June and September immediately following their high school graduation. Applications for these scholarships can be obtained from the guidance departments of participating high schools. These applications must be completed and returned to the College by March 31. Those awarded scholarships are notified by April 30.

Faculty

There are approximately 30 full-time and 25 part-time faculty members at the College, practitioners in their fields of expertise. The average student-faculty ratio is 17:1.

Admission Requirements

Each applicant for admission is assigned an Assistant Director of Admissions who directs the applicant through the steps of the admissions process, providing information on curriculum, policies, procedures, and services and assisting the applicant in setting necessary appointments and interviews. To qualify for admission, each applicant must provide documentation of graduation from an accredited high school or completion of a state-approved secondary education curriculum or provide official documentation of high school graduation equivalency. All transcripts become the property of the College.

Admission to the College is based on the applicant's meeting the stated requirements, a review of the applicant's previous educational records, and a review of the applicant's career interests. If previous academic records indicate that the College's education and training would not benefit the applicant, the College reserves the right to advise the applicant not to enroll. Special requirements for enrollment into certain programs are discussed in the descriptions of those programs.

Application and Information

Applicants must complete and submit an application form along with documentation of graduation from an accredited high school or completion of state-approved secondary education curriculum or provide official documentation of high school graduation equivalency. For additional information, prospective students should contact:

Charles Woods, Director of Admissions
Brown Mackie College–Merrillville
1000 East 80th Place, Suite 101N
Merrillville, Indiana 46410
Phone: 219-769-3321
800-258-3321 (toll-free)
Fax: 219-738-1076
E-mail: bmcmeadm@brownmackie.edu
Web site: http://www.brownmackie.edu

BROWN MACKIE COLLEGE–MICHIGAN CITY

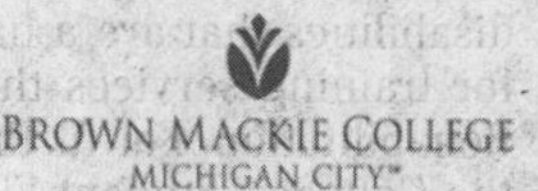

MICHIGAN CITY, INDIANA

The College

Brown Mackie College–Michigan City is dedicated to providing education programs that prepare students for entry-level positions in a competitive, rapidly changing workplace. The College provides bachelor's and associate degrees and certificate programs in the areas of business and accounting, the allied health sciences, legal studies, and computer technology to 313 students.

Founded in 1890 by A. N. Hirons as LaPorte Business College in LaPorte, Indiana, the institution later became known as Commonwealth Business College. In 1919, ownership was transferred to Grace and J. J. Moore, who successfully operated the College under the name of Reese School of Business for several decades. In 1975, the College came under the ownership of Steven C. Smith as Commonwealth Business College. In 1997, the College relocated to its present site in Michigan City, Indiana. The College was acquired by Education Management Corporation on September 2, 2003, and changed its name to Brown Mackie College–Michigan City in November 2004.

Brown Mackie College–Michigan City is accredited by the Accrediting Council for Independent Colleges and Schools (ACICS) to award bachelor's degrees, associate degrees, and certificates. ACICS is listed as a nationally recognized accrediting agency by the U.S. Department of Education. Its accreditation of degree-granting institutions is recognized by the Council for Higher Education Accreditation. ACICS can be reached at 750 First Street NE, Suite 980, Washington, D.C. 20002-4241; phone: 202-336-6780. (AC 0138)

The College's medical assisting degree program is accredited by the Accrediting Bureau of Health Education Schools, 7777 Leesburg Pike, Suite 214 North, Falls Church, Virginia 22046; phone: 703-533-2082.

The College's surgical technology program is accredited by the Commission on Accreditation of Allied Health Education Programs (CAAHEP, 1361 Park Street, Clearwater, Florida 33756; phone: 727-210-2350) on recommendation of the Curriculum Review Board.

The College is a nonresidential, smoke-free institution owned and operated by Education Management Corporation, 210 Sixth Avenue, 33rd floor, Pittsburgh, Pennsylvania 15222-2603; http://www.edmc.edu.

Location

Brown Mackie College–Michigan City is located in northwest Indiana, 1 mile north of Interstate 94, near the intersection of routes 20 and 421. Additional parking spaces were added in 2002, providing students and employees with ample parking at no additional charge.

Majors and Degrees

Brown Mackie College–Michigan City provides higher education to traditional and nontraditional students through bachelor's degree, associate degree, and certificate programs that assist in enhancing their career opportunities, broadening their perspectives through appropriate general education courses, thinking independently and critically, and improving problem-solving abilities. The College strives to develop within its students the desire for lifelong and continued education.

The Bachelor of Science degree (184 credits) is awarded in business administration, criminal justice, and legal studies.

The Associate of Science degree (96 credits) is awarded in accounting technology, business management, computer software technology, criminal justice, early childhood education, medical assisting, medical office management, paralegal studies, surgical technology, and veterinary technology.

The College offers certificate programs (48 credits) in accounting, business, computer software applications, criminal justice, medical assistant studies, and paralegal assistant studies.

Academic Programs

Each College quarter comprises twelve weeks. Bachelor's degree programs require a minimum of sixteen quarters to complete. Associate degree programs require a minimum of eight quarters to complete. Programs are offered on a year-round basis, providing students with the ability to work uninterrupted toward their degrees.

Academic Facilities

In 2002, the College underwent a major renovation and completed the addition of 3,360 square feet, for a total of 10,338 square feet of occupancy. An additional medical laboratory, a larger library, new classrooms, and a bookstore were added. All classrooms and the library are equipped with new technology, including multimedia projectors, surround-sound audio systems, VCRs, and DVD players. Five of the ten new classrooms are equipped with networked computer systems. The two medical laboratories contain newly acquired medical equipment and instructional tools and supplies. Administrative offices are easily accessible to students.

Costs

Tuition is $208 per credit hour. Textbook fees vary according to the program.

Financial Aid

The College maintains a full-time staff of financial aid professionals to assist qualified students in obtaining financial assistance. The College participates in several student aid programs. Forms of financial aid available to qualified students through federal resources include the Federal Pell Grant Program, Federal Supplemental Educational Opportunity Grant (FSEOG) Program, Federal Work-Study Program, Federal Stafford Student Loan Program (subsidized and unsubsidized), and Federal PLUS loan program.

Eligible students may apply for Indiana state awards, such as the Higher Education Award and Twenty-First Century Scholarships for high school students, the Core 40 awards, and veterans' educational benefits. Students with physical or mental disabilities that are a handicap to employment may be eligible for training services through the state's Bureau of Vocational Rehabilitation. For further information, students should contact the College Student Financial Services Office.

Faculty

There are 4 full-time and 18 part-time faculty members at the College. The average student-faculty ratio is 13:1. Each student is assigned a faculty adviser.

Admission Requirements

Each applicant for admission is assigned an Assistant Director of Admissions, who directs the applicant through the steps of the admissions process, providing information on curriculum, policies, procedures, and services and assisting the applicant in setting necessary appointments and interviews. To qualify for admission, each applicant must provide documentation of graduation from an accredited high school or completion of a state-approved secondary education curriculum or provide official documentation of high school graduation equivalency. All transcripts become the property of the College.

Admission to the College is based on the applicant's meeting the stated requirements, a review of the applicant's previous educational records, and a review of the applicant's career interests. If previous academic records indicate that the College's education and training would not benefit the applicant, the College reserves the right to advise the applicant not to enroll. Special requirements for enrollment into certain programs are discussed in the descriptions of those programs.

Application and Information

Applicants must complete and submit an application form along with documentation of graduation from an accredited high school or completion of a state-approved secondary education curriculum or provide official documentation of high school graduation equivalency. For additional information, prospective students should contact:

Director of Admissions
Brown Mackie College–Michigan City
325 East U.S. Highway 20
Michigan City, Indiana 46360
Phone: 219-877-3100
800-519-2416 (toll-free)
Fax: 219-877-3110
E-mail: nspenny@brownmackie.edu
Web site: http://www.brownmackie.edu

COLLEGE DATA CENTER • INDIANA

BROWN MACKIE COLLEGE–SOUTH BEND

SOUTH BEND, INDIANA

The College

Brown Mackie College–South Bend is dedicated to providing education programs that prepare students for entry-level positions in a competitive, rapidly changing workplace. The College provides bachelor's degrees, associate degrees, diplomas, and certificate programs in allied health sciences, business and accounting, computer technology, and legal studies to approximately 800 students.

The College is one of the oldest institutions of its kind in the country and the oldest in the state of Indiana. Established in 1882 as the South Bend Commercial College, the school later changed its name to Michiana College. In 1930, the school was incorporated under the laws of the state of Indiana and was authorized to confer associate degrees and certificates in business. The College relocated to its current location on East Jefferson Boulevard in 1987. Five years later it added a branch location in Fort Wayne, Indiana, now known as Brown Mackie College–Fort Wayne.

Brown Mackie College–South Bend is accredited by the Accrediting Council for Independent Colleges and Schools (ACICS) to award bachelor's degrees, associate degrees, diplomas, and certificates. The Accrediting Council for Independent Colleges and Schools is listed as a nationally recognized accrediting agency by the United States Department of Education. Its accreditation of degree-granting institutions is also recognized by the Council for Higher Education Accreditation. ACICS can be contacted at 750 First Street NE, Suite 980, Washington, D.C. 20002-4241; phone: 202-336-6780.

The medical assisting program is accredited by the Commission on Accreditation of Allied Health Education Programs (CAAHEP), on recommendation of the Curriculum Review Board. The Commission's address is 1361 Park Street, Clearwater, Florida 33756; phone: 727-210-2350.

The occupational therapy assistant program is accredited by the Accreditation Council for Occupational Therapy Education (ACOTE) of the American Occupational Therapy Association (AOTA), 4720 Montgomery Lane, P.O. Box 31220, Bethesda, Maryland 20824-1220; phone: 301-652-2682.

The physical therapist assistant program is accredited by the Commission on Accreditation in Physical Therapy Education (CAPTE) of the American Physical Therapy Association (APTA), 1111 North Fairfax Street, Alexandria, Virginia 22314; phone: 703-706-3241.

The practical nursing program is accredited by the Indiana State Board of Nursing, 402 West Washington Street, Room W066, Indianapolis, Indiana 46204; phone: 317-234-2043.

The College is a nonresidential, smoke-free institution and is owned and operated by Education Management Corporation, 210 Sixth Avenue, 33rd Floor, Pittsburgh, Pennsylvania 15222-2603; phone: 800-275-2440 (toll-free); http://www.edmc.edu. (AC 0110)

Location

Brown Mackie College–South Bend is conveniently located at 1030 East Jefferson Boulevard, South Bend, Indiana 46617. The College has a generous parking area and is also easily accessible by public transportation.

Majors and Degrees

Brown Mackie College–South Bend provides higher education to traditional and nontraditional students through bachelor's degree, associate degree, diploma, and certificate programs that assist in enhancing their career opportunities, broadening their perspectives through appropriate general education courses, thinking independently and critically, and improving problem-solving abilities.

The Bachelor of Science degree (184 credits) is awarded in business administration, criminal justice, and legal studies.

The Associate of Science degree (96 credits) is awarded in accounting technology, business management, computer software technology, criminal justice, early childhood education, health-care administration, information technology, medical assisting, paralegal studies, and veterinary technology.

The Associate of Applied Science degree (100 credits) is awarded in occupational therapy assistant studies and physical therapist assistant studies.

The College offers a diploma program (76 credits) in practical nursing.

The College offers the following certificate programs (48 credits): accounting, business, computer software applications, criminal justice, medical assistant studies, and paralegal assistant studies.

Academic Programs

Each College quarter comprises twelve weeks. Bachelor's degree programs require a minimum of sixteen quarters to complete. Associate degree programs require a minimum of eight quarters to complete. Programs are offered on a year-round basis, providing students with the ability to work uninterrupted toward completion of their programs.

Academic Facilities

Brown Mackie College–South Bend comprises 31,000 square feet of classrooms; medical, computer, occupational, and physical therapy laboratories; and a library, bookstore, and office space.

Costs

Tuition for programs in the 2007–08 academic year was $208 per credit hour, with a $15 per-credit-hour general fee applied to instructional costs for activities and services. Textbooks and other instructional materials varied by program. Tuition for all courses in the practical nursing program was $260 per credit hour, with a $20 per-credit-hour general fee applied to instructional costs for activities and services. Tuition for the physical therapist assistant program courses was $310 per credit hour. Tuition for the occupational therapy assistant program courses was $310 per credit hour.

Financial Aid

The College maintains a full-time staff of financial aid professionals to assist qualified students in obtaining financial assistance. The College participates in several student aid programs. Forms of financial aid available through federal resources include the Federal Pell Grant Program, Federal Supplemental Educational Opportunity Grant (FSEOG) Program, Federal Work-Study Program, Federal Perkins Loan Program, Federal Stafford Student Loan Program (subsidized and unsubsidized), and the Federal PLUS Loan Program.

Eligible students may apply for Indiana state awards, such as the Frank O'Bannon Grant Program (formerly the Indiana Higher Education Grant) and Twenty-First Century Scholars Program for high school students, the Core 40 awards, and veterans' educational benefits. Students with physical or mental disabilities that are a handicap to employment may be eligible for training services through the state's Bureau of Vocational Rehabilitation. For further information, students should contact the College Student Financial Services Office.

Each year, the College makes available President's Scholarships of $1000 each to qualifying seniors from area high schools. No more than one scholarship is awarded per high school. In order to qualify, a senior must be graduating from a participating high school, must be maintaining a cumulative grade point average of at least 2.0, and must submit a brief essay. The student's extracurricular activities and community service are also considered. The President's Scholarship is available only to students enrolling in one of the College's degree programs. Students awarded the scholarship must enroll at Brown Mackie College–South Bend between June and September immediately following their high school graduation. Applications for these scholarships can be obtained from the guidance departments of participating high schools. These applications must be completed and returned to the College by March 31. Those awarded scholarships are notified by April 30.

Faculty

There are 19 full-time and 24 part-time faculty members at the College. The average student-faculty ratio is 12:1. Each student is assigned a program director as an adviser.

Admission Requirements

Each applicant for admission is assigned an Assistant Director of Admissions, who directs the applicant through the steps of the admissions process, providing information on curriculum, policies, procedures, and services and assisting the applicant in setting necessary appointments and interviews. To qualify for admission, each applicant must provide documentation of graduation from an accredited high school or from a state-approved secondary education curriculum or provide official documentation of high school graduation equivalency. All transcripts become the property of the College.

Admission to the College is based on the applicant's meeting the stated requirements, a review of the applicant's previous educational records, and a review of the applicant's career interests. If previous academic records indicate that the College's education and training would not benefit the applicant, the College reserves the right to advise the applicant not to enroll. Special requirements for enrollment into certain programs are discussed in the descriptions of those programs.

In addition to the College's general admission requirements, applicants enrolling in the occupational therapy assistant or physical therapist assistant programs must document one of the following: a high school cumulative grade point average of at least 2.5, a score on the GED examination of at least 57 (557 if taken on or after January 15, 2002), or completion of 12 quarter-credit hours or 8 semester-credit hours of collegiate course work with a grade point average of at least 2.5. Credit hours may not include Professional Development (CF 1100), the Brown Mackie College–South Bend course. Students entering either program must also have completed a biology course with a grade of at least a C (or an average of at least 2.0 on a 4.0 scale).

In addition to the College's general admission requirements, applicants enrolling in the practical nursing program must document the following: fulfillment of Brown Mackie College–South Bend general requirements; complete physical (must be current to within six months of admission); two-step Mantoux TB skin test (must be current throughout schooling); hepatitis B vaccination or signed refusal; up-to-date immunizations, including tetanus and rubella; record of current CPR certification (certification must be current throughout the clinical experience through health-care provider certification or the American Heart Association); and hospitalization insurance or a signed waiver.

Application and Information

Applicants must complete and submit an application form, along with documentation of graduation from an accredited high school or state-approved secondary education curriculum or official documentation of high school graduation equivalency.

For additional information, students should contact:

Director of Admissions
Brown Mackie College–South Bend
1030 East Jefferson Boulevard
South Bend, Indiana 46617
Phone: 574-237-0774
800-743-2447 (toll-free)
Fax: 574-237-3585
E-mail: jkempt@brownmackie.edu
Web site: http://www.brownmackie.edu

BUTLER UNIVERSITY

INDIANAPOLIS, INDIANA

The University

Celebrating more than 150 years of superior academics, Butler University has a proud tradition of excellence and innovation. Challenging and enabling students to meet their personal and professional goals has guided the University since 1855. Today, Butler is an independent, coeducational, nonsectarian university with a total undergraduate enrollment of more than 3,900 students. Butler is accredited by the Higher Learning Commission of the North Central Association of Colleges and Schools.

Butler students represent almost every state in the nation and sixty-three countries, reflecting a diversity of cultures, interests, aspirations, personalities, and experiences. Students can choose from a number of housing options, including a newly built upperclassman residential apartment village, an apartment-style residence hall, one all-women residence hall with an optional living-learning center, two coeducational residence halls with optional living-learning centers, fraternities, and sororities. A health and recreation complex is equipped with recreation courts, an indoor jogging track, an aquatics area, a weight and fitness space, a lounge, and a juice bar. Since opening in 2006, the complex has also won two national awards, including one for innovative architecture and design and one for its outstanding indoor sports facilities.

There are more than 100 student organizations, fifteen Greek organizations, and nineteen Division I varsity athletic teams. Students take advantage of Broadway shows at Butler's Clowes Memorial Hall, the city's premier performing arts center. Basketball fans cheer on the Bulldogs at the 11,000-seat historic Hinkle Fieldhouse, where the final game in the movie *Hoosiers* was filmed.

Located near the center of campus, Atherton Union serves as a natural gathering space for students. Atherton Union has numerous amenities, including e-mail stations, wireless capabilities, a 24-hour computer lab, Starbucks coffee shop, bookstore, food court, dining hall, and convenience store.

Graduate programs include the M.B.A., the M.S. in school counseling, the M.S. in educational administration, the M.S. in education, the M.A. in English, the M.A. in history, and the M.M. in composition, conducting, music education, music history, performance, and piano pedagogy and theory. In addition, Butler offers a dual Pharm.D./M.B.A. program, which allows pharmacy students to develop management skills and entrepreneurial capabilities in conjunction with pharmacy experience while earning both a Pharm.D. and an M.B.A. in six years.

Location

Butler University is located on 290 acres of Indianapolis' historic Butler-Tarkington neighborhood, which is also home to Indiana's governor. The campus maintains its heritage with centuries-old trees; open, landscaped malls; curving sidewalks; and fountains. Most of the University's full-time students live on campus and enjoy a nature preserve, prairie, historical canal, formal botanical garden, an observatory, and jogging paths.

Just 6 miles from downtown Indianapolis, Butler's urban location offers internship opportunities that provide excellent graduate school and career preparation. Indianapolis, Indiana's state capital and the thirteenth-largest city in the nation, boasts a variety of cultural activities, including the Indianapolis Symphony Orchestra, the Indiana Repertory Theatre, the Indianapolis Museum of Art (just two blocks from campus), the Eiteljorg Museum, the Indiana State Museum, and the world's largest children's museum.

The Indianapolis Motor Speedway is the anchor of Indianapolis' professional sports, while basketball, football, hockey, and baseball have homes in three major sports arenas. Indianapolis is home to the NCAA headquarters, its Hall of Champions, and the men's and women's Big Ten basketball championships. Butler has been the proud cohost of the NCAA Final Four championship in 1991, 1997, 2000, and 2006.

Majors and Degrees

As a comprehensive university with a strong liberal arts and sciences tradition, Butler is committed to graduating students who have a well-rounded yet focused education. A core curriculum affords students the opportunity to gain knowledge in the humanities, the arts, social sciences, natural sciences, and mathematics.

Baccalaureate degrees are offered through Butler's five colleges. Unique programs include the engineering dual-degree program, offered jointly by Butler University and the Purdue School of Engineering and Technology at Indianapolis. Students receive both a Butler Bachelor of Science degree in a selected liberal arts and sciences major (biology, chemistry, computer science, economics, mathematics, physics or science, technology and society) and a Purdue Bachelor of Science degree in biomedical computer, electrical, or mechanical engineering.

For students who are undecided about their major field of study, there is an Exploratory Studies Program, where students develop a personalized academic plan to help choose the major that best suits their interests and abilities.

The College of Education is dedicated to preparing outstanding teachers. The administration and the faculty and staff members of the College of Education are committed to providing the best possible learning experience for students. For the past seven years, the College has experienced a 99 percent (or above) placement rate for its students, an indicator that Butler students place first in education. Majors offered through the College are early and middle childhood (kindergarten to grade 6), early adolescence generalist (middle school only)/early adolescence and adolescence young adult (middle and high school)/adolescence young adult (high school only), and early and middle childhood/early adolescence/adolescence young adult (K–12).

The College of Liberal Arts and Sciences creates lifelong learners. The College affirms the central role of liberal arts education while offering opportunities for specialization. Majors include actuarial science, actuarial science/management (five-year B.S./M.B.A.), anthropology, biological sciences, chemistry, communication disorders (speech language pathology), communication studies, computer science, economics, English, exploratory (humanities, natural sciences, social sciences), French, French and business studies, German, German and business studies, Greek, history, international studies, journalism, , mathematics, philosophy, physics, political science, psychology, public and corporate communications, religion, science technology and society, sociology, sociology and criminal justice, software engineering, Spanish, Spanish and business studies, and urban studies.

The College of Business Administration prepares students to be tomorrow's business leaders through classroom work and two required semester-long cooperative education experiences. A new initiative in the College—the Butler Business Accelerator—will allow students to serve as consultants for central Indiana businesses. Majors in the College include accounting, economics, exploratory (business), finance, international management, management information systems, and marketing.

The Jordan College of Fine Arts integrates intensive conservatory training with broad objectives and a strong academic curriculum. The College is well respected for its tradition of educating students as emerging professionals in the arts. Majors offered are arts administration (general, dance, music, theater), dance pedagogy, dance performance, exploratory (fine arts), media arts–Bachelor of Arts (electronic media, multimedia studies, recording industry studies), music–Bachelor of Arts (concentration in jazz studies and lyric theater; emphases in applied music, composition, music history, and piano pedagogy), music–Bachelor of Music (composition, music education, performance, and piano pedagogy), and theater.

College of Pharmacy and Health Sciences graduates serve society as caring, ethical health professionals and community leaders. The College's professional programs combine intensive classroom education with clinical experiences in the professional phases of the degrees. Majors offered are exploratory (pharmacy and health sciences), pharmacy (Pharm.D.), and physician assistant studies. In fall 2005, the College launched a five-year (eleven semesters) Master of Physician Assistant Studies (M.P.A.S.) program.

Butler offers preprofessional programs in dentistry, law, medicine, optometry, physical therapy, seminary, and veterinary medicine.

Academic Programs

All candidates for the baccalaureate degree must complete the University core requirements and at least 45 semester hours of work. At least 30 of the 45 hours must be in the college granting the degree. Eligible students may participate in the honors program. By the end of the sophomore year, honors course work is generally completed. Students then begin the next phase, an independent study to help them research, write, and eventually present their honors thesis. Butler is a sponsoring institution for the National Merit Scholarship Program. Butler also offers advanced placement with appropriate academic credit in most subjects covered by either the AP examinations or the CLEP tests. Students may choose to enroll in Air Force and Army ROTC programs.

Butler students have the chance to originate research projects and participate in them with faculty members and then develop these projects into professional presentations and publications. Hundreds of Butler students present their projects at the Undergraduate Research Conference, hosted by Butler every April. In addition, the Butler Summer Institute awards accepted students a $2000 grant plus housing while they work on summer research projects with faculty members.

Off-Campus Programs

Students may choose to study in one of more than 110 study-abroad programs through Butler's Center for Global Education. Butler students have studied in Argentina, Australia, Chile, Costa Rica, England, Ireland, Mexico, New Zealand, Northern Ireland, and Scotland. Students may also select their overseas study opportunity from programs offered by fifteen other colleges, universities, and well-respected study-abroad organizations.

Academic Facilities

Butler has incorporated state-of-the-art technologies throughout its campus. These include Mac and PC computers, two Ethernet connections per residence hall room, eighteen networked computer labs, electronic and multimedia classrooms, Internet access and e-mail service, wireless capabilities, student home pages, language labs, international studies center, telephone systems with free voicemail, and 24-hour computer labs in Atherton Student Union and each residence hall.

The Richard M. Fairbanks Center for Communication and Technology includes state-of-the-art classrooms, laboratories, conference rooms, television studios, graphics production and editing facilities, recording studios, student newspaper offices, online magazine production space, and speaker labs.

Many student performances, including theater, dance, and music, can be seen in Butler's 2,200-seat Clowes Memorial Hall and the 140-seat Eidson-Duckwall Recital Hall. The Holcomb Observatory and Planetarium houses the largest telescope in the state of Indiana, a 38-inch Cassegrain reflector. Butler's libraries house approximately 250,000 monograph volumes, 110,000 government documents, 1,500 current journal subscriptions, 14,000 audiovisual materials, and more than 17,000 musical scores. The library system also features a searchable computer database, rare books collection, archives, online catalog access, and research tools.

Costs

For the 2007–08 academic year, tuition was $26,070 for full-time undergraduate students. Average room and board were $8735 per year. Books are estimated at $800 per semester, and other fees are estimated at $736. Tuition for the professional pharmacy program was $26,070 and $31,210 for the sixth year. Tuition for the professional physician assistant program was $26,070 and $31,640 for the fifth year.

Financial Aid

Butler University offers a variety of financial assistance programs based on the demonstration of academic excellence, performance talent, or financial need. Butler awards merit-based academic scholarships to students who have displayed outstanding high school achievement and have excelled in leadership and community service. Performance awards are available in the areas of music, dance, theater, and athletics. Academic departments offer scholarships for students in selected majors. On-campus employment and work-study programs are also available. All students who seek need-based financial assistance are required to file the Free Application for Federal Student Aid (FAFSA).

The University offers National Merit, National Achievement, and National Hispanic Recognition Program scholarships. Semifinalists in these programs are guaranteed a minimum Freshman Academic Scholarship. However, based on academic screening, these students may qualify for a higher award. Finalists in these programs who designate Butler as their sponsor and file their FAFSA by March 1 are eligible for an additional award that ranges from $750 to $2000.

The University also offers Dr. John Morton-Finney Leadership Program Awards to students who exhibit leadership and a commitment to diversity in their high schools and communities. Awards are based on class rank, SAT/ACT scores, and leadership roles in school and the community. These awards include an expectation of continued campus and community leadership while at Butler.

Faculty

Teaching is the top priority for Butler's 291 full-time faculty members; 85 percent hold the highest (terminal) degree in their fields. Many are active in national research programs, write for publications, counsel in government and business, and participate in the arts. With a comfortable teaching load, Butler's faculty members have time to work with students individually. The student-faculty ratio is 12:1. All classes are taught by professors; there are no teaching assistants.

Student Government

As the official student governing body, Student Government Association (SGA) is the liaison between faculty and administration members. The organization is also responsible for budgeting funds from the student activity fee. These funds promote SGA's Program Board activities, including the film series, concerts, and all campus special events as well as the purchase of the Butler yearbook, *The Drift*.

Admission Requirements

Applicants are expected to complete a minimum of 17 academic units in high school, including 4 years of English, 3 years each of laboratory sciences and mathematics, 2 years each of history or social studies, and 2 years of the same foreign language. A candidate for admission typically ranks in the upper third of his or her high school class and should submit satisfactory results of the SAT or the ACT, including the optional Writing Test. The Jordan College of Fine Arts requires an audition. In addition to these factors, the Admission Committee considers the applicant's leadership skills, motivation, and writing sample. Students who wish to transfer from another regionally accredited college or university are considered if they are in good standing and have a grade point average of 2.0 or better in their previous academic work. Transfer students must submit official transcripts of all college work.

Application and Information

Butler offers two nonbinding Early Admission (not early decision) programs with specific benefits associated with each program. The application priority date for Early Admission is December 1 of the senior year of high school, and its benefits include early consideration for freshmen academic scholarships and departmental scholarships, early course registration, priority housing, and optional living-learning center participation. The application deadline for Admission I is February 1 and its benefits include early consideration for freshman academic scholarships, early course registration, and priority housing. The application deadline for Admission II is March 1, and applications are processed on a space-available basis. Campus visits and interviews are strongly recommended, though not required, and are arranged on a daily basis. Several open-house programs are also scheduled throughout the year. Interested students and their families are encouraged to visit http://go.butler.edu to make arrangements for campus visits.

Office of Admission
Butler University
4600 Sunset Avenue
Indianapolis, Indiana 46208-3485
Phone: 317-940-8100
888-940-8100 (toll-free)
Fax: 317-940-8150
E-mail: admission@butler.edu
Web site: http://go.butler.edu

DEPAUW UNIVERSITY

GREENCASTLE, INDIANA

DEPAUW UNIVERSITY

The University

"DePauw is not a spectator sport" is the way one graduate described the DePauw experience. Indeed, DePauw students expect and seek a challenge. In small classes, students are challenged by professors who are leading scholars with a passion for teaching. There are countless opportunities to excel in more than forty programs of study, five Programs of Distinction, numerous leadership positions with student organizations and living units, athletic programs, and more. DePauw students have a tradition of volunteerism, as demonstrated by the fact that three fourths of the student body of 2,350 participate in community service each year. In the first annual *Guide to Campuses Where You Can Make a Difference*, DePauw ranked among the top fifteen colleges where students are truly making a difference in terms of service, both on campus and in the community. In brief, DePauw provides a broad, liberal arts education that is intended to serve as a foundation for the student's lifetime of learning and growth.

At DePauw, the traditional liberal arts curriculum is complemented by perhaps the largest per capita student internship program in the country. Eighty percent of DePauw students complete at least one internship during a semester, Winter Term, or summer, and many students complete at least two internships. As a result, DePauw offers a unique opportunity for students to explore various interests and career possibilities, which have a significant impact for students following graduation. More than 90 percent of DePauw graduates are employed or enrolled in graduate/professional school within nine months of graduation. The figure increases to more than 99 percent after one year. Of those students obtaining employment after graduation, approximately 1 out of 4 students accept jobs at companies and organizations where they served a student internship.

Much of DePauw's reputation for excellence can be attributed to the success of its alumni. DePauw ranked eleventh in the nation in terms of the likelihood that its graduates will become chief executive officers of major American companies, according to *Fortune* magazine in 1990. DePauw ranked eighth in the nation and first in the Midwest as the undergraduate origin of the nation's top executives, according to a 1994 study by Standard & Poor's Corp. DePauw also ranked sixteenth as a baccalaureate source for Ph.D. degree recipients in all fields, according to a 1998 survey by Franklin and Marshall College.

DePauw guarantees graduation in four years for students in forty standard programs, or the University waives tuition and fees for any subsequent course work necessary for graduation.

At the graduate level, DePauw offers the Master of Arts in Teaching degree with a leadership emphasis (M.A.T.L.).

Location

DePauw is located in a town of 10,000 people set amid the gently rolling hills of west-central Indiana. The campus is exceptionally well maintained, blending new, state-of-the-art facilities with buildings, such as the historic East College, that exemplify the University's heritage. DePauw students are very active in the community, as indicated by the fact that about three fourths of the student body volunteers each year for public service in numerous community organizations. Greencastle is 45 miles west of Indianapolis and within a 3-hour drive of Chicago, St. Louis, Louisville, Cincinnati, and Columbus.

Majors and Degrees

DePauw offers the Bachelor of Arts (B.A.), Bachelor of Music (B.Mus.), Bachelor of Musical Arts (B.M.A.), and Bachelor of Music Education (B.M.E.).

DePauw offers majors in more than forty areas, including anthropology, art (history), art (studio), biochemistry, biology, black studies, chemistry, classical civilization, communication, computer science, conflict studies, earth science, East Asian studies, economics, education studies, English (literature), English (writing), environmental geoscience, French, geology, German, Greek, history, interdisciplinary, kinesiology (athletic training, sports and exercise science, and sports medicine), mathematics, music, music/business, music performance, music education, philosophy, physics, political science, psychology, religious studies, Romance languages, Russian studies, sociology, sociology and anthropology, Spanish, theater, and women's studies. Preprofessional programs are available in dentistry, law, and medicine. In addition, DePauw offers a 3-2 program in engineering.

Academic Programs

DePauw is committed to providing its students with a traditional, liberal arts education complemented by internship opportunities, and degree requirements reflect this approach. The University follows a 4-1-4 calendar, with four-month fall and spring semesters and a January Winter Term. The normal course load in a semester is four courses, but course loads may vary from three to 4½ courses. During the January Winter Term, first-year and upperclass students study on campus and participate in research, internships, and travel abroad. DePauw's special Programs of Distinction include the Honor Scholar program, the Information Technology Associates Program, Management Fellows, Media Fellows, and Science Research Fellows programs.

In the 1999–2000 academic year, DePauw began a new first-year experience program, called depauw.year1, which is designed to foster a sense of community among first-year students. Through this program, students take a first-year seminar and work with upperclass student mentors; students also take advantage of special programs, speakers, and other activities that are designed to assist them in their transition to college.

Thirty-one courses are required for students earning a Bachelor of Arts, Bachelor of Music, or Bachelor of Musical Arts degree. The Bachelor of Music Education degree requires thirty-two courses. Each student must complete a major, achieve at least a 2.0 GPA (on a 4.0 scale) in that major, and satisfy the senior major requirement. Students must attain a minimum cumulative GPA of 2.0, while students in the B.M.A. and B.M.E. programs need a minimum 2.5 GPA. Fifteen courses leading to a bachelor's degree, including six of the last eight courses, must be completed in residence at DePauw or in a University-approved program. Students in the College of Liberal Arts must achieve certification in writing (W), quantitative reasoning (Q), and oral communication skills (S). Students must complete three Winter Term projects with satisfactory grades, including an on-campus Winter Term for first-year students. A maximum of 3 internship course credits and five internship experiences (including Winter Terms) may be applied toward the bachelor's degree.

Off-Campus Programs

DePauw offers extensive off-campus study programs. Domestic programs include the Washington Semester, New York Arts Program, Newberry Library Program, Oak Ridge Science Semester, and Philadelphia Urban Semester. Study abroad is available in Africa, Asia-Pacific, Australia, Austria, Canada, the Caribbean, China, the Czech Republic, Denmark, England, France, Germany, Greece, Hungary, India, Ireland, Italy, Japan, Latin America, Mexico, the Middle East, the Netherlands, New Zealand, Russia, Samoa, Scotland, Singapore, Spain, Switzerland, Tibet, Vietnam, and Wales. Many students also participate in off-campus Winter Term projects. More than 40 percent of students study off-campus as part of their DePauw experience. In order to receive course credit, a student must have approval from the International Center.

Academic Facilities

The new blends with the old on DePauw's 695-acre campus, which features thirty-six major buildings and a 520-acre nature park. DePauw's facilities provide an excellent environment for teaching and learning. The physical plant is equal to or superior to that of other liberal arts universities.

The centerpiece of the campus is historic East College, built in 1877 and listed on the Register of Historic Landmarks. New buildings on campus include the Indoor Tennis and Track Center, which opened in 2001 and was recognized by the United States Tennis Association as an outstanding public tennis facility for 2002. The Julian Science and Math Center has undergone a $38-million expansion and renovation project, adding 110,000 square feet of new classroom and laboratory space, including the 361° Technology Center. The Peeler Art Center, built in 2002, gives students a state-of-the-art space optimal to the teaching, creation, and presentation of art. The new William Weston Clarke Emison Museum of Art, home to the University's permanent collection of art of more than 2,000 objects, was designed to complement the Peeler Art Center. It also houses teaching spaces, academic departments, and faculty offices. The Pulliam Center for Contemporary Media has superb facilities and equipment for *The DePauw*, the oldest student newspaper in the state; student-operated WGRE-FM radio; and a television unit in which students produce programs for broadcast statewide and nationwide.

The new Manning Environmental Field Station, located in the University's Nature Park, offers laboratory space for the study of biology and environmental geosciences. In fall 2007, DePauw will complete a $29-million renovation of the Green Center for the Performing Arts, home of the School of Music and Communication Department. In addition, the Janet Prindle Institute for Ethics will be constructed in the Nature Park.

Costs

Expenses for the 2007–08 academic year include $29,300 for tuition, $8,100 for room and board, and $400 in fees for health services and activities. Books and supplies are approximately $600 per year, and personal expenses are approximately $1000 per year.

Financial Aid

A significant number of DePauw students receive scholarships, grants, loans, or work-study assistance. The average financial aid package covers more than half of total costs. DePauw's financial aid program is designed to recognize achievement and potential and to assist students who otherwise would be unable to attend the University due to financial constraints. DePauw maintains its own scholarship, work, and loan programs and participates in all traditional forms of state and federal financial aid.

February 15 is the priority filing date for applications for fall financial aid. The FAFSA and an institutional financial aid application are required. Scholarships/grants available include federal and state scholarships/grants, University scholarships/grants, private scholarships/grants, ROTC scholarships and academic merit scholarships. Approximately 40 percent of students work on campus during the academic year. DePauw participates in the Federal Work-Study Program, and 45 percent of students who receive financial aid participate in work-study.

Faculty

DePauw professors are devoted to teaching students. The University has 238 full-time faculty members, and 99 percent have the terminal degree in their field. The student-faculty ratio is 10:1. All classes at DePauw are taught by professors and not by graduate assistants. Ninety-seven percent of full-time faculty members serve as academic advisers to students.

Student Government

Leadership opportunities in a wide variety of organizations are an integral part of the DePauw experience. Students have numerous opportunities to be involved in student government as well as committees and councils representing student concerns. The president of the student body presides over the many committees of the Student Congress; each committee has several student representatives as members. Sororities, fraternities, and residence halls all have annual elections of officers and representatives to various campus organizations.

Admission Requirements

DePauw does not conduct admission by the numbers. Along with grades and SAT or ACT scores, the University strongly considers the quality of courses selected in the high school, the essay, recommendations of high school counselors and teachers, and the personal interview. Also considered are the high school attended, the student's record of extracurricular achievements, and examples of a special talent the student may have. DePauw examines each individual's application carefully.

To be admitted to the first-year class at DePauw, students must have graduated from an accredited secondary school or offer evidence of equivalent education. Students should have completed the following work in a college-preparatory program: 4 units of English, 4 units of mathematics, 3–4 units of a foreign language, 3–4 units of social science, and 3– units of science (2 or more laboratory sciences). In addition, School of Music candidates must audition.

Application and Information

Prospective students are encouraged to apply online. DePauw is a member of the Common Application Group and encourages student use of the Common Application.

Students interested in early decision must submit applications by November 1, students interested in early notification must submit applications by December 1, and students interested in regular decision must submit applications by February 1. Admission decisions are mailed by January 5 for early decision applicants and by February 15 for early notification applicants. Regular decision applicants are notified by April 1. Early decision applicants who are admitted must respond by February 1; other admitted applicants who decide to enroll must submit an enrollment deposit by May 1. Students should contact:

Stefanie D. Niles
Vice President for Admission and Financial Aid
DePauw University
P.O. Box 37
Greencastle, Indiana 46135-0037
Phone: 765-658-4006
800-447-2495 (toll-free)
Fax: 765-658-4007
E-mail: admission@depauw.edu
Web site: http://www.depauw.edu

Historic East College is the centerpiece of DePauw University's campus. The East College bell summons students to class and also signals victories in football.

EARLHAM COLLEGE

RICHMOND, INDIANA

The College

Earlham College offers a challenging intellectual environment that attracts a diverse group of students with a variety of motivations—academic, political, social, athletic, ethical, and career-minded—who want to make an impact on the world. The College's 1,194 students—661 women and 533 men—represent forty-eight states and sixty-eight other countries. Students of many races, religious backgrounds, economic levels, and ethnic traditions join together on this Midwestern campus to create and experience the Earlham Effect. They share an experience rooted in the Quaker values of tolerance, equality, justice, respect, and collaboration. They explore an unending desire to see the world differently and to bring about change when necessary. Earlham's commitment to engaging students in a changing world is at the heart of its own mission.

Students at Earlham get involved in a wide variety of associations and organizations, including numerous extracurricular programs in music, theater, dance, social and political action, ethnic and international awareness, and intramural and varsity athletics. Students manage an FM public radio station, a food co-op, an equestrian program, a newspaper, and a literary magazine. Activities are coordinated by the Student Activities Board, the Earlham Events Committee, and various special interest groups, such as the Black Leadership Action Coalition, Women's Program Committee, International Club, and Earlham Service Learning Center. Students are active in community service and donate more than 50,000 hours of time to the Richmond community each year.

Earlham, an NCAA Division III affiliate, is a member of the North Coast Athletic Conference. The College offers seven intercollegiate sports for men (baseball, basketball, cross-country, football, soccer, tennis, and track) and eight intercollegiate sports for women (basketball, cross-country, field hockey, soccer, tennis, track, and volleyball). Club sports include swimming, Ultimate Frisbee, lacrosse, and men's volleyball. Thirty percent of the students participate in intercollegiate athletics, and 50 percent participate in an extensive intramural program. Earlham athletic facilities include indoor and outdoor tennis courts; football, baseball, soccer, lacrosse, and hockey fields; an all-weather track; and a $13-million athletics and wellness center.

Earlham is a residential college. Students live in the eight residence halls (including the new 45,000-square-foot Mills Hall that opened in 2006) and thirty College-owned houses near the campus.

Earlham offers a Master of Arts in Teaching degree program. This eleven-month program for liberal arts and sciences graduates leads to certification in English/language arts, math, modern foreign languages, science, and social studies, all at the middle and high school levels.

In 2006, the College approved an Earlham Master of Education degree program for licensed teachers.

Location

Earlham's 800-acre tree-shaded campus lies in the southwestern edge of Richmond, Indiana, a city of 40,000. Richmond is 65 miles from Cincinnati, Ohio, and Indianapolis, Indiana, and 40 miles from Dayton, Ohio. Many students find opportunities to join in local activities. The city's arboretum and parks system, symphony orchestra, theater company, and art association all offer extra dimensions to student life.

Majors and Degrees

Earlham College awards the B.A. degree in more than thirty disciplinary and interdisciplinary programs. Academic majors include African and African-American studies, art, biochemistry, biology, business and nonprofit management, chemistry, comparative languages and linguistics, computer science, economics, education, English, environmental programs, French, geosciences, German, history, human development and social relations, international studies, Japanese language and linguistics, Japanese studies, Latin American studies, mathematics, music, peace and global studies, philosophy, physics/astronomy, politics, psychobiology, psychology, religion, sociology/anthropology, Spanish, theater arts, and women's studies. Other special academic programs are offered in film studies, Jewish studies, journalism, languages and literatures, legal studies, medieval studies, museum studies, outdoor education, Quaker studies, studio art, teaching English to speakers of other languages (TESOL), and wilderness. Excellent preprofessional programs are available in law, medicine, and the ministry.

Academic Programs

Earlham aims to educate for depth and breadth, believing that one's success in the twenty-first century depends heavily on an ability to understand and make well-educated connections across different intellectual and experiential boundaries. Earlham's General Education Program encourages students to develop competencies in the arts, quantitative reasoning, scientific inquiry, wellness, and perspectives in diversity (including domestic multiculturalism, interculturalism, or global historical awareness and second language requirements). First- and second-year core courses (Earlham Seminars, Interpretive Practices courses, and Comparative Practices courses) emphasize ways of knowing and critical reading and writing skills.

Students gain an in-depth understanding of one or more disciplines in their major area of academic concentration. An academic major usually consists of eight to ten courses in one department, a senior research project or seminar, and a departmental comprehensive examination. Earlham grants credit for Advanced Placement examinations and higher-level International Baccalaureate subjects. Students may also receive credit for independent studies and academic internships.

The academic year consists of two semesters plus an optional May Term. During the summer, the College sponsors a two-week academic experience for high school students called Explore-A-College.

Off-Campus Programs

Earlham believes that classroom learning must go hand-in-hand with experience in the richness of the wider world. More than 65 percent of Earlham students participate in at least one off-campus study program. Academic credit is earned, and, except for transportation costs, no extra charge is incurred for off-campus study. Earlham students can study abroad in Austria, the Bahamas, China, Curacao, East Africa, England, France, Galapagos (tropical biology), Germany, Greece, Haiti, Japan, Martinique, Menorca, the Middle East, New Zealand, Northern Ireland, Russia, Scotland, Senegal, Sri Lanka, Spain, Turkey, and Vienna. Earlhamites also participate in American programs along the U.S.-Mexico border (Border Studies) and in Philadelphia; New York; Chicago; Woods Hole, Massachusetts; and Oak Ridge, Tennessee. The academic focus of these programs varies, and students in all majors are encouraged to participate in at least one off-campus program. Earlham offers a three-week wilderness experience to incoming first-year students backpacking in the Uinta Mountains of Utah or canoeing in the boundary waters of Canada.

Academic Facilities

Long considered one of the nation's finest teaching libraries, Earlham's Lilly and Wildman Science Libraries received the 2001 Excellence in Academic Libraries Award from the Association of College and Research Libraries. In total, Earlham students and faculty members have ready access to some 3.5 million volumes. Locally, Earlham houses more than 400,000 volumes and currently subscribes to some 1,200 print periodicals and newspapers. Maps, music, and works of art are also available. Another 17,000 periodicals are available online. Special holdings include the Herbert Hoover Peace Studies Collection and the Quaker Collection. Earlham is a Library of Congress selected depository for government documents.

The $13-million Landrum Bolling Center for Interdisciplinary Studies and Social Sciences opened in 2002, providing technologically equipped classrooms, offices, and common areas to enable pursuits in interdisciplinary programs, global outreach, experiential learning, collaborative projects, and networked information resources.

Modern, well-equipped science laboratories for biology, chemistry, geology, and physics are found in Stanley and Dennis Halls. Dennis Hall is also the location of the Joseph Moore Natural History Museum and the Ralph Teetor Planetarium. Earlham's observatory has a 14-inch Schmidt-Cassegrain telescope. Through updated computing and network resources, students have high-speed access to e-mail and the Internet. Eight microcomputer labs with 165 workstations (Macintosh-, Windows-, and UNIX-based) support word processing, programming, research, and Internet and e-mail access. One mixed-platform lab (Macintoshes and Windows) is available to students and faculty and staff members 24 hours a day. All residence hall rooms are wired for Internet access, and wireless networking is available in all academic buildings and campus houses.

Music and art studios are found in the Runyan Student Center, which also houses a modern theater, the campus radio station, and the College bookstore. Other studios and Goddard Auditorium are located in Carpenter Hall.

Costs

Tuition, fees, and room and board charges for 2007–08 totaled $38,018. Students have free admission to the Earlham Artist Series, athletic events, speaker series, and numerous lectures, concerts, and dances.

Financial Aid

Most financial aid is awarded on the basis of demonstrated need; more than 75 percent of Earlham's first-year students receive financial assistance. Earlham usually meets the full need of all accepted students with a combination of Earlham Grants, endowed scholarships, loans, federal and state grants, and campus work. Students must file both the Free Application for Federal Student Aid (FAFSA) and a special Earlham form.

Scholarships are awarded without regard to financial need and recognize academic achievement. Earlham also offers scholarships through the National Merit Scholarship Corporation. Special scholarships are available to members of the Religious Society of Friends (Quakers) and to students who are likely to enhance the diversity of the student body. Scholarships and limited financial aid are available for international students.

Faculty

Earlham's faculty members are dedicated professionals whose first priority is teaching. Ninety-seven percent of the 103 teaching faculty members hold doctoral degrees or terminal degrees in their fields. In recent years their teaching, creative endeavors, and scholarly research have been recognized by numerous grants and fellowships from the Ford Foundation, Danforth Foundation, IBM, Woodrow Wilson Foundation, Fulbright-Hayes Program, Kellogg Foundation, Japan Foundation, Lilly Endowment Inc., National Endowment for the Humanities, National Science Foundation, and Carnegie-Mellon Foundation. The student-faculty ratio is 12:1.

Student Government

Earlham's distinctive approach to consensus governance recalls its Quaker roots. The philosophical system is summarized in a code of principles and practices based on the ideals of respect for individuals and community, integrity, simplicity, peace and justice, and consensus governance. Campus organizations reach decisions by consensus rather than by parliamentary procedure or majority rule. The process emphasizes individual thought, group discussion, listening, and synthesizing.

Admission Requirements

Admission decisions are based on more than SAT and ACT scores or high school grades, as important as these criteria are. Earlham pays close attention to the quality of the academic program, teacher and counselor recommendations, application essays, and personal interviews. Applicants should have had an academic or college-preparatory high school program. The SAT or ACT is required. Interviews are strongly recommended although not required.

Application and Information

Earlham offers several admission options. The early decision deadline is December 1 (notification on December 15), the early action deadline is January 1 (notification on February 1), the regular decision deadline is February 15 (notification on March 15), and the transfer deadline is April 1. International students (non-U.S. citizens) should apply by February 1.

Students wishing additional information or materials on Earlham College should contact:

Office of Admissions
Earlham College
801 National Road West
Richmond, Indiana 47374-4095
Phone: 765-983-1600
800-EARLHAM (toll-free)
Fax: 765-983-1560
E-mail: admission@earlham.edu
Web site: http://www.earlham.edu

From Richmond, Indiana, Earlham College students engage a changing world and strive to make a difference.

FRANKLIN COLLEGE

FRANKLIN, INDIANA

The College

As an innovative scientist, diplomat, thinker, writer, and leader, Benjamin Franklin's remarkable life and accomplishments left a mark on not only a young nation, but the world. Named in the spirit of this extraordinary American icon, Franklin College continues his legacy of exploration and knowledge.

Since it's founding in 1834, Franklin College has a long history of preparing students for lives committed to excellence, leadership, and service. With a comprehensive liberal arts curriculum combined with a leading edge Professional Development Program, Franklin College provides an education that blends thinking with doing, reasoning with acting, and discovering with challenging.

Small classes and dedicated faculty members ensure that students get the attention needed to succeed, and Franklin's career and graduate school admission rates prove this.

Franklin combines liberal arts training with preprofessional development like no other college. Students can develop the competencies and resources necessary to be successful in their personal and professional lives through Franklin's innovative Professional Development Program (PDP). This exciting program gives them the opportunity to dine with corporate executives, network with national and community leaders, learn the finer points of corporate communication, and develop a level of polish and sophistication that sets them apart from other college graduates.

Location

Located in the heart of the Midwest, Franklin College offers students the best of both a small community and a big city's excitement. Franklin, Indiana, only 20 miles south of Indiana's capital city Indianapolis, is the thirteenth largest city in the U.S. It offers a wide variety of internship opportunities, as well as athletic, cultural, and entertainment events that appeal to all students.

Majors and Degrees

Flagship programs at Franklin College include athletic training, business, journalism, pre-med, and education. The Pulliam School of Journalism is one of a few comprehensive journalism schools housed at a small liberal arts institution. Student media opportunities include a student-run PR agency and a student newspaper, magazine, news show, radio show, and yearbook. After graduation, education majors are placed at 97 percent or higher in the classroom, while business students repeatedly score in the top 5 percent on the National College Business Examination. One hundred percent of athletic training majors are employed six months after graduation. Preparation for graduate school is exceptional, with 85 percent of students gaining admission to medical school and 90 percent of applicants accepted to law school.

Franklin College confers more than twenty-five Bachelor of Arts degrees in the following areas: accounting, American studies, art, biology, business (finance, general, international business, management/industrial relations, and marketing), Canadian studies, chemistry, computing/computer information systems, economics, education (elementary, middle school, and secondary), English, French, history, journalism (advertising/public relations, broadcasting, news-editorial, and visual communications), mathematics, music (piano and vocal), philosophy, physical education, political science, psychology, recreation, religious studies, sociology (criminal justice and social work), Spanish, and theater. Minors are also offered in many of these areas, including fine arts, leadership, and physics.

Engineering is offered as a 3+2 program. Students earn a Bachelor of Arts degree from Franklin College and a Bachelor of Science degree in one of the engineering disciplines from the Purdue School of Engineering and Technology (IUPUI).

Students considering a career in dentistry, forestry, medical technology, medicine, nursing, optometry, physical therapy, or veterinary medicine arrange their program with the advice of the preprofessional adviser of the science division. Students seeking a career in law plan their program in consultation with prelaw advisers. Students planning a career in secondary education may elect an academic area of concentration that will satisfy the state requirements for a teaching major. The education department is endorsed and approved by the Indiana Professional Standards Board and the National Council for Accreditation of Teacher Education (NCATE).

Academic Programs

The current academic program is the result of the faculty's plan to meet the express needs of students; the primary emphasis is on the unity of knowledge. Franklin believes in the importance of providing students with a liberal arts background while they develop talents for a particular professional career. Approximately one third of each student's total course work is composed of the prescribed and exploratory courses that make up the general education core curriculum.

All of Franklin's academic departments offer individualized study, allowing a student to pursue his or her field of interest in depth. Students interested in pursuing a major not offered at Franklin may submit a proposal for their individualized major.

As part of the 4-1-4 calendar, students complete up to 8 hours of credit in a special four-week winter-term program in January. The winter term is designed to allow students to study in areas of particular interest to them, either within or outside their major field of study. Some January classes offer students the opportunity to travel to locations such as Belize, England, France, Italy, and Mexico .

A large number of internships are available during the winter term and the summer, offering practical experience under the supervision of a professional. The fall semester ends before Christmas; the spring semester begins in February and ends in May. An eight-week summer session beginning in mid-June allows students to take up to 9 additional credit hours. Ninety-five percent of Franklin College students complete an internship prior to graduation.

Franklin gives credit in seventeen academic areas for successful scores on CLEP subject examinations; credit is also granted for successful scores on the Advanced Placement tests of the College Board. The Running Start Program enables talented high school students to get an early start on their college education.

Off-Campus Programs

Franklin College students participate in a variety of off-campus study experiences, including a year or a semester of study through Acadia University of Nova Scotia, Telemark University of Norway, and Hong Kong Baptist University. Other off-campus study programs include the American University Washington Semester; a junior year abroad; programs at Harlaxton College in England, Franklin College of Switzerland, and Brethren Colleges

Abroad; and specific exchange programs in Japan and Taiwan. Students may also participate in a Semester at Sea program sponsored by the University of Pittsburgh.

Academic Facilities

Franklin College has two campus buildings listed on the National Historic Register. Old Main, the original home of the College, and Shirk Hall, home of the Pulliam School of Journalism, are footholds of the rich past and recent renovation of the Franklin College campus. Classrooms and administrative, business, and professorial offices, along with computer laboratories, occupy Old Main; Shirk Hall also houses classrooms and the radio and television station.

A. A. Barnes Science Building houses all physics, biology, and chemistry department classrooms and laboratories. The Spurlock Center gymnasium and fitness center provides increased classroom and office space along with a weight room.

The Dietz Center for Professional Development is the home of the Professional Development Program. State-of-the-art conference rooms and computer facilities enhance Franklin's career programming commitment to its students.

The B. F. Hamilton Library, containing more than 117,000 volumes and collections of microfilm, slides, art reproductions, recordings, and periodicals, is a member of P.A.L.N.I. (Private Academic Library Network of Indiana). The Johnson Center for Fine Arts provides classrooms and practice and performance accommodations, and it houses the facilities and meeting rooms for the Leadership Program.

Costs

The direct cost of the 2007–08 academic year was $28,065. This amount was derived from tuition, which was $21,150; room and board, which were $6390; student fees of $255; and Winter Term meal fees of $270.

Financial Aid

The Franklin College financial aid program assists students who might not otherwise be able to attend college and also rewards applicants for excellent academic achievement in high school. Awards are based on scholarship, curricular and extracurricular activities, and financial need. Aid involving financial need includes Franklin College grants, loans, and employment. Franklin participates in the Federal Stafford Student Loan, Federal Perkins Loan, and Federal Work-Study programs. Ben Franklin Scholarships, President's Scholarships, Founders Scholarships, and Trustees Scholarships are awarded on the basis of academic performance, activities, and standardized test scores. The Ben Franklin Scholarship covers the full cost of tuition; the President's Scholarship is a $14,000 award; and Academic Excellence and Dean's Scholarships are awarded on the basis of specified criteria. In addition, students identified by the state of Indiana as 21st Century Scholars will be awarded full tuition scholarships. Scholarships are renewable for each of the recipient's four academic years at Franklin, provided students maintain a minimum GPA of 3.0 and advance in class status each year. The Free Application for Federal Student Aid (FAFSA) is required.

Faculty

The 12:1 student-faculty ratio allows Franklin faculty members to provide excellent instruction in small classes that promote participatory learning. Eighty percent of current faculty members have obtained the highest degree in their field. Faculty members serve as advisers and provide supplemental attention outside the classroom. While many faculty members carry on research and publish their work, their main emphasis is teaching. No classes are taught by graduate students or teaching assistants.

Student Government

The Student Congress is composed of representatives elected by the student body. The congress provides a forum for student concerns and is the most important governmental communication link among students, faculty members, and the administration. Student government also includes the Judicial Board and the Residence Hall Council. These groups have jurisdiction over certain questions concerning the social standards and regulations of the College.

Admission Requirements

Applications for admission to Franklin College are evaluated on an individual basis. A student's potential academic and personal contributions to the College, recommendations, school and community activities, academic record, and standardized test scores are taken into consideration by the Admissions Committee. A student should complete a strong college-preparatory program. Candidates for admission are urged to visit the campus in order to experience the College community.

Application and Information

To be considered for admission, an applicant must submit a completed application (paper or online), a transcript of all secondary school and college work attempted, a graded English paper or a personal statement, and either SAT or ACT scores. A decision regarding acceptance is made after the College receives all necessary credentials. Notification is sent immediately after the Enrollment Committee has acted.

Office of Admission
Franklin College
101 Branigin Boulevard
Franklin, Indiana 46131
Phone: 317-738-8062
800-852-0232 (toll-free)
Fax: 317-738-8274
E-mail: admissions@franklincollege.edu
Web site: http://www.franklincollege.edu

The bell tower on top of Old Main on the Franklin College campus.

GOSHEN COLLEGE
GOSHEN, INDIANA

GOSHEN COLLEGE

The College

Goshen College (GC) is a fully accredited national liberal arts college that is known for leadership in international education, service-learning opportunities, and peace and justice issues. Founded in 1894 by the Mennonite Church, one of three historic U.S. peace churches, GC serves nearly 1,000 students and encourages dialogue between students with different perspectives, backgrounds, and beliefs. While students from Mennonite backgrounds represent half of the student body, more than thirty denominations and several world religions are represented. Students come from nearly thirty-five states, Canadian provinces, and more than thirty countries. Goshen College was recognized in *U.S. News & World Report*'s 2007 "America's Best Colleges" rankings as a top national liberal arts college for enrolling a high percentage of international students and for its unique study/service-abroad program. Goshen's record of sustained excellence has attracted other national attention as well. Goshen College was named one of the top twenty-five schools in the country for international education by the highly respected *Open Doors Report* of the Institute for International Education. Goshen is one of 300 schools included in *Barron's Best Buys in College Education* for offering a high-quality education at below-average prices. The *Princeton Review* named GC as a "Best Midwestern College" in 2004. Goshen College is included in the discriminating "Colleges of Distinction" and was named one of *The 100 Best Colleges for African-American Students* in a book by Erlene B. Wilson. A recent study by Franklin and Marshall ranked GC in the top 16 percent of liberal arts colleges in the number of its graduates who go on to complete doctoral degrees. Peterson's lists GC among its 190 *Top Colleges for Science.*

In a highly energetic, Christ-centered environment, students have plenty of opportunities to cultivate leadership skills and assume responsibility. Students edit a weekly newspaper and a yearbook, operate a radio station, produce a campus television program, serve on campus publishing editorial boards, and perform in mainstage theater and opera productions or in the six instrumental and vocal ensembles. Representatives of the student body are elected to serve on the Student Senate and Campus Activities Council. Campus groups also include the Student Women's Association, Black Student Union, Campus Ministries Team and Traveling Worship Team, PAX, Latino Student Union, Nursing Students Association, Eco-PAX, Fellowship of Christian Athletes, Social Work Action Association, International Students Club, Business Club, and Pre-Med Club. GC belongs to the National Association of Intercollegiate Athletics as part of the competitive Mid-Central College Conference, with intercollegiate men's and women's basketball, cross-country, soccer, tennis, and track and field; men's baseball and golf; and women's softball and volleyball. More than half of GC students participate in intramural athletics. All students have free access to the Roman Gingerich Recreation-Fitness Center.

Most Goshen students live in one of the College's six residence halls, all of which were renovated recently. In addition, a new community life area, with lounges and a student-run coffeebar, opened in 2004. A stylish new hall for seniors with apartment-style units opened in fall 2005 and additional units for seniors and juniors opened in late 2007. Small-group housing is a popular option for upper-level students. College-owned houses are available for married students and families.

With longtime emphasis on experiential learning, Goshen's programs encourage partnerships between the College and the community by placing students in practicum, internship, and service experiences. In addition, the College holds an annual Celebrate Service Day; classes are suspended so that students and faculty and members can participate in community service projects. Students also benefit from Multicultural Affairs Office programs that emphasize meaningful ways to address issues of diversity in order to prepare students for life in an increasingly interconnected, multicultural world.

Location

The campus is on the south side of Goshen, a culturally and economically diverse city of 30,000 in north-central Indiana, by car 2 hours east of Chicago and 45 minutes east of South Bend. Known as the Maple City for its shady avenues, Goshen is part of Elkhart County, one of the fastest-growing counties in the nation during the 1990s. The county enjoys its rich Mennonite and Amish heritage as well as a growing Latino community while serving as home to major corporations, with proximity to Chicago and Indianapolis.

Majors and Degrees

Goshen College offers more than sixty programs of study. The Bachelor of Arts is awarded in accounting; American Sign Language interpreting; art; Bible and religion; biology; business; business information systems; chemistry; communication; computer science; computer science and applied mathematics; elementary education; English; environmental science; history; history and investigative skills; management information systems; mathematics; molecular biology; music; natural science; peace, justice, and conflict studies; physical education; physics; psychology; social work; sociology/anthropology; Spanish; special education; teaching English to speakers of other languages (TESOL); and theater. In addition, a Bachelor of Science in Nursing (B.S.N.), a Master of Science (M.S.) degree in nursing, and a Master of Arts in environmental education are awarded. Unique programs include Anabaptist-Mennonite studies, international studies, music and worship, music with business and technology, social policy, women's studies, and youth ministries. Interdisciplinary majors usually combine work in three different departments and allow students to tailor their studies to individual interests. Preprofessional programs in architecture, art therapy, curatorial studies, dentistry, engineering, law, medicine, pharmacy, physical therapy, seminary, and veterinary medicine are available as well. The College also offers minors in more than thirty areas.

Academic Programs

The College calendar consists of two 15-week semesters and a 3½-week May term. A total of 120 semester hours (124 for nursing majors) is required for graduation. One third are usually in general studies courses, including art, Bible and religion, history, literature, philosophy, physical education, science, and social science; another third are courses in the student's major. Most majors require a practicum for graduation. All students must complete a course of international study. Most students choose to participate in the Study-Service Term (SST) program abroad, a thirteen-week term, including course work and field experience in a service assignment, in a significantly different culture. Students also can fulfill the requirement by taking courses on campus or by participating in other study-abroad programs.

Off-Campus Programs

Goshen is one of the few U.S. colleges—and was one of the first—to require international education. Most students (more than 60 percent) choose to fulfill this through SST, while others choose to take classes with an international emphasis on campus. GC's international education program ranks in the top twenty-four both for quality and participation, according to *U.S. News & World Report.* Since the SST program began in 1968, more than 7,000 GC students have benefited from it tremendously, both academically and personally. The program has served as the model for international education programs across the country. In the SST program, students spend six weeks together focusing on the study of one country while immersed in its language and culture. The six-week SST field experience gives students a chance to develop interpersonal skills and to work alongside native residents in service to others. The field experience often relates to the students' major areas of study. During both parts of the program, students live with host families. Most SST units cost the same as a semester on campus. GC students earn 13–14 hours of credit for SST; however, the benefits continue for a lifetime. SST gives students a broader context for living their lives while helping them set an appropriate individual direction. The growing internationalization of U.S. business and culture amplifies SST's benefits; now, more than ever, foreign language skills and knowledge of other cultures are advantages in the job market.

Other off-campus programs include spring term courses in marine biology at the College's center in the Florida Keys and in liberation theology in Central American countries and courses in Europe in theater history, art history, and literature as well as business.

Academic Facilities

On its 135-acre campus, Goshen College has nineteen major buildings and laboratories. The Roman Gingerich Recreation-Fitness Center features a 200-meter indoor track, weight room, three full-size gymnasium courts, racquetball and squash courts, pool and hot tub, climbing wall, and sports medicine training room. In addition, it houses the physical education department, student health center, and intramural and intercollegiate athletics. The new 68,000-square-foot Music Center, which features 1,000- and 300-seat performance halls and a custom-built pipe organ, has some of the best acoustics in the nation. The building also houses an art gallery, rehearsal space, studios, and the Community School of the Arts, which serves hundreds of community students (children through adults) each year.

The Science Building features the Turner Precision X-Ray Measurements Laboratory and the Biological Research Laboratory. The Turner Laboratory gives physics majors a rare opportunity to assist in basic research on crystals; the Biological Research Laboratory is equipped with an electron microscope, Geiger system, climate chambers, incubators, and microtechnique systems. Each summer, students from any discipline may apply to the Maple Scholars Program for undergraduate research, which pays a stipend and pairs students with a faculty member for significant exploration in an area of their interest, such as holography, poetry, genetics, nonviolence, painting, and more. The College regularly does research for larger universities and major industries.

The Harold and Wilma Good Library houses a collection of 130,000 volumes and 800 periodicals as well as the Mennonite Historical Library.

The Merry Lea Environmental Learning Center, and 1,150-acre nature preserve, offers internships in environmental and elementary education and is a key site for the College's environmental science major and minors and the graduate program in environmental education.

Goshen College has a progressive attitude concerning technology in an effort to encourage students to learn how to use technology intelligently and effectively. Computer facilities include three modern student labs, with one computer for every 7.6 students, as well as printers, scanners, digital cameras, wireless Internet access, and other equipment. Computers in student labs are upgraded annually. Multimedia classrooms feature integrated technology as well as media production facilities. All residence hall rooms are connected to the campus network and the Internet; academic registration and account and course information is available on the College intranet.

The John S. Umble Center for the Performing Arts is recognized internationally for its exceptional theater acoustics.

Costs

Tuition for 2007–08 was $21,380 and room and board were $7000. Costs included two 15-week semesters and one 3½-week May term.

Financial Aid

More than ninety-eight percent of the College's students receive some type of financial assistance through federal, state, and Goshen College programs and work-study opportunities. The average award was $17,800. GC offers more than 130 different scholarships. College aid (if applying before February 1) includes the President's Leadership Award, $12,000; Menno Simons Scholarship, $7000, Wens Honors Scholarship, $6000; Yoder Honors Scholarship, $5000, Grebel Honors Scholarship, $4000, and the Kratz Honors Scholarship, $2000 (applications for financial aid received after February 1 receive a slight reduction in scholarship award amount). About 60 percent of incoming students receive renewable academic scholarships. Work-study jobs and other on-campus jobs are available.

Faculty

The faculty includes about 70 full-time and 40 part-time members. Most have lived, served, or worked abroad. The student-faculty ratio is 13:1.

Student Government

The Student Senate acts as an advocate of student concerns and corresponding policy changes and works with the administration, including making significant appointments to campus committees. The Campus Activity Council plans student activities.

Admission Requirements

Applicants should rank in the upper half of their high school graduating class and may apply for admission at any time after the junior year and up to one month before they wish to begin college. ACT or SAT scores are required. Recommended high school work includes 4 years of English, 2 years of science, 2 years of social science, 2 years of mathematics, and 2 to 4 years of a foreign language. Prospective students are encouraged to visit the campus and meet with exceptionally welcoming faculty members and students any Friday during the academic year. Special campus open houses scheduled throughout the year provide excellent opportunities for visits; every Friday is also open for personalized visits.

Application and Information

Students who would like more information may contact:

Office of Admission
Goshen College
1700 South Main Street
Goshen, Indiana 46526
Phone: 574-535-7535
800-348-7422 (toll-free)
Fax: 574-535-7609
E-mail: admission@goshen.edu
Web site: http://www.goshen.edu

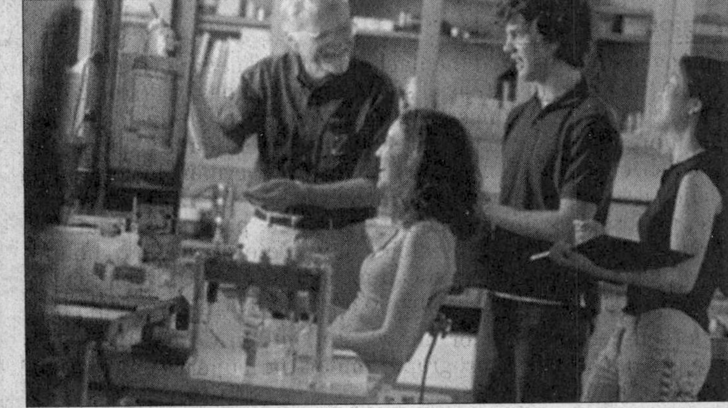

Research and hands-on learning serve students well, especially those who go on to graduate school.

HANOVER COLLEGE

HANOVER, INDIANA

The College

Founded in 1827, Hanover College is Indiana's oldest private college. While the majority of Hanover's approximately 1,000 students come from Indiana, Ohio, and Kentucky, students come from coast to coast, Hawaii, and other countries.

A student's experience at Hanover is characterized by a strong emphasis on a well-rounded liberal arts education, an intimate and personal educational experience that is the result of small classes (average class size is 14) and close contact with faculty members (10:1 student-faculty ratio), a unique college community where 95 percent of students and one third of all faculty and staff members live on campus, active participation outside the classroom in multiple organizations or activities, and being engaged with the world outside the College through travel, internships, community service, and/or academic research.

One third of Hanover students participate in varsity athletics. Hanover offers the following NCAA Division III sports: baseball (men's), basketball (men's and women's), cross-country (men's and women's), football (men's), golf (men's and women's), soccer (men's and women's), softball (women's), tennis (men's and women's), track (men's and women's), and volleyball (women's). Hanover College does not offer athletic scholarships.

Location

Hanover College is located on 650 acres overlooking the Ohio River just outside the historic river town of Madison, Indiana. The campus, referred to by *TIME* and *Princeton Review*'s College Guide as one of the "10 most beautiful college campuses," consists of beautifully landscaped grounds and thirty-eight major buildings of Georgian architectural design.

Madison contains Indiana's largest historic district, with 119 downtown blocks listed on the National Historic Register. The campus community regularly takes advantage of Madison's restaurants, coffeehouses, and shops. Students and faculty and staff members also enjoy access to three major metropolitan areas: Louisville (45 minutes), Cincinnati (70 minutes), and Indianapolis (90 minutes).

Majors and Degrees

Hanover students earn the Bachelor of Arts degree. The College offers the following areas of study: anthropology, art (studio), art history, biology, business, chemistry, classical studies, communication, computer science, economics, elementary education, English, exercise science, French, geology, German, history, international studies, mathematics, medieval-Renaissance studies, music, philosophy, physics, political science, preprofessional programs (dentistry, law, medicine, and veterinary), psychology, secondary education certification, self-designed major, sociology, Spanish, theater, and theological studies.

The self-designed major allows students to design their own major from existing programs under the supervision and approval of the faculty.

Academic Programs

Hanover's academic program includes a 4-4-1 yearly calendar of four courses during each of the fall and winter terms. During the College's one-month Spring Term, students have the opportunity to study a subject in-depth by taking only one class on or off campus. Classes taught on campus during Spring Term include Genetics, Environmental Economics, Urban Sociology, Ceramics, Historical Geology, French Cinema, Abraham Lincoln and the American Dream, Video Production, Physiology of Exercise, and Fiction and Poetry Workshop.

The Center for Business Preparation (CBP) provides M.B.A.-style business education to students in any area of study. Students apply to the CBP as high school seniors or during the freshman year at Hanover. CBP students take six business courses, do a personalized internship during the summer following the junior year, and work on an actual business consulting project during the senior year.

Off-Campus Programs

Hanover offers students a number of options for additional study off campus. The College has established relationships with universities in Australia, Belgium, France, Germany, Mexico, Spain, and Turkey for students interested in spending an entire semester abroad. Individual accommodations can be made for students wishing to study in a country other than those listed.

The College's one-month Spring Term allows students to travel in the U.S. or abroad as part of a class. Classes taught off campus during Spring Term include Roman Philosophy (Italy), Labor Economics (Washington, D.C.), Economics of the European Union (Belgium), History of China (China), Politics and Society in Contemporary Africa (South Africa), Shakespeare in England (England), The Vietnam War (Vietnam), Florence in the Age of Dante and Petrarch (Italy), and Greek Architecture and Classical Athenian Culture (Greece). In addition, various language courses are taught in France, Germany, Spain, and Mexico. The classes and destinations change from year to year; students should check with the Office of Admission to find out current offerings.

Students wishing to study off campus in the U.S. for a semester and get an academic internship are encouraged to look into the programs the College offers in Philadelphia and Washington, D.C. While students are responsible for their travel costs, there are no additional tuition costs for students participating in these programs.

Academic Facilities

Eighty-two percent of Hanover classes contain fewer than 20 students, so the College strives to provide intimate settings as well as the best technology to assist professors and students. Since 1995, the College has invested $51.1 million in the campus with new and renovated buildings. These projects include the Science Center, with its state-of-the-art lab facilities, a human cadaver lab for students in the human anatomy classes, and museum-quality exhibits provided by Hanover faculty members, students, and alumni; the Horner Athletic and Recreation Center, which provides multiple facilities, space, classrooms, and labs for Hanover students, including athletes and exercise science majors, and faculty and staff members; and all academic and residential buildings, which are equipped with wireless computer capabilities.

Costs

Hanover's costs reflect its commitment to providing a high-quality education at a reasonable cost. Direct student expenses in 2007–08 for tuition, room, board, and general fees were $31,370.

Financial Aid

Approximately 95 percent of Hanover students receive some form of direct financial assistance. College aid is available in the form of scholarships, grants, and loans. Every effort is made to meet the demonstrated need of every student. Academic scholarships, music scholarships, and theater scholarships are awarded on merit, regardless of financial need.

U.S. News & World Report, *Princeton Review*, and *Barron's* have all ranked Hanover as a "Best Buy" for its combination of academic excellence and financial assistance.

Faculty

Hanover faculty members are accessible, dedicated, knowledgeable, and, most importantly, hired for their ability to teach. With one third of the faculty living on the campus grounds, students have the ability to develop relationships that would be impossible on other college campuses.

Unlike students at other colleges, Hanover students don't have to worry about graduate students or large numbers of part-time professors teaching their classes. Of *U.S. News & World Report*'s "Top 100 Best Liberal Arts Colleges," Hanover ranks fourth for percentage of full-time faculty members (98 percent) and ranks sixth for percentage of classes under 20 (82 percent).

Though substantial scholars by any standards, Hanover faculty members are not subjected to the "publish or perish" existence found on many campuses. To the contrary, Hanover's small-college experience offers one-on-one academic advising as an integral part of the student-professor relationship.

Student Government

Hanover College's Student Senate is the campuswide organization of student government. Through representative and advisory means, it provides input into the decision-making processes of the College. Student Senate is the governing body that approves and recognizes all official student organizations.

The Interfraternity Council and the Panhellenic Council are the governing bodies for the Greek social organizations (fraternities and sororities) at Hanover College. Composed of representatives of each fraternity and sorority, the councils promote a cooperative spirit and encourage mutual support among the organizations. They collectively serve the campus and wider community through activities and philanthropic projects.

Admission Requirements

To be considered for admission at Hanover, students must show they have prepared themselves academically and be ready for an academic experience that is personal, challenging, engaging, and rewarding.

Students must successfully complete a college-preparatory curriculum that includes English, 4 years, with an emphasis on college-level writing; math, 3 years (a minimum of algebra II and geometry, and a fourth year of math is strongly recommended); science, 3 years (a fourth year of science is strongly recommended); and foreign language, a minimum of 2 years of one language taken in consecutive years (3–4 years of one language is strongly recommended).

Hanover accepts the SAT and/or the ACT for admission purposes. Hanover takes the highest scores from each test, so it may be to a student's benefit to take one or both of the exams more than once. Test scores are accepted directly from the test corporations or as part of an official transcript from the high school. SAT Subject Tests are not required for admission but are considered if submitted. The middle 50 percent of Hanover students scored 1090–1300 (critical reading and math only) on the SAT and 24–30 on the ACT.

Eighty percent of students applying for admission to Hanover submit their application during the fall semester. For application dates and deadlines, students should contact the Office of Admission.

Application and Information

For more information, students should contact:

Office of Admission
Hanover College
P.O. Box 108
Hanover, Indiana 47243-0108
Phone: 812-866-7021
800-213-2178 (toll-free)
Fax: 812-866-7098
E-mail: admission@hanover.edu
Web site: http://www.hanover.edu

Brown Memorial Chapel is a landmark on the Hanover campus and is one of thirty-eight buildings designed in classic Georgian-style architecture that contribute to Hanover's reputation as one of the most beautiful campuses in the country.

HOLY CROSS COLLEGE

NOTRE DAME, INDIANA

The College

Holy Cross College is a Catholic, four-year, coeducational, liberal arts institution founded in 1966. With a campus adjoining St. Mary's College and the University of Notre Dame, Holy Cross College provides the best of both worlds—a close-knit, liberal arts college and the nearby resources and social opportunities of a large university.

A 13:1 faculty-student ratio enables the College to emphasize personal attention and experiential learning. As an institution, Holy Cross believes that experience matters, not only in preparing for careers but in testing one's knowledge, courage, values, and beliefs. The curricular and cocurricular programs at Holy Cross College are designed to emphasize the holistic development of each student—mind, body, and spirit.

Founded and run by the Brothers of Holy Cross, the College is a Catholic community with faith and religious practice as a cornerstone of daily life on campus. Following the Brothers' strong traditions of hospitality and cultural exchange, the College is open and welcoming to followers of all faiths and nonbelievers alike who are open to spiritual growth.

The College encourages a practical, demanding, and comprehensive training of the mind compelled to action by a generous spirit. The professors are known for being available to their students after hours, caring about their students' success, and challenging them to exceed expectations.

Holy Cross College accommodates a broad spectrum of needs, interests, and goals within a challenging, supportive, and experiential environment. The Holy Cross experience prepares students for life, moral leadership, and career or graduate school success through four key programs: an internship to develop real-world career qualifications; a service experience to develop confidence, compassion, and the understanding of how one person can make a positive difference; an international experience to expand horizons and experience other cultures; and a senior capstone project to explain, justify, and summarize the student's learning experiences to a review board consisting of peers, community advisers, mentors, and college administrators.

Local, national, and international students are enrolled at Holy Cross College, including students from more than thirty states and ten countries. The College's residence life program seeks an atmosphere conducive to the intellectual, social, spiritual, and moral growth of its students in a distinctly faith-based environment.

Living in the residence halls is strongly recommended for students who are not from the South Bend area. Residence halls have convenient inside access to full dining services, chapel, laundry facilities, and comfortable student lounge areas. The proximity of the residence halls to classrooms, the library, the computer lab, faculty offices, and the bookstore provides an ideal collegiate environment for undergraduate students.

The campus also features superb new facilities for recreation and competitive athletics. A member of the National Association of Intercollegiate Athletics (NAIA), the College offers men's and women's varsity sports and club teams in basketball, cheerleading, cross-country, golf, hockey, lacrosse, and soccer. A women's intercollegiate volleyball team is planned for the 2009 school year. Intramural sports on campus include basketball, dodgeball, flag football, softball, tennis, and volleyball.

Students are encouraged to attend athletic events and support the HC Saints teams. In addition, many Holy Cross Students also cheer for Notre Dame and St. Mary's sports teams. Tickets for sporting and cultural events are available to Holy Cross students, including Notre Dame football games.

Holy Cross College is very supportive of students who are serious about their Catholic faith. In fact, the College sponsors the Mission Team, a group of student leaders who act as a catalyst for helping other students communicate their spiritual yearnings and practice their faith. Team members immerse themselves in a challenging program of spiritual growth and leadership development grounded in Catholic ideas and practices.

In addition to the Mission Team, Holy Cross College offers a full schedule of activities for students who want to explore and practice their Catholic faith. A full-time director of campus ministry provides pastoral counseling services. Daily mass is celebrated in the campus chapel, and students may participate in mass as part of the liturgical choir, as lectors, as Eucharistic ministers, and by providing logistical support.

The Student Government Association sponsors the Social Concerns Committee, which provides an outlet for students to answer their call to serve. Through this committee and through service-learning components of the curriculum, Holy Cross College promotes its mission by advancing the Gospel and forming compassionate hearts

Location

Holy Cross College is located on the banks of the St. Joseph River just north of the city limits of South Bend in Notre Dame, Indiana. South Bend is the fourth-largest city in the state and offers a variety of fairs and festivals, a top-notch zoo, historical and interactive museums, gardens, parks, the College Football Hall of Fame, and a waterway that is perfect for kayaking. In addition, performing arts include nationally touring Broadway shows, the South Bend Symphony Orchestra, and numerous cultural programs at St. Mary's College and the University of Notre Dame. The campus is located 10 miles south of the Michigan state line, 90 miles from Chicago, and 120 miles from Indianapolis. The South Bend Airport provides regional and international connections, while the Chicago SouthShore and South Bend Railroad provides easy access to Chicago and its airports.

Majors and Degrees

Holy Cross College offers a Bachelor of Arts in elementary education, liberal studies, and theology. The Liberal Studies program offers optional academic concentrations in business and economics, information systems, literature, prelaw, psychology, and theology. Several new majors will be introduced in 2008.

Academic Programs

The Bachelor of Arts in Liberal Studies program is intended for students who desire a flexible, practical, rigorous, Catholic liberal arts education. Graduates are prepared for positions in the business or public sector or for graduate studies in business, law, education, the humanities, or the social and behavioral sciences.

In addition, Holy Cross College offers special academic programs that meet a wide range of student needs. The College Success Program (CSP) is a one-year academic support program that assists students in the transition from high school to college.

Off-Campus Programs

Holy Cross College emphasizes the importance of global and cross-cultural perspectives. All students in the Liberal Studies program must complete an approved international experience. Many students have fulfilled this degree requirement in countries where the Congregation of Holy Cross has ministries. All expenses for the two-week Ghana, India, Mexico, and Peru experiences are covered by students' tuition; there is no extra cost.

Students in the Liberal Studies program must also complete an internship. Students work with their academic advisers and the director of the Lilly Career Development Center to determine appropriate internships based on their career goals. The College has coordinated internships in a variety of professional areas, including business and commerce, government, hospitality and entertainment, and not-for-profit agencies.

Holy Cross students also give back to the South Bend community by completing a community service project before graduation. Many Holy Cross students also take advantage of educational programs that are available to them at the University of Notre Dame, including ROTC, the Notre Dame Marching Band, and the *Observer*, the student newspaper.

Academic Facilities

The Richard and Lucille McKenna Library is a primary learning resource at Holy Cross College, housing approximately 17,000 volumes and 120 periodicals. The library provides access to three online encyclopedias and the LexisNexis database. In addition, Holy Cross College students and faculty members have access to more than 5 million total volumes and 7,500 periodicals through arrangements with libraries that include the Hesburgh Library at the University of Notre Dame, the Cushwa-Leighton Library at Saint Mary's College, and the Bowen Library at Bethel College.

Wireless access is available throughout campus. Off-campus students are provided dial-in access to the College network.

The Learning Resource Center provides writing and math tutoring to groups and individuals.

Costs

Tuition for the 2007–08 academic year was $15,660 for full-time students enrolled in 12 to 19 semester hours. Tuition has not been set for the 2008–09 academic year. For part-time students and for students taking additional credit hours (more than 19), the cost is $520 per credit hour. Room and board ranged from $3500 to $4125 per semester, depending on accommodations. Room and board costs have not been determined for 2008–09.

Financial Aid

The financial aid program offers assistance to students based on financial need, scholarly merit, and outstanding leadership abilities. Financial aid may be in the form of scholarships, grants, loans, employment opportunities, or a combination of sources.

Faculty

The faculty of Holy Cross College comprises religious and laypeople, all of whom hold graduate degrees in their academic disciplines. There is a 13:1 student-teacher ratio. Classes are taught by faculty members, not graduate students.

Student Government

The Student Government Association (SGA) is an organization of student leaders who are elected by and serve the student body. SGA encourages student involvement in campus life, provides leadership development opportunities, and represents the student body outside the College. The standing committees of the SGA conduct student social events, community service opportunities, athletic activities, workshops, and forums.

Admission Requirements

Entering students are expected to have successfully completed a college-preparatory high school program of at least 16 academic units: 4 in English (composition and literature), 3 in college-preparatory mathematics, 1 in a laboratory science, 2 in history or social science, 2 in foreign language, and four college-preparatory electives. A student who has the General Education Development (GED) certificate may be considered for admission to Holy Cross College.

Students should submit the completed Application for Admission form (either paper or electronic), the $50 nonrefundable application fee (waived if the online application is used), an official high school transcript (the GED is also accepted), and SAT or ACT scores. Transfer applicants must submit all previous college transcripts and evaluations from the deans of their previous institutions. Students who are citizens of other countries and for whom English is a second language should submit scores of the TOEFL and certification of finances. All applicants are encouraged to visit the campus for a tour and an admission interview.

Application and Information

A rolling admission policy usually permits notification of the admission decision within several weeks after an application is filed. In order to allow ample time for processing and evaluation, an application should be submitted before August 15 for the fall semester or January 15 for the spring semester. If on-campus housing is required, applicants should apply for admission as early as possible.

In order to qualify for federal and state grants, applicants should complete all financial aid documents before March 1 for admission in the fall semester.

Office of Admissions
Holy Cross College
54515 State Road 933 North
P.O. Box 308
Notre Dame, Indiana 46556-0308
Phone: 574-239-8400
Fax: 574-239-8323
E-mail: admissions@hcc-nd.edu
Web site: http://www.hcc-nd.edu

INDIANA STATE UNIVERSITY

TERRE HAUTE, INDIANA

The University

Indiana State University (ISU) is a publicly assisted, comprehensive, residential institution offering instruction at the associate, bachelor's, master's, and doctoral levels. It was founded in 1865 as the Indiana State Normal School. Through the years, it evolved through successive stages as the Indiana State Teachers College and Indiana State College. It attained university status in 1965. University enrollment stands at 10,543. In fall 2007, undergraduate enrollment was 8,493 students. Graduate enrollment was 2,050. The Indiana State University educational experience is enriched by the presence of a diverse student body drawn from throughout Indiana and the rest of the country and more than sixty other countries.

Indiana State's identity and its vision for the future are based on a historic embrace of the values of opportunity and success for all of its students. In seeking to extend this vision into the twenty-first century, the University, through its Strategic Plan, is promoting excellence in areas such as technology; the student experience, particularly in the first year; teaching and learning; outreach; scholarships; and partnerships with educational institutions, government agencies, business and industry, service learning, and individuals.

ISU is committed to providing a high-quality educational experience in a student-centered learning environment. The student-faculty ratio is 17:1, and approximately 87 percent of classes at ISU have 39 or fewer students. Sixty-six percent of classes are taught by full-time faculty members.

Students can choose from more than 120 majors, ranging from criminology to packaging technology, athletic training to geography, teacher education to insurance and risk management, and safety management to nursing. The School of Graduate Studies offers master's and doctoral programs in a number of the areas listed in the Majors and Degrees section.

Many of ISU's academic programs are nationally known, and some are the only ones of their kind in the state. The insurance and risk management program is listed as one of the top four programs in the nation by the *Journal of Risk and Insurance* in terms of the breadth of courses offered and as one of the top eight programs in the country by *Independent Agent* magazine. The campus's undergraduate and graduate programs in athletic training were the first in the nation to be accredited. ISU is also one of only a few institutions in the country that has accredited undergraduate and accredited master's programs in this field. The Doctor of Psychology in clinical psychology program is the only program of its kind in the state accredited by the American Psychological Association. The criminology program is one of the largest graduate programs in the state and houses one of only two criminalities laboratories in the state that foster education in basic, advanced, and forensic investigation techniques. The College of Education's Professional Development Schools Partnership received the 2002 Christa McAuliffe Award for Leadership and Innovative Teacher Education from the American Association of State Colleges and Universities. In the College of Technology, ISU's programs in industrial automotive technology and packaging technology are the only ones of their kind in the state.

The Hulman Memorial Student Union Board provides cultural, social, educational, and recreational programming for the Student Union and for the entire campus. As the primary all-campus programming board, the Union Board produces events that involve the whole student body, such as Homecoming and Tandemonia, a weeklong spring festival featuring a tandem bike race. Students at ISU can choose from among nearly 200 organizations and clubs. Students can compete in intramural sports. ISU's athletic teams compete in the NCAA Division I.

Location

Indiana State University's scenic campus is adjacent to the downtown area of Terre Haute, which comprises a metropolitan area of 100,000 people in west-central Indiana. The University's proximity to downtown Terre Haute helps to foster a number of partnerships between the campus and local businesses, government agencies, and civic organizations. Terre Haute serves as the fine arts, cultural, and athletic center of west-central Indiana and east-central Illinois. Terre Haute has the Sheldon Swope Art Museum, the Eugene V. Debs Museum, Clabber Girl Museum, the Terre Haute Symphony Orchestra, Community Theatre, and the historic Indiana Theater. The city also has an extensive and excellent parks system. It is convenient to four major metropolitan areas: Indianapolis is within 75 miles, and St. Louis, Chicago, and Cincinnati are each only 180 miles away.

Majors and Degrees

Indiana State's undergraduate academic programs are offered through its College of Arts and Sciences and its professional Colleges of Education, Business, Technology, and Nursing, Health, and Human Services.

College of Arts and Sciences programs include African and African-American studies; anthropology; art; art history; chemistry; clinical laboratory science; communication studies; computer science; criminology; dietetics; ecology and organismal biology; economics; English; English teaching; fine art; food and nutrition; food service management; foreign language concentration (international studies); French; French teaching; general family and consumer science; geography; geology; German; German teaching; history; human development and family studies; information technology; interdisciplinary studies; interior design; journalism; legal studies; liberal studies (two- and four-year programs); life sciences; managerial communications; mathematics; mathematics education; music; music business administration; music composition; music education; music history and literature; music merchandising; music performance; music theory; occupational family and consumer science education; philosophy; physics; political science; pre–dental hygiene; predentistry; pre-engineering; prelaw; premedicine; preoptometry; prepharmacy; pre–veterinary medicine; psychology; public relations; radio/television/film; science education; social studies education; social work; sociology; Spanish; Spanish teaching; speech communication and theater teaching; study of religion; textiles, apparel, and merchandising; theater; visual arts education; and women's studies.

The College of Business offers programs in accounting, business administration, business education, finance, information design and end-user computing, insurance, management, management information systems, marketing, operations management analysis, and quality and decision systems.

The College of Education has programs in child development and early childhood education (two-year program); communication disorders; counseling; curriculum, instruction, and media technology; early childhood education; educational and school psychology; elementary education; kindergarten–primary education; school media services; special education; and speech-language pathology.

The College of Technology offers programs in aerospace administration, biomedical electronics technology, career and technical education (two-year program), career and technical teaching, computer hardware technology, computer-integrated manufacturing technology, construction technology, electronics and computer technology (two-year program), electronics technology, general aviation–flight (two-year program), human resource development, industrial automotive technology, industrial supervision, industrial technology, industrial technology (two-year program), instrumentation and control technology, manufacturing supervision (two-year program), manufacturing technology, mechanical technology, packaging technology, professional aviation flight technology, technology education, and vocational trade-industrial-technical area.

The College of Nursing, Health, and Human Services has programs in athletic training, community health promotion, environmental health sciences, health-safety education, nursing, physical education, recreation and sport management, safety management, and sports studies–fitness and exercise science.

Academic Programs

ISU's academic strength lies in its liberal arts and professional programs of study, its interdependent undergraduate and graduate programs, and its extensive student development programs. Undergraduate programs combine general education with majors and minors. All students working toward a bachelor's degree at Indiana State must take a minimum of 42 to 57 semester hours of general education course work, including 11 to 26 hours of basic studies and 31 hours of liberal studies. Most degree programs require 124 semester hours and a minimum 2.0 grade point average for graduation. Baccalaureate degree candidates must have earned at least 30 semester hours of residence credit at Indiana State. The academic calendar includes fall and spring semesters and summer sessions of varying lengths.

The University Honors Program, which offers special courses, colloquia, seminars, and independent study, is designed to challenge talented students and help them broaden and enhance their education. A variety of distance education programs are available. The transformation of student life through the development of learning communities is the result of the First-Year Experience Program, which was funded by a $2-million grant from the Lilly Endowment. The Student Academic Services Center offers a number of programs for students with special needs. Indiana State's Career Center helps students formulate career goals, gain career-related work experience while in school, and find employment. Air Force and Army ROTC programs are available.

Academic Facilities

Indiana State is committed to providing students with facilities that match the excellence of its academic programs. Over the past several years, the University, through its Campus Master Plan, has completed a number of building projects, including the Center for Fine and Performing Arts, which combines state-of-the-art performance facilities and an art gallery; Stalker Hall, which houses academic units; the John T. Myers Technology Center, which features specially designed laboratories and classrooms in a high-technology setting; and Root Hall, a classroom building for the humanities. The Student Computing Complex offers students access to computers 24 hours a day. Computer clusters are also located in other buildings throughout the campus. All residence hall rooms are wired for Internet access.

With more than 1 million books and more than 5,000 subscriptions to periodicals and journals, the Cunningham Memorial Library ranks as one of the finest collegiate libraries in the Midwest. The library was one of the first in the state to computerize its card catalog and continues to be a leader in making information available in various electronic formats, including CD-ROM and the Internet.

The University also has laboratories and other learning resources such as computer-integrated manufacturing, a remote sensing and geographic information systems laboratory, specially designed rehearsal rooms, fully equipped science laboratories, an observatory, and a human performance laboratory.

Costs

Fees for full-time undergraduate students are $13,134 per year for Indiana residents and $20,988 for nonresidents. On-campus housing costs and board are included in these figures.

Financial Aid

ISU awards financial aid to about 70 percent of its students. Indiana State University offers financial assistance to students in a number of forms, including loans, grants, scholarships, and work-study. Payment plans are also available. ISU awards close to $4 million in scholarships each year. Prestigious scholarship programs such as the President's Scholars and the Academic President's Excellence Scholars are available to outstanding high school students. Those students who meet the minimum academic requirements for a scholarship are mailed a scholarship application after they have been admitted. Students also may be considered for financial assistance such as loans and grants after gaining admission to the University. Those who apply for assistance before March 1 are given priority. Students should file the Free Application for Federal Student Aid (FAFSA).

Faculty

Indiana State's instructional programs are carried out by its 640 faculty members. As a teaching university, ISU expects its faculty members to give highest priority to instruction and the intellectual and personal development of students. Faculty members, however, also are expected to be engaged in meaningful and productive scholarship and professional service and to integrate what is learned from these activities into their teaching. Faculty members also serve as student advisers and assist students in the planning of their academic programs.

Student Government

The Student Government Association (SGA), of which every student is a member, is the governing body for all ISU students. SGA operates under its own constitution and consists of three branches: legislative, executive, and judicial.

Admission Requirements

Admission applications are reviewed as they are received. Students are considered for admission after receipt of complete credentials—an application, a nonrefundable $25 processing fee, and official transcripts from all schools and colleges previously attended. Freshman and transfer students who have completed fewer than 24 transferable semester credit hours must submit scores from either the SAT or ACT. In general, all freshman applicants are expected to rank in the upper 40 percent of their high school graduating class and be in the process of completing a college-preparation curriculum. Indiana residents are expected to complete Indiana Core 40 and to have passed the ISTEP Graduation Qualifying Examination for regular admission. Additional information is available from high school counselors or the ISU Office of Admissions. It is suggested that prospective students visit the campus and talk with a member of the admissions staff.

Application and Information

High school students should complete an application in the fall of their senior year. To ensure full consideration, applications and official transcripts must be received in the Office of Admissions by July 1 for the fall semester, December 1 for the spring semester, May 1 for the first summer session, and July 1 for the second summer session. Indiana State encourages all prospective students to visit the campus. Requests for appointments and information should be addressed to:

Office of Undergraduate Admissions
Erickson Hall
Indiana State University
Terre Haute, Indiana 47809
Phone: 812-237-2121
800-GO-TO-ISU (800-468-6478) (toll-free)
E-mail: admissions@indstate.edu
Web site: http://www.indstate.edu

INDIANA TECH

FORT WAYNE, INDIANA

The University

Indiana Tech is a private, independent, nondenominational university. Indiana Tech provides career-focused degree programs for learners of all ages. With a commitment to relationship-based education, academic programs are designed to offer students hands-on opportunities to learn practical skills for success in their chosen careers. The university was founded in 1930 in Fort Wayne as a small engineering college for men. Since then, it has grown into a coed, private university with programs in engineering, computer studies, business, criminal justice, elementary education, and more. Fall 2007 brought the debut of a bachelor's degree program in computer security and investigation; energy engineering was added in fall 2008.

Indiana Tech's traditional day school targets recent high school graduates and transfer students who are able to take day classes and who may require residential housing on campus. Academic degree programs are divided among the College of Business, the College of Engineering and Computer Studies, and the College of General Studies.

The College of Professional Studies serves nontraditional students by offering an accelerated degree program, with most classes held in the evenings and on weekends in five- or six-week sessions.

Indiana Tech also offers the Master of Business Administration (M.B.A.) with concentrations in accounting, human resources, management, and marketing; the Master of Science in Management (M.S.M.); and the Master of Science in Engineering Management (M.S.E.).

Distance education is also available through Indiana Tech. Independent study and online programs offer course credit through correspondence and via the Internet.

Indiana Tech is accredited by the Higher Learning Commission of the North Central Association of Colleges and Schools, and the mechanical and electrical engineering programs are accredited by the Accreditation Board for Engineering and Technology (ABET).

Most freshmen and sophomores are required to live in campus housing and take meals in the dining hall. A majority of students live in the Pierson Center, a four-story residence hall.

Recreational facilities on campus include the gymnasium, Warrior Fieldhouse, the Wellness Center, and Andorfer Commons. The gymnasium contains basketball, badminton, and volleyball courts and a weight room. The fieldhouse is an indoor facility for soccer, baseball, and softball and also includes a weight room. The Wellness Center contains numerous cardiovascular exercise machines as well as general weight-lifting apparatus. The Wellness Center also offers various courses throughout the year to promote a healthy lifestyle. Andorfer Commons includes a movie theater, a conference center, and a student recreation area that contains a six-lane bowling alley, pool tables, various electronic games, and a student lounge.

Students can participate in a wide variety of clubs and organizations, including fraternities and sororities. Special activities and events are scheduled and publicized on bulletin boards, on the school's Web calendar, and in the *Warrior Legend* (the student newspaper) throughout the year. Indiana Tech is a member of the National Association of Intercollegiate Athletics (NAIA) and the Wolverine-Hoosier Athletic Conference. The university sponsors intercollegiate competition in men's baseball, men's and women's basketball, men's and women's soccer, women's softball, men's and women's tennis, and women's volleyball. Men's and women's cross-country, golf, and track were added in fall 2007. Individual student and campus organizations compete in intramural activities including basketball, bowling, flag football, golf, soccer, softball, table tennis, and volleyball. Spirit teams, which include a cheerleading squad, dance team, and pep band, are also available to Indiana Tech students.

Location

Fort Wayne is a thriving, progressive community with a population of more than 200,000 in the northeastern corner of Indiana. Fort Wayne is a major industrial and commercial center with approximately 400 manufacturing plants in the area, and it offers a variety of recreational and cultural activities. The city is within easy driving distances to Chicago, Cincinnati, Cleveland, Detroit, Indianapolis, and Louisville. The city is served by national and regional airlines, passenger rail service, and bus lines. Indiana Tech is less than an hour's drive from northeast Indiana's beautiful lake region.

Majors and Degrees

Indiana Tech offers the Associate of Science, the Bachelor of Arts, and the Bachelor of Science degrees in the traditional day program. Majors are accounting, biomedical engineering, business administration (health-care administration, human resources, management, management information systems, marketing, production management, and sports management), communication, computer engineering, computer science, computer security and investigation, criminal justice (crime analysis and law enforcement administration), electrical engineering, elementary education, energy engineering, general studies, graphic communications, human services management, industrial and manufacturing engineering, information systems, mechanical engineering, networking, network management, organizational leadership, psychology, recreation management (general and sports management), software engineering, therapeutic recreation, Web design, and Web development. Students can also pursue an individually designed degree. Minors include accounting, athletic training, business administration, coaching, computer science, dance, e-commerce, humanities, industrial and manufacturing engineering, information security, information systems, networking, personal fitness coach, and psychology.

Academic Programs

The number of credits needed to earn each degree varies depending on the program selected. In general, an associate degree requires around 60 credits and a bachelor's degree around 120. Students should consult the undergraduate catalog for program-specific requirements and for a listing of courses.

The general education component is organized around several areas, such as communication skills, cultural and ethical awareness, computer literacy, quantitative skills, and understanding ourselves and society. Many of these components (critical thinking skills, creativity, etc.) are taught across the curriculum. Specific courses required depend upon the degree program.

The fall and spring semesters consist of a fifteen-week session plus final examinations. The ten-week summer term includes final examinations. All freshmen attend an orientation before the start of fall classes. A freshman seminar class also meets once per week for the first half of the fall and spring semesters.

Off-Campus Programs

Indiana Tech enjoys a relationship of mutual pride and cooperation with the City of Fort Wayne. This relationship extends to the many industrial and commercial firms in Fort Wayne that employ Indiana Tech graduates and provide a source of part-time employment for many students. Study-abroad opportunities are also available.

Academic Facilities

The McMillen Library in Andorfer Commons houses a 32,000-volume collection. This state-of-the-art facility includes a fireplace for a nice, cozy atmosphere; computer clusters enabling immediate electronic access to the online catalog, the Internet, and full-text databases; a multimedia room; and a small conference room for study groups or meetings. The open floor plan allows easy access to multiple volumes of books and periodicals that make up the library's collection. The collection is specifically based on the current courses taught at Indiana Tech and, with the help of donations, the leisure-reading section continues to grow.

The McMillen Library is open seven days a week, with reference service available at all times. Since it is impossible for any library to collect all needed information, the library operates an interlibrary loan service to meet the research needs of the students and faculty. Other services available at the McMillen Library include a photocopier, computers, laser printers, a color printer, a scanner, and a TV/VCR.

The Indiana Tech Community Friendship Book Collection is a free resource available to anyone at the university. This collection contains current hardback and paperback books. Readers may contribute to and take items from the collection freely; no book checkout is required. The goal is to maintain the collection by asking that each reader return a book after reading it or replace it with another book.

Costs

The 2007–08 tuition for Indiana Tech's traditional program was $19,200 per academic year. Room and board costs ranged from $5980 to $7300 per year. Tuition for the College of Professional Studies was $290 to $330 per credit hour for undergraduates and $390 to $465 for graduate students.

Financial Aid

Financial assistance is available through federal and state sources, scholarships, Indiana Tech grants and scholarships, and funding provided through outside organizations and foundations. Indiana Tech is a member of National Association of Intercollegiate Athletics (NAIA) and offers athletic scholarships. More than 93 percent of Indiana Tech students receive financial assistance through some combination of merit and/or need-based scholarships, grants, loans, tuition reimbursement, and federal programs. For more information, students should contact the Office of Scholarships and Financial Aid (800-937-2448 Ext. 2342; financialaid@indianatech.edu).

Faculty

Indiana Tech faculty members are more than academic experts. They are men and women who have been out in the workplace and can share their experiences as well as their knowledge. Indiana Tech's full-time faculty includes engineers, entrepreneurs, consultants, authors, editors, certified public accountants, senior professionals in human resources, and other experts. Classroom instruction goes beyond textbooks to include insight on how theories and principles are applied in the real world. In addition to Indiana Tech's full-time faculty members, the school draws on a large network of adjunct professors who also work full-time in their field of expertise and are ready to share that expertise with students.

Student Government

The Student Board members are a select group of Indiana Tech students who volunteer to assist the Office of Student Life with special events, focus groups, recruitment of new board members, and an overall positive representation of the university. The group promotes student life and student activities on, off, and around campus and enhances and improves the overall university experience for Indiana Tech students. This is accomplished through a variety of quality activities, student-focused service, and peer-to-peer mentoring. The board's processes are revisited regularly with the goal of improving systems to establish and build a positive relationship with the student body of Indiana Tech.

Admission Requirements

Students must submit the completed application, the application fee, official high school transcripts, letters of recommendation, and official SAT or ACT scores. Applicants who would like to live in on-campus housing must also send in the completed housing application form. Transfer students apply using the regular application and send secondary school transcripts and transcripts from all colleges or universities previously attended. Applicants from nontraditional high schools are encouraged to apply. Indiana Tech has a rolling admissions policy.

Application and Information

For further information, prospective students should contact:

Monica Chamberlain, Director of Admissions
Indiana Tech
1600 East Washington Boulevard
Fort Wayne, Indiana 46803
Phone: 260-422-5561
800-937-2448 (toll-free)
Fax: 260-422-7696
E-mail: admissions@indianatech.edu
Web site: http://www.indianatech.edu

MANCHESTER COLLEGE

NORTH MANCHESTER, INDIANA

The College

At Manchester College, students find academics that matter. They find their place among students who are motivated to learn and faculty members with top degrees who know what it takes to succeed.

With a rich social life, students become part of the Manchester family that covers the globe. With lasting relationships, their college years will last a lifetime.

Manchester students learn how to give meaning to success. They get the most from their college experience so they can get the most out of life.

Tim Polakowski, a junior from Illinois, says he found success at Manchester College. "In high school, I knew I wanted to make a difference. Today, I feel that Manchester College has not only prepared me to make that difference, but also made a difference in me. The professors want you to succeed and the challenges in and out of the classroom prepare you for a life outside the norm. After a year studying in Spain, a semester south of the border, and working with on-campus groups like Habitat for Humanity, I'm more convinced than ever that there is a place for me after college, much as there is a place for me to succeed—right here at Manchester."

The undergraduate enrollment is 1,050. Most students are between the ages of 18 and 22. Approximately 85 percent of the full-time students are from Indiana. Students from twenty-two states and twenty-three countries were also enrolled during 2006–07. Nine percent of the students are members of the Church of the Brethren. Many different religious backgrounds are represented, and all are welcomed.

Manchester is a member of the National Collegiate Athletic Association Division III and offers nine men's and eight women's sports. The Physical Education and Recreation Center houses physical education classes, a fitness center, intercollegiate and intramural sports, and recreational activities. The College has a very strong intramural program that involves about 80 percent of its students.

Location

Located in the heart of Indiana's beautiful lake country, North Manchester is a thriving community of 6,000 people. It is within a half hour's drive of Indiana's second-largest city, Fort Wayne, and is only 3½ hours from Chicago. Wide streets with large shade trees, graceful homes, and a beautiful park combine to provide a classic setting for college living.

Majors and Degrees

Manchester College grants Bachelor of Arts and Bachelor of Science degrees. Areas of study include accounting, adapted physical education, art, athletic training, biochemistry, biology, biotechnology, business, chemistry, coaching, communication studies, computer science, corporate finance, criminal justice, early childhood education, economics, elementary education, engineering science, English, environmental studies, exercise science, finance, fitness and sport management, French, gender studies, German, gerontology, history, journalism, management, marketing, mathematics, media studies, medical technology, music, nonprofit management, peace studies, philosophy, physical education, physics, political science, prelaw, premedicine, prenursing, pre–occupational therapy, pre–physical therapy, psychology, public relations, religion, secondary education, social work, sociology, Spanish, and sports management. Individualized interdisciplinary majors can also be arranged to meet a student's particular goals.

Academic Programs

The curriculum reflects a commitment to sound training in a specific area of study, the major, and broad development of skills and understanding through the liberal arts. In addition, students may explore interests different from specific career or professional areas through elective courses. This combination prepares students for careers or graduate school immediately after graduation and equips them for the challenges and changes of the future.

Manchester College operates on a 4-1-4 calendar and offers three summer sessions. The College's innovative Fast Forward program allows students to complete a four-year degree in three years on campus and two summers online. Students save as much as $25,000 and enter graduate school or their careers a year earlier than classmates.

Off-Campus Programs

Manchester College students may study abroad for a semester or year in ten countries: at Philipps-Universität Marburg in Marburg/Lahn (Germany), the Institut International d'Études Françaises of the University of Strasbourg (France), the University of Nancy (France), the University of Barcelona (Spain), St. Mary's College in Cheltenham (England), Hokkai Gakuen University in Sapporo (Japan), the Dalian Institute of Foreign Languages in Dalian (People's Republic of China), the Athens Center (Greece), the Catholic University of Ecuador, Cochin (India), and Universidad Veracruzana (Mexico).

During January session, numerous classes are held off campus. In recent years, professors have taken classes to India, Kenya, England, Mexico, Russia, France, Jamaica, Ghana, Vietnam, Nicaragua, Haiti, Germany, Costa Rica, Cuba, and Hawaii as well as destinations in the continental United States.

Field experiences and internships are offered for credit in accounting, broadcasting, business, criminal justice, early childhood education, elementary education, forensic chemistry, gerontology, health sciences practicum, journalism, peace studies, physical education, political science, psychology, secondary education, and social work.

Academic Facilities

Manchester College has more than 160 personal computers in student labs, one for every 6 students. In addition, the Clark Computer Center houses file servers, three computer labs, and an AS400 for student use. PC labs tied to the network are located in each residence hall and the library. A 45-Mbs DS3 line provides high-speed Internet access.

The $17-million Science Center, opened in fall 2005, provides state-of-the-art laboratories and fully wired classrooms. Students in astronomy use the 10-inch Newtonian reflector telescope in the Charles S. Morris Observatory.

The College Union, which was completely renovated in 2007, houses the Success Center, campus store, art gallery, dining facilities, and Oaks coffee bar.

The Funderburg Library is a newly renovated, three-story building that houses more than 170,000 books, 800 periodicals, and 4,500 audio recordings available for student use. Computer connections allow access to major libraries across the country.

Costs

Tuition and fees for 2008–09 are $22,720 for full-time students. Room and board costs for the residence halls (double occupancy) are $8100. The total charges with fees are $30,820 for the academic year.

Financial Aid

Manchester offers extensive scholarship and grant assistance through institutional resources. Academic awards include Honors, Trustee, Presidential, and Dean's Scholarships. Special scholarships based on academic merit and interest are awarded in music and entrepreneurship. International students can receive scholarships based on academic accomplishments and financial need. Manchester awards significant need-based grants. More than $10.5 million in College funds were awarded in 2007–08.

Approximately 98 percent of Manchester's students have some type of financial assistance, whether it is a scholarship, a grant, a loan, or campus employment. Questions about financial aid should be referred to the Office of Admissions.

Faculty

Manchester's faculty consists of 73 full-time and 32 part-time members. Ninety percent of full-time faculty members hold the highest degree in their field, and 94 percent of all courses are taught by full-time faculty members. The primary emphasis of the faculty members is teaching, but many are actively engaged in research as well. Faculty members serve as academic advisers, with a specially trained group of faculty members acting as primary advisers for new students. There is a 13.3:1 student-faculty ratio.

Student Government

Students at Manchester assume responsibility for the governmental and judicial activities of the College. The Student Government Association provides a forum for discussion and investigation of community concerns and a channel for evaluating and solving community problems.

Each of the College's five residence halls elects a governing body, which is responsible for providing leadership.

The Manchester Activities Council organizes programming of student events. Students are offered a wide variety of leadership and participation opportunities as part of the College's student development program.

Admission Requirements

Manchester College seeks to enroll students whose scholastic record, test scores, and personality give promise of success in college. Graduation from an accredited high school or its equivalent is required.

The College recommends that students take 4 years of English, 3 years of laboratory science, 3 years of mathematics, 2 years of foreign language, and 2 years of social studies in high school. Students may take either the ACT or the SAT, and personal recommendations from a high school principal or guidance counselor are required.

For transfer students, transcripts of all previous college work are required.

Application and Information

Students may apply for admission prior to each term. Applications are accepted on a rolling basis. There is a nonrefundable $25 application fee. Online applications are free.

Interested students and their parents are encouraged to visit Manchester College and meet faculty members, coaches, and current students; sit in on classes; and take a campus tour. Arrangements can be made by writing or calling the Office of Admissions.

For application forms and further information, students may contact:

Office of Admissions
Manchester College
North Manchester, Indiana 46962-0365
Phone: 800-852-3648 (toll-free)
E-mail: admitinfo@manchester.edu
Web site: http://www.manchester.edu

Students on the campus of Manchester College.

COLLEGE DATA CENTER • INDIANA

SAINT MARY'S COLLEGE

NOTRE DAME, INDIANA

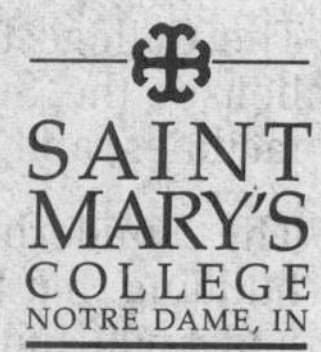

The College

One of the oldest Catholic colleges for women in the United States, Saint Mary's College was founded in 1844 and continues to be sponsored by the Sisters of the Holy Cross. The College has long been recognized as a pioneer in exploring with integrity and imagination the roles of women in society. Today, Saint Mary's enjoys a national reputation for academic excellence and vitality of campus life.

With more than 1,600 students from forty-two states and seven countries, Saint Mary's brings together women from a wide range of geographical areas, social backgrounds, and educational experiences. International and minority students compose 10 percent of the student body.

Saint Mary's College's liberal arts emphasis enhances a comprehensive curriculum. Strong programs in the humanities and sciences are complemented by professional programs in business administration, education, nursing, and social work; majors in the fine and performing arts; and courses of preprofessional study that prepare students for law school, medical school, or advanced study in other health professions.

Small classes (average class size: 16) and a low student-faculty ratio (11:1) encourage student participation in class discussions, collaboration with faculty members, and preparation for real-world challenges. The College enjoys a unique co-exchange program with the University of Notre Dame.

Approximately 80 percent of Saint Mary's students live on campus in five residence halls, each with its own distinctive character. Seniors may choose to live in Opus Hall, which offers apartment-style living on campus. Residence halls offer a full calendar of activities, from twice-yearly dances to discussions with professors. The College has a new student center, a dining hall, and a clubhouse for extracurricular activities. All residence halls have chapels, and the Church of Loretto is on campus.

As an NCAA Division III school and a member of the Michigan Intercollegiate Athletic Association, Saint Mary's sponsors varsity teams in basketball, cross-country, golf, soccer, softball, swimming and diving, tennis, and volleyball. Club sports, cosponsored with Notre Dame, include equestrian, gymnastics, lacrosse, and figure ice skating. In addition, Saint Mary's offers many intramural sports.

The College's Angela Athletic Facility contains multipurpose courts for tennis, volleyball, and basketball; a training and fitness center; and racquetball courts. The campus has tennis courts and athletic fields for both soccer and softball.

Location

Saint Mary's 75-acre campus, set alongside the Saint Joseph River, has great natural beauty. The College is located just across the street from the University of Notre Dame, minutes north of the city of South Bend, and only 90 miles from Chicago. Students from Saint Mary's and Notre Dame form a dynamic intercollegiate community. South Bend provides sites for internships and practicums and opportunities for volunteer service. Seventy-five percent of Saint Mary's students annually contribute their time to a variety of community service efforts.

Majors and Degrees

Saint Mary's College offers programs leading to the Bachelor of Arts, Bachelor of Science, Bachelor of Fine Arts, Bachelor of Business Administration, and Bachelor of Music degrees.

For a Bachelor of Arts degree, students may choose majors in art, biology, chemistry, communication studies, economics, elementary education, English literature, English writing, French, history, humanistic studies, Italian, mathematics, music, philosophy, political science, psychology, religious studies, social work, sociology, Spanish, statistics and actuarial mathematics, and theater.

A Bachelor of Science degree may be obtained in biology (with concentrations in cellular/molecular biology, environmental biology, and general biology), chemistry, computational mathematics, mathematics, nursing, and statistics and actuarial mathematics.

The Bachelor of Music degree program, which is a member of the National Association of Schools of Music, offers concentrations in music education and music performance. For talented art students, Saint Mary's offers a Bachelor of Fine Arts degree with concentrations in several media.

The Bachelor of Business Administration degree program offers majors in accounting, business administration (with concentrations in accounting, finance, international business, management, and marketing), and management information systems.

Superior students who are candidates for either a Bachelor of Arts or a Bachelor of Science degree may design a program of study outside the traditional department structure, called a Student Designed Major.

For women interested in engineering fields, a five-year, dual-degree program offered in cooperation with the University of Notre Dame leads to a bachelor's degree from Saint Mary's College and a Bachelor of Science in Engineering degree from Notre Dame in one of seven areas.

Saint Mary's education department, accredited by the National Council for Accreditation of Teacher Education, offers certification in elementary and secondary education.

In addition, the College offers more than forty minors in a variety of fields, including American history, communicative disorders, information science, justice studies, Latin American studies, and women's studies.

Academic Programs

Graduation from Saint Mary's College requires successful completion of at least 128 semester hours of credit. Every student must also complete a comprehensive examination in her major, which may take the form of a thesis, a research or creative project, or a written or oral examination, depending on the discipline. All students must demonstrate writing proficiency by satisfactorily completing a writing-intensive "W" course, usually in the first year, and an advanced portfolio of writings in the major discipline, usually in the senior year.

Students spend approximately one third of their time in general education courses in humanities, fine arts, foreign language, natural and social sciences, theology, and philosophy. Remaining course hours are devoted to their major and electives or minors. The College assists those students interested in pursuing independent study or research and internships.

Off-Campus Programs

Through Saint Mary's international study programs, students can study with Irish students at the National University of Ireland Maynooth, just outside Dublin. They can absorb Italian art and culture on Saint Mary's campus in the center of Rome or experience Southeast Asia with the India-based program in Mumbai.

Saint Mary's students may also enroll in the Spanish language programs of the Center for Cross-Cultural Study in Seville, Spain, or in the French language and culture study in Dijon, France. A new exchange program with the Australian University of Notre

Dame based in Freemantle is also available, as is a program based in Pietermaritzburg, South Africa. A summer study program in China was recently added.

Saint Mary's students may study in Austria and other countries through a cooperative program with the University of Notre Dame.

A student majoring in political science has the opportunity to spend a semester at the American University in Washington, D.C. Saint Mary's also participates in student and faculty member exchange programs with the University of Notre Dame and members of the Northern Indiana Consortium for Education.

Academic Facilities

Students have abundant access to technology systems, software, and services. Residence halls are wired for network access, and secure wireless network access is available in many public areas on campus, including many classrooms in the new Spes Unica academic building. Computer labs for students are available in several campus buildings as well as computer "collaboratories," where students and faculty members can conduct online research in groups in classroom settings. Extensive support services are available to students and faculty and staff members for instructional, administrative, and network systems. Faculty members make significant use of information technology resources for teaching, research, and scholarship.

The modern Cushwa-Leighton Library houses an outstanding collection of more than 228,000 volumes, and it includes the Trumper Computer Center, the Instructional Technology Resource Center, the College archives, and a rare book room.

In addition to extensive biology, chemistry, and physics lab facilities, laboratories for psychology research and for foreign language study and practice are available to students. Art studios, music practice rooms, the O'Laughlin Auditorium, and Moreau's Little Theatre provide ample space for fine arts creation, practice, and performance. The new Spes Unica academic building is scheduled to open in 2008, providing students with state-of-the-art classrooms and gathering places.

The professionally staffed Early Childhood Development Center provides education and psychology majors with an unusual on-campus opportunity to work with young children. Other facilities include the Madeleva classroom building, Science Hall, Havican nursing facility, and Moreau Art Galleries.

Costs

Expenses for the 2008–09 academic year include tuition and fees, $28,212; room and board, $8675 (double occupancy); and miscellaneous expenses (books, transportation, and living costs), $2625.

Financial Aid

The College strives to make a Saint Mary's education available for every admitted student by offering eligible students financial aid packages that may include grants, scholarships, work-study, and loans. Competitive scholarships, awarded solely on academic merit, as well as grants determined by financial need are available. Last year, more than 90 percent of Saint Mary's students received more than $25 million in financial assistance, more than $13 million from the College alone.

All applicants for financial assistance must complete the College Board PROFILE and the Free Application for Federal Student Aid (FAFSA) each year that they desire assistance. Applications for assistance must be received at the processing center by March 1 to be given priority consideration. Decisions concerning financial aid are made as soon as possible after a student has been accepted and upon receipt of the College Board PROFILE form.

Faculty

Saint Mary's has 129 full-time and 76 part-time faculty members. About 96 percent of the faculty members hold earned doctorates or other terminal degrees; of these, most teach first-year students as well as upper-division students. Faculty members work with students in all phases of college life, including academic counseling. All classes are taught by faculty members, not by teaching assistants.

Student Government

Students are active at every level of campus governance and share in community decision making. There are voting representatives on the president's two highest advisory boards, the Student Affairs Council and the Academic Affairs Council. A student is also a voting member of the College Board of Trustees. Student government sponsors many extracurricular and cocurricular activities.

Admission Requirements

Applicants for admission to Saint Mary's College should be graduates of an accredited high school and have completed a four-year program of 16 or more academic units. These academic units must include 4 units of English, 3 units of college-preparatory mathematics, 2 units of the same foreign language, 2 units of social science, and 2 units of laboratory science. The remaining units should be completed in college-preparatory courses in the previously mentioned areas. An applicant's credentials should include an academic transcript showing current rank and senior-year subjects, a counselor/administrator recommendation, SAT or ACT scores (at least one test should include the writing exam), and an essay. There is no application fee for students who apply online at http://www.saintmarys.edu or by completing the Common Application.

Home-schooled students are encouraged to apply for admission and should contact the Office of Admission for specific details.

An interview with an admission officer is recommended. Saint Mary's encourages students to visit the campus. The Office of Admission can make arrangements for students who wish to attend classes or stay overnight.

Mature, well-qualified students who graduated from high school after three years and who wish to enter college immediately upon graduation may apply for early admission. Saint Mary's College also grants deferred admission upon request to candidates who are accepted in the normal application process.

Application and Information

Saint Mary's has two application and notification programs: Early Decision and modified rolling admission. Highly qualified students who have selected Saint Mary's as their first choice for admission may apply under the Early Decision program. The application deadline is November 15, and the notification date is December 15. Students who apply for modified rolling admission and whose application files are complete on or before December 1 are notified of the admission decision in mid-January. Candidates are encouraged to apply by early fall of their senior year. The priority application deadline for regular admission is February 15. Applications are accepted, however, as long as space is available.

Interested students are encouraged to contact:

Director of Admission
Saint Mary's College
Notre Dame, Indiana 46556-5001
Phone: 574-284-4587
800-551-7621 (toll-free)
Fax: 574-284-4841
E-mail: admission@saintmarys.edu
Web site: http://www.saintmarys.edu

TAYLOR UNIVERSITY

UPLAND, INDIANA

The University

Founded in 1846, Taylor University was named for the missionary statesman Bishop William Taylor and is one of America's oldest evangelical Christian liberal arts colleges.

Education at Taylor is about change—metanoia—a shift in thinking. It's more than taking in information and repeating it for the test. It comes with strings attached—expectations, responsibilities. Learning is not just exercise for the mind; no one ever actually rode a bike simply by reading an instruction manual. People have to do something with the knowledge.

At Taylor, students can anticipate faculty and staff members and administrators who share their journey with them, mentors who gladly offer a hand for balance, urge them on, pick them up, and share their own life experience as instruction. It's what makes Taylor unique—intentional questioning, engaging, exploring, and discovering. It is the beginning of a process that is less about the next four years and more about lifelong learning.

Taylor's large academic community works well partly because its small communities are so healthy. Residence life at Taylor is an intentional experience. For one thing, Taylor has no "freshman dorms." From the first day, students share living space with everyone from freshmen to seniors. The personal accountability begins within the walls of Taylor's residence halls. These buildings are filled with students who are close enough to know daily routines and personal habits, sleeping patterns, study skills, and a mom's voice on the phone. Familiarity is great, but much of the students' closeness comes from their commitment to be scrupulously honest with each other about everything.

The current enrollment at Taylor is approximately 1,900 students. Eighty-one percent live in residence halls and approximately 67 percent of Taylor's students are from out of state and country.

Taylor University's School of Graduate and Professional Studies offers four master's degrees: the Master of Arts in higher education and student development, Master of Arts in religious studies, Master of Business Administration, and Master of Environmental Science (five-year entry program).

Location

Taylor University's campus, located in Upland, Indiana, covers 918 acres and is situated 1 hour north of Indianapolis and 45 minutes south of Fort Wayne. Taylor students enjoy the community life inspired by the University's rural setting, while also taking advantage of the opportunities available from Indiana's two largest cities.

Majors and Degrees

The School of Arts and Humanities offers programs in general education; history (majors in history, international studies, history/systems, social studies education); modern languages (majors in French, French education, Spanish, Spanish education); art (majors in art-new media/ systems, art/systems, art education, visual art-new media); communication arts (majors in communication studies, communication studies/systems, media communication, media communication/systems, theater arts, theater arts/systems); biblical studies, Christian education, and philosophy (majors in biblical literature, Christian educational ministries, philosophy); English (majors in English education, English-literature concentration, English-writing concentration); and music (majors in music, music/composition, music/management, music/marketing, music/performance-instrumental, music/performance-piano, music/performance-vocal, music/theater arts, music education).

The School of Business offers programs in accounting, finance, international business, management, and marketing.

The School of Education offers programs in early childhood education, elementary education, middle school licensure, physical education and human performance (majors in exercise science, health and physical education, sport management), special education licensure, and TESOL licensure.

The School of Science and Mathematics offers programs in biology (majors in biology, biology/premedicine, biology secondary education, biology systems), chemistry (majors in chemistry, chemistry/biochemistry, chemistry/education, chemistry/environmental science, chemistry/premedicine, chemistry/systems, natural science/pre-medical technology, physical science/chemistry), physics (majors in engineering physics, environmental engineering, physics, physical science education/physics, physics science education, physics/mathematics education, physics/systems), math (majors in mathematics, mathematics education, mathematics-interdisciplinary, mathematics-environmental science, mathematics/science education), computer science/systems (majors in computer science, computer science/new media, computer science/systems), environmental science, and geography.

The School of Social Science offers programs in political science (major in political science/systems), psychology (major in psychology/systems), social work, and sociology (major in sociology/systems).

Academic Programs

Taylor University offers preprofessional training and programs leading to the Bachelor of Arts degree, Bachelor of Science degree, Bachelor of Music degree, and Associate of Arts degree. In addition to their specific academic curriculum, every student must meet general requirements and may select from electives to complete his or her studies. A minimum of 128 hours is required for a baccalaureate degree. The Associate of Arts degree requires a minimum of 64 hours, with at least 22 of the last 30 hours taken in residence at Taylor.

The University awards credit for acceptable scores on Advanced Placement, CLEP, and college proficiency examinations and for International Baccalaureate programs.

The University operates on a 4-1-4 academic calendar. A January interterm that lasts 3½ weeks features experimental and conventional courses. In addition, two summer sessions are offered for a total of nine weeks.

Taylor is one of the few Christian liberal arts universities to implement a cohesive research, entrepreneurship, and community collaborative program, the Center for Research and Innovation. But the people at Taylor believe that research shouldn't conjure up images of a lone student sitting in a lab, isolated by test tubes. And they don't believe that it should be limited to the sciences. Taylor's emphasis on teaching translates into a research program that is learner focused. Students in the areas of science, social science, business, communication, and the humanities have opportunities to work alongside professors in the conduct of original research, experiencing one-on-one mentoring with faculty members. In addition to research, students can step beyond the ideas and actually start their own companies or gain experience consulting for other businesses. Students learn to work in interdisciplinary teams with their peers. All of this is offered to them as undergraduates. They are encouraged to begin applying their God-given talents now rather than later, to make an impact, to take a step beyond the mind.

Off-Campus Programs

A Taylor education starts on the campus, broadens to the community, and extends to the world. At Taylor students discover demanding classes and vibrant on-campus ministries enhanced by an education that goes beyond the campus, challenging them to confront the culture while caring for its people. The Spencer Center for Global Engagement helps them move beyond papers to people and beyond statistics to solutions; their calling to love the world compels them to engage it.

Unlike tourists or business persons, students have the unique opportunity to enter another culture without pretense and to absorb, blend, interact, adapt to, and reflect with the people and culture of the area. And at Taylor, studying abroad is not only an available option, it is an encouraged aspect of their education. The Council for Christian Colleges and Universities recognized Taylor twice for it's involvement in its Best Semester programs, first recognizing Taylor for having the highest number of students participate in study-abroad programs, and second for having the highest percentage of its student body participate in study-abroad programs.

To see a complete listing and descriptions of Taylor's off-campus study opportunities, students should visit http://www.taylor.edu/academics/ocp.

Academic Facilities

Each residence hall on the campus has been wired so that the Taylor network and Internet access are available from each student's room. In addition, extensive networking to all academic and administrative buildings provides full network access across the campus. Wireless access continues to expand aggressively throughout the campus.

The Kesler Student Activity Center includes a field house with four playing courts; a fitness/wellness center; an indoor competitive track and field arena, including a 200-meter track; an aerobics room; and support areas, such as individual team and community member locker rooms.

At Taylor, even freshman media communication students are shooting with high definition (HD) video equipment. Five HD cameras and additional professional audio and lighting equipment have been added. There are also four new high-definition video editing suites equipped with Macintosh G5s, Final Cut Pro Software, Apple's Soundtrack, Motion, and LiveType as well as the Adobe Creative Suite that features Photoshop and InDesign.

The science center, which contains laboratories, a greenhouse, and the computing center, serves students majoring in biology, chemistry, computer science, mathematics, and physics. The liberal arts building houses an Educational Technology Center and the Modern Language Department's language labs. The University library has more than 188,925 volumes, 725 print and 6,100 online current periodicals, and twelve newspapers, and houses the Learning Support Center. In addition, Taylor's library belongs to national networks and features an online catalog for electronic searching for all private colleges and universities in Indiana. Taylor also provides online access to thousands of databases, including major library holdings around the world. The music center has a recital hall, practice rooms, and a band rehearsal room. The state-of-the-art Randall Center for Environmental Studies, located on Taylor's 65-acre arboretum, houses fully equipped labs in hydrologic, biotic, and spatial analysis for classroom and field instruction and research.

Other academic facilities include the Center for Biblical Justice and Public Policy, Center for C. S. Lewis and Friends, Center for Environmental Science, Center for Missions Computing, Center for Research and Innovation, and Center for Social Science Research.

Costs

Ranked as a best buy in *Barron's Best Buys in College Education* and as one of *Kiplinger's* "100 Best Private Colleges" for academic excellence and lower total costs, Taylor's tuition and fees for 2007–08 were $23,260. Room and board were $6100, with indirect costs estimated at $2200.

Financial Aid

Scholarships, grants, loans, work-study, and church matching grants are available for students who need assistance in meeting college expenses. Merit scholarships are available to incoming freshmen. In addition, nearly 600 employment opportunities are available through the University. This past year, 88 percent of Taylor's students received some form of financial aid.

Faculty

Taylor University is extremely proud of and thankful for its faculty members. Ninety-two percent have earned a terminal degree and 88 percent are full-time members of the teaching staff. Faculty members are academically recognized, personally committed to the authority of Scripture, and available to and involved with students. The student-faculty ratio is 13.8:1.

Student Government

The Taylor Student Organization (TSO) offers over 400 dynamic and diverse student leadership positions and experiences on campus. Students are encouraged to plug their gifts and passions into an office and team setting that will cultivate their faith, leadership, and calling for service. Student leaders in TSO work to create excellent programs and provide quality services that build Christian community, explore contemporary issues and popular culture through a Christian worldview, and add to the educational and spiritual environment of campus. More information about TSO student offices can be found at http://www.taylor.edu/community/studentlife/leadership/tso.

Admission Requirements

Taylor is committed to enrolling students with high academic motivation, and it continues to honor classroom achievements of applicants in its selection process. However, Taylor also believes that other factors beyond a student's intellectual gifts must guide admission decisions. Leadership skills, extracurricular activities, spiritual motivations, character, and personal aspirations are also considered. While academic preparedness and achievement are key issues (recent freshmen classes average a 3.6 GPA, with average SAT test scores of 1200 or ACT scores of 26), Taylor believes the complete answer includes more factors and looks at the thoughtfully completed personal essays as well as recommendations. In addition, the required interview offers admissions counselors the opportunity to get to know students better while providing meaningful information as students search for the right fit in a college.

Application and Information

Prospective students are encouraged to start the application process early. Students may apply after completing their junior year of high school.

For further information or to apply online, students should contact:

Office of Admissions
Taylor University
236 West Reade Avenue
Upland, Indiana 46989-1001
Phone: 765-998-5511
800-882-3456 (toll-free)
E-mail: admissions@taylor.edu
Web site: http://www.taylor.edu

Taylor distinctives: relentless discovery, global engagement, intentional community.

TRI-STATE UNIVERSITY

ANGOLA, INDIANA

The University

Tri-State University (TSU) is a private, independent, coeducational institution offering associate and baccalaureate degrees in more than thirty-five programs to students in engineering, mathematics, science, computer science, business administration, teacher education, communications, and criminal justice. In 2002, TSU was elevated to a graduate-degree-granting institution and now offers five-year Bachelor of Science/Master of Engineering dual-degree programs. In fall 2006 TSU introduced an interdisciplinary major in entrepreneurship, and a new hospitality and tourism major is planned for fall 2008.

Since its founding in 1884, TSU's emphasis has been on providing an affordable, comprehensive, career-oriented, hands-on education. With a worldwide reputation for being "job-ready," TSU graduates are in demand. That is why each year more than 90 percent of TSU graduates are employed in major-related positions within six months of graduation.

TSU's current undergraduate enrollment is approximately 1,250. Over 800 of these students live on campus in one of nine residence halls. The University's 485-acre campus includes an eighteen-hole championship golf course. In August 2007, TSU opened its new $15.5 million University Center and Center for Online Technology, which houses a new dining hall, deli, bakery, bookstore, game room, climbing wall, sports and wellness center, movie theater, post office, radio station, and library. Three new apartment-style, fully furnished residence halls, at a cost of $7 million, also opened in August 2007, providing new housing options to both freshmen and upperclassmen.

The University's campus offers an informal and friendly atmosphere, which complements the seriousness and determination with which TSU students pursue their academic goals. While focused on pursuing their goals, TSU students enjoy many opportunities to develop friendships and to build leadership and teamwork skills through their participation in athletics and a range of campus organizations.

Men's intercollegiate sports include baseball, basketball, cross-country, football, golf, lacrosse, soccer, tennis, track, and wrestling. Women's sports include basketball, cross-country, golf, lacrosse, soccer, softball, tennis, track, and volleyball. Intramural sports are also a big part of recreational life at TSU.

Student organizations that offer opportunities for participation include the student senate, honor societies, professional organizations, the campus newspaper, the FM radio station, the yearbook, the drama club, and more. In addition, there are a total of twelve social fraternities and sororities on campus, in which approximately 20 percent of the student body participate after their freshman year.

Tri-State University is accredited by the Higher Learning Commission and a member of the North Central Association of Colleges and Schools (Web site: http://www.ncahigherlearningcommission.org; phone: 312-263-0456). TSU's programs in chemical engineering, civil engineering, electrical engineering, and mechanical engineering are accredited by the Engineering Accreditation Commission of the Accreditation Board for Engineering and Technology, Inc. (ABET). ABET's national office is located at 111 Market Place, Suite 1050, Baltimore, Maryland, 21202-4012; phone: 410-347-7700. All teacher preparation programs are accredited by the National Council for Accreditation of Teacher Education (NCATE) and the Indiana Professional Standards Board.

Location

TSU is located in Angola, Indiana, the heart of northeast Indiana's scenic lake resort region and about halfway between the metropolitan areas of Chicago, Illinois, and Cleveland, Ohio. Just a 45-minute drive from Fort Wayne, Indiana, TSU offers the safety and ease of a small-town environment while being close to some of the nation's most vital cities. Pokagon State Park provides year-round recreational opportunities for the community and is just 5 miles from TSU's campus.

Majors and Degrees

The Allen School of Engineering and Technology awards Bachelor of Science degrees in chemical, civil, computer, computer science, electrical, and mechanical engineering; design engineering technology (CADD); and engineering administration. It awards associate degrees in construction management technology, design engineering technology (CADD), and manufacturing technology. An interdisciplinary minor in entrepreneurship is available.

Well-qualified high school graduates may be admitted directly into a five-year mechanical or civil engineering program. Mechanical and civil engineers with the skills necessary to lead the designing of a complex system are highly sought by industry professionals; therefore, the degree is a practice-oriented degree with a heavy design emphasis, as opposed to the research emphasis of a traditional Master of Science degree. On completion of this program, both the Bachelor of Science in mechanical or civil engineering and the Master of Engineering degree are awarded.

The Ketner School of Business awards the Bachelor of Science in Business Administration degree in accounting, business/arts and sciences, entrepreneurship, finance, hospitality and tourism, management, management information systems, and marketing and the Bachelor of Science degree in golf management. Associate degrees are awarded in accounting and business administration.

The Franks School of Education awards Bachelor of Science degrees in elementary education, physical education, and secondary education. Secondary education majors can specialize in mathematics, science, and social studies.

The Jannen School of Arts and Sciences awards Bachelor of Arts degrees in communication and psychology. Bachelor of Science degrees are awarded in biology, chemistry, forensic science, health education (K–12), health education (9–12), health promotion and recreational programming, mathematics, mathematics education, physical education (K–12), physical education (5–12), physical education (9–12), physical science, premed, science education, social studies education, and sport management; and a Bachelor of Science in criminal justice. Associate degrees are awarded in arts, computer technology, criminal justice, and science.

Academic Programs

The graduation requirements for a bachelor's degree are a cumulative grade point average of not less than 2.0 (on a 4.0 scale) and the completion of 120 to 132 semester hours, depending upon the major.

TSU's engineering programs concentrate on providing a fundamental, application-oriented engineering education. In addition to concentrating in a specialized area, students are required to successfully complete courses in communication skills, sociohumanistic studies, and analysis and design.

The University's business programs include a broad range of hands-on practical experience that acquaints the student with the practices, procedures, and problems of the contemporary business professional. Guest lecturers are frequent visitors to the campus, and field trips are considered vital to the total educational experience.

Off-Campus Programs

Co-op and internship opportunities are available. Semesters of classroom study are alternated with professional work experience, giving students the opportunity to integrate theory with practice and gain a competitive edge in the job market. The length of a co-op program depends upon the student's class status when entering the program. Work-study schedules require from three to six semesters on work assignments. During the semesters worked, students are paid directly by the employer.

Academic Facilities

Fawick Hall of Engineering reopened in 1997 after a yearlong $5-million complete interior demolition to load-bearing walls and then full reconstruction to house the University's Departments of Chemical Engineering, Civil and Environmental Engineering, Electrical and Computer Engineering, Mechanical and Aerospace Engineering, and Technology. Because of the University's commitment to a high-quality education, TSU's students use sophisticated equipment such as a scanning electron microscope in their cast metals laboratories and in projects related to industrial consulting. Each department has a computer lab with pertinent software for their students.

Named in honor of John G. Best, a distinguished alumnus and former member of the Board of Trustees, the John G. Best Hall of Science contains classrooms and science laboratories. Best Hall also houses the Fairfield Lecture Room, the Department of Mathematics, the Department of Science, the science laboratories, and the Department of Criminal Justice, Psychology, and Social Sciences.

The University Computer Center houses an academic computer system that consists of Pentium microcomputers running Windows NT Workstation and Windows 2000. The academic system is an Internet site supporting Telnet, the Web, and e-mail to other Internet sites. A Microsoft Exchange server handles the e-mail. There are more than 200 computers dedicated to student access in labs across campus. Every room in each residence hall is wired to the University network and the Internet, and all but one residence hall and Hershey Hall provide wireless Internet service.

Costs

Tuition for the academic year (two semesters) in 2007–08 was $22,250. Room and board for the academic year was $6500.

Financial Aid

Financial aid may be awarded in the form of scholarships, grants, loans, or employment. Any of these aids or any combination may be necessary to supplement family and student resources to meet basic educational expenses. Tri-State requires the use of the Free Application for Federal Student Aid (FAFSA) and recommends its submission by March 1.

Faculty

TSU has a full-time faculty of 70 members, most of whom have doctoral degrees and/or are registered professional engineers. The central mission of the faculty members is teaching. The student-faculty ratio is 13:1.

Student Government

The student senate is organized for the purpose of promoting and coordinating campus activities for students. Representatives elected from campus organizations form the senate, which sponsors social activities and campus projects and aids in formulating policies for student organizations.

Admission Requirements

Graduation from an approved high school or equivalent preparation is required for admission. TSU gives careful consideration to the caliber of the academic records. Selection is made without regard to race, religion, or color. The University requires that applicants for admission arrange to take the ACT or SAT prior to approval for admission (writing sections are optional).

Admission requirements for engineering include 4 years of English, 1 year of chemistry, 1 year of physics, 1 year of social studies, 2 years of algebra, 1 year of geometry, and ½ year of trigonometry.

All other applicants must have the following high school credits: 4 years of English, 3 years of mathematics, 3 years of science, and 3 years of social studies.

Graduates of preprofessional or college-parallel programs at approved community or junior colleges are eligible for transfer into TSU's baccalaureate programs. Qualified graduates of these programs may be granted junior standing upon transfer. In general, credit may be allowed for subjects equivalent to those in the program at TSU, provided that the student earned a C or better in the course.

Application and Information

TSU admits applicants on the basis of scholastic achievement and academic potential. Admission decisions are made on a rolling basis, without regard to race, religion, color, gender, sexual orientation, or age. Applicants are notified of their status within two weeks after the online application and high school record have been received. Transfer students must also submit an official copy of their college transcript(s).

Interested students and their parents are encouraged to visit the campus. Arrangements can be made by writing or calling the Office of Admission.

For additional information, students should call or write:

Office of Admission
Tri-State University
1 University Avenue
Angola, Indiana 46703-1764
Phone: 260-665-4100
800-347-4TSU (toll-free within continental U.S.)
E-mail: admit@tristate.edu
Web site: http://www.tristate.edu

UNIVERSITY OF INDIANAPOLIS

INDIANAPOLIS, INDIANA

The University

The University of Indianapolis is inspiring excellence with a personal approach to education and a commitment to academic quality. Outstanding faculty members inspire students in small classes that allow individual attention, and students are encouraged to apply their knowledge to real-world situations through internships, active learning in the classroom, and community service. A private, residential, comprehensive university founded in 1902 and affiliated with the United Methodist Church, the University of Indianapolis welcomes students of many nations and faiths from around the world. Every year, more than 4,500 full-time and part-time students, both undergraduate and graduate, benefit from the University's commitment to offering outstanding academic programs in more than sixty-five major fields or study. The University of Indianapolis accepts qualified applicants for admission without regard to race, color, sex, sexual orientation, age, religion, creed, marital status, or ethnic or national origin.

Students indicate that they choose the University because of its challenging, yet supportive, atmosphere and relatively small size, combined with the advantages of its location in the southern suburbs of a thriving state capital. As a result, there is a great sense of community and pride on the campus. The University helps students to determine and achieve their individual academic goals. The University has experienced much growth and has instituted many enhancements recently, including the renovation and addition to Esch Hall, which houses a new facility for the communication department.

More than 2,400 Day Division students are enrolled. There are students from sixty countries and thirty-five states. Approximately 82 percent of freshmen live in on-campus housing. The warmth and sensitivity of the faculty and staff members and students alike enable those who are a part of the campus to feel a strong sense of community.

In addition to the undergraduate division, the University is composed of the Graduate and Doctoral Division, including the nationally recognized Krannert School of Physical Therapy. The University of Indianapolis offers twenty-two graduate programs and four doctoral programs, including those in the Schools of Occupational and Physical Therapy, which rank among the finest in the nation. The most popular programs in the undergraduate division include pre–physical therapy, business, athletic training, communication, nursing, education, premedicine, psychology, and music.

Social life is organized through the Campus Program Board, Indianapolis Student Government, and Residence Hall Association, student organizations that plan weekly activities for all students. There are numerous social clubs and interest groups available for students who wish to become involved in extracurricular activities. Five residence halls house students; four house both men and women, and one is only for women. Students must be admitted on a full-time basis in order to be assigned housing. NCAA Division II sports for men include baseball, basketball, cross-country, football, golf, soccer, swimming and diving, tennis, track and field (indoor and outdoor), and wrestling. NCAA Division II sports for women include basketball, cross-country, fast-pitch softball, golf, soccer, swimming and diving, tennis, track and field (indoor and outdoor), and volleyball. Intramural sports are offered for men and women in flag football, basketball, softball, soccer, volleyball, indoor soccer, Ultimate Frisbee, and racquetball.

Location

The University is located in the southern neighborhoods of Indianapolis, the nation's third-largest capital city. Indianapolis and the surrounding area constitute a metropolitan area of nearly 2 million people. As a result, the city offers students valuable internship and service-learning experiences as well as recreational and cultural opportunities too numerous to mention. The campus is extremely accessible, just a few blocks from two major interstate highways (I-65 and I-465). The campus is served by Indygo bus, and Amtrak trains arrive daily at historic Union Station, just 10 minutes from the campus. Indianapolis International Airport is about 15 minutes away.

Majors and Degrees

The undergraduate programs are offered through the College of Arts and Sciences, the School of Business, the School of Nursing, the School of Education, the Krannert School of Physical Therapy, the School of Occupational Therapy, and the School of Psychological Sciences. The degrees awarded are the Associate in Arts, Associate in Science, Associate in Science in Nursing, Bachelor of Arts, Bachelor of Science, and Bachelor of Science in Nursing.

Baccalaureate and preprofessional fields of study include accounting (CMA/CPA), actuarial science, anthropology, archeology, art, athletic training, biology, business administration, chemistry, communication studies, computer engineering (dual degree), computer science, corporate communication, corrections, earth-space sciences, economics, electrical engineering (dual degree), electronic media, elementary education, English, entrepreneurship, environmental science, exercise science, experiential learning (concentrations in applied anthropology, applied history, and applied theater), finance, French, German, history, human biology, human communication, information systems, international business, international relations, journalism, law enforcement, management, marketing, mathematics, mechanical engineering (dual degree), medical technology, music, music performance, nursing, philosophy, physics, political science, pre–art therapy, predentistry, prelaw, premedicine, pre–occupational therapy, pre–physical therapy, pretheology, pre–veterinary science, psychology, public relations, religion, respiratory therapy, secondary education, social work, sociology, Spanish, sports administration, sports information, sports marketing, studio art, theater, youth ministry, and visual communication design.

Teaching majors are offered in business education (all grades), chemistry, earth-space science, English, French, life science, mathematics, music (all grades), physical education (all grades), physics, social studies, Spanish, speech communication, theater, and visual arts (grades 5–12).

Associate degrees are awarded in business administration, chemistry, corrections, information systems, law enforcement, liberal arts, nursing, and physical therapist assistant studies.

Academic Programs

The University of Indianapolis starts with a top-notch education that combines a liberal arts– and career-oriented curriculum that graduates call life-changing. Students find a powerful combination of features designed to inspire them to excellence. Faculty and staff members take a personal interest in students, encouraging them to explore their interests and apply what they learn, so they can excel when it comes time to make their place in the world.

Students can choose from more than sixty-five undergraduate academic programs. The goal of the liberal arts core classes is to provide learning above and beyond the student's major field, so students study topics and cultures that pique their interest in unexpected ways.

Students appreciate the curriculum because they don't have to wait to apply what they learn. At the University of Indianapolis, students have time—before they graduate—to practice what they learn. Most majors offer practical experiences, which give students an edge in the job market. The Indianapolis location is an excellent resource when it comes to finding internships, field experiences, service-learning opportunities, or part-time employment. Internships let students sample their future careers and gain some of the knowledge and experience they admire in their professors. At the University of Indianapolis, there's a host of possibilities for virtually any major.

Off-Campus Programs

The University operates a fully owned branch campus in Athens, Greece, that offers students a unique exchange program. Located within walking distance of the storied Acropolis, the Plaka, Constitution Square, and other historic landmarks, the University of Indianapolis–Athens offers students the opportunity to explore and experience Greece both inside and outside the classroom. Currently, the Athens campus offers thirty-two undergraduate programs in the arts and sciences, business, and psychology. Short-term study trips, as well as full-semester study-abroad programs, are available to students through the Odyssey Program. In addition, students at the main campus have many opportunities to travel to Athens on shorter trips during vacations or during the Spring Term in May. Other partnerships and extension sites for direct credit include Israel, Belize, and the People's Republic of China. Other off-campus study opportunities take place during the Spring Term, including assorted overseas travel openings. The University also has an Office of Career Services, which arranges off-campus internships related to one's field of study.

Academic Facilities

Krannert Memorial Library, which operates an online card catalog, houses more than 175,000 volumes, more than 1,000 periodicals, and more than 19,000 microfilm/microform/microfiche records. The library is home to a full media center. The communication department, with new state-of-the-art equipment for its radio station and television studio, is located in Esch Hall. Martin Hall contains outstanding resources for the Schools of Nursing, Physical Therapy, and Occupational Therapy and is connected to Lilly Science Hall, which recently underwent a major upgrade to all its science labs. Access to computers is available in all of the academic buildings and residence halls. Students have access to the campuswide information system from their rooms in the residence halls, and the whole campus is wireless. Ransburg Auditorium, with seating for nearly 800, is the setting for concerts, recitals, and theatrical productions. The $10-million Christel DeHaan Fine Arts Center features state-of-the-art music and art facilities, an art gallery, and a 450-seat, Viennese-style concert hall.

Costs

Directly billed expenses for the 2007–08 academic year were $19,540 for tuition and $7560 for room and board. Nonbilled indirect expenses were estimated at $800 for books and supplies, an average of $630 for transportation, and $1370 to $1830 for miscellaneous and personal expenses.

Financial Aid

All applicants for admission are eligible to apply for financial aid. Indiana residents should file the Free Application for Federal Student Aid (FAFSA) by March 1 to qualify for state of Indiana financial aid programs. All students should file the FAFSA along with the University of Indianapolis Application for Financial Aid by March 10 for priority consideration. For the 2006–07 academic year, about 88 percent of the enrolled full-time students received more than $37 million from all sources.

Faculty

All Day Division faculty members are assigned teaching (not research) duties, including many administrators and some professional staff personnel. Graduate students do not teach any undergraduate classes. Currently, the student-faculty ratio is 12:1, and the average class size is 18.

Student Government

The Indianapolis Student Government (ISG) consists of students elected to officer positions plus student representatives from each class, chosen for a one-year term in an annual student body election. ISG's main focus is to pass resolutions regarding student concerns.

Admission Requirements

Applicants for admission must be high school graduates or have a GED certificate and are expected to have taken a college-preparatory curriculum in high school. Applicants for regular admission should have completed a minimum of 4 years of English, 3 years of mathematics, 3 years of laboratory science, 2 years of social science (U.S. history, government, and economics), and 2 years of any foreign language. In addition, applicants for full-time admission without restrictions should rank in the upper half of their class and have average to above-average SAT or ACT scores. Essays are not required for admission. For immediate consideration, transfer applicants must have achieved a good overall record and have earned at least a C average in previous college or university work. An on-campus interview is recommended anytime after the junior year of high school. To apply for admission, the Application for Admission, official high school transcript, official college transcript (if applicable), and official SAT or ACT scores should be forwarded to the Office of Admissions.

Application and Information

All applications are reviewed on a rolling basis—an admission decision is made as soon as all documents are received, and notifications are mailed immediately thereafter. There is no deadline for applications, but high school seniors are encouraged to apply during the fall semester of their senior year. Scholarships are also awarded on a rolling basis. Admitted students are notified of scholarships they have been awarded shortly after they have been accepted.

Requests for appointments and information about the University should be directed to:

University of Indianapolis
1400 East Hanna Avenue
Indianapolis, Indiana 46227-3697

Phone: 317-STUDENT
317-788-3216
800-232-8634 (toll-free)
Fax: 317-788-3300
E-mail: admissions@uindy.edu
Web site: http://www.uindy.edu/

Smith Mall, the centerpiece of the University of Indianapolis campus, features a beautifully landscaped water garden canal.

VALPARAISO UNIVERSITY

VALPARAISO, INDIANA

The University

Valparaiso University (Valpo) was founded in 1859 by the citizens of Valparaiso, Indiana, but its recent history dates from 1925, when it was purchased by the Lutheran University Association. Valpo is one of the nation's largest Lutheran-affiliated universities, yet it remains independent and is open to individuals of all faiths. The University's 4,000 students represent most states and more than forty countries; 66 percent come from outside of Indiana. Valparaiso University is a residential community in which activities outside the classroom form an important part of campus life; more than 67 percent of its students live on campus. Over 100 extracurricular and cocurricular programs are open to all, including various NCAA Division I intercollegiate and intramural sports teams for men and women. Approximately 35 percent of the students are members of the University's nine national fraternities and six national sororities. Both in and out of the classroom, students and professors operate a student-initiated honor code in which integrity is assumed to be the norm. If violations occur, they are handled by peers through a student-composed Honor Council. Because of these structures and the University philosophy as a whole, relationships among students, faculty, and administration are remarkably collaborative.

Major divisions at Valparaiso University include the Colleges of Arts and Sciences, Business Administration, Engineering, and Nursing; Christ College (the Honors College); the School of Law; and the Graduate Division. Graduates earned a 97 percent job placement rate last year.

Location

Valparaiso University is located in Valparaiso, a safe community of 31,000 in Indiana. Only 1 hour west, Chicago and its theaters, museums, restaurants, and cultural and sports offerings are accessible by auto, train, or bus. The campus is within walking distance of a vibrant town square and commercial/entertainment center with national chain stores and restaurants. Just 15 miles north is the Indiana Dunes National Lakeshore on Lake Michigan, a famous recreational area and home of the finest ecological laboratory in the nation. Air service is available nearby from Chicago's O'Hare and Midway International Airports and South Bend's Michiana Regional Airport.

Majors and Degrees

Valparaiso University offers the following undergraduate degrees: Associate of Arts, Associate of Science, Bachelor of Arts (B.A.), Bachelor of Music, Bachelor of Music Education, Bachelor of Science (B.S.), Bachelor of Science in Accounting, Bachelor of Science in Business Administration, Bachelor of Science in Civil Engineering, Bachelor of Science in Computer Engineering, Bachelor of Science in Education, Bachelor of Science in Electrical Engineering, Bachelor of Science in Fine Arts, Bachelor of Science in Mechanical Engineering, Bachelor of Science in Nursing, Bachelor of Science in Physical Education, and Bachelor of Social Work. The B.A. or B.S. degree may be earned in accounting, actuarial science, American studies, art, athletic training, biochemistry, biology, business administration, chemistry, Chinese and Japanese studies, church music, civil engineering, classics, communication, communication law, computer engineering, computer science, creative writing, economics, economics and computer analysis, education (elementary, middle, or secondary), electrical engineering, engineering, English, environmental science, exercise science, finance, French, geography, geology, geoscience, German, history, information and decision sciences, international business, international economics and cultural affairs, international service, management, marketing, mathematics, mechanical engineering, meteorology, modern European studies, music, music composition, music education, music performance, new media–journalism, nursing, philosophy, physical education, physics, political science, professional writing, psychology, public and corporate communication, public relations, social work, sociology, Spanish, sports management, television-radio, theater, theology, and youth, family, and education ministry.

Academic Programs

Valparaiso University has a long tradition of combining professional colleges with a strong commitment to the values and broadening experiences of the liberal arts. The University helps students of varied interests and objectives to clarify their goals and explore new possibilities. Connections between students' lives and the classroom are encouraged through an emphasis on hands-on learning programs, including the Valpo Core. Programs are structured to provide a solid base for exploration in various fields, while offering students the freedom to develop depth in a specific interest. This philosophy is extended through the upper division, where students have three options when completing a degree: an individual plan of study involving the major and complementary courses from related fields of study, the election of a second academic major in addition to the first, or a special minor in connection with the major. Career planning is aided through the professional programs and the University's Career Center. Many students also gain professional work experience in their chosen field before graduation by participating in the cooperative education program and internships.

Valparaiso operates on the semester system; the fall semester begins in late August and ends before Christmas, and the spring semester starts in early January and ends during the second week in May. Valpo also has two summer terms that further extend opportunities for study on campus or at various off-campus locations.

The University participates in the Advanced Placement Program, the College-Level Examination Program, and the International Baccalaureate Program. In addition, Valparaiso provides its own placement testing in several academic areas.

All departments of the University offer opportunities for honors work through independent study, seminars, and research. Christ College, the Honors College of Valparaiso, has a well-established but continuously evolving program designed to challenge gifted students. Christ College students enroll concurrently in any other Valpo college.

Off-Campus Programs

Valparaiso University sponsors study-abroad programs in Reutlingen and Tübingen, Germany; Puebla, Mexico; Paris, France; Hangzhou, China; Granada, Spain; and Cambridge, England. Valparaiso also sponsors semester-long study opportunities at two universities in Japan, one in Namibia, and another in Greece. Valpo students may study at other overseas locations through Valparaiso's membership in the Central States College Association. In addition, Valpo grants credit for the following cooperative programs: Urban Studies Semester (Chicago), Urban Affairs Semester and Washington Semester (Washington, D.C.), and Semester on the United Nations (Madison, New Jersey).

Academic Facilities

Opened in 2004, the 115,000-square-foot Christopher Center for Library Information Services is a state-of-the-art facility, which offers a robotic book-retrieval system. In addition to library resources, the four-story structure houses a ninety-one-seat tiered classroom; three fireplace lounges; a sixty-seat computer lab; a snack bar; twenty-four stations for listening to, viewing, and developing multimedia projects; reading rooms; a writing center; electronic information services; and much more. The Neils Science Center houses an astronomical observatory, a greenhouse, and other facilities that have earned the University a citation from the Atomic Energy Commission for having a model undergraduate physics laboratory. The Kade-Duesenberg German House and Cultural Center, Virtual Nursing Learning Center, weather station (which includes Dopplar radar), Center for the Arts, VisBox 3-D scientific learning system, and nonlinear (digital) video editing lab are state-of-the-art facilities. A new 202,000-square-foot Union is currently under construction and slated to open in the 2008–09 academic year.

Costs

Tuition for the 2007–08 academic year at Valparaiso University is $24,360, room is $4430, and board is $2720. General fees are $840. The total cost of tuition, room, board, and fees is $32,350. Students spend approximately $2500 per year for books, supplies, and such miscellaneous expenses as laundry and travel.

Financial Aid

Ninety-two percent of Valparaiso's undergraduate students receive financial aid, totaling more than $55 million. Many scholarships and awards are determined by the admissions application. Students are also encouraged to file the Free Application for Federal Student Aid (FAFSA) to apply for need-based grants, loans, and employment. Valpo awards federal, state, and University need-based aid based on FAFSA results, attempting to make up the difference between the cost of attending Valpo and the amount a family can afford. Early application is recommended for Valpo assistance, since the awarding of aid begins in January of the year of enrollment.

Faculty

Valparaiso's 351 full-time faculty members share a common interest—teaching in ways that encourage students and faculty members to get to know one another. The majority of the faculty members are full-time, and a considerable number serve as advisers to the various academic and social organizations on campus. Classes are led by professors, not teaching assistants. Almost 90 percent of the full-time professors have terminal degrees, and this figure reaches 100 percent in many departments. Each department has a full advising system to help students with course and program selection.

Student Government

Students and faculty members alike are involved in the internal governance of the institution. House Councils in each of the residence halls are composed of representatives elected by the residents. Each council makes decisions and sets standards within the guidelines established by the University. Students in the living units and off-campus students elect representatives to the Student Senate (composed entirely of students) and the University Senate (made up of an equal number of representatives from the student body, faculty, and administration). The functions of these two separate bodies cover most phases of student life.

Admission Requirements

Valparaiso admits candidates who exhibit the potential for academic success at the University. The freshman retention rate averaged 86 percent over the past five years, reflecting in part the high quality of the admission program. Qualified students are admitted without regard to race, color, gender, disability, national origin, or ancestry. The credentials of each applicant are individually and personally evaluated, and consideration is given not only to ACT or SAT scores, but also to grades and trends in the student's record, the nature of the high school and the program followed, outside interests, and recommendations. A campus visit and an interview with an admission counselor are recommended but not required. Students who have taken the ACT or SAT in their junior year and have submitted their high school transcripts, complete through the eleventh grade, may be considered for admission.

Application and Information

An applicant must complete a formal University admission application or the Common Application to be considered for admission. In addition, Valpo requires a high school transcript (complete through the junior year), ACT or SAT scores, a counselor evaluation form, and college transcripts (when applicable). Valpo's nonbinding early action option requires applicants to submit their applications no later than November 1. Regular admission notification begins on a rolling basis after December 1. First priority for scholarship consideration is given to those who apply for admission by the early action deadline; preference is then given to those who apply by January 15.

Information and application forms for admission and financial aid may be obtained from:

Office of Admission
Kretzmann Hall
1700 Chapel Drive
Valparaiso University
Valparaiso, Indiana 46383-6493
Phone: 219-464-5011
888-GO-VALPO (toll-free)
Fax: 219-464-6898
E-mail: undergrad.admissions@valpo.edu
Web site: http://www.valpo.edu

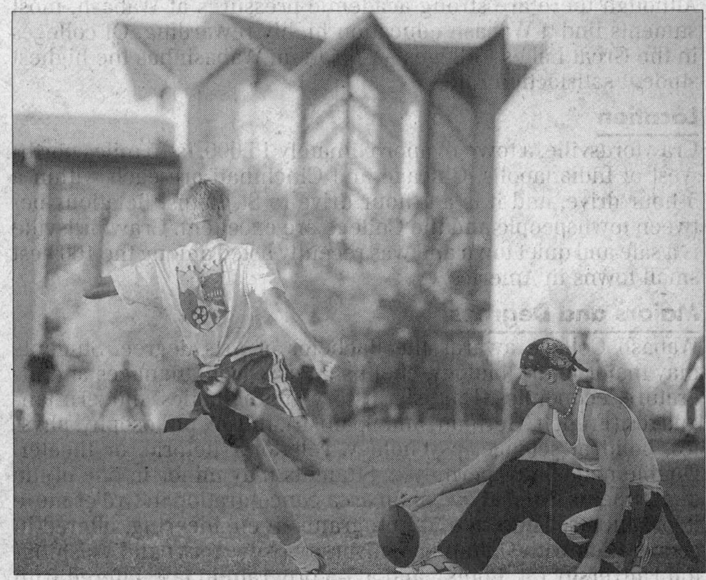

Students on the campus of Valparaiso University.

WABASH COLLEGE

CRAWFORDSVILLE, INDIANA

The College

Founded in 1832, Wabash has remained a liberal arts college educating men to think critically, act responsibly, lead effectively, and live humanely. A common reaction of freshmen to the first semester was expressed in a recent course evaluation: "It's a lot harder than I thought it would be, but I've done a lot better than I expected to." Academic challenges, ample extracurricular activities, and maximum personal autonomy foster independence and versatility in Wabash graduates. Of graduating seniors in the class of 2007, nearly 50 percent enrolled in medical, law, and graduate school programs; about 45 percent took positions in firms like Lehman Brothers, Chevron, Eli Lilly and Company, the Chicago Field Museum, Teach for America, and the Peace Corps, among many others. Approximately 70 percent of the 900 students are from Indiana; the remaining 30 percent come from thirty-four states and two dozen countries.

Outside the classroom, Wabash students have a rich choice of activities to explore. There are workshops, seminars, visiting artists and lecturers, films, music, theater and forensic events, special interest clubs, and intramural sports. About 40 percent of the student body participates in varsity athletics, which include baseball, basketball, cross-country, football, golf, soccer, swimming, tennis, track, and wrestling. Wabash belongs to Division III of the NCAA. Over 230 championships and 15 winners of NCAA Postgraduate Scholarships prove that athletic achievement can accompany academic excellence.

Housing is guaranteed to all entering students, and all students are required to live on campus for their freshman and sophomore years. There are ten national fraternities and four residence halls. The single-sex environment fosters a serious academic routine during the week. Fraternities and other social groups help to organize social events with women at coed institutions in the area.

Although there are strong academic pressures at Wabash, most students find a Wabash education highly rewarding. Of colleges in the Great Lakes Colleges Association, Wabash has the highest student satisfaction rate.

Location

Crawfordsville, a town of approximately 15,000, is 45 miles northwest of Indianapolis. Chicago and Cincinnati are each within a 3-hour drive, and it is a 4-hour drive to St. Louis. Relations between townspeople and the College are excellent. Crawfordsville is a safe and quiet town and was recently listed among the 100 best small towns in America.

Majors and Degrees

Wabash College awards the Bachelor of Arts degree. Students may major in art, biology, chemistry, classical languages and literature, economics, English, history, mathematics, modern languages (French, German, and Spanish), music, philosophy, physics, political science, psychology, religion, rhetoric, or theater. Double majors are permitted. Students may minor in one of the departments listed above or an area concentration in two or more departments. There are 3-2 programs in engineering, offered in cooperation with Columbia University (New York) and Washington University (St. Louis), and a 3-3 program in law, offered with Columbia University.

Academic Programs

To graduate, Wabash students must complete thirty-four courses, including the freshman tutorial and the sophomore course Cultures and Traditions; demonstrate proficiency in English composition and in a foreign language; and pass the senior oral and written comprehensive examinations. With the help of a faculty adviser, students work within a curriculum that allows maximum flexibility as well as a broad base of understanding that is at the core of the liberal arts. In coordination with an adviser, students may arrange special courses of study. Faculty committees and advisers and the Schroeder Center for Career Development assist students who are interested in careers in business, engineering, law, and medicine in planning a program appropriate to their needs.

Wabash measures credits in semester-course units. The academic calendar consists of a fall semester, beginning in August and ending before Christmas, and a spring semester, beginning in January and ending in May.

Off-Campus Programs

One in 4 Wabash students takes advantage of the opportunity to study off campus; a Wabash student's financial aid package travels with him. In addition to the thirteen programs sponsored by the Great Lakes Colleges Association, in recent years students have studied in more than 50 programs around the world. More than half of all Wabash students participate in some form of off-campus program.

Students receive credit, but not grades, for work done in approved programs.

Academic Facilities

The open-stack library collection has over 420,000 books and bound periodicals, nearly 1,700 serial and periodical titles, a 150,000-item government documents section, and more than 11,000 CDs, DVDs, videos, and records. The 10-person library staff provides students and faculty members with reference assistance, information database searching, and computerized interlibrary loan access to over 25 million volumes in more than 5,000 libraries worldwide. Students are free to use the microform facilities and campus computer terminals in the building.

All students have full and free access to more than 350 computers or terminals across campus, including many labs open 24 hours per day. All systems are linked together with an Ethernet WAN with a connection to the Internet so that faculty members and students have access to the same programs and files from any computer classroom, residence hall room, or fraternity room on campus. The entire campus is wireless and every classroom and laboratory is fully equipped with computing and projection equipment. The College's Media Center is state-of-the-art with a full range of digital video and still cameras, powerful computer editing programs, and a range of computers and printers available for student use.

The chemistry department has infrared spectrophotometers, an atomic absorption spectrophotometer, a "Beowulf"-style parallel super computer, and two nuclear magnetic resonance spectrometers. Special equipment and facilities for the biology department include an electron microscope, ultramicrotomes, fluorescence and phase microscopes, scintillation counters, gamma counters, electrophoresis apparatus, physiographs, a 180-acre field station with living facilities and laboratory space, an aquatic field station, and an experimental greenhouse. Special physics department equipment includes an X-ray diffraction machine, a neutron source available for use in the atomic and nuclear physics labs, a multichannel analyzer, a photography darkroom, Mössbauer-effect equipment, a special electronics laboratory, and a range of state-of-the-art computing hardware and software for advanced labs. The chemistry and biology departments are housed in three-year-old Hays Hall, a $30 million, 80,000-square-foot facility, while the physics and mathematics departments are located in a building two years removed from an $8 million renovation.

Another of Wabash's distinctions is Immersion Learning. Each year over 150 students travel to various parts of the world as an integral part of their classroom study. Classics students have traveled to Greece and Rome; history students to France and England; language students to Germany, France, and Russia; and theater students have been backstage in London's most historic theaters.

Wabash's Fine Arts Center houses two art galleries; photography, sculpture, ceramic, painting, and drawing studios; and, for music students, a MIDI lab, a concert hall, and a practice room. Theater patrons and students continue to benefit from the 370-seat proscenium house, scene shop, and 150-seat experimental theater.

Costs

Tuition for 2007–08 is $25,900. Room and board cost $7,200, and there is an activities fee of $450. Most Wabash students spend approximately $1500 per year on books and personal expenses. There are ample opportunities for student employment.

Financial Aid

Wabash College is independent of any direct government funding and has a substantial endowment of nearly $350 million. Cutbacks in government-sponsored financial aid have had no effect on Wabash's generous financial aid and scholarship programs. To apply for financial aid, students must file the Free Application for Federal Student Aid (FAFSA) and the College Scholarship Service (CSS) PROFILE. Students are expected to file the FAFSA by February 15. Wabash College assists families with a combination of scholarships, grants, the Federal Stafford Student Loan, and campus employment.

The Wabash scholarship program is one of the best and oldest in the nation. Scholarships are worth up to full cost for each of four years. Wabash sponsors awards in four general categories: Lilly Awards, Honor Scholarships, Top Ten Scholarships, Top Twenty Scholarships, and President's Scholarships. The Lilly Awards are valued at full cost and are given annually to students who excel in the areas of character, creativity, leadership, and academic achievement. Honor Scholarships that are worth up to $20,000 per year are awarded based on competitive examinations administered on campus in March. The Top Ten Scholarships are worth $12,500 and $15,000 per year and are awarded to students ranking in the top 10 percent and top 5 percent of their classes, respectively, who attend the Top Ten Scholarship visit day in the fall. There is also a Top Twenty Scholarship Program that honors students in the top 20 percent of their graduating class.

Faculty

Ninety-seven percent of Wabash faculty members hold doctorates or other terminal degrees in their fields. While the College encourages faculty research, Wabash is primarily a teaching institution for undergraduates. The faculty-student ratio is 1:10. Approximately 100 students conduct collaborative research with faculty members or work in paid, on-campus internships each summer. The average class size is 15.

Student Government

Wabash has only one rule: Wabash students will conduct themselves as gentlemen and responsible citizens at all times. Beyond diplomatic enforcement of that rule, the College does not undertake to regulate student life. Consequently, Wabash students have a great deal of autonomy. The Student Senate manages and allocates the more than $300,000 collected each year in activity fees. Communication among students, faculty members, and administrators is open and congenial.

Admission Requirements

Wabash seeks academically well-qualified young men from all parts of the United States. The Admissions Committee recommends the following high school courses: 4 years of English, 3 to 4 years of college-preparatory mathematics, 2 years of a foreign language, 2 to 3 years of laboratory science, and 2 years of social studies. In recent years, 70 percent of Wabash's students have ranked in the top quarter of their high school class. The strength of the high school preparation is the most important factor in admission decisions. SAT or ACT scores, counselors' recommendations, and the essay portion of the application form are also important. Personal interviews are not required, but prospective students are strongly encouraged to visit the Wabash campus.

Wabash admits students and gives equal access to its programs and facilities without regard to race, color, national or ethnic origin, or physical or other disabilities.

Application and Information

Students seeking admission to Wabash must submit the Wabash application form, a nonrefundable $40 application fee, and a secondary school report that includes a transcript of grades, SAT or ACT scores, a list of senior-year courses, and the counselor's recommendation. Transfer students must submit transcripts of college courses as well. The application deadline for priority consideration for Wabash merit scholarships and aid is December 15. The final deadline for fall enrollment is March 15. Applicants who are accepted are asked to submit a $250 deposit by May 1.

Application forms and other information may be obtained from:

Steven J. Klein
Dean of Admissions
Wabash College
P.O. Box 352
Crawfordsville, Indiana 47933-0352
Phone: 765-361-6225
800-345-5385 (toll-free)
Web site: http://www.wabash.edu

The heart of the Wabash College campus, the chapel is the site of student gatherings ranging from football rallies to weddings.

IOWA

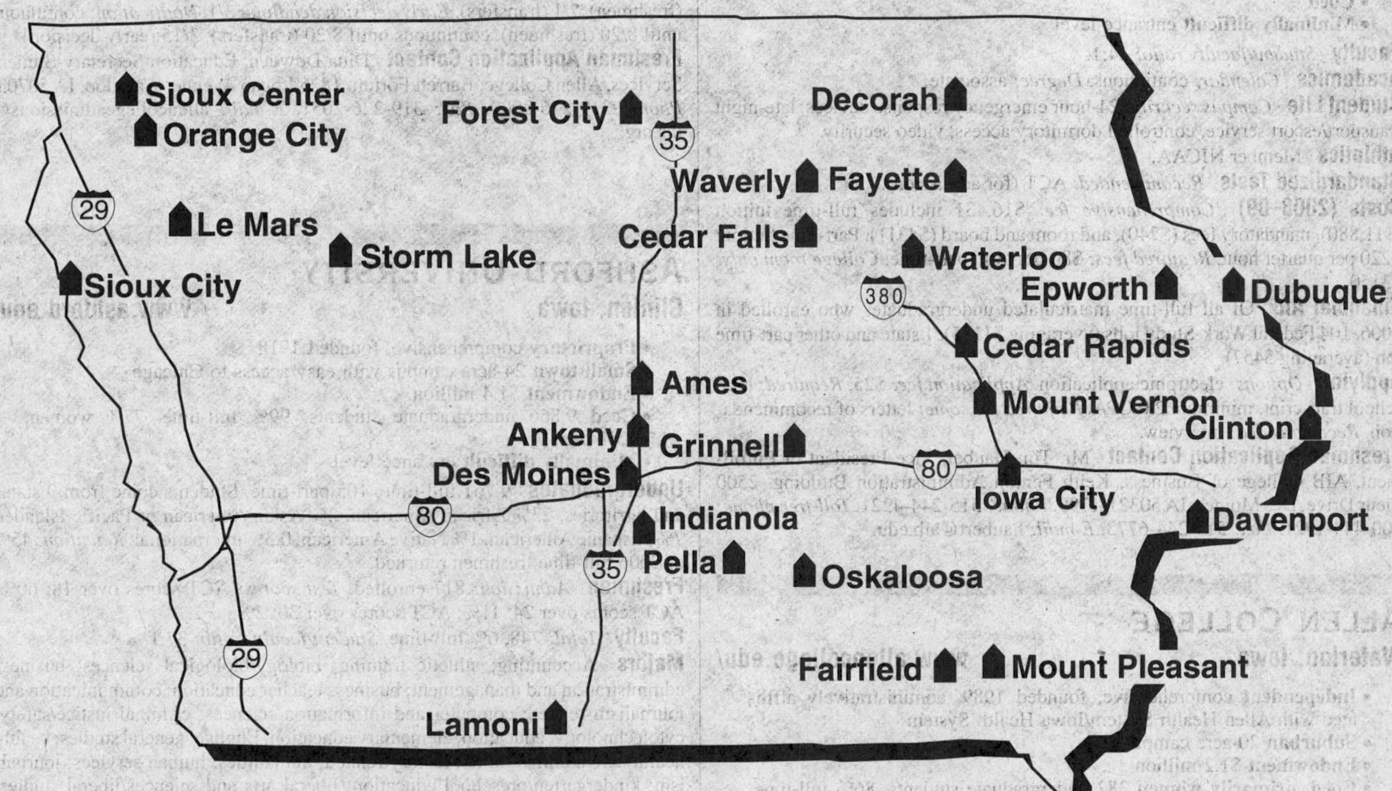

Sioux Center
Orange City
Forest City
Decorah
35
29
Waverly
Fayette
Le Mars
Storm Lake
Cedar Falls
Sioux City
Waterloo
380
Epworth
Dubuque
Cedar Rapids
Ames
Mount Vernon
Ankeny
Clinton
Grinnell
Des Moines
80
Iowa City
80
Indianola
Davenport
35
Pella
Oskaloosa
29
Fairfield
Mount Pleasant
Lamoni

AIB College of Business

Des Moines, Iowa **www.aib.edu/**

- **Independent** 4-year, founded 1921
- **Urban** 20-acre campus
- **Coed**
- **Minimally difficult** entrance level

Faculty *Student/faculty ratio:* 24:1.

Academics *Calendar:* continuous. *Degree:* associate.

Student Life *Campus security:* 24-hour emergency response devices, late-night transport/escort service, controlled dormitory access, video security.

Athletics Member NJCAA.

Standardized Tests *Recommended:* ACT (for admission).

Costs (2008–09) *Comprehensive fee:* $16,431 includes full-time tuition ($11,880), mandatory fees ($240), and room and board ($4311). Part-time tuition: $220 per quarter hour. *Required fees:* $80 per term part-time. *College room only:* $3150.

Financial Aid Of all full-time matriculated undergraduates who enrolled in 2006, 104 Federal Work-Study jobs (averaging $1135). 1 state and other part-time job (averaging $457).

Applying *Options:* electronic application. *Application fee:* $25. *Required:* high school transcript, minimum 2.0 GPA. *Required for some:* letters of recommendation. *Recommended:* interview.

Freshman Application Contact Mr. Tim Hauber, Vice President of Enrollment, AIB College of Business, Keith Fenton Administration Building, 2500 Fleur Drive, Des Moines, IA 50321-1799. *Phone:* 515-244-4221. *Toll-free phone:* 800-444-1921. *Fax:* 515-244-6773. *E-mail:* haubert@aib.edu.

Allen College

Waterloo, Iowa **www.allencollege.edu/**

- **Independent** comprehensive, founded 1989, administratively affiliated with Allen Health System/Iowa Health System
- **Suburban** 20-acre campus
- **Endowment** $1.2 million
- **Coed, primarily women** 382 undergraduate students, 86% full-time, 96% women, 4% men
- **Moderately difficult** entrance level, 76% of applicants were admitted

Undergraduates 330 full-time, 52 part-time. Students come from 9 states and territories, 6% are from out of state, 1% African American, 0.3% Asian American or Pacific Islander, 0.5% Hispanic American, 0.8% Native American, 22% transferred in, 15% live on campus. *Retention:* 94% of 2006 full-time freshmen returned.

Freshmen *Admission:* 88 applied, 67 admitted, 45 enrolled. *Average high school GPA:* 3.62. *Test scores:* ACT scores over 18: 98%; ACT scores over 24: 27%.

Faculty *Total:* 32, 84% full-time, 19% with terminal degrees. *Student/faculty ratio:* 14:1.

Majors Nursing (registered nurse training); radiologic technology/science.

Academics *Calendar:* semesters. *Degrees:* associate, bachelor's, and master's (liberal arts and general education courses offered at either University of North Iowa or Wartburg College). *Special study options:* advanced placement credit, distance learning, independent study, internships, off-campus study, part-time degree program. *ROTC:* Army (c).

Computers on Campus 26 computers/terminals are available on campus for general student use. Campuswide network is available. Wireless service is available via entire campus.

Student Life *Housing options:* coed, men-only, women-only. Campus housing is university owned and is provided by a third party. *Activities and organizations:* student-run newspaper, Allen Student Nurses' Association, Nurses' Christian Fellowship. *Campus security:* 24-hour patrols, controlled dormitory access. *Student services:* health clinic, personal/psychological counseling, women's center.

Standardized Tests *Required:* ACT (for admission).

Costs (2008–09) *Comprehensive fee:* $21,073 includes full-time tuition ($13,359), mandatory fees ($1536), and room and board ($6178). Part-time tuition: $458 per credit hour. *Required fees:* $62 per credit hour part-time. *College room only:* $3089.

Financial Aid Of all full-time matriculated undergraduates who enrolled in 2006, 303 applied for aid, 274 were judged to have need, 18 had their need fully met. 18 Federal Work-Study jobs (averaging $2500). In 2006, 12 non-need-based awards were made. *Average percent of need met:* 51%. *Average financial aid package:* $7827. *Average need-based loan:* $3793. *Average need-based gift aid:* $5214. *Average non-need-based aid:* $589. *Average indebtedness upon graduation:* $20,612.

Applying *Options:* electronic application. *Application fee:* $50. *Required:* essay or personal statement, high school transcript, 1 letter of recommendation. *Required for some:* interview. *Recommended:* minimum 2.7 GPA, rank in upper 50% of high school class, minimum ACT score of 20. *Application deadlines:* 7/1 (freshmen), 7/1 (transfers). *Early decision deadline:* 3/1. *Notification:* continuous until 8/20 (freshmen), continuous until 8/20 (transfers), 3/15 (early decision).

Freshman Application Contact Dina Dowden, Education Secretary-Student Services, Allen College, Barrett Forum, 1825 Logan Avenue, Waterloo, IA 50703. *Phone:* 319-226-2000. *Fax:* 319-226-2051. *E-mail:* allencollegeadmissions@ihs.org.

Ashford University

Clinton, Iowa **www.ashford.edu/**

- **Proprietary** comprehensive, founded 1918
- **Small-town** 24-acre campus with easy access to Chicago
- **Endowment** $1.4 million
- **Coed** 9,866 undergraduate students, 99% full-time, 77% women, 23% men
- **Minimally difficult** entrance level

Undergraduates 9,761 full-time, 105 part-time. Students come from 9 states and territories, 23% African American, 2% Asian American or Pacific Islander, 7% Hispanic American, 1% Native American, 0.3% international. *Retention:* 45% of 2006 full-time freshmen returned.

Freshmen *Admission:* 817 enrolled. *Test scores:* ACT scores over 18: 60%; ACT scores over 24: 11%; ACT scores over 30: 2%.

Faculty *Total:* 748, 6% full-time. *Student/faculty ratio:* 37:1.

Majors Accounting; athletic training; biology/biological sciences; business administration and management; business teacher education; communication and journalism related; computer and information sciences; criminal justice/safety; cytotechnology; education; elementary education; English; general studies; health/health care administration; history related; humanities; human services; journalism; kindergarten/preschool education; liberal arts and sciences/liberal studies; middle school education; multi-/interdisciplinary studies related; music; music teacher education; pre-law studies; pre-medical studies; psychology; religious studies; science teacher education; secondary education; social sciences; visual and performing arts.

Academics *Calendar:* semesters. *Degrees:* bachelor's and master's. *Special study options:* academic remediation for entering students, advanced placement credit, distance learning, double majors, external degree program, freshman honors college, honors programs, independent study, internships, part-time degree program, summer session for credit.

Computers on Campus 109 computers/terminals are available on campus for general student use. Students can access the following: online (class) registration, wireless/laptop campus.

Student Life *Housing:* on-campus residence required through junior year. *Options:* coed. Campus housing is university owned. Freshman campus housing is guaranteed. *Activities and organizations:* drama/theater group, student-run newspaper, choral group, Student Senate, Student Ambassadors, Hall Council, Black Student Union, Student Iowa State Education Association. *Campus security:* 24-hour emergency response devices and patrols, student patrols, late-night transport/escort service, controlled dormitory access, self-defense education, lighted pathways. *Student services:* health clinic, personal/psychological counseling.

Athletics Member NAIA. *Intercollegiate sports:* baseball M (s), basketball M (s)/W (s), cross-country running M (s)/W (s), golf M (s)/W (s), soccer M (s)/W (s), softball W (s), track and field M (s)/W (s), volleyball W (s). *Intramural sports:* football M/W, skiing (downhill) M/W, volleyball M/W.

Standardized Tests *Required for some:* SAT or ACT (for admission).

Costs (2007–08) *Comprehensive fee:* $21,780 includes full-time tuition ($15,430), mandatory fees ($550), and room and board ($5800). Part-time tuition: $447 per credit hour. *Required fees:* $6 per credit hour part-time. *College room only:* $2500.

Applying *Options:* electronic application, early admission, deferred entrance. *Application fee:* $20. *Required:* high school transcript. *Required for some:* letters of recommendation, interview. *Recommended:* minimum 2.0 GPA, interview. *Application deadlines:* rolling (freshmen), rolling (transfers). *Notification:* continuous (freshmen), continuous (transfers).

Director of Admissions Ms. Waunita M. Sullivan, Director of Enrollment, Ashford University, 400 North Bluff Boulevard, PO Box 2967, Clinton, IA 52733-2967. *Phone:* 563-242-4023 Ext. 3401. *Toll-free phone:* 800-242-4153. *E-mail:* admissns@tfu.edu.

BRIAR CLIFF UNIVERSITY

Sioux City, Iowa **www.briarcliff.edu/**

- **Independent Roman Catholic** comprehensive, founded 1930
- **Suburban** 75-acre campus
- **Endowment** $7.8 million
- **Coed**
- **Moderately difficult** entrance level

Briar Cliff University is ranked among the "Best Midwestern Comprehensive Colleges" by *U.S. News & World Report.* Briar Cliff is a community committed to higher education within a liberal arts and Catholic perspective. A student-centered Catholic Franciscan university, Briar Cliff shapes lives. For more information, students should access the Web at http://www.bcuinspired.com/ or http://www.briarcliff.edu or visit the scenic hilltop campus at 3303 Rebecca Street in Sioux City, Iowa.

Faculty *Student/faculty ratio:* 14:1.

Academics *Calendar:* (3 10-week terms plus 2 5-week summer sessions). *Degrees:* associate, bachelor's, and master's.

Student Life *Campus security:* 24-hour emergency response devices and patrols, student patrols, late-night transport/escort service, controlled dormitory access.

Athletics Member NAIA.

Standardized Tests *Required:* SAT or ACT (for admission).

Costs (2007–08) *Comprehensive fee:* $25,983 includes full-time tuition ($19,446), mandatory fees ($549), and room and board ($5988). Part-time tuition: $648 per hour. Part-time tuition and fees vary according to class time and course load. *Required fees:* $18 per hour part-time. *College room only:* $3018. Room and board charges vary according to board plan and housing facility. *Payment plans:* installment, deferred payment.

Financial Aid Of all full-time matriculated undergraduates who enrolled in 2002, 688 applied for aid, 527 were judged to have need, 511 had their need fully met. In 2002, 678 non-need-based awards were made. *Average percent of need met:* 91. *Average financial aid package:* $15,950. *Average need-based loan:* $4775. *Average need-based gift aid:* $4625. *Average non-need-based aid:* $2675. *Average indebtedness upon graduation:* $18,900. *Financial aid deadline:* 3/15.

Applying *Options:* electronic application, early admission, deferred entrance. *Application fee:* $20. *Required:* high school transcript, minimum 2.0 GPA, minimum ACT score of 18. *Required for some:* essay or personal statement, 3 letters of recommendation, interview.

Freshman Application Contact Briar Cliff Admissions, Briar Cliff University, 3303 Rebecca Street, Sioux City, IA 51104. *Phone:* 712-279-5200. *Toll-free phone:* 800-662-3303 Ext. 5200. *Fax:* 712-279-1632. *E-mail:* admissino@briarcliff.edu.

BUENA VISTA UNIVERSITY

Storm Lake, Iowa **www.bvu.edu/**

- **Independent** comprehensive, founded 1891, affiliated with Presbyterian Church (U.S.A.)
- **Small-town** 60-acre campus
- **Endowment** $155.6 million
- **Coed**
- **Moderately difficult** entrance level

Faculty *Student/faculty ratio:* 11:1.

Academics *Calendar:* 4-1-4. *Degrees:* bachelor's and master's.

Student Life *Campus security:* 24-hour emergency response devices, late-night transport/escort service, controlled dormitory access, night security patrols.

Athletics Member NCAA. All Division III.

Standardized Tests *Required:* SAT or ACT (for admission).

Costs (2007–08) *Comprehensive fee:* $30,554 includes full-time tuition ($23,842) and room and board ($6712). Part-time tuition: $801 per semester hour. *Room and board:* Room and board charges vary according to board plan.

Financial Aid Of all full-time matriculated undergraduates who enrolled in 2007, 972 applied for aid, 924 were judged to have need, 452 had their need fully met. 521 Federal Work-Study jobs (averaging $1124). 142 state and other part-time jobs (averaging $995). In 2007, 58 non-need-based awards were made. *Average percent of need met:* 89. *Average financial aid package:* $32,132. *Average need-based loan:* $5074. *Average need-based gift aid:* $8922. *Average non-need-based aid:* $10,645. *Average indebtedness upon graduation:* $31,771.

Applying *Options:* electronic application, deferred entrance. *Required:* high school transcript, letters of recommendation. *Required for some:* essay or personal statement, interview. *Recommended:* minimum 3.0 GPA.

Freshman Application Contact Alan Coheley, Vice President for Enrollment Management, Buena Vista University, 610 West Fourth Street, Storm Lake, IA 50588. *Phone:* 712-749-2235. *Toll-free phone:* 800-383-9600. *E-mail:* admissions@bvu.edu.

CENTRAL COLLEGE

Pella, Iowa **www.central.edu/**

- **Independent** 4-year, founded 1853, affiliated with Reformed Church in America
- **Small-town** 133-acre campus with easy access to Des Moines
- **Endowment** $83.0 million
- **Coed** 1,605 undergraduate students, 97% full-time, 54% women, 46% men
- **Moderately difficult** entrance level, 79% of applicants were admitted

Undergraduates 1,552 full-time, 53 part-time. Students come from 38 states and territories, 15 other countries, 21% are from out of state, 1% African American, 0.9% Asian American or Pacific Islander, 2% Hispanic American, 0.2% Native American, 2% international, 2% transferred in, 86% live on campus. *Retention:* 82% of 2006 full-time freshmen returned.

Freshmen *Admission:* 1,919 applied, 1,522 admitted, 424 enrolled. *Average high school GPA:* 3.46. *Test scores:* SAT critical reading scores over 500: 51%; SAT math scores over 500: 60%; ACT scores over 18: 97%; SAT critical reading scores over 600: 18%; SAT math scores over 600: 20%; ACT scores over 24: 53%; SAT critical reading scores over 700: 1%; SAT math scores over 700: 1%; ACT scores over 30: 7%.

Faculty *Total:* 141, 70% full-time, 70% with terminal degrees. *Student/faculty ratio:* 13:1.

Majors Accounting; art; biology/biological sciences; business administration and management; chemistry; communication/speech communication and rhetoric; computer science; dramatic/theater arts; economics; elementary education; English; environmental studies; French; general studies; German studies; history; information science/studies; interdisciplinary studies; international business/trade/commerce; international/global studies; kinesiology and exercise science; linguistics; mathematics; mathematics and computer science; music; music teacher education; natural sciences; philosophy; physics; political science and government; psychology; religious studies; social sciences; sociology; Spanish.

Academics *Calendar:* semesters. *Degree:* bachelor's. *Special study options:* double majors, English as a second language, honors programs, independent study, internships, off-campus study, part-time degree program, services for LD students, student-designed majors, study abroad, summer session for credit. *Unusual degree programs:* 3-2 engineering with Washington University in St. Louis, Iowa State University of Science and Technology, The University of Iowa.

Computers on Campus 400 computers/terminals and 1,600 ports are available on campus for general student use. Students can access the following: campus intranet, computer help desk, free student e-mail accounts, online (class) grades, online (class) registration, online (class) schedules, student academic records and data. Campuswide network is available. 100% of college-owned or -operated housing units are wired for high-speed Internet access. Wireless service is available via classrooms, learning centers, libraries, student centers.

Student Life *Housing:* on-campus residence required through senior year. *Options:* coed, men-only, women-only, disabled students. Campus housing is university owned. Freshman campus housing is guaranteed. *Activities and organizations:* drama/theater group, student-run newspaper, radio station, choral group, Students Concerned About the Environment, Inter-Varsity, FCA, Coalition for Multicultural Campus, Student Senate. *Campus security:* 24-hour emergency response devices, student patrols, late-night transport/escort service, controlled dormitory access. *Student services:* health clinic, personal/psychological counseling.

Athletics Member NCAA. All Division III. *Intercollegiate sports:* baseball M, basketball M/W, cross-country running M/W, football M, golf M/W, soccer M/W, softball W, tennis M/W, track and field M/W, volleyball W, wrestling M. *Intramural sports:* basketball M/W, football M, racquetball M/W, rugby M, soccer M/W, softball M/W, volleyball M/W.

Standardized Tests *Required:* SAT or ACT (for admission).

Costs (2008–09) *Comprehensive fee:* $31,950 includes full-time tuition ($23,564), mandatory fees ($380), and room and board ($8006). Part-time tuition: $882 per semester hour. *College room only:* $3926.

Financial Aid Of all full-time matriculated undergraduates who enrolled in 2007, 1,267 applied for aid, 1,128 were judged to have need, 214 had their need fully met. 769 Federal Work-Study jobs (averaging $1131). 392 state and other part-time jobs (averaging $1214). In 2007, 292 non-need-based awards were made. *Average percent of need met:* 82%. *Average financial aid package:* $18,863. *Average need-based loan:* $4227. *Average need-based gift aid:* $13,604. *Average non-need-based aid:* $9112. *Average indebtedness upon graduation:* $31,453.

Applying *Options:* electronic application, deferred entrance. *Application fee:* $25. *Required:* high school transcript. *Required for some:* essay or personal statement, 3 letters of recommendation, interview. *Recommended:* minimum 2.5 GPA, interview. *Application deadlines:* rolling (freshmen), rolling (transfers). *Notification:* continuous (transfers).

Freshman Application Contact Ms. Carol Williamson, Dean of Admission and Student Enrollment Services, Central College, 812 University Street, Pella, IA 50219-1999. *Phone:* 641-628-7600. *Toll-free phone:* 877-462-3687 (in-state); 877-462-3689 (out-of-state). *Fax:* 641-628-5316. *E-mail:* admissions@central.edu.

CLARKE COLLEGE

Dubuque, Iowa **www.clarke.edu/**

- **Independent Roman Catholic** comprehensive, founded 1843
- **Urban** 55-acre campus
- **Endowment** $18.5 million
- **Coed** 1,022 undergraduate students, 87% full-time, 71% women, 29% men
- **Moderately difficult** entrance level, 62% of applicants were admitted

Undergraduates 885 full-time, 137 part-time. Students come from 23 states and territories, 5 other countries, 38% are from out of state, 2% African American, 0.5% Asian American or Pacific Islander, 2% Hispanic American, 0.2% Native American, 0.7% international, 9% transferred in, 60% live on campus. *Retention:* 70% of 2006 full-time freshmen returned.

Freshmen *Admission:* 1,020 applied, 636 admitted, 188 enrolled. *Average high school GPA:* 3.73. *Test scores:* SAT critical reading scores over 500: 60%; SAT math scores over 500: 80%; SAT writing scores over 500: 80%; ACT scores over 18: 100%; SAT critical reading scores over 600: 20%; SAT math scores over 600: 10%; SAT writing scores over 600: 20%; ACT scores over 24: 42%; ACT scores over 30: 16%.

Faculty *Total:* 140, 53% full-time, 33% with terminal degrees. *Student/faculty ratio:* 11:1.

Majors Accounting; advertising; art; art history, criticism and conservation; art teacher education; athletic training; biology/biological sciences; business administration and management; chemistry; computer science; dramatic/theater arts; economics; education; elementary education; English; fine/studio arts; French; history; information science/studies; international business/trade/commerce; kindergarten/preschool education; liberal arts and sciences/liberal studies; management information systems; marketing/marketing management; mass communication/media; mathematics; middle school education; music; music teacher education; nursing science; philosophy; physical education teaching and coaching; physical therapy; psychology; public relations/image management; religious studies; secondary education; social work; Spanish; special education; sport and fitness administration/management; voice and opera.

Academics *Calendar:* semesters. *Degrees:* associate, bachelor's, and master's. *Special study options:* accelerated degree program, adult/continuing education programs, advanced placement credit, cooperative education, distance learning, double majors, English as a second language, honors programs, independent study, internships, off-campus study, part-time degree program, student-designed majors, study abroad, summer session for credit. *ROTC:* Army (c).

Computers on Campus 237 computers/terminals are available on campus for general student use. Students can access the following: campus intranet, free student e-mail accounts, online (class) grades, online (class) registration, online (class) schedules. Campuswide network is available. Wireless service is available via learning centers, libraries, student centers.

Student Life *Housing:* on-campus residence required through junior year. *Options:* coed, men-only, women-only. Campus housing is university owned. Freshman campus housing is guaranteed. *Activities and organizations:* drama/theater group, student-run newspaper, radio station, choral group, Admissions Student Team, Student Multicultural Organization, concert choir, campus ministry, student government. *Campus security:* 24-hour emergency response devices and patrols, late-night transport/escort service, controlled dormitory access. *Student services:* health clinic, personal/psychological counseling.

Athletics Member NAIA. *Intercollegiate sports:* baseball M, basketball M/W, cross-country running M/W, golf M/W, soccer M/W, softball W, tennis M/W, volleyball M/W. *Intramural sports:* badminton M/W, basketball M/W, bowling M/W, football M/W, golf M/W, racquetball M/W, skiing (cross-country) M/W, skiing (downhill) M/W, softball M/W, swimming and diving M/W, table tennis M/W, tennis M/W, track and field M/W, volleyball M/W, water polo M/W, weight lifting M/W.

Standardized Tests *Required:* SAT or ACT (for admission).

Costs (2007–08) *Comprehensive fee:* $27,886 includes full-time tuition ($20,666), mandatory fees ($646), and room and board ($6574). Part-time tuition: $523 per credit hour. *College room only:* $3198. Room and board charges vary according to board plan and housing facility. *Payment plans:* installment, deferred payment. *Waivers:* children of alumni, adult students, senior citizens, and employees or children of employees.

Financial Aid Of all full-time matriculated undergraduates who enrolled in 2006, 825 applied for aid, 746 were judged to have need, 159 had their need fully met. 265 Federal Work-Study jobs (averaging $1276). In 2006, 77 non-need-based awards were made. *Average percent of need met:* 85%. *Average financial aid package:* $18,369. *Average need-based loan:* $4866. *Average need-based gift aid:* $13,953. *Average non-need-based aid:* $13,497. *Average indebtedness upon graduation:* $29,638.

Applying *Options:* electronic application, deferred entrance. *Application fee:* $25. *Required:* high school transcript, minimum 2.0 GPA, rank in upper 50% of high school class, minimum ACT score of 21 or SAT score of 1000. *Required for some:* interview. *Application deadlines:* rolling (freshmen), rolling (transfers). *Notification:* continuous until 7/15 (freshmen), continuous until 8/15 (transfers).

Freshman Application Contact Mr. Andy Shroeder, Director of Admissions, Clarke College, 1550 Clarke Drive, Dubuque, IA 52001-3198. *Phone:* 563-588-6316. *Toll-free phone:* 800-383-2345. *Fax:* 563-588-6789. *E-mail:* admissions@clarke.edu.

COE COLLEGE

Cedar Rapids, Iowa **www.coe.edu/**

- **Independent** comprehensive, founded 1851, affiliated with Presbyterian Church
- **Urban** 53-acre campus
- **Endowment** $76.8 million
- **Coed**
- **Moderately difficult** entrance level

Faculty *Student/faculty ratio:* 10:1.

Academics *Calendar:* 4-4-1. *Degrees:* bachelor's and master's.

Student Life *Campus security:* 24-hour emergency response devices and patrols, late-night transport/escort service, controlled dormitory access.

Athletics Member NCAA. All Division III.

Standardized Tests *Required:* SAT or ACT (for admission).

Costs (2007–08) *Comprehensive fee:* $32,990 includes full-time tuition ($26,100), mandatory fees ($290), and room and board ($6600). Part-time tuition: $3300 per course. *College room only:* $2990.

Financial Aid Of all full-time matriculated undergraduates who enrolled in 2007, 1,054 applied for aid, 950 were judged to have need, 279 had their need fully met. 331 Federal Work-Study jobs (averaging $1400). 188 state and other part-time jobs (averaging $1400). In 2007, 268 non-need-based awards were made. *Average percent of need met:* 94. *Average financial aid package:* $23,422. *Average need-based loan:* $7261. *Average need-based gift aid:* $15,899. *Average non-need-based aid:* $13,722. *Average indebtedness upon graduation:* $29,710.

Applying *Options:* electronic application, early admission, early action, deferred entrance. *Application fee:* $30. *Required:* essay or personal statement, high school transcript, 1 letter of recommendation. *Recommended:* minimum 3.0 GPA, interview.

Freshman Application Contact Mr. John Grundig, Dean of Admission, Coe College, 1220 1st Avenue, NE, Cedar Rapids, IA 52402-5070. *Phone:* 319-399-8500. *Toll-free phone:* 877-225-5263. *Fax:* 319-399-8816. *E-mail:* admission@coe.edu.

CORNELL COLLEGE

Mount Vernon, Iowa **www.cornellcollege.edu/**

- **Independent Methodist** 4-year, founded 1853
- **Small-town** 129-acre campus
- **Endowment** $77.6 million
- **Coed** 1,083 undergraduate students, 99% full-time, 51% women, 49% men
- **Moderately difficult** entrance level, 45% of applicants were admitted

Undergraduates 1,067 full-time, 16 part-time. Students come from 46 states and territories, 20 other countries, 71% are from out of state, 3% African American, 2% Asian American or Pacific Islander, 3% Hispanic American, 0.6% Native American, 3% international, 4% transferred in, 91% live on campus. *Retention:* 85% of 2006 full-time freshmen returned.

Freshmen *Admission:* 2,659 applied, 1,209 admitted, 316 enrolled. *Average high school GPA:* 3.44. *Test scores:* SAT critical reading scores over 500: 87%; SAT math scores over 500: 86%; ACT scores over 18: 100%; SAT critical reading scores over 600: 51%; SAT math scores over 600: 46%; ACT scores over 24: 77%; SAT critical reading scores over 700: 18%; SAT math scores over 700: 10%; ACT scores over 30: 20%.

Faculty *Total:* 97, 86% full-time, 91% with terminal degrees. *Student/faculty ratio:* 11:1.

Majors Anthropology; architecture; art; art history, criticism and conservation; biochemistry; biology/biological sciences; chemistry; classics and languages, literatures and linguistics; computer science; cultural studies; dramatic/theater arts; economics; elementary education; English; environmental studies; ethnic, cultural minority, and gender studies related; French; geology/earth science; German; health and physical education related; history; interdisciplinary studies; international business/trade/commerce; international relations and affairs; Latin; Latin American studies; liberal arts and sciences/liberal studies; mathematics; medieval and Renaissance studies; modern Greek; modern languages; multi-/interdisciplinary studies related; music; music teacher education; philosophy; physical education teaching and coaching; physics; political science and government; psychology; religious studies; Russian; secondary education; sociology; Spanish; speech and rhetoric; women's studies.

Academics *Calendar:* 9 3½-week terms. *Degree:* bachelor's. *Special study options:* advanced placement credit, double majors, English as a second language, independent study, internships, off-campus study, services for LD students, student-designed majors, study abroad. *Unusual degree programs:* 3-2 engineering with Washington University in St. Louis; forestry with Duke University; environmental management with Duke University, architecture with Washington University in St. Louis.

Computers on Campus 176 computers/terminals are available on campus for general student use. Students can access the following: campus intranet, computer help desk, free student e-mail accounts, online (class) grades, online (class) schedules. Campuswide network is available. 100% of college-owned or -operated housing units are wired for high-speed Internet access. Wireless service is available via classrooms, computer centers, computer labs, learning centers, libraries, student centers.

Student Life *Housing:* on-campus residence required through senior year. *Options:* coed, men-only, women-only. Campus housing is university owned. Freshman campus housing is guaranteed. *Activities and organizations:* drama/theater group, student-run newspaper, radio station, choral group, social groups, Student-initiated Living-learning Community, Lunch Buddies/Youth Mentoring, Chess and Games Club, PAAC (Performing Arts and Activities Council). *Campus security:* 24-hour emergency response devices and patrols. *Student services:* health clinic, personal/psychological counseling, women's center.

Athletics Member NCAA. All Division III. *Intercollegiate sports:* baseball M, basketball M/W, cross-country running M/W, football M, golf M/W, soccer M/W, softball W, tennis M/W, track and field M/W, volleyball M (c)/W, wrestling M. *Intramural sports:* badminton M/W, basketball M/W, bowling M/W, cheerleading M/W, cross-country running M/W, fencing M/W, football M, golf M/W, racquetball M/W, soccer M/W, softball M/W, table tennis M/W, tennis M/W, track and field M/W, ultimate Frisbee M/W, volleyball M/W, weight lifting M/W, wrestling M/W.

Standardized Tests *Required:* SAT or ACT (for admission). *Recommended:* SAT Subject Tests (for admission).

Costs (2007–08) *Comprehensive fee:* $33,250 includes full-time tuition ($26,100), mandatory fees ($180), and room and board ($6970). Part-time tuition: $816 per credit hour. Part-time tuition and fees vary according to course load and reciprocity agreements. *College room only:* $3250. Room and board charges vary according to board plan and housing facility. *Payment plan:* deferred payment. *Waivers:* employees or children of employees.

Financial Aid Of all full-time matriculated undergraduates who enrolled in 2006, 899 applied for aid, 800 were judged to have need, 362 had their need fully met. 370 Federal Work-Study jobs (averaging $850). 264 state and other part-time jobs (averaging $800). In 2006, 257 non-need-based awards were made. *Average percent of need met:* 91%. *Average financial aid package:* $21,500. *Average need-based loan:* $3505. *Average need-based gift aid:* $16,900. *Average non-need-based aid:* $11,345. *Average indebtedness upon graduation:* $24,622. *Financial aid deadline:* 3/1.

Applying *Options:* electronic application, early admission, early decision, early action, deferred entrance. *Application fee:* $30. *Required:* essay or personal statement, high school transcript, 1 letter of recommendation. *Recommended:* minimum 2.8 GPA, interview. *Application deadlines:* 3/1 (freshmen), 3/1 (transfers), 12/1 (early action). *Early decision deadline:* 11/1. *Notification:* continuous (freshmen), continuous (transfers), 1/15 (early decision), 5/1 (early action).

Freshman Application Contact Todd White, Director of Admissions, Cornell College, 600 First Street West, Mount Vernon, IA 52314-1098. *Phone:* 319-895-4167. *Toll-free phone:* 800-747-1112. *Fax:* 319-895-4451. *E-mail:* twhite@cornellcollege.edu.

See page 968 for the College Close-Up.

DIVINE WORD COLLEGE

Epworth, Iowa **www.dwci.edu/**

Director of Admissions Vice President of Recruitment/Director of Admissions, Divine Word College, 102 Jacoby Drive SW, Epworth, IA 52045-0380. *Phone:* 563-876-3332. *Toll-free phone:* 800-553-3321. *Fax:* 563-876-5515. *E-mail:* svdalum@mwci.net.

DORDT COLLEGE

Sioux Center, Iowa **www.dordt.edu/**

- **Independent Christian Reformed** comprehensive, founded 1955
- **Small-town** 100-acre campus
- **Endowment** $28.0 million
- **Coed** 1,312 undergraduate students, 95% full-time, 49% women, 51% men
- **Moderately difficult** entrance level, 88% of applicants were admitted

Undergraduates 1,241 full-time, 71 part-time. Students come from 38 states and territories, 12 other countries, 63% are from out of state, 0.4% African American, 0.5% Asian American or Pacific Islander, 0.8% Hispanic American, 17% international, 4% transferred in, 90% live on campus. *Retention:* 85% of 2006 full-time freshmen returned.

Freshmen *Admission:* 905 applied, 794 admitted, 382 enrolled. *Average high school GPA:* 3.48. *Test scores:* SAT critical reading scores over 500: 71%; SAT math scores over 500: 75%; SAT writing scores over 500: 63%; ACT scores over 18: 96%; SAT critical reading scores over 600: 38%; SAT math scores over 600: 42%; SAT writing scores over 600: 31%; ACT scores over 24: 54%; SAT critical reading scores over 700: 12%; SAT math scores over 700: 7%; SAT writing scores over 700: 5%; ACT scores over 30: 13%.

Faculty *Total:* 95, 74% full-time, 79% with terminal degrees. *Student/faculty ratio:* 15:1.

Majors Accounting; administrative assistant and secretarial science; agricultural/biological engineering and bioengineering; agricultural teacher education; agriculture; animal/livestock husbandry and production; animal sciences; biology/biological sciences; biology teacher education; business administration and management; business teacher education; chemistry; chemistry teacher education; civil engineering; clinical laboratory science/medical technology; commercial and advertising art; computer engineering; computer/information technology services administration related; computer programming; computer science; computer teacher education; criminal justice/law enforcement administration; data processing and data processing technology; drama and dance teacher education; dramatic/theater arts; education; educational system administration and superintendency; education (K-12); electrical, electronics and communications engineering; elementary education; engineering; engineering mechanics; engineering technology; English; environmental studies; general studies; German; graphic design; health and physical education; history; history teacher education; journalism; kinesiology and exercise science; legal administrative assistant/secretary; management information systems; mass communication/media; mathematics; mechanical engineering; missionary studies and missiology; music; music performance; music teacher education; natural sciences; nursing (registered nurse training); parks, recreation and leisure; philosophy; physical education teaching and coaching; physics; piano and organ; political science and government; pre-dentistry studies; pre-law studies; pre-medical studies; pre-nursing studies; pre-pharmacy studies; pre-veterinary studies; psychology; reading teacher education; religious studies; science teacher education; secondary education; social sciences; social science teacher education; social studies teacher education; social work; sociology; Spanish; Spanish language teacher education; speech teacher education; system administration; teacher assistant/aide; theology; voice and opera; youth ministry.

Academics *Calendar:* semesters. *Degrees:* associate, bachelor's, and master's. *Special study options:* academic remediation for entering students, advanced placement credit, distance learning, double majors, English as a second language, honors programs, independent study, internships, off-campus study, part-time degree program, services for LD students, student-designed majors, study abroad.

Computers on Campus 200 computers/terminals are available on campus for general student use. Students can access the following: campus intranet, computer help desk, free student e-mail accounts, online (class) grades, online (class) registration, online (class) schedules. Campuswide network is available. 100% of college-owned or -operated housing units are wired for high-speed Internet access. Wireless service is available via entire campus.

Student Life *Housing:* on-campus residence required through senior year. *Options:* men-only, women-only, disabled students. Campus housing is university owned. Freshman campus housing is guaranteed. *Activities and organizations:* drama/theater group, student-run newspaper, radio station, choral group, PLIA, Future Teachers, Ag Club, Lacrosse Club, Defenders of Life. *Campus security:* 24-hour emergency response devices, student patrols, late-night transport/escort service, controlled dormitory access. *Student services:* health clinic, personal/psychological counseling.

Athletics Member NAIA. *Intercollegiate sports:* baseball M (s), basketball M (s)/W (s), cross-country running M (s)/W (s), football M (s), golf M (s), ice hockey M (s), lacrosse M, soccer M (s)/W (s), softball W (s), tennis M (s)/W (s), track and field M (s)/W (s), volleyball W (s). *Intramural sports:* basketball M/W, bowling M/W, field hockey M/W, gymnastics M/W, ice hockey M, lacrosse M, racquetball M/W, skiing (cross-country) M/W, soccer M/W, softball M/W, swimming and diving M/W, table tennis M/W, tennis M/W, track and field M/W, volleyball M/W, weight lifting M/W.

Standardized Tests *Required:* SAT or ACT (for admission).

Costs (2007–08) *Comprehensive fee:* $25,360 includes full-time tuition ($19,600), mandatory fees ($300), and room and board ($5460). Full-time tuition and fees vary according to course load. Part-time tuition: $820 per semester hour. *Required fees:* $150 per term part-time. *College room only:* $2880. Room and board charges vary according to board plan and housing facility. *Payment plan:* installment. *Waivers:* senior citizens and employees or children of employees.

Financial Aid Of all full-time matriculated undergraduates who enrolled in 2007, 1,075 applied for aid, 947 were judged to have need, 128 had their need fully met. 555 Federal Work-Study jobs (averaging $1500). 534 state and other part-time jobs (averaging $1500). In 2007, 242 non-need-based awards were made. *Average percent of need met:* 85%. *Average financial aid package:* $17,473. *Average need-based loan:* $5198. *Average need-based gift aid:* $9499. *Average non-need-based aid:* $9568. *Average indebtedness upon graduation:* $18,120.

Applying *Options:* electronic application, deferred entrance. *Application fee:* $25. *Required:* high school transcript, minimum 2.25 GPA, minimum ACT composite score of 19. *Required for some:* essay or personal statement, interview. *Application deadline:* 8/1 (transfers). *Notification:* continuous until 8/1 (freshmen), continuous until 9/1 (transfers).

Freshman Application Contact Mr. Quentin Van Essen, Executive Director of Admissions, Dordt College, 498 4th Avenue, NE, Sioux Center, IA 51250-1697. *Phone:* 712-722-6080. *Toll-free phone:* 800-343-6738. *Fax:* 712-722-1967. *E-mail:* admissions@dordt.edu.

See page 970 for the College Close-Up.

DRAKE UNIVERSITY

Des Moines, Iowa **www.drake.edu/**

- **Independent** university, founded 1881
- **Suburban** 120-acre campus
- **Endowment** $131.5 million
- **Coed** 3,441 undergraduate students, 93% full-time, 57% women, 43% men
- **Moderately difficult** entrance level, 78% of applicants were admitted

Undergraduates 3,202 full-time, 239 part-time. Students come from 46 states and territories, 62 other countries, 60% are from out of state, 3% African American, 5% Asian American or Pacific Islander, 2% Hispanic American, 0.1% Native American, 8% international, 5% transferred in, 67% live on campus. *Retention:* 86% of 2006 full-time freshmen returned.

Freshmen *Admission:* 4,712 applied, 3,692 admitted, 924 enrolled. *Average high school GPA:* 3.62. *Test scores:* SAT critical reading scores over 500: 84%; SAT math scores over 500: 89%; ACT scores over 18: 100%; SAT critical reading scores over 600: 37%; SAT math scores over 600: 52%; ACT scores over 24: 77%; SAT critical reading scores over 700: 8%; SAT math scores over 700: 15%; ACT scores over 30: 19%.

Faculty *Total:* 434, 59% full-time. *Student/faculty ratio:* 14:1.

Majors Accounting; accounting and finance; acting; actuarial science; advertising; anthropology; art; art history, criticism and conservation; astronomy; biochemistry; biology/biological sciences; broadcast journalism; business administration and management; business/commerce; chemistry; commercial and advertising art; computer science; directing and theatrical production; dramatic/theater arts; dramatic/theater arts and stagecraft related; drawing; elementary education; English; environmental science; environmental studies; ethics; finance; fine/studio arts; graphic design; history; international business/trade/commerce; international relations and affairs; jazz/jazz studies; journalism; marketing/marketing management; mass communication/media; mathematics; music; music management and merchandising; music performance; music teacher education; neuroscience; painting; pharmacy; pharmacy administration/pharmaceutics; philosophy; physics; piano and organ; political science and government; pre-dentistry studies; pre-engineering; pre-law studies; pre-medical studies; pre-veterinary studies; printmaking; psychology; public relations/image management; radio and television; radio, television, and digital communication related; religious/sacred music; religious studies; sculpture; secondary education; sociology; speech and rhetoric; voice and opera.

Academics *Calendar:* semesters. *Degrees:* bachelor's, master's, doctoral, first professional, and post-master's certificates. *Special study options:* accelerated degree program, advanced placement credit, cooperative education, distance learning, double majors, English as a second language, honors programs, independent study, internships, off-campus study, services for LD students, student-designed majors, study abroad, summer session for credit. *ROTC:* Army (b), Air Force (c). *Unusual degree programs:* 3-2 journalism and law, arts and sciences and law, accounting.

Computers on Campus 1,000 computers/terminals are available on campus for general student use. Students can access the following: campus intranet, computer help desk, free student e-mail accounts, online (class) grades, online (class) registration, online (class) schedules. Campuswide network is available. 100% of college-owned or -operated housing units are wired for high-speed Internet access. Wireless service is available via classrooms, computer centers, computer labs, dorm rooms, libraries, student centers.

Student Life *Housing:* on-campus residence required through sophomore year. *Options:* coed, disabled students. Campus housing is university owned. Freshman campus housing is guaranteed. *Activities and organizations:* drama/theater group, student-run newspaper, radio and television station, choral group, marching band, Student Activities Board, Drake Magazine, Dog Pound Pep Squad, Alpha Phi Omega Service Organization, Residence Hall Association, national fraternities, national sororities. *Campus security:* 24-hour emergency response devices and patrols, late-night transport/escort service, 24-hour desk attendants in residence halls. *Student services:* health clinic, personal/psychological counseling, legal services.

Athletics Member NCAA. All Division I except football (Division I-AA). *Intercollegiate sports:* basketball M (s)/W (s), cheerleading M (s)/W (s), crew W, cross-country running M (s)/W (s), golf M (s)/W, soccer M (s)/W (s), softball W (s), tennis M (s)/W (s), track and field M (s)/W (s), volleyball W (s). *Intramural sports:* badminton M/W, basketball M/W, football M/W, golf M/W, racquetball M/W, soccer M (c)/W, softball M/W, swimming and diving M/W, tennis M/W, volleyball M/W (c).

Standardized Tests *Required:* SAT or ACT (for admission).

Costs (2007–08) *Comprehensive fee:* $30,612 includes full-time tuition ($23,280), mandatory fees ($412), and room and board ($6920). Full-time tuition and fees vary according to class time, course load, and student level. Part-time tuition: $450 per hour. Part-time tuition and fees vary according to class time. *Required fees:* $40 per hour part-time. *College room only:* $3500. Room and board charges vary according to board plan. *Payment plan:* installment. *Waivers:* children of alumni, senior citizens, and employees or children of employees.

Financial Aid Of all full-time matriculated undergraduates who enrolled in 2006, 2,305 applied for aid, 1,886 were judged to have need, 586 had their need fully met. 1,552 Federal Work-Study jobs (averaging $1553). In 2006, 1077 non-need-based awards were made. *Average percent of need met:* 84%. *Average financial aid package:* $19,827. *Average need-based loan:* $5990. *Average need-based gift aid:* $12,373. *Average non-need-based aid:* $10,443. *Average indebtedness upon graduation:* $29,959.

Applying *Options:* electronic application, early admission, deferred entrance. *Application fee:* $25. *Required:* essay or personal statement, high school transcript. *Recommended:* interview. *Application deadlines:* 3/1 (freshmen), rolling (transfers). *Notification:* continuous (freshmen), continuous (transfers).

Freshman Application Contact Ms. Laura Linn, Director of Admission, Drake University, 2507 University Avenue, Des Moines, IA 50311. *Phone:* 515-271-3181 Ext. 3182. *Toll-free phone:* 800-44DRAKE Ext. 3181. *Fax:* 515-271-2831. *E-mail:* admission@drake.edu.

See page 972 for the College Close-Up.

EMMAUS BIBLE COLLEGE

Dubuque, Iowa **www.emmaus.edu/**

Director of Admissions Mr. Steve Schimpf, Enrollment Services Manager, Emmaus Bible College, 2570 Asbury Road, Dubuque, IA 52001. *Phone:* 563-588-8000 Ext. 1310. *Toll-free phone:* 800-397-2425.

FAITH BAPTIST BIBLE COLLEGE AND THEOLOGICAL SEMINARY

Ankeny, Iowa **www.faith.edu/**

- **Independent** comprehensive, founded 1921, affiliated with General Association of Regular Baptist Churches
- **Small-town** 52-acre campus
- **Endowment** $3.4 million
- **Coed** 326 undergraduate students, 87% full-time, 52% women, 48% men
- **Minimally difficult** entrance level, 86% of applicants were admitted

Undergraduates 285 full-time, 41 part-time. Students come from 26 states and territories, 5 other countries, 42% are from out of state, 0.6% African American, 0.6% Asian American or Pacific Islander, 2% Hispanic American, 0.3% Native American, 0.3% international, 5% transferred in, 90% live on campus. *Retention:* 78% of 2006 full-time freshmen returned.

Freshmen *Admission:* 146 applied, 126 admitted, 98 enrolled. *Average high school GPA:* 3.40. *Test scores:* SAT critical reading scores over 500: 38%; SAT math scores over 500: 50%; SAT writing scores over 500: 86%; ACT scores over 18: 88%; SAT critical reading scores over 600: 13%; SAT math scores over 600: 13%; SAT writing scores over 600: 14%; ACT scores over 24: 39%; ACT scores over 30: 6%.

Faculty *Total:* 35, 57% full-time, 57% with terminal degrees. *Student/faculty ratio:* 14:1.

Majors Administrative assistant and secretarial science; biblical studies; divinity/ministry; elementary education; English/language arts teacher education; missionary studies and missiology; music teacher education; pastoral studies/counseling; religious education; religious/sacred music.

Academics *Calendar:* semesters. *Degrees:* certificates, associate, bachelor's, master's, and first professional. *Special study options:* academic remediation for entering students, adult/continuing education programs, advanced placement credit, double majors, independent study, internships, part-time degree program, summer session for credit.

Computers on Campus 50 computers/terminals are available on campus for general student use. Students can access the following: online (class) registration. Campuswide network is available.

Student Life *Housing:* on-campus residence required through senior year. *Options:* men-only, women-only. Campus housing is university owned. Freshman campus housing is guaranteed. *Activities and organizations:* drama/theater group, choral group, Student Association, Student Missions Fellowship. *Campus security:* 24-hour emergency response devices and patrols, late-night transport/escort service. *Student services:* personal/psychological counseling.

Athletics Member NCCAA. *Intercollegiate sports:* basketball M/W, soccer M/W, ultimate Frisbee M (s)/W (s), volleyball M (s)/W (s). *Intramural sports:* basketball M/W, football M, ultimate Frisbee M/W, volleyball M/W.

Standardized Tests *Required:* SAT or ACT (for admission).

Costs (2007–08) *One-time required fee:* $50. *Comprehensive fee:* $17,716 includes full-time tuition ($12,306), mandatory fees ($400), and room and board ($5010). *College room only:* $2288.

Financial Aid Of all full-time matriculated undergraduates who enrolled in 2004, 311 applied for aid, 290 were judged to have need, 5 had their need fully met. In 2004, 21 non-need-based awards were made. *Average percent of need met:* 48%. *Average financial aid package:* $7124. *Average need-based loan:* $3142. *Average need-based gift aid:* $6299. *Average non-need-based aid:* $2465. *Average indebtedness upon graduation:* $15,006.

Applying *Options:* deferred entrance. *Application fee:* $25. *Required:* essay or personal statement, high school transcript, 2 letters of recommendation. *Required for some:* interview. *Recommended:* minimum 2.0 GPA. *Application deadlines:* 8/1 (freshmen), 8/1 (transfers). *Notification:* continuous until 9/1 (freshmen), continuous until 9/1 (transfers).

Freshman Application Contact Admissions Secretary, Faith Baptist Bible College and Theological Seminary, 1900 NW 4th Street, Ankeny, IA 50023. *Phone:* 515-964-0601. *Toll-free phone:* 888-FAITH 4U. *Fax:* 515-964-1638. *E-mail:* admissions@faith.edu.

GRACELAND UNIVERSITY

Lamoni, Iowa **www.graceland.edu/**

- **Independent Community of Christ** comprehensive, founded 1895
- **Rural** 169-acre campus with easy access to Des Moines
- **Endowment** $56.1 million
- **Coed**
- **Moderately difficult** entrance level

Faculty *Student/faculty ratio:* 15:1.

Academics *Calendar:* 4-1-4. *Degrees:* bachelor's, master's, and post-master's certificates.

Student Life *Campus security:* 24-hour emergency response devices and patrols, late-night transport/escort service, controlled dormitory access.

Athletics Member NAIA.

Standardized Tests *Required:* SAT or ACT (for admission).

Costs (2007–08) *Comprehensive fee:* $23,900 includes full-time tuition ($17,700), mandatory fees ($200), and room and board ($6000). Part-time tuition: $560 per semester hour. *College room only:* $2400.

Financial Aid Of all full-time matriculated undergraduates who enrolled in 2007, 1,018 applied for aid, 880 were judged to have need, 258 had their need fully met. 315 Federal Work-Study jobs (averaging $1783). 402 state and other part-time jobs (averaging $1504). In 2007, 335 non-need-based awards were made. *Average percent of need met:* 83. *Average financial aid package:* $16,873. *Average need-based loan:* $5412. *Average need-based gift aid:* $12,669. *Average non-need-based aid:* $10,420. *Average indebtedness upon graduation:* $26,415.

Applying *Options:* electronic application, early admission, deferred entrance. *Application fee:* $50. *Required:* high school transcript, minimum 2.5 GPA, minimum SAT score of 960 or ACT score of 21. *Required for some:* essay or personal statement, 2 letters of recommendation, interview.

Freshman Application Contact Mr. Greg Sutherland, Interim Vice President for Enrollment, and Dean of Admission, Graceland University, 1 University Place, Lamoni, IA 50140. *Phone:* 641-784-5110. *Toll-free phone:* 866-GRACELAND. *E-mail:* sutherla@graceland.edu.

See page 974 for the College Close-Up.

GRAND VIEW COLLEGE

Des Moines, Iowa **www.gvc.edu/**

- **Independent** 4-year, founded 1896, affiliated with Evangelical Lutheran Church in America
- **Urban** 25-acre campus
- **Endowment** $11.9 million
- **Coed** 1,748 undergraduate students, 77% full-time, 68% women, 32% men
- **Minimally difficult** entrance level, 98% of applicants were admitted

Undergraduates 1,345 full-time, 403 part-time. Students come from 31 states and territories, 6 other countries, 7% are from out of state, 5% African American, 3% Asian American or Pacific Islander, 2% Hispanic American, 0.2% Native American, 0.8% international, 20% transferred in, 34% live on campus. *Retention:* 67% of 2006 full-time freshmen returned.

Freshmen *Admission:* 399 applied, 390 admitted, 172 enrolled. *Average high school GPA:* 3.11. *Test scores:* SAT critical reading scores over 500: 56%; SAT math scores over 500: 44%; ACT scores over 18: 82%; ACT scores over 24: 17%; ACT scores over 30: 2%.

Faculty *Total:* 174, 51% full-time, 44% with terminal degrees. *Student/faculty ratio:* 13:1.

Majors Accounting; applied mathematics; art; biology/biological sciences; business administration and management; computer science; criminal justice/law enforcement administration; dramatic/theater arts; elementary education; English; fine/studio arts; graphic communications; graphic design; history; human services; information science/studies; journalism; liberal arts and sciences/liberal studies; management information systems; mass communication/media; music; nursing (registered nurse training); physical sciences; political science and government; pre-law studies; psychology; radio and television; religious studies; sociology.

Academics *Calendar:* semesters. *Degrees:* certificates, associate, bachelor's, and postbachelor's certificates. *Special study options:* academic remediation for entering students, accelerated degree program, adult/continuing education programs, advanced placement credit, cooperative education, distance learning, double majors, freshman honors college, honors programs, independent study, internships, off-campus study, part-time degree program, services for LD students, student-designed majors, study abroad, summer session for credit. *ROTC:*

Army (c), Air Force (c). *Unusual degree programs:* 3-2 engineering with Iowa State University; hospital administration with The University of Iowa.

Computers on Campus 256 computers/terminals are available on campus for general student use. Students can access the following: campus intranet, free student e-mail accounts, online (class) grades, online (class) schedules. Campuswide network is available. 100% of college-owned or -operated housing units are wired for high-speed Internet access. Wireless service is available via classrooms, computer labs, libraries, student centers.

Student Life *Housing:* on-campus residence required through sophomore year. *Options:* coed. Campus housing is university owned. Freshman applicants given priority for college housing. *Activities and organizations:* drama/theater group, student-run newspaper, radio and television station, choral group, Nursing Student Association, Art Club, Science Club, Education Club, Business Club. *Campus security:* 24-hour emergency response devices and patrols, late-night transport/escort service, controlled dormitory access, night security patrols. *Student services:* health clinic, personal/psychological counseling.

Athletics Member NAIA. *Intercollegiate sports:* baseball M (s), basketball M (s)/W (s), cross-country running M (s)/W (s), football M (s), golf M (s)/W (s), soccer M (s)/W (s), softball W (s), track and field M (s)/W (s), volleyball W (s). *Intramural sports:* basketball M/W, cheerleading W, football M/W, soccer M/W, table tennis M/W, ultimate Frisbee M/W, volleyball M/W.

Standardized Tests *Required:* SAT or ACT (for admission).

Costs (2008–09) *Comprehensive fee:* $24,718 includes full-time tuition ($18,234), mandatory fees ($320), and room and board ($6164). Part-time tuition: $475 per hour.

Financial Aid Of all full-time matriculated undergraduates who enrolled in 2007, 1,227 applied for aid, 1,099 were judged to have need, 325 had their need fully met. 380 Federal Work-Study jobs (averaging $1325). 1 state and other part-time job (averaging $1755). In 2007, 198 non-need-based awards were made. *Average percent of need met:* 91%. *Average financial aid package:* $18,852. *Average need-based loan:* $4325. *Average need-based gift aid:* $9566. *Average non-need-based aid:* $4926. *Average indebtedness upon graduation:* $23,624.

Applying *Options:* electronic application. *Application fee:* $35. *Required:* high school transcript. *Recommended:* minimum 2.0 GPA. *Application deadlines:* 8/15 (freshmen), 8/15 (transfers). *Notification:* continuous until 9/15 (freshmen), continuous until 9/15 (transfers).

Freshman Application Contact Ms. Diane Schaefer, Director of Admissions, Grand View College, 1200 Grandview Avenue, Des Moines, IA 50316-1599. *Phone:* 515-263-2810. *Toll-free phone:* 800-444-6083 Ext. 2810. *Fax:* 515-263-2974. *E-mail:* admissions@gvc.edu.

See page 976 for the College Close-Up.

GRINNELL COLLEGE

Grinnell, Iowa **www.grinnell.edu/**

- **Independent** 4-year, founded 1846
- **Small-town** 120-acre campus
- **Endowment** $1.7 billion
- **Coed** 1,654 undergraduate students, 98% full-time, 53% women, 47% men
- **Very difficult** entrance level, 50% of applicants were admitted

For more than fifteen years, Grinnell College has been named one of the sixteen best liberal arts colleges by *U.S. News & World Report;* it was ranked fourteenth in 2006. Grinnell has an individually advised curriculum, with no general education, core, or distribution requirements. The College has a $1.5-billion endowment and awarded more than $23 million in grants and scholarships last year.

Undergraduates 1,623 full-time, 31 part-time. Students come from 51 states and territories, 51 other countries, 88% are from out of state, 5% African American, 7% Asian American or Pacific Islander, 5% Hispanic American, 0.4% Native American, 11% international, 1% transferred in, 86% live on campus. *Retention:* 94% of 2006 full-time freshmen returned.

Freshmen *Admission:* 3,077 applied, 1,534 admitted, 426 enrolled. *Test scores:* SAT critical reading scores over 500: 94%; SAT math scores over 500: 96%; ACT scores over 18: 100%; SAT critical reading scores over 600: 81%; SAT math scores over 600: 83%; ACT scores over 24: 95%; SAT critical reading scores over 700: 46%; SAT math scores over 700: 37%; ACT scores over 30: 66%.

Faculty *Total:* 198, 83% full-time, 86% with terminal degrees. *Student/faculty ratio:* 9:1.

Majors Anthropology; art; biochemistry; biology/biological sciences; chemistry; Chinese; classics and languages, literatures and linguistics; computer science; dramatic/theater arts; English; French; German; history; interdisciplinary studies; mathematics; music; philosophy; physics; political science and government; psychology; religious studies; Russian; sociology; Spanish.

Academics *Calendar:* semesters. *Degree:* bachelor's. *Special study options:* accelerated degree program, advanced placement credit, double majors, independent study, internships, off-campus study, services for LD students, student-designed majors, study abroad. *Unusual degree programs:* 3-2 engineering with Columbia University, California Institute of Technology, Rensselaer Polytechnic Institute, Washington University in St. Louis; architecture with Washington University in St. Louis, law at Columbia University.

Computers on Campus 212 computers/terminals and 116 ports are available on campus for general student use. Students can access the following: campus intranet, computer help desk, free student e-mail accounts, online (class) grades, online (class) schedules. Campuswide network is available. 100% of college-owned or -operated housing units are wired for high-speed Internet access. Wireless service is available via entire campus.

Student Life *Housing:* on-campus residence required through sophomore year. *Options:* coed, cooperative, disabled students. Campus housing is university owned. Freshman campus housing is guaranteed. *Activities and organizations:* drama/theater group, student-run newspaper, radio station, choral group, Concerned Black Students, International Student Organization, Student Organization of Latinas/Latinos, Campus Democrats, Ultimate Frisbee. *Campus security:* 24-hour emergency response devices and patrols, student patrols, late-night transport/escort service, controlled dormitory access. *Student services:* health clinic, personal/psychological counseling.

Athletics Member NCAA. All Division III. *Intercollegiate sports:* baseball M, basketball M/W, cross-country running M/W, football M, golf M/W, soccer M/W, softball W, swimming and diving M/W, tennis M/W, track and field M/W, volleyball W. *Intramural sports:* badminton M/W, basketball M/W, rugby M (c)/W (c), soccer M/W, softball M/W, tennis M/W, volleyball M/W, water polo M/W.

Standardized Tests *Required:* SAT or ACT (for admission).

Costs (2007–08) *Comprehensive fee:* $42,422 includes full-time tuition ($33,910), mandatory fees ($482), and room and board ($8030). Part-time tuition: $1060 per credit. *College room only:* $3726. Room and board charges vary according to board plan and housing facility. *Payment plans:* tuition prepayment, installment. *Waivers:* employees or children of employees.

Financial Aid Of all full-time matriculated undergraduates who enrolled in 2007, 1,024 applied for aid, 904 were judged to have need, 904 had their need fully met. 455 Federal Work-Study jobs (averaging $1838). 376 state and other part-time jobs (averaging $1984). In 2007, 513 non-need-based awards were made. *Average percent of need met:* 100%. *Average financial aid package:* $28,190. *Average need-based loan:* $5536. *Average need-based gift aid:* $22,176. *Average non-need-based aid:* $10,507. *Average indebtedness upon graduation:* $18,340. *Financial aid deadline:* 2/1.

Applying *Options:* electronic application, early admission, early decision, deferred entrance. *Application fee:* $30. *Required:* essay or personal statement, high school transcript, 3 letters of recommendation. *Recommended:* interview. *Application deadlines:* 1/20 (freshmen), 5/1 (transfers). *Early decision deadline:* 11/20. *Notification:* 4/1 (freshmen), 5/20 (transfers), 12/20 (early decision).

Freshman Application Contact Mr. Seth Allen, Dean for Admission and Financial Aid, Grinnell College, 1103 Park Street, Grinnell, IA 50112. *Phone:* 641-269-3600. *Toll-free phone:* 800-247-0113. *Fax:* 641-269-4800. *E-mail:* askgrin@grinnell.edu.

See page 978 for the College Close-Up.

HAMILTON TECHNICAL COLLEGE

Davenport, Iowa **www.hamiltontechcollege.com/**

Freshman Application Contact Mr. Scott Ervin, Director of Admissions, Hamilton Technical College, 1011 East 53rd Street, Davenport, IA 52807. *Phone:* 563-386-3570. *Fax:* 563-386-6756. *E-mail:* servin@hamiltontechcollege.com.

IOWA STATE UNIVERSITY OF SCIENCE AND TECHNOLOGY

Ames, Iowa **www.iastate.edu/**

- **State-supported** university, founded 1858
- **Suburban** 1788-acre campus
- **Endowment** $592.4 million
- **Coed** 21,004 undergraduate students, 94% full-time, 43% women, 57% men
- **Moderately difficult** entrance level, 89% of applicants were admitted

Undergraduates 19,679 full-time, 1,325 part-time. Students come from 58 states and territories, 106 other countries, 29% are from out of state, 3% African

American, 3% Asian American or Pacific Islander, 3% Hispanic American, 0.3% Native American, 4% international, 7% transferred in, 39% live on campus. *Retention:* 85% of 2006 full-time freshmen returned.

Freshmen *Admission:* 11,058 applied, 9,832 admitted, 4,347 enrolled. *Average high school GPA:* 3.47. *Test scores:* SAT critical reading scores over 500: 79%; SAT math scores over 500: 86%; ACT scores over 18: 97%; SAT critical reading scores over 600: 39%; SAT math scores over 600: 57%; ACT scores over 24: 59%; SAT critical reading scores over 700: 12%; SAT math scores over 700: 18%; ACT scores over 30: 12%.

Faculty *Total:* 1,584, 85% full-time, 89% with terminal degrees. *Student/faculty ratio:* 16:1.

Majors Accounting; advertising; aerospace, aeronautical and astronautical engineering; agricultural/biological engineering and bioengineering; agricultural business and management; agricultural mechanization; agricultural teacher education; agriculture; agronomy and crop science; animal sciences; anthropology; apparel and textiles; applied horticulture; architecture; art; atmospheric sciences and meteorology; biochemistry; biology/biological sciences; biophysics; botany/plant biology; business administration and management; business, management, and marketing related; chemical engineering; chemistry; city/urban, community and regional planning; civil engineering; commercial and advertising art; computer and information sciences; computer engineering; dairy science; design and visual communications; dietetics; dramatic/theater arts; early childhood education; ecology; economics; education; electrical, electronics and communications engineering; elementary education; engineering; engineering related; engineering science; English; entomology; entrepreneurship; environmental science; environmental studies; family and community services; family and consumer economics related; family and consumer sciences/home economics teacher education; family and consumer sciences/human sciences; family resource management; farm and ranch management; fashion/apparel design; finance; fish/game management; food services technology; foods, nutrition, and wellness; forestry; French; genetics; geology/earth science; German; graphic design; health and physical education; health teacher education; history; horticultural science; hotel/motel administration; industrial engineering; interdisciplinary studies; interior design; international agriculture; international business/trade/commerce; international relations and affairs; journalism; landscape architecture; liberal arts and sciences/liberal studies; linguistics; logistics and materials management; management information systems; marketing/marketing management; mass communication/media; materials engineering; mathematics; mechanical engineering; medical illustration; microbiology; multi-/interdisciplinary studies related; music; music teacher education; natural resources management and policy; operations management; ornamental horticulture; philosophy; physics; plant protection and integrated pest management; political science and government; pre-dentistry studies; pre-law studies; pre-medical studies; pre-veterinary studies; psychology; public administration; religious studies; Russian studies; secondary education; sociology; Spanish; special products marketing; speech and rhetoric; statistics; technical and business writing; trade and industrial teacher education; visual and performing arts; women's studies.

Academics *Calendar:* semesters. *Degrees:* bachelor's, master's, doctoral, first professional, and post-master's certificates. *Special study options:* academic remediation for entering students, accelerated degree program, adult/continuing education programs, advanced placement credit, cooperative education, distance learning, double majors, English as a second language, external degree program, freshman honors college, honors programs, independent study, internships, off-campus study, part-time degree program, services for LD students, student-designed majors, study abroad, summer session for credit. *ROTC:* Army (b), Navy (b), Air Force (b). *Unusual degree programs:* 3-2 engineering with William Penn College.

Computers on Campus 2,400 computers/terminals are available on campus for general student use. Students can access the following: campus intranet, computer help desk, free student e-mail accounts, online (class) grades, online (class) registration, online (class) schedules, network services. Campuswide network is available. 100% of college-owned or -operated housing units are wired for high-speed Internet access. Wireless service is available via entire campus.

Student Life *Housing options:* coed, men-only, women-only, disabled students. Campus housing is university owned. Freshman applicants given priority for college housing. *Activities and organizations:* drama/theater group, student-run newspaper, radio and television station, choral group, marching band, student government, Student Alumni Association, Residence Hall Associations, national fraternities, national sororities. *Campus security:* 24-hour emergency response devices and patrols, student patrols, late-night transport/escort service, controlled dormitory access, crime prevention programs, threat assessment team, motor vehicle help van. *Student services:* health clinic, personal/psychological counseling, women's center, legal services.

Athletics Member NCAA. All Division I except football (Division I-A). *Intercollegiate sports:* basketball M (s)/W (s), cross-country running M (s)/W (s), golf M (s)/W (s), gymnastics W (s), soccer W (s), softball W (s), swimming and diving M (s)/W (s), tennis W (s), track and field M (s)/W (s), volleyball W (s), wrestling M (s). *Intramural sports:* archery M (c)/W (c), badminton M (c)/W (c), basketball M/W, bowling M (c)/W (c), cross-country running M/W, equestrian sports M (c)/W (c), fencing M (c)/W (c), football M/W, golf M/W, ice hockey M (c)/W (c), lacrosse M (c)/W (c), racquetball M (c)/W (c), riflery M (c)/W (c), rugby M (c)/W (c), sailing M (c)/W (c), skiing (cross-country) M (c)/W (c), skiing (downhill) M (c)/W (c), soccer M (c)/W (c), softball M/W, squash M/W, swimming and diving M/W, table tennis M (c)/W (c), tennis M/W, volleyball M (c)/W (c), water polo M (c)/W (c), weight lifting M (c)/W (c), wrestling M/W.

Standardized Tests *Required:* SAT or ACT (for admission).

Costs (2008–09) *Tuition:* state resident $5524 full-time, $231 per semester hour part-time; nonresident $16,514 full-time, $689 per semester hour part-time. *Required fees:* $836 full-time.

Financial Aid Of all full-time matriculated undergraduates who enrolled in 2007, 14,510 applied for aid, 10,362 were judged to have need, 4,504 had their need fully met. 1,587 Federal Work-Study jobs (averaging $1304). 8,017 state and other part-time jobs (averaging $1851). In 2007, 5912 non-need-based awards were made. *Average percent of need met:* 82%. *Average financial aid package:* $9798. *Average need-based loan:* $4325. *Average need-based gift aid:* $4916. *Average non-need-based aid:* $1972. *Average indebtedness upon graduation:* $31,501.

Applying *Options:* electronic application, early admission, deferred entrance. *Application fee:* $30. *Required:* high school transcript, rank in upper 50% of high school class. *Application deadlines:* 7/1 (freshmen), 7/1 (transfers). *Notification:* continuous (freshmen), continuous (transfers).

Freshman Application Contact Mr. Phil Caffrey, Associate Director for Freshman Admissions, Iowa State University of Science and Technology, 100 Alumni Hall, Ames, IA 50011-2010. *Phone:* 515-294-5836. *Toll-free phone:* 800-262-3810. *Fax:* 515-294-2592. *E-mail:* admissions@iastate.edu.

IOWA WESLEYAN COLLEGE

Mount Pleasant, Iowa **www.iwc.edu/**

- **Independent United Methodist** 4-year, founded 1842
- **Small-town** 60-acre campus
- **Endowment** $5.9 million
- **Coed** 833 undergraduate students, 76% full-time, 61% women, 39% men
- **Moderately difficult** entrance level, 60% of applicants were admitted

Undergraduates 635 full-time, 198 part-time. Students come from 26 states and territories, 29 other countries, 46% are from out of state, 15% transferred in, 57% live on campus. *Retention:* 56% of 2006 full-time freshmen returned.

Freshmen *Admission:* 796 applied, 478 admitted, 127 enrolled. *Average high school GPA:* 2.94. *Test scores:* ACT scores over 18: 79%; ACT scores over 24: 25%; ACT scores over 30: 2%.

Faculty *Total:* 91, 56% full-time. *Student/faculty ratio:* 14:1.

Majors Accounting; adult and continuing education; art; art teacher education; biological and physical sciences; biology/biological sciences; business administration and management; chemistry; computer programming; computer science; criminal justice/law enforcement administration; education; elementary education; English; environmental biology; environmental health; fine/studio arts; graphic design; history; information science/studies; kindergarten/preschool education; kinesiology and exercise science; liberal arts and sciences/liberal studies; mass communication/media; mathematics; music; music teacher education; natural sciences; nursing (registered nurse training); philosophy and religious studies related; physical education teaching and coaching; pre-dentistry studies; pre-law studies; pre-medical studies; pre-pharmacy studies; pre-veterinary studies; psychology; secondary education; special education; sport and fitness administration/management.

Academics *Calendar:* semesters. *Degree:* bachelor's. *Special study options:* academic remediation for entering students, adult/continuing education programs, advanced placement credit, distance learning, double majors, English as a second language, independent study, internships, off-campus study, part-time degree program, services for LD students, student-designed majors, study abroad, summer session for credit. *Unusual degree programs:* 3-2 forestry with Iowa State University of Science and Technology, Duke University.

Computers on Campus 72 computers/terminals are available on campus for general student use. Students can access the following: campus intranet, computer help desk, free student e-mail accounts, online (class) grades, online (class) registration, online (class) schedules. Campuswide network is available.

Student Life *Housing:* on-campus residence required through senior year. *Options:* coed, men-only, women-only. Campus housing is university owned. Freshman campus housing is guaranteed. *Activities and organizations:* drama/theater group, student-run newspaper, radio station, choral group, Student Union Board, Student Senate, Commuter Club, Choir, Blue Key Society, national fraternities, national sororities. *Campus security:* 24-hour patrols, late-night transport/escort service, controlled dormitory access. *Student services:* health clinic, personal/psychological counseling.

Athletics Member NAIA. *Intercollegiate sports:* baseball M (s), basketball M (s)/W (s), football M (s), golf M (s)/W (s), soccer M (s)/W (s), softball W (s), track and field M (s)/W (s), volleyball W (s). *Intramural sports:* badminton M/W, basketball M/W, bowling M/W, cheerleading M/W, football M/W, soccer M/W, softball M/W, swimming and diving M/W, table tennis M/W, tennis M/W, track and field M/W, volleyball M/W, weight lifting M/W.

Standardized Tests *Required:* SAT or ACT (for admission), SAT or ACT (for placement).

Costs (2007–08) *Comprehensive fee:* $24,750 includes full-time tuition ($18,870) and room and board ($5880). Part-time tuition: $465 per credit hour. *College room only:* $2430.

Financial Aid Of all full-time matriculated undergraduates who enrolled in 2006, 564 applied for aid, 564 were judged to have need, 170 had their need fully met. In 2006, 35 non-need-based awards were made. *Average percent of need met:* 80%. *Average financial aid package:* $14,000. *Average need-based loan:* $5000. *Average need-based gift aid:* $8000.

Applying *Options:* electronic application, early admission, deferred entrance. *Required:* high school transcript, minimum 2.5 GPA. *Required for some:* essay or personal statement. *Application deadlines:* 8/15 (freshmen), 8/15 (transfers). *Notification:* continuous (transfers).

Freshman Application Contact Mr. Mark T. Petty, Dean of Admissions, Iowa Wesleyan College, 601 North Main Street, Mount Pleasant, IA 52641-1398. *Phone:* 319-385-6230. *Toll-free phone:* 800-582-2383 Ext. 6231. *Fax:* 319-385-6240. *E-mail:* mpetty@iwc.edu.

KAPLAN UNIVERSITY-CEDAR FALLS

Cedar Falls, Iowa

www.kucampus.edu/kucampusPortal/kucampusCampuses/Iowa/CedarFalls/

Freshman Application Contact Ms. Jill Lines, Director of Admissions, Kaplan University-Cedar Falls, 7009 Nordic Drive, Cedar Falls, IA 50613. *Phone:* 319-277-0220. *Toll-free phone:* 800-728-1220. *Fax:* 319-268-0978. *E-mail:* jilines@hamiltoncf.com.

KAPLAN UNIVERSITY-CEDAR RAPIDS

Cedar Rapids, Iowa

www.kucampus.edu/kucampusPortal/kucampusCampuses/Iowa/CedarRapids/

Freshman Application Contact Ms. Niki Donahue, Director of Admissions, Kaplan University-Cedar Rapids, 1924 D Street SW, Cedar Rapids, IA 52404. *Phone:* 319-363-0481. *Toll-free phone:* 800-728-0481. *Fax:* 319-363-3812.

KAPLAN UNIVERSITY-DAVENPORT

Davenport, Iowa

www.kucampus.edu/kucampusPortal/default.htm

- **Proprietary** primarily 2-year, founded 1937, part of Kaplan Higher Education
- **Suburban** campus
- **Coed**
- **Minimally difficult** entrance level

Faculty *Student/faculty ratio:* 11:1.

Academics *Calendar:* quarters. *Degrees:* certificates, diplomas, associate, and bachelor's (profile includes both traditional and on-line students).

Costs (2007–08) *Tuition:* $13,680 full-time, $380 per credit hour part-time.

Applying *Options:* early admission, deferred entrance. *Application fee:* $25. *Required:* high school transcript, interview.

Freshman Application Contact Ms. Carla Batchelor, Director of Admissions, Kaplan University-Davenport, 1801 East Kimberly Road, Suite 1, Davenport, IA 52807. *Phone:* 563-441-2496. *Toll-free phone:* 800-747-1035. *Fax:* 563-355-1320. *E-mail:* cbatchelor@kucampus.edu.

LORAS COLLEGE

Dubuque, Iowa **www.loras.edu/**

- **Independent Roman Catholic** comprehensive, founded 1839
- **Suburban** 60-acre campus
- **Endowment** $30.1 million
- **Coed** 1,511 undergraduate students, 97% full-time, 48% women, 52% men
- **Moderately difficult** entrance level, 74% of applicants were admitted

Undergraduates 1,459 full-time, 52 part-time. Students come from 22 states and territories, 7 other countries, 47% are from out of state, 1% African American, 0.5% Asian American or Pacific Islander, 2% Hispanic American, 0.1% Native American, 3% international, 13% transferred in, 66% live on campus. *Retention:* 79% of 2006 full-time freshmen returned.

Freshmen *Admission:* 1,490 applied, 1,109 admitted, 376 enrolled. *Average high school GPA:* 3.28. *Test scores:* ACT scores over 18: 99%; ACT scores over 24: 42%; ACT scores over 30: 6%.

Faculty *Total:* 166, 73% full-time. *Student/faculty ratio:* 11:1.

Majors Accounting; art teacher education; athletic training; biochemistry; biology/biological sciences; business administration and management; business/commerce; chemistry; clinical laboratory science/medical technology; computer science; creative writing; criminal justice/safety; early childhood education; economics; education; elementary education; engineering physics; engineering related; English; finance; fine/studio arts; French; health and physical education; history; human resources management; international business/trade/commerce; international relations and affairs; journalism; kindergarten/preschool education; kinesiology and exercise science; management information systems; marketing/marketing management; mass communication/media; mathematics; music; nuclear medical technology; philosophy; physical education teaching and coaching; physical sciences; physics; political science and government; pre-theology/pre-ministerial studies; psychology; public relations/image management; religious studies; secondary education; social work; sociology; Spanish; special education (emotionally disturbed); special education (mentally retarded); sport and fitness administration/management; visual and performing arts.

Academics *Calendar:* semesters. *Degrees:* associate, bachelor's, and master's. *Special study options:* academic remediation for entering students, adult/continuing education programs, advanced placement credit, cooperative education, double majors, English as a second language, honors programs, independent study, internships, off-campus study, part-time degree program, services for LD students, student-designed majors, study abroad, summer session for credit. *ROTC:* Army (c). *Unusual degree programs:* 3-2 engineering with Iowa State University of Science and Technology, University of Illinois, University of Notre Dame, University of Iowa; nursing with University of Iowa.

Computers on Campus 20 computers/terminals are available on campus for general student use. Students can access the following: campus intranet, computer help desk, free student e-mail accounts, online (class) grades, online (class) registration, online (class) schedules. Campuswide network is available. Wireless service is available via classrooms, computer centers, computer labs, dorm rooms, learning centers, libraries, student centers.

Student Life *Housing:* on-campus residence required through junior year. *Options:* coed. Campus housing is university owned. Freshman campus housing is guaranteed. *Activities and organizations:* drama/theater group, student-run newspaper, radio and television station, choral group, Student Senate, campus ministry, College Activities Board, residence hall councils, national sororities. *Campus security:* 24-hour emergency response devices and patrols, late-night transport/escort service, controlled dormitory access. *Student services:* health clinic, personal/psychological counseling.

Athletics Member NCAA. All Division III. *Intercollegiate sports:* baseball M, basketball M/W, cross-country running M/W, football M, golf M/W, ice hockey M (c), rugby M (c), skiing (downhill) M (c), soccer M/W, softball W, swimming and diving M/W, tennis M/W, track and field M/W, volleyball M (c)/W, water polo M, wrestling M. *Intramural sports:* badminton M/W, baseball M, basketball M/W, cross-country running M/W, football M, golf M/W, ice hockey M, racquetball M/W, rugby M, skiing (cross-country) M/W, skiing (downhill) M/W, soccer M/W, softball M/W, swimming and diving M/W, table tennis M/W, tennis M/W, track and field M/W, volleyball M/W, water polo M/W, weight lifting M/W, wrestling M.

Standardized Tests *Required:* SAT or ACT (for admission).

Costs (2007–08) *Comprehensive fee:* $29,830 includes full-time tuition ($22,140), mandatory fees ($1190), and room and board ($6500). Full-time tuition and fees vary according to course load and degree level. Part-time tuition: $440 per credit. *College room only:* $3320. Room and board charges vary according to board plan and housing facility. *Payment plan:* installment. *Waivers:* senior citizens and employees or children of employees.

Financial Aid Of all full-time matriculated undergraduates who enrolled in 2007, 1,240 applied for aid, 1,116 were judged to have need, 365 had their need fully met. 159 Federal Work-Study jobs (averaging $1500). 290 state and other part-time jobs (averaging $2000). In 2007, 379 non-need-based awards were made. *Average percent of need met:* 88%. *Average financial aid package:* $19,450. *Average need-based loan:* $3896. *Average need-based gift aid:* $8254. *Average non-need-based aid:* $8620. *Average indebtedness upon graduation:* $28,800.

Applying *Options:* electronic application, deferred entrance. *Application fee:* $25. *Required:* high school transcript, minimum 2.5 GPA. *Required for some:* interview. *Recommended:* essay or personal statement, 1 letter of recommendation. *Application deadlines:* rolling (freshmen), rolling (transfers). *Notification:* continuous (freshmen), continuous (transfers).

Freshman Application Contact Ms. Sharon Lyons, Director of Admissions, Loras College, 1450 Alta Vista, Dubuque, IA 52004-0178. *Phone:* 563-588-7829. *Toll-free phone:* 800-245-6727. *Fax:* 563-588-7119. *E-mail:* adms@loras.edu.

LUTHER COLLEGE

Decorah, Iowa **www.luther.edu/**

- **Independent** 4-year, founded 1861, affiliated with Evangelical Lutheran Church in America
- **Small-town** 200-acre campus
- **Endowment** $113.8 million
- **Coed** 2,476 undergraduate students, 98% full-time, 57% women, 43% men
- **Moderately difficult** entrance level, 83% of applicants were admitted

Undergraduates 2,434 full-time, 42 part-time. Students come from 38 states and territories, 43 other countries, 64% are from out of state, 0.9% African American, 2% Asian American or Pacific Islander, 2% Hispanic American, 0.2% Native American, 4% international, 2% transferred in, 84% live on campus. *Retention:* 86% of 2006 full-time freshmen returned.

Freshmen *Admission:* 2,054 applied, 1,696 admitted, 659 enrolled. *Average high school GPA:* 3.6. *Test scores:* SAT critical reading scores over 500: 72%; SAT math scores over 500: 89%; SAT writing scores over 500: 77%; ACT scores over 18: 99%; SAT critical reading scores over 600: 51%; SAT math scores over 600: 54%; SAT writing scores over 600: 43%; ACT scores over 24: 66%; SAT critical reading scores over 700: 17%; SAT math scores over 700: 13%; SAT writing scores over 700: 12%; ACT scores over 30: 18%.

Faculty *Total:* 251, 71% full-time, 71% with terminal degrees. *Student/faculty ratio:* 12:1.

Majors Accounting; African-American/Black studies; ancient Near Eastern and biblical languages; anthropology; art; athletic training; biology/biological sciences; business administration and management; chemistry; communication/speech communication and rhetoric; computer science; dramatic/theater arts; economics; elementary education; English; environmental studies; French; German; health and physical education; history; interdisciplinary studies; international relations and affairs; management information systems; mathematics; music; nursing (registered nurse training); philosophy; physical education teaching and coaching; physics; political science and government; psychology; religious studies; Scandinavian studies; social work; sociology; Spanish; statistics; women's studies.

Academics *Calendar:* 4-1-4. *Degree:* bachelor's. *Special study options:* academic remediation for entering students, advanced placement credit, double majors, honors programs, independent study, internships, off-campus study, part-time degree program, services for LD students, student-designed majors, study abroad, summer session for credit. *Unusual degree programs:* 3-2 engineering with Washington University in St. Louis; University of Minnesota, Twin Cities Campus; environmental management, resource management with Duke University.

Computers on Campus 500 computers/terminals are available on campus for general student use. Students can access the following: campus intranet, computer help desk, free student e-mail accounts, online (class) grades, online (class) registration, online (class) schedules. Campuswide network is available. 100% of college-owned or -operated housing units are wired for high-speed Internet access. Wireless service is available via entire campus.

Student Life *Housing:* on-campus residence required through senior year. *Options:* coed, disabled students. Campus housing is university owned. Freshman campus housing is guaranteed. *Activities and organizations:* drama/theater group, student-run newspaper, radio station, choral group, Alpha Phi Omega, Student Activities Council, intramural clubs and organizations, Campus Ministry. *Campus security:* 24-hour emergency response devices and patrols, late-night transport/escort service, controlled dormitory access. *Student services:* health clinic, personal/psychological counseling, women's center.

Athletics Member NCAA. All Division III. *Intercollegiate sports:* baseball M, basketball M/W, cross-country running M/W, football M, golf M/W, soccer M/W, softball W, swimming and diving M/W, tennis M/W, track and field M/W, volleyball W, wrestling M. *Intramural sports:* archery M/W, badminton M/W, basketball M/W, bowling M/W, football M/W, golf M/W, racquetball M/W, rugby M (c)/W (c), skiing (downhill) M (c)/W (c), soccer M/W, softball M/W, table tennis M/W, tennis M/W, track and field M/W, ultimate Frisbee M/W, volleyball M (c)/W, water polo M/W.

Standardized Tests *Required:* SAT or ACT (for admission).

Costs (2007–08) *Comprehensive fee:* $33,500 includes full-time tuition ($28,840) and room and board ($4660). Full-time tuition and fees vary according to course load. Part-time tuition: $1030 per semester hour. Part-time tuition and fees vary according to course load. *College room only:* $2400. Room and board charges vary according to board plan and housing facility. *Payment plan:* installment. *Waivers:* employees or children of employees.

Financial Aid Of all full-time matriculated undergraduates who enrolled in 2007, 1,982 applied for aid, 1,712 were judged to have need, 515 had their need fully met. 972 Federal Work-Study jobs (averaging $1856). 1,103 state and other part-time jobs (averaging $937). In 2007, 244 non-need-based awards were made. *Average percent of need met:* 88%. *Average financial aid package:* $22,935. *Average need-based loan:* $5257. *Average need-based gift aid:* $15,021. *Average non-need-based aid:* $9039. *Average indebtedness upon graduation:* $19,765.

Applying *Options:* electronic application, deferred entrance. *Application fee:* $25. *Required:* essay or personal statement, high school transcript, 1 letter of recommendation. *Recommended:* interview. *Notification:* continuous (freshmen), continuous (out-of-state freshmen), continuous (transfers).

Freshman Application Contact Kirk Neubauer, Director of Recruiting Services, Luther College, 700 College Drive, Decorah, IA 52101. *Phone:* 563-387-1287. *Toll-free phone:* 800-458-8437. *Fax:* 563-387-2159. *E-mail:* admissions@luther.edu.

See page 980 for the College Close-Up.

MAHARISHI UNIVERSITY OF MANAGEMENT

Fairfield, Iowa **www.mum.edu/**

- **Independent** university, founded 1971
- **Small-town** 272-acre campus
- **Endowment** $9.2 million
- **Coed** 204 undergraduate students, 93% full-time, 43% women, 57% men
- **Moderately difficult** entrance level, 41% of applicants were admitted

Undergraduates 190 full-time, 14 part-time. Students come from 38 states and territories, 72 other countries, 53% are from out of state, 2% African American, 4% Asian American or Pacific Islander, 7% Hispanic American, 17% international, 13% transferred in, 60% live on campus. *Retention:* 61% of 2006 full-time freshmen returned.

Freshmen *Admission:* 126 applied, 52 admitted, 45 enrolled.

Faculty *Total:* 49, 100% full-time, 100% with terminal degrees. *Student/faculty ratio:* 16:1.

Majors Ayurvedic medicine; business administration and management; cinematography and film/video production; computer science; elementary education; English; environmental studies; fine/studio arts; mathematics; secondary education.

Academics *Calendar:* semesters. *Degrees:* certificates, bachelor's, master's, doctoral, and postbachelor's certificates. *Special study options:* academic remediation for entering students, adult/continuing education programs, advanced placement credit, cooperative education, distance learning, double majors, honors programs, independent study, internships, services for LD students, student-designed majors, study abroad.

Computers on Campus 20 computers/terminals are available on campus for general student use. Students can access the following: campus intranet, computer help desk, free student e-mail accounts, online (class) grades, online (class) schedules. Campuswide network is available. 100% of college-owned or -operated housing units are wired for high-speed Internet access.

Student Life *Housing:* on-campus residence required through senior year. *Options:* men-only, women-only, disabled students. Campus housing is university owned. Freshman campus housing is guaranteed. *Activities and organizations:* drama/theater group, student-run newspaper, radio station, choral group, Sustainable Living Club, Soccer Club, Global Student Council, Ultimate Frisbee Club, Business Club. *Campus security:* 24-hour emergency response devices and patrols, late-night transport/escort service, controlled dormitory access. *Student services:* health clinic, personal/psychological counseling, legal services.

Athletics *Intercollegiate sports:* soccer M (c)/W (c), ultimate Frisbee M (c)/W (c), volleyball M (c)/W (c). *Intramural sports:* archery M/W, badminton M/W, basketball M/W, football M/W, gymnastics M/W, rock climbing M/W, sailing M/W, soccer M/W, table tennis M/W, tennis M/W, ultimate Frisbee M/W, volleyball M/W.
Standardized Tests *Recommended:* SAT or ACT (for admission).
Costs (2008–09) *Comprehensive fee:* $30,430 includes full-time tuition ($24,000), mandatory fees ($430), and room and board ($6000). Part-time tuition: $550 per unit.
Financial Aid Of all full-time matriculated undergraduates who enrolled in 2006, 150 applied for aid, 148 were judged to have need, 32 had their need fully met. 120 Federal Work-Study jobs (averaging $1422). 7 state and other part-time jobs (averaging $2729). In 2006, 5 non-need-based awards were made. *Average percent of need met:* 89%. *Average financial aid package:* $23,963. *Average need-based loan:* $8281. *Average need-based gift aid:* $14,082. *Average non-need-based aid:* $9300. *Average indebtedness upon graduation:* $26,800.
Applying *Options:* electronic application, early admission, deferred entrance. *Application fee:* $30. *Required:* essay or personal statement, high school transcript, minimum 2.5 GPA, 2 letters of recommendation. *Recommended:* interview. *Application deadlines:* 8/1 (freshmen), 8/1 (transfers). *Notification:* continuous until 8/15 (freshmen), continuous (transfers).
Freshman Application Contact Ms. Barbara Rainbow, Associate Dean of Admissions, Maharishi University of Management, Office of Admissions, Fairfield, IA 52557. *Phone:* 641-472-1110. *Toll-free phone:* 800-369-6480. *Fax:* 641-472-1179. *E-mail:* admissions@mum.edu.

MERCY COLLEGE OF HEALTH SCIENCES

Des Moines, Iowa **www.mchs.edu/**

- **Independent** 4-year, founded 1995, affiliated with Roman Catholic Church
- **Urban** 5-acre campus
- **Endowment** $1.8 million
- **Coed, primarily women** 680 undergraduate students, 62% full-time, 91% women, 9% men

Undergraduates 422 full-time, 258 part-time. 2% African American, 3% Asian American or Pacific Islander, 3% Hispanic American, 0.7% Native American. *Retention:* 60% of 2006 full-time freshmen returned.
Freshmen *Admission:* 64 enrolled. *Average high school GPA:* 3.02. *Test scores:* ACT scores over 18: 73%; ACT scores over 24: 10%.
Faculty *Total:* 93, 42% full-time, 8% with terminal degrees. *Student/faculty ratio:* 9:1.
Majors Allied health diagnostic, intervention, and treatment professions related; emergency medical technology (EMT paramedic); health/health care administration; medical office assistant; medical radiologic technology; nursing (registered nurse training); nursing science; surgical technology.
Academics *Calendar:* semesters. *Degrees:* certificates, associate, and bachelor's. *Special study options:* academic remediation for entering students, accelerated degree program, advanced placement credit, part-time degree program, services for LD students, summer session for credit.
Computers on Campus 98 computers/terminals are available on campus for general student use. Students can access the following: free student e-mail accounts, online (class) grades. Wireless service is available via entire campus.
Student Life *Housing:* college housing not available. *Activities and organizations:* Professional Organizations, Student senate. *Campus security:* 24-hour emergency response devices and patrols, late-night transport/escort service. *Student services:* health clinic, personal/psychological counseling.
Standardized Tests *Required for some:* ACT (for admission).
Costs (2008–09) *Tuition:* $13,000 full-time, $440 per credit hour part-time.
Financial Aid Of all full-time matriculated undergraduates who enrolled in 2003, 331 applied for aid, 322 were judged to have need, 3 had their need fully met. 11 Federal Work-Study jobs (averaging $1964). In 2003, 9 non-need-based awards were made. *Average percent of need met:* 29%. *Average financial aid package:* $7670. *Average need-based loan:* $2492. *Average need-based gift aid:* $5132. *Average non-need-based aid:* $6697. *Average indebtedness upon graduation:* $17,567. *Financial aid deadline:* 7/1.
Applying *Application fee:* $25. *Required:* high school transcript, minimum 2.25 GPA. *Required for some:* interview. *Application deadline:* rolling (freshmen). *Notification:* continuous (freshmen).
Freshman Application Contact Susan Hill/Sandi Nagel, Admissions Representative, Mercy College of Health Sciences, 928 6th Avenue, Des Moines, IA 50309-1239. *Phone:* 515-643-3180. *Toll-free phone:* 800-637-2994. *Fax:* 515-643-6698. *E-mail:* shill@mercydesmoines.org or snagel@mercydesmoines.org.

MORNINGSIDE COLLEGE

Sioux City, Iowa **www.morningside.edu/**

- **Independent** comprehensive, founded 1894, affiliated with United Methodist Church
- **Suburban** 68-acre campus
- **Endowment** $34.0 million
- **Coed** 1,213 undergraduate students, 96% full-time, 55% women, 45% men
- **Moderately difficult** entrance level, 79% of applicants were admitted

The Morningside College experience cultivates a passion for lifelong learning and a dedication to ethical leadership and civic responsibility. Students develop various dimensions of themselves through the liberal arts core curriculum, a complete range of majors, internships, independent study, and career and graduate school advising services. Typical merit scholarship candidates are students who make a difference in a variety of areas, both in and out of the classroom; those who have an alumni connection; or students with a tie to the United Methodist Church. Within six months of graduation, more than 99 percent are employed or admitted to graduate school.

Undergraduates 1,159 full-time, 54 part-time. Students come from 22 states and territories, 5 other countries, 33% are from out of state, 1% African American, 2% Asian American or Pacific Islander, 3% Hispanic American, 0.7% Native American, 1% international, 6% transferred in, 65% live on campus. *Retention:* 77% of 2006 full-time freshmen returned.
Freshmen *Admission:* 1,375 applied, 1,090 admitted, 290 enrolled. *Average high school GPA:* 3.37. *Test scores:* ACT scores over 18: 97%; ACT scores over 24: 45%; ACT scores over 30: 2%.
Faculty *Total:* 150, 47% full-time, 37% with terminal degrees. *Student/faculty ratio:* 17:1.
Majors Accounting; art; art teacher education; biology/biological sciences; biopsychology; business administration and management; business/corporate communications; business teacher education; chemistry; clinical laboratory science/medical technology; commercial and advertising art; computer science; counseling psychology; dramatic/theater arts; education; elementary education; engineering physics; English; fine/studio arts; history; interdisciplinary studies; literature; management information systems; marketing/marketing management; mass communication/media; mathematics; music; music teacher education; nursing (registered nurse training); philosophy; photography; physics; political science and government; pre-dentistry studies; pre-law studies; pre-medical studies; pre-veterinary studies; psychology; religious studies; science teacher education; secondary education; Spanish; special education.
Academics *Calendar:* semesters. *Degrees:* bachelor's and master's. *Special study options:* academic remediation for entering students, adult/continuing education programs, advanced placement credit, double majors, English as a second language, honors programs, independent study, internships, off-campus study, part-time degree program, services for LD students, student-designed majors, study abroad, summer session for credit. *ROTC:* Army (c).
Computers on Campus 800 computers/terminals are available on campus for general student use. Students can access the following: campus intranet, computer help desk, free student e-mail accounts, online (class) grades, online (class) registration, online (class) schedules, academic and financial records. Campus-wide network is available. Wireless service is available via entire campus.
Student Life *Housing:* on-campus residence required through junior year. *Options:* coed. Campus housing is university owned. Freshman campus housing is guaranteed. *Activities and organizations:* drama/theater group, student-run newspaper, radio and television station, choral group, Student Government/Activities Council, Student Ambassadors, Homecoming Committee, national fraternities, national sororities. *Campus security:* 24-hour emergency response devices, student patrols, late-night transport/escort service, controlled dormitory access, 18-hour patrols by trained security personnel. *Student services:* health clinic, personal/psychological counseling, women's center.
Athletics Member NAIA. *Intercollegiate sports:* baseball M (s), basketball M (s)/W (s), cross-country running M (s)/W (s), football M (s), golf M (s)/W (s), soccer M (s)/W (s), softball W (s), swimming and diving M (s)/W (s), tennis M (s)/W (s), track and field M (s)/W (s), volleyball W (s), wrestling M (s). *Intramural sports:* basketball M/W, bowling M/W, ultimate Frisbee M/W, volleyball M/W.
Standardized Tests *Required:* SAT or ACT (for admission).
Costs (2007–08) *Comprehensive fee:* $26,330 includes full-time tuition ($19,040), mandatory fees ($1124), and room and board ($6166). Full-time tuition and fees vary according to program and student level. Part-time tuition: $610 per semester hour. Part-time tuition and fees vary according to course load. *College room only:* $3180. Room and board charges vary according to housing facility.

Payment plan: installment. *Waivers:* children of alumni, senior citizens, and employees or children of employees.

Financial Aid Of all full-time matriculated undergraduates who enrolled in 2005, 1,012 applied for aid, 928 were judged to have need, 579 had their need fully met. 300 Federal Work-Study jobs (averaging $1161). 1 state and other part-time job (averaging $580). In 2005, 131 non-need-based awards were made. *Average percent of need met:* 77%. *Average financial aid package:* $16,302. *Average need-based loan:* $3585. *Average need-based gift aid:* $5702. *Average non-need-based aid:* $6130. *Average indebtedness upon graduation:* $26,816.

Applying *Options:* electronic application, deferred entrance. *Application fee:* $25. *Required:* high school transcript, minimum SAT score of 930 or ACT score of 20 and rank in top 50% of high school class or achieved GPA of 2.5 or better. *Required for some:* 2 letters of recommendation. *Recommended:* interview. *Application deadlines:* rolling (freshmen), rolling (transfers). *Notification:* continuous (freshmen), continuous (transfers).

Freshman Application Contact Ms. Stephanie Peters, Ms. Amy Williams, Co-Directors of Admissions, Morningside College, 1501 Morningside Avenue, Sioux City, IA 51106. *Phone:* 712-274-5111. *Toll-free phone:* 800-831-0806 Ext. 5111. *Fax:* 712-274-5101. *E-mail:* mscadm@morningside.edu.

See page 982 for the College Close-Up.

MOUNT MERCY COLLEGE

Cedar Rapids, Iowa — www.mtmercy.edu/

- **Independent Roman Catholic** 4-year, founded 1928
- **Suburban** 40-acre campus
- **Endowment** $23.0 million
- **Coed** 1,506 undergraduate students, 62% full-time, 72% women, 28% men
- **Moderately difficult** entrance level, 72% of applicants were admitted

Undergraduates 938 full-time, 568 part-time. Students come from 15 states and territories, 6 other countries, 4% are from out of state, 2% African American, 0.8% Asian American or Pacific Islander, 1% Hispanic American, 0.4% Native American, 0.6% international, 19% transferred in, 29% live on campus. *Retention:* 70% of 2006 full-time freshmen returned.

Freshmen *Admission:* 457 applied, 328 admitted, 142 enrolled. *Average high school GPA:* 3.42. *Test scores:* ACT scores over 18: 100%; ACT scores over 24: 30%; ACT scores over 30: 1%.

Faculty *Total:* 156, 50% full-time, 37% with terminal degrees. *Student/faculty ratio:* 11:1.

Majors Accounting; art; art teacher education; biology/biological sciences; business administration and management; clinical laboratory science/medical technology; communication and journalism related; communication/speech communication and rhetoric; computer and information sciences; computer science; criminal justice/law enforcement administration; elementary education; English; health and medical administrative services related; history; international relations and affairs; journalism; marketing/marketing management; mathematics; middle school education; music; music teacher education; natural resources and conservation related; nursing (registered nurse training); philosophy; political science and government; pre-dentistry studies; pre-law studies; pre-medical studies; pre-veterinary studies; psychology; public relations/image management; religious studies; science teacher education; secondary education; social work; sociology; speech and rhetoric; urban studies/affairs.

Academics *Calendar:* 4-1-4. *Degree:* bachelor's. *Special study options:* academic remediation for entering students, accelerated degree program, adult/continuing education programs, advanced placement credit, double majors, honors programs, independent study, internships, off-campus study, part-time degree program, services for LD students, study abroad, summer session for credit.

Computers on Campus 115 computers/terminals and 200 ports are available on campus for general student use. Students can access the following: campus intranet, computer help desk, free student e-mail accounts, online (class) grades, online (class) registration, online (class) schedules. Campuswide network is available. 100% of college-owned or -operated housing units are wired for high-speed Internet access. Wireless service is available via entire campus.

Student Life *Housing:* on-campus residence required through sophomore year. *Options:* coed, men-only, women-only. Campus housing is university owned. Freshman campus housing is guaranteed. *Activities and organizations:* drama/theater group, student-run newspaper, choral group, Student Government Association, Students in Free Enterprise, Mount Mercy Association of Nursing Students, Student-Iowa State Education Association, Stang Gang. *Campus security:* 24-hour emergency response devices and patrols, student patrols, late-night transport/escort service, controlled dormitory access. *Student services:* health clinic, personal/psychological counseling.

Athletics Member NAIA. *Intercollegiate sports:* baseball M (s), basketball M (s)/W (s), cross-country running M (s)/W (s), golf M (s)/W (s), soccer M (s)/W (s), softball W (s), track and field M (s)/W (s), volleyball W (s). *Intramural sports:* baseball M, basketball M/W, cheerleading W, football M/W, racquetball M/W, tennis M/W, volleyball M/W, weight lifting M/W.

Standardized Tests *Required:* SAT or ACT (for admission).

Costs (2007–08) *Comprehensive fee:* $26,340 includes full-time tuition ($20,070) and room and board ($6270). Full-time tuition and fees vary according to course load. Part-time tuition: $555 per credit hour. Part-time tuition and fees vary according to course load. *Room and board:* Room and board charges vary according to board plan and housing facility. *Payment plan:* installment. *Waivers:* employees or children of employees.

Financial Aid Of all full-time matriculated undergraduates who enrolled in 2006, 925 applied for aid, 818 were judged to have need, 290 had their need fully met. 285 Federal Work-Study jobs (averaging $1419). 127 state and other part-time jobs (averaging $1921). In 2006, 182 non-need-based awards were made. *Average percent of need met:* 77%. *Average financial aid package:* $15,214. *Average need-based loan:* $5289. *Average need-based gift aid:* $10,164. *Average non-need-based aid:* $10,414. *Average indebtedness upon graduation:* $27,083.

Applying *Options:* electronic application, deferred entrance. *Application fee:* $20. *Required:* essay or personal statement, high school transcript, minimum 2.5 GPA, letters of recommendation. *Required for some:* letters of recommendation. *Application deadlines:* 8/15 (freshmen), 8/15 (transfers). *Notification:* continuous (freshmen), continuous (transfers).

Freshman Application Contact Ms. Beth Tjelle, Assistant Director of Admissions, Mount Mercy College, 1330 Elmhurst Drive, NE, Cedar Rapids, IA 52402. *Phone:* 319-368-6460. *Toll-free phone:* 800-248-4504. *Fax:* 319-363-5270. *E-mail:* btjelle@metmercy.edu.

See page 984 for the College Close-Up.

NORTHWESTERN COLLEGE

Orange City, Iowa — www.nwciowa.edu/

- **Independent** 4-year, founded 1882, affiliated with Reformed Church in America
- **Rural** 45-acre campus
- **Endowment** $41.7 million
- **Coed** 1,315 undergraduate students, 97% full-time, 61% women, 39% men
- **Moderately difficult** entrance level, 79% of applicants were admitted

Ranked as a top 20 comprehensive Midwestern college by *U.S. News & World Report*, Northwestern College combines academic rigor with a Christian perspective and numerous opportunities for service and extracurricular preparation. A growing campus has enabled Northwestern to open new state-of-the-art facilities for theater, visual arts, and student services.

Undergraduates 1,271 full-time, 44 part-time. Students come from 30 states and territories, 20 other countries, 46% are from out of state, 0.9% African American, 0.9% Asian American or Pacific Islander, 1% Hispanic American, 0.2% Native American, 3% international, 3% transferred in, 89% live on campus. *Retention:* 76% of 2006 full-time freshmen returned.

Freshmen *Admission:* 1,311 applied, 1,034 admitted, 324 enrolled. *Average high school GPA:* 3.54. *Test scores:* ACT scores over 18: 99%; ACT scores over 24: 61%; ACT scores over 30: 9%.

Faculty *Total:* 128, 64% full-time, 52% with terminal degrees. *Student/faculty ratio:* 15:1.

Majors Accounting; actuarial science; art; art teacher education; athletic training; biology/biological sciences; biology teacher education; business administration and management; business teacher education; chemistry; cinematography and film/video production; clinical laboratory science/medical technology; computer science; dramatic/theater arts; economics; education (K-12); elementary education; English; environmental biology; graphic design; history; humanities; journalism; kinesiology and exercise science; mathematics; music; music teacher education; nursing (registered nurse training); philosophy; physical education teaching and coaching; political science and government; psychology; religious education; religious studies; secondary education; social work; sociology; Spanish; speech and rhetoric; speech/theater education.

Academics *Calendar:* semesters. *Degree:* certificates and bachelor's. *Special study options:* academic remediation for entering students, advanced placement credit, cooperative education, double majors, English as a second language, honors programs, independent study, internships, off-campus study, part-time degree program, services for LD students, student-designed majors, study abroad, summer session for credit. *Unusual degree programs:* 3-2 engineering with Washington University in St. Louis.

Computers on Campus 250 computers/terminals are available on campus for general student use. Students can access the following: campus intranet, computer help desk, free student e-mail accounts, online (class) grades, online (class) registration, online (class) schedules, online degree audits. Campuswide network is available. Wireless service is available via classrooms, computer centers, computer labs, learning centers, libraries, student centers.

Student Life *Housing:* on-campus residence required through senior year. *Options:* men-only, women-only, disabled students. Campus housing is university owned. Freshman campus housing is guaranteed. *Activities and organizations:* drama/theater group, student-run newspaper, television station, choral group, Drama Ministries Ensemble, Acapella Choir, Psi Chi, Fellowship of Christian Athletes, International Club. *Campus security:* 24-hour emergency response devices, controlled dormitory access. *Student services:* health clinic, personal/psychological counseling.

Athletics Member NAIA. *Intercollegiate sports:* baseball M (s), basketball M (s)/W (s), cross-country running M (s)/W (s), football M (s), golf M (s)/W (s), soccer M (s)/W (s), softball W (s), track and field M (s)/W (s), volleyball W (s), wrestling M (s). *Intramural sports:* badminton M/W, basketball M/W, bowling M/W, cheerleading M/W, cross-country running M/W, football M/W, golf M/W, lacrosse M/W, racquetball M/W, softball M, table tennis M/W, tennis M/W, volleyball M/W.

Standardized Tests *Required:* SAT or ACT (for admission).

Costs (2007–08) *Comprehensive fee:* $27,950 includes full-time tuition ($21,648) and room and board ($6302). Part-time tuition and fees vary according to course load. No tuition increase for student's term of enrollment. *Room and board:* Room and board charges vary according to housing facility. *Payment plans:* tuition prepayment, installment. *Waivers:* employees or children of employees.

Financial Aid Of all full-time matriculated undergraduates who enrolled in 2007, 997 applied for aid, 997 were judged to have need, 418 had their need fully met. 354 Federal Work-Study jobs (averaging $1120). 412 state and other part-time jobs (averaging $1120). In 2007, 229 non-need-based awards were made. *Average percent of need met:* 87%. *Average financial aid package:* $16,330. *Average need-based loan:* $4453. *Average need-based gift aid:* $6289. *Average non-need-based aid:* $5562. *Average indebtedness upon graduation:* $23,817.

Applying *Options:* electronic application, early admission, deferred entrance. *Application fee:* $25. *Required:* essay or personal statement, high school transcript, minimum 2.0 GPA, 1 letter of recommendation. *Recommended:* minimum 2.5 GPA, interview. *Application deadlines:* rolling (freshmen), rolling (transfers). *Notification:* continuous (freshmen), continuous (transfers).

Freshman Application Contact Mr. Mark Bloemendaal, Director of Admissions, Northwestern College, 101 7th Street SW, Orange City, IA 51041-1996. *Phone:* 712-737-7130. *Toll-free phone:* 800-747-4757. *Fax:* 712-707-7164. *E-mail:* admissions@nwciowa.edu.

PALMER COLLEGE OF CHIROPRACTIC

Davenport, Iowa **www.palmer.edu/**

- **Independent** comprehensive, founded 1897
- **Urban** campus
- **Coed** 70 undergraduate students, 93% full-time, 51% women, 49% men
- **Moderately difficult** entrance level

Undergraduates 65 full-time, 5 part-time. 4% African American, 3% Asian American or Pacific Islander, 1% Hispanic American.

Freshmen *Admission:* 8 enrolled.

Majors Biological and physical sciences; medical/clinical assistant.

Academics *Calendar:* trimesters. *Degrees:* certificates, associate, incidental bachelor's, master's, and first professional. *Special study options:* academic remediation for entering students, internships, services for LD students, summer session for credit.

Computers on Campus 75 computers/terminals are available on campus for general student use. Students can access the following: campus intranet, free student e-mail accounts, online (class) registration. Campuswide network is available. Wireless service is available via entire campus.

Student Life *Housing:* college housing not available. *Activities and organizations:* student-run newspaper, Gonstead Club, intramural sports, campus guides, Student International Chiropractic Association, Palmer Student Alumni Foundation. *Campus security:* 24-hour emergency response devices and patrols, late-night transport/escort service. *Student services:* health clinic, personal/psychological counseling.

Athletics *Intramural sports:* baseball M (c), basketball M (c)/W (c), golf M, ice hockey M (c), rock climbing M/W, soccer M, softball M/W, table tennis M/W, tennis M/W, volleyball M/W.

Costs (2007–08) *Tuition:* $6420 full-time, $160 per credit part-time. Full-time tuition and fees vary according to course load and degree level. Part-time tuition and fees vary according to course load and degree level. *Required fees:* $430 full-time, $70 per term part-time. *Waivers:* employees or children of employees.

Financial Aid Of all full-time matriculated undergraduates who enrolled in 2006, 4 Federal Work-Study jobs (averaging $2200). *Average indebtedness upon graduation:* $10,895.

Applying *Options:* electronic application, deferred entrance. *Application fee:* $50. *Required:* high school transcript, minimum 2.0 GPA, minimum 2.0 in math, science, and English courses. *Required for some:* essay or personal statement, interview. *Application deadline:* rolling (freshmen). *Notification:* continuous (freshmen).

Freshman Application Contact Ms. Karen Eden, Director of Admissions, Palmer College of Chiropractic, 1000 Brady Street, Davenport, IA 52803-5287. *Phone:* 563-884-5656. *Toll-free phone:* 800-722-3648. *Fax:* 563-884-5414. *E-mail:* pcadmit@palmer.edu.

ST. AMBROSE UNIVERSITY

Davenport, Iowa **www.sau.edu/**

- **Independent Roman Catholic** comprehensive, founded 1882
- **Urban** 50-acre campus
- **Endowment** $51.9 million
- **Coed** 2,893 undergraduate students, 81% full-time, 63% women, 37% men
- **Moderately difficult** entrance level, 70% of applicants were admitted

Undergraduates 2,335 full-time, 558 part-time. Students come from 33 states and territories, 17 other countries, 50% are from out of state, 3% African American, 1% Asian American or Pacific Islander, 3% Hispanic American, 0.7% Native American, 0.9% international, 10% transferred in, 50% live on campus. *Retention:* 79% of 2006 full-time freshmen returned.

Freshmen *Admission:* 2,145 applied, 1,491 admitted, 510 enrolled. *Average high school GPA:* 3.15. *Test scores:* ACT scores over 18: 94%; ACT scores over 24: 32%; ACT scores over 30: 5%.

Faculty *Total:* 335, 50% full-time, 47% with terminal degrees. *Student/faculty ratio:* 11:1.

Majors Accounting; advertising; art; art teacher education; biology/biological sciences; biology teacher education; business administration and management; business/commerce; business teacher education; chemistry; chemistry teacher education; computer science; computer systems analysis; computer systems networking and telecommunications; criminal justice/safety; design and visual communications; dramatic/theater arts; early childhood education; economics; education; education (K-12); elementary education; engineering physics; English; English/language arts teacher education; finance; fine/studio arts; forensic psychology; French; French language teacher education; German; German language teacher education; graphic design; health and physical education; health teacher education; history; history teacher education; industrial engineering; information science/studies; international business/trade/commerce; journalism; management science; marketing/marketing management; mass communication/media; mathematics; mathematics teacher education; multi-/interdisciplinary studies related; music; music teacher education; nursing (registered nurse training); organizational behavior; philosophy; physical education teaching and coaching; physics; physics teacher education; political science and government; psychology; psychology teacher education; public administration; public relations/image management; radio and television; science teacher education; secondary education; security and protective services related; social science teacher education; sociology; Spanish; Spanish language teacher education; speech teacher education; speech/theater education; sport and fitness administration/management; theology.

Academics *Calendar:* 4-1-4. *Degrees:* certificates, bachelor's, master's, doctoral, post-master's, and postbachelor's certificates. *Special study options:* academic remediation for entering students, accelerated degree program, adult/continuing education programs, advanced placement credit, cooperative education, distance learning, double majors, external degree program, independent study, internships, off-campus study, part-time degree program, services for LD students, student-designed majors, study abroad, summer session for credit. *Unusual degree programs:* 3-2 physical therapy, occupational therapy, special education.

Computers on Campus 273 computers/terminals and 505 ports are available on campus for general student use. Students can access the following: campus intranet, computer help desk, free student e-mail accounts, online (class) grades, online (class) registration, online (class) schedules, online course syllabi, online class listings, and online payments. Campuswide network is available. 100% of college-owned or -operated housing units are wired for high-speed Internet access. Wireless service is available via classrooms, libraries, student centers.

Student Life *Housing:* on-campus residence required through sophomore year. *Options:* coed, men-only, women-only, disabled students. Campus housing is university owned. Freshman campus housing is guaranteed. *Activities and organizations:* drama/theater group, student-run newspaper, radio and television station, choral group, Student Government Association, Student Alumni Association, Social Action Group, College Activities Board, Ambrosians for Peace and Justice. *Campus security:* 24-hour emergency response devices and patrols, late-night transport/escort service, controlled dormitory access, police officer on campus 10 p.m. to 6 a.m. *Student services:* health clinic, personal/psychological counseling, women's center.

Athletics Member NAIA. *Intercollegiate sports:* baseball M (s), basketball M (s)/W (s), cheerleading W (s), cross-country running M (s)/W (s), football M (s), golf M (s)/W (s), soccer M (s)/W (s), softball W (s), tennis M (s)/W (s), track and field M (s)/W (s), volleyball M (s)/W (s). *Intramural sports:* badminton M/W, baseball M/W, basketball M/W, bowling M/W, football M/W, golf M/W, racquetball M/W, skiing (downhill) M/W, soccer M/W, softball M/W, table tennis M/W, tennis M/W, volleyball M/W.

Standardized Tests *Required:* SAT or ACT (for admission). *Recommended:* ACT (for admission).

Costs (2008–09) *Comprehensive fee:* $29,435 includes full-time tuition ($21,610) and room and board ($7825). Part-time tuition: $672 per semester hour. *College room only:* $3988.

Financial Aid Of all full-time matriculated undergraduates who enrolled in 2007, 2,256 applied for aid, 1,670 were judged to have need, 526 had their need fully met. 468 Federal Work-Study jobs (averaging $1518). 134 state and other part-time jobs (averaging $1515). In 2007, 586 non-need-based awards were made. *Average percent of need met:* 35%. *Average financial aid package:* $21,025. *Average need-based loan:* $4460. *Average need-based gift aid:* $9723. *Average non-need-based aid:* $6909. *Average indebtedness upon graduation:* $32,444.

Applying *Options:* electronic application, deferred entrance. *Application fee:* $25. *Required:* high school transcript, minimum 2.5 GPA, minimum ACT score of 20 or rank in top 50% of high school class. *Required for some:* letters of recommendation, interview. *Recommended:* interview. *Application deadlines:* rolling (freshmen), rolling (transfers). *Notification:* 10/1 (freshmen), continuous (transfers).

Freshman Application Contact Ms. Meg Halligan, Director of Admissions, St. Ambrose University, 518 West Locust Street, Davenport, IA 52803-2898. *Phone:* 563-333-6300 Ext. 6311. *Toll-free phone:* 800-383-2627. *Fax:* 563-333-6297. *E-mail:* halliganmegf@sau.edu.

See page 986 for the College Close-Up.

SIMPSON COLLEGE

Indianola, Iowa **www.simpson.edu/**

- **Independent United Methodist** 4-year, founded 1860
- **Small-town** 75-acre campus
- **Endowment** $81.6 million
- **Coed** 2,017 undergraduate students, 74% full-time, 58% women, 42% men
- **Moderately difficult** entrance level, 88% of applicants were admitted

Simpson is more than a beautiful campus. The College has an outstanding faculty and renowned curricula, including more than forty majors, minors, and preprofessional programs. A 4-4-1 calendar provides students with many learning opportunities, including internships, career observations, and study programs both abroad and in the United States. The campus is located just 12 miles from Des Moines, Iowa's capital. Simpson's ideal location allows students the opportunity to enjoy a large metropolitan area as well as small-town charm.

Undergraduates 1,500 full-time, 517 part-time. Students come from 21 states and territories, 16 other countries, 8% are from out of state, 2% African American, 1% Asian American or Pacific Islander, 2% Hispanic American, 0.5% Native American, 0.8% international, 4% transferred in, 87% live on campus. *Retention:* 82% of 2006 full-time freshmen returned.

Freshmen *Admission:* 1,346 applied, 1,180 admitted, 385 enrolled. *Test scores:* ACT scores over 18: 99%; ACT scores over 24: 55%; ACT scores over 30: 7%.

Faculty *Total:* 206, 47% full-time, 88% with terminal degrees. *Student/faculty ratio:* 16:1.

Majors Accounting; advertising; art; art teacher education; athletic training; biochemistry; biological and physical sciences; biology/biological sciences; business administration and management; business/corporate communications; chemistry; clinical laboratory science/medical technology; computer science; criminal justice/law enforcement administration; dramatic/theater arts; economics; education; elementary education; English; environmental biology; forensic science and technology; French; German; history; information science/studies; international business/trade/commerce; international relations and affairs; kindergarten/preschool education; mass communication/media; mathematics; music; music performance; music teacher education; philosophy; physical education teaching and coaching; political science and government; pre-dentistry studies; pre-law studies; pre-medical studies; pre-veterinary studies; psychology; religious studies; secondary education; social sciences; sociology; Spanish; sport and fitness administration/management.

Academics *Calendar:* 4-4-1. *Degrees:* diplomas, bachelor's, master's, and postbachelor's certificates. *Special study options:* adult/continuing education programs, advanced placement credit, cooperative education, double majors, external degree program, honors programs, independent study, internships, off-campus study, part-time degree program, services for LD students, study abroad, summer session for credit. *Unusual degree programs:* 3-2 engineering with Washington University in St. Louis; Iowa State University; University of Minnesota.

Computers on Campus 275 computers/terminals are available on campus for general student use. Students can access the following: campus intranet, computer help desk, free student e-mail accounts, online (class) grades, online (class) schedules. Campuswide network is available. 100% of college-owned or -operated housing units are wired for high-speed Internet access. Wireless service is available via classrooms, computer centers, computer labs, learning centers, libraries, student centers.

Student Life *Housing:* on-campus residence required through junior year. *Options:* coed, men-only, women-only. Campus housing is university owned. Freshman campus housing is guaranteed. *Activities and organizations:* drama/theater group, student-run newspaper, radio station, choral group, intramurals, Religious Life Council, Campus Activities Board, student government, Residence Hall Association, national fraternities, national sororities. *Campus security:* 24-hour emergency response devices and patrols, student patrols, late-night transport/escort service, controlled dormitory access. *Student services:* health clinic, personal/psychological counseling, women's center.

Athletics Member NCAA. All Division III. *Intercollegiate sports:* baseball M, basketball M/W, cheerleading M/W, cross-country running M/W, football M, golf M/W, soccer M/W, softball W, swimming and diving W, tennis M/W, track and field M/W, volleyball W, wrestling M. *Intramural sports:* badminton M/W, basketball M/W, bowling M/W, football M/W, golf M/W, racquetball M/W, skiing (downhill) M/W, soccer M/W, softball M/W, swimming and diving M/W, table tennis M/W, tennis M/W, ultimate Frisbee M/W, volleyball M/W, weight lifting M/W.

Standardized Tests *Required:* SAT or ACT (for admission).

Costs (2008–09) *One-time required fee:* $100. *Comprehensive fee:* $31,759 includes full-time tuition ($24,414), mandatory fees ($357), and room and board ($6988). Part-time tuition: $275 per credit hour. *College room only:* $3354.

Financial Aid Of all full-time matriculated undergraduates who enrolled in 2007, 1,491 applied for aid, 1,298 were judged to have need, 347 had their need fully met. 408 Federal Work-Study jobs (averaging $450). 665 state and other part-time jobs (averaging $603). In 2007, 179 non-need-based awards were made. *Average percent of need met:* 86%. *Average financial aid package:* $21,384. *Average need-based loan:* $4195. *Average need-based gift aid:* $14,572. *Average non-need-based aid:* $9615. *Average indebtedness upon graduation:* $29,255.

Applying *Options:* electronic application, early admission, deferred entrance. *Required:* high school transcript, 1 letter of recommendation. *Recommended:* interview, rank in upper 50% of high school class. *Application deadlines:* 8/15 (freshmen), 8/15 (transfers). *Notification:* continuous (freshmen), continuous (transfers).

Freshman Application Contact Ms. Deborah Tierney, Vice President for Enrollment, Simpson College, 701 North C Street, Indianola, IA 50125. *Phone:* 515-961-1624. *Toll-free phone:* 800-362-2454 (in-state); 800-362-2454 Ext. 1624 (out-of-state). *Fax:* 515-961-1870. *E-mail:* admiss@simpson.edu.

See page 988 for the College Close-Up.

UNIVERSITY OF DUBUQUE

Dubuque, Iowa **www.dbq.edu/**

Freshman Application Contact Mr. Jesse James, Director of Admissions, University of Dubuque, 2000 University Avenue, Dubuque, IA 52001-5099. *Phone:* 563-589-3214. *Toll-free phone:* 800-722-5583. *Fax:* 563-589-3690. *E-mail:* admissns@dbq.edu.

See page 990 for the College Close-Up.

THE UNIVERSITY OF IOWA

Iowa City, Iowa **www.uiowa.edu/**

- **State-supported** university, founded 1847
- **Small-town** 1900-acre campus
- **Endowment** $378.4 million
- **Coed** 20,907 undergraduate students, 89% full-time, 53% women, 47% men
- **Moderately difficult** entrance level, 83% of applicants were admitted

Undergraduates 18,669 full-time, 2,238 part-time. Students come from 54 states and territories, 60 other countries, 34% are from out of state, 2% African American, 4% Asian American or Pacific Islander, 3% Hispanic American, 0.5% Native American, 1% international, 5% transferred in, 30% live on campus. *Retention:* 83% of 2006 full-time freshmen returned.

Freshmen *Admission:* 14,678 applied, 12,209 admitted, 4,287 enrolled. *Average high school GPA:* 3.56. *Test scores:* SAT critical reading scores over 500: 83%; SAT math scores over 500: 89%; ACT scores over 18: 99%; SAT critical reading scores over 600: 45%; SAT math scores over 600: 57%; ACT scores over 24: 66%; SAT critical reading scores over 700: 14%; SAT math scores over 700: 15%; ACT scores over 30: 12%.

Faculty *Total:* 1,655, 94% full-time, 97% with terminal degrees. *Student/faculty ratio:* 15:1.

Majors Accounting; actuarial science; African-American/Black studies; African studies; Air Force R.O.T.C./air science; American Indian/Native American studies; American Sign Language related; American studies; ancient/classical Greek; ancient studies; anthropology; applied mathematics related; Army R.O.T.C./military science; art; art history, criticism and conservation; arts management; art teacher education; Asian studies; astronomy; athletic training; audiology and hearing sciences; audiology and speech-language pathology; biochemistry; biology/biological sciences; biology teacher education; biomedical/medical engineering; business administration and management; business/managerial economics; ceramic arts and ceramics; chemical engineering; chemistry; chemistry teacher education; Chinese; cinematography and film/video production; civil engineering; classics and languages, literatures and linguistics; clinical laboratory science/medical technology; communication/speech communication and rhetoric; comparative literature; computer and information sciences; computer science; dance; drama and dance teacher education; dramatic/theater arts; drawing; economics; electrical, electronics and communications engineering; elementary education; engineering; English; English as a second/foreign language (teaching); English language and literature related; entrepreneurship; environmental science; environmental studies; film/cinema studies; film/video and photographic arts related; finance; fine/studio arts; French; French language teacher education; geography; geography teacher education; geology/earth science; German; German language teacher education; history; history teacher education; human resources management; industrial engineering; interdisciplinary studies; international/global studies; Italian; Japanese; jazz/jazz studies; journalism; kinesiology and exercise science; labor and industrial relations; Latin; Latin American studies; Latin teacher education; liberal arts and sciences/liberal studies; linguistics; literature; management information systems; management science; management sciences and quantitative methods related; marketing/marketing management; marketing related; mass communication/media; mathematics; mathematics teacher education; mechanical engineering; medieval and Renaissance studies; metal and jewelry arts; microbiology; modern Greek; museum studies; music; music management and merchandising; music teacher education; music theory and composition; music therapy; nuclear medical technology; nursing (registered nurse training); painting; parks, recreation and leisure; pharmacy; philosophy; photography; physics; physics teacher education; piano and organ; political science and government; Portuguese; pre-dentistry studies; pre-law studies; pre-medical studies; pre-pharmacy studies; pre-veterinary studies; printmaking; psychology; radiologic technology/science; religious studies; Russian; Russian studies; science teacher education; sculpture; secondary education; social studies teacher education; social work; sociology; Spanish; Spanish language teacher education; speech and rhetoric; speech teacher education; sport and fitness administration/management; statistics; theater/theater arts management; therapeutic recreation; violin, viola, guitar and other stringed instruments; voice and opera; wind/percussion instruments; women's studies.

Academics *Calendar:* semesters. *Degrees:* bachelor's, master's, doctoral, first professional, post-master's, and first professional certificates. *Special study options:* academic remediation for entering students, accelerated degree program, adult/continuing education programs, advanced placement credit, cooperative education, distance learning, double majors, English as a second language, external degree program, honors programs, independent study, internships, off-campus study, part-time degree program, services for LD students, student-designed majors, study abroad, summer session for credit. *ROTC:* Army (b), Air Force (b).

Computers on Campus 1,200 computers/terminals are available on campus for general student use. Students can access the following: computer help desk, free student e-mail accounts, online (class) grades, online (class) registration, online (class) schedules, online degree process, financial aid summary, bills. Campuswide network is available. Wireless service is available via classrooms, computer labs, dorm rooms, learning centers, libraries, student centers.

Student Life *Housing options:* coed, disabled students. Campus housing is university owned. Freshman applicants given priority for college housing. *Activities and organizations:* drama/theater group, student-run newspaper, radio station, choral group, marching band, Association of Residence Halls, Graduate Student Senate, National Society of Collegiate Scholars, Organization for the Active Support of International Students (OASIS), Dance Marathon, national fraternities, national sororities. *Campus security:* 24-hour emergency response devices and patrols, late-night transport/escort service, controlled dormitory access. *Student services:* health clinic, personal/psychological counseling, women's center, legal services.

Athletics Member NCAA. All Division I except football (Division I-A). *Intercollegiate sports:* baseball M (s), basketball M (s)/W (s), crew M (c)/W (s), cross-country running M (s)/W (s), field hockey W (s), golf M (s)/W (s), gymnastics M (s)/W (s), ice hockey M (c), lacrosse M (c)/W (c), rugby M (c)/W (c), sailing M (c)/W (c), soccer M (c)/W (s), softball W (s), swimming and diving M (s)/W (s), table tennis M (c)/W (c), tennis M (s)/W (s), track and field M (s)/W (s), ultimate Frisbee M (c)/W (c), volleyball M (c)/W (s), wrestling M (s). *Intramural sports:* badminton M/W, basketball M/W, bowling M/W, fencing M (c)/W (c), football M/W, golf M/W, racquetball M/W, rugby M (c)/W (c), sailing M (c)/W (c), skiing (cross-country) M (c)/W (c), skiing (downhill) M (c)/W (c), soccer M/W, softball M/W, table tennis M/W, tennis M/W, track and field M/W, ultimate Frisbee M/W, volleyball M/W, water polo M (c)/W (c), wrestling M.

Standardized Tests *Required:* SAT or ACT (for admission).

Costs (2008–09) *Tuition:* state resident $5548 full-time; nonresident $19,662 full-time. *Required fees:* $996 full-time. *Room and board:* $7673.

Financial Aid Of all full-time matriculated undergraduates who enrolled in 2007, 13,598 applied for aid, 10,022 were judged to have need, 9,095 had their need fully met. In 2007, 3636 non-need-based awards were made. *Average percent of need met:* 97%. *Average financial aid package:* $7998. *Average need-based loan:* $4058. *Average need-based gift aid:* $4922. *Average non-need-based aid:* $3982. *Average indebtedness upon graduation:* $22,181.

Applying *Options:* electronic application, early admission, deferred entrance. *Application fee:* $40. *Required:* high school transcript, must meet Regent Admission Index (RAI) requirement: residents 245 or above; nonresidents 255 or above. *Application deadlines:* 4/1 (freshmen), 4/1 (transfers). *Notification:* continuous (freshmen), continuous (transfers).

Freshman Application Contact Mr. Michael Barron, Assistant Provost for Enrollment Services and Director of Admissions, The University of Iowa, 107 Calvin Hall, Iowa City, IA 52242. *Phone:* 319-335-3847. *Toll-free phone:* 800-553-4692. *Fax:* 319-335-1535. *E-mail:* admissions@uiowa.edu.

UNIVERSITY OF NORTHERN IOWA

Cedar Falls, Iowa **www.uni.edu/**

- **State-supported** comprehensive, founded 1876, part of Board of Regents, State of Iowa
- **Small-town** 916-acre campus
- **Endowment** $67.3 million
- **Coed** 11,050 undergraduate students, 89% full-time, 57% women, 43% men
- **Moderately difficult** entrance level, 80% of applicants were admitted

Undergraduates 9,849 full-time, 1,201 part-time. Students come from 36 states and territories, 54 other countries, 5% are from out of state, 3% African American, 1% Asian American or Pacific Islander, 2% Hispanic American, 0.3% Native American, 3% international, 10% transferred in, 39% live on campus. *Retention:* 82% of 2006 full-time freshmen returned.

Freshmen *Admission:* 4,722 applied, 3,759 admitted, 1,991 enrolled. *Test scores:* SAT critical reading scores over 500: 63%; SAT math scores over 500: 65%; ACT scores over 18: 96%; SAT critical reading scores over 600: 39%; SAT math scores over 600: 33%; ACT scores over 24: 42%; SAT critical reading scores over 700: 8%; SAT math scores over 700: 2%; ACT scores over 30: 5%.

Faculty *Total:* 811, 77% full-time, 61% with terminal degrees. *Student/faculty ratio:* 16:1.

Majors Accounting; acting; actuarial science; American studies; anthropology; apparel and textiles; applied economics; applied mathematics; art; art history, criticism and conservation; art teacher education; Asian studies; athletic training; biochemistry; bioinformatics; biological and physical sciences; biology/biological sciences; biotechnology; broadcast journalism; business administration and management; business teacher education; chemistry; chemistry related; communication/speech communication and rhetoric; community health services counseling; computer and information sciences and support services related; computer and information sciences related; computer science; construction management; criminology; digital communication and media/multimedia; dramatic/theater arts; driver and safety teacher education; ecology; economics; electromechanical technology; elementary education; engineering physics; English; English as a second/foreign language (teaching); environmental science; European studies; family and community services; family and consumer economics related; finance; fine/studio arts; foods, nutrition, and wellness; foreign languages and literatures; foreign languages related; foreign language teacher education; French; geography; geological and earth sciences/geosciences related; geology/earth science; German; gerontology; graphic communications; health and physical education; health professions related; health teacher education; history; housing and human environments; humanities; industrial technology; interior design; kindergarten/preschool education; Latin American studies; liberal arts and sciences/liberal studies; management information systems; manufacturing technology; marketing/marketing management; mathematics; mathematics teacher education; microbiology; middle school education; music; music performance; music teacher education; music theory and composition; organizational communication; parks, recreation and leisure; philosophy; physical education teaching and coaching; physics related; political science and government; political science and government related; psychology; public administration; public relations/image management; radio and television; reading teacher education; real estate; religious studies; Russian; Russian studies; science teacher education; social science teacher education; social studies teacher education; social work; sociology; Spanish; special education; special education (early childhood); special education (mentally retarded); special education (multiply disabled); speech and rhetoric; speech-language pathology; speech teacher education; system, networking, and LAN/WAN management; technology/industrial arts teacher education.

Academics *Calendar:* semesters. *Degrees:* bachelor's, master's, and doctoral. *Special study options:* academic remediation for entering students, accelerated degree program, adult/continuing education programs, advanced placement credit, cooperative education, distance learning, double majors, English as a second language, external degree program, honors programs, independent study, internships, off-campus study, part-time degree program, services for LD students, student-designed majors, study abroad, summer session for credit. *ROTC:* Army (b). *Unusual degree programs:* 3-2 nursing with University of Iowa; medical technology with St. Luke's Hospital/University of Iowa Medical School, cytotechnology with Mayo School of Health-Related Sciences, Wisconsin State Laboratory of Hygiene and Mercy School of Cytotechnology, chiropractic with Logan College of Chiropractic.

Computers on Campus 1,900 computers/terminals are available on campus for general student use. Students can access the following: computer help desk, free student e-mail accounts, online (class) grades, online (class) registration, online (class) schedules, course registration, student account, degree audit, program of study. Campuswide network is available. 100% of college-owned or -operated housing units are wired for high-speed Internet access. Wireless service is available via classrooms, computer centers, computer labs, learning centers, libraries, student centers.

Student Life *Housing options:* coed, women-only. Campus housing is university owned. *Activities and organizations:* drama/theater group, student-run newspaper, radio station, choral group, marching band, Catholic Student Association, National Society of Collegiate Scholars, Accounting Club, The Navigators, Sigmo Iota, national fraternities, national sororities. *Campus security:* 24-hour emergency response devices and patrols, student patrols, late-night transport/escort service, controlled dormitory access. *Student services:* health clinic, personal/psychological counseling.

Athletics Member NCAA. All Division I except football (Division I-AA). *Intercollegiate sports:* baseball M (s), basketball M (s)/W (s), cross-country running M (s)/W (s), golf M (s)/W (s), soccer W (s), softball W (s), swimming and diving W (s), tennis W (s), track and field M (s)/W (s), volleyball W (s), wrestling M (s). *Intramural sports:* badminton M/W, baseball M (c), basketball M/W, bowling M (c)/W (c), cheerleading M/W, crew M (c)/W (c), cross-country running M (c)/W (c), football M, golf M/W, ice hockey M (c), racquetball M (c)/W (c), rugby M (c)/W (c), skiing (cross-country) M (c)/W (c), skiing (downhill) M (c)/W (c), soccer M (c)/W (c), softball M (c)/W (c), swimming and diving M (c)/W (c), table tennis M/W, tennis M (c)/W (c), track and field M (c)/W (c), ultimate Frisbee M (c)/W (c), volleyball M/W (c), weight lifting M/W, wrestling M.

Standardized Tests *Required:* SAT or ACT (for admission).

Costs (2007–08) *Tuition:* state resident $6246 full-time, $223 per hour part-time; nonresident $14,554 full-time, $561 per hour part-time. Full-time tuition and fees vary according to course load. Part-time tuition and fees vary according to course load. *Required fees:* $838 full-time, $419 per term part-time. *Room and board:* $6280; room only: $2995. Room and board charges vary according to board plan and housing facility. *Payment plan:* installment.

Financial Aid Of all full-time matriculated undergraduates who enrolled in 2006, 7,516 applied for aid, 5,569 were judged to have need, 1,146 had their need fully met. 476 Federal Work-Study jobs (averaging $1829). 122 state and other part-time jobs (averaging $2053). In 2006, 902 non-need-based awards were made. *Average percent of need met:* 65%. *Average financial aid package:* $6992. *Average need-based loan:* $4056. *Average need-based gift aid:* $2888. *Average non-need-based aid:* $3083. *Average indebtedness upon graduation:* $21,561.

Applying *Options:* electronic application, deferred entrance. *Application fee:* $40. *Required:* high school transcript, rank in upper 50% of high school class. *Required for some:* letters of recommendation, interview. *Application deadlines:* 8/15 (freshmen), 8/15 (transfers). *Notification:* 9/1 (freshmen), 9/1 (transfers).

Freshman Application Contact Mr. Philip Patton, Interim Director of Admissions, University of Northern Iowa, 120 Gilchrist Hall, Cedar Falls, IA 50614-0018. *Phone:* 319-273-2281. *Toll-free phone:* 800-772-2037. *Fax:* 319-273-2885. *E-mail:* admissions@uni.edu.

UPPER IOWA UNIVERSITY

Fayette, Iowa **www.uiu.edu/**

- **Independent** comprehensive, founded 1857
- **Rural** 80-acre campus
- **Coed**
- **Moderately difficult** entrance level

Faculty *Student/faculty ratio:* 14:1.

Academics *Calendar:* 4 8-week terms. *Degrees:* associate, bachelor's, and master's (also offers continuing education program with significant enrollment not reflected in profile).

Student Life *Campus security:* late-night transport/escort service, controlled dormitory access.

Athletics Member NCAA. All Division II except softball (Division III), men's and women's track and field (Division III).

Standardized Tests *Required:* SAT or ACT (for admission).

Costs (2007–08) *Comprehensive fee:* $25,700 includes full-time tuition ($19,625) and room and board ($6075). Full-time tuition and fees vary according to course load. Part-time tuition: $680 per credit. *College room only:* $2525. Room and board charges vary according to board plan and housing facility.

Financial Aid *Average financial aid package:* $6000. *Average indebtedness upon graduation:* $17,125.

Applying *Options:* early admission, deferred entrance. *Application fee:* $15. *Required:* high school transcript, minimum 2.0 GPA. *Required for some:* essay or personal statement, letters of recommendation, interview.

Freshman Application Contact Ms. Jobyna Johnston, Interim Director of Admissions, Upper Iowa University, Box 1859, 605 Washington Street, Fayette, IA 52142-1857. *Phone:* 563-425-5393. *Toll-free phone:* 800-553-4150 Ext. 2. *Fax:* 563-425-5323. *E-mail:* admission@uiu.edu.

VATTEROTT COLLEGE

Des Moines, Iowa **www.vatterott-college.edu/**

Freshman Application Contact Mr. Henry Franken, Co-Director, Vatterott College, 6100 Thornton Avenue, Suite 290, Des Moines, IA 50321. *Phone:* 515-309-9000. *Toll-free phone:* 800-353-7264. *Fax:* 515-309-0366.

VENNARD COLLEGE

University Park, Iowa **www.vennard.edu/**

- **Independent interdenominational** 4-year, founded 1996
- **Small-town** 70-acre campus with easy access to Des Moines
- **Endowment** $816,988
- **Coed** 72 undergraduate students, 93% full-time, 49% women, 51% men
- **Moderately difficult** entrance level, 55% of applicants were admitted

Undergraduates 67 full-time, 5 part-time. Students come from 16 states and territories, 2 other countries, 56% are from out of state, 1% Asian American or Pacific Islander, 4% international, 11% transferred in, 76% live on campus. *Retention:* 60% of 2006 full-time freshmen returned.

Freshmen *Admission:* 33 applied, 18 admitted, 11 enrolled. *Average high school GPA:* 2.84. *Test scores:* SAT critical reading scores over 500: 100%; SAT math scores over 500: 50%; ACT scores over 18: 51%; ACT scores over 24: 13%.

Faculty *Total:* 14, 29% full-time, 14% with terminal degrees. *Student/faculty ratio:* 9:1.

Majors Biblical studies; business administration and management; Christian studies; communications technology; computer/information technology services administration related; elementary education; general studies; missionary studies and missiology; multi-/interdisciplinary studies related; pastoral counseling and specialized ministries related; pastoral studies/counseling; psychology; religious education; religious/sacred music; religious studies; secondary education; theology; youth ministry.

Academics *Calendar:* semesters. *Degrees:* certificates, associate, and bachelor's. *Special study options:* academic remediation for entering students, advanced placement credit, cooperative education, distance learning, double majors, independent study, internships, off-campus study, part-time degree program, student-designed majors, summer session for credit.

Computers on Campus 17 computers/terminals are available on campus for general student use. 100% of college-owned or -operated housing units are wired for high-speed Internet access. Wireless service is available via entire campus.

Student Life *Housing:* on-campus residence required through sophomore year. *Options:* men-only, women-only. Campus housing is university owned. Freshman campus housing is guaranteed. *Campus security:* student patrols.

Athletics Member NCCAA. *Intercollegiate sports:* basketball M/W, soccer M, volleyball W. *Intramural sports:* golf M, soccer M/W, volleyball M/W.

Standardized Tests *Required:* SAT or ACT (for admission).

Costs (2007–08) *Comprehensive fee:* $13,800 includes full-time tuition ($8250), mandatory fees ($950), and room and board ($4600). Part-time tuition: $285 per credit hour. *Required fees:* $900 per term part-time.

Financial Aid In 2003, 5 non-need-based awards were made. *Average percent of need met:* 60%. *Average financial aid package:* $7000. *Average indebtedness upon graduation:* $12,000.

Applying *Options:* electronic application, early admission. *Application fee:* $20. *Required:* essay or personal statement, high school transcript, minimum 2.2 GPA, 3 letters of recommendation. *Required for some:* interview. *Notification:* continuous (transfers).

Freshman Application Contact Ms. Rikki Huggett, Administrative Assistance for Admissions, Vennard College, PO Box 29, University Park, IA 52595. *Phone:* 641-673-8391 Ext. 106. *Toll-free phone:* 800-686-8391. *Fax:* 641-673-8365. *E-mail:* rikki.huggett@vennard.edu.

WALDORF COLLEGE

Forest City, Iowa — www.waldorf.edu/

- **Independent Lutheran** 4-year, founded 1903
- **Rural** 29-acre campus
- **Endowment** $4.5 million
- **Coed**
- **Moderately difficult** entrance level

Faculty *Student/faculty ratio:* 14:1.

Academics *Calendar:* semesters. *Degree:* bachelor's.

Student Life *Campus security:* late-night transport/escort service, evening and night patrols by trained security personnel.

Athletics Member NAIA.

Standardized Tests *Required:* SAT or ACT (for admission).

Costs (2007–08) *Comprehensive fee:* $24,110 includes full-time tuition ($17,791), mandatory fees ($785), and room and board ($5534).

Financial Aid Of all full-time matriculated undergraduates who enrolled in 2006, 531 applied for aid, 487 were judged to have need, 153 had their need fully met. 425 Federal Work-Study jobs (averaging $1304). 81 state and other part-time jobs (averaging $941). In 2006, 105 non-need-based awards were made. *Average percent of need met:* 83. *Average financial aid package:* $15,710. *Average need-based loan:* $5348. *Average need-based gift aid:* $10,377. *Average non-need-based aid:* $12,314. *Average indebtedness upon graduation:* $14,782.

Applying *Options:* electronic application, early admission. *Required:* high school transcript, 1 letter of recommendation. *Required for some:* interview. *Recommended:* minimum 2.0 GPA.

Freshman Application Contact Mr. Steve Hall, Assistant Dean of Admission, Waldorf College, 106 South 6th Street, Forest City, IA 50436. *Phone:* 641-585-8119. *Toll-free phone:* 800-292-1903. *E-mail:* admissions@waldorf.edu.

WARTBURG COLLEGE

Waverly, Iowa — www.wartburg.edu/

- **Independent Lutheran** 4-year, founded 1852
- **Small-town** 118-acre campus
- **Endowment** $48.4 million
- **Coed** 1,810 undergraduate students, 96% full-time, 52% women, 48% men
- **Moderately difficult** entrance level, 84% of applicants were admitted

Undergraduates 1,742 full-time, 68 part-time. Students come from 24 states and territories, 43 other countries, 23% are from out of state, 3% African American, 2% Asian American or Pacific Islander, 2% Hispanic American, 0.4% Native American, 6% international, 2% transferred in, 82% live on campus. *Retention:* 81% of 2006 full-time freshmen returned.

Freshmen *Admission:* 1,982 applied, 1,656 admitted, 545 enrolled. *Average high school GPA:* 3.52. *Test scores:* SAT critical reading scores over 500: 75%; SAT math scores over 500: 86%; SAT writing scores over 500: 82%; ACT scores over 18: 97%; SAT critical reading scores over 600: 46%; SAT math scores over 600: 36%; SAT writing scores over 600: 39%; ACT scores over 24: 50%; SAT critical reading scores over 700: 7%; SAT math scores over 700: 11%; SAT writing scores over 700: 11%; ACT scores over 30: 7%.

Faculty *Total:* 163, 66% full-time, 61% with terminal degrees. *Student/faculty ratio:* 12:1.

Majors Accounting; art; arts management; art teacher education; biochemistry; biology/biological sciences; broadcast journalism; business administration and management; chemistry; clinical laboratory science/medical technology; commercial and advertising art; computer science; economics; elementary education; engineering; English; English composition; finance; French; German; history; history teacher education; information science/studies; international business/trade/commerce; international relations and affairs; journalism; kindergarten/preschool education; marketing/marketing management; mass communication/media; mathematics; mathematics teacher education; music; music performance; music teacher education; music theory and composition; music therapy; occupational therapy; philosophy; physical education teaching and coaching; physics; political science and government; psychology; public relations/image management; religious/sacred music; religious studies; secondary education; social science teacher education; social work; sociology; Spanish; speech/theater education; sport and fitness administration/management.

Academics *Calendar:* 4-4-1. *Degree:* bachelor's. *Special study options:* academic remediation for entering students, accelerated degree program, advanced placement credit, double majors, honors programs, independent study, internships, off-campus study, part-time degree program, student-designed majors, study abroad, summer session for credit. *Unusual degree programs:* 3-2 engineering with Iowa State University of Science and Technology, University of Iowa, University of Illinois at Urbana-Champaign, Washington University in St. Louis; occupational therapy with Washington University in St. Louis.

Computers on Campus 250 computers/terminals are available on campus for general student use. Students can access the following: campus intranet, computer help desk, free student e-mail accounts, online (class) registration. Campuswide network is available. 100% of college-owned or -operated housing units are wired for high-speed Internet access. Wireless service is available via classrooms, libraries, student centers.

Student Life *Housing:* on-campus residence required through senior year. *Options:* coed, men-only, women-only, disabled students. Campus housing is university owned. Freshman campus housing is guaranteed. *Activities and organizations:* drama/theater group, student-run newspaper, radio and television station, choral group, Entertainment To Knight, choir, Student Senate, campus ministry, band. *Campus security:* 24-hour emergency response devices and patrols, late-night transport/escort service, controlled dormitory access. *Student services:* health clinic, personal/psychological counseling.

Athletics Member NCAA. All Division III. *Intercollegiate sports:* baseball M, basketball M/W, cheerleading W, cross-country running M/W, football M, golf M/W, soccer M/W, softball W, tennis M/W, track and field M/W, volleyball W, wrestling M. *Intramural sports:* badminton M/W, basketball M/W, golf M/W, racquetball M/W, rugby W, softball M/W, tennis M/W, ultimate Frisbee M/W, volleyball M/W.

Standardized Tests *Required:* SAT or ACT (for admission).

Costs (2007–08) *Comprehensive fee:* $31,285 includes full-time tuition ($23,600), mandatory fees ($700), and room and board ($6985). Part-time tuition: $860 per credit. Part-time tuition and fees vary according to course load. *Required fees:* $50 per term part-time. *College room only:* $3325. Room and board charges vary according to board plan and housing facility. *Payment plan:* installment. *Waivers:* senior citizens and employees or children of employees.

Financial Aid Of all full-time matriculated undergraduates who enrolled in 2006, 1,534 applied for aid, 1,341 were judged to have need, 519 had their need fully met. 421 Federal Work-Study jobs (averaging $948). 701 state and other part-time jobs (averaging $1158). In 2006, 352 non-need-based awards were made. *Average percent of need met:* 89%. *Average financial aid package:* $18,719. *Average need-based loan:* $5938. *Average need-based gift aid:* $13,432. *Average non-need-based aid:* $14,653. *Average indebtedness upon graduation:* $26,835.

Applying *Options:* electronic application, early action, deferred entrance. *Required:* high school transcript, minimum 2.0 GPA. *Required for some:* interview. *Recommended:* letters of recommendation, secondary school report. *Application deadlines:* rolling (freshmen), rolling (transfers), 12/1 (early action). *Notification:* continuous (freshmen), continuous (transfers).

Freshman Application Contact Mr. Todd Coleman, Assistant Vice President for Admissions, Wartburg College, 100 Wartburg Boulevard, PO Box 1003, Waverly, IA 50677-0903. *Phone:* 319-352-8264. *Toll-free phone:* 800-772-2085. *Fax:* 319-352-8579. *E-mail:* admissions@wartburg.edu.

WILLIAM PENN UNIVERSITY

Oskaloosa, Iowa **www.wmpenn.edu/**

- **Independent** 4-year, founded 1873, affiliated with Society of Friends
- **Rural** 60-acre campus with easy access to Des Moines
- **Endowment** $4.2 million
- **Coed**
- **Moderately difficult** entrance level

Faculty *Student/faculty ratio:* 15:1.

Academics *Calendar:* semesters. *Degrees:* associate and bachelor's.

Student Life *Campus security:* 24-hour emergency response devices and patrols, late-night transport/escort service, controlled dormitory access.

Athletics Member NAIA.

Standardized Tests *Required:* SAT or ACT (for admission).

Costs (2007–08) *Comprehensive fee:* $21,922 includes full-time tuition ($16,510), mandatory fees ($370), and room and board ($5042). Part-time tuition: $215 per hour. *Required fees:* $7 per hour part-time.

Financial Aid Of all full-time matriculated undergraduates who enrolled in 2005, 808 applied for aid, 768 were judged to have need, 238 had their need fully met. 511 Federal Work-Study jobs (averaging $1287). 1 state and other part-time job (averaging $1103). In 2005, 2 non-need-based awards were made. *Average percent of need met:* 82. *Average financial aid package:* $17,782. *Average need-based loan:* $4600. *Average need-based gift aid:* $11,300. *Average non-need-based aid:* $4500. *Average indebtedness upon graduation:* $22,169.

Applying *Options:* electronic application, deferred entrance. *Application fee:* $20. *Required:* high school transcript, minimum 2.0 GPA. *Required for some:* essay or personal statement, letters of recommendation, interview.

Freshman Application Contact John Ottosson, Vice President for Enrollment Management, William Penn University, 201 Trueblood Avenue, Oskaloosa, IA 52577-1799. *Phone:* 641-673-1012. *Toll-free phone:* 800-779-7366. *Fax:* 641-673-2113. *E-mail:* admissions@wmpenn.edu.

CORNELL COLLEGE

MOUNT VERNON, IOWA

The College

Cornell College provides students "one extraordinary opportunity after another, in the classroom, on campus, and in the world." Cornell is distinctive in U.S. higher education in that it offers the combination of liberal arts study and preprofessional preparation within the One-Course-At-A-Time (OCAAT) framework, an active residential community, an emphasis on service and leadership, and an ideal, wooded-hilltop setting.

Cornell attracts intellectually curious, motivated students who relish the opportunity to immerse themselves in their programs of study through the College's OCAAT, or block, academic calendar, as well as the opportunity to join an active and diverse college community. OCAAT classes are engaging and discussion-based with class size capped at 25 students. Cornell is one of only two nationally recognized liberal arts colleges that utilize this dynamic and innovative approach to teaching and learning.

A private, independent college founded in 1853, Cornell is historically a place of "firsts." It was the first coeducational college west of the Mississippi, the first college in Iowa to grant a baccalaureate degree to a woman, the first college in the United States to confer upon a woman a full professorship with the same salary received by the male professors, and the first college in the nation to have its entire campus listed on the National Register of Historic Places. The College was among the first schools in the nation to offer its students a choice of degree programs, establish a teacher-education program, and introduce sociology into its curriculum. Cornell offers an exciting civic engagement program and actively promotes community service opportunities. Nearly 70 percent of the student body takes part in volunteer projects.

Enrollment at Cornell is limited to 1,200 students; the current student body is from forty-five states and sixteen other countries. Almost all students reside on the beautiful campus, which is situated atop a hill overlooking the Cedar River valley. Centered on a pedestrian mall, the campus covers 129 acres and has more than forty buildings, including eleven residence halls. A student center, the Commons, houses central dining rooms, a bookstore, meeting rooms, and recreation rooms. Cornell's sports and recreation center has facilities for wellness and fitness programs as well as year-round recreation and athletics space for practice and play. Cornell ranks in the top fifteen nationally in NCAA Postgraduate Scholars among NCAA Division III schools. It competes in the Iowa Intercollegiate Athletic Conference in nineteen sports. Nearly 60 percent of students participate in sixty-six intramural sports. More than seventy clubs and organizations offer a wide range of activities, from participation in the KRNL-FM radio station to Habitat for Humanity and local Greek organizations.

Location

Mount Vernon provides the best of both worlds—a classically beautiful campus in a small college town minutes from Cedar Rapids and Iowa City. These two metropolitan areas contain three additional colleges and universities and 350,000 people. Chicago, Kansas City, Milwaukee, St. Louis, and Minneapolis are within a 3- to 5-hour drive. Palisades–Kepler State Park, site of the annual Pal Day picnic, is 5 miles away. Cornell is 15 minutes from Cedar Rapids, with its Eastern Iowa Airport, movies, and malls, and 20 minutes from Iowa City, home of the University of Iowa, with its Hancher Auditorium, a regular concert and theater tour stop.

Majors and Degrees

Cornell College awards the Bachelor of Arts, Bachelor of Music, Bachelor of Philosophy, and Bachelor of Special Studies degrees. Majors are offered in art, biochemistry and molecular biology, biology, chemistry, classical studies, computer science, economics and business, elementary and secondary education, English, environmental studies, French, geology, German, history, international business, international relations, Latin American studies, mathematics, medieval and Renaissance studies, music education (general, instrumental, and vocal), music performance, philosophy, physical education, physics, politics, psychology, religion, Russian, Russian studies, sociology, sociology and anthropology, Spanish, theater, theater and speech, and women's studies. In addition, students may design their own interdisciplinary majors. Two academic centers, Dimensions: The Center for the Science and Culture of Healthcare and the Berry Center for Business, Economics, and Public Policy, offer exceptional preprofessional opportunities for study and internships. The College also offers an exceptional prelaw program, featuring an outstanding mock trial program.

Combined-degree programs include a 3-2 program in forestry and environmental management offered in cooperation with Duke University, dual-degree programs in engineering and occupational therapy, and a 3-4 program in architecture with Washington University in St. Louis. The College also offers cooperative professional programs in nursing and allied health sciences with Rush University in Chicago and in medical technology with St. Luke's Hospital in Cedar Rapids. For students interested in dentistry, the University of Iowa College of Dentistry offers early acceptance into its program.

Academic Programs

Cornell encourages the creative structuring of students' educational experiences by offering a choice of four degree programs within the framework of a liberal education. Programs range from a traditional curriculum, with course requirements designed to ensure both breadth and depth, to a nontraditional combination of courses, independent studies, and internships that meet specific goals. For the Bachelor of Arts and Bachelor of Music degree programs, faculty members set the goals. The Bachelor of Special Studies degree program permits students to define their own educational objectives and design a curriculum to meet those objectives.

To increase the quality and intensity of a Cornell education, the College's academic calendar incorporates the One-Course-At-A-Time schedule. Cornell divides the traditional September–May academic year into nine 3½-week terms. During each term, students concentrate on one course chosen from the more than sixty offered and take one final examination. After a four-day break, the next term begins. Students take eight terms per year, which leaves a ninth term free for internships, off-campus programs, international study, travel, independent study, rest and relaxation, or another course.

The College's emphasis on One-Course-At-A-Time enhances the quality of liberal education offered by allowing students increased contact with faculty members, no interference from competing courses, and greater efficiency of study. It also provides rapid feedback to students about their progress. The work assigned on one day is discussed on the following day, when the material is fresh for both students and instructor. In addition, the pressure of having to prepare for several courses and examinations at the same time is eliminated.

Another liberalizing feature of One-Course-At-A-Time is the ability for classes to meet for periods longer or shorter than the typical 50-minute period. Professors may opt to divide the day into a series of short meetings, with work assignments given and completed from one session to the next. Laboratories are not necessarily limited to one afternoon. Faculty members are also able to take students on daylong field trips or teach their courses off campus, either in the United States or abroad.

Approximately two thirds of Cornell College graduates achieve an advanced degree within five years of graduation. Recent alumni are studying public health at Harvard, architecture at Washington University in St. Louis, medicine at Iowa, law at Northwestern, and studio art at the Art Institute of Chicago, to name a few. Among the employers of recent graduates are the Peace Corps; Houston Grand Opera; Cheetah Outreach; Visa International; Wells Fargo; AT&T Wireless; U.S. Agency for International Development; New York Life Insurance; RBC Dain Rauscher, Inc.; and the Red Cross.

Off-Campus Programs

Student internship experiences can be central to understanding the realities, demands, and rewards of the workplace. Internships arranged within Cornell's One-Course-At-A-Time academic calendar are distinctly different from those arranged within a semester system.

Students are able to become immersed in the experience every day for an entire month without the distractions of other course demands. Employers/mentors can count on a full-time commitment. This availability earns the attention of many nearby Cedar Rapids businesses and corporations that have offered opportunities from engineering to telecommunications, health-related fields, and art history. The competitive Alumni Fellows program provides distinctive internship experiences with a stipend, enabling Cornell students to pursue their career interests across the nation and around the world.

Through Cornell courses abroad and College-affiliated off-campus programs, students may work and travel in other countries and become acquainted with other cultures. Recent classes have journeyed to Mexico to observe local potters, to Montreal to study French, to Mexico and Spain to study Hispanic and Spanish social development, to London for courses in English literature and drama, and to Brazil and Guatemala to experience firsthand the politics of revolutionary movements.

Cornell students have done tropical field research in Costa Rica, studied Chinese culture in Hong Kong, worked with Hispanic communities in urban Chicago, and visited Europe's great cultural centers through off-campus programs administered by the Associated Colleges of the Midwest, of which Cornell is a charter member, and the School for International Training. Cornell students may elect to have a study-abroad experience for one or two terms, a semester, or a full academic year.

Academic Facilities

Cornell's entire campus has been designated a National Historic District, and its carefully restored nineteenth-century academic architecture is combined with contemporary facilities on a fully wired campus, with Internet access in every residence hall room. King Chapel is the historic landmark of the campus and has a 130-foot clock tower. Armstrong Hall, Kimmel Theatre, and McWethy Hall have recently been renovated and expanded for music, theater, and art, respectively. Law Hall Technology Center opened in 2000, and Cole Library was renovated recently and includes a Center for Teaching and Learning.

Costs

The total cost for the 2007–08 academic year was $33,250. Tuition was $26,100; fees, $180; room, $3250; and full board, $3720. Students generally enroll for eight courses a year but, at no extra cost, they may accelerate or broaden their studies by taking nine courses.

Financial Aid

Cornell is committed to creating financial access for all qualified students. The majority of Cornell's students receive financial assistance, and the average aid package exceeds $18,000. A competitive scholarship program complements an already significant investment in need-based institutional grant assistance and recognizes students with strong academic records or special talents. These awards range from $1000 to $20,000 per year. Federal need-based aid programs include grants, student loans, and campus employment. Additional need-based funds are available through the Iowa Tuition Grant Program and State of Iowa Scholarships, as well as outside scholarships. Need is determined by the Free Application for Federal Student Assistance (FAFSA). An early financial aid evaluation is available from the College upon request.

Faculty

The College's faculty members are distinguished by their desire to teach undergraduates in a small, informal environment. Classes are capped at 25 students. Faculty members are required to have a Ph.D. or other terminal degree and are appointed, retained, and promoted based on their ability to teach. Many also distinguish themselves through scholarly and creative activities. The faculty-student ratio is 1:13, and only faculty members, not teaching assistants, teach classes.

Student Government

Student life at Cornell complements the academic program and provides a feeling of community at the College. Students participate actively in the governance of the College, serving on faculty-student committees, the Student Senate, the Residence Hall Council, and the Performing Arts and Activities Council.

Admission Requirements

The courses and degree programs offered at Cornell are intended for students who have been well prepared at the secondary school level, have obvious motivation and a desire to learn, and have the ability and potential to complete a carefully planned degree program and graduate from Cornell College. Admission to Cornell is very selective. Applicants are judged on their high school records, test scores, interests, and achievements in such cocurricular activities as debate, student government, music, theater, athletics, and school publications as well as through personal recommendations and, in some cases, interviews. These are not exclusive criteria. Motivation, energy, and persistence are basic to Cornell. Students with the desire to succeed at Cornell and the motivation to benefit from a Cornell education may apply with confidence, knowing that these are important factors in the admission decision.

Application and Information

Cornell College offers three application plans. Special consideration is given to students who apply by the early decision and early action deadlines of November 1 and December 1, respectively. The final regular decision deadline is February 1. After submitting all required materials, students are typically notified of their admission status within four to six weeks. To apply for admission to Cornell, prospective students should obtain an application form online or from the Office of Admissions, complete and file the application with Cornell with a $40 application fee, have their high school forward an official transcript and a school recommendation, and have their ACT or SAT scores sent to Cornell. Cornell welcomes transfer students from accredited two- and four-year institutions.

Additional information, catalogs, application forms, and financial aid forms are available from:

Office of Admissions
Cornell College
600 First Street West
Mount Vernon, Iowa 52314-1098
Phone: 319-895-4477
800-747-1112 (toll-free)
E-mail: admissions@cornellcollege.edu
Web site: http://www.cornellcollege.edu

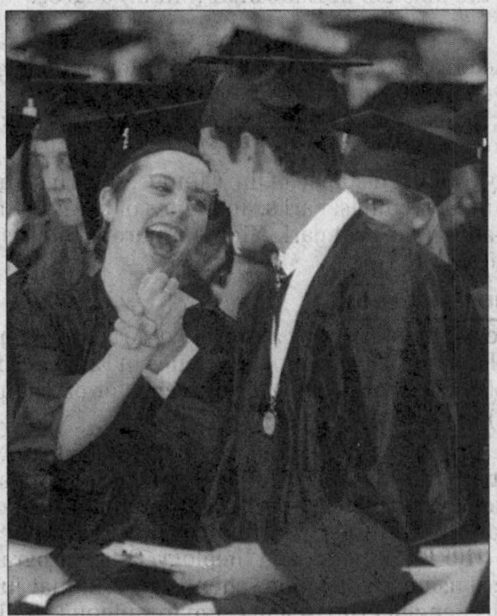

Graduation time at Cornell College.

COLLEGE DATA CENTER • IOWA

DORDT COLLEGE

SIOUX CENTER, IOWA

The College

Dordt College, a Christian liberal arts college, was ranked number 3 this year in *U.S. News & World Report*'s list of "Top Midwest Baccalaureate Colleges."

Dordt College was also one of only ten colleges named to *U.S. News & World Report*'s Midwest baccalaureate colleges "Great Schools, Great Prices" list in which the average tuition paid is weighed against a school's academic quality to determine the best college value. Dordt ranked fourth on this list.

A unique characteristic of Dordt is that in every major, in every classroom, students are encouraged to consider and discuss the spiritual implications of the subjects they are studying. Dordt graduates walk away with more than a degree: they leave knowing they are ready to apply their Christian faith in every walk of life.

A hallmark of a Dordt College education is the personal rapport that develops between students and faculty members during their time together. This is possible because of a low 15:1 student-faculty ratio and special faculty mentoring programs that ensure success. This year, 9 out of 10 members of last year's freshman class returned as sophomores, a retention rate that is 20 percent higher than at other private four-year colleges in Iowa.

In 2007–08, Dordt's student body consisted of 1,316 undergraduate and 64 graduate students who came to Sioux Center from thirty-two states and thirteen other countries.

The College was founded in 1955 and is committed to a Reformed, Christian perspective that embraces the Bible as the word of God. Since its inception, the College has grown to twenty-five buildings located on a spacious 115-acre campus.

In addition to its undergraduate degree programs, Dordt College also offers the Masters in Education (M.Ed.) degree.

Location

Dordt College is located in Sioux Center, Iowa, near the location where Iowa, Minnesota, and South Dakota meet. This community of about 6,300 is 45 miles north of Sioux City, Iowa, and 55 miles southeast of Sioux Falls, South Dakota.

Within easy walking distance of the campus, students find outstanding recreational facilities, parks, and miles of bountiful farmland. A nearby 80-acre industrial park offers numerous internship and job opportunities.

Majors and Degrees

Dordt College offers two-year Associate of Arts (A.A.) and four-year Bachelor of Arts (B.A.), Bachelor of Science in Engineering (B.S. E.), Bachelor of Social Work (B.S.W.), and Bachelor of Science in Nursing (B.S.N.) degrees.

More than thirty-five majors and fifty programs of study are available. Currently the ten largest-enrollment programs are agriculture; art; biology; business administration; communication; elementary education; engineering; health, physical education, and recreation (HPER); nursing; and theology. Other programs include accounting, business education, chemistry, criminal justice, computer science, engineering science, environmental studies, general science, history, individual studies, mathematics, medical technology, music, nursing, philosophy, physical science, physics, political studies, psychology, secondary education, social science, social studies, social work, Spanish, and theater arts. Concentrations are available in many of these majors.

Dordt offers eleven preprofessional programs in architecture, dentistry, law, medicine, nursing, occupational therapy, optometry, pharmacy, physical therapy, seminary studies, and veterinary science. These programs lay the groundwork for further advanced studies.

Two-year Associate of Arts degree programs are available in administrative assistant studies, agriculture, computer networking, general studies, and special education aide/teacher aide studies. These two-year programs offer a wide range of educational options through professionally and occupationally designed programs or through a flexibly designed two-year sequence of relevant courses and educational experiences.

Academic Programs

A core curriculum of general education courses, drawn from various academic disciplines, such as language, natural science, and social science, make up the foundation of every student's education at Dordt. This core curriculum plays a crucial role in the integration of subject matter through which Dordt College seeks to reflect the wholeness of God's creation. In these courses, students are introduced to the character and scope of Christian perspective, and they learn to think more critically about choices and decisions affecting their lifestyle. Courses in the core curriculum provide insight into the nature and demands of contemporary Christian living and help students understand how various aspects of contemporary life are interrelated and how the global culture has developed. These general education courses also supply students with the basic quantitative, analytic, lingual, and physical skills that are essential to the program overall and to their tasks as citizens of God's kingdom.

For a bachelor's degree, students must earn a GPA of at least 2.0 on a 4.0 scale in a minimum of 124 credits, while fulfilling the general education requirements, completing a major, and, in many cases, taking elective or professional courses.

Associate degree programs require a minimum of 60 credits, which include general education courses, an area of concentration, and elective courses. Students must earn a minimum GPA of 2.0 on a 4.0 scale and earn at least 30 credits while attending Dordt.

Dordt operates on a two-semester academic calendar and offers graduate courses in the summer.

Off-Campus Programs

In addition to the numerous majors offered on campus, Dordt College offers more than twenty-five off-campus study opportunities in countries around the world through its affiliation with the Council for Christian Colleges and Universities. These countries include Australia, China, France, Ghana, Great Britain, Honduras, Hungary, Mexico, the Netherlands, Spain, and Uganda. Juniors and seniors also have the opportunity to participate in the Chicago Semester, a semester of living, learning, and working in a major urban center.

Academic Facilities

At the hub of Dordt's campus community is a new $13-million Campus Center, open 24/7 as a gathering place for students. The upper level features enhanced-technology classrooms, conference rooms, and various offices. The entry level consists of a bookstore, an art gallery, meditation rooms, and a student lounge. An activity center, a coffee house, a dining area, a snack bar, and a mail room are located one level down. The final level of the 70,000-square-foot Campus Center features a game room complete with a four-lane regulation-size bowling alley.

Connected to the Campus Center is the John and Louis Hulst Library, which houses a collection of more than 300,000 book volumes, 16,000 print journal volumes, and 163,000 microtext units. The library subscribes to more than 600 journals, magazines, and newspapers and has electronic access to another 10,000 titles. In addition to providing print and electronic resources, the library serves the campus media needs by offering checkout availability of audiotapes and videotapes, DVDs, projectors, laptop computers, recorders, camcorders, digital cameras, GPS units, VCRs, DVD players, CD players, and other media equipment. The library has a significant collection of curriculum and children's literature materials housed in the Learning Resource Center. Other specialized collections include the Dordt College Archives and the Dutch Memorial Collection.

Dordt's B.J. Haan Auditorium/Music Building seats approximately 1,500 people and features one of the Midwest's most outstanding Casavant pipe organs. The auditorium is used for chapel services, concerts, organ recitals, and other regional events, with a mezzanine that accommodates the International Association for the Promotion of Christian Higher Education. The Music Building also has rehearsal rooms, studios and classrooms, vocal and instrumental practice rooms, and music faculty offices.

The Science and Technology Center at Dordt has 180- and 80-seat lecture halls, a greenhouse, laboratories, general-use classrooms, and offices for the agriculture, biology, chemistry, engineering, environmental studies, physics, and planetary science departments. Large and small laboratories for organic and physical chemistry and two physics laboratories are available to students in the physical sciences. Agriculture facilities include animal science and agronomy labs, a surgery room, and a live-animal room. The engineering wing includes labs for mechanical engineering, electronics, electrical engineering, and computer-aided design.

The Health, Physical Education, and Recreation (HPER) facilities are located near the recreation center and include basketball courts, racquetball courts, an aerobics room, a weight room, the indoor track, a batting cage, and volleyball courts.

Adjoining Dordt's spacious 115-acre campus is the All Seasons Center, an indoor swimming pool and ice rink that Dordt College uses in cooperation with the city of Sioux Center and the local public schools.

Costs

Full-time tuition for the 2007–08 academic year was $9800 per semester; part-time students paid $820 per credit. The overload fee for more than 18.5 credits per semester was $200. Summer tuition is $200 per credit. The cost of a residence hall room was $1440 per semester; an apartment-style residence cost $1790 per semester. Students paid $1290 per semester for the College meal plan. The student activity fee was $150 per semester, and other fees may apply, depending on the student's course of study. All fees are subject to change.

Financial Aid

Dordt College is committed to making a Christian education possible, and 98 percent of the student body receives some type of financial aid in the form of scholarships, grants, loans, and work-study opportunities. The College awards scholarships based on academic potential and performance, activities (participation in sports, theater, music, etc.), and demonstrated financial need. Dordt College awards more than $18.5 million in financial aid annually, thanks in large part to private donors and alumni who support the mission of Dordt.

All students are encouraged to apply, regardless of income. The average financial aid package is $12,000 per year. Financial aid applications may be obtained by contacting the Financial Aid Office.

All U.S. citizens who wish to apply for financial aid must submit the Free Application for Federal Student Aid (FAFSA) as well as the Dordt College Supplemental Data Form. Other supplementary information may be requested. All Canadian citizens who wish to apply for financial aid must submit the Canadian Financial Aid Form from Dordt College. All necessary forms may be obtained by writing or calling the financial aid office at Dordt College. Scholarship forms must be completed by January 15.

Faculty

Dordt College has 78 full-time faculty members and a student-faculty ratio of 15:1.

Student Government

The Student Forum is an elected body of 18 students who represent the student body on college committees and in the major decision-making processes of the College. This group of 4 freshman representatives, 3 sophomores, 3 juniors, 3 seniors, and 5 at-large representatives meets regularly to discuss issues of concern to the College community.

Admission Requirements

Dordt College seeks applicants who want to attend a Christian college and who have demonstrated the desire to learn; all students exhibiting these characteristics are considered for admission. Previous academic experience is a large, but not singular, factor in evaluating applications.

Dordt College recommends that applicants have taken 4 years of English/language arts, 3 year of mathematics, 2 years of science, 2 years of social science, 2 years of foreign language, and 4 years of electives chosen from the any of these subject areas. Applicants must have a cumulative high school GPA of at least 2.25. Students taking the ACT should have minimum scores of English, 18; math, 18; and composite, 19. Students who take the SAT should have minimum scores of 460 verbal, 460 math, and 920 combined.

Applicants with incomplete admissions records or applicants with high school records or test scores that do not meet all regular admission standards may be granted admission with special provision.

Students who have attended another accredited institution of collegiate rank may be considered for admission with advanced standing. Students who plan to transfer to Dordt College are encouraged to contact the registrar as soon as possible so course planning can make optimal use of courses and credits. A maximum of 30 semester hours (two semesters) of credit is granted to graduates of community colleges.

For international students, an official TOEFL score of at least 500 (paper-based) or 173 (computer-based) is required for admission of all nonnative English-speaking applicants. With the exception of Canadians, all international and ESL students are required to take the Entrance Interview for International and ESL Students during freshman orientation. International and ESL students meet the foreign language requirement if they receive a passing score on the Entrance Interview.

Application and Information

The application process is free for full-time freshman applicants if their applications are submitted before December 31; for all others, a refundable $25 application fee is required. The Executive Director of Admissions determines admission for all freshman students upon receipt of a complete set of application materials, which consists of a Dordt College application form, the application fee (refundable until May 1 if requested in writing), a final high school transcript, and ACT or SAT test results.

For further information, students should visit the Dordt College Web site at http://www.dordt.edu or talk to an admissions counselor by calling 800-343-6738 (option 1, admissions).

The best way to find out if Dordt College is the right choice is to get information firsthand by visiting the campus. During a campus visit, students are able to meet faculty members, take a tour of the campus, mix with students, and get a feel for Dordt. If this is not a possibility, Dordt has an excellent DVD video that can give a student insight to the College. For more information or to schedule a visit, prospective students should contact:

Dordt College Admissions
Dordt College
498 4th Avenue, NE
Sioux Center, Iowa 51250
Phone: 712-722-6000
800-343-6738 (toll-free)
Fax: 712-722-1198
E-mail: admissions@dordt.edu
Web site: http://www.dordt.edu

DRAKE UNIVERSITY

DES MOINES, IOWA

The University

A Drake University education offers a unique mix of advantages for future success. More than seventy major programs of study—including top-notch professional and preprofessional programs and options for undecided students—create lively and diverse learning opportunities. Drake's outstanding faculty members are renowned scholars and experts whose top priority is teaching. The student-faculty ratio is 14:1, and no graduate assistants teach classes. Drake's 5,618 students, including 3,202 full-time undergraduates, represent forty-five states and more than sixty countries. Approximately 1,790 students live on campus. More than 92 percent of Drake graduates find career employment or enter graduate school within six months of earning their degrees.

In addition to its undergraduate degrees, Drake offers master's degrees in accounting, business administration, communication leadership, education, financial management, and public administration as well as the Doctor of Pharmacy, Doctor of Jurisprudence, and Doctor of Education degrees. The following joint degrees also are offered: M.B.A./Law, M.B.A./Pharm.D., M.P.A./Pharm.D., and Pharm.D./Law.

Location

Drake University's 150-acre campus is located in Des Moines, Iowa's capital and largest city. Des Moines offers numerous internship and employment opportunities in all fields, including government, banking, insurance, publishing, nonprofit organizations, and health care. More than 68 percent of Drake students graduate having had one or more internships. With a metropolitan population of approximately 450,000, Des Moines also offers diverse cultural and entertainment options, a convention center, a nationally known art center, a civic center, professional athletics, parks and bike trails, and a downtown skywalk system.

Majors and Degrees

The College of Arts and Sciences offers degree programs and liberal arts education experiences that equip students to apply knowledge and skills to the scientific, mathematical, literary, and artistic tasks that will confront them in all careers. The college awards Bachelor of Arts and Bachelor of Science degrees with majors in anthropology and sociology; astronomy; biochemistry, cell and molecular biology; biology; chemistry; computer science; English; environmental policy; environmental science; history; international relations; law, politics, and society; mathematics; mathematics education (secondary); neuroscience; philosophy; physics; politics; psychology; religion; rhetoric and communication studies; sociology; study of culture and society; and writing. The college offers individualized majors and an open enrolled (undeclared) option. Preprofessional programs are available in dentistry, engineering, law, medicine, and veterinary medicine. Concentrations are available in anthropology, geography, Latin American studies, women's studies, and most fields that offer majors. Through the School of Fine Arts, the College of Arts and Sciences awards Bachelor of Arts, Bachelor of Fine Arts, Bachelor of Music, and Bachelor of Music Education degrees, offering programs in art, music, and theater arts with a dual focus on teaching excellence and artistic creativity. The Department of Art and Design, which is accredited by the National Association of Schools of Art and Design, provides degree programs in art history, graphic design, and studio art (drawing, painting, printmaking, and sculpture). The Department of Music provides degree programs in applied music (instrumental, piano, and vocal music performance) and music education (instrumental or choral). Students may earn a Bachelor of Arts degree with a major in music or a Bachelor of Music degree with elective studies in business; a jazz studies concentration can be combined with any degree the department offers. The Department of Theatre Arts offers majors in acting, directing, musical theater, theater, theater design, and theater education. The undeclared option is available in art, music, and theater arts.

Drake University's College of Business and Public Administration provides a four-year undergraduate program leading to the Bachelor of Science in Business Administration, with majors in accounting, actuarial science, economics, entrepreneurship, finance, general business, information systems, information technology, international business, management, and marketing. Interdisciplinary majors, combinations of majors, and open business (undeclared) enrollment are also available. Concentrations are offered in human resource management, insurance, and law and business. The college is accredited by AACSB International–The Association to Advance Collegiate Schools of Business.

Drake's School of Education offers professional programs in elementary education and secondary education. The University awards the Bachelor of Science in Education for teaching at the elementary level and the Bachelor of Arts or Bachelor of Science for teaching at the secondary level. Elementary and secondary education majors also may add middle school and coaching endorsements to their teaching credentials. Drake University has been a member of the American Association of Colleges for Teacher Education since the association's inception.

The School of Journalism and Mass Communication offers a Bachelor of Arts in Journalism and Mass Communication, with majors in advertising (management and creative tracks), electronic media (broadcast news and radio/television), magazines, news/Internet, and public relations. A journalism major with a concentration in documentary production is also offered. An open enrolled (undeclared) option is also available. The school is accredited by the Accrediting Council on Education in Journalism and Mass Communication.

With Drake Law School, the College of Arts and Sciences, the College of Business and Public Administration, and the School of Journalism offer combined 3+3 programs. Students in these programs can obtain their undergraduate degrees in three years in one of the aforementioned schools and then pursue a law degree for the next three years at the Law School.

Drake's College of Pharmacy and Health Sciences offers a six-year Pharm.D. degree and a four-year Bachelor of Science in health sciences with tracks in clinical and applied sciences, health services management, and pharmaceutical sciences. First-year students are admitted directly into the Pharm.D. program as prepharmacy majors. The college is accredited by the Accreditation Council for Pharmacy Education and is a member of the American Association of Colleges of Pharmacy.

Academic Programs

What makes the Drake experience so exceptional is the wide variety of accessible, hands-on learning opportunities students have both in class and out of class, beginning in their first year. Drake students conduct real research with top-notch faculty members, and many students present and publish their work. They student-teach in local schools, participate in and lead more than 160 campus organizations, perform in campus and community theater productions and music ensembles, and work on the campus newspaper, radio/TV station, and award-winning magazines. Students also gain invaluable experience in career-related internships in all fields, and they network with Drake's 62,000 alumni worldwide, many of whom are business and civic leaders in central Iowa and beyond.

A Drake education combines a foundation in the liberal arts and sciences with professional programs. The Drake curriculum offers extraordinary preparation for the varied challenges of career and life, with discussion-based first-year seminars, individualized plans for achieving educational goals, and a Senior Capstone—a research project, thesis, or other major work that demonstrates a student's ideas and abilities. Candidates for an undergraduate degree are required to successfully complete a minimum of 124 semester hours. Exceptional students may participate in Drake's Honors Program, a challenging interdisciplinary program of study. Students also have many opportunities for internships, undergraduate research, independent study, and combined bachelor's and master's degree programs.

Qualified Drake students may earn credit through the College Board's Advanced Placement Program, the International Baccalaureate, and the College-Level Examination Program.

The academic year is divided into two semesters; summer terms are also offered.

Off-Campus Programs

Through the Center for International Programs and Services, which maintains affiliations with several institutions and consortia, students can arrange to study overseas for a semester or a year. Programs are available in Argentina, Australia, Austria, the Balkans (four countries), Belgium, Belize, Bolivia, Botswana, Brazil, Cameroon, Chile, China, Costa Rica, Cyprus, Czech Republic, Dominican Republic, Ecuador, El Salvador, England, Fiji, France, Germany, Ghana, Guatemala, Hungary, India, Indonesia (Bali), Ireland, Israel, Italy, Jamaica, Japan, Jordan, Kenya, Madagascar, Mali, Mexico, Mongolia, Morocco, Namibia, Nepal, the Netherlands, New Zealand, Nicaragua, Northern Ireland, Oman, Panama, Peru, Poland, Russia, Samoa, Scotland, Senegal, South Africa, "Southern Cone," Spain, Switzerland, Taiwan, Tanzania, Thailand, Turkey, Uganda, Vietnam, and Wales. The Semester at Sea program is also offered.

Academic Facilities

Cowles Library collections include more than 600,000 books and journals, 100,000 federal and state government documents, 777,000 microform records, 118 electronic databases, and approximately 22,000 scholarly online journals. The collections include DVDs and music CDs as well as a digital repository of scholarship and historical material unique to Drake. The library also provides interlibrary loan and document delivery services to obtain materials not owned by the library. The library Web site serves as a portal to the online catalog and subject sources, including a wide variety of databases, indexes, full-text electronic journals, encyclopedias, and other reference tools. Assistance can also be obtained through the Ask a Librarian virtual reference service. All of these services are accessible through the campus computer network and are available to off-campus users enrolled at Drake. Specialized collections are also maintained by Drake's colleges and schools, including the Law School, College of Pharmacy and Health Sciences, Center for Teacher Education, and School of Fine Arts.

The Dwight D. Opperman Hall and Law Library contains extensive computer and Web resources, numerous study areas and rooms, and more than 330,000 volumes.

The Harmon Fine Arts Center includes the Studio Theater, the Monroe Recital Hall, and the 600-seat Hall of the Performing Arts. The 755-seat Sheslow Auditorium in Old Main also provides a beautiful performance hall.

Costs

For the 2007–08 school year, tuition was $23,280, and room and board were $6920. Full-time students also paid an annual $300 technology fee and $112 student activities fee.

Financial Aid

Drake University's financial aid program is designed to offer, within the University's resources, all capable and deserving students the opportunity for higher education. In 2006–07, the average financial aid package that included grants, scholarships, need-based loans, and need-based work was $18,860. For entering first-year students the average value of scholarships and grants funded by Drake was $10,880. Approximately 98 percent of Drake full-time undergraduate students receive some form of financial aid. Drake awards more than 5,000 scholarships each year, including both merit- and need-based assistance, and more than $50 million in financial assistance annually. Students interested in applying for financial aid should contact Drake's Office of Student Financial Planning and should file the Free Application for Federal Student Aid (FAFSA) by March 1. Students may apply for all federal, state, and institutional awards on this form.

Faculty

Drake's 246 full-time faculty members are accomplished in their fields and dedicated to their professions, yet they are primarily teachers. Full professors, including department chairs, regularly teach introductory-level courses. Each student works with a faculty adviser. The student-faculty ratio is 14:1.

Student Government

Drake offers students a wide variety of opportunities for campus involvement. Students play an active role in academic planning and campus governance through the Student Senate and its committees as well as through representation on some committees of the Faculty Senate. Students are elected to the senate by the student body. Students are also elected to the Student Activities Board, which plans cultural, social, educational, and special events. The Residence Hall Association, a network of student representatives, plans activities, addresses concerns, and provides information about residential life.

Admission Requirements

Admission to Drake University is selective. Because the University prefers students with varied talents and interests, there is no single, inflexible set of admission standards. The admission process involves a comprehensive review of a student's academic background (courses and grades), standardized test scores (ACT or SAT), personal essay, recommendations, and activities in both high school and the community. Drake University admits students without regard to age, sex, sexual orientation, race, religion, color, national or ethnic origin, or disability.

To be considered for admission, first-year applicants must submit a completed application form, the $25 nonrefundable application fee (the fee is waived for those who apply online), the High School Report and Counselor Recommendation Form, an official high school transcript, ACT or SAT scores, and a personal essay. Transfer applicants are considered for admission on the basis of all college work attempted. Transfer students must provide official transcripts from all colleges and universities attended previously; high school transcripts may also be requested.

Application and Information

Application for admission to undergraduate degree programs, except the prepharmacy program, may be made for any fall, spring, or summer term. Beginning October 1, students are notified of admission decisions on a rolling basis as applications become complete. March 1 is the priority deadline for consideration for admission and merit- and need-based financial aid. Applications received after this time are considered on a space-available basis. Freshman applicants to the prepharmacy program in the College of Pharmacy and Health Sciences must meet the December 1 deadline for direct admission. The application must be postmarked no later than December 1, and all required documents must reach the Office of Admission no later than December 10. (Transfer students are considered for admission only to the professional level of the pharmacy program; admission is not offered to transfer applicants at the preprofessional level.)

Candidates should contact:

Tom Delahunt
Vice President for Admission and Financial Aid
Drake University
2507 University Avenue
Des Moines, Iowa 50311
Phone: 515-271-3181
800-44-DRAKE Ext. 3181 (toll-free in U.S.)
Fax: 515-271-2831
Web site: http://www.choose.drake.edu

GRACELAND UNIVERSITY

LAMONI, IOWA

The University

Graceland University (GU) offers a strong academic program firmly rooted in the liberal arts tradition with an emphasis on career preparation. Since its founding in 1895 as a private, coeducational university, Graceland has maintained a tradition of academic excellence based on a commitment to the Christian view of the wholeness, worth, and dignity of every person. The University, sponsored by Community of Christ, is nonsectarian and offers a varied religious life program for those who wish to participate. Of Graceland's fall 2007 freshman class on the Lamoni campus, 17 percent came from Iowa. The remaining 83 percent represent twenty-six states and seventeen countries.

Graceland believes that an important part of a student's learning experience is achieved through association with other students in residence hall living. This belief is supported by an on-campus housing system that provides students with the camaraderie of a fraternity or sorority without the competition. Within the residence halls, there are men's and women's "houses." Members of each house elect a house council to plan social, intramural athletic, religious, and academic support activities. Residence halls are equipped with voice mail, e-mail, Internet connections, and cable TV.

Graceland University is a member of the North Central Association of Colleges and Schools (NCA) and is accredited by the Higher Learning Commission (30 North LaSalle Street, Suite 2400, Chicago, Illinois 60602-2504; 800-621-7440 (toll-free); http://www.ncahigherlearningcommission.org). All teacher-education programs at GU are approved by the Iowa Department of Education. The Bachelor of Arts (B.A.) in education and Master of Education (M.Ed.) programs in collaborative teaching and learning, quality education, and special education are accredited by the National Council for Accreditation of Teacher Education (NCATE; 2010 Massachusetts Avenue NW, Suite 500, Washington, D.C. 20036; 202-466-7496; http://www.ncate.org). All GU nursing programs are accredited by the Iowa and Missouri Departments of Education and the Commission on Collegiate Nursing Education (CCNE; One Dupont Circle NW, Suite 530, Washington, D.C. 20036; http://www.aacn.nche.edu). The athletic training program is accredited by the Commission on Accreditation of Athletic Training Education Programs (CAATE; 2201 Double Creek Drive, Suite 5006, Round Rock, Texas 78664; 512-733-9700; http://www.caate.net). These academic standards ensure that a degree from Graceland University is recognized by educational, business, and professional communities.

Graduate programs include the Master of Arts in Christian Ministries, Master of Arts in Religion, Master of Education, and Master of Science in Nursing. Certificates are offered in American humanics nonprofit management, post-master's family nurse practitioner, post-master's nurse educator, and post-master's health-care administration.

In addition to its traditional programs Graceland offers many options for distance learners. Programs offered online by the School of Nursing include the Bachelor in Healthcare Management, RN-B.S.N., RN-M.S.N., and M.S.N. programs. The M.S.N. program has three tracks: family nurse practitioner, nurse educator, and health-care administrator. The Graceland University School of Education offers a Master of Education with an emphasis in collaborative learning and teaching and special education. The Community of Christ Seminary also offers master's programs in religion and Christian ministries at a distance. The Master of Education program is offered in Cedar Rapids, Des Moines, and Lamoni, Iowa; Independence, Missouri; and online.

The Community of Christ Seminary offers a Master of Arts in Religion and a Master of Arts in Christian Ministries in blended delivery systems. The Community of Christ Seminary also offers master's programs in religion and Christian ministries at a distance.

Location

Lamoni, in south-central Iowa, is on Interstate 35. It is 3 miles north of the Missouri border, 1 hour from Des Moines, 2 hours from Kansas City, and 3 hours from Omaha. Lamoni is the home of Liberty Hall Historic Center, a 6-mile bike trail, an annual Civil War Days Re-Enactment and Living History Event, numerous hometown eateries, and several unique gift and antique shops. A county lake, Slip Bluff County Park, and Nine Eagles State Park are within 10 miles.

Majors and Degrees

Graceland awards the degrees of Bachelor of Arts, Bachelor of Science, and Bachelor of Science in Nursing. These degrees represent study in liberal arts with a concentration of courses in a major.

The majors and concentrations offered in the Bachelor of Arts programs are accounting, art (studio or visual communication), athletic training, business administration (emphases in entrepreneurship and free enterprise, finance, management, marketing, and pre-M.B.A.), chemistry, communications, economics, elementary education, English (concentrations in cinema studies, literature, and writing), fitness leadership, health, health-care administration, history, information technology, international business, international studies, liberal studies, mathematics, modern foreign language, music, music education, philosophy and religion, physical education and health, psychology, publications writing and design, recreation, religion, social science, sociology (concentrations in criminology, general sociology, and human services), Spanish, theater, visual communications (see: art), and wellness program management.

Bachelor of Science programs and majors are basic science, biology (concentrations in animal biology, ecology/environmental biology, molecular/cellular biology, preprofessional, and secondary school teaching), chemistry, clinical laboratory science/medical technology, and computer science.

The first two years of the Bachelor of Science in Nursing program are offered on the Lamoni campus, while the junior and senior years are on the Independence, Missouri, campus.

Graceland also offers degree programs at extended campus locations. Through a partnership with North Central Missouri College, Graceland offers undergraduate degrees in liberal studies and elementary education. Through a partnership with Indian Hills Community College, Graceland offers an undergraduate degree in elementary education. The undergraduate elementary education program is offered at the Graceland Independence campus location.

Academic Programs

Graceland is committed to helping develop the lives of its students—intellectually, socially, physically, and ethically—through a curriculum that is strongly rooted in the liberal arts. General education requirements are based on ten core competencies and can be satisfied by course selections, internships, portfolios, proficiency exams, work experience, independent studies, performance, and achievement. Graceland programs foster conceptual thinking, encourage team building, develop communication skills, and accommodate growth and enrichment.

Two programs at Graceland give attention to the special needs of students. The Honors Program is designed for highly motivated students wanting to expand their learning beyond the regular academic curriculum by developing and completing an honors thesis or project. Chance is a program for bright students who have the aptitude for university education but have experienced learning difficulties. The Lindamood and Bell clinical models are used for remediation in reading, spelling, and language comprehension.

The University operates on a 4-1-4 academic calendar. The regular semesters are separated by a one-month winter term in January. Full tuition for either the fall or the spring semester includes the winter term. This program is geared toward innovative and exceptional approaches and action-oriented learning experiences. On-campus programs vary from dance basics to science fiction to philosophy, and off-campus experiences range from scuba diving in Grand Cayman to touring Italy. Winter term is also the ideal time to explore career interests through an internship.

Off-Campus Programs

Many students see the world during the winter term by visiting such places as Australia, China, England, France, Grand Cayman Island in the British West Indies, Hungary, Italy, India, Israel, Japan, and Mexico. Students who major in a foreign language may study abroad during their junior or senior year under the auspices of a recognized study program. Graceland sponsors an International Health Center that provides opportunities for students to interact with health workers in villages in Africa and Asia.

Academic Facilities

The Helene Center for the Visual Arts includes 29,000 square feet for classrooms, studios, and exhibits. The large north-facing windows, an important feature, provide optimum light for artists.

The Shaw Center for the Performing Arts includes an 800-seat auditorium, a 150-seat studio theater, a 40-foot proscenium stage with orchestra pit, a Casavant pipe organ, a full fly gallery, a spacious scene shop, an art gallery, classrooms, rehearsal rooms, and faculty offices.

Computer facilities include three primary microcomputer laboratories with Macintosh and IBM-compatible computers. Students have access to equipment of commercial quality for desktop publishing and graphics design and to a music laboratory that provides computer-assisted tutoring, synthesis, and composition as well as professional-quality manuscript printing. The centerpiece of this laboratory is the Kurzweil synthesizer. Graceland's Enter.Net.C@fe provides 24-hour Internet access for student research and recreation.

The Frederick Madison Smith Library uses the latest technologies to provide the information services that students need. Ten fully networked computer workstations offer access to the Internet and many research databases, including 7 reference databases and more than 45 periodical databases, many providing access to full-text articles. Access to LIBBIE, the library's online catalog, and to the online reference sources is available to all patrons who use the library on the campus network as well as off-campus users via the Internet. Articles and books may be ordered from a worldwide network of research libraries. Students log on to the library's home page to ask reference questions. Holdings include 113,663 books and bound journals, 3,658 audiovisual materials, 72,866 government documents, 689 magazine and newspaper subscriptions, and 4,533 items in the Teacher Curriculum Lab. Three microcomputer labs and the Iowa Communications Network (ICN) classroom are located in the library.

The Dr. Charles Grabske, Sr. Library on the Independence campus provides resources for both on-campus and distance students in the nursing, education, and business departments. The library contains more than 3,000 nursing, education, and medical books; 250 audiovisual items, and more than 1,000 journal titles. Grabske Library has one of the largest collections of nursing journals in the Kansas City area, with current subscriptions to more than 250 journals online and in print. Books, journal articles, and interlibrary loan services are available to both on-campus and distance students. In addition, Grabske Library received the award for Outstanding Academic Health Science Library from the Health Sciences Library Network of Kansas City in 2006.

Students have the opportunity to use the ABT 52 scanning electron microscope, nuclear magnetic resonance spectroscope, Fourier-transform infrared spectroscope, and a computer lab with PCs that provide access to a multiple-operating system environment in the Platz-Mortimore Science Hall.

The Eugene E. and Judy Travis Closson Physical Education Center includes an indoor junior Olympic-size pool; an indoor track; a weight room; basketball, tennis, and volleyball courts; and a racquetball court. The Bruce Jenner Sports Complex contains the outdoor track, the football stadium, three soccer fields, five intramural fields, and eight tennis courts. The campus borders a nine-hole golf course and two small ponds for fishing and canoeing. Disc golf courses are located throughout the community.

Costs

Full-time tuition for 2007–08 was $23,500. Freshmen and sophomores are required to live on campus.

Financial Aid

Graceland's financial aid program is designed to assist qualified students attending the University. More than 90 percent of Graceland's students receive financial aid such as academic scholarships, performance grants, work-study, federal and state grants, and government loans. Academic scholarships are based on the high school GPA and composite ACT or combined SAT scores for entering freshmen and on cumulative GPA for transfer and continuing students. Grants are available for achievement in athletics and performing arts and for international students. The University matches a grant up to $1500 annually for a contribution made by a congregation and designated for a student attending Graceland. Some financial aid is available for distance learning programs; interested students should contact the Graceland University Financial Aid Services Office for specific information.

Faculty

The majority of faculty members have earned a doctorate or the highest degree in their field. Faculty members are active in their professional fields but consider teaching their primary responsibility. The student-faculty ratio is 15:1.

Student Government

Students are actively involved in the decision-making process of the University. Student-elected executive members of the Graceland Student Government attend faculty meetings and participate with voice and vote. Each academic department has student representatives who participate in business sessions and serve on faculty search committees. Students provide leadership for the housing system and for the campus social program. These and many other avenues are available allowing students to gain practical leadership experience.

Admission Requirements

Admission to Graceland is selective. To be considered, high school graduates must qualify in two of the following three areas: (1) rank in the upper 50 percent of their class; (2) have a minimum 2.5 GPA, based on a 4.0 system; and (3) have either a minimum composite ACT score of 21 or a minimum SAT combined score (Critical Reading and Math) of 960. Applicants who do not meet the above criteria may be considered individually. If accepted, they will be required to take developmental courses. Some applicants may be requested to test for the Chance Program prior to being considered for acceptance. Transfer, international, and home-schooled students should refer to the requirements listed in the catalog on the University's Web site. No one is denied admission to the University on the basis of race, color, religion, age, sex, national origin, disability, or sexual orientation. Prospective students and their families are encouraged to visit the campus.

Application and Information

Students are encouraged to apply as early as possible. For more information and application materials, students should contact:

Admissions Office
Graceland University
1 University Place
Lamoni, Iowa 50140
Phone: 641-784-5196
866-GRACELAND (toll-free in the United States and Canada)
Fax: 641-784-5480
E-mail: admissions@graceland.edu
Web site: http://www.admissions.graceland.edu

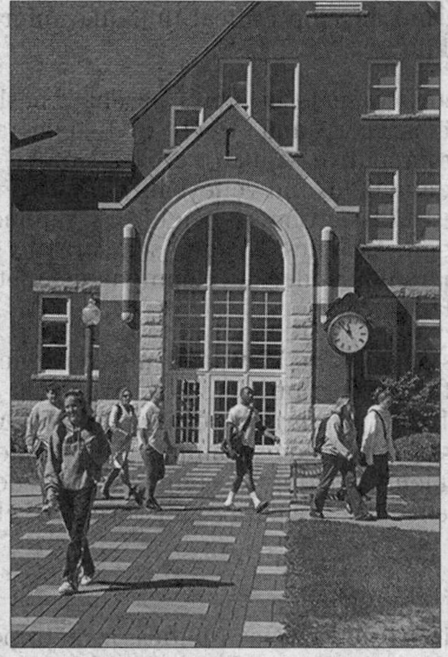

Higdon Administration Building on Graceland's Lamoni Campus.

COLLEGE DATA CENTER • IOWA

GRAND VIEW COLLEGE

DES MOINES, IOWA

The College

Grand View is a four-year liberal arts college affiliated with the Evangelical Lutheran Church in America. Founded more than 100 years ago, Grand View offers a high-quality education to a diverse student body in a career-oriented, liberal arts–grounded curriculum at two campus locations in greater Des Moines. Grand View welcomes traditional students and adult learners representing a wide range of religious and cultural backgrounds.

At Grand View College, students find a winning combination of high-quality programs, experienced professors, and caring individuals. With 1,750 students and an average class size of 14, students get to know their professors and other students well. They learn independence and seek responsibility in Grand View's educational environment. Learning is an interactive process at Grand View—students engage in lively discussions, work on real-world projects, and participate in career-related work experiences.

Grand View College stands out from other colleges because of its partnerships with leading businesses and organizations in Des Moines, which has led to challenging internships and to 100 percent of students finding jobs right after graduation or continuing their education for all but two of the past fourteen years. Grand View is known for its ability to connect students with exciting and challenging career opportunities.

Students are encouraged to develop leadership and team skills through involvement in campus organizations, which include intercollegiate and intramural athletics, speech and theater groups, major department clubs, student government, and the Grand View College Choir. Active honorary societies include Alpha Chi, Alpha Mu Gamma, Alpha Psi Omega, Alpha Sigma Lambda, Beta Beta Beta, Phi Eta Sigma, Sigma Theta Tau, and Theta Alpha Kappa. Grand View's student leadership program provides opportunities for students without leadership experience to seek and develop critical thinking, interpersonal, and networking skills.

Student athletes compete in men's baseball, basketball, cross-country, golf, soccer, and track and field and women's basketball, competitive dance, cross-country, golf, soccer, softball, track and field, and volleyball. Grand View participates in the Midwest Classic Conference of the National Association of Intercollegiate Athletics. Athletic scholarships are available. A football program is under development; competitive play will begin in the fall of 2008.

Two locations offer Grand View students convenient scheduling options for their program of study. Weekend and evening classes are offered at the main campus in Des Moines and at Grand View's Camp Dodge Campus in Johnston, Iowa. For motivated students seeking to complete their degree quickly, accelerated schedules are offered for several of eleven evening majors.

Location

Grand View is located in Des Moines, a metropolitan area of more than half a million people in central Iowa. Des Moines is the state capital and serves as the communications hub for Iowa. Nationally recognized organizations that have their corporate offices in Des Moines include Pioneer Hi-Bred International, Inc.; the Principal Financial Group; Meredith Corporation; and the *Des Moines Register*.

Grand View College's campus is Des Moines—and as part of the Grand View community, students are not limited by the confines of a small college or small town. In a given day, students can catch an Iowa Cubs professional baseball doubleheader, head down to the Court Avenue district for great food and nightlife, or take in a rock concert at Wells Fargo Arena.

A thriving arts program in Des Moines features the Des Moines Metro Opera, Ballet Iowa, the Des Moines Symphony, the Des Moines Art Center, and the Des Moines Playhouse. The summer Des Moines Art Festival is ranked third in the nation.

Des Moines features four distinct and beautiful seasons. Except for a month or so of bundle-up, see-your-breath weather, the climate is ideal for outdoor activities. Grand View students can take advantage of terrific recreational opportunities, including several golf courses, Saylorville Lake, and many city parks and state forests.

Easily accessible from Interstates 35 and 80, Grand View is 4 hours from Minneapolis, 6 hours from Chicago, and 3 hours from Kansas City.

Majors and Degrees

Grand View College grants the Bachelor of Arts degree and offers majors in accounting, art education, biology, broadcast, business administration (with concentrations in agricultural business, finance, human resource management, management, marketing, and real estate), computer science, criminal justice, elementary education, English, general studies–liberal arts, graphic design, graphic journalism, health promotion, history, human services, individualized major, information and technology management, journalism, management information systems, mass communication, math, music, music education, organizational studies, paralegal studies, physical science, political studies (prelaw or public administration), psychology, religion, secondary education, service management, sociology–liberal arts, Spanish for careers and professionals, theater arts, and visual arts. Grand View also offers a Bachelor of Science degree in nursing, as well as an RN to B.S.N. program. In addition, the College offers certificate programs in art therapy, entrepreneurship, human resource management, in-house communication, real estate, Spanish essentials, and sport management, as well as postbaccalaureate certificates in accounting and management in accounting.

Academic Programs

Grand View operates on a 4-4-1 academic calendar. The first semester runs from September to December. The second semester begins in early January and ends in late April. Three 1-month summer sessions are offered in May, June, and July, as is a summer trimester evening program.

Grand View College has adopted a competency-based General Education Core. Requirements for the core are defined in student learning goals. Completion of the educational core enables students to achieve a measurable level of competency in key skill and knowledge areas, such as writing, critical analysis, oral communication, and computer proficiency.

The Logos Honors Program provides an alternative to the General Education Core. By invitation, freshman and sophomore students enrolled in this program complete a series of courses designed to challenge exceptional students.

The Expressions Business Honors Program offers a three-year accelerated option.

The Grand View academic mission is to provide a diverse student body with an academically rigorous education. In order to meet this commitment, Grand View provides a variety of learning environments and teaching techniques. The College's academic support programs and services were lauded as a national model by the examining team from the North Central Association of Colleges and Schools during reaccreditation in 2005, when the College received complete ten-year accreditation with no follow-up required.

Costs

For 2007–08, the comprehensive cost for freshmen on campus is approximately $23,620, which includes tuition, an activity fee, a technology fee, and room and board. Students have several residential and meal plan options that affect cost. Health services and Internet access are also included in the comprehensive fee.

Financial Aid

Typically, most full-time Grand View students received financial assistance. The average freshman full-time award package is usually around $21,000 with about $10,500 in grants and scholarships and the remainder in work-study and student loans. The amount of aid is determined through a combination of merit and analysis of need as determined through the Free Application for Federal Student Aid. The priority deadline for financial aid is March 1. Students receive notification of financial aid packages following acceptance of admission to the College and receipt of their financial aid analysis of need.

Faculty

There are approximately 85 full-time faculty members and 111 part-time faculty members. More than forty percent hold terminal degrees. All classes are taught by professors; no graduate or teaching assistants instruct Grand View classes.

Student Government

Students participate in College governance. The Student Activities Council and Viking Council plan student activities that promote educational, social, cultural, and recreational aspects of student life. Students serve as representatives on faculty and staff search committees, programming committees, and student life committees.

Admission Requirements

Applicants' files are reviewed to determine their preparedness for a Grand View education. Official high school transcripts and submission of ACT or SAT scores are required for applicants with less than 24 semester hours of college credit. Applicants transferring from another college are required to submit official transcripts from all colleges previously attended.

Application and Information

For more information about Grand View, students should contact:

Admissions Office
Grand View College
1200 Grandview Avenue
Des Moines, Iowa 50316
Phone: 515-263-2810
800-444-6083 (toll-free)
Fax: 515-263-2974
E-mail: admissions@gvc.edu
Web site: http://www.gvc.edu

Students on Grand View College's campus.

GRINNELL COLLEGE

GRINNELL, IOWA

The College

Grinnell College has been named one of the sixteen best liberal arts colleges in the country for the past fifteen years by *U.S. News & World Report*. The 130-acre campus is located in the heart of the Midwest, and its student body comes from fifty states and fifty-five countries. Founded in 1846—the first four-year liberal arts college west of the Mississippi to grant a B.A. degree—Grinnell is described today in the Yale publication *The Insider's Guide to the Colleges* as "one of the most enlightened, progressive colleges in the Midwest—or the entire country, for that matter." Innovative from the beginning, Grinnell was the first college to establish an undergraduate department of political science (in 1883), and the school's travel-service program preceded the establishment of the Peace Corps by many years. Examples of current innovations include first-year tutorials, cooperative preprofessional programs, and a comprehensive program in quantitative studies and the societal impacts of technology globally.

The College is a cultural and recreational resource for the local community as well as for its 1,500 students, the faculty, and the staff. More than 500 events during the academic year include plays, concerts, art exhibitions, dance recitals, lectures, discussions, and intramural and intercollegiate sports, all of which are free to the College community and general public. The Rosenfield Program in Public Affairs, International Relations, and Human Rights brings many outside lecturers to the campus to enhance current-events programming. Facilities for sports and recreational activities are provided by the Physical Education Complex and the brand-new Athletic and Fitness Center. The Bucksbaum Center for the Arts, which opened in 1999 with a $22-million addition, more than doubled existing arts space on campus, offering a recital hall, art gallery, theater, scene shop, studio theater, and classroom and studio space.

Location

Named one of the twenty-five best small towns in America, Grinnell is located in central Iowa, 55 minutes east of downtown Des Moines, off Interstate 80, in a prosperous and picturesque agricultural area. Stores, personal and professional services, a modern hospital, churches, restaurants, and other community features are available, in addition to opportunities for community involvement. A landscape of rolling hills is a 10-minute bike ride from the campus, and nearby Rock Creek State Park offers hiking, swimming, and sailing.

Majors and Degrees

Grinnell offers a rigorous and highly interdisciplinary four-year undergraduate liberal arts program leading to the Bachelor of Arts degree. Majors available in the humanities are art, Chinese, classics (Greek and Latin), English, French, German, music, philosophy, religious studies, Russian, Spanish, and theater and dance. In science, the majors are biological chemistry, biology, chemistry, computer science, general science, mathematics and statistics, physics, and psychology. Majors in social studies are anthropology, economics, history, political science, and sociology. Interdepartmental majors and independent majors may be arranged.

Nonmajor programs and concentrations are offered in alternative language studies, education (secondary certification), general literary studies, humanities/social studies, and physical education. Interdisciplinary concentrations include American studies, East Asian studies, environmental studies, gender and women's studies, global development studies, Latin American studies, linguistics, neuroscience, Russian and Eastern European studies, technology studies, and Western European studies.

In cooperation with other institutions, the College offers preprofessional programs in architecture, engineering, and law.

Academic Programs

A Grinnell education is anchored in intense, active learning that occurs in one-on-one interactions between faculty members and students. The school is known for its rigorous academic and diverse extracurricular program. Its individually advised curriculum enables students to learn initiative and leadership by assuming responsibility for their individual courses of study, which are developed under the guidance of a faculty adviser to reflect each student's goals for the future, including graduate school. This process challenges students to define and achieve their academic goals.

Outside of the First-Year Tutorial (a one-semester special-topics seminar that stresses methods of inquiry, critical analysis, and writing skills), there are no core requirements. To graduate, students are expected to complete at least 32 credits in a major field and a total of 124 credits of academic work, with no more than 48 credits in one department and no more than 92 credits in one division. In the humanities, arts, and social and natural sciences at Grinnell, students have opportunities to conduct original research and undertake advanced study through independent and interdisciplinary projects that foster intellectual discovery. Course exemptions and advanced placement are also available. Students usually take 16 credits of course work during each of the two semesters in the academic year, which begins in late August and ends in mid-May.

Off-Campus Programs

Grinnell's commitment to the importance of off-campus study reflects the school's emphasis on social and political awareness and the international nature of its campus. More than 50 percent of all Grinnell students participate in seventy off-campus programs, including the Grinnell-in-London program and study tours of China, France, Greece, and Russia. These study programs in Europe (including Russia), Africa, the Near East, and Asia, as well as programs in Central and South America, provide the opportunity for research and enrichment in many disciplines, from archaeology to education to mathematics. In addition to off-campus programs, Grinnell offers an extensive internship program in such areas as urban studies, art, and marine biology for students interested in field-based learning and experience in professional settings. Second- and third-year students may apply for summer internship grants and receive credit for the experience. Semester programs in the United States include those at the Oak Ridge National Laboratory, Newberry Library, National Theatre Institute, and Grinnell-in-Washington, D.C.

Academic Facilities

The eleven academic buildings on campus include the Grinnell College libraries—consisting of Burling Library, the Windsor Science Library, and the Music Library—which hold 455,000 volumes, 26,100 audio and video recordings, 16,100 microforms, 514,500 state and federal government documents, and subscriptions to 3,597 professional and academic journals, with an online catalog system and CD-ROM databases. In addition to the College archives and rare books collections, the library houses special collections in Africana studies, East Asian studies, and Latina/o studies. A recent $15.3-million renovation and addition to the College's science facilities in the Noyce Science Center has equipped lab facilities and classrooms with research tools that encourage hands-on experience and collaborative work. These include sophisticated laboratories, aquaria, a herbarium, scanning and transmission electron microscope facilities, a nuclear magnetic resonance spectrometer, a physics historical museum, and other specialized resources. An observatory houses a computerized, research-quality, 24-inch reflecting telescope with sophisticated auxiliary devices and a lab, classroom, and darkroom. More than 1,000 PCs, Macintoshes, and workstations, linked to a variety of servers over a campus network, are used for teaching, research, and administrative computing. Near Grinnell, the biology department maintains the widely recognized 365-acre Conard Environmental Research Area, which has a fully equipped field-research laboratory for studies in ecology. Programs in art, music, and theater are housed in the Bucksbaum Center for the Arts. The center includes the Roberts Theatre, the Flanagan Arena Theatre, the Scheaffer Gallery for art exhibitions, a studio for modern dance, music rooms, a scene shop, and art studios. The Joe Rosenfield '25 Center (student union) and the Harris Center, both centers for cultural activity and social and recreational events, serve all members of the College community.

Costs

The comprehensive fee of $42,422 for 2007–08 included $33,910 for tuition, $8030 for room and board, and $482 for activities, health, and other fees. Students should allow for the additional costs of books, supplies, travel, laundry, and personal expenses.

Financial Aid

Students are selected for admission to Grinnell without regard for their ability to pay (a policy called need-blind admission). The school offers generous financial assistance for students in packages that include scholarships, grants, campus employment, and loans, understanding that each family pays as they are able. To that end, more than $23 million is budgeted annually for grants and scholarships. Grinnell also offers further assistance through campus employment opportunities, loans, and numerous payment options. Students who wish to be considered for financial aid should, along with their parents, file the Free Application for Federal Student Aid (FAFSA) and Grinnell's Application for Financial Aid and Scholarships by February 1.

Faculty

The Grinnell faculty consists of 150 men and women. Ninety-three percent hold Ph.D. degrees, and among the members are scholars, writers, and artists of established reputation who are active in producing original, significant scholarship. All classes are taught by professors, not teaching assistants, and the student-faculty ratio of 9:1 means that Grinnell students can work closely with their instructors, who view classroom teaching as their top priority.

Student Government

Self-governance is a guiding principle at Grinnell College. Students serve on departmental educational policy committees and the Faculty Curriculum Committee. Students regulate the residence halls in consultation with residence life coordinators and serve on committees that determine social policy and regulations. The organizational structure of the Student Government Association covers almost all aspects of student activity and campus life. There are no sororities or fraternities.

Admission Requirements

Academic promise and intellectual self-reliance are qualities sought in students applying to Grinnell. Requirements are a scholastic record and class standing that show ability to do college work; graduation from an accredited secondary school with 4 units of English, 4 units of mathematics, 3–4 units of laboratory science, 3–4 units of a foreign language, and 3–4 units of social studies; satisfactory results on the SAT or the American College Testing (ACT) examination; recommendation of the secondary school counselor; and recommendations of 2 secondary school teachers. Interviews on campus or with alumni are strongly recommended.

Application and Information

Students may apply for early decision if Grinnell is their school of first choice. Early decision is a commitment to enroll, and those accepted must withdraw all other applications. Students applying for early decision I should submit their applications by November 20; they are notified by December 20 regarding both admission to the College and financial aid. For early decision II, applications must be submitted by January 1, with notification by February 1.

Students may file applications for regular admission by January 20. Those filing by this date are notified of the decision on admission and financial aid by April 1.

Grinnell College offers early admission to superior college-bound students who have completed the junior year of secondary school. These students neither complete their senior year nor receive a secondary school diploma.

For an application form and more information about Grinnell, students should contact:

Office of Admission
Grinnell College
Grinnell, Iowa 50112-1690
Phone: 641-269-3600
800-247-0113 (toll-free)
E-mail: askgrin@grinnell.edu
Web site: http://www.grinnell.edu

The Grinnell campus is considered to be one of the most attractive of American collegiate landscapes, as depicted in this photograph of North Campus near Gates-Rawson Tower.

COLLEGE DATA CENTER • IOWA

LUTHER COLLEGE

DECORAH, IOWA

The College

Luther College, which was founded in 1861, is a four-year residential liberal arts college of the Evangelical Lutheran Church in America (ELCA). The College, which was founded by Norwegian immigrants, is an academic community of faith and learning where students of promise from all beliefs and backgrounds have the freedom to learn, to express themselves, to perform, to compete, and to grow. The College, which is located in Decorah, Iowa, is home to 2,550 students from thirty-five states and thirty-three countries. Thirty-six percent of the students are from Iowa; 89 percent come from the four-state area of Iowa, Minnesota, Wisconsin, and Illinois. Each year, over 100 international students choose to study at Luther.

In keeping with its liberal arts tradition, the College requires students to develop a depth of knowledge in their chosen major and a breadth of knowledge through exposure to a wide range of subjects and intellectual approaches (general requirements). Learning at Luther is about engagement: faculty members who are passionate in their teaching and scholarship, students who are active and involved, and a College community characterized by personal attention, hands-on experiences, academic challenge, and community support. At Luther, all students become immersed in the liberal arts through the College's common year-long course for first-year students called Paideia. The course, which is uncommon in its approach, helps train students' minds and develop their research and writing skills as they explore human cultures and history. In addition, Luther offers a Phi Beta Kappa chapter and several departmental honor societies, evidence of the quality of teaching and learning on campus.

At Luther, students are encouraged to seek out connections between their lives in the classroom and their lives outside the classroom. The College provides a stimulating cultural and educational atmosphere by bringing distinguished public figures, theater groups, musicians, and educators to the campus. Cocurricular activities are an important part of College life. The College sponsors seven choirs, three orchestras, three bands, two jazz bands, and a full theater and dance program. Numerous student organizations and societies provide ample opportunities for student involvement in meaningful activities. As a community of faith, students can participate in daily chapel, weekly Sunday worship, outreach teams, and midweek Eucharist.

Nineteen intercollegiate sports are offered. Men may participate in ten sports: baseball, basketball, cross-country, football, golf, soccer, swimming, tennis, track and field, and wrestling. Women compete in nine intercollegiate sports: basketball, cross-country, golf, soccer, softball, swimming, tennis, track and field, and volleyball. Club sports include Ultimate Frisbee, rugby, and men's volleyball. Sixty-four percent of the student body is involved in an extensive intramural and recreational sports program. Available for recreational use and for the physical education program are twelve outdoor tennis courts, an eight-lane polyurethane 400-meter track, numerous cross-country running and ski trails, and 15 acres of intramural fields. The well-equipped field house contains a 25-yard indoor pool, three racquetball courts, four hardwood basketball courts, a wrestling complex, and a 3,000-seat gymnasium. A sports forum houses a six-lane, 200-meter indoor track; six indoor tennis courts; locker rooms; and athletic training facilities. The Legends Fitness for Life Center provides the latest fitness equipment and a 30-foot-high rock-climbing wall.

Location

The College is located in Decorah, a city of 8,500 people in the scenic bluff country of northeast Iowa. The Upper Iowa River, which runs through the campus, is designated as a National Scenic and Recreational River. Rich in Scandinavian heritage, Decorah is a popular recreation area, providing opportunities for canoeing, fishing, hunting, cross-country skiing, camping, hiking, cycling, and spelunking. Three airports are located within a 75-mile radius of Decorah: in Rochester, Minnesota; Waterloo, Iowa; and La Crosse, Wisconsin.

Majors and Degrees

Luther College grants the Bachelor of Arts (B.A.) degree and offers majors in accounting, Africana studies, anthropology, art, athletic training, biblical languages, biology, business, chemistry, classical languages (Greek and Latin), classical studies, communication studies, computer science, economics, elementary education, English, environmental studies, health, history, management, management information systems, mathematics, mathematics/statistics, modern languages (Chinese, French, German, Norwegian, and Spanish), music, nursing, philosophy, physical education, physics, political science, psychology, religion, Scandinavian studies, social work, sociology, sociology/political science, speech and theater, theater/dance, and women and gender studies. Interdisciplinary programs are available in arts management, international management, international studies, museum studies, music management, Russian studies, Scandinavian studies, sports management, and theater/dance management. Preprofessional preparation is offered in cytotechnology, dentistry, engineering, environmental management, forestry, law, medical technology, medicine, music therapy, optometry, physical therapy, theology, and veterinary medicine.

Academic Programs

Luther operates on a 4-1-4 academic calendar. The first semester runs from September to December, followed by a three-week January Term and the second semester, which runs from February to May. Two 4-week summer sessions are offered in June and July. Each candidate is required to complete a total of 128 semester hours of credit with a C average or better. At least 76 of the required 128 semester hours must be earned outside the major discipline. Each senior writes a research paper in his or her major. Students are required to complete the following number of semester hours of credit in designated areas: 12 of Paideia, an interdisciplinary course; 9–12 of religion/philosophy; 7–8 of natural science; 6–8 of social science; 3–9 of foreign language (proficiency based); 3–4 of fine arts; 3–4 of global studies; 3–4 of quantitative or symbolic reasoning; and 2 of physical education. Advanced placement and credit by examination are available. A qualified student may develop an interdisciplinary major with a faculty adviser.

Off-Campus Programs

Students may participate in off-campus programs during the fall and spring semesters, the January Term, and summer sessions. All of the programs carry academic credit. Luther participates in the Iowa General Assembly Legislative Intern Program during the spring semester of each year. Urban studies semesters may be arranged in conjunction with other colleges. The Washington Semester gives qualified juniors the opportunity to study at American University and work within one department of the federal government. Luther College also cosponsors a semester program in Washington, D.C., through the Lutheran College Washington Consortium. Students may elect to be exchange students at other colleges for one semester or a January Term.

Luther is an affiliate of the Institute of European Studies, which has centers in more than twenty European and Asian countries; students studying at one of these centers receive credit in accordance with the provisions for transfer credit for study abroad under the Junior Year Abroad programs. A community studies program in Nottingham, England, is staffed by a Luther professor each year. In alternate years, a Luther professor directs on-site programs in Münster, Germany; Lillehammer, Norway; and Sliema, Malta. In addition, opportunities for study are available in a variety of settings, such as the Bahamas, China, Russia, Tanzania, and Norway.

Academic Facilities

The 1,000-acre campus includes the Preus Library, housing 350,000 volumes, 1,100 periodicals, and the College art collection. The library offers five online indexes and ten commercial online services and provides access to more than 480 other libraries. Modern, well-equipped laboratories in the Valders Hall of Science are supplemented by several other science-teaching facilities on campus: a planetarium, a greenhouse, an herbarium, a live-animal center, a human anatomy laboratory, a natural history museum, and a psychology sleep laboratory. Construction of a dynamic new 58,000-square-foot science and research center is expected to be completed in fall 2008. The science facilities also include an extensive field study area and two electron microscopes. Within easy walking distance of the campus, the field study area offers an ideal setting for studies in aquatic biology, ecology, and field biology. Five ponds, two reestablished prairies, marshes, wooded areas, and agricultural lands are available for classwork and independent study. The College has a fiber-based campus network connecting a variety of PC and Macintosh computers (in several environments) to shared computing resources and to the Internet. More than 400 microcomputers and terminals are available for student use throughout the campus.

Luther College maintains radio station KWLC-AM, and the College's affiliate station, KLSE-FM, is part of the Minnesota Public Radio network. Luther also maintains the largest archaeological research center in Iowa. The Norwegian American Museum in Decorah, one of the finest ethnic museums in the country, provides an invaluable resource for museum and Scandinavian studies. The foreign language departments maintain a twenty-five-station electronic classroom, and the psychology department houses a twenty-station IBM interactive computer network.

The impressive F. W. Olin Building houses the economics and business, mathematics, and computer science departments. Among its technological wonders is the Luther Round Table Room, where students experience simultaneous decision making via a computer network.

The award-winning Jenson Hall of Music contains state-of-the-art computer facilities, a recording studio, and four pipe organs: 23-stop/34-rank and 42-stop/61-rank tracker organs for practice and performing and two Schlicker practice organs of 8 and 5 ranks, respectively. Jenson Hall of Music also contains 32,000 square feet of classrooms, studios, practice rooms, and rehearsal rooms for keyboard, vocal, and instrumental music. The Center for Faith and Life (CFL) houses a 42-stop/62-rank organ in the 1,600-seat auditorium for the performing arts. The CFL also houses the offices of the campus ministry, a 24-hour meditation chapel, a 200-seat recital hall, and one of four campus art galleries.

The Center for the Arts serves as the home for theater, dance, and the arts.

Costs

For 2008–09, the comprehensive fee is $35,960, which includes tuition, general fees, facilities fees, room, board, subscription to student publications, and admission to College-supported concerts, lectures, and other events. A room telephone, cable TV, computer access from residence hall rooms, and a health-service program are also included. Private music lessons are $275 per semester. It is estimated that an additional $3000 is adequate for books, clothing, entertainment, and other personal expenses.

Financial Aid

More than 97 percent of all Luther students receive financial aid in the form of grants, such as the Federal Pell Grant; scholarships from Luther and other sources; loans; and jobs on campus. Luther awards Regent and Presidential Scholarships to those demonstrating superior academic achievement. The amount of aid given is determined by the College's analysis of the Free Application for Federal Student Aid (FAFSA). The priority deadline for a financial aid application is March 1. Students receive notification of financial aid awards after their acceptance for admission.

Faculty

There are 177 full-time and 74 part-time faculty members; 89 percent hold a Ph.D., first professional, or other terminal degree. The student-faculty ratio is 12:1.

Student Government

Students share in the governance of the College and participate in social and cultural programming. They have full membership on most College committees, majority representation in the Community Assembly, and nonvoting representation on the Board of Regents.

Admission Requirements

Admission is selective. An applicant must be a graduate of an accredited high school and have completed at least 4 units of English, 3 units of mathematics, 3 units of social science, and 2 units of natural science. It is strongly recommended that the applicant have at least two years of a foreign language. Seventy percent of entering students rank in the top quarter of their high school class. Transfer students may enroll in either semester. Early admission and admission with honors are available. The priority deadline is March 1.

Application and Information

An application, SAT or ACT scores, an educator's reference, a transcript of previous academic work, and a $25 application fee are required for admission. On-campus interviews are recommended but not required. For more information about Luther, students should contact:

Admissions Office
Luther College
Decorah, Iowa 52101-1042
Phone: 563-387-1287
800-458-8437 (toll-free)
Fax: 563-387-2159
563-387-1062 (international)
E-mail: admissions@luther.edu (admissions)
finaid@luther.edu (financial aid)
intladmissions@luther.edu (international)
Web site: http://www.luther.edu

Luther College's spacious 1,000-acre campus in the scenic bluff country of northeast Iowa.

MORNINGSIDE COLLEGE

SIOUX CITY, IOWA

The College

The Morningside College experience cultivates a passion for lifelong learning and a dedication to ethical leadership and civic responsibility. For more than 110 years, the goal of Morningside College has been to provide students with an education of the highest quality. Morningside is rooted in a strong church-related, liberal arts tradition, and its challenge is to prepare students to be flexible in thought, open in attitude, and confident in themselves.

Founded in 1894, Morningside College is a private, four-year, coeducational, liberal arts institution affiliated with the United Methodist Church. The College seeks both students and faculty members representing diverse social, cultural, ethnic, racial, and national backgrounds.

At the graduate level, Morningside confers a Master of Arts in Teaching, with professional educator or special education tracks.

Morningside College's approximately 1,100 full-time students are encouraged to participate in a wide variety of activities, including departmental, professional, and religious organizations; honor societies; and sororities and fraternities. A newspaper, literary magazine, and campus radio station are all student directed. These activities provide students with many opportunities to develop leadership, interpersonal, and social skills. Since nearly all activities on campus are student initiated and student directed, ample opportunities for leadership development exist. Music recitals and concerts, theater productions, and an academic and cultural arts and lecture series are held each semester. Intercollegiate athletics are available for men in baseball, basketball, cross-country, football, golf, soccer, swimming, tennis, track and field, and wrestling and for women in basketball, cross-country, golf, soccer, softball, swimming, tennis, track, and volleyball. A variety of intramural activities are available.

The Hindman-Hobbs Center includes a pool, saunas, racquetball courts, a weight room, basketball courts, a wrestling room, and a jogging track as well as classroom facilities and offices.

Location

Morningside College is located on a 68-acre campus in Sioux City, the fourth-largest city in Iowa. The campus is based in a residential section of the community, adjacent to a city park, swimming pool, and tennis courts and within 5 minutes of a major regional shopping mall and a new shopping center. The Sioux City metropolitan area offers a blend of urban shopping, commerce, and recreation in a scenic setting. Students find Morningside's Sioux City location to be advantageous in seeking internship opportunities and full- or part-time employment.

Majors and Degrees

The five undergraduate degrees conferred by Morningside College are the Bachelor of Arts, Bachelor of Science, Bachelor of Science in Nursing, Bachelor of Music, and Bachelor of Music Education. Career programs consist of accounting, advertising, art, biology, business administration, chemistry, computer science, corporate communications, elementary education, engineering physics, English, graphic arts, history, interdisciplinary studies, marketing, mass communications, mathematics, music, nursing, philosophy, photography, political science, psychology, religious studies, Spanish, special education, and theater. Students choosing to teach in secondary school may be certified in most academic majors.

In cooperation with other institutions, Morningside offers preprofessional programs in dentistry, engineering, law, medical technology, medicine, the ministry, optometry, pharmacy, physical therapy, physician assistant studies, and veterinary medicine.

Academic Programs

Morningside operates on a two-semester system; sessions are held from late August to December and from January to early May. Evening classes are offered each semester. A three-week May Term and a six-week summer session are also available.

The Morningside College experience provides an education that develops the whole person through an emphasis on critical thinking, effective communication, cultural understanding, practical wisdom, spiritual discernment, and ethical action. By working with talented faculty members in a large number of majors, caring college staff members who provide numerous opportunities for valuable cocurricular experiences, and other exceptional and interesting students with whom they will form lifelong connections, Morningside students gain the knowledge, skills, and personal dispositions that will ensure their success.

Special opportunities include a voluntary Interdepartmental Honors Program, in which students meet weekly to discuss ideas that have shaped history from the ancient world into the future. Friday is Writing Day, a weekly discussion format that allows students and faculty members to read aloud and react to one another's writing.

Every entering full-time student is provided with a notebook computer that is used in classroom work. Student technology services include high-speed Internet connection, ports in all residence halls and classrooms, Web-accessible personal e-mail accounts, a digital library accessible day and night, specialized computer labs to support academic programs, and wireless network access points across campus.

Off-Campus Programs

Morningside students who qualify have the opportunity to take advantage of special programs for off-campus study. Programs are available for a semester or the entire school year. The College has agreements with schools in England, Japan, and Northern Ireland.

Students participate in exchange programs with Kansai Gaidai University in Japan; Queen's University, the University of Ulster, Belfast Institute for Further and Higher Education, Stranmillis University College, and St. Mary's University College in Northern Ireland; and Edge Hill University and the Centre for Medieval and Renaissance Studies in England.

In addition, Morningside has opportunities for students to enroll for a semester at American University in Washington, D.C., to study the U.S. government in action. Students may also be nominated for a semester at Drew University in New Jersey to study the United Nations. Students who participate in these programs maintain their enrollment at Morningside College.

Academic Facilities

The Hickman-Johnson-Furrow Learning Center is the home of the library and the Academic Support Services Center. The library has more than 99,000 volumes, nearly 3,000 audio recordings and video materials, and nearly 440 current print periodical subscriptions. Online accessibility includes student/faculty access to more than 18,000 full-text journals. The library's Web-based, integrated online system allows seamless access to numerous subscription databases as well as other online catalogs and Web sites. The library building also houses the Spoonholder Café, classrooms, the Mass Communication Department, and a computer lab.

Charles City College Hall is listed individually on the National Register of Historic Places and houses classrooms and offices for the History and Political Science, Philosophy, Religious Studies, and Theatre Departments.

The Eugene C. Eppley Fine Arts Building is one of the finest music and art facilities in the Midwest. The auditorium seats 1,400 and is noted for its acoustical qualities and the majestic Sanford Memorial Organ. The MacCollin Classroom Building, adjoining the auditorium, houses offices, art studios, practice rooms, and classrooms for music and art students.

The Helen Levitt Art Gallery adjoins the Eppley Auditorium and is home to the Levitt art collection, which includes work by internationally famous artists.

Lewis Hall, the second-oldest building on campus, is the site of the Education, English, Modern Languages, and Nursing Departments as well as administrative offices and Student Services.

The Robert M. Lincoln Center houses the College's division of business administration and economics and contains a library, auditorium, a conference room, several classrooms, and the newly remodeled Center for Entrepreneurship Education.

The James and Sharon Walker Science Center, completely renovated in 2001, features up-to-date laboratories and classrooms and houses offices for the Natural Sciences and Mathematics Division.

Costs

Tuition and fees for 2007–08 were $20,164, and room and board were $6166. These figures do not include books and personal expenses.

Financial Aid

In 2006–07, more than $25.3 million was awarded in financial aid to Morningside students, with an average financial aid package of $20,700. The financial aid resources of federal, state, and College programs are available to Morningside students through a combination of scholarships, grants, loans, and work-study employment. Morningside values students who achieve both in and out of the classroom—people who are thinkers and doers. Morningside Celebration of Excellence Scholarships recognize academic excellence and outstanding service, and awards of up to $10,000 per year are renewable for four years. Morningside also values its ties with alumni and the United Methodist Church, and those awards are also renewable for four years.

Students are encouraged to submit the Free Application for Federal Student Aid (FAFSA) as early as possible. The College's code number is 001879. The annual priority deadline for need-based financial aid is March 1.

Faculty

Seventy-nine percent of Morningside College's 70 full-time faculty members have earned the terminal degree in their chosen field. The College also employs 80 part-time instructors and has a 17:1 student-faculty ratio.

Student Government

Student government is directly responsible for regulation, supervision, and coordination of student campus activities. The president of the student body is a voting member of the Board of Directors, allowing for student input in decisions facing the Board.

Admission Requirements

Morningside College selects students for admission whose scholastic achievement and personal abilities provide a foundation for success at the college level. While the College seeks students who rank in the upper half of their graduating class, each application is considered on an individual basis. The student's academic record, class rank, and test scores are considered. Transfer students must have earned 24 transferable semester hours of a 2.25 or better cumulative GPA on previous college work to qualify for automatic admission. It is the policy and practice of Morningside College to not discriminate against persons on the basis of age, sex, religion, creed, race, color, national or ethnic origin, sexual orientation, or physical or mental disability.

Application and Information

Rolling admission allows for flexibility; however, prospective students are encouraged to apply as early as possible before the semester in which they wish to enroll. Transfer and international students are welcome. Catalogs, application forms, and financial aid forms are available from the Office of Admissions.

For further information, students should contact:

Office of Admissions
Morningside College
1501 Morningside Avenue
Sioux City, Iowa 51106
Phone: 712-274-5111
800-831-0806 (toll-free)
E-mail: mscadm@morningside.edu
Web site: http://www.morningside.edu

Morningside College offers students one-on-one interaction with instructors.

COLLEGE DATA CENTER • IOWA

MOUNT MERCY COLLEGE

CEDAR RAPIDS, IOWA

The College

Mount Mercy College is a Catholic, four-year baccalaureate institution sponsored by the Sisters of Mercy where liberal arts learning and professional preparation are uniquely integrated and strengthened by a special emphasis on leadership and service. Mount Mercy works to promote in its students reflective judgment, purposeful living, strategic communication, and service to the common good. Mount Mercy's distinct student populations—traditional, transfer, and adult-accelerated—participate in a variety of service-learning opportunities and immersion experiences.

Mount Mercy is fully accredited by the North Central Association of Colleges and Schools. Mount Mercy believes strongly in a firm liberal arts foundation of analysis, critical thinking, and communication—skills that help graduates adapt to a global and changing world and find long-term career and personal success. Through its Emerging Leaders, Campus Ministry programs, and Office of Volunteerism, the College supports and encourages the concept of servant leadership and service to the common good. An unwavering tradition of service is a legacy of and testament to the Sisters of Mercy, who founded the College in 1928. Mount Mercy's campus atmosphere is vibrant, engaging, and ecumenical.

Mount Mercy's high academic quality and strong financial aid programs make it one of the best values in Midwest higher education. Mount Mercy offers more than thirty-five major fields of study, including several interdisciplinary majors. Through the Freshman Partnership Program, professors are paired with first-year students to support their transition to college life—academically and socially—and to enhance the intellectual growth needed to ensure future personal and academic success.

Student activities include more than thirty clubs and organizations, a student newspaper, choir, an active Student Government Association, and a pom-pom squad and cheerleaders. Other campus events and activities include those sponsored by the student programming board and student organizations, including entertainment activities like the Roommate Game, Spring Fling, visits by hypnotists and mentalists, coffee house performances, and Mount Mercy Idol. Because of its prime location in Cedar Rapids, Iowa, "The Jewel of the Midwest," Mount Mercy students take advantage of many of the events held in the city of 140,000. The Student Activities Office offers students a significant price reduction on tickets to events such as hockey, baseball, the theater, the movies, and ice skating. The Mount Mercy Cultural Affairs Committee also sponsors a variety of cultural events for students, faculty, staff, and the greater community. Past speakers and presenters include civil rights leader Julian Bond, U.S. Poet Laureate Ted Kooser, internationally renowned filmmaker Gerry Straub, and an annual visit by a Holocaust survivor. Each May, commencement exercises are followed by a celebration for graduates and their families on Mount Mercy's beautiful hilltop campus. During the school year, many student activities, including Club Friday, a Friday afternoon gathering of students, faculty members, and staff members, take place in Lundy Commons, the student union that houses a game room, fitness center, conference rooms, student organization offices, the *Mount Mercy Times* office, lounge areas, and the campus bookstore.

Mount Mercy College is a member of the National Association of Intercollegiate Athletics (NAIA) and the Midwest Collegiate Conference. Mount Mercy offers intercollegiate competition in men's baseball, basketball, cross-country, golf, soccer, and track and field. In women's sports, the College offers basketball, cross-country, golf, soccer, softball, track and field, and volleyball. These programs have combined for more than thirty conference championships. Mount Mercy teams and individuals regularly qualify for regional and national championship events, and Mount Mercy student-athletes are annually recognized as NAIA academic all-Americans. Intramural activities include basketball, cross-country, flag football, golf, softball, and volleyball.

Mount Mercy is committed to providing its traditional residential students a total college experience, and freshman and sophomore students are required to live on campus to fully integrate, academically and socially, to Mount Mercy. Mount Mercy offers a variety of living arrangements, including Andreas House, which houses 144 students in eight home-like, four-bedroom suites, and the Lower Campus Apartments, which offer upperclassmen the opportunity to live in apartments while enjoying proximity to campus. A network of tunnels connects nearly all campus buildings; many students wear shorts and flip-flops all winter!

Location

Located in the heart of historic Cedar Rapids, Iowa, a growing small city of 140,000, Mount Mercy is just minutes from Cedar Rapids' many museums, malls, movie theaters, and restaurants. The 40-acre, tree-lined campus is tucked into a safe residential neighborhood of well-kept homes, neat lawns, and friendly neighbors. Mount Mercy's hilltop, with its sweeping view of the city skyline, is the highest point in Linn County, Iowa. The city bus stops at the College's "front door," providing convenient in-town transportation. Cedar Rapids is served by six major airlines and is a 4-hour drive from Chicago, Minneapolis–St. Paul, Omaha, Kansas City, and St. Louis.

Mount Mercy's location in a thriving Midwestern city helps students explore career possibilities and, when they graduate, find promising opportunities. Mount Mercy and the Cedar Rapids community also provide a wide range of internship opportunities for students, including hands-on work at international corporations such as General Mills, Pillsbury, Quaker Oats, Rockwell Collins, AEGON, and Archer Daniels Midland. Many internships and practicums often result in full-time employment after graduation. Each year, Mount Mercy hosts a career fair that attracts approximately fifty local employers, and separate fairs are held for nursing and education students. More than 96 percent of students report that they are employed or in graduate school within six months of graduation from Mount Mercy. Mount Mercy alumni serve as resources for current students and are easily accessible, since 73 percent of Mount Mercy's graduates reside in Iowa and 44 percent live in Linn County. Both economically and culturally, Cedar Rapids offers an outstanding quality of life.

Majors and Degrees

Mount Mercy awards the Bachelor of Arts, Bachelor of Science, Bachelor of Business Administration, Bachelor of Applied Science, Bachelor of Applied Arts, and Bachelor of Science in Nursing degrees.

The Bachelor of Arts degree is awarded to graduates who major in applied philosophy, art, biology, communication, criminal justice, criminal justice/business administration–interdisciplinary, English, English/business administration–interdisciplinary, English–language arts (teacher education program), history, international studies, mathematics, music, music education (teacher education program), political science, political science/business administration–interdisciplinary, psychology, psychology/business administration–interdisciplinary, religious studies, secondary education, social science–American government (teacher education program), social science–psychology (teacher education program), social work, sociology, sociology/business administration–interdisciplinary, speech/drama, and visual arts/business administration–interdisciplinary.

The Bachelor of Science degree is awarded to graduates who major in biology, biology–education (teacher education program), business, computer information systems, computer science, elementary education, health services administration, mathematics, mathematics–education (teacher education program), medical technology, and secondary education. The Bachelor of Science in Nursing degree is awarded to graduates who major in nursing.

The Bachelor of Business Administration is awarded to graduates who major in accounting, administrative management, business–general (teacher education program), marketing, and secondary education.

The Bachelor of Applied Science and Bachelor of Applied Arts degree programs are designed for students with technical training who wish to broaden their specialized background to include a liberal arts education. The Bachelor of Applied Science degree is awarded to graduates who major in accounting, administrative management, biology, business, computer information systems, computer science, health services administration, marketing, and mathematics. The Bachelor of Applied Arts degree is awarded to graduates who major in art, biology, criminal justice, history, mathematics, music, political science, psychology, religious studies, sociology, and speech/drama.

Elementary education majors may choose from a range of subject-area endorsements, such as reading, early childhood, and special education. Original endorsements, coupled with a secondary education major, may also be completed in a number of subject-area endorsements, ranging from art to speech-communication.

Academic Programs

Mount Mercy requires 123 semester hours for graduation, with a cumulative GPA of at least 2.0. General education requirements include a total of twelve courses in philosophy, religious studies, English, speech, arts, social sciences, natural sciences, history, and multicultural studies. Students apply for admission to their major program in the spring of the sophomore year. Mount Mercy gives credit for related experience based on portfolio presentations and for independent study arranged by the student and the instructor. Graduation requirements may vary according to the major field of study.

Special academic opportunities are offered to outstanding students through special honors sections of general education courses. Students graduating in the honors program receive special recognition at commencement.

Mount Mercy's academic year consists of fall and spring semesters, plus a winter term. This four-week term offers required courses as well as exploratory electives and international travel, allowing students to make more rapid progress toward their degrees. In addition, two 5-week summer sessions are held.

Off-Campus Programs

Mount Mercy College has an exchange program with the University of Palacky in Olomouc, Czech Republic, and is exploring further partnerships with international institutions.

Academic Facilities

The Busse Library provides an inviting study and research environment and access to numerous online databases. Internet access opens other major libraries to students, as well. The library houses the computer center; a computer classroom for instruction in writing, accounting, and computer skills; a media center; individual study carrels; group study rooms; and a variety of other comfortable study areas.

Basile Hall is a state-of-the-art business and biology building that opened in 2003, providing thirteen technology-ready classrooms and teaching labs, four seminar rooms, and a computer teaching laboratory.

All on-campus student rooms and faculty/staff offices are connected to a campus network, and all have wireless Internet capacity. Mount Mercy also has an ICN fiber-optics classroom, making it possible for students in more than one location to take the same course, interacting with other students and the instructor.

Costs

Full-time tuition for the 2007–08 academic year was $20,070. Major fees are included in this figure. Room and board costs average $6270.

Financial Aid

Nearly all Mount Mercy's new, full-time freshmen receive some form of financial aid, including Mount Mercy scholarships or grants, federal or state grants, loans, on-campus employment, or a combination of these sources. Mount Mercy awards a number of academic scholarships based on academic achievement, including Presidential Scholarships, Distinguished Honor Scholarships, and Honor Scholarships. Each year, students who have been admitted to Mount Mercy and identified as Presidential Scholars are invited to the campus to compete for the Holland Scholarship, a full-tuition award named for the first president of Mount Mercy. Students may also apply for the Merit Award, which is given to entering freshman and transfer students on the basis of their demonstrated leadership in school and community activities. In addition to these scholarships, other awards are available to students with records of achievement. Transfer students also qualify for academic awards, including Presidential Scholarships, Distinguished Honor Scholarships, and Honor Scholarships. Transfer students may qualify for an additional Phi Theta Kappa Scholarship. In 2007–08, the College awarded more than $6.2 million in institutional scholarships and grants to qualified students.

Students who show financial need may be eligible for the Federal Pell Grant, Iowa Tuition Grant, Federal Stafford Student Loan, and on-campus employment. Students in work-study positions typically earn from $1000 to $2000 per year. To apply for Mount Mercy scholarships and grants, students must first be admitted to the College. Early application is advised. The priority deadline for filing the FAFSA is March 1. Students should check other deadlines with their high school counselors or call the Mount Mercy financial aid office.

Faculty

Most of Mount Mercy's faculty members hold a terminal degree in their field. Many have been recognized for their achievements, and several faculty members have been Fulbright Fellows or have received grants from the National Endowment for the Humanities and the National Endowment for the Arts; many others have been recognized by their professional organizations. With a student-faculty ratio of 13:1, Mount Mercy offers students the opportunity to know their teachers and to learn from them in an informal, friendly, and supportive environment.

Student Government

The official voice of students at Mount Mercy is the Student Government Association (SGA). Its officers serve on College committees, and SGA is represented at regular faculty meetings. SGA is the body through which all other campus organizations are formed and funded, and the group unanimously supported an amendment to mandate that all campus organizations include a service component each year.

Admission Requirements

Mount Mercy admits students whose academic preparation, abilities, interests, and personal qualities give promise of success in college. Applicants are considered on the basis of academic record, class rank, test scores, and recommendations. An Admission Committee reviews the applications of students with minimum qualifications. To apply, freshman students must submit an application for admission, a transcript of high school credits, ACT or SAT scores, and a $20 application fee. Transfer students must submit an application for admission, official transcripts from all colleges attended, official transcripts from their high school (if not possessing an associate degree), and a $20 application fee. Mount Mercy College has an agreement with several two-year colleges in Iowa through which degree graduates of these colleges may be admitted to Mount Mercy with junior standing.

Prospective students are encouraged to visit the campus, sit in on classes, and meet students and faculty. Special campus visit days are scheduled each year, and individual appointments also may be made. Overnight accommodations in residence halls can be arranged.

Application and Information

Students who wish to be considered for Mount Mercy scholarships and grants should submit their applications for admission as early as possible after their junior year in high school. Admission decisions are made on a rolling basis. Application forms are available online at http://www.mtmercy.edu and may be completed online or printed.

Office of Admissions
Mount Mercy College
1330 Elmhurst Drive, NE
Cedar Rapids, Iowa 52402
Phone: 319-368-6460
800-248-4504 (toll-free)
E-mail: admission@mtmercy.edu
Web site: http://www.mtmercy.edu

Students at Mount Mercy College.

ST. AMBROSE UNIVERSITY

DAVENPORT, IOWA

The University

St. Ambrose University (SAU) offers all of the advantages needed for a successful college experience and a bright future—a great selection of classes, top-of-the-line resources, professors who challenge and encourage, and the kind of people who become friends for life. The student body comprises approximately 3,600 students.

St. Ambrose has been providing an education that nurtures the spirit while training the mind for 125 years. Founded in 1882, the University was named for St. Ambrose, the fourth-century saint and bishop of Milan, who was a doctor, scholar, author, orator, and teacher.

Today, the campus consists of nearly 45 acres in a residential section of Davenport, with about thirty buildings, including historic Ambrose Hall. Newer additions to the campus include a $15.3-million university center and residence halls. Student housing at St. Ambrose, which is widely considered to be the best in the region, combines the comforts of home with the privileges of independence for the more than 1,400 students who live on campus. Some residence halls are apartment style and have kitchen-equipped units with private bedrooms for groups of 4 or 6 students. Other halls provide extras such as semiprivate bathrooms and study rooms on each floor. Housekeeping services are also provided. SAU opened a residence hall for freshmen in 2004 and another new sophomore residence hall in 2005.

At the graduate level, the University offers master's degrees in accounting, business administration, criminal justice, educational administration, information technology management, nursing administration, occupational therapy, organizational leadership, social work, and teaching. Doctoral degrees are offered in business administration and physical therapy.

St. Ambrose has eighteen varsity sports for men and women in a widely varied athletic program. Five hundred undergraduate students, more than one third of all campus residents, participate in NAIA Division II sports. Recreational facilities include a gymnasium, racquetball courts, an indoor track, and weightlifting rooms.

The University sponsors more than fifty clubs and organizations, and the student-run Campus Activities Board (CAB) plans events from major concerts, such as Ben Folds and O.A.R., to family weekends and homecoming activities. Many students participate in intramural athletics, and Campus Ministry provides spiritual recreation through retreats, religious services, social justice activities, and volunteer opportunities, including annual trips to Chicago's inner city and Kentucky's Appalachia.

Location

The Quad Cities, which includes Davenport, is a vibrant metropolitan area with a population of nearly 400,000. The Mississippi River joins the two-state (Iowa and Illinois) community, creating a very affordable, manageable urban setting distinguished by friendly people and unique river vistas. Whether students were born here or come here for the first time to begin their university studies, the Quad Cities is a great place to live and learn.

The area offers several first-class arts and entertainment venues and is host to many museums, theaters, and a symphony orchestra and ballet company. Throughout the year, there are celebrations such as the Bix Beiderbecke Jazz Festival and the Riverssance Fine Arts Festival. There is a range of lively nightspots in the area, and there are many fine restaurants, as well as the i wireless Center, which hosts big-name performers such as Bon Jovi, Nickelback, Tim McGraw, and Avril Lavigne. The shopping is great, too, whether it's in one of the many malls or the historic Village of East Davenport.

Students also find professional sports teams in hockey, baseball, and arena football and major sporting events like the PGA's John Deere Classic and the Quad-City Times Bix 7 road race. The Great River Bike Trail runs along the Mississippi River, Snowstar ski area is nearby, and there are numerous public golf courses in the area.

Majors and Degrees

Programs are offered leading to bachelor's degrees in applied management technology (B.A.M.T.), arts (B.A.), business administration (B.B.A.), elected studies (B.E.S.), music education (B.M.E.), science (B.S.), science in industrial engineering (B.S.I.E.), science in nursing (B.S.N.), and special studies (B.S.S.).

Undergraduate areas of study include accounting, applied management technology, art (art education, book arts, fine arts, and graphic design), biology, business (economics, finance, general business, international business, management, and marketing), Catholic studies, chemistry, computer information systems, computer investigations and criminal justice, computer network administration, computer science, criminal justice, criminalistics, education (early childhood education, elementary education, secondary education, and special education), elected studies, English, environmental studies, exercise science, forensic psychology, history, human performance and fitness, industrial engineering, international accounting and modern language, international studies, Irish studies, journalism, languages (French, German, and Spanish), mass communication, mathematics, media studies, music, nursing, occupational therapy, organizational leadership, peace and justice, philosophy, physical education, physical therapy, physics, political science and leadership studies, psychology, public administration, public relations and marketing communication, radio and television, sociology, special studies, sport management, theater, theology, and women's studies. Preprofessional studies are offered in chiropractic, dentistry, engineering, law, medicine, occupational therapy, osteopathy, physical therapy, social work, and veterinary medicine.

Academic Programs

The best education combines courses that teach students how to think with those that help them apply that thinking to the real world. St. Ambrose has always emphasized liberal arts studies and career education enriched by a Catholic heritage of social justice and service.

Students must complete a minimum of 120 semester credits (usually forty courses). Some bachelor's programs have additional requirements. Ninety-eight percent of graduates are employed or in graduate school within six months of graduation.

Off-Campus Programs

St. Ambrose students may earn up to 44 credits in study-abroad programs around the world. University-sponsored experiential learning opportunities and internships are available in most departments, including business administration, communication, criminal justice, economics, education, industrial engineering, occupational therapy, physical therapy, political science, psychology, and sociology.

Academic Facilities

Studies at St. Ambrose are significantly enhanced by the high quality of the University's facilities and resources, including a state-of-the-art library that houses an extensive collection of materials and the latest information technology. The library has more than 160,000 volumes, 700 journals, and 75 scholarly electronic databases. Thousands of professional journals and archives are available online.

Most of the academic buildings on campus have undergone complete or significant renovation within the past ten years to create comfortable seminar rooms, interactive classrooms, and modern labs. Although substantially upgraded, these facilities have retained their wonderful original architectural character.

Costs

Costs for 2007–08 were $10,580 for tuition and approximately $3450 for room and board per semester.

Financial Aid

Federal, state, and University financial aid programs, scholarships, loans, grants, work-study and cooperative programs, and University employment opportunities are available. Federal programs include the Federal Pell Grant program, the Federal Supplemental Educational Opportunity Grant program, the Federal Work-Study Program, the Federal PLUS Program, and the Federal Stafford Student Loan program. State programs are the Iowa Scholarship and Iowa Tuition Grant programs. The priority deadline for financial aid applications is March 15 for the next fall semester. In addition to submitting an application for admission, applicants for financial aid must submit the Free Application for Federal Student Aid (FAFSA). This form is available in the offices of high school counselors, in the St. Ambrose University Financial Aid Office, or online at http://fafsa.ed.gov/.

Faculty

St. Ambrose's more than 300 distinguished faculty members are a diverse and talented group of individuals. More than 85 percent have earned the highest degree in their fields. Professors, not teaching assistants, teach all classes.

Student Government

All registered students are members of the St. Ambrose Student Government Association (SGA). Organized in 1925, the SGA served as one of the prototypes of such organizations among American colleges. Students are represented on virtually every committee of the University.

Admission Requirements

Admission to St. Ambrose is selective. Students who satisfy at least two of the following requirements are encouraged to apply: a minimum 2.5 cumulative GPA, an ACT composite score of 20 or above or an SAT combined score of 950 or higher, and/or ranking in the upper half of their graduating class. Prospective students must take the ACT or SAT before being admitted. Placement tests in foreign languages and writing are required of most students upon admission.

St. Ambrose's students come from a variety of religious and cultural backgrounds, but they share one thing in common: the desire to fulfill their potential. St. Ambrose welcomes students directly out of high school, transfer students, international students, and those who have postponed their education for various reasons, such as work or family responsibilities.

Application and Information

The completed application for admission, high school transcripts or equivalent credentials, and test scores should be sent to the Director of Admissions. Students can apply online for free at http://www.sau.edu/apply.

For more information or to arrange a campus visit, students should contact:

Meg Halligan
Director of Admissions
St. Ambrose University
518 West Locust Street
Davenport, Iowa 52803
Phone: 563-333-6300
800-383-2627 (toll-free)
E-mail: admit@sau.edu
Web site: http://www.sau.edu/admissions

St. Ambrose's $15.3-million university center opened in 2004.

SIMPSON COLLEGE

INDIANOLA, IOWA

The College

Simpson College was founded in 1860. The institution was named Simpson College to honor Bishop Matthew Simpson (1811–1884), one of the best-known and most influential religious leaders of his day. The College is coeducational; although it is affiliated with the United Methodist Church, it is nonsectarian in spirit and accepts students without regard to race, color, creed, national origin, religion, sex, age, disability, veteran status, sexual orientation, or gender identity.

For more than a century, Simpson has played a vital role in the educational, cultural, intellectual, political, and religious life of the nation. The College has thirty-five buildings on 85 acres of beautiful campus and enrolls more than 2,000 students.

Extracurricular activities at Simpson are designed to supplement and reinforce the academic program and contribute toward a total learning experience. Students may participate in student government, publications, music, theater, and social groups. Simpson competes in eighteen intercollegiate sports and has an extensive intramural program for both men and women. Men's and women's athletics at Simpson are governed by the NCAA. Simpson also has chapters of three national fraternities, one local fraternity, and three national sororities.

Location

Simpson is located in the city of Indianola, a residential community of 14,400 people. Indianola is just 12 miles south of Des Moines, Iowa's capital city, with easy access to Interstates 35, 80, and 235. The Des Moines International Airport is 20 minutes from campus. Five miles south of Indianola is Lake Ahquabi State Park, where swimming, kayaking, hiking, and other recreational facilities are available. Every summer, Indianola is the home of the National Hot Air Balloon Classic and the Des Moines Metropolitan Summer Opera Festival. The location of the residential campus provides the best of both metropolitan and suburban activities.

Majors and Degrees

Simpson College grants Bachelor of Arts and Bachelor of Music degrees in major and career programs, including accounting, applied philosophy, art, athletic training, biochemistry, biology, chemistry, computer information systems, computer science, corporate communication, criminal justice, economics, education, English, environmental science, ethics, exercise science, forensic science/biochemistry, French, German, history, human resource management, international management, international relations, journalism and mass communication, Latin American studies, management, marketing, mathematics, music, music education, music performance, philosophy, physical education/coaching endorsements, physics, political science, psychology, religion, rhetoric and speech communication, sociology, Spanish, sports administration, theater arts, and women's studies.

Simpson also offers preprofessional programs in dentistry, engineering, law, medicine, optometry, physical therapy, theology, and veterinary medicine.

Academic Programs

Simpson College operates on a 4-4-1 academic calendar. The first semester starts in late August and ends in mid-December; the second semester starts in mid-January and ends in late April. A three-week session takes place during the month of May. During this period, students have the opportunity to take one class that focuses on a single subject, to study abroad, or to participate in a field experience or internship.

Students must participate in one May Term class or program for each year of full-time study at Simpson College. All students must complete the requirements of the cornerstone studies in liberal arts and competencies in foreign language, math, and writing. To earn the Bachelor of Arts degree, students may take no more than 42 hours in the major department, excluding May Term programs, and 84 hours in the division of the major, including May Term programs. At least 128 semester hours of course work must be accumulated with a grade point average of C (2.0) or better.

For a Bachelor of Music degree, the same requirements apply, except that 84 hours must be earned in the major, excluding May Terms, and the candidate is limited to 12 additional hours in the division of fine arts. A minimum of 132 hours of course work must be completed with a cumulative grade point average of C (2.0) or better.

The First Year Program is a broadly inclusive program of orientation, group-building, mentoring, community service, advising, and classroom work structured to help new students adapt to their first year of college. The program begins with summer registration and extends throughout the full year.

The academic component of the First Year Program is the Liberal Arts Seminar, a joint classroom and advising concept that is unique among first-year programs. The seminars are small in size—no more than 18 first-year students each—and all are taught by students' faculty advisers.

Off-Campus Programs

A variety of programs are offered for off-campus study. Simpson's semester-long study-abroad programs include London, England; Schorndorf, Germany; and Central America. Students also have the opportunity to study abroad in semester-long programs in France, Spain, Italy, and Australia.

Simpson is an affiliate of the American Institute for Foreign Study, which provides access to carefully planned semester or academic-year study programs in France and Spain. Additional international travel programs are offered on a regular basis during the May Term, including such destinations as Africa, Central America, Great Britain, France, Greece, Ireland, New Zealand, Thailand, and Scandinavia.

The Capitol Hill Internship Program (CHIP) provides students with the opportunity to spend either the fall or spring semester in Washington, D.C., working in an internship. In addition, students participate in two seminars for credit. Also available is the United Nations Semester with Drew University in Madison, New Jersey. Students undertake a course of study at Drew and at the United Nations.

Academic Facilities

The George Washington Carver Science Center provides state-of-the-art research facilities, computer labs, a cadaver lab, and classrooms.

Simpson has a campuswide Ethernet fiber-optic network and high-speed Internet access as well as wireless access in many areas. There are numerous computer labs distributed across the campus where students can use standard office suite applications or specialized, discipline-specific applications.

The Henry H. and Thomas H. McNeill Hall houses classrooms for management, accounting, economics, and communication studies. In addition, the hall houses a seminar room and the Pioneer Hi-Bred International Conference Center.

The Amy Robertson Music Center houses the music department and contains the Sven and Mildred Lekberg Recital Hall, ten studios, twenty-two practice rooms, a music computer lab, and the band rehearsal room. The Salsbury Wing includes a choral rehearsal room, a classroom, and studios.

Dunn Library, a contemporary learning resource center, contains approximately 154,180 volumes, 480 current periodicals, 15,660 electronic journals, 2,705 DVDs and videotapes, 1,075 music CDs, and access to more than 7,485 e-books. Additional materials for research can be obtained through a national computer-based interlibrary loan network. The library also provides audiovisual equipment and services to the campus.

The A. H. and Theo Blank Performing Arts Center accommodates Simpson's well-known programs in theater arts and opera and includes the magnificent 500-seat Pote Theatre, with both proscenium and hydraulically controlled thrust stages; a studio theater; the Barborka Gallery; technical facilities and shops; and classrooms.

Wallace Hall reopened in 1996 after a complete internal renovation. Named to the National Register of Historic Places in 1991, Wallace Hall contains facilities for education, psychology, sociology, applied social science, and a biofeedback/psychology laboratory.

Costs

Tuition and fees for 2007–08 were $23,596; room charges were $3194; and board was $3461. These figures did not include books, music fees, or personal expenses.

Financial Aid

Simpson College seeks to make it financially possible for qualified students to experience the advantages of a Simpson education. Generous gifts from alumni, trustees, and friends of the College—in addition to state and federal student aid programs—make this opportunity possible. Simpson offers financial aid on both a need and non-need basis. Need is determined by filing the Free Application for Federal Student Aid.

Financial aid granted on a non-need basis includes academic scholarships, which are awarded on the basis of prior academic records, and talent scholarships, which are available in theater, music, and art. The talent scholarships are determined by audition/portfolio.

Faculty

Eighty-eight percent of Simpson's 97 full-time faculty members have earned their terminal degrees. At Simpson, faculty members serve as academic advisers as well as teachers and often attend College plays, operas, and athletic events, reinforcing their sincere interest in students. The student-faculty ratio is 16:1.

Student Government

Student involvement in College governance is an integral part of the organization of the College. Students annually elect a president and vice president of the Student Government. The members of each housing unit and the off-campus students elect representatives to the Student Senate. The Student Senate appoints student members to all College committees in which students hold membership. The senate also appoints 3 students-at-large who attend plenary sessions of the Board of Trustees as members on the Student Affairs Committee.

Admission Requirements

Admission to Simpson College is selective and competitive. A strong academic record is essential. Applications are acted upon by an admissions committee, which is elected by the faculty and represents the five academic divisions of the College. These faculty members consider the college-preparatory courses taken, the grades received in those courses, rank in class, and standardized test scores (ACT and/or SAT), including test subscores. A short time after all required credentials are received, the application is reviewed by the Admissions Committee.

Transfer applicants are accepted on the basis of successful completion of academic work at an accredited college or university. In addition, transfer applicants are required to submit official high school transcripts and ACT/SAT results.

Application and Information

Simpson's rolling admission policy allows flexibility; however, early application is recommended. Transfer and international students are welcome. Students are strongly encouraged to visit the campus.

For additional information or to obtain application materials, students should contact:

Office of Admissions
Simpson College
701 North C Street
Indianola, Iowa 50125
Phone: 515-961-1624
800-362-2454 Ext. 1624 (toll-free)
E-mail: admiss@simpson.edu
Web site: http://www.simpson.edu

The George Washington Carver Science Center provides Simpson students with state-of-the-art labs and research facilities.

UNIVERSITY OF DUBUQUE

DUBUQUE, IOWA

The University

The University of Dubuque (UD) is a private, Presbyterian, professional university with a focus in the liberal arts, as well as a theological seminary located in Iowa's first city—Dubuque. The Key City is on the Mississippi River at the point where the borders of Wisconsin, Illinois, and Iowa meet. Founded in 1852, the University is an institution in three parts: the undergraduate college, the graduate theological seminary, and the graduate institute. The University's mission of encouraging intellectual, moral, and spiritual development dates back to its founding.

Throughout its history, the University has been known as a place of educational opportunity. Even today, a large portion of its students are from first-generation or underrepresented populations. The University of Dubuque's welcoming interfaith community of approximately 1,500 students comes from across the country and around the globe.

Because students from many nations attend the University of Dubuque, UD offers students a cosmopolitan atmosphere. The school is convinced that students living in today's world are better prepared for life if they have a global perspective. American and international student interaction on campus, as well as the movement of faculty members and students across international boundaries, is essential for a meaningful education, human enrichment, and intercultural global awareness.

Location

The University of Dubuque, located in eastern Iowa, is in the heart of the Midwest. Dubuque is a city for all seasons. From bluffs blazing with autumn oranges and reds to the river sparkling with summer's blues and greens, the area scenery is spectacular year-round. Dubuque, the oldest city in Iowa, is a dynamic community built along the majestic Mississippi River and surrounded by dramatic bluffs. The setting is ideal for outdoor enthusiasts, with four seasons of ample outlets for recreation, including hiking, biking, boating, skiing, camping, golfing, climbing, and caving.

Dubuque offers the amenities of a larger city with the security and comfort of a smaller town. A lively cultural scene includes the Grand Opera House, the Dubuque Symphony Orchestra, and the Dubuque Museum of Art. The National Farm Toy Museum and the National Mississippi River Museum provide glimpses of the area's past. The city's theater productions, boutiques, and restaurants are wonderful ways to take a study break.

Nearby are some of the Midwest's most interesting cities, an easy drive for a weekend road trip. Historic Galena offers quaint shops and period architecture, while vibrant Chicago is famous for its museums and night life. Madison, Milwaukee, and Minneapolis–St. Paul are only hours away.

Majors and Degrees

With nineteen undergraduate majors, the University prepares students for careers in a variety of fields. From future teachers to corporate leaders to aspiring pilots, the University of Dubuque helps students achieve their career goals. The University's education department has the most majors, and its future teachers graduate with twice as many field-experience hours as required by the state of Iowa.

The University' Nursing Program was reinstated in the fall 2004 semester. The program offers a Bachelor of Science in Nursing (B.S.N.) degree. Nursing began at University of Dubuque in 1976 and, until 1997, the program offered fully accredited RN-to-B.S.N., B.S.N., and M.S.N. nursing preparation. The University has been granted interim approval by the Iowa Board of Nursing and is accredited by the American Association of Colleges of Nursing.

Academic departments encourage internships as an experiential component to complement classroom learning. For example, environmental science majors take advantage of the natural classroom of the Mississippi River, where students study the interaction between people and the environment. Aviation majors complete internships at the Dubuque Regional Airport or major airlines in addition to flying state-of-the-art equipment from UD's Garlick Flight Operations Center.

Academic Programs

The University of Dubuque education aims at helping students develop patterns of scholarship that make them effective learners throughout life. UD students are nurtured in the virtues of scholarship: the desire for understanding different peoples and cultures, an interest in learning, the skills to use multiple resources to explore ideas and find answers for life's questions, an understanding of conceptual connections, and the ability to reason and communicate effectively. Each graduate develops depth of knowledge in a particular field of study based on an integration of this field, the liberal arts, and his or her values.

University of Dubuque students begin to understand their chosen field of study by experiencing how it relates to other areas of knowledge. The process of exploring a variety of interests and possibilities in course work and in University activities results in the choice of a major. Current trends indicate that today's graduates change jobs and/or careers several times during their lifetimes. Therefore, professional preparation is more than a narrow, vocationally oriented process through which students prepare for one specific job. Rather, it is the development of transferable skills and attributes that allow students to succeed in a changing job market.

In the University of Dubuque community, the arts foster intellectual, emotional, and spiritual development. In literature, the visual arts, dance, drama, and music, students not only find aesthetic pleasure but also learn about other people's ideas, beliefs, and experiences and come to deeper understandings of their own.

Because of the University's location near the Mississippi—one of the world's great river systems—students have an appreciation of environmental issues. Through academic endeavors involving formal and experiential learning, students develop an understanding of the basic processes that underpin various ecological communities and of the complex interaction of human activities on the environment. The University of Dubuque encourages individuals to integrate their knowledge of the environment into personal, ethical, and spiritual guidelines, which can be used to improve their lives, their communities, and society.

The Lester G. and Michael Lester Wendt Character Initiative, supported by a substantial endowment, integrates virtues and values such as truthfulness, honesty, fairness, and the Golden Rule across the curriculum and throughout the University.

Off-Campus Programs

As a member of the Dubuque Tri-College Cooperative Effort, the University of Dubuque offers its students the opportunity to attend and receive credit for courses at Clarke College and Loras College, also in the city, thus providing access to the many different faculty members, professional societies, educational opportunities, and social activities of combined campuses of more than 3,500 students.

The University of Dubuque affirms the value of an international/intercultural experience and considers it to be an important component of any student's education. Overseas travel, exchanges, and study programs are available to help increase the global perspective of the students and to promote cross-cultural education.

Academic Facilities

The expanded and renovated University Science Center opened for classes in January 2007. With an additional 21,000 square feet of space, the University can devote the proper resources to its growing science programs. The new facility accommodates efficient laboratories, including state-of-the-art equipment and safety measures, bringing the science programs to the forefront of current teaching methods. Laboratory spaces include geology, zoology, general biology, cell/microbiology, science education, nursing, general chemistry, organic chemistry, geographic information systems (GIS), and five research labs to accommodate student-faculty collaborative research projects.

The Charles and Romona Myers Center, completed in September 2006, has added much-needed classroom and office space to the campus. Designed to be light, airy, and conducive to teaching and learning, the 44,000-square-foot facility houses classrooms, group study rooms, a seminar room, informal study nooks, and a 132-seat auditorium as well as administrative and faculty offices. The President's Office and the Wendt Center for Character Development are located in the building.

Opening in August 2008 is the Chlapaty Recreation and Wellness Center, an 87,000-square-foot facility enveloping the existing football stadium as well as additional construction looking west. Features of the new construction include a 6,900-square-foot, two-level fitness center, including areas for cardiovascular workout and free weights/machines; a 200-meter, six-lane indoor track with synthetic flooring for fitness walking and performance; four multiuse courts nested in the center of the track for intramurals and indoor practices; a training room, including hydrotherapy tubs and examination rooms; home, visitor, officials, and faculty/staff locker rooms; a football stadium, including east side visitor seating and an expanded concessions area; and a lighted field, synthetic field turf surface, and new outdoor track.

Costs

Tuition costs for the 2008–09 academic year are $19,600. Average room and board costs are $6790. These costs do not include books, supplies, personal expenses, and travel.

Financial Aid

Eighty-five percent of the University of Dubuque's students receive financial assistance through scholarships, awards and grants, loans, or work-study programs. The average financial assistance package for 2007–08 was $18,772. All levels of household incomes receive financial assistance.

To apply for financial assistance, applicants must submit a completed application package for admission to the University of Dubuque, file a FAFSA after January 1 and before April 1 (the priority deadline), and send or fax a copy of the completed FAFSA to the University of Dubuque Office of Student Financial Planning. Institutional, federal, state, and alternative loan programs are all available as forms of financial assistance.

Faculty

Seventy percent of University of Dubuque faculty members have earned a Ph.D. or other terminal degree. The student-faculty ratio is 15:1.

Student Government

The Student Government Association (SGA) represents the student body through general election of individual student representatives. The SGA sponsors four campus organizations, the University Program Council (UPC), the Spartan Spirit Club, *Under The Bell Tower* (student newspaper), and *The Key* (student yearbook). SGA provides student representatives for a number of key administrative committees.

Admission Requirements

An applicant for admission to the University of Dubuque undergraduate program is a graduate of a high school or equivalent (GED) and presents a minimum of 15 high school units, of which 10 are from academic fields (English, social studies, natural science, mathematics, foreign language). Either ACT or SAT scores are required. The admission committee looks at the application and transcript for indications of school achievement as well as aspiration, creativity, and adventurousness. Applicants to the University are usually active in cocurricular activities and these, as well as leadership qualities and character, are considered. An on-campus visit is encouraged. Two recommendations and an essay are requested and read with care.

Application and Information

First-year students are admitted to the University on a rolling basis. When the application and all supporting materials (e.g., transcripts and teacher and counselor recommendations) have been received, admission decisions are made by the admission committee and students are advised of the University's decision.

Transfer students who are enrolled or who were previously enrolled at another college or university may apply for transfer to the University of Dubuque. The University considers transfer applications for fall and spring semesters.

In addition to completing the application materials required for first-year applicants, transfer applicants must submit a complete official transcript for all college courses taken and grades received and a complete official transcript for all secondary school courses taken and grades received.

For further information, students should contact:

Office of Admission
University of Dubuque
2000 University Avenue
Dubuque, Iowa 52001
Phone: 563-589-3000
800-722-5583 (toll-free)
E-mail: admssns@dbq.edu
Web site: http://www.dbq.edu

The expanded and renovated University Science Center.

ponent of any student's education. Overseas travel, exchanges, and study programs are available to help increase the global perspective of the students and to promote cross-cultural education.

Academic Facilities

The expanded and renovated University Science Center opened for classes in January 2007. With an additional 31,000 square feet of space, the University can double the physical resources for its growing science programs. The new facility accommodates eighteen laboratories, including state-of-the-art equipment and safety measures, bringing the science programs to the forefront of current teaching methods. Laboratory spaces include geology, zoology, general biology, cell microbiology, science education, nursing, general chemistry, organic chemistry, geographic information systems (GIS), and five research labs to accommodate student-faculty collaborative research projects.

The Charles and Romona Myers Center, completed in September 2006, has added much-needed classroom and office space to the campus. Designed to be light, airy, and conducive to teaching and learning, the 45,000-square-foot facility houses classrooms, group study spaces, a seminar room, informal study nooks, and a 132-seat auditorium as well as administrative and faculty offices. The President's Office and the Wendt Center for Character Development are located in the building.

Opening in August 2008 is the Chlapaty Recreation and Wellness Center, an 41,000-square-foot facility enveloping the existing football stadium as well as additional construction looking west. Features of the new construction include a 6,800-square-foot, two-level fitness center (including areas for cardiovascular workout and free weights machines), a 200-meter six-lane indoor track with synthetic flooring for fitness walking and performance, four multiuse courts nested in the center of the track for intramurals and indoor practices, a training room, including hydrotherapy tubs and examination rooms; home, visitor, officials, and faculty-staff locker rooms; a football stadium, including east side visitor seating and an expanded concessions area; and a lighted field, synthetic field turf surface, and new outdoor track.

Costs

Tuition costs for the 2008–09 academic year are $19,600. Average room and board costs are $6,700. These costs do not include books, supplies, personal expenses, and travel.

Financial Aid

Ninety-nine percent of the University of Dubuque's students receive financial assistance through scholarships, awards and grants, loans, or work-study programs. The average financial assistance package for 2007–08 was $18,772. All levels of household incomes receive financial assistance.

To apply for financial assistance, applicants must submit a completed application package for admission to the University of Dubuque, file a FAFSA after January 1 and before April 1 (the priority deadline), and send or fax a copy of the completed FAFSA to the University of Dubuque Office of Student Financial Planning. Institutional, federal, state, and alternative loan programs are all available as forms of financial assistance.

Faculty

Seventy percent of University of Dubuque faculty members have earned a Ph.D. or other terminal degree. The student-faculty ratio is 16:1.

Student Government

The Student Government Association (SGA) represents the student body through general election of individual student representatives. The SGA sponsors four campus organizations, the University Program Council (UPC), the Spartan Spirit Club, *Under The Bell Tower* (student newspaper), and *The Key* (student yearbook). SGA provides student representatives for a number of key administrative committees.

Admission Requirements

An applicant for admission to the University of Dubuque must meet academic prerequisites, is a graduate of a high school or equivalent (GED), and presents a minimum of 16 high school units, of which 10 are from academic fields (English, social studies, natural science, mathematics, foreign language). Either ACT or SAT scores are required. The admission committee looks at the application and gives careful consideration of school achievements as well as aspiration, creativity, and seriousness. Applicants to the University are usually active in cocurricular activities and there, as well as leadership qualities and character, are considered. An on-campus visit is encouraged. Two recommendations and an essay are requested and read with care.

Application and Information

First-year students are admitted to the University on a rolling basis. When the application and all supporting materials (e.g., transcripts and teacher and counselor recommendations) have been received, admission decisions are made by the admission committee and students are advised of the University's decision.

Transfer students who have applied or who were previously enrolled at another college or university may apply for transfer to the University of Dubuque. The University considers transfer applications for fall and spring semesters.

In addition to completing the application materials required for first-year applicants, transfer applicants must submit a complete official transcript for all college courses taken and grades received and a complete official transcript for all secondary school courses taken and grades received.

For further information, students should contact:

Office of Admission
University of Dubuque
2000 University Avenue
Dubuque, Iowa 52001
Phone: 563-589-3000
800-722-5583 (toll-free)
E-mail: admssns@dbq.edu
Web site: http://www.dbq.edu

The expanded and renovated University Science Center.

KANSAS

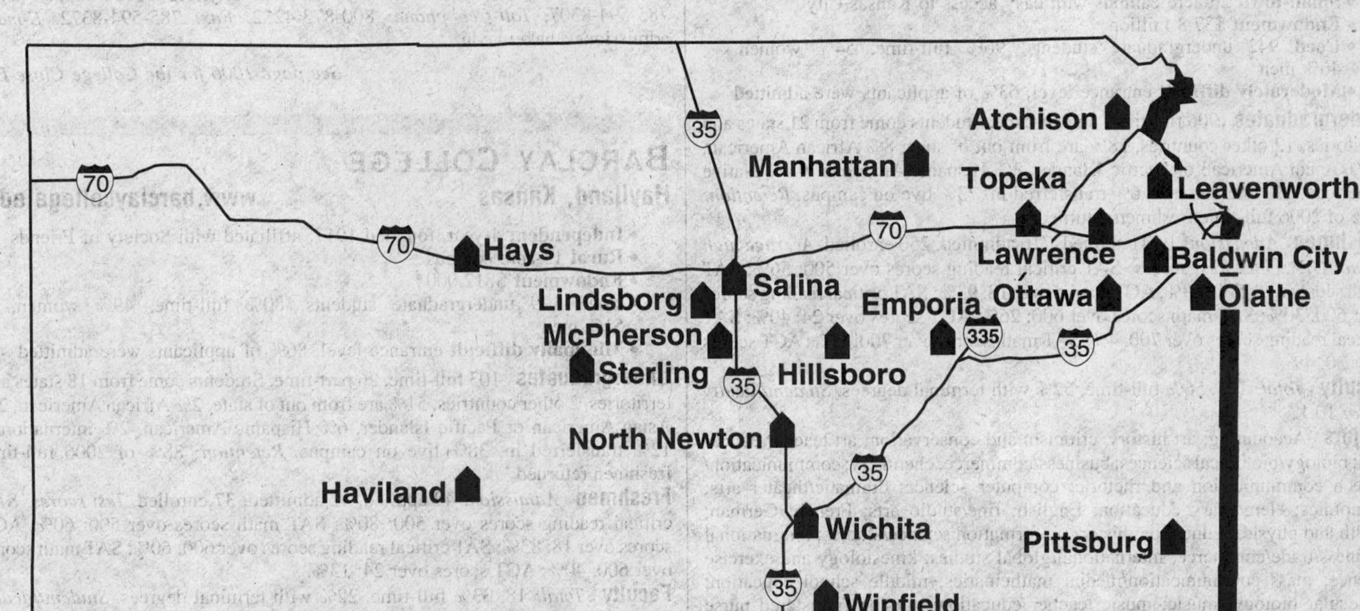

35
70
70
70
Atchison
Manhattan
Topeka
Leavenworth
Hays
Salina
Lawrence
Baldwin City
Lindsborg
Ottawa
Olathe
Emporia
McPherson
335
35
Sterling
Hillsboro
35
North Newton
35
Haviland
Wichita
Pittsburg
35
Winfield

BAKER UNIVERSITY

Baldwin City, Kansas **www.bakeru.edu/**

- **Independent United Methodist** comprehensive, founded 1858
- **Small-town** 26-acre campus with easy access to Kansas City
- **Endowment** $37.8 million
- **Coed** 942 undergraduate students, 96% full-time, 54% women, 46% men
- **Moderately difficult** entrance level, 63% of applicants were admitted

Undergraduates 906 full-time, 36 part-time. Students come from 21 states and territories, 12 other countries, 28% are from out of state, 8% African American, 0.8% Asian American or Pacific Islander, 3% Hispanic American, 0.4% Native American, 1% international, 6% transferred in, 73% live on campus. *Retention:* 78% of 2006 full-time freshmen returned.

Freshmen *Admission:* 1,141 applied, 716 admitted, 250 enrolled. *Average high school GPA:* 3.52. *Test scores:* SAT critical reading scores over 500: 56%; SAT math scores over 500: 59%; ACT scores over 18: 93%; SAT critical reading scores over 600: 30%; SAT math scores over 600: 26%; ACT scores over 24: 40%; SAT critical reading scores over 700: 4%; SAT math scores over 700: 11%; ACT scores over 30: 4%.

Faculty *Total:* 125, 56% full-time, 52% with terminal degrees. *Student/faculty ratio:* 10:1.

Majors Accounting; art history, criticism and conservation; art teacher education; biology/biological sciences; business/commerce; chemistry; communication/speech communication and rhetoric; computer science; dramatic/theater arts; economics; elementary education; English; fine/studio arts; French; German; health and physical education; history; information science/studies; international business/trade/commerce; international/global studies; kinesiology and exercise science; mass communication/media; mathematics; middle school education; molecular biology; music; music teacher education; nursing (registered nurse training); philosophy; physics; political science and government; psychology; religious studies; secondary education; sociology; Spanish; sport and fitness administration/management; wildlife biology.

Academics *Calendar:* 4-1-4, semesters for nursing program. *Degree:* bachelor's. *Special study options:* advanced placement credit, double majors, honors programs, independent study, internships, services for LD students, student-designed majors, study abroad, summer session for credit. *ROTC:* Army (c), Air Force (c). *Unusual degree programs:* 3-2 engineering with Washington University in St. Louis, University of Kansas; forestry with Duke University.

Computers on Campus 222 computers/terminals are available on campus for general student use. Students can access the following: computer help desk, free student e-mail accounts, online (class) grades, online (class) registration, online (class) schedules. Campuswide network is available. 100% of college-owned or -operated housing units are wired for high-speed Internet access. Wireless service is available via classrooms, computer labs, libraries, student centers.

Student Life *Housing:* on-campus residence required through senior year. *Options:* coed, men-only, women-only, disabled students. Campus housing is university owned and is provided by a third party. Freshman campus housing is guaranteed. *Activities and organizations:* drama/theater group, student-run newspaper, radio and television station, choral group, Cardinal Key, Earth We Are, Mungano, Fellowship of Christian Athletes, Student Activities Council, national fraternities, national sororities. *Campus security:* 24-hour emergency response devices and patrols, student patrols, controlled dormitory access. *Student services:* health clinic, personal/psychological counseling, women's center.

Athletics Member NAIA. *Intercollegiate sports:* baseball M (s), basketball M (s)/W (s), cheerleading M (s)/W (s), cross-country running M (s)/W (s), football M (s), golf M (s)/W (s), soccer M (s)/W (s), softball W (s), tennis M (s)/W (s), track and field M (s)/W (s), volleyball W (s). *Intramural sports:* basketball M/W, football M/W, softball M/W, volleyball M/W.

Standardized Tests *Required:* SAT or ACT (for admission).

Costs (2007–08) *One-time required fee:* $80. *Comprehensive fee:* $24,900 includes full-time tuition ($18,750) and room and board ($6150). Full-time tuition and fees vary according to location and program. Part-time tuition: $550 per credit hour. Part-time tuition and fees vary according to course load. *College room only:* $2850. Room and board charges vary according to board plan and housing facility. *Payment plan:* installment. *Waivers:* senior citizens and employees or children of employees.

Financial Aid Of all full-time matriculated undergraduates who enrolled in 2007, 779 applied for aid, 643 were judged to have need, 247 had their need fully met. In 2007, 107 non-need-based awards were made. *Average percent of need met:* 85%. *Average financial aid package:* $13,600. *Average need-based loan:* $5622. *Average need-based gift aid:* $6787. *Average non-need-based aid:* $9006. *Average indebtedness upon graduation:* $28,354.

Applying *Options:* electronic application, deferred entrance. *Required:* high school transcript, minimum 2.75 GPA, 1 letter of recommendation, minimum Composite ACT score of 18. *Required for some:* essay or personal statement, interview. *Application deadlines:* rolling (freshmen), rolling (transfers).

Freshman Application Contact Mr. Daniel McKinney, Director of Admissions, Baker University, PO Box 65, Baldwin City, KS 66006-0065. *Phone:* 785-594-8307. *Toll-free phone:* 800-873-4282. *Fax:* 785-594-8372. *E-mail:* admissions@bakeru.edu.

See page 1006 for the College Close-Up.

BARCLAY COLLEGE

Haviland, Kansas **www.barclaycollege.edu/**

- **Independent** 4-year, founded 1917, affiliated with Society of Friends
- **Rural** 13-acre campus
- **Endowment** $812,000
- **Coed** 129 undergraduate students, 80% full-time, 49% women, 51% men
- **Minimally difficult** entrance level, 86% of applicants were admitted

Undergraduates 103 full-time, 26 part-time. Students come from 18 states and territories, 2 other countries, 51% are from out of state, 2% African American, 2% Asian American or Pacific Islander, 6% Hispanic American, 2% international, 12% transferred in, 38% live on campus. *Retention:* 88% of 2006 full-time freshmen returned.

Freshmen *Admission:* 49 applied, 42 admitted, 37 enrolled. *Test scores:* SAT critical reading scores over 500: 80%; SAT math scores over 500: 60%; ACT scores over 18: 83%; SAT critical reading scores over 600: 60%; SAT math scores over 600: 40%; ACT scores over 24: 13%.

Faculty *Total:* 18, 33% full-time, 22% with terminal degrees. *Student/faculty ratio:* 10:1.

Majors Biblical studies; business administration and management; divinity/ministry; elementary education; general studies; pastoral studies/counseling; psychology; religious education; religious/sacred music.

Academics *Calendar:* semesters. *Degrees:* certificates, associate, and bachelor's. *Special study options:* academic remediation for entering students, accelerated degree program, adult/continuing education programs, advanced placement credit, distance learning, double majors, external degree program, independent study, internships, part-time degree program, student-designed majors. *Unusual degree programs:* 3-2 nursing with Pratt Community College.

Computers on Campus 20 computers/terminals are available on campus for general student use. Students can access the following: campus intranet, computer help desk, free student e-mail accounts, online library catalog. Campuswide network is available. 100% of college-owned or -operated housing units are wired for high-speed Internet access. Wireless service is available via entire campus.

Student Life *Housing:* on-campus residence required through senior year. *Options:* men-only, women-only. Campus housing is university owned. Freshman campus housing is guaranteed. *Activities and organizations:* drama/theater group, choral group, Pep Club, Drama Club, Missions Club. *Campus security:* student patrols. *Student services:* personal/psychological counseling.

Athletics Member NSCAA. *Intercollegiate sports:* baseball M, basketball M/W, cheerleading M/W, soccer M, tennis M/W, volleyball W. *Intramural sports:* baseball M/W, basketball M/W, volleyball M/W.

Standardized Tests *Required:* SAT or ACT (for admission).

Costs (2007–08) *Comprehensive fee:* $18,300 includes full-time tuition ($12,300) and room and board ($6000). Part-time tuition: $350 per hour. Part-time tuition and fees vary according to course load. *Room and board:* Room and board charges vary according to board plan and housing facility. *Payment plan:* installment. *Waivers:* employees or children of employees.

Financial Aid Of all full-time matriculated undergraduates who enrolled in 2003, 163 applied for aid, 163 were judged to have need, 145 had their need fully met. 33 Federal Work-Study jobs (averaging $1200). 67 state and other part-time jobs (averaging $600). In 2003, 4 non-need-based awards were made. *Average percent of need met:* 85%. *Average financial aid package:* $6700. *Average need-based loan:* $3750. *Average need-based gift aid:* $1500. *Average non-need-based aid:* $1500. *Average indebtedness upon graduation:* $10,000.

Applying *Options:* electronic application, early admission, deferred entrance. *Application fee:* $15. *Required:* essay or personal statement, high school transcript, minimum 2.3 GPA, 2 letters of recommendation, interview. *Application deadlines:* 9/1 (freshmen), 9/1 (transfers). *Notification:* continuous (freshmen), continuous (transfers).

Freshman Application Contact Mr. Justin Kendall, Admissions Recruiter, Barclay College, 607 North Kingman, Haviland, KS 67059. *Phone:* 620-862-5252 Ext. 21. *Toll-free phone:* 800-862-0226. *Fax:* 620-862-5242. *E-mail:* jkendall@barclaycollege.edu.

BENEDICTINE COLLEGE

Atchison, Kansas **www.benedictine.edu/**

- **Independent Roman Catholic** comprehensive, founded 1859
- **Small-town** 225-acre campus with easy access to Kansas City
- **Endowment** $9.6 million
- **Coed** 1,753 undergraduate students, 76% full-time, 50% women, 50% men
- **Moderately difficult** entrance level, 27% of applicants were admitted

Benedictine College, in Atchison, Kansas, enjoys nearly 150 years of Catholic Benedictine commitment to learning, tradition, and spirituality. The diverse student body, which comprises more than 1,300 undergraduates, hails from more than forty states and seventeen other countries. In a recent survey, Benedictine College scored in the top 5 percent nationally for student-faculty interaction, supportive campus environment, and enriching educational experiences. Benedictine College has recently been named a *U.S. News & World Report* Top Tier Institution. With forty-one academic majors and three options for graduate schools on campus, success is a way of life at Benedictine College, where more than 95 percent of graduates are immediately placed in graduate schools or careers of their choice.

Undergraduates 1,341 full-time, 412 part-time. Students come from 43 states and territories, 22 other countries, 70% are from out of state, 5% African American, 0.9% Asian American or Pacific Islander, 6% Hispanic American, 0.5% Native American, 3% international, 4% transferred in, 71% live on campus. *Retention:* 75% of 2006 full-time freshmen returned.

Freshmen *Admission:* 1,504 applied, 406 admitted, 364 enrolled. *Average high school GPA:* 3.0.

Faculty *Total:* 118, 60% full-time, 59% with terminal degrees. *Student/faculty ratio:* 15:1.

Majors Accounting; art; arts management; astronomy; athletic training; biochemistry; biology/biological sciences; business administration and management; chemistry; computer science; dramatic/theater arts; economics; elementary education; English; French; history; liberal arts and sciences/liberal studies; mass communication/media; mathematics; music; music teacher education; natural sciences; philosophy; physical education teaching and coaching; physics; political science and government; psychology; religious studies; secondary education; social sciences; sociology; Spanish; special education; youth ministry.

Academics *Calendar:* semesters. *Degrees:* associate, bachelor's, and master's. *Special study options:* academic remediation for entering students, advanced placement credit, cooperative education, double majors, English as a second language, independent study, internships, off-campus study, part-time degree program, student-designed majors, study abroad, summer session for credit. *ROTC:* Army (b). *Unusual degree programs:* engineering with Kansas State University, University of Missouri–Columbia, South Dakota School of Mines and Technology; occupational therapy with Washington University in St. Louis.

Computers on Campus 80 computers/terminals are available on campus for general student use. Students can access the following: computer help desk, free student e-mail accounts, online (class) grades, online (class) registration, online (class) schedules. Campuswide network is available. 100% of college-owned or -operated housing units are wired for high-speed Internet access. Wireless service is available via entire campus.

Student Life *Housing:* on-campus residence required through senior year. *Options:* coed, men-only, women-only. Campus housing is university owned. Freshman campus housing is guaranteed. *Activities and organizations:* drama/theater group, student-run newspaper, choral group, student government, Students in Free Enterprise, Knights of Columbus, Concert Chorale/Chamber Singers, Campus Activities Board. *Campus security:* 24-hour emergency response devices and patrols, late-night transport/escort service. *Student services:* health clinic, personal/psychological counseling.

Athletics Member NAIA. *Intercollegiate sports:* baseball M (s), basketball M (s)/W (s), cheerleading M (s)/W (s), cross-country running M (s)/W (s), football M (s), golf M (s)/W (s), soccer M (s)/W (s), softball W (s), tennis W (s), track and field M (s)/W (s), volleyball W (s). *Intramural sports:* basketball M/W, football M/W, racquetball M/W, soccer M/W, softball M/W, table tennis M/W, volleyball M/W.

Standardized Tests *Required:* SAT or ACT (for admission).

Costs (2007–08) *Comprehensive fee:* $23,910 includes full-time tuition ($17,700) and room and board ($6210). Full-time tuition and fees vary according to course load and degree level. Part-time tuition: $530 per credit hour. Part-time tuition and fees vary according to course load and degree level. *College room only:* $2730. Room and board charges vary according to board plan and housing facility. *Payment plan:* installment. *Waivers:* senior citizens and employees or children of employees.

Financial Aid Of all full-time matriculated undergraduates who enrolled in 2007, 1,068 applied for aid, 937 were judged to have need, 167 had their need fully met. 372 Federal Work-Study jobs (averaging $822). 73 state and other part-time jobs (averaging $547). In 2007, 355 non-need-based awards were made. *Average percent of need met:* 71%. *Average financial aid package:* $16,983. *Average need-based loan:* $4394. *Average need-based gift aid:* $11,975. *Average non-need-based aid:* $7020. *Average indebtedness upon graduation:* $20,823.

Applying *Options:* electronic application, deferred entrance. *Application fee:* $25. *Required:* high school transcript, minimum 2.0 GPA. *Required for some:* interview. *Notification:* continuous (freshmen), continuous (transfers).

Freshman Application Contact Benedictine College, 1020 North 2nd Street, Atchison, KS 66002. *Phone:* 913-367-5340. *Toll-free phone:* 800-467-5340. *Fax:* 913-367-5462. *E-mail:* bcadmiss@benedictine.edu.

See page 1008 for the College Close-Up.

BETHANY COLLEGE

Lindsborg, Kansas **www.bethanylb.edu/**

- **Independent Lutheran** 4-year, founded 1881
- **Small-town** 80-acre campus
- **Endowment** $21.9 million
- **Coed** 537 undergraduate students, 95% full-time, 49% women, 51% men
- **Moderately difficult** entrance level, 61% of applicants were admitted

Undergraduates 512 full-time, 25 part-time. Students come from 30 states and territories, 15 other countries, 43% are from out of state, 10% African American, 1% Asian American or Pacific Islander, 6% Hispanic American, 1% Native American, 3% international, 16% transferred in, 64% live on campus. *Retention:* 61% of 2006 full-time freshmen returned.

Freshmen *Admission:* 632 applied, 388 admitted, 128 enrolled. *Average high school GPA:* 3.36. *Test scores:* SAT critical reading scores over 500: 20%; SAT math scores over 500: 37%; SAT writing scores over 500: 18%; ACT scores over 18: 90%; SAT critical reading scores over 600: 10%; SAT math scores over 600: 13%; SAT writing scores over 600: 3%; ACT scores over 24: 29%; SAT math scores over 700: 3%; ACT scores over 30: 3%.

Faculty *Total:* 87, 49% full-time, 47% with terminal degrees. *Student/faculty ratio:* 9:1.

Majors Accounting; art; arts management; art teacher education; athletic training; biology/biological sciences; biology teacher education; business administration and management; business/managerial economics; business teacher education; ceramic arts and ceramics; chemistry; chemistry teacher education; Christian studies; communication/speech communication and rhetoric; criminal justice/safety; drawing; education; elementary education; English; English/language arts teacher education; financial planning and services; history; international business/trade/commerce; legal professions and studies related; mathematics; mathematics teacher education; music; music teacher education; painting; parks, recreation and leisure; philosophy; physical education teaching and coaching; political science and government; psychology; religious studies; sculpture; social studies teacher education; social work; sociology; sport and fitness administration/management.

Academics *Calendar:* 4-1-4. *Degree:* bachelor's. *Special study options:* academic remediation for entering students, accelerated degree program, advanced placement credit, double majors, honors programs, independent study, internships, off-campus study, services for LD students, student-designed majors, study abroad, summer session for credit. *Unusual degree programs:* 3-2 engineering with Wichita State University.

Computers on Campus 48 computers/terminals are available on campus for general student use. Students can access the following: campus intranet, computer help desk, free student e-mail accounts, online (class) grades, online (class) registration. Campuswide network is available. 99% of college-owned or -operated housing units are wired for high-speed Internet access. Wireless service is available via classrooms, learning centers, libraries, student centers.

Student Life *Housing:* on-campus residence required through junior year. *Options:* coed, women-only. Campus housing is university owned. Freshman campus housing is guaranteed. *Activities and organizations:* drama/theater group, student-run newspaper, choral group, Business Club, Bethany Student Education Association, Multicultural Student Association, Bethany Youth Ministry Team, Bio Chem Club. *Campus security:* 24-hour emergency response devices, student patrols, late-night transport/escort service, controlled dormitory access, night patrols by security personnel. *Student services:* health clinic, personal/psychological counseling.

Athletics Member NAIA. *Intercollegiate sports:* baseball M (s), basketball M (s)/W (s), cross-country running M (s)/W (s), football M (s), golf M (s), soccer M (s)/W (s), softball W (s), tennis M (s)/W (s), track and field M (s)/W (s), volleyball

W (s). *Intramural sports:* archery M/W, badminton M/W, basketball M/W, bowling M/W, cross-country running M/W, field hockey M/W, football M/W, golf M/W, racquetball M/W, soccer M/W, softball M/W, table tennis M/W, tennis M/W, track and field M/W, volleyball M/W, weight lifting M/W.

Standardized Tests *Required:* SAT or ACT (for admission).

Costs (2008–09) *Comprehensive fee:* $23,774 includes full-time tuition ($17,824), mandatory fees ($300), and room and board ($5650). Part-time tuition: $600 per credit hour. *College room only:* $3075.

Financial Aid Of all full-time matriculated undergraduates who enrolled in 2007, 503 applied for aid, 420 were judged to have need, 175 had their need fully met. 115 Federal Work-Study jobs (averaging $1500). In 2007, 28 non-need-based awards were made. *Average percent of need met:* 97%. *Average financial aid package:* $19,074. *Average need-based loan:* $5832. *Average need-based gift aid:* $6560. *Average non-need-based aid:* $6064. *Average indebtedness upon graduation:* $17,717.

Applying *Options:* electronic application, deferred entrance. *Application fee:* $20. *Required:* high school transcript, minimum 2.5 GPA. *Required for some:* essay or personal statement, letters of recommendation, interview. *Application deadlines:* rolling (freshmen), rolling (transfers). *Notification:* continuous (freshmen), continuous (transfers).

Freshman Application Contact Mrs. Tricia Hawk, Dean of Admissions and Financial Aid, Bethany College, 421 North First Street, Lindsborg, KS 67456. *Phone:* 785-227-3311 Ext. 8344. *Toll-free phone:* 800-826-2281. *Fax:* 785-227-8993. *E-mail:* admissions@bethanylb.edu.

BETHEL COLLEGE

North Newton, Kansas www.bethelks.edu/

- **Independent** 4-year, founded 1887, affiliated with Mennonite Church USA
- **Small-town** 60-acre campus with easy access to Wichita
- **Endowment** $20.3 million
- **Coed** 541 undergraduate students, 95% full-time, 50% women, 50% men
- **Moderately difficult** entrance level, 75% of applicants were admitted

Undergraduates 512 full-time, 29 part-time. Students come from 19 other countries, 22% are from out of state, 6% African American, 2% Asian American or Pacific Islander, 4% Hispanic American, 0.6% Native American, 11% international, 16% transferred in, 61% live on campus. *Retention:* 72% of 2006 full-time freshmen returned.

Freshmen *Admission:* 411 applied, 310 admitted, 108 enrolled. *Average high school GPA:* 3.43. *Test scores:* SAT critical reading scores over 500: 40%; SAT math scores over 500: 40%; ACT scores over 18: 95%; SAT critical reading scores over 600: 20%; SAT math scores over 600: 27%; ACT scores over 24: 49%; SAT critical reading scores over 700: 7%; SAT math scores over 700: 7%; ACT scores over 30: 11%.

Faculty *Total:* 71, 69% full-time, 49% with terminal degrees. *Student/faculty ratio:* 9:1.

Majors Athletic training; biology/biological sciences; business/commerce; chemistry; computer science; elementary education; English; Germanic languages; health and physical education; history; mass communication/media; mathematics; music related; natural sciences; nursing (registered nurse training); physics; psychology; religious studies; social work; Spanish; visual and performing arts.

Academics *Calendar:* 4-1-4. *Degree:* certificates and bachelor's. *Special study options:* academic remediation for entering students, advanced placement credit, double majors, independent study, internships, off-campus study, part-time degree program, services for LD students, study abroad, summer session for credit. *Unusual degree programs:* 3-2 engineering with Kansas State University, University of Kansas, Wichita State University.

Computers on Campus 56 computers/terminals are available on campus for general student use. Students can access the following: campus intranet, computer help desk, free student e-mail accounts, online (class) grades, online (class) registration, online (class) schedules. Campuswide network is available. Wireless service is available via entire campus.

Student Life *Housing:* on-campus residence required through senior year. *Options:* coed, disabled students. Campus housing is university owned. Freshman campus housing is guaranteed. *Activities and organizations:* drama/theater group, student-run newspaper, radio and television station, choral group, Bethel College Service Corps, The Collegian (newspaper), Student Alumni Association, Student Senate, Student Activities Board. *Campus security:* 24-hour emergency response devices, student patrols, community police patrols. *Student services:* health clinic, personal/psychological counseling.

Athletics Member NAIA. *Intercollegiate sports:* basketball M (s)/W (s), cross-country running M (s)/W (s), football M (s), golf M (s)/W (s), soccer M (s)/W (s), tennis M (s)/W (s), track and field M (s)/W (s), volleyball W (s). *Intramural sports:* badminton M/W, baseball M, basketball M/W, bowling M/W, cross-country running M/W, golf M/W, soccer M/W, softball M/W, table tennis M/W, tennis M/W, ultimate Frisbee M/W, volleyball M/W.

Standardized Tests *Required:* SAT or ACT (for admission).

Costs (2007–08) *Comprehensive fee:* $24,200 includes full-time tuition ($17,800) and room and board ($6400). Full-time tuition and fees vary according to course load. Part-time tuition: $650 per credit hour. Part-time tuition and fees vary according to course load. *College room only:* $3450. Room and board charges vary according to board plan and housing facility. *Payment plans:* installment, deferred payment. *Waivers:* children of alumni, senior citizens, and employees or children of employees.

Financial Aid Of all full-time matriculated undergraduates who enrolled in 2006, 427 applied for aid, 420 were judged to have need, 159 had their need fully met. 255 Federal Work-Study jobs (averaging $1364). 234 state and other part-time jobs (averaging $860). In 2006, 64 non-need-based awards were made. *Average percent of need met:* 89%. *Average financial aid package:* $17,771. *Average need-based loan:* $6119. *Average need-based gift aid:* $4202. *Average non-need-based aid:* $8271. *Average indebtedness upon graduation:* $20,724.

Applying *Options:* deferred entrance. *Application fee:* $20. *Required:* high school transcript, minimum 2.5 GPA. *Required for some:* essay or personal statement, 2 letters of recommendation. *Recommended:* interview. *Application deadlines:* rolling (freshmen), rolling (transfers). *Notification:* continuous (freshmen), continuous (transfers).

Freshman Application Contact Mr. Allan Bartel, Vice President for Admissions, Bethel College, 300 East 27th Street, North Newton, KS 67117-0531. *Phone:* 316-284-5230. *Toll-free phone:* 800-522-1887 Ext. 230. *Fax:* 316-284-5870. *E-mail:* admissions@bethelks.edu.

CENTRAL CHRISTIAN COLLEGE OF KANSAS

McPherson, Kansas www.centralchristian.edu/

- **Independent Free Methodist** 4-year, founded 1884
- **Small-town** 16-acre campus
- **Endowment** $6.6 million
- **Coed** 362 undergraduate students, 84% full-time, 48% women, 52% men
- **Minimally difficult** entrance level, 99% of applicants were admitted

Undergraduates 305 full-time, 57 part-time. Students come from 34 states and territories, 3 other countries, 69% are from out of state, 13% African American, 0.7% Asian American or Pacific Islander, 5% Hispanic American, 2% Native American, 3% international, 6% transferred in, 80% live on campus. *Retention:* 57% of 2006 full-time freshmen returned.

Freshmen *Admission:* 270 applied, 268 admitted, 104 enrolled. *Average high school GPA:* 3.27. *Test scores:* ACT scores over 18: 81%; ACT scores over 24: 25%; ACT scores over 30: 4%.

Faculty *Total:* 37, 46% full-time, 11% with terminal degrees. *Student/faculty ratio:* 16:1.

Majors Accounting; accounting and finance; acting; airline pilot and flight crew; art; art teacher education; athletic training; biblical studies; biological and physical sciences; biology teacher education; business/commerce; business/corporate communications; business/managerial economics; business teacher education; chemistry teacher education; computer science; computer teacher education; criminal justice/law enforcement administration; criminal justice/safety; divinity/ministry; drama and dance teacher education; economics; elementary education; engineering; English; environmental studies; family and community services; finance; health and physical education; health teacher education; history; history teacher education; human resources management; kindergarten/preschool education; kinesiology and exercise science; legal studies; liberal arts and sciences and humanities related; liberal arts and sciences/liberal studies; marketing/marketing management; mathematics; mathematics teacher education; missionary studies and missiology; music; music history, literature, and theory; music performance; music teacher education; natural sciences; nursing assistant/aide and patient care assistant; nursing (licensed practical/vocational nurse training); nursing (registered nurse training); pastoral studies/counseling; photography; physical education teaching and coaching; physician assistant; pre-dentistry studies; pre-law studies; pre-medical studies; pre-pharmacy studies; pre-theology/pre-ministerial studies; pre-veterinary studies; psychology; psychology teacher education; religious/sacred music; religious studies; sales and marketing/marketing and distribution teacher education; science teacher education; secondary education; social psychology; social sciences; social science teacher education; social studies teacher education; social work; sociology; speech teacher education; sport and fitness administration/management; theology; wildlife biology; youth ministry; zoology/animal biology.

Academics *Calendar:* 4-1-4. *Degrees:* certificates, associate, and bachelor's. *Special study options:* academic remediation for entering students, adult/continuing education programs, advanced placement credit, cooperative education, distance learning, double majors, independent study, internships, off-campus study, part-time degree program, services for LD students, student-designed majors, study abroad.

Computers on Campus 40 computers/terminals are available on campus for general student use. Students can access the following: free student e-mail accounts. Campuswide network is available. 66% of college-owned or -operated housing units are wired for high-speed Internet access. Wireless service is available via computer centers, computer labs, dorm rooms, libraries, student centers.

Student Life *Housing:* on-campus residence required through senior year. *Options:* coed, men-only, women-only. Campus housing is university owned. Freshman campus housing is guaranteed. *Activities and organizations:* drama/theater group, student-run newspaper, choral group, C.O.L.O.R.S. (Cross Over Lines of Racial Stereotype), Performing Arts Club, Student Activities Committee, Fellowship of Christian Athletes, Phi Beta Lambda Business Club. *Campus security:* controlled dormitory access. *Student services:* health clinic, personal/psychological counseling.

Athletics Member NAIA, NCCAA. *Intercollegiate sports:* baseball M (s), basketball M (s)/W (s), cheerleading M (s)/W (s), cross-country running M (s)/W (s), golf M (s)/W (s), soccer M (s)/W (s), softball W (s), tennis M (s)/W (s), volleyball W (s). *Intramural sports:* basketball M/W, football M/W, soccer M/W, softball M/W, table tennis M/W, track and field M/W, ultimate Frisbee M/W, volleyball M/W.

Standardized Tests *Required:* SAT or ACT (for admission).

Costs (2008–09) *Comprehensive fee:* $21,500 includes full-time tuition ($15,800), mandatory fees ($200), and room and board ($5500). Part-time tuition: $450 per credit hour. *College room only:* $2500.

Financial Aid Of all full-time matriculated undergraduates who enrolled in 2007, 267 applied for aid, 244 were judged to have need, 57 had their need fully met. 58 Federal Work-Study jobs (averaging $1000). In 2007, 53 non-need-based awards were made. *Average percent of need met:* 75%. *Average financial aid package:* $13,423. *Average need-based loan:* $5024. *Average need-based gift aid:* $4383. *Average non-need-based aid:* $5284. *Average indebtedness upon graduation:* $20,000.

Applying *Options:* electronic application, deferred entrance. *Application fee:* $20. *Required:* high school transcript, minimum 2.5 GPA, 2 letters of recommendation. *Recommended:* essay or personal statement, interview. *Application deadlines:* rolling (freshmen), rolling (transfers). *Notification:* continuous (freshmen), continuous (transfers).

Freshman Application Contact Dr. David Ferrell, Dean of Admissions, Central Christian College of Kansas, PO Box 1403, McPherson, KS 67460. *Phone:* 620-241-0723 Ext. 380. *Toll-free phone:* 800-835-0078 Ext. 337. *Fax:* 620-241-6032. *E-mail:* admissions@centralchristian.edu.

CLEVELAND CHIROPRACTIC COLLEGE-KANSAS CITY CAMPUS

Overland Park, Kansas **www.cleveland.edu/**

- **Independent** upper-level, founded 1922, administratively affiliated with Cleveland Chriopractic College, Los Angeles Campus
- **Urban** 10-acre campus
- **Coed** 87 undergraduate students, 76% full-time, 32% women, 68% men
- **Noncompetitive** entrance level

Undergraduates 66 full-time, 21 part-time. Students come from 18 states and territories, 3 other countries, 78% are from out of state, 2% African American, 2% Native American, 3% international, 47% transferred in.

Faculty *Total:* 53, 81% full-time, 89% with terminal degrees. *Student/faculty ratio:* 11:1.

Majors Biology/biological sciences.

Academics *Calendar:* trimesters. *Degrees:* bachelor's and first professional. *Special study options:* academic remediation for entering students, accelerated degree program, advanced placement credit, cooperative education, internships, services for LD students, summer session for credit.

Computers on Campus Students can access the following: educational software. Campuswide network is available. Wireless service is available via entire campus.

Student Life *Housing:* college housing not available. *Student services:* health clinic, personal/psychological counseling.

Standardized Tests *Required for some:* SAT or ACT (for admission).

Costs (2007–08) *Tuition:* $5700 full-time, $190 per credit hour part-time. Full-time tuition and fees vary according to course load. Part-time tuition and fees vary according to course load. *Required fees:* $545 full-time. *Payment plan:* installment.

Applying *Options:* electronic application, deferred entrance. *Application fee:* $50.

Application Contact Ms. Melissa Denton, Director of Admissions, Cleveland Chiropractic College-Kansas City Campus, 10850 Lowell Avenue, Overland Park, KS 66210. *Phone:* 913-234-0750. *Toll-free phone:* 800-467-2252. *Fax:* 913-234-0912. *E-mail:* kc.admissions@cleveland.edu.

EMPORIA STATE UNIVERSITY

Emporia, Kansas **www.emporia.edu/**

- **State-supported** comprehensive, founded 1863, part of Kansas State Board of Education
- **Small-town** 207-acre campus with easy access to Wichita
- **Endowment** $65.8 million
- **Coed** 4,320 undergraduate students, 89% full-time, 62% women, 38% men
- **Noncompetitive** entrance level, 87% of applicants were admitted

Undergraduates 3,849 full-time, 471 part-time. Students come from 33 states and territories, 24 other countries, 7% are from out of state, 4% African American, 0.8% Asian American or Pacific Islander, 4% Hispanic American, 0.6% Native American, 5% international, 10% transferred in, 22% live on campus. *Retention:* 71% of 2006 full-time freshmen returned.

Freshmen *Admission:* 1,605 applied, 1,389 admitted, 766 enrolled. *Test scores:* ACT scores over 18: 88%; ACT scores over 24: 33%; ACT scores over 30: 3%.

Faculty *Total:* 291, 89% full-time, 75% with terminal degrees. *Student/faculty ratio:* 18:1.

Majors Accounting; art; athletic training; biology/biological sciences; business administration and management; chemistry; communication/speech communication and rhetoric; computer and information sciences; computer and information systems security; corrections and criminal justice related; dramatic/theater arts; economics; elementary education; English; foreign languages and literatures; general studies; geology/earth science; history; information science/studies; marketing/marketing management; mathematics; multi-/interdisciplinary studies related; music; music teacher education; nursing (registered nurse training); parks, recreation and leisure; physical sciences; physics; political science and government; psychology; secondary education; social sciences; social science teacher education; sociology; vocational rehabilitation counseling.

Academics *Calendar:* semesters. *Degrees:* bachelor's, master's, doctoral, post-master's, and postbachelor's certificates. *Special study options:* academic remediation for entering students, accelerated degree program, adult/continuing education programs, advanced placement credit, distance learning, double majors, English as a second language, honors programs, independent study, internships, off-campus study, part-time degree program, services for LD students, study abroad, summer session for credit. *Unusual degree programs:* 3-2 engineering with Kansas State University, University of Kansas, Wichita State University.

Computers on Campus 410 computers/terminals are available on campus for general student use. Students can access the following: campus intranet, computer help desk, free student e-mail accounts, online (class) grades, online (class) registration, online (class) schedules, various software packages. Campuswide network is available. Wireless service is available via classrooms, computer centers, computer labs, libraries.

Student Life *Housing:* on-campus residence required for freshman year. *Options:* coed, men-only, women-only, disabled students. Campus housing is university owned. Freshman campus housing is guaranteed. *Activities and organizations:* drama/theater group, student-run newspaper, choral group, marching band, Union Activities Council, Associated Student Government, Black Student Union, national fraternities, national sororities. *Campus security:* 24-hour emergency response devices and patrols, student patrols, late-night transport/escort service, controlled dormitory access, 24-hour residence hall monitoring, safety and self-awareness programs. *Student services:* health clinic, personal/psychological counseling, women's center, legal services.

Athletics Member NCAA. All Division II. *Intercollegiate sports:* baseball M (s), basketball M (s)/W (s), cheerleading M (s)/W (s), cross-country running M (s)/W (s), football M (s), soccer W (s), softball W (s), tennis M (s)/W (s), track and field M (s)/W (s), volleyball W (s). *Intramural sports:* badminton M/W, basketball M/W, bowling M (c)/W (c), fencing M (c)/W (c), football M/W, rugby M (c), soccer M (c)/W (c), softball M/W, table tennis M/W, tennis M/W, volleyball M/W.

Standardized Tests *Required:* SAT or ACT (for admission).

Costs (2007–08) *Tuition:* state resident $3140 full-time, $105 per credit hour part-time; nonresident $11,190 full-time, $373 per credit hour part-time. Full-time tuition and fees vary according to degree level. Part-time tuition and fees vary according to degree level. *Required fees:* $786 full-time, $47 per credit hour part-time. *Room and board:* $5581; room only: $2832. Room and board charges vary according to board plan and housing facility. *Payment plans:* installment, deferred payment. *Waivers:* senior citizens and employees or children of employees.

Financial Aid Of all full-time matriculated undergraduates who enrolled in 2006, 3,325 applied for aid, 2,217 were judged to have need, 468 had their need fully met. 200 Federal Work-Study jobs (averaging $1053). 30 state and other part-time jobs (averaging $779). In 2006, 366 non-need-based awards were made. *Average percent of need met:* 72%. *Average financial aid package:* $6131. *Average need-based loan:* $2749. *Average need-based gift aid:* $2274. *Average non-need-based aid:* $946. *Average indebtedness upon graduation:* $16,005.

Applying *Options:* electronic application, early admission, deferred entrance. *Application fee:* $30. *Required:* high school transcript. *Recommended:* minimum 2.0 GPA. *Application deadlines:* rolling (freshmen), rolling (transfers). *Notification:* continuous (freshmen), continuous (transfers).

Freshman Application Contact Ms. Laura Eddy, Director of Admissions, Emporia State University, 1200 Commercial Street, Campus Box 4034, Plumb Hall Room 106, Emporia, KS 66801-5087. *Phone:* 620-341-5465. *Toll-free phone:* 877-GOTOESU (in-state); 877-468-6378 (out-of-state). *Fax:* 620-341-5599. *E-mail:* go2esu@emporia.edu.

FORT HAYS STATE UNIVERSITY

Hays, Kansas **www.fhsu.edu/**

- **State-supported** comprehensive, founded 1902, part of Kansas State Board of Education
- **Small-town** 200-acre campus
- **Endowment** $27.6 million
- **Coed**
- **Noncompetitive** entrance level

Faculty *Student/faculty ratio:* 17:1.

Academics *Calendar:* semesters. *Degrees:* certificates, associate, bachelor's, master's, and post-master's certificates.

Student Life *Campus security:* 24-hour emergency response devices and patrols, late-night transport/escort service, controlled dormitory access.

Athletics Member NCAA. All Division II.

Standardized Tests *Required:* ACT (for admission), SAT or ACT (for admission).

Costs (2007–08) *Tuition:* state resident $3355 full-time, $112 per credit hour part-time; nonresident $10,543 full-time, $351 per credit hour part-time. Full-time tuition and fees vary according to course load and location. Part-time tuition and fees vary according to course load and location. *Room and board:* $6011. Room and board charges vary according to board plan, housing facility, and student level.

Financial Aid Of all full-time matriculated undergraduates who enrolled in 2004, 3,295 applied for aid, 2,717 were judged to have need, 570 had their need fully met. 400 Federal Work-Study jobs. In 2004, 1128 non-need-based awards were made. *Average percent of need met:* 64. *Average financial aid package:* $5749. *Average need-based loan:* $3427. *Average need-based gift aid:* $3174. *Average non-need-based aid:* $2995. *Average indebtedness upon graduation:* $15,077.

Applying *Options:* electronic application. *Application fee:* $30. *Required:* high school transcript.

Freshman Application Contact Ms. Susan Cochran, Office Manager/Campus Visit Coordinator, Office of Admissions, Fort Hays State University, 600 Park Street, Hays, KS 67601-4099. *Phone:* 785-628-5666. *Toll-free phone:* 800-628-FHSU. *E-mail:* tigers@fhsu.edu.

FRIENDS UNIVERSITY

Wichita, Kansas **www.friends.edu/**

Director of Admissions Marla Sexson, Director of Admissions, Friends University, 2100 West University Street, Wichita, KS 67213. *Phone:* 316-295-5100. *Toll-free phone:* 800-577-2233. *E-mail:* sexson@friends.edu.

HASKELL INDIAN NATIONS UNIVERSITY

Lawrence, Kansas **www.haskell.edu/**

Freshman Application Contact Ms. Patty Grant, Recruitment Officer, Haskell Indian Nations University, 155 Indian Avenue #5031, Lawrence, KS 66046. *Phone:* 785-749-8437 Ext. 437.

KANSAS STATE UNIVERSITY

Manhattan, Kansas **www.ksu.edu/**

- **State-supported** university, founded 1863, part of Kansas State Board of Education
- **Suburban** 668-acre campus with easy access to Kansas City
- **Endowment** $344.0 million
- **Coed** 18,545 undergraduate students, 88% full-time, 48% women, 52% men
- **Noncompetitive** entrance level, 95% of applicants were admitted

Undergraduates 16,350 full-time, 2,195 part-time. Students come from 50 states and territories, 100 other countries, 14% are from out of state, 3% African American, 1% Asian American or Pacific Islander, 3% Hispanic American, 0.6% Native American, 2% international, 5% transferred in, 37% live on campus. *Retention:* 79% of 2006 full-time freshmen returned.

Freshmen *Admission:* 6,658 applied, 6,338 admitted, 3,526 enrolled. *Test scores:* ACT scores over 18: 96%; ACT scores over 24: 53%; ACT scores over 30: 11%.

Faculty *Total:* 1,103, 86% full-time, 80% with terminal degrees. *Student/faculty ratio:* 20:1.

Majors Accounting; aeronautics/aviation/aerospace science and technology; agricultural and food products processing; agricultural/biological engineering and bioengineering; agricultural business and management; agricultural economics; agricultural mechanization; agronomy and crop science; airframe mechanics and aircraft maintenance technology; airline pilot and flight crew; animal sciences; anthropology; apparel and textiles; architectural engineering; architecture; art; athletic training; biochemistry; biology/biological sciences; business administration and management; chemical engineering; chemistry; child development; civil engineering; clinical laboratory science/medical technology; communication disorders; communication/speech communication and rhetoric; computer and information sciences; computer engineering; dietetics; dramatic/theater arts; economics; electrical, electronics and communications engineering; elementary education; English; finance; food science; foods, nutrition, and wellness; foreign languages and literatures; geography; geology/earth science; health science; history; horticultural science; hotel/motel administration; human development and family studies; human ecology; humanities; industrial engineering; information science/studies; interdisciplinary studies; interior architecture; interior design; journalism; kinesiology and exercise science; landscape architecture; marketing/marketing management; mathematics; mechanical engineering; music; music teacher education; nuclear engineering; parks, recreation and leisure facilities management; philosophy; physical sciences; physics; political science and government; pre-dentistry studies; pre-medical studies; pre-veterinary studies; psychology; secondary education; social sciences; social work; sociology; statistics; wildlife biology; women's studies.

Academics *Calendar:* semesters. *Degrees:* associate, bachelor's, master's, doctoral, and first professional. *Special study options:* academic remediation for entering students, accelerated degree program, adult/continuing education programs, advanced placement credit, cooperative education, distance learning, double majors, English as a second language, freshman honors college, honors programs, independent study, internships, off-campus study, part-time degree program, services for LD students, study abroad, summer session for credit. *ROTC:* Army (b), Air Force (b). *Unusual degree programs:* 3-2 engineering; agriculture.

Computers on Campus 326 computers/terminals are available on campus for general student use. Students can access the following: online (class) registration. Campuswide network is available.

Student Life *Housing options:* coed, men-only, women-only, cooperative. Campus housing is university owned. *Activities and organizations:* drama/theater group, student-run newspaper, radio and television station, choral group, marching band, athletic department groups, marching band, Union Governing Board, theater productions, debate team, national fraternities, national sororities. *Campus security:* 24-hour emergency response devices and patrols, late-night transport/escort service, controlled dormitory access. *Student services:* health clinic, personal/psychological counseling, women's center, legal services.

Athletics Member NCAA. All Division I except football (Division I-A). *Intercollegiate sports:* baseball M (s), basketball M (s)/W (s), crew W (s), cross-country running M (s)/W (s), golf M (s)/W (s), tennis W (s), track and field M (s)/W (s), volleyball W (s). *Intramural sports:* badminton M/W, basketball M/W, bowling M/W, crew M/W, cross-country running M/W, football M/W, golf M/W, ice hockey M, lacrosse M, racquetball M/W, soccer M/W, softball M/W, table tennis M/W, tennis M/W, track and field M/W, volleyball M/W, water polo M/W, weight lifting M/W, wrestling M.

Standardized Tests *Required for some:* SAT (for admission), ACT (for admission). *Recommended:* SAT (for admission), ACT (for admission).

Costs (2007–08) *Tuition:* state resident $5625 full-time, $188 per credit hour part-time; nonresident $15,360 full-time, $512 per credit hour part-time. *Required fees:* $610 full-time. *Room and board:* $6084. Room and board charges vary according to board plan. *Payment plans:* installment, deferred payment. *Waivers:* employees or children of employees.

Financial Aid Of all full-time matriculated undergraduates who enrolled in 2004, 11,908 applied for aid, 9,266 were judged to have need, 1,202 had their need fully met. 663 Federal Work-Study jobs (averaging $1700). In 2004, 1157 non-need-based awards were made. *Average percent of need met:* 65%. *Average financial aid package:* $6341. *Average need-based loan:* $4015. *Average need-based gift aid:* $3092. *Average non-need-based aid:* $1786. *Average indebtedness upon graduation:* $19,000.

Applying *Options:* electronic application, early admission. *Application fee:* $30. *Required:* high school transcript, minimum 2.0 GPA. *Application deadlines:* rolling (freshmen), rolling (transfers). *Notification:* continuous (freshmen), continuous (transfers).

Freshman Application Contact Ms. Christy Crenshaw, Associate Director of Admissions, Kansas State University, 119 Anderson Hall, Manhattan, KS 66506. *Phone:* 785-532-6250. *Toll-free phone:* 800-432-8270. *Fax:* 785-532-6393. *E-mail:* kstate@ksu.edu.

KANSAS WESLEYAN UNIVERSITY

Salina, Kansas **www.kwu.edu/**

Freshman Application Contact Mr. Jim Allen, Director of Admissions, Kansas Wesleyan University, 100 East Claflin Avenue, Salina, KS 67401-6196. *Phone:* 785-827-5541. *Toll-free phone:* 800-874-1154 Ext. 1285. *Fax:* 785-827-0927. *E-mail:* admissions@kwu.edu.

MANHATTAN CHRISTIAN COLLEGE

Manhattan, Kansas **www.mccks.edu/**

Director of Admissions Director of Admissions, Manhattan Christian College, 1415 Anderson Avenue, Manhattan, KS 66502-4081. *Phone:* 785-539-3571. *Toll-free phone:* 877-246-4622.

MCPHERSON COLLEGE

McPherson, Kansas **www.mcpherson.edu/**

Director of Admissions Ms. Carol L. Williams, Director of Admissions and Financial Aid, McPherson College, 1600 East Euclid, McPherson, KS 67460. *Phone:* 620-241-0731 Ext. 1270. *Toll-free phone:* 800-365-7402.

MIDAMERICA NAZARENE UNIVERSITY

Olathe, Kansas **www.mnu.edu/**

- **Independent** comprehensive, founded 1966, affiliated with Church of the Nazarene
- **Suburban** 105-acre campus with easy access to Kansas City
- **Endowment** $18.1 million
- **Coed** 1,295 undergraduate students, 89% full-time, 56% women, 44% men
- **Minimally difficult** entrance level

Undergraduates 1,147 full-time, 148 part-time. Students come from 40 states and territories, 3 other countries, 33% are from out of state, 7% African American, 1% Asian American or Pacific Islander, 4% Hispanic American, 0.6% Native American, 2% international, 28% transferred in, 55% live on campus. *Retention:* 70% of 2006 full-time freshmen returned.

Freshmen *Admission:* 535 applied, 217 enrolled. *Average high school GPA:* 3.38. *Test scores:* SAT critical reading scores over 500: 43%; SAT math scores over 500: 47%; ACT scores over 18: 88%; SAT critical reading scores over 600: 17%; SAT math scores over 600: 17%; ACT scores over 24: 45%; SAT critical reading scores over 700: 4%; SAT math scores over 700: 4%; ACT scores over 30: 8%.

Faculty *Total:* 179, 26% with terminal degrees. *Student/faculty ratio:* 20:1.

Majors Accounting; athletic training; biology/biological sciences; business administration and management; business teacher education; chemistry; computer science; criminal justice/law enforcement administration; elementary education; English; English/language arts teacher education; graphic design; history; human resources management; international business/trade/commerce; kinesiology and exercise science; liberal arts and sciences/liberal studies; marketing/marketing management; mass communication/media; mathematics; mathematics teacher education; middle school education; missionary studies and missiology; music teacher education; nursing (registered nurse training); physical education teaching and coaching; psychology; public relations/image management; religious education; religious/sacred music; religious studies; secondary education; social studies teacher education; sociology; Spanish; Spanish language teacher education; sport and fitness administration/management; theology; urban studies/affairs; voice and opera.

Academics *Calendar:* semesters. *Degrees:* associate, bachelor's, master's, and post-master's certificates. *Special study options:* academic remediation for entering students, accelerated degree program, adult/continuing education programs, advanced placement credit, double majors, independent study, internships, off-campus study, part-time degree program, services for LD students, study abroad, summer session for credit. *ROTC:* Army (c), Air Force (c).

Computers on Campus 85 computers/terminals are available on campus for general student use. Campuswide network is available. Wireless service is available via entire campus.

Student Life *Housing:* on-campus residence required through senior year. *Options:* men-only, women-only. Campus housing is university owned. Freshman campus housing is guaranteed. *Activities and organizations:* drama/theater group, student-run newspaper, radio and television station, choral group, Associated Student Government, Residence Hall Government, Ministry groups, Gospel Station. *Campus security:* 24-hour emergency response devices and patrols, student patrols, late-night transport/escort service, controlled dormitory access. *Student services:* health clinic, personal/psychological counseling.

Athletics Member NAIA, NCCAA. *Intercollegiate sports:* baseball M (s), basketball M (s)/W (s), cheerleading M (s)/W (s), cross-country running M (s)/W (s), football M (s), soccer M (s)/W (s), softball W (s), track and field M (s)/W (s), volleyball W (s). *Intramural sports:* basketball M/W, bowling M/W, football M/W, golf M/W, soccer M/W, softball M/W, table tennis M/W, tennis M/W, ultimate Frisbee M/W, volleyball M/W.

Standardized Tests *Required:* SAT or ACT (for admission).

Costs (2008–09) *Comprehensive fee:* $24,396 includes full-time tuition ($17,216), mandatory fees ($1000), and room and board ($6180). Part-time tuition: $576 per hour. *Required fees:* $365 per term part-time.

Financial Aid Of all full-time matriculated undergraduates who enrolled in 2005, 978 applied for aid, 838 were judged to have need, 9 had their need fully met. In 2005, 180 non-need-based awards were made. *Average percent of need met:* 60%. *Average financial aid package:* $10,028. *Average need-based loan:* $5861. *Average need-based gift aid:* $6260. *Average non-need-based aid:* $2921. *Average indebtedness upon graduation:* $19,222.

Applying *Options:* electronic application, early admission, deferred entrance. *Application fee:* $25. *Required:* high school transcript, minimum 2.0 GPA, 1 letter of recommendation. *Application deadlines:* 8/1 (freshmen), 8/1 (transfers). *Notification:* continuous (freshmen), continuous (transfers).

Freshman Application Contact Ms. Brigit Mattix, Associate Director of Admissions, MidAmerica Nazarene University, 2030 East College Way, Olathe, KS 66062-1899. *Phone:* 913-791-3380. *Toll-free phone:* 800-800-8887. *Fax:* 913-791-3481. *E-mail:* admissions@mnu.edu.

See page 1010 for the College Close-Up.

NEWMAN UNIVERSITY

Wichita, Kansas **www.newmanu.edu/**

- **Independent Roman Catholic** comprehensive, founded 1933
- **Urban** 61-acre campus
- **Endowment** $21.0 million
- **Coed** 1,560 undergraduate students, 61% full-time, 63% women, 37% men
- **Minimally difficult** entrance level, 64% of applicants were admitted

Undergraduates 952 full-time, 608 part-time. Students come from 31 states and territories, 18 other countries, 15% are from out of state, 6% African American, 4% Asian American or Pacific Islander, 8% Hispanic American, 2%

Native American, 6% international, 14% transferred in, 21% live on campus. *Retention:* 51% of 2006 full-time freshmen returned.

Freshmen *Admission:* 592 applied, 377 admitted, 124 enrolled. *Average high school GPA:* 3.4. *Test scores:* SAT critical reading scores over 500: 63%; SAT math scores over 500: 50%; SAT writing scores over 500: 56%; ACT scores over 18: 95%; SAT critical reading scores over 600: 25%; SAT math scores over 600: 13%; SAT writing scores over 600: 19%; ACT scores over 24: 44%; SAT critical reading scores over 700: 6%; ACT scores over 30: 8%.

Faculty *Total:* 146, 52% full-time. *Student/faculty ratio:* 14:1.

Majors Accounting; art; biology/biological sciences; business administration and management; chemistry; counseling psychology; criminal justice/law enforcement administration; education; elementary education; English; entrepreneurship; finance; health science; history; information science/studies; liberal arts and sciences/liberal studies; management information systems; marketing/marketing management; mass communication/media; mathematics; mental health/rehabilitation; nursing (registered nurse training); paralegal/legal assistant; pastoral studies/counseling; pre-dentistry studies; pre-engineering; pre-law studies; pre-medical studies; pre-veterinary studies; psychology; radiologic technology/science; respiratory care therapy; secondary education; sociology; substance abuse/addiction counseling; theology.

Academics *Calendar:* semesters. *Degrees:* certificates, associate, bachelor's, and master's. *Special study options:* academic remediation for entering students, accelerated degree program, adult/continuing education programs, advanced placement credit, cooperative education, distance learning, double majors, external degree program, independent study, internships, off-campus study, part-time degree program, services for LD students, study abroad, summer session for credit. *Unusual degree programs:* 3-2 occupational therapy with Washington University in St. Louis.

Computers on Campus 130 computers/terminals and 300 ports are available on campus for general student use. Students can access the following: computer help desk, free student e-mail accounts, online (class) grades, online (class) registration, online (class) schedules. Campuswide network is available. 100% of college-owned or -operated housing units are wired for high-speed Internet access. Wireless service is available via computer centers, dorm rooms, learning centers, libraries.

Student Life *Housing:* on-campus residence required through sophomore year. *Options:* coed, men-only, women-only. Campus housing is university owned. Freshman campus housing is guaranteed. *Activities and organizations:* drama/theater group, student-run newspaper, choral group, Student Activities Board, chorale, Multicultural Leadership Organization, Chemistry/Pre-Med Club, Newman Occupational Therapy Student Association. *Campus security:* 24-hour emergency response devices and patrols, student patrols, late-night transport/escort service, controlled dormitory access. *Student services:* personal/psychological counseling.

Athletics Member NCAA. *Intercollegiate sports:* baseball M (s), basketball M (s)/W (s), bowling M (s)/W (s), cross-country running M (s)/W (s), golf M (s)/W (s), soccer M (s)/W (s), softball W (s), tennis M (s)/W (s), volleyball M (s)/W (s), wrestling M (s). *Intramural sports:* baseball M, basketball M/W, bowling M/W, cheerleading M/W, cross-country running M/W, football M/W, golf M/W, soccer M/W, softball M/W, table tennis M/W, volleyball M/W, weight lifting M/W.

Standardized Tests *Required:* SAT or ACT (for admission).

Costs (2008–09) *Comprehensive fee:* $25,374 includes full-time tuition ($18,574), mandatory fees ($300), and room and board ($6500). Part-time tuition: $619 per credit hour. *Required fees:* $10 per credit hour part-time.

Financial Aid Of all full-time matriculated undergraduates who enrolled in 2007, 1,140 applied for aid, 863 were judged to have need, 104 had their need fully met. 72 Federal Work-Study jobs (averaging $1123). 95 state and other part-time jobs (averaging $1222). In 2007, 70 non-need-based awards were made. *Average percent of need met:* 56%. *Average financial aid package:* $11,273. *Average need-based loan:* $3908. *Average need-based gift aid:* $4090. *Average non-need-based aid:* $3163. *Average indebtedness upon graduation:* $20,761.

Applying *Options:* electronic application, early admission, deferred entrance. *Application fee:* $20. *Required:* high school transcript, minimum 2.0 GPA. *Recommended:* interview. *Application deadlines:* rolling (freshmen), rolling (transfers). *Notification:* continuous (freshmen), continuous (transfers).

Freshman Application Contact Jann Reusser, Admissions Recruitment, Newman University, 3100 McCormick Avenue, Wichita, KS 67213. *Phone:* 316-942-4291 Ext. 2144. *Toll-free phone:* 877-NEWMANU Ext. 2144. *Fax:* 316-942-4483. *E-mail:* admissions@newmanu.edu.

OTTAWA UNIVERSITY

Ottawa, Kansas **www.ottawa.edu/**

- **Independent American Baptist Churches in the USA** comprehensive, founded 1865
- **Small-town** 60-acre campus with easy access to Kansas City
- **Endowment** $18.9 million
- **Coed**
- **Moderately difficult** entrance level

Faculty *Student/faculty ratio:* 15:1.

Academics *Calendar:* semesters. *Degrees:* bachelor's (also offers master's, adult, international and on-line education programs with significant enrollment not reflected in profile).

Student Life *Campus security:* 24-hour emergency response devices and patrols, controlled dormitory access, locked residence hall entrances.

Athletics Member NAIA.

Standardized Tests *Required:* SAT or ACT (for admission).

Costs (2007–08) *Comprehensive fee:* $23,280 includes full-time tuition ($17,000), mandatory fees ($350), and room and board ($5930). Part-time tuition: $515 per credit hour. *Required fees:* $15 per credit hour part-time. *College room only:* $2630.

Applying *Options:* electronic application. *Application fee:* $15. *Required:* high school transcript, minimum 2.5 GPA, 18 or higher ACT; rank in upper 50% of class. *Required for some:* essay or personal statement. *Recommended:* 2 letters of recommendation, interview.

Freshman Application Contact Ms. Fola Akande, Director of Admissions, Ottawa University, 1001 South Cedar #17, Ottawa, KS 66067-3399. *Phone:* 785-242-5200 Ext. 5561. *Toll-free phone:* 800-755-5200 Ext. 5559. *Fax:* 785-229-1008. *E-mail:* admiss@ottawa.edu.

PITTSBURG STATE UNIVERSITY

Pittsburg, Kansas **www.pittstate.edu/**

- **State-supported** comprehensive, founded 1903, part of Kansas State Board of Education
- **Small-town** 233-acre campus
- **Endowment** $59.8 million
- **Coed** 5,872 undergraduate students, 91% full-time, 48% women, 52% men
- **Minimally difficult** entrance level, 88% of applicants were admitted

Undergraduates 5,352 full-time, 520 part-time. Students come from 43 states and territories, 26 other countries, 22% are from out of state, 3% African American, 0.8% Asian American or Pacific Islander, 2% Hispanic American, 2% Native American, 5% international, 10% transferred in, 16% live on campus. *Retention:* 75% of 2006 full-time freshmen returned.

Freshmen *Admission:* 2,197 applied, 1,923 admitted, 902 enrolled. *Average high school GPA:* 3.23. *Test scores:* ACT scores over 18: 87%; ACT scores over 24: 29%; ACT scores over 30: 3%.

Faculty *Total:* 408, 74% full-time, 55% with terminal degrees. *Student/faculty ratio:* 18:1.

Majors Accounting; actuarial science; advertising; art; art teacher education; automobile/automotive mechanics technology; automotive engineering technology; biochemistry; biology/biological sciences; biology teacher education; business administration and management; cell and molecular biology; ceramic arts and ceramics; chemistry; chemistry teacher education; child development; clinical/medical laboratory technology; commercial and advertising art; communication/speech communication and rhetoric; computer and information systems security; computer science; construction engineering technology; construction management; counseling psychology; creative writing; diesel mechanics technology; economics; electrical, electronic and communications engineering technology; elementary education; English; English/language arts teacher education; family and consumer sciences/home economics teacher education; family and consumer sciences/human sciences; fashion merchandising; finance; French; French language teacher education; general studies; geography; graphic communications; history; industrial arts; interior design; international business/trade/commerce; international/global studies; journalism; manufacturing technology; marketing/marketing management; mathematics; mathematics teacher education; mechanical engineering/mechanical technology; music performance; music teacher education; nursing (registered nurse training); painting; photojournalism; physical education teaching and coaching; physics; physics teacher education; plant molecular biology; plant physiology; plastics engineering technology; political science and government; polymer chemistry; pre-dentistry studies; pre-engineering; pre-law studies; pre-medical studies; pre-pharmacy studies; pre-veterinary studies; psychology; psychology teacher education; public relations, advertising, and applied communication related; radio and television; radio/television broadcasting technology; social studies teacher education; social work; sociology; Spanish; Spanish language teacher education; technical and business writing; technical teacher education; theater/theater arts management; therapeutic recreation; wood science and wood products/pulp and paper technology.

Academics *Calendar:* semesters. *Degrees:* certificates, associate, bachelor's, and master's (associate, specialist in education). *Special study options:* academic remediation for entering students, adult/continuing education programs, advanced placement credit, cooperative education, distance learning, double majors, English as a second language, external degree program, freshman honors college, honors programs, independent study, internships, off-campus study, part-time degree program, services for LD students, student-designed majors, study abroad, summer session for credit. *ROTC:* Army (b).

Computers on Campus 425 computers/terminals are available on campus for general student use. Students can access the following: campus intranet, computer help desk, free student e-mail accounts, online (class) grades, online (class) registration, online (class) schedules. Campuswide network is available. 100% of college-owned or -operated housing units are wired for high-speed Internet access. Wireless service is available via entire campus.

Student Life *Housing:* on-campus residence required for freshman year. *Options:* coed, disabled students. Campus housing is university owned. Freshman applicants given priority for college housing. *Activities and organizations:* drama/theater group, student-run newspaper, radio and television station, choral group, marching band, Student Government Association, student yearbook, student newspaper, student activities council, national fraternities, national sororities. *Campus security:* 24-hour emergency response devices and patrols, student patrols, controlled dormitory access. *Student services:* health clinic, personal/psychological counseling, legal services.

Athletics Member NCAA. All Division II. *Intercollegiate sports:* baseball M (s), basketball M (s)/W (s), cross-country running M (s)/W (s), football M (s), golf M (s), softball W (s), track and field M (s)/W (s), volleyball W (s). *Intramural sports:* basketball M/W, cheerleading M (c)/W (c), football M, rugby M (c), soccer M/W, softball M/W, table tennis M/W, tennis M/W, ultimate Frisbee M/W, volleyball M/W.

Standardized Tests *Required:* ACT (for admission).

Costs (2007–08) *Tuition:* state resident $3234 full-time, $108 per credit hour part-time; nonresident $11,040 full-time, $368 per credit hour part-time. *Required fees:* $826 full-time, $37 per credit hour part-time. *Room and board:* $5088. Room and board charges vary according to board plan and housing facility. *Payment plan:* installment. *Waivers:* employees or children of employees.

Financial Aid Of all full-time matriculated undergraduates who enrolled in 2006, 3,745 applied for aid, 2,931 were judged to have need, 317 had their need fully met. 260 Federal Work-Study jobs (averaging $1192). 1,146 state and other part-time jobs (averaging $1355). In 2006, 426 non-need-based awards were made. *Average percent of need met:* 85%. *Average financial aid package:* $7699. *Average need-based loan:* $3976. *Average need-based gift aid:* $4047. *Average non-need-based aid:* $1961. *Average indebtedness upon graduation:* $15,776.

Applying *Options:* electronic application. *Application fee:* $30. *Required:* high school transcript. *Required for some:* minimum 2.0 GPA. *Application deadlines:* rolling (freshmen), rolling (transfers).

Freshman Application Contact Director of Admission and Enrollment Services, Pittsburg State University, Pittsburg, KS 66762. *Phone:* 620-235-4251. *Toll-free phone:* 800-854-7488 Ext. 1. *Fax:* 620-235-6003. *E-mail:* psuadmit@pittstate.edu.

SOUTHWESTERN COLLEGE

Winfield, Kansas — www.sckans.edu/

- **Independent United Methodist** comprehensive, founded 1885
- **Small-town** 70-acre campus with easy access to Wichita
- **Endowment** $14.2 million
- **Coed** 1,546 undergraduate students, 37% full-time, 47% women, 53% men
- **Moderately difficult** entrance level, 91% of applicants were admitted

Undergraduates 572 full-time, 974 part-time. Students come from 44 states and territories, 11 other countries, 38% are from out of state, 10% African American, 1% Asian American or Pacific Islander, 5% Hispanic American, 2% Native American, 1% international, 4% transferred in, 70% live on campus. *Retention:* 65% of 2006 full-time freshmen returned.

Freshmen *Admission:* 329 applied, 300 admitted, 138 enrolled. *Average high school GPA:* 3.36. *Test scores:* SAT critical reading scores over 500: 27%; SAT math scores over 500: 32%; ACT scores over 18: 86%; SAT critical reading scores over 600: 9%; SAT math scores over 600: 14%; ACT scores over 24: 35%; ACT scores over 30: 3%.

Faculty *Total:* 201, 24% full-time, 15% with terminal degrees. *Student/faculty ratio:* 9:1.

Majors Athletic training; biochemistry; biology/biological sciences; business administration and management; business/corporate communications; chemistry; communication and media related; computer programming; computer science; computer technology/computer systems technology; criminal justice/law enforcement administration; early childhood education; elementary education; engineering physics; English; general studies; health and physical education; history; human resources management; industrial production technologies related; liberal arts and sciences and humanities related; liberal arts and sciences/liberal studies; management information systems; management science; manufacturing technology; marine biology and biological oceanography; mathematics; music; music teacher education; nursing (registered nurse training); pastoral studies/counseling; philosophy and religious studies related; physics; psychology; purchasing, procurement/acquisitions and contracts management; securities services administration; sport and fitness administration/management.

Academics *Calendar:* semesters. *Degrees:* bachelor's and master's. *Special study options:* adult/continuing education programs, distance learning, double majors, honors programs, independent study, internships, off-campus study, part-time degree program, student-designed majors, study abroad.

Computers on Campus 30 computers/terminals and 100 ports are available on campus for general student use. Students can access the following: computer help desk, free student e-mail accounts, online (class) grades, online (class) registration, online (class) schedules. Campuswide network is available. 100% of college-owned or -operated housing units are wired for high-speed Internet access. Wireless service is available via entire campus.

Student Life *Housing:* on-campus residence required through sophomore year. *Options:* coed, men-only, women-only, disabled students. Campus housing is university owned. Freshman campus housing is guaranteed. *Activities and organizations:* drama/theater group, student-run newspaper, radio and television station, choral group, Student Activities Association, student government, Fellowship of Christian Athletes, Campus Council on Ministries, International Club, national fraternities. *Campus security:* 24-hour emergency response devices and patrols, controlled dormitory access. *Student services:* health clinic, personal/psychological counseling.

Athletics Member NAIA. *Intercollegiate sports:* basketball M (s)/W (s), cheerleading M (s)/W (s), cross-country running M (s)/W (s), football M (s), golf M (s)/W (s), soccer M (s)/W (s), softball W (s), tennis M (s)/W (s), track and field M (s)/W (s), volleyball W (s). *Intramural sports:* baseball M/W, basketball M/W, bowling M/W, softball M/W, ultimate Frisbee M/W.

Standardized Tests *Required:* SAT or ACT (for admission).

Costs (2007–08) *Comprehensive fee:* $23,442 includes full-time tuition ($17,720), mandatory fees ($100), and room and board ($5622). Full-time tuition and fees vary according to course load, degree level, and location. Part-time tuition: $738 per semester hour. Part-time tuition and fees vary according to course load, degree level, and location. *College room only:* $2510. Room and board charges vary according to board plan and housing facility. *Payment plan:* installment. *Waivers:* senior citizens and employees or children of employees.

Financial Aid Of all full-time matriculated undergraduates who enrolled in 2007, 505 applied for aid, 452 were judged to have need, 83 had their need fully met. In 2007, 113 non-need-based awards were made. *Average percent of need met:* 89%. *Average financial aid package:* $13,491. *Average need-based loan:* $4092. *Average need-based gift aid:* $10,730. *Average non-need-based aid:* $7475. *Average indebtedness upon graduation:* $20,589.

Applying *Options:* electronic application, deferred entrance. *Application fee:* $20. *Required:* high school transcript, minimum 2.5 GPA. *Required for some:* letters of recommendation, interview. *Recommended:* essay or personal statement. *Application deadlines:* 8/25 (freshmen), 8/25 (transfers). *Notification:* continuous (freshmen), continuous (transfers).

Freshman Application Contact Mr. Todd Moore, Director of Admission, Southwestern College, 100 College Street, Winfield, KS 67156. *Phone:* 620-229-6236. *Toll-free phone:* 800-846-1543. *Fax:* 620-229-6344. *E-mail:* scadmit@sckans.edu.

STERLING COLLEGE

Sterling, Kansas — www.sterling.edu/

- **Independent Presbyterian** 4-year, founded 1887
- **Rural** 46-acre campus
- **Endowment** $5.6 million
- **Coed** 603 undergraduate students, 91% full-time, 44% women, 56% men
- **Minimally difficult** entrance level, 58% of applicants were admitted

Undergraduates 551 full-time, 52 part-time. Students come from 36 states and territories, 4 other countries, 47% are from out of state, 10% African American,

0.8% Asian American or Pacific Islander, 7% Hispanic American, 2% Native American, 0.7% international, 9% transferred in, 80% live on campus. *Retention:* 52% of 2006 full-time freshmen returned.

Freshmen *Admission:* 804 applied, 466 admitted, 165 enrolled. *Average high school GPA:* 3.2. *Test scores:* SAT critical reading scores over 500: 20%; SAT math scores over 500: 36%; SAT writing scores over 500: 20%; ACT scores over 18: 82%; SAT critical reading scores over 600: 8%; SAT math scores over 600: 12%; SAT writing scores over 600: 4%; ACT scores over 24: 27%; ACT scores over 30: 3%.

Faculty *Total:* 53, 74% full-time, 30% with terminal degrees. *Student/faculty ratio:* 13:1.

Majors Art; athletic training; behavioral sciences; biology/biological sciences; business administration and management; communication and journalism related; computer and information sciences; dramatic/theater arts; elementary education; English; health and physical education; history; interdisciplinary studies; mathematics; music; music teacher education; philosophy and religious studies related; physical education teaching and coaching; religious education.

Academics *Calendar:* 4-1-4. *Degree:* bachelor's. *Special study options:* advanced placement credit, distance learning, double majors, honors programs, independent study, internships, off-campus study, services for LD students, student-designed majors, study abroad. *Unusual degree programs:* 3-2 biology/medical technology; Wichita State University (medical technology portion).

Computers on Campus 115 computers/terminals are available on campus for general student use. Students can access the following: campus intranet, computer help desk, free student e-mail accounts, online (class) grades, online (class) schedules. Campuswide network is available. 100% of college-owned or -operated housing units are wired for high-speed Internet access.

Student Life *Housing:* on-campus residence required through senior year. *Options:* men-only, women-only. Campus housing is university owned. Freshman campus housing is guaranteed. *Activities and organizations:* drama/theater group, student-run newspaper, radio and television station, choral group, Fellowship of Christian Athletes, Student Activities Council, My Brother's Keeper, Habitat for Humanity, youth ministries. *Campus security:* controlled dormitory access, late night security patrol. *Student services:* health clinic, personal/psychological counseling.

Athletics Member NAIA. *Intercollegiate sports:* baseball M (s), basketball M (s)/W (s), cheerleading W (s), cross-country running M (s)/W (s), football M (s), golf M/W, soccer M (s)/W (s), softball W (s), track and field M (s)/W (s), volleyball W (s). *Intramural sports:* basketball M/W, softball M/W, volleyball M/W.

Standardized Tests *Required:* SAT or ACT (for admission).

Costs (2007–08) *One-time required fee:* $100. *Comprehensive fee:* $21,730 includes full-time tuition ($15,500) and room and board ($6230). Part-time tuition: $315 per credit hour. *Room and board:* Room and board charges vary according to board plan. *Payment plan:* installment. *Waivers:* senior citizens and employees or children of employees.

Financial Aid Of all full-time matriculated undergraduates who enrolled in 2004, 449 applied for aid, 363 were judged to have need, 176 had their need fully met. 169 Federal Work-Study jobs (averaging $501). 196 state and other part-time jobs (averaging $808). In 2004, 77 non-need-based awards were made. *Average percent of need met:* 100%. *Average financial aid package:* $15,375. *Average need-based loan:* $4214. *Average need-based gift aid:* $7863. *Average non-need-based aid:* $6817. *Average indebtedness upon graduation:* $9647.

Applying *Options:* electronic application, early action, deferred entrance. *Application fee:* $25. *Required:* high school transcript, minimum 2.2 GPA. *Required for some:* 2 letters of recommendation, audition required for fine arts majors. *Recommended:* essay or personal statement, interview. *Application deadlines:* 7/15 (freshmen), rolling (transfers), 11/15 (early action). *Notification:* continuous (freshmen), continuous (transfers), 12/1 (early action).

Freshman Application Contact Mr. Dennis Dutton, Vice President for Enrollment Services, Sterling College, PO Box 98, Sterling, KS 67579-0098. *Phone:* 620-278-4364. *Toll-free phone:* 800-346-1017. *Fax:* 620-278-4416. *E-mail:* admissions@sterling.edu.

TABOR COLLEGE

Hillsboro, Kansas **www.tabor.edu/**

- **Independent Mennonite Brethren** comprehensive, founded 1908
- **Small-town** 26-acre campus with easy access to Wichita
- **Endowment** $5.4 million
- **Coed** 574 undergraduate students, 82% full-time, 50% women, 50% men
- **Moderately difficult** entrance level, 100% of applicants were admitted

Undergraduates 472 full-time, 102 part-time. Students come from 27 states and territories, 6 other countries, 41% are from out of state, 7% African American, 0.9% Asian American or Pacific Islander, 4% Hispanic American, 0.9% Native American, 1% international, 8% transferred in, 86% live on campus. *Retention:* 65% of 2006 full-time freshmen returned.

Freshmen *Admission:* 241 applied, 241 admitted, 120 enrolled. *Average high school GPA:* 3.36. *Test scores:* ACT scores over 18: 85%; ACT scores over 24: 40%; ACT scores over 30: 3%.

Faculty *Total:* 81, 41% full-time, 38% with terminal degrees. *Student/faculty ratio:* 10:1.

Majors Accounting; actuarial science; administrative assistant and secretarial science; adult and continuing education; agricultural business and management; art teacher education; athletic training; biblical studies; biological and physical sciences; biology/biological sciences; business administration and management; business teacher education; chemistry; clinical laboratory science/medical technology; communication/speech communication and rhetoric; computer science; divinity/ministry; education; education (K-12); elementary education; English; environmental biology; health teacher education; history; humanities; interdisciplinary studies; international relations and affairs; journalism; kindergarten/preschool education; legal administrative assistant/secretary; marketing/marketing management; mass communication/media; mathematics; medical administrative assistant and medical secretary; music; music management and merchandising; music teacher education; natural sciences; pastoral studies/counseling; philosophy; physical education teaching and coaching; piano and organ; pre-dentistry studies; pre-medical studies; psychology; public relations/image management; religious studies; science teacher education; secondary education; social sciences; sociology; special education; voice and opera.

Academics *Calendar:* 4-1-4. *Degrees:* associate, bachelor's, and master's. *Special study options:* academic remediation for entering students, accelerated degree program, adult/continuing education programs, advanced placement credit, cooperative education, distance learning, double majors, honors programs, independent study, internships, off-campus study, part-time degree program, services for LD students, student-designed majors, study abroad.

Computers on Campus 60 computers/terminals and 450 ports are available on campus for general student use. Students can access the following: campus intranet, computer help desk, free student e-mail accounts, online (class) grades, online (class) registration, online (class) schedules. Campuswide network is available. 100% of college-owned or -operated housing units are wired for high-speed Internet access. Wireless service is available via dorm rooms, learning centers, libraries, student centers.

Student Life *Housing:* on-campus residence required through junior year. *Options:* men-only, women-only, disabled students. Campus housing is university owned. Freshman campus housing is guaranteed. *Activities and organizations:* drama/theater group, student-run newspaper, choral group, Student Activities Board, Campus Ministries Council, Multi-Cultural Student Union, Science Club, Public Relations Student Society of America/ American Marketing Association. *Student services:* personal/psychological counseling.

Athletics Member NAIA. *Intercollegiate sports:* baseball M (s), basketball M (s)/W (s), cheerleading M/W (s), cross-country running M (s)/W (s), football M (s), golf M (s)/W (s), soccer M (s)/W (s), softball W (s), tennis M (s)/W (s), track and field M (s)/W (s), volleyball W (s). *Intramural sports:* basketball M/W, football M/W, golf M/W, racquetball M/W, soccer M/W, tennis M/W, track and field M/W, volleyball M/W.

Standardized Tests *Required:* SAT or ACT (for admission).

Costs (2008–09) *One-time required fee:* $100. *Comprehensive fee:* $25,460 includes full-time tuition ($18,300), mandatory fees ($410), and room and board ($6750). Part-time tuition: $720 per credit hour. *Required fees:* $5 per credit hour part-time. *College room only:* $2600.

Financial Aid Of all full-time matriculated undergraduates who enrolled in 2006, 511 applied for aid, 396 were judged to have need, 138 had their need fully met. 147 Federal Work-Study jobs (averaging $667). In 2006, 107 non-need-based awards were made. *Average percent of need met:* 89%. *Average financial aid package:* $15,751. *Average need-based loan:* $7036. *Average need-based gift aid:* $3477. *Average non-need-based aid:* $5075. *Average indebtedness upon graduation:* $20,181. *Financial aid deadline:* 8/15.

Applying *Options:* electronic application, early admission, early decision, deferred entrance. *Application fee:* $30. *Required:* essay or personal statement, high school transcript, minimum 2.5 GPA, minimum ACT score of 18. *Recommended:* interview. *Application deadlines:* 8/1 (freshmen), 8/1 (out-of-state freshmen), 8/1 (transfers). *Notification:* 8/15 (freshmen), 8/15 (out-of-state freshmen), 8/15 (transfers).

Freshman Application Contact Mr. Rusty Allen, Dean of Enrollment Management, Tabor College, 400 South Jefferson, Hillsboro, KS 67063. *Phone:* 620-947-3121. *Toll-free phone:* 800-822-6799. *Fax:* 620-947-6276. *E-mail:* rustya@tabor.edu.

UNIVERSITY OF KANSAS

Lawrence, Kansas **www.ku.edu**

- **State-supported** university, founded 1866
- **Suburban** 1100-acre campus with easy access to Kansas City
- **Endowment** $1.4 billion
- **Coed** 20,828 undergraduate students, 89% full-time, 50% women, 50% men
- **Moderately difficult** entrance level, 92% of applicants were admitted

Undergraduates 18,571 full-time, 2,257 part-time. Students come from 52 states and territories, 81 other countries, 23% are from out of state, 4% African American, 4% Asian American or Pacific Islander, 4% Hispanic American, 1% Native American, 3% international, 6% transferred in, 22% live on campus. *Retention:* 79% of 2006 full-time freshmen returned.

Freshmen *Admission:* 10,367 applied, 9,554 admitted, 4,084 enrolled. *Average high school GPA:* 3.41. *Test scores:* ACT scores over 18: 97%; ACT scores over 24: 59%; ACT scores over 30: 13%.

Faculty *Total:* 1,315, 93% full-time, 95% with terminal degrees. *Student/faculty ratio:* 19:1.

Majors Accounting; aerospace, aeronautical and astronautical engineering; African-American/Black studies; African studies; American studies; ancient studies; anthropology; architectural engineering; architectural history and criticism; architecture; art history, criticism and conservation; art teacher education; astronomy; atmospheric sciences and meteorology; behavioral sciences; biochemistry/biophysics and molecular biology; biological and biomedical sciences related; biology/biological sciences; business/commerce; ceramic arts and ceramics; chemical engineering; chemistry; civil engineering; classics and languages, literatures and linguistics; clinical laboratory science/medical technology; cognitive psychology and psycholinguistics; communication disorders; community health services counseling; computer and information sciences; computer engineering; cytotechnology; dance; design and visual communications; dramatic/theater arts; East Asian languages; economics; electrical, electronics and communications engineering; elementary education; engineering physics; English; environmental studies; European studies; fiber, textile and weaving arts; finance; fine/studio arts; French; geography; geology/earth science; Germanic languages; graphic design; health and physical education; health information/medical records administration; history; humanities; illustration; industrial design; interior design; international relations and affairs; journalism; Latin American studies; liberal arts and sciences/liberal studies; linguistics; logistics and materials management; management information systems; marketing/marketing management; mathematics; mechanical engineering; metal and jewelry arts; microbiology; middle school education; molecular biology; music; musicology and ethnomusicology; music performance; music teacher education; music theory and composition; music therapy; nursing science; occupational therapy; painting; petroleum engineering; pharmacy; philosophy; physical education teaching and coaching; physics; piano and organ; political science and government; printmaking; psychology; public administration; religious studies; respiratory care therapy; Russian studies; sculpture; secondary education; Slavic languages; social work; sociology; Spanish; speech and rhetoric; stringed instruments; theater design and technology; violin, viola, guitar and other stringed instruments; voice and opera; wind/percussion instruments; women's studies.

Academics *Calendar:* semesters. *Degrees:* bachelor's, master's, doctoral, first professional, and post-master's certificates (University of Kansas is a single institution with academic programs and facilities at two primary locations: Lawrence and Kansas City.). *Special study options:* academic remediation for entering students, accelerated degree program, advanced placement credit, cooperative education, distance learning, double majors, English as a second language, honors programs, independent study, internships, part-time degree program, services for LD students, study abroad, summer session for credit. *ROTC:* Army (b), Navy (b), Air Force (b).

Computers on Campus 1,500 computers/terminals are available on campus for general student use. Students can access the following: campus intranet, computer help desk, free student e-mail accounts, online (class) grades, online (class) registration, online (class) schedules. Campuswide network is available. 100% of college-owned or -operated housing units are wired for high-speed Internet access. Wireless service is available via computer centers, computer labs, libraries, student centers.

Student Life *Housing options:* coed, women-only, cooperative. Campus housing is university owned. *Activities and organizations:* drama/theater group, student-run newspaper, radio and television station, choral group, marching band, Association of University Residence Halls, International Student Association, Panhellenic Association, All Scholarship Hall Council, Chinese Students and Scholars Friendship Association, national fraternities, national sororities. *Campus security:* 24-hour emergency response devices and patrols, late-night transport/escort service, controlled dormitory access, University police department. *Student services:* health clinic, personal/psychological counseling, women's center, legal services.

Athletics Member NCAA. All Division I except football (Division I-A). *Intercollegiate sports:* baseball M (s), basketball M (s)/W (s), crew W (s), cross-country running M (s)/W (s), golf M (s)/W (s), ice hockey M (c), rugby M (c)/W (c), soccer W (s), softball W (s), swimming and diving W (s), tennis W (s), track and field M (s)/W (s), ultimate Frisbee M (c)/W (c), volleyball W (s), water polo M (c)/W (c). *Intramural sports:* basketball M/W, bowling M/W, crew M (c)/W (c), fencing M (c)/W (c), football M/W, golf M/W, lacrosse M (c)/W (c), racquetball M/W, rock climbing M (c)/W (c), sailing M (c)/W (c), soccer M (c)/W (c), softball M/W, table tennis M/W, tennis M/W, volleyball M (c)/W (c).

Standardized Tests *Required:* SAT or ACT (for admission).

Costs (2007–08) *Tuition:* state resident $6390 full-time, $213 per credit hour part-time; nonresident $16,800 full-time, $560 per credit hour part-time. Full-time tuition and fees vary according to program, reciprocity agreements, and student level. Part-time tuition and fees vary according to program, reciprocity agreements, and student level. No tuition increase for student's term of enrollment. *Required fees:* $756 full-time, $63 per credit hour part-time. *Room and board:* $6144; room only: $3224. Room and board charges vary according to board plan and housing facility. *Payment plan:* installment. *Waivers:* employees or children of employees.

Financial Aid Of all full-time matriculated undergraduates who enrolled in 2006, 14,143 applied for aid, 7,353 were judged to have need, 1,951 had their need fully met. 440 Federal Work-Study jobs (averaging $3126). 107 state and other part-time jobs (averaging $3769). In 2006, 2210 non-need-based awards were made. *Average percent of need met:* 64%. *Average financial aid package:* $8117. *Average need-based loan:* $3109. *Average need-based gift aid:* $4208. *Average non-need-based aid:* $3137. *Average indebtedness upon graduation:* $20,325.

Applying *Options:* electronic application. *Application fee:* $30. *Required:* high school transcript, minimum 2.0 GPA, Kansas Board of Regents admissions criteria with GPA of 2.0 resident, 2.5 nonresident; or upper third of high school class; or minimum ACT score 21 resident, 24 nonresident; or minimum SAT score 980 resident, 1090 nonresident. *Required for some:* minimum 2.5 GPA. *Application deadlines:* 4/1 (freshmen), 5/1 (transfers). *Notification:* continuous (freshmen), continuous (transfers).

Freshman Application Contact Ms. Lisa Pinamonti Kress, Director of Admissions and Scholarships, University of Kansas, KU Visitor Center, 1502 Iowa Street, Lawrence, KS 66045-7576. *Phone:* 785-864-3911. *Toll-free phone:* 888-686-7323. *Fax:* 785-864-5006. *E-mail:* adm@ku.edu.

UNIVERSITY OF PHOENIX–WICHITA CAMPUS

Wichita, Kansas **www.phoenix.edu/**

- **Proprietary** comprehensive, founded 2003
- **Urban** campus
- **Coed**
- **Noncompetitive** entrance level

Faculty *Student/faculty ratio:* 5:1.

Academics *Calendar:* continuous. *Degrees:* bachelor's and master's.

Student Life *Campus security:* late-night transport/escort service.

Costs (2007–08) *Tuition:* $11,100 full-time, $370 per credit part-time. Full-time tuition and fees vary according to course level.

Financial Aid *Average financial aid package:* $3923. *Average need-based gift aid:* $2054.

Applying *Options:* deferred entrance. *Application fee:* $45. *Required:* 1 letter of recommendation. *Required for some:* high school transcript.

Freshman Application Contact Ms. Beth Barilla, Associate Vice President, Student Admissions and Services, University of Phoenix–Wichita Campus, 4615 East Elwood Street, Mail Stop AA-K101, Phoenix, AZ 85040-1958. *Phone:* 480-894-1758. *Toll-free phone:* 800-776-4867 (in-state); 800-228-7240 (out-of-state). *E-mail:* beth.barilla@phoenix.edu.

UNIVERSITY OF SAINT MARY

Leavenworth, Kansas **www.stmary.edu/**

- **Independent Roman Catholic** comprehensive, founded 1923
- **Small-town** 240-acre campus with easy access to Kansas City
- **Endowment** $9.5 million
- **Coed** 593 undergraduate students, 69% full-time, 62% women, 38% men

• **Moderately difficult** entrance level, 61% of applicants were admitted

Undergraduates 411 full-time, 182 part-time. Students come from 21 states and territories, 2 other countries, 29% are from out of state, 12% African American, 1% Asian American or Pacific Islander, 8% Hispanic American, 0.8% Native American, 0.4% international, 12% transferred in, 23% live on campus. *Retention:* 61% of 2006 full-time freshmen returned.

Freshmen *Admission:* 442 applied, 270 admitted, 66 enrolled. *Test scores:* SAT critical reading scores over 500: 56%; SAT math scores over 500: 78%; ACT scores over 18: 95%; SAT critical reading scores over 600: 11%; SAT math scores over 600: 11%; ACT scores over 24: 40%; SAT math scores over 700: 11%; ACT scores over 30: 1%.

Faculty *Total:* 101, 42% full-time, 28% with terminal degrees. *Student/faculty ratio:* 10:1.

Majors Accounting; art; biology/biological sciences; business administration and management; chemistry; child development; community organization and advocacy; community psychology; computer and information sciences; criminology; curriculum and instruction; dramatic/theater arts; education; elementary education; English; history; information technology; interdisciplinary studies; liberal arts and sciences/liberal studies; mass communication/media; mathematics; multi-/interdisciplinary studies related; nursing (registered nurse training); pastoral studies/counseling; political science and government; psychology; sociology; sport and fitness administration/management; theology; visual and performing arts.

Academics *Calendar:* semesters. *Degrees:* certificates, associate, bachelor's, and master's. *Special study options:* adult/continuing education programs, advanced placement credit, cooperative education, distance learning, double majors, honors programs, independent study, internships, off-campus study, part-time degree program, student-designed majors, study abroad, summer session for credit. *ROTC:* Army (c), Air Force (c).

Computers on Campus 13 computers/terminals are available on campus for general student use. Students can access the following: campus intranet, computer help desk, free student e-mail accounts, online (class) grades, online (class) registration, online (class) schedules. Campuswide network is available. 100% of college-owned or -operated housing units are wired for high-speed Internet access. Wireless service is available via entire campus.

Student Life *Housing:* on-campus residence required through sophomore year. *Options:* coed. Campus housing is university owned. Freshman campus housing is guaranteed. *Activities and organizations:* drama/theater group, student-run newspaper, choral group, Student Government Association, BACCHUS, Theatrical Union, Campus Ministry, Amnesty International. *Campus security:* late-night transport/escort service, controlled dormitory access. *Student services:* health clinic, personal/psychological counseling.

Athletics Member NAIA. *Intercollegiate sports:* baseball M (s), basketball M (s)/W (s), football M (s), soccer M (s)/W (s), softball W (s), volleyball W (s). *Intramural sports:* badminton M/W, basketball M/W, bowling M/W, cross-country running M/W, football M/W, racquetball M/W, soccer M/W, softball M/W, swimming and diving M/W, table tennis M/W, tennis M/W, ultimate Frisbee M/W, volleyball M/W, weight lifting M/W.

Standardized Tests *Required:* SAT or ACT (for admission).

Costs (2007–08) *Comprehensive fee:* $23,670 includes full-time tuition ($16,900), mandatory fees ($370), and room and board ($6400). Full-time tuition and fees vary according to course load. Part-time tuition: $325 per credit. Part-time tuition and fees vary according to class time and course load. *Required fees:* $121 per term part-time. *College room only:* $2700. Room and board charges vary according to student level. *Payment plan:* installment. *Waivers:* minority students, adult students, senior citizens, and employees or children of employees.

Financial Aid *Average percent of need met:* 82%.

Applying *Options:* electronic application. *Application fee:* $25. *Required:* high school transcript, minimum 2.5 GPA. *Recommended:* 1 letter of recommendation, interview. *Application deadlines:* rolling (freshmen), rolling (transfers). *Notification:* continuous (freshmen), continuous (transfers).

Freshman Application Contact Ms. Jessica Goffinet, Director of Admissions, University of Saint Mary, 4100 South Fourth Street, Leavenworth, KS 66048. *Phone:* 913-758-6118. *Toll-free phone:* 800-752-7043. *Fax:* 913-758-6140. *E-mail:* admiss@stmary.edu.

WASHBURN UNIVERSITY

Topeka, Kansas **www.washburn.edu/**

- **City-supported** comprehensive, founded 1865
- **Urban** 160-acre campus with easy access to Kansas City
- **Endowment** $150.2 million
- **Coed** 6,020 undergraduate students, 68% full-time, 61% women, 39% men
- **Noncompetitive** entrance level, 98% of applicants were admitted

Undergraduates 4,084 full-time, 1,936 part-time. Students come from 44 states and territories, 42 other countries, 6% are from out of state, 10% transferred in, 13% live on campus. *Retention:* 61% of 2006 full-time freshmen returned.

Freshmen *Admission:* 1,549 applied, 1,523 admitted, 793 enrolled. *Average high school GPA:* 3.2. *Test scores:* ACT scores over 18: 87%; ACT scores over 24: 34%; ACT scores over 30: 4%.

Faculty *Total:* 527, 50% full-time, 63% with terminal degrees. *Student/faculty ratio:* 16:1.

Majors Accounting; administrative assistant and secretarial science; anthropology; art; art history, criticism and conservation; art teacher education; athletic training; banking and financial support services; biochemistry; biology/biological sciences; biology/biotechnology laboratory technician; business administration and management; business/commerce; business/managerial economics; chemistry; clinical/medical laboratory technology; communication/speech communication and rhetoric; computer and information sciences; computer and information sciences related; corrections; criminal justice/law enforcement administration; criminal justice/police science; criminal justice/safety; design and applied arts related; diagnostic medical sonography and ultrasound technology; drafting and design technology; dramatic/theater arts; early childhood education; economics; education; elementary education; English; finance; food services technology; forensic science and technology; French; German; health/health care administration; health information/medical records technology; health services/allied health/health sciences; history; humanities; industrial technology; legal administrative assistant/secretary; legal studies; liberal arts and sciences/liberal studies; marketing/marketing management; mass communication/media; mathematics; music; music performance; music teacher education; natural sciences; non-profit management; nursing (registered nurse training); office management; philosophy; physical education teaching and coaching; physical therapist assistant; physics; political science and government; pre-dentistry studies; pre-law studies; pre-medical studies; pre-pharmacy studies; pre-theology/pre-ministerial studies; pre-veterinary studies; psychology; public administration; radiologic technology/science; religious studies; respiratory care therapy; secondary education; security and protective services related; social work; sociology; Spanish; substance abuse/addiction counseling; surgical technology.

Academics *Calendar:* semesters. *Degrees:* certificates, associate, bachelor's, master's, first professional, postbachelor's, and first professional certificates. *Special study options:* academic remediation for entering students, adult/continuing education programs, advanced placement credit, cooperative education, distance learning, double majors, English as a second language, honors programs, independent study, internships, off-campus study, part-time degree program, services for LD students, student-designed majors, study abroad, summer session for credit. *ROTC:* Army (b), Navy (c), Air Force (c). *Unusual degree programs:* 3-2 engineering with University of Kansas, Kansas State University.

Computers on Campus 1,200 computers/terminals are available on campus for general student use. Students can access the following: campus intranet, computer help desk, free student e-mail accounts, online (class) grades, online (class) registration, online (class) schedules. Campuswide network is available. 100% of college-owned or -operated housing units are wired for high-speed Internet access. Wireless service is available via entire campus.

Student Life *Housing options:* coed. Campus housing is university owned. *Activities and organizations:* drama/theater group, student-run newspaper, television station, choral group, marching band, national fraternities, national sororities. *Campus security:* 24-hour emergency response devices and patrols, student patrols, late-night transport/escort service. *Student services:* health clinic, personal/psychological counseling, legal services.

Athletics Member NCAA. All Division II. *Intercollegiate sports:* baseball M (s), basketball M (s)/W (s), cheerleading M (s)/W (s), football M (s), golf M (s), soccer W (s), softball W (s), tennis M (s)/W (s), volleyball W (s). *Intramural sports:* badminton M/W, basketball M/W, football M/W, golf M/W, soccer M/W, softball M/W, swimming and diving M/W, table tennis M/W, tennis M/W, ultimate Frisbee M/W, volleyball M/W.

Standardized Tests *Required:* ACT (for admission).

Costs (2007–08) *Tuition:* state resident $5550 full-time, $185 per credit hour part-time; nonresident $12,600 full-time, $420 per credit hour part-time. *Required fees:* $86 full-time, $21 per term part-time. *Room and board:* $5281; room only: $2941. Room and board charges vary according to board plan and housing facility. *Payment plan:* installment. *Waivers:* senior citizens and employees or children of employees.

Financial Aid Of all full-time matriculated undergraduates who enrolled in 2004, 2,540 applied for aid, 1,996 were judged to have need, 402 had their need fully met. In 2004, 1058 non-need-based awards were made. *Average percent of need met:* 39%. *Average financial aid package:* $6766. *Average need-based loan:* $4099. *Average need-based gift aid:* $3306. *Average non-need-based aid:* $2196. *Average indebtedness upon graduation:* $13,125.

Applying *Options:* electronic application, early admission. *Application fee:* $20. *Required:* high school transcript. *Application deadlines:* 8/1 (freshmen), 8/1 (transfers). *Notification:* continuous (freshmen), continuous (transfers).

Freshman Application Contact Mr. Kirk R. Haskins, Director of Admission, Washburn University, 1700 SW College Avenue, Topeka, KS 66621. *Phone:* 785-670-1030. *Toll-free phone:* 800-332-0291. *Fax:* 785-670-1089. *E-mail:* admissions@washburn.edu.

WICHITA STATE UNIVERSITY

Wichita, Kansas **www.wichita.edu/**

- **State-supported** university, founded 1895, part of Kansas State Board of Education
- **Urban** 335-acre campus
- **Endowment** $196.9 million
- **Coed** 11,323 undergraduate students, 66% full-time, 55% women, 45% men
- **Noncompetitive** entrance level, 85% of applicants were admitted

Undergraduates 7,499 full-time, 3,824 part-time. Students come from 44 states and territories, 89 other countries, 4% are from out of state, 6% African American, 6% Asian American or Pacific Islander, 5% Hispanic American, 1% Native American, 6% international, 12% transferred in, 9% live on campus. *Retention:* 67% of 2006 full-time freshmen returned.

Freshmen *Admission:* 2,997 applied, 2,548 admitted, 1,352 enrolled. *Average high school GPA:* 3.35. *Test scores:* SAT critical reading scores over 500: 68%; SAT math scores over 500: 72%; ACT scores over 18: 93%; SAT critical reading scores over 600: 23%; SAT math scores over 600: 31%; ACT scores over 24: 44%; SAT critical reading scores over 700: 7%; SAT math scores over 700: 4%; ACT scores over 30: 5%.

Faculty *Total:* 527, 90% full-time, 75% with terminal degrees. *Student/faculty ratio:* 18:1.

Majors Accounting; aerospace, aeronautical and astronautical engineering; anthropology; art; art history, criticism and conservation; art teacher education; audiology and speech-language pathology; biology/biological sciences; business administration and management; chemistry; clinical laboratory science/medical technology; commercial and advertising art; communication/speech communication and rhetoric; computer and information sciences; computer engineering; criminal justice/safety; dental hygiene; dramatic/theater arts; economics; electrical, electronics and communications engineering; elementary education; English; entrepreneurship; finance; French; geology/earth science; gerontology; health/health care administration; history; human resources management; industrial engineering; international business/trade/commerce; Latin; liberal arts and sciences/liberal studies; management information systems; manufacturing engineering; marketing/marketing management; mathematics; mechanical engineering; music; music teacher education; nursing science; philosophy; physical education teaching and coaching; physician assistant; physics; political science and government; psychology; sales, distribution and marketing; science teacher education; secondary education; social work; sociology; Spanish; visual and performing arts; women's studies.

Academics *Calendar:* semesters. *Degrees:* certificates, associate, bachelor's, master's, doctoral, post-master's, and postbachelor's certificates. *Special study options:* academic remediation for entering students, accelerated degree program, advanced placement credit, cooperative education, distance learning, double majors, English as a second language, freshman honors college, honors programs, independent study, internships, off-campus study, part-time degree program, services for LD students, student-designed majors, study abroad, summer session for credit. *Unusual degree programs:* 3-2 accounting.

Computers on Campus 1,500 computers/terminals are available on campus for general student use. Students can access the following: online (class) registration, online grades, e-mail. Campuswide network is available.

Student Life *Housing:* on-campus residence required for freshman year. *Options:* coed. Campus housing is university owned. *Activities and organizations:* drama/theater group, student-run newspaper, radio and television station, choral group, Association of Malaysian Students, Organization of Pakistani Students, Psychology Club, nursing students organization, Institute of Aeronautics, national fraternities, national sororities. *Campus security:* 24-hour emergency response devices and patrols, student patrols, late-night transport/escort service, controlled dormitory access, bicycle patrols by campus security. *Student services:* health clinic, personal/psychological counseling, women's center, legal services.

Athletics Member NCAA. All Division I. *Intercollegiate sports:* baseball M (s), basketball M (s)/W (s), bowling M (c)/W (c), cheerleading M/W, crew M (c)/W (c), cross-country running M (s)/W (s), golf M (s)/W (s), ice hockey M (c)/W (c), racquetball M (c)/W (c), rugby M (c), soccer M (c)/W (c), softball W (s), swimming and diving M (c)/W (c), tennis M (s)/W (s), track and field M (s)/W (s), volleyball M (c)/W (s), wrestling M (c). *Intramural sports:* badminton M/W, basketball M/W, bowling M/W, football M/W, golf M/W, racquetball M/W, soccer M/W, softball M/W, swimming and diving M/W, table tennis M/W, tennis M/W, ultimate Frisbee M/W, volleyball M/W, weight lifting M/W.

Standardized Tests *Required for some:* SAT or ACT (for admission).

Costs (2007–08) *Tuition:* state resident $3912 full-time, $130 per credit hour part-time; nonresident $11,259 full-time, $375 per credit hour part-time. Full-time tuition and fees vary according to course load. Part-time tuition and fees vary according to course load. *Required fees:* $858 full-time, $29 per credit hour part-time, $17 per term part-time. *Room and board:* $5580. Room and board charges vary according to board plan and housing facility. *Payment plan:* installment. *Waivers:* senior citizens and employees or children of employees.

Financial Aid Of all full-time matriculated undergraduates who enrolled in 2006, 5,835 applied for aid, 3,747 were judged to have need, 2,398 had their need fully met. 195 Federal Work-Study jobs (averaging $2576). In 2006, 691 non-need-based awards were made. *Average percent of need met:* 48%. *Average financial aid package:* $7942. *Average need-based loan:* $3843. *Average need-based gift aid:* $3406. *Average non-need-based aid:* $2533. *Average indebtedness upon graduation:* $20,875.

Applying *Options:* electronic application, deferred entrance. *Application fee:* $30. *Required for some:* minimum 2.0 GPA, minimum ACT score of 21; rank in top 1/3 of high school class, or minimum of 2.00 high school GPA. *Application deadlines:* rolling (freshmen), rolling (transfers). *Notification:* continuous (freshmen), continuous (transfers).

Freshman Application Contact Mr. Bobby Gandu, Director of Admissions, Wichita State University, 1845 Fairmount Street, Wichita, KS 67260-0124. *Phone:* 316-978-3085. *Toll-free phone:* 800-362-2594. *Fax:* 316-978-3174. *E-mail:* admissions@wichita.edu.

BAKER UNIVERSITY

BALDWIN CITY, KANSAS

The University

Baker University was founded in 1858 by a group of Methodist ministers. It was the first University in Kansas and is regarded as the top private school in the state. Guided by principles of integrity, honesty, compassion, and civility, Baker University produces graduates who make a difference in their communities throughout the world.

Baker's reputation is strong. Four Rhodes Scholars and two Pulitzer Prize winners in journalism have graduated from Baker. Two recent graduates have been awarded the prestigious Goldwater Scholarship for their excellence in the area of science. *U.S. News & World Report* and the *Princeton Review* consistently rank the University as a top school in the Midwest. In addition, Baker has been recognized for its value by *Money* magazine and *Barron's Best Buys in College Education.*

Student organizations have a strong presence at the Baldwin City campus, the home of the College of Arts and Sciences (CAS) and the School of Education (SOE) undergraduate programs. Ninety percent of the student body is involved in more than one activity or organization. Half of these students are athletes competing at the NAIA Division II level in the Heart of America Athletic Conference. There are nine men's and ten women's sports offered at Baker. The University has a rich athletic history that includes early-day leadership in founding the NAIA.

The Baldwin City campus is residential, and Greek life involves nearly 50 percent of the student population. There are five houses each for men and women. Students under age 23 who are not living in a Greek house live in one of four residence halls offering suite-style accommodations. Upperclassmen may live in student apartments on campus.

Baker's School of Nursing (SON) began in 1991 when the University and Stormont Vail Health*Care*, a major medical center, entered into a partnership. The close relationship with the hospital provides convenient experiential learning opportunities with state-of-the-art equipment. Students generally are employed before they graduate. Campus housing is not available in Topeka and students are free to choose their own housing arrangements.

The School of Professional and Graduate Studies (SPGS) was established in 1988 to expand opportunities for the adult students Baker had begun serving in 1976. Its nontraditional degree programs are offered in an accelerated format convenient to working adults. The school has produced more than 8,000 graduates in business, education, and liberal arts programs.

There are more than 900 students on the Baldwin City campus, approximately 2,200 in School of Professional and Graduate Studies locations, 145 at the School of Nursing, and 739 graduate students at the School of Education.

Baker is affiliated with the United Methodist Church and is accredited by the Higher Learning Commission of the North Central Association. The nursing program is accredited by the Commission on Collegiate Nursing Education, the Teacher Education Program by the Kansas State Board of Education, music programs by the National Association of Schools of Music, and business programs by AACSB International—the Association to Advance Collegiate Schools of Business.

Location

The College of Arts and Sciences and School of Education's bachelor's degree offerings are at the main campus in Baldwin City, a community of 3,500 people located 40 minutes from Kansas City. The School of Nursing is in Topeka, a city of 128,000, and is an hour's drive from Baldwin City. The school operates in Pozez Education Center, which adjoins Stormont Vail Health*Care*. The School of Professional and Graduate Studies is based in Overland Park, Kansas, a suburb of Kansas City, just 40 minutes from the Baldwin City campus. The location is easily accessible by state and federal highways that provide quick and convenient access for students who travel directly from work. Classes are also offered in Topeka and Wichita, Kansas, and Lee's Summit, Missouri.

Majors and Degrees

Baker University encompasses four schools. The College of Arts and Sciences (CAS) at the main campus in Baldwin City offers more than forty majors and areas of concentration. Students may earn Bachelor of Arts, Bachelor of Science, Bachelor of Music or Bachelor of Music Education degrees.

The School of Education (SOE) offers bachelor's, master's and doctoral degrees through programs at the main campus and at locations throughout Kansas and Missouri. Students may major in elementary, secondary, or middle-level-math education. In addition, a special education component of the program leads to provisional licensure.

Students who graduate from the School of Nursing receive a Bachelor of Science in Nursing degree. The school offers the final two years of preparation for a B.S.N., and its population draws from the CAS campus as well as other universities and community colleges.

The School of Professional and Graduate Studies (SPGS) serves working adults through business, liberal arts, and conflict resolution programs leading to Bachelor of Business Administration, Bachelor of Science in Management, and master's degrees. Courses are conducted at convenient times to best serve working adults. Baker also offers an Associate of Arts in Business degree program designed for adults who are just beginning their academic career path. Students in these programs have class one night each week and work weekly with a study group. Students can earn their degree in as little as two years, though the amount of time depends upon prior course work undertaken.

Academic Programs

Baker emphasizes the liberal arts tradition through a general education program that develops fundamental intellectual skills and provides experiences and ideas that assist the student in making informed decisions as a member of society. The College of Arts and Sciences operates on a 4-1-4 academic calendar with two 5-week sessions of summer school. The month of January is set aside for Interterm, a period when students enroll in only one class. Interterm classes may be taken on campus or abroad, and internships are numerous.

To complete a bachelor's degree at Baker, a student must successfully complete 132 semester hours with a Baker GPA of at least 2.0 (on a 4.0 scale).

The Baker honors program provides an opportunity for highly qualified students to complete advanced work in regular classes for honors credit and take special honors sections of courses. Honors participants are required to have a minimum 3.5 high school GPA and a minimum composite score of 27 on the ACT.

Off-Campus Programs

Many Baker students choose to attend Harlaxton College in Grantham, England, for a semester. They live and study in a Victorian manor while taking classes that apply toward their degree. Long weekends are scheduled so that students may travel throughout Europe. Baker also participates in several other study-abroad programs and has placed students all over the world. In addition, students may study off campus during Interterm with internships or by enrolling in courses that involve national or international travel.

Academic Facilities

The campus in Baldwin City blends historic beauty and modern function. Classroom buildings, offices, the library, and the student union surround a central arboretum with a mixture of greenery that provides beauty all year. In fact, three buildings on campus are listed on the National Historic Register. While preserving Baker's historic landscape, the school is devoted to embracing technology and had spent more than $25 million in facility improvement over the past 15 years. The nursing program is located in the Pozez Education Center at Stormont Vail HealthCare medical center. The building provides modern classrooms, a learning lab, health sciences library, computer lab, and fitness center. Students perform clinical work at the hospital and at other sites in the community. The School of Professional and Graduate Studies offers classes in the metropolitan areas of Kansas and the western edge of Missouri.

Costs

Tuition for the 2007–08 academic year for undergraduates in CAS and SOE is $18,750. Double-occupancy room and board for the year are $5850. Nursing school tuition is $12,150. The cost of SPGS and SOE programs varies depending upon the program.

Financial Aid

Students in all of Baker's schools have the opportunity to receive financial aid. Ninety-five percent of the full-time students in CAS and SOE receive financial assistance. Non-need-based scholarships awarded on academic merit and leadership are available for up to $8000 and are renewable each year. Baker leads the independent colleges in Kansas in the amount of Kansas State Scholar funds awarded to its students.

Financial assistance is available on both a need and non-need basis to full-time students. Aid based on need is given to students who demonstrate genuine need as determined by the Free Application for Federal Student Aid (FAFSA). Applications for financial aid should be submitted as early as possible since aid is awarded on a rolling basis and may be exhausted by the summer months. The University participates in all federally supported student-aid programs.

Faculty

The College's student to faculty ratio is 12:1 with an average class size of 20. Professors are readily available outside of class to assist students and extend a helping hand beyond the classroom. The CAS faculty includes 110 members. Sixty percent are full time. The 16 members of the SON faculty all serve in full-time roles; there is a 9:1 ratio of students to faculty. SPGS is served by 165 faculty members nearly all of whom are professionals working in the fields in which they teach.

Student Government

Members of the official student governing organization, the Student Senate, are elected from organizations on campus. The president of the senate is invited to attend faculty meetings and general sessions of the Board of Trustees. The Student Senate allocates the student activity fund for campus events and student projects and plays a major role in ensuring that student opinion is heard within the University community. Faculty search committees also regularly involve students in the search for new faculty members.

Admission Requirements

Applications for undergraduate admission to the College of Arts and Sciences and School of Education are reviewed by the director of admissions and, in some cases, an admission committee. Readiness is determined by evidence of ability to do college work at Baker and an interest in acquiring a liberal arts education. In most cases applicants who meet two of three academic criteria—an minimum ACT composite score of 18, a minimum 2.75 high school GPA, and/or placement in the top half of the graduating class—are admitted. Other applicants are evaluated on an individual basis. Transfer students are eligible for admission with a minimum 2.3 college GPA in all college-level hours attempted, as determined by the Baker University Office of the Registrar. Applicants not meeting the minimum 2.3 GPA are evaluated on an individual basis.

The School of Nursing admits students in both the fall and spring semesters, with Baker CAS students receiving priority admission. All program prerequisites must be completed with a grade of C or higher on a 4.0 grade point scale, with an overall prerequisite cumulative GPA of at least 2.7. Only required prerequisite courses are considered in calculating the GPA.

To be eligible for admission into the School of Professional and Graduate Studies, bachelor degree programs applicants must have one year of full time work experience, two letters of recommendation, a minimum TOEFL test score (600 paper-based, 250 computer-based, or 100 Internet-based), official transcripts from all colleges attended, and an official high school transcript with a minimum GPA of 2.3 or official GED certificate with a minimum score of 47.

Application and Information

Information and links to applications for all four schools are available at http://www.bakeru.edu or students should contact:

College of Arts and Sciences, School of Education, or School of Nursing Admissions
Baker University
P.O. Box 65
Baldwin City, Kansas 66006-0065
Phone: 800-873-4282 (in the U.S.) (toll-free)
Web site: http://www.bakeru.edu

School of Professional and Graduate Studies Admissions
8001 College Boulevard
Overland Park, Kansas 66210
Phone: 913-491-4432 Ext. 690
Fax: 913-491-0470
Web site: http://www.bakeru.edu

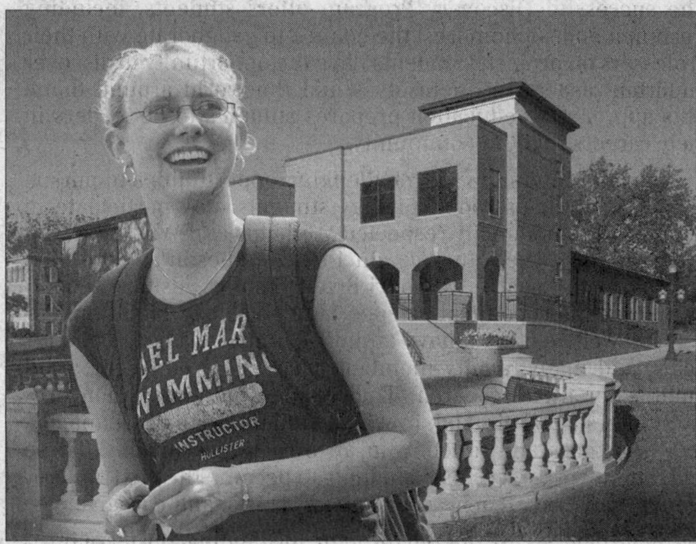

Baker has strong participation in a variety of sports.

BENEDICTINE COLLEGE

ATCHISON, KANSAS

The College

Benedictine College (BC) is a four-year, Catholic, Benedictine, residential, coeducational college that provides an outstanding liberal arts education for students of all backgrounds and faiths. It is located on a wooded, 110-acre campus on the bluffs above the Missouri River near Atchison, Kansas. The College was established as the result of the 1971 merger of St. Benedict's College (founded in 1858) and Mount St. Scholastica College (founded in 1924). The sponsoring monastic communities of Mount St. Scholastica and St. Benedict's Abbey set the tone for the campus, where the dignity of all individuals is respected. Benedictine College is fully accredited by the North Central Association of Colleges and Schools and does not discriminate on the basis of sex, race, color, religion, or national origin. The College has an ethnically diverse student population of 1,300 undergraduates, including students from more than forty states and eighteen other countries.

In a recent survey of approximately 162,000 students at 472 four-year colleges and universities (National Survey of Student Engagement), Benedictine College scored in the top 5 percent nationally for student-faculty interaction, supportive campus environment, and enriching educational experiences. The College has recently been named a *U.S. News & World Report* "Top Tier Institution." Benedictine College fosters scholarship, independent research, and performance in its students and faculty members as a means of participating in and contributing to the broader world of learning.

The successful Discovery Program offers students, including freshmen and sophomores, the chance to collaborate with their professors on projects. Students have the opportunity to discover important aspects of themselves and the world around them. This approach to education prepares students to be leaders in their careers and the community.

Every major offers unique, challenging opportunities to pursue outside of the classroom. Biology students may participate in Benedictine's nationally respected Wetlands and Wildlife Restoration Project, where they conduct field studies in a restoration area along the nearby Missouri River. History, business, chemistry, education, political science, and sociology faculty members, as well as others, have authored numerous books and articles, and many faculty members have received major grant funding for their research. The business administration program offers a learning lab in which students actually manage a small business and function in an ownership capacity. These and other experiences lead students to become the next generation of managers, teachers, scientists, artists, and caregivers.

Graduate degrees are offered through outstanding Master of Business Administration, Executive Master of Business Administration, and Master of Arts in School Leadership Programs.

Benedictine College prides itself on building a sense of family and community. Students find the inviting, spacious residence halls to be convenient and friendly, with a supportive staff in a secure environment. In fact, more than 72 percent of the student body lives on campus, providing the Benedictine student with not only an academic education, but growth of mind, body, and spirit. To meet the needs of growing enrollment, in the last five years Benedictine has renovated all residence halls and built a new hall for women. BC's residential aspect (3 out of 4 students live on campus) is very important to educating the whole student: mind, body, and spirit. A new residence hall is currently under construction.

Benedictine offers more than forty-five clubs and student organizations to meet just about every interest. These include student government, Students in Free Enterprise (SIFE), departmental clubs, International Club, Hunger Coalition, Knights of Columbus, Hispanic American Leadership Organization (HALO), Chamber Singers, Black Student Union, *Loomings* literary magazine, *The Raven* yearbook, and *The Circuit* student newspaper.

The Ravens compete in seventeen varsity intercollegiate sports (NAIA and Heart of America Athletic Conference), with men's teams in baseball, basketball, cross-country, football, soccer, tennis, indoor track, and outdoor track and women's teams in basketball, cross-country, a dance and cheer spirit squad, soccer, softball, tennis, indoor track, outdoor track, and volleyball.

Any student with a passion for athletics can benefit from participating in numerous intramural activities, including competition in men's and women's basketball, flag football, soccer, softball, dodgeball, and volleyball. All students are welcome to exercise at the Student Union, which has a gymnasium, athletic training rooms, and plenty of fitness-oriented equipment along with a comfortable 500-seat auditorium for concerts, plays, and lectures. The Student Union also houses student government and campus life offices, a Career Development Center, and plenty of space to relax and meet friends. Benedictine's Career Development Center offers students a variety of information and services to assist them in career preparation. Services include individual counseling, career testing, workshops, and seminars as well as assistance with graduate and professional school applications, resume writing, interviewing skills, cover-letter writing, and job search strategies. In the natural sciences, 75 percent of the graduates continue their education in graduate or professional schools, a number that is nearly double the national average for liberal arts college graduates. The record of acceptance of BC graduates into medical colleges is among the best in the Midwest. The Raven network of proud Benedictine alumni is a valuable resource for current BC students and new graduates. BC alumni can be found leading others in such prestigious places as the Federal Reserve Bank, the NCAA National Office, Hallmark Cards, NASA, and the Mayo Clinic.

Location

Benedictine College is located on a peaceful, wooded campus in Atchison, Kansas, a picturesque town of 12,000 overlooking the Missouri River. The College is less than 1 hour's drive northwest of Kansas City and only 35 minutes from the Kansas City International Airport. Atchison offers unique shops, beautiful parks, historic Victorian homes, museums, art galleries, and a modern regional hospital near the College campus.

Majors and Degrees

Benedictine currently offers the following accredited degrees: Associate of Arts (business administration), Bachelor of Arts, Bachelor of Science, and Bachelor of Music Education. Every field of study at Benedictine College includes the opportunity for collaborative, hands-on training; a dynamic curriculum; internships; and a supportive faculty. The College offers four-year majors in accounting, art, astronomy, athletic training, biochemistry, biology, business administration, chemistry, computer science, criminology, economics, education (certification, elementary, secondary, special education), English, finance, foreign languages,

French, history, international business, international studies, liberal studies, mass communications, mathematics, music, music education, music marketing, natural science, philosophy, physical education, physics, political science, psychology, sociology, social science, Spanish, theater arts, theater arts management, theology, and youth ministry. In addition, the College offers preprofessional study programs in dentistry, engineering, law, medical technology, medicine, nursing, occupational therapy, optometry, pharmacy, physical therapy, and veterinary studies. The College also offers certification in coaching. The liberal studies major is available for those students who want or need the freedom to design a major to their unique interests.

Academic Programs

Benedictine College divides its academic year into two semesters and one summer session. The semesters are approximately sixteen weeks long. To earn a bachelor's degree from Benedictine College, a student is required to successfully complete 128 semester credit hours of courses numbered above 100. These courses must include courses specified by the student's major department, a total of 40 credit hours in courses numbered 300 or above, and the general education requirements of the College. Students must also achieve a minimum final grade point average of 2.0 in both the major and the overall course work at Benedictine, successfully complete a comprehensive or standardized examination in their major at a level designated by the faculty, and finish the last two semesters of work in residence. The general education requirements for a bachelor's degree are divided into three categories: core requirements, disciplinary requirements, and proficiency requirements. Benedictine College offers opportunities for advanced placement, the College-Level Examination Program (CLEP), and credit for experiential learning to nontraditional students who are at least 23 years of age. The College also has a cross-enrollment agreement with Missouri Western State College and its Reserve Officers' Training Corps (ROTC).

Off-Campus Programs

Benedictine College also has a campus located in Florence, Italy. Each semester, forty Benedictine students live and study at the Florence campus. In addition, Benedictine College participates in the International Student Exchange Program (I.S.E.P.), which allows students to study throughout the world. BC sponsors a study-abroad program in Cuernavaca, Mexico, for students studying Spanish. For French students, the affiliation is with the Catholic University of the West at Angers, France. Benedictine students can also study at the Sorbonne in Paris and at the University of Granada in Spain. BC students also study in China, England, Germany, Ireland, the Netherlands, and Wales.

Academic Facilities

The College enhances every student's educational experience with comprehensive facilities, including modern classrooms, nine science laboratories, and a modern computer network with Internet and e-mail access. The BC library is the designated federal depository for the area's congressional district. It also houses many rare books, including works on monastic history dating from the fifteenth century. Benedictine College is a member of several library consortia, providing students with access to academic and public libraries locally and around the world. The College's Kansas Area Network (KANRAN) is one of the most sophisticated in America.

Costs

For 2007–08, tuition and fees were approximately $17,700 and room and board were $6478. Other estimated expenses included books, $550; personal expenses, $1200; and travel, $800. Tuition and fees usually experience a 3 percent increase each year.

Financial Aid

More than 95 percent of Benedictine students receive some form of financial assistance. Benedictine College annually awards more than $5.3 million in institutional aid and offers a generous number of scholarships based on academic achievement, athletic ability, leadership potential, special talents and abilities, and other merits outside of financial need. The College also participates in the federal grant, work-study, and loan programs as well as ROTC and state of Kansas financial aid programs. Benedictine's priority deadline for financial aid consideration is March 1.

Faculty

Seventy-eight percent of Benedictine College's faculty members hold the highest degree in their fields. With a student-faculty ratio of 16:1, students have greater access to professors, who go out of their way to serve students on a personal level. Students are supported by instructors who are not only respected for their professional achievement but also for their commitment to student development. Professors, not graduate or teaching assistants, teach all Benedictine courses.

Student Government

The Student Government is designed to promote the general welfare of the student body in its academic, social, cultural, and religious needs. The executive officers of the student government and class officers are responsible for formulating and executing student government administrative policy.

Admission Requirements

Applicants must submit scores on the SAT or ACT and all official high school and/or college transcripts. Sixteen units of college-preparatory work are recommended, including 4 units of English, 3 to 4 units of math, 2 to 4 units of foreign language, 2 to 4 units of natural science, 2 units of social science, and 1 unit of history.

Application and Information

The College employs a rolling admission policy. Students are encouraged to apply online (http://www.benedictine.edu/apply). For further information or to request an application, students should contact:

Pete Helgesen
Dean of Enrollment Management
Benedictine College
1020 North Second Street
Atchison, Kansas 66002
Phone: 913-367-5340
800-467-5340 (toll-free)
E-mail: bcadmiss@benedictine.edu
Web site: http://www.benedictine.edu

Located just 35 minutes north of the Kansas City International Airport, Benedictine College overlooks the Missouri River in Atchison, Kansas.

MIDAMERICA NAZARENE UNIVERSITY

OLATHE, KANSAS

The University

MidAmerica Nazarene University (MNU) is a comprehensive liberal arts university of approximately 1,800 students. MNU provides a nurturing environment where students gain broad-based knowledge and skills that can serve them professionally and personally throughout their lives.

Learning to live one's faith is an integral part of the MNU experience. Revitalizing one's spirit, awakening one's concern for others, and helping build deep and lasting relationships are some of the most important objectives at MNU.

The University offers undergraduate academic majors in forty areas, a degree-completion program in management and human relations, a baccalaureate degree affiliation with European Nazarene College in Germany, and graduate-level programs in education, business administration, and counseling.

Sponsored by the North Central Region of the International Church of the Nazarene, the University is committed to serving the church and its global mission. MNU is accredited by the Commission on Institutions of Higher Education of the North Central Association of Colleges and Schools.

Residence halls at MNU are meant to provide more than a place for sleep and studies—they also provide an environment for personal growth. MNU believes that the learning that takes place outside the classroom is of equal value to that within the classroom. Each residence hall has a lobby or shared lobby where students can meet to study, watch television, or just hang out with friends. Each room is equipped for phone, cable television, and Internet service. Coin-operated laundry facilities are available in each residence hall.

Students enjoy a fun and active life through dozens of campuswide events. Special events include Spirit Week, Homecoming, Nerd Day, Beach Bash, Faculty Follies, Mr. MNU contest, Gotcha Week, Colony West Fest, TWIRP weekend, Mock Rock, and Late Night Skates. With more than a dozen clubs and ministries, twelve varsity sports teams, intramurals, music groups, and more, there is always something to do on campus.

MNU is a member of the NAIA and the NCCAA. Scholarships are available in men's baseball and football, women's softball and volleyball, and men's and women's basketball, cheerleading, cross-country running, soccer, and track and field. Intramural sports include basketball, bowling, football, golf, soccer, softball, table tennis, tennis, Ultimate Frisbee, and volleyball.

Location

MidAmerica is in Olathe, Kansas, a residential community of approximately 120,000 located 20 minutes from the heart of Kansas City, with all the cultural advantages of a major metropolitan area. Olathe is the second largest among the twenty-one communities in prosperous Johnson County and the fifth-largest city in the state. Olathe offers a lifestyle of exceptional quality. A drive through Olathe's attractive, gently rolling neighborhoods shows a well-planned, pleasing community. The city's school system is one of the best in the nation. Outdoor recreation offers a variety of activities, including running, jogging, bicycling, fishing, boating, team sports, and just relaxing. The Olathe area is popular for hot-air ballooning and sailboarding. Olathe has two public lakes—Olathe Lake, with 172 acres of water surface, and Cedar Lake, with 45 acres. The city's recreation division maintains year-round activities, including music and dance, sports, and health and fitness programs for all ages. Baseball diamonds, tennis courts, and fitness trails are available throughout the city.

Majors and Degrees

Students can earn an Associate of Arts (A.A.) degree in general business, liberal arts, or music ministry.

The Bachelor of Arts (B.A.) degree is available in accounting, athletic training, the Bible and theology, biology, biology education, business administration, business education, business psychology, chemistry, communication/business, computer science, criminal justice, elementary education, English, English language arts education, graphic design, history, history and government education, international business, marketing, mass communication, mathematics, mathematics education, ministry, missions, music (applied pedagogy, music ministry, and music performance), music ministry, organizational leadership, physical education, psychology, secondary education, sociology, Spanish, Spanish education, speech/theater education, sports management, and youth and family ministry.

MNU also offers the Bachelor of Music Education (B.M.Ed.) degree and the Bachelor of Science in Nursing (B.S.N.) degree.

Academic Programs

The educational experience at MidAmerica Nazarene University is based on certain desired outcomes and consists of several components, including the Freshman Seminar, a program of general education, a comprehensive field of in-depth study, and an optional minor. By these means, the University seeks to achieve its educational mission of developing mature, educated individuals who possess a commitment to service in a Christian lifestyle.

The freshman seminar is a required one-semester, 1-hour course that provides students with an introduction to the traditions of MNU and helps them adjust to the challenges of the higher educational experience. The general education program at MidAmerica Nazarene University exposes students to certain facts, ideas, and values in an attempt to awaken them to their potential and to assist them in developing ways of recognizing and expressing truth through the academic disciplines. A major provides a program of study that enables students to investigate a subject area in considerable depth. The University encourages students to select related minors or secondary interest areas as a part of their comprehensive study plan.

Off-Campus Programs

Because MNU is a member of the Council for Christian Colleges and Universities (CCCU), a national association of more than 100 Christian colleges and universities of the liberal arts and sciences, a number of off-campus learning opportunities are available. Domestic programs are available in Washington, D.C.; Los Angeles; and Martha's Vineyard, Massachusetts. Students can also study abroad in China, Costa Rica, Egypt, Germany, Russia, and the United Kingdom.

Academic Facilities

The new 40,000-square-foot Bell Cultural Events Center features state-of-the-art practice, recital, and performance facilities for the fine arts division, as well as a black-box theater and performance hall for music and drama productions. Osborne Hall houses the Division of Science and Mathematics, while Lunn Hall houses administrative offices. Dobson Hall contains an art studio and a graphic-design computer lab. The largest facility on campus, the Cook Center, houses a basketball/volleyball arena, two practice gyms, the Division of Nursing, the Departments of Athletics and Athletic Training, and several classrooms. Metz Hall houses the Divisions of Behavioral Sciences, Business Administration, and Education; Graduate Studies in Counseling; Graduate Studies in Education; and the Department of Computer Science. A computer lab is an integral part of the facility.

Mabee Library and Learning Resource Center contains more than 481,000 volumes—360,000 in microforms and the balance in bound volumes. Mabee Library also houses a microcomputer laboratory for general use, the Ministry Resource Center, the Kresge Center, a multimedia room, the Teacher Education Resource Center, and the Marge Smith Archives. General science, educational media, business, computer science, reading and learning, and computation laboratories complement the class sessions and provide modern equipment.

Costs

For 2006–07, a typical student paid $21,798. Tuition was $16,090 (for 24 to 34 credit hours). Fees, which include mandatory student insurance and activity and technology fees, are $1000. The residential charge is $6112 (twenty-one meals per week) or $5830 (fourteen meals per week).

Financial Aid

About 92 percent of students receive some form of financial aid. MNU scholarships are available and range between $1000 and full tuition per year. For all full-time matriculated undergraduates who enrolled in 2006–07, the average financial aid package totaled $13,000. Information and applications may be obtained from Student Financial Services at 913-791-3298.

Faculty

MNU students receive personal attention from their instructors. It is not uncommon to find faculty members in residence hall rooms talking with students or even inviting students into their homes for Thanksgiving dinner. MNU has 173 faculty members, 41 percent of whom are full-time, and a student-faculty ratio of 18:1.

Student Government

Associated Student Government exists to discover God's agenda as students serve God and the campus community. The government offers plenty of opportunities for students to get involved.

Admission Requirements

Prospective students should have graduated from an accredited high school and completed at least 15 units of study. While the University does not require specific subjects for entrance, it does recommend that students complete 3 units of math, 4 units of English, 3 units of science, 3 units of social studies, and 1 unit of foreign language. Students over 18 who have not graduated from high school can submit GED scores.

Application and Information

Students must submit the completed application, the $25 nonrefundable application fee, official high school transcripts, ACT or SAT scores, a personal reference, and the housing, parent waiver, and health history forms provided by Admissions. International students must also submit TOEFL scores. The deadline for the fall semester is August 1; the spring semester deadline is December 15.

For more information, prospective students should contact:

Dennis Troyer, Director of Admissions
MidAmerica Nazarene University
2030 East College Way
Olathe, Kansas 66062-1899
Phone: 913-971-3380
800-800-8887 (toll-free)
E-mail: admissions@mnu.edu
Web site: http://www.mnu.edu

KENTUCKY

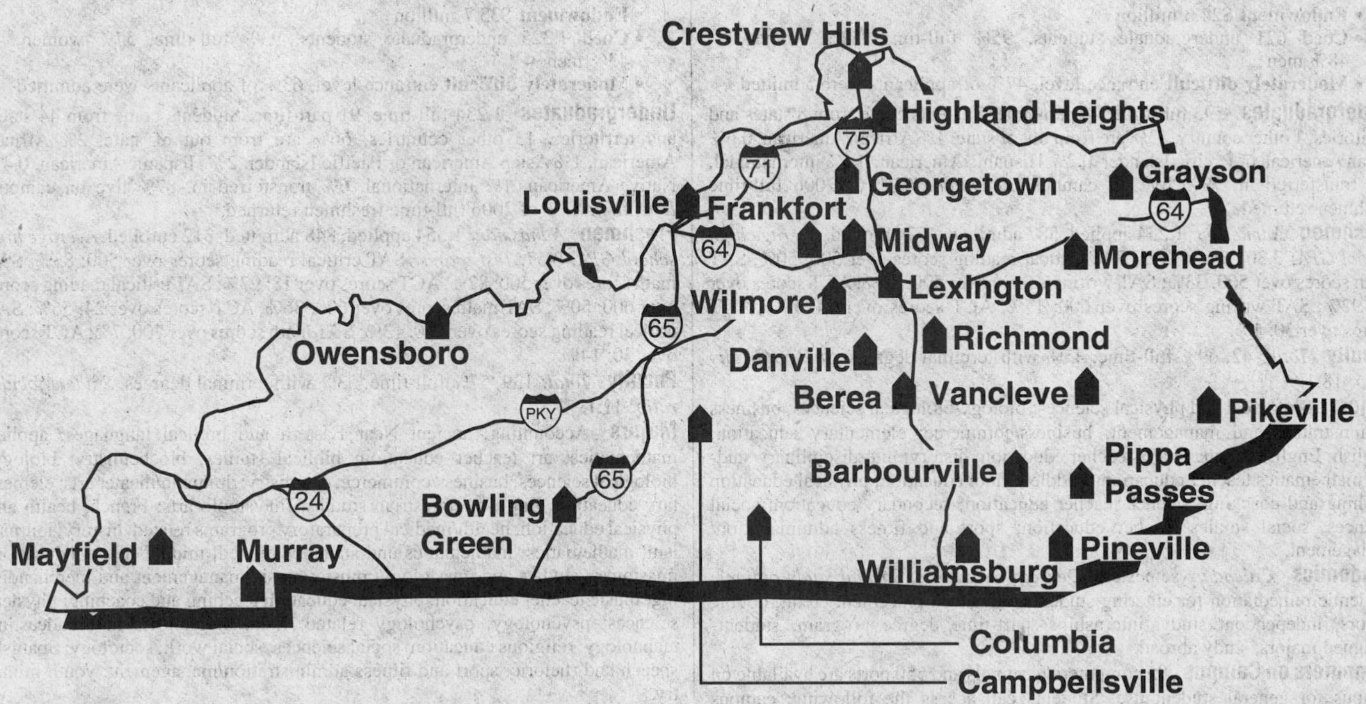
Crestview Hills
Highland Heights
75
71
Georgetown
Grayson
64
Louisville
Frankfort
Midway
Morehead
64
Lexington
Wilmore
65
Richmond
Owensboro
Danville
Berea
Vancleve
Pikeville
PKY
Pippa
Passes
Barbourville
65
24
Bowling
Green
Mayfield
Murray
Pineville
Williamsburg
Columbia
Campbellsville

ALICE LLOYD COLLEGE

Pippa Passes, Kentucky **www.alc.edu/**

- **Independent** 4-year, founded 1923
- **Rural** 175-acre campus
- **Endowment** $24.6 million
- **Coed** 621 undergraduate students, 95% full-time, 52% women, 48% men
- **Moderately difficult** entrance level, 47% of applicants were admitted

Undergraduates 593 full-time, 28 part-time. Students come from 8 states and territories, 1 other country, 13% are from out of state, 1% African American, 0.6% Asian American or Pacific Islander, 0.2% Hispanic American, 0.2% international, 4% transferred in, 79% live on campus. *Retention:* 63% of 2006 full-time freshmen returned.

Freshmen *Admission:* 1,254 applied, 587 admitted, 177 enrolled. *Average high school GPA:* 3.30. *Test scores:* SAT critical reading scores over 500: 50%; SAT math scores over 500: 33%; SAT writing scores over 500: 50%; ACT scores over 18: 92%; SAT writing scores over 600: 17%; ACT scores over 24: 19%; ACT scores over 30: 1%.

Faculty *Total:* 42, 69% full-time, 45% with terminal degrees. *Student/faculty ratio:* 18:1.

Majors Biological and physical sciences; biology/biological sciences; business administration and management; business/commerce; elementary education; English; English/language arts teacher education; history; interdisciplinary studies; mathematics teacher education; middle school education; physical education teaching and coaching; science teacher education; secondary education; social sciences; social studies teacher education; sport and fitness administration/management.

Academics *Calendar:* semesters. *Degree:* bachelor's. *Special study options:* academic remediation for entering students, advanced placement credit, double majors, independent study, internships, part-time degree program, student-designed majors, study abroad.

Computers on Campus 85 computers/terminals and 550 ports are available on campus for general student use. Students can access the following: campus intranet, computer help desk, free student e-mail accounts, online (class) grades. Campuswide network is available. 85% of college-owned or -operated housing units are wired for high-speed Internet access. Wireless service is available via classrooms, computer centers, computer labs, dorm rooms, libraries, student centers.

Student Life *Housing:* on-campus residence required through senior year. *Options:* men-only, women-only. Campus housing is university owned. *Activities and organizations:* drama/theater group, student-run newspaper, radio station, choral group, Phi Beta Lambda, ALC Scholastic Society, Math/Science Club, Allied Health Sciences Club. *Campus security:* 24-hour patrols, late-night transport/escort service. *Student services:* health clinic, personal/psychological counseling.

Athletics Member NAIA. *Intercollegiate sports:* baseball M (s), basketball M (s)/W (s), cheerleading M/W, golf M/W, softball W, tennis M/W. *Intramural sports:* badminton M/W, basketball M/W, bowling M/W, cross-country running M/W, football M, racquetball M/W, rock climbing M/W, soccer M/W, softball M/W, swimming and diving M/W, table tennis M/W, tennis M/W, volleyball M/W, weight lifting M/W.

Standardized Tests *Required:* SAT or ACT (for admission).

Costs (2008–09) *One-time required fee:* $50. *Tuition:* $0 full-time, $212 per credit hour part-time.

Financial Aid Of all full-time matriculated undergraduates who enrolled in 2005, 589 applied for aid, 318 were judged to have need, 100 had their need fully met. 402 Federal Work-Study jobs (averaging $1600). 241 state and other part-time jobs (averaging $1591). In 2005, 242 non-need-based awards were made. *Average percent of need met:* 60%. *Average financial aid package:* $8678. *Average need-based loan:* $501. *Average need-based gift aid:* $7087. *Average non-need-based aid:* $4970. *Average indebtedness upon graduation:* $3495.

Applying *Options:* deferred entrance. *Required:* high school transcript, minimum 2.25 GPA. *Required for some:* essay or personal statement, 2 letters of recommendation, interview. *Application deadlines:* rolling (freshmen), rolling (transfers). *Notification:* continuous (freshmen), continuous (transfers).

Freshman Application Contact Mr. Bryan Swafford, Director of Admissions, Alice Lloyd College, 100 Purpose Road, Pippa Passes, KY 48144. *Phone:* 606-368-6036. *Fax:* 606-368-6215. *E-mail:* bryanswafford@alc.edu.

ASBURY COLLEGE

Wilmore, Kentucky **www.asbury.edu/**

- **Independent nondenominational** comprehensive, founded 1890
- **Small-town** 400-acre campus with easy access to Lexington
- **Endowment** $33.7 million
- **Coed** 1,325 undergraduate students, 93% full-time, 57% women, 43% men
- **Moderately difficult** entrance level, 63% of applicants were admitted

Undergraduates 1,234 full-time, 91 part-time. Students come from 44 states and territories, 13 other countries, 66% are from out of state, 2% African American, 1% Asian American or Pacific Islander, 2% Hispanic American, 0.4% Native American, 1% international, 6% transferred in, 87% live on campus. *Retention:* 87% of 2006 full-time freshmen returned.

Freshmen *Admission:* 1,354 applied, 848 admitted, 312 enrolled. *Average high school GPA:* 3.57. *Test scores:* SAT critical reading scores over 500: 83%; SAT math scores over 500: 82%; ACT scores over 18: 97%; SAT critical reading scores over 600: 50%; SAT math scores over 600: 36%; ACT scores over 24: 56%; SAT critical reading scores over 700: 13%; SAT math scores over 700: 7%; ACT scores over 30: 14%.

Faculty *Total:* 139, 57% full-time, 53% with terminal degrees. *Student/faculty ratio:* 11:1.

Majors Accounting; ancient Near Eastern and biblical languages; applied mathematics; art teacher education; biblical studies; biochemistry; biology/biological sciences; business/commerce; chemistry; dramatic/theater arts; elementary education; English; equestrian studies; fine/studio arts; French; health and physical education; health/medical preparatory programs related; history; journalism; mathematics; mathematics and statistics related; middle school education; missionary studies and missiology; music; music management and merchandising; music teacher education; physical education teaching and coaching; physical sciences; psychology; psychology related; radio and television broadcasting technology; religious education; social sciences; social work; sociology; Spanish; speech and rhetoric; sport and fitness administration/management; youth ministry.

Academics *Calendar:* semesters. *Degrees:* bachelor's and master's. *Special study options:* academic remediation for entering students, adult/continuing education programs, advanced placement credit, double majors, English as a second language, internships, part-time degree program, study abroad, summer session for credit. *ROTC:* Army (c), Air Force (c). *Unusual degree programs:* 3-2 engineering with University of Kentucky.

Computers on Campus 200 computers/terminals are available on campus for general student use. Students can access the following: computer help desk, free student e-mail accounts, online (class) registration, online (class) schedules. Campuswide network is available. 100% of college-owned or -operated housing units are wired for high-speed Internet access. Wireless service is available via libraries, student centers.

Student Life *Housing:* on-campus residence required through senior year. *Options:* men-only, women-only, disabled students. Campus housing is university owned. Freshman campus housing is guaranteed. *Activities and organizations:* drama/theater group, student-run newspaper, radio and television station, choral group, Fellowship of Christian Athletes, Impact (community service), Christian Service Association, ministry teams, Student-Faculty Council. *Campus security:* 24-hour emergency response devices, late-night transport/escort service, controlled dormitory access, late night security personnel. *Student services:* health clinic, personal/psychological counseling.

Athletics Member NAIA, NCCAA. *Intercollegiate sports:* baseball M (s), basketball M (s)/W (s), cross-country running M (s)/W (s), soccer M (s)/W (s), swimming and diving M (s)/W (s), tennis M (s)/W (s), volleyball W (s). *Intramural sports:* basketball M/W, football M/W, golf M/W, racquetball M/W, soccer M/W, softball M/W, ultimate Frisbee M/W, volleyball M/W.

Standardized Tests *Required:* SAT or ACT (for admission).

Costs (2008–09) *Comprehensive fee:* $27,827 includes full-time tuition ($22,242), mandatory fees ($171), and room and board ($5414). Part-time tuition: $855 per semester hour. *College room only:* $3206.

Financial Aid Of all full-time matriculated undergraduates who enrolled in 2007, 980 applied for aid, 833 were judged to have need, 227 had their need fully met. 512 Federal Work-Study jobs (averaging $1078). In 2007, 127 non-need-based awards were made. *Average percent of need met:* 80%. *Average financial aid package:* $15,957. *Average need-based loan:* $3976. *Average need-based gift aid:* $10,053. *Average non-need-based aid:* $11,160. *Average indebtedness upon graduation:* $23,690.

Applying *Options:* electronic application, early admission, deferred entrance. *Application fee:* $30. *Required:* essay or personal statement, high school transcript, minimum 2.5 GPA, 2 letters of recommendation. *Required for some:*

interview. *Application deadlines:* rolling (freshmen), rolling (transfers). *Notification:* continuous (freshmen), continuous (transfers).

Freshman Application Contact Ronald Anderson, Director of Enrollment Management, Asbury College, 1 Macklem Drive, Wilmore, KY 40390. *Phone:* 859-858-3511 Ext. 2142. *Toll-free phone:* 800-888-1818. *Fax:* 859-858-3921. *E-mail:* admissions@asbury.edu.

See page 1030 for the College Close-Up.

BECKFIELD COLLEGE

Florence, Kentucky www.beckfield.edu/

Freshman Application Contact Mrs. Leah Boerger, Director of Admissions, Beckfield College, 16 Spiral Drive, Florence, KY 41042. *Phone:* 859-371-9393. *E-mail:* lboerger@beckfield.edu.

BELLARMINE UNIVERSITY

Louisville, Kentucky www.bellarmine.edu/

- **Independent Roman Catholic** comprehensive, founded 1950
- **Suburban** 144-acre campus
- **Endowment** $30.2 million
- **Coed** 2,325 undergraduate students, 82% full-time, 64% women, 36% men
- **Moderately difficult** entrance level, 63% of applicants were admitted

Undergraduates 1,911 full-time, 414 part-time. Students come from 30 states and territories, 29 other countries, 27% are from out of state, 3% African American, 2% Asian American or Pacific Islander, 2% Hispanic American, 0.3% Native American, 3% international, 3% transferred in, 39% live on campus. *Retention:* 77% of 2006 full-time freshmen returned.

Freshmen *Admission:* 3,481 applied, 2,187 admitted, 569 enrolled. *Average high school GPA:* 3.5. *Test scores:* SAT critical reading scores over 500: 74%; SAT math scores over 500: 72%; ACT scores over 18: 100%; SAT critical reading scores over 600: 27%; SAT math scores over 600: 26%; ACT scores over 24: 53%; SAT critical reading scores over 700: 3%; SAT math scores over 700: 1%; ACT scores over 30: 5%.

Faculty *Total:* 276, 47% full-time, 55% with terminal degrees. *Student/faculty ratio:* 13:1.

Majors Accounting; actuarial science; biochemistry/biophysics and molecular biology; biology/biological sciences; business/commerce; chemistry; clinical laboratory science/medical technology; clinical/medical laboratory science and allied professions related; communication/speech communication and rhetoric; computer and information sciences; computer engineering; criminal justice/safety; economics; elementary education; English; fine/studio arts; foreign languages related; history; international/global studies; liberal arts and sciences/liberal studies; mathematics; middle school education; music; music related; nursing (registered nurse training); nursing science; philosophy; political science and government; psychology; respiratory care therapy; sociology; special education; theology.

Academics *Calendar:* semesters. *Degrees:* certificates, bachelor's, master's, doctoral, and postbachelor's certificates. *Special study options:* accelerated degree program, adult/continuing education programs, advanced placement credit, double majors, honors programs, independent study, internships, off-campus study, part-time degree program, services for LD students, student-designed majors, study abroad, summer session for credit. *ROTC:* Army (c), Air Force (c).

Computers on Campus 430 computers/terminals and 430 ports are available on campus for general student use. Students can access the following: campus intranet, computer help desk, free student e-mail accounts, online (class) registration, online (class) schedules. Campuswide network is available. 100% of college-owned or -operated housing units are wired for high-speed Internet access. Wireless service is available via classrooms, computer centers, computer labs, dorm rooms, learning centers, libraries, student centers.

Student Life *Housing:* on-campus residence required through junior year. *Options:* coed, men-only, women-only, disabled students. Campus housing is university owned. Freshman campus housing is guaranteed. *Activities and organizations:* drama/theater group, student-run newspaper, television station, choral group, Student government, Delta Sigma Pi, Fellowship of Christian Athletes, Campus ministry, Bellarmine Activities Council, national fraternities, national sororities. *Campus security:* 24-hour emergency response devices and patrols, student patrols, late-night transport/escort service, controlled dormitory access, 24-hour locked residence hall entrances, security cameras. *Student services:* health clinic, personal/psychological counseling.

Athletics Member NCAA. All Division II except lacrosse (Division I). *Intercollegiate sports:* baseball M (s), basketball M (s)/W (s), bowling M/W, cross-country running M (s)/W (s), field hockey W (s), golf M (s)/W (s), lacrosse M (s), soccer M (s)/W (s), softball W (s), swimming and diving M (c)/W (c), tennis M (s)/W (s), track and field M (s)/W (s), volleyball W (s). *Intramural sports:* basketball M/W, football M/W, golf M/W, soccer M/W, table tennis M/W, tennis M/W, volleyball M/W, weight lifting M/W.

Standardized Tests *Required:* SAT or ACT (for admission).

Costs (2008–09) *Comprehensive fee:* $36,636 includes full-time tuition ($27,200), mandatory fees ($1030), and room and board ($8406). Part-time tuition: $640 per credit. *Required fees:* $35 per course part-time. *College room only:* $5228.

Financial Aid Of all full-time matriculated undergraduates who enrolled in 2006, 1,472 applied for aid, 1,156 were judged to have need, 296 had their need fully met. In 2006, 502 non-need-based awards were made. *Average percent of need met:* 76%. *Average financial aid package:* $19,000. *Average need-based loan:* $4064. *Average need-based gift aid:* $12,392. *Average non-need-based aid:* $9829. *Average indebtedness upon graduation:* $15,295.

Applying *Options:* electronic application, early admission, early action, deferred entrance. *Application fee:* $25. *Required:* high school transcript, minimum 2.5 GPA, letters of recommendation. *Required for some:* essay or personal statement. *Recommended:* interview. *Application deadlines:* 8/15 (freshmen), 8/15 (transfers), 11/1 (early action). *Notification:* continuous (freshmen), continuous (transfers), 12/1 (early action).

Freshman Application Contact Mr. Timothy A. Sturgeon, Dean of Admission, Bellarmine University, 2001 Newburg Road, Louisville, KY 40205-0671. *Phone:* 502-452-8131. *Toll-free phone:* 800-274-4723 Ext. 8131. *Fax:* 502-452-8002. *E-mail:* admissions@bellarmine.edu.

BEREA COLLEGE

Berea, Kentucky www.berea.edu/

- **Independent** 4-year, founded 1855
- **Small-town** 140-acre campus
- **Endowment** $1.1 billion
- **Coed** 1,582 undergraduate students, 97% full-time, 60% women, 40% men
- **Very difficult** entrance level, 29% of applicants were admitted

Undergraduates 1,532 full-time, 50 part-time. Students come from 40 states and territories, 51 other countries, 57% are from out of state, 17% African American, 2% Asian American or Pacific Islander, 2% Hispanic American, 0.8% Native American, 7% international, 1% transferred in, 87% live on campus. *Retention:* 83% of 2006 full-time freshmen returned.

Freshmen *Admission:* 2,083 applied, 597 admitted, 421 enrolled. *Average high school GPA:* 3.42. *Test scores:* SAT critical reading scores over 500: 64%; SAT math scores over 500: 71%; SAT writing scores over 500: 61%; ACT scores over 18: 99%; SAT critical reading scores over 600: 25%; SAT math scores over 600: 29%; SAT writing scores over 600: 17%; ACT scores over 24: 46%; SAT critical reading scores over 700: 4%; SAT math scores over 700: 4%; SAT writing scores over 700: 4%; ACT scores over 30: 4%.

Faculty *Total:* 171, 75% full-time. *Student/faculty ratio:* 11:1.

Majors Acting/directing; African-American/Black studies; agriculture; art; biology/biological sciences; business administration and management; chemistry; economics; education; elementary education; English; French; German; history; human development and family studies; industrial technology; mathematics; middle school education; music; nursing (registered nurse training); philosophy; physics; political science and government; psychology; religious studies; sociology; Spanish; women's studies.

Academics *Calendar:* 4-1-4. *Degree:* bachelor's. *Special study options:* academic remediation for entering students, advanced placement credit, double majors, honors programs, independent study, internships, off-campus study, services for LD students, student-designed majors, study abroad, summer session for credit. *Unusual degree programs:* 3-2 engineering with Washington University in St. Louis, University of Kentucky.

Computers on Campus 20 computers/terminals and 850 ports are available on campus for general student use. Students can access the following: campus intranet, computer help desk, free student e-mail accounts, online (class) grades, online (class) registration, online (class) schedules. Campuswide network is available. 100% of college-owned or -operated housing units are wired for high-speed Internet access. Wireless service is available via libraries, student centers.

Student Life *Housing:* on-campus residence required through senior year. *Options:* men-only, women-only. Campus housing is university owned. Freshman campus housing is guaranteed. *Activities and organizations:* drama/theater group, student-run newspaper, choral group, Campus Activities Board, Cosmopolitan Club, CELTS (Center for Excellence in Learning through Service), flag football and basketball intramurals, Baptist College Ministry. *Campus security:* 24-hour emergency response devices and patrols, late-night transport/escort service, controlled dormitory access, crime prevention programs. *Student services:* health clinic, personal/psychological counseling, women's center.

Athletics Member NAIA. *Intercollegiate sports:* baseball M, basketball M/W, cross-country running M/W, golf M, soccer M/W, softball W, swimming and diving M/W, tennis M/W, track and field M/W, volleyball W. *Intramural sports:* basketball M/W, football M/W, racquetball M/W, soccer M/W, softball M/W, ultimate Frisbee M/W, volleyball M/W.

Standardized Tests *Required:* SAT or ACT (for admission).

Costs (2007–08) *Comprehensive fee:* includes mandatory fees ($790) and room and board ($5492). financial aid is provided to all students for tuition costs.

Financial Aid Of all full-time matriculated undergraduates who enrolled in 2007, 1,527 applied for aid, 1,527 were judged to have need, 101 had their need fully met. 1,326 Federal Work-Study jobs (averaging $1789). 241 state and other part-time jobs (averaging $1817). *Average percent of need met:* 95%. *Average financial aid package:* $2904. *Average need-based loan:* $384. *Average need-based gift aid:* $27,254. *Average indebtedness upon graduation:* $7705. *Financial aid deadline:* 8/1.

Applying *Options:* electronic application. *Required:* essay or personal statement, high school transcript, interview, financial aid application. *Recommended:* 2 letters of recommendation. *Application deadlines:* 4/30 (freshmen), rolling (transfers). *Notification:* continuous (freshmen), continuous (transfers).

Freshman Application Contact Ms. Erika Smith, Director of Admissions, Berea College, CPO 2220, Berea, KY 40404. *Phone:* 859-985-3500. *Toll-free phone:* 800-326-5948. *Fax:* 859-985-3512. *E-mail:* admissions@berea.edu.

BRESCIA UNIVERSITY

Owensboro, Kentucky **www.brescia.edu/**

Director of Admissions Sr. Mary Austin Blank, Dean of Enrollment, Brescia University, 717 Frederica Street, Owensboro, KY 42301. *Phone:* 270-686-4241 Ext. 241. *Toll-free phone:* 877-273-7242.

CAMPBELLSVILLE UNIVERSITY

Campbellsville, Kentucky **www.campbellsville.edu/**

- **Independent** comprehensive, founded 1906, affiliated with Kentucky Baptist Convention
- **Small-town** 80-acre campus
- **Endowment** $6.1 million
- **Coed**
- **Moderately difficult** entrance level

Faculty *Student/faculty ratio:* 13:1.

Academics *Calendar:* semesters. *Degrees:* certificates, associate, bachelor's, master's, and postbachelor's certificates.

Student Life *Campus security:* 24-hour emergency response devices and patrols, student patrols, late-night transport/escort service, controlled dormitory access.

Athletics Member NAIA.

Standardized Tests *Required:* SAT or ACT (for admission).

Costs (2007–08) *Comprehensive fee:* $23,490 includes full-time tuition ($16,880), mandatory fees ($380), and room and board ($6230). Part-time tuition: $703 per credit. *Room and board:* Room and board charges vary according to board plan and housing facility.

Financial Aid Of all full-time matriculated undergraduates who enrolled in 2006, 1,091 applied for aid, 983 were judged to have need, 178 had their need fully met. 312 Federal Work-Study jobs (averaging $1486). 80 state and other part-time jobs (averaging $1950). In 2006, 88 non-need-based awards were made. *Average percent of need met:* 72. *Average financial aid package:* $13,545. *Average need-based loan:* $3240. *Average need-based gift aid:* $10,712. *Average non-need-based aid:* $7921. *Average indebtedness upon graduation:* $14,524.

Applying *Options:* electronic application, deferred entrance. *Application fee:* $20. *Required:* high school transcript, minimum 2.0 GPA. *Recommended:* essay or personal statement, minimum 3.0 GPA, letters of recommendation, interview.

Freshman Application Contact Mr. David Walters, Vice President for Admissions and Student Services, Campbellsville University, 1 University Drive, Campbellsville, KY 42718-2799. *Phone:* 270-789-5220 Ext. 5007. *Toll-free phone:* 800-264-6014. *Fax:* 270-789-5071. *E-mail:* admissions@campbellsville.edu.

CENTRE COLLEGE

Danville, Kentucky **www.centre.edu/**

- **Independent** 4-year, founded 1819, affiliated with Presbyterian Church (U.S.A.)
- **Small-town** 100-acre campus
- **Endowment** $149.9 million
- **Coed** 1,189 undergraduate students, 100% full-time, 55% women, 45% men
- **Very difficult** entrance level, 61% of applicants were admitted

Undergraduates 1,186 full-time, 3 part-time. Students come from 37 states and territories, 16 other countries, 36% are from out of state, 3% African American, 2% Asian American or Pacific Islander, 2% Hispanic American, 0.3% Native American, 2% international, 0.5% transferred in, 95% live on campus. *Retention:* 94% of 2006 full-time freshmen returned.

Freshmen *Admission:* 2,159 applied, 1,312 admitted, 316 enrolled. *Average high school GPA:* 3.6. *Test scores:* SAT critical reading scores over 500: 94%; SAT math scores over 500: 94%; ACT scores over 18: 100%; SAT critical reading scores over 600: 63%; SAT math scores over 600: 66%; ACT scores over 24: 92%; SAT critical reading scores over 700: 25%; SAT math scores over 700: 10%; ACT scores over 30: 32%.

Faculty *Total:* 125, 82% full-time, 91% with terminal degrees. *Student/faculty ratio:* 11:1.

Majors Anthropology; art; art history, criticism and conservation; biochemistry; biology/biological sciences; chemistry; classics and languages, literatures and linguistics; computer science; dramatic/theater arts; economics; elementary education; English; French; German; history; international relations and affairs; mathematics; molecular biology; music; philosophy; physics; physiological psychology/psychobiology; political science and government; psychology; religious studies; secondary education; sociology; Spanish.

Academics *Calendar:* 4-1-4. *Degree:* bachelor's. *Special study options:* advanced placement credit, double majors, independent study, internships, off-campus study, part-time degree program, services for LD students, student-designed majors, study abroad. *ROTC:* Army (c), Air Force (c). *Unusual degree programs:* 3-2 engineering with Washington University in St. Louis, Columbia University, Vanderbilt University, University of Kentucky.

Computers on Campus 150 computers/terminals are available on campus for general student use. Students can access the following: campus intranet, computer help desk, free student e-mail accounts, online (class) grades, online (class) registration, online (class) schedules. Campuswide network is available. 100% of college-owned or -operated housing units are wired for high-speed Internet access. Wireless service is available via classrooms, computer centers, computer labs, dorm rooms, learning centers, libraries, student centers.

Student Life *Housing:* on-campus residence required through sophomore year. *Options:* coed, men-only, women-only. Campus housing is university owned. Freshman campus housing is guaranteed. *Activities and organizations:* drama/theater group, student-run newspaper, choral group, CARE (Centre Action Reaches Everyone), Christian Fellowship, College Democrats and Republicans, Student Congress, Outdoors Club, national fraternities, national sororities. *Campus security:* 24-hour emergency response devices and patrols, late-night transport/escort service, controlled dormitory access. *Student services:* health clinic, personal/psychological counseling.

Athletics Member NCAA. All Division III. *Intercollegiate sports:* baseball M, basketball M/W, cheerleading W, cross-country running M/W, field hockey W, football M, golf M/W, soccer M/W, softball W, swimming and diving M/W, tennis M/W, track and field M/W, volleyball W. *Intramural sports:* badminton M/W, basketball M/W, bowling M/W, equestrian sports M/W, football M/W, golf M/W, racquetball M/W, soccer M/W, softball M/W, swimming and diving M/W, table tennis M/W, tennis M/W, track and field M/W, ultimate Frisbee M/W, volleyball M/W, weight lifting M/W, wrestling M.

Standardized Tests *Required:* SAT or ACT (for admission).

Costs (2007–08) *Comprehensive fee:* $35,000. Part-time tuition: $1010 per credit hour. Part-time tuition and fees vary according to course load. *Payment plan:* installment. *Waivers:* employees or children of employees.

Financial Aid Of all full-time matriculated undergraduates who enrolled in 2007, 825 applied for aid, 676 were judged to have need, 239 had their need fully met. 285 Federal Work-Study jobs (averaging $1570). 31 state and other part-time jobs (averaging $2060). In 2007, 446 non-need-based awards were made. *Average percent of need met:* 88%. *Average financial aid package:* $21,616. *Average need-based loan:* $4623. *Average need-based gift aid:* $18,447. *Average non-need-based aid:* $11,857. *Average indebtedness upon graduation:* $17,600. *Financial aid deadline:* 3/1.

Applying *Options:* electronic application, early admission, early action, deferred entrance. *Application fee:* $40. *Required:* essay or personal statement, high school transcript, 1 letter of recommendation. *Recommended:* interview. *Application deadlines:* 2/1 (freshmen), 6/1 (transfers), 12/1 (early action). *Notification:* 3/15 (freshmen), continuous until 7/1 (transfers), 1/15 (early action).

Freshman Application Contact Mr. Bob Nesmith, Director of Admission, Centre College, 600 West Walnut Street, Danville, KY 40422-1394. *Phone:* 859-238-5350. *Toll-free phone:* 800-423-6236. *Fax:* 859-238-5373. *E-mail:* admission@centre.edu.

CLEAR CREEK BAPTIST BIBLE COLLEGE

Pineville, Kentucky **www.ccbbc.edu/**

- **Independent Southern Baptist** 4-year, founded 1926
- **Rural** 700-acre campus
- **Coed, primarily men**
- **Noncompetitive** entrance level

Faculty *Student/faculty ratio:* 13:1.

Academics *Calendar:* semesters. *Degree:* certificates, diplomas, and bachelor's.

Student Life *Campus security:* 24-hour emergency response devices, student patrols.

Costs (2007–08) *Comprehensive fee:* $8572 includes full-time tuition ($4972), mandatory fees ($290), and room and board ($3310). Part-time tuition: $226 per semester hour. *Required fees:* $80 per term part-time. *College room only:* $1870.

Financial Aid Of all full-time matriculated undergraduates who enrolled in 2007, 137 applied for aid, 135 were judged to have need. 31 Federal Work-Study jobs (averaging $1228). In 2007, 13 non-need-based awards were made. *Average percent of need met:* 57. *Average financial aid package:* $5586. *Average non-need-based aid:* $595.

Applying *Options:* electronic application, deferred entrance. *Application fee:* $40. *Required:* essay or personal statement, 4 letters of recommendation. *Recommended:* high school transcript, interview.

Freshman Application Contact Mr. Billy Howell, Clear Creek Baptist Bible College, 300 Clear Creek Road, Pineville, KY 40977-9754. *Phone:* 606-337-3196. *Fax:* 606-337-1631. *E-mail:* bhowell@ccbbc.edu.

EASTERN KENTUCKY UNIVERSITY

Richmond, Kentucky **www.eku.edu/**

- **State-supported** comprehensive, founded 1906
- **Small-town** 500-acre campus with easy access to Lexington
- **Endowment** $55.6 million
- **Coed** 13,659 undergraduate students, 81% full-time, 59% women, 41% men
- **Noncompetitive** entrance level, 69% of applicants were admitted

Undergraduates 11,025 full-time, 2,634 part-time. Students come from 46 states and territories, 38 other countries, 13% are from out of state, 5% African American, 0.9% Asian American or Pacific Islander, 0.8% Hispanic American, 0.3% Native American, 0.9% international, 8% transferred in. *Retention:* 62% of 2006 full-time freshmen returned.

Freshmen *Admission:* 6,928 applied, 4,781 admitted, 2,493 enrolled.

Faculty *Total:* 1,039, 56% full-time, 45% with terminal degrees. *Student/faculty ratio:* 17:1.

Majors Accounting; agricultural business and management; agricultural production; agriculture; agriculture and agriculture operations related; airline pilot and flight crew; anthropology; applied mathematics; architectural engineering technology; art; art teacher education; audiology and speech-language pathology; biology/biological sciences; broadcast journalism; business administration and management; business/commerce; business/managerial economics; business teacher education; chemistry; child care/guidance; child care provision; clinical laboratory science/medical technology; clinical/medical laboratory technology; commercial and advertising art; community health liaison; community health services counseling; computer and information sciences; computer engineering technology; computer maintenance technology; computer science; computer technology/computer systems technology; construction engineering technology; consumer merchandising/retailing management; dietetics; dietician assistant; drafting; drafting and design technology; dramatic/theater arts; ecology; economics; education; education (specific subject areas) related; electrical, electronic and communications engineering technology; elementary education; engineering related; English; environmental engineering technology; environmental health; environmental studies; family and community services; family and consumer sciences/home economics teacher education; family and consumer sciences/human sciences; farm and ranch management; fashion merchandising; finance; fine/studio arts; forensic science and technology; French; general studies; geography; geology/earth science; health/health care administration; health teacher education; history; home furnishings; home furnishings and equipment installation; housing and human environments; human development and family studies; information science/studies; insurance; journalism; kindergarten/preschool education; management information systems; marketing/marketing management; mass communication/media; mathematics; medical/clinical assistant; medical microbiology and bacteriology; medical office management; middle school education; music; music teacher education; natural sciences; nursing related; occupational therapy; office management; philosophy; physical education teaching and coaching; physical sciences; physics; political science and government; pre-engineering; psychology; public relations, advertising, and applied communication related; public relations/image management; quality control technology; radio and television; real estate; science teacher education; secondary education; security and loss prevention; sign language interpretation and translation; social work; sociology; Spanish; special education; special education (hearing impaired); special education (speech or language impaired); speech and rhetoric; speech therapy; statistics; technical teacher education; technology/industrial arts teacher education; trade and industrial teacher education; transportation technology; wildlife and wildlands science and management.

Academics *Calendar:* semesters. *Degrees:* associate, bachelor's, master's, post-master's, and postbachelor's certificates. *Special study options:* academic remediation for entering students, accelerated degree program, adult/continuing education programs, advanced placement credit, cooperative education, distance learning, double majors, English as a second language, external degree program, honors programs, independent study, internships, part-time degree program, services for LD students, student-designed majors, study abroad, summer session for credit. *ROTC:* Army (b), Air Force (c). *Unusual degree programs:* 3-2 engineering with University of Kentucky, Auburn University.

Computers on Campus 1,200 computers/terminals are available on campus for general student use. Students can access the following: online (class) registration. Campuswide network is available.

Student Life *Housing options:* coed, men-only, women-only. Campus housing is university owned. Freshman campus housing is guaranteed. *Activities and organizations:* drama/theater group, student-run newspaper, radio station, choral group, marching band, Honor Society, Regular Society, national fraternities, national sororities. *Campus security:* 24-hour emergency response devices and patrols, student patrols, late-night transport/escort service, controlled dormitory access. *Student services:* health clinic, personal/psychological counseling.

Athletics Member NCAA. All Division I. *Intercollegiate sports:* baseball M (s), basketball M (s)/W (s), cheerleading M/W, cross-country running M (s)/W (s), football M (s), golf M (s)/W (s), softball W (s), tennis M (s)/W (s), track and field M (s)/W (s), volleyball W (s). *Intramural sports:* badminton M/W, basketball M/W, fencing M (c)/W (c), football M/W, golf M/W, ice hockey M (c), racquetball M/W, rock climbing M (c)/W (c), soccer M (c)/W (c), softball M/W, tennis M/W, track and field M/W, ultimate Frisbee M/W, volleyball M/W, weight lifting M/W.

Standardized Tests *Required:* SAT or ACT (for admission).

Costs (2007–08) *Tuition:* state resident $5682 full-time, $237 per credit hour part-time; nonresident $15,382 full-time, $641 per credit hour part-time. Part-time tuition and fees vary according to course load. *Room and board:* $5478; room only: $2794. Room and board charges vary according to board plan and housing facility. *Payment plan:* deferred payment. *Waivers:* senior citizens and employees or children of employees.

Financial Aid Of all full-time matriculated undergraduates who enrolled in 2007, 8,127 applied for aid, 6,521 were judged to have need, 698 had their need fully met. 1,000 Federal Work-Study jobs (averaging $1800). 1,000 state and other part-time jobs (averaging $1800). In 2007, 1118 non-need-based awards were made. *Average percent of need met:* 82%. *Average financial aid package:* $8006. *Average need-based loan:* $3736. *Average need-based gift aid:* $6208. *Average non-need-based aid:* $4628. *Average indebtedness upon graduation:* $16,836.

Applying *Options:* electronic application, deferred entrance. *Application fee:* $30. *Required:* high school transcript, minimum 2.0 GPA. *Application deadlines:* 8/1 (freshmen), rolling (transfers). *Notification:* continuous (freshmen), continuous (transfers).

Freshman Application Contact Mr. Stephen Byrn, Director of Admissions, Eastern Kentucky University, SSB CPO 54, 521 Lancaster Avenue, Richmond, KY 40475-3102. *Phone:* 859-622-2106. *Toll-free phone:* 800-465-9191. *Fax:* 859-622-8024. *E-mail:* admissions@eku.edu.

GEORGETOWN COLLEGE

Georgetown, Kentucky **www.georgetowncollege.edu/**

- **Independent** comprehensive, founded 1829, affiliated with Baptist Church
- **Suburban** 110-acre campus with easy access to Cincinnati
- **Endowment** $43.8 million
- **Coed** 1,368 undergraduate students, 96% full-time, 57% women, 43% men
- **Moderately difficult** entrance level, 85% of applicants were admitted

Undergraduates 1,315 full-time, 53 part-time. Students come from 29 states and territories, 10 other countries, 14% are from out of state, 4% African American, 0.5% Asian American or Pacific Islander, 0.7% Hispanic American, 0.1% Native American, 1% international, 2% transferred in, 92% live on campus. *Retention:* 79% of 2006 full-time freshmen returned.

Freshmen *Admission:* 1,452 applied, 1,227 admitted, 368 enrolled. *Average high school GPA:* 3.50. *Test scores:* SAT critical reading scores over 500: 84%; SAT math scores over 500: 72%; ACT scores over 18: 98%; SAT critical reading scores over 600: 24%; SAT math scores over 600: 28%; ACT scores over 24: 43%; SAT critical reading scores over 700: 8%; ACT scores over 30: 7%.

Faculty *Total:* 162, 69% full-time. *Student/faculty ratio:* 12:1.

Majors Accounting; American studies; athletic training; biology/biological sciences; business administration and management; chemistry; communication and media related; computer and information sciences; dramatic/theater arts; ecology; economics; elementary education; English; European studies; fine/studio arts; French; German; history; kinesiology and exercise science; liberal arts and sciences/liberal studies; mathematics; middle school education; multi-/interdisciplinary studies related; music; music teacher education; philosophy; physics; political science and government; psychology; religious studies; sociology; Spanish.

Academics *Calendar:* semesters. *Degrees:* bachelor's and master's. *Special study options:* advanced placement credit, cooperative education, double majors, honors programs, independent study, internships, off-campus study, part-time degree program, student-designed majors, study abroad, summer session for credit. *ROTC:* Army (c), Air Force (c). *Unusual degree programs:* 3-2 engineering with University of Kentucky; nursing with University of Kentucky.

Computers on Campus 175 computers/terminals are available on campus for general student use. Students can access the following: campus intranet, computer help desk, free student e-mail accounts, online (class) grades, online (class) registration, online (class) schedules. Campuswide network is available. 100% of college-owned or -operated housing units are wired for high-speed Internet access. Wireless service is available via classrooms, computer centers, computer labs, dorm rooms, learning centers, libraries.

Student Life *Housing:* on-campus residence required through senior year. *Options:* men-only, women-only. Campus housing is university owned. Freshman campus housing is guaranteed. *Activities and organizations:* drama/theater group, student-run newspaper, radio station, choral group, Campus Ministries, Association of Georgetown Students, Harper-Gatton Leadership Center, President's Ambassadors, Phi Beta Lambda, national fraternities, national sororities. *Campus security:* 24-hour patrols, late-night transport/escort service. *Student services:* health clinic, personal/psychological counseling.

Athletics Member NAIA. *Intercollegiate sports:* baseball M (s), basketball M (s)/W (s), cheerleading W (s), cross-country running M (s)/W (s), football M (s), golf M (s)/W (s), soccer M (s)/W (s), softball W (s), tennis M (s)/W (s), track and field M (s)/W (s), volleyball W (s). *Intramural sports:* basketball M/W, football M/W, golf M/W, racquetball M/W, soccer M/W, softball M/W, table tennis M/W, tennis M/W, ultimate Frisbee M/W, volleyball M/W.

Standardized Tests *Required:* SAT or ACT (for admission). *Recommended:* ACT (for admission).

Costs (2007–08) *Comprehensive fee:* $28,740 includes full-time tuition ($22,360) and room and board ($6380). Part-time tuition: $930 per hour. *College room only:* $3080. Room and board charges vary according to board plan and housing facility. *Payment plan:* deferred payment. *Waivers:* children of alumni and employees or children of employees.

Financial Aid Of all full-time matriculated undergraduates who enrolled in 2007, 1,053 applied for aid, 924 were judged to have need, 448 had their need fully met. 503 Federal Work-Study jobs (averaging $1081). In 2007, 390 non-need-based awards were made. *Average percent of need met:* 87%. *Average financial aid package:* $21,039. *Average need-based loan:* $4834. *Average need-based gift aid:* $17,461. *Average non-need-based aid:* $11,149. *Average indebtedness upon graduation:* $21,969.

Applying *Options:* electronic application, deferred entrance. *Application fee:* $30. *Required:* high school transcript, minimum 2.5 GPA. *Required for some:* essay or personal statement, letters of recommendation, interview. *Application deadlines:* 8/1 (freshmen), rolling (transfers). *Notification:* continuous until 10/1 (freshmen), continuous (out-of-state freshmen), continuous (transfers).

Freshman Application Contact Mr. Johnnie Johnson, Director of Admissions, Georgetown College, 400 East College Street, Georgetown, KY 40324. *Phone:* 502-863-8009. *Toll-free phone:* 800-788-9985. *Fax:* 502-868-7733. *E-mail:* admissions@georgetowncollege.edu.

ITT TECHNICAL INSTITUTE

Lexington, Kentucky **www.itt-tech.edu/**

- **Proprietary** 4-year, founded 2006, part of ITT Educational Services, Inc
- **Coed**

Academics *Degrees:* associate and bachelor's.

Standardized Tests *Required:* Wonderlic aptitude test (for admission).

Applying *Application fee:* $100. *Required:* high school transcript, interview. *Recommended:* letters of recommendation.

Freshman Application Contact Mr. George Nosko, Director of Recruitment, ITT Technical Institute, 2473 Fortune Drive, Suite 180, Lexington, KY 40509. *Phone:* 859-246-3300.

ITT TECHNICAL INSTITUTE

Louisville, Kentucky **www.itt-tech.edu/**

- **Proprietary** primarily 2-year, founded 1993, part of ITT Educational Services, Inc
- **Suburban** campus
- **Coed**
- **Minimally difficult** entrance level

Academics *Calendar:* quarters. *Degrees:* associate and bachelor's.

Standardized Tests *Required:* Wonderlic aptitude test (for admission).

Applying *Options:* deferred entrance. *Application fee:* $100. *Required:* high school transcript, interview. *Recommended:* letters of recommendation.

Freshman Application Contact Mr. Michael Alcorn, Director of Recruitment, ITT Technical Institute, 10509 Timberwood Circle, Louisville, KY 40223. *Phone:* 502-327-7424. *Toll-free phone:* 888-790-7427.

KENTUCKY CHRISTIAN UNIVERSITY

Grayson, Kentucky **www.kcu.edu/**

- **Independent** comprehensive, founded 1919, affiliated with Christian Churches and Churches of Christ
- **Rural** 124-acre campus
- **Endowment** $6.3 million
- **Coed** 613 undergraduate students, 91% full-time, 51% women, 49% men
- **Moderately difficult** entrance level, 66% of applicants were admitted

Undergraduates 555 full-time, 58 part-time. Students come from 18 states and territories, 7 other countries, 52% are from out of state, 6% African American, 0.3% Asian American or Pacific Islander, 1% Hispanic American, 0.3% Native American, 3% international, 6% transferred in, 74% live on campus. *Retention:* 68% of 2006 full-time freshmen returned.

Freshmen *Admission:* 443 applied, 292 admitted, 176 enrolled. *Average high school GPA:* 3.06. *Test scores:* SAT critical reading scores over 500: 27%; SAT math scores over 500: 47%; ACT scores over 18: 66%; SAT critical reading scores over 600: 7%; SAT math scores over 600: 7%; ACT scores over 24: 15%; ACT scores over 30: 1%.

Faculty *Total:* 58, 59% full-time, 47% with terminal degrees. *Student/faculty ratio:* 12:1.

Majors Adult and continuing education; biblical studies; business administration and management; counseling psychology; early childhood education; English/language arts teacher education; history; humanities; intercultural/multicultural and diversity studies; interdisciplinary studies; middle school education; music management and merchandising; music performance; music teacher education; nursing (registered nurse training); religious/sacred music; social studies teacher education; social work; youth ministry.

Academics *Calendar:* semesters. *Degrees:* associate, bachelor's, and master's. *Special study options:* academic remediation for entering students, accelerated degree program, advanced placement credit, cooperative education, distance learning, double majors, independent study, internships, off-campus study, part-time degree program, services for LD students, study abroad, summer session for credit.

Computers on Campus 50 computers/terminals are available on campus for general student use. Students can access the following: computer help desk, free student e-mail accounts, online (class) registration. Campuswide network is available. Wireless service is available via classrooms, dorm rooms, learning centers, libraries, student centers.

Student Life *Housing:* on-campus residence required through senior year. *Options:* men-only, women-only, disabled students. Campus housing is university owned. *Activities and organizations:* drama/theater group, choral group, Global Missions Awareness, Phi Chi Delta, Student Nurses Association, Laos Protos, Collegiate Music Educators National Conference. *Campus security:* 24-hour emergency response devices, late-night transport/escort service, controlled dormitory access, patrols by trained security personnel 6 p.m. to 6 a.m. *Student services:* health clinic, personal/psychological counseling.

Athletics Member NAIA, NCCAA. *Intercollegiate sports:* basketball M/W, cheerleading W, cross-country running M/W, football M/W, soccer M/W, volleyball W. *Intramural sports:* basketball M/W, football M/W, racquetball M/W, softball M/W, table tennis M/W, volleyball M/W.

Standardized Tests *Recommended:* SAT or ACT (for admission).

Costs (2007–08) *Comprehensive fee:* $16,842 includes full-time tuition ($11,700), mandatory fees ($150), and room and board ($4992). Part-time tuition: $390 per credit hour. *Room and board:* Room and board charges vary according to housing facility. *Payment plan:* installment. *Waivers:* employees or children of employees.

Financial Aid Of all full-time matriculated undergraduates who enrolled in 2006, 498 applied for aid, 426 were judged to have need, 78 had their need fully met. 217 Federal Work-Study jobs (averaging $1895). 40 state and other part-time jobs (averaging $1763). In 2006, 96 non-need-based awards were made. *Average percent of need met:* 63%. *Average financial aid package:* $10,772. *Average need-based loan:* $3739. *Average need-based gift aid:* $4988. *Average non-need-based aid:* $5456. *Average indebtedness upon graduation:* $19,200.

Applying *Options:* electronic application, deferred entrance. *Application fee:* $30. *Required:* essay or personal statement, high school transcript, 3 letters of recommendation. *Required for some:* interview. *Recommended:* minimum 2.0 GPA. *Application deadlines:* rolling (freshmen), rolling (transfers). *Notification:* continuous (freshmen), continuous (transfers).

Freshman Application Contact Mr. Brandon Dulaney, Director of Admissions, Kentucky Christian University, 100 Academic Parkway, Box 2021, Grayson, KY 41143-2205. *Phone:* 606-474-3186. *Toll-free phone:* 800-522-3181. *Fax:* 606-474-3155. *E-mail:* bdulaney@kcu.edu.

KENTUCKY MOUNTAIN BIBLE COLLEGE

Vancleve, Kentucky **www.kmbc.edu/**

Freshman Application Contact Mr. Jay Wisler, Director of Recruiting, Kentucky Mountain Bible College, PO Box 10, 855 Route 41, Vancleve, KY 41385. *Phone:* 606-693-5000. *Toll-free phone:* 800-879-KMBC Ext. 130 (in-state); 800-879-KMBC Ext. 136 (out-of-state). *Fax:* 606-693-4884. *E-mail:* jnelson@kmbc.edu.

KENTUCKY STATE UNIVERSITY

Frankfort, Kentucky **www.kysu.edu/**

- **State-related** comprehensive, founded 1886
- **Small-town** 818-acre campus with easy access to Louisville
- **Endowment** $9.8 million
- **Coed** 2,510 undergraduate students, 75% full-time, 58% women, 42% men
- **Minimally difficult** entrance level, 37% of applicants were admitted

Undergraduates 1,876 full-time, 634 part-time. Students come from 35 states and territories, 12 other countries, 40% are from out of state, 60% African American, 0.9% Asian American or Pacific Islander, 0.3% Hispanic American, 0.1% Native American, 3% international, 4% transferred in. *Retention:* 49% of 2006 full-time freshmen returned.

Freshmen *Admission:* 6,644 applied, 2,452 admitted, 678 enrolled. *Average high school GPA:* 2.59. *Test scores:* SAT critical reading scores over 500: 16%; SAT math scores over 500: 15%; ACT scores over 18: 37%; SAT critical reading scores over 600: 4%; SAT math scores over 600: 5%; ACT scores over 24: 4%.

Faculty *Total:* 190, 82% full-time, 59% with terminal degrees. *Student/faculty ratio:* 13:1.

Majors Biology/biological sciences; business/commerce; chemistry; computer and information sciences; criminal justice/safety; drafting and design technology; electrical, electronic and communications engineering technology; elementary education; English; executive assistant/executive secretary; fine/studio arts; human development and family studies; journalism related; liberal arts and sciences/liberal studies; mathematics; music; nursing (registered nurse training); physical education teaching and coaching; political science and government; psychology; public administration; social sciences; social work; web/multimedia management and webmaster.

Academics *Calendar:* semesters. *Degrees:* associate, bachelor's, and master's. *Special study options:* academic remediation for entering students, accelerated degree program, adult/continuing education programs, advanced placement credit, cooperative education, English as a second language, honors programs, independent study, internships, off-campus study, part-time degree program, services for LD students, student-designed majors, study abroad, summer session for credit. *ROTC:* Air Force (c). *Unusual degree programs:* 3-2 engineering with University of Kentucky, University of Maryland College Park.

Computers on Campus 306 computers/terminals are available on campus for general student use. Students can access the following: campus intranet, computer help desk, free student e-mail accounts, online (class) grades, online (class) registration, online (class) schedules. Campuswide network is available. 100% of college-owned or -operated housing units are wired for high-speed Internet access. Wireless service is available via computer labs, libraries, student centers.

Student Life *Housing:* on-campus residence required through sophomore year. *Options:* coed, men-only, women-only. Campus housing is university owned. Freshman applicants given priority for college housing. *Activities and organizations:* drama/theater group, student-run newspaper, choral group, marching band, National Society for Black Engineers, Student Government Association (SGA), Chi Alpha, Baptist Campus Ministries, The Classes—Fr, So, Jr, Sr., national fraternities, national sororities. *Campus security:* 24-hour patrols, controlled dormitory access. *Student services:* health clinic, personal/psychological counseling.

Athletics Member NCAA. All Division II. *Intercollegiate sports:* baseball M (s), basketball M (s)/W (s), cross-country running M (s)/W (s), football M (s), golf M (s), softball W (s), track and field M (s)/W (s), volleyball W (s).

Standardized Tests *Required:* SAT or ACT (for admission).

Costs (2007–08) *Tuition:* state resident $4270 full-time, $175 per hour part-time; nonresident $11,440 full-time, $415 per hour part-time. Full-time tuition and fees vary according to class time, course level, course load, location, program, reciprocity agreements, and student level. Part-time tuition and fees vary according to class time, course level, course load, location, program, reciprocity agreements, and student level. *Required fees:* $1050 full-time. *Room and board:* $6340; room only: $3300. Room and board charges vary according to board plan, housing facility, location, and student level. *Payment plans:* installment, deferred payment. *Waivers:* senior citizens and employees or children of employees.

Financial Aid Of all full-time matriculated undergraduates who enrolled in 2007, 569 Federal Work-Study jobs (averaging $1723). 338 state and other part-time jobs (averaging $1705). *Average financial aid package:* $2613. *Average need-based loan:* $3279. *Average need-based gift aid:* $2305. *Financial aid deadline:* 6/30.

Applying *Application fee:* $30. *Required:* high school transcript. *Required for some:* essay or personal statement, minimum 3.0 GPA, 2 letters of recommendation, interview. *Recommended:* minimum 2.0 GPA. *Application deadlines:* rolling (freshmen), rolling (transfers).

Freshman Application Contact Mr. James Burrell, Director of Admission, Kentucky State University, 400 East Main Street, Frankfort, KY 40601-9957. *Phone:* 502-597-6322. *Toll-free phone:* 800-633-9415 (in-state); 800-325-1716 (out-of-state). *Fax:* 502-597-5814. *E-mail:* james.burrell@kysu.edu.

See page 1032 for the College Close-Up.

KENTUCKY WESLEYAN COLLEGE

Owensboro, Kentucky **www.kwc.edu/**

- **Independent Methodist** 4-year, founded 1858
- **Suburban** 52-acre campus
- **Endowment** $29.4 million
- **Coed** 956 undergraduate students, 94% full-time, 47% women, 53% men
- **Moderately difficult** entrance level, 78% of applicants were admitted

Undergraduates 901 full-time, 55 part-time. Students come from 27 states and territories, 5 other countries, 24% are from out of state, 10% African American, 0.4% Asian American or Pacific Islander, 1% Hispanic American, 0.4% Native American, 0.6% international, 8% transferred in, 48% live on campus. *Retention:* 54% of 2006 full-time freshmen returned.

Freshmen *Admission:* 1,397 applied, 1,085 admitted, 281 enrolled. *Average high school GPA:* 3.13. *Test scores:* SAT critical reading scores over 500: 10%; SAT math scores over 500: 41%; SAT writing scores over 500: 11%; ACT scores over 18: 81%; SAT critical reading scores over 600: 2%; SAT math scores over 600: 10%; SAT writing scores over 600: 2%; ACT scores over 24: 24%; ACT scores over 30: 2%.

Faculty *Total:* 100, 42% full-time, 48% with terminal degrees. *Student/faculty ratio:* 15:1.

Majors Accounting; art teacher education; biology/biological sciences; biology teacher education; business administration and management; chemistry; chemistry teacher education; clinical laboratory science/medical technology; communication/speech communication and rhetoric; computer and information sciences; computer science; criminal justice/safety; elementary education; engineering related; English; English/language arts teacher education; environmental studies; fine arts related; history; human services; interdisciplinary studies; mathematics; mathematics teacher education; middle school education; multi-/interdisciplinary studies related; philosophy; physical education teaching and coaching; physics; political science and government; pre-dentistry studies; pre-law studies; pre-medical studies; pre-veterinary studies; psychology; public administration and social service professions related; secondary education; social studies teacher education; sociology; Spanish; Spanish language teacher education; sport and fitness administration/management.

Academics *Calendar:* semesters. *Degree:* bachelor's. *Special study options:* academic remediation for entering students, advanced placement credit, double majors, independent study, internships, off-campus study, part-time degree program, study abroad, summer session for credit. *ROTC:* Army (c). *Unusual degree programs:* 3-2 engineering with Auburn University, University of Kentucky.

Computers on Campus 125 computers/terminals are available on campus for general student use. Students can access the following: campus intranet, computer help desk, free student e-mail accounts, online (class) grades, online (class) registration, online (class) schedules. Campuswide network is available. 100% of college-owned or -operated housing units are wired for high-speed Internet access. Wireless service is available via entire campus.

Student Life *Housing:* on-campus residence required through junior year. *Options:* coed, men-only, women-only, disabled students. Campus housing is university owned. Freshman campus housing is guaranteed. *Activities and organizations:* drama/theater group, student-run newspaper, radio station, choral group, marching band, Student Government Association, Student Activities Programming Board, Leadership KWC, Pre-Professional Society, Wesley Club, national fraternities, national sororities. *Campus security:* 24-hour emergency response devices, late-night transport/escort service, controlled dormitory access, 12-hour patrols by trained security personnel. *Student services:* health clinic, personal/psychological counseling.

Athletics Member NCAA. All Division II. *Intercollegiate sports:* baseball M (s), basketball M (s)/W (s), cheerleading M/W, cross-country running M (s)/W (s), football M (s), golf M (s)/W (s), soccer M (s)/W (s), softball W (s), tennis W, volleyball W (s). *Intramural sports:* basketball M/W, racquetball M/W, soccer M/W, softball M, table tennis M/W, volleyball M/W.

Standardized Tests *Required:* SAT or ACT (for admission).

Costs (2007–08) *Comprehensive fee:* $20,500 includes full-time tuition ($14,100), mandatory fees ($450), and room and board ($5950). Full-time tuition and fees vary according to course load. Part-time tuition: $420 per credit hour. Part-time tuition and fees vary according to course load. *Required fees:* $50 per term part-time. *College room only:* $2700. *Payment plans:* installment, deferred payment. *Waivers:* children of alumni, senior citizens, and employees or children of employees.

Financial Aid Of all full-time matriculated undergraduates who enrolled in 2006, 891 applied for aid, 792 were judged to have need, 171 had their need fully met. 211 Federal Work-Study jobs (averaging $735). In 2006, 151 non-need-based awards were made. *Average percent of need met:* 70%. *Average financial aid package:* $12,510. *Average need-based loan:* $3104. *Average need-based gift aid:* $10,117. *Average non-need-based aid:* $10,587. *Average indebtedness upon graduation:* $15,100. *Financial aid deadline:* 3/15.

Applying *Options:* electronic application, early admission, deferred entrance. *Required:* high school transcript. *Notification:* continuous (freshmen), continuous (transfers).

Freshman Application Contact Mr. Clayton Daniels, Dean of Admission and Financial Aid, Kentucky Wesleyan College, 3000 Frederica Street, PO Box 1039, Owensboro, KY 42302-1039. *Phone:* 270-852-3120. *Toll-free phone:* 800-999-0592 (in-state); 800-990-0592 (out-of-state). *Fax:* 270-852-3133. *E-mail:* admitme@kwc.edu.

LINDSEY WILSON COLLEGE

Columbia, Kentucky **www.lindsey.edu/**

- **Independent United Methodist** comprehensive, founded 1903
- **Rural** 45-acre campus
- **Endowment** $15.8 million
- **Coed** 1,621 undergraduate students, 91% full-time, 66% women, 34% men
- **Minimally difficult** entrance level, 79% of applicants were admitted

Undergraduates 1,479 full-time, 142 part-time. Students come from 26 states and territories, 30 other countries, 10% are from out of state, 7% African American, 0.4% Asian American or Pacific Islander, 1% Hispanic American, 0.4% Native American, 5% international, 17% transferred in, 42% live on campus. *Retention:* 54% of 2006 full-time freshmen returned.

Freshmen *Admission:* 1,496 applied, 1,184 admitted, 369 enrolled. *Average high school GPA:* 3.03. *Test scores:* ACT scores over 18: 66%; ACT scores over 24: 15%; ACT scores over 30: 1%.

Faculty *Total:* 115, 61% full-time. *Student/faculty ratio:* 23:1.

Majors American studies; art teacher education; biology/biological sciences; biology teacher education; chemistry; computer and information sciences related; computer programming; criminal justice/law enforcement administration; early childhood education; education; elementary education; English; health services/allied health/health sciences; humanities; human services; journalism; management information systems; mass communication/media; mathematics teacher education; middle school education; parks, recreation and leisure; physical education teaching and coaching; pre-dentistry studies; pre-law studies; pre-medical studies; pre-pharmacy studies; pre-veterinary studies; psychology; secondary education; social science teacher education.

Academics *Calendar:* semesters. *Degrees:* associate, bachelor's, and master's. *Special study options:* academic remediation for entering students, accelerated degree program, adult/continuing education programs, advanced placement credit, cooperative education, double majors, English as a second language, independent study, internships, off-campus study, part-time degree program, services for LD students, student-designed majors, study abroad, summer session for credit.

Computers on Campus 80 computers/terminals are available on campus for general student use. Students can access the following: campus intranet, free student e-mail accounts, online (class) grades, online (class) registration, online (class) schedules. Campuswide network is available. 100% of college-owned or -operated housing units are wired for high-speed Internet access. Wireless service is available via entire campus.

Student Life *Housing:* on-campus residence required through senior year. *Options:* men-only, women-only. Campus housing is university owned. Freshman campus housing is guaranteed. *Activities and organizations:* drama/theater group, student-run newspaper, choral group. *Campus security:* 24-hour emergency response devices and patrols. *Student services:* health clinic, personal/psychological counseling, women's center.

Athletics Member NAIA. *Intercollegiate sports:* baseball M (s), basketball M (s)/W (s), bowling M (s)/W (s), cheerleading M (s)/W (s), cross-country running M (s)/W (s), golf M (s)/W (s), soccer M (s)/W (s), softball W (s), tennis M (s)/W (s), track and field M (s)/W (s), volleyball W (s). *Intramural sports:* basketball M, football M/W, softball M/W, table tennis M/W, tennis M/W, volleyball M/W, weight lifting M/W.

Standardized Tests *Required for some:* SAT or ACT (for admission).

Costs (2007–08) *Comprehensive fee:* $22,346 includes full-time tuition ($15,576), mandatory fees ($230), and room and board ($6540). Part-time tuition: $649 per credit hour. *Payment plan:* installment. *Waivers:* senior citizens and employees or children of employees.

Financial Aid Of all full-time matriculated undergraduates who enrolled in 2006, 1,564 applied for aid, 1,450 were judged to have need, 315 had their need fully met. 179 Federal Work-Study jobs (averaging $1404). *Average financial aid package:* $11,351. *Average need-based loan:* $3814. *Average need-based gift aid:* $11,767. *Average indebtedness upon graduation:* $19,955.

Applying *Options:* electronic application. *Required:* high school transcript. *Recommended:* interview. *Application deadlines:* rolling (freshmen), rolling (transfers). *Notification:* continuous (freshmen), continuous (transfers).

Freshman Application Contact Ms. Charity Ferguson, Assistant Director of Admissions, Lindsey Wilson College, 210 Lindsey Wilson Street, Columbia, KY 42728-1298. *Phone:* 270-384-8100. *Toll-free phone:* 800-264-0138. *Fax:* 270-384-8591.

MID-CONTINENT UNIVERSITY

Mayfield, Kentucky www.midcontinent.edu/

- **Independent Southern Baptist** 4-year, founded 1949
- **Small-town** 60-acre campus
- **Endowment** $2.8 million
- **Coed** 1,541 undergraduate students, 86% full-time, 61% women, 39% men
- **Minimally difficult** entrance level, 83% of applicants were admitted

Undergraduates 1,332 full-time, 209 part-time. Students come from 16 states and territories, 14 other countries, 23% are from out of state, 13% African American, 0.2% Asian American or Pacific Islander, 0.9% Hispanic American, 0.3% Native American, 3% international, 22% transferred in, 33% live on campus. *Retention:* 58% of 2006 full-time freshmen returned.

Freshmen *Admission:* 463 applied, 382 admitted, 141 enrolled. *Average high school GPA:* 2.78. *Test scores:* SAT critical reading scores over 500: 23%; SAT math scores over 500: 46%; SAT writing scores over 500: 23%; ACT scores over 18: 66%; SAT critical reading scores over 600: 8%; SAT math scores over 600: 15%; SAT writing scores over 600: 8%; ACT scores over 24: 9%.

Faculty *Total:* 98, 28% full-time, 18% with terminal degrees. *Student/faculty ratio:* 16:1.

Majors Ancient Near Eastern and biblical languages; biblical studies; business administration and management; counseling psychology; elementary education; English; general studies; missionary studies and missiology; multi-/interdisciplinary studies related; organizational behavior; psychology; religious education; social sciences.

Academics *Calendar:* semesters. *Degrees:* certificates, associate, and bachelor's. *Special study options:* academic remediation for entering students, accelerated degree program, advanced placement credit, distance learning, double majors, independent study, off-campus study, part-time degree program, student-designed majors, study abroad, summer session for credit.

Computers on Campus 30 computers/terminals are available on campus for general student use. Campuswide network is available.

Student Life *Housing:* on-campus residence required through sophomore year. *Options:* men-only, women-only. Campus housing is university owned. *Activities and organizations:* student-run newspaper, SGA, Baptist Student Union, Psychology Club, International Club, Ministry Association. *Campus security:* student patrols. *Student services:* personal/psychological counseling.

Athletics Member NAIA, NCCAA. *Intercollegiate sports:* baseball M (s), soccer M (s), softball W (s), volleyball W (s). *Intramural sports:* basketball M/W, bowling M/W, cheerleading W, soccer M.

Standardized Tests *Required:* SAT or ACT (for admission).

Costs (2007–08) *Comprehensive fee:* $18,050 includes full-time tuition ($10,800), mandatory fees ($1250), and room and board ($6000). Full-time tuition and fees vary according to course load and program. Part-time tuition: $360 per credit hour. Part-time tuition and fees vary according to course load and program. *Room and board:* Room and board charges vary according to board plan and housing facility. *Waivers:* employees or children of employees.

Financial Aid Of all full-time matriculated undergraduates who enrolled in 2007, 1,156 applied for aid, 743 were judged to have need, 85 had their need fully met. 48 Federal Work-Study jobs (averaging $1383). In 2007, 110 non-need-based awards were made. *Average percent of need met:* 26%. *Average financial aid package:* $4783. *Average need-based loan:* $3556. *Average need-based gift aid:* $4895. *Average non-need-based aid:* $9369. *Average indebtedness upon graduation:* $8805.

Applying *Options:* electronic application, early admission. *Application fee:* $20. *Required:* essay or personal statement, high school transcript, minimum 2.0 GPA, 1 letter of recommendation. *Required for some:* interview. *Application deadlines:* rolling (freshmen), rolling (transfers). *Notification:* continuous (freshmen), continuous (transfers).

Freshman Application Contact Ms. Debbie Smith, Acting Director of Admissions, Mid-Continent University, 99 Powell Road East, Mayfield, KY 42066. *Phone:* 270-247-8521. *Fax:* 270-247-3115. *E-mail:* admissions@midcontinent.edu.

MIDWAY COLLEGE

Midway, Kentucky www.midway.edu/

- **Independent** 4-year, founded 1847, affiliated with Christian Church (Disciples of Christ)
- **Small-town** 105-acre campus with easy access to Louisville and Lexington
- **Endowment** $17.0 million
- **Coed, primarily women** 1,422 undergraduate students, 73% full-time, 91% women, 9% men
- **Minimally difficult** entrance level, 79% of applicants were admitted

Undergraduates 1,042 full-time, 380 part-time. Students come from 23 states and territories, 1 other country, 9% are from out of state, 7% African American, 0.4% Asian American or Pacific Islander, 0.7% Hispanic American, 0.3% Native American, 0.1% international, 16% transferred in, 14% live on campus. *Retention:* 78% of 2006 full-time freshmen returned.

Freshmen *Admission:* 428 applied, 340 admitted, 202 enrolled. *Average high school GPA:* 3.15. *Test scores:* SAT critical reading scores over 500: 50%; SAT math scores over 500: 38%; ACT scores over 18: 72%; SAT critical reading scores over 600: 13%; SAT math scores over 600: 13%; ACT scores over 24: 20%; SAT critical reading scores over 700: 3%; SAT math scores over 700: 3%; ACT scores over 30: 2%.

Faculty *Total:* 142, 29% full-time, 24% with terminal degrees. *Student/faculty ratio:* 15:1.

Majors Accounting; biology/biological sciences; business administration and management; business/commerce; computer and information sciences; data processing and data processing technology; education; elementary education; English; environmental biology; equestrian studies; health/health care administration; horse husbandry/equine science and management; human resources management; liberal arts and sciences/liberal studies; mathematics; middle school education; multi-/interdisciplinary studies related; nursing (registered nurse training); nursing science; organizational behavior; psychology; secondary education; security and protective services related; special education; sport and fitness administration/management.

Academics *Calendar:* semesters. *Degrees:* associate, bachelor's, and master's. *Special study options:* academic remediation for entering students, adult/continuing education programs, advanced placement credit, distance learning, external degree program, honors programs, independent study, internships, off-campus study, part-time degree program, services for LD students, study abroad, summer session for credit. *ROTC:* Army (c).

Computers on Campus 60 computers/terminals are available on campus for general student use. Students can access the following: campus intranet, computer help desk, free student e-mail accounts, online (class) registration, online (class) schedules. Campuswide network is available. 100% of college-owned or -operated housing units are wired for high-speed Internet access.

Student Life *Housing:* on-campus residence required through sophomore year. *Options:* women-only. Campus housing is university owned. Freshman campus housing is guaranteed. *Activities and organizations:* choral group, Student government, Midway Chorale, Midway Association of Nursing Students, Council on Religious Activities, Midway Horse Women's Association. *Campus security:* 24-hour emergency response devices and patrols, late-night transport/escort service. *Student services:* health clinic, personal/psychological counseling, women's center.

Athletics Member NAIA. *Intercollegiate sports:* basketball W (s), equestrian sports W (s), soccer W (s), softball W (s), tennis W (s).

Standardized Tests *Required:* SAT or ACT (for admission).

Costs (2007–08) *Comprehensive fee:* $22,300 includes full-time tuition ($15,750), mandatory fees ($150), and room and board ($6400). Full-time tuition and fees vary according to class time, location, and program. Part-time tuition: $525 per semester hour. Part-time tuition and fees vary according to class time, location, and program. *Room and board:* Room and board charges vary according to board plan and housing facility. *Payment plan:* deferred payment. *Waivers:* senior citizens and employees or children of employees.

Financial Aid Of all full-time matriculated undergraduates who enrolled in 2004, 771 applied for aid, 705 were judged to have need, 180 had their need fully met. 113 Federal Work-Study jobs (averaging $1372). In 2004, 8 non-need-based awards were made. *Average percent of need met:* 59%. *Average financial aid package:* $12,196. *Average need-based loan:* $3658. *Average need-based gift aid:* $5792. *Average non-need-based aid:* $3756. *Average indebtedness upon graduation:* $15,407.

Applying *Options:* electronic application, early admission, deferred entrance. *Application fee:* $25. *Required:* high school transcript. *Required for some:* essay or personal statement, letters of recommendation, interview. *Recommended:* minimum 2.2 GPA. *Application deadlines:* rolling (freshmen), rolling (transfers). *Notification:* continuous (freshmen), continuous (transfers).

Freshman Application Contact Dr. Jim Wombles, Vice President of Admissions, Chief Enrollment Officer, Midway College, 512 East Stephens Street, Pinkerton Building, Midway, KY 40347-1120. *Phone:* 859-846-5799. *Toll-free phone:* 800-755-0031. *Fax:* 859-846-5823. *E-mail:* admissions@midway.edu.

MOREHEAD STATE UNIVERSITY

Morehead, Kentucky **www.moreheadstate.edu/**

- **State-supported** comprehensive, founded 1922
- **Small-town** 1016-acre campus
- **Endowment** $30.1 million
- **Coed** 7,619 undergraduate students, 76% full-time, 61% women, 39% men
- **Minimally difficult** entrance level, 71% of applicants were admitted

Undergraduates 5,771 full-time, 1,848 part-time. Students come from 44 states and territories, 35 other countries, 13% are from out of state, 3% African American, 0.3% Asian American or Pacific Islander, 0.8% Hispanic American, 0.4% Native American, 0.4% international, 5% transferred in, 34% live on campus. *Retention:* 68% of 2006 full-time freshmen returned.

Freshmen *Admission:* 5,257 applied, 3,740 admitted, 1,409 enrolled. *Average high school GPA:* 3.2. *Test scores:* SAT critical reading scores over 500: 45%; SAT math scores over 500: 43%; ACT scores over 18: 81%; SAT critical reading scores over 600: 4%; SAT math scores over 600: 10%; ACT scores over 24: 26%; ACT scores over 30: 2%.

Faculty *Total:* 516, 73% full-time, 48% with terminal degrees. *Student/faculty ratio:* 16:1.

Majors Accounting; agribusiness; agriculture; biology/biological sciences; business administration and management; business/managerial economics; business teacher education; chemistry; communication/speech communication and rhetoric; computer and information sciences; dramatic/theater arts; ecology; elementary education; English; family and consumer sciences/human sciences related; finance; fine/studio arts; French; general studies; geography; geology/earth science; health teacher education; history; industrial technology; kindergarten/preschool education; kinesiology and exercise science; legal assistant/paralegal; management information systems; marketing/marketing management; mathematics; medical radiologic technology; middle school education; music; nursing (registered nurse training); philosophy; physical education teaching and coaching; physics; political science and government; psychology; real estate; respiratory care therapy; social sciences; social work; sociology; Spanish; special education; speech and rhetoric; sport and fitness administration/management; veterinary/animal health technology.

Academics *Calendar:* semesters. *Degrees:* associate, bachelor's, master's, and post-master's certificates. *Special study options:* academic remediation for entering students, accelerated degree program, adult/continuing education programs, advanced placement credit, cooperative education, distance learning, double majors, honors programs, independent study, internships, off-campus study, part-time degree program, services for LD students, student-designed majors, study abroad, summer session for credit. *ROTC:* Army (b).

Computers on Campus 1,000 computers/terminals and 1,200 ports are available on campus for general student use. Students can access the following: computer help desk, free student e-mail accounts, online (class) registration. Campuswide network is available. 100% of college-owned or -operated housing units are wired for high-speed Internet access. Wireless service is available via entire campus.

Student Life *Housing:* on-campus residence required through sophomore year. *Options:* coed, disabled students. Campus housing is university owned. Freshman applicants given priority for college housing. *Activities and organizations:* drama/theater group, student-run newspaper, radio and television station, choral group, marching band, national fraternities, national sororities. *Campus security:* 24-hour emergency response devices and patrols, late-night transport/escort service, controlled dormitory access. *Student services:* health clinic, personal/psychological counseling.

Athletics Member NCAA. All Division I except football (Division I-AA). *Intercollegiate sports:* baseball M (s), basketball M (s)/W (s), bowling M (c)/W (c), cross-country running M (s)/W (s), equestrian sports M (c)/W (c), golf M (s), riflery M (s)/W (s), soccer W (s), softball W (s), tennis M (s)/W (s), track and field M (s)/W (s), volleyball W (s). *Intramural sports:* archery M/W, badminton M/W, basketball M/W, bowling M/W, football M/W, golf M/W, racquetball M/W, soccer M (c)/W (c), softball M/W, swimming and diving M/W, table tennis M/W, tennis M/W, track and field M/W, volleyball M/W.

Standardized Tests *Required:* SAT or ACT (for admission). *Recommended:* ACT (for admission).

Costs (2007–08) *Tuition:* state resident $5280 full-time, $220 per credit hour part-time; nonresident $13,340 full-time, $560 per credit hour part-time. Full-time tuition and fees vary according to course load and reciprocity agreements. *Room and board:* $5620. Room and board charges vary according to board plan and housing facility. *Payment plans:* installment, deferred payment. *Waivers:* children of alumni, senior citizens, and employees or children of employees.

Financial Aid Of all full-time matriculated undergraduates who enrolled in 2006, 4,675 applied for aid, 3,922 were judged to have need, 1,404 had their need fully met. 438 Federal Work-Study jobs (averaging $1353). 701 state and other part-time jobs (averaging $1572). In 2006, 642 non-need-based awards were made. *Average percent of need met:* 83%. *Average financial aid package:* $8141. *Average need-based loan:* $3324. *Average need-based gift aid:* $4353. *Average non-need-based aid:* $3647. *Average indebtedness upon graduation:* $18,167.

Applying *Options:* electronic application, early admission, deferred entrance. *Required:* high school transcript. *Required for some:* letters of recommendation. *Application deadlines:* rolling (freshmen), rolling (transfers). *Notification:* continuous (freshmen), continuous (transfers).

Freshman Application Contact Mr. Jeffrey Liles, Associate Vice President for Enrollment Services, Morehead State University, Admissions Center, Morehead, KY 40351. *Phone:* 606-783-2000. *Toll-free phone:* 800-585-6781. *Fax:* 606-783-5038. *E-mail:* admissions@moreheadstate.edu.

MURRAY STATE UNIVERSITY

Murray, Kentucky **www.murraystate.edu/**

- **State-supported** comprehensive, founded 1922, part of Kentucky Council on Post Secondary Education
- **Small-town** 238-acre campus
- **Endowment** $40.7 million
- **Coed** 8,354 undergraduate students, 84% full-time, 58% women, 42% men
- **Moderately difficult** entrance level, 85% of applicants were admitted

Undergraduates 6,979 full-time, 1,375 part-time. Students come from 42 states and territories, 46 other countries, 26% are from out of state, 6% African American, 1% Asian American or Pacific Islander, 0.9% Hispanic American, 0.4% Native American, 2% international, 7% transferred in, 40% live on campus. *Retention:* 76% of 2006 full-time freshmen returned.

Freshmen *Admission:* 3,108 applied, 2,636 admitted, 1,415 enrolled. *Average high school GPA:* 3.51. *Test scores:* ACT scores over 18: 98%; ACT scores over 24: 43%; ACT scores over 30: 3%.

Faculty *Total:* 585, 68% full-time, 60% with terminal degrees. *Student/faculty ratio:* 16:1.

Majors Accounting; administrative assistant and secretarial science; agricultural business and management; agricultural teacher education; agriculture; apparel and textiles; art teacher education; audiology and speech-language pathology; biology/biological sciences; biology teacher education; business administration and management; business/commerce; business teacher education; chemical engineering; chemical technology; chemistry; chemistry teacher education; child care provision; civil engineering technology; clinical laboratory science/medical technology; computer and information sciences; computer engineering technology; criminal justice/safety; drafting and design technology; dramatic/theater arts; early childhood education; economics; electromechanical technology; elementary education; engineering physics; engineering technology; English; English as a second/foreign language (teaching); English/language arts teacher education; environmental engineering technology; executive assistant/executive secretary; family and consumer economics related; family and consumer sciences/home economics teacher education; finance; fine/studio arts; fishing and fisheries sciences and management; foodservice systems administration; foods, nutrition, and wellness; foreign language teacher education; French; French language teacher education; general studies; geography; geology/earth science; German; German language teacher education; graphic and printing equipment operation/production; health teacher education; history; history teacher education; human development and family studies; industrial technology; information science/studies; international business/trade/commerce; international relations and affairs; journalism; kinesiology and exercise science; liberal arts and sciences/liberal studies; library science; management information systems; manufacturing technology; marketing/marketing management; mass communication/media; mathematics; mathematics teacher education; mechanical drafting and CAD/CADD; mechanical engineering; mechanical engineering/mechanical technology; middle school education; military technologies; music; music teacher education; nursing (registered nurse training); occupational safety and health technology; office management; parks, recreation and leisure facilities management; perioperative/operating room and surgical nursing; philosophy; physical education teaching and coaching; physics; physics teacher education; political science and government; psychology; public administration; public relations, advertising, and applied communication related; public relations/image management; radio and television; reading teacher education; science teacher education; secondary education; social science teacher education; social studies teacher education; social work; sociology; Spanish; Spanish language teacher education; special education; speech and rhetoric; speech teacher education; speech therapy; technical and business writing; technology/industrial arts teacher education; telecommunications; trade and industrial teacher education; veterinary/animal health technology; water quality and wastewater treatment management and recycling technology; wildlife and wildlands science and management.

Academics *Calendar:* semesters. *Degrees:* certificates, bachelor's, master's, and post-master's certificates. *Special study options:* academic remediation for entering students, accelerated degree program, adult/continuing education programs, advanced placement credit, cooperative education, distance learning, double majors, English as a second language, external degree program, honors programs, independent study, internships, off-campus study, part-time degree program, services for LD students, study abroad, summer session for credit. *ROTC:* Army (c). *Unusual degree programs:* 3-2 business administration; engineering.

Computers on Campus 1,800 computers/terminals are available on campus for general student use. Students can access the following: campus intranet, computer help desk, free student e-mail accounts, online (class) grades, online (class) registration, online (class) schedules, billing accounts. Campuswide network is available. 100% of college-owned or -operated housing units are wired for high-speed Internet access. Wireless service is available via entire campus.

Student Life *Housing:* on-campus residence required through sophomore year. *Options:* coed, women-only, disabled students. Campus housing is university owned. *Activities and organizations:* drama/theater group, student-run newspaper, radio and television station, choral group, marching band, student government, Baptist Student Union, Christ Ambassadors, Residential Colleges, Greek Organizations, national fraternities, national sororities. *Campus security:* 24-hour emergency response devices and patrols, student patrols, late-night transport/escort service, controlled dormitory access. *Student services:* health clinic, personal/psychological counseling, women's center, legal services.

Athletics Member NCAA. All Division I. *Intercollegiate sports:* baseball M (s), basketball M (s)/W (s), bowling M/W, cheerleading M/W, crew M (s)/W (s), cross-country running M (s)/W (s), equestrian sports M (s)/W (s), football M (s), golf M (s)/W (s), riflery M (s)/W (s), skiing (downhill) M/W, soccer W (s), tennis M (s)/W (s), track and field M (s)/W (s), volleyball W (s). *Intramural sports:* basketball M/W, bowling M/W, fencing M/W, field hockey M/W, football M/W, golf M/W, racquetball M/W, rugby M, sailing M/W, skiing (downhill) M/W, soccer M/W, softball M/W, swimming and diving M/W, track and field M/W, volleyball M/W, weight lifting M/W.

Standardized Tests *Required:* ACT (for admission).

Costs (2007–08) *Tuition:* state resident $4650 full-time, $194 per hour part-time; nonresident $6728 full-time, $268 per hour part-time. Full-time tuition and fees vary according to reciprocity agreements. Part-time tuition and fees vary according to reciprocity agreements. *Required fees:* $768 full-time, $32 per hour part-time. *Room and board:* $5670; room only: $3036. Room and board charges vary according to board plan. *Payment plan:* installment. *Waivers:* children of alumni, senior citizens, and employees or children of employees.

Financial Aid Of all full-time matriculated undergraduates who enrolled in 2007, 6,002 applied for aid, 3,361 were judged to have need, 3,030 had their need fully met. 425 Federal Work-Study jobs (averaging $1271). 2,099 state and other part-time jobs (averaging $1681). In 2007, 2373 non-need-based awards were made. *Average percent of need met:* 87%. *Average financial aid package:* $4220. *Average need-based loan:* $1960. *Average need-based gift aid:* $2185. *Average non-need-based aid:* $2557. *Average indebtedness upon graduation:* $16,066.

Applying *Options:* electronic application. *Application fee:* $30. *Required:* high school transcript, minimum 3.0 GPA. *Notification:* continuous until 8/1 (freshmen), continuous until 1/8 (out-of-state freshmen), continuous until 8/1 (transfers).

Freshman Application Contact Ms. Stacy Bell, Undergraduate Admissions Specialist, Murray State University, PO Box 9, Murray, KY 42071-0009. *Phone:* 270-809-3035. *Toll-free phone:* 800-272-4678. *Fax:* 270-809-3050. *E-mail:* admissions@murraystate.edu.

NORTHERN KENTUCKY UNIVERSITY

Highland Heights, Kentucky **www.nku.edu/**

- **State-supported** comprehensive, founded 1968
- **Suburban** 398-acre campus with easy access to Cincinnati
- **Endowment** $42.6 million
- **Coed**
- **Noncompetitive** entrance level

Faculty *Student/faculty ratio:* 14:1.

Academics *Calendar:* semesters. *Degrees:* certificates, associate, bachelor's, master's, and first professional.

Student Life *Campus security:* 24-hour emergency response devices and patrols, late-night transport/escort service, controlled dormitory access.

Athletics Member NCAA. All Division II.

Standardized Tests *Required:* SAT or ACT (for admission). *Recommended:* ACT (for admission).

Costs (2007–08) *Tuition:* state resident $5952 full-time, $248 per semester hour part-time; nonresident $10,776 full-time, $449 per semester hour part-time. Full-time tuition and fees vary according to course load, location, program, and reciprocity agreements. Part-time tuition and fees vary according to location and program. *Room and board:* $6541. Room and board charges vary according to board plan, housing facility, and location.

Financial Aid Of all full-time matriculated undergraduates who enrolled in 2006, 6,212 applied for aid, 4,573 were judged to have need, 874 had their need fully met. In 2006, 722 non-need-based awards were made. *Average percent of need met:* 51. *Average financial aid package:* $7097. *Average need-based loan:* $3503. *Average need-based gift aid:* $4332. *Average non-need-based aid:* $3725. *Average indebtedness upon graduation:* $23,776.

Applying *Options:* electronic application, early admission, early action, deferred entrance. *Application fee:* $40. *Required:* high school transcript. *Recommended:* minimum 2.0 GPA.

Freshman Application Contact Ms. Melissa Gorbandt, Director of Admissions and Outreach, Northern Kentucky University, Administrative Center 400, Highland Heights, KY 41099-7010. *Phone:* 859-572-5220 Ext. 5744. *Toll-free phone:* 800-637-9948. *Fax:* 859-572-6665. *E-mail:* admitnku@nku.edu.

See page 1034 for the College Close-Up.

PIKEVILLE COLLEGE

Pikeville, Kentucky **www.pc.edu/**

- **Independent** comprehensive, founded 1889, affiliated with Presbyterian Church (U.S.A.)
- **Small-town** 25-acre campus
- **Endowment** $19.9 million
- **Coed** 794 undergraduate students, 91% full-time, 52% women, 48% men
- **Noncompetitive** entrance level, 100% of applicants were admitted

Undergraduates 722 full-time, 72 part-time. Students come from 33 states and territories, 5 other countries, 22% are from out of state, 9% African American, 0.6% Asian American or Pacific Islander, 0.8% Hispanic American, 0.9% international, 10% transferred in, 44% live on campus. *Retention:* 49% of 2006 full-time freshmen returned.

Freshmen *Admission:* 731 applied, 731 admitted, 234 enrolled. *Average high school GPA:* 3.19. *Test scores:* ACT scores over 18: 71%; ACT scores over 24: 20%; ACT scores over 30: 1%.

Faculty *Total:* 74, 82% full-time, 45% with terminal degrees. *Student/faculty ratio:* 11:1.

Majors Art; biology/biological sciences; business administration and management; chemistry; communication/speech communication and rhetoric; computer and information sciences; criminal justice/safety; elementary education; English; history; mathematics; middle school education; multi-/interdisciplinary studies related; nursing (registered nurse training); psychology; religious studies; social sciences; social work; sociology.

Academics *Calendar:* semesters. *Degrees:* associate, bachelor's, first professional, and postbachelor's certificates. *Special study options:* academic remediation for entering students, advanced placement credit, double majors, independent study, internships, off-campus study, part-time degree program, services for LD students, student-designed majors, study abroad, summer session for credit.

Computers on Campus 166 computers/terminals are available on campus for general student use. Students can access the following: campus intranet, free student e-mail accounts. Campuswide network is available. Wireless service is available via classrooms, computer centers, computer labs, dorm rooms, libraries.

Student Life *Housing options:* coed, men-only, women-only. Campus housing is university owned and leased by the school. Freshman applicants given priority for college housing. *Activities and organizations:* drama/theater group, student-run newspaper, choral group, Pre-Professional Club, Phi Beta Lambda, Rotaract, Psychology Round Table, Nursing Club. *Campus security:* 24-hour emergency response devices and patrols, controlled dormitory access. *Student services:* personal/psychological counseling.

Athletics Member NAIA. *Intercollegiate sports:* baseball M (s), basketball M (s)/W (s), bowling M (s)/W (s), cheerleading M (s)/W (s), cross-country running M (s)/W (s), football M (s), golf M (s)/W (s), soccer M (s)/W (s), softball W (s), tennis M (s)/W (s), track and field M (s)/W (s), volleyball W (s). *Intramural sports:* basketball M/W, bowling M/W, football M/W, softball M/W, tennis M/W, ultimate Frisbee M/W, volleyball M/W.

Costs (2007–08) *Comprehensive fee:* $19,000 includes full-time tuition ($13,750) and room and board ($5250). Full-time tuition and fees vary according to course load. Part-time tuition: $573 per credit hour. *Payment plan:* installment. *Waivers:* senior citizens and employees or children of employees.

Financial Aid Of all full-time matriculated undergraduates who enrolled in 2007, 713 applied for aid, 708 were judged to have need, 292 had their need fully met. 250 Federal Work-Study jobs (averaging $1713). *Average percent of need met:* 84%. *Average financial aid package:* $14,381. *Average need-based loan:* $3375. *Average need-based gift aid:* $11,699. *Average indebtedness upon graduation:* $14,612.

Applying *Options:* deferred entrance. *Required:* high school transcript. *Application deadlines:* 8/15 (freshmen), 8/15 (transfers). *Notification:* continuous (freshmen), continuous (transfers).

Freshman Application Contact Ms. Melinda Lynch, Dean of Enrollment Management, Pikeville College, 147 Sycamore Street, Pikeville, KY 41501. *Phone:* 606-218-5251. *Toll-free phone:* 866-232-7700. *Fax:* 606-218-5255. *E-mail:* wewantyou@pc.edu.

SOUTHERN BAPTIST THEOLOGICAL SEMINARY

Louisville, Kentucky **www.sbts.edu/**

- **Independent Southern Baptist** comprehensive, founded 1858
- **Coed** 668 undergraduate students, 62% full-time, 29% women, 71% men
- 71% of applicants were admitted

Undergraduates 412 full-time, 256 part-time. 3% African American, 6% Asian American or Pacific Islander, 2% Hispanic American, 0.4% Native American, 12% transferred in. *Retention:* 78% of 2006 full-time freshmen returned.

Freshmen *Admission:* 110 applied, 78 admitted, 62 enrolled.

Majors Biblical studies; Christian studies; divinity/ministry; missionary studies and missiology; pastoral studies/counseling; youth ministry.

Academics *Degrees:* certificates, diplomas, associate, and bachelor's.

Computers on Campus Students can access the following: campus intranet, computer help desk, free student e-mail accounts, online (class) grades, online (class) registration, online (class) schedules. Campuswide network is available. Wireless service is available via entire campus.

Student Life *Housing:* on-campus residence required for freshman year. *Options:* men-only, women-only. Campus housing is university owned. Freshman applicants given priority for college housing. *Activities and organizations:* choral group. *Student services:* health clinic, personal/psychological counseling.

Athletics *Intercollegiate sports:* basketball M.

Standardized Tests *Required for some:* SAT or ACT (for admission).

Costs (2007–08) *Comprehensive fee:* $9236 includes full-time tuition ($5586), mandatory fees ($150), and room and board ($3500). Full-time tuition and fees vary according to course load. Part-time tuition: $241 per credit hour. *Required fees:* $100 per year part-time. *College room only:* $1990. Room and board charges vary according to housing facility.

Financial Aid Of all full-time matriculated undergraduates who enrolled in 2007, 95 applied for aid, 85 were judged to have need. *Average percent of need met:* 8%. *Average financial aid package:* $460. *Average need-based gift aid:* $460. *Average indebtedness upon graduation:* $7803. *Financial aid deadline:* 7/15.

Applying *Application fee:* $35. *Required:* essay or personal statement, high school transcript, minimum 2.0 GPA, letters of recommendation. *Application deadlines:* 7/15 (freshmen), 7/15 (transfers).

Freshman Application Contact Dr. Daniel DeWitt, Southern Baptist Theological Seminary, 2825 Lexington Road, Louisville, KY 40280-0004. *Phone:* 502-897-4011 Ext. 4617.

SPALDING UNIVERSITY

Louisville, Kentucky **www.spalding.edu/**

Freshman Application Contact Mr. Chris Hart, Assistant Director of Admissions, Spalding University, 851 South Fourth Street, Louisville, KY 40203. *Phone:* 502-585-9911. *Toll-free phone:* 800-896-8941 Ext. 2111. *Fax:* 502-992-2418. *E-mail:* admissionsW@spalding.edu.

SULLIVAN UNIVERSITY

Louisville, Kentucky **www.sullivan.edu/**

- **Proprietary** comprehensive, founded 1864, administratively affiliated with Sullivan University System
- **Suburban** 10-acre campus
- **Coed** 4,201 undergraduate students, 85% full-time, 53% women, 47% men
- **Minimally difficult** entrance level

Undergraduates 3,562 full-time, 639 part-time. Students come from 16 states and territories, 11 other countries, 26% are from out of state, 18% African American, 2% Asian American or Pacific Islander, 2% Hispanic American, 0.8% Native American, 0.2% international, 8% transferred in, 9% live on campus. *Retention:* 66% of 2006 full-time freshmen returned.

Freshmen *Admission:* 96 enrolled.

Faculty *Total:* 269, 43% full-time, 18% with terminal degrees. *Student/faculty ratio:* 20:1.

Majors Accounting; business administration and management; criminal justice/safety; culinary arts; early childhood education; finance; human resources management; information technology; legal administrative assistant/secretary; legal assistant/paralegal; logistics and materials management; marketing/marketing management; medical office management; office management; tourism and travel services management.

Academics *Calendar:* quarters. *Degrees:* certificates, diplomas, associate, bachelor's, and master's. *Special study options:* academic remediation for entering students, accelerated degree program, adult/continuing education programs, advanced placement credit, cooperative education, distance learning, double majors, independent study, part-time degree program, summer session for credit.

Computers on Campus 225 computers/terminals are available on campus for general student use. Students can access the following: campus intranet, computer help desk, free student e-mail accounts, online (class) grades, online (class) schedules. Campuswide network is available.

Student Life *Housing options:* men-only, women-only. Campus housing is leased by the school. Freshman campus housing is guaranteed. *Activities and organizations:* student government, Travel Club, Sullivan Student Paralegal Association, American Marketing Association, Society of Hosteurs. *Campus security:* 24-hour patrols. *Student services:* personal/psychological counseling.

Athletics *Intramural sports:* basketball M/W, bowling M/W, football M/W, softball M/W, volleyball M/W.

Standardized Tests *Required:* ACT or CPAt (for admission).

Costs (2008–09) *Tuition:* $14,400 full-time. *Required fees:* $540 full-time. *Room only:* $4320.

Financial Aid Of all full-time matriculated undergraduates who enrolled in 2002, 6,028 applied for aid, 5,247 were judged to have need. 31 Federal Work-Study jobs (averaging $2065). In 2002, 374 non-need-based awards were made. *Average non-need-based aid:* $2000. *Average indebtedness upon graduation:* $15,000.

Applying *Application fee:* $100. *Required:* high school transcript, interview. *Required for some:* essay or personal statement. *Application deadlines:* rolling (freshmen), rolling (transfers). *Notification:* continuous (freshmen), continuous (transfers).

Freshman Application Contact Ms. Terri Thomas, Director of Admissions, Sullivan University, 3101 Bardstown Road, Louisville, KY 40205. *Phone:* 502-456-6505 Ext. 370. *Toll-free phone:* 800-844-1354. *Fax:* 502-456-0040. *E-mail:* admissions@sullivan.edu.

See page 1036 for the College Close-Up.

THOMAS MORE COLLEGE

Crestview Hills, Kentucky **www.thomasmore.edu/**

- **Independent Roman Catholic** comprehensive, founded 1921
- **Suburban** 100-acre campus with easy access to Cincinnati
- **Endowment** $12.9 million
- **Coed** 1,539 undergraduate students, 76% full-time, 52% women, 48% men
- **Moderately difficult** entrance level, 83% of applicants were admitted

Undergraduates 1,166 full-time, 373 part-time. Students come from 11 states and territories, 3 other countries, 36% are from out of state, 4% African American, 0.6% Asian American or Pacific Islander, 0.6% Hispanic American, 0.6% Native American, 0.5% international, 2% transferred in, 34% live on campus. *Retention:* 74% of 2006 full-time freshmen returned.

Freshmen *Admission:* 990 applied, 821 admitted, 247 enrolled. *Average high school GPA:* 3.29. *Test scores:* SAT critical reading scores over 500: 50%; SAT math scores over 500: 52%; ACT scores over 18: 95%; SAT critical reading scores over 600: 17%; SAT math scores over 600: 22%; ACT scores over 24: 37%; SAT critical reading scores over 700: 2%; ACT scores over 30: 7%.

Faculty *Total:* 135, 53% full-time. *Student/faculty ratio:* 14:1.

Majors Accounting; art history, criticism and conservation; art teacher education; biology/biological sciences; business/commerce; business teacher education; chemistry; clinical laboratory science/medical technology; communication/speech communication and rhetoric; computer and information sciences; criminal justice/law enforcement administration; data processing and data processing technology; dramatic/theater arts; economics; education (specific subject areas) related; elementary education; English; fine/studio arts; forensic science and technology; gerontology; history; humanities; international relations and affairs; kinesiology and exercise science; liberal arts and sciences/liberal studies; mathematics; middle school education; music; nursing (registered nurse training); nursing related; philosophy; physics; political science and government; pre-law studies; psychology; religious studies; social studies teacher education; sociology; Spanish; speech and rhetoric; visual and performing arts; web page, digital/multimedia and information resources design.

Academics *Calendar:* semesters. *Degrees:* certificates, associate, bachelor's, and master's. *Special study options:* academic remediation for entering students, accelerated degree program, adult/continuing education programs, advanced placement credit, cooperative education, double majors, external degree program, honors programs, independent study, internships, off-campus study, part-time degree program, services for LD students, student-designed majors, study abroad, summer session for credit. *ROTC:* Army (c), Air Force (c). *Unusual degree programs:* 3-2 engineering with University of Dayton, University of Kentucky, University of Detroit Mercy, University of Cincinnati, University of Notre Dame, University of Louisville.

Computers on Campus 100 computers/terminals are available on campus for general student use. Students can access the following: campus intranet, computer help desk, free student e-mail accounts, online (class) grades, online (class) registration, online (class) schedules. Campuswide network is available. 100% of college-owned or -operated housing units are wired for high-speed Internet access. Wireless service is available via entire campus.

Student Life *Housing options:* coed, men-only, women-only. Campus housing is university owned. *Activities and organizations:* drama/theater group, choral group, Student Government Association, orientation team, ACT More Program Board, Outdoors Club, Business Society, national fraternities, national sororities. *Campus security:* 24-hour patrols, late-night transport/escort service, controlled dormitory access. *Student services:* health clinic, personal/psychological counseling.

Athletics Member NCAA. All Division III. *Intercollegiate sports:* baseball M, basketball M/W, football M, golf M/W, soccer M/W, softball W, tennis M/W, volleyball W. *Intramural sports:* basketball M/W, football M/W, golf M/W, racquetball M/W, softball M/W, volleyball M/W.

Standardized Tests *Required:* SAT or ACT (for admission).

Costs (2007–08) *Comprehensive fee:* $27,470 includes full-time tuition ($20,500), mandatory fees ($720), and room and board ($6250). Full-time tuition and fees vary according to program and student level. Part-time tuition: $490 per credit. Part-time tuition and fees vary according to course load and program. second year student tuition: $20,080; all other returning student tuition: $19,890. *Required fees:* $30 per credit part-time, $15 per term part-time. *College room only:* $2900. Room and board charges vary according to board plan and housing facility. *Payment plans:* installment, deferred payment. *Waivers:* children of alumni and employees or children of employees.

Financial Aid Of all full-time matriculated undergraduates who enrolled in 2005, 828 applied for aid, 828 were judged to have need, 824 had their need fully met. 96 Federal Work-Study jobs (averaging $1235). 47 state and other part-time jobs (averaging $4585). In 2005, 144 non-need-based awards were made. *Average percent of need met:* 82%. *Average financial aid package:* $17,720. *Average need-based loan:* $2301. *Average need-based gift aid:* $4431. *Average non-need-based aid:* $6770. *Average indebtedness upon graduation:* $22,165.

Applying *Options:* electronic application, deferred entrance. *Application fee:* $25. *Required:* high school transcript, minimum 2.0 GPA, rank in upper 50% of high school class, admissions committee may consider those not meeting criteria. *Required for some:* essay or personal statement, 2 letters of recommendation. *Recommended:* interview. *Application deadlines:* 8/15 (freshmen), 8/15 (transfers). *Notification:* continuous (freshmen), continuous (transfers).

Freshman Application Contact Mr. Billy Sarge, Associate Director of Admissions, Thomas More College, 333 Thomas More Parkway, Crestview Hills, KY 41017-3495. *Phone:* 859-344-3332. *Toll-free phone:* 800-825-4557. *Fax:* 859-344-3444. *E-mail:* admissions@thomasmore.edu.

See page 1038 for the College Close-Up.

TRANSYLVANIA UNIVERSITY

Lexington, Kentucky **www.transy.edu/**

- **Independent** 4-year, founded 1780, affiliated with Christian Church (Disciples of Christ)
- **Urban** 40-acre campus with easy access to Cincinnati and Louisville
- **Endowment** $144.5 million
- **Coed** 1,153 undergraduate students, 30% full-time, 19% women, 12% men
- **Very difficult** entrance level, 80% of applicants were admitted

Undergraduates 349 full-time. Students come from 28 states and territories, 2 other countries, 17% are from out of state, 3% African American, 1% Asian American or Pacific Islander, 1% Hispanic American, 0.3% Native American, 0.2% international, 4% transferred in, 76% live on campus. *Retention:* 84% of 2006 full-time freshmen returned.

Freshmen *Admission:* 1,365 applied, 1,095 admitted, 349 enrolled. *Average high school GPA:* 3.56. *Test scores:* SAT critical reading scores over 500: 85%; SAT math scores over 500: 89%; ACT scores over 18: 100%; SAT critical reading scores over 600: 50%; SAT math scores over 600: 45%; ACT scores over 24: 75%; SAT critical reading scores over 700: 13%; SAT math scores over 700: 9%; ACT scores over 30: 22%.

Faculty *Total:* 100, 85% full-time, 84% with terminal degrees. *Student/faculty ratio:* 13:1.

Majors Accounting; anthropology; art; art history, criticism and conservation; art teacher education; biology/biological sciences; business administration and management; business/commerce; chemistry; chemistry teacher education; classics and languages, literatures and linguistics; computer and information sciences; computer science; dramatic/theater arts; economics; elementary education; English; French; history; kinesiology and exercise science; mathematics; middle school education; music performance; music related; music teacher education; philosophy; physical education teaching and coaching; physics; political science and government; psychology; religious studies; social sciences related; sociology; Spanish.

Academics *Calendar:* 4-4-1. *Degree:* bachelor's. *Special study options:* advanced placement credit, double majors, independent study, internships, off-campus study, part-time degree program, student-designed majors, study abroad, summer session for credit. *ROTC:* Army (c), Air Force (c). *Unusual degree programs:* 3-2 engineering with Washington University in St. Louis, University of Kentucky, Vanderbilt University.

Computers on Campus 250 computers/terminals and 250 ports are available on campus for general student use. Students can access the following: campus intranet, computer help desk, free student e-mail accounts, online (class) grades, online (class) schedules. Campuswide network is available. 100% of college-owned or -operated housing units are wired for high-speed Internet access.

Student Life *Housing:* on-campus residence required through junior year. *Options:* coed, men-only, women-only, disabled students. Campus housing is university owned. Freshman campus housing is guaranteed. *Activities and organizations:* drama/theater group, student-run newspaper, radio station, choral group, Student Alumni Association, Student Government Association, Student Activities Board, Crimson Crew, Transylvania Environmental Rights and Responsibility Alliance (TERRA), national fraternities, national sororities. *Campus security:* 24-hour emergency response devices and patrols, late-night transport/escort service, controlled dormitory access. *Student services:* health clinic, personal/psychological counseling.

Athletics Member NCAA. All Division III. *Intercollegiate sports:* baseball M, basketball M/W, cheerleading M/W, cross-country running M/W, field hockey W, golf M/W, soccer M/W, softball W, swimming and diving M/W, tennis M/W, track and field M/W, volleyball W. *Intramural sports:* badminton M/W, basketball M/W, cross-country running M/W, football M/W, golf M/W, racquetball M/W, soccer M/W, softball M/W, swimming and diving M/W, table tennis M/W, tennis M/W, ultimate Frisbee M/W, volleyball M/W.

Standardized Tests *Required:* SAT or ACT (for admission).

Costs (2008–09) *Comprehensive fee:* $31,260 includes full-time tuition ($22,840), mandatory fees ($970), and room and board ($7450). Part-time tuition: $2465 per course.

Financial Aid Of all full-time matriculated undergraduates who enrolled in 2007, 838 applied for aid, 729 were judged to have need, 218 had their need fully met. 416 Federal Work-Study jobs (averaging $1269). 57 state and other part-time jobs (averaging $5913). In 2007, 404 non-need-based awards were made. *Average percent of need met:* 86%. *Average financial aid package:* $18,812. *Average need-based loan:* $4316. *Average need-based gift aid:* $14,546. *Average non-need-based aid:* $12,578. *Average indebtedness upon graduation:* $17,561.

Applying *Options:* electronic application, early admission, early action, deferred entrance. *Application fee:* $30. *Required:* essay or personal statement, high school transcript, minimum 2.75 GPA, 2 letters of recommendation. *Required for some:* interview. *Recommended:* interview. *Application deadlines:* 2/1 (freshmen), rolling (transfers), 12/1 (early action). *Notification:* 3/15 (freshmen), 1/15 (early action).

Freshman Application Contact Mr. Bradley Goan, Director of Admissions, Transylvania University, 300 North Broadway, Lexington, KY 40508-1797. *Phone:* 859-233-4242. *Toll-free phone:* 800-872-6798. *Fax:* 859-281-3642. *E-mail:* admissions@transy.edu.

See page 1040 for the College Close-Up.

UNION COLLEGE

Barbourville, Kentucky **www.unionky.edu/**

- **Independent United Methodist** comprehensive, founded 1879
- **Small-town** 110-acre campus
- **Endowment** $16.0 million
- **Coed** 702 undergraduate students, 92% full-time, 47% women, 53% men
- **Moderately difficult** entrance level, 70% of applicants were admitted

Undergraduates 647 full-time, 55 part-time. Students come from 26 states and territories, 14 other countries, 3% are from out of state, 9% African American, 0.1% Asian American or Pacific Islander, 2% Hispanic American, 0.9% Native American, 5% international, 8% transferred in, 50% live on campus. *Retention:* 51% of 2006 full-time freshmen returned.

Freshmen *Admission:* 701 applied, 493 admitted, 160 enrolled. *Average high school GPA:* 2.9. *Test scores:* SAT critical reading scores over 500: 10%; SAT math scores over 500: 30%; ACT scores over 18: 65%; SAT critical reading scores over 600: 5%; ACT scores over 24: 15%; ACT scores over 30: 2%.

Faculty *Total:* 96, 57% full-time, 54% with terminal degrees. *Student/faculty ratio:* 10:1.

Majors Accounting; biology/biological sciences; business administration and management; business teacher education; chemistry; communication/speech communication and rhetoric; criminal justice/law enforcement administration; education; elementary education; health teacher education; history; mathematics; middle school education; parks, recreation and leisure facilities management; physical education teaching and coaching; psychology; religious studies; secondary education; social sciences; special education; sport and fitness administration/management.

Academics *Calendar:* semesters. *Degrees:* bachelor's and master's. *Special study options:* accelerated degree program, advanced placement credit, cooperative education, distance learning, double majors, independent study, internships, off-campus study, part-time degree program, student-designed majors, study abroad, summer session for credit. *ROTC:* Army (c). *Unusual degree programs:* 3-2 engineering with University of Kentucky.

Computers on Campus 240 computers/terminals and 450 ports are available on campus for general student use. Students can access the following: campus intranet, computer help desk, free student e-mail accounts, online (class) grades, online (class) registration, online (class) schedules. Campuswide network is available. 100% of college-owned or -operated housing units are wired for high-speed Internet access. Wireless service is available via classrooms, computer centers, computer labs, learning centers, libraries, student centers.

Student Life *Housing:* on-campus residence required through sophomore year. *Options:* men-only, women-only. Campus housing is university owned. Freshman campus housing is guaranteed. *Activities and organizations:* drama/theater group, student-run newspaper, choral group, Student Ambassadors, Wilderness Club, Psychology Club, Campus Activities Board. *Campus security:* 24-hour emergency response devices and patrols, late-night transport/escort service, controlled dormitory access. *Student services:* health clinic, personal/psychological counseling.

Athletics Member NAIA. *Intercollegiate sports:* baseball M (s), basketball M (s)/W (s), cheerleading M (s)/W (s), cross-country running M (s)/W (s), football M (s), golf M (s)/W (s), soccer M (s)/W (s), softball W (s), swimming and diving M (s)/W (s), tennis M (s)/W (s), track and field M (s)/W (s), volleyball W (s). *Intramural sports:* basketball M/W, bowling M, football M, softball M/W, table tennis M/W, tennis M/W, volleyball M/W, weight lifting M/W.

Standardized Tests *Required:* SAT or ACT (for admission).

Costs (2007–08) *Comprehensive fee:* $21,020 includes full-time tuition ($15,620), mandatory fees ($400), and room and board ($5000). Full-time tuition and fees vary according to course load and location. Part-time tuition: $270 per hour. *College room only:* $1800. Room and board charges vary according to board plan and student level. *Payment plan:* installment. *Waivers:* senior citizens and employees or children of employees.

Financial Aid Of all full-time matriculated undergraduates who enrolled in 2007, 570 applied for aid, 545 were judged to have need, 174 had their need fully met. 158 Federal Work-Study jobs (averaging $1124). In 2007, 25 non-need-based awards were made. *Average percent of need met:* 84%. *Average financial aid package:* $16,379. *Average need-based loan:* $5919. *Average need-based gift aid:* $10,658. *Average non-need-based aid:* $14,094. *Average indebtedness upon graduation:* $24,344.

Applying *Options:* electronic application, early admission, deferred entrance. *Application fee:* $10. *Required:* high school transcript, minimum 2.0 GPA. *Required for some:* essay or personal statement, letters of recommendation, interview. *Application deadlines:* 8/1 (freshmen), 8/31 (transfers). *Notification:* continuous (freshmen), continuous until 9/1 (transfers).

Freshman Application Contact Mr. Jerry Jackson, Dean for Enrollment Management, Union College, 310 College Street, Barbourville, KY 40906. *Phone:* 606-546-1222. *Toll-free phone:* 800-489-8646. *Fax:* 606-546-1667. *E-mail:* enroll@unionky.edu.

UNIVERSITY OF KENTUCKY

Lexington, Kentucky **www.uky.edu/**

- **State-supported** university, founded 1865
- **Urban** 685-acre campus with easy access to Cincinnati and Louisville
- **Endowment** $916.6 million
- **Coed**
- **Moderately difficult** entrance level

Faculty *Student/faculty ratio:* 17:1.

Academics *Calendar:* semesters. *Degrees:* bachelor's, master's, doctoral, first professional, and post-master's certificates.

Student Life *Campus security:* 24-hour emergency response devices and patrols, late-night transport/escort service, controlled dormitory access.

Athletics Member NCAA. All Division I except football (Division I-A).

Standardized Tests *Required:* SAT or ACT (for admission).

Costs (2007–08) *Tuition:* state resident $6302 full-time, $263 per credit hour part-time; nonresident $14,102 full-time, $588 per credit hour part-time. Full-time tuition and fees vary according to degree level, program, reciprocity agreements, and student level. Part-time tuition and fees vary according to degree level, program, reciprocity agreements, and student level. *Required fees:* $794 full-time, $19 per credit hour part-time. *Room and board:* $7973; room only: $3785. Room and board charges vary according to board plan and housing facility.

Financial Aid Of all full-time matriculated undergraduates who enrolled in 2005, 9,067 applied for aid, 6,602 were judged to have need, 2,932 had their need fully met. 489 Federal Work-Study jobs (averaging $2038). In 2005, 491 non-need-based awards were made. *Average percent of need met:* 81. *Average financial aid package:* $7861. *Average need-based loan:* $3765. *Average need-based gift aid:* $4854. *Average non-need-based aid:* $2821. *Average indebtedness upon graduation:* $17,692.

Applying *Options:* electronic application, early admission. *Application fee:* $40. *Required:* high school transcript, minimum 2.0 GPA.

Freshman Application Contact Ms. Michelle Nordin, Associate Director of Admissions, University of Kentucky, 100 W.D. Funkhouser Building, Lexington, KY 40506-0054. *Phone:* 859-257-2000. *Toll-free phone:* 800-432-0967. *E-mail:* admissio@uky.edu.

UNIVERSITY OF LOUISVILLE

Louisville, Kentucky **www.louisville.edu/**

- **State-supported** university, founded 1798
- **Urban** 169-acre campus
- **Endowment** $796.8 million
- **Coed** 14,962 undergraduate students, 78% full-time, 52% women, 48% men
- **Moderately difficult** entrance level, 70% of applicants were admitted

Undergraduates 11,652 full-time, 3,310 part-time. Students come from 48 states and territories, 60 other countries, 12% are from out of state, 12% African American, 3% Asian American or Pacific Islander, 2% Hispanic American, 0.3% Native American, 2% international, 7% transferred in, 20% live on campus. *Retention:* 78% of 2006 full-time freshmen returned.

Freshmen *Admission:* 7,280 applied, 5,109 admitted, 2,569 enrolled. *Average high school GPA:* 3.47. *Test scores:* SAT critical reading scores over 500: 74%; SAT math scores over 500: 79%; ACT scores over 18: 99%; SAT critical reading scores over 600: 32%; SAT math scores over 600: 39%; ACT scores over 24: 55%; SAT critical reading scores over 700: 9%; SAT math scores over 700: 9%; ACT scores over 30: 11%.

Faculty *Total:* 1,367, 63% full-time, 70% with terminal degrees. *Student/faculty ratio:* 18:1.

Majors Accounting; African-American/Black studies; anthropology; art; art history, criticism and conservation; biology/biological sciences; business administration and management; business administration, management and operations related; business/managerial economics; chemical engineering; chemistry; civil engineering; communication/speech communication and rhetoric; computer engineering; criminal justice/law enforcement administration; dental hygiene; dramatic/theater arts; economics; electrical, electronics and communications engineering; elementary education; engineering; English; finance; fine/studio arts; French; geography; health and physical education; health/medical preparatory programs related; history; industrial engineering; legal assistant/paralegal; liberal arts and sciences and humanities related; liberal arts and sciences/liberal studies; management information systems; marketing/marketing management; mathematics; mechanical engineering; music; music teacher education; music therapy; nursing (registered nurse training); philosophy; physics; political science and government; psychology; sign language interpretation and translation; sociology; Spanish; sport and fitness administration/management; trade and industrial teacher education; women's studies.

Academics *Calendar:* semesters. *Degrees:* certificates, diplomas, associate, bachelor's, master's, doctoral, first professional, post-master's, and postbachelor's certificates. *Special study options:* academic remediation for entering students, accelerated degree program, adult/continuing education programs, advanced placement credit, cooperative education, distance learning, double majors, English as a second language, external degree program, honors programs, independent study, internships, off-campus study, part-time degree program, services for LD students, student-designed majors, study abroad, summer session for credit. *ROTC:* Army (b), Air Force (b).

Computers on Campus 425 computers/terminals are available on campus for general student use. Students can access the following: online (class) registration. Campuswide network is available. 100% of college-owned or -operated housing units are wired for high-speed Internet access. Wireless service is available via classrooms, computer labs, dorm rooms, libraries.

Student Life *Housing options:* coed, disabled students. Campus housing is university owned and is provided by a third party. Freshman applicants given priority for college housing. *Activities and organizations:* drama/theater group, student-run newspaper, radio station, choral group, marching band, Spirit Club—"L" Raisers, Baptist Student Union, Golden Key Society, Sigma Chi, Phi Eta Sigma, national fraternities, national sororities. *Campus security:* 24-hour emergency response devices and patrols, late-night transport/escort service, controlled dormitory access. *Student services:* health clinic, personal/psychological counseling, women's center, legal services.

Athletics Member NCAA. All Division I. *Intercollegiate sports:* baseball M (s), basketball M (s)/W (s), cheerleading M (s)/W (s), crew W (s), cross-country running M (s)/W (s), field hockey W (s), football M (s), golf M (s)/W (s), lacrosse W (s), soccer M (s)/W (s), softball W (s), swimming and diving M (s)/W (s), tennis M (s)/W (s), track and field M (s)/W (s), volleyball W (s). *Intramural sports:* badminton M/W, basketball M/W, bowling M/W, fencing M/W, football M/W, golf M/W, ice hockey M, racquetball M/W, soccer M/W, softball W, swimming and diving M/W, table tennis M/W, tennis M/W, track and field M/W, ultimate Frisbee M/W, volleyball M/W.

Standardized Tests *Required:* SAT or ACT (for admission).

Costs (2007–08) *Tuition:* state resident $6870 full-time, $287 per hour part-time; nonresident $17,664 full-time, $736 per hour part-time. Full-time tuition and fees vary according to reciprocity agreements. Part-time tuition and fees vary according to course load and reciprocity agreements. *Required fees:* $70 full-time, $3 per hour part-time. *Room and board:* $5722; room only: $3732. Room and board charges vary according to board plan and housing facility. *Payment plan:* installment. *Waivers:* senior citizens and employees or children of employees.

Financial Aid Of all full-time matriculated undergraduates who enrolled in 2007, 7,367 applied for aid, 6,380 were judged to have need, 1,032 had their need fully met. In 2007, 1387 non-need-based awards were made. *Average percent of need met:* 60%. *Average financial aid package:* $10,184. *Average need-based loan:* $4429. *Average need-based gift aid:* $7250. *Average non-need-based aid:* $6965. *Average indebtedness upon graduation:* $11,462.

Applying *Options:* electronic application, early admission, deferred entrance. *Application fee:* $40. *Required:* high school transcript, minimum 2.5 GPA. *Application deadline:* rolling (freshmen). *Notification:* continuous (freshmen), continuous (transfers).

Freshman Application Contact Ms. Jenny L. Sawyer, Executive Director for Admissions, University of Louisville, 2211 South Brook, Louisville, KY 40292. *Phone:* 502-852-6531. *Toll-free phone:* 502-852-6531 (in-state); 800-334-8635 (out-of-state). *Fax:* 502-852-4776. *E-mail:* admitme@gwise.louisville.edu.

UNIVERSITY OF THE CUMBERLANDS

Williamsburg, Kentucky **www.ucumberlands.edu/**

- **Independent Kentucky Baptist** comprehensive, founded 1889
- **Rural** 60-acre campus with easy access to Knoxville
- **Endowment** $58.3 million
- **Coed**
- **Moderately difficult** entrance level

Founded in 1889, Cumberland College became University of the Cumberlands on July 1, 2005, reflecting the diversity and excellence of options offered in high-quality education. The University is committed to providing a superior education within a Christian atmosphere emphasizing individual growth and strives to instill in students the desire to be agents of change in the world by using knowledge for the benefit of others.

Faculty *Student/faculty ratio:* 14:1.

Academics *Calendar:* semesters. *Degrees:* associate, bachelor's, and master's.

Student Life *Campus security:* 24-hour emergency response devices and patrols, student patrols, late-night transport/escort service, patrols by trained security personnel 11pm–7am.

Athletics Member NAIA.

Standardized Tests *Required:* SAT or ACT (for admission).

Costs (2007–08) *Comprehensive fee:* $20,284 includes full-time tuition ($13,298), mandatory fees ($360), and room and board ($6626). Part-time tuition: $430 per hour. Part-time tuition and fees vary according to course load. *Required fees:* $65 per term part-time.

Financial Aid Of all full-time matriculated undergraduates who enrolled in 2007, 1,271 applied for aid, 1,182 were judged to have need, 373 had their need fully met. 461 Federal Work-Study jobs (averaging $1625). 169 state and other part-time jobs (averaging $1664). In 2007, 228 non-need-based awards were made. *Average percent of need met:* 94. *Average financial aid package:* $15,520. *Average need-based loan:* $3729. *Average need-based gift aid:* $8698. *Average non-need-based aid:* $10,060. *Average indebtedness upon graduation:* $17,117.

Applying *Application fee:* $30. *Required:* high school transcript, minimum 2.0 GPA, 1 letter of recommendation. *Required for some:* essay or personal statement, interview.

Freshman Application Contact Mrs. Erica Harris, Director of Admissions, University of the Cumberlands, 6178 College Station Drive, Williamsburg, KY 40769. *Phone:* 606-539-4241. *Toll-free phone:* 800-343-1609. *Fax:* 606-539-4303. *E-mail:* admiss@ucumberlands.edu.

See page 1042 for the College Close-Up.

WESTERN KENTUCKY UNIVERSITY

Bowling Green, Kentucky **www.wku.edu/**

- **State-supported** comprehensive, founded 1906
- **Suburban** 223-acre campus with easy access to Nashville
- **Endowment** $102.2 million
- **Coed** 16,501 undergraduate students, 80% full-time, 58% women, 42% men
- **Moderately difficult** entrance level, 95% of applicants were admitted

Undergraduates 13,251 full-time, 3,250 part-time. Students come from 43 states and territories, 40 other countries, 16% are from out of state, 10% African American, 1% Asian American or Pacific Islander, 1% Hispanic American, 0.3% Native American, 2% international, 5% transferred in, 31% live on campus. *Retention:* 73% of 2006 full-time freshmen returned.

Freshmen *Admission:* 6,854 applied, 6,515 admitted, 3,115 enrolled. *Average high school GPA:* 3.16. *Test scores:* SAT critical reading scores over 500: 43%; SAT math scores over 500: 42%; ACT scores over 18: 79%; SAT critical reading scores over 600: 9%; SAT math scores over 600: 13%; ACT scores over 24: 29%; SAT critical reading scores over 700: 2%; SAT math scores over 700: 2%; ACT scores over 30: 4%.

Faculty *Total:* 1,146, 63% full-time, 51% with terminal degrees. *Student/faculty ratio:* 18:1.

Majors Accounting; advertising; agricultural production; agriculture; anthropology; apparel and textiles; architectural drafting and CAD/CADD; architectural technology; biochemistry; biology/biological sciences; business administration and management; business/managerial economics; business teacher education; cartography; cell biology and anatomical sciences related; chemistry; civil engineering; civil engineering technology; clinical laboratory science/medical technology; communication/speech communication and rhetoric; community health services counseling; computer and information sciences; computer/information technology services administration related; dance; data processing and data processing technology; dental hygiene; dramatic/theater arts; early childhood education; economics; electrical, electronics and communications engineering; elementary education; emergency medical technology (EMT paramedic); English; English language and literature related; environmental health; executive assistant/ executive secretary; family and consumer sciences/home economics teacher education; finance; fine/studio arts; French; general studies; geography; geology/ earth science; German; health/health care administration; health information/ medical records technology; health services/allied health/health sciences; history; hospitality administration; industrial technology; information technology; journalism; kindergarten/preschool education; kinesiology and exercise science; legal assistant/paralegal; management information systems; manufacturing technology; marketing/marketing management; mathematics; mechanical engineering; meteorology; middle school education; multi-/interdisciplinary studies related; music; music related; nursing (registered nurse training); organizational communication; paralegal/legal assistant; parks, recreation and leisure facilities management; philosophy; physical education teaching and coaching; physical science technologies related; physics; political communication; political science and government; psychology; public relations/image management; radio and television; religious studies; social sciences; social work; sociology; Spanish; special education; special education (speech or language impaired); speech and rhetoric; sport and fitness administration/management; technical teacher education; trade and industrial teacher education; visual and performing arts.

Academics *Calendar:* semesters. *Degrees:* certificates, associate, bachelor's, master's, doctoral, post-master's, postbachelor's, and first professional certificates. *Special study options:* academic remediation for entering students, accelerated degree program, adult/continuing education programs, advanced placement credit, cooperative education, distance learning, double majors, English as a second language, honors programs, independent study, internships, part-time degree program, services for LD students, student-designed majors, study abroad, summer session for credit. *ROTC:* Army (b), Air Force (c).

Computers on Campus 1,300 computers/terminals are available on campus for general student use. Students can access the following: campus intranet, computer help desk, free student e-mail accounts, online (class) grades, online (class) registration, online (class) schedules. Campuswide network is available. 100% of college-owned or -operated housing units are wired for high-speed Internet access.

Student Life *Housing:* on-campus residence required for freshman year. *Options:* coed, men-only, women-only, disabled students. Campus housing is university owned. Freshman applicants given priority for college housing. *Activities and organizations:* drama/theater group, student-run newspaper, radio and television station, choral group, marching band, Student Government Association, Campus Activities Board, Campus Crusade for Christ, Campus Ministries, Residence Hall Association, national fraternities, national sororities. *Campus security:* 24-hour emergency response devices and patrols, student patrols, late-night transport/escort service, controlled dormitory access. *Student services:* health clinic, personal/psychological counseling, women's center.

Athletics Member NCAA. All Division I except football (Division I-A). *Intercollegiate sports:* baseball M (s), basketball M (s)/W (s), cheerleading M/W, cross-country running M (s)/W (s), golf M (s)/W (s), riflery M (c)/W (c), softball W (s), swimming and diving M (s)/W (s), tennis M (s)/W (s), track and field M (s)/W (s), volleyball W (s). *Intramural sports:* archery M/W, badminton M/W, basketball M/W, bowling M/W, equestrian sports M/W, fencing M (c)/W (c), golf M/W, lacrosse M (c)/W (c), racquetball M/W, rugby M (c)/W (c), soccer M/W, softball M/W (c), swimming and diving M (c)/W (c), table tennis M/W, volleyball M (c)/W (c), water polo M/W, wrestling M.

Standardized Tests *Required:* SAT or ACT (for admission).

Costs (2007–08) *Tuition:* state resident $6416 full-time, $267 per hour part-time; nonresident $15,470 full-time, $645 per hour part-time. Full-time tuition and fees vary according to course load, location, program, and reciprocity agreements. Part-time tuition and fees vary according to course load, location, program, and reciprocity agreements. *Room and board:* $5704; room only: $3360. Room and board charges vary according to board plan and housing facility. *Payment plans:* tuition prepayment, installment. *Waivers:* senior citizens and employees or children of employees.

Financial Aid Of all full-time matriculated undergraduates who enrolled in 2004, 9,293 applied for aid, 7,089 were judged to have need, 2,027 had their need fully met. 833 Federal Work-Study jobs (averaging $1549). 1,674 state and other part-time jobs (averaging $1955). In 2004, 1096 non-need-based awards were made. *Average percent of need met:* 29%. *Average financial aid package:* $7926. *Average need-based loan:* $3342. *Average need-based gift aid:* $3790. *Average non-need-based aid:* $3109. *Average indebtedness upon graduation:* $14,704.

Applying *Options:* electronic application. *Application fee:* $35. *Required:* high school transcript, minimum 2.5 GPA. *Application deadlines:* 8/1 (freshmen), 8/1 (transfers). *Notification:* continuous (freshmen), continuous (transfers).

Freshman Application Contact Western Kentucky University, Potter Hall 117, 1 Big Red Way, Bowling Green, KY 42101-3576. *Phone:* 270-745-2551. *Toll-free phone:* 800-495-8463. *Fax:* 270-745-6133. *E-mail:* admission@wku.edu.

ASBURY COLLEGE

WILMORE, KENTUCKY

The College

Located 20 minutes south of Lexington, Kentucky, Asbury College is a private, residential, liberal arts institution committed to academic excellence and spiritual vitality. Founded in 1890, the College offers forty-nine undergraduate majors, a degree-completion program, several graduate programs in special education, teaching English as a foreign language, and alternative certification programs. An adult degree completion program with three majors is also offered.

The mission of Asbury College, as a Christian liberal arts college in the Wesleyan-Holiness tradition, is to equip men and women, through a commitment to academic excellence and spiritual vitality, for a lifetime of learning, leadership, and service to the professions, society, the family, and the Church, thereby preparing them to engage their cultures and advance the cause of Christ around the world.

A distinguishing mark of Asbury's Christian community is that the members are committed to a set of basic principles that are considered essential to maintain the spirit and health of the community. At Asbury College, the basic tenet of the community is found in Jesus's two great commandments in Matthew 22:37–40: "You shall love the Lord your God with all your heart, and with all your soul, and with all your mind . . . And . . . you shall love your neighbor as yourself." Thus, members of the Asbury community seek to love God and practice self-sacrificial love in relationship to others. Such disciplined community living is inherent preparation for servant-leaders who give their lives to fulfill a cause greater than themselves.

Citing the Christian and academic reputation of the College as their primary reason for selecting Asbury, 316 new freshmen were enrolled in fall 2007. The current undergraduate enrollment is 1,237 students from forty-four states and fourteen other countries. Kentucky, Ohio, Indiana, Pennsylvania, and Florida are the five states that are represented the most. Asbury offers majors and programs of study within the liberal arts curriculum and confers the degrees of Bachelor of Arts and Bachelor of Science in education. The most popular majors are in the departments of communication arts, education, psychology, business management, bible, history, and biology.

Organizations and clubs are an important part of student life at Asbury College. Positions on the *Collegian* (student newspaper) and the *Asburian* (yearbook) are open to all students. Students can become involved in the Ministerial Association, Christian Service Association, Fellowship of Christian Athletes, and Community Involvement, Art, Speech, English, Foreign Student, French, and Spanish Clubs. Students may also participate in the Women's Vocal Ensemble, Men's Glee Club, Jazz Ensemble, Concert Choir, and Concert Band. Student honor societies include Alpha Psi Omega (drama), Phi Alpha Theta (history), Phi Sigma Tau (philosophy), Sigma Zeta (science and mathematics), Sigma Tau Delta (English), and Sigma Delta Pi (Spanish). Among the professional organizations that students may join are the American Guild of Organists, the Music Educators National Conference, the Kentucky Intercollegiate Press Association, the Student National Education Association, and the Student Association for Health, Physical Education and Recreation.

Asbury recognizes the value of athletics and maintains a program of intramural and intercollegiate sports. Intercollegiate sports for men are baseball, basketball, cross-country, soccer, swimming and diving, and tennis. For women, basketball, cross-country, soccer, swimming and diving, tennis, and volleyball are offered. Intramural activities include basketball, flag football, golf, soccer, softball, tennis, volleyball, and walleyball. The College also sponsors a Christian witness gymnastics team that tours each spring semester.

Eighty-five percent of Asbury students reside in College residence halls. Duplexes for married students are available. Counseling and health services are available to all students. Asbury maintains a well-equipped clinic with a competent, experienced staff consisting of registered nurses and a physician.

Location

Wilmore, a safe community of approximately 6,000, is located in the heart of the famous Bluegrass region, 15 miles southwest of Lexington, Kentucky, the second-largest city in the commonwealth. Surrounding Wilmore are reminders of the state's pioneer history, including Fort Harrod, Boonesborough, and Shakertown, a restored religious community dating from the 1800s. Near Lexington is the Kentucky Horse Park. Camping, rock-climbing, boating, and fishing are available at nearby Red River Gorge and Natural Bridge, and Mammoth Cave National Park is less than 2 hours from Wilmore.

Lexington has theaters, an opera house, a symphony orchestra, and Rupp Arena, where programs ranging from performances by well-known musicians to basketball games are presented.

Majors and Degrees

Asbury College confers the degrees of Bachelor of Arts and the Bachelor of Science in education. Undergraduate majors are available in accounting, art, bible and theology (preministry or preseminary), biblical languages, biochemistry, biology, business management, chemistry, Christian ministries, communications, computational mathematics, creative writing, elementary education, engineering (with the University of Kentucky), English, equine management, exercise science, financial mathematics, French, health science, hippotherapy, history, journalism, mathematics, media communication, middle school education, missions, music, music business, P–12 education (art, French, health and physical education, Latin, music, and Spanish), philosophy, physical science, psychology, recreation, secondary education (biological science, chemistry, English, English as a second language, learning and behavior disorders, mathematics, and social studies,), social work, sociology, Spanish, sport management, theater and cinema, and youth ministries.

Academic Programs

Asbury College operates on a sixteen-week semester system with one 4-week summer session. To qualify for graduation, students must complete a minimum of 124 semester hours with an overall grade point average of at least 2.0 and 2.5 in teacher education programs.

The liberal arts core requirements are as follows: Foundations for Spiritual Life and Growth, 9 credits; communication, 3 credits; mathematics, 0–3 credits; English, 3–6 credits; foreign language, 0–9 credits; sciences with a lab, 4 credits; fine arts, 3 credits; social sciences, 3 credits; physical education, 2 credits; cross-cultural experience, 0–3 credits; leadership, 3 credits; and history and philosophy, 3 credits.

Students may be granted college credit for satisfactory performance on AP tests in certain subjects. Advanced standing in foreign language is also available to qualifying students. Further detailed information is available from the College.

Off-Campus Programs

Qualified students may participate in the American Studies Program in Washington, D.C.; the Holy Land Studies Program in Israel; the Wesleyan Urban Coalition Program in Chicago; Martha's Vineyard; Los Angeles Film School; and other bestsemester.com programs, as well as in the Latin American Studies Program.

Academic Facilities

College facilities that are available to students include a computer center and several well-equipped chemistry, biology, physics, computer, and language laboratories. The College also has a radio station and an outstanding TV studio with a 24-hour cable station. The Kinlaw Library, completed in 2001, is a 72,000-square-foot facility that houses the College's 168,000-volume collection, as well as the Kirkland Learning Resources Center. With wireless service available, computer, media, and curriculum labs are included in the building.

Costs

For 2007–08, annual expenses were $21,132 for tuition and $5152 for room and board.

Financial Aid

More than 90 percent of the College's students receive some type of financial assistance. The various aid programs include academic scholarships, Federal Pell Grants, Federal Supplemental Educational Opportunity Grants, Kentucky Higher Education Assistance Authority Grants, Federal Perkins Loans, Federal Stafford Student Loans, state loans, United Methodist Student Loans, institutional grants and loans, institutional employment, and Federal Work-Study Program awards. Asbury offers honor scholarships, including a few full tuition grants. Merit Finalists receive 70 percent tuition scholarships.

To apply for aid, students should complete the Free Application for Federal Student Aid (FAFSA). Priority consideration is given to those who file before March 1. Financial need is defined as the difference between the amount a family can pay and the total expenses for the academic year. If there is a deficit, the student is considered to have financial need. The awards are made on the basis of financial need. Notification of awards begins early in April. For more information, students may contact the financial aid office at 859-858-3511 Ext. 2195 or 800-888-1818 Ext. 2195 (toll-free).

Faculty

Asbury has a full-time faculty of about 80 members. The part-time faculty usually numbers 70 members. Each student has a faculty adviser, who is personally interested in each student and willing to assist advisees in any way possible. Most faculty members are approachable and many open their homes to students, leading Bible studies or homework sessions. Asbury's faculty-student ratio is 1:11. Approximately 75 percent of the full-time faculty members hold earned terminal degrees in their fields.

Student Government

The objectives of the student government organization are to act as a unifying force, bringing the institution as a whole into vital contact with current issues in college life; to help students find opportunities in college life in a mature Christian spirit, through recommendation and administration; and to promote an atmosphere for intellectual, spiritual, and cultural development. Regulations for student life are explained in the student handbook. The use of tobacco, alcoholic beverages, and illegal drugs is strictly prohibited.

Admission Requirements

The Asbury College faculty strongly recommends that applicants should have completed the following requirements in grades 9 through 12: 4 years of English, including 1 year of composition; 3 or 4 years of mathematics (algebra, geometry, advanced algebra, and other advanced math); 2 years of social studies, of which 1 year should be history; 2 or 3 years of laboratory science; and 2 years of the same foreign language. Applicants should have a grade point average of at least 2.5. Students should take the ACT examination (and have a minimum ACT composite score of 22) or the SAT (minimum score of 1020). Freshmen entering Asbury have had an average ACT composite score of 24.6, an SAT combined score of 1163, and a high school grade point average of 3.58. Transfer students must have maintained an average of 2.5 or better at the college or university last attended.

Application and Information

Students may apply for freshman admission during the spring of their junior year or during their senior year in high school. Notification of admission decisions is given within 24 hours after the following have been received: the application and $30 application fee, transcripts and a high school counselor's recommendation (for high school students only). Enrollment is cut off at resident capacity. Admission decisions are made and financial assistance is awarded by Asbury College without regard to race, color, sex, national origin, or handicap.

Further information may be obtained by contacting:

Office of Admissions
Asbury College
Wilmore, Kentucky 40390
Phone: 859-858-3511 Ext. 2142
800-888-1818 Ext. 2142 (toll-free)
Fax: 859-858-3921
Web site: http://www.asbury.edu

In 2006 in Torino, Italy, media communication students participated in the Olympic games as camera operators and loggers.

KENTUCKY STATE UNIVERSITY

FRANKFORT, KENTUCKY

The University

Kentucky State University (KSU) is a liberal studies public institution that offers a friendly, individualized education with excellence as its ultimate goal. Founded in 1886, the University is located in the historic capital city of Frankfort. While the University has changed to meet the needs of the society it serves, its basic goal has remained unchanged since its founding. It is a liberal studies institution of ideal size that is dedicated to the principle of providing the highest-quality education at the lowest possible cost.

Kentucky State University's undergraduate enrollment in 2006–07 was 2,340 students. The primary source of students is the state of Kentucky, but more than thirty-five states and territories are represented on the campus; students also come from fifteen other countries and bring to the campus a regional, national, and global cultural and ethnic diversity. Nontraditional students may earn a degree at Kentucky State University through several programs.

The University believes that the on-campus residential experience is an essential part of student life. Full-time freshman and sophomore students are required to live on campus.

KSU has about thirty student organizations—ranging from social fraternities and sororities to departmental clubs, literary groups, and political organizations. Students enjoy intramural sports as well as intercollegiate men's baseball, football, and golf; women's softball and volleyball; and men's and women's basketball, cross-country, and track. KSU offers convocations, special lectures, art exhibits, fine arts performances, and many other activities designed to complement classroom learning. It also offers personal and career counseling, helps students prepare resumes, arranges job interviews, and provides testing to help students assess their interests and abilities. Placement activities include an annual career fair. Health care is available on campus. KSU offers a Master of Public Administration, a Master of Business Administration, the Master of Science in aquaculture and in computer science, and a Master of Special Education.

Location

KSU is located at the western edge of the Bluegrass region in Kentucky's capital city (population 27,500). The Frankfort area offers historic, scenic, and recreational attractions. Activities in the area include boating, camping, fishing, golfing, horseback riding, and water and snow skiing. Frankfort is between Kentucky's two largest cities, 25 miles west of Lexington and 50 miles east of Louisville. It is on Interstate 64, less than an hour's drive from Interstates 71, 65, and 75, the Bluegrass Parkway, and the Mountain Parkway. Bluegrass Airport, near Lexington, is 20 miles from Frankfort; Standiford Field in Louisville is approximately 55 miles away. Bus transportation to and from both cities is available.

Majors and Degrees

Kentucky State University awards the degrees of Bachelor of Arts, Bachelor of Science, Bachelor of Music Education, and Bachelor of Music in Performance. Majors offered are applied mathematics (3-2 engineering); art (studio); art education; biology (options in general biology or health sciences); business administration (specialization in accounting, business administration, economics, management, management information systems, or marketing); chemistry; child development and family relations; computer science; criminal justice; elementary education; English; history; interdisciplinary early elementary education (grades K–4); liberal studies (including a student-designed liberal studies major); mathematics; music education; music performance (options in vocal or instrumental music); physical education (nonteaching or teaching); political science; psychology; public administration; and social work.

Secondary teacher certification is offered in biology, English, history, mathematics, and social studies.

The Associate in Applied Science degree is offered in drafting and design technology, electronics technology, and nursing, and an Associate of Arts degree is offered in liberal studies.

In cooperation with various professional schools in Kentucky and other states, KSU offers preprofessional study in community health (2-2 program), cytotechnology (2-2 program), dentistry, engineering (3-2 program), law, medicine, nuclear medicine technology (2-3 program), optometry, pharmacy, physical therapy (2-2 program), and veterinary medicine.

Academic Programs

KSU provides a full liberal studies experience. Central to KSU's academic program are courses called the Liberal Studies Requirements. These 53 credit hours, required of all baccalaureate students, provide the broad, basic knowledge necessary in a rapidly changing world. The Liberal Studies Requirements include courses in English, speech, mathematics, and foreign language; in the behavioral, social, and natural sciences; and in health and safety education and physical activity. At least 128 hours are required for a bachelor's degree; at least 64 hours are required for an associate degree. KSU awards up to 64 credit hours based on examinations and certifications. The academic year is divided into two semesters—fall and spring—and a six-week summer session.

KSU's Whitney M. Young, Jr., College of Leadership Studies is believed to be unique in U.S. public higher education. The college is a division in which students study the Great Books—enduring works of literature, including those on history, philosophy, mathematics, and sciences. Intensive work in writing is required. After two years, students may continue the study of the Great Books, which constitutes a liberal studies major, and minor in another area; they may major in an area in one of the University's other colleges and schools and minor in the Great Books study; or they may select both a major and minor in other areas after completing the equivalent of their Liberal Studies Requirements in Whitney Young College.

Students may cross-enroll in Army and Air Force ROTC classes at the University of Kentucky in nearby Lexington. Completion of the ROTC program leads to a commission as a second lieutenant in the appropriate branch of service.

Off-Campus Programs

Some students may qualify for internships in which they can test vocational preferences, develop job skills in work situations, and possibly earn credit toward graduation. KSU also offers cooperative education opportunities that enable students to work off campus as a required part of an academic program. Students receive credit each semester for the paid work assignments. Through the Cooperative Center for Study in England, KSU students can study abroad between semesters, in the summer, or during their junior year.

Academic Facilities

The University has thirty-three buildings on its 511-acre campus. Blazer Library houses nearly 600,000 volumes and subscribes to hundreds of periodicals and journals. Students have access to the nearby Kentucky Historical Society Library, which has 50,000 volumes, and State Library of the Kentucky Department of Libraries and Archives, which has more than 125,000 volumes, 87,000 U.S. government documents, and hundreds of periodicals and journals. KSU also has four auditoriums, used for concerts, plays, lectures, films, and other cultural activities; biology, chemistry, physics, computer, music, and language laboratories; art studios; darkrooms; an art gallery; and a research farm and a fish hatchery.

Costs

In 2007–08, tuition, room (double occupancy), board, and fees totaled $12,238 per year for full-time undergraduate residents of Kentucky. For full-time undergraduate out-of-state students, the total was $19,408 per year. Books, supplies, and personal expenses cost an estimated $700–$1000 per year. KSU offers one meal plan, required of students in residence halls. Certain laboratory courses require small additional fees.

Financial Aid

Eligibility for financial assistance is based on demonstrated financial need, scholastic ability, useful talent, training, and experience. Students can apply for State Student Incentive Grants, Federal Pell Grants, Federal Supplemental Educational Opportunity Grants, Federal Perkins Loans, Kentucky Stafford Student Loans, Federal PLUS loans, part-time employment awards, and Federal Work-Study Program awards. Approximately 85 percent of KSU's students receive some form of financial assistance. To be considered for need-based financial assistance, prospective students must submit a KSU financial aid application and a Free Application for Federal Student Aid (FAFSA) and signed copies of their and their parents' federal income tax return from the previous year. The FAFSA, which can be obtained from high school guidance counselors or the KSU Office of Admission, should be mailed directly to the College Scholarship Service in Cahokia, Illinois. Students who complete the application process by the priority date of March 15 receive consideration for both the fall and spring semesters.

For students who do not qualify for need-based aid but who have demonstrated specific academic, artistic, musical, or athletic skills or talent, scholarships and grants-in-aid are available. Students may qualify for Presidential Scholarships (tuition, room, board, and book stipend), Excellence Scholarships (value of in-state tuition, plus one half the cost of room and board), or Thorobred Scholarships (value of in-state tuition only). Residents of the Kentucky counties of Anderson, Franklin, Scott, Shelby, Owen, and Henry may qualify for Service Area Scholarships. Other scholarships are available as well. Prospective students must submit an application for admission and a FAFSA by March 15 of the year they plan to enter KSU. Application forms can be obtained from the Office of Admissions.

Faculty

KSU has 123 full-time and 7 part-time faculty members; 99 percent hold advanced degrees. Faculty members who teach graduate classes also teach undergraduate classes. Qualified professors, not graduate students, teach all classes. While faculty members represent a broad range at KSU, they share a commitment to close student-teacher relationships and to the value of a liberal education as preparation for graduate and professional school and career employment.

Student Government

The Student Government Association (SGA) gives students a voice in campus affairs, plays a part in scheduling and sponsoring campus activities, and enacts legislation in matters of student concern, subject to ratification by the President's Cabinet and Board of Regents. SGA and the cabinet have joint jurisdiction in regulating and promoting student activities and organizations. An SGA member serves as a voting member of the Board of Regents.

Admission Requirements

KSU seeks serious students who are committed to excelling in college studies. The University requires that all prospective students complete a precollege curriculum of 22 high school units, with at least 4 units in English; 3 in mathematics; 3 in sciences, including at least one laboratory course; 3 in social sciences; 2 in a foreign language; 1 in history and appreciation of visual or performing arts; ½ in health; ½ in physical education; and seven electives. Additional units in foreign languages, mathematics, sciences, arts, and computer literacy are highly desirable.

New freshmen from Kentucky must have graduated from an accredited high school and taken the ACT. Under recently enacted legislation, Kentucky State University may accept up to 10 percent of first-time freshmen enrolled in baccalaureate programs, based on SAT rather than ACT scores. Any graduate of an accredited high school is unconditionally admitted if they meet the precollege curriculum requirements established by the Kentucky Council on Higher Education and have an admission index of 430. The admission index is a numerical score determined by multiplying the cumulative grade point average (on a 4.0 scale) by 100 and the ACT composite (or math and verbal combined SAT) by 10, and adding the two numbers.

Nontraditional applicants (25 years of age or older) may substitute results of the Career Planning and Placement Test (CPP-II) for ACT or SAT results if pursuing an associate degree.

Students applying for admission to the Whitney M. Young, Jr., College of Leadership Studies should have taken sound academic courses in high school and have a strong interest in learning. Transfer students are considered, but they must start at the beginning of the Whitney Young program.

Application and Information

High school students should complete and submit an admission application early in their senior year. An official high school transcript and ACT or SAT scores should be sent to KSU during the senior year. A final high school transcript, including class size and rank, grade point average, and date of graduation, should be sent to KSU after graduation and by July 1. Transfer students must submit official transcripts and statements of good standing from each college attended. Students dismissed less than honorably from other institutions may not enroll at KSU until they qualify for readmission to the college or university from which they were dismissed. Applicants are encouraged to visit the campus. Requests for a student prospectus, application forms, and further information should be directed to:

Office of Admission
Kentucky State University
400 East Main Street
Frankfort, Kentucky 40601-9957
Phone: 502-597-6349 or 6813
877-FOR-KYSU (toll-free)
Fax: 502-597-5814
Web site: http://www.kysu.edu

It is the policy of Kentucky State University not to discriminate against any individual in its educational programs, activities, or employment on the basis of race, color, national origin, sex, disability, veteran status, age, religion, or marital status. KSU is an Equal Educational and Employment Opportunity/Affirmative Action Institution.

NORTHERN KENTUCKY UNIVERSITY

HIGHLAND HEIGHTS, KENTUCKY

The University

Northern Kentucky University (NKU) was founded in 1968 and is the newest of Kentucky's eight state universities. The atmosphere of the campus is futuristic, emphasizing a high-quality education by supporting the liberal arts. Major buildings are of modern, contemporary architectural design and are set on 300 acres of rolling countryside. NKU has an enrollment of approximately 14,900 students from forty-one states and eighty-two countries and is accredited by the Southern Association of Colleges and Schools. The Salmon P. Chase College of Law is accredited by both the American Bar Association and the Association of American Law Schools.

There are more than 179 student organizations. NKU competes in the NCAA Division II Great Lakes Valley Conference. Intercollegiate sports are offered for men and women in basketball, cheerleading, cross-country, golf, soccer, and tennis; for men in baseball; and for women in fast-pitch softball and volleyball. Intramural activities vary by semester, but include basketball, dodgeball, field hockey, flag football, ice hockey, racquetball, soccer, softball, Tae Kwan Do, volleyball, and many others. Students should visit the University's Web site for a complete listing at http://www.nku.edu/~camprec/index.htm.

Location

NKU is located in the largest metropolitan area of any state university in Kentucky. It is located at the junction of U.S. Highway 27 and Interstates 275 and 471 in Highland Heights, Kentucky, 8 miles southeast of Cincinnati, Ohio. NKU is only 60 miles from Dayton, 79 miles from Lexington, 93 miles from Louisville, and 114 miles from Indianapolis. While the immediate surroundings are suburban, NKU is part of the metropolitan area of greater Cincinnati.

Majors and Degrees

Northern Kentucky University awards the Bachelor of Arts, Bachelor of Fine Arts, Bachelor of Music, Bachelor of Science, Bachelor of Science in Nursing, and Bachelor of Social Work degrees. NKU also offers preprofessional programs, secondary education teacher certification, certificates, and the Associate of Applied Science degree.

The B.A. and B.S. degrees are offered in accounting, anthropology, athletic training, art (teaching), biological sciences, business administration, business education, business informatics, chemistry, chemistry/biology, computer education technology, computer information technology, computer science, criminal justice, early childhood education, economics, electronic engineering technology, electronic media and broadcasting, elementary education, English, entrepreneurship, environmental science, finance, French, geography, geology, German, graphic design, health science, history, industrial education, human resources, construction management, international studies, journalism, liberal studies, management, mechanical and manufacturing engineering, marketing, mathematics, media informatics, mental health–human services, middle grades education, organizational leadership, organizational systems technology, organizational systems technology management, philosophy, photography, physical education, physical education recreation, physics, political science, psychology, public relations, radio-TV, recreation-fitness, social studies (teaching), sociology, Spanish, special education, speech communication, sports business, and theater.

The B.F.A. degree is granted in art and in theater arts. The B.Mus. degree is offered in music. The B.S.N. degree is offered in the nursing major and the B.S.W. degree in the social work major.

Preprofessional programs are available in dentistry, engineering, forestry, human resources, law, medicine, optometry, pharmacy, physician assistant studies, physical therapy, veterinary medicine, and wildlife management. In addition, the University offers majors, minors, and areas of discipline for secondary education teacher certification.

The University also awards the A.A.S. degree in construction technology, criminal justice, human services, liberal studies, prebusiness studies, radiologic technology, and respiratory care.

Certificates are also available at the University in architectural drafting, automated manufacturing processes, entrepreneurship, information systems development, information systems management, organizational systems, piano pedagogy, and training and organizational development.

Academic Programs

NKU operates on a semester calendar. To receive a bachelor's degree, students must complete a minimum of 128 credit hours. At least 64 credit hours are required for the associate degree.

The University offers a variety of career planning and placement, internship, independent study, work-study, and cooperative-education programs. There is also an Advising, Counseling, and Testing Center available. Other programs include an honors program, a program that allows for the dual enrollment of high school students, a program where students can combine their career interests in the liberal arts and engineering fields, and University 101, an orientation program for freshmen and transfer students.

NKU recognizes credit earned through the Advanced Placement (AP) Program and the general, subject, and institutional tests of specific College-Level Examination Program (CLEP). A maximum of 45 credit hours may be applied toward the bachelor's degree from the AP and CLEP examinations. The International Baccalaureate Program allows students to earn credit in science, mathematics, psychology, and languages.

Off-Campus Programs

A variety of study-abroad opportunities are available to NKU students through membership in several consortia, through NKU exchange agreements with international universities, and through independent NKU professor-led trips.

Study in Australia, Belize, England, Ghana, Hong Kong, India, Ireland, Jamaica, and Scotland is possible in a wide range of courses and programs available through NKU's membership in the Cooperative Center for Study Abroad (CCSA), which is headquartered at NKU.

The Kentucky Institute for International Studies (KIIS) offers students academic language programs in Argentina, Austria, Brazil, China, Costa Rica, Czech Republic, Denmark, Ecuador, France, Germany, Greece, Italy, Japan, Mexico, Poland, Spain, Turkey, and Ukraine.

The NKU Office of International Programs has student and faculty exchanges with universities in Costa Rica, Denmark, France, Germany, Japan, Korea, Mexico, Russia, Scotland, and Spain.

Academic Facilities

Among the academic facilities at NKU are an anthropology museum, a biology museum, and an art gallery with rotating exhibits. NKU also has a new laser projection planetarium. NKU becomes only the seventh institution worldwide to boast such equipment, joining six major planetariums in cities such as Tokyo, Los Angeles, and London. Additionally, the University has nursing, respiratory care, and radiologic technology laboratories. In spring of 2008, NKU opened a 9000-seat arena called the Bank of Kentucky Center. In fall of 2008, NKU's brand-new Student Union, a student-centered facility, which is a focal point for campus programs and student organizations, opened. The W. Frank Steely Library at NKU contains 311,155 book titles and maintains 1,729 paper periodical subscriptions (additional periodicals are available in electronic format). Computer laboratories offer students opportunities to learn and utilize a variety of software programs. The Computer Science Department and Criminal Justice Department have collaborated to offer students a computer forensics minor to teach students how to handle digital evidence and how to present such evidence in court.

Costs

Tuition and fees for 2007–08 were $5952 for Kentucky residents and $10,776 for out-of-state students per year. Room and board costs were $5080 to $6980 per year. The cost of books and supplies amounted to about $800. Transportation costs were $800, and miscellaneous expenses were $900.

Financial Aid

Last year, 80 percent of undergraduates received some form of financial assistance. To receive financial aid, applicants must complete the Free Application for Federal Student Aid (FAFSA). Academic, athletic, music-drama, and art scholarships and scholarships for members of minority groups are available at Northern Kentucky University.

The application deadline for all academic scholarships is February 1. There is no deadline for the University's financial aid application; however, students who wish to receive institutional aid must apply by March 1 for priority consideration. Applicants are notified of acceptance on a rolling basis.

Faculty

More than 82 percent of the faculty members at NKU hold a doctoral degree or the terminal degree in their field. Classes are small, with an average class size of 24 and a student-faculty ratio of 14:1. All classes are taught by faculty members; no classes are taught by graduate assistants.

Student Government

Student Government (SG) is the elected student assembly at Northern Kentucky University. It is the official student voice on campus and represents the student viewpoint on University committees. All SG meetings are open, and students are encouraged to attend.

Admission Requirements

Incoming freshmen must submit an application for admission; arrange for the official ACT, SAT, or COMPASS score report to be sent; and request that the high school send an official transcript. In order to be considered for regular admission, a student must meet precollege curriculum requirements for Kentucky and institutional admission standards. Out-of-state applicants must also meet the Kentucky precollege curriculum requirements.

Based on the review of official test results and the precollege curriculum, students are admitted into one of two categories: regular admission or admission with conditions. Students who are found to have three or more deficiencies are referred to the NKU Academy, which is a five-week, intensive summer remediation program. Some degree programs require that students meet additional criteria; students should refer to the current catalog for more information (http://www.nku.edu).

Application and Information

The $40 paper application fee or $25 online application fee may be waived for applicants with demonstrated need. The fall semester early action and scholarship deadline is February 1, the priority application deadline is May 1, and the final deadline is August 1. The priority application deadline for the nursing program is January 31. The priority application deadline for the respiratory care program is February 15.

For more information, students should contact:

Office of Admissions
Northern Kentucky University
Highland Heights, Kentucky 41099
Phone: 859-572-5220
800-637-9948 (toll-free)
E-mail: admitnku@nku.edu
Web site: http://www.nku.edu

Northern Kentucky University's modern campus is set in Highland Heights, just minutes from downtown Cincinnati.

SULLIVAN UNIVERSITY

LOUISVILLE, KENTUCKY

The University

In 1962, A. O. Sullivan, a postsecondary educator since 1926, and his son, A. R. Sullivan, formed a postsecondary educational institution founded on the highest ideals and standards to prepare students for successful careers. Since that time, Sullivan University has earned a reputation as one of the leading career institutions in the nation. Accredited by the Commission on Colleges of the Southern Association of Colleges and Schools to offer associate, bachelor's, and master's degrees, Sullivan offers certificate and diploma programs in its Career College Division and associate, bachelor's, and master's degrees in its university offerings. A new College of Pharmacy, offering the Doctor of Pharmacy (Pharm.D.) degree, is scheduled to open in 2008. Sullivan has grown to become Kentucky's largest independent college or university. The University also has a branch campus in Lexington, Kentucky, and an extension campus at Fort Knox, Kentucky; it also attracts students worldwide to its Global Online division.

With a current enrollment of nearly 5,000, Sullivan is a nationally recognized leader in career-focused training. In order for students to get hands-on experience in their chosen fields from the very first day, the University also offers a special "inverted curriculum" in which students take skills courses in their particular career field first and general education courses later in their course of study. At Sullivan, students gain a valuable education along with access to a variety of helpful services. All Sullivan graduates have access to the Graduate Employment Service, which offers fee-free, lifetime, nationwide assistance and has, over the span of more than twenty years, a graduate employment success rate of more than 96 percent.

For students with special physical needs, the University is equipped with special parking facilities, ramped entrances, elevator services, and handicapped-accessible restroom facilities. To whet the student's appetite, the University's award-winning National Center for Hospitality Studies provides delicious meals at the Culinary Food Service Center, its award-winning Winston's Restaurant, and The Bakery, all on campus. Available to students under age 21 are spacious furnished apartments near the campus.

The Vice President for Student Services and his staff coordinate a variety of activities, such as academic advisement, clubs, and organizations—including Phi Beta Lambda, Student Government Association, Baptist Student Union, Summit Club, Travel Club, Rotoract, and clubs related to several academic disciplines. Annual events that bring excitement to the University are a student cruise down the Ohio River on the historic Belle of Louisville Riverboat, a Spring Jam Festival, and special trips that include both camping and skiing. Travel and tourism and hotel and restaurant management students get to travel the world with two major trips to exciting locations.

In addition to ten undergraduate degrees in business, early childhood education, hospitality, justice administration, and legal studies, Sullivan University also offers the Master of Business Administration (M.B.A.) degree, the executive M.B.A. degree (E.M.B.A.), the Master of Science in Managing Information Technology (M.S.M.I.T.) degree, the Master of Science in Dispute Resolution (M.S.D.R.) degree, a dual M.B.A./M.S.M.I.T. degree, a Master of Science in Management and Collaborative Solutions (M.S.M.C.S.) degree, and a Master of Science in Human Resource Leadership (M.S.H.R.L.) degree.

Location

Only minutes from downtown Louisville, Kentucky, Sullivan's 20-acre main campus is conveniently located within a block of one of Louisville's major interstate highways. Students can enjoy the metropolitan environment of Louisville through its symphony, ballet, opera, art museums, theaters, Museum of History and Science with its IMAX theater, Louisville Zoo, Louisville Slugger Museum, historic sites, quaint restaurants, multiple shopping centers, and vivid nightlife. With the flowering of spring comes the thundering excitement of the two-week Kentucky Derby Festival. For nature lovers, the Ohio River as well as nearby lakes and parks provide leisurely activities after a day of studies.

Majors and Degrees

Sullivan University confers the Bachelor of Science degree in business administration (with concentrations in accounting, finance, health-care management, hospitality management, information technology, justice administration, logistics and distribution management, management, and marketing), human resource leadership, information technology, justice and public safety administration, and paralegal studies.

The Associate of Science degree is offered in baking and pastry arts, business administration (with options in accounting, business management, justice and public safety administration, logistics and distribution, and marketing and sales management), culinary arts, hotel/restaurant management, information technology, office administration (with options in executive professional studies, legal professional studies, medical office management, and office administration specialist studies), paralegal studies, professional catering, and travel, tourism, and event management.

Sullivan also offers diplomas in business administration, office administration, professional baker studies, professional cook studies, professional nanny studies, and travel and tourism as well as certificate programs in MCSE, MCSD, and Cisco in its Career College Division and Microsoft Academy.

Academic Programs

All Sullivan students study practical courses that are designed to build a foundation for their careers. Just the opposite of most colleges and universities, Sullivan students begin by concentrating specifically on their areas of interest; then, their general and advanced education courses are taken within the final few months, or quarters, of the degree program. The University operates on an academic quarter system of four 11-week sessions, which allows baccalaureate students to finish their degrees in as little as thirty-six months. Credits are awarded on a quarter-credit-hour basis. Day classes are offered every day of the week except Friday. "Plus Friday" is a free day when students utilize facilities and equipment for individual study and practice and faculty members are available until noon to give students special assistance.

To qualify for graduation in the Bachelor of Science program, students must complete a minimum of 180 quarter credit hours. In addition, all students must attain a minimum cumulative grade point average of 2.0 on a 4.0 scale. The curriculum includes 60 credit hours of core business requirements, 28 credit hours of business support requirements, 16 credit hours of classes in the student's option, 48 hours of general studies, and 60 hours of electives.

Sullivan University offers a number of courses and programs online. This exciting method of delivery is rapidly becoming very popular with Sullivan's busy student population. To learn more about this option, students should visit the University's Web site at http://www.sullivan.edu.

Students may earn credit for certain classes by taking the College-Level Examination Program (CLEP) subject examinations. Students may also receive credit for courses by taking the University by-pass examinations.

Academic Facilities

Sullivan University's multimillion-dollar 20-acre multibuilding campus complex is climate-controlled and houses a variety of training equipment. From numerous personal computer labs utilizing the latest in software packages to the WorldSpan computerized travel reservation system, Sullivan students have outstanding technology right at their fingertips. Sullivan's state-of-the-art library contains a diversity of current reference and circulating materials as well as a high-speed computer network that provides access to the Sullivan University virtual library's (http://www.sullivan.edu/library) latest full-text and full-image electronic databases, such as ABI/Inform, LexisNexis, and WESTLAW. Sullivan University also has resource-sharing agreements with six other area libraries, giving Sullivan students access to more than 50 electronic databases and more than 20,000 e-journals from the campus or by Internet from home.

Costs

Expenses for the 2007–08 academic year ranged from $10,700 to $14,400 for tuition and from $350 to $500 for first-quarter books. The cost for housing was $4320, the general fee was $50 per class, and the parking fee was $84. An additional comprehensive fee is applied for some hospitality programs.

Financial Aid

Students attending Sullivan have access to numerous federal and state financial aid programs, such as all Title IV programs as well as the Kentucky Tuition Grant and the KEES scholarship. Many loans, grants, work-study programs, academic scholarships, and private scholarships are also available. As directed by the Department of Education, federal funds are allotted to the lowest-income families first, but funds are also available for middle- and upper-income families.

Faculty

Sullivan's more than 100 full-time and more than 200 adjunct faculty members share years of education and experience with their students. Faculty members are available daily for student assistance. With a 19:1 student-faculty ratio, the faculty members provide students with the academic guidance that they need and deserve.

Admission Requirements

To be considered for admission to Sullivan University, a student is required to demonstrate the appropriate aptitude and background for his or her anticipated field of study via successful completion of a University-administered entrance test and/or submission of ACT or SAT test scores. Students must also have a high school diploma or its equivalent, such as a General Educational Development (GED) certificate. Sullivan has a rolling admissions policy; those who apply first are accepted first. The University individually interviews and advises each person seeking admission, either at the University or at the student's home. Students from other regions of the United States and international students may complete the application by mail. A University preview CD is available for review if a campus visit is impossible prior to entry. New classes normally begin the first week of January and the last week of March, June, and September of each year.

Application and Information

Students considering applying to the University are strongly encouraged to visit the campus. Included in a weekday visit are an interview with an admissions officer, a tour of the campus, an opportunity to observe classes, and discussions with professors and students. A Sullivan representative assists out-of-town visitors in finding accommodations. Approximately six open houses per year allow prospective students and their families an opportunity to visit the campus and participate in campus activities.

For more information and application materials, prospective students should contact the appropriate campus:

Director of Admissions
Sullivan University (main campus)
3101 Bardstown Road
Louisville, Kentucky 40205
Phone: 502-456-6505
800-844-1354 (toll-free)
Web site: http://www.sullivan.edu

Director of Admissions
Sullivan University, Lexington (Branch Campus)
2355 Harrodsburg Road
Lexington, Kentucky 40504
Phone: 859-276-4357
800-467-6281 (toll-free)

Director of Admissions
Sullivan University, Fort Knox (Extension Center)
P.O. Box 998
Fort Knox, Kentucky 40121
Phone: 502-942-8500
800-562-6713 (toll-free)

Greek revival–style architecture and picturesque grounds characterize the main campus at Sullivan University in Louisville, Kentucky.

THOMAS MORE COLLEGE

CRESTVIEW HILLS, KENTUCKY

The College

Thomas More College is a small, private, Catholic liberal arts college affiliated with the Diocese of Covington, Kentucky. The College was ranked in the top twenty-five best Southern comprehensive colleges by *U.S. News & World Report* in their 2006 "America's Best Colleges" issue. Thomas More College fulfills its liberal arts commitment by maintaining an atmosphere and curriculum that give students the opportunity to grow academically, spiritually, and professionally.

Of the diverse student population of 1,400 undergraduates and graduates, there are 721 traditional undergraduates attending classes full-time; 240 are resident students. The student body is drawn primarily from the states of Kentucky, Ohio, and Indiana, but many other states and a number of countries are also represented. Students who choose to live on campus reside in either the newer suite-style residence hall or one of three town-house-style residence halls. All residence halls offer comfortable, air-conditioned rooms; Internet and cable TV access; and free laundry facilities. The 27,000-square-foot Holbrook Student Center contains a spacious bookstore, computer and study lounges, student activity offices, a TV and game room, food court, and dance rehearsal studio.

The students' college experience is enhanced through their participation in many academic, social, and sports organizations. Intercollegiate athletics are part of the Presidents' Athletic Conference governed by NCAA Division III. Thomas More College competes in men's baseball, basketball, cross-country, football, golf, soccer, and tennis and women's basketball, cross-country, fast-pitch softball, golf, soccer, tennis, and volleyball. Intramural sports offered include, among others, coed flag football, basketball, cornhole, dodgeball, softball, and volleyball. The campus contains a new on-campus football stadium; baseball, soccer, and softball fields; and volleyball and basketball courts as well as training and health facilities. Students can also enjoy world-class facilities for swimming, tennis, racquetball, and basketball and a complete fitness area at the Five Seasons Sports Club, adjacent to the campus.

Location

Thomas More College is located 10 minutes south of Cincinnati, Ohio, in Crestview Hills, Kentucky. The campus is convenient to major highways. The Greater Cincinnati/Northern Kentucky International Airport is just 10 minutes away. All students are permitted to have cars on campus.

The Greater Cincinnati area offers a wide array of cultural and sporting events. Local attractions include the Broadway Series, the Cincinnati Pops, the Cincinnati Zoo, the Newport Aquarium, the Riverbend Music Center, and the Cincinnati Reds and Bengals. Numerous shopping areas and restaurants are also available.

Majors and Degrees

Thomas More College offers bachelor's degrees in accounting, art, biology, business administration, chemistry, computer information systems, communications, criminal justice, drama, economics, education, English, environmental science, forensic science, history, humanities, international studies, Latin American and Caribbean studies, liberal arts, mathematics, medical technology, nursing, philosophy, physics, political science, psychology, sports and entertainment marketing, sociology, speech and theater, and theology.

Preprofessional programs are available in dentistry, law, medicine, occupational therapy, optometry, pharmacy, physical therapy, and veterinary science.

The Associate of Arts degree is available in accounting, art, art history, biology, business administration, chemistry, computer information systems, criminal justice, drama, economics, English, exercise science, French, gerontology, history, humanities, international studies, Latin American and Caribbean studies, liberal arts, management, math, music, philosophy, physics, political science, pre–legal studies, psychology, sociology, Spanish, speech communication, theology, and Web-page design.

Academic Programs

To earn the Bachelor of Arts, Bachelor of Science, or Bachelor of Science in Nursing degree, a student must complete 128 credit hours, including 61 credit hours in liberal arts courses. The Associate of Arts degree requires the completion of 64 credit hours, including a liberal arts component.

The academic calendar is composed of a fall and a spring semester and two summer sessions. The Office of Lifelong Learning offers a full schedule of evening classes.

The Cooperative Education program enables students to gain hands-on professional experience in their field of interest. All students are eligible for this program after the completion of their freshman year. Cooperative Air Force and Army ROTC programs are available in conjunction with nearby universities.

Off-Campus Programs

Nineteen area colleges, including Thomas More College, form the Greater Cincinnati Consortium of Colleges and Universities through which all students at the local member colleges may take courses not available at their home institution. Thomas More encourages full-time students to take advantage of this opportunity for curriculum enrichment through cross-registration. In addition, students who wish to study abroad as part of their undergraduate education have a number of possibilities open to them.

Academic Facilities

The library has a collection of more than 129,000 volumes of books, periodicals, and audiovisual materials and, as a selective depository, it houses more than 8,400 volumes of U.S. government documents. In addition, the library's membership in the Southwest Ohio and Neighboring Libraries gives Thomas More students access to more than 15 million books and more than 75,000 periodicals held by seventy-five other libraries in the region.

Thomas More's computer facilities include a computer classroom and six labs for student use. Student computers are also available in some academic departments and in the library. All PCs are connected to a campuswide Novell network, with access to e-mail, the Internet, and an on-campus Intranet server. There is a laser printer in each lab and a color laser printer and scanner in the PC lab in the main computer center. Software includes Microsoft Windows XP, Office 2003, and Visual Studio; Adobe Photoshop; and additional software used for departmental instruction.

Students in the science programs receive hands-on experience through the use of the newly remodeled advanced biology, chemistry, and physics laboratories. The facilities include an environmental chamber, an aquatic research station, research and measurement labs, a synthesis lab, a light-sensitive project room, and a machine and electronics shop. In addition, Thomas More has an observatory on campus and a biology field station, located near the Ohio River.

The nursing and sociology departments have excellent working relationships with nearby hospitals and social service agencies.

Costs

The 2007–08 annual costs for Thomas More College were $20,080 for tuition and $6250 for room (double occupancy) and board. There is a differential fee of $30 per semester hour for all nursing courses. The Student Government fee is $60 per semester and the computer fee is $300 per semester for full-time students. The cost of books is estimated at $800 per year.

Financial Aid

Thomas More College assists more than 90 percent of its full-time students in meeting college costs. Awards are determined on a rolling basis, with priority consideration given to applications filed by March 15. Financial aid awards are based on economic need, merit, scholastic achievement, and extracurricular activities. ROTC scholarships are also available. The filing of the Free Application for Federal Student Aid (FAFSA) and the Thomas More College Application for Financial Aid and Scholarship is required before any awards are determined. Other Thomas More College awards may require additional applications.

An extensive Federal Work-Study Program is in place, and there are excellent opportunities for outside employment in the immediate area.

Faculty

The faculty is committed to the ideals of a Catholic liberal arts education with the main focus on teaching. The faculty has 135 members, including 71 who are full-time; 66 percent hold tenure and 69 percent hold doctoral or other terminal degrees. Faculty members serve as academic advisers to students in their disciplines. The student-faculty ratio is 14:1.

Student Government

The purpose of the Student Government Association is to serve as the official representative organization of the Thomas More College student body; to serve as the liaison between the student body and the faculty, administration, and Board of Trustees; to promote student projects and activities and improve the quality of student life; to assist the Dean of Students in supervising student organizations and student activities on campus; to protect the rights of the individual; and to preserve the general welfare of the student body of Thomas More College.

Admission Requirements

The admission criteria are as follows: an applicant should have a high school grade point average (based on college-preparatory courses) of 80 percent or better; a high school rank in the top half of the graduating class; and a minimum composite score of 20 on the ACT Assessment, with a minimum of 20 in English, or a minimum combined score of 1010 on the SAT, with a minimum of 480 on the verbal portion. If the applicant does not meet all the admission criteria, the file is forwarded to the Admissions Committee for individual consideration.

Transfer students with 24 or more semester hours of transferable credit and an overall grade point average of at least 2.0 on a 4.0 scale are automatically accepted. Transfer students with fewer than 24 transferable hours must meet the general admission criteria.

The applicant must provide a completed application with a nonrefundable $25 fee (waived for online applicants), high school transcripts, college transcripts (if applicable), and ACT or SAT score reports.

Application and Information

Thomas More College operates under a rolling admission policy, with a final application deadline of August 15. Admission decisions are usually made within two weeks of receiving all application materials. Students can apply online at the Web site listed below. The $25 application fee is waived for online applications.

For further information or to schedule a campus visit, students should contact:

Billy Sarge
Assistant Director for Admissions
Thomas More College
333 Thomas More Parkway
Crestview Hills, Kentucky 41017-3495
Phone: 859-344-3332
800-825-4557 (toll-free)
E-mail: billy.sarge@thomasmore.edu
Web site: http://www.thomasmore.edu

Students on the Thomas More College campus.

TRANSYLVANIA UNIVERSITY

LEXINGTON, KENTUCKY

The University

Transylvania, a small, private liberal arts college of about 1,150 men and women, is consistently ranked among the best in the nation. The name—from the Latin that means across the woods—refers to the heavily forested Transylvania settlement in which the University was founded in 1780. Transylvania was the first college west of the Allegheny Mountains and the sixteenth in the nation. The University established the first schools of medicine and law in what was then the West and educated the doctors, lawyers, ministers, political leaders, and others who helped shape the young nation. Transylvania also founded the first college literary magazine in the West, *The Transylvanian*, still published by students today. Transylvania's link with early Lexington is symbolized by its administration building, Old Morrison, a registered National Historic Landmark and the central feature on the official seal of the city of Lexington.

Transylvania continues as a pioneer in higher education, preparing future leaders in business, government, education, the sciences, and the arts. Students work closely with professors in small classes, many with fewer than 10 students. Due in large part to these close collaborations with faculty members, a high percentage of graduates attend excellent medical, law, and other graduate and professional programs.

Transylvania offers more than seventy cocurricular organizations, covering a range of student interests, and most students participate in several of these. The Lampas Circle of the national leadership honorary society Omicron Delta Kappa, which recently moved its national headquarters to Transylvania, recognizes students for academic excellence and campus leadership. The athletics program includes seven varsity sports for men, nine for women, and more than a dozen intramural sports. Transylvania also has four national sororities and four national fraternities.

Location

Transylvania is located in Lexington, Kentucky, a city of 270,000 and a growing center of commerce, culture, research, and education. Known as the horse capital of the world, Lexington is surrounded by the rolling green pastures of the famous Bluegrass region of central Kentucky. The area is also home to over 30,000 college students. Transylvania's parklike campus is just a 5-minute walk from downtown, with easy access to restaurants, shops, and entertainment. The proximity to downtown is also an advantage for students who want convenient part-time jobs and internship opportunities in law offices, accounting firms, hospitals, and other organizations. Transylvania offers its students a shuttle service between the Transylvania library and the University of Kentucky libraries every day, and the Lexington Public Library is a few blocks from the campus. Lexington is served by major airlines, and Louisville and Cincinnati are only 80 miles away.

Majors and Degrees

The Bachelor of Arts degree is awarded in the following majors: accounting, anthropology, art history, art studio, biology, business administration (concentrations in finance, hospitality management, management, and marketing), chemistry, classics, computer science, drama, economics, education, English, exercise science, French, history, mathematics, music, music technology, philosophy, physical education, physics, political science, psychology, religion, sociology, and Spanish. Individually designed majors also may be arranged. Minors are available in most majors and in classical studies, communication, environmental studies, German, hospitality management, international affairs, multicultural studies, and women's studies. Advising and undergraduate preparation are provided for preprofessional programs in dentistry, engineering, law, medicine, ministry, pharmacy, physical therapy, and veterinary medicine. A cooperative program in engineering allows students to earn a B.A. in physics or liberal studies from Transylvania in three years and a B.S. in engineering from the University of Kentucky or Vanderbilt University in two years. A cooperative program in accounting allows students to earn a B.A. in accounting from Transylvania in four years and an M.S. in accounting from the University of Kentucky in one year; graduates qualify to take the CPA exam.

Academic Programs

The academic year is based on a 4-4-1 academic calendar, with two 14-week terms (fall and winter) and a one-month May term. The fall term begins in early September and ends in mid-December. The winter term begins in mid-January and ends in late April. During the May term, students may participate in a variety of programs on or off campus. Students normally take four courses in each of the fall and winter terms and one course in the May term. Thirty-six courses are required to graduate. Freshmen participate in a two-term program called Foundations of the Liberal Arts, which features small-group discussions with a faculty leader; lectures, films, concerts, and other presentations; and a tutorial program in basic communication, critical thinking, and study skills. Special study-skills clinics and workshops are offered on an optional basis. Students must complete requirements designed to ensure broad familiarity with the major areas of learning and human endeavor in the humanities and fine arts, social sciences, natural sciences and mathematics, logic, and languages.

Transylvania grants credit for scores of 4 or 5 on the Advanced Placement examinations of the College Board and at least 5 on the International Baccalaureate program. Detailed information may be obtained from the Office of the Registrar.

Off-Campus Programs

Experiencing diverse cultures through international study is a vital part of a Transylvania education. It is common for Transylvania students to study abroad for a summer, a term, or a year. Sixty-five percent of the most recent graduating class participated in a study-abroad experience. A program at Regent's College, London, allows students to study there for the same cost and course credit as a semester at Transylvania. Scholarships are available for both semester-long and summer study abroad. Summer study programs, including those in Austria, Brazil, China, Costa Rica, Ecuador, France, Germany, Italy, Japan, Mexico, and Spain, are available through Transylvania's affiliation with the Kentucky Institute for International Studies. Transylvania also cooperates with the English-Speaking Union to offer advanced students scholarships for summer study at Cambridge and Oxford Universities. Students may participate in seminars or internships in Washington, D.C., through the Washington Center and in the Canadian Parliamentary Internship Program in Ottawa. Internships with congressional offices, Kentucky state government, city government, and local firms are easily arranged. Participation in Reserve Officers' Training Corps (Air Force and Army ROTC) is offered in cooperation with the University of Kentucky.

Academic Facilities

Two new Georgian-style buildings combine elegance with high-tech facilities to offer the latest advances in teaching and learning. The Cowgill Center for Business, Economics, and Education includes a multimedia classroom where professors from any discipline can use a large display screen to show the entire class information from one of the twenty-five networked student computers or from a TV, video, CD-ROM, or satellite. A specialized area for education majors includes a laboratory classroom for teacher training. The new Lucille C. Little Theater, used for faculty- and student-directed productions and drama classes, is a technically innovative facility that includes computerized lighting and sound, flexible staging options, and movable seating. The Frances Carrick Thomas/J.

Douglas Gay, Jr. Library offers sophisticated computerized databases, which are invaluable for research and can be accessed from any computer connected to Transylvania's server, including PCs in dorm rooms. The Mitchell Fine Arts Center provides music program facilities, including practice rooms, a recital hall, and an auditorium. It also houses the Career Development Center, which provides free interest testing and helps students research careers, improve job search skills, arrange internships and part-time jobs, and apply to graduate schools and professional positions. Mitchell also houses a teaching laboratory for the hospitality management program. The recently acquired Shearer Art Building is dedicated to instructional space, student and faculty studios, and a student gallery. Other modern facilities include the newly renovated L. A. Brown Science Center, the Haupt Humanities Building, and the Clive M. Beck Athletic and Recreation Center, which opened in January 2002. About 80 percent of students live on campus in six residence halls—two for men, one for women, and three for men and women. These include traditional-style accommodations, apartment-style living for upperclass students, and suite-style rooms. All rooms are air-conditioned and completely furnished and offer private telephone service with voice mail and access to Transylvania's cable television and computer networks. Thomson Hall, a new suite-style hall, is scheduled for completion in fall 2008. Each residence hall has ample lounge and study space and easy access to computer labs and recreational facilities. The William T. Young Campus Center offers a competition-size indoor pool, a gymnasium, a fitness center, and other facilities.

Costs

Transylvania charges an annual tuition that covers fall, winter, and May terms for a normal full-time schedule of courses. Special instruction fees are charged in addition for certain designated courses, such as applied music and May Term travel courses. For 2007–08, tuition and fees were $22,300 and room and board (double occupancy) were $7130.

Financial Aid

Transylvania is committed to providing financial aid to students and their families. Four types of financial assistance are available. Scholarships are based on academic performance, leadership, and citizenship. Grants, loans, and work-study are based on financial need. About 90 percent of Transylvania students receive some form of financial assistance and many receive more than one type of aid. Outstanding entering freshmen may qualify for one of twenty William T. Young Scholarships—each worth more than $90,000 over four years—that cover tuition and fees. Submission of Transylvania's Application for Admission and Scholarships by the appropriate deadline is all that is necessary to be considered for all scholarships at Transylvania. Students who are interested in need-based aid must file the Free Application for Federal Student Aid (FAFSA).

Faculty

Transylvania's relatively small size and low student-faculty ratio of 13:1 allow for close, personal attention in teaching and advising. Ninety-seven percent of full-time faculty members hold a doctorate or the highest degree in their field, and they have come to Transylvania from a variety of graduate and professional schools. Many faculty members are recognized for their scholarship and professional activities, but their central concern is teaching and advising students. In the last six years, four Transylvania professors have been named Kentucky Professor of the Year by the Carnegie Foundation and the Council for the Advancement and Support of Education. In 2006, a Transylvania professor received the Acorn Award as Kentucky's outstanding professor from the Kentucky Advocates for Higher Education and the Council on Postsecondary Education. Transylvania's commitment to outstanding teaching is reflected in its nationally recognized Bingham Program for Excellence in Teaching, the first of its type in the nation to attract and retain gifted teachers through an evaluation process and financial incentives.

Student Government

Students at Transylvania have a high degree of access to the administration and governing board of the University. The Student Government Association serves as a representative government, and students also hold positions on standing committees of the faculty and the Board of Trustees.

Admission Requirements

Each applicant is considered individually on the basis of academic records, SAT scores and/or ACT scores, activities, interests, essays, and recommendations. Admission is also offered to transfer students, international students, and nontraditional students. High school students who graduate at the end of their junior year may also be considered for admission.

Transylvania enrolled 349 new students for the 2007–08 academic year. The middle 50 percent composite ACT score for the freshman class was 23 to 29; the middle 50 percent combined SAT score was 1050 to 1270. Fifty percent were in the top 10 percent of their high school class.

Application and Information

Submission of a Transylvania Application for Admission and Scholarships or submission of the Common Application is all that is necessary to be considered for admission and most merit scholarships at Transylvania. Application deadlines vary with particular scholarships and types of financial aid.

The early action deadline is December 1 for applicants who wish to learn of their admission by January 15 and who want to be considered for all Transylvania scholarships. February 1 is the regular admission and scholarships deadline for applicants who wish to be considered for all Transylvania scholarships except the William T. Young Scholarship. Applicants who apply after February 1 are considered on a space-available basis. The deadline for applications for the winter term, which begins in January, is December 1. The same deadlines apply to electronic applications, which may be submitted on the Internet at the Web address listed below.

Students considering Transylvania are urged to visit the campus, and high school seniors are encouraged to stay overnight in a dorm with a student admissions assistant. Weekday visits may include a customized campus tour and opportunities to attend classes; talk with professors, coaches, students, and admissions and financial aid counselors; and enjoy meals on campus. Visits should be arranged with the Office of Admissions, preferably one to two weeks in advance. Open houses are held in the fall and winter, and a college planning workshop for high school juniors and sophomores is held in the spring.

For more information and application materials, students should contact:

Office of Admissions
Transylvania University
300 North Broadway
Lexington, Kentucky 40508-1797
Phone: 859-233-8242
800-872-6798 (toll-free)
E-mail: admissions@transy.edu
Web site: http://www.transy.edu

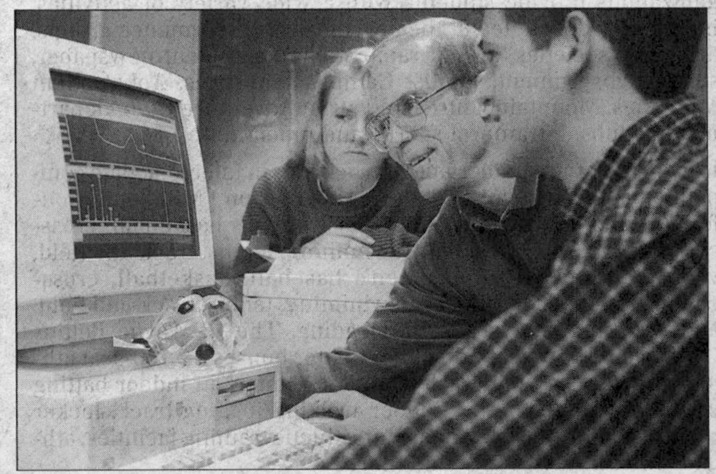

Small class sizes at Transylvania give professors and students the opportunity to work closely together, and many are directly involved in student research projects.

UNIVERSITY OF THE CUMBERLANDS

WILLIAMSBURG, KENTUCKY

The University

Founded in 1889, Cumberland College became University of the Cumberlands on July 1, 2005, reflecting the diversity and excellence of options offered in high-quality education. The University is committed to providing a superior education within an exceptional Christian atmosphere at an affordable cost. Recognition by *U.S. News & World Report* in its list of America's Best Colleges and by the John Templeton Foundation as a member of its Honor Roll of Character Building Colleges signals that a University of the Cumberlands (UC) education is an exceptional value. Emphasizing the growth of the individual student, the University strives to instill in students the desire to be agents of change in the world and to use knowledge for the benefit of others as well as themselves.

UC is one of the few institutions where all students complete a leadership program. One hundred percent of the students participate in community service as a component of this program.

University of the Cumberlands is a four-year, coed, liberal arts institution for higher education that offers a broad curriculum with more than thirty-five programs of undergraduate study, including eight preprofessional programs for professional and health-science careers. Graduates enjoy a high acceptance rate to graduate and professional schools, particularly in science, business, and education. In fact, within five years of graduation, 66 percent of UC's alumni have completed or are pursuing a graduate or professional degree.

Graduate studies at University of the Cumberlands offer individual graduate courses as well as Master of Arts in Teaching and Master of Arts in Education degree programs with certification or concentration in various areas.

One of the largest private institutions in the state of Kentucky, UC serves a diverse body of more than 1,800 students from forty states and fourteen other countries. Primarily a residential campus, UC provides on-campus housing for about 75 percent of its students in the University's ten residence halls. A director, assisted by student staff members, supervises each hall.

Extracurricular activities abound. More than forty clubs and organizations provide students with a wide variety of activities, including a debate team, theater, musical performance groups, academic societies, an FM radio station, a student newspaper, student government, Baptist Campus Ministries, Appalachian Ministries, Mountain Outreach, Patriot Adventure Club, departmental clubs, intramural sports, and much more.

University of the Cumberlands participates in intercollegiate competition and is a member of the NAIA Division I Mid-South Conference and offers opportunities in women's basketball, cross-country, golf, soccer, softball, swimming, tennis, track and field, volleyball, and wrestling; men's baseball, basketball, cross-country, football, golf, soccer, swimming, tennis, track and field, and wrestling; and coed cheerleading. The O. Wayne Rollins Convocation/Physical Education Center houses a 2,700-seat athletic arena, the Dinah Taylor Aquatic Center, an indoor batting cage, a weight room, an indoor walking/jogging track, locker rooms, an intramural gymnasium, athletic training facilities, athletic offices, classrooms, and more.

The James H. Taylor II Stadium complex, which seats 2,400, includes a football field; an eight-lane, 400-meter all-weather track and field; the Patriot Pavilion; and a football practice field.

The Doyle Buhl Stadium and James Keelty Field are the home of Patriot baseball, with dugouts and locker rooms.

UC also has separate golf, soccer, softball, tennis, and wrestling facilities.

Location

One of the state's oldest cities, Williamsburg is located in southern Kentucky, 185 miles south of Cincinnati, Ohio, and 70 miles north of Knoxville, Tennessee. Williamsburg is known for its beautiful homes and the hospitality of its people. The University of the Cumberlands campus is situated on three hills above the town and, about 1 mile from exit 11, is easily accessed from Interstate 75. UC has a well-kept campus that blends stately old buildings with new ones and has a panoramic view of the surrounding mountains and the Cumberland River Valley, an area known throughout the country for its lovely waterfalls, forests, and lakes. Famed Cumberland Falls State Resort Park is just 20 minutes from campus.

Majors and Degrees

University of the Cumberlands is accredited by the Commission on Colleges of the Southern Association of Colleges and Schools (1866 Southern Lane, Decatur, Georgia 30033-4097; telephone: 404-679-4501) to award Bachelor of Arts, Bachelor of General Studies, Bachelor of Music, Bachelor of Science, and Master of Arts in Education degrees. It is approved by the Kentucky State Department of Education for teacher education and certification.

Major fields of study are accounting, art, biology, business administration, chemistry, church music, communication arts, education, English, exercise and sport science, fitness and sport management, history, human services and social work, management information systems, mathematics, music, philosophy, physics, political science, psychology, religion, special education, and theater arts.

Minor fields can be chosen from the major fields or in biblical languages, French, journalism, and Spanish.

Preprofessional and special curricula are offered in military science, predentistry, pre-engineering, prelaw, premedicine, preoptometry, pre–pharmacy, pre–physical therapy, pre–veterinary medicine, and religious vocations.

Academic Programs

University of the Cumberlands seeks to provide academic specialization within a broad framework of a liberal arts education. To supplement the in-depth knowledge acquired within each major, 49 semester hours of general studies from the areas of Christian faith and values, cultural and aesthetic values, the English language, humanities, leadership and community service, natural and mathematical sciences, physical education, and social sciences are required. Students must earn at least 128 semester hours to graduate with a bachelor's degree.

The academic year begins in late August, with the first semester ending in mid-December. The second semester runs from early January to early May. Two 4-week undergraduate summer sessions and two 4-week graduate summer sessions are also offered. Orientation, preregistration, and academic advising by faculty members begin in the summer preceding entrance.

Students may receive credit for successful scores on the Advanced Placement examinations of the College Board, the College-

Level Examination Program (CLEP), and special departmental tests. Through the honors program, highly qualified students have the opportunity to undertake advanced independent study.

Students benefit from such special services as free tutorial assistance and those offered by the Career Services Center, the Center for Leadership Studies, the Student Health Center, and the Academic Resource Center.

Academic Facilities

The University of the Cumberlands campus contains thirty-four buildings reflecting antebellum architectural style. The science building features newly remodeled, well-equipped biology, chemistry, and physics labs providing graduate-level research opportunities.

The McGaw Music Building contains individual rehearsal and studio areas as well as a recital hall. The Norma Perkins Hagan Memorial Library houses more than 150,500 book titles, 1,630 periodical subscriptions, and 715,878 microform titles. Sophisticated computer equipment provides access to an additional 20 million or more items from many of the nation's outstanding libraries. The instructional media center includes a children's library, a computerized language lab, and a listening library.

Other special academic features include a computer center, an art gallery, a word processing center for English composition, a theater, a 600-seat chapel, four large lecture halls, and the Distance Learning Laboratory.

Recent additions to the campus include the Rollins Fine Arts Center, the state-of-the-art Hutton School of Business, and two new residence halls.

Costs

For 2007–08, the basic academic-year expenses were $14,658 for tuition and fees and $6626 for room and board, for a total of $21,284. There are no additional fees for out-of-state students. The average cost for books and supplies is approximately $400 per semester.

Financial Aid

University of the Cumberlands sponsors a large financial aid program that coordinates monies from federal, state, private, and University sources. Ninety-five percent of UC students share more than $22 million in aid.

To apply for financial aid, it is necessary to complete the Free Application for Federal Student Aid (FAFSA). For further information about financial aid opportunities, students should contact the Director of Financial Planning at 800-343-1609 (toll free). Applications made by March 1 are given priority for the fall semester.

Numerous scholarships and grants are available.

Faculty

There are 94 full-time and 18 part-time faculty members who are respected scholars and whose primary responsibility is to teach. Graduate assistants do not teach courses. The student-faculty ratio is 14:1, enabling students to receive ample attention and assistance from professors. Faculty members also serve as advisers to help students in planning their academic programs.

Admission Requirements

In compliance with federal law, including provisions of Title IX of the Educational Amendments of 1972 and Section 504 of the Rehabilitation Act of 1973, University of the Cumberlands does not illegally discriminate on the basis of race, sex, color, national or ethnic origin, age, disability, or military service in its administration of education policies, programs, or activities; admissions policies; or employment. Under federal law, the University reserves the right to discriminate on the basis of sex in its undergraduate admissions programs. Further, the University reserves the right to deny admission to any applicant whose academic preparation, character, or personal conduct is determined to be inconsistent with the purpose and objectives of the University. Where possible, the University will seek to reasonably accommodate a student's disability. However, the University's obligation to reasonably accommodate a student's disability ends where the accommodation would pose an undue hardship on the University or where the accommodation in question would fundamentally alter the academic program. Inquiries or complaints should be directed to the Vice President for Academic Affairs.

The purpose of the admission process is to identify applicants who are likely to succeed academically at University of the Cumberlands and at the same time contribute positively to the campus community. The process considers such factors as high school records (including courses taken, grade trends, and rank in class), college records (if transferring from another institution), scores on the ACT or SAT, extracurricular activities and honors, and personal conduct.

Campus tours are available on weekdays by appointment and on selected Saturdays. Prospective students can take a tour of the beautiful campus; talk with students, professors, and coaches; spend the night in the residence halls; attend an athletic or extracurricular event; and get answers to their questions during a session with an admissions counselor.

Application and Information

Applicants for admission should contact the Office of Admissions for an application form and return the completed form to the University, along with the appropriate application fee, official transcripts of all high school and college work, and a copy of ACT or SAT scores. Each student is notified regarding official admission within ten working days after the application procedure has been completed.

Students accepted for admission must submit the required enrollment deposit.

Additional information can be obtained at:

Office of Admissions
University of the Cumberlands
Williamsburg, Kentucky 40769
Phone: 606-539-4241
800-343-1609 (toll-free)
E-mail: admiss@ucumberlands.edu
Web site: http://www.ucumberlands.edu

Students on the campus of University of the Cumberlands.

LOUISIANA

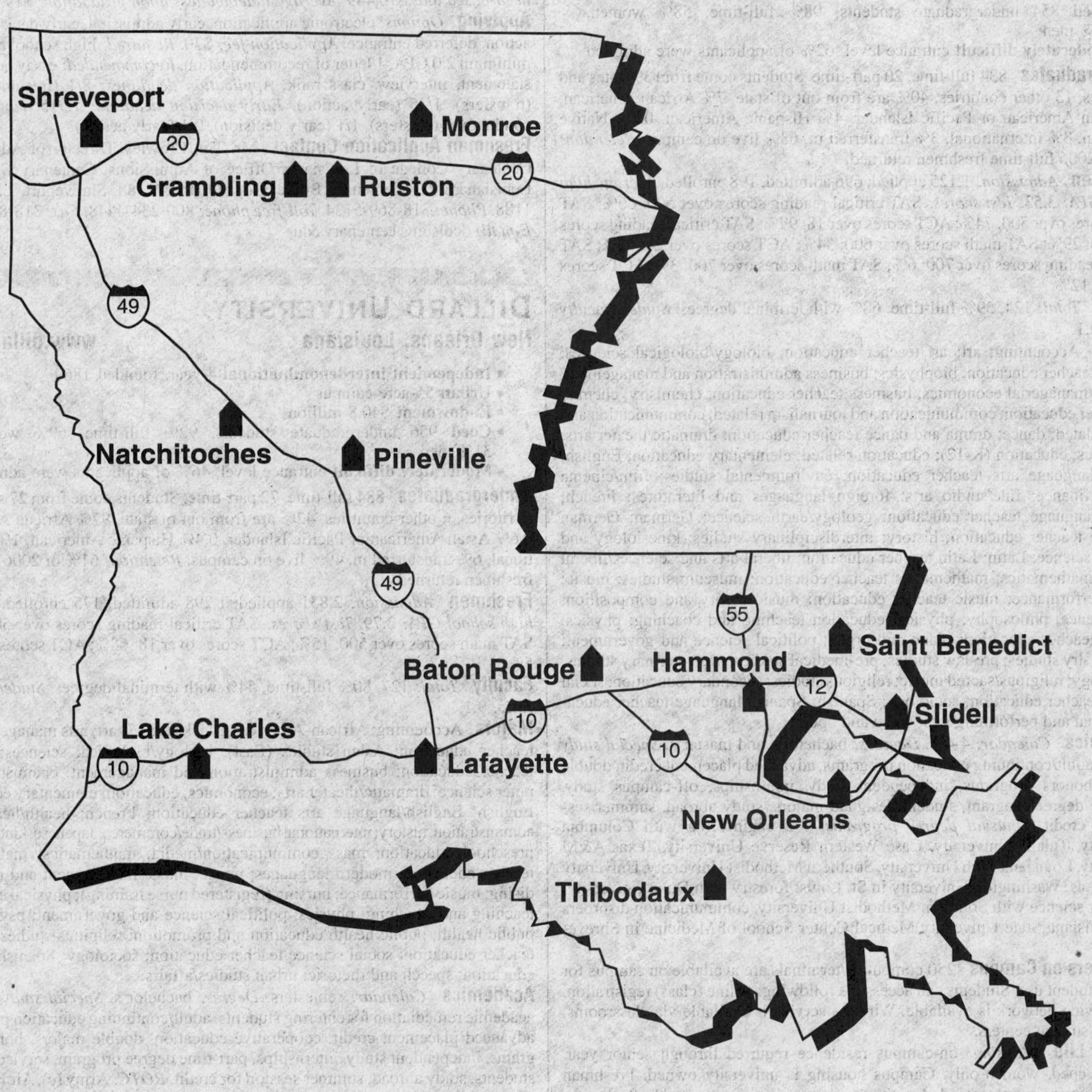

Shreveport
Monroe
20
Grambling
Ruston
20
49
Natchitoches
Pineville
49
55
Saint Benedict
Baton Rouge
Hammond
12
Slidell
10
Lake Charles
10
Lafayette
10
New Orleans
Thibodaux

CENTENARY COLLEGE OF LOUISIANA

Shreveport, Louisiana **www.centenary.edu/**

- **Independent United Methodist** comprehensive, founded 1825
- **Suburban** 65-acre campus
- **Coed** 854 undergraduate students, 98% full-time, 58% women, 42% men
- **Moderately difficult** entrance level, 62% of applicants were admitted

Undergraduates 834 full-time, 20 part-time. Students come from 39 states and territories, 13 other countries, 40% are from out of state, 7% African American, 3% Asian American or Pacific Islander, 4% Hispanic American, 0.2% Native American, 3% international, 3% transferred in, 68% live on campus. *Retention:* 77% of 2006 full-time freshmen returned.

Freshmen *Admission:* 1,125 applied, 696 admitted, 198 enrolled. *Average high school GPA:* 3.53. *Test scores:* SAT critical reading scores over 500: 66%; SAT math scores over 500: 74%; ACT scores over 18: 99%; SAT critical reading scores over 600: 29%; SAT math scores over 600: 34%; ACT scores over 24: 65%; SAT critical reading scores over 700: 6%; SAT math scores over 700: 3%; ACT scores over 30: 12%.

Faculty *Total:* 124, 59% full-time, 68% with terminal degrees. *Student/faculty ratio:* 10:1.

Majors Accounting; art; art teacher education; biology/biological sciences; biology teacher education; biophysics; business administration and management; business/managerial economics; business teacher education; chemistry; chemistry teacher education; communication and journalism related; communication and media related; dance; drama and dance teacher education; dramatic/theater arts; economics; education (K-12); education related; elementary education; English; English/language arts teacher education; environmental studies; film/cinema studies; finance; fine/studio arts; foreign languages and literatures; French; French language teacher education; geology/earth science; German; German language teacher education; history; interdisciplinary studies; kinesiology and exercise science; Latin; Latin teacher education; liberal arts and sciences/liberal studies; mathematics; mathematics teacher education; museum studies; music; music performance; music teacher education; music theory and composition; neuroscience; philosophy; physical education teaching and coaching; physics; physics teacher education; piano and organ; political science and government; pre-dentistry studies; pre-law studies; pre-medical studies; pre-veterinary studies; psychology; religious/sacred music; religious studies; secondary education; social studies teacher education; sociology; Spanish; Spanish language teacher education; visual and performing arts; voice and opera.

Academics *Calendar:* 4-4-1. *Degrees:* bachelor's and master's. *Special study options:* adult/continuing education programs, advanced placement credit, double majors, honors programs, independent study, internships, off-campus study, part-time degree program, student-designed majors, study abroad, summer session for credit. *Unusual degree programs:* 3-2 engineering with Columbia University, Tulane University, Case Western Reserve University, Texas A&M University, Louisiana Tech University, Southern Methodist University, University of Arkansas, Washington University in St. Louis; forestry with Duke University; computer science with Southern Methodist University, communication disorders with Louisiana State University Medical Center School of Medicine in Shreveport.

Computers on Campus 250 computers/terminals are available on campus for general student use. Students can access the following: online (class) registration. Campuswide network is available. Wireless service is available via classrooms, libraries, student centers.

Student Life *Housing:* on-campus residence required through senior year. *Options:* coed, women-only. Campus housing is university owned. Freshman campus housing is guaranteed. *Activities and organizations:* drama/theater group, student-run newspaper, radio station, choral group, intramural sports, Student Activities Board, crew, Church Career/Campus Ministries, student media, national fraternities, national sororities. *Campus security:* 24-hour emergency response devices and patrols, late-night transport/escort service, controlled dormitory access. *Student services:* health clinic, personal/psychological counseling.

Athletics Member NCAA. All Division I. *Intercollegiate sports:* baseball M (s), basketball M (s)/W (s), crew M (c)/W (c), cross-country running M (s)/W (s), golf M (s)/W (s), gymnastics W (s), soccer M (s)/W (s), softball W (s), swimming and diving M (s)/W (s), tennis M (s)/W (s), volleyball W (s). *Intramural sports:* basketball M/W, cheerleading W, football M/W, golf M, lacrosse M, soccer M/W, softball M/W, table tennis M/W, tennis M/W, volleyball M/W.

Standardized Tests *Required:* SAT or ACT (for admission).

Costs (2008–09) *Comprehensive fee:* $29,330 includes full-time tuition ($20,850), mandatory fees ($1150), and room and board ($7330). Part-time tuition: $665 per semester hour. *Required fees:* $60 per term part-time. *College room only:* $3580.

Financial Aid Of all full-time matriculated undergraduates who enrolled in 2006, 661 applied for aid, 470 were judged to have need, 172 had their need fully met. 155 Federal Work-Study jobs (averaging $1671). 67 state and other part-time jobs (averaging $1200). In 2006, 233 non-need-based awards were made. *Average percent of need met:* 83%. *Average financial aid package:* $16,622. *Average need-based loan:* $4382. *Average need-based gift aid:* $13,906. *Average non-need-based aid:* $10,449. *Average indebtedness upon graduation:* $19,206.

Applying *Options:* electronic application, early admission, early decision, early action, deferred entrance. *Application fee:* $30. *Required:* high school transcript, minimum 2.0 GPA, 1 letter of recommendation. *Recommended:* essay or personal statement, interview, class rank. *Application deadlines:* 8/1 (freshmen), 8/15 (transfers), 1/15 (early action). *Early decision deadline:* 12/15. *Notification:* continuous (transfers), 1/1 (early decision), 2/1 (early action).

Freshman Application Contact Mr. Tim Crowley, Director of Admissions, Centenary College of Louisiana, Office of Admissions, Centenary College of Louisiana, 2911 Centenary Boulevard, PO Box 41188, Shreveport, LA 71134-1188. *Phone:* 318-869-5134. *Toll-free phone:* 800-234-4448. *Fax:* 318-869-5005. *E-mail:* dcolson@centenary.edu.

DILLARD UNIVERSITY

New Orleans, Louisiana **www.dillard.edu/**

- **Independent interdenominational** 4-year, founded 1869
- **Urban** 55-acre campus
- **Endowment** $40.8 million
- **Coed** 956 undergraduate students, 92% full-time, 69% women, 31% men
- **Moderately difficult** entrance level, 46% of applicants were admitted

Undergraduates 884 full-time, 72 part-time. Students come from 27 states and territories, 6 other countries, 42% are from out of state, 97% African American, 0.6% Asian American or Pacific Islander, 0.4% Hispanic American, 1% international, 6% transferred in, 49% live on campus. *Retention:* 61% of 2006 full-time freshmen returned.

Freshmen *Admission:* 2,831 applied, 1,298 admitted, 175 enrolled. *Average high school GPA:* 2.79. *Test scores:* SAT critical reading scores over 500: 29%; SAT math scores over 500: 15%; ACT scores over 18: 68%; ACT scores over 24: 5%.

Faculty *Total:* 127, 80% full-time, 54% with terminal degrees. *Student/faculty ratio:* 9:1.

Majors Accounting; African-American/Black studies; art; arts management; art teacher education; Asian studies (East); biology/biological sciences; biology teacher education; business administration and management; chemistry; computer science; dramatic/theater arts; economics; education; elementary education; English; English/language arts teacher education; French; health/health care administration; history; international business/trade/commerce; Japanese; kindergarten/preschool education; mass communication/media; mathematics; mathematics teacher education; modern languages; music; music management and merchandising; music performance; nursing (registered nurse training); physical education teaching and coaching; physics; political science and government; psychology; public health; public health education and promotion; religious studies; science teacher education; social science teacher education; sociology; Spanish; special education; speech and rhetoric; urban studies/affairs.

Academics *Calendar:* semesters. *Degree:* bachelor's. *Special study options:* academic remediation for entering students, adult/continuing education programs, advanced placement credit, cooperative education, double majors, honors programs, independent study, internships, part-time degree program, services for LD students, study abroad, summer session for credit. *ROTC:* Army (c), Air Force (c). *Unusual degree programs:* 3-2 engineering with Auburn University, Columbia University, Georgia Institute of Technology; urban studies with Columbia University, allied health with Howard University, Tuskegee University.

Computers on Campus Students can access the following: computer help desk, free student e-mail accounts, online (class) grades, online (class) registration, online (class) schedules. Campuswide network is available. 100% of college-owned or -operated housing units are wired for high-speed Internet access. Wireless service is available via learning centers, libraries.

Student Life *Housing:* on-campus residence required for freshman year. *Options:* coed, disabled students. Campus housing is university owned, leased by the school and is provided by a third party. Freshman campus housing is guaranteed. *Activities and organizations:* drama/theater group, student-run newspaper, radio station, choral group, Student Government Association, Pre-Alumni Council, KB Clark Psychology Club, National Association for Black Accountants, New Orleans Scholar Activists, national fraternities, national sororities. *Campus security:* 24-hour patrols, late-night transport/escort service, controlled dormitory access. *Student services:* health clinic, personal/psychological counseling.

Athletics Member NAIA. *Intercollegiate sports:* basketball M (s)/W (s), volleyball W (s). *Intramural sports:* basketball M/W, football M/W, softball M/W, tennis M/W, volleyball M/W, weight lifting M.

Standardized Tests *Required:* SAT or ACT (for admission).

Costs (2008–09) *Comprehensive fee:* $17,604 includes full-time tuition ($11,760), mandatory fees ($480), and room and board ($5364). Part-time tuition: $490 per credit.

Financial Aid Of all full-time matriculated undergraduates who enrolled in 2007, 956 applied for aid, 486 were judged to have need, 766 had their need fully met. 207 Federal Work-Study jobs (averaging $1557). 18 state and other part-time jobs (averaging $1174). In 2007, 27 non-need-based awards were made. *Average percent of need met:* 85%. *Average financial aid package:* $14,220. *Average need-based loan:* $3370. *Average need-based gift aid:* $3965. *Average non-need-based aid:* $4120. *Average indebtedness upon graduation:* $26,000.

Applying *Options:* electronic application. *Application fee:* $20. *Required:* high school transcript, 2 letters of recommendation. *Required for some:* essay or personal statement, interview. *Application deadlines:* 7/1 (freshmen), 7/1 (transfers). *Notification:* continuous until 8/1 (freshmen), continuous (transfers).

Freshman Application Contact Ms. Meredith Reed, Director of Admissions, Dillard University, 2601 Gentilly Boulevard, New Orleans, LA 70122. *Phone:* 504-816-4670. *Toll-free phone:* 800-716-8353 (in-state); 800-216-6637 (out-of-state). *Fax:* 504-816-4895. *E-mail:* mreed@dillard.edu.

GRAMBLING STATE UNIVERSITY

Grambling, Louisiana **www.gram.edu/**

- **State-supported** university, founded 1901, part of University of Louisiana System Board of Supervisors
- **Small-town** 380-acre campus
- **Endowment** $3.6 million
- **Coed** 4,753 undergraduate students, 92% full-time, 55% women, 45% men
- **Noncompetitive** entrance level, 30% of applicants were admitted

Undergraduates 4,383 full-time, 370 part-time. Students come from 43 states and territories, 36 other countries, 36% are from out of state, 88% African American, 0.5% Asian American or Pacific Islander, 0.4% Hispanic American, 0.2% Native American, 7% international, 5% transferred in, 44% live on campus. *Retention:* 60% of 2006 full-time freshmen returned.

Freshmen *Admission:* 5,957 applied, 1,793 admitted, 1,211 enrolled. *Average high school GPA:* 2.68. *Test scores:* SAT critical reading scores over 500: 11%; SAT math scores over 500: 12%; ACT scores over 18: 33%; SAT critical reading scores over 600: 2%; ACT scores over 24: 1%.

Faculty *Total:* 288, 86% full-time, 52% with terminal degrees. *Student/faculty ratio:* 17:1.

Majors Accounting; architectural engineering technology; art; art teacher education; biology/biological sciences; business administration and management; business/managerial economics; business teacher education; chemistry; child development; computer science; criminal justice/law enforcement administration; criminal justice/police science; drafting and design technology; dramatic/theater arts; education (multiple levels); electrical, electronic and communications engineering technology; elementary education; English; English/language arts teacher education; family and consumer sciences/home economics teacher education; French; French language teacher education; history; hotel/motel administration; industrial technology; information science/studies; kindergarten/preschool education; legal assistant/paralegal; marketing/marketing management; mass communication/media; mathematics; middle school education; music performance; music teacher education; nursing (registered nurse training); physical education teaching and coaching; physics; physics teacher education; political science and government; pre-law studies; psychology; public administration; science teacher education; secondary education; social science teacher education; social work; sociology; Spanish; special education; speech-language pathology; speech/theater education; technology/industrial arts teacher education.

Academics *Calendar:* semesters. *Degrees:* certificates, associate, bachelor's, master's, doctoral, and post-master's certificates. *Special study options:* academic remediation for entering students, adult/continuing education programs, advanced placement credit, cooperative education, distance learning, honors programs, internships, off-campus study, part-time degree program, study abroad, summer session for credit. *ROTC:* Army (b), Air Force (c).

Computers on Campus 600 computers/terminals and 800 ports are available on campus for general student use. Students can access the following: campus intranet, computer help desk, free student e-mail accounts, online (class) grades, online (class) registration, online (class) schedules. Campuswide network is available. 75% of college-owned or -operated housing units are wired for high-speed Internet access. Wireless service is available via classrooms, computer centers, computer labs, dorm rooms, learning centers, libraries, student centers.

Student Life *Housing:* on-campus residence required for freshman year. *Options:* coed, men-only, women-only, disabled students. Campus housing is university owned. Freshman applicants given priority for college housing. *Activities and organizations:* drama/theater group, student-run newspaper, radio station, choral group, marching band, International Modeling Society, Black Dynasty Modeling Troup, Advent Youth Group, Bayou Boyz, CALYPSO, national fraternities, national sororities. *Campus security:* 24-hour patrols, student patrols, controlled dormitory access. *Student services:* health clinic, personal/psychological counseling.

Athletics Member NCAA. All Division I except football (Division I-AA). *Intercollegiate sports:* baseball M (s), basketball M (s)/W (s), bowling W (s), cross-country running M/W, golf M (s)/W (s), tennis M (s)/W (s), track and field M (s)/W (s), volleyball W (s). *Intramural sports:* bowling W, gymnastics M/W, softball M/W, swimming and diving M/W, table tennis M/W, tennis M, track and field M/W, volleyball M/W, weight lifting M/W.

Standardized Tests *Required:* SAT or ACT (for admission). *Recommended:* SAT Subject Tests (for admission).

Costs (2007–08) *Tuition:* state resident $2232 full-time, $93 per credit hour part-time; nonresident $7582 full-time, $93 per credit hour part-time. Part-time tuition and fees vary according to course load. *Required fees:* $1390 full-time, $430 per term part-time. *Room and board:* $5072; room only: $2600. Room and board charges vary according to housing facility. *Payment plan:* deferred payment. *Waivers:* children of alumni, senior citizens, and employees or children of employees.

Financial Aid Of all full-time matriculated undergraduates who enrolled in 2006, 4,191 applied for aid, 3,931 were judged to have need, 309 had their need fully met. 1,141 Federal Work-Study jobs (averaging $1310). 431 state and other part-time jobs (averaging $1487). In 2006, 200 non-need-based awards were made. *Average percent of need met:* 80%. *Average financial aid package:* $6800. *Average need-based loan:* $3813. *Average need-based gift aid:* $2928. *Average non-need-based aid:* $2328. *Average indebtedness upon graduation:* $29,416. *Financial aid deadline:* 4/1.

Applying *Options:* early admission, early decision. *Application fee:* $20. *Required:* high school transcript, minimum 2.0 GPA. *Application deadlines:* 6/30 (freshmen), 6/30 (transfers). *Early decision deadline:* 4/15. *Notification:* continuous until 8/1 (freshmen), continuous until 8/1 (transfers), 4/20 (early decision).

Freshman Application Contact Ms. Annie Moss, Acting Director of Admissions, Grambling State University, PO Drawer 1165, 100 Main Street, Grambling, LA 71245. *Phone:* 318-274-6183. *E-mail:* mossa@gram.edu.

HERZING COLLEGE

Kenner, Louisiana **www.herzing.edu/**

Director of Admissions Genny Bordelon, Director of Admissions, Herzing College, 2400 Veterans Boulevard, Kenner, LA 70062. *Phone:* 504-733-0074. *Fax:* 504-733-0020.

ITT TECHNICAL INSTITUTE

St. Rose, Louisiana **www.itt-tech.edu/**

- **Proprietary** primarily 2-year, founded 1998, part of ITT Educational Services, Inc
- **Coed**
- **Minimally difficult** entrance level

Academics *Calendar:* quarters. *Degrees:* associate and bachelor's.

Standardized Tests *Required:* Wonderlic aptitude test (for admission).

Applying *Options:* deferred entrance. *Application fee:* $100. *Required:* high school transcript, interview. *Recommended:* letters of recommendation.

Freshman Application Contact Mr. John Richard, Director of Recruitment, ITT Technical Institute, 140 James Drive East, Saint Rose, LA 70087. *Phone:* 504-463-0338. *Toll-free phone:* 866-463-0338.

LOUISIANA COLLEGE

Pineville, Louisiana **www.lacollege.edu/**

- **Independent Southern Baptist** 4-year, founded 1906
- **Small-town** 81-acre campus
- **Endowment** $29.7 million
- **Coed** 1,056 undergraduate students, 81% full-time, 52% women, 48% men

• **Moderately difficult** entrance level, 78% of applicants were admitted

Undergraduates 856 full-time, 200 part-time. Students come from 16 states and territories, 7 other countries, 8% are from out of state, 13% African American, 1% Asian American or Pacific Islander, 2% Hispanic American, 0.9% Native American, 0.9% international, 48% live on campus. *Retention:* 62% of 2006 full-time freshmen returned.

Freshmen *Admission:* 549 applied, 429 admitted.

Faculty *Total:* 96, 65% full-time, 47% with terminal degrees. *Student/faculty ratio:* 13:1.

Majors Accounting; adult and continuing education; advertising; art; art teacher education; athletic training; biology/biological sciences; broadcast journalism; business administration and management; business teacher education; chemistry; clinical laboratory science/medical technology; clinical/medical laboratory technology; commercial and advertising art; criminal justice/police science; dramatic/theater arts; economics; elementary education; English; family and consumer economics related; finance; fine/studio arts; French; health teacher education; history; interdisciplinary studies; journalism; kindergarten/preschool education; kinesiology and exercise science; liberal arts and sciences/liberal studies; marketing/marketing management; mass communication/media; mathematics; modern languages; music; music teacher education; nursing (registered nurse training); philosophy; physical education teaching and coaching; physical therapist assistant; physics; piano and organ; pre-law studies; psychology; public administration; radiologic technology/science; religious education; religious/sacred music; religious studies; respiratory therapy technician; science teacher education; secondary education; social work; sociology; Spanish; special education; speech and rhetoric; theology; voice and opera.

Academics *Calendar:* semesters. *Degree:* bachelor's. *Special study options:* academic remediation for entering students, accelerated degree program, adult/continuing education programs, advanced placement credit, double majors, honors programs, independent study, internships, part-time degree program, services for LD students, student-designed majors, study abroad, summer session for credit. *ROTC:* Army (b).

Computers on Campus 242 computers/terminals are available on campus for general student use. Students can access the following: campus intranet, free student e-mail accounts, online (class) grades. Campuswide network is available. 100% of college-owned or -operated housing units are wired for high-speed Internet access.

Student Life *Housing:* on-campus residence required through senior year. *Options:* men-only, women-only. Campus housing is university owned. Freshman campus housing is guaranteed. *Activities and organizations:* drama/theater group, student-run newspaper, radio station, choral group, marching band, Baptist Student Union, Delta Xi Omega, Student Government Association, Union Board, Lambda Chi Beta. *Campus security:* 24-hour patrols, student patrols, late-night transport/escort service, controlled dormitory access. *Student services:* health clinic, personal/psychological counseling.

Athletics Member NCAA, NCCAA. All NCAA Division III. *Intercollegiate sports:* baseball M, basketball M/W, cheerleading M/W, cross-country running W, football M, golf M, soccer M/W, softball W, tennis W. *Intramural sports:* badminton M/W, basketball M/W, football M/W, racquetball M/W, soccer M/W, softball M/W, table tennis M/W, tennis M/W, ultimate Frisbee M/W, volleyball M/W, water polo M/W.

Standardized Tests *Required:* SAT or ACT (for admission).

Costs (2007–08) *Comprehensive fee:* $15,746 includes full-time tuition ($10,200), mandatory fees ($1290), and room and board ($4256). Part-time tuition: $340 per hour. No tuition increase for student's term of enrollment. *Room and board:* Room and board charges vary according to board plan and housing facility. *Payment plan:* installment. *Waivers:* employees or children of employees.

Financial Aid Of all full-time matriculated undergraduates who enrolled in 2003, 750 applied for aid, 576 were judged to have need, 182 had their need fully met. In 2003, 336 non-need-based awards were made. *Average percent of need met:* 79%. *Average financial aid package:* $10,014. *Average need-based loan:* $3942. *Average need-based gift aid:* $3251. *Average non-need-based aid:* $4063. *Average indebtedness upon graduation:* $5742.

Applying *Options:* electronic application, early admission. *Application fee:* $25. *Required:* high school transcript, minimum 2.0 GPA, letters of recommendation, class rank. *Required for some:* 3 letters of recommendation. *Recommended:* interview. *Application deadline:* 8/15 (freshmen). *Notification:* continuous (freshmen), continuous (transfers).

Freshman Application Contact Mr. Byron McGee, Director of Enrollment Management, Louisiana College, 1140 College Drive, Box 560, Pineville, LA 71359. *Phone:* 318-487-7439. *Toll-free phone:* 800-487-1906. *Fax:* 318-487-7550. *E-mail:* admissions@lacollege.edu.

LOUISIANA STATE UNIVERSITY AND AGRICULTURAL AND MECHANICAL COLLEGE

Baton Rouge, Louisiana **www.lsu.edu/**

- **State-supported** university, founded 1860, part of Louisiana State University System
- **Urban** 2000-acre campus with easy access to New Orleans
- **Endowment** $344.5 million
- **Coed** 23,393 undergraduate students, 93% full-time, 51% women, 49% men
- **Moderately difficult** entrance level, 73% of applicants were admitted

Undergraduates 21,811 full-time, 1,582 part-time. Students come from 49 states and territories, 76 other countries, 14% are from out of state, 9% African American, 3% Asian American or Pacific Islander, 3% Hispanic American, 0.4% Native American, 2% international, 3% transferred in, 23% live on campus. *Retention:* 85% of 2006 full-time freshmen returned.

Freshmen *Admission:* 11,452 applied, 8,332 admitted, 4,596 enrolled. *Average high school GPA:* 3.52. *Test scores:* SAT critical reading scores over 500: 84%; SAT math scores over 500: 92%; SAT writing scores over 500: 74%; ACT scores over 18: 100%; SAT critical reading scores over 600: 43%; SAT math scores over 600: 55%; SAT writing scores over 600: 34%; ACT scores over 24: 67%; SAT critical reading scores over 700: 12%; SAT math scores over 700: 12%; SAT writing scores over 700: 6%; ACT scores over 30: 12%.

Faculty *Total:* 1,437, 88% full-time, 82% with terminal degrees. *Student/faculty ratio:* 20:1.

Majors Accounting; adult and continuing education; agricultural business and management; animal sciences; anthropology; architecture; audiology and speech-language pathology; biochemistry; biology/biological sciences; biomedical/medical engineering; business administration and management; business/managerial economics; chemical engineering; chemistry; civil engineering; computer engineering; computer science; construction management; dietetics; dramatic/theater arts; early childhood education; economics; electrical, electronics and communications engineering; elementary education; English; environmental/environmental health engineering; environmental science; family and consumer sciences/human sciences; fashion merchandising; finance; fine/studio arts; food science; forest/forest resources management; French; general studies; geography; geology/earth science; German; history; industrial engineering; interior architecture; international business/trade/commerce; international/global studies; landscape architecture; Latin; liberal arts and sciences/liberal studies; management science; marketing/marketing management; mass communication/media; mathematics; mechanical engineering; microbiology; music; music performance; music teacher education; natural resources management and policy; petroleum engineering; philosophy; physical education teaching and coaching; physics; plant sciences; political science and government; psychology; secondary education; sociology; Spanish; speech and rhetoric; women's studies.

Academics *Calendar:* semesters. *Degrees:* bachelor's, master's, doctoral, first professional, and post-master's certificates. *Special study options:* accelerated degree program, adult/continuing education programs, advanced placement credit, cooperative education, distance learning, double majors, English as a second language, freshman honors college, honors programs, independent study, internships, off-campus study, part-time degree program, services for LD students, student-designed majors, study abroad, summer session for credit. *ROTC:* Army (b), Navy (c), Air Force (b).

Computers on Campus 7,000 computers/terminals and 8,500 ports are available on campus for general student use. Students can access the following: computer help desk, free student e-mail accounts, online (class) grades, online (class) registration, online (class) schedules, free software for download, personal Web sites, storage, discounts on hardware, virtual computer lab. Campuswide network is available. 100% of college-owned or -operated housing units are wired for high-speed Internet access. Wireless service is available via entire campus.

Student Life *Housing:* on-campus residence required for freshman year. *Options:* coed, men-only, women-only, disabled students. Campus housing is university owned. *Activities and organizations:* drama/theater group, student-run newspaper, radio and television station, choral group, marching band, intramural athletics, student political organizations, student professional organizations, religious organizations, national fraternities, national sororities. *Campus security:* 24-hour emergency response devices and patrols, late-night transport/escort service, controlled dormitory access, self-defense education, crime prevention programs. *Student services:* health clinic, personal/psychological counseling, women's center, legal services.

Athletics Member NCAA. All Division I except football (Division I-A). *Intercollegiate sports:* baseball M (s), basketball M (s)/W (s), cheerleading M/W, cross-country running M (s)/W (s), golf M (s)/W (s), gymnastics W (s), soccer W (s), softball W (s), swimming and diving M (s)/W (s), tennis M (s)/W (s), track and field M (s)/W (s), volleyball W (s). *Intramural sports:* badminton M/W, basketball M/W, bowling M (c)/W (c), crew M (c)/W (c), equestrian sports W (c), football M/W, lacrosse M (c)/W (c), racquetball M/W, rugby M (c), soccer M (c)/W (c), softball M/W, table tennis M/W, tennis M/W, ultimate Frisbee M (c)/W (c), volleyball M (c)/W (c), weight lifting M (c)/W (c), wrestling M (c).

Standardized Tests *Required:* SAT or ACT (for admission).

Costs (2007–08) *Tuition:* state resident $2981 full-time; nonresident $11,281 full-time. Part-time tuition and fees vary according to course load. *Required fees:* $1562 full-time. *Room and board:* $6852; room only: $4130. Room and board charges vary according to board plan and housing facility. *Payment plan:* deferred payment. *Waivers:* children of alumni and employees or children of employees.

Financial Aid Of all full-time matriculated undergraduates who enrolled in 2006, 12,618 applied for aid, 8,948 were judged to have need, 1,170 had their need fully met. 838 Federal Work-Study jobs (averaging $1289). 4,827 state and other part-time jobs (averaging $1977). In 2006, 2790 non-need-based awards were made. *Average percent of need met:* 58%. *Average financial aid package:* $8011. *Average need-based loan:* $3904. *Average need-based gift aid:* $5230. *Average non-need-based aid:* $4003. *Average indebtedness upon graduation:* $16,354.

Applying *Options:* early admission, deferred entrance. *Application fee:* $40. *Required:* high school transcript, minimum 3.0 GPA, minimum ACT score of 22 or SAT score of 1030. *Required for some:* essay or personal statement, interview. *Application deadlines:* 4/15 (freshmen), 4/15 (transfers). *Notification:* continuous (freshmen), continuous (transfers).

Freshman Application Contact Louisiana State University and Agricultural and Mechanical College, 110 Thomas Boyd Hall, Baton Rouge, LA 70803. *Phone:* 225-578-1175.

LOUISIANA STATE UNIVERSITY AT ALEXANDRIA

Alexandria, Louisiana **www.lsua.edu/**

Freshman Application Contact Ms. Shelly Kieffer, Recruiter/Admissions Counselor, Louisiana State University at Alexandria, 8100 Highway 71 South, Alexandria, LA 71302-9121. *Phone:* 318-473-6508. *Toll-free phone:* 888-473-6417. *Fax:* 318-473-6418. *E-mail:* skieffer@isua.edu.

LOUISIANA STATE UNIVERSITY HEALTH SCIENCES CENTER

New Orleans, Louisiana **www.lsuhsc.edu/no/**

- **State-supported** university, founded 1931, part of Louisiana State University System
- **Urban** 80-acre campus with easy access to New Orleans
- **Endowment** $23.0 million
- **Coed** 648 undergraduate students, 51% full-time, 85% women, 15% men

Undergraduates 329 full-time, 319 part-time. Students come from 6 states and territories, 1 other country, 1% are from out of state, 11% live on campus.

Faculty *Total:* 1,044, 75% full-time, 100% with terminal degrees.

Majors Cardiovascular technology; clinical laboratory science/medical technology; dental hygiene; dental laboratory technology; ophthalmic technology; vocational rehabilitation counseling.

Academics *Calendar:* semesters. *Degrees:* associate, bachelor's, master's, doctoral, and first professional. *Special study options:* accelerated degree program, advanced placement credit, cooperative education, distance learning, double majors, independent study, internships, services for LD students, summer session for credit.

Computers on Campus 100 computers/terminals are available on campus for general student use. Students can access the following: campus intranet, computer help desk, free student e-mail accounts. Campuswide network is available. 100% of college-owned or -operated housing units are wired for high-speed Internet access. Wireless service is available via classrooms, learning centers, libraries, student centers.

Student Life *Housing options:* coed. Campus housing is university owned. *Campus security:* 24-hour emergency response devices and patrols, late-night transport/escort service, controlled dormitory access. *Student services:* health clinic, personal/psychological counseling.

Costs (2007–08) *Tuition:* state resident $4577 full-time; nonresident $9482 full-time. Full-time tuition and fees vary according to course load, location, and program. Part-time tuition and fees vary according to course load, location, and program. *Room and board:* $4470; room only: $2370. Room and board charges vary according to board plan and housing facility. *Payment plans:* installment, deferred payment. *Waivers:* children of alumni, senior citizens, and employees or children of employees.

Applying *Application fee:* $50. *Application deadline:* 3/1 (transfers). *Notification:* 8/1 (transfers).

Director of Admissions Mr. W. Bryant Faust IV, Acting Registrar, Louisiana State University Health Sciences Center, 433 Bolivar Street, New Orleans, LA 70112. *Phone:* 504-568-4829. *Fax:* 504-568-5545.

LOUISIANA STATE UNIVERSITY IN SHREVEPORT

Shreveport, Louisiana **www.lsus.edu/**

- **State-supported** comprehensive, founded 1965, part of Louisiana State University System
- **Urban** 200-acre campus
- **Endowment** $11.7 million
- **Coed**
- **Moderately difficult** entrance level

Faculty *Student/faculty ratio:* 18:1.

Academics *Calendar:* semesters plus 8-week and two 4-week summer terms. *Degrees:* bachelor's and master's.

Student Life *Campus security:* 24-hour patrols, student patrols, controlled dormitory access.

Athletics Member NAIA.

Standardized Tests *Required for some:* SAT or ACT (for admission). *Recommended:* ACT (for admission).

Costs (2008–09) *Tuition:* state resident $2628 full-time, $103 per credit hour part-time; nonresident $6954 full-time, $284 per credit hour part-time. *Required fees:* $893 full-time, $36 per credit hour part-time.

Applying *Options:* early admission. *Application fee:* $10. *Required for some:* high school transcript, minimum 2.0 GPA.

Freshman Application Contact Louisiana State University in Shreveport, One University Place, Shreveport, LA 71115-2399. *Phone:* 318-797-5063. *Toll-free phone:* 800-229-5957.

LOUISIANA TECH UNIVERSITY

Ruston, Louisiana **www.latech.edu/**

- **State-supported** university, founded 1894, part of University of Louisiana System
- **Small-town** 247-acre campus
- **Endowment** $39.1 million
- **Coed**
- **Moderately difficult** entrance level

Louisiana Tech University is known for its high graduation rates, entrance exam scores, and overall academic quality. Quarter terms provide an opportunity for flexible scheduling. Support from "The Tech Family" enhances creativity and opportunities for participation in the many student organizations.

Faculty *Student/faculty ratio:* 22:1.

Academics *Calendar:* quarters. *Degrees:* associate, bachelor's, master's, doctoral, and first professional certificates.

Student Life *Campus security:* 24-hour emergency response devices and patrols, student patrols, late-night transport/escort service, controlled dormitory access.

Athletics Member NCAA. All Division I except football (Division I-A).

Standardized Tests *Required:* SAT or ACT (for admission). *Recommended:* ACT (for admission).

Costs (2007–08) *Tuition:* state resident $4577 full-time; nonresident $9482 full-time. Full-time tuition and fees vary according to course load, location, and program. Part-time tuition and fees vary according to course load, location, and program. *Room and board:* $4470; room only: $2370. Room and board charges vary according to board plan and housing facility. *Payment plans:* installment, deferred payment.

Financial Aid Of all full-time matriculated undergraduates who enrolled in 2005, 4,467 applied for aid, 2,911 were judged to have need, 450 had their need fully met. 355 Federal Work-Study jobs (averaging $1308). 1,297 state and other part-time jobs (averaging $1372). In 2005, 1905 non-need-based awards were made. *Average percent of need met:* 57. *Average financial aid package:* $5944.

Average need-based loan: $2734. *Average need-based gift aid:* $4482. *Average non-need-based aid:* $5280. *Average indebtedness upon graduation:* $17,142.

Applying *Options:* early admission. *Application fee:* $20. *Required:* high school transcript, minimum 2.2 GPA.

Freshman Application Contact Mrs. Jan B. Albritton, Director of Admissions, Louisiana Tech University, PO Box 3178, Ruston, LA 71272. *Phone:* 318-257-3036. *Toll-free phone:* 800-528-3241. *Fax:* 318-257-2499. *E-mail:* bulldog@latech.edu.

See page 1058 for the College Close-Up.

LOYOLA UNIVERSITY NEW ORLEANS

New Orleans, Louisiana www.loyno.edu/

- **Independent Roman Catholic (Jesuit)** comprehensive, founded 1912
- **Urban** 26-acre campus
- **Endowment** $327.8 million
- **Coed** 2,645 undergraduate students, 89% full-time, 59% women, 41% men
- **Moderately difficult** entrance level, 61% of applicants were admitted

Loyola's unique combination of high-quality academic programs and outstanding faculty members, an ideal size that fosters a positive learning environment and individual attention, and the centuries-old Jesuit tradition of educating the whole person distinguish it from other institutions. Loyola provides big-school experiences with small-school relationships. Students are British Marshall, Fulbright, Goldwater, Mellon, Mitchell, and Rhodes scholarship recipients.

Undergraduates 2,353 full-time, 292 part-time. Students come from 48 states and territories, 38 other countries, 50% are from out of state, 12% African American, 4% Asian American or Pacific Islander, 12% Hispanic American, 0.6% Native American, 3% international, 4% transferred in, 39% live on campus. *Retention:* 78% of 2006 full-time freshmen returned.

Freshmen *Admission:* 2,980 applied, 1,832 admitted, 496 enrolled. *Average high school GPA:* 3.55. *Test scores:* SAT critical reading scores over 500: 94%; SAT math scores over 500: 89%; ACT scores over 18: 99%; SAT critical reading scores over 600: 55%; SAT math scores over 600: 37%; ACT scores over 24: 66%; SAT critical reading scores over 700: 18%; SAT math scores over 700: 5%; ACT scores over 30: 14%.

Faculty *Total:* 406, 64% full-time, 75% with terminal degrees. *Student/faculty ratio:* 11:1.

Majors Accounting; art; behavioral sciences; biology/biological sciences; business administration and management; business/managerial economics; chemistry; classics and languages, literatures and linguistics; commercial and advertising art; communication/speech communication and rhetoric; computer and information sciences; creative writing; criminal justice/safety; dramatic/theater arts; economics; education; elementary education; English; finance; forensic science and technology; French; general studies; German; history; humanities; information science/studies; international business/trade/commerce; jazz/jazz studies; marketing/marketing management; mathematics; music; music management and merchandising; music performance; music teacher education; music theory and composition; nursing (registered nurse training); philosophy; physics; piano and organ; political science and government; psychology; religious education; religious/sacred music; religious studies; Russian; social sciences; sociology; Spanish; visual and performing arts.

Academics *Calendar:* semesters. *Degrees:* bachelor's, master's, first professional, post-master's, and postbachelor's certificates. *Special study options:* academic remediation for entering students, accelerated degree program, adult/continuing education programs, advanced placement credit, distance learning, double majors, external degree program, honors programs, independent study, internships, off-campus study, part-time degree program, services for LD students, student-designed majors, study abroad, summer session for credit. *ROTC:* Army (c), Navy (c), Air Force (c).

Computers on Campus 458 computers/terminals are available on campus for general student use. Students can access the following: online (class) registration. Campuswide network is available.

Student Life *Housing:* on-campus residence required for freshman year. *Options:* coed, disabled students. Campus housing is university owned. Freshman campus housing is guaranteed. *Activities and organizations:* drama/theater group, student-run newspaper, radio and television station, choral group, University Programming Board, Community Action Program, Black Student Union, Student Government Association, national fraternities, national sororities. *Campus security:* 24-hour emergency response devices and patrols, late-night transport/escort service, controlled dormitory access, self-defense education, bicycle patrols, closed circuit TV monitors, door alarms, crime prevention programs. *Student services:* health clinic, personal/psychological counseling, women's center.

Athletics Member NAIA. *Intercollegiate sports:* baseball M, basketball M (s)/W (s), bowling M (c)/W (c), cheerleading M (c)/W (c), crew M (c)/W (c), cross-country running M/W, golf M (c)/W (c), rugby M (c), soccer M (c)/W, swimming and diving M (c)/W (c), tennis M (c)/W (c), track and field M/W, ultimate Frisbee M (c)/W (c), volleyball W, wrestling M (c). *Intramural sports:* basketball M/W, racquetball M/W, soccer M/W, softball M/W, swimming and diving M/W, tennis M/W, volleyball M/W, water polo M/W, weight lifting M/W.

Standardized Tests *Required for some:* SAT or ACT (for admission), PAA.

Costs (2008–09) *Comprehensive fee:* $37,438 includes full-time tuition ($27,168), mandatory fees ($876), and room and board ($9394). Part-time tuition: $775 per credit hour. *College room only:* $5488.

Financial Aid Of all full-time matriculated undergraduates who enrolled in 2007, 1,496 applied for aid, 1,270 were judged to have need, 376 had their need fully met. 764 Federal Work-Study jobs (averaging $1858). In 2007, 876 non-need-based awards were made. *Average percent of need met:* 83%. *Average financial aid package:* $22,253. *Average need-based loan:* $4267. *Average need-based gift aid:* $18,180. *Average non-need-based aid:* $12,135. *Average indebtedness upon graduation:* $21,020. *Financial aid deadline:* 6/1.

Applying *Options:* electronic application, early admission. *Application fee:* $20. *Required:* essay or personal statement, high school transcript, 1 letter of recommendation. *Required for some:* interview. *Recommended:* interview. *Application deadlines:* 1/15 (freshmen), rolling (transfers). *Notification:* continuous (freshmen).

Freshman Application Contact Ms. Deborah C. Stieffel, Dean of Admission and Enrollment Management, Loyola University New Orleans, 6363 Saint Charles Avenue, Box 18, New Orleans, LA 70118-6195. *Phone:* 504-865-3240. *Toll-free phone:* 800-4-LOYOLA. *Fax:* 504-865-3383. *E-mail:* admit@loyno.edu.

See page 1060 for the College Close-Up.

MCNEESE STATE UNIVERSITY

Lake Charles, Louisiana www.mcneese.edu/

- **State-supported** comprehensive, founded 1939, part of University of Louisiana System
- **Suburban** 766-acre campus
- **Endowment** $45.8 million
- **Coed** 7,053 undergraduate students, 82% full-time, 61% women, 39% men
- **Moderately difficult** entrance level, 78% of applicants were admitted

Undergraduates 5,811 full-time, 1,242 part-time. Students come from 35 states and territories, 46 other countries, 7% are from out of state, 18% African American, 1% Asian American or Pacific Islander, 1% Hispanic American, 0.7% Native American, 3% international, 5% transferred in, 10% live on campus. *Retention:* 64% of 2006 full-time freshmen returned.

Freshmen *Admission:* 2,267 applied, 1,768 admitted, 1,298 enrolled. *Average high school GPA:* 3.16. *Test scores:* ACT scores over 18: 86%; ACT scores over 24: 22%; ACT scores over 30: 1%.

Faculty *Total:* 414, 76% full-time, 56% with terminal degrees. *Student/faculty ratio:* 20:1.

Majors Accounting; agricultural teacher education; agriculture; applied art; art; art teacher education; biology/biological sciences; biology teacher education; business administration and management; business teacher education; ceramic arts and ceramics; chemistry; chemistry teacher education; clinical laboratory science/medical technology; computer typography and composition equipment operation; criminal justice/safety; dramatic/theater arts; drawing; early childhood education; education; educational leadership and administration; education related; electrical, electronic and communications engineering technology; elementary education; engineering; engineering technologies related; engineering technology; English; English/language arts teacher education; environmental science; family and consumer sciences/home economics teacher education; family and consumer sciences/human sciences; finance; foods, nutrition, and wellness; foreign language teacher education; French; general studies; geology/earth science; history; information technology; instrumentation technology; kindergarten/preschool education; kinesiology and exercise science; legal assistant/paralegal; liberal arts and sciences/liberal studies; marketing/marketing management; mass communication/media; mathematics; mathematics teacher education; medical radiologic technology; music; music performance; music teacher education; nursing (registered nurse training); petroleum technology; photography; physical education teaching and coaching; physics; political science and government; printmaking; psychology; secondary education; social studies teacher education; sociology; Spanish; special education; speech and rhetoric; speech teacher education; wildlife and wildlands science and management.

Academics *Calendar:* semesters. *Degrees:* associate, bachelor's, master's, post-master's, and postbachelor's certificates. *Special study options:* academic remediation for entering students, accelerated degree program, adult/continuing education programs, advanced placement credit, cooperative education, distance learning, double majors, English as a second language, freshman honors college, honors programs, independent study, internships, off-campus study, part-time degree program, services for LD students, study abroad, summer session for credit.

Computers on Campus 700 computers/terminals are available on campus for general student use. Students can access the following: computer help desk, free student e-mail accounts, online (class) grades, online (class) registration, online (class) schedules. Campuswide network is available. 100% of college-owned or -operated housing units are wired for high-speed Internet access. Wireless service is available via classrooms, computer centers, computer labs, libraries, student centers.

Student Life *Housing:* on-campus residence required for freshman year. *Options:* coed. Campus housing is university owned and is provided by a third party. *Activities and organizations:* drama/theater group, student-run newspaper, choral group, marching band, Student Government Association, International Students Association, Resident Student Association, national fraternities, national sororities. *Campus security:* 24-hour emergency response devices and patrols, late-night transport/escort service, controlled dormitory access. *Student services:* health clinic, personal/psychological counseling, women's center.

Athletics Member NCAA. All Division I except football (Division I-AA). *Intercollegiate sports:* baseball M (s), basketball M (s)/W (s), cross-country running M (s)/W (s), golf M (s)/W (s), riflery M/W, soccer W (s), softball W (s), tennis W (s), track and field M (s)/W (s), volleyball W (s), weight lifting M (c)/W (c). *Intramural sports:* badminton M/W, baseball M, basketball M/W, football M/W, golf M/W, racquetball M/W, soccer M/W, softball W, swimming and diving M/W, table tennis M/W, tennis M/W, volleyball M/W, water polo M/W, weight lifting M/W.

Standardized Tests *Required:* SAT or ACT (for admission).

Costs (2008–09) *Tuition:* state resident $2226 full-time; nonresident $8292 full-time. *Required fees:* $1036 full-time. *Room and board:* $3460; room only: $1500.

Financial Aid In 2002, 2610 non-need-based awards were made. *Average percent of need met:* 58%.

Applying *Options:* electronic application, early admission. *Application fee:* $20. *Required:* high school transcript. *Application deadlines:* rolling (freshmen), rolling (transfers). *Notification:* continuous (freshmen), continuous (transfers).

Freshman Application Contact Ms. Kara Smith, Director of Admissions, McNeese State University, Box 92495, Kaufman Hall, 4100 Ryan Street, Lake Charles, LA 70609. *Phone:* 337-475-5146. *Toll-free phone:* 800-622-3352. *Fax:* 337-475-5151. *E-mail:* info@mcneese.edu.

See page 1062 for the College Close-Up.

NEW ORLEANS BAPTIST THEOLOGICAL SEMINARY

New Orleans, Louisiana **www.nobts.edu/**

Director of Admissions Dr. Paul E. Gregoire Jr., Registrar/Director of Admissions, New Orleans Baptist Theological Seminary, 3939 Gentilly Boulevard, New Orleans, LA 70126-4858. *Phone:* 504-282-4455 Ext. 3337. *Toll-free phone:* 800-662-8701.

NICHOLLS STATE UNIVERSITY

Thibodaux, Louisiana **www.nicholls.edu**

- **State-supported** comprehensive, founded 1948, part of University of Louisiana System
- **Small-town** 210-acre campus with easy access to New Orleans
- **Endowment** $12.9 million
- **Coed** 6,193 undergraduate students, 79% full-time, 62% women, 38% men
- **Noncompetitive** entrance level, 84% of applicants were admitted

Undergraduates 4,911 full-time, 1,282 part-time. Students come from 35 states and territories, 45 other countries, 6% are from out of state, 18% African American, 1% Asian American or Pacific Islander, 2% Hispanic American, 2% Native American, 1% international, 3% transferred in, 18% live on campus. *Retention:* 66% of 2006 full-time freshmen returned.

Freshmen *Admission:* 2,129 applied, 1,787 admitted, 1,202 enrolled. *Average high school GPA:* 3.14. *Test scores:* ACT scores over 18: 89%; ACT scores over 24: 21%; ACT scores over 30: 1%.

Faculty *Total:* 288, 100% full-time, 55% with terminal degrees. *Student/faculty ratio:* 20:1.

Majors Agricultural business and management; art; art teacher education; audiology and speech-language pathology; biology/biological sciences; business administration and management; business teacher education; cardiopulmonary technology; chemistry; child care and support services management; computer science; culinary arts; dietetics; early childhood education; elementary education; emergency medical technology (EMT paramedic); English; English/language arts teacher education; family and consumer sciences/human sciences; finance; French; French language teacher education; general studies; health services/allied health/health sciences; history; legal assistant/paralegal; liberal arts and sciences/liberal studies; management information systems; marketing/marketing management; mass communication/media; mathematics; mathematics teacher education; mechanical engineering/mechanical technology; middle school education; music; music teacher education; nursing (registered nurse training); petroleum technology; physical education teaching and coaching; political science and government; psychology; science teacher education; social studies teacher education; sociology; survey technology.

Academics *Calendar:* semesters. *Degrees:* associate, bachelor's, master's, and post-master's certificates. *Special study options:* academic remediation for entering students, accelerated degree program, adult/continuing education programs, advanced placement credit, cooperative education, distance learning, double majors, English as a second language, honors programs, independent study, internships, off-campus study, part-time degree program, services for LD students, study abroad, summer session for credit.

Computers on Campus 1,500 computers/terminals and 1,500 ports are available on campus for general student use. Students can access the following: campus intranet, free student e-mail accounts, online (class) grades, online (class) registration, online (class) schedules, course management system—Blackboard. Campuswide network is available. 20% of college-owned or -operated housing units are wired for high-speed Internet access. Wireless service is available via entire campus.

Student Life *Housing options:* coed, men-only, women-only, disabled students. Campus housing is university owned. Freshman campus housing is guaranteed. *Activities and organizations:* drama/theater group, student-run newspaper, radio and television station, choral group, marching band, Student Government Association, Student Programming Association, Residence Hall Association, Food Advisory Association, national fraternities, national sororities. *Campus security:* 24-hour emergency response devices and patrols, student patrols, late-night transport/escort service. *Student services:* health clinic, personal/psychological counseling, women's center, legal services.

Athletics Member NCAA. All Division I except football (Division I-AA). *Intercollegiate sports:* baseball M (s), basketball M (s)/W (s), cross-country running M (s)/W (s), golf M (s)/W (s), soccer W (s), softball W (s), tennis M/W (s), track and field M (s)/W (s), volleyball W (s). *Intramural sports:* basketball M/W, football M/W, softball M/W, volleyball M/W.

Standardized Tests *Required:* SAT or ACT (for admission).

Costs (2007–08) *Tuition:* state resident $2231 full-time; nonresident $7679 full-time. Part-time tuition and fees vary according to course load. *Required fees:* $1392 full-time. *Room and board:* $4556; room only: $2500. Room and board charges vary according to board plan and housing facility. *Payment plans:* installment, deferred payment. *Waivers:* employees or children of employees.

Financial Aid Of all full-time matriculated undergraduates who enrolled in 2006, 4,083 applied for aid, 2,459 were judged to have need, 1,450 had their need fully met. 213 Federal Work-Study jobs (averaging $1100). 590 state and other part-time jobs (averaging $1677). In 2006, 234 non-need-based awards were made. *Average percent of need met:* 85%. *Average financial aid package:* $6116. *Average need-based loan:* $3222. *Average need-based gift aid:* $3046. *Average non-need-based aid:* $2270. *Average indebtedness upon graduation:* $16,710. *Financial aid deadline:* 6/30.

Applying *Options:* electronic application, early admission, deferred entrance. *Application fee:* $20. *Required:* high school transcript. *Application deadlines:* rolling (freshmen), rolling (transfers). *Notification:* 9/1 (freshmen), continuous until 8/28 (transfers).

Freshman Application Contact Mrs. Becky L. Durocher, Director of Admissions, Nicholls State University, PO Box 2004-NSU, Thibodaux, LA 70310. *Phone:* 985-448-4507. *Toll-free phone:* 877-NICHOLLS. *Fax:* 985-448-4929. *E-mail:* nicholls@nicholls.edu.

NORTHWESTERN STATE UNIVERSITY OF LOUISIANA

Natchitoches, Louisiana **www.nsula.edu/**

- **State-supported** comprehensive, founded 1884, part of University of Louisiana System
- **Small-town** 916-acre campus
- **Endowment** $8.9 million
- **Coed** 7,977 undergraduate students, 71% full-time, 68% women, 32% men
- **Moderately difficult** entrance level, 82% of applicants were admitted

Undergraduates 5,651 full-time, 2,326 part-time. Students come from 42 states and territories, 23 other countries, 8% are from out of state, 29% African American, 1% Asian American or Pacific Islander, 2% Hispanic American, 2% Native American, 0.5% international, 7% transferred in, 17% live on campus. *Retention:* 66% of 2006 full-time freshmen returned.

Freshmen *Admission:* 2,872 applied, 2,366 admitted, 1,339 enrolled. *Average high school GPA:* 3.13. *Test scores:* SAT critical reading scores over 500: 51%; SAT math scores over 500: 49%; ACT scores over 18: 83%; SAT critical reading scores over 600: 13%; SAT math scores over 600: 13%; ACT scores over 24: 23%; SAT critical reading scores over 700: 2%; ACT scores over 30: 1%.

Faculty *Total:* 609, 53% full-time, 43% with terminal degrees. *Student/faculty ratio:* 17:1.

Majors Accounting; administrative assistant and secretarial science; anthropology; biology/biological sciences; biology teacher education; business administration and management; business/commerce; business teacher education; chemistry; chemistry teacher education; criminal justice/police science; criminal justice/safety; cultural resource management and policy analysis; dramatic/theater arts; early childhood education; electrical, electronic and communications engineering technology; elementary education; English; English/language arts teacher education; family and consumer sciences/home economics teacher education; family and consumer sciences/human sciences; fine/studio arts; general studies; health and physical education; history; hospitality administration; industrial technology; information science/studies; journalism; liberal arts and sciences/liberal studies; mathematics; mathematics teacher education; middle school education; music performance; music teacher education; nursing (registered nurse training); physical education teaching and coaching; physics; physics teacher education; political science and government; psychology; radiologic technology/science; social studies teacher education; social work; sociology; speech teacher education; substance abuse/addiction counseling; veterinary/animal health technology.

Academics *Calendar:* semesters. *Degrees:* associate, bachelor's, master's, and post-master's certificates. *Special study options:* academic remediation for entering students, adult/continuing education programs, advanced placement credit, cooperative education, distance learning, double majors, freshman honors college, honors programs, independent study, internships, part-time degree program, summer session for credit. *ROTC:* Army (b).

Computers on Campus Students can access the following: computer help desk, free student e-mail accounts, online (class) grades, online (class) registration, online (class) schedules. Campuswide network is available. Wireless service is available via classrooms, computer centers, computer labs, dorm rooms, learning centers, libraries, student centers.

Student Life *Housing:* on-campus residence required through junior year. *Options:* coed. Campus housing is university owned and is provided by a third party. Freshman applicants given priority for college housing. *Activities and organizations:* drama/theater group, student-run newspaper, radio and television station, choral group, marching band, national fraternities, national sororities. *Campus security:* 24-hour emergency response devices and patrols, late-night transport/escort service, controlled dormitory access. *Student services:* health clinic, personal/psychological counseling.

Athletics Member NCAA. All Division I except football (Division I-AA). *Intercollegiate sports:* baseball M (s), basketball M (s)/W (s), cross-country running M (s)/W (s), soccer W (s), softball W (s), tennis W (s), track and field M (s)/W (s), volleyball W (s). *Intramural sports:* badminton M/W, basketball M/W, bowling M/W, cheerleading M (c)/W (c), crew M (c)/W (c), football M/W, golf M/W, racquetball M/W, riflery M/W, soccer M/W, softball M/W, table tennis M/W, tennis M/W, track and field M/W, ultimate Frisbee M/W, volleyball M/W.

Standardized Tests *Required:* SAT or ACT (for admission).

Costs (2007–08) *Tuition:* state resident $2240 full-time, $287 per credit part-time; nonresident $8318 full-time, $542 per credit part-time. Full-time tuition and fees vary according to course load. Part-time tuition and fees vary according to course load. *Required fees:* $1288 full-time. *Room and board:* $5850; room only: $3700. Room and board charges vary according to board plan, housing facility, and location. *Payment plan:* installment. *Waivers:* senior citizens and employees or children of employees.

Financial Aid Of all full-time matriculated undergraduates who enrolled in 2006, 4,637 applied for aid, 4,107 were judged to have need, 852 had their need fully met. 306 Federal Work-Study jobs (averaging $925). 563 state and other part-time jobs (averaging $1307). In 2006, 1264 non-need-based awards were made. *Average percent of need met:* 38%. *Average financial aid package:* $5580. *Average need-based loan:* $5535. *Average need-based gift aid:* $3423. *Average non-need-based aid:* $4211. *Average indebtedness upon graduation:* $19,222.

Applying *Options:* electronic application, deferred entrance. *Application fee:* $20. *Required:* high school transcript, college preparatory curriculum; plus a 2.0 GPA, or a minimum ACT score of 20, or top 50% of class. *Application deadlines:* 7/6 (freshmen), 7/6 (transfers). *Notification:* continuous (freshmen), continuous (transfers).

Freshman Application Contact Ms. Jana Lucky, Director of University Recruiting, Northwestern State University of Louisiana, Roy Hall, Room 209, Natchitoches, LA 71497. *Phone:* 318-357-4503. *Toll-free phone:* 800-327-1903. *Fax:* 318-357-5567. *E-mail:* recruiting@nsula.edu.

OUR LADY OF HOLY CROSS COLLEGE

New Orleans, Louisiana **www.olhcc.edu/**

Director of Admissions Ms. Kristine Hatfield Kopecky, Vice President for Enrollment Services, Our Lady of Holy Cross College, 4123 Woodland Drive, New Orleans, LA 70131. *Phone:* 504-394-7744 Ext. 185. *Toll-free phone:* 800-259-7744 Ext. 175.

OUR LADY OF THE LAKE COLLEGE

Baton Rouge, Louisiana **www.ololcollege.edu/**

- **Independent Roman Catholic** 4-year, founded 1990
- **Suburban** 5-acre campus with easy access to New Orleans
- **Endowment** $5.0 million
- **Coed, primarily women** 1,953 undergraduate students, 33% full-time, 83% women, 17% men
- **Minimally difficult** entrance level, 78% of applicants were admitted

Undergraduates 644 full-time, 1,309 part-time. Students come from 10 states and territories, 1% are from out of state, 22% African American, 3% Asian American or Pacific Islander, 2% Hispanic American, 0.8% Native American, 18% transferred in.

Freshmen *Admission:* 299 applied, 233 admitted, 138 enrolled. *Average high school GPA:* 3.19. *Test scores:* ACT scores over 18: 87%; ACT scores over 24: 11%.

Faculty *Total:* 205, 34% full-time, 42% with terminal degrees. *Student/faculty ratio:* 11:1.

Majors Biological and biomedical sciences related; biology/biological sciences; biomedical sciences; clinical laboratory science/medical technology; clinical/medical laboratory technology; emergency medical technology (EMT paramedic); forensic science and technology; general studies; health/health care administration; humanities; industrial radiologic technology; nursing (registered nurse training); physical therapist assistant; surgical technology.

Academics *Calendar:* semesters. *Degrees:* certificates, associate, bachelor's, and master's. *Special study options:* academic remediation for entering students, adult/continuing education programs, advanced placement credit, external degree program, off-campus study, part-time degree program, services for LD students, summer session for credit. *ROTC:* Army (c), Air Force (c).

Computers on Campus 150 computers/terminals are available on campus for general student use. Students can access the following: free student e-mail accounts, online (class) grades. Campuswide network is available. Wireless service is available via entire campus.

Student Life *Housing:* college housing not available. *Activities and organizations:* student-run newspaper, Student Government Association, Cultural Arts Association, Christian Fellowship Association, Mathematics/Science Association. *Campus security:* 24-hour patrols. *Student services:* health clinic, personal/psychological counseling.

Standardized Tests *Required:* SAT or ACT (for admission), ACT ASSET (for admission). *Recommended:* ACT (for admission).

Costs (2007–08) *Tuition:* $6240 full-time, $260 per credit hour part-time. *Required fees:* $744 full-time, $75 per term part-time. *Payment plans:* installment, deferred payment. *Waivers:* employees or children of employees.

Financial Aid Of all full-time matriculated undergraduates who enrolled in 2003, 25 Federal Work-Study jobs (averaging $3600). *Average indebtedness upon graduation:* $30,000.

Applying *Options:* electronic application. *Application fee:* $35. *Required:* high school transcript, minimum 2.0 GPA. *Application deadlines:* rolling (freshmen), rolling (transfers). *Notification:* 8/1 (freshmen).

Freshman Application Contact Director of Admissions, Our Lady of the Lake College, 7434 Perkins Road, Baton Rouge, LA 70808. *Phone:* 225-768-1718. *Toll-free phone:* 877-242-3509. *E-mail:* admission@ololcollege.edu.

SAINT JOSEPH SEMINARY COLLEGE

Saint Benedict, Louisiana **www.sjasc.edu/**

Freshman Application Contact George J. Binder Jr., Registrar, Saint Joseph Seminary College, 75376 River Road, St. Benedict, LA 70457. *Phone:* 985-867-2248. *Fax:* 985-327-1085. *E-mail:* gbinder@sjasc.edu.

SOUTHEASTERN LOUISIANA UNIVERSITY

Hammond, Louisiana **www.selu.edu/**

- **State-supported** comprehensive, founded 1925, part of University of Louisiana System
- **Small-town** 375-acre campus with easy access to New Orleans
- **Endowment** $17.7 million
- **Coed** 13,253 undergraduate students, 83% full-time, 62% women, 38% men
- **Moderately difficult** entrance level, 88% of applicants were admitted

Undergraduates 11,011 full-time, 2,242 part-time. Students come from 38 states and territories, 55 other countries, 3% are from out of state, 18% African American, 0.9% Asian American or Pacific Islander, 2% Hispanic American, 0.4% Native American, 0.9% international, 5% transferred in, 16% live on campus. *Retention:* 62% of 2006 full-time freshmen returned.

Freshmen *Admission:* 3,603 applied, 3,173 admitted, 2,755 enrolled. *Average high school GPA:* 3.02. *Test scores:* ACT scores over 18: 93%; ACT scores over 24: 21%; ACT scores over 30: 1%.

Faculty *Total:* 681, 77% full-time, 52% with terminal degrees. *Student/faculty ratio:* 25:1.

Majors Accounting; administrative assistant and secretarial science; art; arts management; art teacher education; athletic training; audiology and speech-language pathology; biology/biological sciences; business administration and management; chemistry; communication/speech communication and rhetoric; computer science; computer teacher education; criminal justice/police science; criminal justice/safety; early childhood education; elementary education; English; English/language arts teacher education; family and consumer sciences/home economics teacher education; family and consumer sciences/human sciences; finance; French; French language teacher education; general studies; health professions related; history; horticultural science; industrial technology; liberal arts and sciences/liberal studies; marketing/marketing management; mathematics; mathematics teacher education; middle school education; music performance; music teacher education; nursing (registered nurse training); occupational safety and health technology; occupational therapist assistant; physical education teaching and coaching; physics; political science and government; psychology; public health education and promotion; science teacher education; social studies teacher education; social work; sociology; Spanish; Spanish language teacher education; special education; speech teacher education.

Academics *Calendar:* semesters. *Degrees:* associate, bachelor's, and master's. *Special study options:* academic remediation for entering students, adult/continuing education programs, advanced placement credit, distance learning, double majors, English as a second language, honors programs, independent study, internships, off-campus study, part-time degree program, services for LD students, study abroad, summer session for credit. *ROTC:* Army (c).

Computers on Campus 882 computers/terminals and 568 ports are available on campus for general student use. Students can access the following: campus intranet, computer help desk, free student e-mail accounts, online (class) grades, online (class) registration, online (class) schedules, campus Webmail, student newspaper, transcripts, bookstore. Campuswide network is available. 100% of college-owned or -operated housing units are wired for high-speed Internet access. Wireless service is available via classrooms, computer labs, learning centers, libraries, student centers.

Student Life *Housing:* on-campus residence required through sophomore year. *Options:* coed, men-only, women-only. Campus housing is provided by a third party. Freshman applicants given priority for college housing. *Activities and organizations:* drama/theater group, student-run newspaper, choral group, marching band, Panhellenic Council, Interfraternity Council, Campus Activities Board, Student Government Association, national fraternities, national sororities. *Campus security:* 24-hour emergency response devices and patrols, late-night transport/escort service, controlled dormitory access, video cameras, motorist assistance. *Student services:* health clinic, personal/psychological counseling, legal services.

Athletics Member NCAA. All Division I except football (Division I-AA). *Intercollegiate sports:* baseball M (s), basketball M (s)/W (s), cheerleading M (s)/W (s), cross-country running M (s)/W (s), golf M (s), soccer W (s), softball W (s), tennis M (s)/W (s), track and field M (s)/W (s), volleyball W (s). *Intramural sports:* basketball M/W, football M/W, racquetball M/W, rugby M (c), soccer M (c)/W, softball M/W, volleyball M/W, weight lifting M/W.

Standardized Tests *Required:* SAT or ACT (for admission).

Costs (2007–08) *Tuition:* state resident $2216 full-time, $92 per credit hour part-time; nonresident $8216 full-time, $342 per credit hour part-time. Full-time tuition and fees vary according to course load. Part-time tuition and fees vary according to course load. *Required fees:* $1345 full-time, $56 per credit hour part-time. *Room and board:* $5990; room only: $3780. Room and board charges vary according to board plan and housing facility. *Payment plans:* installment, deferred payment. *Waivers:* senior citizens and employees or children of employees.

Financial Aid Of all full-time matriculated undergraduates who enrolled in 2006, 9,322 applied for aid, 7,178 were judged to have need. 361 Federal Work-Study jobs (averaging $1300). 1,051 state and other part-time jobs (averaging $1056). In 2006, 213 non-need-based awards were made. *Average financial aid package:* $4317. *Average need-based loan:* $3281. *Average need-based gift aid:* $2888. *Average non-need-based aid:* $1564. *Average indebtedness upon graduation:* $16,519.

Applying *Options:* electronic application, early admission, deferred entrance. *Application fee:* $20. *Required:* high school transcript, proof of immunization. *Required for some:* minimum 2.0 GPA. *Application deadlines:* 8/1 (freshmen), 8/1 (transfers). *Notification:* continuous (freshmen), continuous (transfers).

Freshman Application Contact Director of Admissions, Southeastern Louisiana University, SLU 10752, Hammond, LA 70402. *Phone:* 985-549-2066. *Toll-free phone:* 800-222-7358. *Fax:* 985-549-5632. *E-mail:* admissions@selu.edu.

SOUTHERN UNIVERSITY AND AGRICULTURAL AND MECHANICAL COLLEGE

Baton Rouge, Louisiana **www.subr.edu/**

- **State-supported** university, founded 1880, part of Southern University System
- **Suburban** 964-acre campus
- **Endowment** $9.3 million
- **Coed** 6,892 undergraduate students, 89% full-time, 61% women, 39% men
- **Moderately difficult** entrance level, 56% of applicants were admitted

Undergraduates 6,108 full-time, 784 part-time. Students come from 45 states and territories, 37 other countries, 19% are from out of state, 95% African American, 0.4% Asian American or Pacific Islander, 0.1% Hispanic American, 2% international, 3% transferred in, 31% live on campus. *Retention:* 65% of 2006 full-time freshmen returned.

Freshmen *Admission:* 2,179 applied, 1,229 admitted, 1,121 enrolled. *Average high school GPA:* 2.8. *Test scores:* SAT math scores over 500: 19%; ACT scores over 18: 39%; SAT math scores over 600: 2%; ACT scores over 24: 5%.

Faculty *Total:* 546, 74% full-time, 60% with terminal degrees. *Student/faculty ratio:* 16:1.

Majors Accounting; agricultural economics; agricultural teacher education; animal sciences related; architecture; art teacher education; audiology and speech-language pathology; biology/biological sciences; biology teacher education; business administration and management; business/managerial economics; chemistry; chemistry teacher education; civil engineering; communication/speech communication and rhetoric; computer science; computer teacher education; criminal justice/police science; criminal justice/safety; dramatic/theater arts; early childhood education; e-commerce; electrical, electronic and communications engineering technology; electrical, electronics and communications engineering; elementary education; English; English/language arts teacher education; family and consumer sciences/human sciences; finance; fine/studio arts; French; French language teacher education; history; marketing/marketing management; mass communication/media; mathematics; mathematics teacher education; mechanical engineering; middle school education; music performance; music teacher education; nursing (registered nurse training); physical education teaching and coaching; physics; physics teacher education; political science and government; psychology; rehabilitation and therapeutic professions related; rehabilitation therapy; science teacher education; secondary education; social studies teacher education; social work; sociology; Spanish; Spanish language teacher education; special education; speech and rhetoric; therapeutic recreation; urban forestry; vocational rehabilitation counseling.

Academics *Calendar:* semesters. *Degrees:* associate, bachelor's, master's, doctoral, and post-master's certificates. *Special study options:* academic remediation for entering students, adult/continuing education programs, advanced placement credit, cooperative education, distance learning, honors programs, internships, off-campus study, part-time degree program, services for LD students, study abroad, summer session for credit. *ROTC:* Army (b), Navy (b), Air Force (c).

Computers on Campus 1,500 computers/terminals and 2,500 ports are available on campus for general student use. Students can access the following: campus intranet, computer help desk, free student e-mail accounts, online (class) grades, online (class) registration, online (class) schedules. Campuswide network is available. 100% of college-owned or -operated housing units are wired for high-speed Internet access. Wireless service is available via classrooms, computer centers, computer labs, learning centers, libraries, student centers.

Student Life *Housing:* on-campus residence required for freshman year. *Options:* men-only, women-only. Campus housing is university owned. Freshman applicants given priority for college housing. *Activities and organizations:* drama/theater group, student-run newspaper, choral group, marching band, Student Government Association, Association for Women Students, Men's Federation, Collegiate 100 Black Men, Southern University Pan Hellenic Council, national fraternities, national sororities. *Campus security:* 24-hour emergency response devices and patrols, late-night transport/escort service, controlled dormitory access. *Student services:* health clinic, personal/psychological counseling, women's center, legal services.

Athletics Member NCAA. All Division I except football (Division I-AA). *Intercollegiate sports:* baseball M, basketball M (s)/W (s), bowling W (s), cross-country running M (s), golf M (s)/W (s), softball W (s), tennis M (s)/W (s), track and field M (s)/W (s), volleyball W (s). *Intramural sports:* archery M/W, basketball M/W, football M/W, track and field M/W, volleyball M/W, weight lifting M/W.

Standardized Tests *Required:* SAT or ACT (for admission), SAT or ACT (for placement). *Recommended:* SAT (for admission), ACT (for admission).

Costs (2008–09) *Tuition:* state resident $3706 full-time, $367 per credit part-time; nonresident $9498 full-time, $367 per credit part-time. *Room and board:* $6504.

Financial Aid Of all full-time matriculated undergraduates who enrolled in 2006, 6,032 applied for aid, 5,721 were judged to have need, 85 had their need fully met. 900 Federal Work-Study jobs (averaging $1800). 300 state and other part-time jobs (averaging $2500). In 2006, 1209 non-need-based awards were made. *Average percent of need met:* 85%. *Average financial aid package:* $7444. *Average need-based loan:* $3738. *Average need-based gift aid:* $3436. *Average non-need-based aid:* $3151. *Average indebtedness upon graduation:* $23,000.

Applying *Options:* electronic application, early admission. *Application fee:* $20. *Required:* high school transcript, minimum 2.0 GPA, ACT of 20 or better or a SAT of 940 or better, plus Louisiana Board of Regents Core curriculum of 16.5 units of selected courses. See the admissions website for more information. *Application deadlines:* 7/1 (freshmen), 7/1 (transfers). *Notification:* continuous (freshmen), continuous (transfers).

Freshman Application Contact Ms. Tracie Abraham, Director of Admissions, Southern University and Agricultural and Mechanical College, PO Box 9901, Baton Rouge, LA 70813. *Phone:* 225-771-2430. *Toll-free phone:* 800-256-1531. *Fax:* 225-771-2500. *E-mail:* tracie_abraham@subr.edu.

SOUTHERN UNIVERSITY AT NEW ORLEANS

New Orleans, Louisiana **www.suno.edu/**

Director of Admissions Ms. Rene Gill Pratt, Acting Director of Admissions, Recruitment & Retention, Southern University at New Orleans, 6400 Press Drive, New Orleans, LA 70126-1009. *Phone:* 504-286-5033. *Fax:* 504-284-5481. *E-mail:* rgpratt@suno.edu.

TULANE UNIVERSITY

New Orleans, Louisiana **www.tulane.edu/**

- **Independent** university, founded 1834
- **Urban** 110-acre campus
- **Endowment** $1.0 billion
- **Coed** 6,449 undergraduate students, 79% full-time, 54% women, 46% men
- **Very difficult** entrance level, 44% of applicants were admitted

Undergraduates 5,112 full-time, 1,337 part-time. Students come from 53 states and territories, 42 other countries, 67% are from out of state, 9% African American, 5% Asian American or Pacific Islander, 4% Hispanic American, 2% Native American, 2% international, 3% transferred in, 48% live on campus. *Retention:* 87% of 2006 full-time freshmen returned.

Freshmen *Admission:* 16,967 applied, 7,526 admitted, 1,324 enrolled. *Average high school GPA:* 3.39. *Test scores:* SAT critical reading scores over 500: 97%; SAT math scores over 500: 96%; SAT writing scores over 500: 97%; SAT critical reading scores over 600: 80%; SAT math scores over 600: 62%; SAT writing scores over 600: 76%; SAT critical reading scores over 700: 33%; SAT math scores over 700: 16%; SAT writing scores over 700: 22%.

Faculty *Total:* 1,775, 66% full-time. *Student/faculty ratio:* 9:1.

Majors Accounting; African studies; American studies; anatomy; anthropology; architecture; art; art history, criticism and conservation; Asian studies; biochemistry; biology/biological sciences; biomedical/medical engineering; biostatistics; business administration and management; business/commerce; cell biology and anatomical sciences related; cell biology and histology; chemical engineering; chemistry; civil engineering; classics and classical languages related; classics and languages, literatures and linguistics; cognitive psychology and psycholinguistics; communication and journalism related; communication/speech communication and rhetoric; computer and information sciences; computer engineering; computer science; corrections; criminal justice/safety; dramatic/theater arts; ecology; economics; electrical, electronics and communications engineering; engineering science; English; environmental biology; environmental/environmental health engineering; environmental studies; evolutionary biology; finance; fine/studio arts; foreign languages and literatures; French; geology/earth science; German; Hispanic-American, Puerto Rican, and Mexican-American/Chicano studies; history; information science/studies; international relations and affairs; Italian; Jewish/Judaic studies; kinesiology and exercise science; Latin; Latin American studies; legal assistant/paralegal; legal professions and studies related; liberal arts and sciences and humanities related; liberal arts and sciences/liberal studies; linguistics; marketing/marketing management; mass communication/media; mathematics; mathematics and statistics related; mechanical engineering; medieval and Renaissance studies; modern Greek; molecular biology; multi-/interdisciplinary studies related; music; neuroscience; philosophy; physics; political science and government; Portuguese; psychology; religious studies; Russian; Russian studies; sociology; Spanish; women's studies.

Academics *Calendar:* semesters plus 3 summer sessions. *Degrees:* associate, bachelor's, master's, doctoral, first professional, and postbachelor's certificates. *Special study options:* accelerated degree program, adult/continuing education programs, advanced placement credit, cooperative education, double majors, English as a second language, freshman honors college, honors programs, independent study, internships, off-campus study, part-time degree program, services for LD students, student-designed majors, study abroad, summer session for credit. *ROTC:* Army (b), Navy (b), Air Force (b). *Unusual degree programs:* 3-2 business administration; engineering; public health, tropical medicine.

Computers on Campus 592 computers/terminals are available on campus for general student use. Students can access the following: computer help desk, free student e-mail accounts, online (class) grades, online (class) registration, online (class) schedules. Campuswide network is available. 100% of college-owned or -operated housing units are wired for high-speed Internet access. Wireless service is available via entire campus.

Student Life *Housing:* on-campus residence required for freshman year. *Options:* coed, women-only, disabled students. Campus housing is university owned. Freshman campus housing is guaranteed. *Activities and organizations:* drama/theater group, student-run newspaper, radio and television station, choral group, marching band, Community Action Council of Tulane Students (CACTUS), Associated Student Body (ASB), Tulane University Campus Programmin (TUCP), Association of Club Sports (ACS), National Panhellenic Council (NPC), national fraternities, national sororities. *Campus security:* 24-hour emergency response devices and patrols, student patrols, late-night transport/escort service, controlled dormitory access, on and off-campus shuttle service, crime prevention programs, lighted pathways. *Student services:* health clinic, personal/psychological counseling, women's center, legal services.

Athletics Member NCAA. All Division I except football (Division I-A). *Intercollegiate sports:* baseball M (s), basketball M (s)/W (s), crew M (c)/W (c), cross-country running M (s)/W (s), golf M (s)/W (s), gymnastics M (c)/W (c), ice hockey M (c)/W (c), lacrosse M (c)/W (c), rugby M (c), sailing M (c)/W (c), soccer M (c)/W (s), swimming and diving M (c)/W (s), tennis M (s)/W (s), track and field M (c)/W (s), volleyball M (c)/W (s), water polo M (c)/W (c). *Intramural sports:* baseball M (c), cheerleading M (c)/W (c), crew M (c)/W (c), cross-country running M (c), fencing M (c)/W (c), field hockey M (c)/W (c), gymnastics M (c)/W (c), ice hockey M (c), lacrosse M (c)/W (c), racquetball M (c)/W (c), rock climbing M (c)/W (c), rugby M (c), sailing M (c)/W (c), soccer M (c)/W (c), swimming and diving M (c)/W (c), tennis M (c)/W (c), track and field M (c)/W, ultimate Frisbee M (c)/W (c), volleyball M (c)/W (c), water polo M (c)/W (c).

Standardized Tests *Required:* SAT or ACT (for admission).

Costs (2007–08) *Comprehensive fee:* $45,550 includes full-time tuition ($33,500), mandatory fees ($3110), and room and board ($8940). Part-time tuition: $1488 per credit hour. *Required fees:* $60 per term part-time. *College room only:* $5140. Room and board charges vary according to board plan and housing facility. *Payment plans:* tuition prepayment, installment. *Waivers:* employees or children of employees.

Financial Aid Of all full-time matriculated undergraduates who enrolled in 2005, 2,988 applied for aid, 2,310 were judged to have need, 1,134 had their need fully met. 956 Federal Work-Study jobs (averaging $2065). 99 state and other part-time jobs (averaging $6764). In 2005, 1874 non-need-based awards were made. *Average percent of need met:* 88%. *Average financial aid package:* $25,945. *Average need-based loan:* $5765. *Average need-based gift aid:* $19,182. *Average non-need-based aid:* $17,308. *Average indebtedness upon graduation:* $21,202. *Financial aid deadline:* 2/1.

Applying *Options:* electronic application, early admission, early action, deferred entrance. *Required:* essay or personal statement, high school transcript, 1 letter of recommendation. *Application deadlines:* 1/15 (freshmen), 6/1 (transfers), 11/1 (early action). *Notification:* continuous until 4/1 (freshmen), continuous (transfers), 12/15 (early action).

Freshman Application Contact Mr. Earl Retif, Vice President for Enrollment Management and University Registrar, Tulane University, Office of Admissions, 210 Gibson Hall, New Orleans, LA 70118. *Phone:* 504-865-5731. *Toll-free phone:* 800-873-9283. *Fax:* 504-862-8715. *E-mail:* undergrad.admission@tulane.edu.

See page 1064 for the College Close-Up.

UNIVERSITY OF LOUISIANA AT LAFAYETTE

Lafayette, Louisiana **www.louisiana.edu/**

- **State-supported** university, founded 1898, part of University of Louisiana System
- **Urban** 1375-acre campus
- **Endowment** $110.4 million
- **Coed** 14,931 undergraduate students, 84% full-time, 58% women, 42% men
- **Moderately difficult** entrance level, 70% of applicants were admitted

Undergraduates 12,539 full-time, 2,392 part-time. Students come from 46 states and territories, 71 other countries, 4% are from out of state, 18% African American, 2% Asian American or Pacific Islander, 2% Hispanic American, 0.5% Native American, 2% international, 4% transferred in, 13% live on campus. *Retention:* 75% of 2006 full-time freshmen returned.

Freshmen *Admission:* 7,203 applied, 5,059 admitted, 2,763 enrolled. *Average high school GPA:* 3.2. *Test scores:* ACT scores over 18: 94%; ACT scores over 24: 27%; ACT scores over 30: 2%.

Faculty *Total:* 743, 78% full-time, 62% with terminal degrees. *Student/faculty ratio:* 23:1.

Majors Accounting; agribusiness; agriculture; animal sciences; anthropology; apparel and textiles related; architecture; architecture related; art; athletic training; audiology and speech-language pathology; biological specializations related; biology/biological sciences; biology teacher education; business administration and management; business/commerce; business/managerial economics; chemical engineering; chemistry; chemistry teacher education; civil engineering; communication/speech communication and rhetoric; computer and information sciences; computer engineering; computer science; computer systems analysis; criminal justice/safety; dental hygiene; dietetics; dramatic/theater arts; education; education (specific subject areas) related; electrical, electronics and communications engineering; elementary education; engineering; English; fashion/apparel design; fashion merchandising; finance; French; French language teacher education; general studies; geology/earth science; German language teacher education; health information/medical records administration; health professions related; history; horticultural science; hospitality administration related; human development and family studies related; industrial design; industrial technology; insurance; interior architecture; jazz/jazz studies; marketing/marketing management; mass communication/media; mathematics; mechanical engineering; medical microbiology and bacteriology; modern languages; music; music pedagogy; music performance; music related; music teacher education; music theory and composition; natural resources and conservation related; natural resources/conservation; nursing (registered nurse training); petroleum engineering; philosophy; physical education teaching and coaching; physics; physics teacher education; plant sciences; political science and government; pre-law studies; psychology; public relations/image management; science teacher education; secondary education; social studies teacher education; sociology; Spanish; Spanish language teacher education; special education; speech teacher education; visual and performing arts.

Academics *Calendar:* semesters. *Degrees:* bachelor's, master's, doctoral, and post-master's certificates. *Special study options:* academic remediation for entering students, accelerated degree program, adult/continuing education programs, advanced placement credit, cooperative education, distance learning, double majors, honors programs, independent study, internships, part-time degree program, services for LD students, student-designed majors, study abroad, summer session for credit. *ROTC:* Army (b).

Computers on Campus 600 computers/terminals and 855 ports are available on campus for general student use. Students can access the following: campus intranet, computer help desk, free student e-mail accounts, online (class) grades, online (class) registration, online (class) schedules. Campuswide network is available. 67% of college-owned or -operated housing units are wired for high-speed Internet access. Wireless service is available via libraries.

Student Life *Housing options:* men-only, women-only. Campus housing is university owned. Freshman campus housing is guaranteed. *Activities and organizations:* drama/theater group, student-run newspaper, radio station, choral group, marching band, Student Government Association, Resident Hall Association, Newman Club, Union Program Council, Chi Alpha, national fraternities, national sororities. *Campus security:* 24-hour emergency response devices and patrols, late-night transport/escort service, controlled dormitory access. *Student services:* health clinic, personal/psychological counseling, women's center, legal services.

Athletics Member NCAA. All Division I except football (Division I-A). *Intercollegiate sports:* baseball M (s), basketball M (s)/W (s), cross-country running M (s)/W (s), golf M (s), soccer W, softball W (s), tennis M (s)/W (s), track and field M (s)/W (s), volleyball W (s). *Intramural sports:* badminton M (c)/W (c), baseball M, basketball M/W, bowling M (c)/W (c), cross-country running M/W, football M/W, golf M/W, racquetball M/W, rugby M (c)/W (c), sailing M (c)/W (c), soccer M (c)/W (c), softball M/W, swimming and diving M/W, table tennis M/W, tennis M/W, track and field M/W, volleyball M/W, water polo M/W, weight lifting M/W.

Standardized Tests *Required:* SAT or ACT (for admission).

Costs (2007–08) *Tuition:* state resident $3402 full-time, $93 per credit hour part-time; nonresident $9582 full-time, $350 per credit hour part-time. Full-time tuition and fees vary according to course load. Part-time tuition and fees vary according to course load. *Room and board:* $3820. Room and board charges vary according to housing facility. *Payment plan:* deferred payment. *Waivers:* children of alumni, senior citizens, and employees or children of employees.

Financial Aid Of all full-time matriculated undergraduates who enrolled in 2006, 9,498 applied for aid, 6,378 were judged to have need, 689 had their need fully met. 501 Federal Work-Study jobs (averaging $1274). 221 state and other part-time jobs (averaging $1236). In 2006, 700 non-need-based awards were made. *Average percent of need met:* 51%. *Average financial aid package:* $5587. *Average need-based loan:* $3439. *Average need-based gift aid:* $3862. *Average non-need-based aid:* $1479.

Applying *Options:* early admission, deferred entrance. *Application fee:* $25. *Required:* high school transcript, minimum 2.0 GPA, core requirements, no remedials. *Application deadlines:* rolling (freshmen), rolling (transfers).

Freshman Application Contact Mr. Leroy Broussard Jr., Admissions Director, University of Louisiana at Lafayette, PO Drawer 41210, Lafayette, LA 70504. *Phone:* 337-482-6473. *Toll-free phone:* 800-752-6553. *Fax:* 337-482-1317. *E-mail:* admissions@louisiana.edu.

UNIVERSITY OF LOUISIANA AT MONROE

Monroe, Louisiana **www.ulm.edu/**

- **State-supported** university, founded 1931, part of University of Louisana System
- **Urban** 238-acre campus
- **Coed** 7,297 undergraduate students, 80% full-time, 63% women, 37% men
- **Noncompetitive** entrance level, 84% of applicants were admitted

Undergraduates 5,865 full-time, 1,432 part-time. Students come from 41 states and territories, 44 other countries, 7% are from out of state, 26% African American, 2% Asian American or Pacific Islander, 0.9% Hispanic American, 0.3% Native American, 1% international, 6% transferred in, 22% live on campus. *Retention:* 63% of 2006 full-time freshmen returned.

Freshmen *Admission:* 2,909 applied, 2,455 admitted, 1,432 enrolled. *Average high school GPA:* 3.25.

Faculty *Total:* 436, 84% full-time. *Student/faculty ratio:* 17:1.

Majors Accounting; aeronautics/aviation/aerospace science and technology; agricultural business and management; art; atmospheric sciences and meteorology; audiology and speech-language pathology; biology/biological sciences; biology teacher education; business administration and management; business/managerial economics; business systems analysis/design; chemistry; chemistry teacher education; child care services management; clinical laboratory science/medical technology; computer science; construction engineering technology; criminal justice/police science; criminal justice/safety; dental hygiene; education (specific subject areas) related; elementary education; English; English/language arts teacher education; family and consumer sciences/home economics teacher education; family and consumer sciences/human sciences; finance; French; French language teacher education; general studies; health/medical preparatory programs related; history; insurance/risk management; marketing/marketing management; mass communications; mathematics; mathematics teacher education; medical radiologic technology; music performance; music teacher education; nursing (registered nurse training); occupational therapist assistant; occupational therapy; pharmacy; physical education teaching and coaching; physics teacher education; political science and government; psychology; social studies teacher education; social work; sociology; Spanish; Spanish language teacher education; special education; speech and rhetoric; speech teacher education; toxicology.

Academics *Calendar:* semesters. *Degrees:* certificates, associate, bachelor's, master's, doctoral, first professional, post-master's, and postbachelor's certificates. *Special study options:* academic remediation for entering students, advanced placement credit, cooperative education, distance learning, double majors, English as a second language, honors programs, independent study, internships, off-campus study, part-time degree program, study abroad, summer session for credit. *ROTC:* Army (b).

Computers on Campus Students can access the following: online (class) registration. Campuswide network is available.

Student Life *Housing:* on-campus residence required through sophomore year. *Options:* coed, men-only, women-only. Campus housing is university owned and leased by the school. Freshman campus housing is guaranteed. *Activities and organizations:* drama/theater group, student-run newspaper, radio station, choral group, marching band, Union Board, Student Government Association, national fraternities, national sororities. *Campus security:* 24-hour emergency response devices and patrols, student patrols, late-night transport/escort service. *Student services:* health clinic, personal/psychological counseling.

Athletics Member NCAA. All Division I except football (Division I-A). *Intercollegiate sports:* baseball M (s), basketball M (s)/W (s), cheerleading M (s)/W (s), cross-country running M (s)/W (s), golf M (s)/W, soccer W (s), softball W (s), swimming and diving M (s)/W (s), tennis M (s)/W (s), track and field M (s)/W (s), volleyball W (s). *Intramural sports:* archery M/W, badminton M/W, basketball M/W, bowling M/W, cross-country running M/W, football M/W, golf M/W, racquetball M/W, soccer M/W, softball M/W, swimming and diving M/W, table tennis M/W, tennis M/W, track and field M/W, volleyball M/W.

Standardized Tests *Required:* SAT or ACT (for admission).

Costs (2007–08) *Tuition:* state resident $3607 full-time, $93 per credit hour part-time; nonresident $9559 full-time. Full-time tuition and fees vary according to course load and program. Part-time tuition and fees vary according to course load and program. *Required fees:* $503 per term part-time. *Room and board:* $3750. Room and board charges vary according to board plan and housing facility. *Payment plan:* deferred payment. *Waivers:* children of alumni and employees or children of employees.

Applying *Options:* electronic application, early admission, deferred entrance. *Application fee:* $20. *Required:* high school transcript. *Application deadlines:* rolling (freshmen), rolling (transfers). *Notification:* continuous (freshmen), continuous (transfers).

Freshman Application Contact Ms. Susan Duggins, Director, Recruitment and Admissions, University of Louisiana at Monroe, Sandel Hall, Monroe, LA 71209. *Phone:* 318-342-5272. *Toll-free phone:* 800-372-5272 (in-state); 800-372-5127 (out-of-state). *Fax:* 318-342-1915. *E-mail:* admissions@ulm.edu.

UNIVERSITY OF NEW ORLEANS

New Orleans, Louisiana **www.uno.edu/**

- **State-supported** university, founded 1958, part of Louisiana State University System
- **Urban** 345-acre campus
- **Endowment** $17.9 million
- **Coed** 8,653 undergraduate students, 75% full-time, 53% women, 47% men
- **Moderately difficult** entrance level, 81% of applicants were admitted

Undergraduates 6,504 full-time, 2,149 part-time. Students come from 49 states and territories, 66 other countries, 5% are from out of state, 20% African American, 6% Asian American or Pacific Islander, 7% Hispanic American, 0.6% Native American, 3% international, 9% transferred in, 5% live on campus. *Retention:* 69% of 2006 full-time freshmen returned.

Freshmen *Admission:* 1,767 applied, 1,430 admitted, 1,119 enrolled. *Average high school GPA:* 3.06. *Test scores:* SAT critical reading scores over 500: 65%; SAT math scores over 500: 68%; SAT writing scores over 500: 65%; ACT scores over 18: 94%; SAT critical reading scores over 600: 34%; SAT math scores over 600: 34%; SAT writing scores over 600: 25%; ACT scores over 24: 28%; SAT critical reading scores over 700: 4%; SAT math scores over 700: 5%; SAT writing scores over 700: 3%; ACT scores over 30: 2%.

Faculty *Total:* 678, 67% full-time, 56% with terminal degrees. *Student/faculty ratio:* 18:1.

Majors Accounting; anthropology; art history, criticism and conservation; biology/biological sciences; biology teacher education; business administration and management; business/managerial economics; chemistry; chemistry teacher education; civil engineering; clinical laboratory science/medical technology; communication/speech communication and rhetoric; computer science; early childhood education; economics; education (specific subject areas) related; electrical, electronics and communications engineering; elementary education; English; English/language arts teacher education; entrepreneurship; environmental studies; finance; fine/studio arts; French; general studies; geography; geology/earth science; health and physical education; history; hospitality administration; international/global studies; management information systems; marketing/marketing management; mathematics; mathematics teacher education; mechanical engineering; middle school education; music; naval architecture and marine engineering; philosophy; physical education teaching and coaching; physics; political science and government; psychology; social studies teacher education; sociology; Spanish; urban studies/affairs; women's studies.

Academics *Calendar:* semesters. *Degrees:* bachelor's, master's, doctoral, and postbachelor's certificates. *Special study options:* academic remediation for entering students, adult/continuing education programs, advanced placement credit, cooperative education, distance learning, double majors, English as a second language, honors programs, independent study, internships, off-campus study, part-time degree program, services for LD students, student-designed majors, study abroad, summer session for credit. *ROTC:* Army (c), Navy (c), Air Force (c). *Unusual degree programs:* 3-2 engineering with Xavier University of Louisiana, Southern University at New Orleans, Loyola University, New Orleans.

Computers on Campus 1,103 computers/terminals and 1,155 ports are available on campus for general student use. Students can access the following: campus intranet, computer help desk, free student e-mail accounts, online (class) grades, online (class) registration, online (class) schedules, classes in Blackboard. Campuswide network is available. 100% of college-owned or -operated housing units are wired for high-speed Internet access. Wireless service is available via computer centers, libraries, student centers.

Student Life *Housing options:* coed, disabled students. Campus housing is university owned. *Activities and organizations:* drama/theater group, student-run newspaper, choral group, Student Activities Council, Student Government, International Student Organization, Golden Key Honor Society, UNO Ambassadors, national fraternities, national sororities. *Campus security:* 24-hour emergency response devices and patrols, late-night transport/escort service, controlled dormitory access. *Student services:* health clinic, personal/psychological counseling, women's center, legal services.

Athletics Member NCAA. All Division I. *Intercollegiate sports:* baseball M (s), basketball M (s)/W (s), golf M (s), swimming and diving W (s), volleyball W (s). *Intramural sports:* basketball M/W, football M/W, soccer M/W, softball M/W, table tennis M/W, tennis M/W, volleyball M/W.

Standardized Tests *Required:* SAT or ACT (for admission).

Costs (2007–08) *Tuition:* state resident $3292 full-time, $137 per credit hour part-time; nonresident $10,336 full-time, $431 per credit hour part-time. Part-time tuition and fees vary according to course load. *Required fees:* $692 full-time. *Room and board:* $5240. Room and board charges vary according to board plan and housing facility. *Payment plan:* deferred payment. *Waivers:* senior citizens and employees or children of employees.

Financial Aid Of all full-time matriculated undergraduates who enrolled in 2007, 5,030 applied for aid, 4,207 were judged to have need, 424 had their need fully met. 137 Federal Work-Study jobs (averaging $2123). In 2007, 128 non-need-based awards were made. *Average percent of need met:* 62%. *Average financial aid package:* $6238. *Average need-based loan:* $4192. *Average need-based gift aid:* $4113. *Average non-need-based aid:* $2243. *Average indebtedness upon graduation:* $24,657.

Applying *Options:* electronic application, early admission, deferred entrance. *Application fee:* $40. *Required:* high school transcript, Core requirements (17.5 units); ACT or SAT scores. *Required for some:* essay or personal statement, minimum 2.5 GPA. *Application deadlines:* rolling (freshmen), 7/1 (out-of-state freshmen), 7/1 (transfers). *Notification:* continuous (freshmen), continuous (out-of-state freshmen), continuous (transfers).

Freshman Application Contact Mr. Andy Benoit, Director of Admissions, University of New Orleans, Lake Front, New Orleans, LA 70148. *Phone:* 504-280-7013. *Toll-free phone:* 800-256-5866. *E-mail:* admissions@uno.edu.

See page 1066 for the College Close-Up.

UNIVERSITY OF PHOENIX–LOUISIANA CAMPUS

Metairie, Louisiana **www.phoenix.edu/**

Freshman Application Contact Ms. Beth Barilla, Associate Vice President, Student Admissions and Services, University of Phoenix–Louisiana Campus, 4615 East Elwood Street, Mail Stop AA-K101, Phoenix, AZ 85040-1958. *Phone:* 480-317-6000. *Toll-free phone:* 800-776-4867 (in-state); 800-228-7240 (out-of-state). *Fax:* 480-894-1758. *E-mail:* beth.barilla@phoenix.edu.

XAVIER UNIVERSITY OF LOUISIANA

New Orleans, Louisiana **www.xula.edu/**

- **Independent Roman Catholic** comprehensive, founded 1925
- **Urban** 23-acre campus with easy access to New Orleans
- **Endowment** $49.3 million
- **Coed** 2,322 undergraduate students, 96% full-time, 72% women, 28% men
- **Moderately difficult** entrance level, 59% of applicants were admitted

Undergraduates 2,238 full-time, 84 part-time. Students come from 43 states and territories, 8 other countries, 43% are from out of state, 75% African American, 7% Asian American or Pacific Islander, 0.6% Hispanic American, 0.1% Native American, 3% international, 7% transferred in, 43% live on campus. *Retention:* 83% of 2006 full-time freshmen returned.

Freshmen *Admission:* 3,074 applied, 1,821 admitted, 664 enrolled. *Average high school GPA:* 3.1. *Test scores:* SAT critical reading scores over 500: 35%; SAT math scores over 500: 36%; ACT scores over 18: 80%; SAT critical reading scores over 600: 9%; SAT math scores over 600: 11%; ACT scores over 24: 21%; ACT scores over 30: 1%.

Faculty *Total:* 215, 88% full-time, 85% with terminal degrees. *Student/faculty ratio:* 15:1.

Majors Accounting; art; art teacher education; biochemistry; biology/biological sciences; biology teacher education; business administration and management; chemistry; chemistry teacher education; computer and information sciences; computer engineering; computer science; early childhood education; education; elementary education; English; environmental studies; French; French language teacher education; health teacher education; history; history teacher education; marketing/marketing management; mass communication/media; mathematics; medical microbiology and bacteriology; middle school education; music; music performance; music teacher education; philosophy; physical education teaching and coaching; physics; piano and organ; political science and government; pre-dentistry studies; pre-law studies; pre-medical studies; pre-veterinary studies; psychology; science teacher education; secondary education; social studies teacher education; sociology; Spanish; Spanish language teacher education; special education; special education related; speech-language pathology; speech therapy; statistics; theology; violin, viola, guitar and other stringed instruments; wind/percussion instruments.

Academics *Calendar:* semesters. *Degrees:* bachelor's, master's, first professional, and post-master's certificates. *Special study options:* academic remediation for entering students, accelerated degree program, adult/continuing education programs, advanced placement credit, cooperative education, double majors, freshman honors college, honors programs, independent study, internships, off-campus study, part-time degree program, services for LD students, study abroad, summer session for credit. *ROTC:* Army (c), Navy (c), Air Force (c). *Unusual degree programs:* 3-2 business administration with Tulane University; engineering with Tulane University, University of Maryland, University of New Orleans, Georgia Institute of Technology, University of Wisconsin-Madison, Morgan State University, Southern University and Agricultural and Mechanical College; biostatistics with Louisiana State University Medical Center.

Computers on Campus 250 computers/terminals are available on campus for general student use. Campuswide network is available.

Student Life *Housing options:* coed, men-only, women-only, disabled students. Campus housing is university owned. Freshman applicants given priority for college housing. *Activities and organizations:* drama/theater group, student-run newspaper, television station, choral group, Mobilization at Xavier, AWARE, NAACP, California Club, Beta Beta Beta, national fraternities, national sororities. *Campus security:* 24-hour emergency response devices and patrols, student patrols, bicycle patrols. *Student services:* health clinic, personal/psychological counseling.

Athletics Member NAIA. *Intercollegiate sports:* basketball M (s)/W (s), cross-country running M/W, tennis M (s)/W (s). *Intramural sports:* badminton M/W, basketball M/W, football M/W, golf M/W, softball M/W, swimming and diving M/W, table tennis M/W, tennis M/W, track and field M/W, volleyball M/W.

Standardized Tests *Required:* SAT or ACT (for admission).

Costs (2007–08) *One-time required fee:* $150. *Comprehensive fee:* $21,675 includes full-time tuition ($13,700), mandatory fees ($1000), and room and board ($6975). Part-time tuition: $600 per semester hour. Part-time tuition and fees vary according to course load. *Room and board:* Room and board charges vary according to housing facility. *Payment plan:* installment. *Waivers:* employees or children of employees.

Financial Aid Of all full-time matriculated undergraduates who enrolled in 2006, 2,210 applied for aid, 1,952 were judged to have need, 591 had their need fully met. In 2006, 65 non-need-based awards were made. *Average percent of need met:* 22%. *Average financial aid package:* $17,604. *Average need-based loan:* $4442. *Average need-based gift aid:* $5818. *Average non-need-based aid:* $6472. *Average indebtedness upon graduation:* $41,742.

Applying *Options:* electronic application, early action. *Application fee:* $25. *Required:* high school transcript, minimum 2.0 GPA, 1 letter of recommendation. *Required for some:* interview. *Application deadlines:* 7/1 (freshmen), 6/1 (transfers), 1/15 (early action). *Notification:* continuous (freshmen), continuous (transfers), 2/15 (early action).

Freshman Application Contact Mr. Winston Brown, Dean of Admissions, Xavier University of Louisiana, One Drexel Drive, New Orleans, LA 70125. *Phone:* 504-520-7388. *Toll-free phone:* 877-XAVIERU. *Fax:* 504-520-7941. *E-mail:* apply@xula.edu.

LOUISIANA TECH UNIVERSITY

RUSTON, LOUISIANA

The University

"At Tech you'll belong. Tech is family." That is how one graduate described the Louisiana Tech University experience. With a reputation for offering a private-college atmosphere at a public university, this selective-admissions university is dedicated to challenging its students through the efforts of caring faculty members who are passionate about teaching, advising, and research. Founded in 1894, Tech offers more than eighty undergraduate majors and a wide variety of graduate degrees from within thirty-one master's and ten doctoral programs. Tech has the highest retention and graduation rate in the University of Louisiana system.

At this campus, 1,592 freshmen, of a total of 10,607 students, thrive in a safe and supportive environment. Collaborative research opportunities enhance learning alongside extracurricular and NCAA Division I athletic programs that enrich student life. Tech's campus brings together students from every state in the nation and seventy other countries.

The pedestrian-friendly campus revolves around the oak-shaded Quad and its gracious gardens, beckoning benches, and splashing Lady of the Mist fountain. Other campus highlights include a brick walkway that bears the names of all 72,000 Tech graduates, the newly rebuilt Hale Hall (where admissions and architecture are housed), the sixteen-story Wyly Tower of Learning, the cutting-edge Institute for Micromanufacturing, and the striking Thomas Assembly Center.

The 255-acre campus is also home to Tolliver Hall's state-of-the-art cyber café for students, a large T-shaped swimming pool, and the Lambright Sports Center. The Lambright Sports Center houses basketball and racquetball courts, sauna facilities, weight rooms, and an indoor track. The facility includes a nine-hole golf course.

In addition to ten residence halls, including one for honors students, and a new on-campus apartment-style community, campus life is fueled by excellent academic programs, 160 student organizations, and fourteen varsity sports. Students are admitted free of charge to all Tech sporting events.

Tech is a state-supported university that is accredited by the Commission on Colleges of the Southern Association of Colleges and Schools.

Location

Louisiana Tech makes its home in the north-central Louisiana city of Ruston, which sits at the intersection of Interstate 20 and U.S. Highway 167. Students can enjoy local eateries, stores, and entertainment activities, or they can take a drive (70 miles west to Shreveport or 26 miles east to Monroe) for a wider range of dining, shopping, and entertainment experiences. Ruston, a friendly Southern community of 23,000 and the site of the Squire Creek Louisiana Peach Festival, remains close-knit with its university neighbor. Tech students are active in cooperative projects with Ruston businesses and civic organizations.

Majors and Degrees

The College of Business awards the Bachelor of Science (B.S.) degree, with majors in accounting, business administration, business economics, business management entrepreneurship, computer information systems, finance, human resources management, and marketing.

The College of Applied and Natural Sciences awards the Bachelor of Science, Bachelor of Arts (B.A.), and Bachelor of Science in Forestry (B.S.F.) degrees, with majors in agribusiness, animal science, biology, environmental science, family and child studies, family and consumer sciences education (7–12), forestry, health information administration, medical technology, merchandising and consumer studies, nutrition and dietetics, plant sciences, and wildlife conservation.

The College of Education awards the B.A. and B.S. degrees, with majors in art education (K–12), early/elementary education (pre-K–3), educational services, elementary education (1–6), elementary/special education, health and physical education, kinesiology and health promotion, middle school education math/science (4–8), music education (K–12), psychology, secondary education (agriculture, biology, business, chemistry, earth science, English, French, math, physics, social studies, speech), special education (early interventions, mild/moderate elementary, mild/moderate secondary, severe/profound), and speech, language, and hearing therapy (K–12).

The College of Engineering and Science awards the B.S. degree, with majors in biomedical engineering, chemical engineering, chemistry, civil engineering, computer science, construction engineering technology, electrical engineering, electrical engineering technology, geology, industrial engineering, mathematics, mechanical engineering, nanosystems engineering, and physics.

The College of Liberal Arts awards the Bachelor of Architecture (B.Arch.), B.A., Bachelor of Fine Arts (B.F.A.), Bachelor of General Studies (B.G.S.), and Bachelor of Interior Design (B.I.D.) degrees, with majors in architecture (five years), art–graphic design, art-photography, art-studio, aviation management, English, French, general studies, geography, history, interior design, journalism, music, political science, preprofessional speech-language pathology, professional aviation, sociology, Spanish, and speech.

Academic Programs

All baccalaureate degree programs require a minimum of 120 semester hours. Minimum graduation requirements include a 2.0 GPA on all earned curricular course work. Additional GPA performance may be required in certain colleges. All curricula contain a general education core of 45 semester hours. Credit for selected courses may be earned through credit exams administered by the academic departments, through the Advanced Placement Program, and through the College-Level Examination Program (CLEP). Academically qualified students may seek admission to the Honors Program, which features smaller classes taught by prominent faculty members and social and cultural programming. At the Career Center, students can schedule on-campus interviews with employers, get career and graduate school guidance, search job listings, attend resume and interview workshops, and meet company recruiters on Career Days. Tech awards semester hours on a quarter system. The fall, winter, and spring quarters equal two semesters.

Off-Campus Programs

Louisiana Tech offers an on-base degree program at Barksdale Air Force Base in Bossier City, Louisiana. Tech-Barksdale specializes in adult-oriented education for active-duty personnel and anyone seeking evening courses. The University also has a cross-registration program with Grambling State University and the University of Louisiana–Monroe.

Academic Facilities

The Prescott Memorial Library houses a media center, a computer lab with Internet access, classrooms with satellite teleconference downlink capabilities, an electronic reference center, and an electronic instruction classroom. Across the campus, the Innovation Lab, featuring the most advanced information technology available, is a 24-hour-accessible space that encourages interdisciplinary innovation and entrepreneurship. The Honors

Program has a classroom equipped with a plasma board and technology table, which allows for a more interactive learning experience. All classrooms in the College of Business are equipped with LCD projectors, laptop stations, and full multimedia capabilities. Two presentation spaces are dedicated to the performing arts. The 40,000-square-foot School of Art has Macintosh labs that are the industry standard in graphic design and multimedia technology. The Center for Rehabilitation Science and Biomedical Engineering is recognized internationally for research ranging from the study of disabilities to the application of technology to assist disabled individuals.

Costs

Tuition and fees are $4402 for in-state residents and $8197 for out-of-state students. These figures are based on 8 credit hours per quarter, which is full-time status. Average residence hall fees are $2220. The most frequently used meal plan costs $1965.

Financial Aid

Approximately 80 percent of Louisiana Tech students receive some form of financial assistance. Students may qualify for scholarship awards, need-based federal grants, or participation in federal loan programs. Students may also pursue regular or need-based campus job opportunities.

Four-year academic merit scholarships for talented entering freshmen range from $1000 to full tuition and additional incentives. The first step in being considered for financial aid is to complete the Free Application for Federal Student Aid (FAFSA) as early as possible. Tech's code number is 002008.

Faculty

Of the nearly 400 faculty members, 70 percent hold the doctorate or equivalent degree. In addition to being excellent professors and researchers, the faculty members are known for their practical experience outside of academia. Software engineers, civil engineers, published authors, architects, medical doctors, pilots, and other professionals bring hands-on expertise to the classroom to enhance learning. The student-faculty ratio is 23:1.

Student Government

Louisiana Tech's Student Government Association (SGA) serves as the official student voice to the administration, the Louisiana Board of Regents, the University of Louisiana System Board of Supervisors, and the state legislature. Its mission is to continually represent the interests and opinions of students, increase student decision-making power, create and promote student leadership opportunities, improve campus life through the creation and continuation of effective student services, and support students in academic and community endeavors.

Admission Requirements

Freshman applicants must graduate from an approved high school with a minimum 2.5 GPA achieved in at least 17.5 units of prerequisite study, including 4 units of English, 3 units of mathematics (2 of algebra and 1 of geometry or a higher-level math for which algebra is a prerequisite), 3 units of science (biology, chemistry, and 1 other unit of science), 1 additional unit of mathematics or science, 3 units of social science (of which 1 unit must be U.S. history), 2 units of the same foreign language, one fine arts survey, and one computer literacy course. Otherwise, students must rank in the top 25 percent of their graduating class, have a minimum ACT composite score of 23 or combined SAT score of 1060, and require no more than one remedial course. No student with an ACT composite less than 15 will be admitted.

Out-of-state and home-schooled students must have a minimum ACT composite of 23 (SAT, 1060), a minimum grade point average of 2.5, and a high school transcript documenting completion of high school work.

International applicants must have a minimum 2.5 GPA on all course work and an official TOEFL score of 500 or greater on the paper-based test or a score of 173 or higher on the computerized test. Tech must receive the TOEFL score within two years of the test date. A waiver of the TOEFL may be possible if the international student has earned at least 24 hours from another approved U.S. university.

All students are encouraged to apply. The University may admit students not meeting all stated requirements. In such cases, the admission decision is affected by the student's potential for success and the need to enhance the University's population.

Transfer students with fewer than 18 semester hours of course work must meet the same requirements as entering freshmen and be eligible to reenter the institution from which they transferred. Students with 18 hours or more must have a minimum 2.25 GPA on all transfer work.

High school students may be considered for early admission if they have a minimum 3.0 overall GPA on all course work pursued during three years of high school, a minimum ACT composite score of 25 or SAT combined score of 1130 (to be submitted prior to June 1), and a recommendation letter from their high school principal. Upon completing a minimum of 24 semester hours at the University, the student will be issued a diploma by the high school last attended.

Tech's Summer Enrichment Program enables students to pursue college credit between their junior and senior high school years. The Summer Scholars Program for exceptional students awards scholarships to entering freshmen who want to get an early start by enrolling in the summer quarter.

Application and Information

The application and nonrefundable $20 application fee ($30 for an international student) should be submitted to the Office of Admissions. Priority is given to those who apply by August 1 for admission to the fall quarter, November 1 for the winter quarter, February 1 for the spring quarter, and May 1 for the summer quarter.

Campus visits are encouraged. For materials and information, students should contact:

Office of Admissions
Louisiana Tech University
P.O. Box 3178
Ruston, Louisiana 71272-0001
Phone: 318-257-3036
800-LATECH-1 (toll-free)
E-mail: bulldog@latech.edu
Web site: http://www.latech.edu

Louisiana Tech design students have been known to sit on their projects for a while.

LOYOLA UNIVERSITY NEW ORLEANS

NEW ORLEANS, LOUISIANA

The University

Founded by the Jesuits in 1912, Loyola University's more than 35,000 graduates have excelled in innumerable professional fields for over ninety years. More than 3,000 undergraduate students (5,000 students total) enjoy the individual attention of a caring faculty in a university dedicated to creating community and fostering individualism while educating the whole person, not only intellectually, but spiritually, socially, and athletically. Loyola students represent all fifty states and forty-eight countries. This diversity is found in a setting where the average class size is 17–24 students. Almost 70 percent of the students permanently reside outside Louisiana, and 36 percent belong to minority groups.

Loyola's 20-acre main campus and 4-acre Broadway campus are located in the historic uptown area of New Orleans and are hubs of student activity. The University's residence halls, equipped with computer labs, kitchen, laundry, and study facilities, are home to nearly 75 percent of the freshmen who reside on campus. The Joseph A. Danna Center, the student center, houses six food venues, including the Orleans Room, Godfather's Pizza, Smoothie King, the Underground, and a gourmet coffee shop. An art gallery, concierge desk, and post office can also be found in the Danna Center. Nationally affiliated fraternities and sororities are among Loyola's more than 120 student organizations. During the fall's Organizational Fair, students can join the 2006 Pacemaker Award–winning newspaper, the Loyola University Community Action Program (a volunteer community service organization, the largest organization on campus), or one of the many special interest groups. Students can also take this opportunity to sign up for one of Loyola's club sports. Every year, approximately one third of the student body participates in club sports, such as cheerleading, crew, cycling, dance, golf, swimming, and volleyball, as well as in men's lacrosse, rugby, and soccer. Loyola participates in the National Association of Intercollegiate Athletics (NAIA) men's baseball, basketball, cross-country, and track (distance) and women's basketball, cross-country, and volleyball. The Recreational Sports Complex offers six multipurpose courts, an elevated running track, an Olympic-size swimming pool, weight rooms, and aerobics and combat-sports facilities.

The career services offered by the Counseling and Career Services Center include career counseling and testing, assistance with choosing a course of study, recommendations about graduate and professional school, and assistance in securing internships and jobs.

Career development services include individualized consultation and counseling (with personality and career-interest testing), a career exploration course, career-related speakers, and a career information library. Publications include information on a wide range of career choices, graduate school directories, scholarship and financial aid directories, and field-specific directories of employers.

The Joseph A. Butt, S.J., College of Business is fully accredited at both the undergraduate and graduate levels by the Association to Advance Collegiate Schools of Business–AACSB International, and houses the Mildred Soule and Clarence A. Lengendre Chair in Business Ethics. The College of Music and Fine Arts offers students opportunities in music industry studies and music performance areas as well as visual and theater arts. This college also hosts the Thelonious Monk Institute of Jazz Performance. Students in the College of Humanities and Natural Sciences might choose premed preparation, psychology, or areas in the humanities, such as history or modern foreign languages. The College of Social Sciences houses a School of Mass Communication that offers award winning programs in advertising, journalism, and public relations.

Location

Loyola's main campus fronts oak-lined St. Charles Avenue in uptown New Orleans. Its red-brick, Tudor-Gothic buildings overlook Audubon Park, home of the famous Audubon Zoo. The downtown area is a 20-minute streetcar ride away, allowing students to take advantage of the city's broad cultural and artistic environment. Considering that New Orleans enjoys an average temperature of 70 degrees, students can enjoy year-round outdoor activities in a city famous for its food, music, and cultural festivals. Lake Pontchartrain is within the city limits and provides facilities for water sports.

Majors and Degrees

Loyola University grants degrees in four-year undergraduate programs. The College of Humanities and Natural Sciences grants the B.A. degree in classical studies, English, English writing, French, history, philosophy, psychology, psychology (premed), religious studies (Christianity and world religions), and Spanish. It grants the B.S. in biology (predentistry, premedicine, and pre–veterinary studies), chemistry (premedicine), chemistry–forensic science, mathematics, and physics. The College of Business awards the B.B.A. degree in economics, finance, international business, management, marketing, and music industry studies, as well as the Bachelor of Accountancy. The College of Music and Fine Arts grants the B.M. in composition, jazz studies, music education, music industry studies, music therapy and performance (instrumental and vocal), and grants the B.S. in music industry studies. The College also grants a B.A. in graphic arts, theater arts, theater arts–communications, theater arts (with a minor in business administration), and visual arts and a B.F.A. in visual arts. The College of Social Sciences offers the B.A. in criminal justice, political science, and sociology, and the School of Mass Communication offers the B.A. in advertising, journalism, and public relations. Minors are available in all disciplines offered as majors. Africana, African American, American, environmental, film, Latin American, medieval, and women's studies are offered as interdisciplinary minors addressing important areas of national and international concern.

Academic Programs

Once enrolled at Loyola, students are introduced to the Common Curriculum, designed to give them a well-rounded preparation in their major field of concentration, as well as the ability to understand and reflect on disciplines allied to or outside their major. The curriculum is divided into four categories: major, minor, Common Curriculum, and elective courses. Students must meet the requirements of their degree program as specified by their particular college; the minimum four-year program requires 120 hours. Common Curriculum courses include seven introductory courses in English composition, math, science, philosophy, religion, literature, and history and nine upper-division courses in humanities, social science, and natural science. The College of Business requires that all students with junior or senior standing complete a 3-credit-hour internship prior to graduation. Internships provide professional-level experience in area business firms and not-for-profit organizations, along with college credit for semester-long participation. The College of Humanities and Natural Sciences also requires a minimum of one year of study in a modern foreign language. The honors program and independent studies provide special opportunities for qualified students.

Off-Campus Programs

Through the Center for International Education, students may spend their junior year in Rome. Summer programs in Germany, Greece, Ireland, London, and Mexico are also available, as well as opportunities to study in Belgium, France, Japan, and Spain. Through consortium arrangements, students may cross-register for courses for credit at Xavier University, Tulane University, and Notre Dame Seminary and participate with these institutions in joint social-cultural events. In addition, the University offers a rigorous internship program in New Orleans at businesses, institutions, and schools to give students practical experience in their fields, including business, communications, modern foreign languages, music, and writing. Loyola offers a 3-3 program with the Loyola College of Law for students interested in pursuing a prelaw track, an early acceptance program with Tulane University Medical School, and a five-year M.B.A. program through the College of Business.

Academic Facilities

A $13-million Communications/Music Complex includes classrooms, offices, specialized instructional facilities for the College of Music and

Fine Arts and the School of Mass Communication, and a 600-seat performing arts facility for the College of Music and Fine Arts.

Computing is an integral part of campus life at Loyola. The University provides more than 450 computers in seventeen computer labs throughout the campus. These labs consist of Windows- and Macintosh-based computers with a wide variety of application software and access to the Internet. Loyola's high-speed Ethernet network can also be accessed from locations such as residence halls, the library, and other public areas. A noteworthy characteristic of Loyola's computing resources is its student-centered emphasis. For example, specialized computer labs exist in the Writing Across the Curriculum Center, English and Math Basic Skills Labs, Poverty Law Clinic, and Business Solutions Center.

The Broadway campus, approximately two blocks down St. Charles Avenue, houses the Loyola College of Law, the visual arts department, the Division of Institutional Advancement, and a residence hall.

Other facilities on campus include the J. Edgar and Louise S. Monroe Library, the region's most technologically advanced facility and the 2003 recipient of the Association of College and Research Libraries' Excellence in Academic Libraries Award, which contains more than 367,000 volumes and provides access to over 27,000 electronic books and more than 23,000 electronic journals. The Monroe Library also offers more than 660,000 microform units and 2,500 media titles. There are also specialized libraries for music and law. The 150,000-square-foot Monroe Library contains 1,800 computer links, media/instructional technology services, a visual arts center, and the Lindy Boggs National Center for Community Literacy. The library also offers three 24-hour microcomputer labs, two multimedia classrooms, and sixteen group-study rooms.

Costs

For the full-time undergraduate student attending during 2007–08, tuition is $25,631 for the year, plus a $1086 student activity fee. The cost of residence halls (double occupancy) and a complete meal plan is $9028 for the year.

Financial Aid

Loyola University's endowment provides money for financial aid in addition to that provided by federal funding. Assistance in the forms of merit- and talent-based scholarships, loans, work-study program awards, and grants is awarded on the basis of academic achievement and need. More than 450 scholarships are awarded annually to students with competitive grades and test scores. To apply for one of the scholarships, students must have a GPA of at least 3.2 and competitive standardized test scores. Offers of financial aid are not made until after admission. Notifications of awards are sent in early February. Awards of need-based financial aid packages are made on a first-come, first-served basis and are announced in mid-March. Eighty-four percent of Loyola students receive some form of financial aid.

Faculty

Behind every program at Loyola is a faculty of Jesuit and lay professors who are especially well qualified in their particular fields. The Jesuit Order, recognized throughout the world for its educational contributions over the centuries, administers the University's faculty of 259 full-time professors, of whom 90 percent hold the terminal degree in their field. Loyola also employs 137 part-time instructors. No graduate assistants teach classes. The student-faculty ratio of 11:1 emphasizes the University's special quality of personal involvement and concern for each student and his or her particular needs.

Student Government

Loyola's Student Government Association consists of representatives elected by the student body from each of the four colleges and the law school. The association conducts general meetings, elections, and student activities. Student representatives sit on nearly all University committees.

Admission Requirements

Prospective students must submit an application, resume, and essay; have a high school transcript or GED test results sent; submit ACT or SAT scores; and have their counselor or teacher send a recommendation. Individual attention is given to each application form. Final selection is based on high school grades, test scores, and counselor or teacher recommendations. Significant community involvement and demonstrated leadership abilities are recommended. Auditions are required for final acceptance to the College of Music and Fine Arts, which includes the Department of Theatre Arts and Dance. Portfolios are required for final acceptance to the Department of Visual Arts.

December 1 is the priority deadline for freshman admission and scholarship consideration. January 15 is the regular deadline for freshman scholarship consideration. February 15 is the regular deadline for freshman admission consideration.

Transfer students are required to submit an official transcript for each institution previously attended along with their transfer application. Transfer scholarships are available only to students entering in the fall. Transfer students interested in competing for a scholarship should apply by March 1 if possible, and no later than April 15. For nonscholarship admission consideration, transfer students should apply no later than May 15 for the fall semester and no later than December 1 for the spring semester.

Application and Information

Interested students are encouraged to contact:

Office of Admissions
Loyola University New Orleans
6363 St. Charles Avenue, Box 18
New Orleans, Louisiana 70118
Phone: 504-865-3240
800-4-LOYOLA (toll-free)
Fax: 504-865-3383
E-mail: admit@loyno.edu
Web site: http://www.loyno.edu

Loyola is located on beautiful, oak-lined St. Charles Avenue adjacent to Audubon Park.

McNEESE STATE UNIVERSITY

LAKE CHARLES, LOUISIANA

The University

Founded in 1939, McNeese State University is a comprehensive institution that awards undergraduate and graduate degrees. Named after the pioneer John McNeese, a southwest Louisiana educator, the University is committed to providing students with outstanding academic opportunities that prepare them to pursue their educational and career goals. McNeese State University is accredited by the Commission on Colleges of the Southern Association of Colleges and Schools and is a member of the University of Louisiana System, one of the largest public higher education systems in the United States. The system, which includes eight universities, serves more than 80,000 students and employs nearly 4,000 full-time faculty members. More than 8,000 McNeese students choose from more than eighty degree programs offered by the College of Business, Burton College of Education, College of Engineering and Technology, Dore School of Graduate Studies, College of Liberal Arts, College of Nursing, College of Science, and the Department of General and Basic Studies. Dedicated faculty members create an environment where students achieve their full potential, illustrated by McNeese's rating as one of the top schools in the nation for the caring and friendly attitude of the faculty and staff members.

Students have access to state-of-the-art computer labs with convenient hours and locations across the campus. Residence halls provide comfortable and affordable housing for McNeese students and are available year-round. The Recreational Sports Center offers an Olympic-sized swimming pool, free weights, an indoor track, and state-of-the-art exercise equipment free to all students. Students may participate in a wide range of organizations, including student government, newspaper and yearbook staffs, social fraternities and sororities, religious organizations, and numerous honor societies. On-campus dining options range from homemade meals at Rowdy's cafeteria to international fare to fast-food chains. The campus also features a convenience store, coffee shop, bookstore, post office, ATM machine, career services center, student health services center, and counseling center. In addition to the main campus, the current physical plant includes several farms, an athletics plant, a married-student apartment complex, a golf-driving range, and Burton Coliseum.

The College of Business offers a Master of Business Administration degree and is nationally accredited by AACSB International–The Association to Advance Collegiate Schools of Business at both the undergraduate and graduate levels. The College of Engineering and Technology is accredited by the Engineering Accreditation Commission of the Accreditation Board for Engineering and Technology.

The Burton College of Education offers graduate degrees in curriculum and instruction, educational leadership, educational technology leadership, health and human performance, instructional technology, special education, psychology, and school counseling. All teacher education programs are accredited by the National Council for Accreditation of Teacher Education and approved by the Board of Elementary and Secondary Education, state of Louisiana.

The College of Nursing offers a Master of Science in Nursing degree, with concentrations in clinical nurse specialist studies, nurse education, nurse practitioner studies, and nursing administration. The College of Nursing is a member of the Intercollegiate Consortium for a Master of Science in Nursing and is accredited by the National League for Nursing Accrediting Commission (NLNAC). In addition, the College of Nursing is approved by the Louisiana State Board of Nursing.

Location

Lake Charles and southwest Louisiana are historically and culturally rich. The year 2003 marked the bicentennial of the Louisiana Purchase, and Cajun culture is still very much alive in this region. The city of Lake Charles has a population of more than 75,000 and has important petrochemical, entertainment, and shipping industries. Contraband Days, the second-largest festival in Louisiana, is held annually in May, and Mardi Gras is similarly festive in the spring. Perhaps the greatest local attraction is the Cajun food, which is the pride of southwest Louisiana. Lake Charles lies along the I-10 corridor, with Houston, Texas, and Baton Rouge, Louisiana, just over 2 hours away and New Orleans, Louisiana, nearly 4 hours away. This area offers a variety of outdoor activities, cultural events, and entertainment opportunities for students. The city is served by a regional airport with daily flights to Houston.

Majors and Degrees

McNeese State University offers students more than eighty degrees and majors. The degree programs are divided into six different colleges. The College of Business offers a Bachelor of Science degree in accounting, finance, general business administration, management, and marketing.

The Burton College of Education offers a Bachelor of Science degree in business education, early childhood education, elementary education, health and human performance, health and physical education, psychology, and special education.

Many different concentrations in engineering and engineering technology are available in McNeese's College of Engineering and Technology.

The College of Liberal Arts awards a variety of degrees in history, languages, mass communication, music, social sciences, speech, theater arts, and visual arts. Each of these departments offers at least four different areas of concentration.

A Bachelor of Science in Nursing degree is offered by the College of Nursing. An associate degree in nursing is also offered.

Studies in agricultural sciences, biological science, chemistry, computer science and statistics, environmental and chemical sciences, environmental science, family and consumer science, mathematical sciences, mathematics, medical technology, radiologic technology, physics, and wildlife management are made available through the College of Science. Associate degree programs in computer information technology, engineering technology, general studies, nursing, and paralegal studies are also available.

Academic Programs

McNeese operates on a semester system (fall and spring) and summer classes are available. The number of semester hours needed for graduation varies according to degree program, with a minimum of 121 hours. General requirements emphasize the arts, humanities, social sciences, mathematics, and sciences, though students are given a wide variety of choices in selecting core courses. Special programs include the Honors College, which is designed for outstanding students with strong academic records who desire an alternative course of instruction. The program offers a substantial scholarship covering tuition, room and board, and a stipend for students who qualify as well as supplemented honors events, cultural opportunities, and social activities. The women's studies program provides special courses, a resource center, and an established lecture series.

Off-Campus Programs

There are a growing number of off-campus programs at McNeese. Programs are in Rome, Paris, and Greece and are organized directly through the University, allowing students to earn credits in areas such as business, art, literature, and classical studies. There is also a program in New York City through the theater department. Students may qualify for benefits through the CODOFIL program in Louisiana, which provides financial support for students who wish to study in a Francophone country. McNeese also has a Fulbright Advisory Committee dedicated to helping students secure grants to pursue study-abroad opportunities.

Academic Facilities

The Frazar Memorial Library holds more than 400,000 volumes as well as room for study, library offices, and service areas. Several online systems are available through the library, as well as a computer room with Internet access for students, faculty members, and members of the community. Abercrombie Gallery hosts exhibits by students, faculty, and national and international artists. The Business Conference Center hosts seminars, workshops, and other University programs. Hardtner Hall is a $5-million state-of-the-art facility that houses the College of Nursing, a community clinic, and the Department of Mass Communication.

Costs

Tuition and fees at McNeese are $1600 per semester for Louisiana residents and $4605 per semester for nonresidents. Books cost approximately $500 per semester. Costs are subject to change. All students who are enrolled in 7 or more semester hours are covered by the University's student accident and life insurance, which provides $10,000 of coverage.

Financial Aid

More than $3.5 million in scholarships are awarded to McNeese students each year. Academic scholarships are awarded on a competitive basis to qualified full-time students who remain in good standing. Scholarships may be used to pay for University expenses and range from $100 to $3000 per semester. A limited number of scholarships are available to cover residence-hall room fees. The priority deadline for scholarship applications is December 1 for the upcoming academic year. The Office of Financial Aid also offers a variety of grants and loans to meet student needs, and the priority deadline is May 1. Programs such as the Federal Pell Grant and Federal Supplemental Educational Opportunity Grant offer federal money based on demonstrated need and does not have to be repaid. Federal Perkins Loans, Federal Stafford Student Loans, and the Federal PLUS Program offer low-interest-rate loans for students who qualify. For students from the state of Louisiana, the State Student Incentive Grant and Tuition Opportunity Program for Students (TOPS) are available. McNeese also has a Work-on-Campus program that is open to all students regardless of income. However, funds are limited and upperclassmen receive first consideration, subject to deadline dates. Out-of-state students who meet specific criteria are eligible to receive a nonresident fee waiver. In order to be considered for financial aid, students must complete the Free Application for Federal Student Aid (FAFSA).

Faculty

McNeese has a faculty of 392 members, of whom 283 are full-time. Sixty-nine percent of full-time faculty members hold terminal degrees. Qualifying graduate students may serve as undergraduate instructors. The student-faculty ratio is 22:1. The average undergraduate class size is 25 students. McNeese is one of the top-ranked schools in the nation for individual attention to students. Faculty members serve as academic advisers in each degree program. Career and personal counseling, as well as counseling for veterans and international students, are also available. The University prides itself on its dedication to excellence with a personal touch.

Student Government

The Student Government Association (SGA) represents the student body to the faculty, administration, and the community. The SGA is staffed by students and aids the student body through several specific programs. The Student Union Board provides social, recreational, cultural, spiritual, and educational programs for students, faculty members, and alumni.

Admission Requirements

First-time freshmen students seeking admission to undergraduate programs at McNeese are required to submit an application for admission, $20 application fee, proof of immunization, official high school transcripts, official ACT or SAT scores, and proof of Selective Service Registration (men only, ages 18–25). Applicants must complete the Louisiana Regents TOPS/University Core Curriculum, earn a minimum ACT English or math score of 18 (SAT, 450 verbal or 430 math), and have one of the following: an ACT composite score of at least 20 (combined SAT, 940), a final high school GPA of at least 2.0, or a ranking in the top 50 percent of their high school graduating class. Additional information about admission requirements can be found on the University's Web site.

Transfer students should be in good academic standing. In addition to meeting transfer student admission criteria, students transferring to McNeese with fewer than 12 college-level hours must also meet first-time freshmen admission criteria. Transfer students with more than 12 college-level hours must have a minimum 2.0 cumulative GPA on college-level credits, be eligible to return to the institution from which they are transferring, and have earned credit for college-level math or English.

Application and Information

To be considered for admission, students must submit a completed application for admission, nonrefundable $20 application fee, proof of immunization form, official ACT and SAT scores, and all transcripts of previous schooling. Transcripts must be sent directly to the Office of the Registrar by the institutions attended.

For more information, students may contact:

Office of Enrollment Information
McNeese State University
P.O. Box 92895
Lake Charles, Louisiana 70609
Phone: 337-475-5504
800-622-3352 (toll-free)
E-mail: info@mail.mcneese.edu
Web site: http://www.mcneese.edu

TULANE UNIVERSITY

NEW ORLEANS, LOUISIANA

Tulane

The University

Tulane University in New Orleans is known nationally and internationally for its teaching and research. At Tulane a student can get an international education in a European city without leaving America. One of a handful of national independent universities in the South, Tulane was founded in 1834 as the Medical College of Louisiana and reorganized as Tulane in 1884. The University is comprehensive by nature, with more than 10,000 students enrolled in nine schools and colleges ranging from the liberal arts and sciences through a full spectrum of professional schools: law, medicine, business, engineering, architecture, social work, and public health and tropical medicine. Tulane's 5,500 full-time undergraduates choose from more than seventy majors in colleges of liberal arts, sciences and engineering, architecture, business, and public health and continuing studies and may opt for joint-degree programs in Tulane's professional schools to earn undergraduate and graduate degrees in a shorter period of time. Tulane's distinctive arrangement of undergraduate schools gives every student the personal attention and teaching excellence of a small college while providing the interdisciplinary opportunities and research resources of a university that *U.S. News & World Report* ranks in the nation's top quartile. The average class size is 23. Senior faculty members are in the classroom at all levels, and the 8:1 student-teacher ratio ensures individual attention.

On its residential campus about 4 miles from downtown New Orleans, Tulane requires housing for freshmen and sophomores. Students may choose from several special interest floors in the residence halls, with areas for honors students, those interested in international and urban affairs, and women science majors, among others. Students participate in more than 300 campus organizations. About 1 student in 3 joins a fraternity or sorority; 2 in 3 play intramural or intercollegiate club sports, and more than 500 participate in Tulane's community volunteer organization. Tulane fields eight NCAA Division I sports, competing in Conference USA.

More than 80 percent of Tulane students plan to go on eventually to graduate or professional school. Shortly after graduation, 10 percent enter medical school; 16 percent, law school; and 32 percent, other graduate study. Just over one third accept jobs. Tulane students are among the country's most likely to be selected for several prestigious fellowships, including the Fulbright, Marshall, Rhodes, Truman, and Watson scholarships, that support postgraduate study.

Recent additions to Tulane's campus have included a brand new, state-of-the-art student center; a new, larger baseball stadium on campus; an addition to the School of Business; a center for engineering and biotechnology; a law school building; a fine arts complex; residence halls; and a new science facility.

Tulane's programs are shaped by the University's direct experience with the unprecedented natural disaster of Hurricane Katrina. This experience is providing faculty and staff members and students with equally unprecedented research, learning, and community-service opportunities that will have a lasting and profound impact on them, the city of New Orleans, the Gulf Coast region, and other communities around the world.

Location

The University is in a historic New Orleans residential area next to renowned Audubon Park, which offers 440 acres of recreational facilities. While the 110-acre campus maintains a traditional collegiate atmosphere, with Gothic stone and red brick amid blooming azaleas and lawns that are green year-round, new buildings are going up at the rate of one a year. The only remaining streetcar line in the country clatters by the campus, connecting students with downtown New Orleans.

Majors and Degrees

The B.A., B.S., B.F.A., B.S.E, and B/M.Arch. degrees are offered. Programs are for four years, with the exception of the five-year architecture program.

Students may major in more than seventy departmental and interdisciplinary areas, including accounting, African studies, American studies, anthropology, architecture, art history, art studio, Asian studies, biological chemistry, biomedical engineering, cell and molecular biology, chemical engineering, chemistry, classical studies, cognitive studies, communication, consumer behavior–marketing, dance, digital media production, earth sciences, ecology and evolutionary biology, economics, English, environmental biology, environmental geoscience, environmental studies, finance, French, geology, German cultural studies, German language and literature, history, information systems, international development, international relations, Italian, Jewish studies, Latin American studies, legal studies in business, linguistics, literature, management, mathematical economics, mathematics, medieval studies, music composition, music performance, music science and technology, musical theater, neuroscience, philosophy, physics, political economy, political science, Portuguese, psychology, public health (environmental health science, global and community health science, health informatics), religious studies, Russian, Russian studies, sociology, Spanish, theater, and women's studies. Talented students may also design their own majors, and those who meet the requirements may begin professional study in law, medicine, or other professional schools in the senior year, reducing by a year the time spent earning undergraduate and graduate degrees.

Academic Programs

All freshmen enroll in the Undergraduate College that comprises all of the undergraduate programs in Liberal Arts, Science and Engineering, Business, Public Health and Tropical Medicine, and Architecture. All prospective undergraduate students apply to the Undergraduate College for admission. Tulane has a two-semester calendar, with first-semester exams held before the holiday break. While faculty advisers assist in course selection and in planning major requirements, the Tulane University Center for Academic Advising provides a primary point of contact for students who have not declared majors and for upperclassmen to ensure progress toward their degree. The center's staff members assist students to refine their academic goals, understand their choices, and assess their options.

The Tulane Core Curriculum provides a common academic experience for undergraduates across all schools of the University, requiring course work in all areas of knowledge. The Core Curriculum assures the attainment of basic competencies in writing, foreign language, scientific inquiry, cultural knowledge, and interdisciplinary scholarship. Students are offered an integrative, themed first-year seminar experience known as TIDES. The prominent role of public service and leadership reflects the value Tulane places upon developing a lifelong commitment to public service and citizenship.

Every Tulane undergraduate must complete a Senior Capstone Experience related to his or her major. Capstone experiences allow students to demonstrate the capacity to bring information, skills, and ideas acquired from the major and other parts of their education to bear on one significant project.

The School of Liberal Arts is organized into three divisions: humanities, fine arts, and social sciences. Humanities houses African studies, American studies, classical studies, communication, English, French and Italian, Germanic and Slavic studies, Jewish studies, philosophy, and Spanish and Portuguese. The Fine Arts division houses art, music, theater, and dance. The Social Sciences division houses anthropology, economics, history, Latin American studies, political economy, political science, psychology, sociology, and women's studies.

The School of Science and Engineering has five distinct divisions: biological sciences and engineering, chemical sciences and engineering, physical and material sciences, earth and environmental sciences, and mathematics and computational science.

The School of Architecture enrolls about 300 students in the five-year Bachelor/Master of Architecture program. Students graduate fully prepared to become licensed architects with no further study.

The A. B. Freeman School of Business offers majors in accounting, consumer behavior–marketing, entrepreneurship, finance, information systems, legal studies, and management, leading to the Bachelor of Science in Management degree.

The School of Public Health and Tropical Medicine was founded in 1912 and is a leader among the thirty-one such schools accredited in the nation. The undergraduate program in public health integrates study in the humanities, fine arts, social sciences, and sciences, with courses specifically oriented toward public health. Students combine research expertise with the ability to make difficult social choices and devise solutions to individual and population-wide health problems, emphasizing communication skills and cultural sensitivity. Three undergraduate majors are available: environmental health sciences, global and community health, and health informatics.

Tulane's School of Continuing Studies offers degree, certificate, and noncredit programs across a wide range of fields, combining many of Tulane's strengths and extensive resources.

The honors program, with approximately 600 academically outstanding students, emphasizes small seminars during the first three college years and a research-based honors thesis the senior year. More than 100 students choose honors floors in the residence halls.

Off-Campus Programs

With more than 900 students from more than 100 other countries at Tulane, undergraduates don't have to go abroad for an international experience. But many of them choose to take advantage of one of the University's programs for a summer, a semester, or a year of study abroad. Each year, approximately 100 academically talented Tulane students participate in the Tulane/Newcomb Junior Year Abroad (JYA) program, attending universities in Australia, Argentina, Brazil, Chile, Czech Republic, France, Germany, Greece, Great Britain (including Scotland and Wales), Ireland, Italy, Japan, Malta, and Spain. Most scholarships and loans may be applied to JYA costs. Others opt for internships in New Orleans or Washington, D.C. or places as far afield as London and Cambridge, England.

Academic Facilities

Tulane's library system is ranked among the nation's top 100 research collections. University library holdings total more than 2 million volumes, with several special research collections among the best in America: the William Ransom Hogan Jazz Archive; the Newcomb College Center for Research on Women; and the Amistad Research Center, with its collection of primary source materials on the history of America's ethnic minorities, race relations, and civil rights. Other research facilities include the Roger Thayer Stone Center for Latin American Studies and the Murphy Institute for Political Economy. The Newcomb Gallery exhibits a wide range of art work, including shows by students and faculty members. State-of-the-art computing facilities include dozens of public terminals and a fiber-optic network connecting all campus buildings to the Internet.

Costs

In 2007–08, the cost for a year at Tulane was $47,130. Of this amount, tuition and fees were $36,610 and room and board were $8690 for a typical double room and an all-you-can-eat meal plan (cost may vary for upperclass students).

Financial Aid

The University operates a comprehensive aid program; 74 percent of new students receive some form of financial aid. The average financial aid package (through scholarships, federal grants, loans, and work-study jobs) was nearly $24,677 for 2007–08 entering students. Need, determined by family financial information on the Free Application for Federal Student Aid and the PROFILE from the College Scholarship Service, establishes the appropriate amount of assistance. Merit, based on academic record, determines the proportion of Tulane-funded scholarships in the aid package. The University offers assistance to applicants who demonstrate financial need, and 90 percent of freshmen offered aid had their full need met. If financial need continues and the student has an acceptable academic record, aid extends through the normal period of undergraduate study. Notification of the financial aid award follows admission notification. Deans' Honor Scholarships are offered each year to approximately 100 freshmen and cover tuition for the undergraduate career; other merit scholarships, including those for middle-income students, are also available. Tulane also gives at least thirty National Merit Scholarships to National Merit Finalists who have named Tulane as their first-choice college. Tulane offers creative financing options for families that do not qualify for traditional aid but need assistance in meeting costs.

Faculty

The small, personal settings of Tulane classes give students immediate contact with their professors. Some of Tulane's most seasoned faculty members teach introductory and lower-level courses. About 97 percent of the 1,095 full-time faculty members hold the highest academic degrees in their field, and there are broad opportunities for students, from the freshman year to graduation, to work closely with the faculty on research. Endowed chairs bring distinguished visiting lecturers to the campus every semester. Students have access to faculty members and counselors in the Career Services Center, the Newcomb College Center for Research on Women, and the Educational Resources and Counseling Center as well as in their own colleges and departments.

Student Government

Open communication between elected student representatives and the University's administrators makes Tulane responsive to students' needs. All students are members of the Associated Student Body of Tulane University and participate in University-wide elections. They can hold office and serve on a variety of student-faculty administrative committees. Students are also members of student government associations in each University college or division and can participate on a class level within those divisions.

Admission Requirements

Tulane seeks students who have proven academic capabilities combined with talents or achievements that would enrich the quality of life on campus. All applicants are considered without regard to race, sex, color, religion, sexual orientation, national origin, or physical handicap. Secondary school preparation consisting of 16 or more academic units is expected. In general, quality of achievement is more important than the number of units completed. Applicants to the School of Architecture are encouraged to submit evidence of creative interests with their application. Official SAT or ACT scores are required. SAT Subject Tests are not required but may be used for course placement, and four SAT Subject Tests are required of home-schooled applicants. Interviews are not required, but applicants are encouraged to visit the campus. The admission office is open year-round, except on holidays, from 8:30 a.m. to 5 p.m. central time, Monday through Friday.

Application and Information

Regular decision applications should be submitted by January 15 for admission to the fall semester; admission notification is made no later than April 1, with a May 1 deposit deadline. Deans' Honor Scholarship applicants must apply by December 15 and are notified by February 20. Early action candidates should have all credentials on file by November 1 for notification by December 15. The application fee has been eliminated.

Earl Retif
Vice President for Enrollment Management
210 Gibson Hall
Tulane University
6823 St. Charles Avenue
New Orleans, Louisiana 70118-5680
Phone: 504-865-5731
800-873-9283 (toll-free)
Fax: 504-862-8715
E-mail: undergrad.admission@tulane.edu
Web site: http://www.admission.tulane.edu

UNIVERSITY OF NEW ORLEANS

uno

NEW ORLEANS, LOUISIANA

The University

The University of New Orleans (UNO) is part of the rich cultural tapestry of its hometown, which is one of the most extraordinary cities in the world. Established in 1958 to bring publicly supported higher education to the New Orleans area, UNO is fully accredited by the Commission on Colleges of the Southern Association of Colleges and Schools. With an enrollment of nearly 12,000 students (9,000 undergraduates and 3,000 graduate students) in fall 2007, UNO offers both undergraduate and graduate degrees through the doctoral level.

UNO derives its strength from its urban setting and strives to enhance the economic, social, and cultural amenities of New Orleans through its numerous research projects, outreach programs, and special cooperative agreements. The University of New Orleans attracts students from forty-eight states (approximately 10 percent) and 102 countries; a majority of the students are Louisiana residents (approximately 90 percent). The diverse student population (42 percent of students are members of ethnic minorities) provides an excellent opportunity for personal growth and understanding.

For students who are interested in on-campus housing, UNO offers two unique styles of living. Privateer Place overlooks beautiful Lake Pontchartrain and includes a swimming pool and Jacuzzi. Privateer Place contains seventy-two 2-person unfurnished efficiency apartments, 216 furnished two-bedroom apartments, and sixty furnished four-bedroom apartments. In fall 2007, UNO opened a new $38.5-million residence hall complex (Pontchartrain Hall), composed of two 4-story buildings totaling about 220,000 square feet. The facility includes 236 suite-style units that can accommodate 749 students, as well as TV and recreation rooms, study lounges, laundry facilities, and a convenience store. All complexes have disability-accessible rooms available.

Campus dining facilities are conveniently located near all on-campus housing facilities and heavily populated student areas, with various hours of operation. Other student services include six on-campus computer labs that provide free Internet access, a learning resource center that offers additional tutoring services, student counseling services, an on-campus medical office and pharmacy, student legal counseling, and religious centers.

UNO has more than 100 active student organizations on campus, including academic, professional, Greek, social, political, and religious organizations. UNO's newest addition is the University pep band, the UNO Blue Zoo, which performs at all UNO home basketball games and other University-related events. *Bayou* is UNO's annual national literary magazine that collects submissions from writers worldwide. UNO's student newspaper, *Driftwood,* is published weekly, and *Ellipsis,* a literary magazine, is published annually.

As a Division I member of the National Collegiate Athletic Association (NCAA), UNO fields men's teams in basketball, baseball, and tennis and women's teams in basketball, volleyball, and tennis. UNO students can also participate in many recreational and intramural sports. Students have access to a new 85,000-square-foot Recreation and Fitness Center, which features a 12,000-square-foot cardiovascular, circuit, and free-weight-training room; an indoor track; a lap pool; racquetball courts; an outdoor sundeck; a juice bar; and a social lounge.

Location

The University's 195-acre main campus is set in one of the most beautiful residential areas on the south shore of Lake Pontchartrain, only minutes from the fun and excitement of downtown New Orleans and the French Quarter. New Orleans is a cosmopolitan city, known for its great Southern hospitality and its unique tourist attractions. Renowned for Creole and Cajun cuisine, Mardi Gras, and jazz music festivals, New Orleans culture offers a unique environment for students to grow, both socially and academically. Whether exploring the art galleries of the Warehouse District or strolling down stately St. Charles Avenue, New Orleans has something for everyone, and the University of New Orleans is a part of it all.

Many of UNO's hotel, restaurant, and tourism administration majors find internships in the city's best hotels and restaurants. Film students have the opportunity to work at the Nims Center film studio complex as New Orleans becomes the "Hollywood of the South." Naval architecture students have access to the nation's largest undergraduate program in naval architecture and marine engineering as well as to the UNO–Avondale Maritime Center. As New Orleans continues to attract computer technology–based businesses to what has been called "the Silicon Bayou," the UNO Research and Technology Park continues to expand, producing more than 8,000 new jobs. Computer science majors are able to network with potential employers in one of the fastest-growing computer technology markets in the country.

Majors and Degrees

Bachelor of Science degrees are offered in accounting; biological sciences; chemistry; civil and environmental engineering; computer science; earth and environmental science; electrical engineering; entrepreneurship; finance; general business administration; hotel, restaurant, and tourism administration; management; marketing; mathematics; mechanical engineering; naval architecture and marine engineering; physics; psychology; transportation studies; urban studies and planning; and preprofessional programs in dentistry, medicine (with biology, chemistry, and psychology tracks), nursing, pharmacy, physical therapy studies, and veterinary medicine.

Bachelor of Arts degrees are offered in anthropology; early childhood education; elementary education; English; English education; film, theater, and communication arts; fine arts–history; fine arts–studio (with options that include digital media, painting, photography, and sculpture); French; geography; history; international studies; mathematics education; music (with options such as instrumental, jazz studies, theory and composition, and vocal); music education; philosophy; political science; secondary education; social science education; sociology; Spanish; and women's studies.

A four-year Bachelor of General Studies degree program is available for students who wish to design individual curricula. Credit programs in paralegal studies, medical coding, and medical transcripts are also offered. Additional interdisciplinary minors are offered in interdisciplinary studies in African studies, Asian studies, entrepreneurship, environmental studies, Latin American and Caribbean studies, medical coding, Native American studies, paralegal studies, and print journalism.

Academic Programs

All baccalaureate degree programs require a minimum of 128 semester hours with a minimum grade point average of 2.0 (C) in all work attempted in the college major. Also, all students must successfully complete an approved course demonstrating computer literacy. Other course requirements vary according to program. Programs leading to degrees with honors are offered in most academic majors. Credit for selected courses may be earned either through advanced-standing exams administered by the academic departments or through the College Board's Advanced Placement and College-Level Examination Program tests. College credit may also be gained for certain armed services and other nonacademic training. The academic year is composed of sixteen-week fall and spring semesters and three summer sessions.

Off-Campus Programs

The University of New Orleans Metropolitan College coordinates international study programs in Austria, Costa Rica, the Czech Republic, Ecuador, France, Greece, Honduras, and Italy. UNO's partnership with the University of Innsbruck, Austria, affords students an opportunity to participate in the largest international summer school of any American university in Europe. UNO offers college-credit exchange programs in Brazil and Canada. Students may also attend another school within the continental United States via the National Student Exchange (NSE) for one semester or one year.

UNO offers several off-campus facilities throughout the metropolitan New Orleans area, demonstrating UNO's commitment to community outreach. Off-campus locations offer both credit and noncredit courses, with hours varying from sunrise to evening and weekend classes.

Academic Facilities

The Earl K. Long Library's 1.5-million-volume collection includes approximately 12,000 journals, of which 3,800 are current subscriptions. Microform holdings include microfilm, microcard, and microfiche formats; microtext readers and reader-printers are also available. Other facilities include individual study carrels, a music listening room, computer terminals connected to the Computer Research Center, a Kurzweil reader for the visually impaired, and photocopy services. The Office of Educational Support Services includes a media resources center, which provides important media aids for the instructional staff in classroom presentations, and Television Resources, which coordinates a closed-circuit cable system and TV production studio. WWNO, the first public radio station in Louisiana, is located on the UNO campus.

All enrolled students and faculty and staff members receive a LAN and e-mail account. The University's computer network provides connections to approximately 5,000 locations campuswide as well as wireless connections in select buildings. High-speed ResNet service is available to students living in Privateer Place, and a free dial-up Internet modem pool provides access for all off-campus enrolled students and faculty and staff members.

The UNO Lee Circle Center for the Arts includes the Ogden Museum, which houses the largest collection of Southern art in the world. The center also houses the National D-Day Museum, which includes the world's largest collection of World War II color film. The 70,000-square-foot Nims Center, located 20 minutes from the main campus, houses a professional-quality sound stage, including a 10,000-square-foot studio for University film projects. The Nims Center is also available for professional film projects.

Costs

In 2007–08, combined undergraduate fees for full-time students for the fall and spring semesters were $3292 for Louisiana residents and $10,336 for nonresidents; summer session fees for full-time students were $1080 for Louisiana residents and $1630 for nonresidents. Residence hall and board fees totaled $4370 (double occupancy) for the fall and spring semesters. Costs of books and supplies total $800 per year. Additional charges include a $40 application fee, a $10 registration fee, field service and laboratory fees (usually $10 to $35) for some courses, an $80 car registration fee (includes parking pass), a $30 late application fee, a $30 late registration fee, a $5 per credit hour (maximum $75) technology fee, and a $10 per credit hour (maximum $120) academic enhancement fee. All fees are subject to change and can be confirmed by calling the Office of Admissions.

Financial Aid

The Office of Student Financial Aid develops financial aid packages to assist students with their educational expenses. This package is usually a combination of grants, loans, student employment, and/or scholarships, which, along with family contribution, help to finance the student's education. To be eligible for most federal financial aid programs, students must enroll for at least 6 credit hours (half-time) in an eligible program (one that leads to a degree or certificate). More than three quarters of all freshmen in fall 2007 who showed financial need and took at least 6 credit hours were offered some form of financial aid. The priority date for the financial aid application is May 1. All applications postmarked on or before January 15 are considered for UNO's numerous academic scholarships, including those of international students. The University of New Orleans also offers scholarships in jazz studies; classical music; fine arts; film, theater, and communication arts; and creative writing. These scholarships require either an audition or the submission of a portfolio or manuscript along with the scholarship application.

Faculty

UNO has 525 full-time and 175 part-time faculty members, most of whom participate in both graduate and undergraduate instruction and research activity. Graduate students serve as teaching assistants in laboratory courses under the close supervision of the faculty. Approximately 80 percent of the faculty members hold doctorates. Most full-time faculty members devote themselves exclusively to University-related pursuits and are integrally involved in student affairs through counseling, teaching, research, and social activities. The student-faculty ratio is 18:1.

Student Government

Every student enrolled at UNO is a member of the Student Government (SG). SG offers students a way to create effective change, express opinions and concerns, and utilize resources to enhance their educational experiences. Some of the programs SG currently offers and/or sponsors are Student Legal Services, the Academic Travel Fund, 24-hour study hall during finals week, UNO pep band (the Blue Zoo), UNO Soccer Club, the Mechanical Engineering Mini Baja Competition, UNO Jazz Night at the University Center, musical excursions, UNO Ambassadors Fishing Rodeo, the UNO student literary magazine *(Ellipsis)*, recreation and intramural sports, cheerleaders, and the Privateer dance team.

Admission Requirements

Students seeking admission to the University of New Orleans should submit their application as early as possible in their senior year. Admission requirements for Louisiana residents and nonresidents for fall 2008 include the completion of the Board of Regents core curriculum (in years): English (4), mathematics (3), science (3), social studies (3), foreign language (2), fine arts (1), mathematics/science elective (1), and computer science (½). Residents must also have either a high school cumulative GPA of at least 2.5 or an ACT composite score of at least 23 (1060 SAT) or rank in the top 25 percent of their high school graduating class, and students must not require more than one developmental/remedial course. Out-of-state students who do not meet the GPA, test score, and rank requirements must have a minimum ACT composite score of 26 (SAT 1170) for automatic admission.

Transfer requirements include the completion of 18 semester hours of nondevelopmental work, a minimum 2.25 cumulative GPA, and completion of all developmental course work before transferring. Students with fewer than 18 semester hours must meet both freshman and transfer requirements.

Application and Information

The University of New Orleans has a rolling admissions policy. The application fee is $40. Priority deadlines for application are as follows: July 1 for the fall semester, November 15 for the spring semester, and May 1 for the summer semester. Deadlines for international students are June 1, October 1, and March 1, respectively.

Office of Admissions
103 Administration Building
University of New Orleans
2000 Lakeshore Drive
New Orleans, Louisiana 70148

Phone: 504-280-6595
800-256-5-UNO (toll-free)
Fax: 504-280-5522
Web site: http://www.uno.edu

MAINE

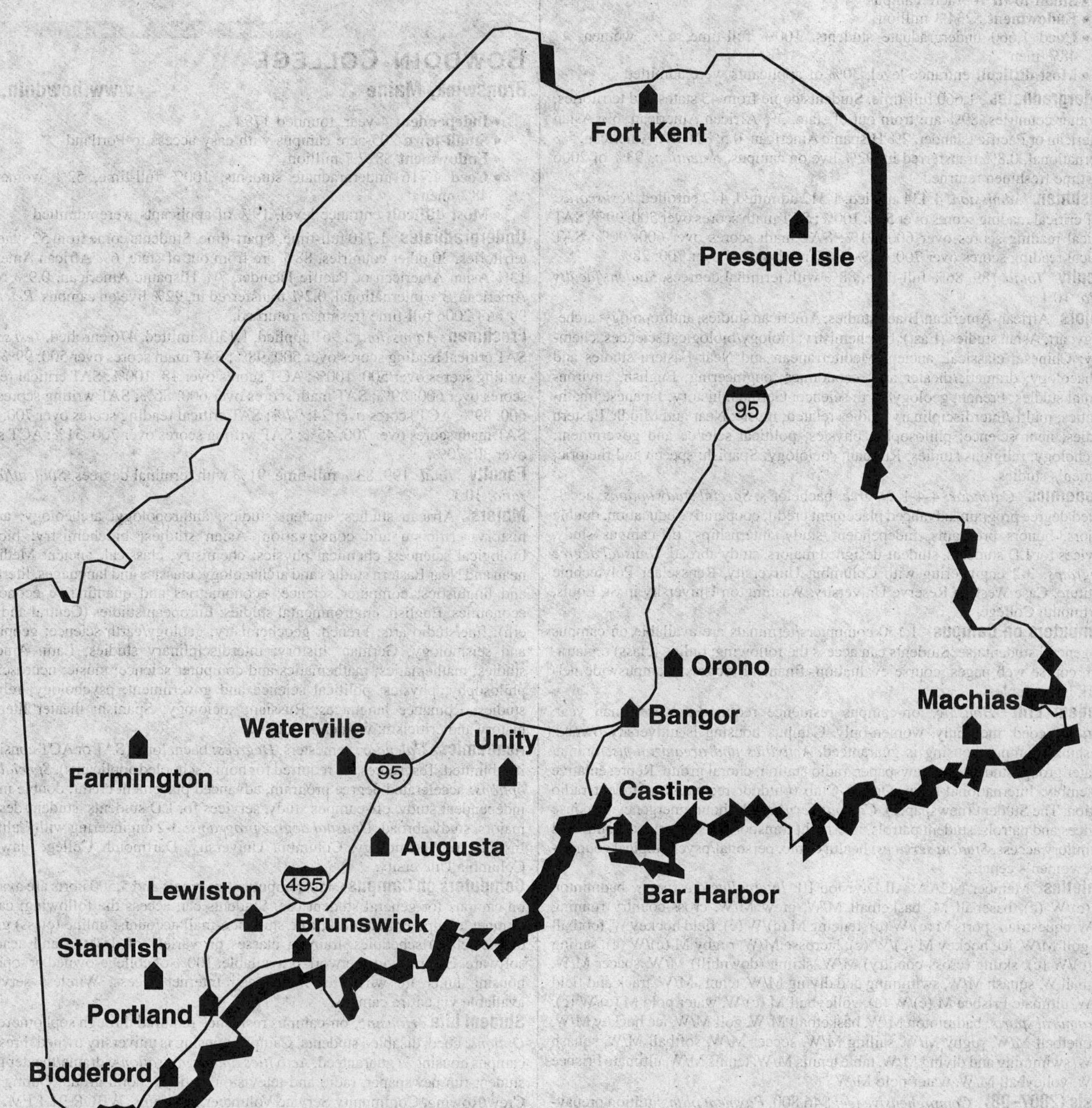

Fort Kent
Presque Isle
95
Orono
Machias
Bangor
Waterville
Unity
Farmington
95
Castine
Augusta
Bar Harbor
Lewiston
495
Brunswick
Standish
Portland
Biddeford
95

Bates College

Lewiston, Maine **www.bates.edu/**

- **Independent** 4-year, founded 1855
- **Small-town** 109-acre campus
- **Endowment** $234.3 million
- **Coed** 1,660 undergraduate students, 100% full-time, 52% women, 48% men
- **Most difficult** entrance level, 30% of applicants were admitted

Undergraduates 1,660 full-time. Students come from 45 states and territories, 78 other countries, 89% are from out of state, 3% African American, 6% Asian American or Pacific Islander, 2% Hispanic American, 0.5% Native American, 5% international, 0.8% transferred in, 92% live on campus. *Retention:* 93% of 2006 full-time freshmen returned.

Freshmen *Admission:* 4,434 applied, 1,312 admitted, 442 enrolled. *Test scores:* SAT critical reading scores over 500: 100%; SAT math scores over 500: 99%; SAT critical reading scores over 600: 91%; SAT math scores over 600: 90%; SAT critical reading scores over 700: 32%; SAT math scores over 700: 28%.

Faculty *Total:* 189, 86% full-time, 88% with terminal degrees. *Student/faculty ratio:* 10:1.

Majors African-American/Black studies; American studies; anthropology; archeology; art; Asian studies (East); biochemistry; biology/biological sciences; chemistry; Chinese; classical, ancient Mediterranean and Near Eastern studies and archaeology; dramatic/theater arts; economics; engineering; English; environmental studies; French; geology/earth science; German; history; Japanese; mathematics; multi-/interdisciplinary studies related; music; Near and Middle Eastern studies; neuroscience; philosophy; physics; political science and government; psychology; religious studies; Russian; sociology; Spanish; speech and rhetoric; women's studies.

Academics *Calendar:* 4-4-1. *Degree:* bachelor's. *Special study options:* accelerated degree program, advanced placement credit, cooperative education, double majors, honors programs, independent study, internships, off-campus study, services for LD students, student-designed majors, study abroad. *Unusual degree programs:* 3-2 engineering with Columbia University, Rensselaer Polytechnic Institute, Case Western Reserve University, Washington University in St. Louis, Dartmouth College.

Computers on Campus 1,150 computers/terminals are available on campus for general student use. Students can access the following: online (class) registration, course web pages, course evaluation, financial records. Campuswide network is available.

Student Life *Housing:* on-campus residence required for freshman year. *Options:* coed, men-only, women-only. Campus housing is university owned. Freshman campus housing is guaranteed. *Activities and organizations:* drama/theater group, student-run newspaper, radio station, choral group, Representative Assembly, International Club, Outing Club (outdoor recreation), student radio station, The Student (newspaper). *Campus security:* 24-hour emergency response devices and patrols, student patrols, late-night transport/escort service, controlled dormitory access. *Student services:* health clinic, personal/psychological counseling, women's center.

Athletics Member NCAA. All Division III. *Intercollegiate sports:* badminton M (c)/W (c), baseball M, basketball M/W, crew M/W, cross-country running M/W, equestrian sports M (c)/W (c), fencing M (c)/W (c), field hockey W, football M, golf M/W, ice hockey M (c)/W (c), lacrosse M/W, rugby M (c)/W (c), sailing M (c)/W (c), skiing (cross-country) M/W, skiing (downhill) M/W, soccer M/W, softball W, squash M/W, swimming and diving M/W, tennis M/W, track and field M/W, ultimate Frisbee M (c)/W (c), volleyball M (c)/W, water polo M (c)/W (c). *Intramural sports:* badminton M/W, basketball M/W, golf M/W, ice hockey M/W, racquetball M/W, rugby M/W, sailing M/W, soccer M/W, softball M/W, squash M/W, swimming and diving M/W, table tennis M/W, tennis M/W, ultimate Frisbee M/W, volleyball M/W, water polo M/W.

Costs (2007–08) *Comprehensive fee:* $46,800. *Payment plans:* tuition prepayment, installment. *Waivers:* employees or children of employees.

Financial Aid Of all full-time matriculated undergraduates who enrolled in 2007, 763 applied for aid, 698 were judged to have need, 619 had their need fully met. 573 Federal Work-Study jobs (averaging $1614). 71 state and other part-time jobs (averaging $1633). *Average percent of need met:* 100%. *Average financial aid package:* $30,341. *Average need-based loan:* $4041. *Average need-based gift aid:* $27,353. *Average indebtedness upon graduation:* $13,636. *Financial aid deadline:* 2/1.

Applying *Options:* electronic application, early admission, early decision, deferred entrance. *Application fee:* $60. *Required:* essay or personal statement, high school transcript, 3 letters of recommendation. *Recommended:* interview. *Application deadlines:* 1/1 (freshmen), 3/1 (transfers). *Early decision deadline:* 11/15 (for plan 1), 1/1 (for plan 2). *Notification:* 3/31 (freshmen), 4/1 (transfers), 12/20 (early decision plan 1), 2/15 (early decision plan 2).

Freshman Application Contact Mr. Wylie Mitchell, Dean of Admissions, Bates College, 23 Campus Avenue, Lewiston, ME 04240-6028. *Phone:* 207-786-6000. *Fax:* 207-786-6025. *E-mail:* admissions@bates.edu.

Bowdoin College

Brunswick, Maine **www.bowdoin.edu/**

- **Independent** 4-year, founded 1794
- **Small-town** 205-acre campus with easy access to Portland
- **Endowment** $827.7 million
- **Coed** 1,716 undergraduate students, 100% full-time, 52% women, 48% men
- **Most difficult** entrance level, 19% of applicants were admitted

Undergraduates 1,710 full-time, 6 part-time. Students come from 52 states and territories, 30 other countries, 88% are from out of state, 6% African American, 13% Asian American or Pacific Islander, 7% Hispanic American, 0.9% Native American, 3% international, 0.2% transferred in, 92% live on campus. *Retention:* 99% of 2006 full-time freshmen returned.

Freshmen *Admission:* 5,961 applied, 1,130 admitted, 476 enrolled. *Test scores:* SAT critical reading scores over 500: 98%; SAT math scores over 500: 99%; SAT writing scores over 500: 100%; ACT scores over 18: 100%; SAT critical reading scores over 600: 89%; SAT math scores over 600: 86%; SAT writing scores over 600: 89%; ACT scores over 24: 97%; SAT critical reading scores over 700: 49%; SAT math scores over 700: 45%; SAT writing scores over 700: 51%; ACT scores over 30: 70%.

Faculty *Total:* 199, 83% full-time, 91% with terminal degrees. *Student/faculty ratio:* 10:1.

Majors African studies; ancient studies; anthropology; archeology; art; art history, criticism and conservation; Asian studies; biochemistry; biology/biological sciences; chemical physics; chemistry; classical, ancient Mediterranean and Near Eastern studies and archaeology; classics and languages, literatures and linguistics; computer science; econometrics and quantitative economics; economics; English; environmental studies; European studies (Central and Eastern); fine/studio arts; French; geochemistry; geology/earth science; geophysics and seismology; German; history; interdisciplinary studies; Latin American studies; mathematics; mathematics and computer science; music; neuroscience; philosophy; physics; political science and government; psychology; religious studies; Romance languages; Russian; sociology; Spanish; theater literature, history and criticism; women's studies.

Academics *Calendar:* semesters. *Degrees:* bachelor's (SAT or ACT considered if submitted. Test scores are required for home-schooled applicants). *Special study options:* accelerated degree program, advanced placement credit, double majors, independent study, off-campus study, services for LD students, student-designed majors, study abroad. *Unusual degree programs:* 3-2 engineering with California Institute of Technology, Columbia University, Dartmouth College; law with Columbia University.

Computers on Campus 450 computers/terminals and 5,500 ports are available on campus for general student use. Students can access the following: campus intranet, computer help desk, free student e-mail accounts, online (class) grades, online (class) schedules, training classes on variety of desktop and academic software. Campuswide network is available. 100% of college-owned or -operated housing units are wired for high-speed Internet access. Wireless service is available via entire campus.

Student Life *Housing:* on-campus residence required through sophomore year. *Options:* coed, disabled students. Campus housing is university owned. Freshman campus housing is guaranteed. *Activities and organizations:* drama/theater group, student-run newspaper, radio and television station, choral group, Outing Club, Crew/Rowing, Community Service Volunteer Programs, WBOR 91.1 FM, Bowdoin Student Government. *Campus security:* 24-hour emergency response devices and patrols, late-night transport/escort service, controlled dormitory access, self-defense education, whistle program, safe ride service (daytime). *Student services:* health clinic, personal/psychological counseling, women's center.

Athletics Member NCAA. All Division III except men's and women's sailing (Division I), men's and women's skiing (cross-country) (Division I), men's and women's squash (Division I). *Intercollegiate sports:* baseball M, basketball M/W, crew M (c)/W (c), cross-country running M/W, equestrian sports M (c)/W (c), fencing M (c)/W (c), field hockey W, football M, golf M/W, ice hockey M/W, lacrosse M/W, rugby M (c)/W, sailing M/W, skiing (cross-country) M/W, skiing (downhill) M (c)/W (c), soccer M/W, softball W, squash M/W, swimming and diving M/W, tennis M/W, track and field M/W, ultimate Frisbee M (c)/W (c), volleyball M (c)/W, water polo M (c)/W (c). *Intramural sports:* badminton M/W, basketball M/W, cheerleading M (c)/W (c), field hockey M/W, football M/W, ice hockey M/W, rock climbing M (c)/W (c), skiing (cross-country) M (c)/W (c), soccer M/W, softball M/W, tennis M/W, ultimate Frisbee M/W, volleyball M/W, water polo M/W.

Costs (2007–08) *One-time required fee:* $100. *Comprehensive fee:* $46,260 includes full-time tuition ($35,990), mandatory fees ($380), and room and board ($9890). *College room only:* $4620. Room and board charges vary according to board plan. *Payment plans:* installment, deferred payment. *Waivers:* employees or children of employees.

Financial Aid Of all full-time matriculated undergraduates who enrolled in 2007, 891 applied for aid, 726 were judged to have need, 726 had their need fully met. 365 Federal Work-Study jobs (averaging $480). 507 state and other part-time jobs (averaging $1843). In 2007, 68 non-need-based awards were made. *Average percent of need met:* 100%. *Average financial aid package:* $31,382. *Average need-based loan:* $4422. *Average need-based gift aid:* $26,424. *Average non-need-based aid:* $1000. *Average indebtedness upon graduation:* $18,300. *Financial aid deadline:* 2/15.

Applying *Options:* electronic application, early admission, early decision, deferred entrance. *Application fee:* $60. *Required:* essay or personal statement, high school transcript, 3 letters of recommendation. *Recommended:* interview. *Application deadlines:* 1/1 (freshmen), 3/1 (transfers). *Early decision deadline:* 11/15 (for plan 1), 1/1 (for plan 2). *Notification:* 4/5 (freshmen), 4/1 (transfers), 12/31 (early decision plan 1), 2/15 (early decision plan 2).

Freshman Application Contact Peter T. Wiley, Associate Dean of Admissions, Bowdoin College, 5000 College Station, Brunswick, ME 04011-8441. *Phone:* 207-725-3190. *Fax:* 207-725-3101. *E-mail:* admissions@bowdoin.edu.

COLBY COLLEGE

Waterville, Maine www.colby.edu/

- **Independent** 4-year, founded 1813
- **Small-town** 714-acre campus
- **Endowment** $598.7 million
- **Coed** 1,867 undergraduate students, 100% full-time, 55% women, 45% men
- **Most difficult** entrance level, 32% of applicants were admitted

Undergraduates 1,867 full-time. Students come from 50 states and territories, 62 other countries, 90% are from out of state, 2% African American, 8% Asian American or Pacific Islander, 3% Hispanic American, 0.5% Native American, 6% international, 0.5% transferred in, 94% live on campus. *Retention:* 93% of 2006 full-time freshmen returned.

Freshmen *Admission:* 4,679 applied, 1,488 admitted, 467 enrolled. *Test scores:* SAT critical reading scores over 500: 99%; SAT math scores over 500: 99%; SAT writing scores over 500: 99%; ACT scores over 18: 100%; SAT critical reading scores over 600: 91%; SAT math scores over 600: 91%; SAT writing scores over 600: 87%; ACT scores over 24: 97%; SAT critical reading scores over 700: 45%; SAT math scores over 700: 38%; SAT writing scores over 700: 34%; ACT scores over 30: 47%.

Faculty *Total:* 228, 70% full-time, 83% with terminal degrees. *Student/faculty ratio:* 10:1.

Majors African-American/Black studies; American studies; anthropology; art; art history, criticism and conservation; Asian studies (East); biochemistry; biology/biological sciences; cell biology and histology; chemistry; classics and languages, literatures and linguistics; computer science; creative writing; dramatic/theater arts; economics; English; environmental science; environmental studies; French; geology/earth science; German; history; interdisciplinary studies; international/global studies; international relations and affairs; Latin American studies; mathematics; molecular biology; music; philosophy; physics; political science and government; psychology; religious studies; Russian studies; science, technology and society; sociology; Spanish; women's studies.

Academics *Calendar:* 4-1-4. *Degree:* bachelor's. *Special study options:* advanced placement credit, double majors, honors programs, independent study, internships, off-campus study, part-time degree program, services for LD students, student-designed majors, study abroad. *ROTC:* Army (c). *Unusual degree programs:* 3-2 engineering with Dartmouth College.

Computers on Campus 350 computers/terminals are available on campus for general student use. Students can access the following: campus intranet, computer help desk, free student e-mail accounts, online (class) grades, online (class) registration, online (class) schedules, Portal. Campuswide network is available. 100% of college-owned or -operated housing units are wired for high-speed Internet access. Wireless service is available via dorm rooms, learning centers, libraries, student centers.

Student Life *Housing:* on-campus residence required through senior year. *Options:* coed. Campus housing is university owned and leased by the school. Freshman campus housing is guaranteed. *Activities and organizations:* drama/theater group, student-run newspaper, radio station, choral group, Outing Club, volunteer center, WMHB-FM (College Radio Station), student government, Powder and Wig (theater). *Campus security:* 24-hour emergency response devices and patrols, late-night transport/escort service, controlled dormitory access, campus lighting, student emergency response team, self-defense class, property id program, party monitors. *Student services:* health clinic, personal/psychological counseling, women's center.

Athletics Member NCAA. All Division III except men's and women's skiing (cross-country) (Division I), men's and women's skiing (downhill) (Division I). *Intercollegiate sports:* badminton M (c)/W (c), baseball M, basketball M/W, crew M/W, cross-country running M/W, equestrian sports M (c)/W (c), fencing M (c)/W (c), field hockey W, football M, golf M/W, ice hockey M/W, lacrosse M/W, rugby M (c)/W (c), sailing M (c)/W (c), skiing (cross-country) M/W, skiing (downhill) M/W, soccer M/W, softball W, squash M/W, swimming and diving M/W, tennis M/W, track and field M/W, ultimate Frisbee M (c)/W (c), volleyball M (c)/W, water polo M (c)/W (c). *Intramural sports:* basketball M/W, football M/W, soccer M/W, softball M/W.

Standardized Tests *Required:* SAT or ACT (for admission).

Costs (2007–08) *Comprehensive fee:* $46,100.

Financial Aid Of all full-time matriculated undergraduates who enrolled in 2006, 795 applied for aid, 690 were judged to have need, 690 had their need fully met. 441 Federal Work-Study jobs (averaging $1533). 98 state and other part-time jobs (averaging $1655). *Average percent of need met:* 100%. *Average financial aid package:* $29,908. *Average need-based loan:* $3423. *Average need-based gift aid:* $28,041. *Average indebtedness upon graduation:* $17,542. *Financial aid deadline:* 2/1.

Applying *Options:* electronic application, early admission, early decision, deferred entrance. *Application fee:* $65. *Required:* essay or personal statement, high school transcript, 2 letters of recommendation. *Recommended:* interview. *Application deadlines:* 1/1 (freshmen), 3/1 (transfers). *Early decision deadline:* 11/15 (for plan 1), 1/1 (for plan 2). *Notification:* 4/1 (freshmen), 5/15 (transfers), 12/15 (early decision plan 1), 2/10 (early decision plan 2).

Freshman Application Contact Mr. Steve Thomas, Director of Admissions, Colby College, Office of Admissions and Financial Aid, 4800 Mayflower Hill, Waterville, ME 04901-8848. *Phone:* 207-859-4800. *Toll-free phone:* 800-723-3032. *Fax:* 207-859-4828. *E-mail:* admissions@colby.edu.

See page 1080 for the College Close-Up.

COLLEGE OF THE ATLANTIC

Bar Harbor, Maine www.coa.edu/

- **Independent** comprehensive, founded 1969
- **Small-town** 35-acre campus
- **Endowment** $20.0 million
- **Coed** 341 undergraduate students, 95% full-time, 64% women, 36% men
- **Very difficult** entrance level, 77% of applicants were admitted

Undergraduates 323 full-time, 18 part-time. Students come from 36 states and territories, 36 other countries, 80% are from out of state, 0.3% African American, 0.6% Asian American or Pacific Islander, 1% Hispanic American, 13% international, 6% transferred in, 31% live on campus. *Retention:* 85% of 2006 full-time freshmen returned.

Freshmen *Admission:* 305 applied, 235 admitted, 84 enrolled. *Average high school GPA:* 3.51. *Test scores:* SAT critical reading scores over 500: 98%; SAT math scores over 500: 94%; SAT writing scores over 500: 98%; ACT scores over 18: 100%; SAT critical reading scores over 600: 81%; SAT math scores over 600: 43%; SAT writing scores over 600: 70%; ACT scores over 24: 88%; SAT critical reading scores over 700: 23%; SAT math scores over 700: 13%; SAT writing scores over 700: 10%; ACT scores over 30: 38%.

Faculty *Total:* 41, 63% full-time, 68% with terminal degrees. *Student/faculty ratio:* 11:1.

Majors Art; biological and physical sciences; biology/biological sciences; botany/plant biology; ceramic arts and ceramics; computer graphics; drawing; economics; education; elementary education; English; environmental biology; environmental design/architecture; environmental education; environmental studies; evolutionary biology; human ecology; interdisciplinary studies; landscape architecture; legal studies; liberal arts and sciences/liberal studies; literature; marine biology and biological oceanography; maritime science; middle school education; museum studies; music; natural sciences; oceanography; philosophy; pre-veterinary studies; psychology; public policy analysis; science teacher education; secondary education; wildlife biology; zoology/animal biology.

Academics *Calendar:* 3 10-week terms. *Degrees:* bachelor's and master's. *Special study options:* academic remediation for entering students, accelerated degree program, advanced placement credit, cooperative education, independent study, internships, off-campus study, part-time degree program, services for LD students, student-designed majors, study abroad.

Computers on Campus 38 computers/terminals and 50 ports are available on campus for general student use. Students can access the following: computer help desk, free student e-mail accounts, online (class) schedules. Campuswide network is available. 100% of college-owned or -operated housing units are wired for high-speed Internet access. Wireless service is available via entire campus.

Student Life *Housing:* on-campus residence required for freshman year. *Options:* coed. Campus housing is university owned. Freshman campus housing is guaranteed. *Activities and organizations:* drama/theater group, student-run newspaper, choral group, Sustain US, All College Meeting, Outdoor Program, Open Mic, Student Meeting. *Campus security:* 24-hour emergency response devices and patrols, late-night transport/escort service. *Student services:* health clinic, personal/psychological counseling, women's center.

Athletics *Intramural sports:* badminton M/W, basketball M, bowling M/W, ice hockey M/W, sailing M/W, skiing (cross-country) M/W, soccer M/W, softball M/W, table tennis M/W, volleyball M/W, water polo M/W.

Standardized Tests *Recommended:* SAT or ACT (for admission).

Costs (2007–08) *Comprehensive fee:* $38,160 includes full-time tuition ($29,520), mandatory fees ($450), and room and board ($8190). Part-time tuition: $3280 per credit. *Required fees:* $150 per term part-time. *College room only:* $5100. Room and board charges vary according to board plan. *Payment plan:* installment. *Waivers:* adult students, senior citizens, and employees or children of employees.

Financial Aid Of all full-time matriculated undergraduates who enrolled in 2007, 264 applied for aid, 257 were judged to have need, 168 had their need fully met. 202 Federal Work-Study jobs (averaging $2288). 48 state and other part-time jobs (averaging $1293). In 2007, 11 non-need-based awards were made. *Average percent of need met:* 97%. *Average financial aid package:* $27,041. *Average need-based loan:* $4294. *Average need-based gift aid:* $20,437. *Average non-need-based aid:* $4518. *Average indebtedness upon graduation:* $19,692.

Applying *Options:* electronic application, early admission, early decision, deferred entrance. *Application fee:* $45. *Required:* essay or personal statement, high school transcript, 3 letters of recommendation. *Required for some:* interview. *Recommended:* minimum 3.0 GPA, interview. *Application deadlines:* 2/15 (freshmen), 4/1 (transfers). *Early decision deadline:* 12/1 (for plan 1), 1/10 (for plan 2). *Notification:* 4/1 (freshmen), 4/25 (transfers), 12/15 (early decision plan 1), 1/25 (early decision plan 2).

Freshman Application Contact Ms. Sarah Baker, Director of Admission, College of the Atlantic, 105 Eden Street, Bar Harbor, ME 04609-1198. *Phone:* 207-288-5015 Ext. 233. *Toll-free phone:* 800-528-0025. *Fax:* 207-288-4126. *E-mail:* inquiry@coa.edu.

See page 1082 for the College Close-Up.

HUSSON COLLEGE

Bangor, Maine **www.husson.edu/**

- **Independent** comprehensive, founded 1898
- **Suburban** 170-acre campus
- **Endowment** $4.8 million
- **Coed** 2,087 undergraduate students, 81% full-time, 59% women, 41% men
- **Moderately difficult** entrance level, 91% of applicants were admitted

Undergraduates 1,695 full-time, 392 part-time. Students come from 23 states and territories, 26 other countries, 15% are from out of state, 4% African American, 2% Asian American or Pacific Islander, 0.6% Hispanic American, 0.6% Native American, 0.8% international, 7% transferred in, 43% live on campus. *Retention:* 69% of 2006 full-time freshmen returned.

Freshmen *Admission:* 1,175 applied, 1,066 admitted, 404 enrolled. *Average high school GPA:* 3.1. *Test scores:* SAT critical reading scores over 500: 26%; SAT math scores over 500: 33%; SAT writing scores over 500: 27%; ACT scores over 18: 67%; SAT critical reading scores over 600: 3%; SAT math scores over 600: 6%; SAT writing scores over 600: 2%; ACT scores over 24: 15%; SAT math scores over 700: 1%; SAT writing scores over 700: 1%; ACT scores over 30: 3%.

Faculty *Total:* 85, 93% full-time, 53% with terminal degrees. *Student/faculty ratio:* 19:1.

Majors Accounting; accounting and computer science; banking and financial support services; biology/biological sciences; biology teacher education; business administration and management; chemistry; chemistry teacher education; clinical psychology; computer programming; computer programming (specific applications); criminal justice/police science; criminal justice/safety; criminology; elementary education; finance; hospitality administration; information science/studies; international business/trade/commerce; legal assistant/paralegal; liberal arts and sciences/liberal studies; management information systems; marketing/marketing management; nursing (registered nurse training); occupational therapy; physical education teaching and coaching; physical therapy; physics teacher education; sales, distribution and marketing; small business administration; sport and fitness administration/management.

Academics *Calendar:* semesters. *Degrees:* associate, bachelor's, master's, post-master's, and postbachelor's certificates. *Special study options:* academic remediation for entering students, adult/continuing education programs, advanced placement credit, cooperative education, double majors, English as a second language, independent study, internships, part-time degree program, services for LD students, student-designed majors, summer session for credit. *ROTC:* Army (c), Navy (c). *Unusual degree programs:* 3-2 business administration.

Computers on Campus 57 computers/terminals are available on campus for general student use. Students can access the following: campus intranet, computer help desk, free student e-mail accounts, online (class) grades, online (class) registration, online (class) schedules. Campuswide network is available. 100% of college-owned or -operated housing units are wired for high-speed Internet access. Wireless service is available via entire campus.

Student Life *Housing:* on-campus residence required through senior year. *Options:* coed. Campus housing is university owned. Freshman campus housing is guaranteed. *Activities and organizations:* drama/theater group, student-run newspaper, radio station, Student Government, Organization of Student Nurses, Organization of Physical Therapy Students, Accounting Society, Criminal Justice Club, national fraternities. *Campus security:* 24-hour emergency response devices and patrols, late-night transport/escort service, controlled dormitory access. *Student services:* health clinic, personal/psychological counseling.

Athletics Member NCAA. All Division III. *Intercollegiate sports:* baseball M, basketball M/W, field hockey W, football M, golf M/W, lacrosse M/W, soccer M/W, softball W, swimming and diving W, tennis W, volleyball W. *Intramural sports:* baseball M, basketball M/W, cheerleading M/W, football M, ice hockey M/W, lacrosse M, soccer M/W, softball M/W, swimming and diving M/W, tennis M/W, volleyball M/W, water polo M/W, wrestling M.

Standardized Tests *Required:* SAT or ACT (for admission).

Costs (2007–08) *Comprehensive fee:* $18,750 includes full-time tuition ($11,970), mandatory fees ($280), and room and board ($6500). Full-time tuition and fees vary according to class time. Part-time tuition: $399 per credit hour. Part-time tuition and fees vary according to class time and course load. *Payment plans:* tuition prepayment, installment. *Waivers:* senior citizens and employees or children of employees.

Financial Aid Of all full-time matriculated undergraduates who enrolled in 2007, 1,471 applied for aid, 1,292 were judged to have need, 151 had their need fully met. 635 Federal Work-Study jobs (averaging $1350). In 2007, 226 non-need-based awards were made. *Average percent of need met:* 73%. *Average financial aid package:* $9952. *Average need-based loan:* $3786. *Average need-based gift aid:* $6581. *Average non-need-based aid:* $9988. *Average indebtedness upon graduation:* $19,380.

Applying *Options:* electronic application, early admission, deferred entrance. *Application fee:* $25. *Required:* essay or personal statement, high school transcript, 1 letter of recommendation. *Recommended:* interview. *Application deadlines:* 9/1 (freshmen), 9/1 (transfers). *Notification:* continuous (freshmen), continuous until 9/1 (transfers).

Freshman Application Contact Mrs. Jane Goodwin, Director of Admissions, Husson College, One College Circle, Bangor, ME 04401-2999. *Phone:* 207-941-7100. *Toll-free phone:* 800-4-HUSSON. *Fax:* 207-941-7935. *E-mail:* admit@husson.edu.

MAINE COLLEGE OF ART

Portland, Maine **www.meca.edu/**

- **Independent** comprehensive, founded 1882
- **Urban** campus with easy access to Boston
- **Endowment** $3.9 million
- **Coed**
- **Moderately difficult** entrance level

Faculty *Student/faculty ratio:* 9:1.

Academics *Calendar:* semesters. *Degrees:* bachelor's, master's, and postbachelor's certificates.

Student Life *Campus security:* 24-hour emergency response devices and patrols, controlled dormitory access.

Standardized Tests *Required:* SAT or ACT (for admission).

Costs (2008–09) *Tuition:* $26,490 full-time, $1104 per credit part-time. *Required fees:* $1250 full-time.

Financial Aid Of all full-time matriculated undergraduates who enrolled in 2005, 323 applied for aid, 292 were judged to have need, 29 had their need fully met. 54 Federal Work-Study jobs (averaging $2151). In 2005, 42 non-need-based awards were made. *Average percent of need met:* 56. *Average financial aid package:* $13,894. *Average need-based loan:* $3965. *Average need-based gift aid:* $10,174. *Average non-need-based aid:* $6860. *Average indebtedness upon graduation:* $33,350.

Applying *Options:* electronic application, early admission, deferred entrance. *Application fee:* $40. *Required:* essay or personal statement, high school transcript, 2 letters of recommendation, portfolio. *Recommended:* minimum 2.0 GPA, interview.

Freshman Application Contact Ms. Blaise MacCarrone, Admissions Coordinator, Maine College of Art, 97 Spring Street, Portland, ME 04101-3987. *Phone:* 207-879-5742 Ext. 726. *Toll-free phone:* 800-639-4808. *Fax:* 207-871-1349. *E-mail:* admissions@meca.edu.

MAINE MARITIME ACADEMY

Castine, Maine **www.mainemaritime.edu/**

- **State-supported** comprehensive, founded 1941
- **Small-town** 35-acre campus
- **Endowment** $20.0 million
- **Coed, primarily men** 842 undergraduate students, 98% full-time, 16% women, 84% men
- **Moderately difficult** entrance level, 65% of applicants were admitted

Undergraduates 822 full-time, 20 part-time. Students come from 35 states and territories, 8 other countries, 31% are from out of state, 0.5% African American, 0.3% Asian American or Pacific Islander, 1% Hispanic American, 0.8% Native American, 0.2% international, 3% transferred in, 80% live on campus. *Retention:* 80% of 2006 full-time freshmen returned.

Freshmen *Admission:* 820 applied, 533 admitted, 250 enrolled. *Average high school GPA:* 2.8.

Faculty *Total:* 90, 77% full-time, 22% with terminal degrees. *Student/faculty ratio:* 12:1.

Majors Business administration and management; engineering; engineering technology; international business/trade/commerce; logistics and materials management; marine biology and biological oceanography; marine science/merchant marine officer; naval architecture and marine engineering; oceanography (chemical and physical); systems engineering; transportation technology.

Academics *Calendar:* semesters. *Degrees:* associate, bachelor's, and master's. *Special study options:* academic remediation for entering students, adult/continuing education programs, advanced placement credit, distance learning, double majors, independent study, internships, off-campus study, student-designed majors, study abroad. *ROTC:* Army (b), Navy (b).

Computers on Campus 40 computers/terminals are available on campus for general student use. Students can access the following: online (class) registration. Campuswide network is available. 100% of college-owned or -operated housing units are wired for high-speed Internet access. Wireless service is available via classrooms, dorm rooms, libraries.

Student Life *Housing:* on-campus residence required through junior year. *Options:* coed. Campus housing is university owned. Freshman campus housing is guaranteed. *Activities and organizations:* drama/theater group, choral group, marching band, Rugby Club, Yacht Club, Alpha Phi Omega, Chess Club, Drill Team. *Campus security:* 24-hour patrols, student patrols. *Student services:* health clinic, personal/psychological counseling, women's center.

Athletics Member NCAA. All Division III. *Intercollegiate sports:* basketball M/W, cross-country running M/W, football M, lacrosse M, sailing M/W, soccer M/W, softball W, volleyball W. *Intramural sports:* basketball M/W, golf M/W, ice hockey M, racquetball M/W, riflery M/W, rock climbing M, rugby M/W, sailing M/W, skiing (downhill) M/W, softball M/W, squash M/W, swimming and diving M/W, tennis M/W, volleyball M, weight lifting M/W.

Standardized Tests *Required:* SAT or ACT (for admission).

Costs (2007–08) *Tuition:* state resident $7000 full-time, $250 per credit hour part-time; nonresident $13,600 full-time, $450 per credit hour part-time. Full-time tuition and fees vary according to course load and program. Part-time tuition and fees vary according to course load and program. *Required fees:* $1805 full-time. *Room and board:* $7400; room only: $2700. Room and board charges vary according to board plan. *Payment plan:* installment.

Financial Aid Of all full-time matriculated undergraduates who enrolled in 2006, 749 applied for aid, 608 were judged to have need, 121 had their need fully met. 152 Federal Work-Study jobs (averaging $704). In 2006, 42 non-need-based awards were made. *Average percent of need met:* 61%. *Average financial aid package:* $8363. *Average need-based loan:* $4529. *Average need-based gift aid:* $1656. *Average non-need-based aid:* $2500. *Average indebtedness upon graduation:* $30,341.

Applying *Options:* electronic application, early admission, early decision, deferred entrance. *Application fee:* $15. *Required:* high school transcript, 1 letter of recommendation, physical examination. *Recommended:* interview. *Application deadlines:* 7/1 (freshmen), 7/1 (transfers). *Early decision deadline:* 12/20. *Notification:* 1/1 (early decision).

Freshman Application Contact Mr. Jeffery Wright, Director of Admissions, Maine Maritime Academy, Castine, ME 04420. *Phone:* 207-326-2215. *Toll-free phone:* 800-464-6565 (in-state); 800-227-8465 (out-of-state). *Fax:* 207-326-2515. *E-mail:* admissions@mma.edu.

NEW ENGLAND SCHOOL OF COMMUNICATIONS

Bangor, Maine **www.nescom.edu/**

- **Independent** 4-year, founded 1981, administratively affiliated with Husson College
- **Small-town** 200-acre campus
- **Coed, primarily men** 393 undergraduate students, 95% full-time, 24% women, 76% men
- **Minimally difficult** entrance level, 66% of applicants were admitted

Undergraduates 375 full-time, 18 part-time. Students come from 11 states and territories, 4 other countries, 19% are from out of state, 2% African American, 0.8% Asian American or Pacific Islander, 3% Hispanic American, 0.5% Native American, 5% transferred in, 54% live on campus.

Freshmen *Admission:* 354 applied, 235 admitted, 146 enrolled. *Average high school GPA:* 2.5.

Faculty *Total:* 57, 19% full-time, 25% with terminal degrees. *Student/faculty ratio:* 15:1.

Majors Advertising; animation, interactive technology, video graphics and special effects; audio engineering; broadcast journalism; cinematography and film/video production; communication and journalism related; communications technologies and support services related; computer graphics; computer software and media applications related; film/video and photographic arts related; graphic communications; intermedia/multimedia; marketing/marketing management; photographic and film/video technology; public relations/image management; radio and television; radio and television broadcasting technology; recording arts technology; web/multimedia management and webmaster; web page, digital/multimedia and information resources design.

Academics *Calendar:* semesters. *Degrees:* associate and bachelor's. *Special study options:* adult/continuing education programs, advanced placement credit, double majors, English as a second language, internships, part-time degree program, services for LD students, student-designed majors, summer session for credit. *ROTC:* Army (c).

Computers on Campus 175 computers/terminals are available on campus for general student use. Students can access the following: campus intranet, computer help desk, free student e-mail accounts. Campuswide network is available. 100% of college-owned or -operated housing units are wired for high-speed Internet access. Wireless service is available via classrooms, computer centers, computer labs, dorm rooms, learning centers, libraries, student centers.

Student Life *Housing options:* coed. Campus housing is university owned. Freshman applicants given priority for college housing. *Activities and organizations:* drama/theater group, student-run newspaper, radio and television station, choral group, marching band, drama, newspaper, student government, radio station, Audio Engineering Society, national fraternities, national sororities. *Campus security:* 24-hour emergency response devices and patrols, late-night transport/escort service. *Student services:* health clinic, personal/psychological counseling.

Athletics *Intramural sports:* basketball M/W, cheerleading M/W, lacrosse M/W, soccer M/W, softball M/W, swimming and diving M/W, table tennis M/W, tennis M/W, volleyball M/W, water polo M/W.

Standardized Tests *Required:* Wonderlic aptitude test (for admission). *Recommended:* SAT or ACT (for admission).

Costs (2008–09) *Comprehensive fee:* $17,405 includes full-time tuition ($10,400), mandatory fees ($280), and room and board ($6725). Part-time tuition: $350 per credit.

Financial Aid Of all full-time matriculated undergraduates who enrolled in 2006, 265 applied for aid, 265 were judged to have need, 37 had their need fully met. 40 Federal Work-Study jobs (averaging $1000). 6 state and other part-time jobs (averaging $2200). *Average percent of need met:* 27%. *Average financial aid package:* $5372. *Average need-based loan:* $3800. *Average need-based gift aid:* $2200. *Average indebtedness upon graduation:* $20,000.

Applying *Options:* electronic application, early admission, deferred entrance. *Application fee:* $15. *Required:* essay or personal statement, high school transcript, 2 letters of recommendation, interview. *Application deadlines:* rolling (freshmen), rolling (transfers). *Notification:* continuous (freshmen), continuous (transfers).

Freshman Application Contact Ms. Louise Grant, Director of Admissions, New England School of Communications, 1 College Circle, Bangor, ME 04401. *Phone:* 207-941-7176 Ext. 1093. *Toll-free phone:* 888-877-1876. *Fax:* 207-947-3987. *E-mail:* info@nescom.edu.

SAINT JOSEPH'S COLLEGE OF MAINE

Standish, Maine **www.sjcme.edu/**

- **Independent** comprehensive, founded 1912, affiliated with Roman Catholic Church
- **Small-town** 350-acre campus
- **Endowment** $9.2 million
- **Coed**
- **Moderately difficult** entrance level

Faculty *Student/faculty ratio:* 15:1.

Academics *Calendar:* semesters. *Degrees:* bachelor's and master's (profile does not include enrollment in distance learning master's program).

Student Life *Campus security:* 24-hour emergency response devices and patrols, late-night transport/escort service, controlled dormitory access.

Athletics Member NCAA. All Division III.

Standardized Tests *Required:* SAT or ACT (for admission).

Costs (2007–08) *Comprehensive fee:* $32,900 includes full-time tuition ($22,500), mandatory fees ($800), and room and board ($9600). Full-time tuition and fees vary according to program. Part-time tuition: $400 per credit. Part-time tuition and fees vary according to course load, degree level, and program. *Required fees:* $140 per term part-time.

Financial Aid Of all full-time matriculated undergraduates who enrolled in 2006, 889 applied for aid, 803 were judged to have need, 297 had their need fully met. 402 Federal Work-Study jobs (averaging $1400). In 2006, 190 non-need-based awards were made. *Average percent of need met:* 82. *Average financial aid package:* $17,436. *Average need-based loan:* $6250. *Average need-based gift aid:* $11,390. *Average non-need-based aid:* $13,262. *Average indebtedness upon graduation:* $36,351.

Applying *Options:* electronic application, early action, deferred entrance. *Application fee:* $50. *Required:* essay or personal statement, high school transcript, minimum 2.0 GPA, 2 letters of recommendation. *Recommended:* interview.

Freshman Application Contact Mr. Vincent J. Kloskowski, Dean of Admission, Saint Joseph's College of Maine, 278 Whites Bridge Road, Standish, ME 04084-5263. *Phone:* 207-893-7746. *Toll-free phone:* 800-338-7057. *Fax:* 207-893-7862. *E-mail:* admission@sjcme.edu.

THOMAS COLLEGE

Waterville, Maine **www.thomas.edu/**

- **Independent** comprehensive, founded 1894
- **Small-town** 70-acre campus
- **Endowment** $5.8 million
- **Coed** 765 undergraduate students, 83% full-time, 49% women, 51% men
- **Minimally difficult** entrance level, 81% of applicants were admitted

Undergraduates 633 full-time, 132 part-time. Students come from 10 states and territories, 1 other country, 20% are from out of state, 2% African American, 0.9% Asian American or Pacific Islander, 0.7% Hispanic American, 0.3% Native American, 0.1% international, 1% transferred in, 64% live on campus. *Retention:* 64% of 2006 full-time freshmen returned.

Freshmen *Admission:* 668 applied, 543 admitted, 230 enrolled. *Average high school GPA:* 2.7. *Test scores:* SAT critical reading scores over 500: 24%; SAT math scores over 500: 29%; SAT writing scores over 500: 25%; ACT scores over 18: 56%; SAT critical reading scores over 600: 2%; SAT math scores over 600: 7%; SAT writing scores over 600: 3%; ACT scores over 24: 12%; SAT critical reading scores over 700: 1%; SAT math scores over 700: 1%.

Faculty *Total:* 81, 26% full-time, 26% with terminal degrees. *Student/faculty ratio:* 18:1.

Majors Accounting; business administration and management; computer and information sciences; computer management; computer science; criminal justice/law enforcement administration; elementary education; finance; hotel/motel administration; human resources management; international business/trade/commerce; liberal arts and sciences/liberal studies; management information systems; marketing/marketing management; psychology; sport and fitness administration/management.

Academics *Calendar:* semesters. *Degrees:* associate, bachelor's, and master's (associate). *Special study options:* academic remediation for entering students, adult/continuing education programs, advanced placement credit, cooperative education, double majors, internships, off-campus study, part-time degree program, study abroad, summer session for credit.

Computers on Campus 120 computers/terminals are available on campus for general student use. Students can access the following: online (class) registration. Campuswide network is available. Wireless service is available via entire campus.

Student Life *Housing options:* coed. Campus housing is university owned. Freshman campus housing is guaranteed. *Activities and organizations:* drama/theater group, student-run newspaper, choral group, Phi Beta Lambda, Students Club, GLOBE, Campus Activity Board, peer advisors, national fraternities, national sororities. *Campus security:* 24-hour emergency response devices and patrols, student patrols, controlled dormitory access. *Student services:* health clinic, personal/psychological counseling.

Athletics Member NCAA, NAIA. All NCAA Division III. *Intercollegiate sports:* baseball M, basketball M/W, field hockey W, golf M, lacrosse M/W, soccer M/W, softball W, tennis M, volleyball W.

Standardized Tests *Required:* SAT (for admission).

Costs (2007–08) *Comprehensive fee:* $26,490 includes full-time tuition ($18,230), mandatory fees ($480), and room and board ($7780). Part-time tuition: $760 per credit hour. *College room only:* $3920. Room and board charges vary according to board plan and housing facility. *Payment plan:* deferred payment. *Waivers:* employees or children of employees.

Financial Aid Of all full-time matriculated undergraduates who enrolled in 2007, 581 applied for aid, 561 were judged to have need, 98 had their need fully met. In 2007, 18 non-need-based awards were made. *Average percent of need met:* 85%. *Average financial aid package:* $18,009. *Average need-based loan:* $4586. *Average need-based gift aid:* $10,472. *Average non-need-based aid:* $8812. *Average indebtedness upon graduation:* $38,734.

Applying *Options:* electronic application, early action, deferred entrance. *Application fee:* $50. *Required:* essay or personal statement, high school transcript, 1 letter of recommendation. *Recommended:* minimum 2.0 GPA, interview, rank in upper 50% of high school class. *Application deadlines:* rolling (freshmen), rolling (transfers), 12/15 (early action). *Notification:* continuous (freshmen), continuous (transfers), 12/31 (early action).

Freshman Application Contact Mr. James Love, Dean of Admissions, Thomas College, 180 West River Road, Waterville, ME 04901. *Phone:* 207-859-1101. *Toll-free phone:* 800-339-7001. *Fax:* 207-859-1114. *E-mail:* admiss@thomas.edu.

UNITY COLLEGE

Unity, Maine **www.unity.edu/**

- **Independent** 4-year, founded 1965
- **Rural** 265-acre campus
- **Endowment** $2.4 million
- **Coed**
- **Moderately difficult** entrance level

Unity College offers more environmental majors than any other college in the country. The curriculum is a unique combination of liberal arts and professional preparation in environmental fields. The emphasis on fieldwork enables students to take classroom theory and find practical applications to tackle environmental issues. This combination of rigorous academics and hands-on experience ensures that Unity graduates become leaders in environmental stewardship.

Faculty *Student/faculty ratio:* 14:1.

Academics *Calendar:* semesters. *Degrees:* associate and bachelor's.

Student Life *Campus security:* 24-hour emergency response devices and patrols.

Athletics Member NSCAA.

Standardized Tests *Required for some:* SAT or ACT (for admission). *Recommended:* SAT or ACT (for admission).

Costs (2007–08) *Tuition:* $18,630 full-time. *Required fees:* $1000 full-time.

Financial Aid Of all full-time matriculated undergraduates who enrolled in 2006, 477 applied for aid, 435 were judged to have need, 155 had their need fully met. 326 Federal Work-Study jobs (averaging $1451). 8 state and other part-time jobs (averaging $1188). In 2006, 83 non-need-based awards were made. *Average percent of need met:* 78. *Average financial aid package:* $14,593. *Average need-based loan:* $6149. *Average need-based gift aid:* $8211. *Average non-need-based aid:* $8706.

Applying *Options:* electronic application, early admission, early action, deferred entrance. *Application fee:* $25. *Required:* essay or personal statement, high school transcript, 2 letters of recommendation. *Required for some:* interview. *Recommended:* minimum 2.0 GPA, interview.

Freshman Application Contact Mr. Gary Zane, Dean of Students, Unity College, PO Box 532, Unity, ME 04988-0532. *Phone:* 207-948-3131. *Fax:* 207-948-6277. *E-mail:* gzane@unity.edu.

UNIVERSITY OF MAINE

Orono, Maine www.umaine.edu/

- **State-supported** university, founded 1865, part of University of Maine System
- **Small-town** 3300-acre campus
- **Endowment** $159.6 million
- **Coed** 9,596 undergraduate students, 82% full-time, 51% women, 49% men
- **Moderately difficult** entrance level, 77% of applicants were admitted

Undergraduates 7,892 full-time, 1,704 part-time. Students come from 48 states and territories, 65 other countries, 16% are from out of state, 1% African American, 1% Asian American or Pacific Islander, 0.9% Hispanic American, 2% Native American, 2% international, 5% transferred in, 42% live on campus.

Freshmen *Admission:* 6,958 applied, 5,387 admitted, 1,935 enrolled. *Average high school GPA:* 3.12. *Test scores:* SAT critical reading scores over 500: 65%; SAT math scores over 500: 70%; SAT writing scores over 500: 64%; ACT scores over 18: 90%; SAT critical reading scores over 600: 22%; SAT math scores over 600: 26%; SAT writing scores over 600: 18%; ACT scores over 24: 38%; SAT critical reading scores over 700: 4%; SAT math scores over 700: 4%; SAT writing scores over 700: 1%; ACT scores over 30: 7%.

Faculty *Total:* 811, 62% full-time, 64% with terminal degrees. *Student/faculty ratio:* 16:1.

Majors Agribusiness; agricultural/biological engineering and bioengineering; agricultural economics; animal sciences; anthropology; art; art history, criticism and conservation; art teacher education; biochemistry; biology/biological sciences; biology teacher education; biomedical sciences; botany/plant biology; business administration and management; business/commerce; cell biology and histology; chemical engineering; chemistry; chemistry teacher education; child development; civil engineering; classics and languages, literatures and linguistics; clinical laboratory science/medical technology; communication disorders; communication/speech communication and rhetoric; computer engineering; computer science; construction engineering technology; drafting and design technology; dramatic/theater arts; ecology; economics; education; educational/instructional media design; education (K-12); electrical, electronic and communications engineering technology; electrical, electronics and communications engineering; elementary education; engineering physics; engineering technology; English; English/language arts teacher education; environmental science; finance; fine/studio arts; food science; foods, nutrition, and wellness; foreign languages and literatures; foreign language teacher education; forest engineering; forestry; French; French language teacher education; geology/earth science; German; health teacher education; history; history teacher education; human development and family studies; international relations and affairs; journalism; labor and industrial relations; landscaping and groundskeeping; Latin; liberal arts and sciences/liberal studies; management information systems; marine biology and biological oceanography; mass communication/media; mathematics; mathematics teacher education; mechanical engineering; mechanical engineering/mechanical technology; medical microbiology and bacteriology; modern languages; molecular biology; music; music teacher education; natural resources management and policy; natural sciences; nursing (registered nurse training); ornamental horticulture; parks, recreation and leisure facilities management; philosophy; physical education teaching and coaching; physics; plant sciences; political science and government; pre-medical studies; pre-veterinary studies; psychology; public administration; Romance languages; science teacher education; secondary education; social studies teacher education; social work; sociology; soil science and agronomy; Spanish; Spanish language teacher education; speech/theater education; surveying engineering; survey technology; systems engineering; wildlife and wildlands science and management; women's studies; wood science and wood products/pulp and paper technology; zoology/animal biology.

Academics *Calendar:* semesters. *Degrees:* bachelor's, master's, doctoral, and post-master's certificates. *Special study options:* accelerated degree program, adult/continuing education programs, advanced placement credit, cooperative education, distance learning, double majors, English as a second language, external degree program, freshman honors college, honors programs, independent study, internships, off-campus study, part-time degree program, services for LD students, student-designed majors, study abroad, summer session for credit. *ROTC:* Army (b), Navy (b).

Computers on Campus 500 computers/terminals are available on campus for general student use. Students can access the following: online (class) registration, online grade and financial aid information, e-mail. Campuswide network is available.

Student Life *Housing:* on-campus residence required for freshman year. *Options:* coed, disabled students. Campus housing is university owned. Freshman campus housing is guaranteed. *Activities and organizations:* drama/theater group, student-run newspaper, radio station, choral group, marching band, Volunteers in Community Efforts/VOICE, Circle K, Campus Crusade for Christ, Outing Club, Wilde Stein, national fraternities, national sororities. *Campus security:* 24-hour emergency response devices and patrols, late-night transport/escort service, controlled dormitory access. *Student services:* health clinic, personal/psychological counseling, women's center, legal services.

Athletics Member NCAA. All Division I except football (Division I-A). *Intercollegiate sports:* baseball M (s), basketball M (s)/W (s), cross-country running M (s)/W (s), field hockey W (s), ice hockey M (s)/W (s), soccer M (s)/W (s), softball W (s), swimming and diving M/W (s), track and field M (s)/W (s), volleyball W (s). *Intramural sports:* badminton M/W, basketball M/W, cross-country running M/W, equestrian sports M (c)/W (c), fencing M (c)/W (c), field hockey M (c)/W (c), golf M/W, lacrosse M (c)/W (c), racquetball M/W, rock climbing M (c)/W (c), rugby M (c)/W (c), skiing (cross-country) M/W, skiing (downhill) M (c)/W (c), soccer M/W, softball M/W, swimming and diving M/W, table tennis M/W, tennis M/W, track and field M/W, ultimate Frisbee M (c)/W (c), volleyball M (c)/W (c), water polo M/W, weight lifting M (c)/W (c), wrestling M (c).

Standardized Tests *Required:* SAT or ACT (for admission).

Costs (2007–08) *Tuition:* state resident $8330 full-time, $218 per credit hour part-time; nonresident $20,540 full-time, $625 per credit hour part-time. Full-time tuition and fees vary according to reciprocity agreements. Part-time tuition and fees vary according to reciprocity agreements. *Room and board:* $7484. Room and board charges vary according to board plan and housing facility. *Payment plan:* installment. *Waivers:* employees or children of employees.

Financial Aid Of all full-time matriculated undergraduates who enrolled in 2006, 6,329 applied for aid, 5,024 were judged to have need, 1,655 had their need fully met. 1,699 Federal Work-Study jobs (averaging $2140). In 2006, 1522 non-need-based awards were made. *Average percent of need met:* 89%. *Average financial aid package:* $10,946. *Average need-based loan:* $4365. *Average need-based gift aid:* $5419. *Average non-need-based aid:* $6752. *Average indebtedness upon graduation:* $21,795.

Applying *Options:* electronic application, early admission, early action, deferred entrance. *Application fee:* $40. *Required:* essay or personal statement, high school transcript, 1 letter of recommendation. *Required for some:* interview. *Application deadlines:* rolling (freshmen), rolling (transfers), 12/15 (early action). *Notification:* continuous (freshmen), continuous (transfers), 1/31 (early action).

Freshman Application Contact Ms. Sharon Oliver, Director of Admissions, University of Maine, 5713 Chadbourne Hall, Orono, ME 04469-5713. *Phone:* 207-581-1561. *Toll-free phone:* 877-486-2364. *Fax:* 207-581-1213. *E-mail:* um-admit@maine.edu.

See page 1084 for the College Close-Up.

THE UNIVERSITY OF MAINE AT AUGUSTA

Augusta, Maine www.uma.maine.edu/

- **State-supported** 4-year, founded 1965, part of University of Maine System
- **Small-town** 159-acre campus
- **Endowment** $1.5 million
- **Coed** 5,101 undergraduate students, 30% full-time, 74% women, 26% men
- **Noncompetitive** entrance level, 57% of applicants were admitted

Undergraduates 1,519 full-time, 3,582 part-time. Students come from 16 states and territories, 2 other countries, 3% are from out of state, 0.7% African American, 0.5% Asian American or Pacific Islander, 0.6% Hispanic American, 3% Native American, 7% transferred in. *Retention:* 55% of 2006 full-time freshmen returned.

Freshmen *Admission:* 1,341 applied, 764 admitted, 540 enrolled.

Faculty *Total:* 253, 41% full-time, 16% with terminal degrees. *Student/faculty ratio:* 18:1.

Majors Accounting; applied horticulture; architectural technology; biology/biological sciences; business administration and management; clinical/medical laboratory assistant; computer and information sciences; criminal justice/law enforcement administration; criminal justice/safety; dental assisting; dental hygiene; English language and literature related; financial planning and services; fine/studio arts; general studies; human services; liberal arts and sciences/liberal studies; library assistant; library science; mental and social health services and allied professions related; music; nursing (registered nurse training); photography; public administration; social sciences; veterinary/animal health technology.

Academics *Calendar:* semesters. *Degrees:* certificates, associate, bachelor's, and postbachelor's certificates (also offers some graduate courses and continuing education programs with significant enrollment not reflected in profile). *Special study options:* academic remediation for entering students, adult/continuing education programs, advanced placement credit, distance learning, double majors, honors programs, independent study, internships, off-campus study, services for LD students, student-designed majors, study abroad, summer session for credit. *ROTC:* Army (c), Navy (c), Air Force (c).

Computers on Campus 142 computers/terminals are available on campus for general student use. Students can access the following: computer help desk, free student e-mail accounts, online (class) grades, online (class) registration, online (class) schedules. Campuswide network is available. Wireless service is available via entire campus.

Student Life *Housing:* college housing not available. *Activities and organizations:* student-run newspaper, Honors Program Student Association, Arts and Architecture Students of UMA, Student Nurse Association, Student-American Dental Hygiene Association, International Student Club. *Campus security:* late-night transport/escort service. *Student services:* personal/psychological counseling.

Athletics *Intercollegiate sports:* basketball M (s)/W (s), soccer W (s). *Intramural sports:* racquetball M/W, soccer M, softball M/W, tennis M/W, volleyball M/W.

Standardized Tests *Recommended:* SAT or ACT (for admission).

Costs (2007–08) *Tuition:* state resident $5220 full-time, $174 per credit hour part-time; nonresident $12,630 full-time, $421 per credit hour part-time. Full-time tuition and fees vary according to reciprocity agreements. Part-time tuition and fees vary according to reciprocity agreements. *Required fees:* $765 full-time, $26 per credit hour part-time. *Payment plan:* installment. *Waivers:* senior citizens and employees or children of employees.

Financial Aid Of all full-time matriculated undergraduates who enrolled in 2007, 1,437 were judged to have need, 274 had their need fully met. 230 Federal Work-Study jobs (averaging $1500). In 2007, 28 non-need-based awards were made. *Average percent of need met:* 74%. *Average financial aid package:* $8620. *Average need-based loan:* $4191. *Average need-based gift aid:* $4879. *Average non-need-based aid:* $4871. *Average indebtedness upon graduation:* $14,473.

Applying *Options:* electronic application, early admission, deferred entrance. *Application fee:* $40. *Required:* high school transcript. *Required for some:* letters of recommendation, interview, music audition. *Recommended:* essay or personal statement. *Application deadlines:* 8/31 (freshmen), rolling (transfers). *Notification:* continuous until 9/15 (freshmen), continuous (transfers).

Freshman Application Contact Jonathan Henry, Director of Admissions and Advising, The University of Maine at Augusta, 46 University Drive, Robinson Hall, Augusta, ME 04330. *Phone:* 207-621-3390. *Toll-free phone:* 877-862-1234 Ext. 3185. *Fax:* 207-621-3333. *E-mail:* umaadm@maine.edu.

UNIVERSITY OF MAINE AT FARMINGTON

Farmington, Maine **www.umf.maine.edu/**

- **State-supported** 4-year, founded 1863, part of University of Maine System
- **Small-town** 50-acre campus
- **Coed** 2,265 undergraduate students, 90% full-time, 67% women, 33% men
- **Moderately difficult** entrance level, 71% of applicants were admitted

Undergraduates 2,033 full-time, 232 part-time. Students come from 20 states and territories, 11 other countries, 17% are from out of state, 0.6% African American, 0.6% Asian American or Pacific Islander, 0.6% Hispanic American, 0.7% Native American, 0.5% international, 4% transferred in, 44% live on campus. *Retention:* 75% of 2006 full-time freshmen returned.

Freshmen *Admission:* 1,817 applied, 1,298 admitted, 482 enrolled. *Test scores:* SAT critical reading scores over 500: 53%; SAT math scores over 500: 48%; SAT critical reading scores over 600: 16%; SAT math scores over 600: 9%; SAT critical reading scores over 700: 2%; SAT math scores over 700: 1%.

Faculty *Total:* 189, 68% full-time, 77% with terminal degrees. *Student/faculty ratio:* 14:1.

Majors Anthropology; art; biology/biological sciences; biology teacher education; business/managerial economics; computer science; creative writing; dramatic/theater arts; early childhood education; elementary education; English; English/language arts teacher education; environmental studies; general studies; geochemistry; geography; geology/earth science; health occupations teacher education; health teacher education; history; interdisciplinary studies; international/global studies; liberal arts and sciences/liberal studies; mathematics; mathematics teacher education; mental health/rehabilitation; music; philosophy and religious studies related; political science and government; psychology; rehabilitation and therapeutic professions related; rehabilitation therapy; science teacher education; secondary education; social science teacher education; sociology; special education; special education (emotionally disturbed); special education (mentally retarded); special education (specific learning disabilities); women's studies.

Academics *Calendar:* semesters plus May term and 2 5-week summer terms. *Degree:* certificates and bachelor's. *Special study options:* academic remediation for entering students, accelerated degree program, advanced placement credit, distance learning, double majors, honors programs, independent study, internships, off-campus study, part-time degree program, services for LD students, student-designed majors, study abroad, summer session for credit.

Computers on Campus 180 computers/terminals are available on campus for general student use. Students can access the following: online (class) registration, laptop initiative. Campuswide network is available. 100% of college-owned or -operated housing units are wired for high-speed Internet access.

Student Life *Housing options:* coed, women-only. Campus housing is university owned and is provided by a third party. Freshman campus housing is guaranteed. *Activities and organizations:* drama/theater group, student-run newspaper, radio station, choral group, Program Board, Intramural Board, Campus Residence Council, campus radio station, Commuter Council. *Campus security:* 24-hour emergency response devices and patrols, late-night transport/escort service, controlled dormitory access, safety whistles. *Student services:* health clinic, personal/psychological counseling.

Athletics Member NCAA, NAIA. All NCAA Division III. *Intercollegiate sports:* baseball M, basketball M/W, cross-country running M/W, field hockey W, golf M, ice hockey M (c), lacrosse M (c)/W (c), soccer M/W, softball W, tennis M (c)/W (c), ultimate Frisbee M (c)/W (c), volleyball W. *Intramural sports:* basketball M/W, cheerleading M (c)/W (c), football M/W, ice hockey M (c)/W (c), rugby M (c)/W (c), skiing (cross-country) M (c)/W (c), skiing (downhill) M (c)/W (c), soccer M/W, softball M/W, swimming and diving M/W, tennis M/W, ultimate Frisbee M/W, volleyball M/W.

Standardized Tests *Required for some:* SAT or ACT (for admission).

Costs (2007–08) *Tuition:* state resident $6528 full-time, $204 per credit hour part-time; nonresident $14,208 full-time, $444 per credit hour part-time. Full-time tuition and fees vary according to course load, reciprocity agreements, and student level. Part-time tuition and fees vary according to course load, reciprocity agreements, and student level. *Required fees:* $815 full-time. *Room and board:* $6722; room only: $3578. Room and board charges vary according to board plan and housing facility. *Payment plan:* installment. *Waivers:* minority students, senior citizens, and employees or children of employees.

Financial Aid Of all full-time matriculated undergraduates who enrolled in 2007, 1,709 applied for aid, 1,418 were judged to have need, 189 had their need fully met. 519 Federal Work-Study jobs (averaging $1448). 406 state and other part-time jobs (averaging $1719). In 2007, 65 non-need-based awards were made. *Average percent of need met:* 73%. *Average financial aid package:* $8719. *Average need-based loan:* $4300. *Average need-based gift aid:* $4210. *Average non-need-based aid:* $1770. *Average indebtedness upon graduation:* $19,490.

Applying *Options:* electronic application, early admission, early action, deferred entrance. *Application fee:* $40. *Required:* essay or personal statement, high school transcript, minimum 2.0 GPA, 1 letter of recommendation. *Required for some:* minimum 2.5 GPA for elementary education majors. *Recommended:* interview. *Application deadlines:* rolling (freshmen), 12/1 (early action). *Notification:* continuous (freshmen), continuous (transfers), 1/8 (early action).

Freshman Application Contact Mr. James G. Collins, Associate Director of Admissions, University of Maine at Farmington, 246 Main Street, Farmington, ME 04938-1994. *Phone:* 207-778-7050. *Fax:* 207-778-8182. *E-mail:* umfadmit@maine.edu.

UNIVERSITY OF MAINE AT FORT KENT

Fort Kent, Maine **www.umfk.maine.edu/**

- **State-supported** 4-year, founded 1878, part of University of Maine System
- **Rural** 52-acre campus
- **Endowment** $1.5 million
- **Coed** 1,269 undergraduate students, 58% full-time, 67% women, 33% men
- **Moderately difficult** entrance level, 81% of applicants were admitted

Undergraduates 738 full-time, 531 part-time. Students come from 30 states and territories, 12 other countries, 4% are from out of state, 0.6% African American, 0.3% Asian American or Pacific Islander, 0.8% Hispanic American, 1% Native American, 22% international, 16% transferred in, 30% live on campus. *Retention:* 59% of 2006 full-time freshmen returned.

Freshmen *Admission:* 394 applied, 321 admitted, 113 enrolled. *Average high school GPA:* 2.43. *Test scores:* SAT critical reading scores over 500: 24%; SAT

math scores over 500: 34%; SAT critical reading scores over 600: 8%; SAT math scores over 600: 14%; SAT math scores over 700: 2%.

Faculty *Total:* 72, 49% full-time, 38% with terminal degrees. *Student/faculty ratio:* 17:1.

Majors Behavioral sciences; bilingual and multilingual education; biology/biological sciences; business administration and management; business teacher education; computer science; criminal justice/law enforcement administration; education; education (K-12); elementary education; English; English/language arts teacher education; environmental studies; forestry; forestry technology; French; French language teacher education; general studies; human services; liberal arts and sciences/liberal studies; mathematics teacher education; nursing (registered nurse training); public administration; social sciences; social science teacher education.

Academics *Calendar:* semesters. *Degrees:* associate and bachelor's. *Special study options:* accelerated degree program, advanced placement credit, distance learning, double majors, English as a second language, external degree program, honors programs, independent study, internships, part-time degree program, services for LD students, student-designed majors, summer session for credit.

Computers on Campus 100 computers/terminals are available on campus for general student use. Students can access the following: free student e-mail accounts, online (class) registration. Campuswide network is available.

Student Life *Housing options:* coed. Campus housing is university owned. *Activities and organizations:* drama/theater group, choral group, Performing Arts Club, Student Teachers Educational Professional Society, Student Nurses Organization, Diversity Club, Dorm Council, national fraternities, national sororities. *Campus security:* controlled dormitory access, 8-hour night patrols by security personnel 11p.m.-7a.m. *Student services:* health clinic, personal/psychological counseling.

Athletics Member NAIA. *Intercollegiate sports:* basketball M/W, cross-country running M/W, golf M/W, skiing (cross-country) M/W, skiing (downhill) M/W, soccer M/W. *Intramural sports:* baseball M, basketball M/W, cross-country running M/W, golf M/W, ice hockey M, racquetball M/W, skiing (cross-country) M/W, skiing (downhill) M/W, soccer M/W, softball M/W, table tennis M/W, tennis M/W, volleyball M/W, weight lifting M/W.

Standardized Tests *Required for some:* SAT (for admission), SAT and SAT Subject Tests or ACT (for admission). *Recommended:* SAT and SAT Subject Tests or ACT (for admission).

Costs (2007–08) *Tuition:* state resident $5100 full-time, $170 per credit hour part-time; nonresident $12,780 full-time, $426 per credit hour part-time. Full-time tuition and fees vary according to course load. Part-time tuition and fees vary according to course load. *Required fees:* $653 full-time. *Room and board:* $6620; room only: $3820. Room and board charges vary according to board plan and housing facility. *Payment plan:* installment. *Waivers:* minority students, senior citizens, and employees or children of employees.

Financial Aid Of all full-time matriculated undergraduates who enrolled in 2007, 499 applied for aid, 423 were judged to have need, 188 had their need fully met. 89 Federal Work-Study jobs (averaging $1800). 58 state and other part-time jobs (averaging $1800). In 2007, 53 non-need-based awards were made. *Average percent of need met:* 87%. *Average financial aid package:* $8326. *Average need-based loan:* $3539. *Average need-based gift aid:* $4744. *Average non-need-based aid:* $5641. *Average indebtedness upon graduation:* $10,483.

Applying *Options:* electronic application, early admission, early decision, deferred entrance. *Application fee:* $40. *Required:* essay or personal statement, high school transcript. *Required for some:* interview. *Recommended:* letters of recommendation. *Application deadlines:* rolling (freshmen), rolling (transfers). *Notification:* continuous (freshmen), continuous (transfers).

Director of Admissions Mrs. Jill B. Cairns, Acting Director of Admissions, University of Maine at Fort Kent, 23 University Drive, Fort Kent, ME 04743. *Phone:* 207-834-7600. *Toll-free phone:* 888-TRY-UMFK. *E-mail:* jillb@maine.edu.

See page 1086 for the College Close-Up.

UNIVERSITY OF MAINE AT MACHIAS

Machias, Maine **www.umm.maine.edu/**

- **State-supported** 4-year, founded 1909, part of University of Maine System
- **Rural** 42-acre campus
- **Endowment** $1.5 million
- **Coed** 1,093 undergraduate students, 40% full-time, 72% women, 28% men
- **Moderately difficult** entrance level, 92% of applicants were admitted

Undergraduates 437 full-time, 656 part-time. Students come from 24 states and territories, 9 other countries, 22% are from out of state, 1% African American, 0.9% Asian American or Pacific Islander, 2% Hispanic American, 4% Native American, 4% international, 3% transferred in, 44% live on campus. *Retention:* 73% of 2006 full-time freshmen returned.

Freshmen *Admission:* 381 applied, 349 admitted, 110 enrolled. *Test scores:* SAT critical reading scores over 500: 48%; SAT critical reading scores over 600: 7%; SAT critical reading scores over 700: 2%.

Faculty *Total:* 77, 38% full-time, 56% with terminal degrees. *Student/faculty ratio:* 16:1.

Majors Accounting; art; behavioral sciences; biology/biological sciences; biology teacher education; business administration and management; business teacher education; conservation biology; creative writing; dramatic/theater arts; ecology; education; elementary education; English; English/language arts teacher education; entrepreneurship; environmental education; environmental studies; family/community studies; general studies; history; history teacher education; hotel/motel administration; human services; marine biology and biological oceanography; marketing/marketing management; mathematics teacher education; music; parks, recreation and leisure; parks, recreation and leisure facilities management; pre-medical studies; psychology; public administration; science teacher education; social science teacher education; tourism and travel services management; visual and performing arts.

Academics *Calendar:* semesters. *Degrees:* associate and bachelor's. *Special study options:* academic remediation for entering students, advanced placement credit, cooperative education, distance learning, double majors, honors programs, independent study, internships, off-campus study, part-time degree program, services for LD students, student-designed majors, study abroad, summer session for credit.

Computers on Campus 185 computers/terminals are available on campus for general student use. Students can access the following: online (class) registration. Campuswide network is available.

Student Life *Housing:* on-campus residence required through sophomore year. *Options:* coed. Campus housing is university owned. *Activities and organizations:* drama/theater group, student-run radio station, choral group, Student Senate, 100% Society, International Club, MRPASS, Softball Club, national fraternities, national sororities. *Campus security:* 24-hour emergency response devices, late-night transport/escort service, controlled dormitory access, night security guard until 3:00 a.m., day security 8-5 p.m. *Student services:* health clinic, personal/psychological counseling.

Athletics Member NAIA. *Intercollegiate sports:* basketball M/W, cross-country running M/W, lacrosse M (c)/W (c), soccer M/W, volleyball W. *Intramural sports:* basketball M/W, cheerleading W, fencing M/W, football M/W, soccer M/W, softball W, water polo M/W.

Standardized Tests *Required:* SAT or ACT (for admission).

Costs (2007–08) *Tuition:* state resident $5100 full-time, $170 per credit hour part-time; nonresident $14,130 full-time, $471 per credit hour part-time.

Financial Aid Of all full-time matriculated undergraduates who enrolled in 2002, 512 applied for aid, 419 were judged to have need, 108 had their need fully met. 140 Federal Work-Study jobs (averaging $1621). 83 state and other part-time jobs (averaging $1660). In 2002, 44 non-need-based awards were made. *Average percent of need met:* 83%. *Average financial aid package:* $8182. *Average need-based loan:* $3356. *Average need-based gift aid:* $4847. *Average non-need-based aid:* $5051. *Average indebtedness upon graduation:* $14,873.

Applying *Options:* electronic application, early admission, early action, deferred entrance. *Application fee:* $40. *Required:* essay or personal statement, high school transcript, 1 letter of recommendation. *Required for some:* minimum 2.0 GPA, interview. *Recommended:* minimum 2.5 GPA, 2 letters of recommendation, interview. *Application deadlines:* 8/15 (freshmen), rolling (transfers), 12/15 (early action). *Notification:* continuous (freshmen), continuous (transfers), 1/15 (early action).

Freshman Application Contact Mr. Stewart Bennett, Director of Admissions, University of Maine at Machias, 9 O'Brien Avenue, Machias, ME 04654. *Phone:* 207-255-1318. *Toll-free phone:* 888-GOTOUMM (in-state); 888-468-6866 (out-of-state). *Fax:* 207-255-1363. *E-mail:* ummadmissions@maine.edu.

See page 1088 for the College Close-Up.

UNIVERSITY OF MAINE AT PRESQUE ISLE

Presque Isle, Maine **www.umpi.maine.edu/**

- **State-supported** 4-year, founded 1903, part of University of Maine System
- **Small-town** 150-acre campus
- **Endowment** $1.1 million
- **Coed**
- **Minimally difficult** entrance level

Faculty *Student/faculty ratio:* 16:1.

Academics *Calendar:* semesters. *Degrees:* certificates, associate, and bachelor's.

Student Life *Campus security:* student patrols, late-night transport/escort service, crime prevention programs, lighted pathways.

Athletics Member NAIA.

Costs (2007–08) *Tuition:* state resident $5100 full-time, $170 per credit hour part-time; nonresident $12,780 full-time, $426 per credit hour part-time. Full-time tuition and fees vary according to course load and reciprocity agreements. Part-time tuition and fees vary according to course load and reciprocity agreements. *Required fees:* $775 full-time, $16 per credit hour part-time. *Room and board:* $5980; room only: $3400. Room and board charges vary according to board plan. *Payment plans:* installment, deferred payment.

Financial Aid Of all full-time matriculated undergraduates who enrolled in 2005, 800 applied for aid, 697 were judged to have need, 266 had their need fully met. 283 Federal Work-Study jobs (averaging $1318). In 2005, 85 non-need-based awards were made. *Average percent of need met:* 89. *Average financial aid package:* $7248. *Average need-based loan:* $3323. *Average need-based gift aid:* $4509. *Average non-need-based aid:* $4046. *Average indebtedness upon graduation:* $11,181.

Applying *Options:* electronic application, early admission, early action, deferred entrance. *Application fee:* $40. *Required:* essay or personal statement, high school transcript, minimum 2.0 GPA, letters of recommendation. *Required for some:* 1 letter of recommendation, interview.

Freshman Application Contact Ms. Erin V. Benson, Director of University Relations and Student Enrollment Services, University of Maine at Presque Isle, 181 Main Street, Presque Isle, ME 04769. *Phone:* 207-768-9536. *Fax:* 207-768-9777. *E-mail:* adventure@umpi.maine.edu.

UNIVERSITY OF NEW ENGLAND

Biddeford, Maine **www.une.edu/**

- **Independent** comprehensive, founded 1831
- **Small-town** 410-acre campus
- **Endowment** $28.5 million
- **Coed** 2,140 undergraduate students, 88% full-time, 73% women, 27% men
- **Moderately difficult** entrance level, 76% of applicants were admitted

Undergraduates 1,893 full-time, 247 part-time. Students come from 44 states and territories, 4 other countries, 55% are from out of state, 0.8% African American, 1% Asian American or Pacific Islander, 1% Hispanic American, 0.3% Native American, 0.2% international, 7% transferred in.

Freshmen *Admission:* 2,904 applied, 2,203 admitted, 594 enrolled. *Test scores:* SAT critical reading scores over 500: 65%; SAT math scores over 500: 69%; SAT critical reading scores over 600: 19%; SAT math scores over 600: 20%; SAT critical reading scores over 700: 3%; SAT math scores over 700: 2%.

Faculty *Total:* 318, 55% full-time, 47% with terminal degrees. *Student/faculty ratio:* 9:1.

Majors American studies; aquaculture; athletic training; biochemistry; biology/biological sciences; biomedical sciences; business administration and management; chemistry; clinical laboratory science/medical technology; dental hygiene; elementary education; English; environmental science; environmental studies; health and physical education related; health/health care administration; health professions related; health science; history; kinesiology and exercise science; liberal arts and sciences/liberal studies; marine biology and biological oceanography; mathematics; medical laboratory technology; nursing (registered nurse training); occupational therapy; physical therapy; physician assistant; physiological psychology/psychobiology; political science and government; pre-dentistry studies; pre-medical studies; psychology; psychology related; social psychology; social sciences related; sociology; sport and fitness administration/management.

Academics *Calendar:* semesters. *Degrees:* associate, bachelor's, master's, first professional, post-master's, and postbachelor's certificates. *Special study options:* academic remediation for entering students, accelerated degree program, advanced placement credit, cooperative education, distance learning, double majors, independent study, internships, off-campus study, part-time degree program, services for LD students, study abroad, summer session for credit. *ROTC:* Army (c).

Computers on Campus 150 computers/terminals are available on campus for general student use. Students can access the following: computer help desk, free student e-mail accounts, online (class) grades, online (class) registration. Campus-wide network is available. Wireless service is available via entire campus.

Student Life *Housing:* on-campus residence required through junior year. *Options:* coed, women-only. Campus housing is university owned. Freshman campus housing is guaranteed. *Activities and organizations:* Student Government, Outing Club, Campus Programming Board, Earth's Eco, Dance Team. *Campus security:* 24-hour emergency response devices and patrols, late-night transport/escort service, controlled dormitory access. *Student services:* health clinic, personal/psychological counseling.

Athletics Member NCAA. All Division III. *Intercollegiate sports:* basketball M/W, cross-country running M/W, field hockey W, golf M, lacrosse M/W, soccer M/W, softball W, swimming and diving W, volleyball W. *Intramural sports:* baseball M (c), basketball M/W, gymnastics M/W, racquetball M/W, soccer M/W, softball M/W, table tennis M/W, ultimate Frisbee M (c)/W (c), volleyball M (c)/W, water polo M/W.

Standardized Tests *Required:* SAT or ACT (for admission).

Costs (2007–08) *Comprehensive fee:* $35,190 includes full-time tuition ($24,440), mandatory fees ($890), and room and board ($9860). Part-time tuition: $880 per credit. *Room and board:* Room and board charges vary according to housing facility and location. *Payment plan:* installment. *Waivers:* children of alumni and employees or children of employees.

Financial Aid Of all full-time matriculated undergraduates who enrolled in 2007, 1,748 applied for aid, 1,618 were judged to have need, 361 had their need fully met. 850 Federal Work-Study jobs (averaging $1946). In 2007, 316 non-need-based awards were made. *Average percent of need met:* 70%. *Average financial aid package:* $19,915. *Average need-based loan:* $6249. *Average need-based gift aid:* $11,979. *Average non-need-based aid:* $7571. *Average indebtedness upon graduation:* $41,645.

Applying *Options:* electronic application, deferred entrance. *Application fee:* $40. *Required:* high school transcript. *Required for some:* interview. *Recommended:* essay or personal statement, interview. *Application deadlines:* 2/15 (freshmen), rolling (transfers). *Notification:* continuous (freshmen), continuous (transfers).

Freshman Application Contact Mr. Robert J. Pecchia, Associate Dean of Admissions, University of New England, Hills Beach Road, Biddeford, ME 04005-9526. *Phone:* 207-283-0170 Ext. 2297. *Toll-free phone:* 800-477-4UNE. *Fax:* 207-602-5900. *E-mail:* admissions@une.edu.

See page 1090 for the College Close-Up.

UNIVERSITY OF SOUTHERN MAINE

Portland, Maine **www.usm.maine.edu/**

- **State-supported** comprehensive, founded 1878, part of University of Maine System
- **Suburban** 144-acre campus
- **Endowment** $25.2 million
- **Coed** 8,133 undergraduate students, 58% full-time, 58% women, 42% men
- **Moderately difficult** entrance level, 80% of applicants were admitted

Combining a small-school atmosphere with the choices of a larger university, University of Southern Maine (USM) is just 2 hours from Boston, with access to the ocean, lakes, and ski resorts. Features include dedicated faculty members, small class sizes, a diverse student body, internships and cooperative education, a field house and ice arena, and a dual residential campus (urban and rural). USM provides students with real value: a high-quality education at an affordable cost.

Undergraduates 4,754 full-time, 3,379 part-time. 2% African American, 2% Asian American or Pacific Islander, 1% Hispanic American, 1% Native American, 0.2% international, 10% transferred in, 40% live on campus. *Retention:* 67% of 2006 full-time freshmen returned.

Freshmen *Admission:* 4,016 applied, 3,220 admitted, 949 enrolled. *Average high school GPA:* 2.83. *Test scores:* SAT critical reading scores over 500: 45%; SAT math scores over 500: 46%; SAT writing scores over 500: 44%; ACT scores over 18: 87%; SAT critical reading scores over 600: 13%; SAT math scores over 600: 10%; SAT writing scores over 600: 9%; ACT scores over 24: 21%; SAT critical reading scores over 700: 1%; SAT math scores over 700: 1%; SAT writing scores over 700: 1%; ACT scores over 30: 2%.

Faculty *Total:* 710, 57% full-time, 51% with terminal degrees. *Student/faculty ratio:* 13:1.

Majors Accounting; anthropology; art; art teacher education; athletic training; biology/biological sciences; biotechnology; business administration and management; chemistry; classics and languages, literatures and linguistics; communication/speech communication and rhetoric; computer science; criminology; dramatic/theater arts; economics; electrical, electronics and communications engineering; English; environmental health; environmental studies; French; geography; geology/earth science; health science; Hispanic-American, Puerto Rican, and Mexican-American/Chicano studies; history; industrial arts; international relations and affairs; linguistics; mass communication/media; mathematics; modern languages; music; music performance; music teacher education; nursing (registered nurse training); philosophy; physics; political science and government; psychology;

Russian studies; social sciences; social work; sociology; therapeutic recreation; trade and industrial teacher education; women's studies.

Academics *Calendar:* semesters. *Degrees:* associate, bachelor's, master's, doctoral, first professional, and post-master's certificates. *Special study options:* academic remediation for entering students, accelerated degree program, adult/continuing education programs, advanced placement credit, cooperative education, distance learning, double majors, English as a second language, external degree program, honors programs, independent study, internships, off-campus study, part-time degree program, services for LD students, student-designed majors, study abroad, summer session for credit. *ROTC:* Army (c), Air Force (c). *Unusual degree programs:* 3-2 education.

Computers on Campus 485 computers/terminals are available on campus for general student use. Students can access the following: online (class) registration. Campuswide network is available.

Student Life *Housing options:* coed. Campus housing is university owned. Freshman applicants given priority for college housing. *Activities and organizations:* drama/theater group, student-run newspaper, radio and television station, choral group, Outing and Ski Clubs, Gorham Events Board, Commuter Student Group, Circle K, national fraternities, national sororities. *Campus security:* 24-hour emergency response devices and patrols, student patrols, late-night transport/escort service, controlled dormitory access, security lighting, preventive programs within residence halls. *Student services:* health clinic, personal/psychological counseling, women's center, legal services.

Athletics Member NCAA. All Division III. *Intercollegiate sports:* baseball M, basketball M/W, cheerleading M/W, cross-country running M/W, field hockey W, golf M/W, ice hockey M/W, lacrosse M/W, sailing M/W, soccer M/W, softball W, tennis M/W, track and field M/W, volleyball W, wrestling M. *Intramural sports:* basketball M/W, cheerleading W, football M/W, ice hockey M/W, lacrosse M (c)/W (c), racquetball M/W, rugby M (c)/W (c), skiing (downhill) M (c)/W (c), soccer M/W, softball M/W, squash M/W, table tennis M/W, tennis M/W, ultimate Frisbee M/W, volleyball M/W, weight lifting M/W.

Standardized Tests *Required:* SAT or ACT (for admission).

Costs (2007–08) *Tuition:* state resident $5940 full-time, $198 per credit hour part-time; nonresident $16,410 full-time, $547 per credit hour part-time. Full-time tuition and fees vary according to course load, degree level, and reciprocity agreements. Part-time tuition and fees vary according to course load, degree level, and reciprocity agreements. *Required fees:* $927 full-time. *Room and board:* $8038; room only: $4140. Room and board charges vary according to board plan, housing facility, and location. *Payment plan:* installment. *Waivers:* minority students and employees or children of employees.

Financial Aid Of all full-time matriculated undergraduates who enrolled in 2007, 3,817 applied for aid, 3,267 were judged to have need, 539 had their need fully met. In 2007, 494 non-need-based awards were made. *Average percent of need met:* 67%. *Average financial aid package:* $9370. *Average need-based loan:* $4761. *Average need-based gift aid:* $4383. *Average non-need-based aid:* $4568. *Average indebtedness upon graduation:* $22,360.

Applying *Options:* electronic application, early admission, deferred entrance. *Application fee:* $40. *Required:* essay or personal statement, high school transcript. *Required for some:* interview, auditions for music majors. *Recommended:* minimum 2.8 GPA, 1 letter of recommendation, interview. *Application deadlines:* 2/15 (freshmen), 2/15 (transfers). *Notification:* continuous (freshmen), continuous (transfers).

Freshman Application Contact Mr. Jonathan Barker, Associate Director, University of Southern Maine, 37 College Avenue, Gorham, ME 04038. *Phone:* 207-780-5724. *Toll-free phone:* 800-800-4USM Ext. 5670. *Fax:* 207-780-5640. *E-mail:* usmadm@usm.maine.edu.

See page 1092 for the College Close-Up.

COLBY COLLEGE

WATERVILLE, MAINE

The College

Colby, founded in 1813 and one of America's best private liberal arts colleges, combines a challenging academic program, an emphasis on undergraduate research, and an active community life—all on one of the nation's most beautiful campuses. Colby's reach is global—in its recruitment of a diverse student body and faculty, in the scope of its curriculum, and in the number of undergraduates who study abroad.

The College is guided by the belief that the best preparation for life, and for professions that require specialized study, is a broad acquaintance with human knowledge. Liberal arts students graduate with the competence and flexibility to thrive in an increasingly complex world. Colby has a superior record of placing students who seek postgraduate study, and career opportunities for graduates are virtually unlimited.

Colby is a national leader at incorporating research into the curriculum in all disciplines. This approach to learning fosters strong critical-thinking skills, a lively imagination, and a capacity for independent work. It also contributes to faculty members' strong and supportive relationships with students. While many colleges lay claim to accessible faculty members, Colby ranks among the best in student-faculty interaction, both in and out of the classroom.

The College has been recognized by the EPA and Maine officials for its commitment to environmental stewardship, both in academic programs and in practices adopted on campus. Through student-led and institutional initiatives, Colby has become a national leader in adopting sustainable practices.

In 2005, Colby became one of the first ten colleges or universities in the U.S. to win a Senator Paul Simon Award for Campus Internationalization. The award recognized Colby's commitment to international content in the curriculum, a 70-percent participation rate in study abroad, and an internationally diverse student body.

The pace of life at Colby is brisk, with a host of clubs, activities, and teams as well as social and cultural events that keep students busy. Colby's 1,800 students, representing nearly every state and more than sixty countries, participate in more than 100 student-run organizations, thirty-two varsity teams, eleven club sports, and more than a half dozen intramural sports. A renovated and expanded student center opened in fall 2007, with a 9,500-square-foot bookstore addition slated for a 2008 opening. Community service is also part of the fabric of the Colby experience. The student-run Colby Volunteer Center coordinates dozens of volunteer programs, and civic engagement is built into many courses.

Almost all students live on campus. A multiyear, $44-million project to add dorms and renovate all residence halls and dining facilities is nearing completion. Notable facilities include the Pugh Center, a hub of multicultural organizations; one of the nation's finest college-based art museums; and the Alfond Athletic Center, one of the largest indoor athletic and fitness facilities in New England. The athletic center features an indoor track, swimming pool, ice arena, gymnasium, fitness center, aerobics studio, squash courts, tennis courts, and climbing wall. Outdoor facilities include a new synthetic turf field, 50 acres of playing fields, cross-country skiing and running trails, tennis courts, and an all-weather track.

Location

Located in Waterville, Maine, Colby is just off Interstate 95, 20 minutes from the state capital and about an hour from Portland, Maine's largest city. Maine's western mountains, including the Sugarloaf/USA ski area, are just over an hour to the north, and the Atlantic Coast is less than an hour to the east. Acadia National Park and Mt. Katahdin are both accessible as day trips. The 714-acre campus includes Johnson Pond and a 128-acre arboretum and bird sanctuary.

Majors and Degrees

Colby awards the Bachelor of Arts degree, with majors in African-American/American studies; American studies; anthropology; art; biology; chemistry; chemistry–ACS (accredited by the American Chemical Society); chemistry–biochemistry; classical civilization; classical civilization–anthropology; classical civilization–English; classics; classics–English; computer science; East Asian studies; economics; economics–mathematics; English; environmental studies–policy; environmental studies–science; French studies; geology; geoscience; German studies; government; history; international studies; Latin American studies; mathematics; mathematical sciences; music; philosophy; physics; psychology; religious studies; Russian language and culture; science, technology, and society; sociology; Spanish; theater and dance; and women's, gender, and sexuality studies. Specific options within the above majors include art–art history, art–studio art, biology–cell and molecular biology/biochemistry, biology–environmental science, biology–neuroscience, chemistry–cell and molecular biology/biochemistry, chemistry–environmental science, economics–financial markets, economics–international economics, economics–public policy, and psychology–neuroscience.

Minors are available in thirty-three fields of study, including administrative science, African studies, Chinese, creative writing, education, environmental studies, German, human development, indigenous peoples of the Americas, Italian studies, Japanese, and Jewish studies.

Academic Programs

Colby's liberal arts program offers a broad educational foundation. In-depth study in a major provides a detailed understanding of at least one discipline's methods and perspectives. In addition to their major, students may complete a minor, a second major, a combined major, or an interdisciplinary major. A self-designed independent major or a senior scholars project of significant independent work may also be approved for qualified students. Secondary school teacher certification may be obtained, and a dual-degree engineering program is offered with Dartmouth College. The 4-1-4 calendar includes a January term that offers opportunities on and off campus to explore special areas of interest and to pursue internships.

Distribution requirements include 4 credit hours of English composition, knowledge of one foreign language, 6 to 8 credit hours in the natural sciences, and 3 to 4 credit hours in each of the following areas: arts, historical studies, literature, quantitative reasoning, and the social sciences. Wellness, residence, and diversity requirements and the requirements of the major also must be filled. A minimum of 128 credit hours with a minimum cumulative 2.0 GPA is required for graduation. Three January terms, including one during the first year, are also required.

In 2004, the Goldfarb Center for Public Affairs and Civic Engagement was formed to connect teaching and research with contemporary political, economic, and social issues. The Goldfarb Center provides a venue in which students and faculty members can think and work across disciplinary boundaries to develop creative approaches to complex local, national, and global challenges.

Off-Campus Programs

More than two thirds of Colby students take advantage of international or off-campus domestic study opportunities. Many participate in Colby's own programs in France, Spain, and Russia. Other students select approved non-Colby programs in countries throughout the world. Domestic off-campus programs include the Washington Semester and exchange programs with Howard University in Washington, D.C., and Clark Atlanta University in Georgia. Colby's financial aid may be applied to any approved off-campus study.

Academic Facilities

Colby is in the midst of an ambitious campus expansion, and a major new facility, the Diamond Building, houses social science departments, interdisciplinary programs, and the Goldfarb Center. In addition, infrastructure is in place for another academic building for natural sciences and, following that, a music and performance building is planned.

Colby has three libraries on campus with access to almost 1 million books, microtexts, and other items, most of which are found in open stacks. The library catalog is online, and many resources are available through the library's Web site.

The Bixler Art and Music Center includes an art and music library, music practice rooms, and a 300-seat auditorium. The Colby College Museum of Art is one of the nation's finest college-based art museums.

The Runnals Building contains the 274-seat Strider Theater, a dance studio, and the Cellar Theater for improvisational workshops and small productions.

Four interconnected buildings contain science facilities, including teaching and research laboratories, animal rooms, research greenhouses, exhibit space, and a science library. A wide range of sophisticated science equipment is accessible to students beginning in their first year. The Collins Observatory features a 14-inch telescope equipped with a high-quality CCD camera and other research-grade equipment.

Computers are available for student use in clusters and teaching labs throughout the campus. Every classroom, dorm room, office, and laboratory is connected to the Colby network and the Internet through high-speed Ethernet connections. A wireless zone is available in Miller Library. All classrooms are served by data-video projectors. An extensive software library is available to students. The Information Technology Services staff helps connect students' computers in the fall, runs a help desk for students, and assists with applications appropriate to each discipline. There are no fees for any of these services.

Costs

For the 2007–08 academic year, the comprehensive fee was $46,100. Personal expenses, books, and supplies average $1500 annually.

Financial Aid

Colby awards financial aid on the basis of need. About 70 percent of students receive some form of financial aid through grants, loans, or on-campus work, and approximately 38 percent receive grant aid from the College's own funds. An average award includes a grant, a loan, and on-campus employment. The average financial aid package in 2006–07 was $31,400.

Faculty

Colby has 226 faculty members, 161 of them full-time. The student-faculty ratio is 10:1, and the median class size is 17. Ninety-five percent of faculty members hold doctorates or final degrees in their fields, and many have national or international reputations. A faculty-in-residence program provides housing for about a dozen faculty families in campus residence halls, and a faculty-associates program fosters further faculty involvement in campus life.

Student Government

Colby students govern many aspects of campus life through the Student Government Association (SGA) and the Student Programming Board (SPB). Students also serve on most College boards and committees, including the Board of Trustees. The SGA deals with academic, cultural, and residential affairs and supports more than 100 clubs and organizations. The Student Judiciary Board has jurisdiction over most incidents that call for possible disciplinary action.

Admission Requirements

Colby seeks applicants from diverse geographical, racial, and economic backgrounds who have special qualities or talents to contribute to the College. Admission is highly selective. Evaluations are made on the basis of academic achievement and ability, interest and excitement in learning, character, and maturity. The quality of a candidate's preparation is judged by his or her academic record, references from school authorities, and College Board or ACT test scores. A minimum of 16 academic preparatory credits is recommended, including 4 years of English, at least 3 years of a foreign language, 3 years of college-preparatory mathematics, 2 years of a laboratory science, 2 years of history or social science, and 2 academic electives.

Colby offers early entrance and early decision options. Advanced standing may be established by examination, taken either through the department or through the Advanced Placement Program of the College Board, the International Baccalaureate, or other standard tests. Some transfer students are considered for admission each year.

Applicants are encouraged to visit the campus for interviews, tours, classes, meals, and, if possible, an overnight stay in the residence halls.

Application and Information

Applications for regular admission must be submitted by January 1. Those wishing to be considered for early decision may choose either the fall or winter option. Fall option applicants must complete the application process by November 15; winter option applicants, by January 1. For applications and admission forms, students should contact:

Admissions and Financial Aid Office
Lunder House
Colby College
4800 Mayflower Hill
Waterville, Maine 04901-8848
Phone: 800-723-3032 (toll-free)
Fax: 207-859-4828
E-mail: admissions@colby.edu
Web site: http://www.colby.edu

The Diamond Building, which opened in February 2007, houses social science departments and interdisciplinary studies.

COLLEGE OF THE ATLANTIC

BAR HARBOR, MAINE

The College

College of the Atlantic (COA) offers a curriculum with a conscience. Founded in 1969, the school provides an ecological, hands-on, problem-solving approach to education, combining academic rigor with practical application. The College is intentionally small, offering close mentoring relationships between faculty members and students. With its one major, human ecology, classes are interdisciplinary, relationships are emphasized, and students are encouraged to go to the source and to do their own creative thinking. Ultimately, students fashion their own course of study, combining classes in all fields with a dose of independent work, off-campus internships, and a capstone project. Enrollment for the 2007–08 school year is 295, about one-third men. COA has a strong international student presence, with 20 percent of its student body from outside the United States. Located between the Atlantic Ocean and Acadia National Park, many students heed the call of the outdoors. The College also sponsors films, speakers, concerts, and dances, and students hold informal parties, musical get-togethers, and recitals. Students, faculty members, and staff members form a close-knit College community.

In addition to its undergraduate degrees, the College also offers a Master of Philosophy (M.Phil.) in human ecology.

Location

The College is located in the town of Bar Harbor on Mount Desert Island, Maine, where Acadia National Park is also situated. Connected to the mainland by a causeway, the large, scenic island lies 300 miles north of Boston and 40 miles east of Bangor. In the summer, Bar Harbor teems with tourists. When students return in the fall, the traffic reverses direction and Bar Harbor becomes a quiet coastal Maine village. The Atlantic Ocean and Acadia National Park provide ample opportunities for such outdoor recreational activities as swimming, fishing, canoeing, kayaking, rock climbing, mountain hiking, cross-country skiing, and snowshoeing. Cooperative programs with the Jackson Laboratory, the Mount Desert Island Biological Laboratory, the national park, and the local public school system helps to broaden the scope of COA's educational activities. The College's two island research stations and 86-acre organic farm expand COA's resources.

Majors and Degrees

College of the Atlantic awards the Bachelor of Arts in Human Ecology. Human ecology emphasizes the understanding of interrelationships between humans and the social, technological, and natural environments. Students may develop individualized programs in many areas, including community development, environmental science, humanities, international and regional studies, landscape design, literature and writing, marine studies, natural-history-museum studies, public policy, sustainable agriculture, teacher certification, and visual arts.

Academic Programs

The academic program is designed to develop an ecological perspective through the understanding of social, biological, and technological interrelationships. Students acquire the skills necessary to enter the fields of science, education, business, law, design, the arts, health, social services, policy and planning, journalism, agriculture, or architecture. Sixty percent of COA's alumni have pursued graduate or professional education at some of the country's leading institutions. Many different forms of study are available at COA, and small and informal classes are the foundation of the curriculum. Student-initiated workshops, independent studies, internships, and senior projects also provide important learning experiences. Applied learning is the norm, not the exception.

To qualify for graduation, students must complete required interdisciplinary course work, write an essay on human ecology, perform community service, and complete a one-term internship and a one-term senior project.

College of the Atlantic accepts up to two years of transfer credits from accredited colleges if the grades earned were C or better and were earned in courses of an academic nature.

Off-Campus Programs

The College's academic program is augmented by exchange agreements with the University of Maine at Orono; the Palacky University in Olomouc, Czech Republic; the Salt Institute for Documentary Studies in Portland, Maine; the Landing School of Boatbuilding in Kennebunk, Maine; the Olin College of Engineering in Needham, Massachusetts; and the Multiversidad Franciscana de Americana Latino in Uruguay. Students may also spend a term in COA's study-abroad program in the Yucatan Peninsula in Mexico or in Guatemala. The Ecoleague consortium allows students to study for up to one year at Alaska Pacific University, Green Mountain College, Northland College, or Prescott College.

Academic Facilities

Thorndike Library has more than 45,000 print and multimedia titles and provides access to a variety of subscription-based electronic resources. Access to material in libraries throughout the world is available via the library's interlibrary loan service. COA has zoology, botany, and chemistry laboratories; a herbarium; greenhouses; design and ceramics studios; state-of-the-art computer facilities, including a Geographic Information Systems Lab and a design/graphics computer lab; research boats for marine research and to ferry students and faculty members to College-owned island research stations in the Gulf of Maine; and an 86-acre working organic farm.

Costs

The total cost for the 2007–08 academic year is about $38,160. This includes $29,970 for tuition, $5100 for room, and $3090 for board.

Financial Aid

More than two thirds of the College's students receive some form of financial aid. The Free Application for Federal Student Aid and the College's own form are required by the College to determine a student's eligibility for assistance. Aid is based on established need and academic merit. Financial aid packages generally consist of a combination of scholarships, work-study awards, and loans.

Faculty

With a faculty of 29 full-time and 13 part-time teachers, the student-faculty ratio is 10:1. Ninety percent of the full-time faculty members have Ph.D.'s or the equivalent. Courses offered

COLLEGE DATA CENTER • MAINE

by regular visiting faculty members supplement the curriculum. The primary commitment of the COA faculty is teaching and advising undergraduate students.

Student Government

The College governance system is a combination of pure and representative democracy. Students participate in all facets of decision making and serve on all standing committees. Major policy decisions are brought for review to the All-College Meeting, where members of the faculty, staff, and student body each have one vote.

Admission Requirements

The Admission Committee, composed of students, staff members, and faculty members, seeks students who have an enthusiastic and active approach to learning, a commitment to community service, a strong record of academic achievement, and accompanying intellectual strengths. These qualities should be supplemented with appropriate personal qualities enabling a student to learn in an environment requiring a high degree of self-motivation.

The COA application form contains a series of essay questions that require students to think carefully about College of the Atlantic's educational focus. The application is designed to encourage prospective students to reflect on and express personal reasons for choosing a small college with a focus on human ecology. The answers to these questions, teacher and counselor references, past academic records, and personal interviews are used by the Admission Committee in arriving at its decision. Standardized test scores are optional.

Admission procedures and standards are the same for transfer students as for freshman applicants. Special emphasis is placed on the transfer applicant's college transcript and recommendations. The transfer of credits is determined on an individual basis. All transferring students are required to complete a minimum of two years of study at COA. Applications are also accepted from students at other institutions who wish to spend time at the College as visiting students.

Application and Information

Prospective students are encouraged to visit the College in order to sit in on classes, talk with students and faculty members, and acquire an understanding of the College's individualized educational style. COA employs a deadline date of February 15 for fall admission for first-year students, but offers two early decision options with a December 1 deadline and a January 10 deadline. Transfer students must apply by April 1. Decisions for first-year students are mailed on or about April 1 and on or about April 25 for transfer students. Applicants for winter term should apply by November 15 and for spring term by February 15. Application materials may be obtained by writing to the College or by telephoning the Admission Office at the number below. The application fee is $45. COA endorses the policy set by the National Association of College Admission Counselors, whereby regular admission students have the right to defer accepting any offer of admission until May 1.

Director of Admission
College of the Atlantic
105 Eden Street
Bar Harbor, Maine 04609
Phone: 207-288-5015
800-528-0025 (toll-free)
Fax: 207-288-4126
E-mail: inquiry@coa.edu
Web site: http://www.coa.edu

Mount Desert Rock, 25 miles off Bar Harbor's coast, is owned by COA and serves as a research station for students.

UNIVERSITY OF MAINE

ORONO, MAINE

The University

The University of Maine, the land-grant university and sea-grant college of the state of Maine, has a mission to provide teaching and public service and to carry out research for the state of Maine and the country. The University was established in 1865 as the Maine State College of Agriculture and the Mechanic Arts. When the institution opened its doors in 1868, it had 12 students and 2 faculty members. Today, as the University of Maine, it has approximately 740 faculty members and 12,000 students who represent forty-eight states and sixty-five countries. The University of Maine is a participant in the New England Regional Program sponsored by the New England Board of Higher Education.

The University of Maine is the flagship institution of the seven-member University of Maine System. Two hundred four buildings sit on the University of Maine's 660-acre central campus. Forests, botanical gardens, and other "green" spaces make up the rest of the 5,500-acre campus, overlooking the Stillwater River. Ivy-covered buildings and pathways shaded by evergreens create a campus that is inviting and picturesque during all four seasons. Students living on campus may select from a variety of housing options, from residence halls to apartment-style complexes to fraternity and sorority houses.

The University has more than 235 student organizations, including honor and professional societies, fraternities, and sororities. Ten women's and nine men's intercollegiate NCAA Division I athletic programs are part of the campus community. Numerous intramural club sports give all students an opportunity to be physically active. Two gymnasiums, a field house, an indoor pool, a sports arena, a domed field, and a 10,000-seat athletic stadium are used for NCAA Division I athletics. A 14,000-square-foot recreation center, which opened in fall 2007, and the Maine Bound Center, with a climbing wall, provide opportunities for recreational sports. For students' creative interests, there are two theaters, excellent music facilities, recital halls, and studios for dance and the visual arts. Community services include a newspaper, a radio station, a police and safety department, and a health facility.

Location

The town of Orono is situated in central Maine, 8 miles north of Bangor, Maine's third-largest city. The University of Maine is 240 miles north of Boston and 306 miles from Montreal. The Bangor area is served by daily air and bus transportation. The local area offers many opportunities for a wide range of recreational activities. Within an easy drive of the campus are many sites of great natural beauty, such as Acadia National Park, Mount Katahdin, and Baxter State Park, as well as several ski resorts, including Sugarloaf/USA and Sunday River.

Majors and Degrees

The University of Maine offers more than eighty 4-year baccalaureate degree programs through five colleges: the College of Business, Public Policy, and Health; the College of Education and Human Development; the College of Engineering; the College of Liberal Arts and Sciences; and the College of Natural Sciences, Forestry, and Agriculture. The Division of Lifelong Learning also offers a Bachelor of University Studies degree for part-time adult learners.

Academic Programs

The University of Maine is a year-round educational institution. The academic year is divided into two 15-week semesters, from early September to early May; a three-week May term; a summer session with two- to eight-week sessions; and a summer field session. The University offers evening as well as day classes.

All students in baccalaureate degree programs must meet the University's General Education requirements. In addition, each academic college sets its own requirements in terms of grades and the number of credits and specific courses required for graduation. Information concerning specific graduation requirements can be found in the undergraduate catalog (http://catalog.umaine.edu). Academic advisers assist all students with completing their degree requirements and fulfilling their personal educational objectives.

The University of Maine provides many opportunities to encourage intellectual curiosity and recognize exceptional achievement. Outstanding entering first-year students are offered the opportunity to participate in the Honors College, one of the country's oldest. Those who successfully complete the honors curriculum and complete the honors thesis graduate with Honors, High Honors, or Highest Honors. Many academic colleges and majors also offer membership in various honor societies. Students and faculty members on campus are members of thirty-nine such societies, including Phi Beta Kappa, Phi Kappa Phi, Tau Beta Pi, Xi Sigma Pi, Kappa Delta Pi, Beta Gamma Sigma, and Alpha Zeta. The University also recognizes top graduates as cum laude, magna cum laude, or summa cum laude.

ROTC programs are available in Army and Navy/Marine Corps.

Off-Campus Programs

At least forty departments of the University offer field-based learning programs, including internships, cooperative education programs, and field experience. Students are given academic credit and/or compensation for on-the-job experience in their major field.

The University of Maine offers a number of national and international student exchanges through the National Student Exchange (NSE), the Council on International Education Exchange (CIEE), the College Consortium for International Studies (CCIS), and the International Student Exchange Program (ISEP). The University also sponsors reciprocal exchanges between the University of Maine and such countries as Australia, France, Germany, Ireland, and Japan and sponsors a Junior Year Abroad Program in Salzburg, Austria. The Canada Year program, which is coordinated by the University's Canadian-American Center, offers students the opportunity to study at various Canadian universities..

The University

Academic Facilities

Fogler Library, which is located at the center of the campus, was built in 1942, and an addition was completed in 1976. It is Maine's largest library collection and the eighteenth-largest library in New England. It contains 1,094,622 volumes and more than 1.64 million microforms, subscribes to 12,412 periodicals, and is a regional depository for more than 2 million government documents. Its departments include Reference Services, the Science and Engineering Center, Special Collections, the Learning Materials Center, Government Documents, and the Listening Center.

All departments on campus have the necessary laboratories and equipment to support student and faculty research. Undergraduates have access to computer facilities through the University's widespread wireless network as well as through computers located throughout the campus. All classroom buildings are wireless and all residence halls are connected to the University's computer system, which provides access to a variety of software programs and network services.

Among the other facilities on campus are the Maine Center for the Arts, which includes the Hutchins Concert Hall (seating capacity of 1,628) and the Hudson Museum, an ethnographic and archeological museum with a permanent collection of 8,000 pieces of pre-Hispanic Mexican, Central American, and Native American artifacts. The University of Maine Museum of Art, which is located in downtown Bangor, is the only museum owned by the citizens of the state of Maine to house a permanent fine arts collection (more than 5,700 works of art), Art Department Galleries, a public observatory (the only one in the state), and a planetarium. Recently completed or renovated buildings include the Advanced Engineered Wood Composites Building, the Wes Jordan Athletic Training Center, and art galleries and studios in Lord Hall.

Costs

Costs are adjusted annually by the University of Maine System Board of Trustees. For the 2007–08 academic year, tuition for state residents was $223 per credit hour; for nonresident students, it was $632 per credit hour. (The average credit load for full-time students is 15 credit hours per semester, or 30 credit hours for the academic year.) Canadian and nonresident students who qualify for the New England Regional Program pay $332 per credit hour. Required University fees ($1494 per year for a full-time student) include the Comprehensive Fee, which provides a variety of health-care services and admission to cultural and recreational events. Books and supplies cost about $700 for the academic year. Room and board (nineteen meals per week) charges for the academic year were $7125. These costs are subject to change by legislative action.

Financial Aid

The University requires all financial aid applicants to file the Free Application for Federal Student Aid (FAFSA). The University of Maine encourages students to file the FAFSA online. The deadline to apply for aid is March 1. Awards usually consist of a combination of several types of aid, ranging from grants and scholarships to work-study jobs and student loans.

Faculty

The University of Maine has approximately 740 full- and part-time faculty members and a student-faculty ratio of 16:1. A number of faculty members teach both undergraduate and graduate courses. Graduate students serve as teaching assistants in some departments. Faculty members are involved in both teaching and research and also serve as academic advisers to undergraduate students. In addition, the faculty takes an active part in the education of students outside of the classroom through seminars, workshops, and discussion groups and by serving as advisers to student organizations. Many faculty members also serve on the Student Advisory Committee, the Student Conduct Committee, and other organizations on campus that serve the needs of students.

Student Government

An elected president, vice president, and vice president of financial affairs direct and coordinate Student Government programs at the University of Maine. Student Government works closely with the Office of the Vice President for Student Affairs and appoints 200 student representatives to the various University committees. These committees are involved with residence hall programs, student discipline, athletics, and cultural activities on campus. The work of the executive budgetary committee of Student Government includes the budgeting of approximately $400,000 in student activity fees. Student Government comprises five governing boards and the General Student Senate.

Admission Requirements

Admission to the University of Maine is a selective process. Successful applicants are those whose scholastic achievement, intellectual curiosity, and established study habits promise success in a comprehensive university environment. The admission committee reviews the strength of the high school curriculum, the grades received, the counselor recommendation, and either SAT or ACT scores as the primary criteria for admission. Student essays and information regarding the applicant's school and community activities provide additional information that may help the committee evaluate potential for success.

The University recognizes advanced work completed in secondary schools by means of Advanced Placement tests. Also, students who demonstrate advanced knowledge may be exempted from certain courses and requirements if they pass examinations specially developed by the University's academic departments.

Application and Information

An application form, which is available from the Admissions Office, any Maine high school guidance office, or online, should be submitted with the nonrefundable application fee. The University of Maine is a member of the Common Application, which may be submitted by paper copy or online, and the online-only Universal College Application. Additional required documents include official high school transcripts along with counselor recommendations. Traditional-age applicants are required to submit scores from either the SAT or ACT.

To be considered for full financial aid, students are encouraged to submit their admission applications by February 1. In addition, the University of Maine has an early action deadline of December 15. Students whose complete applications are postmarked by December 15 are reviewed by the end of January. Early action candidates are given first consideration for merit scholarships awarded by the Admissions Office. Students applying for the spring semester are encouraged to submit applications by December 1. Applications after these dates are processed on a space-available basis. Applications and all supporting documents should be sent to UMS Processing, P.O. Box 412, Bangor, Maine 04402-0412.

Office of Admission
5713 Chadbourne Hall
University of Maine
Orono, Maine 04469-5713
Phone: 207-581-1561
877-486-2364 (toll-free)
Fax: 207-581-1213
E-mail: um-admit@maine.edu
Web site: http://www.go.umaine.edu/

UNIVERSITY OF MAINE AT FORT KENT

FORT KENT, MAINE

The University

The University of Maine at Fort Kent (UMFK) offers the combination of high-quality education and personalized attention today's students are looking for. The small campus population of 1,300 ensures that professors know their students by name. The favorable student-faculty ratio of 18:1 provides many opportunities for interaction. At the same time, the University is large enough to offer a wide variety of academic and extracurricular opportunities. The University's diverse student body includes individuals from small towns and big cities across the United States and Canada, as well as from Europe, Africa, South America, and Asia.

UMFK was founded in 1878 as the Madawaska Training School to educate teachers for what was known as the Madawaska Territory. Over the next century, the school evolved and refined its program into a comprehensive liberal arts–based institution. In 1970, it became part of the seven-campus University of Maine System.

The University's three residence halls, Crocker Hall, Powell Hall, and the Lodge, offer housing; the dining facility, Nowland Hall, provides meal service for the student body. Computer, cable TV, and phone hookups are provided in every room, and the halls also have lounges, game rooms, and free laundry facilities. Resident students and commuters alike participate in a variety of campus activities, including theatrical and musical performances, intercollegiate and intramural athletics, and numerous student organizations.

Location

The town of Fort Kent is situated on the banks of the Fish and St. John Rivers in an area originally settled by French-speaking Acadians from Maritime Canada. The St. John Valley community is noted as one of the country's few truly international, bilingual-bicultural regions, and the University of Maine at Fort Kent is known as a great place to learn and grow within that community.

The campus has convenient access to numerous areas of scenic natural beauty, as well as recreational opportunities, including ski areas and resorts, Baxter State Park, the Allagash Wilderness Waterway, and the Gaspé Peninsula in Canada's Quebec Province.

The University of Maine at Fort Kent is in proximity to the Maine Winter Sports Center, which is the home to Olympic biathlon training. The facility typically offers on-snow training from Thanksgiving to Easter and also offers summer training on its paved roller ski–training and advanced-training loops and cross-country running trails. Mountain-biking trails are also available at the site. The center features a three-story lodge with showers, locker rooms, and waxing facilities. Former Olympians provide world-class coaching in cross-country skiing and biathlon.

Majors and Degrees

The University of Maine at Fort Kent is a four-year baccalaureate-granting institution that offers the Bachelor of Arts in English and French; the Bachelor of Science in behavioral science, biology, business management, computer applications, e-commerce, education (K–12), environmental studies, nursing, rural public safety administration, social sciences, teacher certification (both elementary and secondary education), and University studies; the Associate of Arts in business, computer science, criminal justice, general studies, and human services; and the Associate of Science in forest technology.

Academic Programs

Dedicated to providing a solid liberal arts education within programs designed to equip students for the twenty-first century, the University of Maine at Fort Kent divides the academic year into two 16-week semesters. Both day and evening classes run from early September through early May. Summer classes and workshops are also offered, beginning in May and usually ending in late July. All students, regardless of degree program and major, are required to complete a general education core curriculum and meet certain requirements for graduation. Each degree program and major also has a number of specific requirements that are described in the University catalog.

Entering freshmen are assigned an adviser who is a member of a special advising team devoted to ensuring the success of every student's first year at UMFK.

After the first year, students choose a faculty academic adviser in their field of study, who guides them toward completion of their program requirements.

Off-Campus Programs

UMFK offers opportunities for students to study abroad, including exchange programs with Canadian and European universities. A cooperative agreement between the University of Maine at Fort Kent and Université de Moncton's Edmundston Campus provides students with a unique opportunity for cross-registration at either campus. The French branch of the Université de Moncton is located only 22 miles from Fort Kent in Edmundston, New Brunswick. The universities celebrate the heritage of the original settlers of the Upper St. John River Valley.

Along with approximately 130 other public universities across the United States, the University of Maine at Fort Kent is a member of the National Student Exchange Program as well as the New England–Quebec and the New England–Nova Scotia Student Exchange Programs. These programs allow full-time students to pursue course work at other universities in the United States, Quebec, or Nova Scotia to satisfy part of the credit requirements for a degree at UMFK.

Bachelor of Science in environmental studies students also benefit from a cooperative program that allows them to spend a semester or a year studying at either the University of Maine at Presque Isle or the University of Maine at Machias. In addition, practical field experience is available to UMFK environmental studies students through an agreement with the National Audubon Expedition Institute. Through this program, students in good standing can spend a year on an excursion that takes them across the country and requires that they encounter and deal with an array of environmental issues.

Academic Facilities

UMFK is home to the state-of-the-art Northern Maine Center for Rural Health Sciences and Northern Aroostook Technology

Center. The facilities serve as a home for the University's nursing program and also house the most modern classrooms and teleconferencing center in northern Maine.

Additional buildings on UMFK's 54-acre campus include the Cyr Hall classroom complex and computer laboratory, Fox Auditorium, the Sportscenter, the Old Model School, the Computer Center, and Nadeau Hall, which houses an e-commerce lab, faculty offices, a nursing lab, a music lab, an on-campus health clinic, and a satellite conference center. In addition to its own collections, Blake Library provides students with a variety of available databases and electronic access to more than 1 million volumes in libraries of the University of Maine System. A recently completed construction project is the Acadian Archives Building, which preserves, celebrates, and disseminates information about the region's history and houses documents and artifacts. This building contains a conference room, reading room, work room, reference desk, a bank of computers, and research materials stacks as well as personnel space, a collections area, and an accessioning room.

The University also owns or has access to a number of off-campus facilities that are available to students, and enhance academic programs by providing opportunity for hands-on study. The Elmer Violette Wilderness Camp, located on the Allagash Wilderness Waterway in the famed North Maine Woods, is frequently used by the Environmental Studies and Forestry Programs to conduct fieldwork. The wilderness camp includes housing and classroom facilities. Other academic programs also use the camp at various times throughout the year.

Other off-campus UMFK facilities include a 1,000-acre wooded lot bordering St. Froid Lake, a biological park near the campus, and access points to the Fish and St. John Rivers.

Costs

In 2007–08, tuition was $5100 per year for Maine residents and $12,780 per year for out-of-state students. Nonresident students who qualify for the New England Regional Program paid $7710 per year for tuition. Room and board costs for 2007–08 were $6620. Required University fees for new students were $653, which include application, matriculation, orientation, student activity, and technology fees. Tuition and fee figures listed are based on 15 credit hours per semester.

Financial Aid

The University of Maine at Fort Kent Office of Financial Aid administers scholarships, grants, loans, and work assistance to more than 80 percent of enrolled students. The University requires all applicants for financial aid to file the Free Application for Federal Student Aid (FAFSA), which is available from the UMFK Office of Financial Aid, from high school guidance offices, and online at http://www.fafsa.cd.gov. UMFK has a preferred filing date of March 1. Consideration is given at any time during the year; however, early application is recommended because awards depend on the availability of funds.

Faculty

Excellence has always been the goal of the 38-member UMFK faculty. Its members include accomplished scholars who hold the highest degree in their professional field. Faculty members are active in professional activities, research, and continuing education. Their top priority, however, is always teaching. Classes are generally small, and every faculty member teaches and advises students.

Student Government

UMFK has a long tradition of strong student government. The Student Senate, which represents all students, is a member of the University of Maine Organization of Student Governments.

Admission Requirements

The UMFK Office of Admissions considers each applicant on an individual basis. Consideration is given to academic preparation, maturity, personal motivation, and goals. Particular attention is given to secondary school performance, especially in the junior and senior years. SAT or ACT scores are not required for admission to the University of Maine at Fort Kent.

Application and Information

Application for admission is made by completing a University of Maine System application form or by applying online at the University's Web site. A nonrefundable fee of $40 must be submitted to the UMFK Office of Admissions. The University follows a rolling admissions schedule and accepts applications at any time during the year. Students are usually accepted for entry in either September or January.

Applications and additional information are available from:

Office of Admissions
University of Maine at Fort Kent
23 University Drive
Fort Kent, Maine 04743
Phone: 207-834-7600
888-TRY-UMFK (879-8635; toll-free)
Fax: 207-834-7609
E-mail: umfkadm@maine.edu
Web site: http://www.umfk.maine.edu

Students enjoy the close, family-like atmosphere that the University of Maine at Fort Kent provides. The low student-teacher ratio, personalized attention, and numerous campus events and activities all create the ideal setting for a top-quality learning and life experience.

UNIVERSITY OF MAINE AT MACHIAS

MACHIAS, MAINE

The University

Located on the spectacular coast of Downeast Maine, the University of Maine at Machias (UMM) is a small, residential, undergraduate liberal college of more than 1,200 students. The college was incorporated in 1909 and is a member of the University of Maine system. Small classes (the average is 16 students) and a faculty-student ratio of 1:14 contribute to an academic atmosphere that is intimate and intense and where independent thinking is encouraged.

Although many UMM students are from the state of Maine, the University's distinctive programs and location attract many others from the New England, mid-Atlantic, and Midwest regions of the country.

Location

Machias, Maine, is a classic small New England town located on the tidal Machias River, with a town center that includes a number of retail stores, restaurants (including fast food), a supermarket, a natural foods store, and churches of various denominations. The greater Machias–area population is 5,000. The region is a popular outdoor recreation destination, with ocean beaches, inland lakes and streams, and miles of mountains, forests, and trails.

Downeast Maine has been a source of inspiration for generations of artists, outdoorsmen, mariners, and environmentalists. UMM's coastal location provides a unique learning environment, with excellent opportunities for fieldwork, hands-on learning, and cooperative education and internship experiences.

Majors and Degrees

The University of Maine at Machias awards Bachelor of Arts and Bachelor of Science degrees in behavioral science (concentrations in applied anthropology and applied psychology), biology (concentrations in dentistry, field biology, medicine, optometry, pharmacy, and veterinary medicine), business and entrepreneurial studies (self-designed concentration), college studies (secondary mathematics education and self-designed program option), elementary teacher education, environmental studies (self-designed concentration), English (concentrations in creative writing and literary studies), history, interdisciplinary fine arts (concentrations in creative writing, music, theater, and visual arts), marine biology (concentrations in biological science, mariculture, marine ecology, and self-designed), and recreation management (self-designed concentration).

Academic Programs

Bachelor's degree candidates must complete at least 120 credit hours with a minimum cumulative grade point average of 2.0 and must also complete the core requirements in business studies, fine arts, humanities, physical education, science/mathematics, and social sciences.

Academic Facilities

All of the University's academic buildings are of modern construction and include a well-equipped science building with laboratories, a greenhouse, marine science aquariums, and a GPS computer laboratory. Computer labs, some of which are open 24 hours a day, seven days a week for student use, house the latest in technology hardware and software.

Merrill Library provides a 24-hour study center with computer workstations for students, houses a collection of more than 100,000 volumes, and is linked to other libraries and educational resources throughout the state. A computer center with cross-campus networking and multiple computer labs enhances all of UMM's programs and provides access to the Internet and the Web. Individual computer access is also available in every residence hall room. The University of Maine at Machias Student Support Center provides faculty, peer, and professional assistance as well as computer and audiovisual aids for all students. A residence facility with contemporary suites and single rooms was completed in 2003.

The Center for Lifelong Learning (CLL) includes a large gymnasium, an aquatics center with a competition-size pool, a state-of-the-art fitness center, racquetball/handball courts, and a recreational equipment center, in which students may check out canoes, kayaks, snowshoes, cross-country skis, bicycles, and camping equipment. The Early Care and Education Center provides child-care facilities for the community and the University; it also provides an on-campus site for UMM elementary teacher education students to participate in field studies.

A wide variety of student activities, from meetings to coffeehouses and other social events, are accommodated in the Student Center. Located in the same building, the campus radio station, WUMM, is run entirely by students. The Performing Arts Center, a 358-seat amphitheater auditorium, is host to numerous campus and community meetings, seminars, festivals, and performing arts and theatrical presentations.

Costs

The basic expenses for the 2007–08 academic year (based on a 15-credit-hour load per semester) were $5770 per year for in-state tuition and $14,800 per year for out-of-state tuition. The University of Maine at Machias participates in the New England Board of Higher Education Regional Student program, which allows reduced tuition ($8380 per year) for students from the other New England states who are enrolled in specific academic programs.

Financial Aid

The University of Maine at Machias administers scholarships, loans, grants, and work-study awards. UMM has a Presidential Scholarship Program, a Campus Housing Award Program, and a Travel Grant Program for transfers. Financial aid awards are made on the basis of need, and students must submit the Free

Application for Federal Student Aid (FAFSA) to the College Scholarship Service. March 15 is the University's financial aid priority deadline.

Faculty

Nearly all University of Maine at Machias faculty members hold the highest degree in their professional field. The faculty-student ratio is 1:14. All faculty members work as advisers and mentors to students within their areas of academic expertise. Usually on a first-name basis, faculty members develop a close relationship with students during their years of study at UMM and beyond.

Student Government

The University of Maine at Machias is a member of the University of Maine Organization of Student Governments and operates its own Student Senate. Students are encouraged to become involved and participate.

Admission Requirements

Graduation from secondary school or a high school equivalency diploma is the basic requirement for admission. Applicants to the University should have followed a college-preparatory high school program with 4 years of English, 3 years of math, 3 lab sciences, 2 social sciences, a foreign language, and computer utilization. If a student is entering one of the business programs, consideration is given to business courses taken in high school. However, college-preparatory English, math, science, and social science courses are still necessary. Scores from the SAT or ACT are also required. Applicants should rank in the top half of their high school class and have an overall grade average of B or better.

The University of Maine at Machias does not discriminate on the basis of race, creed, color, sex, or national origin and is an Equal Opportunity/Affirmative Action Employer.

Application and Information

The University of Maine at Machias operates on a rolling admission system. Candidates should complete their applications as early as possible. Students may apply for early admission, through which they may be admitted directly into the University after completing three years of secondary school. Candidates for this program must have recommendations of support from their guidance counselor, principal, superintendent, and/or school board. Their high school grades should place them in the top 15 percent of their class. UMM accepts applications from transfer students. Transfer applicants should complete their applications by June 1 for the fall term or by December 1 for the spring term.

Application materials and additional information may be obtained by contacting:

Director of Admissions
University of Maine at Machias
9 O'Brien Avenue
Machias, Maine 04654
Phone: 207-255-1318
888-468-6866 (toll-free)
Fax: 207-255-1363
E-mail: ummadmissions@maine.edu
Web site: http://www.umm.maine.edu

The University of Maine at Machias is located on the spectacular coast of Downeast Maine.

UNIVERSITY OF NEW ENGLAND

BIDDEFORD AND PORTLAND, MAINE

The University

The University of New England (UNE) is an independent, coeducational, comprehensive university committed to academic excellence and the enhancement of the quality of life for the people, organizations, and communities it serves. The University fosters critical inquiry through a student-centered academic environment rich in research, scholarship, creative activity, and service while providing opportunities for acquiring and applying knowledge in selected clinical, professional, and community settings.

UNE's 3,553 students are enrolled in a wide variety of academic programs at the undergraduate, graduate, and first-professional levels in four colleges: the College of Arts and Sciences, the College of Health Professions, the College of Pharmacy, and the College of Osteopathic Medicine (housing Maine's only medical school). At the undergraduate level, there are approximately 1,986 students enrolled from thirty-five different states and several other countries in over forty undergraduate degree programs.

UNE traces its history to 1831 with the founding of Westbrook College, one of Maine's oldest institutions of learning. Today's university represents the joining of three unique higher education institutions through the combining of St. Francis College and the New England College of Osteopathic Medicine in 1978 and Westbrook College in 1996.

The University has chosen as its primary fields of education business management, education, health sciences (both mental and physical), the humanities, the natural sciences, and social sciences. The University of New England's philosophy of education and student life places emphasis on the quality of instruction and the practical application of academic material.

Each program includes the opportunity for learning in a community-based setting. Internships, co-ops, clinicals, and student teaching add up to the practical experience that allows students at UNE to apply the skills learned in the classroom to real job situations.

The University of New England has two campuses. The University Campus is located on the southern coast of Maine, in Biddeford, 90 miles north of Boston and 20 miles south of Portland, Maine's largest city. UNE's Westbrook College Campus is located in Portland, Maine. As both campuses are geographically placed in areas that afford a high-quality lifestyle, it is only natural that the University of New England consistently engages itself in providing its students with high-quality programming and high-quality education.

The University encourages students to become involved in activities, clubs, and sports. Popular interests include scuba diving, skiing, hiking, biking, varsity and intramural sports, swimming, community service programs, and photography. The University of New England offers a wide range of services on both campuses. Special features include a full health clinic, a dental hygiene clinic, career counseling, personal counseling, learning support services, and an extensive student leadership development program.

Student Support Services provides a wide-range of services to assist students with psychological and emotional health, academic support, educational and career planning, and equal opportunities during their academic experience. The Office of Career Services provides academic and career exploration assistance, assistance in applying to graduate schools, self-assessment and personal interest exploration, resume help, job listings, and job fairs. Learning Assistance Services, another department within Student Support Services, offers a comprehensive array of academic support, including placement testing, courses, workshops, tutoring, and individual consultations.

Both campuses offer a variety of cultural and social events. The Campus Center at the University Campus and the Finley Recreation Center on the Westbrook College Campus provide a setting for many recreational and sports activities. The University of New England Athletic Department operates an NCAA Division III varsity athletics program. Varsity sports for men are basketball, cross-country, golf, lacrosse, and soccer, and a new prevarsity ice hockey program is being developed into a varsity program over the next few years. Varsity sports for women are basketball, cross-country, field hockey, lacrosse, soccer, softball, swimming, and volleyball. Intramural teams in basketball, floor hockey, softball, skiing, and volleyball are popular.

On the University Campus in Biddeford, Decary Hall houses a cafeteria, classrooms, meeting rooms, and faculty and administrative offices. The Campus Center contains a fitness center, bookstore, gym, pool, student union, racquetball courts, an indoor track, a variety of multipurpose rooms, and administrative offices. The University maintains nine dormitories on campus. Marcil Hall houses a variety of classrooms, and faculty offices. The Harold Alfond Center for Health Sciences houses biology and chemistry labs as well as lecture halls, classrooms, a gross anatomy lab, and UNE's medical school facilities. The Marine Science Education and Research Center has classrooms, wet labs, aquaculture labs, and a marine mammal rehabilitation wing.

On the University of New England's Westbrook College Campus, there are three residence halls and the Alexander Hall Student Union, which houses the dining hall, bookstore, the Wing Lounge, and a variety of meeting rooms. The Finley Recreation Center has a full gym and fitness facilities. Ludcke Auditorium, whose main structure was built in 1887, is home to concerts, plays, and a number of workshops and meetings.

Location

The University of New England's two campuses are located in the picturesque southern coastal beach communities of Maine. The 540-acre University Campus in Biddeford, home to the College of Arts and Sciences and the College of Osteopathic Medicine, is situated on a beautiful coastal site where the Saco River flows into the Atlantic Ocean and includes more than 4,000 feet of water frontage. Located 20 miles to the north is the Westbrook College Campus, home to the College of Health Professions and the College of Pharmacy. It is set on 41 acres in a quiet residential setting in Portland. Students at both campuses can enjoy the vibrant social life offered in nearby metropolitan Boston (located 90 miles to the south of Biddeford) or Portland and the dynamic outdoor recreational activities that have made Maine a prime tourist destination. Southern Maine is conveniently serviced by a number of airlines at the Portland International Jetport and by bus and train service with stations in Biddeford/Saco and Portland, making the University's campuses very accessible to all areas of the Northeastern United States and beyond.

Majors and Degrees

UNE offers highly competitive undergraduate and graduate programs in a variety of areas. On the undergraduate level, the University confers Associate of Science, Bachelor of Arts, and Bachelor of Science degrees.

Associate degrees are offered in dental hygiene and nursing. Bachelor's degrees are offered in applied exercise science, aquaculture and aquarium science, art education, athletic training, biochemistry, biological sciences, business, chemistry, communications, dental hygiene, elementary education, English, environmental science, environmental studies, health sciences (for occupational therapy five-year entry-level master's degree), health-services management (bachelor's degree completion program), history, liberal studies (including prelaw), marine biology, mathematics, medical biology (health and medical sciences tracks for predental, premedicine, and pre–veterinary studies), nursing, political science, psychobiology, psychology, psychology and social relations, sociology, and sport management.

Individualized majors, various minors, pre–physical therapy designation, accelerated pre–physician assistant studies programs, prepharmacy with an early assurance path to the Pharm.D. program, and secondary education certification (Teacher Certification Program) are also available at the undergraduate level.

Academic Programs

All undergraduate programs at UNE have a core curriculum as a common thread. Designed to provide a foundation in the liberal arts, the core reflects the values of the college and is designed to prepare students for living informed, thoughtful, and active lives in a complex and changing society. It provides an innovative common learning experience for all UNE undergraduates. It invites students to explore four college-wide themes: Environmental Awareness, Social and Global Awareness, Critical Thinking: Human Responses to Problems and Challenges, and Citizenship. Skills of communications, mathematics, and critical thinking are taught throughout the core.

A bachelor's degree is awarded upon successful completion of at least 120 credit hours and fulfillment of specific program and University requirements.

The University academic year consists of two semesters.

Off-Campus Programs

UNE is committed to supplementing the traditional learning process with practical applications. All students are encouraged to participate in cooperative education programs, field placements, and practicums. These experiences provide valuable learning situations and increase a student's exposure to job-related opportunities, and they are required for graduation by most majors. Students also have the opportunity to arrange a study-abroad experience. The Office for Study Abroad and International Programs promotes the goals of international cooperation and understanding through rigorous academic programs, overseas study opportunities, student-faculty research projects, and a host of special programs designed to address current issues in international relations and cultural studies.

Academic Facilities

On the University Campus, Decary Hall houses classrooms, laboratories, and faculty and administrative offices. The Jack Ketchum Library has been expanded to provide more library and classroom space as well as a media center and special event space. Marcil Hall houses classrooms, faculty offices, and the facility for the occupational therapy program. The Harold Alfond Center for Health Sciences houses labs and classrooms for the medical school, undergraduate health and life science programs, and graduate health programs. The Marine Science Education and Research Center is a $7.5-million facility featuring a marine mammal rehab center as well as classrooms, wet and dry laboratories, and research areas. The marine mammal rehabilitation center works primarily with seals, porpoise, and sea turtles. Gregory Hall is the home of the Department of Creative and Fine Arts. It houses faculty offices and studio space for drawing, painting, print making, sculpting, and photography.

On the University's Westbrook College Campus, Ludcke Auditorium is used for a variety of academic programs. Coleman Dental Hygiene Building houses classroom, clinic, and faculty space. The Blewett Science Center, home of UNE nursing programs, consists of science labs and classrooms, and Alumni Hall is a classroom facility. The University created a Performance Enhancement and Evaluation Center (PEEC) that is an entire center devoted to learning and assessment of patient evaluation skills. The equipment includes two METI Human Patient Simulators and two Laerdal SimMan simulators. Proctor Hall is also a classroom building and is home to the Proctor Learning and Career Center. Josephine S. Abplanalp Library houses study space and computer terminals, along with an outstanding collection of books and periodicals and the Maine Women Writers Collection. The University of New England libraries have over 150,000 volumes and print journals, over 22,000 print and electronic full-text journal titles, and 6,000 electronic books.

Costs

The costs per academic year for 2007–08 were tuition, $24,440; room and board, $9860; and fees, $890.

Financial Aid

In 2007–08, approximately 90 percent of all full-time freshmen received some form of financial assistance. The average package was $22,000. Financial award packages include scholarships, grants, loans, and employment. The University of New England has an extensive scholarship program that is based on academic performance. These scholarships can range from $2000 to $17,000.

Faculty

The men and women who teach at the University of New England are an experienced group of people with more than 85 percent having earned the highest degree in their fields, and they bring to the University varied backgrounds as teachers and practitioners of their disciplines. They are highly competent, demanding, concerned, accessible, and willing to give individual attention to students. Most important, they have come to the University for many of the same reasons that prompt their students to attend. The match between what the faculty has to offer and what the students need and expect is the key to the rare educational environment at the University of New England.

The University has 111 full-time undergraduate faculty members, 85 percent of whom have the terminal degree in their field, and 27 part-time members, a number of whom have doctoral degrees and hold administrative positions.

Student Government

The Student Senate is a vital part of the student life at both campuses of the University of New England. The student government has its own operating budget, which is derived from the student fees. The organization covers student services and public relations.

Admission Requirements

The University welcomes applications from students who are seriously pursuing an education of high quality. Candidates can file their admission application after the completion of their junior year of high school. All applicants are considered on an individual basis.

Students applying for admission are expected to submit a completed application, a $40 nonrefundable application fee, transcripts of all academic work (high school and college), and scores on either the ACT or SAT. Students who do not use English as their primary language must submit TOEFL scores. Students applying for admission should have completed a curriculum that includes English, mathematics, science, and social sciences. International students must also complete the International Student Supplemental Application. Those considering majors in the life or health sciences should show strength and preparation in mathematics and science. All prospective students are strongly encouraged to visit the campuses of the University of New England for an interview and tour. Interviews are held weekdays from 10 a.m. to 4 p.m. An appointment should be requested by letter or telephone.

Application and Information

The undergraduate admission application deadline is February 15; applications received after that date are reviewed on a space-available basis. There is a December 1 priority application deadline with a December 31 notification date. Applications for the spring term are accepted through December 15.

For application information, students should contact:

Office of Admissions
University Campus
University of New England
Hills Beach Road
Biddeford, Maine 04005
Phone: 207-283-0171
800-477-4863 Ext. 2297 (toll-free)
Fax: 207-602-5900
E-mail: admissions@une.edu
Web site: http://www.une.edu/

UNIVERSITY OF SOUTHERN MAINE

PORTLAND, MAINE

The University

Since its founding in 1878 as the Western Maine Normal School, the University of Southern Maine (USM) has evolved into a selective, comprehensive, regional, residential public university. USM undergraduates learn from exceptional professors who give personal attention to students. The average class size at USM is 22 students. Students can enjoy the friendly atmosphere of a small residential New England college campus combined with many opportunities typically available only at large, national, urban universities.

The University of Southern Maine offers students a unique blend of academic and residential life opportunities on two campuses only 8 miles apart in Portland and Gorham. USM's third campus, Lewiston-Auburn College, serves the educational needs for this growing region of the state. The Portland and Gorham campuses enjoy full classroom facilities, library services, athletic facilities, and student centers. The Portland campus is the site of the Southworth Planetarium, which is ranked among the top ten small planetariums in the United States. On the Gorham campus there are seven residence halls, cross-country ski trails, an art gallery, a campus center, a theater, and a concert hall. The sports complex features an Olympic-size ice arena and a field house that features a six-lane, 200-meter track; four tennis courts; basketball courts; and baseball and softball practice areas. The diverse student body of 4,700 full-time undergraduates representing students from thirty-five states and thirty-seven countries includes accomplished artists, musicians, writers, actors, and numerous all-American athletes. Approximately 1,500 students reside in University-owned housing.

The athletic program is a vital part of the USM community and the greater Portland area. In addition to a full intramural program, USM currently fields intercollegiate athletic teams (NCAA Division III) for men in baseball, basketball, cross-country, ice hockey, indoor and outdoor track, lacrosse, soccer, tennis, and wrestling and for women in basketball, cross-country, field hockey, ice hockey, indoor and outdoor track, lacrosse, soccer, softball, tennis, and volleyball. Cheerleading and golf are coeducational offerings.

USM offers master's degrees in the areas of accounting, adult education, American and New England studies, applied immunology, biology, business administration (M.B.A.), community planning and development, computer science, counselor education, creative writing, educational leadership, health policy and management, leadership studies, literacy education, manufacturing systems, music, nursing, occupational therapy, public policy and management, school psychology, social work, special education, and statistics; doctoral degrees are offered in law, public policy and management, and school psychology. The College of Education and Human Development also offers a postbaccalaureate fifth-year program leading to either elementary or secondary teacher certification.

Location

USM's location in southern Maine is an ideal place to be a college student. Students have access to a rich array of social, cultural, and athletic activities in Portland, as well as the endless opportunities provided by proximity to the Atlantic Ocean, mountains, lakes, and woods. Therefore, it is no surprise that Portland is continuously recognized as one of the best cities in the country for outdoor recreation. The coast of Maine, one of the most spectacular scenic regions in the country, offers many fine beaches for relaxing and islands for exploring, while nearby mountains and forests offer skiing and hiking. The city of Portland is a haven for the nearly 35,000 college students from the twelve colleges and universities that are within an hour's drive of USM.

Majors and Degrees

USM offers forty-seven bachelor's degrees, twenty-three master's degrees, and three doctoral degrees through its College of Arts and Sciences, Lewiston-Auburn College, and six professional schools: the College of Education and Human Development; the School of Business; the School of Applied Science, Engineering and Technology; the College of Nursing and Health Professions; the Muskie School of Public Service; and the School of Law.

The College of Arts and Sciences is the heart of USM, comprising twenty-three academic departments. The College offers the following baccalaureate degrees (Bachelor of Arts degrees, except as noted): art (B.A. or B.F.A.), biology, chemistry, communication and media studies, criminology, economics, English, French, geography-anthropology, geosciences, history, linguistics, mathematics and statistics, modern and classical languages and literatures, music, music education, music performance (B.M.), philosophy, physics, political science, psychology, social work, sociology, and theater. Self-designed majors include classical studies, foreign languages, French studies, German studies, Hispanic studies, international studies, and social science. In addition, preprofessional study is offered in dentistry, law, medicine, and veterinary science. The College of Education and Human Development offers an undergraduate teacher certification program, Teachers for Elementary and Middle Schools (TEAMS). It includes course work in an academic major that leads to a degree in a liberal arts field and a professional program of elementary teacher certification (K–8). The School of Business offers Bachelor of Science (B.S.) degree programs in accounting, finance, management information systems, and marketing. These degrees provide the basis for careers in accounting, finance, banking, industry, government, and organizational management. The School of Applied Science, Engineering and Technology offers B.S. degrees in applied technical leadership, computer science, electrical engineering, environmental planning and policy, environmental safety and health, environmental science, industrial technology, and mechanical engineering and technology education. The pre-engineering program provides introductory courses suitable for transfer elsewhere in any engineering discipline. B.S. degrees and teacher certification in technology education and applied technical education are also offered. The College of Nursing and Health Professions offers B.S. degrees in health sciences, nursing, radiation therapy, sports medicine, and therapeutic recreation. The sports medicine program includes three majors: athletic training, exercise physiology, and health fitness. The health sciences and radiation therapy degrees are available to those who have completed a two-year degree in a health field.

Academic Programs

USM's educational programs are designed to meet the needs of a changing society. The curriculum offers a variety of courses in liberal arts that foster creative thinking and communication skills. Undergraduate education at USM is built around a strong, three-component core curriculum. The Basic Competence component develops a foundation of skills necessary for academic success, including the ability to write clearly, the ability to use quantitative information, and the ability to reason effectively. The Methods of Inquiry/Ways of Knowing component introduces the student to different disciplines: their subject matter, methods, and broader purposes. These include the fine arts, humanities, social sciences, and the natural sciences. The Interdisciplinary component seeks to counteract the fragmentation that results from academic specialization. Examples of interdisciplinary courses include Global Enlightenment; the Illuminated Autobiography; and Old and in the Way: Aging in America.

The honors program provides an enriched undergraduate education to students who are outstanding in their ability, curiosity, creativity, and motivation. Approximately 30 to 40 students are admitted to the honors program each year. Students work closely with faculty members in a series of small seminar-type courses. Later, honors students participate in an advanced seminar and undertake a major independent research project under the direction of a faculty member. All honors program work stresses independent learning, original thinking, and the development of skills in research, writing, and oral expression. Speakers, seminars, discussion groups, artistic presentations, and social events are scheduled regularly at Honors House.

The Russell Scholars Program, an innovative living and learning community, features collaborative teaching and learning, interdisciplinary courses, and a residential component. It includes a mentoring program, community service projects, and internships. In addition to the traditional and self-designed majors that are currently offered, motivated students may choose to design an academic program that is specifically suited to their personal career goals. In conjunction with a faculty committee, students have self-designed majors in many areas, including organizational behavior, public relations, and medical technology. USM's Cooperative Education Program provides students with opportunities to apply the knowledge they gain in the classroom.

Off-Campus Programs

USM offers study-abroad programs in cooperation with institutions in Austria, Canada, China, England, France, Ireland, Italy, Japan, the Netherlands, Russia, and Scotland. USM also participates in the National Student Exchange.

Academic Facilities

USM comprises more than 140 acres in Gorham, Portland, and Lewiston. The campus facilities include seventy-eight buildings with more than 130 classrooms and ninety-five laboratories. The library's collection includes more than a million books, documents, journals, and microforms. Full reference, circulation, and interlibrary loan services are available at each location. An online catalog provides access to and remote borrowing from all University of Maine System libraries. Access to the Internet and other computerized indexes and databases is available at workstations in the library and remotely to authorized users. Special collections include the Jean Byers Sampson Center for Diversity in Maine and the renowned Osher Map Library. USM has a variety of computer resources available for student use. Networked microcomputers are available on the Portland, Gorham, and Lewiston-Auburn campuses. Internet access and e-mail services are available from any of the networked computers. Students who own computers can connect from their residence hall rooms. The computer science department offers UNIX on Digital/Compaq Alpha systems and Windows NT. Specialized Windows NT labs are also available for students in electrical engineering, environmental science and policy, geography, and geosciences. Music and foreign language departments have specialized Macintosh labs. Student microlab centers, staffed by student assistants, have been established on all three campuses. The labs have Windows- and Macintosh-compatible computers with many general-purpose and course-specific software packages, including software for work processing, spreadsheets, mathematics/statistics, and databases.

Costs

Expenses for the 2007–08 academic year were $198 per credit hour for in-state tuition and $8038 for room and board. Out-of-state tuition was $547 per credit hour. USM also participates in the New England Regional Program, which allows reduced tuition for some out-of-state New England students. Tuition and fees are set annually.

Financial Aid

Lack of funds should not deter students from applying for admission to USM. During 2005–06, more than $58 million was awarded to students through various financial aid programs, including grants, loans, and employment opportunities. More than 8,800 students received an average of $8200 in financial aid. USM also helped more than 5,500 students borrow more than $34 million in low-interest loans from commercial banks. The average loan was $6600. The Office of Student Financial Aid is available to help students explore funding sources outside USM. All students must complete the Free Application for Federal Student Aid (FAFSA). These forms are available from most high school guidance offices. For priority consideration, students are encouraged to apply by February 15.

Faculty

USM's dedicated faculty members represent a wide range of knowledge and expertise. They include Fulbright Fellows and authors of national note in every academic discipline. In the last ten years, more than 100 faculty members—all with doctoral degrees or the most advanced degrees appropriate to their disciplines—have been recruited from major institutions throughout the country. Faculty members are teachers who can communicate the excitement of learning and the joy of discovery to their students. USM does not employ graduate teaching assistants for undergraduate classes; labs and discussion groups are taught by faculty members themselves. The student-faculty ratio is approximately 13:1.

Student Government

A 21-member Senate, elected by undergraduates, is the principal governing body for student life. Students having problems in any aspect of University life have recourse through the Senate and the Student Grievance Committee.

Admission Requirements

Admission to USM is competitive and based primarily on the applicant's academic background, rigor of the high school program, and grades achieved. USM also considers SAT or ACT scores, individual talents, and activities. Evaluations of transfer students emphasize their most recent college grades. USM recognizes that prospective students may come from differing academic backgrounds, some far removed from high school; therefore, USM has established different admission categories to accommodate the needs of various students. The admission staff members can arrange tours of the campuses, provide information about academic programs, and discuss admission requirements. Music programs require an audition.

Application and Information

To apply to USM, students should submit a completed University of Maine System Application, an online application, or the Common Application and a nonrefundable fee of $40. The application asks for details of their academic, extracurricular, and personal background and an essay on their interest in USM and the degree program to which they are applying. Admission is on a rolling basis. Priority deadlines for admission are February 15 for the fall semester and December 1 for the spring semester. For more information, students should contact:

Director of Admission
University of Southern Maine
37 College Avenue
Portland, Maine 04104-9300
Phone: 207-780-5670
207-780-5646 (TTY)
Fax: 207-780-5640
E-mail: usmadm@usm.maine.edu
Web site: http://www.usm.maine.edu

MARYLAND

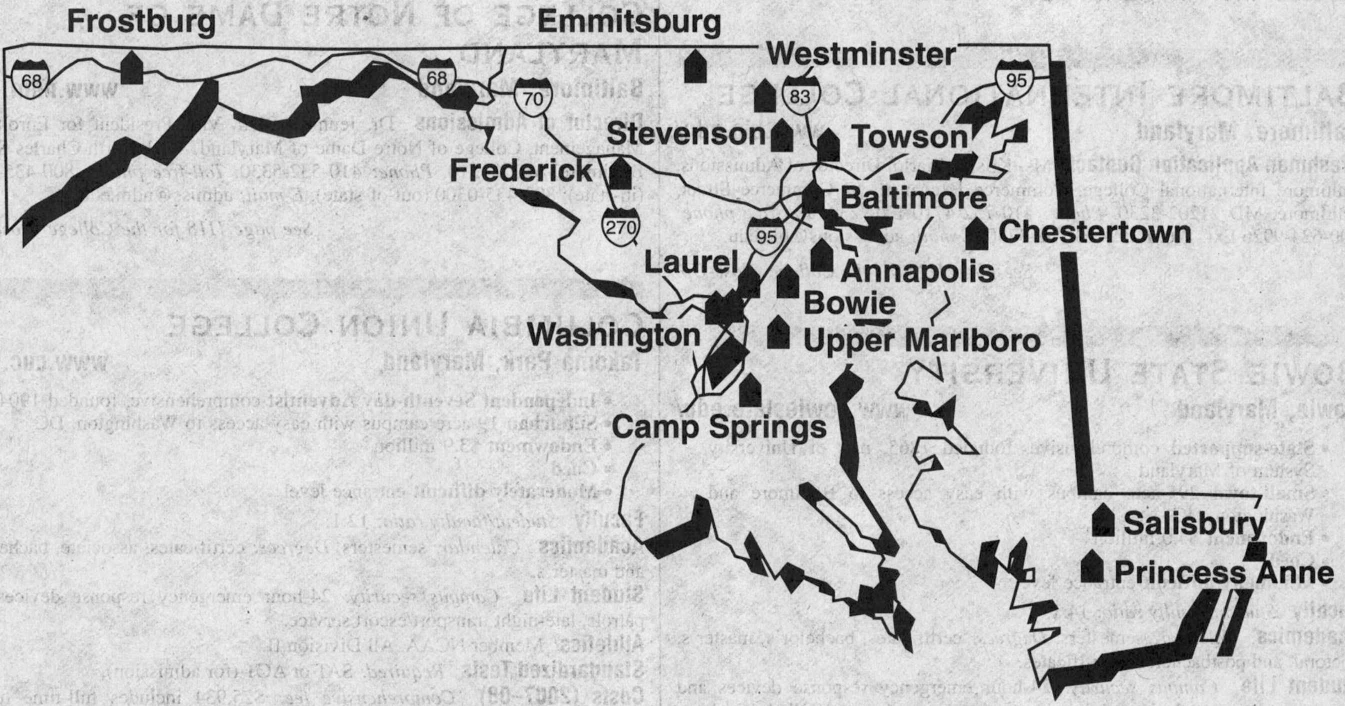

Frostburg
Emmitsburg
Westminster
68
68
70
83
95
Stevenson
Towson
Frederick
Baltimore
270
95
Chestertown
Laurel
Annapolis
Bowie
Washington
Upper Marlboro
Camp Springs
Salisbury
Princess Anne

BALTIMORE HEBREW UNIVERSITY

Baltimore, Maryland **www.bhu.edu/**

Director of Admissions Ms. Essie Keyser, Director of Admissions, Baltimore Hebrew University, 5800 Park Heights Avenue, Baltimore, MD 21209. *Phone:* 410-578-6967. *Toll-free phone:* 888-248-7420. *E-mail:* bhu@bhu.edu.

BALTIMORE INTERNATIONAL COLLEGE

Baltimore, Maryland **www.bic.edu/**

Freshman Application Contact Ms. Kristin Ciarlo, Director of Admissions, Baltimore International College, Commerce Exchange, 17 Commerce Street, Baltimore, MD 21202-3230. *Phone:* 410-752-4710 Ext. 239. *Toll-free phone:* 800-624-9926 Ext. 120. *Fax:* 410-752-3730. *E-mail:* admissions@bic.edu.

See page 1112 for the College Close-Up.

BOWIE STATE UNIVERSITY

Bowie, Maryland **www.bowiestate.edu/**

- **State-supported** comprehensive, founded 1865, part of University System of Maryland
- **Small-town** 295-acre campus with easy access to Baltimore and Washington, DC
- **Endowment** $4.0 million
- **Coed**
- **Minimally difficult** entrance level

Faculty *Student/faculty ratio:* 14:1.

Academics *Calendar:* semesters. *Degrees:* certificates, bachelor's, master's, doctoral, and postbachelor's certificates.

Student Life *Campus security:* 24-hour emergency response devices and patrols, student patrols, late-night transport/escort service, controlled dormitory access.

Athletics Member NCAA. All Division II.

Standardized Tests *Required:* SAT or ACT (for admission).

Costs (2007–08) *Tuition:* state resident $5811 full-time, $189 per credit part-time; nonresident $15,629 full-time, $589 per credit part-time. Part-time tuition and fees vary according to course load. *Required fees:* $1701 full-time. *Room and board:* $6879; room only: $4425. Room and board charges vary according to board plan and housing facility. *Payment plans:* installment, deferred payment.

Financial Aid Of all full-time matriculated undergraduates who enrolled in 2006, 1,911 applied for aid, 1,881 were judged to have need, 168 had their need fully met. 104 Federal Work-Study jobs (averaging $2392). In 2006, 25 non-need-based awards were made. *Average percent of need met:* 46. *Average financial aid package:* $6943. *Average need-based loan:* $3548. *Average need-based gift aid:* $5281. *Average non-need-based aid:* $736.

Applying *Options:* electronic application. *Application fee:* $40. *Required:* high school transcript, minimum 2.0 GPA. *Required for some:* letters of recommendation. *Recommended:* letters of recommendation.

Freshman Application Contact Don Kiah, Director of Admissions, Bowie State University, 14000 Jericho Park Road, Henry Building, Bowie, MD 20715-9465. *Phone:* 301-860-3415. *Toll-free phone:* 877-772-6943. *Fax:* 301-860-3438. *E-mail:* sholt@bowiestate.edu.

See page 1114 for the College Close-Up.

CAPITOL COLLEGE

Laurel, Maryland **www.capitol-college.edu/**

Capitol College is the only independent college in Maryland dedicated to engineering, computer science, information technology, and business. Founded in 1927, Capitol College is a regionally accredited institution offering associate, bachelor's, and master's degrees, as well as professional development training and certificates. The College's 52-acre campus is located in Laurel, Maryland, a suburban setting midway between Washington, D.C., and Baltimore. Full-time undergraduate students are eligible for a five-year tuition lock and job guarantee. All graduate-level degrees are available online, supported by software that delivers live, real-time lectures.

Director of Admissions Mr. Darnell Edwards, Director of Admissions, Capitol College, 11301 Springfield Road, Laurel, MD 20708. *Phone:* 301-953-3200 Ext. 3032. *Toll-free phone:* 800-950-1992. *E-mail:* admissions@capitol-college.edu.

See page 1116 for the College Close-Up.

COLLEGE OF NOTRE DAME OF MARYLAND

Baltimore, Maryland **www.ndm.edu/**

Director of Admissions Dr. Jennifer Blair, Vice President for Enrollment Management, College of Notre Dame of Maryland, 4701 North Charles Street, Baltimore, MD 21210. *Phone:* 410-532-5330. *Toll-free phone:* 800-435-0200 (in-state); 800-435-0300 (out-of-state). *E-mail:* admiss@ndm.edu.

See page 1118 for the College Close-Up.

COLUMBIA UNION COLLEGE

Takoma Park, Maryland **www.cuc.edu/**

- **Independent Seventh-day Adventist** comprehensive, founded 1904
- **Suburban** 19-acre campus with easy access to Washington, DC
- **Endowment** $3.9 million
- **Coed**
- **Moderately difficult** entrance level

Faculty *Student/faculty ratio:* 12:1.

Academics *Calendar:* semesters. *Degrees:* certificates, associate, bachelor's, and master's.

Student Life *Campus security:* 24-hour emergency response devices and patrols, late-night transport/escort service.

Athletics Member NCAA. All Division II.

Standardized Tests *Required:* SAT or ACT (for admission).

Costs (2007–08) *Comprehensive fee:* $25,934 includes full-time tuition ($18,200), mandatory fees ($1175), and room and board ($6559). Part-time tuition: $760 per semester hour. Part-time tuition and fees vary according to class time. *Required fees:* $433 per term part-time.

Financial Aid *Average indebtedness upon graduation:* $16,225.

Applying *Options:* electronic application, early admission, deferred entrance. *Application fee:* $25. *Required:* essay or personal statement, high school transcript, minimum 2.5 GPA, 2 letters of recommendation. *Required for some:* interview.

Freshman Application Contact Elaine Oliver, Associate Vice President, Enrollment Services, Columbia Union College, 7600 Flower Avenue, Takoma Park, MD 20412. *Phone:* 301-891-4502. *Toll-free phone:* 800-835-4212. *Fax:* 301-971-4230. *E-mail:* enroll@cuc.edu.

COPPIN STATE UNIVERSITY

Baltimore, Maryland **www.coppin.edu/**

Freshman Application Contact Ms. Michelle Gross, Director of Admissions, Coppin State University, 2500 W North Avenue, Baltimore, MD 21216. *Phone:* 410-951-3600. *Toll-free phone:* 800-635-3674. *Fax:* 410-523-7351. *E-mail:* mgross@coppin.edu.

DEVRY UNIVERSITY

Bethesda, Maryland **www.devry.edu/**

- **Proprietary** comprehensive, part of DeVry University
- **Coed** 45 undergraduate students, 29% full-time, 40% women, 60% men
- **Minimally difficult** entrance level

Undergraduates 13 full-time, 32 part-time. 9% are from out of state, 49% African American, 27% Hispanic American, 2% international, 16% transferred in. *Retention:* 57% of 2006 full-time freshmen returned.

Freshmen *Admission:* 6 enrolled.

Faculty *Total:* 4, 25% full-time. *Student/faculty ratio:* 26:1.

Majors Business administration and management; business administration, management and operations related; computer systems analysis.

Academics *Calendar:* semesters. *Degrees:* bachelor's and master's. *Special study options:* academic remediation for entering students, accelerated degree program, adult/continuing education programs, advanced placement credit, distance learning, part-time degree program, services for LD students, summer session for credit.
Student Life *Housing:* college housing not available.
Costs (2008–09) *Tuition:* $14,480 full-time, $540 per credit part-time. *Required fees:* $80 full-time.
Applying *Options:* electronic application, early admission, deferred entrance. *Application fee:* $50. *Required:* high school transcript, interview. *Application deadlines:* rolling (freshmen), rolling (transfers). *Notification:* continuous (freshmen), continuous (transfers).
Director of Admissions Admissions Office, DeVry University, 4550 Montgomery Avenue, Suite 100 North, Bethesda, MD 20814-3304.

FROSTBURG STATE UNIVERSITY

Frostburg, Maryland **www.frostburg.edu/**

- **State-supported** comprehensive, founded 1898, part of University System of Maryland
- **Small-town** 260-acre campus with easy access to Baltimore and Washington, DC
- **Endowment** $14.7 million
- **Coed** 4,335 undergraduate students, 94% full-time, 49% women, 51% men
- **Moderately difficult** entrance level, 63% of applicants were admitted

Undergraduates 4,096 full-time, 239 part-time. Students come from 22 states and territories, 19 other countries, 9% are from out of state, 20% African American, 2% Asian American or Pacific Islander, 2% Hispanic American, 0.4% Native American, 0.5% international, 8% transferred in, 35% live on campus. *Retention:* 68% of 2006 full-time freshmen returned.
Freshmen *Admission:* 4,199 applied, 2,634 admitted, 1,063 enrolled. *Average high school GPA:* 3.06. *Test scores:* SAT critical reading scores over 500: 40%; SAT math scores over 500: 42%; SAT writing scores over 500: 36%; ACT scores over 18: 68%; SAT critical reading scores over 600: 8%; SAT math scores over 600: 11%; SAT writing scores over 600: 8%; ACT scores over 24: 13%; SAT critical reading scores over 700: 1%; SAT math scores over 700: 1%.
Faculty *Total:* 344, 68% full-time, 63% with terminal degrees. *Student/faculty ratio:* 17:1.
Majors Accounting; biological specializations related; biology/biological sciences; botany/plant biology related; business administration and management; chemistry; city/urban, community and regional planning; communication/speech communication and rhetoric; computer and information sciences; criminal justice/law enforcement administration; criminal justice/police science; dramatic/theater arts; economics; electrical, electronics and communications engineering; elementary education; English; environmental studies; foreign languages and literatures; geography; history; information science/studies; international relations and affairs; kindergarten/preschool education; kinesiology and exercise science; liberal arts and sciences/liberal studies; mass communication/media; mathematics; mechanical engineering; multi-/interdisciplinary studies related; music; natural resources/conservation; parks, recreation and leisure; philosophy; physical education teaching and coaching; physical sciences related; physics; political science and government; psychology; secondary education; social sciences; social work; sociology; speech and rhetoric; sport and fitness administration/management; visual and performing arts; wildlife and wildlands science and management.
Academics *Calendar:* semesters. *Degrees:* certificates, bachelor's, master's, post-master's, and postbachelor's certificates. *Special study options:* adult/continuing education programs, advanced placement credit, distance learning, double majors, freshman honors college, honors programs, independent study, internships, off-campus study, part-time degree program, services for LD students, study abroad, summer session for credit. *Unusual degree programs:* 3-2 engineering with University of Maryland, College Park.
Computers on Campus 577 computers/terminals are available on campus for general student use. Students can access the following: campus intranet, computer help desk, free student e-mail accounts, online (class) grades, online (class) registration, online (class) schedules. Campuswide network is available. 100% of college-owned or -operated housing units are wired for high-speed Internet access.
Student Life *Housing options:* coed, men-only, women-only. Campus housing is university owned. *Activities and organizations:* drama/theater group, student-run newspaper, radio and television station, choral group, marching band, Student Government Association, Black Student Association, Campus Activities Board, Residence Hall Association, national fraternities, national sororities. *Campus security:* 24-hour emergency response devices and patrols, student patrols, late-night transport/escort service, controlled dormitory access, bicycle patrols. *Student services:* health clinic, personal/psychological counseling, women's center.
Athletics Member NCAA. All Division III. *Intercollegiate sports:* baseball M, basketball M/W, cross-country running M/W, field hockey W, football M, golf M, lacrosse W, soccer M/W, softball W, swimming and diving M/W, tennis M/W, track and field M/W, volleyball W. *Intramural sports:* badminton M/W, basketball M/W, field hockey M/W, football M/W, golf M/W, lacrosse M (c)/W, racquetball M/W, rugby M (c), soccer M/W, softball M/W, squash M/W, table tennis M/W, tennis M/W, volleyball M (c)/W, water polo M/W, weight lifting M/W, wrestling M.
Standardized Tests *Required:* SAT or ACT (for admission).
Costs (2008–09) *Tuition:* state resident $5000 full-time, $207 per credit hour part-time; nonresident $15,196 full-time, $427 per credit hour part-time. *Required fees:* $1614 full-time, $77 per credit hour part-time, $11 per credit hour part-time. *Room and board:* $6746; room only: $3340.
Financial Aid Of all full-time matriculated undergraduates who enrolled in 2007, 3,096 applied for aid, 2,102 were judged to have need, 550 had their need fully met. 242 Federal Work-Study jobs (averaging $1000). 518 state and other part-time jobs (averaging $519). In 2007, 415 non-need-based awards were made. *Average percent of need met:* 73%. *Average financial aid package:* $8080. *Average need-based loan:* $3586. *Average need-based gift aid:* $5140. *Average non-need-based aid:* $2431. *Average indebtedness upon graduation:* $18,035.
Applying *Options:* electronic application, early admission. *Application fee:* $30. *Required:* high school transcript, minimum 2.0 GPA. *Required for some:* essay or personal statement. *Recommended:* letters of recommendation, interview. *Application deadlines:* rolling (freshmen), rolling (transfers).
Freshman Application Contact Ms. Trish Gregory, Director of Admissions, Frostburg State University, 101 Braddock Road, Pullen Hall, Frostburg, MD 21532-1099. *Phone:* 301-687-4201. *Fax:* 301-687-7074. *E-mail:* fsuadmissions@frostburg.edu.

See page 1120 for the College Close-Up.

GEORGE MEANY CENTER FOR LABOR STUDIES-THE NATIONAL LABOR COLLEGE

Silver Spring, Maryland **www.georgemeany.org/**

Director of Admissions Carrie Spruill, Acting Chief Financial Aid Officer/Student Services, George Meany Center for Labor Studies-The National Labor College, 10000 New Hampshire Avenue, Silver Spring, MD 20903. *Phone:* 301-431-5404. *Toll-free phone:* 800-GMC-4CDP. *E-mail:* cspruill@georgemeany.org.

GOUCHER COLLEGE

Baltimore, Maryland **www.goucher.edu/**

- **Independent** comprehensive, founded 1885
- **Suburban** 287-acre campus
- **Endowment** $215.9 million
- **Coed** 1,472 undergraduate students, 98% full-time, 67% women, 33% men
- **Moderately difficult** entrance level, 66% of applicants were admitted

Undergraduates 1,443 full-time, 29 part-time. Students come from 43 states and territories, 7 other countries, 71% are from out of state, 5% African American, 3% Asian American or Pacific Islander, 4% Hispanic American, 0.4% Native American, 0.5% international, 3% transferred in, 80% live on campus. *Retention:* 78% of 2006 full-time freshmen returned.
Freshmen *Admission:* 3,563 applied, 2,361 admitted, 399 enrolled. *Average high school GPA:* 3.2. *Test scores:* SAT critical reading scores over 500: 93%; SAT math scores over 500: 88%; SAT writing scores over 500: 88%; SAT critical reading scores over 600: 63%; SAT math scores over 600: 47%; SAT writing scores over 600: 52%; SAT critical reading scores over 700: 20%; SAT math scores over 700: 9%; SAT writing scores over 700: 12%.
Faculty *Total:* 222, 58% full-time, 66% with terminal degrees. *Student/faculty ratio:* 9:1.
Majors American studies; art; biology/biological sciences; business administration and management; chemistry; computer science; dance; dramatic/theater arts; economics; elementary education; English; French; history; interdisciplinary studies; international relations and affairs; mass communication/media; mathematics; music; peace studies and conflict resolution; philosophy; physics; political

science and government; psychology; religious studies; Russian; sociology; Spanish; special education; women's studies.

Academics *Calendar:* semesters. *Degrees:* bachelor's, master's, and post-bachelor's certificates. *Special study options:* adult/continuing education programs, advanced placement credit, double majors, independent study, internships, off-campus study, services for LD students, student-designed majors, study abroad. *ROTC:* Army (c). *Unusual degree programs:* 3-2 engineering with Johns Hopkins University.

Computers on Campus 170 computers/terminals are available on campus for general student use. Students can access the following: campus intranet, computer help desk, free student e-mail accounts, online (class) grades, online (class) schedules, transcripts, financial aid information, billing, ePortfolios. Campuswide network is available. Wireless service is available via entire campus.

Student Life *Housing:* on-campus residence required through sophomore year. *Options:* coed, women-only. Campus housing is university owned and leased by the school. Freshman campus housing is guaranteed. *Activities and organizations:* drama/theater group, student-run newspaper, radio and television station, choral group, CAUSE (Community Auxiliary for Service), Umoja: The African Alliance, Quindecim (newspaper), PRISM, Hillel. *Campus security:* 24-hour emergency response devices and patrols, late-night transport/escort service, controlled dormitory access. *Student services:* health clinic, personal/psychological counseling, women's center.

Athletics Member NCAA. All Division III. *Intercollegiate sports:* basketball M/W, cross-country running M/W, equestrian sports M/W, field hockey W, lacrosse M/W, soccer M/W, swimming and diving M/W, tennis M/W, track and field M/W, volleyball W. *Intramural sports:* fencing M (c)/W (c), football M/W, racquetball M/W, soccer M/W, softball M/W, squash M/W, tennis M/W, ultimate Frisbee M/W, volleyball M/W, water polo M/W, weight lifting M/W.

Costs (2007–08) *Comprehensive fee:* $40,922 includes full-time tuition ($30,636), mandatory fees ($446), and room and board ($9840). Part-time tuition: $1025 per credit. *College room only:* $5916. Room and board charges vary according to board plan and housing facility. *Payment plans:* tuition prepayment, installment. *Waivers:* adult students, senior citizens, and employees or children of employees.

Financial Aid Of all full-time matriculated undergraduates who enrolled in 2005, 859 applied for aid, 706 were judged to have need, 166 had their need fully met. 297 Federal Work-Study jobs (averaging $1225). 1 state and other part-time job (averaging $1200). In 2005, 399 non-need-based awards were made. *Average percent of need met:* 82%. *Average financial aid package:* $19,917. *Average need-based loan:* $4912. *Average need-based gift aid:* $16,078. *Average non-need-based aid:* $13,674. *Average indebtedness upon graduation:* $17,097.

Applying *Options:* electronic application, early admission, early action, deferred entrance. *Application fee:* $40. *Required:* essay or personal statement, high school transcript, minimum 2.0 GPA. *Recommended:* minimum 2.8 GPA, 3 letters of recommendation, interview. *Application deadlines:* 2/1 (freshmen), 5/1 (transfers), 12/1 (early action). *Notification:* 4/1 (freshmen), 6/1 (transfers), 2/15 (early action).

Freshman Application Contact Mr. Carlton Surbeck III, Director of Admissions, Goucher College, 1021 Dulaney Valley Road, Baltimore, MD 21204-2794. *Phone:* 410-337-6100. *Toll-free phone:* 800-468-2437. *Fax:* 410-337-6354. *E-mail:* admissions@goucher.edu.

See page 1122 for the College Close-Up.

GRIGGS UNIVERSITY

Silver Spring, Maryland **www.griggs.edu/**

- **Independent Seventh-day Adventist** 4-year, founded 1990, part of Seventh-day Adventist Parochial School System
- **Suburban** campus with easy access to Washington D.C.
- **Coed**
- **Minimally difficult** entrance level

Academics *Calendar:* continuous. *Degrees:* associate and bachelor's (offers only external degree programs).

Applying *Options:* early admission, deferred entrance. *Application fee:* $50. *Required:* essay or personal statement, high school transcript, minimum 2.0 GPA.

Freshman Application Contact Ms. Marilyn Riley, Enrollment Officer, Griggs University, PO Box 4437, Silver Spring, MD 20914-4437. *Phone:* 301-680-6593. *Toll-free phone:* 800-782-4769. *Fax:* 301-680-6577. *E-mail:* 74617.74@compuserve.com.

HOOD COLLEGE

Frederick, Maryland **www.hood.edu/**

- **Independent** comprehensive, founded 1893
- **Suburban** 50-acre campus with easy access to Baltimore and Washington, DC
- **Endowment** $59.4 million
- **Coed** 1,448 undergraduate students, 88% full-time, 71% women, 29% men
- **Moderately difficult** entrance level, 71% of applicants were admitted

Undergraduates 1,268 full-time, 180 part-time. Students come from 33 states and territories, 25 other countries, 19% are from out of state, 9% African American, 3% Asian American or Pacific Islander, 3% Hispanic American, 0.3% Native American, 2% international, 11% transferred in, 51% live on campus. *Retention:* 76% of 2006 full-time freshmen returned.

Freshmen *Admission:* 1,719 applied, 1,219 admitted, 295 enrolled. *Average high school GPA:* 3.54. *Test scores:* SAT critical reading scores over 500: 72%; SAT math scores over 500: 70%; ACT scores over 18: 93%; SAT critical reading scores over 600: 30%; SAT math scores over 600: 21%; ACT scores over 24: 51%; SAT critical reading scores over 700: 5%; SAT math scores over 700: 2%; ACT scores over 30: 7%.

Faculty *Total:* 252, 32% full-time, 57% with terminal degrees. *Student/faculty ratio:* 13:1.

Majors Biochemistry; biology/biological sciences; business administration and management; chemistry; communication and media related; computer science; early childhood education; economics; English; environmental science; fine arts related; French; German; history; Latin American studies; legal studies; mathematics; multi-/interdisciplinary studies related; music; philosophy; political science and government; psychology; religious studies; Romance languages related; social work; sociology; Spanish; special education (vision impaired).

Academics *Calendar:* semesters. *Degrees:* bachelor's, master's, and post-bachelor's certificates (also offers adult program with significant enrollment not reflected in profile). *Special study options:* academic remediation for entering students, accelerated degree program, adult/continuing education programs, advanced placement credit, double majors, honors programs, independent study, internships, off-campus study, part-time degree program, services for LD students, student-designed majors, study abroad, summer session for credit. *ROTC:* Army (c). *Unusual degree programs:* 3-2 engineering with George Washington University.

Computers on Campus 283 computers/terminals are available on campus for general student use. Students can access the following: campus intranet, computer help desk, free student e-mail accounts, online (class) grades, online (class) registration, online (class) schedules. Campuswide network is available. 100% of college-owned or -operated housing units are wired for high-speed Internet access. Wireless service is available via entire campus.

Student Life *Housing:* on-campus residence required through sophomore year. *Options:* coed, women-only, disabled students. Campus housing is university owned. Freshman campus housing is guaranteed. *Activities and organizations:* drama/theater group, student-run newspaper, radio station, choral group, Education Club, Black Student Union, Campus Activities Board, International Club, Hood Today (newspaper). *Campus security:* 24-hour emergency response devices and patrols, late-night transport/escort service, controlled dormitory access, residence hall security. *Student services:* health clinic, personal/psychological counseling, women's center.

Athletics Member NCAA. All Division III. *Intercollegiate sports:* basketball M/W, cross-country running M/W, equestrian sports M (c)/W (c), field hockey W, golf M/W, lacrosse M/W, soccer M/W, softball W, swimming and diving M/W, tennis M/W, track and field M/W, volleyball W.

Standardized Tests *Required:* SAT or ACT (for admission).

Costs (2007–08) *Comprehensive fee:* $33,618 includes full-time tuition ($24,720), mandatory fees ($356), and room and board ($8542). Full-time tuition and fees vary according to course load. Part-time tuition: $710 per credit. Part-time tuition and fees vary according to course load. *Required fees:* $111 per term part-time. *College room only:* $4462. Room and board charges vary according to board plan. *Payment plans:* tuition prepayment, installment, deferred payment. *Waivers:* children of alumni, adult students, and employees or children of employees.

Financial Aid Of all full-time matriculated undergraduates who enrolled in 2006, 984 applied for aid, 861 were judged to have need, 323 had their need fully met. 191 Federal Work-Study jobs (averaging $1700). 120 state and other part-time jobs (averaging $1650). In 2006, 230 non-need-based awards were made. *Average percent of need met:* 86%. *Average financial aid package:* $19,463. *Average need-based loan:* $4297. *Average need-based gift aid:* $15,948. *Average non-need-based aid:* $14,203. *Average indebtedness upon graduation:* $21,112.

Applying *Options:* electronic application, early action, deferred entrance. *Application fee:* $35. *Required:* high school transcript, minimum 2.0 GPA. *Required for some:* letters of recommendation. *Recommended:* essay or personal statement, interview. *Application deadlines:* 2/15 (freshmen), 8/10 (transfers), 12/1 (early action). *Notification:* continuous (freshmen), continuous (transfers), 12/15 (early action).

Freshman Application Contact Mr. David Adams, Director of Admissions, Hood College, 401 Rosemont Avenue, Frederick, MD 21701. *Phone:* 301-696-3400. *Toll-free phone:* 800-922-1599. *Fax:* 301-696-3819. *E-mail:* admissions@hood.edu.

ITT TECHNICAL INSTITUTE

Owings Mills, Maryland **www.itt-tech.edu/**

- **Proprietary** primarily 2-year, founded 2005
- **Coed**

Academics *Calendar:* quarters. *Degrees:* associate and bachelor's.

Standardized Tests *Required:* Wonderlic aptitude test (for admission).

Applying *Application fee:* $100. *Required:* high school transcript, interview. *Recommended:* letters of recommendation.

Freshman Application Contact Mr. Tony Owens, Director of Recruitment, ITT Technical Institute, 11301 Red Run Boulevard, Owings Mills, MD 21117. *Phone:* 443-394-7115.

THE JOHNS HOPKINS UNIVERSITY

Baltimore, Maryland **www.jhu.edu/**

- **Independent** university, founded 1876
- **Urban** 140-acre campus with easy access to Washington, DC
- **Endowment** $2.8 billion
- **Coed** 4,591 undergraduate students, 99% full-time, 47% women, 53% men
- **Most difficult** entrance level, 24% of applicants were admitted

Since it was founded in 1876, Johns Hopkins has attracted students and faculty members from every discipline who share the belief that innovative learning means exploration and discovery, both in and outside the classroom. At Johns Hopkins, undergraduates become part of this exhilarating tradition. They are challenged not just to learn but also to advance knowledge itself—and they discover the power of their own ideas.

Undergraduates 4,561 full-time, 30 part-time. Students come from 52 states and territories, 58 other countries, 85% are from out of state, 6% African American, 25% Asian American or Pacific Islander, 7% Hispanic American, 0.6% Native American, 5% international, 0.6% transferred in, 61% live on campus. *Retention:* 97% of 2006 full-time freshmen returned.

Freshmen *Admission:* 14,848 applied, 3,603 admitted, 1,206 enrolled. *Average high school GPA:* 3.7. *Test scores:* SAT critical reading scores over 500: 99%; SAT math scores over 500: 100%; SAT writing scores over 500: 99%; ACT scores over 18: 100%; SAT critical reading scores over 600: 88%; SAT math scores over 600: 92%; SAT writing scores over 600: 86%; ACT scores over 24: 98%; SAT critical reading scores over 700: 42%; SAT math scores over 700: 59%; SAT writing scores over 700: 43%; ACT scores over 30: 65%.

Majors Anthropology; applied mathematics; art history, criticism and conservation; Asian studies (East); behavioral sciences; biological and physical sciences; biology/biological sciences; biomedical/medical engineering; biophysics; business/commerce; chemical engineering; chemistry; civil engineering; classics and languages, literatures and linguistics; cognitive psychology and psycholinguistics; computer and information sciences; computer engineering; creative writing; economics; electrical, electronics and communications engineering; electroneurodiagnostic/electroencephalographic technology; engineering; engineering mechanics; English; environmental/environmental health engineering; environmental studies; film/cinema studies; French; geography; geology/earth science; German; history; history and philosophy of science and technology; industrial engineering; interdisciplinary studies; international relations and affairs; Italian; Latin American studies; liberal arts and sciences and humanities related; liberal arts and sciences/liberal studies; literature; materials engineering; materials science; mathematics; mechanical engineering; music; natural sciences; Near and Middle Eastern studies; neuroscience; nursing (registered nurse training); philosophy; physics; physiological psychology/psychobiology; political science and government; psychology; public health; social sciences; sociology; Spanish.

Academics *Calendar:* 4-1-4. *Degrees:* certificates, diplomas, bachelor's, master's, doctoral, first professional, post-master's, and postbachelor's certificates. *Special study options:* accelerated degree program, adult/continuing education programs, advanced placement credit, double majors, honors programs, independent study, internships, off-campus study, part-time degree program, services for LD students, student-designed majors, study abroad, summer session for credit. *ROTC:* Army (b), Air Force (c). *Unusual degree programs:* 3-2 international studies with Johns Hopkins University, School of Advanced International Studies (Washington, DC); education.

Computers on Campus 140 computers/terminals and 1,000 ports are available on campus for general student use. Students can access the following: campus intranet, computer help desk, free student e-mail accounts, online (class) grades, online (class) registration, online (class) schedules. Campuswide network is available. 100% of college-owned or -operated housing units are wired for high-speed Internet access. Wireless service is available via entire campus.

Student Life *Housing:* on-campus residence required through sophomore year. *Options:* coed, women-only, disabled students. Campus housing is university owned. Freshman campus housing is guaranteed. *Activities and organizations:* drama/theater group, student-run newspaper, radio station, choral group, The Outdoors Club, The Hopkins Organization for Programs, The Barn Stormers (theater group), Inter-Asian Council, Latino Student organization, national fraternities, national sororities. *Campus security:* 24-hour emergency response devices and patrols, student patrols, late-night transport/escort service, controlled dormitory access. *Student services:* health clinic, personal/psychological counseling.

Athletics Member NCAA. All Division III except men's and women's lacrosse (Division I). *Intercollegiate sports:* baseball M, basketball M/W, crew M/W, cross-country running M/W, fencing M/W, field hockey W, football M, lacrosse M (s)/W (s), soccer M/W, swimming and diving M/W, tennis M/W, track and field M/W, volleyball W, water polo M, wrestling M. *Intramural sports:* badminton M/W, basketball M/W, cheerleading M/W, field hockey M/W, football M/W, ice hockey M/W, lacrosse M/W, rock climbing M/W, rugby M/W, sailing M/W, skiing (downhill) M/W, soccer M/W, softball M/W, table tennis M/W, tennis M/W, ultimate Frisbee M/W, volleyball M/W.

Standardized Tests *Required:* SAT or ACT (for admission). *Recommended:* SAT Subject Tests (for admission).

Costs (2007–08) *One-time required fee:* $500. *Comprehensive fee:* $46,992 includes full-time tuition ($35,900) and room and board ($11,092). Part-time tuition: $1200 per credit. *College room only:* $6340. Room and board charges vary according to board plan and housing facility. *Payment plan:* installment. *Waivers:* employees or children of employees.

Financial Aid Of all full-time matriculated undergraduates who enrolled in 2007, 2,475 applied for aid, 2,132 were judged to have need, 206 had their need fully met. 1,565 Federal Work-Study jobs (averaging $2345). In 2007, 68 non-need-based awards were made. *Average percent of need met:* 89%. *Average financial aid package:* $28,765. *Average need-based loan:* $4547. *Average need-based gift aid:* $24,954. *Average non-need-based aid:* $20,273. *Average indebtedness upon graduation:* $18,447. *Financial aid deadline:* 3/1.

Applying *Options:* electronic application, early admission, early decision, deferred entrance. *Application fee:* $70. *Required:* essay or personal statement, high school transcript, letters of recommendation. *Recommended:* interview. *Application deadlines:* 1/1 (freshmen), 3/15 (transfers). *Early decision deadline:* 11/1. *Notification:* 4/1 (freshmen), 5/1 (transfers), 12/15 (early decision).

Freshman Application Contact Dr. John Latting, Dean of Undergraduate Admissions, The Johns Hopkins University, 3400 North Charles Street, Baltimore, MD 21218-2699. *Phone:* 410-516-8341. *Fax:* 410-516-6025. *E-mail:* gotojhu@jhu.edu.

See pages 1124 and 1126 for the College Close-Ups.

LOYOLA COLLEGE IN MARYLAND

Baltimore, Maryland **www.loyola.edu/**

- **Independent Roman Catholic (Jesuit)** comprehensive, founded 1852
- **Urban** 89-acre campus with easy access to Washington, DC
- **Endowment** $178.5 million
- **Coed** 3,580 undergraduate students, 99% full-time, 58% women, 42% men
- **Moderately difficult** entrance level, 60% of applicants were admitted

Undergraduates 3,538 full-time, 42 part-time. Students come from 38 states and territories, 19 other countries, 82% are from out of state, 5% African American, 3% Asian American or Pacific Islander, 3% Hispanic American, 0.1% Native American, 0.8% international, 88% live on campus. *Retention:* 91% of 2006 full-time freshmen returned.

Freshmen *Admission:* 8,594 applied, 5,135 admitted, 983 enrolled. *Average high school GPA:* 3.5. *Test scores:* SAT critical reading scores over 500: 93%; SAT math scores over 500: 93%; ACT scores over 18: 99%; SAT critical reading scores over 600: 52%; SAT math scores over 600: 56%; ACT scores over 24: 77%; SAT critical reading scores over 700: 10%; SAT math scores over 700: 8%; ACT scores over 30: 12%.

Faculty *Total:* 542, 59% full-time, 52% with terminal degrees. *Student/faculty ratio:* 12:1.

Majors Accounting; applied mathematics; art; biology/biological sciences; business/commerce; chemistry; classics and languages, literatures and linguistics; communication/speech communication and rhetoric; computer and information sciences; creative writing; economics; education; electrical, electronics and communications engineering; elementary education; engineering; English; finance; French; German; history; interdisciplinary studies; international business/trade/commerce; mathematics; philosophy; physics; political science and government; psychology; religious studies; sociology; Spanish; special education; speech-language pathology.

Academics *Calendar:* semesters. *Degrees:* bachelor's, master's, doctoral, and post-master's certificates. *Special study options:* accelerated degree program, advanced placement credit, double majors, honors programs, independent study, internships, off-campus study, part-time degree program, services for LD students, study abroad, summer session for credit. *ROTC:* Army (b), Air Force (c).

Computers on Campus 1,667 computers/terminals are available on campus for general student use. Students can access the following: computer help desk, free student e-mail accounts, online (class) grades, online (class) registration, online (class) schedules. Campuswide network is available. 100% of college-owned or -operated housing units are wired for high-speed Internet access. Wireless service is available via classrooms, computer centers, computer labs, dorm rooms, learning centers, libraries, student centers.

Student Life *Housing options:* coed. Campus housing is university owned. Freshman applicants given priority for college housing. *Activities and organizations:* drama/theater group, student-run newspaper, radio station, choral group, Student Government Association (SGA), Resident Affairs Council (RAC), Operation Smile, Relay for Life, Resident Assistants (RA)/Evergreen. *Campus security:* 24-hour emergency response devices and patrols, late-night transport/escort service, controlled dormitory access. *Student services:* health clinic, personal/psychological counseling.

Athletics Member NCAA. All Division I. *Intercollegiate sports:* basketball M/W, crew M/W, cross-country running M/W, golf M, lacrosse M/W, soccer M/W, swimming and diving M/W, tennis M/W, volleyball W.

Standardized Tests *Required:* SAT or ACT (for admission).

Financial Aid Of all full-time matriculated undergraduates who enrolled in 2007, 2,015 applied for aid, 1,672 were judged to have need, 1,606 had their need fully met. 493 Federal Work-Study jobs (averaging $1980). 86 state and other part-time jobs (averaging $7820). In 2007, 342 non-need-based awards were made. *Average percent of need met:* 96%. *Average financial aid package:* $23,705. *Average need-based loan:* $5640. *Average need-based gift aid:* $15,815. *Average non-need-based aid:* $12,760. *Average indebtedness upon graduation:* $19,730. *Financial aid deadline:* 2/15.

Applying *Options:* electronic application, early admission, deferred entrance. *Application fee:* $50. *Required:* essay or personal statement, high school transcript. *Recommended:* interview. *Application deadlines:* 2/1 (freshmen), 7/15 (transfers), 11/15 (early action). *Notification:* 4/1 (freshmen), continuous (transfers), 1/15 (early action).

Freshman Application Contact Ms. Elena Hicks, Director of Undergraduate Admissions, Loyola College in Maryland, 4501 North Charles Street, Baltimore, MD 21210. *Phone:* 410-617-5012. *Toll-free phone:* 800-221-9107 Ext. 2252. *Fax:* 410-617-2176.

See page 1128 for the College Close-Up.

MAPLE SPRINGS BAPTIST BIBLE COLLEGE AND SEMINARY

Capitol Heights, Maryland **www.msbbcs.edu/**

Freshman Application Contact Ms. Mazie Murphy, Assistant Director of Admissions and Records, Maple Springs Baptist Bible College and Seminary, 4130 Belt Road, Capitol Heights, MD 20743. *Phone:* 301-736-3631.

MARYLAND INSTITUTE COLLEGE OF ART

Baltimore, Maryland **www.mica.edu/**

- **Independent** comprehensive, founded 1826
- **Urban** 12-acre campus with easy access to Washington, DC
- **Endowment** $55.9 million
- **Coed** 1,672 undergraduate students, 99% full-time, 66% women, 34% men
- **Very difficult** entrance level, 37% of applicants were admitted

Undergraduates 1,656 full-time, 16 part-time. Students come from 47 states and territories, 44 other countries, 80% are from out of state, 4% African American, 10% Asian American or Pacific Islander, 4% Hispanic American, 0.2% Native American, 4% international, 4% transferred in, 88% live on campus. *Retention:* 84% of 2006 full-time freshmen returned.

Freshmen *Admission:* 2,602 applied, 964 admitted, 400 enrolled. *Average high school GPA:* 3.43. *Test scores:* SAT critical reading scores over 500: 95%; SAT math scores over 500: 84%; SAT writing scores over 500: 89%; SAT critical reading scores over 600: 58%; SAT math scores over 600: 37%; SAT writing scores over 600: 48%; SAT critical reading scores over 700: 13%; SAT math scores over 700: 3%; SAT writing scores over 700: 7%.

Faculty *Total:* 304, 43% full-time, 82% with terminal degrees. *Student/faculty ratio:* 10:1.

Majors Art; art history, criticism and conservation; art teacher education; ceramic arts and ceramics; design and applied arts related; drawing; fiber, textile and weaving arts; film/video and photographic arts related; fine arts related; fine/studio arts; graphic design; illustration; interior design; intermedia/multimedia; painting; photography; printmaking; sculpture; visual and performing arts.

Academics *Calendar:* semesters. *Degrees:* bachelor's, master's, and post-bachelor's certificates. *Special study options:* accelerated degree program, adult/continuing education programs, advanced placement credit, distance learning, double majors, independent study, internships, off-campus study, services for LD students, student-designed majors, study abroad, summer session for credit. *ROTC:* Army (c).

Computers on Campus 440 computers/terminals are available on campus for general student use. Students can access the following: campus intranet, computer help desk, free student e-mail accounts, online (class) grades, online (class) registration, online (class) schedules, campus Portal, online gallery space, network storage space, personal websites. Campuswide network is available. 100% of college-owned or -operated housing units are wired for high-speed Internet access. Wireless service is available via classrooms, computer centers, computer labs, dorm rooms, learning centers, libraries, student centers.

Student Life *Housing options:* coed, disabled students. Campus housing is university owned and leased by the school. Freshman campus housing is guaranteed. *Activities and organizations:* drama/theater group, choral group, Soccer teams, MIQA (Maryland Institute Queer Alliance), Koinonia Christian Fellowship, MICA Playwrights, Knitting Club. *Campus security:* 24-hour emergency response devices and patrols, student patrols, late-night transport/escort service, controlled dormitory access, self-defense education, 24-hour building security, safety awareness programs, campus patrols by city police. *Student services:* health clinic, personal/psychological counseling.

Athletics *Intramural sports:* basketball M (c)/W (c), bowling M (c)/W (c), soccer M (c)/W (c).

Standardized Tests *Required:* SAT or ACT (for admission).

Costs (2007–08) *One-time required fee:* $125. *Comprehensive fee:* $39,070 includes full-time tuition ($29,700), mandatory fees ($980), and room and board ($8390). Part-time tuition: $1238 per credit. *Required fees:* $490 per term part-time. *College room only:* $6230. Room and board charges vary according to board plan and housing facility. *Payment plan:* installment. *Waivers:* employees or children of employees.

Financial Aid *Average indebtedness upon graduation:* $17,472.

Applying *Options:* early admission, early decision, deferred entrance. *Application fee:* $50. *Required:* essay or personal statement, high school transcript, 3 letters of recommendation, art portfolio. *Recommended:* interview. *Application deadlines:* 2/15 (freshmen), 3/3 (transfers). *Early decision deadline:* 11/15. *Notification:* 3/15 (freshmen), 4/18 (transfers), 12/15 (early decision).

Freshman Application Contact Ms. Christine Seese, Director of Undergraduate Admission, Maryland Institute College of Art, 1300 Mount Royal Avenue, Baltimore, MD 21217-4191. *Phone:* 410-225-2222. *Fax:* 410-225-2337. *E-mail:* cgyland@mica.edu.

See page 1130 for the College Close-Up.

MCDANIEL COLLEGE

Westminster, Maryland **www.mcdaniel.edu/**

- **Independent** comprehensive, founded 1867
- **Suburban** 160-acre campus with easy access to Baltimore and Washington, DC
- **Endowment** $89.7 million
- **Coed** 1,731 undergraduate students, 97% full-time, 56% women, 44% men

• **Moderately difficult** entrance level, 73% of applicants were admitted

Undergraduates 1,681 full-time, 50 part-time. Students come from 34 states and territories, 10 other countries, 30% are from out of state, 5% African American, 3% Asian American or Pacific Islander, 2% Hispanic American, 0.5% Native American, 0.1% international, 4% transferred in, 75% live on campus. *Retention:* 84% of 2006 full-time freshmen returned.

Freshmen *Admission:* 2,742 applied, 2,007 admitted, 431 enrolled. *Average high school GPA:* 3.50. *Test scores:* SAT critical reading scores over 500: 76%; SAT math scores over 500: 77%; ACT scores over 18: 100%; SAT critical reading scores over 600: 32%; SAT math scores over 600: 35%; ACT scores over 24: 46%; SAT critical reading scores over 700: 6%; SAT math scores over 700: 7%; ACT scores over 30: 7%.

Faculty *Total:* 240, 58% full-time, 66% with terminal degrees. *Student/faculty ratio:* 12:1.

Majors Art; art history, criticism and conservation; biochemistry; biology/biological sciences; business administration and management; chemistry; communication/speech communication and rhetoric; computer and information sciences; dramatic/theater arts; economics; English; environmental science; French; German; history; kinesiology and exercise science; mathematics; multi-/interdisciplinary studies related; music; philosophy; physical education teaching and coaching; physics; political science and government; psychology; religious studies; social work; sociology; Spanish.

Academics *Calendar:* 4-1-4. *Degrees:* bachelor's, master's, and postbachelor's certificates. *Special study options:* academic remediation for entering students, adult/continuing education programs, advanced placement credit, double majors, honors programs, independent study, internships, off-campus study, part-time degree program, services for LD students, student-designed majors, study abroad, summer session for credit. *ROTC:* Army (b). *Unusual degree programs:* 3-2 engineering with University of Maryland College Park.

Computers on Campus 150 computers/terminals and 1,350 ports are available on campus for general student use. Students can access the following: campus intranet, computer help desk, free student e-mail accounts, online (class) grades, online (class) registration, online (class) schedules. Campuswide network is available. 100% of college-owned or -operated housing units are wired for high-speed Internet access. Wireless service is available via libraries, student centers.

Student Life *Housing:* on-campus residence required through junior year. *Options:* coed, men-only, women-only, disabled students. Campus housing is university owned. Freshman campus housing is guaranteed. *Activities and organizations:* drama/theater group, student-run newspaper, radio and television station, choral group, Gamma Sigma Sigma (service organization), Christian Fellowship, Black Student Union, Beta Beta Beta (Biology Honor Society), Circle K (Kiwanis service group), national fraternities, national sororities. *Campus security:* 24-hour emergency response devices and patrols, late-night transport/escort service, controlled dormitory access. *Student services:* health clinic, personal/psychological counseling.

Athletics Member NCAA. All Division III. *Intercollegiate sports:* baseball M, basketball M/W, cross-country running M/W, field hockey W, football M, golf M/W, lacrosse M/W, soccer M/W, softball W, swimming and diving M/W, tennis M/W, track and field M/W, volleyball W, wrestling M. *Intramural sports:* badminton M/W, basketball M/W, cheerleading M (c)/W (c), football M, golf M/W, racquetball M/W, soccer M/W, softball M/W, swimming and diving M/W, table tennis M/W, tennis M/W, ultimate Frisbee M (c)/W (c), volleyball M/W, weight lifting M/W.

Standardized Tests *Required for some:* SAT or ACT (for admission).

Costs (2007–08) *Comprehensive fee:* $34,840 includes full-time tuition ($28,940) and room and board ($5900). Part-time tuition: $904 per credit. Part-time tuition and fees vary according to reciprocity agreements. *College room only:* $3200. Room and board charges vary according to board plan and housing facility. *Payment plan:* installment. *Waivers:* employees or children of employees.

Financial Aid Of all full-time matriculated undergraduates who enrolled in 2006, 1,261 applied for aid, 1,099 were judged to have need, 328 had their need fully met. 215 Federal Work-Study jobs (averaging $769). 252 state and other part-time jobs (averaging $780). In 2006, 484 non-need-based awards were made. *Average percent of need met:* 95%. *Average financial aid package:* $23,339. *Average need-based loan:* $5106. *Average need-based gift aid:* $10,165. *Average non-need-based aid:* $10,753. *Average indebtedness upon graduation:* $23,283.

Applying *Options:* electronic application, early admission, early action, deferred entrance. *Application fee:* $50. *Required:* essay or personal statement, high school transcript, minimum 2.5 GPA, letters of recommendation. *Required for some:* interview. *Recommended:* interview. *Application deadlines:* 2/1 (freshmen), 4/1 (transfers), 12/1 (early action). *Notification:* 3/15 (freshmen), 4/15 (transfers), 1/1 (early action).

Freshman Application Contact Ms. Florence Hines, Vice President for Enrollment Management and Dean of Admissions, McDaniel College, 2 College Hill, Westminster, MD 21157-4390. *Phone:* 410-857-2230. *Toll-free phone:* 800-638-5005. *Fax:* 410-857-2757. *E-mail:* admissions@mcdaniel.edu.

MORGAN STATE UNIVERSITY

Baltimore, Maryland **www.morgan.edu/**

• **State-supported** university, founded 1867
• **Urban** 143-acre campus with easy access to Washington, DC
• **Coed** 5,990 undergraduate students, 89% full-time, 55% women, 45% men
• **Moderately difficult** entrance level, 34% of applicants were admitted

Undergraduates 5,341 full-time, 649 part-time. 29% are from out of state. *Retention:* 62% of 2006 full-time freshmen returned.

Freshmen *Admission:* 11,804 applied, 3,977 admitted. *Average high school GPA:* 3.0.

Faculty *Total:* 553, 77% full-time, 55% with terminal degrees.

Majors Accounting; African-American/Black studies; African studies; art; art history, criticism and conservation; behavioral sciences; biology/biological sciences; business administration and management; business/managerial economics; business teacher education; chemistry; civil engineering; clinical laboratory science/medical technology; clinical/medical laboratory technology; computer science; dietetics; dramatic/theater arts; economics; education; electrical, electronics and communications engineering; elementary education; engineering; engineering physics; English; family and consumer sciences/human sciences; finance; foods, nutrition, and wellness; health teacher education; history; hospitality administration; hotel/motel administration; human ecology; industrial engineering; information science/studies; management information systems; marketing/marketing management; mass communication/media; mathematics; mental health/rehabilitation; music; parks, recreation and leisure; philosophy; physical education teaching and coaching; physics; political science and government; pre-dentistry studies; pre-law studies; pre-medical studies; psychology; religious studies; secondary education; social work; sociology; speech and rhetoric; sport and fitness administration/management; telecommunications.

Academics *Calendar:* semesters. *Degrees:* bachelor's, master's, and doctoral. *Special study options:* academic remediation for entering students, accelerated degree program, adult/continuing education programs, advanced placement credit, cooperative education, honors programs, independent study, internships, off-campus study, part-time degree program, services for LD students, summer session for credit. *ROTC:* Army (b).

Computers on Campus 285 computers/terminals are available on campus for general student use. Students can access the following: online (class) registration, engineering lab supercomputer. Campuswide network is available.

Student Life *Housing options:* coed. *Activities and organizations:* drama/theater group, student-run newspaper, radio station, choral group, marching band, Student Government Association, choir, band, national fraternities, national sororities. *Campus security:* 24-hour emergency response devices and patrols, late-night transport/escort service, controlled dormitory access. *Student services:* health clinic, personal/psychological counseling.

Athletics Member NCAA. All Division I except football (Division I-AA). *Intercollegiate sports:* basketball M (s)/W (s), bowling W, cheerleading W (s), cross-country running M (s)/W (s), softball W, tennis M (s)/W (s), track and field M (s)/W (s), volleyball W. *Intramural sports:* badminton M/W, basketball M/W, bowling M/W, cross-country running M/W, field hockey M/W, football M, golf M/W, gymnastics M/W, racquetball M/W, soccer M/W, softball M/W, swimming and diving M/W, table tennis M/W, tennis M/W, track and field M/W, volleyball M/W, weight lifting M/W.

Standardized Tests *Required:* SAT or ACT (for admission).

Costs (2007–08) *Tuition:* state resident $4280 full-time, $194 per credit hour part-time; nonresident $12,400 full-time, $458 per credit hour part-time. *Required fees:* $2038 full-time, $58 per credit hour part-time. *Room and board:* $7620; room only: $4900. Room and board charges vary according to board plan and housing facility. *Payment plans:* installment, deferred payment. *Waivers:* senior citizens and employees or children of employees.

Financial Aid *Average percent of need met:* 97%.

Applying *Options:* electronic application, early admission, deferred entrance. *Application fee:* $25. *Required:* high school transcript, minimum 2.0 GPA. *Required for some:* 2 letters of recommendation, interview. *Recommended:* essay or personal statement. *Application deadlines:* 5/1 (freshmen), rolling (transfers). *Notification:* continuous until 6/30 (freshmen), continuous (transfers).

Director of Admissions Mr. Edwin T. Johnson, Director of Admissions and Recruitment, Morgan State University, 1700 East Cold Spring Lane, Baltimore, MD 21251. *Phone:* 443-885-3000. *Toll-free phone:* 800-332-6674. *E-mail:* ejohnson@moac.morgan.edu.

See page 1132 for the College Close-Up.

MOUNT ST. MARY'S UNIVERSITY

Emmitsburg, Maryland **www.msmary.edu/**

- **Independent Roman Catholic** comprehensive, founded 1808
- **Rural** 1400-acre campus with easy access to Baltimore and Washington, DC
- **Endowment** $43.4 million
- **Coed** 1,681 undergraduate students, 92% full-time, 60% women, 40% men
- **Moderately difficult** entrance level, 84% of applicants were admitted

Most Mount students actively engage their interests through exciting internships, research, and study-abroad opportunities for all majors. Through more recent majors in criminal justice, environmental science, information systems, and sports management and established majors in education, business, and biology or in prelaw and premedicine, Mount St. Mary's faculty members help connect the classroom in Emmitsburg, Maryland, with real-world experience. Nearly 90 percent of Mount students live on campus. Students have the opportunity to become involved with more than 100 sports, clubs, and organizations, including the Outdoor Adventure program, which provides exciting, adventurous experiences promoting personal growth and environmental awareness while utilizing the Mount's spectacular setting. Academic scholarships, ranging from $5000 to full tuition annually, are available to qualified students.

Undergraduates 1,547 full-time, 134 part-time. Students come from 33 states and territories, 10 other countries, 43% are from out of state, 6% African American, 3% Asian American or Pacific Islander, 5% Hispanic American, 0.4% Native American, 0.8% international, 2% transferred in, 83% live on campus. *Retention:* 77% of 2006 full-time freshmen returned.

Freshmen *Admission:* 2,549 applied, 2,141 admitted, 449 enrolled. *Average high school GPA:* 3.15. *Test scores:* SAT critical reading scores over 500: 70%; SAT math scores over 500: 65%; SAT critical reading scores over 600: 24%; SAT math scores over 600: 20%; SAT critical reading scores over 700: 4%; SAT math scores over 700: 1%.

Faculty *Total:* 191, 62% full-time, 60% with terminal degrees. *Student/faculty ratio:* 13:1.

Majors Accounting; art; biochemistry; biology/biological sciences; business/commerce; chemistry; communication/speech communication and rhetoric; computer and information sciences; criminal justice/safety; economics; elementary education; English; environmental studies; French; German; history; information resources management; international relations and affairs; mathematics; multi-/interdisciplinary studies related; philosophy; political science and government; psychology; social sciences; sociology; Spanish; sport and fitness administration/management; theology.

Academics *Calendar:* semesters. *Degrees:* bachelor's, master's, first professional, post-master's, and postbachelor's certificates. *Special study options:* academic remediation for entering students, accelerated degree program, adult/continuing education programs, advanced placement credit, double majors, honors programs, independent study, internships, off-campus study, part-time degree program, services for LD students, student-designed majors, study abroad, summer session for credit. *ROTC:* Army (c). *Unusual degree programs:* 3-2 nursing with Johns Hopkins University; physical and occupational therapy with Sacred Heart University.

Computers on Campus 150 computers/terminals are available on campus for general student use. Students can access the following: campus intranet, computer help desk, free student e-mail accounts, online (class) grades, online (class) registration, online (class) schedules, tuition payment, course management system. Campuswide network is available. 100% of college-owned or -operated housing units are wired for high-speed Internet access. Wireless service is available via classrooms, computer centers, computer labs, dorm rooms, libraries, student centers.

Student Life *Housing:* on-campus residence required for freshman year. *Options:* coed, disabled students. Campus housing is university owned. Freshman campus housing is guaranteed. *Activities and organizations:* drama/theater group, student-run newspaper, radio and television station, choral group, Campus Ministry, Rugby Team Club, Ice Hockey Club, Circle K, International Affairs Organization. *Campus security:* 24-hour emergency response devices and patrols, late-night transport/escort service, controlled dormitory access. *Student services:* health clinic, personal/psychological counseling.

Athletics Member NCAA. All Division I. *Intercollegiate sports:* baseball M (s), basketball M (s)/W (s), cheerleading W (c), cross-country running M (s)/W (s), equestrian sports M (c)/W (c), golf M (s)/W (s), ice hockey M (c), lacrosse M (s)/W (s), rugby M (c)/W (c), soccer M (s)/W (s), softball W (s), swimming and diving W (s), tennis M (s)/W (s), track and field M (s)/W (s). *Intramural sports:* basketball M/W, field hockey W, football M, racquetball M/W, skiing (downhill) M/W, soccer M/W, softball M/W, swimming and diving M/W, tennis M/W, volleyball M/W.

Standardized Tests *Required:* SAT or ACT (for admission).

Costs (2007–08) *Comprehensive fee:* $35,020 includes full-time tuition ($25,290), mandatory fees ($600), and room and board ($9130). Part-time tuition: $845 per credit hour. *College room only:* $4600. Room and board charges vary according to board plan. *Payment plan:* installment. *Waivers:* employees or children of employees.

Financial Aid Of all full-time matriculated undergraduates who enrolled in 2007, 1,157 applied for aid, 971 were judged to have need, 291 had their need fully met. 166 Federal Work-Study jobs (averaging $1408). 332 state and other part-time jobs (averaging $959). In 2007, 503 non-need-based awards were made. *Average percent of need met:* 76%. *Average financial aid package:* $17,250. *Average need-based loan:* $4941. *Average need-based gift aid:* $13,009. *Average non-need-based aid:* $13,588. *Average indebtedness upon graduation:* $22,041. *Financial aid deadline:* 3/1.

Applying *Options:* electronic application, early action, deferred entrance. *Application fee:* $35. *Required:* high school transcript, minimum 2.0 GPA, 1 letter of recommendation. *Recommended:* essay or personal statement, minimum 3.0 GPA, interview. *Application deadlines:* rolling (freshmen), 6/1 (transfers), 12/1 (early action). *Notification:* continuous (freshmen), continuous (transfers), 12/15 (early action).

Freshman Application Contact Mr. Stephen Neitz, Dean of Admissions and Enrollment Management, Mount St. Mary's University, 16300 Old Emmitsburg Road, Emmitsburg, MD 21727. *Phone:* 301-447-5214. *Toll-free phone:* 800-448-4347. *Fax:* 301-447-5860. *E-mail:* admissions@msmary.edu.

See page 1134 for the College Close-Up.

NER ISRAEL RABBINICAL COLLEGE

Baltimore, Maryland

Freshman Application Contact Rabbi Berel Weisbord, Dean of Admissions, Ner Israel Rabbinical College, 400 Mount Wilson Lane, Baltimore, MD 21208. *Phone:* 410-484-7200.

PEABODY CONSERVATORY OF MUSIC OF THE JOHNS HOPKINS UNIVERSITY

Baltimore, Maryland **www.peabody.jhu.edu/**

- **Independent** comprehensive, founded 1857, administratively affiliated with Johns Hopkins University
- **Urban** 1-acre campus with easy access to Washington, DC
- **Endowment** $90.0 million
- **Coed** 310 undergraduate students, 97% full-time, 48% women, 52% men
- **Very difficult** entrance level, 40% of applicants were admitted

Undergraduates 301 full-time, 9 part-time. Students come from 35 states and territories, 16 other countries, 70% are from out of state, 4% African American, 7% Asian American or Pacific Islander, 4% Hispanic American, 16% international, 8% transferred in, 40% live on campus. *Retention:* 88% of 2006 full-time freshmen returned.

Freshmen *Admission:* 724 applied, 289 admitted, 58 enrolled. *Test scores:* SAT math scores over 500: 84%; SAT writing scores over 500: 87%; SAT math scores over 600: 57%; SAT writing scores over 600: 53%; SAT math scores over 700: 16%; SAT writing scores over 700: 11%.

Faculty *Total:* 165, 23% with terminal degrees. *Student/faculty ratio:* 4:1.

Majors Audio engineering; jazz/jazz studies; music; music teacher education; piano and organ; violin, viola, guitar and other stringed instruments; voice and opera; wind/percussion instruments.

Academics *Calendar:* semesters. *Degrees:* certificates, diplomas, bachelor's, master's, doctoral, and postbachelor's certificates. *Special study options:* academic remediation for entering students, accelerated degree program, advanced placement credit, double majors, English as a second language, honors programs, independent study, internships, off-campus study, services for LD students.

Computers on Campus 40 computers/terminals are available on campus for general student use. Students can access the following: word processing, music processing. Campuswide network is available.

Student Life *Housing:* on-campus residence required for freshman year. *Options:* coed, women-only. Campus housing is university owned. Freshman campus housing is guaranteed. *Activities and organizations:* choral group. *Cam-*

pus security: 24-hour emergency response devices and patrols, late-night transport/escort service, controlled dormitory access. *Student services:* health clinic, personal/psychological counseling.

Standardized Tests *Required for some:* SAT or ACT (for admission).

Costs (2008–09) *Comprehensive fee:* $43,200 includes full-time tuition ($33,000) and room and board ($10,200). Part-time tuition: $940 per semester hour.

Financial Aid Of all full-time matriculated undergraduates who enrolled in 2005, 200 applied for aid, 181 were judged to have need, 7 had their need fully met. 114 Federal Work-Study jobs (averaging $1919). 103 state and other part-time jobs (averaging $934). In 2005, 11 non-need-based awards were made. *Average percent of need met:* 34%. *Average financial aid package:* $8999. *Average need-based loan:* $5610. *Average need-based gift aid:* $7339. *Average non-need-based aid:* $10,653. *Average indebtedness upon graduation:* $19,196.

Applying *Application fee:* $100. *Required:* essay or personal statement, high school transcript, 3 letters of recommendation, interview, audition. *Recommended:* minimum 3.0 GPA. *Application deadlines:* 12/1 (freshmen), 12/1 (transfers). *Notification:* 4/1 (freshmen), 4/1 (transfers).

Freshman Application Contact Mr. David Lane, Director of Admissions, Peabody Conservatory of Music of The Johns Hopkins University, Peabody Conservatory Admissions Office, One East Mount Vernon Place, Baltimore, MD 21202-2397. *Phone:* 410-659-8110. *Toll-free phone:* 800-368-2521.

ST. JOHN'S COLLEGE

Annapolis, Maryland **www.stjohnscollege.edu/**

- **Independent** comprehensive, founded 1784
- **Small-town** 36-acre campus with easy access to Baltimore and Washington, DC
- **Endowment** $70.7 million
- **Coed** 481 undergraduate students, 100% full-time, 47% women, 53% men
- **Moderately difficult** entrance level, 81% of applicants were admitted

Undergraduates 480 full-time, 1 part-time. Students come from 45 states and territories, 12 other countries, 83% are from out of state, 1% African American, 3% Asian American or Pacific Islander, 3% Hispanic American, 0.2% Native American, 0.4% international, 80% live on campus. *Retention:* 80% of 2006 full-time freshmen returned.

Freshmen *Admission:* 441 applied, 356 admitted, 143 enrolled. *Test scores:* SAT critical reading scores over 500: 100%; SAT math scores over 500: 96%; SAT critical reading scores over 600: 94%; SAT math scores over 600: 65%; SAT critical reading scores over 700: 59%; SAT math scores over 700: 17%.

Faculty *Total:* 83, 92% full-time, 73% with terminal degrees. *Student/faculty ratio:* 8:1.

Majors Interdisciplinary studies; liberal arts and sciences/liberal studies; western civilization.

Academics *Calendar:* semesters. *Degrees:* bachelor's and master's. *Special study options:* internships, off-campus study.

Computers on Campus 16 computers/terminals are available on campus for general student use. Students can access the following: computer help desk, free student e-mail accounts. Campuswide network is available. 100% of college-owned or -operated housing units are wired for high-speed Internet access. Wireless service is available via computer labs, dorm rooms, libraries.

Student Life *Housing:* on-campus residence required for freshman year. *Options:* coed, disabled students. Campus housing is university owned. Freshman campus housing is guaranteed. *Activities and organizations:* drama/theater group, student-run newspaper, choral group, King William Players, Project Politae, Political Forum, Student Committee on Instruction, Rowing Club. *Campus security:* 24-hour emergency response devices and patrols, late-night transport/escort service, controlled dormitory access. *Student services:* health clinic, personal/psychological counseling.

Athletics *Intercollegiate sports:* crew M (c)/W (c), fencing M (c)/W (c). *Intramural sports:* badminton M/W, basketball M/W, fencing M/W, football W, racquetball M/W, sailing M/W, soccer M/W, softball M/W, squash M/W, table tennis M/W, tennis M/W, track and field M/W, volleyball M/W, weight lifting M/W.

Standardized Tests *Required for some:* SAT or ACT (for admission). *Recommended:* SAT or ACT (for admission).

Costs (2007–08) *Comprehensive fee:* $45,280 includes full-time tuition ($36,346), mandatory fees ($250), and room and board ($8684). *Room and board:* Room and board charges vary according to board plan. *Payment plan:* installment. *Waivers:* employees or children of employees.

Financial Aid Of all full-time matriculated undergraduates who enrolled in 2006, 357 applied for aid, 301 were judged to have need, 278 had their need fully met. 177 Federal Work-Study jobs (averaging $2543). *Average percent of need met:* 97%. *Average financial aid package:* $26,029. *Average need-based loan:* $7288. *Average need-based gift aid:* $19,352.

Applying *Options:* electronic application, early admission, deferred entrance. *Required:* essay or personal statement, high school transcript, 2 letters of recommendation. *Recommended:* interview. *Application deadlines:* rolling (freshmen), rolling (transfers). *Notification:* continuous (freshmen), continuous (transfers).

Freshman Application Contact Mr. John Christensen, Director of Admissions, St. John's College, PO Box 2800, 60 College Avenue, Annapolis, MD 21404. *Phone:* 410-626-2522. *Toll-free phone:* 800-727-9238. *Fax:* 410-269-7916. *E-mail:* admissions@sjca.edu.

See page 1136 for the College Close-Up.

ST. MARY'S COLLEGE OF MARYLAND

St. Mary's City, Maryland **www.smcm.edu/**

- **State-supported** 4-year, founded 1840, part of Maryland State Colleges and Universities System
- **Rural** 319-acre campus
- **Endowment** $31.0 million
- **Coed** 1,980 undergraduate students, 96% full-time, 57% women, 43% men
- **Very difficult** entrance level, 55% of applicants were admitted

St. Mary's, with its distinctive identity as Maryland's Public Honors College, is one of the finest liberal arts and sciences colleges in the country. The lively academic atmosphere and stunning beauty of the riverfront campus create a challenging and memorable college experience. Apartment-style residences were completed in 2004, and the new athletic and recreation facilities opened in 2005.

Undergraduates 1,905 full-time, 75 part-time. Students come from 34 states and territories, 37 other countries, 16% are from out of state, 8% African American, 4% Asian American or Pacific Islander, 5% Hispanic American, 0.6% Native American, 2% international, 3% transferred in, 84% live on campus. *Retention:* 91% of 2006 full-time freshmen returned.

Freshmen *Admission:* 2,351 applied, 1,288 admitted, 464 enrolled. *Average high school GPA:* 3.5. *Test scores:* SAT critical reading scores over 500: 93%; SAT math scores over 500: 92%; SAT writing scores over 500: 92%; SAT critical reading scores over 600: 62%; SAT math scores over 600: 58%; SAT writing scores over 600: 57%; SAT critical reading scores over 700: 16%; SAT math scores over 700: 10%; SAT writing scores over 700: 14%.

Faculty *Total:* 214, 64% full-time, 79% with terminal degrees. *Student/faculty ratio:* 12:1.

Majors Anthropology; art; biochemistry; biological and physical sciences; biology/biological sciences; business administration and management; business/commerce; chemistry; communication disorders; communication/speech communication and rhetoric; computer and information sciences; dramatic/theater arts; economics; elementary education; engineering physics; English; fine arts related; foreign languages and literatures; history; journalism; liberal arts and sciences/liberal studies; mass communication/media; mathematics; multi-/interdisciplinary studies related; music; music pedagogy; music performance; music related; music theory and composition; philosophy; physics; political science and government; psychology; psychology related; public policy analysis; religious/sacred music; religious studies; sociology; theology and religious vocations related.

Academics *Calendar:* semesters. *Degrees:* bachelor's and master's. *Special study options:* advanced placement credit, cooperative education, double majors, freshman honors college, honors programs, independent study, internships, off-campus study, part-time degree program, services for LD students, student-designed majors, study abroad, summer session for credit. *Unusual degree programs:* 3-2 engineering with University of Maryland, College Park.

Computers on Campus 325 computers/terminals and 500 ports are available on campus for general student use. Students can access the following: campus intranet, computer help desk, free student e-mail accounts, online (class) grades, online (class) registration, online (class) schedules, Blackboard. Campuswide network is available. 100% of college-owned or -operated housing units are wired for high-speed Internet access. Wireless service is available via classrooms, computer centers.

Student Life *Housing options:* coed, men-only, women-only, disabled students. Campus housing is university owned. Freshman campus housing is guaranteed. *Activities and organizations:* drama/theater group, student-run newspaper, radio and television station, choral group, For Goodness Sake (community service), The Point News (student newspaper), SEAC (Student Environmental Action Coalition), Crew, Dance Club. *Campus security:* 24-hour emergency response devices and patrols, student patrols, late-night transport/escort service, controlled dormitory access. *Student services:* health clinic, personal/psychological counseling, women's center.

Athletics Member NCAA. All Division III. *Intercollegiate sports:* baseball M, basketball M/W, crew M (c)/W (c), cross-country running M (c)/W (c), equestrian sports M (c), fencing M (c)/W (c), field hockey W, golf M (c)/W (c), lacrosse M/W, rock climbing M (c)/W (c), sailing M/W, soccer M/W, swimming and diving M/W, tennis M/W, ultimate Frisbee M (c)/W (c), volleyball W, weight lifting M (c), wrestling M (c). *Intramural sports:* basketball M/W, bowling M/W, football M/W, lacrosse M/W, riflery M/W, rugby M/W, sailing M/W, skiing (downhill) M/W, soccer M/W, softball M/W, swimming and diving M/W, tennis M/W.

Standardized Tests *Required:* SAT or ACT (for admission).

Costs (2008–09) *Tuition:* $160 per credit part-time; state resident $10,472 full-time, $160 per credit part-time; nonresident $21,322 full-time, $160 per credit part-time. *Required fees:* $2132 full-time. *Room and board:* $9225; room only: $5315.

Financial Aid Of all full-time matriculated undergraduates who enrolled in 2006, 1,136 applied for aid, 830 were judged to have need. 110 Federal Work-Study jobs (averaging $900). In 2006, 434 non-need-based awards were made. *Average percent of need met:* 62%. *Average financial aid package:* $6250. *Average need-based loan:* $5500. *Average need-based gift aid:* $4000. *Average non-need-based aid:* $4000. *Average indebtedness upon graduation:* $17,125. *Financial aid deadline:* 3/1.

Applying *Options:* electronic application, early admission, early decision. *Application fee:* $40. *Required:* essay or personal statement, high school transcript, minimum 2.0 GPA. *Recommended:* 2 letters of recommendation, interview. *Application deadlines:* 1/15 (freshmen), 2/15 (transfers). *Early decision deadline:* 12/1 (for plan 1), 1/15 (for plan 2). *Notification:* 4/1 (freshmen), 5/30 (transfers), 1/1 (early decision plan 1), 2/15 (early decision plan 2).

Freshman Application Contact Mr. Richard Edgar, Director of Admissions, St. Mary's College of Maryland, 18952 East Fisher Road, St. Mary's City, MD 20686-3001. *Phone:* 240-895-5000. *Toll-free phone:* 800-492-7181. *Fax:* 240-895-5001. *E-mail:* admissions@smcm.edu.

See page 1138 for the College Close-Up.

SALISBURY UNIVERSITY

Salisbury, Maryland www.ssu.edu/

- **State-supported** comprehensive, founded 1925, part of University System of Maryland
- **Small-town** 154-acre campus
- **Endowment** $52.7 million
- **Coed** 6,941 undergraduate students, 92% full-time, 55% women, 45% men
- **Moderately difficult** entrance level, 56% of applicants were admitted

Nationally recognized for excellence, Salisbury University (SU) has a creative curriculum emphasizing undergraduate research, study abroad, professional internships, and community engagement. In guidebooks and surveys by *U.S. News & World Report*, *The Princeton Review*, and others, SU consistently ranks in the top 10 percent of public and private institutions nationwide. Located on Maryland's beautiful and historic Eastern Shore, the University offers forty-two undergraduate majors and thirteen graduate programs. Enjoying both public and private support, all four of its academic schools are endowed, a rarity among public institutions. Exceptional students, a highly regarded faculty, and dynamic administration have earned SU recognition as a Maryland University of National Distinction.

Undergraduates 6,357 full-time, 584 part-time. Students come from 30 states and territories, 58 other countries, 14% are from out of state, 11% African American, 3% Asian American or Pacific Islander, 2% Hispanic American, 0.6% Native American, 0.6% international, 12% transferred in, 46% live on campus. *Retention:* 81% of 2006 full-time freshmen returned.

Freshmen *Admission:* 6,593 applied, 3,684 admitted, 1,150 enrolled. *Average high school GPA:* 3.50. *Test scores:* SAT critical reading scores over 500: 85%; SAT math scores over 500: 86%; SAT writing scores over 500: 84%; SAT critical reading scores over 600: 24%; SAT math scores over 600: 32%; SAT writing scores over 600: 22%; SAT critical reading scores over 700: 2%; SAT math scores over 700: 3%; SAT writing scores over 700: 2%.

Faculty *Total:* 531, 68% full-time, 59% with terminal degrees. *Student/faculty ratio:* 18:1.

Majors Accounting; art; athletic training; biology/biological sciences; business administration and management; chemistry; clinical laboratory science/medical technology; communication/speech communication and rhetoric; computer and information sciences; dramatic/theater arts; economics; education; elementary education; English; environmental health; finance; fine arts related; French; geography; health and physical education; health/medical preparatory programs related; health teacher education; history; liberal arts and sciences/liberal studies; management information systems; management science; marketing/marketing management; mathematics; music; music performance; nursing (registered nurse training); peace studies and conflict resolution; philosophy; physical education teaching and coaching; physics; political science and government; psychology; respiratory care therapy; secondary education; social work; sociology; Spanish.

Academics *Calendar:* 4-1-4. *Degrees:* bachelor's, master's, post-master's, and postbachelor's certificates. *Special study options:* academic remediation for entering students, adult/continuing education programs, advanced placement credit, distance learning, double majors, English as a second language, honors programs, independent study, internships, off-campus study, part-time degree program, services for LD students, student-designed majors, study abroad, summer session for credit. *ROTC:* Army (c). *Unusual degree programs:* 3-2 engineering with University of Maryland College Park, Old Dominion University, Widener University; social work with University of Maryland Eastern Shore; environmental marine science with University of Maryland Eastern Shore.

Computers on Campus 275 computers/terminals are available on campus for general student use. Students can access the following: computer help desk, free student e-mail accounts, online (class) grades, online (class) registration, online (class) schedules, accounts for all students. Campuswide network is available. 100% of college-owned or -operated housing units are wired for high-speed Internet access. Wireless service is available via classrooms, computer centers, computer labs, learning centers, libraries, student centers.

Student Life *Housing options:* coed, men-only, women-only. Campus housing is university owned. Freshman applicants given priority for college housing. *Activities and organizations:* drama/theater group, student-run newspaper, radio and television station, choral group, Student Government Association, Habitat for Humanity, Saferide, Greek Life, Bowling Club, national fraternities, national sororities. *Campus security:* 24-hour emergency response devices and patrols, student patrols, late-night transport/escort service, controlled dormitory access. *Student services:* health clinic, personal/psychological counseling.

Athletics Member NCAA, NAIA. All NCAA Division III. *Intercollegiate sports:* baseball M, basketball M/W, cross-country running M/W, field hockey W, football M, lacrosse M/W, soccer M/W, softball W, swimming and diving M/W, tennis M/W, track and field M/W, volleyball W. *Intramural sports:* basketball M/W, cross-country running M/W, fencing M (c)/W (c), field hockey W (c), football M/W, golf M (c)/W (c), ice hockey M (c), lacrosse M (c)/W, racquetball M/W, rugby M (c)/W (c), sailing M (c)/W (c), soccer M (c)/W (c), softball W, swimming and diving M/W, tennis M/W, track and field M/W, volleyball W, water polo M/W.

Standardized Tests *Required for some:* SAT and SAT Subject Tests or ACT (for admission).

Costs (2007–08) *Tuition:* state resident $4814 full-time, $200 per credit hour part-time; nonresident $12,902 full-time, $537 per credit hour part-time. *Required fees:* $1598 full-time, $52 per credit hour part-time. *Room and board:* $7601; room only: $3880. Room and board charges vary according to board plan and housing facility. *Payment plan:* installment. *Waivers:* senior citizens and employees or children of employees.

Financial Aid Of all full-time matriculated undergraduates who enrolled in 2006, 3,848 applied for aid, 2,524 were judged to have need, 476 had their need fully met. 69 Federal Work-Study jobs (averaging $1852). In 2006, 940 non-need-based awards were made. *Average percent of need met:* 59%. *Average financial aid package:* $6660. *Average need-based loan:* $3694. *Average need-based gift aid:* $5316. *Average non-need-based aid:* $2611. *Average indebtedness upon graduation:* $17,669.

Applying *Options:* electronic application, early admission, early action. *Application fee:* $45. *Required:* high school transcript, minimum 2.0 GPA. *Application deadlines:* 1/15 (freshmen), rolling (transfers), 12/1 (early action). *Notification:* 3/15 (freshmen), continuous (transfers), 1/15 (early action).

Freshman Application Contact Ms. Laura Thorpe, Director of Admissions, Salisbury University, Admissions House, 1101 Camden Avenue, Salisbury, MD 21801. *Phone:* 410-543-6161. *Toll-free phone:* 888-543-0148. *Fax:* 410-546-6016. *E-mail:* admissions@salisbury.edu.

See page 1140 for the College Close-Up.

SOJOURNER-DOUGLASS COLLEGE

Baltimore, Maryland sdc.edu/

Freshman Application Contact Ms. Diana Samuels, Manager, Office of Admissions, Sojourner-Douglass College, 500 North Caroline Street, Baltimore, MD 21205-1814. *Phone:* 410-276-0306. *Fax:* 410-675-1810.

Towson University

Towson, Maryland **www.towson.edu/**

- **State-supported** university, founded 1866, part of University System of Maryland
- **Suburban** 321-acre campus with easy access to Baltimore and Washington, DC
- **Endowment** $5.6 million
- **Coed** 16,219 undergraduate students, 87% full-time, 60% women, 40% men
- **Moderately difficult** entrance level, 60% of applicants were admitted

Undergraduates 14,180 full-time, 2,039 part-time. Students come from 47 states and territories, 106 other countries, 17% are from out of state, 11% African American, 4% Asian American or Pacific Islander, 2% Hispanic American, 0.4% Native American, 3% international, 10% transferred in, 22% live on campus. *Retention:* 82% of 2006 full-time freshmen returned.

Freshmen *Admission:* 15,464 applied, 9,223 admitted, 2,665 enrolled. *Average high school GPA:* 3.46. *Test scores:* SAT critical reading scores over 500: 72%; SAT math scores over 500: 78%; SAT writing scores over 500: 75%; ACT scores over 18: 91%; SAT critical reading scores over 600: 20%; SAT math scores over 600: 25%; SAT writing scores over 600: 19%; ACT scores over 24: 29%; SAT critical reading scores over 700: 2%; SAT math scores over 700: 2%; SAT writing scores over 700: 2%; ACT scores over 30: 2%.

Faculty *Total:* 1,375, 53% full-time, 54% with terminal degrees. *Student/faculty ratio:* 18:1.

Majors Accounting; art; art history, criticism and conservation; art teacher education; athletic training; biochemistry, biophysics and molecular biology related; biology/biological sciences; business administration and management; business administration, management and operations related; chemistry; chemistry related; communication/speech communication and rhetoric; computer and information sciences; dance; dramatic/theater arts; early childhood education; ecology; economics; education related; elementary education; English; family systems; forensic science and technology; French; geography; geology/earth science; German; gerontology; health and physical education related; health/health care administration; health professions related; history; information science/studies; interdisciplinary studies; international relations and affairs; kinesiology and exercise science; mass communication/media; mathematics; music; music teacher education; nursing (registered nurse training); occupational therapy; philosophy; photographic and film/video technology; physical education teaching and coaching; physics; political science and government; psychology; psychology related; religious studies; social sciences; social sciences related; Spanish; special education; speech-language pathology; sport and fitness administration/management; urban studies/affairs; women's studies.

Academics *Calendar:* semesters. *Degrees:* bachelor's, master's, doctoral, post-master's, and postbachelor's certificates. *Special study options:* academic remediation for entering students, accelerated degree program, adult/continuing education programs, advanced placement credit, cooperative education, distance learning, double majors, English as a second language, freshman honors college, honors programs, independent study, internships, off-campus study, part-time degree program, services for LD students, student-designed majors, study abroad, summer session for credit. *ROTC:* Army (c), Air Force (c). *Unusual degree programs:* 3-2 engineering with University of Maryland College Park; law with University of Baltimore.

Computers on Campus 1,200 computers/terminals are available on campus for general student use. Students can access the following: computer help desk, free student e-mail accounts, online (class) grades, online (class) registration, online (class) schedules. Campuswide network is available. 100% of college-owned or -operated housing units are wired for high-speed Internet access. Wireless service is available via entire campus.

Student Life *Housing options:* coed, disabled students. Campus housing is university owned and is provided by a third party. Freshman campus housing is guaranteed. *Activities and organizations:* drama/theater group, student-run newspaper, radio and television station, choral group, marching band, Student Government Association, Black Student Union, Intramural Sports, Habitat for Humanity, University Residence Government, national fraternities, national sororities. *Campus security:* 24-hour emergency response devices and patrols, late-night transport/escort service, controlled dormitory access. *Student services:* health clinic, personal/psychological counseling, women's center.

Athletics Member NCAA. All Division I. *Intercollegiate sports:* baseball M (s), basketball M (s)/W (s), cheerleading M/W, cross-country running M (s)/W (s), field hockey W (s), football M (s), golf M (s)/W (s), gymnastics W (s), lacrosse M (s)/W (s), soccer M (s)/W (s), softball W (s), swimming and diving M (s)/W (s), tennis M (s)/W (s), track and field M (s)/W (s), volleyball M/W (s). *Intramural sports:* badminton M (c)/W (c), basketball M/W, equestrian sports M (c)/W (c), field hockey W (c), football M/W, golf M (c)/W (c), ice hockey M, lacrosse M/W, racquetball M (c)/W (c), rock climbing M (c)/W (c), rugby M/W (c), sailing M (c)/W (c), soccer M/W, softball M/W, table tennis M/W, tennis M/W, track and field M (c)/W (c), ultimate Frisbee M (c)/W (c), volleyball M/W, wrestling M.

Standardized Tests *Required:* SAT or ACT (for admission).

Costs (2008–09) *Tuition:* state resident $5180 full-time, $225 per credit part-time; nonresident $15,120 full-time, $566 per credit part-time. *Required fees:* $2054 full-time, $80 per credit part-time. *Room and board:* $7986; room only: $4860.

Financial Aid Of all full-time matriculated undergraduates who enrolled in 2007, 8,090 applied for aid, 5,748 were judged to have need, 1,272 had their need fully met. 415 Federal Work-Study jobs (averaging $1711). In 2007, 1400 non-need-based awards were made. *Average percent of need met:* 70%. *Average financial aid package:* $8849. *Average need-based loan:* $4102. *Average need-based gift aid:* $6432. *Average non-need-based aid:* $4795. *Average indebtedness upon graduation:* $11,844. *Financial aid deadline:* 2/15.

Applying *Options:* electronic application, early admission, deferred entrance. *Application fee:* $45. *Required:* high school transcript. *Required for some:* essay or personal statement, interview. *Recommended:* minimum 3.0 GPA, 2 letters of recommendation. *Application deadlines:* 2/15 (freshmen), 2/15 (transfers). *Notification:* continuous (freshmen), continuous (transfers).

Freshman Application Contact Ms. Louise Shulack, Director of Admissions, Towson University, 8000 York Road, Towson, MD 21252. *Phone:* 410-704-2113. *Toll-free phone:* 888-4TOWSON. *Fax:* 410-704-3030. *E-mail:* admissions@towson.edu.

United States Naval Academy

Annapolis, Maryland **www.usna.edu/**

- **Federally supported** 4-year, founded 1845
- **Small-town** 329-acre campus with easy access to Baltimore and Washington, DC
- **Endowment** $135.0 million
- **Coed, primarily men** 4,443 undergraduate students, 100% full-time, 21% women, 79% men
- **Very difficult** entrance level, 10% of applicants were admitted

Undergraduates 4,443 full-time. Students come from 54 states and territories, 24 other countries, 96% are from out of state, 4% African American, 3% Asian American or Pacific Islander, 10% Hispanic American, 0.8% Native American, 1% international, 100% live on campus. *Retention:* 96% of 2006 full-time freshmen returned.

Freshmen *Admission:* 12,003 applied, 1,202 admitted, 1,161 enrolled. *Test scores:* SAT critical reading scores over 500: 95%; SAT math scores over 500: 98%; SAT critical reading scores over 600: 61%; SAT math scores over 600: 77%; SAT critical reading scores over 700: 14%; SAT math scores over 700: 24%.

Faculty *Total:* 525. *Student/faculty ratio:* 8:1.

Majors Aerospace, aeronautical and astronautical engineering; Arabic; chemistry; computer and information sciences; computer hardware engineering; computer science; econometrics and quantitative economics; economics; electrical, electronics and communications engineering; engineering; English; French; history; mathematics; mechanical engineering; naval architecture and marine engineering; ocean engineering; oceanography (chemical and physical); physical sciences; physics; political science and government; systems engineering.

Academics *Calendar:* semesters. *Degree:* bachelor's. *Special study options:* academic remediation for entering students, advanced placement credit, double majors, English as a second language, honors programs, independent study, summer session for credit.

Computers on Campus 6,100 computers/terminals are available on campus for general student use. Students can access the following: campus intranet, computer help desk, free student e-mail accounts, online (class) grades, online (class) registration, online (class) schedules. Campuswide network is available. 100% of college-owned or -operated housing units are wired for high-speed Internet access.

Student Life *Housing:* on-campus residence required through senior year. *Options:* coed. Campus housing is university owned. Freshman campus housing is guaranteed. *Activities and organizations:* drama/theater group, student-run radio station, choral group, marching band, Mountaineering Club, Semper Fi, Black Studies Club, Midshipmen Action Club, Martial Arts Club. *Campus security:* 24-hour emergency response devices and patrols, student patrols, campus gate security. *Student services:* health clinic, personal/psychological counseling, legal services.

Athletics Member NCAA. All Division I except football (Division I-A). *Intercollegiate sports:* baseball M, basketball M/W, cheerleading M/W, crew M/W, cross-country running M/W, golf M, gymnastics M/W (c), ice hockey M (c), lacrosse M/W, riflery M/W, rugby M (c)/W (c), sailing M/W, skiing (downhill) M (c)/W (c), soccer M/W, softball W (c), squash M, swimming and diving M/W, tennis M/W (c), track and field M/W, volleyball M (c)/W, water polo M, weight lifting M (c)/W (c), wrestling M. *Intramural sports:* basketball M/W, cross-country running M/W, football M/W, lacrosse M (c), racquetball M/W, sailing M/W, soccer M/W, softball M/W, volleyball M/W, weight lifting M/W.

Standardized Tests *Required:* SAT or ACT (for admission).

Costs (2008–09) *Tuition:* tuition, room and board, and medical and dental care are provided by the U.S. government. Each midshipman receives a salary from which to pay for uniforms, books, supplies, and personal expenses. Entering freshman are required to deposit $2,500 to defray the initial cost of uniforms and equipment.

Applying *Options:* electronic application. *Required:* essay or personal statement, high school transcript, 2 letters of recommendation, interview, authorized nomination. *Application deadline:* 1/31 (freshmen). *Notification:* 4/15 (freshmen).

Freshman Application Contact Dean of Admissions, United States Naval Academy, 117 Decatur Road, Annapolis, MD 21402-5000. *Phone:* 410-293-4361. *Fax:* 410-293-4348. *E-mail:* webmail@usna.edu.

UNIVERSITY OF BALTIMORE

Baltimore, Maryland **www.ubalt.edu/**

- **State-supported** upper-level, founded 1925, part of University System of Maryland
- **Urban** 49-acre campus
- **Endowment** $18.9 million
- **Coed** 2,411 undergraduate students, 52% full-time, 58% women, 42% men
- **Minimally difficult** entrance level, 34% of applicants were admitted

Undergraduates 1,258 full-time, 1,153 part-time. Students come from 14 states and territories, 62 other countries, 1% are from out of state, 35% African American, 4% Asian American or Pacific Islander, 2% Hispanic American, 0.5% Native American, 1% international, 34% transferred in.

Freshmen *Admission:* 862 applied, 293 admitted.

Faculty *Total:* 352, 47% full-time, 72% with terminal degrees. *Student/faculty ratio:* 16:1.

Majors Accounting; business administration and management; community organization and advocacy; computer and information sciences; criminal justice/law enforcement administration; digital communication and media/multimedia; economics; English; finance; forensic science and technology; health and medical administrative services related; history; human resources management; human services; information science/studies; interdisciplinary studies; international business/trade/commerce; journalism; legal studies; liberal arts and sciences/liberal studies; literature; management information systems; marketing/marketing management; mass communication/media; non-profit management; political science and government; psychology; sales, distribution and marketing; technical and business writing.

Academics *Calendar:* semesters. *Degrees:* certificates, bachelor's, master's, doctoral, first professional, post-master's, and postbachelor's certificates. *Special study options:* academic remediation for entering students, accelerated degree program, adult/continuing education programs, advanced placement credit, cooperative education, distance learning, honors programs, independent study, internships, off-campus study, part-time degree program, services for LD students, student-designed majors, summer session for credit. *ROTC:* Army (c), Air Force (c). *Unusual degree programs:* 3-2 law.

Computers on Campus 135 computers/terminals are available on campus for general student use. Students can access the following: computer help desk, free student e-mail accounts, online (class) grades, online (class) registration, online (class) schedules. Campuswide network is available. Wireless service is available via entire campus.

Student Life *Housing:* college housing not available. *Options:* Campus housing is provided by a third party. *Activities and organizations:* student-run newspaper, Psi Chi, APALSA, International Student Association, African Student Association, Forensics Student Association. *Campus security:* 24-hour emergency response devices and patrols, late-night transport/escort service. *Student services:* health clinic, personal/psychological counseling.

Athletics *Intramural sports:* basketball M/W, golf M/W, racquetball M/W, soccer M, table tennis M/W, volleyball M/W, weight lifting M/W.

Standardized Tests *Required:* SAT or ACT (for admission).

Costs (2007–08) *Tuition:* state resident $5325 full-time, $243 per credit part-time; nonresident $18,107 full-time, $754 per credit part-time. Full-time tuition and fees vary according to course load. Part-time tuition and fees vary according to course load. *Required fees:* $805 full-time, $85 per credit part-time. *Payment plans:* installment, deferred payment. *Waivers:* senior citizens and employees or children of employees.

Financial Aid Of all full-time matriculated undergraduates who enrolled in 2005, 827 applied for aid, 747 were judged to have need, 75 had their need fully met. 105 Federal Work-Study jobs (averaging $3672). In 2005, 29 non-need-based awards were made. *Average percent of need met:* 31%. *Average financial aid package:* $8738. *Average need-based loan:* $4078. *Average need-based gift aid:* $2392. *Average non-need-based aid:* $3143. *Average indebtedness upon graduation:* $18,050.

Applying *Options:* electronic application, deferred entrance. *Application fee:* $30. *Application deadline:* 6/1 (transfers). *Notification:* continuous (transfers).

Application Contact Jenifer Blair, University of Baltimore, 1420 North Charles Street, Baltimore, MD 21201-5779. *Phone:* 410-837-4777. *Toll-free phone:* 877-APPLYUB. *Fax:* 410-837-4793. *E-mail:* admissions@ubalt.edu.

See page 1142 for the College Close-Up.

UNIVERSITY OF MARYLAND, BALTIMORE COUNTY

Baltimore, Maryland **www.umbc.edu/**

- **State-supported** university, founded 1963, part of University System of Maryland
- **Suburban** 530-acre campus with easy access to Washington, D.C.
- **Endowment** $55.5 million
- **Coed** 9,464 undergraduate students, 84% full-time, 46% women, 54% men
- **Moderately difficult** entrance level, 69% of applicants were admitted

UMBC, which is located between Baltimore and Washington, D.C., offers smart, engaged students opportunities to explore the ideas they are passionate about in an honors university setting—providing access to outstanding professors and the individual attention usually found at a smaller, private college. UMBC's leadership in technology and its friendly campus climate, business and industry partnerships, and ability to place students in leading graduate programs and promising careers are just a few of the reasons why students who could attend any college are choosing UMBC.

Undergraduates 7,962 full-time, 1,502 part-time. Students come from 42 states and territories, 81 other countries, 7% are from out of state, 16% African American, 21% Asian American or Pacific Islander, 4% Hispanic American, 0.5% Native American, 4% international, 12% transferred in, 34% live on campus. *Retention:* 85% of 2006 full-time freshmen returned.

Freshmen *Admission:* 5,836 applied, 4,024 admitted, 1,437 enrolled. *Average high school GPA:* 3.6. *Test scores:* SAT critical reading scores over 500: 86%; SAT math scores over 500: 95%; SAT writing scores over 500: 85%; ACT scores over 18: 98%; SAT critical reading scores over 600: 41%; SAT math scores over 600: 55%; SAT writing scores over 600: 38%; ACT scores over 24: 61%; SAT critical reading scores over 700: 11%; SAT math scores over 700: 13%; SAT writing scores over 700: 6%; ACT scores over 30: 11%.

Faculty *Total:* 746, 63% full-time, 68% with terminal degrees. *Student/faculty ratio:* 18:1.

Majors African-American/Black studies; African studies; American studies; ancient studies; anthropology; area, ethnic, cultural, and gender studies related; art; art history, criticism and conservation; biochemistry/biophysics and molecular biology; bioinformatics; biology/biological sciences; business administration and management; business administration, management and operations related; chemical engineering; chemistry; computer engineering; computer/information technology services administration related; computer science; dance; dramatic/theater arts; economics; emergency medical technology (EMT paramedic); engineering; English; environmental science; environmental studies; film/cinema studies; geography; health/health care administration; health professions related; health science; history; information science/studies; interdisciplinary studies; linguistics; mass communication/media; mathematics; mechanical engineering; modern languages; music; philosophy; photography; physical therapy; physics; physics teacher education; political science and government; pre-dentistry studies; pre-medical studies; pre-nursing studies; pre-pharmacy studies; psychology; social work; sociology; statistics; visual and performing arts; women's studies.

Academics *Calendar:* 4-1-4. *Degrees:* bachelor's, master's, doctoral, and postbachelor's certificates. *Special study options:* academic remediation for entering students, adult/continuing education programs, advanced placement credit, cooperative education, distance learning, double majors, English as a second language, external degree program, freshman honors college, honors programs, independent study, internships, off-campus study, part-time degree program, services for LD students, student-designed majors, study abroad, summer session for credit. *ROTC:* Army (c).

Computers on Campus 875 computers/terminals are available on campus for general student use. Students can access the following: campus intranet, computer help desk, free student e-mail accounts, online (class) grades, online (class) registration, online (class) schedules, student account information. Campuswide network is available. 100% of college-owned or -operated housing units are wired for high-speed Internet access. Wireless service is available via classrooms, computer centers, computer labs, libraries, student centers.

Student Life *Housing options:* coed, disabled students. Campus housing is university owned and is provided by a third party. Freshman campus housing is guaranteed. *Activities and organizations:* drama/theater group, student-run newspaper, radio station, choral group, Student Government Association, Student Events Board, Retriever Weekly, Resident Student Association, Black Student Union, national fraternities, national sororities. *Campus security:* 24-hour emergency response devices and patrols, late-night transport/escort service. *Student services:* health clinic, personal/psychological counseling, women's center, legal services.

Athletics Member NCAA. All Division I. *Intercollegiate sports:* baseball M (s), basketball M (s)/W (s), bowling M (c)/W (c), crew M (c)/W (c), cross-country running M (s)/W (s), fencing M (c)/W (c), field hockey W (s), ice hockey M (c), lacrosse M (s)/W (s), rugby M (c)/W (c), sailing M (c)/W (c), skiing (downhill) M (c)/W (c), soccer M (s)/W (s), softball W (s), swimming and diving M (s)/W (s), tennis M (s)/W (s), track and field M (s)/W (s), ultimate Frisbee M (c)/W (c), volleyball M (c)/W (s), wrestling M (c). *Intramural sports:* badminton M/W, basketball M/W, cross-country running M/W, football M/W, lacrosse M (c)/W (c), soccer M (c)/W (c), softball M/W, swimming and diving M/W, tennis M/W, track and field M/W, volleyball M/W (c).

Standardized Tests *Required:* SAT or ACT (for admission).

Costs (2007–08) *Tuition:* state resident $6484 full-time, $270 per credit hour part-time; nonresident $15,216 full-time, $633 per credit hour part-time. Full-time tuition and fees vary according to location and program. Part-time tuition and fees vary according to location and program. *Required fees:* $2224 full-time, $98 per credit hour part-time. *Room and board:* $8658; room only: $5306. Room and board charges vary according to board plan and housing facility. *Payment plan:* installment. *Waivers:* senior citizens and employees or children of employees.

Financial Aid Of all full-time matriculated undergraduates who enrolled in 2005, 4,592 applied for aid, 3,526 were judged to have need, 1,309 had their need fully met. 69 Federal Work-Study jobs (averaging $2083). In 2005, 646 non-need-based awards were made. *Average percent of need met:* 73%. *Average financial aid package:* $9876. *Average need-based loan:* $4338. *Average need-based gift aid:* $6652. *Average non-need-based aid:* $3484. *Average indebtedness upon graduation:* $19,910.

Applying *Options:* electronic application, early admission, early action, deferred entrance. *Application fee:* $50. *Required:* essay or personal statement, high school transcript. *Recommended:* minimum 3.0 GPA, 2 letters of recommendation. *Application deadlines:* 2/1 (freshmen), 5/31 (transfers), 11/1 (early action). *Notification:* continuous (freshmen), continuous (transfers), 12/15 (early action).

Freshman Application Contact Mr. Dale Bittinger, Director of Admissions, University of Maryland, Baltimore County, 1000 Hilltop Circle, Baltimore, MD 21250. *Phone:* 410-455-2291. *Toll-free phone:* 800-UMBC-4U2 (in-state); 800-862-2402 (out-of-state). *Fax:* 410-455-1094. *E-mail:* admissions@umbc.edu.

See page 1144 for the College Close-Up.

UNIVERSITY OF MARYLAND, COLLEGE PARK

College Park, Maryland — www.maryland.edu/

- **State-supported** university, founded 1856, part of University System of Maryland
- **Suburban** 3688-acre campus with easy access to Baltimore and Washington, DC
- **Endowment** $431.6 million
- **Coed** 25,813 undergraduate students, 92% full-time, 48% women, 52% men
- **Moderately difficult** entrance level, 47% of applicants were admitted

Undergraduates 23,756 full-time, 2,057 part-time. Students come from 54 states and territories, 149 other countries, 23% are from out of state, 13% African American, 14% Asian American or Pacific Islander, 6% Hispanic American, 0.4% Native American, 2% international, 8% transferred in, 41% live on campus. *Retention:* 92% of 2006 full-time freshmen returned.

Freshmen *Admission:* 24,172 applied, 11,370 admitted, 4,236 enrolled. *Average high school GPA:* 3.9. *Test scores:* SAT critical reading scores over 500: 92%; SAT math scores over 500: 93%; SAT critical reading scores over 600: 65%; SAT math scores over 600: 76%; SAT critical reading scores over 700: 17%; SAT math scores over 700: 27%.

Faculty *Total:* 2,185, 73% full-time, 82% with terminal degrees. *Student/faculty ratio:* 18:1.

Majors Accounting; aerospace, aeronautical and astronautical engineering; African-American/Black studies; agricultural/biological engineering and bioengineering; agricultural economics; agriculture; agriculture and agriculture operations related; agronomy and crop science; American studies; animal sciences; anthropology; architecture; art history, criticism and conservation; art teacher education; astronomy; biochemistry; biology/biological sciences; business administration and management; business/commerce; business, management, and marketing related; chemical engineering; chemistry; Chinese; civil engineering; classics and languages, literatures and linguistics; communication/speech communication and rhetoric; computer and information sciences; computer engineering; criminology; dance; dietetics; dramatic/theater arts; ecology; economics; education; electrical, electronics and communications engineering; elementary education; engineering; engineering related; English; English/language arts teacher education; family and community services; finance; fine/studio arts; fire protection and safety technology; food science; foods, nutrition, and wellness; foreign languages and literatures; foreign language teacher education; French; geography; geology/earth science; German; health teacher education; history; horticultural science; human resources management; information science/studies; international business/trade/commerce; Italian; Japanese; Jewish/Judaic studies; journalism; kindergarten/preschool education; landscape architecture; Latin; linguistics; logistics and materials management; management science; marketing/marketing management; materials engineering; mathematics; mathematics teacher education; mechanical engineering; medical microbiology and bacteriology; multi-/interdisciplinary studies related; music; music performance; music teacher education; natural resources/conservation; philosophy; physical education teaching and coaching; physical sciences; physics; plant sciences; political science and government; pre-dentistry studies; pre-law studies; psychology; Romance languages; Russian; Russian studies; science teacher education; secondary education; social studies teacher education; sociology; Spanish; special education; speech-language pathology; visual and performing arts; women's studies.

Academics *Calendar:* semesters. *Degrees:* certificates, bachelor's, master's, doctoral, first professional, post-master's, and postbachelor's certificates. *Special study options:* academic remediation for entering students, accelerated degree program, adult/continuing education programs, advanced placement credit, cooperative education, distance learning, double majors, English as a second language, external degree program, honors programs, independent study, internships, off-campus study, part-time degree program, services for LD students, student-designed majors, study abroad, summer session for credit. *ROTC:* Army (b), Navy (c), Air Force (b).

Computers on Campus 11,097 computers/terminals are available on campus for general student use. Students can access the following: campus intranet, computer help desk, free student e-mail accounts, online (class) grades, online (class) registration, online (class) schedules, student account information, financial aid summary. Campuswide network is available. 100% of college-owned or -operated housing units are wired for high-speed Internet access. Wireless service is available via classrooms, computer labs, dorm rooms, libraries, student centers.

Student Life *Housing options:* coed, women-only, cooperative, disabled students. Campus housing is university owned and is provided by a third party. Freshman campus housing is guaranteed. *Activities and organizations:* drama/theater group, student-run newspaper, radio and television station, choral group, marching band, Student Government Association, Residence Hall Association, Black Student Union, Asian-American Student Union/Jewish Student Union, Commuter Students Association, national fraternities, national sororities. *Campus security:* 24-hour emergency response devices and patrols, student patrols, late-night transport/escort service, controlled dormitory access, campus police, video camera surveillance. *Student services:* health clinic, personal/psychological counseling, women's center, legal services.

Athletics Member NCAA. All Division I except football (Division I-A). *Intercollegiate sports:* baseball M (s), basketball M (s)/W (s), cheerleading W (s), cross-country running M (s)/W (s), field hockey W (s), golf M (s)/W (s), gymnastics W (s), lacrosse M (s)/W (s), soccer M (s)/W (s), softball W (s), swimming and diving M (s)/W (s), tennis M (s)/W (s), track and field M (s)/W (s), volleyball W (s), water polo W (s), wrestling M (s). *Intramural sports:* badminton M (c)/W (c), baseball M (c), basketball M/W, bowling M (c)/W (c), crew M (c)/W (c), cross-country running M/W, equestrian sports M (c)/W (c), fencing M (c)/W (c), field hockey W (c), football M/W, golf M/W, ice hockey M (c)/W (c), lacrosse M (c)/W (c), racquetball M (c)/W (c), rock climbing M (c)/W (c), rugby M (c)/W (c), sailing M (c)/W (c), soccer M (c)/W (c), softball W, squash M (c)/W (c), swimming and diving M (c)/W (c), table tennis M/W, tennis M/W, track and field M/W, ultimate Frisbee M/W, volleyball M (c)/W (c), water polo M (c)/W (c), weight lifting M/W, wrestling M.

Standardized Tests *Required:* SAT or ACT (for admission).

Costs (2007–08) *Tuition:* state resident $6566 full-time, $273 per credit hour part-time; nonresident $20,005 full-time, $867 per credit hour part-time. Part-time tuition and fees vary according to course load. *Required fees:* $1403 full-time, $320 per term part-time. *Room and board:* $8854; room only: $5287. Room and board charges vary according to board plan. *Payment plans:* installment, deferred payment. *Waivers:* employees or children of employees.

Financial Aid Of all full-time matriculated undergraduates who enrolled in 2006, 12,501 applied for aid, 9,234 were judged to have need, 619 had their need fully met. 772 Federal Work-Study jobs (averaging $1325). In 2006, 2365 non-need-based awards were made. *Average percent of need met:* 54%. *Average financial aid package:* $8843. *Average need-based loan:* $4219. *Average need-based gift aid:* $5434. *Average non-need-based aid:* $5799. *Average indebtedness upon graduation:* $18,958.

Applying *Options:* early admission, early action, deferred entrance. *Application fee:* $55. *Required:* essay or personal statement, high school transcript, 1 letter of recommendation. *Required for some:* resume of activities, auditions. *Recommended:* 2 letters of recommendation. *Application deadlines:* 1/20 (freshmen), 6/1 (transfers), 12/1 (early action). *Notification:* continuous until 4/1 (freshmen), continuous (transfers), 2/15 (early action).

Freshman Application Contact Ms. Barbara Gill, Director of Undergraduate Admissions, University of Maryland, College Park, Mitchell Building, College Park, MD 20742-5235. *Phone:* 301-314-8385. *Toll-free phone:* 800-422-5867. *Fax:* 301-314-9693. *E-mail:* um-admit@uga.umd.edu.

See page 1146 for the College Close-Up.

University of Maryland Eastern Shore

Princess Anne, Maryland **www.umes.edu/**

- **State-supported** university, founded 1886, part of University System of Maryland
- **Rural** 700-acre campus
- **Coed** 3,326 undergraduate students, 87% full-time, 59% women, 41% men
- **Moderately difficult** entrance level, 58% of applicants were admitted

Undergraduates 2,902 full-time, 424 part-time. Students come from 30 states and territories, 50 other countries, 28% are from out of state, 76% African American, 2% Asian American or Pacific Islander, 0.9% Hispanic American, 0.4% Native American, 11% international, 4% transferred in, 60% live on campus. *Retention:* 65% of 2006 full-time freshmen returned.

Freshmen *Admission:* 3,714 applied, 2,165 admitted, 846 enrolled. *Average high school GPA:* 2.8. *Test scores:* SAT critical reading scores over 500: 19%; SAT math scores over 500: 17%; ACT scores over 18: 3%; SAT critical reading scores over 600: 3%; SAT math scores over 600: 3%.

Faculty *Total:* 283, 61% full-time, 44% with terminal degrees. *Student/faculty ratio:* 20:1.

Majors Accounting; agricultural business and management; agricultural teacher education; agriculture; air traffic control; art teacher education; biology/biological sciences; business administration and management; business teacher education; chemistry; child development; clinical laboratory science/medical technology; clinical/medical laboratory technology; computer science; construction engineering technology; construction management; criminal justice/law enforcement administration; dietetics; ecology; education; electrical, electronic and communications engineering technology; elementary education; engineering technology; English; environmental studies; family and consumer economics related; family and consumer sciences/home economics teacher education; family and consumer sciences/human sciences; fashion/apparel design; fashion merchandising; history; hotel/motel administration; human ecology; industrial arts; industrial radiologic technology; kindergarten/preschool education; liberal arts and sciences/liberal studies; marine biology and biological oceanography; mass communication/media; mathematics; music teacher education; physical education teaching and coaching; physical therapy; poultry science; pre-dentistry studies; pre-law studies; pre-medical studies; rehabilitation therapy; social sciences; social work; sociology; special education; special products marketing.

Academics *Calendar:* semesters. *Degrees:* bachelor's, master's, and doctoral. *Special study options:* academic remediation for entering students, accelerated degree program, adult/continuing education programs, advanced placement credit, cooperative education, honors programs, internships, off-campus study, part-time degree program, services for LD students, student-designed majors, summer session for credit.

Computers on Campus 200 computers/terminals are available on campus for general student use. Campuswide network is available.

Student Life *Housing options:* coed, men-only, women-only. Campus housing is university owned. *Activities and organizations:* drama/theater group, student-run newspaper, choral group, national fraternities, national sororities. *Campus security:* 24-hour emergency response devices and patrols, student patrols, late-night transport/escort service, controlled dormitory access. *Student services:* health clinic, personal/psychological counseling.

Athletics Member NCAA. All Division I. *Intercollegiate sports:* baseball M (s), basketball M (s)/W (s), cheerleading M/W, cross-country running M/W, softball W, tennis M (s)/W, track and field M/W, volleyball W, wrestling M. *Intramural sports:* basketball M/W, bowling W, cheerleading M/W, cross-country running M/W, soccer M/W, softball W, swimming and diving M/W, table tennis M/W, tennis M/W, track and field M/W, volleyball M/W, wrestling M.

Standardized Tests *Required:* SAT or ACT (for admission), ACCUPLACER (for admission).

Costs (2007–08) *Tuition:* state resident $4112 full-time, $171 per credit hour part-time; nonresident $10,679 full-time, $386 per credit hour part-time. Full-time tuition and fees vary according to course load. Part-time tuition and fees vary according to course load. *Required fees:* $1876 full-time, $40 per term part-time. *Room and board:* $6580; room only: $3680. Room and board charges vary according to board plan and housing facility. *Payment plans:* installment, deferred payment. *Waivers:* senior citizens and employees or children of employees.

Financial Aid Of all full-time matriculated undergraduates who enrolled in 2003, 2,425 applied for aid, 1,988 were judged to have need, 317 had their need fully met. 221 Federal Work-Study jobs (averaging $1445). In 2003, 320 non-need-based awards were made. *Average percent of need met:* 73%. *Average financial aid package:* $11,180. *Average need-based loan:* $5000. *Average need-based gift aid:* $6225. *Average non-need-based aid:* $2500. *Average indebtedness upon graduation:* $8500.

Applying *Options:* electronic application, early admission, early action, deferred entrance. *Application fee:* $25. *Required:* essay or personal statement, high school transcript, minimum 2.5 GPA, 2 letters of recommendation. *Recommended:* interview. *Application deadlines:* 7/15 (freshmen), rolling (transfers), 11/15 (early action).

Director of Admissions Tyrone Young, Director of Admissions, University of Maryland Eastern Shore, Princess Anne, MD 21853-1299. *Phone:* 410-651-8410.

University of Maryland University College

Adelphi, Maryland **www.umuc.edu/**

- **State-supported** comprehensive, founded 1947, part of University System of Maryland
- **Suburban** campus with easy access to Washington, DC
- **Coed** 21,853 undergraduate students, 14% full-time, 58% women, 42% men
- **Noncompetitive** entrance level, 100% of applicants were admitted

Undergraduates 3,004 full-time, 18,849 part-time. Students come from 54 states and territories, 49 other countries, 40% are from out of state, 29% African American, 4% Asian American or Pacific Islander, 5% Hispanic American, 0.7% Native American, 2% international, 17% transferred in.

Freshmen *Admission:* 2,889 applied, 2,888 admitted, 901 enrolled.

Faculty *Total:* 1,615, 15% full-time, 68% with terminal degrees. *Student/faculty ratio:* 19:1.

Majors Accounting; business administration and management; communication/speech communication and rhetoric; computer and information sciences; computer science; criminal justice/law enforcement administration; English; environmental studies; fire science; history; humanities; human resources management; information science/studies; legal assistant/paralegal; management science; marketing/marketing management; multi-/interdisciplinary studies related; psychology; social sciences.

Academics *Calendar:* semesters. *Degrees:* certificates, associate, bachelor's, master's, doctoral, and postbachelor's certificates (offers primarily part-time evening and weekend degree programs at more than 30 off-campus locations in Maryland and the Washington, DC area, and more than 180 military communities in Europe and Asia with military enrollment not reflected in this profile; associate of arts program available to military students only). *Special study options:* accelerated degree program, adult/continuing education programs, advanced placement credit, cooperative education, distance learning, double majors, external degree program, off-campus study, part-time degree program, services for LD students, summer session for credit.

Computers on Campus 375 computers/terminals are available on campus for general student use. Students can access the following: campus intranet, computer help desk, free student e-mail accounts, online (class) grades, online (class) registration, online (class) schedules. Campuswide network is available. Wireless service is available via computer labs, libraries.

Student Life *Housing:* college housing not available. *Campus security:* 24-hour emergency response devices and patrols, late-night transport/escort service.

Costs (2007–08) *Tuition:* state resident $5520 full-time, $230 per semester hour part-time; nonresident $11,184 full-time, $466 per semester hour part-time.

Required fees: $120 full-time. *Payment plan:* installment. *Waivers:* senior citizens and employees or children of employees.

Financial Aid Of all full-time matriculated undergraduates who enrolled in 2006, 2,040 applied for aid, 1,970 were judged to have need, 4 had their need fully met. *Average percent of need met:* 21%. *Average financial aid package:* $5836. *Average need-based loan:* $3915. *Average need-based gift aid:* $3167.

Applying *Options:* electronic application, deferred entrance. *Application fee:* $50. *Required:* high school transcript. *Application deadlines:* rolling (freshmen), rolling (transfers). *Notification:* continuous (freshmen), continuous (transfers).

Freshman Application Contact University of Maryland University College, 3501 University Boulevard East, Adelphi, MD 20783. *Phone:* 800-888-UMUC. *Toll-free phone:* 800-888-8682. *E-mail:* admissions@umuc.edu.

UNIVERSITY OF PHOENIX–MARYLAND CAMPUS

Columbia, Maryland **www.phoenix.edu/**

- **Proprietary** comprehensive
- **Urban** campus
- **Coed**
- **Noncompetitive** entrance level

Faculty *Student/faculty ratio:* 11:1.

Academics *Calendar:* continuous. *Degrees:* bachelor's and master's.

Student Life *Campus security:* late-night transport/escort service.

Costs (2007–08) *Tuition:* $11,910 full-time, $397 per credit part-time. Full-time tuition and fees vary according to course level.

Financial Aid *Average financial aid package:* $3797. *Average need-based gift aid:* $2072.

Applying *Options:* deferred entrance. *Application fee:* $45. *Required:* 1 letter of recommendation. *Required for some:* high school transcript.

Freshman Application Contact Ms. Beth Barilla, Associate Vice President, Student Admissions and Services, University of Phoenix–Maryland Campus, 4615 East Elwood Street, Mail Stop AA-K101, Phoenix, AZ 85040-1958. *Phone:* 480-317-6000. *Toll-free phone:* 800-776-4867 (in-state); 800-228-7240 (out-of-state). *Fax:* 480-894-1758. *E-mail:* beth.barilla@phoenix.edu.

VILLA JULIE COLLEGE

Stevenson, Maryland **www.vjc.edu/**

- **Independent** comprehensive, founded 1952
- **Suburban** 150-acre campus with easy access to Baltimore
- **Endowment** $44.8 million
- **Coed** 3,076 undergraduate students, 83% full-time, 70% women, 30% men
- **Moderately difficult** entrance level, 82% of applicants were admitted

Undergraduates 2,546 full-time, 530 part-time. Students come from 13 states and territories, 9 other countries, 6% are from out of state, 15% African American, 3% Asian American or Pacific Islander, 1% Hispanic American, 0.4% Native American, 0.8% international, 8% transferred in, 39% live on campus. *Retention:* 83% of 2006 full-time freshmen returned.

Freshmen *Admission:* 2,461 applied, 2,028 admitted, 605 enrolled. *Average high school GPA:* 3.4. *Test scores:* SAT critical reading scores over 500: 52%; SAT math scores over 500: 45%; ACT scores over 18: 78%; SAT critical reading scores over 600: 13%; SAT math scores over 600: 13%; ACT scores over 24: 27%; SAT critical reading scores over 700: 1%; SAT math scores over 700: 1%.

Faculty *Total:* 386, 29% full-time, 44% with terminal degrees. *Student/faculty ratio:* 14:1.

Majors Accounting; applied art; applied history; art; biological and physical sciences; biology/biological sciences; biology/biotechnology laboratory technician; business administration and management; chemistry; child development; clinical laboratory science/medical technology; clinical/medical laboratory technology; commercial and advertising art; computer and information sciences; computer graphics; computer programming; court reporting; design and visual communications; developmental and child psychology; dramatic/theater arts; early childhood education; elementary education; English; environmental studies; family and community services; film/video and photographic arts related; history; humanities; information science/studies; interdisciplinary studies; journalism; kindergarten/preschool education; legal assistant/paralegal; legal studies; liberal arts and sciences/liberal studies; management information systems; mass communication/media; medical laboratory technology; middle school education; nursing (registered nurse training); photography; physical sciences; political science and government; pre-dentistry studies; pre-law studies; pre-medical studies; pre-veterinary studies; psychology; social sciences; sociology.

Academics *Calendar:* semesters. *Degrees:* bachelor's and master's. *Special study options:* academic remediation for entering students, accelerated degree program, adult/continuing education programs, advanced placement credit, cooperative education, distance learning, double majors, honors programs, independent study, internships, off-campus study, part-time degree program, services for LD students, student-designed majors, study abroad, summer session for credit. *ROTC:* Army (c).

Computers on Campus 300 computers/terminals are available on campus for general student use. Campuswide network is available.

Student Life *Housing options:* men-only, women-only. Campus housing is university owned. Freshman applicants given priority for college housing. *Activities and organizations:* drama/theater group, student-run newspaper, choral group, Student Government Association, Wilderness Club, Black Student Union, National Student Nurses Association, Phi Sigma, national sororities. *Campus security:* 24-hour emergency response devices, late-night transport/escort service, controlled dormitory access, patrols by trained security personnel during campus hours. *Student services:* personal/psychological counseling.

Athletics Member NCAA. All Division III. *Intercollegiate sports:* baseball M, basketball M/W, cheerleading M/W, cross-country running M/W, field hockey W, golf M/W, lacrosse M/W, soccer M/W, softball W, tennis M/W, track and field M/W, volleyball W. *Intramural sports:* badminton M/W, baseball M, basketball M/W, fencing M/W, field hockey W, football M/W, sailing M/W, skiing (cross-country) M/W, skiing (downhill) M/W, softball W, table tennis M/W, tennis M/W, volleyball M.

Standardized Tests *Required:* SAT or ACT (for admission).

Costs (2007–08) *Comprehensive fee:* $26,844 includes full-time tuition ($16,800), mandatory fees ($1144), and room and board ($8900). Part-time tuition: $435 per credit. *Required fees:* $75 per term part-time. *College room only:* $5900. Room and board charges vary according to board plan and housing facility. *Payment plans:* installment, deferred payment. *Waivers:* employees or children of employees.

Financial Aid Of all full-time matriculated undergraduates who enrolled in 2006, 1,768 applied for aid, 1,420 were judged to have need, 410 had their need fully met. In 2006, 618 non-need-based awards were made. *Average percent of need met:* 74%. *Average financial aid package:* $12,883. *Average need-based loan:* $3713. *Average need-based gift aid:* $10,319. *Average non-need-based aid:* $6476. *Average indebtedness upon graduation:* $15,580.

Applying *Options:* electronic application, early admission, deferred entrance. *Application fee:* $25. *Required:* essay or personal statement, high school transcript, 2 letters of recommendation. *Recommended:* interview. *Application deadlines:* rolling (freshmen), rolling (transfers). *Notification:* continuous (freshmen), continuous (transfers).

Freshman Application Contact Mr. Mark Hergan, Vice President, Enrollment Management, Villa Julie College, 1525 Greenspring Valley Road, Stevenson, MD 21153-0641. *Phone:* 410-486-7001. *Toll-free phone:* 877-468-6852 (in-state); 877-468-3852 (out-of-state). *Fax:* 410-352-4440. *E-mail:* admissions@vjc.edu.

See page 1148 for the College Close-Up.

WASHINGTON BIBLE COLLEGE

Lanham, Maryland **www.bible.edu/**

- **Independent nondenominational** 4-year, founded 1938, administratively affiliated with Capital Bible Seminary
- **Suburban** 63-acre campus with easy access to Washington, DC
- **Coed** 254 undergraduate students, 50% full-time, 46% women, 54% men
- **Moderately difficult** entrance level, 65% of applicants were admitted

Undergraduates 126 full-time, 128 part-time. Students come from 14 states and territories, 5 other countries, 21% are from out of state, 44% African American, 7% Asian American or Pacific Islander, 3% Hispanic American, 0.8% Native American, 3% international, 11% transferred in, 27% live on campus. *Retention:* 64% of 2006 full-time freshmen returned.

Freshmen *Admission:* 167 applied, 108 admitted, 29 enrolled. *Average high school GPA:* 2.8.

Faculty *Total:* 14, 100% full-time, 14% with terminal degrees. *Student/faculty ratio:* 13:1.

Majors Elementary education; kindergarten/preschool education; missionary studies and missiology; music; music teacher education; pastoral studies/counseling; youth ministry.

Academics *Calendar:* semesters. *Degrees:* certificates, associate, and bachelor's. *Special study options:* academic remediation for entering students, accelerated degree program, adult/continuing education programs, advanced placement credit, cooperative education, double majors, English as a second language, internships, off-campus study, part-time degree program, summer session for credit. *Unusual degree programs:* 3-2 counseling, divinity, and theology at Capital Bible Seminary.

Computers on Campus 25 computers/terminals are available on campus for general student use.

Student Life *Housing:* on-campus residence required through senior year. *Options:* men-only, women-only. Campus housing is university owned. Freshman applicants given priority for college housing. *Activities and organizations:* drama/theater group, choral group, Student Missions Fellowship, school choir and ensemble, Korean Student Fellowship. *Campus security:* 24-hour patrols, student patrols, late-night transport/escort service, secured campus entrances, trained guards on duty. *Student services:* health clinic, personal/psychological counseling.

Athletics Member NCCAA. *Intercollegiate sports:* basketball M/W, volleyball W. *Intramural sports:* basketball M/W, cheerleading M/W, racquetball M/W, softball M/W, table tennis M/W, volleyball M/W, weight lifting M/W.

Standardized Tests *Required:* SAT or ACT (for admission).

Costs (2007–08) *Comprehensive fee:* $16,150 includes full-time tuition ($9120), mandatory fees ($580), and room and board ($6450). Full-time tuition and fees vary according to course load and location. Part-time tuition: $380 per credit. Part-time tuition and fees vary according to course load and location. *College room only:* $2600. Room and board charges vary according to board plan. *Payment plan:* installment. *Waivers:* employees or children of employees.

Financial Aid Of all full-time matriculated undergraduates who enrolled in 2006, 120 applied for aid, 86 were judged to have need, 7 had their need fully met. 36 Federal Work-Study jobs (averaging $1288). In 2006, 28 non-need-based awards were made. *Average percent of need met:* 46%. *Average financial aid package:* $7656. *Average need-based loan:* $2858. *Average need-based gift aid:* $1175. *Average non-need-based aid:* $1282. *Average indebtedness upon graduation:* $16,928.

Applying *Options:* early admission, deferred entrance. *Application fee:* $25. *Required:* essay or personal statement, high school transcript, 2 letters of recommendation, Christian testimony. *Required for some:* interview. *Application deadlines:* 1/9 (freshmen), rolling (transfers). *Notification:* continuous until 8/15 (freshmen), continuous until 1/15 (transfers).

Freshman Application Contact Mr. Mark D. Johnson, Director of Admissions, Washington Bible College, 6511 Princess Garden Parkway, Lanham, MD 20706. *Phone:* 877-793-7227. *Toll-free phone:* 877-793-7227 Ext. 1212. *Fax:* 301-552-2775. *E-mail:* admissions@bible.edu.

WASHINGTON COLLEGE

Chestertown, Maryland **www.washcoll.edu/**

- **Independent** comprehensive, founded 1782
- **Small-town** 140-acre campus with easy access to Baltimore and Washington, DC
- **Endowment** $144.4 million
- **Coed** 1,222 undergraduate students, 95% full-time, 61% women, 39% men
- **Moderately difficult** entrance level, 64% of applicants were admitted

Washington College (WC) has initiated a $40,000 scholarship program expressly for National Honor Society and Cum Laude Society members. Washington College NHS/CLS Scholarships are $10,000 annual awards renewable through the completion of eight semesters. To be eligible for scholarship consideration, a student must be an honor society member prior to March 1 of the senior year. For more information, students should contact the Admissions Office or visit the WC Web site at http://www.washcoll.edu.

Undergraduates 1,162 full-time, 60 part-time. Students come from 31 states and territories, 45 other countries, 47% are from out of state, 5% African American, 1% Asian American or Pacific Islander, 0.1% Hispanic American, 0.4% Native American, 3% international, 3% transferred in, 77% live on campus. *Retention:* 80% of 2006 full-time freshmen returned.

Freshmen *Admission:* 2,167 applied, 1,377 admitted, 324 enrolled. *Average high school GPA:* 3.34. *Test scores:* SAT critical reading scores over 500: 78%; SAT math scores over 500: 74%; ACT scores over 18: 71%; SAT critical reading scores over 600: 35%; SAT math scores over 600: 25%; ACT scores over 24: 38%; SAT critical reading scores over 700: 7%; SAT math scores over 700: 2%; ACT scores over 30: 4%.

Faculty *Total:* 151, 63% full-time, 52% with terminal degrees. *Student/faculty ratio:* 10:1.

Majors American studies; anthropology; art; biology/biological sciences; business administration and management; chemistry; computer science; dramatic/theater arts; ecology; economics; English; environmental studies; foreign languages and literatures; French; German; history; humanities; international relations and affairs; Latin American studies; liberal arts and sciences/liberal studies; mathematics; multi-/interdisciplinary studies related; music; philosophy; physics; physiological psychology/psychobiology; political science and government; pre-dentistry studies; pre-law studies; pre-medical studies; pre-veterinary studies; psychology; sociology; Spanish.

Academics *Calendar:* semesters. *Degrees:* bachelor's and master's. *Special study options:* advanced placement credit, double majors, English as a second language, independent study, internships, off-campus study, part-time degree program, services for LD students, student-designed majors, study abroad. *Unusual degree programs:* 3-2 engineering with University of Maryland, College Park; nursing with Johns Hopkins University.

Computers on Campus 150 computers/terminals are available on campus for general student use. Students can access the following: campus intranet, computer help desk, free student e-mail accounts, online (class) grades, online (class) registration, online (class) schedules. Campuswide network is available.

Student Life *Housing:* on-campus residence required through sophomore year. *Options:* coed, men-only, women-only, disabled students. Campus housing is university owned. Freshman campus housing is guaranteed. *Activities and organizations:* drama/theater group, student-run newspaper, choral group, Writers Union, Student Government Association, Hands Out, Omicron Delta Kappa, Dale Adams Society, national fraternities, national sororities. *Campus security:* 24-hour emergency response devices and patrols, student patrols, late-night transport/escort service, controlled dormitory access. *Student services:* health clinic, personal/psychological counseling.

Athletics Member NCAA. All Division III. *Intercollegiate sports:* baseball M, basketball M/W, crew M/W, equestrian sports M (c)/W (c), field hockey W, ice hockey M (c), lacrosse M/W, rugby M (c)/W (c), sailing M/W, soccer M/W, softball W, swimming and diving M/W, tennis M/W, volleyball W. *Intramural sports:* rugby M/W, sailing M/W, soccer M/W, tennis M/W.

Standardized Tests *Required:* SAT or ACT (for admission).

Costs (2008–09) *Comprehensive fee:* $41,185 includes full-time tuition ($33,385), mandatory fees ($620), and room and board ($7180). Part-time tuition: $5262 per course. *College room only:* $3650.

Financial Aid Of all full-time matriculated undergraduates who enrolled in 2007, 697 applied for aid, 539 were judged to have need, 230 had their need fully met. 238 Federal Work-Study jobs (averaging $1455). In 2007, 365 non-need-based awards were made. *Average percent of need met:* 89%. *Average financial aid package:* $21,316. *Average need-based loan:* $5000. *Average need-based gift aid:* $15,855. *Average non-need-based aid:* $11,737. *Average indebtedness upon graduation:* $17,125.

Applying *Options:* electronic application, early admission, early decision, early action, deferred entrance. *Application fee:* $45. *Required:* essay or personal statement, high school transcript, 1 letter of recommendation. *Required for some:* interview. *Recommended:* interview. *Application deadlines:* 3/1 (freshmen), 6/1 (transfers), 12/1 (early action). *Early decision deadline:* 11/15. *Notification:* continuous (freshmen), continuous (transfers), 12/15 (early decision), 12/20 (early action).

Freshman Application Contact Mr. Kevin Coveney, Vice President for Admissions and Enrollment Management, Washington College, 300 Washington Avenue, Chestertown, MD 21620-1197. *Phone:* 410-778-7700. *Toll-free phone:* 800-422-1782. *Fax:* 410-778-7287. *E-mail:* admissions_office@washcoll.edu.

See page 1150 for the College Close-Up.

YESHIVA COLLEGE OF THE NATION'S CAPITAL

Silver Spring, Maryland

BALTIMORE INTERNATIONAL COLLEGE

School of Culinary Arts
School of Hotel Restaurant & Catering Management

BALTIMORE, MARYLAND AND VIRGINIA PARK, COUNTY CAVAN, IRELAND

The College

The Baltimore International College, a regionally accredited private college, was founded in 1972 to provide students with the education and experience they need to pursue progressive careers within the international hospitality industry. The College is committed to providing students with the knowledge and ability necessary for employment and success in the hospitality industry.

In 1985 the College was authorized by the state of Maryland to grant associate degrees. In 1987, the Virginia Park Campus in Ireland was founded, enabling students to study under European chefs and hoteliers in Europe. In 1998, the College was authorized by the state of Maryland to grant four-year baccalaureate degrees. In 2000 the State of Maryland and the Commission on Higher Education of the Middle States Association of Colleges and Schools authorized the College to grant a master's degree in hospitality management. In addition to classrooms, offices, and dorms, the College's campus in Baltimore includes a campus bookstore, a student union, a hotel, an inn, a restaurant, parking, student dining facilities, a Career Development Center, and a Learning Resources Center, which includes a library, five academic computer labs, and an art gallery.

Location

The College's main campus located in downtown Baltimore is just two blocks from the city's famous Inner Harbor, a location that puts the College in the midst of numerous hotels and restaurants. The city offers year-round cultural and entertainment opportunities, such as theater, opera, the Baltimore Symphony Orchestra, museums, sporting events, and festivals. Other attractions in Baltimore that are within walking distance of the College are the National Aquarium, the Harborplace, Oriole Park at Camden Yards, Ravens Stadium, Maryland Science Center, and many historic sites, including Fort McHenry, the neighborhood of Mount Vernon, and the Walters Art Museum. Baltimore also offers parks and miles of waterfront for those who enjoy outdoor recreation. Washington, D.C., the nation's capital, is just 30 miles from downtown Baltimore. The city of Baltimore is easily accessed by major highways and bus, rail, and air service. Baltimore/Washington International Airport is a short drive from the campus.

Majors and Degrees

Baltimore International College offers baccalaureate degrees in culinary management, hospitality management, and hospitality management with a concentration in professional marketing. The College also offers associate degrees in professional baking and pastry, professional cooking, and professional cooking and baking. In addition, students can receive a professional certificate in culinary arts.

Academic Programs

The College provides a comprehensive curriculum. The College's professional cooking program and the combined programs in professional cooking and baking and baking and pastry operate throughout the calendar year; new classes begin in the spring, summer, and fall. The College's hospitality management programs accept freshmen in the fall and spring semesters. The culinary arts certificate, which combines cooking and baking, is available through evening classes and begins in the fall and spring semesters.

To earn an associate degree in professional cooking, professional baking and pastry, or professional cooking and baking, the student must complete 62 to 64 credits. The associate degree program combines technical hands-on courses with general education courses (such as nutrition, psychology, English, and mathematics) as well as an internship or externship.

The associate degree is offered separately and as part of the 2+2 program at Baltimore International College. In the 2+2 program, students receive their two-year degree and then continue to complete a four-year bachelor's degree in culinary management or hospitality management. Bachelor's degree programs require 120 to 133 credits.

Off-Campus Programs

All associate and bachelor's degree students will study for five weeks at the College's historic, 100-acre Virginia Park campus in County Cavan, Ireland. Students further enhance their skills in and knowledge of European cuisine, baking and pastry, and in guest service. Students fully enjoy the cross-cultural experience of living in an English-speaking foreign country.

Academic Facilities

The Baltimore campus includes the Culinary Arts Center kitchens, storerooms, cooking demonstration theaters, academic classrooms, multipurpose rooms, a library, two computer labs, a student union, and auxiliary services. Public operations that function as in-house training for students include the Mount Vernon Hotel, the Hopkins Inn, and the Bay Atlantic Club Restaurant.

The Virginia Park Campus is located on 100 acres 50 miles from Dublin and offers student housing with laboratory kitchens and lecture facilities. The complex also includes the Park Hotel, with public operations that function as in-house training for students, including the Marquis Dining Room and the Marchioness Ballroom. The Park Hotel has thirty-six guest rooms. All students enjoy unlimited golf and fishing as well as hiking trails.

The College's Career Development Center offers students access to information about careers in food service and hospitality management. The College's Career Development Services are located in the Career Information Center. There coordinators organize on-campus recruiting and offer workshops and assistance in résumé writing and interviewing skills.

The College's Learning Resource Center is a member of an interlibrary loan network that enables users to borrow from public, academic, and private libraries throughout Maryland. The library's current core collection has approximately 13,000 volumes, 200 periodicals, and almost 500 audiovisual selections. The library offers students access to the Internet, a worldwide network of electronic information. In-house services include two computer labs, electronic databases for research, and a photocopier.

BALTIMORE INTERNATIONAL COLLEGE

School of Culinary Arts
School of Hotel Restaurant & Catering Management

BALTIMORE, MARYLAND, AND VIRGINIA PARK, COUNTY CAVAN, IRELAND

The College

The Baltimore International College, a regionally accredited private college, was founded in 1972 to provide students with the education and experience they need to pursue progressive careers within the international hospitality industry. The College is committed to providing students with the knowledge and ability necessary for employment and success in the hospitality industry.

In 1985, the College was authorized by the state of Maryland to grant associate degrees. In 1987, the Virginia Park Campus in Ireland was founded, enabling students to study under European chefs and hoteliers in Europe. In 1998, the College was authorized by the state of Maryland to grant four-year baccalaureate degrees. In 2006 the State of Maryland and the Commission on Higher Education of the Middle States Association of Colleges and Schools authorized the College to grant a master's degree in hospitality management. In addition to classrooms, offices, and dorms, the College's campus in Baltimore includes a campus bookstore, a student union, a hotel, an inn, a restaurant, parking, student dining facilities, a Career Development Center, and a Learning Resources Center, which includes a library, two academic computer labs, and an art gallery.

Location

The College's main campus, located in downtown Baltimore, is just two blocks from the city's famous Inner Harbor, a location that puts the College in the midst of numerous hotels and restaurants. The city offers year-round cultural and entertainment opportunities, such as theater, opera, the Baltimore Symphony Orchestra, museums, sporting events, and festivals. Other attractions in Baltimore that are within walking distance of the College are the National Aquarium, Harborplace, Oriole Park at Camden Yards, Ravens Stadium, Maryland Science Center, and many historic sites, including Fort McHenry, the neighborhood of Mount Vernon, and the Walters Art Museum. Baltimore also has parks and miles of waterfront for those who enjoy outdoor recreation. Washington, D.C., the nation's capital, is just 30 miles from downtown Baltimore. The city of Baltimore is easily accessed by major highways and bus, rail, and air service. Baltimore/Washington International Airport is a short drive from the campus.

Majors and Degrees

Baltimore International College offers baccalaureate degrees in culinary management, hospitality management, and hospitality management with a concentration in professional marketing. The College also offers associate degrees in professional baking and pastry, professional cooking, and professional cooking and baking. In addition, students can receive a professional certificate in culinary arts.

Academic Programs

The College provides a comprehensive curriculum. The College's professional cooking program and the combined programs in professional cooking and baking and baking and pastry operate throughout the calendar year; new classes begin in the spring, summer, and fall. The College's hospitality management programs accept freshmen in the fall and spring semesters. The culinary arts certificate, which combines cooking and baking, is available through evening classes and begins in the fall and spring semesters.

To earn an associate degree in professional cooking, professional baking and pastry, or professional cooking and baking, the student must complete 62 to 64 credits. The associate degree program combines technical, hands-on courses with general education courses (such as nutrition, psychology, English, and mathematics) as well as an internship or externship.

The associate degree is offered separately and as part of the 2+2 program at Baltimore International College. In the 2+2 program, students receive their two-year degree and then continue to complete a four-year bachelor's degree in culinary management or hospitality management. Bachelor's degree programs require 125 to 133 credits.

Off-Campus Programs

All associate and bachelor's degree students will study for five weeks at the College's historic, 100-acre Virginia Park campus in County Cavan, Ireland. Students further enhance their skills in and knowledge of European cuisine, baking and pastry, and a la carte service. Students fully enjoy the cross-cultural experience of living in an English-speaking foreign country.

Academic Facilities

The Baltimore campus includes the Culinary Arts Center, kitchens, storerooms, cooking demonstration theaters, academic classrooms, multipurpose rooms, a library, two computer labs, a student union, and auxiliary services. Public operations that function as in-house training for students include the Mount Vernon Hotel, the Hopkins Inn, and the Bay Atlantic Club Restaurant.

The Virginia Park Campus is located on 100 acres, 50 miles from Dublin, and offers student housing, with laboratory kitchens and lecture facilities. The complex also includes the Park Hotel, with public operations that function as in-house training for students, including the Marquis Dining Room and the Marchioness Ballroom. The Park Hotel has thirty-six guest rooms. All students enjoy unlimited golf and fishing as well as hiking trails.

The College's Career Development Center offers students access to information about careers in food service and hospitality management. The College's Career Development Services are located in the Career Information Center, where coordinators organize on-campus recruiting and offer workshops and assistance in resume writing and interviewing skills.

The College's Learning Resource Center is a member of an interlibrary loan network that enables users to borrow from public, academic, and private libraries throughout Maryland. The library's current core collection has approximately 13,000 volumes, 200 periodicals, and almost 800 audiovisual selections. The library offers students access to the Internet, a worldwide network of electronic information. In-house services include two computer labs, electronic databases for research, and a photocopier.

The College's art gallery is part of the Learning Resource Center and features a permanent display of edible art. Student participation in all exhibits is encouraged. Culinary competitions are held in the gallery.

The College offers academic counseling for all students, peer tutoring on request, and a variety of referrals for support services. In addition, Student Services provides many recreation and leisure activities, including the student union, a series of activities sponsored by the College, and information about cultural programs around the city. Student Services also provides ongoing support to the College's alumni through surveys, mailings about the College's growth, and involvement in College-sponsored events such as open houses, resume referrals, and career fairs.

Costs

Tuition for 2007–08 was $8131. Fees ranged from $117 to $4173, depending on the student's major. Student housing costs ranged from $3000 to $5400 per semester for dormitory-style housing. Meal plans for housing students range from $1200 to $1680 per semester.

Financial Aid

Students receive financial aid from federal, state, institutional, and private sources and may be employed during their attendance as full-time students. The forms of financial aid available at the College through federal sources include the Federal Pell Grant, the Federal Supplemental Educational Opportunity Grant, the Federal Work-Study Program, the Federal Subsidized and Unsubsidized Stafford Student Loans, PLUS loans, and veterans' educational benefits. Students are encouraged to investigate the scholarship programs in their home state and apply for state scholarships if the grants can be used in Maryland. The College also offers its own series of scholarships and payment options. Students can request a financial aid application from the Student Financial Planning Office. The College employs the Federal Methodology of Need Analysis, approved by the U.S. Department of Education, as a fair and equitable means of determining the family's ability to contribute to the student's educational expenses, as well as eligibility for other financial programs.

Faculty

Baltimore International College faculty members include 29 chefs and academic instructors of high academic distinction. The student-faculty ratio averages 15:1 in culinary labs and 25:1 in academic classes. Each student is assigned to a faculty adviser who oversees the student's progress and answers questions about academic and career concerns. Students are encouraged to discuss program-related issues with the Director of Student Counseling.

Student Government

Many students become junior members of the Greater Baltimore Chapter of the American Culinary Federation. Membership is open to all students in good standing. Meetings, which are held monthly, are announced at the College.

Admission Requirements

Creativity and skill of students must be matched by dedication. The College seeks candidates who desire a professional career in the hospitality industry. Individuals seeking admission to the College must have earned a high school diploma or have passed the GED. Applicants must either pass the College's Admissions Test, take developmental courses during their first semester, or have one of the following: a minimum SAT score of 430 verbal and 420 math, a minimum composite ACT score of 16, minimum CLEP scores in the 50th percentile in math and English composition with essay, a secondary degree, or 16 credit hours at the postsecondary level with a minimum average of C in math and English. Transfer students must submit an official college transcript as well as catalog course descriptions for credits they wish to transfer.

The College affords equally to all students the rights, privileges, programs, activities, scholarships and loan programs, and other programs administered by the College without regard to race, color, creed, sex, age, handicap, or national or ethnic origin.

Application and Information

Applicants are required to submit an application form along with a $40 nonrefundable fee. Requests by the College for additional information must be handled in a timely manner. An admission decision is made as soon as a file is complete. Upon acceptance, applicants are asked to submit a $100 tuition deposit.

For additional information, students should contact:

Office of Admissions
Baltimore International College
17 Commerce Street
Baltimore, Maryland 21202
Phone: 410-752-4710 Ext. 120
800-624-9926 Ext. 120 (toll-free)
E-mail: admissions@bic.edu
Web site: http://www.bic.edu

Small classes at Baltimore International College enable students to receive individual instruction that helps them perfect their skills.

BOWIE STATE UNIVERSITY

BOWIE, MARYLAND

The University

Bowie State University began as a normal school in the city of Baltimore in 1865, and it has evolved over the years into a four-year, coeducational, liberal arts institution. It is currently situated on a beautiful 500-acre campus in Prince Georges County, Maryland, and offers both graduate and undergraduate programs of study. Teacher education programs were established in 1925; in 1935, with state authorization, a four-year program for the training of elementary school teachers was begun and the school became the Maryland State Teachers College at Bowie. In 1951, with the approval of the State Board of Education, its governing body at the time, the college established a teacher-preparation curriculum for the training of teachers for the core program in the junior high schools. Ten years later, permission was granted to institute a teacher-training program for secondary education. A liberal arts program was established in 1963, and the institution's name was changed to Bowie State College. In 1988, Bowie State achieved university status and joined the University System of Maryland (USM).

Bowie State University received its first state funding of $5000 in 1908. Its physical plant is valued at more than $22.5 million, and its current enrollment is approximately 5,400 students, 1,100 of whom are in the Graduate School. The University has twenty-two buildings on campus with the addition of the $21-million state-of-the-art Center for Learning and Technology that opened in 2000, and the $11.8-million Computer Science Center that opened in 2002. In addition, the new $19-million Center for Business and Graduate Studies opened in 2007. Two of the buildings, the Communication Arts Center and the physical education complex, were completed in 1973, and an administration building opened in 1977. Seven residence halls, including Goodloe Hall and Alex Haley Hall, a state-of-the-art residence hall that houses honors students, house approximately 850 students. In addition, a 460-bed apartment-style residence hall, Christa McAuliffe, was completed in 2004. The $2.6-million physical education complex houses a 3,000-seat basketball arena, an Olympic-size swimming pool with underwater viewing windows and facilities for 200 spectators, an apparatus gymnasium, a dance studio, a wrestling room, a weight-training room, eight handball/squash courts, a therapy room, and offices for instructors and coaches. The $5.5-million University Activities Center includes a cafeteria.

Bowie State University considers the student activities program a vital part of the total educational program. Students have access to more than forty different activities. These include student government, the student union, intercollegiate athletics, eight fraternities and sororities, numerous departmental clubs and preprofessional organizations, and music and drama organizations.

The Graduate School grants the Master of Arts in counseling psychology, English, human resource development, mental health counseling, organizational communications, school psychology, and teaching (M.A.T.); the Master of Business Administration; the Master of Education in elementary education, guidance and counseling, reading education, school administration and supervision, secondary education, and special education; the Master of Public Administration; and the Master of Science in applied computational math, computer science, management information systems, and nursing. The Doctor of Education is granted in educational leadership and the Applied Doctor of Science is granted in computer science. The Adler-Dreikurs Institute of Human Relations at Bowie State University is the first fully accredited master's-degree-granting Adlerian institute in the United States.

Bowie State University admits students without regard to sex, religion, or nationality, and the University does not discriminate on the basis of race, creed, color, national or ethnic origin, age, sex, or handicap. The University is accredited by the Middle States Association of Colleges and Schools and approved by the Maryland State Department of Education. Its programs in teacher education, social work education, nursing, business, and computer science are accredited by the National Council for Accreditation of Teacher Education, the National Council on Social Work Education, the National League for Nursing Accrediting Commission, the Maryland Board of Nursing, the Association of Collegiate Business Schools and Programs, and the Computer Science Accreditation Commission of the Computing Sciences Accreditation Board, respectively.

Location

Bowie, Maryland, is in a triangle formed by Annapolis (20 miles east), Baltimore (25 miles north), and Washington, D.C. (17 miles southwest). The suburban setting provides an ideal, safe environment for students and scholars, with access to all of the important cultural, governmental, and business activities in any of the three metropolitan areas.

Majors and Degrees

Bowie State University offers the Bachelor of Arts or Bachelor of Science degree with majors in biology, business administration, communications media, computer science, computer technology, early childhood education, elementary education, English, English education, fine art, government, history, mathematics, nursing, pedology, psychology, science education, social work, sociology/criminal justice, and technology. A dual-degree program is offered in engineering.

Academic Programs

The University operates on a semester calendar. Academic offerings are housed under four schools (School of Arts and Sciences, School of Education, School of Professional Studies, and the new School of Business) and can be divided into four main areas: humanities, science and mathematics, social sciences, and education. To receive a bachelor's degree, a student must earn a minimum of 120 semester hours with a cumulative grade point average of 2.0 or better. Students are provided the opportunity to complete the General Education Program, acquire lifelong learning skills for a competitive world, and make a successful transition into their junior year. General studies requirements include communication skills, 9 hours; humanities, 9 hours; social sciences, 18 hours; science and mathematics, 9 hours; and physical education, 2 hours. The remaining credit hours can be electives or from major and minor areas of interest. Students must also pass the test of Proficiency in the English Language and must take the national standardized test in their major area.

The Honors Program is designed for students with outstanding academic records and potential and provides a special educational opportunity for young adults with exceptional talent. The program is comprehensive and multidisciplinary in structure and interdisciplinary in application. It has been designed to provide a creative approach to the teaching/learning process and to present activities that encourage the shaping of students' own experiences.

The Special Services Project is a federally funded program designed to retain and graduate first-generation, low-income, and disabled students who have been admitted to Bowie State University. The purpose of the project is to help students overcome academic and nonacademic barriers to academic success, through participation in specially designed activities, including counseling, tutoring, and workshops on test taking and study skills.

Through the Cooperative Education Program, a student may choose either the alternate or parallel programs of study and work in business, industry, government, or a social-service agency. This program is open to Bowie State students who have completed at least one academic year with a minimum cumulative grade point average of 2.0.

The University participates in the College-Level Examination Program (CLEP), administered by the Educational Testing Service for the College Board, and in the Defense Activity for Non-Traditional Education Support (DANTES) program. The University also has a program for awarding students credit for learning acquired through life and work experience. Under this program, students document their backgrounds in a portfolio, which is reviewed by the faculty. Through all of these programs, qualified students may receive up to 30 credit hours toward their degree. In addition, the University offers an Army ROTC program. Two-year and three-year scholarships are available.

Academic Facilities

The Communication Arts Center, a $6.5-million building that houses the humanities division, contains classrooms, offices, conference rooms, and studio-laboratories and seats approximately 1,000 patrons. The $8.8-million, 337,543-volume Thurgood Marshall Library is centrally located on campus and provides excellent equipment and reference departments for the student body. The microfilm file contains 458,011 items; periodicals number 764. Campus research facilities include science laboratories, television and radio studios, language laboratories, and the Adler-Dreikurs Institute. Access to the library collection is provided through Victor Web, the electronic catalog that also links users to millions of USM volumes. The new Center for Learning and Technology, the main classroom building, features a new supercomputer (one of the fastest computers in the world), fourteen electronic classrooms, two interactive lecture halls, three computer labs, one speech lab, and a 300-seat auditorium and conference center. In addition, the new Computer Science Center has five classrooms and thirteen labs. Finally, the Center for Business and Graduate Studies, which opened in 2007, provides modern classrooms, labs, study space, offices, and administrative support space for the School of Business and the Division of Graduate Studies.

Costs

In 2007–08, the annual cost of tuition, fees, board, and room for a freshman who is a Maryland resident averaged $13,000; for a non-Maryland resident, the cost averaged $22,500. The annual cost for a commuting student who is a Maryland resident was $5939; the cost for a commuting student who is not a Maryland resident was $15,629.

Financial Aid

Federal Pell Grants, Supplemental Grants, Work-Study, Perkins Loans, and Direct Loans are available. University scholarships, tuition waivers, and diversity grants are awarded. Most awards are based on need. Academic scholarships could be offered to students with cumulative grade point averages of at least 3.0 and minimum SAT (reading and math) scores of 1100. In addition, merit awards are given for athletics, music and fine arts, and ROTC. More than 74 percent of all undergraduate students receive some form of financial aid. Scholarships and assistantships are offered through the Model Institutions for Excellence Program for Science, Engineering, and Mathematics. Deadlines are March 1 for the fall semester and November 15 for the spring semester.

Faculty

More than 85 percent of the 160 full-time faculty members have earned doctoral degrees. The faculty-student ratio is 1:18.

Student Government

All students are members of the Student Government Association, which, in cooperation with the administration, sets the standards for student life. Students are encouraged to assume leadership roles and to participate in the various programs and activities of the University. The Residence Hall Council provides opportunities for students to participate in the administration of residence life and in the cultural growth of the campus community.

Admission Requirements

Maryland residents applying for admission should have a minimum cumulative grade point average in their core high school courses of 2.0 (on a 4.0 scale) and a minimum SAT (reading and math only) score of 900 (or a minimum ACT score of 19). A sliding scale is used for students who have higher grade point averages or SAT scores. Conditional admission may be offered to students with a minimum cumulative grade point average of 2.0 and minimum SAT (reading and math only) scores of 830 to 899 (or a minimum ACT score of 17). Applicants must have earned a high school diploma or a GED certificate. The following courses are required: English, 4 credits; social science/history, 3 credits; mathematics (algebra I, algebra II, and geometry), 3 credits; laboratory sciences, 2 credits; foreign language, 2 credits; and electives, 6 credits. A $40 application fee is charged, and a health certificate must be submitted before entering the University.

Transfer students must have a minimum 2.0 cumulative grade point average for a minimum of 24 transferable credits, or SAT scores are required. International students and mature adults are encouraged to apply.

Application and Information

The application deadline is April 1 for the fall semester and November 1 for spring. For an application form, students should contact:

Admissions Office
Bowie State University
Bowie, Maryland 20715-9465
Phone: 301-860-3415
410-880-4100 Ext. 3415 (from the Baltimore-Columbia area)
877-77-BOWIE (toll-free)
Fax: 301-860-3518
E-mail: undergradadmissions@bowiestate.edu
Web site: http://www.bowiestate.edu

Flags representing the international student population of Bowie State University frame the entrance to the 500-acre campus.

COLLEGE DATA CENTER • MARYLAND

CAPITOL COLLEGE

LAUREL, MARYLAND

The College

Capitol College is the only independent college in Maryland dedicated to engineering, computer science, information technology, and business. Founded in 1927, Capitol College is a regionally accredited institution offering associate, bachelor's, and master's degrees as well as professional development training and certificates. The College's 52-acre campus is located in Laurel, Maryland, a suburban setting midway between Washington, D.C., and Baltimore. Full-time undergraduate students are eligible for a five-year tuition lock and a job guarantee. All graduate-level degrees are available online, supported by software that delivers live, real-time lectures.

Capitol College blends academic excellence with practical learning experiences that prepare students for a range of challenging and competitive careers. Capitol College remains committed to its mission through collaborations with business and government agencies, such as the NASA-supported Space Operations Institute and the National Security Agency and Department of Homeland Security, which designated Capitol College a National Center of Academic Excellence in Information Assurance Education.

The student body is composed of nearly 700 students, who come from fifteen states and twenty-one countries. Capitol College is accredited by the Middle States Association of Colleges and Schools. The electrical engineering and all engineering technology programs are accredited by ABET, Inc., and the business programs are accredited by the International Assembly for Collegiate Business Education (IACBE).

Capitol sponsors a variety of extracurricular activities based on student participation and demand. Basketball, flag football, soccer, softball, and volleyball are offered on an intramural level. Professional clubs include the Institute of Electrical and Electronics Engineers (IEEE), the Society of Women Engineers (SWE), and the National Society of Black Engineers (NSBE), all of which promote educational and social opportunities through trips, guest speakers, and social activities. The Office of Student Life and Retention also plans trips and activities throughout the year. Scholarship and academic achievement are recognized through the Alpha Chi, Tau Alpha Pi, and Eta Kappa Nu national honor societies on campus.

Career development is an integral aspect of the College's mission, and graduates are in great demand by business and industry. Capitol is so certain of the quality of its programs and the market trend for high-technology employees that the College guarantees qualified B.S. degree candidates a job in their field at a nationally competitive salary within ninety days of commencement. For the past twenty-five years, more than 90 percent of Capitol College graduates have been offered full-time jobs in their field of study or have chosen to attend graduate school within ninety days of graduation.

Capitol College's apartment-style residence facilities for men and women provide single- and double-room accommodations. Students who live in the residence halls have access to complete kitchen facilities in each apartment plus Internet access via a T1 line and standard cable included in the room fee.

Location

Capitol College's 52-acre campus is located in Laurel, Maryland, between Baltimore and Washington, D.C. The Baltimore–Washington, D.C., metropolitan area is one of the fastest-growing technology markets in the United States. The campus is close to many high-technology corporations and a host of educational, cultural, and recreational attractions. The Smithsonian museums, the Library of Congress, the Kennedy Center for the Performing Arts, the Verizon Center, FedEx Field, Baltimore's Inner Harbor, the Maryland Science Center, Oriole Park at Camden Yards, and M&T Bank Stadium are just a few of the sites that are a short drive or train ride away.

Majors and Degrees

Capitol College awards Bachelor of Science degrees in astronautical engineering, business administration, computer engineering, computer science, electrical engineering, information assurance, management of information technology, software and Internet applications, and software engineering. Capitol offers both the Associate of Applied Science degree and the Bachelor of Science degree in computer engineering technology, electronics engineering technology, and telecommunications engineering technology. Capitol also offers professional certifications in CompTIA A+/Network+ and Cisco and certification preparation programs in CISSP, SSCP, and Security+.

Academic Programs

Each department has its own sequence requirements for graduation. To earn a bachelor's degree, students must complete between 120 and 136 semester credit hours. To earn an associate degree, students must complete between 64 and 69 credits. Each degree program includes a core of courses in addition to classes within the major. The core curriculum consists of studies in humanities, mathematics, physical sciences, and social sciences. The average course load is 15 credits per semester.

Advanced standing can be earned through Advanced Placement (AP) and College-Level Examination Program (CLEP) tests. Credits can also be earned through institutional validation examinations.

At Capitol College, learning is centered both in and out of the classroom. Professors are available on a one-on-one basis, and tutors and lab aides are available for additional assistance. In the engineering and technology programs, students reinforce their classroom lectures with assigned laboratory projects.

Academic Facilities

The campus is small in size but big in resources. The Campus Center, administrative offices, and classrooms are located in M/A-COM, MCI, and Telecommunications Halls. Also located in these buildings are Capitol's state-of-the-art laboratories. Electronics, computers, telecommunications, and networking—Capitol stays abreast of the ever-changing trends in high technology.

The John G. and Beverly A. Puente Library provides students with 100 monthly periodicals, nearly 10,000 volumes no more than 5 years old, more than twenty-five computer workstations, and a multimedia center with scanner and printer available for student use. The library is also home to the William G. McGowan Center for Innovative Teaching, a multimedia classroom with a network of fifteen interactive computer stations.

The Avrum Gudelsky Memorial Auditorium is where Capitol hosts many special events, including convocations and guest speakers.

The William G. McGowan Academic Center is the newest facility on the campus. The 40,000-square-foot building was designed to combine high-speed multimedia and cutting-edge academic programs that provide an outstanding learning center.

Costs

For the 2008–09 academic year, tuition is $18,784, with the exception of the Bachelor of Science program in business administration, which is $328 per credit hour. Residential costs are $4514 for a double-occupancy room.

Financial Aid

Capitol College maintains an extensive program of financial aid to help students pay for their education. Aid is available in the form of loans, grants, scholarships, and work-study programs. Awards are based on financial need, academic merit, or both. All students who want to apply for aid must submit the Free Application for Federal Student Aid (FAFSA). Students are encouraged to contact the Director of Financial Aid at the College for help or for information about institutional scholarships.

Faculty

Teaching at Capitol College demands a focus on the student. Capitol's faculty members strive to challenge their students, while giving them every opportunity to succeed. Capitol currently has 21 full-time and 63 part-time faculty members, who have amassed extensive teaching credentials and industry experience. Full-time faculty members teach while also serving as academic advisers to assist students with planning their study programs and achieving their academic goals.

Capitol College maintains a student-faculty ratio of 11:1. Individual attention and instruction are key elements of the academic program. Students are constantly encouraged to reach for their potential.

Student Government

The Student-Leadership Advisory Board plays an active role in the academic and social activities of the College. Students elected to the board plan several social events throughout the year while also serving as the voice for students. The board is responsible for ensuring that an effective channel of communication remains open between students, the faculty, and the administration.

Admission Requirements

Capitol College offers rolling admissions. Admission is based on educational preparation and the personal abilities needed for academic success. Applicants must have a high school diploma or its equivalent. Applicants to the technology programs must have completed 4 years of English, 3 years of mathematics (through at least algebra II), 2 years of a laboratory science, and 2 years of social sciences. Engineering majors must have a fourth year of math to prepare for college calculus and a third year of science. SAT or ACT results are required for first-time freshmen. International applicants must submit scores on the Test of English as a Foreign Language (TOEFL). Transfer students must provide all course work completed after high school.

Some applicants may be required to meet with the Admissions Committee. An admissions interview is strongly recommended for all applicants.

Application and Information

An application is considered when the student's file is complete, including a $25 application fee, the required test scores, and transcripts from each school attended. Application forms are available from the Office of Admissions, or students can apply online for free. Capitol College maintains a rolling admission policy, and applicants are notified of the admission decision within one month of the completion of their file. To receive full consideration for financial aid and housing for the fall semester, students should apply by March 1.

For more information, students should contact:

Office of Admissions
Capitol College
11301 Springfield Road
Laurel, Maryland 20708
Phone: 301-953-3200 (from Washington, D.C.)
410-792-8800 (from Baltimore)
800-950-1992 (toll-free outside the Baltimore–Washington, D.C., area)
E-mail: admissions@capitol-college.edu
Web site: http://www.capitol-college.edu

MCI and M/A-COM Halls.

COLLEGE DATA CENTER • MARYLAND

COLLEGE OF NOTRE DAME OF MARYLAND

BALTIMORE, MARYLAND

College of Notre Dame OF MARYLAND

Learn for Life®

The College

College of Notre Dame of Maryland is a vibrant women's college located in northern Baltimore. Founded and sponsored by the School Sisters of Notre Dame, the College was established in 1895 and was the first Catholic college for women to award the baccalaureate degree.

Today's students are achievement-oriented and preparing for rewarding careers. They are deeply involved in their college and their community. At Notre Dame, students are challenged and supported in achieving more than they ever imagined—personally and professionally. They shape their lives for today and for the future. They learn for life.

Notre Dame's mission is to educate women as leaders. Undergraduate and graduate programs challenge students to strive for intellectual and professional excellence, to build inclusive communities, to engage in service to others, and to promote social responsibility. The Women's College has a close-knit community of approximately 600 students, both residents and commuters. About a third of Notre Dame's students are women who are members of minority groups.

Innovative programs for women and men have enabled the College to expand its educational reach. In 1972, the College initiated the Continuing Education (CE) program, offering women age 25 and older the opportunity to study and earn bachelor's degrees. Today, CE has been fully integrated into the Women's College. In 1975, the Weekend College was established to serve employed students by offering conveniently scheduled classes. In 1984, Graduate Studies began offering master's programs. In 2003, the College launched its Accelerated College for working professionals, further establishing partnerships with business and health-care organizations throughout the area. Most recently, the College instituted its first doctoral program, a Ph.D. in instructional leadership for changing populations. The College anticipates enrolling students in its new School of Pharmacy beginning fall 2009. The English Language Institute (ELI), which opened in 1983, offers English as a second language and American culture classes. The Renaissance Institute, a noncredit membership program for students age 50 and older, rounds out the College's educational offerings.

There are approximately 950 women and men in the part-time undergraduate programs in Notre Dame's Weekend College and Accelerated College. Graduate Studies serves more than 1,900 students, both women and men. In fall 2007, the total enrollment (more than 3,400) in all degree programs and ELI represented approximately twenty states, Puerto Rico, and more than thirty other countries. Students may choose to participate in a range of campus groups, including student media, performing arts, service, honor societies, academic interest groups, and more.

Notre Dame's Gators participate in eight NCAA Division III sports: basketball, field hockey, lacrosse, soccer, softball, swimming, tennis, and volleyball. The Marion Burk Knott Sports and Activities Complex houses the gymnasium, a fitness center, a dance and exercise studio, and several racquetball courts.

There also are two residence halls: Doyle Hall for first-year students and sophomores and Mary Meletia Hall for juniors and seniors. The recently renovated Marikle Chapel of the Annunciation is the spiritual center of the campus. Daily masses and special events are held in this beautiful chapel in Theresa Hall.

College of Notre Dame of Maryland is accredited by the Middle State Association of Colleges and Schools and the National Council for Accreditation of Teacher Education.

Location

Located on the North Charles Street college corridor in northern Baltimore, Notre Dame's beautiful campus is situated on 58 wooded and landscaped acres in a residential area. The College also holds classes for part-time students pursuing bachelor's and master's degrees at sites in other regions of Maryland.

The College is just 15 minutes from downtown Baltimore, which is renowned for its vibrant Inner Harbor that features shops and restaurants, the National Aquarium in Baltimore, Maryland Science Center, and more. Annapolis, the state capital, and Washington, D.C., are also nearby.

Baltimore truly is a college town, with a number of diverse colleges and universities in the area. Notre Dame is part of the Baltimore Collegetown Network, a group of fifteen colleges that work together to encourage students to participate in social and academic events and programs on each other's campuses. The network sponsors a free shuttle that has a stop at Notre Dame.

Majors and Degrees

Twenty-seven majors are available to students, many with concentration options so that students can further customize their area of study. The majors are art (art history, photography/graphic design, pre–museum studies, studio art), biology, biology/psychology, business (accounting, computer information systems, finance, management, marketing), chemistry, classical studies, communication arts (advertising and public relations, film and video, human communication, journalism), computer information systems (Internet systems), computer science (Internet systems), criminology and social deviance (forensic psychology, women and social deviance), digital media arts, economics, education (early childhood, elementary, secondary, special education, TESOL), English (drama, creative nonfiction), history (pre–museum studies), international studies (international business, international relations), liberal arts, mathematics, modern foreign languages (French, Spanish, dual language), philosophy, physics, political science (international relations), psychology, radiological sciences, and religious studies. Dual-degree programs are also available in engineering and nursing.

Students may choose to minor in most of the major areas or in Asian studies, Latin American studies, music, women's studies, or writing.

Academic Programs

Students take both general education studies courses and those required for their chosen majors. The general education curriculum provides a coherent yet broad intellectual experience of study in the liberal arts tradition. Through general education studies, students are expected to refine their personal value system, integrate the arts and sciences, develop a global perspective, expand their critical-thinking abilities, and enhance their communication skills.

Courses are required in English composition, fine arts, foreign language, history, literature, mathematics, oral communication, natural science with a lab, philosophy, physical education, social science, and religious studies.

Study and personal behavior are guided by an Honor Code that students pledge to follow beginning early in their first year. Examinations are unsupervised and academic honesty is expected. It is assumed that all work submitted is a student's own. Students and faculty members are deeply committed to the Honor Code, resulting in an academic environment that is grounded in integrity.

Notre Dame is dedicated to experiential learning. Courses integrate service-learning projects that allow students to apply classroom knowledge and skills while meeting community needs. The College's exceptionally strong internship program matches students with credit-bearing experiences in professional settings, helping them to refine career plans and strengthen their resumes.

Exceptionally motivated students of outstanding ability are invited to join the Elizabeth Morrissy Honors Program. Exciting, often interdisciplinary courses bring Notre Dame's excellent liberal arts education to another level and challenge students to stretch themselves intellectually.

In fall 2008, two new programs are planned to be offered to students. The Renaissance Professional Scholars (RP) and Transformational Leaders (TL) Programs will allow students to design programs of study that will be uniquely their own. The RP Scholars Program allows students to combine advanced courses with career-related experiences to expand their major program of study and connect to experiential learning options that will enhance their career potential. The TL Program will give students the chance to earn the certificate in leadership and social change and allow them to gain the knowledge and experience that will empower them to be leaders who can truly make change happen.

Off-Campus Programs

The College is dedicated to providing an education that is truly international, and study abroad is greatly encouraged. The College sponsors academic programs in twenty-one countries in Europe, Asia, Latin America, North America, South America, and Australia. Students receive Notre Dame credit for their work; financial aid is applicable to study abroad.

Short-term experiences, generally two- to three-week study tours during January or the summer, offer another option for students.

Locally, College of Notre Dame of Maryland has cooperative arrangements with Johns Hopkins University, Loyola College in Maryland, Maryland Institute College of Art (MICA), Coppin State University, Morgan State University, Towson University, and Goucher College. This allows students to register for one class per semester at an area college or university and expands academic options for students.

Academic Facilities

The College has several historic and renovated academic buildings. Knott Science Center features state-of-the-art chemistry and biology laboratories. A newly-renovated planetarium and a rooftop greenhouse are special features of Knott. Historic Gibbons Hall, which is recognizable by its landmark tower, has classrooms with hardwood floors and 10-foot windows. The WCND television and radio studios are housed on the fourth floor in the Communication Arts Department.

The College's main computer center is located in Virginia Rice Kelly Hall and hosts both academic and administrative computing. Networked computer labs include a total of eighty-three workstations (PCs and Macs). Students can access the Internet and their e-mail accounts at locations throughout the campus. Residence hall rooms are fully wired. There is also a campus video network for both station access and internal cable television production.

The Loyola/Notre Dame Library supports the education programs of both College of Notre Dame and neighboring Loyola College. The library's Web site is the gateway to a wealth of information, including numerous full-text databases, the library's shared catalog, and the full resources of the Internet. The newly expanded and renovated four-level structure houses 463,000 bound volumes and 989 periodicals, plus thousands of electronic journal titles and microfilm and microfiche units.

The Sister Kathleen Feeley International Center houses ELI and the Office of International Programs. LeClerc Hall is home to the Music Department and a large auditorium for performances and public lectures. Part-time programs for women and men are centralized in Fourier Hall, which features art exhibits in the Gormley Gallery on the second floor.

Costs

The cost for the 2007–08 academic year at College of Notre Dame was $33,100, exclusive of major travel expenses. Tuition was $23,750 and room and board were $8600. Student fees were $750. Additional special academic and nonacademic fees, such as book fees and fees for instrumental lessons, are charged as they apply to a particular student. Fees are subject to change.

Financial Aid

The College works with each student to develop a package that makes Notre Dame an affordable option. Financial assistance consists of scholarships, grants, loans, and paid, part-time employment. Awards are based on need, academic merit, leadership, or achievement. A Free Application for Federal Student Aid (FAFSA) must be completed each year to apply for financial aid.

Faculty

Notre Dame has 83 full-time and 9 half-time faculty members, all of whom hold a master's or doctoral degree. Associate faculty members with exceptional professional and academic experience teach some courses. The faculty–undergraduate student ratio is 1:14.

Student Government

Notre Dame's Student Association provides a vehicle for every Women's College student to participate in the life of the College. Through self-government, participation in college-wide decision making, and planning a vital social life, the Student Association exists to ensure that every student can contribute to a rewarding college experience.

There are five organizations within the Student Association that are coordinated by the Executive Committee: the Student Senate, the Inter-Organizational Council (IOC), the Apportionment Board, the Honor Board, and the Board of Trustees. The Student Senate includes representatives from each class. The Inter-Organizational Council coordinates the programming of more than twenty campus groups. The Honor Board educates the community about the Honor Code and conducts hearings on alleged violations. The Apportionment Board allocates funds for student groups and activities. The student representative to the Board of Trustees is elected by the students to convey their concerns to the board.

Admission Requirements

The Committee on Admissions considers the quality of each student's academic curriculum, grades in academic/college-preparatory or college-level liberal arts and sciences courses, standardized test scores (SAT or ACT for first-year applicants only), essay, resume, and letter of recommendation.

High school students are encouraged to complete courses in English, mathematics, laboratory science, social science, and foreign language in order to be considered favorably. A minimum of 18 units is required for admission for first-year students. Students applying for the Elizabeth Morrissy Honors Program typically have completed numerous Advanced Placement, honors, or International Baccalaureate courses in high school.

Transfer applicants are encouraged to complete at least 12 college credits in liberal arts and science courses prior to submitting an application.

Application and Information

Applications are reviewed and students are accepted on a rolling basis. Students should apply early for best consideration for scholarships and the Morrissy Honors Program. The priority deadline is February 15 for first-year students and March 15 for transfer students for fall admission; December 15 is the deadline for spring admission for first-year and transfer students.

For additional information, students should contact:

Office of Admissions
College of Notre Dame of Maryland
4701 North Charles Street
Baltimore, Maryland 21210
Phone: 410-532-5330
800-435-0200 (toll-free)
E-mail: admiss@ndm.edu
Web site: http://www.ndm.edu

FROSTBURG STATE UNIVERSITY

FROSTBURG, MARYLAND

The University

A state-supported liberal arts institution, Frostburg State University has gone through a series of transitions since its founding in 1898. Established originally as a normal school, the University has expanded to a campus of more than 200 acres and a student body of more than 5,400. During the past decade, the most significant one in the University's history, the academic offerings have been expanded and enrollment has increased. Eleven traditional residence halls as well as an apartment-style residence hall provide ample on-campus housing to meet the needs of entering students.

The University offers extensive extracurricular activities. There are more than 100 student organizations on campus, including sororities and fraternities, honor societies, professional organizations, communications and media-related groups, athletic clubs, and special-interest groups. The University offers thirteen intramural sports. Intercollegiate sports for men are baseball, basketball, cross-country, football, golf, soccer, swimming, tennis, and track and field; 10 percent of the men participate in these. Intercollegiate sports for women are basketball, cross-country, field hockey, golf, lacrosse, soccer, softball, swimming, tennis, track and field, and volleyball; 5 percent of the women participate.

Location

Located in the mountains of western Maryland, the University campus is bordered on one side by the city of Frostburg (population 7,500), an attractive community that offers a range of activities. Neighboring scenic and recreational areas are enjoyed throughout all four seasons of the year. Skiing is a popular winter activity, along with other traditional outdoor sports. The surrounding area has numerous historic sites, such as the C & O Canal and Fort Necessity. The history of the growth of Allegany County can be seen in the Allegany Museum, which is located in Cumberland, Maryland (population 25,000), just a short distance from the campus. Baltimore, Maryland, and Washington, D.C., are 150 miles east of the campus. Pittsburgh, Pennsylvania, is 100 miles to the northeast.

Majors and Degrees

Students completing an undergraduate program of study at the University may earn the Bachelor of Arts (B.A.), the Bachelor of Science (B.S.), or the Bachelor of Fine Arts (B.F.A.) degree. The diversity of the University's academic program is reflected in the majors that are available: accounting, art and design, athletic training, biology, business administration, chemistry, communication studies, computer science, criminal justice, early childhood/elementary education, earth science, economics, elementary education, English, environmental analysis and planning, ethnobotany, exercise and sports science, foreign languages and literature, geography, health and physical education, health science administration, history, information technology management, international studies, interpretive biology and natural history, law and society, liberal studies, mass communication, mathematics, music, philosophy, physics, political science, psychology, recreation and parks management, social science, social work, sociology, theater, urban and regional planning, and wildlife and fisheries.

Frostburg offers preprofessional programs in dentistry, law, medicine, and diverse other areas. Frostburg also participates in cooperative preprofessional programs with the University of Maryland. These include several allied health programs (nursing, pharmacy, and physical therapy). These programs involve preprofessional study at Frostburg and professional training at the University of Maryland. Through a collaborative program with the University of Maryland, a mechanical engineering major is offered at Frostburg. This program offers the opportunity to attend a small university and receive a degree from the University of Maryland, College Park's established and nationally accredited engineering program.

Academic Programs

A student's program of study begins with the General Education Program (GEP), which is designed to provide the foundation for educational development. Through three components, a unified concept of general education is developed to meet the special needs of each student. The first of these components provides a common core of essential tools for further learning; primary among these tools are skills of verbal and symbolic communication. Another component of the GEP offers exposure to broad fields of knowledge through study of the humanities, social sciences, and natural sciences. The third component helps the student gain an understanding of the interrelationship of various disciplines. Each student selects specific courses and develops a common theme to aid in his or her understanding.

The significant distinction of the B.A. degree program is that it requires a student to become competent in a foreign language at the intermediate level. Students who are contemplating additional study beyond an undergraduate degree are strongly encouraged to obtain the B.A. degree, since it is of particular value in a graduate program. Many students are able to combine specific graduate school goals with their major by tailoring their program to meet specific needs. Serious students, with the assistance of their advisers, are able to arrange a program that will help them achieve a high degree of success in acceptance to a variety of professional and graduate schools.

The offering of an honors program provides challenges that make the serious student aware of his or her potential as an individual. Superior performance in a secondary school program will encourage the student to participate in this demanding curriculum.

Off-Campus Programs

Frostburg State University offers students a variety of opportunities for off-campus learning. The largest of these is the internship program. Internships are a required part of several major programs (e.g., education, accounting, and political science) but are also available to students in most other majors. An internship allows students to gain practical experience and earn credit in their chosen fields. An off-campus center is available in Hagerstown. For students who wish to study abroad, Frostburg participates in the International Student Exchange Program, which allows students to select the country in which they wish to study abroad and, if qualified, to be assigned to an institution in that country. Students majoring in education or physical education have the opportunity to study in England through special exchange programs in those majors.

Academic Facilities

As a residential campus, the University has grown physically in order to maintain pace with an expanding academic program.

Academic facilities include eleven classroom buildings. The campus radio station, WFWM, was also renovated and updated recently. An addition to the campus is the new Compton Science Center, which houses the Departments of Biology, Chemistry, Physics, and Engineering. The $33-million structure was completed in the summer of 2003 and features state-of-the-art accommodations.

Costs

In 2007–08, the annual cost of tuition and fees was $6550 for Maryland residents and $16,162 for nonresidents. The cost of room and board ranged from $5994 to $7504 per year.

Financial Aid

Financial aid for eligible students includes need-based grants, merit-based academic scholarships, Federal Stafford Student Loans, and Federal Work-Study Program awards. Approximately 70 percent of the University's students receive financial aid.

Faculty

Frostburg's faculty consists of 233 full-time and 111 part-time members. More than 90 percent of the faculty members hold a Ph.D. degree. The student-faculty ratio is 17:1. Eighty-five percent of classes have fewer than 30 students. All professors have weekly office hours during which they are available to students.

Student Government

A tripartite student government system allows students and members of the faculty and administration to become involved together in deciding the direction the University should take.

Admission Requirements

Applicants are considered for admission on the basis of their high school record and SAT scores. A strong emphasis is placed on the high school transcript. High school equivalency certificates are accepted. An admissions essay is encouraged. An interview is not required, but the Admissions Office encourages students to visit the campus and talk with a member of the admissions staff.

Application and Information

Students may apply to Frostburg State University by submitting an application along with official copies of their SAT scores and high school transcript. Frostburg's admissions office utilizes a rolling admissions program. The University must close admission when no further space is available. Students are strongly advised to make a college choice early in their high school career. Notification of admission decisions begins in mid-November for the fall semester.

For further information, prospective students should contact:

Admissions Office
Frostburg State University
101 Braddock Road
Frostburg, Maryland 21532
Phone: 301-687-4201
Fax: 301-687-7074
E-mail: fsuadmissions@frostburg.edu
Web site: http://www.frostburg.edu

A view of the campus.

GOUCHER COLLEGE

BALTIMORE, MARYLAND

The College

Goucher College is a small, private, coeducational liberal arts and sciences college, where all students are required to study abroad and where the academic program partners classroom learning with real, hands-on experience.

Since it was founded in 1885, Goucher has provided a truly global kind of education that puts learning in perspective against the events and developments of the entire world, encouraging students to test what they've learned against experience in service-learning, study-abroad, and internship programs around the nation and around the globe. It is a small college with a big view of the world—an educational community without boundaries.

Goucher's more than 1,500 undergraduates come from forty states and twenty other countries. They represent a tremendous variety of backgrounds, interests, and points of view. They live together in the center of the campus in six fieldstone residence halls with living spaces designed to blur the lines between the students' educational, cultural, and social lives. Each of the residence halls is divided into "houses" of 40 to 50 students, with each house setting its own rules and regulations based on how the students want to live together. Students can further tailor their residential experience by choosing to live in a special wellness-themed residence hall, on a special foreign language floor, in a quiet area, in a nonsmoking area, or in a single-sex or coed house.

The residence hall buildings also house many of Goucher's academic and social resources, including the dining halls, the student union, a coffeehouse, health and counseling services, music practice rooms, and computer and language labs. Residence on campus is generally required of all students who do not live within 30 miles of the College, and housing space is guaranteed for all four years.

The social center of campus is the Pearlstone Student Center (fully renovated in 1997), which houses a café, lounge, bookstore, post office, commuter study area, student activities office, game room, and the popular Gopher Hole, a coffeehouse offering space for casual conversations and featuring entertainment several nights a week. The campus cultural center is the 1,000-seat Kraushaar Auditorium, where lectures and performances by leading actors, actresses, dancers, musicians, writers, and political and cultural figures attract audiences from the Baltimore-Washington area, around the nation, and around the world.

Athletic facilities include a 50,000-square-foot Sports and Recreation Center, the Welsh Gymnasium, and the von Borries swimming pool. The sports center features a field house, sauna, wellness laboratory, weight-training room, squash and racquetball courts, lockers, and offices. There are two dance studios, 4 miles of wooded riding and jogging trails, six tennis courts, riding rings, and stables. Goucher belongs to NCAA Division III. Varsity sports include basketball, cross-country, equestrian events, field hockey, lacrosse, soccer, swimming, tennis, track and field, and volleyball.

Location

Ideally located on 287 wooded acres just a few miles north of downtown Baltimore, Maryland, and an hour's drive from Washington, D.C., Goucher takes full advantage of its environs with a curriculum and programs that engage students directly in the lives of the communities that surround them—local, national, and international—and bring the best of those communities to the Goucher campus to enrich the cultural and intellectual life of the College.

Majors and Degrees

Goucher awards the Bachelor of Arts degree. Areas of study and concentration include Africana studies, American studies, anthropology and sociology, art, arts administration, biochemistry, biological sciences, chemistry, cognitive studies, communication and media studies, computer science, dance, economics, elementary education, English, environmental studies, European studies, history, international business, international relations, jazz studies, Judaic studies, management, mathematics, modern languages (French, German, Russian, Spanish), music, peace studies, philosophy, physics, political science, prelaw studies, premedical studies, psychology, religion, sociology, special education, theater, and women's studies. Goucher students are encouraged to tailor their studies to their own goals and interests through traditional, double, or individualized majors or by taking a major and a minor. The College also offers a dual-degree program in science and engineering with Johns Hopkins University. Entrance to the Johns Hopkins University Whiting School of Engineering is guaranteed for students with a minimum 3.2 GPA in Goucher science classes.

Academic Programs

Goucher encourages students to plot their own course, offering degrees in thirty-one different areas of study and enabling them to design their own majors. Thoroughly accomplished in all of the areas of study it has embraced, Goucher is particularly noted for its stellar programs in dance, the sciences, and creative writing. All education at Goucher takes an interdisciplinary perspective, encouraging students to assimilate the knowledge they gain throughout their academic careers into a cohesive whole.

Requirements for graduation include a demonstrated proficiency in a foreign language, English composition, and computer technology and successful completion of liberal education core courses in the arts, natural sciences, humanities, social sciences, and mathematics. Degree requirements include 120 semester hours of credit. A departmental major consists of at least 30 credits (about ten courses); a double major requires 60 credits. Goucher's calendar is based on the semester system.

Off-Campus Programs

Education at Goucher extends far beyond the classroom walls. Students test the lessons they learn in class against firsthand experience through internships, service-learning programs, and other off-campus opportunities tailored precisely to their course of study.

More than 75 years old, Goucher's internship program provides students with a view into potential careers, opportunities to apply classroom theory to working reality, and the chance to network with professionals in the field. Supported by advisers who work to ensure a close fit between internships and academic interests, Goucher students have worked with organizations ranging from the *Baltimore Sun* to the European Parliament.

Study-abroad options range from three-week intensive courses to semester-long and yearlong programs. Many students build more than one complementary international experience into their course work. The full-time international studies staff works with students to identify programs that neatly match their interests. Scholarship and other funds make study abroad possible even for students of limited financial means.

Through Goucher's student-founded Community Auxiliary for Service, students tutor at-risk students at area middle schools, serve meals at soup kitchens, and build houses with Habitat for Humanity, often for academic credit. The Hughes Field Politics Center offers high-quality internships in government, politics, and public service in Washington, D.C., and elsewhere, including recent placements with NATO in Brussels, the White House, CNN, and the Sierra Club.

The College has reciprocal agreements with the College of Notre Dame of Maryland, Johns Hopkins University, Loyola College, Maryland Institute College of Art, Morgan State University, and Towson University, to name a few, where qualified students at either institution may elect to take courses at no additional cost.

Academic Facilities

Goucher's campus is home to impressive facilities in technology, the sciences, and the arts, including a scientific visualization laboratory, a nuclear magnetic resonance spectrometer, and several computer, multimedia, and language labs. The campus is fully wired and nearly completely wireless; it features more than a dozen smart classrooms and provides widespread access to the Internet, cable television, and internal networks. Students have access to well-equipped laboratories and research facilities, superb performance and studio art spaces (including the Meyerhoff Arts Center and the Kraushaar Auditorium), and the Hughes Field Politics Center. The Julia Rogers Library includes a collection of more than 295,500 volumes, audiovisual materials, and 1,200 periodical subscriptions, along with several special collections and extensive access to Web-based resources.

Costs

Tuition for 2008–09 is $32,168 for two semesters. The cost for a double room for two semesters is $6034, and the cost for a nineteen-meal board plan is $3703. Fees total $468.

Financial Aid

Goucher's financial aid program is designed to put the College within reach of anyone who has the desire and ability to pursue an academic career there. Students and their families are expected to contribute to the financing of their education to the degree that they are able, but Goucher is committed to working with every qualified student to provide aid in covering the difference between the limits of their financial resources and the total cost of their education.

The College awards financial aid in the form of packages based on each individual student's needs. Aid comes from a variety of resources that may include need-based grants, loans, merit-based scholarships, and work-study opportunities. Goucher makes a sincere effort every year to meet the need of every accepted student who meets the financial aid application deadlines.

Faculty

Goucher's faculty includes Danforth, Fulbright, Guggenheim, Newberry, and Woodrow Wilson fellows and a finalist for the National Book Award. All faculty members develop close, personal relationships with their students, often collaborating with them on nationally recognized, federally funded research projects of the kind most students at other colleges don't get to do until graduate school. With a student-faculty ratio of just 10:1 and 19 or fewer students in the vast majority (nearly 75 percent) of classes, nobody is ever just a face in the classroom at Goucher.

Student Government

The Student Government Association, to which all students belong, coordinates social activities, dispenses student activity funds, and formulates and enforces social regulations and the academic honor code. Students are represented on faculty and administrative committees. Students have founded a variety of departmental clubs in such fields as chemistry, computer science, French, history, math, political science, and Russian. Special interest groups include UMOJA–The African Alliance, Community Auxiliary for Service (CAUSE), International Students' Club, Environmental Concerns Organization (ECO), and Commuting Students' Organization. Student publications include a yearbook, literary magazine, and newspaper.

Admission Requirements

The Goucher Admissions Committee seeks to enroll students with strong academic ability who represent a variety of talents, ambitions, backgrounds, and experiences. Each candidate is considered individually. Goucher offers early action and regular decision classifications for first-year applicants. A complete application, ready for review, consists of the following: a Common Application form; one essay of at least 500 words; a nonrefundable $55 application fee (or fee waiver form); recommendations from 1 teacher who has taught the applicant in an academic subject and from a counselor or school principal; the official school transcript, including senior courses and first-term grades; and the TOEFL for international students. Effective with admission to the fall 2008 semester, Goucher is a test-optional (SAT/ACT) institution. For more details, students should visit the College's Web site, http://www.goucher.edu. Goucher accepts for admission to the freshman class a number of carefully selected students who have completed the eleventh grade and are ready to begin college a year early. Admission criteria are reviewed and weighed in the following order of importance: (1) the quality and level of secondary courses selected (a sound preparation includes at least 15 units of college-preparatory subjects, with AP or honors-level classes carrying more weight than regular classes); (2) grades received in grades 9–12; (3) the essay; (4) letters of recommendation; and (5) activities, special interests, and awards. Applicants are encouraged to apply as early in the fall as possible. The application closing deadline is February 1. Applications are reviewed by the Admissions Committee, and the candidate is notified on or about April 1. The candidate reply date is May 1. Applications from transfer students filed by April 1 are given priority. Those filed after that date are considered on a rolling admissions basis.

Application and Information

Director of Admissions
Goucher College
1021 Dulaney Valley Road
Baltimore, Maryland 21204-2794
Phone: 410-337-6100
800-GOUCHER (toll-free)
E-mail: admissions@goucher.edu
Web site: http://www.goucher.edu

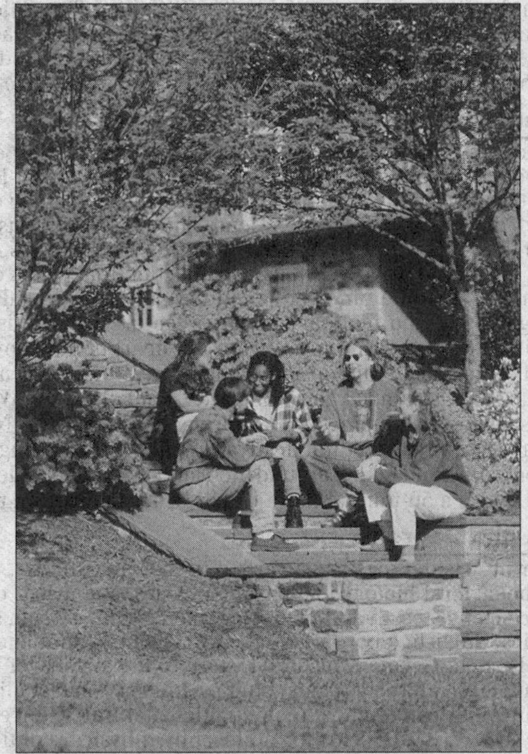

On the campus of Goucher College.

THE JOHNS HOPKINS UNIVERSITY
Krieger School of Arts and Sciences and Whiting School of Engineering
BALTIMORE, MARYLAND

The University

Privately endowed, the Johns Hopkins University (JHU) was founded in 1876 as the first American university committed to the idea that knowledge should be discovered, rather than merely transmitted. Daniel Coit Gilman, the first president of Johns Hopkins, stated that the object of the University was "not so much to impart knowledge as to whet the appetite, exhibit methods, develop powers, strengthen judgment, and invigorate the intellectual and moral forces." Today, Johns Hopkins continues to stress creative scholarship by providing research-oriented education for undergraduates.

Johns Hopkins seeks diversity in its students, who come from all fifty states and from seventy-one other countries. Of the total undergraduate enrollment of approximately 4,400 students, about 47 percent are women and 53 percent are men. All out-of-town freshmen and sophomores must live in campus residence halls. In addition, University-owned housing, located directly across from the University on North Charles Street, is available for juniors and seniors. Upperclassmen may also live in private housing or in Greek housing. Hopkins has eleven fraternities and four sororities.

Films, concerts, seminars, and athletic events are regularly offered on campus. The Student Council runs a number of activities, including an annual Spring Fair featuring outdoor concerts, arts and crafts booths, food, carnival rides, and exhibits. Men's varsity teams compete in fourteen sports. In the fall, there are crew, cross-country, football, soccer, and water polo. In the winter, there are basketball, fencing, swimming, and wrestling. The big sports season at Hopkins is spring, with baseball, crew, indoor track, lacrosse, outdoor track, and tennis. The men's and women's lacrosse teams compete at the Division I level, and the men have won forty-four national championships. Women's varsity sports also include basketball, crew, cross-country, fencing, field hockey, indoor track, outdoor track, soccer, swimming, tennis, and volleyball. An extensive intramural program is also available. The O'Connor Recreation Center contains basketball and volleyball courts, a running track, racquetball courts, a rock-climbing wall, a weight room, and fitness and aerobic areas.

Location

Johns Hopkins University's Homewood campus is on 140 acres of lush greenery, bounded on all sides by residential areas. Hopkins offers the best of both worlds—the tranquil seclusion of the campus plus the adjacent urban environment. The Baltimore Museum of Art is on the southwest corner of the campus. The Walters Art Museum, a 10-minute drive away, has a collection that spans civilization from Egypt to the nineteenth century, and many smaller museums, galleries, and outdoor showings feature local artists. The University is located just 3 miles from the heart of downtown Baltimore; the theater, symphony, and opera are 10 minutes away, as are Oriole Park at Camden Yards and M&T Bank Stadium. Weekend activities include shopping at Harborplace, visiting the National Aquarium, enjoying an ethnic festival by the water, sailing on the Chesapeake Bay, and hiking around the Maryland countryside. Washington, D.C., is a 50-minute drive by car or a 1-hour train ride.

Majors and Degrees

Bachelor of Arts degrees are awarded in Africana studies, anthropology, behavioral biology, biology, biophysics, chemistry, classics, cognitive science, earth and planetary sciences, East Asian studies, economics, English, environmental earth sciences, film and media studies, French, German, history, history of art, history of science and technology, interdisciplinary studies, international studies, Italian, Latin American studies, mathematics, natural sciences, Near Eastern studies, neuroscience, philosophy, physics, political science, psychology, public health studies, Romance languages, sociology, Spanish, and the Writing Seminars. A Bachelor of Arts degree in engineering is available for students who seek preparation for professional careers (such as law or business) with a technological orientation. The B.A. in engineering is awarded in applied mathematics and statistics, biomedical engineering, computer science, electrical engineering, general engineering, and geography. Bachelor of Science degrees are awarded in applied mathematics and statistics, biomedical engineering, chemical and biomolecular engineering, civil engineering, computer engineering, computer science, electrical engineering, environmental engineering, materials science and engineering, mechanical engineering, molecular and cellular biology, and physics.

Accelerated bachelor's/master's degree programs are offered in biology, biophysics, German, history, international studies, mathematics, neuroscience, policy studies, psychology, public health studies, and Spanish. Accelerated B.S./M.S.E. programs are offered in most engineering departments. A dual-degree program leading to a Bachelor of Arts or Bachelor of Science degree and a Bachelor of Music degree is available in cooperation with the University's Peabody Institute and Conservatory of Music.

Academic Programs

The departments in the Krieger School of Arts and Sciences and the Whiting School of Engineering comprise four general areas for undergraduate programs: engineering, humanities, natural sciences, and social sciences. If a student has special interests that fall outside the bounds of the departmental majors, an individual program can be devised, or a student may study independently with the guidance of a faculty member. Qualified students may complete their degree requirements in fewer than four years. In a number of departments, undergraduates of exceptional ability and motivation may in some cases engage in graduate work with the object of qualifying for the simultaneous award of the bachelor's and master's degrees at the end of four years.

Johns Hopkins has an extremely flexible program. There are no required freshman courses. All students must fulfill distribution requirements as well as the requirements for their major; the distribution requirements include a writing element. In most majors, 120 credits are required for graduation. Johns Hopkins has a 4-1-4 calendar.

The University offers the Army ROTC program on campus and the Air Force ROTC program in cooperation with the University of Maryland College Park.

Off-Campus Programs

If qualified, a student may undertake a program for study abroad, normally during the junior year. Programs are offered at Hopkins' international center in Bologna, Italy, and in Paris, France; Madrid, Spain; Berlin, Germany; and Latin America and through independent study-abroad programs with Johns Hopkins credit. The University participates in a cooperative program with the following colleges in the Baltimore area: Goucher College, Loyola College, Morgan State University, College of Notre Dame of Maryland, Towson State University, Baltimore Hebrew University, and Maryland Institute, College of Art. Undergraduates may also take courses at the other divisions of Johns Hopkins University, including the Peabody Conservatory, the School of Nursing, the Bloomberg School of Public Health, the Nitze School of Advanced International Studies, the School of Education, the Carey Business School, and the School of Medicine.

Academic Facilities

The Milton S. Eisenhower Library on the Homewood campus—housing more than 2.8 million volumes—is part of the University's Sheridan Libraries, which comprise the Milton S. Eisenhower Library, the John Work Garrett Library, the Albert D. Hutzler Undergraduate Reading Room, and the George Peabody Library. Together, these libraries provide one of the most comprehensive learning resources in the world, containing more than 3.5 million books, more than 55,000 print and electronic journals, more than 700,000 electronic books, more than 8,000 videos and DVDs, more than 216,000 maps, and significant rare books, manuscripts, and archival resources. The University's other libraries are the Welch Medical Library at the School of Medicine, the Lilienfeld Library at the School of Public Health, the Arthur Friedhem Library at the Peabody Institute, the Mason Library at the School of Advanced International Studies in Washington, D.C., the Montgomery County Campus Library, the Bologna Center Library in Italy, the Hopkins-Nanjing Center for Chinese and American Studies Library in China, and the R. E. Gibson Library at the Applied Physics Laboratory.

Host systems, an academic computer lab, and user support are provided by Information Technology@Johns Hopkins. Students living in University residence halls and apartments can connect directly to the Internet and the JHU network via a high-speed data jack. Wireless network coverage is also available throughout most areas of the campus with the use of a supported wireless LAN card. Those living off campus can remotely access University systems and library resources. The Homewood Academic Computing Lab is open 24 hours a day, has more than 115 computers, and provides student consultants who can assist with problems that arise. The Brown Foundation Digital Media Center offers an environment where students can bring artistic inspiration to life using digital tools. It features twelve high-end computers that enable digital and audio composition and editing, animation, virtual painting, and 3-D modeling. All campus buildings are networked with each other and the other Hopkins campuses.

The Mattin Student Arts Center contains the Swirnow Theater, a dance studio, music practice rooms, film and digital labs, darkrooms, a café, art studios, and spaces for students to gather. The recently constructed Hodson Hall includes classrooms, a meeting room for the Board of Trustees, the archives of the Hodson Trust, and a 500-seat auditorium, in which every seat is wired to the Internet. Clark Hall houses a state-of-the-art research and teaching facility for biomedical engineering. A new building for the chemistry department has also been recently completed, as has an interdisciplinary computational science and engineering building. Charles Commons, a 618-person residential complex, dining facility, and home of the University's two-story Barnes and Noble bookstore, opened its doors in fall 2006.

Costs

Costs for 2007–08 were $35,900 for tuition, $11,092 for room and board, and $2000 for books and personal expenses. Travel expenses vary.

Financial Aid

Financial aid is based on demonstrated eligibility, as determined by the Free Application for Federal Student Aid (FAFSA) at the time of acceptance. Approximately 47 percent of students receive financial assistance. Students must reapply for financial aid each year with the FAFSA and the College Scholarship Service (CSS) Financial Aid PROFILE. Johns Hopkins offers several merit-based scholarships, including the Hodson Trust Scholarship and the Charles R. Westgate Scholarship in Engineering. Hopkins also offers Army ROTC scholarships worth up to full tuition. A new Baltimore Scholars Program provides full-tuition scholarships to eligible Baltimore City public high school graduates.

Faculty

The University's intellectual reputation is based on the strength of its faculty, of whom 92 percent hold a doctorate. The student-faculty ratio is 10:1. The well-known professors at Johns Hopkins teach both undergraduate and graduate students, which means that students receive a great deal of personal attention both in and out of the classroom. Hopkins has a large number of notable professors, including Alice McDermott (professor of the Writing Seminars), winner of the 1998 National Book Award for Fiction; Saul Roseman (professor of biology), a molecular biologist who is a principal authority on the biochemistry of complex carbohydrates and on cell membrane functioning and serves as a consultant to the American Cancer Society and the National Academy of Science; and Charles O'Melia (professor of geography and environmental engineering), who specializes in aquatic chemistry, water and wastewater treatment, and modeling of natural surfaces and subsurface waters and is a member of the National Academy of Engineers. Faculty members are always accessible to advise and assist students and to work with them on research projects.

Student Government

Johns Hopkins students enjoy the benefits of a well organized and far-reaching student government, which is led by a powerful Student Council. The council is composed of elected class representatives and officers, but it relies on the active participation of many students in its numerous committees, boards, and commissions. Through the Student Activities Commission, the University encourages initiative and independence by giving students full responsibility and control of funds for various clubs and organizations.

Admission Requirements

In choosing from a large number of applicants, the University selects those men and women who will benefit from a Johns Hopkins education. A student's intellectual interests and accomplishments are of primary importance, and the Admissions Committee carefully examines each applicant's scholastic record, standardized test results, and recommendations from secondary school officials and other sources about the student's character, intellectual curiosity, seriousness of purpose, and range of extracurricular involvement. The SAT or the ACT with Writing Test is required. For students submitting SAT scores, Johns Hopkins recommends the submission of three SAT Subject Tests. Students should consult the Web site for additional details on test requirements. Counselor and teacher recommendations and two essays must also be submitted. Every year, the University enrolls a first-year class of approximately 1,200 men and women from all parts of the U.S. and a number of other countries. In addition, transfer students from other colleges and universities are admitted to the sophomore and junior classes. Advanced-standing credit is granted from college-level work completed at an accredited college or through the Advanced Placement and International Baccalaureate programs.

Application and Information

Johns Hopkins uses its own application, but also accepts the Common Application and the Universal College Application, both with a Hopkins supplement. The application deadline is January 1. Notification is given by April 1. Students wishing to enroll in the biomedical engineering (BME) program must indicate BME as their first choice of major on their application. Freshmen who are BME majors are admitted specifically as such. If applicants consider Hopkins their first choice, they may apply under the Early Decision Plan. This requires that the application be filed by November 1. Students are notified of the decision of the Admissions Office by December 15. Accepted students who wish to postpone their college studies for one or two years after graduation from high school may do so provided that they notify the director of admissions and submit the nonrefundable $600 deposit by May 1.

Office of Undergraduate Admissions
The Johns Hopkins University
Mason Hall
3400 North Charles Street
Baltimore, Maryland 21218-2683
Phone: 410-516-8171
Fax: 410-516-6025
E-mail: gotojhu@jhu.edu
Internet: http://apply.jhu.edu

THE JOHNS HOPKINS UNIVERSITY
School of Nursing
BALTIMORE, MARYLAND

The University

Since its founding in 1876, The Johns Hopkins University has been in the forefront of higher education. Originally established as an institution oriented toward graduate study and research, it is often called America's first true university. Today, Johns Hopkins' commitment to academic excellence continues in its nine academic divisions: Nursing, Medicine, Public Health, Arts and Sciences, Engineering, Education, Business, Advanced International Studies, and the Peabody Conservatory of Music. With a full-time enrollment of approximately 7,000 students, it is the smallest of the top-ranked universities in the United States and, by its own choice, remains small. The School of Nursing attracts a national and international student body of 622 students.

The School of Nursing was established in 1983 by Johns Hopkins University. By choosing to attend Johns Hopkins University School of Nursing, students can become leaders in the nursing profession. A Hopkins education can provide a solid foundation on which to base a lifelong career in the ever-growing field of nursing. Hopkins students enjoy the advantages of an education at an institution with a worldwide reputation and an outstanding network of alumni who are willing to serve as guides and mentors. Students at the School of Nursing are given the opportunity to participate in designing an educational program tailored to their individual needs. A rigorous academic curriculum, which includes a strong scientific orientation, gives students the background to understand the health-care decisions they are likely to make as professionals. Students learn in an atmosphere where excellence is expected, valued, and reinforced.

The School of Nursing is one of only a few in the country that emphasize baccalaureate-level research. Its graduates are prepared for professional practice through an educational process that emphasizes clinical excellence, critical thinking, and intellectual curiosity. Hopkins is also one of a few schools of nursing that offer resources from four health-related institutions: Johns Hopkins Hospital and the Schools of Nursing, Medicine, and Public Health.

In addition to the baccalaureate program, master's, post-master's, and doctoral programs are also offered. The Ph.D. program in nursing prepares nurse scholars to conduct original research that advances the theoretical foundation of nursing practice and health-care delivery. The School of Nursing has also launched a Doctor of Nursing Practice (D.N.P.) program that is a practice-focused doctoral program designed to prepare expert nurse clinicians, administrators, and executive leaders to improve health and health-care outcomes.

Location

The School of Nursing is located on the campus of Johns Hopkins Medical Institutions, including the School of Medicine, the Bloomberg School of Public Health, and Johns Hopkins Hospital. Located 10 minutes away is the Homewood Campus of Johns Hopkins University, which is accessible to students via a free shuttle service.

Often referred to as "the biggest small town in America," Baltimore has undergone one of the most successful transformations of any city in the nation. Baltimore's famous Inner Harbor and the National Aquarium are focal points of this revitalization. Washington, D.C., is less than an hour away by car or train.

Major and Degrees

The School of Nursing offers an NLNAC-accredited upper-division program that leads to a Bachelor of Science degree with a major in nursing. A 13½-month accelerated option of study makes it possible for students who hold a bachelor's degree in another discipline to receive a bachelor's degree in nursing. Students who hold a bachelor's degree in another discipline are also eligible to apply to the Direct Entry Combined B.S. to M.S.N. option. In addition, students who do not hold a bachelor's degree may consider a traditional twenty-one-month program that leads the B.S. with a major nursing. Students may transfer to the School of Nursing after successful completion of the 60 semester hours of prerequisite course work from any accredited college or university. Those students who hold a previous bachelor's degree may also consider the twenty-one-month option.

Students interested in pursuing the B.S. to M.S.N. option of study may select from a number of master's options, including clinical nurse specialist (in an area of interest, such as, but not limited to, forensic nursing, geriatric nursing, or woman's health), emergency preparedness/disaster response, M.S.N./M.P.H., M.S.N./M.B.A., nurse practitioner, public health nursing, and, in collaboration with Shenandoah University Davison of Nursing, a clinical nurse specialist in women's health and a certificate of completion in midwifery.

Academic Programs

Johns Hopkins University School of Nursing prepares students for professional nursing practice through an educational process that combines a strong academic curriculum with intensive clinical experience. The program is built on the University's commitment to research, teaching, patient service, and educational innovation and the consortium hospitals' commitment to excellence in clinical practice. The School's mission is to prepare its students academically and technologically for challenges of the future and to graduate professional nurses who can participate in all aspects of modern health care.

The upper-division courses in the baccalaureate nursing program are planned to meet the nursing needs of people in a complex and rapidly changing health-care system. The program is built on the liberal and general education prerequisites. The curriculum is planned to provide a balance among technologies, the theories of nursing, and the caring functions of the nurse. A high priority is placed on educating the nurse to practice in a variety of health-care settings, including overseas, as they exist today and in the future.

Johns Hopkins University School of Nursing is the only school of nursing in the country with a Peace Corps Fellows Program. The School of Nursing is world known for the Community Outreach Program, which offers students opportunities to gain additional clinical experiences with underserved populations in East Baltimore. Students may also enroll in the Birth Companions Program—another opportunity to work with underserved populations.

The Army Reserve Officers' Training Corps (ROTC) is the principal source of commissioned officers for the Active Army, Army Reserve, and Army National Guard. All Army nurses are officers. Johns Hopkins University offers two- and three-year scholarships to students enrolled in Army ROTC, which is located on the Homewood Campus of Johns Hopkins University.

Academic Facilities

The William H. Welch Medical Library is the central resource library serving Johns Hopkins Medical Institutions. Students have free 24-hour-per-day access to the Welch Library Gateway, which leads users to local and remote bibliographic databases, full-text journals, and other resources available locally and on the Internet. The Nursing Information Resource Center (NIRC), located in the School of Nursing, is managed by the Welch Library. The NIRC maintains a core collection of books to support student course work, a reprint file of material used in the students' courses, and a pamphlet file of material from the National League for Nursing. In addition, the facilities and 2 million volumes of the University's Milton S. Eisenhower Library, on the Homewood Campus, are available to School of Nursing students.

Three computer laboratories are equipped with a computer network that contains seventy IBM-compatible microcomputers and laser printers. Several classrooms and the auditorium have PC hookup and distance learning capabilities. Additional computer resources are available throughout the campus.

Nursing practice labs are available to provide the student with an opportunity to gain experience and confidence in performing a wide variety of nursing technologies. Students practice basic nursing technologies at numerous patient care stations designed to closely approximate hospital inpatient areas. Practice using actual medical equipment is an integral part of the laboratory experience, and patient simulators are provided to facilitate clinical skill mastery.

Clinical facilities throughout the Baltimore/Washington metropolitan area serve as clinical sites during student clinical rotations. These include the famed Johns Hopkins Hospital as well as a variety of other acute, research, long-term community and specialty health-care institutions. Students also have opportunities with international experiences.

Costs

For the 2007–08 academic year, baccalaureate tuition was $29,280.

Financial Aid

Johns Hopkins University School of Nursing attempts to provide financial assistance to all eligible accepted students. The School of Nursing will assist those students who qualify for need-based aid. Such assistance is usually in the form of loans, grants, scholarships, and work-study programs. While most of the financial aid received by students is based on financial need, many students also benefit from awards based on academic merit and achievement.

Faculty

The faculty members view professional nursing as a unique health service offering effective, humane, and competent care to individuals, families, groups, and communities. Nurses function in independent, interdependent, and dependent roles to promote and improve delivery of health care. The faculty members view education as a process and as an enriching interaction in which both the teacher and learner must actively participate in an atmosphere of mutual trust. They believe that it is the responsibility of the teacher to guide the teaching-learning process and to develop the potential of each individual student to the highest level possible. The student-faculty ratio is 7:1.

Student Government

Each class within the School of Nursing has a government board and a president. There is also the Student Government Association (SGA), which includes all divisions of the entire University. Each class has representatives to the SGA, and anyone may attend the meetings.

Admission Requirements

The School seeks individuals who will bring to the student body the qualities of scholarship, motivation, and commitment. The Admissions Committee is interested in each applicant as an individual and considers both academic potential and personal qualities. Therefore, academic records, test scores, recommendations, and a personal statement about goals and interests are all important. Interviews may be requested.

A complete application consists of an application form and nonrefundable $75 application fee; recommendations from 3 persons, 2 of whom must be instructors in current or recent courses; official college/university transcripts; an official high school transcript (unless the applicant has already completed a college degree); and SAT or ACT scores, if they are not more than five years old and the student does not already hold a bachelor's degree. A GPA of above a 3.0 (on a 4.0 scale) is highly recommended.

First-degree students are required to complete 60 semester hours of prerequisite course work essential for entry into the upper-division nursing curriculum. This course work may be completed at any accredited college or university and includes the natural sciences, humanities, social sciences, statistics, and electives. Students who possess a bachelor's degree must complete prerequisite course work in anatomy and physiology, microbiology, nutrition, human growth and development across the lifespan, and statistics. In addition, the School of Nursing has articulation agreements for direct transfer with the College of Notre Dame of Maryland; Gettysburg College, Pennsylvania; Johns Hopkins University, Maryland; Juniata College, Pennsylvania; Loyola College, Maryland; Mount Holyoke College, Massachusetts; Mount Saint Mary's College, Maryland; Randolph College, Virginia; Virginia Polytechnic Institute and State University, Virginia; Washington College, Maryland; Wheaton College, Illinois; Wittenberg University, Ohio; Yeshiva University, New York; State University of New York at Geneseo, New York; and St. Mary's College, Maryland.

International students must submit official test score reports of the Test of English as a Foreign Language (TOEFL). In order to be considered for admission, nonpermanent residents must establish their ability to finance their education in the United States. International students must have their academic transcripts evaluated course-by-course by World Education Service (WES). International registered nurses may have their transcripts evaluated course-by-course through the Commission on Graduates of Foreign Nursing Schools (CGFNS). WES and CGFNS must then send the official results to Johns Hopkins University School of Nursing.

Johns Hopkins University is an affirmative action/equal opportunity institution.

Application and Information

All inquiries concerning the School of Nursing should be directed to:

Office of Admissions and Student Services
The Johns Hopkins University
School of Nursing
Suite 113
525 North Wolfe Street
Baltimore, Maryland 21205-2110
Phone: 410-955-7548
Fax: 410-614-7086
E-mail: jhuson@son.jhmi.edu
Web site: http://www.son.jhmi.edu

LOYOLA COLLEGE IN MARYLAND

BALTIMORE, MARYLAND

The College

Loyola College is a private liberal arts college with the Catholic traditions of the Jesuits and the Sisters of Mercy. It is an educational community of students and faculty members cooperating for the intellectual, spiritual, and professional enrichment of all its members and for the improvement of the local community and society in general. The intellectual enterprise is a joint creation of the faculty members and the students. Loyola's current full-time undergraduate enrollment is 3,500 men and women; more than 80 percent of the student body lives on campus.

Loyola encourages cocurricular activities that contribute to the academic, social, and spiritual growth of the student. These include social and cultural organizations, Student Government activities, military science activities, national honor societies, and Division I athletic programs such as basketball, crew, cross-country, golf, lacrosse, soccer, swimming and diving, tennis, track, and volleyball. The majority of the student body participates in the wide variety of club and intramural sports offered.

In recent years, the College's campus has undergone significant expansion. Six apartment complexes and three freshman dormitories provide Loyola students with on-campus housing. Completed in fall 1999, the Andrew White Student Center provides more dining choices and expanded meeting and recreational space, making it a popular hub of the remodeled campus. The Student Center also provides facilities for athletics and the fine arts, including the McManus Theatre and the 4,000-seat Reitz Arena. The center also has an art gallery, classrooms, and music, photography, and studio art labs. Adding to Loyola's sports facilities is the Recreation and Sports Complex, which was completed in September 2000. This 110,000-square-foot athletic facility provides an indoor pool, basketball courts, squash courts, a climbing wall, fitness equipment, tracks, and outdoor playing fields.

Location

The Loyola College campus is located in a lovely residential area of north Baltimore, 5 miles from the Inner Harbor area. This location offers the student the advantages of quiet residential living with the attractions of city life. The metropolitan area has a wide variety of theaters, museums, professional and intercollegiate sports events, and historical points of interest. Other colleges and universities in the vicinity help to expand the social calendar and academic life.

Majors and Degrees

Loyola College offers programs in thirty-three majors. The Bachelor of Arts degree is awarded in classical civilization, classics, communication, computer science, economics, education, English, fine arts, global studies, history, journalism, modern languages and literatures, philosophy, political science, psychology, sociology, speech pathology/audiology, theology, and writing. The Bachelor of Business Administration degree is awarded in accounting, business economics, finance, general business, international business, management, management information systems, and marketing. The Bachelor of Science degree is awarded in biology, chemistry, computer science, engineering science, mathematical science, and physics.

Academic Programs

The curriculum at Loyola College is divided into three parts: the core, the major, and electives. The core contains those courses that Loyola College considers essential to the liberal arts curriculum. These courses, which are required of all students regardless of major, are completed during the four years. The core consists of a classical or modern language, English literature, writing, mathematics and natural science, social science, fine arts, history, philosophy, ethics, and theology. The major enables students to pursue in depth their specialized area of study. Electives give students the opportunity to broaden their intellectual and cultural background in areas of special interest. To prepare for graduate study, students may enroll in one of the four preprofessional programs: dental, law, medical, or veterinary.

An honors program and honors housing are available to outstanding students. The honors program stresses independent work by specially grouped students in many of the core courses. Honors housing provides an environment that is conducive to study and close social interaction.

Off-Campus Programs

Loyola College participates in a cooperative program with the College of Notre Dame of Maryland, Johns Hopkins University, Goucher College, Morgan State University, Towson University, the Peabody Conservatory of Music, and the Maryland College Institute of Art. Loyola students may cross-register at any of these area colleges and universities.

Students in good academic standing may pursue studies abroad through Loyola's programs in Leuven, Belgium; Bangkok, Thailand; Alcalá, Spain; Melbourne, Australia; Newcastle, England; Auckland, New Zealand; Beijing, China; Cork, Ireland; Rome, Italy; Paris, France; and San Salvador, El Salvador. Loyola has programs available in twenty-eight other countries in conjunction with other schools.

Academic Facilities

The Donnelly Science Center has recently been expanded, making it the largest academic building on the Evergreen campus. It features state-of-the-art laboratories for tomorrow's scientists and health-care professionals and new classrooms and offices that give faculty members even more space for instruction and research.

In the spring 2000 semester, Loyola welcomed the Sellinger School of Business. For the first time since its formation in 1980, the School of Business and Management is headquartered in one central location on the Evergreen campus. Highlights of this newest academic addition include eleven classrooms, five seminar rooms, fifty-two faculty and departmental offices, and an information center. Also, 90 percent of Sellinger classes are taught in Internet-linked, multimedia classrooms.

Costs

For 2007–08, tuition for all undergraduate students was $33,150 per year. Room for freshmen was $7350; for upperclassmen, room costs ranged from $7350 to $8400. Optional board was estimated at $2400, and student fees were $1100.

Financial Aid

It is the intent of Loyola College to assist qualified students who might not otherwise be able to provide for themselves an opportunity for higher education. Financial aid is awarded on the basis of academic ability and financial need. Two thirds of the student body receive financial assistance in the forms of Loyola College scholarships, state scholarships, Federal Pell Grants, Federal Supplemental Educational Opportunity Grants, Federal Perkins Loans, and Federal Work-Study Program opportunities. To apply for financial assistance, students must submit the Free Application for Federal Student Aid and the Financial Aid PROFILE through the College Scholarship Service in Princeton, New Jersey. The financial aid application deadline is February 15.

Faculty

Loyola College intends to remain a relatively small college and continue to have a faculty-student ratio similar to the current one of 1:12 in order to ensure interest in the individual student. The members of the administration and the full-time faculty of 295 hold degrees from seventy-three different colleges and universities. All of the full-time faculty members serve as student advisers. More than 90 percent of the course work in the Day Division of Loyola College is taught by full-time faculty members. No classes are taught by graduate students.

Student Government

The Student Government serves three chief functions, which make its existence not only valuable but also necessary. These functions are to represent the student body outside the College, to provide leadership within the student body, and to perform services, both social and academic, for the students. Responsibility for budgeting activities also rests with the Student Government. The president of the Student Government is a member of the College Academic Council.

Admission Requirements

Applicants for admission to Loyola College are evaluated according to their academic qualifications. The most important academic criteria include the secondary school record, performance on the College Board's SAT Reasoning Test or the ACT (required for admission), and recommendations from an academic source. The College welcomes applications from men and women of character, intelligence, and motivation, without discrimination on the grounds of race or religious belief.

Application and Information

Interested students seeking to enroll at Loyola College may obtain the application form by writing to the Undergraduate Admission Office; they may also apply online. Each applicant must have his or her SAT or ACT scores sent to the Admission Office. Applicants for all forms of financial aid must submit the Financial Aid PROFILE of the College Scholarship Service and the Free Application for Federal Student Aid. A $50 application fee must accompany the application for admission.

For additional information, students are encouraged to contact:

Undergraduate Admission Office
Loyola College in Maryland
4501 North Charles Street
Baltimore, Maryland 21210-2699
Phone: 410-617-5012
800-221-9107 (toll-free)
Web site: http://www.loyola.edu

Loyola's campus offers the freedom of a residential setting, yet it is only minutes from the resources of a major metropolitan area.

MARYLAND INSTITUTE COLLEGE OF ART

BALTIMORE, MARYLAND

The College

Established in 1826, the Maryland Institute College of Art (MICA) is the oldest independent, fully accredited art college in the nation. Because of its belief in the vital role of art in society, MICA is dedicated to the education of professional artists and to the development of an environment conducive to the creation of art. MICA has a well-equipped network of studio facilities, an exceptional faculty, extensive exhibition space, and an impressive art college library. A unique on-campus residential environment is provided, designed with the artist in mind.

The College offers many options not fully available at a liberal arts college, including a visiting artists program that welcomes more than 100 artists a year to the campus; seven-days-a-week access to some of the most outstanding facilities and best equipped studios in the country; the opportunity to exhibit work in numerous galleries, starting in the freshman year; the opportunity to study, through College-sponsored programs, art and design at colleges throughout the United States and abroad; a challenging liberal arts program that is integrated into and expands upon the studio program; and the advantage of studying with other talented students in a rigorous program of art.

In addition to its undergraduate degrees, MICA offers Master of Fine Arts in painting, multimedia, graphic design, photography, and digital imaging; Master of Arts in Teaching; Master of Arts in Art Education; and Master of Arts in Community Arts degree programs.

The faculty comprises 270 professional artists, designers, art historians, writers, and scholars—an assemblage of dedicated, working professionals who share the insights and experiences they have gained as practicing artists and scholars.

The College's 1,900 students represent forty-seven states and forty-eight other countries. They are marked by their intellectual curiosity, creativity, motivation, and self-discipline. Students develop a body of work that prepares them for a variety of career paths. The MICA experience, which includes internship programs and other reality-based opportunities, develops a firm base upon which students can launch and build their careers.

The Office of Multicultural Affairs coordinates programs, services, and activities for international students and the Black Student Union. The College provides specific services to international students such as orientation, immigration advisement, personal counseling, host families, and a mentoring program to members of the Black Student Union.

MICA is a residential campus providing apartment-style housing that includes dining, laundry, and fitness facilities and is wired for high-speed Internet access. Additional benefits include many private rooms and studio spaces that are incorporated into the residences. MICA housing offers independence, privacy, and a lively sense of activity generated by a community focused on art. Student life is also focused at the Meyerhoff House, which houses the Center Café and meeting rooms for student organizations. The campus also includes a health center, and students have access to an athletic facility.

The College is accredited by the Middle States Association of Colleges and Schools and the National Association of Schools of Art and Design.

Location

MICA is an urban campus of twenty-seven buildings that is located in a historic and beautiful neighborhood, surrounded by many cultural and educational institutions. These include the Meyerhoff Symphony Hall, the Lyric Opera House, and the Theatre Project. Baltimore has been cited as a city especially attractive to artists because of its vibrant and supportive atmosphere and its low cost of living. In addition to four world-class museums—the Contemporary Museum, the Walters Art Museum, the Baltimore Museum of Art, and the American Visionary Art Museum—Baltimore features a wide range of alternative art spaces and galleries that present classical and nontraditional works by acclaimed and emerging artists. It is also ideally situated for an artist because it is at the center of the Washington–New York art corridor. By train, Washington, D.C., is 40 minutes to the south; New York City, less than 3 hours to the north. The College offers inexpensive bus trips to New York studios, galleries, and museums every other week during the academic year.

Majors and Degrees

MICA offers the Bachelor of Fine Arts degree in the following majors: art history, ceramics, drawing, environmental design, experimental animation, fibers, general fine arts, graphic design, illustration, interactive media, painting, photography, printmaking, sculpture, and video. Additional studio concentrations are offered in ten areas, including book arts and fashion design. The Division of Liberal Arts offers minors in art history, literature, and writing. Students may also pursue double majors. A five-year combined Bachelor of Fine Arts/Master of Arts degree is offered in teaching.

Academic Programs

To receive the Bachelor of Fine Arts degree, students must complete a minimum of 126 credits, including 42 liberal arts credits. Students participate in a foundation program during their freshman year and then select a studio major. During the first year, the curriculum is well structured to provide the conceptual and technical skills necessary for further specialized study. By the end of four years, students are expected to be able to work independently in their chosen medium. The program integrates writing and academic inquiry with studio practice. This combination reflects the need for artists to pursue intellectual concepts as well as aesthetic principles.

Off-Campus Programs

MICA participates in a cooperative exchange program with thirteen colleges, including Goucher College, the Johns Hopkins University, Loyola College, the Peabody Conservatory of Music, and the University of Baltimore. This program makes it possible for full-time students at the College to enroll in one course per semester at one of the cooperating institutions without incurring an additional tuition charge. This option has proved to be exceptionally useful in offering studies not available at MICA, such as languages, the sciences, and business.

The Maryland Institute is a member of the Alliance of Independent Colleges of Art and Design (AICAD), which has cooperatively developed a program of study in New York City for eligible second-semester juniors and first-semester seniors. The New York Studio Program's center, a loft facility in the Tribeca area of lower Manhattan, is home base for the semester-long program. Students may pursue either an independent study or, as apprenticeship students, they may work with a professional artist, museum, gallery, or an art-related business.

MICA encourages young artists to work and live in other cultural settings so that they will better understand the universality of the language of art. MICA offers an honors program for juniors in Florence as well as other study-abroad opportunities in England, France, Ireland, Italy, Japan, Korea, the Netherlands, and Scotland that allow third-year students to study for one semester at colleges and universities noted for their strength in the visual arts. Summer study abroad in specialized subjects has been designed to provide students an opportunity to work closely with senior faculty members in locations that offer diverse cultural, environmental, and philosophical experiences. Canada, France, Greece, Italy, Jamaica, Korea, and Spain are the current sites for two- and four-week programs. Exchange programs in twenty countries are also options for students.

The director of career development arranges job internships for juniors and seniors. These internships provide educational experiences that bridge the worlds of academics and work. There are more than 1,000 local and national listings.

Academic Facilities

The campus includes twenty-seven buildings with 430,706 square feet of studio and classroom space, creating a coherent and unified urban campus. The studios are fully furnished with state-of-the-art equipment for each area of concentration. The Decker Library includes more than 50,000 volumes, 300 current periodical subscriptions, and 250,000 slides of artwork. It is one of the largest art college libraries in the country.

MICA has taken a leadership role in integrating new technologies into its programs of study. Within a very short time, the oldest degree-granting college of art in the United States has developed its facilities to provide more than one computer and/or video workstation for approximately every 4 students. The College's faculty has introduced computer-based courses in all of the professional studio majors, and the computer is also an important resource in liberal arts disciplines, whether as a tool for word processing or as a research medium for accessing images and information in a variety of forms. In some departments, such as environmental design, graphic design, animation, interactive media, or photography, competency in the creative use of digital technologies is considered fundamental to the curriculum.

MICA has outstanding instructional facilities with specialized equipment for both traditional and new media. Independent and/or dedicated studio space is provided for seniors. Seven-days-a-week access is provided in all departments. Liberal Arts classrooms and lecture halls are intimately sized. A 550-seat auditorium provides programming for a full schedule of visiting artists and lecturers as well as for film, video, and performing arts.

The Meyerhoff Career Development Center houses a full staff of counselors providing services related to internships, job listings, alumni networking, corporate recruitment, and career development skills.

Exhibitions play a major role in the artistic and intellectual life at the Institute. Each year, more than ninety public exhibitions are featured in the Institute galleries, which are unrivaled by any art college. They bring the work of regional, national, and international artists, as well as faculty members and students, to the public year-round.

Costs

For the 2007–08 academic year, tuition was $29,700. Room was $6230 and board, $2010. Mandatory fees totaled $980.

Financial Aid

Each year approximately 65 percent of the full-time students receive $12 million in financial assistance. The College administers a variety of programs, including need-based grants and scholarships, government-related loans, and college work-study programs. The College also awards more than $500,000 through competitive, merit-based scholarship programs. Students who are not U.S. citizens or permanent residents are not eligible for financial aid.

Faculty

The faculty consists of 140 full-time and 130 part-time professional artists, designers, art historians, writers, and poets. Their work is represented in more than 250 public and private collections from the Museum of Modern Art to the Stedelijk Museum in Amsterdam and the Victoria and Albert Museum in London. They have won individual honors and awards from notable foundations, such as the National Endowment for the Arts and the Guggenheim Foundation. They are Fulbright Scholars and recipients of the Prix de Rome, the Louis Comfort Tiffany Award, and the MacArthur Fellowships. The faculty-student ratio is 1:10.

Student Government

The Student Voice Association represents the interests and viewpoints of students to the faculty, administration, and board of trustees.

Admission Requirements

Students applying to the Maryland Institute must have made a serious commitment to art; therefore, a portfolio of artwork that demonstrates talent, ability, and experience is required for admission to the College. The portfolio is very important; however, evidence of academic ability as determined by level of course work, grades, test scores, and class rank are also weighted heavily in the admission decision. Individual interests and accomplishments, revealed in the personal statement, letters of recommendation, and lists of extracurricular and volunteer activities beyond classroom instruction, strengthen the application. The required personal essay is seriously considered. A minimum TOEFL score of 550 (paper-based test), 213 (computer-based test), or 80 (Internet-based test) is required of students whose native language is not English.

Application and Information

Students interested in early decision must complete all requirements for admission by November 15. Freshmen applicants for the fall term should complete the application process by February 15 for priority admission and to be considered for merit-based scholarships. Transfer students have a March 1 deadline. Applicants for admission to the spring term are asked to complete the application process prior to December 1. For an application, catalog, and further information, students should contact:

Office of Undergraduate Admission
Maryland Institute College of Art
1300 Mount Royal Avenue
Baltimore, Maryland 21217
Phone: 410-225-2222
Fax: 410-225-2337
E-mail: admissions@mica.edu
Web site: http://www.mica.edu

MORGAN STATE UNIVERSITY

BALTIMORE, MARYLAND

The University

Morgan State University, a coeducational institution, is located in a residential area of Baltimore, Maryland. The compact campus of forty-one academic buildings, service facilities, and residence halls covers an area of more than 157 acres. Classified by the Carnegie Foundation as a doctoral research university, Morgan State University has a comprehensive undergraduate curriculum and specialized offerings in thirty master's degree programs and fourteen doctoral programs.

Morgan traditionally has placed strong emphasis on the arts and sciences at the undergraduate level and on the preparation of students for advanced study. This emphasis has also been incorporated into the graduate programs. At the graduate level, the University offers the Master of Arts degree in African American studies, economics, English, history, international studies, mathematics, museum studies, music, sociology, and teaching. The Master of Business Administration is offered in accounting, finance, hospitality management, information systems, international business, management, and marketing and taxation. The Master of Science degree is offered in bioinformatics, education administration and supervision, elementary and middle school education, mathematics education, psychometrics, science, science education, sociology, telecommunications, and transportation. The Master of Science degree program in science is offered in biology, chemistry, and physics. Professional master's degrees are offered in architecture, city and regional planning, engineering, landscape architecture, public health, and social work. Currently, the School of Graduate Studies offers fourteen doctoral programs, including the Doctor of Philosophy (Ph.D.) in bioenvironmental science, business education, English, history, nursing, psychometrics, and social work. The Doctor of Education (Ed.D.) is offered in higher education, mathematics education, science education, and urban educational leadership. Doctorates are also offered in engineering (D.Eng.) and public health (Dr.P.H.).

Morgan State University does not discriminate against applicants because of race, sex, religion, or nationality. The institution was chartered in 1867 and was built on its present site in 1890. From 1867 to 1890, it was known as the Centenary Biblical Institute; from 1890 to 1938 as Morgan College; and from 1938 to 1975 as Morgan State College. In 1975, the college became Morgan State University and was designated as the state's public urban university.

The new student center, often called the "living room of the campus," is the focal point of cultural and social activity for the University community. Its purpose is to provide all members of the University community with programs and facilities to satisfy a variety of out-of-classroom tastes and needs. The center is utilized according to individual interests for meetings, lectures, music, movies, reading, and other forms of indoor recreation, or simply for relaxing over a cup of coffee or casual conversation with friends.

The University is a member institution of several consortia, including the National Student Exchange, a consortium of twenty-two state colleges and universities across the country.

Location

The University has the advantages of both suburban life and proximity to an urban center. Built on two slopes, the campus is strategically located in the picturesque northeastern section of Baltimore, a city with a population of about 650,000, and is surrounded by rapidly growing residential communities. The center of the city is easily accessible from the University campus.

Majors and Degrees

The Bachelor of Arts degree is offered in economics, English, fine art, history, music, philosophy, political science, sociology, speech communication, telecommunications, and theater arts. The Bachelor of Science degree is offered in the fields of accounting, architecture and environmental design, biology, business administration, chemistry, computer science, economics, elementary education, engineering (civil, electrical, and industrial), engineering physics, family and consumer science, finance, food and nutrition, health education, hospitality management, information science and systems, management, marketing, mathematics, medical technology, physical education, physics, psychology, social work, and telecommunications.

Academic Programs

Students admitted to Morgan to study for a Bachelor of Arts or Bachelor of Science degree are expected to adhere to the accepted standards of higher education. Honors programs, independent study, and cooperative education programs are available in most areas. For those students who require special placement and/or special assistance, support services and programs are provided.

To earn a bachelor's degree, students must complete a minimum of 120 semester hours. Some programs require more than the minimum number of semester hours.

Through the Continuing Studies Program, students can pursue an education outside traditional daytime classwork. Participants in the program include part-time students, as well as many full-time students who have been away from a formal educational experience for two or more years and want to pursue courses for personal fulfillment or career advancement. The Continuing Studies Program includes Summer School, Weekend University, Winter Session, noncredit courses, extension programs, conferences, and workshops.

Morgan State's Weekend University is designed for working adults and others who are unable to attend weekday classes. Classes are scheduled on Friday evenings and Saturdays, providing students the opportunity to earn a bachelor's degree in accounting, business administration, social work, or telecommunications in approximately five to six years.

Off-Campus Programs

The Cooperative Education Program is a special program that permits students to extend their chosen major program by working in business, industry, or government agencies, alternating a semester of study with a semester of work while studying for undergraduate and graduate degrees. This program enables students to gain experience in an area close to their chosen field and to understand the requirements of that field. A cooperative work-study program allows students who qualify to gain financial support while learning.

Through cooperative education programs, students may participate in specific seminars cooperatively planned and implemented by the Maryland state colleges or take courses on other state college campuses. In addition, a cooperative program with Goucher College, Towson University, Loyola College, and Johns Hopkins University provides an opportunity for students to enroll in courses not offered on the home campus.

Academic Facilities

The Departments of Biology, Chemistry, Physics, and Mathematics and the School of Engineering have specialized research facilities. The Murphy Fine Arts Center and the renovated Hughes Stadium opened in 2001. The Richard N. Dixon Science Research Center opened in 2003. The new communications building and the Library and Information Technology Center opened in 2006.

A new 212,997-square-foot state-of-the-art library replaced Soper Library. This new facility anticipates planned space for future growth, projected at 5,000 volumes per year for the next twenty years to complement Soper's holdings, which constitute more than 660,000 volumes, including works in special collections. One such collection includes books on Africa, with an emphasis on sub-Saharan Africa. The African American collection is a body of historically significant and current books by and about African Americans and includes papers and memorabilia of such persons as the late Emmett P. Scott, secretary to Booker T. Washington, and Arthur J. Smith, who was associated with the Far East Consular Division of the State Department. The Forbush Collection, named for Dr. Bliss Forbush, is composed of materials associated with the Quakers and slavery. The Martin D. Jenkins Collection was acquired in 1980. Together, these collections provide both a contemporary and historical view of African Americans in education, military service, politics, and religion.

Costs

For 2007–08, tuition and fees were $6318 for residents of Maryland and $14,438 for nonresidents. Room and board with a nineteen-meal plan were $7650. Thus, tuition, fees, and room and board for a student who is a Maryland resident were $13,968; for a nonresident student, they were $22,088. Costs are subject to change without prior notice.

Financial Aid

Scholarships, loans, and campus employment are available. Awards are made on the basis of student merit and financial need. Information on these as well as on Federal Pell Grants, other federal grants, and Federal Work-Study awards may be obtained by writing to the Financial Aid Office.

Faculty

A majority of the University's approximately 400 faculty members hold doctoral degrees. Many faculty members have attained national and international distinction for their research and creative work, and a number are officers of state, regional, national, and international professional organizations.

Student Government

Student government at Morgan State University is part of the student activities program, which is considered a vital element of the total educational program.

Admission Requirements

Applicants are considered on the basis of their high school grades, rank in class, personal recommendations, and scores on the SAT or ACT.

Application and Information

Applications for August entrance should be submitted no later than April 15; those for January entrance should be submitted no later than December 1. Transfer students must submit an official transcript from each college previously attended. All application forms must be accompanied by a $35 application fee and should be forwarded to:

The Office of Admissions
Morgan State University
Cold Spring Lane and Hillen Road
Baltimore, Maryland 21251
Phone: 443-885-3000
Web site: http://www.morgan.edu/

MOUNT ST. MARY'S UNIVERSITY

EMMITSBURG, MARYLAND

The University

As the nation's second-oldest Catholic university, Mount St. Mary's is blessed with a heritage few can match. Founded in 1808, the Mount celebrates its bicentennial in 2008, making it only the second Catholic university in the country to mark this distinction. Mount alumni include a Supreme Court Justice, a president of Mexico, and the founder of Boys' Town. Today, the Most Rev. Harry J. Flynn, Archbishop of St. Paul/Minneapolis; Susan O'Malley, President of the Washington Wizards NBA team; and Matt McHugh, who served nine terms in the U.S. House of Representatives, are counted among the Mount's 14,000 alumni. Most students come from Maryland and other mid-Atlantic states, but, typically, more than half of the U.S. states and nearly a dozen additional countries are represented by the 1,500 undergraduates.

Current Mount students are well prepared to join their predecessors in service to prepare leaders for the church, for the nation and its communities, for the professions, and, most importantly, for social change. The Core Curriculum, which has received national recognition, provides a strong grounding in the liberal arts, developing analytical-reading, significant-writing, and critical-thinking skills—attributes needed for success in any career path. Academic majors and minors add specialized knowledge. Outside the classroom, the Mount offers even more: a full range of extracurricular and cocurricular activities and the opportunity to build people skills in a residential college environment. Among the more than seventy-five clubs and special interest groups are student media (radio, TV, newspaper, yearbook, and literary magazine), drama, music (vocal and instrumental), campus ministry, and community service opportunities. In addition, more than 95 percent of freshmen typically live on campus, and nearly 90 percent of all students live in campus housing.

The Mount has one of the smallest enrollments of colleges competing in athletics at the NCAA Division I level, which gives students many opportunities for participation on the nineteen varsity sports teams. Club sports and intramurals are also available, as are indoor and outdoor recreation facilities. Of particular note is the 105,000-square-foot Knott Athletic Recreation Convocation Complex, with courts for tennis, volleyball, basketball, and handball/racquetball; a swimming pool; an indoor track; and aerobics and weight rooms (both recently outfitted with new weight-training equipment).

Student residences include traditional dormitories, suites, apartments, single rooms, and special interest housing. A new student residence, Bicentennial Hall, is planned to open in 2008. Students are guaranteed housing for all four years. The recently renovated and expanded McGowan Student Center houses the dining hall, Mount Cafe, and social gathering places as well as the bookstore, mailroom, and offices for student organizations.

In addition to the undergraduate university, the Mount includes one of the country's largest and most successful Catholic seminaries, other graduate programs in business and education, and the National Shrine Grotto of Lourdes.

Location

The 1,400-acre campus is in north-central Maryland, just 1 hour west of Baltimore and slightly farther northwest of Washington, D.C. Historic Gettysburg, Pennsylvania, is 12 miles north, and Frederick, Maryland's second-largest city and an attractive shopping and entertainment destination, is 20 miles south. Emmitsburg is a small town with a variety of restaurants and shops. Elizabeth Ann "Mother" Seton, America's first native-born saint, began her religious order and the country's first parochial school here, and both survive to this day. Nearby attractions include skiing at Liberty Mountain, national and state parks (including Catoctin Mountain National Park, home of the Camp David presidential retreat), and golf courses. Horseback riding is also available in the area.

Majors and Degrees

Majors leading to Bachelor of Arts or Bachelor of Science degree are offered in accounting, art education, biochemistry, biology, business (concentrations in finance, international business, management, and marketing), chemistry, communications (concentrations in journalism and mass communications, public relations, and rhetoric and public address), computer science, criminal justice, economics, elementary education (including an option for dual certification in special education), English, environmental science, fine arts (concentrations in art, music, and theater), French, German, history, information systems, international studies, Latin, mathematics, philosophy, political science, psychology, secondary education (certification in English, mathematics, social studies, and other areas), sociology (concentration in criminal justice), Spanish, sports management, and theology. Students may also design their own majors. A 3-2 program in nursing with Johns Hopkins University, a 4-2 B.S./master's in occupational technology with Sacred Heart University, and a 3-3 B.S./Ph.D. in physical therapy with Sacred Heart University are also available. Minors are offered in all major areas and in African American studies, environmental studies, gender studies, Latin American studies, legal studies, and non-Western studies. Predental, prelaw, and premedicine programs are offered.

Academic Programs

The academic majors offer strong preparation for a variety of careers, but Mount students take nearly half of the 120 credit hours required for graduation in the Core Curriculum, a carefully integrated four-year sequence of courses in Western civilization, American and non-Western culture, philosophy and theology, foreign languages, mathematics, and the social and natural sciences. This program helps students gain a broader perspective and a better understanding of themselves and the world around them and fosters the development and strengthening of a rational value system. After core and major requirements, students complete their course work with electives. The Mount accepts Advanced Placement and CLEP credits.

Mount St. Mary's yearlong Freshman Seminar is designed to build reading, writing, and critical-thinking skills. Students are placed in seminar sections of about 18 students each, taught by their faculty advisers. Students with outstanding high school records are invited into the Freshman Honors Program; sophomores enter the College Honors Program. The latter includes an interdisciplinary honors seminar for juniors and a special senior project in a student's major.

The Mount sponsors its own international-study programs in the Czech Republic, Costa Rica, England, France, Germany, Ireland, and Italy, and affiliated programs make it possible to study in other countries. At home, the Mount offers an aggressive internship program (about two thirds of the Mount's graduates have typically participated in an internship) and a variety of career-preparation services.

Academic Facilities

Classes are held in two major academic buildings—the Knott Academic Center and the Coad Science Building—and in several other smaller or multiple-use buildings. Most classrooms are small because most classes are small. The science lab facilities are newly renovated, and continuous improvements are being made to computing facilities. Wireless computer network access is available in Phillips Library, in classrooms, and throughout the campus. Internet access is free. The library contains more than 200,000 books, including a reference collection of 3,000 volumes, CD-ROMs, and electronic databases. More than 2,000 periodicals are available in print, microfilm, or electronic form. Online access provides additional possibilities worldwide. Many special events are held in the 550-seat Marion Burk Knott Auditorium.

Costs

Tuition and fees total $27,560; room and board are $9520. Books, supplies, transportation, and personal expenses average nearly $1700 per year.

Financial Aid

Mount St. Mary's offers financial assistance to qualified students in the form of scholarships, grants, loans, student employment, and special payment plans. Almost 90 percent of students attending the Mount receive some form of financial aid. Through its scholarship program and financial aid packages, the University attempts as much as possible to relieve the financial burden of attending college. The Mount participates in all major federal financial aid programs, including the Federal Pell Grant, Federal Perkins Loan, Federal Stafford Student Loan, and Federal Work-Study programs. Federal PLUS loans may also be used.

The University awards a wide range of merit and merit-and-need scholarships. In 2007–08, about 390 were awarded to entering freshmen (450 total) at an average of more than $9000 per year. Three full-tuition Founder's Scholarships are awarded to qualified candidates on the basis of an essay exam competition. The full-tuition Marion Burk Knott Scholarship, usually one per year, is offered to qualified Catholic students who reside in the Archdiocese of Baltimore. Scholarships and grants are offered to qualified students in amounts typically ranging from $5000 to $15,000 per year. Horning Intercultural Diversity Scholarships are offered to qualified African American and Hispanic American students. All scholarships are renewable annually based on academic performance. In addition, as an NCAA Division I school, the Mount offers athletic scholarships to men and women in all nineteen intercollegiate sports.

The Free Application for Federal Student Aid (FAFSA) and the Mount St. Mary's Financial Aid Application must be submitted by March 1 and should be filed as soon after January 1 as possible.

Faculty

More than 100 full-time faculty members—90 percent with Ph.D. or equivalent degrees—bring the Mount curriculum to life. All faculty members personalize the educational experience by working with and getting to know each student. The student-faculty ratio is 14:1, and the average class size is 21. Most professors serve as academic advisers. No graduate assistants teach class. Faculty members are committed to teaching. Many are also active researchers, and opportunities exist for students to become involved in research projects.

Student Government

The Student Government Association (SGA) provides funding for other student organizations and is a conduit for student feedback to the Mount administration. The SGA President sits on the Mount Council, the University's governing body. The Campus Activities Board schedules dances, concerts, movies, bus trips, and other social events.

Admission Requirements

Candidates for admission to the University must be of good character and must show evidence that they have successfully completed a four-year college-preparatory program in high school. All students applying for admission should have a minimum of 16 academic units, including English, 4; social studies, 3; mathematics, 3; sciences, 3; and a foreign language, 2. Students must also present recommendations from a guidance counselor or a teacher in an academic course as well as scores on the SAT or ACT.

Application and Information

Students applying to the Mount should send test scores, high school transcripts, and recommendations to the Admissions Office along with a $35 application fee. Transfer students in good standing should forward both their college and high school transcripts. Information and forms are also available on the Mount's Web site.

For further information, students may contact:

Director of Admissions
Mount St. Mary's University
Emmitsburg, Maryland 21727
Phone: 301-447-5214
800-448-4347 (toll-free)
E-mail: admissions@msmary.edu
Web site: http://www.msmary.edu

A view of the campus at Mount St. Mary's University.

ST. JOHN'S COLLEGE

ANNAPOLIS, MARYLAND

The College

St. John's College maintains two widely separated campuses, one in Annapolis, Maryland, and another in Santa Fe, New Mexico. Each has its own admissions and financial aid offices. A common curriculum, however, enables students and faculty members to move from one campus to the other. Both campuses are cohesive intellectual communities in which students are eagerly responsive to one another. Students also pursue interests in such activities as publications, dance, dramatics, photography, art, wilderness exploration, and sailing. The social climate is informal and lively, and students enjoy many celebrations each year. Facilities are available for almost any intramural sport; most students participate. There is a bookstore on each campus. In fall 2007, opening enrollment at the Annapolis campus was 229 women and 261 men, for a total of 490 students. The opening enrollment of 436 at the Santa Fe campus consisted of 173 women and 263 men.

The students on both campuses are outstanding, yet they fit no pattern. Though their backgrounds are varied geographically, academically, and otherwise, they are, most typically, young people who habitually read books and value good conversation. Their commitment to ideas and their enthusiasm for the St. John's program are well illustrated by the fact that about one fifth of them on each campus have transferred to St. John's as freshmen after a year or more of college elsewhere.

Location

St. John's is the third-oldest college in the United States. It has been located since 1696 in the Colonial seaport city of Annapolis, the capital of Maryland, 30 miles from Washington, D.C. In 1964, a second campus was opened at the foot of the mountains surrounding Santa Fe, a cultural center and the capital of New Mexico. The campuses are alike in curriculum and methods, but their settings and moods are as different as sailing on the Chesapeake Bay and skiing in the Sangre de Cristo Mountains, as Georgian and Spanish Colonial architecture. St. John's students participate in a number of activities of benefit to their communities at large.

Majors and Degrees

St. John's College is committed to liberal education in the most traditional and yet radical way. It accomplishes this through direct engagement with the books in which the greatest minds of Western civilization have expressed themselves and through translation, mathematical demonstration, musical analysis, and laboratory experimentation. Whether in Annapolis or in Santa Fe, all St. John's students follow the same course of study leading to the B.A. degree. One of the purposes of this program is to emphasize the unity of knowledge; thus the faculty is not divided into departments and there are no majors.

Academic Programs

The academic program is a unified, cohesive whole; instruction takes the form of annual sequences of related seminars, tutorials, and laboratories, in each of which the books that form the core of the curriculum are the basis of study and discussion. To ensure that the intellectual life of the College extends beyond the classroom and that students bring a common frame of reference to the continuing discussion, this academic program is required of everyone, but no two students are expected to approach any subject in the same way or to reach the same conclusions about it. A central purpose of the St. John's program is to give students both the opportunity and the obligation to think for themselves. The books at the heart of the program serve to foster that thinking. They not only illuminate the enduring questions of human existence but also have great relevance to contemporary problems. They can change minds, move hearts, and touch spirits. They help all students to arrive independently at rational opinions and conclusions of their own. From this common curriculum, about 70 percent of the students go on to graduate and professional study in a wide range of fields.

There are two semesters a year. All classes are small discussion groups and range in size from between 12 and 16 students in tutorials to between 18 and 20 in seminars and laboratories. Final examinations are oral and individual. Students are not routinely informed of their grades. Instead, a student's tutors, as members of the faculty are called, evaluate the student's intellectual performance twice a year in his or her presence and with his or her help. St. John's students are participants in their own education. Annual essays and shorter papers, prepared by students without recourse to secondary sources, are based directly on the books of the program.

Seminars are devoted to reading works of the greatest minds and engaging in thoughtful discussion about them. The first-year seminar focuses on Greek authors; the second on the works of the Roman, medieval, and early Renaissance periods; the third on books of the seventeenth and eighteenth centuries; and the fourth on writings from the nineteenth and twentieth centuries. The seminar consists almost exclusively of student conversation. The aim of the discussions is to ascertain not how things were but how things are. Everyone's opinion must be heard and must also be supported by argument and evidence. The role of the tutors is not to give information or to produce the "right" interpretation; it is to guide the discussion, to aid in defining the issues, and to help the students to understand the authors, the issues, and themselves. If tutors do take a definite stand and enter the argument, they are expected to defend their positions just as students do. Reason is the only recognized authority.

Preceptorials replace seminars for eight weeks of the junior and senior years. In the preceptorial, students and tutors gather in groups of 8 or 9 to discuss, with more leisure than the pace and discipline of the seminar permit, books or topics of particular interest to them.

In the language tutorial, Greek is studied in the first two years and French in the last two. By translating works written in Greek and French into English and comparing those languages with each other as well as with English, the student gains an appreciation of all three and learns something of the nature of language in general.

The language of number and figure does not require a special aptitude. Rather, mathematics is an integral and necessary part of comprehending the world. The mathematics tutorial seeks to effect an understanding of the fundamental nature and intention of mathematics. Throughout the four years, the student is in contact not only with the pure science of mathematics but also with the foundations of mathematical physics and astronomy. The blackboard becomes an arena of logical struggle, which brings the imagination constantly into play.

The music tutorial aims at understanding music through study of musical theory and analysis of significant works. Students investigate rhythm, the diatonic system, ratios of musical intervals, melody, counterpoint, and harmony.

In the modern world, the liberal arts are practiced at their best and fullest in the laboratory. This practice puts into serious question the common distinction between the "natural sciences" and the "humanities." The laboratory is a part of the program in all years but the second. It weaves together the main themes of physics, biology, and chemistry with careful scrutiny of the interplay of hypothesis, theory, and observed fact.

On Friday evenings, the College community assembles for a formal lecture or concert by a tutor or visitor. It is the only time the students are lectured to. Afterward, interested students and faculty members engage the speaker or performer in questions and discussion.

Academic Facilities

The library on each campus—about 100,000 volumes in Annapolis, nearly 60,000 in Santa Fe—emphasizes material appropriate to the nature of the academic program, supplemented by a more general collection and by a variety of special collections. Recordings and representative periodicals and newspapers are included. Academic facilities on each campus also include the resources and equipment necessary for study and experimentation in physics, chemistry, and biology (including a planetarium in Annapolis); for audition and performance of music; for display and studio work in art, photography, and other crafts; and for drama productions.

Costs

For 2007–08, annual tuition and fees total $36,346. Room and board are $8684. Books and supplies range in cost from $200 to $275. Personal expenses depend on the student's habits and tastes.

Financial Aid

The criterion for financial assistance is need. On both campuses the application for financial aid is the CSS PROFILE supplemented by the Free Application for Federal Student Aid (FAFSA) and an institutional aid application. More than half of all St. John's students receive aid, usually in a combination of grant, loan, and employment. Federal Perkins Loans, Federal Pell Grants, Federal Supplemental Educational Opportunity Grants, Federal Work-Study Program employment, and College grants and jobs are available.

Faculty

The faculty-student ratio is 1:8 on each campus. Faculty members all hold the same rank. Their intellectual range and vitality come from teaching throughout the curriculum. This breadth and tension and the fact that St. John's is an intellectual community in which all teach and all learn are distinctive characteristics of the St. John's faculty.

Student Government

Inside the classroom and out, the dignity of the students as adults is respected. On both campuses, student government is part of the general College pattern. A Delegate Council and Student Committee on Instruction work with the faculty and administrators on matters of mutual concern.

Admission Requirements

Criteria for admission to either campus are intellectual and academic, though any accomplishment showing initiative and drive may strengthen an application. The written application consists of a series of reflective essays. The academic record and recommendations are considered supplements to it. SAT or ACT scores are optional but may prove helpful. There are no minimums for grades or test scores; both may be made irrelevant by what the candidate writes. On each campus, applicants are judged on their own merits. Although interviews are not required except in special cases, interested students are urged to visit either campus for several days to sit in on seminars and tutorials.

Application and Information

Students may be admitted to either campus for the fall term or, if they are prepared to continue their studies through the following summer, in January. Application must be made to one campus or the other, not to both. Early application is advisable. Each campus seeks to complete its class by mid-May. All applications for admission and financial aid are acted on as soon as they are complete, and the candidate is notified of the decision within two weeks.

In response to inquiries, the College sends a catalog, information on financial aid, an application form, and forms for the school report and for recommendations. Students should contact:

John Christensen
Director of Admissions
St. John's College
Annapolis, Maryland 21404
Phone: 800-727-9238 (toll-free)
E-mail: admissions@sjca.edu
Web site: http://www.stjohnscollege.edu

Larry Clendenin
Director of Admissions
St. John's College
Santa Fe, New Mexico 87501
Phone: 800-331-5232 (toll-free)
E-mail: admissions@sjcsf.edu
Web site: http://www.stjohnscollege.edu

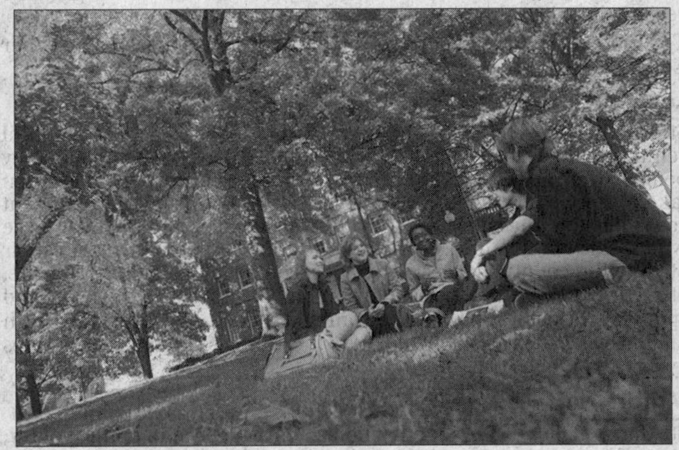

St. John's College at Annapolis.

ST. MARY'S COLLEGE OF MARYLAND

The Public Honors College

ST. MARY'S CITY, MARYLAND

The College

St. Mary's College of Maryland is a public, state-supported, coeducational college dedicated to providing an excellent education in the liberal arts and sciences. There are 1,909 full-time students, of whom 817 are men and 1,092 are women. Almost 83 percent of the students live on campus, where housing is guaranteed for eight semesters.

Designated the State of Maryland's Public Honors College in 1992 in recognition of the academic excellence of its faculty and students, every St. Mary's student participates in the intellectual and social life of the College. St. Mary's combines the educational and personal advantages of a small private college with the affordability of a public institution. Active learning and the development of critical thinking are encouraged in the discussion-oriented format made possible by modest class sizes. Student leadership in academic, cultural, and social spheres is aided by the community atmosphere; opportunities are greater than at larger schools, and involvement is easier.

The campus covers 319 acres, including riverfront, open space, and woodland. Among the waterfront facilities are a boat house, ocean kayaks, rowing shells, and a fleet of sailboats. Other facilities include a field house, lighted tennis courts, a baseball field, an outdoor track, and a stadium for field hockey, soccer, and lacrosse. The new athletic facility includes an aquatic center with an Olympic-sized indoor pool, a basketball stadium, a fitness center, an aerobic center, additional team rooms, and a rock-climbing wall. The College's teams compete in NCAA Division III and the Intercollegiate Sailing Association. Varsity sports for men are baseball, basketball, lacrosse, sailing, soccer, swimming, and tennis; for women, basketball, field hockey, lacrosse, sailing, soccer, swimming, tennis, and volleyball. The College's sailing teams are especially noted for their national recognitions. Club sports available for both men and women include cross-country and track, equestrian, fencing, golf, rowing, rugby, sailing, soccer, and Ultimate Frisbee.

The 2006–07 academic year was the inaugural year for the one-year, full-time Master of Arts in Teaching program at St. Mary's College. Certificates can be obtained for grades 1 through 6 and middle school. Secondary education certificates for grades 7 through 12 are offered in English, math, social studies, biology, chemistry, physics, and modern languages. Certificate programs for K–12 in art, music, and theater and an early childhood education certificate to supplement the elementary certificate are also offered by St. Mary's College of Maryland. All of these certificate programs have been approved through the Maryland State Department of Education and may be eligible for reciprocity with other states.

The College is accredited by the Middle States Commission on Higher Education.

Location

St. Mary's College of Maryland is situated in one of the most beautiful settings in the United States. It is tidewater country, still inhabited by people who make their living from the land and water. Watermen take oysters and crabs from the St. Mary's, Potomac, and Patuxent rivers and the Chesapeake Bay; wild swans, ducks, and Canada Geese winter in the creeks of St. Mary's County. The Patuxent River Naval Air Station, the county's largest employer, is a naval aircraft testing site, attracting many firms that supply technical support to the Navy and sponsor internships. It is an environment that is alive, providing fresh air and space. It is also convenient to the nation's capital, just 75 miles away.

Majors and Degrees

St. Mary's College offers the Bachelor of Arts degree in anthropology; art and art history; biochemistry; biology; chemistry; computer science; economics; English; history; human studies; international languages and cultures (Chinese, French, German, Latin American studies, Spanish, and courses in translation); mathematics; music; natural science; philosophy; physics; political science; psychology; public policy studies; religious studies; sociology; theater, film, and media studies; and student-designed majors. Minors are available in African and African diaspora studies, art history, art studio, biology, computer science, democracy studies, East Asian studies, economics, environmental studies, film and media studies, history, international languages and cultures (Chinese, French, German, Latin American studies, Spanish, and courses in translation), mathematics, museum studies, music, the neurosciences, philosophy, political science, religious studies, theater studies, and women, gender, and sexuality studies. Preprofessional sequences are offered in dentistry, law, medicine, and veterinary medicine.

Academic Programs

The undergraduate course of study at the College provides both diversity and depth, leading to a broad understanding of the liberal arts and sciences and a specific competence in at least one major field. All students must complete the requirements for a major and the general education requirements. The general education requirements are designed to develop skills in communication and analysis, acquaint students with the legacy of the modern world, confront students with the forces and insights that are shaping the modern world, and promote the capacity for integration and synthesis of knowledge.

History, anthropology, and archaeology students can take advantage of the College's location on the site of colonial St. Mary's City, the fourth permanent English settlement in the New World and Maryland's first capital. Many experts consider this area to contain the most abundant and earliest undisturbed artifacts of any American seventeenth-century town.

St. Mary's College offers several courses in aquatic biology as an option within the major program in biology. The College's location on the St. Mary's River, a tributary of the Potomac near the mouth of the Chesapeake Bay, is ideal for the study of estuarine ecology.

A strong music program provides advanced training in composition and piano performance and a jazz ensemble, percussion ensemble, choir, chamber vocal group, wind ensemble, and chamber orchestra for classical performances.

Independent study for credit is possible in every major, allowing students to investigate subjects not covered in normal course offerings. There is also an opportunity for students to design their own majors using components from several majors to create an interdisciplinary, individualized program of study.

Students enrolled in Advanced Placement courses may receive credit for scores of 4 or 5 on the examinations. In addition, St. Mary's may also award credit to students who receive a score of 5, 6, or 7 on the International Baccalaureate higher-level examinations.

Off-Campus Programs

Internship programs for academic credit are available for junior- and senior-level students. Within these semester-long internships, students find ways to explore their career and scholarly interests. In recent years, St. Mary's interns have worked in state and federal government offices and laboratories, in the news media, in museums and art galleries, in commercial organizations, and in positions abroad. In a number of cases, internships have led either to full-time employment after graduation or to graduate or professional study.

Opportunities to study at the Centre for Medieval and Renaissance Studies at Oxford, Fudan University in China, the University of Heidelberg in Germany, the University of the Gambia in The Gambia, and other international universities and colleges are available for qualified St. Mary's students. St. Mary's also participates in the National Student Exchange Program with other colleges throughout the United States.

Academic Facilities

The College's laboratories are equipped for course work in anthropology, biology, chemistry, physics, and psychology. Throughout the campus, there are many general-purpose computer labs with Windows XP Professional and Mac-compatible computers. There are also several smart classrooms and discipline-specific labs in Anne Arundel, Goodpaster, Kent, Montgomery, and Schaefer Halls. All of the computer labs have access to the library system, e-mail, and the Internet. Upon enrollment, every student is given a network account that provides access to e-mail, shared file systems, and other resources.

Students are encouraged but not required to own a computer, since they have access to computers in the College's general purpose and departmental computer labs. However, many students find it more convenient to own a computer so they can complete assignments in their rooms. Residents of all residence halls can connect their computers to the College's gigabit backbone network. There is also wireless access in all academic buildings of the campus for those with laptop computers.

The College library provides access to locally held resources and participates in a state-wide consortium of academic libraries that supports inter-campus borrowing for books and access to more than 70 research databases. The Media Services Department, through its editing lab and loans of video equipment, supports students pursuing multimedia and video projects. The College archive houses documents, photographs, and objects of significance to the history of the College and Southern Maryland.

The Montgomery Fine Arts Center includes facilities for performance in music and theater and also houses the Boyden Gallery. Auerbach Auditorium, located in St. Mary's Hall, is also a popular venue for public lectures, concerts, and other events.

Students have access to a writing center that provides assistance in writing and researching papers.

Costs

Annual costs for 2007–08 included tuition and fees of $9973 for Maryland residents and $20,307 for nonresidents. The most typical residence hall rooms were available for $5060 per year, and the most typical cost for board was $3795 per year. Costs for books and supplies are estimated at $1000 per year. Semester charges for tuition, room, board, and other fees are payable at or prior to registration in the fall and in the spring.

Financial Aid

The Office of Financial Aid provides advice and assistance to students in need of financial aid and joins other College offices in awarding scholarships and loans and in offering part-time employment under the work-study program. Various scholarships are awarded to students on a merit basis, and other scholarships, loans, and grants for students are awarded on the basis of ability and need as determined by the federal government's Free Application for Federal Student Aid, which should be filed no later than March 1.

Faculty

Faculty appointments and promotions are made on the basis of commitment to undergraduate teaching, an interest in new approaches to education, and academic and scholarly achievement. The faculty members have experience in a wide range of activities, including government, business, research, environmental studies, civil rights, theater, musical performance, and writing. Since 1982, St. Mary's College has had 23 Fulbright Scholars on its faculty and staff. Ninety-nine percent of the regular full-time faculty members hold a doctorate or other terminal degree in their field. A student-faculty ratio of 12:1, the relatively small size of the College, and the informal atmosphere all encourage close and personal relationships between students and faculty members. Faculty members serve as academic advisers and also provide much informal counseling and individual attention to students' academic and personal development outside of the formal structure.

Student Government

Student Government Association is the center of many activities and sponsors a variety of social and cultural events, including campus movies, speakers, dances, concerts, and excursions to cultural centers such as Annapolis, Baltimore, and Washington, D.C. Opportunities exist for students to serve as voting members on several faculty committees.

Admission Requirements

The application deadline for freshman admissions is January 15. Strong high school preparation usually includes 4 units of English, 3 units of social science (including U.S. history), 3 units of laboratory science (exclusive of ninth-grade general courses in science), 3 units of mathematics, and 7 units of other academic electives. Upon entrance, the student should have obtained a high school diploma with a minimum of 22 units or should present evidence of equivalent achievement (e.g., a passing score on the high school equivalency examination administered by the student's state department of education). The applicant must present scores on the SAT and/or the ACT examination, which should be taken by the fall of the senior year. In addition, any student whose native language is not English must obtain a minimum score of 550 (paper-based) on the TOEFL. St. Mary's College is interested in evidence of talent and ability as demonstrated in a variety of ways by each student. While the most emphasis is placed on the student's academic record, SAT scores, essay, resume, and letters of recommendation are all considered in the admissions process.

Transfer applicants with at least 24 semester hours of credit are evaluated on the basis of their college transcripts. Students who have earned fewer than 24 semester hours of credit must submit their high school records and SAT or ACT scores. Standardized test scores are required only for individuals who have graduated from high school within the past three years.

The College may grant lower-division credit toward a degree for satisfactory performance on the College Board's Advanced Placement tests or appropriate CLEP tests and International Baccalaureate higher-level courses. Students should consult the College catalog for specific score requirements.

St. Mary's College of Maryland does not discriminate for reasons of age, citizenship, color, disability, gender/gender identity and expression, national origin, race, religion, sex, sexual orientation, or special disabled veteran and Vietnam-era veteran status in the admission of students. The College complies with the Title IX of the Education Amendments of 1972.

Application and Information

An application form, financial aid information, and other materials are available by contacting:

Admissions
St. Mary's College of Maryland
18952 East Fisher Road
St. Mary's City, Maryland 20686
Phone: 240-895-5000
Phone: 800-492-7181 (toll-free)
Fax: 240-895-5001
E-mail: admissions@smcm.edu
Web site: http://www.smcm.edu

A bird's-eye view of St. Mary's College of Maryland.

SALISBURY UNIVERSITY
SALISBURY, MARYLAND

The University

Nationally recognized for excellence, Salisbury University (SU) consistently ranks in the top 10 percent of public and private institutions in national guidebooks and magazines. A member of the University System of Maryland (USM), SU emphasizes undergraduate research, professional internships, community service, and study abroad as pillars of its academic programs.

The foundation of Salisbury's success is the relationship between students and professors. Nearly 7,000 undergraduates are taught by 363 full-time faculty members on a campus of 154 acres. Full professors serve as undergraduate advisers. They often teach freshman courses and routinely lead students on trips and retreats, from exploring the Chesapeake Bay to touring Europe and beyond. Their professional concern for educating the whole student has had measurable results. According to the latest figures, SU has the fastest time-to-degree average and the highest four-, five-, and six-year graduation rates of all comprehensive institutions in the USM. This success has not gone unnoticed. For the eleventh consecutive year, SU is one of *U.S. News & World Report*'s "Top Public Universities–Master's category (North)," the highest-placing public master's-level university in Maryland. Similar kudos come from the *Princeton Review*, *Newsweek*, Kaplan, and *Kiplinger's Personal Finance* magazine.

Salisbury students come from thirty states, the District of Columbia, and fifty-seven other countries. Some 57 percent are from Maryland's western shore (which contains the Metropolitan Baltimore-Washington corridor), 14 percent are from outside the state, and 48 percent live on campus and in University-affiliated housing. Many of SU's 124 student organizations and clubs find a home in the Guerrieri University Center. An NCAA Division III member of intercollegiate athletics, SU has twenty-one varsity sports that compete in the Capital Athletic Conference and in the Atlantic Central Football Conference. Women's sports are basketball, cross-country, field hockey, lacrosse, soccer, swimming, tennis, track and field, and volleyball. Men's sports are baseball, basketball, cross-country, football, lacrosse, soccer, swimming, tennis, and track and field. The Sea Gulls have won eleven national championships, seven in men's lacrosse and four in field hockey. One of the leading Division III programs, Salisbury athletics have been ranked in the top 10 percent of the national Directors' Cup standings the past five seasons. Nearly half of the student body participates in twenty-five intramural programs and thirteen additional sports clubs.

The University has two art galleries; supports film and distinguished lecture series, artist-in-residence programs, and a public access television station; maintains WSCL/WSDL-FM (national public radio affiliates) and WXSU-FM (a student-run radio station); offers performing arts disciplines in music, theater, and dance; and serves as the home of the Salisbury Symphony Orchestra. Beyond the campus are Maryland's scenic Eastern Shore, the pleasures of Ocean City, Maryland (a nearby popular beach resort), and the activities of an energetic Outdoor Club. Faculty members lead trips abroad during winter and summer terms.

The University also offers thirteen graduate programs.

Location

With a population of 89,000, metropolitan Salisbury is the cultural and economic hub of Delmarva (containing portions of Delaware, Maryland, and Virginia), a historically and ecologically rich peninsula located between the Atlantic Ocean and Chesapeake Bay. The city is ½ hour west of the white beaches of Assateague and Ocean City, Maryland; approximately 2 hours from Baltimore, Wilmington, Norfolk, and Washington, D.C.; and 4½ hours from New York City.

Majors and Degrees

Three undergraduate degrees are offered in addition to the Bachelor of Arts and Bachelor of Science: the Bachelor of Arts in Social Work (B.A.S.W.), the Bachelor of Science in Nursing (B.S.N.), and the Bachelor of Fine Arts (B.F.A.) in art. B.A. degrees are awarded in art, communication arts, conflict analysis and dispute resolution, economics, English, English for speakers of other languages, environmental issues, fine arts, French, history, interdisciplinary studies, international studies, music, philosophy, political science, psychology, sociology, Spanish, and theater. Bachelor of Science degrees are awarded in accounting, athletic training, biology, business administration, chemistry, clinical laboratory science/medical technology, computer science, early childhood education, elementary education, environmental health science, exercise science, finance, geography and geosciences, health education, interdisciplinary studies, management, management information systems, marketing, mathematics, nursing, physical education, physics, and respiratory therapy.

Academic Programs

At Salisbury University, majors are designed to educate the whole student. No false distinctions are made between the liberal arts and the professions. While gaining a liberal education, for example, students in preprofessional programs prepare for careers in dentistry, law, medicine, optometry, pharmacy, physical therapy, podiatry, and veterinary science. Certification programs train educators for both elementary and secondary teaching. Dual-degree programs with the University of Maryland Eastern Shore (UMES) enable students to earn two bachelor's degrees in four years in biology/environmental marine science and social work/sociology. SU, UMES, and the University of Maryland College Park also collaborate on an electrical engineering degree. In addition, a newly signed agreement with the University of Delaware will soon allow SU students to take classes for the Army Reserve Officers' Training Corps (ROTC) at Delaware State University. Students may also enroll in the University of Delaware's Air Force ROTC program. Both the graduate and the undergraduate programs of SU's business school are nationally accredited by AACSB International—The Association to Advance Collegiate Schools of Business. Other national accreditations are in chemistry, education, environmental health science, allied health (respiratory therapy, exercise science, and athletic training programs), social work, clinical laboratory science (medical technology program), music, and nursing and through the Middle States Commission on Higher Education.

SU's fifty-five academic programs are administered through four schools: the Franklin P. Perdue School of Business, the Samuel W. and Marilyn C. Seidel School of Education and Professional Studies, the Charles R. and Martha N. Fulton School of Liberal Arts, and the Richard A. Henson School of Science and Technology. All four schools are endowed, a rarity among public institutions nationwide. These recent endowments have enriched the scholastic climate of the campus, providing expanded scholarships, resources, and opportunities.

University planning encourages interdisciplinary study. Students in all majors must take 47 credits in three disciplines: humanities, history and social sciences, and mathematical and general sciences. Nine credits are required in English composition and literature. All courses, from science to business to music, require written assignments in analysis/criticism, research, or creative writing.

SU's advising system has been praised by students in a Maryland Higher Education Commission survey as one of the best in the state. Exceptional orientation programs for students and parents help freshmen make a successful transition from home to college. For example, SU's New Student Seminars offer an orientation-in-the-wilderness experience, which won the Maryland Association for Higher Education Distinguished Program Award. Orientation options include a cycling tour of the Eastern Shore and a hiking trip in Alaska.

Incoming students may earn credit through Advanced Placement and departmental challenge examinations and the College-Level Examination Program (CLEP) for nontraditional educational experiences. Internships have included work abroad; legislative service in Washington, D.C., and Annapolis; and media experience in fields from fine arts to television. Students who relish intellectual challenge are invited to join the honors program housed in the Thomas E. Bellavance Honors Center. Others present research at national and international conferences. SU is also the only university in Maryland to host some 2,800 of the country's top scholars for the Twenty-second National Conference on Undergraduate Research. Study-abroad programs are popular. For example, business majors study economics in China and France, education students teach elementary children in New Zealand, and nursing students provide aid in Africa.

Academic Facilities

Planned to open this year is SU's new $65-million, 165,000-square-foot Teacher Education and Technology Center, lauded as a showcase facility for education in the mid-Atlantic region. With state-of-the-art technology, it will house an Integrated Media Center that includes studios for television production and music recording, editing facilities, a photography center, and a cutting-edge multimedia art exhibition gallery. In 2002, classes began in Henson Science Hall, SU's $42-million science education and research building, one of the largest in Maryland. Blackwell Library is the main research center on campus, with more than a quarter of a million books and bound periodicals and a number of computers. In addition to an online catalog, library users have access to databases, such as FirstSearch. Eight computer labs are part of the campus Novell network, which provides students with various software applications, e-mail, and the Internet. Resident students also have network connections for the Internet and e-mail in their rooms. Fulton Hall is home to the fine and performing arts, and the Center for Conflict Resolution engages students in mediation efforts at home and abroad. The only institution in the USM with an endowed theater program, SU boasts three theaters for performing arts, including the acoustically lauded Holloway Hall Auditorium. Off the main campus, the Edward H. Nabb Research Center for Delmarva History and Culture is a treasure trove of information for students and visitors. SU's Ward Museum of Wildfowl Art was named one of the "10 Great Places to See American Folk Art" by *USA Today*.

Costs

Maryland residents paid undergraduate tuition and fees of $6412 for the academic year. Tuition for out-of-state undergraduates was $14,500. Students living on campus paid about $7600 for room and board; the figure varies, depending on the residence hall and meal plan.

Financial Aid

Financial assistance is available to students through loans, grants, scholarships, and on- and off-campus employment. The University participates in the Federal Perkins Loan, Federal Pell Grant, Federal Supplemental Educational Opportunity Grant, and Federal Work-Study and Direct Loan Programs. Numerous other forms of financial aid on the state and local levels are based exclusively on demonstrated financial need. All students who wish to apply for financial assistance must complete the Free Application for Federal Student Aid (FAFSA) by February 15. Complete details are available through the University's Admissions and Financial Aid Offices.

Through the University's Work Experience Program, which has a budget in excess of $2 million and provides employment for one quarter of the student body, students may be assigned to jobs related to their academic interest. They can earn approximately $1500 to $2000 per semester by working 10 to 20 hours a week. Non-need academic scholarships for incoming freshmen are awarded on the basis of high school performance and SAT scores. Application for admission to the University is the initial step in applying for these scholarships.

Faculty

Faculty members at Salisbury have won national teaching, research, and leadership awards. Ninety-two percent of the tenure-track faculty members, many of whom are National Endowment for the Humanities and Fulbright professors, have the Ph.D. or other highest degree in their field. Professors not only publish but also donate countless hours to community service, thus teaching by deed as well as word. The student-professor ratio is 16:1; smaller classes are not unusual.

Student Government

Shared governance is a hallmark of campus life, and students are actively involved in all its aspects. The Student Government Association (SGA) serves as a liaison between the faculty and administration for students. SGA officers serve on many University committees, both administrative and academic, including the President's Advisory Team. Students are also represented in the University Forum, which includes faculty and administration members and meets regularly to discuss issues facing the University community. The all-student Appropriations Board budgets student activity fees to clubs and organizations. Students are encouraged to participate in a full complement of events, many sponsored by the Student Organization for Activity Planning.

Admission Requirements

The University seeks to admit outstanding students who bring diverse talents, experiences, and points of view to campus. Most successful candidates for admission have earned above-average high school grades in a strong academic program and a score above the national average on the SAT or ACT. The high school record, test scores, essay, and recommendations of the high school principal and guidance counselors are considered. Interviews are not required, but applicants are encouraged to discuss programs and procedures for housing and financial aid with the staff of the Admissions and Financial Aid Offices.

The University has introduced an SAT/ACT optional admissions policy. Applicants who have earned a weighted grade point average of 3.5 or higher on a 4.0 scale have the choice of submitting a standardized test score. The SAT or ACT is required for applicants with a weighted grade point average below 3.5 or who wish to be considered for University scholarships.

Transfer students must have earned at least 24 semester hours at an accredited community college or four-year college or university and have a minimum 2.0 average (on a 4.0 scale). For transfer students who have attempted fewer than 24 hours at another institution, the University's admission policy for entering freshmen applies.

Application and Information

Applications are accepted beginning September 1 for the spring and fall semesters. Applications received by November 1 for the spring semester and by January 15 for the fall semester are given the fullest attention. The University reserves the right to close admissions when the projected enrollment is met. The application is available online at http://www.salisbury.edu/apply. For further information, students should contact:

Admissions Office
Salisbury University
1200 Camden Avenue
Salisbury, Maryland 21801-6862
Phone: 410-543-6161
888-543-0148 (toll-free)
Fax: 410-546-6016
E-mail: admissions@salisbury.edu
Web site: http://www.salisbury.edu

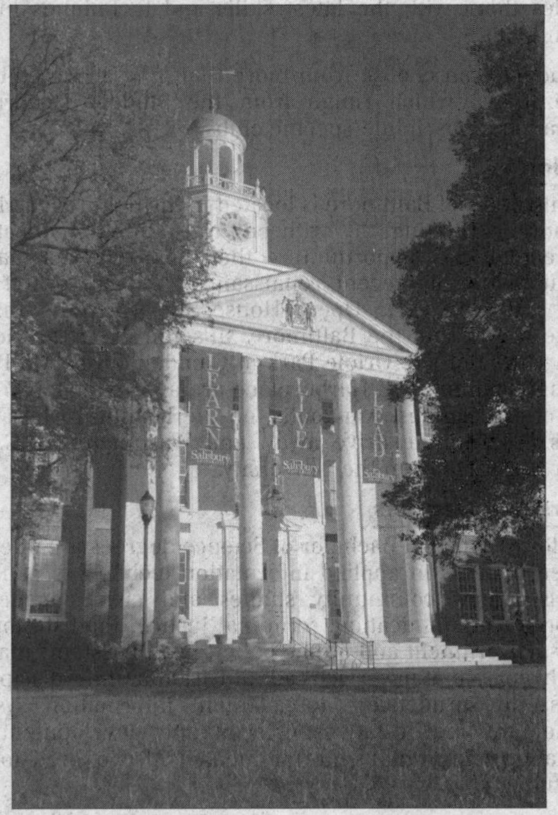

Salisbury University's Holloway Hall is a center for student and University life.

UNIVERSITY OF BALTIMORE

BALTIMORE, MARYLAND

The University

The University of Baltimore (UB) welcomes undergraduate, graduate, and professional students, associate degree recipients, and transfer and reentering students to an urban learning environment where they can benefit from small-college contact with professors and advisers. The preprofessional and undergraduate programs in business and applied liberal arts focus on Knowledge That Works, offering students practical, hands-on experience that prepares them to enter or move up in the career to which they aspire. As UB is a member of the University System of Maryland, students can take advantage of varied, system-wide resources and programs while studying in a city full of inspiration and excitement. UB's commuter campus is easy to get to and easy to get around in; the academic buildings, student center, and library are all within steps of one another. The University of Baltimore offers academic study leading to Bachelor of Arts and Bachelor of Science degrees. In addition to its undergraduate programs, UB offers the J.D. degree through the School of Law as well as graduate degrees in business and liberal arts.

Founded in 1925, UB has a very clear mission: to provide flexible educational programs to professionally oriented students. Approximately 5,400 students study in the University's three schools—the Yale Gordon College of Liberal Arts, the Robert S. Merrick School of Business, and the School of Law. UB traditionally attracts students with strong career ambitions and provides them with the latest skills and techniques in their chosen fields.

UB students can choose from more than fifty active clubs and organizations, which range from the Student Government Association to discipline-specific clubs.

Location

The University of Baltimore is located in the cultural corridor of Baltimore, a thriving city with cultural, athletic, educational, and recreational opportunities that has received national recognition for its recent renaissance. The Meyerhoff Symphony Hall, the Lyric Opera House, the Maryland Institute College of Art, and the Baltimore Museum of Art are located within 1 mile of UB. Oriole Park at Camden Yards, M&T Bank (Ravens) Stadium, and Harborplace are approximately 3 miles south of the campus. Annapolis, on the beautiful Chesapeake Bay, is a 45-minute drive away, and Washington, D.C., is a 1-hour commute from the University.

Majors and Degrees

Bachelor of Arts and Bachelor of Science degrees are offered to transfer students in applied information technology, *business administration, *community studies and civic engagement, *corporate communication, *criminal justice, English, forensic studies, government and public policy, health systems management, history, human services administration, *interdisciplinary studies, *jurisprudence, *management information systems, *psychology, *real estate and economic development, and *simulation and digital entertainment. (*Also offered to first-year students.)

Academic Programs

The University follows a semester system, with fall and spring semesters and a summer session. More than 600 courses are offered during the fall, spring, and summer semesters. Transfer students can attend full-time or part-time during the day or evening, on Saturdays, and on the Web. First-year students attend full-time during the day.

A humanities-centered, interdisciplinary core curriculum is required of all undergraduate students. In these core courses, students examine the relationship between ethics and values while exploring business and public policy, and they trace major themes and ideas in philosophy and the arts. Throughout the core, students are assisted in refining their skills in critical thinking and oral and written communication. To be awarded a bachelor's degree, students must satisfactorily complete a minimum of 120 hours of college credit and have satisfactorily completed a specific curriculum with a grade point average of at least 2.0.

The University's Helen P. Denit Honors Program offers honors-level versions of the core curriculum courses. Honors students are also privy to small grants for honors research projects and participation at national and regional conferences. Students who are interested in the Helen P. Denit Honors Program should visit http://www.ubalt.edu/honors/.

Off-Campus Programs

Several off-campus sites are available for students who desire to take courses closer to home. UB also offers the Web bachelor's, Web M.B.A., and Web M.P.A. degrees. The University offers students opportunities to participate in professional internships, and students from certain majors may also participate in study-abroad opportunities.

Academic Facilities

Located on the corner of Mt. Royal and Charles Streets, the University of Baltimore offers a variety of campus facilities. The Academic Center houses many of the administration offices as well as classrooms, a fitness center, faculty offices, and the dean's offices of the Yale Gordon College of Liberal Arts. The president's suite and a student lounge as well as business, registrar, and student affairs offices and classrooms are also located in the Academic Center.

The Thumel Center houses the Merrick School of Business and the Office of Admissions, with computer laboratories and state-of-the-art communication and computer-capable classrooms; it features a six-story atrium. UB's Langsdale Library compares favorably with those of its peer institutions in Maryland in both breadth and quantity of holdings. The Charles Royal Building is home to the School of Communications Design, and the Schaefer Center Building is the location for the School of Public Affairs. The John and Frances Angelos Law Center houses the law library, classrooms, and administrative offices of the School of Law as well as Poe's House, the University's dining facility.

The brand-new student center, which opened in spring 2006, offers students one convenient location in which to conduct meetings, have a quick lunch, study, conduct forums, catch up on television news, or just socialize. The center allows students and faculty members of different academic disciplines to interact on a daily basis. Computer labs are available for study and research.

Costs

Full-time in-state tuition for the 2007–08 academic year per semester was $2662.50 plus fees; part-time in-state tuition per credit was $243 plus fees. Out-of-state full-time tuition per semester was $9053.50 plus fees; out-of-state part-time tuition per credit was $754 plus fees. Tuition and fees are subject to change.

Financial Aid

Students at the University of Baltimore are eligible to participate in all regular federal financial aid programs, including the Pell Grant, the Supplemental Educational Opportunity Grant, the Perkins Loan, the Stafford Student Loan, the PLUS Program, and the Work-Study Program. Applications for federal aid should be submitted by March 1 for fall and November 1 for spring.

In addition, the University offers an extensive scholarship program for first-year and transfer students. Scholarship and financial aid information is available online at http://www.ubalt.edu/admissions/scholarships/.

Faculty

With a student-faculty ratio of 16:1 and a personalized system of student advising, UB programs emphasize one-on-one interaction and individual attention for all students. The University of Baltimore employs 163 full-time and 200 part-time faculty members; 86 percent of the full-time faculty members hold terminal degrees. All full-time faculty members teach at both the undergraduate and graduate levels and have responsibilities in research and public service. UB does not utilize graduate teaching assistants. Part-time faculty members are expert practitioners who are employed full-time in business, industry, and government.

Student Government

The student government consists of three branches serving as representative bodies for all students at the University of Baltimore. The Undergraduate Student Senate, the Graduate Student Senate, and the Student Bar Association oversee the allotment and expenditure of funds to more than fifty student organizations and are responsible for issues of governance and a variety of programming.

Admission Requirements

First-year students are evaluated on their high school transcript, SAT and/or ACT scores, and an essay. All are required for admission. Optional items include SAT Subject Tests, a resume or list of extracurricular activities, and/or letters of recommendation. Transfer students must have completed a minimum of 24 transferable college credits. All students are evaluated based on college credits completed and grades earned. Students who have earned an associate degree from a Maryland community college are guaranteed admission to UB and can transfer up to 60 credits. Students may also consult the ARTSYS Web site at http://artweb.usmd.edu to determine which credits are transferable.

Applicants who are nonnative speakers of English must demonstrate a satisfactory level of English proficiency. A minimum score of 550 on the paper-based version or 213 on the computer-based version of the Test of English as a Foreign Language (TOEFL) is required of both degree- and non-degree-seeking applicants regardless of citizenship or visa status. Applicants with international transcripts must arrange to have their academic records evaluated by a U.S. credential evaluation service.

Application and Information

Application deadlines for first-year students are November 1 for spring semester (a limited number of students may be accepted for spring) and February 15 for fall semester. Application deadlines for transfer students are December 1 for spring semester and June 1 for fall semester (March 1 for forensics). The deadline for the summer semester is May 1. An online application is available on the Web at http://www.ubalt.edu/admissions, or students may request an application by calling or writing to the Office of Undergraduate Admissions.

Office of Undergraduate Admissions
University of Baltimore
1420 North Charles Street
Baltimore, Maryland 21201-5779
Phone: 410-837-4777
877-ApplyUB (toll-free)
Web site: http://www.ubalt.edu

The new student center at the University of Baltimore.

COLLEGE DATA CENTER • MARYLAND

UNIVERSITY OF MARYLAND, BALTIMORE COUNTY

BALTIMORE, MARYLAND

The University

Located between Baltimore and Washington, D.C., University of Maryland, Baltimore County (UMBC) is a public, medium-sized school offering smart, engaged students opportunities to explore the ideas they are passionate about in an honors university setting—providing access to outstanding professors and the individual attention usually found at a smaller, private college.

The University has been recognized by *Kaplan/Newsweek*'s "How to Get into College" guide as one of the twelve hottest schools in the country. The Carnegie Foundation ranks UMBC in the category of Research Universities with high research activity. The University's academic reputation and industry partnerships help to place students in promising careers and leading graduate programs. One third of UMBC students immediately go on to leading graduate or professional schools such as Harvard, Johns Hopkins, Stanford, and Yale.

At UMBC, students find that learning can take place in many different ways and in a variety of settings. Undergraduates have access to the latest technology in areas from geography to art history to chemistry. The International Media Center offers students multilingual word processing, worldwide databases, and satellite feeds from the International Channel, Deutsche Welle, and French, Russian, and Spanish stations. The Goddard Earth Science and Technology Center brings NASA scientists and UMBC professors and students together to study the earth's surface, atmosphere, and oceans. Students in UMBC's Imaging Research Center (IRC) gain professional experience with companies such as the Discovery Channel, CNN, and PBS; students use the IRC's high-end equipment for applications such as molecular imaging and 3-D cartography. UMBC also has a Howard Hughes Medical Institute laboratory, a privately sponsored research facility dedicated to the study of the structural building blocks of the AIDS virus.

UMBC's 530-acre campus includes more than forty buildings accessed by a 2-mile elliptical drive. UMBC's on-campus research and technology park and nearby incubator and accelerator center attract firms in high-technology fields, including engineering, information technology, and the life sciences and offer students internship opportunities with cutting-edge firms. The U.S. Geological Survey's Maryland-Delaware-Washington, D.C., Water Science Center recently relocated to its new facility in UMBC's research park. Erickson Retirement Communities plans to move its adult-living national broadcast network, Retirement Living TV (RL-TV), into a new building next to the campus.

The UMBC campus climate is friendly and energetic. More than 9,400 undergraduates are involved in over 200 student groups, including Greek organizations; recreational sports clubs, such as fencing and sailing; community outreach efforts, such as Habitat for Humanity; and campus events, including lectures, films, concerts, and plays. Students enthusiastically follow UMBC NCAA Division I athletic teams, such as basketball, lacrosse, and soccer, attending games in the UMBC Stadium and Retriever Activities Center, which includes a multipurpose gym, auxiliary gym, weight room, and classrooms.

UMBC students are from forty-three states, plus Puerto Rico and the District of Columbia, and ninety-five countries. Approximately 72 percent of freshmen live on campus, with nearly 12 percent from out of state. The diverse undergraduate student population is 53 percent Caucasian, 21 percent Asian American, 16 percent African American, 4 percent Hispanic American, and .01 percent Native American; 46 percent are women. UMBC houses nearly 3,900 students, 1,600 of whom live in the three new residence suites and apartment communities. Room layouts are based on a suite concept with a shared living room. Residential communities also feature nine living-learning programs: Center for Women & Information Technology, Emergency Health Services; Exploratory Majors, Honors College, Humanities, Intercultural Living Exchange, Shriver Living Learning Center, Visual and Performing Arts, and Women Involved in Learning and Leadership. Other special-living options include wellness, quiet-lifestyle, continuous-occupancy, and substance-free.

Location

UMBC is 10 minutes from downtown Baltimore and 30 minutes from Washington, D.C. Surrounded by business, government, and metropolitan centers, UMBC places students in over 1,200 co-ops and internships in the Baltimore-Washington area, with 80 percent of the students receiving paid professional experience. UMBC matches students with such major employers as IBM, Northrop Grumman, GE, Social Security Administration, T. Rowe Price, Silicon Graphics, the Smithsonian Institution, U.S. Department of State, Wyeth Pharmaceuticals, NASA, and the National Security Agency. The Baltimore-Washington area is known for its music, sports, museums, restaurants, and historical traditions. Favorite student meeting places include Fells Point, the Inner Harbor, Oriole Park at Camden Yards, M&T Bank Stadium, Patapsco State Park, Annapolis, and Georgetown.

Majors and Degrees

UMBC offers programs leading to Bachelor of Arts, Bachelor of Fine Arts, and Bachelor of Science degrees in the following areas: acting, Africana studies, American studies, ancient studies, biochemistry and molecular biology, bioinformatics and computational biology, biological sciences, business technology administration, chemical engineering, chemistry and biochemistry, computer engineering and computer science, cultural anthropology, dance, economics and financial economics, emergency health services, English, environmental science and environmental studies, gender and women's studies, geography, health administration and policy, history, information systems, interdisciplinary studies, mathematics and statistics, mechanical engineering, media and communication studies, modern languages and linguistics, music, philosophy, physics, physics education, political science, psychology, social work, sociology, theater, visual and performing arts, and visual arts.

In fall 2007, UMBC launched an undergraduate major in media and communication studies where they gain critical media literacy while learning to use relevant new technologies to communicate effectively. An interdisciplinary studies program allows students to design their own course of study according. UMBC offers preprofessional studies programs, including two- and four-year advisement programs to prepare students for clinical training in dental hygiene, medical and research technology, medicine, nursing, pharmacy, physical therapy, and veterinary medicine.

Minor programs include Africana studies, American studies, ancient studies, anthropology, applied politics, art history and theory, astronomy, biological sciences, chemistry, computer science, dance, East Asian history, economics, emergency health services, environmental geography, gender and women's studies, geography, history, international affairs, international economics, Judaic studies, legal policy, literature, mathematics, media and communication studies, modern languages and linguistics, music, philosophy, physics, political science, political thought, psychology, public administration, religious studies, social welfare, sociology, statistics, theater, women's studies, and writing.

Academic Programs

UMBC's academic calendar consists of fall and spring semesters, a four-week mini session in January, and summer sessions ranging from six to eight weeks. To receive a UMBC degree, students complete 120–128 credits plus two physical education courses. In addition to the requirements for the chosen major, a core of courses called the general education program (GEP) provides a solid basis for a lifetime of learning. The GEP courses encompass four broad areas: humanities and fine arts, mathematics and natural sciences, social sciences, and languages and culture.

The Honors College is a special option for students for whom the quest for knowledge is its own reward. Honors College students gain the enlightened perspective that comes with immersion in the liberal arts. Innovative approaches to study, unique internship options, a living-learning community, and emphasis on independent research are among the hallmarks of the program. All Honors College students must take at least one honors course per semester. Students choose from honors versions of core courses, special honors seminars, and many honors courses.

The Shriver Center, named in honor of Eunice Kennedy Shriver and Sargent Shriver, links the resources of the campus to urgent social problems, particularly in the areas of education, criminal justice, health, the environment, and jobs, with special priority given to the needs of citizens with mental retardation. The Shriver Center organizes and manages community service projects and connects students to a wide range of social service projects. It also places students in co-ops and internships at over 1,000 businesses and organizations in the Baltimore/Washington area and abroad. Shriver Center co-op and internship students consistently earn exemplary reviews from host organizations, often followed by an offer of full-time employment when they graduate.

Academic Facilities

UMBC's landmark building, the Albin O. Kuhn Library and Gallery, rises seven stories over the campus. The library contains 1 million books and bound volumes of journals; an extensive reference collection; extensive online journal and database subscriptions; more than 3 million other items, including slides and online images, photographs, maps, musical scores, recordings, and microforms; and more than 200 computers as well as wireless connections for laptops.

The Commons, UMBC's state-of-the-art student center, includes a food court, general lounges, the University bookstore, meeting spaces, a student recreation center, a full-service bank, student organization offices, administrative offices, and other retail-type spaces. It also features wireless computer connectivity and Web-accessible kiosks.

UMBC students have access to outstanding research opportunities and equipment. New facilities include a Public Policy Building and a state-of-the-art Information Technology/Engineering Building. UMBC's Engineering Building contains several general-access computer labs, which offer 320 PC workstations, forty Silicon Graphics workstations, and sixty-four eMac workstations. The University's computer services include a high-speed campus network, remote-access capabilities, powerful networked multiprocessor systems for research, online information, e-mail accounts for all students, and directory services. By 2010, UMBC will open a new Performing Arts and Humanities Facility, which will house seven departments and new performance spaces to showcase the University's strong arts and humanities programs and create a regional and national appreciation of UMBC as a cultural attraction.

Costs

Tuition and fees for 2007–08 were $8708 for Maryland residents and $17,440 for out-of-state students. Room and board averaged $8362. Other expenses, books, and transportation cost about $1500 per year.

Financial Aid

Approximately 46 percent of undergraduate students receive some financial aid in the form of grants, work-study, or loans. UMBC uses the Free Application for Federal Student Aid (FAFSA) to help determine a student's financial need. Aid is awarded to qualified applicants on a first-come, first-served basis. For priority consideration of need-based aid, students are encouraged to submit their FAFSA by February 14. Merit scholarships, ranging from $1000 to $22,000 annually, are awarded to students on the basis of academic or artistic merit. Well-qualified freshmen are automatically considered for general merit scholarships once they are admitted to the University. The Scholars Programs at UMBC provide special opportunities for outstanding entering freshmen who are prepared to focus their education in selected divisions of study. The Scholars Programs at UMBC include the Humanities Scholars, the Linehan Artist Scholars, the Sondheim Public Affairs Scholars, the Meyerhoff Scholarship (for high-achieving high school seniors who have an interest in pursuing doctoral studies in science, mathematics, computer science, and engineering and who are interested in the advancement of minorities in the sciences and related fields), the Center for Women & Information Technology Scholars (open to both men and women), and the Sherman Scholars (for students interested in teaching science, technology, engineering, and math in at-risk schools). Scholars participate in a wide range of academic and cultural enrichment activities, travel abroad, or internships. The selection process for specialty scholarships includes an application, an interview, and, in some cases, nomination from a high school official.

Faculty

UMBC faculty members work at the frontiers of their disciplines, and they are eager to share their expertise with undergraduates. Students have opportunities for research experience, instruction in state-of-the-art techniques, and introductions to prospective employers who partner with UMBC faculty members in research. Leading faculty members, including deans and award-winning professors, teach entry-level classes. The student-faculty ratio is 17.7:1.

Student Government

Elections are held each year for officers in UMBC's Student Government Association (SGA). The SGA represents the student body on a number of administrative committees.

Admission Requirements

In fall 2007, the average incoming freshman had a 3.60 cumulative GPA and a combined SAT score (critical reading and math) of 1191; 58.6 percent ranked in the top quarter of their senior class. Approximately 69 percent of freshman applicants are admitted each year. More than 42.7 percent enter with advanced credit, either through AP, I.B., or other college courses. Academic performance and curriculum strength play an important part in the decision. An essay is required, and a letter of recommendation is strongly encouraged. Transfer students who present at least 30 semester hours of college-level work are admitted based on the strength of college success. A minimum 2.5 cumulative average is recommended for full consideration.

Application and Information

Prospective freshmen are encouraged to submit applications by the early action deadline of November 1 for full consideration for admission, campus housing, financial aid, and scholarships; the final deadline is February 1. The priority deadline for transfer students is March 15 for fall admission and November 1 for spring admission for students seeking admission to special programs or wishing to be considered for campus housing, financial aid, or scholarships. The final deadline for transfer applications is May 31 for fall and December 15 for spring.

Dale Bittinger, Director
Office of Undergraduate Admissions and Orientation
University of Maryland, Baltimore County
1000 Hilltop Circle
Baltimore, Maryland 21250
Phone: 410-455-2291
800-UMBC-4U2 (toll-free)
Fax: 410-455-1094
Web site: http://www.umbc.edu

UMBC's 530-acre campus is just 10 minutes south of Baltimore; 30 minutes from Washington, D.C. Students and visitors have the unlimited resources of two major metropolitan areas at their fingertips.

UNIVERSITY OF MARYLAND, COLLEGE PARK

COLLEGE PARK, MARYLAND

The University

Throughout its 151-year history, the University of Maryland has served as a premier public research university while dedicating itself to providing the highest quality undergraduate education. Designated as the state's flagship university, Maryland attracts the best students and faculty members from across the nation and around the world. Students enroll at Maryland for the reputation and quality of its academic programs, the outstanding and diverse opportunities both in and outside the classroom, and the success of its alumni.

Choosing from among more than 100 academic programs, 23,099 full-time and 2,005 part-time undergraduates are taught by a faculty of more than 3,500. Approximately 9,948 master's- and doctoral-level students are enrolled in the graduate school. About 75 percent of Maryland's undergraduates are state residents, with the remaining quarter coming from all fifty states, the District of Columbia, three territories, and 110 other countries. Maryland's diversity is one of its strongest assets, with 35 percent of students belonging to minority groups.

More than 10,000 undergraduates live on-campus. From traditional halls to apartments with kitchens and from single rooms to special-interest housing, students individualize their housing experience. Many students live near the campus in fraternity and sorority houses, apartments, and private homes. An extensive University shuttle bus system provides free transportation to neighboring communities in ten directions, allowing commuting students easy access to campus. Parking is readily available for both resident and commuter students.

The University sponsors more than 300 student clubs and organizations and hosts dozens of social, athletic, academic, and recreational activities each week. About 10 percent of students are members of twenty-five fraternities and twenty sororities. A full range of intramural and club sports use the University's campus recreation center, which houses indoor and outdoor swimming pools, free weights, fitness machines, courts, and a running track. Outdoor athletic facilities include an eighteen-hole golf course, a soccer/track complex, a 55-foot climbing wall, a ropes course, and playing fields. In addition, Maryland hosts teams in twenty-seven NCAA sports for both men and women, which compete in the Atlantic Coast Conference.

Location

Maryland students step off the campus and into one of the world's most vibrant centers of government, business, research, and culture. The University is located just minutes from the heart of Washington, D.C., and within half an hour of both Baltimore and Annapolis. Maryland's dynamic relationship with these cities gives students access to hands-on experience with government agencies, international corporations, trade associations, and foreign embassies. The Kennedy Center, NASA, the Smithsonian, the NIH, the Environmental Protection Agency, CNN, the National Archives, the FBI, and the *Washington Post* are just a few of the hundreds of places where Maryland students find opportunities for internships, research projects, and jobs. A Metrorail and MARC train station (easily accessible via the ShuttleUM) provide quick and easy public transportation to the entire Washington-Baltimore region. In addition, the city of College Park is a true college town, with dozens of restaurants, clubs, shops, and recreational activities designed for students.

Majors and Degrees

The University of Maryland offers one of the most comprehensive course selections available at any public or private institution. Programs leading to Bachelor of Arts and Bachelor of Science degrees include accounting; aerospace engineering; Afro-American studies; agribusiness, agricultural, and resource economics; agricultural and veterinary medicine; agricultural sciences; American studies; animal sciences: animal management and industry, avian business, equine studies, laboratory animal management, and preprofessional sciences; anthropology; architecture; art education; art history; astronomy; biochemistry; bioengineering; biological sciences; cell biology and genetics; Central European, Russian, and Eurasian studies; chemical engineering; chemistry; Chinese; civil and environmental engineering; classical languages and literature; communication; community health; computer engineering; computer science; conservation of soil, water, and environment; criminology and criminal justice; dance; dietetics; early childhood education; ecology and evolution; economics; education; electrical engineering; elementary education; engineering; English education; English language and literature; environmental, educational, and park management; environmental science and policy; family studies; finance; fire protection engineering; food science; foreign language education; French language and literature; general business and management; geography; geology; German language and literature; government and politics; hearing and speech science; history; horticulture and crop production; information systems; international business; Italian language and literature; Japanese; Jewish studies; journalism; kinesiological sciences; land and water resource management; landscape architecture; landscape management; linguistics; logistics, transportation, and supply chain management; marketing; materials science and engineering; mathematics; mathematics education; mechanical engineering; microbiology; music; music education; nutritional sciences; operations and quality management; philosophy; physical education; physical sciences; physics; physiology and neurobiology; plant and wildlife management; plant sciences; psychology; Romance languages; Russian language and literature; science education; social studies education; sociology; Spanish language and literature; special education; studio art; theater; turf and golf course management; urban forestry; and women's studies.

Preprofessional programs are also available in allied health, dental hygiene, dentistry, law, medical technology, medicine, nursing, occupational therapy, optometry, osteopathic medicine, pharmacy, physical therapy, and podiatry.

Academic Programs

Undergraduate education at Maryland aims to provide students with a sense of identity and purpose, a concern for others, a sense of responsibility for the quality of life around them, a continuing eagerness for knowledge and understanding, and a foundation for a lifetime of personal enrichment and success. Within a research setting such as Maryland's, undergraduate students take strong, interdisciplinary courses taught by renowned researchers and scholars.

Every undergraduate completes at least 120 credit hours to earn a degree, 46 of which are general education or CORE courses. The purpose of CORE is to help students achieve the intellectual integration and awareness they need to meet challenges in their personal, social, political, and professional lives. Although each program is unique, generally 30 to 36 credit hours are earned in the major field. Students may earn a double major, earn a minor in a second area of study, and use AP and IB credit toward a degree.

University Honors offers the most academically talented students the opportunity to join a close-knit community of students and faculty members in small, challenging seminar courses and residential communities. College Park Scholars, an innovative living/learning program that is also designed for academically talented students, encourages students who share common intellectual interests to study and live together. Other special academic opportunities for undergraduates include First Year Learning Communities, Gemstone, Honors Humanities, CIVICUS, Global Communities, Jiménez-Porter Writers' House, Air Force ROTC, and a research assistant program.

The University operates on a semester system and offers two 6-week summer sessions and a three-week winter term. More than 3,000 undergraduate courses are taught at the University of Maryland.

Off-Campus Programs

Students at Maryland have the opportunity to formally study abroad for credit in Argentina; Australia; Austria; Belgium; Belize; Brazil; China; Costa Rica; Cuba; Denmark; Ecuador; France, including Paris; Germany, including Tübingen; Ghana; Great Britain, including England (London, Oxford, and York); Greece; India; Israel; Italy; Japan; Korea; Mexico; Netherlands; South Africa; Spain; and Sweden. The National Student Exchange program allows students to study at one of more than 140 different U.S. colleges and universities for a semester or a year. Internships and cooperative education opportunities are plentiful in and around the nation's capital.

Academic Facilities

Encompassing more than 300 buildings on 1,500 acres, the University of Maryland houses dozens of research laboratories, performance venues, art galleries, and centers of study. Major academic and research facilities include the National Archives II, the Academy of Leadership, the Center for Agricultural Biotechnology, the Astronomy Observatory, the Center for Young Children, the Center of Entrepreneurship, the Engineering Wind Tunnel, the Fire and Rescue Institute, the Institute for Systems Research, a Performing Arts Center, the Space Systems Laboratory, and the Superconductivity Research Center.

A state-of-the-art computer science center and dozens of laboratories across the campus hold more than 800 computer terminals for student use. All residence hall rooms have high-speed (10 MB) Ethernet connections to the Campus Data Network and to the Internet, Web, and e-mail. Seven campus libraries contain 3 million books, 5.4 million microfilm units, 166,000 audiovisual materials, and subscriptions to 30,000 periodicals.

Costs

For the 2007–08 academic year, undergraduate tuition and fees were $7969 for Maryland residents and $22,208 for out-of-state residents. Room and board costs were approximately $8854 for the academic year.

Financial Aid

An array of financial aid programs, including scholarships, grants, loans, and student employment opportunities, are available to undergraduates. To be considered for maximum need-based financial aid, students must submit the completed FAFSA to the FAFSA processor in time for receipt and acceptance by the University's February 15 priority financial aid deadline. The University proudly offers several merit scholarships for academically and creatively talented students; approximately $4 million per year is awarded. To be considered for most merit scholarships, an application for admission must be submitted by December 1. Last year, 68 percent of full-time students who applied for financial aid received it and were awarded an average of $7300.

Faculty

Maryland has a full-time teaching faculty of 2,766 and a part-time teaching faculty of 825 members. Ninety percent hold a Ph.D. or terminal degree in their fields. Faculty honors recipients include Fulbright Scholars, Guggenheim Fellows, NSF Presidential Young Investigators, Sloan Fellows, and members of the National Academy of Sciences and the American Academy of Arts and Sciences. The average class size is 31; the student-faculty ratio is 14:1.

Student Government

Maryland students constitute a self-governing student body, of which every undergraduate is a member. The Student Government Association (SGA) is an integral part of the University's shared governance and regularly provides input and feedback to the University president, campus senate, and state legislature. Student leaders—both executive and legislative—are elected each fall in a multiparty election and are responsible for allocating more than $1 million to student organizations. The SGA also provides funding to a student legal aid office and student entertainment productions. In addition, the students are represented on the University System of Maryland Board of Regents by a student member.

Admission Requirements

The University of Maryland seeks to enroll students who demonstrate that they have potential for academic success and who, the University believes, will help build a talented, diverse, and interesting entering class. Admission to the University of Maryland is competitive. Each year nearly 25,000 applications are received for a fall freshman class of approximately 4,200. Transfer applications are received from approximately 7,500 students, of whom Maryland enrolls 2,100 per year.

Academic potential of freshmen is assessed primarily by examination of high school course work and SAT or ACT scores. All entering freshmen must have completed a minimum of 4 years of English; 3 years of social studies or history; 3 years of mathematics courses (4 years is recommended), including 2 years of algebra and 1 year of geometry; 2 years of a foreign language; and 2 years of science that involves laboratory work. Most successful applicants have also completed several honors and advanced courses during high school. The holistic review includes an assessment of an essay, leadership and extracurricular activities, honors and awards, and counselor and teacher recommendations. Transfer students are assessed primarily by examination of previously completed college-level work.

According to the most recent profile of the enrolled freshmen class, the middle 50 percent have a combined SAT score between 1240 and 1380, have an average high school record of As and Bs, and have taken honors and AP courses.

Application and Information

Applications for fall freshman admission are due by January 20. Students are encouraged to apply by Maryland's priority application deadline of December 1 for best consideration for admission, merit-based scholarships, and invitation to University Honors or College Park Scholars. The spring freshman application deadline is December 1. Applications for fall transfer admission are due by June 1; for the spring semester, November 15. International students and students with any foreign academic records have earlier deadlines.

For application forms and further information about the University of Maryland, students should contact:

Office of Undergraduate Admissions
University of Maryland
Mitchell Building
College Park, Maryland 20742-5235
Phone: 301-314-8385
800-422-5867 (toll-free)
Fax: 301-314-9693
E-mail: um-admit@umd.edu
Web site: http://www.uga.umd.edu

VILLA JULIE COLLEGE

STEVENSON AND OWINGS MILLS, MARYLAND

The College

Villa Julie College (VJC) is a coeducational, independent institution dedicated to providing its 3,000 undergraduate and graduate students with a career-focused liberal arts education. Individual attention from faculty members, extensive career preparation gained through real-world training, and two ideal locations just north of Baltimore, Maryland, in Stevenson and Owings Mills, make the College truly unique.

At Villa Julie, academic quality is viewed as a personalized education that fosters intellectual growth and prepares students to thrive in the working world after graduation. With a student-faculty ratio of 13:1, it is easy to understand why students often site the congenial rapport with faculty members as one of the College's strong points.

Villa Julie College has developed a unique adjunct to its liberal arts, technology, and science programs, an approach known as Career Architecture℠. The process begins in the freshman year with each student developing a vision of personal success. There is support campuswide from the Career Services (Career HQ) team and faculty and staff members who collaborate and care about each student's growth and accomplishments. The success of Career Architecture is reflected by the success of VJC students. During the past five years, on average, 97 percent of Villa Julie students have acquired jobs or gone on to further their education within six months of graduation.

At VJC, students enjoy more than thirty clubs and organizations, multiple honor societies, and NCAA Division III athletics. The following sports are offered: men's and women's basketball, cross-country, golf, indoor track, lacrosse, soccer, tennis, and volleyball; men's baseball; and women's field hockey and softball. Cheerleading, dance, and intramural sports are also extremely popular.

In addition to its undergraduate programs, the College offers the following master's degree programs: advanced information technologies, business and technology management, forensic science, and forensic studies.

Location

Villa Julie College has two beautiful campuses located just north of Baltimore, in Stevenson and Owings Mills, Maryland. Students, faculty and staff members, and visitors enjoy the best of both worlds—the history and beauty of a rural campus (VJC–Stevenson) and the convenience and liveliness of a more urban location (VJC–Owings Mills). Classes are held on both campuses, and the College provides a free shuttle service that runs between these locations.

Villa Julie's original 60-acre Stevenson campus is nestled in the scenic Greenspring Valley, surrounded by horse farms and estate homes, just 12 miles from the attractions of downtown Baltimore.

Located just 6 miles from the Stevenson campus, VJC–Owings Mills offers the utmost in college living and learning. From spacious student apartments and suites to modern classrooms and study lounges, a newly renovated athletic facility, a brand-new dining and student center, and a 10,000-square-foot community center, VJC–Owings Mills is a thriving center of student activity.

Majors and Degrees

Villa Julie College offers the following bachelor's degree programs: accounting; applied mathematics; biology; biotechnology; business administration; business communications; business information systems; chemistry; computer information systems; early childhood education: liberal arts and technology; elementary education: liberal arts and technology; English language and literature; film, video, and theater; human services; interdisciplinary studies; medical technology; nursing; nursing: RN to B.S.; paralegal studies; psychology; public history; and visual communication design.

Villa Julie's B.S. to M.S. degree programs give students the option of earning both a bachelor's and a master's degree in as few as five years. Graduate study begins in the spring semester of the junior year and runs concurrently with undergraduate work until the end of the spring semester of the senior year. All subsequent course work is at the graduate level.

Academic Programs

At VJC, academic quality is regarded as a personalized curriculum that prepares students to enter the working world with the knowledge and skills that employers value. VJC infuses the traditional liberal arts education with a distinct career focus. The College's goal is to offer a synthesis of the liberal arts, current technology, and career preparation in order to prepare students for employment, graduate study, and productive involvement in today's world.

Academic Facilities

From recent enhancements to the Stevenson campus to brand-new facilities at VJC–Owings Mills, the College provides modern facilities that serve the needs of all students.

VJC–Stevenson includes more than 100,000 square feet of facilities that include a 350-seat theater, multiple computer labs and classrooms, video and graphic studios and suites, science laboratories, a student union, and athletic facilities. Each classroom and laboratory on the campus is capable of multimedia projection and computer-assisted learning.

Also at VJC–Stevenson is the Verizon Center for Excellence in Teaching and Learning. The center comprises classrooms equipped with technology that accommodates distance learning via computer transmission.

VJC–Owings Mills hosts the College's newest facilities, including an expansive student center that features an impressive dining hall, a 10,000-square-foot community center, a newly renovated athletic complex, multiple classrooms and study spaces, a fitness center, and additional athletic fields. The College's School of Business is scheduled to open for the fall 2008 semester.

The College's library has an extensive collection of more than 100,000 printed volumes, periodicals, videotapes and audiotapes, CDs, and microfilm and microfiche selections and an interlibrary loan consortium. In addition to the electronic databases it owns, the library has access to thousands of outside databases, such as LexisNexis Academic Universe, WESTLAW, Dialog, and Dow Jones News Retrieval.

Costs

Villa Julie is among the most affordable private colleges in the state of Maryland. For the 2007–08 academic year, tuition and fees for full-time students were $17,944. Part-time tuition and fees were $435 per credit hour, plus a $75 registration and technology fee per semester. Residential expenses range from $5900 to $7150 per year. The College also offers several meal-plan packages, priced at about $3145 per year.

Financial Aid

Villa Julie College offers financial assistance to qualified students in the form of grants, scholarships, loans, student employment, and a special payment plan. On average, approximately 75 percent of the College's students receive some form of financial assistance. The College has a generous scholarship program that grants awards based on academic merit. VJC participates in all major federal aid programs as well as all Maryland state programs. Applicants are required to file the Free Application for Federal Student Aid (FAFSA). The priority deadline for filing is February 15.

Faculty

The faculty at Villa Julie College is first and foremost a teaching faculty. The College's 13:1 student-teacher ratio demonstrates the institutional emphasis on a personalized education. A majority of the full-time faculty members have the doctoral or terminal degree offered in their field, and a significant number are widely published. In addition, many are concurrently employed as professional specialists in their fields.

Student Government

The Student Government Association (SGA) facilitates an environment that encourages students to express their thoughts and opinions concerning Villa Julie College, its policies, and sponsored activities. The SGA serves as the principal governing body of all campus clubs and activities. In conjunction with the Office of Student Affairs, the SGA organizes an array of campuswide events that promote the social aspects of college life. Each student at Villa Julie is welcome and encouraged to participate in all SGA functions.

Admission Requirements

Applications for admission to Villa Julie College are reviewed on a rolling basis. In evaluating each applicant, the College considers the applicant's high school academic record, SAT (critical reading and math) or ACT scores, recommendations, writing sample, and any other special talents or personal interests. Admission to the College is determined without regard for race, color, sex, religion, national or ethnic origin, or handicap. VJC complies with all applicable laws and federal regulations regarding discrimination and accessibility on the condition of handicap, age, veteran status, or otherwise.

Application and Information

Applications for admission to undergraduate programs should be received by March 1 for fall-semester entry and October 1 for spring-semester entry. Scholarship consideration adheres to earlier deadlines. Applications received after these dates are reviewed on a space-available basis. Students applying to the College as freshmen must submit official high school transcripts, standardized test scores, the Counselor Recommendation Form, typed responses to the short answer questions listed on the application, and a $25 nonrefundable application fee. The application fee is waived for all students who apply online (http://www.vjc.edu). Transfer students must submit official transcripts from all colleges or universities they have attended and should contact the Transfer Coordinator to discuss additional credential requirements.

For further information and application forms, students should contact:

Admissions Office
Garrison Hall
Villa Julie College–Owings Mills
10945 Boulevard Circle
Owings Mills, Maryland 21117-7804
Phone: 410-486-7001
877-GO-TO-VJC (877-468-6852) (toll-free)
Fax: 443-352-4440
E-mail: admissions@mail.vjc.edu
Web site: http://www.vjc.edu/admissions

A view of the campus at Villa Julie College.

COLLEGE DATA CENTER • MARYLAND

WASHINGTON COLLEGE

CHESTERTOWN, MARYLAND

The College

Founded in 1782, Washington College is the tenth-oldest college in the United States. George Washington, for whom the College was named, was an early benefactor and member of the College's Board of Visitors and Governors. Today, the College is one of the few nationally recognized selective liberal arts institutions with an enrollment of fewer than 1,350 students. The intimacy of a small-college environment, the tradition of a challenging liberal arts curriculum, and the relaxed informality characteristic of the Chesapeake Bay region continue to exert their influence on the College and all who come to it.

The current enrollment is 1,300 men and women. Although most students come from the Northeast, international students and students from other regions of the country are enrolled in numbers sufficient to add geographic diversity to the student body. Eighty percent of all students live in residences located on the 120-acre campus; special interest housing is available for students interested in science, foreign languages, international studies, creative arts, and Greek organizations.

The College enjoys a high participation rate in intramural sports, in the performing arts, and in student publications, community service clubs, recreational activities, and social organizations. The Division III intercollegiate program offers fifteen varsity sports, including baseball, basketball, lacrosse, rowing, soccer, swimming, and tennis for men and basketball, field hockey, lacrosse, rowing, sailing, softball, swimming, tennis, and volleyball for women.

Location

Chestertown, a community of 4,000 people, is a popular port-of-call for Chesapeake Bay boaters, outdoors enthusiasts, and tourists on day trips from nearby Philadelphia, Baltimore, and Washington, D.C. The center of this eighteenth-century river town, with its historic district, shops, and restaurants, is a 5-minute walk from campus. The "town-gown" relationship is excellent.

Majors and Degrees

The Bachelor of Arts is awarded in American studies, anthropology, art, business management, drama, economics, English, environmental studies, French, German, history, humanities, international studies, mathematics, music, philosophy, political science, psychology, sociology, and Spanish. The Bachelor of Science is awarded in biology, chemistry, physics, and psychology.

Washington College also offers certification programs in elementary and secondary education. Preprofessional programs in dentistry, medicine, or veterinary medicine may be developed within a major in the natural sciences; a preprofessional program in law is also available. A 3-2 dual-degree program in engineering with the University of Maryland, a 3-2 dual-degree program in nursing with Johns Hopkins University, and a 3-4 dual-degree program in pharmacy with the University of Maryland are also offered.

Academic Programs

The College's four-course plan is intended to broaden and deepen a student's education by providing for the intensive study of a limited number of subjects and by encouraging individual responsibility for learning. General education requirements include two freshman seminars and ten semester courses chosen from the following categories: social science, natural science, humanities, fine arts, quantitative studies, and foreign language. Candidates for a degree must satisfactorily complete thirty-two semester courses and must fulfill the senior obligation (for example, a comprehensive examination or thesis).

Washington College offers a nationally renowned creative writing program and awards the prestigious Sophie Kerr Prize every year to the graduating senior who shows the most promise for a career in literary endeavors.

Successful scores (4 or 5) on Advanced Placement examinations can provide exemption from distribution requirements. With the aid of a faculty adviser, students can construct their own major fields of study in some areas or pursue independent study for course credit.

Off-Campus Programs

At Washington College, students have multiple opportunities to become engaged in experiences designed to enhance their learning outside the classroom. The College's proximity to the major cities of Baltimore, Philadelphia, and Washington, D.C., as well as the Delmarva Peninsula, makes it possible for students to gain experience as members of premier governmental, commercial, scientific, and artistic organizations while undertaking internships, research, and participation in a variety of model programs. A study-abroad program is offered at thirty sites worldwide, including sites in England, France, Spain, Germany, Scotland, Mexico, and Japan.

Academic Facilities

The library, which has 200,000 volumes, more than 800 current periodical subscriptions, and extensive microfilm holdings, benefits from an efficient interlibrary loan system and an online card catalog. The new 45,000-square-foot John S. Toll Science Center provides teaching laboratories, research laboratories, and laboratory-support space for science majors. Installation of an artificial playing surface and the construction of the new Roy Kirby Stadium are scheduled to be completed in the spring of 2006. The Gibson Fine Arts Center is scheduled to undergo a $15-million expansion and renovation beginning in the summer of 2006. Full facilities for art majors are located in the Constance S. Larrabee Creative Art Center.

Costs

Tuition and fees for 2007–08 were $32,160 and room and board were $6790, making a total of $38,950. Expenses, including books and transportation, usually range from $600 to $1000 annually.

Financial Aid

Washington College offers financial assistance to approximately 80 percent of its student body. Awards are based on need and academic performance. Financial aid includes scholarships, grants, loans, and jobs. The College participates in the Federal Perkins Loan Program, the Federal Stafford Student Loan Program, and the Federal Work-Study Program. Federal Pell Grants and Federal Supplemental Educational Opportunity Grants are applicable to Washington College. In addition, financial assistance from the Maryland scholarship program and other state programs can be applied to expenses at the College.

Members of the National Honor Society and Cum Laude Society who are admitted to Washington College are awarded $40,000 academic scholarships ($10,000 annually for four years). Other academic scholarships ranging in value from $5000 to $13,750 are offered without regard to financial need.

To be eligible for financial assistance, applicants should file the FAFSA by February 15. An application for admission, with all supporting credentials, should be received by February 15 to establish eligibility. Students interested in Federal Pell Grant assistance or in-state scholarship programs must apply directly to the program concerned.

Faculty

Ninety-five percent of the more than 100 full-time faculty members hold either a doctoral degree or a terminal degree in their discipline. Faculty members engage in professional research and publication but emphasize teaching. Along with performing their classroom duties, faculty members serve as advisers to individuals and student groups. No classes are taught by graduate assistants. Faculty participation in student and College affairs reflects the strong sense of community that characterizes Washington College.

Student Government

The Student Government Association (SGA) is a significant part of the College community. In addition to coordinating social activities, the SGA plays an active role in academic affairs. Students elected by the SGA are voting members of College committees and attend faculty and board meetings.

Admission Requirements

High school students should complete a college-preparatory program, including a minimum of 4 years of English, 4 of social studies, 3 of mathematics, 3 of science, and 2 of a foreign language. SAT or ACT scores and one teacher recommendation are also required. While interviews are not usually required for admission, interested students are strongly encouraged to visit the campus. Both interviews and campus tours are available by appointment on weekdays throughout the year and on selected Saturdays during the fall semester.

Members of the College admission staff visit high schools throughout the United States, seeking above-average students with solid academic backgrounds. There are no quotas based on sex, and there are no religious, geographic, or ethnic restrictions. Indeed, the College seeks the most diverse student body possible, realizing that such diversity is an important aspect of the academic community.

Transfer students are accepted with or without the A.A. degree, and applicants with above-average records are encouraged to apply.

Application and Information

The application, a $45 fee, the high school transcript (and college transcript, for transfer applicants), scores on the SAT or ACT, and one teacher recommendation are required. Applications for early decision must be received by November 15, and candidates are notified of the admission decision by December 15. For regular admission, forms must be submitted prior to February 15. Regular decision candidates are notified of the admission decision on a rolling basis between January 15 and March 1. Applicants for financial assistance must complete the procedures outlined in the Financial Aid section.

Further information and application forms are available from:

Office of Admissions
Washington College
300 Washington Avenue
Chestertown, Maryland 21620-1197
Phone: 410-778-7700
800-422-1782 (toll-free)
E-mail: adm.off@washcoll.edu
Web site: http://www.washcoll.edu

Casey Academic Center at Washington College.

financial assistance from the Maryland scholarship program and other state programs can be applied to expenses at the College.

Members of the National Honor Society and Cum Laude Society who are admitted to Washington College are awarded $40,000 academic scholarships ($10,000 annually for four years). Other academic scholarships ranging in value from $5000 to $13,750 are offered without regard to financial need.

To be eligible for financial assistance, applicants should file the FAFSA by February 15. An application for admission, with all supporting credentials, should be received by February 15 to establish eligibility. Students interested in Federal Pell Grant assistance or in state scholarship programs must apply directly to the program concerned.

Faculty

Ninety-five percent of the more than 100 full-time faculty members hold either a doctoral degree or a terminal degree in their discipline. Faculty members engage in professional research and publication but emphasize teaching. Along with performing their classroom duties, faculty members serve as advisers to individuals and student groups. No classes are taught by graduate assistants. Faculty participation in student and College affairs reflects the strong sense of community that characterizes Washington College.

Student Government

The Student Government Association (SGA) is a significant part of the College community. In addition to coordinating social activities, the SGA plays an active role in academic affairs. Students elected by the SGA are voting members of College committees and attend faculty and board meetings.

Admission Requirements

High school students should complete a college-preparatory program, including a minimum of 4 years of English, 4 of social studies, 3 of mathematics, 3 of science, and 2 of a foreign language. SAT or ACT scores and one teacher recommendation are also required. While interviews are not usually required for admission, interested students are strongly encouraged to visit the campus. Both interviews and campus tours are available by appointment on weekdays throughout the year and on selected Saturdays during the fall semester.

Members of the College admission staff visit high schools throughout the United States, seeking above-average students with solid academic backgrounds. There are no quotas based on sex, and there are no religious, geographic, or ethnic restrictions. Indeed, the College seeks the most diverse student body possible, realizing that such diversity is an important aspect of the academic community.

Transfer students are accepted with or without the A.A. degree, and applicants with above-average records are encouraged to apply.

Application and Information

The application, a $45 fee, the high school transcript (and college transcript for transfer applicants), scores on the SAT or ACT, and one teacher recommendation are required. Applications for early decision must be received by November 15, and candidates are notified of the admission decision by December 15. For regular admission, forms must be submitted prior to February 15. Regular decision candidates are notified of the admission decision on a rolling basis between January 15 and March 1. Applicants for financial assistance must complete the procedures outlined in the Financial Aid section.

Further information and application forms are available from:

Office of Admissions
Washington College
300 Washington Avenue
Chestertown, Maryland 21620-1197
Phone: 410-778-7700
800-422-1782 (toll-free)
E-mail: adm.off@washcoll.edu
Web site: http://www.washcoll.edu

Casey Academic Center at Washington College.

MASSACHUSETTS

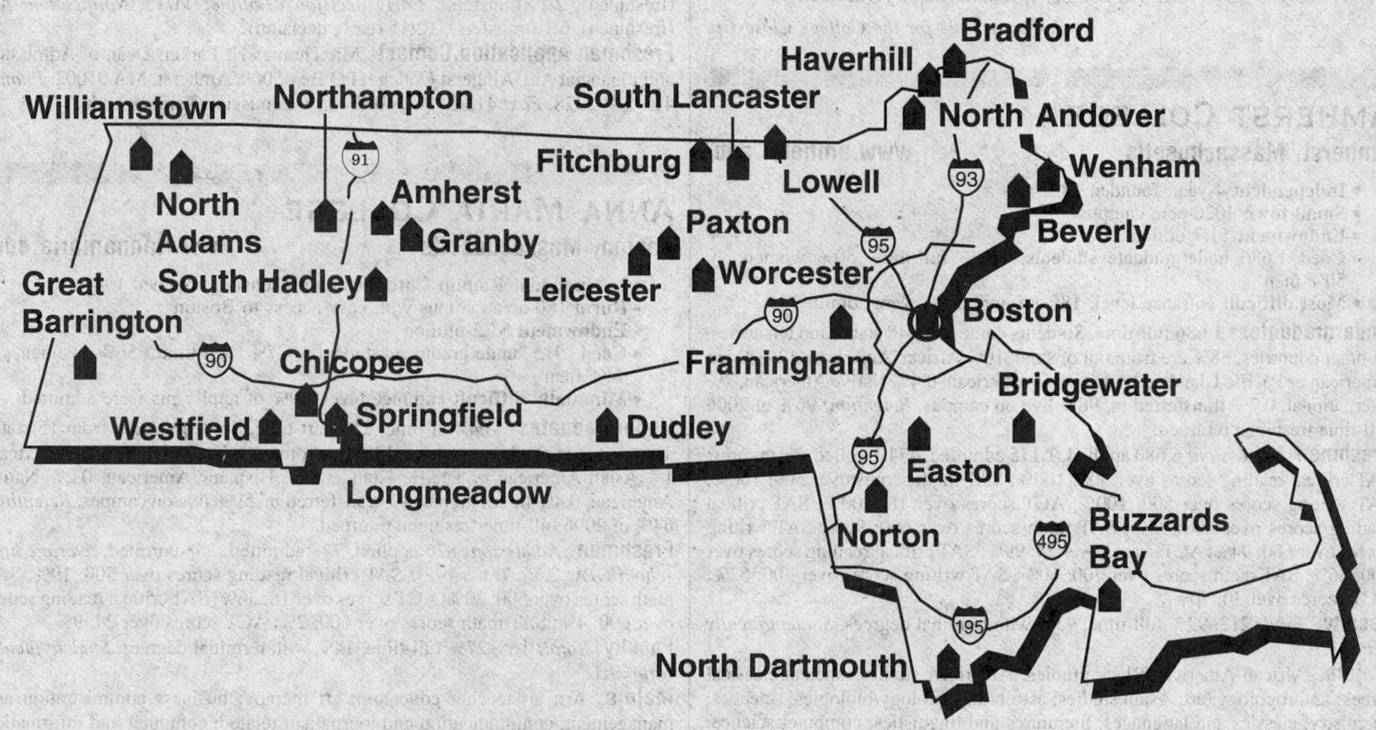

The Boston area includes the towns of Babson Park, Brighton, Brookline, Chestnut Hill, Cambridge, Medford, Milton, Newton, Newton Centre, Quincy, Salem, Waltham, Wellesley, and Weston.

American International College

Springfield, Massachusetts **www.aic.edu/**

Freshman Application Contact Mr. Peter Miller, Dean of Admissions, American International College, 1000 State Street, Springfield, MA 01109-3189. *Phone:* 413-205-3201. *Fax:* 413-205-3051. *E-mail:* inquiry@acad.aic.edu.

See page 1194 for the College Close-Up.

Amherst College

Amherst, Massachusetts **www.amherst.edu/**

- **Independent** 4-year, founded 1821
- **Small-town** 1020-acre campus
- **Endowment** $1.7 billion
- **Coed** 1,686 undergraduate students, 100% full-time, 50% women, 50% men
- **Most difficult** entrance level, 18% of applicants were admitted

Undergraduates 1,686 full-time. Students come from 48 states and territories, 41 other countries, 88% are from out of state, 10% African American, 12% Asian American or Pacific Islander, 9% Hispanic American, 0.4% Native American, 7% international, 0.7% transferred in, 98% live on campus. *Retention:* 96% of 2006 full-time freshmen returned.

Freshmen *Admission:* 6,680 applied, 1,175 admitted, 474 enrolled. *Test scores:* SAT critical reading scores over 500: 100%; SAT math scores over 500: 100%; SAT writing scores over 500: 100%; ACT scores over 18: 100%; SAT critical reading scores over 600: 95%; SAT math scores over 600: 92%; SAT writing scores over 600: 94%; ACT scores over 24: 99%; SAT critical reading scores over 700: 66%; SAT math scores over 700: 60%; SAT writing scores over 700: 62%; ACT scores over 30: 70%.

Faculty *Total:* 212, 92% full-time, 93% with terminal degrees. *Student/faculty ratio:* 8:1.

Majors African-American/Black studies; American studies; ancient/classical Greek; anthropology; art; Asian studies; astronomy; biology/biological sciences; chemistry; classics and languages, literatures and linguistics; computer science; dance; dramatic/theater arts; economics; English; European studies; fine/studio arts; French; geology/earth science; German; history; interdisciplinary studies; Latin; legal studies; mathematics; music; neuroscience; philosophy; physics; political science and government; psychology; religious studies; Russian; sociology; Spanish; women's studies.

Academics *Calendar:* semesters. *Degree:* bachelor's. *Special study options:* double majors, honors programs, independent study, off-campus study, student-designed majors, study abroad.

Computers on Campus 182 computers/terminals are available on campus for general student use. Students can access the following: campus intranet, computer help desk, free student e-mail accounts, online (class) grades, online (class) schedules. Campuswide network is available. 100% of college-owned or -operated housing units are wired for high-speed Internet access. Wireless service is available via entire campus.

Student Life *Housing:* on-campus residence required for freshman year. *Options:* coed, cooperative, disabled students. Campus housing is university owned. Freshman campus housing is guaranteed. *Activities and organizations:* drama/theater group, student-run newspaper, radio station, choral group, choral groups, WAMH (campus radio station), OUTREACH (community service), literary magazines, The Amherst Student (school newspaper). *Campus security:* 24-hour emergency response devices and patrols, student patrols, late-night transport/escort service, controlled dormitory access. *Student services:* health clinic, personal/psychological counseling, women's center.

Athletics Member NCAA. All Division III. *Intercollegiate sports:* baseball M, basketball M/W, crew M (c)/W (c), cross-country running M/W, equestrian sports M (c)/W (c), fencing M (c)/W (c), field hockey W, football M, golf M/W, ice hockey M/W, lacrosse M/W, rugby M (c)/W (c), sailing M (c)/W (c), skiing (downhill) M (c)/W (c), soccer M/W, softball W, squash M/W, swimming and diving M/W, tennis M/W, track and field M/W, ultimate Frisbee M (c)/W (c), volleyball M (c)/W, water polo M (c)/W (c). *Intramural sports:* badminton M/W, basketball M/W, golf M/W, ice hockey M/W, soccer M/W, softball M/W, squash M/W, table tennis M/W, tennis M/W, track and field M/W, volleyball M/W.

Standardized Tests *Required:* SAT and SAT Subject Tests or ACT (for admission).

Costs (2007–08) *Comprehensive fee:* $45,652 includes full-time tuition ($35,580), mandatory fees ($652), and room and board ($9420). *College room only:* $5050. *Payment plans:* installment, deferred payment.

Financial Aid Of all full-time matriculated undergraduates who enrolled in 2007, 1,000 applied for aid, 874 were judged to have need, 873 had their need fully met. 529 Federal Work-Study jobs (averaging $1563). 171 state and other part-time jobs (averaging $1549). *Average percent of need met:* 100%. *Average financial aid package:* $35,055. *Average need-based loan:* $2932. *Average need-based gift aid:* $33,371. *Average indebtedness upon graduation:* $11,655.

Applying *Options:* electronic application, early admission, early decision, deferred entrance. *Application fee:* $60. *Required:* essay or personal statement, high school transcript, 3 letters of recommendation. *Application deadlines:* 1/1 (freshmen), 2/1 (transfers). *Early decision deadline:* 11/15. *Notification:* 4/5 (freshmen), 6/1 (transfers), 12/15 (early decision).

Freshman Application Contact Mr. Thomas H. Parker, Dean of Admission and Financial Aid, Amherst College, PO Box 5000, Amherst, MA 01002. *Phone:* 413-542-2328. *Fax:* 413-542-2040. *E-mail:* admission@amherst.edu.

Anna Maria College

Paxton, Massachusetts **www.annamaria.edu/**

- **Independent Roman Catholic** comprehensive, founded 1946
- **Rural** 180-acre campus with easy access to Boston
- **Endowment** $1.5 million
- **Coed** 915 undergraduate students, 77% full-time, 56% women, 44% men
- **Minimally difficult** entrance level, 89% of applicants were admitted

Undergraduates 704 full-time, 211 part-time. Students come from 15 states and territories, 2 other countries, 13% are from out of state, 5% African American, 1% Asian American or Pacific Islander, 4% Hispanic American, 0.2% Native American, 0.4% international, 4% transferred in, 59% live on campus. *Retention:* 64% of 2006 full-time freshmen returned.

Freshmen *Admission:* 876 applied, 778 admitted, 258 enrolled. *Average high school GPA:* 2.56. *Test scores:* SAT critical reading scores over 500: 19%; SAT math scores over 500: 20%; ACT scores over 18: 36%; SAT critical reading scores over 600: 4%; SAT math scores over 600: 2%; ACT scores over 24: 9%.

Faculty *Total:* 165, 27% full-time, 14% with terminal degrees. *Student/faculty ratio:* 9:1.

Majors Art; art teacher education; art therapy; business administration and management; communication and journalism related; computer and information sciences; criminal justice/safety; English; English/language arts teacher education; environmental science; fire science; graphic design; health services/allied health/health sciences; history; history teacher education; kindergarten/preschool education; legal assistant/paralegal; legal professions and studies related; liberal arts and sciences/liberal studies; management information systems; multi-/interdisciplinary studies related; music; music performance; music teacher education; music therapy; nursing (registered nurse training); political science and government; psychology; public policy analysis; social sciences related; social work; sociology; Spanish; sport and fitness administration/management; theology.

Academics *Calendar:* semesters. *Degrees:* certificates, associate, bachelor's, master's, post-master's, and postbachelor's certificates. *Special study options:* academic remediation for entering students, accelerated degree program, adult/continuing education programs, advanced placement credit, cooperative education, double majors, independent study, internships, off-campus study, part-time degree program, services for LD students, student-designed majors, study abroad, summer session for credit. *ROTC:* Air Force (c).

Computers on Campus 53 computers/terminals are available on campus for general student use. Students can access the following: campus intranet, computer help desk, free student e-mail accounts, online (class) grades, online (class) schedules, student account information. Campuswide network is available. 100% of college-owned or -operated housing units are wired for high-speed Internet access. Wireless service is available via entire campus.

Student Life *Housing options:* coed, disabled students. Campus housing is university owned. Freshman campus housing is guaranteed. *Activities and organizations:* drama/theater group, choral group, Student Government Association, Fire Science, Chamber Choir, Alana, Alternate Spring Break. *Campus security:* 24-hour emergency response devices and patrols, late-night transport/escort service, controlled dormitory access. *Student services:* health clinic, personal/psychological counseling.

Athletics Member NCAA. All Division III. *Intercollegiate sports:* baseball M, basketball M/W, cross-country running M, field hockey W, golf M, soccer M/W, softball W, volleyball W. *Intramural sports:* basketball M, football M, volleyball M/W.

Standardized Tests *Required:* SAT or ACT (for admission).

Costs (2007–08) *Comprehensive fee:* $33,532 includes full-time tuition ($22,360), mandatory fees ($2257), and room and board ($8915). Full-time tuition and fees vary according to program. Part-time tuition: $745 per credit hour. Part-time tuition and fees vary according to class time, course load, and program.

Room and board: Room and board charges vary according to board plan. *Payment plan:* installment. *Waivers:* senior citizens and employees or children of employees.

Financial Aid Of all full-time matriculated undergraduates who enrolled in 2007, 645 applied for aid, 590 were judged to have need, 65 had their need fully met. 107 Federal Work-Study jobs (averaging $1263). In 2007, 114 non-need-based awards were made. *Average percent of need met:* 65%. *Average financial aid package:* $16,473. *Average need-based loan:* $4717. *Average need-based gift aid:* $10,876. *Average non-need-based aid:* $6936. *Average indebtedness upon graduation:* $24,247.

Applying *Options:* electronic application, deferred entrance. *Application fee:* $40. *Required:* essay or personal statement, high school transcript, minimum 2.0 GPA, 1 letter of recommendation. *Required for some:* audition for music programs, portfolio for art programs. *Recommended:* interview. *Application deadlines:* rolling (freshmen), rolling (transfers). *Notification:* continuous (freshmen), continuous (transfers).

Freshman Application Contact Mr. Tim Donahue, Director of Recruitment and Admission, Anna Maria College, 50 Sunset Lane, Box 115, Paxton, MA 01612-1198. *Phone:* 508-849-3360. *Toll-free phone:* 800-344-4586 Ext. 360. *Fax:* 508-849-3362. *E-mail:* admission@annamaria.edu.

See page 1196 for the College Close-Up.

THE ART INSTITUTE OF BOSTON AT LESLEY UNIVERSITY

Boston, Massachusetts www.aiboston.edu/

- **Independent** comprehensive, founded 1912, part of Education Management Corporation, administratively affiliated with Lesley University
- **Urban** 1-acre campus
- **Endowment** $45.6 million
- **Coed** 1,229 undergraduate students, 94% full-time, 75% women, 25% men
- **Moderately difficult** entrance level, 86% of applicants were admitted

Undergraduates 1,160 full-time, 69 part-time. Students come from 56 states and territories, 24 other countries, 42% are from out of state, 5% African American, 4% Asian American or Pacific Islander, 5% Hispanic American, 0.4% Native American, 2% international, 9% transferred in, 48% live on campus. *Retention:* 70% of 2006 full-time freshmen returned.

Freshmen *Admission:* 1,568 applied, 1,342 admitted, 343 enrolled. *Average high school GPA:* 3.0. *Test scores:* SAT critical reading scores over 500: 71%; SAT math scores over 500: 58%; SAT writing scores over 500: 66%; ACT scores over 18: 82%; SAT critical reading scores over 600: 27%; SAT math scores over 600: 16%; SAT writing scores over 600: 21%; ACT scores over 24: 49%; SAT critical reading scores over 700: 4%; SAT math scores over 700: 1%; SAT writing scores over 700: 2%; ACT scores over 30: 7%.

Faculty *Total:* 245, 29% full-time, 39% with terminal degrees. *Student/faculty ratio:* 9:1.

Majors Fine/studio arts; graphic design; illustration; photography.

Academics *Calendar:* semesters. *Degrees:* diplomas, bachelor's, master's, and postbachelor's certificates. *Special study options:* academic remediation for entering students, accelerated degree program, adult/continuing education programs, advanced placement credit, distance learning, double majors, English as a second language, external degree program, freshman honors college, honors programs, independent study, internships, off-campus study, part-time degree program, services for LD students, student-designed majors, study abroad, summer session for credit.

Computers on Campus 175 computers/terminals are available on campus for general student use. Students can access the following: free student e-mail accounts, online (class) registration, graphics programs, software applications. Campuswide network is available. 100% of college-owned or -operated housing units are wired for high-speed Internet access. Wireless service is available via classrooms, student centers.

Student Life *Housing options:* coed, women-only. Campus housing is university owned and leased by the school. Freshman applicants given priority for college housing. *Activities and organizations:* drama/theater group, choral group, Peer Advisors, Ski Club, International Student Association, Student Gallery Committee, Literary Journal. *Campus security:* 24-hour emergency response devices and patrols, late-night transport/escort service, controlled dormitory access, lighted walkways. *Student services:* health clinic, personal/psychological counseling.

Athletics Member NCAA. All Division III. *Intercollegiate sports:* basketball M/W, crew W, cross-country running M/W, soccer M/W, softball W, volleyball M/W. *Intramural sports:* swimming and diving M/W, tennis M.

Standardized Tests *Required:* SAT or ACT (for admission).

Costs (2008–09) *Comprehensive fee:* $37,635 includes full-time tuition ($24,825), mandatory fees ($810), and room and board ($12,000). *College room only:* $7500.

Financial Aid Of all full-time matriculated undergraduates who enrolled in 2007, 1,069 applied for aid, 802 were judged to have need, 23 had their need fully met. 225 Federal Work-Study jobs (averaging $1800). 150 state and other part-time jobs (averaging $1500). In 2007, 210 non-need-based awards were made. *Average percent of need met:* 70%. *Average financial aid package:* $17,634. *Average need-based loan:* $3801. *Average need-based gift aid:* $13,833. *Average non-need-based aid:* $7743. *Average indebtedness upon graduation:* $15,000.

Applying *Options:* electronic application, early action, deferred entrance. *Application fee:* $40. *Required:* essay or personal statement, high school transcript, 3 letters of recommendation, interview, portfolio. *Application deadlines:* rolling (freshmen), rolling (transfers). *Notification:* continuous (freshmen), continuous (transfers).

Director of Admissions Bob Gielow, Director of Admission, The Art Institute of Boston at Lesley University, 700 Beacon Street, Boston, MA 02215-2598. *Phone:* 617-585-6710. *Toll-free phone:* 800-773-0494. *E-mail:* aiboston@aiboston.edu.

See page 1198 for the College Close-Up.

ASSUMPTION COLLEGE

Worcester, Massachusetts www.assumption.edu/

- **Independent Roman Catholic** comprehensive, founded 1904
- **Suburban** 180-acre campus with easy access to Boston
- **Endowment** $68.9 million
- **Coed** 2,198 undergraduate students, 98% full-time, 59% women, 41% men
- **Moderately difficult** entrance level, 67% of applicants were admitted

Undergraduates 2,165 full-time, 33 part-time. Students come from 28 states and territories, 3 other countries, 31% are from out of state, 2% African American, 1% Asian American or Pacific Islander, 3% Hispanic American, 0.1% Native American, 0.4% international, 2% transferred in, 89% live on campus. *Retention:* 83% of 2006 full-time freshmen returned.

Freshmen *Admission:* 3,899 applied, 2,625 admitted, 598 enrolled. *Average high school GPA:* 3.39. *Test scores:* SAT critical reading scores over 500: 69%; SAT math scores over 500: 70%; ACT scores over 18: 96%; SAT critical reading scores over 600: 16%; SAT math scores over 600: 18%; ACT scores over 24: 31%; SAT critical reading scores over 700: 2%; SAT math scores over 700: 1%; ACT scores over 30: 1%.

Faculty *Total:* 223, 68% full-time, 80% with terminal degrees. *Student/faculty ratio:* 12:1.

Majors Accounting; art teacher education; biology/biological sciences; biology teacher education; business administration and management; chemistry; chemistry teacher education; classics and languages, literatures and linguistics; computer and information sciences; economics; elementary education; English; English/language arts teacher education; environmental science; foreign languages and literatures; French; French language teacher education; history; history teacher education; international business/trade/commerce; international/global studies; Italian; Latin American studies; marketing/marketing management; mathematics; mathematics teacher education; middle school education; molecular biology; music; organizational communication; philosophy; political science and government; psychology; rehabilitation and therapeutic professions related; science teacher education; secondary education; sociology; Spanish; Spanish language teacher education; theology; visual and performing arts.

Academics *Calendar:* semesters. *Degrees:* bachelor's, master's, post-master's, and postbachelor's certificates. *Special study options:* adult/continuing education programs, advanced placement credit, double majors, honors programs, independent study, internships, off-campus study, part-time degree program, services for LD students, student-designed majors, study abroad, summer session for credit. *ROTC:* Army (c), Air Force (c). *Unusual degree programs:* 3-2 engineering with Worcester Polytechnic Institute; special education, social rehabilitation counseling, school counseling, accounting.

Computers on Campus 275 computers/terminals and 1,020 ports are available on campus for general student use. Students can access the following: campus intranet, computer help desk, free student e-mail accounts, online (class) grades, online (class) registration, online (class) schedules. Campuswide network is available. 100% of college-owned or -operated housing units are wired for high-speed Internet access. Wireless service is available via classrooms, computer centers, computer labs, learning centers, libraries, student centers.

Student Life *Housing options:* coed, women-only, disabled students. Campus housing is university owned. Freshman campus housing is guaranteed. *Activities and organizations:* drama/theater group, student-run newspaper, television station, choral group, Volunteer Center, Campus Activities Board, student government, Campus Ministry, resident assistants. *Campus security:* 24-hour emergency response devices and patrols, student patrols, late-night transport/escort service, front gate security, well-lit pathways. *Student services:* health clinic, personal/psychological counseling.

Athletics Member NCAA. All Division II. *Intercollegiate sports:* baseball M, basketball M (s)/W (s), crew M/W, cross-country running M/W, field hockey W, football M, golf M, ice hockey M, lacrosse M/W, soccer M/W, softball W, swimming and diving W, tennis M/W, track and field M/W, volleyball W. *Intramural sports:* basketball M/W, football M, golf M/W, ice hockey M/W, racquetball M/W, soccer M/W, softball M/W, volleyball M/W.

Standardized Tests *Required:* SAT or ACT (for admission).

Costs (2007–08) *Comprehensive fee:* $33,462 includes full-time tuition ($27,320), mandatory fees ($165), and room and board ($5977). Full-time tuition and fees vary according to course load and reciprocity agreements. Part-time tuition: $911 per credit hour. Part-time tuition and fees vary according to course load. *Required fees:* $165 per year part-time. *College room only:* $3515. Room and board charges vary according to housing facility. *Payment plan:* installment. *Waivers:* minority students and employees or children of employees.

Financial Aid Of all full-time matriculated undergraduates who enrolled in 2007, 1,722 applied for aid, 1,511 were judged to have need, 297 had their need fully met. In 2007, 458 non-need-based awards were made. *Average percent of need met:* 74%. *Average financial aid package:* $17,915. *Average need-based loan:* $4372. *Average need-based gift aid:* $13,597. *Average non-need-based aid:* $14,886. *Average indebtedness upon graduation:* $32,900. *Financial aid deadline:* 2/1.

Applying *Options:* electronic application, early action, deferred entrance. *Application fee:* $50. *Required:* essay or personal statement, high school transcript, 1 letter of recommendation. *Recommended:* interview. *Application deadlines:* 2/15 (freshmen), 5/1 (transfers), 11/15 (early action). *Notification:* continuous until 5/1 (freshmen), continuous (transfers), 12/15 (early action).

Freshman Application Contact Ms. Kathleen Murphy, Dean of Enrollment, Assumption College, 500 Salisbury Street, Worcester, MA 01609-1296. *Phone:* 508-767-7110. *Toll-free phone:* 888-882-7786. *Fax:* 508-799-4412. *E-mail:* admiss@assumption.edu.

See page 1200 for the College Close-Up.

ATLANTIC UNION COLLEGE

South Lancaster, Massachusetts **www.auc.edu/**

- **Independent Seventh-day Adventist** comprehensive, founded 1882
- **Small-town** 314-acre campus with easy access to Boston
- **Endowment** $2.2 million
- **Coed** 496 undergraduate students, 83% full-time, 63% women, 37% men
- **Moderately difficult** entrance level, 43% of applicants were admitted

Undergraduates 410 full-time, 86 part-time. Students come from 15 states and territories, 22 other countries, 45% are from out of state, 45% African American, 3% Asian American or Pacific Islander, 17% Hispanic American, 10% transferred in, 68% live on campus. *Retention:* 48% of 2006 full-time freshmen returned.

Freshmen *Admission:* 456 applied, 198 admitted, 116 enrolled. *Average high school GPA:* 2.81. *Test scores:* SAT critical reading scores over 500: 20%; SAT math scores over 500: 9%; ACT scores over 18: 50%; SAT critical reading scores over 600: 6%; SAT math scores over 600: 3%.

Faculty *Total:* 61, 57% full-time, 46% with terminal degrees. *Student/faculty ratio:* 11:1.

Majors Accounting; adult and continuing education; art; biology/biological sciences; business administration and management; clinical laboratory science/medical technology; computer programming; computer science; divinity/ministry; education; elementary education; English; history; kindergarten/preschool education; music; music teacher education; natural sciences; nursing (registered nurse training); pre-dentistry studies; pre-law studies; pre-medical studies; preveterinary studies; psychology; religious/sacred music; religious studies; secondary education; theology.

Academics *Calendar:* semesters. *Degrees:* certificates, associate, bachelor's, master's, and postbachelor's certificates. *Special study options:* academic remediation for entering students, adult/continuing education programs, advanced placement credit, cooperative education, English as a second language, external degree program, freshman honors college, honors programs, internships, part-time degree program, study abroad, summer session for credit. *Unusual degree programs:* 3-2 engineering with Walla Walla College.

Computers on Campus 74 computers/terminals are available on campus for general student use. Students can access the following: free student e-mail accounts. Campuswide network is available.

Student Life *Housing:* on-campus residence required through senior year. *Options:* coed, men-only, women-only. Campus housing is university owned. Freshman campus housing is guaranteed. *Activities and organizations:* drama/theater group, student-run newspaper, choral group, Student Association, Black Christian Union, Choir, CHISPA (Hispanic group). *Campus security:* 24-hour patrols, late-night transport/escort service. *Student services:* health clinic, personal/psychological counseling.

Athletics *Intramural sports:* basketball M/W, football M/W, golf M/W, rock climbing M/W, skiing (downhill) M/W, soccer M/W, softball M/W, volleyball M/W.

Standardized Tests *Required:* SAT and SAT Subject Tests or ACT (for admission).

Costs (2007–08) *Comprehensive fee:* $22,640 includes full-time tuition ($16,080), mandatory fees ($1560), and room and board ($5000). Full-time tuition and fees vary according to program. Part-time tuition: $605 per credit. Part-time tuition and fees vary according to class time and program. No tuition increase for student's term of enrollment. *College room only:* $2600. Room and board charges vary according to board plan and housing facility. *Waivers:* senior citizens and employees or children of employees.

Financial Aid Of all full-time matriculated undergraduates who enrolled in 2007, 574 applied for aid, 509 were judged to have need, 47 had their need fully met. 381 Federal Work-Study jobs (averaging $2071). 75 state and other part-time jobs (averaging $2017). In 2007, 96 non-need-based awards were made. *Average percent of need met:* 51%. *Average financial aid package:* $11,596. *Average need-based loan:* $4851. *Average need-based gift aid:* $6113. *Average non-need-based aid:* $8545. *Average indebtedness upon graduation:* $35,888.

Applying *Application fee:* $25. *Required:* high school transcript, minimum 2.0 GPA, 2 letters of recommendation. *Required for some:* essay or personal statement, interview. *Application deadlines:* 8/1 (freshmen), 8/1 (transfers).

Freshman Application Contact Mrs. Rosita Lashley, Director for Admissions, Atlantic Union College, PO Box 1000, South Lancaster, MA 01561. *Phone:* 978-368-2239. *Toll-free phone:* 800-282-2030. *Fax:* 978-368-2015. *E-mail:* rosita.lashley@auc.edu.

BABSON COLLEGE

Wellesley, Massachusetts **www.babson.edu/**

- **Independent** comprehensive, founded 1919
- **Suburban** 370-acre campus with easy access to Boston
- **Endowment** $220.1 million
- **Coed** 1,799 undergraduate students, 100% full-time, 41% women, 59% men
- **Very difficult** entrance level, 38% of applicants were admitted

Undergraduates 1,799 full-time. Students come from 47 states and territories, 69 other countries, 70% are from out of state, 4% African American, 11% Asian American or Pacific Islander, 8% Hispanic American, 0.2% Native American, 18% international, 2% transferred in, 83% live on campus. *Retention:* 93% of 2006 full-time freshmen returned.

Freshmen *Admission:* 3,530 applied, 1,324 admitted, 453 enrolled. *Test scores:* SAT critical reading scores over 500: 96%; SAT math scores over 500: 100%; SAT writing scores over 500: 98%; ACT scores over 18: 100%; SAT critical reading scores over 600: 54%; SAT math scores over 600: 74%; SAT writing scores over 600: 63%; ACT scores over 24: 78%; SAT critical reading scores over 700: 8%; SAT math scores over 700: 20%; SAT writing scores over 700: 10%; ACT scores over 30: 12%.

Faculty *Total:* 239, 63% full-time, 72% with terminal degrees. *Student/faculty ratio:* 16:1.

Majors Accounting; accounting and business/management; accounting and finance; auditing; business administration and management; business administration, management and operations related; business/corporate communications; economics; entrepreneurial and small business related; entrepreneurship; finance; finance and financial management services related; international business/trade/commerce; international finance; investments and securities; management information systems; marketing/marketing management; marketing related; office management; operations management; operations research; pre-law studies; sales, distribution and marketing; small business administration.

Academics *Calendar:* semesters. *Degrees:* bachelor's, master's, and post-master's certificates. *Special study options:* accelerated degree program, advanced placement credit, freshman honors college, honors programs, independent study, internships, off-campus study, services for LD students, student-designed majors, study abroad, summer session for credit. *ROTC:* Army (c), Navy (c), Air Force (c).

Computers on Campus 290 computers/terminals are available on campus for general student use. Students can access the following: campus intranet, computer help desk, free student e-mail accounts, online (class) grades, online (class) registration, online (class) schedules, network drives and folders. Campuswide network is available.

Student Life *Housing:* on-campus residence required for freshman year. *Options:* coed, men-only, disabled students. Campus housing is university owned. Freshman campus housing is guaranteed. *Activities and organizations:* drama/theater group, student-run newspaper, radio station, choral group, student government, Free Press, Dance Ensemble, Asian Pacific Student Association, college radio, national fraternities, national sororities. *Campus security:* 24-hour emergency response devices and patrols, late-night transport/escort service, controlled dormitory access. *Student services:* health clinic, personal/psychological counseling, women's center.

Athletics Member NCAA. All Division III. *Intercollegiate sports:* baseball M, basketball M/W, cheerleading W (c), cross-country running M/W, field hockey W, golf M, ice hockey M/W (c), lacrosse M/W, rugby M (c)/W (c), skiing (downhill) M/W, soccer M/W, softball W, swimming and diving M/W, tennis M/W, track and field M/W, volleyball W. *Intramural sports:* basketball M/W, football M, ice hockey M/W, racquetball M/W, soccer M/W, softball M/W, squash M/W, tennis M/W, ultimate Frisbee M/W, volleyball M/W, wrestling M (c).

Standardized Tests *Required:* SAT or ACT (for admission).

Costs (2007–08) *Comprehensive fee:* $45,782 includes full-time tuition ($34,112) and room and board ($11,670). *College room only:* $7530. Room and board charges vary according to board plan and housing facility. *Payment plan:* installment. *Waivers:* employees or children of employees.

Financial Aid Of all full-time matriculated undergraduates who enrolled in 2007, 790 applied for aid, 741 were judged to have need, 630 had their need fully met. 269 Federal Work-Study jobs (averaging $1215). In 2007, 134 non-need-based awards were made. *Average percent of need met:* 96%. *Average financial aid package:* $29,142. *Average need-based loan:* $4241. *Average need-based gift aid:* $23,469. *Average non-need-based aid:* $15,000. *Average indebtedness upon graduation:* $28,902. *Financial aid deadline:* 2/15.

Applying *Options:* electronic application, early decision, early action, deferred entrance. *Application fee:* $65. *Required:* essay or personal statement, high school transcript, 2 letters of recommendation. *Recommended:* interview. *Application deadlines:* 1/15 (freshmen), 4/1 (transfers), 11/15 (early action). *Early decision deadline:* 11/15. *Notification:* 4/1 (freshmen), 5/15 (transfers), 12/15 (early decision), 1/1 (early action).

Freshman Application Contact Ms. Adrienne Fowkes, Assistant Director of Undergraduate Admission, Babson College, Lunder Undergraduate Admission Center, Babson Park, MA 02457-0310. *Phone:* 781-239-5522. *Toll-free phone:* 800-488-3696. *Fax:* 781-239-4135. *E-mail:* ugradadmission@babson.edu.

See page 1202 for the College Close-Up.

BARD COLLEGE AT SIMON'S ROCK

Great Barrington, Massachusetts **simons-rock.edu/**

- **Independent** 4-year, founded 1964, administratively affiliated with Bard College
- **Rural** 275-acre campus with easy access to Albany and Springfield
- **Endowment** $24.6 million
- **Coed** 408 undergraduate students, 99% full-time, 58% women, 42% men
- **Very difficult** entrance level, 84% of applicants were admitted

Undergraduates 403 full-time, 5 part-time. Students come from 41 states and territories, 11 other countries, 82% are from out of state, 7% African American, 4% Asian American or Pacific Islander, 6% Hispanic American, 0.8% Native American, 4% international, 0.7% transferred in, 81% live on campus. *Retention:* 82% of 2006 full-time freshmen returned.

Freshmen *Admission:* 236 applied, 199 admitted, 182 enrolled. *Test scores:* SAT critical reading scores over 500: 93%; SAT math scores over 500: 84%; ACT scores over 18: 94%; SAT critical reading scores over 600: 61%; SAT math scores over 600: 43%; ACT scores over 24: 88%; SAT critical reading scores over 700: 20%; SAT math scores over 700: 13%; ACT scores over 30: 25%.

Faculty *Total:* 65, 57% full-time, 82% with terminal degrees. *Student/faculty ratio:* 8:1.

Majors Acting; African-American/Black studies; agricultural business and management; American literature; American native/native American education; American studies; anthropology; applied mathematics; art history, criticism and conservation; Asian studies; biology/biological sciences; ceramic arts and ceramics; chemistry; Chinese; Chinese studies; cognitive psychology and psycholinguistics; computer and information sciences; computer graphics; computer science; creative writing; cultural studies; dance; developmental and child psychology; dramatic/theater arts; drawing; ecology; economics related; English composition; environmental studies; ethnic, cultural minority, and gender studies related; European studies; fine/studio arts; foreign languages and literatures; French; French studies; geography; geology/earth science; German; German studies; interdisciplinary studies; jazz/jazz studies; Latin; Latin American studies; liberal arts and sciences/liberal studies; literature; mathematics; metal and jewelry arts; music; music theory and composition; natural sciences; painting; philosophy; photography; physics; playwriting and screenwriting; political science and government; pre-law studies; pre-medical studies; printmaking; psychology; religious studies; sculpture; sociology; Spanish; Spanish and Iberian studies; theater design and technology; theater literature, history and criticism; Ukraine studies; visual and performing arts; visual and performing arts related; women's studies.

Academics *Calendar:* semesters. *Degrees:* associate and bachelor's. *Special study options:* adult/continuing education programs, double majors, external degree program, independent study, internships, off-campus study, part-time degree program, services for LD students, student-designed majors, study abroad. *Unusual degree programs:* engineering with Columbia, Washington University (St. Louis) and Dartmouth.

Computers on Campus 50 computers/terminals are available on campus for general student use. Students can access the following: campus intranet, computer help desk, free student e-mail accounts. Campuswide network is available. 100% of college-owned or -operated housing units are wired for high-speed Internet access. Wireless service is available via classrooms, computer centers, computer labs, dorm rooms, learning centers, libraries, student centers.

Student Life *Housing:* on-campus residence required through sophomore year. *Options:* coed, men-only, women-only, disabled students. Campus housing is university owned. Freshman campus housing is guaranteed. *Activities and organizations:* drama/theater group, student-run newspaper, radio station, choral group, Women's Center, Math and Sciences Club, multicultural student organization, Community Service Program, Green Agers. *Campus security:* 24-hour emergency response devices, late-night transport/escort service, controlled dormitory access, 24-hour weekend patrols by trained security personnel. *Student services:* health clinic, personal/psychological counseling, women's center.

Athletics *Intercollegiate sports:* basketball M/W, cheerleading M/W, cross-country running M/W, fencing M/W, racquetball M/W, soccer M/W, swimming and diving M/W. *Intramural sports:* archery M/W, basketball M/W, cheerleading M/W, cross-country running M/W, fencing M/W, field hockey W, racquetball M/W, rock climbing M/W, soccer M/W, squash M/W, swimming and diving M/W, tennis M/W, volleyball M/W.

Standardized Tests *Required for some:* SAT or ACT (for admission), PSAT.

Costs (2008–09) *Comprehensive fee:* $46,860 includes full-time tuition ($36,550), mandatory fees ($580), and room and board ($9730).

Financial Aid Of all full-time matriculated undergraduates who enrolled in 2007, 319 applied for aid, 231 were judged to have need, 30 had their need fully met. 166 Federal Work-Study jobs (averaging $1200). In 2007, 72 non-need-based awards were made. *Average percent of need met:* 65%. *Average financial aid package:* $19,500. *Average need-based loan:* $4711. *Average need-based gift aid:* $10,100. *Average non-need-based aid:* $17,830. *Average indebtedness upon graduation:* $21,000.

Applying *Options:* electronic application, deferred entrance. *Application fee:* $50. *Required:* essay or personal statement, high school transcript, minimum 2.0 GPA, 2 letters of recommendation, interview, parent application. *Recommended:* minimum 3.0 GPA. *Application deadlines:* 5/31 (freshmen), 7/15 (transfers). *Notification:* continuous (freshmen), continuous (transfers).

Freshman Application Contact Barbara Shultis, Assistant to the Director of Admissions, Bard College at Simon's Rock, 84 Alford Road, Great Barrington, MA 01230. *Phone:* 413-528-7312. *Toll-free phone:* 800-235-7186. *Fax:* 413-528-7334. *E-mail:* admit@simons-rock.edu.

See page 1204 for the College Close-Up.

BAY PATH COLLEGE

Longmeadow, Massachusetts **www.baypath.edu/**

- **Independent** comprehensive, founded 1897
- **Suburban** 48-acre campus with easy access to Boston
- **Endowment** $19.3 million
- **Undergraduate: women only; graduate: coed** 1,322 undergraduate students, 78% full-time, 100% women
- **Moderately difficult** entrance level, 76% of applicants were admitted

Undergraduates 1,025 full-time, 297 part-time. Students come from 17 states and territories, 6 other countries, 37% are from out of state, 11% African American, 1% Asian American or Pacific Islander, 11% Hispanic American, 0.4% Native American, 1% international, 2% transferred in, 66% live on campus. *Retention:* 62% of 2006 full-time freshmen returned.

Freshmen *Admission:* 644 applied, 492 admitted, 222 enrolled. *Average high school GPA:* 3.1. *Test scores:* SAT critical reading scores over 500: 49%; SAT math scores over 500: 37%; SAT writing scores over 500: 53%; ACT scores over 18: 69%; SAT critical reading scores over 600: 6%; SAT math scores over 600: 6%; SAT writing scores over 600: 12%; ACT scores over 24: 15%; SAT critical reading scores over 700: 1%; SAT writing scores over 700: 1%.

Faculty *Total:* 152, 30% full-time, 42% with terminal degrees. *Student/faculty ratio:* 17:1.

Majors Biology/biological sciences; biotechnology; business/commerce; criminal justice/law enforcement administration; elementary education; forensic psychology; kindergarten/preschool education; legal studies; liberal arts and sciences/liberal studies; occupational therapy; pre-law studies; psychology.

Academics *Calendar:* semesters. *Degrees:* certificates, bachelor's, master's, and postbachelor's certificates. *Special study options:* academic remediation for entering students, adult/continuing education programs, advanced placement credit, cooperative education, double majors, English as a second language, freshman honors college, honors programs, independent study, internships, off-campus study, part-time degree program, services for LD students, student-designed majors, study abroad, summer session for credit. *ROTC:* Army (c), Air Force (c).

Computers on Campus 200 computers/terminals are available on campus for general student use. Students can access the following: campus intranet, computer help desk, free student e-mail accounts, online (class) grades, online (class) registration, online (class) schedules. Campuswide network is available. 100% of college-owned or -operated housing units are wired for high-speed Internet access. Wireless service is available via classrooms, computer centers, computer labs, libraries, student centers.

Student Life *Housing:* on-campus residence required through sophomore year. *Options:* women-only. Campus housing is university owned. Freshman campus housing is guaranteed. *Activities and organizations:* drama/theater group, choral group, student government, All Women Excel, Golden Z Service Club, Alliance, Women of Culture. *Campus security:* 24-hour emergency response devices and patrols, late-night transport/escort service, controlled dormitory access. *Student services:* health clinic, personal/psychological counseling.

Athletics Member NCAA. All Division III. *Intercollegiate sports:* basketball W, cross-country running W, soccer W, softball W, tennis W, volleyball W. *Intramural sports:* field hockey W (c), ice hockey W (c), lacrosse W (c).

Standardized Tests *Required:* SAT or ACT (for admission).

Costs (2007–08) *Comprehensive fee:* $31,273 includes full-time tuition ($22,073) and room and board ($9200). Part-time tuition: $444 per credit. *Room and board:* Room and board charges vary according to board plan. *Payment plan:* installment. *Waivers:* employees or children of employees.

Financial Aid Of all full-time matriculated undergraduates who enrolled in 2004, 858 applied for aid, 781 were judged to have need, 81 had their need fully met. 146 Federal Work-Study jobs (averaging $2000). In 2004, 119 non-need-based awards were made. *Average percent of need met:* 66%. *Average financial aid package:* $11,453. *Average need-based loan:* $4045. *Average need-based gift aid:* $7465. *Average non-need-based aid:* $10,982. *Average indebtedness upon graduation:* $18,200.

Applying *Options:* electronic application, early admission, early action, deferred entrance. *Application fee:* $25. *Required:* high school transcript, 2 letters of recommendation. *Required for some:* minimum 3.0 GPA, interview. *Recommended:* essay or personal statement, minimum 2.5 GPA, interview. *Application deadlines:* rolling (freshmen), rolling (transfers), 12/15 (early action). *Notification:* continuous (freshmen), continuous (transfers), 1/2 (early action).

Freshman Application Contact Bay Path College, 588 Longmeadow Street, Longmeadow, MA 01106-2292. *Phone:* 413-565-1000 Ext. 1331. *Toll-free phone:* 800-782-7284 Ext. 1331.

See page 1206 for the College Close-Up.

BAY STATE COLLEGE

Boston, Massachusetts **www.baystate.edu/**

Freshman Application Contact Stephen Lyons M.Ed., Director of Admissions, Bay State College, 122 Commonwealth Avenue, Boston, MA 02116. *Phone:* 617-217-9040. *Toll-free phone:* 800-81-LEARN. *Fax:* 617-536-1735. *E-mail:* admissions@baystate.edu.

See page 1208 for the College Close-Up.

BECKER COLLEGE

Worcester, Massachusetts **www.beckercollege.edu/**

- **Independent** 4-year, founded 1784
- **Rural** 100-acre campus with easy access to Boston
- **Coed** 1,660 undergraduate students, 55% full-time, 80% women, 20% men
- **Minimally difficult** entrance level, 70% of applicants were admitted

Located in the heart of Massachusetts, Becker is a unique New England college. Founded in 1784, Becker is still on the cutting edge; it is entirely wireless and each full-time student receives a laptop. A small, private, four-year coeducational and career-focused college, Becker offers a low student-teacher ratio of 18:1. Becker offers more than twenty-five academic programs. Majors include accounting, business, criminal justice, education, equine management, forensics, graphic design, interior design, prelaw, pre–veterinary medicine, video game design, and video game production. Athletically, Becker College competes nationally at the NCAA Division III level and offers soccer, football, equestrian, tennis, golf, cross-country, basketball, ice hockey, volleyball, baseball, softball, and lacrosse. For further information, prospective students should visit http://www.beckercollege.edu.

Undergraduates 910 full-time, 750 part-time. Students come from 18 states and territories, 2 other countries, 35% are from out of state, 5% African American, 1% Asian American or Pacific Islander, 3% Hispanic American, 0.3% Native American, 0.3% international, 8% transferred in, 50% live on campus. *Retention:* 61% of 2006 full-time freshmen returned.

Freshmen *Admission:* 2,550 applied, 1,794 admitted, 496 enrolled. *Average high school GPA:* 2.60. *Test scores:* SAT critical reading scores over 500: 22%; SAT math scores over 500: 25%; ACT scores over 18: 54%; SAT critical reading scores over 600: 4%; SAT math scores over 600: 4%; ACT scores over 24: 13%; SAT critical reading scores over 700: 1%.

Faculty *Total:* 103, 38% full-time, 17% with terminal degrees. *Student/faculty ratio:* 15:1.

Majors Animal sciences; animal training; business administration and management; business administration, management and operations related; computer graphics; criminal justice/safety; dog/pet/animal grooming; early childhood education; education; elementary education; forensic science and technology; graphic design; horse husbandry/equine science and management; hospitality administration; hotel/motel administration; human resources management and services related; interior design; kinesiology and exercise science; legal studies; liberal arts and sciences/liberal studies; marketing/marketing management; nursing (registered nurse training); pre-veterinary studies; psychology; sport and fitness administration/management; tourism and travel services management; veterinary sciences; veterinary technology.

Academics *Calendar:* semesters. *Degrees:* certificates, associate, and bachelor's (also includes Leicester, MA small town campus). *Special study options:* academic remediation for entering students, accelerated degree program, adult/continuing education programs, advanced placement credit, cooperative education, distance learning, internships, off-campus study, part-time degree program, services for LD students, summer session for credit. *ROTC:* Army (c), Navy (c), Air Force (c). *Unusual degree programs:* 3-2 law with Massachusetts School of Law.

Computers on Campus 155 computers/terminals are available on campus for general student use. Students can access the following: campus intranet, computer help desk, free student e-mail accounts, online (class) grades, online (class) registration, online (class) schedules. Campuswide network is available. 100% of college-owned or -operated housing units are wired for high-speed Internet access. Wireless service is available via dorm rooms, learning centers.

Student Life *Housing options:* coed, men-only, women-only. Campus housing is university owned and leased by the school. Freshman campus housing is guaranteed. *Activities and organizations:* drama/theater group, student-run newspaper, student government, Student Activities Committee, Black Student Union, Animal Health Club, Drama Club. *Campus security:* 24-hour emergency response devices and patrols, late-night transport/escort service, controlled dormitory access. *Student services:* health clinic, personal/psychological counseling.

Athletics Member NCAA. *Intercollegiate sports:* baseball M, basketball M/W, cheerleading M/W, equestrian sports M/W, field hockey W, football M, golf M, ice hockey M/W, lacrosse M/W, soccer M/W, softball W, tennis M/W, volleyball W. *Intramural sports:* badminton M/W, basketball M/W, bowling M/W, skiing (downhill) M (c)/W (c), soccer M/W, table tennis M/W, volleyball M/W.

Standardized Tests *Required:* SAT or ACT (for admission).

Costs (2007–08) *Comprehensive fee:* $34,968 includes full-time tuition ($23,600), mandatory fees ($2068), and room and board ($9300). Part-time tuition: $990 per credit hour. Part-time tuition and fees vary according to program. *Room and board:* Room and board charges vary according to board plan and housing facility. *Payment plan:* installment. *Waivers:* senior citizens and employees or children of employees.

Financial Aid Of all full-time matriculated undergraduates who enrolled in 2005, 1,093 applied for aid, 997 were judged to have need, 83 had their need fully met. 450 Federal Work-Study jobs (averaging $879). In 2005, 149 non-need-based awards were made. *Average percent of need met:* 47%. *Average financial aid package:* $9299. *Average need-based loan:* $2941. *Average need-based gift aid:* $6723. *Average non-need-based aid:* $11,896. *Average indebtedness upon graduation:* $32,121.

Applying *Options:* electronic application, deferred entrance. *Application fee:* $30. *Required:* high school transcript, minimum 2.0 GPA, letters of recommendation. *Required for some:* minimum 2.5 GPA, interview. *Recommended:* essay or personal statement, letters of recommendation. *Application deadlines:* rolling (freshmen), rolling (transfers). *Notification:* continuous (freshmen), continuous (transfers).

Freshman Application Contact Admissions Receptionist, Becker College, 61 Sever Street, Worcester, MA 01609. *Phone:* 508-373-9400. *Toll-free phone:* 877-5BECKER Ext. 245. *Fax:* 508-890-1500. *E-mail:* admissions@beckercollege.edu.

See page 1210 for the College Close-Up.

BENJAMIN FRANKLIN INSTITUTE OF TECHNOLOGY

Boston, Massachusetts **www.bfit.edu/**

Freshman Application Contact Ms. Andrea Dawes, Associate Director of Admissions, Benjamin Franklin Institute of Technology, 41 Berkeley Street, Boston, MA 02116-6296. *Phone:* 617-423-4630 Ext. 190. *Fax:* 617-482-3706. *E-mail:* adawes@bfit.edu.

BENTLEY COLLEGE

Waltham, Massachusetts **www.bentley.edu**

- **Independent** comprehensive, founded 1917
- **Suburban** 163-acre campus with easy access to Boston
- **Endowment** $249.6 million
- **Coed** 4,200 undergraduate students, 94% full-time, 40% women, 60% men
- **Very difficult** entrance level, 38% of applicants were admitted

Undergraduates 3,959 full-time, 241 part-time. Students come from 42 states and territories, 81 other countries, 50% are from out of state, 3% African American, 8% Asian American or Pacific Islander, 4% Hispanic American, 7% international, 2% transferred in, 79% live on campus. *Retention:* 92% of 2006 full-time freshmen returned.

Freshmen *Admission:* 6,689 applied, 2,531 admitted, 934 enrolled. *Test scores:* SAT critical reading scores over 500: 92%; SAT math scores over 500: 98%; SAT writing scores over 500: 93%; ACT scores over 18: 99%; SAT critical reading scores over 600: 47%; SAT math scores over 600: 77%; SAT writing scores over 600: 52%; ACT scores over 24: 80%; SAT critical reading scores over 700: 5%; SAT math scores over 700: 18%; SAT writing scores over 700: 7%; ACT scores over 30: 16%.

Faculty *Total:* 498, 54% full-time, 62% with terminal degrees. *Student/faculty ratio:* 12:1.

Majors Accounting; business administration and management; business/corporate communications; business/managerial economics; computer and information sciences; finance; interdisciplinary studies; liberal arts and sciences/liberal studies; marketing/marketing management; mathematics; philosophy.

Academics *Calendar:* semesters. *Degrees:* associate, bachelor's, master's, post-master's, and postbachelor's certificates. *Special study options:* academic remediation for entering students, accelerated degree program, adult/continuing education programs, advanced placement credit, double majors, English as a second language, honors programs, independent study, internships, off-campus study, part-time degree program, services for LD students, student-designed majors, study abroad, summer session for credit. *ROTC:* Army (c), Air Force (c).

Computers on Campus 4,620 computers/terminals and 13,336 ports are available on campus for general student use. Students can access the following: campus intranet, computer help desk, free student e-mail accounts, online (class) grades, online (class) registration, online (class) schedules, online admission, Blackboard, resume review, student employment, interlibrary loan. Campuswide network is available. 100% of college-owned or -operated housing units are wired for high-speed Internet access. Wireless service is available via entire campus.

Student Life *Housing options:* coed, disabled students. Campus housing is university owned and leased by the school. Freshman campus housing is guaranteed. *Activities and organizations:* drama/theater group, student-run newspaper, radio and television station, choral group, Student Government Association, Campus Activities Board, Hall Council Advisory Board, WBTY, national fraternities, national sororities. *Campus security:* 24-hour emergency response devices and patrols, late-night transport/escort service, controlled dormitory access, security cameras. *Student services:* health clinic, personal/psychological counseling, women's center.

Athletics Member NCAA. All Division II. *Intercollegiate sports:* baseball M (s), basketball M (s)/W (s), cross-country running M (s)/W (s), field hockey W (s), football M, golf W, ice hockey M (s), lacrosse M (s)/W (s), soccer M (s)/W (s), softball W (s), swimming and diving M (s)/W (s), tennis M/W, track and field M (s)/W (s), volleyball W (s). *Intramural sports:* basketball M/W, field hockey W, football M, racquetball M/W, soccer M/W, softball M/W, volleyball M/W.

Standardized Tests *Required:* SAT or ACT (for admission).

Costs (2007–08) *Comprehensive fee:* $43,836 includes full-time tuition ($31,450), mandatory fees ($1446), and room and board ($10,940). Part-time tuition: $1506 per course. Part-time tuition and fees vary according to class time. *Required fees:* $45 per term part-time. *College room only:* $6540. Room and board charges vary according to board plan and housing facility. *Payment plan:* installment. *Waivers:* employees or children of employees.

Financial Aid Of all full-time matriculated undergraduates who enrolled in 2006, 2,751 applied for aid, 2,066 were judged to have need, 649 had their need fully met. 1,254 Federal Work-Study jobs (averaging $1407). 639 state and other part-time jobs (averaging $1835). In 2006, 399 non-need-based awards were made. *Average percent of need met:* 89%. *Average financial aid package:* $24,587. *Average need-based loan:* $4978. *Average need-based gift aid:* $17,928. *Average non-need-based aid:* $13,173. *Average indebtedness upon graduation:* $31,665. *Financial aid deadline:* 2/1.

Applying *Options:* electronic application, early admission, early decision, early action, deferred entrance. *Application fee:* $50. *Required:* essay or personal statement, high school transcript, 2 letters of recommendation. *Recommended:* interview. *Application deadlines:* 1/15 (freshmen), 1/15 (out-of-state freshmen), rolling (transfers), 11/15 (early action). *Early decision deadline:* 11/15. *Notification:* 4/1 (freshmen), 4/1 (out-of-state freshmen), continuous (transfers), 12/15 (early decision), 1/15 (early action).

Freshman Application Contact Bentley College, 175 Forest Street, Waltham, MA 02452. *Phone:* 781-891-2244. *Toll-free phone:* 800-523-2354. *Fax:* 781-891-3414. *E-mail:* ugadmission@bentley.edu.

See page 1212 for the College Close-Up.

BERKLEE COLLEGE OF MUSIC

Boston, Massachusetts **www.berklee.edu/**

- **Independent** 4-year, founded 1945
- **Urban** campus
- **Endowment** $217.0 million
- **Coed** 4,090 undergraduate students, 91% full-time, 28% women, 72% men
- **Moderately difficult** entrance level, 32% of applicants were admitted

Undergraduates 3,739 full-time, 351 part-time. Students come from 54 states and territories, 73 other countries, 78% are from out of state, 5% transferred in, 20% live on campus. *Retention:* 84% of 2006 full-time freshmen returned.

Freshmen *Admission:* 3,710 applied, 1,195 admitted, 612 enrolled.

Faculty *Total:* 514, 43% full-time, 12% with terminal degrees. *Student/faculty ratio:* 8:1.

Majors Audio engineering; jazz/jazz studies; music; music management and merchandising; music performance; music teacher education; music theory and composition; music therapy; piano and organ; violin, viola, guitar and other stringed instruments; voice and opera; wind/percussion instruments.

Academics *Calendar:* semesters. *Degree:* diplomas and bachelor's. *Special study options:* accelerated degree program, advanced placement credit, double majors, English as a second language, internships, off-campus study, services for LD students, student-designed majors, study abroad, summer session for credit.

Computers on Campus 45 computers/terminals are available on campus for general student use. Students can access the following: free student e-mail accounts, online (class) grades, online (class) registration, online (class) schedules. Campuswide network is available. 100% of college-owned or -operated housing units are wired for high-speed Internet access. Wireless service is available via entire campus.

Student Life *Housing options:* coed. Campus housing is university owned. Freshman applicants given priority for college housing. *Activities and organizations:* drama/theater group, student-run newspaper, radio station, choral group,

Musical Theater at Berklee Club, Yoga Society, Black Student Union, Christian Fellowship. *Campus security:* 24-hour patrols. *Student services:* personal/psychological counseling.

Athletics *Intramural sports:* ice hockey M/W, rock climbing M/W, soccer M/W, table tennis M/W.

Costs (2008–09) *One-time required fee:* $650. *Comprehensive fee:* $43,160 includes full-time tuition ($27,500), mandatory fees ($700), and room and board ($14,960). Part-time tuition: $975 per hour.

Financial Aid Of all full-time matriculated undergraduates who enrolled in 2007, 1,971 applied for aid, 1,727 were judged to have need, 107 had their need fully met. 321 Federal Work-Study jobs (averaging $1430). 1,880 state and other part-time jobs. In 2007, 957 non-need-based awards were made. *Average percent of need met:* 26%. *Average financial aid package:* $10,897. *Average need-based loan:* $4909. *Average need-based gift aid:* $7295. *Average non-need-based aid:* $8788.

Applying *Options:* electronic application, early action, deferred entrance. *Application fee:* $150. *Required:* essay or personal statement, high school transcript, 2 letters of recommendation, interview, 2 years of formal music study and audition. *Application deadlines:* 2/1 (freshmen), 2/1 (transfers), 11/1 (early action). *Notification:* 3/31 (freshmen), 3/31 (transfers), 1/31 (early action).

Freshman Application Contact Mr. Damien Bracken, Director of Admissions, Berklee College of Music, 1140 Boyleston Street, Boston, MA 02215-3693. *Phone:* 617-747-2222. *Toll-free phone:* 800-BERKLEE. *Fax:* 617-747-2047. *E-mail:* admissions@berklee.edu.

See page 1214 for the College Close-Up.

BOSTON ARCHITECTURAL COLLEGE

Boston, Massachusetts **www.the-bac.edu/**

- **Independent** comprehensive, founded 1889
- **Urban** 1-acre campus
- **Endowment** $8.6 million
- **Coed** 571 undergraduate students, 97% full-time, 36% women, 64% men
- **Noncompetitive** entrance level, 88% of applicants were admitted

Undergraduates 552 full-time, 19 part-time. Students come from 25 states and territories, 10 other countries, 51% are from out of state, 5% African American, 6% Asian American or Pacific Islander, 12% Hispanic American, 0.4% Native American, 20% transferred in. *Retention:* 63% of 2006 full-time freshmen returned.

Freshmen *Admission:* 310 applied, 274 admitted, 75 enrolled. *Average high school GPA:* 2.8.

Faculty *Total:* 307, 3% full-time, 22% with terminal degrees. *Student/faculty ratio:* 4:1.

Majors Architecture; interior design.

Academics *Calendar:* semesters. *Degrees:* certificates, bachelor's, and master's. *Special study options:* adult/continuing education programs, advanced placement credit, distance learning, independent study, internships, off-campus study, summer session for credit.

Computers on Campus 63 computers/terminals are available on campus for general student use. Students can access the following: computer help desk. Campuswide network is available.

Student Life *Housing:* college housing not available. *Activities and organizations:* student-run newspaper, student government. *Campus security:* 24-hour emergency response devices and patrols, electronically operated building access.

Costs (2008–09) *Tuition:* $10,560 full-time. *Required fees:* $20 full-time.

Financial Aid Of all full-time matriculated undergraduates who enrolled in 2003, 176 applied for aid, 162 were judged to have need. *Average percent of need met:* 17%. *Average financial aid package:* $3525. *Average need-based loan:* $2958. *Average need-based gift aid:* $1657. *Average indebtedness upon graduation:* $25,387.

Applying *Options:* electronic application. *Application fee:* $50. *Required:* high school transcript. *Recommended:* resume. *Application deadlines:* rolling (freshmen), rolling (transfers).

Freshman Application Contact Richard Moyer, Director of Admission, Boston Architectural College, 320 Newbury Street, Boston, MA 02115-2795. *Phone:* 617-585-0256. *Toll-free phone:* 877-585-0100. *Fax:* 617-585-0121. *E-mail:* admissions@the-bac.edu.

See page 1216 for the College Close-Up.

BOSTON BAPTIST COLLEGE

Boston, Massachusetts **www.boston.edu/**

- **Independent Baptist** 4-year, founded 1976
- **Suburban** 8-acre campus with easy access to Providence
- **Coed** 149 undergraduate students, 74% full-time, 40% women, 60% men
- **Moderately difficult** entrance level

Undergraduates 110 full-time, 39 part-time. Students come from 24 states and territories, 5 other countries, 74% are from out of state, 7% African American, 4% Asian American or Pacific Islander, 2% Hispanic American, 1% Native American, 5% international, 10% transferred in, 65% live on campus. *Retention:* 60% of 2006 full-time freshmen returned.

Freshmen *Admission:* 33 enrolled. *Average high school GPA:* 3.0.

Faculty *Total:* 9, 44% full-time, 56% with terminal degrees. *Student/faculty ratio:* 6:1.

Majors Biblical studies.

Academics *Calendar:* semesters. *Degrees:* certificates, diplomas, associate, and bachelor's. *Special study options:* academic remediation for entering students, honors programs, internships, part-time degree program, summer session for credit.

Computers on Campus 12 computers/terminals and 12 ports are available on campus for general student use. Students can access the following: campus intranet, computer help desk, free student e-mail accounts, online (class) grades. Campuswide network is available. 100% of college-owned or -operated housing units are wired for high-speed Internet access. Wireless service is available via entire campus.

Student Life *Housing:* on-campus residence required through senior year. *Options:* men-only, women-only, disabled students. Campus housing is university owned. Freshman campus housing is guaranteed. *Activities and organizations:* drama/theater group, choral group. *Campus security:* 24-hour emergency response devices, student patrols. *Student services:* personal/psychological counseling.

Athletics *Intramural sports:* basketball M/W, soccer M/W, volleyball M/W.

Standardized Tests *Required:* SAT or ACT (for admission).

Costs (2007–08) *Comprehensive fee:* $15,757 includes full-time tuition ($7140), mandatory fees ($1625), and room and board ($6992). Part-time tuition: $297 per hour. *Required fees:* $813 per term part-time. *College room only:* $4252. Room and board charges vary according to board plan. *Payment plan:* installment. *Waivers:* employees or children of employees.

Applying *Options:* deferred entrance. *Application fee:* $40. *Required:* essay or personal statement, high school transcript, letters of recommendation. *Recommended:* interview. *Application deadlines:* rolling (freshmen), rolling (transfers).

Freshman Application Contact Mrs. Karen Fox, Director of Admissions, Boston Baptist College, 950 Metropolitan Avenue, Boston, MA 02136. *Phone:* 617-364-3510 Ext. 217. *Toll-free phone:* 888-235-2014. *Fax:* 775-522-4803. *E-mail:* kfox@boston.edu.

BOSTON COLLEGE

Chestnut Hill, Massachusetts **www.bc.edu/**

- **Independent Roman Catholic (Jesuit)** university, founded 1863
- **Suburban** 379-acre campus with easy access to Boston
- **Endowment** $1.7 billion
- **Coed** 9,081 undergraduate students, 100% full-time, 52% women, 48% men
- **Very difficult** entrance level, 27% of applicants were admitted

Boston College's international stature is strengthened by the more than 450-year tradition of Jesuit education. Students are challenged to fulfill their potential as scholars through honors programs, research with faculty members, independent study, study abroad, and service-learning. Students are also challenged to fulfill their potential as caring, thoughtful individuals and future leaders in society with artistic, cultural, service, social, religious, and athletic opportunities that abound on campus and throughout Boston.

Undergraduates 9,081 full-time. Students come from 54 states and territories, 55 other countries, 71% are from out of state, 6% African American, 10% Asian American or Pacific Islander, 8% Hispanic American, 0.4% Native American, 2% international, 2% transferred in, 82% live on campus. *Retention:* 95% of 2006 full-time freshmen returned.

Freshmen *Admission:* 28,850 applied, 7,869 admitted, 2,291 enrolled. *Test scores:* SAT critical reading scores over 500: 98%; SAT math scores over 500: 98%; SAT writing scores over 500: 97%; ACT scores over 18: 100%; SAT critical reading scores over 600: 82%; SAT math scores over 600: 87%; SAT writing scores over 600: 84%; ACT scores over 24: 95%; SAT critical reading scores over 700: 31%; SAT math scores over 700: 41%; SAT writing scores over 700: 35%; ACT scores over 30: 58%.

Faculty *Total:* 1,246, 54% full-time. *Student/faculty ratio:* 13:1.

Majors Accounting; ancient/classical Greek; art history, criticism and conservation; biochemistry; biology/biological sciences; business administration and management; business/managerial economics; chemistry; classics and languages, literatures and linguistics; communication/speech communication and rhetoric; computer and information sciences; computer science; dramatic/theater arts; economics; elementary education; English; film/cinema studies; finance; fine/studio arts; French; geology/earth science; geophysics and seismology; German; Hispanic-American, Puerto Rican, and Mexican-American/Chicano studies; history; human development and family studies; human resources management; interdisciplinary studies; Italian; kindergarten/preschool education; Latin; management information systems; marketing/marketing management; mathematics; music; nursing (registered nurse training); operations management; philosophy; physics; political science and government; psychology; Russian; Russian studies; secondary education; Slavic languages; sociology; Spanish; theology.

Academics *Calendar:* semesters. *Degrees:* bachelor's, master's, doctoral, first professional, and post-master's certificates (also offers continuing education program with significant enrollment not reflected in profile). *Special study options:* accelerated degree program, adult/continuing education programs, advanced placement credit, double majors, freshman honors college, honors programs, independent study, internships, off-campus study, part-time degree program, services for LD students, student-designed majors, study abroad, summer session for credit. *ROTC:* Army (c), Navy (c), Air Force (c). *Unusual degree programs:* 3-2 engineering with Boston University; education, pastoral ministry.

Computers on Campus 1,000 computers/terminals are available on campus for general student use. Students can access the following: campus intranet, computer help desk, free student e-mail accounts, online (class) grades, online (class) registration, online (class) schedules. Campuswide network is available. Wireless service is available via entire campus.

Student Life *Housing options:* coed, women-only. Campus housing is university owned. Freshman campus housing is guaranteed. *Activities and organizations:* drama/theater group, student-run newspaper, radio and television station, choral group, marching band, UGBC and individual School Senates, Asian Caucus, Appalachia Volunteers, Dance Marathon, 4Boston. *Campus security:* 24-hour emergency response devices and patrols, late-night transport/escort service, controlled dormitory access. *Student services:* health clinic, personal/psychological counseling, women's center.

Athletics Member NCAA. All Division I except football (Division I-A). *Intercollegiate sports:* baseball M, basketball M (s)/W (s), crew W (s), cross-country running M (s)/W (s), fencing M/W, field hockey W (s), golf M (s)/W (s), ice hockey M (s)/W (s), lacrosse W (s), sailing M/W, skiing (downhill) M/W, soccer M (s)/W (s), softball W (s), swimming and diving M (s)/W (s), tennis M (s)/W (s), track and field M (s)/W (s), volleyball W (s), wrestling M. *Intramural sports:* basketball M (c)/W (c), crew M (c), cross-country running M (c)/W (c), equestrian sports M (c)/W (c), field hockey W (c), football W, golf M (c)/W (c), ice hockey M/W, lacrosse M (c)/W (c), racquetball M/W, rugby M (c)/W (c), skiing (downhill) M (c)/W (c), soccer M (c)/W (c), softball M/W, squash M/W, tennis M/W, ultimate Frisbee M (c)/W (c), volleyball M (c)/W, water polo M (c)/W (c).

Standardized Tests *Required:* SAT and SAT Subject Tests or ACT (for admission).

Costs (2007–08) *One-time required fee:* $405. *Comprehensive fee:* $47,727 includes full-time tuition ($35,150), mandatory fees ($524), and room and board ($12,053). *College room only:* $7813. Room and board charges vary according to housing facility. *Payment plan:* installment. *Waivers:* employees or children of employees.

Financial Aid Of all full-time matriculated undergraduates who enrolled in 2006, 4,497 applied for aid, 3,778 were judged to have need, 3,778 had their need fully met. 2,949 Federal Work-Study jobs (averaging $2104). In 2006, 164 non-need-based awards were made. *Average percent of need met:* 100%. *Average financial aid package:* $26,101. *Average need-based loan:* $4855. *Average need-based gift aid:* $21,500. *Average non-need-based aid:* $15,273. *Average indebtedness upon graduation:* $20,350.

Applying *Options:* electronic application, early admission, early action, deferred entrance. *Application fee:* $70. *Required:* essay or personal statement, high school transcript, 2 letters of recommendation. *Application deadlines:* 1/1 (freshmen), 4/1 (transfers), 11/1 (early action). *Notification:* 4/15 (freshmen), 6/1 (transfers), 12/25 (early action).

Freshman Application Contact Office of Undergraduate Admissions, Boston College, 140 Commonwealth Avenue, Devlin 208, Chestnut Hill, MA 02467-3809. *Phone:* 617-552-3100. *Toll-free phone:* 800-360-2522. *Fax:* 617-552-0798. *E-mail:* ugadmis@bc.edu.

See page 1218 for the College Close-Up.

THE BOSTON CONSERVATORY

Boston, Massachusetts **www.bostonconservatory.edu/**

- **Independent** comprehensive, founded 1867
- **Urban** campus
- **Coed** 444 undergraduate students, 100% full-time, 63% women, 37% men
- **Moderately difficult** entrance level, 34% of applicants were admitted

Undergraduates 444 full-time. Students come from 46 states and territories, 65% are from out of state, 3% African American, 6% Asian American or Pacific Islander, 6% Hispanic American, 0.2% Native American, 1% transferred in, 29% live on campus. *Retention:* 82% of 2006 full-time freshmen returned.

Freshmen *Admission:* 1,117 applied, 379 admitted, 181 enrolled.

Faculty *Total:* 171, 26% full-time. *Student/faculty ratio:* 4:1.

Majors Dance; dramatic/theater arts; music; music teacher education; music theory and composition; piano and organ; violin, viola, guitar and other stringed instruments; voice and opera; wind/percussion instruments.

Academics *Calendar:* semesters. *Degrees:* diplomas, bachelor's, master's, post-master's, and postbachelor's certificates. *Special study options:* adult/continuing education programs, advanced placement credit, double majors, English as a second language, off-campus study, summer session for credit.

Computers on Campus 16 computers/terminals are available on campus for general student use. Campuswide network is available.

Student Life *Housing:* on-campus residence required for freshman year. *Options:* coed, women-only. Campus housing is university owned. *Activities and organizations:* drama/theater group, student-run newspaper, choral group, Student Government Association, Korean Student Association, Chinese Student Association, Sigma Alpha Iota, national fraternities, national sororities. *Campus security:* 24-hour emergency response devices and patrols, controlled dormitory access. *Student services:* health clinic, personal/psychological counseling.

Costs (2007–08) *Comprehensive fee:* $45,739 includes full-time tuition ($28,300), mandatory fees ($1799), and room and board ($15,640). Full-time tuition and fees vary according to program. Part-time tuition: $1170 per credit. *Required fees:* $390 per term part-time. *Room and board:* Room and board charges vary according to board plan and housing facility. *Payment plan:* installment. *Waivers:* employees or children of employees.

Financial Aid Of all full-time matriculated undergraduates who enrolled in 2005, 396 applied for aid, 232 were judged to have need, 48 had their need fully met. 90 Federal Work-Study jobs (averaging $1025). 30 state and other part-time jobs (averaging $1335). In 2005, 53 non-need-based awards were made. *Average percent of need met:* 50%. *Average financial aid package:* $15,931. *Average need-based loan:* $4331. *Average need-based gift aid:* $4163. *Average non-need-based aid:* $11,031. *Average indebtedness upon graduation:* $15,000. *Financial aid deadline:* 2/1.

Applying *Options:* deferred entrance. *Application fee:* $105. *Required:* essay or personal statement, high school transcript, minimum 2.7 GPA, 4 letters of recommendation, audition. *Required for some:* interview. *Application deadlines:* 12/1 (freshmen), 12/1 (transfers). *Notification:* 4/1 (freshmen), 4/1 (transfers).

Freshman Application Contact Ms. Halley Shefler, Dean of Enrollment, The Boston Conservatory, 8 The Fenway, Boston, MA 02215. *Phone:* 617-912-9153. *Fax:* 617-536-3176. *E-mail:* admissions@bostonconservatory.edu.

BOSTON UNIVERSITY

Boston, Massachusetts **www.bu.edu/**

- **Independent** university, founded 1839
- **Urban** 132-acre campus
- **Endowment** $1.1 billion
- **Coed** 18,733 undergraduate students, 92% full-time, 59% women, 41% men
- **Very difficult** entrance level, 59% of applicants were admitted

Boston University (BU) is a private teaching and research institution that strongly emphasizes undergraduate education. Throughout its 168-year history, the University has maintained a commitment to providing the highest level of teaching excellence, and fulfillment of this pledge is its highest priority. BU has ten undergraduate schools and colleges offering more than 250 major and minor areas of concentration. Students may choose from programs of study in areas as diverse as biochemistry, theater arts, physical therapy, elementary education, broadcast journalism, international relations, business, and computer engineering. BU has an international student body, with students representing every state and 100 different countries. In addition, Boston University offers sixty-six study-abroad programs on six continents, spanning twenty-two countries, including the U.S.

Undergraduates 17,206 full-time, 1,527 part-time. Students come from 53 states and territories, 100 other countries, 77% are from out of state, 3% African American, 13% Asian American or Pacific Islander, 7% Hispanic American, 0.3% Native American, 6% international, 1% transferred in, 65% live on campus. *Retention:* 91% of 2006 full-time freshmen returned.

Freshmen *Admission:* 33,930 applied, 19,888 admitted, 4,163 enrolled. *Average high school GPA:* 3.45. *Test scores:* SAT critical reading scores over 500: 97%; SAT math scores over 500: 99%; SAT writing scores over 500: 98%; ACT scores over 18: 100%; SAT critical reading scores over 600: 67%; SAT math scores over 600: 75%; SAT writing scores over 600: 71%; ACT scores over 24: 93%; SAT critical reading scores over 700: 17%; SAT math scores over 700: 22%; SAT writing scores over 700: 17%; ACT scores over 30: 26%.

Faculty *Total:* 2,499, 60% full-time. *Student/faculty ratio:* 14:1.

Majors Accounting; acting; aerospace, aeronautical and astronautical engineering; American studies; ancient/classical Greek; animal physiology; anthropology; archeology; area studies related; art history, criticism and conservation; art teacher education; Asian studies (East); astronomy; astrophysics; athletic training; bilingual and multilingual education; biochemistry; biological and biomedical sciences related; biology/biological sciences; biomedical/medical engineering; business administration and management; chemistry; chemistry teacher education; cinematography and film/video production; classics and languages, literatures and linguistics; clinical laboratory science/medical technology; commercial and advertising art; communication disorders; communication/speech communication and rhetoric; computer engineering; computer science; dental laboratory technology; drama and dance teacher education; drawing; ecology; economics; education; education (specific levels and methods) related; electrical, electronics and communications engineering; elementary education; engineering; engineering related; English; English/language arts teacher education; environmental studies; ethnic, cultural minority, and gender studies related; finance; foreign languages and literatures; foreign language teacher education; French; geography; geology/earth science; German; health science; history; hospitality administration; hotel/motel administration; industrial engineering; information science/studies; interdisciplinary studies; international business/trade/commerce; international finance; international relations and affairs; Italian; journalism; journalism related; kindergarten/preschool education; kinesiology and exercise science; Latin; Latin American studies; legal assistant/paralegal; linguistics; management information systems; marine biology and biological oceanography; marketing/marketing management; marketing research; mass communication/media; mathematics; mathematics and computer science; mathematics teacher education; mechanical engineering; modern Greek; molecular biology; music history, literature, and theory; music performance; music teacher education; music theory and composition; neuroscience; nutrition sciences; occupational therapy; operations management; organizational behavior; painting; parks, recreation and leisure; philosophy; physical education teaching and coaching; physical therapy; physics; piano and organ; political science and government; pre-dentistry studies; psychology; public relations/image management; radio and television; rehabilitation therapy; religious studies; Russian; Russian studies; science teacher education; sculpture; social sciences related; social studies teacher education; sociology; Spanish; special education; special education (hearing impaired); speech/theater education; theater design and technology; theater literature, history and criticism; urban studies/affairs; voice and opera.

Academics *Calendar:* semesters. *Degrees:* bachelor's, master's, doctoral, first professional, post-master's, postbachelor's, and first professional certificates. *Special study options:* accelerated degree program, adult/continuing education programs, advanced placement credit, cooperative education, distance learning, double majors, English as a second language, honors programs, independent study, internships, off-campus study, part-time degree program, services for LD students, student-designed majors, study abroad, summer session for credit. *ROTC:* Army (b), Navy (b), Air Force (b). *Unusual degree programs:* 3-2 business administration; forestry; over 30 other programs.

Computers on Campus 750 computers/terminals are available on campus for general student use. Students can access the following: campus intranet, computer help desk, free student e-mail accounts, online (class) registration, research and educational networks. Campuswide network is available. 95% of college-owned or -operated housing units are wired for high-speed Internet access. Wireless service is available via entire campus.

Student Life *Housing:* on-campus residence required for freshman year. *Options:* coed, women-only, cooperative, disabled students. Campus housing is university owned. Freshman campus housing is guaranteed. *Activities and organizations:* drama/theater group, student-run newspaper, radio and television station, choral group, marching band, performing and acappella groups, cultural organizations, service organizations, student government, residence hall associations, national fraternities, national sororities. *Campus security:* 24-hour emergency response devices and patrols, late-night transport/escort service, controlled dormitory access, security personnel at residence hall entrances, self-defense education, well-lit sidewalks. *Student services:* health clinic, personal/psychological counseling, women's center.

Athletics Member NCAA. All Division I. *Intercollegiate sports:* badminton M (c)/W (c), baseball M (c), basketball M (s)/W (s), cheerleading M (c)/W (c), crew M (s)/W (s), cross-country running M (s)/W (s), equestrian sports M (c)/W (c), fencing M (c)/W (c), field hockey W (s), golf M/W, gymnastics M (c)/W (c), ice hockey M (s)/W (s), lacrosse M (c)/W (s), rugby M (c)/W (c), sailing M (c)/W (c), skiing (downhill) M (c)/W (c), soccer M (s)/W (s), softball W (s), swimming and diving M (s)/W (s), tennis M/W (s), track and field M (s)/W (s), ultimate Frisbee M (c)/W (c), volleyball M (c)/W (c), water polo W (c), wrestling M (s). *Intramural sports:* basketball M/W, field hockey W, football M/W, ice hockey M, soccer M/W, softball M/W, swimming and diving M/W, table tennis M/W, tennis M/W, volleyball M/W.

Standardized Tests *Required:* SAT and SAT Subject Tests or ACT (for admission).

Costs (2008–09) *Comprehensive fee:* $48,468 includes full-time tuition ($36,540), mandatory fees ($510), and room and board ($11,418). Part-time tuition: $1142 per credit. *Required fees:* $40 per term part-time. *College room only:* $7420.

Financial Aid Of all full-time matriculated undergraduates who enrolled in 2007, 7,564 applied for aid, 6,813 were judged to have need, 3,456 had their need fully met. 2,866 Federal Work-Study jobs (averaging $2232). 184 state and other part-time jobs (averaging $10,301). In 2007, 1751 non-need-based awards were made. *Average percent of need met:* 90%. *Average financial aid package:* $29,723. *Average need-based loan:* $5556. *Average need-based gift aid:* $19,968. *Average non-need-based aid:* $16,994. *Average indebtedness upon graduation:* $24,939.

Applying *Options:* electronic application, early admission, early decision, deferred entrance. *Application fee:* $75. *Required:* essay or personal statement, high school transcript, 2 letters of recommendation. *Required for some:* interview, audition, portfolio. *Recommended:* minimum 3.0 GPA. *Application deadlines:* 1/1 (freshmen), 4/1 (transfers). *Early decision deadline:* 11/1. *Notification:* continuous until 4/15 (freshmen), 12/15 (early decision).

Freshman Application Contact Ms. Kelly Walter, Director of Undergraduate Admissions, Boston University, 121 Bay State Road, Boston, MA 02215. *Phone:* 617-353-2300. *Fax:* 617-353-9695. *E-mail:* admissions@bu.edu.

See page 1220 for the College Close-Up.

BRANDEIS UNIVERSITY

Waltham, Massachusetts **www.brandeis.edu/**

- **Independent** university, founded 1948
- **Suburban** 235-acre campus with easy access to Boston
- **Coed** 3,233 undergraduate students, 99% full-time, 56% women, 44% men
- **Most difficult** entrance level, 34% of applicants were admitted

A recent major study ranked Brandeis ninth among all United States private research universities, based on the faculty's contribution to the generation of new knowledge. To help students of exceptional scholarly achievement and promise study with this teaching faculty, Brandeis offers a significant number of scholarships of up to full tuition.

Undergraduates 3,216 full-time, 17 part-time. Students come from 48 states and territories, 52 other countries, 75% are from out of state, 4% African American, 9% Asian American or Pacific Islander, 4% Hispanic American, 0.2% Native American, 7% international, 1% transferred in, 77% live on campus. *Retention:* 94% of 2006 full-time freshmen returned.

Freshmen *Admission:* 7,562 applied, 2,601 admitted, 701 enrolled. *Average high school GPA:* 3.8. *Test scores:* SAT critical reading scores over 500: 98%; SAT math scores over 500: 99%; ACT scores over 18: 99%; SAT critical reading scores over 600: 86%; SAT math scores over 600: 89%; ACT scores over 24: 95%; SAT critical reading scores over 700: 42%; SAT math scores over 700: 45%; ACT scores over 30: 61%.

Faculty *Total:* 479, 73% full-time, 89% with terminal degrees. *Student/faculty ratio:* 8:1.

Majors African-American/Black studies; American studies; ancient/classical Greek; anthropology; area, ethnic, cultural, and gender studies related; art history, criticism and conservation; Asian studies (East); biochemistry; biology/biological sciences; biophysics; chemistry; comparative literature; computer science; creative writing; dramatic/theater arts; economics; English; European studies; fine/studio arts; French; German; health/health care administration; history; international/global studies; Jewish/Judaic studies; Latin; Latin American studies; linguistics; mathematics; multi-/interdisciplinary studies related; music; Near and Middle Eastern studies; neuroscience; philosophy; physics; political science and government related; psychology; Russian; sociology; Spanish; women's studies.

Academics *Calendar:* semesters. *Degrees:* bachelor's, master's, doctoral, and postbachelor's certificates. *Special study options:* adult/continuing education

COLLEGE DATA CENTER • MASSACHUSETTS

programs, advanced placement credit, double majors, English as a second language, honors programs, independent study, internships, off-campus study, services for LD students, student-designed majors, study abroad, summer session for credit. *ROTC:* Army (c), Air Force (c).

Computers on Campus 104 computers/terminals are available on campus for general student use. Students can access the following: computer help desk, free student e-mail accounts, online (class) grades, online (class) registration, online (class) schedules, educational software. Campuswide network is available. Wireless service is available via entire campus.

Student Life *Housing options:* coed, men-only, women-only, disabled students. Campus housing is university owned. Freshman campus housing is guaranteed. *Activities and organizations:* drama/theater group, student-run newspaper, radio and television station, choral group, Waltham Group, Student Programming Board, performing groups, student government. *Campus security:* 24-hour emergency response devices and patrols, late-night transport/escort service, controlled dormitory access. *Student services:* health clinic, personal/psychological counseling, women's center.

Athletics Member NCAA. All Division III. *Intercollegiate sports:* baseball M, basketball M/W, crew M (c), cross-country running M/W, fencing M/W, field hockey W (c), golf M, lacrosse M (c)/W (c), rugby M (c)/W (c), sailing M/W, skiing (downhill) M (c)/W (c), soccer W, softball W, squash M (c), swimming and diving M/W, tennis M/W, track and field M/W, volleyball W. *Intramural sports:* basketball M/W, cheerleading W, equestrian sports M/W, football M, golf M/W, ice hockey M, lacrosse M, softball M/W, squash M/W, table tennis M/W, tennis M/W, volleyball M/W, water polo M/W, weight lifting M/W.

Standardized Tests *Required:* SAT and SAT Subject Tests or ACT (for admission).

Costs (2007–08) *Comprehensive fee:* $45,610 includes full-time tuition ($34,566), mandatory fees ($1136), and room and board ($9908). Part-time tuition and fees vary according to course load. *College room only:* $5558. Room and board charges vary according to board plan and housing facility. *Payment plan:* installment. *Waivers:* employees or children of employees.

Financial Aid Of all full-time matriculated undergraduates who enrolled in 2006, 1,937 applied for aid, 1,567 were judged to have need, 486 had their need fully met. In 2006, 721 non-need-based awards were made. *Average percent of need met:* 85%. *Average financial aid package:* $25,928. *Average need-based loan:* $6024. *Average need-based gift aid:* $20,643. *Average non-need-based aid:* $19,915. *Average indebtedness upon graduation:* $19,892.

Applying *Options:* electronic application, early decision, deferred entrance. *Application fee:* $55. *Required:* essay or personal statement, high school transcript, 2 letters of recommendation. *Recommended:* interview. *Application deadlines:* 1/15 (freshmen), 4/1 (transfers). *Early decision deadline:* 11/15 (for plan 1), 1/1 (for plan 2). *Notification:* 4/1 (freshmen), 6/1 (transfers), 12/15 (early decision plan 1), 2/1 (early decision plan 2).

Freshman Application Contact Mr. Gil J. Villanueva, Dean of Admissions, Brandeis University, 415 South Street, Waltham, MA 02254-9110. *Phone:* 781-736-3500. *Toll-free phone:* 800-622-0622. *Fax:* 781-736-3536. *E-mail:* admissions@brandeis.edu.

See page 1222 for the College Close-Up.

BRIDGEWATER STATE COLLEGE

Bridgewater, Massachusetts **www.bridgew.edu/**

- **State-supported** comprehensive, founded 1840, part of Massachusetts Public Higher Education System
- **Suburban** 235-acre campus with easy access to Boston
- **Endowment** $14.4 million
- **Coed** 8,160 undergraduate students, 83% full-time, 59% women, 41% men
- **Moderately difficult** entrance level, 69% of applicants were admitted

Undergraduates 6,771 full-time, 1,389 part-time. Students come from 26 states and territories, 19 other countries, 5% are from out of state, 6% African American, 2% Asian American or Pacific Islander, 2% Hispanic American, 0.4% Native American, 1% international, 10% transferred in, 33% live on campus. *Retention:* 74% of 2006 full-time freshmen returned.

Freshmen *Admission:* 6,498 applied, 4,507 admitted, 1,584 enrolled. *Average high school GPA:* 3.01. *Test scores:* SAT critical reading scores over 500: 53%; SAT math scores over 500: 56%; ACT scores over 18: 88%; SAT critical reading scores over 600: 12%; SAT math scores over 600: 12%; ACT scores over 24: 23%; SAT critical reading scores over 700: 1%; SAT math scores over 700: 1%; ACT scores over 30: 3%.

Faculty *Total:* 587, 51% full-time. *Student/faculty ratio:* 20:1.

Majors Accounting; airline pilot and flight crew; American government and politics; anthropology related; archeology; area studies related; art history, criticism and conservation; art teacher education; athletic training; aviation/airway management; biochemistry; biology/biological sciences; biology teacher education; biomedical sciences; business administration and management; business, management, and marketing related; cell and molecular biology; chemistry; chemistry related; city/urban, community and regional planning; communication disorders; communication/speech communication and rhetoric; computer science; crafts, folk art and artisanry; creative writing; criminal justice/safety; developmental and child psychology; drama and dance teacher education; dramatic/theater arts; early childhood education; economics; elementary education; English; English/language arts teacher education; environmental biology; ethics; finance; fine/studio arts; geochemistry; geography; geography related; geological and earth sciences/geosciences related; geology/earth science; graphic design; health and physical education related; health/medical psychology; health teacher education; history; history related; industrial and organizational psychology; international business/trade/commerce; international relations and affairs; kinesiology and exercise science; kinesiotherapy; legal studies; management information systems; marketing/marketing management; mathematics; music; music teacher education; parks, recreation and leisure; philosophy; photography; physical education teaching and coaching; physics; physics related; political science and government; psychology; science technologies related; social work; sociology; Spanish; special education; sport and fitness administration/management; transportation management.

Academics *Calendar:* semesters. *Degrees:* certificates, bachelor's, master's, post-master's, and postbachelor's certificates. *Special study options:* academic remediation for entering students, accelerated degree program, adult/continuing education programs, advanced placement credit, distance learning, double majors, English as a second language, honors programs, independent study, internships, off-campus study, part-time degree program, services for LD students, study abroad, summer session for credit. *ROTC:* Army (c), Air Force (c).

Computers on Campus 900 computers/terminals are available on campus for general student use. Students can access the following: online (class) registration, student account information, application software. Campuswide network is available. Wireless service is available via entire campus.

Student Life *Housing options:* coed, women-only, disabled students. Campus housing is university owned. Freshman applicants given priority for college housing. *Activities and organizations:* drama/theater group, student-run newspaper, radio station, choral group, marching band, Children's Developmental Clinic, Student Government Association, Afro-American/Latino Club, Program Committee, national fraternities, national sororities. *Campus security:* 24-hour emergency response devices and patrols, late-night transport/escort service, controlled dormitory access. *Student services:* health clinic, personal/psychological counseling, women's center.

Athletics Member NCAA. All Division III. *Intercollegiate sports:* baseball M, basketball M/W, cross-country running M/W, field hockey W, football M, lacrosse M (c)/W, soccer M/W, softball W, swimming and diving M/W, tennis M/W, track and field M/W, volleyball W, water polo M (c)/W (c), wrestling M. *Intramural sports:* basketball M/W, football M/W, soccer M/W, softball M/W, tennis M/W, volleyball M/W.

Standardized Tests *Required:* SAT or ACT (for admission).

Costs (2007–08) *Tuition:* state resident $910 full-time, $38 per credit hour part-time; nonresident $7050 full-time, $294 per credit hour part-time. *Required fees:* $5123 full-time, $208 per credit hour part-time. *Room and board:* $6852. Room and board charges vary according to board plan and housing facility. *Payment plan:* installment. *Waivers:* employees or children of employees.

Financial Aid Of all full-time matriculated undergraduates who enrolled in 2006, 4,725 applied for aid, 3,341 were judged to have need. 450 Federal Work-Study jobs (averaging $1275). In 2006, 76 non-need-based awards were made. *Average percent of need met:* 56%. *Average financial aid package:* $6465. *Average need-based loan:* $3285. *Average need-based gift aid:* $3640. *Average non-need-based aid:* $5280. *Average indebtedness upon graduation:* $16,634.

Applying *Options:* electronic application, early admission, early action, deferred entrance. *Application fee:* $25. *Required:* essay or personal statement, high school transcript, minimum 3.0 GPA. *Required for some:* for applicants whose high school GPA is below 3.0, a sliding SAT scale will be used. *Recommended:* letters of recommendation. *Application deadlines:* 2/15 (freshmen), 6/1 (transfers), 11/15 (early action). *Notification:* continuous (freshmen), 12/15 (early action).

Freshman Application Contact Mr. Gregg Meyer, Director of Admissions, Bridgewater State College, Gates House, Bridgewater, MA 02325. *Phone:* 508-531-1237. *E-mail:* admission@bridgew.edu.

See page 1224 for the College Close-Up.

CAMBRIDGE COLLEGE

Cambridge, Massachusetts **www.cambridgecollege.edu/**

- **Independent** comprehensive, founded 1971
- **Urban** campus with easy access to Boston
- **Endowment** $7.6 million
- **Coed** 1,306 undergraduate students, 27% full-time, 69% women, 31% men
- **Minimally difficult** entrance level

Undergraduates 356 full-time, 950 part-time. Students come from 19 states and territories, 50 other countries, 14% are from out of state, 35% African American, 3% Asian American or Pacific Islander, 22% Hispanic American, 0.5% Native American, 4% international, 46% transferred in. *Retention:* 33% of 2006 full-time freshmen returned.

Freshmen *Admission:* 388 enrolled.

Faculty *Total:* 1,093, 3% full-time, 20% with terminal degrees. *Student/faculty ratio:* 11:1.

Majors Human services; management science; multi-/interdisciplinary studies related; psychology.

Academics *Calendar:* trimesters. *Degrees:* certificates, bachelor's, master's, doctoral, and post-master's certificates. *Special study options:* accelerated degree program, adult/continuing education programs, distance learning, English as a second language, independent study, internships, part-time degree program, services for LD students, summer session for credit.

Computers on Campus Students can access the following: online (class) registration. Campuswide network is available.

Student Life *Housing:* college housing not available.

Costs (2007–08) *Tuition:* $10,350 full-time, $345 per credit part-time. *Required fees:* $130 full-time. *Payment plan:* installment. *Waivers:* employees or children of employees.

Financial Aid Of all full-time matriculated undergraduates who enrolled in 2002, 179 applied for aid, 155 were judged to have need. *Average financial aid package:* $8695. *Average need-based loan:* $3600. *Average need-based gift aid:* $5338. *Average indebtedness upon graduation:* $24,200.

Applying *Options:* deferred entrance. *Application fee:* $30. *Required:* essay or personal statement, high school transcript, letters of recommendation. *Required for some:* interview. *Recommended:* 3 years of work experience. *Application deadlines:* rolling (freshmen), rolling (transfers). *Notification:* continuous (freshmen), continuous (transfers).

Freshman Application Contact Undergraduate Admissions, Cambridge College, 1000 Massachusetts Avenue, Cambridge, MA 02138. *Phone:* 617-868-1000 Ext. 1124. *Toll-free phone:* 800-877-4723. *Fax:* 617-349-3545. *E-mail:* admit@cambridgecollege.edu.

CLARK UNIVERSITY

Worcester, Massachusetts **www.clarku.edu/**

- **Independent** university, founded 1887
- **Urban** 50-acre campus with easy access to Boston
- **Endowment** $290.0 million
- **Coed** 2,320 undergraduate students, 94% full-time, 60% women, 40% men
- **Moderately difficult** entrance level, 56% of applicants were admitted

Undergraduates 2,179 full-time, 141 part-time. Students come from 44 states and territories, 62 other countries, 64% are from out of state, 2% African American, 4% Asian American or Pacific Islander, 2% Hispanic American, 0.3% Native American, 8% international, 3% transferred in, 76% live on campus. *Retention:* 88% of 2006 full-time freshmen returned.

Freshmen *Admission:* 5,201 applied, 2,918 admitted, 574 enrolled. *Average high school GPA:* 3.47. *Test scores:* SAT critical reading scores over 500: 92%; SAT math scores over 500: 92%; ACT scores over 18: 99%; SAT critical reading scores over 600: 57%; SAT math scores over 600: 47%; ACT scores over 24: 78%; SAT critical reading scores over 700: 15%; SAT math scores over 700: 7%; ACT scores over 30: 10%.

Faculty *Total:* 271, 64% full-time. *Student/faculty ratio:* 10:1.

Majors Art history, criticism and conservation; Asian studies; biochemistry; biology/biological sciences; business administration and management; chemistry; classics and languages, literatures and linguistics; commercial and advertising art; comparative literature; computer science; cultural studies; development economics and international development; dramatic/theater arts; ecology; economics; education; elementary education; engineering; English; film/cinema studies; fine/studio arts; French; geography; geology/earth science; history; interdisciplinary studies; international relations and affairs; Jewish/Judaic studies; mass communication/media; mathematics; middle school education; modern languages; molecular biology; music; natural resources management and policy; neuroscience; peace studies and conflict resolution; philosophy; physics; political science and government; pre-dentistry studies; pre-law studies; pre-medical studies; pre-veterinary studies; psychology; secondary education; sociology; Spanish; women's studies.

Academics *Calendar:* semesters. *Degrees:* bachelor's, master's, doctoral, post-master's, and postbachelor's certificates. *Special study options:* academic remediation for entering students, accelerated degree program, adult/continuing education programs, advanced placement credit, double majors, English as a second language, honors programs, independent study, internships, off-campus study, part-time degree program, services for LD students, student-designed majors, study abroad, summer session for credit. *ROTC:* Army (c), Navy (c), Air Force (c). *Unusual degree programs:* 3-2 business administration; engineering with Columbia University, Washington University in St. Louis, Worcester Polytechnic Institute; environmental studies, international development, biology, chemistry, physics, economics, history, communication, public administration, geographic information systems.

Computers on Campus 58 computers/terminals and 4,000 ports are available on campus for general student use. Students can access the following: campus intranet, computer help desk, free student e-mail accounts, online (class) grades, online (class) registration, online (class) schedules, online course support. Campuswide network is available. 100% of college-owned or -operated housing units are wired for high-speed Internet access. Wireless service is available via classrooms, computer centers, computer labs, learning centers, libraries, student centers.

Student Life *Housing:* on-campus residence required through sophomore year. *Options:* coed, women-only, disabled students. Campus housing is university owned. Freshman campus housing is guaranteed. *Activities and organizations:* drama/theater group, student-run newspaper, radio and television station, choral group, marching band, Student Activities Board, Hillel, Pub Entertainment Committee, Massachusetts PIRG, Film Society. *Campus security:* 24-hour emergency response devices and patrols, student patrols, late-night transport/escort service, controlled dormitory access. *Student services:* health clinic, personal/psychological counseling, women's center.

Athletics Member NCAA. All Division III. *Intercollegiate sports:* baseball M, basketball M/W, crew M/W, cross-country running M/W, field hockey W, lacrosse M, soccer M/W, softball W, swimming and diving M/W, tennis M/W, volleyball W. *Intramural sports:* badminton M/W, basketball M/W, bowling M/W, equestrian sports M (c)/W (c), football M/W, golf M (c)/W (c), ice hockey M (c), lacrosse W (c), racquetball M/W, rugby M (c)/W (c), sailing M (c)/W (c), soccer M/W, softball M/W, squash M/W, table tennis M/W, track and field M (c)/W (c), ultimate Frisbee M/W, volleyball M/W, water polo M/W, weight lifting M (c)/W (c).

Standardized Tests *Required:* SAT or ACT (for admission).

Costs (2007–08) *Comprehensive fee:* $39,165 includes full-time tuition ($32,600), mandatory fees ($265), and room and board ($6300). Part-time tuition: $1019 per credit hour. *College room only:* $3700. Room and board charges vary according to board plan and housing facility. *Payment plans:* tuition prepayment, installment. *Waivers:* employees or children of employees.

Financial Aid Of all full-time matriculated undergraduates who enrolled in 2006, 1,521 applied for aid, 1,176 were judged to have need, 827 had their need fully met. In 2006, 504 non-need-based awards were made. *Average percent of need met:* 94%. *Average financial aid package:* $24,581. *Average need-based loan:* $4531. *Average need-based gift aid:* $18,954. *Average non-need-based aid:* $13,451. *Average indebtedness upon graduation:* $21,100. *Financial aid deadline:* 2/1.

Applying *Options:* early admission, early decision, deferred entrance. *Application fee:* $55. *Required:* essay or personal statement, high school transcript, 2 letters of recommendation. *Recommended:* interview. *Application deadlines:* 1/15 (freshmen), 4/15 (transfers). *Early decision deadline:* 11/15. *Notification:* 4/1 (freshmen), 6/1 (transfers), 12/15 (early decision).

Freshman Application Contact Mr. Harold Wingood, Dean of Admissions, Clark University, Admissions House, 950 Main Street, Worcester, MA 01610. *Phone:* 508-793-7431. *Toll-free phone:* 800-GO-CLARK. *Fax:* 508-793-8821. *E-mail:* admissions@clarku.edu.

COLLEGE OF THE HOLY CROSS

Worcester, Massachusetts **www.holycross.edu/**

- **Independent Roman Catholic (Jesuit)** 4-year, founded 1843
- **Suburban** 174-acre campus with easy access to Boston
- **Endowment** $660.6 million
- **Coed** 2,846 undergraduate students, 99% full-time, 56% women, 44% men
- **Very difficult** entrance level, 33% of applicants were admitted

Undergraduates 2,817 full-time, 29 part-time. Students come from 49 states and territories, 13 other countries, 61% are from out of state, 4% African American, 5% Asian American or Pacific Islander, 5% Hispanic American, 0.5% Native American, 1% international, 0.8% transferred in, 90% live on campus. *Retention:* 94% of 2006 full-time freshmen returned.

Freshmen *Admission:* 7,066 applied, 2,331 admitted, 717 enrolled. *Test scores:* SAT critical reading scores over 500: 94%; SAT math scores over 500: 97%; SAT critical reading scores over 600: 76%; SAT math scores over 600: 79%; SAT critical reading scores over 700: 19%; SAT math scores over 700: 20%.

Faculty *Total:* 288, 83% full-time. *Student/faculty ratio:* 11:1.

Majors Accounting; anthropology; art history, criticism and conservation; Asian studies; biology/biological sciences; chemistry; classics and languages, literatures and linguistics; comparative literature; computer science; dramatic/theater arts; economics; English; environmental studies; fine/studio arts; French; German; German studies; history; Italian; literature; mathematics; medieval and Renaissance studies; music; philosophy; physics; political science and government; pre-medical studies; psychology; religious studies; Russian; Russian studies; sociology; Spanish.

Academics *Calendar:* semesters. *Degrees:* bachelor's (standardized tests are optional for admission to the College of Holy Cross). *Special study options:* accelerated degree program, advanced placement credit, double majors, honors programs, independent study, internships, off-campus study, student-designed majors, study abroad. *ROTC:* Army (c), Navy (b), Air Force (c). *Unusual degree programs:* 3-2 engineering with Columbia University, Dartmouth College.

Computers on Campus 485 computers/terminals are available on campus for general student use. Students can access the following: computer help desk, free student e-mail accounts, online (class) registration. Campuswide network is available. 100% of college-owned or -operated housing units are wired for high-speed Internet access. Wireless service is available via classrooms, computer centers, computer labs, dorm rooms, libraries, student centers.

Student Life *Housing:* on-campus residence required through sophomore year. *Options:* coed, disabled students. Campus housing is university owned. Freshman campus housing is guaranteed. *Activities and organizations:* drama/theater group, student-run newspaper, radio station, choral group, marching band, SPUD (community service organization), choral and music groups, Campus Activities Board, Student Government Association, Purple Key Society. *Campus security:* 24-hour emergency response devices and patrols, late-night transport/escort service, controlled dormitory access. *Student services:* health clinic, personal/psychological counseling, women's center.

Athletics Member NCAA. All Division I except football (Division I-AA). *Intercollegiate sports:* baseball M, basketball M (s)/W (s), crew M/W, cross-country running M/W, field hockey W, golf M/W, ice hockey M/W, lacrosse M/W, soccer M/W, softball W, swimming and diving M/W, tennis M/W, track and field M/W, volleyball W. *Intramural sports:* baseball M (c), basketball M/W, equestrian sports M (c)/W (c), football M, ice hockey M (c), lacrosse M (c)/W (c), rugby W (c), sailing M (c)/W (c), skiing (downhill) M (c)/W (c), soccer M (c)/W (c), softball M/W, tennis M/W, ultimate Frisbee M (c)/W (c), volleyball M/W, water polo M (c)/W (c).

Costs (2008–09) *Comprehensive fee:* $47,502 includes full-time tuition ($36,710), mandatory fees ($532), and room and board ($10,260). *College room only:* $5130.

Financial Aid Of all full-time matriculated undergraduates who enrolled in 2007, 1,726 applied for aid, 1,546 were judged to have need, 1,546 had their need fully met. 919 Federal Work-Study jobs (averaging $1664). In 2007, 70 non-need-based awards were made. *Average percent of need met:* 100%. *Average financial aid package:* $27,856. *Average need-based loan:* $4897. *Average need-based gift aid:* $22,217. *Average non-need-based aid:* $18,318. *Average indebtedness upon graduation:* $17,000. *Financial aid deadline:* 2/1.

Applying *Options:* electronic application, early admission, early decision, deferred entrance. *Application fee:* $50. *Required:* essay or personal statement, high school transcript, 2 letters of recommendation. *Recommended:* interview. *Application deadlines:* 1/15 (freshmen), 5/1 (transfers). *Early decision deadline:* 12/15. *Notification:* 4/1 (freshmen), 6/1 (transfers), 1/15 (early decision).

Freshman Application Contact Ms. Ann Bowe McDermott, Director of Admissions, College of the Holy Cross, 105 Fenwick Hall, 1 College Street, Worcester, MA 01610-2395. *Phone:* 508-793-2443. *Toll-free phone:* 800-442-2421. *Fax:* 508-793-3888. *E-mail:* admissions@holycross.edu.

CURRY COLLEGE

Milton, Massachusetts

www.curry.edu/

- **Independent** comprehensive, founded 1879
- **Suburban** 131-acre campus with easy access to Boston
- **Endowment** $32.4 million
- **Coed** 2,832 undergraduate students, 72% full-time, 58% women, 42% men
- **Moderately difficult** entrance level, 66% of applicants were admitted

Undergraduates 2,053 full-time, 779 part-time. Students come from 34 states and territories, 18 other countries, 23% are from out of state, 7% African American, 0.9% Asian American or Pacific Islander, 2% Hispanic American, 0.2% Native American, 0.5% international, 5% transferred in, 75% live on campus. *Retention:* 64% of 2006 full-time freshmen returned.

Freshmen *Admission:* 3,739 applied, 2,472 admitted, 642 enrolled. *Average high school GPA:* 2.7. *Test scores:* SAT critical reading scores over 500: 31%; SAT math scores over 500: 28%; SAT critical reading scores over 600: 6%; SAT math scores over 600: 2%; SAT critical reading scores over 700: 1%.

Faculty *Total:* 438, 26% full-time, 59% with terminal degrees. *Student/faculty ratio:* 12:1.

Majors Biology/biological sciences; business administration and management; commercial and advertising art; criminal justice/law enforcement administration; early childhood education; education; elementary education; English; environmental studies; family/community studies; film/cinema studies; health teacher education; history; information technology; journalism; kindergarten/preschool education; mass communication/media; nursing (registered nurse training); philosophy; physics; political science and government; pre-law studies; psychology; public relations/image management; radio and television; sociology; special education; women's studies.

Academics *Calendar:* semesters. *Degrees:* certificates, bachelor's, and master's. *Special study options:* academic remediation for entering students, accelerated degree program, adult/continuing education programs, advanced placement credit, double majors, external degree program, honors programs, independent study, internships, off-campus study, part-time degree program, services for LD students, student-designed majors, study abroad, summer session for credit. *ROTC:* Army (c).

Computers on Campus 185 computers/terminals and 2,500 ports are available on campus for general student use. Students can access the following: campus intranet, computer help desk, free student e-mail accounts, online (class) grades, online (class) registration, online (class) schedules, library online catalog and research databases. Campuswide network is available. 100% of college-owned or -operated housing units are wired for high-speed Internet access. Wireless service is available via classrooms, computer centers, computer labs, learning centers, libraries, student centers.

Student Life *Housing options:* coed, men-only, women-only. Campus housing is university owned. *Activities and organizations:* drama/theater group, student-run newspaper, radio and television station, choral group, student radio station, student government, Campus Activities Board, student newspaper, Drama Club. *Campus security:* 24-hour emergency response devices and patrols, late-night transport/escort service, controlled dormitory access. *Student services:* health clinic, personal/psychological counseling.

Athletics Member NCAA. All Division III. *Intercollegiate sports:* baseball M, basketball M/W, cross-country running W, football M, ice hockey M, lacrosse M/W, soccer M/W, softball W, tennis M/W. *Intramural sports:* basketball M/W, cheerleading M/W, rugby M/W, skiing (downhill) M/W, softball M/W, tennis M/W, ultimate Frisbee M/W, volleyball M/W.

Standardized Tests *Required for some:* SAT or ACT (for admission).

Costs (2007–08) *Comprehensive fee:* $36,215 includes full-time tuition ($24,975), mandatory fees ($950), and room and board ($10,290). Part-time tuition: $835 per credit hour. Part-time tuition and fees vary according to course load. *College room only:* $6010. Room and board charges vary according to board plan and housing facility. *Payment plan:* installment. *Waivers:* employees or children of employees.

Financial Aid Of all full-time matriculated undergraduates who enrolled in 2007, 1,408 applied for aid, 1,397 were judged to have need, 89 had their need fully met. 560 Federal Work-Study jobs (averaging $1800). In 2007, 70 non-need-based awards were made. *Average percent of need met:* 70%. *Average financial aid package:* $16,571. *Average need-based loan:* $4359. *Average need-based gift aid:* $11,280. *Average non-need-based aid:* $5325. *Average indebtedness upon graduation:* $27,145.

Applying *Options:* electronic application, early admission, early decision, deferred entrance. *Application fee:* $40. *Required:* essay or personal statement, high school transcript, minimum 2.0 GPA, 1 letter of recommendation. *Required for some:* interview. *Recommended:* interview. *Application deadlines:* 4/1 (freshmen), 7/1 (transfers). *Early decision deadline:* 12/1. *Notification:* continuous (freshmen), continuous (transfers), 12/15 (early decision).

Freshman Application Contact Ms. Jane P. Fidler, Dean of Admission, Curry College, 1071 Blue Hill Avenue, Milton, MA 02186. *Phone:* 617-333-2210. *Toll-free phone:* 800-669-0686. *Fax:* 617-333-2114. *E-mail:* curryadm@curry.edu.

See page 1226 for the College Close-Up.

DEAN COLLEGE

Franklin, Massachusetts www.dean.edu/

- **Independent** primarily 2-year, founded 1865
- **Small-town** 100-acre campus with easy access to Boston and Providence
- **Endowment** $22.8 million
- **Coed**
- **Minimally difficult** entrance level

Dean College is a private two- and four-year residential college located in suburban Franklin, Massachusetts. From rigorous academics to unparalleled academic support services to a committed faculty, Dean has a remarkable track record of taking students wherever they want to go.

Faculty *Student/faculty ratio:* 19:1.
Academics *Calendar:* semesters. *Degrees:* certificates, associate, and bachelor's.
Student Life *Campus security:* 24-hour emergency response devices and patrols, late-night transport/escort service, controlled dormitory access.
Athletics Member NJCAA.
Standardized Tests *Required:* SAT or ACT (for admission).
Costs (2007–08) *Comprehensive fee:* $36,380 includes full-time tuition ($25,420) and room and board ($10,960). Part-time tuition: $690 per course. *College room only:* $6930.
Applying *Options:* electronic application, deferred entrance. *Application fee:* $35. *Required:* essay or personal statement, high school transcript, letters of recommendation. *Recommended:* minimum 2.0 GPA, interview.
Freshman Application Contact Mr. Paul Vaccaro, Assistant Vice President for Enrollment Services and Dean of Admission, Dean College, 99 Main Street, Franklin, MA 02038. *Phone:* 508-541-1508. *Toll-free phone:* 877-TRY-DEAN. *Fax:* 508-541-8726. *E-mail:* admission@dean.edu.

See page 1228 for the College Close-Up.

EASTERN NAZARENE COLLEGE

Quincy, Massachusetts www.enc.edu/

- **Independent** comprehensive, founded 1918, affiliated with Church of the Nazarene
- **Suburban** 15-acre campus with easy access to Boston
- **Endowment** $11.0 million
- **Coed**
- **Moderately difficult** entrance level

Faculty *Student/faculty ratio:* 11:1.
Academics *Calendar:* 4-1-4. *Degrees:* associate, bachelor's, and master's.
Student Life *Campus security:* 24-hour emergency response devices and patrols, student patrols, late-night transport/escort service, controlled dormitory access.
Athletics Member NCAA. All Division III.
Standardized Tests *Required:* SAT or ACT (for admission).
Costs (2008–09) *Comprehensive fee:* $29,927 includes full-time tuition ($21,280), mandatory fees ($734), and room and board ($7913). Part-time tuition: $842 per credit hour. *College room only:* $3975.
Financial Aid Of all full-time matriculated undergraduates who enrolled in 2000, 572 applied for aid, 456 were judged to have need, 110 had their need fully met. 179 Federal Work-Study jobs (averaging $1362). In 2000, 106 non-need-based awards were made. *Average percent of need met:* 69. *Average financial aid package:* $10,394. *Average need-based loan:* $4122. *Average need-based gift aid:* $3144. *Average non-need-based aid:* $4275.
Applying *Options:* deferred entrance. *Application fee:* $25. *Required:* essay or personal statement, high school transcript, minimum 2.0 GPA, 1 letter of recommendation, interview.
Freshman Application Contact Mr. Jeffrey Wells, Vice President of Enrollment Management, Eastern Nazarene College, 23 East Elm Avenue, Quincy, MA 02170. *Phone:* 800-883-6288. *Toll-free phone:* 800-88-ENC88. *Fax:* 617-745-3992. *E-mail:* admissions@enc.edu.

ELMS COLLEGE

Chicopee, Massachusetts www.elms.edu/

Freshman Application Contact Mr. Joseph Wagner, Director of Admissions, Elms College, Chicopee, MA 01013-2839. *Phone:* 413-592-3189 Ext. 350. *Toll-free phone:* 800-255-ELMS. *Fax:* 413-594-2781. *E-mail:* admissions@elms.edu.

See page 1230 for the College Close-Up.

EMERSON COLLEGE

Boston, Massachusetts www.emerson.edu/

- **Independent** comprehensive, founded 1880
- **Urban** campus
- **Endowment** $91.5 million
- **Coed** 3,476 undergraduate students, 93% full-time, 56% women, 44% men
- **Very difficult** entrance level, 45% of applicants were admitted

Founded in 1880, Emerson is one of the premier colleges in the United States for the study of communication and the arts. Located on Boston Common in the city's theater district, the College's 3,000 students participate in internships, study abroad, and more than sixty student organizations, performance groups, NCAA teams, student publications, and honor societies. More information can be found online at http://www.emerson.edu/admission.

Undergraduates 3,222 full-time, 254 part-time. Students come from 45 states and territories, 50 other countries, 74% are from out of state, 3% African American, 5% Asian American or Pacific Islander, 7% Hispanic American, 0.6% Native American, 2% international, 4% transferred in, 50% live on campus. *Retention:* 88% of 2006 full-time freshmen returned.
Freshmen *Admission:* 4,981 applied, 2,221 admitted, 776 enrolled. *Average high school GPA:* 3.62. *Test scores:* SAT critical reading scores over 500: 98%; SAT math scores over 500: 94%; SAT writing scores over 500: 97%; ACT scores over 18: 100%; SAT critical reading scores over 600: 70%; SAT math scores over 600: 52%; SAT writing scores over 600: 66%; ACT scores over 24: 84%; SAT critical reading scores over 700: 19%; SAT math scores over 700: 7%; SAT writing scores over 700: 16%; ACT scores over 30: 18%.
Faculty *Total:* 381, 42% full-time, 50% with terminal degrees. *Student/faculty ratio:* 14:1.
Majors Acting; advertising; audiology and speech-language pathology; broadcast journalism; cinematography and film/video production; communication disorders; communication/speech communication and rhetoric; creative writing; drama and dance teacher education; dramatic/theater arts; film/cinema studies; interdisciplinary studies; intermedia/multimedia; journalism; marketing/marketing management; mass communication/media; playwriting and screenwriting; political communication; public relations/image management; publishing; radio and television; radio and television broadcasting technology; radio, television, and digital communication related; special education (speech or language impaired); speech and rhetoric; speech-language pathology; speech therapy; theater design and technology; visual and performing arts.
Academics *Calendar:* semesters. *Degrees:* bachelor's, master's, and doctoral. *Special study options:* adult/continuing education programs, advanced placement credit, double majors, honors programs, independent study, internships, off-campus study, part-time degree program, services for LD students, student-designed majors, study abroad, summer session for credit.
Computers on Campus 466 computers/terminals are available on campus for general student use. Students can access the following: computer help desk, free student e-mail accounts, online (class) registration. Campuswide network is available. 100% of college-owned or -operated housing units are wired for high-speed Internet access. Wireless service is available via classrooms, computer centers, computer labs, dorm rooms, learning centers, libraries, student centers.
Student Life *Housing:* on-campus residence required through sophomore year. *Options:* coed. Campus housing is university owned. Freshman applicants given priority for college housing. *Activities and organizations:* drama/theater group, student-run newspaper, radio and television station, choral group, EIV (Emerson Independent Video), National Broadcasting Society (student chapter), EmComm (student marketing agency), Berkeley Beacon (student newspaper), Emerson Channel (campus TV), national fraternities, national sororities. *Campus security:* 24-hour emergency response devices and patrols, late-night transport/escort service, controlled dormitory access. *Student services:* health clinic, personal/psychological counseling.

Athletics Member NCAA. All Division III. *Intercollegiate sports:* baseball M, basketball M/W, cross-country running M/W, ice hockey M (c), lacrosse M/W, soccer M/W, softball W, tennis M/W, volleyball M/W. *Intramural sports:* weight lifting M/W.

Standardized Tests *Required:* SAT or ACT (for admission).

Costs (2007–08) *Comprehensive fee:* $38,256 includes full-time tuition ($26,880) and room and board ($11,376). Part-time tuition: $840 per credit hour. *Payment plan:* installment. *Waivers:* employees or children of employees.

Financial Aid Of all full-time matriculated undergraduates who enrolled in 2007, 2,016 applied for aid, 1,616 were judged to have need, 1,254 had their need fully met. 382 Federal Work-Study jobs (averaging $2124). 52 state and other part-time jobs (averaging $9673). In 2007, 457 non-need-based awards were made. *Average percent of need met:* 73%. *Average financial aid package:* $15,646. *Average need-based loan:* $4509. *Average need-based gift aid:* $13,120. *Average non-need-based aid:* $14,913. *Average indebtedness upon graduation:* $33,233.

Applying *Options:* electronic application, early admission, early action, deferred entrance. *Application fee:* $65. *Required:* essay or personal statement, high school transcript, letters of recommendation. *Required for some:* interview, Performing Arts candidates must submit a resume of theatre-related activities and either audition or interview, or submit a portfolio or an essay. *Application deadlines:* 1/5 (freshmen), 3/15 (transfers), 11/1 (early action). *Notification:* 4/1 (freshmen), 5/1 (transfers), 12/15 (early action).

Freshman Application Contact Emerson College, 120 Boylston Street, Boston, MA 02116-4624. *Phone:* 617-824-8600.

See page 1232 for the College Close-Up.

EMMANUEL COLLEGE

Boston, Massachusetts **www.emmanuel.edu/**

- **Independent Roman Catholic** comprehensive, founded 1919
- **Urban** 17-acre campus
- **Endowment** $80.1 million
- **Coed** 2,282 undergraduate students, 73% full-time, 73% women, 27% men
- **Moderately difficult** entrance level, 61% of applicants were admitted

Undergraduates 1,658 full-time, 624 part-time. Students come from 32 states and territories, 23 other countries, 30% are from out of state, 6% African American, 2% Asian American or Pacific Islander, 4% Hispanic American, 0.3% Native American, 1% international, 2% transferred in, 75% live on campus. *Retention:* 80% of 2006 full-time freshmen returned.

Freshmen *Admission:* 4,142 applied, 2,518 admitted, 582 enrolled. *Average high school GPA:* 3.38. *Test scores:* SAT critical reading scores over 500: 69%; SAT math scores over 500: 58%; SAT writing scores over 500: 70%; ACT scores over 18: 88%; SAT critical reading scores over 600: 21%; SAT math scores over 600: 15%; SAT writing scores over 600: 18%; ACT scores over 24: 27%; SAT critical reading scores over 700: 3%; SAT math scores over 700: 2%; SAT writing scores over 700: 1%; ACT scores over 30: 5%.

Faculty *Total:* 218, 39% full-time, 57% with terminal degrees. *Student/faculty ratio:* 15:1.

Majors American studies; art; art therapy; biochemistry; biology/biological sciences; biostatistics; business administration and management; business/managerial economics; chemistry; commercial and advertising art; communication/speech communication and rhetoric; developmental and child psychology; economics; education; elementary education; English; English language and literature related; environmental studies; fine/studio arts; graphic design; health services/allied health/health sciences; history; interdisciplinary studies; international/global studies; liberal arts and sciences/liberal studies; mass communication/media; mathematics; neuroscience; nursing administration; political science and government; psychology; religious studies; secondary education; sociology; Spanish.

Academics *Calendar:* semesters. *Degrees:* bachelor's, master's, and post-master's certificates. *Special study options:* academic remediation for entering students, accelerated degree program, adult/continuing education programs, advanced placement credit, double majors, honors programs, independent study, internships, off-campus study, part-time degree program, services for LD students, student-designed majors, study abroad, summer session for credit. *ROTC:* Army (c).

Computers on Campus 145 computers/terminals are available on campus for general student use. Students can access the following: campus intranet, computer help desk, free student e-mail accounts, online (class) grades, online (class) registration, online (class) schedules, software applications. Campuswide network is available. 100% of college-owned or -operated housing units are wired for high-speed Internet access. Wireless service is available via entire campus.

Student Life *Housing options:* coed. Campus housing is university owned. Freshman campus housing is guaranteed. *Activities and organizations:* drama/theater group, student-run newspaper, radio station, choral group, Hellas, Student Government Association, Peace and Justice Club, Theatre Guild, L.E.A.D.E.R.S. *Campus security:* 24-hour emergency response devices and patrols, late-night transport/escort service, controlled dormitory access, 24-hour security personnel on duty at front desk in residence halls. *Student services:* personal/psychological counseling.

Athletics Member NCAA. All Division III. *Intercollegiate sports:* basketball M/W, cross-country running M/W, soccer M/W, softball W, tennis W, track and field M/W, volleyball M/W. *Intramural sports:* baseball M (c), basketball M/W, cheerleading W (c), field hockey W (c).

Standardized Tests *Required:* SAT or ACT (for admission).

Costs (2007–08) *Comprehensive fee:* $37,450 includes full-time tuition ($26,100), mandatory fees ($150), and room and board ($11,200). Full-time tuition and fees vary according to course load, degree level, and program. Part-time tuition: $816 per credit. Part-time tuition and fees vary according to program. *Room and board:* Room and board charges vary according to housing facility. *Payment plan:* installment. *Waivers:* employees or children of employees.

Financial Aid Of all full-time matriculated undergraduates who enrolled in 2007, 1,433 applied for aid, 1,342 were judged to have need, 497 had their need fully met. 698 Federal Work-Study jobs (averaging $1800). 345 state and other part-time jobs (averaging $1000). In 2007, 210 non-need-based awards were made. *Average percent of need met:* 73%. *Average financial aid package:* $17,909. *Average need-based loan:* $4753. *Average need-based gift aid:* $15,684. *Average non-need-based aid:* $10,205. *Average indebtedness upon graduation:* $24,375.

Applying *Options:* electronic application, early admission, early decision, deferred entrance. *Application fee:* $40. *Required:* essay or personal statement, high school transcript, 2 letters of recommendation. *Application deadlines:* 3/1 (freshmen), 4/1 (transfers). *Early decision deadline:* 11/1. *Notification:* 12/1 (freshmen), 12/1 (transfers), 12/1 (early decision).

Freshman Application Contact Ms. Sandra Robbins, Dean for Enrollment, Emmanuel College, Admissions Office, Emmanuel College, 400 The Fenway, Boston, MA 02115. *Phone:* 617-735-9715. *Fax:* 617-735-9801. *E-mail:* enroll@emmanuel.edu.

See page 1234 for the College Close-Up.

ENDICOTT COLLEGE

Beverly, Massachusetts **www.endicott.edu/**

- **Independent** comprehensive, founded 1939
- **Suburban** 240-acre campus with easy access to Boston
- **Endowment** $23.4 million
- **Coed** 2,128 undergraduate students, 92% full-time, 57% women, 43% men
- **Moderately difficult** entrance level, 48% of applicants were admitted

Undergraduates 1,963 full-time, 165 part-time. Students come from 27 states and territories, 27 other countries, 46% are from out of state, 1% African American, 1% Asian American or Pacific Islander, 2% Hispanic American, 0.3% Native American, 2% international, 2% transferred in, 85% live on campus. *Retention:* 83% of 2006 full-time freshmen returned.

Freshmen *Admission:* 3,549 applied, 1,709 admitted, 521 enrolled. *Test scores:* SAT critical reading scores over 500: 72%; SAT math scores over 500: 74%; SAT writing scores over 500: 74%; ACT scores over 18: 97%; SAT critical reading scores over 600: 16%; SAT math scores over 600: 21%; SAT writing scores over 600: 18%; ACT scores over 24: 35%; SAT critical reading scores over 700: 1%; SAT writing scores over 700: 1%; ACT scores over 30: 1%.

Faculty *Total:* 162, 46% full-time, 42% with terminal degrees. *Student/faculty ratio:* 16:1.

Majors Art therapy; athletic training; business administration and management; criminal justice/safety; design and visual communications; early childhood education; elementary education; English; environmental studies; fine/studio arts; hospitality administration; human services; information technology; international/global studies; liberal arts and sciences/liberal studies; mass communication/media; nursing (registered nurse training); physical education teaching and coaching; psychology; Spanish; sport and fitness administration/management.

Academics *Calendar:* semesters. *Degrees:* certificates, associate, bachelor's, and master's. *Special study options:* academic remediation for entering students, accelerated degree program, adult/continuing education programs, advanced placement credit, distance learning, English as a second language, honors programs, independent study, internships, off-campus study, part-time degree program, student-designed majors, study abroad, summer session for credit. *ROTC:* Army (c), Air Force (c).

Computers on Campus 167 computers/terminals are available on campus for general student use. Students can access the following: campus intranet, computer help desk, free student e-mail accounts, online (class) grades, online (class) registration, online (class) schedules. Campuswide network is available. 100% of college-owned or -operated housing units are wired for high-speed Internet access. Wireless service is available via entire campus.

Student Life *Housing options:* coed, women-only, disabled students. Campus housing is university owned. Freshman campus housing is guaranteed. *Activities and organizations:* drama/theater group, student-run newspaper, radio and television station, choral group, Environmental Club, Campus Activities Board, Drama Club, Shipmates, Student Senate. *Campus security:* 24-hour emergency response devices and patrols, late-night transport/escort service, controlled dormitory access. *Student services:* health clinic, personal/psychological counseling.

Athletics Member NCAA. All Division III. *Intercollegiate sports:* baseball M, basketball M/W, crew M (c)/W (c), cross-country running M/W, equestrian sports M/W, field hockey W, football M, golf M/W, lacrosse M/W, soccer M/W, softball W, tennis M/W, volleyball M/W. *Intramural sports:* basketball M/W, cheerleading M (c)/W (c), football M/W, ice hockey M (c), racquetball M/W, sailing M (c)/W (c), soccer M/W, softball M/W, tennis M/W, ultimate Frisbee M/W, volleyball M/W.

Standardized Tests *Required:* SAT or ACT (for admission).

Costs (2008–09) *Comprehensive fee:* $35,910 includes full-time tuition ($24,130), mandatory fees ($400), and room and board ($11,380). Part-time tuition: $740 per credit. *Required fees:* $150 per term part-time. *College room only:* $7930.

Financial Aid Of all full-time matriculated undergraduates who enrolled in 2007, 1,544 applied for aid, 1,109 were judged to have need, 155 had their need fully met. 399 Federal Work-Study jobs (averaging $1500). In 2007, 297 non-need-based awards were made. *Average percent of need met:* 59%. *Average financial aid package:* $14,429. *Average need-based loan:* $4515. *Average need-based gift aid:* $7087. *Average non-need-based aid:* $6215. *Average indebtedness upon graduation:* $29,382.

Applying *Options:* electronic application, deferred entrance. *Application fee:* $40. *Required:* essay or personal statement, high school transcript, minimum 2.5 GPA. *Required for some:* interview. *Recommended:* interview. *Application deadlines:* 2/15 (freshmen), 2/15 (transfers). *Notification:* continuous (freshmen), continuous (transfers).

Freshman Application Contact Mr. Thomas J. Redman, Vice President of Admission and Financial Aid, Endicott College, 376 Hale Street, Beverly, MA 01915. *Phone:* 978-921-1000. *Toll-free phone:* 800-325-1114. *Fax:* 978-232-2520. *E-mail:* admissio@endicott.edu.

FISHER COLLEGE

Boston, Massachusetts **www.fisher.edu/**

- **Independent** primarily 2-year, founded 1903
- **Urban** campus
- **Endowment** $12.9 million
- **Coed**
- **Minimally difficult** entrance level

Faculty *Student/faculty ratio:* 18:1.

Academics *Calendar:* semesters. *Degrees:* associate and bachelor's.

Student Life *Campus security:* 24-hour emergency response devices and patrols, controlled dormitory access.

Athletics Member NAIA.

Costs (2007–08) *One-time required fee:* $50. *Comprehensive fee:* $32,565 includes full-time tuition ($20,065), mandatory fees ($950), and room and board ($11,550). Part-time tuition: $668 per credit.

Applying *Options:* deferred entrance. *Application fee:* $25. *Required:* high school transcript. *Required for some:* essay or personal statement, letters of recommendation, interview. *Recommended:* minimum 2.0 GPA.

Freshman Application Contact Mr. Robert Melaragni, Director Admissions, Fisher College, 118 Beacon Street, Boston, MA 02116. *Phone:* 617-236-8800 Ext. 4401. *Toll-free phone:* 800-821-3050 (in-state); 800-446-1226 (out-of-state). *Fax:* 617-236-5473. *E-mail:* admissions@fisher.edu.

FITCHBURG STATE COLLEGE

Fitchburg, Massachusetts **www.fsc.edu/**

- **State-supported** comprehensive, founded 1894, part of Massachusetts Public Higher Education System
- **Suburban** 45-acre campus with easy access to Boston
- **Endowment** $13.0 million
- **Coed** 3,835 undergraduate students, 83% full-time, 55% women, 45% men
- **Moderately difficult** entrance level, 66% of applicants were admitted

Undergraduates 3,195 full-time, 640 part-time. Students come from 18 states and territories, 4 other countries, 8% are from out of state, 3% African American, 2% Asian American or Pacific Islander, 3% Hispanic American, 0.3% Native American, 0.6% international, 9% transferred in, 40% live on campus. *Retention:* 75% of 2006 full-time freshmen returned.

Freshmen *Admission:* 3,391 applied, 2,230 admitted, 707 enrolled. *Average high school GPA:* 2.98. *Test scores:* SAT critical reading scores over 500: 50%; SAT math scores over 500: 56%; SAT writing scores over 500: 50%; ACT scores over 18: 71%; SAT critical reading scores over 600: 12%; SAT math scores over 600: 11%; SAT writing scores over 600: 8%; ACT scores over 24: 21%; SAT critical reading scores over 700: 1%.

Faculty *Total:* 254, 69% full-time, 70% with terminal degrees. *Student/faculty ratio:* 16:1.

Majors Accounting; architectural technology; biology/biological sciences; biology teacher education; biotechnology; business administration and management; cinematography and film/video production; communication/speech communication and rhetoric; computer and information sciences; computer science; construction engineering technology; creative writing; criminal justice/safety; developmental and child psychology; digital communication and media/multimedia; dramatic/theater arts; early childhood education; economics; education; electrical, electronic and communications engineering technology; elementary education; energy management and systems technology; English; English/language arts teacher education; environmental biology; exercise physiology; finance; geography; geography teacher education; graphic design; history; history teacher education; human services; industrial and organizational psychology; industrial technology; international business/trade/commerce; kinesiology and exercise science; liberal arts and sciences/liberal studies; management science; manufacturing technology; marketing/marketing management; mathematics; mathematics teacher education; middle school education; nursing (registered nurse training); photography; political science and government; psychology; secondary education; sociology; special education; sport and fitness administration/management; technology/industrial arts teacher education; theater design and technology; trade and industrial teacher education.

Academics *Calendar:* semesters. *Degrees:* certificates, bachelor's, master's, post-master's, and postbachelor's certificates. *Special study options:* academic remediation for entering students, accelerated degree program, adult/continuing education programs, advanced placement credit, distance learning, double majors, honors programs, independent study, internships, off-campus study, part-time degree program, services for LD students, student-designed majors, study abroad, summer session for credit. *ROTC:* Air Force (c).

Computers on Campus 150 computers/terminals are available on campus for general student use. Students can access the following: computer help desk, free student e-mail accounts, online (class) grades, online (class) registration, online (class) schedules. Campuswide network is available. 100% of college-owned or -operated housing units are wired for high-speed Internet access. Wireless service is available via entire campus.

Student Life *Housing options:* coed, disabled students. Campus housing is university owned. Freshman applicants given priority for college housing. *Activities and organizations:* drama/theater group, student-run newspaper, radio station, choral group, Student Government Association, Residence Hall Council, student radio station, student newspaper, Dance Club, national fraternities, national sororities. *Campus security:* 24-hour emergency response devices and patrols, student patrols, late-night transport/escort service, controlled dormitory access. *Student services:* health clinic, personal/psychological counseling.

Athletics Member NCAA. All Division III. *Intercollegiate sports:* baseball M, basketball M/W, cross-country running M/W, field hockey W, football M, ice hockey M, lacrosse W, soccer M/W, softball W, track and field M/W. *Intramural sports:* badminton M/W, basketball M/W, bowling M/W, field hockey M/W, football M, golf M/W, racquetball M/W, soccer M/W, softball M/W, table tennis M/W, ultimate Frisbee M/W, volleyball M/W.

Standardized Tests *Required:* SAT or ACT (for admission).

Costs (2007–08) *Tuition:* state resident $970 full-time, $40 per credit part-time; nonresident $7050 full-time, $294 per credit part-time. Full-time tuition and fees vary according to reciprocity agreements. Part-time tuition and fees vary according to course load and reciprocity agreements. *Required fees:* $5022 full-time, $209 per credit part-time. *Room and board:* $6632. Room and board charges vary according to board plan and housing facility. *Payment plan:* installment. *Waivers:* senior citizens and employees or children of employees.

Financial Aid Of all full-time matriculated undergraduates who enrolled in 2005, 2,480 applied for aid, 1,375 were judged to have need, 1,255 had their need fully met. 204 Federal Work-Study jobs (averaging $1050). In 2005, 22 non-need-based awards were made. *Average percent of need met:* 94%. *Average financial* *aid package:* $6559. *Average need-based loan:* $2659. *Average need-based gift aid:* $3265. *Average non-need-based aid:* $1573. *Average indebtedness upon graduation:* $13,228.

Applying *Options:* electronic application, deferred entrance. *Application fee:* $10. *Required:* essay or personal statement, high school transcript, minimum 2.0 GPA, 16 core courses. *Recommended:* letters of recommendation. *Notification:* continuous (freshmen), continuous (transfers).

Freshman Application Contact Director of Admissions, Fitchburg State College, 160 Pearl Street, Fitchburg, MA 01420-2697. *Phone:* 978-665-3140. *Toll-free phone:* 800-705-9692. *Fax:* 978-665-4540. *E-mail:* admissions@fsc.edu.

See page 1236 for the College Close-Up.

FRAMINGHAM STATE COLLEGE

Framingham, Massachusetts www.framingham.edu/

- **State-supported** comprehensive, founded 1839, part of Massachusetts Public Higher Education System
- **Suburban** 73-acre campus with easy access to Boston
- **Endowment** $5.3 million
- **Coed** 3,828 undergraduate students, 82% full-time, 64% women, 36% men
- **Moderately difficult** entrance level, 56% of applicants were admitted

Framingham State College has fully implemented a wireless laptop program, allowing integration of technology-rich tools and resources in the classroom and enabling instructors to expand and deepen the learning experiences of their students. A completely wireless campus allows the student body access to the campus network and Web-based resources anywhere and at any time.

Undergraduates 3,139 full-time, 689 part-time. Students come from 20 states and territories, 12 other countries, 5% are from out of state, 4% African American, 2% Asian American or Pacific Islander, 4% Hispanic American, 0.4% Native American, 0.7% international, 12% transferred in, 44% live on campus. *Retention:* 73% of 2006 full-time freshmen returned.

Freshmen *Admission:* 3,940 applied, 2,208 admitted, 641 enrolled. *Average high school GPA:* 3.05. *Test scores:* SAT critical reading scores over 500: 44%; SAT math scores over 500: 47%; SAT critical reading scores over 600: 10%; SAT math scores over 600: 10%; SAT critical reading scores over 700: 1%; SAT math scores over 700: 1%.

Faculty *Total:* 253, 66% full-time, 69% with terminal degrees. *Student/faculty ratio:* 16:1.

Majors Apparel and textiles; art; biology/biological sciences; business/commerce; chemistry; communications technologies and support services related; computer and information sciences; economics; education; English; family and consumer sciences/human sciences; food science; foreign languages and literatures; geography; history; knowledge management; liberal arts and sciences/liberal studies; mathematics; nursing (registered nurse training); political science and government; psychology; sociology.

Academics *Calendar:* semesters. *Degrees:* bachelor's, master's, and post-bachelor's certificates. *Special study options:* adult/continuing education programs, advanced placement credit, distance learning, double majors, English as a second language, honors programs, independent study, internships, off-campus study, part-time degree program, study abroad, summer session for credit. *ROTC:* Army (c).

Computers on Campus 232 computers/terminals and 3,500 ports are available on campus for general student use. Students can access the following: campus intranet, computer help desk, free student e-mail accounts, online (class) grades, online (class) registration, online (class) schedules. Campuswide network is available. 100% of college-owned or -operated housing units are wired for high-speed Internet access. Wireless service is available via entire campus.

Student Life *Housing options:* coed, women-only. Campus housing is university owned. Freshman applicants given priority for college housing. *Activities and organizations:* drama/theater group, student-run newspaper, radio station, choral group, Dance Club, Student Union Activities Board, Gatepost (student newspaper), Student Government Association, Hilltop Players (theater group). *Campus security:* 24-hour emergency response devices and patrols, student patrols, late-night transport/escort service, controlled dormitory access. *Student services:* health clinic, personal/psychological counseling.

Athletics Member NCAA. All Division III. *Intercollegiate sports:* baseball M, basketball M/W, cross-country running M/W, field hockey W, football M, ice hockey M, lacrosse W, soccer M/W, softball W, volleyball W. *Intramural sports:* basketball M/W, cheerleading M/W, equestrian sports M/W, football M/W, golf M/W, lacrosse M, rugby M/W, skiing (downhill) M/W, soccer M/W, softball M/W, volleyball M/W, weight lifting M/W.

Standardized Tests *Required:* SAT or ACT (for admission).

Costs (2007–08) *Tuition:* state resident $970 full-time, $162 per course part-time; nonresident $7050 full-time, $1175 per course part-time. Full-time tuition and fees vary according to class time. Part-time tuition and fees vary according to class time and course load. *Required fees:* $4829 full-time, $870 per course part-time. *Room and board:* $7127; room only: $4527. Room and board charges vary according to board plan and housing facility. *Payment plan:* installment. *Waivers:* senior citizens and employees or children of employees.

Financial Aid Of all full-time matriculated undergraduates who enrolled in 2005, 2,043 applied for aid, 1,309 were judged to have need, 871 had their need fully met. In 2005, 110 non-need-based awards were made. *Average percent of need met:* 81%. *Average financial aid package:* $6449. *Average need-based loan:* $2889. *Average need-based gift aid:* $3485. *Average non-need-based aid:* $2043. *Average indebtedness upon graduation:* $15,328.

Applying *Options:* electronic application, early admission, early action, deferred entrance. *Application fee:* $25. *Required:* high school transcript, minimum of 16 college preparatory courses in specified areas. *Required for some:* essay or personal statement, interview. *Recommended:* essay or personal statement, minimum 3.0 GPA, letters of recommendation. *Application deadlines:* 5/15 (freshmen), 5/1 (transfers), 11/15 (early action). *Notification:* continuous (freshmen), continuous (transfers), 12/15 (early action).

Freshman Application Contact Ms. Elizabeth J. Canella, Associate Dean of Admissions, Framingham State College, PO Box 9101, Dwight Hall, Room 209, 100 State Street, Framingham, MA 01701-9101. *Phone:* 508-626-4500. *Fax:* 508-626-4017. *E-mail:* admiss@frc.mass.edu.

See page 1238 for the College Close-Up.

FRANKLIN W. OLIN COLLEGE OF ENGINEERING

Needham, Massachusetts www.olin.edu/

- **Independent** 4-year, founded 2002
- **Endowment** $483.0 million
- **Coed** 296 undergraduate students, 100% full-time, 42% women, 58% men
- **Very difficult** entrance level, 11% of applicants were admitted

Undergraduates 296 full-time. Students come from 41 states and territories, 8 other countries, 91% are from out of state, 2% African American, 11% Asian American or Pacific Islander, 4% Hispanic American, 2% international, 100% live on campus. *Retention:* 99% of 2006 full-time freshmen returned.

Freshmen *Admission:* 1,054 applied, 111 admitted, 79 enrolled. *Average high school GPA:* 4.0. *Test scores:* SAT critical reading scores over 500: 100%; SAT math scores over 500: 100%; SAT writing scores over 500: 100%; ACT scores over 18: 100%; SAT critical reading scores over 600: 96%; SAT math scores over 600: 99%; SAT writing scores over 600: 97%; ACT scores over 24: 100%; SAT critical reading scores over 700: 75%; SAT math scores over 700: 99%; SAT writing scores over 700: 62%; ACT scores over 30: 95%.

Faculty *Total:* 39, 79% full-time, 100% with terminal degrees. *Student/faculty ratio:* 9:1.

Majors Computer engineering; engineering; mechanical engineering.

Academics *Degree:* bachelor's. *Special study options:* independent study, internships, student-designed majors, study abroad.

Computers on Campus 15 computers/terminals are available on campus for general student use. Students can access the following: campus intranet, computer help desk, free student e-mail accounts, online (class) grades, online (class) registration, online (class) schedules. Campuswide network is available. 100% of college-owned or -operated housing units are wired for high-speed Internet access. Wireless service is available via entire campus.

Student Life *Housing:* on-campus residence required through senior year. *Options:* coed, disabled students. Campus housing is university owned. Freshman campus housing is guaranteed. *Activities and organizations:* drama/theater group, choral group, Greening Olin, Olin Fire Arts Club, Midnight Riders, Olin Entrepreneurial Group, Open. *Student services:* health clinic, personal/psychological counseling, legal services.

Athletics *Intercollegiate sports:* soccer M/W, ultimate Frisbee M/W. *Intramural sports:* basketball M/W, softball M/W, volleyball M/W.

Standardized Tests *Required:* SAT or ACT (for admission). *Recommended:* SAT Subject Tests (for admission).

Costs (2007–08) *One-time required fee:* $2500. *Comprehensive fee:* $46,825 includes full-time tuition ($33,600), mandatory fees ($1425), and room and board ($11,800). Part-time tuition: $10,050 per credit. all students are awarded full-tuition scholarships. *College room only:* $7800. Room and board charges vary according to board plan. *Payment plan:* installment.

Applying *Options:* deferred entrance. *Application fee:* $70. *Required:* essay or personal statement, high school transcript, 3 letters of recommendation. *Recommended:* interview. *Application deadline:* 12/1 (freshmen). *Notification:* 2/10 (freshmen).

Freshman Application Contact Franklin W. Olin College of Engineering, Olin Way, Needham, MA 02492-1200. *Phone:* 781-292-2250. *Fax:* 781-292-2310. *E-mail:* info@olin.edu.

GORDON COLLEGE

Wenham, Massachusetts **www.gordon.edu/**

- **Independent nondenominational** comprehensive, founded 1889
- **Suburban** 500-acre campus with easy access to Boston
- **Endowment** $35.0 million
- **Coed** 1,530 undergraduate students, 98% full-time, 63% women, 37% men
- **Moderately difficult** entrance level, 71% of applicants were admitted

Undergraduates 1,496 full-time, 34 part-time. Students come from 44 states and territories, 22 other countries, 72% are from out of state, 2% African American, 1% Asian American or Pacific Islander, 3% Hispanic American, 0.3% Native American, 2% international, 3% transferred in, 88% live on campus. *Retention:* 85% of 2006 full-time freshmen returned.

Freshmen *Admission:* 1,574 applied, 1,122 admitted, 457 enrolled. *Average high school GPA:* 3.55. *Test scores:* SAT critical reading scores over 500: 88%; SAT math scores over 500: 84%; SAT writing scores over 500: 87%; SAT critical reading scores over 600: 48%; SAT math scores over 600: 39%; SAT writing scores over 600: 45%; SAT critical reading scores over 700: 10%; SAT math scores over 700: 4%; SAT writing scores over 700: 7%.

Faculty *Total:* 145, 64% full-time, 55% with terminal degrees. *Student/faculty ratio:* 12:1.

Majors Accounting; art; biology/biological sciences; business administration and management; chemistry; Christian studies; communication/speech communication and rhetoric; computer science; economics; elementary education; English; foreign languages and literatures; French; German; history; international relations and affairs; kinesiology and exercise science; mathematics; middle school education; music; music performance; music teacher education; parks, recreation and leisure; philosophy; physics; political science and government; psychology; social work; sociology; Spanish; special education; youth ministry.

Academics *Calendar:* semesters. *Degrees:* bachelor's and master's. *Special study options:* academic remediation for entering students, advanced placement credit, cooperative education, double majors, honors programs, independent study, internships, off-campus study, part-time degree program, services for LD students, student-designed majors, study abroad. *ROTC:* Army (c), Air Force (c). *Unusual degree programs:* 3-2 engineering with University of Massachusetts Lowell; nursing with Thomas Jefferson University.

Computers on Campus 141 computers/terminals are available on campus for general student use. Students can access the following: free student e-mail accounts, online (class) registration, online (class) schedules. Campuswide network is available. 100% of college-owned or -operated housing units are wired for high-speed Internet access. Wireless service is available via learning centers, libraries, student centers.

Student Life *Housing:* on-campus residence required through senior year. *Options:* coed, men-only, women-only, disabled students. Campus housing is university owned. Freshman campus housing is guaranteed. *Activities and organizations:* drama/theater group, student-run newspaper, choral group, Student Government Association, student ministries, diverse music ensembles. *Campus security:* 24-hour emergency response devices and patrols, late-night transport/escort service, controlled dormitory access. *Student services:* health clinic, personal/psychological counseling.

Athletics Member NCAA. All Division III. *Intercollegiate sports:* baseball M, basketball M/W, cheerleading M/W, cross-country running M/W, field hockey W, golf M (c)/W (c), lacrosse M/W, soccer M/W, softball W, swimming and diving M/W, tennis M/W, track and field M/W, volleyball W. *Intramural sports:* basketball M/W, football M/W, ice hockey M (c)/W (c), racquetball M/W, rugby M/W, soccer M/W, softball W, table tennis M/W, tennis M/W, track and field M/W, ultimate Frisbee M/W, volleyball M.

Standardized Tests *Required:* SAT or ACT (for admission). *Recommended:* SAT Subject Tests (for admission).

Costs (2008–09) *Comprehensive fee:* $34,718 includes full-time tuition ($26,132), mandatory fees ($1162), and room and board ($7424).

Financial Aid Of all full-time matriculated undergraduates who enrolled in 2005, 1,189 applied for aid, 1,024 were judged to have need, 183 had their need fully met. 151 Federal Work-Study jobs (averaging $1503). In 2005, 460 non-need-based awards were made. *Average percent of need met:* 70%. *Average financial aid package:* $14,540. *Average need-based loan:* $4473. *Average need-based gift aid:* $10,093. *Average non-need-based aid:* $2383. *Average indebtedness upon graduation:* $11,193.

Applying *Options:* electronic application, early admission, early decision, early action, deferred entrance. *Application fee:* $50. *Required:* essay or personal statement, high school transcript, 2 letters of recommendation, interview, pastoral recommendation, statement of Christian faith. *Recommended:* minimum 3.0 GPA. *Application deadlines:* rolling (freshmen), rolling (transfers), 12/1 (early action). *Early decision deadline:* 11/15. *Notification:* continuous (freshmen), continuous (transfers), 12/15 (early decision), 1/1 (early action).

Freshman Application Contact Barbara Layne, Associate Vice President for Enrollment, Gordon College, 255 Grapevine Road, Wenham, MA 01984-1899. *Phone:* 978-867-4218. *Toll-free phone:* 866-464-6736. *Fax:* 978-867-4682. *E-mail:* admissions@gordon.edu.

HAMPSHIRE COLLEGE

Amherst, Massachusetts **www.hampshire.edu/**

- **Independent** 4-year, founded 1965
- **Small-town** 800-acre campus
- **Endowment** $45.3 million
- **Coed** 1,431 undergraduate students, 100% full-time, 57% women, 43% men
- **Very difficult** entrance level, 55% of applicants were admitted

Undergraduates 1,431 full-time. Students come from 49 states and territories, 27 other countries, 83% are from out of state, 4% African American, 4% Asian American or Pacific Islander, 6% Hispanic American, 0.7% Native American, 4% international, 3% transferred in, 89% live on campus. *Retention:* 78% of 2006 full-time freshmen returned.

Freshmen *Admission:* 2,571 applied, 1,421 admitted, 392 enrolled. *Average high school GPA:* 3.45. *Test scores:* SAT critical reading scores over 500: 98%; SAT math scores over 500: 91%; SAT writing scores over 500: 95%; ACT scores over 18: 99%; SAT critical reading scores over 600: 80%; SAT math scores over 600: 55%; SAT writing scores over 600: 74%; ACT scores over 24: 79%; SAT critical reading scores over 700: 35%; SAT math scores over 700: 10%; SAT writing scores over 700: 26%; ACT scores over 30: 36%.

Faculty *Total:* 145, 65% full-time, 82% with terminal degrees. *Student/faculty ratio:* 12:1.

Majors African-American/Black studies; agriculture; American studies; anthropology; applied art; Asian-American studies; Asian studies; biology/biological sciences; chemistry; cognitive science; comparative literature; computer graphics; computer science; dance; demography and population; dramatic/theater arts; economics; education; English; environmental design/architecture; environmental studies; film/video and photographic arts related; fine/studio arts; geology/earth science; Hispanic-American, Puerto Rican, and Mexican-American/Chicano studies; history; international/global studies; Judaic studies; Latin American studies; legal studies; linguistics; mass communication/media; mathematics; music; nutrition sciences; peace studies and conflict resolution; philosophy; physics; playwriting and screenwriting; political science and government; psychology; public health; religious studies; sociology; urban studies/affairs; women's studies.

Academics *Calendar:* 4-1-4. *Degree:* bachelor's. *Special study options:* accelerated degree program, advanced placement credit, independent study, internships, off-campus study, services for LD students, student-designed majors, study abroad. *ROTC:* Army (c).

Computers on Campus 215 computers/terminals are available on campus for general student use. Students can access the following: campus intranet, computer help desk, free student e-mail accounts, online (class) registration. Campuswide network is available. 100% of college-owned or -operated housing units are wired for high-speed Internet access. Wireless service is available via entire campus.

Student Life *Housing:* on-campus residence required through senior year. *Options:* coed, women-only, cooperative, disabled students. Campus housing is university owned. Freshman campus housing is guaranteed. *Activities and organizations:* drama/theater group, student-run newspaper, radio station, choral group, Alternative Music Collective, Jewish Student Union, Student Action for Radical Change, Theatre Board, Red Scare Ultimate Frisbee. *Campus security:* 24-hour emergency response devices and patrols, student patrols, late-night transport/escort service. *Student services:* health clinic, personal/psychological counseling, women's center.

Athletics *Intercollegiate sports:* basketball M (c)/W (c), fencing M (c)/W (c), soccer M (c)/W (c). *Intramural sports:* archery M (c)/W (c), lacrosse W (c), rock climbing M (c)/W (c), ultimate Frisbee M (c)/W (c).

Costs (2007–08) *Comprehensive fee:* $46,090 includes full-time tuition ($35,785), mandatory fees ($760), and room and board ($9545). *College room* *only:* $6087. Room and board charges vary according to board plan. *Payment plan:* installment. *Waivers:* employees or children of employees.

Financial Aid Of all full-time matriculated undergraduates who enrolled in 2006, 851 applied for aid, 777 were judged to have need, 650 had their need fully met. 587 Federal Work-Study jobs (averaging $2475). 265 state and other part-time jobs (averaging $2475). In 2006, 232 non-need-based awards were made. *Average percent of need met:* 99%. *Average financial aid package:* $29,875. *Average need-based loan:* $4500. *Average need-based gift aid:* $22,900. *Average non-need-based aid:* $5600. *Average indebtedness upon graduation:* $20,300.

Applying *Options:* electronic application, early admission, early decision, early action, deferred entrance. *Application fee:* $55. *Required:* essay or personal statement, high school transcript, 2 letters of recommendation. *Recommended:* interview. *Application deadlines:* 1/15 (freshmen), 3/1 (transfers), 12/1 (early action). *Early decision deadline:* 11/15. *Notification:* 4/1 (freshmen), 4/15 (transfers), 12/15 (early decision), 2/1 (early action).

Freshman Application Contact Ms. Karen S. Parker, Director of Admissions, Hampshire College, 893 West Street, Amherst, MA 01002. *Phone:* 413-559-5471. *Toll-free phone:* 877-937-4267. *Fax:* 413-559-5631. *E-mail:* admissions@hampshire.edu.

HARVARD UNIVERSITY

Cambridge, Massachusetts — www.harvard.edu/

- **Independent** university, founded 1636
- **Urban** 380-acre campus with easy access to Boston
- **Endowment** $34.9 billion
- **Coed** 6,648 undergraduate students, 100% full-time, 50% women, 50% men
- **Most difficult** entrance level, 9% of applicants were admitted

Undergraduates 6,641 full-time, 7 part-time. Students come from 55 states and territories, 97 other countries, 81% are from out of state, 8% African American, 16% Asian American or Pacific Islander, 7% Hispanic American, 0.7% Native American, 10% international, 0.3% transferred in, 98% live on campus. *Retention:* 96% of 2006 full-time freshmen returned.

Freshmen *Admission:* 22,955 applied, 2,108 admitted, 1,668 enrolled.

Faculty *Total:* 2,072, 78% full-time, 99% with terminal degrees. *Student/faculty ratio:* 7:1.

Majors African-American/Black studies; African languages; African studies; American studies; ancient Near Eastern and biblical languages; animal genetics; anthropology; applied mathematics; Arabic; archeology; architectural engineering; art; art history, criticism and conservation; artificial intelligence and robotics; Asian studies; Asian studies (East); Asian studies (South); Asian studies (Southeast); astronomy; astrophysics; atmospheric sciences and meteorology; behavioral sciences; biblical studies; biochemistry; biological and physical sciences; biology/biological sciences; biology/biotechnology laboratory technician; biomedical/medical engineering; biomedical sciences; biometry/biometrics; biophysics; cell biology and histology; chemical engineering; chemistry; Chinese; city/urban, community and regional planning; civil engineering; classics and languages, literatures and linguistics; cognitive psychology and psycholinguistics; cognitive science; comparative literature; computer and information sciences; computer engineering; computer engineering technology; computer graphics; computer programming; computer science; creative writing; cultural studies; dramatic/theater arts; ecology; economics; electrical, electronics and communications engineering; engineering; engineering physics; engineering science; English; entomology; environmental biology; environmental design/architecture; environmental/environmental health engineering; environmental studies; European studies; European studies (Central and Eastern); evolutionary biology; film/cinema studies; fine/studio arts; fluid/thermal sciences; folklore; French; geochemistry; geological/geophysical engineering; geology/earth science; geophysics and seismology; German; Hebrew; Hispanic-American, Puerto Rican, and Mexican-American/Chicano studies; history; history and philosophy of science and technology; history of philosophy; human development and family studies; humanities; information science/studies; interdisciplinary studies; international economics; international relations and affairs; Islamic studies; Italian; Japanese; Jewish/Judaic studies; Latin; Latin American studies; liberal arts and sciences/liberal studies; linguistics; literature; marine biology and biological oceanography; materials engineering; materials science; mathematics; mathematics and computer science; mechanical engineering; medical microbiology and bacteriology; medieval and Renaissance studies; metallurgical engineering; modern Greek; modern languages; molecular biology; music; music history, literature, and theory; natural resources/conservation; Near and Middle Eastern studies; neuroscience; nuclear physics; philosophy; physical sciences; physics; physiological psychology/psychobiology; political science and government; polymer chemistry; Portuguese; pre-dentistry studies; pre-law studies; pre-medical studies; pre-veterinary studies; psychology; public policy analysis; religious studies; Romance languages; Russian; Russian studies; Scandinavian languages; Slavic languages; social sciences; sociobiology; sociology; Spanish; statistics; systems engineering; urban studies/affairs; western civilization; women's studies.

Academics *Calendar:* semesters. *Degrees:* bachelor's, master's, doctoral, and first professional. *Special study options:* academic remediation for entering students, accelerated degree program, adult/continuing education programs, advanced placement credit, double majors, English as a second language, honors programs, independent study, internships, off-campus study, services for LD students, student-designed majors, study abroad, summer session for credit. *ROTC:* Army (c), Navy (c), Air Force (c).

Computers on Campus 405 computers/terminals are available on campus for general student use. Students can access the following: computer help desk, free student e-mail accounts, online (class) grades, online (class) registration, online (class) schedules. Campuswide network is available. 100% of college-owned or -operated housing units are wired for high-speed Internet access. Wireless service is available via entire campus.

Student Life *Housing:* on-campus residence required for freshman year. *Options:* coed, cooperative, disabled students. Campus housing is university owned. Freshman campus housing is guaranteed. *Activities and organizations:* drama/theater group, student-run newspaper, radio and television station, choral group, marching band, Phillips Brooks House Association, Asian-American Association, International Relations Council, Harvard Crimson (newspaper), Harvard/Radcliffe Chorus. *Campus security:* 24-hour emergency response devices and patrols, late-night transport/escort service, controlled dormitory access, required and optional safety courses. *Student services:* health clinic, personal/psychological counseling, women's center, legal services.

Athletics Member NCAA. All Division I except football (Division I-AA). *Intercollegiate sports:* baseball M, basketball M/W, crew M/W, cross-country running M/W, fencing M/W, field hockey W, golf M/W, ice hockey M/W, lacrosse M/W, sailing M/W, skiing (cross-country) M/W, skiing (downhill) M/W, soccer M/W, softball W, squash M/W, swimming and diving M/W, tennis M/W, track and field M/W, volleyball M/W, water polo M/W, wrestling M. *Intramural sports:* badminton M (c)/W (c), baseball M, basketball M/W, crew M/W, cross-country running M/W, equestrian sports M (c)/W (c), fencing M/W, field hockey M/W, football M, gymnastics M (c)/W (c), ice hockey M/W, racquetball M/W, rugby M (c)/W (c), soccer M/W, softball W, squash M/W, swimming and diving M/W, table tennis M (c)/W (c), tennis M/W, track and field M/W, volleyball M/W.

Standardized Tests *Required:* SAT or ACT (for admission), SAT Subject Tests (for admission).

Costs (2007–08) *Comprehensive fee:* $45,620 includes full-time tuition ($31,456), mandatory fees ($3542), and room and board ($10,622). *College room only:* $5856. *Payment plans:* tuition prepayment, installment.

Financial Aid Of all full-time matriculated undergraduates who enrolled in 2007, 3,814 applied for aid, 3,432 were judged to have need, 3,232 had their need fully met. 1,036 Federal Work-Study jobs (averaging $2649). 1,264 state and other part-time jobs (averaging $2777). *Average percent of need met:* 100%. *Average financial aid package:* $35,831. *Average need-based loan:* $4370. *Average need-based gift aid:* $32,850. *Average indebtedness upon graduation:* $9290.

Applying *Options:* deferred entrance. *Application fee:* $65. *Required:* essay or personal statement, high school transcript, 2 letters of recommendation, interview. *Application deadlines:* 1/1 (freshmen), 2/1 (transfers), 11/1 (early action). *Notification:* 4/1 (freshmen), 5/31 (transfers), 12/15 (early action).

Freshman Application Contact Dr. William R. Fitzsimmons, Office of Admissions and Financial Aid, Harvard University, Byerly Hall, 8 Garden Street, Cambridge, MA 02138. *Phone:* 617-495-1551. *E-mail:* college@harvard.edu.

See page 1240 for the College Close-Up.

HEBREW COLLEGE

Newton Centre, Massachusetts — www.hebrewcollege.edu/

- **Independent Jewish** comprehensive, founded 1921
- **Suburban** 3-acre campus with easy access to Boston
- **Endowment** $8.0 million
- **Coed** 6 undergraduate students, 83% full-time, 83% women, 17% men
- **Minimally difficult** entrance level

Undergraduates 5 full-time, 1 part-time. Students come from 6 states and territories, 1 other country, 1% are from out of state.

Freshmen *Admission:* 1 enrolled.

Faculty *Total:* 41, 49% full-time, 73% with terminal degrees.

Majors Education; Jewish/Judaic studies; music; religious education; religious/sacred music.

Academics *Calendar:* semesters. *Degrees:* bachelor's and master's. *Special study options:* adult/continuing education programs, distance learning, internships, off-campus study, part-time degree program, summer session for credit.

Computers on Campus 10 computers/terminals are available on campus for general student use.

Student Life *Housing:* college housing not available.

Costs (2008–09) *Tuition:* $895 per credit part-time. *Required fees:* $100 per semester part-time.

Financial Aid Of all full-time matriculated undergraduates who enrolled in 2006, 3 applied for aid, 3 were judged to have need. *Financial aid deadline:* 4/15.

Applying *Options:* early admission, early decision, deferred entrance. *Application fee:* $50. *Required:* essay or personal statement, high school transcript, 3 letters of recommendation, interview. *Required for some:* GRE, audition. *Application deadlines:* rolling (freshmen), 4/15 (transfers). *Early decision deadline:* 12/15. *Notification:* continuous (freshmen), continuous until 8/1 (transfers).

Freshman Application Contact Ms. Kate Nachman, Admissions, Hebrew College, 160 Herrick Road, Newton Centre, MA 02459. *Phone:* 617-559-8610. *Toll-free phone:* 800-866-4814 Ext. 8619. *Fax:* 617-559-8601. *E-mail:* admissions@lhebrewcollege.edu.

HELLENIC COLLEGE

Brookline, Massachusetts **www.hchc.edu/**

- **Independent Greek Orthodox** 4-year, founded 1937
- **Suburban** 52-acre campus with easy access to Boston
- **Endowment** $24.8 million
- **Coed** 72 undergraduate students, 100% full-time, 32% women, 68% men
- **Minimally difficult** entrance level, 36% of applicants were admitted

Undergraduates 72 full-time. Students come from 39 states and territories, 8 other countries, 85% are from out of state, 1% African American, 1% Native American, 14% international, 10% transferred in, 90% live on campus. *Retention:* 94% of 2006 full-time freshmen returned.

Freshmen *Admission:* 28 applied, 10 admitted, 10 enrolled. *Average high school GPA:* 3.0. *Test scores:* SAT critical reading scores over 500: 75%; SAT math scores over 500: 50%; SAT writing scores over 500: 75%; ACT scores over 18: 100%; SAT critical reading scores over 600: 25%; SAT writing scores over 600: 25%; ACT scores over 24: 33%.

Faculty *Total:* 33, 42% full-time. *Student/faculty ratio:* 9:1.

Majors Business administration and management; classics and languages, literatures and linguistics; elementary education; human development and family studies; religious studies; theology.

Academics *Calendar:* semesters. *Degrees:* bachelor's (also offers graduate degree programs through Holy Cross Greek Orthodox School of Theology). *Special study options:* academic remediation for entering students, advanced placement credit, double majors, independent study, internships, off-campus study, part-time degree program, summer session for credit.

Computers on Campus 9 computers/terminals are available on campus for general student use.

Student Life *Housing:* on-campus residence required through senior year. *Options:* coed. Campus housing is university owned. Freshman campus housing is guaranteed. *Activities and organizations:* student-run newspaper, choral group. *Campus security:* controlled dormitory access. *Student services:* health clinic, personal/psychological counseling.

Athletics *Intramural sports:* baseball M, basketball M/W, football M, golf M, soccer M, table tennis M/W, volleyball M/W.

Standardized Tests *Required:* SAT or ACT (for admission). *Required for some:* SAT Subject Tests (for admission).

Costs (2007–08) *Comprehensive fee:* $28,215 includes full-time tuition ($17,020), mandatory fees ($305), and room and board ($10,890). Part-time tuition: $710 per credit hour. *Payment plans:* installment, deferred payment. *Waivers:* children of alumni and employees or children of employees.

Financial Aid Of all full-time matriculated undergraduates who enrolled in 2005, 69 applied for aid, 67 were judged to have need. 9 Federal Work-Study jobs (averaging $720). In 2005, 3 non-need-based awards were made. *Average percent of need met:* 80%. *Average financial aid package:* $9200. *Average need-based loan:* $5500. *Average need-based gift aid:* $10,100. *Average non-need-based aid:* $1100. *Average indebtedness upon graduation:* $7300.

Applying *Options:* electronic application, early action, deferred entrance. *Application fee:* $50. *Required:* essay or personal statement, high school transcript, minimum 2.0 GPA, letters of recommendation, interview, health certificate. *Application deadlines:* rolling (freshmen), rolling (transfers), 12/1 (early action). *Notification:* continuous (freshmen), continuous (transfers).

Freshman Application Contact Ms. Sonia Daly, Director of Admissions, Hellenic College, 50 Goddard Avenue, Brookline, MA 02445-7496. *Phone:* 617-731-3500 Ext. 1285. *Toll-free phone:* 866-424-2338. *Fax:* 617-850-1460. *E-mail:* admissions@hchc.edu.

LASELL COLLEGE

Newton, Massachusetts **www.lasell.edu/**

Freshman Application Contact Mr. James Tweed, Director of Undergraduate Admission, Lasell College, 1844 Commonwealth Avenue, Newton, MA 02466. *Phone:* 617-243-2225. *Toll-free phone:* 888-LASELL-4. *Fax:* 617-243-2380. *E-mail:* info@lasell.edu.

See page 1242 for the College Close-Up.

LESLEY UNIVERSITY

Cambridge, Massachusetts **www.lesley.edu/**

- **Independent** comprehensive, founded 1909
- **Urban** 5-acre campus with easy access to Boston
- **Endowment** $45.6 million
- **Coed** 1,229 undergraduate students, 94% full-time, 75% women, 25% men
- **Moderately difficult** entrance level, 86% of applicants were admitted

Lesley College prepares men and women for careers that matter and lives that make a difference. Located minutes from downtown Boston and steps from Harvard Square, Lesley offers nearly 1,400 undergraduates small classes; more than fifty majors, minors, and specializations; an honors program; a self-designed major; and, most importantly, field-based internships beginning freshman year.

Undergraduates 1,160 full-time, 69 part-time. Students come from 56 states and territories, 24 other countries, 42% are from out of state, 5% African American, 4% Asian American or Pacific Islander, 5% Hispanic American, 0.4% Native American, 2% international, 9% transferred in, 50% live on campus. *Retention:* 70% of 2006 full-time freshmen returned.

Freshmen *Admission:* 1,568 applied, 1,342 admitted, 343 enrolled. *Average high school GPA:* 3.0. *Test scores:* SAT critical reading scores over 500: 71%; SAT math scores over 500: 58%; SAT writing scores over 500: 66%; ACT scores over 18: 82%; SAT critical reading scores over 600: 27%; SAT math scores over 600: 16%; SAT writing scores over 600: 21%; ACT scores over 24: 49%; SAT critical reading scores over 700: 4%; SAT math scores over 700: 1%; SAT writing scores over 700: 2%; ACT scores over 30: 7%.

Faculty *Total:* 245, 29% full-time, 39% with terminal degrees. *Student/faculty ratio:* 9:1.

Majors American studies; art; art therapy; business administration and management; child development; communications technologies and support services related; counseling psychology; education; elementary education; English; environmental studies; human development and family studies; humanities; human services; interdisciplinary studies; kindergarten/preschool education; liberal arts and sciences/liberal studies; middle school education; natural sciences; secondary education; social sciences; special education.

Academics *Calendar:* semesters. *Degrees:* certificates, diplomas, associate, bachelor's, master's, doctoral, post-master's, and postbachelor's certificates. *Special study options:* academic remediation for entering students, accelerated degree program, adult/continuing education programs, advanced placement credit, distance learning, double majors, external degree program, freshman honors college, honors programs, independent study, internships, off-campus study, part-time degree program, services for LD students, student-designed majors, study abroad, summer session for credit. *Unusual degree programs:* 3-2 counseling psychology, clinical mental health counseling, elementary education, special education.

Computers on Campus 175 computers/terminals are available on campus for general student use. Students can access the following: free student e-mail accounts, online (class) registration. Campuswide network is available. 100% of college-owned or -operated housing units are wired for high-speed Internet access. Wireless service is available via classrooms, student centers.

Student Life *Housing options:* coed, women-only. Campus housing is university owned and leased by the school. Freshman applicants given priority for college housing. *Activities and organizations:* drama/theater group, student-run newspaper, choral group, Student Senate, Women for Social Justice, Hillel, Swim Club, Third Wave. *Campus security:* 24-hour emergency response devices and patrols, late-night transport/escort service, controlled dormitory access, self-defense education, lighted pathways. *Student services:* health clinic, personal/psychological counseling.

Athletics Member NCAA. All Division III. *Intercollegiate sports:* basketball M/W, crew W, cross-country running M/W, soccer M/W, softball W, volleyball M/W. *Intramural sports:* swimming and diving M/W, tennis M.

Standardized Tests *Required:* SAT or ACT (for admission).

Costs (2008–09) *Comprehensive fee:* $39,510 includes full-time tuition ($27,200), mandatory fees ($310), and room and board ($12,000). *College room only:* $7500.

Financial Aid Of all full-time matriculated undergraduates who enrolled in 2006, 814 applied for aid, 706 were judged to have need, 47 had their need fully met. 261 Federal Work-Study jobs (averaging $1724). 122 state and other part-time jobs (averaging $2000). In 2006, 90 non-need-based awards were made. *Average percent of need met:* 70%. *Average financial aid package:* $16,022. *Average need-based loan:* $3286. *Average need-based gift aid:* $11,536. *Average non-need-based aid:* $6686. *Average indebtedness upon graduation:* $15,000.

Applying *Options:* electronic application, early action, deferred entrance. *Application fee:* $40. *Required:* high school transcript, 2 letters of recommendation. *Required for some:* portfolio. *Recommended:* essay or personal statement, minimum 2.5 GPA, interview. *Application deadline:* rolling (transfers). *Notification:* continuous (freshmen), continuous (transfers).

Freshman Application Contact Lesley University, 29 Everett Street, Cambridge, MA 02138-2790. *Phone:* 617-349-8800. *Toll-free phone:* 800-999-1959 Ext. 8800.

See page 1244 for the College Close-Up.

MASSACHUSETTS COLLEGE OF ART AND DESIGN

Boston, Massachusetts **www.massart.edu/**

- **State-supported** comprehensive, founded 1873, part of Massachusetts Public Higher Education System
- **Urban** 5-acre campus
- **Endowment** $6.6 million
- **Coed** 2,157 undergraduate students, 70% full-time, 67% women, 33% men
- **Very difficult** entrance level, 56% of applicants were admitted

Undergraduates 1,516 full-time, 641 part-time. Students come from 30 states and territories, 22 other countries, 29% are from out of state, 3% African American, 6% Asian American or Pacific Islander, 6% Hispanic American, 1% Native American, 3% international, 7% transferred in, 23% live on campus. *Retention:* 82% of 2006 full-time freshmen returned.

Freshmen *Admission:* 1,315 applied, 735 admitted, 287 enrolled. *Average high school GPA:* 3.29. *Test scores:* SAT critical reading scores over 500: 76%; SAT math scores over 500: 67%; SAT writing scores over 500: 75%; SAT critical reading scores over 600: 33%; SAT math scores over 600: 24%; SAT writing scores over 600: 25%; SAT critical reading scores over 700: 7%; SAT math scores over 700: 2%; SAT writing scores over 700: 2%.

Faculty *Total:* 94.

Majors Animation, interactive technology, video graphics and special effects; architecture; art history, criticism and conservation; art teacher education; ceramic arts and ceramics; cinematography and film/video production; commercial and advertising art; fashion/apparel design; fiber, textile and weaving arts; fine/studio arts; industrial design; intermedia/multimedia; metal and jewelry arts; painting; photography; printmaking; sculpture.

Academics *Calendar:* semesters. *Degrees:* certificates, bachelor's, master's, and postbachelor's certificates. *Special study options:* double majors, independent study, internships, off-campus study, part-time degree program, student-designed majors, study abroad, summer session for credit.

Computers on Campus 370 computers/terminals are available on campus for general student use. Students can access the following: campus intranet, computer help desk, free student e-mail accounts, online (class) schedules. Campuswide network is available. Wireless service is available via entire campus.

Student Life *Housing options:* coed. Campus housing is university owned. Freshman campus housing is guaranteed. *Activities and organizations:* drama/theater group, student-run newspaper, radio station, International Students' Club, Design Research Unit, Spectrum, film society, Event Works. *Campus security:* 24-hour emergency response devices and patrols, late-night transport/escort service, security lighting, self-defense workshops. *Student services:* health clinic, personal/psychological counseling, women's center.

Athletics *Intramural sports:* basketball M/W, ice hockey M, sailing M/W, softball M/W, table tennis M/W, volleyball M/W.

Standardized Tests *Required:* SAT or ACT (for admission).

Costs (2007–08) *Tuition:* state resident $7450 full-time; nonresident $21,900 full-time. *Room and board:* $10,900. Room and board charges vary according to housing facility. *Payment plan:* installment. *Waivers:* employees or children of employees.

Financial Aid Of all full-time matriculated undergraduates who enrolled in 2007, 1,136 applied for aid, 887 were judged to have need. 187 Federal Work-Study jobs (averaging $860). In 2007, 16 non-need-based awards were made. *Average financial aid package:* $8490. *Average need-based loan:* $4428. *Average need-based gift aid:* $5471. *Average non-need-based aid:* $3383.

Applying *Options:* electronic application, early admission, early action, deferred entrance. *Application fee:* $65. *Required:* essay or personal statement, high school transcript, minimum 3.0 GPA, letters of recommendation, portfolio. *Application deadlines:* 2/15 (freshmen), 3/15 (transfers), 12/1 (early action). *Notification:* 4/15 (freshmen), 1/5 (early action).

Freshman Application Contact Massachusetts College of Art and Design, 621 Huntington Avenue, Boston, MA 02115. *Phone:* 617-879-7230. *Fax:* 617-879-7250. *E-mail:* admissions@massart.edu.

MASSACHUSETTS COLLEGE OF LIBERAL ARTS

North Adams, Massachusetts **www.mcla.edu/**

- **State-supported** comprehensive, founded 1894, part of Massachusetts Public Higher Education System
- **Small-town** 80-acre campus
- **Endowment** $7.5 million
- **Coed** 1,550 undergraduate students, 86% full-time, 60% women, 40% men
- **Moderately difficult** entrance level, 71% of applicants were admitted

Undergraduates 1,334 full-time, 216 part-time. 25% are from out of state, 4% African American, 0.9% Asian American or Pacific Islander, 4% Hispanic American, 0.1% Native American, 11% transferred in, 61% live on campus. *Retention:* 72% of 2006 full-time freshmen returned.

Freshmen *Admission:* 1,431 applied, 1,018 admitted, 354 enrolled. *Average high school GPA:* 2.94. *Test scores:* SAT critical reading scores over 500: 64%; SAT math scores over 500: 49%; ACT scores over 18: 100%; SAT critical reading scores over 600: 21%; SAT math scores over 600: 11%; ACT scores over 24: 45%; SAT critical reading scores over 700: 3%.

Faculty *Total:* 183, 46% full-time, 45% with terminal degrees. *Student/faculty ratio:* 12:1.

Majors Biology/biological sciences; business administration and management; computer and information sciences; computer science; education; English; environmental studies; history; interdisciplinary studies; mathematics; philosophy; physics; psychology; sociology; visual and performing arts.

Academics *Calendar:* semesters. *Degrees:* bachelor's, master's, and post-bachelor's certificates. *Special study options:* academic remediation for entering students, advanced placement credit, distance learning, double majors, honors programs, independent study, internships, off-campus study, part-time degree program, services for LD students, student-designed majors, study abroad, summer session for credit. *Unusual degree programs:* 3-2 engineering with University of Massachusetts at Amherst.

Computers on Campus 125 computers/terminals are available on campus for general student use. Students can access the following: computer help desk, free student e-mail accounts, online (class) grades, online (class) schedules. Campuswide network is available. 100% of college-owned or -operated housing units are wired for high-speed Internet access. Wireless service is available via entire campus.

Student Life *Housing:* on-campus residence required through junior year. *Options:* coed, disabled students. Campus housing is university owned. *Activities and organizations:* drama/theater group, student-run newspaper, radio and television station, choral group, Student Activities Council, Student Government Association, The Beacon (Student Newspaper), Harlequin-Musical Theatre Company, Lacrosse Club, national fraternities, national sororities. *Campus security:* 24-hour emergency response devices and patrols, late-night transport/escort service, controlled dormitory access, escort service. *Student services:* health clinic, personal/psychological counseling, women's center.

Athletics Member NCAA. All Division III. *Intercollegiate sports:* baseball M, basketball M/W, cross-country running M/W, golf M, soccer M/W, softball W, tennis W. *Intramural sports:* basketball M/W, cross-country running M/W, football M, golf M/W, ice hockey M, lacrosse M (c)/W (c), racquetball M/W, rugby M (c)/W (c), skiing (cross-country) M (c)/W (c), skiing (downhill) M (c)/W (c), soccer M/W, softball M/W, squash M/W, swimming and diving M/W, tennis M/W, volleyball M/W, water polo M/W, weight lifting M (c)/W (c), wrestling M (c)/W (c).

Standardized Tests *Required:* SAT or ACT (for admission). *Recommended:* SAT (for admission).

Costs (2007–08) *One-time required fee:* $140. *Tuition:* state resident $1030 full-time, $43 per credit part-time; nonresident $9975 full-time, $416 per credit part-time. Full-time tuition and fees vary according to student level. Part-time tuition and fees vary according to student level. *Required fees:* $5138 full-time, $174 per credit part-time. *Room and board:* $6804; room only: $3698. Room and board charges vary according to board plan and housing facility. *Waivers:* senior citizens and employees or children of employees.

Financial Aid Of all full-time matriculated undergraduates who enrolled in 2007, 1,151 applied for aid, 826 were judged to have need. In 2007, 136 non-need-based awards were made. *Average need-based loan:* $2894. *Average need-based gift aid:* $4870. *Average non-need-based aid:* $2685. *Average indebtedness upon graduation:* $18,726.

Applying *Options:* electronic application, early action, deferred entrance. *Application fee:* $25. *Required:* essay or personal statement, high school transcript, minimum 2.0 GPA. *Required for some:* interview. *Recommended:* letters of recommendation. *Application deadlines:* rolling (freshmen), rolling (transfers), 12/1 (early action). *Notification:* continuous (freshmen), continuous (transfers), 12/15 (early action).

Freshman Application Contact Massachusetts College of Liberal Arts, 375 Church Street, North Adams, MA 01247-4100. *Phone:* 413-662-5410. *Toll-free phone:* 800-292-6632.

See page 1246 for the College Close-Up.

MASSACHUSETTS COLLEGE OF PHARMACY AND HEALTH SCIENCES

Boston, Massachusetts **www.mcphs.edu/**

- **Independent** university, founded 1823
- **Urban** 3-acre campus
- **Endowment** $100.6 million
- **Coed** 2,462 undergraduate students, 96% full-time, 68% women, 32% men
- **Moderately difficult** entrance level, 65% of applicants were admitted

Founded in 1823, Massachusetts College of Pharmacy and Health Sciences is a private, coeducational college offering graduate, professional, and undergraduate degrees in the health sciences. The College has campuses in Boston and Worcester, Massachusetts, and Manchester, New Hampshire. Professional or undergraduate degrees are offered in chemistry, dental hygiene, environmental sciences, health psychology, nursing, pharmacy and pharmaceutical sciences, physician assistant studies, premedical and health studies, and radiologic sciences. Graduate programs are offered in applied natural products, drug discovery and development, medicinal chemistry, pharmaceutical sciences, pharmacology, and regulatory affairs and health policy.

Undergraduates 2,363 full-time, 99 part-time. Students come from 42 states and territories, 38 other countries, 44% are from out of state, 5% African American, 28% Asian American or Pacific Islander, 3% Hispanic American, 0.2% Native American, 2% international, 9% transferred in, 23% live on campus. *Retention:* 87% of 2006 full-time freshmen returned.

Freshmen *Admission:* 2,517 applied, 1,638 admitted, 577 enrolled. *Average high school GPA:* 3.46. *Test scores:* SAT critical reading scores over 500: 69%; SAT math scores over 500: 82%; SAT writing scores over 500: 72%; ACT scores over 18: 95%; SAT critical reading scores over 600: 17%; SAT math scores over 600: 34%; SAT writing scores over 600: 18%; ACT scores over 24: 43%; SAT critical reading scores over 700: 1%; SAT math scores over 700: 4%; SAT writing scores over 700: 1%; ACT scores over 30: 5%.

Faculty *Total:* 193, 97% full-time, 84% with terminal degrees. *Student/faculty ratio:* 19:1.

Majors Chemistry; dental hygiene; environmental science; health/medical psychology; health professions related; medical radiologic technology; nuclear medical technology; nursing (registered nurse training); pharmacy; pharmacy, pharmaceutical sciences, and administration related; pre-medical studies; radiologic technology/science.

Academics *Calendar:* semesters. *Degrees:* certificates, bachelor's, master's, doctoral, first professional, and postbachelor's certificates. *Special study options:* accelerated degree program, adult/continuing education programs, advanced placement credit, distance learning, double majors, English as a second language, independent study, internships, off-campus study, part-time degree program, services for LD students, summer session for credit.

Computers on Campus 500 computers/terminals are available on campus for general student use. Students can access the following: computer help desk, free student e-mail accounts, online (class) grades. Campuswide network is available. 100% of college-owned or -operated housing units are wired for high-speed Internet access. Wireless service is available via entire campus.

Student Life *Housing options:* coed, women-only. Campus housing is university owned, leased by the school and is provided by a third party. Freshman applicants given priority for college housing. *Activities and organizations:* drama/theater group, student-run newspaper, choral group, Residence Hall Council, Vietnamese Student Association, Student Government Association, Campus Activities Board, Student Indian Organization, national fraternities. *Campus security:* 24-hour emergency response devices and patrols, late-night transport/escort service, controlled dormitory access, electronically operated academic area entrances, security guards at entrance. *Student services:* health clinic, personal/psychological counseling.

Athletics *Intramural sports:* badminton M/W, baseball M/W, basketball M/W, bowling M/W, cross-country running M/W, equestrian sports M/W, field hockey W, golf M/W, racquetball M/W, sailing M/W, skiing (downhill) M/W, soccer M/W, squash M/W, table tennis M/W, tennis M/W, ultimate Frisbee M/W, volleyball M/W, weight lifting M/W.

Standardized Tests *Required:* SAT or ACT (for admission).

Costs (2007–08) *Comprehensive fee:* $34,500 includes full-time tuition ($22,000), mandatory fees ($700), and room and board ($11,800). Full-time tuition and fees vary according to course load, program, and student level. Part-time tuition: $810 per credit hour. *Required fees:* $175 per term part-time. *Room and board:* Room and board charges vary according to housing facility. *Payment plan:* installment. *Waivers:* employees or children of employees.

Financial Aid Of all full-time matriculated undergraduates who enrolled in 2007, 2,105 applied for aid, 1,939 were judged to have need, 112 had their need fully met. In 2007, 257 non-need-based awards were made. *Average percent of need met:* 35%. *Average financial aid package:* $10,812. *Average need-based loan:* $5215. *Average need-based gift aid:* $7648. *Average non-need-based aid:* $15,234. *Average indebtedness upon graduation:* $54,495.

Applying *Options:* electronic application, early admission, early action, deferred entrance. *Application fee:* $70. *Required:* essay or personal statement, high school transcript, 2 letters of recommendation. *Required for some:* 3 letters of recommendation, interview. *Application deadlines:* 2/1 (freshmen), 2/1 (transfers), 11/15 (early action). *Notification:* continuous (freshmen), continuous (transfers), 2/1 (early action).

Freshman Application Contact Mr. Jim Zarakas, Admissions Assistant, Massachusetts College of Pharmacy and Health Sciences, 179 Longwood Avenue, Boston, MA 02115. *Phone:* 617-732-2846. *Toll-free phone:* 617-732-2850 (in-state); 800-225-5506 (out-of-state). *Fax:* 617-732-2118. *E-mail:* admissions@mphs.edu.

See page 1248 for the College Close-Up.

MASSACHUSETTS INSTITUTE OF TECHNOLOGY

Cambridge, Massachusetts **web.mit.edu/**

- **Independent** university, founded 1861
- **Urban** 168-acre campus with easy access to Boston
- **Endowment** $10.0 billion
- **Coed** 4,172 undergraduate students, 99% full-time, 45% women, 55% men
- **Most difficult** entrance level, 12% of applicants were admitted

Undergraduates 4,119 full-time, 53 part-time. Students come from 55 states and territories, 89 other countries, 90% are from out of state, 7% African American, 26% Asian American or Pacific Islander, 12% Hispanic American, 1% Native American, 8% international, 0.4% transferred in, 90% live on campus. *Retention:* 98% of 2006 full-time freshmen returned.

Freshmen *Admission:* 12,445 applied, 1,553 admitted, 1,067 enrolled. *Test scores:* SAT critical reading scores over 500: 99%; SAT math scores over 500: 100%; ACT scores over 18: 100%; SAT critical reading scores over 600: 94%; SAT math scores over 600: 99%; ACT scores over 24: 100%; SAT critical reading scores over 700: 59%; SAT math scores over 700: 87%; ACT scores over 30: 87%.

Faculty *Total:* 1,805, 75% full-time, 87% with terminal degrees. *Student/faculty ratio:* 6:1.

Majors Aerospace, aeronautical and astronautical engineering; anthropology; architecture; biology/biological sciences; biomedical/medical engineering; business/commerce; chemical engineering; chemistry; city/urban, community and regional planning; civil engineering; cognitive psychology and psycholinguistics; computer science; creative writing; economics; electrical, electronics and communications engineering; English; environmental/environmental health engineering; foreign languages and literatures; geology/earth science; history; liberal arts and sciences/liberal studies; linguistics; mass communication/media; materials engineering; mathematics; mathematics and computer science; mechanical engineering; music; neuroscience; nuclear engineering; ocean engineering; philosophy; physics; political science and government; science, technology and society.

Academics *Calendar:* 4-1-4. *Degrees:* bachelor's, master's, and doctoral. *Special study options:* advanced placement credit, cooperative education, English as a second language, internships, off-campus study, services for LD students, study abroad. *ROTC:* Army (b), Navy (b), Air Force (b).

Computers on Campus 1,100 computers/terminals are available on campus for general student use. Students can access the following: campus intranet, computer help desk, free student e-mail accounts, online (class) grades, online (class) registration, online (class) schedules. Campuswide network is available. 85% of college-owned or -operated housing units are wired for high-speed Internet access. Wireless service is available via entire campus.

Student Life *Housing:* on-campus residence required for freshman year. *Options:* coed, women-only, cooperative, disabled students. Campus housing is university owned. Freshman campus housing is guaranteed. *Activities and organizations:* drama/theater group, student-run newspaper, radio and television station, choral group, marching band, Tech Catholic Community, Outing Club, Society of Women Engineers, Hillel, South Asian-American Students, national fraternities, national sororities. *Campus security:* 24-hour emergency response devices and patrols, late-night transport/escort service, controlled dormitory access. *Student services:* health clinic, personal/psychological counseling.

Athletics Member NCAA. All Division III except crew (Division I). *Intercollegiate sports:* baseball M, basketball M/W, cheerleading M (c)/W (c), crew M/W, cross-country running M/W, fencing M/W, field hockey W, football M, golf M, gymnastics M/W, ice hockey M (c)/W, lacrosse M/W, riflery M/W, sailing M/W, skiing (cross-country) M/W, skiing (downhill) M/W, soccer M/W, softball W, squash M, swimming and diving M/W, tennis M/W, track and field M/W, volleyball M/W, water polo M, wrestling M. *Intramural sports:* archery M (c)/W (c), badminton M (c)/W (c), basketball M/W, bowling M/W, cheerleading M (c)/W (c), crew M (c)/W (c), cross-country running M/W, equestrian sports M (c)/W (c), fencing M (c)/W (c), field hockey M (c)/W (c), ice hockey M/W, rugby M (c)/W (c), soccer M/W, softball M/W, squash M/W, table tennis M/W, tennis M/W, ultimate Frisbee M (c)/W (c), volleyball M (c)/W (c), water polo M/W (c).

Standardized Tests *Required:* SAT Subject Tests (for admission). *Required for some:* SAT or ACT (for admission).

Costs (2007–08) *Comprehensive fee:* $45,386 includes full-time tuition ($34,750), mandatory fees ($236), and room and board ($10,400). Part-time tuition: $545 per unit. Part-time tuition and fees vary according to course load. *College room only:* $6000. Room and board charges vary according to board plan and housing facility. *Payment plan:* installment. *Waivers:* employees or children of employees.

Financial Aid Of all full-time matriculated undergraduates who enrolled in 2006, 2,863 applied for aid, 2,542 were judged to have need, 2,542 had their need fully met. 1,034 Federal Work-Study jobs (averaging $2696). 1,058 state and other part-time jobs (averaging $2243). *Average percent of need met:* 100%. *Average financial aid package:* $29,116. *Average need-based loan:* $2389. *Average need-based gift aid:* $27,391. *Average indebtedness upon graduation:* $15,051. *Financial aid deadline:* 2/15.

Applying *Options:* electronic application, early action, deferred entrance. *Application fee:* $65. *Required:* essay or personal statement, high school transcript, 2 letters of recommendation. *Recommended:* interview. *Application deadlines:* 1/1 (freshmen), 3/15 (transfers), 11/1 (early action). *Notification:* 3/20 (freshmen), 5/1 (transfers), 12/15 (early action).

Freshman Application Contact Admissions Counselors, Massachusetts Institute of Technology, Room 3-108, 77 Massachusetts Avenue, Cambridge, MA 02139-4307. *Phone:* 617-253-3400. *Fax:* 617-258-8304. *E-mail:* admissions@mit.edu.

See page 1250 for the College Close-Up.

MASSACHUSETTS MARITIME ACADEMY

Buzzards Bay, Massachusetts **www.maritime.edu/**

- **State-supported** 4-year, founded 1891, part of Massachusetts Public Higher Education System
- **Small-town** 55-acre campus with easy access to Boston
- **Endowment** $5.6 million
- **Coed, primarily men** 1,098 undergraduate students, 94% full-time, 9% women, 91% men
- **Moderately difficult** entrance level, 33% of applicants were admitted

Undergraduates 1,036 full-time, 62 part-time. Students come from 24 states and territories, 4 other countries, 30% are from out of state, 1% African American, 1% Asian American or Pacific Islander, 1% Hispanic American, 0.3% Native American, 0.2% international, 3% transferred in, 100% live on campus. *Retention:* 83% of 2006 full-time freshmen returned.

Freshmen *Admission:* 819 applied, 269 admitted, 263 enrolled. *Average high school GPA:* 2.9. *Test scores:* SAT critical reading scores over 500: 52%; SAT math scores over 500: 64%; ACT scores over 18: 92%; SAT critical reading scores over 600: 10%; SAT math scores over 600: 17%; ACT scores over 24: 2%; SAT critical reading scores over 700: 1%; SAT math scores over 700: 1%.

Faculty *Total:* 70, 84% full-time, 61% with terminal degrees. *Student/faculty ratio:* 15:1.

Majors Engineering; engineering/industrial management; engineering related; engineering technology; environmental/environmental health engineering; environmental science; environmental studies; international business/trade/commerce; marine science/merchant marine officer; maritime science; natural resources management; naval architecture and marine engineering; security and protective services related.

Academics *Calendar:* semesters plus sea term. *Degrees:* bachelor's, master's, and first professional certificates. *Special study options:* academic remediation for entering students, adult/continuing education programs, advanced placement credit, cooperative education, double majors, internships, services for LD students, summer session for credit. *ROTC:* Army (c), Navy (b).

Computers on Campus 100 computers/terminals are available on campus for general student use. Students can access the following: campus intranet, computer help desk, free student e-mail accounts, online (class) grades, online (class) registration, online (class) schedules, Course-supported e-learning. Campuswide network is available. 100% of college-owned or -operated housing units are wired for high-speed Internet access. Wireless service is available via entire campus.

Student Life *Housing:* on-campus residence required for freshman year. *Options:* coed. Campus housing is university owned. Freshman campus housing is guaranteed. *Activities and organizations:* drama/theater group, student-run newspaper, choral group, marching band, Club Hockey, water sports, SAILING/CREW, Rugby Club, Scuba Club. *Campus security:* 24-hour emergency response devices and patrols, late-night transport/escort service. *Student services:* health clinic, personal/psychological counseling, women's center.

Athletics Member NCAA, NAIA. All NCAA Division III. *Intercollegiate sports:* baseball M, crew M/W, cross-country running M/W, football M, lacrosse M, riflery M/W, sailing M/W, soccer M, softball W, ultimate Frisbee M/W, volleyball M/W. *Intramural sports:* basketball M/W, crew M/W, cross-country running M/W, field hockey W, golf M (c)/W (c), ice hockey M (c), racquetball M/W, riflery M/W, rugby M (c), sailing M (c)/W (c), skiing (cross-country) M (c)/W (c), skiing (downhill) M (c)/W (c), soccer M/W, softball M/W, swimming and diving M/W, table tennis M/W, tennis M/W, ultimate Frisbee M/W, volleyball M/W, water polo M/W, weight lifting M (c)/W (c), wrestling M.

Standardized Tests *Required:* SAT or ACT (for admission).

Costs (2007–08) *Tuition:* area resident $1138 full-time, $228 per credit part-time; state resident $1991 full-time, $264 per credit part-time; nonresident $12,712 full-time, $710 per credit part-time. *Required fees:* $5975 full-time. *Room and board:* $7812; room only: $4100.

Financial Aid Of all full-time matriculated undergraduates who enrolled in 2005, 654 applied for aid, 424 were judged to have need, 242 had their need fully met. 147 Federal Work-Study jobs (averaging $1233). In 2005, 137 non-need-based awards were made. *Average percent of need met:* 57%. *Average financial aid package:* $5125. *Average need-based loan:* $3643. *Average need-based gift aid:* $1707. *Average non-need-based aid:* $1707. *Average indebtedness upon graduation:* $12,972.

Applying *Options:* electronic application, early admission, deferred entrance. *Application fee:* $50. *Required:* essay or personal statement, high school transcript, minimum 2.0 GPA, 2 letters of recommendation, physical examination. *Recommended:* interview. *Application deadlines:* rolling (freshmen), rolling (transfers). *Notification:* continuous (freshmen), continuous (transfers).

Freshman Application Contact Roy Fulgueras, Director of Admissions, Massachusetts Maritime Academy, 101 Academy Drive, Blinn Hall, Buzzards Bay, MA 02532. *Phone:* 508-830-5031. *Toll-free phone:* 800-544-3411. *Fax:* 508-830-5077. *E-mail:* admissions@maritime.edu.

See page 1252 for the College Close-Up.

MERRIMACK COLLEGE

North Andover, Massachusetts **www.merrimack.edu/**

- **Independent Roman Catholic** comprehensive, founded 1947
- **Suburban** 220-acre campus with easy access to Boston
- **Endowment** $38.1 million
- **Coed** 2,093 undergraduate students, 87% full-time, 51% women, 49% men
- **Moderately difficult** entrance level, 71% of applicants were admitted

Undergraduates 1,826 full-time, 267 part-time. Students come from 28 states and territories, 9 other countries, 28% are from out of state, 2% African American, 2% Asian American or Pacific Islander, 4% Hispanic American, 0.2% Native American, 1% international, 4% transferred in, 78% live on campus. *Retention:* 80% of 2006 full-time freshmen returned.

Freshmen *Admission:* 3,657 applied, 2,600 admitted, 442 enrolled. *Average high school GPA:* 3.34. *Test scores:* SAT critical reading scores over 500: 63%; SAT math scores over 500: 72%; SAT writing scores over 500: 64%; SAT critical reading scores over 600: 15%; SAT math scores over 600: 22%; SAT writing scores over 600: 18%; SAT critical reading scores over 700: 2%; SAT math scores over 700: 9%; SAT writing scores over 700: 2%.

Faculty *Total:* 211, 66% full-time, 71% with terminal degrees. *Student/faculty ratio:* 12:1.

Majors Athletic training; biochemistry; biology/biological sciences; business/managerial economics; chemistry; civil engineering; communication/speech communication and rhetoric; computer engineering; economics; electrical, electronics and communications engineering; elementary education; engineering science; English; finance; fine/studio arts; French; health science; history; human services; interdisciplinary studies; international business/trade/commerce; liberal arts and sciences/liberal studies; marketing/marketing management; mathematics; middle school education; philosophy; physical therapy; political science and government; psychology; religious studies; Romance languages; Romance languages related; secondary education; sociology; Spanish.

Academics *Calendar:* semesters. *Degrees:* certificates, associate, bachelor's, and master's. *Special study options:* academic remediation for entering students, adult/continuing education programs, advanced placement credit, cooperative education, double majors, English as a second language, honors programs, independent study, internships, off-campus study, part-time degree program, services for LD students, student-designed majors, study abroad, summer session for credit. *ROTC:* Air Force (c).

Computers on Campus 175 computers/terminals are available on campus for general student use. Campuswide network is available. Wireless service is available via classrooms, computer centers, libraries, student centers.

Student Life *Housing options:* coed. Campus housing is university owned. Freshman applicants given priority for college housing. *Activities and organizations:* drama/theater group, student-run newspaper, television station, choral group, Merrimaction Community Outreach, MORE Retreat Program, Merrimack Marketing Association, Orientation Committee Coordinators, Developing Leaders Program, national fraternities, national sororities. *Campus security:* 24-hour emergency response devices and patrols, student patrols, late-night transport/escort service, controlled dormitory access, 24-hour staffed dorm entrances (adult employees). *Student services:* health clinic, personal/psychological counseling.

Athletics Member NCAA. All Division II except ice hockey (Division I). *Intercollegiate sports:* baseball M, basketball M (s)/W (s), cross-country running M/W (s), field hockey W (s), football M, ice hockey M (s), lacrosse M/W (s), soccer M/W (s), softball W (s), tennis M/W (s), track and field M (c)/W (c), volleyball M (c)/W (s). *Intramural sports:* basketball M/W, ice hockey M/W, lacrosse M/W, racquetball M/W, rugby M (c)/W (c), skiing (downhill) M (c)/W (c), softball M/W, tennis M/W, volleyball M/W.

Costs (2007–08) *Comprehensive fee:* $40,515 includes full-time tuition ($29,310), mandatory fees ($500), and room and board ($10,705). Full-time tuition and fees vary according to program and student level. Part-time tuition: $1085 per credit. Part-time tuition and fees vary according to class time, course level, course load, and degree level. No tuition increase for student's term of enrollment. *Required fees:* $55 per term part-time. *College room only:* $6990. Room and board charges vary according to board plan. *Payment plan:* installment. *Waivers:* senior citizens and employees or children of employees.

Financial Aid Of all full-time matriculated undergraduates who enrolled in 2007, 1,426 applied for aid, 1,200 were judged to have need, 1,000 had their need fully met. 138 Federal Work-Study jobs (averaging $1200). 410 state and other part-time jobs (averaging $2000). In 2007, 100 non-need-based awards were made. *Average percent of need met:* 65%. *Average financial aid package:* $20,500. *Average need-based loan:* $5500. *Average need-based gift aid:* $13,500. *Average non-need-based aid:* $12,000. *Average indebtedness upon graduation:* $17,125. *Financial aid deadline:* 2/1.

Applying *Options:* electronic application, early admission, early action, deferred entrance. *Application fee:* $60. *Required:* essay or personal statement, high school transcript, first quarter senior grades. *Required for some:* interview. *Recommended:* minimum 2.8 GPA, 1 letter of recommendation, interview. *Application deadlines:* 2/1 (freshmen), 12/30 (transfers), 11/30 (early action). *Notification:* continuous until 4/1 (freshmen), continuous until 1/10 (transfers), 12/20 (early action).

Freshman Application Contact Director of Admissions, Merrimack College, Austin Hall, A22, North Andover, MA 01845. *Phone:* 978-837-5100. *Fax:* 978-837-5133. *E-mail:* admission@merrimack.edu.

See page 1254 for the College Close-Up.

MONTSERRAT COLLEGE OF ART

Beverly, Massachusetts **www.montserrat.edu/**

- **Independent** 4-year, founded 1970
- **Suburban** 10-acre campus with easy access to Boston
- **Endowment** $715,554
- **Coed** 285 undergraduate students, 91% full-time, 68% women, 32% men
- **Moderately difficult** entrance level, 68% of applicants were admitted

Undergraduates 260 full-time, 25 part-time. Students come from 21 states and territories, 3 other countries, 54% are from out of state, 1% African American, 0.7% Asian American or Pacific Islander, 2% Hispanic American, 1% international, 5% transferred in, 52% live on campus. *Retention:* 77% of 2006 full-time freshmen returned.

Freshmen *Admission:* 303 applied, 205 admitted, 77 enrolled. *Average high school GPA:* 2.69. *Test scores:* SAT critical reading scores over 500: 52%; SAT math scores over 500: 34%; SAT critical reading scores over 600: 19%; SAT math scores over 600: 6%; SAT critical reading scores over 700: 3%.

Faculty *Total:* 48, 42% full-time, 69% with terminal degrees. *Student/faculty ratio:* 12:1.

Majors Art teacher education; drawing; fine arts related; fine/studio arts; graphic design; illustration; painting; photography; printmaking; sculpture.

Academics *Calendar:* semesters. *Degrees:* diplomas, bachelor's, and post-bachelor's certificates. *Special study options:* adult/continuing education programs, advanced placement credit, double majors, English as a second language, independent study, internships, off-campus study, part-time degree program, services for LD students, student-designed majors, study abroad. *ROTC:* Air Force (c).

Computers on Campus 98 computers/terminals and 100 ports are available on campus for general student use. Students can access the following: computer help desk, free student e-mail accounts. Campuswide network is available. 100% of college-owned or -operated housing units are wired for high-speed Internet access. Wireless service is available via entire campus.

Student Life *Housing options:* men-only, women-only. Campus housing is university owned and leased by the school. Freshman applicants given priority for college housing. *Activities and organizations:* drama/theater group, student-run newspaper, radio station, Student Voice, The Radio Station, Bear Gallery, The Newspaper, coed intramural sports. *Campus security:* late-night transport/escort service. *Student services:* personal/psychological counseling.

Athletics *Intramural sports:* badminton M/W, basketball M/W, bowling M/W, football M/W, skiing (downhill) M/W, volleyball M/W.

Costs (2007–08) *Tuition:* $21,500 full-time, $896 per credit part-time. Full-time tuition and fees vary according to course load and reciprocity agreements. Part-time tuition and fees vary according to course load and reciprocity agreements. *Required fees:* $800 full-time, $25 per credit part-time. *Room only:* $5800. Room and board charges vary according to housing facility. *Payment plan:* installment. *Waivers:* employees or children of employees.

Financial Aid Of all full-time matriculated undergraduates who enrolled in 2005, 281 applied for aid, 227 were judged to have need. 65 Federal Work-Study jobs (averaging $847). *Average financial aid package:* $9947. *Average need-based loan:* $4196. *Average need-based gift aid:* $4548.

Applying *Options:* electronic application, deferred entrance. *Application fee:* $50. *Required:* essay or personal statement, high school transcript, minimum 2.25 GPA, 2 letters of recommendation, portfolio. *Recommended:* minimum 2.5 GPA, interview. *Application deadlines:* 8/15 (freshmen), 8/15 (transfers). *Notification:* continuous until 8/20 (freshmen), continuous until 8/20 (transfers).

Freshman Application Contact Mr. Brian Bicknell, Dean of Students, Montserrat College of Art, 23 Essex Street, PO Box 26, Beverly, MA 01915. *Phone:* 978-921-4242 Ext. 1153. *Toll-free phone:* 800-836-0487. *Fax:* 978-921-4241. *E-mail:* bbicknell@montserrat.edu.

See page 1256 for the College Close-Up.

MOUNT HOLYOKE COLLEGE

South Hadley, Massachusetts **www.mtholyoke.edu/**

- **Independent** comprehensive, founded 1837
- **Small-town** 800-acre campus with easy access to Springfield
- **Endowment** $615.4 million
- **Women only** 2,201 undergraduate students, 98% full-time
- **Very difficult** entrance level, 52% of applicants were admitted

Undergraduates 2,152 full-time, 49 part-time. Students come from 50 states and territories, 64 other countries, 75% are from out of state, 5% African

American, 12% Asian American or Pacific Islander, 5% Hispanic American, 0.6% Native American, 16% international, 2% transferred in, 93% live on campus. *Retention:* 94% of 2006 full-time freshmen returned.

Freshmen *Admission:* 3,194 applied, 1,671 admitted, 512 enrolled. *Average high school GPA:* 3.67. *Test scores:* SAT critical reading scores over 500: 99%; SAT math scores over 500: 98%; SAT writing scores over 500: 100%; ACT scores over 18: 100%; SAT critical reading scores over 600: 90%; SAT math scores over 600: 73%; SAT writing scores over 600: 90%; ACT scores over 24: 93%; SAT critical reading scores over 700: 44%; SAT math scores over 700: 25%; SAT writing scores over 700: 37%; ACT scores over 30: 38%.

Faculty *Total:* 236, 88% full-time, 90% with terminal degrees. *Student/faculty ratio:* 10:1.

Majors African-American/Black studies; American studies; ancient/classical Greek; ancient studies; anthropology; architecture related; area, ethnic, cultural, and gender studies related; art history, criticism and conservation; Asian studies; astronomy; biochemistry; biology/biological sciences; chemistry; classics and languages, literatures and linguistics; computer science; dance; dramatic/theater arts; economics; education; education related; engineering; English; environmental studies; European studies; film/cinema studies; fine/studio arts; French; geography; geology/earth science; German; history; interdisciplinary studies; international relations and affairs; Italian; Jewish/Judaic studies; Latin; Latin American studies; mathematics; medieval and Renaissance studies; modern Greek; music; neuroscience; philosophy; physics; political science and government; psychology; psychology related; religious studies; Romance languages; Russian studies; social sciences related; sociology; Spanish; statistics; women's studies.

Academics *Calendar:* 4-1-4. *Degrees:* certificates, bachelor's, master's, and postbachelor's certificates. *Special study options:* adult/continuing education programs, advanced placement credit, cooperative education, double majors, honors programs, independent study, internships, off-campus study, part-time degree program, services for LD students, student-designed majors, study abroad. *ROTC:* Army (c), Air Force (c). *Unusual degree programs:* 3-2 engineering with Dartmouth College, University of Massachusetts; nursing with Johns Hopkins University; public health with University of Massachusetts, Latin American studies with Georgetown University.

Computers on Campus 592 computers/terminals and 500 ports are available on campus for general student use. Students can access the following: campus intranet, computer help desk, free student e-mail accounts, online (class) grades, online (class) registration, online (class) schedules, personal Web pages. Campuswide network is available. 100% of college-owned or -operated housing units are wired for high-speed Internet access. Wireless service is available via classrooms, computer centers, computer labs, dorm rooms, learning centers, libraries, student centers.

Student Life *Housing:* on-campus residence required through senior year. *Options:* women-only, disabled students. Campus housing is university owned. Freshman campus housing is guaranteed. *Activities and organizations:* drama/theater group, student-run newspaper, radio station, choral group, Student Government Association, WMHC (radio station), Mount Holyoke News, cultural organizations, a cappella groups. *Campus security:* 24-hour emergency response devices and patrols, student patrols, late-night transport/escort service, controlled dormitory access, police officers on-campus. *Student services:* health clinic, personal/psychological counseling, women's center.

Athletics Member NCAA. All Division III. *Intercollegiate sports:* basketball W, crew W, cross-country running W, equestrian sports W, field hockey W, golf W, lacrosse W, soccer W, squash W, swimming and diving W, tennis W, track and field W, volleyball W. *Intramural sports:* badminton W, basketball W, equestrian sports W, fencing W (c), ice hockey W (c), rugby W (c), soccer W, tennis W, volleyball W, water polo W (c).

Standardized Tests *Required for some:* SAT Subject Tests (for admission).

Costs (2007–08) *Comprehensive fee:* $46,460 includes full-time tuition ($35,760), mandatory fees ($180), and room and board ($10,520). Part-time tuition: $1120 per credit hour. *College room only:* $5150. Room and board charges vary according to board plan and housing facility. *Payment plans:* tuition prepayment, installment, deferred payment. *Waivers:* employees or children of employees.

Financial Aid Of all full-time matriculated undergraduates who enrolled in 2007, 1,516 applied for aid, 1,367 were judged to have need, 1,367 had their need fully met. 833 Federal Work-Study jobs (averaging $1580). 407 state and other part-time jobs (averaging $1625). In 2007, 142 non-need-based awards were made. *Average percent of need met:* 100%. *Average financial aid package:* $31,077. *Average need-based loan:* $5087. *Average need-based gift aid:* $25,816. *Average non-need-based aid:* $14,262. *Average indebtedness upon graduation:* $22,270. *Financial aid deadline:* 3/1.

Applying *Options:* electronic application, early admission, early decision, deferred entrance. *Application fee:* $60. *Required:* essay or personal statement, high school transcript, 2 letters of recommendation. *Recommended:* interview. *Application deadlines:* 1/15 (freshmen), 5/15 (transfers). *Early decision deadline:* 11/15 (for plan 1), 1/1 (for plan 2). *Notification:* 4/1 (freshmen), continuous (transfers), 1/1 (early decision plan 1), 2/1 (early decision plan 2).

Freshman Application Contact Ms. Diane Anci, Dean of Admission, Mount Holyoke College, 50 College Street, South Hadley, MA 01075. *Phone:* 413-538-2023. *Fax:* 413-538-2409. *E-mail:* admission@mtholyoke.edu.

See page 1258 for the College Close-Up.

MOUNT IDA COLLEGE

Newton, Massachusetts **www.mountida.edu/**

- **Independent** 4-year, founded 1899
- **Suburban** 72-acre campus with easy access to Boston
- **Endowment** $10.6 million
- **Coed** 1,430 undergraduate students, 93% full-time, 67% women, 33% men
- **Moderately difficult** entrance level, 78% of applicants were admitted

Undergraduates 1,329 full-time, 101 part-time. Students come from 29 states and territories, 27 other countries, 40% are from out of state, 9% African American, 2% Asian American or Pacific Islander, 6% Hispanic American, 0.3% Native American, 5% international, 7% transferred in, 62% live on campus. *Retention:* 65% of 2006 full-time freshmen returned.

Freshmen *Admission:* 2,060 applied, 1,614 admitted, 415 enrolled. *Average high school GPA:* 2.6. *Test scores:* SAT critical reading scores over 500: 20%; SAT critical reading scores over 600: 3%.

Faculty *Total:* 170, 36% full-time, 39% with terminal degrees. *Student/faculty ratio:* 13:1.

Majors American studies; animal sciences; business administration and management; child development; commercial and advertising art; consumer merchandising/retailing management; criminal justice/law enforcement administration; dental hygiene; developmental and child psychology; equestrian studies; fashion/apparel design; fashion merchandising; funeral service and mortuary science; horse husbandry/equine science and management; hotel/motel administration; human services; interior design; kindergarten/preschool education; liberal arts and sciences/liberal studies; marketing/marketing management; psychology; social work; teacher assistant/aide; veterinary technology.

Academics *Calendar:* semesters. *Degrees:* certificates, associate, and bachelor's. *Special study options:* academic remediation for entering students, accelerated degree program, adult/continuing education programs, cooperative education, English as a second language, freshman honors college, honors programs, internships, part-time degree program, services for LD students, student-designed majors, study abroad.

Computers on Campus Students can access the following: campus intranet, computer help desk, free student e-mail accounts, online (class) grades, online (class) schedules. Campuswide network is available. Wireless service is available via computer labs, student centers.

Student Life *Housing options:* coed, women-only. Campus housing is university owned. *Activities and organizations:* drama/theater group, student-run newspaper, radio station, choral group, Leadership Students, student government, Phi Theta Kappa, Residence Council, Alpha Chi. *Campus security:* 24-hour emergency response devices and patrols, student patrols, late-night transport/escort service, controlled residence hall entrances, secured campus entrance. *Student services:* health clinic, personal/psychological counseling.

Athletics Member NCAA. except men's and women's basketball (Division III), cross-country running (Division III), football (Division III), lacrosse (Division III), men's and women's soccer (Division III), softball (Division III), men's and women's volleyball (Division III) *Intercollegiate sports:* basketball M/W, cross-country running W, equestrian sports W, football M, lacrosse M, soccer M/W, softball W, volleyball M/W. *Intramural sports:* basketball M/W, football W, lacrosse W, soccer M/W, softball W, tennis W, volleyball M/W, weight lifting M/W.

Standardized Tests *Required:* SAT or ACT (for admission).

Costs (2008–09) *Comprehensive fee:* $33,500 includes full-time tuition ($22,275), mandatory fees ($225), and room and board ($11,000). Part-time tuition: $600 per credit.

Financial Aid Of all full-time matriculated undergraduates who enrolled in 2006, 1,067 applied for aid, 960 were judged to have need, 59 had their need fully met. 299 Federal Work-Study jobs (averaging $1613). 126 state and other part-time jobs (averaging $2010). In 2006, 306 non-need-based awards were made. *Average percent of need met:* 51%. *Average financial aid package:* $12,066. *Average need-based loan:* $3389. *Average need-based gift aid:* $8624. *Average non-need-based aid:* $7994.

Applying *Options:* electronic application, deferred entrance. *Application fee:* $45. *Required:* high school transcript, 1 letter of recommendation. *Required for* *some:* interview. *Recommended:* essay or personal statement, minimum 2.0 GPA, extracurricular activities, leadership, and community service. *Application deadlines:* rolling (freshmen), rolling (transfers). *Notification:* continuous (freshmen), continuous (transfers).

Freshman Application Contact Jay Titus MS, Dean of Admissions, Mount Ida College, 777 Dedham Street, Newton, MA 02459. *Phone:* 617-928-4553. *Fax:* 617-928-4507. *E-mail:* admissions@mountida.edu.

See page 1260 for the College Close-Up.

NEWBURY COLLEGE

Brookline, Massachusetts **www.newbury.edu/**

Freshman Application Contact Newbury College, 129 Fisher Avenue, Brookline, MA 02445-5796. *Phone:* 617-730-7007. *Toll-free phone:* 800-NEWBURY. *Fax:* 617-731-9618. *E-mail:* info@newbury.edu.

NEW ENGLAND CONSERVATORY OF MUSIC

Boston, Massachusetts **www.newenglandconservatory.edu/**

- **Independent** comprehensive, founded 1867
- **Urban** 2-acre campus
- **Endowment** $84.2 million
- **Coed** 389 undergraduate students, 93% full-time, 44% women, 56% men
- **Very difficult** entrance level, 29% of applicants were admitted

Undergraduates 360 full-time, 29 part-time. Students come from 41 states and territories, 22 other countries, 85% are from out of state, 3% African American, 9% Asian American or Pacific Islander, 5% Hispanic American, 0.3% Native American, 22% international, 5% transferred in, 42% live on campus. *Retention:* 91% of 2006 full-time freshmen returned.

Freshmen *Admission:* 1,058 applied, 307 admitted, 96 enrolled.

Faculty *Total:* 211, 43% full-time, 17% with terminal degrees. *Student/faculty ratio:* 6:1.

Majors Jazz/jazz studies; music history, literature, and theory; music performance; music theory and composition; piano and organ; violin, viola, guitar and other stringed instruments; voice and opera; wind/percussion instruments.

Academics *Calendar:* semesters. *Degrees:* certificates, diplomas, bachelor's, master's, doctoral, and postbachelor's certificates. *Special study options:* adult/continuing education programs, advanced placement credit, English as a second language, independent study, internships, off-campus study, part-time degree program, services for LD students, study abroad, summer session for credit. *Unusual degree programs:* music with Tufts University and Harvard.

Computers on Campus 70 computers/terminals and 200 ports are available on campus for general student use. Students can access the following: computer help desk, free student e-mail accounts. Campuswide network is available. Wireless service is available via libraries, student centers.

Student Life *Housing:* on-campus residence required for freshman year. *Options:* coed. Campus housing is university owned. Freshman campus housing is guaranteed. *Activities and organizations:* student-run newspaper, choral group, Fellowship with Christ, Hillel, The Penguin (newspaper), Meditation Group, Penguins in Action (volunteer organization). *Campus security:* 24-hour patrols, late-night transport/escort service. *Student services:* health clinic, personal/psychological counseling.

Standardized Tests *Recommended:* SAT or ACT (for admission).

Costs (2008–09) *Comprehensive fee:* $44,925 includes full-time tuition ($32,900), mandatory fees ($425), and room and board ($11,600). Part-time tuition: $1050 per credit.

Financial Aid Of all full-time matriculated undergraduates who enrolled in 2007, 247 applied for aid, 203 were judged to have need, 30 had their need fully met. 283 Federal Work-Study jobs (averaging $1611). In 2007, 129 non-need-based awards were made. *Average percent of need met:* 62%. *Average financial aid package:* $17,064. *Average need-based loan:* $4720. *Average need-based gift aid:* $12,121. *Average non-need-based aid:* $5212. *Average indebtedness upon graduation:* $23,869.

Applying *Options:* electronic application, deferred entrance. *Application fee:* $100. *Required:* essay or personal statement, high school transcript, minimum 2.75 GPA, 2 letters of recommendation, audition recording, repertoire list. *Application deadlines:* 12/1 (freshmen), 12/3 (transfers). *Notification:* 4/1 (freshmen), 4/1 (transfers).

Freshman Application Contact New England Conservatory of Music, 290 Huntington Avenue, Boston, MA 02115-5000. *Phone:* 617-585-1103.

THE NEW ENGLAND INSTITUTE OF ART

Brookline, Massachusetts **www.neia.aii.edu/**

- **Proprietary** 4-year, part of Education Management Corporation
- **Urban** campus with easy access to Boston
- **Coed** 1,684 undergraduate students
- **Minimally difficult** entrance level, 44% of applicants were admitted

Undergraduates Students come from 36 states and territories, 21 other countries, 65% are from out of state, 15% live on campus. *Retention:* 100% of 2006 full-time freshmen returned.

Freshmen *Admission:* 1,233 applied, 538 admitted. *Average high school GPA:* 2.5.

Faculty *Student/faculty ratio:* 17:1.

Majors Animation, interactive technology, video graphics and special effects; commercial and advertising art; computer graphics; design and applied arts related; digital communication and media/multimedia; fashion merchandising; graphic design; interior design; music management and merchandising; photography; radio and television broadcasting technology; web/multimedia management and webmaster; web page, digital/multimedia and information resources design.

Academics *Calendar:* semesters. *Degrees:* certificates, associate, and bachelor's. *Special study options:* academic remediation for entering students, adult/continuing education programs, advanced placement credit, distance learning, independent study, internships, services for LD students, study abroad.

Computers on Campus 200 computers/terminals are available on campus for general student use. Students can access the following: free student e-mail accounts, Webspace. Campuswide network is available. Wireless service is available via entire campus.

Student Life *Housing options:* coed. Campus housing is leased by the school. *Activities and organizations:* student-run radio station, Graphic Design Club, Naked Truth, Naked Eye Video, Naked Ear Records, Web Raisers. *Campus security:* late-night transport/escort service, controlled dormitory access. *Student services:* personal/psychological counseling.

Costs (2007–08) *Comprehensive fee:* $31,550 includes full-time tuition ($20,250) and room and board ($11,300). Part-time tuition: $675 per credit. tuition cost varies by program. Prospective students should contact the school for current tuition costs. Other charges include a starting kit for all first-quarter students. Kits vary in price depending on the program of study.

Applying *Options:* electronic application. *Application fee:* $50. *Required:* essay or personal statement, high school transcript, interview. *Required for some:* letters of recommendation, portfolio; 3.0 GPA for transfer students. *Application deadlines:* rolling (freshmen), rolling (transfers). *Notification:* continuous (freshmen), continuous (transfers).

Freshman Application Contact Ms. Courtney Nicosia, Second Director of Admissions, The New England Institute of Art, 10 Brookline Place West, Brookline, MA 02445. *Phone:* 617-582-4471. *Toll-free phone:* 800-903=4425. *Fax:* 617-582-4500. *E-mail:* neia.adm@aii.edu.

See page 1262 for the College Close-Up.

NICHOLS COLLEGE

Dudley, Massachusetts **www.nichols.edu/**

- **Independent** comprehensive, founded 1815
- **Suburban** 210-acre campus with easy access to Boston
- **Coed** 1,269 undergraduate students, 83% full-time, 40% women, 60% men
- **Moderately difficult** entrance level, 77% of applicants were admitted

Undergraduates 1,051 full-time, 218 part-time. Students come from 25 states and territories, 5 other countries, 35% are from out of state, 4% African American, 1% Asian American or Pacific Islander, 3% Hispanic American, 0.4% Native American, 0.6% international, 2% transferred in, 80% live on campus. *Retention:* 64% of 2006 full-time freshmen returned.

Freshmen *Admission:* 1,894 applied, 1,456 admitted, 451 enrolled. *Average high school GPA:* 2.61. *Test scores:* SAT critical reading scores over 500: 25%; SAT math scores over 500: 34%; SAT critical reading scores over 600: 2%; SAT math scores over 600: 7%.

Faculty *Total:* 67, 51% full-time, 39% with terminal degrees. *Student/faculty ratio:* 18:1.

Majors Accounting; business administration and management; business/commerce; economics; English; finance; history; human resources management; management information systems; marketing/marketing management; mathematics; psychology; secondary education; sport and fitness administration/management.

Academics *Calendar:* semesters. *Degrees:* certificates, associate, bachelor's, and master's. *Special study options:* academic remediation for entering students, accelerated degree program, adult/continuing education programs, advanced placement credit, cooperative education, distance learning, double majors, honors programs, independent study, internships, off-campus study, part-time degree program, services for LD students, study abroad, summer session for credit. *ROTC:* Army (c).

Computers on Campus 69 computers/terminals are available on campus for general student use. Students can access the following: computer help desk, free student e-mail accounts, online (class) grades, online (class) registration, online (class) schedules. Campuswide network is available. 100% of college-owned or -operated housing units are wired for high-speed Internet access. Wireless service is available via classrooms, computer labs, libraries, student centers.

Student Life *Housing options:* coed, men-only, women-only, disabled students. Campus housing is university owned. Freshman applicants given priority for college housing. *Activities and organizations:* drama/theater group, student-run newspaper, radio station, Rugby Club, Accounting Club, Racquetball Club, Student publications, Theater Club. *Campus security:* 24-hour emergency response devices and patrols, student patrols, late-night transport/escort service. *Student services:* health clinic, personal/psychological counseling.

Athletics Member NCAA. All Division III. *Intercollegiate sports:* baseball M, basketball M/W, cheerleading M/W, field hockey W, football M, golf M/W, ice hockey M/W, lacrosse M/W, racquetball M (c)/W (c), rugby M (c)/W (c), skiing (downhill) M (c), soccer M/W, softball W, tennis M/W, volleyball W (c). *Intramural sports:* baseball M, basketball M/W, cheerleading M/W, field hockey W, golf M/W, ice hockey M/W (c), soccer M/W, softball W, tennis M/W, volleyball M, weight lifting M.

Standardized Tests *Required:* SAT or ACT (for admission).

Costs (2007–08) *Comprehensive fee:* $34,660 includes full-time tuition ($25,400), mandatory fees ($300), and room and board ($8960). Part-time tuition: $255 per credit hour. Part-time tuition and fees vary according to class time and course load. *College room only:* $4800. *Payment plan:* installment. *Waivers:* senior citizens and employees or children of employees.

Financial Aid Of all full-time matriculated undergraduates who enrolled in 2007, 860 applied for aid, 788 were judged to have need, 71 had their need fully met. 284 Federal Work-Study jobs (averaging $1962). In 2007, 51 non-need-based awards were made. *Average percent of need met:* 73%. *Average financial aid package:* $18,348. *Average need-based loan:* $4735. *Average need-based gift aid:* $13,164. *Average non-need-based aid:* $8072. *Average indebtedness upon graduation:* $27,764.

Applying *Options:* electronic application, deferred entrance. *Application fee:* $25. *Required:* essay or personal statement, high school transcript, 1 letter of recommendation. *Required for some:* interview. *Application deadlines:* rolling (freshmen), rolling (transfers). *Notification:* continuous (freshmen), continuous (transfers).

Freshman Application Contact Ms. Marie Keegan, Admissions Assistant, Nichols College, PO Box 5000, Dudley, MA 01571. *Phone:* 508-213-2203. *Toll-free phone:* 800-470-3379. *Fax:* 508-943-9885. *E-mail:* admissions@nichols.edu.

NORTHEASTERN UNIVERSITY

Boston, Massachusetts **www.northeastern.edu/**

- **Independent** university, founded 1898
- **Urban** 67-acre campus
- **Endowment** $698.2 million
- **Coed** 15,339 undergraduate students, 100% full-time, 51% women, 49% men
- **Very difficult** entrance level, 39% of applicants were admitted

Undergraduates 15,339 full-time. Students come from 50 states and territories, 94 other countries, 65% are from out of state, 6% African American, 8% Asian American or Pacific Islander, 5% Hispanic American, 0.4% Native American, 5% international, 4% transferred in, 48% live on campus. *Retention:* 91% of 2006 full-time freshmen returned.

Freshmen *Admission:* 30,339 applied, 11,971 admitted, 2,871 enrolled. *Test scores:* SAT critical reading scores over 500: 95%; SAT math scores over 500: 96%; ACT scores over 18: 99%; SAT critical reading scores over 600: 63%; SAT math scores over 600: 76%; ACT scores over 24: 87%; SAT critical reading scores over 700: 13%; SAT math scores over 700: 20%; ACT scores over 30: 23%.

Faculty *Total:* 1,330, 68% full-time. *Student/faculty ratio:* 16:1.

Majors Accounting; aeronautical/aerospace engineering technology; African-American/Black studies; anthropology; architecture; art; athletic training; audiology and speech-language pathology; behavioral sciences; biochemistry; biology/biological sciences; biology/biotechnology laboratory technician; business administration and management; business/commerce; chemical engineering; chemistry; civil engineering; clinical/medical laboratory technology; commercial and advertising art; communication/speech communication and rhetoric; computer engineering; computer engineering technology; computer science; corrections; criminal justice/police science; criminal justice/safety; dental hygiene; dramatic/theater arts; economics; education; electrical, electronics and communications engineering; elementary education; engineering; English; entrepreneurship; environmental studies; finance; French; geology/earth science; German; health/health care administration; health science; history; human resources management; human services; industrial engineering; information science/studies; international business/trade/commerce; international relations and affairs; Italian; journalism; kindergarten/preschool education; liberal arts and sciences/liberal studies; linguistics; logistics and materials management; management information systems; management science; marine biology and biological oceanography; marketing/marketing management; mass communication/media; mathematics; mechanical engineering; mechanical engineering/mechanical technology; modern languages; music; music history, literature, and theory; music management and merchandising; nursing related; pharmacy; philosophy; physical therapy; physics; political science and government; psychology; public administration; radio and television; rehabilitation therapy; Russian; sign language interpretation and translation; sociology; Spanish; therapeutic recreation; women's studies.

Academics *Calendar:* semesters. *Degrees:* bachelor's, master's, doctoral, first professional, and post-master's certificates. *Special study options:* academic remediation for entering students, accelerated degree program, adult/continuing education programs, advanced placement credit, cooperative education, distance learning, double majors, English as a second language, honors programs, independent study, internships, off-campus study, part-time degree program, services for LD students, student-designed majors, study abroad, summer session for credit. *ROTC:* Army (b), Navy (c), Air Force (c). *Unusual degree programs:* 3-2 engineering; nursing.

Computers on Campus 1,993 computers/terminals are available on campus for general student use. Students can access the following: campus intranet, computer help desk, free student e-mail accounts, online (class) grades, online (class) registration, online (class) schedules. Campuswide network is available. Wireless service is available via classrooms, computer centers, computer labs, learning centers, libraries, student centers.

Student Life *Housing options:* coed, disabled students. Campus housing is university owned and leased by the school. Freshman campus housing is guaranteed. *Activities and organizations:* drama/theater group, student-run newspaper, radio and television station, choral group, Student Government Association, Council for University Programs, Resident Student Association, NU Impovd, national fraternities, national sororities. *Campus security:* 24-hour emergency response devices and patrols, late-night transport/escort service, controlled dormitory access. *Student services:* health clinic, personal/psychological counseling, women's center.

Athletics Member NCAA. All Division I except football (Division I-AA). *Intercollegiate sports:* baseball M (s), basketball M (s)/W (s), crew M (s)/W (s), cross-country running M (s)/W (s), field hockey W (s), ice hockey M (s)/W (s), soccer M (s)/W (s), swimming and diving W (s), tennis M (s), track and field M (s)/W (s), volleyball W (s). *Intramural sports:* basketball M/W, cheerleading M (c)/W (c), fencing M (c)/W (c), field hockey M (c)/W (c), football M/W, ice hockey M/W, lacrosse M (c)/W (c), racquetball M/W, rock climbing M (c)/W (c), sailing M (c)/W (c), skiing (cross-country) M (c)/W (c), skiing (downhill) M (c)/W (c), soccer M/W, softball M/W, squash M/W, swimming and diving M (c)/W (c), table tennis M (c)/W (c), tennis M (c)/W (c), ultimate Frisbee M (c)/W (c), volleyball M (c)/W, water polo M/W, wrestling M (c).

Standardized Tests *Required:* SAT or ACT (for admission).

Costs (2007–08) *Comprehensive fee:* $43,319 includes full-time tuition ($31,500), mandatory fees ($399), and room and board ($11,420). *College room only:* $6040. Room and board charges vary according to board plan and housing facility. *Payment plan:* installment. *Waivers:* senior citizens and employees or children of employees.

Financial Aid Of all full-time matriculated undergraduates who enrolled in 2007, 10,083 applied for aid, 8,489 were judged to have need, 1,382 had their need fully met. In 2007, 3865 non-need-based awards were made. *Average percent of need met:* 61%. *Average financial aid package:* $17,214. *Average need-based loan:* $4996. *Average need-based gift aid:* $12,250. *Average non-need-based aid:* $12,404.

Applying *Options:* electronic application, early admission, early action, deferred entrance. *Application fee:* $75. *Required:* essay or personal statement. *Required for some:* high school transcript, interview. *Recommended:* minimum 2.0 GPA, 2 letters of recommendation. *Application deadlines:* 1/15 (freshmen), 5/1 (transfers), 11/15 (early action). *Notification:* continuous until 4/1 (freshmen), continuous (transfers), 12/31 (early action).

Freshman Application Contact Ronne Turner, Director of Admissions, Northeastern University, 150 Richards Hall, Boston, MA 02115. *Phone:* 617-373-2200. *Fax:* 617-373-8780. *E-mail:* admissions@neu.edu.

See page 1264 for the College Close-Up.

PINE MANOR COLLEGE

Chestnut Hill, Massachusetts www.pmc.edu/

- **Independent** 4-year, founded 1911
- **Suburban** 65-acre campus with easy access to Boston
- **Endowment** $11.2 million
- **Women only**
- **Moderately difficult** entrance level

Faculty *Student/faculty ratio:* 10:1.

Academics *Calendar:* semesters. *Degrees:* certificates, associate, and bachelor's.

Student Life *Campus security:* 24-hour emergency response devices and patrols, student patrols, late-night transport/escort service, controlled dormitory access.

Athletics Member NCAA. All Division III.

Standardized Tests *Required:* SAT or ACT (for admission).

Costs (2007–08) *Comprehensive fee:* $28,320 includes full-time tuition ($17,750) and room and board ($10,570).

Financial Aid Of all full-time matriculated undergraduates who enrolled in 2006, 449 applied for aid, 436 were judged to have need, 21 had their need fully met. In 2006, 33 non-need-based awards were made. *Average percent of need met:* 67. *Average financial aid package:* $15,545. *Average need-based loan:* $3556. *Average need-based gift aid:* $12,008. *Average non-need-based aid:* $8326. *Average indebtedness upon graduation:* $32,875.

Applying *Options:* electronic application, deferred entrance. *Application fee:* $25. *Required:* essay or personal statement, high school transcript, 1 letter of recommendation. *Recommended:* minimum 2.0 GPA, interview.

Freshman Application Contact Mr. Robin Engel, Dean of Admissions and Financial Aid, Pine Manor College, 400 Heath Street, Chestnut Hill, MA 02467-2332. *Phone:* 617-731-7104. *Toll-free phone:* 800-762-1357. *Fax:* 617-731-7102. *E-mail:* admisson@pmc.edu.

See page 1266 for the College Close-Up.

REGIS COLLEGE

Weston, Massachusetts www.regiscollege.edu/

- **Independent Roman Catholic** comprehensive, founded 1927
- **Small-town** 131-acre campus with easy access to Boston
- **Endowment** $12.6 million
- **Coed** 934 undergraduate students, 78% full-time, 91% women, 9% men
- **Moderately difficult** entrance level, 77% of applicants were admitted

Undergraduates 729 full-time, 205 part-time. Students come from 20 states and territories, 10 other countries, 8% are from out of state, 19% African American, 6% Asian American or Pacific Islander, 9% Hispanic American, 0.3% Native American, 1% international, 3% transferred in, 48% live on campus. *Retention:* 70% of 2006 full-time freshmen returned.

Freshmen *Admission:* 1,283 applied, 991 admitted, 263 enrolled. *Average high school GPA:* 2.77. *Test scores:* SAT critical reading scores over 500: 27%; SAT math scores over 500: 27%; SAT writing scores over 500: 32%; ACT scores over 18: 58%; SAT critical reading scores over 600: 4%; SAT math scores over 600: 4%; SAT writing scores over 600: 7%; ACT scores over 24: 19%; ACT scores over 30: 4%.

Faculty *Total:* 124, 48% full-time, 56% with terminal degrees. *Student/faculty ratio:* 14:1.

Majors Biochemistry; biology/biological sciences; business/commerce; chemistry; communication/speech communication and rhetoric; computer and information sciences; computer and information sciences and support services related; dramatic/theater arts; English; graphic design; history; information science/studies; international relations and affairs; liberal arts and sciences/liberal studies; mathematics teacher education; multi-/interdisciplinary studies related; museum studies; nursing (registered nurse training); political science and government; political science and government related; psychology; public relations/image management; radiologic technology/science; social work; sociology; Spanish.

Academics *Calendar:* semesters. *Degrees:* associate, bachelor's, master's, doctoral, and post-master's certificates. *Special study options:* academic remediation for entering students, accelerated degree program, adult/continuing education programs, advanced placement credit, double majors, honors programs, independent study, internships, off-campus study, part-time degree program, services for LD students, student-designed majors, study abroad, summer session for credit. *Unusual degree programs:* 3-2 engineering with Worcester Polytechnic Institute.

Computers on Campus 201 computers/terminals are available on campus for general student use. Students can access the following: campus intranet, computer help desk, free student e-mail accounts, online (class) grades, online (class) registration, online (class) schedules. Campuswide network is available. 100% of college-owned or -operated housing units are wired for high-speed Internet access. Wireless service is available via computer labs, dorm rooms.

Student Life *Housing options:* coed, women-only. Campus housing is university owned. Freshman campus housing is guaranteed. *Activities and organizations:* drama/theater group, student-run radio station, choral group, Tower Activities Board (TAB), student government, Glee Club, Amistades, AHANA. *Campus security:* 24-hour emergency response devices and patrols, late-night transport/escort service. *Student services:* health clinic, personal/psychological counseling.

Athletics Member NCAA. All Division III. *Intercollegiate sports:* basketball M/W, cheerleading M (c)/W (c), crew W, field hockey W, lacrosse M (c)/W, skiing (downhill) M (c)/W (c), soccer M/W, softball W, swimming and diving M/W, tennis M (c)/W, track and field M (c)/W, volleyball M (c)/W. *Intramural sports:* basketball M/W, soccer M/W, softball W, swimming and diving M/W, tennis W, track and field W, ultimate Frisbee W, volleyball M/W.

Standardized Tests *Required:* SAT or ACT (for admission).

Costs (2007–08) *One-time required fee:* $195. *Comprehensive fee:* $37,500 includes full-time tuition ($25,900) and room and board ($11,600). Full-time tuition and fees vary according to course load and student level. Part-time tuition and fees vary according to class time. *College room only:* $5900. *Payment plan:* installment. *Waivers:* employees or children of employees.

Financial Aid Of all full-time matriculated undergraduates who enrolled in 2007, 652 applied for aid, 595 were judged to have need, 66 had their need fully met. 436 Federal Work-Study jobs (averaging $2000). 40 state and other part-time jobs (averaging $1500). In 2007, 61 non-need-based awards were made. *Average percent of need met:* 60%. *Average financial aid package:* $21,871. *Average need-based loan:* $5438. *Average need-based gift aid:* $11,544. *Average non-need-based aid:* $7664. *Average indebtedness upon graduation:* $29,794.

Applying *Options:* electronic application, deferred entrance. *Application fee:* $50. *Required:* essay or personal statement, high school transcript, minimum 2.0 GPA, 2 letters of recommendation. *Required for some:* interview. *Recommended:* minimum 3.0 GPA, interview, rank in upper 50% of high school class. *Application deadlines:* rolling (freshmen), rolling (transfers).

Freshman Application Contact Ms. Emily Keily, Director of Admission, Regis College, 235 Wellesley Street, Weston, MA 02493. *Phone:* 781-768-7100. *Toll-free phone:* 866-438-7344. *Fax:* 781-768-7071. *E-mail:* admission@regiscollege.edu.

SALEM STATE COLLEGE

Salem, Massachusetts www.salemstate.edu/

- **State-supported** comprehensive, founded 1854, part of Massachusetts Public Higher Education System
- **Suburban** 62-acre campus with easy access to Boston
- **Endowment** $12.7 million
- **Coed** 7,607 undergraduate students, 81% full-time, 62% women, 38% men
- **Minimally difficult** entrance level, 60% of applicants were admitted

Undergraduates 6,127 full-time, 1,480 part-time. Students come from 43 other countries, 3% are from out of state, 8% African American, 3% Asian American or Pacific Islander, 7% Hispanic American, 0.4% Native American, 4% international, 11% transferred in, 21% live on campus. *Retention:* 73% of 2006 full-time freshmen returned.

Freshmen *Admission:* 6,890 applied, 4,118 admitted, 1,088 enrolled. *Average high school GPA:* 2.91. *Test scores:* SAT critical reading scores over 500: 43%; SAT math scores over 500: 44%; SAT critical reading scores over 600: 8%; SAT math scores over 600: 7%; SAT critical reading scores over 700: 1%.

Faculty *Total:* 737, 44% full-time. *Student/faculty ratio:* 17:1.

Majors Accounting; administrative assistant and secretarial science; applied mathematics; art; art teacher education; aviation/airway management; biology/biological sciences; business administration and management; business/managerial economics; business teacher education; cartography; chemistry; city/urban, community and regional planning; clinical laboratory science/medical technology; commercial and advertising art; comparative literature; computer science; consumer merchandising/retailing management; criminal justice/law enforcement administration; dramatic/theater arts; drawing; economics; education; elementary education; English; European studies; European studies (Central and Eastern); finance; geography; geology/earth science; health teacher education; history; journalism; kindergarten/preschool education; kinesiology and exercise science; liberal arts and sciences/liberal studies; literature; management information systems; marine biology and biological oceanography; marine science/merchant marine officer; marketing/marketing management; mass communication/media; mathematics; nuclear medical technology; nursing (registered nurse training); parks, recreation and leisure; photography; physical education teaching and coaching; political science and government; pre-dentistry studies; pre-law studies; pre-medical studies; pre-veterinary studies; psychology; public relations/image management; social sciences; social work; sociology; sport and fitness administration/management; tourism and travel services management.

Academics *Calendar:* semesters. *Degrees:* bachelor's, master's, and post-master's certificates. *Special study options:* academic remediation for entering students, adult/continuing education programs, advanced placement credit, distance learning, double majors, English as a second language, honors programs, independent study, internships, off-campus study, part-time degree program, services for LD students, study abroad, summer session for credit. *ROTC:* Army (c), Air Force (c). *Unusual degree programs:* 3-2 occupational therapy.

Computers on Campus 426 computers/terminals are available on campus for general student use. Students can access the following: campus intranet, computer help desk, free student e-mail accounts, online (class) grades, online (class) registration, online (class) schedules. Campuswide network is available. 100% of college-owned or -operated housing units are wired for high-speed Internet access. Wireless service is available via entire campus.

Student Life *Housing options:* coed. Campus housing is university owned. Freshman applicants given priority for college housing. *Activities and organizations:* drama/theater group, student-run newspaper, radio and television station, choral group, Student Government Association, Program Council, Hispanic American Student Association, GLBT Alliance, WMWM Radio. *Campus security:* 24-hour emergency response devices and patrols, late-night transport/escort service, controlled dormitory access. *Student services:* health clinic, personal/psychological counseling, women's center, legal services.

Athletics Member NCAA. All Division III. *Intercollegiate sports:* baseball M, basketball M/W, cross-country running M/W, field hockey W, golf M, ice hockey M, soccer M/W, softball W, swimming and diving M/W, tennis M/W, track and field M/W, volleyball W. *Intramural sports:* archery M/W, badminton M/W, basketball M/W, cross-country running M/W, fencing M/W, field hockey W, football M, golf M/W, gymnastics M/W, ice hockey M/W, lacrosse M/W, racquetball M/W, skiing (cross-country) M/W, skiing (downhill) M/W, soccer M/W, squash M/W, swimming and diving M/W, tennis M/W, volleyball M/W, water polo M/W, weight lifting M/W, wrestling M.

Standardized Tests *Required:* SAT or ACT (for admission).

Costs (2007–08) *Tuition:* state resident $910 full-time, $38 per credit part-time; nonresident $7050 full-time, $294 per credit part-time. Full-time tuition and fees vary according to class time. Part-time tuition and fees vary according to class time. *Required fees:* $5300 full-time, $220 per credit part-time. *Room only:* $5545. Room and board charges vary according to board plan and housing facility. *Payment plan:* installment. *Waivers:* senior citizens and employees or children of employees.

Financial Aid Of all full-time matriculated undergraduates who enrolled in 2004, 2,950 applied for aid, 2,350 were judged to have need, 87 had their need fully met. 726 Federal Work-Study jobs (averaging $2000). *Average percent of need met:* 66%. *Average financial aid package:* $6512. *Average need-based loan:* $8855. *Average need-based gift aid:* $8568.

Applying *Options:* electronic application, early admission. *Application fee:* $25. *Required:* high school transcript, minimum 2.0 GPA. *Required for some:* interview. *Application deadlines:* rolling (freshmen), rolling (transfers). *Notification:* continuous (freshmen), continuous (transfers).

Freshman Application Contact Mr. Nate Bryant, Dean of Student Development, Salem State College, 352 Lafayette Street, Salem, MA 01970. *Phone:* 978-542-6200. *Fax:* 978-542-6893. *E-mail:* admissions@salemstate.edu.

School of the Museum of Fine Arts, Boston

Boston, Massachusetts **www.smfa.edu/**

- **Independent** comprehensive, founded 1876, administratively affiliated with Tufts University; Museum of Fine Arts, Boston
- **Urban** 14-acre campus
- **Endowment** $24.6 million
- **Coed** 710 undergraduate students, 88% full-time, 69% women, 31% men
- **Moderately difficult** entrance level, 82% of applicants were admitted

Undergraduates 625 full-time, 85 part-time. Students come from 34 states and territories, 33 other countries, 50% are from out of state, 2% African American, 4% Asian American or Pacific Islander, 5% Hispanic American, 0.6% Native American, 7% international, 12% transferred in, 9% live on campus. *Retention:* 83% of 2006 full-time freshmen returned.

Freshmen *Admission:* 858 applied, 701 admitted, 135 enrolled. *Test scores:* SAT critical reading scores over 500: 85%; SAT math scores over 500: 68%; SAT writing scores over 500: 75%; ACT scores over 18: 96%; SAT critical reading scores over 600: 37%; SAT math scores over 600: 21%; SAT writing scores over 600: 30%; ACT scores over 24: 54%; SAT critical reading scores over 700: 6%; SAT math scores over 700: 3%; SAT writing scores over 700: 6%; ACT scores over 30: 8%.

Faculty *Total:* 83, 59% full-time, 72% with terminal degrees. *Student/faculty ratio:* 10:1.

Majors Applied art; art; art teacher education; ceramic arts and ceramics; cinematography and film/video production; computer graphics; drawing; film/cinema studies; film/video and photographic arts related; fine arts related; fine/studio arts; graphic design; illustration; intermedia/multimedia; metal and jewelry arts; painting; photography; printmaking; sculpture; visual and performing arts related.

Academics *Calendar:* semesters. *Degrees:* certificates, diplomas, bachelor's, master's, and postbachelor's certificates. *Special study options:* adult/continuing education programs, double majors, English as a second language, independent study, internships, off-campus study, part-time degree program, services for LD students, student-designed majors, study abroad, summer session for credit. *Unusual degree programs:* 3-2 fine arts, art education with Tufts University.

Computers on Campus 86 computers/terminals are available on campus for general student use. Students can access the following: free student e-mail accounts, online (class) grades, online (class) registration, online (class) schedules. Campuswide network is available. 100% of college-owned or -operated housing units are wired for high-speed Internet access. Wireless service is available via classrooms, student centers.

Student Life *Housing options:* coed. Campus housing is university owned. Freshman applicants given priority for college housing. *Activities and organizations:* Gay/Lesbian/Bisexual Alliance, Student Body, Inc., film, video and animation screening nights, Dodgeball, Animation Club. *Campus security:* 24-hour emergency response devices and patrols, late night taxis service between buildings. *Student services:* personal/psychological counseling.

Standardized Tests *Required for some:* SAT or ACT (for admission).

Costs (2007–08) *One-time required fee:* $125. *Tuition:* $26,950 full-time, $1130 per credit hour part-time. Full-time tuition and fees vary according to course load, degree level, and program. Part-time tuition and fees vary according to class time, course load, and program. *Required fees:* $1020 full-time, $450 per semester part-time. *Room only:* $11,600. *Payment plan:* installment. *Waivers:* employees or children of employees.

Financial Aid Of all full-time matriculated undergraduates who enrolled in 2005, 431 applied for aid, 404 were judged to have need. 139 Federal Work-Study jobs (averaging $2173). In 2005, 6 non-need-based awards were made. *Average percent of need met:* 35%. *Average financial aid package:* $15,501. *Average need-based loan:* $4019. *Average need-based gift aid:* $9006. *Average non-need-based aid:* $4290. *Average indebtedness upon graduation:* $23,898.

Applying *Options:* deferred entrance. *Application fee:* $65. *Required:* essay or personal statement, high school transcript, portfolio. *Required for some:* letters of recommendation, interview. *Application deadlines:* 2/1 (freshmen), 3/1 (transfers). *Notification:* continuous (freshmen), continuous (transfers).

Freshman Application Contact Jesse Tarantino, Assistant Dean of Admissions, School of the Museum of Fine Arts, Boston, 230 The Fenway, Boston, MA 02115. *Phone:* 617-369-3626. *Toll-free phone:* 800-643-6078. *Fax:* 617-369-4264. *E-mail:* admissions@smfa.edu.

See page 1268 for the College Close-Up.

Simmons College

Boston, Massachusetts **www.simmons.edu/**

- **Independent** university, founded 1899
- **Urban** 12-acre campus
- **Endowment** $193.6 million
- **Undergraduate: women only; graduate: coed** 2,072 undergraduate students, 90% full-time, 100% women, 0% men
- **Moderately difficult** entrance level, 57% of applicants were admitted

Undergraduates 1,871 full-time, 201 part-time. Students come from 39 states and territories, 25 other countries, 40% are from out of state, 5% African American, 8% Asian American or Pacific Islander, 4% Hispanic American, 0.3%

Native American, 2% international, 4% transferred in, 56% live on campus. *Retention:* 83% of 2006 full-time freshmen returned.

Freshmen *Admission:* 2,937 applied, 1,686 admitted, 479 enrolled. *Average high school GPA:* 3.17. *Test scores:* SAT critical reading scores over 500: 77%; SAT math scores over 500: 72%; SAT writing scores over 500: 81%; ACT scores over 18: 97%; SAT critical reading scores over 600: 27%; SAT math scores over 600: 18%; SAT writing scores over 600: 33%; ACT scores over 24: 52%; SAT critical reading scores over 700: 4%; SAT math scores over 700: 1%; SAT writing scores over 700: 4%; ACT scores over 30: 6%.

Faculty *Total:* 587, 42% full-time. *Student/faculty ratio:* 13:1.

Majors Accounting; advertising; African-American/Black studies; art; arts management; Asian studies (East); biochemistry; biology/biological sciences; business administration and management; chemistry; commercial and advertising art; comparative literature; computer science; consumer merchandising/retailing management; dietetics; economics; education; elementary education; English; English as a second/foreign language (teaching); environmental studies; finance; foods, nutrition, and wellness; French; history; human services; information technology; international relations and affairs; kindergarten/preschool education; management information systems; marketing/marketing management; mass communication/media; mathematics; music; music history, literature, and theory; nursing (registered nurse training); pharmacy; philosophy; physical therapy; physiological psychology/psychobiology; political science and government; pre-dentistry studies; pre-law studies; pre-medical studies; psychology; public policy analysis; public relations/image management; secondary education; sociology; Spanish; special education; women's studies.

Academics *Calendar:* semesters. *Degrees:* bachelor's, master's, doctoral, post-master's, and postbachelor's certificates. *Special study options:* academic remediation for entering students, accelerated degree program, adult/continuing education programs, advanced placement credit, cooperative education, double majors, English as a second language, freshman honors college, honors programs, independent study, internships, off-campus study, part-time degree program, services for LD students, student-designed majors, study abroad, summer session for credit. *ROTC:* Army (c). *Unusual degree programs:* 3-2 nursing; physician assistant, pharmacy with Massachusetts College of Pharmacy and Allied Health Sciences, nutrition with Boston University.

Computers on Campus 455 computers/terminals and 1,000 ports are available on campus for general student use. Students can access the following: campus intranet, computer help desk, free student e-mail accounts, online (class) grades, online (class) registration, online (class) schedules. Campuswide network is available. 100% of college-owned or -operated housing units are wired for high-speed Internet access. Wireless service is available via classrooms, computer labs, learning centers, libraries, student centers.

Student Life *Housing options:* coed, women-only, disabled students. Campus housing is university owned and leased by the school. Freshman applicants given priority for college housing. *Activities and organizations:* drama/theater group, student-run newspaper, choral group, Student Government Association, Black Students Organization, Campus Activities Board, Asian Students Association, Simmons Voice. *Campus security:* 24-hour emergency response devices and patrols, late-night transport/escort service, controlled dormitory access. *Student services:* health clinic, personal/psychological counseling, women's center.

Athletics Member NCAA. All Division III. *Intercollegiate sports:* basketball W, crew W, field hockey W, sailing W, soccer W, softball W, swimming and diving W, tennis W, track and field W, volleyball W. *Intramural sports:* basketball W, field hockey W, golf W, lacrosse W, racquetball W, skiing (cross-country) W, skiing (downhill) W, soccer W, softball W, volleyball W.

Standardized Tests *Required:* SAT or ACT (for admission).

Costs (2007–08) *Comprehensive fee:* $39,440 includes full-time tuition ($27,468), mandatory fees ($834), and room and board ($11,138). Full-time tuition and fees vary according to course load. Part-time tuition: $857 per credit. Part-time tuition and fees vary according to course load. *Room and board:* Room and board charges vary according to board plan. *Payment plan:* installment. *Waivers:* employees or children of employees.

Financial Aid Of all full-time matriculated undergraduates who enrolled in 2006, 1,410 applied for aid, 1,274 were judged to have need, 37 had their need fully met. 451 Federal Work-Study jobs (averaging $2500). In 2006, 39 non-need-based awards were made. *Average percent of need met:* 48%. *Average financial aid package:* $14,473. *Average need-based loan:* $2838. *Average need-based gift aid:* $10,063. *Average non-need-based aid:* $11,235. *Average indebtedness upon graduation:* $26,300.

Applying *Options:* electronic application, early admission, early action, deferred entrance. *Application fee:* $35. *Required:* essay or personal statement, high school transcript, 2 letters of recommendation. *Recommended:* minimum 3.0 GPA, interview. *Application deadlines:* 2/1 (freshmen), 4/1 (transfers), 12/1 (early action). *Notification:* 4/15 (freshmen), continuous (transfers), 1/20 (early action).

Freshman Application Contact Ms. Catherine Childs-Capolupo, Director of Undergraduate Admissions, Simmons College, 300 The Fenway, Boston, MA 02115. *Phone:* 617-521-2057. *Toll-free phone:* 800-345-8468. *Fax:* 617-521-3190. *E-mail:* ugadm@simmons.edu.

See page 1270 for the College Close-Up.

SMITH COLLEGE

Northampton, Massachusetts www.smith.edu/

- **Independent** comprehensive, founded 1871
- **Small-town** 125-acre campus with easy access to Hartford
- **Endowment** $1.4 billion
- **Undergraduate: women only; graduate: coed** 2,596 undergraduate students, 99% full-time, 100% women
- **Very difficult** entrance level, 52% of applicants were admitted

Undergraduates 2,569 full-time, 27 part-time. Students come from 50 states and territories, 72 other countries, 77% are from out of state, 7% African American, 12% Asian American or Pacific Islander, 6% Hispanic American, 0.7% Native American, 7% international, 3% transferred in, 92% live on campus. *Retention:* 90% of 2006 full-time freshmen returned.

Freshmen *Admission:* 3,329 applied, 1,726 admitted, 656 enrolled. *Average high school GPA:* 3.85. *Test scores:* SAT critical reading scores over 500: 95%; SAT math scores over 500: 93%; SAT writing scores over 500: 96%; ACT scores over 18: 100%; SAT critical reading scores over 600: 75%; SAT math scores over 600: 59%; SAT writing scores over 600: 74%; ACT scores over 24: 86%; SAT critical reading scores over 700: 32%; SAT math scores over 700: 17%; SAT writing scores over 700: 27%; ACT scores over 30: 29%.

Faculty *Total:* 309, 91% full-time, 98% with terminal degrees. *Student/faculty ratio:* 9:1.

Majors African-American/Black studies; American studies; ancient/classical Greek; anthropology; architecture; art; art history, criticism and conservation; Asian studies (East); astronomy; biochemistry; biology/biological sciences; chemistry; classics and languages, literatures and linguistics; comparative literature; computer science; dance; dramatic/theater arts; East Asian languages; economics; education; engineering science; English; fine/studio arts; French; French studies; geology/earth science; German; German studies; history; interdisciplinary studies; Italian; Latin; Latin American studies; mathematics; medieval and Renaissance studies; music; Near and Middle Eastern studies; neuroscience; philosophy; physics; political science and government; Portuguese; pre-law studies; pre-medical studies; psychology; religious studies; Russian; Russian studies; sociology; Spanish; women's studies.

Academics *Calendar:* semesters. *Degrees:* bachelor's, master's, doctoral, post-master's, and postbachelor's certificates. *Special study options:* accelerated degree program, adult/continuing education programs, advanced placement credit, double majors, honors programs, independent study, internships, off-campus study, part-time degree program, services for LD students, student-designed majors, study abroad. *ROTC:* Army (c), Air Force (c).

Computers on Campus 585 computers/terminals are available on campus for general student use. Students can access the following: computer help desk, free student e-mail accounts, online (class) registration. Campuswide network is available. 100% of college-owned or -operated housing units are wired for high-speed Internet access. Wireless service is available via classrooms, computer centers, computer labs, dorm rooms, learning centers, libraries, student centers.

Student Life *Housing:* on-campus residence required through senior year. *Options:* women-only, cooperative. Campus housing is university owned. Freshman campus housing is guaranteed. *Activities and organizations:* drama/theater group, student-run newspaper, radio and television station, choral group, Recreation Council, Service Organizations of Smith, Glee Club and choirs, Athletic Association, Black Student Alliance. *Campus security:* 24-hour emergency response devices and patrols, late-night transport/escort service, self-defense workshops, emergency telephones, programs in crime and sexual assault prevention. *Student services:* health clinic, personal/psychological counseling, women's center.

Athletics Member NCAA. All Division III. *Intercollegiate sports:* basketball W, crew W, cross-country running W, equestrian sports W, field hockey W, lacrosse W, skiing (downhill) W, soccer W, softball W, squash W, swimming and diving W, tennis W, track and field W, volleyball W. *Intramural sports:* badminton W (c), crew W, equestrian sports W (c), fencing W (c), golf W (c), ice hockey W (c), rugby W (c), soccer W, squash W, ultimate Frisbee W (c).

Standardized Tests *Required:* SAT or ACT (for admission).

Costs (2007–08) *Comprehensive fee:* $45,606 includes full-time tuition ($33,940), mandatory fees ($246), and room and board ($11,420). Part-time tuition: $1060 per credit hour. *College room only:* $5730. *Payment plan:* installment. *Waivers:* employees or children of employees.

Financial Aid Of all full-time matriculated undergraduates who enrolled in 2006, 2,011 applied for aid, 1,609 were judged to have need, 1,609 had their need fully met. 219 state and other part-time jobs (averaging $1961). In 2006, 187 non-need-based awards were made. *Average percent of need met:* 100%. *Average financial aid package:* $32,659. *Average need-based loan:* $4977. *Average need-based gift aid:* $26,372. *Average non-need-based aid:* $4304. *Average indebtedness upon graduation:* $19,760. *Financial aid deadline:* 2/1.

Applying *Options:* electronic application, early admission, early decision, deferred entrance. *Application fee:* $60. *Required:* essay or personal statement, high school transcript, 3 letters of recommendation. *Recommended:* interview. *Application deadlines:* 1/15 (freshmen), 5/15 (transfers). *Early decision deadline:* 11/15 (for plan 1), 1/2 (for plan 2). *Notification:* 4/1 (freshmen), 6/1 (transfers), 12/15 (early decision plan 1), 2/2 (early decision plan 2).

Freshman Application Contact Ms. Debra Shaver, Director of Admissions, Smith College, 7 College Lane, Northampton, MA 01063. *Phone:* 413-585-2500. *Toll-free phone:* 800-383-3232. *Fax:* 413-585-2527. *E-mail:* admission@smith.edu.

See page 1272 for the College Close-Up.

SPRINGFIELD COLLEGE

Springfield, Massachusetts **www.spfldcol.edu/**

Founded in 1885, Springfield College emphasizes the education of leaders in the allied health sciences, human and social services, sports and movement activities, and arts and sciences. Through its distinctive humanics philosophy—the education of the whole person, consisting of spirit, mind, and body—Springfield College prepares students for leadership in service to others.

Freshman Application Contact Ms. Mary DeAngelo, Director of Undergraduate Admissions, Springfield College, 263 Alden Street, Box M, Springfield, MA 01109. *Phone:* 413-748-3136. *Toll-free phone:* 800-343-1257. *Fax:* 413-748-3694. *E-mail:* admissions@spfldcol.edu.

See page 1274 for the College Close-Up.

STONEHILL COLLEGE

Easton, Massachusetts **www.stonehill.edu/**

- **Independent Roman Catholic** comprehensive, founded 1948
- **Suburban** 375-acre campus with easy access to Boston
- **Endowment** $162.2 million
- **Coed** 2,440 undergraduate students, 96% full-time, 61% women, 39% men
- **Very difficult** entrance level, 52% of applicants were admitted

Located 22 miles south of Boston, Stonehill combines a community atmosphere and a beautiful 375-acre campus with easy access to America's premier college town. Exciting special programs, such as full-time international internships, study abroad, domestic internships, and the Stonehill Undergraduate Research Experience (SURE), complement the College's rigorous education in the liberal arts, sciences, and business. Nearly 70 percent of graduating students take advantage of these enriching programs.

Undergraduates 2,353 full-time, 87 part-time. Students come from 30 states and territories, 8 other countries, 43% are from out of state, 2% African American, 2% Asian American or Pacific Islander, 4% Hispanic American, 0.2% Native American, 0.4% international, 0.8% transferred in, 87% live on campus. *Retention:* 87% of 2006 full-time freshmen returned.

Freshmen *Admission:* 5,704 applied, 2,960 admitted, 659 enrolled. *Average high school GPA:* 3.57. *Test scores:* SAT critical reading scores over 500: 91%; SAT math scores over 500: 92%; ACT scores over 18: 99%; SAT critical reading scores over 600: 43%; SAT math scores over 600: 47%; ACT scores over 24: 79%; SAT critical reading scores over 700: 8%; SAT math scores over 700: 6%; ACT scores over 30: 9%.

Faculty *Total:* 258, 56% full-time, 61% with terminal degrees. *Student/faculty ratio:* 13:1.

Majors Accounting; American studies; biochemistry; biology/biological sciences; business administration and management; chemistry; communication/speech communication and rhetoric; computer engineering; computer science; criminology; early childhood education; economics; elementary education; English; environmental studies; ethnic, cultural minority, and gender studies related; finance; fine/studio arts; foreign languages and literatures; health/health care administration; history; international relations and affairs; marketing/marketing management; mathematics; multi-/interdisciplinary studies related; neuroscience; philosophy; political science and government; psychology; public administration; religious studies; sociology.

Academics *Calendar:* semesters. *Degree:* bachelor's. *Special study options:* adult/continuing education programs, advanced placement credit, double majors, honors programs, independent study, internships, off-campus study, part-time degree program, services for LD students, student-designed majors, study abroad, summer session for credit. *ROTC:* Army (b). *Unusual degree programs:* 3-2 computer engineering with University of Notre Dame.

Computers on Campus 300 computers/terminals and 2,500 ports are available on campus for general student use. Students can access the following: campus intranet, computer help desk, free student e-mail accounts, online (class) grades, online (class) registration, online (class) schedules. Campuswide network is available. 100% of college-owned or -operated housing units are wired for high-speed Internet access. Wireless service is available via classrooms, computer centers, computer labs, learning centers, libraries, student centers.

Student Life *Housing options:* coed, women-only, disabled students. Campus housing is university owned and leased by the school. Freshman applicants given priority for college housing. *Activities and organizations:* drama/theater group, student-run newspaper, radio station, choral group, Into the Streets, Student radio station, Student government, Summit (student newspaper), Sports clubs. *Campus security:* 24-hour emergency response devices and patrols, late-night transport/escort service. *Student services:* health clinic, personal/psychological counseling, women's center.

Athletics Member NCAA. All Division II. *Intercollegiate sports:* baseball M (s), basketball M (s)/W (s), cheerleading M (c)/W (c), cross-country running M (s)/W (s), equestrian sports W, field hockey W (s), golf M (c)/W (c), ice hockey W, lacrosse M (c)/W (s), rock climbing M (c)/W (c), soccer M (s)/W (s), softball W (s), tennis M (s)/W (s), track and field M (s)/W (s), ultimate Frisbee M (c)/W (c), volleyball M (c)/W (s). *Intramural sports:* basketball M/W, field hockey M/W, racquetball M/W, soccer M/W, softball M/W, tennis M/W, volleyball M/W.

Standardized Tests *Recommended:* SAT or ACT (for admission).

Costs (2008–09) *Comprehensive fee:* $41,980 includes full-time tuition ($30,150) and room and board ($11,830). Part-time tuition: $1005 per course. *Required fees:* $25 per term part-time.

Financial Aid Of all full-time matriculated undergraduates who enrolled in 2007, 1,837 applied for aid, 1,517 were judged to have need, 260 had their need fully met. 883 Federal Work-Study jobs (averaging $2272). 300 state and other part-time jobs (averaging $1641). In 2007, 567 non-need-based awards were made. *Average percent of need met:* 75%. *Average financial aid package:* $18,434. *Average need-based loan:* $4638. *Average need-based gift aid:* $14,327. *Average non-need-based aid:* $14,082. *Average indebtedness upon graduation:* $24,120.

Applying *Options:* electronic application, early admission, early decision, early action, deferred entrance. *Application fee:* $60. *Required:* essay or personal statement, high school transcript, 2 letters of recommendation. *Required for some:* interview. *Recommended:* campus visit. *Application deadlines:* 1/15 (freshmen), 4/1 (transfers). *Early decision deadline:* 11/1. *Notification:* 4/1 (freshmen), continuous (transfers), 12/15 (early decision).

Freshman Application Contact Mr. Brian P. Murphy, Dean of Admissions and Enrollment, Stonehill College, 320 Washington Street, Easton, MA 02357-5610. *Phone:* 508-565-1373. *Fax:* 508-565-1545. *E-mail:* admissions@stonehill.edu.

See page 1276 for the College Close-Up.

SUFFOLK UNIVERSITY

Boston, Massachusetts **www.suffolk.edu/**

- **Independent** comprehensive, founded 1906
- **Urban** 2-acre campus
- **Endowment** $104.4 million
- **Coed** 5,488 undergraduate students, 88% full-time, 57% women, 43% men
- **Moderately difficult** entrance level, 80% of applicants were admitted

Undergraduates 4,816 full-time, 672 part-time. Students come from 41 states and territories, 94 other countries, 27% are from out of state, 3% African American, 6% Asian American or Pacific Islander, 5% Hispanic American, 0.3% Native American, 9% international, 7% transferred in, 17% live on campus. *Retention:* 72% of 2006 full-time freshmen returned.

Freshmen *Admission:* 8,044 applied, 6,403 admitted, 1,327 enrolled. *Average high school GPA:* 3.03. *Test scores:* SAT critical reading scores over 500: 53%; SAT math scores over 500: 54%; SAT writing scores over 500: 56%; ACT scores over 18: 94%; SAT critical reading scores over 600: 13%; SAT math scores over 600: 14%; SAT writing scores over 600: 15%; ACT scores over 24: 36%; SAT critical reading scores over 700: 1%; SAT math scores over 700: 1%; SAT writing scores over 700: 2%; ACT scores over 30: 3%.

Faculty *Total:* 911, 46% full-time, 58% with terminal degrees. *Student/faculty ratio:* 12:1.

Majors Accounting; African-American/Black studies; art; biochemistry; biology/biological sciences; biology/biotechnology laboratory technician; biomedical sciences; biomedical technology; biophysics; broadcast journalism; business administration and management; business teacher education; chemistry; clinical laboratory science/medical technology; commercial and advertising art; computer and information sciences; computer science; criminal justice/law enforcement administration; developmental and child psychology; dramatic/theater arts; economics; education; electrical, electronics and communications engineering; elementary education; English; environmental biology; environmental studies; finance; French; history; humanities; human services; information science/studies; interdisciplinary studies; interior design; international economics; journalism; legal assistant/paralegal; legal studies; liberal arts and sciences/liberal studies; management information systems; marine biology and biological oceanography; marketing/marketing management; mass communication/media; mathematics; modern languages; philosophy; physics; political science and government; pre-law studies; psychology; public administration; public policy analysis; public relations/image management; radiologic technology/science; secondary education; social sciences; social work; sociology; Spanish; women's studies.

Academics *Calendar:* semesters. *Degrees:* certificates, diplomas, associate, bachelor's, master's, doctoral, first professional, post-master's, postbachelor's, and first professional certificates (doctoral degree in law). *Special study options:* academic remediation for entering students, accelerated degree program, adult/continuing education programs, advanced placement credit, cooperative education, distance learning, double majors, English as a second language, freshman honors college, honors programs, independent study, internships, off-campus study, part-time degree program, services for LD students, study abroad, summer session for credit. *ROTC:* Army (c).

Computers on Campus 711 computers/terminals are available on campus for general student use. Students can access the following: campus intranet, computer help desk, free student e-mail accounts, online (class) grades, online (class) registration, online (class) schedules. Campuswide network is available. 100% of college-owned or -operated housing units are wired for high-speed Internet access. Wireless service is available via entire campus.

Student Life *Housing options:* coed. Campus housing is university owned. Freshman applicants given priority for college housing. *Activities and organizations:* drama/theater group, student-run newspaper, radio and television station, choral group, Student Government Association, Program Committee, Suffolk Free Radio, Black Student Union', Suffolk University Business Career Organization, national fraternities. *Campus security:* 24-hour emergency response devices, late-night transport/escort service, controlled dormitory access. *Student services:* health clinic, personal/psychological counseling, women's center.

Athletics Member NCAA. All Division III. *Intercollegiate sports:* baseball M, basketball M/W, cross-country running M/W, golf M, ice hockey M, soccer M, softball W, tennis M/W, volleyball W. *Intramural sports:* basketball M/W, soccer M/W, softball M/W, volleyball M/W.

Standardized Tests *Required:* SAT or ACT (for admission).

Costs (2007–08) *Comprehensive fee:* $37,550 includes full-time tuition ($24,170), mandatory fees ($80), and room and board ($13,300). Part-time tuition: $593 per credit. *Required fees:* $10 per term part-time. *College room only:* $11,120. Room and board charges vary according to board plan and housing facility. *Payment plans:* installment, deferred payment. *Waivers:* senior citizens and employees or children of employees.

Financial Aid Of all full-time matriculated undergraduates who enrolled in 2007, 3,197 applied for aid, 2,608 were judged to have need, 312 had their need fully met. 1,360 Federal Work-Study jobs (averaging $2112). 409 state and other part-time jobs (averaging $2434). In 2007, 427 non-need-based awards were made. *Average percent of need met:* 62%. *Average financial aid package:* $14,774. *Average need-based loan:* $4832. *Average need-based gift aid:* $8089. *Average non-need-based aid:* $7526. *Financial aid deadline:* 3/1.

Applying *Options:* electronic application, early action, deferred entrance. *Application fee:* $50. *Required:* essay or personal statement, high school transcript, 2 letters of recommendation. *Required for some:* interview. *Recommended:* minimum 2.5 GPA. *Application deadlines:* 3/1 (freshmen), 3/15 (transfers), 11/15 (early action). *Notification:* continuous until 2/5 (freshmen), continuous (transfers), 12/1 (early action).

Freshman Application Contact Undergraduate Admissions, Suffolk University, 8 Ashburton Place, Boston, MA 02108. *Phone:* 617-573-8460. *Toll-free phone:* 800-6-SUFFOLK. *Fax:* 617-742-4291. *E-mail:* admission@suffolk.edu.

TUFTS UNIVERSITY

Medford, Massachusetts

www.tufts.edu/

- **Independent** university, founded 1852
- **Suburban** 150-acre campus with easy access to Boston
- **Endowment** $1.5 billion
- **Coed** 5,035 undergraduate students, 99% full-time, 51% women, 49% men
- **Most difficult** entrance level, 28% of applicants were admitted

Undergraduates 4,977 full-time, 58 part-time. Students come from 52 states and territories, 93 other countries, 75% are from out of state, 6% African American, 12% Asian American or Pacific Islander, 6% Hispanic American, 0.2% Native American, 6% international, 0.5% transferred in, 75% live on campus. *Retention:* 96% of 2006 full-time freshmen returned.

Freshmen *Admission:* 15,365 applied, 4,229 admitted, 1,370 enrolled. *Test scores:* SAT critical reading scores over 500: 100%; SAT math scores over 500: 100%; SAT writing scores over 500: 49%; ACT scores over 18: 100%; SAT critical reading scores over 600: 95%; SAT math scores over 600: 95%; SAT writing scores over 600: 43%; ACT scores over 24: 99%; SAT critical reading scores over 700: 60%; SAT math scores over 700: 57%; SAT writing scores over 700: 6%; ACT scores over 30: 76%.

Faculty *Total:* 1,047, 63% full-time, 83% with terminal degrees. *Student/faculty ratio:* 7:1.

Majors African-American/Black studies; American studies; anthropology; archeology; architectural engineering; art history, criticism and conservation; Asian studies; Asian studies (Southeast); astronomy; behavioral sciences; biology/biological sciences; chemical engineering; chemistry; child development; Chinese; civil engineering; classics and languages, literatures and linguistics; community health and preventive medicine; computer engineering; computer science; developmental and child psychology; dramatic/theater arts; ecology; economics; electrical, electronics and communications engineering; elementary education; engineering; engineering physics; engineering related; engineering science; English; environmental/environmental health engineering; environmental studies; experimental psychology; French; geological/geophysical engineering; geology/earth science; German; history; industrial engineering; international relations and affairs; Jewish/Judaic studies; kindergarten/preschool education; Latin; mathematics; mechanical engineering; mental health/rehabilitation; modern Greek; music; philosophy; physics; political science and government; psychology; public health; Romance languages; Russian; Russian studies; secondary education; sociobiology; sociology; Spanish; special education; urban studies/affairs; women's studies.

Academics *Calendar:* semesters. *Degrees:* bachelor's, master's, doctoral, first professional, and post-master's certificates. *Special study options:* adult/continuing education programs, advanced placement credit, double majors, honors programs, independent study, internships, off-campus study, services for LD students, student-designed majors, study abroad, summer session for credit. *ROTC:* Army (c), Navy (c), Air Force (c). *Unusual degree programs:* 3-2 with New England Conservatory of Music and the School of the Museum of Fine Arts.

Computers on Campus 300 computers/terminals are available on campus for general student use. Students can access the following: computer help desk, free student e-mail accounts, online (class) registration, online (class) schedules. Campuswide network is available. 100% of college-owned or -operated housing units are wired for high-speed Internet access. Wireless service is available via classrooms, computer centers, computer labs, learning centers, libraries, student centers.

Student Life *Housing:* on-campus residence required through sophomore year. *Options:* coed, women-only, cooperative. Campus housing is university owned. Freshman campus housing is guaranteed. *Activities and organizations:* drama/theater group, student-run newspaper, radio and television station, choral group, marching band, Leonard Carmichael Society, Mountain Club, Intramural Sports, Tufts Daily (newspaper), Admissions Student Outreach, national fraternities, national sororities. *Campus security:* 24-hour emergency response devices and patrols, late-night transport/escort service, controlled dormitory access, security lighting, call boxes to campus police. *Student services:* health clinic, legal services.

Athletics Member NCAA. All Division III. *Intercollegiate sports:* baseball M, basketball M/W, crew M/W, cross-country running M/W, fencing W, field hockey W, football M, golf M, ice hockey M, lacrosse M/W, sailing M/W, soccer M/W, softball W, squash M/W, swimming and diving M/W, tennis M/W, track and field M/W, volleyball W. *Intramural sports:* basketball M/W, cheerleading M/W, cross-country running M/W, equestrian sports M/W, fencing M, football M, racquetball M/W, rugby M/W, skiing (downhill) M/W, soccer M/W, softball M/W, squash M/W, tennis M/W, track and field M/W, ultimate Frisbee M/W, volleyball M, water polo M.

Standardized Tests *Required:* SAT and SAT Subject Tests or ACT (for admission).

Costs (2007–08) *Comprehensive fee:* $46,860 includes full-time tuition ($35,842), mandatory fees ($858), and room and board ($10,160). *College room only:* $5220. Room and board charges vary according to board plan. *Payment plans:* tuition prepayment, installment. *Waivers:* employees or children of employees.

Financial Aid Of all full-time matriculated undergraduates who enrolled in 2007, 2,307 applied for aid, 1,991 were judged to have need, 1,963 had their need fully met. 1,833 Federal Work-Study jobs (averaging $1825). 49 state and other part-time jobs (averaging $1884). In 2007, 48 non-need-based awards were made. *Average percent of need met:* 100%. *Average financial aid package:* $27,828. *Average need-based loan:* $3732. *Average need-based gift aid:* $24,937. *Average non-need-based aid:* $500. *Average indebtedness upon graduation:* $20,668. *Financial aid deadline:* 2/15.

Applying *Options:* electronic application, early admission, early decision, deferred entrance. *Application fee:* $70. *Required:* essay or personal statement, high school transcript, 1 letter of recommendation. *Recommended:* interview. *Application deadlines:* 1/1 (freshmen), 3/1 (transfers). *Early decision deadline:* 11/1 (for plan 1), 1/1 (for plan 2). *Notification:* 4/1 (freshmen), 5/1 (transfers), 12/15 (early decision plan 1), 2/1 (early decision plan 2).

Freshman Application Contact Mr. Lee Coffin, Office of Undergraduate Admissions, Tufts University, Bendetson Hall, Medford, MA 02155. *Phone:* 617-627-3170. *Fax:* 617-627-3860. *E-mail:* admissions.inquiry@ase.tufts.edu.

See page 1278 for the College Close-Up.

UNIVERSITY OF MASSACHUSETTS AMHERST

Amherst, Massachusetts — www.umass.edu/

- **State-supported** university, founded 1863, part of University of Massachusetts
- **Small-town** 1463-acre campus with easy access to Hartford
- **Endowment** $91.2 million
- **Coed** 20,114 undergraduate students, 93% full-time, 50% women, 50% men
- **Moderately difficult** entrance level, 66% of applicants were admitted

Undergraduates 18,646 full-time, 1,468 part-time. 19% are from out of state, 5% African American, 8% Asian American or Pacific Islander, 4% Hispanic American, 0.3% Native American, 0.9% international, 6% transferred in, 60% live on campus. *Retention:* 84% of 2006 full-time freshmen returned.

Freshmen *Admission:* 27,138 applied, 17,815 admitted, 4,395 enrolled. *Average high school GPA:* 3.48. *Test scores:* SAT critical reading scores over 500: 81%; SAT math scores over 500: 86%; SAT critical reading scores over 600: 33%; SAT math scores over 600: 41%; SAT critical reading scores over 700: 6%; SAT math scores over 700: 7%.

Faculty *Total:* 1,361, 86% full-time, 87% with terminal degrees. *Student/faculty ratio:* 17:1.

Majors Accounting; African-American/Black studies; animal sciences; anthropology; applied horticulture/horticultural business services related; art history, criticism and conservation; astronomy; biochemistry/biophysics and molecular biology; biological and physical sciences; biology/biological sciences; business administration and management; chemical engineering; chemistry; Chinese; civil engineering; classics and languages, literatures and linguistics; communication disorders; communication/speech communication and rhetoric; comparative literature; computer engineering; computer science; crop production; dance; dramatic/theater arts; economics; electrical, electronics and communications engineering; engineering; English; environmental design/architecture; environmental science; equestrian studies; finance; fine/studio arts; food science; forestry; French; general studies; geography; geology/earth science; German; history; hospitality administration; humanities; human nutrition; industrial engineering; interior design; Italian; Japanese; Jewish/Judaic studies; journalism; kinesiology and exercise science; landscape architecture; landscaping and groundskeeping; legal studies; liberal arts and sciences and humanities related; linguistics; marketing/marketing management; mathematics; mechanical engineering; microbiology; multi-/interdisciplinary studies related; music; music performance; natural resources management and policy; Near and Middle Eastern studies; nursing (registered nurse training); ornamental horticulture; philosophy; physics; plant sciences; political science and government; Portuguese; pre-dentistry studies; pre-medical studies; pre-veterinary studies; psychology; Russian studies; social sciences related; sociology; Spanish; sport and fitness administration/management; turf and turfgrass management; wildlife and wildlands science and management; women's studies; wood science and wood products/pulp and paper technology.

Academics *Calendar:* semesters. *Degrees:* associate, bachelor's, master's, doctoral, and post-master's certificates. *Special study options:* academic remediation for entering students, adult/continuing education programs, advanced placement credit, cooperative education, distance learning, double majors, English as a second language, freshman honors college, honors programs, independent study, internships, off-campus study, part-time degree program, services for LD students, student-designed majors, study abroad, summer session for credit. *ROTC:* Army (b), Air Force (b).

Computers on Campus 450 computers/terminals are available on campus for general student use. Students can access the following: online (class) grades, online (class) registration. Campuswide network is available.

Student Life *Housing:* on-campus residence required through sophomore year. *Options:* coed, men-only, women-only, disabled students. Campus housing is university owned. Freshman campus housing is guaranteed. *Activities and organizations:* drama/theater group, student-run newspaper, radio and television station, choral group, marching band, Minutemen Marching Band, Theater Guild, Ski Club, Outing Club, student newspaper, national fraternities, national sororities. *Campus security:* 24-hour emergency response devices and patrols, student patrols, controlled dormitory access, residence halls locked nights and weekends. *Student services:* health clinic, personal/psychological counseling, women's center, legal services.

Athletics Member NCAA. All Division I except football (Division I-AA). *Intercollegiate sports:* baseball M (s), basketball M (s)/W (s), cheerleading M/W, crew W (s), cross-country running M (s)/W (s), field hockey W (s), ice hockey M (s), lacrosse M (s)/W (s), skiing (downhill) M (s)/W (s), soccer M (s)/W (s), softball W (s), swimming and diving M (s)/W (s), tennis M (s), track and field M (s)/W (s), volleyball W (s). *Intramural sports:* basketball M/W, crew M (c)/W (c), cross-country running M/W, equestrian sports M (c)/W (c), fencing M (c)/W (c), field hockey W, football M/W, ice hockey M/W, lacrosse M (c)/W, rugby M (c)/W (c), soccer M/W, softball M/W, swimming and diving M/W, tennis M/W, ultimate Frisbee M/W, volleyball M/W, wrestling M/W.

Standardized Tests *Required:* SAT or ACT (for admission).

Costs (2007–08) *Tuition:* state resident $1714 full-time, $72 per credit part-time; nonresident $9937 full-time, $414 per credit part-time. Full-time tuition and fees vary according to course load. Part-time tuition and fees vary according to course load. *Required fees:* $7887 full-time, $1689 per term part-time. *Room and board:* $7274; room only: $3947. Room and board charges vary according to board plan and housing facility. *Payment plan:* installment. *Waivers:* senior citizens and employees or children of employees.

Financial Aid Of all full-time matriculated undergraduates who enrolled in 2006, 13,136 applied for aid, 9,498 were judged to have need, 2,451 had their need fully met. 4,940 Federal Work-Study jobs (averaging $1684). In 2006, 716 non-need-based awards were made. *Average percent of need met:* 86%. *Average financial aid package:* $11,871. *Average need-based loan:* $4161. *Average need-based gift aid:* $7710. *Average non-need-based aid:* $4052. *Average indebtedness upon graduation:* $12,062.

Applying *Options:* electronic application, early action, deferred entrance. *Application fee:* $40. *Required:* essay or personal statement, high school transcript. *Recommended:* minimum 3.0 GPA, letters of recommendation. *Application deadlines:* 1/15 (freshmen), 4/15 (transfers), 11/1 (early action). *Notification:* continuous (freshmen), continuous (transfers), 12/15 (early action).

Freshman Application Contact Mr. Kevin Kelly, Director, Undergraduate Admissions, University of Massachusetts Amherst, 37 Mather Drive, Amherst, MA 01003-9291. *Phone:* 413-545-0222. *Fax:* 413-545-4312. *E-mail:* mail@admissions.umass.edu.

See page 1280 for the College Close-Up.

UNIVERSITY OF MASSACHUSETTS BOSTON

Boston, Massachusetts — www.umb.edu/

- **State-supported** university, founded 1964, part of University of Massachusetts
- **Urban** 177-acre campus
- **Endowment** $9.5 million
- **Coed** 10,008 undergraduate students, 66% full-time, 57% women, 43% men
- **Moderately difficult** entrance level, 61% of applicants were admitted

The University of Massachusetts Boston is a public university campus located just south of downtown Boston on a picturesque peninsula adjacent to the John F. Kennedy Library and Museum. Established in 1964, the campus enrolls more than 12,300 students in its undergraduate and graduate programs.

Undergraduates 6,644 full-time, 3,364 part-time. Students come from 39 states and territories, 138 other countries, 5% are from out of state, 16% African American, 13% Asian American or Pacific Islander, 8% Hispanic American, 0.5% Native American, 3% international, 16% transferred in. *Retention:* 74% of 2006 full-time freshmen returned.

Freshmen *Admission:* 4,213 applied, 2,581 admitted, 997 enrolled. *Average high school GPA:* 3.0. *Test scores:* SAT critical reading scores over 500: 59%; SAT math scores over 500: 68%; SAT critical reading scores over 600: 18%; SAT math scores over 600: 21%; SAT critical reading scores over 700: 2%; SAT math scores over 700: 2%.

Faculty *Total:* 862, 52% full-time, 64% with terminal degrees. *Student/faculty ratio:* 16:1.
Majors African-American/Black studies; American studies; anthropology; art; biochemistry; biology/biological sciences; business administration and management; chemistry; classics and languages, literatures and linguistics; clinical laboratory science/medical technology; communications technology; community organization and advocacy; computer science; computer software and media applications related; criminal justice/safety; dramatic/theater arts; economics; engineering physics; English; French; geography; geology/earth science; German; gerontology; history; human services; interdisciplinary studies; Italian; kinesiology and exercise science; labor and industrial relations; legal studies; mathematics; music; nursing (registered nurse training); philosophy; physical education teaching and coaching; physics; political science and government; psychology; public policy analysis; Russian; sociology; Spanish; women's studies.
Academics *Calendar:* semesters. *Degrees:* certificates, bachelor's, master's, doctoral, post-master's, and postbachelor's certificates. *Special study options:* academic remediation for entering students, accelerated degree program, adult/continuing education programs, advanced placement credit, cooperative education, distance learning, double majors, English as a second language, freshman honors college, honors programs, independent study, internships, off-campus study, part-time degree program, services for LD students, student-designed majors, study abroad, summer session for credit. *Unusual degree programs:* 3-2 engineering with University of Massachusetts Lowell, University of Massachusetts Amherst, Northeastern University.
Computers on Campus 300 computers/terminals are available on campus for general student use. Students can access the following: online (class) registration. Campuswide network is available.
Student Life *Housing:* college housing not available. *Activities and organizations:* drama/theater group, student-run newspaper, radio station, choral group, Women's Center, Black Student Center, Asian Student Center, Veterans Student Center, Disabilities Student Center. *Campus security:* 24-hour emergency response devices and patrols, late-night transport/escort service, crime prevention program, bicycle patrols. *Student services:* health clinic, personal/psychological counseling, women's center, legal services.
Athletics Member NCAA. All Division III. *Intercollegiate sports:* baseball M, basketball M/W, cross-country running M/W, ice hockey M, lacrosse M, soccer M/W, softball W, tennis M/W, track and field M/W, volleyball W. *Intramural sports:* basketball M/W, ice hockey M, racquetball M/W, sailing M/W, soccer M/W, softball M/W, squash M/W, swimming and diving M/W, tennis M/W, volleyball M/W, weight lifting M/W.
Standardized Tests *Required:* SAT or ACT (for admission).
Costs (2007–08) *Tuition:* state resident $1714 full-time, $72 per credit hour part-time; nonresident $9758 full-time, $407 per credit hour part-time. Full-time tuition and fees vary according to class time, course load, program, reciprocity agreements, and student level. Part-time tuition and fees vary according to class time, course load, program, reciprocity agreements, and student level. *Required fees:* $7123 full-time, $296 per credit hour part-time. *Payment plan:* installment. *Waivers:* senior citizens and employees or children of employees.
Financial Aid Of all full-time matriculated undergraduates who enrolled in 2006, 3,925 applied for aid, 3,392 were judged to have need, 2,313 had their need fully met. In 2006, 115 non-need-based awards were made. *Average percent of need met:* 92%. *Average financial aid package:* $11,262. *Average need-based loan:* $5273. *Average need-based gift aid:* $6188. *Average non-need-based aid:* $2196. *Average indebtedness upon graduation:* $17,772.
Applying *Options:* electronic application, deferred entrance. *Application fee:* $40. *Required:* high school transcript, minimum 2.75 GPA. *Required for some:* essay or personal statement, letters of recommendation, interview. *Recommended:* essay or personal statement. *Application deadlines:* 6/1 (freshmen), rolling (transfers). *Notification:* continuous (freshmen), continuous (transfers).
Freshman Application Contact Mrs. Liliana Mickle, Director of Undergraduate Admissions, University of Massachusetts Boston, 100 Morrissey Boulevard, Boston, MA 02125-3393. *Phone:* 617-287-6100. *Fax:* 617-287-5999. *E-mail:* undergrad@umb.edu.

See page 1282 for the College Close-Up.

UNIVERSITY OF MASSACHUSETTS DARTMOUTH

North Dartmouth, Massachusetts **www.umassd.edu/**

- **State-supported** university, founded 1895, part of University of Massachusetts
- **Suburban** 710-acre campus with easy access to Boston and Providence
- **Endowment** $23.5 million
- **Coed** 7,927 undergraduate students, 86% full-time, 49% women, 51% men
- **Moderately difficult** entrance level, 66% of applicants were admitted

The University of Massachusetts Dartmouth enrolls more than 8,500 students on its 710-acre campus in southeastern Massachusetts. Five colleges offer sixty undergraduate and twenty-seven graduate programs. Publicly supported, the University provides affordable options in professional and preprofessional programs as well as in a variety of cocurricular activities, organizations, and teams.

Undergraduates 6,848 full-time, 1,079 part-time. Students come from 26 states and territories, 14 other countries, 4% are from out of state, 7% African American, 3% Asian American or Pacific Islander, 2% Hispanic American, 0.6% Native American, 0.3% international, 6% transferred in, 54% live on campus. *Retention:* 76% of 2006 full-time freshmen returned.
Freshmen *Admission:* 7,422 applied, 4,919 admitted, 1,927 enrolled. *Average high school GPA:* 3.07. *Test scores:* SAT critical reading scores over 500: 63%; SAT math scores over 500: 73%; ACT scores over 18: 93%; SAT critical reading scores over 600: 15%; SAT math scores over 600: 23%; ACT scores over 24: 31%; SAT critical reading scores over 700: 2%; SAT math scores over 700: 2%; ACT scores over 30: 1%.
Faculty *Total:* 616, 59% full-time. *Student/faculty ratio:* 17:1.
Majors Accounting; art history, criticism and conservation; art teacher education; biology/biological sciences; business administration and management; ceramic arts and ceramics; chemistry; chemistry related; civil engineering; clinical laboratory science/medical technology; commercial and advertising art; computer and information sciences; computer engineering; criminology; design and applied arts related; design and visual communications; economics; electrical, electronic and communications engineering technology; electrical, electronics and communications engineering; English; fiber, textile and weaving arts; finance; fine arts related; French; history; interdisciplinary studies; intermedia/multimedia; liberal arts and sciences/liberal studies; management information systems; marketing/marketing management; mathematics; mechanical engineering; mechanical engineering/mechanical technology; metal and jewelry arts; music; nursing (registered nurse training); nursing related; painting; philosophy; photography; physics; political science and government; Portuguese; printmaking; psychology; sculpture; sociology; Spanish; textile sciences and engineering; women's studies.
Academics *Calendar:* semesters. *Degrees:* certificates, bachelor's, master's, doctoral, post-master's, and postbachelor's certificates. *Special study options:* academic remediation for entering students, adult/continuing education programs, advanced placement credit, cooperative education, distance learning, double majors, honors programs, independent study, internships, off-campus study, part-time degree program, services for LD students, student-designed majors, study abroad, summer session for credit. *ROTC:* Army (c).
Computers on Campus 368 computers/terminals are available on campus for general student use. Students can access the following: online (class) registration. Campuswide network is available. 100% of college-owned or -operated housing units are wired for high-speed Internet access. Wireless service is available via classrooms, computer centers, computer labs, dorm rooms, learning centers, libraries, student centers.
Student Life *Housing options:* coed, disabled students. Campus housing is university owned. *Activities and organizations:* drama/theater group, student-run newspaper, radio station, choral group, Student Activities Board, Outing Club, Phi Sigma Sigma, Portuguese Language Club, United Brothers and Sisters, national fraternities, national sororities. *Campus security:* 24-hour emergency response devices and patrols, student patrols, late-night transport/escort service, controlled dormitory access. *Student services:* health clinic, personal/psychological counseling, women's center, legal services.
Athletics Member NCAA. All Division III. *Intercollegiate sports:* baseball M, basketball M/W, cheerleading W, cross-country running M/W, equestrian sports W (c), field hockey W, football M, golf M, ice hockey M, lacrosse M/W, soccer M/W, softball W, swimming and diving M/W, tennis M/W, track and field M/W, volleyball W. *Intramural sports:* badminton M/W, basketball M/W, field hockey W, sailing M/W, soccer M/W, softball M/W, table tennis M/W, tennis M/W, ultimate Frisbee M/W, volleyball M/W.
Standardized Tests *Required:* SAT or ACT (for admission).

Costs (2007–08) *Tuition:* state resident $1417 full-time, $59 per credit part-time; nonresident $11,999 full-time, $458 per credit part-time. Full-time tuition and fees vary according to program and reciprocity agreements. Part-time tuition and fees vary according to course load, program, and reciprocity agreements. *Required fees:* $7175 full-time, $299 per credit part-time. *Room and board:* $8432; room only: $5670. Room and board charges vary according to board plan and housing facility. *Payment plan:* installment. *Waivers:* senior citizens and employees or children of employees.

Financial Aid Of all full-time matriculated undergraduates who enrolled in 2006, 5,200 applied for aid, 4,300 were judged to have need, 2,600 had their need fully met. 1,006 Federal Work-Study jobs (averaging $1215). 1,300 state and other part-time jobs (averaging $3153). In 2006, 294 non-need-based awards were made. *Average percent of need met:* 94%. *Average financial aid package:* $11,200. *Average need-based loan:* $6400. *Average need-based gift aid:* $5850. *Average non-need-based aid:* $2500. *Average indebtedness upon graduation:* $16,214.

Applying *Options:* early admission, early decision, deferred entrance. *Application fee:* $40. *Required:* essay or personal statement, high school transcript, minimum 3.0 GPA. *Recommended:* letters of recommendation. *Application deadlines:* rolling (freshmen), rolling (transfers). *Early decision deadline:* 11/15. *Notification:* continuous (freshmen), continuous (transfers), 12/15 (early decision).

Freshman Application Contact Mr. Steven Briggs, Director of Admissions, University of Massachusetts Dartmouth, 285 Old Westport Road, North Dartmouth, MA 02747-2300. *Phone:* 508-999-8605. *Fax:* 508-999-8755. *E-mail:* admissions@umassd.edu.

See page 1284 for the College Close-Up.

UNIVERSITY OF MASSACHUSETTS LOWELL

Lowell, Massachusetts **www.uml.edu/**

- **State-supported** university, founded 1894, part of University of Massachusetts
- **Urban** 100-acre campus with easy access to Boston
- **Endowment** $32.4 million
- **Coed** 8,879 undergraduate students, 68% full-time, 40% women, 60% men
- **Moderately difficult** entrance level, 69% of applicants were admitted

Undergraduates 6,001 full-time, 2,878 part-time. Students come from 32 states and territories, 19 other countries, 7% are from out of state, 4% African American, 8% Asian American or Pacific Islander, 5% Hispanic American, 0.2% Native American, 0.9% international, 8% transferred in, 40% live on campus. *Retention:* 75% of 2006 full-time freshmen returned.

Freshmen *Admission:* 4,936 applied, 3,419 admitted, 1,243 enrolled. *Average high school GPA:* 3.16. *Test scores:* SAT critical reading scores over 500: 65%; SAT math scores over 500: 78%; SAT critical reading scores over 600: 18%; SAT math scores over 600: 31%; SAT critical reading scores over 700: 2%; SAT math scores over 700: 4%.

Faculty *Total:* 665, 61% full-time. *Student/faculty ratio:* 17:1.

Majors American studies; applied mathematics; biology/biological sciences; business administration and management; chemical engineering; chemistry; civil engineering; civil engineering technology; clinical laboratory science/medical technology; community health and preventive medicine; computer engineering; computer science; criminal justice/law enforcement administration; economics; electrical, electronic and communications engineering technology; electrical, electronics and communications engineering; engineering/industrial management; English; environmental science; fine/studio arts; foreign languages and literatures; history; industrial technology; information technology; kinesiology and exercise science; liberal arts and sciences/liberal studies; mathematics; mechanical engineering; mechanical engineering/mechanical technology; music; music performance; nursing (registered nurse training); philosophy; physics; political science and government; polymer/plastics engineering; psychology; sociology.

Academics *Calendar:* semesters. *Degrees:* associate, bachelor's, master's, doctoral, and post-master's certificates. *Special study options:* accelerated degree program, adult/continuing education programs, advanced placement credit, cooperative education, distance learning, double majors, honors programs, internships, off-campus study, part-time degree program, services for LD students, study abroad, summer session for credit. *ROTC:* Air Force (b).

Computers on Campus 4,000 computers/terminals are available on campus for general student use. Students can access the following: campus intranet, computer help desk, free student e-mail accounts, online (class) grades, online (class) registration, online (class) schedules. Campuswide network is available. Wireless service is available via classrooms, computer centers, computer labs, dorm rooms, learning centers, libraries, student centers.

Student Life *Housing options:* coed, men-only, women-only. Campus housing is university owned. *Activities and organizations:* drama/theater group, student-run newspaper, radio station, choral group, marching band, Student Government Association, Recreational Sports Club, Association of Students of African Origin, WUML Radio Station, Residence Hall Association. *Campus security:* 24-hour emergency response devices and patrols, late-night transport/escort service, controlled dormitory access. *Student services:* health clinic, personal/psychological counseling, women's center.

Athletics Member NCAA. All Division II except ice hockey (Division I). *Intercollegiate sports:* basketball M (s)/W (s), crew M/W, cross-country running M (s)/W (s), field hockey W (s), football M, golf M, ice hockey M (s), soccer M, swimming and diving M (s), tennis M (s)/W (s), track and field M (s)/W (s), volleyball W (s), wrestling M (s). *Intramural sports:* badminton M/W, basketball M/W, bowling M/W, golf M/W, ice hockey M/W, racquetball M/W, soccer M/W, squash M/W, table tennis M/W, tennis M/W, volleyball M/W, water polo M/W.

Standardized Tests *Required:* SAT or ACT (for admission).

Costs (2007–08) *Tuition:* state resident $1454 full-time, $61 per credit part-time; nonresident $8567 full-time, $357 per credit part-time. Part-time tuition and fees vary according to course load. *Required fees:* $7277 full-time, $303 per credit part-time. *Room and board:* $6978; room only: $4331. Room and board charges vary according to board plan and housing facility. *Payment plan:* installment. *Waivers:* senior citizens and employees or children of employees.

Financial Aid Of all full-time matriculated undergraduates who enrolled in 2006, 4,015 applied for aid, 2,887 were judged to have need, 2,123 had their need fully met. 108 Federal Work-Study jobs (averaging $2500). 630 state and other part-time jobs (averaging $2900). In 2006, 433 non-need-based awards were made. *Average percent of need met:* 93%. *Average financial aid package:* $9020. *Average need-based loan:* $4663. *Average need-based gift aid:* $4753. *Average non-need-based aid:* $2840. *Average indebtedness upon graduction:* $17,869.

Applying *Options:* electronic application, deferred entrance. *Application fee:* $60. *Required:* essay or personal statement, high school transcript, minimum 3.0 GPA, audition for music students. *Required for some:* interview. *Application deadlines:* rolling (freshmen), rolling (transfers). *Notification:* continuous (freshmen), continuous (transfers).

Freshman Application Contact Ms. Kerri Mead, Associate Director of Admissions, University of Massachusetts Lowell, 883 Broadway Street, Room 110, Lowell, MA 01854-5104. *Phone:* 978-934-3944. *Toll-free phone:* 800-410-4607. *Fax:* 978-934-3086. *E-mail:* admissions@umi.edu.

See page 1286 for the College Close-Up.

UNIVERSITY OF PHOENIX–BOSTON CAMPUS

Braintree, Massachusetts **www.phoenix.edu/**

- **Proprietary** comprehensive, founded 2001
- **Urban** campus
- **Coed**
- **Noncompetitive** entrance level

Faculty *Student/faculty ratio:* 5:1.

Academics *Calendar:* continuous. *Degrees:* bachelor's and master's.

Student Life *Campus security:* late-night transport/escort service.

Costs (2007–08) *Tuition:* $12,900 full-time, $430 per credit part-time. Full-time tuition and fees vary according to course level.

Financial Aid *Average financial aid package:* $3659. *Average need-based gift aid:* $1732.

Applying *Options:* deferred entrance. *Application fee:* $45. *Required:* 1 letter of recommendation. *Required for some:* high school transcript.

Freshman Application Contact Ms. Beth Barilla, Associate Vice President, Student Admissions and Services, University of Phoenix–Boston Campus, 4615 East Elwood Street, Mail Stop AA-K101, Phoenix, AZ 85040-1958. *Phone:* 480-317-6000. *Toll-free phone:* 800-228-7240. *Fax:* 480-894-1758. *E-mail:* beth.barilla@phoenix.edu.

UNIVERSITY OF PHOENIX–CENTRAL MASSACHUSETTS CAMPUS

Westborough, Massachusetts **www.phoenix.edu/**

- **Proprietary** comprehensive, founded 2003
- **Urban** campus
- **Coed**

• **Noncompetitive** entrance level

Faculty *Student/faculty ratio:* 3:1.

Academics *Calendar:* continuous. *Degrees:* bachelor's and master's.

Student Life *Campus security:* late-night transport/escort service.

Costs (2007–08) *Tuition:* $12,900 full-time, $430 per credit part-time. Full-time tuition and fees vary according to course level.

Financial Aid *Average financial aid package:* $3557. *Average need-based gift aid:* $2322.

Applying *Options:* deferred entrance. *Application fee:* $45. *Required:* 1 letter of recommendation. *Required for some:* high school transcript.

Freshman Application Contact Ms. Beth Barilla, Associate Vice President, Student Admissions and Services, University of Phoenix–Central Massachusetts Campus, 4615 East Elwood Street, Mail Stop AA-K101, Phoenix, AZ 85040-1958. *Phone:* 480-317-6000. *Toll-free phone:* 800-776-4867 (in-state); 800-228-7240 (out-of-state). *Fax:* 480-894-1758. *E-mail:* beth.barilla@phoenix.edu.

WELLESLEY COLLEGE

Wellesley, Massachusetts **www.wellesley.edu/**

• **Independent** 4-year, founded 1870
• **Suburban** 500-acre campus with easy access to Boston
• **Endowment** $1.7 billion
• **Women only** 2,380 undergraduate students, 94% full-time
• **Most difficult** entrance level, 36% of applicants were admitted

Undergraduates 2,238 full-time, 142 part-time. Students come from 53 states and territories, 75 other countries, 83% are from out of state, 6% African American, 26% Asian American or Pacific Islander, 7% Hispanic American, 0.5% Native American, 8% international, 0.8% transferred in, 97% live on campus. *Retention:* 95% of 2006 full-time freshmen returned.

Freshmen *Admission:* 4,017 applied, 1,434 admitted, 590 enrolled. *Test scores:* SAT critical reading scores over 500: 100%; SAT math scores over 500: 100%; SAT writing scores over 500: 100%; ACT scores over 18: 100%; SAT critical reading scores over 600: 92%; SAT math scores over 600: 89%; SAT writing scores over 600: 94%; ACT scores over 24: 98%; SAT critical reading scores over 700: 54%; SAT math scores over 700: 47%; SAT writing scores over 700: 52%; ACT scores over 30: 57%.

Faculty *Total:* 314, 72% full-time, 93% with terminal degrees. *Student/faculty ratio:* 9:1.

Majors African-American/Black studies; African studies; American studies; ancient/classical Greek; anthropology; archeology; architecture; art history, criticism and conservation; Asian studies (East); astronomy; astrophysics; biochemistry; biology/biological sciences; chemistry; Chinese; classics and languages, literatures and linguistics; cognitive psychology and psycholinguistics; comparative literature; computer science; digital communication and media/multimedia; dramatic/theater arts; economics; English; environmental studies; ethnic, cultural minority, and gender studies related; film/cinema studies; fine/studio arts; French; geology/earth science; German; German studies; history; international relations and affairs; Islamic studies; Italian; Italian studies; Japanese; Jewish/Judaic studies; Latin; Latin American studies; linguistics; mathematics; medieval and Renaissance studies; music; Near and Middle Eastern studies; neuroscience; peace studies and conflict resolution; philosophy; physics; political science and government; psychology; religious studies; Russian; Russian studies; sociology; Spanish; women's studies.

Academics *Calendar:* semesters. *Degrees:* bachelor's (double bachelor's degree with Massachusetts Institute of Technology). *Special study options:* adult/continuing education programs, advanced placement credit, double majors, honors programs, independent study, internships, off-campus study, part-time degree program, services for LD students, student-designed majors, study abroad, summer session for credit. *ROTC:* Army (c), Air Force (c). *Unusual degree programs:* 3-2 engineering with Massachusetts Institute of Technology; architecture; aeronautics and astronautics; urban studies and planning—Massachusetts Institute of Technology.

Computers on Campus 200 computers/terminals and 200 ports are available on campus for general student use. Students can access the following: campus intranet, computer help desk, free student e-mail accounts, online (class) registration, online (class) schedules, electronic bulletin boards. Campuswide network is available. 100% of college-owned or -operated housing units are wired for high-speed Internet access. Wireless service is available via computer labs, learning centers, libraries, student centers.

Student Life *Housing options:* women-only, cooperative, disabled students. Campus housing is university owned. Freshman applicants given priority for college housing. *Activities and organizations:* drama/theater group, student-run newspaper, radio and television station, choral group, student government, radio station, cultural clubs, Rugby Club, theater groups. *Campus security:* 24-hour emergency response devices and patrols, late-night transport/escort service, controlled dormitory access. *Student services:* health clinic, personal/psychological counseling, women's center.

Athletics Member NCAA. All Division III. *Intercollegiate sports:* basketball W, crew W, cross-country running W, fencing W, field hockey W, golf W, lacrosse W, rugby W (c), sailing W (c), skiing (downhill) W (c), soccer W, softball W, squash W, swimming and diving W, tennis W, track and field W (c), ultimate Frisbee W (c), volleyball W. *Intramural sports:* archery W, badminton W, basketball W, crew W, equestrian sports W, ice hockey W, racquetball W, sailing W (c), skiing (cross-country) W, soccer W, softball W, squash W, swimming and diving W, table tennis W, tennis W, volleyball W, water polo W, weight lifting W.

Costs (2007–08) *Comprehensive fee:* $45,820 includes full-time tuition ($34,770), mandatory fees ($224), and room and board ($10,826). Part-time tuition: $4346 per course.

Financial Aid Of all full-time matriculated undergraduates who enrolled in 2007, 1,501 applied for aid, 1,312 were judged to have need, 1,312 had their need fully met. 790 Federal Work-Study jobs (averaging $1225). 217 state and other part-time jobs (averaging $1742). *Average percent of need met:* 100%. *Average financial aid package:* $31,530. *Average need-based loan:* $3309. *Average need-based gift aid:* $29,081. *Average indebtedness upon graduation:* $11,902.

Applying *Options:* electronic application, early admission, early decision, deferred entrance. *Application fee:* $50. *Required:* essay or personal statement, high school transcript, 3 letters of recommendation, SAT & 2 SAT Subject Tests or ACT Writing; Midyear Report. *Required for some:* interview. *Recommended:* interview. *Application deadlines:* 1/15 (freshmen), 1/15 (out-of-state freshmen), 3/1 (transfers). *Early decision deadline:* 11/1 (for plan 1), 1/1 (for plan 2). *Notification:* 4/1 (freshmen), 4/1 (out-of-state freshmen), 5/1 (transfers), 12/15 (early decision plan 1), 4/1 (early decision plan 2).

Freshman Application Contact Ms. Heather Ayres, Director of Admission, Wellesley College, 106 Central Street, Green Hall 240, Wellesley, MA 02481-8203. *Phone:* 781-283-2253. *Fax:* 781-283-3678. *E-mail:* admission@wellesley.edu.

WENTWORTH INSTITUTE OF TECHNOLOGY

Boston, Massachusetts **www.wit.edu/**

• **Independent** 4-year, founded 1904
• **Urban** 35-acre campus
• **Endowment** $91.1 million
• **Coed** 3,728 undergraduate students, 89% full-time, 20% women, 80% men
• **Moderately difficult** entrance level, 80% of applicants were admitted

Founded in 1904, Wentworth Institute of Technology offers bachelor's degrees in architecture, biomedical engineering (beginning fall 2009), computer science, construction management, design, engineering, engineering technology, environmental science, and management. Wentworth provides an education that balances classroom theory with laboratory/studio practice and work experience through its strong co-op program. Approximately 3,500 students attend this private coeducational institution, located on a 35-acre campus on Huntington Avenue, across from Boston's Museum of Fine Arts. Wentworth is part of the Colleges of the Fenway consortium.

Undergraduates 3,333 full-time, 395 part-time. Students come from 39 states and territories, 51 other countries, 40% are from out of state, 3% African American, 5% Asian American or Pacific Islander, 3% Hispanic American, 0.1% Native American, 3% international, 5% transferred in, 41% live on campus. *Retention:* 80% of 2006 full-time freshmen returned.

Freshmen *Admission:* 2,329 applied, 1,867 admitted, 895 enrolled. *Average high school GPA:* 3.0. *Test scores:* SAT critical reading scores over 500: 52%; SAT math scores over 500: 73%; SAT writing scores over 500: 50%; ACT scores over 18: 94%; SAT critical reading scores over 600: 10%; SAT math scores over 600: 26%; SAT writing scores over 600: 9%; ACT scores over 24: 34%; SAT critical reading scores over 700: 1%; SAT math scores over 700: 2%; ACT scores over 30: 2%.

Faculty *Total:* 277, 49% full-time, 76% with terminal degrees. *Student/faculty ratio:* 24:1.

Majors Airframe mechanics and aircraft maintenance technology; architecture; avionics maintenance technology; biomedical technology; electrical, electronics and communications engineering; engineering mechanics; environmental engineering technology; environmental/environmental health engineering; industrial technology.

Academics *Calendar:* semesters for freshmen and sophomores, trimesters for juniors and seniors. *Degrees:* certificates, associate, and bachelor's. *Special study options:* academic remediation for entering students, accelerated degree program, advanced placement credit, cooperative education, English as a second language, freshman honors college, internships, off-campus study, part-time degree program, services for LD students, study abroad, summer session for credit. *ROTC:* Army (c), Air Force (c).

Computers on Campus 400 computers/terminals are available on campus for general student use. Campuswide network is available. 100% of college-owned or -operated housing units are wired for high-speed Internet access. Wireless service is available via entire campus.

Student Life *Housing options:* coed. Campus housing is university owned. Freshman campus housing is guaranteed. *Activities and organizations:* drama/theater group, student-run newspaper, radio station, Intramural Sports, Wentworth Events Board, Asian Students Association, Ski and Adventure Club. *Campus security:* 24-hour emergency response devices and patrols, student patrols, late-night transport/escort service, controlled dormitory access. *Student services:* health clinic, personal/psychological counseling, women's center.

Athletics Member NCAA. All Division III. *Intercollegiate sports:* baseball M, basketball M/W, golf M/W, ice hockey M, lacrosse M, riflery M/W, rock climbing M (c), soccer M/W, softball W, tennis M/W, volleyball M/W. *Intramural sports:* skiing (downhill) M (c)/W (c), weight lifting M (c)/W (c).

Standardized Tests *Required:* SAT or ACT (for admission).

Costs (2007–08) *Comprehensive fee:* $29,800 includes full-time tuition ($20,150) and room and board ($9650). Full-time tuition and fees vary according to student level. Part-time tuition: $630 per credit. Part-time tuition and fees vary according to class time, course load, and degree level. *Room and board:* Room and board charges vary according to board plan. *Payment plan:* installment. *Waivers:* employees or children of employees.

Financial Aid Of all full-time matriculated undergraduates who enrolled in 2007, 2,794 applied for aid, 1,866 were judged to have need, 72 had their need fully met. 1,752 Federal Work-Study jobs (averaging $1600). In 2007, 722 non-need-based awards were made. *Average percent of need met:* 38%. *Average financial aid package:* $11,261. *Average need-based loan:* $4294. *Average need-based gift aid:* $2838. *Average non-need-based aid:* $5502. *Average indebtedness upon graduation:* $35,000.

Applying *Options:* electronic application, deferred entrance. *Application fee:* $30. *Required:* essay or personal statement, high school transcript, letters of recommendation. *Recommended:* minimum 2.0 GPA, interview. *Application deadlines:* rolling (freshmen), rolling (transfers). *Notification:* continuous (freshmen), continuous (transfers).

Freshman Application Contact Admissions Office, Wentworth Institute of Technology, 550 Huntington Avenue, Boston, MA 02115-5998. *Phone:* 617-989-4000. *Toll-free phone:* 800-556-0610. *Fax:* 617-989-4010. *E-mail:* admissions@wit.edu.

See page 1288 for the College Close-Up.

WESTERN NEW ENGLAND COLLEGE

Springfield, Massachusetts **www.wnec.edu/**

- **Independent** comprehensive, founded 1919
- **Suburban** 215-acre campus
- **Endowment** $47.8 million
- **Coed** 2,775 undergraduate students, 89% full-time, 39% women, 61% men
- **Moderately difficult** entrance level, 73% of applicants were admitted

Undergraduates 2,456 full-time, 319 part-time. Students come from 31 states and territories, 3 other countries, 61% are from out of state, 3% African American, 2% Asian American or Pacific Islander, 3% Hispanic American, 0.1% Native American, 0.2% international, 3% transferred in, 61% live on campus. *Retention:* 75% of 2006 full-time freshmen returned.

Freshmen *Admission:* 4,693 applied, 3,415 admitted, 721 enrolled. *Average high school GPA:* 3.14. *Test scores:* SAT critical reading scores over 500: 60%; SAT math scores over 500: 69%; ACT scores over 18: 91%; SAT critical reading scores over 600: 13%; SAT math scores over 600: 19%; ACT scores over 24: 31%; SAT critical reading scores over 700: 1%; SAT math scores over 700: 1%.

Faculty *Total:* 314, 56% full-time. *Student/faculty ratio:* 16:1.

Majors Accounting; advertising; applied economics; biology/biological sciences; biomedical/medical engineering; business administration and management; business/commerce; chemistry; communication/speech communication and rhetoric; computer science; creative writing; criminal justice/safety; economics; electrical, electronics and communications engineering; elementary education; English; finance; history; industrial engineering; international/global studies; legal studies; liberal arts and sciences/liberal studies; management information systems; marketing/marketing management; marketing related; mass communication/media; mathematics; mechanical engineering; molecular biology; philosophy; political science and government; psychology; secondary education; social work; sociology; sport and fitness administration/management.

Academics *Calendar:* semesters. *Degrees:* associate, bachelor's, master's, and first professional. *Special study options:* accelerated degree program, adult/continuing education programs, advanced placement credit, distance learning, double majors, honors programs, independent study, internships, off-campus study, part-time degree program, services for LD students, student-designed majors, study abroad, summer session for credit. *ROTC:* Army (b), Air Force (c). *Unusual degree programs:* 3-2 business administration; engineering.

Computers on Campus 460 computers/terminals are available on campus for general student use. Students can access the following: computer help desk, free student e-mail accounts, online (class) registration, online (class) schedules. Campuswide network is available.

Student Life *Housing options:* coed, men-only, women-only. Campus housing is university owned. Freshman campus housing is guaranteed. *Activities and organizations:* drama/theater group, student-run newspaper, radio station, choral group, Student Senate, Residence Hall Association, Campus Activities Board, student radio station, Management Association. *Campus security:* 24-hour emergency response devices and patrols, student patrols, controlled dormitory access, security cameras. *Student services:* health clinic, personal/psychological counseling.

Athletics Member NCAA. All Division III. *Intercollegiate sports:* baseball M, basketball M/W, bowling M/W, cross-country running M/W, field hockey W, football M, golf M, ice hockey M, lacrosse M/W, soccer M/W, softball W, swimming and diving W, tennis M/W, volleyball W, wrestling M. *Intramural sports:* badminton M/W, basketball M/W, football M/W, rugby M/W, soccer M/W, softball M/W, table tennis M/W, volleyball M/W, water polo M/W.

Standardized Tests *Required:* SAT or ACT (for admission).

Costs (2007–08) *Comprehensive fee:* $35,940 includes full-time tuition ($24,224), mandatory fees ($1718), and room and board ($9998). Full-time tuition and fees vary according to program. Part-time tuition: $481 per credit hour. Part-time tuition and fees vary according to location and program. *Room and board:* Room and board charges vary according to board plan and housing facility. *Payment plans:* tuition prepayment, installment. *Waivers:* senior citizens and employees or children of employees.

Financial Aid Of all full-time matriculated undergraduates who enrolled in 2007, 1,980 applied for aid, 1,768 were judged to have need, 218 had their need fully met. 829 Federal Work-Study jobs (averaging $1912). In 2007, 250 non-need-based awards were made. *Average percent of need met:* 68%. *Average financial aid package:* $15,877. *Average need-based loan:* $5119. *Average need-based gift aid:* $10,627. *Average non-need-based aid:* $8417.

Applying *Options:* electronic application. *Application fee:* $50. *Required:* high school transcript, 1 letter of recommendation. *Recommended:* essay or personal statement, interview. *Application deadlines:* rolling (freshmen), rolling (transfers). *Notification:* continuous (freshmen), continuous (transfers).

Freshman Application Contact Dr. Charles R. Pollock, Vice President of Enrollment Management, Western New England College, 1215 Wilbraham Road, Springfield, MA 01119. *Phone:* 413-782-1321. *Toll-free phone:* 800-325-1122 Ext. 1321. *Fax:* 413-782-1777. *E-mail:* ugradmis@wnec.edu.

See page 1290 for the College Close-Up.

WESTFIELD STATE COLLEGE

Westfield, Massachusetts **www.wsc.ma.edu/**

- **State-supported** comprehensive, founded 1838, part of Massachusetts Public Higher Education System
- **Small-town** 227-acre campus
- **Endowment** $5.1 million
- **Coed** 4,699 undergraduate students, 89% full-time, 54% women, 46% men
- **Moderately difficult** entrance level, 56% of applicants were admitted

Undergraduates 4,187 full-time, 512 part-time. Students come from 10 states and territories, 2 other countries, 7% are from out of state, 3% African American, 1% Asian American or Pacific Islander, 4% Hispanic American, 0.3% Native American, 5% transferred in, 54% live on campus. *Retention:* 74% of 2006 full-time freshmen returned.

Freshmen *Admission:* 5,094 applied, 2,875 admitted, 953 enrolled. *Average high school GPA:* 3.07. *Test scores:* SAT critical reading scores over 500: 53%; SAT math scores over 500: 57%; ACT scores over 18: 85%; SAT critical reading scores over 600: 11%; SAT math scores over 600: 12%; ACT scores over 24: 20%; SAT critical reading scores over 700: 1%; ACT scores over 30: 2%.

Faculty *Total:* 370, 49% full-time. *Student/faculty ratio:* 18:1.

Majors Art; art teacher education; biology/biological sciences; business administration and management; business teacher education; city/urban, community and regional planning; computer science; counselor education/school counseling and guidance; criminal justice/safety; dramatic/theater arts; economics; education; elementary education; English; environmental biology; history; information science/studies; kindergarten/preschool education; liberal arts and sciences/liberal studies; mass communication/media; mathematics; music; music teacher education; parks, recreation and leisure; physical education teaching and coaching; physical sciences; political science and government; psychology; science teacher education; social work; sociology; special education; technology/industrial arts teacher education.

Academics *Calendar:* semesters. *Degrees:* bachelor's, master's, post-master's, and postbachelor's certificates. *Special study options:* adult/continuing education programs, advanced placement credit, cooperative education, distance learning, double majors, honors programs, independent study, internships, off-campus study, part-time degree program, services for LD students, student-designed majors, study abroad, summer session for credit. *ROTC:* Army (c), Air Force (c).

Computers on Campus 275 computers/terminals are available on campus for general student use. Students can access the following: computer help desk, free student e-mail accounts, online (class) grades, online (class) registration, online transcripts and billing information. Campuswide network is available. 100% of college-owned or -operated housing units are wired for high-speed Internet access. Wireless service is available via classrooms, computer centers, computer labs, dorm rooms, learning centers, libraries, student centers.

Student Life *Housing options:* coed, disabled students. Campus housing is university owned. Freshman applicants given priority for college housing. *Activities and organizations:* drama/theater group, student-run newspaper, radio and television station, choral group. *Campus security:* 24-hour emergency response devices and patrols, student patrols, late-night transport/escort service. *Student services:* health clinic, personal/psychological counseling, legal services.

Athletics Member NCAA. All Division III. *Intercollegiate sports:* baseball M, basketball M/W, cheerleading M/W, cross-country running M/W, field hockey W, football M, soccer M/W, softball W, swimming and diving W, track and field M/W, volleyball W. *Intramural sports:* badminton M/W, basketball M/W, bowling M/W, football M/W, racquetball M/W, soccer M/W, softball M/W, tennis M/W, volleyball M/W, water polo M/W.

Standardized Tests *Required:* SAT or ACT (for admission).

Costs (2007–08) *Tuition:* state resident $970 full-time, $85 per credit hour part-time; nonresident $7050 full-time, $95 per credit hour part-time. *Required fees:* $5240 full-time, $100 per credit part-time, $145 per semester part-time. *Room and board:* $6458. Room and board charges vary according to board plan, housing facility, and location. *Payment plan:* installment. *Waivers:* senior citizens and employees or children of employees.

Financial Aid Of all full-time matriculated undergraduates who enrolled in 2006, 3,086 applied for aid, 1,915 were judged to have need, 432 had their need fully met. 362 Federal Work-Study jobs (averaging $879). In 2006, 55 non-need-based awards were made. *Average percent of need met:* 78%. *Average financial aid package:* $6435. *Average need-based loan:* $3338. *Average need-based gift aid:* $4018. *Average non-need-based aid:* $4325. *Average indebtedness upon graduation:* $15,307.

Applying *Options:* electronic application, deferred entrance. *Application fee:* $25. *Required:* high school transcript. *Recommended:* letters of recommendation. *Application deadlines:* 3/1 (freshmen), 4/1 (transfers). *Notification:* 5/1 (transfers).

Freshman Application Contact Ms. Emily Gibbings, Associate Director of Admissions, Westfield State College, 577 Western Avenue, Westfield, MA 01086. *Phone:* 413-572-5218. *Toll-free phone:* 800-322-8401.

WHEATON COLLEGE

Norton, Massachusetts www.wheatoncollege.edu/

- **Independent** 4-year, founded 1834
- **Small-town** 385-acre campus with easy access to Boston
- **Endowment** $200.7 million
- **Coed** 1,552 undergraduate students, 100% full-time, 60% women, 40% men
- **Very difficult** entrance level, 37% of applicants were admitted

Undergraduates 1,549 full-time, 3 part-time. Students come from 45 states and territories, 33 other countries, 65% are from out of state, 5% African American, 3% Asian American or Pacific Islander, 3% Hispanic American, 0.3% Native American, 3% international, 0.8% transferred in, 93% live on campus. *Retention:* 88% of 2006 full-time freshmen returned.

Freshmen *Admission:* 3,833 applied, 1,411 admitted, 418 enrolled. *Average high school GPA:* 3.5.

Faculty *Total:* 185, 74% full-time, 75% with terminal degrees. *Student/faculty ratio:* 10:1.

Majors African studies; American studies; ancient/classical Greek; ancient studies; anthropology; art history, criticism and conservation; Asian studies; astronomy; biochemistry; bioinformatics; biology/biological sciences; chemistry; classics and languages, literatures and linguistics; computer science; dance; dramatic/theater arts; economics; English; fine/studio arts; French studies; German; German studies; Hispanic-American, Puerto Rican, and Mexican-American/Chicano studies; history; international relations and affairs; Italian studies; Latin; mathematics; music; philosophy; physics; physiological psychology/psychobiology; political science and government; psychology; religious studies; Russian; Russian studies; sociology; women's studies.

Academics *Calendar:* semesters. *Degree:* bachelor's. *Special study options:* accelerated degree program, advanced placement credit, double majors, honors programs, independent study, internships, off-campus study, part-time degree program, student-designed majors, study abroad. *ROTC:* Army (c). *Unusual degree programs:* 3-2 business administration with University of Rochester, Clark University; engineering with Dartmouth College, George Washington University, Worcester Polytechnic Institute; theology with Andover Newton Theological School, optometry with New England College of Optometry, communications with Emerson College, studio art with School of the Museum of Fine Arts.

Computers on Campus 348 computers/terminals and 274 ports are available on campus for general student use. Students can access the following: campus intranet, computer help desk, online (class) grades, online (class) registration, online (class) schedules. Campuswide network is available. 100% of college-owned or -operated housing units are wired for high-speed Internet access. Wireless service is available via classrooms, computer centers, computer labs, dorm rooms, learning centers, libraries, student centers.

Student Life *Housing:* on-campus residence required through senior year. *Options:* coed, men-only, women-only, disabled students. Campus housing is university owned. Freshman campus housing is guaranteed. *Activities and organizations:* drama/theater group, student-run newspaper, radio station, choral group, Student Government Association, Community Service Network, Amnesty International, a cappella singing groups, Programming Council. *Campus security:* 24-hour emergency response devices and patrols, student patrols, late-night transport/escort service, controlled dormitory access. *Student services:* health clinic, personal/psychological counseling, women's center.

Athletics Member NCAA. All Division III. *Intercollegiate sports:* baseball M, basketball M/W, cross-country running M/W, field hockey W, lacrosse M/W, soccer M/W, softball W, swimming and diving M/W, tennis M/W, track and field M/W, volleyball W. *Intramural sports:* archery M (c)/W (c), badminton M/W, basketball M/W, equestrian sports M (c)/W (c), fencing M (c)/W (c), field hockey M (c)/W (c), golf M (c)/W (c), ice hockey M (c)/W (c), rugby M (c)/W (c), sailing M (c)/W (c), soccer M/W, softball M (c)/W (c), tennis M/W, ultimate Frisbee M (c)/W (c), volleyball M/W.

Costs (2007–08) *One-time required fee:* $50. *Comprehensive fee:* $45,330 includes full-time tuition ($36,430), mandatory fees ($260), and room and board ($8640). *College room only:* $4560. *Payment plans:* tuition prepayment, installment. *Waivers:* employees or children of employees.

Financial Aid Of all full-time matriculated undergraduates who enrolled in 2007, 929 applied for aid, 821 were judged to have need, 630 had their need fully met. 708 Federal Work-Study jobs (averaging $1815). 267 state and other part-time jobs (averaging $1840). In 2007, 238 non-need-based awards were made. *Average percent of need met:* 98%. *Average financial aid package:* $28,347. *Average need-based loan:* $4477. *Average need-based gift aid:* $22,174. *Average non-need-based aid:* $12,809. *Average indebtedness upon graduation:* $23,222. *Financial aid deadline:* 2/1.

Applying *Options:* electronic application, early admission, early decision, deferred entrance. *Application fee:* $55. *Required:* essay or personal statement, high school transcript, 2 letters of recommendation. *Recommended:* interview. *Application deadlines:* 1/15 (freshmen), 4/1 (transfers). *Early decision deadline:* 11/1 (for plan 1), 1/15 (for plan 2). *Notification:* 4/1 (freshmen), 5/15 (transfers), 12/15 (early decision plan 1), 2/15 (early decision plan 2).

Freshman Application Contact Ms. Gail Berson, Vice President For Enrollment and Dean of Admission and Student Aid, Wheaton College, 26 East Main Street, Norton, MA 02766. *Phone:* 508-286-8251. *Toll-free phone:* 800-394-6003. *Fax:* 508-286-8271. *E-mail:* admission@wheatoncollege.edu.

See page 1292 for the College Close-Up.

WHEELOCK COLLEGE

Boston, Massachusetts www.wheelock.edu/

- **Independent** comprehensive, founded 1888
- **Urban** 7-acre campus
- **Endowment** $50.9 million
- **Coed, primarily women** 792 undergraduate students, 93% full-time, 93% women, 7% men

• **Moderately difficult** entrance level, 63% of applicants were admitted

Undergraduates 733 full-time, 59 part-time. Students come from 6 other countries, 40% are from out of state, 9% African American, 3% Asian American or Pacific Islander, 7% Hispanic American, 0.5% Native American, 1% international, 6% transferred in, 69% live on campus. *Retention:* 75% of 2006 full-time freshmen returned.

Freshmen *Admission:* 1,144 applied, 719 admitted, 224 enrolled. *Average high school GPA:* 2.9. *Test scores:* SAT critical reading scores over 500: 44%; SAT math scores over 500: 35%; SAT writing scores over 500: 44%; ACT scores over 18: 78%; SAT critical reading scores over 600: 9%; SAT math scores over 600: 8%; SAT writing scores over 600: 6%; ACT scores over 24: 15%; SAT math scores over 700: 1%.

Faculty *Total:* 143, 44% full-time, 53% with terminal degrees. *Student/faculty ratio:* 10:1.

Majors Child development; early childhood education; education; elementary education; human development and family studies; kindergarten/preschool education; social work; special education.

Academics *Calendar:* semesters. *Degrees:* bachelor's, master's, post-master's, and postbachelor's certificates. *Special study options:* advanced placement credit, double majors, independent study, internships, off-campus study, part-time degree program, services for LD students, study abroad.

Computers on Campus 120 computers/terminals are available on campus for general student use. Students can access the following: campus intranet, computer help desk, free student e-mail accounts, online (class) grades, online (class) registration, online (class) schedules. Campuswide network is available. Wireless service is available via classrooms, dorm rooms, libraries, student centers.

Student Life *Housing options:* coed, women-only, cooperative, disabled students. Campus housing is university owned. Freshman campus housing is guaranteed. *Activities and organizations:* drama/theater group, choral group, Student Government Association, Campus Activities Board, AHANA Club, residence hall councils, class councils. *Campus security:* 24-hour patrols, late-night transport/escort service, controlled dormitory access, self-defense education. *Student services:* health clinic, personal/psychological counseling, women's center.

Athletics Member NCAA. All Division III. *Intercollegiate sports:* basketball W, field hockey W, soccer W, softball W, swimming and diving W, tennis M. *Intramural sports:* basketball M/W, racquetball M/W, soccer M, softball M/W, squash M/W, table tennis M/W, ultimate Frisbee M/W, volleyball M/W, water polo M/W.

Standardized Tests *Required:* SAT or ACT (for admission).

Costs (2007–08) *Comprehensive fee:* $36,480 includes full-time tuition ($25,400), mandatory fees ($680), and room and board ($10,400). Part-time tuition: $794 per credit. *Payment plans:* tuition prepayment, installment. *Waivers:* employees or children of employees.

Financial Aid Of all full-time matriculated undergraduates who enrolled in 2006, 629 applied for aid, 625 were judged to have need, 15 had their need fully met. In 2006, 43 non-need-based awards were made. *Average percent of need met:* 58%. *Average financial aid package:* $16,823. *Average need-based loan:* $4482. *Average need-based gift aid:* $9482. *Average non-need-based aid:* $11,231. *Average indebtedness upon graduation:* $18,231.

Applying *Options:* electronic application, early action, deferred entrance. *Application fee:* $35. *Required:* essay or personal statement, high school transcript, 1 letter of recommendation. *Recommended:* minimum 2.0 GPA, interview. *Application deadlines:* 3/1 (freshmen), 4/15 (transfers), 12/1 (early action). *Notification:* continuous until 4/15 (freshmen), continuous until 5/15 (transfers).

Freshman Application Contact Ms. Lisa Slavin, Dean of Enrollment, Wheelock College, 200 The Riverway, Boston, MA 02215. *Phone:* 617-879-2206. *Toll-free phone:* 800-734-5212. *Fax:* 617-879-2449. *E-mail:* undergrad@wheelock.edu.

See page 1294 for the College Close-Up.

WILLIAMS COLLEGE

Williamstown, Massachusetts www.williams.edu/

• **Independent** comprehensive, founded 1793
• **Small-town** 450-acre campus with easy access to Albany
• **Endowment** $1.9 billion
• **Coed** 1,997 undergraduate students, 98% full-time, 50% women, 50% men
• **Most difficult** entrance level, 18% of applicants were admitted

Undergraduates 1,964 full-time, 33 part-time. Students come from 45 states and territories, 63 other countries, 86% are from out of state, 10% African American, 11% Asian American or Pacific Islander, 9% Hispanic American, 0.4% Native American, 7% international, 0.4% transferred in, 93% live on campus. *Retention:* 97% of 2006 full-time freshmen returned.

Freshmen *Admission:* 6,478 applied, 1,194 admitted, 540 enrolled. *Test scores:* SAT critical reading scores over 500: 100%; SAT math scores over 500: 99%; SAT writing scores over 500: 99%; ACT scores over 18: 100%; SAT critical reading scores over 600: 94%; SAT math scores over 600: 93%; SAT writing scores over 600: 93%; ACT scores over 24: 99%; SAT critical reading scores over 700: 66%; SAT math scores over 700: 61%; SAT writing scores over 700: 61%; ACT scores over 30: 67%.

Faculty *Total:* 305, 84% full-time, 95% with terminal degrees. *Student/faculty ratio:* 7:1.

Majors American studies; anthropology; art history, criticism and conservation; Asian studies; astronomy; astrophysics; biology/biological sciences; chemistry; Chinese; classics and languages, literatures and linguistics; computer science; dramatic/theater arts; economics; English; ethnic, cultural minority, and gender studies related; fine/studio arts; French; geology/earth science; German; history; Japanese; literature; mathematics; music; philosophy; physics; political science and government; psychology; religious studies; Russian; sociology; Spanish; women's studies.

Academics *Calendar:* 4-1-4. *Degrees:* bachelor's and master's. *Special study options:* accelerated degree program, advanced placement credit, double majors, honors programs, independent study, internships, off-campus study, services for LD students, student-designed majors, study abroad. *Unusual degree programs:* 3-2 engineering with Columbia University, Washington University in St. Louis, Oxford-Style tutorials, Dartmouth College.

Computers on Campus 252 computers/terminals are available on campus for general student use. Students can access the following: online (class) registration, wireless network. Campuswide network is available.

Student Life *Housing:* on-campus residence required through senior year. *Options:* coed, cooperative. Campus housing is university owned. Freshman campus housing is guaranteed. *Activities and organizations:* drama/theater group, student-run newspaper, radio station, choral group. *Campus security:* 24-hour emergency response devices and patrols, student patrols, late-night transport/escort service, controlled dormitory access. *Student services:* health clinic, personal/psychological counseling, women's center.

Athletics Member NCAA. All Division III except men's and women's skiing (cross-country) (Division I), men's and women's skiing (downhill) (Division I). *Intercollegiate sports:* baseball M, basketball M/W, crew M/W, cross-country running M/W, equestrian sports M (c)/W (c), field hockey W, football M, golf M/W (c), ice hockey M/W, lacrosse M/W, rugby M (c)/W (c), sailing M (c)/W (c), skiing (cross-country) M/W, skiing (downhill) M/W, soccer M/W, softball W, squash M/W, swimming and diving M/W, tennis M/W, track and field M/W, volleyball M (c)/W, water polo M (c)/W (c), wrestling M. *Intramural sports:* badminton M/W, baseball M (c), basketball M/W, fencing M (c)/W (c), gymnastics M (c)/W (c), ice hockey M/W, skiing (cross-country) M/W, skiing (downhill) M/W, soccer M/W, softball M/W, ultimate Frisbee M (c)/W (c), volleyball M/W, water polo M/W.

Standardized Tests *Required:* SAT and SAT Subject Tests or ACT (for admission).

Costs (2007–08) *Comprehensive fee:* $45,140 includes full-time tuition ($35,438), mandatory fees ($232), and room and board ($9470). *College room only:* $4810. Room and board charges vary according to board plan. *Payment plan:* installment.

Financial Aid Of all full-time matriculated undergraduates who enrolled in 2006, 1,015 applied for aid, 854 were judged to have need, 854 had their need fully met. 444 Federal Work-Study jobs (averaging $1572). 338 state and other part-time jobs (averaging $1589). *Average percent of need met:* 100%. *Average financial aid package:* $32,979. *Average need-based loan:* $3136. *Average need-based gift aid:* $29,713. *Average indebtedness upon graduation:* $9943. *Financial aid deadline:* 2/1.

Applying *Options:* electronic application, early admission, early decision, deferred entrance. *Application fee:* $60. *Required:* essay or personal statement, high school transcript, 2 letters of recommendation. *Application deadlines:* 1/1 (freshmen), 3/15 (transfers). *Early decision deadline:* 11/10. *Notification:* 4/1 (freshmen), 5/1 (transfers), 12/15 (early decision).

Freshman Application Contact Mr. Richard L. Nesbitt, Director of Admission, Williams College, 33 Stetson Court, Williamstown, MA 01267. *Phone:* 413-597-2211. *Fax:* 413-597-4052. *E-mail:* admission@williams.edu.

WORCESTER POLYTECHNIC INSTITUTE

Worcester, Massachusetts www.wpi.edu/

• **Independent** university, founded 1865
• **Suburban** 80-acre campus with easy access to Boston
• **Endowment** $404.7 million
• **Coed** 3,016 undergraduate students, 99% full-time, 26% women, 74% men

• **Very difficult** entrance level, 66% of applicants were admitted

Undergraduates 2,981 full-time, 35 part-time. Students come from 42 states and territories, 70 other countries, 50% are from out of state, 3% African American, 6% Asian American or Pacific Islander, 4% Hispanic American, 0.5% Native American, 8% international, 2% transferred in, 59% live on campus. *Retention:* 94% of 2006 full-time freshmen returned.

Freshmen *Admission:* 5,698 applied, 3,739 admitted, 805 enrolled. *Average high school GPA:* 3.7. *Test scores:* SAT critical reading scores over 500: 94%; SAT math scores over 500: 100%; SAT writing scores over 500: 93%; ACT scores over 18: 100%; SAT critical reading scores over 600: 60%; SAT math scores over 600: 86%; SAT writing scores over 600: 54%; ACT scores over 24: 85%; SAT critical reading scores over 700: 17%; SAT math scores over 700: 35%; SAT writing scores over 700: 12%; ACT scores over 30: 26%.

Faculty *Total:* 314, 76% full-time, 88% with terminal degrees. *Student/faculty ratio:* 13:1.

Majors Actuarial science; aerospace, aeronautical and astronautical engineering; animal genetics; applied mathematics; biochemistry; biology/biological sciences; biology/biotechnology laboratory technician; biomedical/medical engineering; biomedical sciences; business administration and management; cell biology and histology; chemical engineering; chemistry; civil engineering; computer and information sciences; computer engineering; computer science; economics; electrical, electronics and communications engineering; engineering/industrial management; engineering mechanics; engineering physics; engineering related; environmental/environmental health engineering; environmental studies; fluid/thermal sciences; history; history and philosophy of science and technology; humanities; industrial engineering; information science/studies; interdisciplinary studies; intermedia/multimedia; management information systems; materials engineering; materials science; mathematics; mechanical engineering; medical microbiology and bacteriology; medicinal and pharmaceutical chemistry; molecular biology; music; nuclear engineering; philosophy; physical sciences related; physics; robotics; science, technology and society; social sciences; technical and business writing.

Academics *Calendar:* 4 7-week terms. *Degrees:* bachelor's, master's, doctoral, post-master's, and postbachelor's certificates. *Special study options:* accelerated degree program, advanced placement credit, cooperative education, double majors, English as a second language, independent study, internships, off-campus study, part-time degree program, services for LD students, student-designed majors, study abroad, summer session for credit. *ROTC:* Army (b), Navy (c), Air Force (b). *Unusual degree programs:* 3-2 business administration; engineering.

Computers on Campus 500 computers/terminals and 745 ports are available on campus for general student use. Students can access the following: campus intranet, computer help desk, free student e-mail accounts, online (class) grades, online (class) registration, online (class) schedules, online course content. Campuswide network is available. 100% of college-owned or -operated housing units are wired for high-speed Internet access. Wireless service is available via entire campus.

Student Life *Housing options:* coed, men-only, women-only, disabled students. Campus housing is university owned. Freshman campus housing is guaranteed. *Activities and organizations:* drama/theater group, student-run newspaper, radio station, choral group, marching band, Student Government Association, Social Committee (Student Events Programming Board), Music Association (all music-performing groups), Intramural and Club Sports, International Student Council, national fraternities, national sororities. *Campus security:* 24-hour emergency response devices and patrols, student patrols, late-night transport/escort service, controlled dormitory access. *Student services:* health clinic, personal/psychological counseling, women's center.

Athletics Member NCAA. All Division III. *Intercollegiate sports:* baseball M, basketball M/W, crew M/W, cross-country running M/W, field hockey W, football M, soccer M/W, softball W, swimming and diving M/W, track and field M/W, volleyball W, water polo M (c)/W (c), wrestling M. *Intramural sports:* baseball M/W, basketball M/W, bowling M/W, cheerleading M (c)/W (c), cross-country running M (c)/W (c), fencing M (c)/W (c), golf M (c)/W (c), ice hockey M (c)/W (c), lacrosse M (c)/W (c), racquetball M/W, rugby M (c)/W (c), sailing M (c)/W (c), skiing (cross-country) M (c)/W (c), skiing (downhill) M (c)/W (c), soccer M/W, softball M/W, squash M/W, swimming and diving M/W, table tennis M/W, tennis M (c)/W (c), track and field M/W, ultimate Frisbee M (c)/W (c), volleyball M (c)/W, water polo M (c)/W (c), wrestling M (c).

Standardized Tests *Required for some:* SAT or ACT (for admission), TOEFL or IELTS.

Costs (2007–08) *Comprehensive fee:* $45,240 includes full-time tuition ($34,300), mandatory fees ($530), and room and board ($10,410). Full-time tuition and fees vary according to degree level. Part-time tuition and fees vary according to course load and degree level. *College room only:* $6104. Room and board charges vary according to board plan and housing facility. *Payment plans:* installment, deferred payment. *Waivers:* employees or children of employees.

Financial Aid Of all full-time matriculated undergraduates who enrolled in 2006, 2,301 applied for aid, 2,079 were judged to have need, 705 had their need fully met. 560 Federal Work-Study jobs (averaging $1212). In 2006, 681 non-need-based awards were made. *Average percent of need met:* 69%. *Average financial aid package:* $24,552. *Average need-based loan:* $6803. *Average need-based gift aid:* $16,166. *Average non-need-based aid:* $15,430. *Average indebtedness upon graduation:* $37,784. *Financial aid deadline:* 2/1.

Applying *Options:* electronic application, early admission, early action, deferred entrance. *Application fee:* $60. *Required:* essay or personal statement, high school transcript, 2 letters of recommendation. *Required for some:* interview. *Application deadlines:* 2/1 (freshmen), 4/15 (transfers), 11/15 (early action). *Notification:* 4/1 (freshmen), continuous (transfers), 12/15 (early action).

Freshman Application Contact Mr. Edward J. Connor, Director of Admissions, Worcester Polytechnic Institute, 100 Institute Road, Worcester, MA 01609-2280. *Phone:* 508-831-5286. *Fax:* 508-831-5875. *E-mail:* admissions@wpi.edu.

See page 1296 for the College Close-Up.

WORCESTER STATE COLLEGE

Worcester, Massachusetts **www.worcester.edu/**

- **State-supported** comprehensive, founded 1874, part of Massachusetts Public Higher Education System
- **Urban** 58-acre campus with easy access to Boston
- **Endowment** $8.0 million
- **Coed** 4,602 undergraduate students, 73% full-time, 59% women, 41% men
- **Moderately difficult** entrance level, 53% of applicants were admitted

Undergraduates 3,342 full-time, 1,260 part-time. Students come from 16 states and territories, 23 other countries, 5% are from out of state, 4% African American, 3% Asian American or Pacific Islander, 5% Hispanic American, 0.5% Native American, 2% international, 11% transferred in, 25% live on campus. *Retention:* 76% of 2006 full-time freshmen returned.

Freshmen *Admission:* 3,810 applied, 2,030 admitted, 699 enrolled. *Average high school GPA:* 3.00. *Test scores:* SAT critical reading scores over 500: 51%; SAT math scores over 500: 59%; ACT scores over 18: 97%; SAT critical reading scores over 600: 9%; SAT math scores over 600: 10%; ACT scores over 24: 25%; SAT critical reading scores over 700: 1%.

Faculty *Total:* 419, 45% full-time, 33% with terminal degrees. *Student/faculty ratio:* 15:1.

Majors Adult health nursing; biological and physical sciences; biology/biological sciences; biotechnology; business administration and management; chemistry; communication disorders; communication/speech communication and rhetoric; community health services counseling; computer and information sciences; criminal justice/safety; economics; elementary education; English; geography; health professions related; history; kindergarten/preschool education; mass communication/media; mathematics; nursing (registered nurse training); occupational therapy; psychology; sociology; Spanish; urban studies/affairs.

Academics *Calendar:* semesters. *Degrees:* certificates, bachelor's, master's, post-master's, and postbachelor's certificates. *Special study options:* academic remediation for entering students, accelerated degree program, adult/continuing education programs, advanced placement credit, distance learning, double majors, English as a second language, honors programs, independent study, internships, off-campus study, part-time degree program, services for LD students, student-designed majors, study abroad, summer session for credit. *ROTC:* Army (c), Navy (c), Air Force (c).

Computers on Campus 500 computers/terminals and 1,700 ports are available on campus for general student use. Students can access the following: campus intranet, computer help desk, free student e-mail accounts, online (class) grades, online (class) registration, online (class) schedules. Campuswide network is available. 100% of college-owned or -operated housing units are wired for high-speed Internet access. Wireless service is available via entire campus.

Student Life *Housing options:* coed, men-only, women-only, disabled students. Campus housing is university owned. *Activities and organizations:* drama/theater group, student-run newspaper, radio and television station, choral group, Senate, SEC (Student Events Committee), TWA (Third World Alliance), WSCW (Radio Station), Dance Company/Club. *Campus security:* 24-hour emergency response devices and patrols, late-night transport/escort service, controlled dormitory access, well-lit campus, limited access to campus at night. *Student services:* personal/psychological counseling.

Athletics Member NCAA. All Division III. *Intercollegiate sports:* baseball M, basketball M/W, cheerleading M/W, crew W (c), cross-country running M/W, field hockey W, football M, golf M, ice hockey M, lacrosse W, skiing (downhill) M (c)/W (c), soccer M/W, softball W, tennis W, track and field M/W, volleyball M/W. *Intramural sports:* baseball M, basketball M/W, cheerleading M/W, crew

M/W, cross-country running M/W, field hockey W, football M, golf M, ice hockey M, lacrosse W, soccer M/W, softball W, tennis W, track and field M/W, volleyball M/W.

Standardized Tests *Required:* SAT or ACT (for admission). *Required for some:* SAT Subject Tests (for admission).

Costs (2007–08) *Tuition:* state resident $970 full-time, $40 per credit part-time; nonresident $7050 full-time, $294 per credit part-time. Full-time tuition and fees vary according to class time, course load, and reciprocity agreements. Part-time tuition and fees vary according to class time, course load, and reciprocity agreements. *Required fees:* $4894 full-time, $196 per credit part-time. *Room and board:* $7958; room only: $5408. Room and board charges vary according to board plan and housing facility. *Payment plan:* installment. *Waivers:* senior citizens and employees or children of employees.

Financial Aid Of all full-time matriculated undergraduates who enrolled in 2006, 2,418 applied for aid, 1,626 were judged to have need, 788 had their need fully met. 232 Federal Work-Study jobs (averaging $1500). *Average percent of need met:* 84%. *Average financial aid package:* $8849. *Average need-based loan:* $2329. *Average need-based gift aid:* $4110. *Average indebtedness upon graduation:* $17,985.

Applying *Options:* electronic application, deferred entrance. *Application fee:* $20. *Required:* high school transcript, minimum 2.0 GPA. *Required for some:* essay or personal statement, letters of recommendation. *Application deadlines:* 6/1 (freshmen), 6/1 (transfers). *Notification:* continuous (freshmen), continuous (transfers).

Freshman Application Contact Ms. Golda Guella, Clerk of Admissions, Worcester State College, 486 Chandler Street, Administration Building, Room 204, Worcester, MA 01602-2597. *Phone:* 508-929-8040. *Toll-free phone:* 866-WSC-CALL. *Fax:* 508-929-8183. *E-mail:* admissions@worcester.edu.

See page 1298 for the College Close-Up.

AMERICAN INTERNATIONAL COLLEGE

SPRINGFIELD, MASSACHUSETTS

The College

American International College opened in 1885. Today, the College has a wide geographic representation, and the 1,500 students come from twenty-eight states and twenty-five countries; the ratio of men to women is even. The majority are graduates of public high schools. About 48 percent are commuting students; all others live in the five residence halls. Students participate in a wide variety of activities that reflect their interests, ranging from volunteer work in the surrounding community to singing in the Chorale to sports. Varsity athletics include men's baseball, basketball, cross-country, football, golf, hockey, indoor and outdoor track, lacrosse, soccer, tennis, and wrestling and women's basketball, cross-country, field hockey, indoor and outdoor track, lacrosse, soccer, softball, tennis, and volleyball. There are more than forty separate student clubs and organizations.

Location

American International College is located in Springfield, Massachusetts, a city of 165,000 people, which is the seat of Hampden County and the metropolitan center for half a million people. Springfield is also the transportation center of western New England, easily reached by automobile on Interstate 91 and the Massachusetts Turnpike, by rail via major north-south and east-west lines, and by plane via Bradley International Airport. There are many cultural offerings in the area, including the Springfield Symphony, Mass Mutual Center, and City Stage Theatre Company.

Majors and Degrees

The School of Arts, Education, and Sciences offers Bachelor of Arts and Bachelor of Science degrees. Students may select majors for the B.A. degree in the areas of American studies, biology, chemistry, communications, economics, English, history, interdepartmental science, international studies, liberal studies, mathematics, political science, psychology, and sociology. The B.S. is offered in criminal justice, early childhood education, elementary education, secondary education, special education, and speech and language pathology. Massachusetts teacher certification requirements mandate that students seeking certification must also complete the requirements of a second major selected from among those offered in the liberal arts and sciences. Preprofessional programs in dentistry, law, medicine, optometry, physical therapy, podiatry, and veterinary science are also available. Minors are available in these disciplines as well as in the fields of athletic coaching, journalism, and physics.

The School of Business Administration awards the degree of Bachelor of Science in Business Administration. Majors include accounting, economics, finance, international business, management, marketing, and sports and recreation management.

The School of Health Sciences offers majors in health science management, nursing, occupational therapy, and physical therapy.

The nursing program awards a Bachelor of Science in Nursing degree through a four-year undergraduate program as well as through an upper-division program for registered nurses. The Division of Nursing is accredited by the National League for Nursing Accrediting Commission.

The occupational therapy program offers an accredited program leading to a combined Bachelor of Science in occupational science/Master of Science in Occupational Therapy (B.S./M.S.O.T.) degree.

The physical therapy program offers an accredited 6-year program leading to a doctoral degree in physical therapy.

Academic Programs

General requirements are virtually the same for all majors. One year of Freshman Composition is required as are four semesters of physical education. Other general education requirements include 12 semester hours in the social sciences, 3 in literature, 6 in humanities, 8 in a laboratory science, and 3 in a quantitative course as well as one computer-oriented course. To graduate, students are required to complete a minimum total of 120 hours of academic credit with a C average or better.

A special four-year program, the Supportive Learning Services Program, assists students with learning disabilities to function in a regular college curriculum.

An Honors Program is also offered on a selective basis.

Off-Campus Programs

Opportunities for international study are available. Individually designed courses of study can be arranged at the AIC in Ireland campus or at other international universities for a summer, a single semester, or a full year of residence. It is possible to transfer up to one full year of credit for such study.

Qualified students are allowed to participate in off-campus internships under the supervision and guidance of experienced personnel. The type of work and the amount of supervision a student receives are left to the discretion of the faculty member to whom the student is assigned. This program is designed to provide all students with an opportunity to gain practical experience in their field of study and is required of the students in many of the business disciplines and in communications, criminal justice, education, human services, nursing, occupational therapy, and physical therapy.

Academic Facilities

James J. Shea Sr. Memorial Library (1980) houses 125,000 volumes, 519 current periodicals, 14,800 bound periodicals, 12,759 units of microfilm, and 3,423 sound recordings and tapes. An area for group study, a media center, and individual study carrels are provided for students.

Amaron Hall is the primary facility for liberal arts and business classrooms. It also houses microcomputer laboratories and the computer center. Old Science and the newer Breck Hall of Science buildings provide up-to-date classrooms and laboratories for science, mathematics, preprofessional studies, and nursing. The Curtis Blake Child Development Center serves as a diagnostic center for children with learning difficulties and offers graduate-level courses in special education. The center also provides services for specially selected college-age students with learning disabilities.

Courniotes Hall is the academic center for the physical therapy, occupational therapy, and nursing programs. The 30,000-square-foot facility includes an amphitheater, several laboratories, classrooms, and faculty and administrative offices.

Costs

The comprehensive 2008–09 fee for tuition, room, board, and miscellaneous expenses is approximately $34,100. Books and supplies are approximately $800. Personal expenses average $1000 per year.

Financial Aid

American International College provides aid from institutional and external sources to assist nearly 90 percent of the student body. The average financial aid package for the 2007–08 school year was over $18,000. Scholarships and loans are available to those who demonstrate financial need and maintain an acceptable record of academic work and campus citizenship. Campus employment is available, and about 55 percent of the students earn a portion of their expenses. The College participates in the Federal Perkins Loan, Federal Supplemental Educational Opportunity Grant, Federal Pell Grant, and Federal Work-Study programs. Merit-based scholarships are available for eligible freshmen and transfers, and additional College grants are awarded on a need basis. Applications for scholarships and loans should be made to the Office of Financial Aid by March 15 for the following academic year, but they are accepted as long as funds are available. Only the Free Application for Federal Student Aid (FAFSA) is required. Students are urged to file the FAFSA online. Further information about financial aid should be obtained from the Financial Aid Office directly. Students should contact the Admission Office for information about merit-based scholarships.

Faculty

The emphasis of the faculty is on teaching. The full-time faculty members number 86, of whom nearly 70 percent have earned doctorates. All teach freshman courses, and all faculty members, including department chairmen, serve as advisers to undergraduate students. The faculty-student ratio is 1:14.

Student Government

All students are members of the Student Government Association, and the elected officers play an important role in the administration of the College. Serious disciplinary problems are adjudicated by the various levels of the Student Judicial System as well as by the Vice President of Academic Affairs and the Dean of Students. In addition, students are largely responsible for planning the various social activities at the College with the Director of Student Activities.

Admission Requirements

Students applying for admission must be graduates of an approved secondary school and must have successfully completed 16 units of study or show evidence of equivalent education. Among subjects that should be a part of a student's secondary program are English (4 units) and a selection from mathematics, science, social studies, and foreign languages. Applicants should take the SAT Reasoning Test or ACT. Class rank, recommendations, quality of classes taken, and extracurricular involvement are also factors considered in making admission decisions. American International College has no geographic or other quotas. Transfer applications are strongly encouraged.

An interview at the College is recommended but not required of applicants to most of the programs; however, an on-campus interview is required of applicants to the Supportive Service Program. Guides offer campus tours to all guests; class attendance or an overnight stay may be arranged through the Admissions Office. Admission staff members also visit schools throughout the Northeast each year, and candidates who are unable to visit the campus are urged to meet with staff members or talk with alumni in their home area.

Application and Information

A completed application includes the candidate's high school transcript, SAT or ACT scores, and at least one letter of recommendation. Everything should be sent to the address given; a catalog or other information booklets may be requested from the same office. Decision letters are sent on a rolling basis.

The Admissions staff is glad to advise prospective students who wish to write or telephone for additional information.

Vice President for Admission Services
American International College
1000 State Street
Springfield, Massachusetts 01109
Phone: 413-205-3201
800-242-3142 (toll-free)
E-mail: peter.miller@aic.edu
Web site: http://www.aic.edu

Sokolowski Tower, a hub of student activity.

ANNA MARIA COLLEGE

PAXTON, MASSACHUSETTS

The College

Anna Maria College (AMC), a private, comprehensive, four-year, coeducational Catholic college, was founded in 1946 by the Sisters of Saint Anne in Marlboro, Massachusetts. In 1952, AMC moved to its current 180-acre campus in Paxton, Massachusetts. Originally a women's college, AMC has been coeducational since 1973. The 700 full-time undergraduate students come from fifteen states and several countries.

Anna Maria College is a close-knit community. Small class sizes allow for mentor relationships to develop between faculty members and students. Freshman and sophomore classes generally have between 15 and 20 students; some upper-level classes have as few as 5 students. Faculty members teach and advise students based on their knowledge of each person as an individual, and classes are never taught by graduate assistants.

A five-year strategic plan calls for the College to change and enhance its core curriculum and extracurricular activities to ensure that students have access to the programs and services that will help develop their mind, body, and spirit so they can become strong leaders in their communities. New academic programs, such as an honors program, applied history, video game design, and dance and dance therapy are currently being explored.

Anna Maria College is accredited by the New England Association of Schools and Colleges, the Council on Social Work Education, the National League for Nursing Accrediting Commission (RN-B.S.N. program) and is approved by the Board of Registration in Nursing in Massachusetts. AMC is also approved by the Massachusetts Department of Education.

Approximately 50 percent of Anna Maria College's undergraduates reside on campus in the residence halls. Students enjoy a full social life both on campus and within the college-city atmosphere of nearby Worcester. Annual events enjoyed by all students include Winterfest, Harvest and Spring Weekends, President's Christmas Dinner, the 100 Days Party, a semiformal dinner/dance, and Senior Ball.

Anna Maria College's NCAA Division III athletic program offers intercollegiate competition for men (baseball, basketball, cross-country, golf, and soccer) and women (basketball, field hockey, soccer, softball, and volleyball). In the fall of 2008, AMC is introducing men's and women's lacrosse and tennis teams, and in the fall of 2009, the College's first football team will take the field. Intramural athletics and the coed club sport of cheerleading are also available to students who do not wish to participate on varsity teams.

Anna Maria College is linked to the Internet. More than 500 computer hookups link classrooms, offices, the Academic Computing Center, computer labs, the library, and all residence hall rooms. In addition to College-owned computers, students have the opportunity to access the College network to gain access to the Internet from any location on campus through the use of the College wireless network and their personally owned computer.

Location

Anna Maria College is located on a 180-acre wooded campus in Paxton, Massachusetts, 8 miles from downtown Worcester. The city offers numerous professional and cultural opportunities; Boston, Providence, and Hartford are only an hour away.

Local attractions include big-name entertainment and minor league hockey at the DCU Center; art, history, and science museums; classical music performances at Mechanics Hall; theater; and day and night skiing at Wachusett Mountain.

Majors and Degrees

Anna Maria College offers a four-year curriculum of undergraduate instruction leading to bachelor degrees in the following areas: art, art and business, art therapy, business administration, Catholic studies, computer and information science, criminal justice, early childhood education, elementary education, English, environmental science, fire science, graphic design, health science, history, human development/human services, humanities (interdisciplinary program), legal professions, liberal arts/general studies, management information systems, media communications, modern languages, music, music education, music performance, music therapy, nursing, paralegal studies, political science, psychology, public policy, social science, social work, sociology, Spanish, sports management, studio art, teacher preparation/licensure, teacher of visual art, and theology. Associate Degrees are available in nursing, business administration, and paralegal studies.

Criminal justice is the most popular program on campus, followed by fire science, education, social work, and psychology. The Fifth Year Option allows undergraduate students in good academic standing a unique opportunity to earn both their undergraduate and graduate degrees in five years. Fifth-year master's options are available in business administration, counseling psychology, criminal justice, education, emergency management, fire science, pastoral studies/counseling, and visual art.

Academic Programs

When the Sisters of St. Anne founded Anna Maria College in 1946, their mission was to increase access to high-quality education, educational innovation, and respect for service to others through the development of the total human being. That mission has not changed in more than fifty years. As a Catholic college, the relationship between faith and reason is looked at closely. An AMC education is distinct because of its integration of rich tradition, diversity of knowledge, and the understanding of human history, institutions, and societies with Catholic teachings and traditions. The cornerstone of AMC's academic programs is the core curriculum, which integrates the Catholic character with a commitment to liberal arts education.

The academic programs are grouped into five divisions: Division I: Humanities, Arts, and International Studies; Division II: Business, Law, and Public Policy; Division III: Human Development and Human Services; Division IV: Environmental, Natural, and Technological Sciences; and Division V: Fine Arts. Each division serves to illuminate and explore links between related areas of study so that the educational experience is broad-based and interdisciplinary. Students are encouraged to travel beyond their immediate interests to disciplines that may be connected by similar methods, history, theory, or application. The end result is a strong liberal arts foundation with a focused knowledge and professional preparation in a chosen area of concentration. AMC also encourages students to explore their own areas of interest and design their own majors.

While at Anna Maria College, students can gain practical experience and explore career options through internship programs, fieldwork, academic seminars, and summer programs. They also learn through required practicums, part-time work, and community service.

Off-Campus Programs

Anna Maria College is a member of the Colleges of Worcester Consortium. Through this group of thirteen area colleges (Anna Maria College, Assumption College, Atlantic Union College, Becker College, Clark University, College of the Holy Cross, Massachusetts College of Pharmacy and Allied Health, Nichols College, Quinsigamond Community College, Tufts University School of Veterinary Medicine, University of Massachusetts Medical School, Worcester Polytechnic Institute, and Worcester State College), students may enroll in nonmajor courses at any of the member institutions and have credits transferred at no additional cost.

AMC offers several off-campus opportunities for which academic credits are awarded. There are opportunities for study abroad, with programs in a variety of places overseas, including London, Seville, Rome, Latin America, Ireland, Egypt, and Nova Scotia. In addition, there is an Urban Seminar course with travel to various locations worldwide. Students are also eligible to apply for Army and Air Force ROTC programs, available through the Colleges of Worcester Consortium. A Washington, D.C., internship is offered for students in all majors, and a Disney internship is also available.

Academic Facilities

The Mondor-Eagan Library houses Anna Maria College's volumes, stacks, periodicals, study rooms, computer center, resource centers, and language laboratory. The library also houses the main computer terminal, which links the combined material resources of central and western Massachusetts libraries, making more than 4 million books and periodicals accessible to students. Classrooms are located in Trinity Hall, Cardinal Cushing Hall, and Foundress Hall. Foundress Hall houses the Zecco Performing Arts Center. Trinity Hall also houses the learning center. Among the other buildings are Madore Chapel, St. Joseph's Hall for sciences, and Miriam Hall for music, performance, and art.

Costs

Tuition and fees for the 2007–08 academic year included tuition, $22,360; fees, $2257; and room and board, $8915. Tuition for music majors was $25,504.

Financial Aid

Ninety-six percent of the most recent freshman class received financial aid in the form of scholarships, grants, loans, and work-study program awards. Some available sources of funds are the Federal Pell Grant, Federal Supplemental Educational Opportunity Grant, and Federal Perkins Loan programs. To apply for aid, students should submit the Free Application for Federal Student Aid (FAFSA), which can be found at http://www.fafsa.ed.gov. Aid is awarded on the basis of need. Non-need-based scholarships are also available. For further information, students should call 508-849-3366.

Faculty

Anna Maria College has 144 full- and part-time faculty members, 95 percent of whom are lay and 5 percent of whom are religious personnel. Faculty members have a deep respect for scholarship and research and are dedicated to teaching and to the success of the student.

Student Government

The Student Government Association (SGA) is the official representative of the student body, serving as the link between students and the administration. There are more than twenty clubs and organizations under the SGA, offering many activities and opportunities to participate in the extracurricular life of AMC.

Admission Requirements

At Anna Maria College, every application is considered individually and weighed on its own merits. Emphasis is placed on the applicant's transcript, recommendations, and SAT or ACT scores. Extracurricular activities and leadership positions are also important. Successful completion of a four-year college-preparatory program is required. Application for admission to AMC is encouraged for all academically qualified candidates regardless of race, religion, age, gender, or creed.

Application and Information

To apply, students should submit a completed application form and an optional personal essay with the required $40 fee, request that an official high school transcript be sent to the Office of Admission, forward the scores from the SAT or ACT, submit a letter of recommendation, and, if desired, schedule a personal interview. AMC is on rolling admissions; however, the application priority deadline for financial aid is March 1. Students who apply after March 1 do not receive priority for financial aid. To apply as a transfer student, the applicant must submit official transcripts of all postsecondary courses.

Anna Maria College invites students to learn more about AMC's community by visiting the campus. Students should call the Undergraduate Office of Admission to schedule an appointment. For detailed information about Anna Maria College's distinctive programs and campus community, prospective students should contact:

Timothy M. Donahue
Director of Recruitment and Admissions
Anna Maria College
50 Sunset Lane
Paxton, Massachusetts 01612-1198
Phone: 508-849-3360
800-344-4586 Ext. 360 (toll-free)
Fax: 508-849-3362
E-mail: admissions@annamaria.edu
Web site: http://www.annamaria.edu

Socquet House, built in 1750, currently houses the President's Office as well as other administrative offices.

COLLEGE DATA CENTER • MASSACHUSETTS

THE ART INSTITUTE OF BOSTON AT LESLEY UNIVERSITY

BOSTON, MASSACHUSETTS

The Institute

Founded in 1912, The Art Institute of Boston (AIB) is a professional college of visual arts that offers program and course work designed to prepare students to be professional illustrators, animators, graphic designers, Web designers, photographers, exhibiting fine artists, art teachers, and art therapists. AIB provides students with an intimate, challenging, and supportive environment that balances personal artistic expression with practical professional preparation.

AIB's more than 500 students come from thirty states and fifteen other countries, creating a global community of young artists with a stimulating variety of backgrounds and viewpoints. The nature of the college allows students to form close ties with other students and with faculty and staff members, most of whom are practicing professional artists. Studio classes are small and intimate—with an average of 14 students per instructor—which allows for personal attention and an emphasis on self-exploration and the development of an individual style. Students are prepared for professions in the arts by exposure to the most current trends and technology in their fields and internships and freelance opportunities that provide them with professional connections for career opportunities after graduation.

The University also offers activities such as major exhibitions, student exhibits, lectures, art auctions, special event–related parties, as well as a visiting artist program that brings prominent artists to the campus for lectures and workshops.

AIB's strengths as a professional college of the visual arts are combined with the resources of Lesley University, providing students with expanded educational opportunities that are not usually found at most independent colleges of art, yet preserving the character of a small, private art college.

The University provides a variety of dormitory housing options for students, including residences on the Cambridge campus of Lesley University, near Harvard Square (shuttle service provided).

The Career Resource Center at Lesley University provides career development and job search services to AIB degree candidates and alumni. Students are provided individual assistance and training in job search, career assessment, and decision-making skills that are used throughout a lifetime of employment. Workshops and special events are planned throughout the academic year on a variety of topics. The Artists Resource Center at AIB maintains current job listings and provides information on competitions, fellowships and grants, exhibition opportunities, and other resources for artists. Career counseling also takes place informally with faculty members and advisers within each department.

Master's programs in expressive therapies and art education are offered in conjunction with Lesley University.

Location

Boston is an extraordinary college town. Nearly 250,000 students live and study here every year at seventy institutions of higher learning. The city offers all the human and institutional resources expected in a major cultural, educational, and commercial center. World-class art exhibitions, concerts, lectures, theater, sports, and popular entertainment are among its riches. The spirit is cosmopolitan, but the setting is distinctive to Boston, with its historic neighborhoods, parks, and nearby New England rural and coastal areas.

The Art Institute of Boston students use the city's extensive resources as a part of their learning environment in many ways—for artistic and academic research, for internships and job opportunities, and for personal recreation. Full-time students receive free admission to the Museum of Fine Arts, Boston.

Majors and Degrees

The Art Institute of Boston awards the Bachelor of Fine Arts degree in animation, art history, fine arts, graphic design, illustration, and photography. Students may elect to earn a five-year double-major B.F.A./Diploma in fine arts/illustration, graphic design/illustration, illustration/fine arts, or illustration/graphic design. AIB students also have the option to study for a dual B.F.A./M.Ed. in art education or B.F.A./M.A. in art/expressive therapy. An advanced professional certificate two-year studio-intensive program is offered in animation, graphic design, or illustration.

Candidates for the graphic design program can study advertising and corporate communications, package design, publishing and book design, and Web and multimedia design. The illustration program offers specializations in advertising, animation, book, and editorial. Fine arts students choose from drawing, painting, printmaking, and sculpture as concentrations, with courses available in ceramics, installation, and new media. Photography students specialize in either commercial, documentary, fine arts, or media. An intensive precollege program is available for high school students throughout the academic year and the summer.

Academic Programs

AIB's challenging curriculum is structured to provide students with an understanding of the process of visual communication and expression, along with the social, historical, and cultural influences that shape the world and inform their imaginations.

AIB's rigorous first-year foundation includes intensive study in drawing and visual perception. Photography students take a unique foundation, with a direct immersion in the conceptual, technical, and historic aspects of photography. The foundation supplies students with the skills, insights, and fluency of expression that are necessary to meet the challenges of further study in art.

After the foundation year, students choose a major that can include unique specializations, combined majors, and a wide variety of interdisciplinary courses and workshops. Students take core courses in their major and continue with more individualized instruction, working closely with the faculty of working professional artists, toward their personal and professional goals. Students prepare for careers in the visual arts with real world studio assignments and professional internships, giving them valuable firsthand experience in their intended fields.

As an integral part of their study, all degree and diploma students take a blend of required and elective liberal arts courses. These courses are designed to develop effective communication skills, give a firm academic grounding in the history of their major area of study, and allow students to pursue individual interests that stimulate their imaginations and interests.

AIB offers both day and evening degree credit courses during the fall, spring, and summer semesters. In addition, the continuing and professional education program offers evening and weekend courses, workshops, and intensive seminars in the areas of visual arts, liberal arts, and career development to be taken by artists, educators, and professionals.

Off-Campus Programs

AIB students may opt in their junior year to spend a semester abroad. They can choose to study the visual art, history, humanities, language, and culture of Italy at The Art Institute of Florence, of France at Pont-Avon School of Art, or of Ireland at The Burren College of Art. The Illustration and Design Departments offer an exchange with the Willem de Kooning Academy in the Netherlands. Students may take an intensive yearlong course of study and studio work in New York City or spend their junior year at one of thirty schools in the Association of Independent Colleges of Art and Design (AICAD) located across the country. AIB also offers students the opportunity to take classes at the Boston Architectural College and the Maine Photographic Workshop.

Academic Facilities

The Art Institute of Boston's facilities include five state-of-the-art Macintosh computer laboratories, an animation lab, an updated photography lab with color and black-and-white printers, a digital photography lab, a printmaking lab with etching and lithography presses, a wood shop, and a clay lab with kilns. Senior fine arts students have their own individual studios in which to create.

The Art Institute of Boston was selected to join the New Media Centers Program, a consortium of higher education institutions and digital technology companies dedicated to advancing learning through new media. AIB has newly expanded multimedia programs that use state-of-the-art technology and equipment.

The AIB library collection is devoted principally to the visual arts and contains more than 10,000 books, seventy-five serial titles, 45,000 slides, a video viewing room, and more than 500 art-related videos. The AIB library also subscribes to AMICO, the image database. The library has the National Gallery of Art's American Art Collection on videodisc, a visual reference of more than 26,000 images spanning three centuries.

In addition, the Eleanor De Wolfe Ludcke Library at Lesley provides a state-of-the-art multimedia resource center and a collection of 100,000 books, 700 current periodicals, 2,200 computer software and CD-ROM titles, 650 film and video titles, media material, and circulating media equipment. Students have borrowing privileges at six additional libraries through the Fenway Library Online.

The Art Institute of Boston sponsors a full program of exhibitions and lectures by visiting artists. The gallery presents major exhibitions of contemporary and historical work by established and emerging artists, including the alumni of The Art Institute of Boston. Students have the opportunity to assist in mounting exhibitions and to personally meet visiting artists. A student gallery and reserved areas show student work year-round. Gallery South exhibits the work of student photographers throughout the year, including group and senior exhibitions.

Costs

Tuition for the 2007–08 academic year was $23,200. Room and board costs were approximately $11,100 per year. Material and supply costs varied according to individual and departmental requirements. In general, foundation, fine arts, illustration, and design students spend approximately $1700 per year for supplies, while photography students can expect to spend about $3000 per year, with further expenses dependent upon the equipment chosen by the individual student.

Financial Aid

More than 60 percent of students receive aid each year through AIB's active financial aid program. Awards are made on the basis of need as determined by the United States Department of Education, which analyzes all the financial resources of the student. The Financial Aid Office's goal is to help students meet established needs through a combination of Federal Pell Grants, Federal Stafford Student Loans, Federal Work-Study Program awards, other federal grants, scholarships, and state programs.

Various merit-based and need-based scholarships are available. The Art Institute of Boston administers more than $4 million in scholarships, financial aid, and loans for students each year. The application deadline for scholarships is February 15; the deadline is March 15 for need-based awards.

Faculty

The Art Institute of Boston at Lesley University has 113 full- and part-time faculty members, 95 percent of whom have advanced degrees in their field; 90 percent are practicing artists, designers, illustrators, and photographers. The student-faculty ratio is 13:1.

Student Government

Each year, the student peer advisers and office staff are responsible for a full program of social events, lecture and film series, and out-of-town visits to important exhibitions. In addition, students can share their thoughts with the dean in monthly informal round table discussions.

Admission Requirements

In considering applications for admission, The Art Institute of Boston looks for artistic potential and personal commitment. A portfolio of original work is an important part of the application; academic grades, test scores, letters of recommendation, and extracurricular activities are also strongly considered. A school visit is strongly encouraged, giving applicants the opportunity to present their portfolios, discuss their goals and interests with an admissions counselor, and determine how they may benefit from AIB's programs. SAT or ACT scores are required of applicants who have graduated from high school since 1995.

Application and Information

To ensure a place in the desired program of study and in order to meet application deadlines for financial aid, students are encouraged to apply by the priority application deadlines of February 15 for fall and November 15 for spring admittance. After these deadlines, applications are accepted on a rolling basis as long as space allows. A complete application consists of an application form and fee, essay, resume of accomplishments and cocurricular activities, transcript(s) of all courses completed, SAT or ACT test scores (B.F.A. candidates, U.S. only), an interview, and a portfolio. Transfer and international applications are accepted and encouraged.

For further information, students should visit the school's Web site or contact an admissions representative at:

Office of Admission
The Art Institute of Boston at Lesley University
700 Beacon Street
Boston, Massachusetts 02215
Phone: 617-585-6710
800-773-0494 Ext. 6710 (toll-free, U.S. and Canada)
E-mail: admissions@aiboston.edu
Web site: http://www.aiboston.edu

Studio classes are small and intimate, with an average of 13 students per instructor.

ASSUMPTION COLLEGE
WORCESTER, MASSACHUSETTS

The College

Founded in 1904, Assumption College educates students in the liberal arts and professional studies and prepares them for thoughtful and successful lives. Assumption students treasure their close relationships with faculty members and the opportunity to develop their opinions and beliefs within a challenging and supportive Catholic environment. The College supplements the academic life of its students with experiential learning opportunities on and off campus, giving many of the students a competitive edge for graduate school or the job market. The College offers attractive housing options to its students, with 90 percent of students residing on campus all four years.

Location

Assumption College, located on a beautifully landscaped 175-acre campus in the residential Westwood Hills of Worcester, is just a short distance from downtown. Worcester, the second-largest city in New England, is a five-time recipient of the All-America City Award—the nation's oldest and most prestigious community recognition program. The city is a vibrant community, offering students opportunities for internships, service learning, and community service as well as for culture and recreation. Worcester has the nationally acclaimed Worcester DCU Center, one of the country's busiest arenas for concerts, conferences, and shows. It is home to the renowned Worcester Art Museum and Higgins Armory Museum and unique Ecotarium. Nearby facilities for winter and summer sports include Wachusett Mountain and Lake Quinsigamond. Ethnic restaurants and shopping abound. Worcester is also centrally located, with Boston, Providence, Rhode Island, and Hartford, Connecticut, an hour's drive away.

Majors and Degrees

The College offers Bachelor of Arts degrees in accounting, biology, biology with concentration in biotechnology and molecular biology, chemistry, classics, communications (with tracks in organizational communication and in writing and mass communications), computer science, economics, economics with business concentration, economics with international concentration, education (accompanying an appropriate major), English, environmental science, foreign languages, French, French with concentration in Francophone culture and civilization, global studies, global studies with business concentration, history, human services and rehabilitation studies, international business, Italian studies, Latin American studies, management, marketing, mathematics, music, philosophy, political science, psychology, sociology, sociology with concentration in criminology, Spanish, Spanish with concentration in Hispanic culture and civilization, theology, and visual arts.

With the exception of global studies and organizational communication, minors are available in all disciplines. Minors are also available in anthropology, art history, community service learning, comparative literature, finance, foundations of Western civilization, French studies, geography, German studies, law and economics, music, peace and conflict studies, studio arts, theater and television arts, and women's studies. Preprofessional preparation is available for dentistry, medicine, and law. Joint seven-year programs are also available for those interested in physical therapy, podiatry, or optometry. The College offers a First-Year Program, Honors Program, Foundations of Western Civilization Program, study abroad, internships (credit or noncredit), and cross-registration through the Colleges of Worcester Consortium. Air Force and Army ROTC are also available.

Academic Programs

Father Emmanuel d'Alzon, founder of the Assumptionists, dedicated Assumption College to the "pursuit of truth, wherever it may be found." The College continues that pursuit of truth through the liberal education program. The students and faculty come together to contemplate the books, ideas, people, and events that have shaped civilization, so that the students might be better prepared to make their own contributions in the future.

Finding the truth about oneself and the nature of the surrounding world means learning not only how to ask questions but how to find the answers. That is why so many of the classes at Assumption are discussions, not lectures, and why the faculty assigns cooperative projects, frequent writing, and hands-on assignments designed to teach the student how to think, not memorize.

Assumption College follows a traditional two-semester calendar, running from late August to mid-May. The Continuing Education and Graduate School offers two summer sessions for its students. A January intersession is also available.

Students must complete a core curriculum of two courses of English, one of which is composition; two courses of philosophy; two courses of theology; two of the following three courses: mathematics, a laboratory science, and a third year of a foreign language; and one each of literature, history, social science, and either art, music, or theater. A total of 120 semester credit hours must be completed.

Off-Campus Programs

In 1968, Assumption College joined with the other institutions of higher learning in the Worcester area to organize the Colleges of Worcester Consortium. Through the cooperation of thirteen Worcester area colleges, Assumption students may cross-register for academic credit at any of the participating colleges and may enjoy cultural events through those colleges.

Assumption College encourages qualified students to spend a semester or year abroad as an integral part of their undergraduate education. In the past five years, Assumption College students have studied abroad in Australia, Austria, Chile, China, Costa Rica, the Czech Republic, England, France, Germany, Greece, Ireland, Italy, Japan, the Netherlands, and Spain.

Students at Assumption practice classroom theories through internships designed to help them explore their professional choices and broaden their workplace skills. For example, local, national, and international sites where current Assumption students have completed internships in the past few years include PBS, the U.S. House of Representatives, Ralph Lauren, the Hungarian Embassy, Smith Barney, Fidelity, the Late Show with David Letterman, ABC News, Dean Witter Reynolds, AT&T, and SONY Japan.

Academic Facilities

Assumption College has recently completed a six-year, $60-million physical plant expansion program. The flagship of this building program is the new Testa Science Center, which is the home of the Department of Natural Sciences and includes biology, chemistry, environmental science, and physics. The facility features five multiuse classrooms (most of which have state-of-the-art technology), ten teaching laboratories, seven laboratories dedicated for faculty and student research, two conference rooms, a greenhouse, and inviting, open-air lounge areas. To ensure campuswide utilization, the south atrium has been outfitted with a sound system for lectures, receptions, and other special events.

The Information Technology Center houses public-access labs and technology-rich classrooms with more than 150 computers as well as help staff for the community. Equipment and software are available for standard applications and free laser printing as well as Web authoring, graphics and animation, digital video, and multimedia production. The College also has a new digital audio studio available for all students and faculty members. All resident students have broadband Internet access from their rooms as well as in the computer labs. In 2003, Assumption College received a grant from the National Science Foundation for network infrastructure to connect to Internet2. The purpose is to develop and implement a high-performance network connection (Internet2) that is separate from the Internet and dedicated exclusively to research and education in all subject areas.

Costs

For 2007–08, tuition is $27,320 and room and board charges are $9492. The board plan is required for all freshmen and for all residents without cooking facilities. A student government fee and orientation fee is $430. The total for tuition, room and board charges, and the fee is $37,242.

Financial Aid

Assumption College offers financial aid based on demonstrated need and scholastic promise. The College requires the Free Application for Federal Student Aid (FAFSA). This form should be filed by February 1 so that Assumption receives the processed application by the March 1 deadline.

The College offers merit awards up to $16,000 to qualified students. Monies given through this program reflect the College's commitment to upholding a campus culture that champions academic excellence and student leadership. All applicants for admission are considered for these awards.

Faculty

Assumption College faculty members—94 percent of whom hold doctoral or terminal degrees in their field—represent diverse fields of specialization and a wide range of professional experience. They are distinguished by an unusually deep dedication to their students, putting in far more than the minimum requirement of 10 office hours a week.

Student Government

As a very active organization, the Student Government Association (S.G.A.) attempts to move closer to the fulfillment of the ideals of self-government. The elected representatives of the student body constitute the Student Senate of S.G.A. This group is responsible for the recognition and financing of student clubs and activities and for serving as the official means of communication and coordination with the Assumption College student community.

Admission Requirements

Admission to Assumption College is limited to men and women of character, intelligence, and motivation who are selected from applicants who have completed the prescribed secondary school requirements. Assumption College supports the efforts of secondary school officials and governing bodies to have their schools achieve regional accredited status to provide reliable assurance of quality of the education preparation of its applicants for admission.

Application and Information

Campus visits are strongly recommended. Appointments can be scheduled Monday through Friday. Group Information Sessions are held most Saturdays in the fall.

Applicants must submit a completed application, a $50 application fee, official transcripts, SAT or ACT scores, a recommendation, and an essay. All applications for the freshman class, as well as all supporting credentials, must be filed in the Office of Admissions by February 15. Applications for early action must be received by November 15. In addition to the Assumption Application, students may complete the Common Application and Supplement and may apply online at the College's Web site or at http://www.commonapp.org.

For more information, students should contact:

Office of Admissions
Assumption College
500 Salisbury Street
P.O. Box 15005
Worcester, Massachusetts 01609-1296
Phone: 508-767-7285
866-477-7776 (toll-free)
E-mail: admiss@assumption.edu
Web site: http://www.assumption.edu

The flagship of Assumption's six-year, $60-million physical plant expansion program is the Testa Science Center.

BABSON COLLEGE

WELLESLEY, MASSACHUSETTS

The College

Since its founding in 1919, Babson College has focused on educating business leaders capable of initiating and managing change, navigating ethical choices, and solving the problems of today and tomorrow. Students are immersed in an enriching environment that fosters leadership, teamwork, creativity, communication, and diversity. The 2007–08 undergraduate enrollment was 730 women and 1,069 men. An independent, coeducational institution, Babson is accredited by AACSB International–The Association to Advance Collegiate Schools of Business and by the New England Association of Schools and Colleges.

Babson is a residential college and is a 24-hours-a-day, seven days-a-week community alive with intellectual, cultural, athletic, and social activities. Approximately 83 percent of the undergraduate student body live on campus in fourteen residence halls. Housing options include coed residence halls, fraternity and sorority housing, and substance-free, multicultural, entrepreneurial, and other-themed housing.

Babson College is an NCAA Division III school, and most of the College's intercollegiate teams compete in the New England Women's and Men's Athletic Conference (NEWMAC). There are twenty-two men's and women's varsity sports teams, with additional club and intramural sports available to all students.

The Webster Center features an indoor, 200-meter, six-lane track; a field house; a gymnasium with three basketball courts; a racquetball court; a 25-yard, six-lane pool with 1- and 3-meter diving boards; a fitness center; squash courts; and a dance/aerobics studio. The Babson Skating Center features a 600-seat skating arena. Outdoor facilities include eight tennis courts, a new AstroTurf field, a game field, a renovated softball diamond, a baseball field, two sand-based varsity fields, and a club rugby field.

Location

Babson's beautiful 370-acre campus is in Wellesley, Massachusetts, 14 miles west of Boston, a city renowned for its cultural and recreational opportunities. More than sixty colleges and universities bring more than 250,000 college students to the Boston area, making it one of the world's best college towns for cultural exchange and research.

Majors and Degrees

Babson offers a Bachelor of Science degree, a Master of Business Administration degree, custom degree programs, and executive education programs for business professionals.

Academic Programs

The curriculum breaks down the artificial barriers between disciplines by emphasizing an integrated, holistic approach to learning. The curriculum integrates core competencies, key business disciplines, and the liberal arts into foundation, intermediate, and advanced programs. Babson's core competencies include rhetoric, quantitative analysis, entrepreneurial and creative thinking, global and multicultural perspectives, ethics and social responsibility, leadership and teamwork, and critical and integrative thinking.

These learning outcomes are introduced and reinforced as students progress through the undergraduate curriculum. The Foundation Program lays the groundwork, raising students' abilities to formulate, explore, and reflect critically. In the second year, students proceed to the Intermediate Program, which adds breadth, elaborates issues, and exposes them to more disciplinary and interdisciplinary analyses. The Advanced Program challenges students to think about issues with increased confidence, independence, and creativity.

Foundation Program courses may include quantitative methods with calculus, probability and statistics, financial accounting, rhetoric, arts and humanities, history and society, business law, science, and Foundations of Management and Entrepreneurship (FME), a yearlong immersion into the world of start-ups, where student teams actually create their own businesses, receiving grants of up to $3000 to cover costs. Babson is the only U.S. school to teach the management core curriculum as an integrated three-semester course where all aspects of business are covered, including accounting, marketing, finance, management operations, strategy, organizational behavior, IT sales, and economics.

In the Advanced Program, students are free to expand and fine-tune core competencies as they reflect on their own career and life goals. During this time, students take courses in advanced management and liberal arts electives. Babson offers twenty-four optional concentrations in both business and liberal arts disciplines. This way, students may further plan their own course of study by focusing on certain areas of interest while still continuing to benefit from Babson's interdisciplinary approach to learning. Students also have the opportunity to participate in field-based experiences such as an internship or consulting experience. Special programs, such as the Honors Program, the Women's Leadership Program, the Management Consulting Field Experience, the Accelerated Curriculum for Entrepreneurship, the Babson College Fund (student-managed endowment), Master of Science in Accounting (M.S.A.), and Independent Research allow students to take advantage of customized learning opportunities at Babson.

Babson's flexible curriculum allows students to pursue courses that appeal to them and align with their goals. To aid in the decision-making process, students receive guidance from faculty mentors and professional staff throughout their four years.

To earn the Bachelor of Science degree, students are required to complete a minimum of 128 semester hours with a C average or better, with a minimum of 63 credits in the liberal arts (including 20 credits in advanced liberal arts). Transfer students must complete a minimum of 64 semester hours at Babson. Once a student has earned 96 credits, all remaining credits must be earned at Babson, at a Babson-approved cross-registration program, or at a Babson-affiliated Study Abroad Program.

Entering students may be granted credit or advanced course placement for successful scores on Advanced Placement (AP) examinations administered by the College Board as well as some courses in the International Baccalaureate (IB) curriculum.

The College operates on a two-semester academic calendar; semesters run from September to December and from late January through May. An optional credit-bearing three-week winter session is offered in January, and a summer session is offered from late May to mid-July.

Off-Campus Programs

Babson students can also take a course each semester at one of the other area colleges, including Brandeis University and Wellesley College, for full academic credit. These off-campus programs offer greater access to liberal arts courses, including a wide range of foreign languages.

In addition, Babson has a partnership with the Franklin W. Olin College of Engineering, an independent institution that opened in 2001 and is located on a 70-acre site adjacent to Babson. Babson and Olin are collaborating academically in order to provide extraordinary opportunities in technology-based business, including joint academic and research programming, engineering, and entrepreneurial thinking.

Babson's vibrant study-abroad program enables students to spend either a summer or one or both semesters of their junior year overseas at a college or university. Currently, forty-two programs are offered in twenty-three countries, and full academic credit is given for approved management and liberal arts courses.

Academic Facilities

Horn Library houses an extensive business collection of print, media, and computerized information resources. Students have campuswide access to newspapers, journals, investment analyst reports, corporate records, directories, and international information. They also benefit from numerous electronic research and news services that supplement a selection of the best business and liberal arts books, newspapers, journals, CD-ROMs, audiocassettes, videocassettes, and videodiscs.

Horn Computer Center is equipped with a lab that remains open 24 hours a day. Wireless access is available in the library and computer center, Reynolds Center, Olin Hall, and all residence halls. All systems in Horn also have active connections to the Babson network, and the entire campus has access to e-mail, the World Wide Web, and software. Every incoming Babson undergraduate student receives a leased laptop computer with integrated Wi-Fi wireless technology as part of the College's technology initiative.

Other facilities are the Donald W. Reynolds Campus Center, the Richard W. Sorenson Family Visual Arts Center, the Richard W. Sorenson Center for the Arts, the Glavin Family Chapel, and the Arthur M. Blank Center for Entrepreneurship.

Costs

For 2007–08, tuition and fees were $34,112. The total estimated cost for a residential student was $45,782.

Financial Aid

Babson is committed to educating students from diverse backgrounds; applying for financial aid does not affect a student's chances of being admitted to Babson College. Financial assistance is awarded on the basis of merit and demonstrated financial need. Assistance for students begins with consideration for student loans and work-study. Those with need beyond the loan and work-study amounts are also considered for Babson grants.

In 2007–08, nearly 40 percent of all first-year students received need-based Babson grants. More than half of Babson students receive some form of financial assistance. Students should note that need-based financial assistance is available to U.S. citizens and permanent residents of the United States. Babson's merit scholarships include Weissman Scholarships, Presidential Scholarships, the Women's Leadership Awards, and the Diversity Leadership Awards. Application for aid is made by submitting the Free Application for Federal Student Aid (FAFSA) and the Financial Aid PROFILE of the College Scholarship Service. The application deadline for first-year undergraduate students is February 15; for transfer students, April 15.

Faculty

Because of Babson's close-knit community, students are able to form close relationships with the faculty. Of the 235 faculty members, 157 are full-time, and 91 percent of the full-time faculty members hold a doctoral degree or its equivalent. Faculty members are accomplished entrepreneurs, executives, scholars, authors, researchers, poets, and artists who bring an intellectual diversity that adds depth to Babson's educational programs and offers students a rich, challenging experience. Babson's student-faculty ratio is 14:1, with an average class size of 29. Most importantly, faculty members teach 100 percent of the courses.

Student Government

Students are encouraged to take an active role in campus activities and student government. The Student Government Association promotes students' interests; allocates funds to campus organizations for academic, social, and recreational activities; licenses student-run businesses; and helps formulate and maintain student regulations. There are over seventy student clubs and organizations currently on campus.

Admission Requirements

In selecting new students, the admission office considers each candidate's biographical data, transcripts, test scores, personal statements, and references. Evaluation is based upon comparisons of the qualifications of those who apply. To a large extent, the degree of competition is set by the caliber of the applicants themselves. Consideration is given to the depth and rigor of each candidate's academic program, academic motivation and achievement, and progress from one year to the next. Prospective students are strongly encouraged to have completed or be currently enrolled in a precalculus math class.

The Admission Committee carefully reviews courses taken, math aptitude, and standardized test scores. Reading and writing skills as well as verbal expression are measured using English grades, essays, and standardized test scores. Intangible personal qualities are also important—leadership, creativity, enthusiasm, and an overall good fit with Babson that includes a willingness to contribute to the community in meaningful and positive ways. There is no standard format for submitting this information, so Babson relies on letters of recommendation, references, and personal statements. In addition, the College evaluates extracurricular activities and work experience, seeking candidates who have exceptional leadership qualities and have participated in activities that have potential carryover to college. Efforts are made to enroll students with diverse backgrounds and experiences.

The College offers three application plans: regular decision, early decision, and early action. For more information about these plans and their deadlines, prospective students should visit the College's Web site (http://www.babson.edu/ugrad). Campus visits and group information sessions with an admission counselor are strongly recommended.

Application and Information

For further information or application forms, students should contact:

Lunder Undergraduate Admission Center
Babson College
Babson Park, Massachusetts 02457-0310
Phone: 781-239-5522
800-488-3696 (toll-free)
Fax: 781-239-4006
E-mail: ugradadmission@babson.edu
Web site: http://www.babson.edu/ugrad

BARD COLLEGE AT SIMON'S ROCK

GREAT BARRINGTON, MASSACHUSETTS

The College

Simon's Rock is the only four-year residential college of the liberal arts and sciences specifically designed to provide bright, highly motivated students with the opportunity to begin college after the tenth or eleventh grade. Students who successfully complete the requirements receive the Associate of Arts (A.A.) degree after two years of study and the Bachelor of Arts (B.A.) degree after four. Full- and partial-tuition scholarships are available. The average age of entering students is 16.

Simon's Rock challenges the traditional assumption that students must be 18 before they can be asked to develop seriously their intelligence, imagination, and self-discipline. Students at Simon's Rock pursue an academic program that enables them to fulfill their potential at an age when their interest, energy, and curiosity are at a peak.

The College was founded in 1964 by Elizabeth Blodgett Hall, former headmistress of Concord Academy, and first admitted students in 1966. Since its inception, Simon's Rock has based its program on a set of assumptions that over forty years of experience have proved to be valid: that highly motivated students of high school age are fully capable of engaging in college work, that they are best able to develop in a small-college environment, that serving these students well requires a faculty committed to distinction in teaching and scholarship as well as active participation in the students' social and moral development, that a coherent general education in the liberal arts and sciences should be the foundation for such students, and that an early college founded on these assumptions should serve as a model for reform in American education.

In 1979, Simon's Rock became a part of Bard College, located 50 miles away at Annandale-on-Hudson, New York.

Location

The College is built on over 200 rolling and wooded acres 2 miles west of Great Barrington, a town of 8,500, in the Berkshire Hills of western Massachusetts. Boston and New York City are 140 miles away; Albany and Springfield are 40 miles away. The Berkshires' natural beauty and wide variety of cultural attractions make the area an unusually attractive place in which to live. The countryside provides excellent terrain for hiking, bicycling, cross-country and Alpine skiing, canoeing, and climbing. The Tanglewood Music Festival, Jacob's Pillow Dance Festival, and numerous summer theaters are located in nearby towns. Great Barrington itself is a thriving business community with a variety of schools and service agencies in which Simon's Rock students work and volunteer.

Majors and Degrees

Simon's Rock offers programs leading to the A.A. and B.A. degrees in the liberal arts and sciences. Students may complete their B.A. studies with a concentration in most traditional disciplines or choose one of several interdisciplinary concentrations.

Academic Programs

The academic program at Simon's Rock combines a substantial and coherent required core curriculum in the liberal arts and sciences with electives and extensive opportunities for students to pursue their own interests through advanced courses and independent study. The program is designed to engage students in the life of the mind by making them aware of their cultural heritage, introducing them to the spectrum of thought in the arts and sciences, and empowering them to satisfy their curiosity by thinking and learning independently.

Because Simon's Rock students begin college earlier than their peers, the College is particularly conscious of its responsibility to ensure that all students develop the skills and knowledge expected of an educated person. The core curriculum comprises approximately half of students' total academic load during their first two years. Requirements include a writing and thinking workshop, which new students attend during the week before the regular semester begins; first-year, sophomore, and cultural perspectives seminars; and courses in the arts, mathematics, natural science, and foreign language. The College also requires that students participate in a recreational athletics program and attend a series of health and wellness programs.

All new students are assigned a faculty adviser, who meets with them weekly during their first semester and regularly throughout the rest of their career at Simon's Rock. Classes are small, faculty members are accessible, and the opportunities for students to pursue diverse interests are extensive.

The curriculum of the first two years at Simon's Rock leads to the A.A. in liberal arts. Students who successfully complete the A.A. requirements may continue at Simon's Rock for a B.A. or transfer to Bard College or another college or university to complete their baccalaureate degree. About one third of each class remains to complete a B.A. at Simon's Rock in one of thirty-four interdisciplinary concentrations; two thirds choose to transfer. The transfer record of Simon's Rock A.A. graduates is excellent.

Students wishing to stay at Simon's Rock for a B.A. must apply for admission to a major through a process called Moderation. At a formal conference, a faculty Moderation Committee and the student review the student's accomplishments and together plan the remainder of the student's education program. Students suggest and are advised of junior- and senior-year opportunities. These traditionally include advanced seminars, independent study involvement in faculty research projects, specialized tutorials, internships, courses at Bard, and a possible semester or full year of study abroad.

The senior thesis is the focus of each B.A. student's final year. Drawing on the skills in analysis and synthesis acquired during the previous three years, students devote themselves wholeheartedly to the project and to learning, which has been personally defined and developed. Recent theses have taken many forms: critical studies in literature, sociological research, musical compositions, creative fiction, translations, scientific experiments, mathematical problem solving, artistic exhibitions and performances, and various combinations of these forms.

The regular academic program is supplemented by extensive co-curricular offerings, including annual poetry, fiction, concert, humanities, women's studies, and lecture series.

Simon's Rock offers three signature programs. The first is the Simon's Rock/Columbia University Engineering Program. This ambitious program offers three years at Simon's Rock and two years in the engineering school at Columbia University in New York. At the end, students receive both a B.A. from Simon's Rock and a B.S. from Columbia's School of Engineering and Applied Science. Simon's Rock also offers similar arrangements with the engineering schools at Dartmouth University and Washington University in St. Louis.

Through Simon's Rock Scholars at Oxford, a select group of Simon's Rock students are admitted to spend their junior year at Lincoln College of the University of Oxford in England each year. Founded in 1427, Lincoln College is one of the oldest and most esteemed of the Oxford Colleges. Simon's Rock Scholars at Oxford are full members of Lincoln College, live on the grounds at Lincoln, are taught by the regular faculty members at Oxford, and have access to the rich resources and facilities of the University.

Simon's Rock students also have the opportunity to study at Bard College at Annandale. One of the country's most innovative colleges of the liberal arts and sciences is fifty miles down the road—and it is accessible to Simon's Rock students. Upper-college students can take classes at Bard's campus in Annandale-on-Hudson, New York, or work on their senior theses while spending a semester in residence at the Annandale campus. Students can also take advantage of Bard's study-abroad programs; its groundbreaking Manhattan-based Globalization and International Affairs Program; and the Bard Rockefeller Program, a collaborative venture with Rockefeller University offering advanced research opportunities in medicine and the sciences.

Off-Campus Programs

Students pursue a variety of study-abroad programs and options. The Simon's Rock Win Resource Commons works with students to find study-abroad opportunities suited to their goals and interests. They use established independent programs (the School for Field Studies, Semester at Sea, Global Routes), programs through other schools (Oxford University, the Sorbonne, Bogazici University in Istanbul, Turkey), and special Simon's Rock programs (fieldwork in geography in China and in politics and culture in Ghana). The result is something very different from the standard tour of famous sites. Students have recently taken intensive math instruction at Central European University in Budapest, Hungary; helped build a school in a remote village in northern Thailand; and served as apprentices to dancers, drummers, mask carvers, and batik artists in Bali. Students can also take advantage of Bard's study-abroad and international programs, including special arrangements with universities in Germany, Russia, and South Africa and intensive language immersion programs in China, France, Germany, Italy, Japan, Morocco, Mexico, and Russia. Programs can last for a semester, a full academic year, or shorter periods during the breaks

Academic Facilities

The 16,000-square-foot Fisher Science and Academic Center was completed in 1998. The center houses the College's biology, chemistry, ecology, and physics laboratories; research labs for faculty members and students; classrooms and tutorial rooms; a sixty-seat lecture center; and faculty offices. The 50,200-square-foot Daniel Arts Center, which opened in the fall of 2004, incorporates a 350-seat theater and concert hall, a black box theater, a dance studio, and rehearsal facilities; painting, drawing, photography, ceramics, metalworking, printmaking, 3-D, video production, and digital arts studios; exhibit areas; and spaces for large-scale art and set construction. A music hall, a recording studio, and music practice rooms are also available to students in the arts. The campus library houses 68,000 volumes and collections of recordings and periodicals, a listening room, and a language laboratory. Simon's Rock students also have access to the Bard College library. An interlibrary loan system provides access to other college and university collections. The Kilpatrick Athletic Center, a 53,000-square-foot athletic complex with squash courts, a basketball court, an elevated track, a swimming pool, and a full-service fitness center, was completed in 1999.

Costs

For 2007–08, tuition and fees were $36,550, and room and board were $9730. For first-year students, there is also an orientation fee.

Financial Aid

Simon's Rock is committed to making an early college education available to a diverse group of highly motivated, academically qualified students. U.S. citizens and permanent residents are eligible to apply for federal and state financial assistance programs as well as institutional scholarships and grants. International students are eligible to receive Simon's Rock scholarships and grants. Approximately 80 percent of students receive some form of financial aid.

Applicants wishing to be considered for an Acceleration to Excellence Program merit scholarship must submit their applications by February 1.

Faculty

The College has approximately 40 full-time faculty members, most of whom hold either an earned doctorate or an equivalent terminal degree in their field. Simon's Rock supplements this full-time faculty with visiting scholars, regular adjunct faculty members in music and studio arts, and part-time faculty members in other areas as needed. Faculty members are distinguished not only by their excellence in teaching and advising but also by their sensitivity to the particular developmental needs of the College's younger students.

Student Government

Students at Simon's Rock participate in the decision making and governance of the community through elected and appointed positions on College committees that oversee academic and social life. The campus is characterized by respect for individual rights and a strong sense of community.

Admission Requirements

Simon's Rock seeks students who are smart, independent-minded, self-directed, creative, and passionate about learning. The admission staff recognizes its special responsibility to work closely with prospective students and their parents to ensure that the decision to enter Simon's Rock is the right one. For this reason, a personal interview is required of each applicant. The application also requires an official high school transcript, two letters of recommendation, writing samples, and a parent's statement. Standardized test scores are optional for most applicants; however, international students for whom English is not a first language must submit TOEFL scores.

Application and Information

Candidates should submit their materials by May 31 for fall admission. Applications are reviewed on a rolling basis year-round, and early application is strongly encouraged. Applicants are generally notified as to the Admission Committee's decision within several weeks of the time they complete their applications. The application fee is $50.

To schedule an interview or request further information, students should contact:

Office of Admission
Bard College at Simon's Rock
84 Alford Road
Great Barrington, Massachusetts 01230-2499
Phone: 800-235-7186 (toll-free)
Fax: 413-541-0081
E-mail: admit@simons-rock.edu
Web site: http://www.simons-rock.edu

BAY PATH COLLEGE

LONGMEADOW, MASSACHUSETTS

The College

Since its founding in 1897, Bay Path has been known as a place where learning is valued, knowledge is prized, and the leadership and spirit of its students are cultivated and celebrated. The College provides an education for undergraduate women that balances a strong arts and sciences foundation with career and professional preparation. Today, Bay Path offers more than thirty majors and minors to its undergraduates as well as graduate and certificate programs that are open to both men and women. Consistently ranked high by *U.S. News & World Report*, Bay Path College is a diverse campus community, with students from around the globe.

Students who come to Bay Path immediately discover the strong sense of community on campus. The small, supportive environment encourages and challenges students to push their limits academically and personally. All students are required to do an internship, co-op (paid internship), field work, or practicum, which provides them with valuable practical experience for their career and professional goals. Community service and leadership are also woven throughout the Bay Path experience, allowing students to embark on a journey of self-discovery that strengthens confidence while fostering a greater understanding of the world. The College's objective is twofold: to give students every advantage in the job market and graduate school and to educate students to become confident and resourceful contributors to the increasingly interdependent world.

Many of the students and guests who visit Bay Path for the first time immediately notice the tree-lined main driveway, wide green lawns, and immaculate grounds. Approximately 90 percent of first-year students live on campus in attractive residential halls that are wired for high-speed Internet, voice mail, and cable. The Blake Student Commons is the hub of the campus and houses Blake Dining Commons, Sullivan Career Development Center, a media theater, student lounges, a game room, Fleming Book and Gift Store, Carpe Diem Café, and Breck Fitness Center. Breck is equipped with a modern dance studio, cardio and Nautilus equipment, and free weights and also offers classes in yoga, dance, and aerobics.

Bay Path has more than forty student clubs and academic-sponsored organizations—including six NCAA Division III varsity teams (basketball, cross-country, soccer, softball, tennis, and volleyball), performing arts groups, and a literary magazine.

The College is accredited by the New England Association of Schools and Colleges and is a member of the College Entrance Examination Board, the Association of Independent Colleges and Universities in Massachusetts, the College Board, the National Association of College Admission Counselors, the National Association of Independent Colleges and Universities, and the Women's College Coalition. The paralegal programs at associate, baccalaureate, and certificate levels are approved by the American Bar Association. The five-year occupational therapy program is accredited by the Accreditation Council for Occupational Therapy Education of AOTA.

Location

The 48-acre Bay Path College is located in historic Longmeadow, Massachusetts, a residential community just south of Springfield, Massachusetts, and 20 miles north of Hartford, Connecticut. At Bay Path, students have the best of both worlds—a small-town atmosphere minutes from major metropolitan areas offering a multitude of opportunities from entertainment to cultural events to concerts. Both nearby cities have flourishing theaters, fine museums, and attractions (Six Flags New England is 10 minutes away) and civic centers that are the sites of numerous events as well as homes to major sport teams. Students wanting a change of scenery can go to nearby major shopping malls, more than fifty movie screens, and numerous clubs. The College also provides free van service to many off-campus locations.

Air, bus, and rail transportation are conveniently located nearby. Bay Path is 20 minutes from Bradley International Airport, 10 minutes from Amtrak, 1½ driving hours from Boston, and 2½ driving hours from New York City.

Majors and Degrees

Bay Path offers more than thirty majors and minors. Popular majors include accounting, biology, business, criminal justice, elementary/early childhood education, forensic science, interior design, legal studies (approved by the American Bar Association), liberal studies, occupational therapy, and psychology. Students can also declare a minor in fields such as the humanities, performing arts, Web technologies, and women's studies.

Through a dual-degree program, students in the occupational therapy major earn combined bachelor's and master's degrees, fulfilling the requirements of the American Occupational Therapy Association for certification. It also prepares students to take the National Board for Certification in Occupational Therapy in order to become registered occupational therapists.

Students electing to become biology majors with a preprofessional concentration in premedical or pre–veterinary studies can also take advantage of a partnership with Ross University's Schools of Medicine and Veterinary Medicine. This agreement with the largest veterinary and medical schools in the world allows Bay Path students who meet specific academic criteria the opportunity to receive early acceptance into Ross' programs.

Academic Programs

Beginning with the first semester of the first year, students can immediately enroll in courses in their major. This allows students to build and develop a strong knowledge base that, combined with the real-world opportunities of the Bay Path experience, ensures that every student has a competitive edge as they enter their chosen field or graduate school. To this end, each student is assigned an academic adviser in her field of study to assist in developing a plan of courses, offer academic advice, and provide referrals to other campus services.

For academically talented and motivated students, the College has a unique Honors Program that is interdisciplinary and seminar-based for the first two years. In the final two years, under the guidance of a faculty mentor, students explore new areas of knowledge and prepare an Honors thesis.

Internships, practicums, and co-ops (paid internships) are an integral part of all programs, and students are placed with professionals in local, regional, and national businesses, corporations, and organizations. Bay Path interns work in locations ranging from law firms, laboratories, decorating firms, insurance companies, and social service agencies to correctional facilities, schools, and hospitals.

First-year students at Bay Path are connected to the Sullivan Career Center as part of a four-year plan to help them reach career and life goals. Workshops, career counseling, and special events—such as the annual Career Summit—are just some of the services offered by the Career Center.

Off-Campus Programs

Through Bay Path's membership in the Cooperating Colleges of Greater Springfield (including Western New England College,

Springfield College, Elms College, American International College, Holyoke Community College, and Westfield State College), interested Bay Path students may take courses at these neighboring colleges, share networked library resources, and attend seminars or college-sponsored events.

The International Study Abroad Coordinator works with students to plan semester-long exchanges with countries such as France, Ireland, Australia, or England or a destination of choice. Typically, students participate for one semester during their junior year, but they can work with the International Study Abroad Coordinator to develop a plan to fit individual goals. Students may also spend a semester through special arrangements with Chaminade University (Hawaii) or American University in Washington, D.C.

Students also take part in courses, seminars, and projects, such as the Harvard Model United Nations, that offer ways to study other cultures and international issues. In addition, each year during spring break, the College offers the annual weeklong Capitals of the World Trip, which is open to all students.

Academic Facilities

The campus is a blend of traditional and modern, and many of the academic facilities have undergone major renovations to enhance the collaborative and personal learning experience that is a hallmark of a Bay Path education. Carr Hall, one of the main academic buildings, has recently undergone extensive updates. Carr houses a newly renovated and fully equipped theater, presentation and electronic classrooms, computer labs, science laboratories completely redesigned and equipped in the latest in scientific technology (examples include a state-of-the-art gene sequencer for DNA analysis in the forensic science program and high-end gas chromatography and infrared spectrometry for chemical analysis), and study areas with public-access computers. The science labs reflect labs in a typical working environment—whether a crime lab for forensic analysis or a biotechnology lab for testing and analysis.

D'Amour Hall for Business, Communications, and Technology features computer laboratories, a multimedia lab classroom, a video-editing studio, and technology-equipped presentation classrooms.

A preschool on campus provides opportunities for laboratory training for education majors.

Elliott House contains the occupational therapy laboratory, including a specially designed kitchen area and a children's playroom for unique problem solving in occupational therapy.

The Catok Art Center is specifically designed for the study and practice of art and also houses the interior design program.

Hatch Library has extensive book, periodical, tape, and record collections as well as a virtual library with more than sixty full-text online resources available 24 hours a day from any computer with Internet access.

Costs

Costs for 2007–08 were $22,073 for tuition and $9200 for room and board.

Financial Aid

Bay Path is keenly interested in admitting talented students who are serious about their education and encourages students to apply regardless of their financial means. Merit-based scholarships, need-based grants, loans, and employment opportunities are available. The Bay Path Merit Scholarship Program provides scholarship assistance that is renewable for four years. In addition, Bay Path has an aggressive scholarship program for transfer and international students. Financial aid applications are reviewed beginning February 1.

Faculty

The small size of the student population encourages the development of close professional interactions among students and Bay Path faculty members. Faculty members, experts in their fields, have teaching as their primary concern, but they devote many additional hours to participation with students in academic, social, and cultural activities. In fact, in the most recent National Survey of Student Engagement (based on student input from hundreds of colleges and universities), the quality of relationships between Bay Path students and faculty members contributes to an academic experience significantly greater than the national average. Fifty-eight percent of the full-time faculty members have a doctoral degree or a terminal degree in their field.

Student Government

The Student Government, composed of 4 officers and 40 student representatives, assists the administration in deciding a number of matters, leads the way in the observance of regulations, and helps to create a spirit of mutual understanding and cooperation between the student body and the College administration.

Admission Requirements

The satisfactory completion of a college-preparatory high school program or equivalent is required for admission. The Admissions Committee evaluates a student's academic record, class rank, and SAT or ACT test scores. Official transcripts are required, and an interview is encouraged. Transfer students are welcome and should submit transcripts of all previously attended colleges. Students are selected who are best qualified in ability, scholarship, leadership, and motivation to complete the College's program of study.

In accordance with state and federal laws, Bay Path College does not discriminate against any student who applies for admission or is enrolled at the College.

Application and Information

The College follows a rolling admissions policy and encourages students to apply early. Notification of decision is generally within two weeks of receiving the completed application and accompanying materials. The candidate reply is requested on or before May 1 for September enrollment.

Students can apply free online or mail in a copy of the completed application. The completed application should be sent to the Office of Admissions, together with a $25 nonrefundable application fee or fee-waiver request.

Director of Admissions
Bay Path College
588 Longmeadow Street
Longmeadow, Massachusetts 01106
Phone: 413-565-1331
800-782-7284 (toll-free outside 413 area code)
Fax: 413-565-1105
E-mail: admiss@baypath.edu
Web site: http://www.baypath.edu

Blake Student Commons.

BAY STATE COLLEGE

BOSTON, MASSACHUSETTS

The College

Founded in 1946, Bay State College is a private, independent, coeducational institution located in Boston's historic Back Bay. Since its founding, Bay State College has been preparing graduates for outstanding careers and continued education.

The College primarily offers associate degrees and has expanded into bachelor degree offerings. The educational experience offered through the variety of associate and bachelor degree programs prepares students to excel in the career of their choice. Personalized attention is the cornerstone of a Bay State College education. Through the transformative power of its core values of quality, respect, and support, Bay State College has been able to assist students with setting and achieving goals that prepare them for careers and continued education. In fact, with it's First-Year Experience, a 1-credit course all students must complete, Bay State College students are exposed to the concept of "action planning." The Bay State College action plan is designed to help students identify their goals and set about a course of action to achieve those goals. Students review their action plan each semester with their academic adviser and evaluate how they are progressing on their plan. This is just one method Bay State College graduates apply to their lives beyond college. The ability to identify, set, and achieve goals is a trait all people aspire to master.

Recognizing that one of the most important aspects of college is life outside the classroom, the Office of Student Affairs seeks to provide services to Bay State College students from orientation through graduation and beyond. There are many clubs and organizations on the campus, such as the Criminal Justice Society, the Early Childhood Education Club, the Student Government Association, and the Entertainment Management Association. Bay State College students enjoy the opportunity to create clubs and organizations that meet their interests. Special events throughout the year include a fashion show and a host of events produced by the Entertainment Management Association. Students also enjoy sporting teams such as the Boston Red Sox.

To support the overall wellness of the student body, Bay State has partnered with the Body Evolver Fitness Club, where students can take advantage of a wide variety of fitness equipment and classes at a discounted rate.

One of the unique aspects of living at Bay State College is the residence halls. With their location in the historic Back Bay, the buildings are original Victorian townhouses and brownstones. Each building has its own character and charm that makes living on campus a distinctive experience. Each building has a computer lab with free Internet access, coin-operated laundry, vending machines, a house phone with free local calling, and a social lounge that includes cable television and a microwave oven. Each student room also has basic cable service and access to a wireless Internet network.

The Career Services office offers lifetime career assistance to both current students and alumni, continuing to provide assistance and support to them throughout their careers, with career-management counseling, workshops, career panels, guest speakers, resume and cover letter reviews, interview preparation, and job listings.

Bay State College is accredited by the New England Association of Schools and Colleges, is authorized to award the Associate in Science, Associate in Applied Science, and three Bachelor of Science degrees by the Commonwealth of Massachusetts, and is a member of several professional educational associations. Its medical assisting program is accredited by the Accrediting Bureau of Health Education Schools (ABHES). The physical therapist assistant program is accredited by the Commission on Accreditation in Physical Therapy Education (CAPTE) of the American Physical Therapy Association (APTA).

Location

Located in the historic city of Boston, Massachusetts, and surrounded by dozens of colleges and universities, Bay State College is an ideal setting in which to pursue a college degree. Tree-lined streets around the school are mirrored in the skyscrapers of the Back Bay. The College is located within walking distance of several major league sports franchises, concert halls, museums, the Freedom Trail, Boston Symphony Hall, the Boston Public Library, and the Boston Public Garden. World-class shopping and major cultural and sporting events help make college life an experience that students will always remember. The College is accessible by the MBTA, commuter rail, and bus and is near Boston Logan International Airport.

Majors and Degrees

Bay State College is continually reviewing, enhancing, and adding new programs to help graduates remain industry-current in their respective fields.

Bachelor's degrees are offered in entertainment management, fashion merchandising, and management.

Associate degrees are offered in business administration, criminal justice, early childhood education, entertainment management (with a concentration in recording arts production), fashion design, fashion merchandising, health studies, medical assisting, physical therapist assistant studies, retail business management, and travel and hospitality management.

Academic Programs

Bay State College operates on a semester calendar. The fall semester runs from early September to late December. The spring semester runs from late January until mid-May. A satellite campus is located in Middleborough, Massachusetts.

Bay State College also offers courses to working adults in its Continuing and Professional Education Division. The courses, offered in eight-week sessions, allow more flexibility for students who must balance work and family commitments while pursuing their education.

Off-Campus Programs

The internship program, available in all major areas of study, provides practical field experience so that students can gain skills and experience with the technologies used in their respective fields. Field work is a requirement for many majors and is a great opportunity for students to build resumes, apply what they have learned in the classroom, and gain competitive advantages in the job market.

Students from Bay State College are among the 250 students participating in the Walt Disney World College Program. During their stay at Walt Disney World, students receive on-the-job training and classroom experience. This is just one of the many internship possibilities for students each year at Bay State College.

Academic Facilities

The library has a combined book collection of approximately 5,300 books. In addition, Bay State College has 100 periodicals and 200 audiovisual titles. The College's sixty computers have access to the Internet and several databases for magazine and journal articles, including ProQuest Academic, LexisNexis Academic, JSTOR, Infotrac, Newsbank, EBSCO, the Internet Public Library, and the Library of Congress Research Tools. The library also participates in an interlibrary loan program with the Boston Regional Library System.

Costs

Tuition for 2008–09 for full-time students is $18,925 per year; room and board, $11,130 per year; application fee, $40; and student services fee, $375. The cost of books and additional fees varies by major. A residence hall security deposit of $200 is required of all resident students.

Financial Aid

Bay State College offers the following financial aid programs to qualified students: Bay State College grant, which ranges from $500 to $3000; Federal Pell Grant; MASSGrant/State Scholarship; Federal Supplemental Educational Opportunity Grant; Massachusetts No Interest Loan; Federal Perkins Loan; Federal Direct Stafford/Ford Loan. The College also offers numerous part-time employment and work-study opportunities during the academic year.

Faculty

There are 41 faculty members, with the majority holding advanced degrees and several holding doctoral degrees. The student-faculty ratio is 15:1.

Student Government

The Student Association serves as the voice of the Bay State College student body. It consists of a group of elected student representatives from the various academic programs. Roles and responsibilities of Student Association members include providing input on college policies and procedures, assuming leadership roles on campus, acting as a voice of the student body, and planning activities and events.

Elections are held every fall, and all students are encouraged to vote. The group comprises representatives from each College department, club, and organization, and membership spans all four class years.

Admission Requirements

An applicant to Bay State College must be a high school graduate, a current high school student working toward graduation, or a recipient of a GED certificate. The Office of Admissions recommends applicants to the associate degree programs have a minimum 2.0 GPA on a 4.0 scale and, if available, applicants may submit SAT or ACT scores. Applicants must receive the recommendation of a Bay State College Admissions Officer. Applicants to the bachelor's degree programs must have a minimum 2.3 GPA on a 4.0 scale and must also submit SAT or ACT scores. A personal interview is required for all students—parents are encouraged to attend. Students are responsible for arranging for their official high school transcripts, test scores, and letters of recommendation to be submitted to Bay State College. International applicants must also submit high school transcripts translated to English with an explanation of the grading system, a TOEFL score of at least 500 on the paper-based exam or 173 on the computer-based exam if English is not the native language, and financial documentation. Transfer students may transfer up to 30 credits from an accredited institution. The physical therapist assistant program and Evening Division have different or additional admission requirements. For more information about these programs, students should visit the Web site at http://www.baystate.edu.

The Bay State College Admissions Office notifies applicants of a decision within three weeks of receipt of the transcript and other required documents. When a student is accepted to Bay State College, there is a $100 nonrefundable tuition deposit required to ensure a place in the class, which is credited toward the tuition fee. Deposits are due within thirty days of acceptance. Once a student is accepted, a Bay State College representative creates a personalized financial plan that provides payment options for a Bay State College education.

Application and Information

Applications are accepted on a rolling basis. A $40 application fee is due with the application. The fall tuition payment due date is July 1; the spring tuition payment due date is December 1.

Applications should be submitted to:

Admissions Office
Bay State College
122 Commonwealth Avenue
Boston, Massachusetts 02116
Phone: 800-81-LEARN (toll-free)
Fax: 617-536-1735
E-mail: admissions@baystate.edu
Web site: http://www.baystate.edu

BECKER COLLEGE

WORCESTER AND LEICESTER, MASSACHUSETTS

The College

Located in the heart of Massachusetts, Becker College is a distinctive New England college. Becker College encompasses two individual, state-of-the-art wireless campuses that are located only 6 miles apart, each with its academic facilities, residence halls, dining hall, library, and fitness facilities. E. C. A. Becker founded the Worcester campus in 1887. The Leicester campus began as an academy in 1784 and is the nineteenth-oldest campus in the country. Both schools had sustained a long-standing tradition of high-quality education. In 1974, Becker and Leicester began working together to expand academic offerings and provide broader social and recreational opportunities for their students. As a result of their close cooperation, the two were formally consolidated in 1977 as the Worcester campus and Leicester campus of Becker College.

The two beautiful campuses offer students a choice as to the living environment that best suits their personal tastes. On the Worcester campus, gracious older homes have been restored and serve as residence halls. In Leicester, students may choose to live in restored homes or contemporary residence halls. Whether they live on or off campus, students share in the strong sense of community spirit that prevails at Becker.

Today, with an enrollment exceeding more than 1,200 men and women from eighteen states and twelve countries, Becker College continues the tradition of excellence. The innovative programs at Becker College are a carefully crafted blend of professional and liberal arts courses that contribute to the development of competent professionals and informed citizens.

Athletics are an important part of extracurricular activities for Becker students. More than 70 percent participate in some form of extracurricular intramural, recreational, or varsity sport. Becker College is a member of the NCAA Division III, ECAC. Athletics include baseball, basketball, cheerleading, cross-country, equestrian (a member of the Intercollegiate Horse Show Association, IHSA), field hockey, football, golf, ice hockey, lacrosse, soccer, softball, tennis, and volleyball.

Opportunities for extracurricular involvement are plentiful on and off campus. Students are encouraged to participate in numerous activities that enrich learning and enhance personal development. They are encouraged to get involved and have fun. There are several organizations on campus, including ALANA–Multicultural Club, Animal Health Club, B-GLHAAD–Gay Straight Alliance, Black Student Union, Community Service Club, Photography Club, Fitness Club, Music Club, Nursing Club, Residence Life Club, Ski/Snowboard Club, Student Activities Committee (SAC), Student Alumni Society (SAS), Student Government Association (SGA), the student newspaper (The *Becker Journal*), Travel Club, and the Yearbook Club. The school's Student Activities Committee plans student activities directly and through the various student organizations. Movies, comedians, musicians, entertainers, dances, trips, guest speakers, and other special events are hosted on and off campus.

Location

With campuses in Worcester and Leicester, Massachusetts, Becker College enjoys an ideal location and easy access. Becker's Worcester campus is situated in the Elm Park section of Worcester, a quiet area of tree-lined streets and lovely old homes that is a short walk from the downtown business district. With a population of 175,000, the city of Worcester is New England's second-largest urban center. The city is less than 1 hour from Boston, Massachusetts; Hartford, Connecticut; and Providence, Rhode Island and 3 hours from New York City. Air, rail, and bus transportation connect Worcester to all major points. The Worcester Regional Transit Authority provides regular bus service throughout the city.

Becker's Leicester campus surrounds the historic village green at the junction of Routes 9 and 56 in Leicester center. The town of Leicester is located 6 miles from the Worcester campus. Students on the Leicester campus have the opportunity to participate in the cultural, social, and recreational activities of the metropolitan area while living in a small New England town, rich in history that predates the American Revolution.

Becker's two campuses are completely wireless and are linked via campus shuttle.

Majors and Degrees

With more than twenty-three programs of study, Becker College offers programs leading to Bachelor of Science, Bachelor of Arts, and Associate of Science degrees. Majors include accounting, animal care, business administration, computer information, criminal justice, early childhood education, elementary education, equine management, exercise science, graphic design, health and fitness, hospitality and tourism, human resources, interior design, legal studies, liberal arts, management, marketing, nursing, paralegal, pre–veterinary medicine, psychology, sports management, video game design, video game production, veterinary science, and veterinary technology. Prospective students should visit the Web site at http://www.beckercollege.edu to view Becker's extensive list of majors.

Academic Programs

To graduate with a Bachelor of Arts or Bachelor of Science degree, students must complete a minimum of 122 credits with a cumulative GPA of 2.0 or higher. For an Associate in Science degree, a minimum of 60 credits with a GPA of 2.0 or higher is required. Thirty percent of the total credits must be in the area of general studies. Many programs require clinical fieldwork or internships for graduation; student gain invaluable hands-on experience and often outshine other graduates competing in the same field. In addition, all full-time students receive a laptop computer to ensure that they maximize the benefits of information technology.

Becker College operates on a two-semester academic calendar. Classes begin in September and end in May.

Off-Campus Programs

Becker is a member of the Colleges of Worcester Consortium, an association of fourteen Worcester-area colleges and universities that sponsors interlibrary loan services, social events, and a course cross-registration system to broaden course offerings. Full-time students may take one course per semester free of charge at any other consortium institution with permission of their faculty advisers. Member institutions include Anna Maria College, Assumption College, Atlantic Union, Clark University, College of the Holy Cross, Fitchburg State, Massachusetts College of Pharmacy, Nichols College, Quinsigamond Community College, Tufts University School of Veterinary Medicine, the University of Massachusetts Medical School, Worcester Polytechnic Institute, and Worcester State College.

Academic Facilities

Both campuses are entirely wireless.

The Academic Center on the Worcester campus contains the Ruska Library, state-of-the-art computer labs, science labs, classrooms, conference facilities, and a lecture hall.

The Leicester campus academic center contains classrooms, a lecture hall, and science and computer labs. Other facilities include an animal health center, a preschool, and a video production center.

Academic Support Centers are located on both campuses. The centers are dedicated to helping Becker students achieve academic success. Services include one-on-one and group content tutoring, study skills instruction and workshops, and writing seminars. The purpose of the Academic Support Centers is to provide appropriate academic assistance to all students. Professional staff members, peer tutors, and faculty members work together to foster a supportive learning environment. The staff engages in a partnership with students to help them achieve their goals. Academic support is available to all students at no additional cost.

Costs

For current tuition and fees, students should visit the Admissions home page at http://www.beckercollege.edu.

Financial Aid

Financial aid is available for all eligible students through federal, state, and Becker College programs. Approximately 100 percent of all Becker students who apply for aid receive some form of financial assistance. Financial aid comes in the form of grants and scholarships, student loans, and work-study. Most types of financial assistance require that a student demonstrate financial need. All students who wish to apply for aid must complete the Free Application for Federal Student Aid (FAFSA). The application deadline is rolling; however, students are encouraged to apply as soon as possible after January 1. Incoming freshmen receive financial aid award announcements beginning in March.

Faculty

Becker College has a faculty of 126 members. Becker faculty members are committed to personalized teaching and are one of the College's greatest resources. Becker professors have unique field experiences and interweave their classes with an invaluable hands-on perspective. The student-faculty ratio of 18:1 allows students to get the individual attention and recognition they deserve.

Student Government

The Student Government Association (SGA) is charged with overseeing all clubs and organizations and any activities funded by the student activity fee. SGA officers and members hold regular meetings to maintain and improve the quality of campus life, focusing on student needs and expectations. Membership may include elected representatives from each residence hall and the commuter population, as well as student leaders from many organizations.

Admission Requirements

To be considered for admission, students must submit a completed application, a $30 application fee, an official secondary school transcript, and SAT or ACT scores. One letter of recommendation is required and an essay is recommended. Students applying to health science majors are required to demonstrate proficiency in math and science. Becker College recognizes that all students are individuals and considers each applicant's personal strengths and achievements.

Application and Information

Applications are accepted on a rolling basis and reviewed upon receipt of all required materials. Most applicants are notified of admission decisions within two to three weeks of completion of their application. For more information, prospective students should contact:

Office of Admissions
Becker College
61 Sever Street
Worcester, Massachusetts 01609
Phone: 508-791-9241 Ext. 245
877-5BECKER (523-2537) (toll-free)
Fax: 508-890-1500
E-mail: admissions@beckercollege.edu
Web site: http://www.beckercollege.edu

The Student Center.

BENTLEY COLLEGE

WALTHAM, MASSACHUSETTS

The College

Bentley is a national leader in business education. Centered on education and research in business and related professions, Bentley blends the breadth and technological strength of a university with the values and student focus of a small college. A Bentley education combines an unparalleled array of business courses with hands-on technology experience and a strong foundation in liberal arts. Bentley also offers the Liberal Studies Major (LSM), an optional double major in business and liberal studies. The result is that students gain expertise for a competitive edge in today's economy and broad-based skills essential for success in all areas of life. In addition, Bentley has a five-year program that allows students to earn a bachelor's degree and a master's degree in only five years rather than the usual six. Bentley also offers two doctoral programs: accountancy and business.

About 80 percent of Bentley students (97 percent of freshmen) live on the campus, creating a spirited sense of community. Housing includes twenty-three residence halls and apartment-style buildings, featuring a choice of single-, double-, or triple-occupancy dorm rooms; apartments; or suites. Housing is guaranteed to students for all four years. All residence halls have common areas, which typically include study lounges, exercise facilities, TV lounges, and game rooms. Halls are renovated regularly to keep pace with student needs.

Bentley students live and learn in a multicultural environment that reflects and prepares them to thrive in today's diverse work world. International students representing over seventy countries are part of the Bentley community.

All students explore the topic of diversity in courses that promote respect for different perspectives, break down stereotypes, and embrace the vitality that a varied student body adds to the college experience. Supporting this commitment are offices such as the Multicultural Center, Spiritual Life Center, International Services, and the Women's Center.

The Student Center is the hub of campus activity. The center is home to Seasons dining hall, the 1917 Tavern that offers entertainment nearly every night, and more than 100 student clubs and organizations. Opportunities to get involved run the gamut of academic groups, the performing arts, campus media, fraternity and sorority life, and cultural organizations. Sponsored events and informal get-togethers are a regular part of campus life.

The Miller Center for Career Services (CSS) resources include an on-campus recruiting program involving 500 national and international companies, an online job-listing service available to Bentley students and alumni, an online database of student and alumni resumes, career fairs, and workshops on topics such as effective resume writing, interviewing, and job-search strategies. Thanks to these and other programs, more than 90 percent of Bentley students find employment or enroll in graduate school within six months of graduation.

Extensive athletic programs are a Bentley hallmark. Students choose among intramural and recreational sports and twenty-three varsity teams in NCAA Divisions I and II. The Dana Athletic Center houses a weight and fitness complex, an aerobics room, a full-service food court, a suspended track, refurbished locker rooms, and function spaces. It also holds a gym and basketball court, volleyball and racquetball courts, a competition-size pool with a diving tank, and saunas. Outdoor facilities include soccer and baseball fields, a track, lighted tennis courts, and other grass and Astroturf fields.

Location

Bentley's location, just minutes west of Boston, puts the city's many resources within easy reach. Boston is the country's ultimate college town, with the proverbial something for everyone. Options range from theater to art exhibits, dance clubs to alternative rock concerts, and championship sports to championship shopping. Students do not need a car to get around. The free Bentley shuttle makes regular trips to Harvard Square in Cambridge, which is a great location and just a quick subway ride from the heart of Boston. Boston also offers students many opportunities for internships and jobs after college.

Majors and Degrees

Bentley offers a strong curriculum, focusing on business, technology, and the liberal arts, which provides students with many options for shaping an academic program that fits their skills, interests, and career goals. Bachelor of Science (B.S.) degree programs enable students to gain in-depth knowledge and skills in specific business disciplines: accountancy, computer information systems, corporate finance and accounting, economics–finance, finance, information design and corporate communication, information systems audit and control, management, managerial economics, marketing, and mathematical sciences.

Bentley also offers Bachelor of Arts (B.A.) degree programs, with majors in English, history, international studies, liberal arts, media and culture, and philosophy. In addition, students can choose from a number of minors and concentration programs that offer them the opportunity to develop expertise in an area outside their chosen major. Students can choose to pursue the five-year program, which is the combined bachelor's and master's degree program.

In addition, the Liberal Studies Major (LSM), an optional double major in business and liberal studies, allows students to combine courses that fulfill general education requirements with related electives to pursue one of many concentrations. Students take the same number of courses but add another credential to their degree, helping them stand out to future employers.

Academic Programs

The 4,250 undergraduates who study at Bentley benefit from a unique integration of business and the liberal arts. As the largest business school in New England, Bentley offers remarkable depth in subjects such as accountancy, finance, information design and corporate communication, marketing, management, and computer information systems. In addition, there is a strong commitment to the liberal arts, which allows students to build skills in critical thinking, decision making, communication, and other areas essential to becoming a well-rounded, contributing member of the community. Ethics and social responsibility, which are key themes woven into both business and liberal arts offerings, are supported by Bentley's internationally renowned Center for Business Ethics and nationally ranked Service-Learning Center.

Over the course of four years, Bentley students develop a solid understanding of the latest technologies and the ways that businesses use them to stay competitive. They learn how to analyze and manage the mountains of information that drive today's business world.

The focus on information technology begins early, as all Bentley freshmen receive a laptop that is fully loaded and network ready. With computer ports and wireless coverage all over the campus—in classrooms, residence hall rooms, dining halls, and the library—students have incredibly fast and convenient access to the Internet, the Bentley network, and many other information sources. This commitment to high-tech learning is supported by an array of academic resources, including classrooms equipped with multimedia technology, student computer laboratories, and a Virtual Lab that offers online access to specialized software from anywhere on campus. Bentley is also home to six high-tech learning labs that give students hands-on experience with the technology they will use in their careers.

Off-Campus Programs

Hands-on experience is emphasized across the Bentley curriculum. Internships, group consulting projects, study abroad, service-learning assignments, and other opportunities allow students to apply classroom theory in the workplace and community.

Each year, through Bentley's nationally recognized Service-Learning Center, hundreds of students build valuable skills in business, communication, and teamwork while assisting nonprofit and community-based organizations both locally and internationally.

Bentley students can gain valuable insight into different countries and cultures by studying abroad. Programs that run for one week, one semester, or a full academic year take students to places such as Africa, Australia, Brazil, China, France, Italy, and Spain.

Internships in the U.S. and abroad enable students to fine-tune skills, explore interests, and make valuable connections. About 94 percent of students complete at least one internship during their Bentley career. Students can customize the experience to fit their career goals and timetable. CCS works with academic departments to coordinate internships, which typically offer course credit toward a Bentley degree. Many student internships lead to job offers before graduation.

Academic Facilities

Concepts and theories taught in the classroom are put to use in several hands-on, high-tech learning laboratories—each among the first of its kind in higher education—that include the financial Trading Room, Center for Marketing Technology, Accounting Center for Electronic Learning and Business Measurement, Center for Languages and International Collaboration, Media Arts Lab, and Design and Usability Center.

Bentley's financial Trading Room, the largest in higher education, combines state-of-the-art technology and real-time data to offer first-hand exposure to financial concepts. In simulated trading sessions, students build investment portfolios and analyze financial risk. Trading Room resources include Bloomberg, FactSet, DataStream, Wonda, and Thomson One Analytics.

The Center for Marketing Technology (CMT) houses the high-end hardware and software applications that are revolutionizing the marketing of products and services. Students learn the latest strategies for testing consumer preferences, creating ad campaigns, using databases to make marketing decisions, and more. CMT resources include Perseus Survey, SPSS, Qualitap, QuarkExpress, and other tools for exploring the complex forces that drive buying and selling in a global economy.

The Accounting Center for Electronic Learning and Business Management (ACELAB) introduces students to the cutting-edge tools and technologies that are reshaping the accounting profession. Students gain experience with auditing, tax preparation software, and other professional applications—skills they apply to tasks such as developing an accounting system and analyzing operational data for management decision making. Resources include software from industry leaders such as SAP and Oracle.

The Center for Languages and International Collaboration (CLIC) is a key resource for language courses, international studies majors, and all students who have an interest in global issues. The center features two satellite dishes and videoconference technology to promote collaboration among Bentley students and their counterparts overseas.

The Media Arts Lab features state-of-the-art resources for video production and editing as well as digital photography. The lab also provides students with industry-standard software programs for screenwriting, sound mixing, graphic design, and DVD authoring.

The Design and Usability Center (DUC) offers one of the most sophisticated testing facilities in the world. The DUC features two state-of-the-art testing labs ideal for usability testing, focus groups, and design workshops. Students use the same applications employed by technical communicators, Web developers, user-interface designers, and usability specialists. The goal is to create information technology products that users can intuitively understand and easily employ.

The Bentley library supports the school's academic programs with more than 140,000 book titles and 700 periodical subscriptions. The library is also well connected to sophisticated electronic databases such as Dow Jones/Bridge News Retrieval, LexisNexis, Westlaw, and InfoTrac 2000. The library also houses group study rooms, research computers, an art gallery, and a café.

Costs

Tuition for resident and nonresident students in the 2007–08 academic year was $31,450. Room and board (double room, meal plan) costs were $10,940. Additional expenses included books, supplies, laptop computer, and personal and travel expenses.

Financial Aid

Bentley administers about $70 million in undergraduate financial aid every year to ensure that all academically qualified students have access to educational choices regardless of financial resources. Assistance comprises scholarships, grants, loans, employment, and payment plans. Currently, more than 70 percent of Bentley's undergraduates receive some form of financial assistance.

Faculty

Bentley faculty members are respected teacher-scholars known equally well for their classroom skills and cutting-edge research. They bring practical, real-world experience to the classroom, based on years of professional involvement in their chosen fields. Faculty research focuses on issues of prime importance to current business practice, particularly topics where business intersects with technology and/or with the liberal arts. Much of the research is conducted in partnership with leading corporations and organizations. A student-faculty ratio of 12:1 and average class size of 25 ensure a personal experience for Bentley students. All courses are taught by professors; there are no teaching assistants.

Student Government

Bentley has a number of student governing associations, including the Student Government Association, Senior Class Cabinet, Greek Council, Hall Council Advisory Board, Media Board, Panhellenic Council, and the Graduate Student Association.

Admission Requirements

Students applying for admission to Bentley are encouraged to complete a competitive college-preparatory program. Recommendations include 4 years of English, 4 years of mathematics (preferably algebra I and II, geometry, and precalculus or its equivalent), and 3 to 4 years each of history, laboratory science, and a foreign language.

Along with the application, students must submit a secondary school transcript, letters of recommendation from a teacher and a counselor, and official scores of either the SAT or ACT, including the ACT writing test. The College has special applications for international students and transfer students. Applicants who are nonnative speakers of English must also have official scores of the Test of English as a Foreign Language (TOEFL) forwarded to the Office of Undergraduate Admission.

Application and Information

Bentley College accepts the Common Application. The application deadline for students planning to enter in September is January 15. For students planning to begin study in January, the deadline is November 15. Candidates for the fall semester are notified by April 1; spring semester candidates are notified on a rolling basis.

The Early Decision program is designed for academic achievers for whom Bentley is their first choice. Students who are admitted through this binding program agree to withdraw any applications submitted to other colleges. The Early Decision application deadline is November 15.

The Early Action program is designed for students who are seriously considering Bentley but are not prepared to commit through the Early Decision program. This program provides students with an earlier admission decision but gives them the ability to consider other options. The application deadline is November 15.

For more information, students should contact:

Office of Undergraduate Admission
Bentley College
175 Forest Street
Waltham, Massachusetts 02452-4705
Phone: 781-891-2244
800-523-2354 (toll-free)
Fax: 781-891-3414
E-mail: ugadmission@bentley.edu
Web site: http://www.bentley.edu

BERKLEE COLLEGE OF MUSIC

BOSTON, MASSACHUSETTS

The College

Berklee College of Music attracts the most creative music students in the world who know that no other music college or institution offers such a rich diversity of people, music, and programs. Students come here to discover their true music calling, pushing themselves past their own expectations and into the forefront of every aspect of the global music community.

Founded in 1945, Berklee College of Music is the world's largest accredited music college and the premier institution for the study of contemporary music. The College's 3,800 students from seventy-eight other countries and its more than 500 faculty members interact in an environment designed to provide the most complete learning experience possible, including all of the opportunities and challenges presented by a career in the contemporary music industry. Using Berklee's extensive facilities, students develop musical competencies in such areas as composition, performance, and recording/production and also learn to make the informed business decisions necessary for career success.

Berklee was founded on two revolutionary ideas: that musicianship could be taught through the music of the time and that students need practical, professional skills for successful, sustainable music careers. While the bedrock philosophy has not changed, the music has and requires that students evolve with it. For more than half a century, Berklee has demonstrated its commitment to this approach by wholeheartedly embracing change.

Berklee updates its curriculum and technology to make them more relevant and attract diverse students who reflect the multiplicity of influences in today's music. The College prepares its students for a lifetime of professional and personal growth through the study of the arts, sciences, and humanities and is developing new initiatives to reach and influence an ever-widening audience.

More than a college, Berklee has become one of the world's best learning labs for the music of today and tomorrow. It is a microcosm of the music world, reflecting the interplay between music and culture, and is an environment where aspiring music professionals learn how to integrate new ideas, adapt to changing musical genres, and showcase their distinctive skills in an evolving community. Berklee is at the center of a widening network of industry professionals who use their openness, virtuosity, and versatility to take music in surprising new directions. They focus on their musicianship, on the technologies that help shape this art form, on the intricacies and realities of the business and promotion of music, or on the leading thinking in music education and music therapy. Students start bands of their own, participate regularly in ensembles, go on tour, and take advantage of internships throughout the industry. They record student projects, score films, write, practice, and perform. What separates Berklee College of Music from other schools of music is the people—the faculty, the staff, the students, and the alumni who make up this extraordinary community.

Location

Berklee College of Music is located in Boston's Fenway Cultural District. An international hub of intellectual and creative exploration, the neighborhood includes treasure-filled museums and galleries and world-class performing arts centers such as Symphony Hall, the Wang Center, and the Berklee Performance Center. Boston is also home to many of the world's other great colleges and universities. In addition to the music made at Berklee, there is a lively club and concert scene in the area with coffee houses featuring folk and bluegrass music; neighborhood clubs offering jazz, reggae, and world music; and clubs specializing in rock, blues, dance, urban, and country-western music.

Berklee students participate in intramural sports and fitness programs at nearby institutions; watch Boston's professional sports teams play in the new TD Banknorth Garden or at Fenway Park or other area sports venues; attend theater, club, and concert hall events year-round throughout the city; and walk, skate, or bike through the city's many scenic parks and public gardens. The College is located within walking distance of Boston's public transportation system, allowing students to take advantage of all that Boston has to offer.

Majors and Degrees

Berklee offers a Bachelor of Music (B.M.) degree program and a four-year program leading to the professional diploma. Students may choose to major in composition, contemporary writing and production, film scoring, jazz composition, music business/management, music education, music production and engineering, music synthesis, music therapy, performance, professional music, and songwriting. The College also offers a five-year, dual-major option in which students graduate with an even more marketable education that expands their career options in the music industry.

Academic Programs

The Bachelor of Music program offers a complete music curriculum combined with liberal arts courses such as English, history, languages, mathematics, philosophy, and physical or social science. Intensive concentration in music subjects provides students with the necessary tools for developing their musical talents to the fullest and preparing for the multifaceted and ever-changing demands of today's professional music. The degree program is especially appropriate for students who wish to earn a formal degree, are interested in pursuing a career in music education, music therapy, or business/management or want to continue their studies at the graduate level.

The diploma is designed for students who want to focus exclusively on contemporary music studies and still get the benefits of a Berklee experience.

All students must complete the core music curriculum, which consists of harmony, arranging, ear training, and introduction to music technology; instrumental studies; ensembles and instrumental labs; and the concentrate courses designated for each major. All degree candidates must complete the general education curriculum and traditional music studies courses.

Off-Campus Programs

Through the Professional Arts Consortium (ProArts), an association of six area institutions of higher education dedicated to the performing and visual arts, Berklee students can take courses at leading Boston area arts institutions in such areas as communications, modern dance, visual arts, ballet, architectural and graphic design, theater arts, and liberal arts. The other members of the consortium are Boston Architectural Center, the Boston Conservatory, Emerson College, Massachusetts College of Art, and the School of the Museum of Fine Arts.

Students who major in music business/management may be eligible to receive credit for their Berklee course work toward an M.B.A. from Suffolk University.

The Berklee International Network is a shared endeavor designed to promote the effectiveness of contemporary music education among members and to advance the value of contemporary music education internationally. Berklee faculty and staff members visit network member schools annually to conduct workshops and clinics and to audition students for scholarships for full-time study at Berklee. There are currently fifteen members of the network: Fundacio L'Aula de Musica Moderna i Jazz in Barcelona, Spain; Rimon School of Jazz and Contemporary Music in Ramat Hasharon (Tel Aviv), Israel; Phillipos Nakas Conservatory in Athens, Greece; Music Academy International in Nancy, France; American School of Modern Music in Paris, France; Instituto de Musica Contemporanea Universidad San Francisco de Quito in Quito, Ecuador; Pop and Jazz Conservatory in Helsinki, Finland; Koyo Conservatoire in Kobe, Japan; PAN School of Music in Tokyo, Japan; Jazz and Rock Schule in Freiburg, Germany; International College of Music in Kuala Lumpur, Malaysia; Academia de Musica Fermatta, Mexico City, Mexico; Conservatorio Souza Lima in São Paulo, Brazil; Seoul Jazz Academy in Seoul, Korea; and the Newpark Music Centre in Dublin, Ireland.

Academic Facilities

Berklee students have the chance to work in the College's state-of-the-art music technology facilities, using some of the most sophisticated recording and synthesis equipment currently available, in addition to facilities specifically designed for the areas of composition, arranging, and film scoring. The facilities at Berklee are furnished with the instruments and equipment that are being used in the world beyond the classroom. Berklee's performance facilities include the Berklee Performance Center, a 1,200-seat concert hall hosting more than 300 student, faculty, and other concerts each year; four recital halls equipped with a variety of sound reinforcement systems; more than forty ensemble rooms; seventy-five private instruction studios; 300 private practice rooms; and an outdoor concert pavilion.

Technological facilities include the Recording Studio Complex, consisting of twelve studio facilities that include 8-, 16-, and 24-track digital and analog recording capability; synthesis labs, featuring more than 250 MIDI digitally equipped synthesizers, drum machines, sequencers, and computers, including hard-disk recording; Learning Center, equipped with forty computer-based MIDI workstations; Professional Writing Division MIDI Lab; and film scoring labs, providing professional training in the areas of film music composition, editing, sequencing, and computer applications.

Costs

Tuition and fees for the 2007–08 year were $29,831. Room and board fees were $13,550. Although the cost of books tends to vary among students, it is estimated at about $800 per year.

Financial Aid

A very large percentage of the student body receives some form of financial aid, so no student should allow financial barriers to stop him or her from applying to the College. Funds are available from many different sources, including Berklee and federal and state programs. Students are eligible for merit-based scholarships and, in cases of demonstrated need, federal assistance is provided. Subsidized loans, a tuition-installment plan, and campus employment are also available. Financial aid counselors are available to students and their families to discuss the various options available to them. Students should be aware that there are specific deadlines for federal and state fund applications and for scholarships. Berklee awards $14 million in scholarships each year to students from all over the world who demonstrate the potential to succeed in today's music industry.

Berklee's Office of Scholarships and Student Employment provides extensive opportunities for both domestic and international students to apply for merit-based scholarships via in-person or recorded audition (entering students) or submission of an achievement portfolio (continuing and returning students who have successfully completed a minimum of two semesters).

Faculty

The personal attention students receive from teachers at Berklee guides them beyond the theoretical so that they can apply what they've learned in their next ensemble rehearsal, evening jam session, or gig. All instruction is administered by Berklee faculty members. Teachers are talented artists who demonstrate their commitment to music education in the classroom and beyond. Most faculty members also write and arrange music, perform in concert halls and clubs, make recordings, or perform on television and radio, and some do it all. All faculty members bring to the classroom a knowledge of music and the wisdom that comes from professional music experience.

Student Government

In recent years, student leaders have become more involved in the decision making of the College, and the Council of Students was created in response to the students' need for a student-run forum to discuss issues of importance to them as well as to prioritize their needs for presentation to faculty members and administration. The council provides adequate channels for expression of student viewpoints in areas of College life at Berklee and promotes the general welfare, interests, opinions, and activities of Berklee students.

Admission Requirements

To make sure that students are prepared for Berklee's exciting and challenging educational experience, all students must have a minimum of two years of formal music study on their principal instrument, covering standard methods and materials in preparation for college-level music study and/or significant practical experience in musical performance; knowledge of written music fundamentals (including rhythmic notation, melodic notation in treble and bass clefs, key signatures, major and minor scales, intervals, and construction of triads and seventh chords); a diploma from an accredited secondary school with satisfactory marks in college-preparatory courses; and, for degree candidates only, satisfactory scores on either the SAT, ACT, or TOEFL (for international students). An audition and interview are now required for all applicants.

Application and Information

Students intending to begin studies in September must submit their applications prior to the February 1 deadline. This filing date allows applicants to take full advantage of housing, financial aid, and scholarship opportunities at the College. The Office of Admissions (and other offices that serve students) can provide the best service to those who apply earliest. Applications are considered in the order in which they are completed.

Applicants considering the January or May semesters should apply at least three months in advance. International students should apply at least six months to one year in advance. All applicants are encouraged to visit the College and take part in a campus tour and information session; together, they provide an overview of the College and the admission process. Hours of operation are 9 to 5, Monday through Friday. Student-led tours take visitors through administrative buildings, the Berklee Performance Center, the Career Resource Center, and the Learning Center. Information sessions offer insight into Berklee's admission requirements and life at the College. The sessions are presented by admissions representatives. Open Houses are offered on selected Saturdays throughout the year. These include a campus tour, an information session, and special student ensemble performances.

For further information, students should contact:

Office of Admissions
Berklee College of Music
1140 Boylston Street
Boston, Massachusetts 02215
Phone: 617-266-1400 Ext. 2222 (worldwide)
800-BERKLEE (toll-free in the U.S. and Canada)
Fax: 617-747-2047
E-mail: admissions@berklee.edu
Web site: http://www.berklee.edu

Students performing at Berklee College of Music.

BOSTON ARCHITECTURAL COLLEGE

BOSTON, MASSACHUSETTS

The College

Boston Architectural College (BAC) has roots that can be traced to 1889, when the Boston Architectural Club established a formal school of architecture fashioned after the atelier teaching method. The atelier idea was practical: students would learn their profession by working for and being mentored by an architect. Today, the architecture, interior design, landscape architecture, and design studies programs at the BAC still offer this unique learning mode that integrates both academic study and professional experience.

Most degree students work in the design profession during the day and attend classes at night, which allows students to gain professional training in their field while attending school. The BAC faculty consists of respected professionals from design firms in the Boston area. This special relationship between the College and the profession allows the BAC to offer an exceptional education and maintain an affordable tuition.

The fusion of education and practice provides BAC graduates with a solid preparation for a career in design, a professional network, and the most direct route to a professional license. Prior to graduation, architecture students can complete the intern requirements for NCARB (National Council of Architectural Registration Boards) licensing. Interior design students can fulfill most of the intern requirements for NCIDQ (National Council for Interior Design Qualification) certification.

The BAC is a private college that offers bachelor's degrees in architecture, interior design, landscape architecture, and design studies. In addition, the College also awards master's degrees in architecture and interior design, including a new distance-learning Master of Architecture. The College is accredited by the New England Association of Schools and Colleges, and the architecture programs are accredited by the National Architectural Accreditation Board (NAAB). The interior design programs are accredited by the Foundation for Interior Design Education Research (FIDER) accreditation.

Location

Located in Boston's historic Back Bay, known for its abundance of fine restaurants, shops, and art galleries, the BAC is close to many cultural and educational institutions and is easily accessible by public transportation. Within walking distance of the BAC are Symphony Hall, Fenway Park, the Museum of Fine Arts, the Isabella Stewart Gardner Museum, and Boston's Public Garden. Boston is a livable community that is rich in diversity and offers entertainment suitable to a variety of tastes.

Majors and Degrees

BAC awards bachelor's degrees in architecture, design studies, interior design, and landscape architecture. Bachelor of Design Studies concentrations include architectural technology; design computing; design history, theory, and criticism; historic preservation; and sustainable design; degree students may complete this degree and then continue in BAC's Master of Architecture program, if desired.

Academic Programs

Like the careers of professional design, the BAC degree programs are demanding, rewarding, and multidisciplinary. All programs combine classroom and professional learning to unite theory and practice. The BAC follows the traditional semester calendar, and a range of classes is offered in the eight-week summer session.

During the day, most students are employed in paid professional positions to fulfill the practice component of the degree requirement. BAC students enlist their supervisors as mentors, and together they endorse a statement of professional goals and objectives. Practice component skill levels range from entry-level clerical support to design and project management. During the evening, most students participate in the academic portion of the curriculum, which consists of courses in history and theory, visual studies, technology and management, the arts and sciences, and design studios. At the heart of these studies is the design studio sequence. Instead of using terms such as freshman and sophomore, BAC student status is defined by the studio level.

Since fall 2002, the College has been offering to new students with little, if any, academic and experiential background in design the opportunity to enroll in a primarily daytime, academic-only program for the first year. Students begin the concurrent curriculum, academic and practice, at the beginning of their second year at BAC. The Academic-Only First-Year Program includes course work in drawing, design, CAD, and other professional and liberal arts courses. Students benefit by shortening the length of their study by a semester, by gaining important skills and confidence in a concentrated period of time, and by entering practice at a more advanced level.

The academic portion of the curriculum is divided into three segments. In Segment I, or Foundation, students in all majors participate in similar course work. Foundation studios focus on basic design principles and are supported by visual studies and CAD courses. Other Foundation classes focus on design history, construction technology, ethical issues in design practice, computer use, and structural systems. About half of the general education classes are completed in Segment I, including humanities, mathematics, physics, and writing. Segment I concludes with a portfolio review, which a student must pass before progressing to the next level of design studios.

The different degree programs separate to focus on their respective disciplines via Segment II. Architecture design studios emphasize building design but also cover a wide range of topics, including urban design and the theoretical issues of form making and design study. Interior design studios focus on the creation of meaningful interior space through layout and form, color, light, and finish and explore the challenges associated with institutional, commercial, retail, and residential environments. Segment II studios for both programs are complemented by advanced courses in technology and management, history and theory, arts and sciences, and visual studies. Segment II concludes with a second portfolio review.

Segment III begins with advanced design studios and professional electives related to the student's area of concentration. The final phase of Segment III is an intensive Degree Project Studio, a two-semester project joining the goals of general education with those of professional education, actively situating design within cultural contexts beyond the formal limits of the discipline. In achieving these objectives, the Degree Project joins modes of learning, working, and thinking associated with academic work and work in practice. This is also an integrative project in the sense that the student is required to synthesize technical perspectives within the design process.

Progression through the BAC programs is measured by educational progress standards of the academic and practice curriculum, minimum credit requirements, and quantitative grade point average requirements. Students' work is qualitatively evaluated through a series of portfolio and progress reviews. Portfolios are evaluated on the basis of demonstrated growth and progress as well as the ability to synthesize learning from all educational settings and integrate that learning into design work.

Off-Campus Programs

Through the Pro-Arts Consortium, BAC students have the opportunity to register for one course per semester at one of the five nearby art and design schools, including Berklee School of Music, Boston Conservatory, Emerson College, Massachusetts College of Art, and the School of the Museum of Fine Arts. Students also have borrowing privileges at the libraries of all Pro-Arts institutions. The BAC and the Art Institute of Boston have a cross-registration agreement that includes a large selection of courses. The cost of both arrangements is covered by BAC tuition. BAC students may participate in a number of study trips offered periodically throughout the academic year. Recent destinations have included Havana, Cuba; Montreal, Canada; Paris, France; and Charleston, South Carolina.

Academic Facilities

The BAC Library houses an impressive collection of 35,000 books and 120 periodicals. Resources focus on architecture, interior design, urban planning, energy conservation, and architectural history. BAC also maintains a slide library, which contains approximately 40,000 architecture and interior design images that survey historical and contemporary designs. The Interior Design Materials Library houses a collection of reference materials that pertain to interior products and current samples of finishes, furniture, lighting equipment, and construction materials. Students make use of the Materials Library for research, specification, and actual samples.

Fully equipped computer facilities support an array of design-related applications. The facilities support several CAD applications, for both two-dimensional and three-dimensional work; modeling and rendering applications; desktop publishing; multimedia production; and Web development software. Word processing and spreadsheet software, as well as unrestricted high-speed Internet access, are also available. Additional equipment includes large-format plotters, scanners, color and black and white laser printers, and a laser cutter.

Media Services offers a wide range of audiovisual support. Equipment such as slide, overhead, and opaque projectors and videotape and DVD decks is available. Students also have access to a videotape library, photography studio, copy stand, and extensive digital photography capabilities. The BAC Woodshop contains hand and power tools, work benches, and a supply of wood stock suitable for small projects. Classes related to woodworking design are offered in this 700-square-foot facility.

Costs

For the 2007–08 academic year, BAC tuition was $4950 per semester for bachelor's students; tuition for undergraduate students participating in the Academic-Only First-Year Program was $6636 per semester for just that first year. Additional administrative fees may apply. All students must pay a $10 student government fee. Massachusetts state law requires that all full-time students be covered by a qualifying health plan. In case a student does not already have coverage, a comprehensive health insurance package is available through the BAC at an additional cost.

Financial Aid

The BAC provides both institutional and federal or state-funded assistance to qualified students who demonstrate financial need. Sources of aid include federally funded subsidized loans and federal, state, and institutional grants and scholarships. Tuition, fees, food, housing, books, supplies, transportation, and personal costs are taken into account to determine need. Institutional aid is available to qualified students who have completed one semester. Numerous design scholarships and awards are also available.

Faculty

The academic faculty of the BAC consists of 350 dedicated practitioners of the design professions. Approximately 90 percent of the faculty members hold advanced or professional degrees. Students benefit from a tutorial relationship with instructors because of small class size. The overall student-faculty ratio is approximately 10:1 in lecture classes and 6:1 in design studios.

Also unique to the BAC is the Practice Curriculum Faculty, a group of dedicated designers who counsel students on a one-to-one basis. Their function is to review students' progress through the practice component and assess their professional development. This personal advising nurtures the mentoring relationship that exists between BAC students and the profession.

Student Government

All full-time degree students are members of Atelier, the BAC student organization. Atelier's primary purposes are to expand students' educational opportunities through student-initiated activities, advocate concerns and interests of students to the administration of the school, and assist students in achieving their professional goals. Atelier holds the charter for the Boston region AIAS (American Institute of Architecture Students) and organizes social events and exhibits of art and student work. Officers of Atelier are voting members of the BAC Board of Directors and are represented on each of its committees.

All interior design students participate in the Interior Design Student Organization (IDSO). The IDSO develops and coordinates special events such as lectures and exhibits and focuses on issues that explore the students' interests in the design field.

Admission Requirements

The BAC remains dedicated to its founders' goal of allowing an opportunity to all who are interested to pursue a design education. Students may enter upon completion of high school or the equivalent. An official high school transcript or GED certificate, a complete application, a resume, and an application fee are the only admission requirements. Standardized test scores and portfolios are not required. The BAC is only admitting international students at the master's level at this time.

Applicants interested in transferring academic credit from other institutions must submit official transcripts, copies of course descriptions, and a BAC Transfer of Academic Credit application. Although a portfolio is not required for admission, one that demonstrates fine arts and design ability can be submitted for possible advanced standing in the design studio sequence.

Application and Information

Applications are reviewed and letters of admission are issued on a rolling basis. Students are admitted to the entering class of their choice on a space availability basis. It is strongly suggested that students submit their applications to the BAC as early as possible prior to the desired entering semester.

Admissions Office
Boston Architectural College
320 Newbury Street
Boston, Massachusetts 02115
Phone: 617-585-0123
Fax: 617-585-0121
E-mail: admissions@the-bac.edu
Web site: http://www.the-bac.edu

BOSTON COLLEGE

CHESTNUT HILL, MASSACHUSETTS

The University

Boston College (BC) was founded in 1863 by the Jesuits to serve the sons of Boston's Irish immigrants. Today a coeducational university on more than 200 acres in Chestnut Hill, BC may seem a world apart from the small school in the crowded heart of Boston that was its first home. Through more than fourteen decades of growth and change, however, BC has held fast to the Jesuit ideals that inspired its founders. A Jesuit education today, as a century ago, is grounded in the liberal arts and in a commitment to the service of others.

Undergraduates may enroll in the College of Arts and Sciences, the Wallace E. Carroll School of Management, the Connell School of Nursing, or the Lynch School of Education.

BC's more than 9,020 undergraduates come from many backgrounds. The university draws from nearly all fifty states and more than sixty countries. Students' religious and cultural backgrounds are similarly diverse. Today, the university's AHANA (African American, Hispanic, Asian, and Native American) and international students make up nearly 26 percent of the undergraduate student body.

In today's complex and increasingly diverse world, the university believes that the best education is one that broadens a student's capacity to reason, think, and make critical judgments in a wide range of areas. Thus, each BC student fulfills a core of liberal arts courses from which he or she can pursue degrees in more than fifty areas of study and choose from more than 1,400 course offerings throughout the university.

According to several recent national publications, BC is in the top tier of the nation's colleges and universities. The foundation for that achievement is the university's scholars and researchers—675 full-time professionals who make up the faculty. The kinship between teachers and students is one of the hallmarks of a BC education; that relationship is nurtured by a student-teacher ratio of 13:1. The median class size at the university is 24 students.

At BC, learning continues beyond the classroom in more than 200 student-run organizations. These include student government, honor societies, language and cultural organizations, performance ensembles, political groups, preprofessional clubs, publications, and service organizations. BC also sponsors thirteen varsity teams for men and sixteen for women, all of which compete at the NCAA Division I level. The College also supports forty-six club and intramural sports.

Location

Located in the Chestnut Hill section of Newton, BC sits on the doorstep of one of America's great cities, a center of culture and education for more than three centuries. It is an energetic, cosmopolitan city that draws life and enthusiasm from the more than 200,000 college students in residence during the academic year. Located just 6 miles from downtown Boston and with easy access to the city via the trolley system that stops at the foot of the campus, BC offers the best of both worlds: a scenic suburban setting neighboring an exciting metropolitan center.

Majors and Degrees

The College of Arts and Sciences (A&S) is the oldest and largest of the four undergraduate schools at BC. A&S students must complete thirty-eight 1-semester courses, thirty-two of which are in A&S departments. The normal course load is five courses per semester for the first three years and four courses per semester during the senior year. The undergraduate curriculum includes the university Core Curriculum and ten to twelve courses in the major field, with the remainder of courses chosen as electives. A&S offers degrees in the following areas: art history, biochemistry, biology, chemistry, classical studies, communication, computer science, economics, English, environmental geosciences, film studies, French, geology and geophysics, geophysics, German studies, Hispanic studies, history, international studies, Italian, linguistics, mathematics, music, philosophy, physics, political science, psychology, Russian, Slavic studies, sociology, studio art, theater, and theology. Preprofessional advisement is also available in medical, dental, veterinary, and legal programs. Students can also select from twenty interdisciplinary minors or majors.

The Carroll School of Management educates students to be leaders in business and industry and in public agencies, educational institutions, and service organizations. The Carroll School offers concentrations in accounting, computer science, economics, finance, general management, human resource management, information systems, marketing, operations/strategic management, and operations technology.

The Lynch School of Education prepares students for education and human services professions. Programs provide a general education, professional preparation, and specialized education in the major field. Fieldwork in area schools is closely linked to course work in each specialization. The Lynch School awards degrees upon completion of thirty-eight courses, including the University Core, a major field of study in education, and a second major in a subject field or an interdisciplinary area in A&S that complements the student's program. Areas of specialization include early childhood education, elementary education, human development, secondary education, and special education.

The Connell School of Nursing offers a four-year program of study leading to a Bachelor of Science degree. The three major components to the curriculum are nursing major courses, electives, and the required University Core. In all courses, principles of wellness, illness, rehabilitation, and health maintenance serve as a theoretical basis in preparing students for professional nursing practice. Nursing courses include traditional classes, simulated and audiovisual laboratory activities on campus, and clinical learning activities in health-care settings.

Academic Programs

Every BC education is centered on a core curriculum—a set of required courses. BC offers a core curriculum because it believes in the unity of knowledge. While the core, which is continually reviewed by a committee of faculty members, varies somewhat by school, its common elements include literature, natural science, writing, philosophy, theology, social science, modern European history, mathematics, fine arts, and the study of a non-European culture.

There is a wide variety of extraordinary academic programs available to BC students to enhance their educational experience. They include, among others, honors programs within each of the university's four undergraduate schools, Undergraduate Faculty Research Fellows, the Scholar of the College, PULSE, and Perspectives on Western Culture.

Off-Campus Programs

BC encourages all students to take part in internship programs. More than half of BC undergraduates participate in at least one internship or prepracticum placement during their college years. Internships can be paid or unpaid and may take place during the academic year or the summer; some carry academic credit.

BC students may take on the challenge of international study in more than seventy programs administered by BC at universities in more than thirty countries. BC students who study abroad typically do so in their junior year, but there is also a range of full-year and summer-abroad opportunities. The Office of International Programs helps students with program selection and applications and maintains a library of reference books and professional evaluations of international study programs.

Academic Facilities

BC's eight libraries contain more than 2.3 million printed volumes, over 4.1 million items in microform, approximately 222,106 government documents, more than 10,000 serial subscriptions, and a wide collection of films and archival items. The resources of the library system range from some of Europe's earliest printed books to hundreds of computerized databases. Students with personal computers have dorm-room access to these databases as well as to Quest and other library information sources through Agora, the campus information network.

Research laboratories in the state-of-the-art science facilities have been specially designed to accommodate the advanced instrumentation required for modern science and to provide flexibility for accommodating new equipment. The recent $85-million expansion to the Higgins Biology and Physics Center was carefully designed to place classrooms, laboratories, computer facilities, and office space in proximity and to facilitate interaction among faculty members, researchers, and students. In addition to the Center's seventeen new teaching laboratories, special working labs are designed and outfitted for research and teaching in the fields of biology and physics.

Costs

Tuition for the 2007–08 academic year was $35,150. The freshman room rate was $6820. The board plan, which is required for all resident freshmen, was $4240. Freshman mandatory fees, which include a charge for on-campus orientation, totaled $929.

Financial Aid

BC maintains a financial aid program to assist deserving and qualified students who might otherwise not be able to attend the university. Boston College is committed to providing funds to meet the full demonstrated need of every admitted student who applies for financial aid. Overall, 62 percent of students receive some form of financial aid. Assistance for freshmen alone included more than $16 million in need-based grants. The university offers financial aid to students based on need as demonstrated by completion of the College Scholarship Service's Financial Aid PROFILE and the Free Application for Federal Student Aid (FAFSA). All requirements and deadlines and complete instructions are available in BC admission literature. An application for financial aid in no way affects a decision on admission.

Each year, BC chooses 15 incoming freshmen as Presidential Scholars to receive merit-based, full-tuition scholarships. Students are selected from all candidates who apply through the Early Action program.

Faculty

BC has 675 full-time faculty members. Of these faculty members, 98 percent hold doctoral degrees. The nearly 115 Jesuits living on the BC campus make up one of the largest Apostolic Jesuit communities in the world. Nearly half of these members are active in the College's administration and teaching.

Student Government

The Undergraduate Government of Boston College (UGBC), formed in 1968, is led by the president and vice president, who are elected in the spring of each year by the entire student body. UGBC's goal is to serve the students by providing services and opportunities and by representing them in the best manner possible to the university community. To accomplish this goal, UGBC provides many educational, social, and cultural programs, such as concerts, lectures, roundtables, and more.

Admission Requirements

The undergraduate admission staff pays particular attention to students who have done well in a demanding college-preparatory curriculum, including Advanced Placement (AP) and honors courses when available. For the class of 2011, there were nearly 28,500 applications for 2,291 places. The majority of incoming freshmen ranked comfortably in the top 10 percent of their high school class. The SAT scores of the middle half of admitted freshmen were 1860–2120. On the ACT, scores of the middle half were between 27 and 32.

Application and Information

Students applying to Boston College for a place in the freshman class must complete both the Common Application and the Boston College Supplemental Application. All applicants should submit the BC Supplemental Application as soon as they have decided to apply to Boston College. Students are encouraged to apply via BC's Web site at http://www.bc.edu/applications but may also apply at http://www.commonapp.org.

Students applying through the regular admission program must submit the Common Application and all other required forms, along with the $70 application fee, by January 1. Candidates are notified of action taken on their application in early April. Admitted students intending to matriculate are required to forward a confirmation fee to the Admission Office postmarked by May 1.

Students with superior academic credentials who view Boston College as a top choice may apply through the nonbinding early action program. These applicants must submit both application forms, along with the $70 application fee, by November 1. Candidates learn of their admission decision before December 25 but have the standard deadline (May 1) to reserve their places as freshmen. Boston College does permit students to apply under early action if they have applied to an early decision college.

BC accepts transfer applicants each semester. Transfer candidates should request applications for transfer admission from the Office of Undergraduate Admission or via the Web site at http://www.bc.edu/transfer. In addition to high school records and standardized test results, transfer applicants must furnish transcripts from all postsecondary institutions they have attended.

For more information, students should contact:

Office of Undergraduate Admission
Devlin Hall 208
Boston College
Chestnut Hill, Massachusetts 02467
Phone: 617-552-3100
800-360-2522 (toll-free)
Fax: 617-552-0798
Web site: http://www.bc.edu

Located just 6 miles from downtown Boston, Boston College offers the best of both worlds: a scenic suburban setting neighboring an exciting metropolitan center.

BOSTON UNIVERSITY
BOSTON, MASSACHUSETTS

The University

Boston University is a private, coeducational teaching and research university located on the banks of the Charles River in Boston. Boston University is an energizing community, which fosters creativity and innovation in both its students and faculty. The faculty comprises some of the world's foremost experts who are dedicated to the art of teaching. Of the classes held in the freshman and sophomore years, the vast majority contain fewer than 30 students. Together, the ten undergraduate schools and colleges offer more than 250 major and minor areas of concentration. Students may choose from programs of study in areas as diverse as biochemistry, broadcast journalism, business, computer systems engineering, elementary education, international relations, physical therapy, and theater arts. With a student body representing all fifty states and 100 countries, Boston University has one of the most culturally diverse student bodies in the United States. The campus community supports more than 400 different student organizations, ranging from ice broomball teams to performing arts groups, community service activities to student government, and clubs with cultural and professional as well as academic affiliations.

Location

Boston is an international center of cultural and intellectual activity, with a concentration of facilities for higher education unrivaled throughout the world. Home to many fine museums, baseball's Fenway Park, an active theater district, and the Boston Symphony Orchestra, the city has a vibrant energy all its own. During the academic year 1 in 5 residents is a college student, making Boston the ultimate college town.

Majors and Degrees

Boston University grants the B.A., B.S., B.S.B.A., B.S.Ed., B.A.S., B.L.S., B.A.A., Mus.B., and B.F.A. undergraduate degrees. Of the University's sixteen schools and colleges, ten offer opportunities for undergraduate study. The following information indicates the range of undergraduate programs available.

Students in the College of Arts and Sciences may concentrate in American studies, ancient Greek, ancient Greek and Latin, anthropology, anthropology and philosophy, anthropology and religion, archaeology, art history, astronomy, astronomy/physics, biochemistry, biochemistry/molecular biology, biology, biology with a specialization in ecology and conservation biology, biology with a specialization in marine science, biology with a specialization in neuroscience, chemistry, chemistry with a specialization in teaching, classical civilization, classics/philosophy, classics/religion, computer science, computer science and mathematics, earth sciences, East Asian studies, economics, economics/mathematics, English, environmental analysis and policy, environmental earth sciences, environmental science, French/continental European literatures, French language and literature, geography, geography/human, geography/physical, geophysics and planetary sciences, German/continental European literatures, German language and literature, Hispanic/continental European literatures, Hispanic language and literature, history, independent concentration, international relations, Italian/continental European literatures, Italian studies, Japanese language and literature, Latin, Latin American studies, linguistics, mathematics (including statistics), mathematics/philosophy, music (nonperformance), philosophy, philosophy/physics, philosophy/political science, philosophy/psychology, philosophy/religion, physics, political science, predentistry, prelaw, premedicine, preveterinary medicine, psychology, religion, Russian/continental European literatures, Russian language and literature, Russian/Eastern European studies, and sociology. Special curricula include seven-year accelerated programs in liberal arts and dentistry and liberal arts and medicine; the Modular Medical Integrated Curriculum; a dual-degree program; and various combined B.A./M.A. degree programs.

The College of Communication offers major programs of undergraduate study in film and television, journalism (including broadcast journalism, magazine journalism, news-editorial print journalism, and photojournalism), advertising, mass communications, and public relations.

Majors in the College of Engineering include aerospace, biomedical, computer systems, electrical, manufacturing, and mechanical engineering.

Areas of concentration in the School of Education include bilingual education, early childhood education, deaf studies, elementary education, English education, history and social science education, mathematics education, modern foreign language education, science education, and special education.

The School of Hospitality Administration offers a rigorous program in the management of hotels, restaurants, food and beverage service, travel and tourism, and entertainment.

Concentrations in the School of Management include accounting, business law, entrepreneurship, finance, general management, international management, management information systems, marketing, operations and technology management, and organizational behavior.

The College of Fine Arts offers programs in the School of Music (music education, musicology, performance, and theory and composition), the School of Theater (acting, design, stage management, production, and theater arts), and the School of Visual Arts (art education, graphic design, painting, and sculpture).

The College of Health and Rehabilitation Sciences (Sargent College) offers programs in athletic training; health science; human physiology; nutritional science; and speech, language, and hearing sciences as well as a five-year combined B.S./M.S. degree program in occupational therapy, a six-year B.S./D.P.T. program in physical therapy, and a six-year B.S. in athletic training/D.P.T. in physical therapy program.

The College of General Studies offers a two-year liberal-arts-based program that features a core curriculum and intensive team teaching. It is designed so that students continue on at the junior level into select schools and colleges of the University.

The Metropolitan College Science and Engineering Program offers a four-semester program for those students who need additional preparation for studying the sciences or engineering.

Academic Programs

A Boston University education combines the elements of a traditional liberal arts education with training for the professions. In addition, highly qualified freshmen and sophomores may be invited to participate in honors programs in the College of Arts and Sciences or the School of Management.

Boston University has sixty-six programs that take students around the world. Internships, fieldwork, and study-abroad opportunities are offered on six continents within twenty-two countries, including the U.S. The University has a series of programs and internships in a variety of locations, including Auckland, Beijing, Dresden, Dublin, Geneva, Haifa, London, Los Angeles, Madrid, Paris, Sydney, and Washington, D.C. Programs offered include art/architecture, business/economics, human health services, journalism/communications, and visual/performing arts. Fieldwork programs may be found in locations that include Belize, Ecuador, and Spain, with study-abroad options that include programs in Auckland, Burgos, Dresden, Grenoble, Haifa, Madrid, Niamey, Oxford, Padova, Quito, and

Venice. Summer study programs exist in Argentina, Australia, China, England, France, Ireland, Italy, Peru, Senegal, Spain, and the United States.

Boston University operates on a calendar of two semesters and two summer terms. Students generally take four courses each semester; thirty-two courses are required for graduation. Most degree programs are built around a core of humanities and social and natural sciences. Concentrations require eight to thirteen courses. Electives generally total 30–40 percent of the courses taken, allowing for interdisciplinary study.

Academic Facilities

Three of the newest facilities on campus are the School of Hospitality Administration Building, a fully wireless facility with dedicated space for student activities and career recruitment and a hospitality library; the Agganis Arena; and the Fitness and Recreation Center, which opened in the spring of 2005. A life science and engineering facility, with 187,000 square feet of laboratory and research space for the biology, bioinformatics, chemistry, and bioengineering departments, also opened in 2005. Boston University's state-of-the-art Photonics Center features classroom and laboratory space for the College of Engineering as well as labs designed to support industry partners who seek to develop new photonics-based products. The School of Management building represents one of the most technologically advanced educational facilities in the country, with more than 4,000 data and communications ports and a dedicated career center and management library.

Through the Office of Information Technology, students have access to public computing facilities equipped with workstations, terminals, and laser printers as well as a high-speed campus network interconnecting all computer resources and linking them to the Internet. An 890-seat proscenium theater, studio space for visual arts students, practice rooms for music, and a 575-seat music performance center are indicative of Boston University's support for the arts. More than 2.2 million library volumes and more than 4.6 million microform units are contained in Mugar Memorial Library, where the Twentieth-Century Archives are held, including the papers of Martin Luther King Jr., Theodore Roosevelt, Robert Frost, and Bette Davis.

Costs

Tuition for 2007–08 is $34,930; estimated room and board costs are $10,950. University and college fees are $488. These costs are exclusive of books, supplies, travel, and personal expenses.

Financial Aid

The Office of Financial Assistance offers opportunities for grants, scholarships, student loans, and student employment to those who request help in meeting the expenses of attending Boston University. Information about credit-based financing options is also provided to students and parents. Both need-based aid and merit awards are offered to eligible students.

Financial aid offered on the basis of calculated need may be offered in a variety of combinations. Types of aid include Boston University grants, state and federal grants, loans, Federal Work-Study, and other part-time employment. Boston University makes every effort to assist students with calculated need, however, funds are limited and it is not possible to meet the eligibility of all applicants for financial aid. Priority for a Boston University grant is given to those students with the strongest academic records. Nevertheless, all applicants who anticipate the need for financial aid are encouraged to apply. In addition, Boston University believes in recognizing and rewarding outstanding high school seniors for their academic and other accomplishments. The University is therefore committed to offering a variety of merit awards.

Faculty

Students are taught by faculty members who distinguish themselves by their ability, experience, research, and publications. In addition to fulfilling their classroom responsibilities, faculty members are accessible as academic and career advisers who assist students in obtaining internships as well research opportunities.

Student Government

Each school and college has its own student government, which regulates student affairs within the school or college. The University-wide student governing body, the Student Union, has representation from all University schools and colleges. Each residence also has its own student government, composed of elected representatives from each floor.

Admission Requirements

The Board of Admissions considers each candidate individually. Primary emphasis is placed on the strength of the secondary school record, but required test scores (SAT or ACT), character, breadth of interest, school recommendations, and other personal qualifications are also carefully evaluated. Students are required to submit the SAT or the ACT (with Writing Test). Results of the ACT that do not include the Writing Test will not meet the requirement for admission. Students taking the SAT will also be required to submit the results of two SAT Subject Tests in different subject areas. Students taking the ACT (with Writing Test) do not need to submit Subject Tests. Prospective students should see the Requirements and Standards chart at http://www.bu.edu/admissions/apply/fresh_req.html for a full listing of the standardized testing requirements. Secondary school graduation or an equivalency diploma is required of all candidates; for the College of Fine Arts, an audition or a portfolio is required. For certain programs, interviews and additional SAT Subject Test scores are required.

Students with earned credit from other colleges may be admitted. Applicants are considered for September or January entrance. Transfer students are not eligible for admission to the Accelerated Liberal Arts Medical or Dental Programs, the College of General Studies, or the Metropolitan College Science and Engineering Program. January admission to the College of Fine Arts School of Theatre is also not available to transfer students. Boston University offers programs of early decision (binding agreement), early admission, and deferred admission.

Boston University admits qualified students regardless of their race, color, national origin, religion, sex, age, or disability to all its programs and activities.

Application and Information

Boston University requires the Common Application and the Boston University Supplement. Information on applying is available online at http://www.bu.edu/admissions/apply. The deadline for applications is January 1. Applicants for Early Decision must apply by November 1. Accelerated program applicants, Trustee Scholar nominees, Dr. Martin Luther King Jr. Scholarship nominees, and Alexander Graham Bell Scholarship nominees must file by December 1. Candidates for financial aid should complete the College Scholarship Service (CSS) Financial Aid PROFILE and the Free Application for Federal Student Aid (FAFSA) in time for the analysis report to reach the University by February 15. Transfer students applying for September admission should submit their applications, CSS/Financial Aid PROFILE forms, and Free Application for Federal Student Aid (FAFSA) forms by April 1 or by November 1 for January admission.

Office of Admissions
Boston University
121 Bay State Road
Boston, Massachusetts 02215
Phone: 617-353-2300
E-mail: admissions@bu.edu
Web site: http://www.bu.edu/admissions

BRANDEIS UNIVERSITY

WALTHAM, MASSACHUSETTS

The University

Brandeis University combines two important traditions in higher education: a dedication to teaching that is characteristic of a small, selective college and the facilities and renowned faculty members associated with a large research university.

Brandeis is a nonsectarian institution. Founded in 1948 by members of the American Jewish community, the University has endorsed a religious pluralism that attracts bright and highly motivated students from culturally diverse backgrounds. The current student body consists of roughly 3,300 undergraduates, including men and women from nearly every state and fifty-two countries. Seventy-three percent of the students come from out of state. The Graduate School of Arts and Sciences offers programs in twenty-three fields and certificates in three postbaccalaureate programs and attracts an international group of graduate students. The University's two graduate schools, the Heller Graduate School for Social Policy and Management and the International Business School, offer graduate degrees at the master's and doctoral levels.

Students participate in a wide range of activities, from sports to theater and government. Brandeis has more than 250 clubs and organizations that provide unlimited opportunities for a varied and extensive extracurricular life.

Brandeis competes at the NCAA Division III level and is one of eight top private universities that make up the University Athletic Association (UAA). Men compete in varsity baseball, basketball, cross-country, fencing, golf, indoor and outdoor track and field, soccer, swimming and diving, and tennis. Women compete in basketball, cross-country, fencing, indoor and outdoor track and field, soccer, softball, swimming and diving, tennis, and volleyball. There is also a coed varsity sailing team. Club sports include bicycling, crew, field hockey, ice hockey, lacrosse, martial arts, rugby, skiing, softball, squash, tae kwon do, Ultimate Frisbee, volleyball, weight lifting, and wrestling. In addition, students play intramural sports and enjoy recreational activities, which range from football to Frisbee. The Shapiro Athletic Center provides facilities for all of the above, including indoor and outdoor tracks and tennis courts, weight-training facilities, squash courts, a dance/aerobics room, and the largest field house on any New England campus.

More than 85 percent of the students live on campus. First-year students and sophomores are guaranteed on-campus housing in eight of the nine residential quads. Every quad has a live-in professional staff person and upperclass peer advisers. Three dining halls serve the student body; these include a variety of alternate dining options, from kosher and vegetarian meals to Mexican and Middle Eastern fare.

Location

Brandeis is in Waltham, Massachusetts, a community of 58,000 just 9 miles west of Boston. The University's location combines the benefits of urban life with those of a safe, suburban campus. The MBTA train line and campus shuttle provide easy access to cultural, social, and athletic events in Cambridge and downtown Boston. The campus is also convenient to neighboring beach and mountain resorts. Perhaps the greatest advantage of the location is the social and intellectual interaction afforded by proximity to other Boston-area colleges and universities.

Majors and Degrees

Brandeis University offers more than forty different majors. The Bachelor of Arts (B.A.) degree is offered in African and Afro-American studies; American studies; anthropology; art history; biochemistry; biology; chemistry; classical studies; comparative literature; computer science; creative writing; economics; East Asian studies; education studies; English and American literature; environmental studies; European cultural studies; French language and literature; German language and literature; health: science, society, and policy; Hebrew language and literature; history; international and global studies; Islamic and Middle Eastern studies; Italian studies; Latin American studies; Latin language and literature; linguistics; mathematics; music; Near Eastern and Judaic studies; neuroscience; philosophy; physics; politics; psychology; Russian language and literature; sociology; Spanish; studio arts; theater arts; and women's and gender studies.

The Bachelor of Science (B.S.) degree is offered in biochemistry; biology; biological physics; chemistry; computer science; health: science, society, and policy; neuroscience; and physics. Students may pursue double or independent majors.

In addition to choosing a major, undergraduates may follow minors or interdisciplinary programs in several fields: business; East Asian studies; education; environmental studies; film studies; health: science, society, and policy; history of ideas; international and global studies; Internet studies; Islamic and Middle Eastern studies; journalism; Latin American studies; legal studies; medieval and Renaissance studies; peace, conflict, and coexistence studies; religious studies; Russian and Eastern European studies; social justice and social policy; and women's studies. Students may also complete a minor in the following fields: African and Afro-American studies, anthropology, art history, chemistry, classical studies, computer science, creative writing, economics, English and American literature, French, German literature, Hebrew language and literature, linguistics, mathematics, Near Eastern and Judaic studies, neuroscience, philosophy (language, logic, and the philosophy of science; metaphysics and the philosophy of mind; philosophy; or value theory: ethics, politics, society, religion, and art), physics, Russian literature, Spanish, and theater arts. Creative writing is available as a major or minor in the English department.

A combined-degree program is offered with the Columbia University School of Engineering and an engineering certificate program is available in conjunction with the Olin College of Engineering. Preprofessional advising in architecture, business and management, dentistry, law, and medicine prepares students for admission to professional schools after college.

Exceptional undergraduates may enroll in four-year combined B.A./M.A. programs in the departments of American history, anthropology, biochemistry, biology, chemistry, comparative history, mathematics, neuroscience, physics, and politics. Five-year combined B.A./M.A. programs are available in computer science, international economics and finance, and Near Eastern and Judaic studies.

Academic Programs

All first-year students take a seminar taught by Brandeis faculty members, which allows them to discuss fundamental questions about human existence and meaning through the critical study of significant texts or artistic creations. A core curriculum is in place to maintain flexibility while ensuring exposure to course work in each of the four major schools: Creative Arts, Humanities, Sciences, and Social Sciences.

Before the end of their sophomore year, students meet with a faculty adviser in their intended major. To earn a bachelor's degree, undergraduates complete thirty-two semester courses, including the major requirements. Advanced Placement credit, credit for the International Baccalaureate, transfer credit, and other international exams are available upon approval of the University Registrar.

Brandeis offers numerous opportunities for independent research and fieldwork at the undergraduate level. Most departments offer honors and senior thesis programs, and students engaged in approved research work may apply for funding from Brandeis. The Hiatt Career Center, leading the field in career placement, arranges internships in all areas of concentration.

Brandeis operates on a two-semester calendar. Classes for the fall term generally begin in early September, and examinations take place before the winter break. Classes for the spring term begin in late January and end in the middle of May.

Off-Campus Programs

Opportunities exist for study abroad in more than sixty countries under the auspices of a variety of programs sponsored by international and American universities. Brandeis also has a special arrangement for a full-year study program at University College in London.

Through a cross-registration agreement, courses not offered at Brandeis may be taken at Tufts University, Boston University, Boston College, and Wellesley College. Students may also take business courses at Babson College and Bentley College.

Academic Facilities

The Goldfarb and Farber Libraries and the Gerstenzang Science Library together contain more than 1.1 million bound volumes, 893,000 microforms, 16,000 current serial subscriptions, and 500 electronic databases. Brandeis participates in the Boston Library Consortium, which allows undergraduates access to most major university libraries in the Boston area.

Forty-one academic facilities offer undergraduates substantial resources in the arts and sciences. The Berlin Premedical Center contains extensive laboratories devoted to preparing students for careers as physicians. The Volen National Center for Complex Systems hosts research in large, complex systems, with the brain and intelligence as the system of greatest interest. The University maintains twenty-seven technology-enhanced classrooms that are equipped with computers and AV equipment as well as seven public computer classrooms and clusters containing PCs, public printing stations, and selected peripherals. The Instructional Technology Resource Center supports student course-related technology uses. Many laboratories and departments throughout the campus maintain specialized computing facilities and wireless technology. The Computer Science Department has a network of Linux and Mac workstations.

The Spingold Theater Arts Center provides three theaters as well as dance and rehearsal rooms. Shapiro Campus Center, an undergraduate facility, provides opportunities for students to become involved in all aspects of theater production. The Slosberg Music Center hosts more than eighty performances by undergraduate musicians and visiting professionals each year. The permanent collection of American art of the post–World War II era at the Rose Art Museum is considered the finest at any university in the New England area.

Costs

Tuition costs, including fees, were $35,702 for the 2007–08 academic year. The cost of room and board averaged $9908.

Financial Aid

Financial aid at Brandeis is based on need, as determined by information provided on the College Scholarship Service's Financial Aid PROFILE. Need-based aid packages generally include scholarship, loan, and work-study components. However, a number of scholarships up to full tuition annually are available primarily on the basis of merit. Last year, more than 65 percent of the student body received some form of aid. Brandeis realizes that need is not necessarily determined strictly by income and designs each aid package individually.

Faculty

The faculty at Brandeis consists of men and women united by their commitment to undergraduate education. Ninety-eight percent of the 352 full-time and 106 part-time professors hold doctoral degrees or the highest degrees in their field. The student-faculty ratio of approximately 8:1 allows for a rigorous but personal academic environment. Graduate teaching assistants conduct a limited number of entry-level classes. The median class size is 17.

Student Government

The undergraduate student government, the Student Senate, consists of 8 elected class senators, 10 elected residential senators, and an executive board, who represent their constituents' interests to the University administration through the Dean of Student Affairs. The undergraduate student activity fee generates approximately $750,000 for distribution to more than 215 recognized organizations. Ninety undergraduates serve on thirty-four University committees. Two undergraduate students serve as student representatives to the Board of Trustees.

Admission Requirements

Brandeis places the most emphasis on the applicant's secondary school record. Teacher recommendations, the personal statement, and standardized test scores contribute to the evaluation as well. Prospective students should have followed a challenging academic curriculum while in high school, generally having completed 4 years of English; 3 years of a foreign language, including senior study when possible; at least 3 years of mathematics; and a minimum of 1 year each of history and laboratory science.

Brandeis expects its applicants to present scores on the College Board's SAT and on two SAT Subject Tests from different subjects (for example, one math and one language). Applicants may submit scores from the ACT with writing in lieu of the SAT and SAT Subject Tests. The ELPT exam is not an acceptable SAT Subject Test, so if English is not the native language of a student, the Test of English as a Foreign Language (TOEFL) should be taken.

Transfer students, while not required to submit SAT Subject Test scores, are expected to send copies of their SAT scores as well as transcripts of any credit-granting courses taken. High school transcripts are required.

All candidates for admission are reviewed individually. The Office of Admissions encourages each applicant to arrange for an interview on campus or through an Alumni Admissions Council member in the student's home area.

Application and Information

Individuals interested in applying as early decision (EDI) candidates should submit application materials before November 15. A second early decision option (EDII) is available, with an application deadline of January 1. Regular applicants should submit the application by January 15. Transfer students should submit their applications before April 1. The Office of Admissions notifies EDI candidates in mid-December and EDII candidates by mid-February. Regular admission candidates receive notification by April 1 and transfer candidates by June 1.

Requests for information and application materials may be directed to:

Office of Admissions
Brandeis University
Waltham, Massachusetts 02454-9110
Phone: 781-736-3500
800-622-0622 (toll-free outside Massachusetts)
E-mail: admissions@brandeis.edu
Web site: http://www.brandeis.edu/admissions

BRIDGEWATER STATE COLLEGE

BRIDGEWATER, MASSACHUSETTS

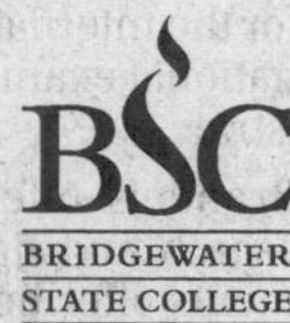

The College

Bridgewater State College was founded in 1840 and has grown from a teacher-preparation school of 28 students to a comprehensive liberal arts institution that enrolls more than 9,000 students each year (7,200 undergraduates) in day, evening, and summer programs.

The College offers students a lively cultural, social, and recreational life to enhance their learning experience. The Adrian Tinsley Center, Rondileau Campus Center, and East Campus Commons are the settings for many of the student-life activities. Cultural, educational, and entertainment programs, including lectures by guest speakers, concerts, exhibits, and movies, are regularly featured at the Campus Center, while a wide selection of fitness activities are available in the Tinsley Center. The College offers more than 100 student clubs and organizations in a variety of interest areas. Intercollegiate varsity athletic teams compete under NCAA Division III. Men's teams include baseball, basketball, cross-country, football, soccer, swimming, tennis, track and field, and wrestling. Teams for women include basketball, cross-country, field hockey, lacrosse, soccer, softball, swimming, tennis, track and field, and volleyball. A number of club sports are open to students, including cheerleading, equestrian, karate, Ultimate Frisbee, men's ice hockey and lacrosse, and women's rugby.

The Bridgewater State College campus has ten residence halls and thirty-four academic/administrative buildings spread over its 235-acre campus. The atmosphere at Bridgewater is friendly and informal, based on the concept that the College is a diverse community of people with shared interests and goals. A number of important student services (including career, academic, and personal counseling; disability and health services; and housing assistance) are available.

The College offers programs leading to the bachelor's degree in more than thirty different areas of study through the Schools of Arts and Sciences, Business, and Education and Allied Studies.

Bridgewater's School of Graduate Studies offers degrees, including the Master of Arts, Master of Arts in Teaching, Master of Public Administration, and Master of Science, in fields such as management, criminal justice, computer science, English, teacher education, physical education, and psychology. Advanced certificates in teaching are also awarded.

Location

Bridgewater State College is located in Bridgewater, Massachusetts, a community of more than 25,000 people approximately 30 miles south of Boston and 25 miles north of Cape Cod. The area is near many cultural, recreational, and historic sites. Commuter train service to and from Boston operates from early morning to late evening, seven days a week. The Bridgewater train station is located in the center of the College's campus.

Majors and Degrees

Bridgewater State College confers the Bachelor of Arts, Bachelor of Science, and Bachelor of Science in Education degrees.

Undergraduate majors are offered in accounting and finance, anthropology, art, aviation science (airport management, aviation management, flight training), biology, business (see "management"), chemistry, chemistry-geology, communication arts and sciences (communication studies, dance education, speech communication, theater arts, theater education), computer science, criminal justice, early childhood education, earth sciences, economics, elementary education, English, geography, health education, history, management (energy and environmental resources management, general management, global management, information systems management, marketing transportation), mathematics, music, philosophy, physical education, physics, political science, psychology, secondary education, social work, sociology, Spanish, and special education (including communication disorders).

Academic Programs

Bridgewater State College offers a full range of study in more than thirty degree areas. The goal of the academic program is to prepare broadly educated individuals in the liberal arts and the professions. The Academic Achievement Center provides academic counseling and assistance to all freshmen and transfer students. All students must complete the Core Curriculum of general education courses to earn a bachelor's degree. Students must complete 120 semester hours of credit, of which at least 30–36 hours must be taken in a major field of study. Selected students may enroll in departmental or College-wide honors programs.

The College operates on a traditional two-semester calendar and offers two 5-week summer sessions and a number of intensive courses over the summer months.

Off-Campus Programs

Bridgewater State College participates in three programs that allow students to take courses for credit at other institutions of higher education. First, College Academic Program Sharing (CAPS) provides full-time students with the opportunity to take courses offered at any of the other state colleges in Massachusetts. The College is also a member of the Southeastern Association for Cooperation of Higher Education in Massachusetts (SACHEM), a consortium of public and private colleges that includes Bristol Community, Cape Cod Community, Dean, Massasoit Community, Stonehill, and Wheaton Colleges; Massachusetts Maritime Academy; and the University of Massachusetts Dartmouth. Finally, Bridgewater participates in the National Student Exchange Program, which allows students to spend a term at other public colleges and universities in the United States.

Students are encouraged to pursue internships within their major field that provide opportunities to earn college credit while gaining practical experience. Faculty advisers assist students in securing internships in which they work with professionals in business, industry, education, and government.

Academic Facilities

The John Joseph Moakley Center for Technological Applications, named in honor of the late congressman from Massachusetts, is the hub of the College's campuswide voice, data, and video network. Technological resources in the building include a series of technology-integrated classrooms, an open-access computer lab, a television studio and control room, a teleconference facility, and a large lecture hall with integrated, computer-based display technology.

The Clement C. Maxwell Library is a four-story facility that seats 2,500 and has more than 300,000 books, 1,102 periodicals, and 19,500 journals on its information network. Other major resources on campus include an astronomy observatory, radio and television production facilities, a Teacher Technology Center, and the new Tinsley Athletic Center, which houses classrooms, laboratories, a fitness center, an NCAA-regulation gymnasium and basketball court, and meeting areas.

Costs

For 2006–07, tuition for full-time study was $910 per year for Massachusetts residents and $7050 per year for out-of-state students. Fees were $4878 per year, books averaged $800, a room averaged $3776, and board averaged $2620. These expenses are all subject to change.

Financial Aid

Many sources of financial aid are available to Bridgewater students, including Federal Pell Grants, Federal Supplemental Educational Opportunity Grants, Federal Perkins Loans, Federal Stafford Student Loans, HELP loans, alumni scholarships, and Federal Work-Study Program awards. The Financial Aid Office has an informative brochure detailing methods of application and guidelines for qualification. For a copy, prospective applicants should write to the Financial Aid Office or telephone 508-531-1341. Students are required to submit the Free Application for Federal Student Aid (FAFSA). Applications for financial aid for the fall semester must be received by March 1.

Faculty

The College faculty has 282 full-time members and 212 part-time members; 93 percent of full-time faculty members hold terminal degrees in their area. Since the student-faculty ratio is 20:1 and the emphasis of the faculty is on classroom instruction, there are many opportunities for personal contact and interaction between faculty members and students at Bridgewater. Students discover that faculty members are interested in them as individuals and are eager to help them succeed. Graduate students do not teach any courses.

Student Government

Every Bridgewater student is automatically a member of the Student Government Association. Bridgewater's special philosophy of maintaining a College community means that all the people who are part of it—students, faculty and staff members, administrators, and alumni—are partners in an educational program whose goal is academic excellence. The Student Government Association is the official representative of the students' point of view, and its officers, elected by the students themselves, organize activities and projects that benefit the student body and the College as a whole.

Admission Requirements

The basic aim of the admission requirements is to ensure the selection of students who have demonstrated intellectual capacity, motivation, and character and who have a record of scholastic achievement. Consideration is given to applicants regardless of their race, religion, national origin, sex, age, color, ethnic origin, or handicap. Three important factors are considered in the freshman admission process: secondary school preparation, SAT or ACT test scores, and personal qualifications. Prior to acceptance, secondary school students are required to pass 16 college-preparatory units: 4 years of English; 3 years of mathematics, including algebra I and II and geometry; 3 years of science, including 2 years of laboratory science; 2 years of history/social science, including 1 year of U.S. history; 2 years of the same foreign language; and two college-preparatory-level electives. High school students are encouraged to elect additional courses in music, art, and computer science. An essay/personal statement is required. Recommendations are not required but may be submitted with other application materials. Transfer students must submit an official transcript from each college previously attended.

The College also encourages qualified international students to apply for admission. The application procedures should be completed at least six months before the desired date of enrollment. Scores on the Test of English as a Foreign Language (TOEFL) are required from students whose first language is not English. An external evaluation of any transcripts from non-U.S. institutions and an Affidavit of Financial Support are also required.

Application and Information

Applications for freshman admission should be filed with the $25 application fee on or before February 15 for priority consideration. Freshmen seeking on-campus housing must apply before February 15. Students who wish to transfer to Bridgewater from another college should apply by November 1 for January entrance or by April 1 for September entrance for priority consideration.

Students choosing the early action option must submit an application and all supporting materials no later than November 15. Early action candidates are sent a decision letter by December 15.

Students are invited to attend on-campus Friday Admission Information Sessions, which are followed by a student-led tour of the campus. General campus tours are also offered Monday through Friday at 11 a.m. and 3 p.m. while classes are in session. Appointments can be scheduled by calling the Office of Admission.

An application form and further information may be obtained by contacting:

Office of Admission
Bridgewater State College
Bridgewater, Massachusetts 02325
Phone: 508-531-1237
Fax: 508-531-1746
E-mail: admission@bridgew.edu
Web site: http://www.bridgew.edu

CURRY COLLEGE

MILTON, MASSACHUSETTS

The College

The mission of Curry College, a private institution, is to develop liberally educated persons who are able to gain and to apply knowledge humanely, intelligently, and effectively in a complex, changing world. To achieve its mission, Curry College promotes individual intellectual and social growth by engaging its students in achieving these educational goals: thinking critically, communicating effectively, understanding context, appreciating aesthetic experience, defining a personal identity, examining value systems, and adapting and innovating. The College's curriculum and programs focus on the two hallmarks of the Curry education: a high respect for the individuality of every student and a developmental approach to learning that maximizes opportunities for achievement. One-on-one faculty-student relationships provide ample opportunities for personalized instruction and close interaction. Full student counseling and other support services are provided.

The current undergraduate enrollment is 2,000 men and women. Curry students have access to a wide range of cocurricular activities, including the Student Government Association, the student-run newspaper, the yearbook, the *Curry Arts Journal,* several organizations for the performing arts, and the award-winning, student-run radio station. The Office of Student Activities and the Campus Activities Board provide a variety of special events. A full schedule of men's and women's Division III and intramural sports is also provided. Varsity sports for men are baseball, basketball, football, ice hockey, lacrosse, soccer, and tennis; women's varsity sports are basketball, cross-country, lacrosse, soccer, softball, and tennis.

Now well into its second century of providing distinguished educational service, Curry College was founded in Boston in 1879. It was named in honor of its founders, Samuel Silas Curry and Anna Baright Curry. The College moved to its present site in Milton in 1952. In 1974, it absorbed the Perry Normal School, and, in 1977, it entered into a collaborative relationship with Children's Hospital Medical Center, which resulted in the establishment of Curry's Division of Nursing Studies. Curry College is accredited by the New England Association of Schools and Colleges; the nursing program is accredited by the National League for Nursing Accrediting Commission. Curry offers a Master of Education (M.Ed.) degree, a master's degree in criminal justice, and a master's degree in business administration.

Location

Curry is ideally situated in Milton, Massachusetts, a largely residential suburb located near the exceptional resources of Boston. The greater Boston area provides students with a diversity of cultural, educational, recreational, and sports activities. A wide variety of corporations, hospitals, agencies, broadcasting stations, and schools provide excellent opportunities for internships and jobs for Curry students. The College operates a shuttle bus to the MBTA trains, which provide easy access to Boston. Curry students have the benefit of a traditional, wooded New England campus and access to the excitement of a large city.

Majors and Degrees

Curry College awards the Bachelor of Arts (B.A.) and Bachelor of Science (B.S.) degrees. Majors are biology; child, youth, and community education; communication (with concentrations in film studies, journalism, organizational communication, public communication, public relations, radio broadcasting, television, and theater); criminal justice; early childhood education; elementary education; English (with concentrations in American literature, creative writing, English literature, journalism, and professional writing); environmental science; graphic design; health; information technology; management (with concentrations in accounting, entrepreneurship, finance, human resources, marketing, residential property management, and sports management); nursing; philosophy; politics and history; psychology (with concentrations in counseling, developmental psychology, education, gerontology, health, and substance-abuse counseling); sociology (with concentrations in ethnic and gender studies and service in the community); special education; and visual arts (with concentrations in graphic design and studio arts). Special minors are available in applied computing, dance, music, religion, Spanish, Web development, women's studies, and writing. Provision is also made for students to design majors in areas in which they have a special interest.

Academic Programs

A central liberal arts curriculum, which is required for all students, incorporates a variety of academic disciplines into every student's plan of study. Curry's programs also integrate theoretical classroom learning with a wide variety of field internships in the greater Boston area.

Curry College operates on a two-semester calendar with a summer session. To graduate, students must complete at least 120 credit hours for a B.A. degree or 121 credit hours for the B.S. In both cases, a minimum 2.0 cumulative average must be achieved.

Curry allows students to gain advanced standing in a variety of ways: through successful scores on College-Level Examination Program (CLEP) tests, through credit earned at other accredited colleges and universities, and through end-of-course proficiency examinations. Credit may also be granted for educational experiences that have occurred outside the traditional academic environment.

Many academic programs enrich and facilitate the Curry education. The First Year Seminar, the Honors Program, the Women's Studies Program, the Essential Skills Center, and the Field Experience Program are representative of that focus on special interests and diverse learning needs.

The Program for Advancement of Learning (PAL) is a credited program designed to help intelligent, motivated, language-based learning-disabled students to achieve at the college level. PAL provides individual or small-group instruction, textbooks on tape, and untimed examinations, as well as other services. Students may take advantage of PAL's services throughout their college careers.

Off-Campus Programs

Curry students may earn up to 30 credit hours for field internships with outside firms, agencies, radio stations, hospitals, schools, or similar organizations. In consultation with faculty members, students develop learning contracts that articulate their educational and personal goals and establish criteria for the evaluation of their field experience. Students may also arrange to study abroad or at another institution within the United States while enrolled at Curry.

Academic Facilities

The Levin Memorial Library houses more than 110,000 volumes, 650 periodicals, and 10,000 microforms. It is a designated depository for U.S. government documents. The library also houses the Essential Skills Center, where students may secure assistance in reading, writing, mathematics, and the development of study skills. Three computer laboratories contain more than 100 Macintosh and IBM computers, laser printers, color printers, and state-of-the-art optical scanning equipment. The entire campus is networked and linked to the Internet.

The Science Building includes five laboratories. The Kennedy Academic Center houses a simulated hospital room for use as a nursing laboratory; the Nursing Resource Center, which is equipped with an interactive video lab; and a laboratory for experimental psychology equipped with biofeedback, computer control, and animal and human learning facilities. The Learning Center, with its own computer lab, maintains a complete tape library of all textbooks used at the College. The Hafer Academic Center houses the Experiential Education Office; the Career Planning and Placement Office; the Academic Advising Office; the Educational Technology Center; the Hirsh Communication Center, which features a state-of-the-art television studio; and the Parent's Lounge, which hosts student art exhibits. In addition, Curry students operate and maintain WMLN-FM, the College's 172-watt radio station.

The newest addition to Curry's campus is the Academic and Performance Center. This brand-new, three-story, 30,000-square-foot facility features a 250-seat multipurpose auditorium, state-of-the-art classrooms equipped with wireless laptop connectivity and Smart Board technology, breakout conference rooms, a stock-trading classroom, and a café-style food court in the main atrium. Recently, the College announced plans to construct a new student center, due to break ground in June 2007. Some features of the new student center will include a gymnasium and fitness center, expanded dining hall facilities, offices for student services, and expanded gathering space for students to either engage in quiet study or simply hang out.

Costs

Tuition for the 2007–08 academic year was $24,975. Room was $6010 and board was $4280 (fourteen-meal plan). The cost of the Program for Advancement of Learning was $5300. The cost of books, supplies, and personal expenses varies from $900 to $1200.

Financial Aid

Curry provides financial assistance for students who need funding in order to attend college. The financial aid program consists of federal, state, and Curry College scholarships, grants, work-study awards, student assistant jobs, and loans. Approximately 75 percent of the student body receives financial aid. All students applying for financial aid must submit the Free Application for Federal Student Aid (FAFSA) by March 1. Students applying for financial aid should contact the financial aid office.

Faculty

There are 113 full-time faculty members at Curry, about half of whom hold earned doctoral degrees. In addition, each year the College hires highly qualified part-time faculty members and visiting lecturers to augment its teaching staff. Although primarily a teaching faculty, many of Curry's faculty members are engaged in writing, research, and consulting.

Student Government

The general purpose of the Student Government Association (SGA) is the advancement of the College community and the promotion of the general welfare of the students. The SGA seeks to increase student involvement in the formulation of College policies, communicate effectively with all constituencies of the College, and promote student participation within the institution. Members of the SGA serve on the Joint Committee on Communication of the Board of Trustees.

Admission Requirements

Curry College accepts all students who have the necessary preparation and educational background to meet the requirements of the College, regardless of race, religion, national or ethnic origin, age, sex, sexual orientation, or physical handicap. Freshman students are selected on the basis of a combination of the following: secondary school record, scores on the SAT or ACT, recommendation of the secondary school, and the candidate's readiness for college. To be considered for admission, students must generally present at least 16 units of high school work from an approved secondary school. A recommended program of studies includes 4 years of English, at least 3 years of mathematics, 2 years of a foreign language, 2 years of science (including at least 1 of a laboratory science), and 2 years of social studies. Applicants should contact the Admission Office to discuss any possible exceptions to these requirements. Nursing applicants are required to have taken high school biology and chemistry. A GED certificate is acceptable in lieu of a high school diploma. Curry College seeks well-rounded students who can contribute to the Curry community in athletic, artistic, and social endeavors as well as in the academic sphere.

Application and Information

Curry's recommended application deadline is April 1. Applicants to the learning disability program (PAL) must apply by March 1. Students are accepted on a rolling basis. Admission options, such as early decision, deferred entrance, and advanced placement, are also available. Students may apply for September or January entrance. Applicants must submit an application and fee, an official high school transcript, scores from the SAT or ACT, and a counselor's recommendation. In addition, transfer students must submit official college transcripts, and international students must submit results of the Test of English as a Foreign Language (TOEFL). An interview is recommended. The Admission Committee evaluates each application as soon as all required credentials are received, beginning in January.

Applicants to the Program for Advancement of Learning must submit the application and fee, an official high school transcript, a counselor's recommendation, and the results of a recently administered Wechsler Adult Intelligence Scale (WAIS-R) test. Achievement testing in reading comprehension, written language, and math must also be submitted. The SAT or ACT requirement is waived for PAL applicants. Final decisions on admission to the program are made once all credentials are complete.

For more information about Curry College, students should contact:

Jane Patricia Fidler
Dean of Admission
Curry College
Milton, Massachusetts 02186
Phone: 617-333-2210
800-669-0686 (toll-free)
Fax: 617-333-2114
E-mail: curryadm@curry.edu
Web site: http://www.curry.edu

The suburban campus of Curry College is only minutes from the city of Boston.

DEAN COLLEGE

FRANKLIN, MASSACHUSETTS

The College

Dean College, accredited by the New England Association of Schools and Colleges, is a private residential college located on 100 pristine acres in Franklin, Massachusetts. Dean College is committed to fostering the academic and personal success of students by offering a variety of associate degree programs, transfer preparation for four-year institutions, and a baccalaureate degree in dance. Students further benefit from the high quality of teaching, personalized academic support, and leadership development opportunities that promote a lifetime of learning and achievement.

The College has 1,000 full- and 500 part-time students. Its diverse student body includes representation from twenty-six states and sixteen countries. Dean College offers a variety of housing options, with approximately 90 percent of full-time students living in residence halls.

Students can choose from over twenty clubs and activities, eleven athletic programs, a thriving theater arts scene, and a renowned dance school. The College also offers dances, concerts, comedy nights, and provocative speakers. Varsity league play and intramural sports are available, with 9 acres of playing fields, a 900-seat gym, a 1,500-seat football arena, and lots of screaming fans.

Location

Franklin, Massachusetts, is a quiet, charming New England town ideally situated between Boston, Massachusetts, and Providence, Rhode Island. As a result, Dean students enjoy the best of both worlds: a small-college atmosphere where there is ample solitude for learning, combined with access to a wealth of cultural and recreational opportunities located in the big city just a 40-mile car or train ride away—not to mention the joys of Cape Cod and New Hampshire, also within easy range.

Day trips from Dean include New England Patriots, Boston Red Sox, Bruins, and Celtics games; Cambridge and Harvard Square; Boston's theater district; the Museum of Fine Arts in Boston; the museum of the Rhode Island School of Design; Newbury Street in Boston's Back Bay; shopping at Wrentham Outlets; concerts at the Providence Dunkin' Donuts Center; Tweeter Center concerts at Great Woods; New York City; Vermont's Green Mountains; and the Maine seacoast.

Majors and Degrees

Dean College offers associate degree programs in sixteen majors, designed to prepare students for baccalaureate degree programs and for transfer to major four-year institutions. Associate degrees are offered in business administration, business technology, communications, criminal justice, dance, early childhood education, English, health sciences, history, liberal studies, math/science, philosophy, psychology, sociology, sport/fitness studies (with concentrations in athletic training, exercise science, physical education, and sports management), and theater arts (with concentrations in musical theater and theater).

Dean College also offers Bachelor of Arts degrees in dance and arts management. The B.A. in dance provides specialized education in the four main dance disciplines—ballet, jazz, modern, and tap—within a broad liberal arts environment. The B.A. in arts management focuses on study related to the business side of the arts and entertainment world.

In addition, students who have satisfied their associate degree requirements may further seek a Bachelor of Science degree in one of three majors—communications, criminal justice, and psychology—through the SUFFOLK/DEAN Partnership, an on-campus program that allows students to continue living at Dean while benefiting from the wide range of courses available through Suffolk University in Boston.

Academic Programs

A full-time student is required to register for a minimum of 12 credits of academic work per semester. For graduation, associate degree candidates must maintain a 2.0 cumulative grade point average (GPA), must take a minimum of 60 credits, and demonstrate competency in reading/writing, mathematics, and computers.

Transfer credit toward a Dean degree may be earned by successfully completing courses at another regionally accredited college or university. Students may also earn credits through Advanced Placement (AP) tests and the College Level Examination Program (CLEP). For an associate degree, a maximum of 30 credits may be transferred; however, 24 of a student's last 36 credits must be earned at Dean College. For a Bachelor of Arts degree in dance, a maximum of 70 credits may be transferred; however, 24 of a student's last 36 credits must be earned at Dean College. In addition, all dance courses must be approved by the department.

The First-Year Seminar (FYS), a course taken during the first semester, helps students make a successful transition to college by teaching the academic and personal strategies necessary for success at Dean and beyond. Students enroll jointly in a section of FYS, which is paired with a liberal arts course. The FYS instructor, a learning specialist, attends the liberal arts course with the students and then directly models effective learning strategies for that course with the students. In addition, FYS students participate in campus events that address critical issues facing college students.

The Honors Program offers academically talented students an opportunity to engage in stimulating and challenging courses, seminars, and colloquia during their tenure at Dean College. Open to students who meet the entrance criteria, honors scholars enroll in honors sections of specific courses and may enhance nonhonors courses through additional intensive reading and analysis with instructors. Exciting academic and cultural activities outside the traditional class environment are also available.

Academic Facilities

The Learning Center at Dean serves as the hub of the College's academic support efforts. Here, academic coaches provide one-on-one professional tutoring through the Personalized Learning Services program. Students also have access to peer tutors and can participate in weekly faculty drop-in sessions where group tutoring takes place across various disciplines.

Dean's E. Ross Anderson Library has a comprehensive collection of print and online resources to support research needs. The library houses more than 44,000 books and 200 periodical subscriptions, including extensive reference and legal materials. The A. W. Pierce Technology and Science Building houses academic computer labs, science labs, and classrooms. The Dean College Children's Center, a laboratory preschool, offers a developmental approach to learning, a wide variety of indoor and outdoor activities, and special annual events.

Costs

In 2007–08, Dean College tuition and fees are $25,420. Room and board total $10,960.

Financial Aid

In 2006–07, Dean provided students with more than $9 million of merit-based aid, with the average Dean financial award ranging from $6000 to $15,000. These awards, which are based solely on the information students provide on their admission application, not on financial need, help to reduce their average cost of attendance by more than 30 percent.

Approximately 90 percent of all full-time students at Dean College receive a scholarship that is not based on demonstrated financial need. Since the mission of Dean College is to nurture the potential within its students, these scholarships focus on current performance as well as future potential. They are based on academic or athletic performance, performing arts talent, place of residence, and academic potential. In addition, most students apply for—and receive—federal and state financial aid, which is separate from (and can be added to) Dean's scholarship awards.

Student financial aid packages are generally a combination of grants, loans, and work-study, contingent upon demonstrated financial need and the availability of funds. Dean College participates in all federal Title IV aid programs and the Federal Family Education Loan Programs. Residents of Massachusetts and other reciprocal states may also be eligible for state scholarships, grants, or loans. In order to be considered for need-based financial aid, students must submit the Free Application for Federal Student Aid (FAFSA). After receipt of a valid FAFSA, full-time students are considered for all of the financial aid programs that Dean administers.

Faculty

Dean's dedicated faculty members, advisers, and educational specialists—some of the best in their respective fields—offer direct, personal involvement to help students obtain the full value of their college experience. The student-faculty ratio is 19:1.

Student Government

The Student Government Association (SGA) at Dean College is the voice of the students. The organization provides a liaison between the student body and the administration through which information regarding Dean policies is channeled, seeks out student opinion, speaks for the student body, allocates funds collected from the student activities fee to clubs and organizations through a budget request process, and coordinates College activities by planning and helping various College clubs and organizations to plan individual, group, and campuswide activities.

Admission Requirements

Every application to Dean College is carefully reviewed by the Admission Committee. In addition to the completed application, students must submit the $35 application fee, an official high school transcript, a letter of recommendation from a guidance counselor or teacher, a written statement or essay, and SAT or ACT scores. Interviews are not required for admission to the College, but they are strongly recommended. Students applying for the B.A. in Dance Program must also submit a resume, a 3-minute video (including 1 minute of barre, in DVD format), and a recent full-length photograph in dance attire. Students applying for the B.A. in Arts Management Program must also submit either a 200-word personal statement that addresses their interest in the field of arts management and their involvement in communications, dance, and/or theater; or a creative, artisitic, or performance piece (presented in the form of a DVD, publication clipping, portfolio, etc.) that relates to communications, dance, and/or theater.

Application and Information

Dean College accepts applications on a rolling basis. Once a completed file is received, a decision is made within two weeks.

Office of Admission
Dean College
99 Main Street
Franklin, Massachusetts 02038
Phone: 508-541-1508
877-TRY-DEAN (toll-free)
E-mail: admission@dean.edu
Web site: http://www.dean.edu

ELMS COLLEGE

CHICOPEE, MASSACHUSETTS

The College

Elms College is a dynamic, Catholic, coeducational liberal arts institution in Chicopee, Massachusetts, educating reflective, principled, and creative learners. Elms College has a 12:1 student-faculty ratio; small classes, all taught by faculty members; a challenging curriculum; successful and dynamic graduates; a thriving, inclusive athletic program; a safe campus; and faculty and staff members who are responsive to individual student's needs. Elms College educates learners for life through an integrated liberal arts curriculum that promotes critical thinking, effective communication, an appreciation of the arts and humanities, an ability to utilize technology for the advancement of knowledge, an understanding of faith, and a willingness to respond to global concerns of justice and peace.

Elms College offers Bachelor of Arts (B.A.) and Bachelor of Science (B.S.) degrees in twenty-eight disciplines as well as master's degrees in education (M.Ed.), teaching (M.A.T.), and applied theology (M.A.A.T.) and Certificates of Advanced Graduate Studies (C.A.G.S.) in education and communication sciences and disorders.

There are a total of 754 full-time students on a beautiful suburban 23-acre campus. The College's nine buildings are situated around a spacious quadrangle. Residential students live in three dorms on the campus, all with wireless Internet access. One dorm, Rose William Hall, was completely renovated in 2002. Also facing the quad is the College Center, which houses the dining hall, a bookstore, a black-box theater and media studio, an art gallery, and the offices of campus ministry and community service, intercultural programming, and career and experiential learning. Elms' modern Maguire Center for Health, Fitness, and Athletics contains a gym with a suspended indoor running track, a 25-meter swimming pool, the Blake Aerobic Center, a weight-training area, and a full Health and Wellness Center.

An active student activities office plans cultural and social programs that provide entertainment, create multicultural and global awareness, and bring students together on campus. Elms College has a vibrant and expanding athletics program that gives students a safe environment in which to risk, compete, and be challenged. Elms belongs to the New England Collegiate Conference (NECC), the Northeast Collegiate Volleyball Association (NECVA), and the New England Women's Lacrosse Alliance in NCAA Division III and has varsity teams in women's basketball, cross-country, field hockey, lacrosse, soccer, softball, swimming, and volleyball and men's baseball, basketball, cross-country, golf, soccer, swimming, and volleyball. Elms College has won conference championships in softball, women's cross-country, men's and women's basketball, and men's and women's soccer. In addition, a popular intramural program and an extensive fitness center offer students who are not varsity athletes a chance to be part of the athletic program and work on their fitness goals.

Elms College is a member of the Cooperating Colleges of Greater Springfield (CCGS), a group of eight private and public colleges in the area that, through the sharing of programs, talents, and facilities, bring to Elms students the educational resources of a large university. CCGS offers students enriching educational experiences through shared library privileges, cultural events and social activities, jointly sponsored courses, and faculty member exchange. Most importantly, the cooperative endeavor provides direct academic exchange so that full-time Elms College students may enroll in undergraduate courses offered by the other seven member colleges.

Location

The Elms College campus is located just 2 miles north of the city of Springfield in the scenic and historic Pioneer Valley. The College's proximity to the city makes available a wide array of off-campus activities. The Springfield Civic Center is the site of many major concerts, sporting events, and other activities. Other nearby attractions include Six Flags New England, the Quadrangle Museum area, Basketball Hall of Fame, the MassMutual Center, City Stage, and Symphony Hall. The College's proximity to the mountains of Vermont and New Hampshire and the Berkshire Hills ensures easy access to great skiing, hiking, and other outdoor recreation. Nearby Northampton and Amherst, a 20-minute drive, are home to a thriving arts community, numerous concert venues, theaters and restaurants, and the active Five College Consortium, which is made up of the University of Massachusetts and Amherst, Smith, Hampshire, and Mount Holyoke Colleges. The nearby junction of the Massachusetts Turnpike (Interstate 90) and Interstate 91 provides easy access from all directions. Boston is 1½ hours away; New York City, 3 hours. Springfield is accessible by Amtrak or by air into Bradley International Airport in Hartford, a ½-hour drive from the College.

Majors and Degrees

Elms College awards bachelor's degrees in accounting, biology, chemistry, communication sciences and disorders, computer information technology, early childhood education, elementary education, English, fine art, health-care management, history, international studies and business, legal studies, liberal arts, management, marketing, mathematics, natural sciences, nursing, paralegal studies, professional studies, psychology, religious studies, secondary education, social services/paralegal studies, social work, sociology, Spanish, speech language pathology assistant studies, teacher of English language learners, and teacher of students with moderate disabilities.

Minor concentrations are offered in most majors as well as in coaching, criminal justice (sociology or legal studies), Irish studies, legal nurse consulting, philosophy, sport management, theater, and writing.

Academic Programs

Elms College offers a student-centered and value-oriented curriculum that teaches students to communicate effectively and think critically and creatively. It makes students aware of global issues and gives them an understanding of science, art, history, and themselves.

A minimum of 120 credits is required for graduation. These credits are distributed among core requirements, major requirements, and general electives that may be used for a minor. The College offers students the opportunity to qualify for credit and/or advanced placement through testing programs and a unique experiential learning program that awards credit for nonclassroom learning.

Elms students develop character as well as intellect and are empowered to use their newfound knowledge to make positive changes in the world. Service learning enables them to gain a better understanding of the needs of the community–and the world–in which they live and develop their feeling of responsibility to help. Social justice is interwoven into every aspect of student life at Elms. Each year, the social justice series conducts a yearlong examination of issues affecting the community and the world today. Past series have focused on diversity, capital punishment, the war in Iraq, and immigration and refugees.

The Elms College campus is home to the Irish Cultural Center and the Polish Center of Discovery and Learning, Academic Resource Center, English as a second language courses, internships, study abroad, Japanese language and culture courses, exchange program with Kochi Women's University in Japan, and international study and service opportunities in France, England, China, Honduras, and Jamaica.

Off-Campus Programs

Elms College recognizes that learning comes from outside as well as inside the classroom. The College has a strong internship program that offers students in all majors a valuable opportunity for field work and career exposure. Elms College has a partnership program with the American Institute for Foreign Study (AIFS), which provides overseas study and travel. Through this affiliation, Elms students can study in France, Ireland, or Spain for a semester, a year, or a summer.

Academic Facilities

Berchmans Hall, the main classroom and administration building, dominates the Elms College campus. Housed in this magnificent Gothic structure are a large auditorium, a gym, and state-of-the-art language, science, and computer laboratories. The Alumnae Library provides an ideal atmosphere for study and research. Its holdings include 109,000 volumes, 750 periodicals, and thousands of audiovisual items, CD-ROMs, and reels of microfilm. Provision is made for computer terminals and personal computers as well as areas for listening to, viewing, and recording various types of media. In addition, the library is one of four Federal Depository Libraries in the area and has a collection of 47,000 government documents. Remote access allows students to access the library's research databases from any computer.

Costs

For the 2007–08 academic year, tuition was $22,590, room and board costs were $8400, and fees were $1155.

Financial Aid

Paying for a college education is a major investment, but Elms College strives to bridge the gap between the cost of attendance and family contribution by offering aid such as need-based and non-need-based scholarships; low-interest, long-term loans from external sources, the Federal Work-Study Program, and part-time jobs. The bottom line is that the cost of an Elms College education is usually not more than that of a public college or university once the generous financial aid is applied. More than 91 percent of the students receive some financial assistance. There are several non-need-based scholarships, including the Presidential Scholarship, for the strongest applicants with superior academic records ($7000 to $14,000 a year); the Elms Scholarship, for students with outstanding academic records ($1000 to $6000 per year); the Transfer Scholarship, offered to the strongest transfer candidates and based on GPA ($1000 to $8000 per year); and the Phi Theta Kappa Scholarship, offered to transfer candidates who are members of Phi Theta Kappa ($6000 to $10,000 per year).

Elms College also offers discounts of up to 50 percent of tuition to students admitted directly from Chicopee High School or Chicopee Comprehensive High School in Chicopee, Massachusetts (based on GPA); diocesan scholarship discounts of up to 50 percent of tuition for students from the Springfield Diocesan Catholic high schools (based on GPA); Catholic school grants of $1000 per year for students from Catholic high schools outside the local diocese; Deanery Awards of 50 percent of tuition for 20 students in the Diocese of Springfield (based on involvement in the life of their parishes); and sibling discounts of 25 percent of tuition for families with more than 1 full-time dependent undergraduate at the College in any given year.

Faculty

Elms College has 63 full-time faculty members, of whom 91 percent hold doctoral or terminal degrees, and 65 part-time faculty members, of whom 23 percent hold doctoral or terminal degrees. Faculty members, many of whom also serve as academic advisers, teach all of the classes. They take a personal interest in guiding each student toward his or her academic and career goals.

Student Government

Students are involved in campus governance through the Faculty-Student Senate (FSS) and the Student Government Association (SGA). Major policy decisions related to student life are made by the FSS, which is composed of 6 students and 6 faculty members, and the SGA, which is composed of an executive board, a student council, and a financial committee. These forms of governance allow for significant student involvement in all matters related to student life.

Admission Requirements

Elms College seeks women and men who have distinguished themselves inside and outside the classroom. In keeping with the College's commitment to a personalized education, the admissions committee carefully reviews the credentials of each applicant, considering the depth and variety of the academic program pursued, GPA, recommendations from teachers and/or guidance counselors, scores on the SAT or ACT, participation in student activities, and part-time employment. Students seeking admission into the nursing program are also reviewed by a Nursing Admission Committee to determine if acceptance directly into that program can be offered.

Application and Information

Elms College requires a completed application, two letters of recommendation, high school transcript, SAT scores, TOEFL scores from international students, and an application fee of $30. A personal interview is not required but is strongly recommended. Interested students are encouraged to visit the campus and discuss their academic and career aspirations with an admission counselor. Several open houses and overnight programs are offered during the academic year, and tours and interviews are available year-round.

For further information and application materials, students should contact:

Joseph Wagner
Director of Admission
Elms College
291 Springfield Street
Chicopee, Massachusetts 01013-2839
Phone: 413-592-3189
800-255-ELMS (3567) (toll-free)
Fax: 413-594-2781
E-mail: admissions@elms.edu
Web site: http://www.elms.edu

Students at Elms College.

EMERSON COLLEGE

BOSTON, MASSACHUSETTS

The College

Founded in 1880, Emerson is one of the premier colleges in the United States for the study of communication and the arts. Students may choose from more than two dozen undergraduate and graduate programs supported by state-of-the-art facilities and a nationally renowned faculty. The campus is home to WERS-FM, the oldest noncommercial radio station in Boston; the historic 1,200-seat Cutler Majestic Theatre; and *Ploughshares,* the award-winning literary journal for new writing.

A pioneer in the fields of communication and performing arts, Emerson was one of the first colleges in the nation to establish a program in children's theater (1919), an undergraduate program in broadcasting (1937), professional-level training in speech pathology and audiology (1935), educational FM radio (1949), closed-circuit television (1955), and a B.F.A. degree program in film as early as 1972. In 1980, the College created the country's first graduate program in professional writing and publishing.

Today, Emerson's 3,000 undergraduate and 900 graduate students come from across the country and more than forty other countries. Approximately 1,200 students live on campus, some in special learning communities, such as the Writers' Block and Digital Culture Floor. Emerson's residence halls are air conditioned with cable television and Internet access. Wireless service is available in several campus locations. There is a fitness center, athletic field, and a new fourteen-story campus center and residence hall that houses a gymnasium, student-services offices, and meeting space for student organizations.

Emerson College is fully accredited by the New England Association of Schools and Colleges.

In addition to its undergraduate programs, Emerson College offers more than a dozen master's degree programs for its graduate students.

Location

With dozens of institutions of higher learning, Boston is the country's best-known college town. The city contains a wealth of diversions ranging from scenic harbor cruises, Boston Pops concerts, and neighborhood festivals to baseball's Fenway Park and the legendary Boston Marathon. Emerson's campus is located on Boston Common in the heart of the city's theater district—within sight of the Massachusetts State House and walking distance from the historic Freedom Trail, Boston Public Garden, Chinatown, financial district, and numerous restaurants and museums. Boston is also an international city with more than thirty foreign consulates, a busy international airport, and several multinational corporations.

Majors and Degrees

Emerson confers Bachelor of Arts, Bachelor of Fine Arts, and Bachelor of Science degrees. Students can major in acting; broadcast journalism; communication sciences and disorders; communication studies; marketing communication: advertising and public relations; media production (animation and motion media, digital postproduction, film, interactive media, radio, sound design, studio television production, writing for film and television); media studies; musical theater; political communication: leadership, politics, and social advocacy; print and multimedia journalism; stage/production management; theater design/technology; theater education; theater studies; and writing, literature, and publishing. Interdisciplinary and self-designed majors, as well as an honors program, are available through the College's Institute for Liberal Arts & Interdisciplinary Studies.

Academic Programs

Emerson's academic calendar consists of two fifteen-week semesters, plus two six-week sessions during the summer months. The requirements for graduation combine general education and liberal arts courses with advanced, specialized classes that are specific to individual departments and majors. Internships for academic credit are available in almost every major and the Institute for Liberal Arts & Interdisciplinary Studies offers exciting first-year seminars, independent study options, and innovative courses that cut across academic disciplines.

Off-Campus Programs

Internships are popular with Emerson students. Hundreds of placements exist throughout Boston and in major cities across the country, including exclusive placements at the College's Los Angeles Center—a residential study and internship program in the heart of the world's entertainment capital.

Emerson also sponsors a semester-long study-abroad program in Kasteel Well, The Netherlands. Students live and study in a restored thirteenth-century castle and take field trips to major cities throughout Europe. In addition, there is a summer film program in Prague and course cross-registration with the six-member Boston ProArts Consortium, whose members include the Berklee College of Music, the Boston Conservatory, Boston Architectural Center, Emerson, the School of the Museum of Fine Arts, and Massachusetts College of Art.

Academic Facilities

Emerson possesses the highest quality visual and media arts equipment, including professionally sound-treated television studios, digital editing labs, audio postproduction suites with analog and digital peripherals, industry-standard software, and a professional marketing-research suite/focus room. In fact, more than half of Emerson's campus has been built new or completely refurbished since 2002. There are two radio stations, seven on-campus facilities and programs to observe speech and hearing therapy, and an integrated digital newsroom for aspiring journalists. The eleven-story Tufte Performance and Production Center houses expanded performance and rehearsal space, a theater design/technology center, makeup lab, and costume shop. Current on-campus projects include renovations to the historic Paramount Theatre complex (to create a cinema, scene shop, sound stage, and residence hall) and Boston's Colonial Building, which houses the city's oldest performance venue.

The Emerson College Library houses more than 175,000 volumes and serial subscriptions, 11,000 microforms, 9,000 audio/visual materials, and 7,000 e-books. The library's Web pages are designed to serve as a gateway for research and can be accessed from the library's workstations, computers located throughout the campus, and dormitory rooms or off-campus apartments, using a student account. Emerson students can also access the resources of a dozen cooperating libraries through the College's membership in the Fenway Library Consortium.

Costs

The basic expenses related to attending Emerson College for the 2007–08 academic year were $26,866 for tuition and $11,376 for room and board. Approximately $2500 should be allotted for books and supplies, fees, health insurance, and personal expenses, including travel.

Financial Aid

Each year, more than two thirds of Emerson's student body receive some form of financial assistance, packaged in awards that typically combine grant and scholarship, loan, and College work-study. Academic scholarships ranging from $8000 to half-tuition are awarded on a limited basis to students who meet high academic standards. Special performance-based scholarships, averaging $4000, are available to exceptional students in the performing arts.

In order to apply for financial assistance, students must complete the Free Application for Federal Student Assistance (FAFSA) and CSS PROFILE form. Deadlines are March 1 for September admission or November 15 for January admission. More information about financial assistance at Emerson can be found online at http://www.emerson.edu/financial_services or by contacting the Office of Student Financial Services at 617-824-8655 or finaid@emerson.edu.

Faculty

With an estimated average class size of 24, students at Emerson develop close relationships with a remarkably talented and active faculty. Faculty members are nationally recognized and award-winning authors, directors, producers, consultants, playwrights, and editors. The vast majority of the faculty have earned doctorates or the highest degree obtainable in their field. The student-teacher ratio is 14:1.

Student Government

Emerson has more than sixty student organizations and performance groups, fourteen NCAA intercollegiate teams, and several student publications and honor societies. The Student Government Association, in cooperation with the Office of Student Affairs staff, plans and executes student activities, allocates and supervises funding for clubs, and serves as a liaison between the student body and the College administration.

Admission Requirements

Emerson accepts the Common Application. Students whose interests and abilities are compatible with the College's specialty in communication and the arts are welcome to apply. Admission is competitive. Each year, more than 5,000 applications are received for a class of 700. Selection is based on academic promise as indicated by secondary school performance, recommendations, writing competency, and SAT or ACT scores (or TOEFL if English is not the first language). The College also considers personal qualities as seen in extracurricular activities, community involvement, and demonstrated leadership.

The academic preparation for successful candidates should include 4 years of English and 3 years each of mathematics, science, social science, and a single foreign language. Candidates for programs offered by the Department of Performing Arts are required to submit a resume of theater-related activities and audition, interview, or submit a portfolio or an essay. Applicants for the media production major with a specialty in film must submit a sample of creative work, either a script or DVD.

Application and Information

First-year candidates for September admission should file their application by January 5. Early Action applications are due November 1. The regular admission deadline for January admission is November 1.

Transfer students should submit their applications and supporting credentials by March 15 for September admission or November 1 for January admission.

Office of Undergraduate Admission
Emerson College
120 Bolyston Street
Boston, Massachusetts 02116-4624
Phone: 617-824-8600
Fax: 617-824-8609
E-mail: admission@emerson.edu
Web site: http://www.emerson.edu

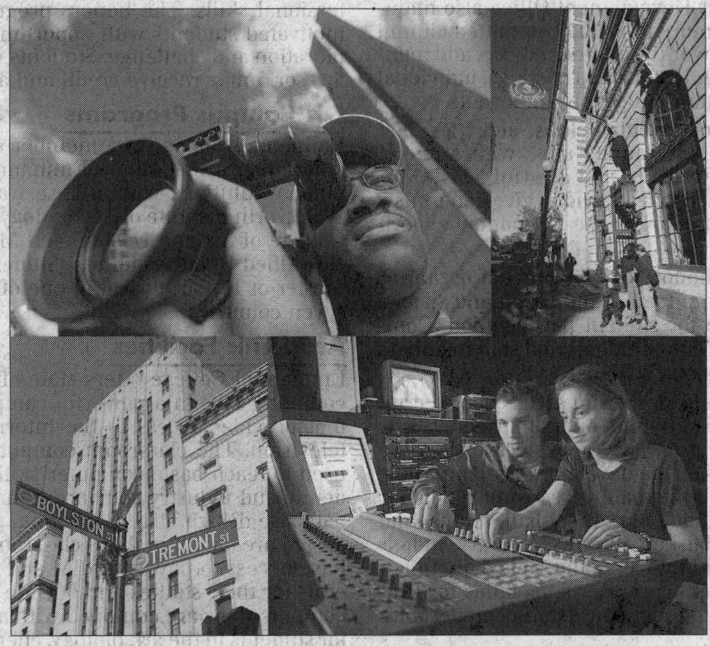

Emerson College: Bringing Innovation to Communication and the Arts.

EMMANUEL COLLEGE

BOSTON, MASSACHUSETTS

The College

Emmanuel College is a coed, residential, Catholic liberal arts and sciences college located on 17 acres in the middle of the excitement, resources, and culture of the city of Boston. Emmanuel's neighbors include a world-class medical center, two major art museums, and Fenway Park.

With a strong liberal arts and sciences core curriculum a proud tradition since 1919, Emmanuel has over 1,700 undergraduate students from twenty-four countries and thirty-two states. Approximately 75 percent of the College's traditional undergraduate students reside in Emmanuel's residence halls on the campus, while the rest commute from the local area.

Students at Emmanuel become active members of the community and participate in internships with the city's most prestigious, leading-edge businesses and nonprofit organizations. A unique partnership with Merck & Co. Inc., which recently opened Merck Research Laboratories-Boston on the Emmanuel campus, provides unprecedented opportunities for students and faculty members.

Supporting the College's mission, the Jean Yawkey Center provides athletic, recreational, and dining facilities and houses the Jean Yawkey Center for Community Leadership. This center focuses on developing service and leadership skills for Emmanuel students and building connections with the young people of the city of Boston through after-school and summer programs. The Carolyn A. Lynch Institute of Emmanuel College strengthens this connection by enabling the development and retention of teachers in urban school systems, focusing on training in math, science, and technology.

The Internship and Career Development Office offers a four-year career-development program for all Emmanuel students. Starting in their first year and continuing until graduation, students are exposed to career planning, assessment, and goal setting. Workshops on resume writing, job/internship search skills, the Internet job search, and interviewing skills are some of the services that are offered to students. The Internship and Career Development Office also maintains a Career Advisory Network of more than 300 committed alumni who are available to students for networking, career advice, and mentorship. Other services include job and internship postings, individual career counseling, and career planning programs and events.

With more than eighty different cocurricular clubs, activities, and organizations on campus, this is a community alive with a strong sense of mission; a vibrant, confident faith; and a joyful spirit. Emmanuel students are challenged to act, to lead, and to give generously to others; community service is a hallmark of the Emmanuel experience.

A wide variety of academic clubs, honor societies, media organizations, performance groups, leadership teams, and social and special interest organizations are available for student participation. Community service is a campus priority. Many students and staff members volunteer in neighborhood agencies and schools.

Emmanuel's NCAA Division III athletics program gives every recruit a chance to make his or her mark. Emmanuel offers fourteen varsity teams. Its strong intramural sports program keeps everyone in the game. The athletics program focuses on the development of the whole person. Women's athletics include basketball, cross-country, indoor track and field, outdoor track and field, soccer, softball, tennis, and volleyball. Men's athletics include basketball, cross-country, indoor track and field, outdoor track and field, soccer, and volleyball. In addition to athletics facilities supporting team sports, facilities for Emmanuel students include a fitness center, a dance studio, an aerobics room, and a nearby swimming pool.

A leader in educating adults for nearly thirty years, Emmanuel College's Graduate and Professional Programs also offer accelerated courses leading to undergraduate and graduate degrees in education, human resources management, management, and nursing. These programs can be taken in flexible format at the Boston campus as well as satellite campuses throughout eastern Massachusetts.

Emmanuel College is accredited by the New England Association of Schools and Colleges.

Location

Emmanuel College's unique location allows student and faculty members the opportunities to explore real-world experiences through internships, research, and strategic partnerships within the Longwood Medical area and the city of Boston, its extended classroom. The College also believes in the transformative power of education through service learning, travel, and opportunities abroad.

Majors and Degrees

Emmanuel College confers bachelor's degrees in American studies, art, biology, biochemistry, biostatistics, chemistry, education (elementary and secondary), English, environmental science, global studies, history, management, mathematics, political science, psychology, sociology, and Spanish. Students may also design individualized majors that reflect particular academic and career interests. The College confers a Bachelor of Fine Arts in graphic design. Tracks within majors allow students with specialized interests to pursue concentrations in art therapy, communications, counseling and health psychology, developmental psychology, global management, marketing–media and design, and medical technology. The education program provides initial licensure for elementary and secondary education.

Academic Programs

The bachelor's degree requires completion of thirty-two courses, divided among general education requirements, major requirements, and electives. Students may choose a minor within any department that offers a major and also in the following areas: applied ethics, art history, biochemistry, Catholic studies, economics, information technology, Latin American studies, music, organizational leadership, philosophy, religious studies, speech, theater arts, and women's studies. Internships are an integral part of most majors and provide students with opportunities for career exploration and the acquisition of professional skills. The honors program provides highly qualified and motivated students with opportunities for additional intellectual exploration and challenge. Students with Advanced Placement scores of 3, 4, or 5 may receive credit and advanced placement.

Off-Campus Programs

Emmanuel College is a member of the Colleges of the Fenway collaboration, which allows Emmanuel students to take courses at five other institutions within close walking distance: Simmons College, Wentworth Institute of Technology, Wheelock College, Massachusetts College of Art and Design, and Massachusetts College of Pharmacy and Allied Health Sciences. Students are encouraged to spend a semester or a year abroad in one of more than 500 programs in sixty-seven countries.

Academic Facilities

Emmanuel College offers state-of-the-art computer classrooms and computer labs in a powerful campuswide communications network that provides access to the Internet, voice mail, e-mail, and cable television. The classroom computers, both IBM and Macintosh, are used to teach basic computer skills as well as a wide variety of academic and industry software. Courses in calculus, communications, database design, digital imaging, graphic design, statistics, and Web design are taught in these classrooms. In the computer labs, students have access to powerful IBM and Macintosh computers and peripherals for their studies and outside interests. Other discipline-specific computer labs are equipped with appropriate hardware and software for students in the art, biology, chemistry, and education departments. The Emmanuel College Wireless Network allows all students and staff and faculty members with active FirstClass e-mail accounts and a laptop containing a wireless networking card to access the Internet and FirstClass wirelessly at most public locations on campus.

In addition to administrative and faculty offices, the administration building houses a chapel, an auditorium, a dance studio, lecture and conference rooms, a bookstore, art and music studios, computer classrooms (IBM and Macintosh platforms), and media classrooms.

The Cardinal Cushing Library, which holds 98,000 volumes, 400 journals, and 39 online databases to support student and faculty member research, also includes listening, viewing, and editing rooms; an art gallery; a language laboratory; and a state-of-the-art lecture hall, complete with satellite technology. The library participates with other local institutions in cooperative alliances to share resources and online catalogs and to exchange information. Library services include reference assistance, bibliographic instruction, interlibrary loan services, and electronic research.

Costs

Tuition for the 2007–08 academic year was $26,100. Room and board costs in the College residence halls were $11,200 per year. There are additional fees of approximately $525 per year.

Financial Aid

Emmanuel College is committed to helping students pay for an Emmanuel College education by providing need-based grants, merit scholarships, low-interest student loans, and employment opportunities. Students' eligibility for need-based financial aid is determined through a careful analysis of information provided by students and their families regardless of race, color, religion, sex, age, national or ethnic origin, or the presence of any handicap. Entering students who seek financial assistance must complete the Free Application for Federal Student Aid (FAFSA) and the Emmanuel College Application for Financial Aid. The FAFSA may be obtained from a secondary school or the College or may be completed online at http://www.fafsa.ed.gov. The Emmanuel College Application for Financial Aid may be obtained from the College or can be printed from the College Web site. The priority filing date for financial aid is April 1.

Students who complete the requirements for admission to Emmanuel College are considered for special scholarships that are awarded on the basis of academic achievement and specific eligibility requirements. These include the Presidential Scholarship (full tuition), the Dean's Scholarship ($15,000), the Academic Achievement Award ($7500–$12,500), the City of Boston Scholarship, and the Phi Theta Kappa Scholarship (for transfer students).

Of special interest is the Sisters of Notre Dame Scholarship program, a $2500 scholarship awarded to students recommended, in writing, by a Sister of Notre Dame. Also of special interest is the $2500 Friends of Emmanuel Scholarship, for which an alumnus or staff or faculty member from Emmanuel College recommends an incoming student. Students must submit the Friends of Emmanuel recommendation form with the written recommendation. Both of these scholarship recommendation forms need to be submitted by the scholarship deadline. In addition, each year, twenty-five $2500 scholarships are awarded to students who demonstrate exemplary leadership or community service experience. Students wishing to be considered for this scholarship must submit a written recommendation that states the type of leadership position or community service activity the student participated in, the length of service, and specific accomplishments.

Faculty

The College has 86 full-time faculty members, 79 percent of whom have a doctorate or other terminal degree. Faculty members hold degrees from prestigious national and international universities. The student-faculty ratio is 15:1. All classes are taught by faculty members, not teaching assistants.

Student Government

Emmanuel students have the opportunity to participate in decision-making processes that affect the College. The student governing body is the Student Government Association (SGA), which comprises student representatives from each class and an Executive Board. The SGA works closely with the College administration and presents the needs and opinions of the students to the College community.

Admission Requirements

An applicant's academic achievement, creativity, initiative, and involvement in the community are considered. No single standard measure for determining ability is used in accepting applicants to the College. The admissions committee reviews each applicant's high school curriculum and record, recommendations, and test results. It is recommended that applicants submit a strong academic program.

Candidates for admission as first-year students are required to take either the SAT or ACT. A personal interview with a representative of the Admissions Office can be scheduled. Applicants are encouraged to visit the campus during their junior or senior year of high school so that they may visit classes and talk with students and faculty members.

Application and Information

To apply, a student must submit an application along with a $40 nonrefundable fee, an essay, SAT or ACT scores, an official high school transcript including first-quarter senior year grades, and two letters of recommendation. International students must submit the TOEFL score and Certification of Finances. The College's application deadline is March 1 for first-year students and April 1 for transfer students. Emmanuel observes the College Board's Candidates Reply Date of May 1. The College also subscribes to the early decision plan. All admissions requirements should be completed before November 1 of the applicant's senior year to be considered for early decision.

Students who apply for transfer admissions must submit an application; an essay; a nonrefundable fee of $40; official secondary school and postsecondary school transcripts, including scores on the SAT or ACT; and two letters of recommendation, at least one from a recent college professor.

For further information or an application, students should contact:

Sandra Robbins
Dean of Enrollment
Emmanuel College
400 The Fenway
Boston, Massachusetts 02115
Phone: 617-735-9715
Fax: 617-735-9801
E-mail: enroll@emmanuel.edu
Web site: http://www.emmanuel.edu

Emmanuel College.

FITCHBURG STATE COLLEGE

FITCHBURG, MASSACHUSETTS

The College

Fitchburg State College is a liberal arts institution where career-oriented and professional education programs thrive. The College guarantees that its graduates are qualified for jobs in their fields and continues to place more than 85 percent of its graduates in their chosen professions within six months of graduation.

Fitchburg State's excellent academic reputation and graduate placement can be attributed to a nationally recognized faculty and a strong commitment to teaching. The College enrolls approximately 3,500 undergraduate students in its day and evening divisions and another 1,500 students in its graduate programs. The average undergraduate class size is 25, and the overall student-teacher ratio remains low at 16:1. Each student is assigned to an academic adviser to assist with the planning of a program of study. In addition, each department has access to state-of-the-art equipment and an internship network that spreads throughout New England.

Student life at Fitchburg State is friendly and informal. There are numerous and varied opportunities for student leadership through the Student Government Association, the Athletic Council, the All-College Committee, the Campus Center Advisory Committee, Residence Hall Councils, publications, and student-faculty-administration committees. More than sixty student-run clubs and organizations are open to all students, including the Dance Club, a student newspaper, the Falcon Players (theater), WXPL (student radio station), and the Black Student Union. Several sororities and fraternities contribute to the social and recreational life of the campus. Hundreds of popular and well-attended activities take place during the year, including films, lectures, concerts, seminars, coffeehouses, pub entertainment, recreational tournaments, a performing arts series, and visual arts exhibits.

In addition to B.A., B.S., and Bachelor of Science in Education degrees, Fitchburg State confers the Master of Arts in Teaching (M.A.T.), the Master in Business Administration (M.B.A.), the Master of Education (M.Ed.) in several disciplines, and the Master of Science (M.S.) in applied communication, computer science, counseling, and management. Several Certificate of Advanced Graduate Studies (C.A.G.S.) programs are available as well.

Location

The College is located in a residential area near the center of Fitchburg, a city with a population of 43,000, which serves as the hub of the commercial and industrial life of north-central Massachusetts. The Wallace Civic Center and Planetarium provides a variety of activities, such as exhibits, fairs, performances, ice skating, hockey, light shows, astronomy demonstrations, and lectures. Fitchburg offers many opportunities for study and practical experience in the areas of sociology, psychology, health, computer technology, business, industry, political organization, and community service. Outdoor activities, including skiing, camping, hiking, canoeing, and fishing, are just minutes from the campus.

The historic and literary centers of Lexington and Concord and the widely varied cultural advantages of Boston are approximately an hour's travel from the College. Worcester is a half hour to the south. Both commuter rail and bus service are available.

Majors and Degrees

Fitchburg State College confers the Bachelor of Arts, Bachelor of Science, and Bachelor of Science in Education degrees and offers the following undergraduate programs: accounting, architectural technology, biology, biotechnology, clinical exercise physiology, computer information systems, computer science, construction technology, criminal justice, developmental psychology, earth science, economics, education (teacher education programs are available in early childhood education; elementary education; middle school education; secondary education, with emphases in biology, earth science, English, history, and mathematics; special education, with emphases in intensive severe disabilities (all levels), moderate disabilities (pre-K–8), and moderate disabilities (5–12); and technology education), electronics engineering technology, English, environmental biology, exercise and sport science, facilities management, film/video production, fitness management, geo/physical sciences, graphic design, history, human services, industrial and organizational psychology, interactive media, interdisciplinary studies–humanities, international business and economics, literature, management, manufacturing engineering technology, marketing, mathematics, nursing, photography, political science, professional communication, professional writing, psychology, sociology, technical theater arts, theater, and the following preprofessional programs: dentistry, law, medicine, and veterinary medicine.

Academic Programs

The College's undergraduate programs operate on a two-semester calendar. The first semester begins in early September and ends in mid-December, and the second semester begins in mid-January and ends in mid-May.

The curriculum has a strong liberal arts and sciences requirement, providing a solid foundation for either further academic study or a career. Students may obtain practical experience through numerous internships in social agencies, government offices, and businesses related to their interests. Some major programs require an extensive supervised practicum to complete degree requirements. For education and nursing majors, a broad spectrum of student-teaching and clinical experiences are incorporated into their respective programs of study. The Leadership Academy (the College's four-year honors program) culminates in a senior thesis or project.

Off-Campus Programs

Fitchburg State is one of nine state colleges under the jurisdiction of the Massachusetts Board of Higher Education. Through this affiliation, students may participate in the College Academic Program Sharing program, which allows study for a semester or a year at another college. The Office of International Education at Fitchburg State provides undergraduate students with the opportunity to study abroad at a variety of colleges and universities overseas. Programs may vary in length from as short as a few weeks to as long as a semester or a year. Over the past several years, Fitchburg State students have studied in Australia, England, Italy, Latin America, Scotland, and Spain.

Academic Facilities

The College has a number of special facilities. An unusually well-equipped Academic Success Center includes offices for academic advising, career services, disability services, math and writing centers, and peer tutoring. The McKay Campus School Teacher Education Center is specifically designed for observing pupil development and instructional techniques. An Instructional Media Center is located in the Conlon Building. Modern, well-equipped shops support the industrial education and industrial technology programs. The nursing program utilizes an on-campus clinical lab that simulates a hospital setting with computerized training models. The communication media program owns a full range of late-model equipment, such as a full-color dye-sublimation printer and CD recording and slide-scanning equipment, and supports multiple editing rooms, a production studio, darkrooms, and graphic design computer labs. Communication students at Fitchburg State have access to appropriate equipment and facilities as early as their freshman year.

Costs

Tuition for residents of Massachusetts was $970 per year in 2007–08; out-of state students paid $7050. Residence hall and meal plan costs were $6830. Required fees, including the student activity fee, Campus Center fee, and athletic fee, totaled $5022. Books and supplies were estimated at $750, depending on the student's major. Fees are subject to change.

The College also participates in a regional compact under the auspices of the New England Board of Higher Education, which provides New England residents with a tuition break when they study certain majors at public colleges and universities in other New England states (not available at public colleges in their home state). In 2007–08, out-of-state Fitchburg State students who met the requirements for this tuition assistance program paid tuition at a rate of 150 percent of the in-state tuition, or approximately $1455 per year.

Financial Aid

Many sources of financial aid are available to Fitchburg State students. The College participates in federal and state programs. Packages consisting of grants, loans, work-study awards, and scholarships are given to students demonstrating financial need and academic merit. Financial aid applications for the fall semester must be completed by the preceding March 1 to be given priority consideration.

Faculty

More than 80 percent of Fitchburg State's 183 full-time faculty members hold earned doctoral or other terminal degrees. Full professors teach freshman sections as well as advanced courses and serve as academic advisers to students majoring in their respective programs.

Student Government

All full-time undergraduate students are members of the Student Government Association (SGA). The purposes of the SGA are to encourage responsibility and cooperation in democratic self-government; to form an official body for expressing the judgments of students and fostering activities and matters of general student interest; and to promote full understanding and cooperation among the students, the faculty members, and the administration in order to further the welfare of the College.

The governing body of the SGA consists of 6 SGA officers and a General Council, which includes these officers and 28 elected representatives of classes and residence halls, as well as the commuter student body. The SGA operates through a number of standing and ad hoc committees, membership on which is open to all students.

An 11-member All-College Committee, representing students, the faculty, and the administration, makes recommendations to the president of the College concerning matters of campuswide policy.

Admission Requirements

The College seeks to admit, without regard to race, religion, or ethnic background, students who are capable of success. To this end, significant attention is given to the student's high school record and SAT or ACT scores. The record of achievement in high school is the single most important item in the applicant's academic credentials. Freshman applicants should have completed a college-preparatory program that includes 16 college-preparatory units, with 4 units in English, 2 units in the same foreign language, 2 units in social studies, 3 units in mathematics (algebra I and II and geometry), 3 units in the natural sciences (2 of which must be laboratory courses), and two college-preparatory electives.

An essay is required; however, interviews are not required. Applicants who have questions about the programs and admission procedures at the College are encouraged to request an interview through the Admissions Office.

Transfer students are welcome to apply to Fitchburg State. An official transcript from each college previously attended must be submitted.

International students are encouraged to apply. Scores on the Test of English as a Foreign Language (TOEFL), evaluations of all international transcripts, and translations of international transcripts must also be submitted. Additional information for international students is available on the College's Web site.

Application and Information

Fitchburg State College reviews applications on a rolling basis, sending its first set of admission decisions for the fall semester by mid-December. The priority deadline for applications is March 1. Applicants to the communications media and nursing programs are strongly encouraged to submit their applications by January 1. In addition, applicants who wish to be considered for merit scholarships and the Leadership Academy must complete their admission and financial aid application process (i.e., submit all required materials) by February 1.

Transfer applicants are encouraged to apply by April 15 for the fall and by December 1 for the spring semester. International applicants must complete the application process by June 1 for the fall semester and by October 1 for the spring.

For further information, students should contact:

Office of Admissions
Fitchburg State College
160 Pearl Street
Fitchburg, Massachusetts 01420
Phone: 800-705-9692 (toll-free)
Fax: 978-665-4540
E-mail: admissions@fsc.edu
Web site: http://www.fsc.edu

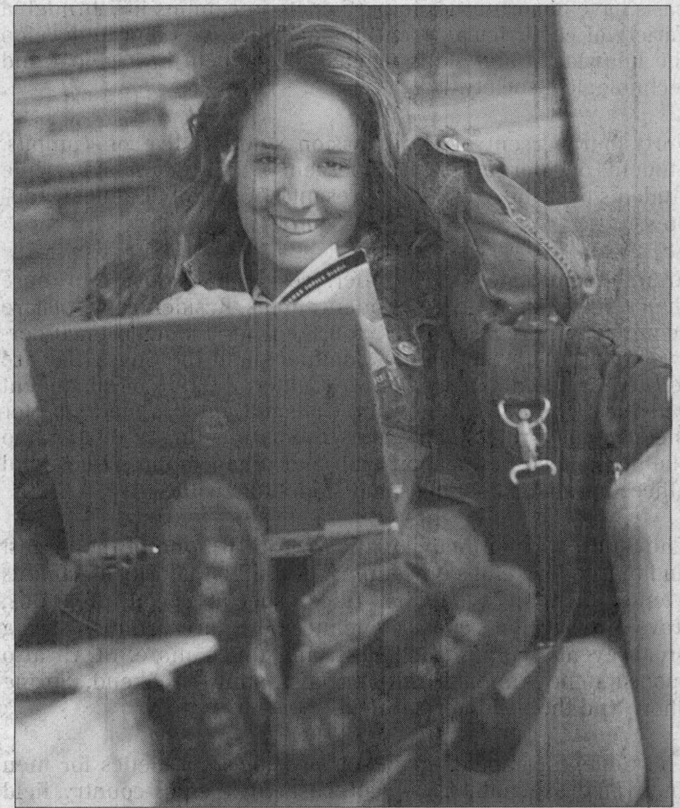

A student works on a laptop in Edgerly Hall at Fitchburg State College. The College began its laptop initiative, which requires all incoming freshmen to purchase laptops, in fall 2006.

FRAMINGHAM STATE COLLEGE

FRAMINGHAM, MASSACHUSETTS

The College

Framingham State College offers small, personalized classes to 6,000 undergraduate and graduate students on a traditional, New England campus. Student success is central to the mission of the College. Many options are available for student support, including programs to help freshmen transition to college. The College also has a robust honors program for exceptional students.

The breadth of programs offered by Framingham State College reflects diverse faculty expertise. Although the College's traditional focus was teacher education, the majority of students today major in fields ranging from business to the sciences to fashion design and retailing, along with a significant number who continue to major in education. The College offers twenty-five majors and many career-related concentrations.

In addition to its undergraduate program, Framingham State College graduates approximately 500 master's students each year. In 2007, the College added an M.B.A. program to its graduate program mix. In addition, the College is a pioneer in undergraduate and graduate online education, having offered online courses since 1998.

Traditional college-age students as well as nontraditional students seeking higher education on either a full- or part-time basis have opportunities to participate in campus life through a variety of cocurricular programs and activities and to develop the knowledge and skills needed to compete in a global and technological society.

Forty-four percent of Day Division students live on campus. Students of color represent 12 percent of the student body, while students over the age of 25 represent 17 percent of undergraduates.

Framingham State College offers residential housing to more than 1,500 students in six residence halls. Resident students are required to purchase a ten-, fourteen-, or nineteen-meal-per-week plan. Both the Dining Commons and the Snack Bar are located in the McCarthy College Center, the hub of all student activities. The newly renovated College Center is the home for the campus art gallery, game room, meeting rooms, radio station, college newspaper, club and organization offices, and offices for student services and student activities.

The Student Union Activities Board (SUAB), one of the largest and most active clubs on campus, plans the majority of campus events, including concerts, films, special social programs, travel, recreation, concerts, dances, lectures, films, spring break events, cultural activities, and much more. SUAB also sponsors the Annual Semi-Formal, Family Weekend, Spring Show, and the Sandbox Carnival.

The College competes in NCAA Division III athletics for men and women, including baseball, basketball, cross-country, field hockey, football, ice hockey, lacrosse, soccer, softball, and volleyball. Intramural sports are also offered, including cheerleading and rugby. A 65,000-square-foot athletic facility opened in 2001.

Location

The College is located in the Commonwealth of Massachusetts' MetroWest area just 20 miles west of Boston. It is the only public four-year college between Route 495 and Route 128, close to the heart of the high-technology industry and within reach of hundreds of professional companies and businesses. The 73-acre campus offers students a small- to medium-sized suburban campus with access to the cultural, recreational, educational, and career opportunities of Boston and New England.

Majors and Degrees

Framingham State College confers the Bachelor of Arts, Bachelor of Science, and Bachelor of Science in Education degrees. Undergraduate majors are offered in art history, biology, business administration, business and information technology, chemistry, communication arts, computer science, early childhood education, economics, elementary education, English, fashion design and retailing, food and nutrition, food science, geography, health and consumer sciences, history, liberal studies, mathematics, modern languages, nursing (post-RN program), politics, psychology, sociology, and studio art. Within the twenty-five major programs are a variety of concentrations and minors. Pre-engineering, prelaw, and premedical professional programs are also offered.

Academic Programs

The mission of Framingham State College is to offer a dynamic and affordable program of educational excellence to its students. The College emphasizes a broad curriculum that blends liberal arts and sciences with several professional fields.

Each student must satisfy a thirty-two-course requirement for completion of any degree program. Up to twenty courses form the basis of a student's major area of study. The remaining twelve courses are used to fulfill the general education requirement, which encompasses writing, mathematics, humanities, social sciences, physical and life sciences, foreign language, and the study of federal and state constitutions. The general education requirement ensures that students experience the benefits of a liberal arts education through familiarity with a variety of curricula. Each student is assigned a faculty member in his or her major as an academic adviser. Undeclared students are assigned advisers through the Center for Academic Support and Advising (CASA). Selected students may participate in departmental and College-wide honors programs.

The College operates on the traditional two-semester calendar, with two optional summer sessions as well as a winter intersession.

Off-Campus Programs

Framingham State College students may choose to participate in one or several college-affiliated programs, allowing them to take credit-bearing courses outside of the College. Among the most popular are internships; the College Academic Program Sharing (CAPS) program; the Massachusetts Bay Marine Studies Consortium; the Washington, D.C., Internship; and study abroad.

Internships are available in most majors. Annually, hundreds of Framingham State College students serve as interns in the Massachusetts State House, town and city governments, museums, and a variety of businesses and high-technology firms in the greater Boston area. Internships allow students the opportunity to gain direct, practical experience while applying the knowledge and skills they have acquired in the classroom.

Through the CAPS program, Framingham State College students may take up to 30 semester hours of college credit at one of the seven other Massachusetts state colleges. Students who participate in the Massachusetts Bay Marine Studies Consortium may also attend a variety of credit-bearing classes and symposia at other schools.

Students who seek an international dimension to enhance their undergraduate program can study abroad for a summer, semester, or academic year. In the past, students have studied in Australia, Canada, England, France, Ireland, Italy, Mexico, New Zealand, and Spain.

Academic Facilities

The Henry Whittemore Library houses more than 200,000 bound volumes, 600,000 volume equivalents in microforms, and 1,600 current periodicals in subscriptions. Electronic databases supplement the library's in-house journal collection, and students have access to a variety of materials shared within the Minuteman Library Network. The College provides extensive computing capabilities for its students, including a wireless network across the campus.

A child-development center, planetarium, and greenhouse provide students with the opportunity to gain practical experience in related studies. Likewise, the radio station and television studios serve as forums to apply textbook knowledge.

The Challenger Learning Center, established in memory of Christa Corrigan McAuliffe, the nation's first teacher astronaut and a 1970 graduate of the College, is located on campus. The center provides a unique hands-on learning experience designed to foster interest in mathematics, science, and technology.

Costs

Tuition and fees for the 2007–08 academic year were $5799 for in-state students and $11,879 for out-of-state students. Yearly residence hall charges were $4527, and the yearly meal plan was $2600. Students should anticipate additional expenses for books, a laptop computer, supplies, transportation, and personal items. All costs are subject to change.

Financial Aid

Sources of financial aid available to Framingham State College students include federal, state, and institutional programs. Framingham State College students were the recipients of more than $17 million last year in loans, scholarships, grants, and work-study.

Federal programs include the Federal Work-Study Program, the Federal Pell Grant, Federal Supplemental Educational Opportunity Grant, the Federal Perkins Loan, and both subsidized and unsubsidized Federal Stafford Student Loans. State-funded aid includes state scholarship grants and a no-interest loan program. Institutional funds mainly provide merit and need-based scholarships.

All students applying for financial aid must file the Free Application for Federal Student Aid (FAFSA), designating Framingham State College as the recipient. Transfer students must submit financial aid transcripts documenting all previous aid received. The priority filing deadline for fall entrance is March 1.

Faculty

One hundred sixty-seven full-time faculty members are dedicated to upholding the undergraduate mission of the College. More than 83 percent of the faculty members hold the terminal degree in their field. The active involvement of many professors in research and writing complements their primary commitment and dedication to teaching excellence at the undergraduate level. With an impressive student-faculty ratio of 16:1, Framingham State College is able to offer a variety of programs in a challenging academic atmosphere.

Student Government

The Student Government Association (SGA) is the center of all political and social activity of the students of Framingham State College. The primary duties of SGA are to provide funding for more than fifty organizations through the student activity fee, to ensure representation of Framingham State College students in the state student organization, and to act on all other matters that concern the students of the College. SGA also plays a major role in the formulation of College policies that are of mutual concern to the students, the faculty, and the administration.

Admission Requirements

Framingham State College seeks to enroll students with a strong academic background who possess the necessary skills to succeed in college. Admission decisions are based primarily on the strength of the high school record and test scores. Secondary school students are required to pass 16 college-preparatory units: 4 years of English; 3 years of math, including algebra I and II and geometry; 3 years of science, including 2 years of laboratory science; 2 years of history/social science, including 1 year of U.S. history; 2 years of the same foreign language; and two college-preparatory-level electives. High school students are encouraged to elect additional courses in music, art, and computer science.

Students in the upper 50 percent of their class with a B average or higher are encouraged to apply. Recommendations, essays, and personal statements are not required but may be submitted as part of the application. International and transfer students, as well as adults returning to college, are also encouraged to apply.

Application and Information

To be considered for admission to a degree program at the College, all applicants must submit a completed application along with the application fee, an official high school transcript, and official complete SAT scores. Transfer students must submit official transcripts from all colleges previously attended.

It is recommended that students apply by the priority filing date of February 15 for fall admission and December 1 for spring admission. Students are encouraged to attend an admissions information session and tour. The information sessions are presented by a member of the admissions staff and are followed by a tour of the campus conducted by a student admissions representative. Students should call the Office of Undergraduate Admissions to arrange an appointment.

For further information and application materials or to schedule a campus visit, students should contact:

Office of Undergraduate Admissions
Framingham State College
100 State Street
P.O. Box 9101
Framingham, Massachusetts 01701-9101
Phone: 508-626-4500
E-mail: admiss@frc.mass.edu
Web site: http://www.framingham.edu

HARVARD UNIVERSITY
Harvard College
CAMBRIDGE, MASSACHUSETTS

The University

Harvard University includes Harvard College and the following graduate and professional schools: the Graduate School of Arts and Sciences, the Business School, the Design School, the Divinity School, the School of Education, the John F. Kennedy School of Government, the Law School, and the Schools of Dental Medicine, Medicine, and Public Health.

The residential plan for undergraduate students is an essential part of the Harvard experience. Every student is assured a place in College housing for four years. Freshmen live in one of the several dormitories in Harvard Yard, the oldest and most central part of the campus. At the end of the freshman year, students move into residential Houses in which they live for the remainder of their undergraduate careers. The House system provides a smaller community for students within the larger University environment. Each House has a resident senior faculty member who is called the master, a senior tutor or dean, a tutorial staff, a library, and dining facilities. All Houses are coeducational, and much of the social, athletic, extracurricular, and academic life centers on the House.

Harvard offers more than 300 student organizations. Some groups are long-established, such as the Hasty Pudding Club and Phillips Brooks House; others reflect the changing interests, attitudes, and politics of the times. Students find organized activities in dance, drama, government, journalism, music, religion, social service, visual arts, and a variety of other special interest areas.

The Department of Athletics offers forty-one intercollegiate sports programs for men and women—more than any other college in the country. In addition, there is a comprehensive system of intramural and recreational sports. The extensive athletic facilities include six basketball courts, forty squash courts, two swimming pools, and forty-eight tennis courts. Also available are facilities for aerobics, baseball, fencing, field hockey, football, hockey, lacrosse, martial arts, racquetball, rowing, soccer, track, water polo, weight lifting, and wrestling. Houses have their own intramural teams, and there are sports clubs run by students.

Location

Harvard College is located in Cambridge, Massachusetts, a city on the banks of the Charles River, across from Boston. Metropolitan Boston is a pleasant mixture of New England culture and urban vitality. Both Boston and Cambridge enjoy a history of tradition and innovation, as illustrated by their concert halls, libraries and bookstores, museums, theaters, coffeehouses, shops, and sports arenas. The cultural and recreational opportunities are countless and easily accessible. Beaches and mountains are within easy reach.

Majors and Degrees

Harvard offers more than forty areas in which an undergraduate may specialize. The following is a sampling of the concentrations offered: African and African American studies, anthropology, applied mathematics, astronomy, biochemical sciences, biology, chemistry, classics, computer science, Earth and planetary sciences, East Asian studies, economics, engineering and applied sciences, English, environmental science and public policy, folklore and mythology, Germanic languages and literatures, government, history, history and literature, history and science, history of art and architecture, linguistics, literature, mathematics, music, Near Eastern languages and literatures, philosophy, physics, psychology, religion, Romance languages and literatures, Sanskrit and Indian studies, Slavic languages and literatures, social studies, sociology, statistics, visual and environmental studies, and women's studies. Within fields, there are various options for further specialization, and it is possible to combine major fields or to devise special concentrations. Almost all undergraduates pursue an A.B. degree (only the engineering and applied sciences concentration offers an S.B. degree program).

Academic Programs

Harvard's goal is to provide students with the freedom to design individual academic programs within the structure of a broadly based liberal arts curriculum. Students must complete at least 32 one-semester courses during their four years, chosen from the more than 3,500 courses available in the humanities, social sciences, and natural sciences. A one-semester course in expository writing is required of all freshmen.

After three semesters, students choose a field of concentration. Over the course of eight semesters, they must complete 16 one-semester courses chosen from that field and related fields. Except in a few subjects, sophomores are assigned a tutor within their chosen field of concentration. The tutorial group meets weekly to investigate assigned topics or areas of special interest. Juniors and seniors may elect to pursue tutorials on an individual basis, thus enabling them to study an issue in depth. The culmination of the tutorial program is the senior thesis. Cross-registration in other faculties of Harvard University and with the Massachusetts Institute of Technology is also available.

The Core Curriculum courses are specially designed to fulfill students' requirements outside of their fields of concentration. Seven one-semester courses are required, chosen from eleven areas of intellectual inquiry that include literature and arts, historical study, social analysis, moral reasoning, science, foreign cultures, and quantitative reasoning. This core program gives students an appreciation of disciplines other than their chosen concentration. Before graduation, students are also required to demonstrate proficiency in a foreign language and competence in certain areas of data analysis.

Harvard's Advanced Standing Program is designed for undergraduates who plan to graduate in three years or plan to complete the A.B./A.M. program in four years. This is a choice made at the end of two years of study at Harvard. To be eligible for this, students who have taken College Board Advanced Placement tests need a total of 4 full credits, earned by scoring a 5 on a minimum of four qualified AP exams.

Each year, freshmen can elect to participate in one of 130 Freshman Seminars. The seminar format is designed for those freshmen who are eager to work independently or within small groups on special topics, under the guidance of a professor well known in his or her field.

Off-Campus Programs

A large number of students receive credit each year for work done away from the Harvard campus under the auspices of a variety of programs that are sponsored by foreign and American universities. Undergraduates interested in study-abroad programs are counseled on an individual basis about program applications, academic credit, and financial assistance.

Courses (including ROTC programs) are also available through the Massachusetts Institute of Technology.

Academic Facilities

The University library system consists of the Harvard College Library and the libraries of the graduate and professional schools. Together these libraries house more than 15 million volumes, constituting the largest university library collection in the world.

The University Museum includes the Peabody Museum of Archaeology and Ethnology, the Botanical Museum, the Museum of Comparative Zoology, and the Mineralogical Museum. The Fogg and Sackler museums house a collection of paintings, drawings, and sculpture. Contemporary exhibits are featured regularly at the Carpenter Center for Visual Arts. The Loeb Drama Center seats 500 in the auditorium and houses a small experimental theater.

More than a dozen buildings are used exclusively for the classrooms, laboratories, and museums of the natural sciences. There are computers available for use in the science center and all residence halls. All student rooms have Internet access.

Costs

Costs for 2007–08 tuition and fees are $34,998, and room and board are $10,622. Estimated personal expenses, books, supplies, and similar costs are $2930; travel expenses vary.

Financial Aid

All admissions decisions at Harvard College are made without consideration of a candidate's financial need, and all financial aid awards at Harvard College are based on need. More than 70 percent of the undergraduates receive some form of financial assistance. Financial aid is provided in the form of scholarships, loans, and term-time employment. Family income and a number of other factors are considered in determining need. Any students who feel they may need financial assistance are encouraged to apply. Financial aid applicants who are U.S. citizens are required to submit the CSS Financial Aid PROFILE, the FAFSA, and copies of their family's tax returns by February 1. International students are required to file the Financial Statement for Students from Foreign Countries (FSSFC) by the same date. Applicants are usually notified of their aid awards at the same time they are notified of the admission decision.

Faculty

Harvard's faculty is an outstanding group of scholars, teachers, and researchers. The Faculty of Arts and Sciences consists of approximately 700 full-time members, all of whom hold the highest degree in their fields; they may be assisted by teaching fellows who are doctoral candidates. Many of the courses with the largest enrollments are taught in small sections of about 20. In contrast, the great majority of classes are taught with very small enrollments, and the tutorial system provides individual instruction. In fact, the median class size is 10. Because teaching and scholarship are both highly valued at Harvard, a freshman may well be taught by a Nobel Prize winner or a distinguished scholar.

Student Government

A freshman may participate in the Freshman Council. Representatives are elected from each dormitory in Harvard Yard. A freshman may also participate in the Undergraduate Council, the main student government organization. Upperclass men and women who reside in the Houses elect members for their respective House committees as well as for the Undergraduate Council, the Committee on Housing and Undergraduate Life, and the Committee on Undergraduate Education.

Admission Requirements

Undergraduates come from every state and nearly 100 countries. More than 22,000 applicants from both public and private schools compete for 1,675 places in the freshman class. The Admissions Committee seeks a diverse group of students who are intellectually capable, socially aware, and mature. The committee considers not only academic achievement but also students' extracurricular talents and potential for contributing to the Harvard community.

Applicants should present a high school transcript, two letters of recommendation from teachers, one letter of recommendation from a school counselor, and scores on the SAT or the ACT and any three SAT Subject Tests. Applicants must also submit a personal essay and, if at all possible, meet with an alumnus or alumna for an interview in their local area. The credentials of all applicants are considered in depth, and full attention is given to each candidate's particular strengths and abilities as well as personal qualities.

Application and Information

Harvard College no longer offers an Early Action program as of fall 2007. The preferred Regular Action deadline is December 15. The final deadline for all materials is January 1; decisions are mailed in late March. Students who apply to transfer into the sophomore or junior year should submit their applications by February 15. They may express a preference to enter in the fall or the spring. The College also accepts a few visiting students each fall and spring from well-qualified candidates who are currently matriculated at another college and wish to spend a term studying at Harvard.

For application forms and additional information, students should contact:

Harvard College Office of Admissions
86 Brattle Street
Cambridge, Massachusetts 02138
Phone: 617-495-1551 (freshman admissions)
617-495-9707 (visiting undergraduate admissions)
617-495-5309 (undergraduate transfer admissions)
617-495-1581 (financial aid)
E-mail: college@fas.harvard.edu
Web site: http://www.admissions.college.harvard.edu

LASELL COLLEGE

NEWTON, MASSACHUSETTS

The College

Founded in 1851, Lasell College is a coeducational, independent, nonsectarian institution of higher education and offers career-oriented bachelor's and master's degree programs. Predominantly a residential college, Lasell seeks to provide its students with the experience of living and learning in a community organized around a central educational purpose that Lasell calls "connected learning." The Lasell plan of education acknowledges that students acquire and retain knowledge most effectively when classroom theory is reinforced by regular application under direct faculty supervision. Students are supervised at any number of Lasell's on- and off-campus laboratories and internship sites.

Lasell students are encouraged to participate in a wide variety of campus organizations and to take an active role in developing new interests. Among the many Lasell College student-run organizations are WCLR–Lasell College Radio, the Donahue Institute, the Performing Arts Council, and the Center for Community-Based Learning. Lasell publications include the *1851Chronicle* (the College's newspaper), yearbook, literary magazine, and fashion magazine. Each year the students and staff of the College plan a series of programs and events designed to inform and involve members of the Lasell community. These include Diversity Week, International Week, and the Academic Symposium. Other annual events include the Commencement Ball, the Torchlight Parade, and River Day. Athletic teams compete in a number of NCAA Division III varsity programs, including men's baseball, basketball, cross-country, lacrosse, soccer, and volleyball and women's basketball, cross-country, field hockey, lacrosse, soccer, softball, and volleyball.

Resident students may choose to live in Victorian houses, modern residence halls, or suite-style residences. All rooms are cable- and Internet-ready. Resident staff members are on hand to provide support when necessary. Special emphasis is placed on the advantages of the College as a close-knit community in proximity to Boston.

At the graduate-level, Lasell offers a Master of Science in management degree program, with concentrations in elder-care administration, elder-care marketing, human resources management, marketing, management, nonprofit management, and project management.

Location

Lasell's campus is 15 minutes from downtown Boston in the suburb of Newton, Massachusetts. The "T," or Mass Transit, is conveniently located within walking distance of the campus. Lasell's 50-acre campus offers forty-nine residential and academic facilities. Students experience the advantages of a suburban setting with all of the social and cultural attractions offered in and around a major metropolitan area.

Majors and Degrees

Lasell offers undergraduate programs in accounting, advertising, athletic training, business administration, communication, criminal justice, early childhood education, elementary education, English, environmental studies, fashion and retail merchandising, fashion design and production, finance, graphic design, history, hospitality and event management, human services, humanities, interdisciplinary studies, international business, journalism and media writing, legal studies, management, marketing, multimedia and Web design, psychology, public relations, radio and television production, secondary education, sociology, sports communication, sport management, and sport science. Students may also enter the College with an undeclared major.

Academic Programs

Candidates for a bachelor's degree complete between 120 and 128 semester hours of course work. Lasell College recognizes that students must be exposed to a wide breadth of liberal arts courses to have a well-rounded education and function in the twenty-first century. Lasell's core curriculum integrates writing across the curriculum, oral communication skills, critical and quantitative reasoning, computer literacy, ethical development, and a commitment to service.

Academic Facilities

All of Lasell's academic and residential buildings are networked with fiber-optic cable, providing high-speed access to the Internet and the College Intranet. In addition, much of Lasell's 50-acre campus is Wi-Fi accessible. Academic buildings include Wolfe Hall, the Wass Science Building, the Brennan Library, the Yamawaki Art and Cultural Center, and the Winslow Academic Center. These buildings house five state-of-the-art computer labs with a wide assortment of software, including graphic design software, business applications, statistical packages, tutorials, and experimental programs.

Brennan Library houses a collection of more than 75,000 books, more than 70 electronic databases, and hundreds of periodicals. Lasell is a member of the Minuteman Library Network, which provides access to more than 5 million volumes from over forty libraries. In addition, the Brennan Library is home to the Center for Academic Achievement, the Kyo Yamawaki Education Library, and Rosen Auditorium.

Wolfe Hall offers the business computer lab, seminar and board rooms, and spacious high-tech classrooms. Wass Hall accommodates laboratories for environmental studies, chemistry, anatomy and physiology, biology, physical sciences, exercise physiology, and athletic training.

The Yamawaki Art and Cultural Center, home of the Lasell theater, chorus, and jazz ensemble, has undergone a multimillion dollar renovation but still retains its 1800s Victorian flair. The center provides an ideal setting for the College's fashion design labs and industry-standard pattern-generation technology, lab space for ceramics and photography, and studios for the College's drawing and painting courses. In addition, the center has an active gallery showcasing works from many media.

Two nationally accredited lab schools—the Holway Child Study Centers—are part of the College campus, and they provide valuable connected learning experiences for education majors.

The Athletic Center and recently completed athletic training labs not only provide a home for Lasell's NCAA Division III athletics, but also serve as experiential learning sites for students majoring in athletic training and sports science.

The Winslow Academic Center has seven classrooms with state-of-the-art audiovisual systems installed to maximize the effectiveness of faculty members and enhance the teaching and learning experience. Each classroom is equipped with an LCD projector, sound system, unified remote control system, and a SMART Board. The SMART Board can be used to project class notes and save them to the College Intranet, enabling students to focus on the lecture and discussion and download class notes later. The interactive technology assists in multiple teaching modalities, thereby enhancing student learning.

The dramatic new Campus Center was designed to meet the needs of the College's growing student population. This state-of-the-art facility offers a host of options for gathering, working, studying, enjoying live performances, and dining. The second floor abounds with student activity. Surrounding the large, modular conference areas that are available for presentations, performances, or learning labs are a bank of offices housing student clubs and organizations—including the Performing Arts Council and Graphic Design League. The third floor provides yet another residential living option for Lasell students and features special interest housing for approximately 22 residents. An underground parking facility connects to the recently completed Bragdon residence hall.

Costs

For the 2007–08 academic year, tuition for full-time students is $20,850. Room and board charges are $9550.

Financial Aid

More than 85 percent of the students at Lasell receive some form of financial assistance from the College. Programs include Lasell grants, Federal Pell Grants, Federal Supplemental Educational Opportunity Grants, Federal Perkins Loans, Federal Stafford Student Loans, Federal Work-Study, awards, state scholarships, and Lasell alumnae scholarships.

Lasell uses the Free Application for Federal Student Aid (FAFSA) and the Lasell Financial Aid Application to determine eligibility for programs. Applicants for aid who wish to enroll in September should mail the FAFSA to the appropriate processing centers as soon as possible after January 1. In 2006–07, the average financial aid package, including loans, grants, and work-study, totaled $14,750. Lasell guarantees the College's portion of all financial aid packages for four years, if a family's financial situation and a student's academic record and status remain consistent.

Faculty

Lasell has a total of 157 faculty members (55 full-time, 102 part-time), many of whom are practicing professionals in their respective fields and bring their experience to the classroom. The student-faculty ratio is 13:1. The student-faculty bond, strengthened by faculty members acting as academic advisers, is considered a vital element in the social, academic, and cultural growth and development of Lasell students. Faculty members serve as role models for success, and particular emphasis is placed on their availability for individual and group conferences.

Student Government

Students are elected in the fall and spring of each year to the association's Executive Council and Executive Board. The elected officials represent the student body and govern and coordinate College activities. All students are encouraged to participate in the association and use it as an effective agency for communicating their concerns and interests.

Admission Requirements

Freshman applicants for admission should complete a rigorous college-preparatory curriculum during their secondary education, including 4 units of English, 3 units of math, 2 units of a lab science, and 2 units each of social studies and history. Applicants are evaluated on the basis of their academic record and achievement, overall initiative, and SAT or ACT scores.

Application and Information

Candidates for admission should submit an application and $40 application fee, a high school transcript, SAT or ACT scores, and at least one letter of recommendation. Lasell offers rolling admission, and applicants receive decisions shortly after their applications have been completed. Transfer applicants must submit all college transcripts in addition to their high school academic information and letter of recommendation.

Prospective students are encouraged to visit the Lasell campus for a tour and interview. Appointments may be scheduled Monday through Saturday by calling the Office of Undergraduate Admissions. For further information, students should contact:

Office of Undergraduate Admission
Lasell College
1844 Commonwealth Avenue
Newton, Massachusetts 02466
Phone: 617-243-2225
888-LASELL4 (toll-free)
Fax: 617-243-2380
E-mail: info@lasell.edu
Web site: http://www.lasell.edu

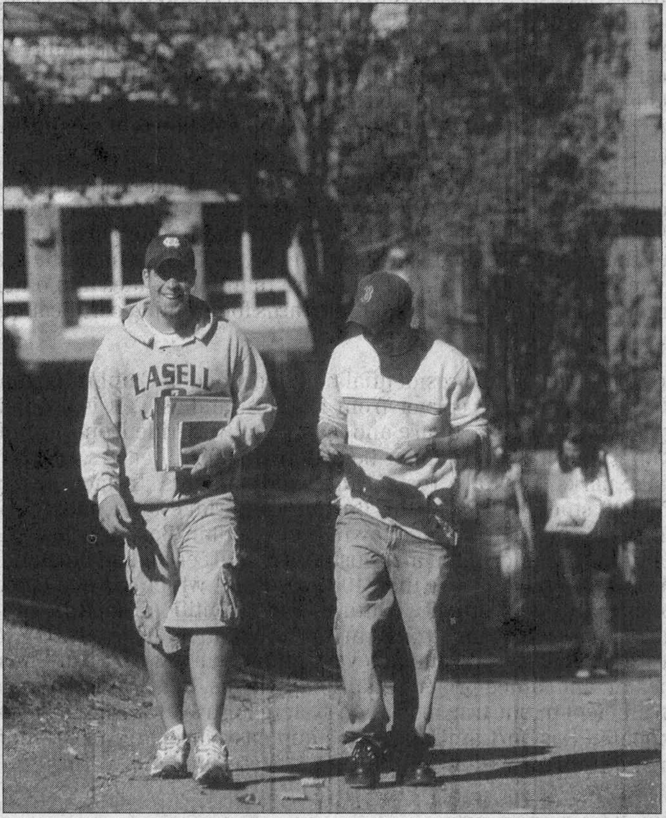

Students on Lasell College's campus.

LESLEY UNIVERSITY
CAMBRIDGE, MASSACHUSETTS

The College

Lesley College prepares young men and women for careers that matter and lives that make a difference. The combination of expert faculty members, stimulating classes, hands-on learning, career-focused internships, and exciting cocurricular activities change, inspire, and prepare students to become catalysts and leaders in their careers and their communities. Whether embarking on professional careers or pursuing further study after graduation, students leave Lesley with a strong commitment to social change, ready to make a difference in the world around them.

As one of four colleges that make up Lesley University, Lesley College integrates the advantages of a small learning community with the academic and cocurricular resources of a large university. Lesley College students are able to cross-register for courses in the other schools at Lesley University, including The Art Institute of Boston. Accelerated bachelor's/master's programs have been developed in conjunction with the School of Education and the Graduate School of Arts and Social Sciences. In addition, the Lesley Dividend offers qualified Lesley College students up to 12 free credits of graduate study in one of Lesley's on-campus master's degree programs.

Located just steps from Harvard Square and minutes from downtown Boston, Lesley College offers the University's nearly 1,400 undergraduates small classes taught by accomplished University faculty members (not graduate students); more than fifty majors, minors, and specializations in the liberal arts and the professions (education, human services, management, the environment, and the arts), including an honors program; and the opportunity to design their own program of study. Most importantly, Lesley students participate in field-based internships beginning in their freshman year and complete between 400 and 650 hours of significant career-related experience.

The University is accredited by the New England Association of Schools and Colleges. The teacher certification programs have been approved by the National Association of State Directors of Teacher Education and Certification (NASDTEC), which offers a reciprocity agreement in which more than forty states and other organizations have established standards for granting certification.

Location

Lesley is located in a residential neighborhood in Cambridge that is right around the corner from Harvard and MIT. It is a quick walk from Harvard Square and a short subway ride from Boston. Cambridge has everything: bookstores, cafés, theaters, concert halls, parks, festivals, restaurants, and students. In fact, nearly 250,000 students live in the Boston/Cambridge area, making it America's ultimate college town. Metropolitan Boston is also famous for its educational and business resources and an outstanding cultural scene. More than 100 museums, which are dedicated to virtually every artistic, cultural, and scientific discipline, provide opportunities for student involvement on many levels. There are shops and restaurants of every ethnic variety, first-run films, theater, and famed professional sports teams. In addition, there is an efficient public transportation system for travel within the metropolitan Boston/Cambridge area and easy, direct transportation to and from all regions of the United States and the world.

Majors and Degrees

Lesley College offers Bachelor of Science and Bachelor of Arts degrees in the following liberal arts and professional areas: American studies, art history, art therapy, child and family studies, communication and technology, counseling, education, English (creative writing, drama, literature), environmental science, environmental studies, European and world studies, expressive arts therapy, global studies, health, history, holistic psychology, an honors program, human services, management (marketing, not-for-profit, sport management), mathematics, natural science, psychology, sociology, and visual studies (design, illustration, photography), as well as self-designed programs of study in such areas as arts management, foreign language, health studies, intercultural relations, leadership and social policy, and prelaw. All undergraduate students at The Art Institute of Boston at Lesley University earn Bachelor of Fine Arts degrees.

Students who are interested in teaching major in one of the following areas: early childhood education, early learning, elementary education, middle school education, secondary education, or special education. These students are also required to elect a double major in one of nine liberal arts areas. Completion of a major in education qualifies a student to be recommended for initial licensure in Massachusetts and the other states that are members of NASDTEC and have signed the Interstate Contract.

In conjunction with Lesley's graduate programs, the following accelerated bachelor's/master's degree programs are offered: a B.S./M.A. in art therapy, clinical mental health counseling, or counseling psychology and a B.S./M.Ed. in early childhood education, elementary education, or middle school education.

Academic Programs

All of Lesley's academic programs are designed to integrate study in the liberal arts with professional course work and significant hands-on internship experience.

Internship experiences begin in the freshman year and are developmentally sequenced to complement classroom instruction throughout the undergraduate program. Internships are designed to show students what the workplace is like, challenge assumptions they may have about themselves and the world, and give the kind of experience that creates exceptional resumes. The internships are linked with seminar classes in which students discuss and evaluate their fieldwork, learning also from fellow students' experiences about workplace issues and emerging trends. It is this careful integration of theory and practice that distinguishes Lesley's curriculum from those at other colleges, providing students with a critical understanding of the real-world demands of their profession and the leadership skills that are needed to succeed.

Through a comprehensive general education program, the students also build a strong liberal arts foundation by taking courses in the arts, humanities, sciences, and social sciences. It is through their liberal arts course work that students develop their ability to think critically and strengthen their writing skills, as well as ensure that they have a breadth of knowledge and skills that leads to success in graduate school and an interest in a life of learning.

Off-Campus Programs

Lesley University offers students the opportunity to participate in a number of Lesley-affiliated programs of off-campus study, in the United States and abroad, through which they may obtain Lesley College credit.

Lesley students may study in Florence, Hong Kong, Madrid, Prague, and Washington, D.C., as well as francophone Africa, China, Costa Rica, England, Ireland, Sweden, Lesley's own Audubon Expedition Institute, and several Lesley-sponsored study/travel opportunities. In addition, planned study/travel tours are led by distinguished members of the faculty and offer students the chance to discover the history, culture, and art of various regions or gain an in-depth understanding of significant world events. Previous tours have included Bali; the British Experience; the Cuban Experience in Education and the Arts; Ecuador: Wisdom of Indigenous Peoples; Learning from the Holocaust; Morocco; People and Culture of Mexico; Tibet; and Traditions and Cultures of the Southwest.

Academic Facilities

The Eleanor DeWolfe Ludcke Library is a state-of-the-art multimedia resource center supporting the academic programs of the University through a collection of books, journals, and multimedia and electronic resources. Located at the center of the campus, the Ludcke Library also houses the Kresge Center for Teaching Resources as well as a computer lab and three computer classrooms.

The Kresge Center for Teaching Resources offers one of the finest collections of juvenile literature in the Northeast, as well as teaching aids; video, audio, and film collections; and media services. Students may produce teaching materials using the center's equipment, and professional staff members offer support in children's literature, media materials, and production of teaching materials.

Ludcke Library offers a wide array of resources through the World Wide Web. On its home page, students may search the library catalog, identify and print journal articles and other documents, and search the Internet. A growing collection of full-text databases offers articles and documents in education, business, management, science, the humanities, and the social sciences. Students may access these resources both on and off campus via the Internet.

Ludcke Library is a member of the Fenway Library Consortium (FLC), a cooperative group of fifteen academic, special, and public libraries that offer reciprocal borrowing to the faculty and staff members and students of its member institutions.

The Instructional Computing Center consists of three classrooms and a lab area, with Macintosh and Windows-compatible computers, full Internet and e-mail access, scanners, laser printers, and other computer peripherals. Instructional Computing's educational software collection has more than 2,000 titles, ranging from pre-K through college level. In addition, the Mollye Lichter Block Computer Lab for word processing is open 24 hours a day.

Costs

Fees in 2008–09 for enrollment in Lesley College include tuition, $27,200; room and board, $12,000; a health services fee, $800 (estimate); and a student activity fee, $250. Costs are subject to change without prior notice. Students should call the University to confirm current expense figures.

Financial Aid

No student should fail to consider Lesley because of financial considerations. More than 80 percent of Lesley College students receive financial aid from one or more sources. The average amount received by newly enrolled students is $15,800 in a combination of scholarships/grants, loans, and work-study jobs. The University participates in all federal aid programs, including the Federal Pell Grant, Federal Supplemental Educational Opportunity Grant, Federal Perkins Loan, and Federal Work-Study programs. Lesley also offers its own grants and need-based scholarships as well as an array of merit scholarships, ranging from $5000 to full tuition.

Students applying for financial aid must submit the Free Application for Federal Student Aid (FAFSA) and request that copies of the analyses be sent to Lesley University. In addition, students must complete the Lesley Financial Aid Application, which is included in the application for admission. Students are advised to file all financial aid forms and documents as early as possible. The FAFSA and the Lesley Financial Aid Application should be filed by February 1.

Faculty

Lesley College faculty members hold the teaching of undergraduates as their highest priority. Even more important to a student's classroom experience, however, is the fact that many members of the faculty are trained practitioners, classroom educators, counselors, social workers, and business professionals. In fact, many continue to work in the field or as consultants and bring a wealth of real-world experience into their classroom teaching.

Of the 245 full- and part-time faculty members, more than two thirds hold a doctorate or other terminal degree. Faculty members serve as academic advisers for students, and the student-faculty ratio of 10:1 allows for a close relationship to develop between students and their professors.

Student Government

The Student Government is the representative governing body of the Lesley College student population. Through its sponsorship, numerous organizations, activities, seminars, and conferences are brought to the Lesley campus.

Admission Requirements

Lesley College has designed the admission process to be reflective of the institution and its values. Lesley is an institution that values community and service to the community. Therefore, the College is interested in students who value making a difference in the lives of others and who have shown a commitment to community service. Lesley also seeks students who, through a strong college-preparatory curriculum, have gained the knowledge and skills that allow them to thrive and be successful in the academic programs. Graduates of accredited secondary schools with a total of 20 college-preparatory units of study are encouraged to apply for admission. Included in the 20 units are the following: English, 4 units; mathematics, at least 3 units; science, at least 3 units (including at least one lab course); and U.S. history, 1 unit. Admitted freshmen typically have a 3.0 average or higher. All freshman applicants must submit SAT or ACT scores. A personal interview is recommended.

Students who have been fully matriculated in a degree program at another college or university may apply for admission as transfers. Transfer applicants must present a minimum cumulative grade point average of 2.5. The maximum number of credit hours that may be transferred is 65. Advanced standing is determined by the nature and quality of the work offered for credit.

Application and Information

Applications are reviewed on a rolling basis beginning December 1, with a first-year early action deadline of December 1, a regular admission deadline of February 15, and a transfer application deadline of May 1 for the fall semester. All applications for the spring semester are due by December 1. A $40 application fee must accompany all freshman and transfer applications.

For further information about Lesley, students should contact:

Office of Admissions
Lesley College
29 Everett Street
Cambridge, Massachusetts 02138-2790
Phone: 617-349-8800
800-999-1959 Ext. 8800 (toll-free)
E-mail: lcadmissions@lesley.edu
Web site: http://www.lesley.edu/lc

MASSACHUSETTS COLLEGE OF LIBERAL ARTS

NORTH ADAMS, MASSACHUSETTS

The College

Nestled in the rolling hills of the Berkshires, Massachusetts College of Liberal Arts (MCLA) offers students the experience of a small, private college at the cost of a public institution. Founded in 1894, MCLA provides students with an ideal learning environment, combining rigorous academic training with broad opportunities for learning outside the classroom. MCLA's small size of 1,475 undergraduate students and a faculty-student ratio of 1:13 foster a tight-knit community among students and faculty members.

MCLA, a four-year, residential, coeducational liberal arts college, offers numerous baccalaureate degrees and a Master of Education degree with concentrations in three areas.

The College is located on 105 acres and includes an athletic complex with softball, baseball, and soccer fields; tennis courts; and a cross-country course. There are three residential facilities that hold more than 1,000 students. Eleven intercollegiate athletic programs, including baseball (men), basketball (men/women), cross-country (men/women), golf (men), soccer (men/women), softball (women), tennis (women), and volleyball (women), are available. In addition, there are forty-five clubs, organizations, and intramural activities.

The Amsler Campus Center, a four-story complex, houses one of the two residence gymnasiums, a modern fitness center, a swimming pool, a dance complex, racquetball and handball courts, dining facilities, a convenience store, and a TV lounge as well as the bookstore and an athletic training center.

Additional programs offered through the College include an honors program, study abroad, internship opportunities, health services, academic support services, and tutorial centers.

Location

MCLA is located in North Adams, Massachusetts, 1 mile from the downtown area of 14,700, in the northwestern corner of the state, bordering both Vermont and New York. Located in the heart of the Berkshires, North Adams offers numerous cultural, historical, and recreational opportunities. Cultural attractions in the Berkshires include the Massachusetts Museum of Contemporary Art (MASS MoCA), Jiminy Peak Mountain Resort, Tanglewood, Jacob's Pillow, the Sterling and Francine Clark Art Institute, and the Williamstown Theatre Festival. Approximate travel time from Boston is 2½ hours; from New York City, 3 hours; from Albany, New York, 1 hour; from Burlington, Vermont, 3 hours; and from Hartford, Connecticut, 2 hours.

Majors and Degrees

MCLA confers the Bachelor of Arts and Bachelor of Science degrees and offers a Masters in Education. Undergraduate programs are offered in arts management, biology, business administration, computer science and information systems, education, English/communications, environmental studies, fine and performing arts, interdisciplinary studies, mathematics, philosophy, physics, psychology, and sociology. Teacher licensure is offered in the areas of early childhood education (grades pre-K–2), elementary education (grades 1–6), middle school education (grades 5–8), and secondary education (grades 8–12).

Concentrations include accounting, anthropology, art, arts management, behavior analysis, biology, broadcast media, business information systems, chemistry, child and family studies, computer science, corporate communications, criminal justice, cytotechnology, environmental science, environment and society, ethics and society, event management, film studies, journalism, law, literature, management, marketing, medical technology, music, political science, prelaw, premed, public relations, social work, sociology, sport management, sports medicine, theater, and writing. There are also thirty minors offered through the College.

Academic Programs

MCLA operates on a two-semester basis, with the first semester running from September through December and the second running from January through May. Classes are available to all students through both day and evening offerings.

A minimum of 120 semester hours of credit, including major requirements and achievement of a quality point average of at least 2.0, is necessary for completion of a bachelor's degree. At least 39 of the 120 credits must be in upper-division work. MCLA offers a course of study divided into three segments: a general education program, major and minor fields of study, and elective areas in which students have the opportunity to pursue additional academic interests. MCLA also has an honors program, which offers a variety of courses with the depth and scope sought by students seeking additional academic challenges. In addition, MCLA places high value on research, which enables students to hone their analytical skills while gaining meaningful hands-on experience. Many MCLA faculty members work one-on-one with students on original research.

College credit is awarded to students with successful scores on the Advanced Placement examinations of the College Board and the College-Level Examination Program (CLEP) tests.

MCLA prepares students with the knowledge, perspective, critical-thinking abilities, and values necessary to become leaders in their chosen profession and active members of their community.

Off-Campus Programs

As a member of the College Consortium for International Studies (CCIS), MCLA offers its students the opportunity to study abroad in sixteen countries throughout the world for a semester or for an entire year. Travel courses are offered during school breaks, and students are encouraged to explore other cultures while earning course credits. Internships are also offered to students in any major program, both on campus and off campus. Local businesses, such as General Electric, Community Development Corporation, Channel 7 in Boston (an NBC-affiliated station), the Massachusetts Museum of Contemporary Art (MASS MoCA), and the Berkshire Medical Center, routinely offer one-semester internships to qualified students.

The College participates in the College Academic Program Sharing (CAPS) program, enabling a student to study at another state college and to earn up to 30 credits while maintaining degree status at MCLA. Students are also offered the opportunity to cross-enroll at neighboring Williams College.

Academic Facilities

The holdings of the Eugene Lawrence Freel Library include 192,000 book volumes, 544 current journal and newspaper subscriptions, more than 300,000 microform units, and approximately 6,500 nonbook items. College facilities also include television and radio production facilities; biology, chemistry, and physics labs; five computer labs; two amphitheaters; a performance theater; the Career Services Center; and the Advising Services Center.

Costs

Estimated annual tuition and fees are $5900 for in-state students, $6400 for residents of New York State and southern Vermont (based on specific criteria), and $14,900 for all other out-of-state students. Room and board are approximately $6950 per year, varying with the choice of housing and meal plans. Additional academic and miscellaneous expenses, including books and travel, average $2500 for the year.

Financial Aid

The Office of Financial Aid helps students remove financial obstacles that stand between them and their educational goals. The College's financial aid philosophy is that it should make every effort to enable attendance for students who have financial need remaining after their families have met as much of the cost as is reasonably possible. Need is calculated by subtracting the family's contribution from the total cost of attendance. Those students whose need is greatest may expect to receive priority in the awarding procedure if they meet published deadlines. Although the financial aid programs operate under specific federal and state constraints, every effort is made to consider each student's family financial situation individually. Typically, the student's financial aid award consists of a package composed of a combination of grants, loans, and part-time employment. The deadline for applying for financial aid is March 1 for priority review; however, applications are accepted on a rolling basis until funds are exhausted.

Faculty

The College currently employs 80 full-time and 42 part-time faculty members; of these, 83 percent hold a doctoral degree. The student-faculty ratio is 13:1, and all classes are taught by faculty members. Working with a diverse student body, the faculty and staff aim to develop liberally educated individuals who have the knowledge, perspectives, critical-thinking abilities, and ethical values necessary to become active citizens and leaders within their chosen field.

Student Government

The Student Government Association (SGA) has been in existence at MCLA since 1909. It was formed in order to coordinate and unify matters of student governance on campus, allowing students to have input in all College policies. The SGA administers the Student Activities Trust Fund to all recognized clubs and organizations and sponsors additional College events.

Admission Requirements

All freshman applicants must submit an official copy of their high school record, including at least the first-quarter senior grades. The primary emphasis in evaluating a candidate is on the applicant's total high school profile, consisting of overall grade point average, curriculum, SAT/ACT scores, and the level of competition in the individual high school. The unit requirements for freshman admission are English, 4; mathematics, 3; science, 3; history/social science, 2; foreign language, 2; and electives, 2.

Transfer students must have a cumulative grade point average of at least 2.0 on a 4.0 scale and submit an official transcript from each college attended. Transfer students are notified at the time of acceptance of the number of credits accepted and how they transfer into their program of study. MCLA has developed transfer articulation agreements with many community and junior colleges to ensure admission and maximum transferability of credit. MCLA offers joint admission to transfer students from Massachusetts community colleges.

International students must submit academic records, SAT/ACT scores, scores on the Test of English as a Foreign Language (TOEFL), and documentation of financial support.

Consideration is given to applicants regardless of their race, religion, national origin, sex, age, color, ethnic origin, or handicap. Admission interviews are recommended for all applicants but not required.

Application and Information

The application for admission to MCLA requests information regarding a student's academic background, extracurricular activities, and personal data.

Applications are reviewed on a rolling admission schedule, with a priority deadline of March 1, and the College accepts students until all spaces are filled. Tours of the campus are provided daily and on specific weekends.

Application materials and additional information, including tour dates and times, may be obtained by contacting:

Office of Admission
Massachusetts College of Liberal Arts
375 Church Street
North Adams, Massachusetts 01247-4100
Phone: 413-662-5410
800-969-MCLA (toll-free)
Fax: 413-662-5179
E-mail: admissions@mcla.edu
Web site: http://www.mcla.edu

Historic Murdock Hall on the Massachusetts College of Liberal Arts campus.

MASSACHUSETTS COLLEGE OF PHARMACY AND HEALTH SCIENCES

BOSTON, MASSACHUSETTS

The College

Founded in 1823, the Massachusetts College of Pharmacy and Health Sciences (MCPHS) is one of the nation's oldest schools of pharmacy. As a private independent institution with a long and distinguished history of specializing in health sciences education, the College offers traditional and nontraditional programs that embody teaching excellence, active scholarship and research, professional service, and community outreach.

MCPHS has a distinguished history and international reputation in pharmacy and health-care programs. With a background of liberal arts, general education, and other courses, graduates are enlightened citizens as well as competent practitioners. MCPHS graduates are in great demand, even before they graduate. Most are employed at or soon after graduation, with salaries that exceed those of most other new college graduates, beginning at $50,000 to $100,000.

The curriculum is designed to develop active thinkers and learners who are prepared for changing professions and a complex world. Developed by educators and working professionals, these courses are often tailored to give students practical information and valuable insights into today's health-care concerns. Students benefit from hands-on learning in the College's well-equipped laboratories and computer centers. Ultimately, the programs, which combine the basic sciences with the humanities, provide an education for lifelong enrichment.

The Department of Sports, Recreation, and Wellness offers opportunities for all students to participate in club sports, intramurals, wellness classes, and the Wellness Center. Baseball, basketball, cross-country, golf, soccer, softball, and volleyball operate as Student Government Association (SGA) clubs on campus. The intramural program is open to all MCPHS students and faculty and staff members and is an ideal way for students to be involved with the College community. Other student activities include the Academy of Students of Pharmacy, the Black Student Union, the Indian Student Organization, the International Student Association, the Republic of China Student Association, the Vietnamese Student Association, the College yearbook, and the *Dispenser* (student newspaper). There are also five professional fraternities—two for men, two for women, and one coed.

In addition to its main campus, in September 2000, MCPHS opened a new campus in Worcester, Massachusetts. The College offers an innovative, accelerated Pharm.D. program for transfer students and a sixteen-month nursing program for students who already hold a bachelor's degree in another major. In 2003, MCPHS opened a third campus, in Manchester, New Hampshire, where it offers a Master of Physician Assistant Studies program. The program awards the M.P.A.S. degree. Manchester's campus also offers an accelerated two-year Pharm.D. program in conjunction with the Worcester campus and offers a sixteen-month Bachelor of Science in Nursing. Programs on these two newer campuses are designed specifically for students holding a bachelor degree in another field looking to transition into the health-care field.

MCPHS is a member of the Colleges of the Fenway (COF). Other participating members are Wentworth, Wheelock, Simmons, Emmanuel, and Massachusetts College of Art. Students can take courses at the other institutions in the consortium.

Location

Dedicated solely to health sciences education, the College is a highly respected institution in Boston's world-renowned Longwood Medical and Academic Area. Its location alone gives MCPHS students resources for enriching their education. The area is home to the nation's premier medical centers and educational and research institutions—a highly stimulating and inspiring environment in which to learn.

Boston is a college town in the best sense of the word—cultural, accessible, and vibrant with activity. Students experience Boston's history along the Freedom Trail, enjoy its seafood on the waterfront, or explore its ethnic neighborhoods. Favorite spots include Faneuil Hall Marketplace; the Esplanade along the Charles River, for outdoor concerts and movies, biking, jogging, and in-line skating; and the Public Gardens and Boston Common, for walks, picnics, and just relaxing. The city's elaborate public transportation network (the "T") connects students to all these places and many more, such as Cambridge and Harvard Square, where students might browse in bookstores and enjoy a sidewalk performance; Newbury Street, for shopping and distinctive galleries; TD Banknorth Garden, where the Celtics and Bruins play; Fenway Park, a 5-minute walk for baseball fans; and Symphony Hall, home of the Boston Pops and the Symphony Orchestra.

Majors and Degrees

Massachusetts College of Pharmacy and Health Sciences is the oldest college in the City of Boston and offers innovative and cutting-edge academic programs that respond to the ever-changing needs of the health-care field. Programs at the College are designed to actively engage students in the learning process and to educate students to become skilled, caring, adaptable professionals who are committed to their own lifelong learning.

MCPHS offers undergraduate and professional degrees in chemistry, health psychology, pharmaceutical marketing and management, pharmaceutical sciences, pharmacy, physician assistant studies, and premedical and health studies with professional pathway opportunities. The College also offers accelerated three-year programs in dental hygiene, radiologic sciences, and nursing as part of the renowned Forsyth School of Dental Hygiene program.

The College offers a distinct advantage over other schools by accepting students directly into the dental hygiene, nursing, pharmacy, and radiologic sciences programs.

Academic Programs

Students in each of the undergraduate programs begin their studies in the basic sciences, humanities, and social sciences. First-year classes include two semesters of English, math, biology, and chemistry. After completing basic science courses, Bachelor of Science degree candidates progress to advanced courses in chemistry, psychology, pharmaceutics, and pharmacology. Students are also required to complete professional development courses, such as interpersonal communications, ethics, and law courses. In addition, students must complete 12 semester hours of elective courses in the humanities, social sciences, and behavioral sciences, as well as 12 semester hours of general elective course work.

Off-Campus Programs

The externship/clinical experience is a very important part of an MCPHS education and is built into most programs. The programs place students in professional settings for firsthand learning and guidance as they work with mentors from a sponsoring institution's staff. Students may choose experiences at more than fifty-five hospitals, 100 community-practice sites, and various research centers throughout New England.

Because the College is located in the heart of Boston's world-renowned Longwood Medical and Academic Area and has affiliations with Boston's high-caliber medical centers, top teaching hospitals, and pharmacies, students are ensured the highest-quality experience. Affiliates include such well-known institutions as Boston Medical Center, Massachusetts General Hospital, Harvard-affiliated hospitals, Dana Farber Cancer Institute, Children's Hospital, Joslin Diabetes Center, Brigham and Women's Hospital, and Genzyme.

Academic Facilities

The Boston campus features the $30-million Ronald A. Matricaria Academic and Student Center. The six-story, 93,000 square-foot building houses a state-of-the art library and chemistry, pharmacy, and computer laboratories. The building also houses four floors of beautiful apartment-style residences for 230 students.

Significant renovations in the White Building in 2005 included state-of-the-art clinics and laboratories for students enrolled in the dental hygiene, nursing, and physician assistant studies programs.

Costs

Tuition in 2007–08 was $22,000 for two semesters for freshmen and transfer students. Fees were $700 and room and board were $11,900. For two semesters and a summer session (accelerated dental hygiene, nursing, and radiologic sciences students), the tuition was $31,900, and room and board (two semesters only) were $14,500. Additional fees may apply for years two and three.

Financial Aid

The College offers a variety of scholarships, grants, loans, and employment opportunities to assist students in meeting costs of education that cannot be met through the family's own resources. The College is committed to making MCPHS an affordable option for its students and in recent years has awarded more than $6.2 million annually to eligible students. It participates in all federal and state college funding programs. Priority consideration is given to students who meet the March 15 financial aid application deadline for all available funds.

MCPHS currently offers incoming freshman students several merit scholarships. All awards are based on academics, regardless of financial need. There is no separate application for these awards; merit scholarships are automatically awarded at the time of admission. In addition, these awards automatically renew each year provided students maintain continuous full-time enrollment and meet a specified grade point average. Students should contact the Admission Office at http://www.admissions@mcphs.edu for the specific requirements of the merit scholarships.

Faculty

MCPHS has 130 outstanding full-time faculty members, with an additional 500-plus adjunct and clinical faculty members who support the programs. Almost 90 percent of the faculty members hold the highest degree possible in their fields. Classes are taught by regular and adjunct faculty members, not by teaching assistants.

Student Government

The Student Government Association is an elective body charged with appropriating funds for and monitoring student activities, overseeing class elections, and functioning as the voice of the students and their interests. Its membership includes the Dean of Students, 18 student representatives, and 2 faculty representatives.

Admission Requirements

Freshman applicants should have a high school diploma or GED credential or have fewer than 12 college credits. In addition, they should have a minimum of 16 units of course work in a challenging college-preparatory program and good to excellent grades in the following subject areas: 4 units of English, 3 in mathematics (algebra 1, algebra 2, and geometry), 2 in laboratory science (1 each in biology and chemistry), 2 in social sciences (including 1 in history), and 5 in additional college-prep courses. Advanced Placement (AP), International Baccalaureate (IB), and honors-level courses are highly desired. Additional science and mathematics courses are highly recommended.

Freshman applicants must provide SAT (including the writing section) and/or ACT scores; a personal essay that cites reasons for choosing the academic program marked on the application, selecting the specific health career to be pursued after graduation, and applying to MCPHS; at least two letters of recommendation, one from a guidance or college counselor and one from a mathematics or science teacher; and a description of extracurricular activities to show a genuine interest, commitment, and involvement in activities outside of the classroom that demonstrate leadership, compassion and dedication—especially activities that are related to health care, including community service positions of leadership, musical instruments played, athletic participation, and any other significant accomplishments.

Transfer applicants are those who have completed 12 or more college credits, with strong performance in math and science courses. They must have a cumulative grade point average of at least 2.5 on a 4.0 scale attained at an accredited college or university and evidence of being able to handle a full-time course load (12–15 credits) at the four-year college or university level

SAT and/or ACT scores are required for transfer candidates with fewer than 30 college or university credits at the time of application. Transfer students must also submit the personal essay and description of extracurricular activities.

Application and Information

For early action admission, freshman candidates with solid academic records who have decided that MCPHS is their top-choice college are encouraged to apply. Applicants must submit the application and all required materials by November 15. The Admission Office makes decisions on early action applications by December 15. Early action is only open to prospective freshmen. Accepted students have until May 1 to respond to the College's offer of admission.

For regular admission, the priority application date is February 1, but students are encouraged to apply as soon as possible. The Admission Office replies on a rolling basis once applications are complete and evaluated by the review committee and faculty members. Review for fall-entry candidates typically begins in early January. Accepted students have until May 1 to respond to offers of admission. Although there are priority filing dates for all programs, MCPHS continues to welcome applications received after these dates until all spaces are filled.

For transfer students, the priority application date is February 1, but students are encouraged to apply as soon as possible. The Admission Office replies on a rolling basis once applications are complete and reviewed by admission counselors and faculty members.

All applicants can visit the Web site at http://www.mcphs.edu to download an application or request one via mail by contacting the Admission Office at admissions@mcphs.edu. MCPHS is a member of the Common Application (http://www.commonapp.org).

For more information, students should contact:

Admission Office
Massachusetts College of Pharmacy and Health Sciences
179 Longwood Avenue
Boston, Massachusetts 02115
Phone: 617-732-2850
800-225-5506 (toll-free outside Massachusetts)
Fax: 617-732-2118
E-mail: admissions@mcphs.edu
Web site: http://www.mcphs.edu

The Massachusetts College of Pharmacy and Health Sciences Ronald A. Matricaria Academic and Student Center.

COLLEGE DATA CENTER • MASSACHUSETTS

MASSACHUSETTS INSTITUTE OF TECHNOLOGY

CAMBRIDGE, MASSACHUSETTS

Massachusetts Institute of Technology

The Institute

Massachusetts Institute of Technology (MIT) was chartered in 1861 to create a new kind of university with a mission to discover and apply knowledge for the benefit of society. Education and related research continue to be MIT's central purpose, with relevance to the practical world as a guiding principle. The campus is located on 168 acres in Cambridge, Massachusetts, bordering the Charles River for a mile and overlooking downtown Boston.

The total undergraduate enrollment at the Institute is 4,127 (1,817 women and 2,310 men). Women represent 46 percent of the entering freshman class. Ninety-one percent of undergraduates live in a mixture of eleven residence halls and thirty-five independent and cooperative living groups. All students are guaranteed campus housing for four years.

Location

Located in Cambridge, directly across the Charles River from Boston, MIT is one of fifty colleges and universities within a 20-mile radius. As a result, in the area there is an extraordinary variety of young people from all over the world as well as an impressive range of facilities and activities available to all students. Within walking distance of the Institute (or easily accessible via public transportation) are the Museum of Fine Arts, the Museum of Science, the New England Aquarium, Fenway Park, the Boston Common, Quincy Market, the Boston Symphony Orchestra, and the Boston Pops. An hour or two from MIT by regional transit are the mountains of Vermont and New Hampshire and the beaches of Cape Cod and Maine. The Boston area is where the American Revolution began, and historic sites are numerous.

Majors and Degrees

MIT offers the S.B. degree in the following fields: aerospace engineering; American studies; ancient and medieval studies; anthropology; archaeology and materials; architecture; biological engineering; biology; brain and cognitive sciences; chemical engineering; chemical-biological engineering; chemistry; civil engineering; comparative media studies; computer science and engineering; earth, atmospheric, and planetary sciences; East Asian studies; economics; electrical engineering and computer science; electrical science and engineering; environmental engineering science; foreign languages and literatures; history; humanities; humanities and engineering; humanities and science; Latin American studies; linguistics; literature; management; materials science and engineering; mathematics; mathematics with computer science; mechanical engineering; mechanical and ocean engineering; music; nuclear science and engineering; philosophy; physics; political science; psychology; Russian studies; theater; urban studies and planning; women's studies; and writing.

Many students earn an S.B. in either a preexisting interdisciplinary program or in one of their own design. Large numbers of MIT graduates go on to medical, law, and business schools.

Academic Programs

The undergraduate programs at MIT are designed to help students develop the understanding, maturity, and capabilities to meet the challenges of modern society. Students base their studies on a core of subjects in science, mathematics, and the humanities, begun the first year, and then slowly go on to concentrate in their departmental or interdepartmental programs. There is considerable time to take elective subjects each year. For most students, the program for the S.B. requires four years of full-time study. The first term at MIT is on a pass/no-record basis.

One of the most exciting features of undergraduate education is the opportunity for students to join with faculty members in ongoing research projects (Undergraduate Research Opportunities Program, or UROP). Approximately 85 percent of all undergraduates are involved in active research in the MIT tradition of learning by doing.

Advanced placement may be granted to entering freshmen through College Board Advanced Placement tests, International Baccalaureate exams, college transcripts, and advanced-standing examinations at MIT.

Air Force, Army, and Naval ROTC are all available at MIT.

There is a cross-registration program with Wellesley College, Harvard University, the Massachusetts College of Art, and the School of the Museum of Fine Arts.

Academic Facilities

At least sixty interdisciplinary and interdepartmental facilities provide opportunities for faculty members, students, and staff members to join together on projects that cross traditional disciplinary lines. Some of these are the Artificial Intelligence Laboratory, Bates Linear Accelerator, Center for Cancer Research, Center for International Studies, Center for Space Research, the Media Laboratory, and Whitehead Institute for Biomedical Research. The Institute has an extensive library system that includes 2.7 million volumes, more than 20,000 current journals and serials, and numerous back files. The Institute has well-equipped facilities to support all its programs.

Costs

The tuition for 2007–08 is $34,986. The standard cost for room and board is $10,400, and $2814 can be estimated for books, materials, clothing, entertainment, and personal expenses. A range of options is available in housing and dining arrangements; the cost before financial aid for most students is about $48,200 per year, excluding travel expenses.

Financial Aid

Financial aid is awarded on the basis of need and is dependent on an objective analysis of family finances. Financial aid packages take into account the family contribution (including the parents' contribution, student's summer earnings, and student's assets), the student's self-help (loan and/or part-time job), and MIT grant/scholarship money, if necessary, to meet the established costs. The CSS Financial Aid PROFILE and the Free Application for Federal Student Aid (FAFSA) are required to apply for financial aid. Approximately 73 percent of the undergraduates received scholarship/grant aid last year.

Faculty

A single faculty of approximately 1,000 members teaches undergraduate and graduate students and engages in research.

Seven members of the current faculty are Nobel laureates, and 20 are MacArthur Fellows. The Institute is characterized by one-on-one interaction between students and professors, and most of the faculty members participate in UROP. All students are assigned to faculty members in their major who serve as their advisers.

Student Government

The Undergraduate Association is the major undergraduate governmental body. Its functions are divided among committees that allocate funds to student organizations, manage social and musical events, operate certain facilities on campus, improve classroom and living conditions in the dormitories, propose educational reforms, sponsor feedback programs, operate free computer services, and recommend student representatives for more than fifty faculty and administrative committees.

Admission Requirements

Ideal preparation for study at MIT includes English (4 years), history/social studies (2 or more years), mathematics through calculus (4 years), laboratory sciences (biology, chemistry, and physics), and a foreign language. Applicants are required to take the SAT or the ACT with the writing test, as well as two SAT Subject Tests: one in math (Level 1 or 2) and one in science (Physics, Chemistry, or Biology E/M). The December testing date is the last one for which SAT, SAT Subject Test, and ACT scores are considered. Interviews are optional but highly recommended and are conducted in the applicant's home area by MIT alumni who belong to the Educational Council. All interviews must be completed by December 15; the deadline for submission of regular admission applications is January 1.

Application and Information

Candidates who wish to apply for early action, which is nonbinding, must submit an application and all materials by November 1 and have tests completed on or by the November testing date. They can expect to hear from the admissions committee by mid-December.

Freshmen are admitted for September only. Transfer students are accepted for September and February after having completed at least one full year at another university.

Requests for additional information and application forms should be addressed to:

Office of Admissions
Massachusetts Institute of Technology
77 Massachusetts Avenue, Room 3-108
Cambridge, Massachusetts 02139-3400
Phone: 617-253-4791
Web site: http://admissions.mit.edu/

Main entrance, Massachusetts Institute of Technology.

MASSACHUSETTS MARITIME ACADEMY

CAPE COD, MASSACHUSETTS

The Academy

As the oldest continuously operating maritime academy in the United States, Massachusetts Maritime Academy (MMA) is a coeducational state college with both maritime and nonmaritime curricula. Graduates of Massachusetts Maritime Academy have traditionally been recognized for their excellence. Naval admirals and government and business leaders are prominent among the Academy's alumni.

In addition to a Bachelor of Science degree and a professional license, students achieve a sense of self-confidence and competence—qualities that are important to success in any career.

A clear statement of approval regarding the Academy is made by employers within both maritime and shoreside industries. Nearly 100 percent of the senior class find high-paying employment within a few months of graduation.

The approximately 1,000 men and women who are attending MMA have in common an interest in hands-on activities, an aptitude for mathematics and science, leadership potential, and an interest in, or experience on, the ocean. They recognize the value of a regimented campus lifestyle for developing decision-making skills, discipline, and the ability to assume responsibility. The Academy attracts most of its students from the Northeastern states, with Massachusetts residents making up two thirds of the total. However, students from across the nation as well as seven other countries are in attendance. The great majority of students live in traditional college dormitories and are proud members of the Regiment of Cadets. Some students commute to the campus as participants in the Facilities Engineering Program.

The Regiment of Cadets is divided into companies and is administered by student leaders as well as by full-time staff members. All students wear uniforms daily and participate in various activities, such as flag formation (morning colors) and inspection of quarters.

MMA has a fine athletics complex, including artificial turf fields, and a highly competitive athletics program. The Academy fields varsity teams in baseball, crew, cross-country, football, lacrosse, rifle marksmanship, sailing, soccer, softball, spring track, and volleyball. Academy teams have won All–New England titles in baseball and football. A vigorous intramural athletics program spans the academic year. The Academy also has active programs through the Catholic Newman, floor hockey, multicultural, photography, pistol and rifle, propeller, rugby, scuba, swimming, and yachting clubs.

Massachusetts Maritime Academy is for the well-directed, environmentally conscientious, motivated young man or woman who loves the ocean and travel and who desires a thorough education to prepare for engineering, business, and maritime-related professions or for the armed forces. For students who are talented in mathematics and science, mature, and self-disciplined and who enjoy travel, the Academy can provide tradition, a fine education, and optimum hands-on training.

Location

The Academy is located on Cape Cod, at the western mouth of the scenic Cape Cod Canal where it joins Buttermilk Bay. Cape Cod is one of the most beautiful resort areas of the United States. Massachusetts Maritime Academy is less than an hour from Boston; Providence, Rhode Island; and the Cape Cod National Seashore.

Majors and Degrees

Massachusetts Maritime Academy provides graduates with a fully accredited Bachelor of Science degree and the option of a professional license, which enables graduates to seek employment within the various maritime industries and within the stationary power-plant industry. To achieve this end, students can major in emergency management, facilities engineering, international maritime business, marine engineering, marine safety and environmental protection, or marine transportation. A five-year dual-major program allows students to obtain both marine transportation and engineering licenses. The marine safety and environmental protection major is designed to present the opportunity for preparation in the scientific, management, and legal foundations of environmental protection. A variety of minor concentrations in such areas as business management, commercial fisheries, environmental/facilities engineering, and mechanical engineering also broaden employment options for graduates.

Academic Programs

Two academic terms on campus separated by a winter Sea Term make up the ten-month academic year. Approximately six months of sea time aboard the Academy's training ship or six months of cooperative education are required. The Sea Term is divided into four cruises of approximately seven weeks each. Countries visited during Sea Term have included Barbados, England, Ireland, Italy, Mexico, Panama, Portugal, and Spain; cadets cruise to twelve to fifteen countries before graduating. During Sea Term, cadets apply classroom lessons to the operation of a large oceangoing vessel. The cadets have the opportunity to ship commercially with a variety of shipping companies or participate in paid co-op programs and internships throughout the world. Cadets have the summer off.

The academic program involves extensive study and emphasizes a blend of mathematics and sciences with technical and professional studies. Each career program provides a solid foundation in mathematics, physical science, humanities, and social studies in addition to a core of required professional subjects. Maritime majors are eligible to sit for U.S. Coast Guard license examinations as a Third Mate (Deck Officer) or Third Assistant Engineer of steam and motor vessels of unlimited tonnage. Facilities engineering majors are eligible for state licensure.

Although there is no military obligation, some students select service in the U.S. Navy, U.S. Army, Coast Guard, or Marine Corps or in other military branches. Courses offered through the Department of Naval Science qualify cadets to apply for an officer's commission in the U.S. Naval or Coast Guard Reserve upon graduation.

Graduates hold positions throughout the maritime industry as well as in government administration and land-based industries, and they have had great success in many fields that are unrelated to the maritime profession, such as power-plant operations and industrial and mechanical engineering.

Academic Facilities

Massachusetts Maritime Academy has facilities representing state-of-the-art technology in order to provide cadets with the finest training available. An All Weather Navigation and Radar Training Simulator coupled with a prototype of a "Schoolship" Full-Function Video Shiphandling Simulator is the most modern instruction device for commercial marine navigation available in the world today. The system features not only video but also realistic radar, loran C, and depth-finding and radio-direction-finding capabilities. The Center for Marine Environmental Protection and Safety provides state-of-the-art emergency response management and tanker liquid cargo simulators for student and industry training. The library computer lab makes personal-application equipment, along with modems, databases, and a wide variety of popular software applications, available to faculty and staff members and cadets.

Costs

For 2007–08, tuition, fees, room, and board were $13,668 for residents of Massachusetts, Connecticut, and Rhode Island. Costs for students from Vermont, New Hampshire, Delaware, Florida, Maryland, New Jersey, North Carolina, Pennsylvania, South Carolina, Virginia, Georgia, and Washington, D.C., were $14,029. Out-of-region tuition and fees came to $24,338. These figures did not include uniforms, books, or incidental personal expenses.

Financial Aid

Massachusetts Maritime Academy offers its 1,000 students more than $500,000 per year in merit awards based on academic achievement, leadership, and community activities. Most of these awards are renewable for four years.

In addition, the Academy assists families with federal and state need-based programs, which include grants, scholarships, work opportunities, and student loan programs. Students apply for the need-based programs by completing the Free Application for Federal Student Aid (FAFSA). Prospective students should contact the Financial Aid Office at 508-830-5087 with any questions concerning the financial aid process.

Faculty

The faculty is known for its high academic standards. Seventy-five percent of the academic faculty members have doctoral degrees or top professional licenses. In the marine transportation department, there are 8 Ship Masters; in the marine engineering department, there are 8 Chief Engineers and 3 Ph.D.'s. These figures compare favorably with those at any similar academy in the country. The student-faculty ratio is a low 14:1 to ensure that all students receive personal attention commensurate with their academic and professional needs. The Academy also provides a strong support and tutorial program to ensure that every student may have an optimum opportunity for success.

Student Government

A student government is elected to help meet the extracurricular needs of the student body, and its members participate with faculty members and administrators on various all-Academy committees. Students are also represented on the Massachusetts Maritime Academy Board of Trustees.

Admission Requirements

Massachusetts Maritime Academy seeks applicants who have demonstrated an aptitude for mathematics and science. SAT or ACT scores are required of all applicants. In making admission decisions, the admission committee considers important criteria to be the applicant's class standing, SAT or ACT scores, and high school average, stressing college-preparatory mathematics and laboratory sciences (such as chemistry and physics). The rest of the evaluation considers the student's leadership potential, athletics or extracurricular participation, church and community involvement, employment, maritime experience, and letters of recommendation. At least two letters of recommendation are required. A personal interview is strongly recommended.

Application and Information

The application should be submitted as soon as possible but no later than June 1 for the class entering in September. The early decision deadline is November 1. Throughout the year, applicants and their families are invited to visit the Academy. Successful applicants receive a timely decision as well as follow-up communication throughout the year.

Application forms may be obtained by contacting:

Office of Admissions
Massachusetts Maritime Academy
101 Academy Drive
Buzzards Bay, Cape Cod, Massachusetts 02532
Phone: 508-830-5000
800-544-3411 (toll-free)
Fax: 508-830-5077
E-mail: admissions@maritime.edu
Web site: http://www.maritime.edu

Located at the gateway to Cape Cod, Massachusetts Maritime Academy is the oldest continuously operating maritime academy in the United States.

MERRIMACK COLLEGE

NORTH ANDOVER, MASSACHUSETTS

The College

Founded by the Order of St. Augustine in 1947, Merrimack College is recognized as a superior Catholic coeducational institution of higher learning. The 2,050 undergraduates come from more than twenty-six states and more than fourteen countries. The College is located just north of Boston, Massachusetts. Merrimack is a college of liberal arts, business, science, and engineering. Eighty percent of the students reside on campus in the College's residence facilities, town houses, suites, or apartment-style housing. The College strives to provide continued growth in its academic, professional, and support services. These services include Academic Support Services; Undergraduate Research Programs; the Career Services and Cooperative Education Office, which provides students with career development and job placement; the Counseling and Health Offices; the Campus Ministry Office, which is involved with social-action projects through its Merrimaction Corps; and the Center for Augustinian Study and Legacy. The Center for the Study of Jewish-Christian Relations is one of the few centers of its kind nationwide and is thoroughly integrated into the academic foundation of the College.

The College offers a full calendar of academic, cultural, ecumenical, athletic, and social activities. The Student Government Association sponsors film series, leading musical artists, and prominent lecturers on campus. Students also may participate in the On-Stagers, one of the College's more than forty cocurricular activities; intramural sports; or such College traditions as Homecoming, Winter Weekend, or the Mr. Merrimack Contest. The College also has a student newspaper, a student chorus, a faculty-student jazz ensemble, and a pep band. As a member of the Hockey East Conference, NCAA, and Northeast Ten Conference, Merrimack has sixteen varsity athletic teams, with eight sports for men and eight sports for women. The S. Peter Volpe Physical Education Center houses exercise rooms, a 3,600-seat hockey rink, and a 1,700-seat gymnasium for basketball. Outdoor facilities include Warrior Field—Merrimack's main outdoor stadium—home to the football, men's and women's soccer, field hockey, and men's and women's lacrosse teams. The field was upgraded to a FieldTurf surface in summer 2005 and included $1.2 million in renovations. Facilities also include baseball and softball fields and tennis courts.

In addition to its undergraduate degrees, Merrimack also offers Master of Education (M.Ed.) degrees in elementary education and in moderate disabilities.

Location

Merrimack College is located in northeastern Massachusetts, 25 miles north of Boston. From the campus, it's a 25-minute drive to the city of Boston, the ocean, or great sport and shopping opportunities. Two hours north are the Lakes Region and White Mountains of New Hampshire. Cape Cod is 2 hours south. New York City is a 4-hour drive. The area provides a wealth of interesting historical sites, cultural opportunities, and recreational pursuits.

The 220-acre campus offers a beautiful New England setting. The College recently opened two new residence halls offering multiple options in housing. The award-winning Rogers Center for the Arts is a 600-seat, state-of-the-art auditorium and art gallery sponsoring hundreds of cultural, musical, film, and lecture offerings for students and the community. The Sakowich Campus Center opened with new dining areas, study lounges, a book store, a chapel, and computer cafés. A multipurpose gymnasium, an indoor running track, and weight and aerobic rooms also enhance this center of student life.

Majors and Degrees

Merrimack College awards the B.A. and B.S. degrees through both day and evening programs. In addition, numerous certificate programs are offered through the Corporate Education Office, including Web design and financial planning. Bachelor of Arts degree programs in the liberal arts include communication, digital media art (graphic and Web design), economics, English, fine arts, French, history, philosophy, political science, psychology, religious studies, Romance languages, self-designed major, sociology (criminology), and Spanish. Teacher certification is available in elementary, middle, and secondary education and in moderate disabilities through a four- or five-year program to attain the M.Ed. in elementary education.

Students in the sciences or engineering may attain the Bachelor of Arts degree in biology (biotechnology) and mathematics and the Bachelor of Science degree in athletic training, chemistry, civil engineering, computer science, electrical engineering, health science, physics, and sports medicine (pre-physical therapy and strength and conditioning).

Bachelor of Science degrees are offered in business administration, with academic concentrations in accounting, finance, international business, management (sports management), and marketing.

The School of Graduate, Continuing, and Professional Education offers programs leading to associate degrees in electrical engineering or the arts and bachelor's degrees in the arts, business administration, communications studies, electrical engineering, and human service administration.

Academic Programs

In the Augustinian tradition, Merrimack's community is committed to scholarship and service to others and provides students myriad opportunities to develop intellectually, spiritually, socially, and ethically. The College seeks to provide sound professional training with a commitment to an integrated liberal arts component in all courses of study.

The Merrimack College academic calendar for day students consists of two 15-week semesters, beginning in early September and mid-January. Summer sessions are also available. The School of Graduate, Continuing, and Professional Education offers four 10-week sessions along with two traditional summer sessions.

To receive a bachelor's degree, all students must complete thirty-two semester courses with a final quality point average of 2.0 or better. Students usually take four academic courses each semester within the 4 credit/course curriculum. All bachelor's degree programs revolve around a liberal arts core curriculum. The remaining semester courses in a student's program, following completion of core, major, and cognate requirements, are open electives. The liberal arts core curriculum consists of courses in religious studies and philosophy, humanities, the social sciences, and mathematics and science.

Merrimack College also offers interdisciplinary courses, study-abroad programs, and internships through the departments of English, history, management, political science, psychology, and sociology. Special academic programs include a double major in the Division of Arts and Sciences; a contract Bachelor of Arts or Bachelor of Science degree, consisting of a special interdepartmental program in two or more fields; and a double-degree program, usually involving five years, through which the student earns two bachelor's degrees (B.A. and B.S.).

Off-Campus Programs

Cooperative education (work-study) provides paid work experiences and may be elected by students majoring in biology, all business programs, chemistry, civil engineering, computer science, electrical and computer engineering, health sciences, math, physics, and select liberal arts. Internships are available and provide students with another avenue of hands-on experiential learning. The Stevens Learning Center provides students the opportunity to learn and develop through active participation in organized service at volunteer community sites while enrolled in traditional course work. International study allows students to immerse themselves in the history and culture of another country and study abroad for a year, semester, or summer. The classes taken abroad are approved for transfer credit and serve as part of the student's academic program.

Academic Facilities

Students find tremendous informational and interactive resources in McQuade Library. It is home to three floors of computer labs; the Media Center; MCTV-10, Merrimack's cable-TV station; a 190-seat auditorium; an art gallery; a reference room; a periodicals room with 900 subscriptions; and more than 130,000 volumes. Through the automated North of Boston Library Exchange (NOBLE) resource-sharing network, students have instant access to twenty-six other libraries. Interlibrary exchanges and a global online library offer convenient access to additional services. The Girard School of Business and International Commerce offers wireless access to the Internet, computer labs, and a technology auditorium with videoconferencing capabilities. The Gregor Johann Mendel, O.S.A., Center for Science, Engineering, and Technology provides students with state-of-the-art laboratory equipment and facilities. All classroom buildings, the McQuade Library, and the Sakowich Campus Center provide wireless Internet access.

Costs

Tuition for the 2007–08 academic year was $29,310. That cost was exclusive of books, supplies, travel, and personal expenses.

Financial Aid

Merrimack College sponsors financial aid through federally and state-funded grants, loans, and work-study awards. Merrimack also provides scholarships and campus employment from College operating funds. To be eligible for any federal, state, or institutional scholarship or financial aid program, an applicant must file the Free Application for Federal Student Aid (FAFSA) by February 1. Students who receive scholarships or other financial aid through Merrimack College are notified between March 15 and April 30. Currently, 75 percent of all Merrimack students receive scholarships and financial assistance through federal, state, and College funds.

Faculty

The Merrimack faculty is committed to the academic and personal growth of undergraduate students. There are 139 full-time faculty members, of whom more than 80 percent hold a Ph.D. degree. More than 100 part-time faculty members, most with terminal degrees, complement the course offerings for students. The faculty-student ratio is 1:13. Faculty interaction with students, through small classes and the availability of personal contact, is a hallmark of Merrimack. Faculty members also participate in a Student-Faculty Advisement Program to provide for students' individual academic guidance; they also serve on many College-wide academic and student affairs committees.

Student Government

The Student Government Association has a twofold purpose. This democratic body represents all students' rights by concerning itself with all policy matters that affect the student body and by serving as a primary liaison between students and the administration. The association also conducts and coordinates a varied program of social and cultural events for the College community.

Admission Requirements

Merrimack College seeks academically prepared students who are eager to improve themselves intellectually and socially within the College community. The Admission Committee considers each applicant on an individual basis and evaluates a candidate's strengths in light of personal accomplishments, motivation, and the academic major selected. The Admission Committee places primary emphasis on the secondary school record (courses and level of courses selected and rank in class when provided) and teacher or guidance counselor recommendations. SAT or ACT scores are now an optional part of the admission process. Applicants are encouraged, but not required, to visit the campus for an interview or tour. The Admission Committee does not discriminate against applicants on the basis of race, sex, religion, or national origin; in fact, the College welcomes diversity among students. Applicants must have earned the following high school units: 4 years of college-preparatory English, 3 years of social studies, 3 years of mathematics (including algebra II), 3 years of science, 2 years of language, and 5 electives. Applicants for the sciences or engineering programs, however, are expected to have at least 4 years of mathematics and 4 years of science (including physics for engineering).

Merrimack offers early action and deferred admission to properly qualified applicants. Merrimack also gives credit and advanced placement for scores of 3 or better on the Advanced Placement examinations sponsored by the College Board in certain academic areas.

Transfer applicants for the fall or spring semester should be in good academic standing at the institution last attended, not be on academic or disciplinary probation at that institution, and have a quality point average of at least 2.5 on the Merrimack College scale.

International applicants must also submit the results of the Test of English as a Foreign Language (TOEFL) or International English Language Testing System (IELTS).

Application and Information

Early-action candidates applying for entrance for the fall term should apply by November 15. Regular-decision candidates should apply by February 1. All applications for the spring term should be made by December 1. Merrimack College adheres to the NACAC deposit deadline of May 1.

For more information, students should contact:

Office of Admission
Merrimack College
North Andover, Massachusetts 01845
Phone: 978-837-5100
Fax: 978-837-5133
E-mail: admission@merrimack.edu
Web site: http://www.merrimack.edu

MONTSERRAT COLLEGE OF ART

BEVERLY, MASSACHUSETTS

The College

Students come to Montserrat College of Art for many reasons—to gain professional competence, to develop their own unique talents, and to engage in new areas of experience. Whatever the personal goal, students find an environment in which their visions, aspirations, and commitments are nurtured and refined.

Founded in 1970 by a group of artists questioning the status quo and seeking new solutions, Montserrat possesses a variety of advantages that distinguish it from the nation's other schools of art and design. With an enrollment of 275 students of diverse cultural and artistic backgrounds, the College is large enough to offer the wide array of courses and concentrations that make up a strong visual arts curriculum, yet small enough to provide the personal attention that is often difficult to find in larger educational environments. Montserrat, with 60 percent of its students living on campus, is the most residential college among its peer institutions. The College is accredited by the New England Association of Schools and Colleges (NEASC) and the National Association of Schools of Art and Design (NASAD).

Location

Beverly, Massachusetts, is a coastal city just 23 miles north of Boston, known for its rich history, picturesque harbor, parks and beaches, and satisfying quality of life

Montserrat's apartment-style housing is nestled among the historic homes of downtown Beverly and is accessible by foot from all college facilities. The Dane Street beach and Lynch Park, site of President Taft's summer White House, are just minutes away. The renowned Peabody Essex Museum, the House of the Seven Gables, and other sites related to the infamous witch hysteria of 1692 are located in the neighboring city of Salem.

The College's main academic building, the Hardie Building, faces the beautiful Beverly Common and the Beverly Public Library. The Cabot Street Cinema Theatre screens popular, foreign, and independent films and is home to Le Grand David and his Spectacular Magic Company. Shops, cafés, restaurants, and churches line nearby Cabot Street, the location of Montserrat's other studio building, which houses the 301 gallery, Sculpture Department and senior studios.

Boston and Cambridge are easily accessible by car or commuter train. More than 100 colleges and universities are located in the Boston metropolitan area. World-class museums, such as Boston's Museum of Fine Arts and Institute of Contemporary Art, galleries, libraries, shopping, sports, and a variety of entertainment options provide a stimulating intellectual, cultural, and social environment in which to live and learn.

Majors and Degrees

Following the first year of art foundation studies, students elect a concentration in one of 6 studio arts: graphic design, illustration, painting and drawing, photography and video, printmaking, or sculpture, or follow a self-designed concentration incorporating various disciplines. To receive a B.F.A. degree a student must earn 120 credits—78 credits of studio course work and 42 credits in liberal arts, including a minimum of 12 credits in art history and 6 credits in English.

The diploma program, also a four-year program, consists of 108 credits—a minimum of 78 credits of studio course work and a minimum of 6 credits in both art history and English. The balance of credits required for the Diploma program may be earned in either studio or liberal art courses.

Students in any studio concentration within the B.F.A. program can elect to take the dual art education concentration. This is a unique artist-based model for training art teachers, with an emphasis on studio practice as the foundation for teaching art. The art education curriculum prepares students to qualify for provisional certification with advanced standing in Massachusetts public schools and other states with reciprocity agreements.

Academic Programs

Art is born of a rich variety of human experience and inquiry. Montserrat's unique curriculum engages both faculty and students in discovering new ways for the liberal and visual arts to work together to educate the total artist. During the first year of foundation studies, students are introduced to the various studio concentrations at Montserrat. The foundation curriculum is a carefully crafted sequence of varied but complementary courses that emphasize the visual, technical, written, and verbal skills essential to a successful art college experience.

Experiential learning provides a unique opportunity for students to gain professional work experience. During the junior year, internships and apprenticeships provide students with opportunities to experience the world of work and to integrate classroom learning with the realities of the workplace. Students explore career options, gain practical experience, and make contacts with potential employers. The Office of Internships and Apprenticeships assists students in locating opportunities and completing field experience relevant to their studies at Montserrat.

Once a student has earned 90 credits, completed required course work, and demonstrated sufficient media skills in their chosen studio concentration, entry into the Senior Seminar is then determined by a faculty panel. Students in Senior Seminar have the opportunity to delve independently into a significant, coherent body of work. Aided by a faculty mentor, students work intensely to articulate their unique voice and visual language. Seniors exhibit seminar work throughout the spring in the Montserrat Gallery at 301 Cabot Street. This revelatory experience helps students mature as artists and designers and, ultimately, make the transition into professional life.

Off-Campus Programs

Montserrat offers students a variety of opportunities to broaden their horizons and earn credits towards the B.F.A. degree or diploma through, local, national, and international study.

The College is a member of the Northeast Consortium of Colleges and Universities in Massachusetts. Students may take classes and use the library facilities of member colleges.

Through Montserrat's affiliation with the Association of Independent Colleges of Art and Design (AICAD), students may spend a semester or a year in comparable studies at a member institution. Students remain registered at Montserrat, retaining residency and student aid eligibility. Montserrat also conducts three study-abroad programs throughout the year: one in Viterbo, Italy; another in Niigata, Japan; and the third in Mali, Africa.

Academic Facilities

Montserrat's main building, the historic Hardie Building, houses four floors of studios, classrooms, exhibition spaces, the Paul Scott Library, and administrative offices. Specially equipped studios for printmaking, photography, painting, and illustration, as well as video and computer labs, are also located in the Hardie Building. Graphic design students work in an environment similar to a professional design studio, with computers, access to the Internet, and a meeting area. The Paul Scott Library contains a collection of more than 14,000 books, numerous art and related periodicals, videos, CD-ROMs, and other resources. The library also offers Internet access and houses a slide collection of more than 60,000 slide images. The library is a member of the North of Boston Library Exchange consortium of academic and public libraries, including the Beverly Public Library located across the street from Montserrat's Hardie Building.

Montserrat has three public art galleries and a vibrant exhibitions program that enhance its students' educational experience. The exhibiting, viewing, and discussion of artwork are important aspects of a Montserrat education. Galleries are the sites of class projects, reflection, and social interaction. The galleries host openings, exhibitions, and artist's lectures throughout the year and bring to campus prominent visiting artists and artists-in-residence.

The 301 Cabot Studio Building offers spacious facilities for sculpture students, including a wood and metal shop and plaster room. Semiprivate studios for seniors are also located in this building.

Across Cabot Street are the newly renovated studios for illustration students, including semiprivate studio spaces for seniors in the department. Adjacent to the studios are reproduction equipment and an extensive collection of research materials.

All students are entitled to free admission to the Boston Museum of Fine Arts, one of the finest collections of art in the world. The museum houses permanent exhibits of art and artifacts representing virtually all periods and civilizations, as well as changing exhibitions of art.

Costs

Tuition for the 2007–08 academic year was $21,500. Other annual direct costs of attendance, including general fees, supplies, health insurance, and on-campus housing in a shared room, were estimated at $9500.

Financial Aid

Nearly 80 percent of Montserrat students receive financial assistance (grants, loans, and employment). Sources include the federal government, state government, the College, and corporate and civic sponsors. Most financial aid is awarded on the basis of demonstrated need. To apply for financial aid, students must complete the Free Application for Federal Student Aid (FAFSA). Applications filed by March 1 receive priority consideration. Each year a number of exceptional applicants are selected for renewable academic achievement and/or talent scholarships. Candidates for merit-based scholarships must complete all requirements and submit their application for admission by the preferred filing dates of February 1 (fall entry) and December 1 (spring entry).

Faculty

The faculty of Montserrat comprises professional artists and designers and accomplished scholars. There are 20 full-time faculty members and 41 part-time instructors. Fifty-nine percent of faculty members have earned a master's degree and 29 percent hold doctorates. The student-teacher ratio is 8:1.

Student Government

Students have a voice in College policies, events, and activities through the Student Council, which maintains close communication with College administrators and faculty members. Each year, a student elected by the Student Council serves as a representative at all faculty meetings. Student Council members are active in the programming and planning of social activities and College events designed to enhance student life.

Admission Requirements

The Admissions Committee is interested in the unique interests, experiences, and abilities of each applicant. The portfolio of artwork is one of the most significant parts of a prospective student's application, and it is highly recommended that it be presented in person during an on-campus interview. Applicants who reside more than 150 miles from the campus may present the portfolio during an off-campus meeting or may mail the portfolio in slide or digital form. Academic achievement is also weighed heavily during the review process, and transcripts, letters of recommendation, and an artist's statement help the Admissions Committee to assess an applicant's potential for success at the College. SAT and ACT test scores are an optional component of the application; applicants are encouraged but are not required to submit test scores.

Application and Information

The preferred application filing date for fall semester is February 1. However, admissions decisions are made on a rolling basis, and applicants are notified of a decision within two to three weeks of completing all application requirements. For complete information on admission, financial aid, studio and academic programs, student and residential life, and campus visits, prospective students may contact:

Admissions Office
Montserrat College of Art
23 Essex Street
Beverly, Massachusetts 01915
Phone: 978-921-4242 Ext. 1153
800-836-0487 (toll-free, within the United States and Canada)
Fax: 978-921-4241
E-mail: admiss@montserrat.edu
Web site: http://www.montserrat.edu

MOUNT HOLYOKE COLLEGE

SOUTH HADLEY, MASSACHUSETTS

The College

Long distinguished for the quality of its curricular and cocurricular life as well as for the diversity of its student body and the success of its alumnae, Mount Holyoke is an independent college of liberal arts and sciences for women. The student body, numbering 2,100, represents forty-eight states and nearly seventy countries. More than 1 out of every 3 students is an international student or an African American, Latina, Asian, or Native American. Ninety-two percent of all graduates are either employed or in graduate/professional school within six months of graduation. Of those who choose to pursue an advanced degree, 20 to 25 percent enroll within five years of graduation.

Mount Holyoke is committed to maintaining small classes and individualized academic advising. The College's student-faculty ratio is 10:1. Half of Mount Holyoke's classes enroll 15 or fewer students, and 28 percent enroll fewer than 10. All students are advised by faculty members. Non-Western cultures are a focus of the College's curricular life. Most students pursue interdisciplinary courses, some taught by teams of faculty members from different fields. Use of computers, proficiency in foreign languages, and development of speaking and writing skills are stressed throughout the curriculum. The College offers first-year students the opportunity to enroll in first-year seminars—small classes designed to introduce first-year students to Mount Holyoke's intellectual community and to help them develop essential skills in writing, speaking, and analytic and critical inquiry.

The College is distinguished in developing women leaders. The Weissman Center for Leadership and the Liberal Arts is devoted to increasing students' understanding of public policy issues and giving them the tools to create change. The work of the center focuses on enhancing students' ability to frame, articulate, and advocate positions constructively and effectively. A major component is the Speaking, Arguing, and Writing Program, which is a nationally recognized model among liberal arts colleges for training students to be powerful communicators. Other Weissman Center initiatives include community-based learning courses, which combine course work with project-based field work in the community.

Mount Holyoke also has long been at the forefront of providing a global education. The McCulloch Center for Global Initiatives was founded in 2004 to unite Mount Holyoke's wealth of international programs and people, and implement a coherent vision for education for global citizenship. The center initiates, promotes, and coordinates educational activities to advance understanding of global problems and solutions from cross-disciplinary, cross-cultural, and cross-national perspectives. Through its programs, students and faculty members engage critically with an increasingly global world.

Mount Holyoke participates in the Five College Consortium, which also includes Amherst, Hampshire, and Smith Colleges and the University of Massachusetts Amherst. Students enrolled at any one of the Five Colleges can take the courses and participate in the cultural and social offerings of the other four. In addition, the five institutions' faculty and classes are coordinated in areas of common interest, such as African studies, Asian/Pacific/American studies, Latin American studies, Middle Eastern studies, and international relations. Dance and astronomy—the two Five College majors—both rank among the largest and most distinguished undergraduate programs nationally in their respective fields.

Forming a vital part of Mount Holyoke's offerings are diverse cocurricular opportunities—concerts, conferences, exhibitions, films, and social events. Noted actors, dancers, and musicians perform at Mount Holyoke and within the Five College area. In addition, there are performance opportunities through instrumental ensembles, dance groups, theater productions, and an active choral program. Groups such as the Five College Dance Department, the Five College Jazz Improvisation Orchestra, and the New World Theatre supplement these opportunities. More than 150 clubs and organizations at Mount Holyoke provide creative outlets, leadership experiences, and service opportunities.

The residence halls complement the liberal arts experience, coordinating cultural and social events and providing a home away from home for all students. Almost all students live on campus in the residence halls, each of which accommodates between 65 and 130 students. All four classes are mixed in each hall, and housing is guaranteed for all four years. A new, 175-bed residence hall offering a variety of living options is planned to open in 2008. Dining options available across campus include a full-service café and several coffee shops. A kosher/halal dining room serves the dietary needs of observant Jews and observant Muslims and is open to the entire campus community.

Other facilities include five cultural houses, a Japanese teahouse and meditation garden, a health clinic and counseling center, and a center for spiritual life and community service. Students of all religious traditions and spiritual paths are made welcome at Mount Holyoke. Four chaplains—Catholic, Jewish, Protestant, and Muslim—and a number of faculty advisers respond to the pastoral and liturgical needs of the College's diverse religious community.

Recent renovation to the Blanchard Campus Center have transformed the building's interior into a center for dining, entertainment, and social activity. Highlights include a cyber café, coffee bar, art gallery, game room, performance space, and campus store. The radio station, student programs offices, and meeting rooms are also located here.

A comprehensive sports and dance complex has 130,000 square feet of facilities. The field house includes basketball, tennis, volleyball, squash, and racquetball courts; a 200-meter track; and an eight-lane swimming pool with a separate diving tank. The field house adjoins the gymnasium and dance studios. There are also twelve outdoor tennis courts, a new eight-lane outdoor track, a synthetic multipurpose turf field with lights, and several grass playing fields. An equestrian center provides a sixty-stall barn and large indoor and outdoor riding arenas as well as three cross-country show courses. This center is widely considered one of nation's finest riding facilities. The College's eighteen-hole golf course, designed by Donald Ross, was the site of the 2004 USGA Women's Open. Mount Holyoke is an NCAA Division III school and offers thirteen intercollegiate teams as well as intramural and club sports.

Location

South Hadley, Massachusetts, is about 20 minutes from Springfield, 1½ hours from Boston, and 3 hours from New York City by car. Convenient bus, plane, and train service to the College is available. Bradley International Airport, 40 minutes away by car, serves Hartford and Springfield; Amtrak train stations are located in Amherst and Springfield. Bookstores, coffee shops, and restaurants are within walking distance of campus, and the nearby towns of Northampton and Amherst are easily reached via the free Five College bus service.

Majors and Degrees

Mount Holyoke offers the Bachelor of Arts degree. Majors include African and African American studies, American studies, ancient studies, anthropology, architectural studies, art (history and studio), Asian studies, astronomy, biochemistry, biological sciences, chemistry, classics, computer science, critical social thought, dance, economics, engineering, English, environmental studies, European studies, film studies, French, gender studies, geography, geology, German studies, Greek, history, international relations, Italian, Latin, Latin American studies, mathematics, medieval studies, music, neuroscience and behavior, philosophy, physics, politics, psychology, psychology and education, religion, Romance languages and literatures, Russian and Eurasian studies, self-designed studies, sociology, Spanish, statistics, and theater arts. Students may also follow prelaw and premedical courses of study. In addition, students can earn both an A.B. from Mount Holyoke and a B.S. in engineering from Caltech, UMass' College of Engineering, or Dartmouth's Thayer School of Engineering in a five-year period.

Academic Programs

Within the framework of the liberal arts and sciences, Mount Holyoke offers students considerable freedom of choice in the academic program. The basic plan of study includes a distribution of courses among at least seven disciplines, courses in language, courses in a major and minor field, and at least one course dealing with an aspect of Africa, Asia, Latin America, the Middle East, or the nonwhite peoples of North America. A normal schedule is four 4-credit courses per semester, each meeting one to four times per week. By graduation, a student has completed 128 credits of academic work in courses that provide exposure to a variety of disciplines, as well as specialization in a major and a minor field. Independent study, honors work, and self-scheduled examinations are among the options available. The Frances Perkins Program is designed for women beyond the traditional undergraduate age who wish to initiate, continue, or enrich their undergraduate education.

The academic calendar consists of two semesters separated by an active January Term program. During January Term, students may take a single intensive course, pursue an independent project, engage in volunteer work, or complete a three-week internship.

Off-Campus Programs

The Mount Holyoke student lives and studies in an area where four independent colleges and a large university enroll a total of more than 30,000 students. Amherst, Hampshire, Mount Holyoke, and Smith Colleges and the University of Massachusetts Amherst participate in an extensive Five College cooperative exchange program. Free buses run among the institutions (all within a 12-mile radius) every 20 minutes from morning to late evening, seven days a week, during the school year.

Mount Holyoke is a member of the Twelve College Exchange, and students can spend a year or semester at any of the other participating institutions (Amherst, Bowdoin, Connecticut, Dartmouth, Smith, Trinity, Vassar, Wellesley, Wheaton, and Williams Colleges and Wesleyan University). The exchange also includes the Williams/Mystic Seaport Program in American Maritime Studies and the O'Neill National Theater Institute Program. Mount Holyoke also has its own exchange programs with Mills College in Oakland, California, and Spelman College in Atlanta, Georgia. Semester programs include the American University Washington Semester and the Semester in Environmental Science at the Marine Biological Laboratory, Woods Hole. Each year, 40 percent of the junior class studies abroad for a semester or a year in such countries as Argentina, Australia, Chile, China, Costa Rica, Denmark, France, Germany, Italy, Japan, Kenya, Korea, Republic of Georgia, Russia, Senegal, and the United Kingdom.

The College's Career Development Center assists students in developing both summer and January internships, which involve full-time work for six to twelve weeks over the summer or for three weeks during January Term. Internships have been undertaken in the fields of the arts, business and banking, communications, education, government, health, public policy, sciences, social services, and technology. Reflecting the College's internationalism and building on the College's extensive overseas ties, Mount Holyoke has a strong network of international internship opportunities around the world. Sponsoring organizations typically include the World Bank, UNESCO, and the United Nations.

Academic Facilities

In recent years, the College has invested $75 million in the renovation and expansion of facilities and technology. The music and art buildings have been fully updated and expanded, including the Mount Holyoke College Art Museum, one of the nation's leading collegiate art museums with an active teaching collection. The new Science Center advances the College's international reputation as a leader in scientific education for women. A multistory, 40,000-square-foot environmentally sound building, Kendade Hall, connects three other science buildings and features a four-story atrium that provides a gathering place for all members of the community. The Science Center houses eight departments—astronomy, biochemistry, biological sciences, chemistry, computer science, earth and environment, mathematics, and physics—and offers classrooms, adjacent labs and offices, common spaces, and shared equipment for students and faculty members with overlapping research interests.

The 800-acre campus includes two lakes, wooded bridle trails, lawns, and forests. An undeveloped nature preserve covers 330 of these acres and serves as an environmental classroom for students and faculty members. Taking advantage of this "outdoor classroom," the Center for the Environment is a resource for students interested in using the campus and surrounding community to advance their studies of ecology and environmental studies.

The College's 740,000-volume library incorporates dedicated science and music libraries and computerized access to 8 million volumes through the Five College Consortium. Within the main library, the Information Commons has forty high-end computers and a Help Desk. The Mediated Educational Work Space (MEWS) has flexible work areas, 52-inch plasma screens, and dual-boot Intel Macs to support multimedia teaching and collaborative projects. The computer and language learning center uses state-of-the-art methods for teaching languages. Technology tools currently in use include wireless networking, video conferencing, and interactive, multimedia-based, curriculum-enhancing Web software. There are ongoing training opportunities for students to learn emerging technologies.

An extensive Career Development Center offers students assistance in clarifying their goals and in identifying internships, jobs, graduate schools, and fellowships.

Costs

For 2007–8, tuition was $35,760, and room and board were $10,520, for a total of $46,280.

Financial Aid

Financial need should not discourage any student from applying to Mount Holyoke. Aid (grants, loans, and campus employment) is based on financial-aid eligibility as determined by the College. Mount Holyoke also offers a limited number of competitive merit aid awards.

Faculty

Mount Holyoke's 200 faculty members are dedicated teachers as well as active scholars, research scientists, and creative artists. Fifty percent are women, and 25 percent are persons of color. All courses are taught by faculty members; professors are also active in advising students about classes, cocurricular opportunities, and careers. Mount Holyoke professors have won numerous national and international awards, including National Science Foundation CAREER awards, MacArthur and Carnegie Corporation fellowships, Guggenheims, Fulbrights, the Pulitzer Prize, the Rome Prize, and the National Book Award.

Student Government

Mount Holyoke students, together with the faculty and administrators, have a strong hand in shaping campus life. Students sit on several committees, including the President's Commission on Diversity, the Academic Policy Committee, and the Board of Admissions. The Student Government Association allows students to govern their cocurricular lives and maintain communication with the faculty and administration. Students have an effective honor code of long standing.

Admission Requirements

Mount Holyoke seeks smart, ambitious students who value a liberal arts education and who are fired by a love of learning. Students who do well here tend to demonstrate a high level of maturity and independence. Mount Holyoke welcomes students of all economic, ethnic, geographic, religious, and social backgrounds. A high school program providing a good preparation for Mount Holyoke includes 4 years of English, 3 years of a foreign language, 3 years each of mathematics and laboratory sciences, and 2 years of history. SAT or ACT scores are optional. The Test of English as a Foreign Language (TOEFL) or the International English Language Testing System (IELTS) is required for students for whom English is not a primary language. Personal interviews are highly recommended for all candidates either on campus or with an alumna admissions representative.

Application and Information

Two rounds of early decision are available: the deadline for Round I is November 15, with notification by January 1; the deadline for Round II is January 1, with notification by February 1. The deadline for regular admission is January 15, with notification by April 1. Other admission options, such as early entrance, deferred entrance, and advanced standing, are available.

The admission office is open all year, Monday through Friday, from 9 a.m. to 5 p.m., and Saturday mornings from 9 a.m. to noon. Visitors may come to the admission office to attend an information session, take a campus tour, obtain admission materials, or meet with a staff member. For more information, students should contact:

Office of Admission
Mount Holyoke College
50 College Street
South Hadley, Massachusetts 01075-1488
Phone: 413-538-2023
Fax: 413-538-2409
E-mail: admission@mtholyoke.edu
Web site: http://www.mtholyoke.edu

MOUNT IDA COLLEGE

NEWTON, MASSACHUSETTS

The College

Mount Ida College, founded in 1899, is an affordable private liberal arts college with more than 1,400 students from over twenty-five states and twenty-five countries around the world and offering degree programs in more than twenty-five fields of study. Mount Ida College is a comprehensive college that combines professional education with a solid liberal arts foundation. Mount Ida campus life offers a supportive learning environment and a diverse, welcoming community.

Mount Ida takes a multidisciplinary approach to learning that emphasizes professional preparation. The All-College Curriculum helps students integrate what they learn in all of their courses, inside and outside of their major. Students learn to think critically and creatively. These transferable skills become the foundation for a lifetime of personal and professional success.

Many of the College's programs offer internships or culminate in a senior capstone project. The veterinary technology program, for instance, requires a minimum of six internships to ensure the widest range of practical knowledge possible. This real-world experience helps Mount Ida students quickly land jobs in their fields upon graduation. Mount Ida graduates understand today's world and how to succeed in it.

The result is quite amazing. Several degree programs have an impressive 100 percent job placement rate within a year of graduation, including interior design, liberal studies, business administration, equine management, funeral home management, and veterinary technology. College-wide, 88 percent of Mount Ida graduates work in a field related to their major within one year of earning a degree, and more than 92 percent have positions that require a bachelor's degree.

At Mount Ida, learning takes place both in and out of the classroom. The College offers a full array of leadership opportunities. For instance, 25 percent of incoming students compete at the NCAA Division III level in one of several varsity sports that foster teamwork and leadership. Plus, Mount Ida students have the opportunity to participate in a variety of intramural programs, clubs, and campus organizations to enrich their education

Location

Beyond its unique approach to learning, Mount Ida literally offers students the best of both worlds. The picturesque, 72-acre campus is located in Newton, Massachusetts, which has twice been named the nation's "safest city." At the same time, Mount Ida is just 8 miles (13 kilometers) from downtown Boston, one of the world's greatest college towns, giving Mount Ida's students easy access to the inexhaustible wealth of cultural resources, internships and professional opportunities, community service opportunities, sports, and nightlife a major city has to offer. The College shuttle bus connects students with the Newton Centre subway service to Boston.

Majors and Degrees

Mount Ida grants B.A., B.S., B.L.S., A.A., and A.S. degrees. Majors and areas of study include American studies, applied forensic science, bereavement studies, biology, business administration, child development, computer animation, criminal justice, dental hygiene, English, equine management, fashion design, fashion merchandising and marketing, funeral home management, funeral service, general studies, graphic design, hotel and tourism management, human services, interior design, liberal studies, management, psychology, sports management, and veterinary technology. Mount Ida also offers a prelaw concentration, pre–dental hygiene studies, and minors in American studies, art/design history, business, child study, coaching, criminalistics, criminal justice, English, forensic psychology, human services, leadership studies, legal studies, marketing, psychology, sociology, and studio art.

Academic Programs

Mount Ida students have access to exceptional academic services, all of which are designed to help them move from potential to achievement. Mount Ida's commitment to its students' success—both at Mount Ida and beyond—is absolute.

In the Academic Success Center, students find content-area tutoring offered by professional and student tutors. In addition, professional writing associates in the comprehensive Writing Center can help students write and revise papers for any of their classes. Students with documented learning disabilities can enhance their academic experience through the Learning Opportunities Program, which provides weekly strategy-based tutorial sessions with a professional learning specialist. The federally funded Learning Circle Program, available to first-generation college students who meet eligibility guidelines, offers academic coaching, financial counseling, topic-based workshops, social events, and cultural opportunities. Altogether, these academic support programs provide an invaluable resource for Mount Ida students.

Students also find support in the Career Services Center, where they find help with resume and cover letter writing, interviewing skills, job research, and identification of their career goals. The Career Services Center also assists with internship and job placements and holds career fairs.

Costs

Tuition for the 2008–09 academic year is $22,275. Room and board charges are $11,100, with books and supplies costing between $500 and $1000, depending on the program of study.

Financial Aid

Need-based and merit-based assistance, including scholarships, grants, loans, and work-study, are available to qualified students. For the 2007–08 school year, $8 million in institutional aid was awarded. Mount Ida has a financial aid priority application deadline of May 1.

Faculty

With approximately 190 full- and part-time faculty members, Mount Ida offers a student-faculty ratio of 13:1, with faculty members available to give each and every student the personalized attention they need to turn their potential into lasting achievement.

Mount Ida's faculty members are well-respected practitioners in their fields of expertise—business, computer animation, veterinary technology, funeral service, and more. As such, the professors bring an invaluable expert perspective to the classroom that adds depth and scope to the learning process

Admission Requirements

A composite evaluation is made of each applicant. Official high school and college transcripts (the latter where applicable) are required, as are SAT or ACT test scores (essay recommended), recommendations, and a personal statement. Transfer students must submit official transcripts of all completed college course work. Transfer credit for fashion design, graphic design, and interior design studio courses may depend on a portfolio review. The TOEFL may be required for students for whom English is not their native language; those applicants should check with the admissions office for more information.

Application and Information

Mount Ida has a rolling admissions policy. Although there is no deadline for the submission of applications, applicants are encouraged to apply as early as possible. Applications are considered as long as there is space in the desired program of study. Applicants are notified within three to four weeks after all credentials have been received

The best way to discover what makes Mount Ida so unique is to visit the campus and see that Mount Ida is a truly special learning community. For more information, to apply for admission, or to schedule a visit, students should contact the admissions office or visit the Web (http://www.mountida.edu).

For further information, students should contact:

Jerry C. Titus, Dean of Admissions
Mount Ida College
777 Dedham Street
Newton, Massachusetts 02459
Phone: 617-928-4553
Fax: 617-928-4507
E-mail: admissions@mountida.edu
Web site: http://www.mountida.edu

Carlson Center at Mount Ida College.

THE NEW ENGLAND INSTITUTE OF ART

BROOKLINE, MASSACHUSETTS

The New England Institute of Art®

The Institute

The New England Institute of Art prepares graduates for entry-level employment in the creative arts. Industry-experienced faculty members use a student-centered approach and market-driven curricula to support students in developing tools and skills consistent with industry needs. The New England Institute of Art offers eight bachelor's degree programs as well as three associate degree programs. Continuing education is available through the Center for Professional Development at The New England Institute of Art.

The school's values include learner-centered education that provides professional and personal development. The New England Institute of Art fosters and rewards creativity and artistic self-expression.

Students at The New England Institute of Art come from throughout the United States and abroad. The student population includes recent high school graduates, transfer students, and those who have left a previous employment situation to study and train for a new career. Students are creative, competitive, and open to new ideas. They place great value on an education that prepares them for an exciting entry-level position in the arts.

Assistance is available to help students with resume writing, networking, and keeping abreast of what employers are looking for in job candidates. The Student Affairs and Career Services departments provide extensive individual services and classroom instruction in areas such as career counseling, job-search assistance, and personal counseling.

Students have many opportunities to participate in student organizations, including an on-campus radio station, record label, literary magazine, and Web development program. School groups include the Audio Engineering Society; Naked Ear Records, the school's record label; *Naked Truth,* the school's literary magazine; and Naked Eye Video, the school's production company. The Web Raisers group helps nonprofit organizations establish an online presence, and the Graphic Design Club gives students the opportunity to work on pro bono and freelance projects outside of the classroom.

Students may live in Domitilla Hall at Regis College, located in Weston, 11 miles from The New England Institute of Art. Domitilla Hall has double and single dorm-style bedrooms and laundry facilities, lounge/study areas, and floor kitchenettes. Free shuttle service is available for students between the residence hall and The New England Institute of Art. The school also assists students seeking independent housing in the area by providing roommate referrals and rental information.

The New England Institute of Art is accredited by the New England Association of Schools and Colleges (NEASC) through its Commission on Institutions of Higher Education (CIHE).

Location

The New England Institute of Art is situated in the greater Boston–area city of Brookline, a blend of busy city streets and rolling countryside. The town features upscale shops and small pubs, a hillside park overlooking Boston with an open-air skating rink, a golf course, and Brookline's very own working farm.

Major retail centers such as Coolidge Corner and Brookline Village contain bookstores, coffee shops, food markets, antique stores, and much more. The New England Institute of Art students find Brookline to be convenient to Boston's radio and television stations, ad agencies, and media production companies.

Majors and Degrees

The school offers bachelor's degree programs in advertising, audio and media technology, digital filmmaking and video production, graphic design, interactive media design, interior design, media arts and animation, and photography. Associate degree programs are available in audio production, broadcasting, and photography.

Academic Programs

The academic year is divided into fall, spring, and summer semesters, beginning in September, January, and May. To receive a bachelor's degree, students must complete a minimum of 120 to 123 credit hours and complete a 120-hour internship or capstone project. To receive an associate degree, students must complete a minimum of 61 credit hours and complete an 80-hour internship or capstone project.

Academic Facilities

The New England Institute of Art facilities house computer labs with industry-related software. The school's library has a collection of communications and design-related books, career-related periodicals, videotapes, computers, and CDs.

Access to production and recording studios is an essential component of the educational process at The New England Institute of Art. The school emphasizes consistent and regular student access beyond the scheduled class hours to all studios. Studio operations personnel are available to assist students during access periods.

Classrooms reserved for radio courses contain reel-to-reel recorder editors, cart machines, a turntable, and cassette recorders. Audio Production Department facilities include music and audio production studios, including digital postproduction studios and a computer music lab. The New England Institute of Art operates a multicamera television studio where students may learn all facets of studio production, including directing, camera operation, lighting, audio, editing, switching, and on-camera performance as well as producing and script writing.

Costs

Tuition cost varies by program. Prospective students should contact the school for current tuition costs. Other charges include a starting kit for all first-quarter students. Kits vary in price, depending on the program of study.

Financial Aid

Financial aid is available for those who qualify. Students who require financial assistance to attend the school should make an appointment with a financial aid officer, who will determine the level of need according to a standard federal formula and cost of attendance. Students must submit a Free Application for Federal Student Aid (FAFSA) in order to receive federal and state aid, which is available in the form of grants, loans, or work-study. Grants include Federal Pell Grants, Federal Supplemental Educational Opportunity Grants, Massachusetts State Grants, and veterans' benefits. Loans include Federal Stafford Student Loans, Federal PLUS loans, and Massachusetts State Loans. The Inabeth Miller Scholarship awards half-tuition scholarships to two applicants who meet Scholarship Committee criteria. Other scholarships may be available from the school or private sources. Application deadlines and eligibility requirements vary.

Faculty

The New England Institute of Art faculty consists of full-time and part-time professors, many of whom have advanced degrees and professional experience in their respective fields.

Admission Requirements

Individuals seeking admission to The New England Institute of Art must have earned a high school diploma or a General Educational Development (GED) certificate. Applications must include an official high school transcript and SAT or ACT scores. Candidates for admission are required to participate in an admission interview to discuss reasons for seeking admission, program preference, and professional and educational objectives. Applications may be submitted anytime prior to the beginning of a new semester.

There is a $50 application fee.

Application and Information

To obtain an application or make arrangements for an interview or tour of the school, students should contact:

The New England Institute of Art
10 Brookline Place West
Brookline, Massachusetts 02445-7295
Phone: 617-739-1700
800-903-4425 (toll-free)
Fax: 617-582-4500
Web site: http://www.artinstitutes.edu/boston

The Art Institute of Atlanta®, GA; The Art Institute of Atlanta®–Decatur, GA; The Art Institute of Austin℠, TX; The Art Institute of California℠–Inland Empire; The Art Institute of California℠–Los Angeles; The Art Institute of California℠–Orange County; The Art Institute of California℠–Sacramento; The Art Institute of California℠–San Diego; The Art Institute of California℠–San Francisco; The Art Institute of California℠–Sunnyvale; The Art Institute of Charleston℠, SC, A branch of The Art Institute of Atlanta, GA; The Art Institute of Charlotte®, NC; The Art Institute of Colorado® (Denver); The Art Institute of Dallas®, TX; The Art Institute of Fort Lauderdale®, FL; The Art Institute of Houston®, TX; The Art Institute of Indianapolis℠, IN*; The Art Institute of Jacksonville℠, FL, A branch of Miami International University of Art & Design; The Art Institute of Las Vegas®, NV; The Art Institute of Michigan℠ (Detroit); The Art Institute of New York City®, NY; The Art Institute of Ohio℠–Cincinnati**; The Art Institute of Philadelphia®, PA; The Art Institute of Phoenix®, AZ; The Art Institute of Pittsburgh®, PA; The Art Institute of Pittsburgh®–Online Division; The Art Institute of Portland®, OR; The Art Institute of Salt Lake City℠, UT; The Art Institute of Seattle®, WA; The Art Institute of Tampa℠, FL, A branch of Miami International University of Art & Design; The Art Institute of Tennessee℠–Nashville, A branch of The Art Institute of Atlanta, GA; The Art Institute of Tucson℠, AZ; The Art Institute of Washington® (Arlington, VA), A branch of The Art Institute of Atlanta, GA; The Art Institute of York–Pennsylvania℠; The Art Institutes International Minnesota℠ (Minneapolis); California Design College℠ (Los Angeles–Wilshire Blvd.); The Illinois Institute of Art®–Chicago; The Illinois Institute of Art®–Schaumburg; Miami International University of Art & Design℠, FL; The New England Institute of Art® (Boston, MA).

*The Art Institute of Indianapolis is licensed by the Indiana Commission on Proprietary Education, 302 West Washington Street, Room E201, Indianapolis, IN 46204, AC-0080.

**The Art Institute of Ohio–Cincinnati, 8845 Governors Hill Drive, Suite 100, Cincinnati, OH 45249-3317, Reg. #04-01-1698B.

NORTHEASTERN UNIVERSITY

BOSTON, MASSACHUSETTS

The University

There is a certain energy about Northeastern. It comes from bright, ambitious students with a sense of purpose. In the classroom, in the workplace, in campus activities, and in the city of Boston—the ultimate college town—Northeastern students stimulate their minds, investigate career options, participate in community affairs, and graduate personally and professionally prepared for their future careers or for graduate school. The Bouvé College of Health Sciences also offers a six-year Doctor of Pharmacy degree and a six-year program leading to a Master of Science in physical therapy.

Northeastern integrates rigorous classroom studies with experiential learning opportunities anchored by the nation's largest, most innovative cooperative education (co-op) program. It is the Northeastern Difference. In addition to co-op, research opportunities, study-abroad programs, and civic engagement options help round out the real-life learning available. Each year, students graduate from Northeastern with a solid sense of themselves and their relationship to the community and with a valuable head start on their careers or graduate school.

Through the co-op program, students alternate classroom learning with periods of full-time, usually paid work or other types of practical learning related to their major or interests. Graduates accumulate as many as two years of professional experience, professional contacts, and the social confidence that gives them a significant edge in the job market over new graduates without experience. By working in varied jobs and settings, students learn what they like—and do not like—before committing to a permanent position. Many Northeastern students even go to work for a co-op employer after graduation. Northeastern students graduate knowing what they could have learned only on the job: how to conduct themselves, what to wear, how to interpret a company's culture, how to get things done, and how to write a resume and interview successfully. Co-op is an education in itself.

The current undergraduate enrollment of 15,339 is made up of students of all backgrounds, interests, and tastes, giving Northeastern its distinctive, urban style. This diversity shows in the range of available activities. Students can join a cultural club, write for the *Northeastern News*, perform with the Silver Masque, go on a ski trip, play basketball, tutor local children, learn to ballroom dance, and much more. Students have many opportunities to make friends, try something new, become a leader, or simply have fun. Students can also find quiet corners of the campus that feel far from city streets where they can read or just relax, sprawled on a wooden bench under a shade tree; sip gourmet coffee from a nearby campus café; or listen to a midday jazz performance behind the Curry Student Center amid the art of Northeastern's sculpture park. The 67-acre campus is dynamic and welcoming, a beautiful stretch of leafy green in the heart of Boston. Its compact size lets students get to class on time or rush back for a forgotten book. Yet it contains many needed services, from a hair salon to a travel agency.

Location

Though in the midst of the hustle and bustle where Boston's Back Bay meets the Fenway, Northeastern is an increasingly residential campus and has built, in the past five years alone, a host of new on-campus residence halls, more than doubling the amount of housing available to undergraduates. The newest residence halls offer apartment-style living with modern kitchens complete with dishwashers, disposals, and full-sized appliances; cable hookups; and data jacks. Many have amazing views of the Boston skyline.

The Back Bay area, known for its many cultural and educational institutions, is steps from Symphony Hall, the New England Conservatory of Music, the Museum of Fine Arts, and the Isabella Stewart Gardner Museum. The Fenway area, with its beautiful rose garden, bicycle and jogging paths, and Fenway Park (home of the Boston Red Sox), is just a few blocks away.

Majors and Degrees

Northeastern's academic programs are divided among six colleges: the College of Arts and Sciences, the Bouvé College of Health Sciences, the College of Business Administration, the College of Computer and Information Science, the College of Criminal Justice, and the College of Engineering. Top-notch faculty members with a variety of research interests personally guide students through their studies.

The College of Arts and Sciences awards undergraduate degrees in art, African-American studies, American Sign Language and English interpreting, anthropology, applied physics, architecture, art (including concentrations in animation and photography), behavioral neuroscience, biochemistry, biology (including a concentration in marine biology), biomedical physics, chemistry, communication studies (including concentrations in media studies, organizational communication, and public communication), economics, English, environmental science, environmental studies, geology, graphic design, history, human services, international affairs, journalism, linguistics, mathematics, modern languages, multimedia studies, music (concentrations in music industry, music literature, music literature and performance, and music technology), philosophy (including concentrations in law and ethics, philosophy generalist, and religious studies), physics, political science (including concentrations in international relations and comparative politics, law and legal issues, and public policy and administration), psychology, sociology, studio art (in collaboration with the School of the Museum of Fine Arts, Boston), and theater (including concentrations in performance, production, and theater generalist). In addition, preparation programs in elementary education and early childhood education (both including a specialization in special education) and a minor in secondary education are available.

The Bouvé College of Health Sciences awards degrees in athletic training, health sciences, nursing, pathways (open option, available to freshmen interested in the health professions who have not yet decided on a specific major), and speech-language pathology and audiology.

The College of Business Administration offers two tracks: the Bachelor of Science in Business Administration (B.S.B.A.) or the Bachelor of Science in International Business (B.S.I.B.). The B.S.I.B. program includes language instruction and international study and work. The College offers concentrations in accounting, entrepreneurship and small business management, finance and insurance, human resources management, management, management information systems, marketing, and supply-chain management.

The College of Computer and Information Science awards degrees in computer science and information science and also offers dual-major degrees combining computer science with cognitive psychology, mathematics, or physics.

The College of Criminal Justice awards an undergraduate degree in criminal justice, with concentrations in criminology and corrections, legal studies, policing and security, and race and justice.

The College of Engineering offers degrees in chemical, civil and environmental, computer, electrical, industrial, and mechanical engineering.

Academic Programs

Northeastern's approach integrates course work in a liberal arts and professional studies with a variety of practical experiences, including the signature cooperative education program. Innovative programs encompass a wide range of majors, concentrations, and interdisciplinary studies along with honors, preprofessional, and study-abroad programs.

The internationally known cooperative education program enables students to gain practical and lively workplace or other experience integrated with their academic studies. Students can alternate semesters of work and study (after completing their freshman year) and can earn their bachelor's degree in either four or five years. Co-op employers include some of the country's largest and most reputable companies, such as Pfizer, John Hancock, Fidelity Investments, General Electric, Massachusetts General Hospital, and the *Boston Globe.* Students also enjoy international placements for a semester or a year abroad; co-op employers recruit from Australia, Scotland, Italy, and Spain, among many other countries.

A University-wide honors program gives students opportunities to participate in enriched educational experiences and offers opportunities that include honors sections of required academic courses, honors seminars, independent research, and study abroad. The University also offers Army, Naval Nursing, and Air Force ROTC. The Disability Resource Center provides many support services that enable students with disabilities to participate fully in the life of the University community.

Academic Facilities

Northeastern is home to a variety of research centers, including the Center for Labor Market Studies, the Institute of Molecular Biotechnology, the Nano Manufacturing Research Institute, the Race and Justice Research Institute, and many others. Students have ample opportunities to work alongside their professors to aid and conduct research on a variety of topics.

University libraries have licensed access to more than 19,600 electronic information sources. A central and branch library contain technologically sophisticated services, including Web-based catalog and circulation systems and a Web portal to licensed electronic resources. The University is a member of the Boston Library Consortium and the Boston Regional Library System, giving students and faculty members access to the region's collections and information resources.

Northeastern University provides a broad range of academic and administrative computer resources available to students and faculty and staff members. Many computing resources are available, including Internet connections for all offices and University-owned residence halls, technology-assisted classrooms, computer labs, and the myNEU portal, which allows student to access many administrative and academic functions online. There is also extensive wireless network access, found in the library, Student Center, and many dorms.

Costs

For 2007–08, tuition was $31,500, and room and board were $11,010. While on co-op, students do not pay tuition but may choose to continue to pay room and board to live in the residence halls.

Financial Aid

The University operates a substantial aid program designed to make attendance at Northeastern feasible for all qualified students. By coordinating the resources of the University and various public and private scholarship programs, the Office of Student Financial Services was able to provide more than $100 million in aid last year. About 83 percent of the freshman class received some form of financial aid. Financial aid is based on need and academic merit and may consist of grants, loans, work-study employment, or any combination of the three. To apply, students must file a Free Application for Federal Student Aid (FAFSA) and a CSS PROFILE form with the College Scholarship Service by the priority filing date of February 15.

Faculty

The University has 839 full-time faculty members with a wide variety of research and teaching interests and specialties and a staff of academic counselors in each college who work closely with students to assist them in developing programs suited to their interests and abilities. Each student is assigned both an academic and a co-op adviser. The co-op adviser aids in resume building, interview skills and tactics, and contacts with business and co-op employers as well as networking and eventual job searches.

Admission Requirements

Students may enter the University with advanced credit on the basis of test scores on Advanced Placement (AP) examinations, the College-Level Examination Program (CLEP), the International Baccalaureate (I.B.), or on successful completion of accredited college-level courses before enrollment at Northeastern. In addition to the application for admission, prospective freshmen must submit official high school transcript(s) (or official GED score reports), including their senior-year grades; official transcripts for any college-level course work taken while a secondary-school student; written recommendations from their secondary school guidance counselor and a teacher; and scores on the SAT (Northeastern's College Board code is 3667) or ACT, including the writing section.

Application and Information

Admission to Northeastern is selective and competitive. For the 2007–08 academic year, the University received more than 30,000 applications for 2,800 places in the freshman class. In building a diverse and talented class, Northeastern seeks to enroll students who have been successful academically and who have shown a strong commitment to school and community through extracurricular activities. Students who have earned strong grades in a rigorous college-preparatory program, are innovative and creative, and who possess leadership abilities are most successful in the admission process.

November 15 is the deadline for the early action admission program. Students who have carefully explored their college options and have decided that Northeastern is where they want to enroll may choose to apply under the early action program. The deadline for the regular admission program is January 15. If accepted for fall admission either through the early action program or the regular admission program, freshmen are required to send a tuition deposit by May 1 to secure a place in the class. For transfer students, the priority deadline for the fall is May 1. March 1 is the deadline for transfer Pharmacy applicants for the fall. Admission decisions for transfer applicants are made on a space-available, rolling basis. November 1 is the deadline for January transfer admission for both freshman and transfer applicants and for international applicants for January admission. Admission decisions for spring applicants are made on a space-available, rolling basis. Campus tours and group information sessions are held daily and are available without an appointment.

For more information, students should contact:

Office of Undergraduate Admissions
150 Richards Hall
Northeastern University
360 Huntington Avenue
Boston, Massachusetts 02115
Phone: 617-373-2211 (visitor information)
617-373-2200 (general information)
E-mail: admissions@neu.edu
Web site: http://www.northeastern.edu/admissions

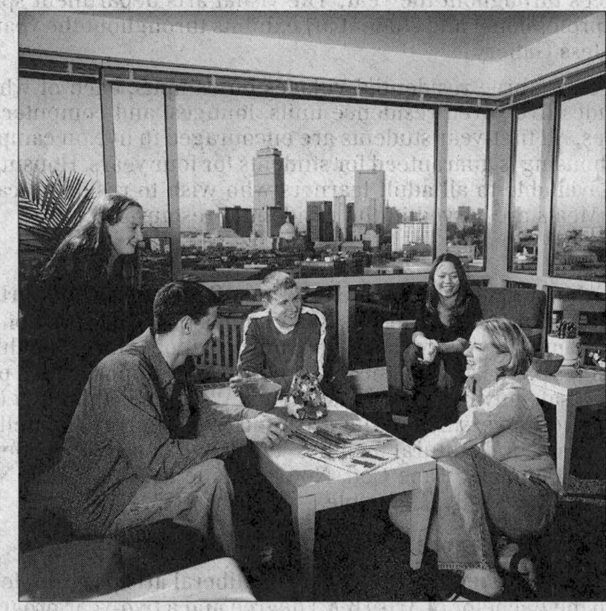

Northeastern University students in a West Village residence hall enjoy spectacular Boston vistas.

PINE MANOR COLLEGE

CHESTNUT HILL, MASSACHUSETTS

The College

Founded in 1911, Pine Manor College (PMC) is a small, private four-year liberal arts college that prepares women for roles of inclusive leadership and social responsibility. PMC enrolls approximately 500 students from a wide range of cultural, racial, educational, and socioeconomic backgrounds. Students come from twenty-four countries and twenty-six states. Pine Manor provides an educational environment that supports individual growth and empowers young women for responsible leadership. The College's small size helps accomplish this, but so do interactive teaching, interdisciplinary study, and active learning techniques such as portfolio development and internships for all students. At Pine Manor, students learn to think critically, act cooperatively, and develop leadership skills in new ways, focusing on inclusiveness and responsibility for the common good. Pine Manor College is accredited by the New England Association of Schools and Colleges.

Student organizations provide many opportunities for cocurricular learning at PMC. Students are sure to find a club, athletic team, performance ensemble, affinity group, or service organization that provides a place to use their talents and expand their abilities. Fun activities abound on campus and there is always room for new groups to form with student interest. Intercollegiate athletics (NCAA Division III) are offered in basketball, cross-country, lacrosse, soccer, softball, tennis, and volleyball. Instruction is available in lifetime fitness activities and other areas of physical education. Members of the performing arts department and their students present musical, dramatic, and dance performances throughout the year. The visual arts department sponsors professional and student art exhibits throughout the year in the Hess Gallery.

There are three residential villages on campus, each of which includes five wired residence units, lounges, and computer facilities. All first-year students are encouraged to live on campus, and housing is guaranteed for students for four years. Housing is also available to all adult learners who wish to reside on campus. Meals are served in the residential restaurant.

Location

Pine Manor College is located in the affluent Boston suburb of Chestnut Hill, Massachusetts, just 5 miles from the heart of the city and minutes away via public transportation. More than thirty buildings are nestled on the 60-acre wooded campus, which provides a safe environment for students. With more than fifty colleges and universities in the area and a wide array of intellectual, social, and cultural facilities, the range of activities offered is almost endless. Cape Cod, New England ski areas, and New York City are easily accessible.

Majors and Degrees

Pine Manor College offers a four-year liberal arts program leading to the Bachelor of Arts (B.A.) degree and a two-year program leading to an Associate in Arts (A.A.) or Associate in Science (A.S.) degree. B.A. majors are offered in biology, communication, economic and financial systems, English, history, management and organizational change, psychology, social and political systems, and visual arts. The College also offers a nursing program in which qualified students study three years at Pine Manor and complete a B.S.N. at the Boston College School of Nursing.

Concentrations within these majors and associated minors include accounting, advertising and public relations, allied health, American political systems, art history, biopsychology, child care, child development, community systems, counseling, creative writing, criminal justice, cultural history, dance, design, drama, electronic media programming and production, entrepreneurship, French, global studies, graphic design, health sciences, history and government, history of race and ethnicity, human resources management, human services, industrial/organizational psychology, international business, international systems, journalism, literature, marine/environmental studies, mathematics, management, marine biology, marketing, music, photography, political science, predental, prelaw, premedical, preveterinary, the school-age child, sociology, Spanish, studio arts, theater arts, and women's studies.

Students seeking licensure in elementary education (1–6) may major in English or history. Students majoring in psychology may elect to pursue teacher certification in early childhood education (pre-K–2). Secondary certification is available in biology, English, and visual arts. Individualized and interdisciplinary majors may be arranged by the student in consultation with her adviser. A certificate program in community health-care outreach is also available.

Academic Programs

For the B.A. degree, students must complete thirty-two full-semester courses, or 132 semester credit hours. To receive the A.A. or A.S. degree, students must successfully complete sixteen full-semester courses, or 64 semester credit hours. Core curriculum requirements create a solid academic foundation for students by framing the major requirements with courses from the following: humanities, social sciences, natural and behavioral sciences, arts and communication, mathematics, and English composition.

Pine Manor College views education as a relationship between and among learners that requires the active engagement of students, faculty members, and others to be successful. These collaborative relationships provide a more focused method of teaching and learning. Classes are open discussions where everyone's contribution matters.

A student's learning portfolio forms the central focus of her educational experience at Pine Manor College. Presentation of a learning portfolio is a graduation requirement for all PMC students. The formal presentation of the portfolio takes place twice, ordinarily during the sophomore and senior years. The portfolio contains evidence of and reflections upon student learning related to the general education outcomes and accomplishments within the major. The portfolio approach promotes leadership skills by providing a holistic perspective on growth by requiring the student to take responsibility for her own learning. A key to leadership development is the ability to be reflective, to establish goals, and to assess progress toward them.

Portfolio Learning Seminars are led by a faculty member and a resource team of peer mentors and student life professionals. This program offers a comprehensive approach that is designed to help students become reflective, self-directed learners. The program offers opportunities to develop effective mentoring and leadership skills, which strengthen the students' capacity to work collaboratively and productively toward common goals.

Recognizing a fundamental link between a liberal arts education and the professional world, Pine Manor College integrates the required fourteen-week internship experience into the curriculum. The PMC internship combines students' academic knowledge with practical experience in the workplace, while students explore career options and develop the leadership skills that employers seek. Many PMC interns are offered permanent positions at their internship sites. After working with top professionals at Boston's best corporations, hospitals, museums, laboratories, publications, and social service agencies, PMC seniors are prepared to make informed career choices.

Adult learners may apply CLEP, transfer credits, or credits for prior learning toward their degrees and may take courses part-time or full-time. A certificate program is offered in community health-care outreach.

The unique Enhanced First-Year Program (EFY) is offered to international women who meet PMC's academic requirements but who need intensive English language training to be successful in their first year of undergraduate studies. Students in the EFY program participate in first-year, credit-bearing college classes and are on track to graduate with a degree in four years. A minimum TOEFL score of 45 iBT or minimum IELTS score of 5.0 is required.

The English Language Institute at Pine Manor is a coed program designed for men and women whose native language is not English. Noncredit instruction in English is offered at the elementary and intermediate levels on a year-round basis. Sessions begin every four weeks and last anywhere from four to forty-eight weeks, depending on the individual needs of each student.

Off-Campus Programs

PMC participates in a program of cross-registration with Boston College, Babson College, and the Marine Studies Consortium. Study-abroad options are available throughout the world, along with the Washington Semester program for juniors sponsored by the American University in Washington, D.C.

Academic Facilities

The Ferry Administration Building accommodates most of the administrative offices and student services; Haldan Hall contains modern classrooms, faculty offices, and language laboratories; the recently renovated Dane Science Center has classrooms, laboratories for science courses, and computer laboratories; and Ellsworth Hall, the performing arts center, has a theater, classrooms, computer facilities, and listening and practice rooms. The Abercrombie Fine Arts Wing has studios for sculpture, printmaking, painting, design, and photography, as well as a state-of-the-art visual arts computer lab. The Annenberg Library and Communications Center houses the library, Learning Resource Center, Cherry Computer Center, radio and TV production studios, Hess Art Gallery, lecture halls, seminar rooms, and music-listening areas. The gymnasium includes basketball, volleyball, and badminton courts; a dance and exercise studio; and a fitness room with multistation exercise equipment. Other athletic facilities include new tennis courts, paddle tennis courts, softball fields, and the Hedley soccer/lacrosse field.

Costs

For 2007–08, tuition was $17,750, the cost of room and board (double-occupancy) was $10,570, and the orientation fee for freshman students was $150. Private music lessons and student parking facilities are available for an extra charge.

Financial Aid

The College's financial aid resources include Pine Manor grants, merit grants, Federal Work-Study Program jobs, Federal Stafford Student Loans, Federal Supplemental Educational Opportunity Grants, Federal Pell Grants, and state scholarships.

To apply for aid, a copy of the Free Application for Federal Student Aid (FAFSA) must be submitted by April 30.

Faculty

Teaching is the number one priority of Pine Manor's faculty members. Sixty-two percent of Pine Manor's full-time professors hold terminal degrees, and 74 percent of faculty members are women. Part-time faculty members are professional practitioners in their fields of expertise. Seventy-five percent of classes have fewer than 20 students, and the low student-faculty ratio of 10:1 allows faculty members to take an active part in every phase of College life.

Student Government

Students participate in decision making at Pine Manor through the Student Government Association. In addition, student representatives sit on the Curriculum Committee, Library Committee, President's Leadership Group, Speakers and Programs Committee, and Academic Ethics Council.

Admission Requirements

Students are selected on the basis of an evaluation of their secondary school performance, SAT or ACT scores, program of studies, school recommendations, and personal essay. While an interview is not required for admission, it is strongly recommended. SAT scores are not required of international students; TOEFL or IELTS scores, however, are required. Applicants are expected to have 16 academic credits, distributed among the following: English, social studies, mathematics, science, and foreign languages. Transfer students must submit transcripts of previous college courses completed. Accepted students may choose to enroll on a part-time basis.

Application and Information

All applications are handled on a rolling admission basis. The College uses the College Board's Candidates Reply Date of May 1. For further information, students should contact:

Dean of Admissions and Financial Aid
Pine Manor College
400 Heath Street
Chestnut Hill, Massachusetts 02467
Phone: 617-731-7104
800-PMC-1357 (toll-free)
Fax: 617-731-7102
E-mail: admissions@pmc.edu
Web site: http://www.pmc.edu

President Gloria Nemerowicz and students.

COLLEGE DATA CENTER • MASSACHUSETTS

SCHOOL OF THE MUSEUM OF FINE ARTS, BOSTON

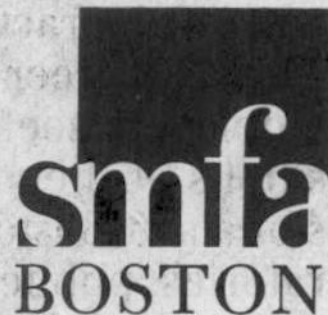

BOSTON, MASSACHUSETTS

The School

The School of the Museum of Fine Arts, Boston (SMFA), or Museum School, is a division of the Museum of Fine Arts, Boston (MFA), and affiliated with Tufts and Northeastern Universities. In partnership with Tufts, the School offers the following degree programs: the Bachelor of Fine Arts, the Bachelor of Fine Arts in Art Education, the five-year Combined-Degree program (B.A./B.F.A. or B.S./B.F.A.), the Master of Fine Arts, and the Master of Arts in Teaching in Art Education. In partnership with Northeastern, the School offers a Bachelor of Fine Arts and a Master of Fine Arts in Studio Art. All students in degree programs are fully enrolled at the School of the Museum of Fine Arts and Tufts or Northeastern University and graduate with a Tufts or Northeastern degree. The School also offers the all-studio Diploma program and the one-year Fifth Year and Post-Baccalaureate Certificate programs.

As in an artists' colony, the Museum School's focus is on creative investigation, risk taking, and the exploration of an individual vision. A truly interdisciplinary institution, the School does not have a mandatory foundations program nor does it have majors. Students are given the freedom to design a program of study that best suits their needs and goals. This freedom comes with strong support and guidance from faculty advisers.

The School's studio curriculum is developed continually in order to incorporate new media and new approaches, concepts, and theories. Dynamic exhibition and visiting artists programs complement the curriculum.

Student Affairs has a knowledgeable staff that is available to assist students in finding living accommodations and to answer questions. A limited amount of residence hall housing is available at a new state-of-the-art dormitory, built exclusively for artists. The office also provides a comprehensive guide to housing in the city and listings of local realtors, studio contacts, and currently available apartments and roommates.

Location

The School of the Museum of Fine Arts, Boston, is tucked among many of Boston's finest academic and cultural institutions, thriving commercial and business centers, and a world of diverse people. The campus is within walking distance of numerous other colleges and major art museums. In addition to the Museum of Fine Arts, Boston, students soon discover the Isabella Stewart Gardner Museum and the Museum of the National Center of Afro-American Artists in the campus neighborhood. The Institute of Contemporary Art and galleries on Newbury Street, the South End, and Fort Point are easily accessible by T, Boston's public transportation. Students also may take the T to Cambridge to explore the Fogg, Sackler, and Busch-Reisinger Museums of Harvard University and the List Visual Arts Center at MIT. SMFA's campus is also bordered on one side by parkland that invites long walks or jogs, picnics, or an afternoon of sketching.

The city responds to and reflects the culture and interests of its residents with venues featuring a world's view of music: alternative, hip-hop, jazz, folk, blues, and Latin. Harvard Square's eclectic range of restaurants, shops, theaters, and street performers are just across the Charles River. The Back Bay boasts a dizzying range of shops and eateries. And the Fenway and Jamaica Plain offer parks, gardens, and quiet spots. Students find a mix of theater—classical and experimental—some of the best independent movie houses around, comedy clubs, people-watching spots, poetry slams, lectures, and great bookstores.

Majors and Degrees

In partnership with Tufts, the School offers the following undergraduate degree programs: the Bachelor of Fine Arts, the Bachelor of Fine Arts in Art Education, and the five-year Combined-Degree program (B.A./B.F.A. or B.S./B.F.A.). In partnership with Northeastern, the School offers the Bachelor of Fine Arts at the undergraduate level. All students in degree programs are fully enrolled at the School of the Museum of Fine Arts and Tufts or Northeastern University and graduate with a Tufts or Northeastern degree. The School also offers the all-studio Diploma program and the one-year Fifth Year and Post-Baccalaureate Certificate programs. The School offers courses in the following areas: artists' books and multiples, ceramics, computer arts, drawing, electronic arts, film and animation, glass, illustration, metals, painting, papermaking, performance, photography, printmaking, sculpture, text and image arts, video, and visual and critical studies.

Academic Programs

All students in the degree programs are enrolled at both the Museum School and Tufts or Northeastern University and graduate with a degree from Tufts or Northeastern. While the academic curriculum is set by Tufts and Northeastern, students design their own programs of studio art study.

The only limitations on this elective system in studio art are the prerequisites stipulated for some courses. The School recommends basic courses for students who need foundation work in any studio area.

Teaching methods range from structured classes, requiring regular attendance, to individual instruction for work done independently outside the School.

Students' studio art work is evaluated at the end of every semester by a review board made up of teachers and students; the student being reviewed participates in this evaluation. Letter grades are not given for studio courses. Students advance on an individual basis. Academic courses are graded in the traditional manner.

Students in the degree programs take courses in studio art at the School and courses in academic areas of study at Tufts or Northeastern.

The School is also a member of the Pro Arts Consortium, which allows students to take classes on a space-available basis at Berklee College of Music, the Boston Architectural Center, Emerson College, the Boston Conservatory, and Massachusetts College of Art. The Museum School also offers selective cross-registration with MIT.

Academic Facilities

The School is a division of the Museum of Fine Arts, Boston. Students and faculty members have special privileges of access to the museum's curatorial departments and library. The collection of the School's W. Van Alan Clark Jr. Library, which is the circulating branch of the Museum of Fine Arts, Boston's William Morris Hunt Library, includes books, periodicals, videotapes, slides, ephemeral materials, and artists' books and generally focuses on contemporary and mid- to late-twentieth-century art. Students also have full access to the William Morris Hunt Collection that is housed in the Clark Library and to the Hunt Library in the Museum of Fine Arts, Boston. This encyclopedic collection of more than 130,000 volumes supports research on collections, new exhibitions, exhibition planning, and interpretation.

Students may also use the collections of eight surrounding colleges and public libraries through the interlibrary loan system and on-site use. Degree students and those taking a class through the Pro Arts Consortium, an association of six schools in Boston, have access to the Tufts and Northeastern University libraries and libraries of Pro Arts member institutions (Berklee College of Music, Boston Architectural Center, The Boston Conservatory, Emerson College, Massachusetts College of Art, and the Museum School).

The Exhibitions Office plans a program of shows covering work accomplished during the entire academic year. Work by students in each area of the School is represented on a rotating basis in the lobby, corridor, and student galleries.

Computers are available throughout the Museum School—including classrooms, print shops, painting and sculpture studios, and hallways. The School also provides computer labs with high-speed T3 Internet connections for all Diploma, Certificate, Degree, and Graduate program students. Each student gets an e-mail account. The Macintosh Lab includes a thirty-six-seat lab with Intel Core 2 Duo iMacs, PowerMac G5s, and PowerMac G4s, most of which are hooked up to flat-bed and film scanners for flat originals and small, medium, and large-format films. The lab also has various DVD and CD writers and printers, including an Epson 9800, which can print up to 3½ by 10-plus feet. There are two black-and-white laser writers and one laser two-color large format printer. The laser writers allow page sizes of up to 11-by-17 inches, and the color printer allows page sizes of up to 3½ by 10-plus feet.

Costs

For 2007–08, the full-year tuition for studio courses is $26,950. Therefore, students enrolled only in studio art courses pay this amount. Tuition for degree-program students in any one semester varies individually with the ratio of academic to studio courses taken in that semester. More information about tuition and fees can be found at http://www.smfa.edu.

Financial Aid

Financial aid is awarded on the basis of demonstrated financial need; approximately 72 percent of students receive some sort of financial aid. Merit scholarships range from $3000 to full tuition scholarships. Students are eligible to apply for Federal Pell Grants, Federal Supplemental Educational Opportunity Grants, Federal Work-Study Program awards, Federal Stafford Student Loans, and SMFA Scholarships. The priority deadline for receipt of completed application forms is March 15. Students should contact the Financial Aid Office to request the necessary forms.

Faculty

All faculty members who teach studio courses are practicing professional artists who have regional, national, and international reputations in their fields. There are approximately 50 full-time and 90 part-time faculty members. Selected members of the undergraduate faculty also work with graduate students. The student-faculty ratio is approximately 9:1.

Student Government

The standing committees of the School, made up of administrative staff members, students, and faculty members, meet regularly to review the School's goals, curriculum, and problems. Each student, teacher, or member of the administration has an equal opportunity to join committees and the Student Government Association.

Admission Requirements

The Admissions Committee endeavors to select for entrance those applicants who appear highly motivated and best suited by apparent creative potential and background to benefit from the professional education offered by the School.

Diploma evaluation criteria are based primarily on the strength of the applicant's portfolio. Degree program evaluation criteria consist of a review of the applicant's portfolio as well as the strength of his or her academic records. The School strongly recommends that prospective students arrange to tour the School or have an interview before a formal application is filed. Qualified secondary school students in their junior year are encouraged to apply at that time for early acceptance for the term beginning in the September following their senior year.

Because of the special structure of the School, the status of transfer students differs from that at other schools. Transfer students are placed at a studio level that the Admissions Committee deems appropriate, based on their portfolio presentation.

Application and Information

Applicants should arrange for all of the following to be delivered to the School: transcripts from the secondary school and any institution of higher education attended, official SAT or ACT scores, an application form and the $65 nonrefundable application fee ($80 for international applicants), and a portfolio. The portfolio of work must be sent to the School to be reviewed by the Admissions Committee. The School intentionally does not designate any specific composition or number of pieces for the portfolio; however a minimum of twenty pieces is recommended. Portfolios should be made up of what the applicant—rather than an art teacher, counselor, or relative—feels best shows a potential for development in visual art.

The admission deadline for the Diploma program is on a rolling basis. Portfolios received from September to May are reviewed within ten days, and diploma applicants are notified of the Admissions Committee's decision by mail within three weeks. Portfolios received from June through August are reviewed on a weekly basis. Students may be accepted to the Diploma program for the second semester beginning in January. The regular procedure is followed, and all application materials should be delivered to the School by October 1. The deadline for application to B.F.A. or B.F.A. in art education programs is February 1 for first-time freshmen; the deadline for spring admission is October 1 for first-time freshmen. The deadline for application to the combined B.A./B.S. and B.F.A. programs is January 1 for first-time freshmen.

Applications from international students are welcome. Applicants from countries other than the United States should offer documentary evidence of financial resources sufficient to satisfy all educational and living expenses for one year of study at the School. Applicants whose native language is not English should also submit scores on the Test of English as a Foreign Language (TOEFL).

For further information, students should contact:

Admissions Office
School of the Museum of Fine Arts, Boston
230 The Fenway
Boston, Massachusetts 02115
Phone: 617-369-3626
800-643-6078 (toll-free)
E-mail: admissions@smfa.edu
Web site: http://www.smfa.edu

The Review Board system, in which students are awarded credit based on a semester's worth of artwork by a panel of faculty members and students, is a hallmark of the SMFA education.

SIMMONS COLLEGE

BOSTON, MASSACHUSETTS

The College

In 1899, decades before women in America gained the right to vote, Simmons College was founded on a revolutionary idea—that women should be able to earn independent livelihoods and lead meaningful lives. Today, Simmons provides a strong liberal arts education for undergraduate women that is integrated with professional career preparation, interdisciplinary study, and global perspectives. Simmons also encompasses the many benefits of a small university, including renowned coeducational graduate programs and the world's only M.B.A. designed specifically for women.

Simmons's interdisciplinary approach offers great advantages: a broader education and view of the world; personalized plans of study; and a chance to develop a range of professional skills and strengths needed for graduate school and an increasingly competitive job market. Every student explores a variety of subjects while gaining an in-depth theoretical and practical understanding of her major. First-year core courses emphasize critical thinking and writing skills, while integrating two or more subjects—ranging from bioethics and Buddhist studies to computational linguistics and visual communication.

Students fulfill their independent learning requirement through internships, fieldwork, and research projects. In doing so, they develop skills, confidence, impressive resumes, and a network of professional contacts. Many students spend one or more semesters interning for businesses and organizations, ranging from Boston Public Schools and *The Boston Globe* to the Museum of Fine Arts, Smash Advertising, and the World Affairs Council. Simmons's Longwood Medical Area partnerships provide outstanding clinical opportunities at Boston's world-renowned hospitals. On campus, students conduct research in state-of-the-art labs in areas such as materials science, gene splicing, and computer modeling. In addition, professors frequently invite undergraduates to collaborate on professional research projects, articles, and presentations.

Acquiring a global outlook is integral at Simmons—including an understanding of languages, cultures, and international politics. Programs such as Africana studies, East Asian studies, international relations, and modern languages offer a direct route to cross-cultural immersion. Simmons encourages students to spend an entire semester or year abroad. Short-term international courses provide unique opportunities to study topics such as journalism in South Africa, music in Austria, or history and civilization in Japan. Students also take part in local and international service-learning projects, ranging from education initiatives in Boston to health care in Nicaragua.

Above all, Simmons offers a learning experience that is highly collaborative and much more personal than that of large universities. A 13:1 student-teacher ratio ensures that every student receives individual attention. The Simmons faculty includes noted researchers, authors, and experts in their respective fields—yet professors passionately uphold their primary obligation to teach. Students say the small classes, intellectual focus, and welcoming environment contribute to their confidence and success.

Students also say that Simmons's location offers the best of both words—an intimate college experience in the heart of a vibrant city. Considered by many to be the best "college town" in the nation, Boston has more than fifty colleges and universities and approximately 300,000 students. Boston is a "walking city" with an exceptional public transportation system. Simmons's 2,072 undergraduates love the fact that they can easily access the city's rich social and cultural resources but also come home to a safe, friendly campus.

Approximately 80 percent of Simmons undergraduates live in college housing two blocks from the main campus. The "quintessential New England" residence campus features nine brick residence halls and a private, landscaped quad, as well as Bartol Dining Hall, the state-of-the-art Holmes Sports Center, a student-run cafe, and the campus health center.

Simmons has more than fifty student organizations and academic liaisons—including eight NCAA Division III varsity teams, honor societies, cultural organizations, volunteer programs, a literary magazine, and more.

Location

Boston is big league in every sense but size—just like Simmons. The historic, tree-lined Simmons campus is located in Boston's eclectic Fenway neighborhood, which is alive with music and fine arts, medical care and research, action and activism, and the resounding cheers of baseball fans at legendary Fenway Park. From campus, it's a safe, easy stroll to other colleges and universities as well as shops, cafes, clubs, museums, movie theaters, parks, and public transportation. Students hop aboard the T to head to destinations such as Downtown Crossing, the Italian North End, Chinatown, Harvard Square, and Greater Boston's many other diverse neighborhoods.

Majors and Degrees

Simmons offers more than forty majors and programs. Popular majors include psychology, nursing, biology, political science, and communications. Faculty advisors help each student create a plan that fulfills requirements and satisfies her personal and professional goals. The OPEN program (Option for Personalized Educational Needs) even allows students to custom design majors. A number of integrated degrees and accelerated programs allow students to go directly from an undergraduate program to earning a graduate degree in areas such as education, health care, liberal arts, physical therapy, and science information technology. Simmons also offers a dual-degree program in chemistry/pharmacy in collaboration with Massachusetts College of Pharmacy and Allied Health Sciences, as well as individually designed preprofessional programs for dentistry, law, medicine, and veterinary medicine. Simmons students typically declare a major by the end of their sophomore year, and nearly a third choose to double major. Interested students may visit http://www.simmons.edu/academics/undergraduate for a complete list of majors.

Academic Programs

Simmons offers a strong liberal arts education integrated with professional preparation, interdisciplinary study, and global perspectives. A minimum of 128 semester hours is required for graduation. Students must demonstrate competence in math and foreign language, complete a core curriculum in the liberal arts and sciences (40 semester hours), complete the courses required for the selected major(s) (20 to 40 semester hours for each major, depending on the program), fulfill an independent learning requirement (8 to 16 semester hours), and round out their program with appropriate electives.

Students may select interdepartmental programs, declare double majors, or participate in an undergraduate-to-graduate degree program. In addition, the OPEN program allows students to design their own program of study, combining courses from several fields. Other special academic opportunities include Simmons' outstanding honors, service-learning, and study-abroad programs.

The Dorothea Lynde Dix Scholars option is available for women who are 24 years or older, or who hold a previous bachelor's degree.

Off-Campus Programs

Simmons is a member of the Colleges of the Fenway consortium, which allows students to cross-register with neighboring colleges, including Emmanuel College, Massachusetts College of Art, Massachusetts College of Pharmacy and Allied Health Sciences, Wentworth Institute of Technology, and Wheelock College. A domestic exchange program allows juniors to spend a semester at Mills College, Spelman College, or Fisk University. Students interested in international study may elect to spend one semester or one year at an approved university exchange or participate in intensive study-abroad programs during the spring semester.

Qualified students, usually juniors, also may apply for the Washington Semester at American University in Washington, D.C. Other opportunities include Success Connection, a mentoring program that matches select seniors with highly successful Simmons alumnae, and the Barbara Lee Internship Fellows program, which places students in Massachusetts legislators' offices and policy advocacy groups for one semester.

Academic Facilities

The beautiful Simmons campus offers an attractive, practical mix of historic and modern architecture, including state-of-the-art facilities and conveniences. The Main College Building houses a dining area and coffee bar, lecture halls and classrooms, administrative and faculty offices, the bookstore, the Student Activities Center, art studios, music practice rooms, and the Trustman Art Gallery.

Park Science Center offers technologically advanced learning environments, including faculty and student research facilities, fully equipped science laboratories, environmental rooms, observation rooms for psychological testing, and food science kitchens.

One Palace Road, the state-of-the-art home for Simmons's School of Social Work and Graduate School of Library and Information Science, features electronic classrooms and also houses the centers for academic support, counseling, career education and resources, media, and technology. Simmons just completed a major renovation and expansion of Beatley Library, which offers a number of high-tech services, including a wireless network, laptop loans, sophisticated online library service, technology-equipped group study rooms, and more. Plans are underway for the construction of a new state-of-the-art "green" building that will house the School of Management.

Costs

Undergraduate tuition and fees for the 2007–08 academic year were $14,151 per semester; room and board charges were $5569 per semester. Total costs, not including books, supplies, and personal expenses, were $39,440.

Financial Aid

Approximately 75 percent of Simmons students receive financial aid. Scholarships, grants, loans, and federal work-study are determined by the Free Application for Federal Student Aid (FAFSA). Simmons also awards academic merit scholarships, ranging from $5000 to full tuition and renewable for four years.

Faculty

Simmons's professors are distinguished experts and practitioners who work closely with students and care about their success. Simmons has 246 full-time and 340 part-time faculty members; 72 percent are women. The student-faculty ratio is 13:1, ensuring a strong tie between students and professors.

Student Government

Simmons has more than fifty student clubs and organizations. The Student Government Association (SGA) coordinates the policies and activities of various student organizations, allocates the student activities funds, and promotes the interests of the student body by working closely with the Simmons faculty and administration. In addition, every academic department has a student liaison that participates in department evaluations and helps promote educational and social activities for students, faculty members, and staff members.

Admission Requirements

There isn't one "type" of Simmons student, but there are common qualities. Simmons women are intellectually motivated and open-minded. They are serious about their personal and professional goals, and they are determined to make a difference in the world. With this in mind, the Simmons admission team reviews applications to see not only what applicants have accomplished, but also who they are and what kind of person they hope to become.

The admission team also evaluates high school performance, SAT or ACT scores, recommendations, and the application essay. If English is not the applicant's first language, TOEFL or IELTS scores are required. Additional English language proficiency exams are accepted on a case by case basis.

Simmons welcomes applications from prospective freshmen, transfer students, international students, and students who are beyond the traditional college age.

Although not required, an interview is highly recommended. This gives admission officers better perspective about an applicant's abilities, interests, and personality—and at the same time, allows the applicant to evaluate Simmons and decide if it's the right place for her.

Application and Information

Students may apply online at the College Web site, use the Common Application, or submit a print application, along with the $35 fee and all supporting credentials. Simmons waives the application fee for students who use the online application. The early action deadline is December 1 and is a nonbinding deadline. The deadline for freshman applicants is February 1. Transfer students are evaluated on a continual basis; the preferred filing date for applications is April 1. Students applying for the semester beginning in January should apply by December 1.

Simmons encourages prospective students and their families to attend an admission event or request an individual visit. They are welcome to tour the campus, sit in on a class, talk to current students, and interview a professor, department chair, or program director.

For further information, interested students should contact:

Office of Undergraduate Admission
Simmons College
300 The Fenway
Boston, Massachusetts 02115
Phone: 800-345-8468 (toll-free)
Fax: 617-521-3190
E-mail: ugadm@simmons.edu
Web site: http://www.simmons.edu

SMITH COLLEGE
NORTHAMPTON, MASSACHUSETTS

The College

Smith College was founded in 1871 as a liberal arts college for women and rapidly became one of the first such institutions to match the standards and facilities of the best colleges of the day. Today, with 2,750 undergraduates, Smith is the largest privately endowed college for women in the country. Graduate degrees (master's, Ph.D.) are offered in a number of departments and in the Smith College School for Social Work. Currently, all fifty states and more than sixty countries are represented in the Smith student body. Ninety percent of the students in each entering class were in the top quarter of their high school class; most chose Smith because of the excellence of its faculty and curriculum. Although most Smith students are between the ages of 18 and 22, Smith's Ada Comstock Scholars Program enables older women whose educations have been interrupted and who meet the College's admission standards to pursue an A.B. degree in part-time or full-time study.

Smith's house system is unusual and highly regarded. Each of the College's thirty-six houses is home to between 12 and 100 women. There are fifteen dining rooms that offer different menus, themes, and types of food. The house system stresses individual freedom, group autonomy, and mutual respect. Other residences, such as a cooperative house, a French house, and apartments, are also available. Smith offers a wide variety of extracurricular activities, ranging from service organizations to musical groups and from student publications to fourteen intercollegiate sports teams. The already varied cultural and social opportunities—lectures, workshops, dance and theatrical performances, art exhibits, concerts, and social events—are increased by participation in Five Colleges, Inc., a consortium that opens to Smith students classes and activities at Amherst, Hampshire, and Mount Holyoke colleges and at the University of Massachusetts. Smith's athletic facilities include two gymnasiums, five squash courts, a 75-foot six-lane swimming pool with 1- and 3-meter diving boards, a human performance laboratory, climbing wall, fitness center, and an indoor track and tennis facility, which houses four tennis courts and a 200-meter track. Outside are 30 acres of athletic fields, a 400-meter track, a 5,000-meter cross-country course, and twelve lighted tennis courts. Smith also has indoor and outdoor Olympic-size riding rings and a forty-two-unit stable.

Location

Northampton, a small cosmopolitan city with a population of more than 30,000, is in the Connecticut River valley of western Massachusetts. It is 93 miles west of Boston and 156 miles northeast of New York City. There are many shops and restaurants within walking distance of the campus and within the service area of a free Five College bus system. Buses run frequently to Boston and New York. Many students are involved in local organizations, and some intern in local city or county offices. Others participate on an extracurricular level in nonprofit agencies.

Majors and Degrees

Smith College awards the Bachelor of Arts (A.B.) degree. Areas of major concentration include Afro-American studies, American studies, anthropology, art, astronomy, biochemistry, biological sciences, chemistry, classical studies, classics, comparative literature, computer science, dance, East Asian languages and cultures, East Asian studies, economics, education and child study, engineering, English language and literature, French studies, geology, German studies, government, Greek, history, Italian language and literature, Italian studies, Latin, Latin American and Latino/Latina studies, mathematics and statistics, medieval studies, music, neuroscience, philosophy, physics, Portuguese-Brazilian studies, psychology, religion, Russian civilization, Russian literature, sociology, Spanish, theater, and women and gender studies. Interdepartmental majors and minors are offered in a variety of fields.

Academic Programs

The academic year is divided into two semesters, the first ending before winter recess. Interterm courses, some for credit, are offered during January. Smith believes in the goals of a liberal arts education. With an open curriculum, students have flexibility to choose from more than 1,000 courses. The only requirement outside a student's field of concentration is one writing-intensive course. The normal course load consists of 16 credits in each of eight semesters, to total the 128 credits of academic work that are required. There are no specific distribution requirements, but 64 credits must be taken outside the major field of study. A student may also complete the requirements of two departmental majors or of one departmental major and another departmental minor.

Through credit earned on Advanced Placement or International Baccalaureate examinations and by summer study, some students may be able to accelerate and complete degree requirements in six or seven semesters. The Departmental Honors Program enables a student with a strong academic background to study a particular topic in depth or undertake research in the field of her major.

Off-Campus Programs

Smith students may take academic courses and participate in social and cultural activities at any of the institutions participating in the Five College consortium, described above. Smith students may also spend a year at another member institution of the Twelve College Exchange Program (Amherst, Bowdoin, Connecticut, Dartmouth, Mount Holyoke, Trinity, Vassar, Wellesley, Wesleyan, Wheaton, and Williams) or spend a year at Spelman College or Pomona College. Some students participate in the Jean Picker Semester-in-Washington Program in public policy, a fall internship program in Washington, D.C., sponsored by the College's Department of Government. The American Studies Program offers an internship at the Smithsonian Institution.

Smith offers Junior Year Abroad programs in Florence, Geneva, Hamburg, and Paris. Students may apply to affiliated programs in more than thirty other countries. Students eligible for financial aid are able to take that aid with them to any approved program.

Academic Facilities

The Smith College Libraries comprise the largest undergraduate library system of any liberal arts college in the country. The 1.4 million holdings are housed in the centrally located William Allan Neilson Library and in the libraries of the fine arts, performing arts, and science centers. The Neilson Library also houses a rare book room, the Nonprint Resource Center, the College archives, and the Sophia Smith Collection, a women's history archive. The Clark Science Center is a five-building complex that accommodates the nearly 30 percent of students who major in the sciences. The facilities include general laboratories, a molecular genetics facility, classrooms, a rooftop astronomy observatory, animal care facilities, scanning and transmission electron microscopes, an analytic ultracentrifuge, and a high-field nuclear magnetic resonance spectrometer. Academic computer facilities include networked Windows and Macintosh computers in public labs, classrooms, the libraries, and the foreign language center. All buildings and student residences are networked, and Internet access is available at no charge. There is wireless access in many buildings. Smith also has a digital design studio and several electronic classrooms. Bass Hall houses the psychology department, the scientific computing center, and Young Library, one of the largest undergraduate science libraries in the country. The Bass laboratories provide numerous facilities for research in neuroscience. The Mendenhall Center for the Performing Arts contains an experimental theater and a traditional theater, dance studios, and television and audio recording rooms. Sage Hall, the music building, includes an electronic music studio, a small recital hall, dozens of practice rooms, and a 750-seat concert hall. The Smith College Museum of Art houses one of the finest teaching collections in the country, and Hillyer Hall contains art studios as well as printmaking, darkroom, and sculpture facilities. Smith's Center for Foreign Languages and Cultures maintains a multimedia laboratory and classroom housing a network of student workstations with integrated and interactive computer, audio, and video components.

Costs

Tuition for 2007–08 was $33,940. The room and board charge for regular student residences was $11,420. The activity fee was $246; books, supplies, and personal expenses were estimated at $1800.

Financial Aid

More than 70 percent of all Smith students receive some form of financial assistance from grants, loans, and/or campus jobs. Aid is awarded on the basis of need, as determined by the College. Each applicant must submit the Free Application for Federal Student Aid (FAFSA), the PROFILE form from the College Scholarship Service, and a copy of the current federal income tax return. Smith meets full demonstrated need for all admitted students who apply for aid by the published deadlines. The first portion of an aid award is an offer of a loan and campus employment; the remaining need is covered by grants from federal, state, and/or College funds. Merit-based aid is also available on a limited and highly competitive basis.

Faculty

The teaching of undergraduate women is the priority of the Smith faculty. There are approximately 290 faculty members; nearly all have earned doctoral degrees and are well-known in their professional fields. Close ties between undergraduates and their teachers are forged through small classes (71 percent have 20 or fewer students) and generous access to faculty members during and outside of regular office hours.

Student Government

Smith students assume much of the responsibility for their personal, social, and academic life at the College through the Student Government Association, which gives students representation on major college-policy committees.

Admission Requirements

Smith seeks students whose motivation, academic preparation, and diversity of interests will enable them to profit from and contribute to the varied possibilities of a liberal arts college. Smith is interested in the woman behind the numbers. As a highly competitive college, Smith gives primary consideration to the academic record of each candidate for admission. Strong high school programs have a basis of 4 years of English, at least 3 years in one foreign language or 2 years in each of two languages, 3 years of mathematics, 3 years of science, and 2 years of history. It is hoped that areas of special interest will have been pursued in depth. Students should submit ACT or SAT scores. Two SAT Subject Tests are strongly recommended but not required. An interview is strongly recommended. A first-choice early decision plan is available.

Applications are also welcomed from students who wish to transfer from other college-level institutions or who wish to enter the Visiting Students Program or the Ada Comstock Scholars Program.

Smith College is committed to maintaining a diverse community in an atmosphere of mutual respect and appreciation of differences. Smith College does not discriminate in its educational and employment policies on the bases of race, color, creed, religion, national/ethnic origin, sex, sexual orientation, or age or with regard to the bases outlined in the Veterans Readjustment Act and the Americans with Disabilities Act. Smith's admission policies and practices are guided by the same principle, concerning women applying to the undergraduate program and all applicants to the graduate programs.

Application and Information

A prospective first-year student interested in applying to Smith has three options: fall early decision, winter early decision, or regular decision. The fall early decision deadline is November 15, and applicants receive a decision on December 15. The deadline for winter early decision is January 2, and students receive a decision in late January. Regular decision applicants must complete the Common Application by January 15; all other parts of the application are due by February 1. These candidates receive their admission decision by April 1. The deadline for January transfer admission is November 15; students receive an admission decision in mid-December. The preferred deadline for September transfer admission is February 1, with notification in early April. Transfer applications are accepted until May 15, and decisions are made on a rolling basis. Applications deadlines for the Visiting Student Programs are July 1 (for September admission) and November 15 (for January admission).

For more information about Smith College, students should contact:

Director of Admission
Smith College
Northampton, Massachusetts 01063
Phone: 413-585-2500
800-383-3232 (toll-free)
Fax: 413-585-2527
E-mail: admission@smith.edu
Web site: http://www.smith.edu

Northampton combines small-town ambiance with big-city offerings.

SPRINGFIELD COLLEGE

SPRINGFIELD, MASSACHUSETTS

The College

Springfield College graduates enter the workforce or advanced education with a competitive advantage—top-quality academic preparation and real-world experience.

Founded in 1885 to train leaders for the YMCA, Springfield College has an international reputation for educating leaders in health sciences, human and social services, sports and movement studies, education, and the arts and sciences. Accredited by the New England Association of Schools and Colleges, it is a private coeducational institution offering forty undergraduate major fields of study. Students perform fieldwork, internships, or service learning as early as their freshman year. It is a learning advantage based on the College's mission—education in spirit, mind, and body for leadership in service to others. Last year, Springfield College was named one of the twenty-five "best neighbor" urban colleges. Recently, it received the Jostens/NADIIIAA Award of Merit for community service by student athletes. The Institute for International Sport named it one of the fifteen most influential educators through sport in America.

An ethnically diverse student body of 3,000 undergraduate and graduate students at the main campus comes from many U.S. states and abroad, with the majority from the Northeast.

Springfield College is a vibrant living and learning environment. The picturesque, 150-acre lakeside campus is technologically up to date. Several new, newly renovated, and under-construction state-of-the-art facilities blend with traditional campus architecture.

Ten campus residence halls provide guaranteed on-campus housing. Options include traditional residence halls and suite-style accommodations with private rooms for 2 to 4 students sharing a lounge, kitchen, and bathrooms. There are single-sex and coeducational residences. Seniors may elect to live off campus. The main student dining facility features a range of fresh food options, and there are snack and other light-fare services around the campus.

Enriching the undergraduate experience is a wide array of cocurricular activities, health and wellness programs, and arts and cultural events; an extensive campus recreation program; and one of the largest athletics programs in the nation for a midsized college. There are more than 100 organizations and opportunities for involvement. More than 80 percent of undergraduates participate in some form of athletics, including varsity teams, intramurals, or club sports. There are men's and women's teams in basketball, cross-country, gymnastics, lacrosse, soccer, swimming, tennis, track, and volleyball. Women's teams also include field hockey and softball, and there are additional men's teams in baseball, football, golf, and wrestling.

Location

On Lake Massasoit in the Pioneer Valley, Springfield College is located in Springfield, the fourth-largest city in Massachusetts. A wide range of social, cultural, and athletic activities enhance the valley, including twelve other colleges and universities. For example, Springfield Symphony Hall is the site of concerts, plays, musicals, and dance performances; the Springfield Civic Center is home to the American Hockey League's Springfield Falcons and the annual Tip-off Classic, the official start of the college basketball season; and the Basketball Hall of Fame is an international attraction.

Nearby cities and towns offer many additional attractions. Northampton bustles with trendy shops, coffeehouses, galleries, theater productions, health-food stores, nightclubs, and restaurants. The Berkshire Hills offer hiking, skiing, biking, and other outdoor activities. Boston lies 90 miles to the east, New York City is less than a 3-hour drive, and Vermont is 1 hour away.

Majors and Degrees

Springfield College offers Bachelor of Science or Bachelor of Arts degrees in American studies, applied exercise science, applied sociology, art, art therapy, athletic training, biology, business management, communication disorders, communications/sports journalism, computer and information sciences, computer graphics, criminal justice, dance, early childhood education, elementary education, emergency medical services management, English, general studies, health services administration, health education, history, human services, mathematics and computer technology, outdoor leadership, physical education, physical therapy (entry-level six-and-a-half year program culminating in a Doctor of Physical Therapy degree), physician assistant studies (entry-level five-year program culminating in a Master of Science degree), psychology, recreation management, rehabilitation and disability studies, secondary education, sport management, sports biology, teacher preparation, therapeutic recreation services, undeclared major, and youth development.

Academic Programs

Consistent with Springfield College's humanics philosophy, undergraduate education is designed to promote an understanding of how the spirit, mind, and body work together in preparing students for a life of leadership in service to others.

The College has a two-semester academic calendar. To graduate, students must complete 130 credits, including required courses for the major field of study, electives, and required courses for all students (writing, computer applications, arts and humanities, analytical and natural sciences, social sciences, international/multicultural studies, social justice, and physical education). Students may also earn credit for successful completion of Advanced Placement (AP) high school courses, the DANTES subject standard test, and the College-Level Examination Program (CLEP) administered by the College Board.

Springfield College has agreements with several medical schools that guarantee acceptance of its qualified students. In addition, many Springfield College programs allow undergraduates to take graduate-level courses.

There are campus chapters of the following honor societies: Beta Beta Beta (biology), Kappa Delta Pi (education), Phi Alpha (social work), Phi Epsilon Kappa (health, physical education, recreation, and safety), and Psi Chi (psychology).

Off-Campus Programs

For fieldwork, internships, and service learning, the College maintains relationships with businesses, not-for-profit organizations, public and private agencies, and schools. Fieldwork sites have included the Basketball Hall of Fame, American Hockey League, the *Boston Globe*, YMCAs, American Heart Association, MassMutual, Boston Children's Hospital, Hilton Head Crowne Plaza, Reebok Health and Fitness Center, Baystate Medical Center, parks and recreation departments, and many other venues.

The cooperative education program links students with work experiences in their fields of study. It is open to second-, third-, and fourth-year students, who average 15 to 20 hours per week of study-related work.

Extensive study-abroad programs are available. Students may also enroll in courses at some of the other colleges in the Springfield area.

Academic Facilities

Technologically up to date, the campus has several wireless zones, smart classrooms, computer labs, a videoconferencing facility, a conference center, and a new language laboratory. There are a new television studio, a journalism lab, and a radio station.

The newly renovated Schoo-Bemis Science Center is state of the art, and the Allied Health Sciences Center contains human anatomy, performance assessment, and neuroscience laboratories.

The 20,000-square-foot Visual Arts Center includes airy, light-filled studios and an exhibition gallery. The multipurpose 300-seat Fuller Performing Arts Center features a proscenium theater and lecture hall. Appleton Auditorium is the site of performances and other programs. Other arts facilities include a black-box theater and Dexter Dance Studio.

The Physical Education Complex combines the Art Linkletter Natatorium; Blake Arena and Athletic Training Facility; Winston Paul Academic Center, with teaching gymnasia and handball/racquetball courts; Stagg Field and the Irv Schmid Sports Complex, with FieldTurf surfaces for football, soccer, lacrosse, and field hockey; eight tennis courts; baseball and softball diamonds; indoor and outdoor tracks; and the Strength and Conditioning Center.

Scheduled to open in August 2008 are a new field house, a wellness center, and the Athletic Training/Exercise Science Complex, all with the latest design and equipment. A new Campus Union is scheduled to open in fall 2009.

The 52-acre East Campus comprises a forest ecosystem with camping facilities and lake shoreline. It is a training ground for students in several academic programs. The Springfield College Child Development Center is an exceptional fieldwork facility for students of education and psychology.

Babson Library, well known for its resources in physical education, psychology, education, and health and human services, contains a rich collection of full-text print and digital materials. Library staff members assist with access to a full range of information sources.

Costs

For 2007–08, tuition and fees were $24,075 and room and board were $8650.

Financial Aid

Students are encouraged to apply for grants, loans, and student employment. Springfield College financial aid is based on need, intellectual promise, leadership, and character. The College gives full consideration to students who submit the Free Application for Federal Student Aid and the College Scholarship Service Financial Aid PROFILE by March 15, 2008, for first-year students and May 1, 2008, for transfer students. Students not eligible for financial aid may be considered for campus employment.

Faculty

Most of the 342 faculty members hold doctorates or other terminal degrees. The student-teacher ratio is 13:1.

Student Government

The Student Government Association, managed by elected students, promotes students' interests and welfare. It guides and finances more than forty student organizations, adopts policies affecting students, and is a liaison between students and the College administration.

Admission Requirements

Springfield College evaluates applicants on the basis of academic and personal factors. Applications for regular admission or early decision must be submitted to the Office of Undergraduate Admissions, including a completed application form, a high school transcript, one personal reference, and SAT scores. Transfer students must also submit a transcript and a dean's report from each college attended.

Springfield College is interested in meeting each applicant and encourages candidates to visit the College and experience campus life. The College offers personal interviews, campus tours, and open-house programs and also facilitates contact with alumni and current students.

Application and Information

Application due dates for the 2008–09 academic year are April 1, 2008, for undergraduate applicants and August 1, 2008, for transfer students; students in athletic training and physical therapy, physician assistant studies, and occupational therapy have earlier deadlines. Students should contact the Office of Admissions for more information.

Springfield College's Admissions Committee reviews applications upon receiving them. Application forms and information may be obtained from:

Office of Admissions
Springfield College
263 Alden Street
Springfield, Massachusetts 01109
Phone: 413-748-3136
800-343-1257 (toll-free)
E-mail: admissions@spfldcol.edu
Web site: http://www.springfieldcollege.edu (online application)

Students on the campus of Springfield College.

COLLEGE DATA CENTER • MASSACHUSETTS

STONEHILL COLLEGE

EASTON, MASSACHUSETTS

The College

Stonehill is a competitive, coeducational, Catholic college located just south of Boston. Established in 1948 by the Congregation of Holy Cross (founders of the University of Notre Dame, Indiana), Stonehill continues the rich Holy Cross tradition of a rigorous liberal education. As a comprehensive undergraduate college of 2,200 full-time degree students, Stonehill offers thirty-three major programs in the liberal arts, natural sciences, and business. The College's programs, through an involved and engaging faculty and a commitment to experiential learning, aim to foster effective communication, critical-thinking, and problem-solving skills in all students.

Stonehill provides its students with a powerful environment for learning where they are safe, known, and valued. The College has a beautiful campus, an enviable location, and state-of-the-art facilities. Stonehill fields varsity teams (NCAA Division II) in twenty sports, in addition to a vibrant intercollegiate club, recreational, and intramural sports program. More than 89 percent of the students live in first-rate on-campus housing and take advantage of the wide range of social and cultural activities offered on campus or in nearby Boston. Housing is guaranteed for four years.

Over seventy organized student groups representing academic societies, multicultural interests, music (as well as performance), community service, and shared interests, in areas such as Amnesty International, the environment, and the EMS Club, enable Stonehill's student population of 2,200 to actually get involved.

Location

Just 22 miles south of Boston, Stonehill is located in the town of Easton (population 23,242). Featuring stunning Georgian-style architecture, the College's thirty main buildings are set among a beautifully landscaped 375-acre campus of ponds, rolling fields, and wooded glens. The beaches of Cape Cod and the mansions and history of Newport and Providence, Rhode Island, are within 45 minutes of the campus, as are major concert (the Tweeter Center for Performing Arts) and sports (Gillette Stadium) venues. The most popular off-campus destination is Boston. Students from more than sixty area colleges and universities converge on Boston to experience its museums, art galleries, shopping and dining, theaters, sporting events, and other exciting nightlife offerings. During the week, Stonehill students enhance their academic experience through internships with the city's plethora of high-tech, medical, and financial institutions.

The College provides a shuttle service that connects to Boston's subway system and area shopping. Stonehill's student government organization also has vans that student clubs can reserve for trips to sporting events, concerts, skiing, and other activities.

Majors and Degrees

The College offers Bachelor of Arts degrees in American studies, chemistry, communication, criminology, economics, education studies (early childhood, elementary, middle, and secondary), English, environmental studies, fine arts, foreign languages (concentrations in French, Spanish, or two languages), gender studies, health-care administration, history, international studies, mathematics, multidisciplinary studies, philosophy, political science, psychology, public administration, religious studies, and sociology. Bachelor of Science degrees are offered in biochemistry, biology, chemistry, computer engineering, computer science, and neuroscience. Bachelor of Science in Business Administration degrees are offered in accounting, finance, international business, management, and marketing. In addition, Stonehill College, in cooperation with the University of Notre Dame, offers a combination five-year B.A./B.S. program in computer science and computer engineering.

Preprofessional programs are offered in dentistry, education, law, medicine, and theology. Students interested in the field of education can receive early childhood, elementary, middle, and secondary school teacher certification. Students may double major as well as design their own major by combining various departmental courses into a comprehensive multidisciplinary program.

Academic Programs

Stonehill's primary mission is to provide a challenging program of academic studies in the liberal arts tradition that engages students in a lifelong quest for intellectual excellence and dedication to service. All students receive a strong foundation in the liberal arts in addition to expertise in one or more fields. The liberal arts courses in the core curriculum are designed to help students understand their culture, find and analyze information, develop critical-thinking skills, and become effective communicators. Developing writing proficiency is a central objective of the core curriculum and is emphasized in all classes.

Interaction with faculty members and academic advisers is a vital part of a Stonehill education. At freshman orientation, each student is assigned an academic adviser. Students who declare a major are assigned a faculty mentor from within their major; students who do not declare a major receive assistance from an adviser who specializes in helping undecided students. Advisers help students choose their major, approve course selections, and give advice on study-abroad, internship, and graduate school opportunities.

Students are encouraged to explore various fields of interest in their first two years, but they must choose a major by the middle of their junior year. They take five courses a semester and must complete forty courses to receive a bachelor's degree.

Off-Campus Programs

In addition to the tremendous on-campus opportunities, the College offers many impressive domestic and international programs to enhance a student's learning experience. One of the most popular is interning. Internships are offered in all majors and over 60 percent of Stonehill students have participated in either an international or domestic work experience by graduation. This hands-on experience in a student's chosen field helps them focus on career objectives and affords each student the opportunity to network with professionals. Students intern at organizations such as Grant Thornton UK, Serono Pharmaceutical, Reebok International, UBS, Marvel Comics, Children's Hospital Boston, NCIS, PriceWaterhouseCoopers, Fidelity Investments, the Boston Globe, and more. Full-time internships are available in New York City, Washington, D.C., Dublin, London, Paris, and Geneva.

Stonehill sponsors study-abroad programs at over 130 institutions in more than forty countries throughout the world. The most popular destinations are Italy, Ireland, England, and Spain.

Academic Facilities

Kaplan's *Insiders Guide to the 320 Most Interesting Colleges* listed Stonehill as one of the colleges with the "Best Freshman Housing." Upper-class housing is equally nice, and that's perhaps why almost everyone lives on campus all four years. Housing is guaranteed, and 89 percent of all students live on-campus.

A new 90,000-square-foot state-of-the-art science center is planned to open in fall 2009. This exciting science facility will include research labs with advanced technology and instrumentation for the biochemistry, biology, chemistry, neuroscience, physics, and psychology departments.

The MacPhaidin Library and Networked Information Center provides students with features such as wireless access, multimedia computers, and electronic resources that include E-Journals, World-Cat (for locating books worldwide), and technology workshops focused on library research skills.

The Joseph W. Martin Institute for Law and Society serves as a regional center for education, research, and public service. The Martin Institute features an archival research center, the Center for Regional and Policy Analysis, the Stonehill Education Project, and the papers of Joseph W. Martin, the former speaker of the U. S. House of Representatives, as well as the papers of Stonehill graduate Michael Novak, recipient of the very prestigious Templeton Award.

Costs

For the 2007–08 academic year, Stonehill's costs were $28,440 for tuition and $11,430 for room and board.

Financial Aid

The College is committed to helping each qualified student find the resources to meet the cost of a Stonehill education. In fact, Stonehill distributes more than $37 million a year in scholarships and financial aid to a full-time student body of 2,200 students. Last year, the average financial aid package awarded to first-year applicants was $18,875. Stonehill also awards a competitive number of merit-based scholarships to outstanding students who do not demonstrate a financial need. Stonehill's merit fund program awards scholarships ranging from $7,500 to $20,000 per year.

To file for Stonehill scholarship and/or financial aid consideration, students should simply complete the online CSS PROFILE form at http://profileonline.collegeboard.com. Stonehill's CSS PROFILE code number is 3770. In addition, students must file the Free Application for Federal Student Aid Assistance (FAFSA) online at http://www.fafsa.ed.gov in order to be considered for government funds. The College's federal code number for the FAFSA form is 002217.

Faculty

Stonehill faculty members are highly credentialed professionals who are committed to the interactive learning process and successful outcomes for students. Serving as teachers, advisers, and mentors, the professors at Stonehill work closely with students to select courses, secure an internship, dispense career advice, assist in the process of studying abroad, and collaborate on research projects. The following statistics say it all—a 1:13 faculty-student ratio with an average class size of 20 students. At Stonehill, classes are never taught by graduate students or teaching assistants.

Student Government

The Student Government Association (SGA) is an influential group of student leaders who represent the voice of Stonehill students to the President, the Board of Trustees, the Alumni Council and the Faculty Senate.

Admission Requirements

Admission to Stonehill is selective. Annually, over 6,000 high school students apply for 610 places. The College actively seeks an academically strong, geographically, culturally, and ethnically diverse student body. In the admissions process, all information on each applicant is carefully considered, but academic performance and curriculum in high school are given the greatest weight. The Admissions Committee evaluates the depth and strength of each applicant's course selection and the consistency of their grades. Competitive students should have completed a strong academic program from among their high school's most challenging offerings. Students may submit testing scores from either the SAT or ACT program. The submission of testing scores is optional for admission. The Admissions Committee also evaluates extracurricular activities, work, volunteer and community activities, recommendations, and writing samples. The College awards credit for strong scores on Advanced Placement, CLEP, and higher-level International Baccalaureate exams.

Application and Information

To apply to Stonehill as a first-year candidate, a transfer student, or an international applicant, students submit the Common Application (CA). Stonehill College is a member of the Common Application Program. The Common Application is available online at https://app.commonapp.org. The application will be securely transmitted electronically to Stonehill along with the student's completed Stonehill Supplement Form and filing fee payment. The CA is also available in paper form at high school guidance offices or online for downloading at http://www.stonehill.edu.

Stonehill offers three admissions plans for first-year candidates: early decision, early action, and the regular decision plan. November 1 is the deadline for early acceptance. Candidates for the regular decision plan must submit an application by January 15.

Dean of Admissions and Enrollment
Stonehill College
320 Washington Street
Easton, Massachusetts 02357-5610
Phone: 508-565-1373
Fax: 508-565-1545
E-mail: admissions@stonehill.edu
Web site: http://www.stonehill.edu

The MacPhaidin Library is a high-tech learning center, with fully networked seating areas for individual and collaborative study.

TUFTS UNIVERSITY
MEDFORD, MASSACHUSETTS

The University

Founded in 1852, Tufts University is recognized as being among the premier universities in the United States. Tufts also enjoys a global reputation for academic excellence and for the preparation of students as leaders in a wide range of professions. Tufts has extensive and highly regarded liberal arts and engineering programs that draw outstanding students with the highest academic achievement and standing from around the world. Tufts University's mission embraces teaching, research, and public service both in the United States and internationally. Tufts believes its focus on its students and the profession of teaching leads to its agile and responsive research efforts and a record of achievement that earned Tufts its Research I rating from the Carnegie Commission, placing it among only thirty-eight private institutions so recognized, and its rank as one of the top universities in the United States by *U.S. News & World Report.*

Sophia Gordon Hall opened in the fall 2006 semester, with 125 beds in thirty suite arrangements. Tufts University received a $500,000 grant from the Massachusetts Renewable Energy Trust to support the design and construction of integrated photovoltaic electricity and high-efficiency features. In addition to providing upperclassmen with more opportunities to live on campus, Sophia Gordon Hall is an important part of a larger initiative to educate Tufts students about energy, energy technologies, and climate change. The Perry and Marty Granoff Music Center opened in January of 2007, featuring an acoustically perfect 300-seat recital hall, as well as a 95-seat performance space, classrooms, practice rooms, rehearsal halls, offices, and library and research space. Tufts also opened a new boathouse by the Malden River in May 2006. This project has attracted national press for its architecture and use of reclaimed land.

Location

Tufts University is situated on a 150-acre site on the boundary between the cities of Medford and Somerville, 5 miles northwest of Boston. The campus occupies a tranquil New England setting that offers easy access by bus and subway to the cultural, social, and entertainment resources of Boston and Cambridge.

Majors and Degrees

Programs include Africa and the New World, American studies, anthropology, applied physics, Arabic, archaeology, architectural studies, art and art history, Asian studies, biochemistry, biology, biomedical engineering, biopsychology, biotechnology, chemical and biological engineering, chemical physics, chemistry, child development, Chinese, civil engineering, classics, clinical psychology, cognitive science, communications and media studies, community health, comparative religion, computer science, computer engineering, dance, drama, economics, education, electrical engineering, engineering psychology, English, environmental engineering, environmental studies, ethnic groups in America, film studies, French, geoengineering, geology, German, Greek, Hebrew, history, international letters and visual studies, international relations, Italian, Italian studies, Japanese, Judaic studies, Latin, Latin American studies, Latino studies, mathematics, mechanical engineering, medieval studies, multimedia arts, music, peace and justice studies, philosophy, physics and astronomy, political science, psychology, quantitative economics, Russian, Russian and East European studies, sociology, Spanish, studio art, urban studies, and women's studies.

Academic Programs

Students in the College of Liberal Arts are required to complete two semesters of college writing, typically Expository Writing and an English Writing seminar. Liberal arts students need a minimum of thirty-four courses to graduate, including those that satisfy foreign language and culture requirements. In addition, students in liberal arts are required to complete distribution requirements in the arts, humanities, social sciences, natural sciences, and mathematical sciences.

In the School of Engineering, students must complete a minimum of thirty-six courses in order to graduate. About 25 percent of those courses are devoted to math and science and another 20 percent to engineering sciences and other foundation courses. In addition to the traditional focus on math and science, first-year engineering students are required to take several half-credit courses that introduce them to all of the engineering disciplines, many of which are taught by senior faculty members.

Off-Campus Programs

Approximately 40 percent of the students at Tufts participate in international study-abroad programs, usually during their junior year. Students may study in a number of programs that Tufts offers through affiliated universities throughout the world, including Tufts-in-London at University College London, Tufts-in-Oxford at Pembroke College, Tufts-in-Madrid at the Autonomous University of Madrid, Tufts-in-Hong Kong at the University of Hong Kong, Tufts-in-China at Zhejiang University in Hangzhou, Tufts-in-Paris at the University of Paris III and IV, Tufts-in-Tübingen at Eberhard-Karls Universität, Tufts-in-Ghana at the University of Ghana, Tufts-in-Japan at Kanazawa University, and Tufts-in-Chile at the University of Chile (Santiago). Students can study for a summer, a semester, or a year and are typically housed in dormitories at their respective host universities or with local families. Tufts also offers study-abroad programs in engineering at the University of Sussex in England and INSA de Lyon in France. In addition, there are more than 200 Tufts-affiliated study-abroad programs in places such as Africa, Asia, Australia, Europe, South America, and the Caribbean, where students can receive credit through programs offered at other colleges and universities.

Through the Tufts-in-Washington program, students have the opportunity to study for a semester at American University in Washington, D.C. The academic schedule includes a seminar, an individual research project, and an internship. A limited number of students may participate in a semester-long exchange with Swarthmore College or Lincoln University, both located near Philadelphia, Pennsylvania. Through Williams College and the Frank C. Munson Institute of Maritime Studies, Tufts offers a semester-long program in American maritime studies at Mystic Seaport, Connecticut. In addition, all full-time undergraduates are eligible to participate in all undergraduate courses and programs in arts and sciences at Boston University, Boston College, and Brandeis University. There are no additional fees, and both course credits and grades transfer to Tufts.

Academic Facilities

The holdings of the University libraries number approximately 2.7 million and include books, microfilms, slides, and government publications. The Tisch Library provides comfortable study space, enhanced access to information technology, new furnishings, and expanded space for collections. The library offers a state-of-the-art audiovisual center with five classrooms, ranging in size from ten to seventy-five seats, and twenty-four viewing carrels. Study spaces include three quiet-study rooms, eleven group-study rooms, and individual study carrels.

Tisch's holdings include nearly 759,000 volumes, 917,400 microtexts, nearly 4,900 print periodicals, 13,000 electronic periodicals, and 33,805 audiovisual materials. The University libraries have a total of 1,046,543 volumes and 1,158,000 microtexts. Undergraduate students also can access the other libraries of Tufts University—the Music Library, located in the Aidekman Arts Center; the Ginn Library of the Fletcher School of Law and Diplomacy on the Medford Campus; the Health Science Library in Boston; and the Veterinary School Library in Grafton, Massachusetts. Tufts is a member of the eleven-college Boston Library Consortium, the OCLO (a computerized support system), and the New England Library Network. The Tufts University Library Information Processing System (TULIPS) provides access to numerous library catalogs from all over the world through the Internet.

Students have access to the newly renovated Eaton Computer Lab, which is operated by Tufts Computing and Communications Services. This lab contains nearly 200 computers, mainly consisting of Dell 866- and 900-MHz Pentium III machines with 256 megabytes of RAM and 400-MHz iMacs running OS/9, in addition to scanners and other multimedia tools. Eaton Lab is open extended hours (until 2 a.m. at certain times) to cater to students' needs and is staffed during these hours.

Costs

In 2006–07, tuition, room, board, and fees totaled $44,500.

Financial Aid

Tufts grants and scholarships, which exceeded $33 million in 2006–07, are by far the largest single source of grant aid received by Tufts undergraduates. When these grants and scholarships are combined with federal and state scholarships, loans, and employment to meet the University's estimate of each student's need, awards may total as much as the full educational and residential costs. A variety of financial aid is available. Federal Supplemental Educational Opportunity Grants (FSEOG) are federal funds allocated to Tufts for exceptionally needy undergraduates. Carl Gilbert Matching Grants are state funds allocated to Tufts for needy Massachusetts undergraduates. Tufts National Merit Scholarships are awarded annually through the National Merit Corporation to finalists who notify the Merit Corporation that Tufts is their first choice if the aid is received. Federal Perkins Loans are awarded to students of exceptional need from funds allocated annually to Tufts by the federal government and from funds repaid by previous borrowers. Federal Stafford Student Loans of up to $2625 in the first year, $3500 in the second year, and $5500 each year in remaining years (up to a maximum of $23,000) are made to undergraduates.

All students, whether receiving aid or not, may obtain information about on- and off-campus work opportunities during term time and the summer. Federal Pell Grants are federal grants of up to $4050 per year to which students from low- and lower-middle-income families are entitled according to their circumstances. Applicants may also be awarded state no-interest loans (NIL), individual state scholarships, and individual state grants. Air Force, Army, or Navy ROTC scholarships may be applied for before admission to Tufts. Students are notified of the aid decision in early April. For more information, students should contact the financial aid office.

Faculty

The student-faculty ratio is 9:1. There are 421 full-time and 263 part-time faculty members in the two undergraduate colleges. Virtually all courses at Tufts are taught by professors, more than 97 percent of whom hold terminal degrees in their field.

Student Government

Students have a voice and vote in those areas that affect their academic, social, and residential lives. Within broad limits, students are allowed to establish operating rules for residential life within their own residence through individual residence hall governments and the Inter-Dormitory Council. Through student government, in the form of the Tufts Community Union Senate, students are provided with a forum for the discussion of all student concerns and the means of responsive action. The Constitution of the Tufts Community Union (TCU), ratified by the student body in 1981, establishes several different branches of student government—the TCU Senate, the TCU Judiciary (TCUJ), and the Elections Board (ELBO). The TCUJ is the student court that exercises the judicial powers of the TCU. The primary purpose of the TCUJ is to decide on the constitutionality of actions of the Senate and other student organizations. The ELBO ensures fairness in all campuswide votes, elections, and referenda. The TCU Senate is the representative government of the entire undergraduate student body. All undergraduate students paying the student activities fee are members of the TCU and are entitled and encouraged to take part in student government by running for elected positions of the various branches, applying for appointment to faculty or trustee committees, and voting in campus elections.

Admission Requirements

The following parts of the application are used by the admissions committee to gain a sense of an applicant's academic accomplishments and potential: course selection and the rigor of those courses, grades since the first year of high school, standardized test results (specific requirements are listed below), letters of recommendation (one from a teacher in a junior or senior academic course and one from the student's guidance counselor), the personal statement, and two required 200-word short-answer essays. Students may also submit an optional essay on one of the topics listed on the Supplemental Form, which accompanies the Common Application. The standardized test requirement is as follows: applicants to the class of 2012 may submit scores from the SAT and two SAT Subject Tests or the ACT with Writing Test.

The admissions committee looks for evidence of involvement and leadership and evaluates the quality and extent of each activity. A student may stand out by demonstrating leadership skills, making meaningful contributions to the school or community, or showing a special talent in a particular area. Thus, in addition to evaluating academic fit, the admissions committee looks for ways in which a student may contribute to the community as a whole. Nearly every first-year applicant to the University has the opportunity for a personal interview in his or her local area with a member of the Tufts Alumni Admissions Program (TAAP). Once the Supplemental Form has been received by the admissions office, the student is contacted by a member of the local alumni committee to schedule an interview. While it is not required, the alumni interview enables students to highlight their interests and achievements and also enables them to talk with someone who attended Tufts and can speak about the University from personal experience.

Application and Information

Tufts requests that students adhere to the application deadlines and make every effort to submit their application as early as possible; early submission of the application helps begin the alumni interview process. The deadline for Early Decision Round I is November 1, and students are notified of Tufts' decision by December 15. The deadline for the Early Decision Round II is January 1, with notification by mid-February. The deadline for Regular Decision is January 1, with a notification date of April 1. For any additional questions regarding the Tufts application, students may contact the Office of Undergraduate Admissions.

Office of Undergraduate Admissions
Bendetson Hall
Tufts University
Medford, Massachusetts 02155
Phone: 617-627-3170
Fax: 617-627-3860
E-mail: admissions.inquiry@ase.tufts.edu
Web site: http://www.tufts.edu

UNIVERSITY OF MASSACHUSETTS AMHERST

AMHERST, MASSACHUSETTS

The University

One of today's leading centers of public higher education in the country, the University of Massachusetts Amherst (UMass Amherst) is a major research university enrolling more than 19,800 undergraduates (about equally divided between genders). The University offers more than eighty-five bachelor's degree programs and six associate degree programs at the undergraduate level as well as seventy-three master's degree programs and fifty-one doctoral programs. The University's size offers a great diversity and choice of academic programs, housing arrangements, and extracurricular involvements. In addition, students can enroll with no extra charge in courses at Amherst, Hampshire, Mount Holyoke, and Smith Colleges through the Five College Consortium.

While many of the undergraduates are Massachusetts residents, students hail from fifty-two states and territories and seventy countries. Nearly 12,000 students reside (in either coed or single-sex accommodations) in forty-five residence halls in six different areas, each with its own unique atmosphere. Residence hall living is required in the freshman and sophomore years. Many students choose to live in residence halls their entire four years. Meal plans are available to fit student lifestyles, including quantity of meals, types of meals (kosher, vegetarian, ethnic offerings), and dining facilities (dining halls, on-campus locations, and even off-campus locations). To ensure a smooth transition to college life, the University has a first-year experience program that welcomes new students to life at UMass Amherst. The University also knows that parents are a key component of a student's success. The Office of Parent Services keeps parents informed and conveniently finds the answer to any question they may have—from how to purchase a birthday cake to advice on navigating their student's independence.

The New Students Orientation (NSO) program welcomes all first-year and transfer students to UMass Amherst for an all-encompassing orientation. Incoming students come to campus during the summer and meet new classmates, decide where to live, discuss academic paths with a faculty adviser, select fall semester courses, and take placement exams. New students participate in workshops, learn about extracurricular activities, and listen as students and faculty and staff members discuss both opportunity and responsibility at the University of Massachusetts Amherst. New student orientation covers all the details and signifies the transition in becoming a member of the UMass Amherst community.

Campus social life revolves around the Five College area, the residence halls, student organizations, sports (intercollegiate and intramural), religious and cultural activities, and a Greek organization of fraternities and sororities. Many social-action, professional, and special interest groups are active in the community. The Center for Student Development (CSD) brings writers, nationally recognized comedians, musicians, and other celebrities to campus. It provides support to more than 150 registered student organizations, including student government and cultural and religious groups. The CSD also supports student-run businesses. About 130 students manage and operate these businesses, which provide vital services to the campus.

The University participates in ten men's and eleven women's NCAA Division I intercollegiate varsity sports as a member of the Atlantic 10 Conference for basketball, football, ice hockey, and other sports. The 9,000-seat Mullins Center, home of UMass Amherst basketball and ice hockey, is a state-of-the-art facility with an Olympic-size ice surface. The arena also has an adjoining practice ice rink and seven racquetball courts. The intramural program, one of the largest in the East, draws more than 11,000 participants annually and runs more than 335 hours a week of recreational programming.

Students are welcome to join the Minuteman Marching Band, which has long been a source of great pride for the University and the surrounding region. At home football games, the "Power and Class" performs its traditional postgame show for its enthusiastic, dedicated fans. In 1998, the Minuteman Marching Band received the Louis C. Sudler Trophy, the highest honor awarded to a collegiate marching band.

Location

Situated on the Connecticut River in the Pioneer Valley of western Massachusetts, 20 miles north of Springfield, the campus of the University of Massachusetts Amherst consists of 1,450 acres of land and buildings. The *New York Times* calls Amherst one of the country's "Ten Best College Towns." The area offers the cultural and educational advantages of an urban environment while also enjoying a rural setting. Amherst is less than 100 miles from Boston, 175 miles from New York City, and only 30 miles from Vermont and New Hampshire. The Five College area in and around Amherst and Northampton offers an impressive array of cultural activities (film, dance, theater, music, and art) while also facilitating outdoor recreation, such as hiking, skiing, and camping in the Berkshire Hills and Vermont's Green Mountains. An extensive, free Five College bus service makes it easy for students to take advantage of academic and extracurricular activities at all five campuses.

Majors and Degrees

A four-year bachelor's degree is offered through nine colleges and schools: Engineering, Natural Resources and the Environment, Humanities and Fine Arts, Management, Natural Sciences and Mathematics, Nursing, Public Health and Health Sciences, Social and Behavioral Sciences, and Commonwealth Honors College. Within many of these, a number of different programs, options, and concentrations are possible. A bachelor's degree with an individualized concentration (BDIC) is also available for upper-division students who wish to create their own faculty-advised major.

A two-year associate degree is offered in six majors in the Stockbridge School of Agriculture. The School of Education offers an undergraduate minor in education.

Academic Programs

The traditional academic calendar includes a fall and a spring semester. The winter break gives students the opportunity to enroll in a unique four-week winter session program. Two summer sessions are also available. Students seeking a bachelor's degree must successfully complete a minimum of 120 credit hours (128 to 136 for engineering majors), including a core of required courses. In addition to the student's main course of study, there are more than a dozen nonmajor curricular programs (e.g., African studies, film studies, and religious studies) and an array of minors to choose from to enhance an academic portfolio.

A variety of special academic programs are also offered: the Commonwealth College Honors Program, community service, legal studies, and women's studies as well as Learning Resource Center, Residential Academic Programs (RAP) for first-year students, and advising for undeclared majors. Options are available for honors study, independent study, credit by examination, and advanced placement. The Division of Continuing Education serves nonmatriculated students.

The University has programs designed especially for the enrollment, retention, and graduation of African, Latino/a, Asian/ Pacific Islander, and Native American (ALANA) students: the Committee for the Collegiate Education of Black and Other Minority Students (CCEBMS), the Bilingual Collegiate Program (BCP), the United Asia Learning Resource Center (UALRC), and the Native American Student Support Services Program (NASSS). The Diversity in Management Education Services for business majors and the Minority Engineering Program provide other special academic opportunities.

Off-Campus Programs

The Five College Consortium (Amherst, Hampshire, Mount Holyoke, and Smith Colleges and the University of Massachusetts Amherst) permits students from the University of Massachusetts Amherst to study at and use the resources of any of the four other colleges in the area. A number of academic and cultural cooperative programs are also offered through the Five College Consortium.

A variety of programs facilitate study off campus. The Field Experience Office is the source for internships and cooperative educational experiences, where students gain firsthand knowledge of their intended industry before graduation. The National Student Exchange Program offers students the opportunity to explore other geographical and cultural environments within the U.S. at one of more than 170 state colleges and universities for one or two semesters, earning transferable credits. The International Programs Office assists students in arranging international exchange and overseas study experiences in more than twenty countries. The University Without Walls features off-campus study arrangements for returning adult students. In addition, specific departments sponsor clinical programs, international study, and internships as part of their individual curricular requirements or offerings.

Academic Facilities

The library system of the University of Massachusetts Amherst is composed of the twenty-eight-story W. E. B. Du Bois Library and several branch libraries. With more than 5.8 million books, periodicals, and government documents, UMass Amherst has the largest library system at any state-supported institution in New England. The Fine Arts Center, a working sculpture in itself, houses the fine arts departments (music, dance, art, and theater), several performance areas (including the main Concert Hall), galleries, and other fine arts facilities. Morrill Science Center, the Graduate Research Center, the computer science complex, and several laboratories serve the sciences and applied sciences.

The University's computing center is one of the largest university-based systems in the Northeast. Students register for classes online and receive free UMass Amherst e-mail accounts. Internet and e-mail access is available from campus terminals in the library, various computer labs, and academic buildings as well as in each residence hall.

Costs

Tuition and fees for 2007–08 were $9921 for in-state students and $20,499 for nonresident students. Room and board cost about $7478, depending on a student's choice of the three available meal plans. Students must be covered by health insurance either through the University's Student Health Insurance Plan or from an outside source, which must be of comparable coverage.

Financial Aid

Financial aid is offered to students who cannot, through their own or their parents' reasonable efforts, meet the full cost of a UMass Amherst college education. Aid consists of scholarships and grants, loans, and work-study employment. Students applying for financial aid are automatically considered for every University-administered program for which they are eligible. The basic financial aid application form required of all applicants is the Free Application for Federal Student Aid (FAFSA). More than half of the students receive some support from the Financial Aid Office. Students should check with their guidance counselor for the most current financial aid information or visit the UMass Amherst financial aid Web Site at http://www.umass.edu/umfa.

Faculty

A total of 1,168 full-time teaching faculty members compose a distinguished group committed to excellence in both teaching and scholarly research. More than 94 percent of the full-time members hold the highest degree in their fields. Most faculty members not only teach and conduct research in their disciplines but also assist in the advising of students. Close interaction between students and faculty members, both in and out of the classroom, is highly encouraged.

Student Government

Most University and student organizations rely on student participation in their decision-making processes. Selected in yearly campuswide elections, student government leaders and representatives participate in the decisions that shape students' educations and futures. The Student Senate is the legislative arm of the Student Government Association, and there is a Student Judiciary whose judges are appointed through the Student Senate and Area Governments. These area residential governments represent students regarding housing, social, cultural, and educational programs and issues. Students are also represented on many of the administrative decision-making bodies of the University, including the Board of Trustees.

Admission Requirements

Undergraduate admission to the University of Massachusetts Amherst is highly selective and competitive. The University receives more than 28,000 applications annually from domestic and international students. All applicants are required to submit a completed application, an official copy of their high school transcript, SAT or ACT scores, an essay, and a nonrefundable application fee. Nonnative speakers of English should include verification of English language proficiency.

The most important criterion for admission to UMass Amherst is academic performance. Academic performance is determined by SAT or ACT scores, college-level preparatory classes, honor courses, and Advance Placement and IB courses. Admission counselors also consider students' special talents, leadership ability, character, ability to overcome adversity, and work and community service experience in the review process. Transfer students are also considered after they have completed at least 12 credits of college work.

UMass Amherst offers an Early Action Admission Program. Applications are due November 1, with notification by mid-December. Regular decision applications are due January 15.

Application and Information

For application forms and additional information, students should contact:

Office of Undergraduate Admissions
University Admissions Center
University of Massachusetts Amherst
37 Mather Drive
Amherst, Massachusetts 01003-9291
Phone: 413-545-0222
Fax: 413-545-4312
Web site: http://www.umass.edu/admissions

UNIVERSITY OF MASSACHUSETTS BOSTON

BOSTON, MASSACHUSETTS

The University

The University of Massachusetts Boston was founded in 1964 by the state legislature to provide the opportunity for superior education at a moderate cost at a public campus located in the state's capital city of Boston. With more than 13,400 commuting students in its undergraduate, graduate, and continuing education programs, UMass Boston is the second-largest campus of the University of Massachusetts system. The University of Massachusetts Boston is a community of scholars who take pride in academic excellence, diversity, research, and service. The fabric of academic research and scholarship is tightly woven into the public and community service needs of Boston and the modern metropolitan center.

The University's students represent an extraordinary range of backgrounds, talents, and interests. Many of them come straight from high school, while others transfer from two- and four-year colleges. Although the majority of students come from the Commonwealth of Massachusetts, many grew up in other states and countries and come from all levels of the economic, political, spiritual, and ethnic spectra.

UMass Boston has a vibrant student life. No matter what a student's interest, he or she can find an activity to engage in—socially and intellectually. From student government to student literary endeavors, from a championship chess team to working with inner-city youth, from academically affiliated clubs and athletic opportunities to a unique course-credit-based leadership-development program, students are sure to find just the right activity to complement their classroom experience.

The UMass Boston student body shares a strong motivation to succeed academically and relate their classroom pursuits to career aspirations. The University Advising Center provides comprehensive academic support, planning, and career advising services. A team of professional counselors provides personalized assistance for students to design their course of study, utilize tutorial and mentoring services, choose a major and career path, and develop interviewing, resume writing, and job-search skills.

Location

From its beautiful landscaped peninsula on Boston Harbor, just south of downtown Boston, the University overlooks Dorchester Bay and the harbor islands. Its neighbors are the John F. Kennedy Presidential Library and the Massachusetts State Archives and Commonwealth Museum.

Located just a half mile off Interstate Route 93, the campus is easily accessed by both motor vehicle and public transportation. The entrance to the campus is a seaside promenade drive. The Office of Undergraduate Admissions provides a number of free parking spaces for visitors in the North Parking Lot. A free shuttle bus runs every few minutes for the half-mile ride from the Massachusetts Bay Transit Authority's (MBTA) JFK/UMass Red Line "T" stop to the front door of the campus. Student MBTA discount "T" passes are available for frequent users.

The University wants students to be at home at UMass Boston. Many students commute from their home communities, while others utilize the Office of Student Housing for free, personalized help with finding a rental property and/or roommates.

Boston itself, with its worldwide standing as a cultural center and well-earned reputation as America's favorite college town, offers UMass Boston students a wealth of resources for exploration and entertainment. Everything from Fenway Park and the Bank of America Garden to Symphony Hall and the Museum of Fine Arts is easily accessible from UMass Boston.

Majors and Degrees

Five undergraduate colleges award bachelor's degrees: the College of Liberal Arts and the College of Science and Mathematics (with thirty-six majors, twenty programs of study, and six certificate programs between them), the College of Management (with two majors and eleven concentrations), the College of Nursing and Health Sciences (with a B.S.N., an online RN-to-B.S.N., and an accelerated B.S.-to-Ph.D. program as well as the Exercise and Health Sciences program), and the College of Public and Community Service (with seven majors and four career concentrations). Premed, prelaw, and teacher licensure for undergraduates programs are also offered, along with programs for honors study, credit by examination, and advanced placement. Students are encouraged to participate fully in designing their own academic plan.

A joint Bachelor of Arts or Science/master's degree program in business is available for high academic achievers as well as a liberal arts or science degree with a minor in management and an engineering program.

Academic Programs

The academic calendar runs from early September through the end of May. There is also a one-month optional winter session in January; summer school is available in June, July, and August. Matriculating students may choose to attend full- or part-time and may adjust their schedules from semester to semester. A minimum of 30 credits must be earned at UMass Boston as a residency requirement for graduation.

For the College of Liberal Arts and the College of Science and Mathematics, 120 credits are required to graduate. The general education curriculum comprises three elements: the distribution requirement, the core curriculum requirement, and the writing requirement. In addition, the requirements of the major must be fulfilled. The Colleges offer both an honors program and an individual major option.

In the College of Management, the 120-credit undergraduate program leads to a B.S. degree in management. By fulfilling the general education, management, and elective course work requirements, graduates build a liberal arts foundation and receive the theoretical, technical, and functional training needed to succeed in the business world. An honors program is also offered.

The College of Nursing and Health Science's B.S. program in nursing requires 123 credits for graduation, including general education courses and 63 credits of intensive study in the principles and practices of nursing. The Exercise and Health Sciences program prepares graduates for the technical aspects of a professional discipline and a solid foundation in liberal arts. Students may also elect to enter the Honors Program in Nursing.

The College of Public and Community Service (CPCS) is a nationally acclaimed model for competency-based education. It offers an innovative curriculum with strong emphasis on social justice. The completion of a total of 40 competencies is required for graduation. Students may draw upon a variety of learning options in pursuit of their degree, including classroom study, self-directed study, project-based learning, and the demonstration of competence gained through relevant prior experience. The University's Honors Program is also open to CPCS students.

Off-Campus Programs

The National Student Exchange Program offers UMass Boston students the opportunity to study at one of more than seventy participating colleges and universities in forty states at a cost comparable to what they pay to attend UMass Boston. The study-abroad program is available for students with a 3.0 GPA or better who seek international travel and academic experiences as well as summer and winter session programs. UMass Boston also participates in the New England Regional Student Program and the Boston Five-College Exchange Program.

The Cooperative Education and Internship programs place students in work assignments related directly to their fields of study so that they may apply what they learn in the classroom to practical work settings. Under the Co-Op Program, students are placed in full-time, paid positions for six-month work periods. Under the Internship Program, students are placed on a part-time basis, usually 15 to 20 hours per week, during a semester or over the summer months. Some are paid internships; others are volunteer opportunities. Both co-op and internship placements combine relevant practical learning, valuable work experience, career awareness, resume enhancement, personal and professional growth, and, in many instances, opportunities for academic credit, good pay, and a permanent job after graduation.

Academic Facilities

The University's Healey Library holds a collection of more than 600,000 volumes, 25,000 electronic and print journals and newspapers, 30,000 electronic books, 85 databases, and more than 2,500 videos, DVDs, and films representing all fields of study on the campus. The library's electronic resources are available on and off campus, 24/7. UMass Boston is a member of three library consortia, including the Boston Library Consortium, and is a participant of the state-wide "virtual catalog," providing wider accessibility to scholarly and study resources. The library also houses an up-to-date Media Center and Language Lab.

The Information Technology Division (ITD) provides seven-day-a-week access to general-purpose computer labs, with some 220 Dell Pentium 4 and sixty Apple Macintosh G5/G4s, as well as other specialized, course-related facilities, including Adaptive Computer, Graduate and Faculty, Media and Language Labs, and a media viewing center. ITD houses equipment from Dell, Sun, and Apple, and operating systems include Windows XP, UNIX, Linux, and Apple OS. With more than seventy smart classrooms, network connections throughout campus, and wireless access in Healey Library and the Campus Center, a wide variety of information technology and data communications resources is available to students. The campus uses the WebCT/Blackboard learning management system, a fiber-optic infrastructure with Gigabit backbone and 10 MB switched connectivity.

The Kennedy Presidential Library is linked to the University by a variety of educational programs, enabling students to conduct research utilizing the more than 28 million pages of documents, 6.5 million feet of film, and more than 100,000 still photographs in the library's archives. Next door, the Archives of the Commonwealth of Massachusetts are a rich depository, covering more than 5½ centuries of Massachusetts history.

The state-of-the-art Campus Center provides easy access to student services, dining services, and spectacular meeting spaces, along with computer terminals and wireless Internet access.

Costs

Tuition and fees for the fall 2007 semester were $4428.50 for Massachusetts residents studying full-time (12 or more credits) or $10,338 for out-of-state students. Students enrolling part-time were charged tuition according to the number of credits taken, with Massachusetts residents paying tuition at $71.50 per credit; out-of-state residents paid tuition of $406.50 per credit. Annual mandatory fees for in-state residents ranged up to $7143 and up to $10,918 for out-of-state students.

Financial Aid

Financial aid is based on need and/or merit. Applicants must complete the Free Application for Federal Student Aid (FAFSA), keeping in mind a priority deadline of March 1 for fall semester and November 1 for spring semester. Need-based aid is awarded to students who demonstrate financial need, as determined by federal methodology. Aid consists of grants, waivers, and merit scholarships as well as self-help in the form of loans and work-study employment. An on-time applicant is automatically considered for all financial aid programs administered by the University's Office of Financial Aid Services.

Faculty

UMass Boston is proud of its distinguished faculty of 862 members, some 90 percent of whom have terminal degrees in their field. UMass Boston has a student-faculty ratio of about 15:1 and a small class size that averages only 28 students. The faculty's top priority is teaching and advising students, although they also conduct research, publish materials, and participate in grant activities and professional organizations. Faculty members maintain office hours for students and make themselves accessible as mentors. Faculty and academic issues are governed by the Faculty Council.

Student Government

The undergraduate Student Senate consists of elected members from the undergraduate colleges and programs, and it participates fully in matters related to the quality of student life and the allocation of the student activities trust fund. Students are also represented on numerous University- and college-based committees and councils that initiate major policy and procedural recommendations, forwarding those recommendations to governance bodies and the administration for enactment.

Admission Requirements

A freshman candidate for admission to the University should have earned a minimum of 16 academic units in high school that include 4 years of English, 3 years of mathematics, 3 years of science (including 2 with laboratory requirements), 2 years of social science (including 1 of U.S. history), 2 years of a single foreign language, and 2 years of electives in the arts or computer science (excluding vocational training). The student must also present satisfactory scores on either the SAT or ACT. The University looks for students with a strong academic background, as determined by a recalculated grade point average, and each candidate's academic program choices, motivation, achievement, and annual progress are closely scrutinized. Reading and writing skills are measured using English grades, the application essay, and standardized test scores.

UMass Boston encourages qualified international students to apply for admission. A separate international application is required. The Test of English as a Foreign Language (TOEFL) is required of all students educated in a non-English educational system.

Transfer students are considered based on a review of all college academic credentials. Several academic majors and programs have specific higher requirements for transfer students, but, in general, a minimum 2.5 GPA is required.

Participation in a campus visit and group informational session with an admissions counselor is strongly encouraged.

Application and Information

For informational materials and an application for admission, students should contact:

Enrollment Information Service
University of Massachusetts Boston
100 Morrissey Boulevard
Boston, Massachusetts 02125-3393
Phone: 617-287-6000
617-287-6010 (TTY/TDD)
Fax: 617-287-6040
E-mail: enrollment.info@umb.edu
Web site: http://www.umb.edu

UMass Boston is located on a beautiful, easily accessed peninsula just south of downtown Boston.

UNIVERSITY OF MASSACHUSETTS DARTMOUTH

NORTH DARTMOUTH, MASSACHUSETTS

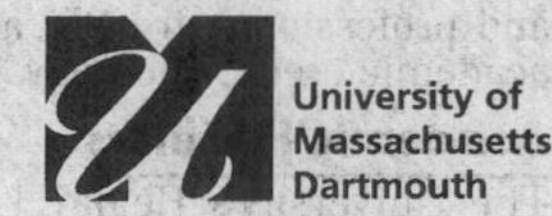

The University

The University of Massachusetts Dartmouth traces its roots to 1895 when the Massachusetts legislature chartered the New Bedford Textile School and the Bradford Durfee Textile School in Fall River. As the region's economic base shifted from textiles to more diverse manufacturing and service industries, the program of the colleges changed. Courses were developed to respond to the needs of new generations of students, stimulated by the clear economic and social advantages of a well-educated citizenry. In 1962, Southeastern Massachusetts Technological Institute (SMTI) was created, and in 1969, out of a need and a clear demand for a comprehensive public university, SMTI became Southeastern Massachusetts University. Then, in 1988, the Swain School of Design merged with the University's College of Visual and Performing Arts.

In 1991, a new University of Massachusetts system was created, which combined the Amherst and Boston campuses with the University of Lowell, Southeastern Massachusetts University, and the Medical Center in Worcester. Today, UMass Dartmouth provides educational programs, research, extension, and continuing education and cyber education in the liberal and creative arts and sciences and in the professions. A broad range of bachelor's, master's, and doctoral degrees are offered. Graduate programs lead to the Master of Arts, Master of Business Administration, Master of Arts in Teaching, Master of Fine Arts, Master of Art Education, and Master of Science. A Ph.D. is offered in electrical engineering, chemical engineering, biomedical engineering, marine science, and physics.

UMass Dartmouth enrolls approximately 8,500 students; 90 percent are from Massachusetts, with a growing number from other states and countries outside the United States. A residential campus with a variety of student organizations, athletic programs, cultural opportunities, and interest groups, the University fosters personal development, diversity, and responsible citizenship.

Location

Located in historic and scenic southeastern Massachusetts, which includes the nearby cities of Fall River and New Bedford and the Cape Cod region to the east, the campus is situated on 710 acres. The dramatic campus is the work of architect Paul Rudolph, former dean of the Yale University School of Art and Architecture. Metropolitan areas, with libraries, museums, theaters, and numerous educational institutions, are within an hour's drive: Boston to the north and Providence, Rhode Island, to the west. Recreational sites are minutes away and include beaches, hiking, and cultural and nightlife opportunities. New York City is 4 hours by car; the mountains of New Hampshire and Vermont are 3 to 4 hours away. Students can walk to homes and shops in the immediate area of the campus, while public transportation is available to nearby communities.

Majors and Degrees

There are five colleges within the University: College of Arts and Sciences (nineteen majors); Charlton College of Business (five majors); Engineering (eight majors); Nursing (one major); and Visual and Performing Arts (twelve majors). In addition, honors programs, interdisciplinary studies, prelaw, premedical advising, and a number of different minors and options are available within various departments. The University offers Bachelor of Arts, Bachelor of Fine Arts, Bachelor of Science, and Bachelor of Science in Nursing degrees at the undergraduate level.

Academic Programs

The University operates on a two-semester calendar, with the fall semester beginning the first week of September and concluding in mid-December and the spring semester beginning in late January and concluding in late May. A five-week intersession is offered between semesters. Summer-term courses are offered in June, July, and early August. Undergraduate students usually enroll in four or five courses each semester, and a typical course earns 3 credits. An undergraduate degree requires a minimum of 120 credits (there are a few majors that require 135 credits); a student can complete degree requirements for a specified major within a department or an approved interdepartmental major (30 credits). Students must also complete requirements according to the degree being sought.

Other learning opportunities include independent study, contract learning, and directed study; study abroad; study at a nearby university through cross-registration; and credit by examination. UMass Dartmouth is a member of SACHEM (Southeastern Association for Cooperation in Higher Education in Massachusetts), allowing for cross-registration at Bridgewater State College, Bristol Community College, Cape Cod Community College, Dean College, Massachusetts Maritime Academy, Massasoit Community College, Stonehill College, and Wheaton College. The University has formal exchange agreements with, among others, the University of Grenoble (France), the Lycée du Grésivaudan at Meylan and the Lycée Aristide Berges, Nottingham Trent University (England), the Baden-Württemberg Universities (Germany), Centro de Arte e Comunicação (Portugal), Nova Scotia College of Art and Design, the École Nationale Supérieure des Industries Textiles, Université de Haute Alsace (France), and Minho University (Portugal). Students may also take initiative in finding other programs in addition to the exchange-agreement institutions.

The College of Engineering provides majors in any of the engineering fields and offers students work experience through cooperative education or internships.

Academic Facilities

Computing is an integral part of the curriculum. All academic buildings, including student residences, are connected to a campuswide network. Computing clusters, located in the library and in most classroom buildings, support the classwork of students. More than 200 microcomputers (Apple Macintosh and IBM) or terminals are readily available. The University library supports all programs of instruction and research with 455,323 volumes and 2,925 periodicals. A large interlibrary loan network and delivery system makes millions of volumes available to the students. Each of the five colleges within the University is housed in academic facilities designed for its purposes with classrooms, laboratories, studies, galleries, faculty offices, and lounges.

Costs

In-state tuition and fees for 2007–08 were $8592; non-Massachusetts resident tuition and fees were $18,174. Room and board expenses ranged from approximately $8000 to more than $9500, depending on the residence and meal plan chosen. Books and supplies cost approximately $1200 a year depending on a student's courses. Specific fees may be assessed, depending on a student's course of study.

Financial Aid

Nearly all students are eligible for some type of financial aid. UMass Dartmouth awards financial aid based on federal, state, and institutional guidelines; students must submit the Free Application for Federal Student Aid (FAFSA). In determining need, the Financial Aid Services Office considers the total costs of attending the University (tuition, fees, books, room and board, the cost of commuting, and an allowance for living and personal expenses). The difference between total University cost and the estimate of expected family contribution is the amount that the financial aid staff considers to be financial need.

Faculty

The faculty, numbering 350 full-time members, is distributed over twenty-nine departments in the five colleges. More than two thirds of the faculty members have a Ph.D., with a significant number holding the terminal degree in their chosen discipline (e.g., business, fine arts, education). A student-faculty ratio of 16:1 ensures that classes are reasonably sized, with an average class size of 30 students. Faculty members are actively engaged in advising students, providing guidance throughout a student's academic career.

Student Government

The Student Senate is the governing body offering a forum for debate on matters of importance to the student body. The Student Judiciary, a system of courts or judicial agencies, provides students and organizations with the protection of due process in all disciplinary matters. A student is also elected to the University of Massachusetts Board of Trustees. Students serve on the Board of Governors, policy makers for the Campus Center; the Resident Hall Congress; and the Student Activities Board. Students are active, voting participants on policymaking committees that regulate both academic and social aspects of the University.

Admission Requirements

Admission is selective. Applicants are evaluated both by the general standards of the University and by the special standards of the academic areas that they request. In addition, the Board of Higher Education sets guidelines governing admission standards for the University. Admission to some colleges or majors may be limited by spaces available. Students are admitted on a rolling basis with no set deadline. Qualified candidates are accepted until the capacity has been reached in the program of choice. Each applicant's record is assessed on the basis of the depth and rigor of the secondary school program, rank in class and grade point average, SAT or ACT results, college-level records for transfer applicants, and other appropriate measures.

The University realizes its commitment to equal access through standard, as well as alternative, admission programs. For College Now, the alternative program, applicants must meet at least one of three eligibility criteria: low-income status, limited English background, or first generation in the family to attend college.

All applicants for freshman admission to the University are required to submit an application form with the appropriate fee ($40 in state and $60 out of state), a transcript of the secondary school record, SAT or ACT results, and any other information that candidates consider important for the admissions committee to review. Transfer students, who compose approximately one third of the new student population every year, are required to submit records for all college-level work completed in addition to the application form. The admission process is virtually the same for transfer candidates, with primary emphasis on the student's previous college/university record.

Application and Information

Students are invited to visit the University for a campus tour and a meeting with an admissions officer; interviews are not required. Some majors, such as nursing, may close early due to enrollment capacity. Admission is rolling except for early decision (freshmen). The early decision deadline is November 15, with notification by December 15. All other decisions are made within three weeks of the completion of an application. For application forms and related information, students may call, write, or e-mail the admissions office.

Office of Admissions
UMass Dartmouth
285 Old Westport Road
North Dartmouth, Massachusetts 02747-2300
Phone: 508-999-8605
Fax: 508-999-8755
E-mail: admissions@umassd.edu
Internet: http://explore.umassd.edu/

The size of UMass Dartmouth appeals to many students.

UNIVERSITY OF MASSACHUSETTS LOWELL

LOWELL, MASSACHUSETTS

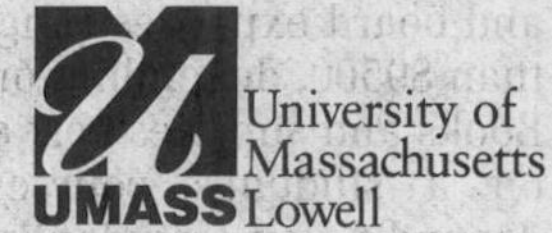

The University

Throughout its 100-year history, the University of Massachusetts (UMass) Lowell has excelled at providing innovative, responsive programs that meet both the needs of its students for a high-quality education and the needs of regional industry for skilled leadership. Formed through the merger of a technical institute and a teacher's college, the University is part of the five-campus University of Massachusetts system.

UMass Lowell students look at the world and society through a wide lens. While they learn the specifics of a major, they also explore its context so they understand how the economy, the environment, and society connect. Courses typically involve a practical component that can range from the political science team that competed nationally in a United Nations Model Assembly to the music business majors who went to a recording industry conference in California to the civil engineering students who helped the city of Lowell inventory and replace all its street signs.

Faculty members are respected researchers who value their commitment to teaching and extend the learning experience beyond the classroom. Undergraduates participate in funded research and college policy committees, and senior faculty members are involved in student projects such as building and racing a solar-powered car. Strong links with local businesses, educational systems, and health-care providers benefit students through an increasing number of internships, part-time jobs, and grants. In short, students graduate with the hands-on experience and practical problem-solving skills employers are looking for.

The University campus covers 100 acres on both sides of the Merrimack River and includes classroom and laboratory buildings, two libraries, a student center, two gymnasiums, three dining halls, a Center for the Performing Arts, an art gallery, and numerous residence halls. A new campus center provides additional social and recreational facilities. State-of-the-art laboratories include such special interest facilities as the six Sound Recording Technology Program studios, an interactive video lab that enables nursing students to simulate medical emergencies, and a manufacturing lab where engineering and management students team up to produce microelectronic components. The University's collaborative relationship with the city of Lowell has resulted in the completion of a nearby hockey arena and a baseball stadium on campus, both shared by UMass Lowell and professional teams.

UMass Lowell's 6,000 undergraduate students are ethnically, culturally, and economically diverse. Students are active in a wide variety of community service activities, including athletics-based programs for local high school students; the Adaptive Technology Program, in which students create modified devices for the disabled; and volunteer work at local shelters and community programs. There are more than 100 campus organizations to choose from: academic, recreational, and special interest groups; the women's center; marching band; the student newspaper; an FM radio station; and the Off-Broadway Players. Campuswide events include University Day and Spring Carnival, and residence hall associations sponsor social and recreational events. The University sponsors fourteen intercollegiate sports teams, including the nationally ranked Division I hockey team, and an active recreational sports program. In conjunction with the five colleges, the Graduate School enrolls nearly 3,000 students in twenty-nine master's degree and twelve doctoral programs.

Location

The University is located in Lowell, a city of 110,000 that has gained national attention by successfully leveraging its history, ethnic diversity, and entrepreneurial spirit to create a vital urban center. The site of a National Historical Park that honors the city as the birthplace of the industrial revolution, Lowell is also home to an acclaimed professional theater company, annual Kerouac and folk festivals, and museums that include the Museum of American Textile History and the Whistler House Museum. Located 26 miles from the cultural and educational riches of Boston and Cambridge, Lowell is also within an hour of ocean beaches and the lakes and mountains of New Hampshire via major highways and regional train and bus service.

Majors and Degrees

The College of Arts and Sciences offers baccalaureate programs in American studies, art, biological sciences, chemistry with an option in forensics science, computer science, criminal justice, design, economics, English, environmental studies, history, liberal arts, mathematics, modern languages, music business, music performance, music studies, philosophy, physics, political science, psychology, sociology, and sound recording technology. Dual majors are permitted. Dual B.A./B.S. and B.S./M.S. degree programs are available in liberal arts, science, and engineering fields. Predental and premedical programs are available.

The James B. Francis College of Engineering offers baccalaureate day programs in chemical, civil and environmental, electrical and computer, mechanical, and plastics engineering. Engineering programs are accredited by the Engineering Accreditation Commission (EAC) of the Accreditation Board for Engineering and Technology, Inc. (ABET). Combined bachelor's/master's programs, internships, and co-op opportunities are available in the College of Engineering.

The School of Health and Environment offers baccalaureate day programs in clinical laboratory sciences, which is accredited by the National Accrediting Agency for Clinical Laboratory Sciences (NAACLS); health education; exercise physiology; medical technology; nursing, which is accredited by the National League for Nursing Accrediting Commission (NLNAC); and nutritional science.

The College of Management offers baccalaureate day programs, all of which are accredited by AACSB International–The Association to Advance Collegiate Schools of Business, in business administration (B.S.B.A.), with concentrations in accounting, entrepreneurship, finance, management, management information systems, and marketing.

The University's Division of Continuing Studies and Corporate Education offers evening programs through the various colleges. Through the College of Arts and Sciences, baccalaureate programs in applied mathematics, criminal justice, information technology, and liberal arts are offered. Through the College of Engineering, associate and baccalaureate degrees are offered in civil engineering technology, electronic engineering technology, and mechanical engineering technology. Through the College of Management, an associate degree program in accounting and a baccalaureate degree program in business administration are available. Certificate programs are offered in accounting, computer-assisted manufacturing, computer engineering technology, data/telecommunications, electrooptics, environmental technology, graphic design and digital imagery, hazardous-waste management, Internet technology, land surveying, manufacturing technology, multimedia applications, nutrition, paralegal studies, plastics engineering technology, quality assurance, Spanish, technical writing, UNIX, wastewater treatment, water treatment, and Web site design and development.

Academic Programs

The University operates on a calendar of two semesters, a condensed two-week intersession in January, and a summer term (with two sessions). Full-time undergraduates generally take five courses each semester. A minimum of 120 credits is required for baccalaureate degrees; the minimum credits required for professional degree programs are generally higher. A University general education requirement is imposed for all baccalaureate curriculums. Majors require 30–60 credits. Elective course options vary widely according to the degree program and major area. Professional degree program options and requirements follow specific accreditation guidelines. Maximum curricular freedom is permitted in B.A. programs. The academic climate is serious and competitive and requires self-motivation. Approximately 50 percent of the undergraduates complete graduation requirements in four years.

Academic Facilities

The University has two comprehensive libraries with online capabilities that can be accessed from networked computers across the campus and from all dormitory rooms.

The University operates a state-of-the-art network facility that includes an OC-3 ATM backbone and 10/100-MBPS switched technology to all desktops. Remote access via PPP or ISDN is also available. Clients to the network include more than 4,000 desktop and laboratory PCs with more than 100 servers. Applications on the network include e-mail, groupware, Microsoft Office products, cybereducation, interactive video, and numerous academic programming applications.

Costs

The annual costs for 2007–08 for full-time undergraduate residents of Massachusetts were $8906 per year; for nonresidents of Massachusetts, they were $20,559 per year. Residence hall charges were $4331 per year. A full meal plan was $2492 per year. Accident insurance is covered by fees; major medical insurance is optional. Books and supplies are estimated at $400 to $600, depending on the program. Quoted rates are subject to change.

Financial Aid

The University is committed to making higher education accessible to all qualified students. The University participates in federal and state programs, assisting students through grants-in-aid, loans, employment opportunities, and scholarships. The amount of an award is determined by need, as indicated by the Free Application for Federal Student Aid (FAFSA), which should be filed by March 1. The University awards a growing number of merit-based scholarships.

Faculty

The full-time resident faculty members number 359. The part-time day faculty members number 235. In addition, 175 part-time faculty members are employed in continuing education programs. Most faculty members teach and conduct research in their disciplines. Graduate teaching assistants also hold part-time instructional positions, particularly as discussion section leaders and laboratory teaching assistants.

Student Government

The Student Government Association and the Residence Hall Association provide opportunities in student government at the all-campus level. Leadership opportunities are provided in residence halls and student organizations. Students also participate in the disciplinary system and in most University committees.

Admission Requirements

All undergraduate day applicants must have a high school diploma or a general equivalency diploma and satisfactory SAT scores. A minimum recalculated high school grade point average of 2.5 (on a 4.0 scale) is recommended, and the University places primary emphasis upon the high school record. Students whose high school average is below the required minimum may be considered for admission if they present SAT verbal and mathematics scores that are higher than those specified for the admission of degree candidates by the college or program to which they wish to apply.

Transfer students are considered for fall- or spring-semester admissions. Transcripts of completed work must be on file prior to acceptance. Depending on the number of transfer credits and college GPA, transfer students who seek admission as matriculating day students may be asked to provide a high school record and SAT scores.

Application and Information

For day programs, the University practices rolling admissions, which means that applications are evaluated as soon as they are complete. Entering freshmen are admitted for the fall or spring semester. The preferred deadline for freshman applications is February 15 for the fall semester and December 1 for the spring semester. The preferred deadline for transfer applications is July 1 for the fall semester and January 7 for the spring semester.

For application forms and further information, students should contact:

Office of Undergraduate Admissions
University of Massachusetts Lowell
883 Broadway Street
Suite 110
Lowell, Massachusetts 01854-5104
Phone: 978-934-3931
Web site: http://www.uml.edu

The main administration building makes a convenient gathering spot between classes.

The University of Massachusetts Lowell is an Equal Opportunity/Affirmative Action, Title IX employer.

WENTWORTH INSTITUTE OF TECHNOLOGY

BOSTON, MASSACHUSETTS

The Institute

Wentworth Institute of Technology was founded in 1904 to provide education in the mechanical arts. Today, it is one of the nation's leading technical institutes, offering study in a variety of disciplines. Wentworth has a current undergraduate day enrollment of approximately 3,500 men and women (3,000 full-time) and graduates more engineering technicians and technologists each year than any other college in the United States. The technical education acquired at Wentworth enables graduates to assume creative and responsible careers in business and industry. Wentworth is located on a 35-acre campus on Huntington Avenue in Boston.

Wentworth provides dormitory and suite-style residence halls on campus for men and women. Students residing in the residence halls are on a full meal plan. Upperclass students have the option of living in on-campus apartments. Students residing in the apartments may prepare their own meals. A cafeteria, snack bar, and new convenience store are available for those wishing to purchase their meals.

Career counseling and placement assistance are available to all alumni and to students who have completed at least one semester of study at the Institute. While many graduates of Wentworth are employed in the Boston area, alumni have secured positions throughout the United States and abroad.

Location

Boston is the educational center of New England. It is a city of charm, tradition, and elegance—a major center of art, science, music, history, medicine, and education. Wentworth is situated near the heart of Boston and is surrounded by institutions that provide the cultural advantages for which the city is famous. The Museum of Fine Arts, with its store of art treasures, is diagonally across the street, and admission is free to any student with a Wentworth ID card. Symphony Hall is just a few blocks away. The Harvard Medical School, the New England Conservatory of Music, Emmanuel College, Simmons College, Massachusetts College of Pharmacy and Allied Health Sciences, Massachusetts College of Art, Roxbury Community College, and Northeastern University are among the many educational institutions within a few blocks of the campus.

Majors and Degrees

Wentworth Institute of Technology is a technical college of great diversity. Degree programs are offered in the fields of architecture, biomedical engineering (beginning in fall 2009), computer science, construction management, design, engineering, engineering technology, environmental science, and management. Specifically, bachelor's degrees are awarded in the following majors: the Bachelor of Architecture and the Bachelor of Science in civil engineering technology, computer engineering technology, computer network and information systems, computer science, construction management, electromechanical engineering (optional concentration in biomedical systems engineering), electronic engineering technology, environmental science, facilities planning and management, industrial design, interior design, management (optional concentrations in communication, project leadership, and technology management), and mechanical engineering technology. Baccalaureate degrees in architecture and interior design are designated as first professional degrees. Completion of a Wentworth baccalaureate degree requires four or five years, depending on the program.

Academic Programs

At Wentworth Institute of Technology, college-level study in technological fundamentals and principles is combined with appropriate laboratory, field, and studio experience. Students apply theory to practical problems, and they acquire skills and techniques by using, operating, and controlling equipment and instruments that are particular to their area of specialization. In addition, study in the social sciences and humanities provides a balanced understanding of the world in which graduates work. Wentworth's programs of study are more practical than theoretical in approach, and the Institute's academic requirements demand extensive time and effort.

During the first two years of study in a degree program at Wentworth, students lay the foundation for more advanced study in the third and fourth (and fifth, where applicable) years. While nearly all majors allow continuous study from the freshman through the senior year, the architecture major requires a petition for acceptance to the baccalaureate program during the sophomore year.

All bachelor's degree programs are conducted as cooperative (co-op) education programs: upon entering their third year, students alternate semesters of academic study at Wentworth with semester-long periods of employment in industry. Two semesters of co-op employment are required; one additional (summer) semester of co-op is optional. Both students and the companies that hire them are enthusiastic about the co-op program and agree that it is a mutually valuable experience.

Academic Facilities

Wentworth's twenty-seven buildings house classrooms, laboratories, studios, administrative offices, and other facilities. Beatty Hall houses the Alumni Library, computer center, classrooms, dining areas, and office space. State-of-the-art laboratories, such as the Richard H. Lufkin Technology Center and the Davis Center for Advanced Graphics and Interactive Learning, are situated throughout the campus.

Costs

For 2008–09, tuition is $21,100, books and supplies are approximately $1000, and room and board are about $10,000 (this figure varies according to accommodation).

Financial Aid

Scholarships are available to students who demonstrate need and academic promise. Merit-based scholarships are also available. Wentworth also provides federal and state financial assistance, such as Federal Pell and Federal Supplemental Educational Opportunity Grants, Federal Perkins Loans, Federal Work-Study Program awards, Gilbert Matching Grants, and Massachusetts No-Interest Loans, to students with financial need in accordance with federal and state guidelines.

Wentworth participates in the Federal Direct Lending program. As a result, students are eligible to borrow under the Federal Direct Stafford Student Loan program and parents may borrow under the Federal Direct PLUS program. Individuals participating in these programs borrow money directly from the federal government rather than through lending institutions.

In addition to these need-based programs, Wentworth also participates in the MEFA loan program sponsored by the Massachusetts Educational Financing Authority. Wentworth offers several payment options through payment plans and alternative loan financing.

To apply for financial aid, new students should complete the Free Application for Federal Student Aid (FAFSA) by March 1. Applications received after this date are considered as funds allow.

Faculty

Wentworth's faculty includes 146 full-time and 123 part-time members. The primary responsibility of every faculty member is teaching. Although professors may engage in some research and related work, student development remains the central mission of Wentworth's faculty. Upon entering Wentworth, every student is assigned a faculty adviser.

Student Government

Wentworth's Student Government performs an essential function as the official representative of the student body. Its purposes are to receive and express student opinion, to advance the best interests of the student body with the administration and faculty and with other institutions and associations, to support all extracurricular activities of the student body, and to serve as a bond between the student body and the faculty to foster mutual cooperation and understanding. The Student Government is made up of elected representatives from each class section and the officers elected by the student body at large. The Student Government sponsors social functions and student organizations and serves as an advocate for student concerns.

Admission Requirements

Applicants must be graduates of secondary schools (or have passed the GED test) and must meet specific entrance requirements. All programs require four years of English, a laboratory science, and mathematics through algebra II in a college-preparatory program. Both the electromechanical engineering and the computer science programs require a background in precalculus or trigonometry. All programs require the submission of SAT or ACT scores. International students and transfers are welcome.

Application and Information

Students are admitted to Wentworth for September and January enrollment. Notification of admission is made on a rolling basis. The preferred method for applying is online at http://www.wit.edu/apply. The online application fee is $10. An application form, the application fee, transcripts from the secondary school and any colleges previously attended, SAT or ACT scores, a personal statement, and a letter of recommendation should be sent to:

Admissions Office
Wentworth Institute of Technology
550 Huntington Avenue
Boston, Massachusetts 02115
Phone: 617-989-4000
800-556-0610 (toll-free)
Fax: 617-989-4010
E-mail: admissions@wit.edu
Web site: http://www.wit.edu

Wentworth Hall.

WESTERN NEW ENGLAND COLLEGE

SPRINGFIELD, MASSACHUSETTS

The College

Western New England College, which was founded in 1919, is a private, independent coeducational institution offering more than thirty undergraduate majors at the baccalaureate level in the Schools of Arts and Sciences, Business, and Engineering. Beginning in fall 2009, Western New England College will admit the first class in the prepharmacy program. Students who graduate from this six-year professional program will earn a Doctor of Pharmacy (Pharm.D.) degree. The College offers a unique combined Bachelor of Arts/Juris Doctor program, a six-year biomedical engineering/law program, a five-year bachelor's/M.B.A. or M.S.A. program, and seven graduate degrees. The American Bar Association–accredited School of Law provides full- and part-time programs leading to a Juris Doctor degree and a Master of Law degree. Western New England College also serves part-time working professionals through its continuing education programs offered in Springfield and at six sites throughout the commonwealth.

In its annual "America's Best Colleges" rankings, *U.S. News & World Report* lists Western New England College in the top tier of its North category among colleges and universities that provide a full range of undergraduate and master's degree programs. In addition, Western New England College is featured in *Colleges of Distinction,* a new college guide and Web site profiling some of America's best bets in higher education. Based on the opinions of guidance counselors, educators, and admissions professionals, *Colleges of Distinction* honors colleges that excel in key areas of educational quality.

Western New England College began as a satellite campus of Northeastern University in rented rooms located in the downtown Springfield YMCA. Its mission was to provide a college education for working people who could not afford the time to attend college classes full-time during the day. The high-quality instruction gave "The Springfield Division," as the College was known, a growing reputation, and by 1951, when Northeastern elected to end its satellite program, there was a demand for the institution to continue. That year, Western New England College was incorporated by the Massachusetts Board of Collegiate Authority.

Western New England College is known for providing strong professionally based programs with a solid liberal arts background to prepare students for entry into professional careers or graduate school. There are approximately 2,500 full-time undergraduates, whereas the total enrollment, including part-time undergraduate, graduate, and law students, is about 4,000. Approximately 61 percent of the full-time undergraduates are men, and about 79 percent of the students live on campus. The College annually enrolls students from about thirty-one states; 60 percent come from out of state.

The College has developed a unique Wholistic Student Development Program that provides a comprehensive educational experience to the student inside and outside of the classroom. In addition to the academic component, other aspects of Learning Beyond the Classroom include personal and social development, career planning, multicultural awareness, physical fitness and health, and artistic and cultural appreciation. The Campus Activities Board is primarily responsible for coordinating a student activities calendar. The Western New England College CareerCenter is staffed with professional career counselors who provide students with the tools they need to obtain internships and succeed professionally—from mock, taped interviews to challenging employment opportunities. The College currently offers students nineteen varsity sports (NCAA Division III) in which to become involved. Men's sports include baseball, basketball, cross-country, football, golf, ice hockey, lacrosse, soccer, tennis, and wrestling. Women's sports include basketball, cross-country, field hockey, lacrosse, soccer, softball, swimming, tennis, and volleyball. Non-NCAA participation sports include men's and women's bowling and martial arts.

The College is accredited by the New England Association of Schools and Colleges; the School of Business is fully accredited by AACSB International; the engineering majors are accredited by the Accreditation Board for Engineering and Technology, Inc. (ABET); the social work major is accredited by the Council on Social Work Education (CSWE); and the School of Law is accredited by the American Bar Association (ABA). Various programs have additional accreditation from specific agencies.

Location

Western New England College's 215-acre campus was developed in a residential section of Springfield, Massachusetts. It is located about 4 miles from downtown Springfield, which is serviced by Greyhound and Peter Pan bus lines, Amtrak, and Bradley International Airport in Windsor Locks, Connecticut. Hartford is just 30 minutes away; Albany, Boston, and Providence are less than 100 miles from the campus; and New York City is a 3-hour drive.

Majors and Degrees

Undergraduate programs offered by the School of Arts and Sciences are majors in biology (concentrations in general and molecular), chemistry, communication (interpersonal and mass media concentrations), computer science, creative writing, criminal justice, economics, education (elementary and secondary), English, forensic biology, forensic chemistry, history, information technology, international studies, law and society, mathematical sciences, philosophy, political science, psychology, social work, and sociology. The prepharmacy program will begin in fall 2009.

The School of Business offers degrees in accounting, business information systems, finance, general business, management, marketing, marketing communication/advertising, and sport management.

The School of Engineering offers majors in biomedical engineering, electrical engineering (concentrations in computer and electrical), industrial engineering, and mechanical engineering (concentrations in mechanical and manufacturing).

Specialized programs include secondary teacher certification (biology, business, chemistry, English, history, mathematics, and political science), elementary education certification (English, history, and psychology), and premed and prelaw programs. The College's 3+3 Law Program offers eligible students the opportunity to earn their bachelor's and Juris Doctor degrees from Western New England College School of Law in just six years instead of seven. Western New England College also offers a six-year biomedical engineering/law program. In addition, eligible students may participate in the five-year bachelor's/M.B.A. or M.S.A. programs.

Academic Programs

The College operates on a two-semester calendar and has a limited summer program. Students normally take five courses each semester. Specific information on the various academic programs is available from the Office of Admissions.

Western New England College participates in the College Board's Advanced Placement (AP) Program, College-Level Examination Program (CLEP), and International Baccalaureate (I.B.). Successful completion of these programs may result in the earning of academic credit and the waiving of certain courses.

Academic Facilities

The Western New England campus contains twenty major buildings and is situated on 215 acres. Classes are held in five classroom-laboratory buildings, which contain more than sixty-five classrooms. The D'Amour Library contains 110,000 volumes, with access to more than 15,000 titles via the Internet, and has wireless access for all students to use. The library is also home to the College's state-of-the-art television studio, the highlight of the 2005 $1.9-million renovation. The College is committed to providing students with access to a wide range of computing hardware and software. The College has a campuswide network linking all buildings to hundreds of PCs in public areas, including the Churchill Hall Lab, the D'Amour Library, the Writing and Math Centers, the Accounting Lab, the School of Law, and the Engineering Labs. In addition, the School of Engineering has a large number of microcomputers, graphic plotters, and other peripherals that may be used to support the laboratory programs. All College residence hall rooms are wired for Internet access and are cable-TV ready. In addition, each semester, faculty members and students use the Manhattan Virtual Classroom, which was developed by Western New England College, to provide safe and secure file transport between faculty members, students, campus organizations, and informal groups.

Costs

Tuition and fees for the 2007–08 academic year for the School of Engineering were $27,034 for commuting students and $37,032 for residential students. For the Schools of Business and Arts and Science, tuition and fees were $25,942 for commuting students and $35,940 for residential students.

Financial Aid

Western New England College offers comprehensive programs of financial assistance to students who demonstrate financial need. The programs include merit- and need-based scholarships, grants, loans, and on-campus employment. Students seeking financial aid must submit the Free Application for Federal Student Aid (FAFSA) and a copy of the federal income tax return and W-2 form. Approximately 90 percent of Western New England College students annually receive assistance.

Faculty

Western New England College has a faculty of 164 full-time instructors, of whom 92 percent have received their terminal degrees. The College also has adjunct instructors, who share important specialized information with the students. The Western New England College School of Law has a distinguished legal faculty numbering 38 full-time and adjunct instructors.

The ratio of students to faculty members is 15:1. The average class size is 20, and students have ample opportunity to meet with faculty members outside of class.

Admission Requirements

Applicants must have graduated from an approved secondary school or have obtained a General Educational Development (GED) credential. The minimum units of high school preparation should include 4 units of English, 2 units of mathematics, 1 unit of laboratory science, and 1 unit of U.S. history. Applicants to the School of Business and those who wish to major in chemistry, computer science, forensic biology, forensic chemistry, or mathematics are required to present 3 units of mathematics. Prospective engineering students must present 1 unit of physics or 1 unit of chemistry as well as 4 units of mathematics.

Application and Information

Admission is offered to students on a rolling basis for all programs. However, students are encouraged to apply early in order to receive complete consideration for admission, financial aid, and housing. Students must submit the Western New England College application, SAT or ACT scores, an official secondary school transcript, and a recommendation from a guidance counselor or teacher. International students can substitute the Test of English as a Foreign Language (TOEFL) for the SAT or ACT. American students for whom English is not the first language are encouraged to submit TOEFL scores. Transfer students must also submit official transcripts for any collegiate work. An essay is not required, but essays and personal statements are welcome. Notification of acceptance begins in late fall.

For further information, students should contact:

Office of Admission
Western New England College
1215 Wilbraham Road
Springfield, Massachusetts 01119-2684
Phone: 413-782-1321
800-325-1122 Ext. 1321 (toll-free)
Fax: 413-782-1777
E-mail: ugradmis@wnec.edu
Web site: http://www.wnec.edu

Students enjoy the beautiful and spacious Western New England College campus.

WHEATON COLLEGE
NORTON, MASSACHUSETTS

The College

Wheaton College is an independent liberal arts college of approximately 1,550 women and men. Founded as a seminary for women in 1834, Wheaton was chartered as a college in 1912 and enrolled its first coeducational class in 1988. Students come from forty-six states and thirty countries. Nearly all students live on campus in both single-sex and coed student-run dormitories.

The vitality of this classic liberal arts college grows out of each student's involvement in the social and academic life of the campus. There are many extracurricular activities and organizations, including intercollegiate and intramural sports, such as baseball, basketball, cross-country, field hockey, lacrosse, soccer, softball, synchronized swimming, tennis, and track; musical groups, such as the Whims, Wheatones, Gentleman Callers, and chamber music ensembles; the Modern Dance Group; the Black Students Association; the Student Government Association; the Christian Fellowship; Hillel; the International Students Association; the Latino Students Association; the Asian Student Association; and the newspaper, yearbook, campus radio station, and literary magazine. Wheaton also has a chapter of Phi Beta Kappa. A number of lecture series are offered, and concerts, plays, films, colloquia, art exhibits, and social events are scheduled regularly. Through the Filene Center for Work and Learning, hundreds of students annually undertake career exploration internships and field placements in local towns as well as in Boston, Providence, and overseas. The Filene Center also provides a full range of career services, graduate and professional school counseling, alumnae networks, and databases of part-time and summer job opportunities. The new Office of Service, Spirituality and Social Responsibility provides an inclusive place for students to participate in community service, explore spirituality, and initiate social activism.

Location

The 385-acre campus with its eighty-seven buildings is in the suburban surroundings of Norton. The newest additions to the campus include a $20-million arts complex with a state-of-the-art studio arts building; 100-bed Beard Hall; two 50-person residence halls; a multipurpose athletics facility, which includes a field house, a pool, and a gymnasium; and Sidell Baseball Stadium. Norton is located 30 minutes from Providence and 45 minutes from Boston. Public buses connect the campus to nearby commuter rail stations serving Boston, Providence, and numerous points in between. The College provides individuals with transportation for academic and internship activities as well as direct service to Boston's center and Providence, Rhode Island, on weekends. The College is also situated within an hour's drive of the beautiful beaches of Cape Cod, Massachusetts, and Newport, Rhode Island. The Tweeter Center for Performing Arts is located 2½ miles away.

Majors and Degrees

Wheaton College grants the Bachelor of Arts degree with formal majors in African, African American, and diaspora studies; American studies; ancient studies; anthropology; art (history and studio); Asian studies; biochemistry; biology; chemistry; classical civilization; classics (Greek and Latin); computer science; economics; economics-mathematics; English (literature, writing, and film studies); environmental science; French studies; German; German studies; Hispanic studies; history; international relations; Italian studies; Latin; mathematics; mathematics and computer science; music; philosophy; physics; physics and astronomy; political science; psychobiology; psychology; religion; religion and history; religion and philosophy; Russian; Russian studies; sociology; theater and English dramatic literature; and women's studies. Students may also create their own interdepartmental majors.

Five-year dual-degree programs are available in engineering with Thayer School of Engineering (Dartmouth), George Washington University, and Worcester Polytechnic Institute; in business and management with Clark University and the University of Rochester; in religion with Andover-Newton Theological School; in optometry with the New England School of Optometry; in communications with Emerson College; and in fine arts with the School of the Museum of Fine Arts in Boston.

Academic Programs

Wheaton's programs reflect the traditional depth and breadth of the liberal arts while going beyond prescribed boundaries. The College's curriculum encourages students to push past one-dimensional views of the world to acquire a deeper understanding of the topics that interest them. Through a series of linked courses, Wheaton students approach the same topic from two or more academic perspectives. Thus, students who examine public policy and politics may also choose to explore environmental management. An art class in figure drawing may be paired with study of human anatomy. Or students investigating evolutionary theory may survey the literature of the Victorian society from which Darwin and his work sprung. This approach helps students discover doorways to new insights and possibilities.

Course credit is granted through the Advanced Placement Program on an individual basis. Independent studies, research, and fieldwork are available to students for academic credit.

In addition to major department offerings, courses may be taken in education, family studies, film, geology, and linguistics.

Off-Campus Programs

Wheaton participates in the Twelve-College Exchange Program, which includes Amherst, Bowdoin, Dartmouth, Mount Holyoke, Smith, Trinity, Wellesley, and Wesleyan. Locally, Wheaton students may cross-register for courses at Brown University and other colleges in the Southeastern Association for Cooperation in Higher Education in Massachusetts (SACHEM).

Wheaton students may study government or economics during a semester in Washington, D.C., sponsored by American University, explore marine ecology at the Marine Biological Laboratory at Woods Hole, or participate in a semester-long program in American maritime studies, sponsored by Williams College at Mystic Seaport. The National Theater Institute Program offers selected students the opportunity to spend a semester at the Eugene O'Neill Theater Center in Waterford, Connecticut. Students may also participate in the Salt Center for Documentary Field Studies in Portland, Maine.

Global education opportunities are coordinated through Wheaton's Center for Global Education. The Center offers study-abroad programs for first-year, sophomore, junior, and senior students during the academic year and semester, as well as short-term faculty-led programs that occur during January, spring break, or summer. Currently the center offers more than eighty academic year and semester programs in more than fifty countries. Wheaton has coordinated ten short-term faculty-led programs to locations such as South Africa, the United Kingdom, Italy, and Russia.

In addition to the traditional model of overseas study through an affiliated university or program, Wheaton students continue to pursue opportunities outside the classroom setting. Students take part in credit-bearing overseas internships in art and architecture, economics, politics, film and television, journalism, international organizations, and health and human services. They are also involved in volunteer work both coordinated directly through a study-abroad program and developed independently with advising support through the Filene Center for Work and Learning.

The Career Exploration Internship Program assists hundreds of students in designing and securing internship positions every summer and awards domestic and international stipends to support unpaid internships, service, and structured independent research in annual amounts exceeding $300,000.

Academic Facilities

Wheaton's library has 371,675 volumes, 7,692 current serial subscriptions, 86,184 microfilm units, 15,099 audiovisual items, and 23,000 e-books; a College Archives/Special Collections area; and the Kollett Center for Collaborative Learning. Wheaton participates in several library consortia, which provide direct access to other regional college libraries and interlibrary loan access to libraries around the country. Automated services include online searching of remote databases, full-text electronic journals, and a fully integrated system containing the Wheaton Library catalog and acquisitions and circulation information. The Library also supports the academic program through bibliographic instruction sessions, including participation in the First-Year Seminars and individual consultations.

The Science Center has fully equipped laboratories for both faculty and student research and two greenhouses. Other facilities include a new studio arts building with public exhibition space and private studio studies for students; the Balfour-Hood Student Center; the Watson Fine Arts Center with a proscenium theater, a black box theater, art studios, and a gallery; a laboratory nursery school; and the Kollett Center for Collaborative Learning. The College also supports twenty-five classrooms on campus, with permanently installed computers, digital projectors and sound systems, and nine computer labs with 130 computers dedicated to specific academic courses and programs, e.g., Geographic Information Systems, Graphic Lab Design, Astronomy, and Language Lab. All academic and administrative buildings and all dormitories are part of a campuswide network. Students are offered accounts for e-mail and Internet access.

Costs

The comprehensive fee for 2006–07 was $42,880, which consisted of tuition, $34,365; room, $4300; board, $3850; Internet and telephone services, $120; and a student activities fee, $245.

Financial Aid

Students who demonstrate financial need normally receive a combination of grants, loans, and opportunities for employment on campus. The decision to award financial aid is made independently of the admission decision. Students applying for financial aid must complete the Free Application for Federal Student Aid (FAFSA) and the CSS PROFILE by January 15. Sixty percent of Wheaton's students receive some form of financial aid.

Faculty

The student-faculty ratio is 11:1. Ninety-eight percent of the full-time faculty members hold the Ph.D. degree. Professors are very accessible to students, act as academic advisers, and often become involved with student activities.

Student Government

The Student Government Association, an active and influential organization, includes all members of the Wheaton community. Students are invited to attend faculty meetings and serve as voting members on most faculty committees. Rules are minimal, based on student self-government and an honor system stressing individual honor and responsibility.

Admission Requirements

Wheaton does not prescribe rigid entrance requirements, but most entering students have had 4 years of English, 4 years of mathematics, 4 years of one or two languages, 3 years of social studies, 3 years of science, and 2 years of history. However, these guidelines are not to be taken as requirements. Applications are reviewed on an individual basis, and the academic achievement, the challenge of the curriculum, evaluations by teachers and counselors, and the extracurricular contributions of each candidate are all taken into account.

The submission of standardized test results is optional for the purposes of admission. Those who wish their scores to be considered should arrange for official score reports to be sent from the appropriate testing agency directly to the Wheaton Office of Admission. Reports must be received no later than the application deadline for the corresponding decision plan. Unofficial test scores (i.e., those reported on high school transcripts) are not considered. A personal interview is expected for all applicants.

Transfer students are admitted to the sophomore and junior classes each year. Transfer applicants must have maintained a promising record and must be eligible for honorable dismissal from the college they are attending. A transfer student must attend Wheaton for at least two years in order to receive a degree from the College. Students who wish to enter in the spring semester must apply by November 1. The regular decision deadline for transfer students is April 1.

Application and Information

Students who consider Wheaton their first choice may apply for early decision by November 15 or early decision 2 by January 15. Decisions are mailed by December 15 and February 15, respectively. The deadline for regular decision applicants is January 15; notification for these students is made during the first week of April.

For more information, students are encouraged to contact:

Dean of Admission and Student Aid
Wheaton College
Norton, Massachusetts 02766
Phone: 508-286-8251
800-394-6003 (toll-free)
E-mail: admission@wheatoncollege.edu
Web site: http://www.wheatoncollege.edu

Park Hall, the administration building (left), and Mary Lyon Hall, a classroom building (right), are among the handsome facilities on Wheaton College's extensive 385-acre campus.

WHEELOCK COLLEGE

BOSTON, MASSACHUSETTS

The College

Wheelock College prepares students for careers that enrich the lives of children and families—and society in general. Founded in 1888, Wheelock has consistently produced progressive and highly respected professionals for such fields as elementary education, preschool and kindergarten teaching, special education, day care, social work, juvenile justice and youth advocacy, and child life work. The 700 undergraduate women and men at Wheelock come from throughout the United States and from several countries. Beginning in their freshman year, students benefit from close contact with outstanding faculty members and from direct fieldwork with children and families.

Wheelock's campus is beautifully kept, and the atmosphere is warm and friendly. Classes are small, and professors are known by their first names. Comfortable residence halls provide housing and many social activities for the two thirds of the College's students who choose to live on campus. The Student Center, with its wide-screen TV, snack bar, and often-used dance floor, is an attraction for the entire Wheelock community and for many students from neighboring schools. Wheelock students enjoy more than twenty-five clubs and organizations and actively participate in a variety of varsity and intramural sports. The College sponsors many cultural and theatrical events as well as traditional activities such as Family Weekend, the Sophomore-Senior Banquet, and Black History Month.

Location

Located in Boston and bordering suburban Brookline, Wheelock is ideally located across from Longwood Park and only a few blocks from the Museum of Fine Arts, several world-renowned hospitals, and many other institutions of higher learning. Students can walk to the shops and restaurants in Coolidge Corner or cheer for the Red Sox in nearby Fenway Park. They can discover the unmatched cultural and historical richness of downtown Boston, which is only a short subway ride away. They can walk the Freedom Trail, attend concerts and plays, or meet friends from other colleges for a day of fun at Faneuil Hall. The entire Boston area provides Wheelock students with exciting opportunities for extracurricular enjoyment and for their practical fieldwork with children and families.

Majors and Degrees

At Wheelock, many students pursue one of four professional directions: teaching, child life, juvenile justice and youth advocacy, or social work, while others choose to major in one of the arts and sciences. Within teaching, there are three separate areas of concentration: early childhood care and education focuses on the comprehensive care and education of children from birth to 8 years old; elementary education prepares students to become teachers of children in grades 1–6; and special education prepares professionals to work with children from prekindergarten through eighth grade with mild to moderate disabilities. The child life program explores the emotional and psychological needs of hospitalized children and their families and prepares students to work as child life specialists with medical teams in hospitals or clinics. The juvenile justice and youth advocacy program prepares students to work with youth and their families in a range of settings, including preventative programs, advocacy programs, and programs for juvenile offenders. Students interested in teaching, juvenile justice and youth advocacy, or child life also major in one of five liberal arts areas: American studies, human development, the arts, the humanities, or mathematics/science. These multidisciplinary majors are designed to form a strong foundation for professional studies and for lifelong learning. Social work majors prepare to work in social service agencies, state agencies, and schools to advocate for and support children and their families. Graduates of Wheelock receive the Bachelor of Arts, Bachelor of Science, or Bachelor of Social Work degree.

Academic Programs

The focus of study at Wheelock is education and human services. Faculty members stress the importance of combining liberal arts, professional studies, and hands-on experience. Students begin work with children and families in their freshman year as part of a required course entitled Human Growth and Development. Juniors and seniors participate in supervised field experiences and student teaching in a variety of settings—elementary schools, daycare centers, nursery schools, museums, hospitals, social service agencies, and clinics—in urban and suburban locations. Professional courses provide preparation for field experience and support to students during their fieldwork. By combining the appropriate courses and field experience, Wheelock graduates are eligible for certification as early childhood, special education, or elementary school teachers and child life specialists.

Off-Campus Programs

Wheelock College is a member of the Colleges of the Fenway, a collaboration among Emmanuel College, Massachusetts College of Art, Massachusetts College of Pharmacy and Health Sciences, Simmons College, Wentworth Institute of Technology, and Wheelock College. Each college maintains its unique identity while providing students with access to academic programs and student services on all six campuses. Wheelock students can cross-register for courses and participate in social and extracurricular activities at any of the other institutions.

Academic Facilities

Wheelock's innovative Resource Center has a fully equipped workshop and holds a large collection of commercially manufactured scrap and natural materials for students to use in the creation of projects and original curriculum tools. Wheelock's library contains 92,000 volumes, providing reference and study facilities, collections in liberal arts areas, and extensive resources in children's literature and curriculum materials. The College also has extensive art studios with facilities for work in ceramics, weaving, and photography. One of the largest and best-equipped theatrical stages in Boston is found in the 700-seat Lucy Wheelock Auditorium in the Activities Building, where the Wheelock Family Theatre produces three shows each year. The Activities Building also houses science and music classrooms, the Little Theatre for theater classes and experimental theater, a music listening room, and an art gallery. All classrooms at Wheelock are equipped with data ports for Internet access and teacher workstations for integrating technology into the classroom. In addition, all students have Internet capabilities in their rooms.

Costs

In 2007–08, tuition was $25,400, room and board were $10,400, and fees were $680, for a total of $36,480. A reasonable estimate for books and supplies is $880 per year and, for personal expenses, $990, exclusive of travel to and from school.

Financial Aid

Wheelock provides financial aid for all applicants who demonstrate need. Currently, about 85 percent of the student body receives financial aid, usually in a combination of grants, loans, and work. Wheelock participates in the Federal Stafford Student Loan, Federal Perkins Loan, Federal Supplemental Educational Opportunity Grant, Federal Pell Grant, and Federal Work-Study programs. The College uses its own funds to provide additional grants, loans, and employment. The Financial Aid Office must receive the Free Application for Federal Student Aid (FAFSA) by February 15 for students who plan to enter in September or by October 15 for midyear students.

Wheelock also offers merit scholarships for eligible first-year and transfer students. New first-year students entering in the fall semester who have earned a high school GPA of 3.0 or higher and have an SAT score of 1050 (critical reading and math combined) or higher automatically receives one of the College's Merit Scholarships ranging from $4000 to $12,000. These scholarships are renewable all four years while the student is enrolled full-time.

New transfer students entering in the fall semester who have earned a college GPA of 3.2 or higher could be eligible for one of the College's Merit Scholarships ranging from $3000 to $5000. These scholarships are renewable while the student is enrolled full-time.

Faculty

All of Wheelock's faculty members, many of whom are nationally recognized for their research and experience in the fields in which they are experts, are actively engaged in classroom teaching. Faculty members also serve as academic advisers, as fieldwork supervisors, and, often, as advisers for student organizations. A student-faculty ratio of only 10:1 allows Wheelock professors to work closely with students both in and out of the classroom.

Student Government

The student government organization is the principal undergraduate governing body on campus. Its members are elected in the spring by the student body. The board meets weekly, often with the dean of students and the president of the College, to discuss issues of concern to the student body. In addition, each residence hall has its own governing body and makes its own policies and regulations. Students sit on many of the administrative committees of the College.

Admission Requirements

Wheelock seeks and admits women and men of all ages from a variety of racial, geographic, ethnic, and economic backgrounds who have the potential for creative, effective work with children and families. Each admission decision is made after careful consideration of an applicant's academic record, SAT and/or ACT scores, graded writing sample, recommendations, and extracurricular activities. On-campus interviews are highly recommended and can be arranged by telephone or online at http://www.wheelock.edu/admissions. A telephone interview can be arranged for those students who are unable to visit the campus. The College has numerous on-campus events throughout the year for prospective students and their families. Students should visit http://www.wheelock.edu/admissions/u_admevents.asp to register for any of the College's events.

Application and Information

A complete Wheelock application consists of the Wheelock application or Common Application with a graded writing sample, one academic recommendation, one guidance counselor recommendation, the high school transcript, SAT and/or ACT scores, and an application fee. The Admissions Committee is glad to review additional information that the candidate feels would be helpful to the committee in making the admission decision. Early Action applications are due by December 1, regular freshman applications on March 1, and transfer applications on April 15. Applicants can expect to hear from the Admissions Office by mid-December for Early Action and within one month after regular applications are completed.

For more information about Wheelock, students should contact:

Lisa Slavin
Dean of Enrollment and Financial Aid
Wheelock College
200 The Riverway
Boston, Massachusetts 02215-4176
Phone: 617-879-2206
800-734-5212 (toll-free)
E-mail: undergrad@wheelock.edu
Web site: http://www.wheelock.edu

Fieldwork in schools, hospitals, and social services settings is one of the focal points of education at Wheelock.

COLLEGE DATA CENTER • MASSACHUSETTS

WORCESTER POLYTECHNIC INSTITUTE

WORCESTER, MASSACHUSETTS

The University

Worcester Polytechnic Institute (WPI) believes in the power of its students to make an impact. They may want to be on the first Mars mission, find alternative energy sources, or work on cancer research. To prepare them for leadership and achievement after college, students do much more than study science and technology in the classroom and lab. They complete projects on campus and around the globe where they connect what they have learned in the classroom with pressing real-life challenges, from human health and the environment to business and engineering as well as the arts and humanities. Students grow personally, professionally, and intellectually as they discover how to apply their talents and turn ideas into tangible solutions.

WPI's aim is to educate students broadly so they can achieve greatly. Though WPI has a more than a 140-year history, the curriculum, like its students, is both innovative and practical. Small classes, a flexible curriculum, and one-on-one interaction with professors at the top of their field make learning at WPI an experience unlike any other.

WPI has been widely recognized for its academic program. WPI was the only technological university out of sixteen national Leadership Institutions selected by the Association of American Colleges and Universities to serve as models of outstanding practices in liberal education. WPI is consistently ranked among the top national universities by *U.S. News & World Report.* In the National Survey of Student Engagement, WPI ranked number one for student-faculty interactions, which is a measure of the quality and quantity of time faculty members spend with undergraduates.

More than thirty-five areas of study in engineering, science, management, and the liberal arts allow many academic options, from molecular biology to music. Exciting new interdisciplinary programs are driven by real-world demand, such as interactive media and game development, robotics engineering, and environmental engineering. The school also offers preprofessional programs and a five-year B.S./M.S. program.

With so many offerings, it is not surprising that more than 40 percent of students change their major at least once. At WPI, a comprehensive academic advising program and a wide array of academic support services help students make the right choices and reach their goals.

WPI students have received some of the nation's highest academic honors: the prestigious Marshall Scholarship, the Goldwater Scholarship, the Rotary Ambassadorial Scholarship, and the Society of Women Engineers Award.

WPI is a member of the Colleges of Worcester Consortium, through which WPI students may register for courses at other colleges within the consortium and may take advantage of a wide range of cultural programming offered by consortium members. A consortium shuttle provides free transportation between campuses.

WPI has twenty varsity (NCAA Division III) athletics teams and thirty-four club and intramural sports. WPI won the Worcester Cup for the three of the last four years for the highest overall winning percentage in all sports in Worcester County. There are eleven fraternities and three sororities, fifteen music or theater ensembles, and dozens of academic clubs, international organizations, religious groups, and other organizations. There are more than 200 student clubs and activities.

Location

With its beautiful architecture, grassy quad, and ivy-covered walls, WPI has a traditional New England campus. Students stop and chat with their friends and professors on tree-lined paths, play pool between classes at the Campus Center, or get a coffee with friends. They study in the sun by the fountain in Reunion Plaza, go cosmic bowling, stop and smell the roses in the formal English garden behind Higgins House, or see a student play at the new Little Theatre.

Home to twelve other colleges and universities and more than 35,000 college students, Worcester is a great college town. Late-night diners, clubs, museums, concert venues, and theaters are right down the hill from WPI in Worcester's vibrant downtown. Boston is less than an hour away by commuter rail, and there are great skiing and snowboarding at nearby Wachusett Mountain. Worcester is centrally located, with easy access to Providence, New York City, the Berkshires, the White Mountains, and Cape Cod.

Majors and Degrees

WPI offers the Bachelor of Science and the Bachelor of Arts degrees. Degree programs are offered in twenty areas of engineering and science: actuarial mathematics, aerospace engineering, biochemistry, biology and biotechnology, biomedical engineering, chemical engineering, chemistry, civil engineering, computer science, electrical and computer engineering, environmental engineering, environmental science, fire protection engineering, industrial engineering, interactive media and game development, manufacturing engineering, mathematical sciences, mechanical engineering, physics, and robotics engineering.

In addition, there are seventeen areas of management and the liberal arts: business/management; economics; environmental policy and development; history; humanities and arts; international studies; literature; management; management engineering; management information systems; music; philosophy and religion; professional writing; psychology/psychological science; society, technology, and policy; system dynamics; and theater.

Three new interdisciplinary majors have been added to the curriculum: interactive media and game development, environmental engineering, and robotics engineering, which is the first undergraduate program in robotics in the nation. WPI offers several preprofessional programs, including dentistry, law, medicine, and veterinary medicine. Students may also design their own majors by combining courses offered in various WPI departments. Undergraduates who wish to continue their studies toward a master's degree at WPI may enroll in a combined, continuous B.S./M.S. program.

Academic Programs

Students take the equivalent of three courses (as either traditional courses or project work) during each of four 7-week terms (two in the fall and two in the spring). At WPI, learning is about more than just theories and ideas. Students learn how to put ideas into practice through the project-enriched curriculum. WPI undergraduates complete two projects before graduation: one directly related to their major and one working with a team of students to solve a problem at the intersection of society and technology—helping to bring electricity to remote villages in Thailand or studying the bioethics of cloning, for example. Students gain valuable professional skills, a talent for team work, and the confidence to dive right in no matter what the challenge.

WPI's academic program encourages collaboration, not competition. Students work closely together in project-oriented classes. Learning how to work in teams prepares students to achieve results and become leaders in life after college, no matter what path they take.

Top-tier employers seek out WPI graduates for their real-world experience and ability to work collaboratively. With a placement rate of more than 90 percent, students are recruited by leading organizations such as Pfizer, General Electric, Fidelity Investments, and IBM. WPI graduates' starting salaries are higher than those of many other college graduates, according to the National Association of Colleges and Employers. Each year, WPI graduates are accepted at many prestigious graduate schools, including MIT, Yale, Princeton, Johns Hopkins, and Tufts University Medical School.

Off-Campus Programs

WPI sends more engineering students abroad than any other university as part of its hands-on, project-enriched curriculum. About half of WPI students complete projects outside the United States and two thirds do projects off campus. With WPI's Global Perspective Program, students experience the challenge of solving real-world problems with their fellow students and immerse themselves in another culture. Students complete projects on campus or at any of the more than twenty project centers located on five continents around the globe, including Thailand, Australia, South Africa, Costa Rica, and the U.S.

Recent project sponsors include NASA Johnson Space Center, Johnson & Johnson, Morgan Stanley, Environmental Protection Agency, and UNESCO. Through their seven-week project experience, students learn valuable professional skills, including communication, team work, and problem solving.

Academic Facilities

Among the many teaching, research, and project facilities available to undergraduates at WPI are a 71,000-square-foot campus center and a new Life Sciences and Bioengineering Center at Gateway Park, which is a state-of-the art facility at the life-sciences-based campus that houses research in regenerative medicine, molecular nanotechnology, biosensors, plant systems, tissue engineering, and untethered health care. A new $11-million Undergraduate Life Sciences Laboratory Center at WPI is scheduled to open in February 2009. The center will become WPI's main facility for undergraduate teaching and research in biology and biotechnology, biomedical engineering, chemistry and biochemistry, and chemical engineering. WPI's other state-of-the-art research facilities include two atomic-force microscopes, medical imaging laboratories, a fire science laboratory, a new team-based chemistry lab, a laser holography lab, a computer music lab, a satellite navigation lab, thirty multimedia classrooms and lecture halls, and a research library with thousands of electronic journals, books, databases, and nearly 300,000 volumes.

The university also has an exceptional computer and networking infrastructure. The facilities include nearly 600 computers in open-access, 24/7 labs; powerful UNIX workstations; a Web-based student information system; a high-speed data network that reaches every building and residence hall; and extensive roaming wireless access. WPI is one of only 208 universities nationwide in the Internet2 (the next-generation Internet) and is one of only six institutions in New England with a node on the Access Grid, a worldwide high-speed multimedia conferencing network.

In addition to these existing facilities, a state-of-the art apartment-style residence hall is scheduled to open in fall 2008. The building features recreation and fitness space, technology suites on the each floor, meeting rooms on the ground floor for group projects, and wireless access.

Plans are also under way for a new athletic, recreation, and wellness complex.

Costs

For 2007–08, full-time tuition was $34,300. Room and board charges were $10,410.

Financial Aid

For families with established financial need, aid, including financial aid packages, on-campus jobs, and loan programs, is available. In addition, all applicants are considered for merit scholarships. More information is available from WPI's Office of Financial Aid (http://www.wpi.edu/+finaid).

Faculty

Besides being passionate about teaching, WPI's 324 full- and part-time faculty members are committed researchers and scholars with world-class credentials. They are leading contributors to the fields of nanotechnology, cryptography, fuel cells, and more. Eleven members of the current faculty are Fulbright Scholars, and more than 40 are fellows of top national and international societies. Since 1994, 17 WPI professors have won the National Science Foundations CAREER Award, which is its most prestigious award for young faculty members. WPI has a 13:1 student-faculty ratio. According to *U.S. News & World Report*, faculty resources, which include salary, class size, and student-faculty ratio, rank thirtieth among national universities.

Student Government

Through the Student Government Association, the Interfraternity Council, the Panhellenic Association, and the International Student Council, students self-govern and develop their own social programs. WPI prides itself on being a caring community that respects the contributions of individuals, appreciates the diversity of the student body, and emphasizes the importance of cooperation and teamwork.

Admission Requirements

Applicants for admission must have completed 4 years of English and mathematics (including precalculus) and 2 years of lab science. Admission requirements include a school transcript, SAT or ACT scores or alternative materials through WPI's Flex Path, recommendations from a science or math teacher and a counselor, and a personal essay. For international students whose first language is not English, a TOEFL or IELTS score is required.

The university has high standards for applicants but also looks for more from a student than just outstanding academic performance. WPI takes care to admit students who will likely thrive at the university. They tend to be creative and curious; like to work in teams to get things done; are comfortable making their own decisions and setting their own courses; love math and science but feel just as passionate about literature, music, movies, and the arts; prefer to be leaders, not followers; and are ready to make a positive impact on the world around them.

Students are encouraged to visit the WPI campus to learn more about the university, see its facilities, and hear firsthand about the WPI experience from students and faculty members. WPI is open most school holidays and offers a wide range of options for tours, group information sessions, open houses, personal interviews, and Saturday visits. Details and schedules may be obtained from the Web site of the Office of Admissions.

The deadline for Early Action Round 1 is November 15, with notification by December 15. The deadline for Early Action Round 2 is January 1, with notification by February 1. The Regular Decision deadline is February 1, with notification by April 1. For transfer admissions, the priority deadline is April 15; students are notified of admission decisions on a rolling basis.

Application and Information

To schedule a visit or request more information, students should contact:

Office of Admissions
Bartlett Center
Worcester Polytechnic Institute
100 Institute Road
Worcester, Massachusetts 01609-2280
Phone: 508-831-5286
Fax: 508-831-5875
E-mail: admissions@wpi.edu
Internet: http://admissions.wpi.edu

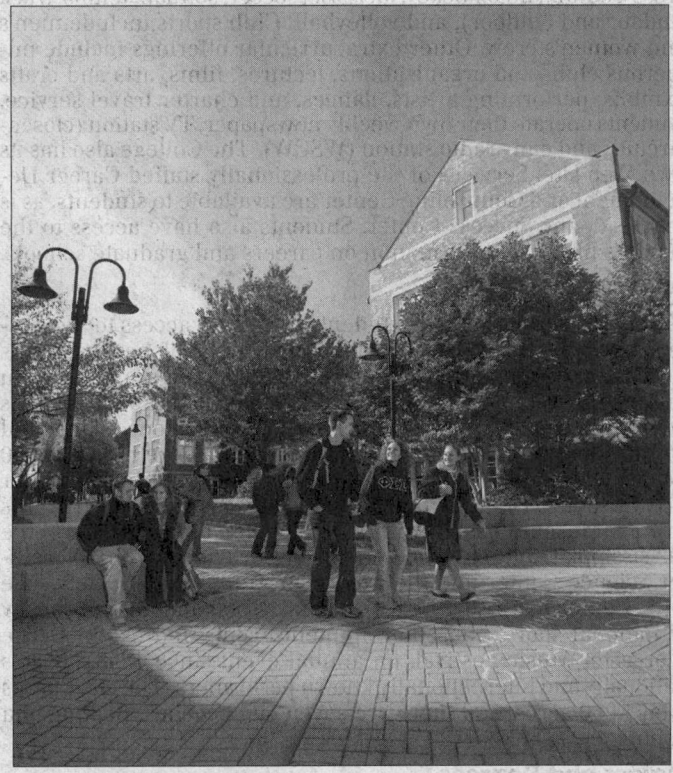

A view of the campus at Worcester Polytechnic Institute.

WORCESTER STATE COLLEGE

WORCESTER, MASSACHUSETTS

The College

Founded in 1874, Worcester State College (WSC) has a long, impressive record of teacher education. Worcester State College has developed into a comprehensive liberal arts institution with more than 3,200 undergraduates and 850 graduate and professional students and a full-time faculty of 173. A wide range of four-year degree programs are offered, as are a number of graduate programs leading to master's degrees. An emphasis on allied health and biotechnology programs leads the College into the twenty-first century. Worcester State's signature program is education, and the College recently embarked on a program to strengthen its leadership in teacher training.

Worcester State College is located on 58 acres on the outskirts of New England's third-largest city and consists of nine major complexes: the Administration Building, the Sullivan Academic Center, the Learning Resource Center, the Ghosh Center for Science and Technology, the gymnasium, the Student Center, Wasylean Hall, Dowden Hall, and Chandler Village. The Student Center provides cultural, social, and personal growth and opportunities and offers many services and conveniences for students. The center serves as the "hearthstone" of the campus community. A 550-space parking garage opened in fall 2007.

The College's athletic department provides numerous opportunities for all students to participate in intercollegiate and intramural athletics. Varsity sports for men are baseball, basketball, cross-country, football, golf, hockey, soccer, tennis, and track (indoor and outdoor). Varsity sports for women are basketball, cross-country, field hockey, lacrosse, soccer, softball, tennis, track (indoor and outdoor), and volleyball. Club sports include men's and women's crew. Other extracurricular offerings include numerous clubs and organizations, lectures, films, arts and crafts exhibits, performing artists, dances, and charter travel service. Students operate their own weekly newspaper, TV station (closed-circuit), and daily radio station (WSCW). The College also has its own Web site. Services of the professionally staffed Career Development and Counseling Center are available to students, as is the Academic Success Center. Students also have access to the center's library of information on careers and graduate schools.

Location

Through a shuttle service, students have easy access to Worcester, which is called the "Heart of New England" because of its location at the geographic center of the six-state region. Rich in history, the city has a population of 170,000 and is about 40 miles west of Boston; 45 miles north of Providence, Rhode Island; and 60 miles northeast of Hartford, Connecticut. More than 700,000 people live less than an hour's drive from the city. The Worcester Art Museum is one of the finest in the country. The Higgins Armory Museum has the greatest collection of armor east of the Mississippi. Other cultural benefits are provided by the Worcester Science Center and the American Antiquarian Society. The DCU Center has a seating capacity of 15,500 and hosts a variety of national sports and entertainment events and exhibits. The Worcester Music Festival, an annual event since 1858, attracts nationally and internationally known performers. The city's parks total 1,290 acres, and there are seven city beaches. Boating and fishing are available in Worcester.

Majors and Degrees

Worcester State College confers the Bachelor of Arts, Bachelor of Science, and Bachelor of Science in Education degrees. Majors are offered in biology, biotechnology, business administration, chemistry, communication sciences and disorders, communications, community health, computer science, criminal justice, economics, education, English, geography, health education, history, mathematics, natural science, nursing (a four-year program and an upper-division program for RNs), occupational therapy, psychology, sociology, Spanish, and urban studies. Minors are available in art, biology, business administration, chemistry, communication disorders, communications, community health, computer science, economics, English, French, geography, health education, history, information technology, mathematics, Middle East studies, music, natural science, philosophy, physics, political science, psychology, sociology, Spanish, theater, urban studies, and Web design. Provisional certification programs are offered in early childhood and elementary education, with a minor available in secondary education.

Academic Programs

The academic year is divided into two semesters, the first beginning in early September and ending in late December and the second beginning in mid-January and ending in late May. The College offers a strong futuristic focus in health and biomedical sciences while continuing its traditional commitment to liberal arts and sciences, business, and teacher education. Volunteer internships, which can be undertaken for college credit, are available in business and social service agencies, in biomedical and biotechnology firms, and in government and the media. Internships are available locally as well as in Washington, D.C., and at Disney World.

Off-Campus Programs

Each semester, full-time students at Worcester State may take one course free of charge on a space-available basis at any of the other institutions in the Colleges of Worcester Consortium. Because Worcester State is one of nine state colleges participating in College Academic Program Sharing (CAPS), students may study for a semester or a year at another of the state colleges. Worcester State College has joint admissions agreements with all of the Massachusetts public community colleges.

Full-time students at Worcester State may spend one semester abroad at Worcester College in Worcester, England, or at the University of Puerto Rico in Cayey as part of a student exchange program. Additional exchange programs are being developed. In addition, opportunities to study abroad in any one of more than twenty different countries are open to students from any public institution of higher education in Massachusetts under the auspices of the Massachusetts Council for International Education, which is headquartered at the University of Massachusetts Amherst.

Academic Facilities

The Science and Technology Building is a state-of-the-art building designed to house the science and allied health programs. The building contains thirty science, therapy, and computer labs; administrative and faculty offices; conference/seminar rooms; and student discussion areas. Also located in the building are a Speech/Language/Hearing Clinic, a 200-seat multimedia classroom, and an eighty-seat general-use computer lab. The Sullivan Academic Center houses state-of-the-art classrooms and administrative and faculty offices. The Administration Building houses administrative and faculty offices and classrooms. In addition to its fitness and athletic facilities, the Gymnasium Building includes general classrooms and art studios.

The Learning Resources Center (LRC) houses the library, a comfortable place for study and research, with more than 150,000 volumes and approximately 800 current periodicals. A CD-ROM network electronically provides ready access to several resources. The library is part of a joint effort of fifteen academic, public, and special-collection libraries that share advanced technologies in library and information sciences. In addition, the building houses the Media Center, which provides student access to television, radio, and film production facilities. The LRC also houses a complex of modern telecommunications and electronic learning facilities. Among these are a writing classroom, a math lab, and several labs for use in computer science classes. In addition, a bank of computers is available for general use by members of the campus community. The College supports both PCs and Macintoshes. All labs are networked and are tied to the campus fiber-optic network; this provides students with Internet connections and access to the Web. Additional computer labs are located in the various academic departments to afford the opportunity to integrate computer technology throughout the curriculum. The College is a completely wireless campus environment.

The Academic Success Center, located in the gymnasium, is dedicated to fostering a healthy academic climate on campus. The Success Center is responsible for academic advising. In addition, the Learning Assistance Center provides individual tutoring services designed to increase student academic effectiveness. The Counseling and Career Service Centers provide services to all students seeking assistance in the areas of personal and career development. They are also responsible for minority affairs, disability services, and the orientation program.

Costs

Tuition for full-time study in 2007–08 is $970 for in-state residents and $7050 for out-of-state students. Yearly fees are $4894, and the cost of books and supplies averages $650. Annual campus housing costs average $6836 (room and board) for a double room and nineteen meals per week. Apartments and single rooms are available at a higher cost. All costs are subject to change.

Financial Aid

Students at Worcester State College may apply for all forms of federal, state, and institutional grant and loan assistance by submitting prior to March 1 a Free Application for Federal Student Aid (FAFSA) and a Worcester State College Financial Aid Application. In addition to need-based financial aid and academic scholarships, the College also offers a tuition payment plan. Academic scholarships, offered to promising freshmen at the time of their acceptance, are also available to upperclass students who demonstrate scholarly excellence.

Faculty

There are 173 full-time faculty members, of whom almost 76 percent hold earned doctorates. With the student-faculty ratio of 17:1, there is ample opportunity for interaction between students and faculty members. Upon matriculation and declaration of a major, each student is assigned a faculty adviser, who assists him or her in developing an educational program. The major adviser also guides students throughout their years at the College.

Student Government

The Student Government Association (SGA) is the representative body of the undergraduate student population. Its goals include advocacy of student concerns and rights, involvement in academic and administrative policy decisions, and facilitation of communications between administration, faculty members, staff members, and students. Payment of the activity fee entitles any undergraduate student to participate in the Association through selection of representation, involvement in legislative and administrative meetings, seeking of elected office, appointment to institutional committees, and involvement in other activities of the Association. The SGA annually elects a student representative to sit as a voting member of the College's Board of Trustees.

Admission Requirements

The College admits applicants who have demonstrated strong academic ability. Acceptance of high school seniors and those who have graduated within the past two years is determined by the high school transcript, academic units, and a minimum grade point average (GPA) of 3.0. This GPA is recalculated using only college-preparatory course work. Applicants with GPAs below 3.0 may be considered for admission by using a sliding scale that includes the GPA and total SAT scores. For those students whose primary language is not English, a minimum TOEFL score of 550 on the paper-based test, 213 on the computer-based test, or 79 on the Internet-based test is required. Additional standards for admission are a minimum of sixteen college-preparatory courses taken in the following subject areas: English (four), mathematics (three), natural science (three), social science (two), foreign language (two), and elective courses (two) from these same disciplines, as well as computer science, visual/performing arts, and humanities.

Worcester State College also welcomes applications from transfer students. In order to be eligible, students must meet one of the following sets of criteria: 12 or more transferable college credits and a 2.5 college GPA; up to 24 transferable college credits, a 2.0 college GPA, and a high school transcript that meets the admission standards for freshman applicants; or 24 or more transferable college credits and a 2.0 college GPA. Transfer applicants should arrange to have all college transcripts as well as a final high school transcript sent directly to the Admissions Office.

Although admission interviews are not required, applicants are urged to visit the College during scheduled information sessions, campus tours, or to seek information from the offices concerned with academic advising, athletics, financial aid, housing, and student activities. For information on campus tours or open campus events, students should contact the Admission Office.

Application and Information

The application deadline for the January semester is December 1. The application priority deadline for September is June 1 for first-time freshmen and July 1 for transfers. Applications received after this date are reviewed on the basis of vacancies. High school candidates are strongly encouraged to apply after the first marking period of the senior year. Applicants are notified of admission decisions on a rolling basis. Letters of notification are forwarded starting in early November for the spring semester and mid-December for the fall semester.

Candidates to either the occupational therapy or nursing programs must submit their applications by January 15; notifications are forwarded starting in mid-December.

International students' deadline to apply for the September semester deadline is April 1. Translations from a professional evaluating agency in the United States must be provided for all international transcripts. Candidates must also submit results of the SAT (or a TOEFL score if English is not the primary language) and an affidavit of financial support.

Application forms may be obtained by contacting:

Admission Office
Worcester State College
486 Chandler Street
Worcester, Massachusetts 01602
Phone: 508-929-8040
866-WSC-CALL (toll-free)
Fax: 508-929-8183
E-mail: admissions@worcester.edu
Web site: http://www.worcester.edu

MICHIGAN

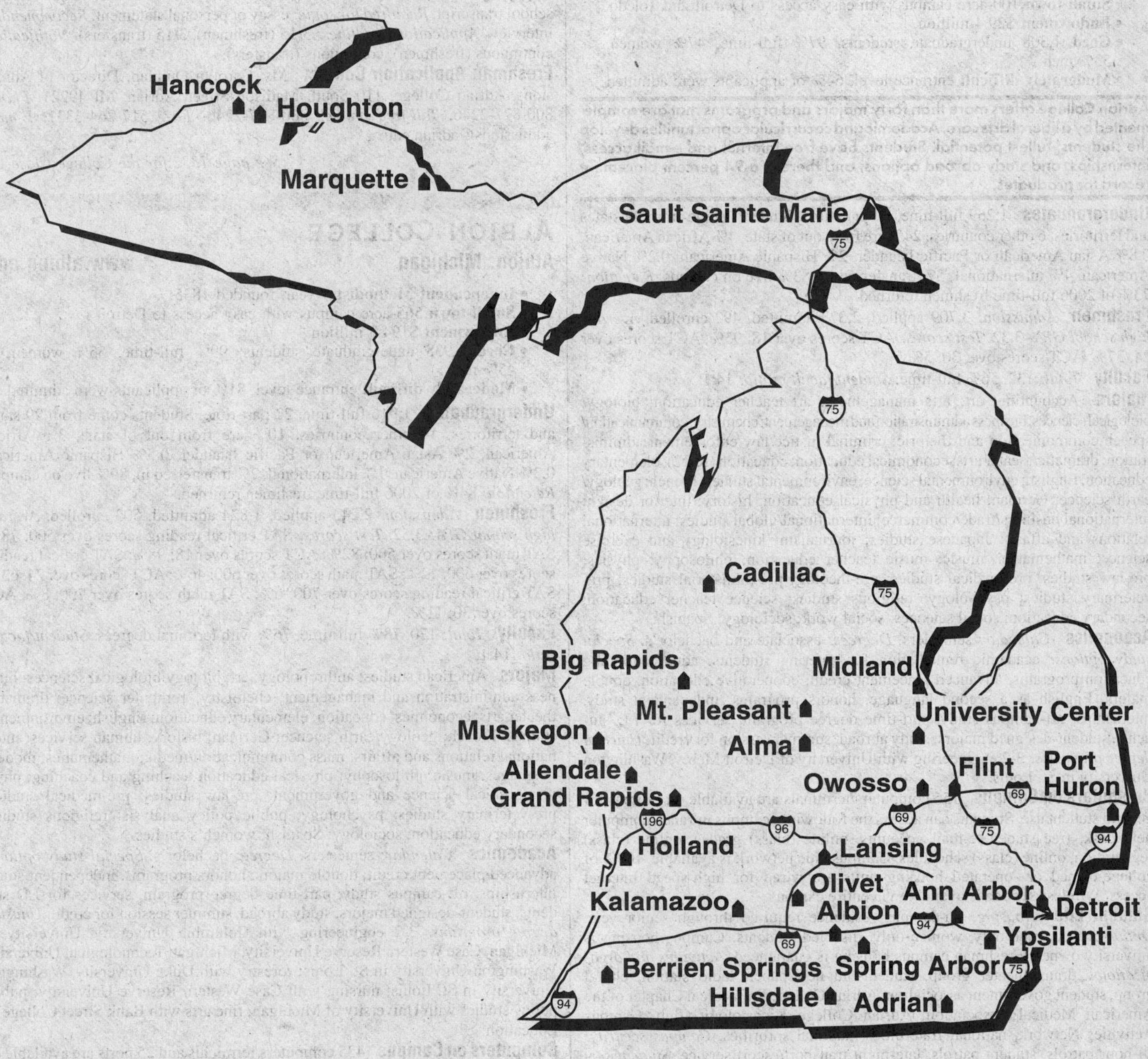

The Detroit area includes the towns of Auburn Hills, Clinton Township, Dearborn, Farmington Hills, Livonia, Oak Park, Orchard Lake, Rochester, Rochester Hills, Southfield, Troy, and Warren.

The Lansing area includes the town of East Lansing.

ADRIAN COLLEGE

Adrian, Michigan **www.adrian.edu/**

- **Independent** 4-year, founded 1859, affiliated with United Methodist Church
- **Small-town** 100-acre campus with easy access to Detroit and Toledo
- **Endowment** $39.4 million
- **Coed** 1,308 undergraduate students, 97% full-time, 47% women, 53% men
- **Moderately difficult** entrance level, 64% of applicants were admitted

Adrian College offers more than forty majors and programs that are complemented by a liberal arts core. Academic and cocurricular opportunities develop the students' fullest potential. Students have free Internet and e-mail access, internships, and study-abroad options, and there is a 94 percent placement record for graduates.

Undergraduates 1,269 full-time, 39 part-time. Students come from 29 states and territories, 6 other countries, 24% are from out of state, 4% African American, 0.8% Asian American or Pacific Islander, 2% Hispanic American, 0.2% Native American, 4% international, 5% transferred in, 83% live on campus. *Retention:* 73% of 2006 full-time freshmen returned.

Freshmen *Admission:* 3,709 applied, 2,373 admitted, 492 enrolled. *Average high school GPA:* 3.32. *Test scores:* ACT scores over 18: 95%; ACT scores over 24: 37%; ACT scores over 30: 5%.

Faculty *Total:* 132, 56% full-time. *Student/faculty ratio:* 14:1.

Majors Accounting; art; arts management; art teacher education; biology/biological sciences; business administration and management; chemistry; communication/speech communication and rhetoric; criminal justice/law enforcement administration; dramatic/theater arts; economics; education; education (K-12); elementary education; English; environmental science; environmental studies; French; geology/earth science; German; health and physical education; history; interior design; international business/trade/commerce; international/global studies; international relations and affairs; Japanese studies; journalism; kinesiology and exercise science; mathematics; music; music teacher education; philosophy; physics; pre-law studies; pre-medical studies; pre-theology/pre-ministerial studies; pre-veterinary studies; psychology; religious studies; science teacher education; secondary education; social sciences; social work; sociology; Spanish.

Academics *Calendar:* semesters. *Degrees:* associate and bachelor's. *Special study options:* academic remediation for entering students, adult/continuing education programs, advanced placement credit, cooperative education, double majors, English as a second language, honors programs, independent study, internships, off-campus study, part-time degree program, services for LD students, student-designed majors, study abroad, summer session for credit. *Unusual degree programs:* 3-2 engineering with University of Detroit Mercy, Washington University in St. Louis.

Computers on Campus 156 computers/terminals are available on campus for general student use. Students can access the following: campus intranet, computer help desk, free student e-mail accounts, online (class) grades, online (class) registration, online (class) schedules. Campuswide network is available. 100% of college-owned or -operated housing units are wired for high-speed Internet access. Wireless service is available via entire campus.

Student Life *Housing:* on-campus residence required through senior year. *Options:* coed, men-only, women-only, disabled students. Campus housing is university owned. Freshman campus housing is guaranteed. *Activities and organizations:* drama/theater group, student-run newspaper, radio station, choral group, student government association, Adrian College Premedical Chapter of the American Medical Association, Adrian College Kinesiology Club, Campus Activities Network, national fraternities, national sororities. *Campus security:* 24-hour patrols, student patrols, late-night transport/escort service. *Student services:* health clinic, personal/psychological counseling.

Athletics Member NCAA. All Division III. *Intercollegiate sports:* baseball M, basketball M/W, bowling W, cross-country running M/W, football M, golf M/W, ice hockey M/W, lacrosse M/W, soccer M/W, softball W, tennis M/W, track and field M/W, volleyball W. *Intramural sports:* badminton M/W, basketball M/W, bowling M/W, cheerleading W (c), football M/W, golf M, ice hockey M (c), lacrosse M/W, racquetball M/W, soccer M/W, softball M/W, tennis M/W, volleyball M/W.

Standardized Tests *Required:* SAT or ACT (for admission). *Recommended:* ACT (for admission).

Costs (2008–09) *Comprehensive fee:* $30,990 includes full-time tuition ($23,090), mandatory fees ($300), and room and board ($7600). Part-time tuition: $670 per credit hour. *Required fees:* $75 per term part-time. *College room only:* $3400.

Financial Aid Of all full-time matriculated undergraduates who enrolled in 2006, 923 applied for aid, 732 were judged to have need, 503 had their need fully met, 102 Federal Work-Study jobs (averaging $1800). 414 state and other part-time jobs (averaging $1747). In 2006, 183 non-need-based awards were made. *Average percent of need met:* 98%. *Average financial aid package:* $17,074. *Average need-based loan:* $4235. *Average need-based gift aid:* $10,282. *Average non-need-based aid:* $8059. *Average indebtedness upon graduation;* $20,849.

Applying *Options:* electronic application, deferred entrance. *Required:* high school transcript. *Required for some:* essay or personal statement. *Recommended:* interview. *Application deadlines:* 3/15 (freshmen), 3/15 (transfers). *Notification:* continuous (freshmen), continuous (transfers).

Freshman Application Contact Ms. Carolyn Quinlan, Director of Admissions, Adrian College, 110 South Madison Street, Adrian, MI 49221. *Phone:* 800-877-2246. *Toll-free phone:* 800-877-2246. *Fax:* 517-264-3331. *E-mail:* admissions@adrian.edu.

See page 1332 for the College Close-Up.

ALBION COLLEGE

Albion, Michigan **www.albion.edu/**

- **Independent Methodist** 4-year, founded 1835
- **Small-town** 565-acre campus with easy access to Detroit
- **Endowment** $194.3 million
- **Coed** 1,938 undergraduate students, 99% full-time, 55% women, 45% men
- **Moderately difficult** entrance level, 81% of applicants were admitted

Undergraduates 1,916 full-time, 22 part-time. Students come from 29 states and territories, 14 other countries, 10% are from out of state, 3% African American, 2% Asian American or Pacific Islander, 0.5% Hispanic American, 0.3% Native American, 1% international, 2% transferred in, 89% live on campus. *Retention:* 84% of 2006 full-time freshmen returned.

Freshmen *Admission:* 2,243 applied, 1,824 admitted, 503 enrolled. *Average high school GPA:* 3.52. *Test scores:* SAT critical reading scores over 500: 78%; SAT math scores over 500: 82%; ACT scores over 18: 98%; SAT critical reading scores over 600: 42%; SAT math scores over 600: 46%; ACT scores over 24: 63%; SAT critical reading scores over 700: 6%; SAT math scores over 700: 8%; ACT scores over 30: 11%.

Faculty *Total:* 170, 78% full-time, 76% with terminal degrees. *Student/faculty ratio:* 14:1.

Majors American studies; anthropology; art; biology/biological sciences; business administration and management; chemistry; computer science; dramatic/theater arts; economics; education; elementary education; English; environmental studies; French; geology/earth science; German; history; human services; international relations and affairs; mass communication/media; mathematics; modern languages; music; philosophy; physical education teaching and coaching; physics; political science and government; pre-law studies; pre-medical studies; pre-veterinary studies; psychology; public policy analysis; religious studies; secondary education; sociology; Spanish; women's studies.

Academics *Calendar:* semesters. *Degree:* bachelor's. *Special study options:* advanced placement credit, double majors, honors programs, independent study, internships, off-campus study, part-time degree program, services for LD students, student-designed majors, study abroad, summer session for credit. *Unusual degree programs:* 3-2 engineering with Columbia University, University of Michigan, Case Western Reserve University, Michigan Technological University, Washington University in St. Louis; forestry with Duke University, Washington University in St. Louis; nursing with Case Western Reserve University; public policy studies with University of Michigan, fine arts with Bank Street College of Education.

Computers on Campus 435 computers/terminals and 25 ports are available on campus for general student use. Students can access the following: campus intranet, computer help desk, free student e-mail accounts, online (class) grades, online (class) registration, online (class) schedules, online student account and financial aid. Campuswide network is available. 100% of college-owned or -operated housing units are wired for high-speed Internet access. Wireless service is available via classrooms, computer centers, computer labs, dorm rooms, learning centers, libraries, student centers.

Student Life *Housing:* on-campus residence required through senior year. *Options:* coed, men-only, women-only, cooperative, disabled students. Campus housing is university owned. Freshman campus housing is guaranteed. *Activities and organizations:* drama/theater group, student-run newspaper, radio station, choral group, marching band, Student Volunteer Bureau, Union Board, Inter-Varsity Christian Fellowship, Student Senate, Frisbee and Disc Club, national fraternities, national sororities. *Campus security:* 24-hour emergency response devices and patrols, student patrols, late-night transport/escort service, controlled dormitory access. *Student services:* health clinic, personal/psychological counseling, women's center.

Athletics Member NCAA. All Division III. *Intercollegiate sports:* baseball M, basketball M/W, cheerleading M/W, cross-country running M/W, equestrian sports M/W, football M, golf M/W, soccer M/W, softball W, swimming and diving M/W, tennis M/W, track and field M/W, volleyball M (c)/W. *Intramural sports:* badminton M/W, basketball M/W, bowling M/W, equestrian sports M (c)/W (c), field hockey W, football M/W, golf W, ice hockey M (c)/W (c), lacrosse M (c)/W (c), racquetball M/W, rugby M (c)/W (c), sailing M (c)/W (c), soccer M/W, softball M/W, swimming and diving M/W, tennis M/W, ultimate Frisbee M/W, volleyball M/W, water polo M (c)/W (c).

Standardized Tests *Required:* SAT or ACT (for admission). *Recommended:* SAT and SAT Subject Tests or ACT (for admission).

Costs (2007–08) *Comprehensive fee:* $35,336 includes full-time tuition ($27,054), mandatory fees ($476), and room and board ($7806). Part-time tuition: $1150 per quarter hour. *Required fees:* $238 per term part-time. *College room only:* $3818. Room and board charges vary according to housing facility. *Payment plans:* installment, deferred payment. *Waivers:* children of alumni and employees or children of employees.

Financial Aid Of all full-time matriculated undergraduates who enrolled in 2007, 1,339 applied for aid, 1,175 were judged to have need, 494 had their need fully met. 640 Federal Work-Study jobs (averaging $1326). In 2007, 692 non-need-based awards were made. *Average percent of need met:* 91%. *Average financial aid package:* $22,108. *Average need-based loan:* $4957. *Average need-based gift aid:* $17,360. *Average non-need-based aid:* $12,322. *Average indebtedness upon graduation:* $25,340.

Applying *Options:* electronic application, early admission, early action, deferred entrance. *Application fee:* $20. *Required:* essay or personal statement, high school transcript, 1 letter of recommendation. *Required for some:* interview. *Recommended:* minimum 3.2 GPA. *Application deadlines:* 3/1 (freshmen), 6/1 (transfers), 12/1 (early action). *Notification:* continuous (freshmen), 8/1 (transfers), 1/1 (early action).

Director of Admissions Mr. Doug Kellar, Associate Vice President for Enrollment, Albion College, 611 East Porter Street, Albion, MI 49224. *Phone:* 517-629-0600. *Toll-free phone:* 800-858-6770. *E-mail:* admissions@albion.edu.

ALMA COLLEGE

Alma, Michigan www.alma.edu/

- **Independent Presbyterian** 4-year, founded 1886
- **Small-town** 125-acre campus
- **Endowment** $112.9 million
- **Coed** 1,355 undergraduate students, 95% full-time, 57% women, 43% men
- **Moderately difficult** entrance level, 78% of applicants were admitted

Undergraduates 1,294 full-time, 61 part-time. Students come from 26 states and territories, 9 other countries, 4% are from out of state, 1% African American, 2% Asian American or Pacific Islander, 2% Hispanic American, 0.4% Native American, 1% international, 2% transferred in, 88% live on campus. *Retention:* 83% of 2006 full-time freshmen returned.

Freshmen *Admission:* 2,044 applied, 1,598 admitted, 423 enrolled. *Average high school GPA:* 3.49. *Test scores:* SAT critical reading scores over 500: 75%; SAT math scores over 500: 86%; SAT writing scores over 500: 76%; ACT scores over 18: 98%; SAT critical reading scores over 600: 43%; SAT math scores over 600: 47%; SAT writing scores over 600: 40%; ACT scores over 24: 51%; SAT critical reading scores over 700: 11%; SAT math scores over 700: 18%; SAT writing scores over 700: 4%; ACT scores over 30: 8%.

Faculty *Total:* 119, 68% full-time, 69% with terminal degrees. *Student/faculty ratio:* 13:1.

Majors Accounting; anthropology; art; art teacher education; biochemistry; biological and physical sciences; biology/biological sciences; biology teacher education; business administration and management; chemistry; chemistry teacher education; communication and media related; computer science; computer teacher education; dance; design and visual communications; dramatic/theater arts; early childhood education; economics; education; elementary education; English; English/language arts teacher education; fine/studio arts; French; French language teacher education; German; German language teacher education; gerontology; graphic design; health science; health teacher education; history; history teacher education; humanities; international business/trade/commerce; kindergarten/preschool education; kinesiology and exercise science; liberal arts and sciences/liberal studies; marketing/marketing management; mathematics; mathematics teacher education; medical illustration; modern languages; music; music performance; music teacher education; philosophy; physical education teaching and coaching; physics; physics teacher education; political science and government; pre-dentistry studies; pre-law studies; pre-medical studies; pre-theology/pre-ministerial studies; pre-veterinary studies; psychology; psychology teacher education; public health; religious studies; science teacher education; secondary education; social sciences; social science teacher education; social studies teacher education; sociology; Spanish; Spanish language teacher education.

Academics *Calendar:* 4-4-1. *Degree:* bachelor's. *Special study options:* academic remediation for entering students, advanced placement credit, double majors, honors programs, independent study, internships, off-campus study, services for LD students, student-designed majors, study abroad, summer session for credit. *ROTC:* Army (c). *Unusual degree programs:* 3-2 engineering with University of Michigan, Michigan Technological University; occupational therapy with Washington University in St. Louis.

Computers on Campus 292 computers/terminals are available on campus for general student use. Students can access the following: campus intranet, computer help desk, free student e-mail accounts, online (class) grades, online (class) registration, online (class) schedules. Campuswide network is available. 100% of college-owned or -operated housing units are wired for high-speed Internet access. Wireless service is available via classrooms, dorm rooms, libraries, student centers.

Student Life *Housing:* on-campus residence required through senior year. *Options:* coed, women-only. Campus housing is university owned. Freshman campus housing is guaranteed. *Activities and organizations:* drama/theater group, student-run newspaper, radio station, choral group, marching band, Ambassadors, Alma College Union Board, New Life Campus Ministries, Student Congress, SOS (Students Offering Service), national fraternities, national sororities. *Campus security:* 24-hour emergency response devices and patrols. *Student services:* health clinic, personal/psychological counseling, women's center.

Athletics Member NCAA. All Division III. *Intercollegiate sports:* baseball M, basketball M/W, cross-country running M/W, football M, golf M/W, soccer M/W, softball W, swimming and diving M/W, tennis M/W, track and field M/W, volleyball W. *Intramural sports:* basketball M/W, cheerleading M (c)/W (c), football M, lacrosse M (c), racquetball M, skiing (downhill) M/W, soccer M/W, softball M/W, tennis M/W, ultimate Frisbee M/W, volleyball M/W.

Standardized Tests *Required:* SAT or ACT (for admission).

Costs (2007–08) *One-time required fee:* $300. *Comprehensive fee:* $31,462 includes full-time tuition ($23,478), mandatory fees ($210), and room and board ($7774). Part-time tuition: $910 per credit. Part-time tuition and fees vary according to course load. *College room only:* $3830. Room and board charges vary according to board plan and housing facility. *Payment plans:* installment, deferred payment. *Waivers:* employees or children of employees.

Financial Aid Of all full-time matriculated undergraduates who enrolled in 2007, 1,298 applied for aid, 1,012 were judged to have need, 339 had their need fully met. 140 Federal Work-Study jobs (averaging $950). 30 state and other part-time jobs (averaging $700). In 2007, 267 non-need-based awards were made. *Average percent of need met:* 85%. *Average financial aid package:* $20,805. *Average need-based loan:* $5933. *Average need-based gift aid:* $15,933. *Average non-need-based aid:* $14,700. *Average indebtedness upon graduation:* $23,736.

Applying *Options:* electronic application, deferred entrance. *Application fee:* $25. *Required:* high school transcript, minimum 3.0 GPA, minimum SAT score of 1030 or ACT score of 22. *Required for some:* essay or personal statement, letters of recommendation. *Recommended:* interview. *Application deadlines:* rolling (freshmen), rolling (transfers). *Notification:* continuous (freshmen), continuous (transfers).

Freshman Application Contact Mr. Evan Montague, Director of Admissions, Alma College, Admissions Office, Alma, MI 48801-1599. *Toll-free phone:* 800-321-ALMA. *Fax:* 989-463-7057. *E-mail:* admissions@alma.edu.

See page 1334 for the College Close-Up.

ANDREWS UNIVERSITY

Berrien Springs, Michigan www.andrews.edu/

- **Independent Seventh-day Adventist** university, founded 1874
- **Small-town** 1650-acre campus
- **Endowment** $28.4 million
- **Coed** 1,777 undergraduate students, 86% full-time, 56% women, 44% men
- **Moderately difficult** entrance level, 57% of applicants were admitted

Undergraduates 1,524 full-time, 253 part-time. Students come from 49 states and territories, 47 other countries, 56% are from out of state, 22% African American, 9% Asian American or Pacific Islander, 11% Hispanic American, 0.5% Native American, 14% international, 9% transferred in, 58% live on campus. *Retention:* 77% of 2006 full-time freshmen returned.

Freshmen *Admission:* 1,298 applied, 735 admitted, 337 enrolled. *Average high school GPA:* 3.41. *Test scores:* SAT critical reading scores over 500: 68%; SAT math scores over 500: 57%; SAT writing scores over 500: 67%; ACT scores over 18: 88%; SAT critical reading scores over 600: 30%; SAT math scores over 600: 28%; SAT writing scores over 600: 22%; ACT scores over 24: 45%; SAT critical reading scores over 700: 8%; SAT math scores over 700: 8%; SAT writing scores over 700: 1%; ACT scores over 30: 2%.

Faculty *Total:* 327, 62% full-time, 63% with terminal degrees. *Student/faculty ratio:* 10:1.

Majors Accounting; agribusiness; anatomy; architectural engineering; architecture; art; art teacher education; audiology and speech-language pathology; behavioral sciences; biblical studies; biochemistry; biology/biological sciences; biomedical technology; biophysics; botany/plant biology; business/managerial economics; chemistry; clinical laboratory science/medical technology; computer and information sciences; computer programming; computer science; dietetics; economics; education; elementary education; English; family and community services; family and consumer economics related; foods, nutrition, and wellness; French; history; horticultural science; information science/studies; journalism; landscaping and groundskeeping; marketing/marketing management; mass communication/media; mathematics; mechanical engineering; music; music teacher education; neurobiology and neurophysiology; nursing (registered nurse training); physical therapy; physics; piano and organ; political science and government; pre-law studies; pre-medical studies; pre-veterinary studies; psychology; public relations/image management; religious education; religious studies; science teacher education; secondary education; social sciences; social work; sociology; Spanish; theology; voice and opera; youth ministry; zoology/animal biology.

Academics *Calendar:* semesters. *Degrees:* associate, bachelor's, master's, doctoral, first professional, and post-master's certificates. *Special study options:* academic remediation for entering students, accelerated degree program, adult/continuing education programs, advanced placement credit, cooperative education, distance learning, double majors, English as a second language, freshman honors college, honors programs, internships, off-campus study, part-time degree program, student-designed majors, study abroad, summer session for credit. *Unusual degree programs:* 3-2 physical therapy and architecture.

Computers on Campus 130 computers/terminals are available on campus for general student use. Students can access the following: campus intranet, computer help desk, free student e-mail accounts, online (class) grades, online (class) registration, online (class) schedules, degree audit. Campuswide network is available. 99% of college-owned or -operated housing units are wired for high-speed Internet access. Wireless service is available via classrooms, computer centers, computer labs, learning centers, libraries, student centers.

Student Life *Housing:* on-campus residence required through senior year. *Options:* men-only, women-only. Campus housing is university owned. Freshman campus housing is guaranteed. *Activities and organizations:* drama/theater group, student-run newspaper, radio station, choral group. *Campus security:* 24-hour emergency response devices and patrols, controlled dormitory access. *Student services:* health clinic, personal/psychological counseling.

Athletics *Intramural sports:* basketball M/W, football M/W, golf M/W, gymnastics M/W, racquetball M/W, soccer M/W, softball M/W, volleyball M/W, water polo M/W.

Standardized Tests *Required:* SAT or ACT (for admission).

Costs (2008–09) *Comprehensive fee:* $26,260 includes full-time tuition ($19,320), mandatory fees ($610), and room and board ($6330). Part-time tuition: $805 per credit hour. *College room only:* $3380.

Financial Aid Of all full-time matriculated undergraduates who enrolled in 2006, 1,086 applied for aid, 989 were judged to have need, 126 had their need fully met. 505 Federal Work-Study jobs (averaging $1320). 233 state and other part-time jobs (averaging $1220). In 2006, 512 non-need-based awards were made. *Average percent of need met:* 86%. *Average financial aid package:* $21,635. *Average need-based loan:* $5162. *Average need-based gift aid:* $7161. *Average non-need-based aid:* $4995. *Average indebtedness upon graduation:* $28,365.

Applying *Options:* electronic application, deferred entrance. *Application fee:* $32. *Required:* essay or personal statement, high school transcript, minimum 2.25 GPA, 2 letters of recommendation. *Application deadlines:* rolling (freshmen), rolling (transfers). *Notification:* continuous (freshmen), continuous (transfers).

Freshman Application Contact Shanna Leak, Undergraduate Admissions Coordinator, Andrews University, Berrien Springs, MI 49104. *Phone:* 800-253-2874. *Toll-free phone:* 800-253-2874. *Fax:* 269-471-3228. *E-mail:* enroll@andrews.edu.

AQUINAS COLLEGE

Grand Rapids, Michigan **www.aquinas.edu/**

- **Independent Roman Catholic** comprehensive, founded 1886
- **Suburban** 107-acre campus with easy access to Detroit
- **Endowment** $27.8 million
- **Coed** 1,827 undergraduate students, 83% full-time, 64% women, 36% men
- **Moderately difficult** entrance level, 81% of applicants were admitted

Undergraduates 1,515 full-time, 312 part-time. Students come from 23 states and territories, 6 other countries, 4% are from out of state, 4% African American, 2% Asian American or Pacific Islander, 3% Hispanic American, 0.5% Native American, 0.2% international, 4% transferred in, 41% live on campus. *Retention:* 74% of 2006 full-time freshmen returned.

Freshmen *Admission:* 2,086 applied, 1,680 admitted, 412 enrolled. *Average high school GPA:* 3.38. *Test scores:* ACT scores over 18: 95%; ACT scores over 24: 40%; ACT scores over 30: 5%.

Faculty *Total:* 183, 50% full-time, 50% with terminal degrees. *Student/faculty ratio:* 14:1.

Majors Accounting; art; art history, criticism and conservation; arts management; art teacher education; athletic training; biology/biological sciences; business administration and management; business/corporate communications; ceramic arts and ceramics; chemistry; clinical laboratory science/medical technology; communication/speech communication and rhetoric; computer and information sciences; computer science; dramatic/theater arts; drawing; economics; education; elementary education; English; English as a second/foreign language (teaching); English/language arts teacher education; environmental science; environmental studies; fine/studio arts; French; general studies; geography; German; health teacher education; history; international business/trade/commerce; international relations and affairs; Japanese; liberal arts and sciences/liberal studies; mathematics; music; music performance; music teacher education; organizational communication; painting; philosophy; photography; physical education teaching and coaching; physics; political science and government; pre-law studies; printmaking; psychology; reading teacher education; religious education; religious/sacred music; religious studies; science teacher education; sculpture; secondary education; social sciences; social studies teacher education; sociology; Spanish; special education (specific learning disabilities); urban studies/affairs.

Academics *Calendar:* semesters. *Degrees:* associate, bachelor's, and master's. *Special study options:* academic remediation for entering students, accelerated degree program, adult/continuing education programs, advanced placement credit, cooperative education, distance learning, double majors, external degree program, honors programs, independent study, internships, off-campus study, part-time degree program, services for LD students, student-designed majors, study abroad, summer session for credit.

Computers on Campus 153 computers/terminals are available on campus for general student use. Students can access the following: campus intranet, computer help desk, free student e-mail accounts. Campuswide network is available. 30% of college-owned or -operated housing units are wired for high-speed Internet access. Wireless service is available via classrooms, dorm rooms, learning centers, libraries, student centers.

Student Life *Housing:* on-campus residence required through sophomore year. *Options:* coed. Campus housing is university owned. Freshman campus housing is guaranteed. *Activities and organizations:* drama/theater group, student-run newspaper, radio station, choral group, Community Senate Programming Board, Aquinas Times, JAMMIN (multicultural group). *Campus security:* 24-hour emergency response devices and patrols, student patrols, late-night transport/escort service, controlled dormitory access. *Student services:* health clinic, personal/psychological counseling, women's center.

Athletics Member NAIA. *Intercollegiate sports:* baseball M (s), basketball M (s)/W (s), cross-country running M (s)/W (s), golf M (s)/W (s), soccer M (s)/W (s), softball W (s), tennis M (s)/W (s), track and field M (s)/W (s), volleyball W (s). *Intramural sports:* basketball M/W, football M/W, golf M, ice hockey M, skiing (cross-country) M/W, skiing (downhill) M/W, soccer M/W, softball M/W, tennis M/W, volleyball M/W.

Standardized Tests *Required:* SAT or ACT (for admission).

Costs (2008–09) *Comprehensive fee:* $27,828 includes full-time tuition ($21,150) and room and board ($6678). Part-time tuition: $428 per credit. *College room only:* $3084.

Financial Aid Of all full-time matriculated undergraduates who enrolled in 2003, 1,181 applied for aid, 1,056 were judged to have need, 430 had their need fully met. 134 Federal Work-Study jobs (averaging $700). In 2003, 416 non-need-based awards were made. *Average percent of need met:* 92%. *Average financial aid package:* $15,461. *Average need-based loan:* $2800. *Average need-based gift aid:* $12,661. *Average non-need-based aid:* $8266. *Average indebtedness upon graduation:* $13,638. *Financial aid deadline:* 8/15.

Applying *Options:* electronic application, early admission, deferred entrance. *Required:* high school transcript, minimum 2.5 GPA. *Required for some:* essay or personal statement, interview. *Application deadlines:* rolling (freshmen), rolling (transfers).

Freshman Application Contact Ms. Erika Davis, Applications Specialist, Aquinas College, 1607 Robinson Road, SE, Grand Rapids, MI 49506-1799. *Phone:* 616-632-2851. *Toll-free phone:* 800-678-9593. *Fax:* 616-732-4469. *E-mail:* admissions@aquinas.edu.

See page 1336 for the College Close-Up.

The Art Institute of Michigan

Novi, Michigan **www.artinstitutes.edu/detroit/**

- **Proprietary** 4-year, part of The Art Institutes International/The Illinois Institute of Art-Chicago
- **Coed**

Majors Advertising; apparel and textile marketing management; culinary arts; design and visual communications; fashion merchandising; graphic design; interior design; restaurant, culinary, and catering management; web page, digital/multimedia and information resources design.

Academics *Degrees:* diplomas, associate, and bachelor's.

Computers on Campus Students can access the following: computer help desk.

Student Life *Housing:* college housing not available.

Costs (2007–08) *Tuition:* $433 per credit hour part-time. tuition cost varies by program. Prospective students should contact the school for current tuition costs. Other charges include a starting kit for all first-quarter students. Kits vary in price depending on the program of study.

Applying *Application fee:* $50. *Required:* essay or personal statement, high school transcript. *Recommended:* interview.

Director of Admissions Ms. Melanie L. Gibson, Senior Director of Admissions, The Art Institute of Michigan, 28125 Cabot Drive, Suite 120, Novi, MI 48377. *Phone:* 248-675-3801. *Toll-free phone:* 800-479-0087. *Fax:* 248-675-3830. *E-mail:* mgibson@aii.edu.

See page 1338 for the College Close-Up.

Ave Maria College

Ypsilanti, Michigan **www.avemaria.edu/**

Freshman Application Contact Ms. Nicole Myshak, Admissions Counselor, Ave Maria College, 300 West Forest Avenue, Ypsilanti, MI 48197. *Phone:* 734-337-4527. *Toll-free phone:* 866-866-3030. *Fax:* 734-337-4140. *E-mail:* admissions@avemaria.edu.

Baker College of Allen Park

Allen Park, Michigan **www.baker.edu/**

- **Independent** 4-year, founded 2003, part of Baker College System
- **Suburban** 13-acre campus with easy access to Detroit
- **Coed, primarily women** 2,204 undergraduate students, 53% full-time, 75% women, 25% men
- 100% of applicants were admitted

Undergraduates 1,168 full-time, 1,036 part-time. Students come from 1 other state, 33% African American, 1% Asian American or Pacific Islander, 5% Hispanic American, 0.5% Native American.

Freshmen *Admission:* 900 applied, 900 admitted.

Faculty *Total:* 88, 2% full-time, 13% with terminal degrees. *Student/faculty ratio:* 34:1.

Majors Accounting; business administration and management; computer and information sciences; computer science; computer systems networking and telecommunications; data entry/microcomputer applications; data entry/microcomputer applications related; early childhood education; executive assistant/executive secretary; interior design; marketing/marketing management; medical/clinical assistant; medical insurance coding; medical insurance/medical billing; medical office computer specialist; receptionist; web page, digital/multimedia and information resources design; word processing.

Academics *Calendar:* quarters. *Degrees:* certificates, diplomas, associate, and bachelor's.

Computers on Campus 100 computers/terminals are available on campus for general student use. Students can access the following: online (class) registration. Campuswide network is available.

Student Life *Housing:* college housing not available. *Campus security:* 24-hour patrols. *Student services:* personal/psychological counseling.

Costs (2008–09) *Tuition:* $6840 full-time, $190 per quarter hour part-time.

Applying *Required:* high school transcript, interview. *Application deadline:* 9/24 (freshmen). *Notification:* continuous (transfers).

Freshman Application Contact Mr. Steve Peterson, Vice President of Admissions, Baker College of Allen Park, 4500 Enterprise Drive, Allen Park, MI 48101. *Phone:* 313-425-3700. *Toll-free phone:* 800-767-4120. *E-mail:* steve.peterson@baker.edu.

Baker College of Auburn Hills

Auburn Hills, Michigan **www.baker.edu/**

- **Independent** 4-year, founded 1911, part of Baker College System
- **Urban** 7-acre campus with easy access to Detroit
- **Coed** 3,702 undergraduate students, 49% full-time, 72% women, 28% men
- **Noncompetitive** entrance level, 100% of applicants were admitted

Undergraduates 1,814 full-time, 1,888 part-time. Students come from 1 other state, 18% African American, 3% Asian American or Pacific Islander, 3% Hispanic American, 0.9% Native American.

Freshmen *Admission:* 1,484 applied, 1,484 admitted.

Faculty *Total:* 155, 7% full-time, 15% with terminal degrees. *Student/faculty ratio:* 41:1.

Majors Accounting; administrative assistant and secretarial science; business administration and management; commercial and advertising art; computer typography and composition equipment operation; data processing and data processing technology; diagnostic medical sonography and ultrasound technology; drafting and design technology; education; health/health care administration; health information/medical records administration; interior design; legal administrative assistant/secretary; marketing/marketing management; medical administrative assistant and medical secretary; medical/clinical assistant; system, networking, and LAN/WAN management.

Academics *Calendar:* quarters. *Degrees:* certificates, diplomas, associate, bachelor's, and postbachelor's certificates. *Special study options:* academic remediation for entering students, accelerated degree program, advanced placement credit, cooperative education, distance learning, double majors, external degree program, independent study, internships, part-time degree program, services for LD students, summer session for credit.

Computers on Campus 110 computers/terminals are available on campus for general student use. Students can access the following: online (class) registration. Campuswide network is available.

Student Life *Housing:* college housing not available. *Activities and organizations:* Baker Business Club, Interior Design Society, Students Action in Engineering, Marketing Club. *Campus security:* 24-hour emergency response devices.

Costs (2008–09) *Tuition:* $6840 full-time, $190 per quarter hour part-time.

Applying *Options:* early admission, deferred entrance. *Application fee:* $20. *Required:* high school transcript. *Application deadlines:* rolling (freshmen), rolling (transfers).

Freshman Application Contact Ms. Jan Bohlen, Vice President for Admissions, Baker College of Auburn Hills, 1500 University Drive, Auburn Hills, MI 48326-1586. *Phone:* 248-340-0600. *Toll-free phone:* 888-429-0410. *Fax:* 248-340-0608. *E-mail:* jan.bohlen@baker.edu.

Baker College of Cadillac

Cadillac, Michigan **www.baker.edu/**

- **Independent** 4-year, founded 1986, part of Baker College System
- **Small-town** 40-acre campus
- **Coed** 1,806 undergraduate students, 55% full-time, 74% women, 26% men
- **Noncompetitive** entrance level, 100% of applicants were admitted

Undergraduates 993 full-time, 813 part-time. Students come from 4 states and territories, 0.2% African American, 0.1% Asian American or Pacific Islander, 0.1% Hispanic American, 0.1% Native American. *Retention:* 69% of 2006 full-time freshmen returned.

Freshmen *Admission:* 595 applied, 595 admitted.

Faculty *Total:* 105, 4% full-time, 5% with terminal degrees. *Student/faculty ratio:* 42:1.

Majors Administrative assistant and secretarial science; computer graphics; computer typography and composition equipment operation; data processing and data processing technology; education; electrical, electronic and communications engineering technology; emergency medical technology (EMT paramedic); health information/medical records administration; marketing/marketing management; medical administrative assistant and medical secretary; medical/clinical assistant; quality control technology; veterinary/animal health technology.

Academics *Calendar:* quarters. *Degrees:* certificates, diplomas, associate, and bachelor's. *Special study options:* academic remediation for entering students, advanced placement credit, cooperative education, distance learning, double majors, external degree program, independent study, internships, part-time degree program, services for LD students, summer session for credit.

Computers on Campus 77 computers/terminals are available on campus for general student use. Students can access the following: online (class) registration. Campuswide network is available.
Student Life *Housing:* college housing not available. *Campus security:* 24-hour emergency response devices.
Standardized Tests *Required for some:* SAT or ACT (for admission).
Costs (2008–09) *Tuition:* $6840 full-time, $190 per quarter hour part-time.
Applying *Options:* early admission, deferred entrance. *Application fee:* $20. *Required:* high school transcript. *Recommended:* interview. *Application deadlines:* rolling (freshmen), rolling (transfers).
Freshman Application Contact Mr. Mike Tisdale, Director of Admissions, Baker College of Cadillac, 9600 East 13th Street, Cadillac, MI 49601. *Phone:* 231-876-3100. *Toll-free phone:* 888-313-3463. *Fax:* 231-775-8505. *E-mail:* mike.tisdale@baker.edu.

BAKER COLLEGE OF CLINTON TOWNSHIP

Clinton Township, Michigan **www.baker.edu/**

- **Independent** 4-year, founded 1990, part of Baker College System
- **Urban** 25-acre campus with easy access to Detroit
- **Coed** 5,608 undergraduate students, 50% full-time, 76% women, 24% men
- **Noncompetitive** entrance level, 100% of applicants were admitted

Undergraduates 2,804 full-time, 2,804 part-time. Students come from 2 states and territories, 20% African American, 2% Asian American or Pacific Islander, 2% Hispanic American, 0.9% Native American.
Freshmen *Admission:* 2,709 applied, 2,709 admitted.
Faculty *Total:* 208, 8% full-time, 12% with terminal degrees. *Student/faculty ratio:* 45:1.
Majors Accounting; administrative assistant and secretarial science; architectural engineering technology; business automation/technology/data entry; commercial and advertising art; computer typography and composition equipment operation; data processing and data processing technology; drafting and design technology; emergency medical technology (EMT paramedic); health information/medical records administration; human services; information science/studies; interior design; kindergarten/preschool education; legal administrative assistant/secretary; marketing/marketing management; medical administrative assistant and medical secretary; medical/clinical assistant; nursing (registered nurse training); radiologic technology/science; surgical technology.
Academics *Calendar:* quarters. *Degrees:* certificates, diplomas, associate, and bachelor's. *Special study options:* academic remediation for entering students, advanced placement credit, cooperative education, external degree program, internships, part-time degree program, services for LD students, summer session for credit.
Computers on Campus 127 computers/terminals are available on campus for general student use. Campuswide network is available.
Student Life *Housing:* college housing not available. *Campus security:* 24-hour emergency response devices and patrols, evening security guard. *Student services:* personal/psychological counseling.
Standardized Tests *Required for some:* SAT or ACT (for admission).
Costs (2008–09) *Tuition:* $6840 full-time, $190 per quarter hour part-time.
Applying *Options:* electronic application, early admission, deferred entrance. *Application fee:* $20. *Required:* high school transcript. *Application deadlines:* rolling (freshmen), rolling (transfers).
Freshman Application Contact Ms. Annette Looser, Vice President for Admissions, Baker College of Clinton Township, 34401 South Gratiot Avenue, Clinton Township, MI 48035. *Phone:* 586-790-3000. *Toll-free phone:* 888-272-2842. *Fax:* 586-791-6811. *E-mail:* annette.looser@baker.edu.

BAKER COLLEGE OF FLINT

Flint, Michigan **www.baker.edu/**

- **Independent** 4-year, founded 1911, part of Baker College System
- **Urban** 30-acre campus with easy access to Detroit
- **Coed** 5,808 undergraduate students, 55% full-time, 71% women, 29% men
- **Noncompetitive** entrance level, 100% of applicants were admitted

Undergraduates 3,194 full-time, 2,614 part-time. Students come from 5 states and territories, 1% are from out of state, 20% African American, 0.7% Asian American or Pacific Islander, 2% Hispanic American, 0.6% Native American, 2% live on campus.
Freshmen *Admission:* 2,536 applied, 2,536 admitted.
Faculty *Total:* 315, 13% full-time, 12% with terminal degrees. *Student/faculty ratio:* 31:1.
Majors Accounting technology and bookkeeping; airline pilot and flight crew; architectural drafting and CAD/CADD; automobile/automotive mechanics technology; avionics maintenance technology; biomedical technology; business administration and management; business/commerce; computer graphics; computer systems networking and telecommunications; computer teacher education; computer typography and composition equipment operation; construction management; data processing and data processing technology; energy management and systems technology; entrepreneurship; environmental engineering technology; executive assistant/executive secretary; family and community services; health/health care administration; health information/medical records administration; health information/medical records technology; hospitality administration; human services; industrial technology; legal administrative assistant/secretary; management information systems; mechanical drafting and CAD/CADD; mechanical engineering; mechanical engineering/mechanical technology; medical administrative assistant and medical secretary; medical/clinical assistant; medical transcription; nursing (registered nurse training); occupational therapy; orthotics/prosthetics; pharmacy technician; physical therapist assistant; quality control technology; sales, distribution and marketing; surgical technology; tourism and travel services management; transportation technology; vehicle/equipment operation.
Academics *Calendar:* quarters. *Degrees:* certificates, diplomas, associate, and bachelor's. *Special study options:* academic remediation for entering students, accelerated degree program, advanced placement credit, cooperative education, distance learning, double majors, external degree program, independent study, internships, part-time degree program, services for LD students, summer session for credit.
Computers on Campus 412 computers/terminals are available on campus for general student use. Campuswide network is available.
Student Life *Housing:* on-campus residence required for freshman year. *Options:* coed. Campus housing is university owned. *Activities and organizations:* Occupational Therapy Club, Interior Design Society, Medical Assistants Student Organization, Physical Therapist Assistant Club. *Campus security:* 24-hour patrols, late-night transport/escort service, controlled dormitory access, video monitoring of high traffic areas. *Student services:* personal/psychological counseling.
Costs (2008–09) *Tuition:* $6840 full-time, $190 per quarter hour part-time. *Room only:* $2650.
Applying *Options:* early admission, deferred entrance. *Application fee:* $20. *Required:* high school transcript. *Application deadlines:* 9/20 (freshmen), 9/20 (transfers).
Freshman Application Contact Ms. Jodi Cunelz, Director of Admissions, Baker College of Flint, 1050 West Bristol Road, Flint, MI 48507-5508. *Phone:* 810-766-4008. *Toll-free phone:* 800-964-4299. *Fax:* 810-766-4049.

BAKER COLLEGE OF JACKSON

Jackson, Michigan **www.baker.edu/**

- **Independent** 4-year, founded 1994, part of Baker College System
- **Urban** 42-acre campus with easy access to Lansing
- **Coed** 1,813 undergraduate students, 51% full-time, 77% women, 23% men
- **Noncompetitive** entrance level, 100% of applicants were admitted

Undergraduates 924 full-time, 889 part-time. Students come from 2 states and territories, 1% are from out of state, 6% African American, 0.7% Asian American or Pacific Islander, 2% Hispanic American, 0.2% Native American.
Freshmen *Admission:* 684 applied, 684 admitted.
Faculty *Total:* 85, 6% full-time, 13% with terminal degrees. *Student/faculty ratio:* 36:1.
Majors Administrative assistant and secretarial science; business/commerce; communication/speech communication and rhetoric; computer typography and composition equipment operation; data processing and data processing technology; early childhood education; health information/medical records administration; health information/medical records technology; legal administrative assistant/secretary; marketing research; medical administrative assistant and medical secretary; medical/clinical assistant; medical transcription; office management; pharmacy technician; sales, distribution and marketing; surgical technology; veterinary/animal health technology.
Academics *Calendar:* quarters. *Degrees:* certificates, diplomas, associate, and bachelor's. *Special study options:* academic remediation for entering students, accelerated degree program, advanced placement credit, cooperative education,

distance learning, double majors, external degree program, independent study, internships, part-time degree program, services for LD students, summer session for credit.

Computers on Campus 110 computers/terminals are available on campus for general student use. Students can access the following: online (class) registration. Campuswide network is available.

Student Life *Housing:* college housing not available. *Campus security:* 24-hour emergency response devices. *Student services:* personal/psychological counseling.

Costs (2008–09) *Tuition:* $6840 full-time, $190 per quarter hour part-time.

Applying *Options:* electronic application, early admission, deferred entrance. *Application fee:* $20. *Required:* high school transcript. *Application deadlines:* 9/19 (freshmen), rolling (transfers). *Notification:* continuous (freshmen).

Freshman Application Contact Ms. Kelli Stepka, Vice President for Admissions, Baker College of Jackson, 2800 Springport Road, Jackson, MI 49202. *Phone:* 517-788-7800. *Toll-free phone:* 888-343-3683. *Fax:* 517-789-7331. *E-mail:* kelli.stepka@baker.edu.

BAKER COLLEGE OF MUSKEGON

Muskegon, Michigan **www.baker.edu/**

- **Independent** 4-year, founded 1888, part of Baker College System
- **Suburban** 40-acre campus with easy access to Grand Rapids
- **Coed** 5,010 undergraduate students, 63% full-time, 71% women, 29% men
- **Noncompetitive** entrance level, 100% of applicants were admitted

Undergraduates 3,156 full-time, 1,854 part-time. Students come from 13 states and territories, 1% are from out of state, 14% African American, 0.4% Asian American or Pacific Islander, 4% Hispanic American, 0.6% Native American, 11% live on campus.

Freshmen *Admission:* 2,247 applied, 2,247 admitted.

Faculty *Total:* 177, 10% full-time, 8% with terminal degrees. *Student/faculty ratio:* 55:1.

Majors Administrative assistant and secretarial science; airline pilot and flight crew; architectural drafting and CAD/CADD; aviation/airway management; commercial and advertising art; computer and information sciences; computer programming; computer science; corrections; culinary arts; data processing and data processing technology; emergency medical technology (EMT paramedic); hotel/motel administration; human services; industrial technology; interior design; kindergarten/preschool education; legal administrative assistant/secretary; medical administrative assistant and medical secretary; medical/clinical assistant; nursing (registered nurse training); occupational therapist assistant; pharmacy technician; physical therapist assistant; quality control technology; radiologic technology/science; rehabilitation therapy; speech-language pathology; surgical technology; tourism and travel services management; veterinary/animal health technology.

Academics *Calendar:* quarters. *Degrees:* certificates, diplomas, associate, and bachelor's. *Special study options:* academic remediation for entering students, accelerated degree program, adult/continuing education programs, advanced placement credit, cooperative education, distance learning, double majors, external degree program, independent study, internships, part-time degree program, services for LD students, summer session for credit.

Computers on Campus 165 computers/terminals are available on campus for general student use. Students can access the following: free student e-mail accounts. Campuswide network is available.

Student Life *Housing:* on-campus residence required for freshman year. *Options:* coed, disabled students. Campus housing is university owned. Freshman applicants given priority for college housing. *Activities and organizations:* Accounting Club, Rehab Club, Travel Club, Culinary Club. *Campus security:* 24-hour emergency response devices and patrols, late-night transport/escort service, controlled dormitory access, 24-hour security camera surveillance. *Student services:* personal/psychological counseling.

Costs (2008–09) *Tuition:* $6840 full-time, $190 per quarter hour part-time. *Room only:* $2600.

Applying *Options:* electronic application, early admission, deferred entrance. *Application fee:* $20. *Required:* high school transcript. *Application deadlines:* 9/24 (freshmen), rolling (transfers). *Notification:* continuous (freshmen).

Freshman Application Contact Ms. Kathy Jacobson, Vice President of Admissions, Baker College of Muskegon, 1903 Marquette Avenue, Muskegon, MI 49442-3497. *Phone:* 231-777-5207. *Toll-free phone:* 800-937-0337. *Fax:* 231-777-5201. *E-mail:* kathy.jacobson@baker.edu.

BAKER COLLEGE OF OWOSSO

Owosso, Michigan **www.baker.edu/**

- **Independent** 4-year, founded 1984, part of Baker College System
- **Small-town** 32-acre campus
- **Coed** 2,911 undergraduate students, 67% full-time, 69% women, 31% men
- **Noncompetitive** entrance level, 100% of applicants were admitted

Undergraduates 1,950 full-time, 961 part-time. Students come from 4 states and territories, 4% African American, 0.3% Asian American or Pacific Islander, 2% Hispanic American, 0.5% Native American, 15% live on campus.

Freshmen *Admission:* 1,321 applied, 1,321 admitted.

Faculty *Total:* 144, 6% full-time, 15% with terminal degrees. *Student/faculty ratio:* 40:1.

Majors Accounting; administrative assistant and secretarial science; architectural engineering technology; business administration and management; clinical/medical laboratory technology; commercial and advertising art; computer engineering technology; computer programming; computer science; construction engineering technology; consumer merchandising/retailing management; data processing and data processing technology; diagnostic medical sonography and ultrasound technology; drafting and design technology; electrical, electronic and communications engineering technology; environmental engineering technology; health/health care administration; hospitality administration; hotel/motel administration; human resources management; industrial radiologic technology; information science/studies; interior design; kindergarten/preschool education; legal administrative assistant/secretary; marketing/marketing management; medical administrative assistant and medical secretary; medical/clinical assistant; nursing (registered nurse training).

Academics *Calendar:* quarters. *Degrees:* certificates, diplomas, associate, and bachelor's. *Special study options:* academic remediation for entering students, accelerated degree program, adult/continuing education programs, advanced placement credit, cooperative education, external degree program, internships, part-time degree program, services for LD students, summer session for credit.

Computers on Campus 190 computers/terminals are available on campus for general student use. Campuswide network is available.

Student Life *Housing options:* coed. *Activities and organizations:* student-run newspaper, Accounting Club, Travel Club, Management Club, Baker Health Information Management Club, RAD Club. *Campus security:* 24-hour emergency response devices and patrols, late-night transport/escort service, controlled dormitory access. *Student services:* personal/psychological counseling.

Costs (2008–09) *Tuition:* $6840 full-time, $190 per quarter hour part-time. *Room only:* $2500.

Applying *Options:* early admission, deferred entrance. *Application fee:* $20. *Required:* high school transcript. *Application deadlines:* rolling (freshmen), rolling (transfers).

Freshman Application Contact Mr. Michael Konopacke, Vice President for Admissions, Baker College of Owosso, Owosso, MI 48867. *Phone:* 989-729-3350. *Toll-free phone:* 800-879-3797. *Fax:* 517-729-3359. *E-mail:* mike.konopacke@baker.edu.

BAKER COLLEGE OF PORT HURON

Port Huron, Michigan **www.baker.edu/**

- **Independent** 4-year, founded 1990, part of Baker College System
- **Urban** 10-acre campus with easy access to Detroit
- **Coed** 1,642 undergraduate students, 65% full-time, 75% women, 25% men
- **Noncompetitive** entrance level, 100% of applicants were admitted

Undergraduates 1,067 full-time, 575 part-time. Students come from 1 other state, 4% African American, 0.3% Asian American or Pacific Islander, 2% Hispanic American, 0.5% Native American.

Freshmen *Admission:* 617 applied, 617 admitted.

Faculty *Total:* 126, 10% full-time, 7% with terminal degrees. *Student/faculty ratio:* 28:1.

Majors Architectural engineering technology; commercial and advertising art; computer programming; data processing and data processing technology; dental hygiene; diagnostic medical sonography and ultrasound technology; drafting and design technology; environmental engineering technology; health/health care administration; health information/medical records administration; hotel/motel administration; interior design; legal administrative assistant/secretary; medical administrative assistant and medical secretary; medical/clinical assistant.

Academics *Calendar:* quarters. *Degrees:* diplomas, associate, and bachelor's. *Special study options:* academic remediation for entering students, accelerated degree program, advanced placement credit, cooperative education, distance learning, double majors, external degree program, independent study, internships, part-time degree program, services for LD students, summer session for credit.

Computers on Campus 145 computers/terminals are available on campus for general student use. Students can access the following: online (class) registration, software. Campuswide network is available.

Student Life *Housing:* college housing not available. *Activities and organizations:* Travel Club, Student Association Dental Hygienists of America. *Campus security:* 24-hour emergency response devices, late-night transport/escort service. *Student services:* personal/psychological counseling.

Costs (2008–09) *Tuition:* $6840 full-time, $190 per quarter hour part-time.

Applying *Options:* early admission, deferred entrance. *Application fee:* $20. *Required:* high school transcript, interview. *Application deadlines:* 9/24 (freshmen), rolling (transfers). *Notification:* continuous (freshmen), continuous (transfers).

Freshman Application Contact Mr. Daniel Kenny, Vice President for Admissions, Baker College of Port Huron, 3403 Lapeer Road, Port Huron, MI 48060-2597. *Phone:* 810-985-7000. *Toll-free phone:* 888-262-2442. *Fax:* 810-985-7066. *E-mail:* kenny_d@porthuron.baker.edu.

CALVIN COLLEGE

Grand Rapids, Michigan **www.calvin.edu/**

- **Independent** comprehensive, founded 1876, affiliated with Christian Reformed Church
- **Suburban** 370-acre campus
- **Endowment** $107.3 million
- **Coed** 4,169 undergraduate students, 97% full-time, 54% women, 46% men
- **Moderately difficult** entrance level, 95% of applicants were admitted

Academic excellence, Christian commitment, reasonable cost, 4,200 students, 100 academic options. Calvin College receives high marks from *U.S. News & World Report's* "America's Best Colleges," *The National Review College Guide*, the *Templeton Guide: Colleges that Encourage Character Development*, the *Fiske Guide to Colleges*, and *Barron's Best Buys in College Education*.

Undergraduates 4,027 full-time, 142 part-time. Students come from 49 states and territories, 45 other countries, 44% are from out of state, 1% African American, 3% Asian American or Pacific Islander, 2% Hispanic American, 0.1% Native American, 7% international, 2% transferred in, 59% live on campus. *Retention:* 89% of 2006 full-time freshmen returned.

Freshmen *Admission:* 2,277 applied, 2,169 admitted, 1,039 enrolled. *Average high school GPA:* 3.59. *Test scores:* SAT critical reading scores over 500: 83%; SAT math scores over 500: 86%; ACT scores over 18: 100%; SAT critical reading scores over 600: 47%; SAT math scores over 600: 47%; ACT scores over 24: 72%; SAT critical reading scores over 700: 14%; SAT math scores over 700: 13%; ACT scores over 30: 17%.

Faculty *Total:* 407, 79% full-time, 71% with terminal degrees. *Student/faculty ratio:* 12:1.

Majors Accounting; art; art history, criticism and conservation; art teacher education; Asian studies; audiology and speech-language pathology; biblical studies; bilingual and multilingual education; biochemistry; biological and physical sciences; biology/biological sciences; biotechnology; business administration and management; business/corporate communications; chemical engineering; chemistry; civil engineering; classics and languages, literatures and linguistics; communication/speech communication and rhetoric; computer science; conducting; development economics and international development; digital communication and media/multimedia; dramatic/theater arts; economics; electrical, electronics and communications engineering; elementary education; engineering; English; English as a second/foreign language (teaching); environmental studies; film/cinema studies; fine/studio arts; French; geography; geology/earth science; German; Germanic languages related; history; interdisciplinary studies; international relations and affairs; kinesiology and exercise science; Latin; management information systems; mass communication/media; mathematics; mechanical engineering; modern Greek; music; music history, literature, and theory; music performance; music teacher education; music theory and composition; natural sciences; nursing (registered nurse training); occupational therapy; parks, recreation and leisure; philosophy; physical education teaching and coaching; physical sciences; physics; piano and organ; political science and government; pre-dentistry studies; pre-law studies; pre-medical studies; pre-veterinary studies; psychology; public administration; religious/sacred music; religious studies; science teacher education; secondary education; social sciences; social work; sociology; Spanish; special education; speech and rhetoric; sport and fitness administration/management; theology; therapeutic recreation; voice and opera.

Academics *Calendar:* 4-1-4. *Degrees:* bachelor's, master's, and postbachelor's certificates. *Special study options:* academic remediation for entering students, accelerated degree program, adult/continuing education programs, advanced placement credit, double majors, honors programs, independent study, internships, off-campus study, part-time degree program, services for LD students, student-designed majors, study abroad, summer session for credit. *ROTC:* Army (c). *Unusual degree programs:* 3-2 occupational therapy with Washington University in St. Louis.

Computers on Campus 800 computers/terminals are available on campus for general student use. Students can access the following: computer help desk, free student e-mail accounts, online (class) grades, online (class) registration, online (class) schedules. Campuswide network is available. 100% of college-owned or -operated housing units are wired for high-speed Internet access. Wireless service is available via classrooms, computer centers, computer labs, dorm rooms, libraries, student centers.

Student Life *Housing:* on-campus residence required through sophomore year. *Options:* men-only, women-only. Campus housing is university owned. Freshman campus housing is guaranteed. *Activities and organizations:* drama/theater group, student-run newspaper, television station, choral group, Social Justice Committee, Environmental Stewardship Coalition, Dance Guild, Chimes, Calvin Video Network. *Campus security:* 24-hour emergency response devices and patrols, student patrols, late-night transport/escort service, controlled dormitory access, crime prevention programs, crime alert bulletins. *Student services:* health clinic, personal/psychological counseling.

Athletics Member NCAA. All Division III. *Intercollegiate sports:* baseball M, basketball M/W, cross-country running M/W, golf M/W, ice hockey M (c), lacrosse M (c)/W (c), rock climbing M (c), soccer M/W, softball W, swimming and diving M/W, tennis M/W, track and field M/W, volleyball M (c)/W. *Intramural sports:* badminton M/W, basketball M/W, cross-country running M/W, football M/W, golf M/W, racquetball M/W, soccer M/W, softball M/W, swimming and diving M/W, tennis M/W, track and field M/W, volleyball M/W, water polo M/W.

Standardized Tests *Required:* SAT or ACT (for admission).

Costs (2007–08) *Comprehensive fee:* $29,145 includes full-time tuition ($21,460), mandatory fees ($225), and room and board ($7460). Full-time tuition and fees vary according to program. Part-time tuition: $510 per credit hour. Part-time tuition and fees vary according to course load. *Room and board:* Room and board charges vary according to board plan. *Payment plans:* tuition prepayment, installment. *Waivers:* employees or children of employees.

Financial Aid Of all full-time matriculated undergraduates who enrolled in 2007, 3,059 applied for aid, 2,434 were judged to have need, 710 had their need fully met. 824 Federal Work-Study jobs (averaging $1220). 1,055 state and other part-time jobs (averaging $1275). In 2007, 1238 non-need-based awards were made. *Average percent of need met:* 82%. *Average financial aid package:* $16,220. *Average need-based loan:* $6710. *Average need-based gift aid:* $9400. *Average non-need-based aid:* $4075. *Average indebtedness upon graduation:* $22,800.

Applying *Options:* deferred entrance. *Application fee:* $35. *Required:* essay or personal statement, high school transcript, minimum 2.5 GPA, 1 letter of recommendation. *Recommended:* interview. *Application deadlines:* 8/15 (freshmen), rolling (transfers). *Notification:* continuous (freshmen).

Freshman Application Contact Mr. Dale D. Kuiper, Director of Admissions, Calvin College, 3201 Burton Street, SE, Grand Rapids, MI 49546-4388. *Phone:* 616-526-6106. *Toll-free phone:* 800-688-0122. *Fax:* 616-526-6777. *E-mail:* admissions@calvin.edu.

See page 1340 for the College Close-Up.

CENTRAL MICHIGAN UNIVERSITY

Mount Pleasant, Michigan **www.cmich.edu/**

- **State-supported** university, founded 1892
- **Small-town** 854-acre campus
- **Endowment** $82.4 million
- **Coed** 20,078 undergraduate students, 89% full-time, 56% women, 44% men
- **Moderately difficult** entrance level, 73% of applicants were admitted

Undergraduates 17,775 full-time, 2,303 part-time. Students come from 52 states and territories, 70 other countries, 2% are from out of state, 6% African American, 1% Asian American or Pacific Islander, 2% Hispanic American, 1% Native American, 2% international, 5% transferred in, 33% live on campus. *Retention:* 76% of 2006 full-time freshmen returned.

Freshmen *Admission:* 15,220 applied, 11,165 admitted, 3,819 enrolled. *Average high school GPA:* 3.30. *Test scores:* SAT critical reading scores over 500:

59%; SAT math scores over 500: 66%; ACT scores over 18: 95%; SAT critical reading scores over 600: 18%; SAT math scores over 600: 27%; ACT scores over 24: 32%; SAT critical reading scores over 700: 2%; SAT math scores over 700: 7%; ACT scores over 30: 3%.

Faculty *Total:* 1,141, 65% full-time, 63% with terminal degrees. *Student/faculty ratio:* 21:1.

Majors Accounting; accounting related; acting; actuarial science; advertising; anthropology; art; art teacher education; astronomy; athletic training; automotive engineering technology; biochemistry; biological and biomedical sciences related; biology/biological sciences; biology teacher education; biomedical sciences; business administration and management; business administration, management and operations related; business teacher education; chemistry; chemistry teacher education; child development; clinical laboratory science/medical technology; cognitive science; communication disorders; communication/speech communication and rhetoric; community organization and advocacy; computer science; computer technology/computer systems technology; construction engineering technology; creative writing; dietetics; dramatic/theater arts; early childhood education; economics; education (specific subject areas) related; electrical, electronic and communications engineering technology; electrical, electronics and communications engineering; elementary education; English; English/language arts teacher education; entrepreneurship; environmental science; environmental studies; European studies; family and consumer sciences/home economics teacher education; family systems; fashion merchandising; finance; financial planning and services; fine/studio arts; foodservice systems administration; French; French language teacher education; geography; geography related; geology/earth science; German; German language teacher education; graphic design; health and physical education; health/health care administration; health teacher education; history; history teacher education; hospitality administration; hotel/motel administration; human resources management; industrial production technologies related; interior architecture; international business/trade/commerce; international relations and affairs; journalism; kinesiology and exercise science; logistics and materials management; management information systems; manufacturing engineering; manufacturing technology; marketing/marketing management; mathematics; mathematics and computer science; mathematics teacher education; mechanical engineering; mechanical engineering/mechanical technology; medical microbiology and bacteriology; meteorology; music; music history, literature, and theory; music related; music teacher education; music theory and composition; natural resources/conservation; neuroscience; oceanography (chemical and physical); operations management; organizational communication; parks, recreation and leisure; parks, recreation and leisure facilities management; philosophy; photojournalism; physical education teaching and coaching; physics; physics teacher education; political science and government; psychology; public health education and promotion; public relations/image management; purchasing, procurement/acquisitions and contracts management; radio, television, and digital communication related; real estate; religious studies; retailing; sales, distribution and marketing; science teacher education; social sciences; social sciences related; social studies teacher education; social work; sociology; Spanish; Spanish language teacher education; special education (emotionally disturbed); special education (mentally retarded); speech teacher education; sport and fitness administration/management; statistics; technology/industrial arts teacher education; theater design and technology; therapeutic recreation; women's studies.

Academics *Calendar:* semesters. *Degrees:* bachelor's, master's, doctoral, post-master's, and postbachelor's certificates. *Special study options:* academic remediation for entering students, accelerated degree program, adult/continuing education programs, advanced placement credit, distance learning, double majors, English as a second language, external degree program, freshman honors college, honors programs, independent study, internships, off-campus study, part-time degree program, student-designed majors, study abroad, summer session for credit. *ROTC:* Army (b).

Computers on Campus 3,000 computers/terminals and 1,000 ports are available on campus for general student use. Students can access the following: campus intranet, computer help desk, free student e-mail accounts, online (class) grades, online (class) registration, online (class) schedules, online bill payment. Campuswide network is available. 100% of college-owned or -operated housing units are wired for high-speed Internet access. Wireless service is available via classrooms, computer centers, computer labs, dorm rooms, libraries, student centers.

Student Life *Housing:* on-campus residence required for freshman year. *Options:* coed, men-only, women-only, disabled students. Campus housing is university owned and is provided by a third party. Freshman campus housing is guaranteed. *Activities and organizations:* drama/theater group, student-run newspaper, radio and television station, choral group, marching band, Residence Hall Assembly, Student Government Association, Program Board, national fraternities, national sororities. *Campus security:* 24-hour emergency response devices and patrols, student patrols, late-night transport/escort service, controlled dormitory access. *Student services:* health clinic, personal/psychological counseling, women's center.

Athletics Member NCAA. All Division I except football (Division I-A). *Intercollegiate sports:* baseball M (s), basketball M (s)/W (s), cross-country running M (s)/W (s), field hockey W (s), gymnastics W (s), soccer W (s), softball W (s), track and field M (s)/W (s), volleyball W (s), wrestling M (s). *Intramural sports:* baseball M (c), basketball M/W, bowling M/W, cross-country running M/W, football M/W, golf M/W, ice hockey M (c), lacrosse M (c)/W (c), racquetball M/W, rock climbing M (c)/W (c), rugby M (c)/W (c), skiing (downhill) M (c)/W (c), soccer M/W, softball M/W, table tennis M/W, tennis M/W, track and field M (c)/W (c), ultimate Frisbee M (c)/W (c), volleyball M (c)/W (c), wrestling M.

Standardized Tests *Required:* ACT (for admission).

Costs (2007–08) *Tuition:* state resident $9120 full-time, $304 per credit part-time; nonresident $21,210 full-time, $707 per credit part-time. Full-time tuition and fees vary according to student level. Part-time tuition and fees vary according to student level. No tuition increase for student's term of enrollment. costs at Central Michigan University are based upon a guaranteed undergraduate tuition plan called the CMU Promise. The CMU Promise to new and transfer undergraduate students is one unchanging tuition rate for up to five years. In addition to fixing the cost of tuition, the CMU Promise guaranteed tuition program eliminates all former mandatory fees, so there are no added fees. The CMU Promise also guarantees that the room and board rate for residence halls will not increase for two years from the date of a student's admission to CMU. *Room and board:* $7236; room only: $3618. Room and board charges vary according to board plan, housing facility, location, and student level. *Payment plan:* installment. *Waivers:* children of alumni, senior citizens, and employees or children of employees.

Financial Aid Of all full-time matriculated undergraduates who enrolled in 2006, 12,712 applied for aid, 9,412 were judged to have need, 4,906 had their need fully met. 875 Federal Work-Study jobs (averaging $1540). 4,616 state and other part-time jobs (averaging $1874). In 2006, 1763 non-need-based awards were made. *Average percent of need met:* 79%. *Average financial aid package:* $9326. *Average need-based loan:* $5636. *Average need-based gift aid:* $4009. *Average non-need-based aid:* $3042. *Average indebtedness upon graduation:* $22,128.

Applying *Options:* electronic application, early admission, early action, deferred entrance. *Application fee:* $35. *Required:* high school transcript. *Required for some:* essay or personal statement, letters of recommendation, interview. *Recommended:* minimum 3.0 GPA. *Application deadlines:* rolling (freshmen), rolling (transfers). *Notification:* continuous (freshmen), continuous (transfers).

Freshman Application Contact Ms. Betty J. Wagner, Director of Admissions, Central Michigan University, Warriner Hall 102, Mt. Pleasant, MI 48859. *Phone:* 989-774-3076. *Toll-free phone:* 888-292-5366. *Fax:* 989-774-7267. *E-mail:* cmuadmit@cmich.edu.

CLEARY UNIVERSITY

Ann Arbor, Michigan **www.cleary.edu/**

- **Independent** comprehensive, founded 1883
- **Suburban** 32-acre campus with easy access to Detroit and Lansing
- **Endowment** $767,361
- **Coed** 716 undergraduate students, 57% full-time, 51% women, 49% men
- **Moderately difficult** entrance level, 90% of applicants were admitted

Undergraduates 410 full-time, 306 part-time. Students come from 4 states and territories, 2 other countries, 1% are from out of state, 7% African American, 0.7% Asian American or Pacific Islander, 2% Hispanic American, 0.6% Native American, 0.4% international. *Retention:* 75% of 2006 full-time freshmen returned.

Freshmen *Admission:* 72 applied, 65 admitted. *Average high school GPA:* 2.72. *Test scores:* ACT scores over 18: 77%; ACT scores over 24: 27%.

Faculty *Total:* 127, 6% full-time, 13% with terminal degrees. *Student/faculty ratio:* 10:1.

Majors Accounting; accounting technology and bookkeeping; business administration and management; computer and information sciences and support services related; finance; financial planning and services; human resources management; information science/studies; management information systems; marketing/marketing management.

Academics *Calendar:* quarters. *Degrees:* associate, bachelor's, and master's. *Special study options:* accelerated degree program, adult/continuing education programs, advanced placement credit, cooperative education, distance learning, independent study, internships, part-time degree program, summer session for credit.

Computers on Campus 60 computers/terminals are available on campus for general student use. Students can access the following: online (class) grades, online (class) schedules, student portal. Campuswide network is available. Wireless service is available via entire campus.

Student Life *Housing:* college housing not available. *Campus security:* 24-hour emergency response devices.

Standardized Tests *Required for some:* SAT or ACT (for admission), SAT Subject Tests (for admission), TOEFL.

Costs (2008–09) *Tuition:* $14,880 full-time, $310 per quarter hour part-time.

Financial Aid Of all full-time matriculated undergraduates who enrolled in 2006, 350 applied for aid, 324 were judged to have need, 4 had their need fully met. 15 Federal Work-Study jobs (averaging $2028). In 2006, 51 non-need-based awards were made. *Average percent of need met:* 27%. *Average financial aid package:* $11,665. *Average need-based loan:* $1484. *Average need-based gift aid:* $1051. *Average non-need-based aid:* $2536.

Applying *Options:* electronic application, early admission, deferred entrance. *Application fee:* $25. *Required:* high school transcript, minimum 2.0 GPA. *Required for some:* essay or personal statement, 2 letters of recommendation. *Recommended:* interview. *Application deadlines:* 8/15 (freshmen), 8/15 (transfers).

Freshman Application Contact Ms. Charlotte Paquette, Admissions Representative, Cleary University, 3750 Cleary Drive, Howell, MI 48843. *Phone:* 517-548-3670 Ext. 2249. *Toll-free phone:* 888-5-CLEARY Ext. 2249. *Fax:* 517-552-7805. *E-mail:* admissions@cleary.edu.

COLLEGE FOR CREATIVE STUDIES

Detroit, Michigan **www.ccscad.edu/**

- **Independent** 4-year, founded 1926
- **Urban** 11-acre campus
- **Endowment** $11.8 million
- **Coed** 1,307 undergraduate students, 85% full-time, 42% women, 58% men
- **Moderately difficult** entrance level, 39% of applicants were admitted

Undergraduates 1,114 full-time, 193 part-time. Students come from 35 states and territories, 18 other countries, 17% are from out of state, 6% African American, 4% Asian American or Pacific Islander, 5% Hispanic American, 0.6% Native American, 4% international, 12% transferred in, 27% live on campus. *Retention:* 73% of 2006 full-time freshmen returned.

Freshmen *Admission:* 1,260 applied, 488 admitted, 251 enrolled.

Faculty *Total:* 206, 25% full-time, 15% with terminal degrees. *Student/faculty ratio:* 8:1.

Majors Animation, interactive technology, video graphics and special effects; art teacher education; commercial and advertising art; crafts, folk art and artisanry; fine/studio arts; graphic design; illustration; industrial design; interior design; photography.

Academics *Calendar:* semesters. *Degrees:* bachelor's and postbachelor's certificates. *Special study options:* academic remediation for entering students, advanced placement credit, cooperative education, double majors, English as a second language, independent study, internships, off-campus study, part-time degree program, services for LD students, summer session for credit.

Computers on Campus Campuswide network is available.

Student Life *Housing options:* coed. Campus housing is university owned. *Campus security:* 24-hour patrols, late-night transport/escort service, controlled dormitory access. *Student services:* personal/psychological counseling.

Standardized Tests *Required:* SAT or ACT (for admission).

Costs (2008–09) *Tuition:* $27,090 full-time. *Required fees:* $1185 full-time. *Room only:* $4300.

Financial Aid *Average indebtedness upon graduation:* $57,980.

Applying *Options:* electronic application, deferred entrance. *Application fee:* $35. *Required:* essay or personal statement, high school transcript, portfolio. *Required for some:* essay or personal statement, letters of recommendation, interview. *Recommended:* minimum 2.5 GPA. *Application deadlines:* 8/1 (freshmen), rolling (transfers). *Notification:* continuous (freshmen).

Freshman Application Contact Office of Admissions, College for Creative Studies, 201 East Kirby, Detroit, MI 48202-4034. *Phone:* 800-952-2787. *Toll-free phone:* 800-952-ARTS. *Fax:* 313-872-2739. *E-mail:* admissions@ccscad.edu.

See page 1342 for the College Close-Up.

CONCORDIA UNIVERSITY

Ann Arbor, Michigan **www.cuaa.edu/**

- **Independent** comprehensive, founded 1963, affiliated with Lutheran Church–Missouri Synod, part of Concordia University System
- **Suburban** 187-acre campus with easy access to Detroit
- **Endowment** $6.0 million
- **Coed** 521 undergraduate students, 82% full-time, 54% women, 46% men
- **Moderately difficult** entrance level, 66% of applicants were admitted

Undergraduates 428 full-time, 93 part-time. Students come from 22 states and territories, 6 other countries, 17% are from out of state, 8% African American, 2% Asian American or Pacific Islander, 2% Hispanic American, 2% Native American, 1% international, 12% transferred in, 59% live on campus. *Retention:* 77% of 2006 full-time freshmen returned.

Freshmen *Admission:* 429 applied, 281 admitted, 94 enrolled. *Average high school GPA:* 3.22. *Test scores:* SAT critical reading scores over 500: 63%; SAT math scores over 500: 72%; SAT writing scores over 500: 57%; ACT scores over 18: 92%; SAT critical reading scores over 600: 42%; SAT math scores over 600: 29%; SAT writing scores over 600: 50%; ACT scores over 24: 44%; SAT critical reading scores over 700: 21%; SAT writing scores over 700: 21%; ACT scores over 30: 5%.

Faculty *Total:* 95, 41% full-time. *Student/faculty ratio:* 17:1.

Majors Ancient/classical Greek; ancient Near Eastern and biblical languages; art; art teacher education; biological and physical sciences; biology/biological sciences; biology teacher education; business administration and management; chemistry; chemistry teacher education; communication/speech communication and rhetoric; criminal justice/law enforcement administration; dramatic/theater arts; early childhood education; elementary education; engineering; English; English/language arts teacher education; general studies; health and physical education; health teacher education; history; history teacher education; hospitality administration; human development and family studies; journalism; mathematics; mathematics teacher education; music; music teacher education; philosophy; physical education teaching and coaching; physical sciences; physics; physics teacher education; pre-law studies; pre-medical studies; pre-nursing studies; pre-theology/pre-ministerial studies; psychology; psychology teacher education; religious education; religious/sacred music; religious studies; science teacher education; secondary education; security and protective services related; social sciences; social studies teacher education; sociology; Spanish; Spanish language teacher education; speech teacher education.

Academics *Calendar:* semesters. *Degrees:* associate, bachelor's, master's, and postbachelor's certificates. *Special study options:* academic remediation for entering students, accelerated degree program, adult/continuing education programs, advanced placement credit, cooperative education, distance learning, double majors, independent study, internships, off-campus study, part-time degree program, services for LD students, student-designed majors, study abroad, summer session for credit. *ROTC:* Army (c), Air Force (c). *Unusual degree programs:* 3-2 engineering with Kettering University (MICH).

Computers on Campus 60 computers/terminals are available on campus for general student use. Students can access the following: campus intranet, computer help desk, free student e-mail accounts, online (class) grades, online (class) registration, online (class) schedules. Campuswide network is available. 100% of college-owned or -operated housing units are wired for high-speed Internet access. Wireless service is available via classrooms, computer centers, computer labs, dorm rooms, learning centers, libraries, student centers.

Student Life *Housing:* on-campus residence required through sophomore year. *Options:* men-only, women-only. Campus housing is university owned. Freshman campus housing is guaranteed. *Activities and organizations:* drama/theater group, student-run newspaper, choral group, Student Activities Committee, Drama Club, Student Senate, Spiritual Life Committee, off-campus ministries. *Campus security:* student patrols, late-night transport/escort service, controlled dormitory access. *Student services:* health clinic, personal/psychological counseling.

Athletics Member NAIA. *Intercollegiate sports:* baseball M (s), basketball M (s)/W (s), cross-country running M (s)/W (s), golf M (s)/W (s), soccer M (s)/W (s), softball W (s), volleyball W (s). *Intramural sports:* badminton M/W, basketball M/W, football M/W, golf M/W, softball M/W, table tennis M/W, tennis M/W, volleyball M/W.

Standardized Tests *Required:* SAT or ACT (for admission). *Recommended:* ACT (for admission).

Costs (2007–08) *One-time required fee:* $100. *Comprehensive fee:* $27,120 includes full-time tuition ($19,700), mandatory fees ($70), and room and board ($7350). Part-time tuition: $650 per credit hour. Part-time tuition and fees vary according to course load. *Required fees:* $35 per term part-time. *College room only:* $5290. *Payment plan:* installment. *Waivers:* employees or children of employees.

Financial Aid Of all full-time matriculated undergraduates who enrolled in 2006, 393 applied for aid, 350 were judged to have need, 126 had their need fully met. 50 Federal Work-Study jobs (averaging $1750). 6 state and other part-time jobs (averaging $1750). In 2006, 50 non-need-based awards were made. *Average percent of need met:* 81%. *Average financial aid package:* $14,968. *Average need-based loan:* $5048. *Average need-based gift aid:* $11,247. *Average non-need-based aid:* $9995. *Average indebtedness upon graduation:* $28,280.

Applying *Options:* electronic application, deferred entrance. *Application fee:* $25. *Required:* high school transcript. *Required for some:* essay or personal statement, interview. *Recommended:* minimum 2.5 GPA, 1 letter of recommendation. *Application deadlines:* rolling (freshmen), rolling (transfers).

Freshman Application Contact Amy Becher, Executive Director of Enrollment Services, Concordia University, 4090 Geddes Road, Ann Arbor, MI 48105. *Phone:* 734-995-7450. *Toll-free phone:* 800-253-0680. *Fax:* 734-995-4610. *E-mail:* admissions@cuaa.edu or bechea@cuaa.edu.

CORNERSTONE UNIVERSITY

Grand Rapids, Michigan **www.cornerstone.edu/**

- **Independent nondenominational** comprehensive, founded 1941
- **Suburban** 132-acre campus
- **Endowment** $6.4 million
- **Coed** 1,841 undergraduate students, 79% full-time, 59% women, 41% men
- **Minimally difficult** entrance level, 62% of applicants were admitted

Undergraduates 1,449 full-time, 392 part-time. Students come from 36 states and territories, 8 other countries, 19% are from out of state, 12% African American, 0.9% Asian American or Pacific Islander, 3% Hispanic American, 0.5% Native American, 1% international, 5% transferred in, 55% live on campus. *Retention:* 70% of 2006 full-time freshmen returned.

Freshmen *Admission:* 981 applied, 611 admitted, 292 enrolled. *Average high school GPA:* 3.4. *Test scores:* ACT scores over 18: 92%; ACT scores over 24: 47%; ACT scores over 30: 6%.

Faculty *Total:* 118, 56% full-time, 29% with terminal degrees. *Student/faculty ratio:* 13:1.

Majors Accounting; airline pilot and flight crew; ancient Near Eastern and biblical languages; biblical studies; biology/biological sciences; biology teacher education; broadcast journalism; business administration and management; business administration, management and operations related; creative writing; early childhood education; education; elementary education; English; English/language arts teacher education; environmental biology; history; history teacher education; information science/studies; interdisciplinary studies; kinesiology and exercise science; management information systems; marketing/marketing management; mass communication/media; mathematics; mathematics teacher education; multi-/interdisciplinary studies related; music; music performance; music teacher education; music theory and composition; pastoral studies/counseling; philosophy; physical education teaching and coaching; political science and government; pre-dentistry studies; pre-law studies; pre-medical studies; pre-theology/pre-ministerial studies; pre-veterinary studies; psychology; religious education; religious studies; science teacher education; secondary education; social science teacher education; social studies teacher education; social work; sociology; Spanish; speech and rhetoric; sport and fitness administration/management.

Academics *Calendar:* semesters. *Degrees:* diplomas, associate, bachelor's, master's, and first professional. *Special study options:* academic remediation for entering students, accelerated degree program, adult/continuing education programs, advanced placement credit, distance learning, double majors, English as a second language, honors programs, independent study, internships, off-campus study, part-time degree program, services for LD students, study abroad, summer session for credit. *ROTC:* Army (c).

Computers on Campus 531 computers/terminals are available on campus for general student use. Students can access the following: campus intranet, computer help desk, free student e-mail accounts, online (class) grades, online (class) registration, online (class) schedules. Campuswide network is available. 100% of college-owned or -operated housing units are wired for high-speed Internet access. Wireless service is available via entire campus.

Student Life *Housing:* on-campus residence required through sophomore year. *Options:* men-only, women-only, disabled students. Campus housing is university owned. Freshman campus housing is guaranteed. *Activities and organizations:* drama/theater group, student-run newspaper, choral group, Student Government, Student Education Association, Breakpoint, Student Activities Council. *Campus security:* 24-hour emergency response devices and patrols, student patrols, late-night transport/escort service, controlled dormitory access. *Student services:* health clinic, personal/psychological counseling.

Athletics Member NAIA. *Intercollegiate sports:* basketball M (s)/W (s), cross-country running M (s)/W (s), golf M (s), soccer M (s)/W (s), softball W (s), track and field M (s)/W (s), volleyball W (s). *Intramural sports:* basketball M/W, football M, soccer M/W, softball M/W, volleyball M/W.

Standardized Tests *Required:* SAT or ACT (for admission).

Costs (2007–08) *Comprehensive fee:* $24,660 includes full-time tuition ($18,040), mandatory fees ($320), and room and board ($6300). Part-time tuition: $698 per credit. Part-time tuition and fees vary according to course load. *Room and board:* Room and board charges vary according to board plan. *Payment plan:* installment. *Waivers:* employees or children of employees.

Financial Aid Of all full-time matriculated undergraduates who enrolled in 2007, 971 applied for aid, 892 were judged to have need, 133 had their need fully met. 189 Federal Work-Study jobs (averaging $1069). 34 state and other part-time jobs (averaging $1911). In 2007, 155 non-need-based awards were made. *Average percent of need met:* 84%. *Average financial aid package:* $16,272. *Average need-based loan:* $740. *Average need-based gift aid:* $8591. *Average non-need-based aid:* $3821. *Average indebtedness upon graduation:* $26,710. *Financial aid deadline:* 3/1.

Applying *Options:* electronic application, deferred entrance. *Application fee:* $25. *Required:* essay or personal statement, high school transcript, minimum 2.5 GPA, 1 letter of recommendation, pastoral letter. *Recommended:* interview. *Application deadlines:* rolling (freshmen), rolling (transfers). *Notification:* continuous (freshmen), continuous (transfers).

Freshman Application Contact Mr. Brent Rudin, Dean of Admissions, Cornerstone University, 1001 East Beltline Avenue, NE, Grand Rapids, MI 49525. *Phone:* 616-222-1426. *Toll-free phone:* 800-787-9778. *Fax:* 616-222-1400. *E-mail:* admissions@cornerstone.edu.

DAVENPORT UNIVERSITY

Alma, Michigan **www.davenport.edu/**

Director of Admissions Admissions, Davenport University, 415 East Fulton Street, Grand Rapids, MI 49503. *Toll-free phone:* 800-632-9569.

DAVENPORT UNIVERSITY

Bad Axe, Michigan **www.davenport.edu/**

Director of Admissions Admissions, Davenport University, 415 East Fulton Street, Grand Rapids, MI 49503. *Toll-free phone:* 800-632-9569.

DAVENPORT UNIVERSITY

Bay City, Michigan **www.davenport.edu/**

Director of Admissions Admissions, Davenport University, 415 East Fulton Street, Grand Rapids, MI 49503. *Toll-free phone:* 800-632-9569.

DAVENPORT UNIVERSITY

Caro, Michigan **www.davenport.edu/**

Director of Admissions Admissions, Davenport University, 415 East Fulton Street, Grand Rapids, MI 49503. *Toll-free phone:* 800-632-9569.

DAVENPORT UNIVERSITY

Dearborn, Michigan **www.davenport.edu/**

- **Independent** comprehensive, founded 1985
- **Suburban** 50-acre campus with easy access to Detroit
- **Endowment** $13.0 million
- **Coed** 10,817 undergraduate students, 30% full-time, 73% women, 27% men
- **Minimally difficult** entrance level, 91% of applicants were admitted

Undergraduates 3,196 full-time, 7,621 part-time. Students come from 49 other countries, 2% are from out of state, 19% African American, 2% Asian American or Pacific Islander, 3% Hispanic American, 0.4% Native American, 0.2% international, 2% live on campus. *Retention:* 61% of 2006 full-time freshmen returned.

Freshmen *Admission:* 1,303 applied, 1,190 admitted, 746 enrolled. *Average high school GPA:* 3.12.

Faculty *Total:* 137. *Student/faculty ratio:* 13:1.

Majors Accounting; bioinformatics; business administration and management; business administration, management and operations related; business/commerce; computer and information sciences; computer and information systems security; computer systems analysis; computer systems networking and telecommunications; executive assistant/executive secretary; finance; health/health care administration; health information/medical records administration; health information/

medical records technology; human resources management; international business/trade/commerce; legal assistant/paralegal; marketing/marketing management; massage therapy; medical/clinical assistant; medical/health management and clinical assistant; medical insurance coding; nursing (registered nurse training); securities services administration; sport and fitness administration/management.

Academics *Calendar:* semesters. *Degrees:* diplomas, associate, bachelor's, master's, post-master's, and postbachelor's certificates. *Special study options:* academic remediation for entering students, accelerated degree program, advanced placement credit, cooperative education, distance learning, double majors, English as a second language, honors programs, independent study, internships, part-time degree program, services for LD students, student-designed majors, study abroad, summer session for credit.

Computers on Campus 3,224 computers/terminals are available on campus for general student use. Students can access the following: campus intranet, computer help desk, free student e-mail accounts, online (class) grades, online (class) registration, online (class) schedules. Campuswide network is available. 100% of college-owned or -operated housing units are wired for high-speed Internet access. Wireless service is available via entire campus.

Student Life *Housing options:* coed. Campus housing is university owned. Freshman applicants given priority for college housing. *Activities and organizations:* Business Professionals of America (BPA), Delta Epsilon Chi (DEX), Davenport Student Ambassadors, Health Occupations Students of America (HOSA). *Campus security:* 24-hour emergency response devices and patrols, late-night transport/escort service, controlled dormitory access.

Athletics Member NAIA. *Intercollegiate sports:* basketball M (s)/W (s), cross-country running M (s)/W (s), golf M (s)/W (s), ice hockey M (s), lacrosse M (s)/W (s), soccer M (s)/W (s), track and field M (s)/W (s), volleyball W (s).

Standardized Tests *Recommended:* SAT or ACT (for admission).

Costs (2007–08) *Tuition:* $9816 full-time, $409 per credit part-time. *Required fees:* $140 full-time. *Room only:* $4750.

Financial Aid Of all full-time matriculated undergraduates who enrolled in 2004, 724 applied for aid, 693 were judged to have need, 15 had their need fully met. 333 Federal Work-Study jobs (averaging $3192). 149 state and other part-time jobs (averaging $3373). In 2004, 37 non-need-based awards were made. *Average percent of need met:* 75%. *Average financial aid package:* $12,223. *Average need-based loan:* $5186. *Average need-based gift aid:* $3818. *Average non-need-based aid:* $8607. *Average indebtedness upon graduation:* $8459.

Applying *Options:* electronic application, deferred entrance. *Application fee:* $25. *Required:* high school transcript. *Recommended:* interview. *Application deadlines:* rolling (freshmen), rolling (out-of-state freshmen), rolling (transfers). *Notification:* continuous (freshmen), continuous (out-of-state freshmen), continuous (transfers).

Freshman Application Contact Ms. Heather Knechtel, Director of Admissions, Davenport University, 415 East Fulton Street, Grand Rapids, MI 49503. *Phone:* 616-451-3511. *Toll-free phone:* 800-632-9569. *E-mail:* heather.knechtel@davenport.edu.

DAVENPORT UNIVERSITY

Grand Rapids, Michigan www.davenport.edu/

- **Independent** comprehensive, founded 1866
- **Urban** campus
- **Endowment** $13.0 million
- **Coed** 10,817 undergraduate students, 30% full-time, 73% women, 27% men
- **Minimally difficult** entrance level, 91% of applicants were admitted

Undergraduates 3,196 full-time, 7,621 part-time. Students come from 49 other countries, 2% are from out of state, 19% African American, 2% Asian American or Pacific Islander, 3% Hispanic American, 0.4% Native American, 0.2% international, 2% live on campus. *Retention:* 61% of 2006 full-time freshmen returned.

Freshmen *Admission:* 1,303 applied, 1,190 admitted, 746 enrolled. *Average high school GPA:* 3.12.

Faculty *Total:* 1,145, 12% full-time. *Student/faculty ratio:* 13:1.

Majors Accounting; animation, interactive technology, video graphics and special effects; bioinformatics; business administration and management; business administration, management and operations related; business/commerce; computer and information sciences; computer and information systems security; computer systems analysis; computer systems networking and telecommunications; executive assistant/executive secretary; finance; health/health care administration; health information/medical records administration; health information/medical records technology; human resources management; international business/trade/commerce; legal assistant/paralegal; marketing/marketing management; massage therapy; medical/clinical assistant; medical/health management and clinical assistant; nursing (registered nurse training); securities services administration; sport and fitness administration/management.

Academics *Calendar:* semesters. *Degrees:* diplomas, associate, bachelor's, master's, post-master's, and postbachelor's certificates. *Special study options:* academic remediation for entering students, accelerated degree program, adult/continuing education programs, advanced placement credit, distance learning, English as a second language, independent study, internships, part-time degree program, student-designed majors, summer session for credit.

Computers on Campus 3,224 computers/terminals are available on campus for general student use. Students can access the following: campus intranet, computer help desk, free student e-mail accounts, online (class) grades, online (class) registration, online (class) schedules. Campuswide network is available. 100% of college-owned or -operated housing units are wired for high-speed Internet access. Wireless service is available via entire campus.

Student Life *Housing options:* coed. Campus housing is university owned. Freshman applicants given priority for college housing. *Activities and organizations:* Business Professionals of America, Delta Epsilon Chi, Davenport Student Ambassadors, Health Occupations Students of America. *Campus security:* 24-hour emergency response devices and patrols, late-night transport/escort service, controlled dormitory access. *Student services:* personal/psychological counseling.

Athletics Member NAIA. *Intercollegiate sports:* basketball M (s)/W (s), cross-country running M (s)/W (s), golf M (s)/W (s), ice hockey M (s), lacrosse M (s)/W (s), soccer M (s)/W (s), track and field M (s)/W (s), volleyball W (s).

Standardized Tests *Recommended:* SAT or ACT (for admission).

Costs (2007–08) *Tuition:* $9816 full-time, $409 per credit part-time. *Required fees:* $140 full-time. *Room only:* $4750.

Financial Aid In 2006, 193 non-need-based awards were made. *Average financial aid package:* $9728. *Average need-based loan:* $3397. *Average need-based gift aid:* $4271. *Average non-need-based aid:* $5685. *Average indebtedness upon graduation:* $8459.

Applying *Options:* electronic application, deferred entrance. *Application fee:* $25. *Required:* high school transcript. *Recommended:* essay or personal statement, interview. *Application deadlines:* rolling (freshmen), rolling (out-of-state freshmen), rolling (transfers). *Notification:* continuous (freshmen), continuous (out-of-state freshmen), continuous (transfers).

Freshman Application Contact Ms. Heather Knechtel, Director of Admissions, Davenport University, 415 East Fulton Street, Grand Rapids, MI 49503. *Phone:* 616-451-3511. *Toll-free phone:* 800-632-9569. *E-mail:* heather.knechtel@davenport.edu.

DAVENPORT UNIVERSITY

Midland, Michigan www.davenport.edu/

Director of Admissions Admissions, Davenport University, 415 East Fulton Street, Grand Rapids, MI 49503. *Toll-free phone:* 800-632-9569.

DAVENPORT UNIVERSITY

Saginaw, Michigan www.davenport.edu/

Freshman Application Contact Admissions, Davenport University, 415 East Fulton Street, Grand Rapids, MI 49503. *Phone:* 616-698-7111. *Toll-free phone:* 800-632-9569. *Fax:* 616-698-0333. *E-mail:* gradmiss@davenport.edu.

EASTERN MICHIGAN UNIVERSITY

Ypsilanti, Michigan www.emich.edu/

- **State-supported** comprehensive, founded 1849
- **Suburban** 460-acre campus with easy access to Detroit
- **Endowment** $44.8 million
- **Coed** 17,808 undergraduate students, 69% full-time, 59% women, 41% men
- **Moderately difficult** entrance level, 75% of applicants were admitted

Undergraduates 12,312 full-time, 5,496 part-time. Students come from 48 states and territories, 55 other countries, 8% are from out of state, 18% African American, 2% Asian American or Pacific Islander, 3% Hispanic American, 0.5% Native American, 1% international, 9% transferred in, 16% live on campus. *Retention:* 71% of 2006 full-time freshmen returned.

Freshmen *Admission:* 9,736 applied, 7,290 admitted, 2,448 enrolled. *Average high school GPA:* 3.04. *Test scores:* SAT critical reading scores over 500: 55%; SAT math scores over 500: 59%; SAT writing scores over 500: 50%; ACT scores over 18: 81%; SAT critical reading scores over 600: 18%; SAT math scores over

600: 21%; SAT writing scores over 600: 13%; ACT scores over 24: 27%; SAT critical reading scores over 700: 3%; SAT math scores over 700: 3%; ACT scores over 30: 3%.

Faculty *Total:* 1,203, 63% full-time. *Student/faculty ratio:* 18:1.

Majors Accounting; actuarial science; African-American/Black studies; airline pilot and flight crew; anthropology; architecture; art; art history, criticism and conservation; arts management; art teacher education; athletic training; aviation/airway management; biochemistry; biological and physical sciences; biology/biological sciences; biology teacher education; business administration and management; business/commerce; business/managerial economics; business teacher education; CAD/CADD drafting/design technology; chemistry; chemistry teacher education; city/urban, community and regional planning; clinical laboratory science/medical technology; communications technology; community organization and advocacy; computer and information sciences; computer engineering technology; computer science; computer teacher education; construction engineering technology; construction management; creative writing; criminology; dance; dietetics; dramatic/theater arts; economics; economics related; electrical, electronic and communications engineering technology; elementary education; engineering technology; English; English composition; English/language arts teacher education; entrepreneurship; facilities planning and management; fashion merchandising; film/cinema studies; finance; foreign language teacher education; French; French language teacher education; geography; geology/earth science; geophysics and seismology; German; Germanic languages; German language teacher education; health and physical education; health/health care administration; history; history teacher education; hospitality administration; industrial technology; information science/studies; interior design; international business/trade/commerce; international economics; Japanese; journalism; labor studies; legal assistant/paralegal; linguistics; management information systems; manufacturing technology; marketing/marketing management; mathematics; mathematics teacher education; mechanical drafting and CAD/CADD; mechanical engineering/mechanical technology; merchandising, sales, and marketing operations related (general); merchandising, sales, and marketing operations related (specialized); music; music performance; music teacher education; music therapy; nursing (registered nurse training); occupational therapy; office management; parks, recreation and leisure facilities management; philosophy; physical education teaching and coaching; physical sciences related; physics; physics teacher education; plastics engineering technology; political science and government; psychology; public administration; public administration and social service professions related; public relations/image management; radio and television broadcasting technology; reading teacher education; sales and marketing/marketing and distribution teacher education; science teacher education; security and protective services related; social sciences; social sciences related; social science teacher education; social studies teacher education; social work; sociology; Spanish; Spanish language teacher education; special education; special education (emotionally disturbed); special education (hearing impaired); special education (mentally retarded); special education (orthopedic and other physical health impairments); special education (specific learning disabilities); special education (speech or language impaired); special education (vision impaired); speech-language pathology; statistics; technical and business writing; technology/industrial arts teacher education; theater/theater arts management; therapeutic recreation; toxicology; women's studies.

Academics *Calendar:* semesters. *Degrees:* bachelor's, master's, doctoral, post-master's, and postbachelor's certificates. *Special study options:* academic remediation for entering students, accelerated degree program, adult/continuing education programs, advanced placement credit, cooperative education, distance learning, double majors, English as a second language, honors programs, independent study, internships, part-time degree program, services for LD students, student-designed majors, study abroad, summer session for credit. *ROTC:* Army (b), Navy (c), Air Force (c).

Computers on Campus 1,500 computers/terminals are available on campus for general student use. Campuswide network is available.

Student Life *Housing:* on-campus residence required through sophomore year. *Options:* coed, disabled students. Campus housing is university owned. *Activities and organizations:* drama/theater group, student-run newspaper, radio and television station, choral group, marching band, national fraternities, national sororities. *Campus security:* 24-hour emergency response devices and patrols, student patrols, late-night transport/escort service, controlled dormitory access, bicycle patrols, local police in dormitories, self-defense education, lighted pathways, bike lock lease program. *Student services:* health clinic, personal/psychological counseling, women's center.

Athletics Member NCAA. All Division I except football (Division I-A). *Intercollegiate sports:* baseball M (s), basketball M (s)/W (s), crew W (s), cross-country running M (s)/W (s), golf M (s)/W (s), gymnastics W (s), soccer W (s), softball W (s), swimming and diving M (s)/W (s), tennis W (s), track and field M (s)/W (s), volleyball W (s), wrestling M (s). *Intramural sports:* badminton M/W, basketball M/W, bowling M/W, cross-country running M/W, fencing M (c)/W (c), golf M/W, gymnastics M (c)/W (c), ice hockey M (c), lacrosse M (c)/W (c), racquetball M/W, skiing (cross-country) M/W, soccer M/W, softball M/W, swimming and diving M/W, table tennis M/W, tennis M/W, track and field M/W, ultimate Frisbee M (c)/W (c), volleyball M/W, water polo W (c), weight lifting M/W.

Standardized Tests *Required:* (for admission). *Required for some:* ACT (for admission).

Costs (2007–08) *One-time required fee:* $82. *Tuition:* state resident $6390 full-time, $213 per credit hour part-time; nonresident $18,825 full-time, $628 per credit hour part-time. *Required fees:* $1100 full-time, $34 per credit hour part-time, $40 per term part-time. *Room and board:* $6942; room only: $3260. Room and board charges vary according to board plan, housing facility, and location. *Payment plan:* installment. *Waivers:* employees or children of employees.

Financial Aid Of all full-time matriculated undergraduates who enrolled in 2006, 8,564 applied for aid, 6,806 were judged to have need, 733 had their need fully met. 521 Federal Work-Study jobs (averaging $1828). 192 state and other part-time jobs (averaging $1628). In 2006, 1830 non-need-based awards were made. *Average percent of need met:* 57%. *Average financial aid package:* $6920. *Average need-based loan:* $4052. *Average need-based gift aid:* $3240. *Average non-need-based aid:* $2853. *Average indebtedness upon graduation:* $25,145.

Applying *Options:* deferred entrance. *Application fee:* $30. *Required:* high school transcript, minimum 2.0 GPA. *Required for some:* 1 letter of recommendation, interview. *Application deadlines:* rolling (freshmen), rolling (transfers). *Notification:* continuous (freshmen), continuous (transfers).

Freshman Application Contact Kathy Orscheln, Interim Director of Admissions, Eastern Michigan University, 400 Pierce Hall, Ypsilanti, MI 48197. *Phone:* 734-487-3060. *Toll-free phone:* 800-GO TO EMU. *Fax:* 734-487-1484. *E-mail:* admissions@emich.edu.

FERRIS STATE UNIVERSITY

Big Rapids, Michigan **www.ferris.edu/**

- **State-supported** comprehensive, founded 1884
- **Small-town** 880-acre campus with easy access to Grand Rapids
- **Endowment** $29.7 million
- **Coed** 11,835 undergraduate students, 75% full-time, 47% women, 53% men
- **Minimally difficult** entrance level

Undergraduates 8,911 full-time, 2,924 part-time. Students come from 47 states and territories, 26 other countries, 4% are from out of state, 7% African American, 2% Asian American or Pacific Islander, 2% Hispanic American, 1% Native American, 0.9% international, 13% transferred in, 29% live on campus. *Retention:* 73% of 2006 full-time freshmen returned.

Freshmen *Admission:* 2,073 enrolled. *Average high school GPA:* 3.17. *Test scores:* ACT scores over 18: 84%; ACT scores over 24: 28%; ACT scores over 30: 3%.

Faculty *Total:* 848, 63% full-time. *Student/faculty ratio:* 15:1.

Majors Accounting technology and bookkeeping; advertising; animation, interactive technology, video graphics and special effects; applied mathematics; architectural engineering technology; art history, criticism and conservation; art teacher education; automobile/automotive mechanics technology; automotive engineering technology; biochemistry; biological and physical sciences; biology/biological sciences; biology teacher education; biotechnology; business administration and management; business/managerial economics; business teacher education; CAD/CADD drafting/design technology; chemical engineering; chemical technology; chemistry; chemistry teacher education; child care and support services management; civil engineering technology; clinical laboratory science/medical technology; clinical/medical laboratory technology; commercial and advertising art; communication/speech communication and rhetoric; construction engineering technology; construction management; criminal justice/police science; dental hygiene; design and applied arts related; design and visual communications; desktop publishing and digital imaging design; diagnostic medical sonography and ultrasound technology; early childhood education; electrical, electronic and communications engineering technology; elementary education; energy management and systems technology; English composition; English language and literature related; English/language arts teacher education; entrepreneurship; family and consumer sciences/home economics teacher education; finance; fine/studio arts; funeral service and mortuary science; general studies; graphic and printing equipment operation/production; graphic design; health/health care administration; health information/medical records administration; health information/medical records technology; health teacher education; heating, air conditioning and refrigeration technology; heavy equipment maintenance technology; history; history teacher education; hospitality administration; hospitality and recreation marketing; hotel/motel administration; human resources management; industrial design; industrial electronics technology; industrial production technologies related; industrial technology; information technology; interior architecture; international business/trade/commerce; legal assistant/paralegal; liberal arts and sciences and humanities related; manufacturing technology; marketing/marketing management; mathematics; mathematics teacher education; mechanical engineering/mechanical technology; medical radiologic technology; metal and jewelry arts; music management and merchandising; nuclear medical technology; nursing (registered nurse training); operations management; ornamental horticulture; painting; parks, recreation and leisure facilities management; photography; plastics engineering technology; pre-engineering; pre-law studies; pre-pharmacy studies; printing management; psychology; public administration; public relations/image management; quality control technology; radio and television broadcasting technology; respiratory care therapy; restaurant, culinary, and catering management; sculpture; secondary education; social science teacher education; social studies teacher education; social work; sociology; speech and rhetoric; survey technology; technical and business writing; technical teacher education; telecommunications technology; tool and die technology; welding technology.

Academics *Calendar:* semesters. *Degrees:* certificates, associate, bachelor's, master's, and first professional (Associate). *Special study options:* academic remediation for entering students, accelerated degree program, adult/continuing education programs, advanced placement credit, cooperative education, distance learning, double majors, English as a second language, freshman honors college, honors programs, independent study, internships, off-campus study, part-time degree program, services for LD students, study abroad, summer session for credit. *ROTC:* Army (c).

Computers on Campus 2,373 computers/terminals are available on campus for general student use. Students can access the following: campus intranet, computer help desk, free student e-mail accounts, online (class) grades, online (class) registration, online (class) schedules. Campuswide network is available. 100% of college-owned or -operated housing units are wired for high-speed Internet access. Wireless service is available via entire campus.

Student Life *Housing:* on-campus residence required through sophomore year. *Options:* coed, disabled students. Campus housing is university owned. Freshman campus housing is guaranteed. *Activities and organizations:* drama/theater group, student-run newspaper, radio and television station, choral group, Student Government of Ferris State University, Intramural Sports Club, University theatre, Music Club, Forensics Club, national fraternities, national sororities. *Campus security:* 24-hour emergency response devices, student patrols, late-night transport/escort service. *Student services:* health clinic, personal/psychological counseling.

Athletics Member NCAA. All Division II. *Intercollegiate sports:* basketball M (s)/W (s), cheerleading M/W, cross-country running M (s)/W (s), football M (s), golf M (s)/W (s), ice hockey M (s), soccer W (s), softball W (s), tennis M (s)/W (s), track and field M (s)/W (s), volleyball W (s). *Intramural sports:* badminton M/W, baseball M, basketball M/W, bowling M/W, football M, golf M/W, ice hockey M, lacrosse M/W, racquetball M/W, rugby M/W, skiing (downhill) M/W, soccer M/W, softball M/W, swimming and diving M/W, tennis M/W, track and field M/W, volleyball M/W, water polo M, weight lifting M.

Standardized Tests *Required:* SAT or ACT (for admission).

Costs (2007–08) *Tuition:* state resident $8700 full-time, $290 per credit hour part-time; nonresident $15,900 full-time, $530 per credit hour part-time. Full-time tuition and fees vary according to reciprocity agreements. *Required fees:* $162 full-time, $162 per term part-time. *Room and board:* $7646; room only: $3884. Room and board charges vary according to board plan and housing facility. *Payment plans:* installment, deferred payment. *Waivers:* employees or children of employees.

Financial Aid Of all full-time matriculated undergraduates who enrolled in 2007, 7,358 applied for aid, 5,698 were judged to have need, 785 had their need fully met. 501 Federal Work-Study jobs (averaging $2095). 81 state and other part-time jobs (averaging $1975). In 2007, 673 non-need-based awards were made. *Average percent of need met:* 89%. *Average financial aid package:* $12,766. *Average need-based loan:* $4114. *Average need-based gift aid:* $3876. *Average non-need-based aid:* $3243. *Average indebtedness upon graduation:* $28,483.

Applying *Options:* electronic application. *Application fee:* $30. *Required:* high school transcript, minimum 2.5 GPA. *Application deadlines:* 8/1 (freshmen), 7/1 (transfers). *Notification:* continuous (freshmen), continuous (transfers).

Freshman Application Contact Troy Tissue, Associate Director of Admissions, Ferris State University, 1201 South State Street, CSS201, Big Rapids, MI 49307-2742. *Phone:* 231-591-2000. *Toll-free phone:* 800-433-7747. *Fax:* 231-591-3944. *E-mail:* admissions@ferris.edu.

FINLANDIA UNIVERSITY

Hancock, Michigan — www.finlandia.edu/

- **Independent** 4-year, founded 1896, affiliated with Evangelical Lutheran Church in America
- **Small-town** 25-acre campus
- **Endowment** $2.5 million
- **Coed** 545 undergraduate students, 89% full-time, 65% women, 35% men
- **Minimally difficult** entrance level, 67% of applicants were admitted

Undergraduates 485 full-time, 60 part-time. Students come from 13 states and territories, 3 other countries, 10% are from out of state, 0.9% African American, 3% Asian American or Pacific Islander, 1% Hispanic American, 2% Native American, 1% international, 10% transferred in, 24% live on campus. *Retention:* 61% of 2006 full-time freshmen returned.

Freshmen *Admission:* 646 applied, 433 admitted, 82 enrolled. *Average high school GPA:* 2.89. *Test scores:* ACT scores over 18: 74%; ACT scores over 24: 23%; ACT scores over 30: 2%.

Faculty *Total:* 70, 60% full-time, 30% with terminal degrees. *Student/faculty ratio:* 10:1.

Majors Art; business administration and management; ceramic arts and ceramics; criminal justice/law enforcement administration; education; education (K-12); fiber, textile and weaving arts; fine/studio arts; general studies; human services; industrial design; international business/trade/commerce; liberal arts and sciences/liberal studies; nursing (registered nurse training); physical therapist assistant.

Academics *Calendar:* semesters. *Degrees:* associate and bachelor's. *Special study options:* academic remediation for entering students, accelerated degree program, adult/continuing education programs, advanced placement credit, cooperative education, distance learning, English as a second language, independent study, internships, off-campus study, part-time degree program, services for LD students, study abroad, summer session for credit. *ROTC:* Army (c), Air Force (c).

Computers on Campus 80 computers/terminals and 250 ports are available on campus for general student use. Students can access the following: free student e-mail accounts, online (class) grades, online (class) registration, online (class) schedules, home directory/network. Campuswide network is available. 100% of college-owned or -operated housing units are wired for high-speed Internet access. Wireless service is available via classrooms, computer centers, computer labs, dorm rooms, learning centers, libraries, student centers.

Student Life *Housing:* on-campus residence required through sophomore year. *Options:* coed, disabled students. Campus housing is university owned. *Activities and organizations:* drama/theater group, student-run newspaper, choral group, Student Senate, Campus Ministry, Student Newspaper, International Club, Artists Coalition. *Campus security:* 24-hour emergency response devices, student patrols.

Athletics Member NSCAA. *Intercollegiate sports:* baseball M, basketball M/W, cross-country running M/W, ice hockey M/W, soccer M/W, softball W, volleyball W. *Intramural sports:* basketball M/W, bowling M/W, cheerleading W, football M/W, ice hockey M/W, skiing (cross-country) M/W, softball M/W, volleyball M/W.

Standardized Tests *Recommended:* SAT or ACT (for admission).

Costs (2007–08) *One-time required fee:* $100. *Comprehensive fee:* $23,714 includes full-time tuition ($17,414), mandatory fees ($500), and room and board ($5800). Full-time tuition and fees vary according to program. Part-time tuition: $580 per credit. Part-time tuition and fees vary according to course load and program. *Room and board:* Room and board charges vary according to housing facility. *Payment plan:* installment. *Waivers:* employees or children of employees.

Financial Aid Of all full-time matriculated undergraduates who enrolled in 2007, 480 applied for aid, 460 were judged to have need, 6 had their need fully met. 154 Federal Work-Study jobs (averaging $1600). 25 state and other part-time jobs (averaging $1200). In 2007, 17 non-need-based awards were made. *Average percent of need met:* 50%. *Average financial aid package:* $16,000. *Average need-based loan:* $3500. *Average need-based gift aid:* $5000. *Average non-need-based aid:* $5000. *Average indebtedness upon graduation:* $17,500.

Applying *Options:* electronic application, early admission. *Application fee:* $30. *Required:* essay or personal statement, high school transcript, minimum 2.0 GPA. *Required for some:* letters of recommendation, interview. *Application deadlines:* 8/25 (freshmen), 8/25 (out-of-state freshmen), 8/25 (transfers). *Notification:* continuous (freshmen), continuous (out-of-state freshmen), continuous (transfers).

Freshman Application Contact Martin Kinard, Finlandia University, 601 Quincy Street, Hancock, MI 49930. *Phone:* 906-487-7352. *Toll-free phone:* 877-202-5491. *Fax:* 906-487-7383. *E-mail:* admissions@finlandia.edu.

GRACE BIBLE COLLEGE

Grand Rapids, Michigan **www.gbcol.edu/**

- **Independent** 4-year, founded 1945, affiliated with Grace Gospel Fellowship
- **Suburban** 16-acre campus
- **Endowment** $180,000
- **Coed** 173 undergraduate students, 93% full-time, 46% women, 54% men
- **Minimally difficult** entrance level, 62% of applicants were admitted

Undergraduates 161 full-time, 12 part-time. Students come from 15 states and territories, 1 other country, 25% are from out of state, 4% African American, 0.6% Asian American or Pacific Islander, 2% Hispanic American, 1% Native American, 0.6% international, 14% transferred in, 53% live on campus. *Retention:* 73% of 2006 full-time freshmen returned.

Freshmen *Admission:* 138 applied, 85 admitted, 42 enrolled. *Average high school GPA:* 3.16. *Test scores:* SAT critical reading scores over 500: 60%; SAT math scores over 500: 60%; SAT writing scores over 500: 60%; ACT scores over 18: 80%; SAT critical reading scores over 600: 20%; SAT writing scores over 600: 20%; ACT scores over 24: 30%.

Faculty *Total:* 28, 29% full-time, 18% with terminal degrees. *Student/faculty ratio:* 11:1.

Majors Accounting; biblical studies; business administration and management; computer and information sciences; digital communication and media/multimedia; early childhood education; elementary education; finance and financial management services related; human services; liberal arts and sciences/liberal studies; management science; marketing/marketing management; missionary studies and missiology; multi-/interdisciplinary studies related; music; music teacher education; pastoral studies/counseling; religious studies; secondary education; theology; youth ministry.

Academics *Calendar:* semesters. *Degrees:* associate and bachelor's. *Special study options:* academic remediation for entering students, advanced placement credit, English as a second language, independent study, internships, off-campus study. *ROTC:* Army (c).

Computers on Campus 25 computers/terminals are available on campus for general student use. Students can access the following: library catalog search. Campuswide network is available.

Student Life *Housing:* on-campus residence required through sophomore year. *Options:* men-only, women-only. Campus housing is university owned. Freshman campus housing is guaranteed. *Activities and organizations:* drama/theater group, choral group, Ambassador Fellowship, Student Activities Committee, Student Council, Ambassador Staff, Campus Ministry Team. *Campus security:* student patrols, controlled dormitory access. *Student services:* personal/psychological counseling.

Athletics Member NCCAA. *Intercollegiate sports:* basketball M/W, soccer M, volleyball W. *Intramural sports:* basketball M, football M, golf M, racquetball M/W, skiing (cross-country) M/W, skiing (downhill) M/W, soccer M/W, table tennis M/W, tennis M/W, volleyball M, weight lifting M/W.

Standardized Tests *Required:* SAT and SAT Subject Tests or ACT (for admission).

Costs (2007–08) *One-time required fee:* $520. *Comprehensive fee:* $18,020 includes full-time tuition ($11,100), mandatory fees ($520), and room and board ($6400). Part-time tuition: $450 per semester hour. Part-time tuition and fees vary according to course load. *College room only:* $2800. Room and board charges vary according to housing facility. *Payment plan:* installment. *Waivers:* employees or children of employees.

Financial Aid Of all full-time matriculated undergraduates who enrolled in 2006, 145 applied for aid, 125 were judged to have need, 10 had their need fully met. 37 Federal Work-Study jobs (averaging $806). 19 state and other part-time jobs (averaging $371). In 2006, 3 non-need-based awards were made. *Average percent of need met:* 57%. *Average financial aid package:* $7762. *Average need-based loan:* $3350. *Average need-based gift aid:* $5532. *Average non-need-based aid:* $1375. *Average indebtedness upon graduation:* $13,640.

Applying *Options:* early admission, deferred entrance. *Required:* high school transcript, 2 letters of recommendation. *Required for some:* interview. *Recommended:* minimum 2.5 GPA. *Application deadline:* 7/15 (freshmen). *Notification:* continuous until 8/1 (freshmen), continuous (transfers).

Freshman Application Contact Mr. Kevin Gilliam, Director of Enrollment, Grace Bible College, 1101 Aldon Street, SW, PO Box 910, Grand Rapids, MI 49509. *Phone:* 616-538-2330 Ext. 239. *Toll-free phone:* 800-968-1887. *Fax:* 616-538-0599. *E-mail:* gbc@gbcol.edu.

GRAND VALLEY STATE UNIVERSITY

Allendale, Michigan **www.gvsu.edu/**

- **State-supported** comprehensive, founded 1960
- **Small-town** 900-acre campus with easy access to Grand Rapids
- **Endowment** $61.7 million
- **Coed** 19,806 undergraduate students, 87% full-time, 60% women, 40% men
- **Moderately difficult** entrance level, 69% of applicants were admitted

Undergraduates 17,294 full-time, 2,512 part-time. Students come from 34 states and territories, 55 other countries, 4% are from out of state, 5% African American, 3% Asian American or Pacific Islander, 3% Hispanic American, 0.6% Native American, 0.8% international, 8% transferred in, 26% live on campus. *Retention:* 84% of 2006 full-time freshmen returned.

Freshmen *Admission:* 13,435 applied, 9,335 admitted, 3,459 enrolled. *Average high school GPA:* 3.57. *Test scores:* SAT critical reading scores over 500: 73%; SAT math scores over 500: 77%; SAT writing scores over 500: 65%; ACT scores over 18: 99%; SAT critical reading scores over 600: 30%; SAT math scores over 600: 31%; SAT writing scores over 600: 20%; ACT scores over 24: 54%; SAT critical reading scores over 700: 6%; SAT math scores over 700: 4%; SAT writing scores over 700: 2%; ACT scores over 30: 7%.

Faculty *Total:* 1,452, 65% full-time, 46% with terminal degrees. *Student/faculty ratio:* 18:1.

Majors Accounting; advertising; anthropology; applied mathematics; art; art history, criticism and conservation; art teacher education; athletic training; behavioral sciences; biochemistry; biological and physical sciences; biology/biological sciences; biomedical sciences; broadcast journalism; business administration and management; cell and molecular biology; ceramic arts and ceramics; chemistry; cinematography and film/video production; classics and languages, literatures and linguistics; clinical laboratory science/medical technology; commercial and advertising art; computer and information sciences; computer engineering; computer programming; computer science; creative writing; criminal justice/law enforcement administration; criminal justice/police science; dramatic/theater arts; drawing; economics; education; electrical, electronics and communications engineering; elementary education; engineering; engineering/industrial management; English; film/cinema studies; finance; fine/studio arts; French; geology/earth science; German; health science; history; hotel/motel administration; humanities; human resources management; hydrology and water resources science; industrial engineering; information science/studies; interdisciplinary studies; international business/trade/commerce; international relations and affairs; journalism; labor and industrial relations; land use planning and management; legal assistant/paralegal; legal studies; liberal arts and sciences/liberal studies; literature; management information systems; marketing/marketing management; mass communication/media; mathematics; mechanical engineering; metal and jewelry arts; music; music teacher education; natural resources management and policy; natural sciences; nursing (registered nurse training); occupational safety and health technology; occupational therapist assistant; parks, recreation and leisure facilities management; philosophy; photography; physical education teaching and coaching; physical sciences; physical therapy; physician assistant; physics; physiological psychology/psychobiology; piano and organ; political science and government; pre-dentistry studies; pre-law studies; pre-medical studies; pre-veterinary studies; printmaking; psychology; public administration; public health; public policy analysis; public relations/image management; radiation biology; radio and television; reading teacher education; Russian studies; sanitation technology; science teacher education; sculpture; secondary education; social sciences; social studies teacher education; social work; sociology; Spanish; special education; statistics; technical and business writing; telecommunications; therapeutic recreation; tourism and travel services management; violin, viola, guitar and other stringed instruments; voice and opera; western civilization; wildlife and wildlands science and management; wildlife biology; wind/percussion instruments; women's studies.

Academics *Calendar:* semesters. *Degrees:* certificates, bachelor's, master's, post-master's, and postbachelor's certificates. *Special study options:* academic remediation for entering students, accelerated degree program, adult/continuing education programs, advanced placement credit, cooperative education, distance learning, double majors, English as a second language, freshman honors college, honors programs, independent study, internships, part-time degree program, services for LD students, study abroad, summer session for credit.

Computers on Campus 2,600 computers/terminals are available on campus for general student use. Students can access the following: online (class) grades, online (class) registration, transcript, degree audit, credit card payments. Campuswide network is available.

Student Life *Housing options:* coed. Campus housing is university owned. Freshman campus housing is guaranteed. *Activities and organizations:* drama/theater group, student-run newspaper, radio and television station, choral group, marching band, Black Student Union, Residence Hall Association, Crew Club, Student Senate, Student Organization Network, national fraternities, national sororities. *Campus security:* 24-hour emergency response devices and patrols, student patrols, late-night transport/escort service, controlled dormitory access. *Student services:* health clinic, personal/psychological counseling, women's center.

Athletics Member NCAA. All Division II. *Intercollegiate sports:* baseball M (s), basketball M (s)/W (s), cheerleading M (c)/W (c), crew M (c)/W (c), cross-country running M (s)/W (s), football M (s), golf M (s)/W (s), ice hockey M (c), rugby M (c)/W (c), sailing M (c)/W (c), skiing (downhill) M (c)/W (c), soccer M (c)/W (s), softball W (s), swimming and diving M (s)/W (s), tennis M (s)/W (s), track and field M (s)/W (s), volleyball M (c)/W (s), water polo M (c)/W (c), wrestling M (c). *Intramural sports:* archery M/W, badminton M/W, basketball M/W, bowling M/W, cheerleading M/W, crew M/W, cross-country running M/W, fencing M/W, field hockey M/W, football M/W, golf M/W, gymnastics M/W, racquetball M/W, skiing (cross-country) M/W, skiing (downhill) M/W, soccer M/W, softball M/W, squash M/W, swimming and diving M/W, tennis M/W, volleyball M/W, water polo M/W, weight lifting M/W, wrestling M.

Standardized Tests *Required:* SAT or ACT (for admission).

Costs (2007–08) *Tuition:* state resident $7240 full-time, $315 per credit hour part-time; nonresident $12,510 full-time, $532 per credit hour part-time. Full-time tuition and fees vary according to program and student level. Part-time tuition and fees vary according to course load, program, and student level. *Room and board:* $6880; room only: $4930. Room and board charges vary according to board plan, housing facility, and location. *Payment plans:* installment, deferred payment. *Waivers:* employees or children of employees.

Financial Aid Of all full-time matriculated undergraduates who enrolled in 2007, 12,543 applied for aid, 8,994 were judged to have need, 2,448 had their need fully met. 865 Federal Work-Study jobs (averaging $1200). 261 state and other part-time jobs (averaging $1340). In 2007, 1885 non-need-based awards were made. *Average percent of need met:* 72%. *Average financial aid package:* $7653. *Average need-based loan:* $4243. *Average need-based gift aid:* $5047. *Average non-need-based aid:* $3629. *Average indebtedness upon graduation:* $19,859.

Applying *Options:* electronic application. *Application fee:* $30. *Required:* high school transcript. *Required for some:* essay or personal statement, interview. *Application deadlines:* 5/1 (freshmen), 7/28 (transfers). *Notification:* continuous until 5/1 (freshmen), continuous until 7/20 (transfers).

Freshman Application Contact Ms. Jodi Chycinski, Director of Admissions, Grand Valley State University, 1 Campus Drive, Allendale, MI 49401. *Phone:* 616-331-2025. *Toll-free phone:* 800-748-0246. *Fax:* 616-331-2000. *E-mail:* go2gvsu@gvsu.edu.

See page 1344 for the College Close-Up.

GREAT LAKES CHRISTIAN COLLEGE

Lansing, Michigan — www.glcc.edu/

- **Independent** 4-year, founded 1949, affiliated with Christian Churches and Churches of Christ
- **Suburban** 50-acre campus
- **Endowment** $818,667
- **Coed** 260 undergraduate students, 71% full-time, 49% women, 51% men
- **Moderately difficult** entrance level

Undergraduates 184 full-time, 76 part-time. 11% African American, 0.8% Asian American or Pacific Islander, 1% Hispanic American, 1% international, 14% transferred in, 68% live on campus. *Retention;* 58% of 2006 full-time freshmen returned.

Freshmen *Admission:* 159 applied, 53 enrolled. *Test scores:* ACT scores over 18: 79%; ACT scores over 24: 19%; ACT scores over 30: 2%.

Faculty *Total:* 27, 37% full-time, 26% with terminal degrees. *Student/faculty ratio:* 14:1.

Majors Biblical studies; communication/speech communication and rhetoric; counseling psychology; divinity/ministry; early childhood education; family and consumer sciences/human sciences; general studies; history; religious education; religious/sacred music; youth ministry.

Academics *Calendar:* semesters. *Degrees:* associate and bachelor's. *Special study options:* adult/continuing education programs, advanced placement credit, double majors, external degree program, independent study, internships, off-campus study, part-time degree program. *Unusual degree programs:* 3-2 business administration with Davenport College of Business; education with Michigan State University.

Computers on Campus 24 computers/terminals are available on campus for general student use. Students can access the following: campus intranet, computer help desk, free student e-mail accounts, online (class) grades, online (class) schedules. Campuswide network is available. 100% of college-owned or -operated housing units are wired for high-speed Internet access. Wireless service is available via entire campus.

Student Life *Housing:* on-campus residence required through senior year. *Options:* men-only, women-only. Campus housing is university owned. Freshman applicants given priority for college housing. *Activities and organizations:* drama/theater group, choral group. *Campus security:* evening security patrols. *Student services:* personal/psychological counseling.

Athletics Member NCCAA. *Intercollegiate sports:* baseball M, basketball M/W, soccer M, volleyball M/W.

Standardized Tests *Required:* SAT or ACT (for admission).

Costs (2008–09) *Comprehensive fee:* $18,327 includes full-time tuition ($10,752), mandatory fees ($975), and room and board ($6600). Part-time tuition: $336 per hour.

Applying *Options:* electronic application. *Application fee:* $30. *Required:* essay or personal statement, high school transcript, minimum 2.25 GPA, 3 letters of recommendation. *Application deadlines:* 8/1 (freshmen), 8/1 (transfers). *Notification:* continuous until 8/15 (freshmen), continuous until 8/15 (transfers).

Freshman Application Contact Mr. Lloyd Scharer, Director of Admissions, Great Lakes Christian College, 6211 West Willow Highway, Lansing, MI 48917-1299. *Phone:* 517-321-0242. *Toll-free phone:* 800-YES-GLCC. *Fax:* 517-321-5902.

HILLSDALE COLLEGE

Hillsdale, Michigan — www.hillsdale.edu/

- **Independent** 4-year, founded 1844
- **Small-town** 200-acre campus
- **Endowment** $245.0 million
- **Coed** 1,326 undergraduate students, 97% full-time, 52% women, 48% men
- **Very difficult** entrance level, 64% of applicants were admitted

Undergraduates 1,284 full-time, 42 part-time. Students come from 48 states and territories, 7 other countries, 62% are from out of state, 1% international, 3% transferred in, 80% live on campus. *Retention:* 88% of 2006 full-time freshmen returned.

Freshmen *Admission:* 1,401 applied, 897 admitted, 346 enrolled. *Average high school GPA:* 3.72. *Test scores:* SAT critical reading scores over 500: 99%; SAT math scores over 500: 96%; SAT writing scores over 500: 98%; ACT scores over 18: 100%; SAT critical reading scores over 600: 87%; SAT math scores over 600: 69%; SAT writing scores over 600: 78%; ACT scores over 24: 84%; SAT critical reading scores over 700: 40%; SAT math scores over 700: 16%; SAT writing scores over 700: 26%; ACT scores over 30: 29%.

Faculty *Total:* 152, 72% full-time, 70% with terminal degrees. *Student/faculty ratio:* 10:1.

Majors Accounting; American studies; art; biology/biological sciences; business administration and management; chemistry; Christian studies; classics and languages, literatures and linguistics; communication/speech communication and rhetoric; comparative literature; computer science; dramatic/theater arts; early childhood education; economics; education; education (K-12); elementary education; English; European studies; finance; French; German; history; interdisciplinary studies; international relations and affairs; kindergarten/preschool education; marketing/marketing management; mathematics; mathematics related; music; philosophy; physical education teaching and coaching; physics; political science and government; pre-dentistry studies; pre-medical studies; pre-veterinary studies; psychology; religious studies; secondary education; sociology; Spanish.

Academics *Calendar:* semesters. *Degree:* bachelor's. *Special study options:* accelerated degree program, advanced placement credit, double majors, honors programs, independent study, internships, part-time degree program, study abroad, summer session for credit. *Unusual degree programs:* 3-2 engineering with Northwestern University, Tri-State University.

Computers on Campus 200 computers/terminals are available on campus for general student use. Students can access the following: computer help desk, free student e-mail accounts. Campuswide network is available. 100% of college-owned or -operated housing units are wired for high-speed Internet access. Wireless service is available via entire campus.

Student Life *Housing:* on-campus residence required through sophomore year. *Options:* men-only, women-only. Campus housing is university owned. Freshman campus housing is guaranteed. *Activities and organizations:* drama/theater group, student-run newspaper, choral group, Inter-Varsity Christian Fellowship, Varsity H-Club, Student Federation, Young Life, College Republicans, national fraternities, national sororities. *Campus security:* 24-hour emergency response devices and patrols, late-night transport/escort service, controlled dormitory access. *Student services:* health clinic, personal/psychological counseling.

Athletics Member NCAA. All Division II. *Intercollegiate sports:* baseball M, basketball M/W, equestrian sports W, football M (s), ice hockey M, lacrosse M, riflery M/W, soccer W, softball W (s), swimming and diving W (s), track and field M (s)/W (s), volleyball W (s). *Intramural sports:* equestrian sports W (c), football M/W, golf W, ice hockey M (c), lacrosse M (c), racquetball M/W, riflery M (c)/W (c), skiing (downhill) M (c)/W (c), soccer W (c), softball M/W, squash M/W, swimming and diving W, table tennis M/W, track and field M/W, ultimate Frisbee M/W, volleyball M/W.

Standardized Tests *Required:* SAT or ACT (for admission). *Recommended:* SAT Subject Tests (for admission).

Costs (2007–08) *Comprehensive fee:* $26,430 includes full-time tuition ($18,600), mandatory fees ($490), and room and board ($7340). Part-time tuition: $730 per semester hour. *College room only:* $3740. Room and board charges vary according to board plan. *Payment plans:* tuition prepayment, installment, deferred payment. *Waivers:* children of alumni and employees or children of employees.

Financial Aid Of all full-time matriculated undergraduates who enrolled in 2006, 600 applied for aid, 521 were judged to have need, 252 had their need fully met. In 2006, 335 non-need-based awards were made. *Average percent of need met:* 80%. *Average financial aid package:* $15,000. *Average need-based loan:* $3000. *Average need-based gift aid:* $8500. *Average non-need-based aid:* $7750. *Average indebtedness upon graduation:* $16,000. *Financial aid deadline:* 4/1.

Applying *Options:* electronic application, early admission, early decision, early action, deferred entrance. *Application fee:* $35. *Required:* essay or personal statement, high school transcript, 2 letters of recommendation. *Required for some:* interview. *Recommended:* minimum 3.3 GPA, interview. *Application deadlines:* 2/15 (freshmen), 2/15 (out-of-state freshmen), 2/15 (transfers), 1/1 (early action). *Early decision deadline:* 11/15. *Notification:* 4/1 (freshmen), 4/1 (out-of-state freshmen), 4/1 (transfers), 12/1 (early decision), 1/25 (early action).

Freshman Application Contact Mr. Jeffrey S. Lantis, Director of Admissions, Hillsdale College, 33 East College Street, Hillsdale, MI 49242-1298. *Phone:* 517-607-2327. *Fax:* 517-607-2223. *E-mail:* admissions@hillsdale.edu.

See page 1346 for the College Close-Up.

HOPE COLLEGE

Holland, Michigan www.hope.edu/

- **Independent** 4-year, founded 1866, affiliated with Reformed Church in America
- **Suburban** 45-acre campus with easy access to Grand Rapids
- **Endowment** $171.4 million
- **Coed** 3,226 undergraduate students, 96% full-time, 59% women, 41% men
- **Moderately difficult** entrance level, 83% of applicants were admitted

Undergraduates 3,084 full-time, 142 part-time. Students come from 45 states and territories, 31 other countries, 30% are from out of state, 2% African American, 2% Asian American or Pacific Islander, 3% Hispanic American, 0.4% Native American, 1% international, 2% transferred in, 81% live on campus. *Retention:* 88% of 2006 full-time freshmen returned.

Freshmen *Admission:* 2,748 applied, 2,275 admitted, 819 enrolled. *Average high school GPA:* 3.74. *Test scores:* SAT critical reading scores over 500: 83%; SAT math scores over 500: 85%; SAT writing scores over 500: 99%; ACT scores over 18: 99%; SAT critical reading scores over 600: 44%; SAT math scores over 600: 51%; SAT writing scores over 600: 73%; ACT scores over 24: 73%; SAT critical reading scores over 700: 10%; SAT math scores over 700: 14%; SAT writing scores over 700: 20%; ACT scores over 30: 20%.

Faculty *Total:* 326, 67% full-time, 61% with terminal degrees. *Student/faculty ratio:* 12:1.

Majors Accounting; ancient Near Eastern and biblical languages; art history, criticism and conservation; art teacher education; athletic training; biology/biological sciences; biology teacher education; business administration and management; business/managerial economics; chemistry; chemistry teacher education; classics and languages, literatures and linguistics; communication/speech communication and rhetoric; computer science; dance; drama and dance teacher education; dramatic/theater arts; economics; education (specific subject areas) related; elementary education; engineering; engineering physics; English; English/language arts teacher education; environmental studies; fine/studio arts; French; French language teacher education; geology/earth science; geophysics and seismology; German; German language teacher education; history; history teacher education; humanities; interdisciplinary studies; international/global studies; Japanese; jazz/jazz studies; kinesiology and exercise science; Latin; Latin teacher education; mathematics; mathematics teacher education; multi-/interdisciplinary studies related; music; music performance; music teacher education; music theory and composition; nursing (registered nurse training); philosophy; physical education teaching and coaching; physics; physics teacher education; piano and organ; political science and government; psychology; religious studies; science teacher education; secondary education; social sciences; social studies teacher education; social work; sociology; Spanish; Spanish language teacher education; special education (emotionally disturbed); special education (specific learning disabilities); theology and religious vocations related; violin, viola, guitar and other stringed instruments; voice and opera.

Academics *Calendar:* semesters. *Degree:* bachelor's. *Special study options:* advanced placement credit, double majors, English as a second language, independent study, internships, off-campus study, part-time degree program, services for LD students, student-designed majors, study abroad, summer session for credit. *ROTC:* Army (c).

Computers on Campus 300 computers/terminals and 5,000 ports are available on campus for general student use. Students can access the following: campus intranet, computer help desk, free student e-mail accounts, online (class) grades, online (class) registration, online (class) schedules. Campuswide network is available. 100% of college-owned or -operated housing units are wired for high-speed Internet access. Wireless service is available via entire campus.

Student Life *Housing:* on-campus residence required through junior year. *Options:* coed, men-only, women-only, disabled students. Campus housing is university owned and leased by the school. Freshman campus housing is guaranteed. *Activities and organizations:* drama/theater group, student-run newspaper, radio and television station, choral group, Fellowship of Christian Athletes, Social Activities Committee, national fraternities, national sororities. *Campus security:* 24-hour emergency response devices and patrols, late-night transport/escort service, controlled dormitory access. *Student services:* health clinic, personal/psychological counseling.

Athletics Member NCAA. All Division III. *Intercollegiate sports:* baseball M, basketball M/W, cheerleading M/W, cross-country running M/W, football M, golf M/W, ice hockey M (c), lacrosse M (c)/W (c), sailing M (c)/W (c), soccer M/W, softball W, swimming and diving M/W, tennis M/W, track and field M/W, volleyball W. *Intramural sports:* basketball M/W, bowling M/W, football M/W, racquetball M/W, soccer M/W, softball M/W, tennis M/W, ultimate Frisbee M/W, volleyball M/W, water polo M/W.

Standardized Tests *Required:* SAT or ACT (for admission).

Costs (2007–08) *Comprehensive fee:* $31,100 includes full-time tuition ($23,660), mandatory fees ($140), and room and board ($7300). Full-time tuition and fees vary according to course load. *College room only:* $3330. Room and board charges vary according to board plan. *Payment plan:* installment. *Waivers:* employees or children of employees.

Financial Aid Of all full-time matriculated undergraduates who enrolled in 2006, 2,040 applied for aid, 1,606 were judged to have need, 539 had their need fully met. 240 Federal Work-Study jobs (averaging $1352). 530 state and other part-time jobs (averaging $1818). In 2006, 867 non-need-based awards were made. *Average percent of need met:* 85%. *Average financial aid package:* $18,771. *Average need-based loan:* $4517. *Average need-based gift aid:* $13,521. *Average non-need-based aid:* $6975. *Average indebtedness upon graduation:* $23,324.

Applying *Options:* electronic application, early admission, deferred entrance. *Application fee:* $35. *Required:* essay or personal statement, high school transcript. *Required for some:* 1 letter of recommendation. *Recommended:* interview. *Application deadlines:* rolling (freshmen), rolling (transfers). *Notification:* continuous (freshmen), continuous (transfers).

Freshman Application Contact Hope College Admissions, Hope College, 69 East 10th Street, PO Box 9000, Holland, MI 49422-9000. *Phone:* 616-395-7850. *Toll-free phone:* 800-968-7850. *E-mail:* admissions@hope.edu.

See page 1348 for the College Close-Up.

KALAMAZOO COLLEGE

Kalamazoo, Michigan www.kzoo.edu/

- **Independent** 4-year, founded 1833, affiliated with American Baptist Churches in the U.S.A.
- **Suburban** 60-acre campus
- **Endowment** $172.0 million
- **Coed** 1,340 undergraduate students, 100% full-time, 58% women, 42% men
- **Very difficult** entrance level, 63% of applicants were admitted

Undergraduates 1,340 full-time. Students come from 38 states and territories, 13 other countries, 29% are from out of state, 4% African American, 6% Asian American or Pacific Islander, 4% Hispanic American, 0.1% Native American, 1% international, 0.4% transferred in, 75% live on campus. *Retention:* 91% of 2006 full-time freshmen returned.

Freshmen *Admission:* 2,092 applied, 1,310 admitted, 363 enrolled. *Average high school GPA:* 3.63. *Test scores:* SAT critical reading scores over 500: 93%;

SAT math scores over 500: 94%; ACT scores over 18: 99%; SAT critical reading scores over 600: 72%; SAT math scores over 600: 66%; ACT scores over 24: 91%; SAT critical reading scores over 700: 25%; SAT math scores over 700: 19%; ACT scores over 30: 30%.

Faculty *Total:* 113, 89% full-time, 81% with terminal degrees. *Student/faculty ratio:* 11:1.

Majors Anthropology; art; art history, criticism and conservation; biology/biological sciences; business/managerial economics; chemistry; classics and languages, literatures and linguistics; computer science; dramatic/theater arts; English; French; German; health science; history; interdisciplinary studies; mathematics; music; philosophy; physics; political science and government; psychology; religious studies; sociology; Spanish.

Academics *Calendar:* quarters. *Degree:* bachelor's. *Special study options:* advanced placement credit, double majors, independent study, internships, off-campus study, services for LD students, study abroad. *ROTC:* Army (c). *Unusual degree programs:* 3-2 engineering with University of Michigan, Washington University in St. Louis; architecture with Washington University in St. Louis education with Michigan State University, University of Michigan.

Computers on Campus 130 computers/terminals are available on campus for general student use. Students can access the following: campus intranet, computer help desk, free student e-mail accounts, online (class) grades, online (class) registration, online (class) schedules. Campuswide network is available. 100% of college-owned or -operated housing units are wired for high-speed Internet access. Wireless service is available via classrooms, computer centers, computer labs, libraries, student centers.

Student Life *Housing:* on-campus residence required through junior year. *Options:* coed, disabled students. Campus housing is university owned. Freshman campus housing is guaranteed. *Activities and organizations:* drama/theater group, student-run newspaper, radio and television station, choral group, Student Activities Committee, Student Commission, Index (college newspaper), Environmental Student Organization, volunteer organization. *Campus security:* 24-hour emergency response devices and patrols, late-night transport/escort service, controlled dormitory access. *Student services:* health clinic, personal/psychological counseling, women's center.

Athletics Member NCAA. All Division III. *Intercollegiate sports:* baseball M, basketball M/W, cross-country running M/W, football M, golf M/W, soccer M/W, softball W, swimming and diving M/W, tennis M/W, volleyball W. *Intramural sports:* badminton M/W, basketball M/W, cheerleading W, fencing M/W, gymnastics W (c), lacrosse W (c), racquetball M/W, rugby M (c)/W (c), skiing (downhill) M (c)/W (c), soccer M (c)/W (c), softball M/W, swimming and diving M/W, table tennis M/W, tennis M/W, track and field M (c)/W (c), ultimate Frisbee M (c)/W (c), volleyball M/W, water polo M/W.

Standardized Tests *Required:* SAT or ACT (for admission).

Costs (2007–08) *Comprehensive fee:* $35,838 includes full-time tuition ($28,716) and room and board ($7122). *College room only:* $3474. Room and board charges vary according to board plan. *Payment plan:* installment. *Waivers:* employees or children of employees.

Financial Aid Of all full-time matriculated undergraduates who enrolled in 2006, 845 applied for aid, 668 were judged to have need. 394 Federal Work-Study jobs (averaging $1583). 9 state and other part-time jobs (averaging $836). In 2006, 501 non-need-based awards were made. *Average financial aid package:* $22,820. *Average need-based loan:* $5329. *Average need-based gift aid:* $16,095. *Average non-need-based aid:* $9290. *Average indebtedness upon graduation:* $25,000.

Applying *Options:* electronic application, early decision, early action, deferred entrance. *Application fee:* $35. *Required:* essay or personal statement, high school transcript, 2 letters of recommendation. *Recommended:* minimum 3.0 GPA, interview. *Application deadlines:* 2/1 (freshmen), 5/1 (transfers), 12/1 (early action). *Early decision deadline:* 11/15. *Notification:* 4/1 (freshmen), 5/15 (transfers), 12/1 (early decision), 12/20 (early action).

Freshman Application Contact Mrs. Linda Wirgau, Records Manager, Kalamazoo College, Mandelle Hall, 1200 Academy Street, Kalamazoo, MI 49006-3295. *Phone:* 269-337-7166. *Toll-free phone:* 800-253-3602. *Fax:* 269-337-7190. *E-mail:* admissions@kzoo.edu.

KETTERING UNIVERSITY

Flint, Michigan — www.kettering.edu/

- **Independent** comprehensive, founded 1919
- **Urban** 85-acre campus with easy access to Detroit
- **Endowment** $65.5 million
- **Coed, primarily men** 2,178 undergraduate students, 100% full-time, 15% women, 85% men
- **Very difficult** entrance level, 72% of applicants were admitted

Undergraduates 2,178 full-time. Students come from 50 states and territories, 8 other countries, 32% are from out of state, 5% African American, 5% Asian American or Pacific Islander, 2% Hispanic American, 0.4% Native American, 2% international, 2% transferred in, 23% live on campus. *Retention:* 85% of 2006 full-time freshmen returned.

Freshmen *Admission:* 1,817 applied, 1,317 admitted, 385 enrolled. *Average high school GPA:* 3.55. *Test scores:* SAT critical reading scores over 500: 83%; SAT math scores over 500: 94%; ACT scores over 18: 100%; SAT critical reading scores over 600: 36%; SAT math scores over 600: 69%; ACT scores over 24: 86%; SAT critical reading scores over 700: 9%; SAT math scores over 700: 18%; ACT scores over 30: 19%.

Faculty *Total:* 138, 91% full-time, 74% with terminal degrees. *Student/faculty ratio:* 9:1.

Majors Applied mathematics; biochemistry; business administration, management and operations related; chemistry; chemistry related; computer engineering; computer science; electrical, electronics and communications engineering; engineering physics; industrial engineering; mechanical engineering; physics.

Academics *Calendar:* semesters (11 weeks of full-time study plus 12 weeks of paid co-op experience per semester). *Degrees:* bachelor's and master's. *Special study options:* accelerated degree program, advanced placement credit, cooperative education, distance learning, double majors, independent study, internships, services for LD students, study abroad.

Computers on Campus 300 computers/terminals and 800 ports are available on campus for general student use. Students can access the following: campus intranet, computer help desk, free student e-mail accounts, online (class) grades, online (class) registration, online (class) schedules. Campuswide network is available. 100% of college-owned or -operated housing units are wired for high-speed Internet access. Wireless service is available via classrooms, computer centers, computer labs, learning centers, libraries, student centers.

Student Life *Housing:* on-campus residence required for freshman year. *Options:* coed. Campus housing is university owned and is provided by a third party. Freshman campus housing is guaranteed. *Activities and organizations:* drama/theater group, student-run newspaper, radio station, choral group, student government, Society of Automotive Engineers, Firebirds, Outdoors Club, International Club, national fraternities, national sororities. *Campus security:* 24-hour emergency response devices and patrols, late-night transport/escort service, controlled dormitory access. *Student services:* health clinic, personal/psychological counseling, women's center.

Athletics *Intercollegiate sports:* ice hockey M (c), lacrosse M (c), soccer M (c), volleyball M (c). *Intramural sports:* basketball M/W, bowling M/W, cross-country running M/W, football M/W, golf M/W, ice hockey M/W, lacrosse M/W, racquetball M/W, riflery M/W, rock climbing M/W, rugby M/W, soccer M/W, softball M/W, squash M/W, swimming and diving M/W, table tennis M/W, tennis M/W, track and field M/W, ultimate Frisbee M/W, volleyball M/W, water polo M/W.

Standardized Tests *Required:* SAT or ACT (for admission).

Costs (2007–08) *Comprehensive fee:* $31,456 includes full-time tuition ($25,248), mandatory fees ($410), and room and board ($5798). Part-time tuition: $789 per credit hour. *College room only:* $3708. *Payment plan:* installment. *Waivers:* employees or children of employees.

Financial Aid Of all full-time matriculated undergraduates who enrolled in 2005, 1,789 applied for aid, 1,651 were judged to have need, 158 had their need fully met. 233 Federal Work-Study jobs (averaging $907). 63 state and other part-time jobs (averaging $356). In 2005, 433 non-need-based awards were made. *Average percent of need met:* 52%. *Average financial aid package:* $13,586. *Average need-based loan:* $3921. *Average need-based gift aid:* $9388. *Average non-need-based aid:* $6915. *Average indebtedness upon graduation:* $47,487.

Applying *Options:* electronic application, deferred entrance. *Application fee:* $35. *Required:* high school transcript. *Required for some:* essay or personal statement. *Recommended:* minimum 3.0 GPA, interview. *Application deadlines:* rolling (freshmen), rolling (transfers). *Notification:* continuous (freshmen), continuous (transfers).

Freshman Application Contact Ms. Barbara Sosin, Director of Admissions, Kettering University, 1700 West Third Avenue, Flint, MI 48504-4898. *Phone:* 810-762-7865. *Toll-free phone:* 800-955-4464 Ext. 7865 (in-state); 800-955-4464 (out-of-state). *Fax:* 810-762-9837. *E-mail:* admissions@kettering.edu.

See page 1350 for the College Close-Up.

KUYPER COLLEGE

Grand Rapids, Michigan — www.kuyper.edu/

- **Independent religious** 4-year, founded 1939
- **Suburban** 34-acre campus
- **Endowment** $8.0 million
- **Coed** 297 undergraduate students, 85% full-time, 51% women, 49% men

• **Moderately difficult** entrance level, 93% of applicants were admitted

Kuyper College is a ministry-focused Christian leadership college that offers degrees in twenty-one fields of study, including social work, youth ministry, music and worship, and communication arts. Kuyper equips students with a biblical, Reformed worldview to effectively serve Christ's church and his world and to bring God's grace into today's culture.

Undergraduates 253 full-time, 44 part-time. Students come from 16 states and territories, 8 other countries, 24% are from out of state, 3% African American, 2% Asian American or Pacific Islander, 4% Hispanic American, 0.3% Native American, 9% international, 16% transferred in, 44% live on campus. *Retention:* 68% of 2006 full-time freshmen returned.

Freshmen *Admission:* 142 applied, 132 admitted, 68 enrolled. *Average high school GPA:* 3.2. *Test scores:* SAT math scores over 500: 67%; SAT writing scores over 500: 67%; ACT scores over 18: 87%; SAT math scores over 600: 17%; SAT writing scores over 600: 17%; ACT scores over 24: 31%; ACT scores over 30: 2%.

Faculty *Total:* 30, 47% full-time, 30% with terminal degrees. *Student/faculty ratio:* 15:1.

Majors Accounting; administrative assistant and secretarial science; biblical studies; broadcast journalism; business administration and management; child development; communication/speech communication and rhetoric; computer and information sciences; divinity/ministry; dramatic/theater arts; elementary education; interdisciplinary studies; international business/trade/commerce; kinesiology and exercise science; liberal arts and sciences/liberal studies; mass communication/media; missionary studies and missiology; nursing (registered nurse training); pastoral studies/counseling; pre-theology/pre-ministerial studies; religious education; religious/sacred music; secondary education; social work; theology; youth ministry.

Academics *Calendar:* semesters. *Degrees:* certificates, associate, bachelor's, and postbachelor's certificates. *Special study options:* academic remediation for entering students, advanced placement credit, cooperative education, double majors, English as a second language, independent study, internships, off-campus study, part-time degree program, services for LD students, study abroad, summer session for credit. *Unusual degree programs:* 3-2 business administration; social work; education.

Computers on Campus 70 computers/terminals are available on campus for general student use. Students can access the following: campus intranet, computer help desk, free student e-mail accounts, online (class) grades, online (class) registration, online (class) schedules. Campuswide network is available. 100% of college-owned or -operated housing units are wired for high-speed Internet access. Wireless service is available via entire campus.

Student Life *Housing:* on-campus residence required through sophomore year. *Options:* men-only, women-only. Campus housing is university owned. Freshman campus housing is guaranteed. *Activities and organizations:* drama/theater group, choral group, Bible study and prayer groups, Student Council, yearbook, Wellspring Drama Club. *Campus security:* student patrols, late-night transport/escort service, controlled dormitory access. *Student services:* health clinic, personal/psychological counseling.

Athletics Member NCCAA. *Intercollegiate sports:* basketball M/W. *Intramural sports:* basketball M/W, football M/W, soccer M/W, softball M/W, table tennis M/W, ultimate Frisbee M/W, volleyball M/W.

Standardized Tests *Required:* SAT or ACT (for admission).

Costs (2008–09) *Comprehensive fee:* $19,609 includes full-time tuition ($13,384), mandatory fees ($525), and room and board ($5700). Part-time tuition: $641 per credit hour.

Financial Aid Of all full-time matriculated undergraduates who enrolled in 2006, 215 applied for aid, 140 were judged to have need, 24 had their need fully met. 29 Federal Work-Study jobs (averaging $1141). 75 state and other part-time jobs (averaging $3000). In 2006, 75 non-need-based awards were made. *Average percent of need met:* 71%. *Average financial aid package:* $10,860. *Average need-based loan:* $3328. *Average need-based gift aid:* $5824. *Average non-need-based aid:* $1550. *Average indebtedness upon graduation:* $12,900.

Applying *Options:* electronic application, deferred entrance. *Application fee:* $25. *Required:* essay or personal statement, high school transcript, minimum 2.5 GPA. *Required for some:* interview. *Application deadline:* rolling (freshmen). *Notification:* continuous (transfers).

Freshman Application Contact Admissions Office, Kuyper College, 3333 East Beltline Avenue, NE, Grand Rapids, MI 49525. *Phone:* 616-222-3000 Ext. 632. *Toll-free phone:* 800-511-3749. *Fax:* 616-222-3045. *E-mail:* admissions@kuyper.edu.

LAKE SUPERIOR STATE UNIVERSITY

Sault Sainte Marie, Michigan **www.lssu.edu/**

- **State-supported** 4-year, founded 1946
- **Small-town** 115-acre campus
- **Endowment** $12.8 million
- **Coed** 2,889 undergraduate students, 71% full-time, 53% women, 47% men
- **Moderately difficult** entrance level, 91% of applicants were admitted

Undergraduates 2,060 full-time, 829 part-time. Students come from 23 states and territories, 4 other countries, 14% are from out of state, 2% African American, 0.3% Asian American or Pacific Islander, 0.9% Hispanic American, 7% Native American, 10% international, 6% transferred in, 26% live on campus. *Retention:* 61% of 2006 full-time freshmen returned.

Freshmen *Admission:* 1,545 applied, 1,403 admitted, 462 enrolled. *Average high school GPA:* 3.06. *Test scores:* ACT scores over 18: 81%; ACT scores over 24: 27%; ACT scores over 30: 2%.

Faculty *Total:* 189, 55% full-time. *Student/faculty ratio:* 17:1.

Majors Accounting; athletic training; business administration and management; business/managerial economics; chemistry; clinical laboratory science/medical technology; computer engineering technology; computer science; construction engineering technology; corrections; criminal justice/law enforcement administration; criminal justice/police science; early childhood education; education; education (multiple levels); electrical, electronic and communications engineering technology; electrical, electronics and communications engineering; elementary education; engineering; engineering/industrial management; engineering technology; English; environmental engineering technology; environmental studies; finance; fire science; fish/game management; French studies; geology/earth science; history; human services; hydrology and water resources science; industrial technology; interdisciplinary studies; kinesiology and exercise science; legal assistant/paralegal; legal studies; liberal arts and sciences/liberal studies; literature; management information systems; mathematics; mathematics and computer science; mechanical engineering; mechanical engineering/mechanical technology; mental health/rehabilitation; middle school education; natural resources management and policy; nursing (registered nurse training); office management; parks, recreation and leisure; parks, recreation and leisure facilities management; political science and government; pre-dentistry studies; pre-law studies; psychiatric/mental health services technology; psychology; robotics technology; secondary education; social sciences; sociology; sport and fitness administration/management; water quality and wastewater treatment management and recycling technology; wildlife and wildlands science and management.

Academics *Calendar:* semesters. *Degrees:* certificates, associate, bachelor's, and master's. *Special study options:* adult/continuing education programs, advanced placement credit, cooperative education, distance learning, double majors, freshman honors college, honors programs, independent study, internships, part-time degree program, services for LD students, student-designed majors, study abroad, summer session for credit.

Computers on Campus 350 computers/terminals are available on campus for general student use. Students can access the following: campus intranet, computer help desk, free student e-mail accounts, online (class) grades, online (class) registration, online (class) schedules. Campuswide network is available. 100% of college-owned or -operated housing units are wired for high-speed Internet access. Wireless service is available via classrooms, libraries, student centers.

Student Life *Housing:* on-campus residence required through sophomore year. *Options:* coed, men-only, women-only. Campus housing is university owned. Freshman campus housing is guaranteed. *Activities and organizations:* drama/theater group, student-run newspaper, radio station, choral group, SIFE—Students Involved in Free Enterprise, SAILS—Student Alumni Involved in Lake State, Political Science Club, LSSNA—Lake State Nursing Association, Anchor House/His House, national fraternities, national sororities. *Campus security:* 24-hour emergency response devices and patrols, student patrols, late-night transport/escort service. *Student services:* health clinic, personal/psychological counseling.

Athletics Member NCAA. All Division II except ice hockey (Division I). *Intercollegiate sports:* basketball M (s)/W (s), cross-country running M (s)/W (s), ice hockey M (s), softball W (s), tennis M (s)/W (s), track and field M (s)/W (s), volleyball W (s). *Intramural sports:* basketball M/W, football M/W, ice hockey M, racquetball M/W, softball M/W, tennis M/W, track and field M/W, volleyball M/W, water polo M/W.

Standardized Tests *Required:* SAT or ACT (for admission).

Costs (2007–08) *Tuition:* state resident $7246 full-time, $299 per credit hour part-time; nonresident $14,422 full-time, $598 per credit hour part-time. Full-time tuition and fees vary according to reciprocity agreements. Part-time tuition and fees vary according to course load and reciprocity agreements. *Required fees:* $70 full-time. *Room and board:* $7172. Room and board charges vary according to board plan and housing facility. *Payment plans:* installment, deferred payment. *Waivers:* minority students, children of alumni, senior citizens, and employees or children of employees.

Financial Aid Of all full-time matriculated undergraduates who enrolled in 2006, 1,864 applied for aid, 1,728 were judged to have need. In 2006, 41 non-need-based awards were made. *Average percent of need met:* 71%. *Average financial aid package:* $9619. *Average need-based loan:* $4815. *Average need-based gift aid:* $3630. *Average non-need-based aid:* $2234. *Average indebtedness upon graduation:* $21,147.

Applying *Options:* electronic application, deferred entrance. *Application fee:* $35. *Required:* high school transcript. *Required for some:* minimum 2.2 GPA. *Application deadlines:* 8/15 (freshmen), rolling (transfers). *Notification:* continuous (freshmen), continuous (transfers).

Freshman Application Contact Ms. Susan Camp, Director of Admissions, Lake Superior State University, 650 West Easterday Avenue, Sault Saint Marie, MI 49783-1699. *Phone:* 906-635-2231. *Toll-free phone:* 888-800-LSSU Ext. 2231. *Fax:* 906-635-6669. *E-mail:* admissions@lssu.edu.

LAWRENCE TECHNOLOGICAL UNIVERSITY

Southfield, Michigan **www.ltu.edu/**

- **Independent** university, founded 1932
- **Suburban** 115-acre campus with easy access to Detroit
- **Endowment** $28.1 million
- **Coed** 3,008 undergraduate students, 55% full-time, 20% women, 80% men
- **Moderately difficult** entrance level, 60% of applicants were admitted

Undergraduates 1,655 full-time, 1,353 part-time. Students come from 28 states and territories, 13 other countries, 2% are from out of state, 10% African American, 2% Asian American or Pacific Islander, 2% Hispanic American, 0.3% Native American, 9% international, 8% transferred in, 17% live on campus. *Retention:* 67% of 2006 full-time freshmen returned.

Freshmen *Admission:* 1,585 applied, 957 admitted, 399 enrolled. *Average high school GPA:* 3.21. *Test scores:* ACT scores over 18: 86%; ACT scores over 24: 50%; ACT scores over 30: 7%.

Faculty *Total:* 375, 30% full-time, 51% with terminal degrees. *Student/faculty ratio:* 13:1.

Majors Architecture; biochemistry; biomedical/medical engineering; business administration and management; chemical technology; chemistry; chemistry related; civil engineering; communications technology; computer engineering; computer science; construction engineering technology; construction management; electrical and electronic engineering technologies related; electrical, electronic and communications engineering technology; electrical, electronics and communications engineering; engineering/industrial management; engineering technology; environmental design/architecture; general studies; humanities; illustration; industrial technology; information technology; interior architecture; manufacturing technology; mathematics; mathematics and computer science; mechanical engineering; mechanical engineering/mechanical technology; physics; physics related; psychology; radio and television.

Academics *Calendar:* semesters. *Degrees:* certificates, associate, bachelor's, master's, doctoral, and postbachelor's certificates. *Special study options:* academic remediation for entering students, adult/continuing education programs, advanced placement credit, cooperative education, distance learning, double majors, English as a second language, independent study, internships, off-campus study, part-time degree program, services for LD students, study abroad, summer session for credit. *ROTC:* Army (c), Navy (c), Air Force (c).

Computers on Campus 60 computers/terminals are available on campus for general student use. Students can access the following: campus intranet, computer help desk, free student e-mail accounts, online (class) grades, online (class) registration, online (class) schedules, degree audit, Blackboard, SCT Banner (student information). Campuswide network is available. 100% of college-owned or -operated housing units are wired for high-speed Internet access. Wireless service is available via entire campus.

Student Life *Housing options:* coed, disabled students. Campus housing is university owned. Freshman applicants given priority for college housing. *Activities and organizations:* drama/theater group, student-run newspaper, American Society of Mechanical Engineers, Institute of Electric and Electronic Engineers, American Institute of Architecture Students, American Society of Civil Engineers, Student Government, national fraternities, national sororities. *Campus security:* 24-hour emergency response devices and patrols, late-night transport/escort service, controlled dormitory access. *Student services:* personal/psychological counseling.

Athletics *Intramural sports:* badminton M/W, basketball M/W, bowling M/W, football M, golf M/W, ice hockey M (c), racquetball M/W, skiing (cross-country) M/W, skiing (downhill) M/W, soccer M (c)/W, softball M/W, table tennis M/W, tennis M/W, volleyball M (c)/W.

Standardized Tests *Required:* SAT or ACT (for admission).

Costs (2007–08) *Comprehensive fee:* $28,368 includes full-time tuition ($20,176), mandatory fees ($320), and room and board ($7872). Full-time tuition and fees vary according to course level, degree level, location, program, and student level. Part-time tuition: $672 per credit hour. Part-time tuition and fees vary according to course level, degree level, location, program, and student level. *Required fees:* $215 per term part-time. *College room only:* $5292. Room and board charges vary according to board plan and housing facility. *Payment plan:* installment. *Waivers:* employees or children of employees.

Financial Aid Of all full-time matriculated undergraduates who enrolled in 2005, 1,455 applied for aid, 1,019 were judged to have need, 193 had their need fully met. 140 Federal Work-Study jobs (averaging $4000). 18 state and other part-time jobs (averaging $2000). In 2005, 295 non-need-based awards were made. *Average percent of need met:* 69%. *Average financial aid package:* $14,891. *Average need-based loan:* $4199. *Average need-based gift aid:* $7180. *Average non-need-based aid:* $6648. *Average indebtedness upon graduation:* $29,224.

Applying *Options:* electronic application, early admission, deferred entrance. *Application fee:* $30. *Required:* high school transcript, minimum 2.5 GPA. *Required for some:* essay or personal statement, letters of recommendation, interview. *Application deadlines:* 8/15 (freshmen), 8/15 (transfers). *Notification:* continuous until 8/26 (freshmen).

Freshman Application Contact Ms. Jane Rohrback, Director of Admissions, Lawrence Technological University, 21000 West Ten Mile Road, Southfield, MI 48075. *Phone:* 248-204-3160. *Toll-free phone:* 800-225-5588. *Fax:* 248-204-3188. *E-mail:* admissions@ltu.edu.

See page 1352 for the College Close-Up.

MADONNA UNIVERSITY

Livonia, Michigan **www.madonna.edu/**

- **Independent Roman Catholic** comprehensive, founded 1947
- **Suburban** 49-acre campus with easy access to Detroit
- **Endowment** $34.0 million
- **Coed** 3,064 undergraduate students, 51% full-time, 75% women, 25% men
- **Moderately difficult** entrance level, 77% of applicants were admitted

Undergraduates 1,551 full-time, 1,513 part-time. Students come from 12 states and territories, 30 other countries, 1% are from out of state, 15% African American, 2% Asian American or Pacific Islander, 3% Hispanic American, 0.4% Native American, 4% international, 59% transferred in, 4% live on campus. *Retention:* 71% of 2006 full-time freshmen returned.

Freshmen *Admission:* 642 applied, 496 admitted, 275 enrolled. *Average high school GPA:* 3.2. *Test scores:* ACT scores over 18: 83%; ACT scores over 24: 26%; ACT scores over 30: 3%.

Faculty *Total:* 334, 34% full-time, 68% with terminal degrees. *Student/faculty ratio:* 13:1.

Majors Accounting; adult development and aging; American Sign Language (ASL); art; art history, criticism and conservation; biochemistry; biological and physical sciences; biology/biological sciences; business administration and management; chemistry; child development; clinical laboratory science/medical technology; clinical/medical laboratory technology; communication/speech communication and rhetoric; computer and information sciences; computer and information sciences related; computer science; consumer merchandising/retailing management; criminal justice/safety; dietetics and clinical nutrition services related; early childhood education; education; education related; education (specific subject areas) related; elementary education; English; environmental science; family and consumer sciences/human sciences; fine arts related; fire science; foods, nutrition, and wellness; forensic science and technology; gerontology; graphic design; health/health care administration; history; hospitality administration; human resources management; industrial and organizational psychology; industrial radiologic technology; information science/studies; international business/trade/commerce; journalism; legal assistant/paralegal; management information systems; management science; marketing/marketing management; mass communication/media; mathematics; mathematics teacher education; music; music pedagogy; natural sciences; nursing (registered nurse training); nursing related; pastoral counseling and specialized ministries related; philosophy; Polish; psychology; psychology related; public relations, advertising, and applied communication related; public relations/image management; quality control and safety technologies related; radio, television, and digital communication related; religious studies; safety/security technology; science teacher education; science technologies related; secondary education; social studies teacher education; social work; sociology; Spanish; special education; special education (specific learning disabilities); speech and rhetoric; theology.

Academics *Calendar:* semesters. *Degrees:* certificates, diplomas, associate, bachelor's, master's, post-master's, and postbachelor's certificates. *Special study options:* academic remediation for entering students, accelerated degree program, adult/continuing education programs, advanced placement credit, cooperative education, distance learning, double majors, English as a second language, independent study, internships, off-campus study, part-time degree program, services for LD students, student-designed majors, study abroad, summer session for credit.

Computers on Campus 175 computers/terminals and 180 ports are available on campus for general student use. Students can access the following: computer help desk, free student e-mail accounts, online (class) grades, online (class) registration, online (class) schedules. Campuswide network is available. 100% of college-owned or -operated housing units are wired for high-speed Internet access. Wireless service is available via classrooms, computer labs, dorm rooms, learning centers, libraries, student centers.

Student Life *Housing options:* coed. Campus housing is university owned. Freshman campus housing is guaranteed. *Activities and organizations:* student-run newspaper, radio station, choral group, Campus Ministry, Gerontology Association, Madonna University Nursing Student Association, Society of Future Teachers, International Students. *Campus security:* 24-hour emergency response devices and patrols, late-night transport/escort service, controlled dormitory access. *Student services:* personal/psychological counseling.

Athletics Member NAIA. *Intercollegiate sports:* baseball M (s), basketball M (s)/W (s), cross-country running M (s)/W (s), golf M (s)/W (s), soccer M (s)/W (s), softball W (s), volleyball W (s).

Standardized Tests *Required:* SAT or ACT (for admission).

Costs (2007–08) *Comprehensive fee:* $17,772 includes full-time tuition ($11,580), mandatory fees ($100), and room and board ($6092). Part-time tuition: $386 per credit hour. *Required fees:* $50 per term part-time. *College room only:* $2652. Room and board charges vary according to board plan. *Payment plan:* deferred payment. *Waivers:* senior citizens and employees or children of employees.

Financial Aid Of all full-time matriculated undergraduates who enrolled in 2007, 862 applied for aid, 698 were judged to have need, 122 had their need fully met. In 2007, 172 non-need-based awards were made. *Average percent of need met:* 56%. *Average financial aid package:* $7396. *Average need-based loan:* $3862. *Average need-based gift aid:* $4508. *Average non-need-based aid:* $2427.

Applying *Options:* electronic application, early admission, deferred entrance. *Application fee:* $25. *Required:* essay or personal statement, high school transcript, minimum 2.75 GPA, ACT composite score greater than 19. *Required for some:* 2 letters of recommendation. *Recommended:* interview. *Application deadlines:* rolling (freshmen), rolling (transfers). *Notification:* continuous (freshmen), continuous (transfers).

Freshman Application Contact Mr. Mike Quattro, Director of Enrollment Management, Madonna University, 36600 Schoolcraft Road, Livonia, MI 48150-1173. *Phone:* 734-432-5317. *Toll-free phone:* 800-852-4951. *Fax:* 734-432-5393. *E-mail:* muinfo@madonna.edu.

MARYGROVE COLLEGE

Detroit, Michigan — www.marygrove.edu/

- **Independent Roman Catholic** comprehensive, founded 1905
- **Urban** 50-acre campus
- **Endowment** $10.4 million
- **Coed, primarily women**
- **Moderately difficult** entrance level

Faculty *Student/faculty ratio:* 22:1.

Academics *Calendar:* semesters. *Degrees:* certificates, diplomas, associate, bachelor's, master's, and postbachelor's certificates.

Student Life *Campus security:* 24-hour emergency response devices and patrols, late-night transport/escort service.

Standardized Tests *Required:* ACT (for admission).

Costs (2007–08) *One-time required fee:* $25. *Comprehensive fee:* $21,290 includes full-time tuition ($14,380), mandatory fees ($310), and room and board ($6600). Part-time tuition: $512 per credit. Part-time tuition and fees vary according to location. *Room and board:* Room and board charges vary according to board plan.

Applying *Options:* early admission, deferred entrance. *Application fee:* $25. *Required:* high school transcript, minimum 2.7 GPA. *Required for some:* letters of recommendation, interview.

Freshman Application Contact Mr. John Ambrose, Director of Undergraduate Admissions, Marygrove College, Office of Admissions, Detroit, MI 48221-2599. *Phone:* 313-927-1236. *Toll-free phone:* 866-313-1297. *Fax:* 313-927-1345. *E-mail:* info@marygrove.edu.

MICHIGAN JEWISH INSTITUTE

Oak Park, Michigan — www.mji.edu/

- **Independent** 4-year, founded 1994
- **Coed** 256 undergraduate students
- **Minimally difficult** entrance level

Undergraduates *Retention:* 63% of 2006 full-time freshmen returned.

Faculty *Total:* 24, 25% full-time, 38% with terminal degrees.

Majors Computer and information sciences; information science/studies; Judaic studies; talmudic studies.

Academics *Calendar:* semesters. *Degrees:* certificates, associate, and bachelor's. *Special study options:* academic remediation for entering students, accelerated degree program, adult/continuing education programs, advanced placement credit, cooperative education, double majors, English as a second language, independent study, internships, services for LD students, study abroad, summer session for credit.

Computers on Campus 11 computers/terminals are available on campus for general student use. Students can access the following: campus intranet, computer help desk, online (class) grades, online (class) registration, online (class) schedules. Campuswide network is available. Wireless service is available via entire campus.

Student Life *Housing:* college housing not available.

Costs (2007–08) *Tuition:* $10,080 full-time. Full-time tuition and fees vary according to course load and program. Part-time tuition and fees vary according to course load and program. *Required fees:* $100 full-time. *Payment plans:* installment, deferred payment.

Applying *Options:* electronic application, early admission, deferred entrance. *Application fee:* $50. *Required:* high school transcript, minimum 2.0 GPA. *Application deadlines:* rolling (freshmen), rolling (transfers). *Notification:* continuous (freshmen), continuous (transfers).

Freshman Application Contact Mr. Dov Stein, Michigan Jewish Institute, 25401 Coolidge Highway, Oak Park, MI 48237. *Phone:* 248-414-6900 Ext. 103. *Fax:* 248-414-6907. *E-mail:* dstein@mji.edu.

MICHIGAN STATE UNIVERSITY

East Lansing, Michigan — www.msu.edu/

- **State-supported** university, founded 1855
- **Suburban** 5192-acre campus with easy access to Detroit
- **Endowment** $1.3 billion
- **Coed** 36,072 undergraduate students, 92% full-time, 53% women, 47% men
- **Moderately difficult** entrance level, 74% of applicants were admitted

Undergraduates 33,088 full-time, 2,984 part-time. Students come from 55 states and territories, 89 other countries, 8% are from out of state, 8% African American, 5% Asian American or Pacific Islander, 3% Hispanic American, 0.7% Native American, 4% international, 4% transferred in, 43% live on campus. *Retention:* 91% of 2006 full-time freshmen returned.

Freshmen *Admission:* 24,436 applied, 18,040 admitted, 7,541 enrolled. *Average high school GPA:* 3.59. *Test scores:* SAT critical reading scores over 500: 70%; SAT math scores over 500: 82%; SAT writing scores over 500: 68%; ACT scores over 18: 97%; SAT critical reading scores over 600: 33%; SAT math scores over 600: 47%; SAT writing scores over 600: 27%; ACT scores over 24: 66%; SAT critical reading scores over 700: 8%; SAT math scores over 700: 11%; SAT writing scores over 700: 5%; ACT scores over 30: 11%.

Faculty *Total:* 2,954, 87% full-time, 88% with terminal degrees. *Student/faculty ratio:* 17:1.

Majors Accounting; advertising; agricultural/biological engineering and bioengineering; agricultural business and management; agricultural communication/journalism; agricultural economics; agriculture and agriculture operations related; American studies; ancient studies; animal sciences; anthropology; apparel and textiles; applied economics; applied mathematics; art; art history, criticism and conservation; art teacher education; astrophysics; audiology and speech-language pathology; biochemistry; biochemistry/biophysics and molecular biology; biological and physical sciences; biology/biological sciences; biomedical/medical engineering; botany/plant biology; business administration and management; chemical engineering; chemical physics; chemistry; chemistry teacher education;

child development; city/urban, community and regional planning; civil engineering; clinical laboratory science/medical technology; communication/speech communication and rhetoric; computational mathematics; computer and information sciences; computer engineering; construction management; criminal justice/law enforcement administration; criminal justice/safety; dietetics; dramatic/theater arts; East Asian languages related; economics; education; electrical, electronics and communications engineering; elementary education; engineering; English; entomology; environmental biology; environmental science; environmental studies; family and community services; family and consumer sciences/home economics teacher education; family and consumer sciences/human sciences; fashion/apparel design; finance; food science; forestry; French; geography; geology/earth science; geophysics and seismology; German; history; horticultural science; hospitality administration; hotel/motel administration; humanities; human resources management; interior design; international/global studies; international relations and affairs; jazz/jazz studies; journalism; kinesiology and exercise science; landscape architecture; logistics and materials management; marketing/marketing management; mass communication/media; materials science; mathematics; mechanical engineering; merchandising; microbiology; music; music pedagogy; music performance; music teacher education; music theory and composition; music therapy; natural resource economics; nursing (registered nurse training); nutrition sciences; operations management; parks, recreation and leisure facilities management; philosophy; physical and theoretical chemistry; physical education teaching and coaching; physical sciences; physics; physiology; plant pathology/phytopathology; political science and government; pre-law studies; pre-medical studies; pre-veterinary studies; psychology; public administration; radio and television; religious studies; Russian; science, technology and society; social sciences; social science teacher education; social work; sociology; soil science and agronomy; Spanish; special education; special education (hearing impaired); special education (specific learning disabilities); statistics; technical and business writing; telecommunications; veterinary/animal health technology; veterinary technology; zoology/animal biology.

Academics *Calendar:* semesters. *Degrees:* certificates, bachelor's, master's, doctoral, first professional, and post-master's certificates. *Special study options:* academic remediation for entering students, accelerated degree program, adult/continuing education programs, advanced placement credit, cooperative education, distance learning, double majors, English as a second language, freshman honors college, honors programs, independent study, internships, off-campus study, part-time degree program, services for LD students, student-designed majors, study abroad, summer session for credit. *ROTC:* Army (b), Air Force (b).

Computers on Campus 2,100 computers/terminals are available on campus for general student use. Students can access the following: campus intranet, computer help desk, free student e-mail accounts, online (class) grades, online (class) registration, online (class) schedules. Campuswide network is available. 100% of college-owned or -operated housing units are wired for high-speed Internet access. Wireless service is available via classrooms, computer centers, computer labs, learning centers, libraries, student centers.

Student Life *Housing:* on-campus residence required for freshman year. *Options:* coed, women-only, cooperative, disabled students. Campus housing is university owned. Freshman campus housing is guaranteed. *Activities and organizations:* drama/theater group, student-run newspaper, radio and television station, choral group, marching band, national fraternities, national sororities. *Campus security:* 24-hour emergency response devices and patrols, late-night transport/escort service, self-defense workshops. *Student services:* health clinic, personal/psychological counseling, women's center, legal services.

Athletics Member NCAA. All Division I except football (Division I-A). *Intercollegiate sports:* baseball M (s), basketball M (s)/W (s), cheerleading M/W, crew W (s), cross-country running M (s)/W (s), equestrian sports M (c)/W (c), field hockey W (s), golf M (s)/W (s), gymnastics W (s), ice hockey M (s)/W (c), lacrosse M (c)/W (c), racquetball M (c)/W (c), rugby M (c)/W (c), sailing M (c)/W (c), skiing (cross-country) M (c)/W (c), skiing (downhill) M (c)/W (c), soccer M (s)/W (s), softball W, swimming and diving M (s)/W (s), tennis M (s)/W (s), track and field M (s)/W (s), volleyball M (c)/W (s), water polo M (c)/W (c), wrestling M (s). *Intramural sports:* archery M/W, badminton M/W, baseball M, basketball M/W, bowling M/W, crew M/W, cross-country running M/W, fencing M/W, field hockey W, football M/W, golf M/W, gymnastics W, ice hockey M/W, lacrosse M/W, racquetball M/W, rugby M/W, sailing M/W, skiing (cross-country) M/W, skiing (downhill) M/W, soccer M/W, softball M/W, squash M/W, swimming and diving M/W, table tennis M/W, tennis M/W, track and field M/W, volleyball M/W, water polo M/W, weight lifting M/W, wrestling M.

Standardized Tests *Required:* SAT or ACT (for admission).

Costs (2007–08) *Tuition:* state resident $8400 full-time, $280 per credit hour part-time; nonresident $22,260 full-time, $742 per credit hour part-time. Full-time tuition and fees vary according to course load, degree level, program, and student level. Part-time tuition and fees vary according to course load, degree level, program, and student level. *Required fees:* $1240 full-time, $620 per term part-time. *Room and board:* $6676; room only: $2756. Room and board charges vary according to board plan, housing facility, and student level. *Payment plan:* deferred payment. *Waivers:* employees or children of employees.

Financial Aid Of all full-time matriculated undergraduates who enrolled in 2006, 19,179 applied for aid, 13,216 were judged to have need, 3,893 had their need fully met. 1,700 Federal Work-Study jobs (averaging $1500). 320 state and other part-time jobs (averaging $900). In 2006, 2004 non-need-based awards were made. *Average percent of need met:* 75%. *Average financial aid package:* $9307. *Average need-based loan:* $4016. *Average need-based gift aid:* $5489. *Average non-need-based aid:* $5241. *Average indebtedness upon graduation:* $22,147.

Applying *Options:* electronic application, deferred entrance. *Application fee:* $35. *Required:* essay or personal statement, high school transcript. *Application deadlines:* rolling (freshmen), rolling (transfers). *Notification:* continuous until 9/1 (freshmen), 9/1 (transfers).

Freshman Application Contact James Cotter, Acting Director of Admissions, Michigan State University, 250 Administration Building, East Lansing, MI 48824. *Phone:* 517-355-8332. *Fax:* 517-353-1647. *E-mail:* admis@msu.edu.

MICHIGAN TECHNOLOGICAL UNIVERSITY

Houghton, Michigan **www.mtu.edu/**

- **State-supported** university, founded 1885
- **Small-town** 925-acre campus
- **Endowment** $66.0 million
- **Coed** 5,846 undergraduate students, 91% full-time, 23% women, 77% men
- **Moderately difficult** entrance level, 84% of applicants were admitted

Undergraduates 5,310 full-time, 536 part-time. Students come from 47 states and territories, 73 other countries, 25% are from out of state, 2% African American, 1% Asian American or Pacific Islander, 1% Hispanic American, 1% Native American, 5% international, 4% transferred in, 45% live on campus. *Retention:* 83% of 2006 full-time freshmen returned.

Freshmen *Admission:* 4,148 applied, 3,485 admitted, 1,223 enrolled. *Average high school GPA:* 3.53. *Test scores:* SAT critical reading scores over 500: 85%; SAT math scores over 500: 96%; SAT writing scores over 500: 77%; ACT scores over 18: 100%; SAT critical reading scores over 600: 49%; SAT math scores over 600: 70%; SAT writing scores over 600: 33%; ACT scores over 24: 70%; SAT critical reading scores over 700: 13%; SAT math scores over 700: 22%; SAT writing scores over 700: 4%; ACT scores over 30: 15%.

Faculty *Total:* 422, 85% full-time, 80% with terminal degrees. *Student/faculty ratio:* 11:1.

Majors Accounting; actuarial science; applied mathematics; audio engineering; biochemistry; bioinformatics; biology/biological sciences; biology/biotechnology laboratory technician; biology teacher education; biomedical/medical engineering; business administration and management; business/managerial economics; business teacher education; chemical engineering; chemical physics; chemistry; civil engineering; civil engineering technology; clinical laboratory science/medical technology; communication/speech communication and rhetoric; computational mathematics; computer engineering; computer programming; computer science; computer software engineering; computer systems networking and telecommunications; computer teacher education; construction engineering; cytotechnology; digital communication and media/multimedia; ecology; economics; electrical, electronic and communications engineering technology; electrical, electronics and communications engineering; electromechanical technology; engineering; engineering mechanics; engineering physics; engineering technology; English; English/language arts teacher education; environmental/environmental health engineering; environmental science; finance; forestry; forestry technology; general studies; geological/geophysical engineering; geology/earth science; geophysics and seismology; histologic technology/histotechnologist; history; humanities; industrial engineering; information science/studies; liberal arts and sciences/liberal studies; management information systems; marine biology; marketing/marketing management; materials engineering; mathematics; mathematics teacher education; mechanical engineering; mechanical engineering/mechanical technology; medical microbiology and bacteriology; medicinal/pharmaceutical chemistry; metallurgical engineering; microbiology; molecular biochemistry; operations management; physical sciences; physics; pre-dentistry studies; pre-law studies; pre-medical studies; pre-pharmacy studies; pre-veterinary studies; psychology; science teacher education; secondary education; social sciences; statistics; survey technology; system administration; technical and business writing; technology/industrial arts teacher education; theater design and technology; wildlife and wildlands science and management.

Academics *Calendar:* semesters. *Degrees:* certificates, associate, bachelor's, master's, doctoral, and postbachelor's certificates. *Special study options:* advanced placement credit, cooperative education, distance learning, double majors, English as a second language, honors programs, internships, off-campus study, part-time degree program, services for LD students, student-designed majors, study abroad, summer session for credit. *ROTC:* Army (b), Air Force (b). *Unusual degree programs:* 3-2 engineering; forestry.

Computers on Campus 1,555 computers/terminals are available on campus for general student use. Students can access the following: online (class) registration. Campuswide network is available.

Student Life *Housing:* on-campus residence required for freshman year. *Options:* coed, disabled students. Campus housing is university owned. Freshman campus housing is guaranteed. *Activities and organizations:* drama/theater group, student-run newspaper, radio station, choral group, Film Board, Undergraduate Student Government, Inter-Residence Hall Council, Blue Key National Honor Fraternity, national fraternities, national sororities. *Campus security:* 24-hour emergency response devices and patrols, late-night transport/escort service, controlled dormitory access. *Student services:* health clinic, personal/psychological counseling.

Athletics Member NCAA. All Division II except ice hockey (Division I). *Intercollegiate sports:* basketball M (s)/W (s), cross-country running M/W, fencing M (c)/W (c), football M (s), ice hockey M (s)/W (c), racquetball M (c)/W (c), riflery M (c)/W (c), skiing (cross-country) M/W, skiing (downhill) M (c)/W (c), soccer M (c)/W (c), squash M (c)/W (c), swimming and diving M (c)/W (c), table tennis M (c)/W (c), tennis M/W (s), track and field M/W, volleyball W (s), water polo M (c)/W (c). *Intramural sports:* badminton M/W, basketball M/W, bowling M/W, cross-country running M/W, football M/W, golf M/W, ice hockey M/W, racquetball M/W, riflery M/W, skiing (cross-country) M (c)/W (c), soccer M/W, softball M/W, squash M/W, swimming and diving M/W, table tennis M/W, tennis M/W, track and field M (c)/W (c), volleyball M/W (c), water polo M/W, weight lifting M/W, wrestling M.

Standardized Tests *Required:* SAT or ACT (for admission).

Costs (2007–08) *Tuition:* state resident $9180 full-time, $306 per credit hour part-time; nonresident $20,940 full-time, $698 per credit hour part-time. Full-time tuition and fees vary according to course load and program. Part-time tuition and fees vary according to course load and program. *Required fees:* $649 full-time, $324 per term part-time. *Room and board:* $7315; room only: $3843. Room and board charges vary according to board plan and housing facility. *Payment plans:* installment, deferred payment. *Waivers:* children of alumni, senior citizens, and employees or children of employees.

Financial Aid Of all full-time matriculated undergraduates who enrolled in 2006, 3,989 applied for aid, 2,881 were judged to have need, 1,046 had their need fully met. 218 Federal Work-Study jobs (averaging $1487). 2,497 state and other part-time jobs (averaging $1600). In 2006, 1448 non-need-based awards were made. *Average percent of need met:* 76%. *Average financial aid package:* $9065. *Average need-based loan:* $4069. *Average need-based gift aid:* $7088. *Average non-need-based aid:* $2424. *Average indebtedness upon graduation:* $13,807.

Applying *Options:* electronic application, deferred entrance. *Required:* high school transcript. *Recommended:* minimum 2.75 GPA, interview. *Application deadlines:* rolling (freshmen), rolling (transfers). *Notification:* continuous (freshmen), continuous (transfers).

Freshman Application Contact Ms. Allison Carter, Director of Admissions, Michigan Technological University, 1400 Townsend Drive, Houghton, MI 49931-1295. *Phone:* 906-487-2335. *Toll-free phone:* 888-MTU-1885. *Fax:* 906-487-2125. *E-mail:* mtu4u@mtu.edu.

See page 1354 for the College Close-Up.

NORTHERN MICHIGAN UNIVERSITY

Marquette, Michigan — www.nmu.edu/

- **State-supported** comprehensive, founded 1899
- **Small-town** 300-acre campus with easy access to Sawyer International
- **Endowment** $33.1 million
- **Coed** 8,488 undergraduate students, 90% full-time, 53% women, 47% men
- **Minimally difficult** entrance level, 78% of applicants were admitted

Undergraduates 7,677 full-time, 811 part-time. Students come from 52 states and territories, 17 other countries, 20% are from out of state, 1% African American, 0.9% Asian American or Pacific Islander, 1% Hispanic American, 2% Native American, 0.6% international, 5% transferred in, 35% live on campus. *Retention:* 70% of 2006 full-time freshmen returned.

Freshmen *Admission:* 5,302 applied, 4,118 admitted, 1,394 enrolled. *Average high school GPA:* 3.07. *Test scores:* ACT scores over 18: 95%; ACT scores over 24: 38%; ACT scores over 30: 5%.

Faculty *Total:* 443, 71% full-time, 55% with terminal degrees. *Student/faculty ratio:* 23:1.

Majors Accounting; accounting and finance; accounting related; administrative assistant and secretarial science; aircraft powerplant technology; architecture related; art; art teacher education; athletic training; automobile/automotive mechanics technology; behavioral sciences; biochemistry; biology/biological sciences; biology teacher education; building/property maintenance and management; business administration and management; business automation/technology/data entry; business/commerce; CAD/CADD drafting/design technology; cartography; ceramic arts and ceramics; chemistry; chemistry related; chemistry teacher education; child development; cinematography and film/video production; clinical laboratory science/medical technology; clinical/medical laboratory technology; commercial and advertising art; communication and journalism related; communication/speech communication and rhetoric; community health services counseling; computer and information sciences; computer systems networking and telecommunications; construction engineering technology; crafts, folk art and artisanry; criminal justice/law enforcement administration; criminal justice/safety; cytogenetics/genetics/clinical genetics technology; cytotechnology; developmental and child psychology; digital communication and media/multimedia; dramatic/theater arts; drawing; ecology; economics; education; education related; electrical and electronic engineering technologies related; electromechanical technology; elementary education; engineering related; English; English/language arts teacher education; entrepreneurship; environmental science; experimental psychology; finance; financial planning and services; fine arts related; foodservice systems administration; French; French language teacher education; general studies; geography; geography teacher education; geology/earth science; graphic design; health and physical education; health/medical preparatory programs related; health teacher education; heating, air conditioning and refrigeration technology; histologic technician; histologic technology/histotechnologist; history; history teacher education; hospitality administration; industrial design; industrial mechanics and maintenance technology; industrial technology; international relations and affairs; kinesiology and exercise science; liberal arts and sciences/liberal studies; machine tool technology; management information systems; manufacturing technology; marketing/marketing management; mathematics; mathematics teacher education; mechanical engineering/mechanical technology; medical administrative assistant and medical secretary; metal and jewelry arts; microbiology; music; music teacher education; natural resources/conservation; nursing (registered nurse training); parks, recreation and leisure; philosophy; photography; physical education teaching and coaching; physics; physics teacher education; physiology; political science and government; pre-dentistry studies; pre-law studies; pre-medical studies; pre-pharmacy studies; pre-veterinary studies; printmaking; psychology; public administration; public relations/image management; radiologic technology/science; respiratory therapy technician; science teacher education; sculpture; secondary education; security and loss prevention; small business administration; social studies teacher education; social work; sociology; Spanish; Spanish language teacher education; special education; special education (mentally retarded); speech-language pathology; sport and fitness administration/management; surgical technology; technology/industrial arts teacher education; zoology/animal biology.

Academics *Calendar:* semesters. *Degrees:* certificates, diplomas, associate, bachelor's, master's, post-master's, and postbachelor's certificates. *Special study options:* academic remediation for entering students, adult/continuing education programs, advanced placement credit, distance learning, double majors, honors programs, independent study, internships, off-campus study, part-time degree program, services for LD students, student-designed majors, study abroad, summer session for credit. *ROTC:* Army (b).

Computers on Campus 9,900 computers/terminals are available on campus for general student use. Students can access the following: campus intranet, computer help desk, free student e-mail accounts, online (class) grades, online (class) registration, online (class) schedules, ThinkPad or MacBook notebook computer included as part of tuition and fees for all students. Notebook computers are replaced every two years. Campuswide network is available. 100% of college-owned or -operated housing units are wired for high-speed Internet access. Wireless service is available via entire campus.

Student Life *Housing:* on-campus residence required through sophomore year. *Options:* coed, disabled students. Campus housing is university owned. Freshman campus housing is guaranteed. *Activities and organizations:* drama/theater group, student-run newspaper, radio station, choral group, marching band, Associated Students of Northern Michigan University, Platform Personalities, campus cinema, Northern Arts and Entertainment, Student Leader Fellowship Program, national fraternities, national sororities. *Campus security:* 24-hour emergency response devices and patrols, student patrols, late-night transport/escort service. *Student services:* health clinic, personal/psychological counseling.

Athletics Member NCAA. All Division II except ice hockey (Division I). *Intercollegiate sports:* basketball M (s)/W (s), cheerleading M (c)/W (c), crew M (c)/W (c), cross-country running W (s), football M (s), golf M (s), ice hockey M (s)/W (c), lacrosse M (c), rugby M (c)/W (c), skiing (cross-country) M (s)/W (s), skiing (downhill) M (c)/W (c), soccer M (c)/W (s), swimming and diving W (s), track and field M (c)/W (s), volleyball W (s). *Intramural sports:* basketball M/W, ice hockey M/W, racquetball M/W, soccer M/W, softball M/W, table tennis M/W, ultimate Frisbee M/W, volleyball M/W, water polo M/W.

Standardized Tests *Required:* SAT or ACT (for admission).

Costs (2007–08) *Tuition:* state resident $6144 full-time, $256 per credit hour part-time; nonresident $10,080 full-time, $420 per credit hour part-time. Full-time tuition and fees vary according to location. Part-time tuition and fees vary according to location. *Required fees:* $565 full-time, $30 per term part-time. *Room and board:* $7220; room only: $3606. Room and board charges vary according to board plan and housing facility. *Payment plans:* installment, deferred payment. *Waivers:* senior citizens and employees or children of employees.

Financial Aid Of all full-time matriculated undergraduates who enrolled in 2006, 6,723 applied for aid, 4,479 were judged to have need, 906 had their need fully met. 567 Federal Work-Study jobs (averaging $1628). 99 state and other part-time jobs (averaging $2216). In 2006, 370 non-need-based awards were made. *Average percent of need met:* 67%. *Average financial aid package:* $7386. *Average need-based loan:* $3700. *Average need-based gift aid:* $3810. *Average non-need-based aid:* $2638. *Average indebtedness upon graduation:* $19,730.

Applying *Options:* electronic application, deferred entrance. *Application fee:* $30. *Required:* high school transcript. *Required for some:* minimum 2.25 GPA. *Application deadlines:* rolling (freshmen), rolling (transfers). *Notification:* continuous (freshmen), continuous (transfers).

Freshman Application Contact Ms. Gerri Daniels, Director of Admissions, Northern Michigan University, 1401 Presque Isle Avenue, Marquette, MI 49855. *Phone:* 906-227-2650. *Toll-free phone:* 800-682-9797. *Fax:* 906-227-1747. *E-mail:* admiss@nmu.edu.

NORTHWOOD UNIVERSITY

Midland, Michigan **www.northwood.edu/**

- **Independent** comprehensive, founded 1959
- **Small-town** 434-acre campus
- **Endowment** $31.1 million
- **Coed** 1,987 undergraduate students, 96% full-time, 35% women, 65% men
- **Moderately difficult** entrance level, 80% of applicants were admitted

Northwood University business students start out with courses that are critical to their chosen career path. Small classes on beautiful campuses foster a friendly, engaged student community where faculty members and experiential learning opportunities prepare students to become leaders in a global, free-enterprise society. Northwood students discover the leader within themselves.

Undergraduates 1,909 full-time, 78 part-time. Students come from 34 states and territories, 34 other countries, 21% are from out of state, 12% African American, 1% Asian American or Pacific Islander, 2% Hispanic American, 0.3% Native American, 9% international, 12% transferred in, 37% live on campus. *Retention:* 74% of 2006 full-time freshmen returned.

Freshmen *Admission:* 1,626 applied, 1,294 admitted, 450 enrolled. *Average high school GPA:* 3.06. *Test scores:* SAT critical reading scores over 500: 38%; SAT math scores over 500: 39%; SAT writing scores over 500: 22%; ACT scores over 18: 86%; SAT critical reading scores over 600: 13%; SAT math scores over 600: 12%; ACT scores over 24: 23%; SAT math scores over 700: 2%; ACT scores over 30: 1%.

Faculty *Total:* 101, 54% full-time, 27% with terminal degrees. *Student/faculty ratio:* 29:1.

Majors Accounting; business administration and management; computer and information sciences; marketing/marketing management; sport and fitness administration/management.

Academics *Calendar:* quarters. *Degrees:* bachelor's and master's. *Special study options:* academic remediation for entering students, accelerated degree program, adult/continuing education programs, advanced placement credit, cooperative education, distance learning, double majors, English as a second language, external degree program, honors programs, independent study, internships, off-campus study, part-time degree program, study abroad, summer session for credit.

Computers on Campus 215 computers/terminals are available on campus for general student use. Students can access the following: campus intranet, computer help desk, free student e-mail accounts, online (class) grades, online (class) registration, online (class) schedules. Campuswide network is available. 100% of college-owned or -operated housing units are wired for high-speed Internet access. Wireless service is available via entire campus.

Student Life *Housing:* on-campus residence required for freshman year. *Options:* coed, men-only, women-only. Campus housing is university owned. Freshman campus housing is guaranteed. *Activities and organizations:* drama/theater group, student-run newspaper, choral group, Student Senate, intramural sports/club sports, campus art, Northwood University International Auto Show (NUTAS), national fraternities, national sororities. *Campus security:* 24-hour emergency response devices and patrols, late-night transport/escort service, controlled dormitory access. *Student services:* health clinic, personal/psychological counseling.

Athletics Member NCAA. All Division II. *Intercollegiate sports:* baseball M (s), basketball M (s)/W (s), cheerleading M (s)/W (s), cross-country running M (s)/W (s), football M (s), golf M (s)/W (s), soccer M (s)/W (s), softball W (s), tennis M (s)/W (s), track and field M (s)/W (s), volleyball W (s). *Intramural sports:* badminton M/W, baseball M (c), basketball M/W, football M, ice hockey M (c), lacrosse M (c), soccer M (c)/W, softball M/W, table tennis M/W, tennis M/W, ultimate Frisbee M/W, volleyball M/W.

Standardized Tests *Required:* SAT or ACT (for admission).

Costs (2007–08) *Comprehensive fee:* $23,649 includes full-time tuition ($15,825), mandatory fees ($630), and room and board ($7194). Part-time tuition: $330 per credit hour. *College room only:* $3474.

Financial Aid Of all full-time matriculated undergraduates who enrolled in 2007, 1,375 applied for aid, 1,186 were judged to have need, 307 had their need fully met. 430 Federal Work-Study jobs (averaging $1733). 110 state and other part-time jobs (averaging $1685). In 2007, 354 non-need-based awards were made. *Average percent of need met:* 52%. *Average financial aid package:* $14,243. *Average need-based loan:* $4094. *Average need-based gift aid:* $5450. *Average non-need-based aid:* $5548. *Average indebtedness upon graduation:* $23,980.

Applying *Options:* electronic application, early admission, deferred entrance. *Application fee:* $25. *Required:* essay or personal statement, high school transcript. *Recommended:* minimum 2.0 GPA, 1 letter of recommendation, interview. *Application deadlines:* rolling (freshmen), rolling (transfers). *Notification:* continuous (freshmen), continuous (transfers).

Freshman Application Contact Mr. Daniel F. Toland, Dean of Admission, Northwood University, 4000 Whiting Drive, Midland, MI 48640. *Phone:* 989-837-4273. *Toll-free phone:* 800-457-7878. *Fax:* 989-837-4490. *E-mail:* miadmit@northwood.edu.

OAKLAND UNIVERSITY

Rochester, Michigan **www.oakland.edu/**

- **State-supported** university, founded 1957
- **Suburban** 1444-acre campus with easy access to Detroit
- **Coed** 14,089 undergraduate students, 72% full-time, 62% women, 38% men
- **Moderately difficult** entrance level, 81% of applicants were admitted

Undergraduates 10,172 full-time, 3,917 part-time. Students come from 25 states and territories, 50 other countries, 1% are from out of state, 8% African American, 4% Asian American or Pacific Islander, 2% Hispanic American, 0.4% Native American, 1% international, 10% transferred in, 13% live on campus. *Retention:* 73% of 2006 full-time freshmen returned.

Freshmen *Admission:* 6,896 applied, 5,593 admitted, 2,340 enrolled. *Average high school GPA:* 3.22. *Test scores:* ACT scores over 18: 87%; ACT scores over 24: 32%; ACT scores over 30: 3%.

Faculty *Total:* 926, 54% full-time, 61% with terminal degrees. *Student/faculty ratio:* 21:1.

Majors Accounting; acting; African studies; anthropology; art history, criticism and conservation; Asian studies (East); Asian studies (South); biochemistry; biology/biological sciences; biophysics; business/commerce; business/managerial economics; chemistry; clinical laboratory science/medical technology; communication/speech communication and rhetoric; comparative literature; computer and information sciences; computer engineering; cytotechnology; dance; dramatic/theater arts; dramatic/theater arts and stagecraft related; drawing; economics; electrical, electronics and communications engineering; elementary education; engineering physics; engineering related; English; environmental health; finance; fine arts related; fine/studio arts; foreign languages and literatures; French; German; health professions related; histologic technology/histotechnologist; history; human resources development; human resources management; industrial engineering; information technology; international relations and affairs; journalism; Latin American studies; liberal arts and sciences/liberal studies; linguistics; management information systems; marketing/marketing management; mathematics; mathematics teacher education; mechanical engineering; medical radiologic technology; music; music performance; music teacher education; music theory and composition; nuclear medical technology; nursing (registered nurse training); occupational health and industrial hygiene; operations management; painting; philosophy; photography; physics; piano and organ; political science and government; psychology; public administration; radiologic technology/science; Slavic studies; social work; sociology; Spanish; statistics; theater design and technology; voice and opera; women's studies.

Academics *Calendar:* semesters. *Degrees:* bachelor's, master's, doctoral, post-master's, and postbachelor's certificates. *Special study options:* academic remediation for entering students, accelerated degree program, advanced placement credit, cooperative education, distance learning, double majors, English as a second language, honors programs, independent study, internships, off-campus study, part-time degree program, services for LD students, student-designed majors, study abroad, summer session for credit. *ROTC:* Air Force (c). *Unusual degree programs:* 3-2 business administration; physical therapy.

Computers on Campus Students can access the following: computer help desk, free student e-mail accounts, online (class) grades, online (class) registration, online (class) schedules. Campuswide network is available. 100% of college-owned or -operated housing units are wired for high-speed Internet access. Wireless service is available via entire campus.

Student Life *Housing options:* coed, cooperative, disabled students. Campus housing is university owned. Freshman applicants given priority for college housing. *Activities and organizations:* drama/theater group, student-run newspaper, radio and television station, choral group, Golden Key National Honor Society, Association of Black Students, SATE (Student Association for Teacher Education), Psi Chi Psychology Club, Student Nurses Association, national fraternities, national sororities. *Campus security:* 24-hour emergency response devices and patrols, student patrols, late-night transport/escort service, controlled dormitory access, security lighting, self-defense classes. *Student services:* health clinic, personal/psychological counseling.

Athletics Member NCAA. All Division I. *Intercollegiate sports:* baseball M (s), basketball M (s)/W (s), cross-country running M (s)/W (s), golf M (s)/W (s), ice hockey M (c)/W (c), soccer M (s)/W (s), softball W (s), swimming and diving M (s)/W (s), tennis W (s), track and field M/W, volleyball W (s). *Intramural sports:* basketball M/W, equestrian sports M (c)/W (c), fencing M (c)/W (c), football M/W, lacrosse M (c)/W (c), racquetball M/W, rock climbing M (c), rugby M (c), soccer M/W, table tennis M/W, volleyball M/W.

Standardized Tests *Recommended:* SAT or ACT (for admission).

Costs (2007–08) *Tuition:* state resident $7575 full-time, $253 per credit part-time; nonresident $17,625 full-time, $588 per credit part-time. Full-time tuition and fees vary according to program and student level. Part-time tuition and fees vary according to program and student level. *Room and board:* $6670. Room and board charges vary according to housing facility. *Payment plans:* installment, deferred payment. *Waivers:* employees or children of employees.

Financial Aid Of all full-time matriculated undergraduates who enrolled in 2003, 4,393 applied for aid, 3,043 were judged to have need, 1,311 had their need fully met. 249 Federal Work-Study jobs (averaging $1260). 77 state and other part-time jobs (averaging $1155). In 2003, 598 non-need-based awards were made. *Average percent of need met:* 88%. *Average financial aid package:* $5674. *Average need-based loan:* $3425. *Average need-based gift aid:* $3226. *Average non-need-based aid:* $2900. *Average indebtedness upon graduation:* $15,513.

Applying *Options:* electronic application, deferred entrance. *Application fee:* $40. *Required:* high school transcript, minimum 2.5 GPA. *Required for some:* minimum 3.0 GPA, letters of recommendation, interview, audition. *Application deadlines:* rolling (freshmen), rolling (transfers). *Notification:* continuous (freshmen), continuous (transfers).

Freshman Application Contact Ms. Eleanor Reynolds, Interim Assistant Vice President, Student Affairs, Oakland University, 101 North Foundation Hall, Rochester, MI 48309-4401. *Phone:* 248-370-3364. *Toll-free phone:* 800-OAK-UNIV. *Fax:* 248-370-4462. *E-mail:* ouinfo@oakland.edu.

OLIVET COLLEGE

Olivet, Michigan **www.olivetcollege.edu/**

Freshman Application Contact Mr. Bernie McConnell, Assistant Vice President for Enrollment Management, Olivet College, 320 South Main Street, Olivet, MI 49076. *Phone:* 269-749-7162. *Toll-free phone:* 800-456-7189. *Fax:* 269-749-6617. *E-mail:* bmcconnell@olivetcollege.edu.

ROCHESTER COLLEGE

Rochester Hills, Michigan **www.rc.edu/**

- **Independent** 4-year, founded 1959, affiliated with Church of Christ
- **Suburban** 83-acre campus with easy access to Detroit
- **Endowment** $1.5 million
- **Coed** 970 undergraduate students, 66% full-time, 62% women, 38% men
- **Minimally difficult** entrance level, 80% of applicants were admitted

Undergraduates 636 full-time, 334 part-time. Students come from 20 states and territories, 6 other countries, 14% are from out of state, 20% African American, 1% Asian American or Pacific Islander, 2% Hispanic American, 0.6% Native American, 2% international, 17% transferred in, 25% live on campus. *Retention:* 55% of 2006 full-time freshmen returned.

Freshmen *Admission:* 210 applied, 167 admitted, 102 enrolled. *Average high school GPA:* 3.00. *Test scores:* SAT critical reading scores over 500: 61%; SAT math scores over 500: 50%; ACT scores over 18: 86%; SAT critical reading scores over 600: 28%; SAT math scores over 600: 11%; ACT scores over 24: 36%; SAT critical reading scores over 700: 6%; ACT scores over 30: 4%.

Faculty *Total:* 159, 29% full-time, 23% with terminal degrees. *Student/faculty ratio:* 6:1.

Majors Accounting; behavioral sciences; biblical studies; biological and physical sciences; biology teacher education; business administration and management; business/corporate communications; communication/speech communication and rhetoric; computer management; counseling psychology; early childhood education; elementary education; English; English/language arts teacher education; history; history teacher education; interdisciplinary studies; liberal arts and sciences/liberal studies; literature; marketing/marketing management; mass communications; mathematics teacher education; missionary studies and missiology; multi-/interdisciplinary studies related; music; psychology; science teacher education; secondary education; social studies teacher education; sport and fitness administration/management; youth ministry.

Academics *Calendar:* semesters. *Degrees:* associate, bachelor's, and master's. *Special study options:* academic remediation for entering students, accelerated degree program, adult/continuing education programs, advanced placement credit, distance learning, double majors, external degree program, independent study, internships, off-campus study, part-time degree program, study abroad, summer session for credit.

Computers on Campus 61 computers/terminals are available on campus for general student use. Campuswide network is available.

Student Life *Housing:* on-campus residence required through sophomore year. *Options:* men-only, women-only, disabled students. Campus housing is university owned. Freshman campus housing is guaranteed. *Activities and organizations:* drama/theater group, student-run newspaper, choral group, Image, Student Government, American Marketing Association. *Campus security:* 24-hour emergency response devices, late-night transport/escort service, controlled dormitory access, evening security guards. *Student services:* personal/psychological counseling.

Athletics Member NCCAA. *Intercollegiate sports:* baseball M (s), basketball M (s)/W (s), golf M (s), soccer M (s)/W (s), softball W (s), volleyball W (s). *Intramural sports:* basketball M/W, football M/W, golf M, softball M/W, ultimate Frisbee M/W, volleyball M/W.

Standardized Tests *Required:* SAT or ACT (for admission).

Costs (2007–08) *Comprehensive fee:* $21,780 includes full-time tuition ($13,420), mandatory fees ($1440), and room and board ($6920). Full-time tuition and fees vary according to course load. Part-time tuition: $435 per credit hour. Part-time tuition and fees vary according to course load. *Required fees:* $230 per term part-time. *College room only:* $1890. Room and board charges vary according to board plan and housing facility. *Payment plan:* installment. *Waivers:* children of alumni, senior citizens, and employees or children of employees.

Financial Aid Of all full-time matriculated undergraduates who enrolled in 2004, 552 applied for aid, 552 were judged to have need. 93 Federal Work-Study jobs (averaging $1500). 106 state and other part-time jobs (averaging $1000). In 2004, 383 non-need-based awards were made. *Average percent of need met:* 82%. *Average financial aid package:* $2539. *Average need-based loan:* $3243. *Average need-based gift aid:* $2967. *Average non-need-based aid:* $4455.

Applying *Options:* electronic application, early admission, deferred entrance. *Application fee:* $25. *Required:* high school transcript, minimum 2.25 GPA. *Required for some:* interview. *Recommended:* essay or personal statement, 2 letters of recommendation. *Application deadlines:* rolling (freshmen), rolling (transfers). *Notification:* continuous (freshmen), continuous (transfers).

Freshman Application Contact Mr. Larry Norman, Dean of Admissions, Rochester College, 800 West Avon Road, Rochester Hills, MI 48307-2764. *Phone:* 248-218-2190. *Toll-free phone:* 800-521-6010. *Fax:* 248-218-2035. *E-mail:* admissions@rc.edu.

SACRED HEART MAJOR SEMINARY

Detroit, Michigan

www.archdioceseofdetroit.org/shms/shms.htm

- **Independent Roman Catholic** comprehensive, founded 1919
- **Urban** 24-acre campus
- **Endowment** $5.0 million
- **Coed** 244 undergraduate students, 15% full-time, 42% women, 58% men
- **Moderately difficult** entrance level, 100% of applicants were admitted

Undergraduates 37 full-time, 207 part-time. Students come from 3 states and territories, 1% are from out of state, 7% transferred in. *Retention:* 25% of 2006 full-time freshmen returned.

Freshmen *Admission:* 4 applied, 4 admitted, 4 enrolled. *Average high school GPA:* 3.21.

Faculty *Total:* 47, 53% full-time, 77% with terminal degrees. *Student/faculty ratio:* 6:1.

Majors Liberal arts and sciences/liberal studies; philosophy; theology.

Academics *Calendar:* semesters. *Degrees:* certificates, associate, bachelor's, master's, first professional, and postbachelor's certificates. *Special study options:* academic remediation for entering students, advanced placement credit, independent study, off-campus study, part-time degree program, services for LD students.

Computers on Campus 23 computers/terminals are available on campus for general student use.

Student Life *Housing:* on-campus residence required through senior year. *Options:* men-only. Campus housing is university owned. Freshman campus housing is guaranteed. *Activities and organizations:* choral group. *Campus security:* 24-hour emergency response devices, late-night transport/escort service. *Student services:* personal/psychological counseling.

Costs (2007–08) *Comprehensive fee:* $19,530 includes full-time tuition ($12,450), mandatory fees ($80), and room and board ($7000). Full-time tuition and fees vary according to course load. Part-time tuition: $295 per credit hour. Part-time tuition and fees vary according to course load. *Required fees:* $40 per term part-time. *Payment plans:* installment, deferred payment. *Waivers:* employees or children of employees.

Financial Aid *Average percent of need met:* 67%. *Average financial aid package:* $3000.

Applying *Options:* deferred entrance. *Application fee:* $30. *Required:* essay or personal statement, high school transcript, minimum 2.0 GPA, 1 letter of recommendation, interview. *Application deadlines:* 7/31 (freshmen), 7/31 (transfers). *Notification:* continuous until 8/15 (freshmen), continuous until 8/15 (transfers).

Freshman Application Contact Fr. Michael Byrnes, Vice Rector, Sacred Heart Major Seminary, 2701 Chicago Boulevard, Detroit, MI 48206. *Phone:* 313-883-8552. *Fax:* 313-868-6400.

SAGINAW VALLEY STATE UNIVERSITY

University Center, Michigan **www.svsu.edu/**

- **State-supported** comprehensive, founded 1963
- **Rural** 782-acre campus
- **Endowment** $43.8 million
- **Coed** 7,984 undergraduate students, 80% full-time, 59% women, 41% men
- **Moderately difficult** entrance level, 89% of applicants were admitted

Undergraduates 6,422 full-time, 1,562 part-time. Students come from 17 states and territories, 35 other countries, 0.6% are from out of state, 7% African American, 0.7% Asian American or Pacific Islander, 2% Hispanic American, 0.4% Native American, 4% international, 7% transferred in, 27% live on campus. *Retention:* 69% of 2006 full-time freshmen returned.

Freshmen *Admission:* 4,821 applied, 4,279 admitted, 1,560 enrolled. *Average high school GPA:* 3.23. *Test scores:* ACT scores over 18: 82%; ACT scores over 24: 29%; ACT scores over 30: 3%.

Faculty *Total:* 582, 48% full-time. *Student/faculty ratio:* 20:1.

Majors Accounting; applied mathematics; art; art teacher education; athletic training; biochemistry; biology/biological sciences; biology teacher education; business administration and management; business/commerce; business/managerial economics; chemical physics; chemistry; chemistry related; chemistry teacher education; clinical laboratory science/medical technology; communication/speech communication and rhetoric; computer and information sciences; computer science; criminal justice/safety; design and visual communications; dramatic/theater arts; economics; education related; electrical, electronics and communications engineering; elementary education; engineering/industrial management; English; English/language arts teacher education; finance; fine/studio arts; French; French as a second/foreign language (teaching); general studies; health services/allied health/health sciences; history; history teacher education; international business/trade/commerce; international relations and affairs; kinesiology and exercise science; marketing/marketing management; mathematics; mathematics teacher education; mechanical engineering; music; music teacher education; nursing (registered nurse training); operations management; optical sciences; physical education teaching and coaching; physics; physics teacher education; political science and government; psychology; public administration; science teacher education; social work; sociology; Spanish; Spanish language teacher education; special education; speech/theater education.

Academics *Calendar:* semesters plus summer session. *Degrees:* bachelor's, master's, and post-master's certificates. *Special study options:* academic remediation for entering students, accelerated degree program, adult/continuing education programs, advanced placement credit, cooperative education, distance learning, double majors, English as a second language, honors programs, independent study, internships, part-time degree program, services for LD students, student-designed majors, study abroad, summer session for credit.

Computers on Campus 1,033 computers/terminals are available on campus for general student use. Students can access the following: online (class) registration. Campuswide network is available.

Student Life *Housing options:* coed, disabled students. Campus housing is university owned. Freshman campus housing is guaranteed. *Activities and organizations:* drama/theater group, student-run newspaper, choral group, marching band, Alpha Sigma Alpha, Sigma Pi, Organization of Black Unity, International Students Association, University Residence Association, national fraternities, national sororities. *Campus security:* 24-hour emergency response devices and patrols, student patrols, late-night transport/escort service, controlled dormitory access, rape prevention program. *Student services:* health clinic, personal/psychological counseling.

Athletics Member NCAA. All Division II. *Intercollegiate sports:* baseball M (s), basketball M (s)/W (s), bowling M (s), cheerleading M/W, cross-country running M (s)/W (s), football M (s), golf M (s), ice hockey M (c), lacrosse M (c)/W (c), soccer M (s)/W (s), softball W (s), tennis W (s), track and field M (s)/W (s), volleyball W (s). *Intramural sports:* badminton M/W, basketball M/W, football M/W, golf M/W, soccer M/W, softball M/W, tennis M/W, volleyball M/W.

Standardized Tests *Required:* ACT (for admission).

Costs (2007–08) *Tuition:* state resident $5832 full-time, $194 per credit hour part-time; nonresident $13,857 full-time, $462 per credit hour part-time. Full-time tuition and fees vary according to course level, course load, location, and program. Part-time tuition and fees vary according to course level, course load, location, and program. *Required fees:* $426 full-time, $14 per credit hour part-time. *Room and board:* $6630; room only: $4000. Room and board charges vary according to board plan, housing facility, and student level. *Payment plan:* installment. *Waivers:* employees or children of employees.

Financial Aid Of all full-time matriculated undergraduates who enrolled in 2002, 4,584 applied for aid, 2,815 were judged to have need, 692 had their need fully met. In 2002, 1046 non-need-based awards were made. *Average percent of need met:* 90%. *Average financial aid package:* $5382. *Average need-based loan:* $3224. *Average need-based gift aid:* $2670. *Average non-need-based aid:* $3420. *Average indebtedness upon graduation:* $16,032.

Applying *Options:* electronic application, deferred entrance. *Application fee:* $25. *Required:* high school transcript. *Recommended:* minimum 2.5 GPA, minimum ACT score of 17. *Application deadlines:* rolling (freshmen), rolling (transfers). *Notification:* continuous (freshmen), continuous (transfers).

Freshman Application Contact Mr. James P. Dwyer, Director of Admissions, Saginaw Valley State University, 7400 Bay Road, University Center, MI 48710-0001. *Phone:* 989-964-4200. *Toll-free phone:* 800-968-9500. *Fax:* 989-790-0180. *E-mail:* admissions@svsu.edu.

SIENA HEIGHTS UNIVERSITY

Adrian, Michigan **www.sienaheights.edu/**

- **Independent Roman Catholic** comprehensive, founded 1919
- **Small-town** 140-acre campus with easy access to Detroit
- **Endowment** $90.0 million
- **Coed** 1,831 undergraduate students, 41% full-time, 58% women, 42% men
- **Moderately difficult** entrance level, 64% of applicants were admitted

Education is a journey. At Siena Heights, students find people and resources, including professors, coaches, advisers, and career service programs, ready to help them discover their destination. A new registered nurse to Bachelor of Science in Nursing (RN to B.S.N.) degree completion program has recently been approved, with classes starting in fall 2008.

Undergraduates 751 full-time, 1,080 part-time. Students come from 8 states and territories, 11 other countries, 10% African American, 0.5% Asian American or Pacific Islander, 3% Hispanic American, 0.5% Native American, 0.6% international, 4% transferred in, 33% live on campus. *Retention:* 63% of 2006 full-time freshmen returned.

Freshmen *Admission:* 979 applied, 631 admitted, 173 enrolled. *Average high school GPA:* 3.25. *Test scores:* ACT scores over 18: 88%; ACT scores over 24: 25%; ACT scores over 30: 1%.

Faculty *Total:* 65. *Student/faculty ratio:* 14:1.

Majors Accounting; applied mathematics; art; art history, criticism and conservation; art teacher education; biology/biological sciences; business administration and management; chemistry; child care and support services management; communication and journalism related; community organization and advocacy; computer and information sciences; creative writing; criminal justice/safety; dramatic/theater arts; elementary education; English; environmental science; general studies; gerontology; history; humanities; human services; kindergarten/preschool education; mathematics; Montessori teacher education; natural sciences; philosophy; pre-engineering; pre-law studies; psychology; public administration; religious studies; secondary education; social sciences; social studies teacher education; social work; Spanish; sport and fitness administration/management.

Academics *Calendar:* semesters. *Degrees:* associate, bachelor's, and master's. *Special study options:* academic remediation for entering students, accelerated degree program, adult/continuing education programs, advanced placement credit, cooperative education, double majors, external degree program, independent study, internships, off-campus study, part-time degree program, services for LD students, student-designed majors, study abroad, summer session for credit.

Computers on Campus 75 computers/terminals are available on campus for general student use. Students can access the following: computer help desk, free student e-mail accounts, online (class) grades, online (class) registration, online (class) schedules. Campuswide network is available. Wireless service is available via entire campus.

Student Life *Housing:* on-campus residence required through sophomore year. *Options:* coed. Campus housing is university owned and is provided by a third party. Freshman campus housing is guaranteed. *Activities and organizations:* drama/theater group, student-run newspaper, choral group, Student Programming Association, Residence Hall Counsel, Student Senate, Siena Heights African American Knowledge Association, national fraternities, national sororities. *Campus security:* 24-hour patrols, student patrols, late-night transport/escort service. *Student services:* health clinic, personal/psychological counseling.

Athletics Member NAIA. *Intercollegiate sports:* baseball M (s), basketball M (s)/W (s), cross-country running M (s)/W (s), golf M (s), lacrosse M (s), soccer M (s)/W (s), softball W (s), track and field M (s)/W (s), volleyball M (s)/W (s). *Intramural sports:* basketball M/W, football M, softball M/W, volleyball M/W.

Standardized Tests *Required:* SAT or ACT (for admission).

Costs (2007–08) *Comprehensive fee:* $12,392 includes full-time tuition ($8947), mandatory fees ($300), and room and board ($3145). Part-time tuition: $345 per hour. *Required fees:* $125 per term part-time.

Financial Aid In 2002, 166 non-need-based awards were made. *Average percent of need met:* 66%. *Average financial aid package:* $12,200. *Average indebtedness upon graduation:* $13,500.

Applying *Options:* electronic application, deferred entrance. *Application fee:* $25. *Required:* high school transcript, transfer GPA 2.0. *Required for some:* essay or personal statement, letters of recommendation, interview. *Recommended:* minimum 2.5 GPA, interview. *Application deadlines:* rolling (freshmen), rolling (out-of-state freshmen), rolling (transfers).

Director of Admissions Mr. Frank Hribar, Vice President of Enrollment Management, Siena Heights University, 1247 East Siena Heights Drive, Adrian, MI 49221-1796. *Phone:* 517-264-7180. *Toll-free phone:* 800-521-0009. *E-mail:* admissions@sienaheights.edu.

See page 1356 for the College Close-Up.

SPRING ARBOR UNIVERSITY

Spring Arbor, Michigan **www.arbor.edu/**

- **Independent Free Methodist** comprehensive, founded 1873
- **Small-town** 123-acre campus
- **Endowment** $10.1 million
- **Coed** 2,734 undergraduate students, 73% full-time, 68% women, 32% men
- **Moderately difficult** entrance level, 78% of applicants were admitted

Undergraduates 1,999 full-time, 735 part-time. Students come from 30 states and territories, 6 other countries, 15% are from out of state, 9% African American, 1% Asian American or Pacific Islander, 2% Hispanic American, 0.6% Native American, 0.7% international, 4% transferred in, 68% live on campus. *Retention:* 72% of 2006 full-time freshmen returned.

Freshmen *Admission:* 1,485 applied, 1,154 admitted, 340 enrolled. *Average high school GPA:* 3.35. *Test scores:* SAT critical reading scores over 500: 64%; SAT math scores over 500: 68%; SAT writing scores over 500: 61%; ACT scores over 18: 88%; SAT critical reading scores over 600: 30%; SAT math scores over 600: 25%; SAT writing scores over 600: 15%; ACT scores over 24: 41%; SAT critical reading scores over 700: 5%; SAT math scores over 700: 2%; ACT scores over 30: 3%.

Faculty *Total:* 128, 63% full-time, 47% with terminal degrees. *Student/faculty ratio:* 15:1.

Majors Accounting; actuarial science; art; biblical studies; biochemistry; biology/biological sciences; business administration and management; chemistry; communication/speech communication and rhetoric; computer science; design and visual communications; dramatic/theater arts; elementary education; English; family systems; film/video and photographic arts related; finance; graphic design; health/health care administration; history; human resources management; international/global studies; kinesiology and exercise science; liberal arts and sciences/liberal studies; management information systems; mathematics; missionary studies and missiology; music; music pedagogy; music teacher education; parks, recreation and leisure; pastoral studies/counseling; philosophy; physical education teaching and coaching; physics; physics related; piano and organ; political science and government; psychology; public relations, advertising, and applied communication related; religious studies; secondary education; social sciences; social work; sociology; Spanish; special education; sport and fitness administration/management; technical and business writing; theology; visual and performing arts related; youth ministry.

Academics *Calendar:* 4-1-4. *Degrees:* associate, bachelor's, and master's. *Special study options:* academic remediation for entering students, accelerated degree program, adult/continuing education programs, advanced placement credit, distance learning, double majors, English as a second language, external degree program, honors programs, independent study, internships, off-campus study, part-time degree program, services for LD students, student-designed majors, study abroad, summer session for credit. *ROTC:* Army (b), Air Force (c). *Unusual degree programs:* 3-2 engineering with University of Michigan, Michigan State University, Western Michigan University, Tri-State University.

Computers on Campus 230 computers/terminals and 1,167 ports are available on campus for general student use. Students can access the following: computer help desk, free student e-mail accounts, online (class) grades, online (class) registration, online (class) schedules. Campuswide network is available. 100% of college-owned or -operated housing units are wired for high-speed Internet access. Wireless service is available via entire campus.

Student Life *Housing:* on-campus residence required through senior year. *Options:* men-only, women-only, disabled students. Campus housing is university owned. Freshman campus housing is guaranteed. *Activities and organizations:* drama/theater group, student-run newspaper, radio station, choral group, Action Jackson, Come Learn With Me, Culture Fest, Blu Butta Cafe, Gospel Fest. *Campus security:* 24-hour emergency response devices, student patrols, late-night transport/escort service, controlled dormitory access. *Student services:* health clinic, personal/psychological counseling.

Athletics Member NAIA, NCCAA. *Intercollegiate sports:* baseball M (s), basketball M (s)/W (s), cross-country running M (s)/W (s), golf M (s), soccer M (s)/W (s), softball W (s), tennis M (s)/W (s), track and field M (s)/W (s), volleyball W (s). *Intramural sports:* basketball M/W, football M, soccer M/W, softball M/W, table tennis M/W, tennis M/W, ultimate Frisbee M/W, volleyball M/W.

Standardized Tests *Required:* SAT or ACT (for admission). *Recommended:* ACT (for admission).

Costs (2007–08) *Comprehensive fee:* $24,730 includes full-time tuition ($17,820), mandatory fees ($540), and room and board ($6370). Full-time tuition and fees vary according to course load and program. Part-time tuition: $450 per credit. Part-time tuition and fees vary according to course load, program, and reciprocity agreements. *Required fees:* $225 per term part-time. *College room only:* $2980. Room and board charges vary according to board plan and housing facility. *Payment plan:* installment. *Waivers:* senior citizens and employees or children of employees.

Financial Aid Of all full-time matriculated undergraduates who enrolled in 2006, 1,233 applied for aid, 1,079 were judged to have need, 763 had their need fully met. 771 Federal Work-Study jobs (averaging $764). 134 state and other part-time jobs (averaging $431). In 2006, 65 non-need-based awards were made. *Average percent of need met:* 96%. *Average financial aid package:* $20,095. *Average need-based loan:* $4802. *Average need-based gift aid:* $10,126. *Average non-need-based aid:* $1235. *Average indebtedness upon graduation:* $14,387.

Applying *Options:* electronic application, early admission, deferred entrance. *Application fee:* $30. *Required:* high school transcript. *Required for some:* essay or personal statement, letters of recommendation, interview. *Recommended:* minimum 2.6 GPA, guidance counselor's evaluation form. *Application deadlines:* 8/1 (freshmen), rolling (transfers). *Notification:* continuous (freshmen), continuous (transfers).

Freshman Application Contact Mr. Randy Comfort, Director of Admissions, Spring Arbor University, 106 East Main Street, Spring Arbor, MI 49283-9799. *Phone:* 517-750-1200 Ext. 1468. *Toll-free phone:* 800-968-0011. *Fax:* 517-750-6620. *E-mail:* admissions@arbor.edu.

UNIVERSITY OF DETROIT MERCY

Detroit, Michigan **www.udmercy.edu/**

Freshman Application Contact Ms. Denise Williams, Dean of Admissions, University of Detroit Mercy, Detroit, MI 48221-3038. *Phone:* 313-993-1245. *Toll-free phone:* 800-635-5020. *Fax:* 313-993-3326. *E-mail:* admissions@udmercy.edu.

UNIVERSITY OF MICHIGAN

Ann Arbor, Michigan **www.umich.edu/**

- **State-supported** university, founded 1817
- **Suburban** 8070-acre campus with easy access to Detroit
- **Endowment** $7.2 billion
- **Coed** 26,083 undergraduate students, 97% full-time, 50% women, 50% men
- **Very difficult** entrance level, 50% of applicants were admitted

Undergraduates 25,179 full-time, 904 part-time. Students come from 55 states and territories, 82 other countries, 32% are from out of state, 6% African American, 12% Asian American or Pacific Islander, 5% Hispanic American, 0.9% Native American, 5% international, 3% transferred in, 37% live on campus. *Retention:* 96% of 2006 full-time freshmen returned.

Freshmen *Admission:* 27,474 applied, 13,826 admitted, 5,992 enrolled. *Average high school GPA:* 3.75. *Test scores:* SAT critical reading scores over 500: 96%; SAT math scores over 500: 98%; ACT scores over 18: 100%; SAT critical reading scores over 600: 73%; SAT math scores over 600: 86%; ACT scores over 24: 93%; SAT critical reading scores over 700: 23%; SAT math scores over 700: 43%; ACT scores over 30: 43%.

Faculty *Total:* 2,971, 80% full-time, 87% with terminal degrees. *Student/faculty ratio:* 15:1.

Majors Actuarial science; aerospace, aeronautical and astronautical engineering; African-American/Black studies; American studies; anthropology; applied mathematics; Arabic; architecture; art history, criticism and conservation; art teacher education; Asian studies; Asian studies (South); Asian studies (Southeast); astronomy; athletic training; atmospheric sciences and meteorology; biochemistry; biology/biological sciences; biomedical sciences; biophysics; biopsychology; botany/plant biology; business administration and management; ceramic arts and ceramics; chemical engineering; chemistry; Chinese; civil engineering; classics and languages, literatures and linguistics; clinical laboratory science/medical technology; commercial and advertising art; comparative literature; computer engineering; computer science; creative writing; dance; dental hygiene; design and visual communications; dramatic/theater arts; drawing; economics; education; electrical, electronics and communications engineering; elementary education; engineering; engineering physics; engineering science; English; environmental/environmental health engineering; environmental studies; European studies; fiber, textile and weaving arts; film/cinema studies; French; general studies; geology/earth science; German; Hebrew; history; humanities; industrial design; industrial engineering; interdisciplinary studies; intermedia/multimedia; international relations and affairs; Islamic studies; Italian; Japanese; jazz/jazz studies; Jewish/Judaic studies; kinesiology and exercise science; landscape architecture; Latin; Latin American studies; linguistics; mass communication/media; materials engineering; materials science; mathematics; mathematics teacher education; mechanical engineering; medieval and Renaissance studies; metal and jewelry arts; Middle/Near Eastern and Semitic languages related; modern Greek; molecular biology; music; music history, literature, and theory; music teacher education; music theory and composition; natural resources management and policy; naval architecture and marine engineering; Near and Middle Eastern studies; nuclear engineering; nursing (registered nurse training); painting; philosophy; photography; physical education teaching and coaching; piano and organ; political science and government; printmaking; psychology; religious studies; Romance languages; Russian; Russian studies; Scandinavian studies; sculpture; secondary education; social sciences; sociology; Spanish; speech and rhetoric; sport and fitness administration/management; statistics; theater design and technology; Turkic, Ural-Altaic, Caucasian, and Central Asian languages related; violin, viola, guitar and other stringed instruments; visual and performing arts; voice and opera; wildlife biology; wind/percussion instruments; women's studies; zoology/animal biology.

Academics *Calendar:* trimesters. *Degrees:* certificates, bachelor's, master's, doctoral, first professional, post-master's, and postbachelor's certificates. *Special study options:* accelerated degree program, adult/continuing education programs, advanced placement credit, cooperative education, distance learning, double majors, English as a second language, honors programs, independent study, internships, off-campus study, part-time degree program, services for LD students, student-designed majors, study abroad, summer session for credit. *ROTC:* Army (b), Air Force (b). *Unusual degree programs:* 3-2 business administration; engineering; architecture, public policy.

Computers on Campus 2,600 computers/terminals and 2,255 ports are available on campus for general student use. Students can access the following: computer help desk, free student e-mail accounts, online (class) grades, online (class) registration, online (class) schedules, personal Websites. Campuswide network is available. 63% of college-owned or -operated housing units are wired for high-speed Internet access. Wireless service is available via classrooms, computer centers, computer labs, libraries, student centers.

Student Life *Housing options:* coed, women-only, cooperative, disabled students. Campus housing is university owned. Freshman campus housing is guaranteed. *Activities and organizations:* drama/theater group, student-run newspaper, radio and television station, choral group, marching band, Hillel Society, Pre-Med Club, Campus Crusade for Christ, Residence Hall Association, Black Student Union, national fraternities, national sororities. *Campus security:* 24-hour emergency response devices and patrols, student patrols, late-night transport/escort service, controlled dormitory access, bicycle patrols. *Student services:* health clinic, personal/psychological counseling, women's center, legal services.

Athletics Member NCAA. All Division I except football (Division I-A). *Intercollegiate sports:* baseball M (s), basketball M (s)/W (s), cheerleading M/W, crew W, cross-country running M (s)/W (s), field hockey W (s), golf M (s)/W (s), gymnastics M (s)/W (s), ice hockey M (s), soccer M/W, softball W (s), swimming and diving M (s)/W (s), tennis M (s)/W (s), track and field M (s)/W (s), volleyball W (s), water polo W, wrestling M (s). *Intramural sports:* archery M (c)/W (c), badminton M/W, basketball M/W, crew M (c)/W (c), cross-country running M/W, fencing M (c)/W (c), field hockey M (c)/W (c), football M/W, golf M/W, gymnastics M (c)/W (c), ice hockey M/W, lacrosse M (c)/W (c), racquetball M/W, riflery M (c)/W (c), rugby M (c)/W (c), sailing M (c)/W (c), skiing (cross-country) M (c)/W (c), skiing (downhill) M (c)/W (c), soccer M/W, softball M/W, swimming and diving M/W, table tennis M/W, tennis M/W, track and field M/W, ultimate Frisbee M/W, volleyball M/W, water polo M (c)/W (c), wrestling M/W.

Standardized Tests *Required:* SAT or ACT (for admission). *Required for some:* SAT Subject Tests (for admission).

Costs (2007–08) *Tuition:* state resident $10,258 full-time, $399 per hour part-time; nonresident $31,112 full-time, $1268 per hour part-time. Full-time tuition and fees vary according to course load, degree level, location, program, and student level. Part-time tuition and fees vary according to course load, degree level, location, program, and student level. *Required fees:* $189 full-time, $451 per term part-time. *Room and board:* $8190. Room and board charges vary according to board plan and housing facility. *Payment plan:* installment. *Waivers:* senior citizens.

Financial Aid Of all full-time matriculated undergraduates who enrolled in 2006, 13,631 applied for aid, 12,216 were judged to have need, 10,094 had their need fully met. 5,163 Federal Work-Study jobs (averaging $2458). 453 state and other part-time jobs (averaging $2160). In 2006, 7120 non-need-based awards were made. *Average percent of need met:* 90%. *Average financial aid package:* $11,174. *Average need-based loan:* $4687. *Average need-based gift aid:* $7786. *Average non-need-based aid:* $5966. *Average indebtedness upon graduation:* $23,754. *Financial aid deadline:* 4/30.

Applying *Options:* electronic application, early action, deferred entrance. *Application fee:* $40. *Required:* essay or personal statement, high school transcript. *Required for some:* interview. *Application deadlines:* 2/1 (freshmen), 2/1 (transfers), 10/31 (early action). *Notification:* continuous until 4/1 (freshmen), continuous until 4/1 (transfers), 12/31 (early action).

Freshman Application Contact Mr. Ted Spencer, Director of Undergraduate Admissions, University of Michigan, 1220 Student Activities Building, 515 East Jefferson, Ann Arbor, MI 48109-1316. *Phone:* 734-764-7433. *Fax:* 734-936-0740. *E-mail:* ugadmiss@umich.edu.

UNIVERSITY OF MICHIGAN–DEARBORN

Dearborn, Michigan **www.umd.umich.edu/**

- **State-supported** comprehensive, founded 1959, part of University of Michigan System
- **Suburban** 210-acre campus with easy access to Detroit
- **Endowment** $28.7 million
- **Coed** 6,447 undergraduate students, 66% full-time, 52% women, 48% men
- **Moderately difficult** entrance level, 66% of applicants were admitted

Undergraduates 4,234 full-time, 2,213 part-time. Students come from 11 states and territories, 28 other countries, 2% are from out of state, 10% African American, 6% Asian American or Pacific Islander, 3% Hispanic American, 0.7% Native American, 1% international, 14% transferred in. *Retention:* 81% of 2006 full-time freshmen returned.

Freshmen *Admission:* 3,438 applied, 2,273 admitted, 893 enrolled. *Average high school GPA:* 3.46. *Test scores:* ACT scores over 18: 92%; ACT scores over 24: 54%; ACT scores over 30: 9%.
Faculty *Total:* 481, 61% full-time, 100% with terminal degrees. *Student/faculty ratio:* 16:1.
Majors Accounting; American studies; anthropology; area studies related; art history, criticism and conservation; biochemistry; biology/biological sciences; business administration and management; business administration, management and operations related; chemistry; chemistry teacher education; communication/speech communication and rhetoric; computer and information sciences; computer programming; criminal justice/safety; early childhood education; economics; education; electrical, electronics and communications engineering; elementary education; engineering related; English; environmental science; environmental studies; finance; French; general studies; geology/earth science; health/health care administration; history; humanities; human resources management; industrial engineering; liberal arts and sciences/liberal studies; management information systems; manufacturing engineering; marketing/marketing management; mathematics; mathematics teacher education; mechanical engineering; microbiology; multi-/interdisciplinary studies related; philosophy; physics; political science and government; psychology; science teacher education; secondary education; social sciences; social studies teacher education; sociology; Spanish; women's studies.
Academics *Calendar:* semesters. *Degrees:* bachelor's, master's, and post-bachelor's certificates. *Special study options:* academic remediation for entering students, accelerated degree program, adult/continuing education programs, advanced placement credit, cooperative education, distance learning, double majors, honors programs, independent study, internships, off-campus study, part-time degree program, services for LD students, student-designed majors, study abroad, summer session for credit. *ROTC:* Army (c), Navy (c), Air Force (c).
Computers on Campus 350 computers/terminals are available on campus for general student use. Campuswide network is available.
Student Life *Housing:* college housing not available. *Activities and organizations:* drama/theater group, student-run newspaper, radio and television station, Dearborn Campus Engineers, student radio station, Association for African-American Students, national fraternities, national sororities. *Campus security:* 24-hour emergency response devices and patrols, late-night transport/escort service. *Student services:* health clinic, personal/psychological counseling, women's center.
Athletics Member NAIA. *Intercollegiate sports:* basketball M (s)/W (s), ice hockey M, volleyball W (s). *Intramural sports:* basketball M/W, cross-country running M (c)/W (c), fencing M (c)/W (c), ice hockey M (c), racquetball M/W, soccer M (c), table tennis M/W, tennis M/W, volleyball M/W.
Standardized Tests *Required:* SAT or ACT (for admission).
Costs (2007–08) *Tuition:* state resident $7832 full-time, $299 per credit hour part-time; nonresident $17,322 full-time, $678 per credit hour part-time. Full-time tuition and fees vary according to course level, course load, program, and student level. Part-time tuition and fees vary according to course level, course load, program, and student level. *Required fees:* $144 full-time, $144 per term part-time. *Payment plan:* installment. *Waivers:* senior citizens and employees or children of employees.
Financial Aid Of all full-time matriculated undergraduates who enrolled in 2006, 3,991 applied for aid, 3,166 were judged to have need, 513 had their need fully met. In 2006, 1945 non-need-based awards were made. *Average percent of need met:* 36%. *Average financial aid package:* $5311. *Average need-based loan:* $4257. *Average need-based gift aid:* $3850. *Average non-need-based aid:* $3116. *Average indebtedness upon graduation:* $18,001.
Applying *Options:* deferred entrance. *Application fee:* $30. *Required:* high school transcript, minimum 3.0 GPA. *Required for some:* interview. *Application deadlines:* rolling (freshmen), rolling (transfers). *Notification:* continuous (freshmen), continuous (transfers).
Freshman Application Contact Mr. Christopher Tremblay, Director of Admissions and Orientation, University of Michigan–Dearborn, 4901 Evergreen Road, Dearborn, MI 48128-1491. *Phone:* 313-593-5100. *Fax:* 313-436-9167. *E-mail:* admissions@umd.umich.edu.

UNIVERSITY OF MICHIGAN–FLINT

Flint, Michigan **www.umflint.edu/**

- **State-supported** comprehensive, founded 1956, part of University of Michigan System
- **Urban** 72-acre campus with easy access to Detroit
- **Endowment** $62.1 million
- **Coed** 5,824 undergraduate students, 62% full-time, 62% women, 38% men
- **Moderately difficult** entrance level, 82% of applicants were admitted

Undergraduates 3,616 full-time, 2,208 part-time. Students come from 43 states and territories, 39 other countries, 2% are from out of state, 12% African American, 2% Asian American or Pacific Islander, 3% Hispanic American, 0.5% Native American, 1% international, 12% transferred in. *Retention:* 71% of 2006 full-time freshmen returned.
Freshmen *Admission:* 1,901 applied, 1,554 admitted, 626 enrolled. *Average high school GPA:* 3.21. *Test scores:* SAT critical reading scores over 500: 60%; SAT math scores over 500: 80%; ACT scores over 18: 83%; SAT critical reading scores over 600: 27%; SAT math scores over 600: 20%; ACT scores over 24: 31%; ACT scores over 30: 3%.
Faculty *Total:* 440, 52% full-time, 43% with terminal degrees. *Student/faculty ratio:* 15:1.
Majors Accounting; actuarial science; African-American/Black studies; anthropology; art teacher education; biochemistry/biophysics and molecular biology; biology/biological sciences; biology teacher education; biomedical sciences; business administration and management; chemistry; chemistry teacher education; clinical laboratory science/medical technology; clinical psychology; computer and information sciences; computer and information sciences and support services related; computer science; corrections and criminal justice related; design and visual communications; dramatic/theater arts; dramatic/theater arts and stagecraft related; early childhood education; ecology; economics; education (specific subject areas) related; elementary education; engineering science; English; English composition; English/language arts teacher education; environmental science; ethics; finance; fine/studio arts; foreign languages related; French; French language teacher education; health and medical administrative services related; health/health care administration; health services/allied health/health sciences; history; history teacher education; human resources management; information science/studies; liberal arts and sciences/liberal studies; marketing/marketing management; mathematics; mathematics teacher education; medical radiologic technology; molecular biology; multi-/interdisciplinary studies related; music; music performance; music teacher education; natural resources/conservation; nursing (registered nurse training); operations management; organizational behavior; organizational communication; philosophy; physics; physics teacher education; political science and government; psychology; psychology related; psychology teacher education; public administration; public health education and promotion; Romance languages related; science teacher education; social sciences; social studies teacher education; social work; sociology; Spanish; Spanish language teacher education; speech teacher education; theater design and technology; Waldorf/Steiner teacher education; wildlife biology.
Academics *Calendar:* semesters. *Degrees:* bachelor's, master's, and first professional. *Special study options:* academic remediation for entering students, adult/continuing education programs, advanced placement credit, cooperative education, distance learning, double majors, honors programs, independent study, internships, off-campus study, part-time degree program, services for LD students, student-designed majors, study abroad, summer session for credit.
Computers on Campus 213 computers/terminals are available on campus for general student use. Students can access the following: computer help desk, free student e-mail accounts, online (class) grades, online (class) registration, online (class) schedules. Campuswide network is available.
Student Life *Housing:* college housing not available. *Activities and organizations:* drama/theater group, student-run newspaper, television station, choral group, Students Moving the UCEN Forward (SMUF), International Student Organization, Muslim Student Association, Kappa Sigma Fraternity, Inter-Varsity Christian Fellowship, national fraternities, national sororities. *Campus security:* 24-hour emergency response devices and patrols, student patrols, late-night transport/escort service. *Student services:* health clinic, personal/psychological counseling, women's center.
Athletics *Intercollegiate sports:* ultimate Frisbee M/W. *Intramural sports:* basketball M/W, football M/W, ice hockey M/W, racquetball M/W, soccer M/W, table tennis M/W, volleyball M/W.
Standardized Tests *Required:* SAT or ACT (for admission).
Costs (2007–08) *Tuition:* state resident $6995 full-time, $276 per credit part-time; nonresident $13,650 full-time, $552 per credit part-time. Full-time tuition and fees vary according to course level, course load, degree level, program, and student level. Part-time tuition and fees vary according to course level, degree level, program, and student level. *Required fees:* $348 full-time, $174 per term part-time. *Payment plan:* installment. *Waivers:* minority students, senior citizens, and employees or children of employees.
Financial Aid Of all full-time matriculated undergraduates who enrolled in 2006, 2,529 applied for aid, 2,020 were judged to have need, 335 had their need fully met. 343 Federal Work-Study jobs (averaging $1755). 85 state and other part-time jobs (averaging $1847). In 2006, 65 non-need-based awards were made. *Average percent of need met:* 60%. *Average financial aid package:* $7228. *Average need-based loan:* $4105. *Average need-based gift aid:* $4278. *Average non-need-based aid:* $2353. *Average indebtedness upon graduation:* $19,315.

Applying *Options:* electronic application, deferred entrance. *Application fee:* $30. *Required:* high school transcript, minimum 2.0 GPA. *Application deadline:* 8/19 (transfers). *Notification:* continuous (freshmen), continuous (transfers).

Freshman Application Contact Ms. Kimberley Buster-Williams, Director of Admissions, University of Michigan–Flint, 303 East Kearsley Street, 245 UPAV, Flint, MI 48502-1950. *Phone:* 810-762-3300. *Toll-free phone:* 800-942-5636. *Fax:* 810-762-3272. *E-mail:* admissions@umflint.edu.

UNIVERSITY OF PHOENIX–METRO DETROIT CAMPUS

Troy, Michigan **www.phoenix.edu/**

- **Proprietary** comprehensive
- **Urban** campus
- **Coed**
- **Noncompetitive** entrance level

Faculty *Student/faculty ratio:* 11:1.

Academics *Calendar:* continuous. *Degrees:* certificates, bachelor's, and master's.

Student Life *Campus security:* late-night transport/escort service.

Costs (2007–08) *Tuition:* $12,180 full-time, $406 per credit part-time. Full-time tuition and fees vary according to course level.

Financial Aid *Average financial aid package:* $4337. *Average need-based gift aid:* $2388.

Applying *Options:* deferred entrance. *Application fee:* $45. *Required:* 1 letter of recommendation. *Required for some:* high school transcript.

Freshman Application Contact Ms. Beth Barilla, Associate Vice President, Student Admissions and Services, University of Phoenix–Metro Detroit Campus, 4615 East Elwood Street, Mail Stop AA-K101, Phoenix, AZ 85040-1958. *Phone:* 480-317-6000. *Toll-free phone:* 800-776-4867 (in-state); 800-228-7240 (out-of-state). *Fax:* 480-894-1758. *E-mail:* beth.barilla@phoenix.edu.

UNIVERSITY OF PHOENIX–WEST MICHIGAN CAMPUS

Walker, Michigan **www.phoenix.edu/**

- **Proprietary** comprehensive, founded 2000
- **Urban** campus
- **Coed**
- **Noncompetitive** entrance level

Faculty *Student/faculty ratio:* 6:1.

Academics *Calendar:* continuous. *Degrees:* bachelor's and master's.

Student Life *Campus security:* late-night transport/escort service.

Costs (2007–08) *Tuition:* $11,640 full-time, $388 per credit part-time. Full-time tuition and fees vary according to course level.

Financial Aid *Average financial aid package:* $4167. *Average need-based gift aid:* $2327.

Applying *Options:* deferred entrance. *Application fee:* $45. *Required:* 1 letter of recommendation. *Required for some:* high school transcript.

Freshman Application Contact Ms. Beth Barilla, Associate Vice President, Student Admissions and Services, University of Phoenix–West Michigan Campus, 4615 East Elwood Street, Mail Stop AA-K101, Phoenix, AZ 85040-1958. *Phone:* 480-317-6000. *Toll-free phone:* 800-776-4867 (in-state); 800-228-7240 (out-of-state). *Fax:* 480-894-1758. *E-mail:* beth.barilla@phoenix.edu.

WALSH COLLEGE OF ACCOUNTANCY AND BUSINESS ADMINISTRATION

Troy, Michigan **www.walshcollege.edu/**

Application Contact Ms. Victoria R. Scavone, Assistant Vice President for Enrollment and Student Services, Walsh College of Accountancy and Business Administration, PO Box 7006, Troy, MI 48007-7006. *Phone:* 248-823-1209. *Toll-free phone:* 800-925-7401. *Fax:* 248-823-1611. *E-mail:* admissions@walshcollege.edu.

WAYNE STATE UNIVERSITY

Detroit, Michigan **www.wayne.edu/**

- **State-supported** university, founded 1868
- **Urban** 203-acre campus
- **Coed** 21,145 undergraduate students, 60% full-time, 59% women, 41% men
- **Moderately difficult** entrance level, 83% of applicants were admitted

Undergraduates 12,645 full-time, 8,500 part-time. Students come from 35 states and territories, 62 other countries, 1% are from out of state, 32% African American, 6% Asian American or Pacific Islander, 3% Hispanic American, 0.5% Native American, 5% international, 12% transferred in, 8% live on campus. *Retention:* 69% of 2006 full-time freshmen returned.

Freshmen *Admission:* 9,004 applied, 7,515 admitted, 3,188 enrolled. *Average high school GPA:* 3.11. *Test scores:* ACT scores over 18: 73%; ACT scores over 24: 26%; ACT scores over 30: 4%.

Faculty *Total:* 1,928, 51% full-time, 42% with terminal degrees. *Student/faculty ratio:* 17:1.

Majors Accounting; African-American/Black studies; American studies; anthropology; apparel and textile marketing management; area studies related; art; art history, criticism and conservation; art teacher education; Asian studies; biology/biological sciences; chemical engineering; chemistry; cinematography and film/video production; civil engineering; classics and languages, literatures and linguistics; clinical laboratory science/medical technology; communication disorders; communication/speech communication and rhetoric; computer and information sciences; computer technology/computer systems technology; criminal justice/safety; dance; dietetics; dramatic/theater arts; economics; electrical, electronic and communications engineering technology; electrical, electronics and communications engineering; electromechanical technology; elementary education; English; English/language arts teacher education; environmental science; film/cinema studies; finance; foods, nutrition, and wellness; foreign languages and literatures; funeral service and mortuary science; geography; geology/earth science; German; health professions related; health teacher education; history; industrial engineering; industrial production technologies related; industrial technology; information science/studies; journalism; labor studies; linguistics; logistics and materials management; management information systems; marketing/marketing management; mathematics; mathematics teacher education; mechanical engineering; mechanical engineering/mechanical technology; medical radiologic technology; Middle/Near Eastern and Semitic languages related; multi-/interdisciplinary studies related; music; nursing (registered nurse training); organizational behavior; pathologist assistant; philosophy; physical education teaching and coaching; physics; political science and government; psychology; public administration; public relations/image management; radio and television; science teacher education; Slavic languages; social studies teacher education; social work; sociology; special education; special education (speech or language impaired); technical teacher education.

Academics *Calendar:* semesters. *Degrees:* certificates, bachelor's, master's, doctoral, first professional, post-master's, and postbachelor's certificates. *Special study options:* academic remediation for entering students, accelerated degree program, adult/continuing education programs, advanced placement credit, cooperative education, distance learning, double majors, English as a second language, honors programs, independent study, internships, off-campus study, part-time degree program, services for LD students, student-designed majors, study abroad, summer session for credit. *ROTC:* Air Force (c). *Unusual degree programs:* 3-2 engineering; nursing.

Computers on Campus 1,800 computers/terminals are available on campus for general student use. Students can access the following: online (class) registration. Campuswide network is available.

Student Life *Housing options:* coed, disabled students. Campus housing is university owned. Freshman applicants given priority for college housing. *Activities and organizations:* drama/theater group, student-run newspaper, choral group, marching band, Muslim Students Association, Honors Students Association, Indian Students Association, American Medical Students Association—Pre-Med Chapter, National Panhellenic Council Groups, national fraternities, national sororities. *Campus security:* 24-hour emergency response devices and patrols, late-night transport/escort service, controlled dormitory access. *Student services:* health clinic, personal/psychological counseling, women's center, legal services.

Athletics Member NCAA. All Division II except men's and women's fencing (Division I), men's and women's ice hockey (Division I). *Intercollegiate sports:* baseball M (s), basketball M (s)/W (s), cross-country running M (s)/W (s), fencing M (s)/W (s), football M (s), golf M (s), ice hockey M (s)/W (s), softball W (s), swimming and diving M (s)/W (s), tennis M (s)/W (s), volleyball W (s). *Intramural sports:* badminton M/W, basketball M/W, bowling M/W, football M/W, racquetball M/W, soccer M/W, softball M/W, tennis M/W, volleyball M/W.

Standardized Tests *Required:* SAT or ACT (for admission).

Costs (2007–08) *Tuition:* state resident $6783 full-time, $226 per credit hour part-time; nonresident $15,534 full-time, $518 per credit hour part-time. Full-time tuition and fees vary according to course load and student level. Part-time tuition and fees vary according to course load and student level. *Required fees:* $1061 full-time, $18 per credit hour part-time, $164 per term part-time. *Room and board:* $6702. Room and board charges vary according to board plan and housing facility. *Payment plan:* installment. *Waivers:* senior citizens and employees or children of employees.

Financial Aid Of all full-time matriculated undergraduates who enrolled in 2006, 8,203 applied for aid, 7,145 were judged to have need, 1,524 had their need fully met. 348 Federal Work-Study jobs (averaging $3004). 160 state and other part-time jobs (averaging $2368). In 2006, 1113 non-need-based awards were made. *Average percent of need met:* 64%. *Average financial aid package:* $10,885. *Average need-based loan:* $3908. *Average need-based gift aid:* $3686. *Average non-need-based aid:* $4702. *Average indebtedness upon graduation:* $19,061.

Applying *Options:* electronic application, deferred entrance. *Application fee:* $30. *Required:* high school transcript, minimum 2.0 GPA. *Required for some:* letters of recommendation, interview, portfolio. *Application deadlines:* 8/1 (freshmen), 8/1 (transfers). *Notification:* continuous until 9/1 (freshmen), continuous until 9/1 (transfers).

Freshman Application Contact Wayne State University, 3E HNJ, Detroit, MI 48202. *Phone:* 313-577-3577. *Toll-free phone:* 877-978 Ext. 4636 (in-state); 800-WSU-INFO (out-of-state).

WESTERN MICHIGAN UNIVERSITY

Kalamazoo, Michigan www.wmich.edu/

- **State-supported** university, founded 1903
- **Urban** 1200-acre campus
- **Endowment** $197.7 million
- **Coed** 19,718 undergraduate students, 88% full-time, 50% women, 50% men
- **Moderately difficult** entrance level, 86% of applicants were admitted

Undergraduates 17,308 full-time, 2,410 part-time. Students come from 34 states and territories, 52 other countries, 5% are from out of state, 6% African American, 2% Asian American or Pacific Islander, 2% Hispanic American, 0.7% Native American, 2% international, 9% transferred in, 26% live on campus. *Retention:* 75% of 2006 full-time freshmen returned.

Freshmen *Admission:* 11,791 applied, 10,179 admitted, 3,506 enrolled. *Average high school GPA:* 3.23. *Test scores:* ACT scores over 18: 91%; ACT scores over 24: 30%; ACT scores over 30: 2%.

Faculty *Total:* 1,354, 67% full-time. *Student/faculty ratio:* 19:1.

Majors Accounting; advertising; aerospace, aeronautical and astronautical engineering; African studies; airline pilot and flight crew; anthropology; apparel and textiles; art; art history, criticism and conservation; Asian studies; athletic training; audiology and speech-language pathology; biochemistry; biology/biological sciences; biomedical sciences; business/commerce; business teacher education; chemical engineering; chemistry; chemistry related; chemistry teacher education; civil engineering; communication and journalism related; communication/speech communication and rhetoric; computer and information sciences; computer engineering; computer science; criminal justice/safety; dance; dietetics; e-commerce; economics; electrical, electronics and communications engineering; engineering/industrial management; English; English composition; English/French as a second/foreign language (teaching) related; English/language arts teacher education; environmental studies; family and consumer sciences/home economics teacher education; family systems; finance; financial planning and services; foodservice systems administration; French; French as a second/foreign language (teaching); French language teacher education; geochemistry; geography; geography teacher education; geology/earth science; geophysics and seismology; German; German language teacher education; graphic design; health teacher education; history; history teacher education; human resources management; hydrology and water resources science; industrial design; industrial engineering; information resources management; interior design; international/global studies; jazz/jazz studies; journalism; kinesiology and exercise science; Latin; Latin teacher education; logistics and materials management; management science; manufacturing engineering; marketing/marketing management; marketing related; mathematics; mathematics teacher education; mechanical engineering; music; music performance; music teacher education; music theory and composition; music therapy; nursing (registered nurse training); occupational therapy; organizational communication; parks, recreation and leisure; philosophy; physical education teaching and coaching; physics; physics teacher education; plastics engineering technology; political science and government; psychology; public/applied history and archival administration; religious studies; science teacher education; sculpture; secondary education; social sciences; social science teacher education; social work; sociology; Spanish; Spanish language teacher education; special education (mentally retarded); special education (vision impaired); statistics; structural engineering; technology/industrial arts teacher education; tourism and travel services management; tourism and travel services marketing; women's studies.

Academics *Calendar:* semesters. *Degrees:* bachelor's, master's, doctoral, post-master's, and postbachelor's certificates (specialist). *Special study options:* academic remediation for entering students, accelerated degree program, adult/continuing education programs, advanced placement credit, cooperative education, distance learning, double majors, English as a second language, freshman honors college, honors programs, independent study, internships, off-campus study, part-time degree program, services for LD students, student-designed majors, study abroad, summer session for credit. *ROTC:* Army (b).

Computers on Campus 2,000 computers/terminals are available on campus for general student use. Students can access the following: computer help desk, free student e-mail accounts, online (class) grades, online (class) registration, online (class) schedules. Campuswide network is available. 100% of college-owned or -operated housing units are wired for high-speed Internet access. Wireless service is available via entire campus.

Student Life *Housing options:* coed, men-only, women-only, disabled students. Campus housing is university owned. *Activities and organizations:* drama/theater group, student-run newspaper, radio station, choral group, marching band, Campus Activities Board, Western Student Association, Young Black Male Support Network, Drive Safe Kalamazoo, Alternative Spring Break, national fraternities, national sororities. *Campus security:* 24-hour emergency response devices and patrols, student patrols, late-night transport/escort service, controlled dormitory access. *Student services:* health clinic, personal/psychological counseling, women's center, legal services.

Athletics Member NCAA. All Division I except football (Division I-A). *Intercollegiate sports:* baseball M (s), basketball M (s)/W (s), cross-country running W (s), golf W (s), gymnastics W (s), ice hockey M (s), soccer M (s)/W (s), softball W (s), tennis M (s)/W (s), track and field W (s), volleyball W (s). *Intramural sports:* badminton M/W, basketball M/W, bowling M/W, equestrian sports M (c)/W (c), fencing M (c)/W (c), football M/W, golf M, ice hockey M (c)/W (c), lacrosse M (c)/W (c), racquetball M/W, rugby M (c)/W, sailing M (c)/W (c), soccer M/W, softball M/W, swimming and diving M/W, table tennis M/W, tennis M/W, volleyball M/W.

Standardized Tests *Required:* SAT or ACT (for admission).

Costs (2007–08) *One-time required fee:* $300. *Tuition:* state resident $6570 full-time, $219 per credit hour part-time; nonresident $16,116 full-time, $537 per credit hour part-time. Full-time tuition and fees vary according to course load, location, and student level. Part-time tuition and fees vary according to course load, location, and student level. *Required fees:* $690 full-time, $181 per term part-time. *Room and board:* $7042; room only: $3725. Room and board charges vary according to board plan. *Payment plan:* installment. *Waivers:* senior citizens and employees or children of employees.

Financial Aid Of all full-time matriculated undergraduates who enrolled in 2003, 11,300 applied for aid, 10,800 were judged to have need, 2,500 had their need fully met. In 2003, 2600 non-need-based awards were made. *Average percent of need met:* 69%. *Average financial aid package:* $7300. *Average need-based loan:* $3800. *Average need-based gift aid:* $4100. *Average non-need-based aid:* $2400. *Average indebtedness upon graduation:* $16,100.

Applying *Options:* electronic application, deferred entrance. *Application fee:* $35. *Required:* high school transcript, minimum 2.0 GPA. *Required for some:* interview. *Application deadlines:* rolling (freshmen), 8/1 (transfers). *Notification:* continuous (freshmen), continuous (transfers).

Freshman Application Contact Ms. Penny Bundy, Director, Office of Admissions, Western Michigan University, 1903 West Michigan Avenue, Kalamazoo, MI 49008-5211. *Phone:* 269-387-2000. *Fax:* 269-387-2096. *E-mail:* ask-wmu@wmich.edu.

See page 1358 for the College Close-Up.

YESHIVA GEDDOLAH OF GREATER DETROIT RABBINICAL COLLEGE

Oak Park, Michigan

Director of Admissions Mr. Eric Krohner, Executive Director, Yeshiva Geddolah of Greater Detroit Rabbinical College, 24600 Greenfield, Oak Park, MI 48237-1544.

ADRIAN COLLEGE

ADRIAN, MICHIGAN

The College

Adrian College, which was chartered in 1859, is a private liberal arts college that is affiliated with the United Methodist Church. Recognized for providing high-quality education by the *College Board Review* and *U.S. News & World Report,* Adrian is characterized by teaching excellence and individual treatment of students. The College's mission is to maintain a learning environment that stimulates individual growth and academic excellence. To fulfill this mission, the College is committed to fostering creativity, encouraging ethical values and the pursuit of truth, and helping students develop the necessary skills to lead satisfying lives and careers within a global society.

In fall 2007, Adrian College enrolled 1,300 students (673 men and 596 women), of whom 1,269 were full-time. Approximately 98 percent of the student body is of traditional college age. Currently, students come from sixteen states, but most come from the surrounding Midwest states of Michigan, Ohio, and Indiana. The international student population represents Canada, Japan, Mexico, Northern Ireland, the United Arab Emirates, and Zimbabwe.

Adrian College students enjoy a lifestyle that combines residential life with academic challenges and social opportunities. With more than sixty-five organizations to choose from, students can apply their talents, interests, and skills in extracurricular activities ranging from academic honoraries and religious, cultural, and social organizations to intercollegiate and intramural athletic teams. Adrian College is a member of the NCAA Division III and the Michigan Intercollegiate Athletics Association. The Merillat Sport and Fitness Center is an 80,000-square-foot multisport forum that includes basketball, volleyball, and tennis courts surrounded by a 1/10-mile indoor track as well as two racquetball courts, an athletic training room, a weight-training and conditioning room, classrooms, a physiology laboratory, and a dance studio. The performance gymnasium, which seats 1,300 people, is host to numerous intercollegiate basketball and volleyball matches. In fall 2006, the College opened a multisport stadium to host the football, men's and women's lacrosse, men's and women's soccer, and women's field hockey teams. Arrington Ice Arena opened in fall 2007.

Location

Adrian College is located in Adrian, Michigan, the county seat of Lenawee County, in the southeastern part of the state. Adrian is a city of approximately 22,000 people, situated in the center of an agricultural, industrial, and recreational area. State and U.S. highways and nearby expressways provide convenient access to the metropolitan areas of Detroit, Toledo, Chicago, Indianapolis, Cleveland, and Pittsburgh. Both the Detroit and Toledo airports are within an hour's drive of the College.

Majors and Degrees

Adrian College is authorized by its Board of Trustees to grant the following degrees: Associate of Arts, Bachelor of Science, Bachelor of Arts, Bachelor of Fine Arts, Bachelor of Music, Bachelor of Music Education, Bachelor of Business Administration, and Bachelor of Social Work. Majors include accountancy; art; arts management; athletic training, biology; business administration (management or marketing); chemistry; communication arts and sciences; criminal justice; earth science; economics; English (journalism, literature, or writing); environmental science; environmental studies; exercise science; French; German; health, physical education, and recreation; history; interior design; international business; international studies; Japanese studies; mathematics; music; musical theater; philosophy/religion; physics; political science; psychology; religion; social work; sociology; Spanish; teacher education; and theater. Students may also choose to design their own major, in consultation with the appropriate department chairpersons, or even major in two or more areas of study. Professional certification areas include elementary and secondary education. Preprofessional programs are offered in architecture, art therapy, dentistry, engineering, law, medicine, optometry, pharmacy, physical therapy, podiatry, seminary, and veterinary studies.

Academic Programs

Distribution requirements are designed to emphasize liberal education through a broad understanding of the liberal arts and have been established in several liberal arts areas (arts, humanities, social sciences, natural and physical sciences, and cross-cultural perspective) and in basic skill areas that indicate education proficiency (communication, linguistics, and physical development). All students must complete at least one course in religion or philosophy and at least one 4-hour laboratory science course. Students must also declare their major during their sophomore year. Successful completion of a minimum of 124 semester hours, with at least 30 hours at the most advanced level, is needed to obtain a baccalaureate degree. An honors program is open to highly motivated students of proven ability. Successful completion of the honors program is noted on the student's transcript and diploma.

Adrian maintains a two-semester calendar. The first semester runs from late August to mid-December, the second semester from early January to the end of April. A May term and summer session are offered for students who wish to intensify or accelerate their studies.

Off-Campus Programs

Participation in approved off-campus and cooperative programs can help students earn academic credit. Adrian offers a variety of ways to visit and study other cultures through established formal arrangements, as well as gain professional experience via cooperative arrangements with a variety of off-campus sites. Formal arrangements for study abroad are available at more than fifty locations in thirty countries. Opportunities for domestic study and living experience are available through the Philadelphia Urban Semester, American University's Washington Semester, and programs offered by the Urban Life Center in Chicago and the Washington Center.

Career internships, which are available in all academic disciplines, provide all students with opportunities to test their career interests and develop job-related skills through College-approved work experiences. Students may earn up to 12 semester hours working for domestic or international employers.

Academic Facilities

Shipman Library includes a complete line of academic library services. The collection numbers more than 82,000 volumes, plus substantial holdings of microforms, art prints, sound recordings, and subscriptions to more than 750 periodicals. The College completed a $6-million library expansion and renovation project in 2000.

Computer terminals and printers for student use are located in Jones Hall, Mahan Hall, North Hall, Peelle Hall, Caine Student Center, and Shipman Library. Access to IBM and IBM-compatible personal computers, printers, scanners, and Internet services is available to students at no charge. Many classrooms and all residence hall rooms are networked for Internet access. In addition, Adrian College's entire campus became wireless in January 2007.

General chemistry and biology laboratories equipped with sophisticated chemical and biochemical instrumentation are provided by the College. Labs for psychology, language study, physics, acoustical studies, and tissue culture provide students with access to a variety of research opportunities. Special facilities include art studios, music practice rooms, greenhouses, and a planetarium.

Downs Hall, the only remaining building from Adrian College's original campus, houses the Stubnitz Gallery of Art and the Downs Studio Theater, a 199-seat facility with a thrust-style stage, where most student theater productions take place. Dawson Auditorium, with its traditional proscenium stage, is used for College musical and theatrical productions, Adrian Symphony concerts, and guest artist appearances.

Costs

Full-time tuition for 2007–08 was $21,300, and room and board were $7610 (waived). The required activity fee of $150 covers the cost of student participation in a variety of campuswide social activities and attendance at Adrian College sports events. The average cost of books and supplies is about $400 per semester.

Financial Aid

Adrian College strives to make a high-quality private liberal arts education affordable to its students through various forms of financial assistance. Approximately 85 percent of the student body receives some form of financial aid through scholarships, grants, loans, and campus employment. The College also participates in all applicable Michigan aid programs, as well as the Federal Work-Study, Federal Pell Grant, and Federal Supplemental Educational Opportunity Grant (FSEOG) programs. The Federal Perkins Loan, Federal Stafford Student Loan, and Federal Parent Loan for Undergraduate Students (PLUS) programs are also available, as are alternative student loans. A number of part-time positions are available for those who wish to work on campus while earning applicable financial assistance. For those with a demonstrated record of high academic ability, merit-based scholarship assistance is available. To be considered for any financial assistance, a student must complete the Free Application for Federal Student Aid (FAFSA) form, which is used to conduct a need analysis for the student. The FAFSA may be obtained from most high school counselors or directly from the Adrian College Office of Financial Aid.

Faculty

Teaching with a personal approach is a top priority at Adrian College. Classes at Adrian are not conducted by teaching assistants. Instead, classes are taught by dedicated faculty members—most of whom hold the terminal degree in their field. With a student-faculty ratio of 13:1 and an average class size of 15, students are assured of a high-quality education that unites challenge and opportunity within a framework of personal and institutional support.

Student Government

Adrian College Student Government is the student organization charged with representing student views on matters of institutional policy and operation at all levels of College organization. As a student organization, it also provides students with a common forum where their individual ideas may be heard, debated, and perhaps adopted. Appropriations and other major decisions are made in full-senate sessions. Other work is carried out through the Campus Activities Network or through the College governance system. Any student who wishes to run for student-elected office may do so.

Admission Requirements

Adrian College enrolls qualified students regardless of age, disability, ethnicity, gender, physical characteristics, race, religion, or sexual orientation. Applicants should present at least 15 units of secondary school preparation, including 4 units of English, 3 units of mathematics, 3 units of sciences, 2 units of social sciences, and 2 units of foreign language.

Students applying for freshman admission must also perform satisfactorily on either the ACT or the SAT and must request that their scores be sent directly to Adrian College. The average high school GPA of entering Adrian College students who have taken college-preparatory courses during their four years of high school is 3.4. The mean ACT composite score is 23. Transfer students must be eligible to return immediately to the last attended college and must have an above-average cumulative GPA. Prospective transfer students must request an official transcript from each college attended to be sent directly to the Office of Admissions at Adrian College. Nontraditional students must complete a different application for admission but are evaluated on the same basis as traditional freshmen. A GED equivalency certificate may be substituted for a full high school transcript.

Students from other countries are always welcome at Adrian College and are encouraged to apply. International applicants must file an international application for admission and must submit complete secondary school records, transcripts of any university credit, and TOEFL test scores demonstrating sufficient fluency in English to participate in the regular instructional program of the College. A minimum TOEFL score of 173 on the computer-based test, 500 on the paper-based test, or 61 on the Internet-based test is required for admission. A full program of services for international students includes English as a second language (ESL) classes for further assistance in English, housing and food service, and initial pick-up service from the airport. The cost of room and board for the academic year is waived for international students.

Application and Information

Application can be made anytime following the completion of the junior year of high school. Students are usually notified of the admissions decision within two weeks after the application file is complete. Campus visits are strongly encouraged but not required.

For more information about Adrian College or to schedule a campus visit, students should contact:

Office of Admissions
Adrian College
110 South Madison Street
Adrian, Michigan 49221-2575
Phone: 517-265-5161 Ext. 4326
800-877-2246 (toll-free)
Fax: 517-264-3878
E-mail: admissions@adrian.edu
Web site: http://www.adrian.edu

ALMA COLLEGE
ALMA, MICHIGAN

The College

Alma College highlights personalized education, social responsibility, and extraordinary achievement.

Alma students work closely with dedicated faculty members. The College has a 12:1 student-faculty ratio and an average class size of 16. Independent study and faculty-sponsored research projects abound, and virtually all students find faculty mentors who help them explore and discover, learn, and grow. In addition to twenty-seven majors, thirty-one minors, several preprofessional programs, and four undergraduate degrees, Alma offers students the ability to create their own personally constructed majors called Programs of Emphasis. Alma encourages students to think independently within the framework of a liberal arts education that can be applied to any task or any profession. Alma graduates enter the job market and graduate schools with a personalized education that serves them well as they continue to learn throughout their lifetime.

The College's one-month intensive spring term supports faculty members and students traveling together across the globe. Some examples include high-altitude physiology in the Rockies; economics, photography, or education in Argentina and Ecuador; Shakespeare or medieval literature in London; cross-border issues between Texas and Mexico; and a host of other innovative courses that cross geographic and disciplinary boundaries. During the regular terms, Alma students pursue applications of their liberal arts foundations through overseas study from India to Scotland to Spain; undertake practicum experiences in nearby jobs or programs in Philadelphia, Chicago, or New York; and embrace uncommonly rich courses that link service with learning. Alma students regularly discover skills, passions, and careers they had not previously imagined.

Every April, Alma College celebrates the extraordinary achievements of its students in a special Honors Day celebration of the liberal arts as students present their own research and study. Despite being a small college, over the past several years Alma has had an unusually large number of nationally competitive scholarships to celebrate. Over the last four years, in fact, Alma students have garnered ten prestigious Fulbright scholarships for international study, five Udall scholarships for work in environmental issues, three Truman Scholarships for study leading toward a career in public service, and the highly esteemed British Marshall Scholarship for study at Cambridge University.

The Center for Responsible Leadership provides opportunities for all students to improve their leadership abilities through guest speakers, seminars, service trips, and other campus programming. In addition, the Center for Responsible Leadership Fellows' Program offers in-depth training and development, including internships, community service opportunities, and international leadership experiences.

A Phi Beta Kappa institution, Alma is classified as a selective "Baccalaureate Arts and Sciences" college by the Carnegie Foundation for the Advancement of Teaching. Alma was selected for inclusion in *Colleges with a Conscience: 81 Great Schools with Outstanding Community Involvement*, published by the Princeton Review and Campus Compact. Alma is one of only 100 colleges and universities to be named to the Templeton Honor Roll in the *Templeton Guide: Colleges that Encourage Character Development.*

With an enrollment of more than 1,200 students, the College employs a full-time teaching faculty of 87 members, of whom 87 percent hold the Ph.D. or other terminal degree. Entering first-year students have an average high school GPA of 3.53 and a mean ACT composite score of 23.8 (approximately equivalent to a combined SAT score of 1160). More than 60 percent of the freshmen students ranked in the top 25 percent of their high school classes, and 31 percent ranked in the top 10 percent.

Eighty-six percent of Alma's students live on campus; first-year students and upperclassmen live together in a complex of residence halls and academic theme houses, including the newest, environmentally friendly, apartment-style Wright Hall. Each residence unit is supervised by a full-time director who is assisted by student staff members.

Nourishment for the body and conversation for the soul can be found at Hamilton Dining Commons, Van Dusen Commons, Joe's Internet Café, and Scottie's Snack Shop. Downtown Alma, a short walk from campus, offers a diverse menu of meals and snacks.

Founded in 1886 by Michigan Presbyterians, Alma College still maintains a relationship with the Presbyterian Church (U.S.A.), but offers an environment that welcomes students of all religious backgrounds. The Alma lifestyle combines academic challenges with favorite activities and opportunities to develop new interests. With nearly 100 student organizations to join, intercollegiate and intramural sports for the competitive spirit, performing and visual arts for creative outlets, and a vital Greek system for active social lives, Alma students have a dynamic cocurricular life. Nearly 40 percent of all Alma students participate in intercollegiate athletics. Alma competes at the NCAA Division III level in nine men's and nine women's sports. In addition, more than a third of all Alma students take part in at least one cultural performance each year. The Heritage Center is the region's premiere performing arts facility.

The Stone Center for Recreation features a climbing wall, a fitness center, four courts, and a suspended three-lane track. The outdoor athletic facilities include a football field with artificial turf, soccer and softball yards, tennis courts, and an eight-lane track. The Klenk Park baseball complex features a scoreboard honoring former Detroit Tiger and Alma Scot great Jim Northrup. Hogan Physical Education Center is home to men's and women's basketball and the College's swimming and diving teams.

Location

Easily reached from Chicago, Cincinnati, Cleveland, Detroit, Indianapolis, and Milwaukee, Alma College is located in the heart of Michigan's lower peninsula. The city of Alma (population of about 10,000) is well-known as Scotland, USA, for its annual Highland Festival. Alma's relaxed, safe, small-town atmosphere enables students to concentrate on educational priorities, while both the metropolitan and recreational areas of Michigan are readily accessible. Tri Cities and Lansing airports are nearby.

Majors and Degrees

Alma offers four degrees: Bachelor of Arts, Bachelor of Fine Arts, Bachelor of Music, and Bachelor of Science. Departmental and interdepartmental majors are possible. Majors include art and design, athletic training, biochemistry, biology, business administration, chemistry, communication, computer science, economics, education, English, exercise and health science, French, German, history, international business, mathematical sciences, mathematics, music, philosophy, physics, political science, psychology, religious studies, sociology and anthropology, Spanish, and theater and dance. Interdisciplinary majors may be designed in such fields as American studies, art history, cognitive science, electronics and computer engineering, environmental studies, foreign service, gerontology, new media studies, public health, and women's studies. Preprofessional programs prepare students for further study and careers in dentistry, engineering, graphic design, law, medical illustration, medicine, the ministry, occupational therapy, and physical therapy. Academic minors are available in American studies, art history, cognitive science, electronics and computer engineering, environmental studies, gerontology, new media studies, public health, and women's studies.

Alma College offers cooperative 3-2 and 4-2 pre-engineering programs with the University of Michigan School of Engineering and Michigan Technological University. A 3-2 program in occupational therapy is offered in conjunction with Washington University in St. Louis.

Academic Programs

The College operates on a 4-4-1 calendar—two 4-month terms in the fall and winter and one 1-month term in the spring. During the spring term, there are opportunities for international study as well as for on-campus instruction and research. In keeping with Alma's philosophy of educating the whole person, the College requires that all students complete liberal arts courses spanning the humanities, the natural sciences, and the social sciences. The B.A. and B.S. degree programs require the completion of 136 credits; the B.F.A. and B.M. degree programs, 148 credits.

Highly qualified students are challenged by Alma's honors program, featuring a specially designed freshman course that explores the methods of communication used in the liberal arts disciplines. The honors concept extends throughout the four years at Alma.

Alma accepts credits earned through the Advanced Placement (AP) Program and the International Baccalaureate Diploma (I.B.) program, and examinations designed by Alma's academic departments.

Off-Campus Programs

Numerous opportunities for international study are available through the College, including offerings in Australia, Austria, Bolivia, Ecuador, England, France, Germany, India, Italy, New Zealand, Peru, Scotland, South Korea, and Spain. A wide variety of options for housing, including placements in private homes, are featured. Alma's Program of Studies in France, a cooperative venture with the prestigious Alliance Française in Paris, can accommodate any student—from beginner to advanced—for periods of time ranging from one month to one year. Students considering careers in international business may enroll in an international marketing or multinational business administration seminar held in Wollongong, Australia. Two spring term courses must be successfully completed, one of which must be a designated "S" course. These courses take advantage of the spring term format and cross-geographical, cultural, or disciplinary boundaries. Internships provide Alma students with experience related to their educational or career goals. On-the-job experience may be arranged in many fields through work in businesses, industries, and government and community agencies.

Academic Facilities

Twenty-six main buildings with up-to-date facilities and an outdoor sports complex are arranged around a scenic central mall on Alma's 125-acre campus. It is a short walk to the fully automated library, which houses more than 271,600 volumes. The Dow and Kapp Science Centers provide research and instructional facilities for biology, biochemistry, chemistry, and physics. Swanson Academic Center houses classrooms and faculty offices. The Eddy Music Building, Clack Art Center, and Remick Heritage Center for the Performing Arts offer exhibition, performance, and rehearsal space for art and design, dance, music, and theater. The McIntyre Center for Exercise and Health Science has labs for cardiovascular physiology, human anatomy, and human performance testing.

Instruction at Alma is supported by computer technology. Students are encouraged to bring their own computers to the campus to best utilize available services. Access to the campus network, e-mail, the Internet, the library, and a variety of printers is available in all of Alma's eight residence halls. Student computer labs in academic departments throughout the campus provide access to Macintosh and IBM-compatible PC systems as well as Sun SPARCstations and Silicon Graphics UNIX systems. Computer classrooms in the library and Swanson Academic Center are staffed by student assistants.

Costs

Tuition for 2007–08 is $23,478. Room and board costs for the fall and winter terms total $7774. Students who attend during the spring term pay a $315 tuition charge and a $535 board charge but no room charge. A student activity fee of $210 is charged each year, and a charge of $300 for the Preterm is added to freshman-year costs. Books, personal expenses (including travel, clothing, and entertainment), and supplies are estimated at $1400 per year.

Financial Aid

At Alma, students can achieve scholarship recognition regardless of need on the basis of outstanding scholastic achievement. Several academically competitive scholarship programs provide awards for eligible students, including a full tuition scholarship for National Merit Finalists. The College also offers performance scholarships in recognition of individual talent, as well as grants, loans, and deferred-payment plans. Approximately 450 campus and community jobs are filled by Alma students yearly. To apply for aid, students are required only to file the Free Application for Federal Student Aid (FAFSA) by March 15 of the year of prospective enrollment at Alma.

Faculty

A look at Alma's faculty shows a diversity of backgrounds; 87 percent of the 87 full-time faculty members hold the highest degree in their field. Superior undergraduate teaching is the first priority of Alma's faculty members; no graduate students teach classes, nor are there television lecture courses at Alma. Classes at Alma are small; the faculty-student ratio is 1:12. Faculty members are accessible and willing to assist students. They are also recognized as scholars in their fields; their research has been supported by such organizations as the Council for the International Exchange of Scholars (Fulbright scholarships), the Michigan Council for the Arts, the National Endowment for the Humanities, and the National Science Foundation.

Student Government

Alma encourages students to build leadership skills through involvement in student government and campus organizations. Members of the Alma College Student Congress represent all major student organizations as well as individual students. This group works as a liaison with the administration to implement or revise campus policies, develop a budget and coordinate the expenditure of student activity fees, manage the campus radio station and student publications, and resolve problems. Alma's Union Board, composed of students representing each residence hall, oversees most of the regular entertainment scheduled on campus. As a residential campus, Alma is governed by rules prohibiting academic dishonesty, gambling, cohabitation, infringements on others' rights, illegal use of alcoholic beverages and drugs, and damage to personal property.

Admission Requirements

To be considered for admission, applicants should have an average of B or higher in high school and a composite score of 22 or higher on the ACT or a combined score of 1030 or higher on the SAT. All applicants are encouraged to schedule an admission interview on campus. Transfer students must have earned an average of C or higher at their previous institution. No more than 62 semester hours or 90 quarter hours of course work completed with a grade of C or better may be transferred to Alma. International students are asked to submit records of previous schooling and must show competence in English through the Test of English as a Foreign Language (TOEFL).

Application and Information

Students may apply at any time after completing their junior year of high school. Freshman applicants should send the completed application for admission along with a $25 nonrefundable application fee, high school transcripts, and ACT or SAT scores. The application fee is waived for students who use the online application. Students are required to submit a recommendation from their high school guidance counselor. Transfer students should submit transcripts from each institution attended, the completed application for admission, a $25 nonrefundable application fee, and a Transfer Recommendation Form from the last institution attended. Applications are handled on a rolling basis; students should hear about admission decisions within three weeks after sending an application and records. Alma College's nondiscrimination policy includes age, color, creed, gender, national origin, physical ability, race, religion, and sexual orientation.

All records and forms should be mailed to:

Admissions Office
Alma College
614 West Superior Street
Alma, Michigan 48801-1599

Phone: 800-321-ALMA (toll-free)
E-mail: admissions@alma.edu
Web site: http://www.alma.edu
http://www.alma.edu/admissions/apply

AQUINAS COLLEGE

GRAND RAPIDS, MICHIGAN

The College

Located on the eastern edge of the city of Grand Rapids, Aquinas enjoys all of the advantages of Michigan's second-largest city and is just a 3-hour drive from Detroit or Chicago. The Aquinas College campus is an interesting blend of early-nineteenth-century architecture coupled with modern-day structures. The campus abounds with natural beauty; it has been called the most beautiful small campus in Michigan. Its ninety species of trees, winding woodland paths, and inviting creeks and ponds create a peaceful 110-acre environment that students of all ages find welcoming. Founded by the Dominican Sisters of Grand Rapids in 1886, Aquinas has a Catholic heritage and a Christian tradition. The Dominican tradition of working and serving remains alive at Aquinas. It is lived out by Aquinas students who volunteer their time and talents in the Grand Rapids community and by those who travel to places such as Oaxaca, Mexico; Appalachia, Kentucky; or any of a dozen other service-learning project sites. An ability to see the world from different perspectives is the hallmark of an Aquinas-educated student. Aquinas, a coeducational liberal arts college, offers an approach to learning and living that teaches students unlimited ways of seeing the world. That is why every Aquinas student enrolls in the humanities program, a two-semester exploration of the best that has been thought, written, composed, and painted. As students find their way in the world of thought, the core curriculum in natural science ensures that they discover the workings of the physical world as well.

An Aquinas education makes graduates more employable. Each year, almost 200 Aquinas students find businesses, government agencies, and other organizations eager to offer field experience and internship opportunities. Students can write press releases, keep sports statistics, and travel around the country with such organizations as Major League Soccer; work on historic preservation projects with the Michigan Bureau of History in Lansing; or learn about politics from the inside as a congressional intern in Washington, D.C. Nine out of 10 applicants recommended by the Aquinas premedical advisory committee are admitted to medical school, and 19 of 20 are accepted into other graduate programs. In all, more than 90 percent of Aquinas seniors find jobs or enroll in graduate school soon after graduation. Aquinas sees a liberal arts education as career preparation. The Aquinas general education plan exposes students to the necessary skills that enable them to become critical thinkers, articulate speakers, strong writers, and effective problem solvers. Aquinas faculty members insist that students carry values as well as skills into the workplace. The College's curriculum, with its more than sixty majors, is designed to provide students with both breadth and depth and to foster a thirst for knowledge and truth and a spirit of intellectual dialogue and inquiry. Coupled with nationally recognized internship programs, it prepares students to both live and work in the rapidly changing world of today and tomorrow.

Arriving from places as near as Grand Rapids, Chicago, and Detroit and as far as Japan and Russia, the 2,100 students include 1,300 full-time, 400 part-time, and 400 graduate students. The Insignis program at Aquinas encourages students of exceptional academic ability to participate in social and intellectual activities such as lectures and receptions for visiting scholars and trips to places of cultural interest. Aquinas offers more than sixty student organizations, ranging from intramural teams and departmental clubs to a wide variety of musical groups, student publications, and service organizations.

In addition to its undergraduate degrees, Aquinas also offers Master in the Art of Teaching, Master in Education, Master in Science Education, and Master of Management degrees.

Location

Aquinas' location in Grand Rapids allows students to reap the benefits of west Michigan's economic, educational, and cultural center. The city is one of the fastest-growing areas in the Great Lakes region. Grand Rapids combines big-city excitement and small-town charm. There are cosmopolitan amenities ranging from four-star hotels and restaurants to top-notch cultural facilities and entertainment venues. In addition to established attractions such as the Gerald R. Ford Presidential Museum, the Van Andel Public Museum, an expanded zoo, the 5,500-seat Fifth Third Park stadium for Whitecaps minor-league baseball, and the 70-acre Fredrik Meijer Gardens, recent attractions include the more than 12,000-seat Van Andel Arena, home to the Grand Rapids Griffins IHL hockey team and a venue for nationally known music concerts and performances. These major facilities add to the list of popular points of interest, festivals, and special events. With nearly half a million residents, there are abundant recreation, arts, and cultural opportunities available.

Majors and Degrees

Aquinas College offers the following undergraduate degree programs: Bachelor of Arts, Bachelor of Fine Arts, Bachelor of Arts in general education, Bachelor of Music Education, Bachelor of Science, Bachelor of Science in Business Administration, Bachelor of Science in sustainable business, and Bachelor of Science in international business. A Bachelor of Science in Nursing degree program is offered in collaboration with the University of Detroit Mercy and St. Mary's Health Care. Majors and programs of study are offered in accounting, accounting/business administration, art, art/business administration, art history, biology, business administration, business administration/communication, business administration/sports management, chemistry, communication, community leadership, computer information systems, drawing, economics, education, English, environmental science, environmental studies, French, geography, German, health, history, international studies, Japanese, journalism/publications, learning disabilities, mathematics, music, not-for-profit management, organizational communication, painting, philosophy, photography, physical education and recreation, physics, political science, pre-engineering, printmaking, psychology, sculpture, social science, sociology, Spanish, studio art, sustainable business, theater, theology, urban studies, and women's studies. Preprofessional courses are available in dentistry, law, and medicine.

Associate degrees are also available, including the Associate of Arts and the Associate of Science.

Academic Programs

In addition to their major and minor fields of study, students take an integrated skills course called Inquiry and Expression. This course spans the first semester of the freshman year and has an emphasis on writing integrated with reading critically, oral communication skills, critical thinking, library/electronic research methods, computer utilization, and basic quantitative reasoning. The thematic content is American Pluralism: The Individual in a Diverse America. Sophomores take a yearlong course in the humanities. As juniors, they are required to take 3 hours in Theological Foundation. Students are also required to be proficient in a second language through the 102 level. There also is a distribution plan in the general education plan covering social science, history/philosophy, natural world, artistic and creative studies, technology, and health, physical education, and recreation. A career/professional development component begins in summer orientation and is apportioned over four years; topics include assessment of students' strengths, skills, and interests; development of goals, a learning plan, and setting a direction; focus on the individual—wellness, personal finances, and leadership/team skills; awareness of careers, professions, and graduate study; information on making and maintaining a professional portfolio and resume; participating in a professional/career mentor program; career fairs and networking; and experiential learning (choices include internship, service learning, service trips, and study abroad). The College follows a two-semester calendar with a summer session. Aquinas also accepts credit through CLEP and Advanced Placement.

Off-Campus Programs

Students have the option of participating in the Dominican College Campus Interchange Program. Cooperating colleges are Barry University in Miami, Florida; Dominican College in San Rafael, California; and St. Thomas Aquinas College in Sparkill, New York. Students can increase their foreign language skills through cultural-immersion programs in Costa Rica, France, Japan, Spain, or Germany. Two Aquinas faculty members accompany 30 students to Aquinas' study center in Tully Cross, Ireland. Students have the opportunity to earn a full semester of credit, travel abroad, and live in a rural Irish community. The curriculum is centered on several aspects of Irish studies.

Academic Facilities

The newly opened Grace Hauenstein Library is a $6-million facility with resources that include a public access catalog, audio-visual materials, circulation and course reserve materials, reference services, and interlibrary loan services (free access to more than 60 million books and documents from libraries across the country). Students find centrally located PC-based labs having more than 150 Pentium computers, with additional PCs in such areas as residence halls and the Cook Carriage House. The lab technology works in a network environment to allow access to standard applications such as Windows XP, Microsoft Office XP, and Web-based e-mail, as well as more than eighty-five discipline-specific applications; printing to high-quality laser printers; and access to multimedia technology. Labs are open seven days a week and are staffed by trained assistants. Albertus Magnus Hall of Science features the handicapped-accessible Baldwin Observatory and a greenhouse. Other facilities include the Cook Carriage House, a student center, and the modern Art and Music Center, featuring a darkroom, a 200-seat recital hall, an art gallery, and a sculpture studio. The Jarecki Center for Advanced Learning offers network plug-ins every few feet and provides the latest in technology. Three new apartment buildings have opened, providing another housing option. The Aquinas Performing Arts Center is a $7-million facility providing a state-of-the-art theater venue.

Costs

For 2007–08, tuition is $20,048 and room and board are $6422, for a total of $26,470. Other expenses, including books, travel, and personal supplies, average $2000.

Financial Aid

Aquinas College awards both merit-based financial assistance and traditional need-based assistance to qualified students. The Spectrum Scholarship Program was developed to recognize students' achievements in academics, leadership, and service. More than 90 percent of entering freshmen receive some form of financial assistance. The College administers the traditional grant and loan programs, including Federal Stafford Student Loans and Federal PLUS loans. Athletic grants are also available. The College participates in the Facts Tuition Management Plan. This plan assists students in paying costs over a period of time. To apply for financial assistance, students must complete the Free Application for Federal Student Aid (FAFSA).

Faculty

Aquinas faculty members are teachers first: while research plays an important part in the Aquinas faculty's development, teaching remains the number-one priority. In addition to teaching, faculty members serve as academic advisers, mentors, and advisers to various clubs and organizations on campus. With a student-professor ratio of 14:1, faculty members give individual attention and assistance to students. All classes and labs are taught by faculty members, not graduate assistants. Approximately 90 percent of Aquinas faculty members have doctoral or terminal degrees.

Student Government

The Student Senate is the governing body of Aquinas students. Senators are chosen by securing twenty-five signatures of students in support of their involvement. These students have both voice and vote on issues facing the College's Academic Assembly. The senate is responsible for many of the academic, social, recreational, and cultural activities that are brought to the campus.

Admission Requirements

Freshman and transfer applications are received on a rolling basis. A candidate for admission to Aquinas is considered on the basis of academic preparation, scholarship, and character. Admission depends on a number of factors, including high school academic record and ACT or SAT test scores. Transfer students must present a minimum 2.0 grade point average on a 4.0 scale. Paper and online applications do not require an application fee. The admissions office reserves the right to review applications on a case-by-case basis. Curriculum, extracurricular activities, and any extenuating circumstances are considered in the decision. Letters of recommendation are encouraged but not required.

Application and Information

For further information, interested students should contact:

Paula Meehan
Dean of Admissions
Aquinas College
1607 Robinson Road, SE
Grand Rapids, Michigan 49506
Phone: 616-632-2900
800-678-9593 (toll-free)
E-mail: admissions@aquinas.edu
Web site: http://www.aquinas.edu

The Aquinas campus was once a private country estate.

THE ART INSTITUTE OF MICHIGAN

NOVI, MICHIGAN

The Institute

The Art Institute of Michigan provides students with an educational environment and dedicated faculty members committed to preparing students for entry-level positions in the creative arts. Under the guidance of industry professionals, students learn by doing the types of tasks they are likely to encounter in the workplace. In addition, assistance is available to help students with resume writing, networking, and keeping aware of what employers are looking for in job candidates. The school offers six bachelor's degree programs, four associate degree programs, and one certificate program.

The school offers assistance in helping students to secure housing.

The student population includes recent high school graduates, transfer students, and those who have left a previous employment situation to study and train for a new career. Students are creative, competitive, and open to new ideas. They place great value on an education that prepares them for an exciting entry-level position in the arts.

The Art Institute of Michigan places a high value on the quality of student life—both in and out of the classroom. Students participate in a wide variety of activities, including clubs and organizations, community service, and various committees designed to enhance the quality of student life.

The Illinois Institute of Art—Chicago is accredited by the Higher Learning Commission of the North Central Association of Colleges and Schools and is a member of the North Central Association. The Illinois Institute of Art—Chicago operates a branch campus, The Art Institute of Michigan, in Novi, Michigan. The Higher Learning Commission may be contacted at 30 North LaSalle Street, Suite 2400, Chicago, Illinois 60602; 800-621-7440; http://www.ncahlc.org. The Art Institute of Michigan is also accredited by the Accrediting Commission of Career Schools and Colleges of Technology (ACCSCT) as a branch of the Illinois Institute of Art—Chicago. ACCSCT may be contacted at 2101 Wilson Blvd., Suite 302, Arlington, Virginia 22201; 703-247- 4212.

Location

Novi, a town of over 52,000, is a suburb of Detroit. One of the fastest-growing cities in Michigan, Novi is home to the Motorsports Hall of Fame of America and Twelve Oaks Mall and is just a short drive from the cultural, entertainment, and sports facilities of Detroit.

Majors and Degrees

The Art Institute of Michigan offers bachelor's degree programs in advertising, culinary management, fashion marketing and management, interior design, visual communications, and Web design and interactive media.

Associate degrees are offered in culinary arts, fashion merchandising, graphic design, and Web design and interactive media.

A certificate program is offered in professional baking and pastry.

Academic Programs

The Art Institute of Michigan operates on a year-round, four-quarter system.

Academic Facilities

The Art Institute of Michigan contains classrooms, Mac and PC computer labs, and a library for student use. There is also a bookstore.

Costs

Tuition cost varies by program. Prospective students should contact the school for current tuition costs. Other charges include a starting kit for all first quarter students. Kits vary in price depending on the program of study.

Financial Aid

Financial aid is available for those who qualify. Students who require financial assistance should first complete and submit a Free Application for Federal Student Aid (FAFSA) and meet with a financial aid officer. The officer determines the level of need based on a required federal formula, the cost of education, and other factors. Gift aid is available in the form of Federal Pell Grants, Federal Supplemental Educational Opportunity Grants, and veterans' benefits. Loans include Federal Stafford Loans, Federal PLUS Loans, and alternative loans. Other scholarships are available from the school and private sources. Application deadlines and eligibility requirements vary by program.

Faculty

Faculty members at The Art Institute of Michigan have professional knowledge that they bring into the classroom. The school's faculty members provide their students with a real-world, relevant educational experience.

Admission Requirements

Applicants must provide proof of high school graduation or achievement of a General Educational Development (GED) certificate as a prerequisite for admission. In lieu of documenting high school graduation or a GED certificate, applicants may provide proof of attaining an associate degree or higher from an accredited institution. An official transcript indicating date of high school graduation, GED certificate (including test scores), or date of college graduation (including degree granted) is required as proof.

All individuals seeking admission to The Art Institute of Michigan are interviewed in person or by phone by an assistant director of admissions, and each applicant must submit an original essay of at least 150 words stating how an education at The Art Institute of Michigan would help the student to achieve career goals. There is a $50 application fee.

Application and Information

To obtain an application, make arrangements for an interview, or tour the school, students should contact:

The Art Institute of Michigan
28125 Cabot Drive, Suite 120
Novi, Michigan 48377
Phone: 248-675-3800
800-479-0087 (toll-free)
Fax: 248-675-3830
Web site: http://www.artinstitutes.edu/detroit

The Art Institute of Atlanta®, GA; The Art Institute of Atlanta®–Decatur, GA; The Art Institute of Austin℠, TX; The Art Institute of California℠–Inland Empire; The Art Institute of California℠–Los Angeles; The Art Institute of California℠–Orange County; The Art Institute of California℠–Sacramento; The Art Institute of California℠–San Diego; The Art Institute of California℠–San Francisco; The Art Institute of California℠–Sunnyvale; The Art Institute of Charleston℠, SC, A branch of The Art Institute of Atlanta, GA; The Art Institute of Charlotte®, NC; The Art Institute of Colorado® (Denver); The Art Institute of Dallas®, TX; The Art Institute of Fort Lauderdale®, FL; The Art Institute of Houston®, TX; The Art Institute of Indianapolis℠, IN*; The Art Institute of Jacksonville℠, FL, A branch of Miami International University of Art & Design; The Art Institute of Las Vegas®, NV; The Art Institute of Michigan℠ (Detroit); The Art Institute of New York City®, NY; The Art Institute of Ohio℠–Cincinnati**; The Art Institute of Philadelphia®, PA; The Art Institute of Phoenix®, AZ; The Art Institute of Pittsburgh®, PA; The Art Institute of Pittsburgh®–Online Division; The Art Institute of Portland®, OR; The Art Institute of Salt Lake City℠, UT; The Art Institute of Seattle®, WA; The Art Institute of Tampa℠, FL, A branch of Miami International University of Art & Design; The Art Institute of Tennessee℠–Nashville, A branch of The Art Institute of Atlanta, GA; The Art Institute of Tucson℠, AZ; The Art Institute of Washington® (Arlington, VA), A branch of The Art Institute of Atlanta, GA; The Art Institute of York–Pennsylvania℠; The Art Institutes International Minnesota℠ (Minneapolis); California Design College℠ (Los Angeles–Wilshire Blvd.); The Illinois Institute of Art®–Chicago; The Illinois Institute of Art®–Schaumburg; Miami International University of Art & Design℠, FL; The New England Institute of Art® (Boston, MA).

*The Art Institute of Indianapolis is licensed by the Indiana Commission on Proprietary Education, 302 W. Washington St., Rm. E201, Indianapolis, IN 46204, AC-0080.

**The Art Institute of Ohio–Cincinnati, 8845 Governors Hill Drive, Suite 100, Cincinnati, OH 45249-3317, OH Reg. #04-01-1698B.

COLLEGE DATA CENTER • MICHIGAN

CALVIN COLLEGE

GRAND RAPIDS, MICHIGAN

The College

Calvin College is an institution that values both intellect and faith; this view affects every area of campus life, from the content of each course to service-learning opportunities and life in the residence halls. Calvin is one of the nation's largest and most respected Christian colleges. The 2007 fall enrollment was 4,224. Calvin maintains a strong affiliation with the Christian Reformed Church, and students from more than fifty other church denominations across North America and the world choose Calvin for its unique curriculum and faith-based mission.

Calvin is deeply committed to being a diverse community and is taking deliberate steps to increase opportunities for women, members of underrepresented minority groups, and students with disabilities. At Calvin, students are challenged not only to obtain an outstanding education and to prepare for a career but also to live lives of commitment and service.

Students come from nearly every state and fifty-three countries. Most students are between 18 and 22 years old; however, those pursuing the Master of Education (M.Ed.) add to the age diversity on campus. The Broene Counseling Center offers career counseling and career resource services as well as personal counseling. Career Development assists students from their first year through their last, equipping them for interviews, internships, and searching for full-time employment upon graduation.

A wide variety of cocurricular opportunities are available, including music, theater, athletics, art, culture, service, and spiritual formation. Calvin's Service-Learning Center provides opportunities for academically based service learning in addition to such programs as big brothers/big sisters, services for the elderly, and school tutoring. Calvin is an NCAA Division III school and participates in the Michigan Intercollegiate Athletic Association; Calvin's athletic teams regularly are ranked nationally in Division III. The men's basketball team won the national championship in 1992 and 2000; the women's cross-country team captured the national championship in 1998 and 1999. In 2000, 2003, 2004, and 2007, the men's cross-country team won the national championship. The men's ice-hockey club won the 2004 ACHA DIII national championship.

The 390-acre campus is a modern, well-planned community; its oldest academic building was erected in 1960. Fifteen residence halls, eleven apartment buildings, and two spacious dining halls accommodate 2,600 resident students. High-speed computing is available throughout the campus, and wireless service is offered in the residence halls and many campus locations. Calvin's new $35-million athletic complex will open in fall 2008, featuring a 5,000-seat arena, an indoor track and tennis center, a health center, and an aquatics center with a 50-meter by 25-yard pool. This facility will provide an exciting new resource for students, faculty members, and the campus community at large. Calvin's outdoor athletic sites include baseball and softball diamonds, a premier soccer field with seating for 1,500 and two practice fields, an eight-lane track, a six-court tennis facility, a paved jogging path, and two sand volleyball courts.

Location

Calvin's beautifully wooded campus, which includes a 100-acre ecosystem preserve, is located in the suburbs of Grand Rapids, a metropolitan area of more than 600,000 people. Hundreds of restaurants, dozens of theaters, seven shopping malls, and a fine selection of museums and parks are within a short drive. Lake Michigan beaches, ski areas, parks, and trails are within a 40-minute drive. Cultural and community activities take place weekly on the Calvin campus, on the campuses of six other local colleges, and at DeVos Hall and VanAndel Arena in downtown Grand Rapids. City buses regularly pass by the Calvin campus.

Majors and Degrees

The Bachelor of Arts and Bachelor of Science degrees are offered, with major concentrations in accounting, art, art history, Asian studies, biochemistry, biology, biotechnology, business, chemistry, classical civilization, classical languages, communication arts and sciences, computer science, Dutch, early childhood education, economics, elementary and secondary education, engineering, English, environmental science, environmental studies, exercise science, film studies, French, geography, geology, German, Greek, history, information systems, international development studies, international relations, Latin, mathematics, music, nursing, philosophy, physical education, physics/astronomy, political science, psychology, public administration, recreation, religious studies, social work, sociology, Spanish, special education, speech pathology and audiology, telecommunications, theater, and theological studies. The Bachelor of Fine Arts (B.F.A.) degree in art is offered in addition to the B.A. degree in art.

Professional programs include engineering (chemical, civil/environmental, electrical/computer, mechanical), natural resources, prearchitecture, prelaw, premedicine/predentistry, prepharmacy, pre–physical therapy, pre–seminary studies, social work, and elementary, secondary, and special education. Minor concentrations are available in African and African diaspora studies, archaeology, Chinese, dance, English as a second language, environmental studies, gender studies, Japanese, journalism, medieval studies, missions, urban studies, writing, and youth ministry leadership.

Academic Programs

Calvin College maintains a strong commitment to a liberal arts curriculum as an integral way to help students understand God's world and their place in it. The College follows a 4-1-4 academic calendar, consisting of two 4-month semesters with a three-week January Interim term. Graduation requires the successful completion of 124 semester hours.

Calvin's core curriculum begins with a first-year gateway course, Developing a Christian Mind, and ends with a capstone course in the senior year. Core curriculum requirements include foreign language, history, literature and arts, mathematics, natural sciences, philosophy, physical education, religion, social sciences, and written and spoken rhetoric. Some requirements can be satisfied by advanced high school work in foreign language, literature, and natural sciences. Qualified students can earn course exemption and/or credit by completing college-level work in high school or by examination. Satisfactory scores on Advanced Placement (AP), International Baccalaureate (I.B.), and/or CLEP exams are also accepted.

Incoming students with an ACT composite of at least 29 or current students with a cumulative grade point average of 3.3 or higher can apply to the Honors Program for advanced-level courses, interdisciplinary courses, and cocurricular opportunities. Students can also benefit from services offered by the Office of Student Academic Services, which provides academic counseling, tutoring, training in study skills, and review courses in key subjects.

Off-Campus Programs

Study-abroad programs for a semester or a year are offered in Austria, Belize, China, Costa Rica, France, Germany, Ghana, Great Britain, Honduras, Hungary, Japan, the Netherlands, and Spain. Students register for courses in various subjects, and the credits earned are applied toward graduation requirements. The Chicago Semester program, the Oregon Extension Program, and the Au Sable Institute of Environmental Studies are offered in cooperation with Calvin and other colleges. Students can also participate in programs of the Council for Christian Colleges and Universities: the American Studies Program in Washington, D.C.; the Latin American Studies Program in Central America; a Film Studies Program in Hollywood; a Middle East Studies Program in Cairo, Egypt; and a Russian Studies Program in Moscow. Calvin's Study in Spain Program is one option students may choose to fulfill their foreign language requirement. Many courses offered during the Interim are also taught abroad.

Academic Facilities

The four-floor Science Complex features a center core of laboratories, an atom trapper, and an observatory. The Engineering Building provides space for engineering students and faculty members to do research and design work. The DeVries Hall of Science includes medical research laboratories and classrooms. The Spoelhof College Center houses administrative offices, a social research center, an art gallery, six art studios, and a 340-seat auditorium. In the Fine Arts Center, classrooms and offices surround a 1,000-seat auditorium.

The Hekman Library–Hiemenga Hall complex includes a five-level, computerized library containing more than 800,000 bound volumes, 2,750 periodicals, an extensive collection of microfiche, records and tapes, and government publications; more than 1,500 students can be comfortably seated at study carrels and tables. The complex also houses the Information Technology Center, the Calvin Center for Christian Scholarship, the Meeter Center for Calvinism Studies, a distance learning classroom, a TV studio, a graphics production lab, and a curriculum center for teacher education students. The 55,000-square-foot DeVos Communications Center is home to a 150-seat video theater, a television studio, an audio studio, digital audio and video editing labs, and a speech pathology and audiology clinic. The Prince Conference Center houses seminars, meetings, and retreats.

Costs

Tuition and fees for 2007–08 were $21,460; tuition for the Interim was free for full-time students enrolled for at least one semester. Room and board charges were $7460 for resident students with a twenty-one-meal-per-week plan (ten- and fifteen-meal-per-week plans are also available). About $800 is needed for textbooks.

Financial Aid

Sixty percent of Calvin students receive need-based financial aid; demonstrated need is the most important criterion in determining eligibility. Students wishing to be considered for financial aid must be admitted to the College and must submit the Free Application for Federal Student Aid (FAFSA) and Calvin's Supplemental Application for Financial Aid. February 15 is the filing deadline for maximum consideration. Financial awards to eligible applicants consist of state and federal grants, loans, Federal Work-Study Program funds, and institutional grants and scholarships. Part-time employment is available on campus, and placement preference is given to students with financial need. Calvin's Job Shop also helps students find off-campus employment.

Faculty

Calvin's outstanding faculty members have distinguished themselves through publication and research, yet each is available 10–15 hours per week outside of class for academic and personal counseling. More than 83 percent have earned the highest academic degree in their field. Each faculty member is a professing Christian, committed to the integration of his or her personal faith and discipline. There are 322 full-time and 85 part-time faculty members; the faculty-student ratio is 1:12.

Student Government

The 27-member Student Senate supervises most student activities and oversees the budgets for student publications, homecoming, the film arts, and the Service-Learning Center. Student members serve on most faculty committees governing the College. Each residence hall has its own governing council and judiciary committee. Campus rules are designed to build a Christian academic community. Calvin attempts to aid student development and responsible action by clearly expressing its expectations and deemphasizing regulations.

Admission Requirements

Applicants should be graduates of an accredited high school program and should have completed satisfactorily at least 15 units of college-preparatory work, including 3 in English and 3 in algebra and geometry. Applicants with high school averages of C+ (2.5) or higher who score above 20 on the ACT composite or above 470 on both the math and critical reading sections of the SAT are normally given regular admission. Applicants with lower grades and scores, or those with deficiencies in their high school preparation, may be admitted under special conditions. International students should refer to http://www.calvin.edu/international for application procedures. Students who come from a non-English-speaking culture must submit results of the TOEFL or IELTS or provide other documentation of English-language proficiency.

Application and Information

Applicants must submit a completed application form, a high school or college transcript, results of either the ACT or SAT, and an educational recommendation completed by a teacher or counselor. Admission decisions are made on a rolling basis beginning in mid-October. Applicants for fall admission are urged to complete their file before February 1; the deadline for admission is August 15 for U.S. and Canadian applicants and April 1 for international applicants, as long as space is available. Students and parents are strongly encouraged to visit the campus. The "Fridays at Calvin" campus visit program provides an excellent opportunity to experience life at Calvin firsthand. For more information about Calvin or to register for a visit, students should contact:

Office of Admissions and Financial Aid
Calvin College
3201 Burton Street, SE
Grand Rapids, Michigan 49546
Phone: 616-526-6106 (admissions)
616-526-6134 (financial aid)
616-526-8480 (TTY)
800-688-0122 (toll-free in North America)
Fax: 616-526-6777
E-mail: admissions@calvin.edu
finaid@calvin.edu
Web site: http://www.calvin.edu

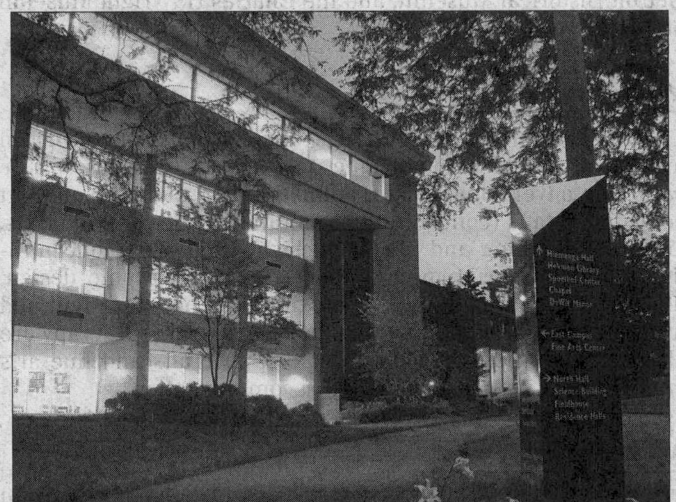

Recognized as one of the finest research libraries in western Michigan, the Hekman Library is a hub of student and faculty activity on the Calvin College campus.

COLLEGE FOR CREATIVE STUDIES

DETROIT, MICHIGAN

COLLEGE *for* Creative STUDIES

The College

The College for Creative Studies (CCS) is one of the nation's leading art and design education institutions. A private, fully accredited, four-year college located in Detroit, CCS offers Bachelor of Fine Arts degrees in eleven majors. The College provides a dynamic learning environment in which students explore issues of art and design and the culture in which they exist while preparing for careers in the professional world. CCS is credited with having one of the world's most recognized programs in transportation design and for placing more graduates in automotive design careers than any other school.

The College is dedicated to providing an educational environment most conducive to the development of outstanding artists and designers. The teaching is directed not only toward developing technical excellence but also toward stimulating intellectual potential. Graduates are well prepared to join the professional world, have the overall ability to carry on their education as desired, are able to communicate effectively, and have a basic understanding of today's artistic, social, and intellectual world and its traditions. The current enrollment is more than 1,300 men and women.

Location

Situated within a 10½-acre complex of award-winning facilities, the College for Creative Studies is appropriately located in Detroit's Cultural Center. Twenty-eight major cultural and educational institutions are within easy walking distance. Students have full access to the Detroit Institute of Arts, one of the largest fine arts museums in the United States, and to the main branch of the Detroit Public Library, which possesses more than 2 million volumes. Other available facilities include the New Detroit Science Center, Detroit Children's Museum, Detroit Historical Museum, and the Charles H. Wright Museum of African American History.

Majors and Degrees

The College for Creative Studies offers a four-year program leading to the Bachelor of Fine Arts degree. Degrees can be earned in advertising design, animation and digital media, art education, crafts (concentrations: ceramics, fiber design, glass, and metalsmithing and jewelry design), fine arts (concentrations: painting, print media, and sculpture), graphic design, illustration, interior design, photography, product design, and transportation design. Minors in art history and art therapy are also available. Interdisciplinary studies in crafts and fine arts are permitted upon departmental recommendation.

Academic Programs

The Bachelor of Fine Arts degree requires the completion of 126 credit hours: 84 in studio areas and 42 in general studies courses. All students are required to take core foundation course work in basic drawing, basic design, and figure drawing during their freshman year. They also begin work in their major department during their freshman year, or they may begin as an undeclared student. Typical weekly schedules for full-time students comprise 18 studio hours and 6 academic hours.

CCS' Continuing Education division offers a rich variety of high-quality art and design programs year-round to students of all ages and artistic backgrounds. High school sophomores, juniors, and seniors can earn college credit in CCS' Summer Experience Pre-College Program. Also available are portfolio preparation courses and professional development programs for teachers.

Off-Campus Programs

Independent study, internships, and study-abroad programs are available. Mobility programs, offered in cooperation with thirty-one other colleges in the Association of Independent Colleges of Art and Design (AICAD), allow students to take advantage of course offerings at other institutions while pursuing a degree at the College. In addition, seniors may study in a studio space in New York City to which CCS has access. Juniors and seniors also have the opportunity to spend a full year of study at an accredited institution abroad.

Academic Facilities

The College's instructional facilities total 597,039 square feet. The Kresge-Ford Building provides classrooms, studios, and workshops for painting, sculpture, printmaking, basic design, basic drawing and figure drawing, illustration, photography, and woodworking and metalworking. The Yamasaki Building houses administrative offices and classrooms, studios, and workshops for ceramics, fabric design, glass, metals, and jewelry. The Walter B. Ford II Building houses the advertising design, animation and digital media, graphic design, interior design, product design, and transportation design departments as well as computer labs and a 250-seat auditorium. Liberal arts courses are conducted in facilities located throughout the campus. The Manoogian Visual Resource Center houses the library and Center Galleries, which encompasses the Main Gallery, the U245 Student Gallery, and the Alumni and Faculty Hall.

Costs

For 2007–08, tuition and fees were $27,090 for the academic year. Average charges for housing were $4200. The estimated cost of materials and supplies is $2500 in most fields of study.

Financial Aid

The College participates in the Federal Pell Grant, Federal Supplemental Educational Opportunity Grant, Federal Work-Study, Federal Stafford Student Loan, Federal PLUS loan, Michigan Tuition Grant, Michigan Competitive Scholarship, Michigan Work Study, Michigan Merit Award, Michigan Educational Trust, and Michigan Educational Savings Plan programs. The College also awards scholarships, based on artistic ability and academic excellence, to currently enrolled and prospective students.

The College attempts to financially assist qualified students who apply, contingent upon the availability of funds.

Faculty

The College has 246 faculty members. All members of the studio art faculty are professionals in their individual fields who bring diverse backgrounds and experiences to the classroom.

Student Government

Students participate in the leadership of the school in several ways. The Student Coalition is composed of representatives from each department and takes an active role in areas affecting student life. The coalition works with the Student Programming Coordinator to organize dances and other events during the year. The coalition was active in the founding of U245, the student-run gallery, and continues to support its activities.

Admission Requirements

The Office of Admissions at the College for Creative Studies is dedicated to assisting students in evaluating educational alternatives and career possibilities in the visual arts. Applicants must have maintained a GPA of at least 2.5 in high school or successfully passed a high school equivalency examination and must submit SAT or ACT scores and a portfolio of representative work. Applicants who have had previous college experience are required to submit an official transcript from each institution attended. Personal interviews are available.

Application and Information

Applications for the fall term are accepted through August 1. Applications for the second semester should be submitted prior to December 1.

For application forms, catalogs, and additional information, students should contact:

Office of Admissions
College for Creative Studies
201 East Kirby
Detroit, Michigan 48202-4034
Phone: 313-664-7425
800-952-ARTS (toll-free)
Web site: http://www.ccscad.edu

The Walter B. Ford II Building of the College for Creative Studies.

GRAND VALLEY STATE UNIVERSITY

ALLENDALE, MICHIGAN

The University

Founded in 1960, Grand Valley State University (GVSU) is a public institution dedicated to providing students with the highest-quality undergraduate and graduate education. A liberal arts education, whether in general arts and sciences or the professional degree programs, has always been at the heart of Grand Valley's educational mission. Students at Grand Valley learn to think for themselves as they develop the skills of inquiry, reflection, critical analysis, knowledge integration, and dialogue for the benefits of lifelong learning and global citizenship. Grand Valley State University is characterized by and known for its superior student-centered teaching and learning. Grand Valley's 23,295 students, 19,578 of whom are undergraduates, experience rich learning environments, an average class size of 28, and classes taught by faculty members, not teaching assistants. Professors collaborate with students on advanced research projects, where they gain knowledge and skills that are more commonly associated with graduate-level study. As an investment, Grand Valley degrees are highly respected and valued by employers and graduate schools. GVSU has been recognized for eleven consecutive years by Educational Research and Evaluation, Inc., as one of "America's 100 Best College Buys." Grand Valley's diverse environment promotes the development of intellect and creativity through teaching, scholarship, service, and a vibrant campus culture.

Grand Valley's residential living centers are some of the newest and most contemporary facilities in the state. More than 5,290 students live on campus, just steps from classes, professors, campus dining, and extracurricular activities. Grand Valley competes and excels in nineteen collegiate sports at the NCAA Division II level. Grand Valley has been recognized for its overall athletic excellence by being awarded the Director's Cup for being the top NCAA Division II athletic program in the nation for the past three years. Grand Valley has also earned the President's Cup and the Great Lakes Intercollegiate Athletic Conference All-Sports trophy for eight consecutive years. More than 240 clubs, societies, groups, and organizations make it simple to connect with other students who share common interests, academic goals, hobbies, ethnic backgrounds, and religious beliefs. Inspiring classroom and research facilities, modern living centers, wireless academic buildings, and convenient student services make Grand Valley a wonderful place to study, learn, and live.

In addition to its undergraduate degree programs, Grand Valley offers twenty-six graduate degree programs: accounting, biology, biostatistics, business/nursing, cell and molecular biology, communications, computer information systems, criminal justice, education, engineering, English language and literature, general business, health administration, health sciences, leadership, medical and bioinformatics, nursing, occupational therapy, physical therapy, physician assistant studies, public administration, reading/language arts, school counseling, social work, special education, and taxation.

Location

Grand Valley State University's vibrant, residential main campus is located on 1,275 acres in Allendale, midway between downtown Grand Rapids (the second-largest city in the state of Michigan) and the Lake Michigan shore. The dynamic, urban Robert C. Pew Grand Rapids Campus, 12 miles to the east, is located in the heart of downtown Grand Rapids. It is a catalyst for interaction between students and the real world, putting students closer to employment, internships, and community outreach programs. The campuses are connected by a convenient, free shuttle service.

Majors and Degrees

Grand Valley State University has eight degree-granting colleges: the College of Community and Public Services, College of Education, Padnos College of Engineering and Computing, College of Health Professions, College of Interdisciplinary Studies, College of Liberal Arts and Sciences, Kirkhof College of Nursing, and Seidman College of Business.

Grand Valley offers undergraduate degree programs in accounting, advertising and public relations, anthropology, art and design, athletic training, behavioral science, biology, biomedical sciences, biopsychology, broadcasting, business economics, cell and molecular biology, chemistry, classical tradition, clinical lab science, communications, computer science, criminal justice, dance, earth science, economics, education–teacher certification, engineering, English language and literature, exercise science, film and video, finance, French, general business, geochemistry, geography, geology, German, Greek, health communication, health professions, health sciences, history, hospitality and tourism management, information systems, integrated science, international business, international relations, journalism, Latin, legal studies, liberal studies, management, marketing, mathematics, medical imaging, music, music education, natural resources management, nursing, occupational safety and health management, philosophy, photography, physical education, physics, political science, predental studies, premedical studies, pre–veterinarian studies, psychology, public administration, Russian studies, social studies, social work, sociology, Spanish, special education psychology, statistics, theater, therapeutic recreation, and writing.

Academic Programs

Grand Valley offers more than 200 areas of study in sixty-eight undergraduate degree programs. At Grand Valley, all students complete the University's general education curriculum, which enriches and complements the student's major and electives and is a significant part of the baccalaureate experience.

The Honors College, which is located on the Allendale campus, offers academically talented students an opportunity to participate in an exclusive community of scholars exemplifying intellectual achievement. Honors students develop high levels of proficiency in research, writing, and critical thinking while taking their classes in the same building they call home, the Neimeyer Living Center.

Off-Campus Programs

The Office of Career Services has teamed up with hundreds of businesses and organizations to offer students internships in nearly every field. Each year, more than 2,000 students gain valuable work experience, often while laying the groundwork for employment after graduation.

Students in every major have opportunities to study in another country. The Barbara H. Padnos International Center offers students more than 3,900 summer, semester, and yearlong study-abroad programs through partnerships with universities in Europe, Asia, South America, and Australia.

Academic Facilities

Grand Valley continually sets new standards for excellence in how its facilities promote academic achievement—including the same leading-edge network technology that runs the Internet, health sciences equipment usually found only in hospitals, and many other unique learning tools. All of Grand Valley's academic buildings are wireless, making connecting to e-mail and the Internet easy and convenient.

On the 1,275-acre Allendale campus, the James H. Zumberge Library houses the 605,879 volumes and other materials that are necessary to effectively support instructional programs at Grand Valley. The Performing Arts Center houses faculty offices, classrooms, practice rooms, teaching studios for the performing arts, a music technology lab (using Macintosh computers), two dance studios, the art gallery, and the 490-seat Louis Armstrong Theatre for presentations of plays, operas, concerts, and other programs. The Alexander Calder Fine Art Center contains two computer graphics labs and facilities for graphic design, painting, printmaking, art education, drawing, and ceramics. The Seymour and Ester Padnos Hall of Science contains modern equipment, sophisticated instruments, and extensive map and specimen collections and is a well-equipped laboratory facility for study, research, and experimentation in the natural sciences. Lake Ontario Hall, new in 2005, contains 50,000 square feet of modern faculty offices, student study areas, and specialized classrooms.

Graduate degree programs and the upper-division courses for majors in business, criminal justice, education, engineering, public administration, and social work are located at the 37-acre Pew Campus in downtown Grand Rapids. The 215,000-square-foot Cook-DeVos Center for Health Science, a $57.1-million state-of-the-art facility that opened in fall 2003, is home to the Kirkhof College of Nursing, the College for Health Professions, and majors within the life sciences. It features cutting-edge training and laboratory facilities, project rooms to encourage group learning and interdisciplinary study, case-study classrooms, and faculty offices. The Richard M. DeVos Center is home to a 242,000-volume library featuring a computer-operated robotic retrieval system and a New York–style reading room. The L. V. Eberhard Center has forty-three classrooms and labs, high-technology teleconference and conference facilities, and two interactive television rooms. The Fred M. Keller Engineering Laboratories Building, which is located adjacent to the Eberhard Center, is a three-story, 27,000-square-foot facility built with its structural, mechanical, and electrical systems exposed to provide students with a living laboratory. The Meijer Public Broadcast Center houses Grand Valley's public television and radio stations.

Costs

GVSU is one of the most affordable public universities in Michigan. During the 2006–07 academic year, freshman residents of Michigan carrying 12–16 credits paid $6588 for tuition; nonresidents paid $12,510. Students on full-service meal plans and living in University-owned on-campus housing paid about $6660 for room and board, depending on accommodations. Books and supplies were about $800 per year. Bus transportation between campuses and the city of Grand Rapids is free. All costs are subject to change.

Financial Aid

Financial aid at Grand Valley State University is awarded in the form of a package and generally consists of grants, scholarships, loans, and college work-study. Grand Valley participates in all applicable federal and state aid programs. During the 2005–06 academic year, Grand Valley students received more than $140 million in total assistance, including more than $40 million in scholarships, grants, and employment. Students should contact the Office of Financial Aid and Scholarships at the toll-free phone number for further information.

Faculty

Grand Valley prides itself on being a teaching institution dedicated to providing the highest possible level of instruction. The most crucial ingredient necessary for the achievement of this goal—the quality of the faculty—was judged "impressive" by the evaluation team of the North Central Association of Colleges and Schools' Higher Learning Commission. Doctoral degrees or other appropriate terminal degrees have been earned by 83 percent of the more than 700 regular faculty members.

The University promotes professional excellence in teaching and research. The Faculty Research and Development Center focuses on the enhancement of faculty and student research and scholarship. Many faculty projects funded by this center actively engage students in research and creative processes to expand their learning experience. These projects include experimentation or observation in the laboratory, field, and library and initiatives in the creative and performing arts.

Student Government

The Student Senate is composed of 50 senators-at-large who represent the students of GVSU. The Resident Housing Association is a programming organization that sponsors campuswide programs for all Grand Valley students. In addition to programming, its members also serve as the governing body for all of the community councils on campus.

Admission Requirements

Admissions decisions are selective and are based on the secondary school record (grades earned and courses selected), the personal data submitted on the application, and SAT or ACT results.

A complete application for freshman admission includes a signed application, the nonrefundable $30 application fee, official high school transcript(s), and SAT or ACT test scores. Freshmen are normally expected to be graduates of accredited high schools or preparatory schools. The University recommends that high school students have taken college-prep courses that include 4 years of English (including composition), 3 years of science (including 2 years of laboratory science), 3 years of mathematics (including 2 years of algebra), 3 years of social sciences, and 2 years of a single foreign language. Elective courses in computer science and the fine arts, as well as a fourth year of math and additional science courses, are strongly recommended.

A complete application for transfer admission includes a signed application, the nonrefundable $30 application fee, and official transcript(s) from all previously attended colleges and/or universities. Transfer admissions are based upon the completion of at least 30 semester credit hours (45 quarter hours) and a cumulative grade point average of 2.5 or higher. If the student has less than 30 earned college credits, official high school transcript(s) and SAT or ACT scores are also required.

Application and Information

For an application or additional information, students should contact:

Admissions Office
Grand Valley State University
1 Campus Drive
Allendale, Michigan 49401-9403
Phone: 616-331-2025
800-748-0246 (toll-free)
E-mail: admissions@gvsu.edu
Web site: http://www.gvsu.edu/admissions

Grand Valley's main campus in Allendale, Michigan.

HILLSDALE COLLEGE

HILLSDALE, MICHIGAN

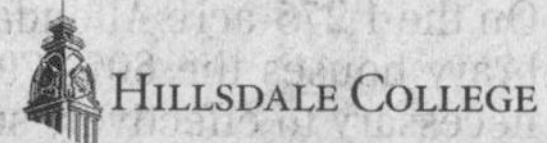

The College

Hillsdale College is a private, independent, nonsectarian institution of higher learning founded in 1844 by men and women who described themselves as "grateful to God for the inestimable blessings" resulting from civil and religious liberty and as "believing that the diffusion of learning is essential to the perpetuity of those blessings." The College has maintained institutional independence since its founding by refusing to accept aid from or control by federal authorities. Far-reaching private support from a national constituency has enabled Hillsdale to continue its trusteeship of the intellectual and spiritual inheritance derived from the Judeo-Christian faith and Greco-Roman culture.

The undergraduate enrollment for fall 2007 was 1,300, of whom 48 percent were men. The College draws students from forty-eight states and eight countries. About 40 percent of the students come from Michigan. The entering freshman class in 2007 had an average high school grade point average of 3.72 and mean ACT (28) and SAT (1940) scores well above the national averages. Hillsdale students are housed in dormitories, fraternity and sorority houses, and various off-campus dwellings. Single and double rooms are available on campus; there are no coed dormitories. Each College-owned residence hall is supervised by a resident director and student staff members. All freshmen (except commuters) are required to live on campus; upperclass students seeking to live off campus must apply to the dean of men or dean of women for this privilege.

Hillsdale's athletes participate in thirteen intercollegiate varsity sports (the College belongs to the NCAA Division II and the Great Lakes Intercollegiate Athletic Conference), and a vigorous intramural program is also available. The College emphasizes the concept of the student-athlete and is proud of the national recognition won by a number of its athletes for academic achievements. Three national fraternities, three national sororities, and about sixty other social, honorary, and service organizations provide Hillsdale students with an array of cocurricular opportunities. A resident drama troupe and dance company, a bagpipe and drum corps, a wind ensemble, a concert choir, a chorale, and a College-community orchestra and band constitute the College's performing arts organizations.

Special student services provided by the College include career planning and placement counseling, academic advising and tutoring, and a health service staffed by a physician and a resident nurse.

Location

Hillsdale College is located amidst the hills and lakes of south-central Michigan. The Indiana and Ohio turnpikes are each 30 minutes away, and the College is easily reached from such metropolitan areas as Detroit, Chicago, Cleveland, Toledo, Ft. Wayne, and Indianapolis. The town of Hillsdale is a county seat with a population of 10,000. Stores, churches, restaurants, and movie theaters are all within walking distance of the campus.

Majors and Degrees

Hillsdale awards the Bachelor of Arts or Bachelor of Science degree in accounting, art, biology, chemistry, classical studies, computational mathematics, economics, education, English, financial management, French, German, history, marketing/management, mathematics, music, philosophy, physical education, physics, political science, psychology, religion, Spanish, speech, and theater. Interdisciplinary majors in American studies, Christian studies, comparative literature, European studies, international studies in business and foreign language, political economy, and sociology and social thought are also available. Preprofessional programs are offered in allied health sciences (including optometry, physical therapy, nursing, and medical technology), dentistry, engineering, environmental sciences, forestry, law, medicine, osteopathy, theology, and veterinary medicine.

Hillsdale offers a 3-2 (B.A./B.S.) or 4-2 (B.A./M.S.) cooperative program in engineering science with Northwestern University and Tri-State University.

Academic Programs

Hillsdale operates on a two-semester schedule, with the fall term beginning in late August and ending in mid-December and the spring term beginning in mid-January and ending in mid-May. Two 3-week summer sessions are also offered.

The College believes that a sound classical liberal arts education includes study in the humanities, natural sciences, and social sciences, and each student is required to complete core courses in these areas. Students are also required to declare a major by the end of their sophomore year. To graduate, they must complete at least 124 hours of course work and fulfill the requirements of at least one major field. It is not unusual for a student to complete two majors or a major and a minor. Each baccalaureate program is based on the completion of four years of study in the liberal arts. The B.A. program stresses language (and includes a foreign language requirement), literature, and the arts. The B.S. program stresses mathematics and the natural sciences. Both programs equally emphasize the social sciences.

The honors program enables exceptionally talented students to develop their intellectual potential through special honors classes, available all four years, and through honors program seminars in the junior and senior years. Honors students are also required to write a thesis on a topic of their choosing.

The Center for Constructive Alternatives conducts four weeklong symposia during the academic year. These programs, dealing with themes that have contemporary significance and application, are of major importance in the intellectual life of the College. Each brings to the campus distinguished scholars and public figures chosen for their ability to contribute to the theme.

Off-Campus Programs

Two internship programs in Washington, D.C., place students at the ERI National Journalism Center or in congressional and government offices for a summer of work and study. Additional internships may be established in the fields of business and communication arts in consultation with the academic department concerned.

Through the College's affiliations with the Center for Medieval and Renaissance Studies and the Oxford Study Abroad Program, Hillsdale students are able to study abroad for a summer or a year at one of the more than thirty colleges of Oxford University. Hillsdale offers a summer business program in cooperation with Regents College in London, England, and the opportunity to study subject areas ranging from ancient history to theoretical physics at the University of St. Andrews in St. Andrews, Scotland. The College also offers qualified students the opportunity to study in Seville, Spain, as well as France and Germany. Qualified individual students who wish to study in another country for a semester or a year are assisted by their faculty adviser and the registrar in planning a program that enables them to gain full credit as well as a rewarding experience. Students majoring in international studies are encouraged to participate in internships abroad.

Academic Facilities

Newly constructed Lane and Kendall Halls contain classrooms, research facilities, language laboratories, faculty offices, and special laboratory facilities for experimental psychology. In the Mossey Learning Resource Center, the main book collection contains more than 300,000 volumes, including over 21,000 electronic books, 61,000 microforms, 8,000 audiovisual items, and more than 1,600 journal subscriptions that include many full-text computer file titles. The

Mossey Library also subscribes to more than twenty local, state, national, and international print newspapers, and hundreds more are available electronically.

In addition to the main study and research collections, the Mossey Library also contains a number of rare and special holdings, including the Ludwig von Mises, Russell Kirk, Richardson Heritage, and Richard Weaver collections. Ludwig von Mises selected Hillsdale College as the recipient of his personal library. This important collection of materials relating to business and economics is housed in the Ludwig von Mises Room in the Mossey Library and is available to Hillsdale faculty members and students. Early American Imprints 1639–1800 (Evans) and Western Americana collections are available in microform. These collections are supplemented by more than 30 million items available from over 3,000 institutional members of the Online Computer Library Center library cooperative.

Strosacker Science Center, with its newly constructed 17,000-square-foot addition, has well-equipped facilities for biology, chemistry, mathematics, and physics. Special research areas and departmental libraries are also available. The 32,000-square-foot Herbert Henry Dow Science Building provides additional classrooms, research laboratories, animal rooms, and a computer lab. Perhaps the most widely known of Hillsdale's academic facilities is the Mary Randall Preschool, a circular laboratory school in which nursery school children are taught by students specializing in early childhood education and psychology. Experts in the field have called this building "a model for the nation." The Hillsdale Academy, a K–12 private model school, provides additional opportunities for classroom observation. The indoor facilities of the Athletic Complex include a field house with a swimming pool, a six-lane indoor track, basketball courts, volleyball courts, tennis courts, and handball and racquetball courts. A prescription turf football field, ringed by an all-weather, Mondo surface, eight-lane running track, is in a lighted stadium that seats 7,000 people. Baseball and softball diamonds, one soccer field, and ten lighted tennis courts complete the outdoor facilities of the College's Athletic Complex.

The Sage Center for the Arts, which houses the departments of art, music, and theater, opened in 1992. The 47,000-square-foot facility features eight practice rooms, a 350-seat auditorium with a complete scene shop, a makeup room, a costume shop, and a hydraulic orchestra pit that can be raised to provide additional seating for nonmusical events. The 29,000-square-foot Howard Music Building houses numerous practice rooms and studios, stately galleries, a large rehearsal hall, and a fine recital hall.

The recently dedicated 53,000-square-foot, two-story Grewcock Student Union provides students with formal and café dining, TV lounges, conference rooms, wireless technology, game rooms, a fireplace, and outdoor patios and houses the College's bookstore. This facility is designed to be the hub of student activity—a warm and inviting place for students.

Costs

Annual tuition for 2007–08 was $18,600, room was $3740, board was $3600, and mandatory fees were $490. Books, supplies, and personal expenses (including travel, recreation, and clothing) are estimated at $2800 per year.

Financial Aid

Financial aid at Hillsdale is available in many forms. Academic scholarships are awarded on a competitive basis, regardless of financial need, to students who rank in the top 10 percent of their high school class and have standardized test scores in the top 10 percent according to national test norms. The priority deadline for academic scholarship consideration is January 1. Athletic scholarships are also available on a competitive basis in men's baseball and football; men's and women's basketball, track, and cross-country; and women's swimming and volleyball. To apply for aid on the basis of financial need, students are required to file Hillsdale's Confidential Family Financial Statement (CFFS) in January or February of the year of prospective enrollment at Hillsdale. Grants and loans are available from the College. Students may also earn up to $1000 per year in various campus jobs.

Faculty

The faculty consists of 104 full-time members, 83 percent of whom have doctorates. No classes are taught by graduate students. The size and closeness of the College community enable faculty members and students to get to know each other well in and out of the classroom. Each student has a faculty adviser, who directs the program of study and provides academic and career counseling. Hillsdale's faculty is dedicated primarily to teaching and to students' personal development. Many faculty members also engage in research and scholarly writing, supported by summer and sabbatical leaves funded by the College.

Student Government

Hillsdale's student government and campus organizations offer students special opportunities to develop leadership skills that enrich their collegiate experience and their lives after graduation. The governing organization of the student body is the Student Federation, which is composed of 18 elected representatives. This group funds student organizations, sponsors all-College entertainment, and acts upon matters of concern to the student community. The Men's Council and Women's Council serve as legislative and judicial bodies within their respective domains in cooperation with members of the administration. The Leadership Workshop, which works closely with the administration, faculty, and community organizations, provides an additional forum for students to cultivate and perfect their leadership skills.

Admission Requirements

Admission is a privilege extended to students who are able to benefit from, and contribute to, the academic, social, and spiritual environments of the College. Important determinants for admission are intellectual curiosity, motivation, and social concern. Accordingly, grade average, test scores, class rank, strength of curriculum, extracurricular activities, interviews, self-evaluations, and recommendations from high school counselors and teachers are all reviewed carefully and are important in the evaluation process. Although some factors are necessarily more important than others, seldom is any single criterion, however important, decisive.

Transfer students must submit the standard application, including the high school record, SAT or ACT scores, transcripts from all colleges previously attended, and a transfer form from the dean of students of the most recent college attended. Applications by transfers are evaluated similarly to nontransfers.

Candidates for admission from other countries follow the regular entrance procedures. Students who come from a non-English-speaking culture must demonstrate proficiency in English by satisfactory performance on the Test of English as a Foreign Language (TOEFL) or the Michigan Test of English Proficiency or at an ESL Center.

Application and Information

Students may apply to Hillsdale College any time after the completion of the junior year of high school. A formal application includes a completed application form accompanied by a nonrefundable fee of $35 (free if submitted online) and all required credentials. Application plans include Early Decision (November 15), Early Action (January 1), and Regular Decision (February 15). Hillsdale College has been distinguished since its founding in 1844 by voluntarily adhering to a nondiscriminatory policy regarding race, religion, sex, and national or ethnic origin—long before the government began regulating such matters.

All records and forms should be mailed to:

Office of Admissions
Hillsdale College
Hillsdale, Michigan 49242-1298
Phone: 517-607-2327
E-mail: admissions@hillsdale.edu
Web site: http://www.hillsdale.edu

HOPE COLLEGE

HOLLAND, MICHIGAN

The College

Founded in 1862, Hope College has always promoted, in a liberal arts setting, the dual concept of preparation for life and vocation. The stimulating academic program is supported by an accepting Christian campus community. Students from all walks of life are welcomed, respected, and given freedom to grow in this vibrant environment. Preparation for a career and for life in general involves both classroom and extracurricular activities. Activities include student publications, musical groups, and political organizations. Students manage an FM radio station, and their cable TV shows are broadcast weekly to the Holland community. There are four major theater productions each year as well as a film series, a Great Performance Series, and lectures by outstanding speakers. Many Christian activities broaden the range of student involvement, including the Campus Ministries Office, Fellowship of Christian Athletes, Intervarsity Christian Fellowship, and similar organizations. Voluntary chapel is offered Monday, Wednesday, and Friday, plus an extended service on Sunday evening, and is well attended. Intercollegiate sports include baseball, basketball, cross-country, football, golf, soccer, swimming, tennis, and track for men and basketball, cross-country, golf, soccer, softball, swimming, tennis, track, and volleyball for women. Club sports include lacrosse, ice hockey, sailing, men's volleyball, and Ultimate Frisbee. An extensive program of intramural sports is also very popular among Hope students. An excellent health and recreation facility is available for student use. As Hope is a residential college, 85 percent of the students reside on the campus. The College has eleven residence halls, with capacity ranging from 40 to 300 students. Styles include corridor, cluster suite, coed, and single-sex residence halls. In addition, upperclass students have the option of living in one of fifteen apartment buildings or seventy-two cottages, which are houses on or near the campus that have been refurbished to accommodate students. The services of a well-developed Career Services Center are available to students and alumni for help with everything from assessing interests to arranging job interviews. The current enrollment is 3,203. Three percent of the students attend on a part-time basis. The student body represents more than forty states and thirty countries.

Location

Hope College's 77-acre wooded campus is in a residential area two blocks from the central business district of Holland, Michigan, a community that was founded by Dutch settlers and now has a population of 35,000 within city limits and a total area population of 100,000. The town is only a 30-minute drive from Grand Rapids and a 2-hour drive from Chicago and Detroit. An 85-acre biological field station is located on the shores of Lake Michigan, 5 miles from the campus. Holland has long been known as a summer resort area, but it is also a fine spot for winter sports. Excellent relations exist between Holland and the College.

Majors and Degrees

Hope College awards the Bachelor of Arts, Bachelor of Science, Bachelor of Music, and Bachelor of Science in Nursing degrees. Major programs include accounting (public accounting), ancient civilization, art** (studio art and art history concentrations), athletic training, biology*, chemistry* (biochemistry emphasis), classical languages, classical studies, communication, computer science, dance**, economics*, engineering (ABET-accredited biochemical, chemical, computer science, electrical, and mechanical emphases), engineering physics, engineering science, English** (literature, writing emphases), French*, geology* (environmental emphasis), German*, history*, Japanese, kinesiology* (physical education, exercise science, and athletic training), Latin*, management, mathematics**, music** (instrumental education, vocal education, jazz studies emphasis, performance), nursing, philosophy, physics*, political science*, psychology, religion*, social work (CSWE approved), sociology* (criminal justice emphasis), Spanish*, special education (emotional impairments and learning disabilities endorsements), and theater*. Hope is fully accredited for certification in elementary, secondary, and special (emotionally impaired and learning disabilities endorsements) education. Preprofessional programs are offered in dance therapy, dentistry, law, library science, medicine, optometry, physical therapy, seminary, and veterinary medicine.

Alternatives to departmental majors include the composite major and contract curriculum major. The composite major is concentrated study in any approved combination of majors related to a particular academic or vocational objective of the student. Some examples include fine arts, communication/English, international studies, and language arts. The contract curriculum major allows the student to develop a plan of study within the educational objectives of the College.

*Secondary teaching certification available; **secondary and/or elementary teaching certification available.

Academic Programs

To graduate, students must pass all College-required courses, earn at least 126 credit hours, and meet minimum GPA requirements. A Phi Beta Kappa institution, Hope is widely respected as a liberal arts college that balances academic excellence with a deep concern for the quality of life of its students and alumni. Hope's commitment to the Christian faith provides an incentive for academic excellence and rigorous inquiry and a perspective on the wholeness and value of life. A core curriculum brings teachers and students together for the purpose of facilitating student growth in seven areas: communication skills, social adaptation, an understanding of American heritage and society, a respect for science and discovery, an awareness of other cultures, an understanding and appreciation of the arts, and an understanding of religion and its impact on society. To accomplish this, students select course work in the following disciplines: English, fine arts, foreign language, kinesiology, mathematics, natural science, philosophy, religion, and social science.

Off-Campus Programs

Hope College participates in off-campus programs that are sponsored and supervised by the Associated Colleges of the Midwest (ACM), the Institute for Asian Studies (IAS), the Institute for European Studies (IES), and the Great Lakes Colleges Association (GLCA). Students may study for a semester or a year in more than sixty countries. Some continents and countries included are Africa, Austria, China, France, Germany, Great Britain, India, Japan, Latin America, Russia, Spain, the Middle East, and the Netherlands. Hope also runs a summer study-abroad program in Vienna, Austria. The College's director of international education assists students in arranging programs in other countries. Domestic programs include the Washington Semester, Urban Semester in Philadelphia, Semester at the Chicago Metropolitan Center, the Oregon Extension, Arts Program in New York City, the New York Center for Arts and Media Studies, Oak Ridge Science Semester, the Border Studies Program, and Newberry Library Program in the Humanities.

Academic Facilities

The campus library contains more than 350,000 volumes. The $36-million science facility contains the most modern laboratory equipment available and facilitates close working relationships

COLLEGE DATA CENTER • MICHIGAN

between faculty members and students. The physics laboratories include an electron particle accelerator. Students from many academic disciplines take advantage of state-of-the-art computer facilities. The theater, music, dance, and art departments are proud to offer excellent facilities as well. The DePree Art Center is a $1.3-million facility that contains a major art gallery, classrooms, and studios. An $11-million center for communication and global studies and a $22-million athletic field house were dedicated in fall 2005. Lubbers Hall, one of the College's most venerable academic buildings, underwent a $3-million renovation project during the summer of 2006. Graves Hall, a centerpiece of the College's identity and early history, is set to undergo renovations beginning in summer 2007. Major renovations to the baseball and softball fields are also underway and are expected to be complete for the 2008 spring seasons.

Costs

Annual charges for the 2007–08 academic year are tuition, $23,660; room, $3300; board (21 meals per week, reduced-cost meal plans are available, $3970; and activity fee, $170 for a total of $31,100.

Financial Aid

Types of aid include academic scholarships, grants, loans, and campus employment. Approximately 60 percent of Hope's students receive need-based aid. All accepted students may be considered for federal and Hope-funded assistance. Michigan residents may apply for state-funded programs. Applicants for aid should be accepted for admission and should submit the Free Application for Federal Student Aid (FAFSA) and a Hope institutional form by March 1 to receive priority consideration for need-based aid. Hope sponsors National Merit Scholars with a $17,000-per-year tuition scholarship. Other academic awards range from $3000 to $17,000. Talent awards of $2500 are also available in the fine arts and creative writing. Sixty-nine percent of freshmen enrolling in fall 2007 received a merit award. Consideration for merit awards requires submission of a complete application for admission by February 15 of the application year.

Faculty

Hope has 215 full-time faculty members, and 77 percent hold a Ph.D. or terminal degree in their field. In addition, there are 107 part-time faculty members who teach in a broad range of disciplines, many of whom also teach, perform, and work outside the campus community. The student-faculty ratio is 13:1. Members of the faculty are dedicated to maintaining excellence in both teaching and scholarship and to taking a personal interest in students. Many conduct research programs in which students actively participate, sometimes as early as their freshman year. Faculty members also serve as academic advisers and frequently host student groups in their homes.

Student Government

Hope has an established community governance system. Decisions that concern the College community are made primarily by boards and committees composed of students, faculty members, and administrators. The Academic Affairs, Administrative Affairs, and Campus Life boards bear the major responsibility for policy decisions, while subcommittees of each deal with more specific areas. Residence hall units elect representatives to Student Congress; these representatives are then appointed to the major boards. A Judicial Board of 7 students, 2 faculty members, and 1 staff person is charged with maintaining high standards of student life.

Admission Requirements

Hope is interested in students who seek the rigors of a proven, demanding academic program and feel comfortable in an open, supportive, Christian campus community. A complete admission file includes the completed application form, the application fee, high school/college transcripts, and either ACT or SAT scores. Primary factors considered are the applicant's high school course selection, grades, rank, test scores, counselor's recommendation, essay, and involvement in extracurricular/leadership activities. The College prefers that its students enroll having completed at least four college-preparatory classes per semester in the ninth through twelfth grades, including a variety of subject areas. The minimum background includes 4 years of English, 2 years of mathematics, 2 years of foreign language, 2 years of history or social studies, and at least 1 year of laboratory science as well as five other college-preparatory classes. For fall 2007, freshmen had a mean GPA of 3.74 (on a 4.0 scale), the average SAT score (critical reading and math) was 1180, and their average rank was in the 80th percentile. Campus visits are not required but are strongly recommended for interested students and their parents.

Application and Information

Most students apply for the fall semester, but applications are accepted for the spring semester or other sessions. The first admission decisions are announced in mid-December. A traditional rolling admission process continues after mid-December until late spring for fall admission. Students must submit the application form, official high school transcript, results of the SAT or ACT, and $35 application fee. Prospective freshmen are encouraged to submit applications during the first semester of their senior year in high school. Completed applications for admission must be on file by February 15 to ensure consideration for merit scholarships. A $300 enrollment deposit is requested by May 1. Prospective students may also apply online; application forms are available on the Web (http://www.hope.edu/admissions).

Hope College Admissions
69 East 10th Street
P.O. Box 9000
Holland, Michigan 49422-9000
Phone: 616-395-7850
800-968-7850 (toll-free)
E-mail: admissions@hope.edu
Web site: http://www.hope.edu

The Pull, an annual tug-of-war between freshmen and sophomores for the past 110 years, has been called "the most unique sporting event in the nation" by *Sports Illustrated*.

KETTERING UNIVERSITY

FLINT, MICHIGAN

The University

Founded in 1919, Kettering University is a private university specializing in technical degrees. The school enrolls about 2,300 undergraduate students and offers a 9:1 student-faculty ratio. Most classes have fewer than 20 students and are taught by Ph.D.-level professors, not teaching assistants. This combination of small class size and highly qualified teaching staff ensures students of a much more personalized learning experience.

Kettering is a highly acclaimed university with the one of the country's most modern cooperative education programs. Whatever major is chosen, students alternate between study terms and full-time work terms—otherwise known as co-op. During study terms, students learn material in small, intense classes taught by University professors. During co-op terms, students work as paid professionals at corporations related to their studies and interests. Kettering co-op students have done everything from test ballistic systems to reengineer crowd management at Disney World. Kettering has the only cooperative program of its kind where students begin working as early as their freshman year. By the time students graduate from Kettering, they have up to 2½ years of professional experience and an impressive resume. Ninety-eight percent of Kettering's students graduate with job offers or grad school acceptances in hand.

Kettering University's cooperative education program pairs hands-on education with real-world experience—all undergraduate students alternate between on-campus study terms and full-time terms of cooperative employment with one of more than 600 corporate partners. This unique system of education prepares students to be technology innovators—professionals with cutting-edge skills who are ready to compete in tomorrow's business environment.

Kettering University is accredited by the North Central Association of Colleges and Schools, the Accreditation Board for Engineering and Technology (ABET), and the Association of Collegiate Business Schools and Programs (ACBSP). Kettering is also a member of the National Commission of Cooperative Education (NCCE) and the Association of Independent Technological Universities.

Besides being academically ahead of the game, Kettering students bring a wide range of skills and interests with them to campus. To make sure that students get a life along with an education, Kettering offers more than fifty student organizations, including fourteen fraternities and six sororities, an active student government, a state-of-the-art recreation and fitness facility, and some competitive intramural sports. Recreation facilities include athletic fields, tennis courts, and a recreation center with an Olympic-size, six-lane swimming pool; aerobic fitness rooms; a full line of Nautilus equipment; and basketball, tennis, and racquetball courts. A public golf course is adjacent to the campus.

Professional counseling, support services, and health-care services are available.

Kettering also offers Master of Science degree programs in engineering, engineering management, information technology, manufacturing management, manufacturing operations, and operations management, in addition to an M.B.A. program.

Location

Kettering University is located in Flint, Michigan, which is 60 miles west of Lake Huron and 60 miles north of Detroit. Flint has approximately 115,000 residents and a metropolitan area population of 450,000.

Flint is particularly proud of its Cultural Center, which is only 10 minutes from Kettering's campus. Built and endowed entirely by the gifts of private citizens, the Cultural Center includes the Alfred P. Sloan Museum, the Whiting Auditorium (home of the Flint Symphony and host to leading stage shows and entertainers), the Robert T. Longway Planetarium (Michigan's largest and best-equipped sky show facility), the Flint Institute of Arts, the F. A. Bower Theater, the Dort Institute of Music, Mott Community College, and the Flint Public Library. Nearby is the University of Michigan–Flint campus.

The area also offers numerous outdoor and indoor recreational opportunities. Within a few minutes' drive are downhill and cross-country skiing facilities, lakes for the entire range of water sports, a wide selection of good public golf courses, excellent indoor and outdoor skating rinks, and plentiful shopping facilities and restaurants

Majors and Degrees

Kettering University offers a 4½-year, professional, cooperative education program with Bachelor of Science degrees in applied mathematics, applied physics, biochemistry, business, chemistry, computer engineering, computer science, electrical engineering, engineering physics, industrial engineering, and mechanical engineering.

Kettering also offers a variety of dual-degree programs and enough minors, specialties, and concentrations to ensure that students' degrees are custom-fit to their interests and career goals.

Academic Programs

Although each program at Kettering University has its own requirements, 160 credit hours are generally required for graduation. The program involves nine academic terms and nine co-op terms, two of which are focused on the capstone thesis project, which is a major work project assigned by the co-op employer. Students alternate between eleven-week periods of academic study on the campus in Flint and twelve-week periods of related work experience with their corporate employer. The academic year consists of two 3-month academic terms on campus and two 3-month terms of paid work experience.

Academic Facilities

Kettering University offers some of the best facilities, labs, and educational resources in the world, and students start using them as early as their freshman year. The Crash Safety Center, for example, is the only one of its kind in the nation used in an undergraduate program. The University also offers labs in areas such as fuel-cell research, polymer optimization, machining, and acoustics.

Kettering is fully networked and allows 24-hour access to computer resources and the Internet from dorms and labs. A 445-student residence hall and a new apartment complex are located on the campus for student housing. The library offers more than 94,000 cataloged volumes and 540 periodicals. And through online resources like Co-op Navigator and Blackboard, students can always be in touch with professors and University staff members.

Costs

2007–08 tuition costs were $25,248, and room and board were $5948.

Financial Aid

Kettering University wants to invest in its students, so it does what it takes to help finance education through scholarships, loans, and work-study opportunities. In fact, more than 92 percent of the students receive some sort of financial aid. Pair that with co-op earnings—between $40,000 and $65,000 over the course of the college career—and students are looking at one of the best values in education today. In addition, Kettering's Merit Scholarship program awards students with scholarships up to $76,500 for 4½ years.

Students should fill out the Free Application for Federal Student Aid (FAFSA) and request a copy of the analysis to be sent to Kettering University. The University works to create a financial aid package for based on those results.

Faculty

Kettering University's 144 full-time faculty members have teaching as their main responsibility. Most professors have industrial experience in addition to academic credentials and maintain contact with industry through consulting, sponsored research, and advising on student thesis projects. More than 80 percent of faculty members hold a doctorate. Because only half of the students are on campus at any one time, class sizes are small, and opportunities for enrichment and extra help are readily available.

Admission Requirements

Admission to Kettering University is competitive and based on scholastic achievement and extracurricular interests, activities, and achievements. Applicants are required to have earned the following: 3 years of English, 2 years algebra, 1 year of geometry, 1 semester of trigonometry, 2 years of lab science (1 must be physics or chemistry; both are recommended). Applicants must submit results of the SAT or ACT (Kettering's ACT code number is 1998 and the SAT code number is 1246).

Most Kettering University students are in the top 10 percent of their graduating class. Kettering University also welcomes students wishing to transfer from other colleges and universities. The transfer alternative is an excellent way to gain admission for students who do not enroll as freshmen.

Application and Information

There is more than one way to apply to Kettering. Students can apply online (free) at http://www.admissions.kettering.edu or print an application and send it by mail. Students should call 800-955-4464 Ext. 7865 for assistance.

Kettering officials review applications and let students know if they have been accepted. Although Kettering accepts and processes applications throughout the year, it is best to apply as early as possible. Once accepted, students receive information on programs and the professional co-op program, which are only available to admitted students. Students should complete the co-op registration (resume) online and pay a $300 tuition deposit (to be credited to the first-semester tuition). The deposit shows that a student is as serious about Kettering as Kettering is about the student and ensures a place in the entering class and eligibility to begin the co-op employment search process.

Admissions Office
Kettering University
1700 West Third Avenue
Flint, Michigan 48504-4898
Phone: 810-762-7865
800-955-4464 (toll-free in the United States and Canada)
E-mail: admissions@kettering.edu
Web site: http://www.admissions.kettering.edu

Kettering has the experts, the labs, and the programs that bring theory and practice together.

COLLEGE DATA CENTER • MICHIGAN

LAWRENCE TECHNOLOGICAL UNIVERSITY

SOUTHFIELD, MICHIGAN

The University

Founded by brothers Russell and E. George Lawrence in 1932 on the site where Henry Ford perfected the moving assembly line, Lawrence Technological University has traditionally provided students a high-quality, affordable education with an emphasis on theory and practice. The University, including the graduate programs in business, architecture, and engineering, is accredited by the Higher Learning Commission and is a member of the North Central Association of Colleges and Schools. Appropriate national professional agencies provide additional accreditation to various degree programs in architecture, interior architecture/design, imaging (digital arts and digital design), administration and management, chemistry, and engineering.

The University offers certificates and associate, bachelor's, master's, and doctoral degrees through the colleges of Architecture and Design, Arts and Sciences, Engineering, and Management. An honors program is available to highly qualified and motivated students. A private university, Lawrence Tech offers a highly competitive tuition rate, modern facilities, and real-world application of textbook knowledge. The 102-acre campus is located at the hub of one of America's great technological and industrial centers and near sites of some of the world's most significant manufacturing and engineering accomplishments.

Nearly 5,000 students attend Lawrence Tech, of whom approximately 600 live in on-campus housing. Women make up 24 percent of the student body, and twenty-five states and twenty-five countries are represented on campus.

Numerous fraternities, sororities, and social and professional organizations sponsor a variety of activities during the year. Recreational facilities include the Don Ridler Field House, which features a fitness track, a gymnasium, racquetball courts, a game room, saunas, and a weight and conditioning room. Intramural and club sports teams in basketball, billiards, curling, flag football, hockey, indoor soccer, racquetball, softball, table tennis, tennis, volleyball, and wallyball are active throughout the academic year. Lawrence Tech's campus includes twelve major buildings, all built since 1955. The campus has more than doubled in size since 1981.

Location

Southfield is a suburb of more than 78,000 people, a center of corporate and industrial activity, and a city that provides a pleasant balance between big-city entertainment opportunities and a quiet residential atmosphere. Southfield's daytime population of commuting workers swells to nearly 175,000. The Lawrence Tech campus is conveniently close to major freeways and about a 30-minute drive north of downtown Detroit. Southeastern Michigan offers a rich variety of recreational and cultural activities, with public transportation making most areas accessible to students.

Within a few miles of the campus, students can find many restaurants, parks, shopping areas, and recreational facilities. Research, manufacturing, scientific, and business enterprises are also located nearby, aiding students in co-op and internship programs as well as those who work full- or part-time while attending classes. More than 200 Fortune 500 companies have headquarters or business operations in the Detroit metropolitan area.

Majors and Degrees

Lawrence Tech offers nearly eighty majors or course concentrations. Most programs are available during the day or evening; some are offered online and on the weekends. Dual majors and customized degree programs combining either associate and bachelor's programs or bachelor's and master's programs are also available. Preprofessional programs are offered in dentistry, law, and medicine.

The College of Architecture and Design offers bachelor's degrees in architecture, imaging (concentrations in digital arts and digital design), interior architecture, and transportation design. Lawrence Tech enrolls more architectural students than any other school in Michigan, and its program is among the top 10 in the nation.

The College of Arts and Sciences awards bachelor's degrees in business management, chemical biology, chemistry, computer science, English and communication arts, environmental chemistry, humanities, mathematics, mathematics and computer science, media communication, molecular and cell biology, physics, physics and computer science, and psychology. Associate degrees are offered in chemical technology, general studies, and radio and television broadcasting. Minors offered are business management, chemistry, computer science, economics, English, general sciences, history, mathematics, philosophy, physics, psychology, Spanish, and technical and professional communication. Certificates can be earned in entrepreneurial strategy, industrial/organizational psychology, leadership and change management, and technical and professional communication.

The College of Arts and Sciences also offers students the opportunity to participate in Quest, an experimental learning program that engages them in unique projects beyond the requirements of their courses and results in an official narrative transcript in addition to their traditional transcript.

The College of Engineering offers bachelor's degrees in biomedical engineering, civil engineering, computer engineering, construction management, electrical engineering (concentrations in computer engineering, electronics engineering, and energy engineering), engineering technology, industrial operations engineering, and mechanical engineering (concentrations in automotive engineering, manufacturing, mechanical system design, and thermal system design).

The College of Engineering offers evening associate programs in communications engineering technology, construction engineering technology, manufacturing engineering technology, and mechanical engineering technology.

Also available in the college are minors in aeronautical engineering and energy engineering and certificates in aeronautical engineering, energy engineering, and entrepreneurship. The Lear Entrepreneurial Center teaches engineering students how to create, promote, and bring to market products and services. Lawrence Tech's mechanical engineering program ranks among the largest 10 percent in the nation.

The College of Management awards a Bachelor of Science degree in information technology.

Academic Programs

Graduation from Lawrence Technological University's undergraduate programs requires the completion of a degree program with an overall GPA of at least 2.0. Most disciplines combine a strong concentration in the major with a core curriculum of natural science, social science, humanities, and mathematics requirements. Also integrated into all undergraduate programs of study is preparation for leadership and entrepreneurship. The University operates on a semester calendar.

Off-Campus Programs

Lawrence Tech chemistry, computer science, engineering, and technology students may participate in co-op programs, alternating semesters of classes and work. Internships are also available.

The University also offers programs at Education Centers in southeastern and northern Michigan as well as international programs in Asia, Canada, Europe, and the Middle East

The Detroit Studio gives architecture students the opportunity to explore community-based architectural, urban design, and community development projects. Architecture students also regularly build homes for Habitat for Humanity.

The Paris Summer Study-Abroad Program is open to junior and senior architecture students. Students explore Paris and study in cooperation with an international architectural design studio and seminar.

The Global Engineering Program arranges for Lawrence Tech engineering students to work and study abroad and brings international engineering students to campus for further study.

Academic Facilities

Lawrence Tech is Michigan's first wireless laptop campus and is ranked among the nation's top 50 unwired universities. All undergraduates are provided high-end laptops customized with the software they need for their academic specialty. Other computers, workstations, terminals, and microcomputers are located in campus labs.

The library houses a broad selection of books, periodical titles, electronic databases, and microforms and is part of a nationwide network of more than 6,000 libraries that share resources via computer. The University also houses the personal library of renowned architect Albert Kahn. Lawrence Tech is surrounded by numerous outstanding municipal and research libraries, many with reciprocal borrowing privileges.

Facilities include architectural and design studios; senior project lab and studio space; fabrication labs; a wind tunnel; wood, metal, and model shops; dedicated labs for constructing Baja- and Formula-style competition vehicles; chemistry, biomedical, and biology labs; an anechoic chamber for sound studies; a structural testing center; alternative energy, mechanical, and electrical labs; a thermal dynamic lab; a graphics lab; a clay modeling studio; and the DENSO Instructional Technology Lab.

Lawrence Tech also owns a nearby Frank Lloyd Wright–designed home that is used as a study center.

The A. Alfred Taubman Student Services Center consolidates all student support services—from admissions through career services—into a convenient one-stop center. This innovative 42,000-square-foot center also utilizes many energy-efficient and environmentally friendly features and technologies, serving as a living laboratory. Students can study its geothermal walls; bioswale; water-recycling system; its exterior skin, designed to reduce heat loss and maximize daylight without succumbing to excessive heat gain; and its multilayer living roof, planted with drought-resistant groundcovers.

The Center for Innovative Materials Research is a state-of-the-art laboratory for the research, development, and testing of composite materials for defense and infrastructure applications. Students participate in related research projects as part of their academic programs.

The Automotive Engineering Institute provides students opportunities to conduct sponsored research on a unique 4 x 4 vehicle chassis dynamometer, which measures many areas of vehicle performance.

Costs

Tuition for all undergrads includes a high-powered laptop computer. The 2007–08 tuition for students majoring in arts and sciences and management was $629 per credit hour for freshmen and $653 per credit hour for sophomores. The tuition for juniors and seniors majoring in arts and sciences and management was $682 per credit hour. In architecture and design and engineering, tuition for freshmen and sophomores was $682 per credit hour; for juniors and seniors, it was $704 per credit hour.

A normal course load is 12–17 credit hours per semester. The undergraduate registration fee is $115 each semester. International students on temporary visas must have sufficient funds to pay for an entire year of tuition, room and board, and books at the time of first registration. Additional fees for specific labs and studio courses vary.

Financial Aid

Approximately 70 percent of full-time students receive some form of financial assistance, and the University awards nearly $30 million in scholarships, grants, loans, and work-study funds each academic year. Many privately funded scholarships are awarded to qualified students, based on need and/or scholastic performance. Part-time employment is available at the University on a first-come, first-served basis for full-time students. Student loans are also available from a variety of sources—state, federal, and private. Prospective students are urged to contact the Office of Financial Aid for information on deadlines and requirements for eligibility at http://www.ltu.edu/financialaid.

Faculty

Approximately 448 full- and part-time faculty members teach at Lawrence Tech. Many part-time faculty members hold full-time jobs in industry and bring their real-world perspective to the classroom. More than 80 percent of the full-time faculty members hold a doctoral degree or the terminal degree in their field. Faculty involvement is extensive in student chapters of professional associations that meet on campus. Many faculty members are active and/or registered professionals in their fields. Lawrence Tech's student-faculty ratio is 13:1. Most classes average 19 or fewer students, and less than 1 percent of the classes have more than 50.

Student Government

The Student Government sponsors and supports a variety of campus activities. It oversees expenditures, meets regularly to plan events, and is authorized to levy fines for minor, on-campus infractions. More than fifty student clubs and organizations, including fraternities, sororities, honor societies, and student chapters of professional groups, are active on campus.

Admission Requirements

A high school diploma or the equivalent is required of all students applying to baccalaureate or associate degree programs. Most baccalaureate applicants must have a minimum 2.5 overall GPA in academic subjects; architecture students must have a minimum 2.75 overall GPA. Applicants to associate degree programs are required to have a minimum 2.0 average in four academic areas (English, mathematics, social science, and natural science) combined. ACT or SAT results are required of all entering freshmen. Required high school courses vary with the curriculum, and Lawrence Tech offers a number of basic studies courses designed to augment incoming students' backgrounds if deficiencies exist.

Application and Information

Programs start in August and January. An optional summer semester begins in May. Entry in the fall semester is advised but not required. Students must submit transcripts from all schools attended, along with a nonrefundable $30 application fee. To obtain a University catalog and an application form, students should contact:

Office of Admissions
Lawrence Technological University
21000 West Ten Mile Road
Southfield, Michigan 48075-1058
Phone: 800-CALL-LTU Ext. 1 (toll-free)
Fax: 248-204-2228
E-mail: admissions@ltu.edu
Web site: http://www.ltu.edu

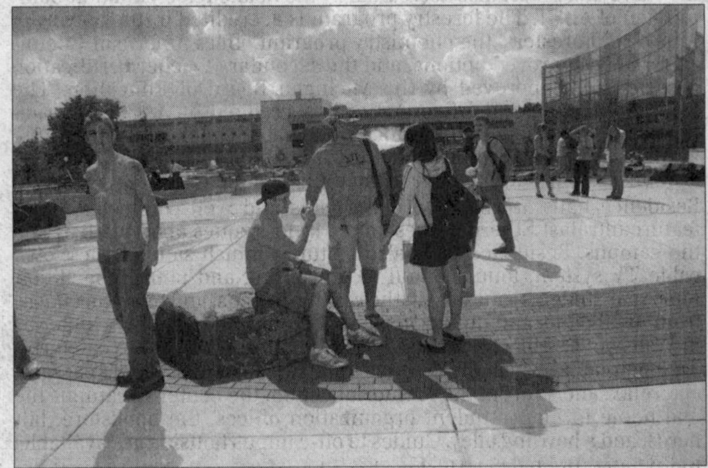

Below Lawrence Tech's new campus quadrangle are eighty-eight geothermal wells sunk 300 feet deep, which heat and cool the adjacent A. Alfred Taubman Student Services Center. *Lawrence Technological University Photo/Justin Munter.*

MICHIGAN TECHNOLOGICAL UNIVERSITY

MichiganTech

HOUGHTON, MICHIGAN

The University

Michigan Technological University students create the future in arts, humanities, and social sciences; business and economics; computing; engineering; forestry and environmental science; sciences; and technology. More than 6,700 students from all fifty states and more than eighty nations enjoy beautiful Upper Michigan while pursuing associate, bachelor's, master's, and Ph.D. degrees. Michigan Tech is rated among the nation's best universities and as a "tech powerhouse" by the *Princeton Review*. In addition, *U.S. News & World Report* has ranked Michigan Tech in the top tier of national universities, and its mechanical and environmental engineering departments are ranked in the top twenty-five. Students from many majors work together on real-world industry projects as part of the Enterprise program, from video games to wireless and from homeland security to hybrid SUVs. Michigan Tech has one of the nation's largest programs in scientific and technical communication and has top-ten enrollments in environmental, mechanical, and geological engineering programs.

The latest improvements on campus include a new computer science hall with numerous high-tech classrooms, a library with meeting rooms and "media wall," and a tech center with plenty of laboratory space (for Enterprise and other programs) to better connect industries with faculty/student research.

More than 55 percent of students are enrolled in the College of Engineering. The College of Sciences and Arts (CSA) accounts for 23 percent; Graduate School, 13 percent; the School of Business and Economics, 7.3 percent; the School of Technology, 7 percent; and the School of Forest Resources and Environmental Science, 3.8 percent. Michigan Tech's graduate programs continue to grow in stature. Enrollment is increasing while students gain access to the latest theories, equipment, and scholarship while working closely with faculty members who are acknowledged leaders in their fields.

Michigan Tech is accredited by the North Central Association of Colleges and Schools. Engineering programs are accredited by the Engineering Accreditation Commission of the Accreditation Board for Engineering and Technology (ABET), Inc.; technology programs are accredited by the Technology Accreditation Commission of ABET; and the surveying program is accredited by the Related Accreditation Commission of ABET. The forestry program is accredited by the Society of American Foresters, the chemistry program offers American Chemical Society–approved options, and the secondary teacher certification programs are approved by the Michigan Board of Education. The School of Business and Economics is accredited by AACSB International–The Association to Advance Collegiate Schools of Business, the premier business accrediting organization in the U.S. Only about 400 U.S. business programs have earned this distinction.

Residence halls are close to classrooms and well connected. They feature ultrafast Ethernet lines, and wireless zones abound all across the campus. Residence halls also feature Finnish saunas, their own cable TV system, lounges, and weight-lifting and laundry facilities. First-year students must live in the residence halls, and they can choose from meal plans and numerous food options and eat at the cafeterias in Wadsworth, McNair, or Douglass Houghton Halls. Some cafeterias are open later, especially during exam weeks, and students can also eat, relax, and study at the Memorial Union, the center of campus life and home to many student organization offices, the bookstore, billiards, and a bowling alley. Guides to off-campus housing are available.

In athletics, the hockey Huskies have been national champions three times and compete in the Western Collegiate Hockey Association, which has produced five of the last six NCAA Division I National Champions. Football, men's and women's basketball, tennis, cross-country, track, and women's volleyball teams compete in the Division II Great Lakes Intercollegiate Athletic Conference against teams from Michigan, Wisconsin, Ohio, Pennsylvania, Indiana, and Illinois. The men's basketball team has been rated number one in NCAA Division II, the women's basketball team has finished as high as third in the nation, and the football team hosted an NCAA Division II playoff game in 2004. Most Michigan Tech students compete in intramural sports in everything from Ultimate Frisbee to wrestling and from water polo to floor hockey. Club sports include lacrosse, women's hockey, and paintball. The biggest game on campus, however, is broomball, where students slide around on ice and hit a volleyball with brooms. The Student Development Complex includes a health center, swimming and diving pools, gyms (one with a running track), a rifle range, an ice arena, a weight room, and more. A community health center and new child-care center are located nearby.

Traditions include K-Day, which is an afternoon to enjoy McLain State Park on the shores of Lake Superior, the world's largest freshwater lake. The Parade of Nations is a celebration (including food) of the eighty nations of the world that have students and faculty and staff members at Michigan Tech. At Homecoming, students dress in their worst attire and parade through the campus in autos that barely run. During homecoming weekend, students enjoy a football game, a Hobo Mixer, and various special events. The biggest event is Winter Carnival, when massive snow statues emerge on campus and in the towns. Skits, queen competitions, first-class entertainment, ice hockey, and tourists everywhere make this a great experience. Before finals, students take a break on the campus mall for Spring Fling and celebrate with games, food booths, music, and more.

Location

Michigan Tech is situated on the Keweenaw Waterway in the hills of Houghton in a safe, friendly environment. The local area offers abundant opportunities for outdoor recreation, including the University's own ski hill; cross-country skiing, running, and biking trails; and golf course. A waterfront jogging and biking trail cuts through the campus. Houghton is located about 4 hours' drive from Green Bay, 7 hours from Minneapolis, and 10 hours from Detroit. The Houghton County Memorial Airport has daily flights to Minneapolis that connect to other major cities; bus service to Houghton is also available.

Majors and Degrees

The School of Technology awards Bachelor of Science degrees in computer network and system administration, construction management, electrical engineering technology, industrial technology, mechanical engineering technology, and surveying engineering.

The College of Engineering offers Bachelor of Science degrees in applied geophysics, biomedical engineering, chemical engineering, civil engineering, computer engineering, electrical engineering, engineering (mechanical design or manufacturing), environmental engineering, geological engineering, geology, materials science and engineering, and mechanical engineering.

The School of Business and Economics awards Bachelor of Science degrees in business administration, with concentrations in accounting, finance, management, management information systems, marketing, and operations and systems management, and economics.

The School of Forest Resources and Environmental Science awards Bachelor of Science degrees in applied ecology and environmental sciences, forestry, and wildlife ecology and management.

The College of Sciences and Arts awards Bachelor of Science degrees in anthropology, applied physics, audio production and technology, biochemistry and molecular biology, bioinformatics, biological sciences, cheminformatics, chemistry, clinical laboratory science, communication and cultural studies, computer science, computer systems science, exercise science, mathematics, pharmaceutical chemistry, physics, preprofessional programs (medicine, dentistry, pharmacy, and law), psychology, scientific and technical communication, social sciences, software engineering, and theater and entertainment technology. The CSA awards the Bachelor of Arts degree in communication and culture studies, liberal arts, scientific and technical communication, sound design, and theater and entertainment technology. The College of Sciences and Arts also awards a two-year associate degree in humanities.

The secondary education program offers certification in biology, business education, chemistry, computer science, earth science, economics, English, mathematics, physics, social studies, and technology and design.

Michigan Tech offers certificate programs in design engineering, industrial forestry, international business, media, mine environmental engineering, modern language and area study, and writing. An advanced certificate in modern language and area study and a graduate certificate in sustainability are also offered.

Michigan Tech's minors are aerospace studies, American studies, applied geophysics, art, astrophysics, biochemistry, biological sciences, chemistry, communication studies, computer science, earth sciences, ecology, economics, electronic materials, engineered wood products, enterprise, environmental studies, ethics and philosophy, geological engineering, historical studies, international modern languages (French, German, or Spanish), international studies, journalism, manufacturing, mathematical sciences, microbiology, military arts and science, mineral processing, mining, modern languages (French, German, or Spanish), municipal engineering, music, physics, plant biotechnology, plant sciences, polymer science and engineering, product design, psychology, remote sensing, social and behavioral studies, state of Michigan secondary teacher certification (see options above), structural materials, technical theater, and theater arts.

Academic Programs

Michigan Tech operates on a fifteen-week fall and spring semester system, and there are three options available for summer: two 7-week tracks and one 14-week track. Typically, it takes 130 credits to graduate, but the amount varies by department. Students must also complete the general education requirements, which seek to develop in each student fundamental scholastic habits of careful reading, communication, critical reasoning, and balanced analysis and argument; the habit of applying multiple disciplinary perspectives in interpretation, analysis, and creative problem solving; respect for diversity and awareness of complex contexts of their study and their work; and knowledge of a broad range of topics and disciplines complementary to the major. Some graduate courses are open to undergraduates with faculty approval. The International Programs and Services Office helps international students adjust to life in Houghton. Nearly 600 students come from approximately eighty other nations to study at Michigan Tech. Students may also study abroad in one of thirty nations, improving their global perspective.

Off-Campus Programs

The Career Center works with more than 200 industries, businesses, and organizations to help students find cooperative, internship, and summer employment opportunities. Job fairs are held on campus and elsewhere in the region. Co-op assignments earn academic credits; internships do not. Michigan Tech students average seven job interviews before they graduate.

Academic Facilities

The J. R. Van Pelt and John and Ruanne Opie Library contains more than 800,000 volumes and regularly receives approximately 10,000 serials and periodicals. The library is a designated depository for official international, U.S. government, and Michigan state documents and for the U.S. Army Map Service. The archives maintain a collection of original materials concerning the history of the Keweenaw region, including the records of various copper-mining companies. The Rozsa Center for the Performing Arts is within walking distance of all residence halls and features nationally known lecturers, musicians, comedians, and theatrical performers as well as Michigan Tech's own productions. The student-run newspaper, the *Lode*, has won national and state awards, and the campus radio station, WMTU, allows students to be disc jockeys. The A. E. Seaman Mineral Museum, the official "Mineralogical Museum of Michigan," is the home of one of the nation's premier collections of crystals, minerals, and ores. The collection contains more than 30,000 specimens, including the world's finest display from Michigan's copper- and iron-mining districts.

Costs

Annual tuition is $9180 for Michigan residents and $20,940 for out-of-state students for an academic year; room and board are $7315. Required fees and computer fees total approximately $1100, and books and supplies total approximately $1000.

Financial Aid

Currently, 87 percent of Michigan Tech's students receive financial aid, totaling nearly $50 million annually. Four kinds of assistance are available to Michigan Tech students, including scholarships, which are awarded on the basis of student potential and, in some cases, financial need; grants, which are provided by the federal or state government or by Michigan Tech and do not need to be repaid; student loans, in which the interest charged is below regular interest rates (payment of the interest and principal on need-based loans does not begin until after students leave Michigan Tech); and part-time employment, which consists of on-campus student employment opportunities. The financial aid process begins with filing an application for admission. Students should apply for admission by January 15 of the year in which they plan to enroll. Michigan Tech students rank in the top twenty-five nationally in the least amount of debt owed when they graduate, according to *U.S. News & World Report*.

Faculty

Most of the 412 faculty members possess terminal degrees. Ninety-five percent of undergraduate classes are taught by faculty members, and the student-faculty ratio is 12:1. Faculty members at Michigan Tech balance teaching and research and have long been known for their student guidance.

Student Government

Undergraduate Student Government and the Graduate Student Council are the two agencies of student involvement in University governance. Fraternities and sororities maintain a strong presence on campus, and there are more than 180 student organizations to choose from, including academic/professional, ethnic/cultural, service, religious, sporting, governmental, media, and honor societies. It is a great way for students to get involved and gain teamwork and leadership experience.

Admission Requirements

Michigan Tech has a selective admissions policy. The University admits only those applicants who give definite evidence that they are qualified through education, academic capability, aptitudes, interests, and character to complete the University's requirements. Once students are accepted for admission, every effort is made by the faculty and staff members to help students realize their potential.

Application and Information

To apply, students may complete the Michigan Tech application for admission any time after June 1 preceding the academic year for which they plan to enroll. Applications received by January 15 are given priority consideration for admission and merit-based scholarships. Undergraduate and graduate applications are free. First-year applicants are required to submit official ACT or SAT test scores. A high school counselor information page must also be completed by a high school counselor or principal and sent to the admissions office with an official high school transcript. Transfer students must have official college transcripts sent directly to Michigan Tech. An official high school transcript and ACT/SAT scores may also be required. International students should contact the International Programs and Services office. Following acceptance by Michigan Tech, students receive a packet containing information regarding on-campus housing and various University deadlines.

Admissions Office
Michigan Technological University
1400 Townsend Drive
Houghton, Michigan 49931-1295
Phone: 888-688-1885 (toll-free)
Internet: http://admissions.mtu.edu

Overlooking the campus of Michigan Tech.

SIENA HEIGHTS UNIVERSITY

ADRIAN, MICHIGAN

The University

Siena Heights University (SHU) was founded in 1919 by the Adrian Dominican Congregation as a Catholic liberal arts college. The name Siena honors Saint Catherine of Siena, a fourteenth-century Italian Dominican who dedicated her life to a quest for truth and social responsibility. Similarly, the mission of the University—to help students become more competent, purposeful, and ethical through a teaching and learning environment that respects the dignity of all—grows out of the philosophy of life exemplified in Saint Catherine of Siena.

Throughout its history, Siena Heights University has built a proud tradition of innovative response to challenging social needs. Originally a university for women who intended to become teachers, Siena broadened its offerings over the years and by the 1950s was recognized as one of the nation's ten best liberal arts colleges for women. Today, Siena continues to be a leading innovator in delivery of educational programs, offering traditional four-year bachelor's degree programs requiring 120 credits.

The mission of Siena Heights University is to assist students to become more competent, purposeful, and ethical through a teaching and learning environment that respects the dignity of all. The University therefore provides an educational process that challenges individuals to identify, to refine, and to achieve their personal goals. Through this process, Siena Heights University expects to engage each of its students in the development of a personal philosophy of life.

The University is accredited by the North Central Association of Colleges and Schools, the Department of Education of the state of Michigan, and the National Association of Schools of Art and Design and is organized into six departments: Art; Business and Management; Computing, Mathematics and the Sciences; Human Services; Humanities; and Performing Arts and Education.

Siena Heights University accommodates 425 students on campus. Hundreds of students live off campus within walking or biking distance. Students also commute from surrounding cities.

The University's Career Planning and Placement Center provides students with excellent placement services. Supported by state-of-the-art technology, the University has a 98 percent placement rate among its students within six months of graduation.

The Fieldhouse, home to the Saints' athletics programs, has five basketball courts, four volleyball courts, two indoor tennis courts, a 200-meter running track, and a training room. Recently, the University completed $1.7 million of renovations on more than 10,000 square feet of space, including completion of a state-of-the-art fitness center with equipment for use by the entire Siena community. Outdoor facilities on campus include a soccer field, baseball fields, two tennis courts, a sand volleyball court, and a softball complex.

Siena Heights University is proud of the accomplishments of its student athletes both in intercollegiate competition and in the classroom. The Saints have won three straight Wolverine-Hoosier Athletic Conference (WHAC) All-Sports competitions. Since 1985, Siena Heights athletic teams have won several conference, district, and regional championships, making SHU one of the finest athletic programs of its size in the nation.

The Saints have produced 62 NAIA All-Americans and 48 All-American Scholar-Athletes over the past two decades. The men's basketball team has advanced to the NAIA National Championship Tournament six times in the past eight years, and the 1997 team went 30–7 and was the national runner-up. In 1995, the men's baseball team became only the third NAIA institution in the state of Michigan to qualify for the NAIA World Series, and the women's soccer team has competed in three NAIA national championship tournaments in its twelve-year history.

More than thirty-five student clubs and organizations are available on the campus. They range from national social organizations to choirs, from Student Senate to intramural sports, and from international student organizations to various honor societies.

In addition to associate and bachelor's degree programs, Siena Heights offers later afternoon and evening graduate courses that lead to the Master of Arts degree.

Location

Siena Heights University is located in Adrian (population 22,000), which serves as the hub of the Lenawee County area. The campus is 75 miles from the Detroit metropolitan area, 30 miles from Ann Arbor, and 30 miles from Toledo, Ohio.

Majors and Degrees

Siena offers Associate of Arts, Associate of Science, Bachelor of Arts, Bachelor of Fine Arts, Bachelor of Science, Bachelor of Social Work, Bachelor of Business Administration, and Bachelor of Applied Science degrees.

The majors offered are accounting; art (ceramics, drawing, graphics, metalsmithing, painting, photography, printmaking, sculpture, watercolor); biology (premedical studies); business administration, with concentrations in accounting, computer information systems, finance, international business, management, and marketing; chemistry; child development; computer and information systems; criminal justice; English (children's literature, communications, creative writing, English general); environmental science; history; humanities; human services; integrated science; language arts; mathematics (pre-actuarial studies); Montessori education; multidisciplinary studies; prelaw studies; philosophy; preprofessional science (dentistry, pharmacy, engineering, veterinary science); psychology; religious studies; social science; social work; Spanish; special education; sport management; theater/speech communications; and special majors, such as a contracted major and inverted major. A nondegree teacher certification program is also available.

Academic Programs

The academic calendar consists of two semesters; a summer session is available. In a typical baccalaureate program, 120 credit hours are required.

COLLEGE DATA CENTER • MICHIGAN

Off-Campus Programs

There are internships in all majors. The cooperative education program allows freshmen and sophomores to test potential career fields while giving upperclass students on-the-job training. The international study program sends students to Florence, Italy; Paris, France; and Mexico.

Academic Facilities

The 140,000-volume library includes a computerized card catalog, automated circulation and book reserve functions, an expanded version of the academic index INFOTRAC to assist in retrieving recent periodical citations by subject, and Internet access. Information and research capabilities are available to students campuswide through the University's wireless computer network, which enables students to access the Internet and Siena Heights network files without plugging in to a hard-wired network connection.

Costs

For the academic year 2007–08, basic expenses were $18,495 for tuition and fees and $6290 for room and board, for a total of $24,785. There are no additional fees for out-of-state students. The average cost for books and supplies is approximately $500 per semester.

Financial Aid

Siena Heights University is committed to making an education affordable for every accepted student. Some form of financial assistance is given to nearly 86 percent of the University's full-time students. Need-based grants, loans, and work-study programs are available through the federal and state governments and the University itself. Siena Heights University also offers various academic scholarships. These awards are made on the basis of academic and leadership excellence, not necessarily because of need.

Students applying for financial aid should file the Free Application for Federal Student Aid (FAFSA) and have the results sent to Siena Heights. Applications are processed on a first-come, first-served basis only after a student has been accepted to the University.

Faculty

Siena Heights University employs more than 130 faculty members. Of the 65 full-time faculty members, more than 50 percent hold a doctorate or other terminal degree. Faculty members conduct recognized research and serve as advisers to aid in course selection and to offer career assistance.

Student Government

The Student Senate is involved with many topical issues touching all areas of University life. Students may serve in University government as elected senators or as volunteers on Student Senate committees. The Student Senate is open to all students of Siena Heights University.

Admission Requirements

Siena Heights admits students who are academically qualified, capable, enthusiastic, motivated, ready to be challenged, and ready to achieve. Admission decisions are based on high school academic performance, ACT or SAT scores, extracurricular activities, leadership potential, class rank, and personal recommendations. The typical profile of a regularly admitted freshman reflects an average high school GPA of 3.3 on a 4.0 scale and an average composite ACT score of 21.2. Conditional admission is available to students who show academic potential.

Application and Information

Admission decisions are made on a rolling basis, and applicants are notified of an admission status within one week after receipt of all application materials. Tours and general information sessions are available Monday through Saturday; annual Campus Visit Days are also scheduled.

For further information, students should contact:

Office of Admissions
Siena Heights University
1247 East Siena Heights Drive
Adrian, Michigan 49221-1796
Phone: 517-264-7180
800-521-0009 Ext. 7180 (toll-free)
Fax: 517-264-7745
E-mail: admissions@sienaheights.edu
Web site: http://www.sienaheights.edu

Dominican Hall on the campus of Siena Heights University.

COLLEGE DATA CENTER • MICHIGAN

WESTERN MICHIGAN UNIVERSITY

KALAMAZOO, MICHIGAN

The University

Western Michigan University (WMU) is one of the country's top public universities and enjoys global recognition for its outstanding programs in aviation, fine arts, communications, and business marketing. WMU is also home to Lee Honors College, which has been in continuous operation longer than almost any other honors program in the country. Nearly 1,100 undergraduates are currently enrolled in Lee Honors College. With an increasing student demand for honors programs, the University plans to continue to enlarge Lee Honors College over the next three years.

Western Michigan University is focused on preparing its graduates for the competitive world of work as well as graduate and professional school. WMU is one of only ninety-seven public universities in the United States to have a chapter of Phi Beta Kappa, the nation's premier honor society. In addition, *U.S. News & World Report* has ranked WMU among America's top 100 public universities for the past eight years.

With 24,433 students, WMU is Michigan's fourth-largest university and one of the nation's fifty largest public universities in the country. Even though it is a large university with a broad range of program offerings at both the undergraduate and graduate level, WMU maintains a comfortable student-faculty ratio of 19:1, although some lectures in general education courses can be larger. Despite its size, complexity, and variety of offerings, WMU is one of the most affordable of Michigan's fifteen public universities.

Founded in 1903, WMU has seven degree-granting colleges: Arts and Sciences, Aviation, the Haworth College of Business, Education, Engineering and Applied Sciences, Fine Arts, and Health and Human Services as well as the Graduate College, to assist students pursuing advanced degrees, and the Lee Honors College. Students have 237 academic programs from which to choose, 140 of them at the undergraduate level. Because it has a vibrant graduate component that includes twenty-nine doctoral programs, the University attracts faculty members who not only enjoy teaching at the undergraduate level but have distinguished themselves nationally through their research.

WMU has focused on enhancing its out-of-class opportunities by expanding its internship opportunities and student engagement in research and service. The Haenicke Institute for Global Education provides access to study-abroad programs all over the world and supports international students coming to study at WMU.

The University is home to a diverse student body that includes students from nearly every state across the United States as well as some 967 international students from eighty-four countries. Minority students also are well represented and make up 11 percent of the student population. The University's main campus enrollment of over 24,000 includes approximately 5,000 students who live in twenty-two campus residence halls that offer a variety of living arrangements.

There are more than 300 registered student organizations, including a wide range of Greek, academic honorary, and professional organizations. In addition, the University has nationally recognized arts programs, a lively cultural calendar, and NCAA Division I-A Mid-American and Central Collegiate Hockey Association sports teams. Its six men's and ten women's varsity sports, intramural teams, and club sports add vitality to campus life.

Location

For more than 100 years, Kalamazoo has been home to WMU. From the dedication of East Hall—the first building on campus—the community has supported Western's growth. Kalamazoo is an ideal college town, where business leaders recognize Western as their second-largest employer and where students and employees contribute more than $500 million annually to the economy of the region. Located just 40 miles from the beautiful eastern shoreline of Lake Michigan, the area embraces all four seasons with cool, sunny summers and moderate winters. Outdoor recreation abounds, from downhill skiing in winter months to every imaginable water sport available from late spring through early fall. Unlike much of eastern Michigan, southwest Michigan is composed of gently rolling hills, small recreational lakes, and dense woodlands. Fall is a particularly beautiful time to enjoy the variety of color while hiking or riding a bike on the Kal-Haven trail that connects Kalamazoo to the Lake Michigan resort town of South Haven. Nearly every weekend throughout the year Kalamazoo has something to offer its students and local residents. It is not unusual on a Saturday afternoon to find faculty members rubbing elbows with students at the annual Art Hop, Blues Festival, or Taste of Kalamazoo.

Kalamazoo, a city of more than 75,000, offers a wide array of lively entertainment including sports, such as professional baseball, hockey, and soccer; music, from jazz to heavy metal; intimate coffee houses and comedy clubs; and dining, from fast food to international cuisine. West Michigan is also home to numerous prosperous businesses, industries, and Fortune 500 companies including Haworth Inc., the Whirlpool Corporation, and the Kellogg Company. Many of these companies offer internships to WMU students.

Majors and Degrees

WMU offers a range of academic majors and programs to meet nearly everyone's needs. The College of Arts and Sciences offers undergraduate degrees in Africana studies; anthropology; biochemistry; biology; biomedical sciences; business-oriented chemistry; chemistry; communication studies; criminal justice; earth science; economics; English; film, video, and media studies; French; geochemistry; geography; geology; geophysics; German; global and international studies; history; hydrogeology; interpersonal communication; journalism; Latin; mathematics; organizational communication; philosophy; physics; political science; psychology; public history; public relations; religion; sociology; Spanish; statistics; student-planned major; telecommunications and information management; tourism and travel; preprofessional programs (dentistry, law, medicine); and coordinate majors (environmental studies, women's studies).

The College of Aviation offers programs in aviation flight science, aviation maintenance technology, and aviation science and administration.

The Haworth College of Business offers programs in accountancy, advertising and promotion, computer information systems, electronic business design, finance, food and consumer package goods marketing, human resource management, integrated supply matrix management, management, marketing, personal financial planning, sales and business marketing, and telecommunications and information management.

The College of Education offers programs in elementary education that emphasize language arts, mathematics, science, and social science. Secondary education students may major in art, biology, business, chemistry, earth science, English, family and consumer science, French, geography, German, health education, history, industrial technology, Latin, marketing, mathematics, music, physical education, physics, political science, school health education, Spanish, and technology and design. Other programs include athletic training, community health education, dietetics, exercise science, family studies, food service administration, industrial technology, interior design, recreation, special education, and textile and apparel studies.

The College of Engineering and Applied Sciences offers programs in aeronautical engineering, chemical engineering, civil engineering, computer engineering, computer science, construction engineering, electrical engineering, engineering graphics and design technology, engineering management technology, imaging, industrial design, industrial engineering, manufacturing engineering, manufacturing engineering technology, mechanical engineering, paper engineering, and paper science.

The College of Fine Arts offers programs in art, art education, art history, dance, graphic design, jazz studies, music, music composition, music education, music history, music performance, music theater performance, music therapy, theater design, theater performance, and theater technology.

The College of Health and Human Services offers programs in interdisciplinary health services, occupational therapy, nursing, nursing (RN), social work, speech pathology and audiology, and travel instruction.

Academic Programs

WMU is committed to student academic success, beginning with the new First-Year Experience program, which utilizes small-group seminars led by senior faculty members and upperclass student mentors. The University's college advisers help students plan their courses of study and consider program options, while advisers in University Curriculum assist undecided students in exploring academic programs and their relationships to various careers and professions. A comprehensive general education program provides the foundation for all fields of study. The Lee Honors College provides an atmosphere of small seminar classes, opportunities for research alongside faculty members, and the chance to explore new horizons through independent study. Student academic success is recognized through University, college, and department honor societies and through the prestigious Presidential Scholar Award given to outstanding graduating seniors.

Off-Campus Programs

A host of U.S. business-industry partnerships and exchange agreements with universities and other organizations around the world provide training, research, and study-abroad opportunities for graduate and undergraduate students. In addition, the University actively assists students seeking internships in their chosen fields of study.

Academic Facilities

Western Michigan University is on Intel's list of the nation's 100 most wireless college campuses. WMU's network provides access to the University libraries, the Internet, and extensive campus information services. Computer labs are available across the campus, including many residence halls. Specialized labs support the work of students in engineering, graphic arts, teacher education, business, and other fields. Western Michigan University's new chemistry building opened in January 2007, and the new James W. and Lois I. Richmond Center for Visual Arts opened in April 2007. New construction is continuously transforming the campus while giving students access to acclaimed fine arts performance spaces, world-class aviation facilities, a leading-edge building for the College of Health and Human Services, and an innovative College of Engineering and Applied Sciences building that is located in a thriving business and research park.

Costs

A college education is one of the best investments a person can make, and, best of all, it never depreciates over time. Over a lifetime of work, WMU's graduates can expect to earn nearly $2 million—more than twice that of someone with a high school diploma. WMU is committed to keeping costs as low as possible to ensure that all qualified students have access to the University. WMU's tuition and fees are among the lowest in the state. For 2007–08, tuition and fee costs were $7260, and room and board costs were $7042. Books and supplies and personal and travel expenses vary based on individual factors.

Financial Aid

The University annually awards more than $200 million in financial assistance to undergraduate students. Students who are qualified for need-based aid usually receive assistance through a combination of gift-aid (grants and scholarships), self-help (student loans), and employment (work-study).

A variety of academic achievement scholarships are available to students who have demonstrated academic success while in high school. These awards vary from $1000 to full tuition, and, in some instances, a combination of awards can be sufficient to cover nearly all direct costs of attendance at WMU. Most merit awards are renewable by enrolling full-time and earning a minimum 3.0 cumulative grade point average while at WMU. The two most recognized awards are the Medallion Scholarship and the Dean's Scholarship. The Dean's Scholarship is awarded to the top academic students (based on high school grades and standardized test scores) who apply for admission in early December, compete in the Medallion competition in January, and enroll the following fall semester as new, first-time students. Medallion recipients receive $10,000 annually, and the scholarship is renewable for up to four years of full-time enrollment.

There are also scholarships for students who have earned associate degrees from state and regional community colleges and who have earned high grade point averages while completing degree requirements.

Faculty

WMU's commitment to academic excellence means that many of its 913 full-time and 441 part-time faculty members conduct research. Tenured professors teach freshman-level courses, and full-time faculty members teach the majority of all courses. Plus, hundreds of these scholars have academic or research experience outside of the United States, bringing a global perspective into the classroom.

Student Government

Governance structures include the Western Student Association and its Student Senate and the Residence Hall Association. Each provides students with a wide variety of opportunities for leadership.

Admission Requirements

Admission to the University is based primarily on a combination of high school cumulative grade point average and standardized test scores (either ACT or SAT). When admission is not conclusive or admission is sought to selective or highly competitive programs, consideration is given to academic rigor of courses taken and counselor/principal recommendations, in addition to grade point averages and test scores.

To ensure academic success at WMU, all students should have completed a minimum of 4 years of English, 3 years of mathematics (through intermediate algebra), 3 years of social sciences, 2 years of natural sciences, and 2 years of the same foreign language.

Offers of admission made to students still in high school are conditional, pending graduation from high school and the University's review of final senior-year grades.

Transfer students with a minimum of 26 transferable hours (39 quarter hours) at the time of application and a grade point average of at least 2.0 (C average) are considered for admission. The trend of the most recent grades is also taken into account. Applicants with fewer than 26 transferable hours (39 quarter hours) at the time of application also must submit a high school transcript. In such cases, admission is based on both college and high school records.

Application and Information

For an application or more information, students should contact:

Office of Admissions and Orientation
Western Michigan University
1903 West Michigan Avenue
Kalamazoo, Michigan 49008-5211
Phone: 269-387-2000
Web site: http://www.wmich.edu/admissions

This impressive Stewart Clock Tower joins Waldo Library, on the right, with the high-tech University Computing Center.

MINNESOTA

Crookston
Bemidji
Moorhead
Duluth
35
94
Collegeville
St Joseph
St. Cloud
Morris
Minneapolis
St. Paul
St. Bonifacius
Marshall
St. Peter
35
Northfield
New Ulm
Winona
Mankato
Owatonna
Rochester
90
90

ACADEMY COLLEGE

Minneapolis, Minnesota **www.academycollege.edu/**

- **Proprietary** 4-year, founded 1936
- **Urban** campus
- **Coed**
- **Minimally difficult** entrance level

Faculty *Student/faculty ratio:* 7:1.

Academics *Calendar:* quarters. *Degrees:* certificates, associate, and bachelor's.

Costs (2007–08) *Tuition:* $19,527 full-time, $305 per credit part-time. *Required fees:* $250 full-time.

Applying *Options:* electronic application, early admission, deferred entrance. *Application fee:* $30. *Required:* high school transcript, interview.

Freshman Application Contact Tracey Schantz, Director, Academy College, 1101 East 78th Street, Suite 100, Minneapolis, MN 55420. *Phone:* 952-851-0066. *Toll-free phone:* 800-292-9149. *Fax:* 952-851-0094. *E-mail:* admissions@academycollege.edu.

ARGOSY UNIVERSITY, TWIN CITIES

Eagan, Minnesota **www.argosy.edu/locations/twin-cities/**

- **Proprietary** university, founded 1961, part of Education Management Corporation
- **Suburban** campus with easy access to Minneapolis–St. Paul, MN
- **Coed**

Majors Business administration and management; criminal justice/law enforcement administration; finance; health/health care administration; international business/trade/commerce; marketing/marketing management; organizational behavior; psychology; substance abuse/addiction counseling.

Academics *Calendar:* semesters. *Degrees:* associate, bachelor's, master's, doctoral, post-master's, and first professional certificates.

Director of Admissions Argosy University, Twin Cities, 1515 Central Parkway, Eagan, MN 55121. *Phone:* 651-846-2882. *Toll-free phone:* 888-844-2004.

See page 1384 for the College Close-Up.

THE ART INSTITUTES INTERNATIONAL MINNESOTA

Minneapolis, Minnesota **www.aim.artinstitutes.edu/**

- **Proprietary** 4-year, founded 1964, part of Education Management Corporation
- **Urban** campus
- **Coed** 1,722 undergraduate students, 56% full-time, 54% women, 46% men
- **Minimally difficult** entrance level, 44% of applicants were admitted

Undergraduates 956 full-time, 766 part-time. Students come from 10 states and territories, 6 other countries, 6% are from out of state, 2% African American, 2% Asian American or Pacific Islander, 1% Hispanic American, 0.5% Native American, 13% live on campus. *Retention:* 50% of 2005 full-time freshmen returned.

Freshmen *Admission:* 840 applied, 367 admitted. *Average high school GPA:* 2.6.

Faculty *Total:* 114, 47% full-time, 7% with terminal degrees. *Student/faculty ratio:* 20:1.

Majors Advertising; animation, interactive technology, video graphics and special effects; computer graphics; fashion merchandising; graphic design; hospitality administration; interior design; photography; restaurant, culinary, and catering management; Web page, digital/multimedia and information resources design.

Academics *Calendar:* quarters. *Degrees:* certificates, associate, and bachelor's. *Special study options:* academic remediation for entering students, advanced placement credit, cooperative education, independent study, internships, part-time degree program, services for LD students, summer session for credit.

Computers on Campus 212 computers/terminals are available on campus for general student use. Students can access the following: campus intranet, computer help desk, free student e-mail accounts, online (class) grades, online (class) registration, online (class) schedules. Campuswide network is available.

Student Life *Housing options:* coed. Campus housing is leased by the school. *Activities and organizations:* student-run newspaper, Siggraph, AIGA, ASID, ACF Jr., Main Frame. *Campus security:* security personnel during hours of operation. *Student services:* personal/psychological counseling.

Standardized Tests *Required:* ACT COMPASS (for admission). *Recommended:* ACT (for admission), ACT (for placement).

Costs (2007–08) *Tuition:* $20,688 full-time, $431 per credit part-time. tuition cost varies by program. Room is $1926 per quarter. Students should contact the school for current tuition costs. Other charges include a starting kit for all first-quarter students. Kits vary in price depending on the program of study.

Financial Aid Of all full-time matriculated undergraduates who enrolled in 2006, 55 Federal Work-Study jobs (averaging $3200).

Applying *Options:* electronic application, deferred entrance. *Application fee:* $50. *Required:* essay or personal statement, high school transcript, interview. *Application deadlines:* rolling (freshmen), rolling (transfers).

Freshman Application Contact Director of Admissions, The Art Institutes International Minnesota, 15 South 9th Street, Minneapolis, MN 55402. *Phone:* 612-332-3361. *Toll-free phone:* 800-777-3643. *Fax:* 612-332-3934.

See page 1386 for the College Close-Up.

AUGSBURG COLLEGE

Minneapolis, Minnesota **www.augsburg.edu/**

- **Independent Lutheran** comprehensive, founded 1869
- **Urban** 23-acre campus
- **Endowment** $32.4 million
- **Coed** 2,921 undergraduate students, 81% full-time, 57% women, 43% men
- **Moderately difficult** entrance level, 61% of applicants were admitted

Augsburg College, a private liberal arts college affiliated with the Evangelical Lutheran Church in America, is located in the heart of the Twin Cities and draws upon the cultural and corporate resources of both Minneapolis and St. Paul. Its challenging academic environment is enhanced by educational and service experiences that transform theory into action, preparing students as leaders for service in a global society. Students at Augsburg come from diverse religious, cultural, and ethnic backgrounds.

Undergraduates 2,357 full-time, 564 part-time. Students come from 39 states and territories, 24 other countries, 17% are from out of state, 5% African American, 4% Asian American or Pacific Islander, 2% Hispanic American, 1% Native American, 1% international, 11% transferred in, 54% live on campus. *Retention:* 84% of 2006 full-time freshmen returned.

Freshmen *Admission:* 1,560 applied, 956 admitted, 401 enrolled. *Average high school GPA:* 3.24. *Test scores:* SAT critical reading scores over 500: 83%; SAT math scores over 500: 80%; ACT scores over 18: 89%; SAT critical reading scores over 600: 37%; SAT math scores over 600: 43%; ACT scores over 24: 40%; SAT critical reading scores over 700: 14%; SAT math scores over 700: 3%; ACT scores over 30: 3%.

Faculty *Total:* 399, 46% full-time, 48% with terminal degrees. *Student/faculty ratio:* 14:1.

Majors Accounting; aeronautics/aviation/aerospace science and technology; art; art history, criticism and conservation; art teacher education; Asian studies (East); astrophysics; athletic training; behavioral sciences; biological and physical sciences; biology/biological sciences; business administration and management; business/managerial economics; chemistry; computer science; criminal justice/safety; dramatic/theater arts; economics; education; elementary education; English; finance; fine/studio arts; French; German; health teacher education; history; humanities; interdisciplinary studies; international business/trade/commerce; international relations and affairs; kindergarten/preschool education; liberal arts and sciences/liberal studies; management information systems; marketing/marketing management; mass communication/media; mathematics; music; music teacher education; music therapy; natural sciences; nursing (registered nurse training); philosophy; physical education teaching and coaching; physician assistant; physics; political science and government; pre-dentistry studies; pre-law studies; pre-medical studies; pre-veterinary studies; psychology; religious studies; Scandinavian languages; secondary education; social sciences; social work; sociology; Spanish; special education (emotionally disturbed); speech and rhetoric; theology; urban studies/affairs; women's studies.

Academics *Calendar:* semesters for undergraduate programs; trimesters for graduate programs and weekend college. *Degrees:* certificates, bachelor's, master's, post-master's, and postbachelor's certificates. *Special study options:* academic remediation for entering students, adult/continuing education programs, advanced placement credit, cooperative education, double majors, English as a second language, freshman honors college, honors programs, independent study, internships, off-campus study, part-time degree program, services for LD students, student-designed majors, study abroad, summer session for credit. *ROTC:*

Army (c), Navy (c), Air Force (c). *Unusual degree programs:* 3-2 engineering with Michigan Technological University, University of Minnesota, Twin Cities Campus.

Computers on Campus 260 computers/terminals are available on campus for general student use. Students can access the following: campus intranet, computer help desk, free student e-mail accounts, online (class) grades, online (class) registration, online (class) schedules. Campuswide network is available. 100% of college-owned or -operated housing units are wired for high-speed Internet access.

Student Life *Housing options:* coed, men-only, women-only, disabled students. Campus housing is university owned. Freshman applicants given priority for college housing. *Activities and organizations:* drama/theater group, student-run newspaper, radio station, choral group, Student Activities Council, student government, newspaper/yearbook, campus ministry, intramurals. *Campus security:* 24-hour emergency response devices and patrols, student patrols, late-night transport/escort service, controlled dormitory access. *Student services:* health clinic, personal/psychological counseling, women's center.

Athletics Member NCAA. All Division III. *Intercollegiate sports:* baseball M, basketball M/W, cross-country running M/W, football M, golf M/W, ice hockey M/W, soccer M/W, softball W, track and field M/W, volleyball W, wrestling M. *Intramural sports:* basketball M/W, football M, skiing (cross-country) M (c)/W (c), skiing (downhill) M (c)/W (c), softball M/W, volleyball M/W, wrestling M.

Standardized Tests *Recommended:* SAT or ACT (for admission).

Costs (2007–08) *Comprehensive fee:* $31,441 includes full-time tuition ($24,046), mandatory fees ($493), and room and board ($6902). Part-time tuition: $3000 per course. Part-time tuition and fees vary according to course load. *Required fees:* $90 per term part-time. *College room only:* $3534. Room and board charges vary according to board plan and housing facility. *Payment plan:* installment. *Waivers:* children of alumni, senior citizens, and employees or children of employees.

Financial Aid Of all full-time matriculated undergraduates who enrolled in 2006, 1,929 applied for aid, 1,412 were judged to have need, 456 had their need fully met. 185 Federal Work-Study jobs (averaging $1380). 415 state and other part-time jobs (averaging $2588). In 2006, 167 non-need-based awards were made. *Average percent of need met:* 69%. *Average financial aid package:* $14,832. *Average need-based loan:* $4923. *Average need-based gift aid:* $10,145. *Average non-need-based aid:* $7261. *Average indebtedness upon graduation:* $25,750. *Financial aid deadline:* 8/15.

Applying *Options:* electronic application, deferred entrance. *Application fee:* $25. *Required:* essay or personal statement, high school transcript, minimum 2.5 GPA, interview. *Required for some:* 2 letters of recommendation. *Application deadlines:* 8/15 (freshmen), 8/15 (transfers). *Notification:* continuous (freshmen), continuous (transfers).

Freshman Application Contact Ms. Carrie Carroll, Director of Undergraduate Day Admissions, Augsburg College, 2211 Riverside Avenue, Minneapolis, MN 55454-1351. *Phone:* 612-330-1001. *Toll-free phone:* 800-788-5678. *Fax:* 612-330-1590. *E-mail:* admissions@augsburg.edu.

BEMIDJI STATE UNIVERSITY

Bemidji, Minnesota **www.bemidjistate.edu/**

- **State-supported** comprehensive, founded 1919, part of Minnesota State Colleges and Universities System
- **Small-town** 89-acre campus
- **Endowment** $13.2 million
- **Coed** 4,456 undergraduate students, 75% full-time, 52% women, 48% men
- **Moderately difficult** entrance level, 86% of applicants were admitted

Undergraduates 3,329 full-time, 1,127 part-time. Students come from 36 states and territories, 40 other countries, 7% are from out of state, 0.6% African American, 0.7% Asian American or Pacific Islander, 0.3% Hispanic American, 4% Native American, 5% international, 8% transferred in, 26% live on campus. *Retention:* 70% of 2006 full-time freshmen returned.

Freshmen *Admission:* 1,955 applied, 1,674 admitted, 752 enrolled. *Test scores:* ACT scores over 18: 84%; ACT scores over 24: 26%; ACT scores over 30: 2%.

Faculty *Total:* 278, 81% full-time, 65% with terminal degrees. *Student/faculty ratio:* 19:1.

Majors Accounting; American Indian/Native American studies; American Native/Native American languages; applied art; art; art teacher education; behavioral sciences; biological and physical sciences; biology/biological sciences; broadcast journalism; business administration and management; chemistry; clinical laboratory science/medical technology; commercial and advertising art; community organization and advocacy; computer science; construction engineering technology; criminal justice/law enforcement administration; criminal justice/police science; data processing and data processing technology; dramatic/theater arts; ecology; economics; education; elementary education; engineering physics; English; environmental studies; fine/studio arts; geography; geology/earth science; German; health teacher education; history; humanities; industrial arts; industrial technology; information science/studies; journalism; liberal arts and sciences/liberal studies; marine biology and biological oceanography; mass communication/media; mathematics; modern languages; music; music teacher education; natural sciences; nursing (registered nurse training); parks, recreation and leisure; philosophy; physical education teaching and coaching; physical sciences; physics; political science and government; pre-law studies; pre-medical studies; pre-veterinary studies; professional studies; psychology; radio and television; religious studies; science teacher education; secondary education; social sciences; social work; sociology; Spanish; speech and rhetoric; speech/theater education; sport and fitness administration/management; technology/industrial arts teacher education; trade and industrial teacher education.

Academics *Calendar:* semesters. *Degrees:* associate, bachelor's, and master's. *Special study options:* academic remediation for entering students, adult/continuing education programs, advanced placement credit, cooperative education, distance learning, double majors, English as a second language, external degree program, honors programs, independent study, internships, off-campus study, part-time degree program, services for LD students, study abroad, summer session for credit.

Computers on Campus 1,200 computers/terminals are available on campus for general student use. Students can access the following: online (class) registration. Campuswide network is available. Wireless service is available via entire campus.

Student Life *Housing options:* coed, men-only, women-only, disabled students. Campus housing is university owned. Freshman applicants given priority for college housing. *Activities and organizations:* drama/theater group, student-run newspaper, radio and television station, choral group, International Students Organization, Jazz Band Club, Madrigal Dinner Club, Student Senate, Council of Indian Students, national fraternities, national sororities. *Campus security:* 24-hour emergency response devices and patrols, late-night transport/escort service, controlled dormitory access. *Student services:* health clinic, personal/psychological counseling, women's center.

Athletics Member NCAA. All Division II. *Intercollegiate sports:* baseball M (s), basketball M (s)/W (s), cross-country running W, football M (s), golf M/W, ice hockey M (s)/W (s), soccer W (s), softball W (s), tennis W (s), track and field M (s)/W (s), volleyball W (s). *Intramural sports:* basketball M/W, football M, ice hockey M/W, racquetball M/W, soccer M/W, softball M/W, tennis M/W, track and field M/W, volleyball M/W, wrestling M.

Standardized Tests *Required:* ACT (for admission).

Costs (2007–08) *Tuition:* state resident $6167 full-time, $208 per semester hour part-time; nonresident $6167 full-time, $208 per semester hour part-time. Full-time tuition and fees vary according to course load, location, program, and reciprocity agreements. Part-time tuition and fees vary according to course load, location, program, and reciprocity agreements. *Required fees:* $810 full-time, $90 per credit part-time. *Room and board:* $5874; room only: $3774. Room and board charges vary according to board plan and housing facility. *Payment plan:* installment. *Waivers:* senior citizens and employees or children of employees.

Financial Aid Of all full-time matriculated undergraduates who enrolled in 2006, 2,578 applied for aid, 2,036 were judged to have need, 526 had their need fully met. 238 Federal Work-Study jobs (averaging $1857). 234 state and other part-time jobs (averaging $1805). In 2006, 511 non-need-based awards were made. *Average percent of need met:* 72%. *Average financial aid package:* $7856. *Average need-based loan:* $3497. *Average need-based gift aid:* $4502. *Average non-need-based aid:* $7179. *Average indebtedness upon graduation:* $18,850.

Applying *Options:* electronic application, deferred entrance. *Application fee:* $20. *Required:* high school transcript. *Required for some:* essay or personal statement, letters of recommendation, interview. *Application deadlines:* rolling (freshmen), rolling (transfers). *Notification:* continuous (freshmen), continuous (transfers).

Freshman Application Contact Mr. Russ Kreager, Director of Admissions, Bemidji State University, Deputy 102, Bemidji State University, 1500 Birchmont Drive, NE, Bemidji, MN 56601. *Phone:* 218-755-2040. *Toll-free phone:* 800-475-2001 (in-state); 800-652-9747 (out-of-state). *Fax:* 218-755-2074. *E-mail:* admissions@bemidjistate.edu.

BETHANY LUTHERAN COLLEGE

Mankato, Minnesota **www.blc.edu/**

- **Independent Lutheran** 4-year, founded 1927
- **Small-town** 50-acre campus with easy access to Minneapolis–St. Paul
- **Endowment** $38.5 million

- **Coed** 617 undergraduate students, 96% full-time, 58% women, 42% men
- **Moderately difficult** entrance level, 83% of applicants were admitted

Undergraduates 591 full-time, 26 part-time. Students come from 25 states and territories, 6 other countries, 28% are from out of state, 2% African American, 2% Asian American or Pacific Islander, 0.8% Hispanic American, 0.3% Native American, 0.5% international, 5% transferred in, 70% live on campus. *Retention:* 71% of 2006 full-time freshmen returned.

Freshmen *Admission:* 404 applied, 336 admitted, 177 enrolled. *Average high school GPA:* 3.43. *Test scores:* ACT scores over 18: 95%; ACT scores over 24: 50%; ACT scores over 30: 6%.

Faculty *Total:* 65, 58% full-time, 31% with terminal degrees. *Student/faculty ratio:* 11:1.

Majors Art; biology/biological sciences; business administration and management; chemistry; communication/speech communication and rhetoric; dramatic/theater arts; elementary education; engineering; English; history; kinesiology and exercise science; mathematics; music; psychology; religious/sacred music; religious studies; social sciences; sociology.

Academics *Calendar:* semesters. *Degree:* bachelor's. *Special study options:* academic remediation for entering students, advanced placement credit, double majors, honors programs, independent study, internships, services for LD students, study abroad. *ROTC:* Army (c). *Unusual degree programs:* 3-2 engineering with University of Minnesota-Twin Cities.

Computers on Campus 100 computers/terminals and 800 ports are available on campus for general student use. Students can access the following: campus intranet, computer help desk, free student e-mail accounts, online (class) grades, online (class) registration, online (class) schedules. Campuswide network is available. 100% of college-owned or -operated housing units are wired for high-speed Internet access. Wireless service is available via entire campus.

Student Life *Housing:* on-campus residence required through sophomore year. *Options:* men-only, women-only. Campus housing is university owned. Freshman campus housing is guaranteed. *Activities and organizations:* drama/theater group, student-run newspaper, television station, choral group, Student Senate, Paul Ylvisaker Center, BLC Scholastic Leadership Society, SIFE Students In Free Enterprise, Lutherans for Life. *Campus security:* 24-hour emergency response devices, late-night transport/escort service, controlled dormitory access. *Student services:* personal/psychological counseling.

Athletics Member NCCAA. *Intercollegiate sports:* baseball M, basketball M/W, golf M/W, soccer M/W, softball W, tennis M/W, volleyball W. *Intramural sports:* basketball M/W, cross-country running M/W, football M/W, racquetball M/W, soccer M/W, softball M/W, table tennis M/W, ultimate Frisbee M/W, volleyball M/W.

Standardized Tests *Required:* SAT or ACT (for admission).

Costs (2007–08) *Comprehensive fee:* $23,038 includes full-time tuition ($17,500), mandatory fees ($260), and room and board ($5278). Part-time tuition: $750 per credit. *Required fees:* $130 per term part-time. *College room only:* $1988. Room and board charges vary according to board plan. *Payment plan:* installment. *Waivers:* employees or children of employees.

Financial Aid Of all full-time matriculated undergraduates who enrolled in 2006, 513 applied for aid, 464 were judged to have need, 157 had their need fully met. 28 Federal Work-Study jobs (averaging $1380). 276 state and other part-time jobs (averaging $766). In 2006, 97 non-need-based awards were made. *Average percent of need met:* 86%. *Average need-based loan:* $3923. *Average need-based gift aid:* $9969. *Average non-need-based aid:* $8212. *Average indebtedness upon graduation:* $22,214.

Applying *Options:* electronic application. *Required:* essay or personal statement, high school transcript, minimum 2.4 GPA. *Required for some:* interview. *Recommended:* minimum 3.2 GPA, interview. *Application deadline:* 7/1 (freshmen). *Notification:* continuous (transfers).

Freshman Application Contact Mr. Donald Westphal, Dean of Admissions, Bethany Lutheran College, 700 Luther Drive, Mankato, MN 56001. *Phone:* 507-344-7320. *Toll-free phone:* 800-944-3066 Ext. 331. *Fax:* 507-344-7376. *E-mail:* dwestpha@blc.edu.

BETHEL UNIVERSITY

St. Paul, Minnesota **www.bethel.edu/**

- **Independent** comprehensive, founded 1871, affiliated with Baptist General Conference
- **Suburban** 248-acre campus with easy access to Twin Cities
- **Endowment** $28.8 million
- **Coed** 3,327 undergraduate students, 82% full-time, 63% women, 37% men
- **Moderately difficult** entrance level, 88% of applicants were admitted

Bethel University is a leader in Christian higher education, with approximately 6,000 students from thirty-five countries and all fifty states enrolled in undergraduate, graduate, seminary, and adult education programs. Based in St. Paul, Minnesota, with additional seminary locations on both coasts, Bethel University offers bachelor's and advanced degrees in nearly 100 relevant fields. Programs are taught by renowned faculty members within a distinctly evangelical Christian framework, equipping women and men for culturally sensitive leadership, scholarship, and service around the world. For further information on Bethel University, prospective students should go to http://www.bethel.edu.

Undergraduates 2,724 full-time, 603 part-time. Students come from 40 states and territories, 18 other countries, 26% are from out of state, 3% African American, 3% Asian American or Pacific Islander, 2% Hispanic American, 0.3% Native American, 0.3% international, 4% transferred in, 71% live on campus. *Retention:* 86% of 2006 full-time freshmen returned.

Freshmen *Admission:* 1,643 applied, 1,447 admitted, 572 enrolled. *Average high school GPA:* 3.52. *Test scores:* SAT critical reading scores over 500: 79%; SAT math scores over 500: 78%; ACT scores over 18: 98%; SAT critical reading scores over 600: 48%; SAT math scores over 600: 46%; ACT scores over 24: 58%; SAT critical reading scores over 700: 11%; SAT math scores over 700: 9%; ACT scores over 30: 15%.

Faculty *Total:* 431, 41% full-time, 54% with terminal degrees. *Student/faculty ratio:* 14:1.

Majors Area, ethnic, cultural, and gender studies related; art; art teacher education; athletic training; biblical studies; biology/biological sciences; biology teacher education; business administration and management; chemistry; chemistry teacher education; communication/speech communication and rhetoric; community health services counseling; computer and information sciences; dramatic/theater arts; early childhood education; economics; elementary education; engineering science; English; English as a second/foreign language (teaching); English composition; English/language arts teacher education; environmental science; French; French language teacher education; health and physical education; health teacher education; history; international relations and affairs; kinesiology and exercise science; liberal arts and sciences/liberal studies; library science related; mass communication/media; mathematics; mathematics teacher education; molecular biology; multi-/interdisciplinary studies related; music; music performance; music teacher education; nursing (registered nurse training); philosophy; physical education teaching and coaching; physics; physics teacher education; political science and government; psychology; religious/sacred music; science teacher education; social sciences; social studies teacher education; social work; Spanish; Spanish language teacher education; youth ministry.

Academics *Calendar:* 4-1-4. *Degrees:* associate, bachelor's, master's, doctoral, first professional, post-master's, and postbachelor's certificates. *Special study options:* academic remediation for entering students, accelerated degree program, adult/continuing education programs, advanced placement credit, double majors, honors programs, independent study, internships, off-campus study, part-time degree program, services for LD students, student-designed majors, study abroad, summer session for credit. *ROTC:* Army (c), Air Force (c). *Unusual degree programs:* 3-2 engineering with dual degree program with the University of Minnesota, Case Western Reserve and Washington University in St. Louis, Missouri. Dual degree agreement can be established with other schools of engineering on an individual basis.

Computers on Campus 375 computers/terminals are available on campus for general student use. Students can access the following: campus intranet, computer help desk, free student e-mail accounts, online (class) grades, online (class) registration, online (class) schedules. Campuswide network is available. 100% of college-owned or -operated housing units are wired for high-speed Internet access. Wireless service is available via classrooms, computer centers, computer labs, dorm rooms, learning centers, libraries, student centers.

Student Life *Housing:* on-campus residence required through sophomore year. *Options:* coed, disabled students. Campus housing is university owned. Freshman applicants given priority for college housing. *Activities and organizations:* drama/theater group, student-run newspaper, radio station, choral group, Twin Cities Outreach, RIOT Leaders, Student Activities, College Republicans, Tri Beta (Biology Honors Society). *Campus security:* 24-hour emergency response devices and patrols, student patrols, late-night transport/escort service, controlled dormitory access. *Student services:* health clinic, personal/psychological counseling.

Athletics Member NCAA. All Division III. *Intercollegiate sports:* baseball M, basketball M/W, cross-country running M/W, football M, golf M/W, ice hockey M/W, soccer M/W, softball W, tennis M/W, track and field M/W, volleyball M (c)/W. *Intramural sports:* badminton M/W, basketball M/W, football M, lacrosse M (c)/W (c), rugby M (c), softball M/W, volleyball M/W.

Standardized Tests *Required:* SAT or ACT (for admission).

Costs (2007–08) *Comprehensive fee:* $31,890 includes full-time tuition ($24,400), mandatory fees ($110), and room and board ($7380). Part-time tuition: $935 per credit. *College room only:* $4400.

Financial Aid Of all full-time matriculated undergraduates who enrolled in 2006, 2,161 applied for aid, 1,811 were judged to have need, 365 had their need fully met. 379 Federal Work-Study jobs (averaging $2200). 1,600 state and other part-time jobs (averaging $2200). In 2006, 680 non-need-based awards were made. *Average percent of need met:* 77%. *Average financial aid package:* $15,186. *Average need-based loan:* $4271. *Average need-based gift aid:* $10,276. *Average non-need-based aid:* $3857. *Average indebtedness upon graduation:* $28,303.

Applying *Options:* electronic application, early admission, early action, deferred entrance. *Application fee:* $25. *Required:* essay or personal statement, 2 letters of recommendation, rank in upper 50% of high school class, minimum ACT score of 21 or SAT score of 920. *Required for some:* high school transcript. *Recommended:* interview. *Application deadlines:* 8/1 (transfers), 11/1 (early action). *Notification:* continuous (freshmen), continuous (transfers), 12/15 (early action).

Freshman Application Contact Mr. Jay Fedje, Director of Admissions, Bethel University, 3900 Bethel Drive, St. Paul, MN 55112. *Phone:* 651-638-6242. *Toll-free phone:* 800-255-8706 Ext. 6242. *Fax:* 651-635-1490. *E-mail:* buadmissions-cas@bethel.edu.

See page 1388 for the College Close-Up.

BROWN COLLEGE

Mendota Heights, Minnesota **www.browncollege.edu/**

Freshman Application Contact Mr. Mark Fredrichs, Registrar, Brown College, 1440 Northland Drive, Mendota Heights, MN 55120. *Phone:* 651-905-3400. *Toll-free phone:* 800-6BROWN6. *Fax:* 651-905-3550.

CAPELLA UNIVERSITY

Minneapolis, Minnesota **www.capella.edu/**

- **Proprietary** upper-level, founded 1993
- **Urban** campus
- **Coed**
- **Minimally difficult** entrance level

Academics *Calendar:* quarters. *Degrees:* certificates, bachelor's, master's, doctoral, first professional, postbachelor's, and first professional certificates (offers only distance learning degree programs).

Costs (2007–08) *Tuition:* $10,440 full-time, $870 per course part-time.

Financial Aid *Average percent of need met:* 90. *Average financial aid package:* $10,500. *Average indebtedness upon graduation:* $8000.

Applying *Options:* electronic application. *Application fee:* $75.

Application Contact Learner Support, Capella University, 225 South Sixth Street, 9th Floor, Minneapolis, MN 55402. *Phone:* 888-277-3552. *Toll-free phone:* 888-CAPELLA. *Fax:* 612-977-5060. *E-mail:* info@capella.edu.

CARLETON COLLEGE

Northfield, Minnesota **www.carleton.edu/**

- **Independent** 4-year, founded 1866
- **Small-town** 955-acre campus with easy access to Minneapolis–St. Paul
- **Endowment** $663.5 million
- **Coed**
- **Very difficult** entrance level

Faculty *Student/faculty ratio:* 9:1.

Academics *Calendar:* three courses for each of three terms. *Degree:* bachelor's.

Student Life *Campus security:* 24-hour emergency response devices and patrols, student patrols, late-night transport/escort service, controlled dormitory access.

Athletics Member NCAA. All Division III.

Standardized Tests *Required:* SAT or ACT (for admission). *Recommended:* SAT Subject Tests (for admission).

Costs (2008–09) *Comprehensive fee:* $43,269 includes full-time tuition ($37,845), mandatory fees ($201), and room and board ($5223). *College room only:* $4770.

Financial Aid Of all full-time matriculated undergraduates who enrolled in 2006, 1,701 applied for aid, 1,083 were judged to have need, 1,083 had their need fully met. 395 Federal Work-Study jobs (averaging $2551). 1,179 state and other part-time jobs (averaging $2442). In 2006, 160 non-need-based awards were made. *Average percent of need met:* 100. *Average financial aid package:* $29,601. *Average need-based loan:* $4849. *Average need-based gift aid:* $24,326. *Average non-need-based aid:* $3443. *Average indebtedness upon graduation:* $19,185. *Financial aid deadline:* 2/15.

Applying *Options:* electronic application, early admission, early decision, deferred entrance. *Application fee:* $30. *Required:* essay or personal statement, high school transcript, 2 letters of recommendation, common application supplement. *Recommended:* interview.

Freshman Application Contact Carleton College, 100 South College Street, Northfield, MN 55057. *Phone:* 507-222-4190. *Toll-free phone:* 800-995-2275.

See page 1390 for the College Close-Up.

COLLEGE OF SAINT BENEDICT

Saint Joseph, Minnesota **www.csbsju.edu/**

- **Independent Roman Catholic** 4-year, founded 1887
- **Small-town** 315-acre campus with easy access to Minneapolis–St. Paul
- **Endowment** $45.3 million
- **Coed, primarily women** 2,087 undergraduate students, 98% full-time, 100% women
- **Moderately difficult** entrance level, 76% of applicants were admitted

Undergraduates 2,051 full-time, 36 part-time. Students come from 34 states and territories, 20 other countries, 16% are from out of state, 0.8% African American, 3% Asian American or Pacific Islander, 2% Hispanic American, 0.3% Native American, 5% international, 2% transferred in, 82% live on campus. *Retention:* 90% of 2006 full-time freshmen returned.

Freshmen *Admission:* 1,677 applied, 1,271 admitted, 537 enrolled. *Average high school GPA:* 3.75. *Test scores:* SAT critical reading scores over 500: 78%; SAT math scores over 500: 73%; ACT scores over 18: 99%; SAT critical reading scores over 600: 35%; SAT math scores over 600: 38%; ACT scores over 24: 67%; SAT critical reading scores over 700: 12%; SAT math scores over 700: 9%; ACT scores over 30: 11%.

Faculty *Total:* 192, 83% full-time, 73% with terminal degrees. *Student/faculty ratio:* 12:1.

Majors Accounting; art; biochemistry; biological and physical sciences; biology/biological sciences; business administration and management; chemistry; classics and languages, literatures and linguistics; clinical/medical laboratory assistant; computer science; dietetics; dramatic/theater arts; economics; education; elementary education; engineering physics; English; environmental studies; fine/studio arts; foods, nutrition, and wellness; forestry; forest sciences and biology; French; German; history; humanities; liberal arts and sciences/liberal studies; mathematics; mathematics and computer science; music; natural sciences; nursing (registered nurse training); nutrition sciences; occupational therapy; peace studies and conflict resolution; philosophy; physical therapy; physics; political science and government; pre-dentistry studies; pre-law studies; pre-medical studies; pre-pharmacy studies; pre-theology/pre-ministerial studies; pre-veterinary studies; psychology; religious education; secondary education; social sciences; social work; sociology; Spanish; speech and rhetoric; theology; women's studies.

Academics *Calendar:* semesters. *Degrees:* certificates and bachelor's (coordinate with Saint John's University for men). *Special study options:* accelerated degree program, advanced placement credit, double majors, English as a second language, honors programs, independent study, internships, off-campus study, services for LD students, student-designed majors, study abroad. *ROTC:* Army (c). *Unusual degree programs:* 3-2 engineering with University of Minnesota, Twin Cities Campus.

Computers on Campus 643 computers/terminals and 3,000 ports are available on campus for general student use. Students can access the following: computer help desk, free student e-mail accounts, online (class) grades, online (class) registration, online (class) schedules, online student accounts. Campuswide network is available. 100% of college-owned or -operated housing units are wired for high-speed Internet access. Wireless service is available via classrooms, computer centers, computer labs, dorm rooms, learning centers, libraries, student centers.

Student Life *Housing:* on-campus residence required through sophomore year. *Options:* women-only, disabled students. Campus housing is university owned. Freshman campus housing is guaranteed. *Activities and organizations:* drama/theater group, student-run newspaper, radio station, choral group, Joint Events Council, Volunteers in Service to Others, Ballroom Dance Club, Students in Free Enterprise, Magis. *Campus security:* 24-hour emergency response devices and patrols, student patrols, late-night transport/escort service, controlled dormitory access, well-lit pathways. *Student services:* health clinic, personal/psychological counseling, women's center.

Athletics Member NCAA. All Division III. *Intercollegiate sports:* basketball W, crew W (c), cross-country running W, golf W, ice hockey W, lacrosse W (c), riflery W (c), rugby W (c), skiing (cross-country) W, soccer W, softball W, swimming and diving W, tennis W, track and field W, ultimate Frisbee W (c), volleyball W. *Intramural sports:* badminton W, basketball W, football W, golf W (c), racquetball W, rock climbing W (c), skiing (cross-country) W (c), skiing (downhill) W (c), soccer W, softball W, table tennis W, tennis W, volleyball W, water polo W (c).
Standardized Tests *Required:* SAT or ACT (for admission).
Costs (2007–08) *One-time required fee:* $40. *Comprehensive fee:* $33,960 includes full-time tuition ($26,038), mandatory fees ($492), and room and board ($7430). Part-time tuition: $1085 per credit. Part-time tuition and fees vary according to course load. *Required fees:* $246 per term part-time. *College room only:* $3546. Room and board charges vary according to board plan and housing facility. *Payment plans:* tuition prepayment, installment. *Waivers:* employees or children of employees.
Financial Aid Of all full-time matriculated undergraduates who enrolled in 2006, 1,499 applied for aid, 1,300 were judged to have need, 493 had their need fully met. 600 Federal Work-Study jobs (averaging $2000). 300 state and other part-time jobs (averaging $2000). In 2006, 639 non-need-based awards were made. *Average percent of need met:* 86%. *Average financial aid package:* $18,940. *Average need-based loan:* $4548. *Average need-based gift aid:* $13,409. *Average non-need-based aid:* $8992.
Applying *Options:* electronic application, early action, deferred entrance. *Required:* essay or personal statement, high school transcript, 1 letter of recommendation. *Recommended:* minimum 3.0 GPA, interview. *Application deadlines:* rolling (freshmen), rolling (transfers), 11/15 (early action). *Notification:* continuous (freshmen), continuous (transfers), 12/15 (early action).
Freshman Application Contact Ms. Karen Backes, Associate Dean of Admissions, College of Saint Benedict, PO Box 7155, 37 South College Avenue, St. Joseph, MN 56374, Collegeville, MN 56321. *Phone:* 320-363-2196. *Toll-free phone:* 800-544-1489. *Fax:* 320-363-2750. *E-mail:* admissions@csbsju.edu.

COLLEGE OF ST. CATHERINE

St. Paul, Minnesota **www.stkate.edu/**

- **Independent Roman Catholic** comprehensive, founded 1905
- **Urban** 110-acre campus with easy access to Minneapolis
- **Endowment** $48.2 million
- **Undergraduate: women only; graduate: coed**
- **Moderately difficult** entrance level

Faculty *Student/faculty ratio:* 11:1.
Academics *Calendar:* 4-1-4. *Degrees:* certificates, associate, bachelor's, master's, doctoral, and postbachelor's certificates.
Student Life *Campus security:* 24-hour emergency response devices and patrols, student patrols, late-night transport/escort service, controlled dormitory access.
Athletics Member NCAA. All Division III.
Standardized Tests *Required:* SAT or ACT (for admission).
Costs (2007–08) *Comprehensive fee:* $32,710 includes full-time tuition ($25,644), mandatory fees ($278), and room and board ($6788). Full-time tuition and fees vary according to class time. Part-time tuition and fees vary according to class time. *College room only:* $3798. Room and board charges vary according to board plan and housing facility.
Financial Aid Of all full-time matriculated undergraduates who enrolled in 2006, 1,508 applied for aid, 1,313 were judged to have need, 178 had their need fully met. 500 Federal Work-Study jobs. In 2006, 265 non-need-based awards were made. *Average percent of need met:* 72. *Average financial aid package:* $23,534. *Average need-based loan:* $5008. *Average need-based gift aid:* $7322. *Average non-need-based aid:* $15,017. *Average indebtedness upon graduation:* $27,519.
Applying *Options:* deferred entrance. *Required:* high school transcript, 1 letter of recommendation. *Required for some:* essay or personal statement, interview. *Recommended:* interview.
Freshman Application Contact Ms. Cory Piper-Hauswirth, Associate Director of Admission and Financial Aid, College of St. Catherine, 2004 Randolph Avenue, F-02, St. Paul, MN 55105. *Phone:* 651-690-6047. *Toll-free phone:* 800-656-5283. *E-mail:* stkate@stkate.edu.

COLLEGE OF ST. CATHERINE–MINNEAPOLIS

Minneapolis, Minnesota **www.stkate.edu/**

Director of Admissions Mr. Cal Mosley, Assistant to the President for Admission, College of St. Catherine–Minneapolis, 601 25th Avenue South, Minneapolis, MN 55454-1494. *Phone:* 651-690-8600. *Toll-free phone:* 800-945-4599 Ext. 7800. *Fax:* 651-690-8119. *E-mail:* careerinfo@stkate.edu.

THE COLLEGE OF ST. SCHOLASTICA

Duluth, Minnesota **www.css.edu/**

- **Independent** comprehensive, founded 1912, affiliated with Roman Catholic Church
- **Suburban** 186-acre campus
- **Endowment** $27.4 million
- **Coed** 2,538 undergraduate students, 90% full-time, 70% women, 30% men
- **Moderately difficult** entrance level, 88% of applicants were admitted

Undergraduates 2,273 full-time, 265 part-time. Students come from 35 states and territories, 33 other countries, 15% are from out of state, 2% African American, 2% Asian American or Pacific Islander, 1% Hispanic American, 2% Native American, 4% international, 8% transferred in, 51% live on campus. *Retention:* 79% of 2006 full-time freshmen returned.
Freshmen *Admission:* 1,461 applied, 1,288 admitted, 448 enrolled. *Average high school GPA:* 3.49. *Test scores:* SAT critical reading scores over 500: 88%; SAT math scores over 500: 84%; ACT scores over 18: 96%; SAT critical reading scores over 600: 42%; SAT math scores over 600: 46%; ACT scores over 24: 45%; SAT critical reading scores over 700: 8%; SAT math scores over 700: 21%; ACT scores over 30: 5%.
Faculty *Total:* 261, 58% full-time, 44% with terminal degrees. *Student/faculty ratio:* 13:1.
Majors Accounting; American native/native American education; applied economics; biochemistry; biology/biological sciences; business administration and management; chemistry; Christian studies; communication/speech communication and rhetoric; computer and information sciences; education (K-12); elementary education; English; exercise physiology; health information/medical records administration; health services/allied health/health sciences; history; humanities; international business/trade/commerce; international/global studies; journalism; liberal arts and sciences/liberal studies; marketing/marketing management; mathematics; music performance; natural sciences; nursing (registered nurse training); organizational behavior; physical sciences related; psychology; public relations, advertising, and applied communication related; religious studies; school librarian/school library media; social sciences; social work.
Academics *Calendar:* semesters. *Degrees:* certificates, bachelor's, master's, first professional, post-master's, and postbachelor's certificates. *Special study options:* accelerated degree program, adult/continuing education programs, advanced placement credit, distance learning, double majors, external degree program, honors programs, independent study, internships, off-campus study, part-time degree program, services for LD students, student-designed majors, study abroad, summer session for credit. *ROTC:* Air Force (c). *Unusual degree programs:* 3-2 occupational therapy.
Computers on Campus 205 computers/terminals are available on campus for general student use. Students can access the following: campus intranet, computer help desk, free student e-mail accounts, online (class) grades, online (class) registration, online (class) schedules, student account information and transcripts online. Campuswide network is available. 100% of college-owned or -operated housing units are wired for high-speed Internet access. Wireless service is available via classrooms, computer centers, computer labs, dorm rooms, learning centers, libraries, student centers.
Student Life *Housing:* on-campus residence required through sophomore year. *Options:* coed, disabled students. Campus housing is university owned. Freshman campus housing is guaranteed. *Activities and organizations:* drama/theater group, student-run newspaper, television station, choral group, Campus Activity Board (CAB), Inter-Varsity, SOTA, SHIMA, Social Work Club. *Campus security:* 24-hour emergency response devices and patrols, late-night transport/escort service, controlled dormitory access, student door monitor at night. *Student services:* health clinic, personal/psychological counseling.
Athletics Member NCAA, NAIA. All NCAA Division III. *Intercollegiate sports:* baseball M, basketball M/W, cross-country running M/W, football M, ice hockey M, soccer M/W, softball W, tennis M/W, track and field M/W, volleyball W. *Intramural sports:* basketball M/W, football M/W, ice hockey W (c), soccer M/W, tennis M/W, volleyball M/W.

Standardized Tests *Required:* SAT or ACT (for admission).

Costs (2007–08) *Comprehensive fee:* $31,674 includes full-time tuition ($24,840), mandatory fees ($150), and room and board ($6684). Full-time tuition and fees vary according to class time. Part-time tuition: $773 per credit hour. Part-time tuition and fees vary according to class time and course load. *College room only:* $3780. Room and board charges vary according to board plan and housing facility. *Payment plan:* installment. *Waivers:* senior citizens and employees or children of employees.

Financial Aid Of all full-time matriculated undergraduates who enrolled in 2007, 1,647 applied for aid, 1,494 were judged to have need, 192 had their need fully met. 227 Federal Work-Study jobs (averaging $2264). 204 state and other part-time jobs (averaging $2254). In 2007, 147 non-need-based awards were made. *Average percent of need met:* 77%. *Average financial aid package:* $19,592. *Average need-based loan:* $4698. *Average need-based gift aid:* $6122. *Average non-need-based aid:* $8786. *Average indebtedness upon graduation:* $34,032.

Applying *Options:* electronic application, early admission, deferred entrance. *Application fee:* $25. *Required:* high school transcript. *Required for some:* minimum 2.0 GPA, interview. *Recommended:* interview. *Application deadlines:* rolling (freshmen), rolling (transfers). *Notification:* continuous (freshmen), continuous (transfers).

Freshman Application Contact Mr. Brian Dalton, Vice President for Enrollment Management, The College of St. Scholastica, 1200 Kenwood Avenue, Duluth, MN 55811-4199. *Phone:* 218-723-6053. *Toll-free phone:* 800-249-6412. *Fax:* 218-723-5991. *E-mail:* admissions@css.edu.

See page 1392 for the College Close-Up.

COLLEGE OF VISUAL ARTS

St. Paul, Minnesota **www.cva.edu/**

- **Independent** 4-year, founded 1924
- **Urban** 2-acre campus with easy access to Minneapolis
- **Endowment** $701,215
- **Coed** 178 undergraduate students, 96% full-time, 58% women, 42% men
- **Moderately difficult** entrance level, 98% of applicants were admitted

Undergraduates 171 full-time, 7 part-time. Students come from 9 states and territories, 2 other countries, 5% are from out of state, 3% African American, 3% Asian American or Pacific Islander, 2% Hispanic American, 1% Native American, 10% transferred in. *Retention:* 54% of 2006 full-time freshmen returned.

Freshmen *Admission:* 115 applied, 113 admitted, 44 enrolled. *Average high school GPA:* 2.85. *Test scores:* ACT scores over 18: 85%; ACT scores over 24: 7%.

Faculty *Total:* 46, 15% full-time, 15% with terminal degrees. *Student/faculty ratio:* 12:1.

Majors Drawing; fine/studio arts; graphic design; photography; printmaking; sculpture; visual and performing arts related.

Academics *Calendar:* semesters. *Degree:* bachelor's. *Special study options:* academic remediation for entering students, advanced placement credit, double majors, honors programs, independent study, internships, part-time degree program, study abroad, summer session for credit.

Computers on Campus 60 computers/terminals and 70 ports are available on campus for general student use. Students can access the following: campus intranet, free student e-mail accounts, free digital tutor for students. Campuswide network is available.

Student Life *Housing:* college housing not available. *Activities and organizations:* AIGA Student Chapter, Board Gaming Club, Anime Club, OASIS (non-traditional students), Intimate Frisbee. *Campus security:* 24-hour emergency response devices, late-night transport/escort service. *Student services:* personal/psychological counseling.

Standardized Tests *Required:* SAT or ACT (for admission).

Costs (2008–09) *Tuition:* $21,926 full-time, $1100 per credit part-time. *Required fees:* $500 full-time, $50 per course part-time.

Financial Aid Of all full-time matriculated undergraduates who enrolled in 2007, 151 applied for aid, 140 were judged to have need, 9 had their need fully met. 44 Federal Work-Study jobs (averaging $806). 32 state and other part-time jobs (averaging $1920). In 2007, 5 non-need-based awards were made. *Average percent of need met:* 69%. *Average financial aid package:* $10,161. *Average need-based loan:* $4187. *Average need-based gift aid:* $6256. *Average non-need-based aid:* $1000. *Average indebtedness upon graduation:* $46,210. *Financial aid deadline:* 6/1.

Applying *Options:* electronic application, deferred entrance. *Application fee:* $40. *Required:* essay or personal statement, high school transcript, portfolio. *Recommended:* minimum 3.0 GPA, letters of recommendation, interview. *Application deadlines:* rolling (freshmen), rolling (transfers). *Notification:* continuous (freshmen), continuous (transfers).

Freshman Application Contact Mr. Paul Gaines, Director of Student Life, College of Visual Arts, 344 Summit Avenue, St. Paul, MN 55102-2124. *Phone:* 651-224-3416. *Toll-free phone:* 800-224-1536. *Fax:* 651-224-8854. *E-mail:* pgaines@cva.edu.

CONCORDIA COLLEGE

Moorhead, Minnesota **www.concordiacollege.edu/**

- **Independent** comprehensive, founded 1891, affiliated with Evangelical Lutheran Church in America
- **Suburban** 120-acre campus
- **Endowment** $85.1 million
- **Coed** 2,805 undergraduate students, 98% full-time, 61% women, 39% men
- **Moderately difficult** entrance level, 85% of applicants were admitted

Undergraduates 2,748 full-time, 57 part-time. 0.6% African American, 2% Asian American or Pacific Islander, 1% Hispanic American, 0.3% Native American, 4% international, 2% transferred in, 68% live on campus. *Retention:* 80% of 2006 full-time freshmen returned.

Freshmen *Admission:* 2,517 applied, 2,152 admitted, 830 enrolled. *Average high school GPA:* 3.72. *Test scores:* SAT critical reading scores over 500: 89%; SAT math scores over 500: 82%; SAT writing scores over 500: 85%; ACT scores over 18: 99%; SAT critical reading scores over 600: 49%; SAT math scores over 600: 50%; SAT writing scores over 600: 47%; ACT scores over 24: 64%; SAT critical reading scores over 700: 14%; SAT math scores over 700: 14%; SAT writing scores over 700: 10%; ACT scores over 30: 12%.

Faculty *Total:* 263, 72% full-time, 57% with terminal degrees. *Student/faculty ratio:* 15:1.

Majors Accounting; advertising; art; art history, criticism and conservation; art teacher education; biology/biological sciences; biology teacher education; broadcast journalism; business administration and management; business/commerce; business teacher education; chemistry; chemistry teacher education; child development; classics and classical languages related; clinical laboratory science/medical technology; communication/speech communication and rhetoric; computer science; creative writing; dietetics; dramatic/theater arts; economics; education; elementary education; English; English/language arts teacher education; environmental studies; fine/studio arts; foods, nutrition, and wellness; French; French language teacher education; German; German language teacher education; health and physical education; health/health care administration; health teacher education; history; humanities; international business/trade/commerce; international/global studies; journalism; kindergarten/preschool education; kinesiology and exercise science; Latin; mass communication/media; mathematics; mathematics teacher education; music; music performance; music teacher education; music theory and composition; nursing (registered nurse training); philosophy; physical education teaching and coaching; physics; physics teacher education; political science and government; pre-dentistry studies; pre-law studies; pre-medical studies; pre-theology/pre-ministerial studies; pre-veterinary studies; psychology; public relations/image management; radio and television; religious studies; Russian studies; Scandinavian languages; science teacher education; secondary education; social studies teacher education; social work; sociology; Spanish; Spanish language teacher education; speech and rhetoric; voice and opera.

Academics *Calendar:* semesters. *Degrees:* certificates, bachelor's, and master's. *Special study options:* adult/continuing education programs, advanced placement credit, cooperative education, double majors, English as a second language, honors programs, independent study, internships, off-campus study, part-time degree program, services for LD students, study abroad, summer session for credit. *ROTC:* Army (c), Air Force (c). *Unusual degree programs:* 3-2 engineering with North Dakota State University.

Computers on Campus 570 computers/terminals and 87 ports are available on campus for general student use. Students can access the following: computer help desk, free student e-mail accounts, online (class) grades, online (class) schedules, online degree audit. Campuswide network is available. 100% of college-owned or -operated housing units are wired for high-speed Internet access. Wireless service is available via computer centers.

Student Life *Housing:* on-campus residence required through sophomore year. *Options:* coed, men-only, women-only. Campus housing is university owned. Freshman applicants given priority for college housing. *Activities and organizations:* drama/theater group, student-run newspaper, radio and television station, choral group, Campus Service Commission, Habitat for Humanity, Lead Now, language clubs, Campus Ministry Commission. *Campus security:* 24-hour emergency response devices and patrols, student patrols, late-night transport/escort service, well-lit campus, 24-hour locked wing doors. *Student services:* health clinic, personal/psychological counseling, women's center.

Athletics Member NCAA. All Division III. *Intercollegiate sports:* baseball M, basketball M/W, cheerleading W (c), cross-country running M/W, football M, golf M/W, ice hockey M/W, skiing (cross-country) M (c)/W (c), soccer M/W, softball W, swimming and diving W, tennis M/W, track and field M/W, volleyball M (c)/W, wrestling M. *Intramural sports:* badminton M/W, baseball M/W, basketball M/W, bowling M/W, cross-country running M/W, football M/W, golf M/W, ice hockey M/W, racquetball M/W, rugby M/W, skiing (cross-country) M/W, soccer M/W, softball M/W, swimming and diving M/W, table tennis M/W, tennis M/W, track and field M/W, ultimate Frisbee M/W, volleyball M/W, water polo M/W, weight lifting M/W.

Standardized Tests *Required:* SAT or ACT (for admission).

Costs (2008–09) *Comprehensive fee:* $30,280 includes full-time tuition ($23,925), mandatory fees ($195), and room and board ($6160). Part-time tuition: $3760 per course. *College room only:* $2760.

Financial Aid Of all full-time matriculated undergraduates who enrolled in 2006, 2,232 applied for aid, 1,875 were judged to have need, 541 had their need fully met. 452 Federal Work-Study jobs (averaging $1592). 1,034 state and other part-time jobs (averaging $977). In 2006, 768 non-need-based awards were made. *Average percent of need met:* 86%. *Average financial aid package:* $15,899. *Average need-based loan:* $4808. *Average need-based gift aid:* $10,465. *Average non-need-based aid:* $10,705. *Average indebtedness upon graduation:* $27,896.

Applying *Options:* electronic application, early admission, deferred entrance. *Application fee:* $20. *Required:* high school transcript, 2 letters of recommendation, references. *Application deadlines:* rolling (freshmen), rolling (transfers).

Freshman Application Contact Mr. Scott E. Ellingson, Director of Admissions, Concordia College, 901 8th Street South, Moorhead, MN 56562. *Phone:* 218-299-3004. *Toll-free phone:* 800-699-9897. *E-mail:* admissions@cord.edu.

CONCORDIA UNIVERSITY, ST. PAUL

St. Paul, Minnesota **www.csp.edu/**

- **Independent** comprehensive, founded 1893, affiliated with Lutheran Church–Missouri Synod
- **Urban** 37-acre campus
- **Endowment** $24.2 million
- **Coed** 1,627 undergraduate students, 84% full-time, 60% women, 40% men
- **Minimally difficult** entrance level, 57% of applicants were admitted

Undergraduates 1,361 full-time, 266 part-time. Students come from 41 states and territories, 5 other countries, 24% are from out of state, 9% African American, 6% Asian American or Pacific Islander, 1% Hispanic American, 0.5% Native American, 0.6% international, 5% transferred in, 25% live on campus. *Retention:* 71% of 2006 full-time freshmen returned.

Freshmen *Admission:* 963 applied, 550 admitted, 201 enrolled. *Average high school GPA:* 3.20. *Test scores:* ACT scores over 18: 82%; ACT scores over 24: 28%; ACT scores over 30: 2%.

Faculty *Total:* 260, 30% full-time, 37% with terminal degrees. *Student/faculty ratio:* 12:1.

Majors Accounting; art teacher education; biology/biological sciences; biology teacher education; business administration and management; chemistry teacher education; child development; computer/information technology services administration related; criminal justice/safety; dramatic/theater arts; early childhood education; education; education related; elementary education; English; English as a second/foreign language (teaching); finance; fine/studio arts; general studies; health teacher education; history; human development and family studies; human resources management; human services; kinesiology and exercise science; marketing/marketing management; mass communication/media; mathematics; mathematics teacher education; middle school education; missionary studies and missiology; music; music teacher education; physical education teaching and coaching; psychology; religious education; religious/sacred music; secondary education; social studies teacher education; sociology; theology.

Academics *Calendar:* semesters. *Degrees:* certificates, associate, bachelor's, master's, and postbachelor's certificates. *Special study options:* academic remediation for entering students, accelerated degree program, adult/continuing education programs, advanced placement credit, distance learning, double majors, honors programs, independent study, internships, off-campus study, part-time degree program, services for LD students, student-designed majors, study abroad, summer session for credit. *ROTC:* Army (c), Navy (c), Air Force (c).

Computers on Campus Students can access the following: campus intranet, computer help desk, free student e-mail accounts, online (class) grades, online (class) registration, online (class) schedules. Campuswide network is available. Wireless service is available via entire campus.

Student Life *Housing options:* coed, men-only, women-only, disabled students. Campus housing is university owned. Freshman campus housing is guaranteed. *Activities and organizations:* drama/theater group, student-run newspaper, television station, choral group. *Campus security:* 24-hour emergency response devices and patrols, student patrols, late-night transport/escort service, controlled dormitory access. *Student services:* health clinic, personal/psychological counseling.

Athletics Member NCAA. All Division II. *Intercollegiate sports:* baseball M (s), basketball M (s)/W (s), cross-country running M (s)/W (s), football M (s), golf M (s)/W (s), soccer W (s), softball W (s), track and field M (s)/W (s), volleyball W (s). *Intramural sports:* basketball M/W, football M/W, lacrosse W, racquetball M/W, softball M/W, volleyball M/W.

Standardized Tests *Required:* ACT (for admission).

Costs (2008–09) *Comprehensive fee:* $31,800 includes full-time tuition ($24,900) and room and board ($6900). Part-time tuition: $520 per credit.

Financial Aid Of all full-time matriculated undergraduates who enrolled in 2007, 1,134 applied for aid, 986 were judged to have need, 141 had their need fully met. 144 Federal Work-Study jobs (averaging $1590). 270 state and other part-time jobs (averaging $1662). In 2007, 104 non-need-based awards were made. *Average percent of need met:* 65%. *Average financial aid package:* $13,757. *Average need-based loan:* $4488. *Average need-based gift aid:* $11,366. *Average non-need-based aid:* $5572. *Average indebtedness upon graduation:* $27,548.

Applying *Options:* electronic application, early admission, deferred entrance. *Application fee:* $30. *Required:* high school transcript, 2 letters of recommendation. *Required for some:* essay or personal statement. *Recommended:* minimum 2.0 GPA. *Application deadlines:* 8/1 (freshmen), 8/1 (transfers). *Notification:* continuous (freshmen), continuous (transfers).

Freshman Application Contact Kristin Schoon, Director of Undergraduate Admission, Concordia University, St. Paul, 275 Syndicate North, St. Paul, MN 55104-5494. *Phone:* 651-641-8230. *Toll-free phone:* 800-333-4705. *Fax:* 651-603-6320. *E-mail:* admission@csp.edu.

CROSSROADS COLLEGE

Rochester, Minnesota **www.crossroadscollege.edu/**

- **Independent** 4-year, founded 1913, affiliated with Christian Churches and Churches of Christ
- **Urban** 40-acre campus with easy access to Minneapolis–St. Paul
- **Endowment** $770,019
- **Coed** 184 undergraduate students, 81% full-time, 52% women, 48% men
- **Noncompetitive** entrance level

Undergraduates 149 full-time, 35 part-time. Students come from 11 states and territories, 2 other countries, 30% are from out of state, 8% African American, 3% Asian American or Pacific Islander, 1% Hispanic American, 1% international, 8% transferred in, 74% live on campus. *Retention:* 58% of 2006 full-time freshmen returned.

Freshmen *Admission:* 39 enrolled. *Average high school GPA:* 3.09. *Test scores:* ACT scores over 18: 72%; ACT scores over 24: 24%.

Faculty *Total:* 31, 23% full-time, 23% with terminal degrees. *Student/faculty ratio:* 9:1.

Majors Biblical studies; business administration and management; business administration, management and operations related; counseling psychology; liberal arts and sciences/liberal studies; missionary studies and missiology; music; pre-theology/pre-ministerial studies; religious education; religious/sacred music; theology; theology and religious vocations related; youth ministry.

Academics *Calendar:* semesters. *Degrees:* associate and bachelor's. *Special study options:* academic remediation for entering students, adult/continuing education programs, advanced placement credit, double majors, external degree program, independent study, internships, student-designed majors.

Computers on Campus 15 computers/terminals are available on campus for general student use. Students can access the following: campus intranet, computer help desk, free student e-mail accounts. Campuswide network is available. 80% of college-owned or -operated housing units are wired for high-speed Internet access. Wireless service is available via dorm rooms, student centers.

Student Life *Housing:* on-campus residence required through sophomore year. *Options:* men-only, women-only, disabled students. Campus housing is university owned. Freshman campus housing is guaranteed. *Activities and organizations:* drama/theater group, student-run newspaper, choral group, Musical Outreach, Ambassadors Mission Group. *Campus security:* student patrols, late-night transport/escort service. *Student services:* personal/psychological counseling.

Athletics *Intercollegiate sports:* baseball M, basketball M/W, golf M/W, softball W, tennis M/W, volleyball M/W. *Intramural sports:* basketball M/W, field hockey M/W, football M/W, golf M/W, racquetball M/W, skiing (cross-country)

COLLEGE DATA CENTER • MINNESOTA

M/W, soccer M, softball M, swimming and diving M/W, table tennis M/W, tennis M/W, volleyball M/W, weight lifting M/W.

Standardized Tests *Required:* SAT or ACT (for admission).

Costs (2008–09) *Tuition:* $12,850 full-time, $375 per semester hour part-time. *Required fees:* $360 full-time, $50 per semester part-time. *Room only:* $3900.

Financial Aid Of all full-time matriculated undergraduates who enrolled in 2007, 182 applied for aid, 131 were judged to have need, 8 had their need fully met. 16 Federal Work-Study jobs (averaging $1450). 9 state and other part-time jobs (averaging $3500). In 2007, 22 non-need-based awards were made. *Average percent of need met:* 67%. *Average financial aid package:* $4120. *Average need-based loan:* $4800. *Average need-based gift aid:* $5820. *Average non-need-based aid:* $2850. *Average indebtedness upon graduation:* $14,941.

Applying *Options:* deferred entrance. *Application fee:* $30. *Required:* essay or personal statement, high school transcript, 3 letters of recommendation. *Recommended:* interview. *Application deadlines:* 8/15 (freshmen), 8/15 (transfers). *Notification:* continuous until 9/1 (freshmen), continuous until 9/1 (transfers).

Freshman Application Contact Mr. Scott Klaehn, Director of Admissions, Crossroads College, 920 Mayowood Road, SW, Rochester, MN 55902-2382. *Phone:* 507-288-4563 Ext. 304. *Toll-free phone:* 800-456-7651. *Fax:* 507-288-9046. *E-mail:* admissions@crossroadscollege.edu.

CROWN COLLEGE

St. Bonifacius, Minnesota **www.crown.edu/**

- **Independent** comprehensive, founded 1916, affiliated with The Christian and Missionary Alliance
- **Suburban** 215-acre campus with easy access to Minneapolis–St. Paul
- **Endowment** $6.7 million
- **Coed** 1,139 undergraduate students, 62% full-time, 62% women, 38% men
- **Minimally difficult** entrance level, 38% of applicants were admitted

Undergraduates 711 full-time, 428 part-time. Students come from 41 states and territories, 4 other countries, 29% are from out of state, 2% African American, 6% Asian American or Pacific Islander, 1% Hispanic American, 0.2% Native American, 0.1% international, 4% transferred in, 48% live on campus. *Retention:* 64% of 2006 full-time freshmen returned.

Freshmen *Admission:* 420 applied, 161 admitted, 142 enrolled. *Average high school GPA:* 3.23. *Test scores:* SAT critical reading scores over 500: 74%; SAT math scores over 500: 74%; ACT scores over 18: 87%; SAT critical reading scores over 600: 37%; SAT math scores over 600: 26%; ACT scores over 24: 33%; SAT critical reading scores over 700: 5%; ACT scores over 30: 1%.

Faculty *Total:* 159, 23% full-time, 28% with terminal degrees. *Student/faculty ratio:* 19:1.

Majors Biological and physical sciences; business/commerce; Christian studies; communication and media related; divinity/ministry; elementary education; English; English/language arts teacher education; history; history teacher education; linguistics; missionary studies and missiology; music teacher education; nursing (registered nurse training); pastoral studies/counseling; physical education teaching and coaching; pre-law studies; religious education; social sciences; social studies teacher education; sport and fitness administration/management; theology.

Academics *Calendar:* semesters. *Degrees:* certificates, associate, bachelor's, and master's. *Special study options:* academic remediation for entering students, accelerated degree program, adult/continuing education programs, advanced placement credit, distance learning, double majors, English as a second language, honors programs, independent study, internships, part-time degree program, services for LD students, study abroad, summer session for credit.

Computers on Campus 95 computers/terminals are available on campus for general student use. Students can access the following: campus intranet, computer help desk, free student e-mail accounts, online (class) grades, online (class) registration, online (class) schedules. Campuswide network is available. 95% of college-owned or -operated housing units are wired for high-speed Internet access. Wireless service is available via classrooms, computer labs, libraries, student centers.

Student Life *Housing:* on-campus residence required through senior year. *Options:* men-only, women-only. Campus housing is university owned. Freshman campus housing is guaranteed. *Activities and organizations:* drama/theater group, student-run newspaper, choral group, Global Impact Team, Hmong Student Fellowship, Married Student Fellowship, Senate/Student Services Board, newspaper/yearbook staff. *Campus security:* 24-hour emergency response devices, late-night transport/escort service, controlled dormitory access. *Student services:* health clinic, personal/psychological counseling.

Athletics Member NCAA, NCCAA. All NCAA Division III. *Intercollegiate sports:* baseball M, basketball M/W, cross-country running M/W, football M, golf M/W, soccer M/W, softball W, track and field M/W, volleyball W. *Intramural sports:* basketball M/W, football M, volleyball M/W.

Standardized Tests *Required:* SAT or ACT (for admission).

Costs (2008–09) *Comprehensive fee:* $26,564 includes full-time tuition ($19,198) and room and board ($7366). Part-time tuition: $777 per credit. *College room only:* $3834.

Financial Aid Of all full-time matriculated undergraduates who enrolled in 2006, 560 applied for aid, 500 were judged to have need, 41 had their need fully met. 178 Federal Work-Study jobs (averaging $2255). 12 state and other part-time jobs (averaging $3697). In 2006, 50 non-need-based awards were made. *Average percent of need met:* 61%. *Average financial aid package:* $12,720. *Average need-based loan:* $4448. *Average need-based gift aid:* $5063. *Average non-need-based aid:* $3969. *Average indebtedness upon graduation:* $30,444. *Financial aid deadline:* 8/1.

Applying *Options:* electronic application, early admission, deferred entrance. *Application fee:* $35. *Required:* essay or personal statement, high school transcript, minimum 2.0 GPA, 2 letters of recommendation, minimum test scores for ACT 18; for SAT 870. *Required for some:* interview. *Application deadlines:* rolling (freshmen), rolling (transfers). *Notification:* continuous (transfers).

Freshman Application Contact Ms. Jill Pautz, Director of Admissions, Crown College, 8700 College View Drive, St. Bonifacius, MN 55375-9001. *Phone:* 952-446-4144. *Toll-free phone:* 800-68-CROWN. *Fax:* 952-446-4149. *E-mail:* info@crown.edu.

DEVRY UNIVERSITY

Edina, Minnesota **www.devry.edu/**

- **Proprietary** comprehensive
- **Coed** 162 undergraduate students, 40% full-time, 39% women, 61% men

Undergraduates 64 full-time, 98 part-time. 6% are from out of state, 10% African American, 5% Asian American or Pacific Islander, 4% Hispanic American, 0.6% Native American, 25% transferred in. *Retention:* 33% of 2006 full-time freshmen returned.

Freshmen *Admission:* 24 enrolled.

Faculty *Total:* 1, 100% full-time. *Student/faculty ratio:* 120:1.

Majors Accounting; business administration and management; business administration, management and operations related; computer software engineering; computer systems analysis; computer systems networking and telecommunications; health information/medical records technology; web page, digital/multimedia and information resources design.

Academics *Degrees:* associate, bachelor's, master's, and postbachelor's certificates. *Special study options:* accelerated degree program, distance learning.

Costs (2008–09) *Tuition:* $13,810 full-time, $515 per credit part-time. *Required fees:* $80 full-time.

Applying *Options:* electronic application, early admission, deferred entrance. *Application fee:* $50. *Required:* high school transcript, interview. *Application deadlines:* rolling (freshmen), rolling (transfers). *Notification:* continuous (freshmen), continuous (transfers).

Director of Admissions Admissions Office, DeVry University, 7700 France Avenue South, Suite 575, Edina, MN 55435-5876.

GLOBE COLLEGE

Oakdale, Minnesota **www.globecollege.com/**

Freshman Application Contact Ms. Christina Hilipipre, Director of Admissions, Globe College, 7166 10th Street North, Oakdale, MN 55128. *Phone:* 651-730-5100. *Fax:* 651-730-5151. *E-mail:* admissions@globecollege.edu.

GUSTAVUS ADOLPHUS COLLEGE

St. Peter, Minnesota **www.gustavus.edu/**

- **Independent** 4-year, founded 1862, affiliated with Evangelical Lutheran Church in America
- **Small-town** 340-acre campus with easy access to Minneapolis–St. Paul
- **Endowment** $115.0 million
- **Coed** 2,628 undergraduate students, 98% full-time, 57% women, 43% men
- **Very difficult** entrance level, 80% of applicants were admitted

Undergraduates 2,582 full-time, 46 part-time. Students come from 38 states and territories, 17 other countries, 18% are from out of state, 2% African American, 4% Asian American or Pacific Islander, 2% Hispanic American, 0.2% Native American, 1% international, 2% transferred in, 77% live on campus. *Retention:* 90% of 2006 full-time freshmen returned.

Freshmen *Admission:* 2,208 applied, 1,759 admitted, 670 enrolled. *Average high school GPA:* 3.64. *Test scores:* SAT math scores over 500: 94%; ACT scores over 18: 100%; SAT math scores over 600: 70%; ACT scores over 24: 81%; SAT math scores over 700: 18%; ACT scores over 30: 18%.

Faculty *Total:* 250, 72% full-time, 72% with terminal degrees. *Student/faculty ratio:* 13:1.

Majors Accounting; anthropology; art; art history, criticism and conservation; art teacher education; athletic training; biochemistry; biology/biological sciences; biology teacher education; business administration and management; business/managerial economics; chemistry; chemistry teacher education; classics and languages, literatures and linguistics; computer science; criminal justice/law enforcement administration; dance; dramatic/theater arts; economics; education; elementary education; English; environmental studies; French; geography; geology/earth science; German; health and physical education related; health teacher education; history; interdisciplinary studies; international business/trade/commerce; Japanese; Japanese studies; Latin American studies; mass communication/media; mathematics; mathematics teacher education; music; music teacher education; nursing (registered nurse training); philosophy; physical education teaching and coaching; physical therapy; physics; physics teacher education; political science and government; pre-dentistry studies; pre-law studies; pre-medical studies; pre-veterinary studies; psychology; religious/sacred music; religious studies; Russian; Russian studies; Scandinavian languages; Scandinavian studies; secondary education; social sciences; social studies teacher education; sociology; Spanish; speech and rhetoric.

Academics *Calendar:* 4-1-4. *Degree:* bachelor's. *Special study options:* accelerated degree program, advanced placement credit, cooperative education, double majors, honors programs, independent study, internships, off-campus study, services for LD students, student-designed majors, study abroad, summer session for credit. *ROTC:* Army (c). *Unusual degree programs:* 3-2 engineering with Minnesota State University, Mankato; University of Minnesota; social work; environmental studies with Duke University.

Computers on Campus 440 computers/terminals and 5,000 ports are available on campus for general student use. Students can access the following: computer help desk, free student e-mail accounts, online (class) grades, online (class) registration, online (class) schedules. Campuswide network is available. 100% of college-owned or -operated housing units are wired for high-speed Internet access. Wireless service is available via entire campus.

Student Life *Housing:* on-campus residence required through sophomore year. *Options:* coed. Campus housing is university owned. Freshman campus housing is guaranteed. *Activities and organizations:* drama/theater group, student-run newspaper, radio and television station, choral group, Proclaim, Big Partner/Little Partner, Study Buddies, I am..We are, Pound Pals, national fraternities, national sororities. *Campus security:* 24-hour emergency response devices and patrols, late-night transport/escort service, controlled dormitory access. *Student services:* health clinic, personal/psychological counseling, women's center.

Athletics Member NCAA. All Division III. *Intercollegiate sports:* baseball M, basketball M/W, cross-country running M/W, football M, golf M/W, gymnastics W, ice hockey M/W, lacrosse M (c), rugby M (c)/W (c), skiing (cross-country) M/W, soccer M/W, softball W, swimming and diving M/W, tennis M/W, track and field M/W, ultimate Frisbee M (c)/W (c), volleyball M (c)/W. *Intramural sports:* badminton M/W, basketball M/W, football M, golf M/W, ice hockey M/W, racquetball M/W, rugby M/W, skiing (cross-country) M/W, skiing (downhill) M/W, soccer M/W, softball M/W, swimming and diving M/W, tennis M/W, track and field M/W, ultimate Frisbee M/W, volleyball M/W, water polo M/W, weight lifting M/W.

Standardized Tests *Recommended:* SAT or ACT (for admission).

Costs (2007–08) *Comprehensive fee:* $35,290 includes full-time tuition ($28,125), mandatory fees ($390), and room and board ($6775). Part-time tuition: $3840 per course. *College room only:* $3775.

Financial Aid Of all full-time matriculated undergraduates who enrolled in 2005, 1,976 applied for aid, 1,639 were judged to have need. 1,000 Federal Work-Study jobs (averaging $1200). 516 state and other part-time jobs (averaging $1000). In 2005, 730 non-need-based awards were made. *Average percent of need met:* 89%. *Average financial aid package:* $18,100. *Average need-based loan:* $4900. *Average need-based gift aid:* $14,100. *Average non-need-based aid:* $6000. *Average indebtedness upon graduation:* $21,300. *Financial aid deadline:* 4/1.

Applying *Options:* electronic application, early admission, early action, deferred entrance. *Required:* essay or personal statement, high school transcript, 2 letters of recommendation. *Recommended:* interview. *Application deadlines:* 4/1 (freshmen), 4/1 (transfers), 11/1 (early action). *Notification:* continuous until 5/1 (freshmen), 5/1 (transfers), 11/20 (early action).

Freshman Application Contact Mr. Mark Anderson, Vice President for Admission and Student Financial Aid, Gustavus Adolphus College, 800 West College Avenue, St. Peter, MN 56082-1498. *Phone:* 507-933-7676. *Toll-free phone:* 800-GUSTAVU (S). *Fax:* 507-933-7474. *E-mail:* admission@gac.edu.

HAMLINE UNIVERSITY

St. Paul, Minnesota **www.hamline.edu/**

- **Independent** comprehensive, founded 1854, affiliated with United Methodist Church
- **Urban** 50-acre campus
- **Endowment** $80.2 million
- **Coed** 2,100 undergraduate students, 94% full-time, 59% women, 41% men
- **Moderately difficult** entrance level, 78% of applicants were admitted

Undergraduates 1,981 full-time, 119 part-time. Students come from 31 states and territories, 41 other countries, 5% African American, 6% Asian American or Pacific Islander, 2% Hispanic American, 0.6% Native American, 3% international. *Retention:* 82% of 2006 full-time freshmen returned.

Freshmen *Admission:* 2,018 applied, 1,570 admitted, 458 enrolled. *Average high school GPA:* 3.4. *Test scores:* SAT critical reading scores over 500: 79%; SAT math scores over 500: 83%; SAT writing scores over 500: 81%; ACT scores over 18: 94%; SAT critical reading scores over 600: 48%; SAT math scores over 600: 56%; SAT writing scores over 600: 31%; ACT scores over 24: 52%; SAT critical reading scores over 700: 19%; SAT math scores over 700: 11%; SAT writing scores over 700: 10%; ACT scores over 30: 10%.

Faculty *Total:* 480, 36% full-time, 56% with terminal degrees. *Student/faculty ratio:* 14:1.

Majors Anthropology; art; art history, criticism and conservation; Asian studies; Asian studies (East); athletic training; biochemistry; biology/biological sciences; business administration and management; chemistry; criminal justice/law enforcement administration; dramatic/theater arts; economics; education; education (K-12); elementary education; English; environmental studies; European studies; European studies (Central and Eastern); fine/studio arts; French; German; health and physical education; health teacher education; history; international business/trade/commerce; international economics; international relations and affairs; Jewish/Judaic studies; kinesiology and exercise science; Latin American studies; legal assistant/paralegal; legal studies; mass communication/media; mathematics; music; music teacher education; occupational therapy; peace studies and conflict resolution; philosophy; physical education teaching and coaching; physical therapy; physics; political science and government; pre-dentistry studies; pre-law studies; pre-medical studies; pre-veterinary studies; psychology; public administration; religious studies; Russian studies; science teacher education; secondary education; social sciences; sociology; Spanish; speech/theater education; urban studies/affairs; women's studies.

Academics *Calendar:* 4-1-4. *Degrees:* bachelor's, master's, doctoral, first professional, and postbachelor's certificates. *Special study options:* academic remediation for entering students, adult/continuing education programs, advanced placement credit, double majors, English as a second language, honors programs, independent study, internships, off-campus study, part-time degree program, services for LD students, student-designed majors, study abroad, summer session for credit. *ROTC:* Air Force (c). *Unusual degree programs:* 3-2 engineering with University of Minnesota, Washington University in St. Louis.

Computers on Campus 150 computers/terminals are available on campus for general student use. Students can access the following: computer help desk, free student e-mail accounts, online (class) grades, online (class) registration, online (class) schedules. Campuswide network is available. 100% of college-owned or -operated housing units are wired for high-speed Internet access.

Student Life *Housing options:* coed. Campus housing is university owned. Freshman campus housing is guaranteed. *Activities and organizations:* drama/theater group, student-run newspaper, radio and television station, choral group, Student Congress (HUSC), Hand in Hand elementary school mentoring program, Minnesota Public Interest Research Group, residential hall councils, Where's the Fun even planning group, national fraternities, national sororities. *Campus security:* 24-hour emergency response devices and patrols, student patrols, late-night transport/escort service, controlled dormitory access. *Student services:* health clinic, personal/psychological counseling, women's center.

Athletics Member NCAA. All Division III. *Intercollegiate sports:* baseball M, basketball M/W, cross-country running M/W, football M, gymnastics W, ice hockey M/W, lacrosse W (c), soccer M/W, softball W, swimming and diving M/W, tennis M/W, track and field M/W, volleyball W. *Intramural sports:* basketball M/W, bowling M/W, football M/W, golf M/W, rock climbing M (c)/W (c), ultimate Frisbee M (c)/W (c), volleyball M/W.

Standardized Tests *Required:* SAT or ACT (for admission).

Costs (2007–08) *One-time required fee:* $190. *Comprehensive fee:* $33,925 includes full-time tuition ($26,060), mandatory fees ($473), and room and board ($7392). Full-time tuition and fees vary according to student level. Part-time tuition: $814 per credit. Part-time tuition and fees vary according to course load and student level. *College room only:* $3832. Room and board charges vary according to board plan and housing facility. *Payment plan:* installment. *Waivers:* employees or children of employees.

Financial Aid Of all full-time matriculated undergraduates who enrolled in 2006, 1,528 applied for aid, 1,349 were judged to have need, 286 had their need fully met. In 2006, 420 non-need-based awards were made. *Average percent of need met:* 80%. *Average financial aid package:* $18,598. *Average need-based loan:* $4425. *Average need-based gift aid:* $12,591. *Average non-need-based aid:* $7908. *Average indebtedness upon graduation:* $30,518.

Applying *Options:* electronic application, early admission, early action, deferred entrance. *Required:* essay or personal statement, high school transcript, 2 letters of recommendation. *Recommended:* interview, activity resume. *Application deadlines:* rolling (freshmen), rolling (transfers), 12/1 (early action). *Notification:* continuous until 12/20 (freshmen), continuous (transfers), 12/20 (early action).

Freshman Application Contact Ms. Ann Kjorstad, Director of Undergraduate Admission, Hamline University, 1536 Hewitt Avenue C1930, St. Paul, MN 55104-1284. *Phone:* 651-523-2207. *Toll-free phone:* 800-753-9753. *Fax:* 651-523-2458. *E-mail:* cla-admis@hamline.edu.

HERZING COLLEGE

Minneapolis, Minnesota **www.herzing.edu/**

- **Proprietary** primarily 2-year, founded 1961, part of Herzing College
- **Suburban** 1-acre campus
- **Coed, primarily women**
- **Moderately difficult** entrance level

Faculty *Student/faculty ratio:* 14:1.

Academics *Calendar:* semesters. *Degrees:* certificates, diplomas, associate, and bachelor's.

Student Life *Campus security:* 24-hour emergency response devices.

Standardized Tests *Required:* ACCUPLACER (for admission).

Costs (2007–08) *Tuition:* $13,186 full-time, $440 per credit part-time. *Required fees:* $25 full-time.

Applying *Required:* high school transcript, interview.

Freshman Application Contact Ms. Shelly Larson, Director of Admissions, Herzing College, 5700 West Broadway, Minneapolis, MN 55428. *Phone:* 763-231-3155. *Toll-free phone:* 800-878-DRAW. *Fax:* 763-535-9205. *E-mail:* info@mpls.herzing.edu.

ITT TECHNICAL INSTITUTE

Eden Prairie, Minnesota **www.itt-tech.edu/**

- **Proprietary** primarily 2-year, founded 2003, part of ITT Educational Services, Inc
- **Coed**

Academics *Calendar:* quarters. *Degrees:* associate and bachelor's.

Standardized Tests *Required:* Wonderlic aptitude test (for admission).

Applying *Application fee:* $100. *Required:* high school transcript, interview. *Recommended:* letters of recommendation.

Freshman Application Contact Mr. Paul Rozeski, ITT Technical Institute, 8911 Columbine Road, Eden Prairie, MN 55347. *Phone:* 952-914-5300. *Toll-free phone:* 888-488-9646.

MACALESTER COLLEGE

St. Paul, Minnesota **www.macalester.edu/**

- **Independent Presbyterian** 4-year, founded 1874
- **Urban** 53-acre campus
- **Endowment** $676.0 million
- **Coed** 1,920 undergraduate students, 98% full-time, 58% women, 42% men
- **Very difficult** entrance level, 41% of applicants were admitted

Undergraduates 1,873 full-time, 47 part-time. Students come from 53 states and territories, 87 other countries, 78% are from out of state, 5% African American, 9% Asian American or Pacific Islander, 4% Hispanic American, 0.9% Native American, 12% international, 1% transferred in, 67% live on campus. *Retention:* 94% of 2006 full-time freshmen returned.

Freshmen *Admission:* 4,967 applied, 2,015 admitted, 485 enrolled. *Test scores:* SAT critical reading scores over 500: 98%; SAT math scores over 500: 97%; SAT writing scores over 500: 97%; ACT scores over 18: 100%; SAT critical reading scores over 600: 87%; SAT math scores over 600: 85%; SAT writing scores over 600: 83%; ACT scores over 24: 96%; SAT critical reading scores over 700: 47%; SAT math scores over 700: 31%; SAT writing scores over 700: 37%; ACT scores over 30: 55%.

Faculty *Total:* 212, 74% full-time, 85% with terminal degrees. *Student/faculty ratio:* 10:1.

Majors Anthropology; art history, criticism and conservation; Asian studies; biology/biological sciences; chemistry; classics and languages, literatures and linguistics; communication/speech communication and rhetoric; computer science; dramatic/theater arts; economics; English; environmental studies; fine/studio arts; French; geography; geology/earth science; German; history; humanities; intercultural/multicultural and diversity studies; international/global studies; Japanese; Latin American studies; linguistics; mathematics; music; neuroscience; philosophy; physics; political science and government; psychology; religious studies; Russian studies; sociology; Spanish; women's studies.

Academics *Calendar:* semesters. *Degree:* bachelor's. *Special study options:* double majors, honors programs, independent study, internships, off-campus study, part-time degree program, student-designed majors, study abroad. *ROTC:* Navy (c), Air Force (c). *Unusual degree programs:* 3-2 engineering with Washington University in St. Louis, University of Minnesota; nursing with Rush University; architecture with Washington University in St. Louis.

Computers on Campus 400 computers/terminals and 2,500 ports are available on campus for general student use. Students can access the following: campus intranet, computer help desk, free student e-mail accounts, online (class) registration, online (class) schedules, Web space. Campuswide network is available. 100% of college-owned or -operated housing units are wired for high-speed Internet access. Wireless service is available via entire campus.

Student Life *Housing:* on-campus residence required through sophomore year. *Options:* coed, men-only, women-only, cooperative. Campus housing is university owned. Freshman campus housing is guaranteed. *Activities and organizations:* drama/theater group, student-run newspaper, radio station, choral group, Community Service Organization, Student Publications, Multicultural Organization, International Organization, Outing Club. *Campus security:* 24-hour emergency response devices and patrols, late-night transport/escort service, controlled dormitory access. *Student services:* health clinic, personal/psychological counseling.

Athletics Member NCAA. All Division III. *Intercollegiate sports:* baseball M, basketball M/W, crew M (c)/W (c), cross-country running M/W, fencing M (c)/W (c), football M, golf M/W, ice hockey M (c)/W (c), rugby M (c)/W (c), skiing (cross-country) M (c)/W (c), soccer M/W, softball W, swimming and diving M/W, tennis M/W, track and field M/W, ultimate Frisbee M (c)/W (c), volleyball M (c)/W, water polo M (c)/W. *Intramural sports:* badminton M/W, basketball M/W, bowling M/W, football M/W, racquetball M/W, soccer M/W, softball M/W, table tennis M/W, tennis M/W, ultimate Frisbee M/W, volleyball M/W, water polo M/W.

Standardized Tests *Required:* SAT or ACT (for admission).

Costs (2008–09) *Comprehensive fee:* $43,176 includes full-time tuition ($34,504), mandatory fees ($200), and room and board ($8472). Part-time tuition: $1135 per semester hour. *College room only:* $4508.

Financial Aid Of all full-time matriculated undergraduates who enrolled in 2005, 1,311 applied for aid, 1,259 were judged to have need, 1,259 had their need fully met. 315 Federal Work-Study jobs (averaging $1591). 936 state and other part-time jobs (averaging $2026). In 2005, 107 non-need-based awards were made. *Average percent of need met:* 100%. *Average financial aid package:* $25,238. *Average need-based loan:* $3627. *Average need-based gift aid:* $19,806. *Average non-need-based aid:* $4686. *Average indebtedness upon graduation:* $14,889.

Applying *Options:* electronic application, early admission, early decision, deferred entrance. *Application fee:* $40. *Required:* essay or personal statement, high school transcript, 3 letters of recommendation. *Recommended:* interview. *Application deadlines:* 1/15 (freshmen), 4/15 (transfers). *Early decision deadline:* 11/15 (for plan 1), 1/2 (for plan 2). *Notification:* 4/1 (freshmen), 5/15 (transfers), 12/15 (early decision plan 1), 2/7 (early decision plan 2).

Freshman Application Contact Mr. Lorne T. Robinson, Dean of Admissions and Financial Aid, Macalester College, 1600 Grand Avenue, St. Paul, MN 55105-1899. *Phone:* 651-696-6357. *Toll-free phone:* 800-231-7974. *Fax:* 651-696-6724. *E-mail:* admissions@macalester.edu.

MARTIN LUTHER COLLEGE

New Ulm, Minnesota **www.mlc-wels.edu/**

- **Independent** 4-year, founded 1995, affiliated with Wisconsin Evangelical Lutheran Synod
- **Small-town** 50-acre campus
- **Coed**
- **Moderately difficult** entrance level

Faculty *Student/faculty ratio:* 14:1.

Academics *Calendar:* semesters. *Degree:* bachelor's.

Student Life *Campus security:* 24-hour emergency response devices, student patrols, controlled dormitory access.

Athletics Member NCAA, NAIA. All NCAA Division III.

Standardized Tests *Required:* ACT (for admission).

Costs (2007–08) *Comprehensive fee:* $13,675 includes full-time tuition ($9850) and room and board ($3825). Part-time tuition: $200 per credit hour.

Financial Aid Of all full-time matriculated undergraduates who enrolled in 2005, 727 applied for aid, 622 were judged to have need, 264 had their need fully met. In 2005, 33 non-need-based awards were made. *Average percent of need met:* 87. *Average financial aid package:* $7789. *Average need-based loan:* $2379. *Average need-based gift aid:* $3209. *Average non-need-based aid:* $555. *Average indebtedness upon graduation:* $15,315. *Financial aid deadline:* 4/15.

Applying *Options:* deferred entrance. *Application fee:* $25. *Required:* high school transcript, minimum 2.0 GPA, letters of recommendation.

Freshman Application Contact Prof. Ronald B. Brutlag, Associate Director of Admissions, Martin Luther College, 1995 Luther Court, New Ulm, MN 56073. *Phone:* 507-354-8221 Ext. 280. *E-mail:* brutlaro@mlc-wels.edu.

MCNALLY SMITH COLLEGE OF MUSIC

Saint Paul, Minnesota **www.mcnallysmith.edu/**

- **Proprietary** 4-year, founded 1985
- **Urban** campus
- **Coed**
- **Noncompetitive** entrance level

Faculty *Student/faculty ratio:* 10:1.

Academics *Calendar:* semesters. *Degrees:* diplomas, associate, and bachelor's.

Student Life *Campus security:* 24-hour emergency response devices.

Standardized Tests *Required for some:* ACT (for admission). *Recommended:* ACT (for admission).

Costs (2008–09) *Tuition:* $18,460 full-time, $710 per credit part-time. *Required fees:* $1800 full-time, $400 per term part-time.

Applying *Options:* electronic application. *Application fee:* $75. *Required:* essay or personal statement, high school transcript, 2 letters of recommendation, interview. *Required for some:* audition.

Freshman Application Contact Mrs. Kathy Hawks, Director of Admissions, McNally Smith College of Music, 19 Exchange Street East, St. Paul, MN 55101. *Phone:* 651-291-0177 Ext. 2373. *Toll-free phone:* 800-594-9500. *Fax:* 651-291-0366. *E-mail:* khawks@mcnallysmith.edu.

METROPOLITAN STATE UNIVERSITY

St. Paul, Minnesota **www.metrostate.edu/**

- **State-supported** comprehensive, founded 1971, part of Minnesota State Colleges and Universities System
- **Urban** campus
- **Endowment** $2.3 million
- **Coed** 6,230 undergraduate students, 35% full-time, 59% women, 41% men
- **Minimally difficult** entrance level, 53% of applicants were admitted

Undergraduates 2,186 full-time, 4,044 part-time. Students come from 18 states and territories, 53 other countries, 2% are from out of state, 12% African American, 9% Asian American or Pacific Islander, 2% Hispanic American, 1% Native American, 2% international, 17% transferred in. *Retention:* 59% of 2006 full-time freshmen returned.

Freshmen *Admission:* 420 applied, 221 admitted, 81 enrolled. *Test scores:* ACT scores over 18: 65%; ACT scores over 24: 16%.

Faculty *Total:* 517, 24% full-time, 44% with terminal degrees. *Student/faculty ratio:* 15:1.

Majors Accounting; advertising; applied mathematics; biology/biological sciences; biology teacher education; business administration and management; communication/speech communication and rhetoric; computer and information systems security; computer science; computer systems analysis; criminal justice/police science; criminal justice/safety; dental hygiene; developmental and child psychology; dramatic/theater arts; economics; elementary education; English; English composition; English/language arts teacher education; ethnic, cultural minority, and gender studies related; finance; general studies; history; hospitality administration; human resources management; human services; information resources management; information science/studies; international business/trade/commerce; kindergarten/preschool education; liberal arts and sciences/liberal studies; management information systems; marketing/marketing management; mathematics teacher education; nursing (registered nurse training); operations management; philosophy; playwriting and screenwriting; psychology; public administration; sales, distribution and marketing; social sciences; social studies teacher education; social work; substance abuse/addiction counseling; technical and business writing; women's studies.

Academics *Calendar:* semesters. *Degrees:* certificates, bachelor's, master's, and doctoral (offers primarily part-time evening degree programs). *Special study options:* adult/continuing education programs, advanced placement credit, distance learning, double majors, English as a second language, external degree program, independent study, internships, off-campus study, part-time degree program, student-designed majors, summer session for credit.

Computers on Campus 550 computers/terminals are available on campus for general student use. Students can access the following: computer help desk, free student e-mail accounts, online (class) grades, online (class) registration, online (class) schedules. Campuswide network is available. Wireless service is available via entire campus.

Student Life *Housing:* college housing not available. *Activities and organizations:* drama/theater group, student-run newspaper, Psychology Club, Lavender Bridge, International Student Organization, Student Senate, African-American Student Association. *Campus security:* 24-hour emergency response devices, late-night transport/escort service. *Student services:* personal/psychological counseling.

Standardized Tests *Required for some:* SAT or ACT (for admission).

Costs (2008–09) *Tuition:* state resident $5160 full-time, $172 per credit part-time; nonresident $10,320 full-time, $344 per credit part-time. *Required fees:* $313 full-time, $10 per credit part-time.

Financial Aid Of all full-time matriculated undergraduates who enrolled in 2002, 1,220 applied for aid, 958 were judged to have need, 129 had their need fully met. 80 Federal Work-Study jobs (averaging $2616). In 2002, 47 non-need-based awards were made. *Average percent of need met:* 72%. *Average financial aid package:* $8671. *Average need-based loan:* $6525. *Average need-based gift aid:* $2181. *Average non-need-based aid:* $1235. *Average indebtedness upon graduation:* $22,700.

Applying *Options:* electronic application, deferred entrance. *Application fee:* $20. *Required:* high school transcript, minimum 2.0 GPA. *Application deadlines:* 6/15 (freshmen), 6/15 (transfers).

Freshman Application Contact Ms. Monir Johnson, Director, Metropolitan State University, 700 East 7th Street, St. Paul, MN 55106-5000. *Phone:* 651-793-1303. *Fax:* 651-793-1310. *E-mail:* monir.johnson@metrostate.edu.

MINNEAPOLIS COLLEGE OF ART AND DESIGN

Minneapolis, Minnesota **www.mcad.edu/**

- **Independent** comprehensive, founded 1886
- **Urban** 7-acre campus
- **Endowment** $37.4 million
- **Coed**
- **Moderately difficult** entrance level

Faculty *Student/faculty ratio:* 13:1.

Academics *Calendar:* semesters. *Degrees:* bachelor's, master's, and post-bachelor's certificates.

Student Life *Campus security:* 24-hour emergency response devices and patrols, late-night transport/escort service.

Standardized Tests *Required:* SAT or ACT (for admission).

Costs (2007–08) *Tuition:* $27,000 full-time, $900 per credit part-time. *Required fees:* $200 full-time, $100 per term part-time. *Room only:* $4160.

Financial Aid Of all full-time matriculated undergraduates who enrolled in 2007, 552 applied for aid, 495 were judged to have need, 42 had their need fully met. 71 Federal Work-Study jobs (averaging $1890). 25 state and other part-time jobs (averaging $1820). In 2007, 87 non-need-based awards were made. *Average*

percent of need met: 56. *Average financial aid package:* $14,586. *Average need-based loan:* $4773. *Average need-based gift aid:* $10,017. *Average non-need-based aid:* $14,407. *Average indebtedness upon graduation:* $53,646. *Financial aid deadline:* 4/1.

Applying *Options:* deferred entrance. *Application fee:* $35. *Required:* essay or personal statement, high school transcript, 1 letter of recommendation. *Required for some:* portfolio. *Recommended:* minimum 2.75 GPA, interview.

Freshman Application Contact Mr. William Mullen, Director of Admissions, Minneapolis College of Art and Design, 2501 Stevens Avenue South, Minneapolis, MN 55404. *Phone:* 612-874-3762. *Toll-free phone:* 800-874-6223. *E-mail:* admissions@mn.mcad.edu.

MINNESOTA SCHOOL OF BUSINESS–BROOKLYN CENTER

Brooklyn Center, Minnesota **www.msbcollege.edu/**

- **Proprietary** primarily 2-year, founded 1989
- **Suburban** campus
- **Coed**

Faculty *Student/faculty ratio:* 13:1.

Academics *Calendar:* quarters. *Degrees:* certificates, diplomas, associate, bachelor's, and master's.

Standardized Tests *Required:* CPAt (for admission).

Costs (2007–08) *Tuition:* $15,750 full-time, $350 per credit hour part-time. Full-time tuition and fees vary according to course load. Part-time tuition and fees vary according to course load.

Applying *Options:* electronic application. *Application fee:* $50. *Required:* high school transcript, interview. *Required for some:* essay or personal statement.

Freshman Application Contact Mr. Bruce Christman, Director of Admissions, Minnesota School of Business–Brooklyn Center, 5910 Shingle Creek Parkway, Brooklyn Center, MN 55430. *Phone:* 763-585-7777. *Fax:* 763-566-7030.

MINNESOTA SCHOOL OF BUSINESS–PLYMOUTH

Minneapolis, Minnesota **www.msbcollege.edu/**

- **Proprietary** primarily 2-year, founded 2002
- **Suburban** 3-acre campus
- **Coed**
- **Minimally difficult** entrance level

Faculty *Student/faculty ratio:* 10:1.

Academics *Calendar:* quarters. *Degrees:* certificates, diplomas, associate, bachelor's, and master's.

Standardized Tests *Required:* CPAt (for admission).

Costs (2007–08) *Tuition:* $15,750 full-time, $350 per credit hour part-time. Full-time tuition and fees vary according to course load. Part-time tuition and fees vary according to course load.

Applying *Options:* electronic application. *Application fee:* $50. *Required:* high school transcript, interview. *Required for some:* essay or personal statement.

Freshman Application Contact Stacy Severson, Minnesota School of Business–Plymouth, 1455 County Road 101 North, Plymouth, MN 55447. *Phone:* 763-476-2000. *Fax:* 763-476-1000.

MINNESOTA SCHOOL OF BUSINESS–RICHFIELD

Richfield, Minnesota **www.msbcollege.edu/**

- **Proprietary** primarily 2-year, founded 1877, administratively affiliated with Globe University
- **Urban** 3-acre campus with easy access to Minneapolis–St. Paul
- **Coed**
- **Minimally difficult** entrance level

Faculty *Student/faculty ratio:* 14:1.

Academics *Calendar:* quarters. *Degrees:* certificates, diplomas, associate, bachelor's, and master's.

Standardized Tests *Required:* CPAt (for admission).

Costs (2007–08) *Tuition:* $15,750 full-time, $350 per credit hour part-time. Full-time tuition and fees vary according to course load. Part-time tuition and fees vary according to course load.

Applying *Options:* electronic application. *Application fee:* $50. *Required:* high school transcript, interview. *Required for some:* essay or personal statement.

Freshman Application Contact Ms. Patricia Murray, Director of Admissions, Minnesota School of Business–Richfield, 1401 West 76th Street, Richfield, MN 55430. *Phone:* 612-861-2000 Ext. 720. *Toll-free phone:* 800-752-4223. *Fax:* 612-861-5548. *E-mail:* pmurray@msbcollege.com.

MINNESOTA SCHOOL OF BUSINESS–ROCHESTER

Rochester, Minnesota **www.msbcollege.edu/**

- **Proprietary** 4-year, administratively affiliated with Minnesota School of Business
- **Small-town** campus
- **Coed**
- 82% of applicants were admitted

Faculty *Student/faculty ratio:* 13:1.

Academics *Calendar:* quarters. *Degrees:* associate, bachelor's, and master's.

Student Life *Campus security:* 24-hour emergency response devices.

Standardized Tests *Required:* CPAt (for admission).

Costs (2007–08) *Tuition:* $15,750 full-time. Full-time tuition and fees vary according to course load. Part-time tuition and fees vary according to course load.

Applying *Application fee:* $50. *Required:* high school transcript, interview.

Freshman Application Contact Mr. Shan Pollitt, Director of Admissions, Minnesota School of Business–Rochestef, 2521 Pennington Drive, NW, Rochester, MN 55901. *Phone:* 507-536-9500. *Toll-free phone:* 888-662-8772. *Fax:* 507-535-8011.

MINNESOTA SCHOOL OF BUSINESS–ST. CLOUD

Waite Park, Minnesota **www.msbcollege.edu/**

- **Proprietary** primarily 2-year, founded 2004
- **Small-town** campus
- **Coed**
- **Minimally difficult** entrance level

Faculty *Student/faculty ratio:* 13:1.

Academics *Calendar:* quarters. *Degrees:* certificates, diplomas, associate, bachelor's, and master's.

Standardized Tests *Required:* CPAt (for admission).

Costs (2007–08) *Tuition:* $15,750 full-time, $350 per credit hour part-time. Full-time tuition and fees vary according to course load. Part-time tuition and fees vary according to course load.

Applying *Options:* electronic application. *Application fee:* $50. *Required:* high school transcript, interview. *Required for some:* essay or personal statement.

Freshman Application Contact Mr. Jim Beck, Director of Admissions, Minnesota School of Business–St. Cloud, 1201 2nd Street S, Waite Park, MN 56387. *Phone:* 320-257-2000. *Toll-free phone:* 866-403-3333. *Fax:* 320-257-0131. *E-mail:* jbeck@msbcollege.edu.

MINNESOTA SCHOOL OF BUSINESS–SHAKOPEE

Shakopee, Minnesota **www.msbcollege.edu/**

- **Proprietary** primarily 2-year, founded 2004
- **Suburban** campus
- **Coed**
- **Minimally difficult** entrance level

Faculty *Student/faculty ratio:* 12:1.

Academics *Calendar:* quarters. *Degrees:* certificates, diplomas, associate, bachelor's, and master's.

Standardized Tests *Required:* CPAt (for admission).

Costs (2007–08) *Tuition:* $15,750 full-time, $350 per credit hour part-time. Full-time tuition and fees vary according to course load. Part-time tuition and fees vary according to course load.

Applying *Options:* electronic application. *Application fee:* $50. *Required:* high school transcript, interview. *Required for some:* essay or personal statement.

Freshman Application Contact Ms. Gretchen Seifert, Director of Admissions, Minnesota School of Business–Shakopee, 1200 Shakopee Town Square, Shakopee, MN 55379. *Phone:* 952-516-7015. *Toll-free phone:* 866-766-1200. *Fax:* 952-345-1201.

MINNESOTA STATE UNIVERSITY MANKATO

Mankato, Minnesota **www.mnsu.edu/**

- **State-supported** comprehensive, founded 1868, part of Minnesota State Colleges and Universities System
- **Small-town** 303-acre campus with easy access to Minneapolis–St. Paul
- **Coed** 12,534 undergraduate students, 89% full-time, 53% women, 47% men
- **Moderately difficult** entrance level, 90% of applicants were admitted

Undergraduates 11,200 full-time, 1,334 part-time. Students come from 44 states and territories, 68 other countries, 13% are from out of state, 3% African American, 2% Asian American or Pacific Islander, 1% Hispanic American, 0.6% Native American, 3% international, 8% transferred in, 22% live on campus. *Retention:* 78% of 2006 full-time freshmen returned.

Freshmen *Admission:* 5,605 applied, 5,035 admitted, 2,163 enrolled. *Test scores:* ACT scores over 18: 91%; ACT scores over 24: 26%; ACT scores over 30: 1%.

Faculty *Total:* 717, 68% full-time, 56% with terminal degrees. *Student/faculty ratio:* 22:1.

Majors Accounting; anatomy; animal physiology; anthropology; applied art; Army R.O.T.C./military science; art; art history, criticism and conservation; art teacher education; astronomy; athletic training; audiology and speech-language pathology; automotive engineering technology; aviation/airway management; behavioral sciences; biochemistry; biological and physical sciences; biology/biological sciences; biology/biotechnology laboratory technician; botany/plant biology; business administration and management; ceramic arts and ceramics; chemistry; child development; city/urban, community and regional planning; civil engineering; clinical laboratory science/medical technology; clothing/textiles; commercial and advertising art; communication disorders; computer engineering; computer engineering technology; computer programming; computer science; construction management; corrections; creative writing; criminal justice/police science; cultural studies; data processing and data processing technology; dental hygiene; developmental and child psychology; dietetics; dramatic/theater arts; drawing; ecology; economics; education; electrical, electronic and communications engineering technology; electrical, electronics and communications engineering; elementary education; English; environmental biology; environmental studies; family and consumer economics related; family and consumer sciences/home economics teacher education; family and consumer sciences/human sciences; fashion/apparel design; finance; fine/studio arts; foods, nutrition, and wellness; French; geography; geology/earth science; German; health science; health teacher education; history; humanities; industrial arts; industrial technology; information science/studies; insurance; interior design; international business/trade/commerce; international relations and affairs; journalism; kindergarten/preschool education; liberal arts and sciences/liberal studies; literature; management science; marketing/marketing management; mass communication/media; mathematics; mechanical engineering; medical microbiology and bacteriology; modern languages; music; music management and merchandising; music teacher education; natural sciences; nursing (registered nurse training); parks, recreation and leisure; parks, recreation and leisure facilities management; philosophy; physical education teaching and coaching; physical sciences; physics; piano and organ; political science and government; pre-dentistry studies; pre-engineering; pre-law studies; pre-medical studies; pre-theology/pre-ministerial studies; pre-veterinary studies; psychology; public administration; public health; public relations/image management; real estate; science teacher education; sculpture; secondary education; social sciences; social studies teacher education; social work; sociology; Spanish; speech and rhetoric; sport and fitness administration/management; therapeutic recreation; toxicology; urban studies/affairs; voice and opera; wind/percussion instruments; women's studies.

Academics *Calendar:* semesters. *Degrees:* associate, bachelor's, master's, doctoral, and post-master's certificates. *Special study options:* academic remediation for entering students, adult/continuing education programs, advanced placement credit, distance learning, double majors, English as a second language, honors programs, independent study, internships, off-campus study, part-time degree program, services for LD students, student-designed majors, study abroad, summer session for credit. *ROTC:* Army (b).

Computers on Campus 900 computers/terminals are available on campus for general student use. Students can access the following: campus intranet, computer help desk, free student e-mail accounts, online (class) grades, online (class) registration, online (class) schedules. Campuswide network is available. Wireless service is available via entire campus.

Student Life *Housing options:* coed. *Activities and organizations:* drama/theater group, student-run newspaper, radio station, choral group, marching band, national fraternities, national sororities. *Campus security:* 24-hour emergency response devices and patrols, student patrols, late-night transport/escort service, Night Owl security program in residence halls, closed circuit cameras in parking lots. *Student services:* health clinic, personal/psychological counseling, women's center, legal services.

Athletics Member NCAA. All Division II except men's and women's ice hockey (Division I). *Intercollegiate sports:* baseball M (s), basketball M (s)/W (s), cheerleading M/W, cross-country running M (s)/W (s), football M (s), golf M (s)/W (s), ice hockey M (s)/W (s), soccer W (s), softball W (s), swimming and diving M (s)/W (s), tennis M (s)/W (s), track and field M (s)/W (s), volleyball W (s), wrestling M (s). *Intramural sports:* archery M/W, basketball M/W, bowling M/W, fencing M/W, football M, ice hockey M/W, lacrosse M/W, racquetball M/W, rock climbing M/W, sailing M/W, skiing (cross-country) M/W, skiing (downhill) M/W, soccer M/W, softball M/W, swimming and diving M/W, table tennis M/W, tennis M/W, track and field M/W, volleyball M/W, wrestling M.

Standardized Tests *Required:* ACT (for admission).

Costs (2007–08) *Tuition:* state resident $5308 full-time, $212 per credit part-time; nonresident $11,370 full-time, $453 per credit part-time. Full-time tuition and fees vary according to course load and reciprocity agreements. Part-time tuition and fees vary according to course load and reciprocity agreements. *Required fees:* $742 full-time, $31 per credit part-time. *Room and board:* $5354. Room and board charges vary according to board plan. *Payment plan:* installment. *Waivers:* senior citizens and employees or children of employees.

Financial Aid Of all full-time matriculated undergraduates who enrolled in 2006, 8,423 applied for aid, 5,594 were judged to have need, 2,431 had their need fully met. 317 Federal Work-Study jobs (averaging $2980). 342 state and other part-time jobs (averaging $3045). In 2006, 347 non-need-based awards were made. *Average percent of need met:* 79%. *Average financial aid package:* $7058. *Average need-based loan:* $3936. *Average need-based gift aid:* $3849. *Average non-need-based aid:* $2924. *Average indebtedness upon graduation:* $20,826.

Applying *Options:* electronic application, early admission, deferred entrance. *Application fee:* $20. *Required:* high school transcript. *Required for some:* essay or personal statement, 3 letters of recommendation, personal statement. *Application deadlines:* rolling (freshmen), rolling (transfers). *Notification:* continuous (freshmen), continuous (transfers).

Freshman Application Contact Office of Admissions, Minnesota State University Mankato, 122 Taylor Center, Mankato, MN 56001. *Phone:* 507-389-1822. *Toll-free phone:* 800-722-0544. *Fax:* 507-389-1511. *E-mail:* admissions@mnsu.edu.

MINNESOTA STATE UNIVERSITY MOORHEAD

Moorhead, Minnesota **www.mnstate.edu/**

Freshman Application Contact Ms. Gina Monson, Director of Admissions, Minnesota State University Moorhead, Owens Hall, Moorhead, MN 56563-0002. *Phone:* 218-477-2161. *Toll-free phone:* 800-593-7246. *Fax:* 218-477-4374. *E-mail:* dragon@mnstate.edu.

NATIONAL AMERICAN UNIVERSITY

Roseville, Minnesota **www.national.edu/**

Director of Admissions Mr. Steve Grunlan, Director of Admissions, National American University, 1500 West Highway 36, Roseville, MN 55113. *Phone:* 651-644-1265.

NORTH CENTRAL UNIVERSITY

Minneapolis, Minnesota **www.northcentral.edu/**

Freshman Application Contact Ms. Amber Stumph, Admissions Secretary, North Central University, 910 Elliot Avenue, Minneapolis, MN 55404. *Phone:* 612-343-4460. *Toll-free phone:* 800-289-6222. *Fax:* 612-343-4146. *E-mail:* admissions@northcentral.edu.

NORTHWESTERN COLLEGE

St. Paul, Minnesota **www.nwc.edu/**

- **Independent nondenominational** 4-year, founded 1902
- **Suburban** 107-acre campus
- **Endowment** $13.4 million
- **Coed** 1,845 undergraduate students, 97% full-time, 59% women, 41% men
- **Moderately difficult** entrance level, 93% of applicants were admitted

Undergraduates 1,794 full-time, 51 part-time. Students come from 35 states and territories, 21 other countries, 32% are from out of state, 3% African American, 4% Asian American or Pacific Islander, 2% Hispanic American, 0.6% Native American, 0.3% international, 5% transferred in, 62% live on campus. *Retention:* 83% of 2006 full-time freshmen returned.

Freshmen *Admission:* 1,109 applied, 1,029 admitted, 502 enrolled. *Average high school GPA:* 3.57. *Test scores:* SAT critical reading scores over 500: 63%; SAT math scores over 500: 77%; ACT scores over 18: 97%; SAT critical reading scores over 600: 40%; SAT math scores over 600: 46%; ACT scores over 24: 58%; SAT critical reading scores over 700: 17%; SAT math scores over 700: 14%; ACT scores over 30: 11%.

Faculty *Total:* 176, 55% full-time, 46% with terminal degrees. *Student/faculty ratio:* 15:1.

Majors Accounting; animation, interactive technology, video graphics and special effects; art teacher education; biblical studies; biology/biological sciences; business administration and management; communication/speech communication and rhetoric; creative writing; criminal justice/safety; dramatic/theater arts; early childhood education; elementary education; engineering; English; English as a second/foreign language (teaching); English/language arts teacher education; finance; fine/studio arts; graphic design; health and physical education; history; international business/trade/commerce; journalism; kinesiology and exercise science; liberal arts and sciences/liberal studies; management information systems; marketing/marketing management; mathematics; mathematics teacher education; missionary studies and missiology; multi-/interdisciplinary studies related; music; music performance; music teacher education; music theory and composition; pastoral counseling and specialized ministries related; physical education teaching and coaching; piano and organ; pre-theology/pre-ministerial studies; psychology; public relations/image management; radio and television; social studies teacher education; technical and business writing; theological and ministerial studies related; violin, viola, guitar and other stringed instruments; voice and opera; youth ministry.

Academics *Calendar:* semesters. *Degrees:* certificates, associate, bachelor's, and master's. *Special study options:* academic remediation for entering students, adult/continuing education programs, advanced placement credit, distance learning, double majors, honors programs, independent study, internships, off-campus study, part-time degree program, services for LD students, student-designed majors, study abroad, summer session for credit. *ROTC:* Army (c), Air Force (c). *Unusual degree programs:* 3-2 engineering with University of Minnesota-Twin Cities.

Computers on Campus 100 computers/terminals and 12 ports are available on campus for general student use. Students can access the following: campus intranet, computer help desk, free student e-mail accounts, online (class) grades, online (class) registration, online (class) schedules. Campuswide network is available. 100% of college-owned or -operated housing units are wired for high-speed Internet access. Wireless service is available via classrooms, computer labs, dorm rooms, learning centers, libraries, student centers.

Student Life *Housing:* on-campus residence required through sophomore year. *Options:* men-only, women-only, disabled students. Campus housing is university owned. Freshman campus housing is guaranteed. *Activities and organizations:* drama/theater group, student-run newspaper, radio station, choral group, Northwestern Student Association (student government), The Gathering (religious group), Student Missions Fellowship, Guardian Angels, It's TIME (coalition of ethnic/multicultural caucuses). *Campus security:* 24-hour patrols, late-night transport/escort service, controlled dormitory access. *Student services:* health clinic, personal/psychological counseling.

Athletics Member NCAA, NCCAA. All NCAA Division III. *Intercollegiate sports:* baseball M, basketball M/W, cheerleading W, cross-country running M/W, football M, golf M, ice hockey M (c), soccer M/W, softball W, tennis M/W, track and field M/W, volleyball M (c)/W. *Intramural sports:* basketball M/W, football M/W, softball M/W, tennis M/W, volleyball M/W.

Standardized Tests *Required:* SAT or ACT (for admission).

Costs (2008–09) *Comprehensive fee:* $29,470 includes full-time tuition ($22,250), mandatory fees ($170), and room and board ($7050). Part-time tuition: $950 per credit. *Required fees:* $45 per term part-time. *College room only:* $3990.

Financial Aid Of all full-time matriculated undergraduates who enrolled in 2006, 1,687 applied for aid, 1,425 were judged to have need, 202 had their need fully met. 230 Federal Work-Study jobs (averaging $1975). 320 state and other part-time jobs (averaging $1750). In 2006, 255 non-need-based awards were made. *Average percent of need met:* 73%. *Average financial aid package:* $14,555. *Average need-based loan:* $4191. *Average need-based gift aid:* $10,690. *Average non-need-based aid:* $5765. *Average indebtedness upon graduation:* $24,449. *Financial aid deadline:* 5/1.

Applying *Options:* electronic application, early admission, deferred entrance. *Application fee:* $30. *Required:* essay or personal statement, high school transcript, minimum 2.0 GPA, 2 letters of recommendation, lifestyle agreement, statement of Christian faith. *Required for some:* interview. *Recommended:* minimum 3.0 GPA. *Application deadlines:* 8/1 (freshmen), 8/1 (transfers). *Notification:* continuous (freshmen), continuous (transfers).

Freshman Application Contact Mr. Kenneth K. Faffler, Director of Admissions, Northwestern College, Office of Admissions, 3003 Snelling Avenue North, Nazareth Hall, St. Paul, MN 55113-1598. *Phone:* 651-631-5111. *Toll-free phone:* 800-827-6827. *Fax:* 651-631-5680. *E-mail:* admissions@nwc.edu.

OAK HILLS CHRISTIAN COLLEGE

Bemidji, Minnesota **www.oakhills.edu/**

- **Independent interdenominational** 4-year, founded 1946
- **Rural** 180-acre campus
- **Endowment** $314,352
- **Coed** 163 undergraduate students, 89% full-time, 45% women, 55% men
- **Minimally difficult** entrance level, 95% of applicants were admitted

Undergraduates 145 full-time, 18 part-time. Students come from 17 states and territories, 1 other country, 29% are from out of state, 2% African American, 2% Asian American or Pacific Islander, 2% Hispanic American, 4% Native American, 0.6% international, 15% transferred in, 80% live on campus. *Retention:* 41% of 2006 full-time freshmen returned.

Freshmen *Admission:* 56 applied, 53 admitted, 33 enrolled. *Average high school GPA:* 2.91. *Test scores:* ACT scores over 18: 65%; ACT scores over 24: 19%.

Faculty *Total:* 23, 30% full-time, 39% with terminal degrees. *Student/faculty ratio:* 7:1.

Majors Counseling psychology; divinity/ministry; general studies; pastoral counseling and specialized ministries related; pastoral studies/counseling; religious education; youth ministry.

Academics *Calendar:* semesters. *Degrees:* certificates, diplomas, associate, and bachelor's. *Special study options:* academic remediation for entering students, advanced placement credit, double majors, honors programs, independent study, internships, off-campus study, part-time degree program, services for LD students.

Computers on Campus 12 computers/terminals and 6 ports are available on campus for general student use. Students can access the following: online (class) schedules. Campuswide network is available. 50% of college-owned or -operated housing units are wired for high-speed Internet access. Wireless service is available via entire campus.

Student Life *Housing:* on-campus residence required through sophomore year. *Options:* coed, men-only, women-only. Campus housing is university owned. Freshman campus housing is guaranteed. *Activities and organizations:* choral group, Student Council (SALT), Students Older Than Average, Student Activity Team, Outreach Program— (20+) Community Service Organizations, Intramural Sports Teams. *Campus security:* 24-hour emergency response devices, controlled dormitory access, evening patrols by trained security personnel. *Student services:* health clinic, personal/psychological counseling.

Athletics *Intercollegiate sports:* basketball M/W. *Intramural sports:* basketball M/W, football M/W, golf M/W, racquetball M/W, soccer M/W, softball M/W, table tennis M/W, volleyball M/W, weight lifting M/W.

Standardized Tests *Required:* SAT or ACT (for admission).

Costs (2008–09) *Comprehensive fee:* $17,540 includes full-time tuition ($12,820) and room and board ($4720). Part-time tuition: $375 per credit.

Financial Aid Of all full-time matriculated undergraduates who enrolled in 2002, 138 applied for aid, 131 were judged to have need, 9 had their need fully met. 22 Federal Work-Study jobs (averaging $1234). 54 state and other part-time jobs (averaging $2188). In 2002, 7 non-need-based awards were made. *Average percent of need met:* 73%. *Average financial aid package:* $9306. *Average need-based loan:* $3099. *Average need-based gift aid:* $6455. *Average non-need-based aid:* $2610. *Average indebtedness upon graduation:* $20,233.

Applying *Options:* electronic application, deferred entrance. *Application fee:* $25. *Required:* essay or personal statement, high school transcript, minimum 2.0

GPA, 2 letters of recommendation. *Required for some:* interview, minimum ACT score of 18. *Application deadlines:* rolling (freshmen), rolling (transfers). *Notification:* continuous (freshmen), continuous (transfers).

Freshman Application Contact Mr. Daniel Hovestol, Admissions Director, Oak Hills Christian College, Bemidji, MN 56601. *Phone:* 218-751-8670 Ext. 1220. *Toll-free phone:* 888-751-8670 Ext. 285. *Fax:* 218-751-8825. *E-mail:* admissions@oakhills.edu.

PILLSBURY BAPTIST BIBLE COLLEGE

Owatonna, Minnesota **www.pillsbury.edu/**

- **Independent Baptist** 4-year, founded 1957
- **Small-town** 14-acre campus with easy access to Minneapolis–St. Paul
- **Coed** 164 undergraduate students, 87% full-time, 60% women, 40% men
- **Noncompetitive** entrance level

Undergraduates 143 full-time, 21 part-time. Students come from 20 states and territories, 2 other countries, 40% are from out of state, 1% African American, 0.6% Asian American or Pacific Islander, 1% Hispanic American, 3% international, 4% transferred in, 76% live on campus. *Retention:* 68% of 2006 full-time freshmen returned.

Freshmen *Admission:* 44 admitted, 44 enrolled. *Test scores:* ACT scores over 18: 75%; ACT scores over 24: 20%; ACT scores over 30: 2%.

Faculty *Total:* 33, 58% full-time, 6% with terminal degrees. *Student/faculty ratio:* 7:1.

Majors Administrative assistant and secretarial science; biblical studies; business administration and management; business teacher education; computer teacher education; education; elementary education; English/language arts teacher education; mathematics teacher education; missionary studies and missiology; music; music teacher education; pastoral studies/counseling; photography; physical education teaching and coaching; religious education; religious/sacred music; science teacher education; secondary education; social studies teacher education; speech teacher education; theological and ministerial studies related; youth ministry.

Academics *Calendar:* semesters. *Degrees:* certificates, diplomas, associate, and bachelor's. *Special study options:* academic remediation for entering students, accelerated degree program, advanced placement credit, double majors, independent study, internships, part-time degree program, services for LD students, study abroad, summer session for credit.

Computers on Campus 33 computers/terminals are available on campus for general student use. Campuswide network is available. Wireless service is available via entire campus.

Student Life *Housing:* on-campus residence required through senior year. *Options:* men-only, women-only. Campus housing is university owned. Freshman campus housing is guaranteed. *Activities and organizations:* student-run newspaper, choral group. *Campus security:* student patrols. *Student services:* personal/psychological counseling.

Athletics Member NCCAA. *Intercollegiate sports:* baseball M, basketball M/W, golf M/W, soccer M, softball W, volleyball W. *Intramural sports:* basketball M/W, table tennis M/W, volleyball M/W.

Standardized Tests *Required:* ACT (for admission).

Costs (2008–09) *Comprehensive fee:* $15,204 includes full-time tuition ($9120), mandatory fees ($1088), and room and board ($4996). Part-time tuition: $285 per semester hour. *Required fees:* $30 per semester hour part-time.

Financial Aid *Average percent of need met:* 50%.

Applying *Options:* deferred entrance. *Application fee:* $25. *Required:* essay or personal statement, high school transcript, 2 letters of recommendation. *Recommended:* interview. *Application deadlines:* 8/20 (freshmen), 8/20 (transfers). *Notification:* continuous (freshmen), continuous (transfers).

Director of Admissions Mr. Jason Nicholson, Admissions Counselor, Pillsbury Baptist Bible College, 315 South Grove Avenue, Owatonna, MN 55060-3097. *Phone:* 507-451-2710 Ext. 279. *Toll-free phone:* 800-747-4557. *E-mail:* jnicholsoln@pillsbury.edu.

ROCHESTER COMMUNITY AND TECHNICAL COLLEGE

Rochester, Minnesota **www.rctc.edu/**

Director of Admissions Mr. Troy Tynsky, Director of Admissions, Rochester Community and Technical College, 851 30th Avenue, SE, Rochester, MN 55904-4999. *Phone:* 507-280-3509.

ST. CLOUD STATE UNIVERSITY

St. Cloud, Minnesota **www.stcloudstate.edu/**

- **State-supported** comprehensive, founded 1869, part of Minnesota State Colleges and Universities System
- **Suburban** 922-acre campus with easy access to Minneapolis–St. Paul
- **Endowment** $18.4 million
- **Coed** 14,137 undergraduate students, 85% full-time, 53% women, 47% men
- **Moderately difficult** entrance level, 76% of applicants were admitted

Undergraduates 11,966 full-time, 2,171 part-time. Students come from 46 states and territories, 89 other countries, 9% are from out of state, 3% African American, 2% Asian American or Pacific Islander, 1% Hispanic American, 0.9% Native American, 5% international, 10% transferred in, 20% live on campus. *Retention:* 71% of 2006 full-time freshmen returned.

Freshmen *Admission:* 6,680 applied, 5,067 admitted, 2,381 enrolled. *Test scores:* ACT scores over 18: 89%; ACT scores over 24: 26%; ACT scores over 30: 1%.

Faculty *Total:* 863, 75% full-time, 65% with terminal degrees. *Student/faculty ratio:* 20:1.

Majors Accounting; acting; advertising; airline pilot and flight crew; air traffic control; American studies; anthropology; applied art; art; art history, criticism and conservation; art teacher education; atmospheric sciences and meteorology; audiology and speech-language pathology; aviation/airway management; behavioral sciences; biology/biological sciences; biology/biotechnology laboratory technician; biomedical sciences; botany/plant biology; broadcast journalism; business administration and management; ceramic arts and ceramics; chemistry; child development; city/urban, community and regional planning; clinical laboratory science/medical technology; communication disorders; communication disorders sciences and services related; comparative literature; computer engineering; computer science; counselor education/school counseling and guidance; creative writing; criminal justice/law enforcement administration; criminology; design and applied arts related; dramatic/theater arts; dramatic/theater arts and stagecraft related; drawing; ecology; economics; education; educational/instructional media design; educational leadership and administration; education (K-12); education (specific levels and methods) related; electrical, electronic and communications engineering technology; electrical, electronics and communications engineering; elementary education; engineering; engineering technology; English; environmental biology; film/cinema studies; finance; fine/studio arts; French; geography; geology/earth science; German; gerontology; health/medical preparatory programs related; health services/allied health/health sciences; health teacher education; history; human resources management; industrial arts; industrial engineering; information science/studies; insurance; interdisciplinary studies; international business/trade/commerce; international relations and affairs; jazz/jazz studies; journalism; kindergarten/preschool education; kinesiology and exercise science; Latin American studies; liberal arts and sciences/liberal studies; library science; linguistics; marketing/marketing management; mass communication/media; mathematics; mechanical engineering; medical microbiology and bacteriology; mental health/rehabilitation; middle school education; multi-/interdisciplinary studies related; music; music history, literature, and theory; music pedagogy; music performance; music teacher education; music theory and composition; natural sciences; nuclear medical technology; nursing (registered nurse training); optometric technician; painting; philosophy; physical education teaching and coaching; physical sciences; physical therapy; physics; piano and organ; political science and government; pre-dentistry studies; pre-law studies; pre-medical studies; pre-pharmacy studies; pre-veterinary studies; printmaking; psychoanalysis and psychotherapy; psychology; public administration; public policy analysis; public relations/image management; radio and television; reading teacher education; real estate; sales, distribution and marketing; science teacher education; sculpture; secondary education; social sciences; social work; sociology; Spanish; special education; speech and rhetoric; speech-language pathology; speech/theater education; speech therapy; statistics; substance abuse/addiction counseling; technology/industrial arts teacher education; theater/theater arts management; therapeutic recreation; tourism and travel services management; tourism promotion; urban studies/affairs; violin, viola, guitar and other stringed instruments; visual and performing arts related; voice and opera; wildlife biology.

Academics *Calendar:* semesters. *Degrees:* certificates, diplomas, associate, bachelor's, master's, doctoral, and postbachelor's certificates. *Special study options:* academic remediation for entering students, accelerated degree program, adult/continuing education programs, advanced placement credit, distance learning, double majors, English as a second language, honors programs, independent study, internships, off-campus study, part-time degree program, services for LD students, student-designed majors, study abroad, summer session for credit. *ROTC:* Army (b).

Computers on Campus 1,495 computers/terminals and 387 ports are available on campus for general student use. Students can access the following: campus intranet, computer help desk, free student e-mail accounts, online (class) grades, online (class) registration, online (class) schedules. Campuswide network is available. 100% of college-owned or -operated housing units are wired for high-speed Internet access. Wireless service is available via entire campus.

Student Life *Housing options:* coed, men-only, women-only. Campus housing is university owned. Freshman applicants given priority for college housing. *Activities and organizations:* drama/theater group, student-run newspaper, radio and television station, choral group, national fraternities, national sororities. *Campus security:* 24-hour emergency response devices and patrols, late-night transport/escort service. *Student services:* health clinic, personal/psychological counseling, women's center.

Athletics Member NCAA. All Division II except men's and women's ice hockey (Division I). *Intercollegiate sports:* baseball M (s), basketball M (s)/W (s), bowling M (c)/W (c), cheerleading M (c)/W (c), crew M (c)/W (c), cross-country running M (s)/W, equestrian sports M (c)/W (c), football M (s), golf M/W (s), ice hockey M (s)/W (s), rock climbing M (c)/W (c), skiing (cross-country) M (c)/W (s), skiing (downhill) M (c)/W (c), soccer M (c)/W (s), softball W (s), swimming and diving M (s)/W (s), tennis M (s)/W (s), track and field M (s)/W (s), ultimate Frisbee M (c)/W (c), volleyball M (c)/W (s), wrestling M (s). *Intramural sports:* badminton M/W, basketball M/W, bowling M/W, crew M/W, football M/W, golf M/W, ice hockey M/W, racquetball M/W, soccer M/W, softball M/W, squash M/W, tennis M/W, volleyball M/W, wrestling M.

Standardized Tests *Required:* SAT or ACT (for admission).

Costs (2007–08) *Tuition:* state resident $5247 full-time, $175 per credit part-time; nonresident $11,389 full-time, $380 per credit part-time. Full-time tuition and fees vary according to course load and reciprocity agreements. Part-time tuition and fees vary according to course load and reciprocity agreements. *Required fees:* $708 full-time, $28 per credit part-time. *Room and board:* $5592; room only: $3596. Room and board charges vary according to board plan and housing facility. *Payment plan:* installment. *Waivers:* senior citizens and employees or children of employees.

Financial Aid Of all full-time matriculated undergraduates who enrolled in 2007, 7,745 applied for aid, 5,716 were judged to have need, 3,959 had their need fully met. In 2007, 307 non-need-based awards were made. *Average percent of need met:* 63%. *Average financial aid package:* $10,992. *Average need-based loan:* $5902. *Average need-based gift aid:* $4507. *Average non-need-based aid:* $1804. *Average indebtedness upon graduation:* $22,721.

Applying *Options:* electronic application, deferred entrance. *Application fee:* $20. *Required:* high school transcript. *Required for some:* letters of recommendation. *Application deadlines:* 6/1 (freshmen), 8/15 (transfers). *Notification:* continuous (freshmen), continuous (transfers).

Freshman Application Contact Mr. Jeff Rhodes, Director of Admissions, St. Cloud State University, 115 AS Building, 720 4th Avenue South, St. Cloud, MN 56301-4498. *Phone:* 320-308-2244. *Toll-free phone:* 877-654-7278. *Fax:* 320-308-2243. *E-mail:* scsu4u@stcloudstate.edu.

SAINT JOHN'S UNIVERSITY

Collegeville, Minnesota **www.csbsju.edu/**

- **Independent Roman Catholic** comprehensive, founded 1857
- **Rural** 2400-acre campus with easy access to Minneapolis–St. Paul
- **Endowment** $139.7 million
- **Coed, primarily men** 1,952 undergraduate students, 98% full-time, 100% men
- **Moderately difficult** entrance level, 74% of applicants were admitted

Undergraduates 1,913 full-time, 39 part-time. Students come from 32 states and territories, 22 other countries, 17% are from out of state, 1% African American, 2% Asian American or Pacific Islander, 1% Hispanic American, 0.2% Native American, 5% international, 2% transferred in, 78% live on campus. *Retention:* 89% of 2006 full-time freshmen returned.

Freshmen *Admission:* 1,527 applied, 1,123 admitted, 515 enrolled. *Average high school GPA:* 3.57. *Test scores:* SAT critical reading scores over 500: 72%; SAT math scores over 500: 78%; ACT scores over 18: 99%; SAT critical reading scores over 600: 37%; SAT math scores over 600: 48%; ACT scores over 24: 72%; SAT critical reading scores over 700: 11%; SAT math scores over 700: 9%; ACT scores over 30: 18%.

Faculty *Total:* 177, 84% full-time, 73% with terminal degrees. *Student/faculty ratio:* 12:1.

Majors Accounting; art; biochemistry; biology/biological sciences; business administration and management; chemistry; classics and languages, literatures and linguistics; computer science; dietetics; dramatic/theater arts; economics; education; elementary education; engineering physics; English; environmental studies; fine/studio arts; foods, nutrition, and wellness; forest sciences and biology; French; German; history; humanities; mathematics; mathematics and computer science; music; natural sciences; nursing (registered nurse training); occupational therapy; peace studies and conflict resolution; philosophy; physical therapy; physics; political science and government; pre-dentistry studies; pre-law studies; pre-medical studies; pre-pharmacy studies; pre-theology/pre-ministerial studies; pre-veterinary studies; psychology; religious education; secondary education; social sciences; social work; sociology; Spanish; speech and rhetoric; theology.

Academics *Calendar:* semesters. *Degrees:* bachelor's, master's, and first professional (coordinate with College of Saint Benedict for women). *Special study options:* accelerated degree program, advanced placement credit, double majors, English as a second language, honors programs, independent study, internships, off-campus study, services for LD students, student-designed majors, study abroad. *ROTC:* Army (b). *Unusual degree programs:* 3-2 engineering with University of Minnesota, Twin Cities Campus.

Computers on Campus 643 computers/terminals and 3,000 ports are available on campus for general student use. Students can access the following: computer help desk, free student e-mail accounts, online (class) grades, online (class) registration, online (class) schedules, online student accounts. Campuswide network is available. 100% of college-owned or -operated housing units are wired for high-speed Internet access. Wireless service is available via classrooms, computer centers, computer labs, dorm rooms, learning centers, libraries, student centers.

Student Life *Housing:* on-campus residence required through sophomore year. *Options:* men-only, disabled students. Campus housing is university owned. Freshman campus housing is guaranteed. *Activities and organizations:* drama/theater group, student-run newspaper, radio station, choral group, Joint Events Council, Volunteers in Service to Others, Ballroom Dance Club, Students in Free Enterprise, Magis. *Campus security:* 24-hour emergency response devices and patrols, student patrols, late-night transport/escort service, well-lit pathways, 911 center on campus, closed circuit TV monitors. *Student services:* health clinic, personal/psychological counseling, women's center.

Athletics Member NCAA. All Division III. *Intercollegiate sports:* baseball M, basketball M, crew M (c), cross-country running M, football M, golf M, ice hockey M, lacrosse M (c), riflery M (c), rugby M (c), skiing (cross-country) M, soccer M, swimming and diving M, tennis M, track and field M, ultimate Frisbee M (c), volleyball M (c), water polo M (c), wrestling M. *Intramural sports:* basketball M, football M, racquetball M, rock climbing M (c), skiing (cross-country) M (c), skiing (downhill) M (c), soccer M, softball M, table tennis M (c), ultimate Frisbee M, volleyball M.

Standardized Tests *Required:* SAT or ACT (for admission).

Costs (2007–08) *One-time required fee:* $40. *Comprehensive fee:* $33,400 includes full-time tuition ($26,038), mandatory fees ($492), and room and board ($6870). Part-time tuition: $1085 per credit. Part-time tuition and fees vary according to course load. *Required fees:* $246 per term part-time. *College room only:* $3458. Room and board charges vary according to board plan and housing facility. *Payment plans:* tuition prepayment, installment. *Waivers:* employees or children of employees.

Financial Aid Of all full-time matriculated undergraduates who enrolled in 2007, 1,276 applied for aid, 1,066 were judged to have need, 411 had their need fully met. 270 Federal Work-Study jobs (averaging $2366). 935 state and other part-time jobs (averaging $2487). In 2007, 740 non-need-based awards were made. *Average percent of need met:* 88%. *Average financial aid package:* $20,628. *Average need-based loan:* $4603. *Average need-based gift aid:* $14,031. *Average non-need-based aid:* $9192.

Applying *Options:* electronic application, early action, deferred entrance. *Required:* essay or personal statement, high school transcript, 1 letter of recommendation. *Recommended:* minimum 3.0 GPA, interview. *Application deadlines:* rolling (freshmen), rolling (transfers), 11/15 (early action). *Notification:* continuous (freshmen), continuous (transfers), 12/15 (early action).

Freshman Application Contact Mr. Matt Beirne, Director of Admission, Saint John's University, PO Box 7155, Collegeville, MN 56321-7155. *Phone:* 320-363-2196. *Toll-free phone:* 800-544-1489. *Fax:* 320-363-2750. *E-mail:* admissions@csbsju.edu.

SAINT MARY'S UNIVERSITY OF MINNESOTA

Winona, Minnesota **www.smumn.edu/**

- **Independent Roman Catholic** comprehensive, founded 1912
- **Small-town** 350-acre campus
- **Endowment** $38.0 million
- **Coed** 2,042 undergraduate students, 70% full-time, 53% women, 47% men

• **Moderately difficult** entrance level, 83% of applicants were admitted

Undergraduates 1,425 full-time, 617 part-time. Students come from 24 states and territories, 13 other countries, 39% are from out of state, 4% African American, 3% Asian American or Pacific Islander, 3% Hispanic American, 0.5% Native American, 1% international, 9% transferred in, 83% live on campus. *Retention:* 78% of 2006 full-time freshmen returned.

Freshmen *Admission:* 1,410 applied, 1,169 admitted, 397 enrolled. *Average high school GPA:* 3.13. *Test scores:* SAT critical reading scores over 500: 60%; SAT math scores over 500: 60%; ACT scores over 18: 89%; SAT critical reading scores over 600: 30%; SAT math scores over 600: 25%; ACT scores over 24: 35%; SAT critical reading scores over 700: 5%; SAT math scores over 700: 15%; ACT scores over 30: 3%.

Faculty *Total:* 595, 18% full-time, 40% with terminal degrees. *Student/faculty ratio:* 12:1.

Majors Accounting; biochemistry; biology/biological sciences; biology teacher education; biophysics; business administration and management; business/commerce; chemistry; chemistry teacher education; clinical laboratory science/medical technology; computer engineering; computer/information technology services administration related; computer science; corrections; criminal justice/law enforcement administration; criminal justice/police science; cytogenetics/genetics/clinical genetics technology; cytotechnology; dramatic/theater arts; elementary education; engineering physics; English; English/language arts teacher education; environmental biology; finance; fine/studio arts; French; French language teacher education; graphic design; history; history related; human resources management; human services; industrial technology; information science/studies; international business/trade/commerce; international/global studies; journalism; marketing/marketing management; mathematics; mathematics and computer science; mathematics teacher education; multi-/interdisciplinary studies related; music; music management and merchandising; music performance; music related; music teacher education; nuclear medical technology; philosophy; physical therapy; physics teacher education; political science and government related; psychology; public relations, advertising, and applied communication related; publishing; religious education; sales, distribution and marketing; social sciences; social science teacher education; sociology; Spanish; Spanish language teacher education; theology; youth ministry.

Academics *Calendar:* semesters. *Degrees:* certificates, diplomas, bachelor's, master's, doctoral, post-master's, and postbachelor's certificates. *Special study options:* academic remediation for entering students, accelerated degree program, adult/continuing education programs, advanced placement credit, cooperative education, double majors, English as a second language, external degree program, honors programs, independent study, internships, off-campus study, part-time degree program, services for LD students, student-designed majors, study abroad, summer session for credit. *ROTC:* Army (c).

Computers on Campus 200 computers/terminals and 50 ports are available on campus for general student use. Students can access the following: campus intranet, computer help desk, free student e-mail accounts, online (class) grades, online (class) registration, online (class) schedules. Campuswide network is available. 100% of college-owned or -operated housing units are wired for high-speed Internet access. Wireless service is available via computer centers, computer labs, dorm rooms, libraries, student centers.

Student Life *Housing:* on-campus residence required through sophomore year. *Options:* coed, men-only, women-only, disabled students. Campus housing is university owned. Freshman campus housing is guaranteed. *Activities and organizations:* drama/theater group, student-run newspaper, radio station, choral group, Student Activity Committee, Habitat for Humanity, Serving Others United in Love (Soul), Colleges Against Cancer, concert choir/chamber singers, national fraternities, national sororities. *Campus security:* 24-hour emergency response devices and patrols, late-night transport/escort service, controlled dormitory access. *Student services:* health clinic, personal/psychological counseling, women's center.

Athletics Member NCAA. All Division III. *Intercollegiate sports:* baseball M, basketball M/W, cross-country running M/W, golf M/W, ice hockey M/W, soccer M/W, softball W, swimming and diving M/W, tennis M/W, track and field M/W, volleyball W. *Intramural sports:* basketball M/W, cheerleading W (c), field hockey M/W, football M/W, ice hockey M, skiing (downhill) M (c)/W (c), soccer M/W, softball M/W, tennis M/W, volleyball W, water polo M (c)/W (c).

Standardized Tests *Required:* SAT or ACT (for admission).

Costs (2008–09) *Comprehensive fee:* $30,530 includes full-time tuition ($23,670), mandatory fees ($480), and room and board ($6380). Part-time tuition: $790 per credit. *Required fees:* $460 per year part-time. *College room only:* $3570.

Financial Aid Of all full-time matriculated undergraduates who enrolled in 2007, 1,078 applied for aid, 912 were judged to have need, 207 had their need fully met. 129 Federal Work-Study jobs (averaging $1439). 308 state and other part-time jobs (averaging $1397). In 2007, 400 non-need-based awards were made. *Average percent of need met:* 80%. *Average financial aid package:* $15,113. *Average need-based loan:* $4223. *Average need-based gift aid:* $11,870. *Average non-need-based aid:* $6654. *Average indebtedness upon graduation:* $26,511.

Applying *Options:* electronic application, early admission, deferred entrance. *Application fee:* $25. *Required:* essay or personal statement, high school transcript, minimum 2.5 GPA. *Required for some:* interview. *Recommended:* 2 letters of recommendation. *Application deadlines:* 5/1 (freshmen), rolling (transfers). *Notification:* continuous (freshmen), continuous (transfers).

Freshman Application Contact Mr. Anthony M. Piscitiello, Vice President for Admission, Saint Mary's University of Minnesota, Admissions, 700 Terrace Heights, Winona, MN 55987-1399. *Phone:* 507-457-1700. *Toll-free phone:* 800-635-5987. *Fax:* 507-457-1722. *E-mail:* admissions@smumn.edu.

ST. OLAF COLLEGE

Northfield, Minnesota **www.stolaf.edu/**

- **Independent Lutheran** 4-year, founded 1874
- **Small-town** 300-acre campus with easy access to Minneapolis-St. Paul
- **Endowment** $321.1 million
- **Coed** 3,040 undergraduate students, 98% full-time, 55% women, 45% men
- **Very difficult** entrance level, 54% of applicants were admitted

Undergraduates 2,986 full-time, 54 part-time. Students come from 45 states and territories, 17 other countries, 43% are from out of state, 1% African American, 5% Asian American or Pacific Islander, 1% Hispanic American, 0.2% Native American, 1% international, 1% transferred in, 96% live on campus. *Retention:* 93% of 2006 full-time freshmen returned.

Freshmen *Admission:* 4,058 applied, 2,208 admitted, 751 enrolled. *Average high school GPA:* 3.65. *Test scores:* SAT critical reading scores over 500: 96%; SAT math scores over 500: 96%; ACT scores over 18: 99%; SAT critical reading scores over 600: 76%; SAT math scores over 600: 77%; ACT scores over 24: 90%; SAT critical reading scores over 700: 35%; SAT math scores over 700: 25%; ACT scores over 30: 43%.

Faculty *Total:* 327, 60% full-time, 80% with terminal degrees. *Student/faculty ratio:* 13:1.

Majors American studies; ancient/classical Greek; ancient studies; art; art history, criticism and conservation; Asian studies; biology/biological sciences; chemistry; classics and languages, literatures and linguistics; computer science; dance; dramatic/theater arts; economics; English; environmental studies; ethnic, cultural minority, and gender studies related; French; German; history; kinesiology and exercise science; Latin; Latin American studies; liberal arts and sciences/liberal studies; mathematics; multi-/interdisciplinary studies related; music; music performance; music related; music teacher education; music theory and composition; Norwegian; nursing (registered nurse training); philosophy; physics; political science and government; psychology; religious studies; Russian; Russian studies; social studies teacher education; social work; sociology; Spanish; women's studies.

Academics *Calendar:* 4-1-4. *Degree:* bachelor's. *Special study options:* advanced placement credit, double majors, independent study, internships, off-campus study, part-time degree program, services for LD students, student-designed majors, study abroad, summer session for credit. *Unusual degree programs:* 3-2 engineering with Washington University at St. Louis.

Computers on Campus 969 computers/terminals and 2,600 ports are available on campus for general student use. Students can access the following: campus intranet, computer help desk, free student e-mail accounts, online (class) grades, online (class) registration, online (class) schedules. Campuswide network is available. 100% of college-owned or -operated housing units are wired for high-speed Internet access. Wireless service is available via entire campus.

Student Life *Housing:* on-campus residence required through senior year. *Options:* coed, disabled students. Campus housing is university owned. Freshman campus housing is guaranteed. *Activities and organizations:* drama/theater group, student-run newspaper, radio and television station, choral group, Student Government Association, Alpha Phi Omega, Habitat for Humanity, College Democrats, College Republicans. *Campus security:* 24-hour emergency response devices and patrols, late-night transport/escort service, controlled dormitory access, lighted pathways and sidewalks, first-year only dorms, quiet halls. *Student services:* health clinic, personal/psychological counseling.

Athletics Member NCAA. All Division III. *Intercollegiate sports:* baseball M, basketball M/W, cross-country running M/W, football M, golf M/W, ice hockey M/W, skiing (cross-country) M/W, skiing (downhill) M/W, soccer M/W, softball W, swimming and diving M/W, tennis M/W, track and field M/W, volleyball W, wrestling M. *Intramural sports:* badminton M/W, basketball M/W, crew M/W, field hockey M, football M/W, golf M/W, ice hockey M, lacrosse M (c)/W (c), rugby M/W, skiing (cross-country) M/W, soccer M/W, softball M/W, swimming and diving M/W, table tennis M/W, tennis M/W, ultimate Frisbee M/W, volleyball M/W, water polo M/W.

Standardized Tests *Required:* SAT or ACT (for admission).

Costs (2008–09) *Comprehensive fee:* $42,200 includes full-time tuition ($34,300) and room and board ($7900). Part-time tuition: $1075 per credit hour. *College room only:* $3650.

Financial Aid Of all full-time matriculated undergraduates who enrolled in 2007, 2,232 applied for aid, 1,936 were judged to have need, 1,936 had their need fully met. 910 Federal Work-Study jobs (averaging $1866). 1,307 state and other part-time jobs (averaging $1632). In 2007, 545 non-need-based awards were made. *Average percent of need met:* 100%. *Average financial aid package:* $22,743. *Average need-based loan:* $5241. *Average need-based gift aid:* $15,471. *Average non-need-based aid:* $7889. *Average indebtedness upon graduation:* $25,501. *Financial aid deadline:* 4/15.

Applying *Options:* electronic application, early decision, early action, deferred entrance. *Required:* essay or personal statement, high school transcript, 2 letters of recommendation. *Recommended:* interview. *Application deadlines:* rolling (freshmen), rolling (transfers), 12/1 (early action). *Early decision deadline:* 11/1. *Notification:* continuous (freshmen), continuous (transfers), 12/1 (early decision), 2/1 (early action).

Freshman Application Contact Derek Gueldenzoph, Dean of Admissions, St. Olaf College, 1520 St. Olaf Avenue, Northfield, MN 55057. *Phone:* 507-786-3025. *Toll-free phone:* 800-800-3025. *Fax:* 507-786-3832. *E-mail:* admissions@stolaf.edu.

SOUTHWEST MINNESOTA STATE UNIVERSITY

Marshall, Minnesota www.southwest.msus.edu/

- **State-supported** comprehensive, founded 1963, part of Minnesota State Colleges and Universities System
- **Small-town** 216-acre campus
- **Coed** 5,721 undergraduate students, 41% full-time, 58% women, 42% men
- **Minimally difficult** entrance level, 78% of applicants were admitted

Undergraduates 2,373 full-time, 3,348 part-time. Students come from 32 states and territories, 33 other countries, 8% are from out of state, 4% African American, 2% Asian American or Pacific Islander, 2% Hispanic American, 0.5% Native American, 9% international, 4% transferred in, 32% live on campus. *Retention:* 67% of 2006 full-time freshmen returned.

Freshmen *Admission:* 1,610 applied, 1,249 admitted, 505 enrolled. *Average high school GPA:* 3.1. *Test scores:* ACT scores over 18: 84%; ACT scores over 24: 23%; ACT scores over 30: 2%.

Faculty *Total:* 202, 62% full-time, 58% with terminal degrees. *Student/faculty ratio:* 23:1.

Majors Accounting; agribusiness; agricultural business and management; art; art teacher education; biology/biological sciences; biology teacher education; business administration and management; chemistry; chemistry teacher education; communication/speech communication and rhetoric; computer science; creative writing; criminal justice/law enforcement administration; criminal justice/safety; dramatic/theater arts; dramatic/theater arts and stagecraft related; education; elementary education; English; English/language arts teacher education; environmental science; finance; general studies; health and physical education; health teacher education; history; hotel/motel administration; information technology; kindergarten/preschool education; literature; management sciences and quantitative methods related; marketing/marketing management; mathematics; mathematics teacher education; music; music management and merchandising; music teacher education; non-profit management; philosophy; physical education teaching and coaching; political science and government; pre-dentistry studies; pre-law studies; pre-medical studies; pre-veterinary studies; psychology; public administration; radio and television; restaurant/food services management; social work; sociology; Spanish; Spanish language teacher education; special education; speech/theater education.

Academics *Calendar:* semesters. *Degrees:* associate, bachelor's, and master's. *Special study options:* academic remediation for entering students, accelerated degree program, adult/continuing education programs, advanced placement credit, distance learning, double majors, English as a second language, external degree program, freshman honors college, honors programs, independent study, internships, off-campus study, part-time degree program, services for LD students, student-designed majors, study abroad, summer session for credit.

Computers on Campus 420 computers/terminals and 200 ports are available on campus for general student use. Students can access the following: campus intranet, computer help desk, free student e-mail accounts, online (class) grades, online (class) registration. Campuswide network is available. 100% of college-owned or -operated housing units are wired for high-speed Internet access. Wireless service is available via classrooms, computer centers, computer labs, dorm rooms, learning centers, libraries, student centers.

Student Life *Housing:* on-campus residence required for freshman year. *Options:* coed, men-only, women-only. Campus housing is university owned. *Activities and organizations:* drama/theater group, student-run newspaper, radio and television station, choral group, marching band, Campus Crusade for Christ, College Republicans, Concert Choir/Vocal Ensemble, Theatre/Drama Club, Student Activities Committee. *Campus security:* 24-hour emergency response devices and patrols, student patrols, late-night transport/escort service, controlled dormitory access. *Student services:* health clinic, personal/psychological counseling, women's center.

Athletics Member NCAA. All Division II. *Intercollegiate sports:* baseball M (s), basketball M (s)/W (s), football M (s), golf W (s), soccer W (s), softball W (s), tennis W (s), volleyball W (s), wrestling M (s). *Intramural sports:* badminton M/W, basketball M/W, football M, ice hockey M, racquetball M/W, softball M/W, tennis M/W, volleyball M/W.

Standardized Tests *Required:* SAT or ACT (for admission). *Recommended:* ACT (for admission).

Costs (2008–09) *Tuition:* state resident $5800 full-time, $186 per credit part-time; nonresident $5800 full-time, $186 per credit part-time. *Required fees:* $950 full-time, $36 per credit part-time. *Room and board:* $5900; room only: $3484.

Financial Aid Of all full-time matriculated undergraduates who enrolled in 2007, 1,735 applied for aid, 1,371 were judged to have need, 443 had their need fully met. 123 Federal Work-Study jobs (averaging $2222). 197 state and other part-time jobs (averaging $2201). In 2007, 342 non-need-based awards were made. *Average percent of need met:* 63%. *Average financial aid package:* $7925. *Average need-based loan:* $3948. *Average need-based gift aid:* $4251. *Average non-need-based aid:* $1707. *Average indebtedness upon graduation:* $17,783.

Applying *Options:* electronic application, early admission, deferred entrance. *Application fee:* $20. *Required:* essay or personal statement, high school transcript, interview. *Application deadlines:* rolling (freshmen), rolling (transfers).

Freshman Application Contact Mr. Richard Shearer, Director of Enrollment Services, Southwest Minnesota State University, 1501 State Street, Marshall, MN 56258. *Phone:* 507-537-6286. *Toll-free phone:* 800-642-0684. *Fax:* 507-537-7145. *E-mail:* shearerr@southwestmsu.edu.

UNIVERSITY OF MINNESOTA, CROOKSTON

Crookston, Minnesota www.umcrookston.edu/

- **State-supported** 4-year, founded 1966, part of University of Minnesota System
- **Rural** 237-acre campus
- **Endowment** $11.3 million
- **Coed** 2,346 undergraduate students, 47% full-time, 50% women, 50% men
- **Moderately difficult** entrance level, 83% of applicants were admitted

Undergraduates 1,100 full-time, 1,246 part-time. Students come from 33 states and territories, 24 other countries, 31% are from out of state, 5% African American, 2% Asian American or Pacific Islander, 2% Hispanic American, 1% Native American, 7% international, 5% transferred in, 40% live on campus. *Retention:* 70% of 2006 full-time freshmen returned.

Freshmen *Admission:* 522 applied, 434 admitted, 241 enrolled. *Test scores:* SAT critical reading scores over 500: 21%; SAT math scores over 500: 46%; ACT scores over 18: 79%; SAT critical reading scores over 600: 9%; SAT math scores over 600: 12%; ACT scores over 24: 20%; ACT scores over 30: 2%.

Faculty *Total:* 103, 50% full-time, 34% with terminal degrees. *Student/faculty ratio:* 16:1.

Majors Accounting; aeronautics/aviation/aerospace science and technology; agribusiness; agricultural business and management; agricultural teacher education; agriculture; agronomy and crop science; animal sciences related; biology/biological sciences; business administration and management; business/commerce; communication/speech communication and rhetoric; computer engineering technology; dietitian assistant; early childhood education; equestrian studies; health and medical administrative services related; health services/allied health/health sciences; horticultural science; hospitality administration; industrial engineering; management information systems; marketing/marketing management; multi-/interdisciplinary studies related; natural resources/conservation; sport and fitness administration/management; turf and turfgrass management.

Academics *Calendar:* semesters. *Degrees:* certificates, associate, and bachelor's. *Special study options:* academic remediation for entering students, adult/

continuing education programs, advanced placement credit, distance learning, double majors, English as a second language, external degree program, independent study, internships, part-time degree program, services for LD students, student-designed majors, study abroad, summer session for credit. *ROTC:* Air Force (c).

Computers on Campus 1,200 computers/terminals are available on campus for general student use. Students can access the following: campus intranet, computer help desk, free student e-mail accounts, online (class) grades, online (class) registration, online (class) schedules, personal Web pages. Campuswide network is available. 100% of college-owned or -operated housing units are wired for high-speed Internet access. Wireless service is available via entire campus.

Student Life *Housing options:* coed. Campus housing is university owned. Freshman applicants given priority for college housing. *Activities and organizations:* drama/theater group, choral group, Students in Free Enterprise, Natural Resources Club, Horseman's Association, Multicultural and International Club, Ag-Arama Planning Club, national fraternities, national sororities. *Campus security:* student patrols, controlled dormitory access. *Student services:* health clinic, personal/psychological counseling, women's center.

Athletics Member NCAA. All Division II except ice hockey (Division III). *Intercollegiate sports:* baseball M (s), basketball M (s)/W (s), equestrian sports W, football M (s), golf M/W, ice hockey M, soccer W (s), softball W (s), tennis W, volleyball W (s). *Intramural sports:* basketball M/W, bowling M/W, cheerleading M/W, football M, racquetball M/W, soccer M/W, softball M/W, table tennis M/W, tennis M/W, volleyball M/W.

Standardized Tests *Required:* SAT (for admission). *Recommended:* ACT (for admission).

Costs (2007–08) *Tuition:* state resident $6448 full-time, $248 per credit part-time; nonresident $6448 full-time, $248 per credit part-time. Full-time tuition and fees vary according to course load. Part-time tuition and fees vary according to course load and reciprocity agreements. No tuition increase for student's term of enrollment. *Required fees:* $2373 full-time. *Room and board:* $5342; room only: $2632. Room and board charges vary according to board plan and housing facility. *Payment plan:* installment. *Waivers:* senior citizens.

Financial Aid Of all full-time matriculated undergraduates who enrolled in 2006, 759 applied for aid, 642 were judged to have need, 260 had their need fully met. In 2006, 94 non-need-based awards were made. *Average percent of need met:* 81%. *Average financial aid package:* $11,369. *Average need-based loan:* $5814. *Average need-based gift aid:* $6377. *Average non-need-based aid:* $1682.

Applying *Options:* electronic application, early admission, deferred entrance. *Application fee:* $30. *Required:* high school transcript. *Application deadlines:* rolling (freshmen), rolling (transfers). *Notification:* continuous (freshmen), continuous (transfers).

Freshman Application Contact Ms. Amber Evans-Dailey, Director of Admissions, University of Minnesota, Crookston, 2900 University Avenue, 170 Owen Hall, Crookston, MN 56716-5001. *Phone:* 218-281-8569. *Toll-free phone:* 800-862-6466. *Fax:* 218-281-8575. *E-mail:* info@UMCrookston.edu.

UNIVERSITY OF MINNESOTA, DULUTH

Duluth, Minnesota **www.d.umn.edu/**

- **State-supported** comprehensive, founded 1947, part of University of Minnesota System
- **Suburban** 250-acre campus
- **Endowment** $126.2 million
- **Coed** 10,093 undergraduate students, 88% full-time, 48% women, 52% men
- **Moderately difficult** entrance level, 70% of applicants were admitted

Undergraduates 8,874 full-time, 1,219 part-time. Students come from 36 states and territories, 38 other countries, 14% are from out of state, 1% African American, 3% Asian American or Pacific Islander, 1% Hispanic American, 1% Native American, 1% international, 4% transferred in, 30% live on campus. *Retention:* 79% of 2006 full-time freshmen returned.

Freshmen *Admission:* 7,653 applied, 5,393 admitted, 2,240 enrolled. *Average high school GPA:* 3.28. *Test scores:* ACT scores over 18: 97%; ACT scores over 24: 43%; ACT scores over 30: 4%.

Faculty *Total:* 564, 74% full-time, 76% with terminal degrees. *Student/faculty ratio:* 22:1.

Majors Accounting; actuarial science; American Indian/Native American studies; anthropology; art; art history, criticism and conservation; art teacher education; audiology and speech-language pathology; biochemistry; biology/biological sciences; business administration and management; cell biology and histology; chemical engineering; chemistry; commercial and advertising art; computer engineering; computer science; criminology; dramatic/theater arts; economics; education; electrical, electronics and communications engineering; elementary education; English; environmental studies; finance; fine/studio arts; French language teacher education; geography; geology/earth science; German language teacher education; health teacher education; history; human resources management; industrial engineering; interdisciplinary studies; international relations and affairs; jazz/jazz studies; kindergarten/preschool education; kinesiology and exercise science; marketing/marketing management; mathematics; mathematics teacher education; middle school education; molecular biology; music; music teacher education; parks, recreation and leisure; philosophy; physical education teaching and coaching; physics; political science and government; pre-dentistry studies; pre-law studies; pre-medical studies; pre-pharmacy studies; pre-veterinary studies; psychology; science teacher education; social studies teacher education; sociology; Spanish; Spanish language teacher education; special education; statistics; urban studies/affairs; women's studies.

Academics *Calendar:* semesters. *Degrees:* bachelor's, master's, doctoral, first professional, and postbachelor's certificates. *Special study options:* academic remediation for entering students, adult/continuing education programs, advanced placement credit, distance learning, double majors, English as a second language, honors programs, independent study, internships, off-campus study, part-time degree program, services for LD students, student-designed majors, study abroad, summer session for credit. *ROTC:* Air Force (b).

Computers on Campus 465 computers/terminals are available on campus for general student use. Students can access the following: campus intranet, computer help desk, free student e-mail accounts, online (class) grades, online (class) registration, online (class) schedules. Campuswide network is available. 100% of college-owned or -operated housing units are wired for high-speed Internet access. Wireless service is available via entire campus.

Student Life *Housing options:* coed, men-only, women-only, disabled students. Campus housing is university owned. Freshman applicants given priority for college housing. *Activities and organizations:* drama/theater group, student-run newspaper, radio station, choral group, marching band, Religious groups, Recreational sports clubs, Departmental clubs, Outdoor recreation clubs, national fraternities, national sororities. *Campus security:* 24-hour emergency response devices and patrols, late-night transport/escort service. *Student services:* health clinic, personal/psychological counseling, women's center.

Athletics Member NCAA. All Division II except men's and women's ice hockey (Division I). *Intercollegiate sports:* baseball M (s), basketball M (s)/W (s), cheerleading W (c), crew M (c)/W (c), cross-country running M (s)/W (s), football M (s), ice hockey M (s)/W (s), lacrosse M (s) (c)/W (c), rock climbing M (c)/W (c), rugby M (c)/W (c), skiing (cross-country) M (c)/W (c), skiing (downhill) M (c)/W (c), soccer M (c)/W (s), softball W (s), swimming and diving M (c)/W (c), tennis W (s), track and field M (s)/W (s), ultimate Frisbee M (c)/W (c), volleyball M (c)/W (s). *Intramural sports:* badminton M/W, basketball M/W, bowling M/W, football M/W, golf M/W, ice hockey M/W, rugby M/W, sailing M/W, skiing (cross-country) M/W, skiing (downhill) M/W, soccer M/W, softball M/W, table tennis M/W, tennis M/W, ultimate Frisbee M/W, volleyball M/W, water polo M/W.

Standardized Tests *Required:* SAT or ACT (for admission).

Costs (2007–08) *Tuition:* state resident $7700 full-time, $296 per credit part-time; nonresident $17,327 full-time, $666 per credit part-time. Full-time tuition and fees vary according to course load, degree level, program, and reciprocity agreements. Part-time tuition and fees vary according to course load, degree level, program, and reciprocity agreements. *Required fees:* $1900 full-time, $50 per credit part-time. *Room and board:* $5904; room only: $3868. *Payment plan:* installment. *Waivers:* children of alumni.

Financial Aid Of all full-time matriculated undergraduates who enrolled in 2007, 6,476 applied for aid, 4,681 were judged to have need, 3,008 had their need fully met. 159 Federal Work-Study jobs (averaging $2431). 249 state and other part-time jobs (averaging $2099). In 2007, 930 non-need-based awards were made. *Average percent of need met:* 68%. *Average financial aid package:* $9222. *Average need-based loan:* $4063. *Average need-based gift aid:* $6967. *Average non-need-based aid:* $2586. *Average indebtedness upon graduation:* $21,933.

Applying *Options:* electronic application. *Application fee:* $35. *Required:* high school transcript. *Application deadlines:* 2/1 (freshmen), 8/1 (transfers). *Notification:* continuous (freshmen), continuous (transfers).

Freshman Application Contact Admissions, University of Minnesota, Duluth, 23 Solon Campus Center, 1117 University Drive, Duluth, MN 55812-3000. *Phone:* 218-726-7171. *Toll-free phone:* 800-232-1339. *Fax:* 218-726-7040. *E-mail:* umdadmis@d.umn.edu.

UNIVERSITY OF MINNESOTA, MORRIS

Morris, Minnesota www.mrs.umn.edu/

- **State-supported** 4-year, founded 1959, part of University of Minnesota System
- **Small-town** 130-acre campus
- **Endowment** $8.8 million
- **Coed**
- **Moderately difficult** entrance level

Faculty *Student/faculty ratio:* 12:1.

Academics *Calendar:* semesters. *Degree:* bachelor's.

Student Life *Campus security:* 24-hour emergency response devices and patrols, late-night transport/escort service, controlled dormitory access.

Athletics Member NCAA. All Division III.

Standardized Tests *Required:* SAT or ACT (for admission).

Costs (2007–08) *Tuition:* state resident $9112 full-time, $311 per credit part-time; nonresident $9112 full-time, $311 per credit part-time. *Room and board:* $6260; room only: $2980.

Financial Aid Of all full-time matriculated undergraduates who enrolled in 2006, 1,238 applied for aid, 1,010 were judged to have need, 442 had their need fully met. 432 Federal Work-Study jobs (averaging $916). 516 state and other part-time jobs (averaging $863). In 2006, 297 non-need-based awards were made. *Average percent of need met:* 82. *Average financial aid package:* $12,660. *Average need-based loan:* $7333. *Average need-based gift aid:* $5885. *Average non-need-based aid:* $3052. *Average indebtedness upon graduation:* $15,490.

Applying *Options:* electronic application, early admission, early action, deferred entrance. *Application fee:* $35. *Required:* essay or personal statement, high school transcript. *Required for some:* 1 letter of recommendation, interview. *Recommended:* minimum 3.0 GPA.

Freshman Application Contact Ms. Jaime Moquin, Director of Admissions, University of Minnesota, Morris, 600 East 4th Street, Morris, MN 56267-2199. *Phone:* 320-539-6035. *Toll-free phone:* 800-992-8863. *Fax:* 320-589-1673. *E-mail:* admissions@morris.umn.edu.

UNIVERSITY OF MINNESOTA, TWIN CITIES CAMPUS

Minneapolis, Minnesota www.umn.edu/tc/

- **State-supported** university, founded 1851, part of University of Minnesota System
- **Urban** 2000-acre campus
- **Coed** 32,294 undergraduate students, 84% full-time, 53% women, 47% men
- **Moderately difficult** entrance level, 57% of applicants were admitted

Undergraduates 27,091 full-time, 5,203 part-time. Students come from 51 states and territories, 77 other countries, 27% are from out of state, 5% African American, 10% Asian American or Pacific Islander, 2% Hispanic American, 1% Native American, 2% international, 6% transferred in, 22% live on campus. *Retention:* 88% of 2006 full-time freshmen returned.

Freshmen *Admission:* 26,097 applied, 14,823 admitted, 5,280 enrolled. *Test scores:* SAT critical reading scores over 500: 85%; SAT math scores over 500: 93%; SAT writing scores over 500: 83%; ACT scores over 18: 97%; SAT critical reading scores over 600: 58%; SAT math scores over 600: 71%; SAT writing scores over 600: 51%; ACT scores over 24: 75%; SAT critical reading scores over 700: 20%; SAT math scores over 700: 26%; SAT writing scores over 700: 14%; ACT scores over 30: 19%.

Faculty *Total:* 2,078, 85% full-time, 85% with terminal degrees.

Majors Accounting; actuarial science; aerospace, aeronautical and astronautical engineering; African-American/Black studies; African studies; agricultural/biological engineering and bioengineering; agricultural business and management; agricultural teacher education; agriculture; agronomy and crop science; American Indian/Native American studies; American studies; animal genetics; animal physiology; animal sciences; anthropology; architecture; art; art history, criticism and conservation; art teacher education; Asian studies (East); Asian studies (South); astronomy; astrophysics; audiology and speech-language pathology; biochemistry; biology/biological sciences; botany/plant biology; business teacher education; cell biology and histology; chemical engineering; chemistry; Chinese; civil engineering; clinical laboratory science/medical technology; clothing/textiles; commercial and advertising art; comparative literature; computer science; construction management; dance; dental hygiene; developmental and child psychology; dramatic/theater arts; ecology; economics; education; electrical, electronics and communications engineering; elementary education; emergency medical technology (EMT paramedic); English; English/language arts teacher education; environmental studies; European studies; family and community services; family and consumer sciences/home economics teacher education; film/cinema studies; finance; fish/game management; foods, nutrition, and wellness; foreign language teacher education; forest/forest resources management; forestry; French; funeral service and mortuary science; geography; geological/geophysical engineering; geology/earth science; geophysics and seismology; German; health and physical education related; Hebrew; Hispanic-American, Puerto Rican, and Mexican-American/Chicano studies; history; industrial engineering; insurance; interior design; international business/trade/commerce; international relations and affairs; Italian; Japanese; Jewish/Judaic studies; journalism; kindergarten/preschool education; landscape architecture; Latin; Latin American studies; linguistics; management information systems; marketing/marketing management; mass communication/media; materials engineering; materials science; mathematics; mathematics teacher education; mechanical engineering; medical microbiology and bacteriology; modern Greek; music; music teacher education; music therapy; natural resources management and policy; Near and Middle Eastern studies; neuroscience; nursing (registered nurse training); occupational therapy; parks, recreation and leisure facilities management; philosophy; physical education teaching and coaching; physical therapy; physics; plant sciences; political science and government; Portuguese; pre-dentistry studies; pre-law studies; pre-medical studies; pre-veterinary studies; psychology; public health; religious studies; Russian; Russian studies; Scandinavian languages; science teacher education; social science teacher education; sociology; soil science and agronomy; Spanish; urban studies/affairs; women's studies; wood science and wood products/pulp and paper technology.

Academics *Calendar:* semesters. *Degrees:* certificates, diplomas, bachelor's, master's, doctoral, first professional, post-master's, postbachelor's, and first professional certificates. *Special study options:* academic remediation for entering students, accelerated degree program, adult/continuing education programs, advanced placement credit, cooperative education, distance learning, double majors, English as a second language, external degree program, freshman honors college, honors programs, independent study, internships, off-campus study, part-time degree program, services for LD students, student-designed majors, study abroad, summer session for credit. *ROTC:* Army (b), Navy (b), Air Force (b).

Computers on Campus Students can access the following: online (class) registration, e-mail. Campuswide network is available.

Student Life *Housing options:* coed, cooperative, disabled students. Campus housing is university owned. Freshman campus housing is guaranteed. *Activities and organizations:* drama/theater group, student-run newspaper, radio and television station, choral group, marching band, sports clubs, student government, religious organizations, departmental/professional organizations, national fraternities, national sororities. *Campus security:* 24-hour emergency response devices and patrols, student patrols, late-night transport/escort service, controlled dormitory access, safety/security orientation, security lighting. *Student services:* health clinic, personal/psychological counseling, women's center, legal services.

Athletics Member NCAA. All Division I except football (Division I-A). *Intercollegiate sports:* baseball M (s), basketball M (s)/W (s), cross-country running M (s)/W (s), golf M (s)/W (s), gymnastics M (s)/W (s), ice hockey M (s)/W (s), soccer W (s), softball W (s), swimming and diving M (s)/W (s), tennis M (s)/W (s), track and field M (s)/W (s), volleyball W (s), wrestling M (s). *Intramural sports:* baseball M/W, basketball M/W, bowling M/W, crew M/W, football M/W, golf M/W, ice hockey M/W, rugby M/W, skiing (cross-country) M/W, skiing (downhill) M/W, soccer M/W, softball M/W, tennis M/W, volleyball M/W, water polo M/W, wrestling M/W.

Standardized Tests *Required:* SAT or ACT (for admission).

Costs (2007–08) *One-time required fee:* $1000. *Tuition:* state resident $7950 full-time, $306 per credit part-time; nonresident $19,580 full-time, $753 per credit part-time. Full-time tuition and fees vary according to program and reciprocity agreements. Part-time tuition and fees vary according to course load, program, and reciprocity agreements. *Room and board:* $7062; room only: $4184. Room and board charges vary according to board plan, housing facility, and location. *Payment plan:* installment. *Waivers:* senior citizens.

Financial Aid Of all full-time matriculated undergraduates who enrolled in 2006, 17,575 applied for aid, 12,747 were judged to have need, 6,425 had their need fully met. In 2006, 3003 non-need-based awards were made. *Average percent of need met:* 85%. *Average financial aid package:* $11,969. *Average need-based loan:* $7742. *Average need-based gift aid:* $7596. *Average non-need-based aid:* $4566.

Applying *Options:* electronic application, early admission, deferred entrance. *Application fee:* $45. *Required:* high school transcript. *Recommended:* minimum 2.0 GPA. *Application deadlines:* rolling (freshmen), rolling (transfers). *Notification:* continuous (freshmen), continuous (transfers).

Freshman Application Contact Rachelle Hernandez, Associate Director of Admissions, University of Minnesota, Twin Cities Campus, 240 Williamson Hall,

231 Pillsbury Drive SE, Minneapolis, MN 55455-0115. *Phone:* 612-625-2008. *Toll-free phone:* 800-752-1000. *Fax:* 612-626-1693. *E-mail:* admissions@tc.umn.edu.

UNIVERSITY OF ST. THOMAS

St. Paul, Minnesota **www.stthomas.edu/**

- **Independent Roman Catholic** university, founded 1885
- **Urban** 78-acre campus with easy access to Minneapolis
- **Endowment** $223.3 million
- **Coed** 6,076 undergraduate students, 94% full-time, 49% women, 51% men
- **Moderately difficult** entrance level, 74% of applicants were admitted

St. Thomas is a coeducational, Catholic liberal arts university with more than 10,000 undergraduate and graduate students. The largest independent university in Minnesota, St. Thomas offers more than ninety majors, including biology, business administration, computer science, engineering, journalism, and a number of preprofessional areas of study. St. Thomas emphasizes values-centered, career-oriented education.

Undergraduates 5,698 full-time, 378 part-time. Students come from 44 states and territories, 7 other countries, 17% are from out of state, 3% African American, 4% Asian American or Pacific Islander, 3% Hispanic American, 0.5% Native American, 0.8% international, 5% transferred in, 42% live on campus. *Retention:* 88% of 2006 full-time freshmen returned.

Freshmen *Admission:* 5,312 applied, 3,921 admitted, 1,315 enrolled. *Average high school GPA:* 3.56. *Test scores:* SAT critical reading scores over 500: 86%; SAT math scores over 500: 89%; ACT scores over 18: 99%; SAT critical reading scores over 600: 47%; SAT math scores over 600: 50%; ACT scores over 24: 69%; SAT critical reading scores over 700: 15%; SAT math scores over 700: 10%; ACT scores over 30: 10%.

Faculty *Total:* 840, 47% full-time. *Student/faculty ratio:* 15:1.

Majors Accounting; actuarial science; ancient/classical Greek; art history, criticism and conservation; Asian studies (East); biochemistry; biology/biological sciences; biology teacher education; broadcast journalism; business administration and management; business administration, management and operations related; business/corporate communications; chemistry; chemistry teacher education; classics and classical languages related; classics and languages, literatures and linguistics; clinical/medical social work; communication/speech communication and rhetoric; computer and information sciences; creative writing; criminology; drama and dance teacher education; dramatic/theater arts; econometrics and quantitative economics; economics; education (K-12); education (specific subject areas) related; electrical, electronics and communications engineering; elementary education; English; English/language arts teacher education; entrepreneurship; finance; foreign languages related; foreign language teacher education; French; geography; geology/earth science; German; health and physical education; health science; health teacher education; history; human resources management; interdisciplinary studies; international business/trade/commerce; international economics; international relations and affairs; Japanese; journalism; journalism related; Latin; legal professions and studies related; liberal arts and sciences and humanities related; marketing/marketing management; mathematics; mathematics teacher education; mechanical engineering; middle school education; multi-/interdisciplinary studies related; music; music teacher education; operations management; peace studies and conflict resolution; philosophy; physical education teaching and coaching; physics; physics teacher education; political science and government; psychology; psychology related; public administration; public health education and promotion; real estate; religious studies; Russian; Russian studies; science teacher education; social sciences; social studies teacher education; social work; sociology; Spanish; speech/theater education; women's studies.

Academics *Calendar:* 4-1-4. *Degrees:* bachelor's, master's, doctoral, first professional, post-master's, and postbachelor's certificates. *Special study options:* advanced placement credit, double majors, English as a second language, honors programs, independent study, internships, off-campus study, part-time degree program, services for LD students, student-designed majors, study abroad, summer session for credit. *ROTC:* Army (c), Navy (c), Air Force (b). *Unusual degree programs:* 3-2 engineering with University of Notre Dame; Washington University in St. Louis; University of Minnesota, Twin Cities Campus; Kettering University.

Computers on Campus 1,549 computers/terminals are available on campus for general student use. Students can access the following: online (class) registration. Campuswide network is available.

Student Life *Housing options:* men-only, women-only. Campus housing is university owned. Freshman applicants given priority for college housing. *Activities and organizations:* drama/theater group, student-run newspaper, radio station, choral group. *Campus security:* 24-hour emergency response devices and patrols, late-night transport/escort service, controlled dormitory access. *Student services:* health clinic, personal/psychological counseling, women's center, legal services.

Athletics Member NCAA. All Division III. *Intercollegiate sports:* baseball M, basketball M/W, crew M (c)/W (c), cross-country running M/W, football M, golf M/W, ice hockey M/W, lacrosse M (c)/W (c), skiing (downhill) M (c)/W (c), soccer M/W, softball W, swimming and diving M/W, tennis M/W, track and field M/W, volleyball W. *Intramural sports:* basketball M/W, golf M/W, racquetball M/W, soccer M/W, softball M/W, squash M/W, table tennis M/W, tennis M/W, volleyball M/W.

Standardized Tests *Required:* SAT or ACT (for admission).

Costs (2008–09) *Comprehensive fee:* $35,436 includes full-time tuition ($27,328), mandatory fees ($494), and room and board ($7614). Part-time tuition: $854 per credit hour. *College room only:* $4872.

Financial Aid Of all full-time matriculated undergraduates who enrolled in 2007, 3,825 applied for aid, 2,171 were judged to have need, 1,169 had their need fully met. 829 Federal Work-Study jobs (averaging $2767). 730 state and other part-time jobs (averaging $2636). In 2007, 960 non-need-based awards were made. *Average percent of need met:* 79%. *Average financial aid package:* $20,620. *Average need-based loan:* $5778. *Average need-based gift aid:* $11,762. *Average non-need-based aid:* $7694. *Average indebtedness upon graduation:* $33,499.

Applying *Options:* electronic application, deferred entrance. *Required:* essay or personal statement, high school transcript. *Recommended:* letters of recommendation, interview. *Application deadlines:* rolling (freshmen), rolling (transfers). *Notification:* continuous (freshmen), continuous (transfers).

Director of Admissions Ms. Marla Friederichs, Associate Vice President of Enrollment Management, University of St. Thomas, 2115 Summit Avenue, Mail #32F-1, St. Paul, MN 55105-1096. *Phone:* 651-962-6150. *Toll-free phone:* 800-328-6819 Ext. 26150. *E-mail:* admissions@stthomas.edu.

See page 1394 for the College Close-Up.

WALDEN UNIVERSITY

Minneapolis, Minnesota **www.waldenu.edu/**

- **Proprietary** upper-level, founded 1970, part of Laureate International Universities Network
- **Coed** 1,502 undergraduate students, 6% full-time, 58% women, 42% men

Undergraduates 87 full-time, 1,415 part-time. Students come from 48 states and territories, 6 other countries, 99% are from out of state, 13% African American, 1% Asian American or Pacific Islander, 3% Hispanic American, 0.1% Native American, 36% international.

Faculty *Total:* 883, 63% full-time. *Student/faculty ratio:* 33:1.

Majors Business administration and management; finance; human resources management; information technology; marketing/marketing management.

Academics *Calendar:* quarter/semester depending on program. *Degrees:* bachelor's, master's, and doctoral. *Special study options:* distance learning.

Costs (2007–08) *One-time required fee:* $50. *Tuition:* $11,250 full-time, $250 per quarter hour part-time. *Waivers:* employees or children of employees.

Director of Admissions Ms. Dawn Wolff, Director of Admissions, Walden University, 155 Fifth Avenue South, Minneapolis, MN 55401. *Phone:* 800-925-3368. *Toll-free phone:* 866-492-5336. *Fax:* 410-843-8780. *E-mail:* request@waldenu.edu.

WINONA STATE UNIVERSITY

Winona, Minnesota **www.winona.edu/**

- **State-supported** comprehensive, founded 1858, part of Minnesota State Colleges and Universities System
- **Small-town** 40-acre campus
- **Endowment** $12.0 million
- **Coed** 7,608 undergraduate students, 92% full-time, 62% women, 38% men
- **Moderately difficult** entrance level, 79% of applicants were admitted

Undergraduates 7,000 full-time, 608 part-time. Students come from 21 states and territories, 48 other countries, 34% are from out of state, 1% African American, 2% Asian American or Pacific Islander, 0.8% Hispanic American, 0.3% Native American, 4% international, 7% transferred in, 28% live on campus. *Retention:* 73% of 2006 full-time freshmen returned.

Freshmen *Admission:* 5,359 applied, 4,246 admitted, 1,727 enrolled. *Average high school GPA:* 3.3. *Test scores:* ACT scores over 18: 99%; ACT scores over 24: 59%; ACT scores over 30: 3%.

Faculty *Total:* 501, 73% full-time, 57% with terminal degrees. *Student/faculty ratio:* 21:1.

Majors Accounting; advertising; applied art; applied mathematics; art; art teacher education; athletic training; aviation/airway management; biological and physical sciences; biology/biological sciences; broadcast journalism; business administration and management; business/managerial economics; business teacher education; chemical engineering; chemistry; clinical laboratory science/medical technology; clinical/medical laboratory technology; commercial and advertising art; computer and information sciences; computer programming; computer science; consumer merchandising/retailing management; corrections; criminal justice/law enforcement administration; criminal justice/police science; cytotechnology; dramatic/theater arts; drawing; ecology; economics; education; elementary education; engineering; English; environmental biology; finance; fine/studio arts; French; geology/earth science; German; health/health care administration; health science; health teacher education; history; human resources management; information science/studies; international relations and affairs; journalism; kindergarten/preschool education; kinesiology and exercise science; labor and industrial relations; legal assistant/paralegal; legal studies; liberal arts and sciences/liberal studies; management information systems; marketing/marketing management; mass communication/media; materials engineering; mathematics; mechanical engineering; middle school education; music; music management and merchandising; music teacher education; natural resources/conservation; natural sciences; nursing (registered nurse training); parks, recreation and leisure; parks, recreation and leisure facilities management; physical education teaching and coaching; physical sciences; physical therapy; physics; political science and government; polymer chemistry; polymer/plastics engineering; pre-dentistry studies; pre-law studies; pre-medical studies; pre-veterinary studies; psychology; public administration; public health; public relations/image management; quality control technology; radio and television; reading teacher education; science teacher education; secondary education; social sciences; social work; sociology; Spanish; special education; speech and rhetoric; sport and fitness administration/management; statistics; telecommunications; therapeutic recreation; voice and opera; wildlife and wildlands science and management; wildlife biology; zoology/animal biology.

Academics *Calendar:* semesters. *Degrees:* associate, bachelor's, master's, and post-master's certificates. *Special study options:* academic remediation for entering students, accelerated degree program, adult/continuing education programs, advanced placement credit, distance learning, double majors, English as a second language, external degree program, honors programs, independent study, internships, off-campus study, part-time degree program, services for LD students, student-designed majors, study abroad, summer session for credit. *ROTC:* Army (c).

Computers on Campus 1,400 computers/terminals are available on campus for general student use. Students can access the following: campus intranet, computer help desk, free student e-mail accounts, online (class) grades, online (class) registration, online (class) schedules. Campuswide network is available. 100% of college-owned or -operated housing units are wired for high-speed Internet access. Wireless service is available via classrooms, computer centers, computer labs, learning centers, libraries, student centers.

Student Life *Housing options:* coed, men-only, women-only. Campus housing is university owned and leased by the school. Freshman campus housing is guaranteed. *Activities and organizations:* drama/theater group, student-run newspaper, radio station, choral group, marching band, University Program Activities Committee, Student Senate, Inter-Residence Hall Council, national fraternities, national sororities. *Campus security:* 24-hour emergency response devices and patrols, student patrols, late-night transport/escort service, controlled dormitory access, security cameras. *Student services:* health clinic, personal/psychological counseling, women's center, legal services.

Athletics Member NCAA. All Division II. *Intercollegiate sports:* baseball M (s), basketball M (s)/W (s), bowling M (c)/W (c), cross-country running M (c)/W (s), fencing M (c)/W (c), football M (s), golf M (s)/W (s), gymnastics W (s), ice hockey M (c), rugby M (c)/W (c), skiing (downhill) M (c)/W (c), soccer M (c)/W (s), softball W (s), tennis M (s)/W (s), track and field W (s), volleyball M (c)/W (s), wrestling M (c). *Intramural sports:* archery M/W, badminton M/W, baseball M, basketball M/W, bowling M/W, cross-country running M/W, fencing M/W, field hockey M/W, football M/W, golf M/W, gymnastics W, ice hockey M/W, racquetball M/W, riflery M/W, rugby M/W, skiing (cross-country) M/W, skiing (downhill) M/W, soccer M/W, softball M/W, swimming and diving M/W, table tennis M/W, tennis M/W, track and field W, volleyball M/W, weight lifting M/W, wrestling M.

Standardized Tests *Required:* SAT or ACT (for admission).

Financial Aid Of all full-time matriculated undergraduates who enrolled in 2006, 4,962 applied for aid, 3,645 were judged to have need, 486 had their need fully met. 204 Federal Work-Study jobs (averaging $1891). 384 state and other part-time jobs (averaging $1933). In 2006, 962 non-need-based awards were made. *Average percent of need met:* 46%. *Average financial aid package:* $6400. *Average need-based loan:* $3545. *Average need-based gift aid:* $3643. *Average non-need-based aid:* $2473. *Average indebtedness upon graduation:* $23,701.

Applying *Options:* electronic application, early admission, early action, deferred entrance. *Application fee:* $20. *Required:* high school transcript, class rank. *Required for some:* essay or personal statement, letters of recommendation, interview. *Application deadlines:* rolling (freshmen), 8/1 (transfers). *Notification:* continuous (freshmen), continuous (transfers).

Freshman Application Contact Carl Stange, Director of Admissions, Winona State University, PO Box 5838, Winona, MN 55987. *Phone:* 507-457-5100. *Toll-free phone:* 800-DIAL WSU. *Fax:* 507-457-5620. *E-mail:* admissions@winona.edu.

ARGOSY UNIVERSITY

ARGOSY UNIVERSITY

The University

Argosy University is a leading institution offering a variety of degree programs that focus on the human side of success alongside professional competence. For students looking for a more personal approach to education, Argosy University may just be the answer. With forty-eight graduate and undergraduate programs, across nineteen campuses and twelve states, Argosy University emphasizes interpersonal skills as well as academic learning. All of its programs are taught by practicing professionals who bring real-world experience into the classroom. So students graduate with both a solid foundation of knowledge and the power to put it to work. To accommodate busy working adults, many programs at Argosy University are structured flexibly—with both campus and online learning and evening, weekend, and daytime classes. There is also a wide range of financial aid options for students who qualify.

Argosy University is a private institution of higher education dedicated to providing high-quality professional education programs at the doctoral, master's, bachelor's, and associate degree levels as well as continuing education to individuals who seek to advance their professional and personal lives. The University emphasizes programs in the behavioral sciences (psychology and counseling), business, education, and the health-care professions. A limited number of preprofessional programs and general education offerings are provided to permit students to prepare for entry into these professional fields. The programs of Argosy University are designed to instill the knowledge, skills, and ethical values of professional practice and to foster values of social responsibility in a supportive, learning-centered environment of mutual respect and professional excellence.

With nineteen campuses nationwide, Argosy University provides students with a network of resources found at larger universities, including a career resources office, an academic resources center, and extensive information access for research. The University's innovative programs feature dynamic, relevant, and practical curricula delivered in flexible class formats. Students enjoy scheduling options that make it easier to fit school into their busy lives. They can choose from day and evening courses, on campus or online. Many students find a combination of both to be an ideal way of continuing their education while meeting family and professional demands.

Most students are full-time working professionals who live within driving distance of the campus. The University does not offer or operate student housing.

Argosy University is accredited by The Higher Learning Commission of the North Central Association (30 North LaSalle Street, Suite 2400, Chicago, Illinois 60602; 800-621-7440; http://ncahlc.org).

Location

Argosy University operates nineteen locations across the U.S. and offers a variety of degree programs online (http://www.argosy.edu). Campus locations include the following:

Atlanta, 980 Hammond Drive, Suite 100, Atlanta, Georgia 30328; phone: 770-671-1200 or 888-671-4777 (toll-free)

Chicago, 225 North Michigan Avenue, Suite 1300, Chicago, Illinois 60601; phone: 312-777-7600 or 800-626-4123 (toll-free)

Dallas, 8080 Park Lane, Suite 400A, Dallas, Texas 75231; phone: 214-890-9900 or 866-954-9900 (toll-free)

Denver, 1200 Lincoln Street, Denver, Colorado 80203; phone: 303-248-2700 or 866-431-5981 (toll-free)

Hawai'i, 400 ASB Tower, 1001 Bishop Street, Honolulu, Hawaii 96813; phone: 808-536-5555 or 888-323-2777 (toll-free)

Inland Empire, 636 East Brier Drive, Suite 235, San Bernardino, California 92408; phone: 909-915-3800 or 866-217-9075 (toll-free)

Nashville, 100 Centerview Drive, Suite 225, Nashville, Tennessee 37214; phone: 615-525-2800 or 866-833-6598 (toll-free)

Orange County, 3501 West Sunflower Avenue, Suite 110, Santa Ana, California 92704; phone: 714-338-6200 or 800-716-9598 (toll-free)

Phoenix, 2233 West Dunlap Avenue, Phoenix, Arizona 85021; phone: 602-216-2600 or 866-216-2777 (toll-free)

Salt Lake City, 121 West Election Road, Suite 300, Draper, Utah 84020; phone: 888-639-4756 (toll-free)

San Diego, 7650 Mission Valley Road, San Diego, California 92108; phone: 858-598-1900 or 866-505-0333 (toll-free)

San Francisco Bay Area, 1005 Atlantic Avenue, Alameda, California 94501; phone: 510-217-4700 or 866-215-2777 (toll-free)

Santa Monica, 2950 31st Street, Santa Monica, California 90405; phone: 310-866-4000 or 866-505-0332 (toll-free)

Sarasota, 5250 17th Street, Sarasota, Florida 34235; phone: 941-379-0404 or 800-331-5995 (toll-free)

Schaumburg, 999 North Plaza Drive, Suite 111, Schaumburg, Illinois 60173-5403; phone: 847-969-4900 or 866-290-2777 (toll-free)

Seattle, 2601-A Elliott Avenue, Seattle, Washington 98121; phone: 206-283-4500 or 888-283-2777 (toll-free)

Tampa, Parkside at Tampa Bay Park, 4401 North Hines Avenue, Suite 150, Tampa, Florida 33614; phone: 813-393-5290 or 800-850-6488 (toll-free)

Twin Cities, 1515 Central Parkway, Eagan, Minnesota 55121; phone: 651-846-2882 or 888-844-2004 (toll-free)

Washington DC, 1550 Wilson Boulevard, Suite 600, Arlington, Virginia 22209; phone: 703-526-5800 or 866-703-2777 (toll-free)

Majors and Degrees

Argosy University's College of Business offers a Bachelor of Science (B.S.) in Business Administration program. Argosy University's College of Psychology and Behavioral Sciences offers the Bachelor of Arts (B.A.) in Psychology degree program.

Academic Programs

The B.S. in Business Administration program prepares students for entry- to mid-level positions within the public or private sector. The curriculum is structured to help students develop competencies in oral and written communication, leadership, team skills, solutions-focused learning, and the analysis and execution of solutions in various business situations. Students may choose one of five optional concentrations: customized professional concentration, finance, health-care management, international business, or marketing.

The B.A. in Psychology program is designed to help students begin human services careers in such capacities as entry-level counselor, case manager, or human resources administrator and

in management and business services roles. The program also lays the foundation for graduate study. Students may choose an optional concentration from the following three options: criminal justice, organizational psychology, or substance abuse. This dynamic program is built around a flexible class approach.

Argosy University's bachelor's degree programs are open to students and working professionals with no college experience, plus those who have already earned college credit at a community college, junior college, or other university.

Academic Facilities

Argosy University libraries provide curriculum support and educational resources including current text materials, diagnostic training documents, reference materials and databases, journals and dissertations, and major and current titles in program areas. There is an online public-access catalog of library resources available throughout the Argosy University system. Students enjoy full remote access to their campus library database, enabling them to study and conduct research at home. Academic databases offer dissertation abstracts, academic journals, and professional periodicals. All library computers are Internet accessible. Software applications include Word, Excel, PowerPoint, SPSS, and various test-scoring programs.

Costs

Tuition varies by program. Students should contact the Argosy University campus of their choice for tuition information.

Financial Aid

A wide range of financial aid options is available to students who qualify. Argosy University offers access to federal and state aid programs, merit-based awards, grants, loans, and a work-study program. As a first step, students should complete the Free Application for Federal Student Aid (FAFSA). Prospective students can apply electronically at http://www.fafsa.ed.gov or at the campus. To receive consideration for financial aid and ensure timely receipt of funds, it is best to submit an application promptly.

Faculty

The Argosy University faculty is composed of working professionals who have a passion to help students succeed. Members bring real-world experience and the latest practice innovations to the academic setting. The diverse faculty is widely recognized for contributions to the field. Most hold doctoral degrees. They provide a substantive education that combines comprehensive knowledge with critical skills and practical workplace relevance. Above all, faculty members are committed to their students' personal and professional development.

Student Government

Argosy University campuses offer unique opportunities for student involvement beyond individual programs of study. Most faculty committees include a student representative. In addition, a student group meets with faculty members and administrators regularly to discuss pertinent campus-related issues.

Admission Requirements

Admission requirements differ depending on the number of college credits completed prior to application.

Students who have earned 12 or fewer semester college credits must provide proof of high school graduation or GED and meet one of the following conditions for admission: ACT composite score of 18 or above, or a combined math and verbal SAT score of 870, or minimum ACCUPLACER scores of 86 in sentence skills and 53 in algebra. Applicants who do not meet any of the above conditions for admission will be admitted with academic support if they provide proof of high school graduation or GED and meet one of the following: ACT composite score of 14 to 17, or a combined math and verbal SAT score of 660 to 869, or minimum ACCUPLACER scores of 54 in sentence skills and 36 in arithmetic.

Applicants who have earned 13 or more semester college credits must provide proof of high school graduation or GED and meet one of the following conditions for admission: cumulative college GPA of 2.0 or above or minimum ACCUPLACER scores of 86 for sentence skills and 53 in algebra. Students who do not meet either of the above criteria will be admitted with academic support if they provide proof of high school graduation or GED and meet the following condition: minimum ACCUPLACER scores of 54 in reading and 36 in arithmetic.

Students admitted with academic support are limited to 12 credit hours of study during their first semester (6 credit hours per session). Students admitted with academic support will be required to complete developmental English and/or math courses unless they meet the following conditions: Writing Review (ENG099)—must meet one of the following: a minimum ACCUPLACER score of 86 in sentence skills, or a minimum ACT verbal score of 18, or a minimum SAT verbal score of 425, or completion of a college-level English composition course with a grade of C or above; Mathematics Review I (MAT096)—must meet one of the following: a minimum ACCUPLACER score of 53 in algebra, or a minimum ACT math score of 18, or a minimum SAT math score of 440, or completion of a college-level English composition course with a grade of C or above.

Other admission requirements may include credit hours of qualified transfer credit with a grade of C- or better from a regionally accredited institution or a nationally accredited institution approved and documented by the faculty and dean of the College of Business, or the College of Professional Psychology, at Argosy University or completion of an Associate of Arts or Associate of Science degree from a regionally accredited institution. A maximum of 78 lower-division or 90 total credit hours may be transferred. A minimum written TOEFL score of 500 (paper-based test), 173 (computer-based test), or 61 (Internet-based test) is required for all applicants whose native language is not English or who have not graduated from an institution in which English is the language of instruction.

Official transcripts from approved postsecondary institutions must include a minimum grade point average of 2.0 (on a scale of 4.0) for all academic work completed. Exceptions may be made for extenuating circumstances. All applications must include a completed application form, proof of high school graduation or successful completion of the GED test, official postsecondary transcripts, and a nonrefundable (except in California) application fee. Additional materials are required prior to matriculation. Some programs have additional application requirements or include exceptions to admission requirements. An admissions representative can provide further information.

Application and Information

Argosy University accepts students on a rolling admissions basis year-round, depending on availability of required courses. Applications for admission are available online at http://www.argosy.edu or by contacting one of the campus locations.

Argosy University
205 North Michigan Avenue, Suite 1300
Chicago, Illinois 60601-2250
Phone: 312-899-9900
800-377-0617 (toll-free)
E-mail: auadmissions@argosy.edu
Web site: http://www.argosy.edu

THE ART INSTITUTES INTERNATIONAL MINNESOTA

The Art Institutes International Minnesota

MINNEAPOLIS, MINNESOTA

The Institute

The Art Institutes International Minnesota teaches students the skills needed to gain entry-level employment in the creative arts, and faculty members bring knowledge from the field to their classroom instruction. The Art Institutes International Minnesota offers eleven bachelor's degree programs, six associate degree programs, and two certificate programs.

Students come to The Art Institutes International Minnesota from throughout the United States and abroad. The student population includes recent high school graduates, transfer students, and those who have left a previous employment situation to study and train for a new career. Students are creative, competitive, and open to new ideas. They place great value on an education that prepares them for an exciting entry-level position in the arts.

Assistance is available to help students with resume writing, networking, and keeping abreast of what employers are looking for in job candidates.

Campus clubs and organizations include the American Society of Interior Designers, American Institute of Graphic Arts, and National Technical Honor Society. Students with interests in animation, baking, and comic books have formed separate groups. There is also an ACF Junior Culinary Competition Team that helps to prepare students for cooking competitions. Students participate in clubs and organizations, including the Student Ambassadors, a group of student leaders who act as school representatives at events such as open houses and orientation. School-sponsored activities include pizza parties, barbecues, a weekly film festival, crime prevention workshops, HTML workshops, software workshops, guest speakers, and even visits by a massage therapist during finals week.

Student housing is available at the Grand Marc in the Seven Corners district of downtown Minneapolis, which is located within 2 miles of the school and accessible by bus. Each apartment is a fully furnished two-bedroom, two-bath unit for 4 students. Utilities, washer/dryer, satellite TV, Internet access, and local phone service are provided at no extra cost. In addition, the Residence Life staff strives to develop events and activities that foster a sense of community. The Housing Department may also provide referrals for independent housing.

The Art Institutes International Minnesota is accredited by the Accrediting Council for Independent Colleges and Schools (ACICS) to award bachelor's degrees, associate degrees, and certificates. ACICS is listed as a nationally recognized accrediting agency by the U.S. Department of Education. Its accreditation of degree-granting institutions is recognized by the Council for Higher Education Accreditation. ACICS can be contacted at 750 First Street NE, Suite 980, Washington, D.C. 20002; phone: 202-336-6780. The Associate in Applied Science in Culinary Arts degree program is accredited by the American Culinary Federation (ACF).

Location

Minneapolis has major art museums, regional theater, and a thriving music scene. The city offers plenty of creative inspiration, from the Sculpture Garden at the Walker Art Center to the Winter Carnival, Renaissance Festival, and the Minneapolis Museum of Arts. The Hennepin Avenue Theatre District is home to Broadway productions. In nearby Bloomington is the Mall of America, the country's largest shopping complex. Minneapolis is on the banks of the Mississippi River and is close to nearly twenty lakes. More than 150 city parks offer hiking, biking, and skating. Students can also cheer on the professional sports teams: the Twins, Vikings, and Timberwolves.

Majors and Degrees

The school offers bachelor's degrees in advertising, culinary management, design management, fashion and retail management, graphic design, hospitality management, interior design, media arts and animation, photography, visual effects and motion graphics, and Web design and interactive media.

Associate degree programs are offered in baking and pastry, culinary arts, graphic design, interior design, interior planning with AutoCAD, and Web design and interactive media. There are certificate programs in the art of cooking and baking and pastry.

Academic Programs

Students are expected not only to complete specific courses but also to develop critical and analytical learning abilities.

The academic year is divided into four quarters of eleven weeks each, starting in January, April, July, and October. Associate degree candidates must complete 112 to 128 credits (twenty-one to twenty-four months). Bachelor's degree candidates must complete 192 credits (thirty-six months).

Academic Facilities

The Art Institutes International Minnesota is conveniently located in the heart of downtown Minneapolis. Inside the school's four-story building, which encompasses approximately 62,500 square feet, are classrooms, studios, laboratories, offices, student lounges, a Learning Resource Center, and an exhibition gallery. The Art Institutes International Minnesota maintains an art supply store for the convenience of students. Equipment provided at the school is specific to the programs of study and includes computers, workstations, printers, and software as well as photo, video, and audio equipment.

Costs

Tuition cost varies by program. Prospective students should contact the school for current tuition costs. Other charges include a starting kit for all first-quarter students. Kits vary in price depending on the program of study.

Financial Aid

Financial aid is available for those who qualify. Students who require financial assistance should first complete and submit a Free Application for Federal Student Aid (FAFSA) and meet with a financial aid officer. The officer determines the level of need based on a required federal formula, the cost of education, and other factors. Gift aid is available in the form of Federal Pell Grants, Federal Supplemental Educational Opportunity Grants, and veterans' benefits. Loans include Federal Stafford Student Loans, Federal PLUS loans, and alternative loans. Other scholarships are available from the school and private sources. Application deadlines and eligibility requirements vary by program.

Faculty

The Art Institutes International Minnesota faculty includes knowledgeable instructors, many of whom are working professionals with achievements in their fields.

Admission Requirements

Prospective students must first meet with an assistant director of admissions for an interview. After a successful interview, an application for admission, proof of high school graduation or its equivalent, and an essay of 150 words explaining how an education at The Art Institutes International Minnesota can help the student to meet creative goals must be submitted to the school. Portfolios are welcome but not required, and students who have taken the SAT or ACT may be asked to submit their test scores.

There is a $50 application fee.

Application and Information

To obtain an application or make arrangements for an interview or tour of the school, students should contact:

The Art Institutes International Minnesota
15 South 9th Street
Minneapolis, Minnesota 55402-3105
Phone: 612-332-3361
800-777-3643 (toll-free)
Fax: 612-332-3934
Web site: http://www.artinstitutes.edu/minneapolis

The Art Institute of Atlanta®, GA; The Art Institute of Atlanta®–Decatur, GA; The Art Institute of Austin[SM], TX; The Art Institute of California[SM]–Inland Empire; The Art Institute of California[SM]–Los Angeles; The Art Institute of California[SM]–Orange County; The Art Institute of California[SM]–Sacramento; The Art Institute of California[SM]–San Diego; The Art Institute of California[SM]–San Francisco; The Art Institute of California[SM]–Sunnyvale; The Art Institute of Charleston[SM], SC, A branch of The Art Institute of Atlanta, GA; The Art Institute of Charlotte®, NC; The Art Institute of Colorado® (Denver); The Art Institute of Dallas®, TX; The Art Institute of Fort Lauderdale®, FL; The Art Institute of Houston®, TX; The Art Institute of Indianapolis[SM], IN*; The Art Institute of Jacksonville[SM], FL, A branch of Miami International University of Art & Design; The Art Institute of Las Vegas®, NV; The Art Institute of Michigan[SM] (Detroit); The Art Institute of New York City®, NY; The Art Institute of Ohio[SM]–Cincinnati**; The Art Institute of Philadelphia®, PA; The Art Institute of Phoenix®, AZ; The Art Institute of Pittsburgh®, PA; The Art Institute of Pittsburgh®–Online Division; The Art Institute of Portland®, OR; The Art Institute of Salt Lake City[SM], UT; The Art Institute of Seattle®, WA; The Art Institute of Tampa[SM], FL, A branch of Miami International University of Art & Design; The Art Institute of Tennessee[SM]–Nashville, A branch of The Art Institute of Atlanta, GA; The Art Institute of Tucson[SM], AZ; The Art Institute of Washington® (Arlington, VA), A branch of The Art Institute of Atlanta, GA; The Art Institute of York–Pennsylvania[SM]; The Art Institutes International Minnesota[SM] (Minneapolis); California Design College[SM] (Los Angeles–Wilshire Blvd.); The Illinois Institute of Art®–Chicago; The Illinois Institute of Art®–Schaumburg; Miami International University of Art & Design[SM], FL; The New England Institute of Art® (Boston, MA).

*The Art Institute of Indianapolis is licensed by the Indiana Commission on Proprietary Education, 302 W. Washington St., Rm. E201, Indianapolis, IN 46204, AC-0080.

**The Art Institute of Ohio–Cincinnati, 8845 Governors Hill Drive, Suite 100, Cincinnati, OH 45249-3317, OH Reg. #04-01-1698B.

BETHEL UNIVERSITY

ST. PAUL, MINNESOTA

The University

Bethel University began its Christian liberal arts program in 1945 but traces its roots to Bethel Seminary, founded in 1871. The University encourages growth and learning in a distinctly Christian environment, continually striving to help students discover and develop the skills God has given them. Campus lifestyle expectations have been designed to build unity within diversity. All Bethel students, faculty members, and staff members are expected to follow those expectations during their time as members of the Bethel community. Bethel's approximately 6,000 students represent a range of national and international cultures. Most of Bethel's undergraduate students are between 18 and 22 years of age, but older and younger students bring a welcome variety to campus life. Bethel students are involved in a wealth of cocurricular activities, from music to ministry, Bible study to broadcasting, theater to tennis, and art to athletics. Bethel sports teams compete in NCAA Division III and the Minnesota Intercollegiate Athletic Conference. The Sports and Recreation Center is used almost continuously for intercollegiate and intramural sports events as well as personal recreation, and the Community Life Center provides a 1,700-seat performance hall and chapel.

The campus, built in the 1970s, is the newest among Minnesota colleges and universities. Versatile buildings are centers for the sciences, humanities, physical education, learning resources, and fine arts. A series of skyways and breezeways connect the facilities and make getting to and from class a pleasure—even in the heart of winter. Residence life at Bethel takes many forms. Traditional college dorm rooms, spacious suites, town houses—whatever their preference, Bethel students find a warm, family atmosphere in the living areas. All freshman and sophomore students, except those who are married or living with their parents while in attendance, are required to live in University housing.

In addition to the seminary programs and undergraduate degree programs, Bethel offers Master of Arts degrees in communication, counseling psychology, education K–12, ethnomusicology, literacy education, nursing, organizational leadership, and teaching; a Master of Education degree in special education; a doctorate in educational administration; and a Master of Business Administration. Classes meet once or twice a week, and course work is integrated with students' professional responsibilities.

Location

The Bethel campus borders Lake Valentine in Arden Hills and comprises 231 acres of beauty and tranquility, conducive to study and leisure. Just 15 minutes from downtown St. Paul and Minneapolis, Bethel enjoys the benefits of both cities, noted nationally for their high quality of life. The Twin Cities are home to the headquarters of most of Minnesota's large corporations as well as more than thirty major shopping centers and one of the world's largest shopping malls, the Mall of America. Culture thrives in the cities with an international array of music, theater, and art. At the all-weather Metrodome, the Target Center, and the Xcel Energy Center, sports fans cheer their favorite pro teams—the Minnesota Vikings, Twins, Timberwolves, and Wild. Abundant recreation exists year-round in this busy metropolis, which has more than 900 lakes and 500 parks.

Majors and Degrees

The Bachelor of Arts (B.A.) degree is offered with majors in art, athletic training, biblical and theological studies, biology, business, business and political science, chemistry, communication studies, community health, computer science, economics, economics and finance, education, engineering science, English literature, English literature and writing, environmental studies, French, history, international relations, journalism, mathematics, media communication, music, philosophy, physics, political science, psychology, reconciliation studies, sacred music, social work, sociocultural studies, Spanish, teaching English as a foreign language, teaching English as a second language, theater arts, Third World studies, and youth ministry.

The Bachelor of Science (B.S.) degree is offered with majors in applied physics, biochemistry/molecular biology, biology, chemistry, computer science, environmental science, nursing, and physics. The Bachelor of Music (B.Mus.) degree is offered in applied performance. The Bachelor of Music Education (B.Mus.Ed.) degree is offered with an emphasis in instrumental K–12 or vocal K–12. Numerous preprofessional programs are offered as well.

Academic minors are available in most of the major disciplines listed above and in the following areas: Asian studies, athletic coaching, biblical languages (Hebrew and Greek), classics, creative writing, cross-cultural mission, entrepreneurship, family studies, film studies, German, leadership studies, management information systems, modern world languages, religious studies, and social welfare studies.

Academic Programs

Bethel was named among the top Midwestern universities by *U.S. News & World Report* for 2007. Students are required to take classes that will give them a broad view of the world and their role in it as Christians. General education classes are grouped around the following themes: personal development; biblical foundations; math, science, and technology; and global perspectives. In addition, in order to graduate, all Bethel students must partake in an off-campus cross-cultural experience and a capstone course in contemporary Christian issues.

Bethel University follows a semester calendar consisting of two 15-week semesters and a three-week interim in January. A full-time academic load for each semester is 12 to 18 credits. To graduate, students must complete a minimum of 122 credits with a cumulative grade point average of at least 2.0 and a minimum 2.25 grade point average in their majors. Also required are 51–52 credits of general education. Bethel awards advanced placement credit in recognition of learning that has been achieved apart from a college or university classroom situation. A maximum of 30 advanced placement credits can be applied toward a degree program. Students may also individualize their academic programs through directed studies with faculty members and through academic internships with off-campus institutions.

Off-Campus Programs

Bethel students may study in almost any country and across the United States as part of their education. Off-campus extension programs include the American Studies Program of the Council for Christian Colleges and Universities, which provides internship opportunities in Washington, D.C. The council also sponsors a Latin American Studies Program, which offers students an opportunity to study in Costa Rica. The Los Angeles Film Studies Center gives students of any major a semester of learning and working experience in Los Angeles, the world's film capital. The Christian College Consortium Visitor Program is designed to allow students to take advantage of course offerings and varied experiences on other Christian college and university campuses throughout the United States. The Au Sable Institute in Michigan offers intensive courses in environmental studies. Through the Upper Midwest Association for Intercultural Education, Bethel students study abroad during interim. In the fall semester of alternate years,

Bethel students can study and travel in France, Great Britain, Ireland, and Northern Ireland under the direction of a faculty member from the Bethel University Department of English. Other Bethel-sponsored programs include Australia Term, Europe Term, Guatemala Term, Spain Term, Thailand Term, South Africa Term, and the New York Center for Art & Media Studies. Additional opportunities available to Bethel students include the Australia Studies Centre, Australia Term, China Studies Program, Creation Care Study Program, Hong Kong Baptist University, Lithuania Christian College, Middle East Studies Program, Russian Studies Program, Scholars' Semester in Oxford, Tokyo Christian University, Uganda Studies Program, Oxford Summer Programme, Contemporary Music Center, The Oregon Extension, and Washington Journalism Center.

Academic Facilities

Bethel's Community Life Center offers a beautiful hall with outstanding acoustical design that makes it one of the best performance facilities in the upper Midwest. The Bethel University Library Web site serves as a portal to more than 179,000 volumes located in the library, including books, music CDs, and nearly 13,000 videos/DVDs; interlibrary loan access to more than 2 million volumes within the consortium; nearly 19,000 full-text periodicals online and 1,150 hard-copy journal titles; 70-plus online databases; a bibliographic manager; an e-mail and chat reference service; a "Research Wizard"; and interactive tutorials. Services in the library include an "Information Commons," which provides research, technical, and multimedia assistance; wireless access to the Internet; laptops for checkout; sixty general use computers; a full-service AV department; individual and small-group study areas; listening/viewing rooms; multimedia production space; reference; faculty technology consulting; and instruction. Bethel students are assigned computer accounts, allowing them access to a wealth of academic and specialized computing services. The Bethel science labs and music practice rooms are modern and well equipped. Approximately four plays are performed each year in the Bethel Theatre.

Costs

For 2007–08, tuition is $24,400, and room and board costs are $7380. Bethel University tuition costs are lower than average for Minnesota private colleges and universities. Housing costs are set each spring for incoming freshmen and transfer students. Freshmen living on campus must purchase the three-meal-per-day basic meal plan; upperclass students may choose from a variety of meal plans. The actual cost of attending Bethel depends on the amount of financial aid a student receives.

Financial Aid

Bethel University strives to make it financially possible for every qualified student to attend. Each year, more than 90 percent of the students receive some kind of financial aid, including scholarships, grants, loans, and assistance in the form of on-campus employment. Students who wish to be considered for financial aid must first be admitted to the University and then submit both the Free Application for Federal Student Aid (FAFSA) and a Bethel University Financial Aid Application. Bethel's priority deadline is April 15 of each year. Students who have completed and mailed all necessary forms by this date receive first consideration.

Faculty

Nothing determines the quality of a university more than the people who teach there. Bethel professors combine strong academic credentials with a commitment to Jesus Christ. Bethel faculty members are known for being warm and caring. It's not hard to receive personal attention, since there are only 15 students to every faculty member. Professors are very accessible to students during regular office hours as well as at other times. Of Bethel's 198 full-time faculty members, the majority have earned doctorates. The Bethel faculty is complemented by 129 part-time instructors.

Student Government

An active and integral part of the Bethel community, the Bethel Student Association functions in a variety of strategic campus areas. In addition to representing student needs to the administration, they oversee student publications and campus social activities as well as provide a forum for influential student-faculty committees. Guiding the affairs of the Bethel Student Association, the Executive Board is composed of the president, the vice president, and 8 executive directors.

Admission Requirements

Bethel University seeks students who desire an education based on strong academics in a Christian environment. To be considered for admission, the student must graduate from an accredited high school or equivalent, rank in the top 50 percent of his or her high school class, and meet minimum test score requirements (92 on the PSAT, 920 on the SAT, or 21 on the ACT). Transcripts, two references, and commitment to Bethel's covenant (lifestyle statement) are also required. Bethel recommends that students take 4 years of English, 3 years of mathematics, 3 years of science, and 2 years of social studies while in high school. Transfer students with a 2.50 or higher cumulative college GPA are also welcome. On-campus interviews are not required but are strongly recommended.

Application and Information

Students wishing to apply for admission to Bethel must send the following: a completed Bethel application form with a $25 nonrefundable application fee (waived before November 1); test scores from the PSAT, SAT, or ACT; essay; transcripts of all course work completed at the high school and college levels; and references from a pastor and a school official. Students considering Bethel should apply in the fall of their senior year. The Office of Admissions reviews applications throughout the year. Early action decisions are made for students who submit applications by November 1.

For further information about specific Bethel programs and campus visit opportunities, students should contact:

Office of Admissions
Bethel University
3900 Bethel Drive
St. Paul, Minnesota 55112
Phone: 651-638-6242
800-255-8706 Ext. 6242 (toll-free)
Fax: 651-635-1490
E-mail: BUadmissions-cas@bethel.edu
Web site: http://www.bethel.edu

Bethel's Community Life Center.

CARLETON COLLEGE

NORTHFIELD, MINNESOTA

The College

Since its inception in 1866, Carleton College has been a coeducational, residential, liberal arts college. Sponsored initially by the Congregationalists, Carleton opened its doors in 1867 as Northfield College. Four years later, William Carleton of Charlestown, Massachusetts, donated $50,000 to the fledgling college, the result of which was the change of name from Northfield to Carleton. Binding church ties were dropped long ago, and the College continues to welcome students from a kaleidoscope of races, religions, and cultures.

Today, first-year classes number about 475 to 500, and the student body is approximately 50 percent men. The on-campus enrollment of about 1,800 includes students from virtually every state and about twenty-five other countries. About a quarter are from Minnesota, and the next most represented states are Illinois, California, Wisconsin, New York, Massachusetts, Oregon, and Washington. About 20 percent are students who are members of minority groups, and 10 percent are the first generation of their families to attend college.

Most first-year students choose to take a first-year seminar, some of which deal with contemporary problems or concerns, others with more esoteric material. Many upperclass students do at least some independent study in their major, and a significant number of students take advantage of internship and work experience.

Though academic work takes top priority, Carleton students are actively involved in nearly 100 organizations, clubs, and other activities, ranging from the Carleton Singers (who performed at Carnegie Hall in 1997) and the improvisational comedy troupe Cujokra to Ultimate Frisbee (Carleton's women's team won the national intercollegiate championship in 2000, and the men's team won in 2001) and one of the top Model United Nations teams in the country. Musicians can play in the orchestra or smaller ensembles or sing in the choir, the Carleton Singers, or one of six a cappella groups. Athletes can participate in one of ten varsity sports for men or eleven for women, one of eighteen competitive club teams, or any of fifteen intramural sports.

Normally, 96 percent of Carleton first-year students return for their sophomore year. The most recent figures available show that 89 percent of first-year students graduated in four years or less, and 93 percent graduated within five years.

Location

Northfield is about 35 miles from the Minneapolis–St. Paul International Airport and 40 miles from the downtown Twin Cities. Once a traditional small agrarian community, Northfield is also the home of St. Olaf College and several multinational businesses, and a number of its residents now commute to the Twin Cities. Most of the buildings in downtown Northfield look much as they did at the turn of the century. A revitalized river bank and a core of downtown businesses and shops make for pleasant afternoon and evening strolls.

Majors and Degrees

Carleton grants only one undergraduate degree, the Bachelor of Arts. Majors offered are African/African American studies, American studies, art history, biology, chemistry, cinema and media studies, classical languages, classical studies, computer science, economics, English, French, French and Francophone studies, geology, German, Greek, history, international relations, Latin, Latin American studies, mathematics, music, philosophy, physics, political science, psychology, religion, Romance languages, Russian, sociology and anthropology, Spanish, studio art, theater arts, and women's studies. Students may also self-design their own majors.

In addition to a major, students may elect to study one of sixteen concentrations, integrated interdisciplinary programs that cut across traditional boundaries of academic disciplines and serve to both strengthen and complement the major: African/African American studies, archaeology, biochemistry, cognitive studies, cross-cultural studies, East Asian studies, educational studies, environmental and technology studies, French and Francophone studies, Latin American studies, media studies, medieval and Renaissance studies, political economy, Russian studies, South Asian studies, and women's studies.

Special programs are available in dance, Hebrew/Judaic studies, linguistics, and literary and cultural studies. Carleton offers a teacher education program leading to a secondary teaching license in art, English, French, German, mathematics, Russian, science, the social studies, or Spanish. Elementary licensure is available only in art and world languages, French, German, and Spanish. The joint liberal arts–engineering program, commonly known as the 3-2 program, is offered in conjunction with either Columbia University or Washington University (St. Louis).

Academic Programs

Carleton's avowed purpose is to provide a liberal arts education of the highest quality. The College teaches the basic skills upon which all higher achievements rest: to read perceptively, to write and speak clearly, and to think analytically. The Carleton education aims to nurture a sense of curiosity and intellectual adventure, an awareness of method and purpose in a variety of fields, and an affinity for quality and integrity wherever they may be found. These values prepare Carleton graduates to lead fully realized lives in a diverse and changing world.

To this end, the Carleton curriculum balances a traditional emphasis upon classic fields of study, or disciplines, with a complementary offering of distribution courses, electives, and interdisciplinary programs. To be awarded the Bachelor of Arts degree, a student must take at least thirty-five courses, two of which must come from arts and literature, two from the humanities, three from the social sciences, and three from mathematics and the natural sciences. In addition, everyone must take at least one course that is centrally concerned with a culture different from his or her own. All students must also satisfy two proficiency requirements: the writing of English and the learning of a second language.

Carleton students normally choose a major during the spring term of their sophomore year. In any given year, 12–18 students graduate with double majors, and about 15 graduate with special majors. All students must complete an integrative exercise, which could include a comprehensive examination, an extensive research project, a major paper, or a public lecture, in their major field, usually in the senior year. Carleton's academic year is composed of three 10-week-long terms: fall, winter, and spring.

Off-Campus Programs

Two thirds of Carleton students spend at least one term completing an off-campus program. During any one academic year, more than 350 students are involved in off-campus study in locations such as Australia, Japan, China, England, India, Mexico, Costa Rica, Western Africa, and Washington, D.C. Each year the College sponsors as many as ten faculty-led off-campus seminars for Carleton students. Through membership in a number of consortia, Carleton students may participate in more than twenty additional international programs lasting from a semester to a full year. Students may also select from a list of programs sponsored by other institutions, consortia, and agencies that Carleton has evaluated and approved for academic credit, or they can request approval of a program that they and their academic advisers believe will further their educational goals.

Academic Facilities

The Carleton campus consists of more than 900 acres of land, about 450 of which are the Cowling Arboretum, a game and nature preserve used regularly as an outdoor laboratory for biology, chemistry, and geology as well as a recreational area. Twenty miles of running and skiing trails crisscross the "arb," which *Runner's World* has named the best place to run in the state of Minnesota.

Approximately forty buildings are found on the College's main campus of nearly 100 acres. Nine are student residence halls ranging in capacity from 110 to 205. Built in 2000, an 80,000-square-foot field house/recreation center offers an indoor track, a climbing wall, and eighty weight-training and fitness machines. The Music and Drama Center offers a concert hall seating 500 and a theater seating 460, joined by a gallery, ensemble rooms, practice rooms, dressing rooms, and scenery and costume storage rooms. Three buildings are devoted to the sciences: Olin (physics and psychology), Mudd (chemistry and geology), and Hulings (biology). Goodsell Observatory houses a 16-inch visual refractor telescope and an 8-inch photographic refractor telescope. The four-story Center for Mathematics and Computing (CMC) offers microcomputing labs open around-the-clock. Along with six other labs distributed around campus, they provide easy access to a wide range of applications, free printing, and specialized multimedia equipment. The campus has more than 600 advanced workstations and personal computers, all of which are linked to the high-speed campus network and Internet2. In the residence halls, every room provides Ethernet connections, allowing students to plug in their own computers for access to the campus network. Wireless networks are also available in many locales.

Costs

For 2007–08, tuition was $35,958; fees, $198; and room and board, $9489. Travel costs vary. Books, supplies, and personal expenses are estimated to be about $1200.

Financial Aid

Carleton meets the full demonstrated financial need of every student admitted to the College and continues meeting each student's need for four years or until graduation. An on-campus job of 8 to 10 hours per week and a loan opportunity are included in nearly every financial aid package. In 2007–08, about 80 percent of Carleton students received a total of more than $25 million in financial aid or scholarships from all sources. Fifty-five percent received grant assistance; the average need-based grant was $21,081. The only non-need scholarships the College offers are sixty-five to seventy-five Carleton-sponsored National Merit, National Achievement, and National Hispanic Scholarships.

Faculty

All Carleton classes are taught by faculty members rather than graduate students or teaching assistants. Of the 207 faculty members, 184 are full-time, resulting in a student-faculty ratio of 9:1. Of those full-time faculty members, 95 percent hold the highest degree in their academic field. The average class size is about 18, and the average lab size is 15. Most faculty members also serve as academic advisers.

Student Government

Students are actively involved in the governance of the College. Directly below the Board of Trustees is the College Council, chaired by the President, which is composed of 5 faculty members, 5 students, 5 staff members, 1 trustee, and 1 alumnus. The three major policy committees, Education and Curriculum, Student Life, and the Budget Committee, are also made up of faculty members, students, and staff members. Every student is a member of the Carleton Student Association (CSA). Three officers and 16 senators are elected annually to serve as the CSA Senate, which, among other duties, manages the student activities budget.

Admission Requirements

Carleton normally receives about 4,900 applications for the approximately 500 places available in the first-year class. Admission is based on several considerations: superior academic achievement, personal qualities and interests, participation in extracurricular activities, and potential for development as a student and a graduate of the College. The Admissions Committee weighs all factors to ensure that those students offered admission are not only adequately prepared for the academic work but also will benefit from their total experience at Carleton and are likely to add significantly to the College through their individual talents and personal qualities.

Application and Information

Students interested in applying for admission should contact the Office of Admissions. Interviews, with either a staff member or an alumni admissions representative, are recommended but not required. A visit to the campus is strongly encouraged. During the academic year, overnight stays, interviews, and class visits are usually available but must be scheduled in advance.

Students who decide that Carleton is their first-choice college are encouraged to apply for early decision by November 15, first round, or by January 15, second round. The application deadline for regular decision is January 15. Regular decision candidates are notified before April 15, and the candidate's reply date is May 1. For more information, prospective students should contact:

Office of Admissions
Carleton College
100 South College Street
Northfield, Minnesota 55057
Phone: 507-222-4190
800-222-2275 (toll-free)
Fax: 507-646-4526
E-mail: admissions@acs.carleton.edu
Web site: http://www.carleton.edu

An aerial view of the Carleton College campus.

THE COLLEGE OF ST. SCHOLASTICA

DULUTH, MINNESOTA

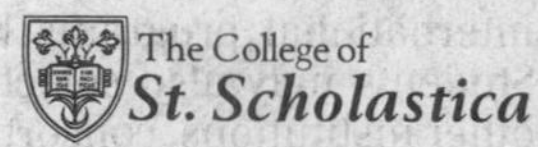

The College

At the tip of Lake Superior on the edge of northern Minnesota's wilderness, St. Scholastica is in the great college town of Duluth. The College's vibrant history is enriched by its Catholic Benedictine heritage. St. Scholastica offers nationally known programs in health sciences and professional career fields. Its low student-faculty ratio provides students with exceptional personal attention from an award-winning faculty.

St. Scholastica offers a Four Year Pledge, guaranteeing that students who enter as first-year students and meet simple guidelines will graduate within four years, or subsequent years are free.

Many think the College's 186-acre campus, with its majestic stone buildings and view of Lake Superior, is the most beautiful in Minnesota. It offers a secure yet stimulating setting for scholarship. The College serves 3,259 students. The small, friendly community enables each student to participate in academics, extracurriculars, and recreational activities. A 13:1 student-faculty ratio makes it easy to seek individualized help and encouragement.

St. Scholastica graduates, who are well known for their academic and professional preparation, enjoy excellent placement opportunities. Graduates over the past five years have enjoyed a 96.4 percent placement rate within six months of degree completion. Saint Scholastica is consistently rated among the Midwest's finest regional universities. *U.S. News & World Report* magazine's 2008 "America's Best Colleges" rankings put St. Scholastica in the top tier of Midwestern colleges for academic excellence and affordability. The *Washington Post* calls the College a "hidden gem."

The College also offers innovative graduate degree programs, including the Master of Education, Master of Education in media and technology, Master of Education in teaching, Master of Arts in computer information systems, Master of Arts in management, Master of Arts in nursing, Master of Arts in occupational therapy, Master of Arts in exercise physiology, Master of Arts in health-care informatics and information management, Doctor of Physical Therapy, and Doctor of Nursing Practice.

Campus residence halls include Cedar Hall, Scanlon Hall, and Kerst Hall student apartment buildings; Somers Residence Hall (featuring a wing of suites); and four modular apartment complexes.

Location

The St. Scholastica campus is on a ridge overlooking Lake Superior in a residential area of Duluth, Minnesota. The location offers a safe and tranquil setting for scholarship amid exceptional natural beauty. The cultural and commercial offerings of Duluth, a regional center for shopping, the arts, and tourism, are only 10 minutes away. Duluth is in northeastern Minnesota, a 2-hour drive from Minneapolis-St. Paul. It is well served by Northwest Airlines as well as commercial bus lines. An intercity bus line provides efficient local transportation.

Duluth's low crime rate, economic stability, and natural beauty regularly earn it high rankings in national quality-of-life surveys. The city is an international seaport and a center of development for the health, education, and tourism industries. There are more than 15,000 college students in the Duluth-Superior metropolitan area.

The College's proximity to the Boundary Waters Canoe Area Wilderness, national parks, ski areas, lakes, and rivers allows St. Scholastica students to enjoy the outdoors in a way few other college students can. A student who values a highly cultured community where extracurricular activities abound will be happy at St. Scholastica. Music students take part in the Duluth-Superior Symphony Orchestra, and theater students feel at home at the Duluth Playhouse, one of the nation's oldest community theaters. Sports enthusiasts can play tennis, racquetball, and golf; use snowmobiles or ice boats; or ice skate, ski, fish, hunt, and sail in St. Scholastica's backyard. Mont du Lac and Spirit Mountain ski areas are only 20 minutes from the campus.

Majors and Degrees

The College of St. Scholastica offers a Bachelor of Arts degree in the following majors: accounting, advertising and public relations, applied economics, behavioral arts and sciences, biochemistry, biology, Catholic studies, chemistry, communication, computer science/information systems, education, educational media and technology, English, exercise physiology, health sciences, health-care informatics and information management, history, humanities, journalism, languages and international studies, management, marketing, mathematics, music, natural sciences, nursing, occupational therapy (entry master's program), Ojibwe language and culture education, organizational behavior, psychology, self-designed major, social science/secondary education, social work, theater management, and theology and religious studies.

Minors are available in most of the major fields as well as in American Indian studies, art, French, German, gerontology, medieval and Renaissance studies, philosophy, photography, political science, Russian, self-designed minor, Spanish, theater, and women's studies.

In addition, St. Scholastica offers preprofessional programs in chiropractic, dentistry, engineering, law, library, medicine, optometry, pharmacy, and veterinary medicine. St. Scholastica has a certificate program in gerontology, and the study of aging is a major initiative throughout the College. St. Scholastica offers a licensure program in teacher education.

Academic Programs

The curriculum prepares students for their responsibilities as working professionals, as citizens of a democracy, and as individuals who seek to live full lives. The program consists of three parts: Benedictine Liberal Arts education requirements, a major, and open electives. The mission of Benedictine Liberal Arts education at The College at St. Scholastica is to engage students in defining and practicing responsible living and meaningful work. The Benedictine program has three components: a first-year experience known as Dignitas, a range of liberal arts courses called Pathways, and a senior-level component called Writing Intensive. Historically, Benedictines have been scholars, caregivers, educators, and artists; the liberal arts mirror the broad pathways that Benedictines have pioneered. The rigor and breadth of the program best prepare St. Scholastica students to meet the present and face the future with wisdom, faith, and imagination. The major prepares the student either for graduate school or for a profession and is normally selected by the end of the sophomore year. Elective courses allow students to pursue particular interests.

The student's last 32 credits before graduation must be earned at St. Scholastica, and a minimum of 16 credits must be earned in a major field at St. Scholastica. The College offers an honors program for students to have enriched learning experiences and to provide a community of support for learners devoted to a vigorous life of the mind. Some majors require an internship that involves work, travel, or study related to a student's academic efforts.

Off-Campus Programs

The College offers its programs throughout the region. Accelerated-degree evening programs for working adults are offered in Duluth, Brainerd, St. Cloud, Rochester, and St. Paul, Minnesota. St. Scholastica also has consortium agreements through which students may enroll in courses at other colleges in the region. Clinical experience in the College's health sciences programs is offered at all health-care facilities in Duluth as well as in many other hospitals and health-care centers throughout the United States. The College also offers students the opportunity to study abroad at its study center in Louisburgh, Ireland; in a Russian language exchange program in Petrozavodsk, Karelia, Russia; in the heart of London; and in exchange programs in Leipzig, Germany, and Lille, France. Service learning opportunities are available in Tanzania, Mexico, and many other countries.

Academic Facilities

St. Scholastica's three-story Romanesque library houses more than 120,000 volumes, with special strengths in the health sciences, nursing, Indian studies, and children's materials. Computer workstations link the library to other state and national libraries, the campus network, and the Internet. Library instruction is provided throughout the curriculum. The Science Center has interactive television classroom capabilities.

College research facilities include general and physical chemistry laboratories, health sciences laboratories, anatomy laboratories, and two state-of-the-art 24-hour computer labs.

Campus facilities also include the Mitchell Auditorium, an acoustically superb 500-seat music hall; Our Lady Queen of Peace Chapel; the Burns Wellness Commons; the St. Scholastica Theatre; and majestic Tower Hall.

Adjoining the campus are St. Scholastica Monastery, home of the Benedictine Sisters; the Benedictine Health Center, which serves the needs of the Duluth area and provides many health science and behavioral arts and sciences students with opportunities to obtain practical experience; and Westwood, a continuous-care facility for senior citizens.

Costs

St. Scholastica's 2007–08 tuition and fees were $24,990. Room and board were $6684.

Financial Aid

The College of St. Scholastica handles a wide variety of financial aid and attempts to meet the needs of any qualified student enrolled. More than 90 percent of full-time students receive some form of aid; the average award is $14,000. The College also offers academic scholarships (Benedictine Scholarships). These awards are made on the basis of academic and leadership excellence, not necessarily because of need.

Students desiring to apply for financial aid should file the Free Application for Federal Student Aid (FAFSA) and have the results sent to St. Scholastica. Applications are processed on a first-come, first-served basis only after a student has been accepted by the College.

Faculty

St. Scholastica faculty members are devoted to personalized instruction, and the 13:1 student-teacher ratio is important to them. Faculty members hold advanced degrees from colleges and universities around the world. Four faculty members have been Fulbright International Scholars.

Student Government

The College trains leaders by encouraging students to hold positions of responsibility. Students manage the Student Senate and are directly involved in policymaking within the College community. They establish policies for the student newspaper and serve on institutional standing committees.

Admission Requirements

The College of St. Scholastica seeks to identify and admit students who have a strong probability of success in a demanding curriculum and rigorous academic major. Historically, the student who successfully demonstrates academic aptitude in high school or in a home school curriculum, has above-average ACT and/or SAT scores, and ranks in the upper half of the senior class is admitted to the College. Transfer students must demonstrate similar success in the college-level environment, with a minimum cumulative GPA of 2.0 for admission consideration. The College is an equal opportunity educator and employer.

Application and Information

The College of St. Scholastica requires each applicant to submit an application and a $25 nonrefundable fee, test scores on the SAT or ACT (required prior to enrollment), and an official high school transcript or GED test score. The College admits students on a rolling basis and notifies the applicant of the admission decision as soon as the file is complete. Online application is free.

For application and financial aid forms, prospective students should contact:

Eric Berg
Associate Vice President for Enrollment Management
The College of St. Scholastica
1200 Kenwood Avenue
Duluth, Minnesota 55811
Phone: 800-249-6412 (toll-free)
E-mail: eberg@css.edu
Web site: http://www.css.edu

Tower Hall is the center of The College of St. Scholastica campus, which is in one of the most beautiful areas of Minnesota. Nearby are the Boundary Waters Canoe Area Wilderness, national forests and parks, ski areas, and pristine lakes and rivers.

UNIVERSITY OF ST. THOMAS

ST. PAUL, MINNESOTA

The University

The University of St. Thomas, founded in 1885, is a Catholic, independent, liberal arts university that emphasizes values-centered and career-oriented education. With 10,984 students, it is Minnesota's largest independent college or university. St. Thomas ranked fifth (and highest among schools) in a newspaper-sponsored survey on "Which Minnesota nonprofit organizations have the most-respected reputations?" St. Thomas has been coeducational at the undergraduate level since 1977; today 49 percent of its 6,076 undergraduates and 53 percent of its 4,908 graduate students are women. St. Thomas welcomes students of all ages, nations, and religions and from a broad range of racial and socioeconomic backgrounds. While 87 percent of St. Thomas students come from Minnesota, during the 2007–08 academic year the University enrolled students from forty-six states and sixty-eight other countries. Overall, 7 percent are international students (1 percent of undergraduate and 4 percent of graduate students).

St. Thomas has both undergraduate and graduate seminaries, and its Center for Catholic Studies is home to the nation's oldest and largest undergraduate program in Catholic studies. Of students who report their religion, 44 percent are Catholic (53 percent of undergraduate and 33 percent of graduate students).

At the undergraduate level, St. Thomas offers ninety-six majors and five bachelor's degrees. At the graduate level, St. Thomas offers forty-six degree programs: thirty-nine master's, two education specialist, one juris doctor, and four doctorates. It also offers six joint- or dual-degree programs that combine a degree in law with degrees in business, psychology, education, or social work. The University offers its degree programs through eight schools and colleges: College of Arts and Sciences, Graduate School of Professional Psychology, Opus College of Business, School of Engineering, St. Paul Seminary School of Divinity, School of Education, School of Law, and School of Social Work.

Entrepreneurship programs at St. Thomas' Opus College of Business are ranked among the top 50 in the nation, according to *Entrepreneur* magazine. St. Thomas was the only Minnesota college or university named to the magazine's top 50 national list. In 2005, the Opus College of Business opened a $22-million facility for the Schulze School of Entrepreneurship, and in 2006 it opened the $25-million McNeely Hall for business education. St. Thomas has won both the National Model Undergraduate Program of the Year and the National Model M.B.A. Program of the Year awards of the U.S. Association for Small Business and Entrepreneurship.

Murray-Herrick Campus Center, the center of student life, contains the University's post office; bookstore and dining facilities; student-life offices, such as Campus Ministry, Multicultural Student Services, and the Career Development Center and Personal Counseling and Testing; and the student government, newspaper, yearbook, and club and student organization offices. More than ninety clubs and professional and social groups thrive on campus. Students produce a weekly newspaper, *The Aquin;* the *Aquinas* yearbook; a literary magazine, *Summit Avenue Review;* and on-campus television and radio programs. Students with musical talent choose from about twenty vocal and instrumental groups. Numerous events, such as homecoming, keep the campus calendar full.

St. Thomas has an extensive intramural sports program and is home to eleven men's and eleven women's varsity teams that compete in the Minnesota Intercollegiate Athletic Conference and the National Collegiate Athletic Association (NCAA) Division III. St. Thomas men have won the conference all-sports trophy for nineteen of the last twenty-five years, while the women have won that honor fifteen of the last twenty years. St. Thomas teams have won eleven national championships over the past twenty-three years. The centerpiece of St. Thomas' sports facilities is a physical education, athletic, and activities complex that includes the 2,200-seat Schoenecker Arena and Coughlan Field House, with an indoor track and basketball, racquetball, tennis, and volleyball courts. Two swimming pools, a 5,000-seat stadium, fitness and weight-room facilities, and an Olympic-caliber track are among the facilities.

The historic Chapel of St. Thomas Aquinas houses the magnificent 2,787-pipe Gabriel Kney organ. The Chapel of St. Thomas Aquinas and the St. Mary's Chapel on the School of Divinity campus are the University's main worship centers. Masses are celebrated daily during the academic year; ecumenical prayer services also are offered.

Ninety-two percent of freshmen and 42 percent of undergraduates reside in eleven campus residence halls. The date of application and class year are among the criteria considered for on-campus housing. Handicapped-accessible facilities are available.

Location

St. Thomas' main campus is located in St. Paul, where the city's historic Summit Avenue meets the Mississippi River. While situated in a quiet, residential neighborhood, the 78-acre parklike campus is only minutes from the downtowns of Minnesota's Twin Cities, St. Paul and Minneapolis. Its three-block downtown Minneapolis campus is home to the University's business law, psychology, and education divisions. St. Thomas' Gainey Conference Center is located in Owatonna, Minnesota. The Bernardi Campus in Rome, Italy, is located on the Tiber River. The Twin Cities are known for a high quality of life.

St. Paul is a winner of a "Most Livable City" award and is the home of the acclaimed Ordway Music Center for the Performing Arts and the Science Museum of Minnesota. Minneapolis, the "City of Lakes," has the renowned Guthrie Theater, Walker Art Center, and Nicollet Mall. The cities also are home to scores of lakes, professional sports teams, and companies with worldwide reputations, such as 3M, Pillsbury, General Mills, and Medtronic.

Majors and Degrees

St. Thomas offers ninety-six undergraduate majors and awards the Bachelor of Arts, Bachelor of Science, Bachelor of Science in Mechanical Engineering, Bachelor of Science in Electrical Engineering, and Bachelor of Music degrees. The majors are available in actuarial science, art history, biochemistry, biology, business administration (accounting, communication, entrepreneurship, financial management, general business management, human resources management, international business, leadership and management, legal studies in business, marketing management, operations management and real estate studies), Catholic studies, chemistry, chemistry (for grades 9–12 teacher licensure with general science 5–8 licensure), classical civilization, classical languages, communication studies, communication arts and literature (for grades 5–12 teacher licensure), community health education, criminal justice, earth and space science (for grades 9–12 teacher licensure with general science 5–8 licensure), economics, electrical engineering, elementary education, elementary education (for grades K–6 teacher licensure with a 5–8 specialty in communication arts and literature), elementary education (for grades K–6 teacher licensure with a 5–8 specialty in general science), elementary education (for grades K–6 teacher licensure with a 5–8 specialty in mathematics), elementary education (for grades K–6 teacher licensure with a 5–8 specialty in social studies), elementary education (for grades K–6 teacher licensure with a K–8 specialty in world languages and cultures—French, German, and Spanish), English, English as a second language (for grades k–12 teacher licensure), English (writing), environmental studies (natural sciences), environmental studies (social science, business, or humanities), French, geographic information systems, geography, geology, German, health education (non-licensure), health education (for grades 5–12 teacher licensure), health promotion, health promotion (science emphasis), history, international studies, journalism and mass communication (in advertising, broadcast journalism, media studies, print journalism, and public relations), justice and peace studies, Latin, life science (for grades 9–12 teacher licensure with general science 5–8), literary studies, mathematics, mathematics (for grades 5–12 teacher licensure), mechanical engineering, music, music business, music education (instrumental—for grades K–12 teacher licensure), music education (vocal—for grades K–12 teacher licensure), music (liturgical), music (performance), philosophy, physical education (for grades K–12 teacher licensure), physics, physics (for grades 9–12 teacher licensure with general science 5–8), political science, psychology, psychology (behavioral neuroscience), quantitative methods and computer science, Russian, science and mathematics for elementary education, secondary education, social sciences, social studies (for grades 5–12 teacher licensure), social work, sociology, Spanish, theater, theater and dance (for grades K–12 teacher licensure), theology, women's studies, and world language and cultures education (for grades K–12 teacher licensure—French, German, and Spanish).

Students may take courses or choose a major field, if not offered at St. Thomas, through the Associated Colleges of the Twin Cities, a consortium of St. Thomas and four other nearby private colleges and universities. Free intercampus bus transportation and a common class schedule make access to other colleges convenient.

St. Thomas undergraduates may elect minors from fifty-eight fields of study. Additional study and licensure programs are offered in Air Force, Army, and Navy ROTC; elementary and secondary school teacher licensure programs; individualized majors; predentistry; pre-engineering; prelaw; premedicine; prepharmacy; pre–physical therapy; preveterinary medicine; social work licensure; and school social worker licensure programs.

Academic Programs

The undergraduate program has two components: core curriculum requirements (in literature and writing, fine arts, social analysis, human diversity, historical studies, moral and philosophical reasoning, faith and the Catholic tradition, natural science and mathematical and quantitative reasoning, language and culture, health and fitness, and computer competency) and course requirements for completion of a major concentration. A total of 132 semester credits is required for a degree. The University operates on a 4-1-4 calendar, with spring and fall semesters and a four-week January Term. St. Thomas also offers summer sessions.

Special programs include the First-Year Program, designed to promote student achievement in college; the Aquinas Scholars Honors Program; study-abroad programs; internships; and the Renaissance Program, which blends a liberal arts major with a business-related minor. In most academic areas, credit is granted to students who have a score of at least 3 or 4, depending on the discipline, on Advanced Placement examinations sponsored by the College Board. Students also may receive credit through qualifying scores on the College-Level Examination Program (CLEP). It is possible to earn credit for scores of 4 or higher on the International Baccalaureate Diploma examination in subjects included in the St. Thomas curriculum.

Off-Campus Programs

Nationally, St. Thomas ranks among the top 10 universities in the doctoral-institutions category for the percentage of students who study abroad. In recent years, just over half of graduating seniors had studied abroad during their years at St. Thomas. Students have access to more than 100 semester or yearlong study-abroad programs and another forty-two short-term programs, in more than forty countries. More than 800 students study abroad under these programs annually. St. Thomas offers several faculty-led programs specifically for its students, including January Term and summer courses as well as the London Business Semester and the Catholic Studies Program in Rome.

Academic Facilities

The University has eighty-six buildings on four campuses, with seventy-seven on its main campus.

St. Thomas is home to four libraries. Three of them—the O'Shaughnessy-Frey Library Center on the main campus, the John Ireland Memorial Library on the St. Paul south campus, and the Charles J. Keffer Library on the Minneapolis campus—collectively house 615,000 volumes and have seating for 2,200 readers. The newest of the four, the Schoenecker Law Library, contains 165,000 volumes in print and microform and provides access to 62,000 electronic books and journals. Library users have access to hundreds of electronic databases and thousands of online resources, including electronic books, newspapers, and journals. CLICNet, the libraries' online catalog, is searchable via the Internet. It serves as the catalog of the holdings of the St. Thomas libraries as well as the collections of an eight-library consortium in the Twin Cities, with a combined collection of 2 million volumes.

Four auditoriums and the Foley Theater provide facilities for student theatrical performances as well as for speakers, forums, and concerts. State-of-the-art equipment in the Frey Science and Engineering Center includes a Fourier-transform infrared spectrometer. A wide range of computing and telecommunication services is available, including several computer labs for student use, wireless Internet access in all residence hall rooms and public spaces on campus, e-mail accounts and server space for all students, and class registration via the Web.

Costs

Tuition for the 2007–08 academic year was $25,808 for full-time students carrying 32 credits a year. The average combined room and board rate was $7312. Student fees (student activities and technology) were $466.

Financial Aid

Federal, state, and institutional aid programs are available for students who demonstrate need. St. Thomas is committed to students who demonstrate academic achievement and who have contributed to their community, school, or church. The University makes that commitment by offering merit scholarships to outstanding students. St. Thomas awards more than $31 million annually in both need- and non-need-based institutional scholarships and grants. More than $2.5 million is awarded annually in University-endowed scholarships from private foundations, individuals, alumni, families and friends of the University. For fall 2007, more than 90 percent of freshmen received some form of aid. For freshmen who applied, the average award was about $16,700.

Faculty

St. Thomas' 776 faculty members make teaching their highest priority. Many involve students in their research efforts as well. Eighty-five percent of full-time St. Thomas faculty members have the highest degree in their field. A low undergraduate student-faculty ratio allows for personal interaction between professors and students both inside and outside the classroom. All classes are taught by professors, not by teaching assistants.

Student Government

The All College Council (ACC) is the main student government board at St. Thomas. It represents student views and interests in academic, financial, and social affairs. The ACC plans numerous campus events, provides a variety of student services, and communicates regularly with the University's administrators and faculty members.

Admission Requirements

Applicants are considered on an individual basis. They are typically in the top 40 percent of their high school class, have a minimum cumulative high school grade point average of 3.0, and have earned an ACT composite score of 20 or higher or an SAT combined math and verbal score of 970 or higher. A GPA of 2.3 or better in transferable credits is required of transfer students. A rolling admission system, which begins October 1, enables applicants to learn of their admission status within one to three weeks after their applications are reviewed.

Application and Information

A completed application, a writing sample, an official high school transcript, and standardized test scores are required. The application fee is waived. Students may request a paper application or download an application from the Web site; completed applications can be sent by mail or submitted electronically. Transfer students are encouraged to contact the Office of Admissions for deadlines and details.

For information and an application form, students should contact:

Office of Admissions
University of St. Thomas
Mail 32F
2115 Summit Avenue
St. Paul, Minnesota 55105-1096

Phone: 651-962-6150
800-328-6819 Ext. 2-6150 (toll-free)
Fax: 651-962-6160
E-mail: admissions@stthomas.edu
Web site: http://www.stthomas.edu/admissions/undergraduate

MISSISSIPPI

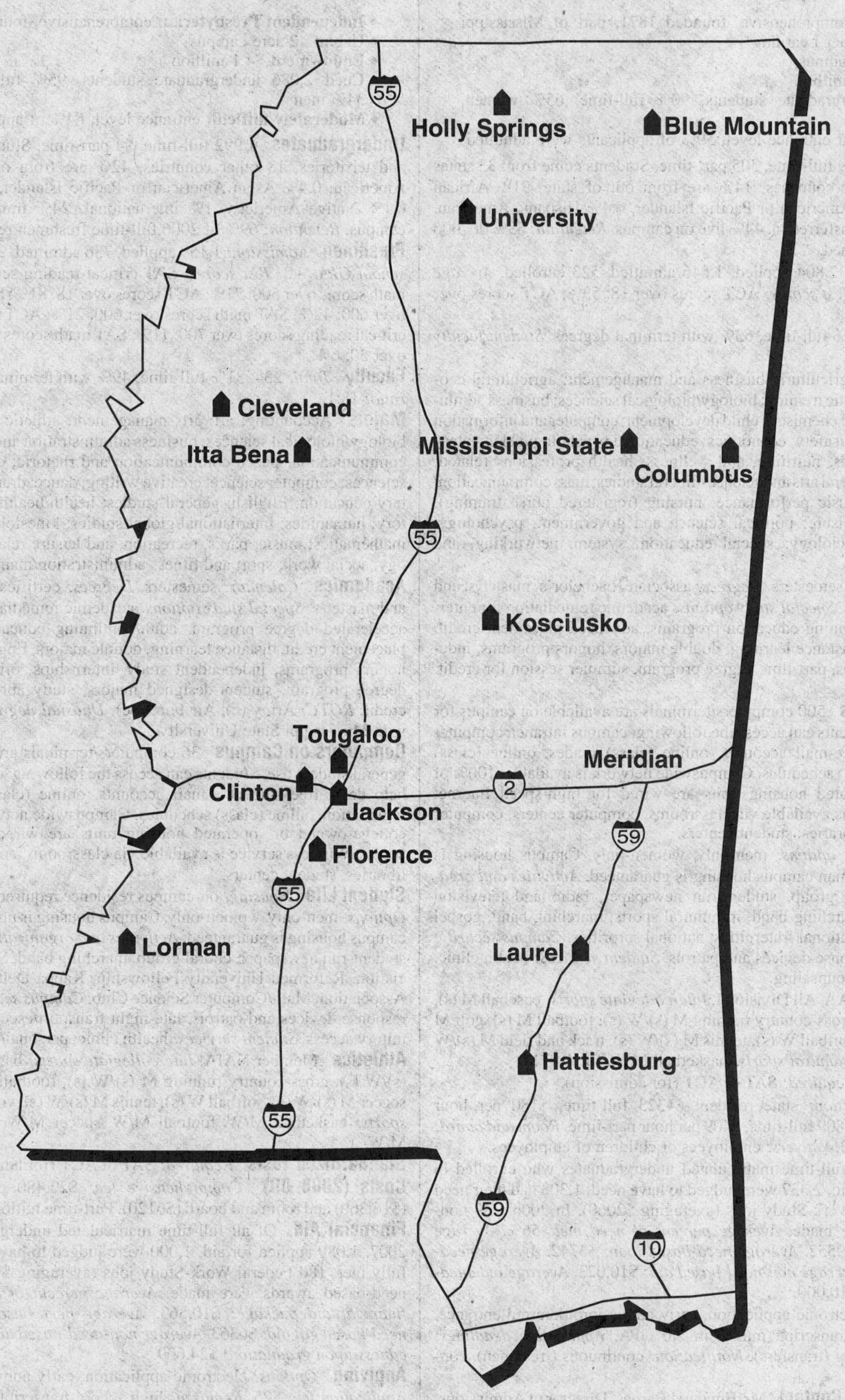

Alcorn State University

Alcorn State, Mississippi **www.alcorn.edu/**

- **State-supported** comprehensive, founded 1871, part of Mississippi Institutions of Higher Learning
- **Rural** 1756-acre campus
- **Endowment** $3.1 million
- **Coed** 3,004 undergraduate students, 90% full-time, 65% women, 35% men
- **Minimally difficult** entrance level, 59% of applicants were admitted

Undergraduates 2,699 full-time, 305 part-time. Students come from 33 states and territories, 14 other countries, 14% are from out of state, 91% African American, 0.3% Asian American or Pacific Islander, 0.4% Hispanic American, 2% international, 9% transferred in, 44% live on campus. *Retention:* 63% of 2006 full-time freshmen returned.

Freshmen *Admission:* 2,804 applied, 1,646 admitted, 523 enrolled. *Average high school GPA:* 2.79. *Test scores:* ACT scores over 18: 53%; ACT scores over 24: 7%.

Faculty *Total:* 219, 79% full-time, 63% with terminal degrees. *Student/faculty ratio:* 17:1.

Majors Accounting; agricultural business and management; agricultural economics; agriculture; athletic training; biology/biological sciences; business administration and management; chemistry; child development; computer and information sciences; criminal justice/safety; economics; educational psychology; elementary education; English; foods, nutrition, and wellness; health professions related; history; industrial arts; liberal arts and sciences/liberal studies; mass communication/media; mathematics; music performance; nursing (registered nurse training); parks, recreation and leisure; political science and government; psychology; robotics technology; sociology; special education; system, networking, and LAN/WAN management.

Academics *Calendar:* semesters. *Degrees:* associate, bachelor's, master's, and post-master's certificates. *Special study options:* academic remediation for entering students, adult/continuing education programs, advanced placement credit, cooperative education, distance learning, double majors, honors programs, independent study, internships, part-time degree program, summer session for credit. *ROTC:* Army (b).

Computers on Campus 500 computers/terminals are available on campus for general student use. Students can access the following: campus intranet, computer help desk, free student e-mail accounts, online (class) grades, online (class) registration, online (class) schedules. Campuswide network is available. 100% of college-owned or -operated housing units are wired for high-speed Internet access. Wireless service is available via classrooms, computer centers, computer labs, learning centers, libraries, student centers.

Student Life *Housing options:* men-only, women-only. Campus housing is university owned. Freshman campus housing is guaranteed. *Activities and organizations:* drama/theater group, student-run newspaper, radio and television station, choral group, marching band, intramural sports, marching band, gospel choir, inter-faith choir, national fraternities, national sororities. *Campus security:* 24-hour emergency response devices and patrols. *Student services:* health clinic, personal/psychological counseling.

Athletics Member NCAA. All Division I. *Intercollegiate sports:* baseball M (s), basketball M (s)/W (s), cross-country running M (s)/W (s), football M (s), golf M (s)/W (s), soccer W (s), softball W (s), tennis M (s)/W (s), track and field M (s)/W (s), volleyball W (s). *Intramural sports:* basketball M/W, football M.

Standardized Tests *Required:* SAT or ACT (for admission).

Costs (2007–08) *Tuition:* state resident $4323 full-time, $180 per hour part-time; nonresident $9809 full-time, $409 per hour part-time. *Room and board:* $4879; room only: $2493. *Waivers:* employees or children of employees.

Financial Aid Of all full-time matriculated undergraduates who enrolled in 2006, 2,710 applied for aid, 2,337 were judged to have need, 1,308 had their need fully met. 244 Federal Work-Study jobs (averaging $2060). In 2006, 239 non-need-based awards were made. *Average percent of need met:* 56%. *Average financial aid package:* $9552. *Average need-based loan:* $3742. *Average need-based gift aid:* $4240. *Average non-need-based aid:* $10,023. *Average indebtedness upon graduation:* $10,000.

Applying *Options:* electronic application, early admission, deferred entrance. *Required:* high school transcript, minimum 2.0 GPA. *Application deadlines:* rolling (freshmen), rolling (transfers). *Notification:* continuous (freshmen), continuous (transfers).

Freshman Application Contact Mr. Emanuel Barnes, Director of Admissions, Alcorn State University, 1000 ASU Drive #300, Alcorn State, MS 39096-7500. *Phone:* 601-877-6147. *Toll-free phone:* 800-222-6790. *Fax:* 601-877-6347. *E-mail:* ebarnes@alcorn.edu.

Belhaven College

Jackson, Mississippi **www.belhaven.edu/**

- **Independent Presbyterian** comprehensive, founded 1883
- **Urban** 42-acre campus
- **Endowment** $4.1 million
- **Coed** 2,086 undergraduate students, 95% full-time, 66% women, 34% men
- **Moderately difficult** entrance level, 64% of applicants were admitted

Undergraduates 1,992 full-time, 94 part-time. Students come from 30 states and territories, 18 other countries, 42% are from out of state, 35% African American, 0.4% Asian American or Pacific Islander, 3% Hispanic American, 0.1% Native American, 1% international, 24% transferred in, 23% live on campus. *Retention:* 69% of 2006 full-time freshmen returned.

Freshmen *Admission:* 1,159 applied, 736 admitted, 243 enrolled. *Average high school GPA:* 3.3. *Test scores:* SAT critical reading scores over 500: 86%; SAT math scores over 500: 71%; ACT scores over 18: 81%; SAT critical reading scores over 600: 42%; SAT math scores over 600: 21%; ACT scores over 24: 42%; SAT critical reading scores over 700: 11%; SAT math scores over 700: 3%; ACT scores over 30: 6%.

Faculty *Total:* 234, 31% full-time, 49% with terminal degrees. *Student/faculty ratio:* 18:1.

Majors Accounting; art; arts management; athletic training; biblical studies; biology/biological sciences; business administration and management; chemistry; communication/speech communication and rhetoric; computer and information sciences; computer science; creative writing; dance; dramatic/theater arts; elementary education; English; general studies; health/health care administration; history; humanities; international/global studies; kinesiology and exercise science; mathematics; music; parks, recreation, and leisure related; philosophy; psychology; social work; sport and fitness administration/management.

Academics *Calendar:* semesters. *Degrees:* certificates, associate, bachelor's, and master's. *Special study options:* academic remediation for entering students, accelerated degree program, adult/continuing education programs, advanced placement credit, distance learning, double majors, English as a second language, honors programs, independent study, internships, off-campus study, part-time degree program, student-designed majors, study abroad, summer session for credit. *ROTC:* Army (c), Air Force (c). *Unusual degree programs:* engineering with Mississippi State University.

Computers on Campus 36 computers/terminals are available on campus for general student use. Students can access the following: campus intranet, computer help desk, free student e-mail accounts, online (class) grades, online (class) registration, online (class) schedules. Campuswide network is available. 100% of college-owned or -operated housing units are wired for high-speed Internet access. Wireless service is available via classrooms, computer labs, dorm rooms, libraries, student centers.

Student Life *Housing:* on-campus residence required through sophomore year. *Options:* men-only, women-only. Campus housing is university owned. Freshman campus housing is guaranteed. *Activities and organizations:* drama/theater group, student-run newspaper, choral group, marching band, Student Government Association, Reformed University Fellowship, Kappa Delta Epsilon, Black Student Association, Math/Computer Science Club. *Campus security:* 24-hour emergency response devices and patrols, late-night transport/escort service, controlled dormitory access. *Student services:* health clinic, personal/psychological counseling.

Athletics Member NAIA. *Intercollegiate sports:* baseball M (s), basketball M (s)/W (s), cross-country running M (s)/W (s), football M (s), golf M (s)/W (s), soccer M (s)/W (s), softball W (s), tennis M (s)/W (s), volleyball W (s). *Intramural sports:* basketball M/W, football M/W, soccer M/W, softball M/W, volleyball M/W.

Standardized Tests *Required:* SAT or ACT (for admission).

Costs (2008–09) *Comprehensive fee:* $22,480 includes full-time tuition ($16,360) and room and board ($6120). Part-time tuition: $350 per semester hour.

Financial Aid Of all full-time matriculated undergraduates who enrolled in 2007, 1,089 applied for aid, 1,000 were judged to have need, 88 had their need fully met. 180 Federal Work-Study jobs (averaging $1432). In 2007, 216 non-need-based awards were made. *Average percent of need met:* 51%. *Average financial aid package:* $10,363. *Average need-based loan:* $4427. *Average need-based gift aid:* $6363. *Average non-need-based aid:* $6832. *Average indebtedness upon graduation:* $24,609.

Applying *Options:* electronic application, early admission, deferred entrance. *Application fee:* $25. *Required:* high school transcript, minimum 2.0 GPA, one academic reference. *Required for some:* essay or personal statement, letters of recommendation, interview, one academic reference. *Application deadlines:*

rolling (freshmen), rolling (out-of-state freshmen), rolling (transfers). *Notification:* continuous (freshmen), continuous (out-of-state freshmen), continuous (transfers).

Freshman Application Contact Mrs. Suzanne T. Sullivan, Director of Admission, Belhaven College, 150 Peachtree Street, Jackson, MS 39202. *Phone:* 601-968-5940. *Toll-free phone:* 800-960-5940. *Fax:* 601-968-8946. *E-mail:* admission@belhaven.edu.

BLUE MOUNTAIN COLLEGE

Blue Mountain, Mississippi **www.bmc.edu/**

Freshman Application Contact Ms. Maria Teel, Director of Admissions, Blue Mountain College, PO Box 160, Blue Mountain, MS 38610-0160. *Phone:* 662-685-4161. *Toll-free phone:* 800-235-0136. *Fax:* 662-685-4776. *E-mail:* eteel@bmc.edu.

DELTA STATE UNIVERSITY

Cleveland, Mississippi **www.deltastate.edu/**

- **State-supported** comprehensive, founded 1924, part of Mississippi Institutions of Higher Learning
- **Small-town** 332-acre campus
- **Endowment** $11.4 million
- **Coed** 3,356 undergraduate students, 82% full-time, 62% women, 38% men
- **Minimally difficult** entrance level, 29% of applicants were admitted

Undergraduates 2,757 full-time, 599 part-time. Students come from 37 states and territories, 14 other countries, 5% are from out of state, 38% African American, 0.8% Asian American or Pacific Islander, 0.7% Hispanic American, 0.2% Native American, 15% transferred in, 30% live on campus. *Retention:* 67% of 2006 full-time freshmen returned.

Freshmen *Admission:* 1,981 applied, 578 admitted, 477 enrolled. *Average high school GPA:* 3.06. *Test scores:* ACT scores over 18: 78%; ACT scores over 24: 18%; ACT scores over 30: 1%.

Faculty *Total:* 255, 70% full-time, 58% with terminal degrees. *Student/faculty ratio:* 16:1.

Majors Accounting; aeronautics/aviation/aerospace science and technology; airline pilot and flight crew; athletic training/sports medicine; audiology and speech-language pathology; biology/biological sciences; biology teacher education; business administration and management; business/commerce; chemistry; chemistry teacher education; communication/speech communication and rhetoric; criminal justice/safety; education; elementary education; English; English/language arts teacher education; environmental science; family and consumer sciences/human sciences; finance; foreign languages and literatures; history; hospitality administration; insurance; insurance/risk management; interdisciplinary studies; journalism; management information systems; marketing/marketing management; mathematics; mathematics teacher education; music; music teacher education; nursing (registered nurse training); office management; physical education teaching and coaching; political science and government; psychology; real estate; social sciences; social science teacher education; social work; special education; speech/theater education; visual and performing arts.

Academics *Calendar:* semesters. *Degrees:* bachelor's, master's, doctoral, and post-master's certificates. *Special study options:* academic remediation for entering students, advanced placement credit, cooperative education, distance learning, double majors, honors programs, independent study, internships, part-time degree program, services for LD students, summer session for credit.

Computers on Campus 350 computers/terminals are available on campus for general student use. Students can access the following: free student e-mail accounts, online (class) registration. Campuswide network is available. 100% of college-owned or -operated housing units are wired for high-speed Internet access.

Student Life *Housing:* on-campus residence required for freshman year. *Options:* men-only, women-only, disabled students. Campus housing is university owned. Freshman campus housing is guaranteed. *Activities and organizations:* drama/theater group, student-run newspaper, choral group, marching band, Student Government Association, Student Alumni Association, Baptist Student Union, Fellowship of Christian Athletes, Delta Volunteers, national fraternities, national sororities. *Campus security:* 24-hour emergency response devices and patrols, late-night transport/escort service, controlled dormitory access. *Student services:* health clinic, personal/psychological counseling.

Athletics Member NCAA. All Division II. *Intercollegiate sports:* baseball M (s), basketball M (s)/W (s), cheerleading M (s)/W (s), cross-country running W (s), football M (s), golf M (s), soccer M (s)/W (s), softball W (s), swimming and diving M (s)/W (s), tennis M (s)/W (s). *Intramural sports:* archery M/W, badminton M/W, basketball M/W, bowling M/W, cross-country running M/W, football M/W, golf M/W, racquetball M/W, riflery M/W, soccer M/W, softball M/W, swimming and diving M/W, table tennis M/W, tennis M/W, volleyball M/W.

Standardized Tests *Required:* SAT or ACT (for admission).

Costs (2007–08) *Tuition:* state resident $4248 full-time, $177 per hour part-time; nonresident $10,258 full-time, $427 per hour part-time. *Room and board:* $4876; room only: $2626. Room and board charges vary according to board plan and housing facility. *Payment plan:* installment. *Waivers:* children of alumni, senior citizens, and employees or children of employees.

Financial Aid Of all full-time matriculated undergraduates who enrolled in 2003, 2,150 applied for aid. 318 Federal Work-Study jobs (averaging $1650). *Average indebtedness upon graduation:* $8750.

Applying *Options:* electronic application, deferred entrance. *Application fee:* $15. *Required:* high school transcript, minimum 3.2 GPA. *Required for some:* interview, interview for art, music majors. *Application deadlines:* 8/1 (freshmen), 8/1 (transfers). *Notification:* continuous (freshmen), continuous (transfers).

Freshman Application Contact Dr. Debbie Heslep, Dean of Enrollment Management, Delta State University, Kent Wyatt Hall 117, Cleveland, MS 38733. *Phone:* 662-846-4655. *Toll-free phone:* 800-468-6378. *Fax:* 662-846-4684. *E-mail:* dheslep@deltastate.edu.

JACKSON STATE UNIVERSITY

Jackson, Mississippi **www.jsums.edu/**

- **State-supported** university, founded 1877, part of Mississippi Institutions of Higher Learning
- **Urban** 250-acre campus
- **Coed** 6,823 undergraduate students, 87% full-time, 62% women, 38% men
- **Minimally difficult** entrance level, 36% of applicants were admitted

Undergraduates 5,917 full-time, 906 part-time. Students come from 35 states and territories, 27 other countries, 16% are from out of state, 96% African American, 0.2% Asian American or Pacific Islander, 0.3% Hispanic American, 0.1% Native American, 0.3% international, 8% transferred in, 31% live on campus. *Retention:* 76% of 2006 full-time freshmen returned.

Freshmen *Admission:* 6,499 applied, 2,341 admitted, 926 enrolled. *Average high school GPA:* 2.88. *Test scores:* ACT scores over 18: 57%; ACT scores over 24: 8%.

Faculty *Total:* 468, 81% full-time, 65% with terminal degrees. *Student/faculty ratio:* 17:1.

Majors Accounting; atmospheric sciences and meteorology; biology/biological sciences; business administration and management; business/managerial economics; chemistry; civil engineering; computer and information sciences; computer engineering; criminal justice/safety; educational/instructional media design; education related; electrical, electronics and communications engineering; elementary education; English; entrepreneurship; finance; foreign languages and literatures; geology/earth science; health/health care administration; history; industrial technology; marketing/marketing management; mass communication/media; mathematics; mathematics teacher education; multi-/interdisciplinary studies related; music performance; music teacher education; physical education teaching and coaching; physics; political science and government; psychology; social science teacher education; social work; sociology; special education; speech and rhetoric; speech-language pathology; technology/industrial arts teacher education; urban studies/affairs; visual and performing arts.

Academics *Calendar:* semesters. *Degrees:* bachelor's, master's, doctoral, and post-master's certificates. *Special study options:* academic remediation for entering students, adult/continuing education programs, advanced placement credit, cooperative education, distance learning, double majors, English as a second language, honors programs, internships, off-campus study, part-time degree program, services for LD students, study abroad, summer session for credit. *ROTC:* Army (b). *Unusual degree programs:* 3-2 engineering with Mississippi State University, Auburn University, Tuskegee University, University of Mississippi, Georgia Institute of Technology, Southern University and Agricultural and Mechanical College, University of Minnesota.

Computers on Campus 300 computers/terminals are available on campus for general student use. Students can access the following: free student e-mail accounts, online (class) grades, online (class) registration, online (class) schedules. Campuswide network is available. Wireless service is available via classrooms, computer centers, dorm rooms, libraries.

Student Life *Housing options:* men-only, women-only. Campus housing is university owned and is provided by a third party. *Activities and organizations:* drama/theater group, student-run newspaper, choral group, marching band, Tiger

Pride Connection, Sonic Boom of the South, Students In Free Enterprise, Interfaith, NAACP, national fraternities, national sororities. *Campus security:* 24-hour emergency response devices and patrols, late-night transport/escort service, controlled dormitory access. *Student services:* health clinic, personal/psychological counseling.

Athletics Member NCAA. All Division I except football (Division I-AA). *Intercollegiate sports:* baseball M (s), basketball M (s)/W (s), bowling W (s), cross-country running M (s)/W (s), golf M (s)/W (s), soccer W (s), softball W (s), tennis M (s)/W (s), track and field M (s)/W (s), volleyball W (s). *Intramural sports:* basketball M/W, bowling M/W, soccer W, tennis M/W, volleyball W.

Standardized Tests *Required:* SAT or ACT (for admission).

Costs (2007–08) *Tuition:* state resident $4432 full-time, $185 per credit hour part-time; nonresident $9974 full-time, $416 per credit hour part-time. Part-time tuition and fees vary according to course load. *Room and board:* $5600; room only: $3400. Room and board charges vary according to board plan. *Payment plan:* installment. *Waivers:* children of alumni and employees or children of employees.

Applying *Options:* electronic application, early admission, deferred entrance. *Required:* high school transcript, minimum 2.0 GPA. *Required for some:* 3 letters of recommendation. *Application deadlines:* 8/1 (freshmen), rolling (transfers). *Notification:* continuous (freshmen), continuous (transfers).

Freshman Application Contact Mrs. Linda Rush, Director, Marketing and Recruitment, Jackson State University, PO Box 17330, 1400 John R. Lynch Street, Jackson, MS 39217. *Phone:* 601-979-2911. *Toll-free phone:* 800-682-5390 (in-state); 800-848-6817 (out-of-state). *E-mail:* schatman@ccaix.jsums.edu.

MAGNOLIA BIBLE COLLEGE

Kosciusko, Mississippi www.magnolia.edu/

- **Independent** 4-year, founded 1976, affiliated with Church of Christ
- **Small-town** 5-acre campus
- **Endowment** $332,238
- **Coed, primarily men** 35 undergraduate students, 66% full-time, 23% women, 77% men
- **Noncompetitive** entrance level, 100% of applicants were admitted

Undergraduates 23 full-time, 12 part-time. 3% are from out of state, 31% African American, 29% transferred in, 31% live on campus. *Retention:* 100% of 2006 full-time freshmen returned.

Freshmen *Admission:* 2 applied, 2 admitted, 2 enrolled.

Faculty *Total:* 11, 18% full-time, 36% with terminal degrees. *Student/faculty ratio:* 7:1.

Majors Biblical studies.

Academics *Calendar:* semesters. *Degree:* bachelor's. *Special study options:* academic remediation for entering students, independent study, internships, part-time degree program, summer session for credit.

Computers on Campus 8 computers/terminals are available on campus for general student use. 100% of college-owned or -operated housing units are wired for high-speed Internet access. Wireless service is available via entire campus.

Student Life *Housing options:* coed. Campus housing is university owned. *Campus security:* 24-hour emergency response devices. *Student services:* personal/psychological counseling.

Standardized Tests *Required:* SAT or ACT (for admission).

Costs (2008–09) *Tuition:* $6450 full-time, $215 per semester hour part-time. *Required fees:* $90 full-time, $45 per term part-time. *Room only:* $1500.

Financial Aid Of all full-time matriculated undergraduates who enrolled in 2006, 13 applied for aid, 12 were judged to have need, 5 had their need fully met. 2 Federal Work-Study jobs (averaging $1250). In 2006, 10 non-need-based awards were made. *Average percent of need met:* 77%. *Average financial aid package:* $7543. *Average need-based gift aid:* $6811. *Average non-need-based aid:* $2578.

Applying *Required:* essay or personal statement, high school transcript, 3 letters of recommendation. *Application deadlines:* 8/31 (freshmen), 8/31 (transfers). *Notification:* continuous (freshmen), continuous (transfers).

Freshman Application Contact Mr. Travis Brown, Director of Admissions, Magnolia Bible College, PO Box 1109, 822 South Huntington Street, Kosciusko, MS 39090. *Phone:* 662-289-2896 Ext. 109. *Toll-free phone:* 800-748-8655. *Fax:* 662-289-1850. *E-mail:* tbrown@magnolia.edu.

MILLSAPS COLLEGE

Jackson, Mississippi www.millsaps.edu/

- **Independent United Methodist** comprehensive, founded 1890
- **Urban** 100-acre campus
- **Endowment** $101.4 million
- **Coed** 1,043 undergraduate students, 98% full-time, 51% women, 49% men
- **Moderately difficult** entrance level, 77% of applicants were admitted

Undergraduates 1,020 full-time, 23 part-time. Students come from 32 states and territories, 16 other countries, 52% are from out of state, 11% African American, 4% Asian American or Pacific Islander, 1% Hispanic American, 0.1% Native American, 1% international, 3% transferred in, 81% live on campus. *Retention:* 81% of 2006 full-time freshmen returned.

Freshmen *Admission:* 1,253 applied, 968 admitted, 296 enrolled. *Average high school GPA:* 3.5. *Test scores:* SAT critical reading scores over 500: 88%; SAT math scores over 500: 86%; ACT scores over 18: 100%; SAT critical reading scores over 600: 58%; SAT math scores over 600: 48%; ACT scores over 24: 74%; SAT critical reading scores over 700: 16%; SAT math scores over 700: 11%; ACT scores over 30: 24%.

Faculty *Total:* 109, 83% full-time, 86% with terminal degrees. *Student/faculty ratio:* 11:1.

Majors Accounting; anthropology; art history, criticism and conservation; biology/biological sciences; business administration and management; chemistry; classics and languages, literatures and linguistics; computer science; dramatic/theater arts; economics; education; English; European studies; fine/studio arts; French; geology/earth science; German; history; mathematics; multi-/interdisciplinary studies related; music; philosophy; philosophy and religious studies related; physics; political science and government; psychology; public administration; religious studies; sociology; Spanish.

Academics *Calendar:* semesters. *Degrees:* bachelor's and master's. *Special study options:* accelerated degree program, adult/continuing education programs, advanced placement credit, double majors, honors programs, independent study, internships, off-campus study, part-time degree program, services for LD students, student-designed majors, study abroad, summer session for credit. *ROTC:* Army (c). *Unusual degree programs:* 3-2 engineering with Auburn University, Columbia University, Vanderbilt University, Washington University in St. Louis; nursing with University of Mississippi School of Nursing.

Computers on Campus 150 computers/terminals are available on campus for general student use. Students can access the following: campus intranet, computer help desk, free student e-mail accounts, online (class) grades, online (class) registration, online (class) schedules, online transcripts. Campuswide network is available. 100% of college-owned or -operated housing units are wired for high-speed Internet access. Wireless service is available via entire campus.

Student Life *Housing:* on-campus residence required through sophomore year. *Options:* coed, men-only, women-only, cooperative. Campus housing is university owned. Freshman campus housing is guaranteed. *Activities and organizations:* drama/theater group, student-run newspaper, choral group, Campus Ministry Team, Student Body Association, Black Student Association, SAPS (Socializing Activities and Programs for Students)..formerly Major Productions, Outdoor Adventure Club, national fraternities, national sororities. *Campus security:* 24-hour emergency response devices and patrols, student patrols, late-night transport/escort service, controlled dormitory access, self-defense education, lighted pathways. *Student services:* health clinic, personal/psychological counseling.

Athletics Member NCAA. All Division III. *Intercollegiate sports:* baseball M, basketball M/W, cheerleading M/W, cross-country running M/W, football M, golf M/W, soccer M/W, softball W, tennis M/W, volleyball W. *Intramural sports:* basketball M/W, bowling M/W, fencing M/W, football M/W, golf M/W, lacrosse W, racquetball M/W, soccer M/W, softball M/W, table tennis M/W, tennis M/W, ultimate Frisbee M/W, volleyball M/W, weight lifting M/W.

Standardized Tests *Required:* SAT or ACT (for admission).

Costs (2008–09) *Comprehensive fee:* $33,554 includes full-time tuition ($23,214), mandatory fees ($1540), and room and board ($8800). Part-time tuition: $720 per credit hour. *Required fees:* $32 per credit hour part-time. *College room only:* $4956.

Financial Aid Of all full-time matriculated undergraduates who enrolled in 2006, 658 applied for aid, 531 were judged to have need, 155 had their need fully met. 293 Federal Work-Study jobs (averaging $1256). In 2006, 395 non-need-based awards were made. *Average percent of need met:* 83%. *Average financial aid package:* $18,892. *Average need-based loan:* $3805. *Average need-based gift aid:* $15,617. *Average non-need-based aid:* $14,212. *Average indebtedness upon graduation:* $21,495.

Applying *Options:* electronic application, early admission, early action, deferred entrance. *Required:* essay or personal statement, high school transcript, minimum

2.5 GPA, letters of recommendation. *Required for some:* interview. *Application deadlines:* rolling (freshmen), rolling (out-of-state freshmen), rolling (transfers), 1/8 (early action). *Notification:* continuous until 10/1 (freshmen), continuous until 10/1 (out-of-state freshmen), continuous until 10/1 (transfers).

Freshman Application Contact Mr. Mathew Cox, Dean of Enrollment Management, Millsaps College, 1701 North State Street, Jackson, MS 39210-0001. *Phone:* 601-974-1050. *Toll-free phone:* 800-352-1050. *Fax:* 601-974-1059. *E-mail:* admissions@millsaps.edu.

MISSISSIPPI COLLEGE

Clinton, Mississippi **www.mc.edu/**

- **Independent Southern Baptist** comprehensive, founded 1826
- **Suburban** 320-acre campus
- **Endowment** $50.7 million
- **Coed** 2,921 undergraduate students, 86% full-time, 60% women, 40% men
- **Moderately difficult** entrance level, 65% of applicants were admitted

Undergraduates 2,515 full-time, 406 part-time. Students come from 28 states and territories, 18 other countries, 16% are from out of state, 24% African American, 1% Asian American or Pacific Islander, 0.6% Hispanic American, 0.4% Native American, 4% international, 16% transferred in, 56% live on campus. *Retention:* 77% of 2006 full-time freshmen returned.

Freshmen *Admission:* 1,642 applied, 1,064 admitted, 541 enrolled. *Average high school GPA:* 3.42. *Test scores:* SAT critical reading scores over 500: 54%; SAT math scores over 500: 59%; ACT scores over 18: 98%; SAT critical reading scores over 600: 24%; SAT math scores over 600: 20%; ACT scores over 24: 42%; SAT critical reading scores over 700: 3%; SAT math scores over 700: 3%; ACT scores over 30: 7%.

Faculty *Total:* 378, 44% full-time, 60% with terminal degrees. *Student/faculty ratio:* 16:1.

Majors Accounting; art; art history, criticism and conservation; art teacher education; biochemistry; biology/biological sciences; business administration and management; business teacher education; chemistry; Christian studies; communication and journalism related; communication/speech communication and rhetoric; computer and information sciences; computer science; criminal justice/law enforcement administration; education; elementary education; English; foreign languages and literatures; foreign languages related; French; graphic design; health and physical education; history; interior design; kinesiology and exercise science; language interpretation and translation; legal assistant/paralegal; liberal arts and sciences/liberal studies; marketing/marketing management; mass communication/media; mathematics; music; music performance; music teacher education; music theory and composition; nursing (registered nurse training); physics; piano and organ; political science and government; pre-dentistry studies; pre-law studies; pre-medical studies; pre-pharmacy studies; pre-veterinary studies; psychology; public relations/image management; religious/sacred music; science teacher education; secondary education; social sciences; social sciences related; social science teacher education; social studies teacher education; social work; sociology; Spanish; special education; sport and fitness administration/management; voice and opera.

Academics *Calendar:* semesters. *Degrees:* bachelor's, master's, doctoral, first professional, and postbachelor's certificates. *Special study options:* academic remediation for entering students, accelerated degree program, adult/continuing education programs, advanced placement credit, cooperative education, distance learning, double majors, English as a second language, honors programs, independent study, internships, part-time degree program, services for LD students, study abroad, summer session for credit. *ROTC:* Army (c). *Unusual degree programs:* 3-2 engineering with Auburn University, University of Mississippi; law, medicine-University of Mississippi.

Computers on Campus 250 computers/terminals are available on campus for general student use. Students can access the following: campus intranet, computer help desk, free student e-mail accounts, online (class) grades, online (class) registration, online (class) schedules. Campuswide network is available. 60% of college-owned or -operated housing units are wired for high-speed Internet access. Wireless service is available via classrooms, dorm rooms, libraries, student centers.

Student Life *Housing:* on-campus residence required through senior year. *Options:* men-only, women-only, disabled students. Campus housing is university owned. Freshman applicants given priority for college housing. *Activities and organizations:* drama/theater group, student-run newspaper, radio station, choral group, marching band, Baptist Student Union, Nenamoosha Social Tribe, Laguna Social Tribe, Civitan Service Club, Shawreth Service Club. *Campus security:* 24-hour emergency response devices and patrols, late-night transport/escort service, controlled dormitory access. *Student services:* health clinic, personal/psychological counseling.

Athletics Member NCAA. All Division III. *Intercollegiate sports:* baseball M, basketball M/W, cheerleading W, cross-country running M/W, equestrian sports W, football M, golf M, soccer M/W, softball W, tennis M/W, track and field M/W, volleyball W, wrestling M. *Intramural sports:* basketball M/W, football M/W, soccer M/W, softball M/W, tennis M/W, ultimate Frisbee M/W, volleyball M/W.

Standardized Tests *Required:* SAT or ACT (for admission).

Costs (2008–09) *Comprehensive fee:* $18,600 includes full-time tuition ($12,200), mandatory fees ($600), and room and board ($5800). Part-time tuition: $382 per credit hour. *Required fees:* $150 per term part-time.

Financial Aid Of all full-time matriculated undergraduates who enrolled in 2007, 2,432 applied for aid, 1,456 were judged to have need, 441 had their need fully met. 222 Federal Work-Study jobs (averaging $1816). In 2007, 940 non-need-based awards were made. *Average percent of need met:* 71%. *Average financial aid package:* $14,463. *Average need-based loan:* $6757. *Average need-based gift aid:* $8835. *Average non-need-based aid:* $9641. *Average indebtedness upon graduation:* $22,145.

Applying *Options:* electronic application, early admission, early decision, deferred entrance. *Required:* high school transcript, 1 letter of recommendation. *Recommended:* minimum 2.0 GPA, interview. *Application deadlines:* rolling (freshmen), rolling (transfers). *Early decision deadline:* 12/1. *Notification:* continuous (freshmen), continuous (transfers), 12/15 (early decision).

Freshman Application Contact Mr. Chad Phillips, Director of Admissions, Mississippi College, PO Box 4026, 200 South Capitol Street, Clinton, MS 39058. *Phone:* 601-925-3800. *Toll-free phone:* 800-738-1236. *Fax:* 601-925-3804. *E-mail:* enrollment-services@mc.edu.

MISSISSIPPI STATE UNIVERSITY

Mississippi State, Mississippi **www.msstate.edu/**

- **State-supported** university, founded 1878, part of Mississippi Institutions of Higher Learning
- **Small-town** 4200-acre campus
- **Endowment** $240.1 million
- **Coed** 13,208 undergraduate students, 89% full-time, 47% women, 53% men
- **Moderately difficult** entrance level, 70% of applicants were admitted

Undergraduates 11,753 full-time, 1,455 part-time. Students come from 50 states and territories, 34 other countries, 17% are from out of state, 21% African American, 1% Asian American or Pacific Islander, 1% Hispanic American, 0.5% Native American, 0.6% international, 12% transferred in, 26% live on campus. *Retention:* 83% of 2006 full-time freshmen returned.

Freshmen *Admission:* 6,141 applied, 4,276 admitted, 2,281 enrolled. *Average high school GPA:* 3.2. *Test scores:* SAT critical reading scores over 500: 74%; SAT math scores over 500: 76%; ACT scores over 18: 92%; SAT critical reading scores over 600: 38%; SAT math scores over 600: 41%; ACT scores over 24: 50%; SAT critical reading scores over 700: 11%; SAT math scores over 700: 11%; ACT scores over 30: 11%.

Faculty *Total:* 1,053, 81% full-time, 75% with terminal degrees. *Student/faculty ratio:* 15:1.

Majors Accounting; aerospace, aeronautical and astronautical engineering; agribusiness; agricultural/biological engineering and bioengineering; agricultural economics; agricultural teacher education; agriculture; agronomy and crop science; animal sciences; anthropology; architecture; biochemistry; biological and physical sciences; biology/biological sciences; biomedical/medical engineering; business administration and management; business/managerial economics; business teacher education; chemical engineering; chemistry; civil engineering; clinical laboratory science/medical technology; communication/speech communication and rhetoric; computer and information sciences; computer engineering; construction management; economics; educational psychology; electrical, electronics and communications engineering; elementary education; engineering related; English; family and consumer sciences/human sciences; finance; food science; foreign languages and literatures; forestry; geology/earth science; history; horticultural science; industrial engineering; industrial technology; insurance; landscape architecture; landscaping and groundskeeping; liberal arts and sciences/liberal studies; management information systems; marketing/marketing management; mathematics; mechanical engineering; medical microbiology and bacteriology; multi-/interdisciplinary studies related; music teacher education; philosophy; physical education teaching and coaching; physics; plant protection and integrated pest management; political science and government; poultry science; psychology; real estate; secondary education; social work; sociology; special education; technical teacher education; technology/industrial arts teacher education; visual and performing arts; wildlife and wildlands science and management; wood science and wood products/pulp and paper technology.

Academics *Calendar:* semesters. *Degrees:* bachelor's, master's, doctoral, first professional, and post-master's certificates. *Special study options:* academic remediation for entering students, accelerated degree program, adult/continuing education programs, advanced placement credit, cooperative education, distance learning, double majors, English as a second language, freshman honors college, honors programs, independent study, internships, off-campus study, part-time degree program, services for LD students, student-designed majors, study abroad, summer session for credit. *ROTC:* Army (b), Air Force (b).

Computers on Campus 1,000 computers/terminals and 1,000 ports are available on campus for general student use. Students can access the following: campus intranet, computer help desk, free student e-mail accounts, online (class) grades, online (class) registration, online (class) schedules, campus-wide wireless Internet access. Campuswide network is available. 100% of college-owned or -operated housing units are wired for high-speed Internet access. Wireless service is available via entire campus.

Student Life *Housing options:* coed, men-only, women-only, disabled students. Campus housing is university owned. Freshman applicants given priority for college housing. *Activities and organizations:* drama/theater group, student-run newspaper, radio and television station, choral group, marching band, Student Association, Black Student Alliance, Residence Hall Association, Fashion Board, Campus Activities Board, national fraternities, national sororities. *Campus security:* 24-hour emergency response devices and patrols, late-night transport/escort service, controlled dormitory access, bicycle patrols, crime prevention program, RAD program, general law enforcement services. *Student services:* health clinic, personal/psychological counseling.

Athletics Member NCAA. All Division I except football (Division I-A). *Intercollegiate sports:* baseball M (s), basketball M (s)/W (s), cheerleading M (s)/W (s), cross-country running M (s)/W (s), golf M (s)/W (s), soccer W (s), softball W (s), tennis M (s)/W (s), track and field M (s)/W (s), volleyball W (s). *Intramural sports:* badminton M (c)/W (c), basketball M/W, bowling M/W, cross-country running M (c)/W (c), fencing M (c)/W (c), football M/W, golf M/W, lacrosse M (c), racquetball M/W, rugby M (c)/W (c), soccer M (c)/W (c), softball M/W, swimming and diving M (c)/W (c), table tennis M/W, tennis M/W, ultimate Frisbee M/W, volleyball M/W, water polo M/W.

Standardized Tests *Required:* SAT or ACT (for admission).

Costs (2007–08) *Tuition:* state resident $4978 full-time, $206 per hour part-time; nonresident $11,469 full-time, $476 per hour part-time. Part-time tuition and fees vary according to course load. *Room and board:* $6951; room only: $3716. Room and board charges vary according to board plan, housing facility, and student level. *Waivers:* children of alumni, senior citizens, and employees or children of employees.

Financial Aid Of all full-time matriculated undergraduates who enrolled in 2006, 6,606 applied for aid, 5,393 were judged to have need, 1,652 had their need fully met. 735 Federal Work-Study jobs (averaging $2556). In 2006, 1926 non-need-based awards were made. *Average percent of need met:* 67%. *Average financial aid package:* $8980. *Average need-based loan:* $4169. *Average need-based gift aid:* $4686. *Average non-need-based aid:* $2693. *Average indebtedness upon graduation:* $20,828.

Applying *Options:* electronic application, early admission, deferred entrance. *Application fee:* $25. *Required:* high school transcript, minimum 2.0 GPA. *Application deadlines:* 8/1 (freshmen), 8/1 (transfers). *Notification:* continuous (freshmen), continuous (transfers).

Freshman Application Contact Ms. Cheryl Dill, Associate Director of Admissions and Scholarships, Mississippi State University, PO Box 6305, Mississippi State, MS 39762. *Phone:* 662-325-2224. *Fax:* 662-325-1MSU. *E-mail:* admit@msstate.edu.

MISSISSIPPI UNIVERSITY FOR WOMEN

Columbus, Mississippi **www.muw.edu/**

- **State-supported** comprehensive, founded 1884, part of Mississippi Institutions of Higher Learning
- **Small-town** 110-acre campus
- **Endowment** $32.7 million
- **Coed, primarily women** 2,222 undergraduate students, 75% full-time, 84% women, 16% men
- **Moderately difficult** entrance level, 46% of applicants were admitted

Undergraduates 1,662 full-time, 560 part-time. Students come from 22 states and territories, 13 other countries, 9% are from out of state, 34% African American, 2% Asian American or Pacific Islander, 0.8% Hispanic American, 0.4% Native American, 1% international, 14% transferred in, 21% live on campus. *Retention:* 66% of 2006 full-time freshmen returned.

Freshmen *Admission:* 1,356 applied, 627 admitted, 241 enrolled. *Average high school GPA:* 3.3. *Test scores:* SAT critical reading scores over 500: 63%; SAT math scores over 500: 75%; ACT scores over 18: 79%; SAT critical reading scores over 600: 13%; ACT scores over 24: 25%; ACT scores over 30: 1%.

Faculty *Total:* 210, 65% full-time, 45% with terminal degrees. *Student/faculty ratio:* 12:1.

Majors Accounting; art; art teacher education; audiology and speech-language pathology; biological and physical sciences; biology/biological sciences; business administration and management; chemistry; clothing/textiles; communication/speech communication and rhetoric; culinary arts; dramatic/theater arts; drawing; education; elementary education; English; history; human development and family studies; information science/studies; kinesiology and exercise science; legal assistant/paralegal; marketing/marketing management; mathematics; medical microbiology and bacteriology; music management and merchandising; music teacher education; parks, recreation and leisure; physical education teaching and coaching; physical sciences; political science and government; printmaking; psychology; science teacher education; secondary education; social sciences; Spanish; special education; sport and fitness administration/management.

Academics *Calendar:* semesters. *Degrees:* associate, bachelor's, master's, and post-master's certificates. *Special study options:* academic remediation for entering students, accelerated degree program, adult/continuing education programs, advanced placement credit, cooperative education, distance learning, double majors, English as a second language, freshman honors college, honors programs, internships, off-campus study, part-time degree program, services for LD students, study abroad, summer session for credit. *ROTC:* Army (c), Air Force (c). *Unusual degree programs:* 3-2 engineering with Auburn University, Mississippi State University.

Computers on Campus 300 computers/terminals are available on campus for general student use. Students can access the following: campus intranet, computer help desk, free student e-mail accounts, online (class) grades, online (class) registration, online (class) schedules, various software packages. Campuswide network is available. 100% of college-owned or -operated housing units are wired for high-speed Internet access. Wireless service is available via computer centers, computer labs, learning centers.

Student Life *Housing options:* men-only, women-only, disabled students. Campus housing is university owned. Freshman campus housing is guaranteed. *Activities and organizations:* drama/theater group, student-run newspaper, radio station, choral group, Student Government Association, Residence Hall Association, Class Council, Modeling Squad, Student Programming Board, national fraternities, national sororities. *Campus security:* 24-hour patrols, student patrols, late-night transport/escort service. *Student services:* health clinic, personal/psychological counseling, women's center.

Athletics *Intramural sports:* badminton M/W, basketball M/W, football M/W, golf M/W, racquetball M/W, soccer M/W, softball M/W, swimming and diving M/W, table tennis M/W, tennis M/W, ultimate Frisbee M/W, volleyball M/W.

Standardized Tests *Required for some:* SAT or ACT (for admission). *Recommended:* SAT or ACT (for admission).

Costs (2007–08) *Tuition:* state resident $4209 full-time, $175 per credit hour part-time; nonresident $10,723 full-time, $447 per credit hour part-time. *Room and board:* $4740; room only: $2780.

Financial Aid Of all full-time matriculated undergraduates who enrolled in 2006, 1,367 applied for aid, 1,154 were judged to have need, 735 had their need fully met. 111 Federal Work-Study jobs (averaging $1180). 268 state and other part-time jobs (averaging $1123). In 2006, 316 non-need-based awards were made. *Average percent of need met:* 65%. *Average financial aid package:* $7459. *Average need-based loan:* $3737. *Average need-based gift aid:* $3257. *Average non-need-based aid:* $4614. *Average indebtedness upon graduation:* $14,847.

Applying *Options:* electronic application, early admission, early decision. *Required:* high school transcript. *Required for some:* minimum 2.0 GPA, rank in upper 50% of high school class. *Application deadlines:* rolling (freshmen), rolling (transfers). *Notification:* continuous (freshmen), continuous (transfers).

Director of Admissions Ms. Cassie Derden, Manager of Admissions, Mississippi University for Women, PO Box 1613, Columbus, MS 39701-9998. *Phone:* 601-329-7106. *Toll-free phone:* 877-GO 2 THE W. *E-mail:* cderden@admissions.muw.edu.

MISSISSIPPI VALLEY STATE UNIVERSITY

Itta Bena, Mississippi **www.mvsu.edu/**

- **State-supported** comprehensive, founded 1946, part of Mississippi Institutions of Higher Learning
- **Small-town** 450-acre campus
- **Endowment** $2.1 million
- **Coed** 2,574 undergraduate students, 90% full-time, 65% women, 35% men
- **Minimally difficult** entrance level, 25% of applicants were admitted

Undergraduates 2,309 full-time, 265 part-time. Students come from 33 states and territories, 2 other countries, 12% are from out of state, 94% African American, 0.2% Asian American or Pacific Islander, 0.4% Hispanic American, 9% transferred in, 36% live on campus. *Retention:* 65% of 2006 full-time freshmen returned.

Freshmen *Admission:* 3,341 applied, 848 admitted, 490 enrolled. *Average high school GPA:* 2.58. *Test scores:* ACT scores over 18: 36%; ACT scores over 24: 3%.

Faculty *Total:* 179, 76% full-time, 40% with terminal degrees. *Student/faculty ratio:* 17:1.

Majors Accounting; art; biology/biological sciences; business administration and management; chemistry; computer science; criminal justice/law enforcement administration; education; elementary education; English; English/language arts teacher education; history; industrial technology; kindergarten/preschool education; mass communication/media; mathematics; mathematics teacher education; music; music teacher education; office management; physical education teaching and coaching; political science and government; public administration; recording arts technology; science teacher education; social science teacher education; social work; sociology; speech and rhetoric; water quality and wastewater treatment management and recycling technology.

Academics *Calendar:* semesters. *Degrees:* bachelor's and master's. *Special study options:* academic remediation for entering students, cooperative education, distance learning, double majors, freshman honors college, honors programs, internships, part-time degree program, summer session for credit. *ROTC:* Army (b).

Computers on Campus 250 computers/terminals are available on campus for general student use. Students can access the following: online (class) registration. Campuswide network is available.

Student Life *Housing options:* men-only, women-only. Campus housing is university owned. *Activities and organizations:* drama/theater group, student-run newspaper, radio and television station, choral group, marching band, Student Government Association, Baptist Student Union, Black Student Fellowship, National Education Association, national fraternities, national sororities. *Campus security:* 24-hour emergency response devices and patrols, controlled dormitory access. *Student services:* health clinic, personal/psychological counseling.

Athletics Member NCAA. All Division I except football (Division I-AA). *Intercollegiate sports:* baseball M (s), basketball M (s)/W (s), bowling W, cross-country running M (s)/W (s), golf M (s)/W (s), softball W (s), tennis M (s)/W (s), track and field M (s)/W (s). *Intramural sports:* baseball M, basketball M/W, cross-country running M/W, football M, golf M/W, softball M/W, tennis M/W, track and field M/W.

Standardized Tests *Required:* SAT or ACT (for admission).

Costs (2007–08) *Tuition:* area resident $4417 full-time, $184 per hour part-time; nonresident $10,198 full-time, $241 per hour part-time. Full-time tuition and fees vary according to course load and degree level. Part-time tuition and fees vary according to course load and degree level. *Required fees:* $50 full-time, $184 per hour part-time. *Room and board:* $4542. Room and board charges vary according to board plan and housing facility. *Payment plans:* tuition prepayment, installment, deferred payment. *Waivers:* employees or children of employees.

Financial Aid *Average percent of need met:* 80%. *Average financial aid package:* $7000.

Applying *Options:* deferred entrance. *Required:* high school transcript. *Required for some:* 2.5 GPA for non-residents. *Recommended:* interview. *Application deadlines:* rolling (freshmen), rolling (transfers). *Notification:* continuous (freshmen), continuous (transfers).

Freshman Application Contact Ms. Nora Taylor, Director of Admissions and Recruitment, Mississippi Valley State University, 14000 Highway 82 West, Itta Bena, MS 38941-1400. *Phone:* 662-254-3344. *Toll-free phone:* 800-844-6885. *Fax:* 662-254-7900. *E-mail:* nbtaylor@mvsu.edu.

RUST COLLEGE

Holly Springs, Mississippi — www.rustcollege.edu/

- **Independent United Methodist** 4-year, founded 1866
- **Rural** 126-acre campus with easy access to Memphis
- **Coed**
- **Moderately difficult** entrance level

Faculty *Student/faculty ratio:* 20:1.

Academics *Calendar:* semesters. *Degrees:* associate and bachelor's.

Student Life *Campus security:* 24-hour emergency response devices and patrols, late-night transport/escort service, controlled dormitory access.

Athletics Member NCAA. All Division III.

Standardized Tests *Required:* ACT (for admission).

Costs (2007–08) *Comprehensive fee:* $9700 includes full-time tuition ($6600) and room and board ($3100). Part-time tuition: $283 per credit hour. Part-time tuition and fees vary according to class time and course load. *Room and board:* Room and board charges vary according to board plan. *Payment plans:* installment, deferred payment.

Financial Aid Of all full-time matriculated undergraduates who enrolled in 2004, 806 applied for aid, 806 were judged to have need, 481 had their need fully met. 492 Federal Work-Study jobs (averaging $714). 189 state and other part-time jobs (averaging $546). In 2004, 112 non-need-based awards were made. *Average percent of need met:* 60. *Average financial aid package:* $5067. *Average need-based loan:* $2158. *Average need-based gift aid:* $4281. *Average non-need-based aid:* $2795. *Average indebtedness upon graduation:* $9314.

Applying *Options:* deferred entrance. *Application fee:* $10. *Required:* high school transcript, minimum 2.0 GPA, 2 letters of recommendation. *Required for some:* essay or personal statement.

Freshman Application Contact Mr. Johnny McDonald, Director of Enrollment Services, Rust College, 150 Rust Avenue, Holly Springs, MS 38635-2328. *Phone:* 601-252-8000. *Toll-free phone:* 888-886-8492 Ext. 4065. *Fax:* 662-252-8895. *E-mail:* admissions@rustcollege.edu.

SOUTHEASTERN BAPTIST COLLEGE

Laurel, Mississippi

Freshman Application Contact Mrs. Emma Bond, Director of Admissions, Southeastern Baptist College, 4229 Highway 15 North, Laurel, MS 39440-1096. *Phone:* 601-426-6346.

TOUGALOO COLLEGE

Tougaloo, Mississippi — www.tougaloo.edu/

- **Independent** 4-year, founded 1869, affiliated with United Church of Christ
- **Suburban** 500-acre campus
- **Endowment** $4.7 million
- **Coed** 856 undergraduate students, 95% full-time, 68% women, 32% men
- **Minimally difficult** entrance level, 99% of applicants were admitted

Undergraduates 816 full-time, 40 part-time. Students come from 26 states and territories, 2 other countries, 18% are from out of state, 99% African American, 0.1% Asian American or Pacific Islander, 0.2% Hispanic American, 4% transferred in. *Retention:* 71% of 2006 full-time freshmen returned.

Freshmen *Admission:* 627 applied, 621 admitted, 200 enrolled. *Average high school GPA:* 3.0. *Test scores:* ACT scores over 18: 58%; ACT scores over 24: 8%.

Faculty *Total:* 103, 68% full-time. *Student/faculty ratio:* 13:1.

Majors Accounting; African-American/Black studies; art; biology/biological sciences; business administration and management; chemistry; child guidance; computer science; economics; education; elementary education; English; history; interdisciplinary studies; kindergarten/preschool education; mathematics; music; physics; political science and government; pre-dentistry studies; psychology; secondary education; sociology.

Academics *Calendar:* semesters. *Degrees:* associate and bachelor's. *Special study options:* academic remediation for entering students, accelerated degree program, adult/continuing education programs, cooperative education, honors programs, internships, off-campus study, part-time degree program, student-designed majors, study abroad. *ROTC:* Army (b). *Unusual degree programs:* 3-2 engineering with Brown University, Georgia Institute of Technology.

Computers on Campus 100 computers/terminals are available on campus for general student use. Students can access the following: campus intranet, computer help desk, free student e-mail accounts, online (class) grades, online (class) registration, online (class) schedules. Campuswide network is available. Wireless service is available via entire campus.

Student Life *Housing options:* men-only, women-only. Campus housing is university owned. *Activities and organizations:* drama/theater group, student-run newspaper, choral group, concert choir, Student Government Association, gospel choir, NAACP, Pre-Alumni Club, national fraternities, national sororities. *Campus security:* 24-hour emergency response devices and patrols. *Student services:* health clinic, personal/psychological counseling.

Athletics Member NAIA. *Intercollegiate sports:* basketball M (s)/W (s), cross-country running M (s)/W (s), golf M, softball W. *Intramural sports:* basketball M/W, bowling M, cross-country running M/W, golf M/W, softball M/W, tennis M/W, volleyball M/W.

Standardized Tests *Required:* SAT or ACT (for admission).

Costs (2007–08) *Comprehensive fee:* $16,047 includes full-time tuition ($9240), mandatory fees ($477), and room and board ($6330). Part-time tuition: $385 per credit. *College room only:* $4400.

Financial Aid In 2002, 110 non-need-based awards were made. *Average percent of need met:* 80%. *Average financial aid package:* $10,500. *Average indebtedness upon graduation:* $25,000.

Applying *Options:* early admission. *Application fee:* $25. *Required:* high school transcript, minimum 2.0 GPA. *Application deadlines:* rolling (freshmen), rolling (transfers). *Notification:* continuous (freshmen), continuous (transfers).

Freshman Application Contact Ms. Juno Jacobs, Director of Admissions, Tougaloo College, Student Enrollment Management Center, 500 West County Line Road, Tougaloo, MS 39174. *Phone:* 601-977-7765. *Toll-free phone:* 888-42GALOO. *Fax:* 601-977-4501. *E-mail:* jjacobs@tougaloo.edu.

UNIVERSITY OF MISSISSIPPI

Oxford, Mississippi **www.olemiss.edu/**

- **State-supported** university, founded 1844, part of Mississippi Institutions of Higher Learning
- **Small-town** 2500-acre campus with easy access to Memphis
- **Endowment** $495.0 million
- **Coed** 12,682 undergraduate students, 91% full-time, 53% women, 47% men
- **Moderately difficult** entrance level, 90% of applicants were admitted

Undergraduates 11,540 full-time, 1,142 part-time. Students come from 49 states and territories, 65 other countries, 34% are from out of state, 13% African American, 1% Asian American or Pacific Islander, 1% Hispanic American, 0.3% Native American, 1% international, 9% transferred in, 33% live on campus. *Retention:* 81% of 2006 full-time freshmen returned.

Freshmen *Admission:* 7,365 applied, 6,628 admitted, 2,473 enrolled. *Average high school GPA:* 3.17. *Test scores:* SAT critical reading scores over 500: 60%; SAT math scores over 500: 61%; ACT scores over 18: 95%; SAT critical reading scores over 600: 21%; SAT math scores over 600: 22%; ACT scores over 24: 41%; SAT critical reading scores over 700: 6%; SAT math scores over 700: 2%; ACT scores over 30: 8%.

Faculty *Total:* 749, 90% full-time. *Student/faculty ratio:* 20:1.

Majors Accounting; advertising; American studies; anthropology; art; art history, criticism and conservation; audiology and speech-language pathology; biology/biological sciences; biomedical sciences; business administration and management; business/commerce; business/managerial economics; chemical engineering; chemistry; civil engineering; clinical laboratory science/medical technology; computer and information sciences; court reporting; dramatic/theater arts; economics; electrical, electronics and communications engineering; elementary education; engineering; English; English/language arts teacher education; family and consumer sciences/human sciences; finance; forensic science and technology; French; geological/geophysical engineering; geology/earth science; German; history; insurance; international business/trade/commerce; international relations and affairs; journalism; kinesiology and exercise science; liberal arts and sciences/liberal studies; linguistics; management information systems; marketing/marketing management; mathematics; mathematics teacher education; mechanical engineering; music; parks, recreation and leisure; pharmacy; philosophy; physics; political science and government; psychology; radio and television; real estate; science teacher education; secondary education; social studies teacher education; social work; sociology; Spanish; special education.

Academics *Calendar:* semesters. *Degrees:* bachelor's, master's, doctoral, and first professional. *Special study options:* academic remediation for entering students, accelerated degree program, adult/continuing education programs, advanced placement credit, double majors, English as a second language, freshman honors college, honors programs, independent study, internships, part-time degree program, services for LD students, study abroad, summer session for credit. *ROTC:* Army (b), Navy (b), Air Force (b).

Computers on Campus 3,500 computers/terminals are available on campus for general student use. Students can access the following: campus intranet, computer help desk, free student e-mail accounts, online (class) grades, online (class) registration, online (class) schedules, application for admission, registration for orientation. Campuswide network is available. 100% of college-owned or -operated housing units are wired for high-speed Internet access. Wireless service is available via classrooms, computer centers, learning centers, libraries, student centers.

Student Life *Housing:* on-campus residence required for freshman year. *Options:* men-only, women-only. Campus housing is university owned, leased by the school and is provided by a third party. Freshman campus housing is guaranteed. *Activities and organizations:* drama/theater group, student-run newspaper, radio and television station, choral group, marching band, Associated Student Body, School Spirit Club, sport clubs, Black Student Union, Student Programming Board, national fraternities, national sororities. *Campus security:* 24-hour emergency response devices and patrols, late-night transport/escort service, controlled dormitory access, crime prevention programs. *Student services:* health clinic, personal/psychological counseling, women's center, legal services.

Athletics Member NCAA. All Division I except football (Division I-A). *Intercollegiate sports:* baseball M (s), basketball M (s)/W (s), cheerleading M (s)/W (s), cross-country running M (s)/W (s), fencing M (c)/W (c), golf M (s)/W (s), lacrosse M (c), riflery W (s), rugby M (c), soccer M (c)/W (s), softball W (s), tennis M (s)/W (s), track and field M (s)/W (s), volleyball M (c)/W (s). *Intramural sports:* badminton M/W, basketball M/W, bowling M/W, crew M (c)/W (c), football M/W, golf M/W, racquetball M/W, riflery M (c), soccer M/W, softball M/W, swimming and diving M/W, table tennis M (c)/W (c), tennis M/W, track and field M/W, ultimate Frisbee M/W, volleyball M/W, water polo M/W.

Standardized Tests *Required:* SAT or ACT (for admission).

Costs (2007–08) *Tuition:* state resident $4932 full-time, $206 per credit part-time; nonresident $11,436 full-time, $477 per credit part-time. *Room and board:* $6578; room only: $3300. Room and board charges vary according to board plan and housing facility. *Payment plan:* tuition prepayment. *Waivers:* children of alumni, senior citizens, and employees or children of employees.

Financial Aid Of all full-time matriculated undergraduates who enrolled in 2006, 6,804 applied for aid, 4,792 were judged to have need, 841 had their need fully met. 416 Federal Work-Study jobs (averaging $1492). In 2006, 3283 non-need-based awards were made. *Average percent of need met:* 65%. *Average financial aid package:* $8681. *Average need-based loan:* $4661. *Average need-based gift aid:* $4746. *Average non-need-based aid:* $3748. *Average indebtedness upon graduation:* $19,183.

Applying *Options:* electronic application, early admission. *Application fee:* $50. *Required:* high school transcript, minimum 2.0 GPA. *Notification:* continuous until 8/16 (freshmen), continuous until 8/16 (transfers).

Freshman Application Contact Mr. Jody Lowe, Associate Director of Admissions, University of Mississippi, 145 Martindale Student Services Center, University, MS 38677. *Phone:* 662-915-7226. *Toll-free phone:* 800-653-6477. *Fax:* 662-915-5869. *E-mail:* admissions@olemiss.edu.

UNIVERSITY OF MISSISSIPPI MEDICAL CENTER

Jackson, Mississippi **www.umc.edu/**

- **State-supported** upper-level, founded 1955, administratively affiliated with University of Mississippi
- **Urban** 164-acre campus
- **Endowment** $33.5 million
- **Coed** 512 undergraduate students, 75% full-time, 80% women, 20% men

Undergraduates 383 full-time, 129 part-time. Students come from 1 other state, 22% African American, 2% Asian American or Pacific Islander, 1% Hispanic American, 0.4% Native American, 64% transferred in.

Faculty *Total:* 836, 83% full-time, 81% with terminal degrees. *Student/faculty ratio:* 2:1.

Majors Clinical laboratory science/medical technology; cytotechnology; dental hygiene; health information/medical records administration; nursing (registered nurse training).

Academics *Calendar:* semesters. *Degrees:* certificates, bachelor's, master's, doctoral, and first professional. *Special study options:* distance learning, internships, services for LD students, study abroad.

Computers on Campus 90 computers/terminals are available on campus for general student use. Campuswide network is available.

Student Life *Housing options:* women-only. Campus housing is university owned. *Activities and organizations:* student-run newspaper. *Campus security:* 24-hour emergency response devices and patrols, late-night transport/escort service, controlled dormitory access. *Student services:* health clinic, personal/psychological counseling.

Athletics *Intramural sports:* basketball M/W, football M/W, golf M, rugby M, soccer M/W, softball M/W, volleyball M/W.

Financial Aid Of all full-time matriculated undergraduates who enrolled in 2001, 368 applied for aid, 191 were judged to have need, 41 had their need fully met. In 2001, 32 non-need-based awards were made. *Average percent of need met:* 47%. *Average financial aid package:* $6300. *Average need-based loan:* $4200. *Average need-based gift aid:* $2500. *Average non-need-based aid:* $1000. *Average indebtedness upon graduation:* $8000.

Applying *Application fee:* $10. *Application deadline:* 2/15 (transfers). *Notification:* continuous until 5/1 (transfers).

Application Contact Ms. Barbara Westerfield, Director of Student Records and Registrar, University of Mississippi Medical Center, 2500 North State Street, Jackson, MS 39216-4505. *Phone:* 601-984-1080. *Fax:* 601-984-1079.

UNIVERSITY OF SOUTHERN MISSISSIPPI

Hattiesburg, Mississippi **www.usm.edu/**

- **State-supported** university, founded 1910, part of Mississippi Institutions of Higher Learning
- **Suburban** 1090-acre campus with easy access to New Orleans
- **Coed** 11,924 undergraduate students, 86% full-time, 60% women, 40% men
- **Moderately difficult** entrance level, 58% of applicants were admitted

Undergraduates 10,205 full-time, 1,719 part-time. Students come from 39 states and territories, 44 other countries, 11% are from out of state, 29% African American, 1% Asian American or Pacific Islander, 1% Hispanic American, 0.4% Native American, 0.8% international, 13% transferred in, 21% live on campus. *Retention:* 74% of 2006 full-time freshmen returned.

Freshmen *Admission:* 4,648 applied, 2,675 admitted, 1,396 enrolled. *Average high school GPA:* 3.0. *Test scores:* SAT critical reading scores over 500: 56%; SAT math scores over 500: 64%; ACT scores over 18: 87%; SAT critical reading scores over 600: 26%; SAT math scores over 600: 21%; ACT scores over 24: 30%; SAT critical reading scores over 700: 13%; ACT scores over 30: 5%.

Faculty *Total:* 901, 80% full-time, 68% with terminal degrees. *Student/faculty ratio:* 17:1.

Majors Accounting; advertising; American studies; anthropology; apparel and textiles; architectural engineering technology; athletic training; audiology and speech-language pathology; biological and physical sciences; biology/biological sciences; business administration and management; business/managerial economics; business teacher education; chemistry; chemistry related; clinical laboratory science/medical technology; communication/speech communication and rhetoric; computer and information sciences; computer engineering technology; criminal justice/safety; dance; data processing and data processing technology; dietetics; dramatic/theater arts; electrical, electronic and communications engineering technology; elementary education; English; family systems; finance; foreign languages and literatures; geography; geology/earth science; health and physical education; health services/allied health/health sciences; history; hospitality administration related; hotel/motel administration; human resources management; industrial technology; interior architecture; international business/trade/commerce; international relations and affairs; journalism; legal assistant/paralegal; library science; management information systems; marine biology and biological oceanography; marketing/marketing management; mathematics; music; music management and merchandising; music teacher education; nursing (registered nurse training); parks, recreation and leisure; philosophy; physical education teaching and coaching; physics; political science and government; psychology; public health; radio and television; religious studies; social work; sociology; special education; special education (hearing impaired); technology/industrial arts teacher education; visual and performing arts.

Academics *Calendar:* semesters. *Degrees:* certificates, bachelor's, master's, doctoral, and post-master's certificates. *Special study options:* academic remediation for entering students, accelerated degree program, adult/continuing education programs, advanced placement credit, cooperative education, distance learning, double majors, English as a second language, honors programs, off-campus study, part-time degree program, services for LD students, study abroad, summer session for credit. *ROTC:* Army (b), Air Force (b).

Computers on Campus 600 computers/terminals are available on campus for general student use. Students can access the following: computer help desk, free student e-mail accounts, online (class) grades, online (class) registration, online (class) schedules. Campuswide network is available. 100% of college-owned or -operated housing units are wired for high-speed Internet access. Wireless service is available via entire campus.

Student Life *Housing options:* men-only, women-only, disabled students. Campus housing is university owned. *Activities and organizations:* drama/theater group, student-run newspaper, radio station, choral group, marching band, University Activities Council, residence halls associations, national fraternities, national sororities. *Campus security:* 24-hour emergency response devices and patrols, late-night transport/escort service, controlled dormitory access. *Student services:* health clinic, personal/psychological counseling, women's center, legal services.

Athletics Member NCAA. All Division I. *Intercollegiate sports:* baseball M (s), basketball M (s)/W (s), cheerleading M/W, cross-country running W (s), football W (s), golf M (s)/W (s), soccer W (s), softball W (s), tennis M (s)/W (s), track and field M (s)/W (s), volleyball W (s). *Intramural sports:* badminton M/W, basketball M/W, bowling M/W, fencing M/W, racquetball M/W, riflery M/W, soccer W, softball M/W, table tennis M/W, tennis M/W, ultimate Frisbee M/W.

Standardized Tests *Required:* SAT or ACT (for admission). *Required for some:* SAT and SAT Subject Tests or ACT (for admission).

Costs (2008–09) *Tuition:* state resident $4914 full-time, $205 per credit part-time; nonresident $11,692 full-time, $488 per credit part-time. *Room and board:* $5040; room only: $2826.

Financial Aid Of all full-time matriculated undergraduates who enrolled in 2006, 7,945 applied for aid, 6,688 were judged to have need, 2,106 had their need fully met. 140 Federal Work-Study jobs (averaging $1275). In 2006, 889 non-need-based awards were made. *Average percent of need met:* 85%. *Average financial aid package:* $7839. *Average need-based loan:* $4372. *Average need-based gift aid:* $3654. *Average non-need-based aid:* $3243. *Average indebtedness upon graduation:* $17,646.

Applying *Options:* electronic application, early admission. *Application fee:* $25. *Required:* high school transcript, minimum 2.0 GPA. *Required for some:* interview. *Application deadlines:* 7/1 (freshmen), 7/1 (transfers).

Freshman Application Contact Mr. Jason Beverly, Senior Admissions Counselor, University of Southern Mississippi, 118 college Drive, # 5166, Hattiesburg, MS 39406-1000. *Phone:* 601-266-5000. *Fax:* 601-266-5148. *E-mail:* admissions@usm.edu.

WESLEY COLLEGE

Florence, Mississippi **www.wesleycollege.com/**

- **Independent Congregational Methodist** 4-year, founded 1944
- **Small-town** 40-acre campus with easy access to Jackson
- **Endowment** $353,038
- **Coed**
- **Noncompetitive** entrance level

Faculty *Student/faculty ratio:* 6:1.

Academics *Calendar:* semesters. *Degree:* certificates and bachelor's.

Student Life *Campus security:* 24-hour emergency response devices.

Athletics Member NCCAA.

Standardized Tests *Required:* SAT or ACT (for admission).

Financial Aid Of all full-time matriculated undergraduates who enrolled in 2007, 72 applied for aid, 57 were judged to have need, 5 had their need fully met. 16 Federal Work-Study jobs (averaging $1581). In 2007, 5 non-need-based awards were made. *Average percent of need met:* 58. *Average financial aid package:* $6400. *Average need-based loan:* $2100. *Average need-based gift aid:* $200. *Average non-need-based aid:* $6650. *Average indebtedness upon graduation:* $8700.

Applying *Application fee:* $20. *Required:* essay or personal statement, high school transcript, 3 letters of recommendation. *Recommended:* interview.

Freshman Application Contact Mr. Chris Garcia, Director of Admissions, Wesley College, PO Box 1070, Florence, MS 39073-1070. *Phone:* 601-845-2265 Ext. 21. *Toll-free phone:* 800-748-9972. *Fax:* 601-845-2266. *E-mail:* cgarcia@admin.wesleycollege.edu.

WILLIAM CAREY UNIVERSITY

Hattiesburg, Mississippi **www.wmcarey.edu/**

- **Independent Southern Baptist** comprehensive, founded 1906
- **Small-town** 110-acre campus with easy access to New Orleans
- **Endowment** $8.3 million
- **Coed**
- **Moderately difficult** entrance level

Faculty *Student/faculty ratio:* 15:1.

Academics *Calendar:* trimesters. *Degrees:* bachelor's and master's.

Student Life *Campus security:* 24-hour patrols, controlled dormitory access.

Athletics Member NAIA.

Standardized Tests *Required:* SAT or ACT (for admission).

Costs (2007–08) *Comprehensive fee:* $12,825 includes full-time tuition ($8700), mandatory fees ($315), and room and board ($3810). Full-time tuition and fees vary according to degree level and location. Part-time tuition: $290 per hour. Part-time tuition and fees vary according to degree level and location. *College room only:* $1500. Room and board charges vary according to board plan, housing facility, and location.

Financial Aid Of all full-time matriculated undergraduates who enrolled in 2006, 1,680 applied for aid, 1,672 were judged to have need, 1,601 had their need fully met. 302 Federal Work-Study jobs (averaging $1700). 100 state and other part-time jobs (averaging $1700). In 2006, 220 non-need-based awards were made. *Average percent of need met:* 90. *Average financial aid package:* $13,400. *Average need-based loan:* $6000. *Average need-based gift aid:* $6500. *Average non-need-based aid:* $7200. *Average indebtedness upon graduation:* $17,000.

Applying *Options:* early admission, deferred entrance. *Application fee:* $20. *Required:* high school transcript. *Required for some:* letters of recommendation. *Recommended:* minimum 2.0 GPA.

Freshman Application Contact Mr. William N. Curry, Dean of Enrollment Management, William Carey University, 498 Tuscan Avenue, Hattiesburg, MS 39401-5499. *Phone:* 601-318-6051. *Toll-free phone:* 800-962-5991. *Fax:* 601-318-6154. *E-mail:* admissions@wmcarey.edu.

MISSOURI

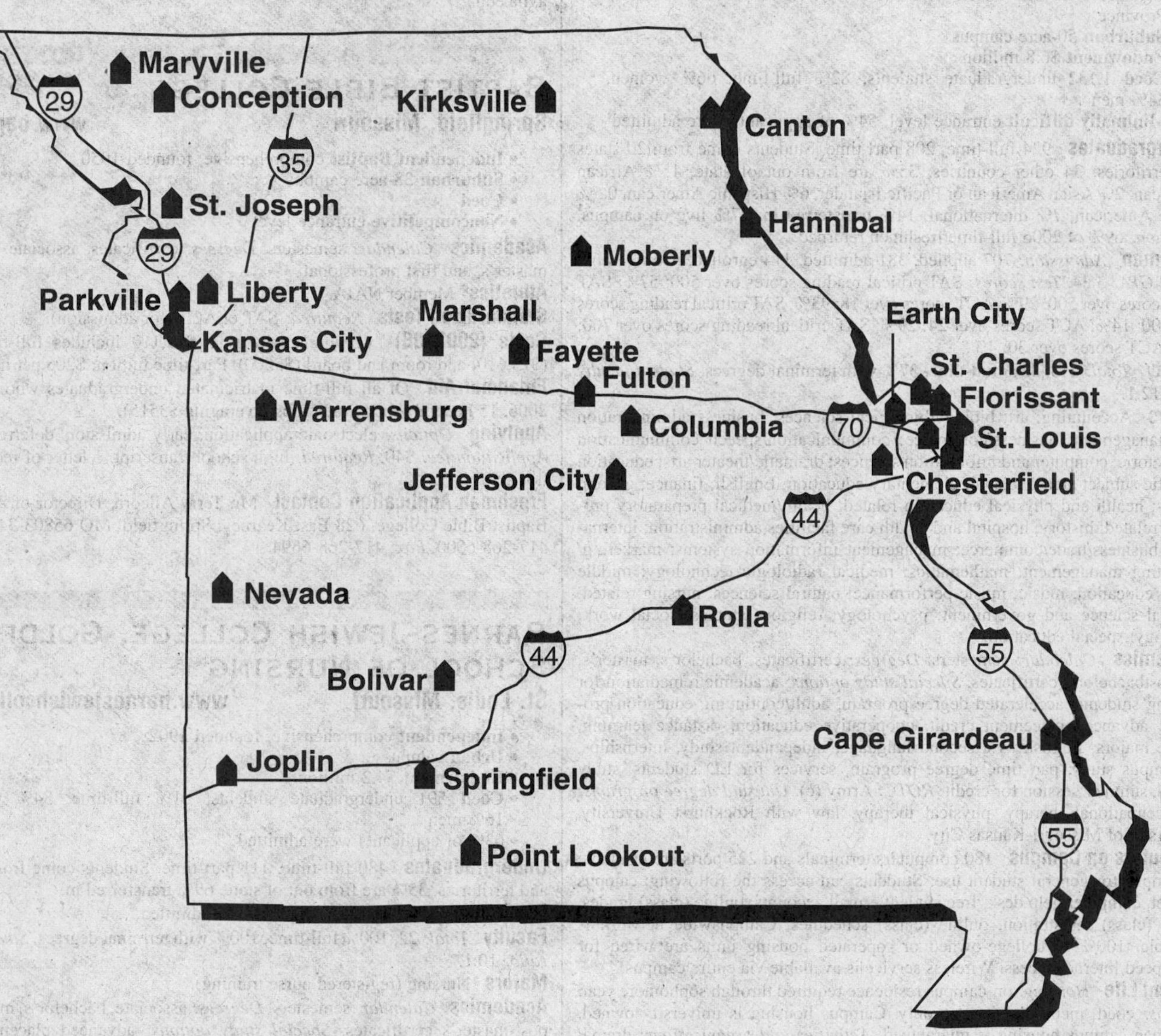
Maryville
Conception
Kirksville
Canton
29
35
St. Joseph
Hannibal
29
Moberly
Parkville
Liberty
Marshall
Earth City
Kansas City
Fayette
St. Charles
Fulton
Florissant
Warrensburg
70
Columbia
St. Louis
Jefferson City
Chesterfield
44
Nevada
Rolla
55
44
Bolivar
Cape Girardeau
Joplin
Springfield
55
Point Lookout

AVILA UNIVERSITY

Kansas City, Missouri **www.avila.edu/**

- **Independent Roman Catholic** 4-year, founded 1916, administratively affiliated with The Sisters of Saint Joseph of Carondelet, St. Louis Province
- **Suburban** 50-acre campus
- **Endowment** $6.8 million
- **Coed** 1,132 undergraduate students, 82% full-time, 66% women, 34% men
- **Minimally difficult** entrance level, 54% of applicants were admitted

Undergraduates 924 full-time, 208 part-time. Students come from 20 states and territories, 34 other countries, 35% are from out of state, 15% African American, 2% Asian American or Pacific Islander, 6% Hispanic American, 0.5% Native American, 7% international, 14% transferred in, 27% live on campus. *Retention:* 69% of 2006 full-time freshmen returned.

Freshmen *Admission:* 707 applied, 381 admitted, 114 enrolled. *Average high school GPA:* 3.34. *Test scores:* SAT critical reading scores over 500: 57%; SAT math scores over 500: 29%; ACT scores over 18: 93%; SAT critical reading scores over 600: 14%; ACT scores over 24: 29%; SAT critical reading scores over 700: 14%; ACT scores over 30: 4%.

Faculty *Total:* 215, 32% full-time, 37% with terminal degrees. *Student/faculty ratio:* 12:1.

Majors Accounting; art; biology/biological sciences; business administration and management; business/commerce; communication/speech communication and rhetoric; computer and information sciences; dramatic/theater arts; education (specific subject areas) related; elementary education; English; finance; general studies; health and physical education related; health/medical preparatory programs related; history; hospital and health care facilities administration; international business/trade/commerce; management information systems; marketing/marketing management; mathematics; medical radiologic technology; middle school education; music; music performance; natural sciences; nursing related; political science and government; psychology; religious studies; social work; sociology; special education.

Academics *Calendar:* semesters. *Degrees:* certificates, bachelor's, master's, and postbachelor's certificates. *Special study options:* academic remediation for entering students, accelerated degree program, adult/continuing education programs, advanced placement credit, cooperative education, distance learning, double majors, English as a second language, independent study, internships, off-campus study, part-time degree program, services for LD students, study abroad, summer session for credit. *ROTC:* Army (c). *Unusual degree programs:* 3-2 occupational therapy, physical therapy, law with Rockhurst University, University of Missouri-Kansas City.

Computers on Campus 180 computers/terminals and 225 ports are available on campus for general student use. Students can access the following: campus intranet, computer help desk, free student e-mail accounts, online (class) grades, online (class) registration, online (class) schedules. Campuswide network is available. 100% of college-owned or -operated housing units are wired for high-speed Internet access. Wireless service is available via entire campus.

Student Life *Housing:* on-campus residence required through sophomore year. *Options:* coed, men-only, women-only. Campus housing is university owned. Freshman campus housing is guaranteed. *Activities and organizations:* drama/theater group, student-run newspaper, choral group, Group Activities Programming, Avila Student Nurses Association, Residence Hall Association, Student Senate, Black Student Union. *Campus security:* 24-hour emergency response devices, student patrols, late-night transport/escort service, controlled dormitory access. *Student services:* health clinic, personal/psychological counseling.

Athletics Member NAIA. *Intercollegiate sports:* baseball M (s), basketball M (s)/W (s), cheerleading W (s), football M (s), golf W (s), soccer M (s)/W (s), softball W (s), volleyball W (s). *Intramural sports:* bowling M/W, table tennis M/W.

Standardized Tests *Required:* SAT or ACT (for admission).

Costs (2008–09) *One-time required fee:* $200. *Comprehensive fee:* $26,050 includes full-time tuition ($19,500), mandatory fees ($650), and room and board ($5900). Part-time tuition: $495 per credit hour. *Required fees:* $23 per credit hour part-time. *College room only:* $3000.

Financial Aid Of all full-time matriculated undergraduates who enrolled in 2005, 1,912 applied for aid, 1,679 were judged to have need, 165 had their need fully met. In 2005, 279 non-need-based awards were made. *Average percent of need met:* 25%. *Average financial aid package:* $11,751. *Average need-based loan:* $5221. *Average need-based gift aid:* $7465. *Average non-need-based aid:* $8933. *Average indebtedness upon graduation:* $16,398.

Applying *Options:* electronic application, early admission. *Application fee:* $25. *Required:* high school transcript, minimum 2.5 GPA, minimum ACT score of 20 and Secondary School Report. *Required for some:* essay or personal statement, letters of recommendation. *Recommended:* interview. *Application deadlines:* 8/15 (freshmen), 8/15 (transfers). *Notification:* 8/15 (freshmen), 8/15 (transfers).

Freshman Application Contact Ms. Patricia Harper, Director of Admission, Avila University, 11901 Wornall Road, Kansas City, MO 64145. *Phone:* 816-501-2400. *Toll-free phone:* 800-GO-AVILA. *Fax:* 816-501-2453. *E-mail:* patti.harper@avila.edu.

BAPTIST BIBLE COLLEGE

Springfield, Missouri **www.baptist.edu/**

- **Independent Baptist** comprehensive, founded 1950
- **Suburban** 38-acre campus
- **Coed**
- **Noncompetitive** entrance level

Academics *Calendar:* semesters. *Degrees:* certificates, associate, bachelor's, master's, and first professional.

Athletics Member NAIA.

Standardized Tests *Required:* SAT or ACT (for admission).

Costs (2007–08) *Comprehensive fee:* $19,110 includes full-time tuition ($13,610) and room and board ($5500). Part-time tuition: $206 per hour.

Financial Aid Of all full-time matriculated undergraduates who enrolled in 2006, 15 Federal Work-Study jobs (averaging $3515).

Applying *Options:* electronic application, early admission, deferred entrance. *Application fee:* $40. *Required:* high school transcript, 1 letter of recommendation.

Freshman Application Contact Mr. Terry Allcorn, Director of Admissions, Baptist Bible College, 628 East Kearney, Springfield, MO 65803-3498. *Phone:* 417-268-6000. *Fax:* 417-268-6694.

BARNES-JEWISH COLLEGE, GOLDFARB SCHOOL OF NURSING

St. Louis, Missouri **www.barnesjewishcollege.edu/**

- **Independent** comprehensive, founded 1902
- **Urban** campus
- **Endowment** $4.2 million
- **Coed** 591 undergraduate students, 81% full-time, 84% women, 16% men
- 63% of applicants were admitted

Undergraduates 480 full-time, 111 part-time. Students come from 29 states and territories, 35% are from out of state, 69% transferred in.

Freshmen *Admission:* 227 applied, 142 admitted.

Faculty *Total:* 22, 100% full-time, 100% with terminal degrees. *Student/faculty ratio:* 10:1.

Majors Nursing (registered nurse training).

Academics *Calendar:* semesters. *Degrees:* associate, bachelor's, master's, and post-master's certificates. *Special study options:* advanced placement credit, double majors, independent study, off-campus study, part-time degree program, services for LD students, summer session for credit.

Computers on Campus 85 computers/terminals are available on campus for general student use. Students can access the following: software, research databases. Campuswide network is available. Wireless service is available via entire campus.

Student Life *Housing:* college housing not available. *Activities and organizations:* student-run newspaper, Student Nurses Association. *Campus security:* 24-hour patrols, late-night transport/escort service, controlled dormitory access. *Student services:* health clinic, personal/psychological counseling.

Athletics *Intercollegiate sports:* ultimate Frisbee M/W, volleyball M/W. *Intramural sports:* soccer W, ultimate Frisbee M/W, volleyball M/W.

Costs (2007–08) *Tuition:* $19,728 full-time, $411 per credit hour part-time. *Required fees:* $150 full-time.

Financial Aid Of all full-time matriculated undergraduates who enrolled in 2003, 150 applied for aid, 150 were judged to have need, 21 had their need fully met. 10 Federal Work-Study jobs (averaging $3300). In 2003, 21 non-need-based awards were made. *Average financial aid package:* $16,000. *Average need-based loan:* $4000. *Average need-based gift aid:* $4000. *Average non-need-based aid:* $9000. *Average indebtedness upon graduation:* $10,000.

Applying *Options:* deferred entrance. *Application fee:* $50. *Required:* 2 letters of recommendation. *Application deadline:* rolling (transfers). *Notification:* continuous (transfers).

Freshman Application Contact Office of Admissions, Barnes-Jewish College, Goldfarb School of Nursing, 306 South Kings Highway Boulevard, St. Louis, MO 63110. *Phone:* 314-454-7057. *Toll-free phone:* 800-832-9009.

CALVARY BIBLE COLLEGE AND THEOLOGICAL SEMINARY

Kansas City, Missouri **www.calvary.edu/**

- **Independent nondenominational** comprehensive, founded 1932
- **Suburban** 55-acre campus
- **Endowment** $207,512
- **Coed**
- **Minimally difficult** entrance level

Faculty *Student/faculty ratio:* 12:1.

Academics *Calendar:* semesters. *Degrees:* certificates, diplomas, associate, bachelor's, master's, and first professional.

Student Life *Campus security:* late-night transport/escort service, night patrols by trained security personnel.

Athletics Member NCCAA.

Standardized Tests *Required:* SAT or ACT (for admission).

Costs (2007–08) *Comprehensive fee:* $12,500 includes full-time tuition ($7800), mandatory fees ($700), and room and board ($4000). Part-time tuition: $260 per hour. *Required fees:* $25 per hour part-time, $50 per term part-time. *College room only:* $1800. *Payment plans:* installment, deferred payment.

Financial Aid Of all full-time matriculated undergraduates who enrolled in 2004, 168 applied for aid, 145 were judged to have need, 31 had their need fully met. 10 Federal Work-Study jobs (averaging $1368). *Average percent of need met:* 5. *Average financial aid package:* $5054. *Average need-based loan:* $2280. *Average need-based gift aid:* $2622. *Average indebtedness upon graduation:* $17,098. *Financial aid deadline:* 4/1.

Applying *Options:* early admission, deferred entrance. *Application fee:* $25. *Required:* essay or personal statement, high school transcript, 2 letters of recommendation, statement of faith. *Required for some:* interview.

Freshman Application Contact Rev. Robert Reinsch, Director of Admissions, Calvary Bible College and Theological Seminary, 15800 Calvary Road, Kansas City, MO 64147-1341. *Phone:* 816-322-0110 Ext. 1326. *Toll-free phone:* 800-326-3960. *Fax:* 816-331-4474. *E-mail:* admissions@calvary.edu.

CENTRAL BIBLE COLLEGE

Springfield, Missouri **www.cbcag.edu/**

Director of Admissions Mrs. Eunice A. Bruegman, Director of Admissions and Records, Central Bible College, 3000 North Grant Avenue, Springfield, MO 65803-1096. *Phone:* 417-833-2551 Ext. 1184. *Toll-free phone:* 800-831-4222 Ext. 1184.

CENTRAL CHRISTIAN COLLEGE OF THE BIBLE

Moberly, Missouri **www.cccb.edu/**

Freshman Application Contact Mr. Jason Rodenbeck, Director of Admissions, Central Christian College of the Bible, 911 Urbandale Drive East, Moberly, MO 65270-1997. *Phone:* 660-263-3900. *Toll-free phone:* 888-263-3900. *Fax:* 660-263-3936. *E-mail:* iwant2be@cccb.edu.

CENTRAL METHODIST UNIVERSITY

Fayette, Missouri **www.centralmethodist.edu/**

- **Independent Methodist** comprehensive, founded 1854
- **Small-town** 80-acre campus
- **Endowment** $20.9 million
- **Coed**
- **Moderately difficult** entrance level

Faculty *Student/faculty ratio:* 14:1.

Academics *Calendar:* semesters. *Degrees:* associate, bachelor's, and master's.

Student Life *Campus security:* 24-hour emergency response devices, late-night transport/escort service, controlled dormitory access.

Athletics Member NAIA.

Standardized Tests *Required:* SAT or ACT (for admission). *Recommended:* ACT (for admission).

Costs (2007–08) *Comprehensive fee:* $22,880 includes full-time tuition ($16,430), mandatory fees ($730), and room and board ($5720). Part-time tuition: $170 per semester hour. Part-time tuition and fees vary according to course load. *Required fees:* $31 per semester hour part-time. *College room only:* $2820. Room and board charges vary according to board plan and housing facility.

Financial Aid Of all full-time matriculated undergraduates who enrolled in 2007, 893 applied for aid, 843 were judged to have need, 21 had their need fully met. 145 Federal Work-Study jobs (averaging $1000). 90 state and other part-time jobs (averaging $1619). In 2007, 89 non-need-based awards were made. *Average percent of need met:* 58. *Average financial aid package:* $13,986. *Average need-based loan:* $4286. *Average need-based gift aid:* $5404. *Average non-need-based aid:* $8832. *Average indebtedness upon graduation:* $25,463.

Applying *Options:* electronic application, deferred entrance. *Application fee:* $20. *Required:* high school transcript, minimum 2.5 GPA. *Required for some:* 2 letters of recommendation.

Freshman Application Contact Mr. Larry Anderson, Director of Admissions, Central Methodist University, 411 Central Methodist Square, Fayette, MO 65248-1198. *Phone:* 660-248-6247. *Toll-free phone:* 888-CMU-1854. *Fax:* 660-248-1872. *E-mail:* admissions@centralmethodist.edu.

CHAMBERLAIN COLLEGE OF NURSING

St. Louis, Missouri **www.chamberlain.edu/**

Freshman Application Contact Ms. Michelle McGrail, Dean of Enrollment and Marketing, Chamberlain College of Nursing, 6150 Oakland Avenue, St. Louis, MO 63139-3215. *Phone:* 314-768-7528. *Toll-free phone:* 800-942-4310. *Fax:* 314-768-5673.

COLLEGE OF THE OZARKS

Point Lookout, Missouri **www.cofo.edu/**

- **Independent Presbyterian** 4-year, founded 1906
- **Small-town** 1000-acre campus
- **Endowment** $366.2 million
- **Coed** 1,351 undergraduate students, 97% full-time, 56% women, 44% men
- **Moderately difficult** entrance level, 12% of applicants were admitted

Undergraduates 1,309 full-time, 42 part-time. Students come from 38 states and territories, 14 other countries, 37% are from out of state, 1% African American, 0.7% Asian American or Pacific Islander, 1% Hispanic American, 1% Native American, 1% international, 4% transferred in, 84% live on campus. *Retention:* 84% of 2006 full-time freshmen returned.

Freshmen *Admission:* 2,709 applied, 321 admitted, 282 enrolled. *Average high school GPA:* 3.5. *Test scores:* ACT scores over 18: 98%; ACT scores over 24: 32%; ACT scores over 30: 2%.

Faculty *Total:* 129, 68% full-time, 43% with terminal degrees. *Student/faculty ratio:* 13:1.

Majors Accounting; acting; agribusiness; agricultural mechanization; agricultural mechanization related; agricultural teacher education; agronomy and crop science; animal sciences; apparel and textiles; applied horticulture; art; art teacher education; biology/biological sciences; biology teacher education; broadcast journalism; business administration and management; business/managerial economics; business teacher education; chemistry; chemistry teacher education; child care/guidance; child development; child guidance; clinical laboratory science/medical technology; communication and journalism related; computer and information sciences; computer science; consumer services and advocacy; corrections; criminal justice/law enforcement administration; criminal justice/police science; criminology; dietetics; dramatic/theater arts; education; elementary education; engineering; English; English/language arts teacher education; family and consumer sciences/home economics teacher education; family and consumer sciences/human sciences; family/community studies; fine/studio arts; foods, nutrition, and wellness; forensic science and technology; French; French language teacher education; German; gerontology; graphic/printing equipment; health and physical education; health/medical preparatory programs related; health science; history; history related; history teacher education; horticultural science; hotel and restaurant management; industrial arts; information technology; interdisciplinary studies; international business/trade/commerce; journalism; marketing/marketing management; mass communication/media; mathematics; mathematics teacher education; middle school education; multi-/interdisciplinary studies related; music;

music management and merchandising; music related; music teacher education; nursing (registered nurse training); parks, recreation and leisure facilities management; philosophy; philosophy and religious studies related; physical education teaching and coaching; political science and government; pre-law studies; premedical studies; pre-pharmacy studies; pre-veterinary studies; psychology; public relations/image management; religious/sacred music; science teacher education; science, technology and society; secondary education; social work; sociology; Spanish; speech and rhetoric; technology/industrial arts teacher education; wildlife and wildlands science and management.

Academics *Calendar:* semesters. *Degree:* bachelor's. *Special study options:* academic remediation for entering students, accelerated degree program, advanced placement credit, cooperative education, double majors, English as a second language, honors programs, independent study, internships, part-time degree program, student-designed majors. *ROTC:* Army (b). *Unusual degree programs:* 3-2 law.

Computers on Campus 164 computers/terminals and 1,097 ports are available on campus for general student use. Students can access the following: campus intranet, computer help desk, free student e-mail accounts, online (class) grades, online (class) registration, online (class) schedules, intranet/campus Web. Campuswide network is available. 100% of college-owned or -operated housing units are wired for high-speed Internet access. Wireless service is available via dorm rooms, libraries, student centers.

Student Life *Housing:* on-campus residence required through junior year. *Options:* men-only, women-only. Campus housing is university owned. *Activities and organizations:* drama/theater group, student-run newspaper, radio station, choral group, Aviation Club, Student Senate, Baptist Student Union, Aggie Club, Business Undergraduate Society. *Campus security:* 24-hour emergency response devices and patrols, controlled dormitory access, front gate closed 1 a.m. to 6 a.m., gate security 5:30 p.m. to 1 a.m. *Student services:* health clinic, personal/psychological counseling.

Athletics Member NAIA. *Intercollegiate sports:* baseball M (s), basketball M (s)/W (s), cheerleading M/W, volleyball W (s). *Intramural sports:* basketball M/W, fencing M/W, football M/W, golf M/W, racquetball M/W, soccer M, softball M/W, volleyball M/W, weight lifting M/W.

Standardized Tests *Required:* SAT or ACT (for admission).

Costs (2008–09) *Required fees:* $390 full-time, $185 per term part-time. *Room and board:* $4700.

Financial Aid Of all full-time matriculated undergraduates who enrolled in 2007, 1,424 applied for aid, 1,343 were judged to have need, 510 had their need fully met. 740 Federal Work-Study jobs (averaging $3682). 727 state and other part-time jobs (averaging $3682). In 2007, 124 non-need-based awards were made. *Average percent of need met:* 87%. *Average financial aid package:* $15,227. *Average need-based gift aid:* $12,332. *Average non-need-based aid:* $14,606. *Average indebtedness upon graduation:* $6770.

Applying *Options:* electronic application. *Required:* high school transcript, 2 letters of recommendation, interview, medical history, financial statement. *Recommended:* minimum 3.0 GPA. *Application deadlines:* 3/15 (freshmen), 3/15 (transfers). *Notification:* continuous (freshmen), continuous (transfers).

Freshman Application Contact Mrs. Gayle Groves, Admissions Secretary, College of the Ozarks, PO Box 17, Point Lookout, MO 65726. *Phone:* 417-334-6411 Ext. 4217. *Toll-free phone:* 800-222-0525. *Fax:* 417-335-2618. *E-mail:* admiss4@cofo.edu.

COLORADO TECHNICAL UNIVERSITY—NORTH KANSAS CITY

North Kansas City, Missouri **kc.coloradotech.edu/**

- **Proprietary** primarily 2-year, founded 1992, administratively affiliated with Colorado Technical University
- **Suburban** campus
- **Coed**
- **Minimally difficult** entrance level

Majors Accounting; accounting and finance; business administration and management; computer engineering; computer science; computer software technology; computer systems analysis; computer technology/computer systems technology; criminal justice/law enforcement administration; e-commerce; electrical, electronic and communications engineering technology; electrical, electronics and communications engineering; finance; general studies; graphic design; health/health care administration; health information/medical records technology; human resources management; information science/studies; information technology; management information systems; marketing/marketing management; massage therapy; medical/clinical assistant; medical radiologic technology; surgical technology.

Academics *Calendar:* quarters. *Degrees:* diplomas, associate, and bachelor's. *Special study options:* internships, services for LD students.

Computers on Campus Campuswide network is available. Wireless service is available via classrooms, computer centers, computer labs, learning centers, libraries, student centers.

Student Life *Housing:* college housing not available. *Campus security:* 24-hour patrols.

Costs (2008–09) *Tuition:* Contact campus for cost.

Applying *Options:* electronic application, deferred entrance. *Application fee:* $50. *Required:* interview. *Application deadlines:* rolling (freshmen), rolling (transfers). *Notification:* continuous (freshmen), continuous (transfers).

Director of Admissions Director of Admissions, Colorado Technical University—North Kansas City, 520 East 19th Avenue, North Kansas City, MO 80907. *Phone:* 816-472-7400.

COLUMBIA COLLEGE

Columbia, Missouri **www.ccis.edu/**

- **Independent** comprehensive, founded 1851, affiliated with Christian Church (Disciples of Christ)
- **Small-town** 29-acre campus
- **Endowment** $22.4 million
- **Coed**
- **Moderately difficult** entrance level

Faculty *Student/faculty ratio:* 13:1.

Academics *Calendar:* semesters. *Degrees:* associate, bachelor's, and master's (offers continuing education program with significant enrollment not reflected in profile).

Student Life *Campus security:* 24-hour emergency response devices and patrols, late-night transport/escort service, controlled dormitory access.

Athletics Member NAIA.

Standardized Tests *Required:* SAT or ACT (for admission).

Costs (2007–08) *Comprehensive fee:* $18,354 includes full-time tuition ($13,034) and room and board ($5320). Full-time tuition and fees vary according to class time and course load. Part-time tuition: $279 per credit hour. Part-time tuition and fees vary according to class time, course load, and location. *College room only:* $3346. Room and board charges vary according to board plan.

Financial Aid Of all full-time matriculated undergraduates who enrolled in 2006, 621 applied for aid, 445 were judged to have need, 126 had their need fully met. 92 Federal Work-Study jobs (averaging $555). In 2006, 147 non-need-based awards were made. *Average percent of need met:* 71. *Average financial aid package:* $12,096. *Average need-based loan:* $4291. *Average need-based gift aid:* $3364. *Average non-need-based aid:* $8759. *Average indebtedness upon graduation:* $12,707.

Applying *Options:* early admission, deferred entrance. *Application fee:* $25. *Required:* high school transcript, minimum 2.5 GPA. *Required for some:* essay or personal statement, letters of recommendation, interview. *Recommended:* rank in upper 50% of high school class.

Freshman Application Contact Ms. Regina Morin, Director of Admissions, Columbia College, 1001 Rogers Street, Columbia, MO 65216. *Phone:* 573-875-7354. *Toll-free phone:* 800-231-2391 Ext. 7366. *Fax:* 573-875-7508. *E-mail:* admissions@ccis.edu.

CONCEPTION SEMINARY COLLEGE

Conception, Missouri **www.conceptionabbey.org/**

- **Independent Roman Catholic** 4-year, founded 1886
- **Rural** 30-acre campus
- **Men only**
- **Noncompetitive** entrance level

Faculty *Student/faculty ratio:* 3:1.

Academics *Calendar:* semesters. *Degree:* certificates and bachelor's.

Student Life *Campus security:* 24-hour emergency response devices.

Standardized Tests *Required:* ACT (for admission).

Costs (2007–08) *Comprehensive fee:* $22,292 includes full-time tuition ($13,872), mandatory fees ($180), and room and board ($8240). Part-time tuition: $180 per credit. *College room only:* $3486.

Financial Aid Of all full-time matriculated undergraduates who enrolled in 2005, 34 applied for aid, 30 were judged to have need, 16 had their need fully met. 13 Federal Work-Study jobs (averaging $729). 35 state and other part-time jobs (averaging $691). In 2005, 11 non-need-based awards were made. *Average*

percent of need met: 78. *Average financial aid package:* $16,500. *Average need-based loan:* $2254. *Average need-based gift aid:* $5825. *Average non-need-based aid:* $1708. *Average indebtedness upon graduation:* $16,375.

Applying *Options:* electronic application. *Required:* essay or personal statement, high school transcript, minimum 2.0 GPA, 2 letters of recommendation, church certificate, medical history.

Freshman Application Contact Br. Victor Schinstock OSB, Director of Recruitment and Admissions, Conception Seminary College, PO Box 502, Highway 136 and VV, 37174 State Highway VV, Conception, MO 64433. *Phone:* 660-944-2886. *Fax:* 660-944-2829. *E-mail:* vocations@conception.edu.

COX COLLEGE OF NURSING AND HEALTH SCIENCES

Springfield, Missouri **www.coxcollege.edu/**

Freshman Application Contact Ms. Stacy Danaher, Admission Coordinator, Cox College of Nursing and Health Sciences, 1423 North Jefferson, Springfield, MO 65802. *Phone:* 417-269-3038. *Toll-free phone:* 866-898-5355. *Fax:* 417-269-3581. *E-mail:* admissions@coxcollege.edu.

CULVER-STOCKTON COLLEGE

Canton, Missouri **www.culver.edu/**

- **Independent** 4-year, founded 1853, affiliated with Christian Church (Disciples of Christ)
- **Rural** 143-acre campus
- **Endowment** $22.4 million
- **Coed** 849 undergraduate students, 90% full-time, 60% women, 40% men
- **Moderately difficult** entrance level, 76% of applicants were admitted

Undergraduates 765 full-time, 84 part-time. Students come from 21 states and territories, 4 other countries, 45% are from out of state, 6% African American, 0.8% Asian American or Pacific Islander, 1% Hispanic American, 0.5% Native American, 0.6% international, 9% transferred in, 68% live on campus. *Retention:* 70% of 2006 full-time freshmen returned.

Freshmen *Admission:* 1,233 applied, 932 admitted, 203 enrolled. *Average high school GPA:* 3.24. *Test scores:* ACT scores over 18: 91%; ACT scores over 24: 27%; ACT scores over 30: 2%.

Faculty *Total:* 54, 94% full-time, 65% with terminal degrees. *Student/faculty ratio:* 15:1.

Majors Accounting; art; arts management; art teacher education; athletic training; biology/biological sciences; business administration and management; business administration, management and operations related; criminal justice/law enforcement administration; dramatic/theater arts; elementary education; English; English/language arts teacher education; finance; history; history teacher education; information science/studies; management information systems; mass communication/media; mathematics; mathematics teacher education; music; music teacher education; nursing (registered nurse training); physical education teaching and coaching; psychology; religious studies; science teacher education; special education; speech teacher education; speech/theater education; sport and fitness administration/management.

Academics *Calendar:* semesters. *Degree:* bachelor's. *Special study options:* advanced placement credit, double majors, honors programs, independent study, internships, off-campus study, part-time degree program, student-designed majors, study abroad, summer session for credit. *Unusual degree programs:* 3-2 engineering; occupational therapy with Washington University in St. Louis.

Computers on Campus 100 computers/terminals and 50 ports are available on campus for general student use. Students can access the following: campus intranet, computer help desk, free student e-mail accounts, online (class) grades, online (class) registration, online (class) schedules. Campuswide network is available. 100% of college-owned or -operated housing units are wired for high-speed Internet access. Wireless service is available via entire campus.

Student Life *Housing:* on-campus residence required through senior year. *Options:* coed, men-only, women-only. Campus housing is university owned. Freshman campus housing is guaranteed. *Activities and organizations:* drama/theater group, student-run newspaper, radio station, choral group, Culver-Stockton Teachers Organization, Institute of Management Accountants, Fellowship of Christian Athletes, Student Government Association, Student Nurses Organization, national fraternities, national sororities. *Campus security:* 24-hour emergency response devices and patrols, student patrols, late-night transport/escort service, controlled dormitory access. *Student services:* personal/psychological counseling.

Athletics Member NAIA. *Intercollegiate sports:* baseball M (s), basketball M (s)/W (s), cheerleading M (s)/W (s), cross-country running M (s)/W (s), football M (s), golf M (s)/W (s), soccer M (s)/W (s), softball W (s), track and field M (s)/W (s), volleyball W (s). *Intramural sports:* basketball M/W, soccer M/W, volleyball M/W.

Standardized Tests *Required:* SAT or ACT (for admission).

Costs (2007–08) *Comprehensive fee:* $23,450 includes full-time tuition ($16,600) and room and board ($6850). Part-time tuition: $450 per credit hour. *Required fees:* $125 per term part-time. *College room only:* $3100. Room and board charges vary according to board plan. *Payment plan:* installment. *Waivers:* senior citizens and employees or children of employees.

Financial Aid Of all full-time matriculated undergraduates who enrolled in 2007, 674 applied for aid, 619 were judged to have need, 144 had their need fully met. 101 Federal Work-Study jobs (averaging $1599). 185 state and other part-time jobs (averaging $1656). In 2007, 85 non-need-based awards were made. *Average percent of need met:* 75%. *Average financial aid package:* $14,058. *Average need-based loan:* $4096. *Average need-based gift aid:* $10,164. *Average non-need-based aid:* $12,172. *Average indebtedness upon graduation:* $22,509. *Financial aid deadline:* 6/1.

Applying *Options:* electronic application, deferred entrance. *Required:* high school transcript, minimum 2.0 GPA, rank in upper 50% of high school class. *Required for some:* interview. *Recommended:* essay or personal statement, letters of recommendation, interview. *Application deadlines:* rolling (freshmen), rolling (transfers). *Notification:* continuous (freshmen), continuous (transfers).

Freshman Application Contact Mr. Jim Lynes, Director of Admissions, Culver-Stockton College, One College Hill, Canton, MO 63435-1299. *Phone:* 573-288-6467. *Toll-free phone:* 800-537-1883. *Fax:* 573-288-6618. *E-mail:* enrollment@culver.edu.

See page 1436 for the College Close-Up.

DEVRY UNIVERSITY

Kansas City, Missouri **www.devry.edu/**

- **Proprietary** comprehensive, founded 1931, part of DeVry University
- **Urban** 12-acre campus
- **Coed** 951 undergraduate students, 54% full-time, 29% women, 71% men
- **Minimally difficult** entrance level

Undergraduates 515 full-time, 436 part-time. 35% are from out of state, 19% African American, 3% Asian American or Pacific Islander, 3% Hispanic American, 2% Native American, 0.2% international, 16% transferred in. *Retention:* 35% of 2006 full-time freshmen returned.

Freshmen *Admission:* 144 enrolled.

Faculty *Total:* 82, 40% full-time. *Student/faculty ratio:* 15:1.

Majors Biomedical technology; business administration and management; business administration, management and operations related; computer engineering technology; computer systems analysis; computer systems networking and telecommunications; electrical, electronic and communications engineering technology; web page, digital/multimedia and information resources design.

Academics *Calendar:* semesters. *Degrees:* associate, bachelor's, master's, and postbachelor's certificates. *Special study options:* academic remediation for entering students, accelerated degree program, adult/continuing education programs, advanced placement credit, distance learning, part-time degree program, services for LD students, summer session for credit.

Computers on Campus 334 computers/terminals are available on campus for general student use. Students can access the following: online (class) registration. Campuswide network is available.

Student Life *Housing:* college housing not available. *Activities and organizations:* Phi Beta Lambda, Institution of Electrical and Electronic Engineers, Tau Alpha Pi, Association of Information Technology Professionals, Cutting Edge Bible Club. *Campus security:* 24-hour emergency response devices and patrols, lighted pathways/sidewalks.

Athletics *Intramural sports:* basketball M/W, football M, golf M, volleyball M/W.

Costs (2008–09) *Tuition:* $13,810 full-time, $515 per credit part-time. *Required fees:* $180 full-time.

Financial Aid Of all full-time matriculated undergraduates who enrolled in 2002, 1,496 applied for aid, 1,413 were judged to have need, 49 had their need fully met. In 2002, 122 non-need-based awards were made. *Average percent of need met:* 42%. *Average financial aid package:* $8714. *Average need-based loan:* $6437. *Average need-based gift aid:* $3982. *Average non-need-based aid:* $10,431.

Applying *Options:* electronic application, early admission, deferred entrance. *Application fee:* $50. *Required:* high school transcript, interview. *Application* *deadlines:* rolling (freshmen), rolling (transfers). *Notification:* continuous (freshmen), continuous (transfers).

Freshman Application Contact Admissions Office, DeVry University, 11224 Holmes Road, Kansas City, MO 64131.

DEVRY UNIVERSITY
Kansas City, Missouri

DEVRY UNIVERSITY
St. Louis, Missouri

DRURY UNIVERSITY
Springfield, Missouri www.drury.edu/

- **Independent** comprehensive, founded 1873
- **Urban** 80-acre campus
- **Endowment** $83.6 million
- **Coed** 1,608 undergraduate students, 98% full-time, 53% women, 47% men
- **Moderately difficult** entrance level, 76% of applicants were admitted

Undergraduates 1,568 full-time, 40 part-time. Students come from 35 states and territories, 33 other countries, 17% are from out of state, 2% African American, 2% Asian American or Pacific Islander, 2% Hispanic American, 0.9% Native American, 5% international, 7% transferred in, 55% live on campus. *Retention:* 82% of 2006 full-time freshmen returned.

Freshmen *Admission:* 1,193 applied, 903 admitted, 398 enrolled. *Average high school GPA:* 4.0. *Test scores:* ACT scores over 18: 99%; ACT scores over 24: 67%; ACT scores over 30: 15%.

Faculty *Total:* 173, 72% full-time, 73% with terminal degrees. *Student/faculty ratio:* 13:1.

Majors Accounting; advertising; architecture; art history, criticism and conservation; arts management; biology/biological sciences; business administration and management; chemistry; communication/speech communication and rhetoric; computer and information sciences; computer science; criminology; design and visual communications; dramatic/theater arts; economics; education; elementary education; engineering; English; environmental studies; finance; fine/studio arts; French; German; history; kinesiology and exercise science; marketing/marketing management; mathematics; music; music performance; music teacher education; music theory and composition; occupational therapy; philosophy; physics; political science and government; pre-dentistry studies; pre-law studies; pre-medical studies; pre-pharmacy studies; pre-veterinary studies; psychology; public relations/image management; religious studies; secondary education; sociology; Spanish; sport and fitness administration/management.

Academics *Calendar:* semesters. *Degrees:* bachelor's and master's (also offers evening program with significant enrollment not reflected in profile). *Special study options:* accelerated degree program, adult/continuing education programs, advanced placement credit, cooperative education, distance learning, double majors, English as a second language, honors programs, independent study, internships, off-campus study, part-time degree program, services for LD students, student-designed majors, study abroad, summer session for credit. *ROTC:* Army (c). *Unusual degree programs:* 3-2 engineering with Washington University in St. Louis; international management with American Graduate School of International Management, occupational therapy with Washington University in St. Louis.

Computers on Campus 323 computers/terminals are available on campus for general student use. Students can access the following: campus intranet, computer help desk, free student e-mail accounts, online (class) grades, online (class) registration, online (class) schedules, digital imaging lab, online bill payment/student information. Campuswide network is available. 100% of college-owned or -operated housing units are wired for high-speed Internet access. Wireless service is available via entire campus.

Student Life *Housing:* on-campus residence required through senior year. *Options:* coed, men-only, women-only. Campus housing is university owned and leased by the school. Freshman campus housing is guaranteed. *Activities and organizations:* drama/theater group, student-run newspaper, radio and television station, choral group, Student Union Board, Community Outreach/Taking a Stand for Kids, choral groups and bands, International Student Organization, academic department clubs, national fraternities, national sororities. *Campus security:* 24-hour emergency response devices and patrols, student patrols, late-night transport/escort service, controlled dormitory access, security cameras in parking areas. *Student services:* health clinic, personal/psychological counseling.

Athletics Member NCAA. All Division II. *Intercollegiate sports:* baseball M (s), basketball M (s)/W (s), cheerleading M (s)/W (s), cross-country running M (s)/W (s), golf M (s)/W (s), soccer M (s)/W (s), softball W (s), swimming and diving M (s)/W (s), tennis M (s)/W (s), volleyball W (s). *Intramural sports:* basketball M/W, football M/W, racquetball M/W, soccer M/W, softball M/W, table tennis M/W, tennis M/W, volleyball M/W.

Standardized Tests *Required:* SAT or ACT (for admission).

Costs (2008–09) *Comprehensive fee:* $24,793 includes full-time tuition ($17,900), mandatory fees ($509), and room and board ($6384). Part-time tuition: $600 per semester hour.

Financial Aid Of all full-time matriculated undergraduates who enrolled in 2007, 1,587 applied for aid, 1,501 were judged to have need, 1,311 had their need fully met. 787 Federal Work-Study jobs (averaging $3000). 91 state and other part-time jobs (averaging $2000). In 2007, 107 non-need-based awards were made. *Average percent of need met:* 84%. *Average financial aid package:* $7642. *Average need-based loan:* $5880. *Average need-based gift aid:* $6930. *Average non-need-based aid:* $3465. *Average indebtedness upon graduation:* $18,225.

Applying *Options:* electronic application, deferred entrance. *Application fee:* $25. *Required:* essay or personal statement, high school transcript, minimum 2.7 GPA, 1 letter of recommendation, minimum ACT score of 21. *Recommended:* interview. *Application deadlines:* 8/1 (freshmen), rolling (transfers). *Notification:* continuous (freshmen), continuous (transfers).

Freshman Application Contact Mr. Chip Parker, Director of Admission, Drury University, 900 North Benton, Bay Hall, Springfield, MO 65802. *Phone:* 417-873-7205. *Toll-free phone:* 800-922-2274. *Fax:* 417-866-3873. *E-mail:* druryad@drury.edu.

EVANGEL UNIVERSITY
Springfield, Missouri www.evangel.edu/

- **Independent** comprehensive, founded 1955, affiliated with Assemblies of God
- **Urban** 80-acre campus
- **Endowment** $6.3 million
- **Coed** 1,534 undergraduate students, 95% full-time, 60% women, 40% men
- **Moderately difficult** entrance level, 76% of applicants were admitted

Prominent alumni include Congressman Todd Tiahrt (R-KS); Dr. Fred Mihm, Professor of Anesthesia, Stanford University Medical School; Dr. James Long, Director, Utah Artificial Heart Program; Sara Groves, CCM singer/songwriter; Kevin Compton, owner, San Jose Sharks (NHL); Steve Poppen, VP/CFO, Minnesota Vikings (NFL); Beverly Lewis, *New York Times* bestselling author of inspirational fiction; and Phil Stanton, founding member of Blue Man Group.

Undergraduates 1,462 full-time, 72 part-time. Students come from 50 states and territories, 11 other countries, 47% are from out of state, 3% African American, 2% Asian American or Pacific Islander, 4% Hispanic American, 0.5% Native American, 0.1% international, 8% transferred in, 81% live on campus. *Retention:* 65% of 2006 full-time freshmen returned.

Freshmen *Admission:* 769 applied, 584 admitted, 344 enrolled. *Average high school GPA:* 3.26. *Test scores:* ACT scores over 18: 90%; ACT scores over 24: 41%; ACT scores over 30: 7%.

Faculty *Total:* 145, 71% full-time, 42% with terminal degrees. *Student/faculty ratio:* 16:1.

Majors Art; art teacher education; behavioral sciences; biblical studies; biology/biological sciences; biology teacher education; broadcast journalism; business administration and management; business teacher education; chemistry; chemistry teacher education; child development; clinical laboratory science/medical technology; computer science; criminal justice/law enforcement administration; early childhood education; elementary education; English; health and physical education; history; history teacher education; intercultural/multicultural and diversity studies; kindergarten/preschool education; marketing/marketing management; mathematics; medical laboratory technology; middle school education; music; music teacher education; parks, recreation and leisure; physical education teaching and coaching; political science and government; pre-dentistry studies; pre-law studies; pre-medical studies; pre-veterinary studies; psychology; public administration; radio and television; religious/sacred music; science teacher education; secondary education; social work; sociology; Spanish; Spanish language teacher education; special education; speech and rhetoric; speech teacher education.

Academics *Calendar:* semesters. *Degrees:* associate, bachelor's, and master's. *Special study options:* academic remediation for entering students, accelerated degree program, adult/continuing education programs, advanced placement credit,

COLLEGE DATA CENTER • MISSOURI

double majors, internships, part-time degree program, services for LD students, summer session for credit. *ROTC:* Army (b). *Unusual degree programs:* 3-2 engineering with Washington University in St. Louis, University of Missouri-Rolla.

Computers on Campus 400 computers/terminals are available on campus for general student use. Students can access the following: campus intranet, computer help desk, free student e-mail accounts, online (class) grades, online (class) registration, online (class) schedules, online payment. Campuswide network is available. 90% of college-owned or -operated housing units are wired for high-speed Internet access. Wireless service is available via learning centers, student centers.

Student Life *Housing:* on-campus residence required through senior year. *Options:* coed, men-only, women-only. Campus housing is university owned. Freshman campus housing is guaranteed. *Activities and organizations:* drama/theater group, student-run newspaper, radio station, choral group, Evangel Student Government Association, Student Missouri State Teachers Association, Crosswalk, Students in Free Enterprise. *Campus security:* 24-hour emergency response devices and patrols, student patrols, late-night transport/escort service, controlled dormitory access. *Student services:* health clinic, personal/psychological counseling.

Athletics Member NAIA. *Intercollegiate sports:* baseball M (s), basketball M (s)/W (s), cross-country running M (s)/W (s), football M (s), golf M (s)/W (s), softball W (s), tennis M (s)/W (s), track and field M (s)/W (s), volleyball W (s). *Intramural sports:* baseball M, basketball M/W, football M, golf M/W, soccer M/W, softball W, tennis M/W, volleyball W.

Standardized Tests *Required:* SAT or ACT (for admission).

Costs (2007–08) *Comprehensive fee:* $19,420 includes full-time tuition ($13,530), mandatory fees ($770), and room and board ($5120). Part-time tuition: $528 per credit hour. *Required fees:* $384 per term part-time. *College room only:* $2580.

Financial Aid Of all full-time matriculated undergraduates who enrolled in 2006, 1,460 applied for aid, 1,250 were judged to have need, 116 had their need fully met. 358 Federal Work-Study jobs (averaging $949). 89 state and other part-time jobs (averaging $663). In 2006, 334 non-need-based awards were made. *Average percent of need met:* 41%. *Average financial aid package:* $8409. *Average need-based loan:* $4025. *Average need-based gift aid:* $5535. *Average non-need-based aid:* $7259. *Average indebtedness upon graduation:* $22,105.

Applying *Options:* electronic application, deferred entrance. *Application fee:* $25. *Required:* high school transcript. *Recommended:* minimum 2.0 GPA. *Application deadlines:* 8/1 (freshmen), 8/1 (transfers). *Notification:* continuous (freshmen), continuous (transfers).

Freshman Application Contact Ms. Cheri Meyer, Director of Admissions, Evangel University, 1111 North Glenstone, Springfield, MO 65802. *Phone:* 417-865-2811 Ext. 7262. *Toll-free phone:* 800-382-6435. *Fax:* 417-865-9599. *E-mail:* admissions@evangel.edu.

EVEREST COLLEGE

Springfield, Missouri **www.everest.edu/campus/springfield**

Freshman Application Contact Admissions Office, Everest College, 1010 West Sunshine Street, Springfield, MO 65807. *Phone:* 417-864-7220. *Toll-free phone:* 800-864-5697 (in-state); 800-475-2669 (out-of-state).

FONTBONNE UNIVERSITY

St. Louis, Missouri **www.fontbonne.edu/**

- **Independent Roman Catholic** comprehensive, founded 1917
- **Suburban** 13-acre campus
- **Endowment** $18.0 million
- **Coed** 2,078 undergraduate students, 74% full-time, 70% women, 30% men
- **Moderately difficult** entrance level, 75% of applicants were admitted

Undergraduates 1,532 full-time, 546 part-time. Students come from 22 states and territories, 23 other countries, 12% are from out of state, 34% African American, 1% Asian American or Pacific Islander, 1% Hispanic American, 0.3% Native American, 0.8% international, 11% transferred in, 10% live on campus. *Retention:* 58% of 2006 full-time freshmen returned.

Freshmen *Admission:* 600 applied, 452 admitted, 200 enrolled. *Average high school GPA:* 3.05.

Faculty *Total:* 414, 18% full-time. *Student/faculty ratio:* 16:1.

Majors Accounting; advertising; art; arts management; art teacher education; audiology and speech-language pathology; biology/biological sciences; broadcast journalism; business administration and management; civil engineering technology; commercial and advertising art; communication/speech communication and rhetoric; computer science; consumer merchandising/retailing management; dietetics; dramatic/theater arts; education; elementary education; engineering; English; family and consumer sciences/home economics teacher education; family and consumer sciences/human sciences; fashion merchandising; finance; fine/studio arts; history; human services; kindergarten/preschool education; liberal arts and sciences/liberal studies; management information systems; marketing/marketing management; mathematics; middle school education; pre-law studies; premedical studies; psychology; religious studies; secondary education; social sciences; sociology; special education; speech therapy; sport and fitness administration/management.

Academics *Calendar:* semesters. *Degrees:* certificates, bachelor's, master's, and postbachelor's certificates. *Special study options:* academic remediation for entering students, accelerated degree program, adult/continuing education programs, advanced placement credit, cooperative education, distance learning, double majors, English as a second language, honors programs, independent study, internships, off-campus study, services for LD students, student-designed majors, study abroad, summer session for credit. *ROTC:* Army (c), Air Force (c). *Unusual degree programs:* 3-2 engineering with Washington University in St. Louis; social work with Washington University in St. Louis.

Computers on Campus 133 computers/terminals are available on campus for general student use. Students can access the following: computer help desk, free student e-mail accounts, online (class) grades, online (class) registration, online (class) schedules. Campuswide network is available.

Student Life *Housing options:* coed, women-only. Campus housing is university owned. Freshman campus housing is guaranteed. *Activities and organizations:* drama/theater group, student-run newspaper, choral group, Future Teachers Association, Students for the Enhancement of Black Awareness, Fontbonne Athletic Association, Fontbonne in Service and Humility, Student Government Association. *Campus security:* 24-hour patrols, late-night transport/escort service, controlled dormitory access. *Student services:* health clinic, personal/psychological counseling.

Athletics Member NCAA, NAIA. All NCAA Division III. *Intercollegiate sports:* baseball M, basketball M/W, bowling W, cheerleading W, cross-country running M/W, golf M/W, lacrosse M/W, soccer M/W, softball W, tennis M/W, volleyball W. *Intramural sports:* basketball M/W, bowling M, soccer M, volleyball M/W.

Standardized Tests *Required:* SAT or ACT (for admission).

Costs (2008–09) *Comprehensive fee:* $26,527 includes full-time tuition ($19,000), mandatory fees ($320), and room and board ($7207). Part-time tuition: $508 per credit hour. *Required fees:* $16 per credit hour part-time.

Financial Aid In 2003, 502 non-need-based awards were made. *Average percent of need met:* 86%. *Average financial aid package:* $15,600.

Applying *Options:* electronic application, early admission, deferred entrance. *Application fee:* $25. *Required:* high school transcript, minimum 2.5 GPA. *Recommended:* 2 letters of recommendation, interview. *Application deadlines:* 8/1 (freshmen), rolling (transfers). *Notification:* continuous (freshmen), continuous (transfers).

Freshman Application Contact Ms. Peggy Musen, Vice President for Enrollment Management, Fontbonne University, 6800 Wydown Boulevard, St. Louis, MO 63105-3098. *Phone:* 314-889-1400. *Fax:* 314-889-1451. *E-mail:* pmusen@fontbonne.edu.

GLOBAL UNIVERSITY OF THE ASSEMBLIES OF GOD

Springfield, Missouri **www.globaluniversity.edu/**

- **Independent** comprehensive, founded 1948, affiliated with Assemblies of God
- **Small-town** campus
- **Coed**
- **Noncompetitive** entrance level

Faculty *Student/faculty ratio:* 21:1.

Academics *Calendar:* continuous. *Degrees:* certificates, diplomas, associate, bachelor's, master's, first professional, and postbachelor's certificates (offers only external degree programs).

Student Life *Campus security:* 24-hour emergency response devices.

Costs (2007–08) *Tuition:* $2970 full-time, $99 per hour part-time. Part-time tuition and fees vary according to class time.

Applying *Application fee:* $35. *Required:* high school transcript. *Required for some:* 1 letter of recommendation. *Recommended:* essay or personal statement.

Freshman Application Contact Ms. Jessica Dorn, Director of US Enrollments, Global University of the Assemblies of God, 1211 South Glenstone

Avenue, Springfield, MO 65804. *Phone:* 417-862-9533 Ext. 2335. *Toll-free phone:* 800-443-1083. *Fax:* 417-862-0863. *E-mail:* studentinfo@globaluniversity.edu.

GRANTHAM UNIVERSITY

Kansas City, Missouri **www.grantham.edu/**

- **Proprietary** 4-year, founded 1951
- **Urban** campus
- **Coed** 8,000 undergraduate students
- **Noncompetitive** entrance level

Faculty *Total:* 119, 24% with terminal degrees.

Majors Business administration and management; computer engineering technology; computer science; criminal justice/law enforcement administration; criminal justice/safety; electrical, electronic and communications engineering technology; general studies; interdisciplinary studies.

Academics *Calendar:* continuous. *Degrees:* associate, bachelor's, and master's (offers only external degree programs). *Special study options:* accelerated degree program, adult/continuing education programs, advanced placement credit, distance learning, external degree program, independent study, part-time degree program.

Computers on Campus Students can access the following: online (class) grades, online (class) registration.

Student Life *Housing:* college housing not available.

Costs (2008–09) *Tuition:* $7950 full-time, $265 per credit hour part-time.

Applying *Options:* electronic application. *Required:* high school transcript. *Application deadlines:* rolling (freshmen), rolling (out-of-state freshmen), rolling (transfers). *Notification:* continuous (freshmen), continuous (out-of-state freshmen), continuous (transfers).

Freshman Application Contact Ms. DeAnn Wandler, Director of Admissions, Grantham University, 7200 NW 86th Street, Suite M, Kansas City, MO 64153. *Phone:* 800-955-2527. *Toll-free phone:* 800-955-2527. *Fax:* 816-595-5757. *E-mail:* admissions@grantham.edu.

HANNIBAL-LAGRANGE COLLEGE

Hannibal, Missouri **www.hlg.edu/**

- **Independent Southern Baptist** 4-year, founded 1858
- **Small-town** 110-acre campus
- **Coed** 1,139 undergraduate students, 72% full-time, 65% women, 35% men
- **Moderately difficult** entrance level, 96% of applicants were admitted

Undergraduates 816 full-time, 323 part-time. Students come from 20 states and territories, 25 other countries, 20% are from out of state, 3% African American, 0.2% Asian American or Pacific Islander, 1% Hispanic American, 0.8% Native American, 5% international, 43% live on campus. *Retention:* 74% of 2006 full-time freshmen returned.

Freshmen *Admission:* 338 applied, 324 admitted. *Test scores:* ACT scores over 18: 94%; ACT scores over 24: 30%.

Faculty *Total:* 140, 39% full-time, 17% with terminal degrees. *Student/faculty ratio:* 12:1.

Majors Accounting; art; art teacher education; biblical studies; biology/biological sciences; business administration and management; business teacher education; child development; communication and journalism related; communication/speech communication and rhetoric; computer and information sciences; criminal justice/law enforcement administration; dramatic/theater arts; early childhood education; education; elementary education; emergency medical technology (EMT paramedic); English; English/language arts teacher education; history; history teacher education; human services; kindergarten/preschool education; liberal arts and sciences/liberal studies; marketing/marketing management; mathematics; mathematics teacher education; missionary studies and missiology; music; music teacher education; nursing (registered nurse training); parks, recreation and leisure facilities management; physical education teaching and coaching; piano and organ; pre-law studies; psychology; religious education; religious/sacred music; respiratory care therapy; science teacher education; secondary education; sociology; speech and rhetoric; voice and opera.

Academics *Calendar:* semesters. *Degrees:* associate, bachelor's, and master's. *Special study options:* academic remediation for entering students, accelerated degree program, adult/continuing education programs, advanced placement credit, cooperative education, distance learning, double majors, honors programs, independent study, internships, part-time degree program, services for LD students, study abroad, summer session for credit.

Computers on Campus 76 computers/terminals are available on campus for general student use. Students can access the following: online (class) grades, online (class) registration, online (class) schedules. Campuswide network is available.

Student Life *Housing:* on-campus residence required for freshman year. *Options:* men-only, women-only. Campus housing is university owned. Freshman campus housing is guaranteed. *Activities and organizations:* drama/theater group, student-run newspaper, choral group, Phi Beta Lambda, Student Government, Student Teachers Organization, Phi Beta Delta, Association of Women Students. *Campus security:* 24-hour emergency response devices and patrols. *Student services:* health clinic, personal/psychological counseling.

Athletics Member NAIA, NCCAA. *Intercollegiate sports:* baseball M (s), basketball M (s)/W (s), cheerleading M (s)/W (s), cross-country running M (s)/W (s), golf M (s), soccer M (s)/W (s), softball W (s), swimming and diving M (s)/W (s), track and field M (s)/W (s), volleyball M (s)/W (s), wrestling M (s). *Intramural sports:* basketball M/W, racquetball M/W, soccer M/W, softball M/W, swimming and diving M/W, table tennis M/W, tennis M/W, volleyball M/W, water polo M/W.

Standardized Tests *Required:* SAT or ACT (for admission).

Costs (2007–08) *One-time required fee:* $50. *Comprehensive fee:* $18,410 includes full-time tuition ($13,064), mandatory fees ($416), and room and board ($4930). Full-time tuition and fees vary according to class time, course load, and program. Part-time tuition: $436 per hour. Part-time tuition and fees vary according to class time, course load, and program. *Required fees:* $100 per term part-time. *Room and board:* Room and board charges vary according to housing facility. *Payment plan:* installment. *Waivers:* employees or children of employees.

Financial Aid Of all full-time matriculated undergraduates who enrolled in 2007, 560 were judged to have need. 85 Federal Work-Study jobs (averaging $550). In 2007, 214 non-need-based awards were made. *Average financial aid package:* $11,379. *Average need-based loan:* $4314. *Average need-based gift aid:* $4678. *Average non-need-based aid:* $5099. *Average indebtedness upon graduation:* $16,689.

Applying *Options:* electronic application, early admission, deferred entrance. *Application fee:* $25. *Required:* high school transcript, minimum 2.0 GPA. *Required for some:* GED. *Application deadlines:* rolling (freshmen), rolling (transfers). *Notification:* continuous (freshmen).

Freshman Application Contact Dr. Raymond Carty, Vice President for Enrollment Management, Hannibal-LaGrange College, 2800 Palmyra Road, Hannibal, MO 63401-1999. *Phone:* 573-629-2278. *Toll-free phone:* 800-HLG-1119. *E-mail:* admissio@hlg.edu.

HARRIS-STOWE STATE UNIVERSITY

St. Louis, Missouri **www.hssu.edu/**

- **State-supported** 4-year, founded 1857, part of Missouri Coordinating Board for Higher Education
- **Urban** 22-acre campus
- **Coed** 1,882 undergraduate students, 66% full-time, 69% women, 31% men
- **Noncompetitive** entrance level, 76% of applicants were admitted

Undergraduates 1,234 full-time, 648 part-time. Students come from 14 states and territories, 10 other countries, 10% are from out of state, 90% African American, 0.1% Asian American or Pacific Islander, 0.4% Hispanic American, 0.1% Native American, 0.6% international, 11% transferred in, 12% live on campus. *Retention:* 39% of 2006 full-time freshmen returned.

Freshmen *Admission:* 1,114 applied, 842 admitted, 448 enrolled. *Average high school GPA:* 2.36. *Test scores:* ACT scores over 18: 26%; ACT scores over 24: 3%.

Faculty *Total:* 181, 31% full-time. *Student/faculty ratio:* 25:1.

Majors Accounting; business administration and management; business/commerce; criminal justice/law enforcement administration; early childhood education; elementary education; health/health care administration; information science/studies; interdisciplinary studies; juvenile corrections; kindergarten/preschool education; marketing/marketing management; middle school education; public administration; secondary education; urban education and leadership; urban studies/affairs.

Academics *Calendar:* semesters. *Degrees:* bachelor's and postbachelor's certificates. *Special study options:* academic remediation for entering students, advanced placement credit, cooperative education, internships, off-campus study, part-time degree program, services for LD students, student-designed majors, summer session for credit. *ROTC:* Air Force (c).

Computers on Campus 251 computers/terminals are available on campus for general student use. Students can access the following: free student e-mail accounts, online (class) registration. Campuswide network is available. Wireless service is available via student centers.

Student Life *Housing options:* coed. Campus housing is university owned. *Activities and organizations:* drama/theater group, choral group, Drama Club, Concert chorale, Student Government Association, Multicultural Council, Student Ambassadors, national fraternities, national sororities. *Campus security:* 24-hour emergency response devices and patrols, student patrols, late-night transport/escort service, controlled dormitory access, 16-hour patrols by trained security personnel Monday through Friday, 24-hour weekend and holiday patrols. *Student services:* health clinic, personal/psychological counseling.

Athletics Member NAIA. *Intercollegiate sports:* baseball M (s), basketball M (s)/W (s), cheerleading M (s)/W (s), soccer M (s)/W (s), softball W (s), volleyball W (s).

Standardized Tests *Recommended:* SAT or ACT (for admission).

Costs (2007–08) *Tuition:* state resident $4740 full-time, $158 per hour part-time; nonresident $9338 full-time, $311 per hour part-time. Full-time tuition and fees vary according to course load. Part-time tuition and fees vary according to course load. *Required fees:* $350 full-time, $175 per term part-time. *Room and board:* $7200; room only: $5250. Room and board charges vary according to board plan.

Financial Aid Of all full-time matriculated undergraduates who enrolled in 2002, 800 applied for aid, 787 were judged to have need, 130 had their need fully met. 70 Federal Work-Study jobs (averaging $1958). 90 state and other part-time jobs (averaging $2000). In 2002, 89 non-need-based awards were made. *Average percent of need met:* 82%. *Average financial aid package:* $7350. *Average need-based loan:* $4000. *Average need-based gift aid:* $4000. *Average non-need-based aid:* $2000. *Average indebtedness upon graduation:* $16,000.

Applying *Options:* early admission, deferred entrance. *Application fee:* $15. *Required:* high school transcript. *Application deadlines:* rolling (freshmen), rolling (transfers). *Notification:* continuous (freshmen), continuous (transfers).

Freshman Application Contact Ms. LaShanda Boone, Executive Director of Enrollment Management, Harris-Stowe State University, 3026 Laclede Avenue, St. Louis, MO 63103. *Phone:* 314-340-3300. *Fax:* 314-340-3555. *E-mail:* admissions@hssu.edu.

HICKEY COLLEGE

St. Louis, Missouri **www.hickeycollege.edu/**

Founded in 1933, Hickey College provides business and technology programs that prepare students to enter the business world in the shortest possible time. Diploma, associate, and bachelor's degree programs are available. Programs are offered in accounting, administrative assistant studies, applied management, computer programming, computer specialist studies, graphic design, legal administrative assistant studies, medical administrative assistant studies, network management, paralegal studies, and veterinary technician studies. For more information, prospective students should call 314-434-2212 Ext. 150 or 800-777-1544 Ext. 150 (toll-free) or visit the College Web site at http://www.hickeycollege.edu.

Freshman Application Contact Admissions Office, Hickey College, 940 West Port Plaza Drive, St. Louis, MO 63146. *Phone:* 314-434-2212. *Toll-free phone:* 800-777-1544. *Fax:* 314-434-1974.

ITT TECHNICAL INSTITUTE

Arnold, Missouri **www.itt-tech.edu/**

- **Proprietary** primarily 2-year, founded 1997, part of ITT Educational Services, Inc
- **Coed**
- **Minimally difficult** entrance level

Academics *Calendar:* quarters. *Degrees:* associate and bachelor's.

Standardized Tests *Required:* Wonderlic aptitude test (for admission).

Applying *Options:* deferred entrance. *Application fee:* $100. *Required:* high school transcript, interview. *Recommended:* letters of recommendation.

Freshman Application Contact Mr. Brad Coleman, Director of Recruitment, ITT Technical Institute, 1930 Meyer Drury Drive, Arnold, MO 63010. *Phone:* 636-464-6600. *Toll-free phone:* 888-488-1082.

ITT TECHNICAL INSTITUTE

Earth City, Missouri **www.itt-tech.edu/**

- **Proprietary** primarily 2-year, founded 1936, part of ITT Educational Services, Inc
- **Suburban** 2-acre campus with easy access to St. Louis
- **Coed**
- **Minimally difficult** entrance level

Academics *Calendar:* quarters. *Degrees:* associate and bachelor's.

Standardized Tests *Required:* Wonderlic aptitude test (for admission).

Applying *Options:* deferred entrance. *Application fee:* $100. *Required:* high school transcript, interview. *Recommended:* letters of recommendation.

Freshman Application Contact Mr. Arlen K. Freeman, Director of Recruitment, ITT Technical Institute, 13505 Lakefront Drive, Earth City, MO 63045. *Phone:* 314-298-7800. *Toll-free phone:* 800-235-5488.

ITT TECHNICAL INSTITUTE

Kansas City, Missouri **www.itt-tech.edu/**

- **Proprietary** primarily 2-year, founded 2004, part of ITT Educational Services, Inc
- **Coed**

Academics *Calendar:* quarters. *Degrees:* associate and bachelor's.

Standardized Tests *Required:* Wonderlic aptitude test (for admission).

Applying *Application fee:* $100. *Required:* high school transcript, interview. *Recommended:* letters of recommendation.

Freshman Application Contact Mr. William Vinson, Director of Recruitment, ITT Technical Institute, 9150 East 41st Terrace, Kansas City, MO 64133. *Phone:* 816-276-1400. *Toll-free phone:* 877-488-1442.

KANSAS CITY ART INSTITUTE

Kansas City, Missouri **www.kcai.edu/**

- **Independent** 4-year, founded 1885
- **Urban** 18-acre campus
- **Endowment** $30.8 million
- **Coed** 676 undergraduate students, 99% full-time, 55% women, 45% men
- **Moderately difficult** entrance level, 63% of applicants were admitted

Undergraduates 669 full-time, 7 part-time. Students come from 37 states and territories, 6 other countries, 59% are from out of state, 3% African American, 4% Asian American or Pacific Islander, 5% Hispanic American, 1% Native American, 0.9% international, 8% transferred in, 25% live on campus. *Retention:* 78% of 2006 full-time freshmen returned.

Freshmen *Admission:* 537 applied, 338 admitted, 152 enrolled. *Average high school GPA:* 3.19. *Test scores:* SAT critical reading scores over 500: 78%; SAT math scores over 500: 71%; SAT writing scores over 500: 68%; ACT scores over 18: 96%; SAT critical reading scores over 600: 39%; SAT math scores over 600: 32%; SAT writing scores over 600: 27%; ACT scores over 24: 45%; SAT critical reading scores over 700: 10%; SAT math scores over 700: 2%; SAT writing scores over 700: 4%; ACT scores over 30: 5%.

Faculty *Total:* 104, 49% full-time, 81% with terminal degrees. *Student/faculty ratio:* 12:1.

Majors Animation, interactive technology, video graphics and special effects; art history, criticism and conservation; ceramic arts and ceramics; creative writing; fiber, textile and weaving arts; film/cinema studies; graphic design; interdisciplinary studies; painting; photography; printmaking; sculpture.

Academics *Calendar:* semesters. *Degree:* bachelor's. *Special study options:* academic remediation for entering students, adult/continuing education programs, advanced placement credit, cooperative education, double majors, English as a second language, independent study, internships, off-campus study, services for LD students, study abroad, summer session for credit.

Computers on Campus 145 computers/terminals and 1,000 ports are available on campus for general student use. Students can access the following: campus intranet, computer help desk, free student e-mail accounts, online (class) grades, online (class) registration, online (class) schedules. Campuswide network is available. 100% of college-owned or -operated housing units are wired for high-speed Internet access. Wireless service is available via classrooms, computer centers, computer labs, learning centers, libraries, student centers.

Student Life *Housing:* on-campus residence required for freshman year. *Options:* coed. Campus housing is university owned. Freshman applicants given priority for college housing. *Activities and organizations:* Student Assembly (council), Student Gallery Committee, Ethnic Student Association. *Campus security:* 24-hour emergency response devices and patrols, late-night transport/escort service, controlled dormitory access. *Student services:* personal/psychological counseling.

Standardized Tests *Required:* SAT or ACT (for admission).

Costs (2007–08) *Comprehensive fee:* $35,480 includes full-time tuition ($27,220) and room and board ($8260). Full-time tuition and fees vary according to program. Part-time tuition: $1134 per credit hour. Part-time tuition and fees vary according to program. *Room and board:* Room and board charges vary according to board plan and housing facility. *Waivers:* employees or children of employees.

Financial Aid Of all full-time matriculated undergraduates who enrolled in 2005, 539 applied for aid, 483 were judged to have need, 50 had their need fully met. 124 Federal Work-Study jobs (averaging $997). 30 state and other part-time jobs (averaging $1000). In 2005, 121 non-need-based awards were made. *Average percent of need met:* 59%. *Average financial aid package:* $15,004. *Average need-based loan:* $4830. *Average need-based gift aid:* $10,366. *Average non-need-based aid:* $11,786. *Average indebtedness upon graduation:* $30,000.

Applying *Options:* electronic application, deferred entrance. *Application fee:* $35. *Required:* essay or personal statement, high school transcript, minimum 2.5 GPA, 2 letters of recommendation, portfolio, statement of purpose. *Recommended:* interview. *Application deadlines:* rolling (freshmen), rolling (transfers). *Notification:* continuous until 8/1 (freshmen), continuous until 8/1 (transfers).

Freshman Application Contact Mr. Gerald Valet, Director of Admission Technology, Kansas City Art Institute, 4415 Warwick Boulevard, Kansas City, MO 64111-1874. *Phone:* 816-474-5224. *Toll-free phone:* 800-522-5224. *Fax:* 816-802-3309. *E-mail:* admiss@kcai.edu.

LINCOLN UNIVERSITY

Jefferson City, Missouri **www.lincolnu.edu/**

- **State-supported** comprehensive, founded 1866, part of Missouri Coordinating Board for Higher Education
- **Small-town** 165-acre campus
- **Endowment** $1.4 million
- **Coed** 2,952 undergraduate students, 68% full-time, 60% women, 40% men
- **Noncompetitive** entrance level, 95% of applicants were admitted

Undergraduates 2,009 full-time, 943 part-time. Students come from 35 states and territories, 23 other countries, 16% are from out of state, 45% African American, 0.8% Asian American or Pacific Islander, 1% Hispanic American, 0.4% Native American, 4% international, 5% transferred in, 31% live on campus. *Retention:* 53% of 2006 full-time freshmen returned.

Freshmen *Admission:* 1,549 applied, 1,477 admitted, 606 enrolled. *Average high school GPA:* 2.63. *Test scores:* SAT critical reading scores over 500: 12%; SAT math scores over 500: 15%; ACT scores over 18: 45%; SAT critical reading scores over 600: 4%; ACT scores over 24: 8%.

Faculty *Total:* 240, 52% full-time, 32% with terminal degrees. *Student/faculty ratio:* 15:1.

Majors Accounting; agricultural business and management; agriculture; art teacher education; biology/biological sciences; biology teacher education; business administration and management; business teacher education; chemistry; chemistry teacher education; civil engineering; clinical laboratory science/medical technology; computer science; criminal justice/law enforcement administration; drafting and design technology; early childhood education; economics; elementary education; English; English/language arts teacher education; fine/studio arts; history; information science/studies; journalism; marketing/marketing management; mathematics; mathematics teacher education; mechanical design technology; middle school education; music teacher education; nursing (registered nurse training); physical education teaching and coaching; physics; physics teacher education; political science and government; pre-engineering; psychology; public administration; sociology; Spanish; special education.

Academics *Calendar:* semesters. *Degrees:* associate, bachelor's, master's, and post-master's certificates. *Special study options:* academic remediation for entering students, accelerated degree program, adult/continuing education programs, advanced placement credit, distance learning, double majors, honors programs, independent study, internships, off-campus study, part-time degree program, services for LD students, summer session for credit. *ROTC:* Army (b), Navy (c), Air Force (c).

Computers on Campus 250 computers/terminals and 1,100 ports are available on campus for general student use. Students can access the following: free student e-mail accounts, online (class) grades, online (class) registration, online (class) schedules. Campuswide network is available. 100% of college-owned or -operated housing units are wired for high-speed Internet access. Wireless service is available via entire campus.

Student Life *Housing:* on-campus residence required through sophomore year. *Options:* coed, men-only, women-only. Campus housing is university owned. *Activities and organizations:* drama/theater group, student-run newspaper, radio and television station, choral group, marching band, national fraternities, national sororities. *Campus security:* 24-hour emergency response devices and patrols, student patrols, late-night transport/escort service, controlled dormitory access. *Student services:* health clinic, personal/psychological counseling, women's center.

Athletics Member NCAA. All Division II. *Intercollegiate sports:* baseball M (s), basketball M (s)/W (s), cross-country running W (s), football M (s), golf M (s)/W (s), softball W (s), tennis W (s), track and field M (s)/W (s). *Intramural sports:* basketball M/W, bowling M/W.

Standardized Tests *Required:* SAT or ACT (for admission).

Costs (2007–08) *Tuition:* state resident $5520 full-time, $184 per credit hour part-time; nonresident $10,050 full-time, $335 per credit hour part-time. Full-time tuition and fees vary according to location. Part-time tuition and fees vary according to location. *Required fees:* $490 full-time, $15 per credit hour part-time, $20 per term part-time. *Room and board:* $4590; room only: $2358. Room and board charges vary according to board plan and housing facility. *Payment plan:* installment. *Waivers:* senior citizens and employees or children of employees.

Financial Aid Of all full-time matriculated undergraduates who enrolled in 2007, 1,574 applied for aid, 1,399 were judged to have need, 175 had their need fully met. 221 Federal Work-Study jobs (averaging $775). 202 state and other part-time jobs (averaging $2549). In 2007, 15 non-need-based awards were made. *Average percent of need met:* 74%. *Average financial aid package:* $8252. *Average need-based loan:* $3788. *Average need-based gift aid:* $4176. *Average non-need-based aid:* $4427. *Average indebtedness upon graduation:* $20,845.

Applying *Options:* deferred entrance. *Application fee:* $20. *Required:* high school transcript. *Required for some:* minimum 2.0 GPA, audition for sacred music and music education. *Application deadlines:* 7/15 (freshmen), 6/15 (transfers). *Notification:* continuous (freshmen), continuous (transfers).

Freshman Application Contact Mr. Mike Kosher, Director of Admissions, Lincoln University, 820 Chestnut Street, PO Box 29, Jefferson City, MO 65102-0029. *Phone:* 573-681-5599. *Toll-free phone:* 800-521-5052. *Fax:* 573-681-5889. *E-mail:* enroll@lincolnu.edu.

LINDENWOOD UNIVERSITY

St. Charles, Missouri **www.lindenwood.edu/**

- **Independent Presbyterian** comprehensive, founded 1827
- **Suburban** 420-acre campus with easy access to St. Louis
- **Endowment** $64.3 million
- **Coed** 5,895 undergraduate students, 96% full-time, 57% women, 43% men
- **Moderately difficult** entrance level, 58% of applicants were admitted

Undergraduates 5,639 full-time, 256 part-time. Students come from 42 states and territories, 69 other countries, 18% are from out of state, 12% African American, 0.8% Asian American or Pacific Islander, 1% Hispanic American, 0.3% Native American, 9% international, 22% transferred in, 68% live on campus. *Retention:* 62% of 2006 full-time freshmen returned.

Freshmen *Admission:* 2,584 applied, 1,511 admitted, 884 enrolled. *Average high school GPA:* 3.17. *Test scores:* SAT critical reading scores over 500: 37%; SAT math scores over 500: 62%; SAT writing scores over 500: 39%; ACT scores over 18: 98%; SAT critical reading scores over 600: 9%; SAT math scores over 600: 23%; SAT writing scores over 600: 6%; ACT scores over 24: 28%; SAT critical reading scores over 700: 2%; SAT math scores over 700: 1%; ACT scores over 30: 5%.

Faculty *Total:* 598, 34% full-time, 56% with terminal degrees. *Student/faculty ratio:* 18:1.

Majors Accounting; applied art; art; art history, criticism and conservation; art teacher education; athletic training; biology/biological sciences; biology teacher education; broadcast journalism; business administration and management; business teacher education; cell biology and histology; chemistry; chemistry teacher education; Christian studies; clinical laboratory science/medical technology; computer/information technology services administration related; computer science; consumer merchandising/retailing management; criminal justice/law enforcement administration; criminology; dance; digital communication and media/multimedia; dramatic/theater arts; drawing; economics; education; educational/instructional media design; educational leadership and administration; education (K-12); elementary education; English; environmental science; fashion/apparel

COLLEGE DATA CENTER • MISSOURI

design; fashion merchandising; finance; fine/studio arts; French; French language teacher education; funeral service and mortuary science; gerontology; health and physical education; health/health care administration; history; history teacher education; human resources management; human services; international relations and affairs; journalism; kindergarten/preschool education; liberal arts and sciences/liberal studies; management information systems; marketing/marketing management; mass communication/media; mathematics; mathematics teacher education; middle school education; music; music teacher education; pastoral studies/counseling; physical education teaching and coaching; political science and government; pre-dentistry studies; pre-law studies; pre-medical studies; pre-nursing studies; pre-veterinary studies; psychology; public administration; public relations/image management; radio and television; religious studies; restaurant, culinary, and catering management; science teacher education; secondary education; social science teacher education; social work; sociology; Spanish; Spanish language teacher education; special education; sport and fitness administration/management; technology/industrial arts teacher education; youth ministry.

Academics *Calendar:* 4-1-4 for daytime programs; quarters and trimesters for evening programs. *Degrees:* bachelor's, master's, doctoral, post-master's, and postbachelor's certificates (education specialist). *Special study options:* academic remediation for entering students, accelerated degree program, adult/continuing education programs, advanced placement credit, cooperative education, double majors, freshman honors college, honors programs, independent study, internships, off-campus study, part-time degree program, services for LD students, student-designed majors, study abroad, summer session for credit. *ROTC:* Army (b), Air Force (c). *Unusual degree programs:* 3-2 engineering with University of Missouri-Columbia.

Computers on Campus 160 computers/terminals are available on campus for general student use. Students can access the following: free student e-mail accounts, WebCT. Campuswide network is available. Wireless service is available via libraries.

Student Life *Housing options:* men-only, women-only. Campus housing is university owned. Freshman campus housing is guaranteed. *Activities and organizations:* drama/theater group, student-run newspaper, radio and television station, choral group, marching band, Alpha Phi Omega, American Humanics, A Cross Between Campus Ministry, Campus YMCA, Alpha Sigma Phi, national fraternities, national sororities. *Campus security:* 24-hour emergency response devices and patrols, late-night transport/escort service, controlled dormitory access.

Athletics Member NAIA. *Intercollegiate sports:* baseball M (s), basketball M (s)/W (s), bowling M (s)/W (s), cheerleading M (s)/W (s), cross-country running M (s)/W (s), field hockey W (s), football M (s), golf M (s)/W (s), ice hockey M (s)/W (s), riflery M (s)/W (s), soccer M (s)/W (s), softball W (s), swimming and diving M (s)/W (s), tennis M (s)/W (s), track and field M (s)/W (s), volleyball M (s)/W (s), water polo M (s) (c)/W (s) (c), wrestling M (s). *Intramural sports:* basketball M/W, bowling M/W, football M/W, lacrosse M/W, soccer M/W, softball M/W, tennis M/W, volleyball M/W.

Standardized Tests *Required:* SAT or ACT (for admission).

Costs (2008–09) *Comprehensive fee:* $19,500 includes full-time tuition ($12,700), mandatory fees ($300), and room and board ($6500). Part-time tuition: $360 per credit hour. *College room only:* $3400.

Applying *Options:* early admission, deferred entrance. *Application fee:* $30. *Required:* high school transcript, minimum ACT score of 20 or minimum SAT score of 900. *Required for some:* essay or personal statement, 2 letters of recommendation, interview. *Recommended:* minimum 2.25 GPA, interview. *Application deadlines:* rolling (freshmen), rolling (transfers). *Notification:* continuous (freshmen), continuous (transfers).

Freshman Application Contact Lindenwood University, 209 South Kings Highway, St. Charles, MO 63301-1695. *Phone:* 636-949-4949.

See page 1438 for the College Close-Up.

LOGAN UNIVERSITY-COLLEGE OF CHIROPRACTIC

Chesterfield, Missouri **www.logan.edu/**

- **Independent** upper-level, founded 1935
- **Suburban** 111-acre campus with easy access to St. Louis
- **Endowment** $9.8 million
- **Coed** 121 undergraduate students, 60% full-time, 37% women, 63% men
- **Moderately difficult** entrance level

Undergraduates 72 full-time, 49 part-time. Students come from 6 other countries, 8% African American, 2% Asian American or Pacific Islander, 3% Hispanic American, 2% international.

Faculty *Total:* 96, 50% full-time.

Majors Biological and biomedical sciences related; biology/biological sciences.

Academics *Calendar:* trimesters. *Degrees:* bachelor's, master's, and first professional. *Special study options:* adult/continuing education programs, advanced placement credit, distance learning, independent study, internships, part-time degree program, services for LD students.

Computers on Campus 85 computers/terminals are available on campus for general student use. Students can access the following: campus intranet, computer help desk, free student e-mail accounts, online (class) grades, online (class) registration, online (class) schedules, on-line classes, course homepages, wireless technologies, Academic Software Solutions for teaching and learning. Campuswide network is available.

Student Life *Housing:* college housing not available. *Activities and organizations:* student-run newspaper, Pi Kappa Chi, Lambda Kappa Chi, Chiro Sigma, Student American Chiropractic Association, Omega Sigma Pi, national fraternities, national sororities. *Campus security:* 24-hour patrols, late-night transport/escort service. *Student services:* health clinic, personal/psychological counseling.

Athletics *Intramural sports:* basketball M/W, football M, golf M/W, ice hockey M, soccer M, softball M/W, swimming and diving M/W, tennis M/W, volleyball M/W.

Costs (2007–08) *Tuition:* $4500 full-time, $125 per credit hour part-time. Full-time tuition and fees vary according to program. Part-time tuition and fees vary according to program. *Required fees:* $330 full-time, $110 per term part-time. *Waivers:* employees or children of employees.

Financial Aid Of all full-time matriculated undergraduates who enrolled in 1999, 160 applied for aid, 160 were judged to have need, 130 had their need fully met. 130 Federal Work-Study jobs (averaging $2693). *Average percent of need met:* 100%. *Average need-based loan:* $3500. *Average need-based gift aid:* $3000.

Applying *Options:* electronic application, deferred entrance. *Application fee:* $40. *Application deadline:* rolling (transfers). *Notification:* continuous (transfers).

Application Contact Robert Smith, Associate Director of Admissions, Logan University-College of Chiropractic, 1851 Schoettler Road, Chesterfield, MO 63006-1065. *Phone:* 636-227-2100. *Toll-free phone:* 800-533-9210. *Fax:* 636-207-2425. *E-mail:* loganadm@logan.edu.

MARYVILLE UNIVERSITY OF SAINT LOUIS

St. Louis, Missouri **www.maryville.edu/**

- **Independent** comprehensive, founded 1872
- **Suburban** 130-acre campus
- **Endowment** $41.8 million
- **Coed** 2,801 undergraduate students, 60% full-time, 77% women, 23% men
- **Moderately difficult** entrance level, 65% of applicants were admitted

Undergraduates 1,674 full-time, 1,127 part-time. Students come from 22 states and territories, 10 other countries, 17% are from out of state, 7% African American, 2% Asian American or Pacific Islander, 1% Hispanic American, 0.6% Native American, 0.4% international, 17% transferred in, 30% live on campus. *Retention:* 82% of 2006 full-time freshmen returned.

Freshmen *Admission:* 1,167 applied, 764 admitted, 303 enrolled. *Average high school GPA:* 3.53. *Test scores:* ACT scores over 18: 100%; ACT scores over 24: 56%; ACT scores over 30: 8%.

Faculty *Total:* 369, 29% full-time, 40% with terminal degrees. *Student/faculty ratio:* 12:1.

Majors Accounting; accounting related; actuarial science; applied mathematics; art teacher education; biological and physical sciences; biology/biological sciences; biology teacher education; biomedical sciences; business administration and management; business/commerce; chemistry; chemistry teacher education; clinical laboratory science/medical technology; computer science; criminology; e-commerce; elementary education; English; English/language arts teacher education; environmental science; environmental studies; fine/studio arts; graphic design; health/medical preparatory programs related; health science; history; history teacher education; industrial and organizational psychology; interdisciplinary studies; interior design; kindergarten/preschool education; legal assistant/paralegal; liberal arts and sciences/liberal studies; management information systems; marketing/marketing management; mass communication/media; mathematics; mathematics teacher education; middle school education; music therapy; nursing (registered nurse training); psychology; public health; secondary education; social psychology; sociology; sport and fitness administration/management; vocational rehabilitation counseling.

Academics *Calendar:* semesters. *Degrees:* bachelor's, master's, and doctoral. *Special study options:* accelerated degree program, adult/continuing education programs, advanced placement credit, cooperative education, distance learning, double majors, freshman honors college, honors programs, independent study, internships, off-campus study, part-time degree program, services for LD students, student-designed majors, study abroad, summer session for credit. *ROTC:* Army (c). *Unusual degree programs:* 3-2 business administration; engineering with Washington University in St. Louis; social work with Saint Louis University; education.

Computers on Campus 425 computers/terminals are available on campus for general student use. Students can access the following: campus intranet, computer help desk, free student e-mail accounts, online (class) grades, online (class) registration, online (class) schedules, specialized software, university catalog. Campuswide network is available. Wireless service is available via entire campus.

Student Life *Housing options:* coed. Campus housing is university owned. *Activities and organizations:* drama/theater group, student-run newspaper, choral group, Campus Activity Board, Physical Therapy Club, Maryville University Student Government, Community Service Club, Campus Crusade for Christ. *Campus security:* 24-hour emergency response devices and patrols, late-night transport/escort service, controlled dormitory access, video security system in residence halls, self-defense and education programs. *Student services:* health clinic, personal/psychological counseling.

Athletics Member NCAA. All Division III. *Intercollegiate sports:* baseball M, basketball M/W, cross-country running M/W, golf M/W, soccer M/W, softball W, tennis M/W, track and field M/W, volleyball W. *Intramural sports:* basketball M/W, bowling M/W, football M/W, soccer M/W, softball M/W, table tennis M/W, volleyball M/W.

Standardized Tests *Required:* SAT or ACT (for admission).

Costs (2007–08) *Comprehensive fee:* $26,550 includes full-time tuition ($18,600), mandatory fees ($450), and room and board ($7500). Full-time tuition and fees vary according to course load. Part-time tuition: $565 per credit hour. Part-time tuition and fees vary according to class time. *Required fees:* $75 per term part-time. *Room and board:* Room and board charges vary according to housing facility. *Payment plans:* installment, deferred payment. *Waivers:* senior citizens and employees or children of employees.

Financial Aid Of all full-time matriculated undergraduates who enrolled in 2006, 1,415 applied for aid, 1,236 were judged to have need, 179 had their need fully met. 168 Federal Work-Study jobs (averaging $1613). 110 state and other part-time jobs (averaging $1632). In 2006, 351 non-need-based awards were made. *Average percent of need met:* 65%. *Average financial aid package:* $15,055. *Average need-based loan:* $6268. *Average need-based gift aid:* $8521. *Average non-need-based aid:* $5400. *Average indebtedness upon graduation:* $21,363.

Applying *Options:* electronic application, early admission, deferred entrance. *Application fee:* $25. *Required:* high school transcript, minimum 2.5 GPA. *Required for some:* essay or personal statement, letters of recommendation, interview, audition, portfolio. *Application deadlines:* 8/15 (freshmen), rolling (transfers). *Notification:* continuous (freshmen), continuous (transfers).

Freshman Application Contact Ms. Shani Lenore, Admissions Director, Maryville University of Saint Louis, 13550 Conway Road, St. Louis, MO 63141-7299. *Phone:* 314-529-9350. *Toll-free phone:* 800-627-9855. *Fax:* 314-529-9927. *E-mail:* admissions@maryville.edu.

MESSENGER COLLEGE

Joplin, Missouri **www.messengercollege.edu/**

- **Independent Pentecostal** 4-year, founded 1987
- **Suburban** 16-acre campus with easy access to Springfield
- **Endowment** $289,532
- **Coed**
- **Moderately difficult** entrance level

Faculty *Student/faculty ratio:* 8:1.

Academics *Calendar:* semesters. *Degrees:* associate and bachelor's.

Student Life *Campus security:* 24-hour emergency response devices, student patrols.

Athletics Member NCCAA.

Standardized Tests *Required:* SAT or ACT (for admission).

Financial Aid Of all full-time matriculated undergraduates who enrolled in 2006, 84 applied for aid, 80 were judged to have need. 18 Federal Work-Study jobs (averaging $493). *Average percent of need met:* 49. *Average financial aid package:* $7655. *Average need-based loan:* $4002. *Average need-based gift aid:* $2696. *Average indebtedness upon graduation:* $20,344.

Applying *Options:* electronic application. *Application fee:* $35. *Required:* essay or personal statement, high school transcript, minimum 2.0 GPA, 3 letters of recommendation, health form. *Required for some:* interview.

Freshman Application Contact Ron Cannon, Vice President of Academic Affairs, Messenger College, 300 East 50th, Joplin, MO 64804. *Phone:* 417-624-7070 Ext. 108. *Toll-free phone:* 800-385-8940. *Fax:* 417-624-5070. *E-mail:* info@messengercollege.edu.

METRO BUSINESS COLLEGE

Cape Girardeau, Missouri **www.metrobusinesscollege.edu/**

Director of Admissions Ms. Kyla Evans, Admissions Director, Metro Business College, 1732 North Kingshighway, Cape Girardeau, MO 63701. *Phone:* 573-334-9181. *Fax:* 573-334-0617.

MIDWEST UNIVERSITY

Wentzville, Missouri

MISSOURI BAPTIST UNIVERSITY

St. Louis, Missouri **www.mobap.edu/**

- **Independent Southern Baptist** comprehensive, founded 1964
- **Suburban** 65-acre campus
- **Endowment** $2.9 million
- **Coed** 3,406 undergraduate students, 33% full-time, 60% women, 40% men
- **Moderately difficult** entrance level, 72% of applicants were admitted

Undergraduates 1,140 full-time, 2,266 part-time. Students come from 29 states and territories, 20 other countries, 7% are from out of state, 9% African American, 0.5% Asian American or Pacific Islander, 2% Hispanic American, 0.6% Native American, 4% international, 7% transferred in, 14% live on campus. *Retention:* 70% of 2006 full-time freshmen returned.

Freshmen *Admission:* 432 applied, 313 admitted, 186 enrolled. *Average high school GPA:* 3.11. *Test scores:* ACT scores over 18: 90%; ACT scores over 24: 33%; ACT scores over 30: 5%.

Faculty *Total:* 203, 33% full-time, 28% with terminal degrees. *Student/faculty ratio:* 14:1.

Majors Accounting; behavioral sciences; biology/biological sciences; biotechnology; business administration and management; business administration, management and operations related; business teacher education; chemistry; child development; Christian studies; communication/speech communication and rhetoric; computer and information sciences; criminal justice/safety; elementary education; English; health teacher education; history; human services; kindergarten/preschool education; marketing/marketing management; mathematics; middle school education; multi-/interdisciplinary studies related; music performance; music teacher education; nursing science; operations management; physical education teaching and coaching; psychology; religious education; religious/sacred music; religious studies; science teacher education; social sciences; sport and fitness administration/management; theology; theology and religious vocations related.

Academics *Calendar:* semesters. *Degrees:* certificates, associate, bachelor's, master's, post-master's, and postbachelor's certificates. *Special study options:* accelerated degree program, adult/continuing education programs, advanced placement credit, distance learning, double majors, independent study, internships, off-campus study, part-time degree program, services for LD students, student-designed majors, study abroad, summer session for credit. *ROTC:* Army (c). *Unusual degree programs:* 3-2 engineering with University of Missouri-Columbia.

Computers on Campus 122 computers/terminals are available on campus for general student use. Students can access the following: campus intranet, computer help desk, free student e-mail accounts. Campuswide network is available. Wireless service is available via entire campus.

Student Life *Housing options:* men-only, women-only. Campus housing is university owned and leased by the school. *Activities and organizations:* drama/theater group, student-run radio station, choral group, Baptist Collegiate Ministry, Students in Free Enterprise (SIFE), Missouri State Teacher's Association, Fellowship of Christian Athletes, Ministerial Alliance. *Campus security:* 24-hour emergency response devices and patrols, late-night transport/escort service, controlled dormitory access, self-defense classes. *Student services:* personal/psychological counseling.

Athletics Member NAIA. *Intercollegiate sports:* baseball M (s), basketball M (s)/W (s), bowling M (s) (c)/W (c), cross-country running M (s)/W (s), golf M (s)/W, lacrosse M (s) (c)/W (s) (c), soccer M (s)/W (s), softball W (s), tennis M (s)/W (s), track and field M (s)/W (s), volleyball M (s) (c)/W (s), wrestling M (s). *Intramural sports:* basketball M/W, football M/W, soccer M/W, softball M/W, volleyball M/W.

Standardized Tests *Required for some:* SAT or ACT (for admission).

Costs (2007–08) *Comprehensive fee:* $22,128 includes full-time tuition ($15,120), mandatory fees ($658), and room and board ($6350). Full-time tuition and fees vary according to course load and location. Part-time tuition: $525 per credit. Part-time tuition and fees vary according to course load and location. *Required fees:* $12 per credit part-time, $25 per term part-time. *Room and board:* Room and board charges vary according to housing facility. *Payment plan:* installment. *Waivers:* children of alumni, senior citizens, and employees or children of employees.

Financial Aid Of all full-time matriculated undergraduates who enrolled in 2005, 1,509 applied for aid, 1,509 were judged to have need. 68 Federal Work-Study jobs (averaging $1224). 15 state and other part-time jobs (averaging $3394). In 2005, 112 non-need-based awards were made. *Average percent of need met:* 27%. *Average financial aid package:* $8120. *Average need-based loan:* $3959 *Average need-based gift aid:* $5116. *Average non-need-based aid:* $3004. *Average indebtedness upon graduation:* $18,358.

Applying *Application fee:* $30. *Required:* high school transcript, minimum 2.0 GPA, letters of recommendation, interview. *Application deadlines:* rolling (freshmen), rolling (transfers). *Notification:* continuous (freshmen), continuous (transfers).

Freshman Application Contact Mr. Terry Dale Cruse, Director of Admissions, Missouri Baptist University, One College Park Drive, St. Louis, MO 63141-8660. *Phone:* 877-434-1115. *Toll-free phone:* 877-434-1115 Ext. 2290. *Fax:* 314-434-7596. *E-mail:* admissions@mobap.edu.

MISSOURI SOUTHERN STATE UNIVERSITY

Joplin, Missouri **www.mssu.edu/**

- **State-supported** comprehensive, founded 1937
- **Small-town** 350-acre campus
- **Endowment** $25.0 million
- **Coed** 5,563 undergraduate students, 71% full-time, 60% women, 40% men
- **Moderately difficult** entrance level, 99% of applicants were admitted

Undergraduates 3,933 full-time, 1,630 part-time. Students come from 31 states and territories, 34 other countries, 15% are from out of state, 3% African American, 1% Asian American or Pacific Islander, 2% Hispanic American, 2% Native American, 2% international, 9% transferred in, 12% live on campus. *Retention:* 62% of 2006 full-time freshmen returned.

Freshmen *Admission:* 1,425 applied, 1,404 admitted, 818 enrolled. *Average high school GPA:* 3.24. *Test scores:* ACT scores over 18: 94%; ACT scores over 24: 65%; ACT scores over 30: 11%.

Faculty *Total:* 295, 72% full-time, 47% with terminal degrees. *Student/faculty ratio:* 16:1.

Majors Accounting; art; biochemistry; biology/biological sciences; business/commerce; chemistry; clinical laboratory science/medical technology; communication/speech communication and rhetoric; computer and information sciences; computer programming; criminal justice/law enforcement administration; criminal justice/police science; dental hygiene; dramatic/theater arts; education; elementary education; engineering technologies related; English; French; German; health and medical administrative services related; health and physical education related; health professions related; history; industrial engineering; international relations and affairs; legal professions and studies related; liberal arts and sciences/liberal studies; machine shop technology; mathematics; medical radiologic technology; music performance; nursing (registered nurse training); physics; political science and government; secondary education; sociology; Spanish.

Academics *Calendar:* semesters. *Degrees:* certificates, associate, bachelor's, and master's. *Special study options:* academic remediation for entering students, accelerated degree program, adult/continuing education programs, advanced placement credit, cooperative education, distance learning, double majors, English as a second language, external degree program, honors programs, independent study, internships, off-campus study, part-time degree program, services for LD students, study abroad, summer session for credit.

Computers on Campus 560 computers/terminals and 900 ports are available on campus for general student use. Students can access the following: campus intranet, computer help desk, free student e-mail accounts, online (class) grades, online (class) registration, online (class) schedules. Campuswide network is available. 100% of college-owned or -operated housing units are wired for high-speed Internet access. Wireless service is available via entire campus.

Student Life *Housing:* on-campus residence required for freshman year. *Options:* coed, men-only, women-only, disabled students. Campus housing is university owned. Freshman campus housing is guaranteed. *Activities and organizations:* drama/theater group, student-run newspaper, radio and television station, choral group, marching band, Koinonia, Campus Activities Board, Residence Hall Association, Baptist Student Union, Student Senate, national fraternities, national sororities. *Campus security:* 24-hour emergency response devices and patrols, late-night transport/escort service, controlled dormitory access, security at campus events, emergency vehicle assistance, safety awareness information to students. *Student services:* health clinic, personal/psychological counseling.

Athletics Member NCAA. All Division II. *Intercollegiate sports:* baseball M (s), basketball M (s)/W (s), cross-country running M (s)/W (s), football M (s), golf M (s), soccer M (s)/W (s), softball W (s), tennis W (s), track and field M (s)/W (s), volleyball W (s). *Intramural sports:* baseball M/W, basketball M/W, football M/W, golf M/W, racquetball M/W, soccer M/W, softball M/W, swimming and diving M/W, table tennis M/W, tennis M/W, ultimate Frisbee M/W, volleyball M/W.

Standardized Tests *Required:* SAT or ACT (for admission). *Required for some:* Michigan Test of English Language Proficiency. *Recommended:* ACT (for admission).

Costs (2008–09) *Tuition:* state resident $4290 full-time, $143 per credit part-time; nonresident $8580 full-time, $286 per credit part-time. *Required fees:* $526 full-time, $83 per term part-time. *Room and board:* $5440.

Financial Aid Of all full-time matriculated undergraduates who enrolled in 2006, 3,209 applied for aid, 2,804 were judged to have need. 149 Federal Work-Study jobs (averaging $1575). 438 state and other part-time jobs (averaging $1401). In 2006, 602 non-need-based awards were made. *Average percent of need met:* 69%. *Average financial aid package:* $6722. *Average need-based loan:* $3249. *Average need-based gift aid:* $4636. *Average non-need-based aid:* $2560. *Average indebtedness upon graduation:* $16,137.

Applying *Options:* electronic application, deferred entrance. *Application fee:* $15. *Required:* high school transcript, standardized test scores; class rank. *Required for some:* 2 letters of recommendation. *Application deadlines:* 8/1 (freshmen), 8/1 (transfers). *Notification:* continuous (freshmen), continuous (transfers).

Freshman Application Contact Mr. Derek Skaggs, Director of Enrollment Services, Missouri Southern State University, 3950 East Newman Road, Joplin, MO 64801-1595. *Phone:* 417-625-9537. *Toll-free phone:* 866-818-MSSU. *Fax:* 417-659-4429. *E-mail:* admissions@mssu.edu.

MISSOURI STATE UNIVERSITY

Springfield, Missouri **www.missouristate.edu/**

- **State-supported** comprehensive, founded 1905
- **Suburban** 225-acre campus
- **Endowment** $52.1 million
- **Coed** 16,255 undergraduate students, 78% full-time, 56% women, 44% men
- **Moderately difficult** entrance level, 75% of applicants were admitted

Undergraduates 12,760 full-time, 3,495 part-time. Students come from 47 states and territories, 81 other countries, 6% are from out of state, 3% African American, 2% Asian American or Pacific Islander, 2% Hispanic American, 0.9% Native American, 2% international, 8% transferred in, 25% live on campus. *Retention:* 74% of 2006 full-time freshmen returned.

Freshmen *Admission:* 7,677 applied, 5,755 admitted, 2,649 enrolled. *Average high school GPA:* 3.44. *Test scores:* ACT scores over 18: 98%; ACT scores over 24: 49%; ACT scores over 30: 8%.

Faculty *Total:* 1,047, 69% full-time, 59% with terminal degrees. *Student/faculty ratio:* 19:1.

Majors Accounting; agribusiness; agricultural teacher education; agriculture; agronomy and crop science; ancient studies; animal sciences; anthropology; apparel and textiles; art; art history, criticism and conservation; art teacher education; athletic training; audiology and speech-language pathology; biology/biological sciences; biology teacher education; business administration and management; business administration, management and operations related; business/commerce; business teacher education; cartography; cell and molecular biology; chemistry; chemistry teacher education; city/urban, community and regional planning; clinical laboratory science/medical technology; communication/speech communication and rhetoric; computer science; construction management; criminology; dance; design and visual communications; dietetics; dramatic/theater arts; early childhood education; economics; education (specific subject areas) related; elementary education; engineering/industrial management; English; English/language arts teacher education; entrepreneurship; family and consumer

COLLEGE DATA CENTER • MISSOURI

sciences/home economics teacher education; finance; fine/studio arts; French; French language teacher education; geography; geology/earth science; German; German language teacher education; gerontology; history; history teacher education; horticultural science; hospitality administration; housing and human environments; human development and family studies; insurance; intermedia/multimedia; journalism; Latin; logistics and materials management; management information systems; marketing/marketing management; mass communication/media; mathematics; mathematics teacher education; middle school education; molecular biology; music; music performance; music teacher education; nursing (registered nurse training); parks, recreation and leisure; philosophy; physical education teaching and coaching; physical science technologies related; physics; physics teacher education; political science and government; psychology; public administration; radiologic technology/science; religious studies; respiratory care therapy; science teacher education; social work; sociology; Spanish; Spanish language teacher education; special education; technical and business writing; visual and performing arts; wildlife and wildlands science and management.

Academics *Calendar:* semesters. *Degrees:* bachelor's, master's, doctoral, post-master's, and postbachelor's certificates. *Special study options:* accelerated degree program, advanced placement credit, cooperative education, distance learning, double majors, English as a second language, freshman honors college, honors programs, independent study, internships, off-campus study, part-time degree program, services for LD students, student-designed majors, study abroad, summer session for credit. *ROTC:* Army (b).

Computers on Campus 1,800 computers/terminals are available on campus for general student use. Students can access the following: online (class) registration. Campuswide network is available.

Student Life *Housing:* on-campus residence required for freshman year. *Options:* coed, disabled students. Campus housing is university owned. Freshman campus housing is guaranteed. *Activities and organizations:* drama/theater group, student-run newspaper, radio and television station, choral group, marching band, Residence Hall Association, Campus Crusade, Gamma Sigma Sigma, Student Government Association, national fraternities, national sororities. *Campus security:* 24-hour emergency response devices and patrols, late-night transport/escort service, controlled dormitory access, on-campus police substation. *Student services:* health clinic, personal/psychological counseling, legal services.

Athletics Member NCAA. All Division I except football (Division I-AA). *Intercollegiate sports:* baseball M (s), basketball M (s)/W (s), bowling M (c)/W (c), cross-country running W (s), equestrian sports M (c)/W (c), field hockey W (s), golf M (s)/W (s), ice hockey M (c), lacrosse M (c), racquetball M (c)/W (c), soccer M (s)/W (s), softball W (s), swimming and diving M (s)/W (s), track and field W (s), ultimate Frisbee M (c)/W (c), volleyball M (c)/W (s), wrestling M (c). *Intramural sports:* basketball M/W, bowling M/W, football M/W, golf M/W, racquetball M/W, soccer M/W, softball M/W, table tennis M/W, tennis M/W, track and field W, ultimate Frisbee M/W, volleyball M/W, weight lifting M/W.

Standardized Tests *Required:* SAT or ACT (for admission).

Costs (2007–08) *Tuition:* state resident $5988 full-time, $179 per credit hour part-time; nonresident $11,088 full-time, $349 per credit hour part-time. Full-time tuition and fees vary according to course load, degree level, location, and program. Part-time tuition and fees vary according to course load, degree level, location, and program. *Required fees:* $618 full-time. *Room and board:* $5312. Room and board charges vary according to board plan and housing facility. *Payment plans:* tuition prepayment, deferred payment. *Waivers:* children of alumni, senior citizens, and employees or children of employees.

Financial Aid Of all full-time matriculated undergraduates who enrolled in 2007, 15,060 applied for aid, 9,058 were judged to have need, 1,801 had their need fully met. 449 Federal Work-Study jobs (averaging $1748). 1,336 state and other part-time jobs (averaging $2924). In 2007, 4937 non-need-based awards were made. *Average percent of need met:* 55%. *Average financial aid package:* $6579. *Average need-based loan:* $3963. *Average need-based gift aid:* $4467. *Average non-need-based aid:* $7332. *Average indebtedness upon graduation:* $16,921.

Applying *Options:* electronic application, deferred entrance. *Application fee:* $35. *Required:* high school transcript. *Required for some:* essay or personal statement, letters of recommendation, interview. *Application deadlines:* 7/20 (freshmen), 7/20 (transfers). *Notification:* continuous (freshmen), continuous (transfers).

Freshman Application Contact Ms. Jill Duncan, Associate Director of Admissions, Missouri State University, 901 South National, Springfield, MO 65804. *Phone:* 417-836-5517. *Toll-free phone:* 800-492-7900. *Fax:* 417-836-6334. *E-mail:* info@missouristate.edu.

MISSOURI TECH

St. Louis, Missouri **www.motech.edu/**

Freshman Application Contact Mr. Bob Honaker, Director of Admissions, Missouri Tech, 1167 Corporate Lake Drive, St. Louis, MO 63132. *Phone:* 314-569-3600. *Fax:* 314-569-1167.

MISSOURI UNIVERSITY OF SCIENCE AND TECHNOLOGY

Rolla, Missouri **www.mst.edu/**

- **State-supported** university, founded 1870, part of University of Missouri System
- **Small-town** 284-acre campus
- **Endowment** $107.5 million
- **Coed, primarily men** 4,753 undergraduate students, 92% full-time, 22% women, 78% men
- **Very difficult** entrance level, 67% of applicants were admitted

Undergraduates 4,375 full-time, 378 part-time. Students come from 46 states and territories, 27 other countries, 20% are from out of state, 5% African American, 2% Asian American or Pacific Islander, 2% Hispanic American, 0.6% Native American, 3% international, 6% transferred in, 58% live on campus. *Retention:* 87% of 2006 full-time freshmen returned.

Freshmen *Admission:* 2,317 applied, 1,563 admitted, 977 enrolled. *Average high school GPA:* 3.71. *Test scores:* SAT math scores over 500: 95%; ACT scores over 18: 100%; SAT math scores over 600: 71%; ACT scores over 24: 84%; SAT math scores over 700: 21%; ACT scores over 30: 33%.

Faculty *Total:* 403, 84% full-time, 79% with terminal degrees. *Student/faculty ratio:* 15:1.

Majors Aerospace, aeronautical and astronautical engineering; agricultural/biological engineering and bioengineering; applied mathematics; architectural engineering; biology/biological sciences; business administration and management; business/commerce; ceramic sciences and engineering; chemical engineering; chemistry; civil engineering; computer and information sciences and support services related; computer engineering; computer science; economics; electrical, electronics and communications engineering; engineering/industrial management; English; environmental/environmental health engineering; geological/geophysical engineering; geology/earth science; geophysics and seismology; history; industrial engineering; information science/studies; manufacturing engineering; materials engineering; mechanical engineering; metallurgical engineering; mining and mineral engineering; nuclear engineering; petroleum engineering; philosophy; physics; pre-dentistry studies; pre-law studies; pre-medical studies; psychology; secondary education; systems engineering.

Academics *Calendar:* semesters. *Degrees:* bachelor's, master's, doctoral, and postbachelor's certificates. *Special study options:* academic remediation for entering students, accelerated degree program, adult/continuing education programs, advanced placement credit, cooperative education, distance learning, double majors, English as a second language, freshman honors college, honors programs, independent study, internships, off-campus study, part-time degree program, services for LD students, study abroad, summer session for credit. *ROTC:* Army (b), Navy (c), Air Force (b).

Computers on Campus 980 computers/terminals and 25 ports are available on campus for general student use. Students can access the following: campus intranet, computer help desk, free student e-mail accounts, online (class) grades, online (class) registration, online (class) schedules. Campuswide network is available. 100% of college-owned or -operated housing units are wired for high-speed Internet access. Wireless service is available via entire campus.

Student Life *Housing:* on-campus residence required through sophomore year. *Options:* coed, men-only, women-only. Campus housing is university owned and leased by the school. *Activities and organizations:* drama/theater group, student-run newspaper, radio station, choral group, marching band, student government, service organizations, academic organizations, national fraternities, national sororities. *Campus security:* 24-hour emergency response devices and patrols, student patrols, late-night transport/escort service, controlled dormitory access, crime prevention programs. *Student services:* health clinic, personal/psychological counseling, legal services.

Athletics Member NCAA. All Division II. *Intercollegiate sports:* baseball M (s), basketball M (s)/W (s), cross-country running M (s)/W (s), football M (s), soccer M (s)/W (s), softball W (s), swimming and diving M (s), track and field M (s)/W (s), volleyball W. *Intramural sports:* badminton M/W, basketball M/W, bowling M/W, cross-country running M/W, football M, golf M/W, racquetball

M/W, soccer M/W, softball M/W, swimming and diving M/W, table tennis M/W, tennis M/W, track and field M/W, volleyball M/W, water polo M, weight lifting M/W.

Standardized Tests *Required:* SAT or ACT (for admission).

Costs (2008–09) *Tuition:* state resident $7077 full-time, $236 per credit hour part-time; nonresident $17,733 full-time, $591 per credit hour part-time. *Required fees:* $1095 full-time. *Room and board:* $6660.

Financial Aid Of all full-time matriculated undergraduates who enrolled in 2006, 2,799 applied for aid, 2,594 were judged to have need, 581 had their need fully met. 198 Federal Work-Study jobs (averaging $1180). 1,185 state and other part-time jobs (averaging $1338). In 2006, 871 non-need-based awards were made. *Average percent of need met:* 46%. *Average financial aid package:* $8675. *Average need-based loan:* $4971. *Average need-based gift aid:* $4640. *Average non-need-based aid:* $6180.

Applying *Options:* electronic application, early admission, early action, deferred entrance. *Application fee:* $35. *Required:* high school transcript. *Application deadlines:* 7/1 (freshmen), 7/1 (transfers). *Notification:* continuous (freshmen), continuous (transfers).

Director of Admissions Ms. Lynn Stichnote, Director of Admissions, Missouri University of Science and Technology, 106 Parker Hall, Rolla, MO 65409. *Phone:* 573-341-4164. *Toll-free phone:* 800-522-0938. *E-mail:* umrolla@mst.edu.

MISSOURI VALLEY COLLEGE

Marshall, Missouri **www.moval.edu/**

- **Independent** 4-year, founded 1889, affiliated with Presbyterian Church
- **Small-town** 140-acre campus with easy access to Kansas City
- **Endowment** $3.4 million
- **Coed** 1,639 undergraduate students, 85% full-time, 43% women, 57% men
- **Minimally difficult** entrance level, 57% of applicants were admitted

Undergraduates 1,394 full-time, 245 part-time. Students come from 42 states and territories, 29 other countries, 28% are from out of state, 17% African American, 4% Asian American or Pacific Islander, 6% Hispanic American, 0.3% Native American, 10% international, 8% transferred in, 73% live on campus. *Retention:* 55% of 2006 full-time freshmen returned.

Freshmen *Admission:* 1,543 applied, 876 admitted, 444 enrolled. *Average high school GPA:* 2.86. *Test scores:* SAT critical reading scores over 500: 29%; SAT math scores over 500: 36%; ACT scores over 18: 68%; SAT critical reading scores over 600: 3%; SAT math scores over 600: 4%; ACT scores over 24: 9%; ACT scores over 30: 1%.

Faculty *Total:* 90, 66% full-time, 44% with terminal degrees. *Student/faculty ratio:* 18:1.

Majors Accounting; art; athletic training; biology/biological sciences; computer science; criminal justice/law enforcement administration; dramatic/theater arts; economics; education; elementary education; English; health teacher education; history; human services; marketing/marketing management; mass communication/media; mathematics; music; parks, recreation and leisure; parks, recreation and leisure facilities management; philosophy; physical education teaching and coaching; political science and government; pre-dentistry studies; pre-law studies; pre-medical studies; pre-nursing studies; pre-pharmacy studies; pre-veterinary studies; psychology; public administration; religious studies; science teacher education; secondary education; sociology; special education; speech and rhetoric; sport and fitness administration/management.

Academics *Calendar:* semesters plus 2 summer sessions. *Degrees:* associate and bachelor's. *Special study options:* academic remediation for entering students, adult/continuing education programs, advanced placement credit, cooperative education, distance learning, double majors, English as a second language, independent study, internships, part-time degree program, services for LD students, student-designed majors, study abroad, summer session for credit. *ROTC:* Army (b).

Computers on Campus 250 computers/terminals are available on campus for general student use. Students can access the following: campus intranet, computer help desk, free student e-mail accounts, online (class) grades, online (class) registration, online (class) schedules. Campuswide network is available. Wireless service is available via computer centers, computer labs, learning centers, libraries.

Student Life *Housing options:* coed, men-only, women-only. Campus housing is university owned. Freshman campus housing is guaranteed. *Activities and organizations:* drama/theater group, student-run newspaper, radio and television station, choral group, student government, Valley players, American Humanics, national fraternities, national sororities. *Campus security:* 24-hour emergency response devices, student patrols, late-night transport/escort service, controlled dormitory access, evening patrol by trained security personnel. *Student services:* health clinic, personal/psychological counseling.

Athletics Member NAIA. *Intercollegiate sports:* baseball M (s), basketball M (s)/W (s), cheerleading M (s)/W (s), cross-country running M (s)/W (s), football M (s), golf M (s)/W (s), soccer M (s)/W (s), softball W (s), tennis M (s)/W (s), track and field M (s)/W (s), volleyball M (s)/W (s), wrestling M (s)/W (s). *Intramural sports:* badminton M/W, baseball M, basketball M/W, bowling M/W, football M/W, soccer M/W, softball M/W, table tennis M/W, tennis M/W, volleyball M/W.

Standardized Tests *Required:* SAT or ACT (for admission).

Costs (2008–09) *Comprehensive fee:* $22,000 includes full-time tuition ($15,450), mandatory fees ($500), and room and board ($6050). Part-time tuition: $350 per credit hour. *College room only:* $3100.

Financial Aid Of all full-time matriculated undergraduates who enrolled in 2006, 1,176 applied for aid, 940 were judged to have need, 342 had their need fully met. 176 Federal Work-Study jobs (averaging $1285). 463 state and other part-time jobs (averaging $1248). In 2006, 444 non-need-based awards were made. *Average percent of need met:* 78%. *Average financial aid package:* $12,175. *Average need-based loan:* $3200. *Average need-based gift aid:* $10,510. *Average non-need-based aid:* $7809. *Average indebtedness upon graduation:* $17,600.

Applying *Options:* electronic application, early admission, deferred entrance. *Application fee:* $15. *Required:* high school transcript. *Required for some:* essay or personal statement, 3 letters of recommendation, interview. *Recommended:* minimum 2.0 GPA, interview. *Application deadlines:* rolling (freshmen), rolling (transfers). *Notification:* continuous (freshmen), continuous (transfers).

Freshman Application Contact Ms. Debi Bultmann, Admissions Office Manager, Missouri Valley College, Admissions Office, 500 East College, Marshall, MO 65340. *Phone:* 660-831-4125. *Fax:* 660-831-4233. *E-mail:* admissions@moval.edu.

MISSOURI WESTERN STATE UNIVERSITY

St. Joseph, Missouri **www.missouriwestern.edu/**

- **State-supported** 4-year, founded 1915
- **Suburban** 744-acre campus with easy access to Kansas City
- **Endowment** $2.6 million
- **Coed**
- **Noncompetitive** entrance level

Missouri Western State University affords high-quality instruction with a wide range of programs, affordable costs, scholarships, and a well-rounded university experience. A friendly, personal atmosphere pervades both classroom and campus. The University serves a four-state area and attracts students nationwide. Its small student-faculty ratio allows hands-on emphasis in all academic areas.

Faculty *Student/faculty ratio:* 19:1.

Academics *Calendar:* semesters. *Degrees:* certificates, associate, and bachelor's.

Student Life *Campus security:* 24-hour emergency response devices and patrols, student patrols, late-night transport/escort service, controlled dormitory access.

Athletics Member NCAA. All Division II.

Costs (2007–08) *Tuition:* state resident $4800 full-time, $160 per credit part-time; nonresident $8760 full-time, $292 per credit part-time. *Required fees:* $530 full-time, $18 per credit part-time, $30 per term part-time. *Room and board:* $5784. Room and board charges vary according to board plan and housing facility. *Payment plans:* installment, deferred payment.

Financial Aid *Average indebtedness upon graduation:* $15,200.

Applying *Options:* early admission. *Application fee:* $15. *Required:* high school transcript.

Freshman Application Contact Mr. Howard McCauley, Director of Admissions, Missouri Western State University, 4525 Downs Drive, St. Joseph, MO 64507-2294. *Phone:* 816-271-4267. *Toll-free phone:* 800-662-7041 Ext. 60. *Fax:* 816-271-5833. *E-mail:* admission@missouriwestern.edu.

NATIONAL AMERICAN UNIVERSITY

Kansas City, Missouri **www.national.edu/**

Director of Admissions Chuck Wolfe, Vice President, National American University, 4200 Blue Ridge Boulevard, Kansas City, MO 64133-1612. *Phone:* 816-353-4554. *Fax:* 816-353-1176. *E-mail:* jjoy@national.edu.

NORTHWEST MISSOURI STATE UNIVERSITY

Maryville, Missouri www.nwmissouri.edu/

- **State-supported** comprehensive, founded 1905, part of Missouri Coordinating Board for Higher Education
- **Small-town** 240-acre campus with easy access to Kansas City
- **Coed** 5,661 undergraduate students, 89% full-time, 56% women, 44% men
- **Moderately difficult** entrance level, 75% of applicants were admitted

Undergraduates 5,037 full-time, 624 part-time. Students come from 38 states and territories, 25 other countries, 26% are from out of state, 4% African American, 0.9% Asian American or Pacific Islander, 2% Hispanic American, 0.5% Native American, 2% international, 5% transferred in, 40% live on campus. *Retention:* 73% of 2006 full-time freshmen returned.

Freshmen *Admission:* 4,433 applied, 3,306 admitted, 1,534 enrolled. *Average high school GPA:* 3.33. *Test scores:* SAT critical reading scores over 500: 56%; SAT math scores over 500: 66%; ACT scores over 18: 91%; SAT critical reading scores over 600: 13%; SAT math scores over 600: 16%; ACT scores over 24: 32%; SAT math scores over 700: 3%; ACT scores over 30: 3%.

Faculty *Total:* 303, 83% full-time, 59% with terminal degrees. *Student/faculty ratio:* 21:1.

Majors Accounting; administrative assistant and secretarial science; advertising; agricultural business and management; agricultural economics; agricultural mechanization; agricultural teacher education; agriculture; agronomy and crop science; animal sciences; Army R.O.T.C./military science; art; art teacher education; behavioral sciences; biological and physical sciences; biology/biological sciences; biomedical technology; botany/plant biology; broadcast journalism; business administration and management; business/managerial economics; business teacher education; chemistry; child development; clinical laboratory science/medical technology; clinical/medical laboratory technology; clothing/textiles; commercial and advertising art; computer management; computer programming; computer science; consumer merchandising/retailing management; counselor education/school counseling and guidance; data processing and data processing technology; developmental and child psychology; dietetics; dramatic/theater arts; drawing; ecology; economics; education; educational leadership and administration; elementary education; English; family and consumer economics related; family and consumer sciences/home economics teacher education; family and consumer sciences/human sciences; farm and ranch management; fashion/apparel design; fashion merchandising; fiber, textile and weaving arts; finance; fine/studio arts; food science; foods, nutrition, and wellness; forestry; French; geography; geology/earth science; health science; health teacher education; history; horticultural science; hospitality and recreation marketing; humanities; information science/studies; interior design; international business/trade/commerce; journalism; kindergarten/preschool education; landscape architecture; legal administrative assistant/secretary; literature; management information systems; marketing/marketing management; mass communication/media; mathematics; metal and jewelry arts; middle school education; music; music management and merchandising; music teacher education; natural resources/conservation; parks, recreation and leisure; philosophy; physical education teaching and coaching; physical sciences; physics; piano and organ; political science and government; predentistry studies; pre-law studies; pre-medical studies; pre-veterinary studies; psychology; public administration; public relations/image management; radio and television; reading teacher education; Romance languages; science teacher education; sculpture; secondary education; social sciences; sociology; Spanish; special education; speech and rhetoric; sport and fitness administration/management; therapeutic recreation; violin, viola, guitar and other stringed instruments; voice and opera; wildlife and wildlands science and management; wildlife biology; wind/percussion instruments; zoology/animal biology.

Academics *Calendar:* trimesters. *Degrees:* certificates, bachelor's, master's, and post-master's certificates. *Special study options:* academic remediation for entering students, accelerated degree program, advanced placement credit, distance learning, double majors, English as a second language, honors programs, independent study, internships, off-campus study, part-time degree program, services for LD students, study abroad, summer session for credit. *ROTC:* Army (b).

Computers on Campus 5 computers/terminals and 4,000 ports are available on campus for general student use. Students can access the following: campus intranet, computer help desk, free student e-mail accounts, online (class) grades, online (class) registration, online (class) schedules, online courses with library and databases. Campuswide network is available. 100% of college-owned or -operated housing units are wired for high-speed Internet access. Wireless service is available via learning centers, libraries, student centers.

Student Life *Housing:* on-campus residence required for freshman year. *Options:* coed, disabled students. Campus housing is university owned. Freshman campus housing is guaranteed. *Activities and organizations:* drama/theater group, student-run newspaper, radio and television station, choral group, marching band, student government, national fraternities, national sororities. *Campus security:* 24-hour emergency response devices and patrols, student patrols, late-night transport/escort service, controlled dormitory access, security personnel are all police officers. *Student services:* health clinic, women's center.

Athletics Member NCAA. All Division II. *Intercollegiate sports:* baseball M (s), basketball M (s)/W (s), cross-country running M (s)/W (s), football M (s), soccer W (s), softball W (s), tennis M (s)/W (s), track and field M (s)/W (s), volleyball W (s). *Intramural sports:* badminton M/W, basketball M/W, cross-country running M/W, football M/W, golf M/W, racquetball M/W, skiing (cross-country) M/W, soccer W (c), softball M/W, swimming and diving M/W, table tennis M/W, tennis M/W, track and field M/W, volleyball M/W, wrestling M (c).

Standardized Tests *Required:* SAT or ACT (for admission).

Costs (2007–08) *Tuition:* state resident $6228 full-time, $208 per credit hour part-time; nonresident $10,686 full-time, $356 per credit hour part-time. Full-time tuition and fees vary according to reciprocity agreements. *Required fees:* $210 full-time. *Room and board:* $6276; room only: $4006. Room and board charges vary according to board plan and housing facility. *Payment plans:* installment, deferred payment. *Waivers:* senior citizens and employees or children of employees.

Financial Aid Of all full-time matriculated undergraduates who enrolled in 2001, 3,320 applied for aid, 2,455 were judged to have need, 838 had their need fully met. 402 Federal Work-Study jobs (averaging $1374). 595 state and other part-time jobs (averaging $970). In 2001, 398 non-need-based awards were made. *Average percent of need met:* 82%. *Average financial aid package:* $6047. *Average need-based loan:* $3252. *Average need-based gift aid:* $2560. *Average non-need-based aid:* $1706. *Average indebtedness upon graduation:* $13,799.

Applying *Options:* electronic application, deferred entrance. *Application fee:* $25. *Required:* high school transcript, minimum 2.0 GPA. *Required for some:* letters of recommendation, interview. *Application deadlines:* rolling (freshmen), rolling (out-of-state freshmen), rolling (transfers). *Notification:* continuous (freshmen), continuous (out-of-state freshmen), continuous (transfers).

Freshman Application Contact Ms. Tami Grow, Associate Director of Admission, Northwest Missouri State University, 800 University Drive, Maryville, MO 64468. *Phone:* 660-562-1146. *Toll-free phone:* 800-633-1175. *E-mail:* admissions@nwmissouri.edu.

OZARK CHRISTIAN COLLEGE

Joplin, Missouri www.occ.edu/

- **Independent Christian** 4-year, founded 1942
- **Small-town** 110-acre campus
- **Coed**
- **Noncompetitive** entrance level

Undergraduates 63% live on campus.

Faculty *Total:* 60, 50% full-time, 17% with terminal degrees. *Student/faculty ratio:* 19:1.

Majors Ancient Near Eastern and biblical languages; biblical studies; elementary education; religious education; religious/sacred music; sign language interpretation and translation; theology.

Academics *Calendar:* semesters. *Degrees:* certificates, associate, and bachelor's. *Special study options:* academic remediation for entering students, adult/continuing education programs, distance learning, double majors, English as a second language, internships, part-time degree program, services for LD students, summer session for credit.

Computers on Campus 28 computers/terminals are available on campus for general student use.

Student Life *Housing:* on-campus residence required through senior year. *Options:* men-only, women-only. Campus housing is university owned. Freshman campus housing is guaranteed. *Activities and organizations:* drama/theater group, student-run radio station, choral group, Family Outreach Group, God's Spokesman, Imagine. *Campus security:* 24-hour emergency response devices, controlled dormitory access, 12-hour patrols by trained security personnel. *Student services:* health clinic, personal/psychological counseling.

Athletics Member NCCAA. *Intercollegiate sports:* basketball M/W, cheerleading M/W, soccer M, volleyball W. *Intramural sports:* basketball M, racquetball M/W, soccer M, softball M/W, volleyball M/W.

Standardized Tests *Required:* SAT or ACT (for admission).

Costs (2007–08) *One-time required fee:* $32. *Comprehensive fee:* $12,870 includes full-time tuition ($7840), mandatory fees ($480), and room and board ($4550). Full-time tuition and fees vary according to course load and program.

Part-time tuition: $245 per hour. Part-time tuition and fees vary according to course load and program. *College room only:* $2060. Room and board charges vary according to board plan. *Payment plan:* installment. *Waivers:* senior citizens and employees or children of employees.

Financial Aid Of all full-time matriculated undergraduates who enrolled in 2001, 55 Federal Work-Study jobs (averaging $1078). *Financial aid deadline:* 4/1.

Applying *Options:* electronic application. *Application fee:* $30. *Required:* essay or personal statement, high school transcript, 2 letters of recommendation. *Required for some:* interview. *Application deadlines:* 8/5 (freshmen), rolling (transfers).

Freshman Application Contact Mr. Troy B. Nelson, Executive Director of Admissions, Ozark Christian College, 1111 North Main Street, Joplin, MO 64801-4804. *Phone:* 417-624-2518. *Toll-free phone:* 800-299-4622. *Fax:* 417-624-0090. *E-mail:* oecadmin@occ.edu.

PARK UNIVERSITY

Parkville, Missouri **www.park.edu/**

- **Independent** comprehensive, founded 1875
- **Suburban** 800-acre campus with easy access to Kansas City
- **Endowment** $50.0 million
- **Coed** 12,681 undergraduate students, 9% full-time, 49% women, 51% men
- **Moderately difficult** entrance level, 73% of applicants were admitted

Undergraduates 1,163 full-time, 11,518 part-time. Students come from 50 states and territories, 112 other countries, 82% are from out of state, 20% African American, 3% Asian American or Pacific Islander, 16% Hispanic American, 0.9% Native American, 2% international, 19% transferred in, 1% live on campus. *Retention:* 63% of 2006 full-time freshmen returned.

Freshmen *Admission:* 523 applied, 383 admitted, 175 enrolled. *Average high school GPA:* 3.3. *Test scores:* ACT scores over 18: 90%; ACT scores over 24: 49%; ACT scores over 30: 9%.

Faculty *Total:* 972, 16% full-time. *Student/faculty ratio:* 15:1.

Majors Accounting; athletic training; biological and biomedical sciences related; biology/biological sciences; building/property maintenance and management; business administration and management; business, management, and marketing related; business/managerial economics; chemistry; communication/speech communication and rhetoric; computer and information sciences; computer and information sciences and support services related; computer science; dramatic/theater arts; early childhood education; economics; education related; elementary education; engineering related; English; finance and financial management services related; fine/studio arts; geography; graphic design; health/health care administration; health information/medical records administration; history; human development and family studies related; human resources development; human resources management and services related; human services; interior design; legal studies; liberal arts and sciences/liberal studies; logistics and materials management; management information systems; marketing/marketing management; mathematics; multi-/interdisciplinary studies related; music; natural sciences; nursing (registered nurse training); office management; political science and government; psychology; public administration; sociology; Spanish.

Academics *Calendar:* semesters. *Degrees:* associate, bachelor's, master's, and postbachelor's certificates. *Special study options:* academic remediation for entering students, adult/continuing education programs, advanced placement credit, distance learning, double majors, English as a second language, external degree program, honors programs, independent study, internships, off-campus study, part-time degree program, services for LD students, student-designed majors, summer session for credit. *ROTC:* Army (b).

Computers on Campus 143 computers/terminals are available on campus for general student use. Students can access the following: online (class) registration. Campuswide network is available.

Student Life *Housing:* on-campus residence required through junior year. *Options:* coed. Campus housing is university owned. Freshman campus housing is guaranteed. *Activities and organizations:* drama/theater group, student-run newspaper, radio station, choral group, World Student Union, Student Senate, Radio Club, Latin American Student Organization, Marketing Club. *Campus security:* 24-hour patrols, student patrols, late-night transport/escort service. *Student services:* health clinic, personal/psychological counseling.

Athletics Member NAIA. *Intercollegiate sports:* baseball M (s), basketball M (s)/W (s), cross-country running M (s)/W (s), golf W, soccer M (s)/W (s), softball W (s), track and field M (s)/W (s), volleyball M (s)/W (s). *Intramural sports:* basketball M/W, softball M/W, volleyball M/W.

Standardized Tests *Required:* SAT or ACT (for admission).

Costs (2007–08) *Comprehensive fee:* $12,662 includes full-time tuition ($7280), mandatory fees ($60), and room and board ($5322). Part-time tuition: $260 per credit hour. *Required fees:* $15 per term part-time. *College room only:* $2142.

Financial Aid Of all full-time matriculated undergraduates who enrolled in 2007, 3,967 applied for aid, 2,767 were judged to have need, 3,171 had their need fully met. 209 Federal Work-Study jobs (averaging $2875). 103 state and other part-time jobs (averaging $2675). In 2007, 281 non-need-based awards were made. *Average percent of need met:* 84%. *Average financial aid package:* $3811. *Average need-based loan:* $1478. *Average need-based gift aid:* $1713. *Average non-need-based aid:* $3690. *Average indebtedness upon graduation:* $12,800.

Applying *Options:* electronic application, early admission, deferred entrance. *Application fee:* $25. *Required:* high school transcript, minimum 2.0 GPA. *Required for some:* 2 letters of recommendation, interview. *Recommended:* essay or personal statement. *Application deadlines:* 8/1 (freshmen), 8/1 (transfers). *Notification:* continuous (freshmen), continuous (transfers).

Freshman Application Contact Cathy Colapietro, Director of Admissions and Student Financial Services, Park University, 8700 NW River Park Drive, Campus Box 1, Parkville, MO 64152. *Phone:* 816-584-6728. *Toll-free phone:* 800-745-7275. *Fax:* 816-741-4462. *E-mail:* admissions@mail.park.edu.

PATRICIA STEVENS COLLEGE

St. Louis, Missouri **www.patriciastevenscollege.edu/**

- **Proprietary** 4-year, founded 1947
- **Urban** campus
- **Coed** 145 undergraduate students, 64% full-time, 90% women, 10% men
- **Moderately difficult** entrance level, 61% of applicants were admitted

Undergraduates 93 full-time, 52 part-time. Students come from 2 states and territories, 34% are from out of state, 45% African American, 0.7% Asian American or Pacific Islander, 0.7% Hispanic American. *Retention:* 81% of 2006 full-time freshmen returned.

Freshmen *Admission:* 57 applied, 35 admitted. *Average high school GPA:* 2.5.

Faculty *Total:* 18, 22% full-time, 11% with terminal degrees. *Student/faculty ratio:* 9:1.

Majors Business administration and management; interior design; paralegal/legal assistant; tourism and travel services management.

Academics *Calendar:* quarters. *Degrees:* diplomas, associate, and bachelor's. *Special study options:* academic remediation for entering students, adult/continuing education programs, advanced placement credit, cooperative education, honors programs, independent study, internships, part-time degree program, summer session for credit.

Computers on Campus 42 computers/terminals are available on campus for general student use. Students can access the following: wireless internet.

Student Life *Housing:* college housing not available. *Campus security:* 24-hour emergency response devices and patrols. *Student services:* personal/psychological counseling.

Standardized Tests *Required for some:* SAT or ACT (for admission).

Costs (2008–09) *Tuition:* $15,120 full-time, $210 per quarter hour part-time.

Applying *Options:* electronic application. *Application fee:* $15. *Required:* essay or personal statement, high school transcript, interview. *Required for some:* minimum 2.75 GPA. *Recommended:* letters of recommendation. *Application deadline:* rolling (freshmen).

Freshman Application Contact Mr. John Willmon, Director of Admissions, Patricia Stevens College, 330 North Fourth Street, Suite 306, St. Louis, MO 63102. *Phone:* 314-421-0949. *Toll-free phone:* 800-871-0949. *Fax:* 314-421-0304. *E-mail:* admission@patriciastevenscollege.com.

RANKEN TECHNICAL COLLEGE

St. Louis, Missouri **www.ranken.edu/**

Director of Admissions Ms. Elizabeth Keserauskis, Director of Admissions, Ranken Technical College, 4431 Finney Avenue, St. Louis, MO 63113. *Phone:* 314-371-0233 Ext. 4811. *Toll-free phone:* 866-4RANKEN.

RESEARCH COLLEGE OF NURSING

Kansas City, Missouri **www.researchcollege.edu/**

- **Independent** comprehensive, founded 1980, part of Rockhurst University
- **Urban** 66-acre campus
- **Coed, primarily women** 280 undergraduate students, 99% full-time, 93% women, 7% men
- **Moderately difficult** entrance level, 68% of applicants were admitted

Undergraduates 276 full-time, 4 part-time. Students come from 7 states and territories, 6% African American, 5% Asian American or Pacific Islander, 5% Hispanic American, 0.4% Native American, 1% international, 4% transferred in.

Freshmen *Admission:* 244 applied, 165 admitted, 53 enrolled. *Average high school GPA:* 3.46. *Test scores:* ACT scores over 18: 100%; ACT scores over 24: 85%; ACT scores over 30: 35%.

Faculty *Total:* 29, 90% full-time, 14% with terminal degrees. *Student/faculty ratio:* 7:1.

Majors Nursing (registered nurse training).

Academics *Calendar:* semesters. *Degrees:* bachelor's and master's (bachelor's degree offered jointly with Rockhurst College). *Special study options:* accelerated degree program, advanced placement credit, double majors, honors programs, independent study, services for LD students, study abroad, summer session for credit. *ROTC:* Army (c).

Computers on Campus 125 computers/terminals are available on campus for general student use. Students can access the following: online (class) registration. Campuswide network is available.

Student Life *Housing options:* coed, men-only, women-only. Campus housing is university owned. Freshman campus housing is guaranteed. *Activities and organizations:* drama/theater group, student-run newspaper, radio station, choral group, national fraternities, national sororities. *Campus security:* 24-hour emergency response devices and patrols, late-night transport/escort service, controlled dormitory access. *Student services:* health clinic, personal/psychological counseling.

Athletics Member NCAA. All Division II. *Intercollegiate sports:* baseball M (s), basketball M (s)/W (s), golf M (s)/W (s), soccer M (s)/W (s), softball W (s), tennis M (s)/W (s), volleyball W (s). *Intramural sports:* badminton M/W, basketball M/W, cross-country running M/W, field hockey M/W, football M/W, golf M/W, lacrosse M/W, racquetball M/W, rugby M/W, soccer M/W, softball M/W, table tennis M/W, tennis M/W, volleyball M/W, weight lifting M.

Standardized Tests *Required:* SAT or ACT (for admission).

Costs (2007–08) *Comprehensive fee:* $29,120 includes full-time tuition ($22,000), mandatory fees ($720), and room and board ($6400). Part-time tuition: $733 per credit hour. Part-time tuition and fees vary according to class time. *Required fees:* $50 per credit hour part-time. *College room only:* $3500. Room and board charges vary according to board plan, housing facility, and location. *Payment plan:* installment. *Waivers:* employees or children of employees.

Financial Aid Of all full-time matriculated undergraduates who enrolled in 2004, 90 applied for aid, 81 were judged to have need, 19 had their need fully met. In 2004, 39 non-need-based awards were made. *Average percent of need met:* 60%. *Average financial aid package:* $21,196. *Average need-based loan:* $4580. *Average need-based gift aid:* $2000. *Average non-need-based aid:* $15,700. *Average indebtedness upon graduation:* $12,740.

Applying *Options:* electronic application, deferred entrance. *Application fee:* $20. *Required:* high school transcript, 1 letter of recommendation, minimum ACT score of 21. *Recommended:* minimum 2.8 GPA, interview. *Application deadlines:* 6/30 (freshmen), 2/15 (transfers). *Notification:* continuous until 8/15 (freshmen), 3/15 (transfers).

Freshman Application Contact Mr. Lane Ramey, Director of Transfer Admission, Research College of Nursing, 1100 Rockhurst Road, Kansas City, MO 64110. *Phone:* 816-501-4102. *Toll-free phone:* 800-842-6776. *E-mail:* lane.ramey@rockhurst.edu.

ROCKHURST UNIVERSITY

Kansas City, Missouri **www.rockhurst.edu/**

- **Independent Roman Catholic (Jesuit)** comprehensive, founded 1910
- **Urban** 35-acre campus
- **Endowment** $41.2 million
- **Coed** 2,318 undergraduate students, 63% full-time, 60% women, 40% men
- **Moderately difficult** entrance level, 76% of applicants were admitted

Undergraduates 1,459 full-time, 859 part-time. Students come from 26 states and territories, 38% are from out of state, 4% transferred in, 61% live on campus. *Retention:* 86% of 2006 full-time freshmen returned.

Freshmen *Admission:* 1,833 applied, 1,388 admitted, 369 enrolled. *Average high school GPA:* 3.60. *Test scores:* SAT critical reading scores over 500: 77%; SAT math scores over 500: 75%; ACT scores over 18: 100%; SAT critical reading scores over 600: 35%; SAT math scores over 600: 35%; ACT scores over 24: 64%; SAT critical reading scores over 700: 10%; ACT scores over 30: 11%.

Faculty *Total:* 210, 57% full-time, 64% with terminal degrees. *Student/faculty ratio:* 13:1.

Majors Biochemistry; bioinformatics; biology/biological sciences; business administration and management; business/corporate communications; chemistry; communication/speech communication and rhetoric; community organization and advocacy; computer programming; computer science; creative writing; economics; education; elementary education; English; French; history; international relations and affairs; mathematics; medical laboratory technology; nursing (registered nurse training); philosophy; physics; political science and government; psychology; secondary education; social sciences; sociology; Spanish; speech-language pathology; theology.

Academics *Calendar:* semesters. *Degrees:* certificates, bachelor's, master's, doctoral, and postbachelor's certificates. *Special study options:* academic remediation for entering students, accelerated degree program, adult/continuing education programs, advanced placement credit, cooperative education, distance learning, double majors, freshman honors college, honors programs, independent study, internships, off-campus study, part-time degree program, services for LD students, study abroad, summer session for credit. *ROTC:* Army (c). *Unusual degree programs:* 3-2 engineering with University of Missouri-Rolla, University of Detroit Mercy, Marquette University, University of Missouri–Columbia.

Computers on Campus 500 computers/terminals are available on campus for general student use. Campuswide network is available.

Student Life *Housing:* on-campus residence required through sophomore year. *Options:* coed, men-only, women-only. Campus housing is university owned. *Activities and organizations:* drama/theater group, student-run newspaper, choral group, Student Activities Board, Organization of Collegiate Women, Black Student Union, Student Organization of Latinos, College Players, national fraternities, national sororities. *Campus security:* 24-hour emergency response devices and patrols, student patrols, late-night transport/escort service, controlled dormitory access, closed-circuit TV monitors. *Student services:* health clinic, personal/psychological counseling.

Athletics Member NCAA. All Division II. *Intercollegiate sports:* baseball M (s), basketball M (s)/W (s), golf M (s)/W (s), soccer M (s)/W (s), softball W (s), tennis M (s)/W (s), volleyball W (s). *Intramural sports:* badminton M/W, basketball M/W, cheerleading M/W, cross-country running M/W, field hockey M/W, football M/W, golf M/W, racquetball M/W, soccer M/W, softball M/W, tennis M/W, ultimate Frisbee M/W, volleyball M/W, weight lifting M, wrestling M.

Standardized Tests *Required:* SAT or ACT (for admission).

Costs (2007–08) *Comprehensive fee:* $29,040 includes full-time tuition ($22,000), mandatory fees ($840), and room and board ($6200). Part-time tuition: $733 per credit hour. *Required fees:* $30 per term part-time. *College room only:* $3500.

Financial Aid Of all full-time matriculated undergraduates who enrolled in 2007, 1,528 applied for aid, 1,344 were judged to have need, 219 had their need fully met. In 2007, 152 non-need-based awards were made. *Average percent of need met:* 99%. *Average financial aid package:* $21,667. *Average need-based loan:* $3918. *Average need-based gift aid:* $5769. *Average non-need-based aid:* $11,358. *Average indebtedness upon graduation:* $16,579.

Applying *Options:* electronic application, deferred entrance. *Application fee:* $25. *Required:* high school transcript, minimum 2.0 GPA, 1 letter of recommendation. *Required for some:* essay or personal statement, interview. *Application deadlines:* 6/30 (freshmen), rolling (transfers). *Notification:* continuous (freshmen), continuous (transfers).

Freshman Application Contact Mr. Lane Ramey, Director of Freshman Admissions, Rockhurst University, 1100 Rockhurst Road, Kansas City, MO 64110-2561. *Phone:* 816-501-4100. *Toll-free phone:* 800-842-6776. *Fax:* 816-501-4142. *E-mail:* admission@rockhurst.edu.

See page 1440 for the College Close-Up.

ST. LOUIS CHRISTIAN COLLEGE

Florissant, Missouri **www.slcconline.edu/**

- **Independent Christian** 4-year, founded 1956
- **Suburban** 20-acre campus with easy access to St. Louis
- **Endowment** $577,910

- **Coed** 321 undergraduate students, 85% full-time, 39% women, 61% men
- **Minimally difficult** entrance level, 76% of applicants were admitted

Undergraduates 273 full-time, 48 part-time. Students come from 17 states and territories, 3 other countries, 34% are from out of state, 31% African American, 0.6% Asian American or Pacific Islander, 0.6% Hispanic American, 0.6% Native American, 2% international, 11% transferred in, 38% live on campus. *Retention:* 65% of 2006 full-time freshmen returned.

Freshmen *Admission:* 55 applied, 42 admitted, 54 enrolled. *Average high school GPA:* 2.95. *Test scores:* ACT scores over 18: 90%; ACT scores over 24: 45%.

Faculty *Total:* 33, 27% full-time, 24% with terminal degrees. *Student/faculty ratio:* 12:1.

Majors Biblical studies; liberal arts and sciences/liberal studies; religious education; religious/sacred music; theology.

Academics *Calendar:* semesters. *Degrees:* associate and bachelor's. *Special study options:* academic remediation for entering students, accelerated degree program, adult/continuing education programs, advanced placement credit, internships, part-time degree program, services for LD students.

Computers on Campus 11 computers/terminals are available on campus for general student use.

Student Life *Housing:* on-campus residence required through senior year. *Options:* men-only, women-only. Campus housing is university owned. *Activities and organizations:* drama/theater group, choral group, World Christians Unlimited, Drama Club, pep band. *Campus security:* 24-hour emergency response devices and patrols, controlled dormitory access, night security. *Student services:* personal/psychological counseling.

Athletics Member NCCAA. *Intercollegiate sports:* baseball M, basketball M, ultimate Frisbee M (s)/W (s), volleyball M (s)/W (s). *Intramural sports:* basketball M/W, ultimate Frisbee M/W, volleyball M/W.

Standardized Tests *Required:* ACT (for admission).

Costs (2008–09) *Comprehensive fee:* $12,800 includes full-time tuition ($8850), mandatory fees ($650), and room and board ($3300). Part-time tuition: $295 per credit hour.

Financial Aid Of all full-time matriculated undergraduates who enrolled in 2007, 235 applied for aid, 214 were judged to have need, 43 had their need fully met. 16 Federal Work-Study jobs (averaging $1583). 23 state and other part-time jobs (averaging $4800). In 2007, 19 non-need-based awards were made. *Average percent of need met:* 76%. *Average financial aid package:* $10,856. *Average need-based loan:* $3540. *Average need-based gift aid:* $8039. *Average non-need-based aid:* $6152. *Average indebtedness upon graduation:* $8901.

Applying *Options:* early admission. *Required:* essay or personal statement, high school transcript, 2 letters of recommendation. *Required for some:* interview. *Recommended:* minimum 2.0 GPA. *Application deadlines:* 8/15 (freshmen), 8/15 (transfers). *Notification:* continuous (freshmen), continuous (transfers).

Freshman Application Contact Carrie Chapman, Admissions Director, St. Louis Christian College, 1360 Grandview Drive, Florissant, MO 63033-6499. *Phone:* 314-837-6777 Ext. 1500. *Toll-free phone:* 800-887-SLCC. *E-mail:* cchapman@slcconline.edu.

St. Louis College of Pharmacy

St. Louis, Missouri **www.stlcop.edu/**

- **Independent** comprehensive, founded 1864
- **Urban** 5-acre campus
- **Endowment** $90.2 million
- **Coed** 648 undergraduate students, 100% full-time, 55% women, 45% men
- **Moderately difficult** entrance level, 53% of applicants were admitted

Undergraduates 648 full-time. Students come from 19 states and territories, 3 other countries, 50% are from out of state, 2% African American, 17% Asian American or Pacific Islander, 0.8% Hispanic American, 0.5% international, 0.8% transferred in, 40% live on campus. *Retention:* 90% of 2006 full-time freshmen returned.

Freshmen *Admission:* 565 applied, 299 admitted, 241 enrolled. *Average high school GPA:* 3.88. *Test scores:* ACT scores over 18: 100%; ACT scores over 24: 100%; ACT scores over 30: 17%.

Faculty *Total:* 101, 63% full-time, 93% with terminal degrees. *Student/faculty ratio:* 18:1.

Majors Pharmacy.

Academics *Calendar:* semesters. *Degree:* first professional. *Special study options:* academic remediation for entering students, advanced placement credit, internships, summer session for credit. *ROTC:* Army (c), Air Force (c).

Computers on Campus 10 computers/terminals are available on campus for general student use. Students can access the following: campus intranet, computer help desk, free student e-mail accounts, online (class) grades, online (class) registration, online (class) schedules. Campuswide network is available. 100% of college-owned or -operated housing units are wired for high-speed Internet access. Wireless service is available via entire campus.

Student Life *Housing options:* coed. Campus housing is university owned. Freshman applicants given priority for college housing. *Activities and organizations:* drama/theater group, student-run newspaper, choral group, Gateway Academy of Student Pharmacists, Student Council, International Student Council, student ambassadors, Student Alumni Association, national fraternities, national sororities. *Campus security:* 24-hour emergency response devices and patrols, late-night transport/escort service, controlled dormitory access. *Student services:* personal/psychological counseling.

Athletics Member NAIA. *Intercollegiate sports:* basketball M/W, cross-country running M/W, volleyball W. *Intramural sports:* basketball M/W, cheerleading W, cross-country running M/W, football M/W, golf M/W, soccer M/W, softball M/W, table tennis M/W, tennis M/W, volleyball M/W, weight lifting M/W.

Standardized Tests *Required:* SAT or ACT (for admission).

Costs (2008–09) *Comprehensive fee:* $28,855 includes full-time tuition ($20,475), mandatory fees ($350), and room and board ($8030). Part-time tuition: $800 per credit.

Financial Aid Of all full-time matriculated undergraduates who enrolled in 2007, 570 applied for aid, 498 were judged to have need, 32 had their need fully met. 105 Federal Work-Study jobs (averaging $1200). In 2007, 154 non-need-based awards were made. *Average percent of need met:* 51%. *Average financial aid package:* $13,028. *Average need-based loan:* $6259. *Average need-based gift aid:* $8230. *Average non-need-based aid:* $8895. *Average indebtedness upon graduation:* $101,300.

Applying *Options:* electronic application, early decision. *Application fee:* $50. *Required:* essay or personal statement, high school transcript, minimum 3.0 GPA, 2 letters of recommendation. *Required for some:* interview. *Application deadlines:* 2/1 (freshmen), 2/1 (transfers). *Early decision deadline:* 12/15. *Notification:* 3/1 (freshmen), 7/1 (transfers), 1/15 (early decision).

Freshman Application Contact Connie Horrall, Administrative Assistant, St. Louis College of Pharmacy, 4588 Parkview Place, St. Louis, MO 63110-1088. *Phone:* 314-446-8328. *Toll-free phone:* 800-278-5267. *Fax:* 314-446-8310. *E-mail:* chorrall@stlcop.edu.

See page 1442 for the College Close-Up.

Saint Louis University

St. Louis, Missouri **www.slu.edu/**

- **Independent Roman Catholic (Jesuit)** university, founded 1818
- **Urban** 244-acre campus
- **Endowment** $959.5 million
- **Coed** 7,556 undergraduate students, 93% full-time, 58% women, 42% men
- **Moderately difficult** entrance level, 80% of applicants were admitted

Undergraduates 6,991 full-time, 565 part-time. Students come from 53 states and territories, 48 other countries, 57% are from out of state, 7% African American, 6% Asian American or Pacific Islander, 3% Hispanic American, 0.3% Native American, 3% international, 5% transferred in, 53% live on campus. *Retention:* 82% of 2006 full-time freshmen returned.

Freshmen *Admission:* 9,169 applied, 7,340 admitted, 1,740 enrolled. *Average high school GPA:* 3.67. *Test scores:* SAT critical reading scores over 500: 87%; SAT math scores over 500: 89%; ACT scores over 18: 99%; SAT critical reading scores over 600: 52%; SAT math scores over 600: 54%; ACT scores over 24: 76%; SAT critical reading scores over 700: 12%; SAT math scores over 700: 14%; ACT scores over 30: 23%.

Faculty *Total:* 952, 64% full-time, 63% with terminal degrees. *Student/faculty ratio:* 13:1.

Majors Aeronautical/aerospace engineering technology; aerospace, aeronautical and astronautical engineering; airline pilot and flight crew; American studies; art history, criticism and conservation; atmospheric sciences and meteorology; audiology and speech-language pathology; aviation/airway management; biochemistry; biology/biological sciences; biomedical/medical engineering; business administration and management; chemistry; city/urban, community and regional planning; classics and classical languages related; clinical laboratory science/medical technology; clinical/medical laboratory science and allied professions related; communication/speech communication and rhetoric; computer and information sciences; computer engineering; corrections; criminal justice/law enforcement administration; cytotechnology; dramatic/theater arts; economics; education; education (multiple levels); electrical, electronics and communications engineering; engineering/industrial management; engineering physics; English; environmental science; fine/studio arts; foods, nutrition, and wellness; foreign languages and literatures; French; geology/earth science; geophysics and seismology; German; health/health care administration; health information/medical records administration; history; humanities; human resources management; international business/trade/commerce; international relations and affairs; kinesiology and exercise science; management information systems; management science; marketing/marketing management; mathematics; mechanical engineering; meteorology; modern Greek; music; nuclear medical technology; nursing (registered nurse training); occupational therapy; organizational behavior; philosophy; physical therapy; physics; political science and government; psychology; purchasing, procurement/acquisitions and contracts management; religious studies related; Russian; social work; sociology; Spanish; theology; urban studies/affairs; women's studies.

Academics *Calendar:* semesters. *Degrees:* certificates, bachelor's, master's, doctoral, first professional, post-master's, and postbachelor's certificates. *Special study options:* academic remediation for entering students, accelerated degree program, adult/continuing education programs, advanced placement credit, cooperative education, distance learning, double majors, English as a second language, honors programs, independent study, internships, off-campus study, part-time degree program, services for LD students, student-designed majors, study abroad, summer session for credit. *ROTC:* Army (c), Air Force (b).

Computers on Campus 750 computers/terminals and 4,500 ports are available on campus for general student use. Students can access the following: campus intranet, computer help desk, free student e-mail accounts, online (class) grades, online (class) registration, online (class) schedules. Campuswide network is available. 100% of college-owned or -operated housing units are wired for high-speed Internet access. Wireless service is available via entire campus.

Student Life *Housing options:* coed, men-only, women-only, disabled students. Campus housing is university owned. *Activities and organizations:* drama/theater group, student-run newspaper, radio and television station, choral group, Alpha Phi Omega, Student Activities Board, Oriflamme, Interfraternity Council, Panhelenic Council, national fraternities, national sororities. *Campus security:* 24-hour emergency response devices and patrols, late-night transport/escort service, controlled dormitory access, crime prevention program, bicycle patrols, pamphlets, posters, films. *Student services:* health clinic, personal/psychological counseling, women's center.

Athletics Member NCAA. All Division I. *Intercollegiate sports:* baseball M (s), basketball M (s)/W (s), crew M (c)/W (c), cross-country running M (s)/W (s), equestrian sports M (c)/W (c), fencing M (c), field hockey W (s), golf M (c), ice hockey M (c), lacrosse M (c)/W (c), racquetball M (c)/W (c), rugby M (c), soccer M (s) (c)/W (s) (c), softball W (s), swimming and diving M (s)/W (s), tennis M (s)/W (s), track and field M (s)/W (s), ultimate Frisbee M (c)/W (c), volleyball M (c)/W (s). *Intramural sports:* badminton M/W, basketball M/W, bowling M/W, football M/W, golf M/W, racquetball M/W, soccer M/W, softball M/W, squash M/W, swimming and diving M/W, table tennis M/W, tennis M/W, ultimate Frisbee M/W, volleyball M/W.

Standardized Tests *Required:* SAT or ACT (for admission).

Costs (2007–08) *Comprehensive fee:* $37,428 includes full-time tuition ($28,480), mandatory fees ($398), and room and board ($8550). Full-time tuition and fees vary according to location and program. Part-time tuition: $995 per credit hour. Part-time tuition and fees vary according to location and program. *Required fees:* $120 per semester part-time. *College room only:* $4840. Room and board charges vary according to board plan, housing facility, and location. *Payment plan:* installment. *Waivers:* employees or children of employees.

Financial Aid Of all full-time matriculated undergraduates who enrolled in 2006, 4,580 applied for aid, 3,904 were judged to have need, 645 had their need fully met. 1,505 Federal Work-Study jobs (averaging $2964). 70 state and other part-time jobs (averaging $1885). In 2006, 1898 non-need-based awards were made. *Average percent of need met:* 62%. *Average financial aid package:* $18,773. *Average need-based loan:* $4719. *Average need-based gift aid:* $12,560. *Average non-need-based aid:* $8803. *Average indebtedness upon graduation:* $27,013.

Applying *Options:* electronic application, deferred entrance. *Application fee:* $25. *Required:* essay or personal statement, high school transcript, minimum 2.5 GPA, secondary school report form. *Recommended:* 2 letters of recommendation, interview. *Application deadlines:* 8/1 (freshmen), 8/1 (out-of-state freshmen), rolling (transfers). *Notification:* 9/15 (freshmen), 9/15 (out-of-state freshmen), continuous until 9/15 (transfers).

Freshman Application Contact Director, Saint Louis University, 221 North Grand Boulevard, St. Louis, MO 63103-2097. *Phone:* 314-977-3415. *Toll-free phone:* 800-758-3678. *Fax:* 314-977-7136. *E-mail:* admitme@slu.edu.

Saint Luke's College

Kansas City, Missouri www.saintlukescollege.edu/

- **Independent Episcopal** upper-level, founded 1903, administratively affiliated with Saint Luke's Hospital
- **Urban** 3-acre campus
- **Endowment** $2.8 million
- **Coed**
- **Very difficult** entrance level

Faculty *Student/faculty ratio:* 8:1.

Academics *Calendar:* semesters. *Degree:* bachelor's.

Student Life *Campus security:* 24-hour emergency response devices and patrols.

Costs (2008–09) *Tuition:* $8850 full-time. *Required fees:* $670 full-time.

Financial Aid Of all full-time matriculated undergraduates who enrolled in 2006, 88 applied for aid, 87 were judged to have need, 6 had their need fully met. In 2006, 6 non-need-based awards were made. *Average percent of need met:* 76. *Average financial aid package:* $6600. *Average need-based loan:* $5000. *Average need-based gift aid:* $2000. *Average non-need-based aid:* $1000.

Applying *Options:* early admission, early decision. *Application fee:* $35.

Application Contact Assistant Director of Admissions, Saint Luke's College, 8320 Ward Parkway, Suite 300, Kansas City, MO 64114. *Phone:* 816-932-3372. *Fax:* 816-932-9064.

Sanford-Brown College

Fenton, Missouri www.sanford-brown.edu/

Director of Admissions Ms. Judy Wilga, Director of Admissions, Sanford-Brown College, 1203 Smizer Mill Road, Fenton, MO 63026. *Phone:* 636-349-4900 Ext. 102. *Toll-free phone:* 800-456-7222. *Fax:* 636-349-9170.

Southeast Missouri State University

Cape Girardeau, Missouri www.semo.edu/

- **State-supported** comprehensive, founded 1873, part of Missouri Coordinating Board for Higher Education
- **Small-town** 400-acre campus with easy access to St. Louis
- **Endowment** $43.5 million
- **Coed** 9,209 undergraduate students, 75% full-time, 60% women, 40% men
- **Moderately difficult** entrance level, 88% of applicants were admitted

Undergraduates 6,892 full-time, 2,317 part-time. Students come from 37 states and territories, 34 other countries, 12% are from out of state, 9% African American, 0.6% Asian American or Pacific Islander, 1% Hispanic American, 0.5% Native American, 1% international, 6% transferred in, 30% live on campus. *Retention:* 71% of 2006 full-time freshmen returned.

Freshmen *Admission:* 4,111 applied, 3,618 admitted, 1,805 enrolled. *Average high school GPA:* 3.21. *Test scores:* SAT critical reading scores over 500: 60%; SAT math scores over 500: 60%; ACT scores over 18: 95%; SAT critical reading scores over 600: 29%; SAT math scores over 600: 33%; ACT scores over 24: 34%; SAT critical reading scores over 700: 13%; SAT math scores over 700: 2%; ACT scores over 30: 5%.

Faculty *Total:* 614, 67% full-time, 56% with terminal degrees. *Student/faculty ratio:* 17:1.

Majors Accounting; administrative assistant and secretarial science; agribusiness; agriculture; animal sciences; anthropology; art; art teacher education; biology/biological sciences; business administration and management; business teacher education; chemistry; child care and support services management; clinical laboratory science/medical technology; communication disorders; communication/speech communication and rhetoric; computer and information sciences; computer technology/computer systems technology; corrections; dramatic/theater arts; economics; education; elementary education; engineering physics; engineering technology; English; English/language arts teacher education; environmental studies; family and consumer sciences/home economics teacher education; family and consumer sciences/human sciences; finance; foreign language teacher education; French; general studies; German; health and physical education; history; horticultural science; humanities; industrial technology; international/global studies; kindergarten/preschool education; marketing/marketing management; mathematics; mathematics teacher education; middle school education; multi-/

interdisciplinary studies related; music; music teacher education; nursing (registered nurse training); office management; parks, recreation and leisure; philosophy; physical education teaching and coaching; physics; plant sciences; political science and government; psychology; science teacher education; social studies teacher education; social work; Spanish; special education; speech and rhetoric; speech teacher education; sport and fitness administration/management; technology/ industrial arts teacher education; visual and performing arts.

Academics *Calendar:* semesters. *Degrees:* certificates, associate, bachelor's, master's, and post-master's certificates. *Special study options:* academic remediation for entering students, accelerated degree program, adult/continuing education programs, advanced placement credit, distance learning, double majors, English as a second language, honors programs, independent study, internships, part-time degree program, services for LD students, student-designed majors, study abroad, summer session for credit. *ROTC:* Air Force (b).

Computers on Campus 1,311 computers/terminals are available on campus for general student use. Students can access the following: campus intranet, computer help desk, free student e-mail accounts, online (class) grades, online (class) registration, online (class) schedules. Campuswide network is available. 100% of college-owned or -operated housing units are wired for high-speed Internet access. Wireless service is available via classrooms, computer centers, computer labs, learning centers, libraries, student centers.

Student Life *Housing:* on-campus residence required through sophomore year. *Options:* coed, men-only, women-only. Campus housing is university owned. Freshman campus housing is guaranteed. *Activities and organizations:* drama/ theater group, student-run newspaper, radio station, choral group, marching band, Student Activities Council, Residence Hall Association, student government, Baptist Student Union, Up 'til Dawn, national fraternities, national sororities. *Campus security:* 24-hour emergency response devices and patrols, late-night transport/escort service, controlled dormitory access. *Student services:* health clinic, personal/psychological counseling.

Athletics Member NCAA. All Division I except football (Division I-AA). *Intercollegiate sports:* baseball M (s), basketball M (s)/W (s), cheerleading M (s)/W (s), cross-country running M (s)/W (s), gymnastics W (s), soccer W (s), softball W (s), tennis W (s), track and field M (s)/W (s), volleyball W (s). *Intramural sports:* badminton M/W, basketball M/W, bowling M/W, fencing M (c)/W (c), golf M (c)/W (c), lacrosse M (c)/W (c), racquetball M/W, rock climbing M (c)/W (c), soccer M (c)/W (c), softball M/W, swimming and diving M/W, table tennis M/W, tennis M/W, ultimate Frisbee M/W, volleyball M/W, wrestling M/W.

Standardized Tests *Required:* SAT or ACT (for admission).

Costs (2007–08) *Tuition:* state resident $5304 full-time, $177 per credit hour part-time; nonresident $9699 full-time, $323 per credit hour part-time. Full-time tuition and fees vary according to course load and location. Part-time tuition and fees vary according to course load and location. *Required fees:* $621 full-time, $21 per credit hour part-time. *Room and board:* $5923; room only: $3661. Room and board charges vary according to board plan and housing facility. *Payment plans:* installment, deferred payment. *Waivers:* senior citizens and employees or children of employees.

Financial Aid Of all full-time matriculated undergraduates who enrolled in 2006, 4,792 applied for aid, 3,557 were judged to have need, 595 had their need fully met. 192 Federal Work-Study jobs (averaging $1305). 1,100 state and other part-time jobs (averaging $2450). In 2006, 905 non-need-based awards were made. *Average percent of need met:* 62%. *Average financial aid package:* $6477. *Average need-based loan:* $3642. *Average need-based gift aid:* $4249. *Average non-need-based aid:* $4053. *Average indebtedness upon graduation:* $17,142.

Applying *Options:* electronic application. *Application fee:* $25. *Required:* high school transcript, minimum 2.0 GPA. *Application deadlines:* 5/1 (freshmen), 5/1 (transfers). *Notification:* continuous until 9/1 (freshmen), continuous (transfers).

Freshman Application Contact Dr. Deborah Below, Director of Admissions, Southeast Missouri State University, MS 3550, Cape Girardeau, MO 63701. *Phone:* 573-651-2590. *Fax:* 573-651-5936. *E-mail:* admissions@semo.edu.

SOUTHWEST BAPTIST UNIVERSITY

Bolivar, Missouri www.sbuniv.edu/

- **Independent Southern Baptist** comprehensive, founded 1878
- **Small-town** 152-acre campus
- **Endowment** $18.5 million
- **Coed** 2,752 undergraduate students, 66% full-time, 66% women, 34% men
- **Moderately difficult** entrance level, 65% of applicants were admitted

Southwest Baptist University (SBU) is a Christ-centered, caring academic community that prepares students to be servant-leaders in a global society. Integrating faith with every academic pursuit is the cornerstone of an SBU education. No matter which of the more than forty-five areas of study students choose to pursue, they are well-prepared to excel in their field. As an established leader in higher education, SBU has been named to *America's 100 Best College Buys* since 1996 and to *America's Best Christian Colleges* since 1997. It was recently named to *America's Best College Scholarships*. To learn more about SBU's excellent academics and student life opportunities, students should visit http://www.SBUniv.edu.

Undergraduates 1,822 full-time, 930 part-time. Students come from 45 states and territories, 15 other countries, 28% are from out of state, 4% African American, 0.6% Asian American or Pacific Islander, 1% Hispanic American, 1% Native American, 1% international, 4% transferred in, 66% live on campus. *Retention:* 72% of 2006 full-time freshmen returned.

Freshmen *Admission:* 1,674 applied, 1,081 admitted, 448 enrolled. *Average high school GPA:* 3.39. *Test scores:* SAT critical reading scores over 500: 60%; SAT math scores over 500: 44%; ACT scores over 18: 90%; SAT critical reading scores over 600: 26%; SAT math scores over 600: 18%; ACT scores over 24: 42%; SAT critical reading scores over 700: 8%; ACT scores over 30: 9%.

Faculty *Total:* 256, 43% full-time, 39% with terminal degrees. *Student/faculty ratio:* 13:1.

Majors Accounting; art; art teacher education; athletic training; biblical studies; biology/biological sciences; biology teacher education; business administration and management; business/commerce; chemistry; chemistry teacher education; clinical laboratory science/medical technology; commercial and advertising art; communication/speech communication and rhetoric; computer and information sciences; computer science; criminal justice/law enforcement administration; customer service management; dramatic/theater arts; early childhood education; elementary education; emergency medical technology (EMT paramedic); English; English/language arts teacher education; finance; general studies; health and physical education; health teacher education; history; human services; marketing/ marketing management; mathematics; mathematics teacher education; middle school education; missionary studies and missiology; music; music teacher education; nursing (registered nurse training); occupational safety and health technology; office management; parks, recreation and leisure; pastoral studies/ counseling; physical education teaching and coaching; political science and government; psychology; religious education; religious studies; science teacher education; social science teacher education; sociology; Spanish; speech teacher education; sport and fitness administration/management; theology.

Academics *Calendar:* 4-1-4. *Degrees:* certificates, associate, bachelor's, master's, doctoral, and post-master's certificates. *Special study options:* academic remediation for entering students, advanced placement credit, cooperative education, distance learning, double majors, honors programs, independent study, internships, off-campus study, part-time degree program, services for LD students, student-designed majors, study abroad, summer session for credit. *ROTC:* Army (c).

Computers on Campus 261 computers/terminals are available on campus for general student use. Students can access the following: computer help desk, free student e-mail accounts, online (class) grades, online (class) registration, online (class) schedules. Campuswide network is available. 90% of college-owned or -operated housing units are wired for high-speed Internet access. Wireless service is available via entire campus.

Student Life *Housing:* on-campus residence required through junior year. *Options:* men-only, women-only. Campus housing is university owned. Freshman campus housing is guaranteed. *Activities and organizations:* drama/theater group, student-run newspaper, choral group, Students in Free Enterprise (SIFE), Student Government Association, Fellowship of Christian Athletes, Student Missouri State Teachers Association, PSY CHI. *Campus security:* 24-hour emergency response devices and patrols, controlled dormitory access. *Student services:* health clinic, personal/psychological counseling.

Athletics Member NCAA. All Division II. *Intercollegiate sports:* baseball M (s), basketball M (s)/W (s), cheerleading M/W, cross-country running M (s)/W (s), football M (s), golf M (s), soccer M/W (s), softball W (s), tennis M (s)/W (s), track and field M (s)/W (s), volleyball W (s). *Intramural sports:* basketball M/W, football M/W, soccer M/W, softball M/W, table tennis M/W, volleyball M/W.

Standardized Tests *Required:* SAT or ACT (for admission).

Costs (2008–09) *Comprehensive fee:* $20,870 includes full-time tuition ($15,000), mandatory fees ($870), and room and board ($5000). *Required fees:* $500 per hour part-time. *College room only:* $2500.

Financial Aid Of all full-time matriculated undergraduates who enrolled in 2007, 1,489 applied for aid, 1,235 were judged to have need, 342 had their need fully met. 396 Federal Work-Study jobs (averaging $1762). In 2007, 416 non-need-based awards were made. *Average percent of need met:* 75%. *Average financial aid package:* $12,575. *Average need-based loan:* $4494. *Average need-based gift aid:* $4334. *Average non-need-based aid:* $5735. *Average indebtedness upon graduation:* $22,234.

Applying *Options:* electronic application. *Application fee:* $30. *Required:* high school transcript, minimum 2.5 GPA. *Required for some:* 3 letters of recommendation. *Recommended:* essay or personal statement, interview. *Application deadlines:* rolling (freshmen), rolling (transfers). *Notification:* continuous (freshmen), continuous (transfers).

Freshman Application Contact Mr. Darren Crowder, Director of Admissions, Southwest Baptist University, 1600 University Avenue, Bolivar, MO 65613-2597. *Phone:* 417-328-1817. *Toll-free phone:* 800-526-5859. *Fax:* 417-328-1808. *E-mail:* dcrowder@sbuniv.edu.

STEPHENS COLLEGE

Columbia, Missouri **www.stephens.edu/**

- **Independent** comprehensive, founded 1833
- **Urban** 86-acre campus
- **Endowment** $24.1 million
- **Undergraduate: women only; graduate: coed** 890 undergraduate students, 78% full-time, 97% women, 3% men
- **Moderately difficult** entrance level, 71% of applicants were admitted

Undergraduates 691 full-time, 199 part-time. Students come from 43 states and territories, 1 other country, 50% are from out of state, 9% African American, 2% Asian American or Pacific Islander, 3% Hispanic American, 1% Native American, 0.3% international, 6% transferred in, 72% live on campus. *Retention:* 68% of 2006 full-time freshmen returned.

Freshmen *Admission:* 735 applied, 522 admitted, 225 enrolled. *Average high school GPA:* 3.31. *Test scores:* SAT critical reading scores over 500: 88%; SAT math scores over 500: 72%; ACT scores over 18: 99%; SAT critical reading scores over 600: 34%; SAT math scores over 600: 24%; ACT scores over 24: 59%; SAT critical reading scores over 700: 2%; SAT math scores over 700: 2%; ACT scores over 30: 6%.

Faculty *Total:* 113, 47% full-time, 29% with terminal degrees. *Student/faculty ratio:* 12:1.

Majors Accounting; advertising; biology/biological sciences; biomedical sciences; broadcast journalism; business administration and management; creative writing; dance; dramatic/theater arts; early childhood education; elementary education; English; equestrian studies; fashion/apparel design; fashion merchandising; film/cinema studies; graphic design; health information/medical records administration; horse husbandry/equine science and management; human development and family studies; interdisciplinary studies; interior design; kindergarten/preschool education; liberal arts and sciences/liberal studies; marketing/marketing management; mass communication/media; occupational therapy; pre-law studies; psychology; public relations/image management; radio and television.

Academics *Calendar:* semesters. *Degrees:* bachelor's, master's, and post-bachelor's certificates. *Special study options:* academic remediation for entering students, accelerated degree program, adult/continuing education programs, advanced placement credit, cooperative education, distance learning, double majors, English as a second language, external degree program, freshman honors college, honors programs, independent study, internships, off-campus study, part-time degree program, services for LD students, student-designed majors, study abroad. *ROTC:* Army (c), Air Force (c). *Unusual degree programs:* 3-2 animal science with University of Missouri–Columbia, occupational therapy with Washington University in St. Louis.

Computers on Campus 104 computers/terminals and 80 ports are available on campus for general student use. Students can access the following: computer help desk, free student e-mail accounts. Campuswide network is available. 33% of college-owned or -operated housing units are wired for high-speed Internet access.

Student Life *Housing:* on-campus residence required through senior year. *Options:* women-only. Campus housing is university owned and is provided by a third party. Freshman campus housing is guaranteed. *Activities and organizations:* drama/theater group, student-run newspaper, radio and television station, choral group, IFA, Warehouse Theater, Student Government, PRSSA, national sororities. *Campus security:* 24-hour emergency response devices and patrols, student patrols, late-night transport/escort service, controlled dormitory access. *Student services:* health clinic, personal/psychological counseling.

Athletics Member NAIA. *Intercollegiate sports:* basketball W (s), cross-country running W (s), softball W (s), swimming and diving W (s), tennis W (s), volleyball W (s).

Standardized Tests *Required:* SAT or ACT (for admission).

Costs (2008–09) *Comprehensive fee:* $31,730 includes full-time tuition ($23,000) and room and board ($8730). Part-time tuition: $265 per credit. *College room only:* $5080.

Financial Aid Of all full-time matriculated undergraduates who enrolled in 2007, 579 applied for aid, 524 were judged to have need, 120 had their need fully met. 40 Federal Work-Study jobs (averaging $1502). 190 state and other part-time jobs (averaging $1306). In 2007, 144 non-need-based awards were made. *Average percent of need met:* 83%. *Average financial aid package:* $19,161. *Average need-based loan:* $4948. *Average need-based gift aid:* $6575. *Average non-need-based aid:* $8472. *Average indebtedness upon graduation:* $21,178.

Applying *Options:* electronic application, deferred entrance. *Application fee:* $25. *Required:* essay or personal statement, high school transcript, minimum 2.5 GPA, 1 letter of recommendation. *Recommended:* interview. *Application deadline:* 8/1 (freshmen). *Notification:* continuous until 8/15 (freshmen), continuous until 8/15 (transfers).

Freshman Application Contact Mr. David Adams, Director of Enrollment, Stephens College, 1200 East Broadway, Box 2121, Columbia, MO 65215-0002. *Phone:* 573-876-7207. *Toll-free phone:* 800-876-7207. *Fax:* 573-876-7237. *E-mail:* apply@stephens.edu.

See page 1444 for the College Close-Up.

TRUMAN STATE UNIVERSITY

Kirksville, Missouri **www.truman.edu/**

- **State-supported** comprehensive, founded 1867
- **Small-town** 140-acre campus
- **Endowment** $25.0 million
- **Coed** 5,608 undergraduate students, 98% full-time, 57% women, 43% men
- **Moderately difficult** entrance level, 81% of applicants were admitted

Undergraduates 5,473 full-time, 135 part-time. Students come from 41 states and territories, 40 other countries, 24% are from out of state, 4% African American, 2% Asian American or Pacific Islander, 2% Hispanic American, 0.8% Native American, 4% international, 2% transferred in, 51% live on campus. *Retention:* 88% of 2006 full-time freshmen returned.

Freshmen *Admission:* 4,076 applied, 3,300 admitted, 1,405 enrolled. *Average high school GPA:* 3.75. *Test scores:* SAT critical reading scores over 500: 92%; SAT math scores over 500: 95%; ACT scores over 18: 100%; SAT critical reading scores over 600: 65%; SAT math scores over 600: 57%; ACT scores over 24: 85%; SAT critical reading scores over 700: 25%; SAT math scores over 700: 17%; ACT scores over 30: 31%.

Faculty *Total:* 369, 92% full-time, 80% with terminal degrees. *Student/faculty ratio:* 16:1.

Majors Accounting; agricultural business and management; agriculture; agronomy and crop science; animal sciences; applied art; art; art history, criticism and conservation; athletic training; biology/biological sciences; business administration and management; chemistry; classics and languages, literatures and linguistics; commercial and advertising art; communication disorders; communication/speech communication and rhetoric; computer and information sciences; criminal justice/police science; criminal justice/safety; design and visual communications; dramatic/theater arts; economics; English; equestrian studies; exercise physiology; finance; fine/studio arts; French; German; health science; health services/allied health/health sciences; history; horticultural science; journalism; kinesiology and exercise science; linguistics; management information systems; marketing/marketing management; mass communication/media; mathematics; multi-/interdisciplinary studies related; music; music performance; nursing (registered nurse training); philosophy; physics; piano and organ; political science and government; pre-dentistry studies; pre-law studies; pre-medical studies; pre-pharmacy studies; pre-veterinary studies; psychology; public health; religious studies; Romance languages; Russian; sociology; Spanish; speech and rhetoric; visual and performing arts; voice and opera.

Academics *Calendar:* semesters. *Degrees:* bachelor's and master's. *Special study options:* advanced placement credit, double majors, honors programs, internships, off-campus study, part-time degree program, services for LD students, student-designed majors, study abroad, summer session for credit. *ROTC:* Army (b). *Unusual degree programs:* 3-2 engineering with University of Missouri-Rolla.

Computers on Campus 1,081 computers/terminals are available on campus for general student use. Students can access the following: computer help desk, free student e-mail accounts, online (class) grades, online (class) registration, online (class) schedules. Campuswide network is available. 100% of college-owned or -operated housing units are wired for high-speed Internet access. Wireless service is available via entire campus.

Student Life *Housing:* on-campus residence required for freshman year. *Options:* coed, disabled students. Campus housing is university owned. Freshman campus housing is guaranteed. *Activities and organizations:* drama/theater group, student-run newspaper, radio and television station, choral group, marching band, Campus Christian Fellowship, Alpha Phi Omega, Student Ambassadors, Alpha Sigma Gamma, Delta Zeta, national fraternities, national sororities. *Campus security:* 24-hour emergency response devices and patrols, student patrols, late-night transport/escort service, patrols by commissioned officers. *Student services:* health clinic, personal/psychological counseling, women's center.

Athletics Member NCAA. All Division II. *Intercollegiate sports:* baseball M (s), basketball M (s)/W (s), cheerleading M (c)/W (c), cross-country running M (s)/W (s), equestrian sports M (c)/W (c), football M (s), golf M (s)/W (s), lacrosse W (c), rugby M (c)/W (c), soccer M (s)/W (s), softball W (s), swimming and diving M (s)/W (s), tennis M (s)/W (s), track and field M (s)/W (s), ultimate Frisbee M (c)/W (c), volleyball M (c)/W (s), weight lifting M (c)/W (c), wrestling M (s). *Intramural sports:* badminton M/W, basketball M/W, bowling M/W, cross-country running M/W, football M/W, golf M/W, racquetball M/W, soccer M/W, softball M/W, swimming and diving M/W, table tennis M/W, tennis M/W, track and field M/W, ultimate Frisbee M/W, volleyball M/W.

Standardized Tests *Required:* SAT or ACT (for admission). *Recommended:* ACT (for admission).

Costs (2007–08) *One-time required fee:* $250. *Tuition:* state resident $6210 full-time, $259 per credit part-time; nonresident $10,820 full-time, $450 per credit part-time. Part-time tuition and fees vary according to course load. *Required fees:* $222 full-time. *Room and board:* $5815. Room and board charges vary according to housing facility. *Payment plan:* installment. *Waivers:* senior citizens and employees or children of employees.

Financial Aid Of all full-time matriculated undergraduates who enrolled in 2006, 3,227 applied for aid, 2,117 were judged to have need, 1,423 had their need fully met. 394 Federal Work-Study jobs (averaging $996). 1,674 state and other part-time jobs (averaging $938). In 2006, 2406 non-need-based awards were made. *Average percent of need met:* 80%. *Average financial aid package:* $6848. *Average need-based loan:* $4163. *Average need-based gift aid:* $3018. *Average non-need-based aid:* $4697. *Average indebtedness upon graduation:* $17,091.

Applying *Options:* electronic application, deferred entrance. *Required:* essay or personal statement, high school transcript. *Recommended:* minimum 3.0 GPA, interview. *Application deadlines:* 3/1 (freshmen), rolling (transfers). *Notification:* continuous (freshmen), continuous (transfers).

Freshman Application Contact Mr. Brad Chambers, Director of Admissions, Truman State University, 205 McClain Hall, 100 East Normal Street, Kirksville, MO 63501-4221. *Phone:* 660-785-4114. *Toll-free phone:* 800-892-7792. *Fax:* 660-785-7456. *E-mail:* admissions@truman.edu.

See page 1446 for the College Close-Up.

UNIVERSITY OF CENTRAL MISSOURI

Warrensburg, Missouri **www.ucmo.edu/**

- **State-supported** comprehensive, founded 1871
- **Small-town** 1561-acre campus with easy access to Kansas City
- **Endowment** $26.7 million
- **Coed** 8,919 undergraduate students, 79% full-time, 55% women, 45% men
- **Moderately difficult** entrance level, 81% of applicants were admitted

The University of Central Missouri (UCM) is a comprehensive, public institution located 35 miles from the Kansas City metro area. Within its 150 different areas of study, UCM has achieved national recognition for many of its academic programs, including aviation, criminal justice, and education. The University is also a leader among Missouri's public universities in program-specific accreditations. Founded in 1871, UCM takes ongoing pride in providing a student-centered learning environment where tenured professors teach the majority of classes. The University has a 16:1 student-faculty ratio and a graduate job placement rate of 94 percent, exceeding the national average for fourteen consecutive years. UCM received additional distinction recently when it was named one of "America's Best Colleges" by *U.S. News & World Report* and a "Best Midwestern College" by *The Princeton Review*. Prospective students should visit the University's Web site at http://www.ucmo.edu.

Undergraduates 7,070 full-time, 1,849 part-time. Students come from 39 states and territories, 51 other countries, 6% are from out of state, 6% African American, 1% Asian American or Pacific Islander, 2% Hispanic American, 0.5% Native American, 3% international, 9% transferred in, 25% live on campus. *Retention:* 71% of 2006 full-time freshmen returned.

Freshmen *Admission:* 3,887 applied, 3,132 admitted, 1,554 enrolled. *Average high school GPA:* 3.29. *Test scores:* ACT scores over 18: 94%; ACT scores over 24: 33%; ACT scores over 30: 4%.

Faculty *Total:* 443, 68% with terminal degrees. *Student/faculty ratio:* 17:1.

Majors Administrative assistant and secretarial science; aeronautical/aerospace engineering technology; agribusiness; agricultural business and management; agricultural economics; apparel and textiles; art teacher education; biology/biological sciences; business administration and management; business statistics; business teacher education; chemistry; clinical laboratory science/medical technology; commercial and advertising art; communication and media related; computer and information sciences; criminal justice/law enforcement administration; dietetics; dramatic/theater arts; economics; education; electrical, electronic and communications engineering technology; elementary education; English; family and consumer sciences/human sciences; finance; fine/studio arts; French; geography; geology/earth science; German; history; hotel/motel administration; human resources management; interior architecture; interior design; journalism; management information systems; marketing/marketing management; mathematics; middle school education; music; music teacher education; music theory and composition; nursing (registered nurse training); occupational safety and health technology; office management; parks, recreation and leisure; photography; physical education teaching and coaching; physics; physics teacher education; political science and government; pre-dentistry studies; pre-medical studies; pre-pharmacy studies; pre-veterinary studies; printing management; psychology; public relations/image management; radio and television; reading teacher education; secondary education; social work; sociology; Spanish; special education; speech and rhetoric; speech-language pathology; tourism and travel services marketing.

Academics *Calendar:* semesters. *Degrees:* associate, bachelor's, master's, post-master's, and postbachelor's certificates. *Special study options:* academic remediation for entering students, adult/continuing education programs, advanced placement credit, cooperative education, distance learning, double majors, English as a second language, honors programs, internships, off-campus study, part-time degree program, services for LD students, student-designed majors, study abroad, summer session for credit. *ROTC:* Army (b), Air Force (c). *Unusual degree programs:* 3-2 engineering with University of Missouri-Columbia, University of Missouri-Rolla, University of Missouri-Kansas City; law, medical.

Computers on Campus 1,729 computers/terminals are available on campus for general student use. Students can access the following: campus intranet, computer help desk, free student e-mail accounts, online (class) grades, online (class) registration, online (class) schedules. Campuswide network is available.

Student Life *Housing:* on-campus residence required for freshman year. *Options:* coed, men-only, women-only, disabled students. Campus housing is university owned. Freshman campus housing is guaranteed. *Activities and organizations:* drama/theater group, student-run newspaper, radio and television station, choral group, marching band, Student Government Association, Campus Activities Board, Association of Black Collegiates, International Student Organization, national fraternities, national sororities. *Campus security:* 24-hour emergency response devices and patrols, student patrols, late-night transport/escort service, controlled dormitory access, canine patrol. *Student services:* health clinic, personal/psychological counseling, women's center.

Athletics Member NCAA. All Division II. *Intercollegiate sports:* baseball M (s), basketball M (s)/W (s), bowling M (c)/W (c), cross-country running M (s)/W (s), football M (s), golf M (s), rock climbing M (c)/W (c), soccer M (c)/W (s), softball W (s), track and field M (s)/W (s), volleyball W (s), wrestling M (s). *Intramural sports:* archery M, badminton M/W, basketball M/W, bowling M/W, cheerleading M/W, cross-country running M/W, football M/W, golf M/W, racquetball M/W, riflery M/W, rock climbing M/W, soccer M/W, softball M/W, swimming and diving M/W, table tennis M/W, tennis M/W, track and field M/W, volleyball M/W, water polo M/W, weight lifting M, wrestling M.

Standardized Tests *Required:* ACT (for admission).

Costs (2007–08) *Tuition:* state resident $6225 full-time, $207 per credit part-time; nonresident $11,845 full-time, $395 per credit part-time. Full-time tuition and fees vary according to course load and location. *Required fees:* $604 full-time, $20 per credit part-time. *Room and board:* $5846; room only: $3746. Room and board charges vary according to board plan and housing facility. *Payment plans:* installment, deferred payment. *Waivers:* children of alumni, senior citizens, and employees or children of employees.

Financial Aid Of all full-time matriculated undergraduates who enrolled in 2006, 5,364 applied for aid, 3,560 were judged to have need, 792 had their need fully met. 281 Federal Work-Study jobs (averaging $1250). 1,136 state and other part-time jobs (averaging $1367). In 2006, 1085 non-need-based awards were made. *Average percent of need met:* 72%. *Average financial aid package:* $6975. *Average need-based loan:* $4069. *Average need-based gift aid:* $3024. *Average non-need-based aid:* $2180. *Average indebtedness upon graduation:* $18,099.

Applying *Options:* electronic application, deferred entrance. *Application fee:* $30. *Required:* high school transcript, rank in upper two-thirds of high school class, minimum ACT score of 20. *Required for some:* letters of recommendation. *Application deadlines:* rolling (freshmen), rolling (transfers). *Notification:* continuous (freshmen), continuous (transfers).

Freshman Application Contact Ms. Ann Nordyke, Chief Admission Officer, University of Central Missouri, 1401 Ward Edwards, Warrensburg, MO 64093. *Phone:* 660-543-4170. *Toll-free phone:* 800-729-2678. *Fax:* 660-543-8517. *E-mail:* admit@ucmovmb.cmsu.edu.

UNIVERSITY OF MISSOURI–COLUMBIA

Columbia, Missouri www.missouri.edu/

- **State-supported** university, founded 1839, part of University of Missouri System
- **Suburban** 1358-acre campus
- **Endowment** $590.9 million
- **Coed** 21,654 undergraduate students, 94% full-time, 52% women, 48% men
- **Moderately difficult** entrance level, 86% of applicants were admitted

Undergraduates 20,295 full-time, 1,359 part-time. Students come from 53 states and territories, 84 other countries, 14% are from out of state, 6% African American, 3% Asian American or Pacific Islander, 2% Hispanic American, 0.6% Native American, 1% international, 5% transferred in, 29% live on campus. *Retention:* 84% of 2006 full-time freshmen returned.

Freshmen *Admission:* 12,089 applied, 10,346 admitted, 4,982 enrolled. *Test scores:* SAT critical reading scores over 500: 85%; SAT math scores over 500: 87%; ACT scores over 18: 99%; SAT critical reading scores over 600: 49%; SAT math scores over 600: 48%; ACT scores over 24: 67%; SAT critical reading scores over 700: 11%; SAT math scores over 700: 10%; ACT scores over 30: 17%.

Faculty *Total:* 1,325, 96% full-time, 91% with terminal degrees. *Student/faculty ratio:* 17:1.

Majors Accounting; advertising; agricultural business and management; agricultural communication/journalism; agricultural economics; agricultural mechanization; agricultural teacher education; agriculture; animal sciences; anthropology; apparel and textiles; archeology; art; art history, criticism and conservation; art teacher education; Asian studies (East); Asian studies (South); atmospheric sciences and meteorology; behavioral sciences; biochemistry; biology/biological sciences; biology teacher education; broadcast journalism; business administration and management; business/managerial economics; business teacher education; chemical engineering; chemistry; chemistry teacher education; civil engineering; classics and languages, literatures and linguistics; communication disorders sciences and services related; communication/speech communication and rhetoric; computer and information sciences; computer engineering; computer science; diagnostic medical sonography and ultrasound technology; dietetics; dramatic/theater arts; early childhood education; economics; education; education related; electrical, electronics and communications engineering; elementary education; English; environmental studies; European studies; European studies (Central and Eastern); family and consumer economics related; finance; fish/game management; fishing and fisheries sciences and management; food science; foods, nutrition, and wellness; forestry; French; general studies; geography; geology/earth science; German; health/medical preparatory programs related; history; hotel/motel administration; housing and human environments; human development and family studies; human nutrition; industrial engineering; interdisciplinary studies; interior architecture; international agriculture; international business/trade/commerce; international economics; journalism; kindergarten/preschool education; Latin; Latin American studies; linguistics; management information systems; marketing/marketing management; mass communication/media; mathematics; mathematics teacher education; mechanical engineering; medical radiologic technology; microbiology; middle school education; modern Greek; music; music teacher education; natural resources/conservation; nuclear medical technology; nursing (registered nurse training); nutrition sciences; occupational therapy; parks, recreation and leisure; peace studies and conflict resolution; philosophy; photojournalism; physics; physics teacher education; plant sciences; political science and government; psychology; publishing; radio and television; radiologic technology/science; real estate; religious studies; respiratory care therapy; restaurant/food services management; Russian; Russian studies; science teacher education; secondary education; social studies teacher education; social work; sociology; Spanish; special education related; statistics; technical teacher education; tourism and travel services marketing; wildlife and wildlands science and management.

Academics *Calendar:* semesters. *Degrees:* bachelor's, master's, doctoral, first professional, post-master's, and first professional certificates. *Special study options:* accelerated degree program, adult/continuing education programs, advanced placement credit, cooperative education, distance learning, double majors, English as a second language, external degree program, freshman honors college, honors programs, independent study, internships, off-campus study, part-time degree program, services for LD students, student-designed majors, study abroad, summer session for credit. *ROTC:* Army (b), Navy (b), Air Force (b). *Unusual degree programs:* 3-2 accountancy, physical therapy, occupational therapy.

Computers on Campus 1,080 computers/terminals are available on campus for general student use. Students can access the following: computer help desk, free student e-mail accounts, online (class) registration, online (class) schedules, telephone registration. Campuswide network is available. Wireless service is available via entire campus.

Student Life *Housing:* on-campus residence required for freshman year. *Options:* coed, men-only, women-only, disabled students. Campus housing is university owned. Freshman campus housing is guaranteed. *Activities and organizations:* drama/theater group, student-run newspaper, radio and television station, choral group, marching band, Student Governance, Greek Organizations, Academic Organizations, Religious Organizations, Sports Clubs, national fraternities, national sororities. *Campus security:* 24-hour emergency response devices and patrols, late-night transport/escort service, controlled dormitory access. *Student services:* health clinic, personal/psychological counseling, women's center, legal services.

Athletics Member NCAA. All Division I except football (Division I-A). *Intercollegiate sports:* baseball M (s), basketball M (s)/W (s), cheerleading M (c)/W (c), cross-country running M (s)/W (s), golf M (s)/W (s), gymnastics W (s), soccer W (s), softball W (s), swimming and diving M (s)/W (s), tennis W (s), track and field M (s)/W (s), volleyball W (s), wrestling M (s). *Intramural sports:* basketball M/W, fencing M (c)/W (c), football M/W, golf M/W, ice hockey M (c)/W (c), lacrosse M (c)/W (c), racquetball M (c)/W (c), riflery M (c)/W (c), rock climbing M (c)/W (c), rugby M (c)/W (c), soccer M (c)/W (c), softball M/W, tennis M (c)/W (c), ultimate Frisbee M (c)/W (c), volleyball M (c)/W (c), water polo M (c)/W (c).

Standardized Tests *Required:* SAT or ACT (for admission). *Recommended:* ACT (for admission).

Costs (2007–08) *Tuition:* state resident $7077 full-time, $236 per credit hour part-time; nonresident $17,733 full-time, $591 per credit hour part-time. Full-time tuition and fees vary according to course load, program, and reciprocity agreements. Part-time tuition and fees vary according to course load, program, and reciprocity agreements. *Required fees:* $1022 full-time, $34 per credit hour part-time. *Room and board:* $7002; room only: $3752. Room and board charges vary according to board plan and housing facility. *Payment plan:* installment. *Waivers:* senior citizens and employees or children of employees.

Financial Aid Of all full-time matriculated undergraduates who enrolled in 2006, 12,547 applied for aid, 8,716 were judged to have need, 1,873 had their need fully met. 1,188 Federal Work-Study jobs (averaging $1528). In 2006, 4672 non-need-based awards were made. *Average percent of need met:* 86%. *Average financial aid package:* $11,452. *Average need-based loan:* $4001. *Average need-based gift aid:* $6154. *Average non-need-based aid:* $4310. *Average indebtedness upon graduation:* $18,983.

Applying *Options:* electronic application, deferred entrance. *Application fee:* $45. *Required:* high school transcript, specific high school curriculum. *Application deadlines:* rolling (freshmen), rolling (transfers). *Notification:* continuous (freshmen), continuous (transfers).

Freshman Application Contact Ms. Barbara Rupp, Director of Admissions, University of Missouri–Columbia, 230 Jesse Hall, Columbia, MO 65211. *Phone:* 573-882-7786. *Toll-free phone:* 800-225-6075. *Fax:* 573-882-7887. *E-mail:* mu4u@missouri.edu.

UNIVERSITY OF MISSOURI–KANSAS CITY

Kansas City, Missouri www.umkc.edu/

- **State-supported** university, founded 1929, part of University of Missouri System
- **Urban** 191-acre campus
- **Endowment** $256.1 million
- **Coed** 9,094 undergraduate students, 61% full-time, 58% women, 42% men
- **Moderately difficult** entrance level, 60% of applicants were admitted

Undergraduates 5,537 full-time, 3,557 part-time. Students come from 47 states and territories, 55 other countries, 26% are from out of state, 12% African American, 5% Asian American or Pacific Islander, 4% Hispanic American, 0.7% Native American, 2% international, 14% transferred in, 12% live on campus. *Retention:* 71% of 2006 full-time freshmen returned.

Freshmen *Admission:* 3,458 applied, 2,088 admitted, 959 enrolled. *Average high school GPA:* 3.33. *Test scores:* SAT critical reading scores over 500: 86%; SAT math scores over 500: 91%; ACT scores over 18: 92%; SAT critical reading scores over 600: 56%; SAT math scores over 600: 66%; ACT scores over 24: 56%; SAT critical reading scores over 700: 14%; SAT math scores over 700: 25%; ACT scores over 30: 15%.

Faculty *Total:* 1,522, 64% full-time, 66% with terminal degrees. *Student/faculty ratio:* 9:1.

Majors Accounting; American studies; art; art history, criticism and conservation; biology/biological sciences; business administration and management; chemistry; civil engineering; clinical/medical laboratory technology; communication/speech communication and rhetoric; computer science; criminal justice/law enforcement administration; criminology; dance; dental hygiene; dramatic/theater arts; early childhood education; economics; electrical, electronics and communications engineering; elementary education; English; fine/studio arts; French; geography; geology/earth science; German; history; information technology; interdisciplinary studies; liberal arts and sciences/liberal studies; mass communication/media; mathematics; mechanical engineering; middle school education; music; music performance; music teacher education; music theory and composition; nursing (registered nurse training); pharmacy; philosophy; physics; political science and government; psychology; secondary education; sociology; Spanish; statistics; urban education and leadership; urban studies/affairs.

Academics *Calendar:* semesters. *Degrees:* bachelor's, master's, doctoral, first professional, post-master's, and first professional certificates. *Special study options:* accelerated degree program, adult/continuing education programs, advanced placement credit, cooperative education, distance learning, double majors, English as a second language, honors programs, independent study, internships, off-campus study, part-time degree program, services for LD students, student-designed majors, study abroad, summer session for credit. *ROTC:* Army (b), Air Force (c). *Unusual degree programs:* education.

Computers on Campus 728 computers/terminals are available on campus for general student use. Students can access the following: campus intranet, computer help desk, free student e-mail accounts, online (class) grades, online (class) registration, online (class) schedules. Campuswide network is available. 88% of college-owned or -operated housing units are wired for high-speed Internet access. Wireless service is available via classrooms, computer labs, dorm rooms, libraries.

Student Life *Housing options:* coed. Campus housing is university owned. *Activities and organizations:* drama/theater group, student-run newspaper, choral group, African-American Student Association, International Student Council, Alpha Phi Omega, Activities and Programs Council, Intramural Organizations, national fraternities, national sororities. *Campus security:* 24-hour emergency response devices and patrols, late-night transport/escort service, controlled dormitory access. *Student services:* health clinic, personal/psychological counseling, women's center, legal services.

Athletics Member NCAA. All Division I. *Intercollegiate sports:* basketball M (s)/W (s), cheerleading W, cross-country running M (s)/W (s), golf M (s)/W (s), riflery M (s)/W (s), soccer M (s), softball W (s), tennis M (s)/W (s), track and field M (s)/W (s), volleyball W (s). *Intramural sports:* badminton M/W, basketball M/W, football M/W, golf M/W, racquetball M/W, soccer M/W, softball M/W, squash M/W, swimming and diving M/W, table tennis M/W, track and field M/W, ultimate Frisbee M/W, volleyball M/W, water polo M/W, weight lifting M/W.

Standardized Tests *Required:* SAT or ACT (for admission).

Costs (2008–09) *Tuition:* state resident $7368 full-time, $246 per credit hour part-time; nonresident $18,459 full-time, $615 per credit hour part-time. *Required fees:* $1028 full-time, $33 per credit hour part-time, $15 per term part-time. *Room and board:* $7841; room only: $5460.

Financial Aid Of all full-time matriculated undergraduates who enrolled in 2007, 4,166 applied for aid, 3,608 were judged to have need, 332 had their need fully met. In 2007, 1885 non-need-based awards were made. *Average percent of need met:* 55%. *Average financial aid package:* $9318. *Average need-based loan:* $8405. *Average need-based gift aid:* $6137. *Average non-need-based aid:* $2148. *Average indebtedness upon graduation:* $19,137.

Applying *Options:* electronic application, deferred entrance. *Application fee:* $35. *Required:* high school transcript. *Required for some:* essay or personal statement, interview. *Application deadlines:* rolling (freshmen), rolling (transfers). *Notification:* continuous (freshmen), continuous (transfers).

Freshman Application Contact Ms. Jennifer DeHaemers, Director of Admissions, University of Missouri–Kansas City, Office of Admissions, 5100 Rockhill Road, Kansas City, MO 64110-2499. *Phone:* 816-235-1111. *Toll-free phone:* 800-775-8652. *Fax:* 816-235-5544. *E-mail:* admit@umkc.edu.

UNIVERSITY OF MISSOURI–ST. LOUIS

St. Louis, Missouri **www.umsl.edu/**

- **State-supported** university, founded 1963, part of University of Missouri System
- **Suburban** 350-acre campus
- **Endowment** $54.2 million
- **Coed** 12,448 undergraduate students, 48% full-time, 59% women, 41% men
- **Moderately difficult** entrance level, 46% of applicants were admitted

Undergraduates 5,943 full-time, 6,505 part-time. Students come from 35 states and territories, 60 other countries, 6% are from out of state, 18% African American, 3% Asian American or Pacific Islander, 2% Hispanic American, 0.3% Native American, 2% international, 15% transferred in, 8% live on campus. *Retention:* 72% of 2006 full-time freshmen returned.

Freshmen *Admission:* 2,272 applied, 1,056 admitted, 498 enrolled. *Test scores:* SAT math scores over 500: 73%; ACT scores over 18: 94%; SAT math scores over 600: 27%; ACT scores over 24: 43%; SAT math scores over 700: 5%; ACT scores over 30: 5%.

Faculty *Total:* 818, 55% full-time, 54% with terminal degrees. *Student/faculty ratio:* 17:1.

Majors Accounting; anthropology; applied mathematics; art history, criticism and conservation; biochemistry; biology/biological sciences; biology teacher education; business administration and management; business/commerce; business teacher education; chemistry; chemistry teacher education; civil engineering; communication/speech communication and rhetoric; computer and information sciences; criminology; drawing; early childhood education; economics; education; electrical, electronics and communications engineering; elementary education; English; English/language arts teacher education; finance; fine/studio arts; French; French language teacher education; general studies; German; German language teacher education; graphic design; history; international business/trade/commerce; liberal arts and sciences/liberal studies; literature; management information systems; management science; marketing/marketing management; mass communication/media; mathematics; mathematics teacher education; mechanical engineering; music; music performance; music teacher education; nursing (registered nurse training); painting; philosophy; photography; physical education teaching and coaching; physics; physics teacher education; political science and government; pre-dentistry studies; pre-law studies; pre-medical studies; pre-pharmacy studies; pre-veterinary studies; printmaking; psychology; psychology teacher education; public administration; secondary education; social studies teacher education; social work; sociology; Spanish; Spanish language teacher education; special education.

Academics *Calendar:* semesters. *Degrees:* bachelor's, master's, doctoral, first professional, and postbachelor's certificates. *Special study options:* accelerated degree program, adult/continuing education programs, advanced placement credit, cooperative education, distance learning, double majors, English as a second language, freshman honors college, honors programs, independent study, internships, off-campus study, part-time degree program, services for LD students, student-designed majors, study abroad, summer session for credit. *ROTC:* Army (c), Air Force (c). *Unusual degree programs:* 3-2 economics, history, philosophy, political science and sociology.

Computers on Campus 1,280 computers/terminals and 1,280 ports are available on campus for general student use. Students can access the following: campus intranet, computer help desk, free student e-mail accounts, online (class) grades, online (class) registration, online (class) schedules. Campuswide network is available. 90% of college-owned or -operated housing units are wired for high-speed Internet access. Wireless service is available via classrooms, computer centers, computer labs, learning centers, libraries, student centers.

Student Life *Housing options:* coed, women-only, disabled students. Campus housing is university owned and is provided by a third party. *Activities and organizations:* drama/theater group, student-run newspaper, radio station, choral group, Student Government Association, Associated Black Collegians, Pierre laclede Honors College Student Association, Residence Hall Council, International Student Association, national fraternities, national sororities. *Campus security:* 24-hour emergency response devices and patrols, late-night transport/escort service, controlled dormitory access. *Student services:* health clinic, personal/psychological counseling, women's center.

Athletics Member NCAA. All Division II. *Intercollegiate sports:* baseball M (s), basketball M (s)/W (s), golf M (s)/W (s), ice hockey M (c), soccer M (s)/W (s), softball W (s), tennis M (s)/W (s), volleyball W (s). *Intramural sports:* badminton M/W, basketball M/W, bowling M/W, cross-country running M/W, football M/W, golf M/W, racquetball M/W, rugby M/W, soccer M/W, softball W, table tennis M/W, tennis M/W, ultimate Frisbee M/W, volleyball M/W, weight lifting M/W.

Standardized Tests *Required:* SAT or ACT (for admission).

Costs (2007–08) *Tuition:* state resident $7077 full-time, $236 per credit hour part-time; nonresident $17,733 full-time, $591 per credit hour part-time. Full-time tuition and fees vary according to course load, program, and reciprocity agreements. Part-time tuition and fees vary according to course load, program, and reciprocity agreements. *Required fees:* $1187 full-time, $46 per credit hour part-time. *Room and board:* $7394; room only: $5458. Room and board charges vary according to board plan and housing facility. *Payment plan:* installment. *Waivers:* senior citizens and employees or children of employees.

Financial Aid Of all full-time matriculated undergraduates who enrolled in 2007, 3,844 applied for aid, 3,377 were judged to have need, 409 had their need fully met. 64 Federal Work-Study jobs (averaging $3293). In 2007, 606 non-need-based awards were made. *Average percent of need met:* 66%. *Average financial* *aid package:* $11,047. *Average need-based loan:* $4532. *Average need-based gift aid:* $4856. *Average non-need-based aid:* $4768. *Average indebtedness upon graduation:* $21,956.

Applying *Options:* electronic application. *Application fee:* $35. *Required:* high school transcript, CBHE core requirements. *Application deadlines:* rolling (freshmen), rolling (out-of-state freshmen), rolling (transfers). *Notification:* continuous (freshmen), continuous (out-of-state freshmen), continuous (transfers).

Freshman Application Contact Mr. Dennis Saunders, Associate Director of Admissions, University of Missouri–St. Louis, 301 Woods Hall, One University Boulevard, St. Louis, MO 63121. *Phone:* 314-516-5451. *Toll-free phone:* 888-GO2-UMSL. *Fax:* 314-516-5310. *E-mail:* admissions@umsl.edu.

UNIVERSITY OF PHOENIX–KANSAS CITY CAMPUS

Kansas City, Missouri **www.phoenix.edu/**

- **Proprietary** comprehensive, founded 2002
- **Urban** campus
- **Coed**
- **Noncompetitive** entrance level

Faculty *Student/faculty ratio:* 8:1.

Academics *Calendar:* continuous. *Degrees:* bachelor's and master's.

Student Life *Campus security:* late-night transport/escort service.

Costs (2007–08) *Tuition:* $11,520 full-time, $384 per credit part-time. Full-time tuition and fees vary according to course level.

Financial Aid *Average financial aid package:* $4111. *Average need-based gift aid:* $2209.

Applying *Options:* deferred entrance. *Application fee:* $45. *Required:* 1 letter of recommendation. *Required for some:* high school transcript.

Freshman Application Contact Ms. Beth Barilla, Associate Vice President, Student Admissions and Services, University of Phoenix–Kansas City Campus, 4615 East Elwood Street, Mail Stop AA-K101, Phoenix, AZ 85040-1958. *Phone:* 480-317-6000. *Toll-free phone:* 800-776-4867 (in-state); 800-228-7240 (out-of-state). *Fax:* 480-894-1758. *E-mail:* beth.barilla@phoenix.edu.

UNIVERSITY OF PHOENIX–ST. LOUIS CAMPUS

St. Louis, Missouri **www.phoenix.edu/**

- **Proprietary** comprehensive, founded 2000
- **Urban** campus
- **Coed**
- **Noncompetitive** entrance level

Faculty *Student/faculty ratio:* 7:1.

Academics *Calendar:* continuous. *Degrees:* bachelor's and master's.

Student Life *Campus security:* late-night transport/escort service.

Costs (2007–08) *Tuition:* $12,180 full-time, $406 per credit part-time. Full-time tuition and fees vary according to course level.

Financial Aid *Average financial aid package:* $3888. *Average need-based gift aid:* $2123.

Applying *Options:* deferred entrance. *Application fee:* $45. *Required:* 1 letter of recommendation. *Required for some:* high school transcript.

Freshman Application Contact Ms. Beth Barilla, Associate Vice President, Student Admissions and Services, University of Phoenix–St. Louis Campus, 4615 East Elwood Street, Mail Stop AA-K101, Phoenix, AZ 85040-1958. *Phone:* 480-317-6000. *Toll-free phone:* 800-776-4867 (in-state); 800-228-7240 (out-of-state). *Fax:* 480-894-1758. *E-mail:* beth.barilla@phoenix.edu.

UNIVERSITY OF PHOENIX–SPRINGFIELD CAMPUS

Springfield, Missouri **www.phoenix.edu/**

- **Proprietary** comprehensive
- **Urban** campus
- **Coed**
- **Noncompetitive** entrance level

Faculty *Student/faculty ratio:* 5:1.

Academics *Degrees:* bachelor's and master's.

Student Life *Campus security:* late-night transport/escort service.

Costs (2007–08) *Tuition:* $10,140 full-time, $338 per credit part-time. Full-time tuition and fees vary according to course level.

Financial Aid *Average financial aid package:* $4044. *Average need-based gift aid:* $2251.

Applying *Options:* deferred entrance. *Application fee:* $45. *Required:* 1 letter of recommendation. *Required for some:* high school transcript.

Freshman Application Contact Ms. Beth Barilla, Associate Vice President, Student Admissions and Services, University of Phoenix–Springfield Campus, 4615 East Elwood Street, Phoenix, AZ 58040-1958. *Phone:* 480-317-6000. *Toll-free phone:* 800-776-4867 (in-state); 800-228-7240 (out-of-state). *Fax:* 480-894-1758. *E-mail:* beth.barilla@phoenix.edu.

VATTEROTT COLLEGE

St. Ann, Missouri **www.vatterott-college.edu/**

Director of Admissions Mrs. Shari H. Cobb, Director of Admissions, Vatterott College, 3925 Industrial Drive, St. Ann, MO 63074-1807. *Phone:* 314-428-5900 Ext. 215. *Toll-free phone:* 800-345-6018.

VATTEROTT COLLEGE

Sunset Hills, Missouri **www.vatterott-college.edu/**

Director of Admissions Ms. Michelle Tinsley, Director of Admission, Vatterott College, 12970 Maurer Industrial Drive, St. Louis, MO 63127. *Phone:* 314-843-4200.

WASHINGTON UNIVERSITY IN ST. LOUIS

St. Louis, Missouri **www.wustl.edu/**

- **Independent** university, founded 1853
- **Suburban** 169-acre campus
- **Endowment** $5.7 billion
- **Coed** 7,253 undergraduate students, 85% full-time, 51% women, 49% men
- **Most difficult** entrance level, 17% of applicants were admitted

Undergraduates 6,141 full-time, 1,112 part-time. Students come from 54 states and territories, 57 other countries, 90% are from out of state, 10% African American, 13% Asian American or Pacific Islander, 3% Hispanic American, 0.1% Native American, 4% international, 1% transferred in, 73% live on campus. *Retention:* 97% of 2006 full-time freshmen returned.

Freshmen *Admission:* 22,428 applied, 3,887 admitted, 1,338 enrolled. *Test scores:* SAT critical reading scores over 500: 100%; SAT math scores over 500: 100%; ACT scores over 18: 100%; SAT critical reading scores over 600: 97%; SAT math scores over 600: 98%; ACT scores over 24: 100%; SAT critical reading scores over 700: 64%; SAT math scores over 700: 74%; ACT scores over 30: 85%.

Faculty *Total:* 1,066, 83% full-time, 81% with terminal degrees. *Student/faculty ratio:* 7:1.

Majors Accounting; advertising; African-American/Black studies; African studies; American literature; American studies; ancient/classical Greek; ancient studies; anthropology; applied art; applied mathematics; Arabic; archeology; architectural engineering technology; architectural technology; architecture; architecture related; area, ethnic, cultural, and gender studies related; area studies related; art; art history, criticism and conservation; art teacher education; Asian studies; Asian studies (East); biochemistry; biological and biomedical sciences related; biological and physical sciences; biology/biological sciences; biology teacher education; biomedical/medical engineering; biophysics; biopsychology; business administration and management; business administration, management and operations related; business/commerce; business/managerial economics; ceramic arts and ceramics; chemical engineering; chemistry; chemistry related; chemistry teacher education; Chinese; civil engineering; classics and languages, literatures and linguistics; cognitive psychology and psycholinguistics; commercial and advertising art; communication and journalism related; communication/speech communication and rhetoric; comparative literature; computer and information sciences; computer and information sciences and support services related; computer engineering; computer/information technology services administration related; computer science; creative writing; cultural studies; dance; design and visual communications; drama and dance teacher education; dramatic/theater arts; drawing; East Asian languages related; economics; education; education (K-12); education (specific levels and methods) related; electrical, electronics and communications engineering; elementary education; engineering; English; English language and literature related; English/language arts teacher education; English literature (British and Commonwealth); entrepreneurship; environmental studies; ethnic, cultural minority, and gender studies related; European studies; fashion/apparel design; film/cinema studies; finance; fine/studio arts; French; French language teacher education; geology/earth science; German; Germanic languages; German language teacher education; graphic design; health professions related; Hebrew; history; history teacher education; humanities; human resources management; illustration; industrial and organizational psychology; information science/studies; international business/trade/commerce; international economics; international finance; international relations and affairs; Islamic studies; Italian; Japanese; Jewish/Judaic studies; Latin; Latin American studies; liberal arts and sciences/liberal studies; literature; marketing/marketing management; marketing related; mathematics; mathematics and computer science; mathematics teacher education; mechanical engineering; medieval and Renaissance studies; merchandising, sales, and marketing operations related (general); middle school education; modern languages; multi-/interdisciplinary studies related; music; music history, literature, and theory; music theory and composition; natural resources/conservation; natural sciences; Near and Middle Eastern studies; neuroscience; operations management; painting; philosophy; philosophy and religious studies related; photography; physics; physics teacher education; political science and government; pre-dentistry studies; pre-medical studies; pre-pharmacy studies; pre-veterinary studies; printmaking; psychology; regional studies; religious studies; Romance languages; Russian; Russian studies; science teacher education; science, technology and society; sculpture; secondary education; social and philosophical foundations of education; social sciences; social sciences related; social science teacher education; social studies teacher education; Spanish; Spanish language teacher education; statistics; systems engineering; systems science and theory; theater literature, history and criticism; urban studies/affairs; voice and opera; women's studies.

Academics *Calendar:* semesters. *Degrees:* certificates, bachelor's, master's, doctoral, first professional, and postbachelor's certificates. *Special study options:* accelerated degree program, adult/continuing education programs, advanced placement credit, cooperative education, double majors, English as a second language, independent study, internships, off-campus study, part-time degree program, services for LD students, student-designed majors, study abroad, summer session for credit. *ROTC:* Army (b), Air Force (c). *Unusual degree programs:* 3-2 business administration; engineering; social work; art, occupational therapy, physical therapy.

Computers on Campus 2,500 computers/terminals are available on campus for general student use. Students can access the following: campus intranet, computer help desk, free student e-mail accounts, online (class) grades, online (class) registration, online (class) schedules. Campuswide network is available. 90% of college-owned or -operated housing units are wired for high-speed Internet access. Wireless service is available via classrooms, computer centers, computer labs, dorm rooms, learning centers, libraries, student centers.

Student Life *Housing:* on-campus residence required for freshman year. *Options:* coed, men-only, women-only, cooperative. Campus housing is university owned. Freshman campus housing is guaranteed. *Activities and organizations:* drama/theater group, student-run newspaper, radio and television station, choral group, community service organizations, student government/programming groups, performing arts groups, multicultural interest groups, intramural sports groups, national fraternities, national sororities. *Campus security:* 24-hour emergency response devices and patrols, student patrols, late-night transport/escort service, controlled dormitory access. *Student services:* health clinic, personal/psychological counseling, women's center.

Athletics Member NCAA. All Division III. *Intercollegiate sports:* baseball M, basketball M/W, crew M (c)/W (c), cross-country running M/W, equestrian sports M (c)/W (c), fencing M (c)/W (c), field hockey W (c), football M, golf M (c)/W (c), gymnastics M (c)/W (c), ice hockey M (c), lacrosse M (c)/W (c), rugby M (c)/W (c), sailing M (c)/W (c), soccer M/W, softball W, swimming and diving M/W, table tennis M (c)/W (c), tennis M/W, track and field M/W, ultimate Frisbee M (c)/W (c), volleyball M (c)/W, water polo M (c)/W (c). *Intramural sports:* badminton M/W, basketball M/W, bowling M/W, cross-country running M/W, football M/W, golf M/W, racquetball M/W, soccer M (c)/W (c), softball M/W, swimming and diving M/W, table tennis M/W, tennis M/W, track and field M/W, ultimate Frisbee M/W, volleyball M/W, water polo M/W.

Standardized Tests *Required:* SAT or ACT (for admission).

Costs (2008–09) *Comprehensive fee:* $48,884 includes full-time tuition ($36,200), mandatory fees ($1048), and room and board ($11,636). *College room only:* $7360.

Financial Aid Of all full-time matriculated undergraduates who enrolled in 2007, 4,274 applied for aid, 2,556 were judged to have need, 2,528 had their need fully met. 1,003 Federal Work-Study jobs (averaging $1863). In 2007, 880 non-need-based awards were made. *Average percent of need met:* 100%. *Average financial aid package:* $28,725. *Average need-based loan:* $6251. *Average need-based gift aid:* $24,286. *Average non-need-based aid:* $5740. *Financial aid deadline:* 2/15.

Applying *Options:* electronic application, early admission, early decision, deferred entrance. *Application fee:* $55. *Required:* essay or personal statement, high school transcript, 2 letters of recommendation. *Recommended:* minimum 3.0 GPA, portfolio for art and architecture programs. *Application deadlines:* 1/15 (freshmen), 4/15 (transfers). *Early decision deadline:* 11/15. *Notification:* 4/1 (freshmen), continuous (transfers), 12/15 (early decision).

Freshman Application Contact Ms. Nanette Tarbouni, Director of Admissions, Washington University in St. Louis, Campus Box 1089, One Brookings Drive, St. Louis, MO 63130-4899. *Phone:* 314-935-6000. *Toll-free phone:* 800-638-0700. *Fax:* 314-935-4290. *E-mail:* admissions@wustl.edu.

WEBSTER UNIVERSITY

St. Louis, Missouri **www.webster.edu/**

- **Independent** comprehensive, founded 1915
- **Suburban** 47-acre campus
- **Endowment** $68.5 million
- **Coed** 3,623 undergraduate students, 73% full-time, 58% women, 42% men
- **Moderately difficult** entrance level, 56% of applicants were admitted

Undergraduates 2,653 full-time, 970 part-time. Students come from 41 states and territories, 40 other countries, 19% are from out of state, 11% African American, 2% Asian American or Pacific Islander, 2% Hispanic American, 0.2% Native American, 3% international, 13% transferred in, 26% live on campus. *Retention:* 81% of 2006 full-time freshmen returned.

Freshmen *Admission:* 1,677 applied, 934 admitted, 499 enrolled. *Average high school GPA:* 3.47. *Test scores:* ACT scores over 18: 97%; ACT scores over 24: 54%; ACT scores over 30: 8%.

Faculty *Total:* 1,223, 14% full-time. *Student/faculty ratio:* 10:1.

Majors Accounting; advertising; anthropology; art; art history, criticism and conservation; art therapy; biology/biological sciences; broadcast journalism; business administration and management; business/commerce; cinematography and film/video production; communication and journalism related; computer science; dance; dramatic/theater arts; economics; education; elementary education; English; English language and literature related; film/cinema studies; fine/studio arts; French; German; history; interdisciplinary studies; international business/trade/commerce; international relations and affairs; journalism; legal studies; liberal arts and sciences/liberal studies; literature; marketing/marketing management; mathematics; music; music performance; music teacher education; music theory and composition; nursing (registered nurse training); philosophy; photography; political science and government; psychology; public relations/image management; radio and television; religious studies; social sciences; Spanish; technical and business writing; theater design and technology.

Academics *Calendar:* semesters. *Degrees:* certificates, bachelor's, master's, doctoral, post-master's, and postbachelor's certificates. *Special study options:* academic remediation for entering students, accelerated degree program, adult/continuing education programs, advanced placement credit, cooperative education, distance learning, double majors, English as a second language, independent study, internships, off-campus study, part-time degree program, services for LD students, student-designed majors, study abroad, summer session for credit. *ROTC:* Army (c), Air Force (c). *Unusual degree programs:* 3-2 engineering with University of Missouri-Columbia, Washington University in St. Louis; architecture with Washington University in St. Louis.

Computers on Campus 450 computers/terminals are available on campus for general student use. Students can access the following: computer help desk, free student e-mail accounts, online (class) grades, online (class) registration, online (class) schedules. Campuswide network is available. 100% of college-owned or -operated housing units are wired for high-speed Internet access. Wireless service is available via classrooms, computer labs, libraries, student centers.

Student Life *Housing options:* coed. Campus housing is university owned. Freshman applicants given priority for college housing. *Activities and organizations:* drama/theater group, student-run newspaper, radio and television station, choral group, Student Government Association, Habitat for Humanity, Big Brothers/Big Sisters, Marketing Communications Club, Residential Housing Association. *Campus security:* 24-hour emergency response devices and patrols, student patrols, late-night transport/escort service. *Student services:* health clinic, personal/psychological counseling, women's center.

Athletics Member NCAA. All Division III. *Intercollegiate sports:* baseball M, basketball M/W, cross-country running W, golf M, soccer M/W, softball W, swimming and diving M/W, tennis M/W, volleyball W. *Intramural sports:* bowling M (c)/W (c), soccer M (c)/W (c), table tennis M (c)/W (c), volleyball M (c).

Standardized Tests *Required:* SAT or ACT (for admission).

Costs (2007–08) *Comprehensive fee:* $27,550 includes full-time tuition ($19,330) and room and board ($8220). Full-time tuition and fees vary according to program. Part-time tuition: $495 per credit hour. Part-time tuition and fees vary according to location. *College room only:* $4100. Room and board charges vary according to board plan and housing facility. *Payment plan:* installment. *Waivers:* employees or children of employees.

Financial Aid Of all full-time matriculated undergraduates who enrolled in 2007, 2,133 applied for aid, 1,824 were judged to have need. 424 Federal Work-Study jobs (averaging $1943). 826 state and other part-time jobs (averaging $1637). In 2007, 529 non-need-based awards were made. *Average financial aid package:* $19,911. *Average need-based loan:* $4625. *Average need-based gift aid:* $6229. *Average non-need-based aid:* $7088. *Average indebtedness upon graduation:* $23,183.

Applying *Options:* electronic application, early admission, deferred entrance. *Application fee:* $35. *Required:* essay or personal statement, high school transcript, minimum 2.5 GPA, 1 letter of recommendation. *Required for some:* minimum 3.0 GPA, audition. *Recommended:* minimum 3.0 GPA, interview. *Application deadlines:* 6/1 (freshmen), 8/1 (transfers). *Notification:* continuous (freshmen), continuous (transfers).

Freshman Application Contact Mr. Andrew Laue, Associate Director of Undergraduate Admission, Webster University, 470 East Lockwood Avenue, St. Louis, MO 63119-3194. *Phone:* 314-961-2660. *Toll-free phone:* 800-75-ENROL. *Fax:* 314-968-7115. *E-mail:* admit@webster.edu.

WESTMINSTER COLLEGE

Fulton, Missouri **www.westminster-mo.edu/**

- **Independent** 4-year, founded 1851, affiliated with Presbyterian Church
- **Small-town** 80-acre campus
- **Endowment** $49.6 million
- **Coed** 972 undergraduate students, 98% full-time, 44% women, 56% men
- **Moderately difficult** entrance level, 80% of applicants were admitted

Undergraduates 952 full-time, 20 part-time. Students come from 17 states and territories, 65 other countries, 24% are from out of state, 4% African American, 2% Asian American or Pacific Islander, 2% Hispanic American, 1% Native American, 14% international, 3% transferred in, 74% live on campus. *Retention:* 83% of 2006 full-time freshmen returned.

Freshmen *Admission:* 931 applied, 744 admitted, 224 enrolled. *Average high school GPA:* 3.31. *Test scores:* SAT critical reading scores over 500: 71%; SAT math scores over 500: 79%; ACT scores over 18: 99%; SAT critical reading scores over 600: 31%; SAT math scores over 600: 34%; ACT scores over 24: 66%; SAT critical reading scores over 700: 5%; ACT scores over 30: 15%.

Faculty *Total:* 91, 60% full-time, 51% with terminal degrees. *Student/faculty ratio:* 14:1.

Majors Accounting; anthropology; biochemistry; biology/biological sciences; business administration and management; chemistry; computer science; economics; elementary education; English; environmental science; environmental studies; French; history; international business/trade/commerce; international relations and affairs; management information systems; mathematics; middle school education; philosophy; physical education teaching and coaching; physics; political science and government; pre-law studies; psychology; religious studies; secondary education; sociology; Spanish.

Academics *Calendar:* semesters. *Degree:* bachelor's. *Special study options:* academic remediation for entering students, advanced placement credit, cooperative education, double majors, honors programs, independent study, internships, off-campus study, part-time degree program, services for LD students, student-designed majors, study abroad, summer session for credit. *ROTC:* Army (c), Air Force (c). *Unusual degree programs:* 3-2 engineering with Washington University in St. Louis, University of Missouri-Columbia.

Computers on Campus 188 computers/terminals are available on campus for general student use. Students can access the following: computer help desk, free student e-mail accounts, online (class) grades, online (class) registration, online (class) schedules. Campuswide network is available. 100% of college-owned or -operated housing units are wired for high-speed Internet access.

Student Life *Housing:* on-campus residence required through junior year. *Options:* coed, women-only. Campus housing is university owned. Freshman campus housing is guaranteed. *Activities and organizations:* drama/theater group, student-run newspaper, choral group, Student Government Association, Environmentally Concerned Students, International Student Club, Habitat for Humanity, Little Brother/Little Sister, national fraternities, national sororities. *Campus security:* 24-hour emergency response devices and patrols, late-night transport/escort service, controlled dormitory access, well-lit campus. *Student services:* health clinic, personal/psychological counseling, women's center.

Athletics Member NCAA. All Division III. *Intercollegiate sports:* baseball M, basketball M/W, football M, golf M/W, soccer M/W, softball W, tennis M/W, volleyball W. *Intramural sports:* basketball M/W, football M, softball M/W, table tennis M/W, volleyball M/W.

Standardized Tests *Required:* SAT or ACT (for admission).

Costs (2008–09) *Comprehensive fee:* $23,970 includes full-time tuition ($16,650), mandatory fees ($600), and room and board ($6720). *College room only:* $3500.

Financial Aid Of all full-time matriculated undergraduates who enrolled in 2007, 632 applied for aid, 526 were judged to have need, 319 had their need fully met. 139 Federal Work-Study jobs (averaging $573). 152 state and other part-time jobs (averaging $1566). In 2007, 411 non-need-based awards were made. *Average percent of need met:* 93%. *Average financial aid package:* $13,993. *Average need-based loan:* $3512. *Average need-based gift aid:* $10,499. *Average non-need-based aid:* $7882. *Average indebtedness upon graduation:* $18,958.

Applying *Options:* electronic application, early admission, deferred entrance. *Required:* high school transcript, 1 letter of recommendation, minimum ACT score of 21 or minimum SAT score of 970. *Required for some:* interview. *Recommended:* essay or personal statement, minimum 2.5 GPA. *Notification:* continuous until 8/1 (freshmen), continuous (transfers).

Freshman Application Contact Dr. George Wolf, Vice President and Dean of Enrollment Services, Westminster College, 501 Westminster Avenue, Fulton, MO 65251-1299. *Phone:* 573-592-5251. *Toll-free phone:* 800-475-3361. *Fax:* 573-592-5255. *E-mail:* admissions@westminster-mo.edu.

See page 1448 for the College Close-Up.

WILLIAM JEWELL COLLEGE

Liberty, Missouri **www.jewell.edu/**

- **Independent Baptist** 4-year, founded 1849
- **Small-town** 200-acre campus with easy access to Kansas City
- **Endowment** $86.3 million
- **Coed** 1,329 undergraduate students, 83% full-time, 60% women, 40% men
- **Moderately difficult** entrance level, 92% of applicants were admitted

Undergraduates 1,108 full-time, 221 part-time. Students come from 29 states and territories, 2 other countries, 29% are from out of state, 4% African American, 1% Asian American or Pacific Islander, 3% Hispanic American, 2% Native American, 0.5% international, 3% transferred in, 62% live on campus. *Retention:* 81% of 2006 full-time freshmen returned.

Freshmen *Admission:* 990 applied, 911 admitted, 288 enrolled. *Average high school GPA:* 3.62. *Test scores:* SAT critical reading scores over 500: 87%; SAT math scores over 500: 78%; ACT scores over 18: 99%; SAT critical reading scores over 600: 54%; SAT math scores over 600: 43%; ACT scores over 24: 64%; SAT critical reading scores over 700: 17%; SAT math scores over 700: 18%; ACT scores over 30: 16%.

Faculty *Total:* 158, 49% full-time. *Student/faculty ratio:* 11:1.

Majors Accounting; art; art teacher education; biochemistry; biology/biological sciences; business administration and management; business/managerial economics; cell biology and histology; chemistry; chemistry teacher education; clinical laboratory science/medical technology; computer science; drama and dance teacher education; dramatic/theater arts; economics; elementary education; English; English/language arts teacher education; foreign language teacher education; French; French language teacher education; history; information science/studies; international business/trade/commerce; international relations and affairs; mathematics; middle school education; molecular biology; music; music performance; music teacher education; music theory and composition; nursing (registered nurse training); parks, recreation and leisure; philosophy; physical education teaching and coaching; physics; physics teacher education; political science and government; psychology; religious/sacred music; religious studies; secondary education; Spanish; Spanish language teacher education; speech and rhetoric; speech teacher education.

Academics *Calendar:* semesters. *Degrees:* bachelor's (also offers evening program with significant enrollment not reflected in profile). *Special study options:* academic remediation for entering students, adult/continuing education programs, advanced placement credit, cooperative education, double majors, honors programs, independent study, internships, off-campus study, part-time degree program, services for LD students, student-designed majors, study abroad, summer session for credit. *Unusual degree programs:* 3-2 engineering with

Columbia University, Washington University in St. Louis, University of Kansas, Vanderbilt University; forestry with Duke University.

Computers on Campus 232 computers/terminals are available on campus for general student use. Students can access the following: campus intranet, computer help desk, free student e-mail accounts, online (class) grades, online (class) registration, online (class) schedules. Campuswide network is available. 100% of college-owned or -operated housing units are wired for high-speed Internet access. Wireless service is available via classrooms, learning centers, libraries, student centers.

Student Life *Housing:* on-campus residence required through junior year. *Options:* coed, men-only, women-only, disabled students. Campus housing is university owned. Freshman campus housing is guaranteed. *Activities and organizations:* drama/theater group, student-run newspaper, radio station, choral group, Christian student ministries, College Union activities, Fellowship of Christian Athletes, UNITY, Amnesty International, national fraternities, national sororities. *Campus security:* 24-hour emergency response devices and patrols, late-night transport/escort service, controlled dormitory access. *Student services:* health clinic, personal/psychological counseling.

Athletics Member NAIA. *Intercollegiate sports:* baseball M (s), basketball M (s)/W (s), cheerleading M (s)/W (s), cross-country running M (s)/W (s), football M (s), golf M (s)/W (s), soccer M (s)/W (s), softball W (s), tennis M (s)/W (s), track and field M (s)/W (s), volleyball W (s). *Intramural sports:* racquetball M/W, soccer M/W, softball M/W, tennis M/W, ultimate Frisbee M/W, volleyball M/W.

Standardized Tests *Required:* SAT or ACT (for admission).

Costs (2008–09) *Comprehensive fee:* $29,430 includes full-time tuition ($23,000), mandatory fees ($300), and room and board ($6130). Part-time tuition: $700 per credit hour. *College room only:* $2610.

Financial Aid Of all full-time matriculated undergraduates who enrolled in 2007, 863 applied for aid, 745 were judged to have need, 239 had their need fully met. 337 Federal Work-Study jobs (averaging $1485). 163 state and other part-time jobs (averaging $800). *Average percent of need met:* 90%. *Average financial aid package:* $16,372. *Average need-based loan:* $5249. *Average need-based gift aid:* $12,020. *Average indebtedness upon graduation:* $24,240.

Applying *Options:* electronic application, deferred entrance. *Application fee:* $25. *Required:* essay or personal statement, high school transcript. *Required for some:* interview. *Recommended:* letters of recommendation, interview. *Application deadlines:* 8/15 (freshmen), rolling (transfers). *Notification:* continuous (transfers).

Freshman Application Contact Ms. Bridget Gramling, Dean of Admission, William Jewell College, 500 College Hill, Liberty, MO 64068. *Phone:* 816-415-7511. *Toll-free phone:* 888-2JEWELL. *E-mail:* gramblingb@william.jewell.edu.

WILLIAM WOODS UNIVERSITY

Fulton, Missouri **www.williamwoods.edu/**

- **Independent** comprehensive, founded 1870, affiliated with Christian Church (Disciples of Christ)
- **Small-town** 170-acre campus with easy access to St. Louis
- **Endowment** $12.9 million
- **Coed** 975 undergraduate students, 81% full-time, 73% women, 27% men
- **Moderately difficult** entrance level, 85% of applicants were admitted

Undergraduates 786 full-time, 189 part-time. Students come from 42 states and territories, 13 other countries, 47% are from out of state, 3% African American, 0.1% Asian American or Pacific Islander, 1% Hispanic American, 0.7% Native American, 3% international, 13% transferred in, 80% live on campus. *Retention:* 75% of 2006 full-time freshmen returned.

Freshmen *Admission:* 613 applied, 520 admitted, 186 enrolled. *Average high school GPA:* 3.3. *Test scores:* SAT critical reading scores over 500: 51%; SAT math scores over 500: 44%; ACT scores over 18: 92%; SAT critical reading scores over 600: 26%; SAT math scores over 600: 19%; ACT scores over 24: 36%; SAT critical reading scores over 700: 2%; ACT scores over 30: 7%.

Faculty *Total:* 249, 22% full-time, 28% with terminal degrees. *Student/faculty ratio:* 14:1.

Majors Accounting; advertising; art; art teacher education; athletic training; biology/biological sciences; broadcast journalism; business administration and management; business/managerial economics; commercial and advertising art; communication/speech communication and rhetoric; comparative literature; computer and information sciences; design and visual communications; dramatic/theater arts; education; elementary education; English; English composition; English/language arts teacher education; equestrian studies; fine/studio arts; French language teacher education; history; interdisciplinary studies; interior design; international business/trade/commerce; international relations and affairs; legal assistant/paralegal; liberal arts and sciences/liberal studies; management information systems; mathematics; mathematics teacher education; middle school education; physical education teaching and coaching; political science and government; psychology; public relations/image management; radio and television; science teacher education; secondary education; sign language interpretation and translation; social work; Spanish; special education; speech/theater education; theater design and technology.

Academics *Calendar:* semesters. *Degrees:* associate, bachelor's, master's, post-master's, and first professional certificates. *Special study options:* academic remediation for entering students, accelerated degree program, adult/continuing education programs, advanced placement credit, double majors, honors programs, independent study, internships, off-campus study, part-time degree program, student-designed majors, study abroad, summer session for credit. *ROTC:* Army (c), Navy (c), Air Force (c).

Computers on Campus 105 computers/terminals and 50 ports are available on campus for general student use. Students can access the following: campus intranet, computer help desk, free student e-mail accounts, online (class) grades, online (class) registration, online (class) schedules. Campuswide network is available. 100% of college-owned or -operated housing units are wired for high-speed Internet access. Wireless service is available via classrooms, computer labs, learning centers, libraries.

Student Life *Housing:* on-campus residence required through senior year. *Options:* coed, men-only, women-only. Campus housing is university owned. Freshman campus housing is guaranteed. *Activities and organizations:* drama/theater group, student-run newspaper, radio station, choral group, Campus Crusade for Christ, Leader Scholars, Hunter Jumper Show Team, national fraternities, national sororities. *Campus security:* 24-hour emergency response devices and patrols, late-night transport/escort service, controlled dormitory access. *Student services:* health clinic, personal/psychological counseling.

Athletics Member NAIA. *Intercollegiate sports:* baseball M (s), basketball M (s)/W (s), cross-country running M (s)/W (s), golf M (s)/W (s), soccer M (s)/W (s), softball W (s), track and field M (s)/W (s), volleyball M (s)/W (s). *Intramural sports:* badminton M/W, baseball M, basketball M/W, equestrian sports M/W, football M/W, rugby M/W, softball M/W, table tennis M/W, tennis M/W, volleyball M/W, weight lifting M/W.

Standardized Tests *Required:* SAT or ACT (for admission).

Costs (2007–08) *Comprehensive fee:* $22,480 includes full-time tuition ($15,650), mandatory fees ($430), and room and board ($6400). Full-time tuition and fees vary according to degree level and program. Part-time tuition: $520 per credit. Part-time tuition and fees vary according to course load, degree level, and program. *Required fees:* $15 per term part-time. *Room and board:* Room and board charges vary according to board plan and housing facility. *Payment plan:* installment. *Waivers:* children of alumni, senior citizens, and employees or children of employees.

Financial Aid Of all full-time matriculated undergraduates who enrolled in 2005, 733 applied for aid, 515 were judged to have need, 160 had their need fully met. 302 Federal Work-Study jobs (averaging $1278). 169 state and other part-time jobs (averaging $847). In 2005, 271 non-need-based awards were made. *Average percent of need met:* 79%. *Average financial aid package:* $12,617. *Average need-based loan:* $3931. *Average need-based gift aid:* $9235. *Average non-need-based aid:* $9356. *Average indebtedness upon graduation:* $13,865.

Applying *Options:* electronic application, deferred entrance. *Application fee:* $25. *Required:* high school transcript, minimum 2.5 GPA, 16 hours college prep. *Required for some:* essay or personal statement, 2 letters of recommendation. *Recommended:* interview. *Application deadlines:* rolling (freshmen), rolling (transfers). *Notification:* continuous (freshmen), continuous (transfers).

Freshman Application Contact Ms. Sharon Horn, Admissions Data Analyst, William Woods University, One University Avenue, Fulton, MO 65251. *Phone:* 573-592-4221. *Toll-free phone:* 800-995-3159 Ext. 4221. *Fax:* 573-592-1146. *E-mail:* admissions@williamwoods.edu.

CULVER-STOCKTON COLLEGE

CANTON, MISSOURI

The College

Students at Culver-Stockton College (C-SC) receive a superb education that extends far beyond the classroom. The four-year experience at C-SC expands not only the student's academic knowledge but also an awareness of the world in which they live. Besides achieving their academic goals, students receive an opportunity to develop their leadership skills, discover new interests, and form lasting relationships with classmates and faculty and staff members. These opportunities play a major part in the College's goal of creating an active learning environment.

C-SC was founded in 1853 as the first coeducational institution of higher learning west of the Mississippi River. Affiliated with the Christian Church (Disciples of Christ), the College is personal (about 850 students) and provides a strong liberal arts foundation with practical learning experiences.

Primarily residential in character, the College offers a full array of extracurricular activities, including course-related clubs and organizations, an active national fraternity and sorority system, an intramural program, and a strong intercollegiate athletics program featuring men's teams in baseball, basketball, cross-country, football, golf, soccer, and track and field; and women's teams in basketball, cross-country, golf, soccer, softball, track and field, and volleyball. The College also features a coed spirit squad team and an award-winning dance team. Performance opportunities in the fine arts include outstanding choral and instrumental ensembles as well as several theater productions each year, which are open to nonmajors as well.

Culver-Stockton College has more than 10,000 living alumni, many of whom have achieved distinction in the arts, government, medicine, law, education, and other professional fields. With more than 150 years of history, Culver-Stockton College moves into the twenty-first century as one of the truly distinctive small liberal arts colleges in the Midwest.

Culver-Stockton College is fully accredited by the Higher Learning Commission of the North Central Association of Colleges and Schools, the Missouri Department of Elementary and Secondary Education, the International Assembly for Collegiate Business Education, the National Association of Schools of Music, the Commission on Accreditation of Allied Health Education Programs, the National League of Nursing, and the Commission on Collegiate Nursing Education.

Location

Canton, Missouri, a town of 2,600 on the Mississippi River, sits in the rolling farmland of northeast Missouri. The College has close ties with Quincy, Illinois, a progressive, arts-oriented community of approximately 45,000. Canton is located on U.S. 61, the "Avenue of the Saints," 30 miles north of historic Hannibal, Missouri, the boyhood home of the famous American author Mark Twain. St. Louis is within a 2½-hour drive, and Chicago and Kansas City are close enough to be significant factors in the cultural life of the College. Culver-Stockton sits atop a hill that overlooks Canton and the Mississippi River. Canton exhibits a strong sense of community pride, civic involvement, and a very low crime rate. Canton and Culver-Stockton work closely together on common issues such as emergency preparedness and economic development.

Majors and Degrees

Culver-Stockton offers an array of bachelor's degrees: the Bachelor of Fine Arts (in art, arts management, music, musical theater, and theater), the Bachelor of Music Education, and the Bachelor of Science in Nursing. Study areas include accounting, art education, athletic training, biology, business administration, communication, criminal justice, education, English, finance, history and political science, management, management information systems, mathematics, psychology, religion and philosophy, speech and theater education, and sports management. Culver-Stockton also accepts students who are undecided and works with them in selecting a major.

Academic Programs

The Culver-Stockton emphasis on career preparation is enhanced by the liberal arts. The development of student skills in writing, speaking, critical thinking, and problem solving is a critical element in the liberal arts emphasis. In addition, core courses in composition, religious studies, and speech combine with student choices from among five areas to ensure a wide breadth of study. Students must complete 124 credit hours for the bachelor's degree. Major programs require from 30 to 62 credits. Double majors and minors are encouraged, adding further diversity and breadth to graduates' qualifications as they approach the job market.

The College has committed itself to academic distinction. Students are challenged to achieve their maximum potential in learned skills, breadth and depth of knowledge, and understanding their own values. Students are assigned an academic adviser, who is prepared to assist students in achieving their educational goals. An individualized plan is developed and then updated each semester until graduation.

For highly motivated students, including freshmen, the Honors Scholars Program provides the opportunity to participate in certain specially designated courses and events, culminating in an opportunity for independent study or research in an area of the student's special interest. The program is especially helpful for students planning for graduate programs.

Exploratory and professional internships are available in all majors and are viewed as an important part of the career selection process. More than 700 internship sites are available. Combined with an active career counseling and placement service that includes computerized interest and preference testing, on- and off-campus internships are a key element in the Culver-Stockton approach to preparing students for employment after graduation.

Work completed at other colleges and universities is transferable toward Culver-Stockton graduation requirements, and various testing procedures (e.g., CLEP, AP, PEP) allow credit for equivalent knowledge or experience. Individualized learning options are plentiful; they range from individually negotiated independent study to the option of developing an individualized major.

The College operates on a two-semester calendar, with the first semester concluding before Christmas and the spring semester ending in early to mid-May. Summer sessions of varying lengths are also available. All programs and classes are characterized by individual attention.

In January 2006, the College began offering online courses for nontraditional students through the Connected Campus program. The degree-completion programs include the Bachelor of Science in business administration and Bachelor of Science in management information systems.

Off-Campus Programs

Students at Culver-Stockton College may pursue a variety of study-abroad opportunities. For example, each January, students and faculty members travel together on study-abroad trips. Recent trips have included such destinations as Austria, Greece, Great Britain, Italy, and China. C-SC also offers a Semester Study and International Program in London in association with the Missouri Consortium for International Programs and Studies and International Enrichment Inc. The College's wind ensemble and concert choir also take concert tours annually.

Academic Facilities

C-SC is a wireless campus. Not only are all buildings and some green spaces accessible by wireless devices, there are also several computer labs and a cyber café. Culver-Stockton maintains four general computer labs, as well as four specialized labs. Faculty members have integrated computers into the classroom in almost every field, using dedicated computer labs equipped with major-specific software. Several SMART classrooms were added in 2007.

The computerized Johann Memorial Library has a collection of 151,979 volumes and also presents comprehensive collections of periodicals, journals, and other materials in both hard copy and microform. Extensive interlibrary loan and electronic bibliographical search capabilities are available to both students and the faculty. C-SC belongs to the MOBIUS Consortium, which provides open access to the holdings of every academic library in Missouri. Students also have access to more than 6 million volumes through the College's link to a statewide library database.

The Robert W. Brown Performing Arts Center and Mabee Art Gallery house professional-quality art and performance studios, computer laboratories, and three performance stages where 200 to nearly 1,000 guests can attend theater and music performances.

The five-year-old Science Center is home to the departments of biology, chemistry, clinical laboratory sciences, and mathematics. Students can benefit from its state-of-the-art labs and technology, classrooms with full multimedia capabilities, and facilities designed specifically for student research.

Costs

The 2007–08 school year costs at Culver-Stockton College were $16,600 for tuition, $6850 for room and board, approximately $800 for books and supplies, and a $125 unified student fee. With the exception of students who are married or living with parents, all students receiving financial aid from the College are required to participate in the College's room and board plan. Variable board plans are available for the dining hall and Cat's Pause, the campus snack bar and cyber café.

Financial Aid

Culver-Stockton College understands the financial needs of students and their families and works to make a C-SC education affordable. The College assists every qualified student to meet the costs of earning a C-SC degree. Through scholarships, grants, work-study opportunities, and loans, the College works to offset the cost of a college education for qualified students. Through careful tuition pricing and a variety of financial aid options, C-SC is a great value for a superb educational experience.

The College participates in all federal and state financial aid programs, presenting aid packages that are based on need and merit. Merit awards are based on academic achievement as well as performance—theater, music, art, leadership, and athletics. The College requires the Free Application for Federal Student Aid (FAFSA). Vision and Pillars for Excellence full-tuition scholarships are awarded on a competitive basis each year for high-achieving students who meet certain GPA and ACT criteria.

Faculty

The strength of the College's academic program is the outstanding faculty. Faculty members provide instruction of high quality and individualized attention to students. Faculty members are active in scholarship, professional activity, and service. Faculty members also take an active role in many aspects of college life, including the advising and sponsorship of student organizations.

Student Government

An active Student Government Association deals with significant issues of student interest and communicates information about them to the faculty and administration. Students have voting representation on key faculty committees, such as the Academic Council, the Student Development Council, the Academic and Cultural Events Committee, and others that have a direct impact upon the nature and quality of student life. The Student Government Association president also serves as the student representative on the College's board of trustees. An active Campus Programming Council regularly plans student events.

Admission Requirements

Prospective students are expected to have completed a college-preparatory course of study of 15 units at an accredited secondary school. A proper foundation to facilitate success in college studies includes 4 units of English, 3 units of history, at least 2 units of mathematics (algebra and geometry), and 2 to 4 units of science. Students who intend to major in scientific disciplines may wish to select additional high school courses in science and mathematics, and those interested in the humanities and social studies areas typically present additional course work in literature, foreign language, and social studies. Applicants must submit ACT or SAT scores. Each applicant for admission is given personal attention and is considered on the basis of academic performance, test scores, and personal attributes. An electronic application is available on the College's Web site at http://www.culver.edu.

Application and Information

Early application is recommended, as residence halls and classroom space may be limited. For further information, students should contact:

Admissions Office
Culver-Stockton College
One College Hill
Canton, Missouri 63435
Phone: 800-537-1883 (toll-free)
E-mail: admissions@culver.edu
Web site: http://www.culver.edu

Students on the Culver-Stockton College campus.

LINDENWOOD UNIVERSITY

ST. CHARLES, MISSOURI

The University

An independent teaching university founded in 1827, Lindenwood is the oldest university west of the Missouri River. Lindenwood is a dynamic four-year liberal arts institution dedicated to excellence, delivering a high-quality education that leads to the development of the whole person and preparation for life and work after graduation, through more than eighty values-centered programs.

Lindenwood University (LU) is accredited by the Higher Learning Commission of the North Central Association of Colleges and Schools and the Missouri Department of Elementary and Secondary Education and is a member of the Teacher Education Accreditation Council. Lindenwood University is authorized to grant associate, bachelor's, master's, Education Specialist, and Doctor of Education degrees. Lindenwood is an independent, public-serving, liberal arts university that has a historical relationship with the Presbyterian Church and is committed to the values inherent in the Judeo-Christian tradition. Lindenwood welcomes students from all religious denominations.

The University's athletic teams compete in the Heart of America Athletic Conference and the National Association of Intercollegiate Athletics (NAIA). Lindenwood's men and women athletes participate in baseball, basketball, bowling, cross-country, football, golf, ice hockey, indoor and outdoor track, lacrosse, soccer, softball, swimming and diving, tennis, volleyball, water polo, and wrestling. The men's wrestling team won the 2007 NAIA National Championship and finished as the national runner-up in the 2006 tournament. The men's indoor track team was the national champion in the spring of 2006. In addition, the University offers women's field hockey and men's roller hockey. The teams use the Robert F. Hyland Performance Arena, Harlen C. Hunter Stadium, baseball and softball fields, and a new eight-lane all-weather track. Students also participate in an assortment of intramural sports at the University's Fitness Center.

Student organizations and clubs provide avenues for extended personal growth, leadership, and community service. The University radio station, 35,000-watt KCLC-FM, and LUHE-TV, Lindenwood's new television station, are staffed by students.

Students wishing to live on campus may choose from residence halls, houses, and apartment-style living. Six new residence halls have opened since 2000. Sibley Hall, named in honor of founders Mary Easton and Major George C. Sibley, was built in 1856 to replace the original log cabin that served as the first University building. It is listed on the National Register of Historic Places and is now a women's residence hall. All residential buildings have easy access to University facilities.

Location

The 500-acre campus is located in St. Charles, Missouri, a city of about 55,000 people, situated 20 miles from downtown St. Louis. Resting on the banks of the Missouri River, just south of the Mississippi, St. Charles is the site of Missouri's first state capital. The area offers a wide range of opportunities for all types of interests and is particularly rich in state heritage and attractions associated with the history of America's westward expansion. Lindenwood's proximity to a major city allows students to enjoy theme parks, a world-class zoo, professional sporting events, Broadway plays and theater, performances of a world-renowned symphony orchestra, state parks, and lakes. St. Louis–Lambert International Airport is located just 5 miles from Lindenwood University on Interstate 70.

Majors and Degrees

With a foundation as solid as the campus' century-old linden trees, the academic programs of Lindenwood University have a tradition of excellence and innovation. Lindenwood awards Bachelor of Arts, Bachelor of Fine Arts, and Bachelor of Science degrees with majors in accounting, agribusiness, art history, art management, art (studio), athletic training, biology, business administration, chemistry, computer science, corporate communications, criminal justice, dance, early childhood education, elementary education, English, fashion design, fashion merchandising, finance, French, general studies, history, human resource management, human service agency management, information technology, international studies, management, management information systems, marketing, mass communication, mathematics, medical technology, music, nonprofit administration, performing arts, physical education, political science, psychology, public administration, religion, retail marketing, secondary education, social work, sociology, Spanish, special education, theater, theater management, and writing.

Preprofessional courses are offered in dentistry, engineering, law, medicine, and veterinary medicine. Also, programs in engineering are available in conjunction with Washington University in St. Louis, the University of Missouri–Columbia, and the University of Missouri–Rolla.

Academic Programs

The emphasis at Lindenwood University is on an individualized liberal arts education with career-oriented preparation. Students fulfill general education requirements, participate in the University's Work and Learn Program when qualified, and acquire an in-depth knowledge of at least one area of study as a major. Lindenwood requires the completion of 128 credit hours to earn a bachelor's degree.

Academic Facilities

The newly renovated Margaret Leggat Butler Library houses volumes, microfilm items, and a computer lab and subscribes to 450 periodicals. Roemer Hall serves as the main administration building and has classrooms and faculty offices on the upper floors. Roemer Hall is also home to the 450-seat Jelkyl Theatre. Young Science Hall houses an auditorium, laboratories, and classrooms for natural science, mathematics, and computer science, as well as a state-of-the-art television studio. Harmon Hall provides students with art, photography, dance, music, and performing arts studios; classrooms; practice rooms; a recital and lecture hall; the Harmon Theatre; and the Harry D. Hendren Gallery, which attracts local and national art exhibits. The Lindenwood University Cultural Center provides a 750-seat auditorium, classrooms, meeting rooms, and offices. It is home to the University's music department and is the site of theatrical productions, concerts, convocations, and lectures. In addition, the Spellmann Campus Center opened in 2002. The Campus Center serves as a student union and houses a state-of-the-art cafeteria, Macintosh and PC computer labs, conference rooms, networking and campus life offices, and career planning and placement services. Currently, a 132,000-square-foot Fine and Performing Arts Center is under construction and is set to be completed in 2008.

Costs

For the academic year 2007–08, tuition is $12,400. Students who choose to live on campus pay $6200 for room and board, plus $360 for communications service. There are a refundable $300 room deposit and a $240 activity fee. Books and other supplies are extra.

Financial Aid

Financial aid is available to all qualified students. A student must submit the Free Application for Federal Student Aid (FAFSA). To qualify for the full amount of financial aid, students must submit their federal financial aid forms before March 15. As determined by the evaluation, a student's financial need may be met with a combination of federal, state, and institutional sources of aid. In addition, institutional awards are available in the areas of academics, leadership, athletics, drama, yearbook/newspaper, and music. Resident students may earn $2400 toward their expenses by working on campus.

Faculty

Lindenwood has 228 full-time faculty members, who serve as teachers, mentors, and advisers to their students. Faculty members advise students regarding majors and other matters to help them succeed academically.

Student Government

The Lindenwood Student Government Association (LSGA) is made up of representatives elected by the student body. LSGA has the responsibility of providing a balanced program of cultural, social, and recreational events and activities throughout the year.

Admission Requirements

To apply for admission, a student should submit a completed application form with a nonrefundable $30 application fee, a transcript of high school and/or college work, and ACT or SAT scores.

Applicants are evaluated on an individual basis, and admission is based on an analysis of the student's grade point average, ACT or SAT scores, extracurricular activities, recommendations, and personal qualifications. Students are admitted without regard to race, sex, or national origin.

Application and Information

Although admission to Lindenwood is on a rolling basis, students are encouraged to apply by April 15 for the fall semester and by December 1 for the spring semester. Notification of the admission decision is mailed soon after all required materials are received and evaluated by the Director of Undergraduate Admissions.

Applications for admission, financial aid, and scholarships and other information about Lindenwood University can be obtained by contacting:

Undergraduate Admissions
Lindenwood University
209 South Kingshighway
St. Charles, Missouri 63301-1695
Phone: 636-949-4949
Fax: 636-949-4989
Web site: http://www.lindenwood.edu

Students look over class notes in the shade of the linden trees at Lindenwood University.

COLLEGE DATA CENTER • MISSOURI

ROCKHURST UNIVERSITY

KANSAS CITY, MISSOURI

The University

Rockhurst University believes in experience-based learning. The goal is to help students confront the challenges they will encounter in the real world by using the wide range of resources available in Kansas City as a learning laboratory. Through activities such as professional internships, research projects, and community service work throughout the city, students learn by doing. This approach to education helps students clarify their professional interests as well as acquire a deeper sense of confidence in themselves, their skills, and their life choices.

The intellectual community of 3,000 students encourages students to find their own capacity for original thinking and to approach new challenges as questioning, open-minded thinkers. This ability is one of the great gifts of a Jesuit education. Rockhurst is one of the most intimate, manageable, and affordable of the nation's twenty-eight Jesuit colleges and universities. It has been consistently ranked among the top master's universities in the Midwest by *U.S. News & World Report.*

Rockhurst enjoys an excellent reputation that translates into outstanding employment opportunities for graduates. Rockhurst graduates serve as executive leaders for major companies and organizations in Kansas City and throughout the country.

Activities outside of class are a critical component of the Rockhurst experience. Rockhurst freshmen begin their college careers doing community service through the Finucane Service Project during orientation; seniors complete their education by participating in the Van Ackeren Service Project. In addition, many students spend spring break on a service project.

Classroom work is linked to service and extracurricular achievement. A few examples: one organizational behavior class studied a social service agency and eventually became the agency's consulting team; students have received National Science Foundation grants for undergraduate research; 2 students have been the only undergraduate presenters at the 7,000-person American Political Science Association convention; and students take leading roles in developing the campus master plan and the University's strategic plan.

Rockhurst recognizes that campus life involves more than academics and cocurricular activities. The Town House Village student residence complex provides an apartment-style residence experience for juniors and seniors. About half of Rockhurst's full-time undergraduate students live on campus, located just a few blocks south of the famed Country Club Plaza.

Men's and women's basketball and soccer and women's volleyball teams have regularly participated in NCAA national tournaments. Men's baseball, women's softball, and men's and women's tennis and golf teams continue Rockhurst's strong athletic traditions at the NCAA Division II level. Construction recently was completed on a new $5.5-million athletic complex named Loyola Park.

Students can also take advantage of the Rockhurst network in Kansas City's thriving business community. The Career Center offers the Cooperative Education program, placing students in full- or part-time jobs for a semester, where they earn both pay and credit.

Rockhurst also provides opportunities for learning after students receive a bachelor's degree by offering Doctor of Physical Therapy, Master of Occupational Therapy, Master of Education, Master in Communication Sciences and Disorders, traditional and executive Master of Business Administration, and five-year bachelor's degree/Master of Business Administration programs. A postbaccalaureate premed program is also available.

Rockhurst's emphasis on values and lifelong learning leads students to new definitions of success. The process of being a successful person has been mastered by many famous "Rocks," as Rockhurst alumni are known. From space scientists to entrepreneurs to founders of a clinic for crack babies to college presidents, famous Rocks are found in nearly every state, making a difference in their fields and in their communities.

Location

The 55-acre Rockhurst campus is in the cultural heart of thriving Kansas City. Rustic stone classroom buildings surrounded by beautiful, shaded walkways provide the perfect atmosphere for study and relaxation. The campus is a short stroll from Kansas City's brightest cultural attractions, including the Nelson-Atkins Museum of Art and the Country Club Plaza. All of the metropolitan area's attractions, such as the Truman Sports Complex (home to the Chiefs and Royals), Sprint Center, Crown Center, and jazz and rock concert halls, are easily accessible.

Majors and Degrees

Rockhurst University offers Bachelor of Arts, Bachelor of Science, Bachelor of Science in Business Administration, and Bachelor of Science in Nursing degrees. Rockhurst offers programs and majors in accounting, biochemistry, biology, business administration, business communication, chemistry, clinical laboratory sciences, communication, communication sciences and disorders (speech pathology), economics, education (elementary and secondary), English, finance/accounting, finance/economics, French, global studies, history, international business, management, marketing, mathematics, nonprofit leadership studies, nursing, organizational leadership studies, philosophy, physics, political science, psychology, Spanish, sports science, and theology and religious studies. The Evening Program offers bachelor's degrees in business administration, elementary education, English, nonprofit leadership studies, and organizational leadership studies.

Preprofessional programs are available in dentistry, engineering, law, medicine, occupational therapy, optometry, osteopathic medicine, pharmacy, physical therapy, physician's assistant studies, and veterinary medicine. Minors and certificate programs include American humanics, art, Catholic studies, German, journalism, music, paralegal studies, theater arts, women's studies, and writing.

Academic Programs

Depending upon their intended major, beginning students are advised in the College of Arts and Sciences, the Helzberg School of Management, the Research College of Nursing, or the School of Graduate and Professional Studies. Students eventually declare a major in one of these four schools. The Research College of Nursing provides an accelerated program for students with degrees in other fields. The Evening Program offers opportunities for working adults to complete the bachelor's degree through part-time study. The University has an excellent honors program. A minimum of 128 credit hours is required for graduation; there are specific requirements for each degree area.

The University's programs in occupational therapy and physical therapy respond to the growing need for health-care professionals. Students entering Rockhurst as freshmen may pursue a program that leads to a bachelor's degree in a related field and a master's degree in occupational therapy after five years or a bachelor's degree in a related field and a doctorate of physical therapy after six years.

The Cooperative Education Program enables students to earn college credit while gaining valuable work experience in major companies. Cooperative education provides students with an opportunity to match academic learning with workplace experience, testing career choices and potential employers. By alternating semesters of study and work, students can complete course work in four years (including summers) and have a year's experience in real-world jobs. Many co-op students are offered permanent positions with firms for which they have worked in the program.

Off-Campus Programs

The study-abroad program coordinates course work in nine European cities: Madrid, Spain; Rome and Florence, Italy; Aix-en-Provence, Avignon, and Toulon, France; and Richmond, Surrey, and Kensington, England. In addition, scholarships have funded dozens of students on study trips to Russia, and a study in Mexico program is offered every summer in Xalapa, Mexico. Rockhurst students regularly find internships in government and in the nonprofit and private sectors through the Washington Center, in the nation's capital. Special scholarships have also provided internships in Congress for Rockhurst students. Students may also take courses at other local institutions, such as the Kansas City Art Institute and the Conservatory of Music of the University of Missouri at Kansas City, through an exchange program.

Academic Facilities

The Greenlease Library houses more than 100,000 volumes and is a repository for a variety of government documents, including the *Federal Register,* Congressional reports, Supreme Court decisions, and presidential papers. Rockhurst students also have access to the renowned Linda Hall Science Library, which is just a few blocks from the campus. The Science Center houses science programs.

Costs

In 2007–08, the cost of tuition was $20,000; room and board costs averaged $6100.

Financial Aid

Rockhurst University arranges significant financial aid packages, which include scholarships, grants, loans, and part-time jobs, for eligible students. Nearly half of the entering freshman class receives partial to full scholarship awards based on academic, talent, service, and athletic achievements. Federal, state, Rockhurst University, and research grants are available. Low-interest student loans include the Federal Stafford Student and Federal Perkins Loans; Federal PLUS loans are available for parents. The Federal Work-Study Program provides campus jobs. The Career Center helps students find part-time jobs throughout the Kansas City area. A monthly payment plan allows students to pay all or part of their fees in installments without interest. Students must file a Free Application for Federal Student Aid (FAFSA) to be considered for financial assistance.

Faculty

Rockhurst's outstanding faculty includes 119 full-time and 91 part-time professors. Approximately 84 percent of full-time faculty members hold a Ph.D. or the terminal degree in their field. All classes and labs, including those on the freshman level, are taught by professors or instructors, not teaching assistants. Faculty members also act as academic advisers to students. Rockhurst's student-faculty ratio of 13:1 ensures close interaction between students, from freshmen to seniors, and faculty members.

Student Government

All full-time students can participate in the Student Senate. Students elect senate representatives and officers annually. The Student Activities Board, which is also elected, organizes social activities and allocates student activity fees. Resident students elect Residence Hall Councils to plan activities and help administer the residence halls. Students may also serve on tripartite committees that include students, faculty members, and administrators. These committees advise the President and others on policy issues. The Interfraternity Council and the Panhellenic Council provide leadership for the fraternities and sororities on campus.

Admission Requirements

Applicants must submit scores on the ACT or SAT examination. Sixteen units of college-preparatory work are required, and an interview is recommended.

Application and Information

There is a $25 application fee, but it is waived for those who apply online. For further information, students should contact:

Office of Admission
Rockhurst University
1100 Rockhurst Road
Kansas City, Missouri 64110-2561
Phone: 816-501-4100
800-842-6776 (toll-free)
Fax: 816-501-4241
E-mail: admission@rockhurst.edu
Web site: http://www.rockhurst.edu

The distinctiveness of a Rockhurst University education stems from its Jesuit heritage, which calls for students to find their unique gifts and talents and become leaders in service to others.

ST. LOUIS COLLEGE OF PHARMACY

ST. LOUIS, MISSOURI

The College

Ranking among the top pharmacy colleges in the nation, St. Louis College of Pharmacy (StLCoP) offers its students a strong liberal arts and professional degree program. Founded in 1864, St. Louis College of Pharmacy is the oldest and largest private, independent college in the nation whose sole degree is in pharmacy. A recent $42-million, campuswide transformation makes it one of the most modern. Students can access the College's wireless computer network from virtually anywhere on campus. An eight-story residence hall features suite and efficiency-style units and is connected to a spacious dining facility that serves both fast food and plate meals. Upper-level students may elect to live on campus in Rabe Hall, a fifty-seven-unit apartment building featuring studio and one-bedroom and two-bedroom units.

The total enrollment for 2007–08 was 684 women and 492 men. The students of the College maintain chapters of the Academy of Students in Pharmacy, the student National Community Pharmacy Association (NCPA), and the Student National Pharmaceutical Association. These chapters conduct programs of professional and general interest that are directed toward advancing pharmacy practice. The College recognizes national professional fraternal organizations. In addition to their professional functions, these groups provide social activities. Groups are governed by an Interfraternity Council. A national honor pharmaceutical society, Rho Chi, is open to fourth- through sixth-year students who are both academically and professionally outstanding.

Extracurricular activities include the College band; chorus; theater and musical programs; dances; movies; lecture programs; the student newspaper, the *Pharmakon;* and the student yearbook, the *Prescripto.* Student ambassadors act as hosts at College functions.

St. Louis College of Pharmacy offers an athletic program for both varsity and intramural sports. The College is a member of NAIA Division III in men's and women's basketball, women's volleyball, and men's and women's cross-country. The College's student center has excellent facilities for weight training, aerobics, and body conditioning.

Location

Known for generations as the Gateway to the West, St. Louis is a center for cultural, educational, and industrial activities. It has many fine museums, a symphony orchestra, theaters, professional sports, historic landmarks, zoological and botanical gardens, and one of the nation's foremost medical centers. A number of these outstanding attractions are within a 2-mile radius of the College. St. Louis College of Pharmacy is located in the Washington University medical complex of St. Louis, one block from Forest Park and two blocks from Barnes-Jewish Hospital.

Majors and Degrees

The College offers a six-year program leading to the Doctor of Pharmacy (Pharm.D.) degree.

Academic Programs

The Doctor of Pharmacy program includes intensive courses in biology, chemistry, mathematics, and physics, as well as electives. Courses in literature, humanities, and social and behavioral sciences constitute a significant portion of the curriculum. Introductory practice experiences throughout the curriculum give students the opportunity to apply nearly all facets of their education and enable students to develop communicative and professional interactions with other health-care practitioners and with patients. The six-year Pharm.D. program comprises specialized didactic courses and includes a calendar year of clinical clerkship rotations.

Off-Campus Programs

St. Louis College of Pharmacy offers clinical training in cooperation with the Washington University and Saint Louis University schools of medicine and in other facilities that include Barnes-Jewish, St. Louis Children's, St. John's Mercy, and St. Louis State hospitals. In addition, numerous clerkship rotations are available in a variety of community retail settings.

Academic Facilities

The O. J. Cloughly Alumni Library, located adjacent to Jones Hall, is an integral supplement to the instructional program and contains a continually increasing number of volumes in the field of pharmacy, its allied sciences, and the liberal arts. It receives the leading pharmaceutical and scientific periodicals, journals, bulletins, and reports. The library is open throughout the day and most evenings and weekends under the administration of a professional librarian. Jones Hall contains classrooms, lecture halls, laboratories, research laboratories, and faculty/ administrative offices. Whelpley Hall contains a 300-seat auditorium in addition to small- and medium-size classrooms.

Costs

For 2007–08, tuition and fees for students in the first and second year were $19,710; third, fourth, and fifth year were $21,470; and sixth year was $21,730. Notebook computer (issued to all new students) and laboratory fees are included in tuition costs. Room and board costs were $7650 for the academic year. Additional costs, including books, vary each year but average $500 per semester.

Financial Aid

The awarding of financial aid is based on merit, need, and availability of funds. The College participates in all applicable federal and state financial aid programs. Scholarships, grants, loans, and student employment are offered to help qualified students pay for their college expenses. Financial aid may be funded by the federal or state government, the College, benefactors and friends of the College, or other sponsoring organizations or agencies. Merit-based scholarships are offered to qualified students regardless of need.

Students planning to attend the College in the fall semester should submit the Free Application for Federal Student Aid (FAFSA) along with signed copies of student and parent federal tax returns as early as possible during the previous spring semester. The College begins awarding financial aid in February and continues until all funds are exhausted. Further information on student financial aid may be obtained from the College's Financial Aid Office.

Faculty

An outstanding faculty teaches and counsels students at the College throughout their course of study. No classes are taught by graduate students. Sixty-two of the 65 full-time campus-based faculty members hold a doctoral degree. More than 200 registered pharmacists serve as adjunct instructors in the externship-clerkship program.

Student Government

The Student Council represents the interests of all students. It is composed of representatives elected by the various classes and is sponsored by two faculty advisers. The council budgets and supervises the expenditure of funds provided by the student activities fee and sponsors numerous student activities and social events.

Admission Requirements

All students applying for admission to the Pharm.D. program must present evidence of the satisfactory completion of a four-year course of study in, and graduation from, a high school approved by a recognized accrediting body. A transcript of the high school record, including class standing, should be sent by the high school directly to the director of admissions. The high school course of study should include 4 units of English; 3 units of math, including algebra 1 and 2 and geometry; and at least 3 units of science, including biology/lab and chemistry lab. The College requires that the SAT or ACT examination be completed.

Advanced credit may be earned through Advanced Placement examinations. Further details are available from the Office of Admissions.

Students transferring into the Pharm.D. program must present transcripts of their college records and must have taken the PCAT. Such records must demonstrate satisfactory academic status. Transfer students must apply for admission through the Pharmacy College Application Service (PharmCAS) Web site at http://www.pharmcas.org. Applications and subsequent admission materials sent to St. Louis College of Pharmacy will not be accepted—all materials for admission must be submitted directly to PharmCAS. For more information, students should go to the PharmCAS Web site.

Application and Information

Students applying to the Pharm.D. program should recognize that applications are no longer considered after the freshman class has been filled. Application deadlines can be found at the Web site (http://www.stlcop.edu). StLCoP participates in early decision as well as regular decision.

The application deadline for transfer students is March 1. However, the PharmCAS deadline for submission of all admission materials is February 1. StLCoP takes very few transfer students into the Pharm.D. program, and as a result admission is extremely competitive. Transfer students are only accepted into the third year of the six-year program, without exception.

For application forms or additional information, students should contact:

Registrar/Director of Admissions
St. Louis College of Pharmacy
4588 Parkview Place
St. Louis, Missouri 63110
Phone: 314-367-8700 Ext. 8313
800-278-5267 (toll-free)
E-mail: pbryant@stlcop.edu
Web site: http://www.stlcop.edu

STEPHENS COLLEGE

COLUMBIA, MISSOURI

The College

Stephens College was founded in 1833 as the nation's second-oldest women's college. Stephens is ranked nationally in *U.S. News & World Report* and has repeatedly been selected to the *Princeton Review*'s list of the best colleges in the country (listed one of the Best in the Midwest, 2006, and sixth on the list of best college theater programs in the nation).

Students from around the globe enrich Stephens with their varied talents, interests, and backgrounds. Stephens students may choose to join one of ten honorary societies on campus, including Psi Chi, Alpha Epsilon Rho, and Mortar Board, or become involved in student government. Leadership experience is emphasized in all aspects of life at Stephens.

Stephens' residence halls provide much of the focus for campus activity. The Honors House Plan offers a living/learning environment in the humanities to a select group of freshmen each year. Since it began in the 1960s as an experiment funded by the Ford Foundation, the program has served as a model for similar living/learning communities in colleges and universities across the nation.

In addition to undergraduate degrees, Stephens offers master's degrees.

Location

Stephens College is located in Columbia, Missouri. Situated halfway between Kansas City and St. Louis, Columbia is the cultural, medical, and business center of mid-Missouri. Often called "College Town, USA," Columbia is also the home of Columbia College and the University of Missouri. Stephens students have easy access to Columbia's shopping, dining, and entertainment offerings.

Majors and Degrees

Stephens College awards the Associate in Arts, Bachelor of Arts, Bachelor of Fine Arts, and Bachelor of Science. Majors include accounting; biology; creative writing; dance; digital filmmaking; education; English; entrepreneurship and business management; equestrian business management; equestrian science; fashion communication; fashion design and product development; fashion marketing and management; graphic design; human development; interior design; legal studies; liberal studies; marketing: public relations and advertising; mass media (electronic media production, print media production, or public relations); psychology; student-initiated majors; theater arts; theater management; and theatrical costume design. The B.F.A. program includes professional-level work in the fine or performing arts plus a strong component in liberal studies.

Academic Programs

The B.A. degree is generally completed in four years. Students pursue depth of study in an academic area, breadth in liberal arts study, and elective course work with guidance from faculty advisers. Academic departments require relevant internships and often provide opportunities for research projects in field settings. Stephens has introduced many innovative educational concepts into its programs. Stephens emphasizes personalized teaching and development of the individual. Small classes are offered, and most departments offer tutorial projects and readings.

Students in the bachelor's degree programs—B.A., B.F.A., or B.S.—must complete the residency requirement of seven semesters. Students take a total of 30 hours in the liberal arts program throughout their three or four years at the College. These courses provide an interdisciplinary platform for the study of the behavioral/social sciences, literature, humanities, history, science, ethics, math, and digital literacy. All liberal arts courses, regardless of the topics they cover, provide opportunities for students to sharpen their critical thinking and communication skills.

Degree requirements for the Bachelor of Arts include completion of at least 24 semester hours in a department. At least 15 of these hours must be at or above the 300 level. As many as 45 semester hours may be required in the major, but no more than 45 may count toward a 120-semester-hour degree program. Students also may elect to design an interdisciplinary student-initiated Bachelor of Arts major.

The Bachelor of Science degree program requires completion of 45 to 57 hours, including a minimum of 15 hours at or above the 300 level. Bachelor of Science candidates may elect additional courses in the major, but no more than 60 hours may count toward a 120-semester-hour degree program. Students also may elect to design an interdisciplinary student-initiated Bachelor of Science major.

Degree requirements for the Bachelor of Fine Arts include completion of 60 to 75 semester hours, including at least 15 hours at or above the 300 level. B.F.A. candidates may elect additional courses in their major, up to a maximum of 78 hours within a 120-semester-hour degree program. The B.F.A. degree programs in theater and in dance are completed in three years and two summers. Students also may elect to design an interdisciplinary student-initiated Bachelor of Fine Arts major.

Through Stephens College Division of Graduate and Continuing Studies, nontraditional students have the opportunity to complete degrees through programs that build on prior and current learning. The Division of Graduate and Continuing Studies offers undergraduate programs in business administration, and health information administration (the first accredited external degree program in medical record administration in the country). In addition, Stephens offers a Master of Business Administration (M.B.A.), a Master of Education (M.Ed.) in counseling, and a Master of Education in curriculum and instruction. Undergraduates in accounting, entrepreneurship and business management, fashion marketing/management, equestrian business management, and marketing: public relations and advertising may apply for a tuition-paid fellowship to complete the M.B.A degree. Certain requirements apply.

Stephens also offers numerous partnerships with other institutions wherein students may earn a bachelor's degree from Stephens in three years and a master's degree from another college or university after two or three additional years. Partnerships currently exist in occupational therapy, physical therapy, physician assistant studies, accounting, and law.

Off-Campus Programs

Stephens sponsors summer seminars in several countries, including France, Italy, and Japan, as extensions of courses that are regularly offered at the College. Summer-study programs include drama and musical theater at Lake Okoboji, Spirit Lake, Iowa. Stephens also offers study opportunities in Ireland, Sweden, Ecuador, Korea, and Cambridge, England.

Many other study opportunities are available through global partnerships with other universities.

Academic Facilities

The Hugh Stephens Resources Library contains more than 120,000 volumes. The library is the central building of a quadrangle that includes the Helis Communication Center and the Patricia Barry Television Studio. The E. S. Pillsbury Science Center houses science and mathematics classrooms and laboratories, and the Ellis Learning Laboratories provide modern equipment for individual and group study of foreign languages. Other working laboratories include the student-run Warehouse Theatre, the Johnson Plant Laboratory, and the Audrey Webb Child Study Center, which has an enrollment of approximately 100 children in preschool through fifth grade.

Costs

For 2007–08, tuition is $21,730; room and board are $8240. Costs for room and board are subject to change. Additional costs for books, supplies, and personal expenses range between $750 and $1000. The enrollment deposit is $100.

Financial Aid

More than 95 percent of the student body receive some form of assistance through scholarships, grants, loans, or employment. Stephens participates in the Federal Pell Grant, Federal Supplemental Educational Opportunity Grant, Federal Perkins Loan, Federal Stafford Student Loan, and Federal Work-Study programs. Missouri residents are encouraged to apply for aid under the Missouri Student Grant Program. The Free Application for Federal Student Aid (FAFSA) is required for financial aid consideration. Applications for financial aid should be received by March 15. Stephens also offers an early financial aid estimate service.

Faculty

Though most faculty members have come to college teaching via the recognized route of graduate study and scholarship, some have prepared for teaching through work experience, particularly those in applied and performing arts with careers as actors, dancers, musicians, and artists. The faculty is primarily a teaching faculty, and many of the instructors include students in independent scholarly research. Men and women join the Stephens faculty with a commitment to individualized education. They are actively engaged in academic advising and tutorial relationships and frequently spend many more hours working with students outside the classroom than in formal teaching situations. The student-faculty ratio is 13:1.

Student Government

Each student is a member of the Student Government Association (SGA). Working in the SGA provides women with experience in planning and administering cultural, social, and recreational activities and in dealing with academic, residential, and community concerns. The association has executive and legislative powers to govern student activities and to develop and maintain group-living standards. Students also serve as voting members of established faculty committees and in advisory capacities to committees of the Board of Trustees. Stephens has been nationally recognized for the many leadership opportunities it provides for students.

Admission Requirements

Applicants are considered by the Dean of Enrollment Management and the Admission Committee on an individual basis without regard to race, religion, geographic origin, or handicap. Major factors for admission consideration are the recommendations and academic record, including rank in class, subjects studied, grade point average, proficiency in English, and test scores (SAT and ACT).

Application and Information

Candidates for admission should submit the application with the $25 application fee and arrange to have transcripts and recommendations mailed to the Office of Admission. Students who apply online at http://www.stephens.edu/admission/apply can waive the application fee. Upon receipt of the application, any additional material is mailed to the student. Qualified students are accepted on a rolling admission basis upon receipt of all necessary credentials.

Office of Admission
Campus Box 2121
Stephens College
Columbia, Missouri 65215
Phone: 573-876-7207
800-876-7207 (toll-free)
Fax: 573-876-7237
E-mail: apply@stephens.edu
Web site: http://www.stephens.edu

On the Stephens College campus.

TRUMAN STATE UNIVERSITY

KIRKSVILLE, MISSOURI

The University

Truman has forged a national reputation for offering an exceptionally high-quality undergraduate education at a competitive price. For the eleventh consecutive year, *U.S. News & World Report* has ranked Truman as the number one master's-level public institution in the Midwest offering bachelor's and master's degrees. In addition, Truman is ranked as the second-best public college value in the nation by Princeton Review's 2008 edition of *America's Best Value Colleges.*

A commitment to student achievement and learning is at the core of everything Truman does. This commitment is evidenced by faculty and staff members who recognize the importance of providing students with the opportunity to interact with their professors both in and out of the classroom. With class sizes averaging only 24 students and 93 percent of freshman-level academic courses being taught by instructional faculty members, students find ample opportunity to ask questions of professors as well as interact with their multitalented peers. Truman's academic environment is enhanced by a student body that achieves at remarkable levels. The 2006 freshman class had an ACT midrange of 25 to 30 and an average GPA of 3.78 on a 4.0 scale. In addition, numerous opportunities exist for students to engage in undergraduate research. Each year, approximately 1,200 students work side by side with professors on University research projects, gaining greater confidence, knowledge, and skill in their chosen disciplines. The University offers these students the opportunity to present the results of their research at the annual Student Research Conference. In addition, selected students travel to the National Undergraduate Research Symposium to present their research findings. Undergraduate research stipends are also available.

The teaching degree at Truman is the Master of Arts in Education (M.A.E.). Students wishing to pursue a teaching career first complete a bachelor's degree in an academic discipline and then apply for admission into professional study at the master's level. Through this program, certification can be achieved for early childhood education, middle school education, special education, elementary education, and secondary education.

With more than 250 University organizations available to students, encompassing service, Greek, honorary, professional, religious, social, political, and recreational influences, Truman students have tremendous opportunities to become involved while enrolled at the University. Truman's Student Activities Board provides special events such as Mythbusters: Adam and Jamie, comic acts such as Lewis Black and the Laughing Irish Comedy Tour, and musical artists like Cake, Yellowcard, and MXPX. In addition, admission to all varsity athletic events, Truman theater productions, and Lyceum Series events is free to Truman students. Recent theater productions have included *Cabaret, One Flew Over the Cuckoo's Nest,* and *The Real Inspector Hound.*

Location

Truman is located in Kirksville, a town of approximately 17,000 nestled in the northeast corner of Missouri. The town square, located within walking distance of the Truman campus, provides a connection to Kirksville's past. A multiplex movie theater is located on the town square; local merchants operate specialized gift, book, and clothing stores; and several restaurants offer a wide selection of American and international cuisine.

The Kirksville Aquatic Center is a great place to have fun and get fit. This indoor/outdoor pool complex offers a variety of activities, classes, and programs designed to appeal to people of all ages. Inside the complex is a six-lane indoor swimming pool, perfect for swimming, relaxing, or playing a game of water-basketball. The outdoor pool is designed with a zero-depth entry, a 1-meter diving board, and four 25-yard outdoor lap lanes as well as a 20-foot water slide.

The northeast region of Missouri is also home to Thousand Hills State Park. A 3,252-acre state park and 573-acre lake for camping, hiking, biking, fishing, swimming, boating, and waterskiing is located within 10 minutes of the Truman campus.

Majors and Degrees

Undergraduate degrees offered by Truman include the Bachelor of Arts (B.A.), Bachelor of Science (B.S.), Bachelor of Music: Performance (B.M.), Bachelor of Fine Arts (B.F.A.), and Bachelor of Science in Nursing (B.S.N.). Truman offers more than forty areas of study in the following disciplines: accounting, agricultural science, art, art history, biology, business administration, chemistry, classics, communication, communication disorders, computer science, economics, English, exercise science, French, German, health science, history, interdisciplinary studies, justice systems, linguistics, mathematics, music, music: performance, nursing, philosophy and religion, physics, political science, psychology, Russian, sociology/anthropology, Spanish, and theater.

Professional paths include but are not limited to dentistry, engineering, law, medicine, optometry, pharmacy, physical therapy, and veterinary medicine.

Academic Programs

Truman is Missouri's premier liberal arts and sciences university and the only highly selective public institution in the state. The Liberal Studies Program is the heart of Truman's curriculum and is intended to serve as a foundation for all major programs of study offered by the University. Truman's mission is to "offer an exemplary undergraduate education, grounded in the liberal arts and sciences, in the context of a public institution of higher learning." Therefore, Truman is providing the kind of education in the liberal arts and sciences that has historically been offered only at private colleges. The program is a blend of two intellectual traditions in higher education, one that emphasizes the traditional thought and learning of the culture, as reflected in the classical works produced by it, and the other that emphasizes personal investigation and freedom of discovery. The philosophy behind the Liberal Studies Program is based upon a commitment that Truman has made to provide students with essential skills needed for lifelong learning, breadth across the traditional liberal arts and sciences through exposure to various discipline-based modes of inquiry, and interconnecting perspectives that stress interdisciplinary thinking and integration as well as linkage to other cultures and experiences. All students graduating from Truman must complete 63 or more credit hours in liberal arts and sciences courses.

Truman's Residential College Program brings the University learning community inside the student residence halls. Historically, residential colleges have been places where faculty members and students join together as "friends of learning." At Truman, this living/learning tradition is honored as one means of furthering its specific goals as a public liberal arts university. The Residential College Program seeks to make liberal arts education personally vital and engaging to the whole person.

Truman also offers an especially challenging General Honors Program. This program provides students with the opportunity to select the most rigorous honors courses to satisfy the liberal arts component of their respective programs. Students who successfully complete this program not only benefit from an even richer academic experience at Truman but also receive special recognition at graduation. Departmental honors are also available in several disciplines.

Off-Campus Programs

Each year, approximately 500 Truman students participate in enriching and life-changing study-abroad experiences. Truman's own study-abroad programs, combined with programs offered through Truman's membership in the College Consortium for International Studies, International Student Exchange Program, Australearn, and the Council on International Educational Exchange, provide students with study-abroad opportunities in more than forty countries worldwide, including Australia, China, England, Finland, France, Italy, Russia, Spain, and Thailand.

In addition, there are two cooperative programs affiliated with biology. Truman is affiliated with the Gulf Coast Research Laboratory at Ocean Springs, Mississippi. Marine biology courses may be taken at the laboratory during the summer, with credit awarded at Truman. In-depth study of the Ozark habitats is also available through Truman's affiliation with Reis Biological Station located near Steelville, Missouri.

In cooperation with the Washington Center for Internships and Academic Seminars, Truman offers a wide variety of experiential internships in Washington, D.C. Included are work-experience opportunities in such areas as public administration, the fine and performing arts, foreign affairs/diplomacy, government affairs, criminal justice, international relations, health and human services, environmental policy, business administration, and communications as well as other areas. Placement sites include nonprofit groups, media organizations, the State Department, Congress, museums, and much more.

Truman requires internships in education, health science, and exercise science and annually offers internship opportunities with the Missouri State Legislature. In recent years, students have completed internships with United States senators, the governor of Missouri, business and industry managers, zoos, broadcast and print media professionals, accountants, advertising agencies, physical therapists, musicians, artists, and the United States Supreme Court.

Academic Facilities

The Truman campus is beautifully situated on an expanse of 140 acres near downtown Kirksville. Featured among the forty facilities on campus is Pickler Memorial Library. This 460,116-volume facility provides a state-of-the-art library resource for students and faculty members alike. Materials not available in Pickler Memorial Library can be obtained through the Interlibrary Loan Office and MOBIUS.

Improvements to campus facilities recently include the $20-million renovation and 80,000-square-foot addition to the Ophelia Parrish Building that transformed this facility into the new Fine Arts Center housing art studios, practice facilities, a performing arts center, and a black-box theater. The $20-million renovation and expansion of Truman's science facility, Magruder Hall, was completed for the spring 2006 semester and included new research labs, a greenhouse, classrooms, meeting areas, and a cyber café. The brand-new West Campus Suites opened to students in fall 2006. Each suite is equipped with a living room, two bedrooms housing 2 students each, closet space, a large bathroom, and central air conditioning. Renovations are being completed on Missouri Hall. Improvements include a 2,500-square-foot addition, laundry facilities on every floor, and individually controlled heating and cooling in each room.

Additional facilities include a student media center with a TV studio, a radio station, print media production facilities, a speech-and-hearing clinic for students in communication disorders, a biofeedback laboratory, an organic chemistry lab, an analytical chemistry lab, an independent learning center for nursing students, an observatory, a greenhouse, a 5,000-seat football stadium, a soccer field, tennis and racquetball courts, softball and baseball diamonds, a 3,000-seat arena with three basketball courts, an Olympic-size swimming pool, a multicultural affairs center, a writing center, and a career center.

Costs

Tuition for Missouri residents for the 2007–08 academic year is $6210; out-of-state tuition is $10,820. Room and board totals for both Missouri residents and nonresidents start at $5480. Additional fees include a $250 freshman orientation fee, an annual $72 activities fee, a $50 Student Health Center fee, an annual $100 athletic fee, a $50 parking fee for those with a vehicle, and the costs of books and personal expenses.

Financial Aid

Truman offers automatic scholarships ranging from $1000 to $2000. Competitive scholarship awards vary from $500 up to full tuition, room, and board plus a $4000 study-abroad stipend. The application for admission also serves as the application for the automatic and competitive scholarship programs.

Several scholarships are awarded to students for excellence in music, theater, or art. These scholarships are available for instrumental, strings, or vocal music; acting or dramatic production; and studio art or art history. Of special interest to piano students is the Truman Piano Fellowship Competition.

The National Collegiate Athletic Association and the University authorize a limited number of grants to outstanding athletes. The value of this aid may vary with each individual recipient.

Truman accepts the Free Application for Federal Student Aid (FAFSA) and participates in all Federal Title IV financial aid programs. Financial aid estimates are available upon request.

Faculty

Truman State University is committed to teaching the academically talented undergraduate student. The University has 338 full-time faculty members and 25 part-time faculty members. Of these, 98 percent teach undergraduates and 81 percent hold a doctoral degree or the highest terminal degree in their discipline. Most major graduate institutions are represented among the Truman faculty, including Harvard, Princeton, Yale, Berkeley, Oxford, and the Sorbonne. The student-faculty ratio at Truman is 16:1.

Student Government

Student Senate is the official elected governing body of the Student Association, representing approximately 5,800 students. Its mission is to represent the views of the Student Association in the formulation of the University policy through legislation and membership on all University committees; to facilitate communication and mutual understanding among the Student Association, faculty and staff members, and administration; to maintain a cohesive vision for the future of the University; and to actively participate in the fulfillment of the University's mission as an exemplary public liberal arts and sciences university.

Admission Requirements

Admission to Truman is competitive. Each applicant is evaluated for admission based upon academic and cocurricular record, ACT or SAT results, and the admission essay. Truman requires the following high school core: 4 units of English, 3 units of mathematics (4 recommended), 3 units of social studies/history, 3 units of natural science, 1 unit of fine arts, and 2 units of the same foreign language.

Application and Information

The priority deadline for admission is December 15. Students who have applied by this date are considered for all applicable competitive scholarships. Applications are processed on a rolling basis. There is no application fee. Students may apply online at the University's Web site. For further information or to schedule a campus visit, students should contact:

Admission Office
205 McClain Hall
Truman State University
100 East Normal
Kirksville, Missouri 63501
Phone: 660-785-4114
800-892-7792 (toll-free, Missouri only)
Fax: 660-785-7456
E-mail: admissions@truman.edu
Web site: http://admissions.truman.edu

COLLEGE DATA CENTER • MISSOURI

WESTMINSTER COLLEGE

FULTON, MISSOURI

The College

Founded in 1851, Westminster is a private, coeducational, liberal arts and sciences college that has a proven record of preparing its graduates for promising careers in business, public service, and in the professional area. Westminster College currently enrolls just under 1,000 students, and 35 percent of these students come from outside Missouri. States strongly represented are Oklahoma, Arkansas, Texas, Kansas, and Illinois. Ten percent of Westminster's students are international.

Facilities include the Hunter Activity Center, which houses a gymnasium, an indoor running track, racquetball courts, student mailboxes, a recreation room, student activity offices, and the campus grill. The expanded Priest Athletic Complex includes varsity and practice facilities for soccer, softball, baseball, tennis, and football, including new lights for night events. The Wetterau Field Sports Facility includes athletic offices, varsity locker rooms, training rooms, and a varsity weight room. The Mueller Student Center is a popular place for student parties, special College events, and athletic practices.

Westminster's Center for Leadership and Service promotes leadership and character development and community service on the campus and in the community. The Center for Leadership and Service works closely with the Center for Teaching Excellence to promote service-learning opportunities and greater interaction between academics and community service.

Whether students plan to enter the professional world immediately or pursue a graduate program, they are given encouragement, advice, and guidance in preparing for life after Westminster. Included in Career Services is an important linking of current students with graduates who are now in influential positions in society. In addition, Westminster's formalized internship program is designed to extend the student's learning opportunities beyond the traditional classroom setting into professional work environments.

The Green Lecture Series, a distinguished series on economic, social, and international affairs, was established in 1936 as a memorial to John Findley Green, an 1884 Westminster graduate. The roster of past speakers includes former Presidents Bush, Reagan, and Truman; former British Prime Minister Edward Heath; former CIA Director William Casey; former U.S. Ambassador to Russia Robert S. Strauss; former President of the Soviet Union Mikhail Gorbachev; and former President of Poland and Nobel laureate Lech Walesa. The 1996 Green Lecture, presented by Lady Margaret Thatcher, commemorated the fiftieth anniversary of Winston Churchill's famous "Iron Curtain" address held in the historic Westminster Gym.

Held in 2006, the sixtieth anniversary weekend celebration of Churchill's Iron Curtain speech and the grand reopening of the newly renovated $4-million Winston Churchill Memorial and Library in the United States were commemorated by keynote speaker Chris Matthews, host of the popular MSNBC program *Hardball with Chris Matthews* and the NBC program *The Chris Matthews Show.*

Westminster College uses as its chapel a seventeenth-century English Church, which was dismantled in London and rebuilt on the campus. The lower level of the church houses the Winston Churchill Memorial and Library, which contains memorabilia of Sir Winston Churchill and World War II. The church, originally designed by Sir Christopher Wren, is a national landmark that attracts 30,000 visitors annually.

Westminster College is a member of the National Collegiate Athletic Association (Division III) and the St. Louis Intercollegiate Athletic Conference. Westminster fields teams for men in baseball, basketball, golf, soccer, and tennis and for women in basketball, golf, soccer, softball, tennis, and volleyball. Westminster's football team plays in the Upper Midwest Athletic Conference.

Location

Fulton is a safe, historic community of more than 12,000 people, situated in the rolling hills and trees of central Missouri. Nearly 15 percent of Fulton's population are college students. Westminster is located a little more than an hour north of the Lake of the Ozarks, a beautiful recreational area. Within 25 minutes to the west is Columbia, a college town of more than 80,000 people. Just to the south of Fulton is Jefferson City, Missouri's state capital. Kansas City is 2½ hours west, and St. Louis is located 2 hours east on Interstate 70.

Majors and Degrees

Westminster grants the Bachelor of Arts degree in the following major fields: accounting; anthropology; biology; business administration; chemistry; computer science; economics; elementary, middle school, and secondary education; English; environmental studies; French; history; international business; international studies/sciences; management information systems; mathematics; philosophy; physical education; physics; political science; psychology; religious studies; sociology; and Spanish.

Preprofessional tracks are offered in the health professions and law. An individualized five/six-year engineering program is available to Westminster students in cooperation with Washington University in St. Louis.

Students who wish to design their own academic majors may do so through the self-designed major, which brings together an interdisciplinary committee of faculty members to serve as advisers. Examples include advertising, communications, hospital management, public administration, and sports management.

Academic Programs

Westminster is a selective college with an innovative curriculum based on the liberal arts that emphasizes breadth as well as depth. The College's general education program reflects a commitment to liberal learning in the arts and sciences and to providing its students with opportunities to explore the aesthetic, cultural, ethical, historical, scientific, and social contexts in which they will live, work, and learn in the twenty-first century. Requirements for the baccalaureate degree are usually completed in four years. Students must satisfy general course requirements as well as departmental requirements in courses outside of their major. Academic advisers guide all students through the four years of their enrollment.

The Westminster Seminar Program is designed to bridge the gap between high school and college and introduce students to campus facilities, resources, faculty members, and other students. The program begins prior to the start of classes and continues for the remainder of the semester for all first-year students. The professor of this class is the students' faculty adviser until the student declares a major.

Westminster operates on a traditional two-semester calendar. A three-week term is available after the spring semester for special travel and field study courses or internships.

Off-Campus Programs

The College's Center for Off-Campus and International Programs assists students seeking overseas study opportunities or pursuing exchange opportunities with sister institutions. Westminster participates in the Institutes of European and Asian Studies, which provide twenty campuses throughout the world for Westminster students to spend a semester or a year studying abroad. The College's strong historical relationship with England has led to several educational opportunities, including exchange programs with Queen Mary and Westfield College and the University of East Anglia School of English and American Studies, which allows study in Norwich, located 2 hours from London. Other overseas exchange programs are available at Kansai Gaidai University (Osaka, Japan) and with L'Ecole Supérieure des Sciences Commerciales (ESSCA: School for Business Study) in Angers, France; the latter allows French majors the opportunity to study abroad in a French-speaking environment. Other off-campus programs include the United Nations Semester, the Washington Semester, and the Chicago Urban Studies Semester.

Academic Facilities

The 80,000-square-foot Wallace H. Coulter Science Center provides space for modern classrooms and laboratories for biology, chemistry, computer science, mathematics, physics, and psychology. Most other classes meet in Newnham Hall and Westminster Hall. Reeves Library includes ample space for study and research, with four computer classrooms, a language lab, multimedia classrooms and facilities, additional computers, and student workstations. Students also have computer connections available in all residence halls and fraternity rooms, allowing 24-hour access to computers and the Internet, as well as wireless hot spots all over campus. A brand-new Mueller Leadership and Dining Hall facility opened in fall 2007, and a new dormitory is scheduled to open in fall 2008.

Costs

The basic cost for the 2008–09 academic year is $23,970 for tuition, room, board, student activity, health center, and technology fees. The College estimates that students should allow $2400 annually for books, supplies, and personal expenses.

Financial Aid

More than 97 percent of the College's students receive assistance through scholarships, grants, loans, or employment. Federal aid programs include the Federal Pell Grant, Federal Supplemental Educational Opportunity Grant, Federal Perkins Loan, and Federal Work-Study programs. To determine eligibility for need-based aid, students should complete the Free Application for Federal Student Aid (FAFSA) after January 1.

A merit-based aid program recognizes and rewards outstanding students. Academic scholarships and other awards, ranging from $1000 to full tuition, are awarded based on grades, test scores, competition results, and leadership activities.

Faculty

The 57 faculty members are part of a unique learning environment where students and teachers work together to discover answers to the complex problems faced in and out of the classroom and, in the process, establish lifelong relationships. Approximately 75 percent of the distinguished faculty members hold the doctorate or equivalent terminal degree, many are published authors, and others are engaged in advanced research and scholarly study. Although faculty members are involved in research and writing, they primarily constitute a teaching faculty whose main concern is the education of the undergraduate student.

Student Government

The Westminster College Student Government Association is composed of all students of the College. Its officers are elected by the entire student body. The Student Government Association serves the interests of the individual student and student groups and sponsors and supports activities and events on their behalf. The activity fee charged each student gives the Student Government Association a sizable budget to carry out such programs as intramurals, community relations, publications, entertainment, and other special events.

Admission Requirements

Each application is considered individually by the Enrollment Services staff and the Admissions Committee, who evaluate a number of factors, including courses taken in secondary school, a counselor's recommendation, test scores (either ACT or SAT), grade point average, and activities. Transfer students must submit a transcript from each college previously attended. International students must submit the TOEFL score report.

Application and Information

To apply to Westminster College a student should submit the application for admission along with an official copy of the secondary school transcript, test scores on either the ACT or SAT, and a recommendation from a high school official. The College operates on a rolling admissions calendar. While there is no application deadline, students are encouraged to apply by February 1 of their senior year.

Westminster College does not discriminate on the basis of race, sex, color, national or ethnic origin, sexual orientation, or physical handicap in the administration of its educational policies, admissions policies, scholarship and loan programs, or other school-administered programs.

For further information regarding admissions, financial assistance, academic programs, and campus visits, students should write or call:

Office of Enrollment Services (Admissions and Financial Aid)
Westminster College
501 Westminster Avenue
Fulton, Missouri 65251-1299
Phone: 573-592-5251
800-475-3361 (toll-free)
Fax: 573-592-5255
E-mail: admissions@westminster-mo.edu
Web site: http://www.westminster-mo.edu

Westminster College just completed construction of the New Mueller Leadership Dining Hall in September 2007. This new state-of-the-art facility is now a favorite student destination.

MONTANA

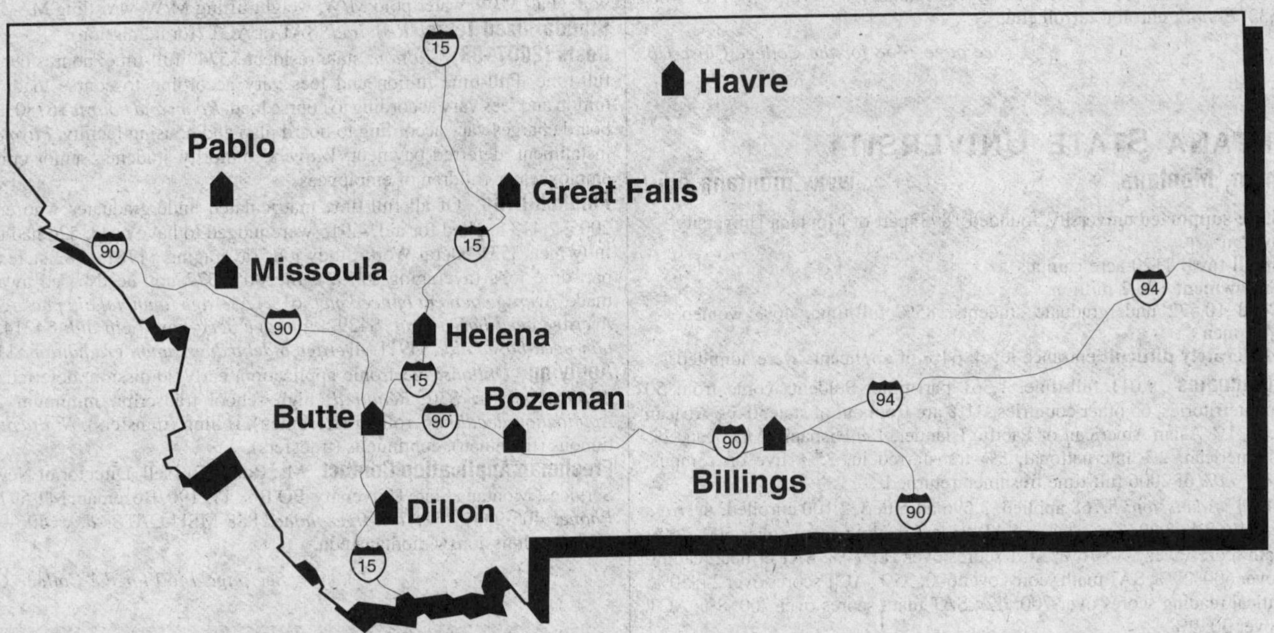
15
Havre
Pablo
Great Falls
90
15
Missoula
94
90
Helena
15
94
Bozeman
Butte
90
90
Billings
Dillon
90
15

CARROLL COLLEGE

Helena, Montana **www.carroll.edu/**

Freshman Application Contact Ms. Cynthia Thornquist, Director of Admissions and Enrollment, Carroll College, 1601 North Benton Avenue, Helena, MT 59625-0002. *Phone:* 406-447-4384. *Toll-free phone:* 800-992-3648. *Fax:* 406-447-4533. *E-mail:* enroll@carroll.edu.

See page 1458 for the College Close-Up.

MONTANA STATE UNIVERSITY

Bozeman, Montana **www.montana.edu/**

- **State-supported** university, founded 1893, part of Montana University System
- **Small-town** 1170-acre campus
- **Endowment** $76.2 million
- **Coed** 10,572 undergraduate students, 85% full-time, 46% women, 54% men
- **Moderately difficult** entrance level, 64% of applicants were admitted

Undergraduates 9,011 full-time, 1,561 part-time. Students come from 50 states and territories, 65 other countries, 31% are from out of state, 0.5% African American, 1% Asian American or Pacific Islander, 1% Hispanic American, 2% Native American, 2% international, 5% transferred in, 25% live on campus. *Retention:* 71% of 2006 full-time freshmen returned.

Freshmen *Admission:* 5,768 applied, 3,696 admitted, 2,100 enrolled. *Average high school GPA:* 3.29. *Test scores:* SAT critical reading scores over 500: 70%; SAT math scores over 500: 76%; ACT scores over 18: 94%; SAT critical reading scores over 600: 29%; SAT math scores over 600: 35%; ACT scores over 24: 50%; SAT critical reading scores over 700: 6%; SAT math scores over 700: 8%; ACT scores over 30: 9%.

Faculty *Total:* 802, 69% full-time, 65% with terminal degrees. *Student/faculty ratio:* 16:1.

Majors Agricultural business and management; agricultural mechanization; agricultural teacher education; animal sciences; anthropology; art; biology/biological sciences; biotechnology; business/commerce; cell biology and anatomy; chemical engineering; chemistry; cinematography and film/video production; civil engineering; computer engineering; computer science; construction engineering technology; design and visual communications; dramatic/theater arts; economics; electrical, electronics and communications engineering; elementary education; English; environmental design/architecture; environmental science; environmental studies; family and consumer sciences/human sciences; fine/studio arts; foreign languages and literatures; geology/earth science; health and physical education; health/health care administration; history; horticultural science; human development and family studies; industrial engineering; mathematics; mechanical engineering; mechanical engineering/mechanical technology; medical microbiology and bacteriology; music; music teacher education; natural resources/conservation; neuroscience; nursing (registered nurse training); philosophy; physics; plant sciences; political science and government; psychology; range science and management; secondary education; sociology; sport and fitness administration/management; technology/industrial arts teacher education.

Academics *Calendar:* semesters. *Degrees:* certificates, bachelor's, master's, doctoral, and post-master's certificates. *Special study options:* academic remediation for entering students, adult/continuing education programs, advanced placement credit, distance learning, double majors, English as a second language, honors programs, independent study, internships, off-campus study, part-time degree program, services for LD students, student-designed majors, study abroad, summer session for credit. *ROTC:* Army (b), Air Force (b).

Computers on Campus 850 computers/terminals are available on campus for general student use. Students can access the following: computer help desk, free student e-mail accounts, online (class) registration, online (class) schedules. Campuswide network is available. Wireless service is available via entire campus.

Student Life *Housing:* on-campus residence required for freshman year. *Options:* coed, men-only, women-only. Campus housing is university owned. Freshman campus housing is guaranteed. *Activities and organizations:* drama/theater group, student-run newspaper, radio and television station, choral group, marching band, Spurs, Inter-Varsity Christian Fellowship, Campus Crusade for Christ, Fangs, Mortar Board, national fraternities, national sororities. *Campus security:* 24-hour emergency response devices and patrols, student patrols, late-night transport/escort service, 24-hour residence hall monitoring. *Student services:* health clinic, personal/psychological counseling, women's center, legal services.

Athletics Member NCAA. All Division I except football (Division I-AA). *Intercollegiate sports:* basketball M (s)/W (s), cheerleading M (s)/W (s), cross-country running M (s)/W (s), golf W (s), skiing (cross-country) M (s)/W (s), skiing (downhill) M (s)/W (s), tennis M (s)/W (s), track and field M (s)/W (s), volleyball W (s). *Intramural sports:* archery W, badminton M/W, baseball M, basketball M/W, bowling M/W, cross-country running M/W, fencing M/W, football M, golf M/W, gymnastics M/W, racquetball M/W, rugby M/W, skiing (cross-country) M/W, skiing (downhill) M/W, soccer M/W, softball M/W, swimming and diving M/W, table tennis M/W, tennis M/W, track and field M/W, ultimate Frisbee M/W, volleyball M/W, water polo M/W, weight lifting M/W, wrestling M.

Standardized Tests *Required:* SAT or ACT (for admission).

Costs (2007–08) *Tuition:* state resident $5749 full-time; nonresident $16,274 full-time. Full-time tuition and fees vary according to course load. Part-time tuition and fees vary according to course load. *Room and board:* $6780. Room and board charges vary according to board plan and housing facility. *Payment plans:* installment, deferred payment. *Waivers:* minority students, senior citizens, and employees or children of employees.

Financial Aid Of all full-time matriculated undergraduates who enrolled in 2005, 7,413 applied for aid, 4,915 were judged to have need, 526 had their need fully met. 353 Federal Work-Study jobs (averaging $1781). 282 state and other part-time jobs (averaging $1792). In 2005, 577 non-need-based awards were made. *Average percent of need met:* 61%. *Average financial aid package:* $7444. *Average need-based loan:* $4292. *Average need-based gift aid:* $4214. *Average non-need-based aid:* $4911. *Average indebtedness upon graduation:* $18,081.

Applying *Options:* electronic application, early admission, deferred entrance. *Application fee:* $30. *Required:* high school transcript, minimum 2.5 GPA. *Application deadlines:* rolling (freshmen), rolling (transfers). *Notification:* continuous (freshmen), continuous (transfers).

Freshman Application Contact Ms. Ronda Russell, Director of New Student Services, Montana State University, PO Box 172190, Bozeman, MT 59717-2190. *Phone:* 406-994-2452. *Toll-free phone:* 888-MSU-CATS. *Fax:* 406-994-1923. *E-mail:* admissions@montana.edu.

See page 1460 for the College Close-Up.

MONTANA STATE UNIVERSITY–BILLINGS

Billings, Montana **www.msubillings.edu/**

- **State-supported** comprehensive, founded 1927, part of Montana University System
- **Urban** 92-acre campus
- **Endowment** $15.6 million
- **Coed** 4,425 undergraduate students, 74% full-time, 63% women, 37% men
- **Moderately difficult** entrance level, 100% of applicants were admitted

Undergraduates 3,265 full-time, 1,160 part-time. Students come from 45 states and territories, 19 other countries, 9% are from out of state, 0.6% African American, 1% Asian American or Pacific Islander, 4% Hispanic American, 5% Native American, 0.5% international, 10% transferred in, 11% live on campus. *Retention:* 62% of 2006 full-time freshmen returned.

Freshmen *Admission:* 1,415 applied, 1,410 admitted, 828 enrolled. *Average high school GPA:* 3.1. *Test scores:* SAT critical reading scores over 500: 51%; SAT math scores over 500: 60%; ACT scores over 18: 87%; SAT critical reading scores over 600: 13%; SAT math scores over 600: 9%; ACT scores over 24: 27%; SAT critical reading scores over 700: 2%; ACT scores over 30: 1%.

Faculty *Total:* 268, 56% full-time. *Student/faculty ratio:* 21:1.

Majors Accounting; accounting related; accounting technology and bookkeeping; administrative assistant and secretarial science; art; art teacher education; autobody/collision and repair technology; automobile/automotive mechanics technology; biology/biological sciences; biology teacher education; business administration and management; business automation/technology/data entry; business/commerce; business/managerial economics; chemistry; chemistry teacher education; community psychology; computer and information sciences; computer and information sciences and support services related; data processing and data processing technology; dental hygiene; diesel mechanics technology; drafting and design technology; dramatic/theater arts; education; elementary education; emergency medical technology (EMT paramedic); English; English/language arts teacher education; environmental studies; finance; fire protection and safety technology; general studies; health and physical education; health/health care administration; health information/medical records administration; health teacher education; heating, air conditioning, ventilation and refrigeration maintenance technology; history; history teacher education; human resources management; legal administrative assistant/secretary; liberal arts and sciences/liberal studies; marketing/marketing management; mass communication/media; mathematics; mathematics teacher education; medical administrative assistant and medical secretary; medical/clinical assistant; multi-/interdisciplinary studies related; music; music teacher education; nursing (licensed practical/vocational nurse training); petroleum technology; physical education teaching and coaching; pre-engineering; pre-law studies; pre-medical studies; pre-nursing studies; pre-pharmacy studies; psychology; public relations/image management; rehabilitation and therapeutic professions related; rehabilitation therapy; science teacher education; secondary education; sheet metal technology; social science teacher education; sociology; Spanish; Spanish language teacher education; special education; sport and fitness administration/management; surgical technology.

Academics *Calendar:* semesters. *Degrees:* certificates, associate, bachelor's, master's, post-master's, and postbachelor's certificates. *Special study options:* academic remediation for entering students, accelerated degree program, adult/continuing education programs, advanced placement credit, cooperative education, distance learning, double majors, English as a second language, external degree program, honors programs, independent study, internships, off-campus study, part-time degree program, services for LD students, study abroad, summer session for credit.

Computers on Campus 1,000 computers/terminals are available on campus for general student use. Students can access the following: campus intranet, computer help desk, free student e-mail accounts, online (class) grades, online (class) registration, online (class) schedules, online degree programs. Campuswide network is available. 95% of college-owned or -operated housing units are wired for high-speed Internet access. Wireless service is available via classrooms, computer labs, libraries, student centers.

Student Life *Housing:* on-campus residence required for freshman year. *Options:* coed, men-only, women-only, disabled students. Campus housing is university owned. Freshman applicants given priority for college housing. *Activities and organizations:* drama/theater group, student-run newspaper, radio station, choral group, Art Student League, Band Club, Inter-Varsity Christian Fellowship, Residence Hall Association, Student Council for Exceptional Children. *Campus security:* 24-hour emergency response devices and patrols, late-night transport/escort service, controlled dormitory access. *Student services:* health clinic, personal/psychological counseling, women's center, legal services.

Athletics Member NCAA. All Division II. *Intercollegiate sports:* baseball M, basketball M (s)/W (s), cross-country running M (s)/W (s), golf M/W, soccer M (s)/W (s), softball W, tennis M (s)/W (s), volleyball W (s). *Intramural sports:* baseball M/W, basketball M/W, bowling M/W, cheerleading M/W, cross-country running M/W, football M/W, golf M/W, racquetball M/W, skiing (cross-country) M/W, soccer M/W, softball M/W, swimming and diving M/W, table tennis M/W, tennis M/W, track and field M/W, volleyball M/W.

Standardized Tests *Required:* SAT or ACT (for admission).

Costs (2007–08) *Tuition:* state resident $3988 full-time, $143 per credit hour part-time; nonresident $13,707 full-time, $381 per credit hour part-time. Full-time tuition and fees vary according to course load, degree level, and location. Part-time tuition and fees vary according to course load, degree level, and location. *Required fees:* $1144 full-time. *Room and board:* $4882. Room and board charges vary according to board plan and housing facility. *Payment plan:* installment. *Waivers:* minority students, senior citizens, and employees or children of employees.

Financial Aid Of all full-time matriculated undergraduates who enrolled in 2006, 2,741 applied for aid, 2,398 were judged to have need, 433 had their need fully met. 214 Federal Work-Study jobs (averaging $1406). 67 state and other part-time jobs (averaging $1432). In 2006, 165 non-need-based awards were made. *Average percent of need met:* 63%. *Average financial aid package:* $7886. *Average need-based loan:* $3351. *Average need-based gift aid:* $4409. *Average non-need-based aid:* $8843. *Average indebtedness upon graduation:* $16,748.

Applying *Options:* electronic application, early admission, deferred entrance. *Application fee:* $30. *Required:* high school transcript, minimum 2.5 GPA. *Application deadlines:* 7/1 (freshmen), rolling (transfers). *Notification:* continuous (freshmen), continuous (transfers).

Freshman Application Contact Ms. Shelly Andersen, Associate Director of Admissions, Montana State University–Billings, 1500 University Drive, Billings, MT 59101. *Phone:* 406-657-2158. *Toll-free phone:* 800-565-6782. *Fax:* 406-657-2302. *E-mail:* sandersen@msubillings.edu.

MONTANA STATE UNIVERSITY–NORTHERN

Havre, Montana **www.msun.edu/**

Director of Admissions Ms. Rosalie Spinler, Director of Admissions, Montana State University–Northern, PO Box 7751, Havre, MT 59501-7751. *Phone:* 406-265-3704. *Toll-free phone:* 800-662-6132.

MONTANA TECH OF THE UNIVERSITY OF MONTANA

Butte, Montana **www.mtech.edu/**

- **State-supported** comprehensive, founded 1895, part of Montana University System
- **Small-town** 56-acre campus
- **Endowment** $23.8 million
- **Coed** 2,243 undergraduate students
- **Moderately difficult** entrance level

Undergraduates Students come from 33 states and territories, 19 other countries, 12% are from out of state, 15% live on campus. *Retention:* 68% of 2006 full-time freshmen returned.

Freshmen *Average high school GPA:* 3.2. *Test scores:* SAT critical reading scores over 500: 67%; SAT math scores over 500: 75%; SAT writing scores over 500: 47%; ACT scores over 18: 87%; SAT critical reading scores over 600: 23%; SAT math scores over 600: 30%; SAT writing scores over 600: 16%; ACT scores over 24: 40%; SAT critical reading scores over 700: 4%; SAT writing scores over 700: 1%; ACT scores over 30: 4%.

Faculty *Total:* 175, 69% full-time, 39% with terminal degrees. *Student/faculty ratio:* 16:1.

Majors Accounting; administrative assistant and secretarial science; applied mathematics; architectural drafting and CAD/CADD; artificial intelligence and robotics; autobody/collision and repair technology; automobile/automotive mechanics technology; biological and physical sciences; biology/biological sciences; business administration and management; business automation/technology/data entry; business/commerce; chemistry; civil drafting and CAD/CADD; civil engineering; communication/speech communication and rhetoric; computer and information sciences; computer engineering; computer programming; computer science; computer systems analysis; data processing and data processing technology; drafting and design technology; electrical, electronics and communications engineering; engineering; engineering science; engineering technology; environmental/environmental health engineering; executive assistant/executive secretary; finance; geological/geophysical engineering; geotechnical engineering; health science; human resources management; information science/studies; legal administrative assistant/secretary; liberal arts and sciences/liberal studies; materials engineering; materials science; mathematics; mechanical drafting and CAD/CADD; mechanical engineering; medical administrative assistant and medical secretary; medical informatics; metallurgical engineering; mining and mineral engineering; nursing assistant/aide and patient care assistant; nursing (registered nurse training); occupational health and industrial hygiene; occupational safety and health technology; petroleum engineering; petroleum technology; systems engineering; technical and business writing; welding technology.

Academics *Calendar:* semesters. *Degrees:* certificates, diplomas, associate, bachelor's, master's, and postbachelor's certificates. *Special study options:* academic remediation for entering students, adult/continuing education programs, advanced placement credit, cooperative education, distance learning, double majors, independent study, internships, part-time degree program, services for LD students, student-designed majors, summer session for credit. *ROTC:* Army (b).

Computers on Campus 500 computers/terminals are available on campus for general student use. Students can access the following: campus intranet, computer help desk, free student e-mail accounts, online (class) grades, online (class) registration, online (class) schedules. Campuswide network is available. 100% of college-owned or -operated housing units are wired for high-speed Internet access. Wireless service is available via classrooms, computer centers, computer labs, learning centers, libraries, student centers.

Student Life *Housing:* on-campus residence required for freshman year. *Options:* coed, disabled students. Campus housing is university owned. Freshman campus housing is guaranteed. *Activities and organizations:* student-run newspaper, radio station, choral group, Environmental Engineering Club, SH/IH Club, Petroleum Club SPE, Marcus Daly Mining, Chemistry Club. *Campus security:* 24-hour patrols, controlled dormitory access. *Student services:* health clinic, personal/psychological counseling.

Athletics Member NAIA. *Intercollegiate sports:* basketball M (s)/W (s), cross-country running M (c)/W (c), football M (s), golf M (s)/W (s), rugby M (c)/W (c), soccer M (c)/W (c), swimming and diving M (c)/W (c), volleyball W (s). *Intramural sports:* basketball M/W, cheerleading M/W, football M/W, ice hockey M (c)/W (c), racquetball M/W, skiing (cross-country) M/W, skiing (downhill) M/W, softball M/W, swimming and diving M/W, tennis M/W, ultimate Frisbee M/W, volleyball M/W, water polo M/W, weight lifting M/W.

Standardized Tests *Required:* SAT or ACT (for admission).

Costs (2007–08) *Tuition:* state resident $5644 full-time, $271 per credit hour part-time; nonresident $15,076 full-time, $664 per credit hour part-time. Full-time tuition and fees vary according to course level, course load, degree level, and location. Part-time tuition and fees vary according to course level, course load, degree level, and location. *Required fees:* $72 per credit part-time. *Room and board:* $5860; room only: $2530. Room and board charges vary according to board plan. *Payment plans:* installment, deferred payment. *Waivers:* employees or children of employees.

Financial Aid Of all full-time matriculated undergraduates who enrolled in 2006, 1,500 applied for aid, 1,300 were judged to have need, 700 had their need fully met. 100 Federal Work-Study jobs (averaging $2000). 25 state and other part-time jobs (averaging $2000). In 2006, 100 non-need-based awards were made. *Average percent of need met:* 70%. *Average financial aid package:* $7000. *Average need-based loan:* $5000. *Average need-based gift aid:* $1000. *Average non-need-based aid:* $4000. *Average indebtedness upon graduation:* $20,000.

Applying *Options:* electronic application, early admission, deferred entrance. *Application fee:* $30. *Required:* high school transcript, minimum 2.5 GPA, proof of immunization, standardized test scores. *Application deadlines:* rolling (freshmen), rolling (transfers). *Notification:* continuous (freshmen), continuous (transfers).

Freshman Application Contact Montana Tech of The University of Montana, 1300 West Park Street, Butte, MT 59701-8997. *Phone:* 406-496-4178. *Toll-free phone:* 800-445-TECH Ext. 1. *Fax:* 406-496-4170. *E-mail:* admissions@mtech.edu.

ROCKY MOUNTAIN COLLEGE

Billings, Montana **www.rocky.edu/**

- **Independent interdenominational** comprehensive, founded 1878
- **Urban** 60-acre campus
- **Endowment** $19.2 million
- **Coed**
- **Moderately difficult** entrance level

Faculty *Student/faculty ratio:* 13:1.

Academics *Calendar:* semesters. *Degrees:* associate, bachelor's, and master's.

Student Life *Campus security:* 24-hour emergency response devices, student patrols, controlled dormitory access, security cameras.

Athletics Member NAIA.

Standardized Tests *Required:* SAT or ACT (for admission).

Financial Aid Of all full-time matriculated undergraduates who enrolled in 2003, 661 applied for aid, 552 were judged to have need, 102 had their need fully met. 353 Federal Work-Study jobs (averaging $387). 216 state and other part-time jobs (averaging $1335). In 2003, 67 non-need-based awards were made. *Average percent of need met:* 74. *Average financial aid package:* $13,276. *Average need-based loan:* $4233. *Average need-based gift aid:* $8476. *Average non-need-based aid:* $6869. *Average indebtedness upon graduation:* $20,571.

Applying *Options:* electronic application, early admission, deferred entrance. *Application fee:* $25. *Required:* high school transcript, minimum 2.5 GPA. *Required for some:* essay or personal statement, 2 letters of recommendation, interview.

Freshman Application Contact Ms. Laurie Rodriguez, Director of Admissions, Rocky Mountain College, 1511 Poly Drive, Billings, MT 59102. *Phone:* 406-657-1026. *Toll-free phone:* 800-877-6259. *Fax:* 406-259-9751. *E-mail:* admissions@rocky.edu.

SALISH KOOTENAI COLLEGE

Pablo, Montana **www.skc.edu/**

- **Independent** primarily 2-year, founded 1977
- **Rural** 4-acre campus
- **Coed**
- **Noncompetitive** entrance level

Academics *Calendar:* quarters. *Degrees:* certificates, associate, and bachelor's.

Standardized Tests *Required:* TABE (for placement).

Costs (2007–08) *Tuition:* area resident $2664 full-time, $74 per credit part-time; state resident $4572 full-time, $127 per credit part-time; nonresident $9144 full-time, $254 per credit part-time. Full-time tuition and fees vary according to course load. Part-time tuition and fees vary according to course load. *Required fees:* $897 full-time, $131 per credit part-time. *Room and board:* $6975.

Financial Aid Of all full-time matriculated undergraduates who enrolled in 2006, 54 Federal Work-Study jobs (averaging $1450).

Applying *Options:* deferred entrance. *Required:* high school transcript, proof of immunization, tribal enrollment.

Freshman Application Contact Ms. Jackie Moran, Admissions Officer, Salish Kootenai College, 52000 Highway 93, PO Box 70, Pablo, MT 59855. *Phone:* 406-275-4866. *Fax:* 406-275-4810. *E-mail:* jackie_moran@skc.edu.

UNIVERSITY OF GREAT FALLS

Great Falls, Montana **www.ugf.edu/**

- **Independent Roman Catholic** comprehensive, founded 1932, administratively affiliated with Providence Services
- **Urban** 40-acre campus
- **Endowment** $6.9 million
- **Coed** 640 undergraduate students, 75% full-time, 64% women, 36% men
- **Noncompetitive** entrance level, 57% of applicants were admitted

Undergraduates 482 full-time, 158 part-time. Students come from 27 states and territories, 3 other countries, 20% are from out of state, 4% African American, 2% Asian American or Pacific Islander, 6% Hispanic American, 5% Native American, 2% international, 20% transferred in, 29% live on campus. *Retention:* 59% of 2006 full-time freshmen returned.

Freshmen *Admission:* 351 applied, 200 admitted, 137 enrolled. *Average high school GPA:* 3.37. *Test scores:* SAT math scores over 500: 29%; ACT scores over 18: 86%; SAT math scores over 600: 4%; ACT scores over 24: 52%; ACT scores over 30: 2%.

Faculty *Total:* 103, 33% full-time, 34% with terminal degrees. *Student/faculty ratio:* 11:1.

Majors Accounting; accounting and business/management; American literature; art; art teacher education; biology/biological sciences; biology teacher education; botany/plant biology; business administration and management; chemistry; chemistry teacher education; computer and information sciences; computer and information sciences and support services related; computer and information sciences related; computer and information systems security; computer graphics; computer/information technology services administration related; computer management; computer programming; computer science; computer software and media applications related; computer systems analysis; computer systems networking and telecommunications; corrections; corrections administration; corrections and criminal justice related; counseling psychology; creative writing; criminal justice/law enforcement administration; criminal justice/police science; criminal justice/safety; early childhood education; education (multiple levels); elementary education; English; English composition; English language and literature related; English/language arts teacher education; fine/studio arts; forensic science and technology; health and physical education; health/health care administration; health teacher education; history; history teacher education; human services; information science/studies; information technology; kindergarten/preschool education; legal assistant/paralegal; library science related; management science; marketing/marketing management; mathematics; mathematics teacher education; middle school education; physical education teaching and coaching; political science and government; psychology; reading teacher education; religious studies; school librarian/school library media; science teacher education; secondary education; social sciences; social science teacher education; social studies teacher education; sociology; special education; special education (gifted and talented); substance abuse/addiction counseling; system administration; system, networking, and LAN/WAN management; theology; web/multimedia management and webmaster; web page, digital/multimedia and information resources design.

Academics *Calendar:* semesters. *Degrees:* certificates, associate, bachelor's, and master's. *Special study options:* academic remediation for entering students, adult/continuing education programs, advanced placement credit, cooperative education, distance learning, double majors, external degree program, independent study, internships, off-campus study, part-time degree program, services for LD students, summer session for credit.

Computers on Campus 110 computers/terminals are available on campus for general student use. Students can access the following: campus intranet, computer help desk, free student e-mail accounts, online (class) grades, online (class) registration, online (class) schedules. Campuswide network is available. Wireless service is available via classrooms, computer centers, computer labs, dorm rooms, learning centers, libraries, student centers.

Student Life *Housing:* on-campus residence required through sophomore year. *Options:* coed, disabled students. Campus housing is university owned and leased by the school. Freshman campus housing is guaranteed. *Activities and organizations:* drama/theater group, student-run newspaper, radio station, choral group, Student Montana Education Association, Student Senate, International Law and Justice Club, Students In Free Enterprise, Science Club (medical, forensic and computer science students). *Campus security:* 24-hour emergency response devices and patrols, late-night transport/escort service, controlled dormitory access. *Student services:* health clinic, personal/psychological counseling, women's center.

Athletics Member NAIA. *Intercollegiate sports:* basketball M (s)/W (s), cheerleading M (s)/W (s), cross-country running M/W, golf M/W, soccer W (s), softball W, volleyball W (s), wrestling M (s). *Intramural sports:* basketball M/W, football M/W, golf M/W, skiing (downhill) M/W, soccer M, softball W, table tennis M/W, ultimate Frisbee M/W, volleyball M/W, wrestling M.

Standardized Tests *Recommended:* SAT or ACT (for admission).

Costs (2008–09) *Comprehensive fee:* $21,990 includes full-time tuition ($15,500) and room and board ($6490). Part-time tuition: $490 per credit.

Financial Aid Of all full-time matriculated undergraduates who enrolled in 2007, 409 applied for aid, 320 were judged to have need, 5 had their need fully met. 52 Federal Work-Study jobs (averaging $1992). In 2007, 15 non-need-based awards were made. *Average percent of need met:* 55%. *Average financial aid package:* $12,985. *Average need-based loan:* $4596. *Average need-based gift aid:* $4451. *Average non-need-based aid:* $4773. *Average indebtedness upon graduation:* $26,450.

Applying *Options:* electronic application, early admission, deferred entrance. *Application fee:* $35. *Required:* high school transcript. *Recommended:* essay or personal statement, interview. *Application deadlines:* 8/1 (freshmen), 8/1 (transfers). *Notification:* 8/31 (freshmen), 8/31 (transfers).

Freshman Application Contact April Clutter, Director of Admissions, University of Great Falls, 1301 20th Street South, Great Falls, MT 59405. *Phone:* 406-791-5200. *Toll-free phone:* 800-856-9544. *Fax:* 406-791-5209. *E-mail:* enroll@ugf.edu.

See page 1462 for the College Close-Up.

THE UNIVERSITY OF MONTANA

Missoula, Montana **www.umt.edu/**

- **State-supported** university, founded 1893, part of Montana University System
- **Urban** 220-acre campus
- **Endowment** $126.3 million
- **Coed** 11,799 undergraduate students, 84% full-time, 54% women, 46% men
- **Moderately difficult** entrance level, 95% of applicants were admitted

Undergraduates 9,940 full-time, 1,859 part-time. Students come from 52 states and territories, 61 other countries, 27% are from out of state, 0.5% African American, 1% Asian American or Pacific Islander, 2% Hispanic American, 4% Native American, 2% international, 7% transferred in, 25% live on campus. *Retention:* 72% of 2006 full-time freshmen returned.

Freshmen *Admission:* 4,756 applied, 4,536 admitted, 2,149 enrolled. *Average high school GPA:* 3.2. *Test scores:* SAT critical reading scores over 500: 68%; SAT math scores over 500: 66%; SAT writing scores over 500: 58%; ACT scores over 18: 86%; SAT critical reading scores over 600: 29%; SAT math scores over 600: 25%; SAT writing scores over 600: 21%; ACT scores over 24: 42%; SAT critical reading scores over 700: 5%; SAT math scores over 700: 2%; SAT writing scores over 700: 1%; ACT scores over 30: 6%.

Faculty *Total:* 771, 71% full-time, 68% with terminal degrees. *Student/faculty ratio:* 19:1.

Majors Accounting; accounting technology and bookkeeping; administrative assistant and secretarial science; African-American/Black studies; American government and politics; American Indian/Native American studies; anthropology; apparel and accessories marketing; applied mathematics; area studies; art; art history, criticism and conservation; art teacher education; Asian studies; Asian studies (East); astronomy; audiology and speech-language pathology; biochemistry; biology/biological sciences; botany/plant biology; business/commerce; business teacher education; chemistry; Chinese; city/urban, community and regional planning; classics and languages, literatures and linguistics; clinical laboratory science/medical technology; clinical/medical laboratory technology; communication/speech communication and rhetoric; computer and information sciences; computer science; creative writing; culinary arts; curriculum and instruction; dance; dramatic/theater arts; drawing; economics; education; electrical, electronic and communications engineering technology; elementary education; English; English as a second/foreign language (teaching); environmental education; environmental studies; executive assistant/executive secretary; fashion merchandising; finance; foreign languages and literatures; forest/forest resources management; forestry; French; geography; geology/earth science; German; health teacher education; heavy equipment maintenance technology; history; industrial arts; information science/studies; information technology; interdisciplinary studies; international business/trade/commerce; Japanese; journalism; Latin; legal administrative assistant/secretary; legal assistant/paralegal; legal studies; liberal arts and sciences/liberal studies; linguistics; marketing/marketing management; mathematics; mathematics teacher education; medical administrative assistant and medical secretary; medical microbiology and bacteriology; medical pharmacology and pharmaceutical sciences; music; music performance; music teacher education; natural resources/conservation; natural resources management and policy; nursing (licensed practical/vocational nurse training); parks, recreation and leisure; pharmacy; pharmacy technician; philosophy; physical education teaching and coaching; physical therapy; physics; pre-engineering; pre-law studies; pre-medical studies; pre-pharmacy studies; psychology; radio and television; radiologic technology/science; reading teacher education; receptionist; respiratory care therapy; Russian; Russian studies; science teacher education; secondary education; small engine mechanics and repair technology; social sciences; social science teacher education; social work; sociology; Spanish; speech and rhetoric; statistics; surgical technology; technical and business writing; vehicle/equipment operation; welding technology; wildlife and wildlands science and management; women's studies; zoology/animal biology.

Academics *Calendar:* semesters. *Degrees:* certificates, associate, bachelor's, master's, doctoral, first professional, and post-master's certificates. *Special study options:* academic remediation for entering students, adult/continuing education programs, advanced placement credit, cooperative education, distance learning, double majors, English as a second language, external degree program, freshman honors college, honors programs, independent study, internships, off-campus study, part-time degree program, services for LD students, study abroad, summer session for credit. *ROTC:* Army (b).

Computers on Campus 545 computers/terminals are available on campus for general student use. Students can access the following: computer help desk, free student e-mail accounts, online (class) grades, online (class) registration, online (class) schedules. Campuswide network is available. Wireless service is available via entire campus.

Student Life *Housing:* on-campus residence required for freshman year. *Options:* coed, men-only, women-only, disabled students. Campus housing is university owned. Freshman campus housing is guaranteed. *Activities and organizations:* drama/theater group, student-run newspaper, radio and television station, choral group, marching band, Forestry Club, Honors Student Association, Campus Outdoor Program, International Organization, Kyi-Yo Native American Student Association, national fraternities, national sororities. *Campus security:* 24-hour emergency response devices and patrols, student patrols, late-night transport/escort service, controlled dormitory access. *Student services:* health clinic, personal/psychological counseling, women's center, legal services.

Athletics Member NCAA. All Division I except football (Division I-AA). *Intercollegiate sports:* baseball M (c), basketball M (s)/W (s), crew M (c)/W (c), cross-country running M (s)/W (s), equestrian sports M (c)/W (c), fencing M (c)/W (c), field hockey W (c), golf W (s), gymnastics W (c), ice hockey M (c)/W (c), lacrosse M (c)/W (c), rugby M (c)/W (c), skiing (downhill) M (c)/W (c), soccer W, tennis M (s)/W (s), track and field M (s)/W (s), ultimate Frisbee M (c)/W (c), volleyball W (s). *Intramural sports:* archery M/W, badminton M/W, baseball M, basketball M/W, bowling M/W, cross-country running M/W, football M/W, ice hockey M, racquetball M/W, rugby M/W, skiing (cross-country) M/W, soccer W, softball M/W, swimming and diving M/W, table tennis M/W, tennis M/W, track and field M/W, volleyball M/W, water polo M/W, weight lifting M/W.

Standardized Tests *Required:* SAT or ACT (for admission).

Costs (2008–09) *Tuition:* state resident $3739 full-time, $156 per credit part-time; nonresident $15,014 full-time, $669 per credit part-time. *Required fees:* $1441 full-time, $87 per credit part-time. *Room and board:* $6258; room only: $2808.

Financial Aid Of all full-time matriculated undergraduates who enrolled in 2005, 7,752 applied for aid, 5,924 were judged to have need, 992 had their need fully met. 1,098 Federal Work-Study jobs (averaging $1977). In 2005, 1672 non-need-based awards were made. *Average percent of need met:* 75%. *Average financial aid package:* $7866. *Average need-based loan:* $5012. *Average need-based gift aid:* $3504. *Average non-need-based aid:* $4195. *Average indebtedness upon graduation:* $15,185.

Applying *Options:* electronic application, early admission, deferred entrance. *Application fee:* $30. *Required:* high school transcript, minimum 2.5 GPA, SAT 1540 (M-V-Wr) or ACT 22; and SAT Math 440 or ACT Math 18. *Application deadlines:* rolling (freshmen), rolling (transfers). *Notification:* continuous (freshmen), continuous (transfers).

Freshman Application Contact Ms. Juana Alcala, Manager, Enrollment Services, The University of Montana, Missoula, MT 59812-0002. *Phone:* 406-243-6266. *Toll-free phone:* 800-462-8636. *Fax:* 406-243-5711. *E-mail:* admiss@umontana.edu.

THE UNIVERSITY OF MONTANA–WESTERN

Dillon, Montana **www.umwestern.edu/**

- **State-supported** 4-year, founded 1893, part of Montana University System
- **Small-town** 36-acre campus
- **Endowment** $7.0 million
- **Coed** 1,148 undergraduate students, 84% full-time, 54% women, 46% men
- **Minimally difficult** entrance level, 97% of applicants were admitted

Undergraduates 962 full-time, 186 part-time. Students come from 36 states and territories, 5 other countries, 26% are from out of state, 0.7% African American, 3% Asian American or Pacific Islander, 1% Hispanic American, 4% Native American, 0.6% international, 9% transferred in, 35% live on campus. *Retention:* 66% of 2006 full-time freshmen returned.

Freshmen *Admission:* 463 applied, 449 admitted, 252 enrolled. *Average high school GPA:* 3.05. *Test scores:* SAT critical reading scores over 500: 26%; SAT math scores over 500: 31%; ACT scores over 18: 66%; SAT critical reading scores over 600: 5%; SAT math scores over 600: 4%; ACT scores over 24: 17%; ACT scores over 30: 1%.

Faculty *Total:* 83, 72% full-time, 67% with terminal degrees. *Student/faculty ratio:* 17:1.

Majors Art teacher education; biology teacher education; business administration and management; business/commerce; business teacher education; dramatic/theater arts; education; education (K-12); elementary education; English; English/language arts teacher education; environmental studies; equestrian studies; general studies; health teacher education; history teacher education; industrial arts; kindergarten/preschool education; liberal arts and sciences/liberal studies; literature; mathematics teacher education; multi-/interdisciplinary studies related; music teacher education; physical education teaching and coaching; pre-dentistry studies; pre-law studies; pre-medical studies; pre-veterinary studies; science teacher education; secondary education; social sciences; social science teacher education; teacher assistant/aide; technology/industrial arts teacher education; tourism and travel services management.

Academics *Calendar:* semesters. *Degrees:* certificates, associate, and bachelor's. *Special study options:* academic remediation for entering students, accelerated degree program, adult/continuing education programs, advanced placement credit, cooperative education, distance learning, double majors, honors programs, independent study, internships, off-campus study, part-time degree program, services for LD students, student-designed majors, summer session for credit.

Computers on Campus 140 computers/terminals are available on campus for general student use. Students can access the following: computer help desk, free student e-mail accounts, online (class) registration. Campuswide network is available. Wireless service is available via entire campus.

Student Life *Housing:* on-campus residence required for freshman year. *Options:* coed, men-only, women-only, disabled students. Campus housing is university owned. Freshman campus housing is guaranteed. *Activities and organizations:* drama/theater group, student-run newspaper, radio station, choral group, Rodeo Club, Chi Alpha (Christian Fellowship), Catholic Campus Ministries, Equestrian Club, Polynesian Club. *Campus security:* 24-hour emergency response devices and patrols, student patrols, late-night transport/escort service. *Student services:* personal/psychological counseling.

Athletics Member NAIA. *Intercollegiate sports:* basketball M (s)/W (s), football M (s), golf M (s)/W (s), volleyball W (s). *Intramural sports:* archery M (c)/W (c), basketball M/W, cheerleading W, crew W (c), equestrian sports M (c)/W (c), football M/W, golf M/W, softball M/W, tennis M/W, volleyball M/W, wrestling M.

Standardized Tests *Required:* SAT or ACT (for admission).

Costs (2008–09) *Tuition:* state resident $3355 full-time, $148 per credit part-time; nonresident $11,794 full-time, $514 per credit part-time. *Required fees:* $873 full-time, $14 per credit part-time, $71 per term part-time. *Room and board:* $5350; room only: $2120.

Financial Aid Of all full-time matriculated undergraduates who enrolled in 2004, 875 applied for aid, 807 were judged to have need, 16 had their need fully met. 210 Federal Work-Study jobs (averaging $1178). 187 state and other part-time jobs (averaging $1671). In 2004, 3 non-need-based awards were made. *Average percent of need met:* 18%. *Average financial aid package:* $2649. *Average need-based loan:* $3485. *Average need-based gift aid:* $2256. *Average non-need-based aid:* $667. *Average indebtedness upon graduation:* $20,703.

Applying *Options:* electronic application, early admission, deferred entrance. *Application fee:* $30. *Required:* high school transcript, minimum 2.5 GPA, immunization record, 2 doses of MMR. *Application deadlines:* rolling (freshmen), rolling (transfers). *Notification:* continuous (freshmen), continuous (transfers).

Freshman Application Contact Admissions, The University of Montana–Western, 710 South Atlantic, Dillon, MT 59725. *Phone:* 406-683-7331. *Toll-free phone:* 866-869-6668 (in-state); 877-683-7493 (out-of-state). *Fax:* 406-683-7493. *E-mail:* admissions@umwestern.edu.

See page 1464 for the College Close-Up.

CARROLL COLLEGE

HELENA, MONTANA

The College

Student centered and affordable, Carroll College is a private, Catholic liberal arts college nationally recognized for excellence in academics, athletics, and extracurricular competition. With a student body of 1,500 and most classes averaging 20 or fewer students, Carroll offers each student personalized attention and mentoring from outstanding expert faculty members, not graduate assistants. As Carroll English Professor Kay Satre says, "Because of our small size, every one of our students who wants to get a front row seat in their education can. There are no long lines where you just hope and wait."

In national competition, Carroll also wins high honors. One example: Carroll's Fighting Saints football team has won five NAIA national championships in the past six years, all while maintaining a record number of nationally recognized scholar-athletes. The Carroll Talking Saints forensics team, a training ground for future attorneys and business professionals, is ranked in the top five of all colleges and universities of all sizes nationwide and has reigned as the Northwest regional champion for the past eighteen years. Eighty-four percent of Carroll pre-med students applying to medical school are accepted, while the national average for medical school acceptance hovers near 50 percent. Carroll students taking all sections of the nationwide Uniform Certified Public Accountant Examination enjoy a first-time pass rate three times the national average, and 90 percent of Carroll nursing majors pass their national professional examinations on the first attempt.

Resume building is as important as academic performance in the competition for graduate school admissions and jobs, and Carroll undergraduates benefit from experience far beyond what is typical for undergraduates at other institutions. Carroll students can join faculty members in their research and in publishing their groundbreaking discoveries in professional journals.

Carroll students have discovered more than ten new species; contributed to first-ever studies of species ranges and health; produced new studies of plant, animal, and human genetics; uncovered environmental contamination; and had their findings published internationally and used by professional scientists in their research.

Unique to Carroll is its dedication to service learning and social justice. Starting from the first semester of freshman year, students embark on professor-led projects to help the less fortunate while examining the deeper issues surrounding poverty, hunger, illiteracy, violence, health-care access, and other problems. Service learning continues in regular courses across disciplines throughout all four years at Carroll. Each year, the College offers several service-immersion trips out of state and overseas and, locally, the College hosts several annual social justice days devoted to hands-on service for the less fortunate in Helena. Students can also create their own social justice project. In 2006, a student-led fund-raiser to benefit St. Jude Children's Research Hospital earned Carroll the School of the Year award out of a pool of over 250 colleges and universities.

The College's unique commitment to service is also embodied in Carroll's Human-Animal Bond Program, the first of its kind in the nation, which educates students to train dogs and horses as service and therapy animals.

The College's rigorous and highly respected Honors Scholars Program stands apart, with dedicated honors courses, rigorous study of the world's great books and ideas across all disciplines, off-campus involvement in cultural and arts events, and a capstone honors thesis.

Founded in 1909, Carroll College is a private, Catholic college, accredited by the Northwest Association of Schools and Colleges. The College is a member of the National Association of Independent Colleges and Universities, the American Council on Education, the Council of Independent Colleges, the Association of Catholic Colleges and Universities, and the Western Independent College Fund.

Location

Helena, the state capital, nestles in the heart of southwestern Montana's Rocky Mountains. Just 5 minutes from the campus, hikers and mountain bikers can access Mount Helena City Park, part of Helena's over 2,000 acres of open-space land and one of the most expansive city park trail systems in the nation. The Missouri River and six pristine recreational lakes are short rides from the campus. Wilderness backpacking and camping opportunities, within short drives of Helena, are almost limitless. Students can have outdoor fun on their own or guided through Carroll's Adventures and Mountaineering Program, which brings hundreds of students out to hike, camp, kayak, raft, rock and ice climb, ski, snowshoe, learn outdoor survival, and more.

For winter sports, the Great Divide Ski Area is a 45-minute trek from campus. Two internationally top-rated world-class ski resorts are easy day trips and boast the "biggest" skiing in America. Four other outstanding ski hills lie within about a two hour's drive of the campus.

Majors and Degrees

Carroll College offers a four-year Bachelor of Arts degree program. Its majors and areas of concentration include accounting; biology; business administration (with concentrations in economics, finance, international business, management, and marketing); chemistry; civil engineering; classical studies; communication studies; computer information systems; computer science (with concentrations in computer networking and in computer programming for biological sciences, business, mathematics, and physical sciences, or an individually designed program); elementary education; engineering (3-2 program); English; English writing; environmental studies (with concentrations in community, culture, and science; ethics and value studies); French; health and physical education (with concentrations in community health, K–12, and sports management); history; international relations; mathematics (with a cognate concentration); nursing; performing arts/theater (with concentrations in acting/directing and performing arts technology); philosophy; political science; psychology; public administration; public relations (with concentrations in business and journalism); secondary education (with concentrations in biology, chemistry, communication studies, English, history, mathematics, political science, and social studies); sociology; Spanish; Spanish education (K–12); teaching English to speakers of other languages (TESOL); TESOL (K–12); and theology (with concentrations in contextual and systematic).

Under the 3-2 engineering program, students attend Carroll for three years and then transfer to an affiliate school to complete specialized studies. Upon completion of the program, students receive two degrees, one from Carroll and one from the affiliate school. Affiliate schools are Columbia, Gonzaga, Montana State–Bozeman, Montana Tech, and the Universities of Minnesota, Notre Dame, and Southern California.

Carroll offers preprofessional programs in dentistry, law, medicine, optometry, pharmacy, physical therapy, physician's assistant studies, seminary, and veterinary medicine. Carroll also offers various two-year Associate of Arts degrees.

Academic Programs

The academic year consists of fall and spring semesters and a limited summer term. Carroll's Bachelor of Arts degree program requires that all students study the arts, sciences, humanities, and social sciences for at least four of their eight semesters at Carroll.

New programs include athletic trainer preparation, gender studies, geographic information system (GIS) certification, and health science. Special programs, minors, and course offerings include broadcast journalism, Carroll Intensive Language Institute (CILI), cooperative education and internships, the Honors Scholars Program, Human-Animal Bond, languages (including French, German, Greek, Latin, linguistics, and Spanish), Latin American studies, military science, physics, and study abroad.

Off-Campus Programs

Study-abroad opportunities round out Carroll's academic offerings. Carroll has provided students professor-led study-abroad opportunities to every continent except Antarctica. Carroll offers exchange programs with Kumamoto-Gakuen University, Japan, and the Universidad Internacional, Mexico. Carroll's Study Abroad Office also arranges for students to perform independent study abroad at colleges and universities worldwide.

Academic Facilities

Carroll College offers "smart classrooms" with the latest technology, including real-time classroom voting to gauge student learning and evaluate effective teaching methods. The Fortin Science Center provides outstanding chemistry and biology laboratories equipped with the latest analytical tools. In Simperman Hall, the Nursing Department's training facility is the regional leader, with a realistic ER triage unit, a new Holistic Healing Lab, and an extensive array of the most advanced patient-simulation equipment available, including SimMan and SimBaby. The Civil Engineering Laboratory houses professional-grade machinery and materials, including hydraulics-, machinery-, and structures-testing capabilities and a model water-treatment plant. Carroll's four coed residence halls provide classrooms, computer labs, chapels, and art galleries.

Costs

For the 2007–08 academic year, Carroll's tuition and fees totaled $19,290; room and board fees were $6608. Other general personal expenses included books, supplies, and transportation.

Financial Aid

Because of its generous financial aid packages, Carroll students graduate with slightly less debt than state-school alumni. On average, a Carroll student receives a 42 percent discount on tuition in the form of College gift aid. In the 2007–08 academic year, Carroll awarded an average of over $17,000 in financial aid packages to freshmen. Ninety-nine percent of Carroll's full-time, degree-seeking students receive College-sponsored, state, and federal financial aid. Carroll's merit scholarships range from $4000 to $10,500 annually.

The average four-year graduation rate of Carroll College students is 86 percent, compared the national private college average of 79 percent and the national state university average of 49 percent. An earlier graduation lowers graduates' debts and advances their earnings. As a result, Carroll's student loan repayment default rate remains one of the lowest in the nation. Carroll was recently recognized with an award from the Montana Guaranteed Student Loan Program for achieving the lowest loan default rate in Montana.

More information on Carroll scholarships is available at the College Web site at http://www.carroll.edu/finaid/index.cc. To receive priority consideration for scholarships, students must have a complete admission file by March 1. Carroll requires students interested in need-based financial assistance to submit the Free Application for Federal Student Aid (FAFSA), available from high school counselors or at http://www.fafsa.ed.gov, as early as possible after January 1.

Faculty

Carroll's 83 full-time and 52 adjunct faculty members are expert teachers and experts in their fields, with almost all holding doctorate or terminal degrees. Professors, not graduate students, instruct all Carroll courses.

Carroll's faculty members are consistently recognized for their excellence, earning Fulbright Scholarships and awards for leadership and scholarship in their fields. In the sciences, Carroll professors perform groundbreaking research across the globe and lead student research in biology, chemistry, history, psychology, and many other disciplines. Widely published in the humanities and sciences, Carroll professors are also student-centered, placing a particular emphasis on mentoring students and maintaining extensive office hours and other opportunities for students seeking academic help and personal guidance. Every month, students can take advantage of opportunities to dine with professors in their homes and participate in activities such as game nights and music sessions at professors' residences. Professors are on-call to assist students applying for employment and graduate school and often play pivotal roles in their students' obtaining their first job offers, internships, graduate school scholarships, and research fellowships.

Student Government

The Associated Students of Carroll College helps students communicate with the administration and make important decisions about campus activities and student life. Each class (freshman, sophomore, junior, and senior) elects its own student officers, with each vice president serving as a student senator. Carroll's Student Senate consists of elected representatives from each floor of the residence halls, off-campus students, and nontraditional students. Students may also serve on a variety of committees through the Carroll Activities Board, start their own clubs, and lead their own projects, including a variety of campus events like concerts, film festivals, comedy nights, and charity fundraisers. Editing Carroll's monthly newspaper and yearly literary magazine, hosting a Carroll KROL-FM radio show, interning for Saints TV, and independent filmmaking are always open to students.

Admission Requirements

Degree candidates are those who have applied through the Office of Admission for a course of study leading to the Bachelor of Arts degree. Degree candidates may be enrolled on a full-time or part-time basis. Admission decisions are based upon a student's performance during high school, verbal and quantitative skills, a secondary school report, letters of recommendation, demonstrated commitment to intellectual achievement, and performance on standardized college entrance examinations.

When applying for admission, candidates must submit the application form, official transcripts from the high school and all colleges previously attended, a secondary school report and/or a letter of recommendation, ACT or SAT scores, and a $35 nonrefundable application fee. There is no fee for online applications at http://www.carroll.edu/prostudents. Transfer students who have successfully completed more than 30 college semester credits with at least a C (2.5) grade average are not required to submit high school transcripts or ACT or SAT scores.

Application and Information

Carroll College has a rolling admission policy with a priority admission deadline of March 1. Within three weeks of submission of all materials, the Office of Admission notifies candidates of acceptance, conditional acceptance, or denial. Students should note that late submission of material may jeopardize financial aid awards and course registration. Students can apply online at the College Web site.

For application forms or more information, students should contact:

Director of Admission
Carroll College
1601 North Benton Avenue
Helena, Montana 59625-0002
Phone: 406-447-4384
800-992-3648 (toll-free)
E-mail: admit@carroll.edu
Web site: http://www.carroll.edu

The Carroll College campus.

MONTANA STATE UNIVERSITY

BOZEMAN, MONTANA

The University

Montana State University (MSU) is home to 12,170 students and offers a comprehensive array of programs and opportunities for students to study in one of America's most spectacular outdoor environments. Undergraduate and graduate programs are offered in the Colleges of Agriculture; Arts and Architecture; Business; Education, Health, and Human Development; Engineering; Letters and Science; and Nursing. Undecided students can explore MSU's newest college, University College, which offers students a chance for a rigorous, broad education in the arts, humanities, and sciences and allows them to pursue interdisciplinary interests, such as international or environmental studies.

"Mountains and minds" is a slogan especially appropriate to Montana State University. Nestled in the beautiful ranges and wilderness areas of the Rocky Mountains, the campus environment of clean air, uncrowded classes, and wide-open spaces creates a collegiate atmosphere that is unrivaled in most of the United States.

MSU is unique in that it is not an overgrown and impersonal institution. The enrollment of 12,170 students (10,572 undergraduates) allows for much closer student-faculty interaction than is possible at many schools, ensuring each student the individual attention and academic counseling that are so important in achieving a meaningful college education. Its 1,170-acre campus and the surrounding area offer unlimited opportunities for combining academic and recreational experiences.

Location

Few geographical locations offer the broad range of recreational opportunities found in Bozeman. A community of about 63,000 people in a broad valley surrounded by the magnificence of the northern Rockies, Bozeman is a university town, the social and economic center for a large agricultural area, and a major tourist destination. Outstanding outdoor recreation is at the town's doorstep. Three challenging ski areas (Big Sky, Moonlight Basin, and Bridger Bowl), world-class fly-fishing streams, and a multitude of hunting, hiking, camping, mountain climbing, ice-skating, snowmobiling, boating, swimming, and waterskiing opportunities are within minutes of Bozeman. In addition, the gateway to the phenomenally breathtaking Yellowstone National Park is less than an hour away. The community, in cooperation with the University, offers a variety of cultural activities throughout the year, including opera, symphony, ballet, and various festivals. The Museum of the Rockies, which houses nationally known dinosaur exhibits, is also located on the campus.

Majors and Degrees

The College of Agriculture offers degrees in agricultural business, agricultural education (options in agricultural education broadfield teaching and agricultural relations), agricultural operations technology, animal science (options in equine science, livestock management and industries, and science), biotechnology (options in animal systems, microbial systems, and plant systems), environmental science (options in environmental biology and soil and water science), horticulture (options in horticulture and landscape design), land rehabilitation, land resource sciences (options in agroecology and land resources analysis and management), natural resources and rangeland ecology (options in rangeland ecology/management and wildlife habitat ecology/management), and plant science (options in crop science and plant biology). The college also offers a nondegree program in pre–veterinary medicine.

The College of Arts and Architecture offers degrees in architecture (five-year master's), arts (options in art education K–12 broadfield, art history, and liberal arts studio), environmental design, fine arts (options in graphic design and studio arts), media and theater arts (options in motion picture/video/theater and photography), music, and music education.

The College of Business offers degrees in business, with options in accounting, finance, management, and marketing.

The College of Education, Health and Human Development offers degrees in elementary education (options in early childhood education, K–8 education, library media K–12, mathematics, reading K–12, science education, and special education), health and human development (options in community health, exercise science, family and consumer sciences, food and nutrition, health enhancement K–12, and pre–physical therapy studies), health promotion, secondary education (options in general science broadfield, social studies broadfield, and technology education broadfield), technology education (options in industrial technology and technology education broadfield), and departmental teaching options.

The College of Engineering offers degrees in chemical engineering, civil engineering (options in bioresources and civil engineering), computer engineering, computer science, construction engineering technology, electrical engineering, industrial engineering, mechanical engineering, and mechanical engineering technology.

The College of Letters and Science offers degrees in anthropology, biological sciences (options in biology teaching, ecology and evolution, organismal biology, and fish and wildlife management), cell biology and neuroscience (options in biomedical science and cell biology and neuroscience), chemistry (options in biochemistry, chemistry professional, and chemistry teaching), earth sciences (options in geography, geohydrology, geology, GIS/planning, paleontology, and snow science), economics, English (options in literature and English teaching), history (options in history; history teaching; Japan studies; religious studies; and science, the environment, technology and society), mathematics (options in applied mathematics, mathematics, mathematics teaching, and statistics), microbiology (options in environmental health, medical laboratory science, and microbiology), modern languages and literatures (options in commerce, French, French teaching, German, German teaching, Spanish, and Spanish teaching), philosophy (options in philosophy and philosophy and religion), physics (options in interdisciplinary physics, physics teaching, and professional physics), political science, (options in international relations and political science), psychology (options in applied psychology and psychological science), and sociology (option in sociology).

The College of Nursing offers degrees in nursing.

University College offers a degree in liberal studies.

Bachelor of Arts and Bachelor of Science degrees are also offered in directed interdisciplinary studies. Nondegree programs are offered in military aerospace studies (Air Force), military science (Army), and university studies for students who are undecided about a major. In addition, minors are offered in Japan studies, Native American studies, and women's studies, as well as many other teaching and nonteaching disciplines.

Montana State University offers direction in several preprofessional disciplines, including dentistry, medicine, optometry, physical therapy, and veterinary science.

An intensive English language program is also available to students.

The three smaller units of the Montana State University system, MSU–Billings, MSU–Northern, and the Great Falls College of Technology, offer a wide variety of additional academic programs.

Academic Programs

Core 2.0 is the new general education requirement at MSU, and its features include a freshman seminar, a diversity course, and an undergraduate research/creative experience for all students. Beyond the usual math and English requirements, students also choose a research or inquiry course in the fine arts, social sciences, natural sciences, and humanities. The new core's mission is to enhance the students' use of multiple perspectives in making informed critical and ethical judgments in their personal, public, and professional lives through inquiry and research experiences.

An interdisciplinary University honors program is a significant addition to the curricular and community life of Montana State. Students from various academic fields take part in innovative seminars and research projects. Teaching is primarily Socratic in method.

Montana State University was recently ranked in the top tier of research universities by the Carnegie Foundation for the Advancement of Teaching and is ranked among the top in the nation for the number of Goldwater Fellowships in the sciences.

Included among the special programs at MSU are various internships and cooperative education opportunities.

The University operates on a semester system, and a summer session is available.

Off-Campus Programs

MSU offers opportunities for off-campus study, including the National Student Exchange Program, which allows students to attend one of more than 160 other colleges and universities for up to one year, and an international study program, which offers opportunities for study in 220 locations in fifty countries.

Academic Facilities

The University has many special facilities that are used for undergraduate education and research. The foremost of these is a recently renovated 712,241-volume library that receives more than 8,757 periodicals on a regular basis and also serves as a depository for U.S. government documents. Montana State posted a record of more than $102 million in research expenditures in 2007, putting MSU in the top 100 public universities based on its research volume. The University is home to numerous nationally and internationally acclaimed faculties, laboratories, institutes, and research centers, including the Center for Biofilm Engineering, the Center for Bio-Inspired Nanomaterials, the Center for Computational Biology, the Big Sky Institute, the Western Transportation Institute, the Geographic Information and Analysis Center, the Spectrum Lab, the Thermal Biology Institute, the Ag/BioScience Building (which houses one of the two largest biocontainment facilities in the nation), and the Molecular Bioscience Building. In addition, the area surrounding the University is utilized as a natural laboratory by students in many academic areas. Hundreds of students each year participate in cutting-edge research opportunities through the Undergraduate Scholarship Program. Projects range from developing experiments to be put on a satellite to studying thermal features in Yellowstone Park to original research on the history of Bozeman.

Costs

University tuition and fees for the 2007–08 academic year for out-of-state students were $16,274; board and a double room, $6780; and books and supplies, about $1050. Personal expenses and transportation costs were estimated at $2750. The estimated total for an out-of-state student was $26,854 per year. Residents of Montana pay one third the cost in tuition and fees, with all other expenses remaining constant.

Financial Aid

Montana State University maintains a comprehensive program of financial assistance for both freshmen and upperclass students, including scholarships, loans, grants, and work-study opportunities. Such aid is intended to recognize and assist students who otherwise would not be able to begin or continue their education. Approximately 75 percent of the students attending Montana State receive some form of financial aid. Approximately 25 percent earn part of their expenses through part-time employment.

Faculty

There are 828 resident faculty members at Montana State who are teachers and hold their scholarly relationship with their students as a priority above all else. For example, 5.1 percent of lectures/seminars are taught by graduate teaching assistants (GTAs) and 36.1 percent of labs are taught by GTAs. Members of the faculty serve as advisers to undergraduate and graduate students, and many also serve as faculty advisers for student clubs, organizations, and committees.

Student Government

Student government at MSU has a long history of responsible leadership and service to the campus. As a result, students actively participate in the administration of the University as well as of student organizations.

Admission Requirements

All applicants must file an application for admission with a nonrefundable $30 fee. Freshmen must submit their high school record (posting date of graduation and rank in class) and scores from either the SAT or ACT. Transfer applicants must submit official transcripts from each college or university attended. Transfer applicants who have earned fewer than 12 postsecondary quarter or semester credits must also submit an official high school transcript and test scores.

A graduate of any high school that is accredited by the Board of Public Education is eligible for admission as a first-time full-time undergraduate student, provided he or she has obtained a minimum score of 22 on the ACT or 1050 on the SAT (math and critical reading scores combined) or at least a 2.5 high school grade point average or ranks in the upper half of the school's graduating class and has completed the prescribed college-preparatory curriculum. Entering students are required to have completed the following courses in high school in order to be eligible for admission: 4 years of English, 3 years of mathematics (algebra I and II and geometry), 3 years of social studies, 2 years of laboratory science, and 2 years of electives chosen from foreign languages, computer science, visual or performing arts, or vocational education.

Transfer students must present at least a 2.0 (C) cumulative GPA based on transferable credits from all colleges or universities previously attended.

Students should visit the University's Web site for more specific admission requirements regarding math and writing proficiencies that apply to incoming freshmen.

Application and Information

Students should contact:

Office of Admissions
Montana State University
P.O. Box 172190
Bozeman, Montana 59717-2190
Phone: 406-994-2452
888-MSU-CATS (toll-free)
E-mail: admissions@montana.edu
Web site: http://www.montana.edu/wwwnss/

Montana State University in Bozeman.

COLLEGE DATA CENTER • MONTANA

UNIVERSITY OF GREAT FALLS

GREAT FALLS, MONTANA

The University

The University of Great Falls (UGF) is a private, Catholic liberal arts university sponsored by the Sisters of Providence within the jurisdiction of the Catholic Bishop of Great Falls–Billings. UGF is open to qualified men and women of every race and creed. UGF offers the Corps of Discovery, a distinctive four-year, outside-of-the-classroom, personal-formation program. Students develop their leadership and team abilities through a variety of physical challenges, collaborative efforts, artistic endeavors, and spiritual and service activities.

UGF's academic programs are designed to educate students through curricula featuring liberal arts courses combined with career and professional preparation. The University's mission is to provide students with the opportunity to obtain a liberal arts education for lifelong learning and a successful career or profession. The faculty and staff members of the University join with students in a cooperative and enthusiastic search for truth, meaning, and the analytical skills to resolve moral and ethical dilemmas. The low student-faculty ratio (14:1) equates to more individual attention and help with both academic and personal development. Although faculty members participate in applied research, the focus is on teaching. Because teaching students is the primary concern of faculty members, they combine traditional classroom instruction with education using multimedia computer technology and learning through internships, field experiences, and community service.

The University was founded in 1932 by Bishop Edwin V. O'Hara to fill the need for an institution of higher education in Great Falls and the central Montana area. The present campus opened in 1960. Providence Tower, the main campus landmark, was constructed in 1964, and McLaughlin Memorial Center, a spacious physical education and recreation facility, was added in 1965. The campus consists of more than a dozen buildings, including Sullivan Hall, Emilie Hall, the DiRocco-Peressini Science Center, a theater/music building, an art building, Galerie Trinitas, Trinitas Chapel, and the library. The library, which was doubled in size in 1999, provides additional study room for students. The University of Great Falls has been accredited by the Northwest Association of Schools and Colleges since 1935.

The University's athletic programs include men's and women's basketball, cross-country, golf, soccer, and track; men's wrestling; and softball and volleyball. Playing in the Frontier Conference, the Argonauts enhance the community's quality of life and offer student athletes opportunities to be a part of a highly competitive, nationally recognized program. "Jason the Argonaut" has been the school's mascot since UGF started athletic programs in 1967. UGF's chosen mascot stems from Greek mythology and the story of Jason and his band of courageous men, called the Argonauts, in their quest for the Golden Fleece.

Student-life activities abound in the UGF community. The Argo Café and lounge in the Student Center are a popular socializing and studying place that is central to the campus. The spacious campus offers a year-round setting for student-initiated activities. On a winter day, it is quite common to see students snowboarding on the large hill next to Emilie Hall. On fall and spring days, many students enjoy flag football, Frisbee, FOLF, and, of course, the seasonal water fights and Slip 'N' Slide. Students also have opportunities throughout the semester to participate in intramural sports, attend community events, and engage in a wide variety of outdoor recreation.

Location

The city of Great Falls is located in north-central Montana. Situated next to the five waterfalls of the Missouri River at an elevation of 3,300 feet, the city lies between the Rocky Mountains and Great Plains. The river, a historically significant waterway explored by the Lewis and Clark Expedition in 1805, provides abundant recreational opportunities such as boating, canoeing, and fishing its blue-ribbon trout waters. Great Falls is also home to the Lewis and Clark National Historic Trail Interpretive Center and the Charlie Russell Museum, which showcases the treasured works of the famous Western artist Charles M. Russell. On the museum grounds sit the Russell home and the artist's log studio. Great Falls exemplifies the Western heritage and ethos of the Big Sky Country of Montana.

Nestled near the Big Belt, Little Belt, and Highwood Mountain Ranges, Great Falls is centrally located in one of the nation's most scenic regions. For skiing enthusiasts, the Little Belt Mountains, an hour south of Great Falls, offer excellent downhill skiing at Showdown Ski Area and 17 miles of groomed cross-country trails at Silver Crest. In addition to skiing, the surrounding area provides extensive outdoor recreational activities, including biking, hiking, camping, technical rock climbing, white-water rafting, archaeological exploration, fishing, and hunting. About an hour west of the city lies the Rocky Mountain Front Range, which extends northward to one of the country's crown jewels, Glacier National Park. The majestic peaks of this area provide outdoor enthusiasts with hundreds of miles of trails and pristine lakes and streams. Four hours to the south of Great Falls is Yellowstone National Park, where abundant herds of bison and elk roam the vast spaces. Many other species of wildlife call Yellowstone home, including the reintroduced wolf.

The central location of Great Falls gives students the opportunity to explore numerous surrounding communities with local attractions and shops.

Majors and Degrees

At the undergraduate level, the University of Great Falls offers curricular programs in forty-five areas, including bachelor's degrees in twenty-three majors and associate degrees in three majors. Through the integration of liberal arts and professional preparation, the University helps students prepare for lifelong learning and rewarding careers.

Academic Programs

The University develops professional/career programs designed to meet society's present and future needs, as well as traditional academic degrees in appropriate fields. As part of the undergraduate core curriculum, students acquire fundamental skills and experiences that facilitate comprehension, information processing, and communication within particular disciplines. Beyond the learning required for their chosen majors, students embark on a path of self-discovery and learn to apply meaning to the world around them from historical, contemporary, and future perspectives. All students are required to complete courses in communications, composition, computer science, fine arts, history, literature, mathematics, natural science, social sciences, and theology and religion.

As part of the Freshman Experience, the University of Great Falls introduces its Corps of Discovery Program. Like the 1804 adventure lead by Captains William Clark and Meriwether Lewis, the Corps of Discovery at the University takes students on an extraordinary journey of adventure, discovery, and accomplishments. The Corps of Discovery at UGF is an opportunity for students to learn outside of the classroom while gaining the skills necessary to be successful academically and professionally. It is a life experience where lessons are learned from the desktop to the mountaintop.

UGF serves students of all beliefs while offering a foundation for actively implementing spiritual values and a variety of religious teachings that are rooted in the Catholic tradition. Students are strongly encouraged to complement classroom learning with nonacademic learning in the areas of community service, wellness activities, and cultural arts.

Off-Campus Programs

The Distance Learning Program provides instruction to students throughout the country and around the world, enabling them to complete four undergraduate degrees and one master's degree from their home or work. Many students choose to begin their lower-division course work at home and then move to the campus to complete their degree. Distance learning students receive instruction through a variety of media technologies, such as videotapes, e-mail, and Internet conferencing. Students benefit from a mix of self-study and live Internet classroom sessions for a uniquely personal distance learning environment. The UGF Distance Learning Program offers high-quality educational opportunities to students who would not otherwise have access to the campus.

Academic Facilities

The University library provides informational resources for students and faculty and staff members. The collection contains more than 106,000 books and 400 journal subscriptions. Services include access to reference materials, interlibrary loan, and more than 50 online databases from InfoTrac, ProQuest, OCLC First Search, and LexisNexis. In addition, fax services, copiers, and workstations for the disabled are available for student use. Special collections include the McDonald Collection of Business Resources, the Bertsche Collection of Montana History, and the Korontzos Law Library. An audiovisual collection with videocassettes, records, CDs, scores, and other media can be checked out or used in the library.

The main computer lab, which is centrally located in Sullivan Hall, houses more than forty personal computers, while other labs on campus house more than thirty-five additional personal computers. These computers are upgraded yearly and are available for use by all students. UGF students take advantage of the wireless Internet connection in the student center, Sullivan Hall, and the library. Students can access the Internet and e-mail through the UGFNET from on-campus residence halls. The lab supports one of the most widely used Windows-based software suites, and peripheral equipment is always available.

The University offers student support services to help students achieve academic success. The Center for Academic Excellence serves first-generation students, students with limited income, and students with disabilities and is strongly committed to both their academic success and personal growth. To accomplish this goal, the center provides a wide range of services and activities to all eligible students, including academic support, personal counseling, minority student support, and support for students with disabilities. Tutoring, academic support, and personal counseling are also available in the Grandma Rice Retention Center.

The University partnered with the Montana State University–Bozeman College of Nursing to establish a student health center. The center offers limited primary care to UGF students and faculty and staff members. It is staffed by an advanced-practice registered nurse/family practitioner with prescriptive authority. The clinic focuses on treating acute illnesses as well as promoting wellness and education about at-risk behaviors.

The McLaughlin Memorial Center is a site used for health and physical education classes, as well as athletic competition. Facilities include a large gymnasium, a wellness exercise center, a large conference room, and academic classrooms. A high- and low-element ropes course, which is known as Adventure Quest, is located in the building and in the surrounding grounds. In the fall of 2007, the McLaughlin Memorial Center began a huge transformation. When completed, it will house a state-of-the-art fitness and recreation area and will include a place to eat for those late night study sessions.

With seating for 357 people, the University Theater is used frequently by the campus and the community. Theater students produce one play per semester as part of their course requirement. Musicians, comedians, and local groups also perform regularly in the building.

Costs

Undergraduate tuition for the 2006–07 school year was $15,600. Room and board for students living in University housing were $5530. Books and supplies were estimated to cost $900 per year. Emilie Hall, a newly renovated residence hall on campus, is designated for first year students. A growing university population has opened the door for new student housing options. Most notable is the conversion of Providence Hall to student living quarters. A scenic courtyard, large kitchen facility, recently renovated lounge, and free wireless Internet access in rooms are just a few of the amenities Providence Hall has to offer. The on-campus location offers security and extreme proximity to important student services. Providence Hall is handicapped accessible and many of the rooms have sinks. The Villa, an off-campus apartment complex, is designated for students age 21 and older, married students, or students with children.

Financial Aid

Approximately 90 percent of students at UGF receive some form of financial assistance. The University offers more than $2 million annually in merit-based, athletic, and fine arts scholarships. Information on need-based financial assistance programs is available from the Financial Aid Office. Scholarship information for new students is available from the Admissions Office. To be considered for financial aid, students should submit a Free Application for Federal Student Aid (FAFSA) form electronically at http://www.fafsa.ed.gov with UGF's school code of 002527. To be considered for scholarships, students should submit an application for admission along with academic transcripts.

Faculty

UGF has a student-faculty ratio of 14:1 and features faculty members who possess personal philosophies that are compatible with a Catholic learning environment. These experienced teachers, of whom 57 percent possess terminal degrees, are not only highly competent in their academic fields but also persons of integrity to whom students can look for example, inspiration, and information. Since a faculty member's influence is of paramount significance in education, an ability and willingness to mentor students about academic concerns and lifelong goals are traits that are expected of each teacher.

Student Government

The University's students are represented by the Associated Students of the University of Great Falls. The governing body is an elected Student Senate. The University student government was the first in Montana to eliminate the class structure in favor of giving greater representation to all students. One student is a full voting member of the Board of Trustees.

Admission Requirements

The University of Great Falls Admissions Office accepts applicants on a rolling basis. Applicants may apply for admission at any time; however, all applicants are strongly urged to apply at least one month prior to the first day of classes of the term during which they intend to enter the University. Students are encouraged to submit their test scores from the ACT or the SAT whenever possible. The scores from these tests are used in scholarship consideration, academic counseling, and course placement. The University also has an early admission program for students in high school. The University of Great Falls grants advanced standing credit for AP, CLEP, and ACE military programs.

Application and Information

The University of Great Falls is committed to a program of equal opportunity for education, employment, and participation in University activities without regard to race, color, gender, age, religion, marital status, sexual orientation, physical handicap, national origin, or mental handicap. For additional information about the University of Great Falls, including an admission packet, students should contact:

Office of Admissions
University of Great Falls
1301 20th Street South
Great Falls, Montana 59405
Phone: 406-791-5200
800-856-9544 (toll-free)
Fax: 406-791-5209
E-mail: enroll@ugf.edu
Web site: http://www.ugf.edu

Students enjoy a fall class in the UGF Scholar's Circle.

THE UNIVERSITY OF MONTANA WESTERN

DILLON, MONTANA

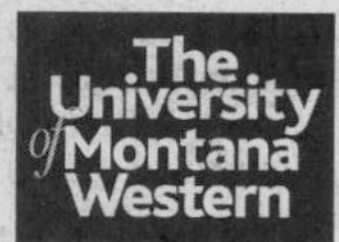

The University

The University of Montana Western (UMW) is a small, public baccalaureate university that was originally established in 1893 in beautiful southwestern Montana. UMW nurtures scholarship, creativity, lifelong learning, and high standards. The intimate size of Montana Western's campus provides accessibility to all aspects of academic and extracurricular life.

With a current enrollment of 1,200 students, Montana Western specializes in providing individual attention, personalized caring, commitment, hands-on classroom experiences using state-of-the-art technology, and, most important, field experiences and research at the undergraduate level. Montana Western offers classes by block scheduling, one class every eighteen days for 3 hours a day; UMW refers to this innovative approach to education as "EXPERIENCE ONE." Montana Western is the only public institution to offer classes in this manner. With "EXPERIENCE ONE," faculty members teach just one class every eighteen academic days and students take just one class every eighteen academic days, creating small, interactive learning communities. Courses are rarely lecture based and are experiential by nature. All classes are taught by professors, not graduate students, and class size is capped at 30, with an average student-faculty ratio of 14:1. The 36-acre campus is friendly and beautiful and is surrounded by three mountain ranges and the Continental Divide.

Athletics are an important part of campus life at Montana Western. One in every 5 UMW students participates in a sport. Montana Western is affiliated with the National Association of Intercollegiate Athletics (NAIA) and participates in the Frontier Conference. Varsity sports are offered for women in basketball, golf, and volleyball. Men compete in basketball, football, and golf. The University also fields very competitive men's and women's NIRA rodeo teams each year and an IHSA equestrian team for men and women.

Location

Located at the southwestern tip of Big Sky Country, the quiet town of Dillon is home to Montana Western. Dillon has a population of 4,000. The town has excellent medical facilities and a lively downtown business area. Dillon is the seat of Beaverhead County, Montana's largest county. The 3.3-million-acre Beaverhead-Deer Lodge National Forest is known for its all-season outdoor recreational opportunities. Fishing, hunting, boating, downhill and cross-country skiing, climbing, backpacking, horseback riding, and camping are all available within an hour's drive. The area is also rich in Western history. The region's temperatures average daily highs of 25 degrees Fahrenheit in the winter months and 85 degrees Fahrenheit in the summer months. Annual precipitation averages 10 inches. Rich farmland, rugged mountains, and wide expanses of the old frontier surround Dillon, yet major Montana and Idaho cities are easily accessible by interstate highways.

Majors and Degrees

Montana Western offers the Bachelor of Science, Bachelor of Applied Science, Bachelor of Arts, Associate of Arts, Associate of Science, and Associate of Applied Science degrees.

The Bachelor of Science offers majors in business (options in equine management, health and fitness, industrial technology management, information technology/network administration, office systems technology, small business management, and tourism), early childhood education, elementary education, natural horsemanship (options in management, psychology, and science), and secondary education (options in art (K–12), biology, business and computer applications, drama, earth science, English, general science, history, industrial arts technology, mathematics, music (K–12), physical education and health, social science, and special education (K–12)).

The Bachelor of Arts offers majors in biology, with options in cell/molecular biology, health and human performance, mathematical biology, preprofessional health sciences, veterinary science, and wildlife biology; environmental interpretation, with options in biology, geology, and preprofessional fish and wildlife; environmental science, with options in applied mathematical science, biology, environmental geochemistry, geology, sustainable natural resource management, and wildlife therapy; literature and writing, with options in creative writing, professional communications, and Western culture; social science, with options in history, political science, prelaw, psychology, restorative justice, society and culture, sociology, and women's studies; and visual and performing arts, with options in business, crafts, drama, illustration, music, pre–art therapy, and studio art.

The Associate of Arts and Associate of Science provide two-year degrees with a full general education curriculum. Other two-year degrees include the Associate of Applied Science in business (with options in business management, computer-aided manufacturing, and office systems technology), early childhood education, education studies, equine studies (with options in equine management, equine psychology, and equine science), natural horsemanship, and tourism and recreation.

Minors are offered in all major areas. Preprofessional programs may be planned to meet the needs of individual students.

Academic Programs

Each graduate of any associate or baccalaureate degree program is expected to demonstrate competency in both oral and written communication as applied to the particular major and minor fields. The foundation of the general education requirements is oral and written communication. Completion of 32 to 40 credits of general education core is required for all four-year degree programs.

The baccalaureate degree is conferred upon completion of the proper curriculum, with a minimum of 120 to 128 semester credits and an overall scholastic grade point average (institutional plus transfer) of at least 2.0. Some baccalaureate degrees may require a higher cumulative grade point average.

All baccalaureate degrees require completion of a cooperative education/internship/student teaching experience or a senior project/thesis.

Montana Western's honors program is designed to enrich and challenge a small number of students who apply and are chosen to participate. Classes in the honors program are thematically based interdisciplinary seminars that emphasize independent research. Students who successfully complete a sequence of honors classes throughout their college career are designated as Honors Graduates. Some honors classes may be substituted for general education requirements.

Montana Western operates on the semester system. The block scheduling system offers classes for eighteen days, 3 hours a day, and then the student switches to a new class. Each academic year has two semesters, fall and spring. There are four blocks in the fall semester and four blocks in the spring semester. Four-week courses during May Interim and four- and six-week courses during the summer are also available. Outreach offers online, evening, and weekend classes and workshops throughout the academic year.

Academic Facilities

The campus is guarded by Old Main Hall, which was built in 1895. The historic, architecturally impressive building houses many faculty offices, newly renovated classrooms, and an art gallery/museum. The library, which is located at the heart of the campus, is the focal point for academics at UMW. It contains more than 65,000 books, 26,000 microform titles, 550 periodicals, and 500 records, tapes, and CDs. The library houses a telecommunications lab with PCs, modems, and printers that allow access to the Internet, databases, and utilities. An audiovisual laboratory is also available.

The University's Swysgood Technology Center (STC) has state-of-the-art computers and equipment. There are three computer labs on the main floor, housing seventy-five new Dell computers for student use. The computer labs are fully mediated and can be used as classrooms. On the lower level is a new, fifteen-computer Macintosh lab with dual-platform capabilities and a smart board. In addition to the computer labs, there are three mediated classrooms on the lower level of the center that are equipped with a projector, a CPU, and a DVD/VCR player. The STC also provides a wireless environment for students on all three levels of the building. Computers are also located in the residence halls, the Learning Center, the office-simulation center, the library, and the math/science center. All residence halls are equipped with computer hookups and can be networked to the campus computer system.

The Learning Center provides students with individualized programs to assist in reading, writing, math, or science. Tutors are available to assist with these subjects. Workshops geared toward helping students succeed academically are also held in the Learning Center.

Costs

Montana Western prides itself on providing an outstanding education for a relatively low cost. For the 2007–08 academic year, state resident tuition and fees were $3700; nonresident tuition and fees were $12,400. The cost of board and a double room was $5000. Books and supplies are estimated at $750. Living expenses, including estimated costs of phone, personal transportation, and other miscellaneous expenses, are estimated to be $3400. Residents of states participating in the Western Undergraduate Exchange (WUE) program (Alaska, Arizona, California, Colorado, Hawaii, Idaho, Nevada, New Mexico, North Dakota, Oregon, South Dakota, Utah, Washington, and Wyoming) pay approximately 150 percent of Montana-resident tuition plus fees, or approximately $5100. Eligibility for WUE is through an application process and selection based on merit.

Financial Aid

More than 85 percent of UMW students receive some form of financial assistance while working toward a degree. The more than $3 million awarded includes scholarships, grants, loans, and work-study opportunities. Applicants must submit the Free Application for Federal Student Aid (FAFSA) for priority consideration by March 1.

Faculty

Fifty-one resident, full-time faculty members teach at Montana Western. All full-time faculty members are academic advisers for students. No courses are taught by graduate assistants. Nearly 85 percent of faculty members hold terminal degrees. The faculty-student ratio of 1:14 allows considerable interaction and personal attention. All faculty members are expected to incorporate experiential learning into their teaching. In addition, faculty members participate actively in student-oriented activities, serve as advisers to student clubs, and conduct extracurricular workshops and field trips.

Student Government

All students registered at Western are members of the Associated Students of the University of Montana Western (ASUMW). ASUMW is governed by student officers who are elected each spring. The president serves as a member of the Chancellor's Council. The ASUMW Activities Board is responsible for organizing a balanced calendar of social, recreational, educational, and cultural programs that are appropriate to the goals and needs of the campus community. Funding for activities is allocated annually by the Student Senate from student activities fees.

Admission Requirements

All applicants must file an application for admission with a nonrefundable $30 fee. Freshmen must submit their high school transcript (with date of graduation and rank in class), scores from either the ACT or SAT, and proof of immunization. Transfer applicants must submit official transcripts from all colleges or universities attended. Transfer applicants who have earned fewer than 12 post-secondary quarter or semester credits must also submit an official high school transcript and standardized test scores.

Graduates of fully accredited high schools are eligible for admission as first-time undergraduate students, provided they have a minimum score of 20 on the ACT or 1440 on the SAT, have at least a 2.5 high school grade point average, or rank in the upper half of their graduating class and have completed the prescribed college-preparatory curriculum. Applicants are also required to have a score of 18 or better on the math section of the ACT or 440 or better on the math section of the SAT. Students submitting the ACT are required to provide the writing score if they wish to be placed in a four-year degree program. Freshman applicants' college-preparatory curriculum must include 4 years of English, 3 years of mathematics (algebra I and higher), 3 years of social studies, 4 years of a laboratory science, and 2 years of electives chosen from foreign language, computer science, visual or performing arts, or vocational education.

Transfer students normally are required to have a minimum cumulative grade point average of at least 2.0 (on a 4.0 scale) from the most recently attended school.

Application and Information

Montana Western has a rolling admission policy. Students are informed of acceptance approximately two weeks after their admission files have been completed. The Admissions Office is open Monday through Friday, 8 a.m. to 5 p.m. (Mountain Time). Visitors are welcome to contact the office to schedule a campus tour, obtain admission materials, or meet with an admissions representative. Prospective students are also invited to see UMW during the campus visitation programs (X Days), which are held every fall and spring. For further information, students should contact:

Admissions Office
The University of Montana Western
710 South Atlantic Street
Dillon, Montana 59725-3598
Phone: 406-683-7331
877-683-7331 (toll-free)
Fax: 406-683-7493
E-mail: admissions@umwestern.edu
Web site: http://www.umwestern.edu

There's a big difference
at Montana Western.
experience
one

COLLEGE DATA CENTER • MONTANA

NEBRASKA

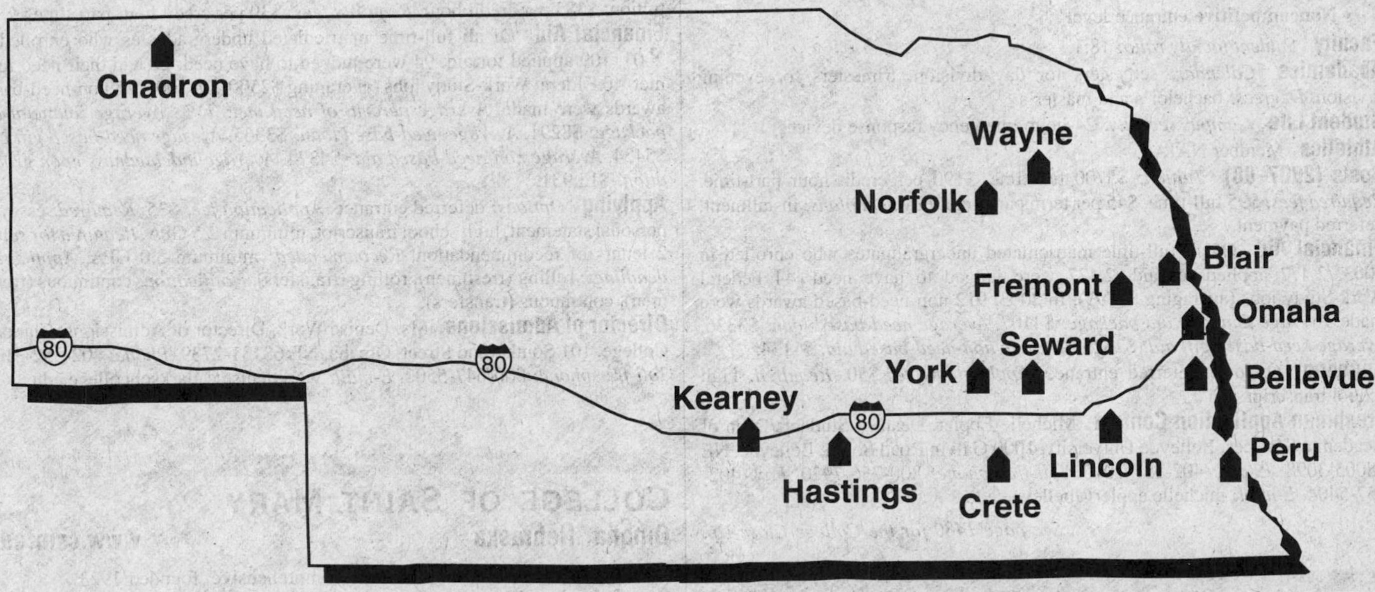

Chadron
Wayne
Norfolk
Blair
Fremont
Omaha
Seward
York
Bellevue
Kearney
Lincoln
Peru
Hastings
Crete
80
80
80

BELLEVUE UNIVERSITY

Bellevue, Nebraska **www.bellevue.edu/**

- **Independent** comprehensive, founded 1965
- **Suburban** 50-acre campus with easy access to Omaha
- **Coed**
- **Noncompetitive** entrance level

Faculty *Student/faculty ratio:* 18:1.

Academics *Calendar:* semesters for day division, trimesters for evening division. *Degrees:* bachelor's and master's.

Student Life *Campus security:* 24-hour emergency response devices.

Athletics Member NAIA.

Costs (2007–08) *Tuition:* $5700 full-time, $190 per credit hour part-time. *Required fees:* $95 full-time, $45 per term part-time. *Payment plans:* installment, deferred payment.

Financial Aid Of all full-time matriculated undergraduates who enrolled in 2003, 2,477 applied for aid, 2,477 were judged to have need. 44 Federal Work-Study jobs (averaging $1793). In 2003, 912 non-need-based awards were made. *Average financial aid package:* $4107. *Average need-based loan:* $3326. *Average need-based gift aid:* $2325. *Average non-need-based aid:* $1134.

Applying *Options:* deferred entrance. *Application fee:* $50. *Required:* high school transcript.

Freshman Application Contact Michelle Eppler, Dean of Students/Dean of Academic Services, Bellevue University, 1000 Galvin Road South, Bellevue, NE 68005-3098. *Phone:* 402-557-7010. *Toll-free phone:* 800-756-7920. *Fax:* 402-557-5404. *E-mail:* michelle.eppler@bellevue.edu.

See page 1480 for the College Close-Up.

CHADRON STATE COLLEGE

Chadron, Nebraska **www.csc.edu/**

Freshman Application Contact Ms. Tena Cook Gould, Director of Admissions, Chadron State College, 1000 Main Street, Chaddron State College, Chadron, NE 69337-2690. *Phone:* 308-432-6263. *Toll-free phone:* 800-242-3766. *Fax:* 308-432-6229. *E-mail:* inquire@csc1.csc.edu.

See page 1482 for the College Close-Up.

CLARKSON COLLEGE

Omaha, Nebraska **www.clarksoncollege.edu/**

- **Independent** comprehensive, founded 1888, part of Nebraska Health System
- **Urban** 3-acre campus
- **Endowment** $2.5 million
- **Coed, primarily women** 706 undergraduate students
- **Moderately difficult** entrance level, 60% of applicants were admitted

Undergraduates Students come from 35 states and territories, 33% are from out of state, 4% African American, 2% Asian American or Pacific Islander, 2% Hispanic American, 0.6% Native American, 20% live on campus. *Retention:* 85% of 2006 full-time freshmen returned.

Freshmen *Admission:* 613 applied, 367 admitted. *Average high school GPA:* 3.39. *Test scores:* ACT scores over 18: 94%; ACT scores over 24: 29%.

Faculty *Total:* 95, 44% full-time, 7% with terminal degrees. *Student/faculty ratio:* 12:1.

Majors Business administration and management; nursing administration; nursing (registered nurse training); nursing science; physical therapy; radiologic technology/science.

Academics *Calendar:* semesters. *Degrees:* certificates, associate, bachelor's, master's, and post-master's certificates. *Special study options:* accelerated degree program, adult/continuing education programs, advanced placement credit, cooperative education, distance learning, double majors, external degree program, independent study, internships, part-time degree program, study abroad, summer session for credit. *ROTC:* Army (c), Air Force (c).

Computers on Campus 40 computers/terminals are available on campus for general student use. Students can access the following: campus intranet, computer help desk, free student e-mail accounts, online (class) grades, online (class) registration, online (class) schedules. Campuswide network is available. Wireless service is available via entire campus.

Student Life *Housing options:* coed. Campus housing is university owned. *Activities and organizations:* Clarkson Student Nurses Association, Clarkson Radiology Student Association, Student Government Association, Student Ambassadors, Clarkson Fellows Program. *Campus security:* 24-hour emergency response devices and patrols, late-night transport/escort service, controlled dormitory access. *Student services:* health clinic, personal/psychological counseling.

Standardized Tests *Required for some:* SAT or ACT (for admission).

Costs (2007–08) *One-time required fee:* $100. *Comprehensive fee:* $17,270 includes full-time tuition ($11,070) and room and board ($6200). Part-time tuition: $385 per credit hour. *Required fees:* $39 per credit hour part-time.

Financial Aid Of all full-time matriculated undergraduates who enrolled in 2001, 109 applied for aid, 94 were judged to have need, 22 had their need fully met. 40 Federal Work-Study jobs (averaging $2500). In 2001, 15 non-need-based awards were made. *Average percent of need met:* 71%. *Average financial aid package:* $8291. *Average need-based loan:* $3365. *Average need-based gift aid:* $5434. *Average non-need-based aid:* $4374. *Average indebtedness upon graduation:* $13,931.

Applying *Options:* deferred entrance. *Application fee:* $35. *Required:* essay or personal statement, high school transcript, minimum 2.5 GPA. *Required for some:* 2 letters of recommendation. *Recommended:* minimum 3.0 GPA. *Application deadlines:* rolling (freshmen), rolling (transfers). *Notification:* continuous (freshmen), continuous (transfers).

Director of Admissions Ms. Denise Work, Director of Admissions, Clarkson College, 101 South 42nd Street, Omaha, NE 68131-2739. *Phone:* 402-552-3100. *Toll-free phone:* 800-647-5500. *E-mail:* workdenise@clarksoncollege.edu.

COLLEGE OF SAINT MARY

Omaha, Nebraska **www.csm.edu/**

- **Independent Roman Catholic** comprehensive, founded 1923
- **Suburban** 25-acre campus
- **Endowment** $7.8 million
- **Women only** 818 undergraduate students, 76% full-time
- **Minimally difficult** entrance level, 42% of applicants were admitted

Undergraduates 620 full-time, 198 part-time. Students come from 22 states and territories, 4 other countries, 12% are from out of state, 10% African American, 0.9% Asian American or Pacific Islander, 8% Hispanic American, 1% Native American, 1% international, 19% transferred in, 22% live on campus. *Retention:* 61% of 2006 full-time freshmen returned.

Freshmen *Admission:* 650 applied, 275 admitted, 98 enrolled. *Average high school GPA:* 3.27. *Test scores:* ACT scores over 18: 64%; ACT scores over 24: 27%; ACT scores over 30: 1%.

Faculty *Total:* 159, 36% full-time, 30% with terminal degrees. *Student/faculty ratio:* 9:1.

Majors Accounting; art; biology/biological sciences; business administration and management; chemistry; clinical laboratory science/medical technology; computer and information sciences; early childhood education; education; education (K-12); elementary education; English; humanities; legal assistant/paralegal; mathematics; natural sciences; nursing (registered nurse training); pre-dentistry studies; pre-law studies; pre-medical studies; pre-veterinary studies; psychology; science teacher education; secondary education; social sciences; Spanish language teacher education; special education; theology.

Academics *Calendar:* semesters. *Degrees:* certificates, associate, bachelor's, master's, doctoral, and postbachelor's certificates. *Special study options:* academic remediation for entering students, accelerated degree program, adult/continuing education programs, advanced placement credit, double majors, independent study, internships, part-time degree program, services for LD students, study abroad, summer session for credit. *ROTC:* Army (c), Air Force (c).

Computers on Campus 170 computers/terminals and 150 ports are available on campus for general student use. Students can access the following: campus intranet, computer help desk, free student e-mail accounts, online (class) grades, online (class) registration, online (class) schedules. Campuswide network is available. 100% of college-owned or -operated housing units are wired for high-speed Internet access. Wireless service is available via entire campus.

Student Life *Housing:* on-campus residence required through sophomore year. *Options:* women-only. Campus housing is university owned. Freshman campus housing is guaranteed. *Activities and organizations:* choral group, Student Senate, Campus Activities Board, Student Education Association of Nebraska, Student Occupational Therapy Club, Student Nurse's Association. *Campus security:* 24-hour emergency response devices and patrols, late-night transport/escort service, controlled dormitory access, surveillance cameras at residence hall entrances. *Student services:* health clinic, personal/psychological counseling.

Athletics Member NAIA. *Intercollegiate sports:* basketball W (s), cross-country running W (s), soccer W (s), softball W (s), volleyball W (s).

Standardized Tests *Required:* SAT or ACT (for admission).

Costs (2007–08) *Comprehensive fee:* $26,520 includes full-time tuition ($19,800), mandatory fees ($420), and room and board ($6300). Part-time tuition: $660 per credit hour. Part-time tuition and fees vary according to class time. *Required fees:* $14 per credit hour part-time. *Room and board:* Room and board charges vary according to housing facility. *Payment plans:* installment, deferred payment. *Waivers:* senior citizens and employees or children of employees.

Financial Aid Of all full-time matriculated undergraduates who enrolled in 2007, 574 applied for aid, 533 were judged to have need, 79 had their need fully met. 139 Federal Work-Study jobs (averaging $1200). 10 state and other part-time jobs (averaging $6200). In 2007, 63 non-need-based awards were made. *Average percent of need met:* 65%. *Average financial aid package:* $14,609. *Average need-based loan:* $6189. *Average need-based gift aid:* $8884. *Average non-need-based aid:* $13,879. *Average indebtedness upon graduation:* $15,551.

Applying *Options:* electronic application. *Application fee:* $30. *Required:* high school transcript, minimum 2.0 GPA. *Required for some:* essay or personal statement, minimum 3.0 GPA, 2 letters of recommendation, interview. *Application deadlines:* rolling (freshmen), rolling (transfers). *Notification:* continuous until 8/24 (freshmen), continuous until 8/24 (transfers).

Freshman Application Contact Ms. Erika Pritchard, College of Saint Mary, 1901 South 72nd Street, Omaha, NE 68124-2377. *Phone:* 402-399-2406. *Toll-free phone:* 800-926-5534. *Fax:* 402-399-2412. *E-mail:* enroll@csm.edu.

CONCORDIA UNIVERSITY, NEBRASKA

Seward, Nebraska **www.cune.edu/**

- **Independent** comprehensive, founded 1894, affiliated with Lutheran Church–Missouri Synod
- **Small-town** 120-acre campus with easy access to Omaha
- **Endowment** $27.7 million
- **Coed** 1,079 undergraduate students, 97% full-time, 55% women, 45% men
- **Moderately difficult** entrance level, 77% of applicants were admitted

Undergraduates 1,045 full-time, 34 part-time. Students come from 42 states and territories, 6 other countries, 59% are from out of state, 1% African American, 0.5% Asian American or Pacific Islander, 0.8% Hispanic American, 0.3% Native American, 1% international, 4% transferred in, 72% live on campus. *Retention:* 77% of 2006 full-time freshmen returned.

Freshmen *Admission:* 1,409 applied, 1,080 admitted, 264 enrolled. *Average high school GPA:* 3.51. *Test scores:* SAT critical reading scores over 500: 59%; SAT math scores over 500: 64%; ACT scores over 18: 94%; SAT critical reading scores over 600: 20%; SAT math scores over 600: 15%; ACT scores over 24: 51%; SAT critical reading scores over 700: 7%; ACT scores over 30: 8%.

Faculty *Total:* 140, 40% full-time, 50% with terminal degrees. *Student/faculty ratio:* 14:1.

Majors Accounting; art; art teacher education; behavioral sciences; biology/biological sciences; biology teacher education; business administration and management; business/commerce; business teacher education; chemistry; chemistry teacher education; commercial and advertising art; communication/speech communication and rhetoric; computer and information sciences; computer science; computer teacher education; drama and dance teacher education; dramatic/theater arts; early childhood education; education; elementary education; English; English as a second/foreign language (teaching); English/language arts teacher education; family and consumer sciences/home economics teacher education; fine/studio arts; geography; geography teacher education; health and physical education; health/medical preparatory programs related; health teacher education; history; history teacher education; kindergarten/preschool education; kinesiology and exercise science; management information systems; mass communication/media; mathematics; mathematics teacher education; middle school education; music; music teacher education; natural sciences; pastoral studies/counseling; physical education teaching and coaching; physical sciences; physics teacher education; piano and organ; pre-dentistry studies; pre-law studies; pre-medical studies; pre-nursing studies; pre-pharmacy studies; pre-theology/pre-ministerial studies; pre-veterinary studies; psychology; religious education; religious/sacred music; science teacher education; secondary education; social sciences; social science teacher education; sociology; Spanish; Spanish language teacher education; special education; speech and rhetoric; speech teacher education; sport and fitness administration/management; technology/industrial arts teacher education; theology; trade and industrial teacher education; voice and opera.

Academics *Calendar:* 4-4-1. *Degrees:* bachelor's, master's, and postbachelor's certificates. *Special study options:* academic remediation for entering students, accelerated degree program, adult/continuing education programs, advanced placement credit, distance learning, double majors, English as a second language, independent study, internships, off-campus study, part-time degree program, services for LD students, study abroad, summer session for credit. *ROTC:* Army (c), Air Force (c).

Computers on Campus 186 computers/terminals and 1,000 ports are available on campus for general student use. Students can access the following: campus intranet, computer help desk, free student e-mail accounts, online (class) grades, online (class) registration, online (class) schedules, academic plans, human resource data. Campuswide network is available. 100% of college-owned or -operated housing units are wired for high-speed Internet access. Wireless service is available via computer centers, computer labs, dorm rooms, learning centers, libraries, student centers.

Student Life *Housing:* on-campus residence required through junior year. *Options:* men-only, women-only, disabled students. Campus housing is university owned. Freshman campus housing is guaranteed. *Activities and organizations:* drama/theater group, student-run newspaper, choral group, Student Activities Council, musical groups, Curtain/Drama Club, Student Senate, Concordia Youth Ministry. *Campus security:* 24-hour emergency response devices and patrols, controlled dormitory access. *Student services:* health clinic, personal/psychological counseling.

Athletics Member NAIA. *Intercollegiate sports:* baseball M (s), basketball M (s)/W (s), cross-country running M (s)/W (s), football M (s), golf M (s)/W (s), soccer M (s)/W (s), softball W (s), tennis M (s)/W (s), track and field M (s)/W (s), volleyball W (s). *Intramural sports:* badminton M/W, basketball M/W, bowling M/W, cross-country running M/W, soccer M/W, softball M/W, table tennis M/W, tennis M/W, volleyball M/W.

Standardized Tests *Required:* SAT or ACT (for admission).

Costs (2008–09) *Comprehensive fee:* $25,980 includes full-time tuition ($20,580), mandatory fees ($120), and room and board ($5280). Part-time tuition: $610 per credit. *College room only:* $2240.

Financial Aid Of all full-time matriculated undergraduates who enrolled in 2006, 941 applied for aid, 818 were judged to have need, 214 had their need fully met. 150 Federal Work-Study jobs (averaging $679). In 2006, 213 non-need-based awards were made. *Average percent of need met:* 74%. *Average financial aid package:* $14,097. *Average need-based loan:* $3953. *Average need-based gift aid:* $8935. *Average non-need-based aid:* $5881. *Average indebtedness upon graduation:* $18,923.

Applying *Options:* electronic application, deferred entrance. *Required:* high school transcript, minimum 2.5 GPA. *Required for some:* letters of recommendation. *Recommended:* interview. *Application deadline:* 8/1 (freshmen). *Notification:* continuous (freshmen), continuous (transfers).

Freshman Application Contact Concordia University, Nebraska, 800 North Columbia Avenue, Seward, NE 68434-1599. *Phone:* 800-535-5494 Ext. 7233. *Toll-free phone:* 800-535-5494.

CREIGHTON UNIVERSITY

Omaha, Nebraska **www.creighton.edu/**

- **Independent Roman Catholic (Jesuit)** university, founded 1878
- **Urban** 110-acre campus
- **Endowment** $313.4 million
- **Coed** 4,104 undergraduate students, 93% full-time, 60% women, 40% men
- **Moderately difficult** entrance level, 81% of applicants were admitted

Undergraduates 3,828 full-time, 276 part-time. Students come from 52 states and territories, 33 other countries, 57% are from out of state, 3% African American, 8% Asian American or Pacific Islander, 4% Hispanic American, 1% Native American, 1% international, 2% transferred in, 64% live on campus. *Retention:* 86% of 2006 full-time freshmen returned.

Freshmen *Admission:* 4,274 applied, 3,476 admitted, 950 enrolled. *Average high school GPA:* 3.78. *Test scores:* SAT critical reading scores over 500: 87%; SAT math scores over 500: 89%; SAT writing scores over 500: 84%; ACT scores over 18: 99%; SAT critical reading scores over 600: 47%; SAT math scores over 600: 52%; SAT writing scores over 600: 46%; ACT scores over 24: 78%; SAT critical reading scores over 700: 11%; SAT math scores over 700: 15%; SAT writing scores over 700: 7%; ACT scores over 30: 25%.

Faculty *Total:* 681, 74% full-time, 77% with terminal degrees. *Student/faculty ratio:* 12:1.

Majors Accounting; American Indian/Native American studies; American studies; ancient/classical Greek; anthropology; applied mathematics; art; athletic training; atmospheric sciences and meteorology; biology/biological sciences; chemistry; classical, ancient Mediterranean and Near Eastern studies and archaeology; communication/speech communication and rhetoric; computer science; dramatic/theater arts; economics; elementary education; emergency medical technology (EMT paramedic); English; environmental studies; finance; French; German; graphic design; health/health care administration; history; international business/trade/commerce; international relations and affairs; journalism; kinesiology and exercise science; Latin; management information systems; marketing/

marketing management; mathematics; music; nursing (registered nurse training); organizational communication; philosophy; physics; political science and government; pre-law studies; psychology; social work; sociology; Spanish; speech and rhetoric; theological and ministerial studies related; theology.

Academics *Calendar:* semesters. *Degrees:* certificates, diplomas, bachelor's, master's, doctoral, first professional, and postbachelor's certificates. *Special study options:* accelerated degree program, adult/continuing education programs, advanced placement credit, distance learning, double majors, English as a second language, freshman honors college, honors programs, independent study, internships, off-campus study, part-time degree program, services for LD students, study abroad, summer session for credit. *ROTC:* Army (b), Air Force (c). *Unusual degree programs:* 3-2 engineering with Marquette University, University of Detroit Mercy.

Computers on Campus 505 computers/terminals are available on campus for general student use. Students can access the following: campus intranet, computer help desk, free student e-mail accounts, online (class) grades, online (class) registration, online (class) schedules, financial aid information. Campuswide network is available. 100% of college-owned or -operated housing units are wired for high-speed Internet access. Wireless service is available via entire campus.

Student Life *Housing:* on-campus residence required through sophomore year. *Options:* coed, women-only, disabled students. Campus housing is university owned. Freshman campus housing is guaranteed. *Activities and organizations:* drama/theater group, student-run newspaper, radio station, choral group, Birdcage (Athletic Boosters), Pre-Medical Society, Student Nurses Association, Alpha Kappa Psi (Business majors), Omicron Delta Kappa (Greek Leadership), national fraternities, national sororities. *Campus security:* 24-hour emergency response devices and patrols, student patrols, late-night transport/escort service, controlled dormitory access. *Student services:* health clinic, personal/psychological counseling, women's center, legal services.

Athletics Member NCAA. All Division I. *Intercollegiate sports:* baseball M (s), basketball M (s)/W (s), crew W (s), cross-country running M (s)/W (s), golf M (s)/W (s), soccer M (s)/W (s), softball W (s), tennis M (s)/W (s), volleyball W (s). *Intramural sports:* badminton M/W, basketball M/W, bowling M/W, crew M (c), football M/W, golf M/W, racquetball M/W, rugby M (c)/W (c), soccer M/W, softball M/W, tennis M/W, volleyball M/W, weight lifting M (c)/W (c).

Standardized Tests *Required:* SAT or ACT (for admission).

Costs (2007–08) *Comprehensive fee:* $34,814 includes full-time tuition ($25,616), mandatory fees ($1018), and room and board ($8180). Full-time tuition and fees vary according to student level. Part-time tuition: $801 per semester hour. Part-time tuition and fees vary according to student level. *Required fees:* $168 per term part-time. *College room only:* $4620. Room and board charges vary according to board plan and housing facility. *Payment plan:* installment. *Waivers:* adult students and employees or children of employees.

Financial Aid Of all full-time matriculated undergraduates who enrolled in 2007, 2,372 applied for aid, 1,937 were judged to have need, 673 had their need fully met. 1,045 Federal Work-Study jobs (averaging $1810). In 2007, 1178 non-need-based awards were made. *Average percent of need met:* 88%. *Average financial aid package:* $26,932. *Average need-based loan:* $6854. *Average need-based gift aid:* $17,048. *Average non-need-based aid:* $12,049. *Average indebtedness upon graduation:* $29,074.

Applying *Options:* electronic application, deferred entrance. *Application fee:* $40. *Required:* essay or personal statement, high school transcript, minimum 2.75 GPA, 1 letter of recommendation. *Application deadlines:* 2/15 (freshmen), 8/1 (transfers). *Notification:* continuous (freshmen), continuous (transfers).

Freshman Application Contact Ms. Mary Chase, Assistant Vice President for Enrollment Management and Director of Admissions and Scholarships, Creighton University, 2500 California Plaza, Omaha, NE 68178-0001. *Phone:* 402-280-3105. *Toll-free phone:* 800-282-5835. *Fax:* 402-280-2685. *E-mail:* admissions@creighton.edu.

DANA COLLEGE

Blair, Nebraska **www.dana.edu/**

- **Independent** 4-year, founded 1884, affiliated with Evangelical Lutheran Church in America
- **Small-town** 150-acre campus with easy access to Omaha
- **Endowment** $12.9 million
- **Coed** 634 undergraduate students, 95% full-time, 47% women, 53% men
- **Moderately difficult** entrance level, 72% of applicants were admitted

Undergraduates 605 full-time, 29 part-time. Students come from 31 states and territories, 38% are from out of state, 3% African American, 0.8% Asian American or Pacific Islander, 4% Hispanic American, 0.5% Native American, 0.3% international, 5% transferred in, 64% live on campus. *Retention:* 65% of 2006 full-time freshmen returned.

Freshmen *Admission:* 899 applied, 647 admitted, 185 enrolled. *Average high school GPA:* 3.24. *Test scores:* SAT critical reading scores over 500: 18%; SAT math scores over 500: 64%; ACT scores over 18: 99%; ACT scores over 24: 34%; ACT scores over 30: 2%.

Faculty *Total:* 68, 51% full-time, 50% with terminal degrees. *Student/faculty ratio:* 13:1.

Majors Accounting; art; art teacher education; biology/biological sciences; business administration and management; business teacher education; chemistry; criminal justice/law enforcement administration; education; elementary education; English; English/language arts teacher education; foreign language teacher education; history; history teacher education; interdisciplinary studies; journalism related; management information systems; mathematics; mathematics teacher education; music; music teacher education; organizational communication; physical education teaching and coaching; psychology; religious studies; science teacher education; secondary education; social science teacher education; social work; Spanish; special education; sport and fitness administration/management; visual and performing arts related; web page, digital/multimedia and information resources design.

Academics *Calendar:* 4-1-4. *Degree:* bachelor's. *Special study options:* accelerated degree program, adult/continuing education programs, advanced placement credit, double majors, English as a second language, honors programs, independent study, internships, off-campus study, part-time degree program, services for LD students, student-designed majors, study abroad, summer session for credit. *ROTC:* Army (c), Air Force (c).

Computers on Campus 110 computers/terminals are available on campus for general student use. Students can access the following: campus intranet, computer help desk, free student e-mail accounts, online (class) registration, online (class) schedules, campus events. Campuswide network is available. 100% of college-owned or -operated housing units are wired for high-speed Internet access. Wireless service is available via entire campus.

Student Life *Housing:* on-campus residence required through junior year. *Options:* coed, women-only. Campus housing is university owned. Freshman campus housing is guaranteed. *Activities and organizations:* drama/theater group, student-run newspaper, radio and television station, choral group, Business Club, Campus Crusade for Christ, Student Education Association, Social Awareness Organization, Nebraska's for Peace. *Campus security:* 24-hour emergency response devices and patrols, late-night transport/escort service, controlled dormitory access. *Student services:* health clinic, personal/psychological counseling.

Athletics Member NAIA. *Intercollegiate sports:* baseball M (s), basketball M (s)/W (s), cross-country running M (s)/W (s), football M (s), golf W (s), soccer M (s)/W (s), softball W (s), track and field M (s)/W (s), volleyball W (s), wrestling M (s). *Intramural sports:* basketball M/W, bowling M/W, football M/W, softball M/W, swimming and diving M/W, table tennis M/W, volleyball M/W, weight lifting M/W.

Standardized Tests *Required:* SAT or ACT (for admission). *Recommended:* ACT (for admission).

Costs (2007–08) *Comprehensive fee:* $24,930 includes full-time tuition ($18,570), mandatory fees ($800), and room and board ($5560). Part-time tuition: $520 per credit hour. Part-time tuition and fees vary according to course load. *Required fees:* $35 per term part-time. *College room only:* $2230. Room and board charges vary according to board plan and housing facility. *Payment plans:* installment, deferred payment. *Waivers:* children of alumni and employees or children of employees.

Financial Aid Of all full-time matriculated undergraduates who enrolled in 2006, 551 applied for aid, 478 were judged to have need, 145 had their need fully met. In 2006, 73 non-need-based awards were made. *Average percent of need met:* 88%. *Average financial aid package:* $16,241. *Average need-based loan:* $4578. *Average need-based gift aid:* $4473. *Average non-need-based aid:* $4500. *Average indebtedness upon graduation:* $17,029.

Applying *Options:* electronic application, deferred entrance. *Required:* high school transcript, minimum 2.0 GPA. *Required for some:* essay or personal statement, 1 letter of recommendation, interview. *Application deadline:* rolling (freshmen). *Notification:* continuous (freshmen), continuous (transfers).

Freshman Application Contact Gretchen Foster, Dean of Enrollment Management, Dana College, 2848 College Drive, Blair, NE 68008-1099. *Phone:* 402-426-7220. *Toll-free phone:* 800-444-3262. *Fax:* 402-426-7386. *E-mail:* admissions@dana.edu.

DOANE COLLEGE

Crete, Nebraska **www.doane.edu/**

- **Independent** comprehensive, founded 1872, affiliated with United Church of Christ
- **Small-town** 300-acre campus with easy access to Omaha
- **Endowment** $92.7 million

- **Coed** 921 undergraduate students, 99% full-time, 53% women, 47% men
- **Moderately difficult** entrance level, 75% of applicants were admitted

Undergraduates 909 full-time, 12 part-time. Students come from 25 states and territories, 3 other countries, 20% are from out of state, 4% African American, 1% Asian American or Pacific Islander, 3% Hispanic American, 0.1% Native American, 0.8% international, 4% transferred in, 86% live on campus. *Retention:* 77% of 2006 full-time freshmen returned.

Freshmen *Admission:* 1,027 applied, 773 admitted, 259 enrolled. *Average high school GPA:* 3.33. *Test scores:* ACT scores over 18: 93%; ACT scores over 24: 39%; ACT scores over 30: 9%.

Faculty *Total:* 132, 55% full-time, 46% with terminal degrees. *Student/faculty ratio:* 10:1.

Majors Accounting; art; biochemistry; biology/biological sciences; business administration and management; business teacher education; chemistry; computer and information sciences; computer science; dramatic/theater arts; economics; elementary education; English; English as a second/foreign language (teaching); English language and literature related; environmental studies; French; German; health and physical education; history; human services; information science/studies; international/global studies; journalism; mathematics; music; natural sciences; philosophy; physical education teaching and coaching; physical sciences; physics; political science and government; psychology; public administration; religious studies; social sciences; sociology; Spanish; special education; theater design and technology.

Academics *Calendar:* 4-1-4. *Degrees:* bachelor's and master's (non-traditional undergraduate programs and graduate programs offered at Lincoln campus). *Special study options:* advanced placement credit, cooperative education, double majors, English as a second language, honors programs, independent study, internships, off-campus study, student-designed majors, study abroad, summer session for credit. *ROTC:* Army (c), Air Force (c). *Unusual degree programs:* 3-2 engineering with Columbia University, Washington University in St. Louis; forestry with Duke University; environmental studies with Duke University.

Computers on Campus 246 computers/terminals and 900 ports are available on campus for general student use. Students can access the following: campus intranet, computer help desk, free student e-mail accounts, online (class) grades, online (class) registration, online (class) schedules. Campuswide network is available. 100% of college-owned or -operated housing units are wired for high-speed Internet access. Wireless service is available via classrooms, computer centers, dorm rooms, learning centers, libraries, student centers.

Student Life *Housing:* on-campus residence required through senior year. *Options:* coed, women-only. Campus housing is university owned. Freshman campus housing is guaranteed. *Activities and organizations:* drama/theater group, student-run newspaper, radio and television station, choral group, marching band, Student Activities Council, Hansen Leadership Program, band/choir, Doane Ambassadors, Doane Art League. *Campus security:* student patrols, evening patrols by trained security personnel. *Student services:* health clinic, personal/psychological counseling.

Athletics Member NAIA. *Intercollegiate sports:* baseball M (s), basketball M (s)/W (s), cross-country running M (s)/W (s), football M (s), golf M (s)/W (s), soccer M (s)/W (s), softball W (s), tennis M/W, track and field M (s)/W (s), volleyball W (s). *Intramural sports:* baseball M (c)/W (c), basketball M/W, bowling M/W, football M/W, golf M/W, ice hockey M, racquetball M (c)/W (c), softball M/W, swimming and diving M/W, table tennis M (c)/W (c), tennis M/W, volleyball M/W, water polo M/W.

Standardized Tests *Required:* SAT or ACT (for admission).

Costs (2007–08) *Comprehensive fee:* $24,560 includes full-time tuition ($18,800), mandatory fees ($350), and room and board ($5410). Full-time tuition and fees vary according to location. Part-time tuition: $630 per credit hour. Part-time tuition and fees vary according to course load, degree level, and location. *Required fees:* $125 per term part-time. *College room only:* $1950. Room and board charges vary according to board plan, housing facility, and location. *Payment plan:* installment. *Waivers:* senior citizens and employees or children of employees.

Financial Aid Of all full-time matriculated undergraduates who enrolled in 2007, 769 applied for aid, 690 were judged to have need, 479 had their need fully met. In 2007, 122 non-need-based awards were made. *Average percent of need met:* 96%. *Average financial aid package:* $18,745. *Average need-based loan:* $4288. *Average need-based gift aid:* $11,720. *Average non-need-based aid:* $9828. *Average indebtedness upon graduation:* $14,171.

Applying *Options:* electronic application, early admission, deferred entrance. *Required:* high school transcript, 2 letters of recommendation. *Required for some:* interview. *Recommended:* minimum 2.0 GPA. *Application deadlines:* rolling (freshmen), rolling (transfers). *Notification:* continuous (freshmen), continuous (transfers).

Freshman Application Contact Mr. Cezar Mesquita, Director of Admission, Doane College, Crete, NE 68333. *Phone:* 402-826-8222. *Toll-free phone:* 800-333-6263. *Fax:* 402-826-8600. *E-mail:* admissions@doane.edu.

GRACE UNIVERSITY

Omaha, Nebraska **www.graceuniversity.edu/**

- **Independent interdenominational** comprehensive, founded 1943
- **Urban** 15-acre campus
- **Endowment** $890,668
- **Coed** 363 undergraduate students, 84% full-time, 56% women, 44% men
- **Moderately difficult** entrance level, 64% of applicants were admitted

Undergraduates 306 full-time, 57 part-time. Students come from 13 states and territories, 6 other countries, 34% are from out of state, 7% African American, 2% Asian American or Pacific Islander, 2% Hispanic American, 0.3% Native American, 2% international, 10% transferred in, 60% live on campus. *Retention:* 67% of 2006 full-time freshmen returned.

Freshmen *Admission:* 228 applied, 146 admitted, 90 enrolled. *Average high school GPA:* 3.36.

Faculty *Total:* 50, 50% full-time, 90% with terminal degrees. *Student/faculty ratio:* 18:1.

Majors Accounting; agricultural business and management; airline pilot and flight crew; avionics maintenance technology; biblical studies; broadcast journalism; business administration and management; business teacher education; communication/speech communication and rhetoric; computer and information sciences; computer and information sciences related; computer programming; computer science; divinity/ministry; education (K-12); elementary education; humanities; human resources management; liberal arts and sciences/liberal studies; marriage and family therapy/counseling; mass communication/media; middle school education; missionary studies and missiology; music; music teacher education; music theory and composition; nursing (licensed practical/vocational nurse training); nursing (registered nurse training); pastoral studies/counseling; piano and organ; pre-theology/pre-ministerial studies; psychology; religious education; religious/sacred music; secondary education; social science teacher education; voice and opera; web/multimedia management and webmaster; youth ministry.

Academics *Calendar:* semesters. *Degrees:* certificates, associate, bachelor's, and master's. *Special study options:* accelerated degree program, adult/continuing education programs, advanced placement credit, cooperative education, distance learning, double majors, external degree program, independent study, internships, off-campus study, part-time degree program, services for LD students, student-designed majors, study abroad, summer session for credit. *ROTC:* Army (c), Air Force (c). *Unusual degree programs:* 3-2 nursing with Clarkson College; social work with University of Nebraska at Omaha.

Computers on Campus 45 computers/terminals are available on campus for general student use. Students can access the following: campus intranet, computer help desk, free student e-mail accounts, online (class) grades, online (class) registration, online (class) schedules. Campuswide network is available. 100% of college-owned or -operated housing units are wired for high-speed Internet access. Wireless service is available via entire campus.

Student Life *Housing:* on-campus residence required through junior year. *Options:* men-only, women-only. Campus housing is university owned. Freshman applicants given priority for college housing. *Activities and organizations:* drama/theater group, student-run radio station, choral group, choral group, band, radio station, yearbook. *Campus security:* student patrols, late-night transport/escort service, controlled dormitory access. *Student services:* health clinic, personal/psychological counseling.

Athletics Member NCCAA. *Intercollegiate sports:* basketball M/W, soccer M, volleyball W. *Intramural sports:* basketball M/W, volleyball M/W.

Standardized Tests *Required:* SAT or ACT (for admission).

Costs (2008–09) *Comprehensive fee:* $20,140 includes full-time tuition ($14,110), mandatory fees ($380), and room and board ($5650). Part-time tuition: $390 per credit hour. *Required fees:* $35 per term part-time. *College room only:* $2500.

Financial Aid Of all full-time matriculated undergraduates who enrolled in 2006, 236 applied for aid, 216 were judged to have need, 26 had their need fully met. 85 Federal Work-Study jobs (averaging $1103). In 2006, 29 non-need-based awards were made. *Average percent of need met:* 54%. *Average financial aid package:* $8443. *Average need-based loan:* $3825. *Average need-based gift aid:* $5104. *Average non-need-based aid:* $7708. *Average indebtedness upon graduation:* $14,805.

Applying *Options:* electronic application, early admission, deferred entrance. *Application fee:* $20. *Required:* essay or personal statement, high school transcript, minimum 2.0 GPA. *Required for some:* letters of recommendation, interview. *Application deadlines:* rolling (freshmen), rolling (transfers).

Freshman Application Contact Angela Wayman, Director of Admissions, Grace University, 1311 South Ninth Street, Omaha, NE 68108. *Phone:* 402-449-2831. *Toll-free phone:* 800-383-1422. *Fax:* 402-341-9587. *E-mail:* admissions@graceuniversity.com.

HASTINGS COLLEGE

Hastings, Nebraska www.hastings.edu/

- **Independent Presbyterian** comprehensive, founded 1882
- **Small-town** 109-acre campus
- **Endowment** $66.0 million
- **Coed** 1,091 undergraduate students, 98% full-time, 46% women, 54% men
- **Moderately difficult** entrance level, 78% of applicants were admitted

Undergraduates 1,068 full-time, 23 part-time. Students come from 27 states and territories, 4 other countries, 27% are from out of state, 2% African American, 0.7% Asian American or Pacific Islander, 3% Hispanic American, 0.4% Native American, 0.9% international, 6% transferred in, 67% live on campus. *Retention:* 76% of 2006 full-time freshmen returned.

Freshmen *Admission:* 1,564 applied, 1,225 admitted, 304 enrolled. *Average high school GPA:* 3.2. *Test scores:* SAT critical reading scores over 500: 82%; SAT math scores over 500: 82%; ACT scores over 18: 95%; SAT critical reading scores over 600: 25%; SAT math scores over 600: 25%; ACT scores over 24: 41%; SAT critical reading scores over 700: 5%; SAT math scores over 700: 5%; ACT scores over 30: 6%.

Faculty *Total:* 123, 71% full-time, 55% with terminal degrees. *Student/faculty ratio:* 12:1.

Majors Accounting; advertising; art; art history, criticism and conservation; art teacher education; biology/biological sciences; biology teacher education; biopsychology; broadcast journalism; business administration and management; business teacher education; chemistry; chemistry teacher education; communication/speech communication and rhetoric; communications technology; computer and information sciences; computer science; corrections and criminal justice related; creative writing; drama and dance teacher education; dramatic/theater arts; early childhood education; economics; education; elementary education; English; English language and literature related; English/language arts teacher education; foreign languages and literatures; foreign language teacher education; German; German language teacher education; health and physical education; health/health care administration; history; history teacher education; human resources management; human services; international relations and affairs; journalism; kinesiology and exercise science; liberal arts and sciences/liberal studies; literature; marketing/marketing management; mass communication/media; mathematics; mathematics teacher education; music; music history, literature, and theory; music pedagogy; music performance; music teacher education; parks, recreation and leisure facilities management; philosophy; physical education teaching and coaching; physics; physics teacher education; piano and organ; political science and government; pre-dentistry studies; pre-law studies; pre-medical studies; pre-veterinary studies; psychology; public administration; public relations/image management; radio and television; religious studies; science teacher education; secondary education; social science teacher education; social studies teacher education; sociology; Spanish; Spanish language teacher education; special education; speech and rhetoric; speech teacher education; sport and fitness administration/management; violin, viola, guitar and other stringed instruments; voice and opera.

Academics *Calendar:* 4-1-4. *Degrees:* bachelor's and master's. *Special study options:* adult/continuing education programs, advanced placement credit, double majors, independent study, internships, off-campus study, part-time degree program, services for LD students, student-designed majors, study abroad, summer session for credit. *Unusual degree programs:* 3-2 engineering with Columbia University, Georgia Institute of Technology, Washington University in St. Louis, University of Colorado at Boulder, Colorado State University; occupational therapy with Washington University in St. Louis, Boston University.

Computers on Campus 181 computers/terminals are available on campus for general student use. Students can access the following: e-mail. Campuswide network is available.

Student Life *Housing:* on-campus residence required through junior year. *Options:* coed, men-only, women-only. Campus housing is university owned. Freshman campus housing is guaranteed. *Activities and organizations:* drama/theater group, student-run newspaper, radio and television station, choral group, marching band, Student Association, Student Alumni Ambassadors, Fellowship of Christian Athletes, Phi Mu Alpha Sinfonia, Hastings College Singers. *Campus security:* 24-hour emergency response devices, student patrols, late-night transport/escort service, controlled dormitory access, security cameras at entrances and parking lots. *Student services:* health clinic, personal/psychological counseling.

Athletics Member NAIA. *Intercollegiate sports:* baseball M (s), basketball M (s)/W (s), cheerleading W (s), cross-country running M (s)/W (s), football M (s), golf M (s)/W (s), soccer M (s)/W (s), softball W (s), tennis M (s)/W (s), track and field M (s)/W (s), volleyball W (s). *Intramural sports:* basketball M/W, bowling M/W, football M/W, racquetball M/W, softball M/W, table tennis M/W, ultimate Frisbee M/W, volleyball M/W.

Standardized Tests *Required:* SAT or ACT (for admission).

Costs (2007–08) *Comprehensive fee:* $25,036 includes full-time tuition ($18,822), mandatory fees ($782), and room and board ($5432). Full-time tuition and fees vary according to course level and program. Part-time tuition: $779 per semester hour. Part-time tuition and fees vary according to course level, course load, and program. *Required fees:* $206 per term part-time. *College room only:* $2322. Room and board charges vary according to board plan and housing facility. *Payment plans:* installment, deferred payment. *Waivers:* adult students.

Financial Aid Of all full-time matriculated undergraduates who enrolled in 2007, 912 applied for aid, 783 were judged to have need, 227 had their need fully met. In 2007, 294 non-need-based awards were made. *Average percent of need met:* 75%. *Average financial aid package:* $13,933. *Average need-based loan:* $4536. *Average need-based gift aid:* $10,261. *Average non-need-based aid:* $9070. *Average indebtedness upon graduation:* $17,634. *Financial aid deadline:* 9/1.

Applying *Application fee:* $20. *Required:* high school transcript, minimum 2.0 GPA, counselor's recommendation. *Required for some:* essay or personal statement, 2 letters of recommendation, interview. *Application deadlines:* 8/1 (freshmen), 8/1 (transfers). *Notification:* continuous (freshmen), continuous (transfers).

Freshman Application Contact Ms. Mary Molliconi, Director of Admissions, Hastings College, 710 North Turner Avenue, Hastings, NE 68901-7621. *Phone:* 402-461-7320. *Toll-free phone:* 800-532-7642. *Fax:* 402-461-7490. *E-mail:* mmolliconi@hastings.edu.

ITT TECHNICAL INSTITUTE

Omaha, Nebraska www.itt-tech.edu/

- **Proprietary** primarily 2-year, founded 1991, part of ITT Educational Services, Inc
- **Urban** 1-acre campus
- **Coed**
- **Minimally difficult** entrance level

Academics *Calendar:* quarters. *Degrees:* associate and bachelor's.

Standardized Tests *Required:* Wonderlic aptitude test (for admission).

Applying *Options:* deferred entrance. *Application fee:* $100. *Required:* high school transcript, interview. *Recommended:* letters of recommendation.

Freshman Application Contact Schon Nielson, Director of Recruitment, ITT Technical Institute, 9814 M Street, Omaha, NE 68127. *Phone:* 402-331-2900. *Toll-free phone:* 800-677-9260.

KAPLAN UNIVERSITY-OMAHA

Omaha, Nebraska
www.kucampus.edu/kucampusortal/kucampuscampuses/nebraska/omaha/

Director of Admissions Mr. Mark Stoltenberger, Director of Admissions, Kaplan University-Omaha, 3350 North 90 Street, Omaha, NE 68134. *Phone:* 402-572-8500. *Toll-free phone:* 800-642-1456.

MIDLAND LUTHERAN COLLEGE

Fremont, Nebraska www.mlc.edu/

- **Independent Lutheran** 4-year, founded 1883
- **Small-town** 27-acre campus with easy access to Omaha
- **Endowment** $21.0 million
- **Coed** 827 undergraduate students, 98% full-time, 56% women, 44% men
- **Moderately difficult** entrance level, 88% of applicants were admitted

Undergraduates 808 full-time, 19 part-time. Students come from 18 states and territories, 1 other country, 26% are from out of state, 3% African American, 1% Asian American or Pacific Islander, 2% Hispanic American, 0.3% Native American, 5% transferred in, 62% live on campus. *Retention:* 80% of 2006 full-time freshmen returned.

Freshmen *Admission:* 920 applied, 808 admitted, 215 enrolled. *Average high school GPA:* 3.26.
Faculty *Total:* 81, 67% full-time, 43% with terminal degrees. *Student/faculty ratio:* 14:1.
Majors Accounting; administrative assistant and secretarial science; art; art teacher education; athletic training; behavioral sciences; biological and physical sciences; biology/biological sciences; broadcast journalism; business administration and management; business teacher education; chemistry; community organization and advocacy; computer programming; computer science; criminal justice/law enforcement administration; criminology; dramatic/theater arts; economics; education; education (K-12); elementary education; English; environmental studies; history; humanities; human services; journalism; kindergarten/preschool education; legal administrative assistant/secretary; liberal arts and sciences/liberal studies; management information systems; marketing/marketing management; mass communication/media; mathematics; medical administrative assistant and medical secretary; middle school education; music; music teacher education; natural sciences; nursing (registered nurse training); parks, recreation and leisure; physical education teaching and coaching; physical sciences; pre-dentistry studies; pre-law studies; pre-medical studies; pre-veterinary studies; psychology; religious studies; respiratory care therapy; science teacher education; secondary education; social sciences; sociology; speech/theater education; tourism and travel services management.
Academics *Calendar:* 4-1-4. *Degrees:* associate and bachelor's. *Special study options:* academic remediation for entering students, accelerated degree program, advanced placement credit, cooperative education, double majors, English as a second language, honors programs, independent study, internships, off-campus study, part-time degree program, services for LD students, student-designed majors, study abroad, summer session for credit.
Computers on Campus 190 computers/terminals are available on campus for general student use. Students can access the following: campus intranet, computer help desk, free student e-mail accounts, online (class) grades, online (class) registration, online (class) schedules. Campuswide network is available. 100% of college-owned or -operated housing units are wired for high-speed Internet access. Wireless service is available via entire campus.
Student Life *Housing:* on-campus residence required through sophomore year. *Options:* coed, men-only, women-only. Campus housing is university owned. *Activities and organizations:* drama/theater group, student-run newspaper, choral group, marching band, Student Nurses Association, Student Education Association, Phi Beta Lambda, Fellowship of Christian Athletics, Circle K. *Campus security:* 24-hour emergency response devices, student patrols, late-night transport/escort service, controlled dormitory access. *Student services:* health clinic, personal/psychological counseling.
Athletics Member NAIA. *Intercollegiate sports:* baseball M (s), basketball M (s)/W (s), cross-country running M (s)/W (s), football M (s), golf M (s)/W (s), soccer M (s)/W (s), softball W (s), tennis M (s)/W (s), track and field M (s)/W (s), volleyball W (s). *Intramural sports:* basketball M/W, football M, golf M/W, gymnastics M/W, racquetball M/W, soccer M/W, swimming and diving M/W, tennis M/W, track and field M/W, volleyball M/W, weight lifting M.
Standardized Tests *Required:* SAT or ACT (for admission).
Costs (2007–08) *Comprehensive fee:* $25,675 includes full-time tuition ($20,525) and room and board ($5150). Full-time tuition and fees vary according to class time, course load, and program. Part-time tuition: $515 per credit. Part-time tuition and fees vary according to class time, course load, and program. *Required fees:* $10 per credit part-time. *College room only:* $2255. Room and board charges vary according to board plan and housing facility. *Payment plan:* installment. *Waivers:* children of alumni, senior citizens, and employees or children of employees.
Financial Aid Of all full-time matriculated undergraduates who enrolled in 2004, 856 applied for aid, 775 were judged to have need, 362 had their need fully met. 196 Federal Work-Study jobs (averaging $904). 139 state and other part-time jobs (averaging $1480). In 2004, 53 non-need-based awards were made. *Average percent of need met:* 95%. *Average financial aid package:* $15,639. *Average need-based loan:* $6038. *Average need-based gift aid:* $9311. *Average non-need-based aid:* $8083. *Average indebtedness upon graduation:* $19,698.
Applying *Options:* electronic application, early admission. *Application fee:* $30. *Required:* high school transcript. *Required for some:* interview. *Recommended:* essay or personal statement, minimum 3.0 GPA, letters of recommendation. *Application deadlines:* rolling (freshmen), rolling (transfers). *Notification:* continuous until 9/1 (freshmen), continuous until 9/1 (transfers).
Freshman Application Contact Mr. Todd Hansen, Associate Director of Admissions, Midland Lutheran College, Admissions Office, Fremont, NE 68025-4200. *Phone:* 402-941-6504. *Toll-free phone:* 800-642-8382 Ext. 6501. *Fax:* 402-941-6513. *E-mail:* admissions@mlc.edu.

NEBRASKA CHRISTIAN COLLEGE

Papillon, Nebraska **www.nechristian.edu/**

- **Independent** 4-year, founded 1944, affiliated with Christian Churches and Churches of Christ
- **Small-town** 85-acre campus
- **Endowment** $324,000
- **Coed** 146 undergraduate students, 96% full-time, 43% women, 57% men
- **Minimally difficult** entrance level

Undergraduates 140 full-time, 6 part-time. Students come from 12 states and territories, 4 other countries, 42% are from out of state, 0.7% Asian American or Pacific Islander, 1% Hispanic American, 0.7% international, 8% transferred in, 90% live on campus. *Retention:* 30% of 2006 full-time freshmen returned.
Freshmen *Admission:* 154 applied, 48 enrolled. *Test scores:* ACT scores over 18: 23%; ACT scores over 24: 6%.
Faculty *Total:* 20, 15% with terminal degrees. *Student/faculty ratio:* 7:1.
Majors Administrative assistant and secretarial science; divinity/ministry; elementary education; pastoral studies/counseling; religious education; religious/sacred music; religious studies; secondary education; sign language interpretation and translation; theology.
Academics *Calendar:* semesters. *Degrees:* associate and bachelor's. *Special study options:* internships, off-campus study, part-time degree program.
Computers on Campus 12 computers/terminals and 153 ports are available on campus for general student use. Students can access the following: campus intranet, free student e-mail accounts. Campuswide network is available. 100% of college-owned or -operated housing units are wired for high-speed Internet access. Wireless service is available via entire campus.
Student Life *Housing:* on-campus residence required through junior year. *Options:* men-only, women-only. Campus housing is university owned. Freshman campus housing is guaranteed. *Activities and organizations:* choral group.
Athletics Member NCCAA. *Intercollegiate sports:* basketball M/W, soccer M, volleyball W. *Intramural sports:* basketball M/W, soccer M, volleyball M/W.
Standardized Tests *Required:* ACT (for admission).
Costs (2008–09) *Tuition:* $275 per credit part-time.
Financial Aid Of all full-time matriculated undergraduates who enrolled in 2003, 147 applied for aid, 129 were judged to have need. 13 Federal Work-Study jobs (averaging $1183). In 2003, 16 non-need-based awards were made. *Average need-based loan:* $2958. *Average non-need-based aid:* $2215. *Average indebtedness upon graduation:* $11,593.
Applying *Options:* electronic application. *Application fee:* $25. *Required:* high school transcript, 2 letters of recommendation. *Required for some:* interview. *Application deadlines:* rolling (freshmen), rolling (transfers). *Notification:* continuous until 9/1 (freshmen), continuous until 9/1 (transfers).
Freshman Application Contact Ms. Alisha Livengood, Associate Director of Admissions, Nebraska Christian College, 1800 Syracuse Avenue, Norfolk, NE 68701. *Phone:* 402-935-9407.

NEBRASKA METHODIST COLLEGE

Omaha, Nebraska **www.methodistcollege.edu/**

- **Independent** comprehensive, founded 1891, affiliated with United Methodist Church
- **Urban** 5-acre campus
- **Endowment** $30.2 million
- **Coed, primarily women** 446 undergraduate students, 69% full-time, 89% women, 11% men
- **Moderately difficult** entrance level, 39% of applicants were admitted

Undergraduates 309 full-time, 137 part-time. Students come from 6 states and territories, 1 other country, 25% are from out of state, 4% African American, 2% Asian American or Pacific Islander, 0.7% Hispanic American, 0.4% Native American, 0.2% international, 29% transferred in, 20% live on campus. *Retention:* 83% of 2006 full-time freshmen returned.
Freshmen *Admission:* 64 applied, 25 admitted, 20 enrolled. *Average high school GPA:* 3.42. *Test scores:* ACT scores over 18: 90%; ACT scores over 24: 20%.
Faculty *Total:* 57, 58% full-time, 23% with terminal degrees. *Student/faculty ratio:* 10:1.
Majors Cardiovascular technology; diagnostic medical sonography and ultrasound technology; emergency medical technology (EMT paramedic); nursing (registered nurse training); radiologic technology/science; respiratory care therapy.

Academics *Calendar:* semesters. *Degrees:* certificates, associate, bachelor's, master's, and post-master's certificates. *Special study options:* academic remediation for entering students, accelerated degree program, advanced placement credit, distance learning, independent study, internships, services for LD students, summer session for credit. *ROTC:* Army (c), Air Force (c).

Computers on Campus 45 computers/terminals are available on campus for general student use. Campuswide network is available.

Student Life *Housing options:* coed. Campus housing is university owned. Freshman applicants given priority for college housing. *Activities and organizations:* Student Senate, Student Nurses Association, Methodist Allied Health Student Association, Student Ambassadors, Residence Hall Council. *Campus security:* 24-hour emergency response devices, late-night transport/escort service, controlled dormitory access. *Student services:* health clinic, personal/psychological counseling.

Standardized Tests *Required:* SAT or ACT (for admission).

Costs (2008–09) *Tuition:* $13,440 full-time, $428 per credit hour part-time. *Required fees:* $600 full-time, $20 per credit hour part-time. *Room only:* $6150.

Financial Aid Of all full-time matriculated undergraduates who enrolled in 2005, 170 applied for aid, 142 were judged to have need, 26 had their need fully met. In 2005, 48 non-need-based awards were made. *Average percent of need met:* 56%. *Average financial aid package:* $6789. *Average need-based loan:* $3855. *Average need-based gift aid:* $3752. *Average non-need-based aid:* $8642. *Average indebtedness upon graduation:* $24,901.

Applying *Options:* electronic application, deferred entrance. *Application fee:* $25. *Required:* essay or personal statement, high school transcript, minimum 2.0 GPA, 3 letters of recommendation, interview. *Application deadlines:* 4/1 (freshmen), 4/1 (transfers). *Notification:* 4/15 (freshmen), 4/15 (transfers).

Freshman Application Contact Ms. Deann Sterner, Director of Admissions, Nebraska Methodist College, Omaha, NE 68114. *Phone:* 402-354-7200. *Toll-free phone:* 800-335-5510. *Fax:* 402-354-7020. *E-mail:* deann.sterner@methodistcollege.edu.

NEBRASKA WESLEYAN UNIVERSITY

Lincoln, Nebraska **www.nebrwesleyan.edu/**

- **Independent United Methodist** comprehensive, founded 1887
- **Suburban** 50-acre campus with easy access to Omaha
- **Endowment** $47.4 million
- **Coed** 1,888 undergraduate students, 89% full-time, 57% women, 43% men
- **Moderately difficult** entrance level, 80% of applicants were admitted

Undergraduates 1,671 full-time, 217 part-time. Students come from 23 states and territories, 14 other countries, 9% are from out of state, 2% African American, 1% Asian American or Pacific Islander, 1% Hispanic American, 0.2% Native American, 0.2% international, 3% transferred in, 62% live on campus. *Retention:* 82% of 2006 full-time freshmen returned.

Freshmen *Admission:* 1,632 applied, 1,300 admitted, 439 enrolled. *Test scores:* ACT scores over 18: 100%; ACT scores over 24: 63%; ACT scores over 30: 10%.

Faculty *Total:* 173, 59% full-time, 64% with terminal degrees. *Student/faculty ratio:* 13:1.

Majors Accounting; art; athletic training; biochemistry; biochemistry/biophysics and molecular biology; biology/biological sciences; biopsychology; business administration and management; business, management, and marketing related; chemistry; communication/speech communication and rhetoric; computer science; dramatic/theater arts; dramatic/theater arts and stagecraft related; economics; elementary education; English; English/language arts teacher education; French; German; health and physical education; history; industrial and organizational psychology; information science/studies; interdisciplinary studies; international business/trade/commerce; international/global studies; kinesiology and exercise science; mathematics; middle school education; music; music performance; music teacher education; nursing administration; philosophy; physical education teaching and coaching; physics; political communication; political science and government; psychology; religious studies; science teacher education; social science teacher education; social work; sociology; Spanish; special education; speech and rhetoric; sport and fitness administration/management; women's studies.

Academics *Calendar:* semesters. *Degrees:* certificates, bachelor's, master's, post-master's, and postbachelor's certificates. *Special study options:* adult/continuing education programs, advanced placement credit, double majors, independent study, internships, off-campus study, part-time degree program, services for LD students, study abroad, summer session for credit. *ROTC:* Army (c), Air Force (c). *Unusual degree programs:* 3-2 engineering with Washington University in St. Louis, Columbia University, University of Nebraska-Lincoln; physical therapy with University of Nebraska Medical Center, Mayo Medical School.

Computers on Campus 360 computers/terminals are available on campus for general student use. Students can access the following: computer help desk, free student e-mail accounts, online (class) grades, online (class) registration, online (class) schedules. Campuswide network is available. 100% of college-owned or -operated housing units are wired for high-speed Internet access. Wireless service is available via classrooms, computer centers, computer labs, learning centers, libraries, student centers.

Student Life *Housing:* on-campus residence required through junior year. *Options:* coed, women-only. Campus housing is university owned. Freshman campus housing is guaranteed. *Activities and organizations:* drama/theater group, student-run newspaper, choral group, Student Affairs Senate, Union programs, Ambassadors, FCA, national fraternities, national sororities. *Campus security:* 24-hour emergency response devices, late-night transport/escort service, controlled dormitory access. *Student services:* health clinic, personal/psychological counseling, women's center.

Athletics Member NCAA, NAIA. All NCAA Division III. *Intercollegiate sports:* baseball M, basketball M/W, cheerleading W, cross-country running M/W, football M, golf M/W, soccer M/W, softball W, tennis M/W, track and field M/W, volleyball W. *Intramural sports:* basketball M/W, bowling M/W, football M/W, racquetball M/W, soccer M/W, softball M/W, table tennis M/W, ultimate Frisbee M/W, volleyball M/W.

Standardized Tests *Required:* SAT or ACT (for admission).

Costs (2007–08) *One-time required fee:* $120. *Comprehensive fee:* $25,592 includes full-time tuition ($19,930), mandatory fees ($322), and room and board ($5340). Full-time tuition and fees vary according to class time, course load, degree level, location, and program. Part-time tuition: $750 per credit hour. Part-time tuition and fees vary according to class time, course load, degree level, location, and program. *Room and board:* Room and board charges vary according to board plan. *Payment plans:* installment, deferred payment. *Waivers:* adult students, senior citizens, and employees or children of employees.

Financial Aid Of all full-time matriculated undergraduates who enrolled in 2007, 1,266 applied for aid, 1,092 were judged to have need, 163 had their need fully met. In 2007, 405 non-need-based awards were made. *Average percent of need met:* 72%. *Average financial aid package:* $14,913. *Average need-based loan:* $4479. *Average need-based gift aid:* $10,252. *Average non-need-based aid:* $6789. *Average indebtedness upon graduation:* $19,534.

Applying *Options:* electronic application, early action, deferred entrance. *Application fee:* $20. *Required:* high school transcript, minimum 2.0 GPA. *Required for some:* essay or personal statement, resume of activities. *Recommended:* interview. *Application deadlines:* 8/15 (freshmen), 8/15 (transfers), 11/15 (early action). *Notification:* continuous (freshmen), 12/15 (early action).

Freshman Application Contact Nebraska Wesleyan University, 5000 Saint Paul Avenue, Lincoln, NE 68504. *Phone:* 402-465-2218. *Toll-free phone:* 800-541-3818.

PERU STATE COLLEGE

Peru, Nebraska **www.peru.edu/**

- **State-supported** comprehensive, founded 1867, part of Nebraska State College System
- **Rural** 104-acre campus
- **Coed** 1,891 undergraduate students, 60% full-time, 55% women, 45% men
- **Noncompetitive** entrance level, 42% of applicants were admitted

Undergraduates 1,130 full-time, 761 part-time. Students come from 41 states and territories, 7 other countries, 18% are from out of state, 5% African American, 0.9% Asian American or Pacific Islander, 2% Hispanic American, 0.9% Native American, 12% transferred in, 30% live on campus. *Retention:* 50% of 2006 full-time freshmen returned.

Freshmen *Admission:* 774 applied, 327 admitted, 206 enrolled. *Average high school GPA:* 2.76. *Test scores:* ACT scores over 18: 72%; ACT scores over 24: 20%; ACT scores over 30: 1%.

Faculty *Total:* 139. *Student/faculty ratio:* 20:1.

Majors Accounting; applied art; art; art teacher education; biological and physical sciences; biology/biological sciences; business administration and management; chemistry; clinical laboratory science/medical technology; commercial and advertising art; criminal justice/law enforcement administration; education; elementary education; English; health teacher education; history; kindergarten/preschool education; management information systems; marketing/marketing management; mathematics; middle school education; music; music management and merchandising; music teacher education; natural resources/conservation; natural sciences; nuclear medical technology; physical education teaching and coaching; physician assistant; pre-dentistry studies; pre-law studies; pre-medical studies; pre-veterinary studies; psychology; science teacher education; secondary

COLLEGE DATA CENTER • NEBRASKA

education; social sciences; special education; voice and opera; wildlife and wildlands science and management; wind/percussion instruments.

Academics *Calendar:* semesters. *Degrees:* certificates, bachelor's, and master's. *Special study options:* academic remediation for entering students, accelerated degree program, adult/continuing education programs, advanced placement credit, cooperative education, distance learning, double majors, external degree program, freshman honors college, honors programs, internships, off-campus study, part-time degree program, services for LD students, summer session for credit. *ROTC:* Army (c), Air Force (c).

Computers on Campus 120 computers/terminals are available on campus for general student use. Students can access the following: campus intranet, free student e-mail accounts, online (class) grades, online (class) registration, online (class) schedules. Campuswide network is available. 90% of college-owned or -operated housing units are wired for high-speed Internet access.

Student Life *Housing:* on-campus residence required through sophomore year. *Options:* coed, men-only, women-only. Campus housing is university owned. Freshman applicants given priority for college housing. *Activities and organizations:* drama/theater group, student-run newspaper, choral group, marching band, Peru Chorus, Campus Activities Board, Marching band, Student government, Peru Players. *Campus security:* 24-hour patrols. *Student services:* health clinic, personal/psychological counseling.

Athletics Member NAIA. *Intercollegiate sports:* baseball M (s), basketball M (s)/W (s), cheerleading M (s)/W (s), cross-country running W (s), football M (s), golf W (s), softball W (s), volleyball W (s). *Intramural sports:* basketball M/W, bowling M/W, football M/W, softball M/W, swimming and diving M/W, table tennis M/W, ultimate Frisbee M/W, volleyball M/W, weight lifting M/W.

Standardized Tests *Required for some:* SAT or ACT (for admission).

Costs (2008–09) *Room and board:* $4816.

Applying *Options:* electronic application. *Required:* high school transcript. *Required for some:* minimum 2.0 GPA, ACT/SAT. *Application deadlines:* rolling (freshmen), rolling (transfers). *Notification:* continuous (freshmen), continuous (transfers).

Freshman Application Contact Ms. Micki Willis, Director of Recruitment and Admissions, Peru State College, PO Box 10, Peru, NE 68421. *Phone:* 402-872-2221. *Toll-free phone:* 800-742-4412. *Fax:* 402-872-2296. *E-mail:* mwillis@oakmail.peru.edu.

UNION COLLEGE

Lincoln, Nebraska **www.ucollege.edu/**

- **Independent Seventh-day Adventist** comprehensive, founded 1891
- **Suburban** 26-acre campus with easy access to Omaha
- **Coed** 944 undergraduate students, 81% full-time, 56% women, 44% men
- **Moderately difficult** entrance level, 43% of applicants were admitted

Undergraduates 763 full-time, 181 part-time. Students come from 48 states and territories, 26 other countries, 82% are from out of state, 2% African American, 3% Asian American or Pacific Islander, 6% Hispanic American, 1% Native American, 8% international, 7% transferred in, 58% live on campus. *Retention:* 72% of 2006 full-time freshmen returned.

Freshmen *Admission:* 903 applied, 386 admitted, 164 enrolled. *Average high school GPA:* 3.33. *Test scores:* ACT scores over 18: 92%; ACT scores over 24: 33%; ACT scores over 30: 5%.

Faculty *Total:* 101, 58% full-time, 29% with terminal degrees. *Student/faculty ratio:* 13:1.

Majors Accounting; art; art teacher education; biochemistry; biology/biological sciences; biology teacher education; business administration and management; business teacher education; chemistry; chemistry teacher education; clinical laboratory science/medical technology; commercial and advertising art; computer science; computer teacher education; education; elementary education; engineering; English; English/language arts teacher education; entrepreneurship; fine/studio arts; French; German; graphic design; health/medical preparatory programs related; health science; history; history teacher education; information science/studies; international relations and affairs; journalism; kinesiology and exercise science; mathematics; mathematics teacher education; music; music performance; music teacher education; nursing (registered nurse training); pastoral studies/counseling; physical education teaching and coaching; physician assistant; physics; physics teacher education; psychology; public relations/image management; religious education; religious studies; secondary education; social sciences; social science teacher education; social work; Spanish; sport and fitness administration/management; theology.

Academics *Calendar:* semesters. *Degrees:* associate, bachelor's, and master's. *Special study options:* accelerated degree program, adult/continuing education programs, advanced placement credit, cooperative education, double majors, English as a second language, honors programs, independent study, internships, off-campus study, part-time degree program, services for LD students, student-designed majors, study abroad, summer session for credit.

Computers on Campus 520 computers/terminals are available on campus for general student use. Campuswide network is available.

Student Life *Housing:* on-campus residence required through sophomore year. *Options:* men-only, women-only. Campus housing is university owned. Freshman campus housing is guaranteed. *Activities and organizations:* drama/theater group, student-run newspaper, choral group. *Campus security:* 24-hour emergency response devices, student patrols, late-night transport/escort service. *Student services:* health clinic, personal/psychological counseling.

Athletics *Intercollegiate sports:* basketball M/W, volleyball W. *Intramural sports:* badminton M/W, baseball M/W, basketball M/W, field hockey M/W, football M/W, golf M/W, gymnastics M/W, racquetball M/W, sailing M/W, soccer M/W, softball M/W, swimming and diving M/W, tennis M/W, volleyball M/W.

Standardized Tests *Required:* SAT or ACT (for admission).

Costs (2007–08) *Comprehensive fee:* $21,400 includes full-time tuition ($15,670), mandatory fees ($460), and room and board ($5270). *College room only:* $3070. *Payment plan:* installment. *Waivers:* employees or children of employees.

Financial Aid Of all full-time matriculated undergraduates who enrolled in 2005, 172 Federal Work-Study jobs (averaging $1663). *Average percent of need met:* 71%. *Average financial aid package:* $12,234. *Average need-based loan:* $4442. *Average need-based gift aid:* $7056. *Average non-need-based aid:* $3699. *Average indebtedness upon graduation:* $23,379.

Applying *Options:* electronic application. *Required:* high school transcript, minimum 2.5 GPA, 3 letters of recommendation. *Required for some:* essay or personal statement, interview. *Application deadlines:* rolling (freshmen), rolling (transfers). *Notification:* continuous (freshmen), continuous (transfers).

Freshman Application Contact Huda McClelland, Director of Admissions, Union College, 3800 South 48th Street, Lincoln, NE 68506. *Phone:* 402-486-2504. *Toll-free phone:* 800-228-4600. *Fax:* 402-486-2895. *E-mail:* ucenroll@ucollege.edu.

See page 1484 for the College Close-Up.

UNIVERSITY OF NEBRASKA AT KEARNEY

Kearney, Nebraska **www.unk.edu/**

- **State-supported** comprehensive, founded 1903, part of University of Nebraska System
- **Small-town** 235-acre campus
- **Endowment** $65,712
- **Coed** 5,183 undergraduate students, 89% full-time, 53% women, 47% men
- **Moderately difficult** entrance level, 79% of applicants were admitted

Undergraduates 4,632 full-time, 551 part-time. Students come from 43 states and territories, 45 other countries, 7% are from out of state, 1% African American, 0.5% Asian American or Pacific Islander, 4% Hispanic American, 0.3% Native American, 9% international, 6% transferred in, 32% live on campus. *Retention:* 79% of 2006 full-time freshmen returned.

Freshmen *Admission:* 2,646 applied, 2,092 admitted, 996 enrolled. *Average high school GPA:* 3.3. *Test scores:* SAT critical reading scores over 500: 37%; SAT math scores over 500: 50%; ACT scores over 18: 91%; SAT critical reading scores over 600: 25%; ACT scores over 24: 35%; ACT scores over 30: 5%.

Faculty *Total:* 380, 81% full-time, 68% with terminal degrees. *Student/faculty ratio:* 16:1.

Majors Agricultural business and management; art; aviation/airway management; biology/biological sciences; business administration and management; business teacher education; chemistry; communication disorders; computer and information sciences; criminal justice/safety; dietetics; dramatic/theater arts; economics; elementary education; English; family and consumer economics related; French; general studies; geography; German; history; international relations and affairs; journalism; mass communication/media; mathematics; music; operations management; parks, recreation and leisure; physical education teaching and coaching; physics; political science and government; psychology; social work; sociology; Spanish; special education; speech and rhetoric; sport and fitness administration/management; statistics; technical teacher education; therapeutic recreation.

Academics *Calendar:* semesters. *Degrees:* bachelor's, master's, and post-master's certificates. *Special study options:* academic remediation for entering students, advanced placement credit, cooperative education, distance learning, double majors, English as a second language, honors programs, independent study, internships, off-campus study, part-time degree program, services for LD students, study abroad, summer session for credit.

Computers on Campus 277 computers/terminals are available on campus for general student use. Students can access the following: computer help desk, free student e-mail accounts, online (class) grades, online (class) registration, online (class) schedules, online degree audit, online update personal information, online bill viewing and payment, online financial aid awards and acceptance. Campuswide network is available.

Student Life *Housing:* on-campus residence required for freshman year. *Options:* coed, men-only, women-only. Campus housing is university owned. Freshman campus housing is guaranteed. *Activities and organizations:* drama/theater group, student-run newspaper, radio and television station, choral group, marching band, Student Activities Council, Intramurals Council, Residence Hall Association, International Student Association, national fraternities, national sororities. *Campus security:* 24-hour emergency response devices and patrols, late-night transport/escort service. *Student services:* health clinic, personal/psychological counseling.

Athletics Member NCAA. All Division II. *Intercollegiate sports:* baseball M (s), basketball M (s)/W (s), cross-country running M (s)/W (s), football M (s), golf M (s)/W (s), softball W (s), swimming and diving W (s), tennis M (s)/W (s), track and field M (s)/W (s), volleyball W (s), wrestling M (s). *Intramural sports:* badminton M/W, basketball M/W, cross-country running M/W, football M/W, golf M/W, racquetball M/W, soccer M/W, softball M/W, tennis M/W, volleyball M/W, water polo M/W, wrestling M/W.

Standardized Tests *Required:* SAT and SAT Subject Tests or ACT (for admission).

Costs (2007–08) *Tuition:* state resident $4118 full-time, $137 per hour part-time; nonresident $8438 full-time, $281 per hour part-time. Full-time tuition and fees vary according to course level, course load, degree level, and location. Part-time tuition and fees vary according to course level, course load, degree level, and location. *Required fees:* $903 full-time, $18 per hour part-time, $69 per term part-time. *Room and board:* $6000; room only: $3100. Room and board charges vary according to board plan and housing facility. *Payment plan:* installment. *Waivers:* employees or children of employees.

Financial Aid Of all full-time matriculated undergraduates who enrolled in 2006, 3,598 applied for aid, 2,878 were judged to have need, 886 had their need fully met. 325 Federal Work-Study jobs (averaging $1088). In 2006, 1478 non-need-based awards were made. *Average percent of need met:* 79%. *Average financial aid package:* $7227. *Average need-based loan:* $3590. *Average need-based gift aid:* $3176. *Average non-need-based aid:* $1994. *Average indebtedness upon graduation:* $16,175.

Applying *Options:* electronic application. *Application fee:* $45. *Required:* high school transcript, rank in upper 50% of high school class, minimum SAT score of 950, or ACT score of 20. *Required for some:* 3 letters of recommendation. *Application deadlines:* rolling (freshmen), rolling (transfers). *Notification:* continuous (freshmen), continuous (transfers).

Freshman Application Contact Mr. Dusty Newton, Director of Admissions, University of Nebraska at Kearney, 905 West 25th Street, Kearney, NE 68849-0001. *Phone:* 308-865-8702. *Toll-free phone:* 800-532-7639. *Fax:* 308-865-8987. *E-mail:* admissionsug@unk.edu.

UNIVERSITY OF NEBRASKA AT OMAHA

Omaha, Nebraska **www.unomaha.edu/**

- **State-supported** university, founded 1908, part of University of Nebraska System
- **Urban** 158-acre campus
- **Endowment** $191.6 million
- **Coed** 11,331 undergraduate students, 76% full-time, 52% women, 48% men
- **Minimally difficult** entrance level, 86% of applicants were admitted

Undergraduates 8,660 full-time, 2,671 part-time. Students come from 40 states and territories, 65 other countries, 7% are from out of state, 6% African American, 3% Asian American or Pacific Islander, 4% Hispanic American, 0.5% Native American, 2% international, 11% transferred in, 9% live on campus. *Retention:* 74% of 2006 full-time freshmen returned.

Freshmen *Admission:* 3,891 applied, 3,341 admitted, 1,677 enrolled. *Average high school GPA:* 3.3. *Test scores:* SAT critical reading scores over 500: 40%; SAT math scores over 500: 20%; ACT scores over 18: 92%; SAT critical reading scores over 600: 20%; SAT math scores over 600: 20%; ACT scores over 24: 40%; ACT scores over 30: 8%.

Faculty *Total:* 880, 55% full-time, 55% with terminal degrees. *Student/faculty ratio:* 18:1.

Majors Accounting; aeronautics/aviation/aerospace science and technology; African-American/Black studies; architectural engineering; art; art history, criticism and conservation; banking and financial support services; biology/biological sciences; biotechnology; broadcast journalism; business administration and management; business/commerce; business/managerial economics; chemistry; civil engineering; communication/speech communication and rhetoric; community health services counseling; computer engineering; computer science; construction engineering technology; creative writing; criminal justice/safety; dramatic/theater arts; electrical, electronics and communications engineering; elementary education; engineering physics; English; environmental studies; family and consumer sciences/human sciences; family and consumer sciences/human sciences communication; family resource management; finance; fine/studio arts; French; general studies; geography; geology/earth science; German; gerontology; health and physical education; history; human resources management; industrial technology; international/global studies; journalism; Latin American studies; library science; management information systems; manufacturing technology; marketing/marketing management; mathematics; multi-/interdisciplinary studies related; music; music performance; music teacher education; music theory and composition; natural sciences; parks, recreation and leisure; philosophy; physical education teaching and coaching; physics; political science and government; psychology; real estate; religious studies; secondary education; social work; sociology; Spanish; special education (speech or language impaired); speech and rhetoric; voice and opera; women's studies.

Academics *Calendar:* semesters. *Degrees:* bachelor's, master's, doctoral, post-master's, and postbachelor's certificates. *Special study options:* adult/continuing education programs, advanced placement credit, cooperative education, distance learning, double majors, English as a second language, honors programs, independent study, internships, off-campus study, part-time degree program, services for LD students, student-designed majors, study abroad, summer session for credit. *ROTC:* Army (c), Air Force (b).

Computers on Campus 2,000 computers/terminals are available on campus for general student use. Students can access the following: computer help desk, free student e-mail accounts, online (class) grades, online (class) registration. Campuswide network is available. 100% of college-owned or -operated housing units are wired for high-speed Internet access.

Student Life *Housing options:* coed. Campus housing is university owned and leased by the school. *Activities and organizations:* drama/theater group, student-run newspaper, radio and television station, choral group, marching band, Student Programming Organization, Student Government, Greek Life, Emerging Leaders, national fraternities, national sororities. *Campus security:* 24-hour emergency response devices and patrols, late-night transport/escort service, controlled dormitory access. *Student services:* health clinic, personal/psychological counseling, women's center, legal services.

Athletics Member NCAA. All Division II except ice hockey (Division I). *Intercollegiate sports:* baseball M (s), basketball M (s)/W (s), cross-country running W (s), football M (s), golf W, ice hockey M (s), soccer W, softball W (s), swimming and diving W, tennis W, volleyball W (s), wrestling M (s). *Intramural sports:* baseball M/W, basketball M/W, bowling M/W, field hockey M/W, football M/W, golf M/W, racquetball M/W, soccer M/W, softball M/W, swimming and diving M/W, table tennis M/W, tennis M/W, volleyball M/W, weight lifting M/W, wrestling M/W.

Standardized Tests *Required:* SAT or ACT (for admission). *Required for some:* SAT or ACT (for placement).

Costs (2007–08) *Tuition:* state resident $4643 full-time, $155 per semester hour part-time; nonresident $13,680 full-time, $456 per semester hour part-time. Full-time tuition and fees vary according to course load and reciprocity agreements. Part-time tuition and fees vary according to course load and reciprocity agreements. *Required fees:* $888 full-time, $51 per hour part-time, $307 per term part-time. *Room and board:* $6810; room only: $4610. Room and board charges vary according to board plan. *Payment plans:* installment, deferred payment. *Waivers:* children of alumni and employees or children of employees.

Financial Aid Of all full-time matriculated undergraduates who enrolled in 2007, 5,435 applied for aid, 3,927 were judged to have need. 400 Federal Work-Study jobs (averaging $1500). *Average financial aid package:* $2564. *Average need-based loan:* $3210. *Average need-based gift aid:* $2236. *Average indebtedness upon graduation:* $19,000.

Applying *Options:* deferred entrance. *Application fee:* $45. *Required:* high school transcript, minimum ACT score of 20 or rank in upper 50% of high school class. *Application deadlines:* 8/1 (freshmen), 8/1 (transfers). *Notification:* continuous (freshmen), continuous (transfers).

Freshman Application Contact Ms. Jolene Adams, Associate Director of Admissions, University of Nebraska at Omaha, 6001 Dodge Street, Omaha, NE 68182. *Phone:* 402-554-2393. *Toll-free phone:* 800-858-8648. *Fax:* 402-554-3472. *E-mail:* jadams@mail.unomaha.edu.

UNIVERSITY OF NEBRASKA–LINCOLN

Lincoln, Nebraska www.unl.edu/

- **State-supported** university, founded 1869, part of University of Nebraska System
- **Urban** 623-acre campus with easy access to Omaha
- **Endowment** $224.1 million
- **Coed** 18,053 undergraduate students, 93% full-time, 46% women, 54% men
- **Moderately difficult** entrance level, 62% of applicants were admitted

Undergraduates 16,757 full-time, 1,296 part-time. Students come from 50 states and territories, 75 other countries, 17% are from out of state, 2% African American, 3% Asian American or Pacific Islander, 3% Hispanic American, 0.7% Native American, 3% international, 5% transferred in, 41% live on campus. *Retention:* 83% of 2006 full-time freshmen returned.

Freshmen *Admission:* 9,598 applied, 5,978 admitted, 4,235 enrolled. *Test scores:* SAT critical reading scores over 500: 76%; SAT math scores over 500: 85%; ACT scores over 18: 98%; SAT critical reading scores over 600: 47%; SAT math scores over 600: 54%; ACT scores over 24: 60%; SAT critical reading scores over 700: 14%; SAT math scores over 700: 17%; ACT scores over 30: 17%.

Faculty *Total:* 1,082, 99% full-time, 97% with terminal degrees. *Student/faculty ratio:* 19:1.

Majors Accounting; actuarial science; advertising; agricultural and food products processing; agricultural/biological engineering and bioengineering; agricultural business and management; agricultural communication/journalism; agricultural economics; agricultural mechanization; agricultural teacher education; agriculture; agronomy and crop science; ancient/classical Greek; ancient studies; animal sciences; anthropology; apparel and textiles; architectural engineering; architecture; art history, criticism and conservation; art teacher education; athletic training; atmospheric sciences and meteorology; audiology and hearing sciences; biochemistry; biology/biological sciences; biology teacher education; biomedical/medical engineering; botany/plant biology; broadcast journalism; business administration and management; business/managerial economics; business teacher education; chemical engineering; chemistry; chemistry teacher education; civil engineering; classics and languages, literatures and linguistics; communication/speech communication and rhetoric; community health services counseling; computer and information sciences; computer engineering; computer teacher education; construction engineering technology; dance; dramatic/theater arts; economics; education (multiple levels); education (specific subject areas) related; electrical, electronics and communications engineering; elementary education; engineering related; English; English as a second/foreign language (teaching); English/language arts teacher education; entomology; environmental studies; European studies (Western); family and consumer economics related; film/cinema studies; finance; fine/studio arts; fire protection and safety technology; food science; foods, nutrition, and wellness; foreign language teacher education; forensic science and technology; French; French language teacher education; geography; geology/earth science; German; German language teacher education; health teacher education; history; history teacher education; horticultural science; hospitality administration; industrial engineering; industrial production technologies related; interior architecture; international business/trade/commerce; international relations and affairs; journalism related; landscape architecture; landscaping and groundskeeping; Latin; Latin American studies; law and legal studies related; legal professions and studies related; liberal arts and sciences/liberal studies; management science; marketing/marketing management; mathematics; mathematics teacher education; mechanical engineering; medieval and Renaissance studies; middle school education; music; natural resources/conservation; natural resources management and policy; philosophy; physical education teaching and coaching; physics; physics teacher education; plant protection and integrated pest management; political science and government; pre-dentistry studies; pre-medical studies; pre-pharmacy studies; pre-veterinary studies; psychology; range science and management; reading teacher education; Russian; sales and marketing/marketing and distribution teacher education; science teacher education; social science teacher education; sociology; soil science and agronomy; Spanish; Spanish language teacher education; special education (hearing impaired); special education related; speech-language pathology; technology/industrial arts teacher education; trade and industrial teacher education; veterinary/animal health technology; women's studies.

Academics *Calendar:* semesters. *Degrees:* associate, bachelor's, master's, doctoral, first professional, post-master's, and postbachelor's certificates. *Special study options:* accelerated degree program, adult/continuing education programs, advanced placement credit, cooperative education, distance learning, double majors, English as a second language, honors programs, independent study, internships, off-campus study, part-time degree program, services for LD students, student-designed majors, study abroad, summer session for credit. *ROTC:* Army (b), Navy (b), Air Force (b).

Computers on Campus 650 computers/terminals are available on campus for general student use. Students can access the following: online (class) registration. Campuswide network is available.

Student Life *Housing:* on-campus residence required for freshman year. *Options:* coed, men-only, women-only, cooperative, disabled students. Campus housing is university owned. Freshman campus housing is guaranteed. *Activities and organizations:* drama/theater group, student-run newspaper, radio station, choral group, marching band, Student Alumni Association, University Ambassadors, University Program Council, Golden Key, national fraternities, national sororities. *Campus security:* 24-hour emergency response devices and patrols, student patrols, late-night transport/escort service, controlled dormitory access. *Student services:* health clinic, personal/psychological counseling, women's center, legal services.

Athletics Member NCAA. All Division I except football (Division I-A). *Intercollegiate sports:* baseball M (s), basketball M (s)/W (s), bowling M, crew M (c)/W (c), cross-country running M (s)/W (s), fencing M (c)/W (c), golf M (s)/W (s), gymnastics M (s)/W (s), riflery W (s), soccer W (s), softball W (s), swimming and diving W (s), tennis M (s)/W (s), track and field M (s)/W (s), volleyball W (s), wrestling M (s). *Intramural sports:* archery M/W, badminton M/W, basketball M/W, bowling M/W, crew M/W, cross-country running M/W, equestrian sports W, fencing M/W, football M/W, golf M/W, ice hockey M (c)/W (c), racquetball M/W, riflery M/W, rugby M (c)/W (c), soccer M/W, softball M/W, squash M/W, swimming and diving W, table tennis M/W, tennis M/W, track and field M/W, volleyball M/W, water polo M/W, weight lifting M/W, wrestling M/W.

Standardized Tests *Required:* SAT or ACT (for admission). *Recommended:* ACT (for admission).

Costs (2007–08) *Tuition:* state resident $5085 full-time, $170 per semester hour part-time; nonresident $15,105 full-time, $504 per semester hour part-time. Full-time tuition and fees vary according to course load. Part-time tuition and fees vary according to course load. *Required fees:* $1130 full-time, $9 per semester hour part-time, $233 per term part-time. *Room and board:* $6523; room only: $3441. Room and board charges vary according to board plan and housing facility. *Payment plan:* installment. *Waivers:* employees or children of employees.

Financial Aid Of all full-time matriculated undergraduates who enrolled in 2004, 9,785 applied for aid, 7,445 were judged to have need, 2,039 had their need fully met. 1,364 Federal Work-Study jobs (averaging $2121). In 2004, 966 non-need-based awards were made. *Average percent of need met:* 85%. *Average financial aid package:* $8245. *Average need-based loan:* $4011. *Average need-based gift aid:* $4867. *Average non-need-based aid:* $4999. *Average indebtedness upon graduation:* $16,909.

Applying *Options:* electronic application. *Application fee:* $45. *Required:* high school transcript. *Required for some:* rank in upper 50% of high school class. *Application deadlines:* 5/1 (freshmen), 6/30 (transfers). *Notification:* continuous (freshmen), continuous (transfers).

Freshman Application Contact Pat McBride, Director, New Student Enrollment, University of Nebraska–Lincoln, 313 North 13th Street, Ross Van Brunt Building, Lincoln, NE 68588-0256. *Phone:* 402-472-2023. *Toll-free phone:* 800-742-8800. *Fax:* 402-472-0670. *E-mail:* admissions@unl.edu.

See page 1486 for the College Close-Up.

UNIVERSITY OF NEBRASKA MEDICAL CENTER

Omaha, Nebraska www.unmc.edu/

- **State-supported** upper-level, founded 1869, part of University of Nebraska System
- **Urban** 51-acre campus
- **Endowment** $9.0 million
- **Coed** 829 undergraduate students, 92% full-time, 88% women, 12% men
- **Moderately difficult** entrance level

Undergraduates 759 full-time, 70 part-time. Students come from 24 states and territories, 4 other countries, 10% are from out of state, 1% African American, 2% Asian American or Pacific Islander, 3% Hispanic American, 0.8% Native American, 0.7% international, 28% transferred in.

Faculty *Total:* 1,053, 82% full-time, 88% with terminal degrees.

Majors Clinical laboratory science/medical technology; dental hygiene; diagnostic medical sonography and ultrasound technology; medical radiologic technology; nuclear medical technology; nursing (registered nurse training); radiologic technology/science.

Academics *Calendar:* semesters. *Degrees:* bachelor's, master's, doctoral, first professional, post-master's, postbachelor's, and first professional certificates. *Special study options:* accelerated degree program, distance learning, honors programs, internships, off-campus study, part-time degree program, services for LD students, summer session for credit. *ROTC:* Army (c), Air Force (c).

Computers on Campus 100 computers/terminals are available on campus for general student use. Students can access the following: campus intranet, computer help desk, free student e-mail accounts, online (class) grades, online (class) schedules, various software packages. Campuswide network is available. Wireless service is available via classrooms, computer centers, computer labs, libraries, student centers.

Student Life *Housing:* college housing not available. *Activities and organizations:* student government, Toastmasters, Student Alliance for Global Health, Christian Medical Society, Student Research Group, national fraternities, national sororities. *Campus security:* 24-hour emergency response devices and patrols, late-night transport/escort service. *Student services:* health clinic, personal/psychological counseling.

Costs (2007–08) *Tuition:* state resident $4800 full-time, $160 per semester hour part-time; nonresident $14,250 full-time, $475 per semester hour part-time. Full-time tuition and fees vary according to program. *Required fees:* $365 full-time, $2 per semester hour part-time, $47 per semester part-time. *Payment plan:* installment.

Financial Aid Of all full-time matriculated undergraduates who enrolled in 2006, 863 applied for aid, 729 were judged to have need, 103 had their need fully met. 53 Federal Work-Study jobs (averaging $663). In 2006, 181 non-need-based awards were made. *Average percent of need met:* 56%. *Average financial aid package:* $8239. *Average need-based loan:* $4871. *Average need-based gift aid:* $4760. *Average non-need-based aid:* $8607. *Average indebtedness upon graduation:* $29,188.

Applying *Options:* electronic application. *Application fee:* $45. *Application deadline:* rolling (transfers).

Application Contact Ms. Tymaree Tonjes, Administrative Technician, University of Nebraska Medical Center, 984265 Nebraska Medical Center, Omaha, NE 68198-4230. *Phone:* 402-559-6468. *Toll-free phone:* 800-626-8431 Ext. 6468. *Fax:* 402-559-6796. *E-mail:* ttonjes@unmc.edu.

WAYNE STATE COLLEGE

Wayne, Nebraska **www.wsc.edu/**

- **State-supported** comprehensive, founded 1910, part of Nebraska State College System
- **Small-town** 128-acre campus
- **Endowment** $10.8 million
- **Coed** 2,802 undergraduate students, 92% full-time, 54% women, 46% men
- **Noncompetitive** entrance level, 100% of applicants were admitted

Undergraduates 2,580 full-time, 222 part-time. Students come from 22 states and territories, 18 other countries, 15% are from out of state, 3% African American, 0.6% Asian American or Pacific Islander, 2% Hispanic American, 1% Native American, 0.8% international, 8% transferred in, 48% live on campus. *Retention:* 75% of 2006 full-time freshmen returned.

Freshmen *Admission:* 1,356 applied, 1,356 admitted, 661 enrolled. *Average high school GPA:* 3.19. *Test scores:* ACT scores over 18: 82%; ACT scores over 24: 29%; ACT scores over 30: 2%.

Faculty *Total:* 209, 63% full-time, 53% with terminal degrees. *Student/faculty ratio:* 19:1.

Majors Art; art teacher education; athletic training; biology/biological sciences; biology teacher education; business administration and management; business teacher education; chemistry; chemistry teacher education; child care provision; communication/speech communication and rhetoric; computer and information sciences; counseling psychology; criminal justice/safety; drama and dance teacher education; dramatic/theater arts; early childhood education; education (specific subject areas) related; elementary education; English; English/language arts teacher education; family and consumer sciences/home economics teacher education; family and consumer sciences/human sciences; foreign languages and literatures; foreign language teacher education; geography; geography teacher education; graphic design; health and physical education related; history; history teacher education; industrial production technologies related; information science/studies; interdisciplinary studies; mass communication/media; mathematics; mathematics teacher education; middle school education; music; music teacher education; physical education teaching and coaching; political science and government; psychology; psychology teacher education; science teacher education; social sciences; social science teacher education; sociology; Spanish; special education; speech teacher education; sport and fitness administration/management; technology/industrial arts teacher education.

Academics *Calendar:* semesters. *Degrees:* bachelor's, master's, and post-master's certificates. *Special study options:* adult/continuing education programs, advanced placement credit, cooperative education, distance learning, double majors, honors programs, independent study, internships, off-campus study, part-time degree program, services for LD students, student-designed majors, study abroad, summer session for credit. *ROTC:* Army (b).

Computers on Campus 365 computers/terminals are available on campus for general student use. Students can access the following: campus intranet, computer help desk, free student e-mail accounts, online (class) grades, online (class) registration, online (class) schedules. Campuswide network is available. 100% of college-owned or -operated housing units are wired for high-speed Internet access. Wireless service is available via classrooms, computer centers, computer labs, learning centers, libraries, student centers.

Student Life *Housing:* on-campus residence required for freshman year. *Options:* coed. Campus housing is university owned. Freshman campus housing is guaranteed. *Activities and organizations:* drama/theater group, student-run newspaper, radio and television station, choral group, marching band, national fraternities, national sororities. *Campus security:* 24-hour emergency response devices and patrols, student patrols, late-night transport/escort service, controlled dormitory access. *Student services:* health clinic, personal/psychological counseling.

Athletics Member NCAA. All Division II. *Intercollegiate sports:* baseball M (s), basketball M (s)/W (s), cross-country running M (s)/W (s), football M (s), golf M (s)/W (s), rock climbing M (c)/W (c), soccer M (c)/W (s), softball W (s), track and field M (s)/W (s), volleyball W (s). *Intramural sports:* archery M/W, badminton M/W, basketball M/W, bowling M/W, football M/W, golf M/W, racquetball M/W, softball M/W, swimming and diving M/W, table tennis M/W, tennis M/W, track and field M/W, volleyball M/W, weight lifting M/W, wrestling M.

Costs (2007–08) *Tuition:* state resident $3300 full-time, $110 per credit hour part-time; nonresident $6600 full-time, $220 per credit hour part-time. Full-time tuition and fees vary according to course level and course load. Part-time tuition and fees vary according to course level and course load. *Required fees:* $1022 full-time, $41 per credit hour part-time. *Room and board:* $4800; room only: $2280. Room and board charges vary according to board plan and housing facility. *Payment plan:* installment. *Waivers:* minority students and employees or children of employees.

Financial Aid Of all full-time matriculated undergraduates who enrolled in 2006, 2,053 applied for aid, 1,576 were judged to have need, 464 had their need fully met. 112 Federal Work-Study jobs (averaging $1200). In 2006, 132 non-need-based awards were made. *Average percent of need met:* 36%. *Average financial aid package:* $4027. *Average need-based loan:* $1855. *Average need-based gift aid:* $1597. *Average non-need-based aid:* $1150.

Applying *Options:* electronic application, deferred entrance. *Application fee:* $30. *Required:* high school transcript. *Application deadlines:* rolling (freshmen), rolling (out-of-state freshmen), rolling (transfers). *Notification:* continuous (freshmen), continuous (out-of-state freshmen), continuous (transfers).

Freshman Application Contact Ms. Tammy Young, Director of Admissions, Wayne State College, 1111 Main Street, Wayne, NE 68787. *Phone:* 402-375-7234. *Toll-free phone:* 800-228-9972. *Fax:* 402-375-7204. *E-mail:* admit1@wsc.edu.

YORK COLLEGE

York, Nebraska **www.york.edu/**

- **Independent** 4-year, founded 1890, affiliated with Church of Christ
- **Small-town** 44-acre campus
- **Endowment** $6.6 million
- **Coed** 402 undergraduate students, 90% full-time, 51% women, 49% men
- **Moderately difficult** entrance level, 57% of applicants were admitted

Undergraduates 362 full-time, 40 part-time. Students come from 30 states and territories, 4 other countries, 66% are from out of state, 4% African American, 2% Asian American or Pacific Islander, 4% Hispanic American, 1% international, 8% transferred in, 76% live on campus. *Retention:* 55% of 2006 full-time freshmen returned.

Freshmen *Admission:* 531 applied, 302 admitted, 90 enrolled. *Average high school GPA:* 3.26. *Test scores:* SAT critical reading scores over 500: 50%; SAT math scores over 500: 50%; ACT scores over 18: 74%; SAT critical reading scores over 600: 10%; SAT math scores over 600: 10%; ACT scores over 24: 34%; ACT scores over 30: 7%.

Faculty *Total:* 57, 58% full-time, 26% with terminal degrees. *Student/faculty ratio:* 9:1.

Majors Accounting; ancient Near Eastern and biblical languages; art teacher education; biblical studies; biological and physical sciences; biology/biological sciences; biology teacher education; business administration and management; business teacher education; education; education (multiple levels); elementary education; English; English/language arts teacher education; finance; general studies; history; history teacher education; human resources management; liberal arts and sciences/liberal studies; mathematics teacher education; middle school education; music; music teacher education; natural sciences; physical education teaching and coaching; physiological psychology/psychobiology; psychology; psychology teacher education; reading teacher education; religious education; religious studies; science teacher education; secondary education; social science teacher education; social studies teacher education; special education; speech teacher education; speech/theater education; sport and fitness administration/management.

Academics *Calendar:* semesters. *Degrees:* associate and bachelor's. *Special study options:* academic remediation for entering students, adult/continuing education programs, advanced placement credit, cooperative education, double majors, external degree program, honors programs, independent study, internships, part-time degree program, services for LD students, study abroad, summer session for credit. *ROTC:* Army (c), Navy (c), Air Force (c). *Unusual degree programs:* 3-2 engineering with Oklahoma Christian University; nursing with Harding University.

Computers on Campus 57 computers/terminals and 394 ports are available on campus for general student use. Students can access the following: free student e-mail accounts. Campuswide network is available. 100% of college-owned or -operated housing units are wired for high-speed Internet access. Wireless service is available via libraries, student centers.

Student Life *Housing:* on-campus residence required through senior year. *Options:* men-only, women-only. Campus housing is university owned. Freshman campus housing is guaranteed. *Activities and organizations:* drama/theater group, student-run newspaper, choral group, concert choir, Student Association, Promethians, Marksmen. *Campus security:* 24-hour patrols, student patrols, controlled dormitory access. *Student services:* personal/psychological counseling.

Athletics Member NAIA, NCCAA. *Intercollegiate sports:* baseball M (s), basketball M (s)/W (s), soccer M (s)/W (s), softball W (s), volleyball W, wrestling M. *Intramural sports:* badminton M/W, basketball M/W, football M/W, soccer M/W, softball M/W, table tennis M/W, tennis M/W, volleyball M/W.

Standardized Tests *Required:* SAT or ACT (for admission).

Costs (2007–08) *Comprehensive fee:* $18,500 includes full-time tuition ($12,500), mandatory fees ($1500), and room and board ($4500). Full-time tuition and fees vary according to course load. Part-time tuition: $390 per credit hour. Part-time tuition and fees vary according to course load. *Required fees:* $220 per credit hour part-time. *Room and board:* Room and board charges vary according to board plan and housing facility. *Payment plan:* installment. *Waivers:* children of alumni, adult students, and employees or children of employees.

Financial Aid Of all full-time matriculated undergraduates who enrolled in 2006, 315 applied for aid, 286 were judged to have need, 1 had their need fully met. 108 Federal Work-Study jobs (averaging $1080). In 2006, 28 non-need-based awards were made. *Average percent of need met:* 66%. *Average financial aid package:* $12,201. *Average need-based loan:* $5039. *Average need-based gift aid:* $6661. *Average non-need-based aid:* $5444. *Average indebtedness upon graduation:* $19,700.

Applying *Options:* electronic application, early admission, deferred entrance. *Application fee:* $20. *Required:* high school transcript, minimum 2.0 GPA. *Required for some:* letters of recommendation. *Application deadlines:* rolling (freshmen), rolling (transfers). *Notification:* continuous (transfers).

Freshman Application Contact Ms. Judy Rinard, York College, 1125 East 8th Street, York, NE 68467-2699. *Phone:* 402-363-5627. *Toll-free phone:* 800-950-9675. *Fax:* 402-363-5623. *E-mail:* enroll@york.edu.

BELLEVUE UNIVERSITY

BELLEVUE, NEBRASKA

The University

The community leaders who founded Bellevue College in 1966 had a vision that still resonates today: to provide high-quality, cost-effective business and liberal arts degree programs that meet the needs of busy working students, employers, and society.

From a small, one-building campus in the Omaha suburb of Bellevue, Nebraska, that original, down-to-earth vision has expanded worldwide. Today, Bellevue University attracts students from seventy-two countries and has more than 20,000 alumni spread around the world. The University is recognized globally as an educational leader that values individual achievement, high productivity, and applied critical thinking in creating opportunities for undergraduate and graduate students. The University actively facilitates a network of strategic alliances and partnerships that builds on its core strengths and enriches what it offers students. Among educators and employers, the University has established itself as an important national force for high quality, growth, and innovation in classroom and online graduate degree programs.

Bellevue University is accredited by the Higher Learning Commission of the North Central Association of Colleges and Schools, 30 North LaSalle Street, Suite 2400, Chicago, Illinois 60602-2504. Its College of Business is accredited by the International Assembly for College Business Education.

The University is structured in five colleges, each targeting specific needs. The College of Arts and Sciences meets a need for high-quality, affordable degree programs in the arts, sciences, communication, and humanities. The Kirkpatrick Signature Series, General Education Core Curriculum, and Master of Human Services are offered by the College.

The College of Business provides undergraduate majors in accounting and business administration and offers a flexible M.B.A. degree with several concentration areas, as well as a Master of Arts in management, Master of Science in acquisition management, and Master of Science in human capital management.

The College of Professional Studies provides accelerated bachelor's degree-completion programs for students with a two-year degree or equivalent earned college credit and accelerated-format master's degree programs in health-care administration, leadership, public administration, public health, and security management.

The College of Distributed Learning assists with online degree programs and courses in a variety of disciplines incorporating the University's expertise in Cyber-Active® Learning. Online instructional design, technical support, and faculty training are within the purview of the College.

The College for Information Technology actively engages learners to pursue a high-quality technical and business education and offers undergraduate degrees in computer information systems (CIS) as well as graduate degrees in CIS and management of information systems.

Location

The Bellevue University main campus features some of the most modern facilities in the region. A historic river town nudging the banks of the Missouri River, Bellevue is a small, safe, and friendly city, nestled amid a 1,300-acre forest.

Classes are offered everywhere online through the University's award-winning Cyber-Active Learning platform; at the Bellevue University main campus in Bellevue; the Lozier Professional Center in west Omaha; the Lakeside Center in west Omaha; the Taylor Meadow Office Park in Lincoln; Central Community College in Grand Island; Western Iowa Tech Community College in Sioux City, Iowa; Iowa Western Community College in Council Bluffs, Iowa; two locations in the Kansas City, Missouri, area; corporate locations; and other satellite centers throughout Nebraska, Iowa, and South Dakota.

Majors and Degrees

Bellevue University offers a variety of majors and degrees, including more than twenty accelerated bachelor's degree-completion programs offered entirely online. Programs include leadership, business, management, health care, IT, and security management. The College of Information Technology offers five information systems degrees online, including business information systems and management of information systems.

In the College of Arts and Sciences, Bachelor of Arts degree candidates may choose from more than twenty majors, including art, biology, communications, and psychology. Bachelor of Science degree candidates may select from twelve majors, including psychology and sociology.

The College of Business offers a Bachelor of Science degree in accounting and business administration.

Although some majors are not offered entirely online, all Bellevue University bachelor's degree programs include an online component.

Academic Programs

Most online programs are offered in the accelerated format, which means students can complete their bachelor's degree in as little as fifteen months if they enter the program with an associate degree, or roughly 60 credit hours. Traditional programs are offered in a format following ten-week fall, winter, spring, and summer terms. The programs leading to a Bachelor of Arts degree are offered in the humanities and related disciplines. The Bachelor of Science degree programs place more emphasis on research and scientific method. For traditional programs, students are required to follow the General Education Core Curriculum, which furnishes background and foundation knowledge to build academic excellence and career flexibility. In addition to the General

Education Core Curriculum, students complete a major in at least one academic area. Courses taken in a major area are accepted, where applicable, in meeting the requirements of the General Education Core Curriculum. The General Education Core can be completed in as little as a year. A minimum of 127 hours is required for Bachelor of Arts and Bachelor of Science degrees.

Academic Facilities

The Bellevue University main campus features the University's Riley Technology Center, which houses the heart of the computer network where all campus data, communications, and Internet traffic converge. Classrooms in the Riley Technology Center house more than 170 computers that are connected by 9 miles of wire. The University also recently finished construction of its state-of-the-art 70,000-square-foot Educational Services Building, which includes classrooms and three of the University's colleges.

The recently renovated Freeman/Lozier Library offers many services to its customers and is the primary center for support of academic research and information services. The collection includes more than 122,000 volumes in a variety of formats, including books, periodicals, microfilms, CD-ROMs, videotapes, and other media.

The library's collection is arranged according to the Library of Congress classification system and is shelved in open stacks to facilitate customer access to the collection. The library's collection is available through an online catalog, VTLS, which may be accessed through any of the library's workstations.

The library also is an active participant in Online Computer Library Center (OCLC), an international computer network of library holdings. Customers can search a variety of databases on CD-ROM and through OCLC's First Search service. As an active participant in ICON, a consortium of health science libraries in Nebraska and Iowa, the library provides an electronic connection to databases housed at the University of Nebraska Medical Center.

Costs

For 2008–09, undergraduate tuition for traditional programs is $220 per credit hour. Application and general college fees total $95 (for noninternational students). In addition, specialized instruction fees generally cover equipment, supplies, and access to all laboratories and are listed in the schedule of classes with the course listing. Some courses may require additional expenditures for materials. Undergraduate online cohort programs are $330 per credit hour.

Financial Aid

Financial aid is money available to assist students with the costs of attending college. This assistance comes from the federal and state government, the institution, and private sources. Financial aid includes grants, scholarships, work-study programs, and student loans. Grants and scholarships do not have to be repaid. Federal Work-Study allows a student to work and earn money. Student loans and loans to parents for the student must be repaid.

In general, all U.S. citizens and eligible noncitizens enrolled in an approved degree program may apply for financial aid. The student eligibility criteria are listed on the front of the Free Application for Federal Student Aid (FAFSA). Some scholarships are available to students who may not qualify for other forms of financial aid.

Faculty

The Bellevue University full-time and adjunct faculty consists of 246 men and 152 women teaching students from the freshman to the graduate level. The student-faculty ratio is 22:1.

Admission Requirements

Graduation from high school, preparatory school, or the equivalent is required, and submission of an official high school transcript, official GED transcript, or certification of home or high school completion is necessary.

Students seeking admission more than two years after graduation from high school must submit an official high school transcript, official GED credential, or certification of home or high school completion.

Students transferring from another institution of higher education must submit an official transcript from each learning institution previously attended and transfer in good standing from the last institution of higher education attended (associate and bachelor degrees, however, are transferred in full). To satisfy the minimum residency requirements for the degree, transfer students must complete a minimum of 30 hours at Bellevue University. Students dismissed from another institution during the past five years for academic or disciplinary reasons may be accepted for admission after one year has elapsed since dismissal from the other institution. In all cases of transfer, the credit evaluation is completed by the Registrar's Office under guidance of the Council for Higher Education Accreditation (CHEA).

Application and Information

The Bellevue University Admissions Office is open from 8 to 5 weekdays. Prospective students may find additional information at the University's Web site or by contacting:

Bellevue University
1000 Galvin Road South
Bellevue, Nebraska 68005
Phone: 800-756-7920
E-mail: infocenter@bellevue.edu
Web site: http://www.bellevue.edu

CHADRON STATE COLLEGE

CHADRON, NEBRASKA

The College

Chadron State College (CSC) challenges and prepares students to realize academic, personal, and professional success. These successes are developed through experiences in activities on and off campus. Founded in 1911 as Nebraska State Normal School, Chadron State has a proven record of graduates who excel. The professors are approachable and work closely with the students. The total fall 2006 enrollment was slightly over 2,400 students. The majority of the student population comes from Nebraska, Wyoming, South Dakota, and Colorado; twelve other countries are also represented on the campus. Approximately 40 percent of the undergraduate students are men and 60 percent are women.

A combination of academic offerings and faculty expertise enhances the rewards from students' efforts at Chadron State College. Chadron State offers Bachelor of Arts, Bachelor of Science, Bachelor of Applied Sciences, and Bachelor of Science in education programs (four-year degrees) as well as the Master of Arts in Education, Master of Business Administration, Master of Science in Education, Specialist in Education, and Master of Science in Organizational Management. The College is accredited by the Higher Learning Commission of the North Central Association of Colleges and Schools, the National Council for Accreditation of Teacher Education, the Council on Social Work Education, and the Nebraska State Department of Education.

A college campus environment in beautiful northwest Nebraska makes the location a great place to live and study. Tall, pine-covered buttes extend across the south end of the campus. A national forest is nearby and two state parks are within driving distance of the College. Chadron State College has six spacious residence halls, a physical activity center with an indoor track, three versatile basketball/tennis/volleyball courts, a weight-training room, five racquetball courts, and specialized classrooms for dance, cardiovascular exercise, and gymnastics. Chadron State also has a student center, a fine arts building with two theaters, an educational technology and distance learning center, and a Starbucks coffee shop in the basement of the library. More than sixty campus clubs and organizations, numerous intramural leagues, and eleven intercollegiate NCAA Division II athletic teams offer opportunities for involvement and entertainment. The newest addition is women's softball.

Location

Chadron is a community of approximately 6,000 people. Located at the junction of U.S. Highways 385 and 20, Chadron has a low crime rate. The national forest and state parks surrounding the city of Chadron provide a beautiful recreational aspect to the College. Students enjoy hiking, mountain biking, hunting, fishing, and camping as favorite pastimes. Fort Robinson, 28 miles west, was once a colorful frontier military post. The Hudson-Meng Bison Kill Site, the Agate Fossil Beds, and the Mammoth Site are close by. Nearby Cherry County produces more high-grade beef cattle than any other county in this country. The Black Hills of South Dakota are only an hour's drive to the north.

A commuter airline connects Denver, Colorado, and Chadron. The Denver Coach is also available in and out of Chadron. Six major fast food businesses and several fine dining restaurants provide numerous dining opportunities. Four theater screens provide movies each night of the week. The College brings nationally and internationally known entertainers and fine arts attractions to the city of Chadron regularly.

Majors and Degrees

Bachelor of Arts degrees are awarded in applied history/museum studies, art (with options in graphic design and art studio), business administration (with options in accounting, agribusiness, economics, finance, management, management information systems, and marketing), communication arts (with options in public relations, journalism, and communication), English and literature, family and consumer sciences (with options in child development, design and merchandising, hospitality management, and human services), history, industrial management, justice studies (with options in criminal justice and legal studies), library media, music (with options in music performance and commercial music business), psychology (with options in general psychology and substance abuse), recreation, social work, and theater.

Bachelor of Science degrees are awarded in biology (with options in environmental studies, general biology, and human biology), chemistry, clinical laboratory science (medical technology), health sciences, information science and technology, mathematics, physical science (with options in chemistry, geoscience, and physics), and range management (with options in rangeland livestock production, and range management). A minor in wildlife management is now available.

A Bachelor of Applied Sciences (B.A.S.) degree is now available. This program is designed for individuals who have completed an Associate of Science or Associate of Applied Science degree from an accredited technical or community college. The B.A.S. degree is intended to enhance technical learning with general education courses and advanced technical support courses to meet the student's individual career and education goals. Options may be selected in agricultural operations, computers and electronics, health care, industrial trades, or management services.

The Bachelor of Science in Education is offered in art (K–12), basic business education, biology, chemistry, earth science, economics, English, English (4–9), extended health education, family and consumer sciences (4–9 and 7–12), health and physical education (7–12), health education (7–12), history, industrial technology (7–12), language arts (7–12), mathematics (4–9 and 7–12), middle grades (4–9), music (K–12) and vocal music (K–8), natural science, physical education (K–8 and 7–12), physical science, physics, social science, Spanish, theater, trade and industrial education (10–12), and vocational business education.

Academic Programs

Chadron State College has an academic year that is divided into fall, spring, and summer semesters. Students seeking a baccalaureate degree from Chadron State College must complete the requirements for the program in addition to the general studies requirements. Bachelor of Arts and Bachelor of Science in education degrees are granted upon completion of a minimum total of 125 credit hours—45 of which must be at the 300 or 400 (junior or senior) level. A grade point average of at least 2.0 (on a 4.0 scale) must be maintained for the Bachelor of

Arts programs, and a GPA of at least 2.5 must be maintained for the Bachelor of Science in education programs. No more than 66 credit hours may be transferred or applied toward a baccalaureate degree from a two-year institution.

Students who possess either an A.S. or A.A.S. degree may pursue the Bachelor of Applied Science degree. Degree requirements for the B.A.S. degree include a minimum of 125 credit hours, 45 credit hours of upper-division course work (24 of the last 30 credit hours must be from CSC), 40 credit hours of CSC general studies, 36 credit hours of upper-division courses to support the student's chosen option, and a cumulative GPA of at least 2.0 (on a 4.0 scale). Prospective students should contact the Extended Campus Programs Office for an application.

Chadron State College offers alternative options for earning credit. Course work may be supplemented by internships and a cooperative learning program. Travel opportunities for credit during the school year and the summers are available. Independent studies and the College-Level Examination Program (CLEP) are available as well.

Off-Campus Programs

Several low-cost tours and field trips are arranged by the College, usually in the spring and summer months. Internships are encouraged for junior and senior students. Summer travel opportunities are developed, for which students may receive credit. In the past, tours have gone to Europe, Japan, Canada, Nassau, and Mexico as well as various parts of the United States, including Alaska and Hawaii.

Academic Facilities

The Reta King Library currently contains 211,758 books, 361,172 microform titles, and 730 periodicals. The library provides a computer laboratory, duplicating machines, and microfilm/microfiche readers for student and faculty use. Students also have access to the card catalogs of the two other state colleges in Nebraska and an electronic database with access to 3,500 full-text and 6,000 indexed periodicals. The Internet is readily accessible in the residence halls and classroom buildings. Wireless Internet access is provided on a restricted basis in the library and the student center. The College has more than 175 computers, including PCs and Macintosh computers for student use in the computer labs, classrooms, library, and residence halls.

Costs

For the 2007–08 academic year, the cost of tuition for 15 credit hours, fees, room, and board for Nebraska residents is $8424. For nonresident students, the cost is $11,724. Other expenses such as books, travel, and supplies cost approximately $2925. Nonresidents may become eligible to pay resident tuition by either qualifying for the Non-Resident Scholars Program, the Student Opportunity Award, proof of tribal enrollment, or completing requirements for obtaining legal Nebraska residency.

Financial Aid

Undergraduate students should file the Free Application for Federal Student Aid (FAFSA) online. After receiving the results from the processor, students should forward them to the College Director of Financial Aid. Undergraduate applications for financial assistance provide consideration for the Federal Pell Grant, Federal Work-Study, Federal Perkins Loan, Federal Supplemental Educational Opportunity Grant, Federal PLUS, and Federal Family Education Loan Programs as well as the State Scholarship Award Program and Student Assistance Program. A monthly payment plan is available through the Business Office. CSC provides electronic FAFSA processing.

Faculty

The College currently has a teaching faculty of 118 members (97 full-time, 70 percent of whom have terminal degrees). Faculty members are involved in student activities, and the vast majority of the undergraduate classes are taught by faculty members. The student–undergraduate faculty ratio of 17:1 allows close relationships between faculty members and students.

Student Government

A large number of students are actively involved in the student government. Numerous committees and organizations, including Student Senate, make an impact on the College. Students take part in decisions concerning scholastic, collegiate, intellectual, recreational, social, and cultural activities on and off campus.

Admission Requirements

The College has an open-admission policy for all students. Free tutoring is available to all students. Chadron State College welcomes inquiries regarding the College's programs and admission requirements. To ensure a more successful college career, Chadron State recommends that a student pursue the following courses in high school: 4 units of English; 3 units of mathematics; 3 units of social studies, including 1 unit of American history and 1 unit of global studies; 2 units of laboratory science; and other academic courses selected from areas such as foreign language, visual or performing arts, and computer literacy. Applications for admission should be submitted by currently enrolled high school students between the beginning of their last year and one month prior to the beginning of the term for which they seek admission. Individuals who have completed high school should submit their application materials at least one month prior to the beginning of the term for which they wish to be admitted.

Application and Information

Freshman applicants should submit a completed application for admission; a $15 application fee; an official high school transcript reflecting a graduation date, class rank, and overall grade point average; and ACT or SAT scores. Scores from the ACT/SAT are not required for students who graduated from high school five or more years prior to enrollment at Chadron State. Home-schooled students are accepted with a home school transcript and ACT/SAT scores.

Freshmen who have earned college credit and transfer students should submit a completed application for admission, a $15 application fee, and official transcripts from all colleges or universities previously attended. If the student has attempted fewer than 12 semester hours of credit, he or she must also submit an official high school transcript, including ACT or SAT scores. Campus visits are encouraged. For more information, students should contact:

Ms. Tena Cook
Director of Admissions
Chadron State College
1000 Main Street
Chadron, Nebraska 69337-2690
Phone: 308-432-6263
800-242-3766 (toll-free)
Fax: 308-432-6229
E-mail: inquire@csc.edu
Web site: http://www.csc.edu

UNION COLLEGE

LINCOLN, NEBRASKA

The College

Established in 1891, Union College is an accredited, comprehensive institution of higher education. Union College is rated top tier among Midwestern colleges in it's category by *U.S. News & World Report*. Union offers bachelor's degrees in more than fifty majors, collaboration agreements in engineering and other specialized fields, an honors program, a Master of Physician Assistant degree program, and the only U.S. bachelor's-level degree in international rescue and relief. Union enrolls over 1,000 students from all fifty states and twenty-six countries. Union's location in Lincoln, Nebraska, offers students recreation, internships, and part-time employment.

Union's Christian values, undergraduate emphasis, low student-teacher ratio, focus on service, and nurturing culture provide students with unique opportunities for intellectual, personal, and spiritual development. Union is a Seventh-day Adventist college that welcomes students of diverse backgrounds.

Union is renowned for the humanitarian service of its students. Each August for the last twenty-five years, approximately 80 percent of the student body voluntarily takes part in Project Impact, Union's annual community service day. This is the longest-running event of its kind, with the highest participation rate, on any college campus. In addition, each year 25 to 35 students volunteer a year of service in North America or overseas.

Union's percentage of alumni contribution is among the highest in the nation and allows for major campus improvements, such as the newly completed Ortner Center, a dining services and conference facility.

Location

Union is perched on the highest point in Lincoln, the capital of Nebraska. The 114-year-old campus features more than 100 species of trees in a beautiful parklike setting. The 50 surrounding acres of property are a part of the statewide arboretum system. The College is an eclectic blend of ivy-covered neo-Greco brick buildings, brick walkways, and modern academic and student service structures. Near the campus are connections to more than 80 miles of scenic biking and walking trails within the city and the surrounding area.

With a population of more than 250,000, Lincoln is small enough to have a sense of community yet large enough to have its own culture. Downtown Lincoln contains galleries, museums, playhouses, state and federal offices, gardens, fountains, banking centers, the Davany Sports Complex, and the Lied Center for the Performing Arts. The historic Haymarket district offers shopping, bistros, galleries, boutiques, and ethnic restaurants. As a college town, Lincoln is home to two universities: Nebraska Wesleyan University and the University of Nebraska–Lincoln.

Majors and Degrees

Union College grants the following undergraduate degrees: Associate in Science, Bachelor of Arts, Bachelor of Music, Bachelor of Science, Bachelor of Science in Nursing, Bachelor of Social Work, Bachelor of Technology, and Bachelor of Arts in Theology.

Four-year majors include art, biology, business administration (accounting, finance, management, marketing, science, small-business management), chemistry (biochemistry), clinical laboratory science, communication (journalism, public relations), computing (business, computer information systems, computer science, graphic design), education (elementary, secondary—see endorsements), English (literature, writing and speaking), exercise science, general studies, graphic design, health and human performance (business/sport management), history, institutional development, international language studies (French, German, Spanish), international rescue and relief (business communication, dental preprofessional, human services and counseling, medical preprofessional, paramedical, physician assistant preprofessional, project development), international studies, mathematics, music (music education—instrumental, keyboard, and vocal; music performance—conducting, instrumental, keyboard, and vocal), natural science education, nursing, pastoral care, physician assistant studies, physics, psychology, religion, social science, social work, and theology.

Two-year majors include accounting,* art, business administration, English as a second language, graphic design, music pedagogy, and pre–allied health.

Many of the four-year majors listed above are also offered as minors. Minors in additional areas include biblical languages, disaster preparedness (nursing majors only), drama, emergency management, missions and evangelism, prelaw, sociology, survival and rescue, and youth ministry.

Secondary education endorsements include art, biology, business, chemistry, elementary education, English, English as a second language, history, information technology, language arts, mathematics, music, physical education, physics, psychology, religious education, and social science.

Preprofessional programs are available in chiropractic, clinical laboratory science, cytotechnology, dental assistant studies, dental hygiene, dentistry, dietetic technology, emergency medical care, engineering, health information management, law, medical radiography, medical technology, medicine, naturopathic medicine, nursing, nutrition, nutrition and dietetics, occupational therapy, optometry, osteopathic medicine, pharmacy, physical therapy, physical therapy assistant studies, physician assistant studies, podiatric medicine, public health, radiography/radiation technology, respiratory care, respiratory therapy, speech, speech pathology, and veterinary medicine.

Union's Best of Both Worlds Program allows students to develop a personalized degree in many disciplines that are offered by other colleges and universities in Lincoln.

Academic Programs

Union offers a traditional liberal arts education combined with practical experiences such as internships, career counseling, study abroad, and leadership opportunities.

Baccalaureate degrees are awarded after students complete all graduation requirements, including general education, major, and contextual requirements and electives, for a minimum of 128 semester hours (64 for associate degrees). At least 40 of the 128 hours must be courses numbered at the 300 level or above. A minimum of 56 hours must be completed in four-year colleges or universities. Three writing-designated (WR) courses are required after successful completion of freshman composition (ENGL 111 and ENGL 112). A minimum grade point average (GPA) of 2.0 is required in all course work attempted at Union College and all transferred credits. (Students should consult an academic bulletin for further details.)

Union Scholars, the College's honors program, offers an enriched academic experience with a global focus, innovative classes, volunteer service, an independent research project in the senior year, and substantial scholarship awards. Students in the program are required to complete one honors course abroad.

The Teaching Learning Center provides academic assistance for students with disabilities, students on academic probation, first-year freshmen with low GPAs or test scores, and struggling students who desire personal assistance. Services include personal coaching/advising, study-skills training, time management and organization assistance, and reasonable accommodations for students with verified disabilities.

Union offers three levels of English as a second language (ESL), from beginning conversation to university-level preparation. Students with TOEFL scores between 475 and 549 may take selected university-level courses. The TOEFL or a satisfactory ACT score is required of all nonnative English speakers upon arrival. Completion of the ESL program occurs when the student is able to score at least 550 on the TOEFL.

Academic Facilities

The Engel Hall fine arts complex houses both visual and musical arts programs. The Everett Dick Building includes the divisions of humanities, business and computer science, human development, and religion. Microcomputer labs use cutting-edge software and hardware and provide access to the Internet and advanced business, art, and desktop publishing programs. Jorgensen Hall houses engineering, chemistry, biology, mathematics, and physics. Science students use an in-house HP 5890 capillary gas chromatography unit and other advanced analytical equipment. The Ella Johnson Crandall Memorial Library holdings include 175,000 volumes (books, audiovisual items, microforms, etc.), with additional access to 9,000 electronic periodicals and subscriptions to approximately 600 print periodical titles. In addition to health science classrooms, offices, and labs, the Larson Lifestyle Center houses a 25-meter pool, weight rooms, a Jacuzzi, tennis courts, and sand volleyball courts. Classroom buildings contain computer and scientific/health science laboratories. Residence halls and other key campus buildings feature wireless networks and online connectivity.

The Career Center hosts on-campus career fairs and offers resources to assist students in making career decisions, writing resumes and cover letters, conducting job searches, perfecting interview techniques, and arranging career shadowing and internships.

Costs

Annual estimated expenses for the 2008–09 academic year total $23,530 (tuition, $16,440; general fee, $480; room and board, $5610; and textbooks and supplies, $1000). Tuition is based on 12 to 17 credit hours.

Financial Aid

Union College tailors financial aid packages to fit individual student needs. Proceeds from more than $7.9 million in endowments (150 endowed scholarship funds), federal and institutional scholarships, student loans, grants, and work-study programs are available to qualified students. On- and off-campus employment may also defray costs and provide career experience. Grants and loans are available from federal and state agencies.

Students who have finished a four-year degree at Union and later decide to change careers may return for another degree, tuition free. (Interested students should consult the Academic Bulletin for details of the Guaranteed Degree Program.)

Students apply for financial aid by completing the Free Application for Federal Student Aid (FAFSA), which is available at any local college, many libraries, and high school guidance counselors' offices or on the Internet. March 15 is the priority FAFSA deadline at Union.

Faculty

The Union College faculty includes 58 full-time faculty members and additional part-time faculty members. Nearly half of the full-time faculty members hold terminal degrees.

In addition to being qualified professionals, Union's professors are Christian role models who portray their values through their actions and speech. They are committed to the art of teaching and to caring for each student. Professors, not graduate assistants, teach classes and supervise labs.

Student Government

Students participate in College governance through elected positions in the Associated Student Body (ASB). Students are also members of most campus committees. Regularly scheduled town hall assemblies are held to allow students direct interaction with administrators. In addition to the ASB, other recognized campus clubs and organizations meet regularly.

Admission Requirements

Specific admission requirements include a GPA of at least 2.5 (for native English speakers) and a minimum ACT score of 18 or SAT score of 870 (old SAT) or 1290 (new SAT). Some applicants with lower GPAs or test scores may be accepted into the Freshman Development Program. Applicants also need three references; high school transcripts, home school transcripts, or a GED certificate; and transcripts from other colleges (if applicable). Special assistance and admission is available to students with certified learning differences; interested students should call the Teaching Learning Center at 402-486-2506.

Union College does not discriminate on the basis of race, religion, disability, age, or gender.

Application and Information

Applications may be submitted year-round. Notification of acceptance occurs approximately two weeks after all requirements are met. Prospective applicants should contact:

Office of Admissions
Union College
3800 South 48th Street
Lincoln, Nebraska 68506
Phone: 402-486-2504 (outside North America)
800-228-4600 (toll-free inside North America)
Fax: 402-486-2566
E-mail: ucenroll@ucollege.edu
Web site: http://www.ucollege.edu

Located at the center of the campus, Union's Ortner Center includes the Campus Welcome Center, Union Market Dining Services, McClelland Art Gallery, a conference center, and many other features.

UNIVERSITY OF NEBRASKA–LINCOLN
LINCOLN, NEBRASKA

The University

The University of Nebraska–Lincoln is one of today's most dynamic universities. Over the past decade, the University has developed a national reputation for undergraduate education grounded in technology, research, innovation, and student engagement. Undergraduates have the opportunity to work with world-renowned researchers, dedicated professors, and accomplished peers.

Established in 1869, the University of Nebraska–Lincoln has a rich tradition of excellence. Students join more than 200,000 alumni who have made their mark as industry leaders in business, engineering, the arts, journalism, education, and the sciences. A degree from Nebraska opens doors. Nebraska graduates recently interviewed on campus with major national companies such as Abercrombie & Fitch, the Central Intelligence Agency (CIA), IBM, Microsoft, Sprint, Target, and the *Washington Post.* While attending Nebraska, students have built-in connections with 116 graduate degree programs, including those in the University of Nebraska law, dental, and medical centers located either on campus or 50 miles east in Omaha.

The University of Nebraska–Lincoln is a major research university. Nebraska is one of sixteen schools nationwide to be recognized as innovators in undergraduate education and one of only five major research universities to be named to the "first tier" for its innovative programs for students. Nebraska has also been a member of the Association of American Universities since 1909; it is one of only sixty-two universities to claim this prestigious membership. This gives students an advantage. Classes are taught by faculty members who are experts in their fields, and students find a diverse variety of academic choices.

At Nebraska, technology is invented, and real-world problems are solved. Researchers and students at Nebraska have developed everything from turfgrass that can survive with very little water to eggs that contain less cholesterol to a highway guard rail that helps stop the impact of a car crash.

Nebraska's community is local and global. More than 18,000 undergraduate students from a wide range of ethnic, cultural, and economic backgrounds make their college home at Nebraska. Many students choose to live in one of Nebraska's sixteen residence halls, including the new apartment-style the Village and Courtyards. Each residence hall has high-speed Internet access, cable television, air conditioning, and local phone service in every room and a resident assistant and health aid on every floor. Greek organizations at Nebraska offer social, academic, community-service, and campus-living opportunities. Nebraska has twenty-one fraternities, fourteen sororities, four National Pan-Hellenic Council fraternities, two National Pan-Hellenic Council sororities, one Multicultural Greek Council fraternity, and two Multicultural Greek Council sororities. Greek recruitment information is mailed to students in the spring prior to enrollment.

Location

The University is located in the capital city of Lincoln, a community of 250,000 that combines a friendly college-town atmosphere with the cultural and employment opportunities of a larger city. Students looking for cultural experiences and internship possibilities find art, music, theater, state government, and industry all within walking distance of the campus. On campus, students receive ticket discounts for major Broadway performances such as *Hairspray* and *Chicago* at one of the Midwest's premier venues, the Lied Center for Performing Arts. Lincoln has more parks per capita than any other city in the U.S. and a network of bike paths that extends far beyond the city limits. There are sixteen golf courses, hundreds of restaurants, more than thirty movie screens, major shopping malls, and a restored downtown historic district complete with specialty shops, coffeehouses, and a dinner theater. Major metropolitan cities—such as Kansas City, Chicago, Minneapolis–St. Paul, and Denver—are within a day's drive, and Lincoln is easily accessible by plane, train, and bus.

Majors and Degrees

The University of Nebraska–Lincoln offers 150 undergraduate majors, providing students the opportunity to choose a challenging course of study and gain a solid background of fundamentals, critical thinking, and experience. With more than 87 percent of the classes under 50 students, there is a balance between lecture and lab and practice and theory, and the classes are taught by faculty members who are highly respected in their fields. Degree programs are distributed over eight Colleges: Agricultural Sciences and Natural Resources, Architecture, Arts and Sciences, Business Administration, Education and Human Sciences, Engineering, Fine and Performing Arts, and Journalism and Mass Communications.

Academic Programs

Nebraska offers classes during the fall and spring semesters and during the summer sessions, which consist of a three-week presession, two 5-week sessions, and one 8-week session. Undergraduates must take a minimum of 12 hours to be full-time. Most undergraduate degree programs require 120 to 130 credit hours for graduation. Each degree program at Nebraska has specific course requirements, and some require a minimum grade point average.

The University Honors Program provides motivated students with academic challenges, opportunities to learn from and do research with top faculty members, and a community of supportive peers. Students admitted to the highly selective J. D. Edwards Honors Program in Computer Science and Management become tomorrow's leaders in technology applications and solutions.

Outside the classroom, students can participate in various experiences, including study abroad, internships, cooperative educational programs, ROTC, and research opportunities with faculty members. Students may also participate in tutoring and mentoring programs such as supplemental instruction, the Husker Teammates program, and the English conversation program.

Off-Campus Programs

Students gain professional experience through an extensive internship and cooperative education program, connecting them to industry leaders in the U.S. government, NASA, General Motors, Microsoft, Gannett Newspapers, and Gallup. Through Nebraska's study-abroad programs, students can choose to study in one of more than fifty countries and at 140 universities. Financial aid often applies to study-abroad programs. Field courses are held at on-site locations to give students hands-on experience. Examples of popular courses include excavation of earth lodges at Fontenelle Forest and the study of parasitology specimens at Cedar Point Biological Station in western Nebraska.

Academic Facilities

The University is housed on 616 acres of land across two campuses, City Campus and East Campus. City Campus is the home of the nationally renowned Sheldon Memorial Art Gallery and Sculpture Garden, the Christlieb Collection of Western Art, and several other galleries. The Lied Center for Performing Arts draws big-name acts in contemporary entertainment, and the University of Nebraska State Museum boasts a world-class fossil collection. A number of specialized centers offer assistance to the state's citizens, including the Bureau of Business Research, the Food Processing Center, and the Technology Transfer Office, which expedites the movement of University-developed knowledge into real-world products and processes.

Nebraska also offers students a variety of research libraries. Love Library is the main library located on City Campus and contains about half of the University's collection of 3 million volumes. C. Y. Thompson Library on East Campus and the various departmental libraries offer students excellent research facilities.

Costs

For the 2007–08 academic year, in-state tuition and fees were $6315.50 and out-of-state tuition and fees were $16,335.50 (based on a single undergraduate student taking 15 credit hours per semester for two semesters). Room and board were $6653 for a double room for two semesters. Books and supplies are estimated at $900.

Financial Aid

The University of Nebraska offers one of the most affordable, high-quality educations in the country. It has one of the lowest total costs among Big 12, Big 10, and AAU institutions. In addition, about 75 percent of full-time undergraduate students at the University receive some type of scholarship or financial aid. During the 2005–06 school year, full-time freshman students received nearly $8 million in scholarships. Nebraska offers a wide range of scholarships based on academic achievement, leadership and involvement, and specific academic interests such as engineering, mathematics, computer science, business, and agricultural sciences. While scholarship awards are made on a rolling basis, full consideration for freshman scholarships is given to students whose admissions application materials are complete and on file in the Office of Admissions by January 15 (March 15 for transfer students).

Faculty

Nebraska has a strong reputation for excellence in teaching. Highly respected in their fields, Nebraska faculty members conduct research that leads to new discoveries and pass on their new knowledge to the students. Some of the recent achievements by Nebraska faculty members include professor Ron Bonnstetter being named as Outstanding Science Teacher Educator of the Year by the Association for the Education of Teachers of Science; James Van Etten being elected to the National Academy of Sciences, one of the highest honors for a U.S. scientist; Susan Sheridan earning a $5-million children and family education grant; and Michael Meagher earning a $6.5-million botulism grant to help the fight against bioterrorism.

Student Government

The Association for Students at the University of Nebraska (ASUN) serves as the representative voice for Nebraska students by gathering input from all students, advocating student concerns to the administration, and providing essential student services, ultimately working to improve the campus and enhance student life. The functions of ASUN are carried out by elected student senators representing each of the nine academic colleges, the divisions of general studies and graduate studies, and the professional schools.

Admission Requirements

In order to be eligible for assured admission to the University of Nebraska–Lincoln, students who graduated from high school after 1997 must have completed a set of 16 units of core courses, including 4 units of English, 4 units of math, 3 units of natural science, 3 units of social science, and 2 units of foreign language (1 unit = one high school year). In addition, students must have graduated in the upper half of their graduating class or earned a combined score of 950 or higher on the SAT (Critical Reading and Math only) or a composite of 20 or higher on the ACT. Transfer students must also have a minimum 2.0 cumulative grade point average and at least a 2.0 GPA in their final semester of attendance at another postsecondary institution. Some academic programs may require higher test scores and class ranks than these minimums. Students are encouraged to apply for admission even if they do not meet one or more of the above requirements.

Application and Information

Students interested in applying for the fall semester should apply and pay the $250 enrollment deposit by the May 1 deadline, and those interested in applying for the spring semester should apply by December 1. While scholarship awards are made on a rolling basis, full consideration for freshman scholarships is given to students whose admissions application materials are complete and on file in the Office of Admissions by January 15 (March 15 for transfer students). A $45 application fee is required as are official transcripts from the student's high school and/or postsecondary institution and official ACT or SAT scores. Students whose first language is not English should also send official TOEFL scores.

To make arrangements to visit the University or to receive an application and admissions information, students should contact:

Office of Admissions
University of Nebraska–Lincoln
313 North 13th Street
Lincoln, Nebraska 68588-0256
Phone: 402-472-2023
800-742-8800 (toll-free)
Fax: 402-472-0670
E-mail: admissions@unl.edu
Web site: http://www.unl.edu
http://www.admissions.unl.edu

Students participating in the J. D. Edwards Honors Program live in the Kauffman Center, one of the many living and learning communities offered at Nebraska. Opened in 2001, the center contains 82,500 square feet of classrooms, living space, and social areas.

NEVADA

THE ART INSTITUTE OF LAS VEGAS

Henderson, Nevada **www.ailv.artinstitutes.edu/**

- **Proprietary** 4-year, founded 2002, part of Education Management Corporation
- **Suburban** campus
- **Coed**
- **Moderately difficult** entrance level

Faculty *Student/faculty ratio:* 19:1.

Majors Animation, interactive technology, video graphics and special effects; cinematography and film/video production; fashion merchandising; graphic design; interior design; photography; restaurant, culinary, and catering management; restaurant/food services management; retail management; Web page, digital/multimedia and information resources design.

Academics *Calendar:* quarters. *Degrees:* certificates, diplomas, associate, and bachelor's.

Student Life *Campus security:* 24-hour emergency response devices.

Costs (2007–08) *Tuition:* for the 2007–08 academic year, tuition is $19,872. Housing is $5850. Other costs include a first-quarter supply kit and other course necessities. Culinary arts students also pay a lab fee. *Payment plans:* tuition prepayment, installment, deferred payment.

Applying *Options:* electronic application. *Application fee:* $50. *Required:* essay or personal statement, high school transcript, interview.

Freshman Application Contact The Art Institute of Las Vegas, 2350 Corporate Circle, Henderson, NV 89074. *Phone:* 702-369-9944. *Fax:* 702-992-8494.

See page 1494 for the College Close-Up.

DEVRY UNIVERSITY

Henderson, Nevada **www.devry.edu/**

- **Proprietary** comprehensive, part of DeVry University
- **Coed** 127 undergraduate students, 45% full-time, 43% women, 57% men
- **Minimally difficult** entrance level

Undergraduates 57 full-time, 70 part-time. 2% are from out of state, 20% African American, 14% Asian American or Pacific Islander, 22% Hispanic American, 0.8% international, 18% transferred in. *Retention:* 17% of 2006 full-time freshmen returned.

Freshmen *Admission:* 27 enrolled.

Faculty *Total:* 6. *Student/faculty ratio:* 52:1.

Majors Business administration and management; business administration, management and operations related; electrical, electronic and communications engineering technology.

Academics *Calendar:* semesters. *Degrees:* associate, bachelor's, and master's. *Special study options:* academic remediation for entering students, accelerated degree program, adult/continuing education programs, advanced placement credit, distance learning, part-time degree program, services for LD students, summer session for credit.

Student Life *Housing:* college housing not available.

Costs (2008–09) *Tuition:* $13,810 full-time, $515 per credit part-time. *Required fees:* $80 full-time.

Applying *Options:* electronic application, early admission, deferred entrance. *Application fee:* $50. *Required:* high school transcript, interview. *Application deadlines:* rolling (freshmen), rolling (transfers). *Notification:* continuous (freshmen), continuous (transfers).

Freshman Application Contact DeVry University, 2490 Paseo Verde Parkway, Suite 150, Henderson, NV 89074.

GREAT BASIN COLLEGE

Elko, Nevada **www.gbcnv.edu/**

- **State-supported** primarily 2-year, founded 1967, part of University and Community College System of Nevada
- **Small-town** 45-acre campus
- **Endowment** $150,000
- **Coed**
- **Noncompetitive** entrance level

Academics *Calendar:* semesters. *Degrees:* certificates, associate, and bachelor's.

Student Life *Campus security:* evening patrols by trained security personnel.

Costs (2007–08) *Tuition:* state resident $1643 full-time; nonresident $4335 full-time. *Room and board:* $4520; room only: $1900.

Financial Aid Of all full-time matriculated undergraduates who enrolled in 2006, 35 Federal Work-Study jobs (averaging $1000). 50 state and other part-time jobs (averaging $1800).

Applying *Options:* electronic application, early admission, deferred entrance. *Application fee:* $5. *Required:* high school transcript.

Freshman Application Contact Ms. Julie Byrnes, Director of Enrollment Management, Great Basin College, 1500 College Parkway, Elko, NV 89801-3348. *Phone:* 775-753-2271. *Fax:* 775-753-2311. *E-mail:* stdsvc@gbcnv.edu.

ITT TECHNICAL INSTITUTE

Henderson, Nevada **www.itt-tech.edu/**

- **Proprietary** primarily 2-year, founded 1997, part of ITT Educational Services, Inc
- **Coed**
- **Minimally difficult** entrance level

Academics *Degrees:* associate and bachelor's.

Standardized Tests *Required:* Wonderlic aptitude test (for admission).

Financial Aid Of all full-time matriculated undergraduates who enrolled in 2006, 6 Federal Work-Study jobs (averaging $5000).

Applying *Options:* deferred entrance. *Application fee:* $100. *Required:* high school transcript, interview. *Recommended:* letters of recommendation.

Freshman Application Contact Ms. Anne Buzak, Director of Recruitment, ITT Technical Institute, 168 North Gibson Road, Henderson, NV 89014. *Phone:* 702-558-5404. *Toll-free phone:* 800-488-8459.

MORRISON UNIVERSITY

Reno, Nevada **www.morrison.neumont.edu/**

- **Proprietary** comprehensive, founded 1902
- **Urban** 2-acre campus
- **Coed**
- **Noncompetitive** entrance level

Academics *Calendar:* 5 sessions per year. *Degrees:* certificates, diplomas, associate, bachelor's, and master's.

Student Life *Campus security:* 24-hour emergency response devices, late-night transport/escort service, evening patrols by security.

Costs (2007–08) *Tuition:* $8000 full-time, $800 per course part-time. *Required fees:* $25 full-time.

Applying *Options:* early admission, deferred entrance. *Application fee:* $25. *Required:* high school transcript, interview. *Required for some:* essay or personal statement. *Recommended:* CPAt of 160 for paralegal program.

Freshman Application Contact Mr. Charles Timinsky, Director of Enrollment, Morrison University, 10315 Professional Circle, Reno, NV 89521. *Phone:* 775-850-0700 Ext. 101. *Toll-free phone:* 800-369-6144. *Fax:* 775-850-0711. *E-mail:* ctiminsky@morrison.neumont.edu.

NEVADA STATE COLLEGE AT HENDERSON

Henderson, Nevada **www.nsc.nevada.edu/**

- **State-supported** 4-year, founded 2002, part of Nevada System of Higher Education
- **Suburban** 520-acre campus with easy access to Las Vegas
- **Coed**
- 39% of applicants were admitted

Faculty *Student/faculty ratio:* 9:1.

Academics *Calendar:* semesters. *Degree:* bachelor's.

Student Life *Campus security:* late-night transport/escort service.

Standardized Tests *Recommended:* SAT or ACT (for admission).

Costs (2007–08) *One-time required fee:* $20. *Tuition:* state resident $0 full-time; nonresident $8097 full-time, $90 per credit part-time. *Required fees:* $2262 full-time, $94 per credit part-time.

Applying *Application fee:* $30. *Required:* high school transcript, minimum 2.0 GPA.

Freshman Application Contact Ms. Patricia Ring, Registrar, Nevada State College at Henderson, 1125 Nevada State Drive, Henderson, NV 89107. *Phone:* 702-992-2114. *Fax:* 702-992-2111. *E-mail:* patricia.ring@nsc.nevada.edu.

SIERRA NEVADA COLLEGE

Incline Village, Nevada **www.sierranevada.edu/**

- **Independent** comprehensive, founded 1969
- **Small-town** 20-acre campus with easy access to Reno
- **Endowment** $3.5 million
- **Coed**
- **Moderately difficult** entrance level

Faculty *Student/faculty ratio:* 10:1.

Academics *Calendar:* semesters. *Degrees:* bachelor's and master's.

Student Life *Campus security:* 24-hour emergency response devices and patrols, controlled dormitory access.

Standardized Tests *Required:* SAT or ACT (for admission).

Costs (2007–08) *Tuition:* $976 per unit part-time.

Financial Aid Of all full-time matriculated undergraduates who enrolled in 2003, 203 applied for aid, 203 were judged to have need. 63 Federal Work-Study jobs (averaging $2000). 2 state and other part-time jobs (averaging $2500). In 2003, 36 non-need-based awards were made. *Average percent of need met:* 60. *Average financial aid package:* $14,000. *Average need-based gift aid:* $6000. *Average non-need-based aid:* $8000. *Average indebtedness upon graduation:* $18,000.

Applying *Options:* electronic application, early admission, deferred entrance. *Required:* essay or personal statement, high school transcript, minimum 2.0 GPA. *Required for some:* letters of recommendation, school report form for high school seniors. *Recommended:* interview.

Freshman Application Contact Matt Delekta, James McMaster, Dean of Enrollment Services and Registrar, Sierra Nevada College, 999 Tahoe Boulevard, David Hall II, Incline Village, NV 89451. *Phone:* 866-412-4636. *Toll-free phone:* 775-831-1314. *Fax:* 775-831-6223. *E-mail:* admissions@sierranevada.edu.

See page 1496 for the College Close-Up.

UNIVERSITY OF NEVADA, LAS VEGAS

Las Vegas, Nevada **www.unlv.edu/**

- **State-supported** university, founded 1957, part of Nevada System of Higher Education
- **Urban** 358-acre campus
- **Endowment** $134.3 million
- **Coed** 21,962 undergraduate students, 71% full-time, 56% women, 44% men
- **Moderately difficult** entrance level, 68% of applicants were admitted

The University of Nevada, Las Vegas (UNLV), offers 220 undergraduate, master's, and doctoral degree programs. The University serves more than 28,000 students from the U.S. and abroad. The average class size is 30, and the student-teacher ratio is 21:1. A premier metropolitan research university, UNLV is located on a beautifully landscaped 350-acre campus that is just minutes from McCarran International Airport and the world-famous Las Vegas Strip. All programs are accredited by the Northwest Commission on Colleges and Universities.

Undergraduates 15,677 full-time, 6,285 part-time. Students come from 51 states and territories, 68 other countries, 20% are from out of state, 9% African American, 17% Asian American or Pacific Islander, 13% Hispanic American, 1% Native American, 4% international, 9% transferred in, 10% live on campus. *Retention:* 71% of 2006 full-time freshmen returned.

Freshmen *Admission:* 7,875 applied, 5,348 admitted, 2,859 enrolled. *Average high school GPA:* 3.28. *Test scores:* SAT critical reading scores over 500: 55%; SAT math scores over 500: 59%; ACT scores over 18: 86%; SAT critical reading scores over 600: 14%; SAT math scores over 600: 19%; ACT scores over 24: 29%; SAT critical reading scores over 700: 1%; SAT math scores over 700: 2%; ACT scores over 30: 2%.

Faculty *Total:* 1,677, 57% full-time. *Student/faculty ratio:* 18:1.

Majors Accounting; adult and continuing education; African-American/Black studies; anthropology; applied mathematics; architecture; art; art history, criticism and conservation; athletic training; athletic training/sports medicine; biochemistry; biology/biological sciences; business administration and management; chemistry; city/urban, community and regional planning; civil engineering; clinical laboratory science/medical technology; communication/speech communication and rhetoric; comparative literature; computer engineering; computer science; construction engineering; criminal justice/law enforcement administration; culinary arts; culinary arts related; cultural studies; dance; dramatic/theater arts; dramatic/theater arts and stagecraft related; economics; education; electrical, electronics and communications engineering; elementary education; English; entrepreneurship; environmental studies; film/cinema studies; finance; fine/studio arts; French; geological and earth sciences/geosciences related; geology/earth science; German; gerontology; health/health care administration; health/medical physics; health science; health teacher education; history; hospitality administration; hospitality administration related; hotel/motel administration; human resources management; human services; interdisciplinary studies; interior architecture; international business/trade/commerce; jazz/jazz studies; kindergarten/preschool education; kinesiology and exercise science; landscape architecture; management information systems; marketing/marketing management; marriage and family therapy/counseling; mass communication/media; mathematics; mechanical engineering; medical laboratory technology; medical radiologic technology; music; music theory and composition; nuclear medical technology; nursing (registered nurse training); nutrition sciences; parks, recreation and leisure; philosophy; physical education teaching and coaching; physics; physics related; political science and government; psychology; real estate; Romance languages; secondary education; social sciences; social work; sociology; Spanish; special education; sport and fitness administration/management; statistics; tourism and travel services management; women's studies.

Academics *Calendar:* semesters. *Degrees:* certificates, bachelor's, master's, doctoral, first professional, post-master's, postbachelor's, and first professional certificates. *Special study options:* academic remediation for entering students, accelerated degree program, adult/continuing education programs, advanced placement credit, cooperative education, distance learning, double majors, English as a second language, honors programs, independent study, internships, off-campus study, part-time degree program, services for LD students, student-designed majors, study abroad, summer session for credit.

Computers on Campus 2,100 computers/terminals and 3,000 ports are available on campus for general student use. Students can access the following: online (class) registration. Campuswide network is available. 100% of college-owned or -operated housing units are wired for high-speed Internet access. Wireless service is available via entire campus.

Student Life *Housing:* on-campus residence required for freshman year. *Options:* coed, disabled students. Campus housing is university owned. Freshman applicants given priority for college housing. *Activities and organizations:* drama/theater group, student-run newspaper, radio and television station, choral group, marching band, Inter-Varsity Christian Fellowship, Rebel Ski Club, Student Organization of Latinos, Latter Day Saints, Hawaii Club, national fraternities, national sororities. *Campus security:* 24-hour emergency response devices and patrols, late-night transport/escort service, controlled dormitory access. *Student services:* health clinic, personal/psychological counseling, women's center.

Athletics Member NCAA. All Division I except football (Division I-A). *Intercollegiate sports:* baseball M (s), basketball M (s)/W (s), cheerleading M (s)/W (s), cross-country running W (s), equestrian sports W, golf M (s), soccer M (s)/W (s), softball W (s), swimming and diving M (s)/W (s), tennis M (s)/W (s), track and field W (s), volleyball W (s). *Intramural sports:* badminton M/W, basketball M/W, bowling M/W, cross-country running M/W, football M/W, golf M/W, racquetball M/W, soccer M/W, softball M/W, swimming and diving M/W, tennis M/W, track and field M/W, volleyball M/W.

Standardized Tests *Recommended:* SAT or ACT (for admission).

Costs (2008–09) *Tuition:* state resident $4005 full-time, $130 per credit hour part-time; nonresident $15,100 full-time, $272 per credit hour part-time. *Required fees:* $578 full-time, $4 per credit part-time, $229 per term part-time. *Room and board:* $9808; room only: $6232.

Financial Aid Of all full-time matriculated undergraduates who enrolled in 2006, 7,960 applied for aid, 5,933 were judged to have need, 449 had their need fully met. In 2006, 659 non-need-based awards were made. *Average percent of need met:* 64%. *Average financial aid package:* $6037. *Average need-based loan:* $3979. *Average need-based gift aid:* $4280. *Average non-need-based aid:* $2091. *Average indebtedness upon graduation:* $17,944.

Applying *Options:* deferred entrance. *Application fee:* $60. *Required:* high school transcript, minimum 2.75 GPA. *Required for some:* 2 letters of recommendation. *Application deadline:* 7/20 (freshmen). *Notification:* continuous (freshmen), continuous (transfers).

Freshman Application Contact Ms. Kristi Rodriguez, Director for Undergraduate Recruitment, University of Nevada, Las Vegas, 4505 Maryland Parkway, Box 451021, Las Vegas, NV 89154-1021. *Phone:* 702-774-8001. *Fax:* 702-774-8008. *E-mail:* undergraduate.recruitment@unlv.edu.

See page 1498 for the College Close-Up.

UNIVERSITY OF NEVADA, RENO

Reno, Nevada **www.unr.edu/**

- **State-supported** university, founded 1874, part of Nevada System of Higher Education
- **Urban** 200-acre campus
- **Endowment** $231.4 million
- **Coed** 13,205 undergraduate students, 78% full-time, 53% women, 47% men
- **Moderately difficult** entrance level, 88% of applicants were admitted

Undergraduates 10,342 full-time, 2,863 part-time. Students come from 47 states and territories, 42 other countries, 17% are from out of state, 3% African American, 7% Asian American or Pacific Islander, 8% Hispanic American, 1% Native American, 2% international, 7% transferred in, 11% live on campus. *Retention:* 78% of 2006 full-time freshmen returned.

Freshmen *Admission:* 4,683 applied, 4,111 admitted, 2,278 enrolled. *Average high school GPA:* 3.35. *Test scores:* SAT critical reading scores over 500: 60%; SAT math scores over 500: 63%; SAT writing scores over 500: 53%; ACT scores over 18: 91%; SAT critical reading scores over 600: 20%; SAT math scores over 600: 23%; SAT writing scores over 600: 14%; ACT scores over 24: 40%; SAT critical reading scores over 700: 2%; SAT math scores over 700: 3%; SAT writing scores over 700: 1%; ACT scores over 30: 5%.

Faculty *Total:* 891, 66% full-time, 72% with terminal degrees. *Student/faculty ratio:* 19:1.

Majors Accounting; advertising; agricultural animal breeding; agricultural economics; agricultural teacher education; animal sciences; anthropology; art; art history, criticism and conservation; art teacher education; biochemistry; biology/biological sciences; biotechnology; broadcast journalism; business/commerce; business/managerial economics; business teacher education; chemical engineering; chemistry; child development; civil engineering; communication/speech communication and rhetoric; computer and information sciences; computer engineering; computer science; construction engineering technology; criminology; dramatic/theater arts; education (specific subject areas) related; electrical, electronics and communications engineering; elementary education; engineering physics; English; English composition; English language and literature related; English/language arts teacher education; entrepreneurship; environmental/environmental health engineering; family and consumer sciences/home economics teacher education; finance; foods, nutrition, and wellness; foreign language teacher education; forestry; French; general studies; geography; geological/geophysical engineering; geology/earth science; geophysics and seismology; German; health/medical preparatory programs related; health professions related; health teacher education; history; hospitality administration; housing and human environments related; human development and family studies; human resources management; international business/trade/commerce; international relations and affairs; journalism; logistics and materials management; marketing/marketing management; mathematics; mathematics teacher education; mechanical engineering; metallurgical engineering; mining and mineral engineering; music; music performance; music teacher education; natural resources/conservation; natural resources management and policy; nursing (registered nurse training); parks, recreation and leisure; philosophy; physical education teaching and coaching; physics; political science and government; pre-medical studies; pre-veterinary studies; psychology; science teacher education; science, technology and society; social psychology; social science teacher education; social studies teacher education; social work; sociology; Spanish; special education; speech-language pathology; technology/industrial arts teacher education; trade and industrial teacher education; water resources engineering; wildlife and wildlands science and management; women's studies.

Academics *Calendar:* semesters. *Degrees:* bachelor's, master's, doctoral, first professional, post-master's, postbachelor's, and first professional certificates. *Special study options:* academic remediation for entering students, adult/continuing education programs, advanced placement credit, distance learning, double majors, English as a second language, honors programs, independent study, internships, off-campus study, part-time degree program, services for LD students, study abroad, summer session for credit. *ROTC:* Army (b). *Unusual degree programs:* 3-2 biotechnology.

Computers on Campus 500 computers/terminals are available on campus for general student use. Students can access the following: computer help desk, free student e-mail accounts, online (class) registration, online (class) schedules. Campuswide network is available. Wireless service is available via learning centers, libraries, student centers.

Student Life *Housing options:* coed, men-only, women-only, disabled students. Campus housing is university owned. Freshman applicants given priority for college housing. *Activities and organizations:* drama/theater group, student-run newspaper, radio station, choral group, marching band, Intervarsity Christian Fellowship, Student Ambassadors, Young Democrats, Asian American Association, Blue Crew, national fraternities, national sororities. *Campus security:* 24-hour emergency response devices and patrols, late-night transport/escort service, controlled dormitory access. *Student services:* health clinic, personal/psychological counseling, women's center, legal services.

Athletics Member NCAA. All Division I except football (Division I-A). *Intercollegiate sports:* baseball M (s), basketball M (s)/W (s), cheerleading M/W, cross-country running W (s), golf M (s)/W (s), riflery M (s)/W (s), skiing (cross-country) M (s)/W (s), skiing (downhill) M (s)/W (s), soccer W (s), softball W (s), swimming and diving W (s), tennis M (s)/W (s), track and field W (s), volleyball W (s). *Intramural sports:* basketball M/W, bowling M/W, cross-country running M/W, equestrian sports M/W, football M, golf M/W, racquetball M/W, rock climbing M/W, rugby M/W, skiing (cross-country) M/W, skiing (downhill) M/W, soccer M/W, softball M/W, swimming and diving M/W, table tennis M/W, tennis M/W, track and field M/W, ultimate Frisbee M/W, volleyball M/W, water polo M/W.

Standardized Tests *Required for some:* SAT or ACT (for admission).

Costs (2008–09) *Tuition:* state resident $4005 full-time, $134 per credit part-time; nonresident $15,100 full-time, $276 per credit part-time. *Required fees:* $406 full-time. *Room and board:* $9989; room only: $5890.

Financial Aid Of all full-time matriculated undergraduates who enrolled in 2006, 4,357 applied for aid, 2,381 were judged to have need, 533 had their need fully met. In 2006, 4864 non-need-based awards were made. *Average percent of need met:* 60%. *Average financial aid package:* $6754. *Average need-based loan:* $4194. *Average need-based gift aid:* $5032. *Average non-need-based aid:* $2420. *Average indebtedness upon graduation:* $13,657.

Applying *Options:* electronic application, deferred entrance. *Application fee:* $60. *Required:* high school transcript, minimum 3.0 GPA. *Application deadlines:* rolling (freshmen), rolling (transfers). *Notification:* continuous (freshmen), continuous (transfers).

Freshman Application Contact Dr. Melissa Choroszy, Associate Vice President of Enrollment Services, University of Nevada, Reno, Mail Stop 120, Reno, NV 89557. *Phone:* 775-784-4700. *Toll-free phone:* 866-263-8232. *Fax:* 775-784-4283. *E-mail:* asknevada@unr.edu.

See page 1500 for the College Close-Up.

UNIVERSITY OF PHOENIX–LAS VEGAS CAMPUS

Las Vegas, Nevada **www.phoenix.edu/**

- **Proprietary** comprehensive, founded 1994
- **Urban** campus
- **Coed**
- **Noncompetitive** entrance level

Faculty *Student/faculty ratio:* 11:1.

Academics *Calendar:* continuous. *Degrees:* bachelor's, master's, and post-master's certificates.

Student Life *Campus security:* late-night transport/escort service.

Costs (2007–08) *Tuition:* $10,410 full-time, $347 per credit part-time. Full-time tuition and fees vary according to course level.

Financial Aid *Average financial aid package:* $4273. *Average need-based gift aid:* $2217.

Applying *Options:* deferred entrance. *Application fee:* $45. *Required:* 1 letter of recommendation. *Required for some:* high school transcript.

Freshman Application Contact Ms. Beth Barilla, Associate Vice President, Student Admissions and Services, University of Phoenix–Las Vegas Campus, 4615 East Elwood Street, Mail Stop AA-K101, Phoenix, AZ 85040-1958. *Phone:* 480-317-6000. *Toll-free phone:* 800-776-4867 (in-state); 800-228-7240 (out-of-state). *Fax:* 480-894-1758. *E-mail:* beth.barilla@phoenix.edu.

THE ART INSTITUTE OF LAS VEGAS

HENDERSON, NEVADA

The Institute

The Art Institute of Las Vegas provides programs that prepare students for entry-level positions in the creative arts. Located in the prestigious Green Valley area of Henderson in the Las Vegas Valley, the school occupies approximately 48,000 square feet and currently offers twelve bachelor's degree programs and six associate degree programs.

Each program is offered on a year-round basis, allowing students to work uninterrupted toward their degrees. The faculty members strive to strengthen the students' skills and cultivate their talents through programs carefully designed with the support and contributions of leading members of the professional community. Instructional methods include lectures, demonstrations, labs, one-on-one tutorials, and periodic examinations. Courses may include internships, field trips, online courses, and independent studies. The curricula are reviewed periodically to ensure that they meet the needs of a changing marketplace.

Students come to The Art Institute of Las Vegas from across the United States and abroad. The student population includes recent high school graduates, transfer students, and those who have left a previous employment situation to study and train for a new career. Students are creative, competitive, and open to new ideas. They place great value on an education that prepares them for an exciting entry-level position in the arts.

Students are expected to gain an understanding of theoretical and practical knowledge appropriate to their degree objectives, complete specific courses, and develop critical and analytical learning abilities along with values that contribute to lifelong learning.

The Career Services Department helps students to launch a job search and assists in locating part-time employment while students are still in school. The department assists students with resume writing, networking, and keeping abreast of what employers are looking for in job applicants.

The Art Institute of Las Vegas school-sponsored housing facility offers a variety of living accommodations in a fully-equipped, partially furnished, apartment-style complex. A resident adviser lives in the housing facility and assists students in coordinating activities, meeting each other, and learning about the school.

The Student Affairs Office is the key contact for all international students. This office provides a variety of support services and enrichment activities to meet the needs of international students.

The Art Institute of Las Vegas holds film festivals, portfolio shows, and other activities for students. Counseling services are available to all students while attending the school. The school provides confidential short-term counseling for individuals and groups in accordance with professional, legal, and ethical codes of the counseling profession.

The Art Institute of Las Vegas is accredited by the Accrediting Commission of Career Schools and Colleges of Technology (ACCSCT) and is licensed by the Nevada Commission on Postsecondary Education (CPE).

Location

Las Vegas provides sunny days, museums, libraries, parks, gift shops, and historical sights. Just outside the city are some of the world's most beautiful natural wonders, including the Grand Canyon, Red Rock Canyon, Death Valley, Hoover Dam, and Valley of Fire State Park. Nearly 1.5 million residents enjoy the strong economy and climate of this growing city.

Majors and Degrees

The school offers bachelor's degree programs (thirty-six months) in audio production, culinary management, digital filmmaking and video production, digital photography, fashion and retail management, food and beverage management, game art and design, graphic design, interior design, media arts and animation, visual effects and motion graphics, and Web design and interactive media. Associate degree programs (twenty-one months) are available in baking and pastry, culinary arts, drafting technology with AutoCAD, home furnishings merchandising, interior design, and kitchen and bath design.

Academic Programs

To receive an associate degree, a student must complete a minimum of 112 quarter credits, with 28 quarter credits in general education courses and 84 quarter credits in a specialty area. To receive a bachelor's degree, a student must complete a minimum of 192 quarter credits, with 48 quarter credits in general education courses and 114 quarter credits in a specialty area. For both degrees, the student must achieve a cumulative GPA of 2.0 or higher, meet portfolio or other requirements, and satisfy all financial obligations to the school. A limited number of courses are available online for an additional fee per course.

Academic Facilities

The Art Institute of Las Vegas houses classrooms, studios, offices, a student lounge, a supply store, Mac and PC labs, faculty and staff offices, and the Learning Resource Center, with library and reference materials. In addition, program-specific equipment, including projectors, editing decks, camcorders, printers, drafting tables, and kitchen appliances are provided to help students complete their projects. Students also have access to the public libraries and the University of Nevada–Las Vegas campus library.

Costs

Tuition cost varies by program. Prospective students should contact the school for current tuition costs. Other charges include a starting kit for all first quarter students. Kits vary in price depending on the program of study.

Financial Aid

Financial aid is available for those who qualify. Students who require financial assistance should first complete and submit a Free Application for Federal Student Aid (FAFSA) and meet with a financial aid officer. The officer determines the student's level of need based on a required federal formula, the cost of education, and other factors. Gift aid is available in the form of Federal Pell Grants, Federal Supplemental Educational Opportunity Grants, and veterans' benefits. Loans include Federal Stafford Loans, Federal PLUS Loans, and alternative loans.

Scholarships are available from the school and private sources. Application deadlines and eligibility requirements vary by program.

Faculty

The Art Institute of Las Vegas faculty includes full-time and part-time instructors, many of whom have advanced degrees and professional experience in their respective fields of study.

Admission Requirements

As a prerequisite for admission, a prospective student must be a high school graduate, hold a General Educational Development (GED) certificate, or have earned a bachelor's degree or higher from an accredited institution of postsecondary education. Each prospective student is interviewed, either in person or by telephone, by an assistant director of admissions to determine whether the student and school are a good fit. Portfolios may qualify the student for advanced placement, and applications may be submitted any time prior to the start of the next quarter.

There is a $50 application fee.

Application and Information

To obtain an application, make arrangements for an interview, or tour the school, students should contact:

The Art Institute of Las Vegas
2350 Corporate Circle
Henderson, Nevada 89074-7737
Phone: 702-369-9944
800-833-2678 (toll-free)
Fax: 702-992-8458
Web site: http://www.artinstitutes.edu/lasvegas

The Art Institute of Atlanta®, GA; The Art Institute of Atlanta®–Decatur, GA; The Art Institute of Austin℠, TX; The Art Institute of California℠–Inland Empire; The Art Institute of California℠–Los Angeles; The Art Institute of California℠–Orange County; The Art Institute of California℠–Sacramento; The Art Institute of California℠–San Diego; The Art Institute of California℠–San Francisco; The Art Institute of California℠–Sunnyvale; The Art Institute of Charleston℠, SC, A branch of The Art Institute of Atlanta, GA; The Art Institute of Charlotte®, NC; The Art Institute of Colorado® (Denver); The Art Institute of Dallas®, TX; The Art Institute of Fort Lauderdale®, FL; The Art Institute of Houston®, TX; The Art Institute of Indianapolis℠, IN*; The Art Institute of Jacksonville℠, FL, A branch of Miami International University of Art & Design; The Art Institute of Las Vegas®, NV; The Art Institute of Michigan℠ (Detroit); The Art Institute of New York City®, NY; The Art Institute of Ohio℠–Cincinnati**; The Art Institute of Philadelphia®, PA; The Art Institute of Phoenix®, AZ; The Art Institute of Pittsburgh®, PA; The Art Institute of Pittsburgh®–Online Division; The Art Institute of Portland®, OR; The Art Institute of Salt Lake City℠, UT; The Art Institute of Seattle®, WA; The Art Institute of Tampa℠, FL, A branch of Miami International University of Art & Design; The Art Institute of Tennessee℠–Nashville, A branch of The Art Institute of Atlanta, GA; The Art Institute of Tucson℠, AZ; The Art Institute of Washington® (Arlington, VA), A branch of The Art Institute of Atlanta, GA; The Art Institute of York–Pennsylvania℠; The Art Institutes International Minnesota℠ (Minneapolis); California Design College℠ (Los Angeles–Wilshire Blvd.); The Illinois Institute of Art®–Chicago; The Illinois Institute of Art®–Schaumburg; Miami International University of Art & Design℠, FL; The New England Institute of Art® (Boston, MA).

*The Art Institute of Indianapolis is licensed by the Indiana Commission on Proprietary Education, 302 W. Washington St., Rm. E201, Indianapolis, IN 46204, AC-0080.

**The Art Institute of Ohio–Cincinnati, 8845 Governors Hill Drive, Suite 100, Cincinnati, OH 45249-3317, OH Reg. #04-01-1698B.

SIERRA NEVADA COLLEGE

INCLINE VILLAGE, NEVADA

The College

Sierra Nevada College (SNC), established in 1969, is a four-year private liberal arts college with postbaccalaureate teacher certification and Master of Arts in teaching programs in Incline Village, Reno, and Las Vegas. The liberal arts focus at SNC is enhanced by an entrepreneurial spirit throughout the curriculum. The College offers intellectual, educational, and cultural resources to its graduates and the communities of Nevada. Sierra Nevada College is accredited by the Northwest Commission on Colleges and Universities (NWCCU) and licensed by Nevada Commission on Postsecondary Education. The College's Teacher Education Programs are state approved through the Nevada State Board of Education. With an enrollment of 300 undergraduate students, approximately 300 graduate students enrolled in the College's Master of Arts in Teaching program, and a student-faculty ratio of 12:1, students can expect to work closely with their professors and classmates. Small, intimate classes—one of the hallmarks of the SNC educational experience—allow *all* students the chance to actively participate and thrive in their classrooms.

Information on graduate schools and entrance exams such as the GRE, LSAT, PRAXIS, MCAT, and GMAT, as well as career exploration and job-seeking skills, are available to students through the Student Career Center. The Director of Student Services meets with students for private appointments in career counseling.

A residential college nestled in the community of Incline Village at Lake Tahoe, Sierra Nevada College is welcoming and friendly. Student residences are spacious and bright, with views of surrounding forests and snowy peaks. Common areas have fireplaces and well-lit nooks. The campus is within walking distance of exercise equipment, an indoor swimming pool, and ball courts in the 37,000-square-foot Incline Village Recreation Center.

Location

The Lake Tahoe region enjoys more than 300 days of sun a year, making it a perfect venue for backpacking, rock climbing, kayaking, river rafting, skiing, and snowboarding. Eight ski and snowboard resorts are within 45 minutes of the College, with the nearest resort only one mile from campus. The campus is a short 35 miles from the city of Reno (The Biggest Little City in the World) and the Reno-Tahoe International Airport. The College also has branch campuses in Reno and Henderson, Nevada.

Majors and Degrees

The Departments of Fine Arts, Humanities and Social Sciences, Business, and Science and Technology offer fourteen majors. Sierra Nevada College offers undergraduate programs that lead to the Bachelor of Arts (B.A.), the Bachelor of Science (B.S.), the Bachelor of Science in Business Administration (B.S.B.A.), and the Bachelor of Fine Arts (B.F.A). in more than thirty majors, minors, and concentrations, including ski business and resort management, entrepreneurship, entertainment technology, environmental sciences, and international studies. A general education core curriculum is required of all students. Honors, Summer Arts, and study-abroad programs are offered, as well as evening courses and a summer session. The Summer Visiting Artist Workshops feature well-known artists and attract students from all parts of the United States, Europe, and the Far East.

Academic Programs

With the motto "Freedom, wisdom, and responsibility" reflecting a progressive, forward-looking approach to academics, Sierra Nevada College offers more than thirty undergraduate majors, minors, and concentrations. With a liberal arts education, students have the opportunity to experiment in other areas of interest—taking a class in sketching, testing research in a chemistry lab, or exploring their musical talent. The goal of a great liberal arts college is to craft a curriculum that ensures students are exposed to the best of human thought and ideals. At Sierra Nevada College, this liberal arts education and professional preparedness are combined through an interdisciplinary curriculum that emphasizes environmental, social, economic, and cultural responsibility and sustainability.

The Sierra Nevada College faculty recently approved a new mission statement: "Our graduates will be scholars of and contributors to a sustainable world. SNC combines the liberal arts and professional preparedness through an interdisciplinary curriculum which emphasizes environmental, social, economic, and educational responsibility." The move toward sustainability was the organizing factor in the development of a new cohesive series of interdisciplinary core requirements for the College. During the first semester, incoming freshmen participate in a highly kinesthetic learning experience in a course entitled Ecopsychology. This class is team taught by senior members of the psychology and computer science programs. Concurrently, incoming students take a Writing and the Environment class. During the second semester, students take a Creativity, Innovation, and Sustainability course, team taught by members of the business and art departments. They also take a math class that emphasizes applied math (such as how to assess interest rates and terms when buying a car, or geometry as it applies to half-pipe tricks).

In the second year, the core requirements include a studio art course and an environmental science course, team taught by the natural sciences and mathematics programs. In the third year, the common experience is in the course Civilization. Seniors then take a Capstone Ethics course. Each of the core requirements is arranged to introduce core competencies, develop core competencies, and, finally, to master them. For example, "active citizenship" is introduced in the Ecopsychology class, developed during the Environmental Science class, and mastered by the Capstone Ethics course. All core requirements have a strong emphasis on active learning, and courses were developed with full faculty participation, ensuring that the core is both imaginative and rigorous.

Students at SNC are thus prepared to think critically and communicate effectively in order to pursue a lifetime of achievement and success. Sierra Nevada College entrepreneurship student teams, for instance, have won first place in the highly competitive, statewide Nevada Donald W. Reynolds Governor's Cup Business Plan Competition in both 2006 and 2007.

Off-Campus Programs

Sierra Nevada College has agreements for internship placement with a number of businesses, schools, resorts, and public service agencies. The internship experience complements and reinforces the College's classroom-based curriculum by allowing SNC students to earn academic credit by putting their creative and problem-solving skills to work in professional situations. Interns observe firsthand the realities and requirements of potential careers. In many cases, SNC graduates return to their intern placement sites for full-time employment.

SNC has strategic alliances with entrepreneurial startup companies, growth-oriented organizations, entrepreneurial-minded individuals, professional service organizations in support of new ventures, and even governmental agencies dedicated to supporting the "spirit of entrepreneurship" in each and every one of us. Coaching, mentoring, internships, applied field experiences, entrepreneurial teamwork, and networking embedded in on-campus and off-campus academic activities are all offered.

SNC encourages students in all majors to consider studying abroad and participating in approved off-campus field experiences or internships during their undergraduate experience. Studying abroad for a semester or year can be the most meaningful way to experience other cultures, and the experience can have a profound impact on students academically, personally, and professionally. Financial aid can apply to approved study-abroad programs.

The SNC Outdoor Adventure Program was launched in an effort to create more program options for students. The trips are built around weekends and include backpacking in Yosemite, rock climbing near Bishop, and sea kayaking on Lake Tahoe as well as river rafting along the American River. The goal of the program is multifaceted and designed to promote wilderness adventures in the Sierra Nevada, team building, and leadership development. Overall, the program reaches more than 100 SNC students and provides unique experiences for those involved in the program. The sense of adventure, camaraderie, and support generated during these trips is significant. As the College moves forward with this program, there will be several enhancements to the program, including the addition of advanced trips and leadership training courses. Furthermore, an inclusive schedule that leads into the spring will be included as the year unfolds. This program provides several significant contributions to student life at SNC. Primarily, this program offers students options other than staying on campus during the weekends. Secondly, it helps students become acquainted with the challenging environment presented to an 18- or 19-year-old who has just moved to Lake Tahoe. Lastly, it provides an opportunity for experienced students to excel in the outdoors and develop their wilderness leadership skills.

Academic Facilities

The College comprises six campus buildings on 18 acres, including two residence halls, a dining hall, a library, an administrative center for student services, and the new Tahoe Center for the Environmental Sciences, a "green" LEED-certified Platinum-rated laboratory building. The library holds more than 45,000 books, with additional new resource materials. The campus network provides accounts, e-mail services, and high-speed Internet access over T1 lines. The on-campus bookstore carries textbooks, related materials for SNC classes, insignia items, school and office supplies, art supplies, gift items, and snacks.

Costs

The approximate nine-month academic year cost projection for a full-time, undergraduate, residential student is $22,168 for tuition; $8825 for room and board; $300, SGA student body fee; and $1386 for books and supplies, for a total of $32,679.

Financial Aid

Financial aid for students of Sierra Nevada College is available from a variety of sources in many forms; awards are based on students' merit and financial need. These include Federal Pell Grants, Federal Supplemental Educational Opportunity Grants (FSEOG), Nevada State Incentive Grants (NSIG), Academic Competitiveness Grants (ACG), National SMART Grants, Sierra Nevada College Grants (SNCG), Federal Direct Stafford Loans, and Federal Direct Parent Loans for Undergraduate Students (PLUS). In addition, Nevada high school students can apply for the Nevada Millennium Scholarship.

Faculty

The faculty includes full-time/salaried and part-time members. Over 71 percent of full-time faculty members at Sierra Nevada College have a Ph.D. or equivalent. The student-faculty ratio is 12:1

Student Government

The College's Student Government Association (SGA) is the planning and implementing board for student activities, programs, and services. Most of the activities are conceived, planned, and implemented by the student government and interested students. All SNC students are invited to attend SGA meetings, which are customarily held on a weekday afternoon at a predetermined place. Candidacy for an SGA officer position is open to all students as specified by the SGA bylaws. The SGA undertakes a number of student and community campaigns each year and organizes various campus events, including concerts, speakers, and parties. In addition, the SGA hosts a monthly student forum where students develop leadership skills by participating in the College's policymaking process. The SGA is financially supported by the College and through the student activity fees. Student clubs and organizations also receive funding through the student activity fees. After clubs and organizations present activities they would like to sponsor, SGA approves and assists in funding those activities.

Admission Requirements

Sierra Nevada College employs a rolling admissions policy; it is recommended that students submit required documents by the priority application date of February 15. Freshman/transfer admission requirements include the application, official high school transcript for freshmen or official college/university transcripts from previously attended institutions for transfer applicants, SAT or ACT scores for freshman applicants or transfer applicants with fewer than 15 units of college credit, admission essay, and the School Report Form for freshman applicants completed by applicant's guidance counselor or a letter of recommendation (recommended). International student applicants follow the same guidelines for freshman or transfer admission, and they must also submit an international credential evaluation of all course work previously completed outside the U.S., proof of financial support, a personal statement detailing the student's reasons for wishing to study in the U.S. in general and SNC in particular, TOEFL results (SAT results can be used in place of TOEFL by native English speakers), and a completed International Student Form.

Application and Information

For application forms, a catalog, or further information, students should contact:

Office of Admissions
Sierra Nevada College
999 Tahoe Boulevard
Incline Village, Nevada 89451
Phone: 866-412-4636 (toll-free)
E-mail: admissions@sierranevada.edu
Web site: http://www.sierranevada.edu

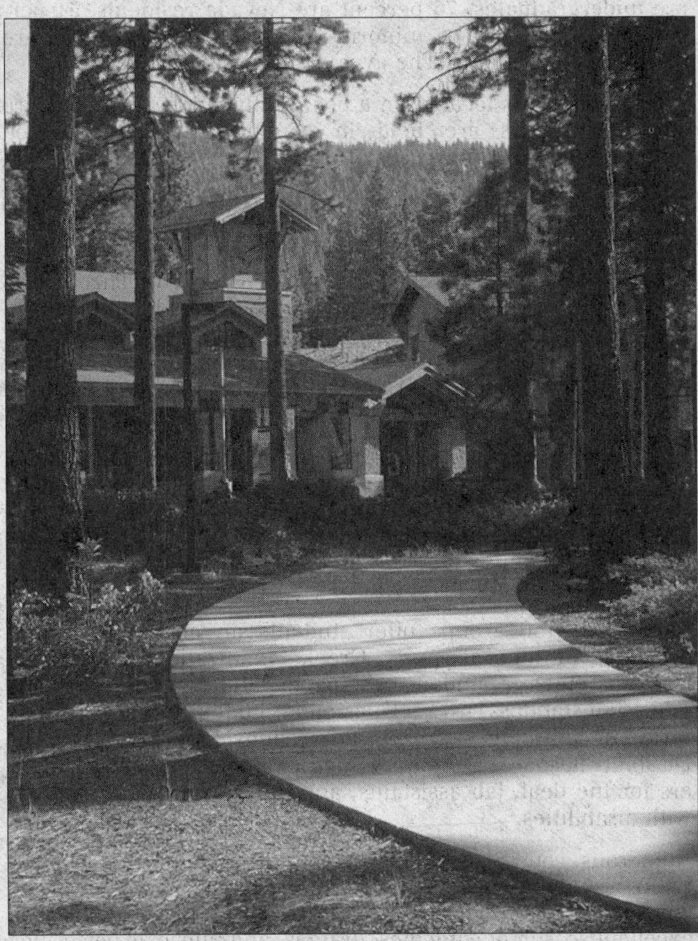

A residential college nestled in the community of Incline Village at Lake Tahoe, Sierra Nevada College is welcoming and friendly.

UNIVERSITY OF NEVADA, LAS VEGAS

LAS VEGAS, NEVADA

The University

The University of Nevada, Las Vegas (UNLV), is recognized nationally as a comprehensive teaching and research university that provides students with an excellent education at a reasonable cost. UNLV has established an agenda for the next decade to become a premier metropolitan research university. All UNLV programs are accredited by the Northwest Association of Schools and Colleges. Individual programs have further accreditation from professional accrediting organizations.

Since its founding in 1957, UNLV has seen dramatic growth in both its academic programs and its facilities. There are 220 undergraduate, master's, and doctoral degree programs offered to more than 28,000 students. Of UNLV's students, 79 percent are undergraduates, 76 percent are Nevada residents, 31 percent are members of minority groups, and 4 percent are international students. The average class size is 30.

The University is located on a beautifully landscaped 350-acre campus. Classes are held in comfortable, well-equipped buildings that are showcases of modern architecture.

Since 1995, UNLV has completed, or currently has in design or construction, thirty-two major facilities and real estate projects. These total approximately $567 million. Of that amount, the state has contributed $217 million or 38 percent. Through its own resources, federal grants, or private donations, the University has managed to fund 62 percent of these projects with nonstate monies. In calendar year 2007 alone, four major construction projects were planned for the Maryland Parkway campus, totaling more than $129 million.

UNLV's residential life program provides students with a secure, convenient place to live on the University campus. The modern residence halls are organized into suites of two rooms joined by a bathroom. Four students share a suite, with 2 per room. UNLV's dining facilities are excellent, providing students with quality, quantity, and choice.

More than 150 groups offer students an active social life, including intramural sports, Greek organizations, ethnic and religious clubs, a student newspaper, and campus radio and television stations. UNLV's Division of Student Life provides an array of advising, tutorial, and counseling services. The Disability Resource Center provides textbooks on tape, interpreters for the deaf, lab assistants, and other services to students with disabilities.

Numerous concerts are performed throughout the year by UNLV's student music groups, choirs, dance companies, and ensembles. The Department of Theatre Arts also offers an excellent season of comedies, dramas, and musicals performed by students and community members, as well as performances by national professional touring companies. The student government sponsors lectures, films, concerts, and entertainment throughout the year.

Location

Las Vegas, touted by historian Hal Rothman as the First City of the Twenty-First Century, is located at the southern tip of Nevada in a desert valley surrounded by mountains. The Las Vegas metropolitan area is a rapidly growing community of more than 2 million residents with a strong sense of family and community pride. The surrounding area is one of the Southwest's most picturesque, offering residents outdoor recreation year-round. Within a 50-mile radius lie the shores of Lake Mead, Hoover Dam, and the Colorado River recreation area; the snow-skiing and hiking trails of 12,000-foot Mount Charleston; and a panoramic view of rugged rock mountains. Las Vegas has an average of 320 days of sunshine per year. The average daytime winter temperature is 60 degrees Fahrenheit. Summer daytime temperatures are usually more than 100 degrees Fahrenheit.

Majors and Degrees

Undergraduate programs are offered by the Colleges of Business, Honors, Education, Fine Arts, Health Sciences, Liberal Arts, University Studies, and Sciences; the School of Nursing, Health and Human Sciences, and the Greenspun College of Urban Affairs; the Howard R. Hughes College of Engineering; and the William F. Harrah College of Hotel Administration.

Majors include accounting, Afro-American studies, anthropology, applied physics, architecture, art, art history, Asian studies, athletic training, beverage management, biochemistry, biological sciences (including preprofessional), chemistry, civil and environmental engineering, clinical lab sciences, communications studies, comprehensive medical imaging, computational physics, computer engineering, computer science, construction management, criminal justice, culinary arts management, dance, early childhood education, earth science, economics, electrical engineering, elementary education, English, environmental studies, film, finance, fitness and sports management, forensic science, French, geoscience, German, gerontology, health-care administration, health education, health physics, health sciences, history, hotel administration, human resources management, interior architecture and design, international business, jazz studies, journalism, kinesiological sciences, landscape architecture, Latin American studies, liberal studies, library science, linguistic studies, management, management information systems, marketing, mathematics, mechanical engineering, multidisciplinary studies, music, musical theater, nuclear medicine, nursing, nutritional sciences, philosophy, physical education, physics, political science, psychology, radiography, real estate, recreation, Romance languages, secondary education, senior adult theater, social science studies, social work, sociology, Spanish, special education, theater arts, urban and regional planning, women's studies, workforce education, and university studies.

Academic Programs

The UNLV General Education Core requirement, which must be completed by all baccalaureate degree candidates, consists of courses in English composition and literature, international and multicultural studies, logic, mathematics, computer science or statistics, U.S. and Nevada constitutions, social sciences, natural sciences, fine arts, and humanities. The balance of baccalaureate degree programs consists of college and departmental requirements. The number of credit hours required for baccalaureate degrees varies between 124 and 136, depending on the program of study. Numerous special academic opportunities are available, such as dual majors, dual baccalaureates, approved minors, internships, international studies, interdisciplinary programs, honors programs, and nontraditional credit (military credits, Advanced Placement Program, College-Level Examination Program, and correspondence credits).

The UNLV academic calendar has two semesters (fall and spring), each lasting approximately sixteen weeks. Three summer sessions are held from mid-May through August.

Off-Campus Programs

International study-abroad programs are available throughout the year, with opportunities to spend one semester, one academic year, or a summer abroad. Academic credits earned in UNLV study-abroad programs are part of regular authorized course offerings. Students can make normal progress toward their UNLV degree while utilizing international resources and experiencing a different culture.

Academic Facilities

The campus has an excellent Curriculum Materials Library, which is used extensively by local school teachers and University students. The National Supercomputing Center for Energy and the Environment facilitates study of the engineering, socioeconomic, transportation, and social impacts of energy and hazardous waste management along with other appropriate studies. The center includes a Cray YMP 2/215 supercomputer and a Sun 4/490 front-end computer, ten color graphics workstations, and a Silicon Graphics workstation. There are seven public computer labs on the UNLV campus with various types of equipment, including IBM PCs, Spool Printers, Gateways, NEC machines, Macintoshes, Image Writers, letter quality and laser printers, Apple II's, and DEC workstations.

Costs

For the 2008–09 academic year, average room and board costs are $9810 per year. Nonresident tuition and fees are $15,291 per year (14 credits per semester), and in-state tuition and fees are $4196 per year (14 credits per semester). UNLV has a Good Neighbor Policy for the Arizona and California counties that border Nevada. High school graduates and transfer students from these counties may be eligible for reduced tuition. Residents of fourteen states (Alaska, Arizona, California, Colorado, Hawaii, Idaho, Montana, New Mexico, North Dakota, Oregon, South Dakota, Utah, Washington, and Wyoming) may also qualify for reduced tuition rates through the Western Undergraduate Exchange (WUE) Nonresident Scholarship Program. Children of alumni (bachelor's degree graduates only) are also eligible for a reduction in nonresident tuition.

Financial Aid

UNLV provides a variety of financial assistance to qualified students. Loans, grants, scholarships, and employment are all awarded to help students meet their educational expenses while attending UNLV. All students should explore every possible resource. A student's eligibility may be determined by financial need, scholastic achievement, special skills, or service. Prospective students may complete a scholarship application prior to or at the same time as the application for admission. The deadline to apply for scholarships is February 1. It is recommended that the Free Application for Federal Student Aid (FAFSA) is submitted by the February 1 priority deadline.

Faculty

More than 850 full-time instructional faculty members are involved in teaching, research, and community service. The scholars and scientists at UNLV are warm, caring people committed as much to excellence in teaching as they are to their research. Academic advising is available to every degree-seeking student at UNLV. Graduate assistants have limited teaching and laboratory assignments.

Student Government

All undergraduate students are automatically members of the Consolidated Students of the University of Nevada, Las Vegas (CSUN). CSUN is a self-governing body and is recognized by UNLV's faculty and the Nevada System of Higher Education. All officers are elected by the student body. CSUN has many boards and committees in which students are encouraged to get involved. CSUN provides students an opportunity to practice their communication skills and enrich their education both socially and academically.

Admission Requirements

Regular admission to UNLV is based on a student's academic record and placement examination scores. Incoming freshman students must earn a minimum 3.0 weighted grade point average (GPA) in the academic core in order to be considered for admission. The academic core consist of 4 years of English; 3 years of algebra or higher-level mathematics, such as algebra II, geometry, precalculus, or calculus; 3 years of natural science, with at least 2 years in a lab science; and 3 years of social studies. A minimum composite score of 22 on the ACT or a score of at least 1040 (critical reading and math) on the SAT can be used to waive the GPA requirement, however all students must meet the core course requirement. Official ACT or SAT test scores are also required for scholarship consideration and English and math placement.

Transfer students must earn a minimum of 24 transferable credits and earn a cumulative GPA of 2.5 or higher from a regionally accredited university or college to be considered for admission. The applicant must be in good standing and eligible to return to the educational institution last attended. Students with less than 24 transferable credits must apply as a freshman transfer and submit their college and high school transcripts for evaluation.

Students who do not meet the minimum requirements may be eligible to appeal through the Faculty Senate appeals committee.

Application and Information

Priority application deadlines are February 1 for the fall and summer semester and October 1 for the spring semester. The nonrefundable application fee of $60 for domestic students and $95 for international students cannot be waived.

Prospective students may access the UNLV applications and catalog on the University's Web site.

For further assistance, students may contact:

Office of Undergraduate Recruitment
University of Nevada, Las Vegas
Box 451021
4505 Maryland Parkway
Las Vegas, Nevada 89154-1021
Phone: 702-774-UNLV or TOUR
702-895-2970 (orientation)
702-895-3011 (main university number)
702-895-3424 (financial aid)
702-895-3131 (UNLV events)
Fax: 702-774-8008
Web site: http://www.unlv.edu

UNIVERSITY OF NEVADA, RENO

RENO, NEVADA

The University

The University of Nevada, Reno, ranks among the top 150 research institutions nationally according to the Carnegie Foundation's listing of colleges and universities. This is further evidence of Nevada's growing reputation as one of the nation's best universities. Funds for sponsored research, training, and public service totaled nearly $130 million during the fiscal year 2006. Nevada's Reynolds School of Journalism has produced 6 Pulitzer Prize winners. Fortune 500 companies rate the University's supply chain management program in the College of Business Administration among the nation's top 10. The Chemistry Department was ranked "Very Best" for its size in the U.S. and Canada by the National Science Foundation; the Geography Department, fifth in the U.S. for its size for undergraduate teaching; the Honors Program among the fifty-five best nationally in "a state's major university" category; and the hydrologic sciences program, eighth nationally.

Accredited by the Northwest Association of Schools and Colleges, the University has 12,500 acres of field laboratories and research areas statewide. Nevada is internationally known for its research in earthquakes, stem cells, heap leach mining, Basque studies, remote sensing, watershed preservation, and structural engineering. The University's Center for Environmental Sciences and Engineering prepares students for the growing demand for environmental scientists. Nevada is also known for having strong programs in agriculture, biochemistry, geriatrics, heart disease research, theoretical chemistry, and speech pathology and audiology.

Within the past eight years, the 255-acre campus has opened the $8-million Fitzgerald Student Services Building, the $17-million Argenta Residence Hall with a parking garage and a full-service dining center, and the $63-million Joe Crowley Student Union. By 2010, $300 million in construction will have been completed, with current projects including Davidson Mathematics and Science Education Center, Mathewson-IGT Knowledge Center Library, and the Petersen Athletic Academic Center. Students and visitors enjoy the University's historic brick buildings and tree-lined walkways.

Students at Nevada may live in one of seven residence halls on the campus or at one of fourteen fraternity and sorority houses nearby. They come from all seventeen Nevada counties, all fifty states, and more than eighty countries. For extracurricular activities, students may participate in more than 180 student organizations that are recognized by the Associated Students of the University of Nevada (ASUN). Support services include intensive orientation sessions for new students, a freshman and sophomore success center, academic advisement, counseling, tutoring, financial aid, health services, and special programs.

Mackay Stadium is home to the Wolf Pack football and soccer teams, and Lawlor Events Center is home to the Wolf Pack basketball teams. In 2006, Nevada was ranked in the top 10 NCAA Division I-A athletic departments in overall diversity excellence. The Wolf Pack is also a winner on the fields of competition as a member of the nine-team Western Athletic Conference (WAC). The Kennedy Index, a study released in 2005 by Penn State York professor Charles Kennedy, rated Nevada as "best in the nation" overall for providing opportunities for women in sports. The Nevada football team won a share of the WAC title and the Sheraton Hawaii Bowl in 2005, and the men's basketball team has captured back-to-back conference championships and NCAA tournament appearances, including a spot in the Sweet 16 in 2004. The women's volleyball team qualified for the NCAA tournament for the second straight season in 2005. The Wolf Pack has also had 11 athletes compete in the Olympics and 2 Olympic medalists, both in swimming.

A land-grant university that opened in 1874, Nevada has an enrollment of more than16,000 students. Approximately 13,000 are undergraduates. Degree programs at the University include seventy-five undergraduate majors and seventy-six master's degree programs, thirty-nine Ph.D. programs, five Ed.D. programs, and the M.D. and M.D./Ph.D. programs.

Location

The University is four blocks from downtown Reno and serves as both an educational and cultural resource for the community. It is easily accessible from Interstate 80.

Reno itself has one of the most attractive locations in the country. Situated in northern Nevada's Truckee Meadows at an elevation of 4,600 feet, it is on the eastern slope of the Sierra Nevada Mountains. The climate is cool and dry, and there are four distinct seasons. The six counties of northwestern Nevada have a population of 550,000. Reno is only a 45-minute drive from scenic Lake Tahoe, with its world-class skiing and limitless summer recreation; a 2-hour drive from Sacramento; and a 4-hour drive from San Francisco. Reno offers cultural events, including the symphony, ballet, theater, and opera and a summer celebration of the arts called Artown. Many University facilities, such as the Fleischmann Planetarium and Science Center and the Sheppard Fine Arts Gallery, are open to the public. The University also sponsors concerts, lectures, films, plays, and many other events for the community.

Majors and Degrees

Undergraduate degrees are awarded in the following academic units and majors: College of Agriculture, Biotechnology, and Natural Resources: agricultural and applied economics, agricultural education, animal biotechnology, animal science (equine and rangeland production), biochemistry, environmental science, environmental policy analysis, forest and rangeland management, nutrition, pre–veterinary science, and wildlife ecology and conservation; College of Business Administration: accounting, economics, finance, information systems, international business, management, marketing, and supply chain management; College of Education: early childhood education (cooperative program), elementary education, elementary/special education, secondary education, and special education; College of Engineering: chemical engineering, civil engineering, computer science, computer and information engineering, construction sciences, electrical engineering, engineering physics, environmental engineering, materials science and engineering, and mechanical engineering; College of Human and Community Sciences: early childhood education (cooperative program), health ecology, human development and family studies, nursing, and social work; Reynolds School of Journalism: journalism; College of Liberal Arts: anthropology, art, criminal justice, English, French, German, general studies, history, interior design, international affairs, music, music education, philosophy, political science, psychology, sociology, Spanish, speech communication, theater, and women's studies; School of Medicine: speech pathology and audiology; and College of Science: biology, chemistry, chemical engineering, geography, geological engineering, geology, geophysics, hydrogeology, mathematics, mining engineering, and physics.

The University also offers preparatory programs for law, medicine, dentistry, and several other health-related fields.

Academic Programs

Students must complete a core curriculum of English, mathematics, natural sciences, social sciences, fine arts, core humanities, capstone courses, and diversity in addition to completing specific requirements for their degree. The number of credit hours required for graduation is typically 128 to 134. Credit by examination is available. The University also offers an honors program for exceptional students and an active Army ROTC program. The school calendar includes two 15-week semesters, beginning in August for the fall and January for the spring. The Independent Learning department offers an early summer minisession and two 5-week summer sessions.

Off-Campus Programs

The University offers a number of study-abroad programs for credit in twenty-five countries, including Australia, the Basque Country in Spain, Chile, China, Costa Rica, Ghana, India, Japan, Korea, Malta, Mexico, New Zealand, Thailand, and several European sites. The University is also a member of the National Student Exchange Program, which gives undergraduates from Nevada an opportunity to study in other parts of the country. Similarly, the Western Interstate Commission for Higher Education (WICHE) provides grants to Nevada scholars to pursue disciplines that are not available in Nevada.

Academic Facilities

The Getchell Library is one of the largest libraries in Nevada. It contains more than 1 million books and bound periodicals and offers access to government documents, patents, microforms, newspapers, online databases, full-text electronic journals, and e-books. Getchell is the main library facility, and there are also four branch libraries located near the academic units they serve.

Scheduled to open in fall 2008, the Mathewson-IGT Knowledge Center is a state-of-the-art facility that will be one of the most technologically advanced libraries in the country, combining the resources of the University library with computing and information technologies to provide an outstanding learning environment for students, faculty members, and researchers. The College of Agriculture, Biotechnology, and Natural Resources houses a number of world-class facilities, such as the Proteomics Facility that has high-tech equipment not found in most universities, and the Jay Dow Wetlands, a field laboratory that provides an ideal high-desert setting for learning about the interactions between wildlife and agriculture. The College of Engineering maintains fifteen laboratories and research centers, including Computer Vision and Robotics, Bridge Engineering, Virtual Reality, and Earthquake Engineering, which is among the top ten facilities in the nation.

Costs

The per-credit cost for Nevada residents was $133.50 for 2007–08; thus, the total estimated cost for a student taking an average 15-credit load for two semesters was $4005. Out-of-state students paid $7550.00 per semester in addition to per-credit fees. Students from certain California counties, however, are eligible for a reduction in out-of-state tuition under the University's Good Neighbor policy. The University of Nevada, Reno, also participates in the Western Undergraduate Exchange (WUE) program that allows eligible students from fourteen Western states (Alaska, Arizona, California, Colorado, Hawaii, Idaho, Montana, New Mexico, North Dakota, Oregon, South Dakota, Utah, Washington, and Wyoming) to pay a reduced nonresident tuition for all programs of study. Fall 2007 WUE students paid $211.25 per credit and did not pay any additional out-of-state tuition. This reduced nonresident tuition is available for all programs of study. More information on these policies can be obtained by contacting the Office for Prospective Students. Though residence hall and meal plan fees vary, new students should budget about $7600 per year for room and board. Books and supplies are approximately $1000 per year. Students should also budget extra money for personal needs and expenses.

Financial Aid

The University administers more than $88 million annually in grants, scholarships, student employment, and loans. To be eligible for financial aid, a student must be admitted into a degree program at the University.

To access all need-based programs, the Free Application for Federal Student Aid (FAFSA) must be filed with the federal processor as soon as possible after January 1 for the upcoming academic year. Early filers with the greatest financial need have the best opportunity for grant and work-study programs. The FAFSA can be filed on the Internet or in a paper format.

Students should apply for admission early in the fall to maximize the opportunity for University scholarships. The University of Nevada awards merit scholarships to incoming freshmen based upon grade point average (GPA) and ACT or SAT test scores. New transfer students are evaluated by college GPA. For priority consideration for scholarships, students must be admitted by February 1; awards are made based upon available funds. Students admitted by November 15 are considered for early awarding of merit scholarships.

Faculty

In fall 2007, the University had a total of 999 full-time-equivalent faculty members. Students benefit from studying at a school where approximately 94 percent of tenured faculty members and 79 percent of full-time faculty members hold the highest degrees attainable in their fields, and more than 90 percent of classes are taught by professors, not graduate students. Since the University of Nevada, Reno, is a land-grant institution, faculty members are expected to teach, conduct research, and provide public service to the state. The student-faculty ratio is 17:1.

Student Government

The ASUN government represents students in all University affairs. The ASUN Senate is composed of students from every school and college on campus. Students appointed by the ASUN president serve on University-wide committees and represent the students' viewpoints on all issues. ASUN recognizes more than 180 organizations, ranging from the advertising and international clubs to the peace and human rights group and wildlife organizations. It also provides the financial support for concerts, lecture series, and dining events. Students participate in annual major events, such as Homecoming, Mackay Week, and Winter Carnival, which are sponsored by ASUN and the Greek organizations. ASUN also operates the campus bookstore.

Admission Requirements

To be admitted as a freshman, a potential student must be a graduate of an accredited high school and have an academic GPA of 3.00 (weighted) or above in the following courses: 4 years of English, 3 years of mathematics (algebra 1 or higher), 3 years of natural science (with at least 2 years of laboratory sciences), and 3 years of social science. Prospective freshmen may submit college entrance examination (ACT/SAT) scores. The state of Nevada also requires that all applicants have had a tetanus-diphtheria immunization in the last ten years and two doses of measles-mumps-rubella vaccine prior to admittance.

To be admitted as a transfer, a potential student must have completed a minimum of 24 transferable credits with a GPA of at least 2.5.

International students must have a score of at least 61 on the Internet-based or 500 on the paper-based Test of English as a Foreign Language (TOEFL) or a recommendation from the Intensive English Language Center (IELC). They must also provide financial verification equivalent to tuition, fees, and living expenses for one academic year. For more information, students should contact International Application Services/074, University of Nevada, Reno, Reno, Nevada 89557 U.S.A. or call 775-784-6318 or visit the University's Web site at http://www.unr.edu/oiss.

Application and Information

Application for admission can be made at any time but should be completed no later than February 1 for the fall semester and November 1 for the spring semester. To apply, individuals must submit a completed application form, a nonrefundable $60 application fee, immunization records, and official transcripts sent directly from the high school or each college the student attended. ACT or SAT scores are used for math and English placement and scholarship consideration. Transfer students are not required to submit ACT or SAT scores. Online applications are available via the University's Web site. Students may register for classes beginning in April for summer and fall semesters and November for spring.

For a campus tour and other information, students should contact:

Office for Prospective Students/110
University of Nevada, Reno
Reno, Nevada 89557-0002
Phone: 775-784-4700 Option 1
866-2NEVADA (toll-free)
E-mail: asknevada@unr.edu
Web site: http://www.unr.edu

NEW HAMPSHIRE

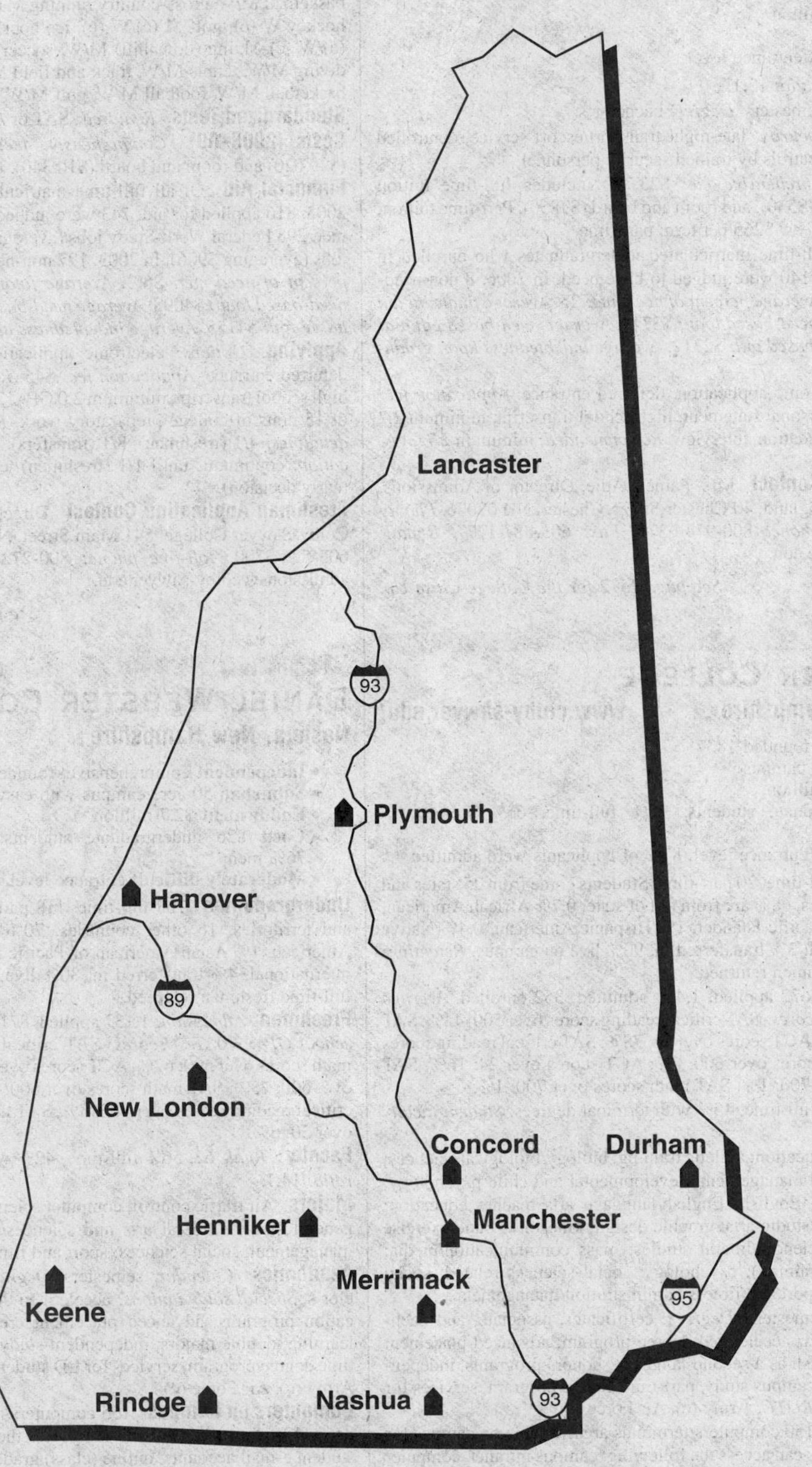

CHESTER COLLEGE OF NEW ENGLAND

Chester, New Hampshire **www.chestercollege.edu/**

- **Independent** 4-year, founded 1965
- **Rural** 75-acre campus with easy access to Boston
- **Endowment** $3.1 million
- **Coed**
- **Moderately difficult** entrance level

Faculty *Student/faculty ratio:* 12:1.

Academics *Calendar:* semesters. *Degree:* bachelor's.

Student Life *Campus security:* late-night transport/escort service, controlled dormitory access, regular patrols by trained security personnel.

Costs (2007–08) *Comprehensive fee:* $23,780 includes full-time tuition ($15,400), mandatory fees ($530), and room and board ($7850). Part-time tuition: $640 per credit. *Required fees:* $265 per term part-time.

Financial Aid Of all full-time matriculated undergraduates who enrolled in 2006, 148 applied for aid, 140 were judged to have need. In 2006, 8 non-need-based awards were made. *Average percent of need met:* 25. *Average financial aid package:* $7200. *Average need-based loan:* $3713. *Average need-based gift aid:* $2545. *Average non-need-based aid:* $2312. *Average indebtedness upon graduation:* $32,915.

Applying *Options:* electronic application, deferred entrance. *Application fee:* $35. *Required:* essay or personal statement, high school transcript, minimum 2.2 GPA, 2 letters of recommendation, interview. *Recommended:* minimum 2.7 GPA, portfolio.

Freshman Application Contact Mrs. Pamela Adie, Director of Admissions, Chester College of New England, 40 Chester Street, Chester, NH 03036. *Phone:* 603-887-7400. *Toll-free phone:* 800-974-6372. *Fax:* 603-887-1777. *E-mail:* admissions@chestercollege.edu.

See page 1512 for the College Close-Up.

COLBY-SAWYER COLLEGE

New London, New Hampshire **www.colby-sawyer.edu/**

- **Independent** 4-year, founded 1837
- **Small-town** 200-acre campus
- **Endowment** $28.2 million
- **Coed** 948 undergraduate students, 98% full-time, 65% women, 35% men
- **Moderately difficult** entrance level, 87% of applicants were admitted

Undergraduates 928 full-time, 20 part-time. Students come from 25 states and territories, 11 other countries, 68% are from out of state, 0.7% African American, 0.6% Asian American or Pacific Islander, 1% Hispanic American, 0.4% Native American, 1% international, 3% transferred in, 90% live on campus. *Retention:* 71% of 2006 full-time freshmen returned.

Freshmen *Admission:* 1,672 applied, 1,454 admitted, 352 enrolled. *Average high school GPA:* 3.0. *Test scores:* SAT critical reading scores over 500: 44%; SAT math scores over 500: 46%; ACT scores over 18: 78%; SAT critical reading scores over 600: 9%; SAT math scores over 600: 8%; ACT scores over 24: 16%; SAT critical reading scores over 700: 1%; SAT math scores over 700: 1%.

Faculty *Total:* 127, 47% full-time, 45% with terminal degrees. *Student/faculty ratio:* 11:1.

Majors Art; art teacher education; athletic training; biology/biological sciences; business administration and management; developmental and child psychology; early childhood education; English; English/language arts teacher education; environmental studies; fine/studio arts; graphic design; kinesiology and exercise science; liberal arts and sciences/liberal studies; mass communication/media; nursing (registered nurse training); psychology; social sciences related; social studies teacher education; sport and fitness administration/management.

Academics *Calendar:* semesters. *Degrees:* certificates, associate, and bachelor's. *Special study options:* accelerated degree program, advanced placement credit, double majors, English as a second language, honors programs, independent study, internships, off-campus study, part-time degree program, services for LD students, study abroad. *ROTC:* Army (c), Air Force (c).

Computers on Campus 150 computers/terminals are available on campus for general student use. Students can access the following: campus intranet, computer help desk, free student e-mail accounts. Campuswide network is available. 100% of college-owned or -operated housing units are wired for high-speed Internet access. Wireless service is available via entire campus.

Student Life *Housing:* on-campus residence required for freshman year. *Options:* coed, women-only, disabled students. Campus housing is university owned. Freshman campus housing is guaranteed. *Activities and organizations:* drama/theater group, student-run newspaper, radio station, choral group, Student Government Association, campus radio station, Alpha Chi Honor Society, Outing Club. *Campus security:* 24-hour emergency response devices and patrols, late-night transport/escort service, controlled dormitory access, awareness seminars. *Student services:* health clinic, personal/psychological counseling.

Athletics Member NCAA. All Division III. *Intercollegiate sports:* baseball M, basketball M/W, cross-country running M (c)/W (c), equestrian sports M/W, field hockey W (c), golf M (c)/W (c), ice hockey M (c)/W (c), lacrosse W, rugby M (c)/W (c), skiing (downhill) M/W, soccer M/W, softball W (c), swimming and diving M/W, tennis M/W, track and field M/W, volleyball W. *Intramural sports:* basketball M/W, football M/W, golf M/W, volleyball M/W.

Standardized Tests *Required:* SAT or ACT (for admission).

Costs (2008–09) *Comprehensive fee:* $39,960 includes full-time tuition ($29,620) and room and board ($10,340). Part-time tuition: $990 per credit hour.

Financial Aid Of all full-time matriculated undergraduates who enrolled in 2003, 816 applied for aid, 743 were judged to have need, 16 had their need fully met. 298 Federal Work-Study jobs (averaging $939). 78 state and other part-time jobs (averaging $906). In 2003, 127 non-need-based awards were made. *Average percent of need met:* 86%. *Average financial aid package:* $15,250. *Average need-based loan:* $4098. *Average need-based gift aid:* $7500. *Average non-need-based aid:* $4155. *Average indebtedness upon graduation:* $18,050.

Applying *Options:* electronic application, early admission, early decision, deferred entrance. *Application fee:* $45. *Required:* essay or personal statement, high school transcript, minimum 2.0 GPA, 2 letters of recommendation, minimum of 15 units of college preparatory work. *Recommended:* interview. *Application deadlines:* 4/1 (freshmen), 8/1 (transfers). *Early decision deadline:* 12/1. *Notification:* continuous until 1/1 (freshmen), continuous until 1/1 (transfers), 12/15 (early decision).

Freshman Application Contact Director of Admissions and Financial Aid, Colby-Sawyer College, 541 Main Street, New London, NH 03257-4648. *Phone:* 603-526-3700. *Toll-free phone:* 800-272-1015. *Fax:* 603-526-3452. *E-mail:* admissions@colby-sawyer.edu.

See page 1514 for the College Close-Up.

DANIEL WEBSTER COLLEGE

Nashua, New Hampshire **www.dwc.edu/**

- **Independent** comprehensive, founded 1965
- **Suburban** 50-acre campus with easy access to Boston
- **Endowment** $2.7 million
- **Coed** 826 undergraduate students, 86% full-time, 24% women, 76% men
- **Moderately difficult** entrance level, 77% of applicants were admitted

Undergraduates 708 full-time, 118 part-time. Students come from 23 states and territories, 16 other countries, 70% are from out of state, 4% African American, 1% Asian American or Pacific Islander, 3% Hispanic American, 3% international, 4% transferred in, 80% live on campus. *Retention:* 69% of 2006 full-time freshmen returned.

Freshmen *Admission:* 1,137 applied, 871 admitted, 229 enrolled. *Average high school GPA:* 3.0. *Test scores:* SAT critical reading scores over 500: 60%; SAT math scores over 500: 62%; ACT scores over 18: 78%; SAT critical reading scores over 600: 25%; SAT math scores over 600: 26%; ACT scores over 24: 21%; SAT critical reading scores over 700: 5%; SAT math scores over 700: 5%; ACT scores over 30: 5%.

Faculty *Total:* 62, 56% full-time, 42% with terminal degrees. *Student/faculty ratio:* 14:1.

Majors Air traffic control; computer science; engineering; engineering science; general studies; liberal arts and sciences/liberal studies; marketing/marketing management; social sciences; sport and fitness administration/management.

Academics *Calendar:* semesters. *Degrees:* certificates, associate, and bachelor's. *Special study options:* accelerated degree program, adult/continuing education programs, advanced placement credit, cooperative education, distance learning, double majors, independent study, internships, off-campus study, part-time degree program, services for LD students, summer session for credit. *ROTC:* Army (c), Air Force (c).

Computers on Campus 155 computers/terminals are available on campus for general student use. Students can access the following: computer help desk, free student e-mail accounts, online (class) grades, online (class) schedules. Campuswide network is available. 100% of college-owned or -operated housing units are wired for high-speed Internet access. Wireless service is available via entire campus.

Student Life *Housing:* on-campus residence required through sophomore year. *Options:* coed, men-only, women-only, disabled students. Campus housing is university owned. Freshman campus housing is guaranteed. *Activities and orga-*

nizations: drama/theater group, student-run newspaper, choral group, Student Activities Board, OAK (Outdoor Adventure Klub), Ice Hockey Club, student government, jazz band. *Campus security:* 24-hour emergency response devices and patrols, student patrols, late-night transport/escort service, controlled dormitory access. *Student services:* health clinic, personal/psychological counseling, women's center.

Athletics Member NCAA. All Division III. *Intercollegiate sports:* baseball M, basketball M/W, cross-country running M/W, field hockey W, golf M/W, ice hockey M (c)/W (c), lacrosse M/W, soccer M/W, softball W, volleyball M/W. *Intramural sports:* basketball M/W, cross-country running M/W, football M/W, golf M/W, rock climbing M/W, skiing (cross-country) M/W, skiing (downhill) M (c)/W (c), soccer M/W, softball M/W, tennis M/W, ultimate Frisbee M/W, volleyball M/W, weight lifting M/W.

Standardized Tests *Required:* SAT or ACT (for admission).

Costs (2008–09) *Comprehensive fee:* $36,651 includes full-time tuition ($26,357), mandatory fees ($925), and room and board ($9369). Part-time tuition: $1036 per credit. *Required fees:* $275 per credit part-time. *College room only:* $4622.

Financial Aid Of all full-time matriculated undergraduates who enrolled in 2006, 567 applied for aid, 566 were judged to have need. 369 Federal Work-Study jobs (averaging $2000). In 2006, 31 non-need-based awards were made. *Average percent of need met:* 72%. *Average financial aid package:* $15,371. *Average need-based loan:* $4257. *Average need-based gift aid:* $6114. *Average non-need-based aid:* $8287. *Average indebtedness upon graduation:* $45,000.

Applying *Options:* electronic application, early admission, early decision, deferred entrance. *Application fee:* $35. *Required:* high school transcript. *Recommended:* essay or personal statement, 2 letters of recommendation, interview. *Application deadlines:* rolling (freshmen), rolling (transfers). *Notification:* continuous (freshmen), continuous (transfers).

Freshman Application Contact Daniel Webster College, 20 University Drive, Nashua, NH 03063. *Phone:* 603-577-6600. *Toll-free phone:* 800-325-6876.

See page 1516 for the College Close-Up.

DARTMOUTH COLLEGE

Hanover, New Hampshire **www.dartmouth.edu/**

- **Independent** university, founded 1769
- **Small-town** 265-acre campus
- **Endowment** $3.8 billion
- **Coed** 4,164 undergraduate students, 99% full-time, 50% women, 50% men
- **Most difficult** entrance level, 15% of applicants were admitted

Undergraduates 4,109 full-time, 55 part-time. Students come from 54 states and territories, 47 other countries, 96% are from out of state, 7% African American, 14% Asian American or Pacific Islander, 6% Hispanic American, 4% Native American, 6% international, 0.7% transferred in, 86% live on campus. *Retention:* 98% of 2006 full-time freshmen returned.

Freshmen *Admission:* 14,176 applied, 2,166 admitted, 1,119 enrolled. *Test scores:* SAT critical reading scores over 500: 99%; SAT math scores over 500: 100%; SAT writing scores over 500: 99%; ACT scores over 18: 100%; SAT critical reading scores over 600: 91%; SAT math scores over 600: 93%; SAT writing scores over 600: 91%; ACT scores over 24: 94%; SAT critical reading scores over 700: 65%; SAT math scores over 700: 65%; SAT writing scores over 700: 64%; ACT scores over 30: 67%.

Faculty *Total:* 647, 76% full-time, 87% with terminal degrees. *Student/faculty ratio:* 8:1.

Majors African-American/Black studies; African studies; American Indian/Native American studies; ancient/classical Greek; animal genetics; anthropology; Arabic; archeology; art history, criticism and conservation; Asian studies; astronomy; biochemistry; biology/biological sciences; chemistry; chemistry related; Chinese; classics and languages, literatures and linguistics; cognitive psychology and psycholinguistics; comparative literature; computer science; creative writing; dramatic/theater arts; East Asian languages related; ecology; economics; engineering; engineering physics; English; environmental studies; evolutionary biology; film/cinema studies; fine/studio arts; French; geography; geology/earth science; German; Hebrew; Hispanic-American, Puerto Rican, and Mexican-American/Chicano studies; history; Italian; Japanese; Latin; Latin American studies; linguistics; mathematics; molecular biology; multi-/interdisciplinary studies related; music; Near and Middle Eastern studies; philosophy; physics; political science and government; psychology; religious studies; Romance languages; Russian; Russian studies; sociology; Spanish; women's studies.

Academics *Calendar:* quarters. *Degrees:* bachelor's, master's, doctoral, and first professional. *Special study options:* advanced placement credit, double majors, honors programs, independent study, internships, off-campus study, services for LD students, student-designed majors, study abroad, summer session for credit. *ROTC:* Army (c).

Computers on Campus 200 computers/terminals are available on campus for general student use. Students can access the following: campus intranet, computer help desk, free student e-mail accounts, online (class) grades, online (class) registration, online (class) schedules. Campuswide network is available. 100% of college-owned or -operated housing units are wired for high-speed Internet access. Wireless service is available via entire campus.

Student Life *Housing:* on-campus residence required for freshman year. *Options:* coed, cooperative. Campus housing is university owned. Freshman campus housing is guaranteed. *Activities and organizations:* drama/theater group, student-run newspaper, radio and television station, choral group, marching band, student government, Outing Club, intramural sports, community service, performing arts organizations, national fraternities, national sororities. *Campus security:* 24-hour emergency response devices and patrols, student patrols, late-night transport/escort service, controlled dormitory access. *Student services:* health clinic, personal/psychological counseling, women's center.

Athletics Member NCAA. All Division I except football (Division I-AA). *Intercollegiate sports:* badminton M (c)/W (c), baseball M, basketball M/W, cheerleading M (c)/W (c), crew M/W, cross-country running M/W, equestrian sports M/W, fencing M (c)/W (c), field hockey W, golf M/W, gymnastics M (c)/W (c), ice hockey M/W, lacrosse M/W, rugby M (c)/W (c), sailing M/W, skiing (cross-country) M/W, skiing (downhill) M/W, soccer M/W, softball W, squash M/W, swimming and diving M/W, table tennis M (c)/W (c), tennis M/W, track and field M/W, ultimate Frisbee M (c)/W (c), volleyball M (c)/W, water polo M (c)/W (c), wrestling M (c). *Intramural sports:* baseball M, basketball M/W, cross-country running M/W, football M/W, golf M/W, ice hockey M/W, lacrosse M/W, racquetball M/W, riflery M/W, rugby M/W, skiing (cross-country) M/W, skiing (downhill) M/W, soccer M/W, softball M/W, squash M/W, swimming and diving M/W, table tennis M/W, tennis M/W, track and field M/W, volleyball M/W, water polo M/W, weight lifting M/W, wrestling M.

Standardized Tests *Required:* SAT and SAT Subject Tests or ACT (for admission).

Costs (2007–08) *Comprehensive fee:* $45,483 includes full-time tuition ($34,965), mandatory fees ($213), and room and board ($10,305). *College room only:* $6165.

Financial Aid Of all full-time matriculated undergraduates who enrolled in 2006, 2,489 applied for aid, 2,082 were judged to have need, 2,082 had their need fully met. 1,564 Federal Work-Study jobs (averaging $1787). 429 state and other part-time jobs (averaging $1762). In 2006, 10 non-need-based awards were made. *Average percent of need met:* 100%. *Average financial aid package:* $31,802. *Average need-based loan:* $4279. *Average need-based gift aid:* $27,785. *Average non-need-based aid:* $450. *Average indebtedness upon graduation:* $21,561. *Financial aid deadline:* 2/1.

Applying *Options:* electronic application, early admission, early decision, deferred entrance. *Application fee:* $70. *Required:* essay or personal statement, high school transcript, 2 letters of recommendation, peer evaluation. *Recommended:* interview. *Application deadlines:* 1/1 (freshmen), 3/1 (transfers). *Early decision deadline:* 11/1. *Notification:* 4/10 (freshmen), 4/25 (transfers), 12/15 (early decision).

Freshman Application Contact Maria Laskaris, Dean of Admissions and Financial Aid, Dartmouth College, 6016 McNutt Hall, Hanover, NH 03755. *Phone:* 603-646-2875. *Toll-free phone:* 603-646-2875. *E-mail:* admissions.office@dartmouth.edu.

FRANKLIN PIERCE UNIVERSITY

Rindge, New Hampshire **www.franklinpierce.edu/**

- **Independent** comprehensive, founded 1962
- **Rural** 1000-acre campus
- **Endowment** $9.2 million
- **Coed**
- **Moderately difficult** entrance level

Faculty *Student/faculty ratio:* 17:1.

Academics *Calendar:* semesters. *Degrees:* bachelor's (profile does not reflect significant enrollment at 6 continuing education sites; master's degree is only offered at these sites).

Student Life *Campus security:* 24-hour emergency response devices and patrols, student patrols, late-night transport/escort service, controlled dormitory access.

Athletics Member NCAA. All Division II.

Standardized Tests *Required:* SAT or ACT (for admission).

Costs (2007–08) *Comprehensive fee:* $35,456 includes full-time tuition ($25,516), mandatory fees ($1300), and room and board ($8640). Full-time tuition and fees vary according to course load and location. Part-time tuition: $851 per credit. *College room only:* $4860. Room and board charges vary according to board plan, housing facility, and student level.

Financial Aid Of all full-time matriculated undergraduates who enrolled in 2006, 1,306 applied for aid, 1,182 were judged to have need, 128 had their need fully met. 758 Federal Work-Study jobs (averaging $1467). 183 state and other part-time jobs (averaging $2128). In 2006, 305 non-need-based awards were made. *Average percent of need met:* 67. *Average financial aid package:* $16,346. *Average need-based loan:* $4486. *Average need-based gift aid:* $11,888. *Average non-need-based aid:* $11,589. *Average indebtedness upon graduation:* $28,036.

Applying *Options:* electronic application, early admission, deferred entrance. *Required:* essay or personal statement, high school transcript, 1 letter of recommendation. *Recommended:* minimum 2.0 GPA, interview.

Freshman Application Contact Office of Admissions, Franklin Pierce University, Box 60, 20 College Road, Rindge, NH 03461. *Phone:* 603-899-4050. *Toll-free phone:* 800-437-0048. *Fax:* 603-899-4394. *E-mail:* admissions@fpc.edu.

See page 1518 for the College Close-Up.

GRANITE STATE COLLEGE

Concord, New Hampshire **www.granite.edu/**

- **State and locally supported** 4-year, founded 1972, part of University System of New Hampshire
- **Small-town** campus
- **Endowment** $20,374
- **Coed** 1,334 undergraduate students, 38% full-time, 77% women, 23% men
- **Noncompetitive** entrance level, 100% of applicants were admitted

Undergraduates 503 full-time, 831 part-time. Students come from 19 states and territories, 1 other country, 9% are from out of state, 0.6% African American, 0.7% Asian American or Pacific Islander, 0.9% Hispanic American, 1% Native American, 12% transferred in. *Retention:* 50% of 2006 full-time freshmen returned.

Freshmen *Admission:* 80 applied, 80 admitted, 49 enrolled.

Faculty *Total:* 142. *Student/faculty ratio:* 10:1.

Majors Behavioral sciences; business administration and management; computer management; computer programming; computer systems analysis; corrections and criminal justice related; criminal justice/law enforcement administration; early childhood education; finance; general studies; health/health care administration; human resources management; liberal arts and sciences/liberal studies.

Academics *Calendar:* semesters. *Degrees:* associate, bachelor's, and post-bachelor's certificates (offers primarily part-time degree programs; courses offered at 50 locations in New Hampshire). *Special study options:* academic remediation for entering students, accelerated degree program, adult/continuing education programs, advanced placement credit, cooperative education, distance learning, double majors, independent study, internships, off-campus study, part-time degree program, services for LD students, student-designed majors, summer session for credit.

Computers on Campus 128 computers/terminals are available on campus for general student use. Students can access the following: campus intranet, computer help desk, free student e-mail accounts, online (class) grades, online (class) registration, online (class) schedules. Campuswide network is available. Wireless service is available via entire campus.

Student Life *Housing:* college housing not available. *Activities and organizations:* Alumni Learner Association.

Costs (2007–08) *Tuition:* state resident $5328 full-time, $222 per credit part-time; nonresident $5760 full-time, $240 per credit part-time. *Required fees:* $195 full-time, $65 per term part-time. *Payment plan:* deferred payment. *Waivers:* senior citizens and employees or children of employees.

Applying *Options:* electronic application. *Application fee:* $45. *Required:* essay or personal statement, self-certify high school grad/GED. *Application deadlines:* rolling (freshmen), rolling (transfers). *Notification:* continuous (freshmen), continuous (transfers).

Freshman Application Contact Ms. Tessa McDonnell, Dean of Learner Services, Granite State College, 125 North State Street, Concord, NH 03301. *Phone:* 603-513-1308. *Toll-free phone:* 800-582-7248 Ext. 313. *Fax:* 603-513-1386. *E-mail:* tessa.mcdonnell@granite.edu.

HESSER COLLEGE

Manchester, New Hampshire **www.hesser.edu/**

- **Proprietary** primarily 2-year, founded 1900, part of Quest Education Corporation
- **Urban** 1-acre campus with easy access to Boston
- **Coed**
- **Moderately difficult** entrance level

Academics *Calendar:* semesters. *Degrees:* certificates, diplomas, associate, and bachelor's.

Student Life *Campus security:* 24-hour emergency response devices and patrols, student patrols, late-night transport/escort service, controlled dormitory access.

Standardized Tests *Recommended:* SAT (for admission).

Financial Aid Of all full-time matriculated undergraduates who enrolled in 2006, 700 Federal Work-Study jobs (averaging $1000).

Applying *Options:* electronic application, deferred entrance. *Application fee:* $10. *Required:* high school transcript, interview. *Required for some:* essay or personal statement, letters of recommendation. *Recommended:* minimum 2.0 GPA.

Freshman Application Contact Director of Admissions, Hesser College, 3 Sundial Avenue, Manchester, NH 03103. *Phone:* 888-234-4000 Ext. 266.

See page 1520 for the College Close-Up.

KEENE STATE COLLEGE

Keene, New Hampshire **www.keene.edu/**

- **State-supported** comprehensive, founded 1909, part of University System of New Hampshire
- **Small-town** 160-acre campus
- **Endowment** $11.2 million
- **Coed** 5,002 undergraduate students, 91% full-time, 57% women, 43% men
- **Moderately difficult** entrance level, 73% of applicants were admitted

Keene State College celebrates its centennial in 2009 as a dynamic public institution with an enrollment of 5,200, offering forty majors in the liberal arts and sciences, professional programs, and selected graduate degrees. Keene State emphasizes academic excellence, integrative learning, community engagement, faculty scholars, and a tradition of small classes and spirited inquiry.

Undergraduates 4,541 full-time, 461 part-time. Students come from 28 states and territories, 4 other countries, 46% are from out of state, 0.6% African American, 0.5% Asian American or Pacific Islander, 0.9% Hispanic American, 0.2% international, 4% transferred in, 60% live on campus. *Retention:* 80% of 2006 full-time freshmen returned.

Freshmen *Admission:* 4,676 applied, 3,425 admitted, 1,301 enrolled. *Average high school GPA:* 2.99. *Test scores:* SAT critical reading scores over 500: 46%; SAT math scores over 500: 46%; SAT writing scores over 500: 48%; SAT critical reading scores over 600: 9%; SAT math scores over 600: 9%; SAT writing scores over 600: 8%; SAT critical reading scores over 700: 1%; SAT writing scores over 700: 1%.

Faculty *Total:* 425, 44% full-time, 41% with terminal degrees. *Student/faculty ratio:* 18:1.

Majors Acting; American studies; applied mathematics; architectural technology; art; athletic training; biology/biological sciences; biology teacher education; business administration and management; chemistry; chemistry related; chemistry teacher education; cinematography and film/video production; clinical psychology; commercial and advertising art; communication/speech communication and rhetoric; computer and information sciences; computer science; computer teacher education; counselor education/school counseling and guidance; curriculum and instruction; dance; developmental and child psychology; dietetics; drafting and design technology; dramatic/theater arts; early childhood education; ecology; economics; education; educational leadership and administration; education (specific subject areas) related; electrical, electronic and communications engineering technology; electromechanical and instrumentation and maintenance technologies related; elementary education; engineering technologies related; English; English/language arts teacher education; environmental science; environmental studies; experimental psychology; family and consumer sciences/home economics teacher education; fine/studio arts; foods, nutrition, and wellness; French; French language teacher education; general studies; geography; geography teacher education; geology/earth science; graphic design; health and physical education; health teacher education; history; history teacher education; industrial arts; industrial technology; interdisciplinary studies; journalism; kindergarten/preschool education; liberal arts and sciences/liberal studies; mass communication/media; mathematics; mathematics and computer science; mathematics teacher education; multi-/interdisciplinary studies related; music; music history, literature, and theory; music related; music teacher education; natural resources/conservation; occupational safety and health technology; physical education teaching and coaching; pre-engineering; psychology; safety/security technology; science teacher education; secondary education; social sciences; social science teacher education; social studies teacher education; sociology; Spanish; Spanish language teacher education; special education; special education related; sport and fitness administration/management; substance abuse/addiction counseling; technology/industrial arts teacher education; theater design and technology; trade and industrial teacher education.

Academics *Calendar:* semesters. *Degrees:* certificates, bachelor's, master's, post-master's, and postbachelor's certificates. *Special study options:* advanced placement credit, cooperative education, double majors, English as a second language, honors programs, independent study, internships, off-campus study, part-time degree program, services for LD students, student-designed majors, study abroad, summer session for credit. *ROTC:* Air Force (c). *Unusual degree programs:* 3-2 engineering with Clarkson University, University of New Hampshire.

Computers on Campus 500 computers/terminals are available on campus for general student use. Students can access the following: campus intranet, computer help desk, free student e-mail accounts, online (class) grades, online (class) registration, online (class) schedules, personal Web pages. Campuswide network is available. 100% of college-owned or -operated housing units are wired for high-speed Internet access. Wireless service is available via classrooms, computer centers, computer labs, dorm rooms, learning centers, libraries, student centers.

Student Life *Housing options:* coed, women-only, disabled students. Campus housing is university owned. Freshman campus housing is guaranteed. *Activities and organizations:* drama/theater group, student-run newspaper, radio and television station, choral group, Social Activities Council, Concerned Students Coalition, Pride, Habitat for Humanity, Sports Club, national fraternities, national sororities. *Campus security:* 24-hour emergency response devices and patrols, late-night transport/escort service, controlled dormitory access. *Student services:* health clinic, personal/psychological counseling, women's center.

Athletics Member NCAA. All Division III. *Intercollegiate sports:* baseball M, basketball M/W, cross-country running M/W, field hockey W, lacrosse M/W, rock climbing M (c)/W (c), skiing (downhill) M (c)/W (c), soccer M/W, softball W, swimming and diving M/W, track and field M/W, volleyball W. *Intramural sports:* badminton M/W, basketball M/W, cheerleading M/W, fencing M (c), football M/W, racquetball M/W, soccer W, softball M/W, squash M/W, tennis M/W, volleyball M/W, water polo M/W.

Standardized Tests *Required:* SAT or ACT (for admission).

Costs (2007–08) *Tuition:* state resident $6180 full-time, $258 per credit part-time; nonresident $13,730 full-time, $572 per credit part-time. Part-time tuition and fees vary according to course load. *Required fees:* $2118 full-time, $84 per credit part-time. *Room and board:* $7460; room only: $5030. Room and board charges vary according to board plan and housing facility. *Payment plan:* installment. *Waivers:* senior citizens and employees or children of employees.

Financial Aid Of all full-time matriculated undergraduates who enrolled in 2005, 2,985 applied for aid, 2,139 were judged to have need, 491 had their need fully met. 604 Federal Work-Study jobs (averaging $870). 522 state and other part-time jobs (averaging $878). In 2005, 338 non-need-based awards were made. *Average percent of need met:* 71%. *Average financial aid package:* $7802. *Average need-based loan:* $3753. *Average need-based gift aid:* $4241. *Average non-need-based aid:* $2658. *Average indebtedness upon graduation:* $20,992. *Financial aid deadline:* 3/1.

Applying *Options:* electronic application, deferred entrance. *Application fee:* $35. *Required:* essay or personal statement, high school transcript, 1 letter of recommendation. *Required for some:* interview. *Recommended:* interview. *Application deadlines:* 4/1 (freshmen), rolling (transfers). *Notification:* continuous (freshmen), continuous (transfers).

Freshman Application Contact Ms. Margaret Richmond, Director of Admissions, Keene State College, 229 Main Street, Keene, NH 03435-2604. *Phone:* 603-358-2273. *Toll-free phone:* 800-KSC-1909. *Fax:* 603-358-2767. *E-mail:* admissions@keene.edu.

See page 1522 for the College Close-Up.

MAGDALEN COLLEGE

Warner, New Hampshire **www.magdalen.edu/**

Freshman Application Contact Mr. Justin Fout, Admissions Counselor, Magdalen College, 511 Kearsarge Mountain Road, Warner, NH 03278. *Phone:* 603-456-2656 Ext. 12. *Toll-free phone:* 877-498-1723. *Fax:* 603-456-2660. *E-mail:* admissions@magdalen.edu.

NEW ENGLAND COLLEGE

Henniker, New Hampshire **www.nec.edu/**

- **Independent** comprehensive, founded 1946
- **Small-town** 225-acre campus with easy access to Boston
- **Endowment** $7.3 million
- **Coed** 1,059 undergraduate students, 97% full-time, 47% women, 53% men
- **Moderately difficult** entrance level, 70% of applicants were admitted

Undergraduates 1,029 full-time, 30 part-time. Students come from 37 states and territories, 19 other countries, 68% are from out of state, 3% African American, 0.6% Asian American or Pacific Islander, 2% Hispanic American, 0.2% Native American, 7% international, 6% transferred in, 67% live on campus. *Retention:* 63% of 2006 full-time freshmen returned.

Freshmen *Admission:* 2,150 applied, 1,511 admitted, 306 enrolled. *Average high school GPA:* 2.66. *Test scores:* SAT critical reading scores over 500: 25%; SAT math scores over 500: 26%; SAT writing scores over 500: 24%; ACT scores over 18: 34%; SAT critical reading scores over 600: 6%; SAT math scores over 600: 5%; SAT writing scores over 600: 2%.

Faculty *Total:* 149, 41% full-time, 40% with terminal degrees. *Student/faculty ratio:* 13:1.

Majors Accounting; art; art history, criticism and conservation; biology/biological sciences; business administration and management; comparative literature; computer management; creative writing; criminal justice/law enforcement administration; dramatic/theater arts; drawing; education; education (K-12); elementary education; English; environmental science; environmental studies; finance; fine/studio arts; health and physical education; health/health care administration; history; journalism; liberal arts and sciences/liberal studies; marketing/marketing management; mass communication/media; parks, recreation and leisure; parks, recreation and leisure facilities management; philosophy; photography; physical education teaching and coaching; political science and government; pre-law studies; psychology; public relations/image management; secondary education; sociology; special education; sport and fitness administration/management.

Academics *Calendar:* semesters. *Degrees:* associate, bachelor's, and master's. *Special study options:* academic remediation for entering students, adult/continuing education programs, advanced placement credit, distance learning, double majors, English as a second language, external degree program, honors programs, independent study, internships, off-campus study, part-time degree program, services for LD students, student-designed majors, study abroad, summer session for credit. *ROTC:* Army (c), Air Force (c). *Unusual degree programs:* 3-2 business administration with Union College; engineering with Clarkson University.

Computers on Campus 151 computers/terminals and 300 ports are available on campus for general student use. Students can access the following: computer help desk, free student e-mail accounts, online (class) grades, online (class) registration, online (class) schedules. Campuswide network is available. 100% of college-owned or -operated housing units are wired for high-speed Internet access. Wireless service is available via entire campus.

Student Life *Housing:* on-campus residence required through sophomore year. *Options:* coed. Campus housing is university owned. Freshman campus housing is guaranteed. *Activities and organizations:* drama/theater group, student-run newspaper, radio station, choral group, Student Senate, Campus Activities Board, Role Playing Association, International Student Association, History Club, national fraternities, national sororities. *Campus security:* 24-hour emergency response devices and patrols, student patrols, late-night transport/escort service, controlled dormitory access. *Student services:* health clinic, personal/psychological counseling.

Athletics Member NCAA. All Division III. *Intercollegiate sports:* baseball M, basketball M/W, cross-country running M/W, field hockey W, ice hockey M/W, lacrosse M/W, skiing (downhill) M/W, soccer M/W, softball W. *Intramural sports:* badminton M/W, basketball M/W, cheerleading W, ice hockey M/W, rugby M/W, skiing (downhill) M/W, soccer M/W, softball W, tennis M/W, volleyball M/W.

Costs (2008–09) *Comprehensive fee:* $35,748 includes full-time tuition ($26,270), mandatory fees ($200), and room and board ($9278). Part-time tuition: $821 per credit. *College room only:* $4826.

Financial Aid Of all full-time matriculated undergraduates who enrolled in 2006, 855 applied for aid, 637 were judged to have need, 386 had their need fully met. 455 Federal Work-Study jobs (averaging $1788). 46 state and other part-time jobs (averaging $1100). In 2006, 300 non-need-based awards were made. *Average percent of need met:* 90%. *Average financial aid package:* $28,694. *Average* *need-based loan:* $9515. *Average need-based gift aid:* $13,054. *Average non-need-based aid:* $10,259. *Average indebtedness upon graduation:* $29,874.

Applying *Options:* electronic application, deferred entrance. *Application fee:* $30. *Required:* essay or personal statement, high school transcript, 3 letters of recommendation. *Recommended:* interview. *Application deadlines:* rolling (freshmen), rolling (transfers). *Notification:* continuous (freshmen), continuous (transfers).

Freshman Application Contact Diane Raymond, Director of Admissions, New England College, 24 Bridge Street, Henniker, NH 03242. *Phone:* 603-428-2223. *Toll-free phone:* 800-521-7642. *Fax:* 603-428-7230. *E-mail:* admission@nec.edu.

See page 1524 for the College Close-Up.

NEW HAMPSHIRE INSTITUTE OF ART

Manchester, New Hampshire **www.nhia.edu/**

- **Proprietary** 4-year, founded 1898
- **Urban** campus with easy access to Boston, MA
- **Coed**
- **Minimally difficult** entrance level

Faculty *Student/faculty ratio:* 10:1.

Academics *Calendar:* semesters. *Degree:* certificates and bachelor's.

Standardized Tests *Recommended:* SAT or ACT (for admission).

Costs (2007–08) *Tuition:* $12,960 full-time, $432 per credit part-time. Part-time tuition and fees vary according to course load. *Required fees:* $1440 full-time, $320 per term part-time. *Room only:* $6300. Room and board charges vary according to housing facility.

Applying *Application fee:* $25. *Required:* essay or personal statement, high school transcript, letters of recommendation, portfolio. *Recommended:* interview.

Freshman Application Contact Ms. Amanda Abbott, Admissions Administrator, New Hampshire Institute of Art, 148 Concord Street, Manchester, NH 03104-4858. *Phone:* 603-623-0313 Ext. 576. *Toll-free phone:* 866-241-4918. *E-mail:* admissions@nhia.edu.

See page 1526 for the College Close-Up.

PLYMOUTH STATE UNIVERSITY

Plymouth, New Hampshire **www.plymouth.edu/**

- **State-supported** comprehensive, founded 1871, part of University System of New Hampshire
- **Small-town** 170-acre campus
- **Endowment** $6.2 million
- **Coed** 4,253 undergraduate students, 95% full-time, 47% women, 53% men
- **Moderately difficult** entrance level, 66% of applicants were admitted

Undergraduates 4,040 full-time, 213 part-time. Students come from 29 states and territories, 17 other countries, 40% are from out of state, 0.5% African American, 0.7% Asian American or Pacific Islander, 1% Hispanic American, 0.2% Native American, 0.5% international, 5% transferred in, 58% live on campus. *Retention:* 76% of 2006 full-time freshmen returned.

Freshmen *Admission:* 4,247 applied, 2,788 admitted, 1,012 enrolled. *Average high school GPA:* 2.79. *Test scores:* SAT critical reading scores over 500: 39%; SAT math scores over 500: 41%; ACT scores over 18: 77%; SAT critical reading scores over 600: 6%; SAT math scores over 600: 8%; ACT scores over 24: 10%.

Faculty *Total:* 452, 39% full-time, 50% with terminal degrees. *Student/faculty ratio:* 17:1.

Majors Accounting; applied economics; art; art teacher education; athletic training; atmospheric sciences and meteorology; biology/biological sciences; biotechnology; business administration and management; business/commerce; chemistry; city/urban, community and regional planning; communication/speech communication and rhetoric; computer science; criminal justice/safety; dramatic/theater arts; early childhood education; education (specific subject areas) related; elementary education; English; environmental biology; fine/studio arts; French; geography; health and physical education; history; humanities; information technology; marketing/marketing management; mathematics; multi-/interdisciplinary studies related; music; music teacher education; parks, recreation, and leisure related; philosophy; political science and government; psychology; public administration; public health education and promotion; social sciences; social sciences related; social work; Spanish.

Academics *Calendar:* semesters. *Degrees:* bachelor's, master's, post-master's, and postbachelor's certificates. *Special study options:* accelerated degree program, advanced placement credit, double majors, honors programs, independent study, internships, off-campus study, part-time degree program, services for LD students, student-designed majors, study abroad, summer session for credit. *ROTC:* Army (c), Air Force (c).

Computers on Campus 500 computers/terminals are available on campus for general student use. Students can access the following: online (class) registration, degree audit, academic history, account status. Campuswide network is available.

Student Life *Housing:* on-campus residence required for freshman year. *Options:* Campus housing is university owned. Freshman applicants given priority for college housing. *Activities and organizations:* drama/theater group, student-run newspaper, radio station, choral group, Programming Activities in College Environment, Student Senate, alternative spring break, Childhood Studies Club, Health, Physical Ed, & Recreation Club, national fraternities, national sororities. *Campus security:* 24-hour emergency response devices and patrols, student patrols, late-night transport/escort service, controlled dormitory access, shuttle bus service, crime prevention programs, self-defense education. *Student services:* health clinic, personal/psychological counseling, women's center.

Athletics Member NCAA. All Division III. *Intercollegiate sports:* baseball M, basketball M/W, cheerleading M (c)/W, field hockey W, football M, ice hockey M/W, lacrosse M/W, skiing (downhill) M/W, soccer M/W, softball W, swimming and diving W, tennis W, volleyball M (c)/W, wrestling M. *Intramural sports:* basketball M/W, football M/W, golf M/W, racquetball M/W, rugby M (c)/W (c), soccer M/W, softball M/W, table tennis M/W, tennis M/W, ultimate Frisbee M/W, volleyball M/W.

Standardized Tests *Required:* SAT or ACT (for admission).

Costs (2008–09) *Tuition:* state resident $6600 full-time, $375 per credit hour part-time; nonresident $14,450 full-time, $602 per credit hour part-time. *Required fees:* $1824 full-time. *Room and board:* $8150; room only: $5850.

Financial Aid Of all full-time matriculated undergraduates who enrolled in 2004, 3,050 applied for aid, 2,051 were judged to have need, 78 had their need fully met. 1,458 Federal Work-Study jobs (averaging $1460). In 2004, 289 non-need-based awards were made. *Average percent of need met:* 62%. *Average financial aid package:* $6993. *Average need-based loan:* $3704. *Average need-based gift aid:* $4091. *Average non-need-based aid:* $1792. *Average indebtedness upon graduation:* $23,088.

Applying *Options:* electronic application, deferred entrance. *Application fee:* $35. *Required:* essay or personal statement, high school transcript, 1 letter of recommendation. *Required for some:* interview. *Application deadlines:* 4/1 (freshmen), 4/1 (transfers). *Notification:* continuous until 4/15 (freshmen), continuous until 4/15 (transfers).

Freshman Application Contact Mr. Eugene Fahey, Senior Associate Director of Admission, Plymouth State University, 17 High Street, MSC #52, Plymouth, NH 03264-1595. *Toll-free phone:* 800-842-6900. *Fax:* 603-535-2714. *E-mail:* plymouthadmit@plymouth.edu.

RIVIER COLLEGE

Nashua, New Hampshire **www.rivier.edu/**

- **Independent Roman Catholic** comprehensive, founded 1933
- **Suburban** 68-acre campus with easy access to Boston
- **Endowment** $19.0 million
- **Coed**
- **Moderately difficult** entrance level

Rivier's School of Undergraduate Studies enrolls approximately 1,000 full-time day students and 600 undergraduate evening students. Rivier's programs combine academic achievement in the liberal arts and professional studies with hands-on preparation for the future. Special opportunities, such as the honors program, offer added challenges and enrichment.

Faculty *Student/faculty ratio:* 11:1.

Academics *Calendar:* semesters. *Degrees:* certificates, associate, bachelor's, master's, post-master's, and postbachelor's certificates.

Student Life *Campus security:* 24-hour emergency response devices and patrols, late-night transport/escort service, controlled dormitory access.

Athletics Member NCAA. except baseball (Division III), men's and women's basketball (Division III), men's and women's cheerleading (Division III), men's and women's cross-country running (Division III), men's and women's golf (Division III), men's and women's soccer (Division III), softball (Division III), men's and women's volleyball (Division III)

Standardized Tests *Required:* SAT or ACT (for admission). *Required for some:* nursing exam.

Costs (2007–08) *Comprehensive fee:* $30,920 includes full-time tuition ($21,810), mandatory fees ($850), and room and board ($8260). Full-time tuition and fees vary according to program. Part-time tuition: $727 per credit. Part-time tuition and fees vary according to class time, course level, course load, and program. *Required fees:* $25 per year part-time. *Room and board:* Room and board charges vary according to board plan and housing facility. *Payment plans:* installment, deferred payment.

Financial Aid Of all full-time matriculated undergraduates who enrolled in 2005, 810 applied for aid, 736 were judged to have need, 240 had their need fully met. 393 Federal Work-Study jobs (averaging $1107). 153 state and other part-time jobs (averaging $1304). In 2005, 142 non-need-based awards were made. *Average percent of need met:* 74. *Average financial aid package:* $14,606. *Average need-based loan:* $6666. *Average need-based gift aid:* $8193. *Average non-need-based aid:* $11,974. *Average indebtedness upon graduation:* $25,959.

Applying *Options:* early action, deferred entrance. *Application fee:* $25. *Required:* essay or personal statement, high school transcript, 1 letter of recommendation. *Required for some:* interview. *Recommended:* minimum 2.3 GPA, interview.

Freshman Application Contact David A. Boisvert, Vice President of Enrollment, Rivier College, 420 South Main Street, Nashua, NH 03060. *Phone:* 603-897-8507. *Toll-free phone:* 800-44RIVIER. *Fax:* 603-891-1799. *E-mail:* rivadmit@rivier.edu.

See page 1528 for the College Close-Up.

SAINT ANSELM COLLEGE

Manchester, New Hampshire **www.anselm.edu/**

Director of Admissions Ms. Nancy Davis Griffin, Director of Admission, Saint Anselm College, 100 Saint Anselm Drive, Manchester, NH 03102-1310. *Phone:* 603-641-7500. *Toll-free phone:* 888-4ANSELM. *E-mail:* admission@anselm.edu.

See page 1530 for the College Close-Up.

SOUTHERN NEW HAMPSHIRE UNIVERSITY

Manchester, New Hampshire **www.snhu.edu/**

- **Independent** comprehensive, founded 1932
- **Suburban** 288-acre campus with easy access to Boston
- **Endowment** $17.3 million
- **Coed** 1,982 undergraduate students, 98% full-time, 55% women, 45% men
- **Moderately difficult** entrance level, 65% of applicants were admitted

Southern New Hampshire University (SNHU) is a premier private northeastern university that offers more than forty majors in business, education, hospitality, and liberal arts disciplines. Master's and doctoral degrees are also awarded. The students and faculty members at SNHU enjoy the resources of a university while maintaining the personal approach of a small college.

Undergraduates 1,933 full-time, 49 part-time. Students come from 28 states and territories, 38 other countries, 55% are from out of state, 1% African American, 1% Asian American or Pacific Islander, 2% Hispanic American, 0.4% Native American, 4% international, 7% transferred in, 75% live on campus. *Retention:* 75% of 2006 full-time freshmen returned.

Freshmen *Admission:* 3,565 applied, 2,306 admitted, 545 enrolled. *Average high school GPA:* 2.92. *Test scores:* SAT critical reading scores over 500: 56%; SAT math scores over 500: 50%; SAT writing scores over 500: 41%; ACT scores over 18: 79%; SAT critical reading scores over 600: 9%; SAT math scores over 600: 9%; SAT writing scores over 600: 5%; ACT scores over 24: 15%; ACT scores over 30: 2%.

Faculty *Total:* 397, 33% full-time, 24% with terminal degrees. *Student/faculty ratio:* 15:1.

Majors Accounting; accounting and computer science; accounting and finance; advertising; baking and pastry arts; business administration and management; business, management, and marketing related; child development; communication and media related; computer and information sciences; corrections and criminal justice related; creative writing; culinary arts; digital communication and media/multimedia; early childhood education; economics; education; elementary education; English; English/language arts teacher education; environmental studies; fashion merchandising; general studies; graphic design; history; hospitality administration; international business/trade/commerce; liberal arts and sciences and humanities related; marketing/marketing management; political science and government; psychology; public administration; public relations, advertising, and applied communication related; retailing; social sciences; social studies teacher education; sport and fitness administration/management; tourism and travel services management.

Academics *Calendar:* semesters. *Degrees:* certificates, associate, bachelor's, master's, doctoral, and postbachelor's certificates. *Special study options:* academic remediation for entering students, accelerated degree program, adult/continuing education programs, advanced placement credit, cooperative education, distance learning, double majors, English as a second language, honors programs, independent study, internships, off-campus study, part-time degree program, services for LD students, study abroad, summer session for credit. *ROTC:* Army (c), Air Force (c). *Unusual degree programs:* 3-2 business administration.

Computers on Campus 557 computers/terminals and 1,500 ports are available on campus for general student use. Students can access the following: computer help desk, free student e-mail accounts, online (class) grades, online (class) registration, online (class) schedules. Campuswide network is available. 100% of college-owned or -operated housing units are wired for high-speed Internet access. Wireless service is available via classrooms, dorm rooms, libraries, student centers.

Student Life *Housing:* on-campus residence required for freshman year. *Options:* coed, disabled students. Campus housing is university owned. Freshman campus housing is guaranteed. *Activities and organizations:* drama/theater group, student-run newspaper, radio and television station, choral group, Student Government Association, Student Programming Board, Association Cultural Exchange, Commuter Club, national fraternities, national sororities. *Campus security:* 24-hour emergency response devices and patrols, student patrols, late-night transport/escort service, controlled dormitory access. *Student services:* health clinic, personal/psychological counseling.

Athletics Member NCAA. All Division II. *Intercollegiate sports:* baseball M (s), basketball M (s)/W (s), cheerleading M/W, cross-country running M (s)/W (s), golf M, ice hockey M, lacrosse M (s)/W (s), soccer M (s)/W (s), softball W (s), tennis M (s)/W (s), volleyball W (s). *Intramural sports:* basketball M/W, crew M (c)/W (c), field hockey M (c)/W (c), football M, racquetball M/W, soccer M (c)/W (c), softball W, table tennis M/W, tennis M/W, volleyball W.

Standardized Tests *Required:* SAT or ACT (for admission).

Costs (2007–08) *Comprehensive fee:* $32,316 includes full-time tuition ($23,016), mandatory fees ($330), and room and board ($8970). Full-time tuition and fees vary according to class time. Part-time tuition: $959 per credit. Part-time tuition and fees vary according to class time. *College room only:* $6400. Room and board charges vary according to board plan and housing facility. *Payment plan:* installment. *Waivers:* employees or children of employees.

Financial Aid Of all full-time matriculated undergraduates who enrolled in 2007, 1,560 applied for aid, 1,392 were judged to have need, 173 had their need fully met. 568 Federal Work-Study jobs (averaging $695). In 2007, 330 non-need-based awards were made. *Average percent of need met:* 67%. *Average financial aid package:* $15,514. *Average need-based loan:* $5174. *Average need-based gift aid:* $10,223. *Average non-need-based aid:* $3599.

Applying *Options:* electronic application, early action, deferred entrance. *Application fee:* $40. *Required:* essay or personal statement, high school transcript, minimum 2.0 GPA, 1 letter of recommendation from guidance counselor or 2 letters from teachers. *Recommended:* interview. *Application deadlines:* rolling (freshmen), rolling (transfers), 11/15 (early action). *Notification:* continuous (freshmen), continuous (transfers), 12/15 (early action).

Freshman Application Contact Mr. Steve Soba, Director of Admission, Southern New Hampshire University, 2500 North River Road, Manchester, NH 03106-1045. *Phone:* 603-645-9611. *Toll-free phone:* 800-642-4968. *Fax:* 603-645-9693. *E-mail:* admission@snhu.edu.

See page 1532 for the College Close-Up.

THOMAS MORE COLLEGE OF LIBERAL ARTS

Merrimack, New Hampshire **www.thomasmorecollege.edu/**

Freshman Application Contact Teddy Sifert, Director of Admissions, Thomas More College of Liberal Arts, 6 Manchester Street, Merrimack, NH 03054-4818. *Toll-free phone:* 800-880-8308. *Fax:* 603-880-9280. *E-mail:* admissions@thomasmorecollege.edu.

UNIVERSITY OF NEW HAMPSHIRE

Durham, New Hampshire **www.unh.edu/**

- **State-supported** university, founded 1866, part of University System of New Hampshire
- **Small-town** 2600-acre campus with easy access to Boston
- **Endowment** $243.4 million

- **Coed** 12,067 undergraduate students, 95% full-time, 56% women, 44% men
- **Moderately difficult** entrance level, 59% of applicants were admitted

Undergraduates 11,467 full-time, 600 part-time. Students come from 47 states and territories, 86 other countries, 38% are from out of state, 1% African American, 2% Asian American or Pacific Islander, 2% Hispanic American, 0.3% Native American, 0.9% international, 5% transferred in, 45% live on campus. *Retention:* 87% of 2006 full-time freshmen returned.

Freshmen *Admission:* 14,382 applied, 8,497 admitted, 2,646 enrolled. *Test scores:* SAT critical reading scores over 500: 76%; SAT math scores over 500: 80%; SAT critical reading scores over 600: 28%; SAT math scores over 600: 33%; SAT critical reading scores over 700: 4%; SAT math scores over 700: 4%.

Faculty *Total:* 933, 68% full-time, 62% with terminal degrees. *Student/faculty ratio:* 18:1.

Majors Accounting; adult and continuing education; agricultural business and management; agricultural teacher education; agriculture; agronomy and crop science; animal/livestock husbandry and production; animal sciences; anthropology; art; art history, criticism and conservation; art teacher education; astronomy; athletic training; audiology and speech-language pathology; biochemistry; bioinformatics; biological and physical sciences; biology/biological sciences; biomedical technology; botany/plant biology; business administration and management; cell biology and histology; chemical engineering; chemistry; chemistry teacher education; child development; city/urban, community and regional planning; civil engineering; civil engineering technology; classics and languages, literatures and linguistics; clinical/medical laboratory technology; community organization and advocacy; computer engineering; computer science; computer software technology; construction engineering technology; construction management; criminal justice/law enforcement administration; culinary arts; dairy science; dance; dietetics; dietetic technician; dramatic/theater arts; ecology; economics; electrical, electronics and communications engineering; elementary education; English; English/language arts teacher education; English literature (British and Commonwealth); environmental/environmental health engineering; environmental science; environmental studies; equestrian studies; European studies; evolutionary biology; family and consumer economics related; family and consumer sciences/human sciences; finance; fine/studio arts; foods, nutrition, and wellness; forestry; forestry technology; French; general studies; geography; geology/earth science; German; health/health care administration; history; horticultural science; hospitality administration; hotel/motel administration; humanities; hydrology and water resources science; interdisciplinary studies; international/global studies; international relations and affairs; journalism; kindergarten/preschool education; kinesiology and exercise science; landscape architecture; landscaping and groundskeeping; Latin; liberal arts and sciences/liberal studies; linguistics; literature; marine biology and biological oceanography; marine science/merchant marine officer; mass communication/media; materials science; mathematics; mathematics teacher education; mechanical engineering; medical microbiology and bacteriology; modern Greek; modern languages; molecular biology; music; music performance; music teacher education; natural resources/conservation; natural resources management and policy; natural sciences; nursing (registered nurse training); occupational therapy; ocean engineering; oceanography (chemical and physical); parks, recreation and leisure; philosophy; physical education teaching and coaching; physics; piano and organ; political science and government; pre-engineering; pre-medical studies; pre-veterinary studies; psychology; restaurant, culinary, and catering management; restaurant/food services management; Romance languages; Russian; science teacher education; secondary education; social work; sociology; soil conservation; Spanish; speech therapy; statistics; survey technology; therapeutic recreation; tourism and travel services management; trade and industrial teacher education; violin, viola, guitar and other stringed instruments; voice and opera; wildlife and wildlands science and management; wildlife biology; wind/percussion instruments; women's studies; zoology/animal biology.

Academics *Calendar:* semesters. *Degrees:* associate, bachelor's, master's, doctoral, post-master's, and postbachelor's certificates. *Special study options:* adult/continuing education programs, advanced placement credit, cooperative education, double majors, English as a second language, external degree program, honors programs, independent study, internships, off-campus study, part-time degree program, services for LD students, student-designed majors, study abroad, summer session for credit. *ROTC:* Army (b), Air Force (b). *Unusual degree programs:* 3-2 business administration; accounting.

Computers on Campus 389 computers/terminals are available on campus for general student use. Students can access the following: campus intranet, computer help desk, free student e-mail accounts, online (class) registration, online (class) schedules. Campuswide network is available. 100% of college-owned or -operated housing units are wired for high-speed Internet access. Wireless service is available via classrooms, computer centers, computer labs, libraries, student centers.

Student Life *Housing options:* coed, women-only, disabled students. Campus housing is university owned. Freshman campus housing is guaranteed. *Activities and organizations:* drama/theater group, student-run newspaper, radio and television station, choral group, marching band, Campus Activity Board, The Outing Club, SCOPE, Freshman Camp, Memorial Union Student Organization, national fraternities, national sororities. *Campus security:* 24-hour emergency response devices and patrols, student patrols, late-night transport/escort service, controlled dormitory access, lighted pathways and sidewalks. *Student services:* health clinic, personal/psychological counseling, women's center, legal services.

Athletics Member NCAA. All Division I except football (Division I-AA). *Intercollegiate sports:* archery M (c)/W (c), badminton M (c)/W (c), baseball M (c), basketball M (s)/W (s), crew M (c)/W, cross-country running M (s)/W (s), fencing M (c)/W (c), field hockey W (s), golf M (c)/W (c), gymnastics W (s), ice hockey M (s)/W (s), lacrosse M (c)/W (s), rock climbing M (c)/W (c), rugby M (c), sailing M (c)/W (c), skiing (cross-country) M (s)/W (s), skiing (downhill) M (s)/W (s), soccer M (s)/W (s), softball W (c), swimming and diving W (s), tennis M/W (s), track and field M (s)/W (s), volleyball M (c)/W (s), wrestling M (c). *Intramural sports:* badminton M (c)/W (c), basketball M/W, field hockey W, football M/W, ice hockey M/W, racquetball M/W, riflery M (c)/W (c), soccer M/W, softball M/W, table tennis M/W, tennis M/W, ultimate Frisbee M/W, volleyball M/W.

Standardized Tests *Required:* SAT or ACT (for admission).

Costs (2007–08) *Tuition:* state resident $8810 full-time, $367 per credit part-time; nonresident $21,770 full-time, $907 per credit part-time. Part-time tuition and fees vary according to course load. No tuition increase for student's term of enrollment. *Required fees:* $2260 full-time, $15 per term part-time. *Room and board:* $8168; room only: $5042. Room and board charges vary according to board plan and housing facility. *Payment plan:* installment. *Waivers:* employees or children of employees.

Financial Aid Of all full-time matriculated undergraduates who enrolled in 2006, 8,087 applied for aid, 6,366 were judged to have need, 1,322 had their need fully met. 3,676 Federal Work-Study jobs (averaging $2116). 3,016 state and other part-time jobs (averaging $1906). In 2006, 2443 non-need-based awards were made. *Average percent of need met:* 79%. *Average financial aid package:* $16,852. *Average need-based loan:* $3275. *Average need-based gift aid:* $2604. *Average non-need-based aid:* $6930. *Average indebtedness upon graduation:* $25,145.

Applying *Options:* electronic application, early action, deferred entrance. *Application fee:* $50. *Required:* essay or personal statement, high school transcript, 1 letter of recommendation. *Recommended:* minimum 3.0 GPA. *Application deadlines:* 2/1 (freshmen), 3/1 (transfers), 11/15 (early action). *Notification:* 4/15 (freshmen), 4/15 (transfers), 1/15 (early action).

Director of Admissions Mr. Robert McGann, Director of Admissions, University of New Hampshire, Grant House, 4 Garrison Avenue, Durham, NH 03824. *Phone:* 603-862-1360. *Fax:* 603-862-0077. *E-mail:* admissions@unh.edu.

See page 1534 for the College Close-Up.

UNIVERSITY OF NEW HAMPSHIRE AT MANCHESTER

Manchester, New Hampshire **www.unhm.unh.edu/**

- **State-supported** comprehensive, founded 1967, part of University System of New Hampshire
- **Urban** 800-acre campus with easy access to Boston
- **Coed** 998 undergraduate students, 56% full-time, 53% women, 47% men
- **Moderately difficult** entrance level, 66% of applicants were admitted

Undergraduates 558 full-time, 440 part-time. Students come from 4 states and territories, 5 other countries, 2% are from out of state, 1% African American, 2% Asian American or Pacific Islander, 3% Hispanic American, 0.1% Native American, 0.6% international, 12% transferred in.

Freshmen *Admission:* 217 applied, 143 admitted, 117 enrolled. *Test scores:* SAT critical reading scores over 500: 53%; SAT math scores over 500: 52%; ACT scores over 18: 80%; SAT critical reading scores over 600: 20%; SAT math scores over 600: 12%; SAT critical reading scores over 700: 1%.

Faculty *Total:* 91, 36% full-time, 48% with terminal degrees. *Student/faculty ratio:* 12:1.

Majors Biology/biological sciences; business administration and management; electrical, electronic and communications engineering technology; English; fine/studio arts; history; humanities; liberal arts and sciences/liberal studies; mass communication/media; mechanical engineering/mechanical technology; nursing science; psychology; sign language interpretation and translation.

Academics *Calendar:* semesters. *Degrees:* certificates, associate, bachelor's, and master's. *Special study options:* academic remediation for entering students, adult/continuing education programs, advanced placement credit, double majors, independent study, internships, off-campus study, part-time degree program, services for LD students, student-designed majors, study abroad, summer session for credit. *ROTC:* Army (c), Air Force (c).

Computers on Campus 47 computers/terminals are available on campus for general student use. Students can access the following: online (class) registration. Campuswide network is available. Wireless service is available via entire campus.

Student Life *Housing:* college housing not available. *Activities and organizations:* student-run radio station, Student Council. *Campus security:* 24-hour emergency response devices, late-night transport/escort service.

Standardized Tests *Required:* SAT or ACT (for admission).

Costs (2007–08) *Tuition:* state resident $8250 full-time, $344 per credit part-time; nonresident $20,880 full-time, $870 per credit part-time. Full-time tuition and fees vary according to course load and program. Part-time tuition and fees vary according to course load and program. *Required fees:* $345 full-time. *Waivers:* senior citizens and employees or children of employees.

Financial Aid Of all full-time matriculated undergraduates who enrolled in 2006, 474 applied for aid, 352 were judged to have need, 35 had their need fully met. 95 Federal Work-Study jobs (averaging $2042). In 2006, 4 non-need-based awards were made. *Average percent of need met:* 57%. *Average financial aid package:* $8437. *Average need-based loan:* $3356. *Average need-based gift aid:* $942. *Average non-need-based aid:* $875. *Average indebtedness upon graduation:* $18,456.

Applying *Options:* electronic application, deferred entrance. *Application fee:* $45. *Required:* essay or personal statement, high school transcript, 1 letter of recommendation. *Recommended:* interview. *Application deadlines:* 6/15 (freshmen), 6/15 (transfers). *Notification:* continuous (freshmen), continuous (transfers).

Freshman Application Contact Ms. Susan Miller, Administrative Assistant, University of New Hampshire at Manchester, 400 Commercial Street, Manchester, NH 03101. *Phone:* 603-641-4150. *Fax:* 603-641-4125. *E-mail:* unhm@unh.edu.

CHESTER COLLEGE OF NEW ENGLAND

CHESTER, NEW HAMPSHIRE

The College

Chester College of New England is a close-knit community of visual and language artists. The College offers students a foundation in the liberal and fine arts and a thorough preparation for careers in the professional arts. Chester College of New England offers majors in creative writing, professional writing, graphic design, fine art, and photography and media arts; an interdisciplinary arts major is offered through the Department of Interdisciplinary Studies. The College also offers minors in creative writing, illustration, photojournalism, and professional writing–publishing. The programs are complementary. Students specialize in intersections among art, graphic design, photography, and the written word.

The low faculty-student ratio (12:1); artist/writer-in-residence programs; a robust program of visiting artists, exhibitions, art contests, and shows; internships; and relationships with professional associations complement and strengthen the College's offerings. The College's aim is to provide all students with the education, knowledge, skills, and experiences they need to become both thoughtful citizens and successful professionals.

Students at Chester College of New England find that the tranquil setting of the campus provides them with the kind of environment that is essential for creative inspiration. The College is close to Manchester and Portsmouth, New Hampshire, and Boston, Massachusetts. The College also offers a study-abroad program that is linked to the majors cited above.

Chester College of New England is a private, coeducational, nonsectarian institution. It is accredited to award the Bachelor of Arts degree by the New Hampshire Postsecondary Education Commission and by the New England Association of Schools and Colleges.

The College has an enrollment of approximately 250 students. Although the ages of students range from 17 to 35, the average age of students is 19. Most of these students live on campus, but a number of students enroll as commuters. All resident students are full-time. Commuters may choose to enroll on a full-time or part-time basis. The classroom student-teacher ratio is very low, approximately 12:1, which allows for a great deal of personalized instruction. The College believes that this sort of interaction is critical, given its focus on visual and language arts.

A new residence hall opened in 2002. This coeducational residence houses the majority of the College's resident students and has lounge areas, meeting rooms, laundry facilities, a small kitchen, a study room, and an art studio open 24/7. To accommodate the growing resident student population, Adams Hall was completely renovated in summer 2006, providing a second residence hall on campus. This smaller residential building houses 30 students, in double rooms. All student rooms provide broadband Internet access.

The Dining Commons provides meals for students, faculty and staff members, and visitors. Breakfast, lunch, and dinner are served in this facility seven days a week during the academic year.

Extracurricular programs are designed to enhance and enrich the learning experience, and students are expected to be active members of the campus community, both in and out of the classroom.

Location

Chester College of New England offers the aspiring artist a natural setting that nurtures both artistic and intellectual development. The campus is situated on 75 acres in the center of Chester, New Hampshire, a classic rural New England town near Manchester, New Hampshire, and just a short drive from the state's beaches and ski resorts. The campus buildings are a mixture of restored eighteenth-century houses and new buildings that preserve the feel of Colonial New England while providing modern conveniences and spaces appropriate for classroom learning and artistic creation. Many of the houses in the vicinity of the College are beautifully maintained antique homes from the Colonial, Federal, and Victorian periods. The town square, only a few hundred yards from the campus, includes a classic white Colonial church, the town hall, and a general store. Chester, New Hampshire, is very close to both Manchester and Portsmouth, New Hampshire, and less than an hour from Boston, Massachusetts—cities that are rich in history and culture. Students frequently travel to these cities to work at internship sites, visit galleries and museums, and attend an assortment of performances and exhibits.

Majors and Degrees

The College offers a Bachelor of Arts degree with majors in creative writing, fine art, graphic design, interdisciplinary arts, photography and media arts, and professional writing. Minors are offered in creative writing, illustration, photojournalism, and professional writing–publishing.

Academic Programs

An artist cannot be fully prepared to create without an understanding of the depth and breadth of human experience and inquiry. New movements and ideas cannot evolve in a vacuum. The artist must have an appreciation of the intellectual, cultural, and historical context in which he or she works. That is, the artist needs a solid foundation in order to be able to create. Chester College of New England is committed to the liberal arts as one means of providing this necessary foundation. Close acquaintance with the liberal arts sharpens students' oral and written communication skills; provides them with opportunities to explore historical, social, and scientific concepts; and develops an appreciation of ideas and experiences that form the basis of all human endeavors.

The General Education Core courses integrate liberal arts courses with courses in the creative arts to provide students with an interdisciplinary approach to their education. This core program views courses as a continuum rather than a set of isolated experiences. The faculty at Chester College of New England is committed to preparing its students to face the multidisciplinary needs of the work world, integrating what students have learned in disparate fields. In addition, interdisciplinary modes expose students to a greater variety of teaching perspectives and opinions about society, enabling students to think critically from a great number of vantage points.

The liberal arts component begins by establishing a foundation in English composition, art history, and the humanities. Students then move on to three traditional and challenging areas of study: the sciences, the social sciences, and history. Finally, they explore the liberal arts in greater depth by choosing from among a variety of course offerings, some of them at the upper level. The result is a unique blend of courses that helps students discover how the liberal arts and the visual arts work together to educate the whole person.

The creative arts elements of the General Education Core introduce students to the majors offered and provide the concepts, vocabularies, and insight that are essential preparation for further study. Core courses emphasize verbal, visual, technical, and written skills. The curriculum is carefully sequenced to provide varied and complementary courses that interact with other foundation courses—as well as with the liberal arts component of the curriculum. Requirements include a 6-credit senior project that may be satisfied in various ways, depending on the student's interests, skill level, and the program requirements. For example, a student may complete this requirement with an internship or by combining the senior project with an advanced-level seminar.

Professional Practices is another creative arts requirement that underscores the College's commitment to graduating artists with a practical knowledge of their field. Students may choose from a variety of courses with similar learning objectives, depending on their areas of interest. These courses include Small Press Publishing, Visiting Artists Seminar, Professional Practices in Art and Illustration, and Galleries. All of these courses are designed to expose students to aspects of life in the working world as professional artists.

The curriculum integrates courses in the liberal arts, fine arts, and professional arts throughout the undergraduate experience, along with opportunities to learn from and interact with a faculty of practicing professional artists, poets, designers, photographers, and writers. The College's internship program and Student Success Center prepare students to enter their chosen professional fields with the appropriate knowledge, skills, experience, and preparation to succeed.

The programs leading to the Bachelor of Arts degree require a minimum of 120 credits.

Chester College of New England follows a traditional academic calendar of two semesters. Summer-session courses are optional. Fall semester generally begins at the end of August; spring semester begins in early January.

Academic Facilities

Office, classroom, and living spaces on campus are relatively compact and create a comfortable environment for highly personalized interaction. The largest classroom holds no more than 40 people, and classes at the College rarely exceed 15 students.

The Photography Studios are located in the Photo Barn and include a darkroom with multiple workstations for black-and-white and color printing. Separate studio areas are provided. In the exhibit areas, each student has the opportunity to have photographs selected for display for the benefit and enjoyment of fellow students and the College community. The Photo Barn also houses a Mac lab, where students learn digital video technologies and techniques. The Visionaries Institute International (VII), a center for the creation and study of media that inspires positive social change, is also housed in the Photo Barn.

Douglas Hall, a renovated governor's mansion, currently houses art, drawing, illustration, and sculpture studios as well as three general-purpose classrooms and "senior space," small, private studio space reserved just for students with senior status.

The Wadleigh Library provides academic research support for the programs offered on campus. The library also provides individual study space, meeting spaces for study groups, a large classroom for lectures and presentations, and three computer labs. The College's Student Success Center, also housed in the library, is intended to help students succeed not only academically, but also in their decisions about future career paths.

The three computer labs housed in Wadleigh Library are equipped with Macintosh computers for graphic design, digital imaging, and advertising classes, using state-of-the-art software. In addition, Wadleigh Library houses networked personal computers and printers specifically for student use. These machines are equipped with current releases of word processing software and provide students with Internet access.

Each student is permitted to have one car on campus, and parking is provided for a $35 annual fee. The College provides occasional transportation to Manchester, Portsmouth, and Boston and to recreational sites.

Costs

In 2007–08, tuition for full-time students is $15,400. Room and board (double room) are $7850. Tuition per credit hour for full-time students and part-time students (8 to 11 credits per semester) is $640. Photography majors should anticipate book and supply expenditures of $650 per semester ($350 per semester for other majors). Other charges included a semester service fee of $135, a technology fee of $130, a summer session fee of $445 per credit hour, a parking fee of $35, and a freshman-orientation fee of $90.

Financial Aid

Chester College of New England is dedicated to helping its students determine the best possible means for financing their educations and offers advice to students and their families regardless of income level. Through its programs of need- and merit-based financial assistance, the College makes every effort possible to assist students who wish to attend. These programs consist of loans, grants, work-study jobs, and scholarships. The College offers opportunities through federal financial aid programs that include the Federal Pell Grant, Federal Supplemental Educational Opportunity Grant (FSEOG), Federal Stafford Student Loan, Federal Work-Study Program, and PLUS loans. The College also offers merit-based scholarships to incoming students, which range from $1000 to full tuition for up to four years of study. More than 85 percent of the students at Chester College receive some form of financial aid.

Faculty

The faculty is made up of both full- and part-time instructors who are master teachers and working artists and professionals. Faculty members participate in advising students in curriculum and career planning and act in supervisory capacities for internships.

Student Government

Student Government members, in consultation with the coordinator of student activities, plan and schedule activities and events for the academic year. The campus calendar offers numerous events, including dramatic performances, skiing and snowboarding trips, art and photography exhibits, dances, on-campus musical performances, and lectures and discussion groups concerning important social and political issues.

Admission Requirements

Chester College of New England is a small college by design and enrolls limited-size classes of highly talented women and men in its Bachelor of Arts programs. The College admits freshmen and transfer students and seeks a diverse student body. Students may be admitted for the September and January semesters. Applicants for admission are judged by many criteria, including academic performance, artistic achievements and potential, extracurricular accomplishments and activities, communication skills (both oral and written), standardized test scores (SAT or ACT), energy and determination, and portfolio quality.

The College recommends but does not require the submission of SAT or ACT scores. Students who do not submit test scores are not penalized in the admission process.

Admission requirements include submitting a completed application form (either paper or the online version, which is available at http://www.chestercollege.edu/apply), the $35 application fee, official copies of transcripts from all secondary schools and any colleges or universities attended, two letters of recommendation, and a written personal statement. A personal interview is required, either in person or via telephone.

Depending on the student's choice of major, artistic achievement may be a significant factor in the admission decision. Also, a number of merit-based scholarships are available, and only students who have submitted a portfolio are given consideration for these scholarships. For these reasons, while the College does not require the submission of a portfolio, it is strongly recommended.

Students are encouraged to arrange for a campus visit and tour, which provides an important opportunity to gain valuable firsthand knowledge of Chester College.

Application and Information

Chester College of New England operates on a rolling admissions basis. Students are notified of a decision within two weeks after they have completed the admission requirements. There is no application deadline; however, students are encouraged to submit applications no later than May 1 for fall admission and no later than December 15 for spring admission.

For more information, students should contact:

Director of Admissions
Chester College of New England
40 Chester Street
Chester, New Hampshire 03036
Phone: 603-887-7400
800-974-6372 (toll-free)
E-mail: admissions@chestercollege.edu
Web site: http://www.chestercollege.edu

COLBY–SAWYER COLLEGE

NEW LONDON, NEW HAMPSHIRE

The College

Colby-Sawyer College, a coeducational, residential, undergraduate college founded in 1837, evolved from the New England academy tradition and has been engaged in higher education since 1928. The College provides programs of study that innovatively integrate the liberal arts and sciences with professional preparation. Through all of its programs, the College encourages students of varied backgrounds and abilities to realize their full intellectual and personal potential so they may gain understanding about themselves, others, and the major forces shaping our rapidly changing world. At present, students come from all over the United States and eight other countries, with nearly 70 percent of the students coming from outside of New Hampshire. Within the last ten years, two suite-style residence halls have been built to accommodate the College's steady growth in enrollment.

Student athletic involvement occurs at the varsity, club, intramural, and recreational levels. There are nine varsity sports for women (NCAA Division III basketball, lacrosse, soccer, swimming and diving, tennis, track and field, and volleyball; ECSC Alpine ski racing; and IHSA riding) and eight for men (NCAA Division III baseball, basketball, soccer, swimming and diving, tennis, and track and field; ECSC Alpine ski racing; and IHSA riding). Athletic successes include a nationally ranked men's basketball team that competed in the NCAA tournaments from 2001 to 2003; a track and field team that produced 2 All-Americans in 2004 and 2005 and sent individual qualifiers to the NCAA Championships in 2000, 2002, 2004, 2005, and 2006; and conference championships for men's baseball in 1998 and 1999, men's basketball in 2001–03, women's volleyball in 1999, 2003, and 2005, and women's basketball in 1997–99 and 2005–06. The women's basketball team also competed in the 2001–03 ECAC tournaments as well as the NCAA tournaments in 1997–99 and 2005. The women's volleyball team also made appearances at the NCAA tournaments in 1999, 2003, and 2005. Colby-Sawyer's equestrian team was the national champion in 1989 and 1994 as well as the reserve national champion in 1998 and has sent riders to the IHSA national team every year since 1987. For the past nine seasons, the Alpine ski racing team has competed in the USCSA National Championships, where, in 2005, they placed both teams within the top three, a school record. The Alpine ski racing team has produced 65 All-American citations since 1988. The Colby-Sawyer Chargers compete as a member of the Commonwealth Coast Conference.

The College is accredited by the New England Association of Schools and Colleges, and professional programs also carry the appropriate accreditations. Colby-Sawyer has consistently received recognition as one of the top colleges in its category.

Location

Colby-Sawyer's 200-acre campus is located on the crest of a hill in New London, New Hampshire. Its beautifully maintained grounds and stately Georgian architecture create a picturesque and safe environment that is conducive to learning. The College is located in the heart of the Dartmouth–Lake Sunapee region, a four-season recreational and cultural community known for the natural beauty of its lakes and mountains. Boston is only 1½ hours south and Montreal is 3½ hours north. Students have access to major cities by College van or public bus. The nearby seacoast at Portsmouth, and surrounding lakes, mountains, and state parks provide opportunities for biking, camping, canoeing, golf, hiking, ice skating, Nordic and Alpine skiing, swimming, and tennis. Arts and cultural opportunities can be found in New London as well as in nearby Concord, the state capital, and Hanover, the home of Dartmouth College.

Majors and Degrees

Colby-Sawyer offers bachelor's degrees in many fields. The Bachelor of Arts degree is awarded in studio art; biology; communication studies; English; history, society, and culture; and psychology. The Bachelor of Fine Arts degree is awarded in studio art and graphic design. The Bachelor of Science degree is awarded in business administration, child development, community and environmental studies, exercise and sport sciences (specializations offered in athletic training, exercise science, and sport management), and nursing. Major advising tracks are available in predentistry, prelaw, premedicine, and pre–physical therapy. In addition, Colby-Sawyer offers sixteen academic minors.

Academic Programs

Colby-Sawyer College faculty and staff are excellent at working with students who are undecided on a major and they are highly qualified to help students explore their values, talents, and academic and career interests. At Colby-Sawyer College, it is believed that knowledge and experience nurture each other. Therefore, the combination of classroom learning and professional experience is an integral part of each student's education.

All students begin their liberal education at Colby-Sawyer by selecting a Pathway Seminar. Students choose a topic they are interested in learning more about, pose questions that are personally relevant, and search for answers through experiences in several liberal arts areas. They return to these themes in a seminar in their sophomore year, applying all they have learned to answer their own questions and share insights with classmates on such topics as "Sound: From Physics to Fantasia" and "Rituals, Excellence, and Challenge: The Ancient and Modern Games."

Colby-Sawyer's Wesson Honors Program offers an environment conducive to intellectual exploration and creativity beyond that which is available in the general curriculum. This program is carefully designed to advance and polish critical skills of each participating student.

Through a carefully crafted program offered by the Harrington Center for Career Development, all students are encouraged throughout their four years of study to continue to clarify their interests and goals and to gain practical experiences through student employment, internships, and voluntary service to the community.

Internships are a key element in career development and are required for almost all majors. Colby-Sawyer has an impressive roster of internship opportunities available, and through the internship experience, students often receive their first offer of a permanent position. During the internship, students have an opportunity to work directly with professionals in their field of study while developing valuable contacts who can serve as references and career mentors. Organizations that have recently accepted Colby-Sawyer interns include Merrill Lynch, the Minnesota Twins, Continental Cable, Beth Israel Hospital, Blue Cross/Blue Shield, Harvard University Athletic Department, the Buffalo Bisons, the New England Patriots, Nantucket Nectars, the Currier Gallery of Art, the Basketball Hall of Fame, the Olympic Regional Development Authority, Channel 7 (Boston), the Appalachian Mountain Club, and CNN.

Off-Campus Programs

Colby-Sawyer encourages students to study abroad for a semester or a year. The study-abroad adviser works closely with students to select an experience and a school best suited to their individual needs and interests. Students have studied in England, Poland, Australia, Spain, New Zealand, France, Italy, Ireland, Scotland, Switzerland, and many other countries.

Colby-Sawyer's membership in the fourteen-college New Hampshire College and University Council (NHCUC) allows students to enroll in other NHCUC institutions for a course or for an entire semester.

Academic Facilities

The Susan Colgate Cleveland Library/Learning Center contains 92,116 volumes, 4,148 periodicals, and 197,625 microforms. Access to these materials is provided by a Dynix automated catalog system and more than 35 online and CD-ROM databases for periodical research. The library is housed in a unique five-level structure constructed from two pre–Civil War dairy barns masterfully transformed into a warm and inviting facility that has won regional and national architectural awards. The library/learning center also houses a curriculum lab, an audiovisual room, thirty PC workstations for Internet and library database access, a twelve-station wireless lab, and a networked computer classroom with twenty-five PCs and interactive multimedia teaching equipment. Interlibrary loan service provides access to an extensive array of library holdings throughout New England and the nation.

The magnificent 63,000-square-foot Dan and Kathleen Hogan Sports Center was designed to meet the athletic and recreational needs of Colby-Sawyer College students and members of the local community. This sports center contains a large field house with newly installed maple-wood floors; a suspended walking/jogging track; a six-lane, competition-size swimming pool; and a fitness center furnished with equipment such as StairMasters, Body Master stations, treadmills, rowing ergometers, Nordic cross-country skiing tracks, a Universal gym, stationary bicycles, and a complete selection of free weights. The Hogan Center also houses the Sports Medicine Clinic, which is fully equipped with the latest technology to support the Exercise and Sport Sciences Program.

Opened in 2004, the Curtis L. Ivey Science Center is one of Colby-Sawyer's finest academic facilities and houses the Natural Science and Environmental Studies Programs. Set against nearby Mt. Kearsarge, this beautiful two-story, 33,000-square foot building consists of a variety of classrooms, laboratories, and offices as well as a 180-seat lecture hall. One of these laboratories focuses on spatial ecology and performs grant-funded research utilizing Geographic Information Systems (GIS) and Global Positioning Systems (GPS) technology.

The Academic Development Center at James House provides academic support services for all students. The staff consists of faculty members, learning specialists, and student academic counselors who work with students to strengthen their writing, math, and research skills, as well as their study skills, such as time management, note-taking, and exam preparation. Colby-Sawyer's English Language and American Culture Program provides support for international students and others whose first language is not English. Among the services available to students with diagnosed learning differences are classroom modifications, personal counseling, and professional as well as peer tutoring.

The nursing program features a Nursing and Health Laboratory containing resources that simulate clinical practice settings. Students also have access to a computer laboratory with software that helps to prepare them for clinical experiences. The nursing program is enriched by its relationship with Dartmouth Hitchcock Medical Center, one of the most well-equipped and technologically advanced teaching hospitals in North America.

The Colby-Sawyer campus computing array includes a campus network with wireless Internet access, five computer laboratory/classrooms, and six mobile multimedia teaching stations, which provide computer graphics, audio, and video capabilities employing the latest digital technology. Computing facilities are equipped with the latest Microsoft Windows applications and laser printers for student use. The College now has a 5:1 student-computer ratio.

The Frances Lockwood Bailey Graphic Design Studios are the center of the graphic design facilities. These studios are equipped with computers loaded with the latest versions of graphic design software programs and desktop publishing capability. Students create graphic images while working with digital scanning and optical character recognition, still-video photography, and VCR, video camera, and other state-of-the-practice images. Advanced student projects are sent to professional imaging centers to create high-resolution hard copy.

Costs

Tuition, room, and board for 2008–09 are $39,960. Approximately $1750 should be allowed for books, supplies, personal expenses, and travel, depending on where students live.

Financial Aid

Through its Financial Aid Program, Colby-Sawyer encourages the attendance of students from a variety of ethnic and cultural backgrounds, economic levels, and geographic regions. Currently, 91 percent of the students receive some form of financial assistance, and Colby-Sawyer provides more than $9 million a year in financial aid and scholarships. Both need-based and merit awards are available, including merit awards for outstanding academic achievement, community service, student leadership, and special talent in art, creative writing, or original research. Each applicant for need-based aid must submit the Free Application for Federal Student Aid (FAFSA). Priority is given to students whose completed forms are received before March 1. A modest amount of financial assistance is available for international students.

Faculty

Colby-Sawyer has a distinguished faculty and staff dedicated to undergraduate teaching, and a personalized education is ensured by a 12:1 student-faculty ratio and average class size of 18. At Colby-Sawyer, senior faculty members teach first-year students as well as students in the upper classes.

Student Government

The Student Government Association (SGA) is structured to provide considerable interaction among students, faculty members, and staff, and the SGA allocates the resources that fund a multitude of involvement and leadership opportunities outside the classroom. Campus activities include the Campus Activities Board, Dance Club, Alpha Chi Honor Society, yearbook, radio station (WSCS 90.9 FM), Drama Club, Admissions Key Association, Art Students Society, Student Nurses Association, *The Courier* (student newspaper), community service, and numerous clubs and intramural teams.

Admission Requirements

The College requires prospective students to present at least 15 units of college-preparatory work. This would usually include 4 years of English, 3 years of mathematics, 3 or more years of social studies, 2 years of a foreign language, and 2 or more years of a laboratory science.

While an admissions interview is not required, every applicant is strongly encouraged to visit Colby-Sawyer for a tour and interview. Interviews often play an important part in the final admissions decision.

Application and Information

Colby-Sawyer College receives and considers applications throughout the year. Beginning in December, applications are reviewed as soon as they become complete, and candidates are notified as soon as the admissions decision is finalized. A completed application includes a transcript of the candidate's high school work (including first-quarter grades for the senior year), SAT or ACT scores, one letter of recommendation (from a teacher or a guidance professional), a personal statement, and a $50 nonrefundable application fee. Application forms and additional information may be obtained by contacting:

Office of Admissions
Colby-Sawyer College
541 Main Street
New London, New Hampshire 03257
Phone: 603-526-3700
800-272-1015 (toll-free)
Fax: 603-526-3452
E-mail: admissions@colby-sawyer.edu
Internet: http://www.colby-sawyer.edu

DANIEL WEBSTER COLLEGE

NASHUA, NEW HAMPSHIRE

The College

Daniel Webster College (DWC) prepares its students for individual excellence through a commitment to individual attention. The College's innovative curricula in aviation, business, computer science, engineering, information systems, and social science equip students with the knowledge and skills necessary to become tomorrow's industry leaders.

Daniel Webster College is accredited by the New England Association of Schools and Colleges and is a member of the New Hampshire College and University Council. The College holds Federal Aviation Administration Air Agency Certification PSE 15-21 as an approved pilot school. Courses are operated under Part 141 and Part 61 of the FAA regulations. Daniel Webster College's Air Traffic Management Program is one of thirteen recognized by the FAA as part of their Collegiate Training Initiative (CTI).

There is a diverse student population at Daniel Webster College, with twenty-five states and twelve countries currently represented. A variety of living options promote comfort and enjoyment. Residential students are housed in five residence halls and in contemporary town house–style apartments on campus.

The College Center houses the dining hall, the After Hours Café, and the Student Affairs Offices. The Residence Life Office is in Fremont Hall, conveniently located for student access. Movies, concerts, and other special events are held at the Common Thread, which contains a piano and pool tables and houses a coffee bar. The Mario J. Vagge Gymnasium has facilities for volleyball and basketball, a weight room, and an aerobics facility.

There are plenty of extracurricular activities, including the Student Activities Board, the student yearbook, Student Senate, the Gaming Guild, the Jazz Band, Theater Group, Outdoor Adventure Klub, Film Society, a variety of intramural athletics, and other exciting programs. The Leadership Initiative and Student Life Office annually bring nationally renowned speakers and visual and performing artists to the campus. A rigorous two- and four-year Air Force ROTC program is also available.

Home of the Eagles, Daniel Webster College's men's and women's sports teams compete in the Great Northeast Athletic Conference at the NCAA Division III level. Men's sports include baseball, basketball, cross-country, lacrosse, and soccer. Women compete in basketball, cross-country, soccer, softball, and volleyball. Ice hockey is currently available as an intercollegiate sport in the ACHA league.

Location

The College is conveniently located in Nashua, New Hampshire, the state's second-largest city and twice named "America's Best Place to Live." The city's municipal airport is adjacent to the campus. Nashua is home to a symphony orchestra, theater guild, arts center, and several fine restaurants, shopping areas, and craft centers. Several Fortune 500 companies are nearby, providing employment and internships.

Boston is just 46 miles to the south, and Manchester, New Hampshire, is 18 miles to the north. Excellent skiing, snowboarding, hiking, and boating and the scenic New Hampshire seacoast are all within an hour's drive.

Majors and Degrees

Daniel Webster College awards Bachelor of Science degrees in aeronautical engineering; aviation/air traffic management; aviation flight operations (professional pilot training); aviation management; business management; computer science in information systems engineering; computer science in networking/Web management; computer science in software engineering, gaming, simulation, and robotics; marketing management; mechanical engineering; psychology; social science; and sport management.

Associate in Science degrees are awarded in aeronautical engineering, aviation operations, business management, engineering science, general studies, and information systems.

Academic Programs

The College operates on a semester system. Courses are designed to provide the highest-quality educational opportunities. Independent study, a customized internship program, and advanced-placement programs are available to qualified students. The College is known for its commitment to individual attention.

The College's Aviation Division provides one of the country's most innovative and respected aviation programs and is one of only a few to introduce glider and aerobatic flight into its educational programs. Students can qualify for private single-engine, private glider, instrument, commercial, multiengine, and instructor ratings. A student instructor internship is available to qualified juniors and seniors.

Academic Facilities

Daniel Webster Hall houses several classrooms, laboratories, the College Store, and administrative and faculty offices. The 25,000-square-foot Anne-Bridge Baddour Library and Success Center houses the College's extensive library, the Academic Support Center, the Center for Career Planning and Placement as well as computer labs. There are also conference and seminar rooms, audiovisual labs, classrooms, and staff offices. The Eaton-Richmond Center houses faculty offices, multimedia classrooms, and a 350-seat auditorium and features five new, state-of-the-art Windows computer labs.

The Tamposi Aviation Center is adjacent to Nashua Airport/Boire Field, an FAA Class-D airport with a 5,500-foot paved and lighted runway, operating control tower, and ILS, VOR, GPS, and NDB instrument approaches. The College's fleet of aircraft includes Cessna 172 trainers, Grob G109B motor gliders, Piper PA-28 Arrow complex aircraft, and multiengine Piper PA-44 Seminoles. The Center is fully equipped with a flight dispatch area, classrooms, offices, and flight-planning stations. The Flight Simulation Lab is equipped with new Elite iGate 500 flight simulators configurable to the single-engine Cessna 172 and Piper Arrow and the multiengine Piper Seneca IV. The simulation lab also contains the new Precision Flight Controls' (PFC) jet trainer flight simulator/procedures trainer that represents a Boeing 737-800 or next generation–style cockpit. It is used for Part 121 airline simulation, advanced systems, and cockpit resource management training. The Air Traffic Control Lab features the Adacel MaxSim tower-control simulator, the UFA radar control simulators that are used for TRACON, and Center ATC simulations for en-route and approach control.

Costs

Tuition for 2007–08 is $24,865. Residence costs, including room and board, are $9052. Books, supplies, and miscellaneous personal expenses are estimated at $3500. First-year flight students can expect to pay approximately $10,200 in flight fees.

Financial Aid

The College is committed to helping students make a Daniel Webster College education a reality. It offers more than $5.6 million annually in institutional funds through a variety of financial assistance programs based on analysis of the Free Application for Federal Student Aid (FAFSA), which can be obtained through high school guidance offices. DWC also offers four-year renewable academic performance scholarships to students exhibiting high academic achievement through high school GPA and other test scores. These scholarships range from $500 to full-tuition scholarship opportunities. More than 90 percent of the students at Daniel Webster College receive some form of financial assistance.

In addition to providing aid through its own scholarship and work programs, the College administers both federal and local financial assistance programs. For more information, students should call or write the Director of Financial Assistance at the College.

Faculty

The student-faculty ratio at Daniel Webster College is 13:1. This provides the opportunity for individual attention and instruction, tutoring, and advising. While scholarship is encouraged and applauded, the prime focus of the faculty is high-quality teaching.

Student Government

The Student Activities Board and Office of Student Life coordinate a wide variety of student activities. Student Senate represents students' views and facilitates meaningful dialog between the students and the College administration. The Student Senate represents all full-time day students. The Student Senate strives to construct and promote a common voice; encourage the continuous exchange of ideas between students, faculty members, and administrators; make recommendations regarding college policies and procedures concerning students' academic and social environments; and promote the welfare of the student body. The Student Senate works very closely with recognized student organizations by allocating and monitoring funds generated by the student activity fee.

Admission Requirements

A student who has graduated from an accredited high school program is considered for admission. The SAT or ACT is required for all students interested in earning a Bachelor of Science degree. Consideration is based on high school performance and a letter of recommendation. Students may be admitted to the September and January semesters. Admission decisions are made without regard to race, color, creed, sex, physical handicap, or national origin.

Although not required for acceptance, a personal admission interview is strongly recommended. A campus visit, including an optional tour by air for students interested in the flight program, provides an important opportunity to gain valuable firsthand knowledge of Daniel Webster College.

Application and Information

The application fee is $35. The College operates on a rolling admission basis, and students are notified of a decision within two weeks after their file is complete. Interested students are urged to arrange a campus visit while the College is in session.

For further information, students should contact:

Daniel Webster College
20 University Drive
Nashua, New Hampshire 03063-1300
Phone: 800-325-6876 (toll-free)
Fax: 603-577-6001
E-mail: admissions@dwc.edu
Web site: http://www.dwc.edu

Daniel Webster College is located in Nashua, New Hampshire—the only city in America twice rated "Number One Place to Live" by *Money* magazine.

FRANKLIN PIERCE UNIVERSITY

RINDGE, NEW HAMPSHIRE

The University

Franklin Pierce University is a four-year, coeducational nonsectarian university located in the Monadnock region of New Hampshire. The University enrolls approximately 1,700 undergraduates on its main campus in Rindge and more than 2,500 adult learners at its five graduate and professional studies campuses across the state and through distance learning. The diverse student population represents twenty-two states and eight countries. Franklin Pierce is accredited by the New England Association of Schools and Colleges, Inc. (NEASC).

Physical facilities of the main campus include modern classroom buildings (including a laboratory facility), the library, an academic services center, a campus center, residence halls and apartment houses, town-house complexes, a field house, an air frame recreation complex, a dance studio, a health center, a boat house, the Lakeside Educational Center, a glass-blowing facility, and a theater. A wide range of services are offered to the students, including health-care services, counseling, and career planning and placement assistance.

Campus activities include a number of academic and special interest clubs, such as the Campus Activities Board; groups centered around common political, arts, and academic interests; *Pierce Arrow* (newspaper); *Raven* (yearbook); *Northern New England Review* (literary magazine); the Student Government Association; and many others. Bus trips to special events are offered on weekends. The University's active Adventure Recreation and intramural programs offer a wide variety of activities on both the University's 1,200-acre campus and throughout the region's many natural recreational facilities. At the intercollegiate level, men compete in baseball, basketball, crew, golf, ice hockey, lacrosse, soccer, and tennis. For women, basketball, cross-country, rowing, lacrosse, field hockey, soccer, softball, tennis, and volleyball are available. In addition, the University offers a rugby program.

Location

The main campus in Rindge, New Hampshire, is situated on 1,200 wooded acres on the shore of Pearly Pond near the base of Mount Monadnock. Rindge, which is in southwestern New Hampshire, is 65 miles from Boston, 112 miles from Hartford, and 236 miles from New York City. The area is an ideal setting for outdoor activities. There are many lakes and streams, including the Pearly Pond beach facility, which is ideal for fishing, swimming, and sailing, and there are also numerous trails for hiking, mountaineering, biking, and cross-country skiing.

Majors and Degrees

Franklin Pierce University offers Bachelor of Science and Bachelor of Arts degrees through five academic divisions. The Division of Behavioral Sciences offers majors in anthropology/archaeology, art education, criminal justice, elementary education, psychology, secondary education, and social work and counseling. In the Division of Business Administration, students can major in accounting-finance, arts management, management, marketing, and sports and recreation management. The Division of Natural Sciences offers majors in biology, computer information technology, and environmental science. In the Division of Visual and Performing Arts, students major in fine arts, graphic communications, mass communication (journalism, media production, and media studies), music, and theater arts. Majors in the Division of Humanities are American studies, English, history, and political science. The University also offers preprofessional programs in dentistry, law, medicine, physical therapy, and veterinary medicine. In addition to a major, students may also complete a minor area of study, and they also have the option of designing their own interdisciplinary majors.

Academic Programs

Franklin Pierce University's curriculum is a blend of traditional liberal arts, preprofessional study, teacher preparation programs, and a nationally recognized core curriculum, The Individual and Community. In 1997, the University was the recipient of the Templeton Award for Character Building Colleges. Students receive much personal attention at Franklin Pierce University; the average class size is 19, and the student-faculty ratio is 15:1.

A total of 120 semester hours are required for graduation. These include the courses in the student's chosen major (generally 30 to 54 credits); and the required 38-credit Individual and Community Integrated Curriculum. The purpose of the Individual and Community program is to foster a common understanding of the questions and issues that lie at the heart of contemporary American life. The Integrated Curriculum begins with a one-semester freshman seminar called Individual and Community and continues with a sequence of courses culminating in the Senior Liberal Arts Seminar.

Franklin Pierce offers an Honors Program, which was established to help provide challenge and intellectual community to participants. The program offers honors sections of core courses, occasional honors electives, and honors options in major courses designed to appeal to the more academically committed student. Students are invited to participate in the freshman honors program based on their high school academic records.

Off-Campus Programs

Credit-bearing internships are available for qualified upperclassmen in several academic divisions, and students may participate in the Washington Center for Internships and Academic Seminars, a comprehensive, credit-bearing learning experience in Washington, D.C.

Franklin Pierce University is one of sixteen member colleges of the New Hampshire College and University Council (NHCUC). The NHCUC Student Exchange Agreement allows students to take courses at other NHCUC colleges at no extra tuition cost. Students may take courses at Franklin Pierce University and another member college during the same semester, or they may spend up to two semesters in residence at a member school. Members of the NHCUC are Chester College of New England, Colby-Sawyer College, Daniel Webster College, Dartmouth College, Franklin Pierce University, Granite State College, Keene State College, Massachusetts College of Pharmacy and Health Sciences–Manchester, New England College, New Hampshire Community Technical College System, New Hampshire Institute of Art, Plymouth State University, Rivier College, St. Anselm College, Southern New Hampshire University, and the University of New Hampshire, Durham.

Franklin Pierce offers opportunities for academic programs abroad and international studies on campus. The Global Citizenship Program and the University's own program in Vienna, Austria, are two additions to the curriculum that give students the chance to engage in studies with a global focus. In addition to its own programs abroad, Franklin Pierce has formed affiliations with a variety of institutions that allow students from any academic discipline to fulfill their program requirements while studying at an affiliated university or program abroad. Students have the opportunity to take part in programs in Australia, New Zealand, Spain, Belgrade, Scotland, England, and Ireland.

Another study-abroad opportunity is the Walk in Europe. This is a project that is unique to Franklin Pierce University and has been part of the curriculum since 1969. Approximately 25 students are chosen to participate in the semester-long project: a long-distance walk through several European countries. The sheer adventure and vitality of the project profoundly changes the participants' outlook on the world. The Walk is structured to facilitate engagement with Europeans and their cultures and with each member of the group. Students who have participated have described the Walk as the single most valuable learning experience of their years at Franklin Pierce.

Academic Facilities

The Franklin Pierce University Library provides a comfortable, open-stack environment for study and research. The 135,653-volume collection includes books, microforms, compact discs, DVDs, software, and audio and videocassettes. More than 30 licensed Web-based databases, including EBSCOhost and LexisNexis, provide full-text access to more than 19,410 electronic and print periodical titles. The Curriculum Library supports the education curriculum of the University and includes a wealth of resources related to K–12 teaching and learning and children's literature.

Costs

Basic charges for the 2007–08 academic year were $25,516 for tuition, $4860 for a double room, and $3780 for board. Other fees and deposits brought the total to $35,456 per year.

Financial Aid

Both need-based and merit-based financial aid is available in the forms of loans, grants, scholarships, and on-campus employment. Students should visit the University's Web site for details about the various aid programs.

Faculty

There are 74 full-time and 76 part-time professors at the undergraduate residential campus in Rindge, 74 percent of whom have terminal degrees in their field. All Franklin Pierce University students are taught by faculty members who are active professionally in organizations that span the academic disciplines. Over the years, their work has received the support of the Council for the International Exchange of Scholars (Fulbright Scholars), the Hewlett Foundation, the Whiting Foundation, the Lilly Endowment for the Arts, the National Endowment for the Humanities, the National Science Foundation, the Carnegie Foundation for the Advancement of Teaching, the Council for Advancement and Support of Education, and the Kettering Foundation. Faculty members regularly contribute their work as researchers, writers, presenters, editors of professional journals, and performing artists.

Student Government

The Franklin Pierce University Student Government Association (SGA) is made up of dedicated student representatives working to make positive change for the student body. In addition to being an advocate for the student body, the SGA also funds the various clubs and organizations that enrich campus life and the Pierce experience.

Admission Requirements

Applicants are evaluated on an individual basis, with the student's potential and seriousness of purpose of primary concern. The trend toward improved grades, more difficult course work, and greater school involvement are weighed heavily in the student's behalf. Counselor support and supplementary recommendations are valued and are given special consideration. Class size and the campus environment are such that SAT Reasoning Test or ACT results are generally a less valid predictor of success at Franklin Pierce University than ongoing classroom achievement.

Each entering student must submit evidence of adequate preparation for college. Sixteen credits of secondary school work are required of each candidate. The preferred distribution is English, 4 credits; mathematics, 3 credits; laboratory sciences, 2 credits; social sciences, 3 credits; and electives, 4 credits. Candidates deemed to have potential and motivation, yet not meeting all the admission requirements, may be accepted provisionally.

The application consists of the completed application form, official secondary school transcripts, official transcripts from each college attended, an official secondary school recommendation (guidance counselor, principal, or teacher), and SAT Reasoning Test or ACT scores. An on-campus interview is recommended. Students whose native language is not English must also submit the Certification of Finances and an acceptable TOEFL score.

Application and Information

Students may apply to enter in the fall, spring, or summer sessions. Applications are processed on a rolling basis, but students are encouraged to apply and have their transcripts and recommendations sent early in their senior year.

Department of Admissions
Franklin Pierce University
40 University Drive
Rindge, New Hampshire 03461-0060
Phone: 603-899-4050
800-437-0048 (toll-free)
Fax: 603-899-4394
E-mail: admissions@franklinpierce.edu
Web site: http://www.franklinpierce.edu

HESSER COLLEGE

MANCHESTER, NEW HAMPSHIRE

The College

The primary purpose of Hesser College is to provide a high-quality education that is personalized and employment oriented. Hesser College's approach to higher education provides students with increased flexibility. After two years of college, students earn an associate degree and are prepared to enter the workplace, or, if they prefer, students can continue their studies in one of Hesser College's bachelor's degree programs.

Hesser College was established in 1900 as Hesser Business College, a private, nonsectarian college. Since 1972, Hesser College has expanded and enriched its curriculum in keeping with its tradition of providing an affordable career education of high quality.

Hesser College is accredited by the New England Association of Schools and Colleges.

Many students work in the afternoons, evenings, or weekends while attending Hesser College. The men and women currently enrolled represent several states and more than fifteen countries. A large part of the student population is from the New England region.

Hesser College offers intercollegiate sports in men's and women's basketball and soccer, men's baseball, and women's softball. The basketball team has consistently been a major power in the Northern New England Small College Conference. Students also participate in a number of intramural sports programs. Extracurricular activities are varied and include social activities, clubs, trips, and programs in the residence halls.

Hesser College has developed a number of learning assistance programs to help students succeed in their studies. Tutoring and special classes are provided by the faculty throughout each semester. In addition, several departments offer honors programs and special opportunities for independent study. The College also sponsors an active chapter of the national honor society, Phi Theta Kappa, which promotes scholarship and service to the College and the community.

Location

Hesser College is located in Manchester, New Hampshire. With a population of more than 100,000, Manchester is a medium-sized city that offers many cultural, historical, and social events. Hesser's central location provides easy access to entertainment, shopping, and a variety of part-time jobs and academic work experiences.

Manchester was recently named by *Money* magazine as the number-one small city in the northeastern United States. In addition, Manchester was recently named one of the best cities in the United States for business. According to *U.S. News & World Report,* it is "at the hub of things" in the fast-growing high-technology and financial industries of southern New Hampshire.

Manchester has been called the "Gateway to Northern New England," and several major carriers serve the Manchester Airport. Manchester is within 1 hour of Boston, and the mountains and major ski resorts are within 1 to 2 hours of Hesser's campus.

Majors and Degrees

Hesser offers a wide range of programs that prepare students for high-demand careers. Associate degree programs include accounting, business administration, communications and public relations, criminal justice, early childhood education, graphic design, interior design, liberal studies, medical assistant studies, paralegal studies, physical therapist assistant studies, psychology, radio and video production and broadcasting, and small business and management/entrepreneurship.

In addition, Hesser College offers Bachelor of Science degree programs in accounting, business administration, and criminal justice.

Academic Programs

The primary goal of the curriculum is to prepare students for success in specific career areas. The general education requirements are designed to provide the skills necessary for career growth and lifelong learning. Externships, practicums, and opportunities for part-time work experience are available in all majors. An education from Hesser College provides a solid career foundation. Hesser College's goal is quite simple: to prepare people for careers and career advancement.

Many of Hesser College's programs are for the career-minded student who wants to concentrate on the skills required to be successful in the workplace. Most of the courses that students take are directly related to their career choices.

Hesser College follows a traditional semester calendar.

Off-Campus Programs

The College offers opportunities for cooperative education and externships in most of its academic programs. The early childhood education program includes practicums and supervised fieldwork in a variety of child-care facilities. In addition, the curricula of several programs may incorporate short-term study trips to places such as Walt Disney World and Washington, D.C.

Academic Facilities

The academic facilities include five computer labs, a Macintosh-based graphic design lab, medical assistant labs, physical therapist assistant labs, and a radio/video production lab. The

College library contains more than 30,000 titles. The Center for Teaching, Learning, and Assessment provides special tutoring and programs in study skills, reading, writing, math, and computer skills.

Costs

Costs vary by program. Students should contact Hesser College for more information.

Financial Aid

Hesser College offers financial assistance to students who qualify. Many students receive some form of aid. Scholarships are awarded each year to selected students based on academic and financial standing. Hesser College also offers loans and grants. Students should contact Hesser College for more information.

Faculty

The faculty members of Hesser College consistently receive high student evaluations for their interest in each student's success and for the high quality of their teaching. The majority of the faculty members have completed programs of advanced study; many hold doctoral degrees, and all have practical experience in business or other career fields.

Admission Requirements

Hesser College has a rolling admissions policy. Students may apply for admission at any time and should contact the Hesser College admissions team for more information.

Application and Information

Applicants must submit an application form with a $10 nonrefundable fee. Applications are reviewed on a first-come, first-served basis and normally take seven to fourteen days to be fully reviewed upon receipt of all required information.

Requests for additional information and application forms should be addressed to:

Director of Admissions
Hesser College
3 Sundial Avenue
Manchester, New Hampshire 03103
Phone: 888-234-4000 Dept. 266 (toll-free)
Web site: http://www.hesser.edu/

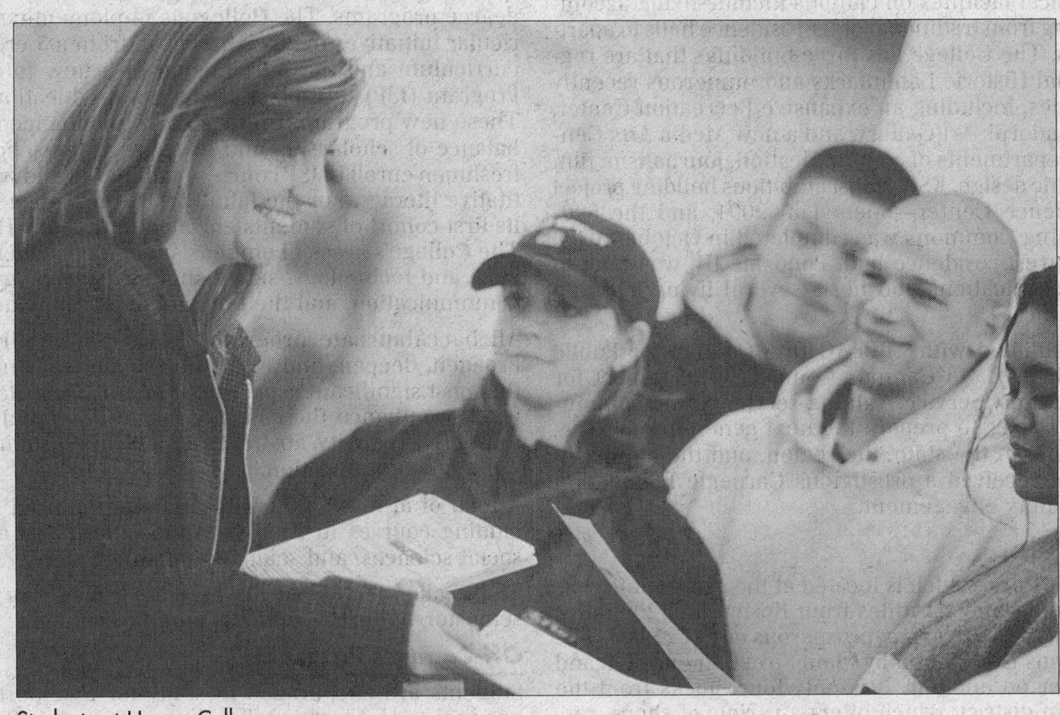

Students at Hesser College.

COLLEGE DATA CENTER • NEW HAMPSHIRE

KEENE STATE COLLEGE
KEENE, NEW HAMPSHIRE

The College

The public liberal arts college of New Hampshire, Keene State College (KSC) is a vibrant educational community that provides an extensive range of opportunities, awarding associate, bachelor's, and master's degrees. Students come to Keene State College for its small size and friendly atmosphere, the choice of forty major programs, a location in the heart of New England, and a private feeling at a public price.

A member of the University System of New Hampshire, Keene State College is a coeducational, residential college with an enrollment of approximately 4,400 full-time, undergraduate students and 1,000 part-time and graduate students. Founded in 1909, the College enrolled 27 students in its first year. From its original 20 acres, the campus has expanded to 170 acres and more than seventy-six buildings that feature a remarkable blend of traditional and contemporary architecture.

The superb physical facilities on campus include living accommodations ranging from traditional older residence halls to apartments and suites. The College has three buildings that are registered as National Historic Landmarks and numerous recently completed facilities, including an expansive Recreation Center, the Thorne-Sagendorph Art Gallery, and a new Media Arts Center housing the departments of communication, journalism, film studies, and graphic design. KSC's most ambitious building project ever—a new Science Center—opened in 2004, and the $20-million Zorn Dining Commons was completed in October 2005. The College's newest residence hall, Pondside III, was built to LEED "silver" specifications and hosts several living/learning student communities.

Keene State is affiliated with CoPLAC (the Council for Public Liberal Arts Colleges) and Campus Compact: The Project for Public and Community Service. Valuing service to the community, the College strives to prepare the next generation for service and leadership in the state, the region, and the nation. In 2006, the College received a prestigious Carnegie Foundation Award for community engagement.

Location

Keene, New Hampshire, which is located at the geographic center of New England—only 84 miles from Boston and 200 miles from New York City—is a thriving, prosperous city of 23,000. The Keene State campus is bordered by Main Street on one side and the Ashuelot River on another. It is only four blocks from the historic downtown district, which offers a variety of shops, restaurants, and theaters. The surrounding New England landscape includes Mount Monadnock (the most-climbed mountain in the world), which is only 18 miles to the southeast of Keene. Opportunities for camping, hiking, mountain climbing, skiing, and swimming are all within a short drive of the campus.

Majors and Degrees

Bachelor of Arts, Fine Arts, Music, and Science degrees are granted in American studies, applied computer science, architecture, art, biology, chemistry, chemistry-physics, communication, computer mathematics, economics, education, English, engineering (transfer programs), environmental studies, film studies, French, general science, geography, geology, graphic design, health science, history, journalism, management, mathematics, mathematics-physics, music, physical education, psychology, safety studies, social science, sociology, Spanish, technology studies, and theater and dance. An individualized B.A. or B.S. major is available for students who wish to design their own interdisciplinary program. Music education and music performance students are awarded the Bachelor of Music degree. Minors in thirty-seven areas, including Holocaust studies and women's studies, make it possible for students to supplement and strengthen their program. A strong cooperative education program provides work/credit opportunities in many majors.

Two-year degree programs offered are the Associate in Arts in general studies and Associate in Science in applied computer science, chemical dependency, general studies, and technology studies.

The College also offers a master's degree in education and post-master's certification programs.

Academic Programs

Education in the liberal arts and sciences and in several professional fields is provided through associate and baccalaureate degree programs. The College is implementing two major curricular initiatives in 2007: the move from a 3-credit to a 4-credit curriculum and the introduction of a new Integrative Studies Program (ISP) to replace the general education requirements. These new programs are designed to enhance the breadth and balance of scholarship and learning at the school. All entering freshmen enroll in ISP courses on thinking and writing and quantitative literacy. For the fall of 2007, the College also welcomes its first cohort of students enrolled in the new Honors Program. The College's areas of emphasis include teacher education, science and technology, safety studies, psychology, management, communication, and the fine and performing arts.

All baccalaureate programs have ISP requirements, which broaden, deepen, and integrate the student's understanding of the most significant aspects of humanity's heritage. These studies also enhance the capacity for aesthetic enjoyment, critical thinking, creativity, abstract and logical reasoning, and oral and written communication.

A total of at least 120 credit hours is required to graduate, including courses in English composition, arts and humanities, social sciences, and science/mathematics.

The academic year at Keene State consists of fall and spring semesters, plus two optional summer sessions.

Off-Campus Programs

Students are encouraged to study for a semester or a year in national and international exchange programs. The National Student Exchange is a domestic alternative to study abroad, with programs at 175 colleges and universities in the U.S., Guam, the Virgin Islands, and Puerto Rico. Keene State has eleven Direct Exchange Programs with institutions in Ecuador, England, France, Ireland, and Russia and more than sixty consortium programs in such popular destinations as China, Costa Rica, Greece, Italy, Scotland, and Spain.

Academic Facilities

The Wallace E. Mason Library houses more than 300,000 paper volumes; has active subscriptions to more than 1,200 periodicals, newspapers, and annual publications; and has a microform collection of more than 550,000 items. Students also have access to the 100,000 volumes that are available nearby at Keene Public Library. Mason Library has direct online access to thousands of other libraries and also subscribes to EBSCOhost, FirstSearch, and JSTOR for access to additional online resources. Mason Library houses the Cohen Center for Holocaust Studies, with resources for scholars and teachers; it also houses the Curriculum Materials Library, which is used by student and classroom teachers across the state.

The library is also home to the Orang Asli Archive, with materials from the indigenous peoples of peninsular Malaysia.

Keene State's new Science Center prepares graduates for professional life in business, industry, and the public sector and trains science teachers on all levels. The $23-million, state-of-the-art building is a center for interactive learning and research in science and mathematics.

Other academic resources include the Media Arts Center, the BodyWorks Fitness Center, the Film Studies Center, the Language Learning Center, and the Writing and Math Centers.

The Redfern Arts Center on Brickyard Pond, which serves as a major regional performing arts center, houses classrooms and performance spaces for the art, dance, music, and theater programs. The Thorne-Sagendorph Art Gallery hosts exhibits by KSC students and faculty members as well as regional, national, and international artists.

Computer equipment, both wired and wireless, is available in all academic areas. A network connects student rooms and the offices of full-time faculty members and administrative personnel to the online library catalog, e-mail, and the Web.

Costs

Tuition for the 2007–08 academic year is $6180 for New Hampshire residents and $13,730 for out-of-state students. Room and board cost $7430, and mandatory fees totaled $2118. Books and supplies cost about $600 per year.

Financial Aid

Financial assistance is available in three basic forms: grants and scholarships, loans, and part-time employment. Grants and scholarships do not have to be repaid. Educational loans must be repaid, but such loans are made on a long-term, low-interest basis. Additional aid consists of part-time, on-campus employment. At Keene State, aid can be based on merit or need or a combination of both. Matriculated students are eligible to apply for assistance if they are enrolled in at least 6 credits per semester. Currently, approximately 70 percent of Keene State students receive some sort of financial aid. Interested students should write to Student Financial Services for more information.

Faculty

The resident faculty numbers 405 men and women (181 full-time and 224 part-time), who value personal attention to students and a commitment to academic advising. They are also active in their academic fields—writing books and articles, serving as consultants, presenting papers and seminars, participating in exhibits, and performing in concerts. The full-time student-faculty ratio is 18:1.

Student Government

The 27-member Student Assembly is the official student government organization of Keene State College. Its members are elected by the student body, with representatives for each academic class, off-campus students, and adult learners. A student body president and vice president are elected by the entire student body, while the chair of the Student Assembly, the secretary, and the treasurer are elected by Student Assembly members. Members of the Student Assembly serve on student committees and College Senate committees. The Student Assembly allocates student activity fee money and recognizes and sets policies for official student organizations.

Admission Requirements

The following requirements apply to all undergraduate programs except the Associate in Science in technology studies. Applicants should provide an application accompanied by the application fee, an official high school transcript and evidence of high school graduation or a satisfactory high school equivalency certificate, scores on the SAT (applicants are responsible for making arrangements to take the test and for having the results forwarded to Keene State College), and a satisfactory evaluation from a high school guidance counselor, principal, or teacher. Applicants who have been out of high school for several years do not need to submit the evaluation; questions regarding this requirement should be addressed to the Director of Admissions.

Applicants should have completed college-preparatory course work, ensuring competence in English grammar and composition, college-level reading speed and comprehension, and a distribution of courses in the humanities (English literature, a modern language, history, and philosophy), the social sciences (political science, sociology, anthropology, psychology, economics, and geography), the sciences (three years required, one of which must be a lab), and mathematics (algebra I, algebra II, and geometry).

A personal interview is not required, although all applicants are encouraged to visit the campus. Visits are arranged through the Admissions Office.

Application and Information

To receive an application form and additional information, students should contact:

Peggy Richmond
Director of Admissions
Elliot Hall
Keene State College
Keene, New Hampshire 03435-2604
Phone: 603-358-2276
800-KSC-1909 (toll-free)
Fax: 603-358-2767
E-mail: admissions@keene.edu
Web site: http://www.keene.edu

Appian Gateway serves as a gathering place for students and welcomes visitors to Keene State College's traditional New England campus.

NEW ENGLAND COLLEGE

HENNIKER, NEW HAMPSHIRE

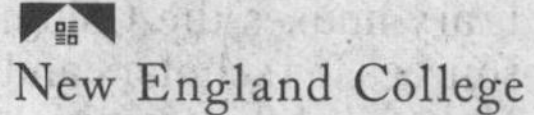

The College

New England College (NEC) is a place where students amaze themselves with what they learn and with what they can accomplish. A college that prepares students for the professional world, NEC also empowers its graduates with a broad knowledge base that results from a focus on the liberal arts and hands-on learning. In addition, students develop strong analytical and communication skills that are vital to success in any career. The College's current enrollment stands at about 1,580 students (1,040 are undergraduates). The diverse student body, representing thirty states and twenty other countries, enriches the College curriculum's multicultural focus and global perspective. New England College prides itself on its commitment to each individual student and provides a strong support network to assist students with a variety of learning styles. The Pathways Center plays a key role in the academic and professional achievements of all students. It is an innovative combination of academic advising, study skills and support services, and career planning and placement. The Pathways Center is an integral part of academic life at NEC; students begin honing their academic and professional skills, planning for their future, and building their resumes from the moment they arrive on campus. Thus, NEC graduates are extremely successful in finding employment upon graduation. As an example, education majors have enjoyed 100 percent job placement over the last eleven years.

The campus, which is nestled in the center of Henniker, a classic small New England town, consists of thirty-two buildings. Students take advantage of the many extracurricular activities available at NEC, ranging from outdoor recreation to theater productions and the student newspaper. There are thirteen Division III intercollegiate sports teams at NEC in addition to numerous club and recreational sports options. The campus offers 26 acres of playing fields, a fitness center with the latest exercise and strength-building equipment, a gymnasium, and an indoor field house for student athletic activities. The Lee Clement Ice Arena, home to the NEC Pilgrims, provides some of the best hockey games in the region.

Location

New England College's location offers students the best of all worlds. Students have easy access to vibrant cities and the incomparable recreation and wilderness regions of New Hampshire. The College is located a short drive from the state capital, Concord, and about 30 minutes from the state's largest city, Manchester, and its airport. Portsmouth, Boston, and some of the best ocean beaches in New England can be reached in just 90 minutes. Alpine and Nordic skiing opportunities abound. Pats Peak, located only 3 miles from the campus, provides free skiing and snowboarding to all NEC students. The College's 225-acre campus offers excellent trails for cross-country skiing and hiking. The Contoocook River flows through the center of the campus, spanned by the College's historic covered bridge, a popular subject for photographers, especially during autumn. Almost all NEC students reside on campus in the six residence halls located adjacent to classroom buildings and the student center.

Majors and Degrees

The College offers twenty-nine majors, a remarkable number for a small college. Such variety permits students to consider a number of options before selecting a major, which is encouraged. Graduates of the undergraduate program are awarded the Bachelor of Arts or the Bachelor of Science, depending upon their major. A number of concentrations are offered within the majors, further permitting students to develop expertise based upon their specific career goals. For instance, a student can major in art with a concentration in photography.

Majors available at NEC include art, art history, biological studies, biology, business administration, communication, comparative literature, creative writing, criminal justice, educational studies, elementary education, engineering (3+2 program with Clarkson University), English, environmental chemistry, environmental science, environmental studies, health sciences, history, kinesiology, mathematics, outdoor leadership, philosophy, physical education, political science, psychology, secondary education, sociology, special education, sport and recreation management, theater, and theater education.

In addition, New England College offers a 3+3 program in conjunction with New York Law School that allows students to obtain their undergraduate and law degrees in six years. There are also a 4+1 M.B.A. program with Union University and a 4+3 Doctor of Physical Therapy program with Franklin Pierce University, giving students postgraduate opportunities to look forward to. In conjunction with Massachusetts College of Pharmacy and Health Sciences, NEC also offers Bachelor of Science in Nursing (B.S.N.), Master of Physician Assistant, and Doctor of Pharmacy programs.

Students may elect an individually designed major, combining elements from several majors, subject to faculty approval. Many students pursue internship options (required for 70 percent of majors) in a wide range of disciplines, including business, fine and performing arts, government, health care and human services, law, media and communications, professional sports, and many others. Recent internship sites have included National Public Radio, Disney World, the Verizon Wireless Center, the Army Corps of Engineers, the Manchester Monarchs, and Edge Sports. In addition, a joint venture between Edge Sports and the College has allowed students to manage the Edge Sports Magazine and Web site (http://www.edgesportsonline.com). This cross-curriculum project has provided students hands-on experience in the full production of these publications, from sales calls to marketing to layout and print.

Education majors have many opportunities to interact with children and adolescents, from early on in their programs to their capstone student-teaching experience.

Academic Programs

A comprehensive liberal arts college that also offers professional programs, NEC aims for its students to develop certain abilities: to think and communicate effectively, to understand the methods of the broad academic disciplines, to develop a strong sense of ethics, to respect other identities and cultures, and to develop a lifelong love of learning.

The First-Year Experience at NEC introduces students to college-level learning. It includes two writing courses, a computer technology course, seminars on human rights and cultural diversity, a course in science, and a course in basic mathematics. The New England College curriculum is rooted in the belief that students learn best when actively involved with their subject matter; thus, NEC courses focus on learning by doing. Students may also elect to participate in the honors program, where they work one-on-one with faculty members on research and student projects that earn extra credits. The academic year is divided into two main semesters, fall and spring. Additional sessions during January and the summer months offer students opportunities to take courses online or on campus. To graduate, students are required to complete a minimum of 120 credits as part of an approved program of study. CLEP and AP credits are accepted.

Off-Campus Programs

New England College encourages students to consider study-abroad options available to them via consortia agreements with a wide range of institutions located throughout the world. Students generally spend one semester when studying abroad, although some opt for a yearlong program. Participating institutions are located in Australia, Canada, England, France, Japan, and South Africa. Students may also choose to participate in travel courses, which are generally offered during the January term.

NEC's membership in the New Hampshire College and University Consortium (NHCUC) enables NEC students to take courses at any of the NHCUC member institutions and apply these credits to their degree program at the College.

Academic Facilities

The College's Center for Educational Innovation (CEI) was opened in 2001. A state-of-the art facility, the CEI provides networked data ports, Internet access, videoconferencing, and the full range of electronic and broadcast media access that enables professors to enhance their teaching by connecting to today's global network of information. The Simon Center, at the heart of the NEC campus, serves as the student center for the College. The entire campus is wireless, enabling students to access the College's network and the Internet from laptop computers at any location on campus. The H. Raymond Danforth Library provides a comprehensive research facility in addition to housing the Academic Support Center, where students may receive comprehensive subject tutoring and organizational and time management skill training from professional tutors. The library holds more than 100,000 volumes as well as a new thirty-three-station computer laboratory with Internet access. The science building serves as the home of the science departments, although classes for many other disciplines are scheduled in this large facility. Also located in the science building is the newly renovated Mainstage Theatre, where a number of plays are presented each year by NEC's outstanding Theatre Department.

Costs

For the 2007–08 year, tuition and fees were $24,900. Room and board were $8794.

Financial Aid

New England College offers a wide range of scholarships and grants for incoming students, ranging from $1500 to $17,000. The majority of these awards are merit-based, taking into account the student's academic achievement or other talents and accomplishments, such as participation in the arts, community service, and student government. Some need-based grants are available as well and are awarded to students based upon information provided on the Free Application for Federal Student Aid (FAFSA). All awards are renewable on an annual basis, depending upon the student's academic record and/or documented financial need.

Faculty

There are 62 full-time faculty members at New England College. More than 75 percent hold terminal degrees in their fields. The NEC faculty is highly accomplished and active professionally, publishing books and articles, participating in national conferences, conducting scientific research, and creating works of art. The main focus of the NEC faculty members is teaching. They understand that students learn best by doing and so incorporate practical projects and activities into their course syllabi. The low student-teacher ratio (14:1) contributes to the friendly, highly personalized classroom experience. Students benefit from regular, personalized interaction with their professors, which helps them develop their knowledge and abilities beyond what they had ever thought possible.

Student Government

New England College's student government is actively involved in the academic, cultural, social, and organizational life of the institution. The Student Senate functions as a liaison between students and the NEC faculty, administration, alumni, and trustees. The Student Senate is responsible for its own budget, which funds numerous student-run clubs, organizations, social events, and recreational activities.

Admission Requirements

Freshman applicants must have received their high school diplomas (or equivalent) before attending New England College. A basic college-preparatory program is recommended, with course work in English, mathematics, science, social studies, and other academic electives. The Office of Admission takes into account the student's academic record, extracurricular activities and achievements, personal statement, and letters of recommendation, as well as the student's maturity and determination to succeed. Standardized tests (SAT or ACT) are not required, although most students submit scores. Students are encouraged to arrange an interview, conducted either in person or via telephone, with an admission counselor.

Application and Information

New England College has a rolling admission system; applications are reviewed as they become complete. All applicants must submit a completed application form, a $30 application fee, official high school transcripts covering at least the first marking period of the senior year, a personal essay, and two letters of recommendation from high school teachers or guidance counselors. Most students receive decisions within two weeks of their file's completion. Students are encouraged to apply early, as scholarship decisions are made shortly after admission, and they are considered for the full range of scholarship opportunities at the early part of the application cycle. Students whose native language is not English must submit TOEFL scores. Those students who do not meet TOEFL score minimums may participate in the English language learner (ELL) program at NEC. Transfer students must also provide official college transcripts and a supporting letter from their college's dean of students.

Application forms may be obtained from the Office of Admission or at the New England College Web site. Students may submit their applications online. For further information, interested students should contact:

Diane Raymond
Director of Admission
New England College
102 Bridge Street
Henniker, New Hampshire 03242-3297
Phone: 800-521-7642 (toll-free)
Fax: 603-428-3155
E-mail: admission@nec.edu
Web site: http://www.nec.edu/

Students walking by New England College's Center for Educational Innovation.

COLLEGE DATA CENTER • NEW HAMPSHIRE

NEW HAMPSHIRE INSTITUTE OF ART

MANCHESTER, NEW HAMPSHIRE

The Institute

The New Hampshire Institute of Art has been devoted to the education of artists for more than 100 years. Founded in 1898 as the Manchester Institute of Arts and Sciences, the Institute provides educational opportunities for a broad regional audience to learn about and experience the arts. In 1996, the Institute's Board of Trustees voted to rename the organization the New Hampshire Institute of Art. In that same year, the Institute was authorized by the state of New Hampshire to grant the Bachelor of Fine Arts (B.F.A.) degree. The Institute received national accreditation through the National Association of Schools of Art and Design in November 2001.

The Institute functions as an important cultural resource for the state of New Hampshire. Several fully accessible gallery spaces support a free and widely varied exhibition schedule throughout each year, featuring student, faculty member, special artist, and community exhibits. The Institute's French Auditorium offers significant opportunities for visiting artist presentations and political and critical forums of regional and national importance. In recent years, speakers have included Bob Smith, Dan Quayle, Pat Buchanan, John Sununu, Al Gore, Bill Clinton, and Richard Gephardt.

Housing is available for students at three locations, Institute Hall, the Hampshire, and the Plaza. The Hampshire is an all-female dormitory set in a residential community. Institute Hall is a coed dormitory that is conveniently located just two blocks from the campus in downtown Manchester and offers all residents a free Y membership. The Plaza is a coed dormitory that offers a 24-hour studio space, a quiet study area, an indoor garden, a lounge area with a flat-screen television, and a pool table. All residence halls offer many single rooms, kitchen facilities, laundry facilities, and common areas.

Location

The Institute is located in Manchester, New Hampshire, a medium-sized, cosmopolitan city of 110,000 people, with a lively downtown. Manchester, which was recently named the number-one city in America by *Money Magazine,* is a northern New England cultural center, featuring the Currier Gallery of Art, the Verizon Wireless Arena, the Manchester Historic Association, Millyard Museum, and the SEE Science Center. In addition, Manchester offers the Palace Theatre, the New Hampshire Symphony Orchestra, the Granite State Opera, the New Hampshire Philharmonic Orchestra, and the Opera League of New Hampshire. There are eleven other colleges in the greater Manchester area. Students can hike, fish, golf, and ski without leaving the city. Manchester is centrally located, allowing easy access to Boston, Portland, and the seacoast areas.

Majors and Degrees

The Institute offers a four-year Bachelor of Fine Arts degree in ceramics, illustration, interdisciplinary studies, painting, and photography. Students can also take B.F.A. classes in art education, metals, printmaking, sculpture, digital imaging, and graphic design. Certificate programs and lifelong-learning classes are also available.

Academic Programs

The mission of the New Hampshire Institute of Art's Bachelor of Fine Arts degree program is to provide a traditional program of study in the fine arts, emphasizing the importance of integrating creative, aesthetic, technical, and critical skills in artistic expression. The creation and study of art is central to the mission and to the student's educational experience at the Institute.

The B.F.A. degree allocates 75 percent to course work in studio and art history courses and 25 percent to liberal arts courses. All of the Institute's resources, programs, faculty members, facilities, and student services focus on the needs of the developing artist. Liberal arts courses support the studio programs and develop an understanding of creative expression. For example, a science course may focus on color in light and pigment, or a philosophy course may explore the thought and inner reflection of the creative process.

During a student's first year in the B.F.A. program, required courses focus on drawing, two- and three-dimensional design, color theory, art history, and writing. Specific introductory studio, art history, and liberal arts courses are required in the sophomore year to prepare students for the intermediate- and advanced-level courses to follow.

The student's final year at the Institute focuses on the student's ability to create a culminating body of work and a senior paper addressing the issues posed in the student's original entrance essay. This serves as the capstone to the student's experience in the B.F.A. program.

Academic Facilities

The Main Building is home to the drawing, painting, printmaking, liberal arts, and sculpture programs and a metalsmithing studio, in addition to two exhibition galleries, a student lounge, and the main administration offices. Studio 7 is reserved for the Institute's artist in residence.

Fuller Hall houses an up-to-date studio and digital photography facility, liberal arts classrooms, a writing studio, the Institute's library, and gallery space. The student gallery, lounge, café, and student service and admissions offices are on the main floor.

The Amherst Street Building opened in September 2005, adding 80 percent more studio classroom space for painting, drawing, illustration, and foundation classes. It is also the location of student mailboxes, a new gallery, and the Institute Shop, which carries art supplies and books and offers a photography service.

Costs

For the 2007–08 academic year, tuition for full-time B.F.A. students was $6480 per semester. A full-time course load is 12 to 18 credits per semester. Estimated fees for full-time students are $720 per semester. Rooms were available during the 2007–08 academic year for $3150 per semester for a single and $2350 per semester for a double. Costs are subject to change.

Financial Aid

The Institute offers federal financial aid programs to its B.F.A. students. In addition, the Institute offers several merit- and need-based scholarship opportunities to help students and their families defray the cost of education. All B.F.A. students seeking financial aid at the Institute must complete the Free Application for Federal Student Aid (FAFSA). The Institute's FAFSA priority deadline is May 1. Students are encouraged to submit their FAFSA online at http://www.fafsa.ed.gov.

Faculty

Most faculty members have terminal degrees and have achieved significant recognition in their fields. Their extensive studio experience and strong educational backgrounds enable them to assist students in the development of artistic skills and the professional skills required to be a practicing artist. Institute faculty members serve both as mentors and as academic advisers to students.

The faculty members of the New Hampshire Institute of Art are a diverse group of practicing artists who are highly experienced in their fields and dedicated to the educational experience. Works by Institute faculty members are exhibited in major museum collections, including the Art Institute of Chicago; the Museum of Fine Arts, Boston; the Museum of Quebec; the Currier Gallery of Art; and the De Cordova Museum and Sculpture Garden. Museum and gallery exhibitions include Dartmouth College's Hood Museum; the Renwick Gallery in Washington, D.C.; New York City's American Craft Museum; the Whistler House Museum; the Fitchburg Art Museum; McGowan Fine Art; and numerous Boston, New York, and San Francisco galleries. Faculty members' works also appear in many private and corporate collections all over the world.

Student Government

Through the Student Activities Council (SAC), students participate in a wide variety of college and community activities. SAC officers are elected and serve as exhibition coordinators for the student-run gallery. They plan social activities and museum trips, identify student initiatives, and improve the quality of the student experience at the Institute.

Admission Requirements

The New Hampshire Institute of Art is a private, not-for-profit educational institution that maintains a policy of equal opportunity for all. The Institute does not discriminate on the basis of race, color, religion, national origin, sex, sexual orientation, age, veteran status, or disability in admission to, access to, or employment in its educational programs. Students who demonstrate artistic promise, potential, and aptitude for successful artistic endeavor are encouraged to apply for admission. A student's potential for success at the Institute is judged by the submission of a complete application, which includes a portfolio interview.

A complete application contains two letters of recommendation from a present or former teacher and/or guidance counselor or person who is familiar with the student on a professional basis, a 500-word essay on what inspires the student to make art and why they want to attend a fine arts college, official transcripts from every high school or college attended, and a nonrefundable $25 application fee. Transcripts must be requested from each institution and sent directly to the Institute's Admissions Office. Applicants who are currently in high school are encouraged to submit either SAT or ACT scores. Applicants who have not graduated from high school must submit GED forms.

Portfolios usually contain between ten and twenty examples of the student's actual artwork and observe the following guidelines: drawings made from direct observation (not copied from photographs of published artwork); two or more self-portrait drawings ranging from representational to conceptual or expressive renderings; still-life drawings in any medium; interior studies, architectural renderings, or any other drawings that demonstrate the use of perspective; works that demonstrate the use of color; landscape, cityscape, portrait, or still-life paintings; and works that refer to the student's personal interests and strengths, including works in photography, digital imaging, printmaking, ceramics, sculpture, metalsmithing, or other mediums.

A slide portfolio can be submitted if necessary and should observe the following guidelines: 2" x 2", 35mm slides (standard mount) in a clear plastic slide page; the student's name, address, and phone number and an identification number and a notation indicating the top of the slide in permanent marker on each slide; and a slide identification sheet listing the size, the medium, and the year each work was created (titles and a brief description of each piece are optional). Two different views should be submitted of three-dimensional work (these two slides equal the representation of one work). Students should prepare their slide portfolios carefully and include postage if they want them to be returned. Portfolios may also be submitted via digital formats.

The New Hampshire Institute of Art also accepts transfer students. Transfer students must follow the same application criteria as traditional students, with the addition of all college-level transcripts.

Application and Information

The Institute has a rolling admissions policy; however, it is recommended that applications be completed by April 1 to be considered for merit-based and need-based financial aid. Applications are available online through the Institute's Web site. The Institute offers application fee waivers; for more information, students should contact the Admissions Office.

To be considered for admission, students must submit the completed application and the required nonrefundable $25 application fee to:

Admissions Department
New Hampshire Institute of Art
148 Concord Street
Manchester, New Hampshire 03104-4858
Phone: 603-623-0313 Ext. 576
866-241-4918 (toll-free)
E-mail: admissions@nhia.edu
Web site: http://www.nhia.edu

On the campus of the New Hampshire Institute of Art.

RIVIER COLLEGE

NASHUA, NEW HAMPSHIRE

The College

Rivier College, a private Catholic college founded in 1933, has gained a reputation for academic excellence in more than forty programs. The College has adapted to changing needs by developing liberal arts/career-oriented programs designed to prepare graduates in many fields.

The programs in the School of Undergraduate Studies enroll approximately 1,500 students, including 900 full-time day students. With an 18:1 student-faculty ratio, students have plenty of opportunities to connect with faculty members and become active members of the academic community.

Most full-time undergraduate traditional day students are between 18 and 22 years old. The majority are residents of New England, although other states are represented, including Texas and Virginia. International students represent countries in Africa, Asia, Europe, the Middle East, and South America. Students who live on campus reside in four modern residence halls. Most rooms are doubles, with some triples, quads, and singles available. Rivier also provides substance-free housing in Presentation Hall. The newest hall offers suite-style living, with several double and triple rooms sharing a kitchenette and common area. The Dion Center houses the dining room, the commuter lounge, the mail room, a campus store, student development offices, and meeting rooms. All students are permitted to have cars on the campus.

Orientation sessions for new students are sponsored by the Office of Student Development. Academic and personal counseling are available throughout the year. A full-time chaplain and Campus Ministry team coordinate spiritual activities and service opportunities, while a comprehensive career development service helps students prepare for employment after graduation. Students' health needs are met by a Health Services Center. The Office of Student Development, the Student Government Association, and more than twenty-five student clubs and organizations provide a calendar of social, cultural, and recreational activities, including concerts, live entertainment, films, and sporting events. The College and student organizations frequently organize outings, including trips to Boston and New York and abroad. Students also enjoy a variety of performances by the Rivier Theater Company.

Rivier offers a wide range of team and individual sports, including NCAA Division III men's baseball, basketball, cross-country, soccer, and volleyball and women's basketball, cross-country, soccer, softball, and volleyball. The men's volleyball team has been nationally ranked every year since 2001. The Muldoon Health and Fitness Center is home to Rivier's varsity athletics and to many intramural sports and fitness activities, including volleyball, floor hockey, basketball, weight training, aerobics, self-defense, and more. The campus also has soccer and softball fields, as well as a beach volleyball court and cross-country trail. Student athletes and others can take advantage of an on-campus rehabilitation clinic offering free injury assessment, physical and occupational therapy, and athletic training.

Location

Nashua (population 87,000) is located in southern New Hampshire. The city of Boston lies within easy access 40 miles to the south. Local access to public transportation provides for easy travel to and from the campus. Recreational activities abound year-round at nearby lakes and ski areas, in the White Mountains to the north, and at the seacoast, just an hour's drive to the east.

Majors and Degrees

Rivier College awards Bachelor of Arts and Bachelor of Science degrees in the following areas of concentration: art (drawing and painting, graphic design, and photography and digital media); biology (allied health and environmental science) and biology education; business (business management, information technology management, and marketing); communications (advertising/public relations, journalism, photojournalism, scriptwriting, video production, and Web design/online publishing); computer science; education (early childhood/special education, elementary education/special education, and human development/interdisciplinary); English and English education; history, law, and political science (criminal justice, history, political science, and social studies education); human development; international studies; liberal studies; mathematics and mathematics education; modern languages (modern languages education and Spanish); nursing; psychology; and sociology. Preprofessional programs are offered in law, dentistry, medicine, and veterinary medicine. Associate degrees are offered in art, business management, computer science, early childhood education, information technology management, liberal studies, and nursing.

Academic Programs

Rivier College takes special pride in its curriculum, which offers both professional studies and liberal arts in order to prepare students for a fast-changing, highly technological society. The curriculum is broad-based, with emphasis on preparing students for challenging and rewarding careers and furthering their personal growth. Core curriculum requirements may vary slightly, depending on the degree to be obtained, but generally include courses in the areas of English, mathematics and/or natural sciences, modern language and literature, philosophy, religious studies, social science, and Western civilization. No fewer than ten courses must be taken in the major field. Electives may be chosen according to the student's interests. For the bachelor's degree, a minimum of 120 credits with a grade point average of at least 2.0 is required. For the associate degree, the student must complete a minimum of 60 credits with a grade point average of at least 2.0.

All departments encourage qualified students to pursue internships in their field of study during their junior or senior year. Education specialists student teach in local schools. Nursing majors complete clinical rotations in health-care facilities throughout southern New Hampshire and Boston. History, law, and political science majors may work in a law office, business, legal-assistance agency, or government agency. Sociology and psychology majors work with local social service agencies. English and communications majors work in public relations, broadcasting, or corporate communications positions. Art majors work in advertising or graphic design or at local galleries. Business majors work in such areas as marketing, management, and technology.

Honors awards include placement on the dean's list, membership in Kappa Gamma Pi, listing in *Who's Who Among Students in American Universities and Colleges,* listing in *The National Dean's List,* and degrees with honors. Academically talented students may also apply to the four-year honors program.

The college year is divided into two 15-week semesters, with first-semester examinations held before Christmas recess. Students usually take five courses each semester. Academic credit may be granted to incoming freshmen on the basis of scores on Advanced Placement tests and CLEP examinations. Students may also "challenge" courses and receive credit by special examination.

Off-Campus Programs

Through Rivier College's membership in the New Hampshire College and University Council, a sixteen-member consortium of senior and two-year colleges, Rivier students may register for courses at any of the member colleges and receive transfer credits.

Academic Facilities

Academic facilities include Memorial Hall, which houses fourteen classrooms, faculty offices, a lecture hall, a fully equipped digital imaging studio, a communications lab offering the most recent software and video/sound editing equipment, a behavioral science lab, the studio of community television station tv13 Nashua (WYCN), and art department facilities that include a gallery, a slide library, and studios. The Academic Computer Center features up to sixty-eight workstations with a full range of cutting-edge software and Internet/e-mail access. Regina Library houses more than 100,000 volumes and provides access to more than 3 million volumes in twelve area libraries, as well as online access to licensed databases in virtually every academic subject. The Writing and Resource Center is staffed by professional writing consultants as well as student tutors. Other academic facilities include nursing and science laboratories; a physical assessment lab and nursing skills simulation lab, which provide nursing students with practical experience using blood pressure cuffs, ophthalmoscopes, IV pumps, and more; the McLean Center for Finance and Economics; the BAE Student Research Lab; electronic classrooms offering multimedia learning tools; and the Education Center, which houses an eight-classroom Early Childhood Center, observation rooms, and an educational resource center.

Costs

Tuition and fees for the academic year 2007–08 were $21,810; room and board, $8260; and books and supplies, approximately $700. Students should expect to pay a $100 activities fee and a $25 registration fee each semester.

Financial Aid

Financial aid is awarded on the basis of the financial need of the student and family. Approximately 80 percent of Rivier's students receive financial aid from the College or from government or private sources. Federal aid includes Federal Pell Grants, Federal Supplemental Educational Opportunity Grants, Federal Perkins Loans, Federal Stafford Student Loans, the Federal PLUS loan program, and the Federal Work-Study Program. To be considered for financial aid, a student must file the Free Application for Federal Student Aid (FAFSA) with the federal government as soon as possible after January 1 for the coming year. FAFSA results should be on file with the College Financial Aid Office prior to March 1 for the following academic year. Each applicant is assessed individually to determine the best combination of grant, work, scholarship, and loan amounts to meet the need of the student. The College awards more than $5 million worth of merit-based scholarships and grants, ranging in value from $1000 to full tuition. For more information, students should contact the Office of Financial Aid.

Faculty

The College employs 71 full-time faculty members. The full-time student–faculty ratio is 11:1. Part-time instructors in specialized areas are working professionals who bring current knowledge and expertise in their field to their classes. All classes are taught by faculty members, and department chairs serve as academic advisers to students in their major programs.

Student Government

Every full-time day student automatically becomes a member of the Student Government Association (SGA) upon registration and payment of the student activity fee. The main goals of the SGA are to stimulate active participation in all College functions, to establish and maintain effective channels of communication among members of the College community and the community at large, and to foster a mutual trust, encourage a spirit of cooperation, and initiate new endeavors. The SGA also supervises student clubs and organizations and oversees their finances. The SGA Executive Board serves as the channel of communication through which the views of the students on institutional policies reach the College administration.

Admission Requirements

Applicants for admission should ordinarily have completed, in an accredited high school, a minimum of 16 academic units, including 4 in English, 2 in a modern foreign language, 3 in mathematics, 2 in social science, 2 in science, and 3 in electives. The most successful candidates are in the upper half of their class, with at least a B average. Combined SAT scores average 1410–1500. A personal interview is strongly recommended but not required.

Rivier welcomes applications from qualified transfer candidates from accredited institutions, as well as applications from international students. Transfer students must forward transcripts of all previous college work and a high school transcript. International students must fulfill the requirements for general admission; they may also be required to submit Test of English as a Foreign Language (TOEFL) scores. Deferred admission may be granted to students who wish to postpone entrance for up to one year, provided they have not been enrolled full-time at another postsecondary institution.

Application and Information

Applications must be accompanied by a nonrefundable $25 application fee, SAT scores, one letter of recommendation, and a high school transcript. The School of Undergraduate Studies employs a system of rolling admission that allows qualified students to be admitted approximately one month after their application is completed. Transfers should apply by June 1 for fall admission and by December 1 for spring admission. Those applying for financial aid should observe the March 1 deadline. Interviews are arranged through the Admissions Office. Students may apply online at the College's Web site.

More specific information and application forms can be obtained by contacting:

Director of Undergraduate Admissions
Rivier College
420 South Main Street
Nashua, New Hampshire 03060
Phone: 603-897-8507
800-44-RIVIER (toll-free)
Fax: 603-891-1799
E-mail: rivadmit@rivier.edu
Web site: http://www.rivier.edu

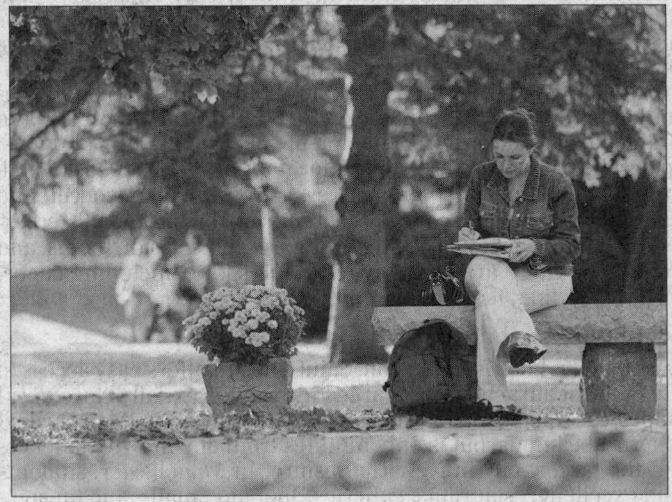

The campus of Rivier College in Nashua, New Hampshire.

SAINT ANSELM COLLEGE

MANCHESTER, NEW HAMPSHIRE

The College

Saint Anselm is a small liberal arts college in the hills of southern New Hampshire, less than an hour north of Boston. Founded in 1889 by the Catholic Order of Saint Benedict, it maintains the family spirit that is characteristic of a Benedictine institution. By choosing to remain small (fewer than 2,000 students), it provides a friendly and supportive environment for students of all backgrounds and faiths and allows for close interaction between students and faculty members. The College has earned a reputation for high academic standards. It prides itself on offering a challenging intellectual environment while encouraging the students' intellectual, social, spiritual, and physical development. Saint Anselm is also well-known for its strong commitment to community service and civic engagement. A large percentage of students volunteer on campus and in the community, gaining valuable work and leadership experience.

All Saint Anselm College students pursue specialized major courses of study in such areas as liberal arts, business, the sciences, nursing, and preprofessional preparation. A curriculum that emphasizes critical thinking, communication, research, and analysis skills leads to strong placement in graduate and professional schools. The College's primary goal, however, is to offer an educational experience that produces well-rounded graduates with a creative and open-minded spirit.

The beauty of Saint Anselm College's 400-acre campus changes with the seasons. Buildings surrounding the "quad" range from original ivy-covered brick to contemporary architecture, and the grounds include a church and an abbey that is home to 30 monks. In addition to student housing, administration, and academic facilities, the campus includes a multipurpose activities center; Davison Hall dining commons; Stoutenburgh Gymnasium, home of Saint Anselm varsity athletics; the new Thomas F. Sullivan hockey arena; and Cushing Student Center, which houses academic and career counseling offices, student organizations, health services, and an academic resource center. A short drive away is a 100-acre tract used for retreats and environmental study and research.

Saint Anselm College has students from twenty-eight states and thirteen countries, more than 86 percent of whom live on campus in traditional dormitories and modern apartments. The list of more than eighty clubs and organizations that match the students' diverse interests is constantly evolving and includes music, community service, theater, outdoor recreation, debating, prelaw and premedicine, and a local chapter of the Knights of Columbus. Intercollegiate sports are offered for men in baseball, basketball, cross-country, football, golf, hockey, lacrosse, skiing, soccer, and tennis. For women, teams are organized in basketball, cross-country, field hockey, lacrosse, skiing, soccer, softball, tennis, and volleyball. There are nearly twenty club sports, including cheerleading, cycling, ice skating, and rugby.

Location

Less than an hour from Boston, Saint Anselm offers easy access to the cultural attractions of a large city, yet it is equally close to ski slopes, the Appalachian Trail, and the Atlantic coast. It has the feel of a rural campus, but is only minutes from downtown Manchester, the largest city in New Hampshire. In Manchester, students find excellent restaurants, galleries, shopping malls, and theaters as well as professional offices with internship and employment opportunities.

Majors and Degrees

Saint Anselm awards the Bachelor of Arts degree in thirty-one majors: accounting, biochemistry, biology, business, chemistry, classics, computer science, computer science with business, computer science with mathematics, criminal justice, economics, English, environmental science, financial economics, fine arts, French, history, international business, international relations, liberal studies in the great books, mathematics, mathematics with economics, natural science, nursing, philosophy, physics, politics, psychology, sociology, Spanish, and theology. It also offers a program leading to the Bachelor of Science in Nursing (B.S.N.) degree.

The College offers preprofessional programs in dentistry, education (secondary), law, medicine, and theology.

A 3-2 program in engineering is available in cooperation with the University of Notre Dame, Catholic University of America, Manhattan College, and the University of Massachusetts Lowell.

Academic Programs

Saint Anselm College provides students with a strong liberal arts background, including required courses in philosophy, theology, and foreign language. Students generally take ten to fifteen courses in their majors, while the liberal arts core courses and a wide range of electives make up the remainder of the forty courses required for graduation. Honors program participants distinguish themselves by taking additional courses in order to graduate with honors.

All Saint Anselm students participate in a nationally recognized humanities program, Portraits in Human Greatness, during their freshman and sophomore years. The program's nondisciplinary approach to Western culture integrates science, sociology, history, philosophy, and the arts. The heart of the program is its seminar component, which strengthens skills in reasoning, articulating ideas, and debating.

Saint Anselm College participates in the Advanced Placement Program of the College Board. Students who receive a score of 3 or better on the Advanced Placement examinations may obtain advanced placement and credit in the pertinent subject matter. Applicants who have completed examinations under the College-Level Examination Program may receive advanced placement and credit if the scores they receive are acceptable.

Off-Campus Programs

More than 40 percent of Saint Anselm students complete an internship related to their major field of study, usually during their junior or senior year. Internships help students apply theoretical knowledge, explore careers and graduate school choices, and improve employment prospects. Internships are arranged locally and in major cities such as Boston, New York, and Washington, D.C.

The College provides access to several approved semester-long study-abroad programs, and Saint Anselm faculty members often lead summer study trips abroad. Service trips sponsored by the Office of Campus Ministry take place from Arizona to Maine as well as in Latin America.

Academic Facilities

Among the College's fifty-one buildings are facilities for classes, research, arts performances and exhibits, and campus events. Geisel Library holds 230,000 bound volumes and 68,000 microform titles and maintains a collection of 4,000 periodical titles and 1,700 video recordings, as well as CDs and audiotapes. Goulet Science Center has been expanded and renovated to meet the students' needs, and contains its own library. The 20,000-square-foot New Hampshire Institute of Politics is a center for civic education and engagement. It attracts diplomats, candidates, and political experts throughout the year and is in the national and international spotlight during presidential primary and election seasons. The Charles A. Dana Center houses a 700-seat theater and serves as the home of the humanities program. Poisson Computer Science Center contains more than 200 PCs and specially equipped classrooms and offices. Fine arts studios and a small theater are located in the Comiskey Center.

Costs

Tuition for the 2008–09 school year is $28,440, and room and board charges are $10,760. Books and other miscellaneous fees cost approximately $1850.

Financial Aid

Saint Anselm College offers financial aid through various federal and private programs. Assistance is awarded as a supplement to the reasonable financial sacrifice that the College expects will be made by the interested student and his or her parents. Eighty-five percent of Saint Anselm's students receive some form of financial assistance to help defray the cost of their education. Financial aid packages consist of scholarships, grants, loans, and work opportunities. Merit awards (Presidential Scholarships) of up to $12,500 are awarded to outstanding students.

Two forms are required in applying for aid. The student must submit the CSS Financial Aid PROFILE and the Free Application for Federal Student Aid (FAFSA) to the College Scholarship Service by March 1.

Faculty

The College's faculty consists of full-time and part-time members. Ninety-six percent of the faculty members have earned doctorates or the appropriate terminal degrees in their fields. With a student-teacher ratio of 12:1, professors are extremely accessible. In addition to teaching, the faculty members serve as advisers to students in their departments. No classes are taught by graduate students or teaching assistants.

Student Government

Students participate in the affairs of the college in a variety of ways. Students are elected to positions as class officers and serve on the Student Senate and Campus Activities Board. They serve as student body representatives on the Board of Trustees and on administrative committees, including the college judiciary board, curriculum committee, and health committee. Saint Anselm encourages students to express their opinions and take active roles in shaping the life of their college and to be aware of their potential as active and engaged citizens to effect change in the world around them.

Admission Requirements

In selecting a freshman class, the admission committee considers each candidate personally and thoroughly, evaluating their high school record, SAT scores, letters of recommendation, and essay (part of the application). Of greatest importance is the student's high school transcript, in terms of both the quality of courses taken and the grades earned.

Transfer and international students are welcome to apply. The same general admission procedures are required, along with at least a C average in all transferable courses and, for international students, a satisfactory score on the TOEFL.

Application and Information

The College follows a rolling admission policy, with a priority date of March 1, but international students must apply by February 1, and students applying to the nursing program must apply by January 15. The Office of Admission is open from 8:30 to 4:30 on weekdays and, during the fall, from 9 to 12:30 on Saturday. The College strongly recommends a campus visit and an interview in order to discover the many benefits of Saint Anselm.

For more information, students should contact:

Office of Admission
Saint Anselm College
100 Saint Anselm Drive
Manchester, New Hampshire 03102
Phone: 603-641-7500
888-426-7356 (toll-free)
E-mail: admission@anselm.edu
Web site: http://www.anselm.edu

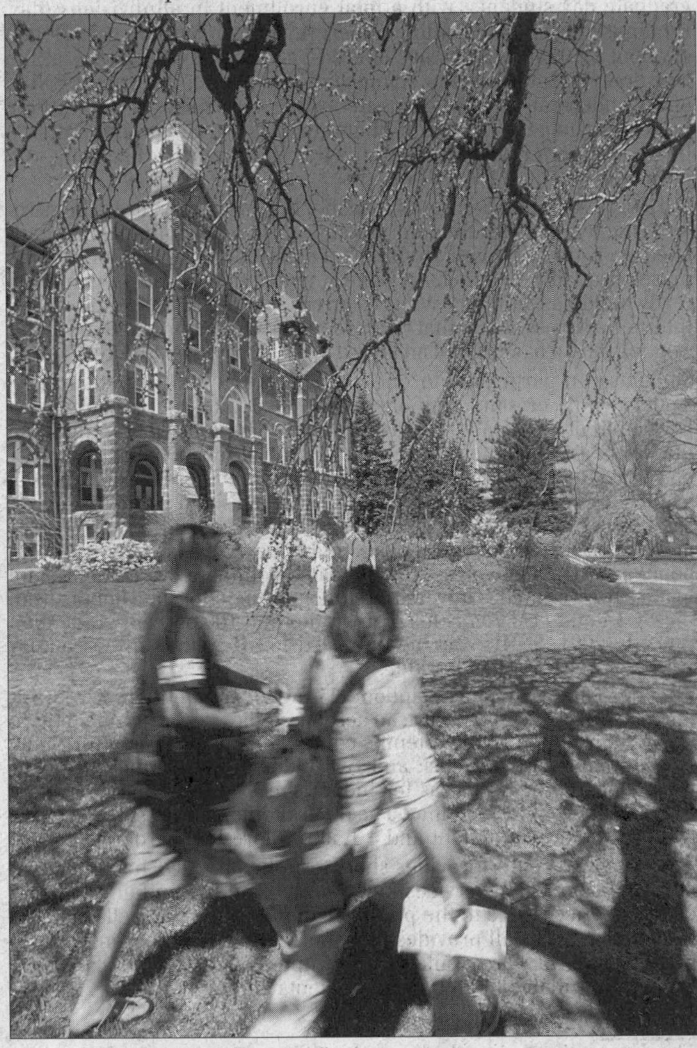

Saint Anselm College Alumni Hall.

COLLEGE DATA CENTER • NEW HAMPSHIRE

SOUTHERN NEW HAMPSHIRE UNIVERSITY

MANCHESTER, NEW HAMPSHIRE

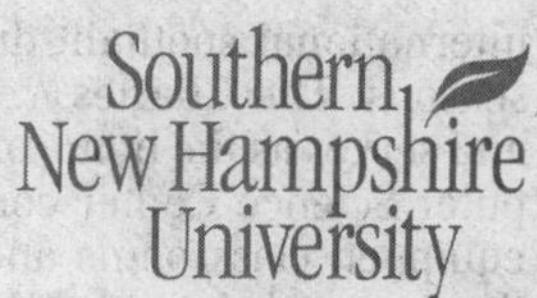

The University

At Southern New Hampshire University (SNHU), there are no limits to what students can achieve. With a culture that inspires every person, every day, to do more, learn more, try harder, and exceed expectations, the University is dedicated to helping students realize their potential. SNHU goes the extra mile—and so do its students. SNHU blends the best elements of its small-college heritage with the power and prestige that come with university status.

The University has approximately 1,900 traditional, full-time undergraduate day students, with a total enrollment in all divisions (day, evening, weekend, and online undergraduate and graduate students) of about 9,400. Programs are offered on campus, on location at the University's centers in New Hampshire and Maine, and online. SNHU offers undergraduate programs in business, culinary arts, education, hospitality management, and liberal arts and graduate programs in business, community economic development, education, and hospitality.

SNHU is the first carbon-neutral school in New Hampshire. The wireless campus features new dorms and apartment buildings, a simulated stock trading room, multimedia classrooms, an auditorium, the museum-quality McIninch Art Gallery, virtual science labs, technology-ready buildings, a library with resources that can be accessed via the Internet, a fitness center that rivals members-only gyms, athletic fields, cooking labs, a bakery, and an award-winning, student-run restaurant.

Students can participate in one of the University's more than forty student clubs or start new ones. Intercollegiate teams compete in Division II of the NCAA, the Eastern College Athletic Conference, and the Northeast-10 Conference. Sports include baseball, men's and women's basketball, cheerleading, men's and women's cross-country, golf, ice hockey, men's and women's lacrosse, men's and women's soccer, softball, men's and women's tennis, and volleyball. Intramural sports, including basketball, flag football, and volleyball, also are extremely popular. SNHU's powerful athletic teams dominate on the field—and in the classroom. The University's student-athletes earned honors from the NCAA and *USA Today* for high grades and 100 percent graduation rates. In 2001, SNHU was the only Division II school in the country with a perfect graduation rate.

Athletic facilities include an indoor, 25-meter, competition-size swimming pool; a racquetball court; an aerobic studio; cardiovascular equipment; four outdoor lighted tennis courts; a soccer/lacrosse turf field; baseball and softball fields; and two indoor gymnasiums with four basketball courts and areas for indoor soccer, indoor tennis, volleyball, and many other activities. The fitness center features 4,000 square feet of strength equipment and a 1,500-square-foot cardio deck.

The Wellness Center provides short-term health care, health education, and counseling services for students, and the buildings and facilities are accessible to the physically handicapped. A well-qualified student-services staff provides personal, career, and academic counseling; counselors are available on campus. A lifetime job placement service is available to all current students and to alumni.

Location

The University is ideally located, with easy access to downtown Manchester, New Hampshire's largest city and the most livable city in the East, according to *Money* magazine. Public transportation is available, and students may keep cars on campus. The mountains, beaches, and Boston are only an hour away. In 2005, Morgan Quinto Press named New Hampshire the nation's most livable state for the second straight year.

Majors and Degrees

The University has four schools: the School of Business, the School of Community Economic Development, the School of Education, and the School of Liberal Arts. The University offers associate, bachelor's, master's, and doctoral degrees. Undergraduate programs provide students with a strong liberal arts foundation and the knowledge and skills they need to succeed in their careers.

The School of Business majors include accounting, accounting/finance, advertising, business administration, business studies, computer information technology, fashion merchandising, finance/economics, hospitality management (with concentrations in convention and event management, hotel and resort management, and restaurant management), international business, management advisory services, marketing, retailing, sport management, technical management, and the unique 3-Year Honors Program, with majors in business administration and marketing—the only three-year programs of their kind in the country. Students save a full year of tuition by acquiring a bachelor's degree in just three years. Customized and outcomes-based, it is not a condensed four-year degree program and does not require night, weekend, or summer course work. The six-semester, 120-credit program features an interdisciplinary course of study.

The School of Liberal Arts offers degrees in advertising; communication; creative writing; digital media; English language and literature; environment, ethics, and public policy; graphic design; history; liberal arts; political science; psychology; public service and policy; and social science. Students in any major within the School of Liberal Arts may participate in the prelaw program.

The School of Education majors include business teacher education, child development, early childhood education, elementary education, English teacher education, justice studies, marketing teacher education, and social studies teacher education.

The University also offers associate degrees in baking and culinary arts and a bachelor's degree in culinary arts that emphasizes industry experience and provides an opportunity for study abroad.

An honors program, a prelaw program, and a pre-M.B.A. program are also available for students seeking additional challenges.

Academic Programs

At Southern New Hampshire University, undergraduate students receive a broad education in the liberal arts and intense practice in oral and written communication coupled with the specific knowledge and skills they need to succeed in their chosen fields.

Recognizing that successful leaders must be able to view problems from a variety of perspectives, the University mandates that all students complete courses in writing, the fine arts, the social sciences, mathematics, science, and public speaking. First-year students must take SNHU 101, a critical-thinking seminar to help them make the transition to University life. Students also have the opportunity to take elective courses in whatever areas capture their curiosity and may elect to concentrate their electives to earn a minor. The University curriculum offers both structure and flexibility.

Off-Campus Programs

Southern New Hampshire University is adept at mixing academic theory with practical experience inside and outside the classroom. Half of the undergraduates participate in off-campus cooperative education experiences/internships, earning 3 to 12 academic credits. Such opportunities are based on a student's major and career goals and typically are taken during a student's junior or senior year. Students work with faculty members and the Career Development Office to find appropriate assignments. About 70 percent of those who complete co-ops/internships are offered positions by their employers.

Students also work with real-world off-campus partners in their courses. For example, advertising students have created media campaigns for area businesses, marketing students have conducted market research for external groups, and education students have assisted preschool teachers in their classrooms. The University's graduates are in demand because businesses know they have been prepared to contribute to their employers and their communities.

Opportunities for studying abroad are available at partnering institutions, which include Huron University in London, SIT in Malaysia, Christelijke Hogesschool in the Netherlands, and Trinity International Hospitality Studies in Crete. Students may choose from thirty-six schools in twenty-six countries. Closer to home, students are eligible to take courses at New Hampshire College and University Council–member institutions during the regular academic year. Courses must be approved in advance by the registrar and are subject to available space. Participating schools include Colby-Sawyer College, Daniel Webster College, Franklin Pierce College, Keene State College, New England College, Plymouth State University, Rivier College, Saint Anselm College, the University of New Hampshire, and the University of New Hampshire–Manchester.

Academic Facilities

The main campus features new dormitory and apartment buildings, state-of-the-art classrooms, wireless Internet access, auditoriums, technology labs, multimedia rooms, computer labs, a graphic arts lab, a student-run gourmet restaurant, a student-run bakery, a simulated stock trading room, a museum-quality art gallery, and more.

The University is home to a novel outdoor experiential-learning facility called Camp Synergy, which is primarily used for teamwork and leadership training sessions. The Harry A. B. and Gertrude C. Shapiro Library features the Education Resource Center, networked computers, conference rooms, a career and placement resource center, and a growing collection of bound volumes, microfilm, microfiche, and ultrafiche; materials are available online as well. A recording studio, a listening room, and a closed-circuit television network that covers the entire campus are among the school's audiovisual assets.

Costs

Undergraduate tuition for the 2007–08 academic year is $23,016. Typical room and board charges are an additional $8970. Students must pay $330 in student activity fees each year and should plan to budget funds for books, supplies, travel, and personal expenses.

All students are required to bring wireless laptop computers. Culinary arts students are required to purchase uniforms and knife sets.

Financial Aid

More than 90 percent of the University's students receive some form of financial aid, which may include need-based grants, academic and commuter scholarships, work-study funds, and loans. Aid packages range from $250 to the full cost of attending the University. The average aid package has a value of more than $17,500 and includes a combination of scholarships, grants, loans, and employment sources.

The University participates in the Federal Work-Study Program, the Federal Perkins Loan Program, and the Federal Supplemental Educational Opportunity Grant Program. The school is also eligible under the Federal Stafford Student Loan Program and the Federal Pell Grant Program. Aid applicants must complete the Free Application for Federal Student Aid (FAFSA). The Office of Financial Aid can provide the appropriate forms, or students can go online to http://www.fafsa.ed.gov. Academic, athletic, and leadership scholarships are available for students who qualify.

Faculty

The University has more than 116 full-time faculty members and more than 200 part-time instructors. The student-faculty ratio is 9:1. Nearly 75 percent of the full-time faculty members hold Ph.D.'s or the equivalent in their areas of expertise.

The instructional programs blend theory with practice to stimulate students' professional development and personal growth. Faculty members bring extensive academic, work, travel, and life experiences to their classrooms. Although their primary goal is teaching, faculty members remain current in their disciplines. Outside the classroom, faculty members are management consultants, CPAs, analysts, small-business owners, economists, accountants, marketing professionals, entrepreneurs, innkeepers, chefs, world travelers, artists, poets, novelists, and much more.

Student Government

The Student Government Association is led by 25 students, including 5 officers, who represent all the students at the University. Its primary function is to represent the student body in campus affairs and to dispense student activity funds. One student is appointed to represent the student body on the Board of Trustees. Students are also appointed to most other standing committees, including the Financial Aid Advisory Committee, the Curriculum Advisory Committee, the Library Committee, and judiciary committees.

Admission Requirements

Applicants for admission are evaluated individually on the basis of academic credentials and personal characteristics. When reviewing applicants, primary emphasis is placed on a student's academic record, as demonstrated by the quality and level of college-preparatory course work and achievement attained. Most successful candidates admitted to SNHU present a program of study consisting of sixteen college-preparatory courses, including 4 years of English, 3 or more years of mathematics, 2 or more years of science, and 2 or more years of social science. Separate consideration is given to admission decisions for freshmen, transfer, culinary arts, 3-Year Honors Program, nontraditional, and international applicants. Students may complete a paper application for admission or apply online.

Application and Information

Applicants for undergraduate day programs must submit an application for admission, an up-to-date official high school transcript, a personal essay, and high school recommendations. SAT or ACT scores are required of freshman applicants. Test scores are optional for students applying to the culinary arts programs but are required in order to be considered for academic scholarship awards. Candidates for the 3-Year Honors Program are also required to have an interview. Transfer students must also submit official transcripts from all schools previously attended. International students whose native language is other than English must prove proficiency in the English language through the TOEFL examination. Admission decisions are based on the quality of academic performance, but a campus visit and interview are strongly recommended for all candidates. The University operates on a rolling admission basis, and applicants can expect a decision within one month of the receipt of their complete credentials. Applicants may also apply as Early Action candidates by submitting their application prior to November 15. There is a $40 application fee.

For more information about Southern New Hampshire University, students should contact:

Office of Admission
Southern New Hampshire University
2500 North River Road
Manchester, New Hampshire 03106-1045
Phone: 603-645-9611
800-642-4968 (toll-free)
Fax: 603-645-9693
Web site: http://www.snhu.edu

Students on the campus of Southern New Hampshire University.

UNIVERSITY OF NEW HAMPSHIRE

DURHAM, NEW HAMPSHIRE

The University

The University of New Hampshire (UNH) is a rising star among American research universities, a community of exceptional faculty members and talented and energetic students from forty-five states and twenty-eight countries. The University has a sizeable undergraduate population of approximately 11,500 but still feels cozy and intimate. This is due in part to a campus layout that is manageable and beautiful—with college greens, water, and a pleasing mix of classic and modern buildings that gradually give way to 2,600 acres of woods, fields, and farms. It is also due to the school's traditions of strong student-faculty interaction and active student culture. As one student put it, "It's easy to meet people and get involved in campus activities here. You need to have some initiative, but student leaders, residence hall staff, and others also seek you out."

The University offers students a variety of housing options, including halls of 100 to 600 students and two on-campus apartment complexes. Themed housing, such as honors, first-year experience, or international, is offered by dorm or floor. Holloway Commons, a spectacular dining and conference facility with seating for 850 and an after-hours café, opened in fall 2003, and Southeast Residential Community (SERC) Buildings A & B, 326- and 227-bed residence halls, opened this fall. Kingsbury Hall, the home of the engineering school, just completed a $50-million renovation.

The Memorial Union Building (MUB) is the University's community center. Housed in the MUB are two movie theaters, the UNH Copy Center, the UNH Bookstore, the Ticket Office, specific lounge/study space for both nontraditional and graduate students, and Granite Square Station, the undergraduate mail center. Computing and Information Services provides a computer cluster and a help desk with walk-in service. The MUB Food Court offers expanded dining options, and food service is also available in the Coffee Office. The Student Senate Office; the Office of Multicultural Student Affairs; WUNH-radio; *The New Hampshire*, the student newspaper; and nearly 160 other student organizations originate in the MUB. Students at the University can participate in a rich cultural life. Numerous lectures, films, concerts, exhibitions, meet-the-artist receptions, master classes, dance performances, and theatrical productions are offered throughout the year. The UNH Celebrity Series, the Art Gallery, and the Departments of Music, Theater and Dance, and Art and Art History bring artists of international stature to campus. Most events are free for students.

Many opportunities for athletics and recreation, regardless of skill or ability, are offered through Campus Recreation. The Hamel Student Recreation Center is available to all full-time matriculating students and Rec Pass holders. The center offers participants two multipurpose courts, a group exercise studio, a club/martial art studio, an 8,000-square-foot fitness center with more than 100 exercise stations, three basketball/volleyball courts, an indoor track, a lounge, several classrooms, locker rooms, towel and lock service at the equipment room, and saunas. Campus Recreation offers a variety of activities designed to make it easier to reach personal fitness goals and have fun. Participants may take part in one of the many group exercise classes, such as step aerobics, Reebok cycling, or cardio kickboxing. Other opportunities include Pilates, yoga, tai chi, a climbing wall, racquetball, personal training, or massage therapy. Noncredit courses are also offered, including CPR and first aid. The intramural sports program consists of twenty-four different sports and activities offered to co-rec and men's and women's teams. Campus Recreation forms and assists special interest groups or sport club teams to reflect the varied recreation and cultural preferences of campus community members. Some clubs are intensely competitive, requiring a daily commitment to workouts and conditioning. They compete either on an inter-collegiate basis with New England teams or sponsor University tournaments. Other clubs meet on a casual come-when-you-can basis. In addition, Campus Recreation offers ice skating, manages a large outdoor recreation facility with its own sailing and canoe center, runs a children's camp (Camp Wildcat) in the summer, and supports the men's and women's sport club crew boat house.

Location

Nestled in New Hampshire's seacoast region, the town of Durham is an outdoor-lover's dream, with ocean, ski and hiking mountains, and charming working-port cities nearby. Popular road trips for students include Boston (about an hour), Portsmouth (about 20 minutes), and the White Mountains (about an hour). With a nonstudent population of 8,000, Durham is a classic college town that caters to the student clientele. Main Street includes restaurants, coffeehouses, a bookstore, pizza shops, and other student hangouts.

Majors and Degrees

The University of New Hampshire comprises seven colleges and schools: College of Engineering and Physical Sciences, College of Liberal Arts, College of Life Sciences and Agriculture, College of Health and Human Services, Thompson School of Applied Science, Whittemore School of Business and Economics, and the University of New Hampshire at Manchester, the University's urban campus. The University offers more than 100 majors through these fully accredited academic divisions. New Hampshire enjoys a strong reputation in a wide range of academic fields, with child and family studies, creative writing, engineering, environmental studies, history, hospitality management, journalism, marine and animal sciences, occupational therapy, and performing arts among those topping the list. The business school offers several options under the business administration major that include accounting, entrepreneurial venture creation, information systems, international business and economics, management, and a student-designed track. First-year students take introduction to business and introduction to information systems, which blend classroom theory with direct industry exposure.

Academic Programs

The University's general education requirements provide students with a broad foundation in the liberal arts and an introduction to the methods of inquiry needed for academic success. All students must complete ten courses from eight categories: writing skills; quantitative reasoning; biological, physical, and technological sciences; historical perspectives; foreign culture; fine arts; social science; and works of philosophy, literature, and ideas. Four intensive writing courses are required but are usually satisfied by completing the ten core courses. Depending on their academic program, students may begin course work in their major as early as their first year.

A major research university, UNH prides itself on producing students who have had meaningful research experiences with a world-class faculty. Programs such as the Undergraduate Research Opportunities Program and International Research Opportunities Program provide research grants each year for undergraduates to work closely with faculty members, on campus or abroad, on original projects. Students majoring in a wide range of subjects can access a wealth of research centers and facilities, some on the campus itself, others in surrounding towns. As New Hampshire's major public institution, the University is involved in a wide range of outreach programs with state and industry groups. These partnerships provide abundant opportunities for students interested in internships.

Academic Facilities

The Dimond Library is the state's only public university research library. The library offers three grand reading rooms, seating for 1,200 students, and state-of-the-art technology, including wireless and Internet. The Parker Adaptive Technology Room provides an array of technological options for patrons who have learning, mobility, or vision disabilities. Through ResNet, students who live on-campus have high-speed Internet access to UNH library resources, class software and information, e-mail, and other services. The Environmental Technology Building is a multidisciplinary science and engineering research facility with a focus on environmental technology development. Most of the University's cultural events take place in the Paul Creative Arts Center, which houses two theaters, dressing rooms, a well-equipped scene shop, a costume shop, a green room, storage facilities, classrooms, and the faculty and staff offices. New Hampshire Hall contains the Newman Dance Studio and a smaller stage studio.

Costs

The 2007–08 tuition and fees for undergraduate in-state students were $11,070. For out-of-state students, tuition was $24,030. Room (double) and board (unlimited meal plan) cost $8168.

Financial Aid

Approximately 70 percent of students receive some form of financial assistance from UNH. University scholarships ranging from $1000 to $10,000 are awarded automatically to qualified students who apply for admission. Amounts are subject to change. Other scholarships are awarded by individual academic departments. The average student's financial aid package, including gift, loan, and employment assistance, is $8231 for in state and $13,156 for out of state. The University participates in the Federal Pell Grant program, the Federal Supplemental Educational Opportunity Grant program, the Federal Perkins Loan program, the Federal Work-Study Program, and the Federal Stafford Student Loan program. Students are required to submit the Free Application for Federal Student Aid (FAFSA) by March 1.

Faculty

The University of New Hampshire has 681 full-time and 267 part-time faculty members, 86 percent of whom hold doctoral degrees, with 11 percent at the master's level. The student-faculty ratio is 17:1. The UNH faculty includes winners of the Pulitzer Prize, Guggenheim awards, and many other prestigious awards and honors, while the University ranks among the top campuses in the nation in the percentage of faculty members who have won Fulbright scholarships. This research productivity has a powerful effect on students, who can share the experience of discovery.

Student Government

The Student Senate comprises a governing body of student officers and senators. They are the voice of the student body, representing student opinion to members of the faculty, staff, and administration as well as the University community and the state legislature. The Senate believes that all students have the right to participate in University decisions and policy making. Committees of the Senate include areas in academics, residential life, commuters, health and human services, judicial affairs, and community change. They also approve and monitor the rates and uses of all mandatory student fees.

Admission Requirements

Admission to a bachelor's degree program is based upon successful completion of a strong secondary school program of college-preparatory course work. Primary consideration is given to the academic record, as demonstrated by the quality of the candidate's secondary school course selection and achievement, recommendation, and SAT or ACT with writing component results. Consideration is also given to character, initiative, leadership, and special talents. Most successful candidates present at least four years of English and mathematics and three or more years of laboratory science, social science, and foreign language. Recommended mathematics preparation includes the equivalent of algebra I, geometry, algebra II, and trigonometry or advanced math. Students who plan to specialize in health, the physical sciences, life sciences, or mathematics should present at least four years of mathematics, including trigonometry as well as laboratory course work in chemistry and/or physics. Students pursuing business-related studies should also have completed four years of mathematics, including trigonometry.

All candidates for admission to bachelor's degree programs are required to submit SAT Reasoning Test or ACT scores with writing component results. SAT Subject Tests are not required. A foreign language SAT Subject Test may satisfy the foreign language requirement of the Bachelor of Arts degree programs. Required scores vary by test. International students whose primary language is not English must submit TOEFL results. The recommended minimum TOEFL score is 213 (computer-based) or 550 (paper-based) or 80 (Internet-based).

Candidates applying for programs in the Department of Music must make arrangements with the department chairperson for an audition (603-862-2404).

Application and Information

High school students who seek fall-semester admission may apply anytime after the start of the senior year and before the February 1 priority deadline. Admission notifications are provided on a continuous basis through April 15. Admitted first-year students have until May 1 to confirm their intent to enroll at the University. The review of candidates begins with the receipt of all review application materials. The Early Action (EA) Program allows candidates to receive a response by mid-January of their senior year; EA candidates must submit admission applications by November 15. In some cases, the Admission Committee requests senior mid-year grade reports in order to make a final admission decision. All positive admission decisions made prior to the completion of a candidate's course work in progress are considered provisional and are subject to the verification of satisfactory senior-year achievement when final high school transcripts are reviewed.

Office of Admissions
University of New Hampshire
4 Garrison Avenue
Durham, New Hampshire 03824-3501
Phone: 603-862-1360
Fax: 603-862-0077
Web site: http://www.unh.edu/admissions

NEW JERSEY

The Upper Montclair area includes the towns of Bloomfield and Caldwell.

BERKELEY COLLEGE

West Paterson, New Jersey **www.berkeleycollege.edu/**

- **Proprietary** primarily 2-year, founded 1931, administratively affiliated with Berkeley College
- **Suburban** 25-acre campus with easy access to New York City
- **Coed**
- **Minimally difficult** entrance level

Faculty *Student/faculty ratio:* 22:1.
Academics *Calendar:* quarters. *Degrees:* certificates, associate, and bachelor's.
Student Life *Campus security:* 24-hour emergency response devices, controlled dormitory access, security patrols.
Standardized Tests *Required:* SAT or ACT (for admission).
Costs (2007–08) *Comprehensive fee:* $27,150 includes full-time tuition ($17,400), mandatory fees ($750), and room and board ($9000). Full-time tuition and fees vary according to course load. Part-time tuition: $425 per credit. Part-time tuition and fees vary according to course load. *Room and board:* Room and board charges vary according to housing facility.
Financial Aid Of all full-time matriculated undergraduates who enrolled in 2006, 150 Federal Work-Study jobs (averaging $1200).
Applying *Options:* electronic application, deferred entrance. *Application fee:* $50. *Required:* high school transcript. *Recommended:* interview.
Freshman Application Contact Mr. David Bertone, Senior Director of Enrollment, Berkeley College, 44 Rifle Camp Road, West Paterson, NJ 07424. *Phone:* 973-278-5400. *Toll-free phone:* 800-446-5400. *Fax:* 973-328-9141. *E-mail:* info@berkeleycollege.edu.

BETH MEDRASH GOVOHA

Lakewood, New Jersey

Director of Admissions Rabbi Yehuda Jacobs, Director of Admissions, Beth Medrash Govoha, 617 Sixth Street, Lakewood, NJ 08701-2797. *Phone:* 908-367-1060.

BLOOMFIELD COLLEGE

Bloomfield, New Jersey **www.bloomfield.edu/**

- **Independent** 4-year, founded 1868, affiliated with Presbyterian Church (U.S.A.)
- **Suburban** 12-acre campus with easy access to New York City
- **Endowment** $9.1 million
- **Coed** 2,056 undergraduate students, 77% full-time, 66% women, 34% men
- **Moderately difficult** entrance level, 41% of applicants were admitted

Bloomfield College students come from a rich mixture of backgrounds and experiences. Reflecting the contemporary world, students learn together, share interests, build friendships to last a lifetime, and graduate fully prepared for careers and continued education. New majors and concentrations include game development, allied health technology, network engineering, education, and special education. A Latino/Latin American and Caribbean studies minor is also offered.

Undergraduates 1,577 full-time, 479 part-time. Students come from 18 states and territories, 18 other countries, 4% are from out of state, 49% African American, 4% Asian American or Pacific Islander, 20% Hispanic American, 0.1% Native American, 2% international, 12% transferred in, 20% live on campus. *Retention:* 70% of 2006 full-time freshmen returned.
Freshmen *Admission:* 2,750 applied, 1,133 admitted, 354 enrolled. *Average high school GPA:* 2.74. *Test scores:* SAT critical reading scores over 500: 16%; SAT math scores over 500: 20%; SAT critical reading scores over 600: 2%; SAT math scores over 600: 2%.
Faculty *Total:* 234, 30% full-time, 30% with terminal degrees. *Student/faculty ratio:* 14:1.
Majors Accounting; allied health diagnostic, intervention, and treatment professions related; applied mathematics; biology/biological sciences; business administration and management; chemistry; clinical/medical laboratory science and allied professions related; computer and information sciences; computer programming; computer systems networking and telecommunications; education; English; fine/studio arts; history; mathematics; multi-/interdisciplinary studies related; nursing (registered nurse training); philosophy; political science and government; psychology; religious studies; sociology; special education (specific learning disabilities); visual and performing arts.
Academics *Calendar:* semesters. *Degree:* certificates and bachelor's. *Special study options:* academic remediation for entering students, accelerated degree program, advanced placement credit, cooperative education, distance learning, double majors, English as a second language, honors programs, independent study, internships, part-time degree program, services for LD students, student-designed majors, study abroad, summer session for credit. *ROTC:* Army (c).
Computers on Campus 300 computers/terminals and 50 ports are available on campus for general student use. Students can access the following: computer help desk, free student e-mail accounts, online (class) grades, online (class) registration, online (class) schedules. Campuswide network is available. 100% of college-owned or -operated housing units are wired for high-speed Internet access.
Student Life *Housing options:* coed, men-only, women-only. Campus housing is university owned and is provided by a third party. *Activities and organizations:* student-run newspaper, radio station, Humanities on the go, Team Infinite, Residence Life Development, Association of Latin American Students, Sisters in Support, national fraternities, national sororities. *Campus security:* 24-hour emergency response devices and patrols, security cameras in high-traffic areas. *Student services:* health clinic, personal/psychological counseling.
Athletics Member NCAA. All Division II. *Intercollegiate sports:* baseball M (s), basketball M (s)/W (s), cross-country running M (s)/W (s), soccer M (s)/W (s), softball W (s), tennis M (s), volleyball W (s). *Intramural sports:* basketball M/W.
Standardized Tests *Required:* SAT or ACT (for admission).
Costs (2007–08) *Comprehensive fee:* $26,650 includes full-time tuition ($17,500), mandatory fees ($500), and room and board ($8650). Part-time tuition: $1790 per course. Part-time tuition and fees vary according to course load. *Required fees:* $80 per term part-time. *College room only:* $4325. *Payment plans:* installment, deferred payment. *Waivers:* senior citizens and employees or children of employees.
Financial Aid Of all full-time matriculated undergraduates who enrolled in 2007, 1,483 applied for aid, 1,317 were judged to have need, 415 had their need fully met. 358 Federal Work-Study jobs (averaging $1930). In 2007, 80 non-need-based awards were made. *Average percent of need met:* 56%. *Average financial aid package:* $18,501. *Average need-based loan:* $6121. *Average need-based gift aid:* $11,107. *Average non-need-based aid:* $9673. *Average indebtedness upon graduation:* $19,476. *Financial aid deadline:* 6/1.
Applying *Options:* electronic application, early admission, early action, deferred entrance. *Application fee:* $40. *Required:* essay or personal statement, high school transcript, minimum 2.7 GPA, 2 letters of recommendation, graded essay/term paper. *Required for some:* interview. *Application deadlines:* 7/1 (freshmen), 8/1 (transfers), 1/7 (early action). *Notification:* continuous (freshmen), continuous (transfers), 1/21 (early action).
Freshman Application Contact Mr. Adam Castro, Director of Admissions, Bloomfield College, Office of Enrollment Management and Admission, Bloomfield, NJ 07003-9981. *Phone:* 973-748-9000. *Toll-free phone:* 800-848-4555 Ext. 230. *Fax:* 973-748-0916. *E-mail:* admission@bloomfield.edu.

See page 1556 for the College Close-Up.

CALDWELL COLLEGE

Caldwell, New Jersey **www.caldwell.edu/**

- **Independent Roman Catholic** comprehensive, founded 1939
- **Suburban** 70-acre campus with easy access to New York City
- **Endowment** $5.0 million
- **Coed**
- **Moderately difficult** entrance level

Caldwell College offers the only master's degree program in the state of New Jersey in applied behavior analysis (ABA), a science-based teaching approach that is highly effective in the treatment of autism. Caldwell also offers a Post-Baccalaureate Certificate Program in ABA. The course work in both programs is approved by the Behavior Analyst Certification Board. For more information on Caldwell's ABA programs, students should visit http://www.caldwell.edu/graduate.

Faculty *Student/faculty ratio:* 12:1.
Academics *Calendar:* semesters. *Degrees:* bachelor's, master's, post-master's, and postbachelor's certificates.
Student Life *Campus security:* 24-hour patrols, late-night transport/escort service, controlled dormitory access, dusk-to-dawn patrols by trained security personnel.
Athletics Member NCAA. All Division II.
Standardized Tests *Required:* SAT or ACT (for admission).

Costs (2007–08) *Comprehensive fee:* $30,300 includes full-time tuition ($21,400), mandatory fees ($600), and room and board ($8300). Part-time tuition: $529 per credit. Part-time tuition and fees vary according to course load. *Required fees:* $50 per year part-time. *Room and board:* Room and board charges vary according to board plan and housing facility.

Financial Aid Of all full-time matriculated undergraduates who enrolled in 2006, 763 applied for aid, 655 were judged to have need, 285 had their need fully met. 183 Federal Work-Study jobs (averaging $1000). In 2006, 186 non-need-based awards were made. *Average percent of need met:* 44. *Average financial aid package:* $8518. *Average need-based loan:* $2074. *Average need-based gift aid:* $5476. *Average non-need-based aid:* $6350. *Average indebtedness upon graduation:* $21,873.

Applying *Options:* electronic application, early admission, early action, deferred entrance. *Application fee:* $40. *Required:* essay or personal statement, high school transcript, minimum 2.0 GPA, 1 letter of recommendation. *Required for some:* interview.

Freshman Application Contact Ms. Kathryn Reilly, Director of Admissions, Caldwell College, 9 Ryerson Avenue, Caldwell, NJ 07006. *Phone:* 973-618-3226. *Toll-free phone:* 888-864-9516. *Fax:* 973-618-3600. *E-mail:* admissions@caldwell.edu.

See page 1558 for the College Close-Up.

CENTENARY COLLEGE

Hackettstown, New Jersey **www.centenarycollege.edu/**

- **Independent** comprehensive, founded 1867, affiliated with United Methodist Church
- **Suburban** 42-acre campus with easy access to New York City
- **Endowment** $3.0 million
- **Coed** 2,238 undergraduate students, 88% full-time, 66% women, 34% men
- **Moderately difficult** entrance level, 70% of applicants were admitted

Undergraduates 1,976 full-time, 262 part-time. Students come from 21 states and territories, 14 other countries, 15% are from out of state, 9% African American, 2% Asian American or Pacific Islander, 7% Hispanic American, 0.2% Native American, 3% international, 9% transferred in, 59% live on campus. *Retention:* 73% of 2006 full-time freshmen returned.

Freshmen *Admission:* 1,244 applied, 874 admitted, 333 enrolled. *Average high school GPA:* 2.66. *Test scores:* SAT critical reading scores over 500: 28%; SAT math scores over 500: 32%; ACT scores over 18: 87%; SAT critical reading scores over 600: 4%; SAT math scores over 600: 7%; ACT scores over 24: 7%; SAT math scores over 700: 1%.

Faculty *Total:* 328, 20% full-time, 12% with terminal degrees. *Student/faculty ratio:* 16:1.

Majors Accounting; biology/biological sciences; business administration and management; commercial and advertising art; criminology; education; elementary education; English; equestrian studies; fashion/apparel design; history; information science/studies; international relations and affairs; liberal arts and sciences/liberal studies; marketing/marketing management; mass communication/media; mathematics; political science and government; psychology; secondary education; sociology; special education; sport and fitness administration/management; theater design and technology.

Academics *Calendar:* semesters. *Degrees:* associate, bachelor's, master's, and postbachelor's certificates. *Special study options:* academic remediation for entering students, accelerated degree program, adult/continuing education programs, advanced placement credit, double majors, English as a second language, honors programs, independent study, internships, off-campus study, part-time degree program, services for LD students, student-designed majors, study abroad, summer session for credit.

Computers on Campus 100 computers/terminals are available on campus for general student use. Students can access the following: campus intranet, computer help desk, free student e-mail accounts, online (class) grades, online (class) schedules. Campuswide network is available. 100% of college-owned or -operated housing units are wired for high-speed Internet access. Wireless service is available via entire campus.

Student Life *Housing options:* coed, women-only. Campus housing is university owned. Freshman applicants given priority for college housing. *Activities and organizations:* drama/theater group, student-run newspaper, radio and television station, Student Activities Council, equestrian teams, Quill, student government, Kappa Delta Epsilon. *Campus security:* 24-hour emergency response devices and patrols, late-night transport/escort service, controlled dormitory access, patrols by trained security personnel 4 p.m. to 8 a.m. *Student services:* health clinic, personal/psychological counseling, women's center.

Athletics Member NCAA, NSCAA. All NCAA Division III. *Intercollegiate sports:* baseball M, basketball M/W, cross-country running M/W, equestrian sports M/W, golf M/W, lacrosse M/W, soccer M/W, softball W, volleyball W, wrestling M. *Intramural sports:* ice hockey M (c)/W (c).

Standardized Tests *Required:* SAT or ACT (for admission).

Costs (2007–08) *Comprehensive fee:* $33,000 includes full-time tuition ($22,930), mandatory fees ($1170), and room and board ($8900). Full-time tuition and fees vary according to course load and program. Part-time tuition: $445 per credit. Part-time tuition and fees vary according to course load and program. *Room and board:* Room and board charges vary according to board plan. *Payment plan:* installment.

Financial Aid Of all full-time matriculated undergraduates who enrolled in 2007, 1,388 applied for aid, 1,182 were judged to have need, 264 had their need fully met. 230 Federal Work-Study jobs (averaging $808). 209 state and other part-time jobs (averaging $780). In 2007, 197 non-need-based awards were made. *Average percent of need met:* 68%. *Average financial aid package:* $14,862. *Average need-based loan:* $5139. *Average need-based gift aid:* $11,515. *Average non-need-based aid:* $13,713. *Average indebtedness upon graduation:* $22,351.

Applying *Options:* electronic application, deferred entrance. *Application fee:* $30. *Required:* essay or personal statement, high school transcript. *Required for some:* interview, portfolio. *Recommended:* minimum 2.0 GPA, interview. *Application deadlines:* rolling (freshmen), rolling (transfers). *Notification:* continuous (freshmen), continuous (transfers).

Freshman Application Contact Ms. Diane Finnan, Vice President for Enrollment Management and Strategic Branding, Centenary College, 400 Jefferson Street, Hackettstown, NJ 07840-2100. *Phone:* 908-852-1400 Ext. 2217. *Toll-free phone:* 800-236-8679. *Fax:* 908-852-3454. *E-mail:* admissions@centenarycollege.edu.

THE COLLEGE OF NEW JERSEY

Ewing, New Jersey **www.tcnj.edu/**

- **State-supported** comprehensive, founded 1855
- **Suburban** 255-acre campus with easy access to Philadelphia
- **Endowment** $14.4 million
- **Coed** 6,205 undergraduate students, 97% full-time, 58% women, 42% men
- **Very difficult** entrance level, 47% of applicants were admitted

The College of New Jersey (TCNJ) is one of New Jersey's most competitive colleges, attracting high-achieving students from throughout the region. The College has created a challenging and dynamic learning environment, which is located on an elegant campus. Small classes ensure that students and faculty members collaborate in a transformative educational process.

Undergraduates 6,028 full-time, 177 part-time. Students come from 19 states and territories, 12 other countries, 5% are from out of state, 6% African American, 8% Asian American or Pacific Islander, 8% Hispanic American, 0.1% Native American, 0.1% international, 4% transferred in, 48% live on campus. *Retention:* 95% of 2006 full-time freshmen returned.

Freshmen *Admission:* 8,607 applied, 4,005 admitted, 1,297 enrolled. *Test scores:* SAT critical reading scores over 500: 91%; SAT math scores over 500: 93%; SAT writing scores over 500: 92%; SAT critical reading scores over 600: 59%; SAT math scores over 600: 68%; SAT writing scores over 600: 59%; SAT critical reading scores over 700: 12%; SAT math scores over 700: 17%; SAT writing scores over 700: 12%.

Faculty *Total:* 733, 46% full-time, 52% with terminal degrees. *Student/faculty ratio:* 13:1.

Majors Accounting; art; art teacher education; biology/biological sciences; biology teacher education; biomedical/medical engineering; business administration and management; business/managerial economics; chemistry; chemistry teacher education; commercial and advertising art; computer and information sciences; computer engineering; criminal justice/law enforcement administration; economics; education; electrical, electronics and communications engineering; elementary education; engineering science; English; English/language arts teacher education; finance; fine/studio arts; history; history teacher education; intermedia/multimedia; international business/trade/commerce; international relations and affairs; kindergarten/preschool education; mathematics; mathematics teacher education; mechanical engineering; multi-/interdisciplinary studies related; music; music teacher education; nursing (registered nurse training); philosophy; physical education teaching and coaching; physics; physics teacher education; political science and government; pre-law studies; pre-medical studies; psychology; secondary education; sociology; Spanish; Spanish language teacher education; special education; special education (hearing impaired); speech and rhetoric; statistics; technology/industrial arts teacher education; women's studies.

Academics *Calendar:* semesters. *Degrees:* bachelor's, master's, post-master's, and postbachelor's certificates. *Special study options:* academic remediation for entering students, advanced placement credit, double majors, honors programs, independent study, internships, off-campus study, part-time degree program, services for LD students, student-designed majors, study abroad, summer session for credit. *ROTC:* Army (c), Air Force (c). *Unusual degree programs:* 3-2 5 year BS/MA in education of the deaf and hard of hearing and elementary education; 5 year BS/MA in special education and a liberal arts major; 5 year BS/MA in criminal justice with Rutgers University.

Computers on Campus 800 computers/terminals are available on campus for general student use. Students can access the following: online (class) grades, online (class) registration, online (class) schedules. Campuswide network is available. 100% of college-owned or -operated housing units are wired for high-speed Internet access. Wireless service is available via classrooms, computer labs, learning centers, libraries, student centers.

Student Life *Housing:* on-campus residence required for freshman year. *Options:* coed. Campus housing is university owned. Freshman campus housing is guaranteed. *Activities and organizations:* drama/theater group, student-run newspaper, radio and television station, choral group, Student Government Association, College Union Board, Intramurals, The Signal, national fraternities, national sororities. *Campus security:* 24-hour emergency response devices and patrols, student patrols, late-night transport/escort service, controlled dormitory access. *Student services:* health clinic, personal/psychological counseling, women's center, legal services.

Athletics Member NCAA. All Division III. *Intercollegiate sports:* baseball M, basketball M/W, cross-country running M/W, field hockey W, football M, golf M, lacrosse W, soccer M/W, softball W, swimming and diving M/W, tennis M/W, track and field M/W, wrestling M. *Intramural sports:* baseball M (c), basketball M (c)/W, bowling M (c)/W (c), cheerleading M (c)/W (c), crew M (c)/W (c), fencing M (c)/W (c), field hockey M/W, football M/W, golf M (c)/W (c), ice hockey M (c), lacrosse M (c)/W (c), racquetball M/W, rugby M (c)/W (c), skiing (cross-country) M (c)/W (c), skiing (downhill) M (c)/W (c), soccer M (c)/W (c), softball M/W (c), swimming and diving M (c)/W (c), table tennis M (c)/W (c), tennis M (c)/W (c), ultimate Frisbee M (c)/W (c), volleyball M (c)/W (c), wrestling M (c)/W (c).

Standardized Tests *Required:* SAT (for admission).

Costs (2007–08) *Tuition:* state resident $8072 full-time, $286 per credit part-time; nonresident $15,295 full-time, $542 per credit part-time. Part-time tuition and fees vary according to course load. *Required fees:* $3235 full-time, $129 per credit part-time. *Room and board:* $9242; room only: $6680. Room and board charges vary according to board plan. *Payment plan:* installment. *Waivers:* senior citizens and employees or children of employees.

Financial Aid Of all full-time matriculated undergraduates who enrolled in 2007, 3,980 applied for aid, 2,599 were judged to have need, 612 had their need fully met. 319 Federal Work-Study jobs (averaging $1226). In 2007, 1234 non-need-based awards were made. *Average percent of need met:* 55%. *Average financial aid package:* $9207. *Average need-based loan:* $4288. *Average need-based gift aid:* $9486. *Average non-need-based aid:* $4106. *Average indebtedness upon graduation:* $19,459. *Financial aid deadline:* 10/1.

Applying *Options:* electronic application, early admission, early decision, deferred entrance. *Application fee:* $60. *Required:* essay or personal statement, high school transcript. *Required for some:* interview, art portfolio or music audition. *Recommended:* minimum 3.5 GPA, 3 letters of recommendation. *Application deadlines:* 2/15 (freshmen), 2/15 (transfers). *Early decision deadline:* 11/15. *Notification:* continuous until 4/1 (freshmen), continuous (transfers), 12/15 (early decision).

Freshman Application Contact Ms. Lisa Angeloni, Dean of Admissions, The College of New Jersey, PO Box 7718, Ewing, NJ 08628. *Phone:* 609-771-2131. *Toll-free phone:* 800-624-0967. *Fax:* 609-637-5174. *E-mail:* admiss@tcnj.edu.

See page 1560 for the College Close-Up.

COLLEGE OF SAINT ELIZABETH

Morristown, New Jersey **www.cse.edu/**

- **Independent Roman Catholic** comprehensive, founded 1899
- **Suburban** 188-acre campus with easy access to New York City
- **Endowment** $22.5 million
- **Undergraduate: women only; graduate: coed** 1,190 undergraduate students, 59% full-time, 93% women, 7% men
- **Moderately difficult** entrance level, 82% of applicants were admitted

An independent, four-year Catholic liberal arts college founded in 1899 by the Sisters of Charity of Saint Elizabeth, the College of Saint Elizabeth (CSE) was one of the first colleges in New Jersey to award degrees to women. Today, the College has a unique and critical role in higher education—not only as one of the preeminent Catholic colleges for women on the East Coast but also as a leader in the education of working adults, both women and men, at the graduate and undergraduate levels and through programs and speakers sponsored by the nationally recognized Center for Theological and Spiritual Development of Catholic laity.

Undergraduates 699 full-time, 491 part-time. Students come from 13 states and territories, 21 other countries, 3% are from out of state, 15% African American, 4% Asian American or Pacific Islander, 17% Hispanic American, 0.3% Native American, 5% international, 3% transferred in, 66% live on campus. *Retention:* 75% of 2006 full-time freshmen returned.

Freshmen *Admission:* 451 applied, 369 admitted, 160 enrolled. *Test scores:* SAT critical reading scores over 500: 27%; SAT math scores over 500: 19%; SAT writing scores over 500: 27%; SAT critical reading scores over 600: 5%; SAT math scores over 600: 1%; SAT writing scores over 600: 4%; SAT critical reading scores over 700: 1%.

Faculty *Total:* 205, 33% full-time, 48% with terminal degrees. *Student/faculty ratio:* 12:1.

Majors American studies; art; biochemistry; biology/biological sciences; business administration and management; chemistry; clinical laboratory science/medical technology; communication/speech communication and rhetoric; computer and information sciences; computer science; dietetics; economics; education (multiple levels); English; history; human resources management; international/global studies; mathematics; multi-/interdisciplinary studies related; music; nursing science; philosophy; psychology; sociology; Spanish; theology.

Academics *Calendar:* semesters. *Degrees:* certificates, bachelor's, master's, doctoral, and postbachelor's certificates (also offers coed adult undergraduate degree program and coed graduate programs). *Special study options:* academic remediation for entering students, accelerated degree program, advanced placement credit, distance learning, double majors, English as a second language, honors programs, independent study, internships, off-campus study, part-time degree program, services for LD students, student-designed majors, study abroad, summer session for credit. *Unusual degree programs:* 3-2 business administration; counseling psychology.

Computers on Campus 127 computers/terminals and 20 ports are available on campus for general student use. Students can access the following: campus intranet, computer help desk, free student e-mail accounts, online (class) grades. Campuswide network is available. 100% of college-owned or -operated housing units are wired for high-speed Internet access. Wireless service is available via classrooms, computer labs, dorm rooms, libraries.

Student Life *Housing options:* women-only. Campus housing is university owned. Freshman campus housing is guaranteed. *Activities and organizations:* drama/theater group, student-run newspaper, choral group, Student Government Association, Students Take Action Committee, International/Intercultural Club, College Activities Board, campus ministry. *Campus security:* 24-hour emergency response devices and patrols, late-night transport/escort service, controlled dormitory access. *Student services:* health clinic, personal/psychological counseling.

Athletics Member NCAA. All Division III. *Intercollegiate sports:* basketball W, equestrian sports W, soccer W, softball W, swimming and diving W, tennis W, volleyball W. *Intramural sports:* volleyball W.

Standardized Tests *Required:* SAT or ACT (for admission).

Costs (2007–08) *Comprehensive fee:* $32,537 includes full-time tuition ($21,347), mandatory fees ($1200), and room and board ($9990). Part-time tuition: $667 per credit. Part-time tuition and fees vary according to course load and location. *Required fees:* $140 per course part-time. *Payment plan:* installment. *Waivers:* children of alumni, senior citizens, and employees or children of employees.

Financial Aid Of all full-time matriculated undergraduates who enrolled in 2006, 613 applied for aid, 518 were judged to have need, 86 had their need fully met. In 2006, 120 non-need-based awards were made. *Average percent of need met:* 75%. *Average financial aid package:* $18,190. *Average need-based loan:* $3792. *Average need-based gift aid:* $15,241. *Average non-need-based aid:* $12,926.

Applying *Options:* electronic application, early admission, deferred entrance. *Application fee:* $35. *Required:* high school transcript, minimum 2.0 GPA, 2 letters of recommendation. *Recommended:* essay or personal statement, interview. *Application deadlines:* 8/15 (freshmen), rolling (transfers). *Notification:* 11/15 (freshmen), continuous (transfers).

Freshman Application Contact Ms. Donna Tatarka, Dean of Admissions, College of Saint Elizabeth, 2 Convent Road, Morristown, NJ 07960-6989. *Phone:* 973-290-4700. *Toll-free phone:* 800-210-7900. *Fax:* 973-290-4710. *E-mail:* apply@csa.edu.

See page 1562 for the College Close-Up.

DEVRY UNIVERSITY

North Brunswick, New Jersey **www.devry.edu/**

- **Proprietary** 4-year, founded 1969, part of DeVry University
- **Urban** 10-acre campus with easy access to New York City
- **Coed** 1,382 undergraduate students, 64% full-time, 26% women, 74% men
- **Minimally difficult** entrance level

Undergraduates 880 full-time, 502 part-time. 9% are from out of state, 24% African American, 8% Asian American or Pacific Islander, 20% Hispanic American, 0.4% Native American, 2% international, 11% transferred in.

Freshmen *Admission:* 348 enrolled.

Faculty *Total:* 144, 28% full-time. *Student/faculty ratio:* 14:1.

Majors Biomedical technology; business administration and management; business administration, management and operations related; computer systems analysis; computer systems networking and telecommunications; electrical, electronic and communications engineering technology; electroneurodiagnostic/electroencephalographic technology; health information/medical records technology.

Academics *Calendar:* semesters. *Degrees:* associate and bachelor's. *Special study options:* academic remediation for entering students, accelerated degree program, adult/continuing education programs, advanced placement credit, distance learning, part-time degree program, services for LD students, summer session for credit.

Computers on Campus 575 computers/terminals are available on campus for general student use. Students can access the following: online (class) registration. Campuswide network is available.

Student Life *Housing:* college housing not available. *Activities and organizations:* Phi Theta Kappa, Data Processing Management Association, Telecommunications Management Association, Institute of Electrical and Electronics Engineering. *Campus security:* 24-hour emergency response devices and patrols, late-night transport/escort service.

Costs (2008–09) *Tuition:* $14,480 full-time, $540 per credit part-time. *Required fees:* $180 full-time.

Financial Aid Of all full-time matriculated undergraduates who enrolled in 2003, 1,809 applied for aid, 1,695 were judged to have need, 43 had their need fully met. In 2003, 148 non-need-based awards were made. *Average percent of need met:* 45%. *Average financial aid package:* $8488. *Average need-based loan:* $5111. *Average need-based gift aid:* $5448. *Average non-need-based aid:* $9674.

Applying *Options:* electronic application, early admission, deferred entrance. *Application fee:* $50. *Required:* high school transcript, interview. *Application deadlines:* rolling (freshmen), rolling (transfers). *Notification:* continuous (freshmen), continuous (transfers).

Freshman Application Contact DeVry University, 630 US Highway One, North Brunswick, NJ 08902-3362.

DREW UNIVERSITY

Madison, New Jersey **www.drew.edu/**

- **Independent** university, founded 1867, affiliated with United Methodist Church
- **Suburban** 186-acre campus with easy access to New York City
- **Endowment** $241.5 million
- **Coed** 1,676 undergraduate students, 96% full-time, 61% women, 39% men
- **Moderately difficult** entrance level, 77% of applicants were admitted

Drew is educating students to help shape the world of tomorrow. With its roots in the best traditions of the arts and sciences, Drew blends inspired teaching on a technologically integrated campus. There are numerous opportunities for academic internships in nearby corporate headquarters and research centers. For example, Drew's innovative international seminars program and semesters in New York City on Wall Street and at the United Nations provide students with an understanding of issues that affect a global society.

Undergraduates 1,612 full-time, 64 part-time. Students come from 45 states and territories, 16 other countries, 41% are from out of state, 6% African American, 5% Asian American or Pacific Islander, 7% Hispanic American, 0.3% Native American, 2% international, 2% transferred in, 86% live on campus. *Retention:* 83% of 2006 full-time freshmen returned.

Freshmen *Admission:* 3,816 applied, 2,940 admitted, 456 enrolled. *Average high school GPA:* 3.35. *Test scores:* SAT critical reading scores over 500: 82%; SAT math scores over 500: 79%; SAT writing scores over 500: 84%; ACT scores over 18: 97%; SAT critical reading scores over 600: 46%; SAT math scores over 600: 36%; SAT writing scores over 600: 46%; ACT scores over 24: 48%; SAT critical reading scores over 700: 12%; SAT math scores over 700: 6%; SAT writing scores over 700: 10%; ACT scores over 30: 9%.

Faculty *Total:* 222, 71% full-time. *Student/faculty ratio:* 11:1.

Majors African studies; anthropology; art; art history, criticism and conservation; behavioral sciences; biochemistry; biology/biological sciences; chemistry; Chinese studies; classics and languages, literatures and linguistics; computer science; dramatic/theater arts; economics; English; French; German; history; mathematics; mathematics and computer science; music; neuroscience; philosophy; physics; political science and government; psychology; religious studies; Russian; sociology; Spanish; women's studies.

Academics *Calendar:* semesters. *Degrees:* bachelor's, master's, doctoral, first professional, and postbachelor's certificates. *Special study options:* academic remediation for entering students, accelerated degree program, adult/continuing education programs, advanced placement credit, double majors, honors programs, independent study, internships, off-campus study, part-time degree program, services for LD students, student-designed majors, study abroad, summer session for credit. *Unusual degree programs:* 3-2 engineering with Washington University in St. Louis, Stevens Institute of Technology, Columbia University; forestry with Duke University.

Computers on Campus 200 computers/terminals are available on campus for general student use. Students can access the following: online (class) registration. Campuswide network is available.

Student Life *Housing options:* coed, disabled students. Campus housing is university owned. Freshman campus housing is guaranteed. *Activities and organizations:* drama/theater group, student-run newspaper, radio and television station, choral group, The Acorn (student newspaper), Student Government Association, Volunteer Resource Center, University Program Board, WMNJ (student radio station). *Campus security:* 24-hour emergency response devices and patrols, late-night transport/escort service, controlled dormitory access. *Student services:* health clinic, personal/psychological counseling.

Athletics Member NCAA. All Division III. *Intercollegiate sports:* baseball M, basketball M/W, cross-country running M/W, equestrian sports M/W, fencing M/W, field hockey W, lacrosse M/W, rugby M (c)/W (c), soccer M/W, softball W, swimming and diving M/W, tennis M/W. *Intramural sports:* basketball M/W, football M/W, racquetball M/W, soccer M/W, softball M/W, squash M/W, table tennis M/W, ultimate Frisbee M/W, volleyball M/W.

Costs (2007–08) *Comprehensive fee:* $44,266 includes full-time tuition ($34,230), mandatory fees ($560), and room and board ($9476). Full-time tuition and fees vary according to course load. Part-time tuition: $1426 per credit. Part-time tuition and fees vary according to course load. *Required fees:* $23 per credit part-time. *College room only:* $6126. Room and board charges vary according to board plan and housing facility. *Payment plans:* tuition prepayment, installment, deferred payment. *Waivers:* senior citizens and employees or children of employees.

Financial Aid Of all full-time matriculated undergraduates who enrolled in 2006, 1,014 applied for aid, 788 were judged to have need, 230 had their need fully met. 322 Federal Work-Study jobs (averaging $1192). 33 state and other part-time jobs (averaging $9222). In 2006, 515 non-need-based awards were made. *Average percent of need met:* 81%. *Average financial aid package:* $25,488. *Average need-based loan:* $4803. *Average need-based gift aid:* $20,194. *Average non-need-based aid:* $11,531. *Average indebtedness upon graduation:* $16,777. *Financial aid deadline:* 2/15.

Applying *Options:* early admission, early decision, deferred entrance. *Application fee:* $50. *Required:* essay or personal statement, high school transcript, 1 letter of recommendation. *Recommended:* interview. *Application deadlines:* 2/15 (freshmen), 8/1 (transfers). *Early decision deadline:* 12/1 (for plan 1), 1/15 (for plan 2). *Notification:* 3/15 (freshmen), continuous until 4/1 (transfers), 12/24 (early decision plan 1), 2/15 (early decision plan 2).

Freshman Application Contact Ms. Mary Beth Carey, Dean of Admissions and Financial Assistance, Drew University, 36 Madison Avenue, Madison, NJ 07940-1493. *Phone:* 973-408-3739. *Fax:* 973-408-3068. *E-mail:* cadm@drew.edu.

See page 1564 for the College Close-Up.

FAIRLEIGH DICKINSON UNIVERSITY, COLLEGE AT FLORHAM

Madison, New Jersey **www.fdu.edu/**

- **Independent** comprehensive, founded 1942
- **Suburban** 178-acre campus with easy access to New York City
- **Coed** 2,545 undergraduate students, 90% full-time, 53% women, 47% men
- **Moderately difficult** entrance level, 63% of applicants were admitted

Undergraduates 2,298 full-time, 247 part-time. Students come from 28 states and territories, 20 other countries, 14% are from out of state, 8% African American, 3% Asian American or Pacific Islander, 7% Hispanic American, 0.4% Native American, 1% international, 5% transferred in, 58% live on campus. *Retention:* 76% of 2006 full-time freshmen returned.

Freshmen *Admission:* 2,706 applied, 1,693 admitted, 488 enrolled. *Test scores:* SAT critical reading scores over 500: 56%; SAT math scores over 500: 59%; SAT writing scores over 500: 40%; SAT critical reading scores over 600: 16%; SAT math scores over 600: 17%; SAT writing scores over 600: 6%; SAT critical reading scores over 700: 2%; SAT math scores over 700: 2%; SAT writing scores over 700: 1%.

Majors Accounting; allied health diagnostic, intervention, and treatment professions related; biology/biological sciences; business administration and management; business/managerial economics; chemistry; cinematography and film/video production; clinical laboratory science/medical technology; communication/speech communication and rhetoric; computer and information sciences; creative writing; dramatic/theater arts; economics; English; finance; French; general studies; health services/allied health/health sciences; history; hotel and restaurant management; humanities; marine biology and biological oceanography; marketing/marketing management; mathematics; medical radiologic technology; nursing (registered nurse training); philosophy; political science and government; psychology; sales, distribution and marketing; sociology; Spanish; visual and performing arts.

Academics *Calendar:* semesters. *Degrees:* bachelor's, master's, post-master's, and postbachelor's certificates. *Special study options:* academic remediation for entering students, accelerated degree program, adult/continuing education programs, advanced placement credit, cooperative education, distance learning, double majors, external degree program, honors programs, independent study, internships, off-campus study, part-time degree program, services for LD students, study abroad, summer session for credit. *ROTC:* Army (c), Air Force (c).

Computers on Campus 170 computers/terminals are available on campus for general student use. Students can access the following: computer help desk, free student e-mail accounts, online (class) grades, online (class) registration, online (class) schedules. Campuswide network is available. Wireless service is available via entire campus.

Student Life *Housing options:* coed, disabled students. Campus housing is university owned. Freshman applicants given priority for college housing. *Activities and organizations:* student-run newspaper, radio station, choral group, Green Club, Florham Programming Committee, Latin American Student Organization, Colleges Against Cancer, Student Government, national fraternities, national sororities. *Campus security:* 24-hour emergency response devices and patrols, late-night transport/escort service, controlled dormitory access, trained law enforcement personnel on staff. *Student services:* health clinic, personal/psychological counseling, women's center.

Athletics Member NCAA. All Division III. *Intercollegiate sports:* baseball M, basketball M/W, cross-country running M/W, field hockey W, football M, golf M, lacrosse M/W, soccer M/W, softball W, swimming and diving M/W, tennis M/W, volleyball W. *Intramural sports:* basketball M/W, bowling M/W, cross-country running W, football M/W, golf M, racquetball M/W, soccer M/W, softball M/W, tennis M/W, volleyball M/W.

Standardized Tests *Required:* SAT or ACT (for admission).

Costs (2007–08) *Comprehensive fee:* $38,210 includes full-time tuition ($27,620), mandatory fees ($608), and room and board ($9982). Part-time tuition: $797 per credit. Part-time tuition and fees vary according to course load. *College room only:* $6074. Room and board charges vary according to board plan and housing facility. *Payment plans:* installment, deferred payment. *Waivers:* employees or children of employees.

Financial Aid Of all full-time matriculated undergraduates who enrolled in 2003, 1,772 applied for aid, 1,567 were judged to have need. In 2003, 681 non-need-based awards were made. *Average financial aid package:* $15,806. *Average need-based loan:* $3653. *Average need-based gift aid:* $8290. *Average non-need-based aid:* $6952.

Applying *Options:* electronic application, deferred entrance. *Application fee:* $40. *Required:* high school transcript, 2 letters of recommendation. *Required for some:* interview. *Application deadline:* rolling (freshmen). *Notification:* continuous (freshmen), continuous (transfers).

Freshman Application Contact Mr. Jonathan Wexler, Fairleigh Dickinson University, College at Florham, 285 Madison Avenue, M-MS1-03, Madison, NJ 07940. *Phone:* 201-692-7304. *Toll-free phone:* 800-338-8803. *Fax:* 201-692-7319. *E-mail:* globaleducation@fdu.edu.

See page 1566 for the College Close-Up.

FAIRLEIGH DICKINSON UNIVERSITY, METROPOLITAN CAMPUS

Teaneck, New Jersey **www.fdu.edu/**

- **Independent** comprehensive, founded 1942
- **Suburban** 88-acre campus with easy access to New York City
- **Coed** 6,024 undergraduate students, 37% full-time, 52% women, 48% men
- **Moderately difficult** entrance level, 49% of applicants were admitted

Undergraduates 2,223 full-time, 3,801 part-time. Students come from 33 states and territories, 67 other countries, 6% are from out of state, 16% African American, 6% Asian American or Pacific Islander, 18% Hispanic American, 0.3% Native American, 7% international, 8% transferred in, 22% live on campus. *Retention:* 72% of 2006 full-time freshmen returned.

Freshmen *Admission:* 3,019 applied, 1,481 admitted, 453 enrolled. *Test scores:* SAT critical reading scores over 500: 40%; SAT math scores over 500: 55%; SAT writing scores over 500: 40%; SAT critical reading scores over 600: 6%; SAT math scores over 600: 15%; SAT writing scores over 600: 6%; SAT critical reading scores over 700: 1%; SAT math scores over 700: 3%; SAT writing scores over 700: 1%.

Majors Accounting; allied health diagnostic, intervention, and treatment professions related; biochemistry; biological and physical sciences; biology/biological sciences; business administration and management; business/managerial economics; chemistry; civil engineering technology; clinical laboratory science/medical technology; clinical/medical laboratory technology; communication and media related; communication/speech communication and rhetoric; computer science; construction engineering technology; criminal justice/safety; dramatic/theater arts; economics; electrical, electronic and communications engineering technology; electrical, electronics and communications engineering; English; entrepreneurial and small business related; environmental science; French; general studies; history; hotel/motel administration; humanities; information technology; international relations and affairs; liberal arts and sciences/liberal studies; marine biology and biological oceanography; marketing research; mathematics; mechanical engineering/mechanical technology; multi-/interdisciplinary studies related; nursing (registered nurse training); nursing science; philosophy; physics; political science and government; psychology; radiologic technology/science; sociology; Spanish; visual and performing arts.

Academics *Calendar:* semesters. *Degrees:* certificates, associate, bachelor's, master's, doctoral, post-master's, and postbachelor's certificates. *Special study options:* academic remediation for entering students, accelerated degree program, adult/continuing education programs, advanced placement credit, cooperative education, distance learning, double majors, English as a second language, honors programs, independent study, internships, off-campus study, part-time degree program, services for LD students, student-designed majors, study abroad, summer session for credit. *ROTC:* Army (c), Air Force (c).

Computers on Campus 190 computers/terminals are available on campus for general student use. Students can access the following: computer help desk, free student e-mail accounts, online (class) grades, online (class) registration, online (class) schedules. Campuswide network is available. Wireless service is available via entire campus.

Student Life *Housing options:* coed. Campus housing is university owned. *Activities and organizations:* drama/theater group, student-run newspaper, radio station, choral group, Indian Cultural Experience, Student Program Board, Residence Hall Student Association, International Student Association, Business Leaders of Tomorrow, national fraternities, national sororities. *Campus security:* 24-hour emergency response devices and patrols, late-night transport/escort service, controlled dormitory access, trained law enforcement personnel on staff. *Student services:* health clinic, personal/psychological counseling.

Athletics Member NCAA. All Division I. *Intercollegiate sports:* baseball M (s), basketball M (s)/W (s), bowling W (s), cross-country running M (s)/W (s), fencing W (s), golf M (s)/W (s), soccer M (s)/W (s), softball W (s), tennis M (s)/W (s), track and field M (s)/W (s), volleyball W (s). *Intramural sports:* badminton M/W, baseball M, basketball M/W, bowling M/W, cheerleading M/W, football M/W, golf M, racquetball M/W, skiing (downhill) M/W, soccer M/W, table tennis M/W, tennis M/W, volleyball M/W.

Standardized Tests *Required:* SAT or ACT (for admission).

Costs (2007–08) *Comprehensive fee:* $36,560 includes full-time tuition ($25,624), mandatory fees ($608), and room and board ($10,328). Part-time tuition: $797 per credit. Part-time tuition and fees vary according to course load. *College room only:* $6420. Room and board charges vary according to board plan and housing facility. *Payment plans:* installment, deferred payment. *Waivers:* senior citizens and employees or children of employees.

Financial Aid Of all full-time matriculated undergraduates who enrolled in 2003, 1,599 applied for aid, 1,510 were judged to have need. In 2003, 272 non-need-based awards were made. *Average financial aid package:* $16,556. *Average need-based loan:* $3666. *Average need-based gift aid:* $7279. *Average non-need-based aid:* $3658.

Applying *Options:* electronic application, early admission, deferred entrance. *Application fee:* $40. *Required:* high school transcript, 2 letters of recommendation. *Required for some:* interview. *Application deadline:* rolling (freshmen). *Notification:* continuous (freshmen), continuous (transfers).

Freshman Application Contact Mr. Jonathan Wexler, Associate Vice President of Enrollment Management, Fairleigh Dickinson University, Metropolitan Campus, 1000 River Road, H-DH3-10, Teaneck, NJ 07666. *Phone:* 201-692-7304. *Toll-free phone:* 800-338-8803. *Fax:* 201-692-7319. *E-mail:* globaleducation@fdu.edu.

See page 1566 for the College Close-Up.

FELICIAN COLLEGE

Lodi, New Jersey **www.felician.edu/**

- **Independent Roman Catholic** comprehensive, founded 1942
- **Suburban** 37-acre campus with easy access to New York City
- **Endowment** $716,953
- **Coed** 1,615 undergraduate students, 78% full-time, 78% women, 22% men
- **Moderately difficult** entrance level, 61% of applicants were admitted

Undergraduates 1,257 full-time, 358 part-time. Students come from 10 states and territories, 5% are from out of state, 15% African American, 11% Asian American or Pacific Islander, 17% Hispanic American, 0.5% Native American, 20% transferred in. *Retention:* 60% of 2006 full-time freshmen returned.

Freshmen *Admission:* 1,561 applied, 948 admitted, 322 enrolled.

Faculty *Total:* 173, 55% full-time. *Student/faculty ratio:* 11:1.

Majors Accounting; art; behavioral sciences; biochemistry; biology/biological sciences; business administration and management; clinical laboratory science/medical technology; clinical/medical laboratory technology; commercial and advertising art; computer science; cytotechnology; education; education (K-12); elementary education; English; environmental studies; fine/studio arts; gerontology; history; humanities; interdisciplinary studies; liberal arts and sciences/liberal studies; marketing/marketing management; mass communication/media; mathematics; mathematics teacher education; medical laboratory technology; mental health/rehabilitation; natural sciences; nursing (registered nurse training); philosophy; political science and government; pre-law studies; pre-medical studies; psychology; religious studies; social sciences; sociology; special education; toxicology.

Academics *Calendar:* semesters. *Degrees:* certificates, associate, bachelor's, master's, and postbachelor's certificates. *Special study options:* academic remediation for entering students, accelerated degree program, adult/continuing education programs, advanced placement credit, cooperative education, distance learning, double majors, English as a second language, external degree program, honors programs, independent study, internships, off-campus study, part-time degree program, services for LD students, student-designed majors, study abroad, summer session for credit. *Unusual degree programs:* 3-2 clinical lab sciences with University of Medicine and Dentistry of New Jersey.

Computers on Campus 100 computers/terminals are available on campus for general student use. Campuswide network is available.

Student Life *Housing options:* coed, men-only, women-only, disabled students. Campus housing is university owned. Freshman applicants given priority for college housing. *Activities and organizations:* drama/theater group, student-run radio station, choral group, Student Nurses Association, Zeta Alpha Zeta teaching sorority, Campus Activity Board, Students In Free Enterprise, Student Government Association. *Campus security:* 24-hour patrols, student patrols, late-night transport/escort service. *Student services:* health clinic, personal/psychological counseling.

Athletics Member NCAA, NAIA. All NCAA Division II. *Intercollegiate sports:* baseball M (s), basketball M (s)/W (s), cross-country running M (s)/W (s), soccer M (s)/W (s), softball W (s), track and field M (s)/W (s). *Intramural sports:* soccer M/W, softball W, volleyball M/W, weight lifting M/W.

Standardized Tests *Required:* SAT or ACT (for admission). *Required for some:* ACT (for admission), SAT Subject Tests (for admission).

Costs (2008–09) *Comprehensive fee:* $31,700 includes full-time tuition ($22,200), mandatory fees ($1300), and room and board ($8200). Part-time tuition: $730 per credit.

Financial Aid Of all full-time matriculated undergraduates who enrolled in 2006, 1,075 applied for aid, 956 were judged to have need, 124 had their need fully met. 84 Federal Work-Study jobs (averaging $1300). 116 state and other part-time jobs (averaging $1300). In 2006, 221 non-need-based awards were made. *Average percent of need met:* 86%. *Average financial aid package:* $15,442. *Average need-based loan:* $4300. *Average need-based gift aid:* $7400. *Average non-need-based aid:* $5700. *Average indebtedness upon graduation:* $19,500.

Applying *Options:* deferred entrance. *Application fee:* $30. *Required:* high school transcript, minimum 2.0 GPA. *Required for some:* essay or personal statement, interview. *Application deadlines:* rolling (freshmen), rolling (transfers). *Notification:* continuous (freshmen), continuous (transfers).

Freshman Application Contact College Admissions Office, Felician College, 262 South Main Street, Lodi, NJ 07644. *Phone:* 201-559-6131.

See page 1568 for the College Close-Up.

GEORGIAN COURT UNIVERSITY

Lakewood, New Jersey **www.georgian.edu/**

- **Independent Roman Catholic** comprehensive, founded 1908
- **Suburban** 150-acre campus with easy access to New York City and Philadelphia
- **Endowment** $46.9 million
- **Undergraduate: women only; graduate: coed** 1,955 undergraduate students, 72% full-time, 92% women, 8% men
- **Moderately difficult** entrance level, 77% of applicants were admitted

Founded in 1908 on the dreams of the Sisters of Mercy, Georgian Court University today makes it possible for thousands of students to realize their own dreams of a high-quality, affordable private education. Deeply rooted in a liberal arts curriculum and with an emphasis on service-learning, GCU offers a personalized, supportive learning environment within a technologically advanced university setting. With a student body of 3,000 and an average class size of just 14, GCU students work side by side with dedicated professors who are leaders in their respective fields. GCU offers thirty undergraduate and nine graduate majors, state-of-the-art facilities, seven NCAA sports teams, numerous student activities, generous financial aid, and a beautiful 156-acre campus. For more information, students should call 732-987-2760 or visit http://www.georgian.edu.

Undergraduates 1,399 full-time, 556 part-time. Students come from 17 states and territories, 14 other countries, 2% are from out of state, 7% African American, 1% Asian American or Pacific Islander, 7% Hispanic American, 0.2% Native American, 0.5% international, 11% transferred in, 28% live on campus. *Retention:* 72% of 2006 full-time freshmen returned.

Freshmen *Admission:* 563 applied, 433 admitted, 226 enrolled. *Average high school GPA:* 3.00.

Faculty *Total:* 307, 33% full-time, 34% with terminal degrees. *Student/faculty ratio:* 14:1.

Majors Accounting; allied health diagnostic, intervention, and treatment professions related; art; art history, criticism and conservation; biochemistry; biology/biological sciences; business administration and management; chemistry; communication/speech communication and rhetoric; computer and information sciences; criminal justice/law enforcement administration; elementary education; English; history; humanities; liberal arts and sciences/liberal studies; mathematics; natural sciences; physics; psychology; religious studies; social work; sociology; Spanish.

Academics *Calendar:* semesters. *Degrees:* certificates, bachelor's, master's, post-master's, and postbachelor's certificates. *Special study options:* academic remediation for entering students, accelerated degree program, adult/continuing education programs, advanced placement credit, distance learning, double majors, English as a second language, honors programs, independent study, internships, off-campus study, part-time degree program, services for LD students, study abroad, summer session for credit.

Computers on Campus 172 computers/terminals are available on campus for general student use. Students can access the following: campus intranet, computer help desk, free student e-mail accounts, online (class) grades, online (class) registration, online (class) schedules. Campuswide network is available. 100% of college-owned or -operated housing units are wired for high-speed Internet access. Wireless service is available via classrooms, computer centers, computer labs, dorm rooms, learning centers, libraries, student centers.

Student Life *Housing options:* women-only. Campus housing is university owned. Freshman campus housing is guaranteed. *Activities and organizations:* student-run newspaper, choral group, Women in Leadership Development, Student Government Association, Latin American Student Organization, Social Work Club, Golden Z. *Campus security:* 24-hour emergency response devices and patrols, late-night transport/escort service, controlled dormitory access. *Student services:* health clinic, personal/psychological counseling.

Athletics Member NCAA. All Division II. *Intercollegiate sports:* basketball W (s), cross-country running W (s), lacrosse W (s), soccer W (s), softball W (s), tennis W (s), volleyball W (s).

Standardized Tests *Recommended:* SAT or ACT (for admission).

Costs (2007–08) *Comprehensive fee:* $30,214 includes full-time tuition ($20,928), mandatory fees ($1150), and room and board ($8136). Part-time tuition: $563 per credit hour. *Required fees:* $290 per term part-time. *Payment plan:* installment. *Waivers:* employees or children of employees.

Financial Aid Of all full-time matriculated undergraduates who enrolled in 2007, 1,230 applied for aid, 1,101 were judged to have need, 195 had their need fully met. 104 Federal Work-Study jobs (averaging $1880). 199 state and other part-time jobs (averaging $1836). In 2007, 169 non-need-based awards were made. *Average percent of need met:* 72%. *Average financial aid package:* $16,424. *Average need-based loan:* $4937. *Average non-need-based aid:* $12,595. *Average indebtedness upon graduation:* $25,988.

Applying *Options:* electronic application, early action. *Application fee:* $40. *Required:* high school transcript, minimum 2.5 GPA, letters of recommendation. *Recommended:* essay or personal statement, interview. *Application deadlines:* 8/1 (freshmen), 8/1 (transfers), 11/15 (early action). *Notification:* continuous (transfers), 12/30 (early action).

Freshman Application Contact Ms. Kathie Gallant, Director of Admissions, Georgian Court University, Office of Admissions, 900 Lakewood Avenue, Lakewood, NJ 08701-2697. *Phone:* 732-987-2760. *Toll-free phone:* 800-458-8422. *Fax:* 732-987-2000. *E-mail:* admissions@georgian.edu.

See page 1570 for the College Close-Up.

KEAN UNIVERSITY

Union, New Jersey **www.kean.edu/**

- **State-supported** comprehensive, founded 1855, part of New Jersey State College System
- **Suburban** 150-acre campus with easy access to New York City
- **Endowment** $12.9 million
- **Coed** 10,441 undergraduate students, 76% full-time, 63% women, 37% men
- **Moderately difficult** entrance level, 67% of applicants were admitted

Undergraduates 7,976 full-time, 2,465 part-time. Students come from 23 states and territories, 70 other countries, 2% are from out of state, 20% African American, 6% Asian American or Pacific Islander, 20% Hispanic American, 0.2% Native American, 2% international, 12% transferred in, 14% live on campus. *Retention:* 77% of 2006 full-time freshmen returned.

Freshmen *Admission:* 5,455 applied, 3,633 admitted, 1,478 enrolled. *Average high school GPA:* 2.88. *Test scores:* SAT critical reading scores over 500: 27%; SAT math scores over 500: 35%; SAT critical reading scores over 600: 2%; SAT math scores over 600: 5%.

Faculty *Total:* 1,289, 29% full-time. *Student/faculty ratio:* 15:1.

Majors Accounting; acting; art; art history, criticism and conservation; athletic training; biology/biological sciences; business administration and management; chemistry; clinical laboratory science/medical technology; communication/speech communication and rhetoric; computer and information sciences; computer systems networking and telecommunications; criminal justice/law enforcement administration; design and visual communications; dramatic/theater arts; economics; electrical, electronic and communications engineering technology; elementary education; English; finance; fine/studio arts; geology/earth science; health information/medical records administration; history; industrial design; interior design; kindergarten/preschool education; liberal arts and sciences/liberal studies; manufacturing technology; marketing/marketing management; mathematics; music; music teacher education; nursing science; parks, recreation and leisure facilities management; philosophy and religious studies related; physical education teaching and coaching; political science and government; printing management; psychology; psychology related; public administration; science technologies related; social work; sociology; Spanish; special education; special education related; speech teacher education; technology/industrial arts teacher education; theater design and technology.

Academics *Calendar:* semesters. *Degrees:* bachelor's, master's, and post-master's certificates. *Special study options:* academic remediation for entering students, accelerated degree program, adult/continuing education programs, advanced placement credit, cooperative education, distance learning, double majors, English as a second language, honors programs, independent study, internships, off-campus study, part-time degree program, services for LD students, study abroad, summer session for credit. *ROTC:* Army (c), Air Force (c). *Unusual degree programs:* 3-2 BA/MPA public administration, BS science & technology/MS science & technology, BS science & technology/MA instruction & curriculum.

Computers on Campus 1,650 computers/terminals and 2,000 ports are available on campus for general student use. Students can access the following: free student e-mail accounts, online (class) grades, online (class) registration, online (class) schedules. Campuswide network is available. 100% of college-owned or -operated housing units are wired for high-speed Internet access.

Student Life *Housing options:* coed, women-only, disabled students. Campus housing is university owned, leased by the school and is provided by a third party. Freshman applicants given priority for college housing. *Activities and organizations:* drama/theater group, student-run newspaper, radio station, choral group, Student Organization, Council for Part-Time Students, Pan African Student Union, Association of Látin American Students, Kean Dance Theatre, national fraternities, national sororities. *Campus security:* 24-hour emergency response devices and patrols, student patrols, late-night transport/escort service, controlled dormitory access, 24-hour patrols by campus police. *Student services:* health clinic, personal/psychological counseling.

Athletics Member NCAA. All Division III. *Intercollegiate sports:* baseball M, basketball M/W, cheerleading M/W, cross-country running M/W, field hockey W, football M, lacrosse M/W, soccer M/W, softball W, tennis W, track and field M/W, volleyball W. *Intramural sports:* basketball M/W, soccer M/W, softball M/W, table tennis M/W, tennis M/W, volleyball M/W, weight lifting M/W.

Standardized Tests *Required:* SAT or ACT (for admission).

Costs (2007–08) *Tuition:* state resident $5550 full-time, $185 per credit part-time; nonresident $9690 full-time, $323 per credit part-time. Part-time tuition and fees vary according to course load. *Required fees:* $2955 full-time, $99 per credit part-time. *Room and board:* $9190; room only: $6490. Room and board charges vary according to board plan and housing facility. *Payment plans:* installment, deferred payment. *Waivers:* senior citizens and employees or children of employees.

Financial Aid Of all full-time matriculated undergraduates who enrolled in 2006, 5,438 applied for aid, 4,260 were judged to have need, 622 had their need fully met. 250 Federal Work-Study jobs (averaging $1985). In 2006, 124 non-need-based awards were made. *Average percent of need met:* 55%. *Average financial aid package:* $7931. *Average need-based loan:* $3846. *Average need-based gift aid:* $6159. *Average non-need-based aid:* $2219. *Average indebtedness upon graduation:* $20,037. *Financial aid deadline:* 3/15.

Applying *Options:* electronic application. *Application fee:* $50. *Required:* essay or personal statement, high school transcript, minimum 2.0 GPA. *Required for some:* interview. *Recommended:* 2 letters of recommendation. *Application deadlines:* 5/31 (freshmen), 8/1 (transfers). *Notification:* continuous (freshmen), continuous (transfers).

Freshman Application Contact Mr. Audley Bridges, Director of Undergraduate Admissions, Kean University, PO Box 411, Union, NJ 07083. *Phone:* 908-737-7100. *Fax:* 908-737-7105. *E-mail:* admitme@kean.edu.

See page 1572 for the College Close-Up.

MONMOUTH UNIVERSITY

West Long Branch, New Jersey **www.monmouth.edu/**

- **Independent** comprehensive, founded 1933
- **Suburban** 156-acre campus with easy access to New York City and Philadelphia
- **Endowment** $51.3 million
- **Coed** 4,744 undergraduate students, 91% full-time, 58% women, 42% men
- **Moderately difficult** entrance level, 57% of applicants were admitted

Undergraduates 4,300 full-time, 444 part-time. Students come from 27 states and territories, 14 other countries, 10% are from out of state, 4% African American, 2% Asian American or Pacific Islander, 5% Hispanic American, 0.2% Native American, 0.4% international, 8% transferred in, 44% live on campus. *Retention:* 80% of 2006 full-time freshmen returned.

Freshmen *Admission:* 6,982 applied, 4,014 admitted, 946 enrolled. *Average high school GPA:* 3.17. *Test scores:* SAT critical reading scores over 500: 72%; SAT math scores over 500: 76%; SAT writing scores over 500: 67%; ACT scores over 18: 100%; SAT critical reading scores over 600: 12%; SAT math scores over 600: 21%; SAT writing scores over 600: 15%; ACT scores over 24: 41%; SAT critical reading scores over 700: 1%; SAT math scores over 700: 2%; SAT writing scores over 700: 1%.

Faculty *Total:* 534, 47% full-time, 51% with terminal degrees. *Student/faculty ratio:* 15:1.

Majors Anthropology; art; biology/biological sciences; business administration and management; chemistry; clinical laboratory science/medical technology; communication/speech communication and rhetoric; computer and information sciences; computer software engineering; criminal justice/safety; dramatic/theater arts; education; English; fine arts related; foreign languages and literatures; general studies; health services/allied health/health sciences; history; international business/trade/commerce; marine biology; mathematics; music; nursing science; political science and government; psychology; real estate; secondary education; social sciences related; social work; special education.

Academics *Calendar:* semesters. *Degrees:* certificates, associate, bachelor's, master's, and post-master's certificates. *Special study options:* academic remediation for entering students, accelerated degree program, advanced placement credit, cooperative education, distance learning, double majors, honors programs, independent study, internships, part-time degree program, services for LD students, student-designed majors, study abroad, summer session for credit. *ROTC:* Air Force (c).

Computers on Campus 695 computers/terminals are available on campus for general student use. Students can access the following: computer help desk, free student e-mail accounts, online (class) grades, online (class) registration, online (class) schedules. Campuswide network is available. Wireless service is available via entire campus.

Student Life *Housing options:* coed. Campus housing is university owned and leased by the school. Freshman applicants given priority for college housing. *Activities and organizations:* drama/theater group, student-run newspaper, radio and television station, choral group, student-run radio station, Student Government Association, student newspaper (Outlook), Student Activities Board, Shadows (yearbook), national fraternities, national sororities. *Campus security:* 24-hour emergency response devices and patrols, late-night transport/escort service, controlled dormitory access. *Student services:* health clinic, personal/psychological counseling, women's center, legal services.

Athletics Member NCAA. All Division I except football (Division I-AA). *Intercollegiate sports:* baseball M (s), basketball M (s)/W (s), cross-country running M (s)/W (s), field hockey W (s), golf M (s)/W (s), ice hockey M (c), lacrosse W (s), sailing M (c)/W (c), soccer M (s)/W (s), softball W (s), tennis M (s)/W (s), track and field M (s)/W (s), wrestling M (c). *Intramural sports:* badminton M/W, basketball M/W, cheerleading M/W, field hockey W (c), football M/W, soccer M/W, softball M/W, volleyball M/W.

Standardized Tests *Required:* SAT or ACT (for admission).

Costs (2007–08) *One-time required fee:* $200. *Comprehensive fee:* $31,938 includes full-time tuition ($22,406), mandatory fees ($628), and room and board ($8904). Part-time tuition: $649 per credit hour. *Required fees:* $157 per term part-time. *College room only:* $5056. Room and board charges vary according to housing facility. *Payment plan:* installment. *Waivers:* senior citizens and employees or children of employees.

Financial Aid Of all full-time matriculated undergraduates who enrolled in 2006, 3,153 applied for aid, 2,531 were judged to have need, 454 had their need fully met. 549 Federal Work-Study jobs (averaging $1200). In 2006, 1372 non-need-based awards were made. *Average percent of need met:* 76%. *Average financial aid package:* $16,739. *Average need-based loan:* $4631. *Average need-based gift aid:* $7515. *Average non-need-based aid:* $5526. *Average indebtedness upon graduation:* $33,092.

Applying *Options:* electronic application, early action, deferred entrance. *Application fee:* $50. *Required:* high school transcript, resume of activities including community involvement and leadership positions. *Recommended:* essay or personal statement, letters of recommendation. *Application deadlines:* 3/1 (freshmen), 7/15 (transfers), 12/1 (early action). *Notification:* 4/1 (freshmen), continuous (transfers), 1/15 (early action).

Freshman Application Contact Ms. Lauren Cifelli, Director of Undergraduate Admission, Monmouth University, 400 Cedar Avenue, West Long Branch, NJ 07764-1898. *Phone:* 732-571-3456. *Toll-free phone:* 800-543-9671. *Fax:* 732-263-5166. *E-mail:* admission@monmouth.edu.

See page 1574 for the College Close-Up.

MONTCLAIR STATE UNIVERSITY

Montclair, New Jersey **www.montclair.edu/**

- **State-supported** comprehensive, founded 1908
- **Suburban** 275-acre campus with easy access to New York City
- **Coed** 13,017 undergraduate students, 84% full-time, 62% women, 38% men
- **Moderately difficult** entrance level, 57% of applicants were admitted

Undergraduates 10,880 full-time, 2,137 part-time. Students come from 33 states and territories, 130 other countries, 6% are from out of state, 10% African American, 6% Asian American or Pacific Islander, 19% Hispanic American, 0.2% Native American, 5% international, 10% transferred in, 27% live on campus. *Retention:* 82% of 2006 full-time freshmen returned.

Freshmen *Admission:* 10,114 applied, 5,732 admitted, 2,098 enrolled. *Average high school GPA:* 3.29. *Test scores:* SAT critical reading scores over 500: 47%; SAT math scores over 500: 56%; SAT writing scores over 500: 50%; SAT critical reading scores over 600: 10%; SAT math scores over 600: 12%; SAT writing scores over 600: 10%; SAT critical reading scores over 700: 1%; SAT math scores over 700: 1%; SAT writing scores over 700: 1%.

Faculty *Total:* 1,275, 40% full-time, 40% with terminal degrees. *Student/faculty ratio:* 17:1.

Majors Animation, interactive technology, video graphics and special effects; anthropology; athletic training; biochemistry; biology/biological sciences; broadcast journalism; business administration and management; chemistry; cinematography and film/video production; classics; communication/speech communication and rhetoric; computer science; criminal justice/safety; dance; drama and dance teacher education; dramatic/theater arts; economics; English; family and consumer sciences/human sciences; fashion/apparel design; fine/studio arts; food/nutrition; foods, nutrition, and wellness; French; geography; geological and earth sciences/geosciences related; geology/earth science; graphic design; health services/allied health/health sciences; health teacher education; history; hospitality administration; humanities; information technology; Italian; Latin; legal professions and studies related; legal studies; linguistics; mathematics; medical informatics; molecular biology; music; music therapy; parks, recreation and leisure; philosophy; physical education teaching and coaching; physics; political science and government; psychology; religious studies; social work; sociology; Spanish; women's studies.

Academics *Calendar:* semesters. *Degrees:* bachelor's, master's, doctoral, post-master's, and postbachelor's certificates. *Special study options:* academic remediation for entering students, accelerated degree program, adult/continuing education programs, advanced placement credit, cooperative education, double majors, English as a second language, freshman honors college, honors programs, independent study, internships, off-campus study, part-time degree program, services for LD students, study abroad, summer session for credit. *ROTC:* Air Force (c).

Computers on Campus 218 computers/terminals are available on campus for general student use. Students can access the following: online (class) registration. Campuswide network is available.

Student Life *Housing options:* coed, women-only. Campus housing is university owned and is provided by a third party. Freshman applicants given priority for college housing. *Activities and organizations:* drama/theater group, student-run newspaper, radio station, choral group, Latin American Student Organization, Campus Recreation, MSU Gamers, Unified Asian American Student Organization, Human Relations and Leadership Association, national fraternities, national sororities. *Campus security:* 24-hour emergency response devices and patrols, late-night transport/escort service, controlled dormitory access, video surveillance, student escorts. *Student services:* health clinic, personal/psychological counseling, women's center.

Athletics Member NCAA. All Division III. *Intercollegiate sports:* baseball M, basketball M/W, field hockey W, football M, golf M/W, lacrosse M/W, soccer M/W, softball W, swimming and diving M/W, tennis M, track and field M/W, volleyball W. *Intramural sports:* baseball M, basketball M/W, bowling M/W, football M/W, ice hockey M (c), skiing (downhill) M (c)/W (c), soccer M, softball M/W, tennis M/W, volleyball M/W.

Standardized Tests *Required:* SAT or ACT (for admission).

Costs (2007–08) *Tuition:* state resident $6390 full-time, $213 per credit part-time; nonresident $13,659 full-time, $455 per credit part-time. *Required fees:* $2505 full-time, $122 per credit part-time, $23 per term part-time. *Room and board:* $9500; room only: $6350. Room and board charges vary according to board plan and housing facility. *Payment plan:* installment. *Waivers:* senior citizens and employees or children of employees.

Financial Aid Of all full-time matriculated undergraduates who enrolled in 2007, 7,030 applied for aid, 5,707 were judged to have need, 2,182 had their need fully met. 374 Federal Work-Study jobs (averaging $1161). 1,563 state and other part-time jobs (averaging $2070). In 2007, 316 non-need-based awards were made. *Average percent of need met:* 66%. *Average financial aid package:* $7964. *Average need-based loan:* $4301. *Average need-based gift aid:* $6950. *Average non-need-based aid:* $4629.

Applying *Options:* electronic application, deferred entrance. *Application fee:* $55. *Required:* essay or personal statement, high school transcript. *Required for some:* interview. *Application deadlines:* 3/1 (freshmen), 6/15 (transfers). *Notification:* continuous (freshmen), continuous (transfers).

Freshman Application Contact Director of Admissions, Montclair State University, One Normal Avenue, Montclair, NJ 07043-1624. *Phone:* 973-655-5116. *Toll-free phone:* 800-331-9205. *Fax:* 973-655-7700. *E-mail:* undergraduate.admissions@montclair.edu.

See page 1576 for the College Close-Up.

NEW JERSEY CITY UNIVERSITY

Jersey City, New Jersey **www.njcu.edu/**

- **State-supported** comprehensive, founded 1927
- **Urban** 46-acre campus with easy access to New York City
- **Coed** 6,285 undergraduate students, 71% full-time, 62% women, 38% men
- **Moderately difficult** entrance level, 48% of applicants were admitted

Undergraduates 4,471 full-time, 1,814 part-time. Students come from 16 states and territories, 15 other countries, 1% are from out of state, 19% African American, 7% Asian American or Pacific Islander, 35% Hispanic American, 0.1% Native American, 1% international, 12% transferred in, 4% live on campus. *Retention:* 73% of 2006 full-time freshmen returned.

Freshmen *Admission:* 3,529 applied, 1,687 admitted, 804 enrolled. *Test scores:* SAT critical reading scores over 500: 20%; SAT math scores over 500: 25%; SAT critical reading scores over 600: 3%; SAT math scores over 600: 3%.

Faculty *Total:* 674, 37% full-time. *Student/faculty ratio:* 13:1.

Majors Art; art teacher education; biology/biological sciences; business administration and management; chemistry; communication/speech communication and rhetoric; computer and information sciences; criminal justice/safety; economics; elementary education; English; geology/earth science; health science; history; kindergarten/preschool education; mathematics; music; music teacher education; nursing science; philosophy; physics; political science and government; psychology; sociology; Spanish; special education; urban studies/affairs.

Academics *Calendar:* semesters. *Degrees:* certificates, bachelor's, master's, post-master's, and postbachelor's certificates. *Special study options:* academic remediation for entering students, accelerated degree program, adult/continuing education programs, advanced placement credit, cooperative education, distance learning, double majors, English as a second language, honors programs, independent study, internships, off-campus study, part-time degree program, services for LD students, study abroad, summer session for credit.

Computers on Campus 1,400 computers/terminals are available on campus for general student use. Students can access the following: online (class) registration. Campuswide network is available.

Student Life *Housing options:* coed. Campus housing is university owned. *Activities and organizations:* drama/theater group, student-run newspaper, radio station, choral group, International Student Association, Black Freedom Society, Latin Power Association, national fraternities. *Campus security:* 24-hour emergency response devices and patrols, late-night transport/escort service. *Student services:* health clinic, personal/psychological counseling, women's center, legal services.

Athletics Member NCAA. All Division III. *Intercollegiate sports:* baseball M, basketball M/W, bowling W, cross-country running W, soccer M/W, softball W, track and field M/W, volleyball M/W. *Intramural sports:* basketball M/W, bowling W, soccer M/W, softball M/W, swimming and diving M/W, table tennis M/W, tennis M/W, volleyball M/W, weight lifting M/W.

Standardized Tests *Required:* SAT or ACT (for admission).

Costs (2007–08) *Tuition:* state resident $5936 full-time, $198 per credit part-time; nonresident $12,540 full-time, $418 per credit part-time. Full-time tuition and fees vary according to course load. Part-time tuition and fees vary according to course load. *Required fees:* $2218 full-time, $72 per credit part-time. *Room and board:* $8558; room only: $5426. *Payment plan:* deferred payment. *Waivers:* senior citizens.

Financial Aid Of all full-time matriculated undergraduates who enrolled in 2006, 3,539 applied for aid, 3,301 were judged to have need, 291 had their need fully met. In 2006, 51 non-need-based awards were made. *Average percent of need met:* 63%. *Average financial aid package:* $7942. *Average need-based loan:* $3904. *Average need-based gift aid:* $6380. *Average non-need-based aid:* $4502. *Average indebtedness upon graduation:* $28,833.

Applying *Options:* electronic application, deferred entrance. *Application fee:* $35. *Required:* essay or personal statement, high school transcript, minimum 2.0 GPA. *Required for some:* interview. *Recommended:* 1 letter of recommendation. *Application deadlines:* 4/1 (freshmen), rolling (transfers). *Notification:* continuous (freshmen).

Freshman Application Contact Ms. Carmen Panlilio, New Jersey City University, 2039 Kennedy Boulevard, Jersey City, NJ 07305. *Phone:* 201-200-3234. *Toll-free phone:* 888-441-NJCU. *E-mail:* admissions@nicu.edu.

See page 1578 for the College Close-Up.

NEW JERSEY INSTITUTE OF TECHNOLOGY

Newark, New Jersey **www.njit.edu/**

- **State-supported** university, founded 1881
- **Urban** 45-acre campus with easy access to New York City
- **Endowment** $73.0 million
- **Coed** 5,428 undergraduate students, 78% full-time, 20% women, 80% men
- **Moderately difficult** entrance level, 64% of applicants were admitted

Recognized by *U.S News & World Report* as a top-tier national research university offering bachelor's, master's, and doctoral degrees, New Jersey Institute of Technology (NJIT) has been a leader in the field of engineering education for almost ninety years. NJIT's Newark College of Engineering is one of the largest professional engineering schools in the U.S., and among its more than 40,000 alumni are pioneers and leaders in such fields as aerospace, telecommunications, plastics, electronics, and environmental engineering.

Undergraduates 4,213 full-time, 1,215 part-time. Students come from 14 states and territories, 98 other countries, 8% are from out of state, 10% African American, 20% Asian American or Pacific Islander, 17% Hispanic American, 0.6% Native American, 5% international, 8% transferred in, 28% live on campus. *Retention:* 80% of 2006 full-time freshmen returned.

Freshmen *Admission:* 3,027 applied, 1,941 admitted, 783 enrolled. *Test scores:* SAT critical reading scores over 500: 68%; SAT math scores over 500: 93%; SAT writing scores over 500: 64%; SAT critical reading scores over 600: 23%; SAT math scores over 600: 52%; SAT writing scores over 600: 19%; SAT critical reading scores over 700: 3%; SAT math scores over 700: 11%; SAT writing scores over 700: 3%.

Faculty *Total:* 696, 56% full-time. *Student/faculty ratio:* 12:1.

Majors Actuarial science; applied mathematics; architecture; biology/biological sciences; biomedical/medical engineering; business administration and management; chemical engineering; chemistry; civil engineering; computer and information sciences; computer and information sciences and support services related; computer engineering; electrical, electronics and communications engineering; engineering science; engineering technologies related; engineering technology; environmental/environmental health engineering; geological/geophysical engineering; history; industrial engineering; information science/studies; manufacturing engineering; mechanical engineering; natural resources/conservation; nursing (registered nurse training); nursing science; physics related; science, technology and society; technical and business writing.

Academics *Calendar:* semesters. *Degrees:* bachelor's, master's, doctoral, and postbachelor's certificates. *Special study options:* academic remediation for entering students, accelerated degree program, adult/continuing education programs, advanced placement credit, cooperative education, distance learning, double majors, English as a second language, freshman honors college, honors programs, independent study, internships, off-campus study, part-time degree program, services for LD students, study abroad, summer session for credit. *ROTC:* Air Force (b). *Unusual degree programs:* 3-2 business administration; engineering.

Computers on Campus 1,938 computers/terminals are available on campus for general student use. Students can access the following: online (class) registration. Campuswide network is available. Wireless service is available via entire campus.

Student Life *Housing options:* coed. Campus housing is university owned. *Activities and organizations:* drama/theater group, student-run newspaper, radio station, Student Senate, Student Activities Council, Microcomputer Users Group, Chess Club, national fraternities, national sororities. *Campus security:* 24-hour emergency response devices and patrols, late-night transport/escort service, controlled dormitory access, bicycle patrols. *Student services:* health clinic, personal/psychological counseling, women's center.

Athletics Member NCAA. All Division I except track and field (Division II). *Intercollegiate sports:* baseball M, basketball M/W, cross-country running M/W, fencing M/W, golf M, soccer M/W, softball W, swimming and diving W, tennis M/W, track and field W, volleyball M (c)/W (c). *Intramural sports:* archery M/W, badminton M/W, basketball M/W, bowling M/W, football M, golf M/W, racquetball M/W, soccer M/W, softball M/W, swimming and diving M/W, tennis M/W, track and field M/W, volleyball M/W, water polo M/W, weight lifting M/W.

Standardized Tests *Required:* SAT or ACT (for admission). *Required for some:* SAT Subject Tests (for admission).

Costs (2007–08) *Tuition:* state resident $9700 full-time, $370 per credit part-time; nonresident $18,432 full-time, $788 per credit part-time. Full-time tuition and fees vary according to course load and degree level. Part-time tuition and fees vary according to course load and degree level. *Required fees:* $1650 full-time, $80 per credit part-time, $102 per term part-time. *Room and board:*

$9108; room only: $6330. Room and board charges vary according to board plan and housing facility. *Payment plan:* installment. *Waivers:* employees or children of employees.

Financial Aid Of all full-time matriculated undergraduates who enrolled in 2006, 2,615 applied for aid, 2,306 were judged to have need, 229 had their need fully met. In 2006, 453 non-need-based awards were made. *Average percent of need met:* 81%. *Average financial aid package:* $10,089. *Average need-based loan:* $2802. *Average need-based gift aid:* $7153. *Average non-need-based aid:* $6654. *Average indebtedness upon graduation:* $13,000. *Financial aid deadline:* 5/15.

Applying *Options:* electronic application, deferred entrance. *Application fee:* $50. *Required:* high school transcript. *Required for some:* essay or personal statement, interview. *Recommended:* 1 letter of recommendation. *Application deadlines:* 4/1 (freshmen), 6/1 (transfers). *Notification:* continuous (freshmen), continuous (transfers).

Freshman Application Contact Ms. Kathy Kelly, Director of Admissions, New Jersey Institute of Technology, University Heights, Newark, NJ 07102-1982. *Phone:* 973-596-3300. *Toll-free phone:* 800-925-NJIT. *Fax:* 973-596-3461. *E-mail:* admissions@njit.edu.

PRINCETON UNIVERSITY

Princeton, New Jersey **www.princeton.edu/**

- **Independent** university, founded 1746
- **Suburban** 600-acre campus with easy access to New York City and Philadelphia
- **Endowment** $12.8 billion
- **Coed** 4,918 undergraduate students, 99% full-time, 47% women, 53% men
- **Most difficult** entrance level, 10% of applicants were admitted

Undergraduates 4,845 full-time, 73 part-time. Students come from 54 states and territories, 95 other countries, 84% are from out of state, 9% African American, 14% Asian American or Pacific Islander, 8% Hispanic American, 0.7% Native American, 9% international, 98% live on campus. *Retention:* 98% of 2006 full-time freshmen returned.

Freshmen *Admission:* 18,942 applied, 1,838 admitted, 1,242 enrolled. *Average high school GPA:* 3.87. *Test scores:* SAT critical reading scores over 500: 100%; SAT math scores over 500: 97%; ACT scores over 18: 100%; SAT critical reading scores over 600: 97%; SAT math scores over 600: 95%; ACT scores over 24: 99%; SAT critical reading scores over 700: 73%; SAT math scores over 700: 72%; ACT scores over 30: 82%.

Faculty *Total:* 1,015, 81% full-time, 87% with terminal degrees. *Student/faculty ratio:* 8:1.

Majors Anthropology; architecture; art history, criticism and conservation; Asian studies (East); astrophysics; chemical engineering; chemistry; civil engineering; classics and languages, literatures and linguistics; comparative literature; computer engineering; ecology; economics; electrical, electronics and communications engineering; English; French; geological and earth sciences/geosciences related; German; history; mathematics; mechanical engineering; molecular biology; multi-/interdisciplinary studies related; music; Near and Middle Eastern studies; operations research; philosophy; physics; political science and government; psychology; public policy analysis; religious studies; Slavic languages; sociology; Spanish.

Academics *Calendar:* semesters. *Degrees:* bachelor's, master's, and doctoral. *Special study options:* adult/continuing education programs, advanced placement credit, independent study, off-campus study, services for LD students, student-designed majors, study abroad. *ROTC:* Army (b), Air Force (c).

Computers on Campus 500 computers/terminals are available on campus for general student use. Students can access the following: campus intranet, computer help desk, free student e-mail accounts, online (class) grades, online (class) registration, online (class) schedules, academic applications and courseware. Campuswide network is available. 100% of college-owned or -operated housing units are wired for high-speed Internet access.

Student Life *Housing:* on-campus residence required through sophomore year. *Options:* coed, men-only, women-only, disabled students. Campus housing is university owned. Freshman campus housing is guaranteed. *Activities and organizations:* drama/theater group, student-run newspaper, radio station, choral group, marching band. *Campus security:* 24-hour emergency response devices and patrols, student patrols, late-night transport/escort service, controlled dormitory access. *Student services:* health clinic, personal/psychological counseling, women's center, legal services.

Athletics Member NCAA. All Division I except football (Division I-AA). *Intercollegiate sports:* baseball M, basketball M/W, cheerleading M/W, crew M/W, cross-country running M/W, fencing M/W, field hockey W, golf M/W, ice hockey M/W, lacrosse M/W, soccer M/W, softball W, squash M/W, swimming and diving M/W, tennis M/W, track and field M/W, volleyball M/W, water polo M/W, wrestling M. *Intramural sports:* badminton M (c)/W (c), baseball M (c), basketball M (c)/W (c), equestrian sports M (c)/W (c), field hockey W (c), ice hockey M (c)/W (c), lacrosse M (c)/W (c), riflery M (c)/W (c), rugby M (c)/W (c), sailing M (c)/W (c), skiing (cross-country) M (c)/W (c), softball M (c)/W (c), squash M (c)/W (c), table tennis M (c)/W (c), ultimate Frisbee M (c)/W (c), volleyball M (c)/W (c).

Standardized Tests *Required:* SAT or ACT (for admission), SAT Subject Tests (for admission).

Costs (2008–09) *Comprehensive fee:* $45,695 includes full-time tuition ($34,290) and room and board ($11,405). *College room only:* $6205.

Financial Aid Of all full-time matriculated undergraduates who enrolled in 2006, 2,734 applied for aid, 2,490 were judged to have need, 2,490 had their need fully met. 792 Federal Work-Study jobs (averaging $1297). 1,004 state and other part-time jobs (averaging $1278). *Average percent of need met:* 100%. *Average financial aid package:* $30,242. *Average need-based gift aid:* $28,673. *Average indebtedness upon graduation:* $5592.

Applying *Options:* electronic application, early admission, deferred entrance. *Application fee:* $65. *Required:* essay or personal statement, high school transcript, 3 letters of recommendation. *Recommended:* interview. *Application deadline:* 1/1 (freshmen). *Notification:* 4/1 (freshmen).

Freshman Application Contact Ms. Janet Rapelye, Dean of Admission, Princeton University, PO Box 430, Princeton, NJ 08544. *Phone:* 609-258-3060. *Fax:* 609-258-6743. *E-mail:* uaoffice@princeton.edu.

See page 1580 for the College Close-Up.

RABBI JACOB JOSEPH SCHOOL

Edison, New Jersey

RABBINICAL COLLEGE OF AMERICA

Morristown, New Jersey

- **Independent Jewish** 4-year, founded 1956
- **Small-town** 81-acre campus with easy access to New York City
- **Men only** 259 undergraduate students
- **Minimally difficult** entrance level, 100% of applicants were admitted

Undergraduates Students come from 24 states and territories, 10 other countries.

Freshmen *Admission:* 60 applied, 60 admitted.

Faculty *Total:* 16, 100% full-time, 100% with terminal degrees. *Student/faculty ratio:* 12:1.

Majors Religious studies.

Academics *Calendar:* semesters. *Degree:* bachelor's. *Special study options:* academic remediation for entering students, accelerated degree program, internships, off-campus study, study abroad, summer session for credit.

Student Life *Housing:* on-campus residence required through senior year. *Options:* men-only. Campus housing is university owned. *Student services:* health clinic, personal/psychological counseling.

Athletics *Intercollegiate sports:* ultimate Frisbee M, volleyball M. *Intramural sports:* ultimate Frisbee M, volleyball M.

Costs (2007–08) *Comprehensive fee:* $16,500 includes full-time tuition ($9700) and room and board ($6800).

Applying *Application fee:* $150. *Required:* interview. *Required for some:* letters of recommendation. *Application deadline:* rolling (freshmen).

Director of Admissions Sharon Miller, Registrar, Rabbinical College of America, Box 1996, Morristown, NJ 07962. *Phone:* 973-267-9404. *E-mail:* rca079@aol.com.

RAMAPO COLLEGE OF NEW JERSEY

Mahwah, New Jersey **www.ramapo.edu/**

- **State-supported** comprehensive, founded 1969, part of New Jersey State College System
- **Suburban** 300-acre campus with easy access to New York City
- **Endowment** $7.5 million
- **Coed** 5,393 undergraduate students, 89% full-time, 48% women, 52% men
- **Moderately difficult** entrance level, 49% of applicants were admitted

As "the College of Choice for a Global Education," Ramapo College provides students with the opportunity to encounter the world beyond the campus through study-abroad and cooperative education programs and teleconferences. Undergraduate experiences through these programs have taken students to faraway countries such as China, Costa Rica, Czech Republic, England, Germany, Italy, and Kenya and to corporate offices in the U.S. and abroad.

Undergraduates 4,795 full-time, 598 part-time. Students come from 17 states and territories, 52 other countries, 6% are from out of state, 6% African American, 4% Asian American or Pacific Islander, 9% Hispanic American, 0.3% Native American, 3% international, 11% transferred in, 62% live on campus. *Retention:* 90% of 2006 full-time freshmen returned.

Freshmen *Admission:* 4,983 applied, 2,421 admitted, 902 enrolled. *Average high school GPA:* 3.5. *Test scores:* SAT critical reading scores over 500: 90%; SAT math scores over 500: 95%; SAT writing scores over 500: 90%; SAT critical reading scores over 600: 35%; SAT math scores over 600: 42%; SAT writing scores over 600: 35%; SAT critical reading scores over 700: 5%; SAT math scores over 700: 6%; SAT writing scores over 700: 5%.

Faculty *Total:* 434, 45% full-time. *Student/faculty ratio:* 18:1.

Majors Accounting; allied health and medical assisting services related; American studies; area studies related; biochemistry; bioinformatics; biological and physical sciences; biology/biological sciences; business administration and management; chemistry; clinical laboratory science/medical technology; communication/speech communication and rhetoric; comparative literature; computer and information sciences; dramatic/theater arts; economics; environmental science; environmental studies; history; humanities; information science/studies; interdisciplinary studies; intermedia/multimedia; international business/trade/commerce; legal professions and studies related; mathematics; medical basic sciences related; multi-/interdisciplinary studies related; music; nursing (registered nurse training); physics; political science and government; psychology; social sciences; social work; sociology; Spanish; visual and performing arts.

Academics *Calendar:* semesters. *Degrees:* certificates, bachelor's, and master's. *Special study options:* academic remediation for entering students, accelerated degree program, adult/continuing education programs, advanced placement credit, cooperative education, distance learning, double majors, English as a second language, external degree program, freshman honors college, honors programs, independent study, internships, off-campus study, part-time degree program, services for LD students, student-designed majors, study abroad, summer session for credit. *ROTC:* Air Force (c). *Unusual degree programs:* 3-2 nursing with The University of Medicine and Dentistry of New Jersey (for Dentistry and for Osteopathic Medicine); biology, chemistry with Rutgers, The State University of New Jersey; NY University College of Dentistry; SUNY State College of Optometry.

Computers on Campus 977 computers/terminals and 1,500 ports are available on campus for general student use. Students can access the following: campus intranet, computer help desk, free student e-mail accounts, online (class) grades, online (class) registration, online (class) schedules. Campuswide network is available. 100% of college-owned or -operated housing units are wired for high-speed Internet access. Wireless service is available via classrooms, computer centers, computer labs, learning centers, libraries, student centers.

Student Life *Housing options:* coed, disabled students. Campus housing is university owned. Freshman campus housing is guaranteed. *Activities and organizations:* drama/theater group, student-run newspaper, radio and television station, choral group, Student Government Association, Ramapo Pride, Sci-Fi Club, Organization for African Unity, Future Educators of America, national fraternities, national sororities. *Campus security:* 24-hour emergency response devices and patrols, late-night transport/escort service, controlled dormitory access, surveillance cameras, patrols by trained security personnel. *Student services:* health clinic, personal/psychological counseling, women's center.

Athletics Member NCAA. All Division III. *Intercollegiate sports:* baseball M, basketball M/W, cheerleading W, cross-country running M/W, field hockey W, lacrosse W, soccer M/W, softball W, swimming and diving M/W, tennis M/W, track and field M/W, volleyball M/W. *Intramural sports:* basketball M/W, bowling M/W, football M, soccer M/W, softball M/W, swimming and diving M/W, tennis M/W, ultimate Frisbee M/W, volleyball M/W.

Standardized Tests *Required:* SAT (for admission). *Required for some:* ACT (for admission).

Costs (2007–08) *Tuition:* state resident $6904 full-time, $216 per credit part-time; nonresident $12,475 full-time, $390 per credit part-time. *Required fees:* $3061 full-time, $96 per credit part-time. *Room and board:* $10,310; room only: $7480. Room and board charges vary according to board plan and housing facility. *Payment plan:* installment. *Waivers:* senior citizens and employees or children of employees.

Financial Aid Of all full-time matriculated undergraduates who enrolled in 2006, 2,828 applied for aid, 2,136 were judged to have need, 113 had their need fully met. 137 Federal Work-Study jobs (averaging $1846). 655 state and other part-time jobs (averaging $1870). In 2006, 530 non-need-based awards were made. *Average percent of need met:* 72%. *Average financial aid package:* $9965. *Average need-based loan:* $3746. *Average need-based gift aid:* $7349. *Average non-need-based aid:* $9295. *Average indebtedness upon graduation:* $15,937.

Applying *Options:* electronic application, early admission, early action, deferred entrance. *Application fee:* $55. *Required:* essay or personal statement, high school transcript. *Recommended:* minimum 3.0 GPA, letters of recommendation. *Application deadlines:* 3/1 (freshmen), 5/1 (transfers). *Notification:* continuous until 3/1 (freshmen), continuous until 7/1 (transfers).

Freshman Application Contact Mr. Michael DiBartolomeo, Associate Director for Freshmen Admissions, Ramapo College of New Jersey, Office of Admissions, 505 Ramapo Valley Road, Mahwah, NJ 07430-1680. *Phone:* 201-684-7300. *Toll-free phone:* 800-9RAMAPO. *Fax:* 201-684-7964. *E-mail:* admissions@ramapo.edu.

See page 1582 for the College Close-Up.

THE RICHARD STOCKTON COLLEGE OF NEW JERSEY

Pomona, New Jersey **www.stockton.edu/**

- **State-supported** comprehensive, founded 1969, part of New Jersey State College System
- **Suburban** 1600-acre campus with easy access to Philadelphia
- **Endowment** $3.0 million
- **Coed** 6,766 undergraduate students, 87% full-time, 59% women, 41% men
- **Very difficult** entrance level, 54% of applicants were admitted

The Richard Stockton College is a selective, midsized, highly ranked public liberal arts college in southern New Jersey, with programs in business, liberal arts and humanities, professional studies, and social, behavioral, and natural sciences. Students enjoy small class sizes, modern facilities, exceptional educational experiences, an environmentally friendly campus, a great location, and reasonable tuition.

Undergraduates 5,873 full-time, 893 part-time. Students come from 27 states and territories, 10 other countries, 2% are from out of state, 8% African American, 5% Asian American or Pacific Islander, 6% Hispanic American, 0.4% Native American, 0.4% international, 16% transferred in, 38% live on campus. *Retention:* 83% of 2006 full-time freshmen returned.

Freshmen *Admission:* 3,962 applied, 2,158 admitted, 799 enrolled. *Test scores:* SAT critical reading scores over 500: 66%; SAT math scores over 500: 71%; SAT writing scores over 500: 64%; ACT scores over 18: 69%; SAT critical reading scores over 600: 16%; SAT math scores over 600: 20%; SAT writing scores over 600: 13%; ACT scores over 24: 15%; SAT critical reading scores over 700: 2%; SAT math scores over 700: 1%; SAT writing scores over 700: 1%; ACT scores over 30: 2%.

Faculty *Total:* 457, 57% full-time, 50% with terminal degrees. *Student/faculty ratio:* 18:1.

Majors Audiology and speech-language pathology; biochemistry; biology/biological sciences; business administration and management; chemistry; communication/speech communication and rhetoric; computer and information sciences; computer science; criminology; economics; education (multiple levels); English; environmental studies; foreign languages and literatures; geology/earth science; history; hospitality administration; liberal arts and sciences/liberal studies; marine biology and biological oceanography; mathematics; multi-/interdisciplinary studies related; nursing (registered nurse training); philosophy; physics; political science and government; psychology; public health; social work; sociology; visual and performing arts.

Academics *Calendar:* semesters. *Degrees:* bachelor's, master's, and post-bachelor's certificates. *Special study options:* academic remediation for entering students, adult/continuing education programs, advanced placement credit, distance learning, double majors, freshman honors college, honors programs, independent study, internships, off-campus study, part-time degree program, services for LD students, student-designed majors, study abroad, summer session for credit. *Unusual degree programs:* 3-2 engineering with New Jersey Institute of Technology; Rutgers, The State University of New Jersey.

Computers on Campus 865 computers/terminals are available on campus for general student use. Students can access the following: campus intranet, computer help desk, free student e-mail accounts, online (class) grades, online (class) registration, online (class) schedules. Campuswide network is available. 100% of college-owned or -operated housing units are wired for high-speed Internet access. Wireless service is available via classrooms, computer centers, computer labs, learning centers, libraries, student centers.

Student Life *Housing options:* coed. Campus housing is university owned. Freshman campus housing is guaranteed. *Activities and organizations:* drama/

theater group, student-run newspaper, radio and television station, choral group, Stockton Action Volunteers for the Environment, Stockton Entertainment Team, Los Latinos Unidos, Unified Black Student Society, Stockton Residents Association, national fraternities, national sororities. *Campus security:* 24-hour emergency response devices and patrols, late-night transport/escort service, controlled dormitory access, on-campus sworn/commissioned police force. *Student services:* health clinic, personal/psychological counseling, women's center.

Athletics Member NCAA. All Division III. *Intercollegiate sports:* baseball M, basketball M/W, cheerleading M/W, crew W, cross-country running M/W, field hockey W, lacrosse M, soccer M/W, softball W, tennis W, track and field M/W, volleyball W. *Intramural sports:* basketball M/W, bowling M (c)/W (c), crew M (c), fencing M (c)/W (c), football M/W, golf M (c)/W (c), skiing (downhill) M (c)/W (c), softball M/W, swimming and diving M/W, tennis M/W, volleyball M/W.

Standardized Tests *Required:* SAT or ACT (for admission).

Costs (2007–08) *Tuition:* state resident $6353 full-time, $199 per credit part-time; nonresident $11,253 full-time, $352 per credit part-time. *Required fees:* $3344 full-time, $105 per credit part-time. *Room and board:* $9077; room only: $6388. Room and board charges vary according to board plan and housing facility. *Payment plans:* installment, deferred payment. *Waivers:* senior citizens and employees or children of employees.

Financial Aid Of all full-time matriculated undergraduates who enrolled in 2007, 4,277 applied for aid, 3,438 were judged to have need, 1,666 had their need fully met. 212 Federal Work-Study jobs (averaging $1735). 610 state and other part-time jobs (averaging $1297). In 2007, 315 non-need-based awards were made. *Average percent of need met:* 74%. *Average financial aid package:* $12,714. *Average need-based loan:* $4510. *Average need-based gift aid:* $6957. *Average non-need-based aid:* $3212.

Applying *Options:* electronic application, early admission, early action. *Application fee:* $50. *Required:* high school transcript, minimum 2.0 GPA. *Recommended:* minimum 3.0 GPA, letters of recommendation. *Application deadlines:* 5/1 (freshmen), 6/1 (transfers). *Notification:* continuous until 5/15 (freshmen), continuous until 6/15 (transfers).

Freshman Application Contact Mr. John Iacovelli, Dean of Admissions, The Richard Stockton College of New Jersey, PO Box 195, Pomona, NJ 08240-0195. *Phone:* 609-652-4261. *Fax:* 609-626-5541. *E-mail:* admissions@stockton.edu.

See page 1584 for the College Close-Up.

RIDER UNIVERSITY

Lawrenceville, New Jersey **www.rider.edu/**

- **Independent** comprehensive, founded 1865
- **Suburban** 280-acre campus with easy access to New York City and Philadelphia
- **Endowment** $61.6 million
- **Coed** 4,733 undergraduate students, 82% full-time, 60% women, 40% men
- **Moderately difficult** entrance level, 75% of applicants were admitted

Undergraduates 3,896 full-time, 837 part-time. Students come from 35 states and territories, 50 other countries, 23% are from out of state, 9% African American, 3% Asian American or Pacific Islander, 5% Hispanic American, 0.2% Native American, 3% international, 4% transferred in, 57% live on campus. *Retention:* 83% of 2006 full-time freshmen returned.

Freshmen *Admission:* 6,213 applied, 4,672 admitted, 993 enrolled. *Average high school GPA:* 3.24. *Test scores:* SAT critical reading scores over 500: 60%; SAT math scores over 500: 68%; SAT writing scores over 500: 64%; ACT scores over 18: 94%; SAT critical reading scores over 600: 17%; SAT math scores over 600: 20%; SAT writing scores over 600: 17%; ACT scores over 24: 30%; SAT critical reading scores over 700: 2%; SAT math scores over 700: 1%; SAT writing scores over 700: 2%; ACT scores over 30: 2%.

Faculty *Total:* 545, 45% full-time, 67% with terminal degrees. *Student/faculty ratio:* 14:1.

Majors Accounting; actuarial science; advertising; American studies; bilingual and multilingual education; biochemistry; biology/biological sciences; biopsychology; business administration and management; business/managerial economics; business operations support and secretarial services related; business teacher education; chemistry; computer science; economics; elementary education; English; entrepreneurship; environmental studies; finance; fine/studio arts; French; geology/earth science; German; history; human resources management; information science/studies; international business/trade/commerce; international relations and affairs; journalism; liberal arts and sciences/liberal studies; management science; marketing/marketing management; mathematics; music; music teacher education; music theory and composition; oceanography (chemical and physical); organizational behavior; philosophy; physics; piano and organ; political science and government; psychology; public relations/image management; religious/sacred music; Russian; science teacher education; secondary education; sociology; Spanish; speech and rhetoric; voice and opera.

Academics *Calendar:* semesters. *Degrees:* certificates, associate, bachelor's, master's, and post-master's certificates. *Special study options:* academic remediation for entering students, adult/continuing education programs, advanced placement credit, cooperative education, double majors, English as a second language, honors programs, independent study, internships, part-time degree program, services for LD students, study abroad, summer session for credit. *ROTC:* Army (c).

Computers on Campus 300 computers/terminals are available on campus for general student use. Students can access the following: computer help desk, free student e-mail accounts, online (class) grades, online (class) registration, online (class) schedules. Campuswide network is available. 100% of college-owned or -operated housing units are wired for high-speed Internet access. Wireless service is available via entire campus.

Student Life *Housing options:* coed, women-only. Campus housing is university owned. Freshman campus housing is guaranteed. *Activities and organizations:* drama/theater group, student-run newspaper, radio and television station, choral group, Student Government Association, Student Entertainment Council, Association of Commuter Students, Black Student Union, Residence Hall Association, national fraternities, national sororities. *Campus security:* 24-hour emergency response devices and patrols, student patrols, late-night transport/escort service, controlled dormitory access. *Student services:* health clinic, personal/psychological counseling.

Athletics Member NCAA. All Division I. *Intercollegiate sports:* baseball M (s), basketball M (s)/W (s), cheerleading M/W, cross-country running M (s)/W (s), field hockey W (s), golf M (s), soccer M (s)/W (s), softball W (s), swimming and diving M (s)/W (s), tennis M (s)/W (s), track and field M (s)/W (s), volleyball W (s), wrestling M (s). *Intramural sports:* basketball M/W, cheerleading M/W, equestrian sports W (c), golf M, ice hockey M (c), lacrosse M (c)/W, soccer M/W, softball M/W, track and field M/W, volleyball M/W, water polo M/W.

Standardized Tests *Required:* SAT or ACT (for admission).

Costs (2007–08) *Comprehensive fee:* $36,010 includes full-time tuition ($25,650), mandatory fees ($580), and room and board ($9780). Full-time tuition and fees vary according to course load and program. Part-time tuition: $465 per credit. Part-time tuition and fees vary according to course load and program. *Required fees:* $35 per course part-time. *College room only:* $5640. Room and board charges vary according to board plan, housing facility, and location. *Payment plan:* installment. *Waivers:* employees or children of employees.

Financial Aid Of all full-time matriculated undergraduates who enrolled in 2007, 2,865 applied for aid, 2,475 were judged to have need, 392 had their need fully met. 1,717 Federal Work-Study jobs (averaging $2093). In 2007, 779 non-need-based awards were made. *Average percent of need met:* 71%. *Average financial aid package:* $19,318. *Average need-based loan:* $4375. *Average need-based gift aid:* $12,883. *Average non-need-based aid:* $9218. *Average indebtedness upon graduation:* $32,132.

Applying *Options:* electronic application, early admission, early decision, early action, deferred entrance. *Application fee:* $50. *Required:* essay or personal statement, high school transcript, letters of recommendation. *Required for some:* interview. *Application deadlines:* rolling (freshmen), rolling (transfers), 12/15 (early action). *Early decision deadline:* 11/15. *Notification:* continuous (freshmen), continuous (transfers), 12/15 (early decision), 1/15 (early action).

Freshman Application Contact William Larrousse, Director of Admissions, Rider University, 2083 Lawrenceville Road, Lawrenceville, NJ 08648-3099. *Phone:* 609-896-5177. *Toll-free phone:* 800-257-9026. *Fax:* 609-895-6645. *E-mail:* wlarrousse@rider.edu.

See page 1586 for the College Close-Up.

ROWAN UNIVERSITY

Glassboro, New Jersey **www.rowan.edu/**

- **State-supported** comprehensive, founded 1923, part of New Jersey State College System
- **Suburban** 200-acre campus with easy access to Philadelphia
- **Endowment** $176.4 million
- **Coed** 8,912 undergraduate students, 86% full-time, 53% women, 47% men
- **Moderately difficult** entrance level, 52% of applicants were admitted

Rowan University is a selective, medium-sized public institution combining liberal education with professional preparation in business, communication, education, engineering, fine and performing arts, and liberal arts and sciences. A collaborative, learning-centered environment joins a diverse faculty,

staff, and student body with integrated teaching, research, scholarship, creative activity, and community service.

Undergraduates 7,675 full-time, 1,237 part-time. Students come from 22 states and territories, 12 other countries, 2% are from out of state, 8% African American, 3% Asian American or Pacific Islander, 7% Hispanic American, 0.4% Native American, 10% transferred in, 35% live on campus. *Retention:* 86% of 2006 full-time freshmen returned.

Freshmen *Admission:* 8,088 applied, 4,178 admitted, 1,381 enrolled. *Average high school GPA:* 3.4. *Test scores:* SAT critical reading scores over 500: 73%; SAT math scores over 500: 78%; SAT writing scores over 500: 70%; SAT critical reading scores over 600: 21%; SAT math scores over 600: 32%; SAT writing scores over 600: 18%; SAT critical reading scores over 700: 2%; SAT math scores over 700: 4%; SAT writing scores over 700: 1%.

Faculty *Total:* 912, 44% full-time, 35% with terminal degrees. *Student/faculty ratio:* 15:1.

Majors Accounting technology and bookkeeping; art; biochemistry; biology/biological sciences; business administration and management; chemical engineering; chemistry; civil engineering; communication/speech communication and rhetoric; computer and information sciences; criminal justice/police science; dramatic/theater arts; economics; education; education (specific levels and methods) related; electrical, electronics and communications engineering; elementary education; English; environmental studies; fine/studio arts; geography; history; kindergarten/preschool education; liberal arts and sciences/liberal studies; mathematics; mechanical engineering; music; music performance; music theory and composition; nursing (registered nurse training); physical education teaching and coaching; physical sciences; political science and government; psychology; sociology; Spanish; special education.

Academics *Calendar:* semesters. *Degrees:* bachelor's, master's, and doctoral. *Special study options:* academic remediation for entering students, adult/continuing education programs, advanced placement credit, double majors, English as a second language, freshman honors college, honors programs, independent study, internships, part-time degree program, services for LD students, study abroad, summer session for credit. *ROTC:* Army (c). *Unusual degree programs:* 3-2 optometry with Pennsylvania College of Optometry, podiatry with Temple University College of Podiatric Medicine, pharmacy with University of the Sciences in Philadelphia.

Computers on Campus 1,200 computers/terminals are available on campus for general student use. Students can access the following: computer help desk, free student e-mail accounts, online (class) registration, online (class) schedules, online library. Campuswide network is available. Wireless service is available via classrooms, computer centers, computer labs, libraries, student centers.

Student Life *Housing:* on-campus residence required for freshman year. *Options:* coed, disabled students. Campus housing is university owned. Freshman campus housing is guaranteed. *Activities and organizations:* drama/theater group, student-run newspaper, radio and television station, choral group, marching band, Student Council for Exceptional Children, PRSSA, Health and Exercise Science Club, RTN, Elementary Education Club, national fraternities, national sororities. *Campus security:* 24-hour emergency response devices and patrols, late-night transport/escort service, controlled dormitory access. *Student services:* health clinic, personal/psychological counseling, women's center, legal services.

Athletics Member NCAA. All Division III. *Intercollegiate sports:* baseball M, basketball M/W, cross-country running M/W, field hockey W, football M, lacrosse W, soccer M (s)/W, softball W (s), swimming and diving M/W, tennis M/W, track and field M/W, volleyball W (s). *Intramural sports:* basketball M/W, bowling M/W, cheerleading W (c), field hockey W (c), golf M/W, ice hockey M (c), lacrosse M (c), racquetball M/W, rock climbing M (c), skiing (downhill) M (c)/W (c), soccer M/W, softball M/W, table tennis M/W, tennis M (c)/W (c), ultimate Frisbee W, volleyball M/W, wrestling M (c).

Standardized Tests *Required:* SAT or ACT (for admission).

Costs (2007–08) *Tuition:* state resident $7308 full-time, $282 per credit hour part-time; nonresident $14,616 full-time, $564 per credit hour part-time. Full-time tuition and fees vary according to degree level. Part-time tuition and fees vary according to degree level. *Required fees:* $2760 full-time, $119 per credit hour part-time. *Room and board:* $9242; room only: $5862. Room and board charges vary according to board plan and housing facility. *Payment plan:* deferred payment. *Waivers:* employees or children of employees.

Financial Aid Of all full-time matriculated undergraduates who enrolled in 2006, 5,583 applied for aid, 3,749 were judged to have need, 1,013 had their need fully met. 750 Federal Work-Study jobs (averaging $1270). 597 state and other part-time jobs (averaging $3382). In 2006, 479 non-need-based awards were made. *Average percent of need met:* 86%. *Average financial aid package:* $7183. *Average need-based loan:* $3949. *Average need-based gift aid:* $6869. *Average non-need-based aid:* $4179. *Average indebtedness upon graduation:* $19,643.

Applying *Options:* deferred entrance. *Application fee:* $50. *Required:* high school transcript. *Required for some:* interview. *Recommended:* minimum 3.0 GPA, letters of recommendation, interview. *Application deadlines:* 3/1 (freshmen), 3/1 (transfers). *Notification:* continuous (freshmen), continuous (transfers).

Freshman Application Contact Mr. Albert Betts, Director of Admissions, Rowan University, 201 Mullica Hill Road, Glassboro, NJ 08028. *Phone:* 856-256-4200. *Toll-free phone:* 800-447-1165. *Fax:* 856-256-4430. *E-mail:* admissions@rowan.edu.

See page 1588 for the College Close-Up.

RUTGERS, THE STATE UNIVERSITY OF NEW JERSEY, CAMDEN

Camden, New Jersey **camden-www.rutgers.edu/**

- **State-supported** university, founded 1927, part of Rutgers, The State University of New Jersey
- **Endowment** $496.3 million
- **Coed** 3,690 undergraduate students, 79% full-time, 56% women, 44% men
- **Moderately difficult** entrance level, 51% of applicants were admitted

Rutgers, The State University of New Jersey, Camden (Rutgers-Camden), is a vibrant intellectual community located on a tree-lined, 40-acre campus in the heart of the bustling metropolitan Philadelphia region. The closest university to the Liberty Bell, Rutgers-Camden offers thirty-five undergraduate majors, the Honors College, exceptional internship and clinical programs, and much more. As part of the internationally respected Rutgers system, Rutgers-Camden students enjoy world-class faculty members, libraries, and technology, all in an intimate campus setting.

Undergraduates 2,909 full-time, 781 part-time. 2% are from out of state, 17% African American, 8% Asian American or Pacific Islander, 7% Hispanic American, 0.3% Native American, 0.3% international, 11% transferred in, 13% live on campus.

Freshmen *Admission:* 7,788 applied, 3,989 admitted, 380 enrolled. *Test scores:* SAT critical reading scores over 500: 73%; SAT math scores over 500: 80%; SAT critical reading scores over 600: 24%; SAT math scores over 600: 31%; SAT critical reading scores over 700: 4%; SAT math scores over 700: 5%.

Faculty *Total:* 408, 56% full-time, 99% with terminal degrees. *Student/faculty ratio:* 11:1.

Majors Accounting; African-American/Black studies; art; biology/biological sciences; biomedical technology; business administration and management; chemistry; clinical laboratory science/medical technology; computer and information sciences; criminal justice/safety; dramatic/theater arts; economics; engineering; English; finance; French; German; history; hospitality administration; liberal arts and sciences/liberal studies; marketing/marketing management; mathematics; multi-/interdisciplinary studies related; music; nursing (registered nurse training); philosophy; physics; political science and government; psychology; social work; sociology; Spanish; urban studies/affairs.

Academics *Calendar:* semesters. *Degrees:* bachelor's, master's, and first professional. *Special study options:* academic remediation for entering students, accelerated degree program, advanced placement credit, cooperative education, distance learning, double majors, English as a second language, freshman honors college, honors programs, independent study, internships, part-time degree program, services for LD students, student-designed majors, study abroad, summer session for credit. *ROTC:* Army (c), Air Force (c).

Computers on Campus 184 computers/terminals are available on campus for general student use. Students can access the following: online grade reports. Campuswide network is available.

Student Life *Housing options:* coed, disabled students. *Activities and organizations:* drama/theater group, student-run radio station.

Standardized Tests *Required:* SAT or ACT (for admission).

Costs (2007–08) *Tuition:* state resident $8541 full-time, $275 per credit hour part-time; nonresident $17,709 full-time, $574 per credit hour part-time. Part-time tuition and fees vary according to course level. *Required fees:* $1991 full-time, $281 per term part-time. *Room and board:* $9024; room only: $6424. Room and board charges vary according to board plan and housing facility. *Payment plan:* installment. *Waivers:* employees or children of employees.

Financial Aid Of all full-time matriculated undergraduates who enrolled in 2006, 1,826 were judged to have need, 730 had their need fully met. In 2006, 180 non-need-based awards were made. *Average percent of need met:* 72%. *Average financial aid package:* $10,706. *Average need-based loan:* $1388. *Average need-based gift aid:* $7670. *Average non-need-based aid:* $4725. *Average indebtedness upon graduation:* $19,439.

Applying *Options:* electronic application. *Application fee:* $60. *Required:* high school transcript. *Application deadline:* rolling (freshmen). *Notification:* 2/28 (freshmen), 5/15 (transfers).

Director of Admissions Ms. Diane Williams Harris, Associate Director of University Undergraduate Admissions, Rutgers, The State University of New Jersey, Camden, 406 Penn Street, Camden, NJ 08102. *Phone:* 732-932-4636.

See page 1590 for the College Close-Up.

RUTGERS, THE STATE UNIVERSITY OF NEW JERSEY, NEWARK

Newark, New Jersey **www.newark.rutgers.edu/**

- **State-supported** university, founded 1892, part of Rutgers, The State University of New Jersey
- **Urban** 38-acre campus
- **Endowment** $497.9 million
- **Coed** 6,685 undergraduate students, 78% full-time, 55% women, 45% men
- **Moderately difficult** entrance level, 49% of applicants were admitted

Undergraduates 5,212 full-time, 1,473 part-time. Students come from 25 states and territories, 65 other countries, 3% are from out of state, 20% African American, 24% Asian American or Pacific Islander, 19% Hispanic American, 0.2% Native American, 2% international, 9% transferred in, 25% live on campus.

Freshmen *Admission:* 13,085 applied, 6,442 admitted, 989 enrolled. *Test scores:* SAT critical reading scores over 500: 73%; SAT math scores over 500: 79%; SAT critical reading scores over 600: 24%; SAT math scores over 600: 28%; SAT critical reading scores over 700: 4%; SAT math scores over 700: 5%.

Faculty *Total:* 625, 65% full-time, 99% with terminal degrees. *Student/faculty ratio:* 12:1.

Majors Accounting; African-American/Black studies; allied health diagnostic, intervention, and treatment professions related; American studies; anthropology; applied mathematics; art; biological and biomedical sciences related; biology/biological sciences; botany/plant biology; business administration and management; chemistry; classics and classical languages related; classics and languages, literatures and linguistics; clinical laboratory science/medical technology; computer and information sciences; criminal justice/safety; cultural studies; dramatic/theater arts; economics; engineering; English; environmental studies; finance; fine arts related; French; geological/geophysical engineering; geology/earth science; German; Hispanic-American, Puerto Rican, and Mexican-American/Chicano studies; history; information science/studies; Italian; journalism; marketing/marketing management; mathematics; multi-/interdisciplinary studies related; music; nursing (registered nurse training); philosophy; physics; physics related; political science and government; psychology; science, technology and society; Slavic, Baltic, and Albanian languages related; social work; sociology; Spanish; women's studies; zoology/animal biology.

Academics *Calendar:* semesters. *Degrees:* bachelor's, master's, doctoral, and first professional. *Special study options:* academic remediation for entering students, accelerated degree program, adult/continuing education programs, advanced placement credit, cooperative education, distance learning, double majors, English as a second language, freshman honors college, honors programs, independent study, off-campus study, part-time degree program, services for LD students, student-designed majors, study abroad, summer session for credit. *ROTC:* Army (b), Air Force (b). *Unusual degree programs:* 3-2 business administration; criminal justice.

Computers on Campus 708 computers/terminals are available on campus for general student use. Students can access the following: online grade reports. Campuswide network is available.

Student Life *Housing options:* coed, disabled students. *Activities and organizations:* drama/theater group, student-run newspaper, radio station, choral group.

Standardized Tests *Required:* SAT or ACT (for admission).

Costs (2007–08) *Tuition:* state resident $8541 full-time, $275 per credit hour part-time; nonresident $17,709 full-time, $574 per credit hour part-time. Part-time tuition and fees vary according to course level. *Required fees:* $1726 full-time, $281 per term part-time. *Room and board:* $10,034; room only: $6348. Room and board charges vary according to board plan and housing facility. *Payment plan:* installment. *Waivers:* employees or children of employees.

Financial Aid Of all full-time matriculated undergraduates who enrolled in 2006, 3,450 applied for aid, 3,262 were judged to have need, 818 had their need fully met. In 2006, 185 non-need-based awards were made. *Average percent of need met:* 80%. *Average financial aid package:* $10,851. *Average need-based loan:* $4014. *Average need-based gift aid:* $8230. *Average non-need-based aid:* $3883. *Average indebtedness upon graduation:* $17,473.

Applying *Options:* electronic application. *Application fee:* $60. *Required:* high school transcript. *Application deadlines:* rolling (freshmen), rolling (transfers). *Notification:* 3/1 (freshmen), 5/15 (transfers).

Freshman Application Contact Mr. Jason Hand, Director of Admissions, Rutgers, The State University of New Jersey, Newark, 249 University Avenue, Newark, NJ 07102-1896. *Phone:* 973-353-5205. *Fax:* 973-353-1440. *E-mail:* admissions@ugadm.rutgers.edu.

RUTGERS, THE STATE UNIVERSITY OF NEW JERSEY, NEW BRUNSWICK

New Brunswick, New Jersey **www.rutgers.edu/**

- **State-supported** university, founded 1766, part of Rutgers, The State University of New Jersey
- **Urban** 2682-acre campus
- **Endowment** $497.9 million
- **Coed** 26,829 undergraduate students, 93% full-time, 49% women, 51% men
- **Moderately difficult** entrance level, 56% of applicants were admitted

Rutgers–New Brunswick, which was established in 1766, is both traditional and revolutionary. At Rutgers, students can choose from one of more than 100 majors in the liberal arts or professional areas such as pharmacy, engineering, business, the arts, and the life sciences; participate in research with internationally prominent faculty members; enjoy a dynamic student life on campus and in town; play in the mountains or at the shore; and hop the train into New York or Philadelphia.

Undergraduates 24,876 full-time, 1,953 part-time. Students come from 48 states and territories, 112 other countries, 7% are from out of state, 9% African American, 24% Asian American or Pacific Islander, 8% Hispanic American, 0.2% Native American, 2% international, 6% transferred in, 49% live on campus.

Freshmen *Admission:* 28,208 applied, 15,877 admitted, 5,519 enrolled. *Test scores:* SAT critical reading scores over 500: 90%; SAT math scores over 500: 93%; SAT critical reading scores over 600: 42%; SAT math scores over 600: 58%; SAT critical reading scores over 700: 9%; SAT math scores over 700: 17%.

Faculty *Total:* 2,366, 65% full-time, 99% with terminal degrees. *Student/faculty ratio:* 14:1.

Majors Accounting; African studies; agricultural/biological engineering and bioengineering; agriculture; American studies; ancient/classical Greek; animal genetics; animal/livestock husbandry and production; animal physiology; animal sciences; anthropology; art; art history, criticism and conservation; Asian studies (East); astrophysics; atmospheric sciences and meteorology; biochemistry; biology/biological sciences; biomedical/medical engineering; biomedical sciences; biometry/biometrics; biotechnology; business administration and management; cell biology and anatomical sciences related; cell biology and histology; ceramic arts and ceramics; ceramic sciences and engineering; chemical engineering; chemistry; Chinese; civil engineering; classics and languages, literatures and linguistics; clinical laboratory science/medical technology; commercial and advertising art; communication/speech communication and rhetoric; comparative literature; computer engineering; computer science; criminal justice/law enforcement administration; cultural studies; dance; dramatic/theater arts; drawing; ecology; economics; electrical, electronics and communications engineering; engineering science; English; environmental design/architecture; environmental studies; equestrian studies; European studies (Central and Eastern); evolutionary biology; film/cinema studies; finance; food science; foreign languages and literatures; French; geography; geology/earth science; German; Hispanic-American, Puerto Rican, and Mexican-American/Chicano studies; history; human ecology; industrial engineering; information science/studies; interdisciplinary studies; Italian; jazz/jazz studies; Jewish/Judaic studies; journalism; kinesiology and exercise science; labor and industrial relations; Latin; Latin American studies; liberal arts and sciences/liberal studies; linguistics; management science; management sciences and quantitative methods related; marine biology and biological oceanography; marketing/marketing management; mass communication/media; mathematics; mechanical engineering; medical microbiology and bacteriology; medieval and Renaissance studies; molecular biology; music; music teacher education; natural resources/conservation; natural resources management; Near and Middle Eastern studies; nursing (registered nurse training); nutrition sciences; painting; pharmacy; philosophy; photography; physics; plant sciences; political science and government; Portuguese; pre-dentistry studies; pre-law studies; pre-medical studies; printmaking; psychology; public health; religious studies; Russian; Russian studies; sculpture; social sciences related; social work; sociology; Spanish; statistics; turf and turfgrass management; urban studies/affairs; veterinary sciences; visual and performing arts; women's studies.

Academics *Calendar:* semesters. *Degrees:* bachelor's, master's, doctoral, first professional, and post-master's certificates. *Special study options:* academic remediation for entering students, accelerated degree program, advanced placement credit, cooperative education, distance learning, double majors, English as a second language, honors programs, independent study, student-designed majors, study abroad. *ROTC:* Army (b), Air Force (b). *Unusual degree programs:* 3-2 planning and public policy, education, criminal justice.

Computers on Campus 1,450 computers/terminals are available on campus for general student use. Students can access the following: online grade reports. Campuswide network is available.

Student Life *Housing options:* coed, men-only, women-only, cooperative. *Activities and organizations:* drama/theater group, student-run newspaper, radio and television station, choral group, marching band, national fraternities, national sororities. *Student services:* health clinic.

Athletics Member NCAA. All Division I except football (Division I-A). *Intercollegiate sports:* baseball M, basketball M/W, crew M/W, cross-country running M/W, fencing M/W, golf M/W, gymnastics W, lacrosse M/W, soccer M/W, softball W, swimming and diving M/W, tennis M/W, track and field M/W, volleyball W, wrestling M. *Intramural sports:* badminton M/W, baseball M (c), basketball M/W, bowling M/W, cross-country running M/W, equestrian sports M (c)/W (c), field hockey W (c), football M, golf M/W, ice hockey M (c), lacrosse M/W, racquetball M/W, rugby M (c)/W (c), sailing M (c)/W (c), skiing (cross-country) M (c)/W (c), skiing (downhill) M (c)/W (c), soccer M/W, softball M/W, squash M (c)/W (c), swimming and diving M/W, table tennis M (c)/W (c), tennis M/W, track and field M/W, volleyball M/W, water polo M/W, wrestling M.

Standardized Tests *Required:* SAT or ACT (for admission).

Costs (2007–08) *Tuition:* state resident $8541 full-time, $275 per credit hour part-time; nonresident $17,709 full-time, $574 per credit hour part-time. Part-time tuition and fees vary according to course level. *Required fees:* $2145 full-time, $281 per term part-time. *Room and board:* $9762; room only: $5952. Room and board charges vary according to board plan and housing facility. *Payment plan:* installment. *Waivers:* employees or children of employees.

Financial Aid Of all full-time matriculated undergraduates who enrolled in 2006, 16,239 applied for aid, 12,635 were judged to have need, 4,446 had their need fully met. In 2006, 1886 non-need-based awards were made. *Average percent of need met:* 69%. *Average financial aid package:* $12,305. *Average need-based loan:* $4061. *Average need-based gift aid:* $8807. *Average non-need-based aid:* $2670. *Average indebtedness upon graduation:* $16,609.

Applying *Options:* electronic application. *Application fee:* $60. *Required:* high school transcript. *Application deadlines:* rolling (freshmen), rolling (transfers). *Notification:* 3/1 (freshmen), 5/15 (transfers).

Director of Admissions Ms. Diane Williams Harris, Associate Director of University Undergraduate Admissions, Rutgers, The State University of New Jersey, New Brunswick, 65 Davidson Road, Room 202, Piscataway, NJ 08854-8097. *Phone:* 732-932-4636.

See page 1592 for the College Close-Up.

SAINT PETER'S COLLEGE

Jersey City, New Jersey **www.spc.edu/**

- **Independent Roman Catholic (Jesuit)** comprehensive, founded 1872
- **Urban** 15-acre campus with easy access to New York City
- **Coed**
- **Moderately difficult** entrance level

Faculty *Student/faculty ratio:* 16:1.

Academics *Calendar:* semesters. *Degrees:* certificates, associate, bachelor's, and master's.

Student Life *Campus security:* 24-hour emergency response devices and patrols, late-night transport/escort service, controlled dormitory access, ID checks at residence halls and library.

Athletics Member NCAA. All Division I except football (Division I-AA).

Standardized Tests *Required:* SAT or ACT (for admission).

Costs (2007–08) *Comprehensive fee:* $33,776 includes full-time tuition ($23,426), mandatory fees ($600), and room and board ($9750). Full-time tuition and fees vary according to course load. Part-time tuition: $784 per credit. Part-time tuition and fees vary according to course load. *Required fees:* $5 per credit part-time. *College room only:* $6250. Room and board charges vary according to board plan, housing facility, and student level. *Payment plans:* installment, deferred payment.

Financial Aid Of all full-time matriculated undergraduates who enrolled in 2002, 1,731 applied for aid, 1,548 were judged to have need, 233 had their need fully met. 214 Federal Work-Study jobs (averaging $1655). 219 state and other part-time jobs (averaging $2689). In 2002, 170 non-need-based awards were made. *Average percent of need met:* 73. *Average financial aid package:* $14,637. *Average need-based loan:* $3276. *Average need-based gift aid:* $9557. *Average non-need-based aid:* $9364. *Average indebtedness upon graduation:* $13,625.

Applying *Options:* early admission, deferred entrance. *Required:* essay or personal statement, high school transcript, minimum 2.0 GPA, 2 letters of recommendation. *Required for some:* interview. *Recommended:* interview.

Freshman Application Contact Saint Peter's College, 2641 Kennedy Boulevard, Jersey City, NJ 07306-5944. *Phone:* 201-761-7106. *Toll-free phone:* 888-SPC-9933.

See page 1594 for the College Close-Up.

SETON HALL UNIVERSITY

South Orange, New Jersey **www.shu.edu/**

Seton Hall University has been preparing students to assume leadership roles for more than 150 years. A Catholic university founded with the purpose of "enriching the mind, the heart, and the spirit," Seton Hall offers more than sixty majors and concentrations as well as honors and leadership programs. With a 15:1 student-faculty ratio and an average class size of 25, Seton Hall offers all the advantages of a big school; however, with just 5,200 undergraduate students, the University also provides the personal attention of a small college. Seton Hall's mission of "preparing student leaders for a global society" is evidenced through its high academic standards, values-centered curriculum, and cutting-edge technology.

Freshman Application Contact Mr. Robert Herr, Director of Admissions, Seton Hall University, Enrollment Services, Bayley Hall, South Orange, NJ 07079-2697. *Phone:* 973-275-2576. *Toll-free phone:* 800-THE HALL. *Fax:* 973-275-2040. *E-mail:* thehall@shu.edu.

See page 1596 for the College Close-Up.

SOMERSET CHRISTIAN COLLEGE

Zarephath, New Jersey **www.somerset.edu/**

- **Independent Pillar of Fire International** 4-year, founded 1908
- **Coed**
- **Minimally difficult** entrance level

Faculty *Student/faculty ratio:* 12:1.

Academics *Calendar:* semesters plus "FastTrack" semesters. *Degree:* associate.

Standardized Tests *Required for some:* SAT or ACT (for admission).

Costs (2007–08) *Tuition:* $8400 full-time, $300 per credit part-time. Part-time tuition and fees vary according to course load. *Required fees:* $220 full-time, $110 per term part-time.

Financial Aid *Financial aid deadline:* 8/1.

Applying *Options:* electronic application, deferred entrance. *Application fee:* $35. *Required:* essay or personal statement, letters of recommendation. *Required for some:* high school transcript, minimum 2.5 GPA, interview.

Freshman Application Contact Ms. Coleen Klein, Director of Recruitment, Somerset Christian College, 10 College Way, P. O. Box 9188, Zarephath, NJ 08890. *Phone:* 732-356-1595. *Toll-free phone:* 800-234-9305. *Fax:* 732-356-4846. *E-mail:* info@somerset.edu.

STEVENS INSTITUTE OF TECHNOLOGY

Hoboken, New Jersey **www.stevens.edu/**

- **Independent** university, founded 1870
- **Urban** 55-acre campus with easy access to New York City
- **Endowment** $158.8 million
- **Coed**
- **Very difficult** entrance level

Stevens Institute of Technology is among the nation's leading universities, combining a broad-based curriculum with hands-on laboratory experience, cooperative education, and internship opportunities, which foster critical analysis and creativity. Students graduate to career placements and starting salaries well above the national average. The residential campus is located in vibrant Hoboken, just minutes from the cultural and professional advantages of New York City.

Faculty *Student/faculty ratio:* 8:1.

Academics *Calendar:* semesters. *Degrees:* bachelor's, master's, doctoral, and postbachelor's certificates.

Student Life *Campus security:* 24-hour emergency response devices and patrols, late-night transport/escort service, controlled dormitory access.

Athletics Member NCAA. All Division III.

Standardized Tests *Required:* SAT or ACT (for admission). *Required for some:* SAT Subject Tests (for admission).
Costs (2008–09) *Comprehensive fee:* $47,700 includes full-time tuition ($34,900), mandatory fees ($1600), and room and board ($11,200). Part-time tuition: $1164 per credit. *Required fees:* $700 per term part-time.
Financial Aid Of all full-time matriculated undergraduates who enrolled in 2005, 1,645 applied for aid, 1,431 were judged to have need, 245 had their need fully met. 818 Federal Work-Study jobs (averaging $1269). In 2005, 296 non-need-based awards were made. *Average percent of need met:* 85. *Average financial aid package:* $21,139. *Average need-based loan:* $4203. *Average need-based gift aid:* $12,871. *Average non-need-based aid:* $9973. *Average indebtedness upon graduation:* $14,113.
Applying *Options:* electronic application, early admission, early decision, deferred entrance. *Application fee:* $55. *Required:* essay or personal statement, high school transcript, letters of recommendation, interview.
Freshman Application Contact Mr. Daniel Gallagher, Dean of University Admissions, Stevens Institute of Technology, Castle Point on Hudson, Hoboken, NJ 07030. *Phone:* 201-216-5197. *Toll-free phone:* 800-458-5323. *E-mail:* admissions@stevens.edu.

TALMUDICAL ACADEMY OF NEW JERSEY
Adelphia, New Jersey

Director of Admissions Rabbi G. Finkel, Director of Admissions, Talmudical Academy of New Jersey, Route 524, Adelphia, NJ 07710. *Phone:* 201-431-1600.

THOMAS EDISON STATE COLLEGE
Trenton, New Jersey www.tesc.edu/

- **State-supported** comprehensive, founded 1972
- **Urban** 2-acre campus with easy access to Philadelphia
- **Coed** 15,963 undergraduate students, 38% women, 62% men
- **Noncompetitive** entrance level

Undergraduates 15,963 part-time. Students come from 55 states and territories, 72 other countries, 67% are from out of state, 15% African American, 2% Asian American or Pacific Islander, 7% Hispanic American, 1% Native American, 2% international.
Majors Accounting; airframe mechanics and aircraft maintenance technology; air traffic control; air transportation related; allied health and medical assisting services related; allied health diagnostic, intervention, and treatment professions related; applied horticulture; architectural drafting and CAD/CADD; art; biology/biological sciences; biomedical technology; business administration and management; business administration, management and operations related; child care and support services management; clinical laboratory science/medical technology; community organization and advocacy; computer engineering technologies related; computer science; construction engineering technology; criminal justice/law enforcement administration; cytotechnology; dental hygiene; drafting/design engineering technologies related; electrical, electronic and communications engineering technology; engineering technologies related; English; environmental science; environmental studies; fire protection and safety technology; foreign languages and literatures; forestry; gerontology; health/health care administration; health services administration; health services/allied health/health sciences; history; hospitality administration; humanities; human resources management; human services; international business/trade/commerce; journalism; legal assistant/paralegal; liberal arts and sciences/liberal studies; management information systems and services related; manufacturing technology; mathematics; mechanical engineering/mechanical technology; mechanical engineering technologies related; medical radiologic technology; military technologies; music; natural sciences; nuclear engineering technology; nuclear medical technology; nursing (registered nurse training); operations management; parks, recreation and leisure; perfusion technology; philosophy; photography; political science and government; psychology; public administration; public health education and promotion; radiation protection/health physics technology; real estate; religious studies; respiratory care therapy; security and protective services related; social sciences; sociology; survey technology; veterinary/animal health technology.
Academics *Calendar:* continuous. *Degrees:* certificates, associate, bachelor's, master's, post-master's, and postbachelor's certificates (offers only distance learning degree programs). *Special study options:* adult/continuing education programs, advanced placement credit, distance learning, double majors, external degree program, independent study, part-time degree program, services for LD students, student-designed majors, summer session for credit.
Computers on Campus Students can access the following: online (class) grades, online (class) registration, online (class) schedules. Campuswide network is available. Wireless service is available via entire campus.
Student Life *Housing:* college housing not available. *Campus security:* 24-hour emergency response devices and patrols, late-night transport/escort service, security officer from 7 a.m. to 11 p.m., local police patrol.
Costs (2007–08) *Tuition:* state resident $4300 full-time, $1275 per year part-time; nonresident $6150 full-time, $2300 per year part-time. Part-time tuition and fees vary according to student level. *Required fees:* $97 per year part-time. *Waivers:* employees or children of employees.
Applying *Options:* electronic application. *Application fee:* $75. *Required:* age 21 or older and a high school graduate. *Application deadline:* rolling (transfers).
Freshman Application Contact Thomas Edison State College, 101 West State Street, Trenton, NJ 08608-1176. *Phone:* 888-442-8372. *Toll-free phone:* 888-442-8372.

See page 1598 for the College Close-Up.

WILLIAM PATERSON UNIVERSITY OF NEW JERSEY
Wayne, New Jersey ww2.wpunj.edu/

- **State-supported** comprehensive, founded 1855, part of New Jersey State College System
- **Suburban** 300-acre campus with easy access to New York City
- **Coed** 8,830 undergraduate students, 83% full-time, 56% women, 44% men
- **Moderately difficult** entrance level, 70% of applicants were admitted

Committed to student success, William Paterson University seeks ambitious students who are up to its challenge. Small classes and a distinguished faculty; thirty-five majors; preprofessional programs in engineering, law, medicine (which includes dentistry, optometry, podiatry, and veterinary science), pharmacy, physical therapy, and speech-language pathology; and seven distinctive honors programs provide a rewarding educational experience that far exceeds its cost.

Undergraduates 7,321 full-time, 1,509 part-time. Students come from 39 states and territories, 2% are from out of state, 14% African American, 6% Asian American or Pacific Islander, 17% Hispanic American, 0.2% Native American, 0.8% international, 10% transferred in, 23% live on campus. *Retention:* 77% of 2006 full-time freshmen returned.
Freshmen *Admission:* 5,992 applied, 4,206 admitted, 1,437 enrolled. *Test scores:* SAT critical reading scores over 500: 39%; SAT math scores over 500: 46%; SAT critical reading scores over 600: 7%; SAT math scores over 600: 9%; SAT critical reading scores over 700: 1%; SAT math scores over 700: 1%.
Faculty *Total:* 974, 38% full-time.
Majors Accounting; African-American/Black studies; African studies; anthropology; applied art; applied mathematics; art; art history, criticism and conservation; art teacher education; behavioral sciences; biology/biological sciences; business administration and management; business/managerial economics; commercial and advertising art; computer science; dramatic/theater arts; ecology; education; elementary education; English; environmental studies; fine/studio arts; geography; health science; health teacher education; history; humanities; international business/trade/commerce; jazz/jazz studies; kinesiology and exercise science; literature; mass communication/media; mathematics; music; music management and merchandising; music teacher education; nursing (registered nurse training); parks, recreation and leisure; philosophy; physical education teaching and coaching; physical sciences; political science and government; pre-dentistry studies; pre-law studies; pre-medical studies; psychology; public health; secondary education; social sciences; sociology; Spanish; special education; voice and opera.
Academics *Calendar:* semesters. *Degrees:* bachelor's, master's, post-master's, and postbachelor's certificates. *Special study options:* academic remediation for entering students, accelerated degree program, adult/continuing education programs, advanced placement credit, distance learning, double majors, English as a second language, honors programs, independent study, internships, off-campus study, part-time degree program, services for LD students, study abroad, summer session for credit. *ROTC:* Air Force (c).
Computers on Campus 700 computers/terminals are available on campus for general student use. Students can access the following: online (class) registration. Campuswide network is available.
Student Life *Housing options:* coed, disabled students. *Activities and organizations:* drama/theater group, student-run newspaper, radio and television station, choral group, Caribbean Student Association, Organization of Latin American Students (OLAS), Sisters of Awareness, Student Activities Committee, national

fraternities, national sororities. *Campus security:* 24-hour emergency response devices and patrols, controlled dormitory access. *Student services:* health clinic, personal/psychological counseling, women's center, legal services.

Athletics Member NCAA. All Division III. *Intercollegiate sports:* baseball M, basketball M/W, bowling M (c)/W (c), cheerleading M/W, cross-country running M/W, fencing M/W, field hockey W, football M, golf M, ice hockey M (c), skiing (downhill) M (c)/W (c), soccer M/W, softball W, swimming and diving M/W, track and field M/W, volleyball W. *Intramural sports:* basketball M, equestrian sports M/W, football M, golf M, lacrosse M, racquetball M/W, softball M/W, tennis M (c)/W (c), volleyball M/W, wrestling M.

Standardized Tests *Required:* SAT or ACT (for admission).

Costs (2007–08) *Tuition:* state resident $6072 full-time, $195 per credit part-time; nonresident $12,318 full-time, $399 per credit part-time. *Required fees:* $3924 full-time, $126 per credit part-time. *Room and board:* $9650; room only: $6400. Room and board charges vary according to board plan and housing facility. *Payment plan:* installment. *Waivers:* senior citizens and employees or children of employees.

Financial Aid Of all full-time matriculated undergraduates who enrolled in 2007, 4,897 applied for aid, 3,700 were judged to have need, 1,626 had their need fully met. In 2007, 465 non-need-based awards were made. *Average financial aid package:* $12,515. *Average need-based loan:* $4182. *Average need-based gift aid:* $7057. *Average non-need-based aid:* $7700. *Average indebtedness upon graduation:* $19,600.

Applying *Options:* electronic application, deferred entrance. *Application fee:* $50. *Required:* essay or personal statement, high school transcript. *Required for some:* letters of recommendation, interview. *Recommended:* minimum 2.5 GPA. *Application deadlines:* 5/1 (freshmen), 6/1 (transfers). *Notification:* continuous (freshmen), continuous (transfers).

Freshman Application Contact Mr. Anthony Leckey, Acting Director of Admissions, William Paterson University of New Jersey, 300 Pompton Road, Wayne, NJ 07470. *Phone:* 973-720-2906. *Toll-free phone:* 877-WPU-EXCEL. *Fax:* 973-720-2910. *E-mail:* admissions@wpunj.edu.

See page 1600 for the College Close-Up.

BLOOMFIELD COLLEGE

BLOOMFIELD, NEW JERSEY

The College

Founded in 1868 as a Presbyterian seminary, Bloomfield College (BC) is an independent, four-year, nonsectarian liberal arts college enrolling more than 2,300 men and women from all over the world. The College's mission is to prepare students to attain academic, personal, and professional excellence in a multicultural and global society. Bloomfield College offers programs in the liberal arts and sciences, creative arts and technology, and professional studies, which include accounting, business administration, computer information systems, criminal justice, education, game development, network engineering, nursing, prechiropractic, and the sciences.

Bloomfield is accredited by the Middle States Association of Colleges and Schools, and the nursing program is accredited by the Commission on Collegiate Nursing Education and the New Jersey Board of Nursing. The College is chartered by the state of New Jersey, and its academic programs are approved by the New Jersey Commission on Higher Education. The accounting program is a Registered Accounting Curriculum for Public Accountancy in the state of New Jersey and meets the state's educational requirements for candidates applying to sit for the CPA examination.

With about forty organizations to choose from, students have many opportunities to engage in cocurricular programs that enrich their educational experience. In addition to student government, activities include the Nursing Student Association, the Association of Latin American Students, the International Student Association, and a variety of departmental clubs and ethnic and social organizations. Campus publications include *In Print,* the College yearbook, and *On the Green,* a magazine for alumni and friends.

The Student Center is the social and recreational focus of the College community and houses meeting rooms, a snack bar, lounges, and the Center for Student Leadership and Engagement, which provides opportunities for student socialization, leadership, and cocurricular learning. Also located in the Student Center, the bookstore is a convenient place to buy textbooks, school supplies, gifts, clothes, snacks, and personal items.

Bloomfield College has a full program of intercollegiate and intramural sports and recreational activities. Men's intercollegiate sports are baseball, basketball, cross-country, soccer, and tennis. Women's intercollegiate sports are basketball, cross-country, soccer, softball, and volleyball. Bloomfield College is a member of NCAA Division II as part of the Central Atlantic Collegiate Conference (CACC).

In addition to general on-campus housing, the College provides special residence halls for first-year students. Theme houses are also available on campus. Housing priority is given to first-year students and students who live beyond a reasonable commuting distance. A complete residence-life program provides academic, social, and recreational programs for resident students.

The Center for Academic Development offers individual tutoring and group workshops to all students. Academic advising is ongoing, and students meet with their adviser before registering each semester.

Other support services include the Honors Program, Support for Achievement in Graduate Education, First Year Experience, Educational Opportunity Fund Program, career counseling and placement, women's services, and the Wellness Center, which includes health services, the chaplain, and personal counseling. An extensive English for Academic Purposes program for students for whom English is a second language is also offered.

Location

Located in Bloomfield, New Jersey, a suburban, residential community just 15 miles from New York City, the College attracts resident students from many geographic areas as well as commuter students from the New Jersey/New York metropolitan area. Bloomfield is accessible by bus, train, or car from northern New Jersey and from the boroughs of Manhattan, the Bronx, Staten Island, and Brooklyn as well as Rockland and Westchester counties in New York.

Majors and Degrees

Bloomfield College offers the Bachelor of Arts and Bachelor of Science degrees. Majors and their concentrations include accounting (professional accounting and general accounting), allied health technology (diagnostic medical sonography, nuclear medicine technology, respiratory care, and vascular technology), biology (environmental studies, general biology, prechiropractic studies, premedical studies, and prepodiatric studies), business administration (with specializations in economics, finance, human resource management, human resource training, international business management, management, management information systems, marketing, and supply chain management), chemistry (biochemistry, general chemistry, and premedical), clinical laboratory sciences (cytotechnology and medical technology), computer information systems (database, networks/security, programming), creative arts and technology (animation, digital video, fine arts, game development, graphics for print and digital media, interactive multimedia and the World Wide Web, music technology, and theater), education (elementary/early childhood, secondary, and special education), English (communications, literature, and writing), history, network engineering (Internet technology, LAN specialist), mathematics (applied mathematics), nursing (generic nursing, RN/B.S.N.), philosophy, political science (general, human services, public administration, and public policy), psychology (general psychology and human services), religion, and sociology (criminal justice, human services, and general sociology).

Bloomfield College maintains a joint Bachelor of Science/Doctor of Chiropractic degree program with twelve accredited chiropractic colleges. Three versions of the prechiropractic program are offered, each preparing students for admission to colleges offering the Doctor of Chiropractic (D.C.) degree. (More information is available in the Academic Programs section.) Bloomfield offers certificate programs in digital media, diversity training, game design, game programming, and supply chain management.

Academic Programs

Degree candidacy requires the successful completion of at least 33 course units; a full course unit is equivalent to 4 semester hours. A minimum of 16 course units must be completed at an advanced level. Four categories of courses are offered at the College: general education courses, distribution courses, specific major and major required courses, and elective courses.

Course requirements for the degree vary among majors. The prechiropractic program is a sequence of courses preparing the student for study for the Doctor of Chiropractic degree. The student may either complete graduation requirements for a bachelor's degree or transfer from Bloomfield College directly into a D.C. program after three years.

Other special programs available at Bloomfield include an RN/B.S.N. transfer program for registered nurses who already have a two-year degree; the Educational Opportunity Fund Program, a state-funded program of educational and special services for disadvantaged students; English as a second language; an honors program; a circus program, under the auspices of the division of creative arts and technology; Weekend College, a complete degree program for adults that is offered on weekends; and various internship programs.

The Bloomfield College academic calendar consists of fifteen-week fall and spring semesters and an optional summer session consisting of a fourteen-week term or two 7-week terms.

Off-Campus Programs

Bloomfield College is a member of the College Consortium for International Studies (CCIS). Students have the choice of more than seventy-five study-abroad programs in thirty countries around the world, for a semester, a summer, or a full academic year.

Academic Facilities

Renovated Talbott Hall is the technology hub and media center of the College. The lower level houses classrooms featuring laptop and desktop computers, conference rooms, a general computer lab, and a comfortable lounge area. A Web-based radio station, which is part of the College's communications program, occupies the lower mezzanine area level.

The Bloomfield College library opened in 2000 and houses a collection of more than 64,000 titles, including subscriptions to more than 400 periodicals and 1,000 electronic journals, an up-to-date reference collection, and thousands of reels of microfilm and microfiche as well as musical recordings and scores, films, and videotapes. The library is particularly proud of its extensive audiovisual collection. The library has an online card catalog, offers access to 15 databases on the Internet, and holds a variety of CD-ROMs in the humanities, nursing, and social sciences. Library instruction and research assistance make the library a complete learning center. The library is open Monday through Friday from 7:30 a.m. to 11 p.m., Saturday from 7:30 a.m. to 7 p.m., and Sunday from 4 p.m. to 11 p.m. The library also houses the Media Center, which consists of three electronic classrooms, a distance learning room, and a screening room.

Academic computing facilities consist of four laboratories in the Science Building with more than seventy computers. The library houses six laboratories with more than 130 computers, including the Pollack Computer Center. The College has wireless connectivity in a number of buildings on campus, including the library, the Student Center, and student residences, with plans for many more locations. Students who register their wireless network card can use their laptops in any of these facilities.

All campus computers are networked, and all computers are updated every three years. The College has a campuswide Microsoft licensing agreement as well as popular database and statistics packages and programming languages and packages used by specific disciplines, such as biology, mathematics, and nursing. Graphics and desktop publishing packages are also available. Technical support is available, and laptops may be rented through the Media Center.

Costs

Tuition in 2007–08 for full-time students is $18,000 per year. Tuition for part-time students is $1650 per course. Room and board for resident students are $8650 per year. Fees total approximately $300.

Financial Aid

In 2004–05, Bloomfield College students received approximately $19 million in scholarships and financial aid, with more than 90 percent of the full-time day student population receiving some form of financial assistance. Academic scholarships are administered by the Office of Enrollment Management and Admission; athletic scholarships are administered by the athletics department. College, state, and federal programs, such as grants, loans, and work-study, are administered by the Financial Aid Office. The priority deadline for filing the FAFSA for Bloomfield College financial aid is March 15. Applicants who meet the March 15 deadline are considered for Bloomfield College scholarships and campus-based financial aid, including PACE, a new interest-free loan for parents.

Faculty

A highly qualified and diverse faculty instructs more than 2,300 students of all ages in day, evening, and weekend sessions, with a student-faculty ratio of 15:1. Approximately 80 percent of the full-time faculty members have earned doctorates or terminal degrees.

Student Government

The Bloomfield College Day Student Government represents registered day students, all organized student groups and clubs, and the College's academic divisions. It also serves as a vehicle of communication for student concerns and interests. The Bloomfield College Evening/Weekend Student Government provides a means of communication among evening students, faculty members, and members of the administration and assists the College in meeting the educational needs of the evening student. The administrative staff and the College faculty serve as advisers to all student government activities and enterprises.

Admission Requirements

Bloomfield College admits qualified applicants who demonstrate the motivation, desire, and potential to benefit from and contribute to programs of study in the liberal arts and sciences, creative arts and technology, and professional studies. The College evaluates applicants in a comprehensive manner, with emphasis placed on the applicant's academic history, quality of curriculum, performance on standardized tests such as SAT and/or ACT, extracurricular involvement, results of one-on-one interviews, and recommendations from teachers and counselors. Once admitted, students are placed according to their academic preparation and achievement. Bloomfield's admission criteria remain unaffected by the new SAT format. The College, like many other area colleges, is waiting to assess the true value and impact of the new writing section of the SAT on the first cohort of students to experience it and will then determine its role in the admission process.

Application and Information

All applicants are encouraged to visit the College to discuss their academic and career plans with an admission counselor. Applicants may also spend a day on campus attending classes and talking with students, faculty members, and administrators about academic programs and student activities, as well as the issues of admission and financial assistance. Applications are accepted throughout the year, with a priority application deadline of March 14 for the fall and November 15 for the spring semester. Applicants are notified within two weeks of the College's receipt of required materials. Applications received after these dates are considered on a space-available basis. Admission is open to all qualified students without regard to race, color, creed, religion, national or ethnic origin, sex, age, or physical disability. The College welcomes applications from high school seniors, transfer students, and adult students returning to school. Students may apply online at http://www.bloomfield.edu/admissions/apply.aspx. For further information, students should contact:

Kristin Cohen
Vice President for Enrollment Management
and Dean of Admission
Bloomfield College
One Park Place
Bloomfield, New Jersey 07003
Phone: 973-748-9000 Ext. 230
800-848-4555 (toll-free)
Fax: 973-748-0916
E-mail: admission@bloomfield.edu
Web site: http://www.bloomfield.edu/admissions

CALDWELL COLLEGE

CALDWELL, NEW JERSEY

The College

Caldwell College is a Catholic, coeducational four-year liberal arts institution rooted in a proud 800-year Dominican tradition of rigorous scholarship, committed teaching, and ethical values. Founded in 1939 by the Sisters of St. Dominic, Caldwell College helps students achieve their full intellectual and personal potential in a supportive community.

The College's most popular offerings include undergraduate degrees in business, psychology, and education. Caldwell has twenty-nine undergraduate degrees, seventeen graduate programs, and a Caldwell Scholars Program. The adult undergraduate program encourages adults to return to college to complete their degree, earn a new degree, or simply learn for pleasure. Day, evening, Saturday, and distance learning courses highlight the importance of lifelong learning. Accelerated options combine the curricular opportunities of the distance education program with traditional on-campus offerings. Postbaccalaureate programs in applied behavior analysis (ABA), special education, and teacher certification are available.

The Center for Graduate and Continuing Studies meets the academic needs of the College's adult students. The center provides adult learners, in undergraduate or graduate programs, with excellence in teaching, caring academic support, and learning options that work with their busy lives.

Master's degrees are offered in ABA, business administration (accounting, nonprofit management), counseling psychology (art therapy, school counseling), curriculum and instruction (educational technology, special education, supervisor certification), educational administration, pastoral ministry (church administration), and special education (ABA, general teacher certification, learning disabilities). Educational administration is also offered in a fast-track Off-Campus Leadership Development Program. Post-master's programs in art therapy, educational supervisor's certification, professional counselor licensing credits, and school counseling are offered. Combined bachelor's-master's programs are available to qualified students in art therapy, business, psychology, school counseling, and theology.

The Office of Career Development provides ongoing career counseling, a career library, career education and planning, interest testing, and graduate-study information to assist students in clarifying personal goals and in exploring academic and career opportunities.

Caldwell College sponsors work-based internship and cooperative education opportunities that encourage students to integrate work experience with classroom learning. Approximately 40 percent of the program's participants are offered full-time positions upon graduation. The Office of Experiential Learning assists students and alumni who are seeking full- and part-time employment. The College's Business Advisory Council, which includes about 40 members from major corporations throughout New Jersey, helps business leaders and educators share their resources so both students and the business community can prepare for the challenges of the global marketplace. Through guest lectures by corporate leaders, mentoring programs, and interaction during business conferences, students learn how to be successful in today's workplace.

Caldwell College enrolls more than 2,300 full-time, part-time, and graduate students. Approximately 84 percent of the full-time students are from New Jersey. In addition, the College's rich cultural diversity attracts individuals from northeastern and mid-Atlantic states and from more than twenty-six other countries. The cultural mix of students includes African American (13 percent), Hispanic (10 percent), Asian American (2 percent), and international (4 percent) students. Fully qualified faculty members and a 13:1 student-faculty ratio provide close, personal attention.

About 45 percent of full-time students live on campus. Single, double, triple, and a few quad rooms are available. A new 200-bed, apartment-style residence hall opened in August 2007. The food service features extended hours and an expanded menu, with both American and international food selections. All students may have a car on campus. A variety of clubs and organizations are available. Guest artists, musicians, authors, and speakers appear on campus regularly, and there are dances and other activities. An on-campus fitness center, equipped with cardiovascular equipment, provides students with health and exercise opportunities. Caldwell fields NCAA Division II teams in men's baseball, basketball, golf, soccer, and tennis and in women's basketball, cross-country, soccer, softball, tennis, and volleyball and sponsors a variety of intramural sports. The 60,000-square-foot George R. Newman Student Activities and Recreation Center opened in 2002.

Location

Located on a beautiful, secure 70-acre campus 20 miles west of New York City, students participate in numerous educational, cultural, and social experiences while enjoying the relaxed atmosphere of campus life. A variety of shops and restaurants are within walking distance. Area attractions include theaters, museums, parks, ski resorts, malls, the New Jersey Performing Arts Center, and the New Jersey shore. Many corporate headquarters are easily accessible and provide a variety of internship opportunities. The College can be reached by public transportation and is near major highways, including the Garden State Parkway, the New Jersey Turnpike, and Interstates 80, 280, and 287.

Majors and Degrees

Caldwell College offers twenty-nine undergraduate Bachelor of Arts (B.A.), Bachelor of Science (B.S.), and Bachelor of Fine Arts (B.F.A.) degrees. A multidisciplinary major is offered. The College also offers an individualized major for students seeking to design their own course work with administrative approval. The B.A. is offered in art, biology, chemistry, communication arts, criminal justice, elementary education, English, French, history, an individualized major, mathematics, music, political science, psychology, social studies, sociology, Spanish, and theology. The B.S. is offered in accounting, business administration, computer information systems, computer science, financial economics, international business, management, marketing, and medical technology. The B.F.A. is offered in art. The education department offers teacher certification programs in elementary education (nursery–grade 8) and for teaching grades K–12 in art, biology, English, French, mathematics, music, social studies, Spanish, and special education as well as a P–3 certification. A dual certification program is available to registered nurses who wish to obtain school nurse certification and teacher of health endorsement.

Academic Programs

Eligibility for a degree requires completion of a minimum of 120 credits and a GPA of at least 2.0 (C). Students must also complete major courses with a minimum grade of C and satisfy all other departmental requirements. All programs require that students successfully pass a form of outcomes assessment in the senior year. Liberal arts requirements include courses in computer literacy, English, fine arts, foreign language, history, mathematics, natural sciences, philosophy, physical education, public speaking, religious studies, and social sciences. A Writing Across the Curriculum program systematically develops a student's ability to write well, regardless of his or her major. Opportunities for independent study, internships, co-ops, double majors, minors, and certificate programs are available. The Caldwell Scholars Program challenges exceptional students with both interdisciplinary studies and a directed honors project and is supplemented by guest lecturers.

Scores of 3, 4, or 5 on the College Board's Advanced Placement tests earn advanced placement or credit for completed work. Students may receive credit for knowledge gained through independent study or experience through the College-Level Examination Program (CLEP). Adult students can earn credit through Caldwell's Prior Learning Assessment Policy, provided they can demonstrate acquired knowledge that corresponds to course requirements. Course selection is determined by placement test results, and international students may be required to enroll in credit-bearing, advanced-level English for nonnative speakers (ENNS) courses.

Caldwell College currently has ten joint health-degree programs, which give students the opportunity to attain health profession degrees in an accelerated period of time and to save a year of Caldwell College tuition. Some of the affiliated schools include St. George's University's School of Medicine and Veterinary Medicine in Grenada, UMDNJ's Dental School and School of Nursing, and New York Chiropractic College. An affiliation with Rutgers University enables qualified students to earn a B.A. degree in sociology from Caldwell and an M.S.W. from Rutgers School of Social Work in five years. Caldwell College also has an affiliation agreement with Columbia University for a combined B.A. in psychology or biology and an M.S. in occupational therapy. This five-year program enables Caldwell College psychology or biology majors to take three years of course work at Caldwell, then two years at Columbia, earning both B.A. and M.S. degrees. Affiliation programs also include seven-year accelerated programs and eight-year traditional routes. The seven-year programs are highly competitive, and students must be accepted by both the affiliated institution and Caldwell and maintain the mandatory GPAs and test scores.

Off-Campus Programs

The College has exchange-program agreements with Duksung Women's University and Catholic University of Korea that provide students with broad opportunities to better prepare themselves for the global marketplace. Caldwell also offers short-term travel experiences, usually up to three weeks in length and during the winter or summer session, to numerous locations throughout the world. Students are accompanied by faculty members, who design and present courses in a variety of academic disciplines. Caldwell is also affiliated with the Washington Semester Program of American University, Washington, D.C.

Academic Facilities

To better focus on its desire to excel in the teaching of math and science, Caldwell College used nearly $2 million in federal grants to help establish the Center for Excellence for Teaching on the campus. The College renovated the biology, physics, and chemistry labs and plans to serve as a regional hub to implement innovative teacher preparation programs that will emphasize the effective use of classroom technology, refinement of math and science training, special education teacher training, and developing programs for disadvantaged students.

Campus facilities include a library, four classroom and administrative buildings, and a theater. An academic building, which opened in 1997, features a 120-seat lecture hall and faculty and administrative offices. A psychology lab is equipped with computers and specialized state-of-the-art hardware and software for conducting psychological studies related to class work and for independent student and faculty psychological research. The lab provides equipment for observing and collecting behavioral data, student role-playing, and developing counseling skills. Wide-screen video and computer graphics capability and satellite reception are available. Jennings Library contains 146,350 volumes, subscribes to 443 periodicals, and provides access to more than 21,500 journal titles in 53 full-text databases. Off-campus access to the online public-access catalog and online databases is available. Full-text databases support the major curricular areas. A curriculum lab has texts for grades K–12, visual aids, and other resources. The Media Center is equipped with VHS, DVD, and CD listening equipment for use in classroom assignments.

The art department contains a gallery studio featuring professional and student work. The Communication Arts Department's facilities include a television studio, a digital editing suite, a public speaking lab, and a radio studio. Students may produce and perform TV and radio shows, which are broadcast to the entire campus community.

Computer labs, with up-to-date personal computers, software, and multimedia equipment, offer free scanning and laser printing. Other computer labs are dedicated to specific areas of study, including art, education, ENNS, math, music, the sciences, video editing, and writing. There are two technology-rich classrooms, the Academic Computer Classroom and the Business Computer Classroom, and twelve technology-enhanced classrooms that are equipped with digital audio and video and computer equipment. All offices, classrooms, labs, and dorm rooms are connected to the campus network and the Internet.

Costs

For the 2007–08 academic year, full-time tuition and fees were $22,000 and campus room and board were approximately $8300. Adult undergraduate tuition was $529 per credit hour.

Financial Aid

Approximately 80 percent of the current full-time undergraduate students receive financial aid from federal sources that include the Pell Grant, Stafford Student Loan, Work-Study, and Supplemental Educational Opportunity Grant programs. Caldwell College offers scholarships for academic and athletic excellence, special interest and privately sponsored scholarships, tuition grants, and campus employment. New Jersey offers tuition aid grants for state residents. The New Jersey Educational Opportunity Fund (EOF) makes it possible for all students, especially the educationally and economically disadvantaged for whom college might otherwise be an unrealistic goal, to pursue higher education. All financial aid applicants must file the Free Application for Federal Student Aid (FAFSA). The priority filing deadline is April 1.

Faculty

There are 79 full-time faculty members, with 84 percent having earned their doctoral/terminal degree, and 14 part-time faculty members. There are 4 full-time ENNS and Academic Support Center instructors and 105 adjunct faculty members.

Student Government

Caldwell College's students, through the Student Government Association and the Resident Council, shape many nonacademic policies and regulations. Students help determine total College policy through representation on several College standing committees.

Admission Requirements

The Office of Undergraduate Admissions individually reviews each applicant's high school record, SAT or ACT scores (with essay score), essay, letters of recommendation, and class rank (when available) to determine the student's ability to succeed at Caldwell College. International students must submit proof of their TOEFL score with their applications. Students must complete at least 16 high school academic units, including 4 years of English, 2 of foreign language, 2 of mathematics, 2 of science, and 1 of history. Transfer applicants must submit an official transcript from each college and university attended. If they have earned fewer than 30 credits, they must also submit a high school transcript and SAT/ACT scores with the essay score. Caldwell College does not discriminate against applicants on the basis of race, color, creed, age, national or ethnic origin, or handicap.

Application and Information

Caldwell College works with a rolling admissions policy, accepting applicants throughout the year, based on availability. An early action admissions program allows students who apply by December 1 to have a decision by January 1. The priority application deadline for freshmen is April 1 (July 15 for transfer students). There is a nonrefundable $40 application fee. Applicants are notified of their admission eligibility after their credentials have been received and evaluated. For further information, students should contact:

Office of Admissions
Caldwell College
9 Ryerson Avenue
Caldwell, New Jersey 07006-6195
Phone: 973-618-3500
888-864-9516 (toll-free outside New Jersey)
Fax: 973-618-3600
E-mail: admissions@caldwell.edu
Web site: http://www.caldwell.edu

Caldwell College provides a caring atmosphere and develops goal-oriented students who can achieve their full intellectual and personal potential.

THE COLLEGE OF NEW JERSEY

EWING TOWNSHIP, NEW JERSEY

The College

The College of New Jersey (TCNJ) welcomes students who have the talent and motivation to succeed in a highly rigorous academic environment. A public institution founded in 1855, the College enrolls about 5,600 full-time undergraduates, two thirds of whom reside on campus. Today it is heralded by *U.S. News & World Report* as well as *Barron's* as one of the most competitive schools in the nation, public or private. TCNJ serves a diverse student body, preparing graduates to be leaders in their chosen fields.

TCNJ has set the standard for public higher education. Students report they find TCNJ large enough to provide a full range of academic and extracurricular choices, yet small enough to be a genuine residential community of friends and fellow learners. With professors easily available in and out of class and facilities of enviable quality, TCNJ today represents an exceptional value in higher education.

The College of New Jersey's academic approach combines those of both traditional liberal arts schools and professional schools. A liberal learning curriculum ensures that all students are grounded in the beliefs and values of a civic responsibility and intellectual and scholarly growth and that they receive a well-rounded education in the liberal arts. Interdisciplinary studies, internships, research, and faculty mentoring all are part of an educational approach designed to produce successful leaders. While a very high percentage of graduates find immediate employment related to their fields of study, more than 20 percent go directly into graduate schools across the country.

All first- and second-year students are guaranteed on-campus housing, and most juniors and seniors continue to live on campus. Rooming arrangements are quite flexible, from doubles in freshman residence halls to suites and single rooms in campus town houses or apartments for upperclass students. A nationally recognized residence life program and more than 150 student organizations offer numerous opportunities for friendship, personal growth, and leadership. An exceptional 96 percent of first-year students return for their sophomore year.

The arts flourish in two theaters, a recital hall, an art gallery, and numerous other campus venues. Student performances, professional groups on tour, and a large variety of films, lectures, local bands, and solo entertainers fill the academic year with cultural options—many of them free, the rest at low cost.

Student wellness has a high priority, with many facilities for recreation and physical conditioning. In Packer Hall, the campus has access to a larger fitness center, a 25-meter swimming and diving pool, and a basketball court. The Student Recreation Center offers racquetball courts, four tennis courts that are convertible to basketball or volleyball use, a weight room, and an indoor track. Other facilities include a lighted Astroturf field, eight lighted outdoor tennis courts, an outdoor "beach" volleyball court, and numerous athletic fields.

As a Division III member of the National Collegiate Athletic Association, TCNJ offers twenty-one sports: eleven for men and ten for women. Since 1979, TCNJ student-athletes have amassed thirty-six national championships and twenty-nine runner-up awards, more than any other Division III institution in the country. In addition to its NCAA athletics, TCNJ offers a wide variety of recreation programs for intramural competition and self-governing sports clubs. More than 3,500 students play with these less demanding, but spirited and competitive teams, each year, some of which have intercollegiate schedules.

The College's undergraduate programs are accredited by the Middle States Association of Colleges and Schools and by professional associations in engineering, nursing, chemistry, music, education, education of the deaf, computer science, and business.

Location

The College of New Jersey is set on 289 acres in suburban Ewing Township, approximately 15 minutes from downtown Princeton; 10 minutes from Bucks County, Pennsylvania; and 5 miles from the state capital of Trenton. Woodlands and lakes surround the thirty-nine major academic and residential buildings. The campus is 30 miles from the theaters and museums of Philadelphia and 60 miles from those in New York City.

Majors and Degrees

The College of New Jersey offers programs leading to the Bachelor of Arts, Bachelor of Fine Arts, Bachelor of Music, Bachelor of Science, and Bachelor of Science in Nursing degrees.

The B.A. is awarded in art education; art history; communication studies; economics; English, including journalism and professional writing options; history; interactive multimedia; international studies; mathematics and statistics; philosophy; political science; psychology; sociology; Spanish; and women's and gender studies. The B.F.A. is awarded in digital arts, and fine art and graphic design. The B.M. is awarded in music (performance and education). The B.S. is granted in accountancy, biology, biomedical engineering, business administration (finance, general business, information systems management, international business, management, and marketing), chemistry, computer engineering, computer science, early childhood education, economics, education for the hearing-impaired, electrical engineering, elementary education, engineering science, health and physical education, law and justice, mechanical engineering, physics, special education, and technology education. Teacher preparation is available in many arts and science majors.

TCNJ offers a five-year combined Master of Arts in Teaching degree with dual certification in deaf and hard-of-hearing and elementary education. Students may also enroll in a seven-year B.S./M.D. degree program with UMDNJ—New Jersey Medical School (Newark) or a seven-year B.S./O.D. degree program with the State University of New York College of Optometry. Students may apply to TCNJ for a 4½-year combined B.S./M.A. program in law and justice with Rutgers, The State University of New Jersey (Newark). The College also offers a Medical Careers Advisory Committee for premed students and a Pre-Law Advisement Committee for students planning a career in law.

Academic Programs

In 2004, the College completed a transformation of its curriculum, requiring fewer, more in-depth courses. All courses contain a significant out-of-class requirement and provide for even more student-faculty interaction. All baccalaureate degrees require at least thirty-two courses, including a core curriculum in the traditional arts and sciences.

The thirty-week year is divided into fall and spring semesters; the summer session offers courses in two 5-week sessions and one 6-week session. The average class size for freshman-level lectures is 24 students and for upper-division lectures, 22 students.

All first-year students participate in a program linking residential learning in small classes taught by full-time faculty members. Seminars, independent studies, and capstone courses give many students the opportunity for challenging advanced study in close collaboration with faculty members. TCNJ students publish the results of these endeavors or present them at national and regional conferences.

The honors program offers students the particularly challenging academic experiences that allow normal progress toward the degree. Whenever possible, honors courses have an interdisciplinary perspective and curriculum, concentrating on central themes within significant periods in the cultural development of civilization. Honors courses in the major consist of either specially designated sections or independent study. All honors classes are small, personal, and stimulating.

Off-Campus Programs

TCNJ offers students a variety of full-year and one-semester programs of study abroad as well as study at other state colleges and universities within the United States. Exchange programs are available in Australia, Austria, Canada, Denmark, France, Germany, Greece, Israel, Japan, Mexico, the United Kingdom, and twenty-three other countries. National exchanges are available at more than 130 participating institutions in the United States, the U.S. Virgin Islands, Puerto Rico, and Guam. The College of New Jersey hosts the New Jersey State Consortium for International Studies.

Academic Facilities

The College of New Jersey is nearing the end of a ten-year, $250-million campus-planning initiative. Within the past several years, TCNJ has built and opened a Science Complex, Biology Building, Social Science Building, College Spiritual Center, and state-of-the-art library, which serves as the intellectual and social hub of the campus. Campuswide networking provides full Internet accessibility from all residence hall rooms and more than twenty student computing laboratories.

Costs

Costs are relatively low because of state funding. For 2006–07, full-time undergraduate tuition and fees were $9500 for New Jersey residents and $14,500 for out-of-state students. Room and board charges for the academic year, with a middle meal plan, averaged $8093.

Financial Aid

Approximately half of the full-time undergraduates receive some form of financial aid, such as federal, state, and institutional grants; merit scholarships; student employment; and loan assistance. The Free Application for Federal Student Aid (FAFSA) or Renewal FAFSA is used to apply for all types of aid.

Scholarships and grants include the College of New Jersey Merit Scholars Program, the New Jersey Edward J. Bloustein Distinguished Scholars Program, the New Jersey Tuition Aid Grant, Federal Pell Grants, Federal Supplemental Educational Opportunity Grants (FSEOG), Educational Opportunity Fund (EOF) Promise Award, and Army and Air Force ROTC Scholarships, as well as other institutional scholarships. Loans include the Federal Subsidized and Unsubsidized Stafford Loans, the Federal Perkins Loan, the Federal Parent Loan for Undergraduate Students (PLUS), the New Jersey CLASS Loan, nursing loans, and short-term emergency loan funds. Student employment options include the need-based Federal Work-Study Program (on- and off-campus positions) as well as institutionally supported campus jobs.

Faculty

The approximately 335 full-time members of the College of New Jersey faculty are teachers and scholars. While teaching is their primary commitment, they are also active researchers, authors, artists, performers, and regular contributors in their academic disciplines. No classes are taught by graduate assistants. The student-faculty ratio is 12:1. From their first day, students study with faculty members who may be researching new ways to use solar energy; writing a new text, play, or novel; or investigating the life cycle of desert ferns. Members of the faculty have attracted many significant grants, fellowships, and awards, including the Bancroft Prize in history, Fulbright Scholarships, and grants from the National Science Foundation, the National Institute for Advanced Study, the Guggenheim Foundation, and the National Endowment for the Humanities. Faculty members mentor their students, preparing them for careers, graduate and professional schools, and prestigious fellowships such as the Fulbright, Truman, and Marshall Fellowships recently awarded to TCNJ students.

Student Government

The Student Government Association, comprising all undergraduate students at the College, is governed by elected representatives. The Residence Hall Association provides the mechanism for student input into campus housing policies, and members of the Student Finance Board oversee and administer approximately $500,000 in student funds. The College Union Board sponsors a wide range of special events, including visits by John Leguizamo, Cornel West, and George Carlin.

Admission Requirements

The College of New Jersey seeks students who can succeed in a highly selective academic program and who show intellectual curiosity, academic talent, and the potential to contribute to the life of the College. The College is committed to attracting students from diverse economic, racial, social, and geographic backgrounds. A high school record of at least 16 college-preparatory credits, high school class rank, SAT scores, and special interests, skills, and qualities of all kinds can be influential. Certain departments, such as art and music, use additional criteria to evaluate candidates seeking admission into their programs.

Application and Information

The College of New Jersey is a member of the Common Application. The deadline for applications for January admission is November 15 and for September admission, February 15. There is a $50 application fee. Candidates who apply only to the College of New Jersey under the early decision plan may apply before November 15 and will be notified on or before December 15. For September admission, the College subscribes to the candidates' reply date of May 1 for payment of a $100 tuition deposit and a $100 room and board deposit.

For more information, students should contact:

Dean of Admissions
The College of New Jersey
P.O. Box 7718
Ewing, New Jersey 08628-0718
Phone: 609-771-2131
800-624-0967 (toll-free)
Web site: http://www.tcnj.edu

Students take a break in front of Green Hall.

COLLEGE OF SAINT ELIZABETH

MORRISTOWN, NEW JERSEY

The College

The College of Saint Elizabeth (CSE), which celebrated its centennial year in 1999–2000, is the oldest college for women in New Jersey. In addition, CSE is one of the first Catholic colleges in the U.S. to award degrees to women. A Catholic college in the liberal arts tradition, the College now includes a women's college, coeducational adult undergraduate degree programs, and coeducational graduate degree programs. An enrollment of more than 2,000 students fosters considerable student-faculty interaction and a spirit of campuswide encouragement and support. An emphasis is placed on opportunities for individual growth through academic, spiritual, cultural, leadership, and civic experiences.

Located on a 200-acre campus, CSE's buildings command a wide view of the surrounding hills. Sixty-five percent of the women's college students live on campus. The majority come from New Jersey, 2 percent from other Northeastern states, 1 percent from other states, and 6 percent from other countries. About 60 percent of those who begin as freshmen graduate, and about 47 percent go on to graduate study within five years of leaving college. Two attractive residence halls provide ample private and double rooms. Each residence hall has kitchenettes, laundry facilities, a mail room, lounges, and conference rooms. The student center contains a swimming pool, a gymnasium, a fitness center, a drama studio, an art studio, a dining room, and the College store.

Students may belong to extracurricular organizations associated with their academic interests, such as the cocurricular leadership program, the Elizabeth Singers, the International/Intercultural Club, the College Activities Board, Campus Ministry, the Students Take Action Committee, Volunteer Services, Student Government, and varsity athletics. NCAA Division III team sports include basketball, soccer, softball, swimming, tennis, and volleyball. Other organizations include a number of Greek-letter honor and professional societies and student affiliates of the American Chemical Society. A rich calendar of social, cultural, and recreational events is available at the College of Saint Elizabeth. Students frequently socialize with their peers from Drew University and Fairleigh Dickinson University, two nearby coeducational institutions within walking distance of the campus. Career Services provides assistance with career preparation, internships, and graduate study.

In addition to the undergraduate majors and degrees listed, the College offers the M.A. degree in counseling psychology, education, educational leadership, forensic psychology, and theology; the M.S. degree in health-care management, management, nursing, and nutrition; and the Ed.D. degree in educational leadership.

Location

Morristown is located in the rapidly growing corporate center of historical Morris County. Neighboring towns and cities, only minutes from the campus, offer facilities for shopping and recreation. The College is an hour from the cultural and social opportunities of New York City by car, train, or bus and is near the campuses of Fairleigh Dickinson, Seton Hall, Drew, and the County College of Morris. Newark Liberty International Airport is approximately 30 minutes and two New York airports are approximately 1 hour from the campus. Local bus routes are easily accessible, and New Jersey Transit, which has a stop at the campus gate, provides excellent rail commuter service from New York City, Hoboken, Newark, the Oranges, Short Hills, Maplewood, Millburn, Summit, Chatham, Madison, and Dover. Routes 287, 80, 280, 46, 78, 24, and 10 are located close by.

Majors and Degrees

The Bachelor of Arts is offered in American studies, applied science, art, biology, chemistry, communication, economics, education (early childhood and elementary education, secondary education, or special education), English, history, individualized major, international studies, justice studies (criminal justice, legal studies), mathematics, music, philosophy, psychology, sociology, Spanish, and theology. The Bachelor of Science is offered in biochemistry, biology (options for cytotechnology and medical technology), business administration (options for accounting, computer information systems, management, and marketing), chemistry, computer science, and foods and nutrition. The Bachelor of Science in Nursing degree is offered as an upper-division nursing program.

Academic Programs

The requirements for a B.A., B.S., or B.S.N. degree are 128 semester hours of academic credit, competency in writing, First Year Seminar (not required of adult students), 2 credits in fitness/wellness, and successful completion of the comprehensive examination in the major subject. A minimum of 32 credits is required in the major. The core curriculum requires that students take between 36 and 44 credits distributed among five cluster areas: Literature/Fine Arts/Language; Social and Behavioral Sciences; Natural and Physical Sciences and Mathematics and Computer Science; Philosophy, Theology, and History; and Perspectives on an Interdependent World. The remaining courses are free electives.

Career preparation includes studies in accounting, business management, computer information systems, computer science, criminal justice and legal studies, foods and nutrition, gerontology, human resource management, management, marketing, premedicine, pre–veterinary studies, secondary education, and social work. Education majors may obtain state certification and/or endorsement in early childhood or special education. The College has a highly successful leadership program.

Students interested in becoming registered dietitians may enroll in the dietetic internship program if they hold a baccalaureate degree and meet the current American Dietetic Association course work requirements.

Independent study, field experience, internships, study-abroad opportunities, honors, leadership, and accelerated programs, minors, and double majors are available for qualified students. Successful scores on Advanced Placement tests are honored for placement or credit. Credit is given for successful scores on CLEP subject examinations with essays; on the Thomas Edison College Examination Program (TECEP) examinations; on the Regents College Examination in nursing, DANTES, and ACE College Credit Recommendation; and on portfolio assessment of prior learning.

Seven-week courses are offered in the evenings. Courses are also given during the summer and winter intersessions through the School of Graduate and Continuing Studies. Undergraduate degree programs in the School of Graduate and Continuing Studies are offered in business administration, computer science, justice studies, nursing, psychology, and theology. Fast-track programs are offered in communication and business administration.

Off-Campus Programs

A cross-registration policy exists with nearby Fairleigh Dickinson and Drew Universities. Qualified students may study abroad during the junior year or in the summer. A January intersession program and summer sessions provide opportunities for short-term courses and off-campus experiences. Students have opportunities in Morris County for volunteer service, field experience, and internships in local agencies, institutions, and the corporate headquarters of numerous multinational corporations.

Academic Facilities

Students majoring in biology and chemistry conduct independent research projects under the guidance of highly qualified professors and in conjunction with local research companies. The College has several well-equipped microcomputer laboratories and extensive software. Mahoney Library is a 300-seat, air-conditioned facility that provides group and individual study areas. The library's collection includes 109,352 volumes, 2,148 audiovisual titles, 153,213 microforms, 561 periodical subscriptions, and a 610-volume curriculum collection for education students. The Phillips Library of Rare Books and Manuscripts houses a variety of special collections. The library is a selective depository for U.S. government documents. Nine Internet workstations provide access to the World Wide Web and to more than 100 online subscription databases, many of which include full text. A TV production studio, an editing suite, and a videoconferencing classroom are housed in the Media Services area.

Costs

Tuition and fees in 2007–08 for incoming full-time freshmen were $21,347, and room and board were $9990. Other incidental expenses, such as travel, entertainment, clothes, books, and personal expenses, are estimated at about $3350. Part-time undergraduate students paid $623 per credit.

Financial Aid

Approximately 95 percent of full-time undergraduate students at the College of Saint Elizabeth receive financial aid. Aid is available from the College itself in the form of scholarships, grants-in-aid, and campus employment and from the federal and state governments in the form of scholarships, grants, loans, and employment. Students who wish to be considered for grants, loans, and campus employment should apply to the College by March 1 for the fall semester and by November 1 for the spring semester. Campus employment is available in the residence halls, laboratories, the library, and College offices, and a limited number of work-study opportunities for qualified students are available both on and off campus. Transfer scholarships are also available.

Faculty

The faculty-student ratio is 1:12. Full-time instructional faculty members for 2007–08 included approximately 87 percent with doctorates and 13 percent with master's degrees. Several faculty members hold additional professional credentials. The goals of the faculty are to teach effectively, to be readily available to students, and to pursue research.

Student Government

Students participate in the governance of the College through the Student Organization. The Student Organization elects members to the student government, which serves as the student executive branch. Student views on student activities, clubs, and organizations are expressed and acted on through a committee structure. The academic life, student life, and lectures and concerts committees of the College are composed of both faculty members and students and are engaged in determining methods of implementing institutional goals and increasing student satisfaction with campus life. Students are encouraged to participate fully in the academic community and to exercise considerable influence in social and extracurricular activities. There is an open atmosphere on campus, and students have access to the deans and the president.

Admission Requirements

The College looks for students whose aptitude and academic record demonstrate the ability to meet academic challenges. Normally, a student interested in admission to the College should complete 16 academic units by the end of her senior year, including 3 years of English; 2 years of college-preparatory mathematics, including algebra; 2 years of the same foreign language; 1 year of U.S. history; 1 unit of laboratory science and 1 additional unit of science; and six upper-level academic electives. Applicants must submit either SAT or ACT scores. International students must send scores on the Test of English as a Foreign Language (TOEFL). Students applying to the College should submit a secondary school transcript, including courses currently in progress, plus two letters of recommendation from persons who can attest to their academic potential. Students are encouraged to have an on-campus interview and visit the campus. Open houses are held each spring and fall. Well-qualified students who are recommended by their high school principals may be accepted after three years of high school. Transfers from two- and four-year colleges are accepted for the fall and spring semesters. Through articulation agreements, an applicant who has earned an A.A. degree in a transfer program at an accredited two-year college is eligible for admission with junior-class standing. Adult students must submit secondary and previous college transcripts (if any) in addition to the application.

Application and Information

For further information, students may contact:

College of Saint Elizabeth
2 Convent Road
Morristown, New Jersey 07960-6989
Phone: 973-290-4700 (Women's College)
800-210-7900 (Women's College, toll-free)
973-290-4600 (School of Graduate and Continuing Studies)
Fax: 973-290-4710 (Women's College)
E-mail: apply@cse.edu (Women's College)
Web site: http://www.cse.edu

Students at the College of Saint Elizabeth.

The College of Saint Elizabeth has filed compliance with the Department of Education (formerly Department of Health, Education, and Welfare) under Title VI–Civil Rights Act of 1964, Title IX–Education Amendment of 1972, and the regulations issued by the then Department of Health, Education, and Welfare in implementation thereof, and Section 504 of the Rehabilitation Act of 1973, as amended.

DREW UNIVERSITY

MADISON, NEW JERSEY

The University

Drew prepares students for personal and professional growth in a rapidly changing world. It provides a rigorous liberal arts education characterized by inspiring teaching, close student-faculty relationships, the integration of modern technology into the study of the traditional arts and sciences, widespread opportunities for hands-on learning, and the cultivation of interdisciplinary and global perspectives. Students become fluent in the use of electronic information systems, explore the ideas and methodologies of diverse fields of study, sharpen the critical thinking and communications skills essential to success in all professions, and learn to place subjects of inquiry into larger intellectual and cultural contexts.

Ubiquitous computing, in which every student has a laptop computer and access to the campus network and the Internet, has been the foundation of the College's technology program for many years. Drew recently received a Pioneer Award from Educause for this program. The campus network includes ATTIC (Academic Technology Tools for Instructional Computing), an award-winning program that automatically provides shared network space as well as course management. Specialized facilities include mediated classrooms, a Multimedia Lab and a multimedia Language Resource Center, user labs and a computer classroom in the Academic Computer Center, a networked writing classroom, and many departmental facilities. Technology is used for teaching and learning throughout the curriculum, from music to statistics, and many faculty members participate in technology workshops and use a faculty lab to prepare digitized course materials. Students can also register and check their grades online. Residence halls offer students access to voice mail and cable TV.

Drew is committed to providing students with a global perspective through special off-campus programs, a variety of area studies programs, and curricular opportunities to investigate the history, economics, politics, literature, religions, and cultures of other nations and heritages. In addition, student-organized clubs and activities promote and celebrate the multicultural and international diversity of the campus community. Along with the faculty and staff members, Drew students (coming from thirty-nine states and eleven countries) help create a stimulating and supportive campus community. Drew's enrollment totals more than 2,400 students, of whom more than 1,600 are undergraduates.

Ninety percent of Drew students live on campus in traditional residence halls or in special theme/language houses (ASIA Tree House, Umoja House, Environmental Concerns House, La Casa, Spirituality House, and Womyn's Concerns House). Fourteen percent of Drew students are members of American ethnic minority groups. Drew students exert extraordinary influence on student affairs and provide leadership in more than eighty clubs and organizations, including an award-winning newspaper, a radio station, a television station, a literary magazine, a prelaw society and law journal, cultural clubs, a social committee, service organizations, an environmental action group, political clubs, fine and performing arts groups, and intramural sports programs. In addition, students may attend more than 300 free lectures, concerts, exhibits, conferences, films, dances, parties, and performances each year. Speakers appearing in Drew's Forum have included Presidents George H. Bush, George W. Bush, William J. Clinton, and Gerald Ford; Shimon Peres; Colin Powell; Leah Rabin; Mike Wallace; Henry Kissinger; Barbara Bush; Bill Moyers; Rudolph Giuliani; Walter Cronkite; and Tim Russert. The University also sponsors varsity sports (NCAA Division III), which include men's and women's basketball, cross-country, lacrosse, soccer, swimming, and tennis; women's field hockey and softball; men's baseball; and coed equestrian riding (IHSA) and fencing.

Drew also has a graduate school, which offers eleven master's and eight doctoral programs in the humanities, as well as a theological school, which offers five professional degrees.

Location

Drew's undergraduates enjoy a location that affords a wide variety of academic, cultural, and recreational opportunities. Just 30 miles west of New York City, the quaint, small town of Madison, New Jersey, provides a safe home to Drew's beautiful, heavily wooded, 186-acre campus. The immediate area has the highest concentration of headquarters for international corporations and research companies in the nation. Proximity to these resources and to those provided by New York City makes special semesters, academic internships, research assistantships, field trips, and guest speakers important parts of all department curricula. In addition, numerous parks and recreational areas, including the Jersey Shore, several ski resorts, Giants Stadium, and the Meadowlands, are all within a 1-hour ride by car, commuter train, or bus.

Majors and Degrees

The College of Liberal Arts awards the Bachelor of Arts degree in anthropology, art history, behavioral science, biochemistry, biology, chemistry, Chinese studies, classics, computer science, economics, English, French, German, history, mathematics, mathematics and computer science, music, neurosciences, Pan-African studies, philosophy, physics, political science, psychology, religious studies, sociology, Spanish, studio art, theater arts, and women's studies. Interdisciplinary and other special majors may be arranged. Minors are available in major subject areas (except behavioral science and neurosciences) as well as in American studies, archaeology, arts administration and museology, Asian studies, business, comparative literature, environmental studies, European studies, Holocaust studies, humanities, Italian, Jewish studies, Latin American studies, linguistic studies, Middle East studies, Russian, Western heritage, and writing.

A seven-year, dual-degree program (including three years of study at Drew) leads to a B.A. from Drew and a medical degree (M.D.) from the University of Medicine and Dentistry of New Jersey–New Jersey Medical School (UMDNJ–NJMS) in Newark. An articulation agreement with the Graduate School of Management of Rutgers University offers qualified Drew graduates guaranteed admission to the M.B.A. program in professional accounting. Five-year cooperative programs lead to a B.A. from Drew and a master's degree in forestry or environmental management from Duke University, a B.S. in engineering from Washington University in St. Louis or Columbia University in New York, or a B.S. in chemical engineering from Stevens Institute of Technology. Through a cross-registration agreement with the College of St. Elizabeth, students may earn teacher certification in several areas.

Academic Programs

Drew operates on a two-semester calendar. To graduate with the bachelor's degree, students must complete 128 credit hours, including a major, the First-Year Seminar, and, as part of the general education program, a minor. The major is chosen by the end of the sophomore year. Independent study, a regular offering in some departments, is an option in all departments. Up to 8 semester hours may be earned in off-campus internships for academic credit. General and specialized honors are awarded in the major field. Drew has one of New Jersey's three Phi Beta Kappa chapters as well as chapters of twelve other national honor societies: Alpha Kappa Delta (sociology), Beta Beta Beta (biology), Omicron Delta Epsilon (economics), Delta Phi Alpha (German), Phi Alpha Theta (history), Pi Delta Phi (French), Pi Mu Epsilon (mathematics), Pi Sigma Alpha (political science), Sigma Pi Sigma (physics), Psi Chi (psychology), Sigma Delta Pi (Spanish), and Dobro Slovo (Russian). There is also

Epsilon Omega Psi, Drew's Educational Opportunity Scholars honors program, and Pinnacle, for nontraditional continuing education students.

Off-Campus Programs

The Drew International Seminars Program was established to allow as many students as possible to study, on location, a culture other than their own. In small groups, students and faculty members engage in course work on campus combined with three to four weeks of on-site, interdisciplinary study during January or May. Subjects and locations vary each year, depending on interest. In recent years, programs were held in China, Egypt, Ghana, Greece, Iceland, Italy, and Peru. Students receive 8 credits for the entire program. The University subsidizes all travel, room, and board costs for the seminar; students are only charged tuition. Drew sponsors summer programs in West Africa; Venice, Italy; Barcelona, Spain; and Harbin, China. Drew also offers semester-long programs in London, Brussels, and Eritrea; American politics and public policy in Washington, D.C.; and theater, contemporary art, the United Nations, or Wall Street in New York City. Several of these programs include internship opportunities. Students may also participate in off-campus programs sponsored and supervised by other recognized American colleges and universities. University-approved marine biology programs are available at Duke University and the Marine Biological Laboratory at Woods Hole. Closer to campus, credit-bearing internship opportunities in business, communication, industry, government, social service, and the arts and entertainment provide students with professional experiences to complement their studies.

Academic Facilities

The University library complex, which houses more than 500,000 volumes, 3,000 periodicals, and 363,077 microforms, is a federal, state, and United Nations depository. Drew's library is automated. Students and faculty have 24-hour direct access to the Drew library card catalog and selected journal indexes as well as to other bibliographic databases across the nation. In addition to the personal computer system given to each student, Drew maintains open computer labs for multimedia, foreign languages, computer graphics, and general use. The Hall of Sciences contains impressive research-grade equipment, including a scanning electron microscope; an observatory with solar radio and optical telescopes; a greenhouse; a laser holography laboratory; nuclear magnetic resonance, infrared, ultraviolet-visible, and mass spectrometers; and a chemistry and physics library. The William E. and Carol G. Simon Forum and Athletic Center is open to the entire University community. There is seating capacity for 4,000 people in its indoor forum, featuring a Cybex fitness room; an eight-lane, 25-yard pool; a six-lane, 200-meter indoor track; an indoor area with four multipurpose courts for basketball, tennis, or volleyball; and racquetball and squash courts. Other major facilities include the Lena C. Coburn Media Resource Center, the Elizabeth Korn Art Gallery, the Commons Theater, and the Kirby Shakespeare Theatre.

The Dorothy Young Center for the Arts, completed in 2005, provides spacious state-of-the-art facilities that significantly expand the already strong offerings of the theater and art departments. The new facility holds a 400-seat performance hall; advanced art studios, including a large sculpture room; an exhibition gallery; and a black-box theater.

Costs

Tuition for the 2007–08 academic year is $34,230, fees are $560, and room and board are $9476.

Financial Aid

Drew offers a comprehensive program of need-based and merit-based financial assistance. Last year, more than 80 percent of the first-year class received some form of assistance. Need-based aid is available in the form of University grants, campus employment, loans, or a combination of these. The Federal Pell Grant, Federal Supplemental Educational Opportunity Grant, Federal Work-Study, state grant, and federal and state loan programs are also sources of aid. A completed Free Application for Federal Student Aid (FAFSA) and a completed PROFILE form of the College Scholarship Service are required of all applicants for need-based aid. The on-time filing deadline is February 15; aid applicants are notified in early April. No special application is necessary for most of Drew's academic merit awards, which are offered in various increments. Students who hope to be considered for the Presidential Scholarship in the Arts must submit a portfolio to Drew. Students should visit the Drew Web site for specific requirements.

Faculty

Of the University's more than 120 full-time faculty members, 95 percent hold the Ph.D. or highest degree in their fields. All college faculty members teach undergraduates. In addition, the Charles A. Dana Research Institute for Scientists Emeriti (RISE) has brought 10 prominent scientists, who recently retired from the area's corporate community, to campus to continue their work. With hundreds of patents and publications to their credit, RISE scientists serve as mentors and provide research assistantships for undergraduates.

Student Government

The student government is active in shaping institutional policy, academic and nonacademic. Students sit as voting members on the University Senate and on many college faculty committees, administer their own social program, manage the extracurricular budget, and participate in the judicial process.

Admission Requirements

Applicants for admission are strongly encouraged to complete a minimum of 16 academic units, including 4 in English, 3 in mathematics, 2 in foreign language, 2 in laboratory sciences, 2 in social studies, and 3 in other academic areas. SAT or ACT scores are optional. Students who choose not to submit SAT or ACT scores must instead submit a graded paper from a high school class. The graded paper should be critical or analytical in nature, not merely a summary of a work. Admission is based principally on academic performance in high school. Nearly one quarter of Drew's first-year students graduated in the top 5 percent of their high school class; approximately 40 percent in the top tenth; and 75 percent graduated in the top 25 percent. Personal qualities and special talents are also considered. About 20 percent of each freshman class enter under Drew's Early Decision Plan, and early admission is also available. Applications from transfer and international students are encouraged. A campus interview is required for transfer students and is strongly recommended for first-year candidates. Interviews are offered between mid-April and January. Overnight accommodations are available on campus for visiting candidates. Tours are offered throughout the year.

Application and Information

The application deadline for first-year admission is February 15. Candidates are notified after mid-March. Accepted students are expected to respond to an offer of admission by May 1. The early decision application deadlines are December 1 and January 15. Transfer applications are reviewed on a rolling basis beginning April 1. The final deadline for transfer students for the fall semester is August 1.

Dean of College Admissions
Drew University
Madison, New Jersey 07940
Phone: 973-408-DREW (3739)
Fax: 973-408-3068
E-mail: cadm@drew.edu
Web site: http://www.drew.edu

FAIRLEIGH DICKINSON UNIVERSITY

COLLEGE AT FLORHAM, MADISON, NEW JERSEY
METROPOLITAN CAMPUS, TEANECK, NEW JERSEY

The University

Founded in 1942, Fairleigh Dickinson University (FDU) is a center of academic excellence dedicated to the creation of world citizens through global education. It comprises two strategically located and uniquely different campuses in northern New Jersey—the College at Florham in Madison and the Metropolitan Campus in Teaneck—offering both undergraduate and graduate programs. Building on its long history of international outreach and its proximity to New York City, the University provides students with the multidisciplinary, intercultural, and ethical understandings necessary to participate, lead, and prosper in the global marketplace of ideas, commerce, and culture. Fairleigh Dickinson is the first university in the nation to require that all undergraduates complete at least one distance learning course a year as part of their educational requirements.

Location

Fairleigh Dickinson University's two campuses in northern New Jersey provide undergraduates with the choice of distinctively different living and learning environments.

The University's College at Florham, located on the former Vanderbilt-Twombly estate in suburban Madison (Morris County) about 45 minutes from New York City, offers undergraduates a classic experience for the contemporary world in a smaller college setting. Its focus is on providing outstanding on-campus and residential living opportunities, hands-on learning experiences, strong graduate and professional school preparation, and customized educational options—all framed by a global perspective.

The University's Metropolitan Campus for professional and international studies, located in the dynamic New York–New Jersey corridor less than 10 miles from New York City in Teaneck (Bergen County), features a university atmosphere with an international perspective, attracting students from the U.S. and around the world. Undergraduates have access to the resources of a major graduate center, and nearby New York City is an integral part of their learning experience. Accelerated bachelor's/master's options are among its many professional preparation programs.

Both campuses offer students a distinctive living and learning environment and a wide range of academic choices within an intimate university setting. Residence halls and off-campus housing are available on both campuses. There are nearly 100 active academic, social, political, and professional student organizations; sororities and fraternities; and sports at the varsity, intramural, club, and intercampus levels. Lectures, seminars, concerts, performances, and special events are also an intrinsic part of University life.

The University also owns and operates two international campuses—Wroxton College, in Oxfordshire, England, and FDU-Vancouver in British Columbia, Canada.

Majors and Degrees

Bachelor of Arts degrees are offered in art, communication, communication studies, creative writing, criminal justice, economics, English language and literature, film and animation, filmmaking, fine arts, French language and literature, history, humanities, interdisciplinary studies, international studies, literature, mathematics, philosophy, political science, psychology, religion and philosophy, sociology, Spanish language and literature, and theater arts.

Bachelor of Science degrees are offered in accounting, allied health technologies, biochemistry, biology, business management, chemistry, civil engineering technology, clinical laboratory sciences, computer science, construction engineering technology, electrical engineering, electrical engineering technology, entrepreneurial studies, environmental science, finance, hotel and restaurant management, information technology, marine biology, marketing, mathematics, mechanical engineering technology, medical technology, nursing (including a one-year accelerated program), radiologic technology, and science.

The QUEST five-year teacher certification program allows students to earn a bachelor's degree in a field of their choosing in the liberal arts or sciences as well as dual teacher certification in one or two high-demand specifications and a Master of Arts in Teaching (M.A.T.) degree. Preprofessional studies are offered in chiropractic, dentistry, law, medicine, optometry, pharmacy, physical therapy, and veterinary medicine.

In addition, the University offers dozens of concentrations and minors in such marketable fields as actuarial science, biotechnology, computer engineering, forensic psychology, information systems, pharmaceutical biostatistics, toxicology, and visual communication. Fairleigh Dickinson also offers many combined degree programs, which enable students to earn both their undergraduate and graduate degrees in just five years in such fields as accounting, biology, business administration, chemistry, civil engineering or construction technology/systems science, communication/corporate and organizational communication, computer science, computer science/computer engineering, criminal justice/public administration, electrical engineering, electrical engineering/computer engineering, environmental science/systems science, hotel and restaurant management/hospitality management, political science, psychology, and public administration.

in collaboration with leading professional schools, 6½- or 7-year combined bachelor's/doctoral programs are also offered in chiropractic, dental medicine, dental surgery, medicine, pharmacy, physical therapy, and veterinary medicine.

An Associate in Arts degree in liberal arts and an Associate in Science in radiography are also offered.

Academic Programs

Candidates for the degree of Bachelor of Arts or Bachelor of Science must complete a minimum of 128 credit-hours of course work, maintain a minimum 2.0 CGPR (individual colleges have minimum CGPRs for course work within their majors), and complete the University Core Curriculum—a sequence of four courses designed to provide all FDU undergraduates with a solid foundation in the liberal arts, sciences, and humanities. The core provides students with a common base of knowledge; improves skills in communications and analysis; promotes understanding of individual, societal, and international perspectives; and instills an appreciation for the interrelationship among bodies of knowledge. Candidates for the B.A. must take 30 to 44 credits in the major, 40 to 63 credits in distribution requirements (19 to 23 credits in foundation courses, 15 to 30 credits in humanities and social and behavioral sciences, and 6 to 10 credits in laboratory science), and the University Core; the remainder of credits may be taken as free electives. Candidates for the B.S. degree must complete 54 to 60 credits in the major and the University Core; the remaining credits are taken in foundation and free elective courses. The undergraduate program includes all courses needed to meet graduate and professional school requirements.

The University offers a variety of specialized honors programs and a cooperative education program, and many departments have internships and work-experience programs. Mature adult students may participate in a variety of specialized programs, including the Bachelor of Arts in individualized studies, that are offered on campus and at over fifty off-site locations. An all-online degree-completion program is also available for adult learners.

Through the University's Regional Center for College Students with Learning Disabilities, students can receive academic support within the regular college curriculum (enrollment is selective and limited). The Freshmen Intensive Studies and Enhanced Freshman Experience programs are designed to assist a limited number of promising students who require focused support as they begin their college careers. The University also offers English Language Centers (a division of Berlitz, Inc.) at the Metropolitan Campus as a service to international students.

Off-Campus Programs

The University strongly encourages all students to incorporate an international learning experience into their education. For example, students can spend a semester or summer at Wroxton College, the historic British campus located 70 miles from London that Fairleigh Dickinson has owned and operated since 1965. Summer-study opportunities are also offered at FDU-Vancouver. A variety of other international experiences are also based on student interests and career goals. The University's requirements in distance learning further expand students' international learning experiences, enabling them to study with its Global Virtual Faculty of scholars and professionals around the world.

Domestic learning experiences available to students include the well-known Semester in Washington. In addition, the marine biology curriculum includes laboratory field experiences at Samana Station, the University's own marine biology research and learning facility in the Tambora Beach resort in the Dominican Republic.

Academic Facilities

The University maintains comprehensive libraries on each campus as well as a business reference library on the Metropolitan Campus. The libraries have combined holdings of 470,000 volumes and subscriptions to 2,585 periodicals. Each library provides computer search services and access to subject CD-ROMs to augment in-house print resources. The University is a participating member of the Online Computer Library Center and maintains a University-wide online catalog to facilitate intracampus library loans. Each library has a number of distinguished special collections on subjects such as the Columbia film archives, the Kahn Memorial Collection on the History of Photography, and the Harry Chesler Collection of comic art, graphic satire, and illustration.

Students have access to nearly 2,000 minicomputers and microcomputers on campus as well as to programming languages and software. In addition, there are state-of-the-art computer graphics laboratories for the production of professional-quality, computer-generated art. Computer, software, and Internet training are offered through the campus computer centers. Resident students with their own computers can link to the campus computer network from their rooms. Student e-mail and Internet access accounts are offered to all students. Many buildings throughout the University offer wireless computer access.

Costs

Educational costs (including the estimated cost of residence and meals) for 2007–08 for the College at Florham were $27,620 for tuition, a $608 technology fee, $6074 for residence (based on standard double occupancy), and $3528 for meals (based on an eleven-meal plan plus a $300 flex plan). For the Metropolitan Campus, costs included $25,624 for tuition, a $608 technology fee, $6420 for residence (based on standard double occupancy), and $3508 for meals (based on an eleven-meal plan plus a $300 flex plan).

Financial Aid

More than $30 million in financial aid is awarded annually, including a generous program offering annually renewable academic scholarships ranging from $7000 to $20,000 for academically outstanding students. To be considered for financial aid, students should file the Free Application for Federal Student Aid (FAFSA) and Fairleigh Dickinson's University Financial Aid Application. Applications for aid should be filed by February 15 for priority consideration. Applications filed after this date are processed subject to availability of funds.

Faculty

There are 362 full-time and 575 part-time faculty members at Fairleigh Dickinson University. Of the full-time faculty members, most hold a doctorate or the highest terminal degree in their field. The student-faculty ratio is 15:1 at the Metropolitan Campus and 16:1 at the College at Florham. All courses are taught by faculty members, not graduate assistants. Members of the faculty and administration participate in advising students as well as in planned activities that concern the student body as a whole. All first-year students are assigned faculty mentors to help develop class schedules and assess students' academic progress.

Student Government

Each campus has a student council that acts as the governing body to enforce student regulations and to plan social club activities. The student council serves as a liaison with the faculty and administration of both the campus and the University. It offers students' opinions as an aid in developing University curricular and extracurricular policies. The University Senate, which formulates University policies, includes voting representatives from the student body.

Admission Requirements

The University recommends at least 16 units of full-credit work from an accredited secondary school, including 4 years of English, 2 years of history, 3 years of science (two units of laboratory science minimum), 3 years of college-preparatory mathematics, 4 elective units (at least 3 of which should be academic), and 2 years of a foreign language. Additional science and mathematics units are required for some majors. The criteria that are used for University-wide admission are the high school record, SAT or ACT scores, and counselor recommendations. SAT Subject Test scores are used for placement only. Foreign Language Subject Test scores may be submitted by those applicants who intend to continue study of the language they took in high school. The Mathematics Level I or II Subject Test may be taken by prospective chemistry, physics, mathematics, and engineering majors. The SAT may be taken as early as July preceding the senior year and as late as March of the senior year, but the October, November or December test dates are preferred. Campus visits are strongly recommended. Interviews are encouraged for all students and may be required in select cases.

Application and Information

Students must submit a completed and signed application form, a secondary school record form listing all courses and grades, SAT or ACT scores, and a nonrefundable $40 application fee (which can be waived in cases of hardship). Freshmen and transfer students are admitted in September and January and during summer sessions. Applicants for regular admission are reviewed on a rolling basis and are notified after receipt of all credentials. Information on filing an online application can be found by visiting the University's Web site.

For application forms, financial aid information, and other materials, students should contact:

Office of University Admissions
Fairleigh Dickinson University
1000 River Road, H-DH3-10
Teaneck, New Jersey 07666
Phone: 800-338-8803 (toll-free)
E-mail: globaleducation@fdu.edu
Web site: http://www.fdu.edu

FELICIAN COLLEGE

LODI, NEW JERSEY

The College

Felician College is a Catholic/Franciscan college serving more than 2,000 men and women. Its mission is to provide a values-oriented education based in the liberal arts while it prepares students for meaningful lives and careers in contemporary society. To meet the needs of students and to provide personal enrichment courses to matriculated and nonmatriculated students, Felician College offers day, evening, weekend, and online programs. The College is accredited by the Middle States Association of Colleges and Schools, and carries program accreditation from the National League for Nursing Accrediting Commission, the National Accrediting Agency for Clinical Laboratory Sciences, and the International Assembly for Collegiate Business Education.

In addition to its undergraduate degree programs, Felician College offers the Master of Science in Nursing (M.S.N.), Master of Business Administration (M.B.A.), Master of Arts in Religious Education, and Master of Arts in Teacher Education.

Felician College competes in Division II of the National Collegiate Athletic Association (NCAA). The Felician teams, called the Golden Falcons, compete in men's baseball, men's and women's basketball, men's and women's soccer, men's and women's cross-country, men's golf, and women's softball and volleyball. The Athletic Department also sponsors numerous intramural sports activities, such as indoor soccer, faculty-student softball and volleyball games on the quad.

Students may elect to reside in one of the spacious suites in Elliott Hall or Milton Court Residence, both located on the Rutherford Campus, a 10-minute shuttle bus ride from the campus in Lodi. The campuses offer comfortable student lounge areas, student meeting rooms, dining halls, a gymnasium, a fitness center, and grassy areas for outdoor recreation.

Location

Felician College is located on two beautifully landscaped campuses in Lodi and Rutherford, in Bergen County, in northern New Jersey. Both campuses, nestled in suburban towns, are 12 miles from New York City and a few miles from the New Jersey Meadowlands sports complex.

Majors and Degrees

Felician College offers programs of study in the arts and sciences, business and management sciences, nursing and health management, and teacher education.

A liberal arts program leading to the Bachelor of Arts, Bachelor of Science, Bachelor of Science in Nursing, or Associate in Arts degree is designed to provide students with a broad general education and concentrated preparation in a major area. For the B.A. degree, a student may choose a departmental major in art, biology, business administration, communications, computer information systems, criminal justice, English, history, management and marketing, mathematics, philosophy, psychology, or religious studies. A student may choose an interdisciplinary major in one of three liberal arts areas: humanities, natural sciences and mathematics, or social and behavioral sciences. Concentrations are available in accounting, communications, fine arts, general science, graphic design, international education and foreign languages, journalism, mathematical sciences, political science, sociology, and teaching math P–12 certification. Bachelor of Arts degree programs are available in elementary education (K–5), early childhood education (P–3), elementary education with content area specializations (5–8), mathematics education, and teacher of students with disabilities (K–12).

The Bachelor of Science degree is offered in nursing and in business administration. A program leading to the Bachelor of Science degree in clinical laboratory science and eligibility for national certification is offered in collaboration with the University of Medicine and Dentistry of New Jersey's School of Health-Related Professions (UMDNJ–SHRP). For this degree, a student may concentrate in cytotechnology or medical technology. Also offered in conjunction with UMDNJ–SHRP is a Bachelor of Science program in allied-health technology. Students may study medical sonography, nuclear medicine technology, respiratory care, or vascular technology. Joint degree programs that lead to a master's or doctoral degree are offered for the following preprofessional programs: audiology, chiropractic studies, medicine, occupational therapy, optometry, physical therapy, physician assistant studies, and podiatry.

Two-year programs are offered leading to the Associate in Arts degree in liberal arts, with a concentration in business.

Academic Programs

A candidate for the B.A. in liberal arts is required to complete an organized program of study comprising a minimum of 120 semester hours distributed among prescribed and elective courses. Four interdisciplinary courses in the College's Core Curriculum are mandatory for all students. Each baccalaureate degree student in arts and sciences is required to prepare a written and oral senior research project. A minimum of 30 credit hours must be earned at the College. A student who pursues an A.A. degree is required to complete 64 to 66 credits in an approved program of study.

A candidate for the B.A. in elementary or special education is required to complete a program of 126 to 131 semester hours, including credits in general education, professional education, and a major in the arts and sciences. Field experience begins in the freshman year, students participate in a practicum in the junior year, and there is supervised teaching during the senior year in a public elementary school. The education programs are approved by the National Association of State Directors of Teacher Education and Certification (NASDTEC).

Evening and weekend classes provide adults with the opportunity to earn associate and baccalaureate degrees offered at Felician College. Students may take courses through the traditional semester format and through an accelerated trimester format. Distance learning courses are also offered.

The Honors Program, for students with strong academic records, provides an opportunity to conduct scholarly research and develop leadership skills through service learning. Upon successful completion of the program students graduate as Honors Scholars.

The Service Learning Program allows students to be of service to others while learning the value of citizenship and responsibility through action and reflection.

Academic Facilities

Seminar rooms, multimedia and learning resource centers, and laboratories in accounting, computers, psychology, science, and writing are updated annually the latest instructional technology. Through the Internet Laboratories, all students have access to e-mail and the World Wide Web. The College auditorium comfortably seats 1,500 people; its large stage with modern theatrical features hosts performing groups from all parts of the country. The College library has a selective collection of more than 110,000 volumes, as well as periodicals, cassettes, records, microfilms, and ultrafiche. A curriculum library serves as a resource center for the teacher education programs. The Child Care Center, the Felician School for Exceptional Children, the Lourdes Health Care Center, and the Nursing Skills Laboratory, all located on the Lodi campus, furnish convenient facilities for observation, application of learning, and field experiences.

Costs

Undergraduate tuition in 2007–08 is $20,500 per year for full-time students. The annual cost of room and board is $8900 (double occupancy). There are additional student fees, commuter fees, and resident fees.

Financial Aid

Felician College participates in federal, state, and institutional programs of financial assistance. To determine the amount and type of aid needed, applicants must file a Free Application for Federal Student Aid (FAFSA) with the Department of Education. The College participates in the Federal Work-Study, Federal Pell Grant, and Federal Supplemental Educational Opportunity Grant programs. Students who do not receive state scholarships may be considered for New Jersey tuition aid grants. Through a state-guaranteed loan program, students may also take out low-interest bank loans. A number of institutional scholarships are available for qualified students in need of financial assistance. The Office of Undergraduate Admission also awards merit-based scholarships to those who are eligible, regardless of need. Monies range from $4500 to full tuition based on GPA and SAT scores. To take advantage of federal financial aid programs exclusively for veterans, a certificate of eligibility should be submitted to the director of financial aid at Felician College. More than half of the students attending Felician receive some form of financial aid.

Faculty

All courses are taught by fully qualified faculty members with advanced degrees, who are dedicated primarily to teaching, advising, and continued involvement in their disciplines. The student-faculty ratio of 13:1 facilitates a close working relationship, as well as individualized programs of instruction. The faculty is composed of lay and religious men and women.

Student Government

All students participate in the Student Government Organization (SGO). The governing body of the SGO, composed of elected representatives from various student groups, coordinates activities on and off campus, including community service, campus ministry, and social, cultural, civic, and athletic events. Student representatives also serve on College committees with faculty members and administrators.

Admission Requirements

Applicants must be graduates of an accredited high school or have the high school equivalency certificate and satisfactory SAT or ACT scores. A personal interview is strongly recommended.

Students graduating with an associate degree from a recognized junior college are eligible for admission into the upper division of Felician College. Applications for transfer are considered for both fall and spring semesters. Admission requirements may be adjusted for adults on the basis of maturity and experience.

Felician College offers credit and advanced placement for acceptable scores on the College Board Advanced Placement tests and the College-Level Examination Program tests. Through Felician's Project Forward program, qualified students who have completed their junior year may take college-level courses upon recommendation by their high school principal and guidance counselor.

Application and Information

Applications, accompanied by a $30 fee, should be submitted during the fall of the senior year. The Office of Undergraduate Admission evaluates applicants' credentials on a rolling basis. However, applicants for the fall semester are strongly encouraged to apply before April 15.

Office of Undergraduate Admission
Felician College
262 South Main Street
Lodi, New Jersey 07644
Phone: 201-559-6131
Fax: 201-559-6138
Web site: http://www.felician.edu

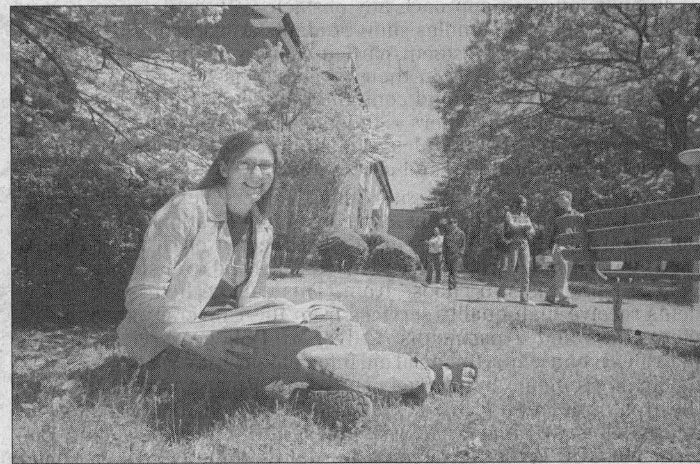

On the Rutherford campus of Felician College.

GEORGIAN COURT UNIVERSITY

LAKEWOOD, NEW JERSEY

The University

Founded in 1908 on the dreams of the Sisters of Mercy, Georgian Court University (GCU) today makes it possible for thousands of students, of all faiths and backgrounds, to realize their own dreams of a high-quality, affordable private education. Georgian Court is the only Mercy University in New Jersey and one of only two Catholic universities in the state. This means that the Mercy core values of respect, integrity, compassion, service, and justice are a distinctive part of a Georgian Court University education.

Deeply rooted in a liberal arts curriculum and anchored by the core values, GCU offers a personalized and supportive learning environment within a technologically advanced university setting. With a student body of 3,000 and an average class size of just 14, GCU students work side by side with dedicated professors. Faculty members are leaders in their respective fields, including scientific researchers, school administrators, musicians, business and industry leaders, and world-renowned experts in criminal justice and history.

A National Historic Landmark, the stunning 156-acre campus borders Lake Carasaljo in suburban Lakewood, New Jersey, and is distinguished by impressive Georgian architecture, prompting its name, Georgian Court. With magnificent statuary, lush gardens, and striking architecture, GCU is truly a breathtaking and inspiring place to learn, study, and live.

Georgian Court University students can choose from among thirty undergraduate programs—including three new majors in dance; tourism, hospitality, and recreation management; and exercise science, wellness, and sports—through two highly regarded colleges.

The first college, the Women's College, is dedicated to the success of women, both personally and professionally. The college offers a comprehensive liberal arts education tailored to women's learning styles. The emphasis is on building strong women leaders who excel in their careers; contribute to the greater good of their communities, state, and nation; and can approach any obstacle with confidence. It is no surprise to GCU that studies show students at women's colleges like GCU develop high self-esteem, participate fully in and out of the classroom, and enjoy success in their careers. The Women's College is open to both residential and commuter students. University College helps nontraditional learners—students who have family obligations, hectic employment schedules, and limited time to attend class—achieve their educational and career goals.

The second college, University College, offers flexible scheduling, technology-enhanced courses, and convenient locations, all while upholding the high caliber of education expected of GCU. There are over nine graduate programs and certificates and over sixteen undergraduate programs to choose from. This college helps ensure students receive high-quality services from the University's many support offices and departments. University College services include individual counseling, financial aid information, tutoring services, academic advisement, and career counseling. Programs are offered in the evening at the GCU main campus in Lakewood and during the day and evening at GCU at Woodbridge, GCU at Cumberland County College, and GCU at the New Jersey Coastal Communiversity in Wall.

Both residents and commuters enjoy a variety of activities, including trips to museums, theater events, and concerts. Campus social activities are planned throughout the year, and more than thirty cultural, academic, and service organizations involve students in activities on and off campus. The offices of Special Events and Student Development bring notable personalities to campus throughout the year to entertain, educate, and enlighten.

Committed to empowering students through education, GCU fosters academic leadership through the honors program, while professional growth is nurtured through Women in Leadership Development, an innovative program that cultivates the students' professional skills through hands-on workshops; seminars led by notable professional women, such as author Naomi Wolf; and discussions with women who are leaders in business, education, and government, such as former Maryland Lieutenant Governor Kathleen Kennedy Townsend.

The University also participates in seven NCAA Division II sports: basketball, cross-country, lacrosse, soccer, softball, tennis, and volleyball.

GCU's athletic teams will soon be enjoying a state-of-the-art sports complex. The $26-million Wellness Center is scheduled to open in fall 2008. The Wellness Center will have a new arena and athletic fields—two softball fields, two soccer fields, new tennis courts, an eight-lane track surrounding new lacrosse and field hockey fields, dance studios, exercise facilities, and the University bookstore.

There are three residence halls on campus: Maria Hall, St. Joseph Hall, and St. Catherine Hall, as well as a new chapel, a residence hall for visiting faculty members and Sisters of Mercy, and the Gilded Age mansion, now home to a series of interactive history theater productions.

Location

Georgian Court University is located in Lakewood, New Jersey, a suburban town midway between the urban excitement of New York City and Philadelphia, and only minutes from the spectacular beaches of the Jersey Shore. The campus is easily accessible from Route 9, the Garden State Parkway, and Interstate 195. New Jersey Transit bus access is within walking distance, giving students quick, inexpensive transportation to points of interest throughout the tristate area.

Majors and Degrees

The four prestigious schools of Georgian Court University, the School of Arts and Humanities, the School of Sciences and Mathematics, the School of Business, and the School of Education, are seamlessly integrated into both the Women's College and University College. GCU regularly reviews its academic offerings, based on recommendations from faculty members, students, and industry and community leaders.

The Bachelor of Arts is awarded in applied arts and sciences, art, art history, biology, chemistry, communications, computer information systems, criminal justice, dance, elementary education, English, history, humanities, mathematics, music, physics, psychology, religious studies, sociology, and Spanish. The Bachelor of Science is awarded in accounting; allied health technologies; biochemistry; biology; business administration; chemistry; clinical laboratory sciences; exercise science, wellness, and sports; natural sciences; tourism, hospitality, and recreation management; and physics. Students planning a career in social work may earn a Bachelor of Social Work, and future fine and graphic artists may participate in the Bachelor of Fine Arts program.

There are more than fifty minor field sequences, certification programs, and concentrations available, including anthropology, bilingual/bicultural studies, communications, criminal justice, economics, English as a second language, general fine art, gerontology, graphic design/illustration, holistic health, human resource management, marketing, medical technology, nuclear medicine technology, philosophy, political science, toxicology, and more. Preprofessional programs include chiropractic, dentistry, law, medicine, and veterinary medicine. Interdisciplinary minors are offered in international area studies, Latin American studies, and women's studies. Internships and practicums are offered in most majors, and independent study is available.

Academic Programs

Georgian Court University is concerned with developing the whole person. A well-rounded, wide-ranging liberal arts education develops the mind, and participating in service learning develops the spirit. With this dual approach, GCU graduates become successful professionals as well as compassionate neighbors, concerned citizens, and civic leaders.

The undergraduate curriculum is designed to capitalize on the student's college preparation as well as embrace the aptitudes, talents, and interests particular to the individual. Service learning opportunities, such as working hand in hand with Honduran villagers to build a new school or install clean water systems or helping disadvantaged segments of society in Lakewood to access social services, challenge GCU students to put classroom learning into action.

Candidates for a bachelor's degree at Georgian Court must complete 120 credit hours. With departmental approval, students may elect a second major. Elementary education majors are required to choose a second liberal arts major. A minimum cumulative GPA of 2.0 and a minimum cumulative major GPA of 2.5 are required for graduation.

Georgian Court University hosts seventeen academic honor society chapters, including chapters for the national biological, business administration, chemistry, education, English, mathematics, physics, psychology, social work, and sociology honor societies.

Off-Campus Programs

In addition to offering students opportunities to study abroad in several Spanish-speaking countries, Georgian Court University offers joint-degree programs through which students take courses at both Georgian Court and a partner institution, such as the University of Medicine and Dentistry of New Jersey.

Academic Facilities

The Arts and Science Center is Georgian Court's largest academic building, providing classrooms, seminar rooms, offices, art studios, and a computer lab. Construction was recently completed on the state-of-the-art Audrey Birish George Science Center, which added a two-story addition, with the latest laboratory and instruction space for scientific study.

Other campus buildings include the Sister Mary Joseph Cunningham Library, Raymond Hall Complex, which houses the School of Education, the Raymond Hall Computer Center, and the GCU Dining Hall. The School of Business and the Department of Psychology reside in Farley Center, a recently remodeled building with a computer lab, student lounge, and conference center.

Costs

Full-time tuition for the 2007–08 academic year was $20,928. Residence and board for the Women's College were $8136 (seven-day meal plan) or $7980 (five-day meal plan). General fees were $750. Instructional materials (textbooks and other items) cost extra and vary depending on the course.

Financial Aid

As a private university, Georgian Court endeavors to keep the cost of attendance affordable. Ninety-nine percent of first-year, full-time students at GCU receive financial aid in the form of scholarships, grants, loans, and work-study. The average financial aid package for a first-year student is more than $22,000. GCU also offers the Women's Leadership Award, a $5000 grant given to qualified full-time resident students in recognition of outstanding leadership and service to school, community, or church. It also participates in the New Jersey Educational Opportunity Fund. To be considered for financial aid, candidates must submit a Free Application for Federal Student Aid (FAFSA) to the Office of Financial Aid online at http://www.fafsa.ed.gov.

Faculty

Eighty-three percent of the full-time faculty members hold doctoral degrees. All courses are taught by faculty members, not graduate assistants. From the freshman year on, students have the opportunity to take classes taught by department chairs, even school deans. Georgian Court features a student-faculty ratio of 14:1 and an average class size of 14. This promotes individual attention and open, thoughtful discourse among students and professors. All students receive individual counseling by a faculty adviser.

Student Government

The Student Government Association, composed of elected students, organizes extracurricular activities, charity fund-raisers, and other events. Through the student government structure, students take leadership roles in shaping student life and participate in all major University committees, along with members of the faculty and administration.

Admission Requirements

Georgian Court University welcomes applications from qualified students of all faiths and backgrounds who desire a liberal arts education. The University strives to enroll students who can benefit most from its academic program. Entrance is based on individual merit. The high school record of achievement is of primary importance and must reflect solid performance. Candidates for admission must have completed 16 academic (Carnegie) units. The majority of students at Georgian Court ranked in the upper half of their senior high school class.

Submission of SAT or ACT scores is optional. Further consideration is given to the applicant's extracurricular activities and the letters of recommendation submitted by teachers, counselors, employers, or similarly qualified people. A campus interview is highly recommended, and a guided tour of the campus is available at the interview.

Qualified applicants whose first choice is Georgian Court University and who apply no later than November 15 may be considered for early decision. A mature, well-qualified student who wishes to enter the University after three years of high school may apply for early entrance.

Transfer students are accepted into the freshman, sophomore, and junior classes for fall and spring semesters. All transfer applicants must be in good standing at their previous college. Applicants with fewer than 24 credits must fulfill all requirements for admission to the freshman class. International students in need of a student visa must present official documents at least six months prior to the semester start and must have a minimum TOEFL score of 550 on the paper-based test or 213 on the computer-based test. International students must also complete a GCU financial support form and should be prepared to assume full financial responsibility for their educational and personal expenses in the United States.

Application and Information

To apply for admission, first-time freshman applicants should send an application, high school transcript, and nonrefundable $40 application fee payable to Georgian Court University to the Office of Admissions. Transfer students should submit those materials as well as transcripts from all colleges previously attended. Freshman applicants are urged to submit an application as early as possible during their senior year of high school. Completed applications must be received by August 1 for the fall semester and December 15 for the spring semester. Printable and electronic applications are available at http://www.georgian.edu. Schedules and registration for campus visits are available at http://www.georgian.edu/admissions.

For further information, prospective students should contact:

Office of Admissions
Georgian Court University
900 Lakewood Avenue
Lakewood, New Jersey 08701-2697
Phone: 732-987-2760
800-458-8422 Ext. 2760 (toll-free)
Fax: 732-987-2000
E-mail: admissions@georgian.edu
Web site: http://www.georgian.edu/admissions

Georgian Court University students.

KEAN UNIVERSITY

UNION, NEW JERSEY

The University

Founded in 1855, Kean University has grown to become one of New Jersey's largest institutions of higher learning. In 1958, Kean moved from Newark to Union and currently occupies more than 150 acres in Union and Hillside Townships. Kean was granted university status on September 26, 1997. While maintaining its significant role in the training of teachers, Kean has become a comprehensive institution, offering more than fifty undergraduate and thirty graduate degree programs serving more than 13,000 students. With its four undergraduate colleges, the School of Visual and Performing Arts, and the Nathan Weiss Graduate College, Kean's academic programs cover an exceptional range of disciplines.

Kean is a metropolitan, comprehensive, interactive teaching university. A campus dedicated to the pursuit of excellence in higher education, Kean University supports a student-centered learning environment that nurtures the development of the whole student for rewarding careers, lifelong learning, and fulfilling lives in a global society. It maintains a commitment to excellence and equity in enrollment, instruction, and administration.

There are 130 different clubs and organizations on the Kean University campus. These include fraternities and sororities, religious clubs, cultural organizations, and departmental clubs.

Kean is accredited by all major accrediting organizations. Many majors have accreditation in their field.

Location

Kean University is in a great location—metropolitan Union County. The campus is a short distance from Newark Liberty International Airport, New Jersey Transit trains, and major highways. Just 10 miles outside of New York City, the campus is conveniently reached by road, sea, or air.

Majors and Degrees

Kean University grants bachelor's degrees in nearly fifty majors and more than seventy options and collateral programs.

Students can pursue Bachelor of Arts degrees in art history, biology, chemistry, communications, early childhood education, earth science, economics, elementary education, English, fine arts, foreign languages (Spanish), history, mathematics, music, music education, philosophy and religion, physical education, political science, psychology, public administration, recreation administration, sociology, special education, speech and hearing, and theater. The University has recently added Bachelor of Arts programs in criminal justice administration, finance, graphic communications, industrial education, interior design, marketing, speech, studio art, theater arts, and visual communication.

Bachelor of Science degrees can be earned in accounting, computer science, health information management, industrial technology, management science, medical technology, occupational therapy, and psychology/psychiatric rehabilitation. Students may also work toward their Bachelor of Fine Arts, Bachelor of Social Work, and Bachelor of Science in Nursing (for RNs only) degrees.

Undergraduates may undertake the dual M.S. program in physical therapy and the Physician's Assistant Program. Both programs are available through an alliance with the University of Medicine and Dentistry of New Jersey (UMDNJ). Undergraduates may also undertake a dual B.A./M.S. program in occupational therapy, which is available through the Nathan Weiss Graduate College.

Kean now offers an exciting opportunity for students dedicated to pursuing a career in medicine. Kean University, Drexel University College of Medicine, and St. Peter's University Hospital have formed a partnership offering a 4-4 Bachelor of Science/Doctor of Medicine (B.S./M.D.) Scholars Program to highly qualified undergraduate students. Preference is given to candidates primarily from northeast and central New Jersey who are inclined toward careers in family medicine, general internal medicine, and general pediatrics. Students must meet all requirements of this joint program during their bachelor's degree in order to remain in the program and then proceed to medical school at Drexel University College of Medicine upon graduation from Kean University.

Academic Programs

To complete a degree, students must complete the general education requirements, totaling 52 units. Eighteen of these credits are earned in the humanities-based core curriculum. The remaining 34 are distributed between departments to lay a broad liberal arts background on which to base later specialized study. Each department specifies major requirements, with a minimum of 30 units, and students also take elective courses.

Most departments can arrange internships for juniors and seniors. Some subject areas also provide course options that students can complete from off-campus locations.

Two semesters make up the academic year, along with two summer sessions.

Off-Campus Programs

Kean University offers a variety of travel/study programs in which students may participate for a semester or for shorter periods of time. Programs include travel to all areas of the world and may be taken for credit or for personal enrichment. Selected courses are also offered in nontraditional formats, such as distance education and service learning.

Academic Facilities

Among the resources available at Kean University's Nancy Thompson Library are 270,000 volumes (including rare books), 11,164 serial subscriptions, CD-ROMs, online databases, and 14,200 bound periodicals and microfilms. Resources are located using the online catalog, VOYAGER, or CD-ROM databases. To access books not available at Kean, students can utilize the interlibrary loan system. For a small fee, students may use the journal document delivery service. Nonprint materials, such as multimedia items and media services, are located in the Instructional Resource Center (IRC).

Kean University hosts laboratory facilities such as the Reading Institute, the Institute of Child Study, and the Clinic in Learning Disabilities. Other research tools include the electron microscope and meteorological station. In addition, the extensive statewide computer network is always available.

Costs

Tuition and fees for full-time undergraduates with New Jersey residency for fall 2007 were $4252.50. Out-of-state students paid $6322.50 in fall 2007. (These figures may be adjusted for the fall 2008 semester.) In addition to tuition and fees, indirect costs for books and supplies vary but usually average $1119 per year. Personal expenses average $1399 per year, and transportation expenses range from $912 (on campus) to $1820 (off campus) per year. Room and board expenses for students living away from home average $11,456 (on and off campus) per year, while the average room and board expenses for students living at home (with parents or relatives) are $2239 per year.

Financial Aid

Kean University remains one of the most affordable universities in the nation. It recognizes that financial aid is an integral part of the financial planning process for students and their families. The University is committed to assisting students with financial aid programs and services to supplement the resources of the family. The goal of Kean's financial aid programs is to keep the University affordable for all students, regardless of financial need, by offering a wide variety of grant, loan, scholarship, work, alternative loan, and installment payment programs.

Financial aid, which may be Federal Perkins Loans, Federal Pell Grants, Federal Supplemental Educational Opportunity Grants, Federal Work-Study Program awards, or Federal Direct Loans, is awarded to about 50 percent of full-time undergraduates. The state of New Jersey offers Garden State Scholarships, Educational Opportunity Fund awards, and Tuition Aid Grants. To be considered, applicants must submit the Free Application for Federal Student Aid (FAFSA) to the University no later than March 15.

Faculty

Kean has 375 full-time faculty members, 21 part-time faculty members, and 894 adjunct faculty members. The faculty's regularly scheduled office hours and participation in virtually all areas of campus governance and operations ensure that they have continual interaction with students. Part-time and adjunct faculty members, including elected officials, business leaders, and industry representatives, provide valuable links with the community at large. Graduate assistants are not given primary instructional responsibility for any undergraduate course.

Student Government

The Student Organization of Kean University, Inc., a truly autonomous body, is incorporated and is composed entirely of students chosen through campuswide elections. Student officers administer an annual budget that is derived from student activity fees and receipts. The Student Organization supports the undergraduate student body with a wide array of service, culture, and media programming, activities, and entertainment.

The University wholly supports the concept of students' rights of self-determination, and student participation in all areas of campus governance is traditional.

Admission Requirements

The admissions committee evaluates students' apparent capacity to succeed at Kean. Decisions are not based on age, sex, race, color, creed, or national origin. High school transcripts should display a minimum cumulative GPA of 2.8 and a minimum of 16 academic units completed. Applications must include letters of recommendation from a guidance counselor, teacher, or employer, and an essay is required. Students may enter Kean with advanced standing through consideration of CLEP scores or substantial life experience.

Most transfer students must have a minimum 2.0 GPA for admission. Certain departments, such as physical therapy, demand a higher GPA.

Application and Information

Those applying to enter their freshman year must submit their application by May 31 for fall admission and December 1 for spring admission. Kean employs a rolling admissions system. International students must submit their application and all supporting documentation by May 31 for fall admission and November 1 for spring admission. Complete application packets include the following items: the Kean University application, a $50 nonrefundable application fee, official high school transcripts, and official SAT results. For those wishing to visit the campus, the information session and campus tours are Fridays at 10 a.m. from mid-September through mid-May and Thursdays at 10 a.m. from May 15 through mid-August. For other times, students should contact the office to arrange an appointment.

For additional information and application forms, students should refer to the Kean University Web site or contact:

Office of Undergraduate Admissions
Kean University
1000 Morris Avenue
Union, New Jersey 07083
Phone: 908-737-7100
Fax: 908-737-7105
E-mail: admitme@kean.edu
Web site: http://www.kean.edu

Kean students learn while enjoying the University's unique environment.

MONMOUTH UNIVERSITY

WEST LONG BRANCH, NEW JERSEY

The University

Monmouth University is a private, moderate-sized coeducational school committed to providing a learning environment that enables men and women to pursue their educational goals and realize their full potential for making significant contributions to their community and society. Small classes, which allow for individual attention and student-faculty dialogue, together with careful academic advising and career counseling, are hallmarks of a Monmouth education.

The student body is diverse, with a population of more than 4,700 undergraduates and 1,750 graduate students. Although most are from the Northeast, thirty states and thirty nations are represented, and there is a rich ethnic mix. Of the nearly 4,300 full-time undergraduate students enrolled, approximately 1,600 live on campus in traditional residence halls and garden apartment complexes. Both resident and commuting students have a wide variety of extracurricular activities to choose from: an active Student Government Association; the campus newspaper *(Outlook)*, FM radio station (WMCX), and television station (Hawk TV); the yearbook *(Shadows)* and the literary magazine *(Monmouth Review)*; the African American Student Union; a vast array of special-interest groups; theater; intramurals; and sororities and fraternities that engage in service work on behalf of the University and of the community. Many special events are planned each year, including art exhibits, concerts, lectures, sightseeing trips, and more.

The University's NCAA Division I intercollegiate athletics program includes nine men's teams—baseball, basketball, cross-country, football (Division I-AA), golf, indoor track, outdoor track and field, soccer, and tennis—and ten women's teams—basketball, cross-country, field hockey, golf, indoor track, lacrosse, outdoor track and field, soccer, softball, and tennis. The gymnasium has an indoor pool, regulation-size basketball courts, and a training room and fitness center. Outdoor facilities include tennis courts, an all-weather track, and baseball, football, soccer, and softball fields.

Monmouth students are accorded many special services, including the full resources of the First-year Experience Office and the Life and Career Advising Center, which offers academic advising and individual personal and career counseling. Academic skills services, including the Math Center, the Writing Center, and the Peer Tutoring Office, provide personalized academic assistance. Employment counseling is available through the Placement Office.

In addition to its undergraduate degree programs, Monmouth offers numerous graduate degree programs in business administration, computer science, corporate and public communication, criminal justice, education, English, health-care management, history, liberal arts, mental health counseling, nursing, psychological counseling, public policy, social work, and software engineering. There are also graduate certificate programs in numerous areas of academic interest.

Location

The University is located in a residential area of an attractive community near the Atlantic Ocean, slightly more than a 1-hour drive from the metropolitan attractions of New York City and Philadelphia. The University's safe and secure 156-acre campus, considered to be one of the most beautiful in New Jersey, includes among its fifty-five buildings a harmonious blending of traditional and contemporary architectural styles.

The centerpiece building is Woodrow Wilson Hall, a National Historic Landmark that houses administrative offices and humanities classrooms. The University has completed the construction of the state-of-the-art Jules L. Plangere Jr. Center for Communication and Instructional Technology and commenced construction of a Multipurpose Activity Center in fall 2007. Restaurants, shops, and theaters are within easy reach, and several large shopping malls and the PNC Bank Arts Center (an entertainment hub) are only a few miles away.

Another advantage is proximity to many high-technology firms, financial institutions, and a thriving business-industrial sector. These provide not only employment possibilities for graduates but also the opportunity for undergraduates to gain practical experience through various internships and the cooperative education program conducted by the University.

Majors and Degrees

Monmouth University offers twenty-nine baccalaureate degree programs within five schools. The School of Business Administration awards bachelor's degrees in business administration with concentrations in accounting, economics, finance, management, marketing, and real estate. The School of Education awards bachelor's degrees that allow students to earn certification as elementary teachers (K–5), as elementary teachers (K–5) with middle school endorsement (5–8), as secondary teachers (9–12), or as special education teachers. The Wayne D. McMurray School of Humanities and Social Sciences awards bachelor's degrees in the areas of anthropology, art, communication, criminal justice, English, fine arts, foreign language, history, history/political science, music, political science, psychology, social work, and theater. A Spanish and international business bachelor's degree is awarded jointly through the School of Business Administration and the School of Humanities and Social Sciences. The School of Science, Technology and Engineering awards bachelor's degrees in biology, chemistry, clinical laboratory sciences, computer science, marine and environmental biology and policy, mathematics, medical technology, and software engineering. The Marjorie K. Unterberg School of Nursing and Health Studies awards the Bachelor of Science in health studies and the Bachelor of Science in Nursing to upper-division transfer students. A preprofessional advising program is available for students who intend to pursue careers in medicine, dentistry, or other health-care fields. Monmouth also offers the Five-Year Baccalaureate/Master's Program, which enables students to achieve both a bachelor's and a master's degree in just five years in the areas of business, computer science, criminal justice, public policy, social work, or software engineering.

Academic Programs

The curriculum is attuned to today's globally oriented, technological society while retaining a strong grounding in the liberal arts. Under the general education curriculum, students in all degree programs acquire a breadth of knowledge beyond their major fields of study, including an appreciation of world culture. Monmouth University also emphasizes writing, speaking, and other interpersonal skills that are critical to personal and professional success. Monmouth requires all students to fulfill a technology literacy component and an experiential education component that is a real-world experience related to the student's academic major.

Monmouth University believes that in addition to providing sound preparation for successful careers, a major goal of higher education is to help students develop values. These include a keen sense of citizenship and social responsibility and the leadership qualities that equip graduates to contribute actively to the democratic society in which they live. Academic programs at Monmouth prepare students for life in an increasingly complex, multicultural world.

The Honors School at Monmouth University allows qualified students to participate in an educational environment that encourages and supports intellectual and personal excellence. Courses are clustered, with professors developing common themes and assignments. Honors classes are distinguished by in-depth coverage of material through discussion and writing, smaller class size, and a heightened student/faculty rapport. Extracurricular activities like cultural excursions to New York City are scheduled to reinforce the themes of the program.

Cooperative education is available to students, enabling them to gain practical experience in jobs related to their majors while completing their studies. All education majors are required to complete a semester of student teaching. The University also participates in the Washington Center, which is a partnership through which students may earn credit for experiential learning gained through internships and symposia in the nation's capital.

Genuine concern for the individual student characterizes the Monmouth University educational program. Professors—not teaching assistants—conduct all courses and supervise all laboratories. Students benefit from direct interaction with professors who are recognized for their scholarly expertise.

Academic Facilities

The Monmouth University Library holds approximately 271,000 volumes and more than 25,000 electronic and print journal subscriptions. Academic programs are amply supported by state-of-the-art computer hardware and software and classroom/laboratory facilities. The major components supporting Monmouth's academic programs include UNIX and Windows 2003 server systems connected by a sophisticated campus Ethernet network spanning twenty-three buildings and encompassing more than 1,400 workstations campus-wide. Workstations that are specifically dedicated to student use are distributed among many instructional and open-use laboratories and include Pentium-class workstations and Macintosh workstations. Laptop plug-in ports and wireless connectivity are available in convenient locations across campus. A campus communications network (HawkNet) connects all Monmouth University computing resources to the Internet. All students receive a computer account that provides them with e-mail, World Wide Web browsing and authoring tools, and electronic access to the Monmouth University Library catalog.

The Lauren K. Woods Theatre offers students an opportunity to experience all phases of the theater arts, from acting to lighting. Control of all aspects of a theatrical performance is maintained by students. The University supports communications facilities for both radio and television, a student-run FM radio station, a student-run greenhouse, and studios for art and music majors.

Costs

For 2007–08, tuition and fees were approximately $23,035 per year. Room and board costs were approximately $8900 per year; actual costs are determined by the type of room and meal plan selected. Costs are subject to change for 2008–09.

Financial Aid

Monmouth University believes that qualified students should not be denied an educational opportunity due to lack of financial resources. The financial aid staff counsels students and their families and assists them in obtaining the maximum financial aid to which they are entitled. In a cooperative effort, the University utilizes institutional, federal, and state resources and expects a reasonable family contribution toward the student's cost of attendance. In developing each student's award package, all resources available are utilized to address individual circumstances and to provide equitable treatment for all applicants.

A wide range of University scholarships and grants is offered to the incoming class each year. These scholarship and grant programs are available to all prospective full-time, first-year and transfer students and are offered without regard to financial need. Eligibility for University scholarship and grant funding varies according to the quality of the student's previous academic record. Award amounts range from $2000 to $15,500. Scholarships and grants are renewed at the same amount for each year of the student's undergraduate career, provided the student maintains satisfactory levels of academic performance. Scholarship recipients are required to maintain a minimum 3.0 cumulative GPA; academic excellence grant recipients must maintain a minimum 2.5 cumulative GPA; incentive grant recipients must maintain a minimum 2.0 cumulative GPA. The University also participates in all federal and state grant and loan programs. To establish eligibility for these programs and capitalize on the assistance available to them, students must complete the Free Application for Federal Student Aid (FAFSA) and are encouraged to do so as soon after January 1 as possible. Students and their families are invited to call 732-571-3463, send e-mail to finaid@monmouth.edu, or visit the Office of Financial Aid for assistance.

Faculty

The University's professors are leaders in their fields and contribute through research, publishing, and consulting to their respective academic areas. There are 251 full-time and 283 part-time faculty members. Approximately 85 percent of the full-time instructional faculty members have doctorates or other terminal degrees in their fields. The average class size is 22, and the student-faculty ratio is 15:1. Professors often know each student by name, and faculty members are available to students for office consultation and extra help.

Student Government

Monmouth's Student Government Association is an important and necessary voice in the University community. Six senators from each class, 2 commuter senators, 4 senators-at-large, and members who have been installed by the executive leadership express clear and definite opinions and cast votes on University policy as it affects the student community. Senators actively meet with campus administrators and faculty members in an effort to present the opinions of the student body and take part in resolution-adopting events. The Student Government Association hosts a number of events annually, including Homecoming, the Big Event/Day of Community Service, Springfest, the SGA Auction, and the Student Awards Ceremony. All students are strongly encouraged to participate in these activities.

Admission Requirements

Many factors are considered when candidates are evaluated for admission. For freshman applicants, the committee evaluates grades and test scores. High school transcripts, a resume of activities including leadership positions held, and SAT or ACT scores are required. Counselor recommendations and other information supporting the application are welcome. Admission interviews and campus tours are available. Transfer students must submit official transcripts from all colleges attended. If they have earned fewer than 24 transferable credits, they must fulfill freshman admission requirements as well.

Application and Information

The early action option is for students with a strong desire to enroll at Monmouth. The application deadline for early action is December 1. The admission decision notification date is January 15. The application deadline for regular decision is March 1. The admission decision notification date is prior to April 1. Applications received after March 1 are considered on a space-available basis. Freshman housing is guaranteed for the first 700 students who submit the required enrollment and housing deposits and housing contract. Housing historically fills by mid-April. Students who submit their deposits and contract after housing is full are placed on a housing waitlist. Housing is prioritized by the date on which Monmouth University is in receipt of the student's enrollment deposit, housing contract, and housing deposit. Out-of-state students who submit all required documents and fees needed to reserve housing by May 1 are accommodated.

For further information, students should contact:

Office of Undergraduate Admission
Monmouth University
400 Cedar Avenue
West Long Branch, New Jersey 07764-1898
Phone: 732-571-3456
800-543-9671 (toll-free)
Fax: 732-263-5166
E-mail: admission@monmouth.edu
Web site: http://www.monmouth.edu

MONTCLAIR STATE UNIVERSITY

MONTCLAIR, NEW JERSEY

The University

Founded in 1908 as a normal school for the education of future teachers, Montclair State University has evolved into a four-year comprehensive public university that offers a broad range of educational and cultural opportunities. Montclair State is composed of the School of Business, the School of the Arts, the College of Humanities and Social Sciences, the College of Science and Mathematics, the College of Education and Human Services, and the Graduate School and confers degrees in forty-eight undergraduate majors and forty-two graduate majors. Through its diverse programs and services, Montclair State seeks to develop educated men and women who are inquiring, creative, and responsible contributors to society.

Montclair State has been designated a Center of Excellence in the fine and performing arts in New Jersey. It is accredited by the Middle States Association of Colleges and Schools, and its teacher education, administrative, and school service personnel programs are approved by the National Council for Accreditation of Teacher Education. The School of Business is also accredited by AACSB International–The Association to Advance Collegiate Schools of Business.

The total enrollment was 16,736 in fall 2007, 13,017 of whom were enrolled as undergraduates, 8,039 women and 4,978 men. The majority of students are from New Jersey, and approximately 67 percent commute. Other students live in campus residence halls or apartments or in off-campus housing. Students participate in more than 115 campus organizations. Some of the organizations that are involved in student life are the College Life Union Board, which is responsible for coordinating all social, cultural, educational, and recreational student programs; the Intercollegiate Athletic Council, which provides men and women of all the schools with the opportunity to participate in many varsity sports; and the Department of Campus Recreation, which runs the student intramural programs.

Location

Montclair State has the advantage of being situated on a 246-acre suburban campus only 14 miles west of New York City. The campus has its own New Jersey Transit train station—the Montclair State University train station—that provides direct access to Penn Station in New York City via the Boonton-Montclair line. This proximity to the city gives students the opportunity to take advantage of the unusually rich cultural, social, and educational environment of the metropolitan area, while Montclair's suburban setting offers a nice contrast to city life. Convenient access to all major New Jersey highways makes day trips to nearby mountain resorts and ocean beaches an easy option.

Majors and Degrees

Montclair State offers programs of study leading to the Bachelor of Arts degree in anthropology, broadcasting, classics, communication studies, economics, English, family and child studies, fine arts, French, general humanities, geography, history, human ecology, Italian, jurisprudence, justice studies, Latin, linguistics, music, music therapy, philosophy, political science, psychology, religious studies, sociology, Spanish, theater studies, and women's studies. The Bachelor of Science degree is offered in allied health services, athletic training, biochemistry, biology, business administration, chemistry, computer science, geosciences, health education, mathematics, molecular biology, nutrition and food science, physical education, physics, and science informatics. The Bachelor of Fine Arts degree is awarded in dance, fine arts, and theater. The Bachelor of Music is awarded in music, and there is a five-year combined B.A./B.Mus. program. There is a four-year/five-year combined B.S./M.S. program in aquatic and coastal sciences. Combined Bachelor of Science/Doctor of Dental Medicine and Bachelor of Science/Doctor of Medicine degrees are also offered with the University of Medicine and Dentistry of New Jersey–New Jersey Dental School and University of Medicine and Dentistry of New Jersey–New Jersey Medical School, respectively. Articulated programs in physical therapy and physician assistant studies with the University of Medicine and Dentistry of New Jersey are offered, as is an articulation leading to a Pharm.D. with Rutgers.

A teacher certification program is offered in many of the subject areas mentioned above, generally for grades K through 12. Nursery school and elementary certification (N–8) is also available through several majors.

Minors are available in many of the majors listed. There are also several interdisciplinary academic programs, such as African American studies, archaeology, criminal justice, film, Hispanic community affairs, international studies, paralegal studies, prelaw studies, public administration, Russian, Russian area studies, and women's studies. Part-time bachelor's degree programs are available.

Academic Programs

Successful completion of a minimum of 120 semester hours is necessary for graduation. Course requirements include general education (34–58 semester hours), comprising communication, humanities and the arts, pure and applied sciences, social and behavioral sciences, a physical education requirement, a multicultural awareness requirement, and courses in the major field of study (32–82 semester hours).

The academic calendar is organized into two semesters (fall and spring) and summer sessions.

Montclair State also offers undergraduate degrees through the Center for Academic Advising and Adult Learning for students 25 years of age or older.

Off-Campus Programs

Through the Cooperative Education Program, a student may receive academic credit for a full-time job and earn a full-time salary. This program gives a student the opportunity to receive on-the-job training in his or her prospective career area. Internships—work for credit, not pay—are available through many major departments.

Through programs offered by the New Jersey State College Council for International Education, the International Student Exchange Program, and the College Consortium for International Studies, students have the opportunity to study abroad in the continent of Australia and such countries as Argentina, Austria, Belize, China, Colombia, Denmark, Ecuador, France, Germany, Great Britain, Greece, Hungary, Ireland, Israel, Italy, Jamaica, Korea, Mexico, the Netherlands, Portugal, Spain, and Uruguay. In addition, foreign language majors may spend a year, a semester, or a summer in French-, German-, Italian-, or Spanish-speaking countries.

The University is a charter member of the New Jersey Marine Sciences Consortium, through which students may take field-oriented courses in the marine sciences. The New Jersey School of Conservation, located in Stokes State Forest, is the largest university-operated environmental education center in the world. Through this facility, students may take courses relating to the environment in the humanities, social sciences, and natural and physical sciences and in outdoor pursuits.

Academic Facilities

The recently opened University Hall is the largest and most sophisticated building in Montclair State University's history. This significant addition has more than sixty instructional spaces for use by all of the University's colleges and schools, including one 200-seat and six 100-seat lecture halls, thirty-nine general classrooms, eleven specialized classrooms and laboratories, and a number of student study lounges and gathering spaces, including a Mission-style outdoor courtyard.

The south wing of University Hall provides a state-of-the-art new home for the University's nationally recognized College of Education and Human Services, including the ADP Center for Teacher Preparation and Learning Technologies, the Center of Pedagogy, the Literacy Enrichment Center, the Institute for the Advancement of Philosophy for Children, and offices and conference rooms for the more than 150 faculty and staff members in the College of Education and Human Services.

Two floors of the north wing of the building are dedicated to the University's information technology services and house the University's Information Commons and Technology Solutions Center for students and faculty members. Located on the seventh floor of University Hall is the region's newest and most sophisticated conference center, with meeting, conference, and event space for groups of up to 500.

The holdings of the Harry A. Sprague Library include 430,968 books, 18,000 periodical subscriptions, 117,413 government publications, and more than 1.3 million nonprint items. The Multimedia Resources Department has equipment for viewing and listening to videocassettes, records, audiocassettes, compact discs, soundslide sets, and a variety of microforms. As a designated government publications depository, the library receives and makes available for use its collections of federal and New Jersey publications. Sprague Library provides computerized access to its holdings, interlibrary services, and information retrieval. Online database searching and compact disc database searching are available for most subjects and disciplines. Café Diem, a sleek and modern 4,300-square-foot Internet café at Sprague Library, offers food, beverages, and wireless access to the Internet for students and staff members. The café is supported by library staff members, who also assist patrons with research queries.

Students are also encouraged to use the resources of the Technology Solutions Center, which provides audiovisual materials, equipment, and services. The center contains a film library, videotaping equipment, and a wide range of other audiovisual equipment and provides custom graphic and photographic services. The Information Technology Center offers computer services to students and incorporates the latest advances in technology in its facilities. Also included among the University's facilities are two modern theaters, a recital hall, a theater-arts workshop, and science, language, and computer laboratories as well as a new state-of-the-art academic building.

Costs

In 2007–08, full-time tuition and fees were assessed at a yearly rate of $8895 for New Jersey residents and $16,165 for out-of-state students. Part-time tuition and fees were $280 per credit for New Jersey residents and $460 per credit for out-of-state students. Approximate annual room and board for dormitory students were $8695 (costs are subject to change).

Financial Aid

Four major types of financial aid programs are available at Montclair State: loans, grants, scholarships, and employment. Within each of these categories, funding may be available through federal, state, and/or institutional sources. State aid programs include Tuition Aid Grants, Educational Opportunity Fund Grants, Bloustein Distinguished Scholars awards, Public Tuition Benefits awards, and NJCLASS Loans. Federal sources of aid include Federal Pell Grants, Federal Supplemental Educational Opportunity Grants, Federal Perkins Loans, the Federal Work-Study Program, Federal Stafford Student Loans, Federal PLUS Program loans, and programs for veterans. Approximately 71 percent of undergraduates receive financial aid. Students should contact the Financial Aid Office regarding application materials and deadline dates.

Faculty

Faculty members teach both graduate and undergraduate courses, with few departments employing graduate assistants. Approximately 94 percent of the faculty members hold doctorates or the appropriate terminal degree in their disciplines. A faculty-student ratio of 1:21 permits considerable interaction between students and professors. All faculty members have posted office hours in order to provide students with assistance in course material and in planning a program of study. In addition, faculty members participate actively in student-oriented activities, serve as advisers to student clubs, and conduct extracurricular workshops and field trips.

Student Government

The Student Government Association (SGA), a parent corporation that includes within its structure various class organizations and services for the student body, is composed of all undergraduates. The substantial budget of the SGA allows for the development and financing of student activities and services, such as concerts, film series, intramural sports, a drop-in center, legal aid services, a student-run radio station, and a student newspaper. The Student Government Association Legislature acts as the final representative for the entire undergraduate student body and is composed of elected representatives from each class and major curriculum.

Admission Requirements

Montclair State is an Equal Opportunity/Affirmative Action institution and does not discriminate on the basis of sex, race, color, national origin, age, or physical handicap in providing access to its benefits and services, in compliance with relevant federal and state legislation.

Applicants must present a certificate of graduation from an approved secondary school (or a high school equivalency certificate), showing the following minimum college-preparatory units: English, 4; history, 2; mathematics, 3; laboratory science, 2; foreign language, 2; and electives in English, social studies, science, mathematics, or foreign languages, 3. Freshman applicants must take the SAT or ACT; Subject Tests are not required. Admission to the programs in broadcasting, communication studies, dance, fine arts, music, and theater depends upon successful completion of departmental auditions, interviews, or portfolio reviews.

Application and Information

Applicants must submit a completed application form, a nonrefundable application fee of $55, a copy of their official high school transcript, and copies of their SAT or ACT scores. Admission decisions are announced on a rolling basis until all spaces are filled.

For application forms and additional admission information, students should contact:

Office of Admissions
Montclair State University
1 Normal Avenue
Montclair, New Jersey 07043-1624
Phone: 973-655-4444
800-331-9205 (toll-free)
E-mail: undergraduate.admissions@montclair.edu
Web site: http://www.montclair.edu

NEW JERSEY CITY UNIVERSITY

JERSEY CITY, NEW JERSEY

The University

There is much to discover at New Jersey City University (NJCU). This vital, 78-year-old liberal arts institution (formerly Jersey City State College) offers an incomparable educational experience at an affordable price. At the heart of the University is a strong academic program that is recognized by a host of accrediting institutions. NJCU has an esteemed and caring faculty and extensive student support services. Thirty-six undergraduate major degree programs are offered, as are twenty-three graduate degree programs and teacher certification programs. NJCU provides unparalleled opportunity for academic and personal growth through such study options as its nationally recognized Cooperative Education Program, which enables undergraduates in all majors to earn income and academic credit while experiencing field study at one of hundreds of participating corporations, agencies, and organizations.

There is a sense of excitement on the 47-acre, tree-lined campus, which is located in the midst of one of the world's largest metropolitan areas. The University community is rich in diversity; people from many cultures come together and learn from each other. The student population includes high school graduates pursuing the four-year degree sequence, part-time and weekend students, nontraditional older students, and students seeking job retraining, all of whom are able to take advantage of the University's flexible class scheduling and online learning opportunities. Although drawn primarily from northern New Jersey and the New York metropolitan area, students from ten other states, some as distant as California and Florida, are enrolled. International students, who come to the University from more than fifty-two other countries, enrich the multicultural nature of the campus.

The total undergraduate and graduate enrollment for full- and part-time students at the University is 10,000. With an average class size of 20 students can work closely and directly with faculty members and classmates, encouraging intellectual exchange and fostering successful mentoring relationships.

To continue to provide NJCU students with first-rate facilities that encourage intellectual success and ensure a rich quality of life on the campus and in the community, NJCU is moving ahead with capital construction projects, renovation, and maintenance of its Main Campus as well as the development of its West Campus. In addition, the University continues to have a leadership role in Jersey City's Bayside Redevelopment Vision Plan revitalizing 700 acres on the west side of the city. The West Campus, a 21-acre mixed-use site located several blocks west of the Main Campus, will include several academic buildings, a performing arts center, upgraded athletic fields and an indoor field house, student and staff housing, parking, and retail stores. In November 2005, NJCU's West Campus Redevelopment Plan received the Smart Growth Award in Urban Design from the New Jersey Department of Community Affairs and the New Jersey chapter of the American Institute of Architects.

The Michael B. Gilligan Student Union has just undergone a complete renovation and redesign. The interior features a central atrium with mall-style social space. The University Service Center, a cyber lounge, a number of other services, and an auditorium are located on the first floor. Special areas include quiet study lounges, a game room, a TV lounge, the University bookstore, a cafeteria, indoor parking, small and large meeting rooms, a private dining room, and a multipurpose room that can accommodate banquets, special events, lectures, festivals, and fairs. The Gilligan Student Union is also home to the Student Government Organization, the student newspaper, the radio station, and many clubs, organizations, fraternities, and sororities.

Students can participate in varsity sports through the University's intercollegiate athletics program, which includes men's and women's basketball, cross-country, indoor and outdoor track, soccer, and volleyball; men's baseball; and women's bowling and softball. The University's John J. Moore Athletics and Fitness Center is a 72,000-square-foot state-of-the-art facility that houses a 25-yard, six-lane swimming pool; saunas; a 2,000-seat basketball/volleyball arena; an elevated jogging track; a fitness center and training facility; and three racquetball courts. The Thomas M. Gerrity Athletic Complex, home to NJCU's outdoor sports and located a mile southwest of the Main Campus, is a 14-acre facility that features a 3,000-seat stadium, an enclosed press box, and a natural-grass surface.

Location

NJCU is located in Jersey City, New Jersey, minutes away from New York City. Although the University's location in the urban center of the Northeast affords students all the cultural and intellectual stimulation of the metropolitan area, the campus has retained a quiet atmosphere for study. The University's setting also makes travel to and from the campus convenient, providing easy access by car, train, and bus. Newark Liberty International Airport is located minutes away.

Majors and Degrees

Undergraduate programs at New Jersey City University lead to the Bachelor of Arts (B.A.), Bachelor of Science (B.S.), Bachelor of Music (B.M.), Bachelor of Fine Arts (B.F.A.), or Bachelor of Science in Nursing (B.S.N.) degrees.

NJCU's William J. Maxwell College of Arts and Sciences offers major programs leading to a bachelor's degree in art (B.A. or B.F.A.), biology (B.A. or B.S.), chemistry and computer science (B.S.), geoscience/geography (B.A. or B.S.), physics (B.A. or B.S.), and economics, English, history, mathematics, media arts, music, philosophy, political science, psychology, sociology, and Spanish (B.A.). A B.S. in clinical laboratory sciences is offered jointly with the University of Medicine and Dentistry of New Jersey (UMDNJ). The Deborah Cannon Partridge Wolfe College of Education offers major programs leading to a Bachelor of Arts degree in early childhood education, elementary education, and special education. Also offered are undergraduate programs that lead to certification, such as New Jersey Department of Education certification in secondary education. The College of Professional Studies offers major programs leading to a Bachelor of Science degree in business administration, criminal justice, fire science, health sciences, and security. The University's Department of Fire Science is the only university-based fire science program in New Jersey and one of few in the nation. A Bachelor of Science in Nursing (B.S.N.) is also offered.

New Jersey City University and New Jersey Institute of Technology (NJIT) offer a dual-degree program that enables undergraduates to study for five years and earn two Bachelor of Science degrees: a Bachelor of Science in applied physics from NJCU and a Bachelor of Science in electrical engineering from NJIT.

Academic Programs

As an institution committed to the liberal arts, New Jersey City University expects all incoming students to satisfy 18 credits of all University requirements and 48 credits of general studies area requirements. Students take 48 credits from each of six clusters: natural sciences, social sciences, art and media arts, humanities, multicultural disciplines and languages, and quantitative and computer literacy. There are specific major requirements as well as electives in each degree program. In addition, students may use general electives to complete a minor or a second major, strengthen a major, or pursue areas of personal interest. In their junior and senior years of study, students have ample opportunity to engage in fieldwork in their major. Online learning opportunities are available to undergraduates. The University calendar is based on a two-semester system with two summer sessions.

The Honors Program is an innovative and intellectually rigorous course of study offering an advanced core curriculum that emphasizes in-depth investigation rather than broad surveys, as well as the opportunity to do independent research. Class sizes are small and personalized, so there is more opportunity to interact with faculty members within a community of learners from a variety of disciplines. Acceptance into the Honors Program is based on a combination of standing in the high school class, high school GPA, combined scores on the SAT, placement scores in writing and math, and the application essay. Current NJCU and transfer students with a GPA of higher than 3.0 may also be eligible for admission to the Honors Program.

Off-Campus Programs

NJCU, the premier cooperative education university in New Jersey, offers sophomores, juniors, and seniors in all academic areas the opportunity to study for a degree while working in salaried positions in related fields. NJCU's Cooperative Education Program places students with more than 550 local and international employers.

Academic Facilities

On the Main Campus, the most imposing new structure is the seven-story George Karnoutsos Arts and Sciences Hall, designed by the renowned architect Michael Graves. The 77,000-square-foot building opened in fall 2006. The academic building houses fourteen state-of-the-art classrooms, nine computer labs, faculty offices for nine departments, and the Office of the Dean of Arts and Sciences.

The Congressman Frank J. Guarini Library, a state-of-the-art research facility, houses 250,000 books and monographs, subscribes to 1,579 periodicals and journals and more than 22,500 e-journals in about 100 online databases, receives approximately 5,000 selected U.S. government publications per year, and maintains a collection of official state of New Jersey publications. The library has a complete file of microfiche issued by the Educational Research Information Center, which is a clearinghouse for research in all areas of education, and more than 500,000 fully indexed publications on microfilm. NJCU provides computer laboratory support services to students through its Office of Academic Computing.

NJCU's Media Arts Center is a 16,000-square-foot facility that houses two full-color broadcast-quality television studios, a radio and audio production studio, a complete 16-mm production studio and processing laboratory, two large projection/seminar rooms, an animation laboratory, a graphic-production studio, individual student editing space, and work rooms. Since 1991, the Media Arts Center has been the home of the Black Maria Film Festival.

The University administers the A. Harry Moore Laboratory School, which is a special education facility. The University Academy Charter High School is also located on the University's West Campus. The University is home to the NJCU Business Development Incubator, a campus resource that assists potential entrepreneurs with innovative ideas or commercially attractive technology by providing reasonably priced office space, a library, conference rooms, and marketing and managerial assistance.

The NJCU Speicher-Rubin Women's Center offers a range of services to women and presents programs on women's issues for NJCU and the community. The center provides a supportive atmosphere, informal counseling and referrals, and various education services. Both NJCU's Health and Wellness Center and Counseling and Psychological Services Center provide medical care, counseling, and psychotherapy services on the campus. The Academic Career Planning and Placement Center provides career counseling services and job placement assistance. NJCU's Early Childhood Learning Center provides educationally focused child care for the children of students.

Costs

Undergraduate tuition and fees for the 2007–08 academic year are $8155 for New Jersey residents and $14,759 for nonresidents. Room and board in NJCU's Vodra Hall Dormitory, Cooperative Education Dormitory, or apartment complex are $8200.

Financial Aid

NJCU offers students maximum opportunities for financial aid. Financial aid for eligible students includes needs-based federal grants, state grants, and scholarships; merit-based Corporate Scholarships; Federal Perkins Loans; Federal Stafford Student Loans; and jobs provided under the Federal Work-Study Program. Applicants for financial aid must submit the Free Application for Federal Student Aid (FAFSA). Approximately 75 percent of NJCU full-time undergraduates receive financial aid.

Faculty

Seventy-nine percent of NJCU's faculty members hold the highest degrees attainable in their fields. A student-faculty ratio of 14:1 supports the development of close mentoring relationships and fosters the academic, social, and cultural growth of undergraduates. This student-faculty ratio also enables NJCU professors to be very accessible to their students.

Student Government

NJCU's Student Government Organization (SGO) charters and regulates all student clubs and organizations funded by student activity fees, providing a necessary degree of leadership and coordination. The SGO is administered by the Student Council, which is composed of the Student Executive Committee and class representatives. Members of the SGO serve in the University Senate to represent the interests and concerns of students.

Admission Requirements

Admission to New Jersey City University is based on a student's projected ability to complete a degree program. All admission decisions are made without regard to race, religion, sex, age, handicap, or national origin. It is desirable that freshman applicants rank in the top half of their high school class and complete a college-preparatory program that includes 4 units of English, 3 units of mathematics, 2 units of social science, and 2 units of laboratory science. A student's combined SAT score or ACT score is taken into account in determining acceptance in individual cases. In addition, New Jersey residents who demonstrate financial need and do not meet traditional admissions requirements but have the academic potential and motivation to succeed in college may apply for admission through NJCU's Opportunity Scholarship Program (OSP). The University also accepts students who have been identified as learning disabled through its Project Mentor Program. Transfer applicants are required to have a minimum grade point average of 2.0. Transfer students are also required to have a minimum of 12 college-level credits. Every applicant must submit a required personal statement along with a completed application.

Application and Information

Application for admission may be made by submitting a completed application, a $35 application fee, an official high school transcript, and SAT or ACT scores. Transfer students must submit all college transcripts. Applications for the fall semester should be received by April 1; applications for the spring semester should be received by November 1. These dates are subject to change. Admission decisions are made on a rolling basis.

For additional information and application forms, students should contact:

Director of Admissions
New Jersey City University
2039 Kennedy Boulevard
Jersey City, New Jersey 07305
Phone: 201-200-3234
888-441-NJCU (toll-free)
Web site: http://www.njcu.edu

The Gothic tower of Hepburn Hall at New Jersey City University.

COLLEGE DATA CENTER • NEW JERSEY

PRINCETON UNIVERSITY

PRINCETON, NEW JERSEY

The University

The fourth-oldest college in the country, Princeton was chartered in 1746 and has roots that extend deep into America's past. Woodrow Wilson, a former president of Princeton (as well as a former governor of New Jersey and president of the United States), coined the phrase "Princeton in the Nation's Service" during his address at the University's 150th anniversary of its founding in 1896. It has served as Princeton's unofficial motto ever since, recently expanding to include "and in the Service of All Nations." It nicely summarizes the commitment of Princetonians to various kinds of public service around the nation and throughout the world.

Princeton owns more than 2,000 acres of land, of which, about 200 make up the main campus. A wealth of architectural styles are displayed, ranging from the oldest Colonial buildings to the predominantly Gothic dormitories to modern structures by such eminent architects as Minoru Yamasaki, Edward Larrabee Barnes, Lew Davis, I. M. Pei, Robert Venturi, and Frank Gehry.

The total enrollment is 7,085, of whom 4,790 are undergraduates. In the three most recent entering classes, the ratio of men to women was about 52:48. Students at Princeton come from all fifty states, Puerto Rico, the Virgin Islands, Guam, and more than seventy countries. They come from a wide variety of ethnic and socioeconomic backgrounds. The University sponsors multicultural and women's centers, which are open to all students. Interaction among students of different backgrounds is an important part of a Princeton education.

The Frist Campus Center is a hub of activity at Princeton. It offers the entire campus community a convenient place to eat, socialize, and connect with each other. Other services at Frist include theater and performance space, computer clusters, game rooms, and shopping. The Community Service Center (home of the Student Volunteers Council, Princeton's largest student organization) and Undergraduate Student Government are housed in Frist, as well as dining venues, mail services, ATM machines, computer connection ports, and a convenience store. Frist also hosts film series, lectures, and special events. Princeton has more than 200 student clubs and organizations, including a radio station, daily newspaper and other publications, and numerous cultural, ethnic, political, religious, and service organizations. Performing arts facilities include McCarter Theatre (home to a professional company and performing arts center as well as Princeton's famed Triangle Club), Richardson Auditorium, Taplin Auditorium, and 185 Nassau Street, which is home to a variety of studios for the fine and performing arts, including the James Stewart Film Center.

Princeton has two gymnasiums. Jadwin Gym provides 250,000 square feet of indoor space for basketball, track, wrestling, fencing, squash, and tennis, in addition to large practice areas for outdoor field sports. Dillon Gym has facilities for swimming, diving, dance, weight training, and volleyball, plus additional space for basketball, wrestling, fencing, and squash. Other sports facilities include Princeton Stadium (multiuse), 1952 Stadium for lacrosse and field hockey, William Weaver Memorial Stadium for track and field, the DeNunzio Pool swimming and diving complex, Baker Rink for hockey and skating, Lake Carnegie's Olympic-quality racing course for crew and sailing, outdoor tennis courts, an eighteen-hole golf course, and numerous playing fields.

The University guarantees housing for all undergraduates. All freshmen and sophomores live and dine in six residential colleges. Juniors and seniors may choose to live and eat in the residential colleges as well; some juniors and seniors opt to live in the upperclass dorms, and more than half dine in the nonresidential independent eating clubs. The Center for Jewish Life offers a kosher dining facility open to all students and sponsors a wide array of social, educational, and religious programs.

Location

The town of Princeton, adjoining the University campus, has a population of 30,000. New York and Philadelphia are easily accessible by public transportation, and there are hourly departures throughout most of the day. The University regularly subsidizes and otherwise facilitates students' attendance at cultural, sports, and social events in both cities. Boston and Washington, D.C., are near enough for weekend visits by trains that stop in Princeton.

Majors and Degrees

Princeton University awards a Bachelor of Arts (A.B.) degree in anthropology, architecture, art and archaeology, astrophysical sciences, chemistry, classics, comparative literature, computer science, East Asian studies, ecology and evolutionary biology, economics, English, French and Italian, geosciences, Germanic languages and literatures, history, mathematics, molecular biology, music, Near Eastern studies, philosophy, physics, politics, psychology, religion, Slavic languages and literatures, sociology, and Spanish and Portuguese. An A.B. degree in public and international affairs is offered through the Woodrow Wilson School of Public and International Affairs. In addition, Princeton offers courses in more than thirty interdepartmental programs, many of which award a certificate of study. These programs include African-American studies, creative writing, environmental studies, musical performance, theater and dance, visual arts, and women's studies.

The Bachelor of Science in Engineering (B.S.E.) degree is awarded in chemical engineering, civil engineering, computer science, electrical engineering, mechanical and aerospace engineering, and operations research and financial engineering. Interdepartmental and topical programs are offered in areas such as engineering biology, engineering physics, geological engineering, materials science and engineering, and robotics and intelligent systems.

Academic Programs

Princeton endeavors to provide a broad education with emphasis in a particular field of study. Consequently, A.B. students are required to fulfill distribution, foreign language, and writing requirements, and every A.B. student is required to complete a total of thirty courses with at least eight in his or her concentration. In addition, students are expected to do independent research, which takes the form of junior papers and a senior thesis under the guidance of a departmental faculty adviser.

The School of Engineering and Applied Science requires thirty-six courses for graduation, and at least seven of these must be liberal arts electives. While specific prerequisites and requirements within each department may vary, all emphasize independent work during the junior and senior years.

Freshmen with scores of 4 or 5 on the Advanced Placement tests given by the College Board or scores of 6 or 7 on the International Baccalaureate Higher Level exams may, with the approval of the appropriate department, be granted advanced placement/standing.

Academic Facilities

The Princeton University library system consists of the Harvey S. Firestone Memorial Library, one of the country's major university libraries, which houses the largest portion of Princeton's collection, and eighteen special libraries, including fifteen academic department collections. Firestone Library's open-stack collections include more than 6 million books, records, and 6 million microforms. There are reading spaces for 2,000, study carrels for 500, and a number of offices and conference rooms.

The Engineering Quadrangle, home of the School of Engineering and Applied Science, contains numerous laboratories and classrooms, a library, a machine shop, a convocation room, more than 125 faculty offices and graduate-study spaces, and an energy-research facility.

The Art Museum has an extensive permanent collection that ranges from artifacts of the ancient world to paintings and sculpture of the Renaissance, modern Europe, and America.

Princeton students are given access to a varied and powerful computing environment. The cornerstone is DormNet, a fiber-optic-based network that brings a high-speed data connection to every dorm room on campus.

Costs

The basic 2007–08 academic-year expenses for all students are $33,000 for tuition and fees and $10,980 for room and board.

Financial Aid

Admission decisions are need-blind. Princeton provides assistance to meet the full demonstrated financial need of all admitted students. Once admitted with aid, a student receives assistance for succeeding undergraduate years, as long as the family continues to demonstrate need and the student makes normal progress toward a degree. Financial aid packages consist of a combination of the University scholarship and federal assistance in the form of grant and work-study opportunities. Beginning in 2001, Princeton removed student loans from the award packages for aid students, replacing them with additional University scholarships.

Approximately 75 percent of the student body receives financial aid from outside sources and/or the University each year; about 54 percent receive financial aid from the University.

Faculty

One of Princeton's outstanding assets is its faculty. A single faculty teaches both undergraduate and graduate students, all of whom have close contact with scholars of national and international reputation. The current student-faculty ratio is 5:1.

Student Government

The Undergraduate Student Government (USG) is the undergraduate representative body that advocates students' interests to other groups. Other purposes of the USG include the exercise of leadership in undergraduate activities and the running of services for members of the University community.

Admission Requirements

Princeton does not require a specific set of secondary school courses for admission. It does, however, strongly recommend the following as a basic preparation for study at the University: 4 years each of English (including continued practice in writing), mathematics, and a single foreign language; 2 years each of laboratory science and history (including that of the United States and another country or area); some study of art or music; and, if possible, a second foreign language.

All candidates must submit the results of the SAT Reasoning Test or the ACT with writing. In addition, all candidates must submit the results of three different SAT Subject Tests. Students interested in pursuing a B.S.E. degree should take SAT Subject Tests in either physics or chemistry and in either level I or level II mathematics in addition to a third Subject Test of their choice.

Interviews on campus are not available. Applicants are encouraged to have an interview in their home area with a member of one of Princeton's Alumni Schools Committees and to visit the campus to attend group information sessions and take guided tours.

Application and Information

Students may apply to Princeton on an application form provided by the University, or they may use the Common Application. Applicants can submit applications electronically or by mail. The application deadline is January 1, and notification is in early April.

Requests for additional information and application forms should be sent to:

Admission Office
Princeton University
110 West College
P.O. Box 430
Princeton, New Jersey 08544-0430
Phone: 609-258-3060
Web site: http://www.princeton.edu

Blair Hall, with its distinctive arch, is a landmark building at Princeton University.

RAMAPO COLLEGE OF NEW JERSEY

MAHWAH, NEW JERSEY

The College

Ramapo College of New Jersey has been recognized by the State Legislature as New Jersey's "public liberal arts college." Offering a diverse student body and the educational ambience associated with liberal arts colleges, Ramapo has fulfilled its promise as one of the more distinguished institutions of moderate size. In recognition of Ramapo College of New Jersey's strong commitment to character-building programs, the John Templeton Foundation, which publishes a reference guide for students, families, and high schools, named Ramapo to its Honor Roll. The Honor Roll program recognizes and promotes colleges and universities that emphasize character building as an integral part of the college experience.

Ramapo offers bachelor's degrees in the arts, business, humanities, social sciences, and sciences as well as in professional studies that include nursing and social work. In addition, Ramapo offers programs leading to teacher certification at the elementary and secondary levels. The student body reflects the diversity of the regions served by the College, including eighteen states and fifty-two countries as of fall 2007. This diversity, the talents of the faculty, the expectations the College has of its students, and the proximity of the College to some of the world's major multinational organizations give Ramapo an edge in meeting its objective of preparing students of all ages for an increasingly interdependent and multicultural world. For these reasons, Ramapo is called "the college of choice for a global education."

Ramapo College takes pride in four distinctive features that enhance each student's education: concern for student development in and out of the classroom, an exemplary faculty committed to a curricular emphasis on the international and multicultural dimensions of all fields of study, an interdisciplinary orientation in its philosophy and programs, and a collaborative association with local corporations, communities, and educational institutions in the development of experiential educational opportunities and other new ventures both nationally and globally.

The fall 2007 undergraduate enrollment was 5,393 men and women. During the academic year, the campus is alive with exciting cultural events, such as music festivals, plays, art exhibits, and film and lecture series. The Student Center, with recreation rooms, lounges, and club offices, is the hub of on-campus activity. Students take an active part in planning the calendar of events for the College community. The campus contains attractive residential units housing more than 2,900 students. A 116,684-square-foot sports and recreation center opened in fall 2004, and Laurel Hall, a new 432-bed dormitory, opened in fall 2006. In addition, a sports complex has twelve lighted tennis courts; baseball, soccer, and softball fields; and a track. The gym is equipped with a full-size basketball court, an Olympic-size indoor pool, and a fitness center. At Ramapo, sports facilities are available for all students, not just the varsity athletes, who participate in seventeen intercollegiate sports in the most challenging NCAA Division III conference in the country. The College offers a rewarding blend of academic, social, and cultural experiences in the students' daily routine.

In addition to bachelor's degrees, the College offers the Master of Arts in Liberal Studies, the Master of Science in Educational Technology, and the Master of Science in Nursing.

Location

Ramapo College's barrier-free campus, more than 300 acres in size, is located in the foothills of the Ramapo Mountains in Mahwah, New Jersey, just 25 miles from New York City and all of its cultural advantages.

Majors and Degrees

Ramapo College offers programs of study leading to the Bachelor of Arts degree in American studies, communication arts, contemporary arts, economics, environmental studies, history, international business, international studies, law and society, literature, music, political science, psychology, social science, sociology, Spanish language studies, theater, and visual arts. The Bachelor of Science degree is awarded in accounting, allied health, biochemistry, bioinformatics, biology, biology/physical therapy track, biology/physician assistant track, business administration (including finance, management, and marketing), chemistry, clinical laboratory sciences, computer science, environmental science, information systems, integrated science studies, mathematics, physics, and psychology. The Bachelor of Social Work and Bachelor of Science in Nursing degrees are also offered.

Ramapo also offers state-approved teacher education programs to train and certify teachers. Students seeking teacher certification take a sequence of professional education courses in subjects relating to elementary, middle school, junior high, and senior high curricula. Subjects include, but are not limited to, art, biology, business, chemistry, drama, earth science, elementary education, English, foreign languages, mathematics, music, physical science, physics, and social studies.

Academic Programs

Each course at Ramapo is offered through one of five academic units, called schools. These units are relatively small groupings of faculty members, organized around individual themes considered to be important and useful areas of study.

The five schools include the Anisfield School of Business, American and International Studies, Contemporary Arts, Social Science and Human Services, and Theoretical and Applied Science. Each student is associated with one of these schools while at Ramapo. This association brings the student in contact with others who have the same or similar academic interests and provides the student with easy access to academic advisement and to the courses needed to satisfy degree requirements.

Academic Facilities

A construction boom during recent years has resulted in the completion of the Bill Bradley Sports and Recreation Center, with a main arena of 1,516 bleecher seats and 914 floor seats, a skybox, a fitness center, a jogging track, and a climbing wall; the Angelica and Russ Berrie Center for Performing and Visual Arts that houses performance theaters, art galleries, and specialized spaces devoted to fine arts, computer art, photography, theater, dance, and music; residence facilities that include a suite-style residence hall, a townhouse-style apartment complex, and two traditional-style residence halls; and newly renovated classrooms and computer labs. A five-story academic facility to house the Anisfield School of Business is substantially complete. Groundbreaking for a new 1,787-square-foot Sustainability Education Center commenced in October 2007, with completion targeted for the fall 2008 semester.

Costs

Full-time tuition and fees in 2007–08 were $9965 for New Jersey residents and $15,536 for out-of-state students. The combined cost of tuition and fees was $311.40 per credit for New Jersey residents and $485.50 for out-of-state students. Other charges, depending on circumstances, included $10,310 per year for room and board and a parking fee of $200 per year. Books and supplies cost about $1200 per year.

Financial Aid

Most financial aid is awarded on the basis of a student's financial need. To qualify for aid at Ramapo, students must complete the Free Application for Federal Student Aid (FAFSA). A student should apply for financial aid prior to March 1 to receive preferential consideration. Federal Perkins Loans, Federal Pell Grants, and Federal Work-Study Program funds are vital parts of the College financial aid program. New Jersey residents should also apply for a state-supported tuition-aid grant. In addition, Ramapo College offers scholarships for high-achieving incoming freshman students. These awards include tuition and fees, housing, or both. Merit awards are offered for eight semesters as long as the student maintains the required grade point average. New student applicants are automatically considered for these scholarships. Continuing students not receiving an initial scholarship award may apply for additional merit awards based on their academic achievement at the College.

Faculty

Ramapo College has 434 full- and part-time faculty members as of fall 2007. Most have been at the College for a number of years and have played a significant role in shaping the College and building strong academic programs. Faculty members have been recruited principally for their effectiveness as teachers of undergraduate students. The College believes it has a distinguished faculty in this regard. Of the full-time faculty members teaching academic courses, 95 percent have a doctoral or equivalent final degree. Their graduate research training—from Ivy League institutions, from the great state universities of the nation, and from universities abroad—as well as their professional experience—indicate that faculty members possess high quality and diverse experience in the subject matter of their courses.

Student Government

There is an active student government. Each spring, students are elected to this body. The group meets on a weekly basis to discuss any issues that it feels affect the welfare of the student body. Executive officers of the student government meet regularly with the College president and participate actively on committees of the Board of Trustees. Each year students elect a student trustee and student trustee alternate. A member of the Faculty Assembly is designated as liaison to the group so students and others are aware of issues being discussed by the faculty. The president of the Student Government Association makes presentations to both the Faculty Assembly and the trustees at their regular meetings. Students also participate actively in the governance of the College's schools as members of the unit councils. It is here that students have the greatest opportunity to influence decisions on personnel and academic programs.

Admission Requirements

High school seniors generally are expected to have completed a minimum of 18 academic units (although most have more), distributed as follows: 4 units of English, 3 units of social studies/history, 3 units of mathematics (including algebra, algebra II, and geometry), 3 units of science (including 3 of laboratory science), 2 units of a foreign language, and 3 units of academic electives. In addition, students applying from high school must take the SAT or the ACT and have their test scores sent to Ramapo.

Admission of candidates is made on the basis of the academic record, SAT or ACT scores, a school counselor's evaluation, and evidence of motivation and community and school contributions. Rank in the top quarter of the student's secondary school class is expected. Transfer students are also admitted. Deferred admission is possible.

Immediate Decision Day, Ramapo College of New Jersey's antidote to the stress of the college selection and application process, is an opportunity to apply and receive a notice of acceptance in just one day. On the appointed day, high school seniors submit their applications and supporting materials, have an admissions interview, and receive a decision notice, all on the same day. In addition, students who are eligible for a scholarship are offered one at that time.

On the day of their visit, students and their families receive information about the College, tour the campus (including the residence halls), attend a class, and then have lunch in the student dining hall. They also meet individually with an admissions officer. At the end of the day, students receive the College's decision regarding their application. Immediate Decision Days are scheduled in August, September, October, November, and December.

The College hosts open house programs during the fall and spring that give students and their families the opportunity to learn about academic programs, admissions, and financial aid; to meet faculty and staff members and students; and to tour the campus. Students are encouraged to visit during these special events. Weekday tours of the campus are available as well and personal interviews are available during the Immediate Decision Days in the fall. Interested students should contact the Office of Admissions at 201-684-7300 or 7301 or visit Ramapo's Web site for further details about campus visits.

Application and Information

Students may enter in September or January. Freshmen are encouraged to apply during the fall of their senior year. Applications for the freshman year are accepted until March 1. Applications from transfer students are accepted until May 1. Applying for admission as a matriculating (degree-seeking) student involves completing an application, having the high school and college (if a transfer student) forward transcripts, and sending a $55 nonrefundable fee to the admissions office. Students may obtain the forms and instructions by visiting or contacting the admissions office or by visiting the Ramapo Web site. Admission decisions are made on a rolling basis. The College Board Candidates Reply Date of May 1 is used for confirming an offer of admission.

For a viewbook, application forms, and additional information, including current costs, students should contact:

Director of Admissions
Ramapo College of New Jersey
505 Ramapo Valley Road
Mahwah, New Jersey 07430
Phone: 201-684-7300 or 7301
E-mail: admissions@ramapo.edu
Web site: http://www.ramapo.edu

The Russ and Angelica Berrie Center for the Performing and Visual Arts on the campus of Ramapo College of New Jersey.

THE RICHARD STOCKTON COLLEGE OF NEW JERSEY

POMONA, NEW JERSEY

STOCKTON COLLEGE
THE RICHARD STOCKTON COLLEGE OF NEW JERSEY

The College

The Richard Stockton College of New Jersey (RSCNJ) is a selective, medium-sized, highly-ranked, public liberal arts college within the New Jersey system of higher education, offering programs in the arts and humanities, business, professional studies, and social, behavioral, and natural sciences. Founded in 1969, the College was named for Richard Stockton, one of the New Jersey signers of the Declaration of Independence.

Stockton enrolls more than 7,000 students from New Jersey and the surrounding mid-Atlantic states, providing distinctive traditional educational programs and alternative educational experiences that extend learning beyond the classroom. Stockton seeks to develop the analytic and creative capabilities of its students and encourages them to undertake individually planned courses of study that promote self-reliance, acceptance of change, and an educated response to change.

The College's campus provides an excellent natural setting for a wide range of outdoor recreational activities, including sailing, canoeing, hiking, jogging, and fishing. Students and faculty and staff members join together in an extensive intramural and club sports program that includes aikido, crew, flag football, golf, ice hockey, soccer, softball, street hockey, swimming, and volleyball. At the intercollegiate level, Stockton fields NCAA Division III sports teams in men's baseball, basketball, lacrosse, and soccer; women's basketball, crew, field hockey, soccer, softball, tennis, and volleyball; and men's and women's cross-country and track and field. The new multipurpose Sports and Recreation Center has fitness facilities, a glass-enclosed indoor swimming pool, racquetball courts, weight rooms, a gymnasium, and outdoor recreational facilities that include a field house, NCAA track, field-event venues, and four playing fields for soccer and lacrosse.

College Center I is the hub for social, recreational, cultural, and leisure activities. More than eighty clubs and organizations have their offices in the center: social clubs, such as the Film Committee, Concert Committee, and Performing Arts Committee; service clubs, including the Social Work Club, Speech and Hearing Association, and Unified Black Students' Society; special interest clubs, such as the Accounting and Finance Society, Dance Club, and Photography Club; and independent organizations, including the Jewish Student Union, New Life Christian Fellowship, and twenty-one sororities and fraternities. Participation in cocurricular activities can be documented through the College's student development program, ULTRA (Undergraduate Learning, Training and Awareness), culminating in a cocurricular transcript issued to students.

College Center II, which is connected to the main academic complex, is an open living room–type area featuring a dining facility for students and staff members, a wide-screen television, a game room, lounge areas, and several conference rooms.

A new Campus Center is being constructed and will include student services, student meeting rooms, classrooms, computer labs, dining services, and large meeting and conference facilities.

The Residential Life Center provides a curricular/cocurricular facility within two student housing areas. With its large and small meeting rooms, convenience store, and computer lab, the center encourages activities and programs for both organized and informal student groups.

The Lakeside Center, located in the garden apartment housing area, contains a convenience store, snack bar, outdoor concert area, computer lab, multipurpose room for large programs, and a small meeting room for student groups.

Stockton provides on-campus housing for almost 2,500 students in traditional residence hall–style arrangements and apartment-style living. All complexes are completely furnished and air conditioned, with cable TV, telephone service, and Internet access (port-per-pillow) provided. Students choosing to live off campus can find a number of nearby complexes as well as summer shore homes not used during the academic year that are rented to Stockton students.

The Richard Stockton College of New Jersey is accredited by the Commission on Higher Education of the Middle States Association of Colleges and Schools. In addition, the social work program is accredited by the Council on Social Work Education; the teacher education sequence is approved by the New Jersey Department of Education and the National Association of State Directors of Teacher Education and Certification; the nursing program is accredited by the New Jersey Board of Nursing and the Commission on Collegiate Nursing Education; the chemistry program (B.S.) is accredited by the American Chemical Society; the physical therapy program is accredited by the Commission on Accreditation in Physical Therapy Education (CAPTE) of the American Physical Therapy Association; the environmental health/public health program is accredited by the National Environmental Health Sciences and Protection Accreditation Council; the health administration/public health program is accredited by the Association of University Programs in Health Administration; and the occupational therapy program is accredited by the Accreditation Council for Occupational Therapy Education (ACOTE) of the American Occupational Therapy Association (AOTA).

In addition to undergraduate bachelor's degrees, Stockton offers graduate studies in Doctor of Physical Therapy, Master of Arts in criminal justice, Holocaust and genocide studies, education, and instructional technology; Master of Business Administration; and Master of Science in computational science, Nursing, and Occupational Therapy as well as certificate programs in education, ESL (English as a second language), NJ Standard Supervisor Endorsement, and paralegal studies.

Location

The Richard Stockton College of New Jersey is located on a stunning 1,600-acre campus in Pomona, New Jersey, nestled in the Pinelands National Reserve 12 miles from Atlantic City, with easy access to Philadelphia and New York City. The environmentally friendly campus has a rural parklike setting, yet is close to a variety of cultural and recreational activities with nearby opportunity for shopping and dining.

A full schedule of concerts, art exhibitions, lectures, recreation, and sports on campus is complemented by the nearby Jersey Shore resort destinations. Within a 15-minute drive, students find fishing, boating, swimming, and cultural attractions as well as the entertainment of Atlantic City.

Majors and Degrees

The Bachelor of Arts degree is offered in applied physics, biology, business studies, chemistry, communication, computer science and information systems, criminal justice (forensic science), economics, education, environmental studies, geology, historical studies, languages and culture studies, liberal studies, literature, marine science, mathematics, philosophy and religion, political science, psychology, sociology and anthropology, and studies in the arts.

The Bachelor of Science degree is offered in applied physics, biochemistry/molecular biology, biology, business studies (accounting, finance, hospitality and tourism management, international business, management, marketing), chemistry, computational science, computer science and information systems, environmental studies, geology, marine science, mathematics, nursing, psychology, public health, social work, and speech pathology and audiology.

Stockton's flexible curriculum allows students to prepare for professional careers, such as dentistry, law, medicine, and veterinary medicine, while pursuing a traditional major. The College also offers preprofessional preparation in occupational therapy, optometry, pharmacy, physical therapy, and podiatry, with the Master of Science in Occupational Therapy and the doctorate in physical therapy completed at Stockton.

Stockton has accelerated seven-year dual-degree articulation agreements with the University of Medicine and Dentistry of New Jersey (Robert Wood Johnson Medical School, New Jersey Medical School, School of Osteopathic Medicine, New Jersey Dental School), the Pennsylvania College of Podiatric Medicine, the New York College of Podiatric Medicine, the New York State College of Optometry, and Rutgers School of Pharmacy. Stockton also has an articulation program with Cornell University for veterinary medicine as well as five-year, dual-degree programs with New Jersey Institute of Technology (NJIT) and Rutgers University for students interested in engineering. Students participating in the engineering program earn a Bachelor of Science degree in chemistry, physics, or math from Stockton and a Bachelor of Science degree in engineering from NJIT or Rutgers. A dual degree in pharmacy allows students to graduate from Stockton with a Bachelor of Science degree in biochemistry/molecular biology and finish their Doctor of Pharmacy degree at the Ernest Mario School of Pharmacy at Rutgers University.

Academic Programs

To earn a baccalaureate degree at Stockton, a student must satisfactorily complete a minimum of 128 semester credits. Degree programs include a combination of general studies and program (major field) studies. The Bachelor of Arts student must earn a total of 64 credits in general studies; the Bachelor of Science student must earn 48. General studies courses are broad cross-disciplinary courses designed to introduce students to all major areas of the curriculum and to the broadly applicable intellectual skills necessary for success in college. Students must select some courses from each major curricular area. The only required courses within general studies are the basic studies courses (up to three), but students may be exempt from these courses based on diagnostic testing. The Bachelor of Arts student must earn a total of 64 credits in program studies; the Bachelor of Science student must earn 80. Program studies requirements are carefully structured and emphasize sequences of specific courses.

Stockton students have special opportunities to influence what and how they learn by participating in the major decisions that shape their academic lives. The opportunities of the preceptorial system enable students to work on a personalized basis with an assigned faculty-staff preceptor in planning and evaluating individual courses of study and in exploring various career alternatives. Stockton's academic programs emphasize curricular organization and methods of instruction that promote independent learning and research, cross-disciplinary study, problem solving, and decision making through analysis and synthesis.

Off-Campus Programs

Off-campus educational experiences for credit are a key feature of most degree programs at Stockton. Internships, research projects, and field studies extend the principles and methods learned beyond the classroom. Study abroad, Semester at Sea, and four-year independent study with the One-on-One Connect mentor/scholar program are also available.

The Washington, D.C., Internship Program gives students the opportunity to gain professional work experience. Stockton sends more students to the program than any other college or university outside the Washington, D.C., area.

Coordination of off-campus internship programs is provided by the academic divisional offices; coordination of foreign study is provided by the coordinator of international education.

Academic Facilities

Stockton's award-winning academic complex serves as a living-learning center. Academic, recreational, and living spaces are mixed to promote interaction among students and faculty and staff members. The facilities, all constructed since 1971, include several large classroom/office buildings, a library, a lecture hall/auditorium, and the 550-seat Performing Arts Center.

The library contains more than 300,000 volumes, more than 2,600 periodical subscriptions, 280,000 government documents, more than 19,000 reels of microfilm, and about 68,000 other units of microtext. The media collection includes films, slides, videotapes, audiotapes, compact discs, and phonograph records. The library also houses a special collection on the New Jersey Pine Barrens and is a depository for federal, state, and Atlantic City documents.

Costs

Costs for the 2007–08 academic year, including flat-rate tuition and fees based on 32 credits per year, were $9697 for in-state students and $14,597 for out-of-state students; on-campus housing and board was $8993 (double-occupancy residence room and the 180-meal Block Plan). Books, supplies, transportation, and personal items are extra. All costs are subject to change.

Financial Aid

Financial aid is available in the form of scholarships, grants, loans, and work-study. Need-based financial aid is awarded according to student and family need. Students seeking financial aid should file the Free Application for Federal Student Aid (FAFSA) by March 1. Merit-based aid is awarded to recognize academic excellence. Stockton offers aggressive and generous scholarship opportunities for academically talented freshmen and transfer students based on standardized test scores, grade point average, high school class rank, and college-level performance.

Faculty

Stockton's 265 full-time and 80 part-time and adjunct faculty members represent highly diverse academic, training, and social backgrounds, with 95 percent holding the terminal degree in their field. Faculty members work closely with students through small class sizes and individual research opportunities and share with students and staff members the initiative and responsibility for the College's social, recreational, athletic, and cultural programs and activities. This arrangement supports the exceptional rapport and learning relationships among students and faculty members.

Student Government

The RSCNJ Student Senate consists of 25 student members. The advisory council is made up of 1 faculty member and 2 staff members. Student senators hold office for one year, with elections held every spring. Among other duties, the Student Senate reviews and makes recommendations on budgets of funded student organizations and acts as the official representative of the student body.

Admission Requirements

Stockton operates on a rolling admission basis. For most freshman majors, the deadline for fall admission is May 1. Students should check the Web site for special program deadlines. Transfer student deadline for fall admission is June 1. Spring term (January) admission deadline for all students is December 1. Students may apply for admission to the fall or spring term and are notified of the admission decision as soon as their application file has been completed. Freshman applicants must submit ACT or SAT scores. All students must submit official transcripts from all educational institutions attended. Admission is selective.

Stockton offers early acceptance programs for high school students in their junior year. Armed Services veterans and those who have been away from formal education for some time are also invited to apply for admission on an individual basis. Stockton makes no distinction between part- and full-time students in offering admission.

Stockton offers special admission access to a limited number of New Jersey students from educationally and financially disadvantaged backgrounds. Students wishing to explore this opportunity should contact the Admissions Office.

Application and Information

For more information, students should contact:

Dean of Enrollment Management
The Richard Stockton College of New Jersey
P.O. Box 195
Pomona, New Jersey 08240-0195
Phone: 609-652-4261
866-RSC-2885 (toll-free)
Fax: 609-626-5541
E-mail: admissions@stockton.edu
Web site: http://www.stockton.edu

RIDER UNIVERSITY

LAWRENCEVILLE AND PRINCETON, NEW JERSEY

The University

Founded in 1865, Rider University is an independent, coeducational, nonsectarian institution accredited by the Middle States Association of Colleges and Schools. Rider's business programs are accredited by AACSB International–The Association to Advance Collegiate Schools of Business, and its education programs are recognized by the National Council for the Accreditation of Teacher Education (NCATE). Rider has campuses in Lawrenceville and Princeton, New Jersey.

Rider comprises four academic schools and colleges: the College of Business Administration; the College of Liberal Arts, Education, and Sciences; the College of Continuing Studies; and Westminster College of the Arts.

Ninety-six percent of Rider's faculty members hold a doctorate or other appropriate advanced degree. Primarily a teaching institution, Rider University selects instructors who are committed to imparting the knowledge and skills of a particular discipline. Full professors teach at all levels. There are no teaching assistants in the classrooms or laboratories.

Rider University's Lawrenceville campus is home to academic, recreational, and housing facilities. A state-of-the-art recreational facility opened in 2005 and features an indoor track, basketball courts, and exercise equipment. Approximately 65 percent of the 4,700 undergraduates live in University residence halls or in fraternities or sororities on the campus.

Rider participates in NCAA Division I in all of its intercollegiate sports. Women's sports are basketball, cross-country, field hockey, soccer, softball, swimming and diving, tennis, track and field, and volleyball. Men's sports are baseball, basketball, cross-country, golf, soccer, swimming and diving, tennis, track and field, and wrestling.

Preparation for career success goes beyond the classroom at Rider. The Office of Career Services enables students and alumni to increase career awareness through assessment, research, experiential learning, and the development of job-search competencies, resulting in informed decision making. Career Services encourages the ongoing documentation of acquired skills, experiences, achievements, and leadership development and is committed to building partnerships with students, alumni, faculty members, administrators, and employers.

Location

Rider University is located in New Jersey, with suburban campuses in Lawrenceville and Princeton. It is approximately 35 miles northeast of Philadelphia and 65 miles southwest of New York City. The location combines the advantages of accessibility to the cultural and recreational facilities of major urban areas and to the peaceful surroundings of a suburban community.

Westminster Choir College, a subsidiary of Westminster College of the Arts, is ideally located in picturesque Princeton, within walking distance of Princeton's Palmer Square, and is an outstanding atmosphere for living, performing, and learning.

All students have full access to the academic and recreational services available on both campuses.

Majors and Degrees

The College of Business Administration awards the Bachelor of Science in Business Administration (B.S.B.A.) degree in accounting, actuarial science, advertising, business administration, computer information systems, economics, entrepreneurial studies, finance, human resource management, international business, management and leadership, and marketing.

The College of Liberal Arts, Education, and Sciences (CLAES) awards the Bachelor of Arts (B.A.) degree in elementary education and secondary education and the Bachelor of Science (B.S.) degree in business education.

The CLAES also awards the B.A. degree in American studies, communications, economics, English, French, German, global and multinational studies, history, journalism, mathematics, philosophy, physics, political science, psychology, Russian, sociology, and Spanish. It offers the B.S. degree in biochemistry, biology, biopsychology, chemistry, environmental sciences, geosciences, integrated sciences, and marine sciences.

The Westminster College of the Arts is composed of two divisions: Westminster Choir College and the School of Fine and Performing Arts. Westminster Choir College, located on the Princeton campus, awards the Bachelor of Music degrees in sacred music, music education, theory/composition, voice, piano, and organ.

Located on Rider's Lawrenceville campus, the School of Fine and Performing Arts currently offers a Bachelor of Arts in Fine Arts with tracks in dance, music, theater, and art. Beginning in the 2008–09 academic year, the School will offer a Bachelor of Arts in Music and a Bachelor of Music in Music Theater. A Bachelor of Arts in Arts Administration is also being planned for fall 2008. New students accepted into these programs will live and study on the Lawrenceville campus.

Rider's postbaccalaureate premedical studies program is geared toward career changers who have not taken the undergraduate course prerequisites for admission to medical, dental, and veterinary schools.

Academic Programs

Rider University operates on the semester system. Each college requires a minimum of 120 semester hours of credit for graduation; the last 30 semester hours of credit must be earned at Rider University. The College of Business Administration requires that a student earn at least 45 semester hours, including the last 30, at Rider University.

The Baccalaureate Honors Program is available to students in all programs. To be considered for the program, incoming freshmen must be in the top 10 percent of their high school class, have a minimum combined SAT score (for critical reading and math only) of 1230, and a minimum 3.3 high school grade point average.

Rider University recognizes the Advanced Placement (AP) Program and offers credit and placement for scores of 3, 4, or 5 on most AP tests. Credit is awarded for the College-Level Examination Program (CLEP) tests, provided that the minimum required score is obtained. The minimum score varies according to the specific area covered by the examination.

Off-Campus Programs

Rider University offers semester-long and academic-year programs at a variety of international sites through an extensive study-abroad program. Sites include Argentina, Australia, Austria, Chile, England, France, Germany, Ghana, Greece, Ireland, Italy, Mexico, and Spain.

Academic Facilities

The Franklin F. Moore Library contains 409,414 volumes and 66,823 microforms, among many other resources. The library is automated and has a computerized catalog and circulation system. To complement its on-campus holdings, the library offers 117 online database searches of holdings of other libraries. The Talbott Library/Learning Center on the Princeton campus houses 73,666 books, scores, periodicals, and microforms; an electronic piano is provided for in-house score study. The media collection includes more than 30,000 recordings and videos, with facilities for student playback. The library supports the music education curriculum with over 1,000 school-music textbooks, recordings, charts, and other resource materials. The Performance Collection contains approximately 5,300 titles in multiple copies for student study, class assignments, student teaching, and church choirs; a single-copy reference file of approximately 80,000 supplements this collection. Special collections include the Erik Routley Collections of Books and Hymnals, D. DeWitt Wasson Reference Collection of Organ Music, and the Organ Historical Society's American Organ Archives.

The Office of Information Technology (OIT) is to ensure a pervasive, state-of-the-art, and well-utilized environment for the University. OIT is responsible for all university technology services including but not limited to computing, voice network, cable television, electronic classrooms, and instructional technology. There are two general access computer labs and computer kiosks for Internet access. Teaching computer labs are located on both campuses.

Other academic facilities include well-equipped laboratories for biochemistry, biology, biopsychology, chemistry, communications, environmental sciences, geology, physics, and psychology and performance facilities.

Costs

The total annual tuition charge for new students who began their studies in 2007–08 was $25,650, plus applicable mandatory fees. Room (standard double room) and board charges totaled $9780 for the academic year.

Financial Aid

Rider University offers merit-based scholarships for qualified applicants. These scholarships are for up to full tuition and are renewable for up to four years of study if the student maintains the minimum grade point average specified by the Scholarship Committee. Scholarships range from $5000 to $15,000 annually.

Other financial aid is based on demonstrated financial need. Students and their parents are required to file the Free Application for Federal Student Aid (FAFSA) prior to March 1 to be considered for financial assistance administered by Rider University. Students are eligible for consideration for Federal Pell Grants, Federal Supplemental Educational Opportunity Grants, Federal Work-Study Program awards, Federal Perkins Loans, New Jersey Tuition Aid Grants, New Jersey Distinguished Scholar Scholarships, Rider University grants, Trustee Scholarships, Alumni Scholarships, and other forms of institutional aid.

Faculty

There are 277 full-time and 301 part-time faculty members, 96 percent of whom hold a doctorate or terminal degree in their field. The same faculty members teach both graduate and undergraduate courses; graduate assistants do not teach classes at Rider University. The student-faculty ratio is approximately 13:1. Faculty members serve on student affairs committees and as faculty advisers to all student organizations.

Student Government

The active Student Government Association (SGA) sponsors concerts, lectures, plays, and other events. All social rules and regulations are made, enforced, and adjudicated by students. Each class, each residence hall, and many other student organizations are represented in the Student Government Association.

Admission Requirements

Students applying for admission to Rider University are expected to have completed a minimum of 16 acceptable college-preparatory units of study by the end of their senior year in high school. These 16 units must include 4 in English and 3 in mathematics, including algebra I, algebra II, and geometry. The other 9 units should be selected from traditional academic areas, including history, mathematics, science, social studies, foreign languages, and literature. Business or vocational courses completed in high school are not considered college-preparatory units. Students are required to submit official SAT or ACT results, a personal statement, and two letters of recommendation in support of their application. Most successful applicants rank in the upper half of their high school senior class.

Rider University seeks a diverse student body and encourages applications from students from varied ethnic, economic, and geographic backgrounds. Campus interviews are strongly recommended but not required for most candidates.

Application and Information

Rider University works on a rolling admissions basis, but it encourages applications for the fall semester to be submitted by February 15 if the student wishes to obtain housing on the campus. Applications for the spring semester should be submitted by December 15. The application fee is $50. The Early Decision option is available for freshmen applying for the fall semester. The application deadline for Early Decision is November 15, and students are notified of a decision by December 15. Early Decision is a binding option. The Early Action option is available for fall applicants. Students interested in the Early Action option must submit all necessary documentation by December 1 and are notified of an admissions decision by January 15. Students are notified of the admission decision approximately three to four weeks after the completed application is received. Transfer applicants receive the same priority for admission, housing, and financial aid as freshman applicants. More information can be found at http://www.rider.edu/applynow.

Interested students are encouraged to contact:

Director of Undergraduate Admissions
Rider University
2083 Lawrenceville Road
Lawrenceville, New Jersey 08648-3099
Phone: 609-896-5042
800-257-9026 (toll-free)
E-mail: admissions@rider.edu
Web site: http://www.rider.edu/admissions

Centennial Lake and Franklin F. Moore Library.

ROWAN UNIVERSITY

GLASSBORO, NEW JERSEY

The University

Founded in 1923, Rowan University has become a regional center for education, business, technology, and the arts and humanities. With state-of-the-art facilities, nationally ranked academic and athletic programs, and talented professors, Rowan offers an outstanding educational experience at an exceptional value. Currently, the University is the home of nearly 10,000 students in forty-two majors, twenty-six minors, and twenty-eight graduate programs across six academic colleges—Business, Communication, Education, Engineering, Fine and Performing Arts, and Liberal Arts and Sciences—and the College of Professional & Continuing Education. Rowan's admission standards are competitive, attracting applicants from the top quarter of their high school classes. All courses are taught by professors without the aid of teaching assistants, and the average class size is 20.

Rowan's tree-lined campus features student residence halls, apartments and townhouses; a brand-new $28.5 million education hall; a new $45 million science center; a $28 million engineering building; a $16.7 million library; an $8.6 million Student Recreation Center; theatres; galleries; and thirty-three student computer labs.

Rowan's eighteen varsity athletic teams compete in NCAA Division III, the New Jersey Athletic Conference, and the Eastern College Athletic Conference. More than 100 clubs, preprofessional organizations, honor societies, and fraternities and sororities foster a sense of community life.

Rowan University, established for teacher training and later known as Glassboro State College, made philanthropic history with the 1992 Rowan $100 million donation.

Location

The University is located on 200 acres in the historic southern New Jersey town of Glassboro, less than 30 minutes from Philadelphia, Pennsylvania, less than an hour from the New Jersey shore. Because of the University's location halfway between New York and Washington, D.C., it was chosen as the site of the historic 1967 conference between President Johnson and Soviet Premier Kosygin. Facilities for all forms of surface and air transportation, including Philadelphia International Airport, are within minutes of the campus.

Just 20 minutes from the main campus, the Rowan University Camden Campus, in Camden, New Jersey, serves the urban community with an emphasis on nontraditional students in three degree programs, plus English as a second language studies.

Majors and Degrees

The Bachelor of Arts degree is offered in accounting, advertising, art (general fine arts), communication studies, early childhood education, economics, education (K–12 subject matter in art, biology, chemistry, English, history, mathematics, music, physical science, physics, Spanish, theater/speech/dramatic arts), elementary education, English, environmental studies, geography, health and exercise science (athletic training, health promotion and fitness management, K–12 teacher certification), history, journalism, law and justice studies, liberal studies: American studies, liberal studies: math/science, mathematics, music, political science, psychology, public relations, radio/TV/film, sociology, Spanish, theater (theater, child drama), and writing arts. The Bachelor of Science degree is offered in accounting, biochemistry, biological sciences, business (entrepreneurship, finance, human resource management, management, management information systems, marketing), chemistry, computer science, engineering (chemical, civil and environmental, electrical and computer, mechanical), mathematics, physical sciences, and physics. The Bachelor of Science in Nursing degree is also offered. The Bachelor of Fine Arts degree is offered in studio arts (drawing and painting, ceramics, computer art, graphic design, illustration, jewelry/metalry, photography, printmaking, puppetry, and sculpture). The Bachelor of Music degree is offered in composition, jazz studies, music education, and performance.

Academic Programs

All degree programs include a general education requirement (approximately 60 semester hours) from the areas of communication, science and mathematics, social and behavioral sciences, humanities and languages, and fine arts. In addition, most academic majors have specific general education courses that students in that major must take. Each degree program includes individual major requirements and free electives. A minimum of thirty semester hours is required in a major program; many departments require more.

Students are encouraged to use free electives to establish a second major, minor, or concentration; strengthen their major program; pursue personal interests; or study abroad.

Internships are available in all majors, and some type of internship or academic field experiences are required in most of them.

The University calendar is based on the two-semester system with a summer session.

Off-Campus Programs

Rowan University offers the opportunity to spend a semester or a year living and learning in a new country and culture through study abroad, with destinations to more than 200 programs in fifty nations in Africa, Asia, Australia, Europe, and South and Central America. Students can also earn work-study dollars while exploring careers and building credentials and experience through Off-Campus Work-Study.

Academic Facilities

In just the past decade, Rowan has added a number of new buildings that are notable for their modern architecture, bright open spaces, and state-of-the-art equipment. They include the Student Recreation Center, a full-service health club for students, faculty members, and alumni; the Campbell Library, which combines spacious new study areas with a rich collection of print and electronic resources for research; and Henry M. Rowan Hall, a $28-million engineering building with a technology spine and modular classrooms and laboratories. The $45-million, state-of-the-art Science Hall, which opened in fall 2003, is the home of the biological sciences, chemistry, and physics departments and features a fully equipped laser laboratory, a rooftop greenhouse and telescope, a planetarium, twenty-two research laboratories, and twenty-seven teaching laboratories. Education Hall, the new home for the College of Education, featuring state-of-the-art technology, learning centers, classrooms, and office space, opened in spring 2006. Rowan is also expanding its campus to accommodate the building of the South Jersey Technology Park, a facility that will be shared by students, faculty members, and private industry.

Costs

In 2007–08, tuition and fees were $10,068 for New Jersey residents and $17,376 for out-of-state students, based on flat-rate tuition for full-time undergraduates taking 24 to 36 semester hours per year. Room and board costs for 2007–08 were $9242, based on the double-residence room rate and a primary meal plan. All freshmen are required to live in residence halls, with guaranteed housing. Apartment-style housing is available on the campus for upperclass students in any one of the three University-owned apartment complexes and brand-new townhouses.

Financial Aid

Nearly 70 percent of all Rowan students receive some form of financial aid, such as grants, loans, or scholarships, from federal and state sources, alumni, friends of the University, and various other organizations. In 2007, Rowan awarded $68 million in total financial assistance to undergraduates. Students should submit a Free Application for Federal Student Aid (FAFSA) as soon as possible after January 1 and no later than March 15 to be evaluated for the earliest consideration.

Faculty

Rowan University has 401 full-time faculty members. The faculty's regularly scheduled office hours, participation in virtually all areas of campus governance and operations, and individual guidance and support for every student who needs them, ensures a truly personal education. Part-time and adjunct faculty members, including business leaders, industry representatives, and practicing professionals, provide valuable links with the community and offer knowledge of practical experiences to Rowan University students. The student-faculty ratio is 13:1, and all classes are taught by professors. There are no teaching assistants.

Student Government

The Student Government Association (SGA) is composed entirely of students chosen through campuswide elections. In 2007–08, student officers administered a budget of more than $800,000, derived from student activity fees and receipts. All students paying student activity fees are members of the SGA. Free legal advice, personal property insurance, and a tenants' association are some of the SGA's projects. The SGA oversees more than 100 chartered clubs on campus and sponsors intercollegiate athletics, social events, and service activities.

The University administration wholly supports the concept of student rights and student participation in all areas of campus governance.

Admission Requirements

Rowan University carefully considers each application it receives and selects candidates who will be academically successful, contribute to student life on campus, and benefit most from the Rowan experience. Rowan's admissions standards are competitive. The 2007 freshman class posted a mean SAT score of 1135, a top-20 percent class rank, and an average GPA of 3.6. The average transfer student GPA is 3.07.

Admission decisions are based on the strength and quality of the high school record, SAT or ACT scores, class rank, and letters of recommendation. An essay or interview is not required.

Applicants are expected to have completed a minimum of 16 college preparatory units: 4 of English, 2 of laboratory science, 3 of college preparatory mathematics (algebra I and II, geometry), 2 of social studies, and 5 of additional work in at least two of the following areas: English, social studies, languages, mathematics, or sciences. The College of Engineering seeks applicants with 3 units of laboratory science, including chemistry and physics, and 4 units of college preparatory mathematics, including precalculus (calculus preferred).

Admission for transfer students is competitive and is based on college transcripts and available space in the desired major.

Application and Information

The University application, $50 application fee, high school and/or college transcript, and SAT or ACT scores should be forwarded to the Admissions Office. For September entrance, freshman and transfer applications are due March 1, with notification no later than April 15. Because admission to those programs is highly competitive, a February 15 application deadline applies. The fall-enrollment deposit must be received by May 1. The application deadline for spring semester (January entrance) is November 1 for freshmen and transfers. Campus visits are highly recommended.

Prospective students should visit http://ru.rowan.edu. For additional information, students should contact:

Albert Betts
Director of Admissions
Rowan University
Glassboro, New Jersey 08028-1701
Phone: 856-256-4200
877-RU-ROWAN (toll-free)
E-mail: admissions@rowan.edu
Web site: http://www.rowan.edu

Science Hall, Rowan's state-of-the-art science center, is one of the most advanced undergraduate research facilities at a public university on the East coast.

COLLEGE DATA CENTER • NEW JERSEY

RUTGERS, THE STATE UNIVERSITY OF NEW JERSEY, CAMDEN

RUTGERS
CAMDEN

CAMDEN, NEW JERSEY

The University

Located in the heart of the University District on the exciting Camden Waterfront, Rutgers-Camden is a vibrant academic community of 5,383 undergraduate and graduate students who work closely with professors who are among the top scholars in their fields. These students enjoy strong success with national employers and in gaining admission to the nation's most prestigious graduate programs.

Rutgers-Camden is the southernmost of the three campuses that comprise New Jersey's flagship public research university: Rutgers, The State University of New Jersey. Faculty members at Rutgers-Camden are selected and promoted based on the same high standards as their peers across every Rutgers campus, and Camden students enjoy the same access to Rutgers' system-wide research library and state-of-the-art computing network.

Founded in 1926 as the South Jersey Law School and joined by the College of South Jersey in 1927, the Camden campus joined Rutgers in 1950. Today, Rutgers is a member of the prestigious Association of American Universities (a group comprising the top research universities in North America) and is accredited by the Middle States Association of Colleges and Schools. Rutgers-Camden is home to southern New Jersey's only law school and its first internationally accredited business school.

Students seeking the opportunity to work closely with world-class scholars select Rutgers-Camden for its unique combination of "small college" ambience, with day and evening classes offered during the traditional fall and spring semesters and a smaller schedule of offerings during winter and summer sessions.

Located at the foot of the Benjamin Franklin Bridge, Rutgers-Camden is directly across the Delaware River from Philadelphia; in fact, Rutgers-Camden is the four-year college closest to the Liberty Bell. On-campus housing is available for 550 students on a first-come basis. Some students choose to live in the comfortable southern New Jersey communities located along the PATCO Speedline, which has a station located one block from campus and offers a very convenient option for commuting; the train also brings Philadelphia residents to campus. A light-rail system stops on campus and is an easy commuting option for residents of northern counties. The campus is accessible by all major regional transportation arteries.

A spacious Campus Center offers dining areas as well as offices for student organizations. A University District bookstore offers comprehensive service directly adjacent to the campus. The gymnasium offers a complete health club experience, including squash and racquetball courts and strength and cardio conditioning.

On-campus dining is available through a dining hall and the Courtyard Café restaurant. An on-campus Starbucks provides a relaxing gathering spot for students. In addition, a number of small eateries surround the campus.

The Rutgers-Camden Center for the Arts brings established and emerging performers to the campus and offers a series of intriguing exhibitions in the Stedman Gallery and the Gordon Theater. The Office of Student Affairs works with students to provide a diverse schedule of activities throughout the year. The Rutgers-Camden Scarlet Raptors compete in NCAA Division III sports, with thirteen competitive men's and women's teams. The women's softball team won the NCAA Division III championship in 2006.

Location

The metro Philadelphia/Delaware Valley region is a thriving area with many opportunities for careers, research, and social activities. The city of Camden is home to such notable attractions as the Tweeter Center, which books top headline performers on a regular basis; Campbell's Field, a Rutgers-owned stadium that is home to the Camden Riversharks minor league baseball team; and the Adventure Aquarium, just to name a few. Philadelphia is an easy commute by car, train, and ferry and offers world-class museums, cafés, restaurants, shops, clubs, theaters, and much more. Atlantic City and New Jersey's spectacular beaches are less than an hour away, and New York City and Washington, D.C., are both within a 3-hour drive. International travel is easy, courtesy of Philadelphia International Airport, which is located 15 minutes from campus.

Majors and Degrees

Rutgers-Camden awards the following baccalaureate degrees: Bachelor of Arts, Bachelor of Science, and Bachelor of Hospitality Management. The College of Arts and Sciences offers dual-degree programs in several fields, which allow students to earn both a baccalaureate and a master's degree in five years. In addition, highly qualified undergraduates can begin graduate studies during their senior year in some selected programs.

First-year students may apply to a program that allows transition to Rutgers' College of Engineering.

Majors and programs are offered in accounting, African-American studies, American studies, anthropology, art, art history, biology, biomedical technology, chemistry, childhood studies, computer science, criminal justice, dance, economics, English, film studies, finance, fine arts, French, German, history, hospitality management, human resource management, independent/individualized studies, Latin American studies, liberal studies, management, marketing, mathematics, music, nursing, philosophy, physics, political science, psychology, religion, general science, social work, sociology, Spanish, statistics, statistics/mathematics, theater arts, urban studies, visual arts, and women's and gender studies.

Dual-degree programs include bachelor's/M.P.A, bachelor's/J.D., bachelor's/D.O., bachelor's/M.A. in childhood studies, English, history, liberal studies, or psychology and bachelor's/M.S. in biology, chemistry, computer science, or mathematics.

Academic Programs

Each college or school establishes its own admission, scholastic standing, and graduation requirements, and each offers specific academic programs that reflect the mission and philosophy of the college or school. Highly qualified students are invited to participate in the Honors College, a college within a college. Special academic programs include honors courses, tracks, and programs; ROTC; national honors societies; undergraduate research; graduate course work; internships; cooperative education; and service learning. The academic year runs on a two-semester schedule, from September to December and from January to May. Selected class offerings are also available during summer and winter sessions.

Students are encouraged to participate in independent research under the guidance of a faculty member and may qualify for grants to support their research.

Off-Campus Programs

Students can earn credit through the International Studies Program, which offers classes in numerous countries in Africa, Europe, Asia, and South America. Internships and other off-campus learning and research arrangements are routinely made between Rutgers and area businesses, nonprofits, and colleges and universities. The School of Business offers an aggressive internship program, while the Department of Nursing places students in clinical rotations at metro Philadelphia's top hospitals and health centers. An Arts and Sciences internship course offers students experiences in a wide variety of settings.

Academic Facilities

Rutgers-Camden is home to the Paul Robeson Library. It offers direct access to the Rutgers University Library system, which has holdings of more than 3 million volumes and is ranked among the nation's top research libraries. The library also offers online access to thousands of digital research resources. An on-campus Law Library serves the Rutgers-Camden School of Law. The RUNet communications infrastructure project continues to upgrade the University's communications network to support instruction, research, and outreach. Through RUNet, residence halls are wired for Internet, phone, and cable TV. Wireless service is available for students in the Campus Center, Armitage Hall, Paul Robeson Library, Business and Science Building, residence halls, and the Law Building, with plans to extend this service elsewhere on campus. Numerous student computing labs are located in virtually every academic building on campus. A Language Resource Center houses a fully computerized language lab that incorporates audio, video, and digital materials of all kinds into language learning at all levels.

Rutgers-Camden's outstanding academic facilities include an excellent performing arts theater; a state-of-the-art focus-group study facility; numerous technology-enhanced classrooms; computer graphic arts and animation labs; and a research facility in the heart of New Jersey's Pine Barrens. Technology available to assist undergraduate research includes a scanning electron microscope, a 300-MHz nuclear magnetic resonance spectrometer, and an upgraded fiber-optic network for student and faculty research.

Costs

Costs for the 2007–08 academic year included state-resident annual tuition and fees of $10,614. For nonresidents, annual tuition and fees were $20,096. Typical room and board charges were $9482. Part-time tuition was $275 per credit for residents and $574 per credit for nonresidents.

Financial Aid

A wide variety of merit and need-based financial aid is available to students at Rutgers. University-wide, undergraduate students received more than $292 million in federal and state grants and loans, work/study jobs, and university scholarships in 2006–07. Seventy-three percent of Rutgers-Camden undergraduates receive financial assistance. Merit and need-based scholarships are offered by the University and by individual colleges and schools.

Faculty

There are a total of 260 full-time faculty members, 98 percent of whom hold terminal degrees. The student-faculty ratio is 22:1. Senior faculty members regularly teach undergraduate courses and often include undergraduates in their research projects.

Student Government

The Student Governing Association is a student-run association comprising representatives from the School of Business, Camden College of Arts and Sciences, and University College. Representatives serve as the voice for the students of these schools and provide funding for student organizations from these schools.

Admission Requirements

Admission to Rutgers' colleges and schools is competitive and selective, with primary emphasis on academic promise as demonstrated by grades; grade point average; rank in class; strength of the candidate's academic program as evidenced by the number of academic, honors, and Advanced Placement courses completed; and standardized test scores. High school course requirements vary by the individual college or school, but all require a combination of sixteen academic courses. In addition to SAT and/or ACT test scores, a completed undergraduate application form and official high school transcript are required. Advanced Placement and/or degree credit are awarded for AP grades of 5 and 4.

Application and Information

Candidates for admission submit a single application for consideration at any three Rutgers colleges or schools. Applying online to meet priority application dates is strongly urged. Priority dates are October 15 for spring admission for first-year and transfer students, December 1 for fall admission for first-year students, and January 15 for fall admission for transfer students. Letters of recommendation are not required. Personal interviews are not required and are not granted. Candidates may track the status of their applications and required credentials online. Campus tours are encouraged; for more information, students should visit http://www.admissions.rutgers.edu.

Office of University Undergraduate Admissions
Rutgers, The State University of New Jersey
406 Penn Street
Camden, New Jersey 08102-1400
Phone: 856-225-6104
Web site: http://camden.rutgers.edu

RUTGERS, THE STATE UNIVERSITY OF NEW JERSEY, NEW BRUNSWICK

NEW BRUNSWICK, NEW JERSEY

The University

Chartered in 1766 as Queen's College, Rutgers is one of the original nine colonial colleges and the eighth-oldest institution of higher education in the nation. Today, seven (Brown, Columbia, Dartmouth, Harvard, Princeton, the University of Pennsylvania, and Yale) of the nine colonial colleges are private and two (Rutgers and the College of William and Mary) are public. Rutgers is New Jersey's flagship public research university, is a member of the prestigious Association of American Universities (a group comprising the top research universities in North America), and is accredited by the Middle States Association of Colleges and Schools.

With ten schools offering more than 100 undergraduate majors and five residential campus communities, students choose Rutgers for all the advantages of a small school and all the resources of a leading research university. The liberal arts college is the School of Arts and Sciences. The professional schools are the School of Environmental and Biological Sciences, Mason Gross School of the Arts, Ernest Mario School of Pharmacy, Rutgers Business School, School of Engineering, Edward J. Bloustein School of Planning and Public Policy, School of Social Work, College of Nursing, and School of Communication, Information, and Library Studies. Each school has a unique culture, personality, and undergraduate enrollment, which ranges from approximately 600 at Mason Gross School of the Arts to 20,000 at the School of Arts and Sciences, where students are served by five smaller residential campus communities.

In fall 2007, 24,878 full-time undergraduates were enrolled at the New Brunswick campus, including 12,156 women and 12,722 men, 54 percent of whom were between the ages of 18 and 21. University-wide, 92 percent of Rutgers undergraduates are New Jersey residents. Residents of all twenty-one New Jersey counties, forty-six states, and 119 nations of the world are enrolled at Rutgers.

Rutgers has an extensive network of housing, restaurants, museums, student centers, cultural centers, student clubs and organizations, parks, hiking trails, recreational facilities, and more. The Division of Housing in New Brunswick houses approximately 14,000 undergraduate and graduate students on five residential campuses. Campus housing is allocated on a first-come, first-served basis and is generally assigned according to the undergraduate school in which one enrolls. On-campus housing is complemented by a lively fraternity and sorority scene and by off-campus housing in privately owned apartments and houses.

The campus offers a wide array of dining options that include meal-plan dining halls, food courts, snack bars, cafés, and concessions. Meal plan options include location, menu, and the number of meals. Take-out service is available. Valid meal cards may be used at any of the five dining halls on campus. Weekday hours of operation are from 7 a.m. to 8 p.m. Weekend hours vary.

The birthplace of college football, Rutgers has a proud past in producing outstanding scholar-athletes and is the alma mater of dozens of athletes who have distinguished themselves on America's national, Olympic, and professional sports teams. Recreational and athletic activities are available on every campus. Rutgers–New Brunswick participates in the NCAA Division I Big East Conference with twenty-five competitive men's and women's teams.

Rutgers offers numerous services to help students get the most out of their time spent "on the banks of the Old Raritan." Career counseling, learning resource centers, health services, academic advising, undergraduate research, and leadership training are just a small sampling of available services. Alumni say of Rutgers that its academic, cultural, recreational, and social opportunities are endless; students just have to jump in and take Rutgers for all they can.

Location

The greater New Brunswick area provides a perfect complement to Rutgers' academic environment. The city of New Brunswick, with its small-city feel, has fine restaurants, theaters, shops, clubs, cafés, and more, while some of Rutgers' academic, residential, and sports facilities are located just across the Raritan River in suburban Piscataway. New Brunswick is easily accessible by train from all eastern corridor cities, 50 minutes by train from New York or Philadelphia, less than an hour from the New Jersey shore, and a short 30-minute trip by train or car from Newark Liberty International Airport.

Majors and Degrees

Rutgers awards the following baccalaureate degrees: Bachelor of Arts, Bachelor of Fine Arts, Bachelor of Music, and Bachelor of Science.

Majors are offered in accounting; Africana studies; agricultural science; American studies; animal science; anthropology; applied sciences in engineering; art history; astrophysics; biochemistry; biological sciences; biomathematics; biotechnology; cell biology and neuroscience; chemistry; Chinese; classics; communication; comparative literature; computer science; criminal justice; dance; East Asian languages and area studies; economics; engineering (biomedical, bioresource, ceramic, chemical, civil, electrical and computer, industrial, and mechanical); English; environmental and business economics; environmental planning and design; environmental policy, institutions, and behavior; environmental sciences; European studies; evolutionary anthropology; exercise science and sport studies; finance; food science; French; genetics; geography; geological sciences; German; history; history/French; history/political science; independent/individualized; information technology and informatics; Italian; Jewish studies; journalism and media studies; labor studies and employment relations; Latin American studies; Latino and Hispanic Caribbean studies; linguistics; management; management science and information systems; marine sciences; marketing; mathematics; medical technology; medieval studies; meteorology; microbiology; Middle Eastern studies; molecular biology and biochemistry; music; natural resource management; nursing; nutritional sciences; philosophy; physics; planning and public policy; plant science; political science; Portuguese; psychology; public health; religion; Russian; social work; sociology; Spanish; statistics; statistics/mathematics; theater arts; visual arts; and women's and gender studies.

Certificate programs are offered in twenty-seven areas, ranging from behavioral pharmacology to international studies to urban planning. Dual-degree programs include bachelor's/M.D., bachelor's/M.B.A., bachelor's/M.Ed., bachelor's/M.P.A., bachelor's/M.P.H., bachelor's/M.P.P., B.A./B.S., B.A./B.S. (engineering), and bachelor's/M.A. in criminal justice.

Academic Programs

Each college or school offers specific academic programs that reflect its mission and philosophy. Special academic programs include honors courses, tracks, and programs; ROTC; national honor societies; undergraduate research; graduate course work; internships; cooperative education; and service learning. The academic year runs on a two-semester schedule, from September to December and from January to May. Limited class offerings are also available during summer and winter sessions.

Off-Campus Programs

Students can earn credit during study abroad offered in eighteen countries. The nationally acclaimed Citizenship and Service Education program offers a wide array of credit-bearing service-learning experiences. Cooperative Education offers paid work experience that is also credit bearing. Internships and other off-campus learning and research arrangements are routinely made between Rutgers and area businesses, nonprofit organizations, and colleges and universities.

Academic Facilities

Every Rutgers campus in New Brunswick has a library, a student center, a recreational center, a health center, computer labs, and dining halls. With holdings of more than 3 million volumes, the Rutgers University libraries rank among the nation's top research libraries. The system includes twenty-six libraries, centers, reading rooms, and RU-Online, a digital library. The RUNet communications infrastructure project continues to upgrade the University's communications network to support instruction, research, and outreach. Through RUNet, most residence halls are wired for Internet, phone, and cable TV. Rutgers' outstanding academic facilities run the gamut, from a state-of-the-art spinal cord injury research center to supercomputers to performing arts venues to experimental agricultural fields.

Costs

Costs for the 2007–08 academic year included state-resident annual tuition and fees of $10,686 (slightly higher for the professional schools) and typical room and board of $9762. For nonresidents, annual tuition and fees were $19,854 (slightly higher for the professional schools) and typical room and board were $10,686. Part-time tuition was $275 per credit for residents and $574 per credit for nonresidents.

Financial Aid

A wide variety of merit- and need-based financial aid is available to students at Rutgers, offered by the University and its individual colleges and schools. University-wide, undergraduate students received more than $308 million in federal and state grants and loans, work-study jobs, and University scholarships in 2006–07, with an average first-year award of $11,800. More than 85 percent of Rutgers undergraduates receive financial assistance.

Faculty

There are 3,367 faculty members at Rutgers; 67 percent are full-time and 99 percent have terminal degrees in their field. The student-faculty ratio is 14:1. Senior faculty members regularly teach undergraduate courses and include undergraduates in their research projects.

Student Government

The University-wide Rutgers University Senate is a deliberative body of faculty members, students, administrators, and alumni that meets seven or eight times during the academic year to consider matters of general University interest and make recommendations to the University administration. Student-run governing associations have their own missions, goals, and operating procedures.

Admission Requirements

Admission to Rutgers' colleges and schools is competitive and selective, with primary emphasis on academic promise, as demonstrated by grades; grade point average; rank in class; strength of the candidate's academic program, as evidenced by the number of academic, honors, and Advanced Placement (AP) courses completed; and standardized test scores. High school course requirements vary by the individual college or school, but all require a minimum combination of sixteen academic courses. In addition to SAT and/or ACT test scores, a completed undergraduate application form and official high school transcript are required. Advanced Placement and/or degree credit are awarded for AP grades of 5 and 4.

Application and Information

Candidates for admission submit a single application for consideration at any three Rutgers colleges or schools. Applying online to meet priority application dates is strongly urged. Priority dates are October 15 for spring first-year and transfer students, December 1 for fall first-year students, and January 15 for fall transfer students. Letters of recommendation are not required. Personal interviews are not required and are not granted, except for Mason Gross School of the Arts, which requires a portfolio review or talent assessment. Candidates may apply online and track the status of their applications and required credentials online.

Office of University Undergraduate Admissions
Room 202
Rutgers, The State University of New Jersey
65 Davidson Road
Piscataway, New Jersey 08854-8097
Phone: 732-932-INFO (Campus Information Services)
Web site: http://admissions.rutgers.edu

SAINT PETER'S COLLEGE

JERSEY CITY, NEW JERSEY

The College

Saint Peter's College (SPC) offers a strong liberal arts education focused on the holistic, personal development of the individual student; the advantages of its international, New York City metropolitan location; and affordable tuition. Located within minutes of New York City and the Statue of Liberty, the College has offered academic excellence in the Jesuit, Catholic tradition since its founding in 1872. Saint Peter's students can participate in class, internship, and cooperative education experiences in a variety of international, cultural, business, and communication institutions and corporations. Saint Peter's participates in NCAA Division I athletics, with strongly competitive teams in both men's and women's sports. The diverse, international student body is composed of students from throughout the Northeast, America, and the world.

Saint Peter's offers a curriculum based on students' developing a breadth of knowledge in the core curriculum of the liberal arts and sciences and depth of knowledge, skills, and proficiencies within the major area of study. The College seeks to develop graduates of competence and conscience by emphasizing ethical and moral decision making throughout the entire course of study. Students may choose to prepare for positions in professional fields such as business or education; preprofessional programs in fields such as medicine and dentistry; or graduate study in many disciplines.

The goal of a Saint Peter's College education is to equip students to succeed in learning, leadership, and service. The *ethos* of the College is reflected in the motto of the twenty-eight American Jesuit colleges and universities, which is to develop "men and women for others." The College serves as a significant educational, religious, cultural, social, and economic resource for Jersey City and the surrounding area. Its main campus is located in Jersey City, New Jersey, with additional branch campuses in Englewood Cliffs and South Amboy, New Jersey. Total enrollment is 3,000, including 2,200 full-time undergraduates in the College of Arts and Sciences and the School of Business Administration, 500 adult undergraduates in the School for Professional and Continuing Studies, and 700 graduate students. SPC alumni, over 31,000 strong, are successful professionals in the arts, business, humanities, law, medicine, education, politics, public service, and the sciences.

The College offers more than thirty-eight major programs leading to the baccalaureate degree as well as graduate programs in accountancy, business, education, and nursing.

Location

Saint Peter's College is easily accessible by all major forms of transportation. Midtown Manhattan is a short ride on the PATH subway system from Journal Square. Liberty International Airport is only 20 minutes away, and there are numerous trains (including Amtrak) and Greyhound buses leaving from Penn Station in Newark and New York City, the Erie-Lackawanna Railroad Terminal in Hoboken, and Port Authority and Grand Central Station in New York City. SPC is also accessible from the New Jersey Turnpike and other major highways.

Majors and Degrees

Saint Peter's College offers baccalaureate degrees in accountancy, American studies, art history, biological chemistry, biology, business management, chemistry, classical civilizations, classical languages, communications, computer science, computer science/CIS, computer science/MIS, criminal justice, economics, education, English literature, fine arts, history, humanities*, international business and trade, marketing management, mathematical economics, mathematics, modern languages and literature, natural science, nursing, philosophy, physics, political science, prelaw, psychology, social sciences*, sociology, Spanish, theology, urban studies, and visual arts. Five-year bachelor's degree programs in cytotechnology, medical technology, and toxicology are offered in affiliation with the University of Medicine and Dentistry of New Jersey (UMDNJ). Preprofessional programs in accountancy (3-3 at SPC), dentistry (3-4 with UMDNJ), law (3-3 with Seton Hall), medicine (3-4 with UMDNJ), pharmacy (3-4 with the Rutgers School of Pharmacy), physician assistant studies (3-3 with UMDNJ), and physical therapy (3-3 with UMDNJ) are available. Associate degrees are offered in banking*, business management, finance, humanities, information systems, international business and trade, marketing management, public policy*, social sciences, and theater arts. (*School for Professional and Continuing Studies only.)

Academic Programs

The liberal arts core curriculum, required for all degrees, comprises 60 semester hours and includes study in composition and fine arts (a minimum of 3 semester hours each), history, literature, mathematics (6–8 semester hours), modern language, natural sciences (9 semester hours), philosophy, social sciences, theology (6 semester hours each), and a core elective in ethical values (3 semester hours). The baccalaureate degree requires the completion of 120 semester hours. Approximately half of the courses required for the degree are in the core curriculum, one quarter are in the major area of study, and one quarter are in elective courses. Students may complete majors in two areas by meeting all degree requirements or design a composite major to meet individual interests following consultation with and approval from the academic dean. Summer sessions are available on both campuses. Sessions for full-time undergraduates are based on a semester system.

The Honors Program provides an opportunity for academically talented students to participate in challenging classes and to do research with a faculty mentor. Students who complete the entire Honors Program successfully are awarded degrees *in cursu honorum.* The College participates in both the Army and Air Force ROTC programs. The College recognizes the Advanced Placement (AP) Program as well as the College-Level Examination Program (CLEP).

Under the direction of the freshman dean, the College offers a number of summer and freshman-year programs in order to foster the successful transition of students to college life. All freshmen are assigned faculty advisers. SPC participates in the Educational Opportunity Fund (EOF) program in partnership with the state of New Jersey. This program offers a six-week summer study program and individual support and guidance throughout the entire College experience. The Summer Academy is offered to all students who would benefit from structure and directed study in order to successfully acclimate to the demands of college-level study. During the year, the Academic Success Program fosters student success through individual attention and mentoring. Additional resources are available to meet students' needs, such as the Tutoring Center, Counseling Center, Campus Ministry, Residence Life, and Freshman Seminar.

Off-Campus Programs

Supervised, off-campus cooperative education opportunities and internships are available in all fields. Students in SPC's nationally ranked Cooperative Education Program may earn a maximum of 9 academic credits and up to $10,000. Up to 15 credits are awarded through the Washington Center Program in Washington, D.C., which provides experience working in the nation's capital in a wide range of internship positions. Study abroad is arranged through the International Student Exchange Program, which conducts programs in more than sixty universities in Europe, Asia, Africa, and Latin America.

Academic Facilities

The Edward and Theresa O'Toole Library houses a large collection of volumes, periodicals, and information databases. Students also benefit from interlibrary loan arrangements as well as access to the New Jersey state-supported university library system. Students may obtain referral cards to other metropolitan-area libraries, including the New York Public Library and the Science, Industry, and Business Library, both located in midtown Manhattan, minutes from the campus.

Saint Peter's was one of the first colleges in the nation to adopt a wireless Ethernet throughout the campus. Wireless access is available to all students free of charge. The College is also implementing a new information infrastructure that supports the Student Information System, instruction in the classrooms, student computer labs, and faculty and student research. Students are offered individual e-mail accounts and Internet connectivity through the campus local area network (LAN).

Costs

Annual tuition for 2007–08 was $24,251 for full-time study (12–18 semester hours each semester), and student fees were $550. Typical housing costs for room and board were $9750. Personal expenses, books, supplies, and transportation were estimated to be $3850 for residential students and $2200 for commuter students.

Financial Aid

Saint Peter's College admits students without regard to financial status. Ninety percent of SPC students receive financial assistance. For the 2007–08 academic year, the average award was $20,000. The only form required is the Free Application for Federal Student Aid (FAFSA). It is recommended that students file the FAFSA by March 15 for full consideration for all federal, state, and institutional funds available.

Federal sources include Federal Pell Grants, Federal Supplemental Educational Opportunity Grants (FSEOG), the Federal Work-Study Program (FWS), Federal Stafford Student Loans, and Parent Loans for Undergraduate Students (PLUS). New Jersey state sources include Tuition Aid Grants (TAG) and the Educational Opportunity Fund (EOF). All applications for admission are reviewed for academic scholarships, grants, athletic scholarships, and need-based grants. Prospective students should call the Student Financial Aid Office at 201-761-6060 for more information.

Faculty

All classes at Saint Peter's are taught by faculty members rather than graduate students or teaching assistants. Faculty members in every discipline are expected to meet high standards for teaching. Faculty members work with students as advisers and mentors in the classroom and in supervised areas of study, such as research or internships and cooperative education experiences. Faculty members are expected to maintain currency in their fields of instruction through a scholarly agenda of research and/or through continued development as active professionals. Saint Peter's offers small classes so that students can obtain the maximum benefit from their interaction with the faculty members. The 118 full-time faculty members have completed advanced degrees at some of the nation's finest institutions of higher learning. All of Saint Peter's faculty members are committed to *cura personalis,* or personal attention, and to the success of each student individually.

Student Government

The Student Senate consists of an elected executive committee and 5 elected student senators from each class. The objectives of the Student Senate are to coordinate student activities, provide effective means of communication between the student body and the College administration, and strive to maintain and further the spirit and ideals of Saint Peter's College.

Admission Requirements

Admission to Saint Peter's College is based upon a student's demonstrated academic performance, academic preparation, and potential for success in college-level study. Each application is reviewed on an individual basis, and SAT scores, class rank, high school record, personal statement, letters of recommendation, part-time employment, leadership positions, athletics/extracurricular activities, and community service are all considered. Interviews are not required but are strongly recommended for all applicants. Students are expected to have a solid preparation for college. Saint Peter's requires a minimum of 16 units of high school academic courses for admission: 4 units in English, 2 units in history, 2 units in a modern language, 3 units of college-preparatory mathematics, and 2 units of science (including at least 1 unit of a laboratory science). In addition to these 13 basic units, students must have completed at least 3 more units in any combination of the subject areas listed above. One unit is the equivalent of one year of study in a high school subject.

Application and Information

Students are encouraged to submit their applications in the fall of their senior year of high school. Admission is on a rolling basis. Students who wish to be considered for an academic scholarship should apply by February 15. When a student's completed application and records are on file, they are reviewed by the committee. Students are ordinarily notified of the admission decision within two weeks of receipt of the complete admission file, which must include the completed application form, a personal statement, a high school transcript with official SAT scores, and recommendations. Transfer students must submit official copies of all college transcripts by December 1 for admission to the spring semester and before August 1 for admission to the fall semester.

To complete their admission file, international students should submit the results of the Test of English as a Foreign Language (TOEFL) or the equivalent, all official documents of education, an affidavit of financial support, and the completed application form, including a personal statement. International students are encouraged to apply before March 1 for the fall term and before October 1 for the spring term.

For more information, students should contact:

Office of Admission
Saint Peter's College
2641 Kennedy Boulevard
Jersey City, New Jersey 07306-5944
Phone: 201-761-7100
888-SPC-9933 (toll-free)
Fax: 201-761-7105
E-mail: admissions@spc.edu
Web site: http://www.spc.edu

SETON HALL UNIVERSITY

SOUTH ORANGE, NEW JERSEY

The University

Seton Hall University has been preparing students to assume leadership roles for 150 years. A Catholic university founded with the purpose of becoming "a home for the mind, the heart and the spirit," Seton Hall offers more than sixty majors and concentrations, as well as honors and leadership programs. With a 14:1 student-faculty ratio and an average class size of 25, Seton Hall offers all the advantages of a big school; however, with just 5,300 undergraduate students, the University also provides the personal attention of a small college. Seton Hall's mission of "preparing student leaders for a global society" is evident through its high academic standards, values-centered curriculum, and cutting-edge technology. Recently cited by the Intercollegiate Studies Institute's critically acclaimed college guide *Choosing the Right College* as "a Catholic university evolving from being a regional treasure to a national resource," Seton Hall was listed among 110 of the nation's top colleges.

The University comprises eight schools and colleges: the College of Arts and Sciences, the Stillman School of Business, the College of Education and Human Services, the College of Nursing, the Whitehead School of Diplomacy and International Relations, the Immaculate Conception Seminary School of Theology, and the School of Graduate Medical Education, all on the South Orange campus. The School of Law is in nearby Newark.

Emphasizing Judeo-Christian intellectual traditions and values, the University was founded by Bishop James Roosevelt Bayley, the first Catholic bishop of Newark. Seton Hall was named after Bishop Bayley's aunt, St. Elizabeth Ann Seton, the founder of the first American community of the Sisters of Charity. Established as the first diocesan college in the United States in 1856 and organized into a University in 1950, Seton Hall continues to operate under the auspices of the Roman Catholic Diocese of Newark. As such, Seton Hall is both a Catholic university and a catholic university—meaning that the school fosters the values and traditions of the Catholic faith while also universally welcoming students of all denominations.

At Seton Hall, technology is integrated into the curriculum. Every undergraduate is issued a laptop computer with wireless Internet access to facilitate learning through technology both inside and outside the classroom. Seton Hall has integrated technology into course work by including the use of streaming video to increase learning, note-taking, and collaborative work online. The state-of-the-art laptop is upgraded after two years, and students who graduate in four years keep their laptops after graduation. Seton Hall is leading the way in wireless technology, allowing virtually limitless access to online learning.

Seton Hall's on-campus recruiting events and career fairs help students find paid internships at companies like CNN, Prudential, AT&T, Pfizer, Johnson & Johnson, the United Nations, the FBI, ESPN, and the New Jersey Devils. More than 600 employers and alumni come to the campus each year to mentor and recruit students for internships and employment after graduation.

The relationships forged with these companies are so solid that more than 90 percent of the University's employers report that they would hire their Seton Hall interns after graduation if they had appropriate openings. Graduates of Seton Hall University join the ranks of the more than 70,000 alumni who work in leadership positions in business, industry, law, health care, and education nationally and internationally.

Seton Hall graduates are also successful doctors, dentists, optometrists, and veterinarians. Faculty members combine personal attention with strong academic advice to students wishing to enter medical and dental school, and, as a result, approximately 78 percent of students gain entry to medical school and about 100 percent into dental school. Unique opportunities with the Graduate School of Medical Education allow students to enter dual-degree programs to earn advanced degrees in athletic training, physical therapy, occupational therapy, and physician assistant studies.

Location

The suburban village of South Orange, New Jersey, is home to the University's 58-acre parklike campus. With the village center a short walk away, students find practically anything they need. Just beyond the border of the suburban residential community of South Orange is New York City—the Big Apple—the capital of finance, fashion, art, theater, and international relations. Travel to New York is convenient via a midtown direct train from the village center. Just 14 miles away, New York City provides students with opportunities for cultural exploration and internships. Career opportunities also abound throughout northern New Jersey, which is the site of an extensive pharmaceutical, chemical, and financial center. Social, cultural, and recreational opportunities are available throughout the area, with the New Jersey Performing Arts Center, the Meadowlands sports complex, numerous state parks, and the beautiful New Jersey shore all close by.

Majors and Degrees

The College of Arts and Sciences offers the Bachelor of Arts (B.A.) in Africana and Diaspora studies, anthropology, art (art history, fine art, graphic design and advertising art, theater), Asian studies, athletic training, broadcasting and visual media, Catholic studies, classical studies, communication studies, criminal justice, economics, English, environmental studies, French, history, Italian, journalism and public relations, liberal studies, modern languages, music, occupational therapy, philosophy, physical therapy, physician assistant studies, political science, psychology, religious studies, social and behavioral sciences, social work, sociology, Spanish, and theater studies and performance. It offers the Bachelor of Science (B.S.) in biochemistry, biology, chemistry, computer science, mathematics, and physics.

The College of Education and Human Services offers the B.S. in a unique integrated early childhood, elementary, and special education program and in secondary education.

The College of Nursing offers the Bachelor of Science in Nursing (B.S.N.).

The Stillman School of Business offers the B.S. in accounting, economics, finance, management, management information systems, marketing, and sport management. It also offers the B.A. in business administration with concentrations in arts and sciences, diplomacy, international studies, and occupational therapy.

The Whitehead School of Diplomacy and International Relations offers the B.S. in diplomacy and international relations.

Preprofessional programs are available in dentistry, law, medicine, optometry, seminary, and veterinary science. A dual-admission program with Seton Hall University School of Law is offered to qualified undergraduates. Engineering students participate in a five-year program (chemical, civil, computer, electrical, industrial, or mechanical) offered jointly with New Jersey Institute of Technology. Combination undergraduate and postgraduate programs in athletic training, occupational therapy, physical therapy, physician assistant studies, and speech-language pathology are also offered.

Academic Programs

The University uses a semester calendar. It also offers day, evening, and summer sessions.

Select students are invited to participate in the University Honors Program, which consists of four semester-long colloquia devoted to the history of civilization, from ancient through medieval and early modern cultures to contemporary civilization.

With the oldest college of nursing in New Jersey, Seton Hall provides nursing education that prepares its graduates for a variety of health-care settings. Clinical experience is provided in hospitals, public health agencies, schools, nursing homes, industrial organizations, and other community agencies. More than 97 percent of Seton Hall nursing students pass the national nursing exam. Graduates of Seton Hall hold leadership positions in nursing throughout the state.

Seton Hall's Stillman School of Business is accredited by AACSB International—The Association to Advance Collegiate Schools of Business, which puts it among the most rigorous business programs in the United States. Founded on a background of liberal arts courses, the Stillman School offers specialized programs in leadership studies, international business, and sport management.

The Whitehead School of Diplomacy and International Relations is the only school affiliated with the United Nations Association of the United States of America and offers a Bachelor of Science degree in international relations. This program emphasizes ethnopolitical studies or world cultures and the development of management and leadership skills, as well as a high degree of competency in a second language. Requirements include study abroad.

The University offers an Army ROTC program on campus.

Off-Campus Programs

Seton Hall offers study-abroad programs in the People's Republic of China, Japan, Korea, the Dominican Republic, and Puerto Rico. Through the international student exchange program, students may study at any of the 101 universities in thirty-five countries for one academic year. Students have several opportunities for cooperative learning and internships in the metropolitan area. Many co-op positions are with Fortune 500 companies, while others are with leading government, cultural, charitable, and scientific organizations. A semester in Washington, D.C., is also available for students to obtain internships and to take classes at exchange universities.

Academic Facilities

At Seton Hall, there is an emphasis on the use of state-of-the-art technology and available facilities to aid in the overall development and college experience for all students. Seton Hall's award-winning Mobile Computing Program provides all incoming, full-time freshmen with a brand-new, fully loaded laptop. The Department of Information Technology also supports and maintains numerous public computer labs around campus. The Richie Regan Recreation Center serves the recreational and fitness needs of the Seton Hall community with cardio machines, an Olympic-sized pool, an indoor track, and six indoor basketball courts. The brand-new fitness center features a free-weight center, new cardiovascular equipment, plasma screen televisions, and wireless headsets to listen to the TVs.

The University's Walsh library is a twenty-first-century research center with a computerized card catalog, four electronic multimedia rooms, ten CD-ROM information search and retrieval stations, 200 computer workstations for students, nearly 1 million holdings, and the University Gallery. The University Center houses most of Seton Hall's cultural, social, and recreational activities. The University Center is the hub of student activity and includes the Galleon Dining Room/food court, the Pirate's Cove (lounge and coffee house), Theatre-in-the-Round, an art gallery, a study lounge, and the student government office as well as a wide variety of student clubs and organizations. Services such as aptitude testing, career counseling, career services, health services, and personal counseling are also provided for all Seton Hall students. Fahy Hall contains classrooms and offices, a TV studio, two classroom amphitheaters, and language and journalism laboratories. McNulty Hall, renovated in October 2007, is a state-of-the-future science and technology center. The new center is home to more than thirty research and teaching laboratories, a confocal microscope laboratory, a computational chemistry laboratory, a radiochemistry laboratory, and a rooftop observatory and greenhouse. The Art Center (a registered National Historic landmark) houses an art gallery, studios, classrooms, and offices of the Department of Art and Music. The College of Nursing has multipurpose and audiovisual laboratories. Jubilee Hall, completed in 1997, contains state-of-the-art lecture halls, computer rooms, faculty offices, a 300-seat auditorium, conference rooms, and the University's new Trading Room, where students learn about stocks, bonds, and trading. There are also microcomputer laboratories in several locations on campus, and a large University-operated mainframe computer is located in the Computer Center. The University also has various centers and research institutes, including the Center for Catholic Studies, the G.K. Chesterton Institute, the Center for Jewish Christian Studies, and the 50-year-old Asia Center.

Costs

For the 2007–08 academic year, tuition and fees were $28,150 per year. This amount covers 31 credits and all fees, including a mobile-computing fee. The charge for room and board was $9710.

Financial Aid

The University offers federal, state, and institutional aid. Most aid is based on need, but many scholarships are based on outstanding scholastic ability and achievement. Athletic grants are also available. Currently, about 90 percent of the students receive financial aid, with 75 percent receiving aid directly from Seton Hall. All applicants for aid are required to file the Free Application for Federal Student Aid (FAFSA) by March 1 for the fall semester and by October 1 for the spring semester.

Faculty

The University has 860 faculty members, and 92 percent of the full-time faculty members have doctoral degrees. The ratio of full-time students to full-time faculty members is 14:1. Faculty members serve as advisers to students in their respective departments.

Student Government

The Student Government Association consists of students who make up two legislative bodies that have the responsibility of representing their fellow students and providing programs of interest to the campus community. Students are elected to seats on the University Senate, which deals with all legislative matters pertinent to the University. In addition, the Resident Student Association represents the interests of resident students, and the Commuter Council represents the interests of commuter students.

Admission Requirements

Applicants are selected on the basis of their school achievement record, SAT or ACT scores, personal essay, and teacher and counselor recommendations. Students must graduate from an accredited high school or have passing scores on the GED test. Sixteen high school units are required: 4 in English, 3 in mathematics, 2 in social studies, 2 in a foreign language (taken consecutively), 1 in a laboratory science, and 4 in approved academic electives. Special admission policies exist for students who have been out of high school for an extended period of time. There is also a $55 application fee (free if applying online). The application fee may be waived for applicants with financial need.

Transfer applicants must have a minimum 2.5 grade point average and must be in good standing at the last institution attended. Applicants must submit transcripts from all colleges and universities attended. Credit is usually given for grades of 2.0 or higher in University-equivalent courses taken at approved institutions; a maximum of 100 semester hours of transferable credit are allowed toward a bachelor's degree.

Application and Information

The University uses rolling admission. Admission decisions are announced on a rolling basis; however, Seton Hall's early action deadline is November 15. Students applying nonbinding early action receive an admission decision on or before December 30. The preferred application deadlines are March 1 for freshman and June 1 for transfers.

Peter Nacy, Assistant Vice President for Admissions
Seton Hall University
400 South Orange Avenue
South Orange, New Jersey 07079-2680
Phone: 800-THE-HALL (toll-free)
E-mail: thehall@shu.edu
Web site: http://www.shu.edu

THOMAS EDISON STATE COLLEGE

TRENTON, NEW JERSEY

The College

Thomas Edison State College provides flexible, high-quality, collegiate learning opportunities for self-directed adults. Identified by *Forbes* magazine as one of the top twenty colleges and universities in the nation in the use of technology to create learning opportunities for adults, Thomas Edison State College is a national leader in the assessment of adult learning and a pioneer in the use of educational technologies. Founded in 1972, Thomas Edison State College enables adults to complete associate, baccalaureate, and master's degrees through a wide variety of rigorous and high-quality academic methods that can be customized to meet their individual needs.

The College's convenient programs are designed to help students pursue their educational goals while attending to the challenges and priorities of adult life. Accredited by the Commission on Higher Education of the Middle States Association of Colleges and Schools, Thomas Edison State College offers a distinguished academic program for the self-motivated adult learner. The College has approximately 25,000 alumni worldwide.

Academic advisement is provided to enrolled students by the College's Advisement Center, which assists students in integrating their learning style, background, and educational goals with the credit-earning methods and programs available. Students may access advisement through telephone and in-person appointments through the Advisement Phone Center, and they have 24-hour-a-day access through fax and e-mail.

In addition to the undergraduate programs highlighted in this description, the College offers four online master's programs. These online degrees are designed to have broad appeal for those who are not served by conventional graduate study programs.

The Master of Science in Human Resources Management (M.S.H.R.M.) degree serves human resources professionals who wish to become strategic partners in their organizations. This online program uses a cohort model and is designed to position human resources professionals as leaders within their organizations. The 36-semester-hour program provides practitioners with technical human resources skills in staffing, providing professional development, managing organizational culture, and measuring and rewarding performance.

The Master of Science in Management (M.S.M.) degree serves employed adults who have had professional experience in the management field. The M.S.M. program integrates the theory and practice of management as it applies to diverse organizations, educational institutions, and nonprofit agencies. The emphasis is on theory and practice in the management of organizations.

The Master of Arts in Liberal Studies (M.A.L.S.) degree enables students to study and apply the liberal arts to their professional lives. The M.A.L.S. program serves practitioners who are interested in broadening and deepening their professional skills, knowledge, and competencies through an intensive exposure to the liberal arts. The focus is on a deeper appreciation of the value and relevance of the arts, sciences, and humanities to the practical concerns of the workplace.

The Master of Science in Nursing (M.S.N.) degree in nurse education serves registered nurses (with current RN licenses that are valid in the United States) who have completed a Bachelor of Science in Nursing degree. Graduates of the 36-credit M.S.N. degree program are awarded a Nurse Educator Certificate in addition to the diploma and are prepared for teaching positions in schools of nursing and health-care settings. Furthermore, the School of Nursing at Thomas Edison State College offers an RN-B.S.N./M.S.N. degree program that is designed for experienced RNs who want a high-quality education with the convenience and flexibility that an online program can provide.

During the 2007–08 academic year, Thomas Edison State College plans to launch a new graduate-level degree, the Master of Arts in educational leadership (MAEL), which will serve adults who wish to prepare for roles as school leaders.

Location

Thomas Edison State College is located in Trenton, New Jersey.

Majors and Degrees

Thomas Edison State College offers sixteen associate, baccalaureate, and master's degree programs in more than 100 areas of study. Undergraduate degrees offered include Associate in Applied Science, Associate in Science in Business Administration, Associate in Science in Applied Science and Technology, Associate in Arts, Associate in Science in Natural Sciences and Mathematics, Associate in Science in Public and Social Services, Bachelor of Arts, Bachelor of Science in Applied Science and Technology, Bachelor of Science in Business Administration, Bachelor of Science in Health Sciences (a joint-degree program with the University of Medicine and Dentistry of New Jersey (UMDNJ) School of Health Related Professions (SHRP)), Bachelor of Science in Human Services, and Bachelor of Science in Nursing. The College's Undergraduate Prospectus contains a list of the more than 100 areas of study available within these degrees. To obtain the Undergraduate Prospectus, students should contact the College at its toll-free number or by e-mail.

Academic Programs

At Thomas Edison State College, students have the opportunity to earn degrees through traditional and nontraditional methods. These methods take into consideration personal needs and interests while ensuring both breadth and depth of knowledge within the degree program. Thomas Edison State College offers one of the most highly regarded, comprehensive distance learning programs in the United States. Students at Thomas Edison State College may use several convenient methods of meeting degree requirements, depending upon their individual learning styles and preferences. Thomas Edison State College courses, examinations, Prior Learning Assessment, corporate or military education, and credits earned at other accredited colleges may be combined in a number of ways to earn credits toward an undergraduate degree.

Each undergraduate degree requires work in general education, a major area of study, and elective subjects. Students are encouraged to familiarize themselves with the requirements of their chosen degree and work in conjunction with one of the College's knowledgeable program advisers to develop a program plan that best meets their individual needs, goals, and interests.

Thomas Edison State College's Military Degree Completion Program (MDCP) serves military personnel worldwide. The MDCP was developed to accommodate the special needs of military personnel, whose location, relocation, and time constraints make traditional college attendance difficult, if not impossible. The program allows students to engage in a degree program wherever they may be stationed. The program allows maximum credit for military training and education. As a result of its long-standing commitment to providing access to educational options for military personnel, Thomas Edison State College participates in the Navy College Program Distance Learning Partnership (NCPDLP) and the Navy College Program for Afloat College Education (NCPACE) and is a participant in the Army University Access Online (eArmyU) program.

In addition, the College welcomes community and county college students and graduates and values their educational experience. Thomas Edison State College works closely with community and county colleges to assure maximum credit transfer for students. Up to 80 credits from a community or county college may be transferred to Thomas Edison State College toward the 120 credits needed for a baccalaureate degree. Furthermore, the College accepts an unlimited number of four-year college credits toward degree requirements.

In addition, students are able to take distance learning courses through Thomas Edison State College, and they may earn credit for what they already know through testing, Prior Learning Assessment, and other methods of earning credit that are available through the College.

Thomas Edison State College also provides services for individuals who are not seeking a degree. These are credit-earning options for non-degree-seeking students, credit banking, and credit for licenses and certificates.

Credit-earning options for non-degree-seeking students benefit individuals who would like to earn credits through examinations, Prior Learning Assessment, Guided Study, and online courses. They may do so by paying the appropriate fee for these programs. An application to Thomas Edison State College is not required to take advantage of these credit-earning options.

Credit banking is for students who wish to document college-level learning gained through military experience, professional licenses, college proficiency examinations, college-level corporate training programs, or American Council on Education (ACE) recommendations. Thomas Edison State College offers a credit-banking service for individuals who wish to consolidate college-level work into a Thomas Edison State College transcript. Credits transcripted under the credit-banking program may or may not apply to a degree program at Thomas Edison State College.

Thomas Edison State College grants credit for current professional licenses or certificates that have been approved for credit by ACE and the College's Academic Council. Students who have earned one of these licenses or certificates must submit notarized copies of the license or certificate and a current renewal card, if appropriate, to receive credit. A list of licenses and certificates approved for credit may be found in the College's Undergraduate Prospectus.

Academic Facilities

Distance education courses are provided through several venues, including Internet-based online courses via myEdison, print-based Guided Study courses, standardized TECEP® examinations, *e*-Pack® courses, and assessment of prior learning through the College's unique Prior Learning Assessment (PLA) program. The College's distance learning program is administered through its Center for Directed Independent Adult Learning (DIAL).

Thomas Edison State College students utilize the rich library research facilities of the New Jersey State Library, which is an affiliate of Thomas Edison State College. Students have access to the Virtual Academic Libraries Environment (VALE), a system that provides access to a network of research libraries.

Costs

Tuition is payment for all costs that are directly associated with the academic delivery of a Thomas Edison State College education to registered students. Fees are designated as payment for administrative services associated with other activities in support of that educational process and for materials used by students for courses and other activities undertaken by them. Thomas Edison State College offers one annual tuition plan, the Comprehensive Tuition Plan, for students who want access to all components of the tuition package. Students who determine that they require only some components of the Comprehensive Tuition Plan are offered the Enrolled Options Plan. A complete listing of tuition and fees is included in the College's information packet, which may be obtained by calling the toll-free number or visiting the College Web site.

Financial Aid

Thomas Edison State College participates in a number of federal and state aid programs. Eligible students may receive Federal Pell Grants or federal education loans, such as the Federal Stafford Student Loan (subsidized and unsubsidized), for courses offered by the College. Eligible New Jersey residents may also tap a variety of state grant and loan programs. Students may use state aid to meet all or part of their College costs, provided they are taking at least 12 credits per semester.

Students interested in using financial assistance, including student loans, should file an application as well as the Free Application for Federal Student Aid (FAFSA) and submit all required documentation at least two months prior to the start of the first semester for which they plan to enroll in the College. Once a student's financial aid file is complete, a letter is sent to the student indicating what aid has been awarded.

Detailed information about the financial aid process may be found in the financial aid packet, which is available from the Office of Financial Aid & Veterans' Affairs. To receive this information, students should call the toll-free number listed in this description or send e-mail to finaid@tesc.edu.

Faculty

There are approximately 230 mentors at Thomas Edison State College. Drawn from other highly regarded colleges and universities, mentors provide many services to Thomas Edison State College, including assessment of knowledge adults already have, advisement, and other special assignments.

Admission Requirements

Adults seeking an associate or baccalaureate degree who are high school graduates and at least 21 years of age are eligible to become Thomas Edison State College students. Adults seeking a graduate degree must have a baccalaureate degree from a regionally accredited college or university, and must submit a current resume, provide two letters of recommendation, and complete and submit all appropriate essay questions. Because Thomas Edison State College delivers high-quality education directly to students wherever they live or work, students may complete degree requirements at their convenience. There are two brief residency requirements for the organizational leadership professional focus area of the Master of Science in Management degree. A computer is required to complete graduate degrees and to take online courses. Once a student has applied for a specific degree program, an evaluator determines the number of credits the student has already earned and fits those into the degree program requirements.

Application and Information

Students may apply to Thomas Edison State College any day of the year by mail or fax or through the College Web site. The Office of Admissions assists potential applicants in determining whether Thomas Edison State College suits their particular academic goals. For more information, students should contact:

David Hoftiezer
Assistant Director of Admissions
Thomas Edison State College
101 West State Street
Trenton, New Jersey 08608-1176
Phone: 888-442-8372 (toll-free)
Fax: 609-984-8447
E-mail: info@tesc.edu
Web site: http://www.tesc.edu

WILLIAM PATERSON UNIVERSITY OF NEW JERSEY

WAYNE, NEW JERSEY

WILLIAM PATERSON UNIVERSITY

The University

Since its founding in 1855, William Paterson University has grown into a comprehensive state institution whose programs reflect the area's need for challenging, affordable educational options. Ideally midsized (the total enrollment is 10,443, of whom 8,863 are degree-seeking undergraduates), William Paterson offers a wider variety of academic programs than smaller universities, yet provides students with a more personalized atmosphere than larger institutions. Once the site of the family estate of Garret Hobart, the twenty-fourth vice president of the United States, William Paterson's 370-acre spacious campus, with its wooded areas and waterfalls, offers an environment in which students may develop both intellectually and socially. Although the majority of the University's students come from the New Jersey and New York vicinity, some international and out-of-state students enroll each year. Twenty-three percent of undergraduates reside on campus in ten residence halls or apartment-style facilities, which accommodate 2,700 students. On-campus housing is offered on a first-come, first-served basis. Portions of the residence halls are dedicated to dynamic "learning communities" centered around students' shared interests and themes, such as the University's Honors College and health and wellness.

Social, cultural, and recreational activities complement the academic programs. Cultural events take place throughout the year, featuring both William Paterson's own talent as well as renowned professional artists. Among the programs are concerts presenting jazz, classical, and contemporary music; theater productions; gallery exhibits; and a distinguished-lecturer series. The brand new University Commons complex, including the redesigned John Victor Machuga Student Center, is the heart of the campus, where the entire University community gathers and interacts. This state-of-the-art campus center provides students with an exquisite setting for a vast array of social and extracurricular activities, dining venues, and student support services, all under one roof. The Student Activities Programming Board helps the more than fifty clubs and organizations to develop diverse activities for the entire student body. William Paterson has twenty-two social fraternities and sororities and sixteen honor societies. Students staff the campus radio station (WPSC) and the television station (WPC-TV), which develops a number of widely distributed television programs for local and statewide cable networks. The Recreation Center serves as the focal point for physical recreation. In addition to the main courts, which accommodate badminton, basketball, indoor tennis, and volleyball, the 4,000-seat facility has racquetball courts, an exercise room, saunas, and Jacuzzis. The University has twelve intercollegiate sports teams, five for men and seven for women, including successful NCAA teams in men's baseball and women's softball. In 2002, the Pioneers won the coed cheerleading and dance team national championship. In addition, bowling, dance, horseback riding, and ice hockey are organized as club sports. The University has a competition-size indoor pool, outdoor tennis courts, and a lighted athletics field complex.

Guided by the University's mission to provide community outreach with opportunities for lifelong learning, the Center for Continuing and Professional Education brings the University to students and students to the University. From noncredit courses to corporate training and advanced computer skills training, the center offers today's working adults professional development as well as flexible scheduling.

Location

William Paterson University is located in northern New Jersey in the busy suburban town of Wayne. Several major recreational and cultural centers are nearby. New York City is just 20 miles to the east, the seacoast is an hour's drive south, skiing is 30 miles north, and the Meadowlands Sports Complex is a half-hour drive away.

Majors and Degrees

William Paterson University grants four undergraduate degrees—the B.A., B.S., B.F.A., and B.M.—and offers degree programs through its five colleges: Arts and Communication; the Christos M. Cotsakos College of Business, which in 2005 became one of 15 percent of schools internationally to achieve prestigious accreditation from AACSB International–The Association to Advance Collegiate Schools of Business; Education; Humanities and Social Sciences; and Science and Health.

The Bachelor of Arts degree is awarded in African, African American, and Caribbean studies; anthropology; art; Asian studies; communication; economics; English; French and Francophone studies; geography; history; Latin American studies; liberal studies; mathematics; music; philosophy; political science; psychology; sociology; Spanish; and women's studies. The Bachelor of Science degree is conferred in accounting, applied chemistry, athletic training; biology, biotechnology, business administration, community health/school health education, computer science, environmental science, exercise science; nursing, physical education, and professional sales. The Bachelor of Fine Arts degree in fine arts and the Bachelor of Music degree in music are also offered. Urban studies, a cross-disciplinary minor, is part of the curriculum, as well. In addition, the Christos M. Cotsakos College of Business allows students to pursue several noteworthy offerings, including a one-of-a-kind academic program in professional sales; the Financial Learning Center, one of the few, advanced, simulated electronic trading rooms found in an academic environment; and the Russ Berrie Institute for Professional Sales, which advances professional sales for both students and business professionals.

Certification is available in early childhood, elementary, secondary, and special education. Preprofessional programs in engineering, law, medicine (dentistry, optometry, podiatry, and veterinary science), pharmacy, physical therapy, and speech-language pathology are arranged at the request of students. Students who have completed the premedical program in the College of Science and Health have consistently been accepted by American medical schools for more than a decade.

Academic Programs

Students must complete a minimum of 128 credits to earn a baccalaureate degree. Degree programs include a 60-credit general education requirement, 30–60 credits in a major, and 20–40 credits in elective courses. (In specialized degree programs, such as the B.F.A. and the B.M., general education and major course requirements may differ.) Students uncertain of which career path to follow may take advantage of advisement and counseling programs. In addition, the general education requirements enable students to take up to 60 credits before declaring a major, so that they can acquire a basic understanding of all major fields of knowledge before having to choose a specific area. Diagnostic testing and career seminars, provided by the Career Development Office, also ensure that students receive the guidance necessary to make wise course selections and career decisions.

William Paterson offers a variety of special programs. Its Honors College is designed for those ambitious and well-qualified students who want to add a challenging dimension to their majors. Currently, there are seven program tracks—biopsychology, cognitive science, humanities, life science and environmental ethics, music, performing and literary arts, and social sciences.

Students who successfully complete Advanced Placement tests and/or College-Level Examination Program tests may receive credit for acceptable scores. Credit may also be awarded for military training and experience. William Paterson University operates on a two-semester and two-summer-session system.

Off-Campus Programs

William Paterson offers a special opportunity for off-campus study. Semester Abroad, a 15-credit program, is open to sophomores and juniors who wish to study for a semester at selected institutions in Australia, Denmark, Great Britain, Greece, Israel, Spain, and other countries around the world.

Academic Facilities

Situated on a 370-acre campus set in the hills of suburban Wayne, New Jersey, William Paterson's facilities are easily accessible, promote interaction among students, and encourage participation by all students in the various academic, cultural, and recreational programs. The University has recently expanded the David and Lorraine Cheng Library's bound collection area by 33 percent and increased the seating capacity by 100 percent. The library contains a collection of more than 360,000 volumes, more than 17,000 audiovisual items, and access to over 23,000 electronic and print periodicals and journals. A special-collections room houses rare and out-of-print items on New Jersey and valuable editions of literary works. Media services, group studies, carrels, and computer labs provide space for a variety of student uses. An extensive collection of online journals and resources is accessible campuswide from the library Web site. Supporting William Paterson's varied cultural and artistic offerings are the Power Arts Center, an extensive, 42,600-square-foot facility accommodating an array of studio arts, such as design, photography, sculpture, ceramics, printmaking, woodworking, and painting; the Ben Shahn Center for Visual Arts, which contains art galleries, studios, and classrooms; and the Shea Center for Performing Arts, which contains a 922-seat theater as well as band, choral, and orchestra practice rooms and classrooms.

Hobart Hall, a state-of-the-art communication facility, is designed to educate communication majors in the most contemporary communication technology, including teleconferences. The facility houses two broadcast-quality TV studios, a multipurpose computer lab, a film studio, an FCC-licensed FM radio station, an uplink and four downlink satellite dishes, audio and video digital nonlinear editing systems, a cable system linking nearly all of the buildings on campus, and a computerized telephone system for voice and data transmission. In addition, William Paterson is finalizing the process of creating fiberoptic links throughout the campus. The Atrium, a two-story academic building, contains a writing center, multimedia language lab, tutorial center, and computing support facilities.

Among the other academic resources are extensive computer facilities, a filmmaking laboratory, a professionally equipped television production truck, a child-care center, a nursing instructional center, a language lab, and a speech and hearing clinic. William Paterson University has dual accreditation from the American Speech-Language-Hearing Association for its speech and hearing clinic and its graduate program in communication disorders. The science research facilities contain two electron microscopes and various specialized labs.

Costs

Annual tuition (including fees) for the 2006–07 academic year was $9422 for full-time (12 credits or more) students who are New Jersey residents and $15,370 for full-time nonresident students. Room and board cost approximately $9380 per year. All charges are subject to change per the Board of Trustees.

Financial Aid

Financial aid is available through a number of federal and state grant, loan, scholarship, and work-study programs. To apply for need-based aid, students must file the Free Application for Federal Student Aid (FAFSA) with the United States Department of Education by the priority date of April 1.

Both the University and the Alumni Association award a number of competitive scholarships, based solely on academic merit, to entering freshmen. They are the Scholarships for Academic Excellence, Educational Enrichment Scholarships, Trustee and Presidential Scholarships, and New Jersey's Outstanding Scholars Recruitment Program. Academic Achievement Scholarships are awarded only on a competitive basis to continuing students. Each year, more than 1,000 scholarships are awarded, which total more than $4.8 million.

Faculty

William Paterson's 366 full-time and 699 part-time faculty members bring to the classroom a valuable blend of accomplished scholarship and practical, applied experience. Faculty members assist students with curriculum and career planning, which engenders open, personal communication between the students and faculty.

Through a formal reciprocal exchange relationship with various institutions worldwide, and through the Fulbright Scholarship Program, William Paterson University often receives visiting international scholars. Among the University faculty are more than 30 Fulbright scholars, one of the most prestigious academic distinctions in the world.

Student Government

The Student Government Association (SGA), of which all full-time and part-time students are automatically members, has become an influential voice in University decision making. Elected officers and various committees convey students' perspectives to the administration and advance their causes. The SGA is also responsible for chartering more than fifty campus organizations and allocating student activity fees among them.

Admission Requirements

Admission to William Paterson University is competitive. Admissions decisions for entering freshmen are based on a complete review of the students' academic record (course of study, grades, and rank) as well as the results of the SAT or ACT. Applicants are considered eligible if they have taken a minimum of 16 Carnegie units and have demonstrated strong academic ability. The students' secondary school record must show the following courses: English, 4 years (composition and literature); mathematics, 3 years (algebra I and II and geometry); laboratory science, 2 years (biology, chemistry, or physics); social science, 2 years (American history, world history, or political science); and additional college-preparatory subjects, 5 units (advanced mathematics, literature, foreign language, or social sciences). In addition, students selecting a major in art or music (except musical studies) must submit a portfolio for review by the Art Department or must audition for the Music Department.

Transfer students must present at least 12 college-level credits with a minimum 2.0 GPA; science and nursing majors must have a minimum 2.5 GPA; and teacher certification program applicants must have a minimum 2.75 GPA. Applicants with fewer than 12 college credits must submit a high school transcript. Application review is completed only upon receipt of official transcripts from high schools and especially colleges and universities. Unofficial transcripts or transcripts sent by students will not be used for admissions.

Application and Information

Application forms and transcripts from candidates for freshman status must be received by May 1 for fall admission and November 1 for spring admission. Transfer students, readmitted students, and students seeking a second bachelor's degree must submit their materials by May 1 and November 1 for fall and spring entry, respectively. However, the University closes the application process earlier when the number of new and continuing students strains its ability to provide effective programs and services. A $50 application fee is required. Applications are reviewed on a rolling basis. Campus tours are available during the fall and spring semesters on weekdays by appointment when classes are in session.

Office of Admissions
William Paterson University of New Jersey
Wayne, New Jersey 07470
Phone: 973-720-2125
877-WPU-EXCEL (978-3923; toll-free)
E-mail: admissions@wpunj.edu
Web site: http://www.wpunj.edu

William Paterson University's hilltop suburban campus offers an environment where students may develop both intellectually and socially.

NEW MEXICO

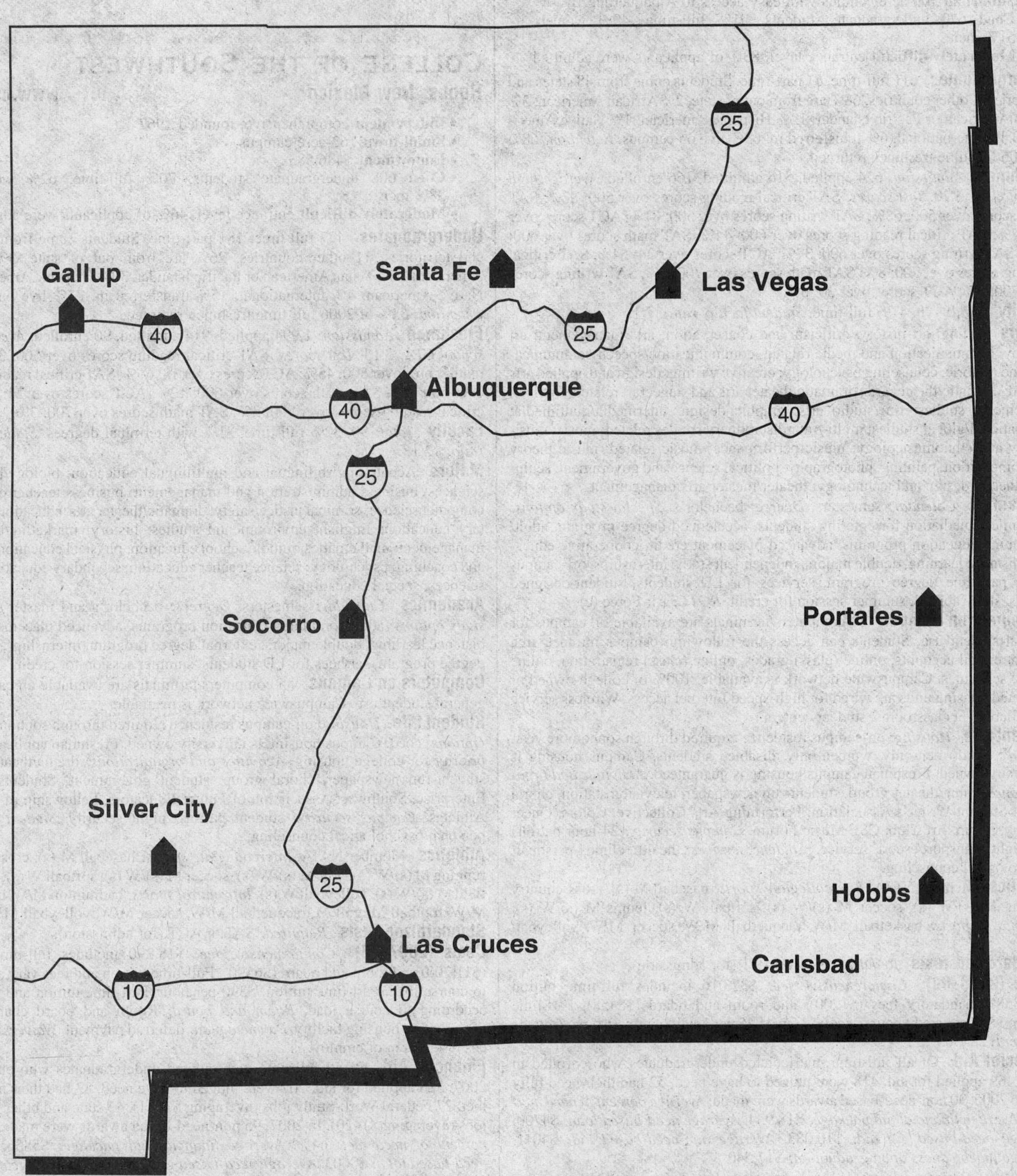

Gallup
Santa Fe
Las Vegas
Albuquerque
Socorro
Portales
Silver City
Hobbs
Las Cruces
Carlsbad
25
40
10

COLLEGE OF SANTA FE

Santa Fe, New Mexico **www.csf.edu**

- **Independent** comprehensive, founded 1947
- **Suburban** 100-acre campus with easy access to Albuquerque
- **Coed** 672 undergraduate students, 91% full-time, 49% women, 51% men
- **Moderately difficult** entrance level, 83% of applicants were admitted

Undergraduates 611 full-time, 61 part-time. Students come from 48 states and territories, 4 other countries, 68% are from out of state, 2% African American, 3% Asian American or Pacific Islander, 12% Hispanic American, 1% Native American, 0.4% international, 6% transferred in, 63% live on campus. *Retention:* 68% of 2006 full-time freshmen returned.

Freshmen *Admission:* 624 applied, 516 admitted, 166 enrolled. *Average high school GPA:* 3.20. *Test scores:* SAT critical reading scores over 500: 82%; SAT math scores over 500: 68%; SAT writing scores over 500: 81%; ACT scores over 18: 97%; SAT critical reading scores over 600: 44%; SAT math scores over 600: 23%; SAT writing scores over 600: 37%; ACT scores over 24: 54%; SAT critical reading scores over 700: 8%; SAT math scores over 700: 1%; SAT writing scores over 700: 3%; ACT scores over 30: 6%.

Faculty *Total:* 178, 41% full-time. *Student/faculty ratio:* 7:1.

Majors Acting; art history, criticism and conservation; arts management; art therapy; communication and media related; communication/speech communication and rhetoric; counseling psychology; creative writing; design and applied arts related; dramatic/theater arts; dramatic/theater arts and stagecraft related; English; film/cinema studies; fine/studio arts; graphic design; intermedia/multimedia; international/global studies; multi-/interdisciplinary studies related; music; musicology and ethnomusicology; music performance; music related; music theory and composition; painting; photography; political science and government; sculpture; theater design and technology; theater/theater arts management.

Academics *Calendar:* semesters. *Degree:* bachelor's. *Special study options:* academic remediation for entering students, accelerated degree program, adult/continuing education programs, advanced placement credit, cooperative education, distance learning, double majors, independent study, internships, off-campus study, part-time degree program, services for LD students, student-designed majors, study abroad, summer session for credit. *ROTC:* Air Force (c).

Computers on Campus 84 computers/terminals are available on campus for general student use. Students can access the following: campus intranet, free student e-mail accounts, online (class) grades, online (class) registration, online (class) schedules. Campuswide network is available. 100% of college-owned or -operated housing units are wired for high-speed Internet access. Wireless service is available via classrooms, student centers.

Student Life *Housing:* on-campus residence required through sophomore year. *Options:* coed, men-only, women-only, disabled students. Campus housing is university owned. Freshman campus housing is guaranteed. *Activities and organizations:* drama/theater group, student-run newspaper, television station, choral group, Student Writer's Association, Performing Arts Collective, Colors: Queer Identity Group, Art Club, CSF Music Forum. *Campus security:* 24-hour patrols, late-night transport/escort service. *Student services:* health clinic, personal/psychological counseling.

Athletics Member NAIA. *Intercollegiate sports:* baseball M (s), cross-country running M (s)/W (s), soccer M (s)/W (s), softball W (s), tennis M (s)/W (s). *Intramural sports:* basketball M/W, racquetball M/W, soccer M/W, volleyball M/W.

Standardized Tests *Required:* SAT or ACT (for admission).

Costs (2008–09) *Comprehensive fee:* $37,016 includes full-time tuition ($27,358), mandatory fees ($1200), and room and board ($8458). Part-time tuition: $835 per credit hour. *Required fees:* $25 per credit hour part-time. *College room only:* $4565.

Financial Aid Of all full-time matriculated undergraduates who enrolled in 2005, 469 applied for aid, 418 were judged to have need, 52 had their need fully met. In 2005, 90 non-need-based awards were made. *Average percent of need met:* 77%. *Average financial aid package:* $18,934. *Average need-based loan:* $4700. *Average need-based gift aid:* $10,083. *Average non-need-based aid:* $4011. *Average indebtedness upon graduation:* $17,540.

Applying *Options:* electronic application, early admission, early decision, deferred entrance. *Application fee:* $35. *Required:* essay or personal statement, high school transcript, 2 letters of recommendation, interview. *Required for some:* portfolio or audition for visual and performing arts programs. *Recommended:* minimum 3.0 GPA. *Application deadlines:* rolling (freshmen), rolling (transfers). *Notification:* continuous (freshmen), continuous (transfers).

Freshman Application Contact Mr. Joseph Fitzpatrick, College of Santa Fe, 1600 Saint Michael's Drive, Santa Fe, NM 87505-7634. *Phone:* 505-473-6133. *Toll-free phone:* 800-456-2673. *Fax:* 505-473-6129. *E-mail:* admissions@csf.edu.

COLLEGE OF THE SOUTHWEST

Hobbs, New Mexico **www.csw.edu/**

- **Independent** comprehensive, founded 1962
- **Small-town** 162-acre campus
- **Endowment** $486,583
- **Coed** 608 undergraduate students, 70% full-time, 62% women, 38% men
- **Moderately difficult** entrance level, 46% of applicants were admitted

Undergraduates 427 full-time, 181 part-time. Students come from 11 states and territories, 11 other countries, 26% are from out of state, 3% African American, 0.5% Asian American or Pacific Islander, 30% Hispanic American, 3% Native American, 4% international, 15% transferred in, 23% live on campus. *Retention:* 63% of 2006 full-time freshmen returned.

Freshmen *Admission:* 1,994 applied, 914 admitted, 90 enrolled. *Average high school GPA:* 3.13. *Test scores:* SAT critical reading scores over 500: 30%; SAT math scores over 500: 45%; ACT scores over 18: 61%; SAT critical reading scores over 600: 6%; SAT math scores over 600: 12%; ACT scores over 24: 8%; SAT critical reading scores over 700: 3%; SAT math scores over 700: 3%.

Faculty *Total:* 90, 32% full-time, 31% with terminal degrees. *Student/faculty ratio:* 12:1.

Majors Accounting; bilingual and multilingual education; biology/biological sciences; business administration and management; business teacher education; computer science; criminal justice/safety; dramatic/theater arts; education; elementary education; English; environmental studies; history; marketing/marketing management; mathematics; middle school education; physical education teaching and coaching; psychology; science teacher education; secondary education; social sciences; special education.

Academics *Calendar:* semesters. *Degrees:* bachelor's and master's. *Special study options:* adult/continuing education programs, advanced placement credit, distance learning, double majors, external degree program, internships, part-time degree program, services for LD students, summer session for credit.

Computers on Campus 35 computers/terminals are available on campus for general student use. Campuswide network is available.

Student Life *Housing:* on-campus residence required through sophomore year. *Options:* coed. Campus housing is university owned. Freshman applicants given priority for college housing. *Activities and organizations:* drama/theater group, student-run newspaper, choral group, student government, Students in Free Enterprise, Southwest Association of Future Educators, Fellowship of Christian Athletes. *Campus security:* student patrols, night security. *Student services:* personal/psychological counseling.

Athletics Member NAIA. *Intercollegiate sports:* baseball M (s), cross-country running M (s)/W (s), golf M (s)/W (s), soccer M (s)/W (s), softball W (s), track and field M (s)/W (s), volleyball W (s). *Intramural sports:* badminton M/W, basketball M/W, football M, golf M, racquetball M/W, soccer M/W, volleyball M/W.

Standardized Tests *Required:* SAT or ACT (for admission).

Costs (2007–08) *Comprehensive fee:* $18,290 includes full-time tuition ($11,700) and room and board ($6590). Full-time tuition and fees vary according to course load. Part-time tuition: $390 per hour. Part-time tuition and fees vary according to course load. *Room and board:* Room and board charges vary according to housing facility. *Payment plan:* deferred payment. *Waivers:* employees or children of employees.

Financial Aid Of all full-time matriculated undergraduates who enrolled in 2007, 328 applied for aid, 207 were judged to have need, 83 had their need fully met. 27 Federal Work-Study jobs (averaging $1581). 43 state and other part-time jobs (averaging $1420). In 2007, 95 non-need-based awards were made. *Average percent of need met:* 64%. *Average financial aid package:* $5856. *Average need-based loan:* $3603. *Average need-based gift aid:* $3132. *Average non-need-based aid:* $4769. *Financial aid deadline:* 8/1.

Applying *Options:* electronic application, early admission, deferred entrance. *Application fee:* $25. *Required:* high school transcript, minimum 2.0 GPA. *Application deadlines:* rolling (freshmen), rolling (transfers). *Notification:* continuous (freshmen), continuous (transfers).

Freshman Application Contact Dr. Steve Hill, Dean of Recruitment, College of the Southwest, 6610 Lovington Highway, Hobbs, NM 88240. *Phone:* 505-392-6563. *Toll-free phone:* 800-530-4400. *Fax:* 505-392-6006. *E-mail:* shill@csw.edu.

Eastern New Mexico University

Portales, New Mexico **www.enmu.edu/**

- **State-supported** comprehensive, founded 1934, part of Eastern New Mexico University System
- **Rural** 240-acre campus
- **Endowment** $8.8 million
- **Coed** 3,443 undergraduate students, 69% full-time, 54% women, 46% men
- **Minimally difficult** entrance level, 70% of applicants were admitted

Undergraduates 2,371 full-time, 1,072 part-time. Students come from 43 states and territories, 15 other countries, 19% are from out of state, 6% African American, 1% Asian American or Pacific Islander, 31% Hispanic American, 3% Native American, 3% international, 10% transferred in, 30% live on campus. *Retention:* 60% of 2006 full-time freshmen returned.

Freshmen *Admission:* 1,634 applied, 1,136 admitted, 555 enrolled. *Average high school GPA:* 3.22. *Test scores:* SAT critical reading scores over 500: 39%; SAT math scores over 500: 49%; ACT scores over 18: 69%; SAT critical reading scores over 600: 12%; SAT math scores over 600: 7%; ACT scores over 24: 14%; SAT critical reading scores over 700: 5%; SAT math scores over 700: 1%; ACT scores over 30: 1%.

Faculty *Total:* 281, 55% full-time, 49% with terminal degrees. *Student/faculty ratio:* 15:1.

Majors Accounting; agricultural business and management; agricultural teacher education; anthropology; audiology and speech-language pathology; aviation/airway management; biology/biological sciences; business administration and management; business administration, management and operations related; business teacher education; chemistry; child care and support services management; clinical laboratory science/medical technology; communication/speech communication and rhetoric; computer and information sciences; criminal justice/safety; dairy science; dramatic/theater arts; elementary education; engineering technology; English; environmental science; family and consumer sciences/human sciences; finance; forensic science and technology; general studies; geology/earth science; history; human resources management; kindergarten/preschool education; liberal arts and sciences/liberal studies; management information systems; marketing/marketing management; multi-/interdisciplinary studies related; music; music teacher education; nursing (registered nurse training); physical education teaching and coaching; physics; political science and government; religious studies; sales and marketing/marketing and distribution teacher education; social sciences; sociology; Spanish; special education; statistics; wildlife and wildlands science and management.

Academics *Calendar:* semesters. *Degrees:* associate, bachelor's, and master's. *Special study options:* academic remediation for entering students, accelerated degree program, adult/continuing education programs, advanced placement credit, cooperative education, distance learning, double majors, English as a second language, external degree program, honors programs, internships, part-time degree program, services for LD students, student-designed majors, study abroad, summer session for credit.

Computers on Campus 475 computers/terminals are available on campus for general student use. Students can access the following: free student e-mail accounts, online (class) registration, online (class) schedules. Campuswide network is available.

Student Life *Housing:* on-campus residence required for freshman year. *Options:* coed, women-only, disabled students. Campus housing is university owned. Freshman campus housing is guaranteed. *Activities and organizations:* drama/theater group, student-run newspaper, radio and television station, choral group, marching band, Student Government Association, Student Activities Board, Residence Hall Association, IFC, national fraternities, national sororities. *Campus security:* 24-hour emergency response devices and patrols, late-night transport/escort service, controlled dormitory access. *Student services:* health clinic, personal/psychological counseling.

Athletics Member NCAA. All Division II. *Intercollegiate sports:* baseball M (s), basketball M (s)/W (s), cross-country running M (s)/W (s), football M (s), soccer W (s), softball W (s), track and field M (s)/W (s), volleyball W (s). *Intramural sports:* badminton M/W, basketball M/W, cross-country running M/W, football M/W, racquetball M/W, rugby M (c), soccer M/W, softball M/W, volleyball M/W, wrestling M (c).

Standardized Tests *Required:* SAT or ACT (for admission).

Costs (2007–08) *Tuition:* state resident $2232 full-time, $93 per credit hour part-time; nonresident $7776 full-time, $324 per credit hour part-time. *Required fees:* $924 full-time, $39 per credit hour part-time. *Room and board:* $4888; room only: $2330. Room and board charges vary according to housing facility. *Payment plan:* installment. *Waivers:* senior citizens and employees or children of employees.

Financial Aid *Average financial aid package:* $5866.

Applying *Options:* electronic application, early admission, deferred entrance. *Required:* high school transcript, minimum 2.0 GPA. *Application deadlines:* rolling (freshmen), rolling (transfers).

Freshman Application Contact Ms. Donna Kittrell, Director, Eastern New Mexico University, Station #7 ENMU, Portales, NM 88130. *Phone:* 505-562-2178. *Toll-free phone:* 800-367-3668. *Fax:* 505-562-2118. *E-mail:* donna.kittrell@enmu.edu.

Institute of American Indian Arts

Santa Fe, New Mexico **www.iaia.edu/**

Director of Admissions Myra Garro, Manager of Enrollment and Admissions, Institute of American Indian Arts, 83 Avan Nu Po Road, Santa Fe, NM 87508. *Phone:* 505-424-2328.

International Institute of the Americas

Albuquerque, New Mexico **www.iia-online.com/site/**

- **Independent** primarily 2-year
- **Urban** campus
- **Coed**
- **Noncompetitive** entrance level

Faculty *Student/faculty ratio:* 12:1.

Academics *Calendar:* continuous. *Degrees:* diplomas, associate, and bachelor's.

Student Life *Campus security:* 24-hour emergency response devices.

Costs (2007–08) *Tuition:* $10,250 full-time. Full-time tuition and fees vary according to degree level and program. *Required fees:* $200 full-time.

Applying *Application fee:* $200. *Required:* interview.

Freshman Application Contact Campus Director, International Institute of the Americas, 4201 Central Avenue NW, Suite J, Albuquerque, NM 87105-1649. *Phone:* 505-880-2877. *Toll-free phone:* 888-660-2428. *Fax:* 505-352-0199. *E-mail:* esigman@iia.edu.

ITT Technical Institute

Albuquerque, New Mexico **www.itt-tech.edu/**

- **Proprietary** primarily 2-year, founded 1989, part of ITT Educational Services, Inc
- **Coed**
- **Minimally difficult** entrance level

Academics *Calendar:* quarters. *Degrees:* associate and bachelor's.

Standardized Tests *Required:* Wonderlic aptitude test (for admission).

Applying *Options:* deferred entrance. *Application fee:* $100. *Required:* high school transcript, interview. *Recommended:* letters of recommendation.

Freshman Application Contact Mr. John Crooks, Director of Recruitment, ITT Technical Institute, 5100 Masthead Street NE, Albuquerque, NM 87109. *Phone:* 505-828-1114. *Toll-free phone:* 800-636-1114.

National American University

Albuquerque, New Mexico **www.national.edu/**

Freshman Application Contact Ms. Kim Hauser, Executive Admissions Representative, National American University, 4775 Indian School, NE, Albuquerque, NM 87110. *Phone:* 505-265-7517 Ext. 3019. *Toll-free phone:* 800-843-8892.

National College of Midwifery

Taos, New Mexico **www.midwiferycollege.org/**

Director of Admissions Ms. Beth Enson, Dean of Students, National College of Midwifery, 209 State Road 240, Taos, NM 87571. *Phone:* 505-758-8914.

NEW MEXICO HIGHLANDS UNIVERSITY

Las Vegas, New Mexico **www.nmhu.edu/**

- **State-supported** comprehensive, founded 1893
- **Small-town** 120-acre campus
- **Endowment** $2.2 million
- **Coed** 2,046 undergraduate students, 70% full-time, 60% women, 40% men
- **Minimally difficult** entrance level, 79% of applicants were admitted

Undergraduates 1,435 full-time, 611 part-time. Students come from 32 states and territories, 9 other countries, 17% are from out of state, 6% African American, 2% Asian American or Pacific Islander, 58% Hispanic American, 7% Native American, 2% international, 15% transferred in, 10% live on campus. *Retention:* 45% of 2006 full-time freshmen returned.

Freshmen *Admission:* 1,598 applied, 1,263 admitted, 353 enrolled. *Average high school GPA:* 2.94. *Test scores:* SAT critical reading scores over 500: 50%; SAT math scores over 500: 50%; ACT scores over 18: 53%; SAT math scores over 600: 50%; ACT scores over 24: 8%; ACT scores over 30: 1%.

Faculty *Total:* 87, 100% full-time.

Majors Accounting; art; biology/biological sciences; business administration and management; chemistry; cinematography and film/video production; clinical/medical social work; communication/speech communication and rhetoric; computer and information sciences; criminal justice/safety; design and visual communications; electrical, electronics and communications engineering; elementary education; engineering; English; environmental studies; family and consumer sciences/human sciences; finance; forensic science and technology; forestry; geology/earth science; health teacher education; history; information science/studies; kindergarten/preschool education; management information systems; marketing/marketing management; mathematics; music; natural resources management and policy; nursing (registered nurse training); parks, recreation and leisure; parks, recreation and leisure facilities management; physical education teaching and coaching; physics; political science and government; psychology; science teacher education; social sciences related; Spanish; special education; technology/industrial arts teacher education; visual and performing arts.

Academics *Calendar:* semesters. *Degrees:* associate, bachelor's, and master's. *Special study options:* academic remediation for entering students, accelerated degree program, advanced placement credit, cooperative education, distance learning, double majors, honors programs, independent study, internships, off-campus study, part-time degree program, services for LD students, summer session for credit.

Computers on Campus 500 computers/terminals are available on campus for general student use. Students can access the following: online (class) registration. Campuswide network is available.

Student Life *Housing options:* coed, men-only, women-only. Campus housing is university owned. *Activities and organizations:* drama/theater group, student-run newspaper, radio station, choral group, marching band, Salsa Club, TKE, NMHU Soccer Club, Delta Sigma Zeta, Undergraduate Social Work Association, national fraternities. *Campus security:* 24-hour emergency response devices and patrols, late-night transport/escort service, controlled dormitory access. *Student services:* health clinic, personal/psychological counseling.

Athletics Member NCAA. All Division II. *Intercollegiate sports:* baseball M (s), basketball M (s)/W (s), cross-country running M (s)/W (s), football M (s), soccer W (s), softball W (s), track and field M/W, volleyball W (s). *Intramural sports:* badminton M/W, basketball M/W, football M, golf M/W, racquetball M/W, rugby M, skiing (cross-country) M/W, skiing (downhill) M/W, softball W, swimming and diving M/W, table tennis M/W, tennis M/W, volleyball M/W, weight lifting M/W.

Standardized Tests *Recommended:* SAT or ACT (for admission), Compass.

Costs (2007–08) *Tuition:* state resident $2516 full-time, $105 per credit hour part-time; nonresident $3775 full-time, $105 per credit hour part-time. Full-time tuition and fees vary according to course load and location. Part-time tuition and fees vary according to course load and location. *Room and board:* $3431; room only: $1826. Room and board charges vary according to board plan and housing facility. *Payment plan:* installment. *Waivers:* senior citizens and employees or children of employees.

Financial Aid Of all full-time matriculated undergraduates who enrolled in 2006, 1,131 applied for aid, 1,010 were judged to have need, 92 had their need fully met. 270 Federal Work-Study jobs (averaging $2628). 108 state and other part-time jobs (averaging $2791). In 2006, 83 non-need-based awards were made. *Average percent of need met:* 67%. *Average financial aid package:* $8183. *Average need-based loan:* $2867. *Average need-based gift aid:* $4588. *Average non-need-based aid:* $2015. *Average indebtedness upon graduation:* $12,147.

Applying *Options:* electronic application, early admission, deferred entrance. *Application fee:* $15. *Required:* high school transcript, minimum 2.0 GPA. *Required for some:* 2 letters of recommendation, interview. *Application deadlines:* rolling (freshmen), rolling (transfers). *Notification:* continuous (freshmen), continuous (transfers).

Freshman Application Contact Ms. Judy Cordova, Vice President for Student Affairs, New Mexico Highlands University, Box 9000, Las Vegas, NM 87701. *Phone:* 505-454-3566. *Toll-free phone:* 800-338-6648. *E-mail:* judycordova@nmhu.edu.

NEW MEXICO INSTITUTE OF MINING AND TECHNOLOGY

Socorro, New Mexico **www.nmt.edu/**

- **State-supported** university, founded 1889
- **Small-town** 320-acre campus with easy access to Albuquerque
- **Endowment** $16.2 million
- **Coed** 1,327 undergraduate students, 82% full-time, 33% women, 67% men
- **Moderately difficult** entrance level, 55% of applicants were admitted

Undergraduates 1,092 full-time, 235 part-time. Students come from 24 states and territories, 29 other countries, 13% are from out of state, 1% African American, 3% Asian American or Pacific Islander, 25% Hispanic American, 3% Native American, 2% international, 4% transferred in, 49% live on campus. *Retention:* 73% of 2006 full-time freshmen returned.

Freshmen *Admission:* 763 applied, 419 admitted, 240 enrolled. *Average high school GPA:* 3.6. *Test scores:* SAT critical reading scores over 500: 83%; SAT math scores over 500: 89%; ACT scores over 18: 98%; SAT critical reading scores over 600: 52%; SAT math scores over 600: 58%; ACT scores over 24: 70%; SAT critical reading scores over 700: 15%; SAT math scores over 700: 17%; ACT scores over 30: 20%.

Faculty *Total:* 145, 82% full-time, 84% with terminal degrees. *Student/faculty ratio:* 11:1.

Majors Biology/biological sciences; business administration and management; chemical engineering; chemistry; civil engineering; computer science; electrical, electronics and communications engineering; engineering mechanics; environmental/environmental health engineering; environmental studies; general studies; geology/earth science; geophysics and seismology; information technology; materials engineering; mathematics; mechanical engineering; mining and mineral engineering; petroleum engineering; physical sciences; physical sciences related; physics; psychology; technical and business writing.

Academics *Calendar:* semesters. *Degrees:* associate, bachelor's, master's, and doctoral. *Special study options:* accelerated degree program, advanced placement credit, cooperative education, distance learning, double majors, independent study, internships, part-time degree program, services for LD students, student-designed majors, summer session for credit.

Computers on Campus 225 computers/terminals are available on campus for general student use. Students can access the following: computer help desk, free student e-mail accounts, online (class) registration, online (class) schedules. Campuswide network is available. Wireless service is available via computer centers, learning centers, student centers.

Student Life *Housing options:* coed, men-only, women-only. Campus housing is university owned. *Activities and organizations:* drama/theater group, student-run newspaper, radio station, choral group, Search and Rescue, Society for Creative Anachronism, Amateur Astronomers, Ski Club. *Campus security:* 24-hour emergency response devices and patrols, late-night transport/escort service. *Student services:* health clinic, personal/psychological counseling.

Athletics *Intercollegiate sports:* golf M (c)/W (c), rugby M (c)/W (c), soccer M (c)/W (c). *Intramural sports:* badminton M/W, basketball M/W, cross-country running M/W, fencing M/W, racquetball M/W, riflery M/W, skiing (downhill) M/W, softball M/W, squash M/W, table tennis M/W, tennis M/W, volleyball M/W, weight lifting M/W.

Standardized Tests *Required:* SAT or ACT (for admission). *Recommended:* ACT (for admission).

Costs (2007–08) *Tuition:* state resident $3543 full-time, $148 per credit hour part-time; nonresident $11,199 full-time, $467 per credit hour part-time. Part-time tuition and fees vary according to course load. *Required fees:* $562 full-time. *Room and board:* $5300. Room and board charges vary according to board plan and housing facility. *Payment plan:* deferred payment. *Waivers:* senior citizens and employees or children of employees.

Financial Aid Of all full-time matriculated undergraduates who enrolled in 2004, 941 applied for aid, 442 were judged to have need, 236 had their need fully met. In 2004, 382 non-need-based awards were made. *Average percent of need met:* 94%. *Average financial aid package:* $7849. *Average need-based loan:* $4120. *Average need-based gift aid:* $4094. *Average non-need-based aid:* $4097. *Average indebtedness upon graduation:* $8788.

Applying *Options:* electronic application, deferred entrance. *Application fee:* $15. *Required:* high school transcript, minimum 2.5 GPA. *Required for some:* 2 letters of recommendation. *Recommended:* interview. *Application deadlines:* 8/1 (freshmen), 8/1 (transfers). *Notification:* continuous (freshmen), continuous (transfers).

Freshman Application Contact Mr. Mike Kloeppel, Director of Admissions, New Mexico Institute of Mining and Technology, 801 Leroy Place, Socorro, NM 87801. *Phone:* 575-835-5424. *Toll-free phone:* 800-428-TECH. *Fax:* 575-835-5989. *E-mail:* admission@admin.nmt.edu.

NEW MEXICO STATE UNIVERSITY

Las Cruces, New Mexico **www.nmsu.edu/**

- **State-supported** university, founded 1888, part of New Mexico State University System
- **Suburban** 900-acre campus with easy access to El Paso
- **Endowment** $74.3 million
- **Coed**
- **Moderately difficult** entrance level

Faculty *Student/faculty ratio:* 19:1.

Academics *Calendar:* semesters. *Degrees:* associate, bachelor's, master's, doctoral, and post-master's certificates.

Student Life *Campus security:* 24-hour emergency response devices and patrols, late-night transport/escort service, controlled dormitory access.

Athletics Member NCAA. All Division I except football (Division I-A).

Standardized Tests *Required:* SAT or ACT (for admission).

Costs (2007–08) *Tuition:* state resident $3274 full-time, $186 per credit part-time; nonresident $13,002 full-time, $591 per credit part-time. *Required fees:* $1178 full-time. *Room and board:* $5766; room only: $3322. Room and board charges vary according to board plan and gender. *Payment plans:* installment, deferred payment.

Financial Aid Of all full-time matriculated undergraduates who enrolled in 2007, 8,157 applied for aid, 6,769 were judged to have need, 676 had their need fully met. 349 Federal Work-Study jobs (averaging $2273). 350 state and other part-time jobs (averaging $2315). In 2007, 2463 non-need-based awards were made. *Average percent of need met:* 65. *Average financial aid package:* $8040. *Average need-based loan:* $4439. *Average need-based gift aid:* $4993. *Average non-need-based aid:* $3530.

Applying *Options:* electronic application, early admission, deferred entrance. *Application fee:* $20. *Required:* high school transcript, minimum 2.0 GPA.

Freshman Application Contact Mr. Tyler Pruett, Director of Admissions, New Mexico State University, Box 30001, MSC 3A, Las Cruces, NM 88003-8001. *Phone:* 505-646-3121. *Toll-free phone:* 800-662-6678. *Fax:* 505-646-6330. *E-mail:* admssions@nmsu.edu.

NORTHERN NEW MEXICO COLLEGE

Española, New Mexico **www.nnmc.edu/**

- **State-supported** primarily 2-year, founded 1909, part of New Mexico Commission on Higher Education
- **Rural** 35-acre campus
- **Endowment** $829,791
- **Coed**
- **Noncompetitive** entrance level

Academics *Calendar:* semesters. *Degrees:* certificates, associate, and bachelor's.

Student Life *Campus security:* 24-hour emergency response devices and patrols.

Costs (2007–08) *Tuition:* state resident $864 full-time, $36 per credit part-time; nonresident $2088 full-time, $85 per credit part-time. Full-time tuition and fees vary according to course level and reciprocity agreements. Part-time tuition and fees vary according to course level. *Required fees:* $156 full-time. *Room and board:* $3860; room only: $1300.

Financial Aid Of all full-time matriculated undergraduates who enrolled in 2006, 150 Federal Work-Study jobs (averaging $3000). 140 state and other part-time jobs (averaging $3000).

Applying *Options:* early admission, deferred entrance. *Required:* high school transcript.

Freshman Application Contact Mr. Mike L. Costello, Registrar, Northern New Mexico College, 921 Paseo de Oñate, Española, NM 87532. *Phone:* 505-747-2193. *Fax:* 505-747-2191. *E-mail:* dms@nnmc.edu.

ST. JOHN'S COLLEGE

Santa Fe, New Mexico **www.stjohnscollege.edu/**

- **Independent** comprehensive, founded 1964, administratively affiliated with St. John's College (MD)
- **Suburban** 250-acre campus
- **Endowment** $81.9 million
- **Coed** 436 undergraduate students, 100% full-time, 40% women, 60% men
- **Very difficult** entrance level, 79% of applicants were admitted

Undergraduates 434 full-time, 2 part-time. Students come from 46 states and territories, 7 other countries, 95% are from out of state, 0.7% African American, 3% Asian American or Pacific Islander, 6% Hispanic American, 1% Native American, 2% international, 6% transferred in.

Freshmen *Admission:* 344 applied, 271 admitted, 134 enrolled. *Test scores:* SAT critical reading scores over 500: 100%; SAT math scores over 500: 96%; ACT scores over 18: 100%; SAT critical reading scores over 600: 91%; SAT math scores over 600: 70%; ACT scores over 24: 88%; SAT critical reading scores over 700: 46%; SAT math scores over 700: 22%; ACT scores over 30: 29%.

Faculty *Total:* 74, 99% full-time, 82% with terminal degrees. *Student/faculty ratio:* 8:1.

Majors Ancient/classical Greek; classics and languages, literatures and linguistics; English; ethics; foreign languages and literatures; French; general studies; history; history of philosophy; humanities; liberal arts and sciences and humanities related; liberal arts and sciences/liberal studies; literature; mathematics; philosophy; philosophy and religious studies related; philosophy related; physical sciences; physics; pre-medical studies; religious studies; western civilization.

Academics *Calendar:* semesters. *Degrees:* bachelor's and master's. *Special study options:* internships, off-campus study, summer session for credit.

Computers on Campus Campuswide network is available.

Student Life *Housing:* on-campus residence required for freshman year. *Options:* coed, women-only, disabled students. Campus housing is university owned. Freshman campus housing is guaranteed. *Activities and organizations:* drama/theater group, student-run newspaper, choral group, student government, film society, Search and Rescue Team, student newspaper, theatre group. *Campus security:* 24-hour emergency response devices and patrols, student patrols, late-night transport/escort service. *Student services:* health clinic, personal/psychological counseling.

Athletics *Intercollegiate sports:* fencing M/W, soccer M/W. *Intramural sports:* badminton M/W, basketball M/W, cross-country running M/W, fencing M/W, football M/W, golf M/W, racquetball M/W, rock climbing M/W, skiing (cross-country) M/W, skiing (downhill) M/W, soccer M/W, softball M/W, squash M/W, swimming and diving M/W, table tennis M/W, tennis M/W, track and field M/W, ultimate Frisbee M/W, volleyball M/W, water polo M/W, weight lifting M/W.

Costs (2007–08) *Comprehensive fee:* $45,280 includes full-time tuition ($36,346), mandatory fees ($250), and room and board ($8684).

Financial Aid Of all full-time matriculated undergraduates who enrolled in 2006, 282 applied for aid, 270 were judged to have need, 248 had their need fully met. 140 Federal Work-Study jobs (averaging $2427). 19 state and other part-time jobs (averaging $2376). *Average percent of need met:* 94%. *Average financial aid package:* $24,858. *Average need-based loan:* $3390. *Average need-based gift aid:* $19,137. *Average indebtedness upon graduation:* $26,263. *Financial aid deadline:* 2/15.

Applying *Options:* early admission, deferred entrance. *Required:* essay or personal statement, high school transcript, 2 letters of recommendation. *Required for some:* interview. *Recommended:* 3 letters of recommendation, interview. *Application deadlines:* rolling (freshmen), rolling (transfers). *Notification:* continuous (freshmen), continuous (transfers).

Freshman Application Contact Mr. Larry Clendenin, Director of Admissions, St. John's College, 1160 Camino Cruz Blanca, Santa Fe, NM 87505. *Phone:* 505-984-6060. *Toll-free phone:* 800-331-5232. *Fax:* 505-984-6162. *E-mail:* admissions@stjohnscollege.edu.

UNIVERSITY OF NEW MEXICO

Albuquerque, New Mexico **www.unm.edu/**

- **State-supported** university, founded 1889
- **Urban** 875-acre campus with easy access to Albuquerque
- **Endowment** $336.9 million
- **Coed**
- **Moderately difficult** entrance level, 71% of applicants were admitted

Undergraduates Students come from 52 states and territories, 56 other countries, 10% are from out of state, 10% live on campus. *Retention:* 77% of 2006 full-time freshmen returned.

Freshmen *Admission:* 7,404 applied, 5,252 admitted. *Average high school GPA:* 3.34. *Test scores:* SAT critical reading scores over 500: 66%; SAT math scores over 500: 63%; ACT scores over 18: 87%; SAT critical reading scores over 600: 29%; SAT math scores over 600: 25%; ACT scores over 24: 34%; SAT critical reading scores over 700: 7%; SAT math scores over 700: 4%; ACT scores over 30: 4%.

Faculty *Total:* 1,453, 63% full-time, 70% with terminal degrees. *Student/faculty ratio:* 19:1.

Majors African-American/Black studies; American studies; anthropology; architecture; art; art history, criticism and conservation; art teacher education; Asian studies; astrophysics; audiology and speech-language pathology; biochemistry; biology/biological sciences; business administration and management; chemical engineering; chemistry; civil engineering; classics and languages, literatures and linguistics; clinical/medical laboratory technology; comparative literature; computer and information sciences; computer engineering; corrections; dance; dramatic/theater arts; early childhood education; economics; electrical, electronics and communications engineering; elementary education; engineering science; English; environmental design/architecture; environmental science; European studies; family and consumer sciences/human sciences; film/cinema studies; foods, nutrition, and wellness; foreign languages and literatures; French; general studies; geography; geology/earth science; German; health teacher education; history; human development and family studies; humanities; journalism; Latin American studies; liberal arts and sciences/liberal studies; linguistics; mass communication/media; mathematics; mechanical engineering; medical radiologic technology; music performance; music teacher education; nuclear engineering; nursing (registered nurse training); parks, recreation and leisure; pharmacy; philosophy; physical education teaching and coaching; physician assistant; physics; political science and government; Portuguese; psychology; religious studies; Russian; Russian studies; secondary education; sign language interpretation and translation; sociology; Spanish; special education; speech and rhetoric; statistics; technology/industrial arts teacher education; theater design and technology; women's studies.

Academics *Calendar:* semesters. *Degrees:* associate, bachelor's, master's, doctoral, first professional, and post-master's certificates. *Special study options:* academic remediation for entering students, accelerated degree program, adult/continuing education programs, advanced placement credit, cooperative education, distance learning, double majors, English as a second language, honors programs, independent study, internships, off-campus study, part-time degree program, services for LD students, student-designed majors, study abroad, summer session for credit. *ROTC:* Army (b), Navy (b), Air Force (b). *Unusual degree programs:* 3-2 engineering; Latin American studies, business.

Computers on Campus 479 computers/terminals are available on campus for general student use. Students can access the following: free student e-mail accounts, online (class) grades, online (class) registration, online (class) schedules. Campuswide network is available.

Student Life *Housing options:* coed, disabled students. Campus housing is university owned. *Activities and organizations:* drama/theater group, student-run newspaper, radio and television station, choral group, marching band, Associated Students of UNM, Graduate and Professional Students Association, Golden Key National Honor Society, national fraternities, national sororities. *Campus security:* 24-hour emergency response devices and patrols, student patrols, late-night transport/escort service, controlled dormitory access. *Student services:* health clinic, personal/psychological counseling, women's center.

Athletics Member NCAA. All Division I except football (Division I-A). *Intercollegiate sports:* baseball M, basketball M (s)/W (s), cross-country running M (s)/W (s), golf M (s)/W (s), skiing (cross-country) M (s)/W (s), skiing (downhill) M (s)/W (s), soccer M (s)/W (s), softball W (s), swimming and diving W (s), tennis M (s)/W (s), track and field M (s)/W (s), volleyball W (s). *Intramural sports:* archery M/W, badminton M/W, basketball M/W, bowling M/W, cross-country running M/W, fencing M/W, football M/W, golf M/W, ice hockey M (c), racquetball M/W, rugby M (c)/W (c), skiing (downhill) M/W, soccer M/W, softball M/W, swimming and diving W, table tennis M/W, tennis M/W, volleyball M/W, water polo M/W.

Standardized Tests *Required:* SAT or ACT (for admission).

Costs (2007–08) *Tuition:* state resident $4571 full-time, $190 per credit hour part-time; nonresident $14,942 full-time. Part-time tuition and fees vary according to course load. *Room and board:* $7020; room only: $4100. Room and board charges vary according to board plan and housing facility. *Payment plan:* deferred payment. *Waivers:* senior citizens and employees or children of employees.

Financial Aid Of all full-time matriculated undergraduates who enrolled in 2001, 7,598 applied for aid, 6,570 were judged to have need, 1,051 had their need fully met. 1,521 Federal Work-Study jobs, 865 state and other part-time jobs. In 2001, 4124 non-need-based awards were made. *Average percent of need met:* 75%. *Average financial aid package:* $7829. *Average need-based loan:* $3261. *Average need-based gift aid:* $4796. *Average non-need-based aid:* $3173. *Average indebtedness upon graduation:* $16,595.

Applying *Options:* electronic application, early admission, deferred entrance. *Application fee:* $20. *Required:* high school transcript, minimum 2.25 GPA. *Required for some:* essay or personal statement, letters of recommendation. *Application deadlines:* 6/15 (freshmen), 6/15 (transfers). *Notification:* continuous (freshmen), continuous (transfers).

Freshman Application Contact Ms. Kathleen Roberts, Coordinator of Freshmen Admissions, University of New Mexico, Office of Admissions, PO Box 4895, Albuquerque, NM 87196-4895. *Phone:* 505-277-2447. *Toll-free phone:* 800-CALLUNM. *Fax:* 505-277-6686. *E-mail:* apply@unm.edu.

UNIVERSITY OF NEW MEXICO–GALLUP

Gallup, New Mexico **www.gallup.unm.edu/**

- **State-supported** primarily 2-year, founded 1968, part of New Mexico Commission on Higher Education
- **Small-town** 80-acre campus
- **Coed**
- **Noncompetitive** entrance level

Faculty *Student/faculty ratio:* 25:1.

Academics *Calendar:* semesters. *Degrees:* certificates, diplomas, associate, and bachelor's.

Student Life *Campus security:* late-night transport/escort service.

Standardized Tests *Required for some:* SAT (for admission), ACT (for admission).

Costs (2007–08) *Tuition:* state resident $1438 full-time, $60 per credit part-time; nonresident $3190 full-time, $133 per credit part-time. Full-time tuition and fees vary according to course level. Part-time tuition and fees vary according to course level and course load. *Required fees:* $25 full-time.

Applying *Options:* early admission. *Application fee:* $15. *Required for some:* high school transcript.

Director of Admissions Ms. Pearl A. Morris, Admissions Representative, University of New Mexico–Gallup, 200 College Road, Gallup, NM 87301-5603. *Phone:* 505-863-7576.

UNIVERSITY OF PHOENIX–NEW MEXICO CAMPUS

Albuquerque, New Mexico **www.phoenix.edu/**

- **Proprietary** comprehensive
- **Urban** campus
- **Coed**
- **Noncompetitive** entrance level

Faculty *Student/faculty ratio:* 10:1.

Academics *Calendar:* continuous. *Degrees:* certificates, bachelor's, and master's.

Student Life *Campus security:* late-night transport/escort service.

Costs (2007–08) *Tuition:* $10,110 full-time, $337 per credit part-time. Full-time tuition and fees vary according to course level.

Financial Aid *Average financial aid package:* $5497. *Average need-based gift aid:* $2748.

Applying *Options:* deferred entrance. *Application fee:* $45. *Required:* 1 letter of recommendation. *Required for some:* high school transcript.

Freshman Application Contact Ms. Beth Barilla, Associate Vice President, Student Admissions and Services, University of Phoenix–New Mexico Campus, 4615 East Elwood Street, Mail Stop AA-K101, Phoenix, AZ 85040-1958. *Phone:* 480-317-6000. *Toll-free phone:* 800-776-4867 (in-state); 800-228-7240 (out-of-state). *Fax:* 480-894-1758. *E-mail:* beth.barilla@phoenix.edu.

WESTERN NEW MEXICO UNIVERSITY

Silver City, New Mexico **www.wnmu.edu/**

- **State-supported** comprehensive, founded 1893
- **Rural** 83-acre campus
- **Endowment** $5.0 million
- **Coed** 2,219 undergraduate students
- **Noncompetitive** entrance level, 100% of applicants were admitted

Undergraduates Students come from 33 states and territories, 14 other countries, 4% African American, 1% Asian American or Pacific Islander, 46% Hispanic American, 2% Native American, 1% international. *Retention:* 48% of 2006 full-time freshmen returned.

Freshmen *Admission:* 788 applied, 788 admitted. *Average high school GPA:* 2.5. *Test scores:* ACT scores over 18: 49%; ACT scores over 24: 6%; ACT scores over 30: 1%.

Faculty *Total:* 259, 49% full-time. *Student/faculty ratio:* 17:1.

Majors Accounting; art; art teacher education; biological and physical sciences; biology/biological sciences; botany/plant biology; business administration and management; business teacher education; chemistry; clinical laboratory science/medical technology; computer science; computer technology/computer systems technology; criminal justice/law enforcement administration; criminal justice/police science; digital communication and media/multimedia; early childhood education; e-commerce; education; electrical/electronics maintenance and repair technology related; elementary education; English; financial planning and services; geology/earth science; graphic design; Hispanic-American, Puerto Rican, and Mexican-American/Chicano studies; history; humanities; interdisciplinary studies; international business/trade/commerce; kindergarten/preschool education; kinesiology and exercise science; liberal arts and sciences/liberal studies; marketing/marketing management; mathematics; music; music teacher education; nursing (registered nurse training); occupational therapist assistant; occupational therapy; physical education teaching and coaching; physical sciences; pre-law studies; pre-veterinary studies; psychology; public administration; science teacher education; secondary education; social sciences; social work; sociology; Spanish; special education; special products marketing; teacher assistant/aide; trade and industrial teacher education; welding technology; wildlife and wildlands science and management; zoology/animal biology.

Academics *Calendar:* semesters. *Degrees:* certificates, diplomas, associate, bachelor's, and master's. *Special study options:* academic remediation for entering students, accelerated degree program, adult/continuing education programs, advanced placement credit, cooperative education, internships, part-time degree program, services for LD students, student-designed majors, summer session for credit.

Computers on Campus 85 computers/terminals are available on campus for general student use. Students can access the following: computer help desk, free student e-mail accounts, online (class) registration, online classes in Spanish. Campuswide network is available. Wireless service is available via computer centers, computer labs, libraries.

Student Life *Housing:* on-campus residence required for freshman year. *Options:* coed, men-only, women-only. Campus housing is university owned. Freshman campus housing is guaranteed. *Activities and organizations:* drama/theater group, student-run newspaper, choral group. *Campus security:* 24-hour emergency response devices and patrols, student patrols, late-night transport/escort service. *Student services:* personal/psychological counseling, women's center.

Athletics Member NCAA. All Division II. *Intercollegiate sports:* basketball M (s)/W (s), cheerleading M/W, cross-country running M (s)/W (s), football M (s), golf M (s)/W (s), rock climbing M/W, softball W (s), tennis M (s)/W (s), volleyball W (s). *Intramural sports:* basketball M/W, golf M/W, racquetball M/W, soccer M/W, softball W, swimming and diving M/W, tennis M/W, volleyball M/W.

Standardized Tests *Recommended:* ACT (for admission).

Costs (2008–09) *Tuition:* state resident $2544 full-time; nonresident $11,832 full-time. *Required fees:* $887 full-time. *Room and board:* $5060; room only: $1940.

Financial Aid Of all full-time matriculated undergraduates who enrolled in 2003, 1,349 applied for aid, 1,265 were judged to have need, 204 had their need fully met. 134 Federal Work-Study jobs (averaging $1825). 82 state and other part-time jobs (averaging $1937). In 2003, 121 non-need-based awards were made. *Average percent of need met:* 68%. *Average financial aid package:* $5915. *Average need-based loan:* $2980. *Average need-based gift aid:* $2434. *Average non-need-based aid:* $2457. *Average indebtedness upon graduation:* $17,000.

Applying *Options:* electronic application, early admission, deferred entrance. *Required:* high school transcript. *Application deadlines:* 8/1 (freshmen), 8/1 (transfers). *Notification:* continuous (freshmen), continuous (transfers).

Freshman Application Contact Mr. Dan Tressler, Director of Admissions, Western New Mexico University, College Avenue, Silver City, NM 88062-0680. *Phone:* 505-538-6106. *Toll-free phone:* 800-872-WNMU. *Fax:* 505-538-6127. *E-mail:* tresslerd@wnmu.edu.

NEW YORK

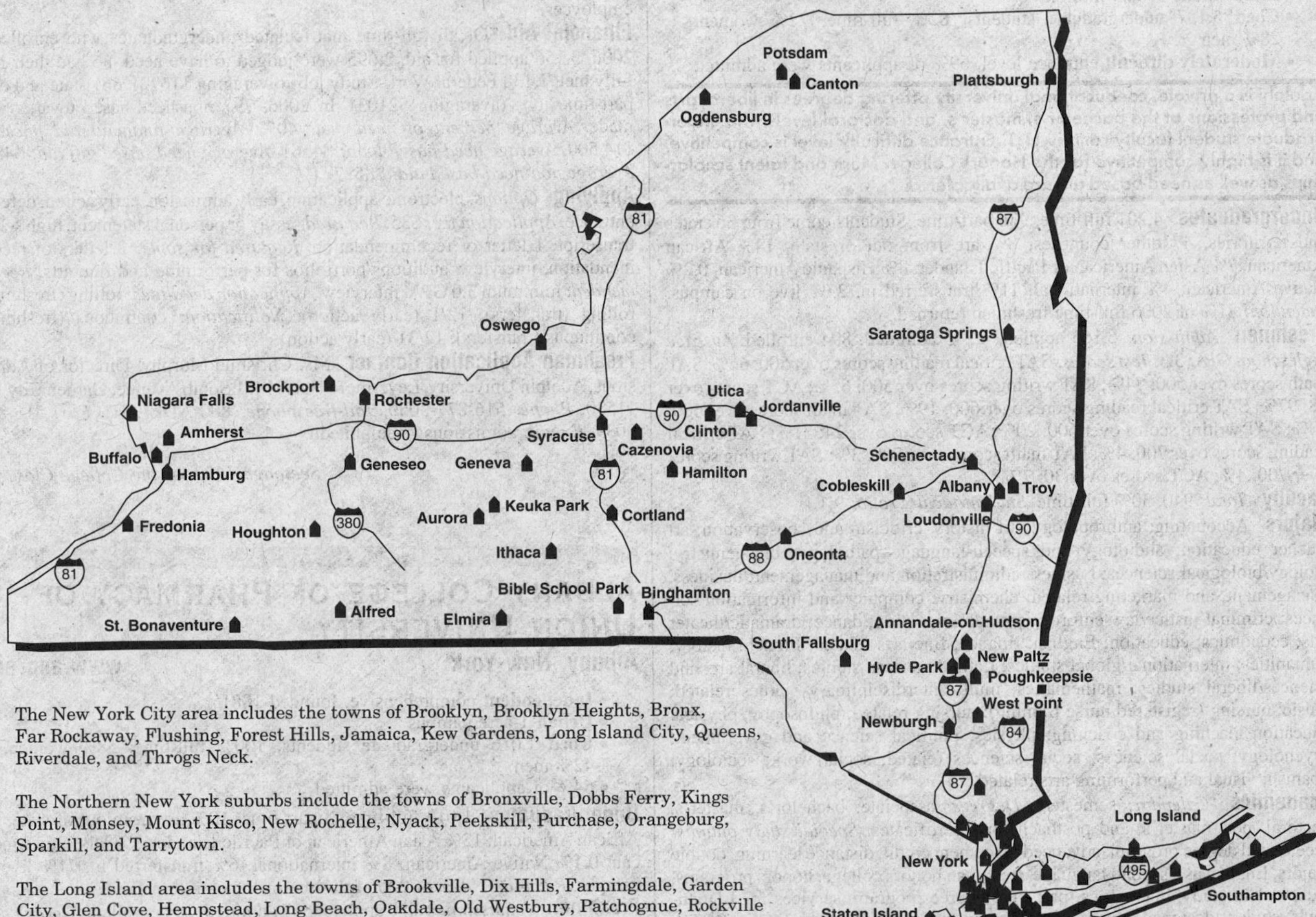

The New York City area includes the towns of Brooklyn, Brooklyn Heights, Bronx, Far Rockaway, Flushing, Forest Hills, Jamaica, Kew Gardens, Long Island City, Queens, Riverdale, and Throgs Neck.

The Northern New York suburbs include the towns of Bronxville, Dobbs Ferry, Kings Point, Monsey, Mount Kisco, New Rochelle, Nyack, Peekskill, Purchase, Orangeburg, Sparkill, and Tarrytown.

The Long Island area includes the towns of Brookville, Dix Hills, Farmingdale, Garden City, Glen Cove, Hempstead, Long Beach, Oakdale, Old Westbury, Patchognue, Rockville Center, and Stony Brook.

ADELPHI UNIVERSITY

Garden City, New York **www.adelphi.edu/**

- **Independent** university, founded 1896
- **Suburban** 75-acre campus with easy access to New York City
- **Endowment** $106.5 million
- **Coed** 5,137 undergraduate students, 82% full-time, 72% women, 28% men
- **Moderately difficult** entrance level, 69% of applicants were admitted

Adelphi is a private, coeducational university offering degrees in liberal arts and professions at the bachelor's, master's, and doctoral levels. The undergraduate student-faculty ratio is 11:1. Entrance difficulty level is competitive, and it is highly competitive for the Honors College. Merit and talent scholarships as well as need-based aid are available.

Undergraduates 4,201 full-time, 936 part-time. Students come from 36 states and territories, 47 other countries, 8% are from out of state, 14% African American, 7% Asian American or Pacific Islander, 8% Hispanic American, 0.2% Native American, 4% international, 11% transferred in, 23% live on campus. *Retention:* 81% of 2006 full-time freshmen returned.

Freshmen *Admission:* 6,165 applied, 4,245 admitted, 894 enrolled. *Average high school GPA:* 3.3. *Test scores:* SAT critical reading scores over 500: 66%; SAT math scores over 500: 74%; SAT writing scores over 500: 65%; ACT scores over 18: 97%; SAT critical reading scores over 600: 19%; SAT math scores over 600: 23%; SAT writing scores over 600: 20%; ACT scores over 24: 31%; SAT critical reading scores over 700: 4%; SAT math scores over 700: 3%; SAT writing scores over 700: 4%; ACT scores over 30: 7%.

Faculty *Total:* 940, 30% full-time. *Student/faculty ratio:* 9:1.

Majors Accounting; anthropology; art history, criticism and conservation; art teacher education; audiology and speech-language pathology; biochemistry; biology/biological sciences; business administration and management; business, management, and marketing related; chemistry; computer and information sciences; criminal justice/law enforcement administration; dance; dramatic/theater arts; economics; education; English; finance; fine arts related; French; history; humanities; international/global studies; Latin American studies; liberal arts and sciences/liberal studies; mathematics; multi-/interdisciplinary studies related; music; nursing (registered nurse training); nursing related; philosophy; physical education teaching and coaching; physics; political science and government; psychology; social sciences; social sciences related; social work; sociology; Spanish; visual and performing arts related.

Academics *Calendar:* semesters. *Degrees:* associate, bachelor's, master's, doctoral, post-master's, and postbachelor's certificates. *Special study options:* accelerated degree program, advanced placement credit, distance learning, double majors, English as a second language, freshman honors college, honors programs, independent study, internships, part-time degree program, services for LD students, student-designed majors, study abroad, summer session for credit. *ROTC:* Army (c), Air Force (c). *Unusual degree programs:* 3-2 engineering with Columbia University, Rensselaer Polytechnic University, Stevens Institute of Technology; physical therapy with New York Medical College; dentistry with Tufts; law with New York Law School; optometry with SUNY College of Optometry; environmental studies with Columbia.

Computers on Campus 772 computers/terminals are available on campus for general student use. Students can access the following: computer help desk, free student e-mail accounts, online (class) grades, online (class) registration, online (class) schedules, payment, drop/add classes, check application status. Campuswide network is available. 100% of college-owned or -operated housing units are wired for high-speed Internet access. Wireless service is available via entire campus.

Student Life *Housing options:* coed, disabled students. Campus housing is university owned. Freshman campus housing is guaranteed. *Activities and organizations:* drama/theater group, student-run newspaper, radio station, choral group, Student Activities Board, Caribbean Cultural Awareness Club, Student Activities Board, Accounting Society, African Peoples Organization, national fraternities, national sororities. *Campus security:* 24-hour emergency response devices and patrols, late-night transport/escort service, controlled dormitory access. *Student services:* health clinic, personal/psychological counseling.

Athletics Member NCAA. All Division II except soccer (Division I). *Intercollegiate sports:* baseball M (s), basketball M (s)/W (s), cross-country running M (s)/W (s), golf M (s), lacrosse M (s)/W (s), soccer M (s)/W (s), softball W (s), swimming and diving M (s)/W (s), tennis M (s)/W (s), track and field M (s)/W (s), volleyball W (s). *Intramural sports:* badminton M/W, basketball M/W, football M/W, racquetball M/W, soccer M/W, softball M/W, volleyball M/W, water polo M/W.

Standardized Tests *Required:* SAT or ACT (for admission).

Costs (2007–08) *Comprehensive fee:* $33,155 includes full-time tuition ($21,800), mandatory fees ($1455), and room and board ($9900). Full-time tuition and fees vary according to course level, location, and program. Part-time tuition: $700 per credit. Part-time tuition and fees vary according to course level, location, and program. *Required fees:* $600 per year part-time. *Room and board:* Room and board charges vary according to board plan and housing facility. *Payment plans:* installment, deferred payment. *Waivers:* employees or children of employees.

Financial Aid Of all full-time matriculated undergraduates who enrolled in 2006, 3,156 applied for aid, 2,695 were judged to have need, 36 had their need fully met. 1,138 Federal Work-Study jobs (averaging $1672). 661 state and other part-time jobs (averaging $2103). In 2006, 797 non-need-based awards were made. *Average percent of need met:* 40%. *Average financial aid package:* $14,500. *Average need-based loan:* $4361. *Average need-based gift aid:* $4804. *Average non-need-based aid:* $8527.

Applying *Options:* electronic application, early admission, early action, deferred entrance. *Application fee:* $35. *Required:* essay or personal statement, high school transcript, 1 letter of recommendation. *Required for some:* 2 letters of recommendation, interview, auditions/portfolios for performing and fine arts. *Recommended:* minimum 3.0 GPA, interview. *Application deadlines:* rolling (freshmen), rolling (transfers), 12/1 (early action). *Notification:* continuous (freshmen), continuous (transfers), 12/31 (early action).

Freshman Application Contact Ms. Christine Murphy, Director of Admissions, Adelphi University, Levermore Hall 114, 1 South Avenue, Garden City, NY 11530. *Phone:* 516-877-3050. *Toll-free phone:* 800-ADELPHI. *Fax:* 516-877-3039. *E-mail:* admissions@adelphi.edu.

See page 1690 for the College Close-Up.

ALBANY COLLEGE OF PHARMACY OF UNION UNIVERSITY

Albany, New York **www.acp.edu/**

- **Independent** comprehensive, founded 1881
- **Urban** 1-acre campus
- **Coed** 1,016 undergraduate students, 100% full-time, 58% women, 42% men
- 54% of applicants were admitted

Undergraduates 1,013 full-time, 3 part-time. 10% are from out of state, 2% African American, 13% Asian American or Pacific Islander, 1% Hispanic American, 0.1% Native American, 8% international, 6% transferred in, 71% live on campus. *Retention:* 79% of 2006 full-time freshmen returned.

Freshmen *Admission:* 1,050 applied, 567 admitted, 264 enrolled. *Average high school GPA:* 3.7. *Test scores:* SAT critical reading scores over 500: 87%; SAT math scores over 500: 97%; SAT writing scores over 500: 84%; ACT scores over 18: 100%; SAT critical reading scores over 600: 38%; SAT math scores over 600: 57%; SAT writing scores over 600: 28%; ACT scores over 24: 78%; SAT critical reading scores over 700: 4%; SAT math scores over 700: 6%; SAT writing scores over 700: 4%; ACT scores over 30: 14%.

Faculty *Total:* 103, 80% full-time, 59% with terminal degrees. *Student/faculty ratio:* 16:1.

Majors Clinical laboratory science/medical technology; cytotechnology; pharmacy, pharmaceutical sciences, and administration related.

Academics *Calendar:* semesters. *Degrees:* certificates, bachelor's, and first professional. *Special study options:* academic remediation for entering students, accelerated degree program, advanced placement credit, internships, off-campus study, services for LD students, summer session for credit. *ROTC:* Army (c), Navy (c), Air Force (c).

Computers on Campus 30 computers/terminals are available on campus for general student use. Students can access the following: computer help desk, free student e-mail accounts, online (class) grades, online (class) registration, online (class) schedules. Campuswide network is available. 100% of college-owned or -operated housing units are wired for high-speed Internet access. Wireless service is available via entire campus.

Student Life *Housing:* on-campus residence required through sophomore year. *Options:* coed. Campus housing is university owned and is provided by a third party. Freshman campus housing is guaranteed. *Activities and organizations:* student-run newspaper, choral group, American Pharmacy Association—Student Chapter, Orthodox Christian Student Association, Intra Fraternity Council, Student Government Association, Colleges Against Cancer, national fraternities, national sororities. *Campus security:* 24-hour emergency response devices and patrols, controlled dormitory access. *Student services:* health clinic, personal/psychological counseling.

Athletics *Intercollegiate sports:* basketball M/W, soccer M/W. *Intramural sports:* basketball M/W, cross-country running M/W, golf M (c)/W (c), lacrosse M (c), softball W (c), tennis M (c)/W (c), ultimate Frisbee M/W, volleyball M/W.

Standardized Tests *Required:* SAT or ACT (for admission). *Recommended:* ACT (for admission).

Costs (2007–08) *Comprehensive fee:* $28,450 includes full-time tuition ($20,650), mandatory fees ($500), and room and board ($7300). Part-time tuition: $688 per credit. *College room only:* $5500. Room and board charges vary according to board plan and housing facility. *Payment plan:* installment. *Waivers:* employees or children of employees.

Financial Aid Of all full-time matriculated undergraduates who enrolled in 2002, 567 applied for aid, 498 were judged to have need, 186 had their need fully met. 202 Federal Work-Study jobs (averaging $450). 12 state and other part-time jobs (averaging $432). In 2002, 74 non-need-based awards were made. *Average percent of need met:* 78%. *Average financial aid package:* $12,320. *Average need-based loan:* $8238. *Average need-based gift aid:* $5247. *Average non-need-based aid:* $8933. *Average indebtedness upon graduation:* $9397.

Applying *Options:* electronic application, early decision, deferred entrance. *Application fee:* $75. *Required:* essay or personal statement, high school transcript, 2 letters of recommendation. *Required for some:* interview. *Recommended:* minimum 3.0 GPA. *Application deadlines:* 2/1 (freshmen), 2/1 (transfers). *Early decision deadline:* 11/1. *Notification:* 3/15 (freshmen), 3/15 (transfers), 12/15 (early decision).

Freshman Application Contact Ms. Carly Connors, Director of Admissions, Albany College of Pharmacy of Union University, 106 New Scotland Avenue, Albany, NY 12208-3425. *Phone:* 518-694-7221. *Toll-free phone:* 888-203-8010. *Fax:* 518-694-7322. *E-mail:* admissions@acp.edu.

ALFRED UNIVERSITY

Alfred, New York **www.alfred.edu/**

- **Independent** university, founded 1836
- **Rural** 232-acre campus with easy access to Rochester
- **Endowment** $114.3 million
- **Coed** 2,030 undergraduate students, 95% full-time, 51% women, 49% men
- **Moderately difficult** entrance level, 74% of applicants were admitted

Undergraduates 1,927 full-time, 103 part-time. Students come from 45 states and territories, 31% are from out of state, 4% African American, 2% Asian American or Pacific Islander, 2% Hispanic American, 0.4% Native American, 1% international, 4% transferred in, 71% live on campus. *Retention:* 79% of 2006 full-time freshmen returned.

Freshmen *Admission:* 2,355 applied, 1,736 admitted, 518 enrolled. *Average high school GPA:* 3.13. *Test scores:* SAT critical reading scores over 500: 74%; SAT math scores over 500: 78%; SAT writing scores over 500: 66%; ACT scores over 18: 99%; SAT critical reading scores over 600: 30%; SAT math scores over 600: 33%; SAT writing scores over 600: 21%; ACT scores over 24: 57%; SAT critical reading scores over 700: 4%; SAT math scores over 700: 2%; SAT writing scores over 700: 3%; ACT scores over 30: 9%.

Faculty *Total:* 211, 82% full-time. *Student/faculty ratio:* 12:1.

Majors Accounting; art; art teacher education; athletic training; biological and physical sciences; biology/biological sciences; biomedical/medical engineering; business administration and management; business teacher education; ceramic arts and ceramics; ceramic sciences and engineering; chemistry; communication/speech communication and rhetoric; criminal justice/law enforcement administration; dramatic/theater arts; economics; electrical, electronics and communications engineering; elementary education; engineering related; English; environmental studies; finance; fine/studio arts; French; general studies; geology/earth science; German; gerontology; history; interdisciplinary studies; international/global studies; literature; marketing/marketing management; materials engineering; mathematics; mechanical engineering; modern languages; philosophy; physics; political science and government; psychology; public administration; science teacher education; secondary education; sociology; Spanish.

Academics *Calendar:* semesters. *Degrees:* bachelor's, master's, doctoral, and post-master's certificates. *Special study options:* academic remediation for entering students, accelerated degree program, advanced placement credit, cooperative education, double majors, honors programs, independent study, internships, off-campus study, part-time degree program, services for LD students, student-designed majors, study abroad, summer session for credit. *ROTC:* Army (c). *Unusual degree programs:* 3-2 engineering with Columbia University; forestry with Duke University; dentistry with New York University.

Computers on Campus 450 computers/terminals are available on campus for general student use. Students can access the following: computer help desk, free student e-mail accounts, online (class) grades, online (class) registration, online (class) schedules. Campuswide network is available. 100% of college-owned or -operated housing units are wired for high-speed Internet access. Wireless service is available via classrooms, computer labs, libraries, student centers.

Student Life *Housing:* on-campus residence required through junior year. *Options:* coed. Campus housing is university owned. Freshman campus housing is guaranteed. *Activities and organizations:* drama/theater group, student-run newspaper, radio and television station, choral group, Student Activities Board, Spectrum, WALF, Student Senate, Fiat Lux. *Campus security:* 24-hour emergency response devices, student patrols, late-night transport/escort service. *Student services:* health clinic, personal/psychological counseling, women's center.

Athletics Member NCAA. All Division III. *Intercollegiate sports:* basketball M/W, cross-country running M/W, equestrian sports M/W, football M, lacrosse M/W, skiing (cross-country) M (c)/W (c), skiing (downhill) M/W, soccer M/W, softball W, swimming and diving M/W, tennis M/W, track and field M/W, volleyball W. *Intramural sports:* baseball M (c), basketball M/W, cheerleading W (c), field hockey W (c), football M/W, ice hockey M (c), lacrosse M/W, racquetball M/W, rock climbing M (c)/W (c), soccer M/W, softball M/W, squash M/W, tennis M/W, ultimate Frisbee M (c)/W (c), volleyball M/W.

Standardized Tests *Required:* SAT or ACT (for admission).

Costs (2008–09) *Comprehensive fee:* $35,074 includes full-time tuition ($23,428), mandatory fees ($850), and room and board ($10,796). Part-time tuition: $760 per credit hour. *Required fees:* $70 per term part-time. *College room only:* $5596.

Financial Aid Of all full-time matriculated undergraduates who enrolled in 2006, 1,611 applied for aid, 1,410 were judged to have need, 276 had their need fully met. In 2006, 168 non-need-based awards were made. *Average percent of need met:* 86%. *Average financial aid package:* $19,697. *Average need-based loan:* $5118. *Average need-based gift aid:* $14,194. *Average non-need-based aid:* $8794. *Average indebtedness upon graduation:* $23,292. *Financial aid deadline:* 3/15.

Applying *Options:* electronic application, early admission, early decision, deferred entrance. *Application fee:* $40. *Required:* essay or personal statement, high school transcript, 1 letter of recommendation. *Required for some:* interview, portfolio. *Recommended:* interview. *Application deadlines:* 2/1 (freshmen), 8/1 (transfers). *Early decision deadline:* 12/1. *Notification:* continuous (freshmen), continuous (transfers), 12/15 (early decision).

Freshman Application Contact Mr. Jeremy Spencer, Director of Admissions, Alfred University, Alumni Hall, Alfred, NY 14802-1205. *Phone:* 607-871-2115. *Toll-free phone:* 800-541-9229. *Fax:* 607-871-2198. *E-mail:* admissions@alfred.edu.

BARD COLLEGE

Annandale-on-Hudson, New York **www.bard.edu/**

- **Independent** comprehensive, founded 1860
- **Rural** 600-acre campus
- **Coed** 1,801 undergraduate students, 95% full-time, 56% women, 44% men
- **Very difficult** entrance level, 27% of applicants were admitted

Undergraduates 1,707 full-time, 94 part-time. Students come from 48 states and territories, 46 other countries, 70% are from out of state, 2% African American, 3% Asian American or Pacific Islander, 3% Hispanic American, 0.6% Native American, 10% international, 2% transferred in, 77% live on campus. *Retention:* 88% of 2006 full-time freshmen returned.

Freshmen *Admission:* 4,980 applied, 1,350 admitted, 491 enrolled. *Average high school GPA:* 3.5. *Test scores:* SAT math scores over 500: 100%; SAT writing scores over 500: 100%; SAT math scores over 600: 73%; SAT writing scores over 600: 83%; SAT math scores over 700: 22%; SAT writing scores over 700: 36%.

Faculty *Total:* 250, 56% full-time, 93% with terminal degrees. *Student/faculty ratio:* 9:1.

Majors Acting; African studies; American government and politics; American history; American studies; ancient/classical Greek; anthropology; Arabic; archeology; area studies; art; Asian history; Asian studies; biology/biological sciences; chemistry; Chinese; cinematography and film/video production; comparative literature; computer science; creative writing; dance; dramatic/theater arts; economics; English; environmental studies; European history; European studies; film/cinema studies; fine/studio arts; French; German; Hebrew; history; history and philosophy of science and technology; interdisciplinary studies; international relations and affairs; Italian; jazz/jazz studies; Jewish/Judaic studies; Latin; Latin American studies; liberal arts and sciences/liberal studies; literature; mathematics; medieval and Renaissance studies; music; music history, literature, and theory; music performance; music theory and composition; philosophy; photography; physics; playwriting and screenwriting; political science and government;

pre-medical studies; psychology; religious studies; Romance languages; Russian; Russian studies; sociology; Spanish; theater literature, history and criticism; voice and opera.

Academics *Calendar:* semesters. *Degrees:* associate, bachelor's, master's, and doctoral. *Special study options:* adult/continuing education programs, advanced placement credit, double majors, independent study, internships, off-campus study, part-time degree program, services for LD students, student-designed majors, study abroad. *Unusual degree programs:* 3-2 business administration; engineering with Columbia University, Washington University in St. Louis, Dartmouth College; forestry with Duke University; social work; Master of Arts in teaching with Bard College.

Computers on Campus 425 computers/terminals are available on campus for general student use. Students can access the following: campus intranet, computer help desk, free student e-mail accounts, online (class) grades, online (class) registration, online (class) schedules. Campuswide network is available. 100% of college-owned or -operated housing units are wired for high-speed Internet access. Wireless service is available via classrooms, computer centers, dorm rooms, libraries, student centers.

Student Life *Housing:* on-campus residence required for freshman year. *Options:* coed, women-only, cooperative. Campus housing is university owned. Freshman campus housing is guaranteed. *Activities and organizations:* drama/theater group, student-run newspaper, radio station, choral group, student government, Social Action Workshop, Model United Nations, student newspaper, International Student Organization. *Campus security:* 24-hour emergency response devices and patrols, student patrols, late-night transport/escort service, controlled dormitory access. *Student services:* health clinic, personal/psychological counseling, women's center, legal services.

Athletics Member NCAA, NAIA. All NCAA Division III. *Intercollegiate sports:* basketball M/W, cross-country running M/W, soccer M/W, squash M, tennis M/W, track and field M/W, volleyball M/W. *Intramural sports:* baseball M (c), basketball M/W, equestrian sports M (c)/W (c), fencing M (c)/W (c), ice hockey M (c), rugby W (c), soccer M/W, softball M/W, squash M/W, swimming and diving M (c)/W (c), ultimate Frisbee M (c)/W (c).

Costs (2007–08) *One-time required fee:* $620. *Comprehensive fee:* $46,880 includes full-time tuition ($35,784), mandatory fees ($750), and room and board ($10,346). Part-time tuition: $1120 per credit. *Payment plans:* tuition prepayment, installment.

Financial Aid Of all full-time matriculated undergraduates who enrolled in 2007, 1,097 applied for aid, 958 were judged to have need, 489 had their need fully met. 589 Federal Work-Study jobs (averaging $1518). 70 state and other part-time jobs (averaging $1650). In 2007, 56 non-need-based awards were made. *Average percent of need met:* 90%. *Average financial aid package:* $26,224. *Average need-based loan:* $3791. *Average need-based gift aid:* $23,932. *Average non-need-based aid:* $10,986. *Average indebtedness upon graduation:* $19,507. *Financial aid deadline:* 2/15.

Applying *Options:* electronic application, early admission, early action, deferred entrance. *Application fee:* $50. *Required:* essay or personal statement, high school transcript, minimum 3.0 GPA, 3 letters of recommendation. *Required for some:* interview. *Recommended:* interview. *Application deadlines:* 1/15 (freshmen), 3/15 (transfers), 11/1 (early action). *Notification:* 4/1 (freshmen), 5/15 (transfers), 1/1 (early action).

Freshman Application Contact Ms. Mary Backlund, Director of Admissions, Bard College, PO Box 5000, 51 Ravine Road, Annandale-on-Hudson, NY 12504-5000. *Phone:* 845-758-7472. *Fax:* 845-758-5208. *E-mail:* admission@bard.edu.

BARNARD COLLEGE

New York, New York

www.barnard.edu/

- **Independent** 4-year, founded 1889, part of Columbia University
- **Urban** 4-acre campus
- **Endowment** $204.8 million
- **Women only** 2,346 undergraduate students, 98% full-time
- **Most difficult** entrance level, 29% of applicants were admitted

Undergraduates 2,295 full-time, 51 part-time. Students come from 48 states and territories, 40 other countries, 68% are from out of state, 5% African American, 16% Asian American or Pacific Islander, 9% Hispanic American, 0.3% Native American, 4% international, 3% transferred in, 90% live on campus. *Retention:* 95% of 2006 full-time freshmen returned.

Freshmen *Admission:* 4,574 applied, 1,315 admitted, 559 enrolled. *Average high school GPA:* 3.91. *Test scores:* SAT critical reading scores over 500: 99%; SAT math scores over 500: 98%; SAT writing scores over 500: 99%; ACT scores over 18: 100%; SAT critical reading scores over 600: 91%; SAT math scores over 600: 84%; SAT writing scores over 600: 91%; ACT scores over 24: 96%; SAT critical reading scores over 700: 49%; SAT math scores over 700: 28%; SAT writing scores over 700: 51%; ACT scores over 30: 55%.

Faculty *Total:* 325, 61% full-time, 90% with terminal degrees. *Student/faculty ratio:* 10:1.

Majors African studies; American studies; ancient/classical Greek; anthropology; applied mathematics; architectural history and criticism; architecture; art history, criticism and conservation; Asian studies; biochemistry; biology/biological sciences; chemistry; classics; comparative literature; computer and information sciences; dance; dramatic/theater arts; economics; education; English; environmental biology; environmental science; European studies; film/cinema studies; French; French studies; German; German studies; history; interdisciplinary studies; Italian; Jewish/Judaic studies; Latin; Latin American studies; mathematical statistics and probability; mathematics; medieval and Renaissance studies; music; Near and Middle Eastern studies; neuroscience; philosophy; physics; political science and government; pre-law studies; pre-medical studies; psychology; religious studies; Russian; Russian studies; Slavic studies; sociology; Spanish; Spanish and Iberian studies; statistics; urban studies/affairs; visual and performing arts; women's studies.

Academics *Calendar:* semesters. *Degree:* bachelor's. *Special study options:* accelerated degree program, advanced placement credit, double majors, independent study, internships, off-campus study, services for LD students, student-designed majors, study abroad. *Unusual degree programs:* 3-2 engineering with Columbia University, The Fu Foundation School of Engineering and Applied Science; joint degrees with Columbia University, School of International and Public Affairs; School of Law; School of Dentistry. Double degree programs with Julliard School; double degree and exchange program with the Jewish Theological Seminary. Exchange program with the Manhattan School of Music.

Computers on Campus 210 computers/terminals are available on campus for general student use. Students can access the following: campus intranet, computer help desk, free student e-mail accounts, online (class) grades, online (class) registration, online (class) schedules. Campuswide network is available. 100% of college-owned or -operated housing units are wired for high-speed Internet access. Wireless service is available via computer centers, computer labs, dorm rooms, libraries, student centers.

Student Life *Housing options:* women-only, disabled students. Campus housing is university owned and leased by the school. Freshman campus housing is guaranteed. *Activities and organizations:* drama/theater group, student-run newspaper, radio and television station, choral group, marching band, Community Impact (community service), Student Government Association, Take Back the Night, Student Activities Council, College Democrats. *Campus security:* 24-hour emergency response devices and patrols, late-night transport/escort service, gated campus with permanent security posts. *Student services:* health clinic, personal/psychological counseling, women's center.

Athletics Member NCAA. All Division I. *Intercollegiate sports:* archery W, basketball W, crew W, cross-country running W, equestrian sports W (c), fencing W, field hockey W, golf W, ice hockey W (c), lacrosse W, rugby W (c), sailing W (c), skiing (downhill) W (c), soccer W, softball W, squash W (c), swimming and diving W, tennis W, track and field W, volleyball W. *Intramural sports:* archery W, badminton W, basketball W, equestrian sports W, ice hockey W, rugby W, sailing W, soccer W, squash W, tennis W, volleyball W, water polo W.

Standardized Tests *Required:* SAT with writing and two subject tests or ACT with writing (for admission).

Costs (2007–08) *Comprehensive fee:* $46,736 includes full-time tuition ($33,776), mandatory fees ($1414), and room and board ($11,546). Part-time tuition: $1130 per credit. *College room only:* $7142. Room and board charges vary according to board plan and housing facility. *Payment plans:* tuition prepayment, installment, deferred payment. *Waivers:* employees or children of employees.

Financial Aid Of all full-time matriculated undergraduates who enrolled in 2007, 1,128 applied for aid, 1,005 were judged to have need, 1,005 had their need fully met. 322 Federal Work-Study jobs (averaging $1789). 704 state and other part-time jobs (averaging $1689). *Average percent of need met:* 100%. *Average financial aid package:* $32,153. *Average need-based loan:* $4292. *Average need-based gift aid:* $28,262. *Average indebtedness upon graduation:* $17,630. *Financial aid deadline:* 2/1.

Applying *Options:* early admission, early decision, deferred entrance. *Application fee:* $55. *Required:* essay or personal statement, high school transcript, 3 letters of recommendation, Common Application with Barnard supplement. *Recommended:* interview. *Application deadlines:* 1/1 (freshmen), 4/1 (transfers). *Early decision deadline:* 11/15. *Notification:* 4/1 (freshmen), 5/15 (transfers), 12/15 (early decision).

Freshman Application Contact Ms. Jennifer Gill Fondiller, Dean of Admissions, Barnard College, 3009 Broadway, New York, NY 10027. *Phone:* 212-854-2014. *Fax:* 212-854-6220. *E-mail:* admissions@barnard.edu.

See page 1692 for the College Close-Up.

BEIS MEDRASH HEICHAL DOVID

Far Rockaway, New York

BERKELEY COLLEGE-NEW YORK CITY CAMPUS

New York, New York **www.berkeleycollege.edu/**

- **Proprietary** primarily 2-year, founded 1936, administratively affiliated with Berkeley College
- **Urban** campus
- **Coed**
- **Minimally difficult** entrance level

Faculty *Student/faculty ratio:* 26:1.

Academics *Calendar:* quarters. *Degrees:* certificates, associate, and bachelor's.

Student Life *Campus security:* 24-hour emergency response devices.

Standardized Tests *Required:* SAT or ACT (for admission).

Costs (2007–08) *Tuition:* $17,400 full-time, $425 per credit part-time. Full-time tuition and fees vary according to course load. Part-time tuition and fees vary according to course load. *Required fees:* $750 full-time.

Financial Aid Of all full-time matriculated undergraduates who enrolled in 2006, 120 Federal Work-Study jobs (averaging $1500).

Applying *Options:* electronic application, deferred entrance. *Application fee:* $50. *Required:* high school transcript. *Recommended:* interview.

Freshman Application Contact Ms. Linda Pinsky, Associate Vice President, Enrollment, Berkeley College-New York City Campus, 3 East 43rd Street, New York, NY 10017. *Phone:* 212-986-4343 Ext. 4117. *Toll-free phone:* 800-446-5400. *Fax:* 212-818-1079. *E-mail:* info@berkeleycollege.edu.

BERKELEY COLLEGE-WESTCHESTER CAMPUS

White Plains, New York **www.berkeleycollege.edu/**

- **Proprietary** primarily 2-year, founded 1945
- **Suburban** campus with easy access to New York City
- **Coed**
- **Minimally difficult** entrance level

Faculty *Student/faculty ratio:* 22:1.

Academics *Calendar:* quarters. *Degrees:* certificates, associate, and bachelor's.

Student Life *Campus security:* 24-hour emergency response devices, controlled dormitory access, monitored entrance with front desk security guard.

Standardized Tests *Required:* SAT or ACT (for admission).

Costs (2007–08) *Tuition:* $17,400 full-time, $425 per credit part-time. Full-time tuition and fees vary according to course load. Part-time tuition and fees vary according to course load. *Required fees:* $750 full-time. *Room only:* $7200.

Financial Aid Of all full-time matriculated undergraduates who enrolled in 2006, 40 Federal Work-Study jobs (averaging $1100).

Applying *Options:* electronic application, deferred entrance. *Application fee:* $50. *Required:* high school transcript. *Recommended:* interview.

Freshman Application Contact Mr. John Wool, Assistant Director of Admissions, Berkeley College-Westchester Campus, 99 Church Street, White Plains, NY 10601. *Phone:* 914-694-1122 Ext. 3110. *Toll-free phone:* 800-446-5400. *Fax:* 914-328-9469. *E-mail:* info@berkeleycollege.edu.

BERNARD M. BARUCH COLLEGE OF THE CITY UNIVERSITY OF NEW YORK

New York, New York **www.baruch.cuny.edu/**

- **State and locally supported** comprehensive, founded 1919, part of City University of New York System
- **Urban** campus
- **Coed** 12,863 undergraduate students, 75% full-time, 52% women, 48% men
- **Very difficult** entrance level, 26% of applicants were admitted

Undergraduates 9,588 full-time, 3,275 part-time. Students come from 151 other countries, 3% are from out of state, 11% African American, 30% Asian American or Pacific Islander, 16% Hispanic American, 0.1% Native American, 13% international, 11% transferred in. *Retention:* 88% of 2006 full-time freshmen returned.

Freshmen *Admission:* 17,114 applied, 4,414 admitted, 1,479 enrolled. *Average high school GPA:* 3.0. *Test scores:* SAT critical reading scores over 500: 68%; SAT math scores over 500: 91%; SAT critical reading scores over 600: 20%; SAT math scores over 600: 47%; SAT critical reading scores over 700: 2%; SAT math scores over 700: 11%.

Faculty *Total:* 964, 52% full-time, 58% with terminal degrees. *Student/faculty ratio:* 19:1.

Majors Accounting; actuarial science; advertising; arts management; business administration and management; business/managerial economics; creative writing; economics; education; English; finance; history; human resources management; information science/studies; interdisciplinary studies; international business/trade/commerce; journalism; literature; management information systems; marketing/marketing management; mathematics; music; natural sciences; operations research; philosophy; political science and government; psychology; public administration; public policy analysis; Romance languages; sociology; Spanish; statistics.

Academics *Calendar:* semesters. *Degrees:* bachelor's, master's, and post-master's certificates. *Special study options:* accelerated degree program, adult/continuing education programs, advanced placement credit, distance learning, double majors, English as a second language, honors programs, independent study, internships, part-time degree program, services for LD students, student-designed majors, study abroad, summer session for credit.

Computers on Campus 1,300 computers/terminals are available on campus for general student use. Students can access the following: campus intranet, computer help desk, free student e-mail accounts, online (class) grades, online (class) registration, online (class) schedules. Campuswide network is available. Wireless service is available via classrooms, computer centers, computer labs, libraries, student centers.

Student Life *Housing:* college housing not available. *Activities and organizations:* drama/theater group, student-run newspaper, radio station, choral group, Accounting Society, Computer Information Systems Society, Association of Latino Professionals in Finance and Accounting, Golden Key International Society, Helpline, national fraternities, national sororities. *Campus security:* 24-hour emergency response devices and patrols, late-night transport/escort service, controlled access by ID card. *Student services:* health clinic, personal/psychological counseling, legal services.

Athletics Member NCAA. All Division III. *Intercollegiate sports:* baseball M, basketball M/W, cheerleading W, cross-country running M/W, soccer M, softball W, swimming and diving M/W, tennis M/W, volleyball M/W. *Intramural sports:* badminton M/W, basketball M/W, cross-country running M/W, racquetball M/W, table tennis M/W, volleyball M/W, weight lifting M/W.

Standardized Tests *Required:* SAT or ACT (for admission).

Costs (2008–09) *Tuition:* state resident $4000 full-time, $170 per credit part-time; nonresident $8640 full-time, $360 per credit part-time. *Required fees:* $320 full-time, $160 per term part-time.

Financial Aid Of all full-time matriculated undergraduates who enrolled in 2006, 7,758 applied for aid, 6,983 were judged to have need, 777 had their need fully met. 520 Federal Work-Study jobs (averaging $647). 640 state and other part-time jobs (averaging $925). In 2006, 87 non-need-based awards were made. *Average percent of need met:* 60%. *Average financial aid package:* $5120. *Average need-based loan:* $3803. *Average need-based gift aid:* $3921. *Average non-need-based aid:* $3300. *Average indebtedness upon graduation:* $14,159.

Applying *Options:* early admission, early decision, early action. *Application fee:* $65. *Required:* high school transcript, minimum 2.5 GPA, 16 academic units. *Required for some:* letters of recommendation, interview. *Application deadlines:* 2/1 (freshmen), 3/1 (transfers), 12/15 (early action). *Early decision deadline:* 12/13. *Notification:* continuous until 5/15 (freshmen), continuous until 5/1 (transfers), 1/7 (early decision), 1/7 (early action).

Director of Admissions Ms. Marybeth Murphy, Assistant Vice President for Undergraduate Admissions and Financial Aid, Bernard M. Baruch College of the City University of New York, Box H-0720, New York, NY 10010-5585. *Phone:* 646-312-1400. *E-mail:* marybeth_murphy@baruch.cuny.edu.

See page 1694 for the College Close-Up.

BETH HAMEDRASH SHAAREI YOSHER INSTITUTE

Brooklyn, New York

Director of Admissions Mr. Menachem Steinberg, Director of Admissions, Beth HaMedrash Shaarei Yosher Institute, 4102-10 Sixteenth Avenue, Brooklyn, NY 11204. *Phone:* 718-854-2290.

BETH HATALMUD RABBINICAL COLLEGE

Brooklyn, New York

Director of Admissions Rabbi Osina, Director of Admissions, Beth Hatalmud Rabbinical College, 2127 Eighty-second Street, Brooklyn, NY 11214. *Phone:* 718-259-2525.

BORICUA COLLEGE

New York, New York **www.boricuacollege.edu/**

- **Independent** comprehensive, founded 1974
- **Urban** campus
- **Endowment** $626,808
- **Coed** 1,004 undergraduate students, 100% full-time, 79% women, 21% men
- **Moderately difficult** entrance level, 40% of applicants were admitted

Undergraduates 1,004 full-time. Students come from 2 states and territories, 12% African American, 0.5% Asian American or Pacific Islander, 80% Hispanic American, 0.1% Native American. *Retention:* 53% of 2006 full-time freshmen returned.

Freshmen *Admission:* 924 applied, 369 admitted.

Faculty *Total:* 133, 43% full-time, 100% with terminal degrees. *Student/faculty ratio:* 20:1.

Majors Business administration and management; elementary education; human services; liberal arts and sciences/liberal studies.

Academics *Calendar:* 15-15-8. *Degrees:* associate, bachelor's, and master's. *Special study options:* accelerated degree program, adult/continuing education programs, honors programs, internships, study abroad, summer session for credit.

Computers on Campus 120 computers/terminals are available on campus for general student use. Wireless service is available via entire campus.

Student Life *Housing:* college housing not available. *Activities and organizations:* choral group. *Campus security:* 24-hour emergency response devices.

Athletics *Intramural sports:* basketball M/W.

Standardized Tests *Required:* Boricua College Exam (for admission).

Costs (2007–08) *One-time required fee:* $25. *Tuition:* $9200 full-time. *Payment plan:* installment. *Waivers:* employees or children of employees.

Financial Aid Of all full-time matriculated undergraduates who enrolled in 2005, 1,472 applied for aid, 1,453 were judged to have need, 590 had their need fully met. 121 Federal Work-Study jobs (averaging $1900). In 2005, 6 non-need-based awards were made. *Average percent of need met:* 40%. *Average financial aid package:* $5200. *Average need-based loan:* $3937. *Average need-based gift aid:* $443. *Average non-need-based aid:* $700.

Applying *Options:* deferred entrance. *Application fee:* $25. *Required:* essay or personal statement, high school transcript, 2 letters of recommendation, interview, proficiency in English. *Application deadlines:* rolling (freshmen), rolling (transfers).

Freshman Application Contact Miriam Pfeiffer, Director of Student Services, Boricua College, 3755 Broadway, New York, NY 10032-1560. *Phone:* 718-782-2200. *Fax:* 718-782-2025. *E-mail:* mpfeffer@boricuacollege.edu.

BRIARCLIFFE COLLEGE

Bethpage, New York **www.briarcliffe.edu/**

- **Proprietary** 4-year, founded 1966, part of Career Education Corporation
- **Suburban** campus with easy access to New York City
- **Coed**
- **Noncompetitive** entrance level

Academics *Calendar:* semesters. *Degrees:* diplomas, associate, and bachelor's.

Student Life *Campus security:* late-night transport/escort service.

Athletics Member NJCAA.

Applying *Options:* electronic application, deferred entrance. *Application fee:* $35. *Required:* high school transcript. *Recommended:* interview.

Freshman Application Contact Ms. Theresa Donohue, Vice President of Marketing and Admissions, Briarcliffe College, Bethpage, NY 11714. *Phone:* 516-918-3705. *Toll-free phone:* 888-333-1150. *Fax:* 516-470-6020. *E-mail:* info@bcl.edu.

BROOKLYN COLLEGE OF THE CITY UNIVERSITY OF NEW YORK

Brooklyn, New York **www.brooklyn.cuny.edu/**

- **State and locally supported** comprehensive, founded 1930, part of City University of New York System
- **Urban** 26-acre campus
- **Coed**
- **Moderately difficult** entrance level

Faculty *Student/faculty ratio:* 15:1.

Academics *Calendar:* semesters. *Degrees:* certificates, bachelor's, master's, post-master's, and postbachelor's certificates.

Student Life *Campus security:* 24-hour emergency response devices and patrols, late-night transport/escort service.

Athletics Member NCAA. All Division III.

Standardized Tests *Required:* SAT or ACT (for admission). *Recommended:* SAT Subject Tests (for admission).

Costs (2007–08) *Tuition:* state resident $4000 full-time, $170 per credit part-time; nonresident $8762 full-time, $360 per credit part-time. *Required fees:* $150 full-time, $38 per term part-time.

Financial Aid Of all full-time matriculated undergraduates who enrolled in 2003, 6,300 applied for aid, 5,977 were judged to have need, 5,800 had their need fully met. 1,100 Federal Work-Study jobs (averaging $1200). In 2003, 750 non-need-based awards were made. *Average percent of need met:* 99. *Average financial aid package:* $5400. *Average need-based loan:* $2850. *Average need-based gift aid:* $3300. *Average non-need-based aid:* $4000. *Average indebtedness upon graduation:* $13,750.

Applying *Options:* early admission, deferred entrance. *Application fee:* $65. *Required:* high school transcript, minimum 3.0 GPA. *Required for some:* essay or personal statement, letters of recommendation, interview.

Freshman Application Contact Admissions Information Center, Brooklyn College of the City University of New York, 2900 Bedford Avenue, 1103 James Hall, Brooklyn, NY 11210-2889. *Phone:* 718-951-5001. *Fax:* 718-951-4506. *E-mail:* adminqry@brooklyn.cuny.edu.

See page 1696 for the College Close-Up.

BRYANT AND STRATTON COLLEGE, AMHERST CAMPUS

Clarence, New York **www.bryantstratton.edu/**

Freshman Application Contact Mr. Paul Kehr, WNY Market Admissions Director, Bryant and Stratton College, Amherst Campus, 40 Hazelwood Drive, Amherst, NY 14228. *Phone:* 716-677-9500. *Fax:* 716-677-9599. *E-mail:* jaweslowskiy@bryantstratton.edu.

BUFFALO STATE COLLEGE, STATE UNIVERSITY OF NEW YORK

Buffalo, New York **www.buffalostate.edu/**

- **State-supported** comprehensive, founded 1867, part of State University of New York System
- **Urban** 115-acre campus
- **Endowment** $19.0 million
- **Coed** 9,139 undergraduate students, 88% full-time, 59% women, 41% men
- **Moderately difficult** entrance level, 47% of applicants were admitted

Undergraduates 8,052 full-time, 1,087 part-time. Students come from 29 states and territories, 12 other countries, 1% are from out of state, 14% African

American, 2% Asian American or Pacific Islander, 5% Hispanic American, 0.5% Native American, 0.7% international, 12% transferred in, 20% live on campus. *Retention:* 76% of 2006 full-time freshmen returned.

Freshmen *Admission:* 9,762 applied, 4,631 admitted, 1,401 enrolled. *Average high school GPA:* 3.1. *Test scores:* SAT critical reading scores over 500: 46%; SAT math scores over 500: 50%; SAT critical reading scores over 600: 8%; SAT math scores over 600: 8%; SAT critical reading scores over 700: 1%; SAT math scores over 700: 1%.

Faculty *Total:* 787, 55% full-time, 51% with terminal degrees. *Student/faculty ratio:* 17:1.

Majors Anthropology; applied art; art; art history, criticism and conservation; art teacher education; audiology and speech-language pathology; biology/biological sciences; broadcast journalism; business administration and management; business teacher education; chemistry; city/urban, community and regional planning; commercial and advertising art; communication/speech communication and rhetoric; criminal justice/law enforcement administration; design and visual communications; dietetics; dramatic/theater arts; drawing; economics; electrical, electronic and communications engineering technology; electromechanical technology; elementary education; engineering; engineering technology; English; English/language arts teacher education; fashion/apparel design; fashion merchandising; fine/studio arts; foreign language teacher education; forensic science and technology; French; general studies; geography; geology/earth science; history; hospitality administration; hotel/motel administration; humanities; industrial arts; industrial technology; information science/studies; journalism; kindergarten/preschool education; kinesiology and exercise science; liberal arts and sciences/liberal studies; mass communication/media; mathematics; mathematics teacher education; mechanical engineering/mechanical technology; multi-/interdisciplinary studies related; music; music teacher education; painting; philosophy; photography; physics; political science and government; pre-dentistry studies; pre-law studies; pre-medical studies; pre-veterinary studies; printmaking; psychology; public relations/image management; radio and television; science teacher education; sculpture; secondary education; social studies teacher education; social work; sociology; Spanish; special education; special education (speech or language impaired); special products marketing; technology/industrial arts teacher education; trade and industrial teacher education; urban studies/affairs.

Academics *Calendar:* semesters. *Degrees:* bachelor's, master's, and post-master's certificates. *Special study options:* academic remediation for entering students, adult/continuing education programs, advanced placement credit, cooperative education, distance learning, double majors, English as a second language, freshman honors college, honors programs, independent study, internships, off-campus study, part-time degree program, services for LD students, study abroad, summer session for credit. *ROTC:* Army (c). *Unusual degree programs:* 3-2 engineering with State University of New York at Binghamton, Clarkson University, State University of New York at Buffalo.

Computers on Campus 1,700 computers/terminals are available on campus for general student use. Students can access the following: computer help desk, free student e-mail accounts, online (class) registration, online (class) schedules. Campuswide network is available. Wireless service is available via classrooms, libraries, student centers.

Student Life *Housing:* on-campus residence required through sophomore year. *Options:* coed. Campus housing is university owned. Freshman campus housing is guaranteed. *Activities and organizations:* drama/theater group, student-run newspaper, radio station, choral group, United Student Government, African-American Student Organization, Caribbean Student Organization, The Record, WBNY radio, national fraternities, national sororities. *Campus security:* 24-hour emergency response devices and patrols, student patrols, late-night transport/escort service, controlled dormitory access. *Student services:* health clinic, personal/psychological counseling, women's center, legal services.

Athletics Member NCAA. All Division III. *Intercollegiate sports:* baseball M (c), basketball M/W, bowling M (c)/W (c), cheerleading W (c), cross-country running M/W, fencing M (c), football M, ice hockey M/W, lacrosse M (c)/W, rugby M (c)/W (c), skiing (cross-country) M (c)/W (c), skiing (downhill) M (c)/W (c), soccer M/W, softball W, swimming and diving M/W, tennis W, track and field M/W, volleyball M (c)/W. *Intramural sports:* basketball M, football M, racquetball M/W, softball M/W, volleyball M/W, water polo M (c)/W (c).

Standardized Tests *Required:* SAT (for admission), SAT or ACT (for admission), SAT and SAT Subject Tests or ACT (for admission). *Recommended:* SAT (for admission).

Costs (2007–08) *Tuition:* state resident $4350 full-time, $181 per credit hour part-time; nonresident $10,610 full-time, $442 per credit hour part-time. Part-time tuition and fees vary according to course load. *Required fees:* $1025 full-time, $43 per credit hour part-time. *Room and board:* $8314; room only: $5028. Room and board charges vary according to board plan, housing facility, and student level. *Payment plan:* installment. *Waivers:* employees or children of employees.

Financial Aid Of all full-time matriculated undergraduates who enrolled in 2003, 6,587 applied for aid, 5,624 were judged to have need, 12 had their need fully met. *Average percent of need met:* 62%. *Average financial aid package:* $3037. *Average need-based loan:* $1559. *Average need-based gift aid:* $1043. *Average non-need-based aid:* $1298. *Average indebtedness upon graduation:* $15,776.

Applying *Options:* electronic application, early admission, early decision, deferred entrance. *Application fee:* $40. *Required:* high school transcript, minimum 3.0 GPA. *Required for some:* essay or personal statement, letters of recommendation, interview. *Application deadlines:* rolling (freshmen), rolling (transfers). *Early decision deadline:* 11/15. *Notification:* continuous (freshmen), continuous (transfers), 12/15 (early decision).

Freshman Application Contact Ms. Lesa Loritts, Director of Admissions, Buffalo State College, State University of New York, 110 Moot Hall, Buffalo, NY 14222. *Phone:* 716-878-4017. *Fax:* 716-878-6100. *E-mail:* admissions@buffalostate.edu.

See page 1698 for the College Close-Up.

CANISIUS COLLEGE

Buffalo, New York **www.canisius.edu/**

- **Independent Roman Catholic (Jesuit)** comprehensive, founded 1870
- **Urban** 36-acre campus
- **Endowment** $81.9 million
- **Coed** 3,490 undergraduate students, 93% full-time, 55% women, 45% men
- **Moderately difficult** entrance level, 79% of applicants were admitted

Undergraduates 3,233 full-time, 257 part-time. Students come from 35 states and territories, 12 other countries, 8% are from out of state, 6% African American, 1% Asian American or Pacific Islander, 2% Hispanic American, 0.3% Native American, 4% international, 5% transferred in, 45% live on campus. *Retention:* 81% of 2006 full-time freshmen returned.

Freshmen *Admission:* 3,695 applied, 2,914 admitted, 846 enrolled. *Average high school GPA:* 3.44. *Test scores:* SAT critical reading scores over 500: 71%; SAT math scores over 500: 78%; ACT scores over 18: 97%; SAT critical reading scores over 600: 23%; SAT math scores over 600: 29%; ACT scores over 24: 57%; SAT critical reading scores over 700: 4%; SAT math scores over 700: 3%; ACT scores over 30: 7%.

Faculty *Total:* 485, 44% full-time, 53% with terminal degrees. *Student/faculty ratio:* 13:1.

Majors Accounting; accounting and finance; accounting technology and bookkeeping; anthropology; art history, criticism and conservation; athletic training; biochemistry; bioinformatics; biological and physical sciences; business administration and management; business administration, management and operations related; chemistry; communication and media related; computer science; creative writing; criminal justice/law enforcement administration; digital communication and media/multimedia; dramatic/theater arts; early childhood education; economics; education; engineering related; English; entrepreneurship; environmental science; European studies; finance; fine/studio arts; forest sciences and biology; French; general studies; German; Germanic languages; history; information technology; international business/trade/commerce; international relations and affairs; marketing/marketing management; marketing related; mathematics and statistics related; neuroscience; philosophy; physical education teaching and coaching; physics; political science and government; psychology; religious studies; science teacher education; secondary education; sociology; Spanish; special education (early childhood); urban studies/affairs; women's studies.

Academics *Calendar:* semesters. *Degrees:* associate, bachelor's, master's, and post-master's certificates. *Special study options:* academic remediation for entering students, advanced placement credit, distance learning, double majors, English as a second language, honors programs, independent study, internships, off-campus study, part-time degree program, services for LD students, study abroad, summer session for credit. *ROTC:* Army (b). *Unusual degree programs:* 3-2 business administration.

Computers on Campus 500 computers/terminals are available on campus for general student use. Students can access the following: computer help desk, free student e-mail accounts, online (class) grades, online (class) registration, online (class) schedules, online accounts. Campuswide network is available. 100% of college-owned or -operated housing units are wired for high-speed Internet access. Wireless service is available via entire campus.

Student Life *Housing options:* coed. Campus housing is university owned. Freshman applicants given priority for college housing. *Activities and organizations:* drama/theater group, student-run newspaper, radio and television station, choral group, Campus Programming Board, Undergraduate Student Association, Afro-American Society, Residence Hall Association, Student Association, national fraternities, national sororities. *Campus security:* 24-hour emergency response devices and patrols, late-night transport/escort service, controlled dormitory access, crime prevention programs, closed-circuit television monitors. *Student services:* health clinic, personal/psychological counseling.

Athletics Member NCAA. All Division I. *Intercollegiate sports:* baseball M (s), basketball M (s)/W (s), cross-country running M (s)/W (s), golf M (s), ice hockey M (s), lacrosse M (s)/W (s), rugby M (c), soccer M (s)/W (s), softball W (s), swimming and diving M (s)/W (s), volleyball M (c)/W (s). *Intramural sports:* basketball M/W, cheerleading M (c)/W (c), crew M (c)/W (c), field hockey W, racquetball M/W, riflery M (c)/W (c), soccer M/W, softball M (c)/W (c), tennis M/W, volleyball M/W.

Standardized Tests *Required:* SAT or ACT (for admission).

Costs (2007–08) *Comprehensive fee:* $36,197 includes full-time tuition ($25,370), mandatory fees ($1057), and room and board ($9770). Full-time tuition and fees vary according to course load. Part-time tuition: $724 per hour. Part-time tuition and fees vary according to course load. *Required fees:* $13 per credit part-time, $41 per term part-time. *College room only:* $5790. Room and board charges vary according to board plan and housing facility. *Payment plans:* tuition prepayment, installment, deferred payment. *Waivers:* employees or children of employees.

Financial Aid Of all full-time matriculated undergraduates who enrolled in 2007, 2,648 applied for aid, 2,439 were judged to have need, 617 had their need fully met. 537 Federal Work-Study jobs (averaging $1659). In 2007, 665 non-need-based awards were made. *Average percent of need met:* 79%. *Average financial aid package:* $21,447. *Average need-based loan:* $4367. *Average need-based gift aid:* $15,597. *Average non-need-based aid:* $11,246. *Average indebtedness upon graduation:* $29,512.

Applying *Options:* electronic application, early admission, deferred entrance. *Application fee:* $40. *Required:* high school transcript, minimum 2.5 GPA. *Required for some:* interview. *Recommended:* essay or personal statement, letters of recommendation, interview. *Application deadlines:* 5/1 (freshmen), rolling (transfers). *Notification:* continuous (freshmen), continuous (transfers).

Freshman Application Contact Ms. Ann Marie Moscovic, Director of Admissions, Canisius College, 2001 Main Street, Buffalo, NY 14208-1098. *Phone:* 716-888-2200. *Toll-free phone:* 800-843-1517. *Fax:* 716-888-3230. *E-mail:* admissions@canisius.edu.

See page 1700 for the College Close-Up.

CAZENOVIA COLLEGE

Cazenovia, New York **www.cazenovia.edu/**

- **Independent** 4-year, founded 1824
- **Small-town** 40-acre campus with easy access to Syracuse
- **Endowment** $27.0 million
- **Coed**
- **Minimally difficult** entrance level

Cazenovia College, named one of "America's Best Colleges" by *U.S. News & World Report*, is an independent, coeducational baccalaureate college. Located near Syracuse, New York, Cazenovia College offers a unique blend of professional and liberal arts education in an exceptional community environment, with academic and cocurricular programs devoted to developing successful graduates. For more information, students should visit http://www.cazenovia.edu.

Faculty *Student/faculty ratio:* 11:1.

Academics *Calendar:* semesters. *Degrees:* associate and bachelor's.

Student Life *Campus security:* 24-hour emergency response devices and patrols, late-night transport/escort service, controlled dormitory access.

Athletics Member NCAA.

Standardized Tests *Recommended:* SAT or ACT (for admission).

Costs (2007–08) *Comprehensive fee:* $30,440 includes full-time tuition ($21,280), mandatory fees ($220), and room and board ($8940). Full-time tuition and fees vary according to class time and course load. Part-time tuition: $450 per credit. Part-time tuition and fees vary according to class time and course load. *Required fees:* $105 per term part-time. *Room and board:* Room and board charges vary according to board plan and housing facility.

Financial Aid Of all full-time matriculated undergraduates who enrolled in 2007, 860 applied for aid, 788 were judged to have need, 123 had their need fully met. In 2007, 98 non-need-based awards were made. *Average percent of need met:* 77. *Average financial aid package:* $18,614. *Average need-based loan:* $4258. *Average need-based gift aid:* $13,813. *Average non-need-based aid:* $12,204.

Applying *Options:* early admission, deferred entrance. *Application fee:* $30. *Required:* essay or personal statement, high school transcript, letters of recommendation. *Recommended:* minimum 2.0 GPA, interview, portfolio for art and design students.

Freshman Application Contact Office of Admission and Enrollment Services, Cazenovia College, Cazenovia, NY 13035. *Phone:* 315-655-7208. *Toll-free phone:* 800-654-3210. *Fax:* 315-655-4860. *E-mail:* admission@cazenovia.edu.

See page 1702 for the College Close-Up.

CENTRAL YESHIVA TOMCHEI TMIMIM-LUBAVITCH

Brooklyn, New York

Director of Admissions Moses Gluckowsky, Director of Admissions, Central Yeshiva Tomchei Tmimim-Lubavitch, 841-853 Ocean Parkway, Brooklyn, NY 11230. *Phone:* 718-859-7600.

CITY COLLEGE OF THE CITY UNIVERSITY OF NEW YORK

New York, New York **www.ccny.cuny.edu/**

- **State and locally supported** university, founded 1847, part of City University of New York System
- **Urban** 35-acre campus
- **Coed** 11,314 undergraduate students
- **Moderately difficult** entrance level, 40% of applicants were admitted

For more than 160 years, the City College of New York (CUNY) has provided an excellent higher education to generations of New Yorkers. City College offers degree programs in architecture, the arts, biomedical education, computer science, education, engineering, humanities, sciences, and social sciences. Conveniently located in New York City, the College lets students take advantage of an environment that is diverse, politically and socially active, and artistically and intellectually stimulating. For more information, students may visit the Web site at http://www.ccny.cuny.edu.

Undergraduates Students come from 130 other countries, 4% are from out of state, 24% African American, 20% Asian American or Pacific Islander, 33% Hispanic American, 0.1% Native American, 12% international, 1% live on campus. *Retention:* 81% of 2006 full-time freshmen returned.

Freshmen *Admission:* 17,816 applied, 7,204 admitted. *Average high school GPA:* 2.81. *Test scores:* SAT critical reading scores over 500: 40%; SAT math scores over 500: 56%; SAT critical reading scores over 600: 14%; SAT math scores over 600: 22%; SAT critical reading scores over 700: 3%; SAT math scores over 700: 6%.

Faculty *Total:* 1,129, 46% full-time, 59% with terminal degrees. *Student/faculty ratio:* 13:1.

Majors African-American/Black studies; anthropology; architecture; art; art history, criticism and conservation; art teacher education; Asian studies; biochemistry; biology/biological sciences; biology teacher education; biomedical/medical engineering; biomedical sciences; business administration and management; chemical engineering; chemistry; chemistry teacher education; cinematography and film/video production; civil engineering; computer science; creative writing; dramatic/theater arts; early childhood education; economics; education; electrical, electronics and communications engineering; elementary education; English; environmental engineering technology; environmental studies; French; geography; geology/earth science; graphic design; history; intermedia/multimedia; international/global studies; international relations and affairs; jazz/jazz studies; Jewish/Judaic studies; Latin American studies; linguistics; literature; mass communication/media; mathematics; mathematics teacher education; mechanical engineering; music; music performance; music teacher education; music theory and composition; philosophy; physician assistant; physics; physics teacher education; political science and government; pre-dentistry studies; pre-law studies; pre-medical studies; pre-veterinary studies; psychology; Romance languages; science teacher education; secondary education; social studies teacher education; sociology; Spanish; women's studies.

Academics *Calendar:* semesters. *Degrees:* bachelor's, master's, first professional, and post-master's certificates. *Special study options:* academic remediation for entering students, accelerated degree program, adult/continuing education programs, advanced placement credit, cooperative education, English as a second language, freshman honors college, honors programs, independent study, internships, off-campus study, part-time degree program, services for LD students, student-designed majors, study abroad, summer session for credit. *ROTC:* Army (c), Air Force (c). *Unusual degree programs:* 3-2 BS/OD optometry with SUNY Optometry.

Computers on Campus 4,000 computers/terminals are available on campus for general student use. Students can access the following: campus intranet,

computer help desk, free student e-mail accounts, online (class) grades, online (class) registration, online (class) schedules. Campuswide network is available. 100% of college-owned or -operated housing units are wired for high-speed Internet access. Wireless service is available via entire campus.

Student Life *Housing options:* coed. Campus housing is provided by a third party. *Activities and organizations:* drama/theater group, student-run newspaper, radio station, LAESA-SHPE, NSBE, BSA, Salsa-Mambo, IVCF, national fraternities. *Campus security:* 24-hour patrols, late-night transport/escort service, controlled dormitory access. *Student services:* health clinic, personal/psychological counseling.

Athletics Member NCAA. All Division III. *Intercollegiate sports:* baseball M, basketball M/W, cross-country running M/W, fencing W, lacrosse M, soccer M/W, softball W, tennis M/W, track and field M/W, volleyball W. *Intramural sports:* basketball M/W, fencing W, soccer M, softball W, tennis M/W, track and field M/W, volleyball M/W.

Standardized Tests *Required:* SAT or ACT (for admission).

Costs (2007–08) *Tuition:* state resident $4080 full-time, $170 per credit part-time; nonresident $8640 full-time, $360 per credit part-time. Full-time tuition and fees vary according to class time, course load, and program. Part-time tuition and fees vary according to class time, course load, and program. *Required fees:* $279 full-time. *Room only:* $8250. *Payment plan:* deferred payment. *Waivers:* senior citizens.

Financial Aid Of all full-time matriculated undergraduates who enrolled in 2006, 6,212 applied for aid, 5,570 were judged to have need, 3,326 had their need fully met. 2,155 Federal Work-Study jobs (averaging $1558). In 2006, 1083 non-need-based awards were made. *Average percent of need met:* 77%. *Average financial aid package:* $8400. *Average need-based loan:* $3310. *Average need-based gift aid:* $6005. *Average non-need-based aid:* $2570. *Average indebtedness upon graduation:* $16,080.

Applying *Options:* early admission, deferred entrance. *Application fee:* $65. *Required:* high school transcript, minimum high school GPA requirements. *Required for some:* essay or personal statement, letters of recommendation. *Application deadlines:* 3/1 (freshmen), 3/1 (transfers). *Notification:* continuous until 8/1 (freshmen), continuous until 8/1 (transfers).

Freshman Application Contact Joseph A. Fantozzi, Director of Admissions, City College of the City University of New York, Convent Avenue at 138th Street, New York, NY 10031-9198. *Phone:* 212-650-6977. *Fax:* 212-650-6417. *E-mail:* admissions@ccny.cuny.edu.

See page 1704 for the College Close-Up.

CLARKSON UNIVERSITY

Potsdam, New York **www.clarkson.edu/**

- **Independent** university, founded 1896
- **Small-town** 640-acre campus
- **Endowment** $178.0 million
- **Coed** 2,540 undergraduate students, 99% full-time, 26% women, 74% men
- **Very difficult** entrance level, 82% of applicants were admitted

Undergraduates 2,525 full-time, 15 part-time. Students come from 41 states and territories, 25 other countries, 28% are from out of state, 3% African American, 3% Asian American or Pacific Islander, 2% Hispanic American, 0.3% Native American, 3% international, 4% transferred in, 83% live on campus. *Retention:* 85% of 2006 full-time freshmen returned.

Freshmen *Admission:* 2,943 applied, 2,408 admitted, 682 enrolled. *Average high school GPA:* 3.52. *Test scores:* SAT critical reading scores over 500: 81%; SAT math scores over 500: 93%; ACT scores over 18: 99%; SAT critical reading scores over 600: 32%; SAT math scores over 600: 57%; ACT scores over 24: 64%; SAT critical reading scores over 700: 4%; SAT math scores over 700: 13%; ACT scores over 30: 11%.

Faculty *Total:* 211, 87% full-time, 84% with terminal degrees. *Student/faculty ratio:* 15:1.

Majors Accounting; aerospace, aeronautical and astronautical engineering; American literature; American studies; applied mathematics; biochemistry; biology/biological sciences; biophysics; biotechnology; business administration and management; cell biology and histology; chemical engineering; chemistry; civil engineering; communication/speech communication and rhetoric; computer and information sciences; computer engineering; computer science; computer software engineering; construction engineering; digital communication and media/multimedia; ecology; e-commerce; electrical, electronics and communications engineering; engineering; entrepreneurship; environmental/environmental health engineering; environmental health; environmental studies; finance; history; humanities; human resources management; industrial and organizational psychology; information resources management; interdisciplinary studies; international business/trade/commerce; liberal arts and sciences/liberal studies; logistics and materials management; management information systems; manufacturing engineering; marketing/marketing management; materials engineering; materials science; mathematics; mechanical engineering; molecular biology; non-profit management; occupational health and industrial hygiene; operations management; physics; political science and government; pre-dentistry studies; pre-law studies; pre-medical studies; pre-veterinary studies; psychology; social sciences; sociology; statistics; structural engineering; technical and business writing; toxicology.

Academics *Calendar:* semesters. *Degrees:* bachelor's, master's, doctoral, and first professional. *Special study options:* accelerated degree program, advanced placement credit, cooperative education, double majors, English as a second language, honors programs, independent study, internships, off-campus study, part-time degree program, services for LD students, student-designed majors, study abroad, summer session for credit. *ROTC:* Army (b), Air Force (b). *Unusual degree programs:* 3-2 engineering.

Computers on Campus 400 computers/terminals and 10,000 ports are available on campus for general student use. Students can access the following: campus intranet, computer help desk, free student e-mail accounts, online (class) grades, online (class) registration, online (class) schedules. Campuswide network is available. 100% of college-owned or -operated housing units are wired for high-speed Internet access. Wireless service is available via classrooms, computer centers, computer labs, learning centers, libraries, student centers.

Student Life *Housing:* on-campus residence required through senior year. *Options:* coed, men-only, women-only. Campus housing is university owned. Freshman campus housing is guaranteed. *Activities and organizations:* drama/theater group, student-run newspaper, radio and television station, choral group, Ski Club, Outing Club, Pep Band, ISO (International Students Organization), Theatre, national fraternities, national sororities. *Campus security:* 24-hour emergency response devices and patrols, late-night transport/escort service, controlled dormitory access. *Student services:* health clinic, personal/psychological counseling, legal services.

Athletics Member NCAA. All Division III except men's and women's ice hockey (Division I). *Intercollegiate sports:* baseball M, basketball M/W, cross-country running M/W, golf M, ice hockey M (s)/W (s), lacrosse M/W, skiing (cross-country) M/W, skiing (downhill) M/W, soccer M/W, swimming and diving M/W, volleyball M (c)/W. *Intramural sports:* archery M (c)/W (c), basketball M/W, bowling M (c)/W (c), crew M (c), football M, ice hockey M/W, racquetball M (c)/W (c), rugby M (c)/W (c), soccer M/W, softball M/W, ultimate Frisbee M (c)/W (c), volleyball M/W.

Standardized Tests *Required:* SAT or ACT (for admission). *Recommended:* SAT Subject Tests (for admission).

Costs (2007–08) *Comprehensive fee:* $39,290 includes full-time tuition ($28,470), mandatory fees ($690), and room and board ($10,130). Full-time tuition and fees vary according to course load. Part-time tuition: $949 per credit. Part-time tuition and fees vary according to course load. *College room only:* $5320. Room and board charges vary according to housing facility. *Payment plans:* tuition prepayment, installment. *Waivers:* employees or children of employees.

Financial Aid Of all full-time matriculated undergraduates who enrolled in 2006, 2,195 applied for aid, 1,992 were judged to have need, 119 had their need fully met. 1,300 Federal Work-Study jobs (averaging $1365). 150 state and other part-time jobs (averaging $2800). In 2006, 201 non-need-based awards were made. *Average percent of need met:* 87%. *Average financial aid package:* $22,572. *Average need-based loan:* $6000. *Average need-based gift aid:* $15,783. *Average non-need-based aid:* $12,248. *Average indebtedness upon graduation:* $33,774.

Applying *Options:* early admission, early decision, deferred entrance. *Application fee:* $50. *Required:* high school transcript, 2 letters of recommendation. *Recommended:* interview. *Application deadline:* 1/15 (freshmen). *Early decision deadline:* 12/1. *Notification:* continuous (freshmen), continuous (transfers), 12/15 (early decision).

Freshman Application Contact Mr. Brian Grant, Director of Admission, Clarkson University, Holcroft House, Potsdam, NY 13699-5605. *Phone:* 315-268-6480. *Toll-free phone:* 800-527-6577. *Fax:* 315-268-7647. *E-mail:* admission@clarkson.edu.

See page 1706 for the College Close-Up.

COLGATE UNIVERSITY

Hamilton, New York **www.colgate.edu/**

- **Independent** comprehensive, founded 1819
- **Rural** 515-acre campus
- **Coed** 2,780 undergraduate students, 99% full-time, 53% women, 47% men
- **Most difficult** entrance level, 26% of applicants were admitted

Undergraduates 2,747 full-time, 33 part-time. Students come from 40 states and territories, 33 other countries, 71% are from out of state, 0.8% transferred in, 93% live on campus. *Retention:* 94% of 2006 full-time freshmen returned.

Freshmen *Admission:* 8,759 applied, 2,242 admitted, 694 enrolled. *Average high school GPA:* 3.7. *Test scores:* SAT critical reading scores over 500: 98%; SAT math scores over 500: 98%; ACT scores over 18: 100%; SAT critical reading scores over 600: 85%; SAT math scores over 600: 86%; ACT scores over 24: 98%; SAT critical reading scores over 700: 38%; SAT math scores over 700: 36%; ACT scores over 30: 63%.

Faculty *Total:* 318, 80% full-time, 88% with terminal degrees. *Student/faculty ratio:* 10:1.

Majors African-American/Black studies; African studies; American Indian/Native American studies; anthropology; art; art history, criticism and conservation; Asian studies; Asian studies (East); astronomy; astrophysics; biochemistry; biology/biological sciences; chemistry; Chinese; classics and languages, literatures and linguistics; dramatic/theater arts; economics; education; English; environmental biology; environmental studies; French; geography; geology/earth science; German; history; humanities; international relations and affairs; Japanese; Latin; Latin American studies; mathematics; modern Greek; molecular biology; music; natural sciences; neuroscience; peace studies and conflict resolution; philosophy; physical sciences; physics; political science and government; psychology; religious studies; Romance languages; Russian; Russian studies; social sciences; sociology; Spanish; women's studies.

Academics *Calendar:* semesters. *Degrees:* bachelor's and master's. *Special study options:* advanced placement credit, double majors, honors programs, independent study, internships, off-campus study, services for LD students, student-designed majors, study abroad. *ROTC:* Army (c). *Unusual degree programs:* 3-2 engineering with Rensselaer Polytechnic Institute, Columbia University, Washington University in St. Louis.

Computers on Campus Students can access the following: campus intranet, computer help desk, free student e-mail accounts, online (class) registration, online (class) schedules, software applications. Campuswide network is available. 100% of college-owned or -operated housing units are wired for high-speed Internet access.

Student Life *Housing:* on-campus residence required through junior year. *Options:* coed, men-only, women-only, cooperative. Campus housing is university owned. Freshman campus housing is guaranteed. *Activities and organizations:* drama/theater group, student-run newspaper, radio and television station, choral group, Volunteer Colgate, student government, cultural/ethnic interest groups, student publications, Outdoor Education, national fraternities, national sororities. *Campus security:* 24-hour emergency response devices and patrols, student patrols, late-night transport/escort service, controlled dormitory access. *Student services:* health clinic, personal/psychological counseling, women's center, legal services.

Athletics Member NCAA. All Division I except football (Division I-AA). *Intercollegiate sports:* baseball M (c), basketball M (s)/W (s), cheerleading M (c)/W (c), crew M/W, cross-country running M/W, equestrian sports M (c)/W (c), fencing M (c)/W (c), field hockey W (s), golf M/W (c), ice hockey M (s)/W (s), lacrosse M (s)/W (s), rugby M (c)/W (c), sailing M (c)/W (c), skiing (downhill) M (c)/W (c), soccer M (s)/W (s), softball W (s), squash M (c)/W (c), swimming and diving M/W, table tennis M (c)/W (c), tennis M/W, track and field M/W, volleyball M (c)/W (s), water polo M (c)/W (c), wrestling M (c)/W (c). *Intramural sports:* basketball M/W, bowling M/W, football M/W, golf M/W, ice hockey M/W, racquetball M/W, riflery M/W, soccer M/W, softball M/W, squash M/W, tennis M/W, ultimate Frisbee M/W, volleyball M/W.

Standardized Tests *Required:* SAT or ACT (for admission).

Costs (2007–08) *Comprehensive fee:* $46,830 includes full-time tuition ($37,405), mandatory fees ($255), and room and board ($9170). Full-time tuition and fees vary according to course load. Part-time tuition: $4676 per course. Part-time tuition and fees vary according to course load. *College room only:* $4430. Room and board charges vary according to board plan and housing facility. *Payment plans:* tuition prepayment, installment, deferred payment. *Waivers:* employees or children of employees.

Financial Aid Of all full-time matriculated undergraduates who enrolled in 2007, 991 applied for aid, 951 were judged to have need, 951 had their need fully met. 502 Federal Work-Study jobs (averaging $2060). 299 state and other part-time jobs (averaging $2006). *Average percent of need met:* 100%. *Average financial aid package:* $34,659. *Average need-based loan:* $3102. *Average need-based gift aid:* $30,203. *Average indebtedness upon graduation:* $16,666. *Financial aid deadline:* 1/15.

Applying *Options:* electronic application, early decision, deferred entrance. *Application fee:* $55. *Required:* essay or personal statement, high school transcript, 3 letters of recommendation. *Application deadlines:* 1/15 (freshmen), 3/15 (transfers). *Early decision deadline:* 11/15 (for plan 1), 1/15 (for plan 2). *Notification:* 4/1 (freshmen), 5/1 (transfers), 12/15 (early decision).

Freshman Application Contact Mr. Gary L. Ross, Dean of Admission, Colgate University, 13 Oak Drive, Hamilton, NY 13346-1383. *Phone:* 315-228-7401. *Fax:* 315-228-7544. *E-mail:* admission@mail.colgate.edu.

THE COLLEGE AT BROCKPORT, STATE UNIVERSITY OF NEW YORK

Brockport, New York **www.brockport.edu/**

- **State-supported** comprehensive, founded 1867, part of State University of New York System
- **Small-town** 435-acre campus with easy access to Rochester
- **Endowment** $4.9 million
- **Coed** 6,926 undergraduate students, 90% full-time, 57% women, 43% men
- **Moderately difficult** entrance level, 42% of applicants were admitted

Undergraduates 6,257 full-time, 669 part-time. Students come from 29 states and territories, 21 other countries, 1% are from out of state, 6% African American, 1% Asian American or Pacific Islander, 3% Hispanic American, 0.4% Native American, 0.8% international, 13% transferred in, 40% live on campus. *Retention:* 84% of 2006 full-time freshmen returned.

Freshmen *Admission:* 8,522 applied, 3,571 admitted, 1,038 enrolled. *Average high school GPA:* 3.47. *Test scores:* SAT critical reading scores over 500: 77%; SAT math scores over 500: 67%; SAT writing scores over 500: 56%; ACT scores over 18: 96%; SAT critical reading scores over 600: 25%; SAT math scores over 600: 16%; SAT writing scores over 600: 13%; ACT scores over 24: 45%; SAT critical reading scores over 700: 2%; SAT math scores over 700: 2%; SAT writing scores over 700: 1%; ACT scores over 30: 2%.

Faculty *Total:* 573, 55% full-time, 60% with terminal degrees. *Student/faculty ratio:* 18:1.

Majors Accounting; acting; African-American/Black studies; African studies; American literature; anthropology; art; Asian studies; astronomy; athletic training; atmospheric sciences and meteorology; bilingual, multilingual, and multicultural education related; biochemistry; biology/biological sciences; biology/biotechnology laboratory technician; biology teacher education; biotechnology; broadcast journalism; business administration and management; cell and molecular biology; cell biology and histology; ceramic arts and ceramics; chemistry; chemistry teacher education; clinical laboratory science/medical technology; communication and journalism related; communication and media related; communication/speech communication and rhetoric; computer science; corrections; corrections and criminal justice related; creative writing; criminal justice/law enforcement administration; criminal justice/police science; criminology; dance; dramatic/theater arts; drawing; early childhood education; economics; education; elementary education; English; English/language arts teacher education; environmental biology; environmental studies; European studies; exercise physiology; finance; fine/studio arts; foreign language teacher education; French; French language teacher education; geological and earth sciences/geosciences related; geology/earth science; health and physical education; health and physical education related; health/health care administration; health science; health teacher education; history; history teacher education; hydrology and water resources science; interdisciplinary studies; international business/trade/commerce; international relations and affairs; journalism; kinesiology and exercise science; Latin American studies; literature; marketing/marketing management; mass communication/media; mathematics; mathematics teacher education; metal and jewelry arts; meteorology; middle school education; molecular biology; nursing (registered nurse training); organizational communication; painting; parks, recreation and leisure; parks, recreation, and leisure related; philosophy; physical education teaching and coaching; physics; physics related; physics teacher education; political science and government; pre-dentistry studies; pre-law studies; premedical studies; pre-veterinary studies; psychology; public relations, advertising, and applied communication related; public relations/image management; radio and television; radio, television, and digital communication related; science teacher education; sculpture; secondary education; securities services administration; social studies teacher education; social work; sociology; Spanish; Spanish language teacher education; speech and rhetoric; sport and fitness administration/management; substance abuse/addiction counseling; therapeutic recreation; women's studies.

Academics *Calendar:* semesters. *Degrees:* bachelor's, master's, post-master's, and postbachelor's certificates. *Special study options:* academic remediation for entering students, accelerated degree program, advanced placement credit, cooperative education, distance learning, double majors, freshman honors college, honors programs, independent study, internships, off-campus study, part-time degree program, services for LD students, student-designed majors, study abroad, summer session for credit. *ROTC:* Army (b), Navy (c), Air Force (c).

Computers on Campus 700 computers/terminals and 100 ports are available on campus for general student use. Students can access the following: campus intranet, computer help desk, free student e-mail accounts, online (class) grades, online (class) registration, online (class) schedules. Campuswide network is available. 100% of college-owned or -operated housing units are wired for high-speed Internet access. Wireless service is available via entire campus.

Student Life *Housing:* on-campus residence required for freshman year. *Options:* coed, disabled students. Campus housing is university owned. Freshman campus housing is guaranteed. *Activities and organizations:* drama/theater group, student-run newspaper, radio and television station, choral group, Fine arts clubs, Organization for Students of African Descent, Communication Club, Student radio station, Sports clubs, national fraternities, national sororities. *Campus security:* 24-hour emergency response devices and patrols, student patrols, late-night transport/escort service, controlled dormitory access. *Student services:* health clinic, personal/psychological counseling, women's center, legal services.

Athletics Member NCAA. All Division III. *Intercollegiate sports:* baseball M, basketball M/W, cross-country running M/W, field hockey W, football M, gymnastics W, ice hockey M, lacrosse M/W, soccer M/W, softball W, swimming and diving M/W, tennis W, track and field M/W, volleyball W, wrestling M. *Intramural sports:* badminton M/W, basketball M/W, bowling M/W, cheerleading M/W, football M/W, golf M (c), ice hockey W (c), racquetball M/W, rugby M/W, soccer M/W, softball M/W, table tennis M/W, tennis M/W, ultimate Frisbee M/W, volleyball M/W.

Standardized Tests *Required:* SAT or ACT (for admission).

Costs (2008–09) *Tuition:* state resident $4350 full-time; nonresident $10,610 full-time. *Required fees:* $1092 full-time. *Room and board:* $8597; room only: $5682.

Financial Aid Of all full-time matriculated undergraduates who enrolled in 2004, 4,520 applied for aid, 3,576 were judged to have need, 1,110 had their need fully met. 636 Federal Work-Study jobs (averaging $1280). 1,392 state and other part-time jobs (averaging $1378). In 2004, 126 non-need-based awards were made. *Average percent of need met:* 80%. *Average financial aid package:* $8403. *Average need-based loan:* $4551. *Average need-based gift aid:* $3658. *Average non-need-based aid:* $4363. *Average indebtedness upon graduation:* $19,082.

Applying *Options:* electronic application, deferred entrance. *Application fee:* $40. *Required:* high school transcript. *Required for some:* letters of recommendation, interview. *Recommended:* essay or personal statement, minimum 3.1 GPA, letters of recommendation. *Application deadlines:* rolling (freshmen), 8/1 (transfers). *Notification:* continuous (freshmen), continuous (transfers).

Freshman Application Contact Mr. Bernard Valento, Director of Undergraduate Admissions, The College at Brockport, State University of New York, 350 New Campus Drive, Brockport, NY 14420-2997. *Phone:* 585-395-2751. *Fax:* 585-395-5452. *E-mail:* admit@brockport.edu.

COLLEGE OF MOUNT SAINT VINCENT

Riverdale, New York **www.mountsaintvincent.edu/**

- **Independent** comprehensive, founded 1911
- **Suburban** 70-acre campus with easy access to New York City
- **Endowment** $7.3 million
- **Coed** 1,519 undergraduate students, 86% full-time, 73% women, 27% men
- **Moderately difficult** entrance level, 71% of applicants were admitted

Undergraduates 1,308 full-time, 211 part-time. Students come from 24 states and territories, 3 other countries, 13% are from out of state, 11% African American, 11% Asian American or Pacific Islander, 30% Hispanic American, 0.1% Native American, 0.5% international, 5% transferred in, 57% live on campus. *Retention:* 77% of 2006 full-time freshmen returned.

Freshmen *Admission:* 2,092 applied, 1,486 admitted, 394 enrolled. *Test scores:* SAT critical reading scores over 500: 44%; SAT math scores over 500: 38%; SAT critical reading scores over 600: 8%; SAT math scores over 600: 6%; SAT math scores over 700: 1%.

Faculty *Total:* 185, 39% full-time, 50% with terminal degrees. *Student/faculty ratio:* 14:1.

Majors Biochemistry; biology/biological sciences; business/managerial economics; chemistry; economics; education; elementary education; English; French; history; liberal arts and sciences/liberal studies; mass communication/media; mathematics; modern languages; nursing (registered nurse training); philosophy; pre-dentistry studies; pre-law studies; pre-medical studies; psychology; religious studies; social sciences; sociology; Spanish; urban studies/affairs.

Academics *Calendar:* semesters. *Degrees:* certificates, associate, bachelor's, master's, and post-master's certificates. *Special study options:* academic remediation for entering students, accelerated degree program, adult/continuing education programs, advanced placement credit, double majors, English as a second language, freshman honors college, honors programs, independent study, internships, off-campus study, part-time degree program, services for LD students, student-designed majors, study abroad, summer session for credit. *Unusual degree programs:* 3-2 occupational therapy with Columbia University, physical therapy with New York Medical College.

Computers on Campus 200 computers/terminals are available on campus for general student use. Students can access the following: campus intranet, computer help desk, free student e-mail accounts, online (class) grades, online (class) registration, online (class) schedules. Campuswide network is available. 100% of college-owned or -operated housing units are wired for high-speed Internet access. Wireless service is available via libraries.

Student Life *Housing options:* coed, women-only, disabled students. Campus housing is university owned. Freshman campus housing is guaranteed. *Activities and organizations:* drama/theater group, student-run newspaper, radio and television station, choral group, Casa Latina, Players, Dance Club, Student Nurse Association. *Campus security:* 24-hour emergency response devices and patrols, late-night transport/escort service, controlled dormitory access, emergency call boxes. *Student services:* health clinic, personal/psychological counseling.

Athletics Member NCAA. All Division III. *Intercollegiate sports:* baseball M, basketball M/W, cheerleading W, cross-country running M/W, lacrosse M/W, soccer M/W, softball W, swimming and diving W, tennis M/W, track and field W, volleyball M/W. *Intramural sports:* basketball M/W, football M/W, soccer M/W, track and field W, volleyball M/W.

Standardized Tests *Required:* SAT or ACT (for admission).

Costs (2008–09) *Comprehensive fee:* $33,870 includes full-time tuition ($23,170), mandatory fees ($1330), and room and board ($9370). Part-time tuition: $700 per credit. *Required fees:* $200 per term part-time.

Financial Aid Of all full-time matriculated undergraduates who enrolled in 2004, 1,019 applied for aid, 881 were judged to have need. *Average percent of need met:* 74%. *Average financial aid package:* $17,000. *Average need-based loan:* $4100. *Average need-based gift aid:* $7500. *Average indebtedness upon graduation:* $17,000.

Applying *Options:* electronic application, early admission, early decision, deferred entrance. *Application fee:* $35. *Required:* essay or personal statement, high school transcript, minimum 2.0 GPA, 1 letter of recommendation. *Required for some:* interview. *Recommended:* 2 letters of recommendation, interview. *Application deadlines:* rolling (freshmen), rolling (transfers), 11/15 (early action). *Notification:* continuous (freshmen), continuous (transfers), 12/1 (early action).

Freshman Application Contact Mr. Roland Pinzon, Director of Admissions, College of Mount Saint Vincent, 6301 Riverdale Avenue, Riverdale, NY 10471-1093. *Phone:* 718-405-3268. *Toll-free phone:* 800-665-CMSV. *Fax:* 718-549-7945. *E-mail:* roland.pinzon@mountsaintvincent.edu.

See page 1708 for the College Close-Up.

THE COLLEGE OF NEW ROCHELLE

New Rochelle, New York **cnr.edu/**

- **Independent** comprehensive, founded 1904
- **Suburban** 20-acre campus with easy access to New York City
- **Coed, primarily women** 1,011 undergraduate students, 11% full-time, 12% women, 1% men
- **Moderately difficult** entrance level, 43% of applicants were admitted

Undergraduates 116 full-time, 12 part-time. Students come from 14 states and territories, 10 other countries, 12% are from out of state, 33% African American, 4% Asian American or Pacific Islander, 14% Hispanic American, 0.6% Native American, 0.5% international, 14% transferred in, 37% live on campus. *Retention:* 71% of 2006 full-time freshmen returned.

Freshmen *Admission:* 1,784 applied, 765 admitted, 128 enrolled. *Average high school GPA:* 3.25. *Test scores:* SAT critical reading scores over 500: 94%; SAT math scores over 500: 95%; SAT critical reading scores over 600: 53%; SAT math scores over 600: 53%; SAT critical reading scores over 700: 1%; SAT math scores over 700: 1%.

Faculty *Total:* 232, 38% full-time. *Student/faculty ratio:* 12:1.

Majors Art history, criticism and conservation; art teacher education; art therapy; biology/biological sciences; broadcast journalism; business administration and management; chemistry; classics and languages, literatures and linguistics; economics; education; elementary education; English; environmental studies; fine/studio arts; foreign languages related; French; history; international/global studies; Latin; liberal arts and sciences/liberal studies; mass communication/media; mathematics; multi-/interdisciplinary studies related; nursing (registered nurse training); philosophy; physics; political science and government; pre-law studies; pre-medical studies; psychology; religious studies; social work; sociology; Spanish; special education; women's studies.

Academics *Calendar:* semesters. *Degrees:* bachelor's, master's, post-master's, and postbachelor's certificates (also offers a non-traditional adult program with significant enrollment not reflected in profile). *Special study options:* academic remediation for entering students, accelerated degree program, adult/continuing education programs, advanced placement credit, cooperative education, double majors, honors programs, independent study, internships, off-campus study, part-time degree program, services for LD students, student-designed majors, study abroad, summer session for credit.

Computers on Campus 120 computers/terminals are available on campus for general student use. Students can access the following: campus intranet, computer help desk, free student e-mail accounts, online (class) registration. Campuswide network is available. 100% of college-owned or -operated housing units are wired for high-speed Internet access. Wireless service is available via entire campus.

Student Life *Housing options:* women-only. Campus housing is university owned. Freshman campus housing is guaranteed. *Activities and organizations:* drama/theater group, student-run newspaper, choral group, Drama Club, Science and Math Society, Latin-American Women's Society. *Campus security:* 24-hour emergency response devices and patrols, late-night transport/escort service, controlled dormitory access, 24-hour monitored security cameras at residence hall entrances. *Student services:* health clinic, personal/psychological counseling, women's center.

Athletics Member NCAA. All Division III. *Intercollegiate sports:* basketball W, cross-country running W, softball W, swimming and diving W, tennis W, volleyball W.

Standardized Tests *Required:* SAT or ACT (for admission).

Costs (2007–08) *Comprehensive fee:* $32,400 includes full-time tuition ($23,200), mandatory fees ($500), and room and board ($8700). Full-time tuition and fees vary according to course load and program. Part-time tuition: $781 per credit. Part-time tuition and fees vary according to course load. *Required fees:* $90 per term part-time. *Room and board:* Room and board charges vary according to housing facility. *Payment plan:* installment. *Waivers:* senior citizens and employees or children of employees.

Financial Aid Of all full-time matriculated undergraduates who enrolled in 2006, 610 applied for aid, 578 were judged to have need, 97 had their need fully met. 455 Federal Work-Study jobs (averaging $2376). In 2006, 58 non-need-based awards were made. *Average percent of need met:* 78%. *Average financial aid package:* $19,219. *Average need-based loan:* $4815. *Average need-based gift aid:* $10,382. *Average non-need-based aid:* $13,115. *Average indebtedness upon graduation:* $25,288.

Applying *Options:* early admission, early decision, deferred entrance. *Application fee:* $20. *Required:* high school transcript. *Recommended:* essay or personal statement, 1 letter of recommendation, interview. *Application deadlines:* rolling (freshmen), rolling (transfers). *Early decision deadline:* 11/1. *Notification:* continuous (freshmen), continuous (transfers), 12/15 (early decision).

Freshman Application Contact Ms. Stephanie Decker, Director of Admission, The College of New Rochelle, 29 Castle Place, New Rochelle, NY 10805-2339. *Phone:* 914-654-5452. *Toll-free phone:* 800-933-5923. *Fax:* 914-654-5464. *E-mail:* admission@cnr.edu.

See page 1710 for the College Close-Up.

THE COLLEGE OF SAINT ROSE

Albany, New York **www.strose.edu/**

- **Independent** comprehensive, founded 1920
- **Urban** 28-acre campus
- **Endowment** $18.8 million
- **Coed** 3,165 undergraduate students, 93% full-time, 71% women, 29% men
- **Moderately difficult** entrance level, 67% of applicants were admitted

Undergraduates 2,933 full-time, 232 part-time. Students come from 20 states and territories, 7% are from out of state, 3% African American, 1% Asian American or Pacific Islander, 4% Hispanic American, 0.3% Native American, 9% transferred in, 36% live on campus. *Retention:* 82% of 2006 full-time freshmen returned.

Freshmen *Admission:* 3,842 applied, 2,558 admitted, 624 enrolled. *Average high school GPA:* 3.6. *Test scores:* SAT critical reading scores over 500: 64%; SAT math scores over 500: 66%; ACT scores over 18: 100%; SAT critical reading scores over 600: 19%; SAT math scores over 600: 22%; ACT scores over 24: 49%; SAT critical reading scores over 700: 1%; SAT math scores over 700: 4%; ACT scores over 30: 10%.

Faculty *Total:* 481, 41% full-time. *Student/faculty ratio:* 14:1.

Majors Accounting; American studies; art teacher education; audiology and speech-language pathology; biochemistry; biology/biological sciences; biology teacher education; business administration and management; cell biology and histology; chemistry; chemistry teacher education; clinical laboratory science/medical technology; commercial and advertising art; communication disorders; communication/speech communication and rhetoric; communications technology; computer and information sciences; criminal justice/law enforcement administration; cytotechnology; elementary education; English; English/language arts teacher education; environmental studies; fine/studio arts; history; information science/studies; interdisciplinary studies; liberal arts and sciences/liberal studies; mathematics; mathematics teacher education; music; music teacher education; political science and government; psychology; religious studies; social studies teacher education; social work; sociology; Spanish; Spanish language teacher education; special education; trade and industrial teacher education.

Academics *Calendar:* semesters. *Degrees:* bachelor's, master's, post-master's, and postbachelor's certificates. *Special study options:* academic remediation for entering students, accelerated degree program, adult/continuing education programs, advanced placement credit, double majors, external degree program, independent study, internships, off-campus study, part-time degree program, services for LD students, student-designed majors, study abroad, summer session for credit. *Unusual degree programs:* 3-2 engineering with Alfred University, Clarkson University, Union College (NY), Rensselaer Polytechnic Institute.

Computers on Campus 322 computers/terminals are available on campus for general student use. Students can access the following: online (class) registration. Campuswide network is available.

Student Life *Housing options:* coed, men-only, women-only. Campus housing is university owned. Freshman applicants given priority for college housing. *Activities and organizations:* drama/theater group, student-run newspaper, radio and television station, choral group, Student Association, Student Events Board, Circle K, Student Education Association, Student Speech, Hearing and Language Association. *Campus security:* 24-hour emergency response devices and patrols, student patrols, late-night transport/escort service, controlled dormitory access. *Student services:* health clinic, personal/psychological counseling.

Athletics Member NCAA. All Division II. *Intercollegiate sports:* baseball M (s), basketball M (s)/W (s), cross-country running M (s)/W (s), soccer M (s)/W (s), softball W (s), swimming and diving M (s)/W (s), volleyball W (s). *Intramural sports:* basketball M/W, soccer M/W, softball W, volleyball M/W.

Standardized Tests *Required:* SAT or ACT (for admission).

Costs (2007–08) *Comprehensive fee:* $28,518 includes full-time tuition ($19,960) and room and board ($8558).

Financial Aid Of all full-time matriculated undergraduates who enrolled in 2006, 2,658 applied for aid, 2,244 were judged to have need, 89 had their need fully met. In 2006, 272 non-need-based awards were made. *Average percent of need met:* 47%. *Average financial aid package:* $7945. *Average need-based loan:* $1926. *Average need-based gift aid:* $3408. *Average non-need-based aid:* $1720. *Average indebtedness upon graduation:* $24,920.

Applying *Options:* electronic application, early admission, early action, deferred entrance. *Application fee:* $35. *Required:* essay or personal statement, high school transcript, 1 letter of recommendation. *Required for some:* interview. *Recommended:* minimum 3.0 GPA, interview. *Application deadlines:* 5/1 (freshmen), 5/1 (transfers), 12/1 (early action). *Notification:* continuous (freshmen), continuous (transfers), 12/15 (early action).

Freshman Application Contact Ms. Mary Elizabeth Amico, Director of Undergraduate Admissions, The College of Saint Rose, 432 Western Avenue, Albany, NY 12203. *Phone:* 518-454-5150. *Toll-free phone:* 800-637-8556. *E-mail:* admit@strose.edu.

See page 1712 for the College Close-Up.

COLLEGE OF STATEN ISLAND OF THE CITY UNIVERSITY OF NEW YORK

Staten Island, New York **www.csi.cuny.edu/**

- **State and locally supported** comprehensive, founded 1955, part of City University of New York System
- **Urban** 204-acre campus with easy access to New York City
- **Endowment** $4.9 million
- **Coed** 11,588 undergraduate students, 70% full-time, 60% women, 40% men
- **Moderately difficult** entrance level, 100% of applicants were admitted

Undergraduates 8,096 full-time, 3,492 part-time. Students come from 32 states and territories, 109 other countries, 0.6% are from out of state, 8% African American, 8% Asian American or Pacific Islander, 11% Hispanic American, 0.1% Native American, 3% international, 6% transferred in. *Retention:* 82% of 2006 full-time freshmen returned.

Freshmen *Admission:* 7,399 applied, 7,399 admitted, 2,478 enrolled. *Average high school GPA:* 2.97. *Test scores:* SAT critical reading scores over 500: 50%; SAT math scores over 500: 56%; SAT writing scores over 500: 46%; SAT critical reading scores over 600: 12%; SAT math scores over 600: 14%; SAT writing scores over 600: 10%; SAT critical reading scores over 700: 2%; SAT math scores over 700: 1%; SAT writing scores over 700: 1%.

Faculty *Total:* 881, 39% full-time, 50% with terminal degrees. *Student/faculty ratio:* 18:1.

Majors Accounting; African-American/Black studies; American studies; architectural technology; biochemistry; biology/biological sciences; business/commerce; chemistry; cinematography and film/video production; clinical laboratory science/medical technology; clinical/medical laboratory technology; communication/speech communication and rhetoric; computer and information sciences and support services related; computer programming; dramatic/theater arts; economics; electrical, electronic and communications engineering technology; engineering; English; fine arts related; history; information science/studies; international relations and affairs; liberal arts and sciences/liberal studies; mathematics; music; nursing (registered nurse training); nursing related; philosophy; physics; political science and government; psychology; social work; sociology; Spanish; women's studies.

Academics *Calendar:* semesters. *Degrees:* associate, bachelor's, master's, doctoral, and post-master's certificates. *Special study options:* academic remediation for entering students, accelerated degree program, adult/continuing education programs, advanced placement credit, cooperative education, distance learning, double majors, English as a second language, freshman honors college, honors programs, independent study, internships, off-campus study, part-time degree program, services for LD students, student-designed majors, study abroad, summer session for credit.

Computers on Campus 1,000 computers/terminals and 1,000 ports are available on campus for general student use. Students can access the following: campus intranet, computer help desk, free student e-mail accounts, online (class) grades, online (class) registration, online (class) schedules. Campuswide network is available. Wireless service is available via entire campus.

Student Life *Housing:* college housing not available. *Activities and organizations:* drama/theater group, student-run newspaper, radio station, choral group, Latin Club, Spanish Club, South Asian Student Association, Apostolic Christian Life Center. *Campus security:* 24-hour emergency response devices and patrols, late-night transport/escort service, emergency call boxes, blue light system, bicycle patrols, radar-controlled traffic monitoring, lighted pathways. *Student services:* health clinic, personal/psychological counseling, women's center.

Athletics Member NCAA. All Division III. *Intercollegiate sports:* baseball M, basketball M/W, cross-country running M/W, soccer M/W, softball W, swimming and diving M/W, tennis M/W, volleyball W. *Intramural sports:* badminton M/W, basketball M/W, football M/W, racquetball M/W, soccer M/W, softball M/W, table tennis M/W, tennis M/W, track and field M/W, volleyball M/W.

Standardized Tests *Recommended:* SAT or ACT (for admission).

Costs (2007–08) *Tuition:* state resident $4000 full-time, $170 per credit part-time; nonresident $8640 full-time, $360 per credit part-time. Full-time tuition and fees vary according to course load. Part-time tuition and fees vary according to course load. *Required fees:* $328 full-time, $101 per term part-time. *Payment plan:* installment. *Waivers:* senior citizens and employees or children of employees.

Financial Aid Of all full-time matriculated undergraduates who enrolled in 2006, 5,715 applied for aid, 4,280 were judged to have need, 88 had their need fully met. 337 Federal Work-Study jobs (averaging $1300). In 2006, 469 non-need-based awards were made. *Average percent of need met:* 59%. *Average financial aid package:* $8194. *Average need-based loan:* $3714. *Average need-based gift aid:* $5355. *Average non-need-based aid:* $2000.

Applying *Options:* electronic application, deferred entrance. *Application fee:* $65. *Required:* high school transcript, minimum 2.0 GPA. *Required for some:* essay or personal statement, letters of recommendation, interview. *Application deadlines:* rolling (freshmen), rolling (transfers). *Notification:* 12/15 (freshmen), continuous (transfers).

Freshman Application Contact College of Staten Island of the City University of New York, 2800 Victory Boulevard, Building 2A Room 404, Staten Island, NY 10314. *Phone:* 718-982-2010. *Fax:* 713-982-2500. *E-mail:* admissions@mail.cuny.csi.edu.

See page 1714 for the College Close-Up.

COLUMBIA UNIVERSITY

New York, New York **www.columbia.edu/**

- **Independent** 4-year, founded 1754, part of Columbia University
- **Endowment** $7.2 billion
- **Coed** 5,602 undergraduate students, 100% full-time, 46% women, 54% men
- **Most difficult** entrance level, 11% of applicants were admitted

Undergraduates 5,602 full-time. Students come from 53 states and territories, 66 other countries, 75% are from out of state, 9% African American, 18% Asian American or Pacific Islander, 10% Hispanic American, 0.7% Native American, 9% international, 1% transferred in, 94% live on campus. *Retention:* 97% of 2006 full-time freshmen returned.

Freshmen *Admission:* 21,343 applied, 2,255 admitted, 1,333 enrolled. *Test scores:* SAT critical reading scores over 500: 100%; SAT math scores over 500: 100%; SAT writing scores over 500: 99%; ACT scores over 18: 100%; SAT critical reading scores over 600: 92%; SAT math scores over 600: 94%; SAT writing scores over 600: 91%; ACT scores over 24: 98%; SAT critical reading scores over 700: 60%; SAT math scores over 700: 63%; SAT writing scores over 700: 58%; ACT scores over 30: 65%.

Faculty *Total:* 1,057, 75% full-time. *Student/faculty ratio:* 6:1.

Academics *Calendar:* semesters. *Degrees:* bachelor's, master's, and doctoral.

Computers on Campus 400 computers/terminals are available on campus for general student use. Students can access the following: campus intranet, computer help desk, free student e-mail accounts, online (class) grades, online (class) registration, online (class) schedules. Campuswide network is available.

Student Life *Housing:* on-campus residence required for freshman year. *Options:* coed, men-only, women-only, disabled students. Campus housing is university owned. Freshman campus housing is guaranteed. *Activities and organizations:* drama/theater group, student-run newspaper, radio and television station, choral group, marching band, community service, cultural organizations, performing arts, national fraternities, national sororities. *Student services:* health clinic, personal/psychological counseling, women's center.

Athletics Member NCAA. All Division I except football (Division I-AA). *Intercollegiate sports:* archery M (c)/W, badminton M (c)/W (c), baseball M, basketball M/W, crew M/W, cross-country running M/W, fencing M/W, field hockey W, golf M, ice hockey W (c), lacrosse M (c)/W, racquetball M (c)/W (c), riflery M (c)/W (c), rugby M (c)/W (c), skiing (cross-country) M (c)/W (c), skiing (downhill) M (c)/W (c), soccer M (c)/W (c), softball W, squash M (c)/W (c), swimming and diving M/W, table tennis M (c)/W (c), tennis M (c)/W (c), track and field M/W, ultimate Frisbee M (c)/W (c), volleyball M (c)/W (c), water polo M (c)/W (c), wrestling M. *Intramural sports:* archery W (c), badminton M/W, basketball M (c)/W (c), cross-country running M (c)/W (c), field hockey W, lacrosse W (c), racquetball M/W, soccer M/W, softball M/W, squash M/W, swimming and diving M/W, tennis M/W, volleyball M/W, water polo W.

Standardized Tests *Required:* SAT and SAT Subject Tests or ACT (for admission).

Costs (2007–08) *Comprehensive fee:* $47,153 includes full-time tuition ($35,516), mandatory fees ($1700), and room and board ($9937).

Applying *Options:* electronic application, early admission, early decision, deferred entrance. *Application fee:* $65. *Required:* essay or personal statement, high school transcript, 3 letters of recommendation. *Application deadlines:* 1/2 (freshmen), 3/15 (transfers). *Early decision deadline:* 11/1. *Notification:* 4/1 (freshmen), 5/15 (transfers), 12/15 (early decision).

Director of Admissions Ms. Jessica Marinaccio, Dean of Undergraduate Admissions, Columbia University, 116th Street and Broadway, New York, NY 10027.

See page 1716 for the College Close-Up.

COLUMBIA UNIVERSITY, SCHOOL OF GENERAL STUDIES

New York, New York **www.gs.columbia.edu/**

- **Independent** 4-year, founded 1754, part of Columbia University
- **Urban** 36-acre campus
- **Endowment** $6.2 billion
- **Coed**
- **Most difficult** entrance level

Faculty *Student/faculty ratio:* 7:1.

Academics *Calendar:* semesters. *Degrees:* bachelor's and postbachelor's certificates.

Student Life *Campus security:* 24-hour emergency response devices and patrols, late-night transport/escort service.

Athletics Member NCAA. All Division I except football (Division I-AA).

Standardized Tests *Required:* SAT or ACT (for admission). Applicants may also take the General Studies Admissions Exam (for admission). *Recommended:* SAT and SAT Subject Tests or ACT (for admission), SAT Subject Tests (for admission).

Costs (2007–08) *Comprehensive fee:* $47,792 includes full-time tuition ($34,380), mandatory fees ($1508), and room and board ($11,904). Full-time tuition and fees vary according to course load. Part-time tuition: $1146 per credit.

Part-time tuition and fees vary according to course load. *College room only:* $8618. Room and board charges vary according to board plan and housing facility. *Payment plans:* tuition prepayment, installment.

Financial Aid *Financial aid deadline:* 6/1.

Applying *Options:* electronic application, deferred entrance. *Application fee:* $65. *Required:* essay or personal statement, high school transcript, letters of recommendation, General Studies Admissions Exam. *Required for some:* interview.

Freshman Application Contact Mr. Curtis M. Rodgers, Dean of Admissions, Enrollment Management, and Communications, Columbia University, School of General Studies, Mail Code 4101, Lewisohn Hall, 2970 Broadway, New York, NY 10027-9829. *Phone:* 212-854-2772. *Toll-free phone:* 800-895-1169. *Fax:* 212-854-6316. *E-mail:* gsdegree@columbia.edu.

See page 1718 for the College Close-Up.

CONCORDIA COLLEGE–NEW YORK

Bronxville, New York **www.concordia-ny.edu/**

- **Independent Lutheran**, 4-year, founded 1881, part of Concordia University System
- **Suburban** 33-acre campus with easy access to New York City
- **Endowment** $6.4 million
- **Coed** 748 undergraduate students, 86% full-time, 62% women, 38% men
- **Moderately difficult** entrance level, 67% of applicants were admitted

Undergraduates 643 full-time, 105 part-time. Students come from 46 states and territories, 35 other countries, 29% are from out of state, 11% African American, 0.4% Asian American or Pacific Islander, 8% Hispanic American, 0.4% Native American, 10% international, 6% transferred in, 68% live on campus. *Retention:* 73% of 2006 full-time freshmen returned.

Freshmen *Admission:* 682 applied, 455 admitted, 128 enrolled. *Average high school GPA:* 2.7. *Test scores:* SAT critical reading scores over 500: 36%; SAT math scores over 500: 40%; SAT writing scores over 500: 35%; ACT scores over 18: 66%; SAT critical reading scores over 600: 8%; SAT math scores over 600: 9%; SAT writing scores over 600: 6%; ACT scores over 24: 21%; SAT critical reading scores over 700: 1%; SAT math scores over 700: 1%; ACT scores over 30: 3%.

Faculty *Total:* 77, 43% full-time, 79% with terminal degrees. *Student/faculty ratio:* 12:1.

Majors Administrative assistant and secretarial science; biology/biological sciences; business administration and management; early childhood education; ecology; education; elementary education; English; history; international relations and affairs; liberal arts and sciences/liberal studies; mathematics; middle school education; music; pre-law studies; religious/sacred music; religious studies; science teacher education; secondary education; social sciences; social work.

Academics *Calendar:* semesters. *Degrees:* associate and bachelor's. *Special study options:* academic remediation for entering students, accelerated degree program, adult/continuing education programs, advanced placement credit, distance learning, double majors, English as a second language, honors programs, independent study, internships, off-campus study, part-time degree program, services for LD students, student-designed majors, study abroad.

Computers on Campus 50 computers/terminals are available on campus for general student use. Students can access the following: campus intranet, computer help desk, free student e-mail accounts, online (class) grades, online (class) registration, online (class) schedules. Campuswide network is available. Wireless service is available via entire campus.

Student Life *Housing options:* men-only, women-only. Campus housing is university owned. Freshman campus housing is guaranteed. *Activities and organizations:* drama/theater group, student-run newspaper, choral group, Campus Christian Ministries, Drama Club, Student Government Association, International and Afro/Latin American Club, yearbook and newspaper, national fraternities, national sororities. *Campus security:* 24-hour emergency response devices and patrols, late-night transport/escort service, controlled dormitory access. *Student services:* health clinic, personal/psychological counseling.

Athletics Member NCAA. All Division II. *Intercollegiate sports:* baseball M (s), basketball M (s)/W (s), cross-country running M (s)/W (s), soccer M (s)/W (s), softball W (s), tennis M (s)/W (s), volleyball W (s). *Intramural sports:* basketball M/W, cheerleading W, equestrian sports W, racquetball M/W, squash M/W, table tennis M/W, tennis M/W, volleyball W.

Standardized Tests *Required:* SAT or ACT (for admission).

Costs (2007–08) *Comprehensive fee:* $30,970 includes full-time tuition ($21,950), mandatory fees ($500), and room and board ($8520). Part-time tuition: $612 per credit hour. Part-time tuition and fees vary according to course load. *College room only:* $4820. Room and board charges vary according to board plan. *Payment plan:* installment. *Waivers:* senior citizens and employees or children of employees.

Financial Aid Of all full-time matriculated undergraduates who enrolled in 2006, 533 applied for aid, 448 were judged to have need, 89 had their need fully met. In 2006, 100 non-need-based awards were made. *Average percent of need met:* 71%. *Average financial aid package:* $22,309. *Average need-based loan:* $4133. *Average need-based gift aid:* $11,129. *Average non-need-based aid:* $6170. *Average indebtedness upon graduation:* $24,153.

Applying *Options:* electronic application, early admission, early action, deferred entrance. *Application fee:* $50. *Required:* essay or personal statement, high school transcript, 1 letter of recommendation, common application supplement. *Required for some:* interview. *Recommended:* minimum 2.7 GPA. *Application deadlines:* 3/15 (freshmen), 7/15 (transfers), 11/15 (early action). *Notification:* continuous until 6/15 (freshmen), continuous until 8/15 (transfers), 12/1 (early action).

Freshman Application Contact Ms. Donna J. Hoyt, Dean of Enrollment, Concordia College–New York, Bronxville, NY 10708. *Phone:* 914-337-9300 Ext. 2149. *Toll-free phone:* 800-YES-COLLEGE. *Fax:* 914-395-4636. *E-mail:* admission@concordia-ny.edu.

See page 1720 for the College Close-Up.

COOPER UNION FOR THE ADVANCEMENT OF SCIENCE AND ART

New York, New York **www.cooper.edu/**

- **Independent** comprehensive, founded 1859
- **Urban** campus
- **Endowment** $601.1 million
- **Coed** 906 undergraduate students, 100% full-time, 37% women, 63% men
- **Most difficult** entrance level, 11% of applicants were admitted

Undergraduates 905 full-time, 1 part-time. Students come from 44 states and territories, 25 other countries, 40% are from out of state, 5% African American, 17% Asian American or Pacific Islander, 8% Hispanic American, 0.4% Native American, 16% international, 4% transferred in, 20% live on campus. *Retention:* 95% of 2006 full-time freshmen returned.

Freshmen *Admission:* 2,551 applied, 274 admitted, 219 enrolled. *Average high school GPA:* 3.6. *Test scores:* SAT critical reading scores over 500: 95%; SAT math scores over 500: 96%; SAT critical reading scores over 600: 84%; SAT math scores over 600: 86%; SAT critical reading scores over 700: 29%; SAT math scores over 700: 56%.

Faculty *Total:* 215, 23% full-time, 67% with terminal degrees. *Student/faculty ratio:* 8:1.

Majors Architecture; chemical engineering; civil engineering; electrical, electronics and communications engineering; engineering; fine/studio arts; mechanical engineering; visual and performing arts.

Academics *Calendar:* semesters. *Degrees:* certificates, bachelor's, and master's (also offers master's program primarily made up of currently-enrolled students). *Special study options:* advanced placement credit, honors programs, independent study, internships, off-campus study, student-designed majors, study abroad, summer session for credit.

Computers on Campus 400 computers/terminals are available on campus for general student use. Campuswide network is available. 100% of college-owned or -operated housing units are wired for high-speed Internet access.

Student Life *Housing options:* coed. Campus housing is university owned. Freshman applicants given priority for college housing. *Activities and organizations:* drama/theater group, student-run newspaper, choral group, Athletic Association, Chinese Students Association, Kesher, Campus Crusade for Christ, Muslim Students Organization, national fraternities, national sororities. *Campus security:* 24-hour emergency response devices and patrols, controlled dormitory access, security guards. *Student services:* personal/psychological counseling.

Athletics *Intercollegiate sports:* badminton M/W, basketball M, cross-country running M/W, football M, soccer M, table tennis M/W, tennis M/W, volleyball M/W. *Intramural sports:* basketball M/W, bowling M/W, fencing M/W, sailing M/W, skiing (downhill) M/W, soccer M, softball M/W, table tennis M/W, tennis M/W, ultimate Frisbee M/W, volleyball M/W.

Standardized Tests *Required:* SAT or ACT (for admission). *Required for some:* SAT and SAT Subject Tests or ACT (for admission).

Costs (2008–09) *Comprehensive fee:* includes mandatory fees ($1450) and room and board ($13,700). *College room only:* $9700.

Financial Aid Of all full-time matriculated undergraduates who enrolled in 2006, 386 applied for aid, 279 were judged to have need, 185 had their need fully met. 40 Federal Work-Study jobs (averaging $1001). 428 state and other part-time jobs (averaging $844). In 2006, 621 non-need-based awards were made. *Average percent of need met:* 93%. *Average financial aid package:* $30,000. *Average need-based loan:* $2810. *Average need-based gift aid:* $3087. *Average non-need-based aid:* $30,000. *Financial aid deadline:* 6/1.

Applying *Options:* electronic application, early admission, early decision, deferred entrance. *Application fee:* $65. *Required:* essay or personal statement, high school transcript, minimum 2.0 GPA, 2 letters of recommendation. *Required for some:* minimum 3.5 GPA, 3 letters of recommendation, interview, portfolio, home examination. *Recommended:* minimum 3.0 GPA. *Application deadlines:* 1/1 (freshmen), 1/1 (transfers). *Early decision deadline:* 12/1 (for plan 1), 12/1 (for plan 2). *Notification:* 4/1 (freshmen), 5/1 (transfers), 12/24 (early decision plan 1), 2/1 (early decision plan 2).

Freshman Application Contact Mr. Mitchell L. Lipton, Dean of Admissions and Records and Registrar, Cooper Union for the Advancement of Science and Art, 30 Cooper Square, New York, NY 10003. *Phone:* 212-353-4120. *Fax:* 212-353-4342. *E-mail:* admissions@cooper.edu.

CORNELL UNIVERSITY

Ithaca, New York **www.cornell.edu/**

- **Independent** university, founded 1865
- **Small-town** 745-acre campus with easy access to Syracuse
- **Endowment** $5.2 billion
- **Coed** 13,510 undergraduate students, 100% full-time, 49% women, 51% men
- **Most difficult** entrance level, 21% of applicants were admitted

Undergraduates 13,510 full-time. Students come from 58 states and territories, 76 other countries, 62% are from out of state, 5% African American, 16% Asian American or Pacific Islander, 6% Hispanic American, 0.5% Native American, 8% international, 4% transferred in, 46% live on campus. *Retention:* 96% of 2006 full-time freshmen returned.

Freshmen *Admission:* 30,383 applied, 6,503 admitted, 3,010 enrolled. *Test scores:* SAT critical reading scores over 500: 99%; SAT math scores over 500: 99%; ACT scores over 18: 100%; SAT critical reading scores over 600: 87%; SAT math scores over 600: 92%; ACT scores over 24: 95%; SAT critical reading scores over 700: 42%; SAT math scores over 700: 59%; ACT scores over 30: 57%.

Faculty *Total:* 1,910, 90% full-time, 90% with terminal degrees. *Student/faculty ratio:* 9:1.

Majors African-American/Black studies; agribusiness; agricultural and horticultural plant breeding; agricultural/biological engineering and bioengineering; agricultural business and management; agricultural economics; agricultural teacher education; agriculture; agronomy and crop science; American studies; animal genetics; animal physiology; animal sciences; anthropology; archeology; architecture; art history, criticism and conservation; Asian studies; astronomy; atmospheric sciences and meteorology; biochemistry; biological and biomedical sciences related; biology/biological sciences; biology teacher education; biometry/biometrics; chemical engineering; chemistry; chemistry teacher education; city/urban, community and regional planning; civil engineering; classics and languages, literatures and linguistics; communication/speech communication and rhetoric; community organization and advocacy; comparative literature; computer science; consumer economics; dance; dramatic/theater arts; ecology; economics; education; educational psychology; electrical, electronics and communications engineering; engineering; engineering physics; English; entomology; environmental design/architecture; environmental/environmental health engineering; environmental science; family and consumer sciences/home economics teacher education; family and consumer sciences/human sciences; fiber, textile and weaving arts; film/cinema studies; fine/studio arts; food science; foods, nutrition, and wellness; French; gay/lesbian studies; geology/earth science; German; German studies; history; horticultural science; hotel/motel administration; human development and family studies; human services; information technology; interdisciplinary studies; international agriculture; Italian; labor and industrial relations; landscape architecture; liberal arts and sciences/liberal studies; linguistics; materials engineering; mathematics; mathematics teacher education; mechanical engineering; microbiology; multi-/interdisciplinary studies related; music; natural resource economics; natural resources/conservation; Near and Middle Eastern studies; nutrition sciences; operations research; ornamental horticulture; philosophy; physics; physics teacher education; plant pathology/phytopathology; plant sciences; political science and government; pre-medical studies; psychology; public policy analysis; religious studies; restaurant/food services management; Russian; Russian studies; science teacher education; science, technology and society; social sciences; social sciences related; sociology; Spanish; theater design and technology; women's studies.

Academics *Calendar:* semesters. *Degrees:* bachelor's, master's, doctoral, and first professional. *Special study options:* academic remediation for entering students, accelerated degree program, advanced placement credit, cooperative education, distance learning, double majors, English as a second language, honors programs, independent study, internships, off-campus study, services for LD students, student-designed majors, study abroad, summer session for credit. *ROTC:* Army (b), Air Force (b). *Unusual degree programs:* 3-2 business administration; engineering; law.

Computers on Campus 2,650 computers/terminals and 1,000 ports are available on campus for general student use. Students can access the following: campus intranet, computer help desk, free student e-mail accounts, online (class) grades, online (class) registration. Campuswide network is available. 100% of college-owned or -operated housing units are wired for high-speed Internet access.

Student Life *Housing options:* coed, men-only, women-only, cooperative, disabled students. Campus housing is university owned. Freshman campus housing is guaranteed. *Activities and organizations:* drama/theater group, student-run newspaper, radio and television station, choral group, marching band, Student Assembly, Residence Hall Association, Catholic Community, Hillel, Concert Commission, national fraternities, national sororities. *Campus security:* 24-hour emergency response devices and patrols, late-night transport/escort service, controlled dormitory access, escort service. *Student services:* health clinic, personal/psychological counseling, women's center.

Athletics Member NCAA. All Division I except football (Division I-AA). *Intercollegiate sports:* baseball M, basketball M/W, crew M/W, cross-country running M/W, equestrian sports W, fencing W, field hockey W, golf M, gymnastics W, ice hockey M/W, lacrosse M/W, soccer M/W, softball W, squash M/W, swimming and diving M/W, tennis M/W, track and field M/W, volleyball W, wrestling M. *Intramural sports:* badminton M/W, basketball M/W, bowling M/W, cheerleading W (c), crew M (c)/W (c), cross-country running M/W, equestrian sports M (c)/W (c), fencing M/W, field hockey M (c)/W (c), football M/W, golf M/W, gymnastics M (c), ice hockey M/W, rock climbing M (c)/W (c), rugby M (c)/W (c), sailing M (c)/W (c), skiing (cross-country) M (c)/W (c), skiing (downhill) M/W, soccer M/W, softball M/W, squash M/W, table tennis M/W, tennis M/W, track and field M/W, ultimate Frisbee M (c), volleyball M/W, water polo M/W, wrestling M/W.

Standardized Tests *Required:* SAT or ACT (for admission). *Required for some:* SAT Subject Tests (for admission).

Costs (2007–08) *Comprehensive fee:* $45,971 includes full-time tuition ($34,600), mandatory fees ($181), and room and board ($11,190). *College room only:* $6680. Room and board charges vary according to board plan and housing facility. *Payment plan:* installment. *Waivers:* employees or children of employees.

Financial Aid Of all full-time matriculated undergraduates who enrolled in 2007, 6,026 applied for aid, 5,614 were judged to have need, 5,614 had their need fully met. *Average percent of need met:* 100%. *Average financial aid package:* $28,577. *Average need-based loan:* $5523. *Average need-based gift aid:* $20,492. *Average indebtedness upon graduation:* $23,936. *Financial aid deadline:* 2/11.

Applying *Options:* electronic application, early admission, early decision, deferred entrance. *Application fee:* $65. *Required:* essay or personal statement, high school transcript, 2 letters of recommendation. *Required for some:* interview. *Application deadlines:* 1/1 (freshmen), 3/15 (transfers). *Early decision deadline:* 11/1. *Notification:* 4/3 (freshmen), continuous until 6/15 (transfers), 12/15 (early decision).

Freshman Application Contact Mr. Jason Locke, Director of Undergraduate Admissions, Cornell University, 410 Thurston Avenue, Ithaca, NY 14850. *Phone:* 607-255-1446. *Fax:* 607-255-0659. *E-mail:* admissions@cornell.edu.

See page 1722 for the College Close-Up.

THE CULINARY INSTITUTE OF AMERICA

Hyde Park, New York **www.ciachef.edu/**

- **Independent** 4-year, founded 1946
- **Suburban** 170-acre campus
- **Endowment** $67.1 million
- **Coed**
- **Moderately difficult** entrance level

Faculty *Student/faculty ratio:* 18:1.

Academics *Calendar:* semesters plus 18 or 21 week externship program. *Degrees:* certificates, associate, and bachelor's.

Student Life *Campus security:* 24-hour emergency response devices and patrols, late-night transport/escort service, controlled dormitory access.

Standardized Tests *Recommended:* SAT or ACT (for admission).

Costs (2007–08) *Comprehensive fee:* $31,760 includes full-time tuition ($21,280), mandatory fees ($990), and room and board ($9490). Full-time tuition and fees vary according to degree level. *College room only:* $5170. Room and board charges vary according to housing facility.

Financial Aid Of all full-time matriculated undergraduates who enrolled in 2005, 2,604 applied for aid, 2,340 were judged to have need, 124 had their need fully met. 900 Federal Work-Study jobs (averaging $435). In 2005, 400 non-need-based awards were made. *Average percent of need met:* 42. *Average financial aid package:* $11,507. *Average need-based loan:* $3495. *Average need-based gift aid:* $3529. *Average non-need-based aid:* $2500. *Average indebtedness upon graduation:* $18,000. *Financial aid deadline:* 2/15.

Applying *Options:* electronic application, deferred entrance. *Application fee:* $50. *Required:* essay or personal statement, high school transcript, 2 letters of recommendation. *Required for some:* an Affidavit of Support.

Freshman Application Contact Ms. Rachel Birchwood, Director of Admissions, The Culinary Institute of America, 1946 Campus Drive, Hudson Hall, Hyde Park, NY 12538. *Phone:* 845-451-1459. *Toll-free phone:* 800-CULINARY. *Fax:* 845-451-1068. *E-mail:* admissions@culinary.edu.

See page 1724 for the College Close-Up.

DAEMEN COLLEGE

Amherst, New York **www.daemen.edu/**

- **Independent** comprehensive, founded 1947
- **Suburban** 35-acre campus with easy access to Buffalo
- **Endowment** $5.2 million
- **Coed** 1,674 undergraduate students, 81% full-time, 73% women, 27% men
- **Moderately difficult** entrance level, 68% of applicants were admitted

Undergraduates 1,360 full-time, 314 part-time. Students come from 17 states and territories, 8 other countries, 3% are from out of state, 10% African American, 1% Asian American or Pacific Islander, 2% Hispanic American, 0.4% Native American, 0.7% international, 15% transferred in, 42% live on campus. *Retention:* 70% of 2006 full-time freshmen returned.

Freshmen *Admission:* 1,780 applied, 1,203 admitted, 363 enrolled. *Average high school GPA:* 3.5. *Test scores:* SAT critical reading scores over 500: 52%; SAT math scores over 500: 66%; ACT scores over 18: 95%; SAT critical reading scores over 600: 9%; SAT math scores over 600: 14%; ACT scores over 24: 41%; SAT math scores over 700: 2%; ACT scores over 30: 2%.

Faculty *Total:* 275, 32% full-time, 34% with terminal degrees. *Student/faculty ratio:* 13:1.

Majors Accounting; applied art; art; art teacher education; biochemistry; biology/biological sciences; biology teacher education; business administration and management; early childhood education; elementary education; English; English/language arts teacher education; fine/studio arts; French; French language teacher education; graphic design; history; mathematics; mathematics teacher education; natural sciences; nursing (registered nurse training); political science and government; psychology; religious studies; social studies teacher education; social work; Spanish; Spanish language teacher education.

Academics *Calendar:* semesters. *Degrees:* certificates, bachelor's, master's, first professional, and post-master's certificates. *Special study options:* academic remediation for entering students, accelerated degree program, adult/continuing education programs, advanced placement credit, double majors, honors programs, independent study, internships, off-campus study, part-time degree program, services for LD students, student-designed majors, study abroad, summer session for credit. *ROTC:* Army (c). *Unusual degree programs:* 3-2 physician assistant program.

Computers on Campus 99 computers/terminals are available on campus for general student use. Students can access the following: campus intranet, free student e-mail accounts. Campuswide network is available. 100% of college-owned or -operated housing units are wired for high-speed Internet access. Wireless service is available via libraries, student centers.

Student Life *Housing:* on-campus residence required for freshman year. *Options:* coed. Campus housing is university owned. Freshman campus housing is guaranteed. *Activities and organizations:* drama/theater group, student-run newspaper, choral group, Multi-Cultural Association, Daemen Blue Crew, Voices of Zion, Cynergy, Environmental Club. *Campus security:* 24-hour emergency response devices and patrols, late-night transport/escort service, 24-hour security cameras. *Student services:* personal/psychological counseling.

Athletics Member NAIA. *Intercollegiate sports:* basketball M (s)/W (s), cross-country running M (s)/W (s), golf M (s), soccer M (s)/W (s), volleyball W (s). *Intramural sports:* basketball M/W, ice hockey M (c), lacrosse M (c), soccer M (c), softball M/W.

Standardized Tests *Required:* SAT or ACT (for admission).

Costs (2007–08) *Comprehensive fee:* $27,360 includes full-time tuition ($18,300), mandatory fees ($450), and room and board ($8610). Part-time tuition: $610 per credit. Part-time tuition and fees vary according to course load. *Required fees:* $4 per credit part-time, $68 per term part-time. *Room and board:* Room and board charges vary according to board plan and housing facility. *Payment plans:* installment, deferred payment. *Waivers:* senior citizens and employees or children of employees.

Financial Aid Of all full-time matriculated undergraduates who enrolled in 2007, 1,360 applied for aid, 1,166 were judged to have need, 199 had their need fully met. 262 Federal Work-Study jobs (averaging $1165). 45 state and other part-time jobs (averaging $1248). In 2007, 46 non-need-based awards were made. *Average percent of need met:* 71%. *Average financial aid package:* $12,693. *Average need-based loan:* $4552. *Average need-based gift aid:* $7492. *Average non-need-based aid:* $7766. *Average indebtedness upon graduation:* $20,465.

Applying *Options:* electronic application, early admission, early action, deferred entrance. *Application fee:* $25. *Required:* high school transcript, minimum 2.0 GPA. *Required for some:* essay or personal statement, 3 letters of recommendation, interview. *Application deadlines:* rolling (freshmen), rolling (transfers), 8/30 (early action). *Notification:* continuous (freshmen), continuous (transfers), 9/1 (early action).

Freshman Application Contact Mr. Frank Williams, Associate Director of Admissions, Daemen College, Amherst, NY 14226-3592. *Phone:* 716-839-8225. *Toll-free phone:* 800-462-7652. *Fax:* 716-839-8229. *E-mail:* admissions@daemen.edu.

See page 1726 for the College Close-Up.

DARKEI NOAM RABBINICAL COLLEGE

Brooklyn, New York

Director of Admissions Rabbi Pinchas Horowitz, Director of Admissions, Darkei Noam Rabbinical College, 2822 Avenue J, Brooklyn, NY 11210. *Phone:* 718-338-6464.

DAVIS COLLEGE

Johnson City, New York **www.davisny.edu/**

- **Independent nondenominational** 4-year, founded 1900
- **Suburban** 22-acre campus with easy access to Syracuse
- **Coed** 323 undergraduate students, 63% full-time, 54% women, 46% men
- **Minimally difficult** entrance level, 68% of applicants were admitted

Undergraduates 202 full-time, 121 part-time. Students come from 9 states and territories, 5 other countries, 24% are from out of state, 6% African American, 2% Asian American or Pacific Islander, 2% Hispanic American, 0.3% Native American, 3% international, 61% live on campus. *Retention:* 84% of 2006 full-time freshmen returned.

Freshmen *Admission:* 60 applied, 41 admitted. *Average high school GPA:* 3.18. *Test scores:* ACT scores over 18: 62%; ACT scores over 24: 26%; ACT scores over 30: 5%.

Faculty *Total:* 24, 29% full-time, 42% with terminal degrees. *Student/faculty ratio:* 14:1.

Majors Biblical studies; divinity/ministry; early childhood education; education; English as a second/foreign language (teaching); international/global studies; pastoral counseling and specialized ministries related; pastoral studies/counseling; youth ministry.

Academics *Calendar:* semesters. *Degrees:* certificates, diplomas, associate, and bachelor's. *Special study options:* academic remediation for entering students, adult/continuing education programs, advanced placement credit, cooperative education, English as a second language, independent study, internships, part-time degree program, services for LD students, summer session for credit.

Computers on Campus 12 computers/terminals are available on campus for general student use. Campuswide network is available. 100% of college-owned or -operated housing units are wired for high-speed Internet access. Wireless service is available via entire campus.

Student Life *Housing options:* men-only, women-only. Campus housing is university owned. *Activities and organizations:* drama/theater group, student-run newspaper, choral group, Student Missionary Fellowship, Student Wives Fellowship, Student Life Committee, Married Couples Fellowship. *Campus security:* 24-hour emergency response devices and patrols, student patrols, late-night transport/escort service. *Student services:* health clinic, personal/psychological counseling.

Athletics Member NCCAA. *Intercollegiate sports:* basketball M/W, soccer M, volleyball W. *Intramural sports:* skiing (downhill) M/W, soccer M/W, table tennis M/W, volleyball M/W, weight lifting M/W.

Standardized Tests *Required:* SAT or ACT (for admission).

Costs (2007–08) *Comprehensive fee:* $16,070 includes full-time tuition ($9450), mandatory fees ($800), and room and board ($5820).

Financial Aid Of all full-time matriculated undergraduates who enrolled in 2002, 182 applied for aid, 175 were judged to have need, 27 had their need fully met. 77 Federal Work-Study jobs (averaging $898). In 2002, 10 non-need-based awards were made. *Average percent of need met:* 37%. *Average financial aid package:* $5120. *Average need-based loan:* $4893. *Average need-based gift aid:* $4360. *Average non-need-based aid:* $610. *Average indebtedness upon graduation:* $5360.

Applying *Options:* electronic application, deferred entrance. *Application fee:* $45. *Required:* high school transcript, 2 letters of recommendation, references. *Required for some:* essay or personal statement. *Recommended:* minimum 2.0 GPA, interview. *Application deadlines:* rolling (freshmen), rolling (transfers). *Notification:* continuous (freshmen), continuous (transfers).

Freshman Application Contact Director of Admissions, Davis College, PO Box 601, Bible School Park, NY 13737-0601. *Phone:* 607-729-1581 Ext. 406. *Toll-free phone:* 800-331-4137 Ext. 406. *Fax:* 607-729-2962. *E-mail:* admissions@davisny.edu.

DeVry College of New York

Long Island City, New York **www.devry.edu/**

- **Proprietary** 4-year, founded 1998, part of DeVry University
- **Urban** 4-acre campus
- **Coed** 882 undergraduate students, 71% full-time, 25% women, 75% men
- **Minimally difficult** entrance level

Undergraduates 624 full-time, 258 part-time. 3% are from out of state, 34% African American, 10% Asian American or Pacific Islander, 29% Hispanic American, 0.6% Native American, 1% international, 10% transferred in. *Retention:* 36% of 2006 full-time freshmen returned.

Freshmen *Admission:* 200 enrolled.

Faculty *Total:* 103, 37% full-time. *Student/faculty ratio:* 14:1.

Majors Biomedical technology; business administration and management; business administration, management and operations related; computer engineering technology; computer systems analysis; computer systems networking and telecommunications; electrical, electronic and communications engineering technology.

Academics *Calendar:* semesters. *Degrees:* associate, bachelor's, and master's. *Special study options:* academic remediation for entering students, accelerated degree program, adult/continuing education programs, advanced placement credit, distance learning, part-time degree program, summer session for credit.

Computers on Campus 478 computers/terminals are available on campus for general student use. Students can access the following: online (class) registration. Campuswide network is available.

Student Life *Housing:* college housing not available. *Activities and organizations:* International Students Club, Video Games Club, DeVry Student Association, Chess Club, Muslim Student Association. *Campus security:* 24-hour emergency response devices and patrols, student patrols, late-night transport/escort service, lighted pathways/sidewalks.

Costs (2008–09) *Tuition:* $14,480 full-time, $510 per credit part-time. *Required fees:* $180 full-time.

Financial Aid Of all full-time matriculated undergraduates who enrolled in 2003, 1,596 applied for aid, 1,571 were judged to have need, 24 had their need fully met. In 2003, 63 non-need-based awards were made. *Average percent of need met:* 48%. *Average financial aid package:* $10,384. *Average need-based loan:* $5123. *Average need-based gift aid:* $6127. *Average non-need-based aid:* $8252.

Applying *Options:* electronic application, early admission, deferred entrance. *Application fee:* $50. *Required:* high school transcript, interview. *Application deadlines:* rolling (freshmen), rolling (transfers). *Notification:* continuous (freshmen), continuous (transfers).

Freshman Application Contact DeVry College of New York, 3020 Thomson Avenue, Long Island City, NY 11101-3051.

Dominican College

Orangeburg, New York **www.dc.edu/**

- **Independent** comprehensive, founded 1952
- **Suburban** 62-acre campus with easy access to New York City
- **Endowment** $355,126
- **Coed** 1,745 undergraduate students, 73% full-time, 68% women, 32% men
- **Noncompetitive** entrance level, 75% of applicants were admitted

Undergraduates 1,267 full-time, 478 part-time. Students come from 18 states and territories, 8 other countries, 23% are from out of state, 18% African American, 8% Asian American or Pacific Islander, 18% Hispanic American, 0.3% Native American, 0.9% international, 10% transferred in, 51% live on campus. *Retention:* 66% of 2006 full-time freshmen returned.

Freshmen *Admission:* 1,474 applied, 1,107 admitted, 332 enrolled. *Average high school GPA:* 2.74. *Test scores:* SAT critical reading scores over 500: 23%; SAT math scores over 500: 24%; SAT writing scores over 500: 19%; SAT critical reading scores over 600: 2%; SAT math scores over 600: 2%; SAT writing scores over 600: 2%.

Faculty *Total:* 204, 33% full-time. *Student/faculty ratio:* 14:1.

Majors Accounting; American studies; athletic training; biology/biological sciences; biology teacher education; business administration and management; computer and information sciences; criminal justice/safety; economics; education; elementary education; English; English/language arts teacher education; finance; health/health care administration; history; history teacher education; humanities; human resources management; international business/trade/commerce; liberal arts and sciences/liberal studies; management information systems; marketing/marketing management; mathematics; mathematics teacher education; nursing (registered nurse training); occupational therapy; pre-law studies; psychology; secondary education; social sciences; social science teacher education; social work; Spanish; special education; special education (multiply disabled).

Academics *Calendar:* semesters. *Degrees:* certificates, associate, bachelor's, master's, and doctoral. *Special study options:* academic remediation for entering students, accelerated degree program, adult/continuing education programs, advanced placement credit, cooperative education, distance learning, double majors, honors programs, independent study, internships, part-time degree program, services for LD students, summer session for credit. *Unusual degree programs:* 3-2 engineering with Manhattan College.

Computers on Campus 120 computers/terminals are available on campus for general student use. Students can access the following: computer help desk, free student e-mail accounts, online (class) schedules, Web portal, Black Board. Campuswide network is available. 100% of college-owned or -operated housing units are wired for high-speed Internet access. Wireless service is available via dorm rooms, libraries.

Student Life *Housing options:* coed. Campus housing is university owned, leased by the school and is provided by a third party. Freshman campus housing is guaranteed. *Activities and organizations:* drama/theater group, student-run newspaper, choral group, Student Government Association, Business Club, Aquin Players, school newspaper, Nursing Association. *Campus security:* 24-hour emergency response devices and patrols, student patrols, late-night transport/escort service, controlled dormitory access. *Student services:* health clinic, personal/psychological counseling.

Athletics Member NCAA, NAIA. All NCAA Division II. *Intercollegiate sports:* baseball M (s), basketball M (s)/W (s), cross-country running M (s)/W (s), golf M (s), lacrosse M (s)/W (s), soccer M (s)/W (s), softball W (s), volleyball W (s).

Standardized Tests *Required:* SAT or ACT (for admission).

Costs (2007–08) *One-time required fee:* $35. *Comprehensive fee:* $28,867 includes full-time tuition ($18,830), mandatory fees ($680), and room and board ($9357). Part-time tuition: $565 per credit. Part-time tuition and fees vary according to program. *Required fees:* $165 per term part-time. *Room and board:* Room and board charges vary according to housing facility. *Payment plans:* installment, deferred payment. *Waivers:* senior citizens and employees or children of employees.

Financial Aid Of all full-time matriculated undergraduates who enrolled in 2007, 1,101 applied for aid, 1,070 were judged to have need, 188 had their need fully met. 250 Federal Work-Study jobs (averaging $1180). 60 state and other part-time jobs (averaging $2917). In 2007, 181 non-need-based awards were made. *Average percent of need met:* 61%. *Average financial aid package:* $13,891. *Average need-based loan:* $4342. *Average need-based gift aid:* $10,288. *Average non-need-based aid:* $12,077. *Average indebtedness upon graduation:* $25,521.

Applying *Options:* electronic application, deferred entrance. *Application fee:* $35. *Required:* high school transcript. *Required for some:* essay or personal statement, interview. *Recommended:* interview. *Application deadlines:* rolling (freshmen), rolling (transfers). *Notification:* continuous (freshmen), continuous (transfers).

Freshman Application Contact Ms. Joyce Elbe, Director of Admissions, Dominican College, Orangeburg, NY 10962-1210. *Phone:* 845-359-7900. *Toll-free phone:* 866-432-4636. *Fax:* 845-365-3150. *E-mail:* admissions@dc.edu.

See page 1728 for the College Close-Up.

DOWLING COLLEGE

Oakdale, New York **www.dowling.edu/**

- **Independent** comprehensive, founded 1955
- **Suburban** 157-acre campus with easy access to New York City
- **Endowment** $11.4 million
- **Coed** 3,428 undergraduate students, 64% full-time, 58% women, 42% men
- **Moderately difficult** entrance level, 76% of applicants were admitted

Undergraduates 2,182 full-time, 1,246 part-time. Students come from 31 states and territories, 61 other countries, 13% are from out of state, 10% African American, 2% Asian American or Pacific Islander, 10% Hispanic American, 0.3% Native American, 5% international, 9% transferred in, 17% live on campus. *Retention:* 64% of 2006 full-time freshmen returned.

Freshmen *Admission:* 2,607 applied, 1,987 admitted, 496 enrolled. *Average high school GPA:* 2.86. *Test scores:* SAT critical reading scores over 500: 26%; SAT math scores over 500: 32%; SAT critical reading scores over 600: 4%; SAT math scores over 600: 8%; SAT math scores over 700: 1%.

Faculty *Total:* 532, 23% full-time, 34% with terminal degrees. *Student/faculty ratio:* 15:1.

Majors Accounting; aerospace, aeronautical and astronautical engineering; anthropology; applied art; applied mathematics; art teacher education; biological and physical sciences; biology/biological sciences; biology teacher education; business administration and management; business, management, and marketing related; business teacher education; commercial and advertising art; communication/speech communication and rhetoric; computer and information sciences; computer and information sciences and support services related; economics; education; elementary education; engineering related; English; English/language arts teacher education; finance; fine arts related; fine/studio arts; foreign languages and literatures; health professions related; history; humanities; interdisciplinary studies; international business/trade/commerce; liberal arts and sciences/liberal studies; marine biology and biological oceanography; mathematics; mathematics teacher education; music; music teacher education; natural sciences; philosophy; political science and government; psychology; Romance languages; sales, distribution and marketing; secondary education; social sciences; social studies teacher education; sociology; Spanish language teacher education; special education; speech and rhetoric; tourism and travel services management; transportation and materials moving related; transportation technology.

Academics *Calendar:* semesters. *Degrees:* bachelor's, master's, doctoral, post-master's, and postbachelor's certificates. *Special study options:* academic remediation for entering students, accelerated degree program, advanced placement credit, cooperative education, double majors, English as a second language, honors programs, independent study, internships, off-campus study, part-time degree program, services for LD students, student-designed majors, summer session for credit. *ROTC:* Air Force (c).

Computers on Campus 202 computers/terminals are available on campus for general student use. Students can access the following: campus intranet, computer help desk, free student e-mail accounts, online (class) grades, online (class) registration, online (class) schedules. Campuswide network is available. 100% of college-owned or -operated housing units are wired for high-speed Internet access. Wireless service is available via classrooms, computer centers, computer labs, learning centers, libraries, student centers.

Student Life *Housing options:* coed. Campus housing is university owned and leased by the school. *Activities and organizations:* drama/theater group, student-run newspaper, choral group, Student Government Association, Dormitory Councils, Aviation Organization, Cultural Organization, Religious Organization. *Campus security:* 24-hour emergency response devices and patrols, late-night transport/escort service. *Student services:* health clinic, personal/psychological counseling.

Athletics Member NCAA. All Division II. *Intercollegiate sports:* baseball M (s), basketball M (s)/W (s), crew M (c)/W (c), equestrian sports W, lacrosse M, soccer M (s), softball W (s), tennis M (s)/W (s), volleyball W (s). *Intramural sports:* bowling M/W, cross-country running M/W, track and field M/W, weight lifting M/W.

Standardized Tests *Required:* SAT or ACT (for admission).

Costs (2007–08) *Comprehensive fee:* $28,177 includes full-time tuition ($18,180), mandatory fees ($1090), and room and board ($8907). Full-time tuition and fees vary according to course load and degree level. Part-time tuition: $606 per credit. Part-time tuition and fees vary according to course load and degree level. *Required fees:* $238 per term part-time. *Room and board:* Room and board charges vary according to housing facility and location. *Payment plans:* installment, deferred payment. *Waivers:* minority students, children of alumni, adult students, senior citizens, and employees or children of employees.

Financial Aid Of all full-time matriculated undergraduates who enrolled in 2007, 1,364 applied for aid, 1,307 were judged to have need, 167 had their need fully met. In 2007, 834 non-need-based awards were made. *Average percent of need met:* 29%. *Average financial aid package:* $2375. *Average need-based loan:* $4400. *Average need-based gift aid:* $23,333. *Average non-need-based aid:* $4435. *Average indebtedness upon graduation:* $28,585.

Applying *Options:* electronic application, deferred entrance. *Application fee:* $25. *Required:* high school transcript. *Application deadlines:* rolling (freshmen), rolling (transfers). *Notification:* continuous (freshmen), continuous (transfers).

Freshman Application Contact Ms. Ronnie Lee MacDonald, Assistant Vice President for Student Affairs, Dowling College, 150 Idle Hour Boulevard, Oakdale, NY 11769. *Phone:* 631-244-3662. *Toll-free phone:* 800-DOWLING. *Fax:* 631-244-1078. *E-mail:* admissions@dowling.edu.

D'YOUVILLE COLLEGE

Buffalo, New York **www.dyc.edu/**

- **Independent** comprehensive, founded 1908
- **Urban** 7-acre campus
- **Endowment** $24.8 million
- **Coed** 1,654 undergraduate students, 81% full-time, 75% women, 25% men
- **Moderately difficult** entrance level, 64% of applicants were admitted

The College offers a chiropractic program, a physical therapy program in both bachelor's and doctoral degrees, and an exercise and sports studies (B.S.) program. The five-year combined bachelor's/master's degree is offered in dietetics, education, information technology, international business, nursing, occupational therapy, and physician assistant studies. Many dual-degree students pay undergraduate full-time tuition all five years. The Instant Scholarship Program offers scholarships with total values up to $55,000. D'Youville automatically rewards applicants in recognition of their high school or college accomplishments. The Honors Scholarship requires a minimum score of 1100 on the SAT (math and verbal) or 24 on the ACT and gives 50 percent off tuition and 25 percent off total room and board. The Academic Scholarship requires a minimum score of 1000 on the SAT (math and verbal) or 21 on the ACT and a minimum average grade of 85 percent and gives 25 percent off tuition and 50 percent off total room and board. These scholarships are renewable based on program specifics. Other scholarships are available.

Undergraduates 1,345 full-time, 309 part-time. Students come from 29 states and territories, 43 other countries, 5% are from out of state, 15% African American, 1% Asian American or Pacific Islander, 5% Hispanic American, 0.5% Native American, 10% international, 15% transferred in, 19% live on campus. *Retention:* 68% of 2006 full-time freshmen returned.

Freshmen *Admission:* 1,606 applied, 1,025 admitted, 216 enrolled. *Test scores:* SAT critical reading scores over 500: 51%; SAT math scores over 500: 56%; ACT scores over 18: 93%; SAT critical reading scores over 600: 11%; SAT math scores over 600: 13%; ACT scores over 24: 31%; SAT critical reading scores over 700: 1%; SAT math scores over 700: 1%.

Faculty *Total:* 274, 54% full-time, 34% with terminal degrees. *Student/faculty ratio:* 13:1.

Majors Accounting; biology/biological sciences; business administration and management; dietetics; English; health/health care administration; health professions related; health services/allied health/health sciences; history; history related; information technology; interdisciplinary studies; international business/trade/commerce; liberal arts and sciences/liberal studies; marketing/marketing management; nursing (registered nurse training); occupational therapy; philosophy; psychology; sociology.

Academics *Calendar:* semesters plus summer session. *Degrees:* bachelor's, master's, doctoral, first professional, post-master's, and postbachelor's certificates. *Special study options:* academic remediation for entering students, accelerated degree program, adult/continuing education programs, distance learning, double majors, independent study, internships, off-campus study, part-time degree program, services for LD students, study abroad, summer session for credit. *ROTC:* Army (c). *Unusual degree programs:* 3-2 nursing; education, dietetics, international business, occupational therapy.

Computers on Campus 72 computers/terminals are available on campus for general student use. Students can access the following: free student e-mail accounts, online (class) grades, online (class) registration, online (class) schedules. Campuswide network is available. Wireless service is available via libraries, student centers.

Student Life *Housing options:* coed, men-only, women-only, disabled students. Campus housing is university owned. Freshman campus housing is guaranteed. *Activities and organizations:* drama/theater group, student-run newspaper, choral group, Student Association, Occupational Therapy Student Association, Physical Therapy Student Association, Student Nurses Association, Black Student Union. *Campus security:* 24-hour emergency response devices and patrols, late-night transport/escort service, controlled dormitory access. *Student services:* health clinic, personal/psychological counseling.

Athletics Member NCAA, NSCAA. All NCAA Division III. *Intercollegiate sports:* baseball M, basketball M/W, cross-country running W, golf M/W, soccer M/W, softball W, volleyball M/W. *Intramural sports:* basketball M/W, cheerleading W, crew W, cross-country running M, football M/W, golf M/W, skiing (downhill) M/W, soccer M/W, softball M, swimming and diving M/W, table tennis M/W, tennis M/W, volleyball M/W.

Standardized Tests *Required:* SAT or ACT (for admission).

Costs (2007–08) *Comprehensive fee:* $26,550 includes full-time tuition ($17,600), mandatory fees ($200), and room and board ($8750). Full-time tuition and fees vary according to course level, degree level, and program. Part-time tuition: $485 per credit hour. Part-time tuition and fees vary according to course load. No tuition increase for student's term of enrollment. *Required fees:* $2 per credit hour part-time, $30 per term part-time. *Room and board:* Room and board charges vary according to board plan and housing facility. *Payment plans:* tuition prepayment, installment, deferred payment. *Waivers:* children of alumni, senior citizens, and employees or children of employees.

Financial Aid Of all full-time matriculated undergraduates who enrolled in 2005, 989 applied for aid, 895 were judged to have need, 201 had their need fully met. 72 state and other part-time jobs (averaging $2000). In 2005, 164 non-need-based awards were made. *Average percent of need met:* 73%. *Average financial aid package:* $13,295. *Average need-based loan:* $5317. *Average need-based gift aid:* $8380. *Average non-need-based aid:* $9979. *Average indebtedness upon graduation:* $26,897.

Applying *Options:* electronic application, deferred entrance. *Application fee:* $25. *Required:* high school transcript, minimum 2.0 GPA. *Required for some:* essay or personal statement, minimum 3.0 GPA, letters of recommendation, interview. *Application deadlines:* rolling (freshmen), rolling (transfers). *Notification:* continuous (freshmen), continuous (transfers).

Freshman Application Contact Mr. Ronald Dannecker, Director of Admissions, D'Youville College, 320 Porter Avenue, Buffalo, NY 14201-1084. *Phone:* 716-829-7600. *Toll-free phone:* 800-777-3921. *Fax:* 716-829-7790. *E-mail:* admissions@dyc.edu.

See page 1730 for the College Close-Up.

ELMIRA COLLEGE

Elmira, New York **www.elmira.edu/**

Freshman Application Contact Mr. Gary Fallis, Dean of Admissions, Elmira College, Office of Admissions, Elmira, NY 14901. *Phone:* 607-735-1724. *Toll-free phone:* 800-935-6472. *Fax:* 607-735-1718. *E-mail:* admissions@elmira.edu.

See page 1732 for the College Close-Up.

EUGENE LANG COLLEGE THE NEW SCHOOL FOR LIBERAL ARTS

New York, New York **www.lang.edu/**

- **Independent** 4-year, founded 1978, part of The New School
- **Urban** 5-acre campus
- **Coed** 1,294 undergraduate students, 95% full-time, 69% women, 31% men
- **Moderately difficult** entrance level, 63% of applicants were admitted

Undergraduates 1,225 full-time, 69 part-time. Students come from 49 states and territories, 36 other countries, 68% are from out of state, 4% African American, 5% Asian American or Pacific Islander, 6% Hispanic American, 0.6% Native American, 3% international, 11% transferred in, 27% live on campus. *Retention:* 73% of 2006 full-time freshmen returned.

Freshmen *Admission:* 1,670 applied, 1,056 admitted, 321 enrolled. *Average high school GPA:* 3.19. *Test scores:* SAT critical reading scores over 500: 92%; SAT math scores over 500: 73%; SAT writing scores over 500: 91%; ACT scores over 18: 100%; SAT critical reading scores over 600: 61%; SAT math scores over 600: 30%; SAT writing scores over 600: 57%; ACT scores over 24: 67%; SAT critical reading scores over 700: 14%; SAT math scores over 700: 4%; SAT writing scores over 700: 15%; ACT scores over 30: 11%.

Faculty *Total:* 136, 39% full-time. *Student/faculty ratio:* 15:1.

Majors Anthropology; communication and media related; creative writing; cultural studies; dance; dramatic/theater arts; economics; education; English; foreign languages and literatures; history; humanities; journalism; liberal arts and sciences/liberal studies; literature; music history, literature, and theory; philosophy; political science and government; psychology; religious studies; social sciences; sociology; urban studies/affairs; women's studies.

Academics *Calendar:* semesters. *Degree:* bachelor's. *Special study options:* accelerated degree program, adult/continuing education programs, advanced placement credit, distance learning, English as a second language, independent study, internships, off-campus study, part-time degree program, student-designed majors, study abroad, summer session for credit. *Unusual degree programs:* 3-2 media studies, education, social science, management and urban policy.

Computers on Campus 1,200 computers/terminals are available on campus for general student use. Students can access the following: computer help desk, free student e-mail accounts, online (class) grades, online (class) registration, online (class) schedules, online portal. Campuswide network is available. 94% of college-owned or -operated housing units are wired for high-speed Internet access. Wireless service is available via entire campus.

Student Life *Housing options:* coed, disabled students. Campus housing is university owned and leased by the school. Freshman applicants given priority for college housing. *Activities and organizations:* drama/theater group, student-run newspaper, choral group, Student Union, Theater Club, student newspaper, literary journal, ethnic organizations. *Campus security:* 24-hour emergency response devices, controlled dormitory access, 24-hour desk attendants in residence halls. *Student services:* health clinic, personal/psychological counseling.

Standardized Tests *Required:* SAT or ACT (for admission).

Costs (2007–08) *Comprehensive fee:* $43,060 includes full-time tuition ($30,660), mandatory fees ($650), and room and board ($11,750). Full-time tuition and fees vary according to program. Part-time tuition: $1046 per credit. Part-time tuition and fees vary according to course load, program, and reciprocity agreements. *College room only:* $8750. Room and board charges vary according to board plan and housing facility. *Payment plan:* installment. *Waivers:* employees or children of employees.

Financial Aid Of all full-time matriculated undergraduates who enrolled in 2006, 839 applied for aid, 682 were judged to have need, 100 had their need fully met. In 2006, 44 non-need-based awards were made. *Average percent of need met:* 80%. *Average financial aid package:* $19,478. *Average need-based loan:* $4281. *Average need-based gift aid:* $15,393. *Average non-need-based aid:* $2153. *Average indebtedness upon graduation:* $21,293.

Applying *Options:* early admission, early decision, deferred entrance. *Application fee:* $50. *Required:* essay or personal statement, high school transcript, 2 letters of recommendation, interview. *Recommended:* minimum 3.0 GPA. *Application deadlines:* 2/1 (freshmen), 5/15 (transfers). *Early decision deadline:* 11/15. *Notification:* 3/25 (freshmen), 6/1 (transfers), 12/15 (early decision).

Director of Admissions Nicole Curvin, Director of Admissions, Eugene Lang College The New School for Liberal Arts, 65 West 11th Street, New York, NY 10011-8601. *Phone:* 212-229-5665. *Toll-free phone:* 877-528-3321. *E-mail:* lang@newschool.edu.

See page 1734 for the College Close-Up.

EXCELSIOR COLLEGE

Albany, New York **www.excelsior.edu/**

- **Independent** comprehensive, founded 1970
- **Urban** campus
- **Endowment** $412,550
- **Coed** 33,769 undergraduate students, 60% women, 40% men
- **Noncompetitive** entrance level

Undergraduates 33,769 part-time. Students come from 50 states and territories, 51 other countries, 90% are from out of state, 16% African American, 4% Asian American or Pacific Islander, 5% Hispanic American, 0.8% Native American, 0.7% international, 36% transferred in.

Faculty *Total:* 692, 4% full-time.

Majors Accounting; area studies; avionics maintenance technology; biology/biological sciences; chemistry; criminal justice/law enforcement administration; economics; finance; foreign languages and literatures; geography; geology/earth science; history; human resources management; information science/studies; insurance; international business/trade/commerce; literature; management information systems; manufacturing technology; marketing/marketing management; mass communication/media; mathematics; music; operations management; philosophy; physics; political science and government; psychology; sociology; welding technology.

Academics *Calendar:* continuous. *Degrees:* associate, bachelor's, master's, and postbachelor's certificates (offers only external degree programs). *Special study options:* accelerated degree program, adult/continuing education programs, advanced placement credit, distance learning, external degree program, honors programs, independent study, part-time degree program, student-designed majors.

Computers on Campus Students can access the following: online (class) registration. Campuswide network is available.

Student Life *Housing:* college housing not available.

Costs (2007–08) *Tuition:* $290 per credit hour part-time. *Required fees:* $440 per year part-time. *Payment plan:* installment. *Waivers:* employees or children of employees.

Financial Aid *Average indebtedness upon graduation:* $5410.

Applying *Options:* electronic application. *Application fee:* $75. *Application deadlines:* rolling (freshmen), rolling (transfers). *Notification:* continuous (freshmen), continuous (transfers).

Freshman Application Contact Admissions, Excelsior College, 7 Columbia Circle, Albany, NY 12203-5159. *Phone:* 518-464-8500. *Toll-free phone:* 888-647-2388. *Fax:* 518-464-8777. *E-mail:* admissions@excelsior.edu.

See page 1736 for the College Close-Up.

FARMINGDALE STATE COLLEGE

Farmingdale, New York **www.farmingdale.edu/**

- **State-supported** 4-year, founded 1912, part of State University of New York System
- **Small-town** 380-acre campus with easy access to New York City
- **Endowment** $4.0 million
- **Coed** 6,447 undergraduate students, 69% full-time, 44% women, 56% men
- **Moderately difficult** entrance level, 52% of applicants were admitted

Undergraduates 4,455 full-time, 1,992 part-time. Students come from 13 states and territories, 29 other countries, 10% African American, 4% Asian American or Pacific Islander, 9% Hispanic American, 0.2% Native American, 0.9% international, 9% transferred in, 10% live on campus. *Retention:* 74% of 2006 full-time freshmen returned.

Freshmen *Admission:* 4,643 applied, 2,407 admitted, 1,023 enrolled. *Average high school GPA:* 2.89. *Test scores:* SAT critical reading scores over 500: 34%; SAT math scores over 500: 53%; SAT critical reading scores over 600: 5%; SAT math scores over 600: 9%; SAT critical reading scores over 700: 1%; SAT math scores over 700: 1%.

Faculty *Total:* 512, 36% full-time, 27% with terminal degrees. *Student/faculty ratio:* 18:1.

Majors Airline pilot and flight crew; applied economics; applied horticulture; applied mathematics; architectural engineering technology; aviation/airway management; biological and biomedical sciences related; business administration and management; clinical/medical laboratory technology; computer engineering technology; computer programming; computer programming related; computer science; construction engineering technology; construction management; criminal justice/law enforcement administration; data processing and data processing technology; dental hygiene; design and visual communications; electrical, electronic and communications engineering technology; engineering/industrial management; history and philosophy of science and technology; industrial and organizational psychology; information science/studies; landscaping and groundskeeping; liberal arts and sciences/liberal studies; manufacturing technology; nursing (registered nurse training); operations management; ornamental horticulture; safety/security technology; security and loss prevention; technical and business writing.

Academics *Calendar:* semesters. *Degrees:* certificates, associate, and bachelor's. *Special study options:* academic remediation for entering students, advanced placement credit, distance learning, double majors, internships, part-time degree program, services for LD students, study abroad, summer session for credit.

Computers on Campus 950 computers/terminals are available on campus for general student use. Students can access the following: online (class) registration. Campuswide network is available.

Student Life *Housing options:* coed. Campus housing is university owned. *Activities and organizations:* drama/theater group, student-run newspaper, radio station, Liberal Arts Club, Campus Activities Board, Farmingdale Student Government, student radio station, Rambler Newspaper. *Campus security:* 24-hour emergency response devices and patrols, controlled dormitory access. *Student services:* health clinic, personal/psychological counseling.

Athletics Member NCAA. All Division III. *Intercollegiate sports:* baseball M, basketball M/W, cross-country running M/W, golf M, lacrosse M, soccer M/W, softball W, track and field M/W, volleyball W. *Intramural sports:* basketball M/W, football M, golf M/W, racquetball M/W, soccer M/W, softball M/W, squash M/W, swimming and diving M/W, tennis M/W, volleyball M/W, weight lifting M/W.

Standardized Tests *Required:* SAT or ACT (for admission).

Costs (2008–09) *Tuition:* state resident $4350 full-time, $180 per credit part-time; nonresident $10,610 full-time, $442 per credit part-time. *Required fees:* $995 full-time, $35 per credit part-time. *Room and board:* $11,410; room only: $5985.

Financial Aid Of all full-time matriculated undergraduates who enrolled in 2000, 1,872 applied for aid, 1,480 were judged to have need, 257 had their need fully met. 134 Federal Work-Study jobs, 78 state and other part-time jobs. In 2000, 213 non-need-based awards were made. *Average percent of need met:* 63%. *Average financial aid package:* $5127. *Average need-based gift aid:* $3786. *Average non-need-based aid:* $3198.

Applying *Options:* electronic application, early admission. *Application fee:* $40. *Required:* high school transcript, minimum 2.0 GPA. *Required for some:* interview, portfolio. *Application deadlines:* rolling (freshmen), rolling (transfers). *Notification:* continuous (freshmen).

Freshman Application Contact Mr. Jim Hall, Director of Admissions, Farmingdale State College, 2350 Broadhollow Road, Farmingdale, NY 11735-1021. *Phone:* 631-420-2457. *Toll-free phone:* 877-4-FARMINGDALE. *Fax:* 631-420-2633. *E-mail:* admissions@farmingdale.edu.

FASHION INSTITUTE OF TECHNOLOGY

New York, New York **www.fitnyc.edu/**

- **State and locally supported** comprehensive, founded 1944, part of State University of New York System
- **Urban** 5-acre campus
- **Endowment** $30.4 million
- **Coed, primarily women** 9,736 undergraduate students, 69% full-time, 85% women, 15% men
- **Moderately difficult** entrance level, 42% of applicants were admitted

Undergraduates 6,747 full-time, 2,989 part-time. Students come from 52 states and territories, 59 other countries, 27% are from out of state, 6% African American, 9% Asian American or Pacific Islander, 11% Hispanic American, 0.2% Native American, 11% international, 10% transferred in, 30% live on campus. *Retention:* 86% of 2006 full-time freshmen returned.

Freshmen *Admission:* 3,913 applied, 1,658 admitted, 1,097 enrolled. *Average high school GPA:* 3.2.

Faculty *Total:* 929, 25% full-time. *Student/faculty ratio:* 17:1.

Majors Advertising; animation, interactive technology, video graphics and special effects; apparel and textile manufacturing; apparel and textiles; art history, criticism and conservation; arts management; commercial and advertising art; commercial photography; fashion/apparel design; fashion merchandising; fashion modeling; fine/studio arts; graphic design; illustration; industrial design; interior design; international marketing; marketing research; merchandising, sales, and marketing operations related (specialized); metal and jewelry arts; special products marketing.

Academics *Calendar:* 4-1-4. *Degrees:* certificates, associate, bachelor's, and master's. *Special study options:* academic remediation for entering students, adult/continuing education programs, advanced placement credit, cooperative education, distance learning, English as a second language, honors programs, internships, part-time degree program, services for LD students, study abroad, summer session for credit.

Computers on Campus 1,500 computers/terminals are available on campus for general student use. Students can access the following: computer help desk, free student e-mail accounts, online (class) grades, online (class) registration, online (class) schedules. Campuswide network is available. 100% of college-owned or -operated housing units are wired for high-speed Internet access. Wireless service is available via classrooms, computer centers, computer labs, learning centers, libraries, student centers.

Student Life *Housing options:* coed, women-only. Campus housing is university owned and is provided by a third party. Freshman applicants given priority for college housing. *Activities and organizations:* drama/theater group, student-run newspaper, radio station, choral group, FITSA/Student Government, Merchandising Society, Delta Epilson Chi: Promoting Leadership in Marketing, Merchandising, and Advertising, PRSSA: Public Relations Student Society of America, Student Ambassadors. *Campus security:* 24-hour emergency response devices and patrols, controlled dormitory access. *Student services:* health clinic, personal/psychological counseling.

Athletics Member NJCAA. *Intercollegiate sports:* basketball M, bowling M/W, cross-country running M/W, table tennis M/W, volleyball W. *Intramural sports:* basketball M/W, bowling M/W, table tennis M/W, tennis M/W, volleyball M/W.

Costs (2007–08) *Tuition:* state resident $4567 full-time, $190 per credit part-time; nonresident $11,140 full-time, $464 per credit part-time. *Required fees:* $440 full-time. *Room and board:* $10,095; room only: $9705.

Financial Aid Of all full-time matriculated undergraduates who enrolled in 2006, 4,572 applied for aid, 3,063 were judged to have need, 392 had their need fully met. 644 Federal Work-Study jobs (averaging $2126). In 2006, 145 non-need-based awards were made. *Average percent of need met:* 65%. *Average financial aid package:* $8365. *Average need-based loan:* $3630. *Average need-based gift aid:* $3926. *Average non-need-based aid:* $1563. *Average indebtedness upon graduation:* $12,869.

Applying *Options:* electronic application, early action, deferred entrance. *Application fee:* $40. *Required:* essay or personal statement, high school transcript. *Required for some:* portfolio for art and design programs. *Application deadlines:* 2/1 (freshmen), 1/1 (transfers), 11/15 (early action). *Notification:* continuous (freshmen), continuous (transfers), 1/31 (early action).

Freshman Application Contact Ms. Dolores Lombardi, Director of Admissions, Fashion Institute of Technology, Seventh Avenue at 27th Street, New York, NY 10001-5992. *Phone:* 212-217-3760. *Toll-free phone:* 800-GOTOFIT. *Fax:* 212-217-3761. *E-mail:* fitinfo@fitnyc.edu.

See page 1738 for the College Close-Up.

FIVE TOWNS COLLEGE

Dix Hills, New York **www.fivetowns.edu/**

- **Independent** comprehensive, founded 1972
- **Suburban** 40-acre campus with easy access to New York City
- **Coed** 1,093 undergraduate students, 92% full-time, 38% women, 62% men
- **Moderately difficult** entrance level, 71% of applicants were admitted

Five Towns College offers associate, bachelor's, master's, and doctoral degree programs. Students may select from nearly thirty different programs, including audio recording technology, broadcasting, elementary teacher education, film/video, jazz/commercial music, journalism, music business, music teacher education, and theater arts. The College is accredited by the Middle States Association of Colleges and Schools, National Council for Accreditation of Teacher Education, and New York State Board of Regents.

Undergraduates 1,006 full-time, 87 part-time. Students come from 12 states and territories, 5 other countries, 14% are from out of state, 19% African American, 0.8% Asian American or Pacific Islander, 11% Hispanic American, 0.1% Native American, 2% international, 8% transferred in, 15% live on campus. *Retention:* 67% of 2006 full-time freshmen returned.

Freshmen *Admission:* 710 applied, 501 admitted, 240 enrolled. *Average high school GPA:* 2.6.

Faculty *Total:* 129, 26% full-time. *Student/faculty ratio:* 13:1.

Majors Audio engineering; broadcast journalism; business administration and management; cinematography and film/video production; computer management; data processing and data processing technology; dramatic/theater arts; elementary education; film/video and photographic arts related; jazz/jazz studies; liberal arts and sciences/liberal studies; marketing/marketing management; mass communication/media; music; music management and merchandising; music teacher education; theater design and technology; violin, viola, guitar and other stringed instruments; voice and opera; wind/percussion instruments.

Academics *Calendar:* semesters. *Degrees:* associate, bachelor's, master's, and doctoral. *Special study options:* academic remediation for entering students, advanced placement credit, cooperative education, distance learning, independent study, internships, off-campus study, services for LD students, summer session for credit.

Computers on Campus 110 computers/terminals are available on campus for general student use. Campuswide network is available.

Student Life *Housing options:* coed. Campus housing is university owned. Freshman applicants given priority for college housing. *Activities and organizations:* drama/theater group, student-run newspaper, radio station, choral group, Film Video Club, Audio Club, Dance Club, Ski Club, Yearbook. *Campus security:* 24-hour emergency response devices and patrols, late-night transport/escort service, controlled dormitory access. *Student services:* health clinic, personal/psychological counseling.

Standardized Tests *Required:* SAT or ACT (for admission).

Costs (2008–09) *Comprehensive fee:* $29,875 includes full-time tuition ($17,400), mandatory fees ($725), and room and board ($11,750). Part-time tuition: $725 per credit.

Financial Aid Of all full-time matriculated undergraduates who enrolled in 2007, 829 applied for aid, 725 were judged to have need, 422 had their need fully met. 100 Federal Work-Study jobs (averaging $1100). In 2007, 75 non-need-based awards were made. *Average percent of need met:* 48%. *Average financial aid package:* $8100. *Average need-based loan:* $5167. *Average need-based gift aid:* $6000. *Average non-need-based aid:* $2000. *Average indebtedness upon graduation:* $18,000.

Applying *Options:* electronic application, early admission, early decision, deferred entrance. *Application fee:* $35. *Required:* essay or personal statement, high school transcript, minimum 2.3 GPA, letters of recommendation, minimum SAT score of 1250 or ACT score of 18, immunization records. *Required for some:* interview. *Application deadlines:* rolling (freshmen), rolling (transfers). *Notification:* continuous (freshmen), continuous (transfers).

Freshman Application Contact Mr. Jerry Cohen, Dean of Enrollment, Five Towns College, 305 North Service Road, Dix Hills, NY 11746-6055. *Phone:* 631-424-7000 Ext. 2110. *Fax:* 631-656-2172.

See page 1740 for the College Close-Up.

FORDHAM UNIVERSITY

New York, New York **www.fordham.edu/**

- **Independent Roman Catholic (Jesuit)** university, founded 1841
- **Urban** 85-acre campus
- **Endowment** $357.3 million
- **Coed**
- **Very difficult** entrance level

Fordham, the Jesuit University of New York, has two residential campuses in New York City. The 85-acre Rose Hill campus is one of the largest green campuses in the city and is located in the Bronx, adjacent to the Botanical Gardens and the Bronx Zoo. The Lincoln Center campus, with a twenty-story residence hall, is in the cultural heart of Manhattan.

Faculty *Student/faculty ratio:* 12:1.

Academics *Calendar:* semesters. *Degrees:* bachelor's, master's, doctoral, first professional, and post-master's certificates (branch locations at Rose Hill and Lincoln Center).

Student Life *Campus security:* 24-hour emergency response devices and patrols, student patrols, late-night transport/escort service, controlled dormitory access, security at each campus entrance and at residence halls.

Athletics Member NCAA. All Division I except football (Division I-AA).

Standardized Tests *Required:* SAT or ACT (for admission). *Recommended:* SAT Subject Tests (for admission).

Costs (2007–08) *Comprehensive fee:* $45,157 includes full-time tuition ($31,800), mandatory fees ($1057), and room and board ($12,300). *Room and board:* Room and board charges vary according to board plan and location.

Financial Aid Of all full-time matriculated undergraduates who enrolled in 2004, 4,936 applied for aid, 4,374 were judged to have need, 930 had their need fully met. 1,295 Federal Work-Study jobs (averaging $2676). 99 state and other part-time jobs (averaging $9328). In 2004, 586 non-need-based awards were made. *Average percent of need met:* 77. *Average financial aid package:* $19,953. *Average need-based loan:* $4396. *Average need-based gift aid:* $15,096. *Average non-need-based aid:* $8005. *Average indebtedness upon graduation:* $16,590. *Financial aid deadline:* 2/1.

Applying *Options:* electronic application, early admission, early action, deferred entrance. *Application fee:* $50. *Required:* essay or personal statement, high school transcript, 1 letter of recommendation.

Freshman Application Contact Mr. Peter Farrell, Director of Admission, Fordham University, Duane Library, 441 East Fordham Road, New York, NY 10458. *Phone:* 718-817-4000. *Toll-free phone:* 800-FORDHAM. *Fax:* 718-367-9404. *E-mail:* enroll@fordham.edu.

See page 1742 for the College Close-Up.

GLOBAL COLLEGE OF LONG ISLAND UNIVERSITY

Brooklyn, New York **www.liu.edu/globalcollege/**

- **Independent** 4-year, founded 1965, part of Long Island University
- **Urban** campus
- **Coed** 98 undergraduate students, 100% full-time, 68% women, 32% men
- **Minimally difficult** entrance level, 73% of applicants were admitted

Undergraduates 98 full-time. Students come from 20 states and territories, 76% are from out of state, 8% African American, 6% Asian American or Pacific Islander, 8% Hispanic American, 1% Native American, 15% transferred in. *Retention:* 59% of 2006 full-time freshmen returned.

Freshmen *Admission:* 88 applied, 64 admitted, 32 enrolled. *Average high school GPA:* 3.48.

Faculty *Total:* 20. *Student/faculty ratio:* 4:1.

Majors Interdisciplinary studies; liberal arts and sciences/liberal studies; multi-/interdisciplinary studies related.

Academics *Calendar:* semesters. *Degree:* bachelor's. *Special study options:* advanced placement credit, external degree program, independent study, internships, off-campus study, study abroad.

Computers on Campus Students can access the following: free student e-mail accounts. Campuswide network is available.

Student Life *Housing options:* coed. Campus housing is provided by a third party. Freshman campus housing is guaranteed. *Activities and organizations:* Activist Club, P.E.A.C.E., LaFuenza Latina, Caribbean Student Association, Women's Issues Collective. *Student services:* health clinic, personal/psychological counseling.

Costs (2007–08) *Comprehensive fee:* $34,872 includes full-time tuition ($26,272), mandatory fees ($4800), and room and board ($3800). Full-time tuition and fees vary according to location. Part-time tuition: $821 per credit. Part-time tuition and fees vary according to location. *Required fees:* $2770 per year part-time. *Room and board:* Room and board charges vary according to location. *Payment plans:* installment, deferred payment. *Waivers:* employees or children of employees.

Applying *Options:* electronic application, early admission, deferred entrance. *Application fee:* $30. *Required:* essay or personal statement, high school transcript, letters of recommendation, interview. *Recommended:* minimum 3.0 GPA. *Application deadlines:* rolling (freshmen), rolling (transfers). *Notification:* continuous (freshmen), continuous (transfers).

Freshman Application Contact Global College of Long Island University, Brooklyn Campus, 9 Hanover Place, 4th Floor, Brooklyn, NY 11201-5882. *Phone:* 718-780-4320.

GLOBE INSTITUTE OF TECHNOLOGY

New York, New York **www.globe.edu/**

- **Proprietary** 4-year
- **Urban** campus
- **Coed**
- **Minimally difficult** entrance level

Faculty *Student/faculty ratio:* 10:1.

Academics *Calendar:* semesters. *Degrees:* associate and bachelor's.

Athletics Member NJCAA.

Standardized Tests *Recommended:* SAT or ACT (for admission).

Costs (2007–08) *Tuition:* $11,950 full-time. *Required fees:* $200 full-time.

Applying *Options:* electronic application. *Application fee:* $50. *Required:* high school transcript, interview.

Freshman Application Contact Ms. Tanya Garelik, Admissions Director, Globe Institute of Technology, 291 Broadway, New York, NY 10007. *Phone:* 212-349-4330 Ext. 1624. *Toll-free phone:* 877-394-5623. *Fax:* 212-227-5920. *E-mail:* admissions@globe.edu.

See page 1744 for the College Close-Up.

HAMILTON COLLEGE

Clinton, New York **www.hamilton.edu/**

- **Independent** 4-year, founded 1812
- **Small-town** 1200-acre campus
- **Endowment** $780.2 million
- **Coed** 1,842 undergraduate students, 98% full-time, 52% women, 48% men
- **Very difficult** entrance level, 28% of applicants were admitted

Undergraduates 1,810 full-time, 32 part-time. Students come from 20 states and territories, 46 other countries, 66% are from out of state, 4% African American, 7% Asian American or Pacific Islander, 5% Hispanic American, 0.9% Native American, 5% international, 0.4% transferred in, 98% live on campus. *Retention:* 93% of 2006 full-time freshmen returned.

Freshmen *Admission:* 4,962 applied, 1,376 admitted, 468 enrolled. *Test scores:* SAT critical reading scores over 500: 97%; SAT math scores over 500: 99%; SAT critical reading scores over 600: 87%; SAT math scores over 600: 91%; SAT critical reading scores over 700: 49%; SAT math scores over 700: 39%.

Faculty *Total:* 217, 79% full-time, 85% with terminal degrees. *Student/faculty ratio:* 10:1.

Majors African studies; American studies; anthropology; archeology; art; art history, criticism and conservation; Asian studies; Asian studies (East); biochemistry; biology/biological sciences; chemistry; classics and languages, literatures and linguistics; comparative literature; computer science; creative writing; dance; dramatic/theater arts; economics; English; fine/studio arts; French; geology/earth science; German; history; history related; international relations and affairs; Latin; mass communication/media; mathematics; medieval and Renaissance studies; modern Greek; modern languages; molecular biology; music; neuroscience; philosophy; physics; physiological psychology/psychobiology; political science and government; psychology; public policy analysis; religious studies; Russian studies; sociology; Spanish; women's studies.

Academics *Calendar:* semesters. *Degree:* bachelor's. *Special study options:* accelerated degree program, adult/continuing education programs, advanced placement credit, double majors, English as a second language, independent study, internships, off-campus study, part-time degree program, services for LD students, student-designed majors, study abroad. *ROTC:* Army (c), Air Force (c). *Unusual degree programs:* 3-2 engineering with Columbia University, Rensselaer Polytechnic Institute, Washington University in St. Louis; social work; public policy analysis with University of Rochester.

Computers on Campus 625 computers/terminals and 6,000 ports are available on campus for general student use. Students can access the following: computer help desk, free student e-mail accounts, online (class) grades, online (class) registration. Campuswide network is available. 100% of college-owned or -operated housing units are wired for high-speed Internet access. Wireless service is available via entire campus.

Student Life *Housing:* on-campus residence required through senior year. *Options:* coed, disabled students. Campus housing is university owned. Freshman campus housing is guaranteed. *Activities and organizations:* drama/theater group, student-run newspaper, radio and television station, choral group, community service groups, Outing Club, student newspaper, club/intramural sports, performing arts groups, national fraternities. *Campus security:* 24-hour emergency response devices and patrols, late-night transport/escort service, controlled dormitory access, student safety program. *Student services:* health clinic, personal/psychological counseling, women's center.

Athletics Member NCAA. All Division III. *Intercollegiate sports:* baseball M, basketball M/W, crew W, cross-country running M/W, fencing M (c)/W (c), field hockey W, football M, golf M/W (c), ice hockey M/W, lacrosse M/W, rugby M (c)/W (c), sailing M (c)/W (c), skiing (downhill) M (c)/W (c), soccer M/W, softball W, squash M/W, swimming and diving M/W, tennis M/W, track and field M/W, ultimate Frisbee M (c)/W (c), volleyball M (c)/W, water polo M (c)/W (c). *Intramural sports:* basketball M/W, bowling M/W, cross-country running M/W, equestrian sports M/W, field hockey W, football M, golf M/W, ice hockey M/W, lacrosse M/W, racquetball M/W, skiing (cross-country) M/W, skiing (downhill) M/W, soccer M/W, softball M, squash M/W, table tennis M/W, tennis M/W, volleyball M/W, water polo M/W.

Standardized Tests *Required:* SAT and SAT Subject Tests or ACT (for admission).

Costs (2007–08) *Comprehensive fee:* $46,210 includes full-time tuition ($36,500), mandatory fees ($360), and room and board ($9350). *College room only:* $5100. Room and board charges vary according to board plan. *Payment plan:* installment. *Waivers:* employees or children of employees.

Financial Aid Of all full-time matriculated undergraduates who enrolled in 2007, 963 applied for aid, 856 were judged to have need, 856 had their need fully met. In 2007, 58 non-need-based awards were made. *Average percent of need met:* 100%. *Average financial aid package:* $31,003. *Average need-based loan:* $3735. *Average need-based gift aid:* $26,773. *Average non-need-based aid:* $8667. *Average indebtedness upon graduation:* $16,808. *Financial aid deadline:* 2/8.

Applying *Options:* electronic application, early decision, deferred entrance. *Application fee:* $50. *Required:* essay or personal statement, high school transcript, 1 letter of recommendation, sample of expository prose. *Recommended:* interview. *Application deadlines:* 1/1 (freshmen), 4/15 (transfers). *Early decision deadline:* 11/15 (for plan 1), 1/1 (for plan 2). *Notification:* 4/1 (freshmen), 6/1 (transfers), 12/15 (early decision plan 1), 2/15 (early decision plan 2).

Freshman Application Contact Ms. Monica Inzer, Dean of Admission and Financial Aid, Hamilton College, 198 College Hill Road, Clinton, NY 13323. *Phone:* 315-859-4421. *Toll-free phone:* 800-843-2655. *Fax:* 315-859-4457. *E-mail:* admission@hamilton.edu.

HARTWICK COLLEGE

Oneonta, New York **www.hartwick.edu/**

- **Independent** 4-year, founded 1797
- **Small-town** 425-acre campus with easy access to Albany
- **Endowment** $66.9 million
- **Coed** 1,537 undergraduate students, 96% full-time, 56% women, 44% men
- **Moderately difficult** entrance level, 84% of applicants were admitted

Undergraduates 1,483 full-time, 54 part-time. Students come from 36 states and territories, 43 other countries, 34% are from out of state, 5% African American, 2% Asian American or Pacific Islander, 5% Hispanic American, 0.4%

Native American, 3% international, 3% transferred in, 86% live on campus. *Retention:* 79% of 2006 full-time freshmen returned.

Freshmen *Admission:* 2,422 applied, 2,034 admitted, 452 enrolled. *Test scores:* SAT critical reading scores over 500: 71%; SAT math scores over 500: 79%; SAT writing scores over 500: 69%; ACT scores over 18: 94%; SAT critical reading scores over 600: 30%; SAT math scores over 600: 25%; SAT writing scores over 600: 21%; ACT scores over 24: 49%; SAT critical reading scores over 700: 3%; SAT math scores over 700: 2%; SAT writing scores over 700: 3%; ACT scores over 30: 11%.

Faculty *Total:* 169, 64% full-time. *Student/faculty ratio:* 11:1.

Majors Accounting; anthropology; art; art history, criticism and conservation; biochemistry; biology/biological sciences; business administration and management; chemistry; clinical laboratory science/medical technology; computer and information sciences; computer science; dramatic/theater arts; economics; English; environmental science; French; geology/earth science; German; history; mathematics; music; music teacher education; nursing (registered nurse training); philosophy; physics; political science and government; pre-law studies; premedical studies; pre-veterinary studies; psychology; religious studies; sociology; Spanish.

Academics *Calendar:* 4-1-4. *Degree:* bachelor's. *Special study options:* accelerated degree program, advanced placement credit, double majors, honors programs, independent study, internships, off-campus study, part-time degree program, services for LD students, student-designed majors, study abroad. *Unusual degree programs:* 3-2 engineering with Clarkson University, Columbia University.

Computers on Campus 80 computers/terminals are available on campus for general student use. Students can access the following: computer help desk, free student e-mail accounts, online (class) grades, online (class) schedules. Campuswide network is available. 100% of college-owned or -operated housing units are wired for high-speed Internet access. Wireless service is available via entire campus.

Student Life *Housing:* on-campus residence required through junior year. *Options:* coed, women-only. Campus housing is university owned. Freshman campus housing is guaranteed. *Activities and organizations:* drama/theater group, student-run newspaper, radio station, choral group, Student Union, student radio station, Student Senate, Hilltops, Cardboard Alley Players, national fraternities, national sororities. *Campus security:* 24-hour emergency response devices and patrols, late-night transport/escort service, controlled dormitory access. *Student services:* health clinic, personal/psychological counseling, women's center.

Athletics Member NCAA. All Division III except soccer (Division I), water polo (Division I). *Intercollegiate sports:* basketball M/W, cheerleading W, cross-country running M/W, equestrian sports W, field hockey W, football M, ice hockey M (c), lacrosse M/W, rugby M (c), soccer M (s)/W, swimming and diving M/W, tennis M/W, volleyball W, water polo M (c)/W (s). *Intramural sports:* basketball M/W, cross-country running M/W, football M, golf M/W, racquetball M/W, soccer M/W, squash M/W, swimming and diving M/W, table tennis M/W, tennis M/W, track and field M/W, volleyball M/W, water polo M/W.

Standardized Tests *Required for some:* SAT (for admission).

Costs (2007–08) *One-time required fee:* $300. *Comprehensive fee:* $39,100 includes full-time tuition ($30,125), mandatory fees ($605), and room and board ($8370). Part-time tuition: $927 per hour. *College room only:* $4285. Room and board charges vary according to board plan and housing facility. *Payment plan:* installment. *Waivers:* employees or children of employees.

Financial Aid Of all full-time matriculated undergraduates who enrolled in 2006, 1,205 applied for aid, 1,082 were judged to have need, 139 had their need fully met. 723 Federal Work-Study jobs (averaging $1542). In 2006, 330 non-need-based awards were made. *Average percent of need met:* 83%. *Average financial aid package:* $22,964. *Average need-based loan:* $4019. *Average need-based gift aid:* $15,808. *Average non-need-based aid:* $9140. *Average indebtedness upon graduation:* $25,044. *Financial aid deadline:* 2/15.

Applying *Options:* electronic application, early admission, early decision, deferred entrance. *Application fee:* $35. *Required:* essay or personal statement, high school transcript, 2 letters of recommendation, audition for music program. *Recommended:* minimum 3.0 GPA, interview. *Application deadlines:* 2/15 (freshmen), 8/1 (transfers). *Early decision deadline:* 11/15 (for plan 1), 1/15 (for plan 2). *Notification:* 3/5 (freshmen).

Freshman Application Contact Ms. Jacqueline Gregory, Director of Admissions, Hartwick College, PO Box 4022, Oneonta, NY 13820-4022. *Phone:* 607-431-4150. *Toll-free phone:* 888-HARTWICK. *Fax:* 607-431-4102. *E-mail:* admissions@hartwick.edu.

HILBERT COLLEGE

Hamburg, New York www.hilbert.edu/

- **Independent** 4-year, founded 1957
- **Small-town** 40-acre campus with easy access to Buffalo
- **Endowment** $2.9 million
- **Coed** 1,046 undergraduate students, 76% full-time, 61% women, 39% men
- **Minimally difficult** entrance level, 85% of applicants were admitted

With four new apartment-style residence halls, high-tech communications labs, and new athletic facilities, Hilbert College is an active and growing campus. This past year saw the opening of Hilbert's new academic building and auditorium. An expansion and refurbishment of the original academic building is scheduled to take place during the new school year, providing smart classrooms and new forensic science labs. Program offerings continue to expand along with the campus; Hilbert has introduced unique new programs in digital media and communication, rehabilitation services, and forensic science/crime scene investigation.

Undergraduates 798 full-time, 248 part-time. Students come from 5 states and territories, 1 other country, 75% are from out of state, 6% African American, 0.1% Asian American or Pacific Islander, 2% Hispanic American, 2% Native American, 0.2% international, 9% transferred in, 25% live on campus. *Retention:* 64% of 2006 full-time freshmen returned.

Freshmen *Admission:* 722 applied, 614 admitted, 210 enrolled. *Average high school GPA:* 3.20. *Test scores:* SAT critical reading scores over 500: 27%; SAT math scores over 500: 41%; ACT scores over 18: 71%; SAT critical reading scores over 600: 6%; SAT math scores over 600: 8%; ACT scores over 24: 18%.

Faculty *Total:* 115, 42% full-time, 85% with terminal degrees. *Student/faculty ratio:* 12:1.

Majors Accounting; banking and financial support services; criminal justice/police science; digital communication and media/multimedia; English; finance; forensic science and technology; liberal arts and sciences/liberal studies; management information systems; psychology; rehabilitation and therapeutic professions related.

Academics *Calendar:* semesters. *Degrees:* associate and bachelor's. *Special study options:* academic remediation for entering students, advanced placement credit, cooperative education, distance learning, honors programs, independent study, internships, part-time degree program, services for LD students, study abroad, summer session for credit. *ROTC:* Army (c).

Computers on Campus 146 computers/terminals are available on campus for general student use. Students can access the following: online (class) registration. Campuswide network is available.

Student Life *Housing options:* coed. Campus housing is university owned and leased by the school. Freshman campus housing is guaranteed. *Activities and organizations:* drama/theater group, student-run newspaper, Student Government Association, Student Business and Accounting Association, SADD, Students in Free Enterprise (SIFE), Criminal Justice Association. *Campus security:* 24-hour emergency response devices and patrols, student patrols, late-night transport/escort service, controlled dormitory access. *Student services:* personal/psychological counseling.

Athletics Member NCAA. All Division III. *Intercollegiate sports:* baseball M, basketball M/W, cross-country running M/W, golf M/W, soccer M/W, softball W, volleyball M/W. *Intramural sports:* baseball M, basketball M/W, bowling M/W, cheerleading W, football M/W, golf M, ice hockey M (c), lacrosse M (c), skiing (downhill) M (c)/W (c), soccer M/W, softball W, table tennis M/W, volleyball M/W.

Standardized Tests *Recommended:* SAT or ACT (for admission).

Costs (2007–08) *Comprehensive fee:* $23,200 includes full-time tuition ($16,000), mandatory fees ($600), and room and board ($6600).

Financial Aid Of all full-time matriculated undergraduates who enrolled in 2006, 797 applied for aid, 709 were judged to have need, 205 had their need fully met. 54 Federal Work-Study jobs (averaging $1665). In 2006, 103 non-need-based awards were made. *Average percent of need met:* 74%. *Average financial aid package:* $10,601. *Average need-based loan:* $4758. *Average need-based gift aid:* $6380. *Average non-need-based aid:* $9997. *Average indebtedness upon graduation:* $22,282. *Financial aid deadline:* 5/1.

Applying *Options:* electronic application, early admission, deferred entrance. *Application fee:* $20. *Required:* high school transcript. *Required for some:* interview. *Recommended:* essay or personal statement, letters of recommendation, interview. *Application deadlines:* 9/1 (freshmen), 8/1 (transfers). *Notification:* continuous (freshmen), continuous (transfers).

Freshman Application Contact Mr. Timothy Lee, Director of Admissions, Hilbert College, 5200 South Park Avenue, Hamburg, NY 14075-1597. *Phone:* 716-649-7900. *Fax:* 716-649-0702. *E-mail:* tlee@hilbert.edu.

See page 1746 for the College Close-Up.

HOBART AND WILLIAM SMITH COLLEGES

Geneva, New York **www.hws.edu/**

- **Independent** 4-year, founded 1822
- **Small-town** 200-acre campus with easy access to Rochester and Syracuse
- **Coed** 2,001 undergraduate students, 100% full-time, 54% women, 46% men
- **Very difficult** entrance level, 55% of applicants were admitted

Hobart and William Smith (HWS) Colleges are dedicated to providing a liberal arts education that is not merely informative but also transformative—emphasizing ideals as well as knowledge. In other words, HWS is committed to nurturing the whole person and not just the academic student. To achieve this goal, HWS melds an interdisciplinary curriculum with a worldview of learning, the highlights of which are an extensive and vibrant study-abroad program; local, national, and global internships; and a strong community service component.

Undergraduates 1,998 full-time, 3 part-time. Students come from 48 states and territories, 13 other countries, 58% are from out of state, 4% African American, 3% Asian American or Pacific Islander, 3% Hispanic American, 0.4% Native American, 2% international, 0.9% transferred in, 90% live on campus. *Retention:* 85% of 2006 full-time freshmen returned.

Freshmen *Admission:* 4,165 applied, 2,270 admitted, 619 enrolled. *Average high school GPA:* 3.39. *Test scores:* SAT critical reading scores over 500: 96%; SAT math scores over 500: 96%; SAT critical reading scores over 600: 50%; SAT math scores over 600: 54%; SAT critical reading scores over 700: 10%; SAT math scores over 700: 12%.

Faculty *Total:* 212, 86% full-time. *Student/faculty ratio:* 11:1.

Majors African-American/Black studies; African studies; American studies; ancient/classical Greek; anthropology; architecture; art; art history, criticism and conservation; Asian studies; biochemistry; biology/biological sciences; chemistry; Chinese; classics and languages, literatures and linguistics; comparative literature; computer science; dance; dramatic/theater arts; economics; English; environmental studies; European studies; fine/studio arts; French; gay/lesbian studies; geology/earth science; history; interdisciplinary studies; international relations and affairs; Japanese; Latin; Latin American studies; liberal arts and sciences/liberal studies; mass communication/media; mathematics; medieval and Renaissance studies; modern languages; music; philosophy; physics; political science and government; pre-dentistry studies; pre-law studies; pre-medical studies; pre-veterinary studies; psychology; public policy analysis; religious studies; Russian; Russian studies; sociology; Spanish; urban studies/affairs; women's studies.

Academics *Calendar:* semesters. *Degrees:* bachelor's and master's. *Special study options:* accelerated degree program, adult/continuing education programs, advanced placement credit, double majors, English as a second language, honors programs, independent study, internships, off-campus study, services for LD students, student-designed majors, study abroad. *Unusual degree programs:* 3-2 business administration with Clarkson University, Rochester Institute of Technology; engineering with Columbia University, Rensselaer Polytechnic Institute, Dartmouth College; architecture with Washington University in St. Louis.

Computers on Campus 250 computers/terminals are available on campus for general student use. Students can access the following: campus intranet, computer help desk, free student e-mail accounts, online (class) grades, online (class) registration, online (class) schedules. Campuswide network is available. 100% of college-owned or -operated housing units are wired for high-speed Internet access. Wireless service is available via entire campus.

Student Life *Housing:* on-campus residence required through junior year. *Options:* coed, men-only, women-only, cooperative. Campus housing is university owned. Freshman campus housing is guaranteed. *Activities and organizations:* drama/theater group, student-run newspaper, radio station, choral group, Student Life and Leadership, student government, Campus publications, Service Network, sports clubs, national fraternities. *Campus security:* 24-hour emergency response devices and patrols, late-night transport/escort service, controlled dormitory access. *Student services:* health clinic, personal/psychological counseling, women's center, legal services.

Athletics Member NCAA. All Division III except lacrosse (Division I). *Intercollegiate sports:* basketball M/W, crew M/W, cross-country running M/W, equestrian sports M (c)/W (c), field hockey W, football M, golf M/W, ice hockey M/W (c), lacrosse M/W, rock climbing M (c)/W (c), rugby M (c)/W (c), sailing M/W, skiing (downhill) M (c)/W (c), soccer M/W, squash M/W, swimming and diving W, tennis M/W, ultimate Frisbee M (c)/W (c). *Intramural sports:* badminton M/W, baseball M, basketball M/W, fencing M/W, football M, golf M/W, ice hockey M/W, lacrosse M/W, racquetball M/W, skiing (cross-country) M/W, skiing (downhill) M/W, soccer M/W, softball M/W, squash M/W, swimming and diving M/W, table tennis M/W, tennis M/W, track and field M/W, ultimate Frisbee M/W, volleyball M/W, water polo M/W, weight lifting M/W.

Standardized Tests *Required for some:* SAT or ACT (for admission).

Costs (2008–09) *Comprehensive fee:* $48,546 includes full-time tuition ($37,820), mandatory fees ($1040), and room and board ($9686).

Financial Aid Of all full-time matriculated undergraduates who enrolled in 2006, 1,403 applied for aid, 1,173 were judged to have need, 934 had their need fully met. 911 Federal Work-Study jobs (averaging $1725). 385 state and other part-time jobs (averaging $1863). In 2006, 369 non-need-based awards were made. *Average percent of need met:* 80%. *Average financial aid package:* $25,054. *Average need-based loan:* $3676. *Average need-based gift aid:* $21,108. *Average non-need-based aid:* $17,765. *Average indebtedness upon graduation:* $25,924. *Financial aid deadline:* 3/15.

Applying *Options:* electronic application, early admission, early decision, deferred entrance. *Application fee:* $45. *Required:* essay or personal statement, high school transcript, 1 letter of recommendation. *Recommended:* interview. *Application deadlines:* 2/1 (freshmen), 7/1 (transfers). *Early decision deadline:* 11/15 (for plan 1), 1/1 (for plan 2). *Notification:* 4/1 (freshmen), continuous (transfers), 12/15 (early decision plan 1), 2/1 (early decision plan 2).

Director of Admissions Don W. Emmons, Dean of Admissions and Vice President of Enrollment, Hobart and William Smith Colleges, 629 South Main Street, Geneva, NY 14456-3397. *Phone:* 315-781-3622. *Toll-free phone:* 800-245-0100. *Fax:* 315-781-3914. *E-mail:* emmons@hws.edu.

See page 1748 for the College Close-Up.

HOFSTRA UNIVERSITY

Hempstead, New York **www.hofstra.edu/**

- **Independent** university, founded 1935
- **Suburban** 240-acre campus with easy access to New York City
- **Endowment** $230.4 million
- **Coed** 8,444 undergraduate students, 91% full-time, 53% women, 47% men
- **Moderately difficult** entrance level, 54% of applicants were admitted

Undergraduates 7,718 full-time, 726 part-time. Students come from 49 states and territories, 50 other countries, 34% are from out of state, 9% African American, 5% Asian American or Pacific Islander, 7% Hispanic American, 0.6% Native American, 1% international, 8% transferred in, 50% live on campus. *Retention:* 79% of 2006 full-time freshmen returned.

Freshmen *Admission:* 18,471 applied, 9,986 admitted, 1,735 enrolled. *Average high school GPA:* 3.37. *Test scores:* SAT critical reading scores over 500: 94%; SAT math scores over 500: 95%; ACT scores over 18: 100%; SAT critical reading scores over 600: 45%; SAT math scores over 600: 46%; ACT scores over 24: 65%; SAT critical reading scores over 700: 5%; SAT math scores over 700: 4%; ACT scores over 30: 8%.

Faculty *Total:* 1,193, 46% full-time, 62% with terminal degrees. *Student/faculty ratio:* 14:1.

Majors Accounting; acting; actuarial science; African studies; allied health diagnostic, intervention, and treatment professions related; American studies; anthropology; applied mathematics; area studies related; art history, criticism and conservation; art teacher education; Asian studies; athletic training; audiology and speech-language pathology; biochemistry; biology/biological sciences; biology teacher education; biomedical/medical engineering; broadcast journalism; business administration and management; business administration, management and operations related; business/commerce; business/managerial economics; business teacher education; Caribbean studies; ceramic arts and ceramics; chemistry; chemistry teacher education; Chinese; civil engineering; classics and languages, literatures and linguistics; communication/speech communication and rhetoric; community health and preventive medicine; comparative literature; computer and information sciences and support services related; computer engineering; computer science; creative writing; dance; design and applied arts related; directing and theatrical production; dramatic/theater arts; early childhood education; econometrics and quantitative economics; economics; education (multiple levels); electrical, electronics and communications engineering; elementary education; engineering science; English; English language and literature related; English/language arts teacher education; English literature (British and Commonwealth); entrepreneurship; environmental/environmental health engineering; environ-

COLLEGE DATA CENTER • NEW YORK

mental studies; finance; finance and financial management services related; fine/studio arts; foreign language teacher education; forensic science and technology; French; French language teacher education; geography; geology/earth science; German; German language teacher education; health teacher education; Hebrew; Hispanic-American, Puerto Rican, and Mexican-American/Chicano studies; history; humanities; industrial engineering; international business/trade/commerce; Italian; jazz/jazz studies; Jewish/Judaic studies; journalism; labor studies; Latin; Latin American studies; liberal arts and sciences and humanities related; liberal arts and sciences/liberal studies; linguistics; management information systems; manufacturing engineering; marketing/marketing management; mass communication/media; mathematics; mathematics and computer science; mathematics and statistics related; mathematics teacher education; mechanical engineering; metal and jewelry arts; multi-/interdisciplinary studies related; music; music history, literature, and theory; music management and merchandising; music performance; music teacher education; music theory and composition; natural sciences; painting; philosophy; photography; physical education teaching and coaching; physician assistant; physics; physics teacher education; political science and government; pre-dentistry studies; pre-law studies; pre-medical studies; pre-veterinary studies; psychology; public relations/image management; radio and television; radio, television, and digital communication related; religious studies; Russian; science teacher education; secondary education; social sciences; social studies teacher education; sociology; Spanish; Spanish language teacher education; women's studies.

Academics *Calendar:* 4-1-4. *Degrees:* bachelor's, master's, doctoral, first professional, post-master's, and postbachelor's certificates. *Special study options:* accelerated degree program, adult/continuing education programs, advanced placement credit, double majors, English as a second language, external degree program, freshman honors college, honors programs, independent study, internships, part-time degree program, services for LD students, student-designed majors, study abroad, summer session for credit. *ROTC:* Army (b). *Unusual degree programs:* 3-2 business administration.

Computers on Campus 1,694 computers/terminals and 1,900 ports are available on campus for general student use. Students can access the following: campus intranet, computer help desk, free student e-mail accounts, online (class) grades, online (class) registration, online (class) schedules, Gmail/Google Apps for students; Emergency Notification System; Online course management system; Online card services balance update; Online portfolio. Campuswide network is available. 100% of college-owned or -operated housing units are wired for high-speed Internet access. Wireless service is available via classrooms, computer centers, computer labs, learning centers, libraries, student centers.

Student Life *Housing options:* coed, women-only, disabled students. Campus housing is university owned. Freshman applicants given priority for college housing. *Activities and organizations:* drama/theater group, student-run newspaper, radio and television station, choral group, Student Government Association, Hillel, Entertainment Unlimited, Danceworks, NAACP, national fraternities, national sororities. *Campus security:* 24-hour emergency response devices and patrols, student patrols, late-night transport/escort service, controlled dormitory access, security booths and cameras at each residence hall entrance. *Student services:* health clinic, personal/psychological counseling.

Athletics Member NCAA. All Division I except football (Division I-AA). *Intercollegiate sports:* baseball M (s), basketball M (s)/W (s), cross-country running M (s)/W (s), field hockey W (s), golf M (s)/W (s), lacrosse M (s)/W (s), soccer M (s)/W (s), softball W (s), tennis M (s)/W (s), volleyball W (s), wrestling M (s). *Intramural sports:* badminton M/W, baseball M (c), basketball M/W, cheerleading M (c)/W (c), crew M (c)/W (c), equestrian sports M (c)/W (c), ice hockey M (c), lacrosse M (c)/W (c), rugby M (c)/W (c), soccer M (c)/W, softball M/W, table tennis M/W, tennis M/W, ultimate Frisbee M (c)/W (c), volleyball M/W.

Standardized Tests *Required for some:* SAT or ACT (for admission). *Recommended:* SAT Subject Tests (for admission).

Costs (2007–08) *Comprehensive fee:* $37,030 includes full-time tuition ($25,700), mandatory fees ($1030), and room and board ($10,300). Full-time tuition and fees vary according to course load and program. Part-time tuition: $785 per credit hour. Part-time tuition and fees vary according to course load and program. *Required fees:* $155 per term part-time. *College room only:* $6900. Room and board charges vary according to board plan and housing facility. *Payment plans:* installment, deferred payment. *Waivers:* senior citizens and employees or children of employees.

Financial Aid Of all full-time matriculated undergraduates who enrolled in 2006, 5,626 applied for aid, 4,557 were judged to have need, 664 had their need fully met. 1,307 Federal Work-Study jobs (averaging $3022). 2,104 state and other part-time jobs (averaging $2259). In 2006, 1250 non-need-based awards were made. *Average percent of need met:* 74%. *Average financial aid package:* $13,519. *Average need-based loan:* $4113. *Average need-based gift aid:* $8070. *Average non-need-based aid:* $7194.

Applying *Options:* electronic application, early admission, early action, deferred entrance. *Application fee:* $50. *Required:* essay or personal statement, high school transcript, proof of degree required for all; TOEFL required for international students. *Required for some:* interview, proof of degree required for all; TOEFL required for international students. *Application deadlines:* rolling (freshmen), 12/15 (early action). *Notification:* 2/1 (freshmen), continuous (transfers), 1/15 (early action).

Freshman Application Contact Mr. Sunil Samuel, Senior Associate Dean of Admissions, Hofstra University, 100 Hofstra University, Hempstead, NY 11549. *Phone:* 516-463-6700. *Toll-free phone:* 800-HOFSTRA. *Fax:* 516-463-5100. *E-mail:* admitme@hofstra.edu.

See page 1750 for the College Close-Up.

HOLY TRINITY ORTHODOX SEMINARY

Jordanville, New York **www.hts.edu/**

- **Independent Russian Orthodox** 5-year, founded 1948
- **Rural** 900-acre campus
- **Men only** 28 undergraduate students, 89% full-time
- **Noncompetitive** entrance level, 80% of applicants were admitted

Undergraduates 25 full-time, 3 part-time. Students come from 3 states and territories, 11 other countries, 80% are from out of state, 4% Hispanic American, 75% international, 14% transferred in, 100% live on campus. *Retention:* 100% of 2006 full-time freshmen returned.

Freshmen *Admission:* 10 applied, 8 admitted, 3 enrolled.

Faculty *Total:* 15, 67% full-time, 7% with terminal degrees. *Student/faculty ratio:* 2:1.

Majors Theology.

Academics *Calendar:* semesters. *Degree:* certificates and bachelor's. *Special study options:* accelerated degree program, distance learning, English as a second language.

Computers on Campus 8 computers/terminals and 3 ports are available on campus for general student use.

Student Life *Housing:* on-campus residence required through senior year. *Options:* men-only. Campus housing is university owned. Freshman campus housing is guaranteed. *Activities and organizations:* student-run newspaper, choral group, Student Union. *Campus security:* 24-hour emergency response devices. *Student services:* health clinic, personal/psychological counseling.

Costs (2007–08) *Comprehensive fee:* $5525 includes full-time tuition ($3000), mandatory fees ($25), and room and board ($2500). Part-time tuition: $300 per course.

Applying *Required:* essay or personal statement, high school transcript, letters of recommendation, special examination, proficiency in Russian, Eastern Orthodox baptism. *Recommended:* minimum 3.0 GPA. *Application deadlines:* 5/1 (freshmen), 5/1 (transfers).

Freshman Application Contact Fr. Vladimir Tsurikov, Assistant Dean, Holy Trinity Orthodox Seminary, PO Box 36, Jordanville, NY 13361. *Phone:* 315-858-0945. *Fax:* 315-858-0945. *E-mail:* info@hts.edu.

HOUGHTON COLLEGE

Houghton, New York **www.houghton.edu/**

- **Independent Wesleyan** comprehensive, founded 1883
- **Rural** 1300-acre campus with easy access to Buffalo and Rochester
- **Endowment** $40.4 million
- **Coed** 1,368 undergraduate students, 95% full-time, 64% women, 36% men
- **Moderately difficult** entrance level, 84% of applicants were admitted

Undergraduates 1,297 full-time, 71 part-time. Students come from 32 states and territories, 17 other countries, 32% are from out of state, 2% African American, 2% Asian American or Pacific Islander, 0.7% Hispanic American, 0.4% Native American, 3% international, 7% transferred in, 86% live on campus. *Retention:* 82% of 2006 full-time freshmen returned.

Freshmen *Admission:* 1,005 applied, 843 admitted, 265 enrolled. *Average high school GPA:* 3.5. *Test scores:* SAT critical reading scores over 500: 79%; SAT math scores over 500: 75%; SAT writing scores over 500: 80%; ACT scores over 18: 97%; SAT critical reading scores over 600: 41%; SAT math scores over 600: 34%; SAT writing scores over 600: 36%; ACT scores over 24: 58%; SAT critical reading scores over 700: 12%; SAT math scores over 700: 7%; SAT writing scores over 700: 7%; ACT scores over 30: 15%.

Faculty *Total:* 115, 76% full-time, 70% with terminal degrees. *Student/faculty ratio:* 14:1.

Majors Accounting; art; biblical studies; biochemistry; biological and physical sciences; biology/biological sciences; business administration and management;

chemistry; clinical laboratory science/medical technology; computer science; creative writing; cultural studies; elementary education; English; English as a second/foreign language (teaching); environmental biology; French; health and physical education; history; humanities; information technology; international relations and affairs; liberal arts and sciences/liberal studies; literature; mathematics; music; music performance; music teacher education; music theory and composition; natural sciences; parks, recreation and leisure; pastoral studies/counseling; philosophy; physical education teaching and coaching; physics; piano and organ; political science and government; pre-dentistry studies; pre-law studies; pre-medical studies; pre-veterinary studies; psychology; religious education; religious studies; secondary education; sociology; Spanish; special education; theology; violin, viola, guitar and other stringed instruments; voice and opera; wind/percussion instruments.

Academics *Calendar:* semesters. *Degrees:* associate, bachelor's, and master's. *Special study options:* adult/continuing education programs, advanced placement credit, double majors, honors programs, independent study, internships, off-campus study, part-time degree program, services for LD students, study abroad, summer session for credit. *ROTC:* Army (c). *Unusual degree programs:* 3-2 engineering with Clarkson University, Washington University in St. Louis.

Computers on Campus 25 computers/terminals and 820 ports are available on campus for general student use. Students can access the following: computer help desk, free student e-mail accounts, online (class) grades, online (class) registration, online (class) schedules. Campuswide network is available. 100% of college-owned or -operated housing units are wired for high-speed Internet access. Wireless service is available via entire campus.

Student Life *Housing:* on-campus residence required through senior year. *Options:* men-only, women-only. Campus housing is university owned. Freshman campus housing is guaranteed. *Activities and organizations:* drama/theater group, student-run newspaper, choral group, International Student Association, Gospel Choir, Global Christian Fellowship, American Choral Directors Association, Army ROTC. *Campus security:* 24-hour patrols, late-night transport/escort service, controlled dormitory access, phone connection to security patrols. *Student services:* health clinic, personal/psychological counseling.

Athletics Member NAIA. *Intercollegiate sports:* basketball M (s)/W (s), cross-country running M (s)/W (s), field hockey W (s), soccer M (s)/W (s), track and field M (s)/W (s), volleyball W (s). *Intramural sports:* basketball M/W, equestrian sports M/W, racquetball M/W, rock climbing M/W, skiing (cross-country) M/W, skiing (downhill) M/W, soccer M/W, softball M/W, swimming and diving M/W, table tennis M/W, ultimate Frisbee M/W, volleyball M/W, water polo M/W, weight lifting M/W.

Standardized Tests *Required:* SAT or ACT (for admission).

Costs (2007–08) *Comprehensive fee:* $28,480 includes full-time tuition ($21,620) and room and board ($6860). Full-time tuition and fees vary according to class time, program, and reciprocity agreements. Part-time tuition: $900 per credit. *College room only:* $3640. Room and board charges vary according to board plan and housing facility. *Payment plan:* installment. *Waivers:* senior citizens and employees or children of employees.

Financial Aid Of all full-time matriculated undergraduates who enrolled in 2007, 1,136 applied for aid, 1,042 were judged to have need, 216 had their need fully met. 766 Federal Work-Study jobs (averaging $2153). 5 state and other part-time jobs (averaging $2250). In 2007, 183 non-need-based awards were made. *Average percent of need met:* 74%. *Average financial aid package:* $16,899. *Average need-based loan:* $4742. *Average need-based gift aid:* $8080. *Average non-need-based aid:* $7517. *Average indebtedness upon graduation:* $28,515.

Applying *Options:* electronic application, deferred entrance. *Application fee:* $40. *Required:* essay or personal statement, high school transcript, 1 letter of recommendation, Christian character recommendation. *Recommended:* minimum 2.5 GPA, interview. *Application deadlines:* rolling (freshmen), rolling (transfers). *Notification:* continuous (freshmen), continuous (transfers).

Freshman Application Contact Mr. Wayne MacBeth, Vice President for Enrollment Management and Market Relations, Houghton College, PO Box 128, Houghton, NY 14744. *Phone:* 585-567-9353. *Toll-free phone:* 800-777-2556. *Fax:* 585-567-9522. *E-mail:* admission@houghton.edu.

HUNTER COLLEGE OF THE CITY UNIVERSITY OF NEW YORK

New York, New York **www.hunter.cuny.edu/**

- **State and locally supported** comprehensive, founded 1870, part of City University of New York System
- **Urban** campus
- **Coed** 15,718 undergraduate students, 68% full-time, 68% women, 32% men
- **Moderately difficult** entrance level, 30% of applicants were admitted

Undergraduates 10,764 full-time, 4,954 part-time. Students come from 35 states and territories, 60 other countries, 6% are from out of state, 12% African American, 18% Asian American or Pacific Islander, 19% Hispanic American, 0.2% Native American, 10% international, 10% transferred in, 1% live on campus. *Retention:* 80% of 2006 full-time freshmen returned.

Freshmen *Admission:* 24,701 applied, 7,470 admitted, 1,906 enrolled. *Average high school GPA:* 3.0. *Test scores:* SAT critical reading scores over 500: 69%; SAT math scores over 500: 81%; SAT critical reading scores over 600: 21%; SAT math scores over 600: 28%; SAT critical reading scores over 700: 4%; SAT math scores over 700: 5%.

Faculty *Total:* 1,550, 43% full-time, 59% with terminal degrees. *Student/faculty ratio:* 15:1.

Majors Accounting; African-American/Black studies; ancient/classical Greek; anthropology; archeology; art; art history, criticism and conservation; audiology and speech-language pathology; biology/biological sciences; biology teacher education; biotechnology research; chemistry; Chinese; cinematography and film/video production; classics; classics and languages, literatures and linguistics; clinical/medical laboratory science and allied professions related; comparative literature; computer science; dance; dramatic/theater arts; economics; elementary education; English; English literature (British and Commonwealth); environmental science; film/cinema studies; fine/studio arts; foods, nutrition, and wellness; French; geography; German; German language teacher education; health teacher education; Hebrew; Hispanic-American, Puerto Rican, and Mexican-American/Chicano studies; history; humanities; Italian; Jewish/Judaic studies; kindergarten/preschool education; Latin; Latin American studies; literature; mass communication/media; mathematics; mathematics teacher education; music; nursing (registered nurse training); philosophy; physical education teaching and coaching; physics; political science and government; psychology; public health; religious studies; Romance languages; Russian; science teacher education; secondary education; sociology; Spanish; statistics; urban studies/affairs; women's studies.

Academics *Calendar:* semesters. *Degrees:* bachelor's, master's, and post-master's certificates. *Special study options:* advanced placement credit, distance learning, double majors, English as a second language, freshman honors college, honors programs, independent study, internships, off-campus study, part-time degree program, services for LD students, student-designed majors, study abroad, summer session for credit. *Unusual degree programs:* 3-2 anthropology, economics, English, history, mathematics, music, physics, sociology.

Computers on Campus 750 computers/terminals are available on campus for general student use. Campuswide network is available.

Student Life *Housing options:* coed. *Activities and organizations:* drama/theater group, student-run newspaper, radio and television station, choral group. *Campus security:* 24-hour emergency response devices and patrols. *Student services:* personal/psychological counseling, women's center.

Athletics Member NCAA. All Division III. *Intercollegiate sports:* basketball M/W, cross-country running M/W, fencing M/W, gymnastics W, soccer M, swimming and diving W, tennis M/W, track and field M/W, volleyball M/W, wrestling M. *Intramural sports:* basketball M/W, cross-country running M/W, gymnastics M/W, racquetball M/W, rugby M, soccer M/W, swimming and diving M/W, tennis M/W, volleyball M/W.

Standardized Tests *Required:* SAT or ACT (for admission).

Costs (2008–09) *Tuition:* state resident $4000 full-time; nonresident $10,800 full-time. *Required fees:* $349 full-time. *Room only:* $5311.

Financial Aid *Average financial aid package:* $4809. *Average indebtedness upon graduation:* $7200.

Applying *Options:* early admission. *Application fee:* $65. *Required:* high school transcript. *Application deadlines:* 3/15 (freshmen), 3/15 (transfers). *Notification:* continuous until 1/3 (freshmen), continuous (transfers).

Freshman Application Contact Mr. William Zlata, Director of Admissions, Hunter College of the City University of New York, 695 Park Avenue, New York, NY 10021-5085. *Phone:* 212-772-4490. *Fax:* 212-650-3472. *E-mail:* bill.zlata@hunter.cuny.edu.

See page 1752 for the College Close-Up.

IONA COLLEGE

New Rochelle, New York **www.iona.edu/**

- **Independent** comprehensive, founded 1940, affiliated with Roman Catholic Church
- **Suburban** 35-acre campus with easy access to New York City
- **Endowment** $26.5 million
- **Coed** 3,507 undergraduate students, 95% full-time, 54% women, 46% men
- **Moderately difficult** entrance level, 59% of applicants were admitted

Undergraduates 3,343 full-time, 164 part-time. Students come from 40 states and territories, 32 other countries, 20% are from out of state, 6% African American, 2% Asian American or Pacific Islander, 11% Hispanic American, 0.2% Native American, 1% international, 4% transferred in, 30% live on campus. *Retention:* 86% of 2006 full-time freshmen returned.

Freshmen *Admission:* 6,017 applied, 3,550 admitted, 908 enrolled. *Average high school GPA:* 3.4. *Test scores:* SAT critical reading scores over 500: 57%; SAT math scores over 500: 56%; SAT writing scores over 500: 57%; SAT critical reading scores over 600: 11%; SAT math scores over 600: 12%; SAT writing scores over 600: 11%; SAT critical reading scores over 700: 2%; SAT math scores over 700: 2%; SAT writing scores over 700: 2%.

Faculty *Total:* 403, 44% full-time, 60% with terminal degrees. *Student/faculty ratio:* 13:1.

Majors Accounting; advertising; applied mathematics; audiology and speech-language pathology; biochemistry; biology/biological sciences; biology teacher education; business administration and management; chemistry; clinical laboratory science/medical technology; communication/speech communication and rhetoric; computer science; computer systems networking and telecommunications; criminal justice/law enforcement administration; dramatic/theater arts; early childhood education; economics; education; education (multiple levels); elementary education; English; English/language arts teacher education; environmental biology; finance; French; French language teacher education; health/health care administration; history; interdisciplinary studies; international business/trade/commerce; international/global studies; Italian; journalism; liberal arts and sciences/liberal studies; management information systems; marketing/marketing management; mass communication/media; mathematics; mathematics teacher education; organizational communication; philosophy; physics; political science and government; psychology; public relations/image management; radio and television; radio and television broadcasting technology; religious studies; school psychology; science teacher education; secondary education; social sciences; social studies teacher education; social work; sociology; Spanish; Spanish language teacher education; Web page, digital/multimedia and information resources design.

Academics *Calendar:* semesters. *Degrees:* certificates, bachelor's, master's, post-master's, and postbachelor's certificates. *Special study options:* accelerated degree program, adult/continuing education programs, advanced placement credit, distance learning, double majors, honors programs, independent study, internships, off-campus study, part-time degree program, services for LD students, study abroad, summer session for credit. *ROTC:* Army (c), Air Force (c). *Unusual degree programs:* 3-2 4-1 Degree Programs resulting in a Bachelor's and Master's degree in: computer science, telecommunications, English, history and psychology.

Computers on Campus 500 computers/terminals and 10,000 ports are available on campus for general student use. Students can access the following: campus intranet, computer help desk, free student e-mail accounts, online (class) grades, online (class) registration, online (class) schedules, online courses. Campuswide network is available. 100% of college-owned or -operated housing units are wired for high-speed Internet access. Wireless service is available via entire campus.

Student Life *Housing options:* coed, disabled students. Campus housing is university owned and leased by the school. Freshman applicants given priority for college housing. *Activities and organizations:* drama/theater group, student-run newspaper, radio and television station, choral group, marching band, Council of Multicultural Leaders, Student government, The Ionian, LASO, WICR, national fraternities, national sororities. *Campus security:* 24-hour emergency response devices and patrols, controlled dormitory access. *Student services:* health clinic, personal/psychological counseling.

Athletics Member NCAA. All Division I except football (Division I-AA). *Intercollegiate sports:* baseball M (s), basketball M (s)/W (s), crew M/W, cross-country running M (s)/W (s), golf M (s), lacrosse W (s), rock climbing M (c)/W (c), soccer M (s)/W (s), softball W (s), swimming and diving M (s)/W (s), track and field M (s)/W (s), volleyball W (s), water polo M/W (s). *Intramural sports:* basketball M/W, cheerleading M (c)/W (c), soccer M/W, table tennis M/W, ultimate Frisbee M/W, volleyball M/W.

Standardized Tests *Required:* SAT or ACT (for admission). *Recommended:* SAT Subject Tests (for admission).

Costs (2007–08) *Comprehensive fee:* $35,224 includes full-time tuition ($23,024), mandatory fees ($1700), and room and board ($10,500). Full-time tuition and fees vary according to class time. Part-time tuition: $764 per credit. Part-time tuition and fees vary according to class time and course load. *Required fees:* $400 per term part-time. *Room and board:* Room and board charges vary according to housing facility. *Payment plan:* installment. *Waivers:* senior citizens and employees or children of employees.

Financial Aid Of all full-time matriculated undergraduates who enrolled in 2006, 3,073 applied for aid, 2,404 were judged to have need, 491 had their need fully met. 417 Federal Work-Study jobs (averaging $753). 258 state and other part-time jobs (averaging $906). In 2006, 638 non-need-based awards were made. *Average percent of need met:* 22%. *Average financial aid package:* $14,433. *Average need-based loan:* $2200. *Average need-based gift aid:* $3055. *Average non-need-based aid:* $10,297. *Average indebtedness upon graduation:* $19,457. *Financial aid deadline:* 4/15.

Applying *Options:* early action, deferred entrance. *Application fee:* $50. *Required:* high school transcript. *Recommended:* essay or personal statement, minimum 2.5 GPA, letters of recommendation, interview. *Application deadlines:* 2/15 (freshmen), 8/15 (transfers), 12/1 (early action). *Notification:* 3/20 (freshmen), 12/21 (early action).

Freshman Application Contact Mr. Kevin Cavanagh, Assistant Vice President for College Admissions, Iona College, Admissions, 715 North Avenue, New Rochelle, NY 10801. *Phone:* 914-633-2502. *Toll-free phone:* 800-231-IONA. *Fax:* 914-637-2778. *E-mail:* icad@iona.edu.

See page 1754 for the College Close-Up.

ITHACA COLLEGE

Ithaca, New York **www.ithaca.edu/**

- **Independent** comprehensive, founded 1892
- **Small-town** 757-acre campus with easy access to Syracuse
- **Endowment** $233.6 million
- **Coed** 6,260 undergraduate students, 98% full-time, 55% women, 45% men
- **Moderately difficult** entrance level, 74% of applicants were admitted

Undergraduates 6,140 full-time, 120 part-time. Students come from 50 states and territories, 67 other countries, 54% are from out of state, 3% African American, 4% Asian American or Pacific Islander, 4% Hispanic American, 0.5% Native American, 2% international, 2% transferred in, 70% live on campus. *Retention:* 87% of 2006 full-time freshmen returned.

Freshmen *Admission:* 11,235 applied, 8,326 admitted, 1,798 enrolled. *Test scores:* SAT critical reading scores over 500: 88%; SAT math scores over 500: 91%; SAT critical reading scores over 600: 43%; SAT math scores over 600: 44%; SAT critical reading scores over 700: 8%; SAT math scores over 700: 6%.

Faculty *Total:* 673, 68% full-time, 80% with terminal degrees. *Student/faculty ratio:* 12:1.

Majors Accounting; acting; anthropology; applied economics; applied mathematics; art; art history, criticism and conservation; arts management; art teacher education; athletic training; audiology and speech-language pathology; biochemistry; biology/biological sciences; biology teacher education; broadcast journalism; business administration and management; business/commerce; business/managerial economics; chemistry; chemistry teacher education; cinematography and film/video production; communication and journalism related; computer and information sciences; computer science; creative writing; dance; dramatic/theater arts; economics; educational/instructional media design; education (K-12); education (multiple levels); English; English/language arts teacher education; environmental studies; film/cinema studies; finance; fine/studio arts; foods, nutrition, and wellness; French; French language teacher education; German; German language teacher education; German studies; gerontology; health and physical education; health and physical education related; health/health care administration; health/medical preparatory programs related; health teacher education; history; history teacher education; hospital and health care facilities administration; industrial and organizational psychology; interdisciplinary studies; international business/trade/commerce; jazz/jazz studies; journalism; kinesiology and exercise science; labor and industrial relations; liberal arts and sciences/liberal studies; marketing/marketing management; marketing research; mass communication/media; mathematics; mathematics and computer science; mathematics teacher education; middle school education; multi-/interdisciplinary studies related; music; music performance; music teacher education; music theory and composition; occupational therapy; parks, recreation and leisure; philosophy; photography; physical education teaching and coaching; physical therapy; physics; physics teacher education; piano and organ; political science and government; pre-law studies; pre-medical studies; psychology; public health education and promotion; public relations/image management; radio and television; recording arts technology; rehabilitation therapy; science teacher education; secondary education; social sciences; social studies teacher education; sociology; Spanish; Spanish language teacher education; special education (speech or language impaired); speech and rhetoric; sport and fitness administration/management; telecommunications; theater design and technology; therapeutic recreation; visual and performing arts; voice and opera.

Academics *Calendar:* semesters. *Degrees:* certificates, bachelor's, master's, and doctoral. *Special study options:* accelerated degree program, adult/continuing education programs, advanced placement credit, distance learning, double majors, freshman honors college, honors programs, independent study, internships, off-campus study, part-time degree program, services for LD students, student-designed majors, study abroad, summer session for credit. *ROTC:* Army (c), Air Force (c). *Unusual degree programs:* 3-2 engineering with Cornell University, Rensselaer Polytechnic Institute, Clarkson University, State University of New York at Binghamton.

Computers on Campus 640 computers/terminals and 20 ports are available on campus for general student use. Students can access the following: campus intranet, computer help desk, free student e-mail accounts, online (class) grades, online (class) registration, online (class) schedules. Campuswide network is available. 100% of college-owned or -operated housing units are wired for high-speed Internet access.

Student Life *Housing:* on-campus residence required through junior year. *Options:* coed, women-only, disabled students. Campus housing is university owned and leased by the school. Freshman campus housing is guaranteed. *Activities and organizations:* drama/theater group, student-run newspaper, radio and television station, choral group, student government association, African-Latino Society, Residence Hall Association, Habitat for Humanity, Senior Class, national fraternities, national sororities. *Campus security:* 24-hour emergency response devices, student patrols, late-night transport/escort service, controlled dormitory access, patrols by trained security personnel 11 p.m. to 7 a.m. *Student services:* health clinic, personal/psychological counseling.

Athletics Member NCAA. All Division III. *Intercollegiate sports:* baseball M, basketball M/W, crew M/W, cross-country running M/W, field hockey W, football M, gymnastics W, lacrosse M/W, soccer M/W, softball W, swimming and diving M/W, tennis M/W, track and field M/W, volleyball W, wrestling M. *Intramural sports:* basketball M/W, bowling M (c)/W (c), crew M (c)/W (c), football M, golf M/W, ice hockey M (c), rugby W (c), skiing (downhill) M (c)/W (c), soccer M/W, softball M/W, tennis M/W, volleyball M/W.

Standardized Tests *Required:* SAT or ACT (for admission).

Costs (2007–08) *Comprehensive fee:* $39,398 includes full-time tuition ($28,670) and room and board ($10,728). Part-time tuition: $955 per credit hour. *College room only:* $5604. *Payment plan:* installment. *Waivers:* employees or children of employees.

Financial Aid Of all full-time matriculated undergraduates who enrolled in 2006, 4,611 applied for aid, 4,007 were judged to have need, 1,650 had their need fully met. 2,801 Federal Work-Study jobs (averaging $2337). 1,832 state and other part-time jobs (averaging $2397). In 2006, 856 non-need-based awards were made. *Average percent of need met:* 86%. *Average financial aid package:* $23,786. *Average need-based loan:* $5107. *Average need-based gift aid:* $16,130. *Average non-need-based aid:* $10,027.

Applying *Options:* electronic application, early admission, early decision, deferred entrance. *Application fee:* $60. *Required:* essay or personal statement, high school transcript, 1 letter of recommendation. *Required for some:* audition. *Recommended:* minimum 3.0 GPA. *Application deadlines:* 2/1 (freshmen), 3/1 (transfers). *Notification:* continuous until 4/15 (freshmen), continuous until 4/15 (transfers).

Freshman Application Contact Gerard Turbide, Director of Admission, Ithaca College, 100 Job Hall, Ithaca, NY 14850-7020. *Phone:* 607-274-3124. *Toll-free phone:* 800-429-4274. *Fax:* 607-274-1900. *E-mail:* admission@ithaca.edu.

See page 1756 for the College Close-Up.

THE JEWISH THEOLOGICAL SEMINARY

New York, New York **www.jtsa.edu/**

- **Independent Jewish** university, founded 1886
- **Urban** 1-acre campus
- **Endowment** $113.3 million
- **Coed** 182 undergraduate students, 94% full-time, 61% women, 39% men
- **Very difficult** entrance level, 61% of applicants were admitted

The Albert A. List College of Jewish Studies, the undergraduate school of the Jewish Theological Seminary, offers students a unique opportunity to pursue two bachelor's degrees simultaneously. Students earn a degree from List in one of a dozen areas of Jewish study and a second degree in the liberal arts field of their choice from Columbia University or Barnard College. This exciting four-year program enables students to experience an intimate and supportive Jewish community as well as a diverse and dynamic campus life.

Undergraduates 171 full-time, 11 part-time. Students come from 25 states and territories, 3 other countries, 78% are from out of state, 2% Hispanic American, 1% transferred in, 75% live on campus. *Retention:* 92% of 2006 full-time freshmen returned.

Freshmen *Admission:* 102 applied, 62 admitted, 40 enrolled. *Average high school GPA:* 3.7. *Test scores:* SAT critical reading scores over 500: 100%; SAT math scores over 500: 100%; SAT writing scores over 500: 100%; ACT scores over 18: 100%; SAT critical reading scores over 600: 94%; SAT math scores over 600: 88%; SAT writing scores over 600: 91%; ACT scores over 24: 100%; SAT critical reading scores over 700: 44%; SAT math scores over 700: 22%; SAT writing scores over 700: 57%; ACT scores over 30: 77%.

Faculty *Total:* 131, 48% full-time, 84% with terminal degrees. *Student/faculty ratio:* 6:1.

Majors Ancient Near Eastern and biblical languages; biblical studies; Hebrew; history; Jewish/Judaic studies; literature; music; philosophy; religious education; religious studies; talmudic studies; women's studies.

Academics *Calendar:* semesters. *Degrees:* bachelor's, master's, doctoral, and first professional (double bachelor's degree with Barnard College, Columbia University, joint bachelor's degree with Columbia University). *Special study options:* academic remediation for entering students, adult/continuing education programs, advanced placement credit, distance learning, double majors, freshman honors college, honors programs, internships, off-campus study, part-time degree program, services for LD students, student-designed majors, study abroad, summer session for credit. *ROTC:* Army (c), Navy (c), Air Force (c).

Computers on Campus 50 computers/terminals are available on campus for general student use. Students can access the following: computer help desk, free student e-mail accounts, online (class) registration. Campuswide network is available. 100% of college-owned or -operated housing units are wired for high-speed Internet access. Wireless service is available via classrooms, computer labs, dorm rooms, learning centers, libraries, student centers.

Student Life *Housing options:* coed. Campus housing is university owned and leased by the school. Freshman campus housing is guaranteed. *Activities and organizations:* drama/theater group, student-run newspaper, radio station, choral group. *Campus security:* 24-hour emergency response devices and patrols, late-night transport/escort service, controlled dormitory access. *Student services:* health clinic, personal/psychological counseling, women's center.

Athletics *Intramural sports:* basketball M, softball M/W.

Standardized Tests *Required:* SAT or ACT (for admission).

Costs (2008–09) *Tuition:* $14,200 full-time, $750 per credit part-time. *Required fees:* $800 full-time.

Financial Aid Of all full-time matriculated undergraduates who enrolled in 2007, 75 applied for aid, 73 were judged to have need, 56 had their need fully met. In 2007, 21 non-need-based awards were made. *Average percent of need met:* 92%. *Average financial aid package:* $18,639. *Average need-based loan:* $4256. *Average need-based gift aid:* $18,639. *Average non-need-based aid:* $1520. *Average indebtedness upon graduation:* $18,444. *Financial aid deadline:* 3/1.

Applying *Options:* early admission, early decision, deferred entrance. *Application fee:* $65. *Required:* essay or personal statement, high school transcript, 2 letters of recommendation. *Recommended:* minimum 3.0 GPA, interview. *Application deadlines:* 2/15 (freshmen), 5/1 (transfers). *Early decision deadline:* 11/15 (for plan 1), 1/15 (for plan 2). *Notification:* continuous until 4/15 (freshmen), continuous until 6/1 (transfers), 12/15 (early decision plan 1), 2/15 (early decision plan 2).

Freshman Application Contact Ms. Reina Cohen, Director List Collect Admissions, The Jewish Theological Seminary, 3080 Broadway, New York, NY 10027. *Phone:* 212-678-8820. *E-mail:* lcadmissions@jtsa.edu.

JOHN JAY COLLEGE OF CRIMINAL JUSTICE OF THE CITY UNIVERSITY OF NEW YORK

New York, New York **www.jjay.cuny.edu/**

Director of Admissions Richard Saulnier PhD, Dean for Enrollment Services, John Jay College of Criminal Justice of the City University of New York, 445 West 59th Street, Room 4205, New York, NY 10019. *Phone:* 212-237-8878. *Toll-free phone:* 877-JOHNJAY.

See page 1758 for the College Close-Up.

THE JUILLIARD SCHOOL

New York, New York **www.juilliard.edu/**

- **Independent** comprehensive, founded 1905
- **Urban** campus
- **Endowment** $478.1 million
- **Coed** 491 undergraduate students, 100% full-time, 45% women, 55% men
- **Most difficult** entrance level, 6% of applicants were admitted

Undergraduates 489 full-time, 2 part-time. Students come from 41 states and territories, 29 other countries, 9% African American, 16% Asian American or Pacific Islander, 5% Hispanic American, 0.2% Native American, 17% international, 4% transferred in. *Retention:* 95% of 2006 full-time freshmen returned.
Freshmen *Admission:* 2,311 applied, 149 admitted, 106 enrolled.
Faculty *Total:* 265, 43% full-time. *Student/faculty ratio:* 3:1.
Majors Dance; dramatic/theater arts; music; music performance.
Academics *Calendar:* semesters. *Degrees:* diplomas, bachelor's, master's, doctoral, post-master's, and postbachelor's certificates. *Special study options:* accelerated degree program, adult/continuing education programs, double majors, English as a second language, off-campus study, study abroad. *Unusual degree programs:* 3-2 music/liberal arts with Columbia University.
Computers on Campus 34 computers/terminals are available on campus for general student use. Campuswide network is available.
Student Life *Housing:* on-campus residence required for freshman year. *Options:* coed. Campus housing is university owned. Freshman campus housing is guaranteed. *Activities and organizations:* drama/theater group, choral group, ArtREACH, Korean Campus Crusade for Christ, Julliard Christian Fellowship, The Forum, Artists Inspired. *Campus security:* 24-hour emergency response devices and patrols, controlled dormitory access, electronically operated main building entrances. *Student services:* health clinic, personal/psychological counseling, legal services.
Costs (2007–08) *Comprehensive fee:* $37,890 includes full-time tuition ($27,150) and room and board ($10,740).
Financial Aid Of all full-time matriculated undergraduates who enrolled in 2007, 459 applied for aid, 375 were judged to have need, 102 had their need fully met. 204 Federal Work-Study jobs (averaging $1936). 265 state and other part-time jobs (averaging $2147). In 2007, 27 non-need-based awards were made. *Average percent of need met:* 82%. *Average financial aid package:* $25,242. *Average need-based loan:* $5217. *Average need-based gift aid:* $20,431. *Average non-need-based aid:* $12,035. *Average indebtedness upon graduation:* $23,304. *Financial aid deadline:* 3/1.
Applying *Options:* electronic application. *Application fee:* $100. *Required:* essay or personal statement, high school transcript, audition. *Application deadlines:* 12/1 (freshmen), 12/1 (transfers). *Notification:* 4/1 (freshmen), 4/1 (transfers).
Freshman Application Contact Ms. Lee Cioppa, Associate Dean for Admissions, The Juilliard School, 60 Lincoln Center Plaza, New York, NY 10023-6588. *Phone:* 212-799-5000. *Fax:* 212-724-0263. *E-mail:* admissions@julliard.edu.

KEHILATH YAKOV RABBINICAL SEMINARY
Brooklyn, New York

Director of Admissions Rabbi Zalman Gombo, Admissions Officer, Kehilath Yakov Rabbinical Seminary, 206 Wilson Street, Brooklyn, NY 11211-7207. *Phone:* 718-963-1212.

KEUKA COLLEGE
Keuka Park, New York — www.keuka.edu/

- **Independent** comprehensive, founded 1890, affiliated with American Baptist Churches in the U.S.A.
- **Rural** 173-acre campus with easy access to Rochester
- **Endowment** $5.7 million
- **Coed** 1,444 undergraduate students, 78% full-time, 71% women, 29% men
- **Moderately difficult** entrance level, 75% of applicants were admitted

Undergraduates 1,120 full-time, 324 part-time. Students come from 22 states and territories, 3 other countries, 5% are from out of state, 6% African American, 0.7% Asian American or Pacific Islander, 2% Hispanic American, 1% Native American, 0.3% international, 5% transferred in, 81% live on campus. *Retention:* 65% of 2006 full-time freshmen returned.
Freshmen *Admission:* 889 applied, 666 admitted, 285 enrolled. *Average high school GPA:* 3.0. *Test scores:* SAT critical reading scores over 500: 38%; SAT math scores over 500: 55%; ACT scores over 18: 70%; SAT critical reading scores over 600: 8%; SAT math scores over 600: 16%; ACT scores over 24: 17%; SAT critical reading scores over 700: 1%; SAT math scores over 700: 1%.
Faculty *Total:* 101, 56% full-time, 57% with terminal degrees. *Student/faculty ratio:* 14:1.
Majors Accounting; biochemistry; biology/biological sciences; biology teacher education; biomedical sciences; business administration and management; clinical laboratory science/medical technology; communication/speech communication and rhetoric; criminal justice/law enforcement administration; elementary education; English; English/language arts teacher education; environmental science; history; hotel/motel administration; interdisciplinary studies; liberal arts and sciences/liberal studies; marketing/marketing management; mathematics; mathematics teacher education; nursing (registered nurse training); occupational therapy; pre-dentistry studies; pre-law studies; pre-medical studies; pre-veterinary studies; psychology; secondary education; social sciences; social studies teacher education; social work; sociology; special education; special education (early childhood).
Academics *Calendar:* 4-1-4. *Degrees:* bachelor's and master's. *Special study options:* academic remediation for entering students, accelerated degree program, adult/continuing education programs, advanced placement credit, cooperative education, double majors, independent study, internships, off-campus study, part-time degree program, services for LD students, student-designed majors, study abroad, summer session for credit. *Unusual degree programs:* 3-2 occupational therapy-4 years undergraduate and one year graduate.
Computers on Campus 120 computers/terminals are available on campus for general student use. Campuswide network is available.
Student Life *Housing options:* coed, women-only, cooperative. Campus housing is university owned. Freshman campus housing is guaranteed. *Activities and organizations:* drama/theater group, student-run newspaper, radio station, choral group, Student Senate, Campus Activities Board, OTTERS (occupational therapy club), Education Club, BAKU. *Campus security:* 24-hour emergency response devices and patrols, late-night transport/escort service. *Student services:* health clinic, personal/psychological counseling.
Athletics Member NCAA. All Division III. *Intercollegiate sports:* baseball M, basketball M/W, cross-country running M/W, lacrosse M, soccer M/W, softball W, swimming and diving W, track and field M, volleyball W. *Intramural sports:* badminton M/W, basketball M/W, cheerleading M/W, crew M/W, lacrosse W, skiing (cross-country) M/W, skiing (downhill) M/W, soccer M/W, softball M/W, table tennis M/W, tennis M/W, volleyball W, water polo M/W.
Standardized Tests *Recommended:* SAT or ACT (for admission).
Costs (2007–08) *Comprehensive fee:* $29,080 includes full-time tuition ($19,960), mandatory fees ($590), and room and board ($8530). Full-time tuition and fees vary according to program. Part-time tuition: $650 per credit hour. Part-time tuition and fees vary according to program. *College room only:* $4050. Room and board charges vary according to board plan and housing facility. *Payment plan:* installment. *Waivers:* employees or children of employees.
Financial Aid Of all full-time matriculated undergraduates who enrolled in 2006, 1,098 applied for aid, 1,007 were judged to have need, 259 had their need fully met. 401 Federal Work-Study jobs (averaging $1365). 261 state and other part-time jobs (averaging $1083). In 2006, 100 non-need-based awards were made. *Average percent of need met:* 77%. *Average financial aid package:* $16,681. *Average need-based loan:* $6301. *Average need-based gift aid:* $10,893. *Average non-need-based aid:* $14,057. *Average indebtedness upon graduation:* $18,645.
Applying *Options:* electronic application, early admission, deferred entrance. *Application fee:* $30. *Required:* essay or personal statement, high school transcript, letters of recommendation. *Required for some:* interview. *Recommended:* minimum 2.75 GPA, interview. *Application deadlines:* rolling (freshmen), rolling (transfers).
Freshman Application Contact Fred Hoyle, Associate Vice President of Admissions, Keuka College, Wagner House, Keuka Park, NY 14478. *Phone:* 315-279-5254. *Toll-free phone:* 800-33-KEUKA. *Fax:* 315-279-5386. *E-mail:* admissions@mail.keuka.edu.

THE KING'S COLLEGE
New York, New York — www.tkc.edu/

- **Independent nondenominational** 4-year, founded 1939
- **Urban** campus
- **Endowment** $406,695
- **Coed** 216 undergraduate students, 100% full-time, 63% women, 38% men
- **Very difficult** entrance level, 75% of applicants were admitted

Undergraduates 215 full-time, 1 part-time. Students come from 39 states and territories, 11 other countries, 82% are from out of state, 2% African American, 2% Asian American or Pacific Islander, 3% Hispanic American, 6% international, 3% transferred in, 87% live on campus. *Retention:* 64% of 2006 full-time freshmen returned.
Freshmen *Admission:* 166 applied, 125 admitted, 44 enrolled. *Average high school GPA:* 3.83. *Test scores:* SAT critical reading scores over 500: 100%; SAT math scores over 500: 91%; SAT writing scores over 500: 100%; ACT scores over

18: 100%; SAT critical reading scores over 600: 69%; SAT math scores over 600: 37%; SAT writing scores over 600: 69%; ACT scores over 24: 86%; SAT critical reading scores over 700: 23%; SAT math scores over 700: 3%; SAT writing scores over 700: 14%; ACT scores over 30: 18%.

Faculty *Total:* 25, 48% full-time, 92% with terminal degrees. *Student/faculty ratio:* 13:1.

Majors Business administration and management; interdisciplinary studies.

Academics *Calendar:* semesters. *Degree:* bachelor's. *Special study options:* advanced placement credit, independent study, study abroad, summer session for credit.

Computers on Campus 20 computers/terminals are available on campus for general student use. Students can access the following: computer help desk, free student e-mail accounts, online (class) grades, online (class) registration, online (class) schedules. Campuswide network is available. 100% of college-owned or -operated housing units are wired for high-speed Internet access. Wireless service is available via entire campus.

Student Life *Housing options:* men-only, women-only. Campus housing is leased by the school. *Activities and organizations:* drama/theater group, student-run newspaper, student newspaper, artisan's guild, sports clubs, BreadBreakers, The Tent. *Campus security:* 24-hour emergency response devices, late-night transport/escort service.

Athletics *Intramural sports:* table tennis M/W.

Standardized Tests *Required:* SAT or ACT (for admission).

Costs (2008–09) *Tuition:* $22,500 full-time, $950 per credit part-time. *Required fees:* $350 full-time, $175 per term part-time. *Room only:* $8750.

Applying *Options:* electronic application, early action, deferred entrance. *Application fee:* $30. *Required:* essay or personal statement, high school transcript, interview. *Recommended:* minimum 3.0 GPA, letters of recommendation. *Application deadlines:* 2/1 (freshmen), 2/1 (transfers), 11/15 (early action). *Notification:* 12/15 (early action).

Freshman Application Contact The King's College, Empire State Building, 350 Fifth Avenue, Lower Lobby, New York, NY 10118. *Phone:* 212-659-7217. *Toll-free phone:* 888-969-7200 Ext. 3610.

See page 1760 for the College Close-Up.

KOL YAAKOV TORAH CENTER

Monsey, New York **horizons.edu/**

Freshman Application Contact Assistant Director of Admissions, Kol Yaakov Torah Center, 29 West Maple Avenue, Monsey, NY 10952-2954. *Phone:* 914-425-3871. *E-mail:* horizonss@aol.com.

LABORATORY INSTITUTE OF MERCHANDISING

New York, New York **www.limcollege.edu/**

- **Proprietary** 4-year, founded 1939
- **Urban** campus
- **Coed, primarily women** 1,107 undergraduate students, 96% full-time, 95% women, 5% men
- **Moderately difficult** entrance level, 63% of applicants were admitted

The Laboratory Institute of Merchandising (LIM) is a private, Middle States–accredited college that offers bachelor's degrees in fashion merchandising, management, marketing, and visual merchandising and an associate degree in fashion merchandising. Students receive a unique education through a combination of academics and industry work-study/co-ops. The school prepares them for careers in areas such as fashion marketing, buying, product development, retail management, production, cosmetics, and magazine publishing. Weekly field trips and guest lectures broaden the educational experience. In addition, the campus is set in one of the finest areas of New York City, near business, fashion, and cultural centers. A summer session and a Saturday program are also available for high school students.

Undergraduates 1,062 full-time, 45 part-time. Students come from 37 states and territories, 15 other countries, 54% are from out of state, 9% African American, 6% Asian American or Pacific Islander, 16% Hispanic American, 0.3% Native American, 1% international, 14% transferred in, 32% live on campus. *Retention:* 68% of 2006 full-time freshmen returned.

Freshmen *Admission:* 837 applied, 525 admitted, 286 enrolled. *Average high school GPA:* 2.83. *Test scores:* SAT critical reading scores over 500: 28%; SAT math scores over 500: 29%; ACT scores over 18: 61%; SAT critical reading scores over 600: 4%; SAT math scores over 600: 4%; SAT critical reading scores over 700: 1%.

Faculty *Total:* 144, 18% full-time. *Student/faculty ratio:* 17:1.

Majors Business/commerce; design and visual communications; fashion merchandising; marketing/marketing management.

Academics *Calendar:* semesters. *Degrees:* associate and bachelor's. *Special study options:* academic remediation for entering students, accelerated degree program, advanced placement credit, cooperative education, internships, part-time degree program, study abroad, summer session for credit.

Computers on Campus 270 computers/terminals are available on campus for general student use. Students can access the following: campus intranet, computer help desk, free student e-mail accounts, online (class) grades, online (class) registration, online (class) schedules. Campuswide network is available. 100% of college-owned or -operated housing units are wired for high-speed Internet access. Wireless service is available via entire campus.

Student Life *Housing options:* coed. Campus housing is leased by the school. *Activities and organizations:* student government, LIMlight Club (yearbook), Fashion Club, Fashion Show, Marketing Club/SIFE. *Student services:* personal/psychological counseling.

Standardized Tests *Required:* SAT or ACT (for admission).

Costs (2007–08) *Comprehensive fee:* $34,425 includes full-time tuition ($18,100), mandatory fees ($525), and room and board ($15,800). Part-time tuition: $575 per credit. *Required fees:* $313 per term part-time. *Room and board:* Room and board charges vary according to board plan and housing facility.

Financial Aid Of all full-time matriculated undergraduates who enrolled in 2006, 798 applied for aid, 597 were judged to have need. 40 Federal Work-Study jobs (averaging $1640). In 2006, 98 non-need-based awards were made. *Average financial aid package:* $7326. *Average need-based loan:* $3666. *Average need-based gift aid:* $5182. *Average non-need-based aid:* $2746. *Average indebtedness upon graduation:* $19,593.

Applying *Options:* electronic application, early action, deferred entrance. *Application fee:* $40. *Required:* essay or personal statement, high school transcript, 2 letters of recommendation, interview. *Recommended:* minimum 2.5 GPA. *Application deadlines:* rolling (freshmen), rolling (transfers), 11/15 (early action). *Notification:* continuous (freshmen), continuous (transfers), 12/15 (early action).

Freshman Application Contact Ms. Kristina Gibson, Director of Admissions, Laboratory Institute of Merchandising, 12 East 53rd Street, New York, NY 10022. *Phone:* 212-752-1530 Ext. 217. *Toll-free phone:* 800-677-1323. *Fax:* 212-317-8602. *E-mail:* admissions@limcollege.edu.

See page 1762 for the College Close-Up.

LEHMAN COLLEGE OF THE CITY UNIVERSITY OF NEW YORK

Bronx, New York **www.lehman.cuny.edu/**

- **State and locally supported** comprehensive, founded 1931, part of City University of New York System
- **Urban** 37-acre campus
- **Endowment** $7.2 million
- **Coed** 8,864 undergraduate students, 63% full-time, 71% women, 29% men
- **Moderately difficult** entrance level, 32% of applicants were admitted

Undergraduates 5,602 full-time, 3,262 part-time. Students come from 2 states and territories, 112 other countries, 1% are from out of state, 32% African American, 4% Asian American or Pacific Islander, 49% Hispanic American, 0.1% Native American, 5% international, 12% transferred in. *Retention:* 74% of 2006 full-time freshmen returned.

Freshmen *Admission:* 14,155 applied, 4,474 admitted, 887 enrolled. *Test scores:* SAT critical reading scores over 500: 23%; SAT math scores over 500: 26%; SAT critical reading scores over 600: 5%; SAT math scores over 600: 5%; SAT critical reading scores over 700: 1%; SAT math scores over 700: 1%.

Faculty *Total:* 826, 45% full-time, 45% with terminal degrees. *Student/faculty ratio:* 15:1.

Majors Accounting; African-American/Black studies; American studies; anthropology; art; art history, criticism and conservation; art teacher education; audiology and speech-language pathology; biochemistry; biology/biological sciences; business administration and management; business teacher education; chemistry; classics and languages, literatures and linguistics; communication and journalism related; computer and information sciences; computer management; computer science; creative writing; dance; dietetics; dramatic/theater arts; economics; English; foods, nutrition, and wellness; French; geography; geology/earth science; health/health care administration; health teacher education; Hebrew; history; interdisciplinary studies; Italian; Jewish/Judaic studies; Latin; Latin American studies; linguistics; mass communication/media; mathematics; modern Greek; music; nursing (registered nurse training); philosophy; physics; political science and government; psychology; Russian; social work; sociology; Spanish; speech and rhetoric; speech-language pathology.

Academics *Calendar:* semesters. *Degrees:* bachelor's, master's, and post-master's certificates. *Special study options:* adult/continuing education programs, advanced placement credit, cooperative education, distance learning, double majors, English as a second language, freshman honors college, honors programs, independent study, internships, off-campus study, part-time degree program, services for LD students, student-designed majors, study abroad, summer session for credit. *ROTC:* Army (c). *Unusual degree programs:* 3-2 mathematics.

Computers on Campus 600 computers/terminals are available on campus for general student use. Students can access the following: campus intranet, computer help desk, free student e-mail accounts, online (class) grades, online (class) registration, online (class) schedules. Campuswide network is available. Wireless service is available via entire campus.

Student Life *Housing:* college housing not available. *Activities and organizations:* drama/theater group, student-run newspaper, radio and television station, choral group, Club Mac, African Students Association, Dominican Student Association, The Sociology Club, Club Live. *Campus security:* 24-hour emergency response devices and patrols, student patrols, late-night transport/escort service. *Student services:* health clinic, personal/psychological counseling, women's center.

Athletics Member NCAA. All Division III. *Intercollegiate sports:* baseball M, basketball M/W, cross-country running M/W, racquetball M/W, soccer M/W, softball M/W, swimming and diving M/W, table tennis M/W, tennis M/W, track and field M/W, volleyball M/W, water polo M, wrestling M. *Intramural sports:* badminton M/W, baseball M/W, basketball M/W, cross-country running M/W, racquetball M/W, soccer M, softball M/W, swimming and diving M/W, tennis M/W, volleyball M/W, wrestling M.

Standardized Tests *Required:* SAT or ACT (for admission).

Costs (2008–09) *Tuition:* state resident $4000 full-time, $170 per credit part-time. *Required fees:* $290 full-time.

Financial Aid Of all full-time matriculated undergraduates who enrolled in 2006, 4,275 applied for aid, 4,217 were judged to have need, 119 had their need fully met. 510 Federal Work-Study jobs (averaging $950). In 2006, 116 non-need-based awards were made. *Average percent of need met:* 68%. *Average financial aid package:* $3537. *Average need-based loan:* $1559. *Average need-based gift aid:* $1361. *Average non-need-based aid:* $1400. *Average indebtedness upon graduation:* $10,500.

Applying *Options:* deferred entrance. *Application fee:* $65. *Required:* high school transcript, minimum 3.0 GPA. *Required for some:* essay or personal statement, interview. *Application deadlines:* rolling (freshmen), rolling (transfers). *Notification:* continuous (freshmen), continuous (transfers).

Freshman Application Contact Mr. Clarence Wilkes, Director of Admissions, Lehman College of the City University of New York, 250 Bedford Park Boulevard West, Bronx, NY 10468. *Phone:* 718-960-8713. *Toll-free phone:* 877-Lehman1. *Fax:* 718-960-8712. *E-mail:* enroll@lehman.cuny.edu.

See page 1764 for the College Close-Up.

LE MOYNE COLLEGE

Syracuse, New York **www.lemoyne.edu/**

- **Independent Roman Catholic (Jesuit)** comprehensive, founded 1946
- **Suburban** 161-acre campus
- **Endowment** $49.7 million
- **Coed** 2,797 undergraduate students, 82% full-time, 62% women, 38% men
- **Moderately difficult** entrance level, 69% of applicants were admitted

Le Moyne is a coeducational, residential college founded in the Jesuit tradition of academic excellence. Offering a comprehensive program rooted in the liberal arts and sciences, Le Moyne's shared mission of learning and service stresses education of the whole person. Strong academic programs, committed faculty members, a reassuring Jesuit presence, and career advisement/internship opportunities prepare Le Moyne students for leadership and service in their personal and professional lives. Le Moyne is consistently recognized for outstanding value in *U.S. News & World Report*'s annual college rankings.

Undergraduates 2,287 full-time, 510 part-time. Students come from 24 states and territories, 14 other countries, 6% are from out of state, 4% African American, 2% Asian American or Pacific Islander, 4% Hispanic American, 0.5% Native American, 0.8% international, 6% transferred in, 61% live on campus. *Retention:* 84% of 2006 full-time freshmen returned.

Freshmen *Admission:* 3,968 applied, 2,738 admitted, 578 enrolled. *Average high school GPA:* 3.29. *Test scores:* SAT critical reading scores over 500: 70%; SAT math scores over 500: 77%; ACT scores over 18: 98%; SAT critical reading scores over 600: 25%; SAT math scores over 600: 31%; ACT scores over 24: 42%; SAT critical reading scores over 700: 3%; SAT math scores over 700: 4%; ACT scores over 30: 4%.

Faculty *Total:* 327, 48% full-time, 60% with terminal degrees. *Student/faculty ratio:* 13:1.

Majors Accounting; biochemistry; biological and physical sciences; biology/biological sciences; biology teacher education; business administration and management; business administration, management and operations related; chemistry; chemistry teacher education; communication/speech communication and rhetoric; computer and information sciences; criminology; dramatic/theater arts; ecology; economics; elementary education; engineering related; English; English as a second/foreign language (teaching); English/language arts teacher education; finance; French; French language teacher education; history; human resources management; labor and industrial relations; management information systems; marketing/marketing management; mathematics; mathematics teacher education; middle school education; nursing (registered nurse training); operations management; peace studies and conflict resolution; philosophy; physics; physics teacher education; political science and government; pre-dentistry studies; pre-law studies; pre-medical studies; pre-pharmacy studies; pre-veterinary studies; psychology; religious studies; science teacher education; secondary education; social studies teacher education; sociology; Spanish; Spanish language teacher education; special education.

Academics *Calendar:* semesters. *Degrees:* bachelor's, master's, and post-master's certificates. *Special study options:* academic remediation for entering students, accelerated degree program, adult/continuing education programs, advanced placement credit, double majors, honors programs, independent study, internships, off-campus study, part-time degree program, services for LD students, study abroad, summer session for credit. *ROTC:* Army (c), Air Force (c). *Unusual degree programs:* 3-2 engineering with Manhattan College, Clarkson University, University of Detroit Mercy.

Computers on Campus 325 computers/terminals are available on campus for general student use. Students can access the following: campus intranet, computer help desk, free student e-mail accounts, online (class) grades, online (class) registration, online (class) schedules, ECHO (campus-wide portal). Campuswide network is available. 100% of college-owned or -operated housing units are wired for high-speed Internet access. Wireless service is available via classrooms, computer centers, computer labs, dorm rooms, learning centers, libraries, student centers.

Student Life *Housing:* on-campus residence required through senior year. *Options:* coed, men-only, women-only, disabled students. Campus housing is university owned. Freshman campus housing is guaranteed. *Activities and organizations:* drama/theater group, student-run newspaper, radio and television station, choral group, Student Programming Board, Outing Club, Performing Arts groups, Student Dancers, New Student Orientation Committee. *Campus security:* 24-hour emergency response devices and patrols, late-night transport/escort service, controlled dormitory access, self-defense education, lighted pathways, closed-circuit security cameras, and emergency code blue phones. *Student services:* health clinic, personal/psychological counseling.

Athletics Member NCAA. All Division II except baseball (Division I), lacrosse (Division I). *Intercollegiate sports:* baseball M (s), basketball M (s)/W (s), cross-country running M (s)/W (s), golf M (s), lacrosse M (s)/W (s), soccer M (s)/W (s), softball W (s), swimming and diving M/W, tennis M (s)/W (s), volleyball W (s). *Intramural sports:* basketball M/W, cross-country running M/W, field hockey W (c), football M, ice hockey M (c), racquetball M/W, rugby M (c)/W (c), soccer M/W, softball M/W, volleyball M/W.

Standardized Tests *Required:* SAT or ACT (for admission).

Costs (2007–08) *Comprehensive fee:* $32,790 includes full-time tuition ($23,040), mandatory fees ($720), and room and board ($9030). Part-time tuition: $489 per credit hour. Part-time tuition and fees vary according to class time. *College room only:* $5720. Room and board charges vary according to board plan and housing facility. *Payment plans:* installment, deferred payment. *Waivers:* employees or children of employees.

Financial Aid Of all full-time matriculated undergraduates who enrolled in 2006, 2,030 applied for aid, 1,816 were judged to have need, 414 had their need fully met. 297 Federal Work-Study jobs (averaging $1112). In 2006, 258 non-need-based awards were made. *Average percent of need met:* 75%. *Average financial aid package:* $17,385. *Average need-based loan:* $4471. *Average need-based gift aid:* $13,386. *Average non-need-based aid:* $9907. *Average indebtedness upon graduation:* $19,392.

Applying *Options:* electronic application, early admission, early decision, deferred entrance. *Application fee:* $35. *Required:* essay or personal statement, high school transcript, 2 letters of recommendation. *Recommended:* interview.

Application deadlines: 2/1 (freshmen), 6/1 (transfers). *Early decision deadline:* 12/1. *Notification:* continuous (freshmen), continuous (transfers), 12/15 (early decision).

Freshman Application Contact Mr. Dennis J. Nicholson, Director of Admission, Le Moyne College, 1419 Salt Spring Road, Syracuse, NY 13214-1399. *Phone:* 315-445-4300. *Toll-free phone:* 800-333-4733. *Fax:* 315-445-4711. *E-mail:* admission@lemoyne.edu.

See page 1766 for the College Close-Up.

LONG ISLAND UNIVERSITY, BRENTWOOD CAMPUS

Brentwood, New York **www.liu.edu/**

Director of Admissions Mr. John P. Metcalfe, Director of Admissions, Long Island University, Brentwood Campus, 100 Second Avenue, Brentwood, NY 11717. *Phone:* 631-273-5112 Ext. 26.

LONG ISLAND UNIVERSITY, BROOKLYN CAMPUS

Brooklyn, New York **www.liu.edu/**

Freshman Application Contact Elizabeth Storinge, Dean of Admissions, Long Island University, Brooklyn Campus, 1 University Plaza, Brooklyn, NY 11201. *Phone:* 718-488-1011. *Toll-free phone:* 800-LIU-PLAN. *Fax:* 718-797-2399. *E-mail:* admissions@brooklyn.liu.edu.

See page 1768 for the College Close-Up.

LONG ISLAND UNIVERSITY, C.W. POST CAMPUS

Brookville, New York **www.liu.edu/**

- **Independent** comprehensive, founded 1954, part of Long Island University
- **Suburban** 308-acre campus with easy access to New York City
- **Coed**
- **Moderately difficult** entrance level

Academics *Calendar:* semesters. *Degrees:* bachelor's, master's, doctoral, post-master's, and postbachelor's certificates.

Student Life *Campus security:* 24-hour emergency response devices and patrols, late-night transport/escort service, controlled dormitory access.

Athletics Member NCAA. All Division II.

Standardized Tests *Required:* SAT or ACT (for admission).

Costs (2007–08) *Comprehensive fee:* $35,550 includes full-time tuition ($24,700), mandatory fees ($1250), and room and board ($9600). Part-time tuition: $771 per credit. *Required fees:* $230 per term part-time. *College room only:* $6320. Room and board charges vary according to board plan and housing facility. *Payment plans:* installment, deferred payment.

Financial Aid Of all full-time matriculated undergraduates who enrolled in 2002, 3,390 applied for aid, 2,881 were judged to have need, 430 had their need fully met. 823 Federal Work-Study jobs (averaging $1620). In 2002, 960 non-need-based awards were made. *Average percent of need met:* 75. *Average financial aid package:* $8500. *Average need-based loan:* $4000. *Average need-based gift aid:* $4500. *Average non-need-based aid:* $7000. *Average indebtedness upon graduation:* $12,500. *Financial aid deadline:* 3/1.

Applying *Options:* electronic application, deferred entrance. *Application fee:* $30. *Required:* essay or personal statement, high school transcript, minimum 2.5 GPA. *Required for some:* interview. *Recommended:* letters of recommendation.

Freshman Application Contact Mr. Gary Bergman, Associate Provost for Enrollment Services, Long Island University, C.W. Post Campus, 720 Northern Boulevard, Brookville, NY 11548-1300. *Phone:* 516-299-2900. *Toll-free phone:* 800-LIU-PLAN. *Fax:* 516-299-2137. *E-mail:* enroll@cwpost.liu.edu.

See page 1770 for the College Close-Up.

MACHZIKEI HADATH RABBINICAL COLLEGE

Brooklyn, New York

Director of Admissions Rabbi Abraham M. Lezerowitz, Director of Admissions, Machzikei Hadath Rabbinical College, 5407 Sixteenth Avenue, Brooklyn, NY 11204-1805. *Phone:* 718-854-8777.

MANHATTAN COLLEGE

Riverdale, New York **www.manhattan.edu/**

- **Independent** comprehensive, founded 1853, affiliated with Roman Catholic Church
- **Urban** 31-acre campus with easy access to New York City
- **Endowment** $43.8 million
- **Coed**
- **Moderately difficult** entrance level

For more than 150 years, there has been one principle that has guided Manhattan College to its present day: a commitment to excellence in the classroom. At Manhattan, students study under excellent teachers in a personalized atmosphere that promises big opportunities—a learning environment that spells success. Manhattan College's nationally acclaimed science and engineering programs and comprehensive arts, education, and business programs equip students with the knowledge and resources for a successful career in their chosen field of interest. Manhattan combines the resources of a university with the caring, close-knit atmosphere of a private liberal arts college. Manhattan College encourages students to succeed.

Faculty *Student/faculty ratio:* 14:1.

Academics *Calendar:* semesters. *Degrees:* bachelor's, master's, and post-master's certificates.

Student Life *Campus security:* 24-hour patrols, late-night transport/escort service, controlled dormitory access.

Athletics Member NCAA. All Division I.

Standardized Tests *Required:* SAT or ACT (for admission).

Costs (2007–08) *Comprehensive fee:* $32,240 includes full-time tuition ($21,640), mandatory fees ($1300), and room and board ($9300). Full-time tuition and fees vary according to course load and program. Part-time tuition: $610 per credit hour. Part-time tuition and fees vary according to course load and program. *Room and board:* Room and board charges vary according to board plan.

Financial Aid Of all full-time matriculated undergraduates who enrolled in 2006, 1,919 applied for aid, 1,896 were judged to have need, 362 had their need fully met. 501 Federal Work-Study jobs (averaging $1118). 224 state and other part-time jobs (averaging $893). In 2006, 196 non-need-based awards were made. *Average percent of need met:* 69. *Average financial aid package:* $14,828. *Average need-based loan:* $4405. *Average need-based gift aid:* $10,265. *Average non-need-based aid:* $7859. *Average indebtedness upon graduation:* $35,130.

Applying *Options:* early admission, early decision, deferred entrance. *Application fee:* $50. *Required:* essay or personal statement, high school transcript, minimum 2.5 GPA, 1 letter of recommendation. *Required for some:* interview. *Recommended:* minimum 3.0 GPA, interview.

Freshman Application Contact Mr. William Bisset, Assistant Vice President for Enrollment Management, Manhattan College, 4513 Manhattan College Parkway, Riverdale, NY 10471. *Phone:* 718-862-7200. *Toll-free phone:* 800-622-9235. *Fax:* 718-862-8019. *E-mail:* admit@manhattan.edu.

See page 1772 for the College Close-Up.

MANHATTAN SCHOOL OF MUSIC

New York, New York **www.msmnyc.edu/**

- **Independent** comprehensive, founded 1917
- **Urban** 1-acre campus
- **Endowment** $14.1 million
- **Coed** 415 undergraduate students, 99% full-time, 50% women, 50% men
- **Very difficult** entrance level, 37% of applicants were admitted

Undergraduates 410 full-time, 5 part-time. Students come from 25 states and territories, 36 other countries, 69% are from out of state, 4% African American, 9% Asian American or Pacific Islander, 4% Hispanic American, 0.2% Native American, 23% international, 7% transferred in, 54% live on campus. *Retention:* 87% of 2006 full-time freshmen returned.

Freshmen *Admission:* 945 applied, 346 admitted, 121 enrolled. *Average high school GPA:* 3.55.

Faculty *Total:* 389, 19% full-time, 24% with terminal degrees. *Student/faculty ratio:* 5:1.

Majors Jazz/jazz studies; music; piano and organ; violin, viola, guitar and other stringed instruments; voice and opera; wind/percussion instruments.

Academics *Calendar:* semesters. *Degrees:* diplomas, bachelor's, master's, doctoral, post-master's, and postbachelor's certificates. *Special study options:* academic remediation for entering students, advanced placement credit, English as a second language, off-campus study, services for LD students.

Computers on Campus 14 computers/terminals and 14 ports are available on campus for general student use. Students can access the following: campus intranet, free student e-mail accounts. Campuswide network is available. 100% of college-owned or -operated housing units are wired for high-speed Internet access. Wireless service is available via computer labs, libraries.

Student Life *Housing:* on-campus residence required through sophomore year. *Options:* coed. Campus housing is university owned. *Activities and organizations:* choral group, Pan-African Student Union, International Student Association, Student Council, Resident Community Council, Gay/Lesbian/Bisexual Students Association. *Campus security:* 24-hour patrols, controlled dormitory access.

Standardized Tests *Recommended:* SAT or ACT (for admission).

Costs (2008–09) *Tuition:* $1200 per credit part-time.

Financial Aid Of all full-time matriculated undergraduates who enrolled in 2004, 291 applied for aid, 291 were judged to have need, 11 had their need fully met. 82 Federal Work-Study jobs (averaging $1303). In 2004, 19 non-need-based awards were made. *Average percent of need met:* 32%. *Average financial aid package:* $12,080. *Average need-based loan:* $4080. *Average need-based gift aid:* $10,576. *Average non-need-based aid:* $8583. *Average indebtedness upon graduation:* $17,658.

Applying *Options:* electronic application, deferred entrance. *Application fee:* $100. *Required:* essay or personal statement, high school transcript, minimum 2.8 GPA, 1 letter of recommendation, audition. *Recommended:* minimum 3.0 GPA, interview. *Application deadlines:* 12/1 (freshmen), 12/1 (transfers). *Notification:* 4/1 (freshmen), 4/1 (transfers).

Freshman Application Contact Mrs. Amy Anderson, Director of Admission and Financial Aid, Manhattan School of Music, 120 Claremont Avenue, New York, NY 10027. *Phone:* 917-493-4501. *Fax:* 212-749-3025. *E-mail:* admission@msmnyc.edu.

See page 1774 for the College Close-Up.

MANHATTANVILLE COLLEGE

Purchase, New York www.manhattanville.edu/

- **Independent** comprehensive, founded 1841
- **Suburban** 100-acre campus with easy access to New York City
- **Endowment** $20.3 million
- **Coed** 1,842 undergraduate students, 93% full-time, 67% women, 33% men
- **Moderately difficult** entrance level, 50% of applicants were admitted

On its 100-acre campus 30 minutes north of New York City, Manhattanville College has created a small global village. The private, coeducational college, founded in 1841, draws its 1,600 students from seventy-six different countries and forty states. This richly diverse community embodies the College's mission: to educate ethically and socially responsible leaders for the global community. Manhattanville offers more than fifty academic concentrations in a curriculum that nurtures intellectual curiosity and independent thinking.

Undergraduates 1,709 full-time, 133 part-time. Students come from 39 states and territories, 59 other countries, 39% are from out of state, 7% African American, 2% Asian American or Pacific Islander, 15% Hispanic American, 0.6% Native American, 8% international, 4% transferred in, 76% live on campus. *Retention:* 74% of 2006 full-time freshmen returned.

Freshmen *Admission:* 3,927 applied, 1,951 admitted, 469 enrolled. *Average high school GPA:* 3.0. *Test scores:* SAT critical reading scores over 500: 73%; SAT math scores over 500: 71%; SAT critical reading scores over 600: 26%; SAT math scores over 600: 21%; SAT critical reading scores over 700: 5%; SAT math scores over 700: 3%.

Faculty *Total:* 268, 38% full-time. *Student/faculty ratio:* 11:1.

Majors American studies; art history, criticism and conservation; art teacher education; Asian studies; biochemistry; biology/biological sciences; biology teacher education; business administration and management; chemistry; chemistry teacher education; classics and languages, literatures and linguistics; computer science; dance; economics; education; elementary education; English; English/language arts teacher education; finance; fine/studio arts; French; French language teacher education; German studies; history; international relations and affairs; legal studies; mathematics; mathematics teacher education; music; music teacher education; philosophy; physics; political science and government; premedical studies; psychology; religious studies; Romance languages; secondary education; social studies teacher education; sociology; Spanish; Spanish language teacher education.

Academics *Calendar:* semesters. *Degrees:* bachelor's and master's. *Special study options:* academic remediation for entering students, accelerated degree program, adult/continuing education programs, advanced placement credit, distance learning, double majors, English as a second language, freshman honors college, honors programs, independent study, internships, off-campus study, part-time degree program, services for LD students, student-designed majors, study abroad, summer session for credit. *Unusual degree programs:* 3-2 business administration; education.

Computers on Campus 240 computers/terminals are available on campus for general student use. Students can access the following: computer help desk, free student e-mail accounts, online (class) grades, online (class) registration, online (class) schedules. Campuswide network is available. 100% of college-owned or -operated housing units are wired for high-speed Internet access. Wireless service is available via classrooms, computer centers, computer labs, libraries.

Student Life *Housing options:* coed, disabled students. Campus housing is university owned. Freshman campus housing is guaranteed. *Activities and organizations:* drama/theater group, student-run newspaper, radio and television station, choral group, Latin American Student Organization, International Student Organization, Black Student Union, WMVL (radio station), Connie Hogarth Center. *Campus security:* 24-hour emergency response devices and patrols, late-night transport/escort service, controlled dormitory access. *Student services:* health clinic, personal/psychological counseling, women's center.

Athletics Member NCAA. All Division III. *Intercollegiate sports:* baseball M, basketball M/W, field hockey W, golf M, ice hockey M/W, lacrosse M/W, soccer M/W, softball W, swimming and diving W, tennis M/W, volleyball W. *Intramural sports:* basketball M/W, cheerleading M/W.

Standardized Tests *Required:* SAT or ACT (for admission). *Required for some:* ACT (for admission).

Costs (2008–09) *Comprehensive fee:* $44,660 includes full-time tuition ($30,400), mandatory fees ($1220), and room and board ($13,040). Part-time tuition: $700 per credit. *Required fees:* $45 per semester hour part-time. *College room only:* $7740.

Financial Aid Of all full-time matriculated undergraduates who enrolled in 2005, 1,302 applied for aid, 1,168 were judged to have need, 205 had their need fully met. 305 Federal Work-Study jobs (averaging $1075). 651 state and other part-time jobs (averaging $1500). In 2005, 381 non-need-based awards were made. *Average percent of need met:* 79%. *Average financial aid package:* $24,548. *Average need-based loan:* $4183. *Average need-based gift aid:* $12,366. *Average non-need-based aid:* $8325. *Average indebtedness upon graduation:* $23,253.

Applying *Options:* electronic application, early admission, early decision, deferred entrance. *Application fee:* $65. *Required:* essay or personal statement, high school transcript, minimum 2.0 GPA, 2 letters of recommendation. *Recommended:* minimum 3.0 GPA, interview. *Application deadlines:* 3/1 (freshmen), 3/1 (transfers). *Early decision deadline:* 12/1. *Notification:* continuous (freshmen), continuous (transfers), 12/31 (early decision).

Freshman Application Contact Ms. Erica Padilla, Director of Admissions, Manhattanville College, 2900 Purchase Street, Purchase, NY 10577. *Phone:* 914-323-5129. *Toll-free phone:* 800-328-4553. *Fax:* 914-694-1732. *E-mail:* admissions@mville.edu.

See page 1776 for the College Close-Up.

MANNES COLLEGE THE NEW SCHOOL FOR MUSIC

New York, New York www.newschool.mannes.edu/

- **Independent** comprehensive, founded 1916, part of The New School
- **Urban** campus
- **Coed** 197 undergraduate students, 84% full-time, 57% women, 43% men
- **Very difficult** entrance level, 34% of applicants were admitted

A small, distinguished conservatory in the heart of New York City, Mannes College The New School for Music features faculty members from New York City's most prominent and internationally known ensembles. Students receive rigorous professional training as members of a friendly, supportive community dedicated to the highest artistic achievement.

Undergraduates 165 full-time, 32 part-time. Students come from 25 states and territories, 13 other countries, 58% are from out of state, 3% African American, 9% Asian American or Pacific Islander, 5% Hispanic American, 32% international, 6% transferred in, 14% live on campus. *Retention:* 91% of 2006 full-time freshmen returned.

Freshmen *Admission:* 473 applied, 163 admitted, 59 enrolled. *Average high school GPA:* 3.1.

Faculty *Total:* 156, 3% full-time. *Student/faculty ratio:* 6:1.

Majors Conducting; music; music performance; music theory and composition; piano and organ; violin, viola, guitar and other stringed instruments; voice and opera.

Academics *Calendar:* semesters. *Degrees:* diplomas, bachelor's, master's, and postbachelor's certificates. *Special study options:* academic remediation for entering students, adult/continuing education programs, advanced placement credit, double majors, English as a second language, summer session for credit.

Computers on Campus 1,200 computers/terminals are available on campus for general student use. Students can access the following: computer help desk, free student e-mail accounts, online (class) grades, online (class) registration, online (class) schedules, online portal. Campuswide network is available. 94% of college-owned or -operated housing units are wired for high-speed Internet access. Wireless service is available via entire campus.

Student Life *Housing options:* coed, disabled students. Campus housing is university owned and leased by the school. Freshman applicants given priority for college housing. *Activities and organizations:* student-run newspaper, choral group. *Campus security:* 24-hour emergency response devices, controlled dormitory access. *Student services:* health clinic, personal/psychological counseling.

Costs (2007–08) *Comprehensive fee:* $42,160 includes full-time tuition ($29,800), mandatory fees ($610), and room and board ($11,750). Part-time tuition: $984 per credit. *College room only:* $8750. Room and board charges vary according to board plan.

Financial Aid Of all full-time matriculated undergraduates who enrolled in 2006, 116 applied for aid, 50 were judged to have need, 16 had their need fully met. In 2006, 39 non-need-based awards were made. *Average percent of need met:* 34%. *Average financial aid package:* $12,162. *Average need-based loan:* $3884. *Average need-based gift aid:* $4335. *Average non-need-based aid:* $9876. *Average indebtedness upon graduation:* $18,025.

Applying *Options:* deferred entrance. *Application fee:* $100. *Required:* essay or personal statement, high school transcript, 1 letter of recommendation, interview, audition, written test. *Application deadlines:* 12/1 (freshmen), 5/15 (transfers). *Notification:* 4/1 (freshmen), 6/1 (transfers).

Director of Admissions Ms. Georgia Schmitt, Director of Admissions, Mannes College The New School for Music, 150 West 85th Street, New York, NY 10024. *Phone:* 212-580-0210 Ext. 4862. *Toll-free phone:* 800-292-3040. *Fax:* 212-580-1738. *E-mail:* mannesadmissions@newschool.edu.

See page 1778 for the College Close-Up.

MARIST COLLEGE

Poughkeepsie, New York **www.marist.edu/**

- **Independent** comprehensive, founded 1929
- **Small-town** 180-acre campus with easy access to Albany and New York City
- **Endowment** $24.5 million
- **Coed** 4,851 undergraduate students, 92% full-time, 57% women, 43% men
- **Very difficult** entrance level, 42% of applicants were admitted

Undergraduates 4,481 full-time, 370 part-time. Students come from 39 states and territories, 9 other countries, 41% are from out of state, 3% African American, 2% Asian American or Pacific Islander, 5% Hispanic American, 0.2% Native American, 0.3% international, 3% transferred in, 72% live on campus. *Retention:* 91% of 2006 full-time freshmen returned.

Freshmen *Admission:* 8,328 applied, 3,488 admitted, 1,019 enrolled. *Average high school GPA:* 3.3. *Test scores:* SAT critical reading scores over 500: 87%; SAT math scores over 500: 89%; SAT writing scores over 500: 87%; ACT scores over 18: 97%; SAT critical reading scores over 600: 36%; SAT math scores over 600: 42%; SAT writing scores over 600: 36%; ACT scores over 24: 60%; SAT critical reading scores over 700: 2%; SAT math scores over 700: 5%; SAT writing scores over 700: 2%; ACT scores over 30: 9%.

Faculty *Total:* 593, 37% full-time. *Student/faculty ratio:* 15:1.

Majors Accounting; advertising; American studies; applied mathematics; art; art history, criticism and conservation; athletic training; biochemistry; biology/biological sciences; biology teacher education; biomedical sciences; business administration and management; chemistry; chemistry teacher education; clinical laboratory science/medical technology; computational mathematics; computer programming; computer programming (vendor/product certification); computer science; criminal justice/law enforcement administration; digital communication and media/multimedia; dramatic/theater arts; economics; English; English/language arts teacher education; environmental studies; fashion/apparel design; fashion merchandising; fine/studio arts; French; French language teacher education; general studies; history; information science/studies; information technology; journalism; mathematics; mathematics teacher education; organizational communication; philosophy; political science and government; psychology; public relations/image management; radio and television; secondary education; social studies teacher education; social work; Spanish; Spanish language teacher education; special education.

Academics *Calendar:* semesters. *Degrees:* certificates, bachelor's, master's, and postbachelor's certificates. *Special study options:* academic remediation for entering students, accelerated degree program, adult/continuing education programs, advanced placement credit, cooperative education, distance learning, double majors, English as a second language, honors programs, independent study, internships, off-campus study, part-time degree program, services for LD students, study abroad, summer session for credit. *ROTC:* Army (b). *Unusual degree programs:* 3-2 psychology, computer science.

Computers on Campus 646 computers/terminals and 1,000 ports are available on campus for general student use. Students can access the following: campus intranet, computer help desk, free student e-mail accounts, online (class) grades, online (class) registration, online (class) schedules, admissions application, billing, transcript, degree audit, online financial aid summary, online library database search. Campuswide network is available. 100% of college-owned or -operated housing units are wired for high-speed Internet access. Wireless service is available via entire campus.

Student Life *Housing options:* coed. Campus housing is university owned. Freshman campus housing is guaranteed. *Activities and organizations:* drama/theater group, student-run newspaper, radio and television station, choral group, marching band, Marist Singers, Dance Club, Student Government, Theater Club, Community Service and Campus Ministry, national fraternities. *Campus security:* 24-hour emergency response devices and patrols, student patrols, late-night transport/escort service, controlled dormitory access, night residence hall monitors. *Student services:* health clinic, personal/psychological counseling.

Athletics Member NCAA. All Division I. *Intercollegiate sports:* baseball M (s), basketball M (s)/W (s), bowling M (c)/W (c), cheerleading M (c)/W (c), crew M/W (s), cross-country running M (s)/W (s), equestrian sports M (c)/W (c), fencing M (c)/W (c), football M, ice hockey M (c), lacrosse M (s)/W (s), rugby M (c)/W (c), skiing (downhill) M (c)/W (c), soccer M (s)/W (s), softball W (s), swimming and diving M (s)/W (s), tennis M (s)/W (s); track and field M (s)/W (s), volleyball M (c)/W (s), water polo W (s). *Intramural sports:* basketball M/W, soccer M/W, softball M/W, ultimate Frisbee M/W, volleyball M/W.

Standardized Tests *Required:* SAT or ACT (for admission).

Costs (2007–08) *Comprehensive fee:* $34,290 includes full-time tuition ($23,560), mandatory fees ($480), and room and board ($10,250). Part-time tuition: $550 per credit. *Required fees:* $80 per term part-time. *College room only:* $6580. Room and board charges vary according to board plan and housing facility. *Payment plan:* installment. *Waivers:* employees or children of employees.

Financial Aid Of all full-time matriculated undergraduates who enrolled in 2007, 3,380 applied for aid, 2,700 were judged to have need, 524 had their need fully met. 649 Federal Work-Study jobs (averaging $1969). 605 state and other part-time jobs (averaging $1000). In 2007, 997 non-need-based awards were made. *Average percent of need met:* 67%. *Average financial aid package:* $19,790. *Average need-based loan:* $4959. *Average need-based gift aid:* $10,016. *Average non-need-based aid:* $6562. *Average indebtedness upon graduation:* $28,374. *Financial aid deadline:* 5/1.

Applying *Options:* electronic application, early admission, early decision, early action, deferred entrance. *Application fee:* $50. *Required:* essay or personal statement, high school transcript, 2 letters of recommendation. *Application deadlines:* 2/15 (freshmen), 6/1 (transfers), 12/1 (early action). *Early decision deadline:* 11/15. *Notification:* 3/15 (freshmen), continuous (transfers), 12/15 (early decision), 1/30 (early action).

Freshman Application Contact Mr. Kenton Rinehart, Dean of Undergraduate Admissions, Marist College, 3399 North Road, Poughkeepsie, NY 12601. *Phone:* 845-575-3226. *Toll-free phone:* 800-436-5483. *Fax:* 845-575-3215. *E-mail:* admission@marist.edu.

See page 1780 for the College Close-Up.

MARYMOUNT MANHATTAN COLLEGE

New York, New York **www.mmm.edu/**

- **Independent** 4-year, founded 1936
- **Urban** 3-acre campus
- **Endowment** $15.1 million

- **Coed** 1,895 undergraduate students, 83% full-time, 75% women, 25% men
- **Moderately difficult** entrance level, 74% of applicants were admitted

Undergraduates 1,579 full-time, 316 part-time. Students come from 46 states and territories, 26 other countries, 54% are from out of state, 11% African American, 3% Asian American or Pacific Islander, 11% Hispanic American, 0.5% Native American, 3% international, 7% transferred in, 47% live on campus. *Retention:* 58% of 2006 full-time freshmen returned.

Freshmen *Admission:* 2,565 applied, 1,896 admitted, 490 enrolled. *Average high school GPA:* 3.17. *Test scores:* SAT critical reading scores over 500: 74%; SAT math scores over 500: 62%; ACT scores over 18: 100%; SAT critical reading scores over 600: 27%; SAT math scores over 600: 14%; ACT scores over 24: 46%; SAT critical reading scores over 700: 3%; SAT math scores over 700: 1%.

Faculty *Total:* 285, 32% full-time, 55% with terminal degrees. *Student/faculty ratio:* 11:1.

Majors Accounting; acting; art; art history, criticism and conservation; biology/biological sciences; business administration and management; commercial and advertising art; communication/speech communication and rhetoric; dance; dramatic/theater arts; English; fine/studio arts; history; international relations and affairs; liberal arts and sciences/liberal studies; philosophy and religious studies related; photography; political science and government; psychology; sociology; speech-language pathology; theater literature, history and criticism.

Academics *Calendar:* semesters plus summer and January mini-semesters. *Degree:* certificates and bachelor's. *Special study options:* academic remediation for entering students, accelerated degree program, adult/continuing education programs, advanced placement credit, double majors, English as a second language, honors programs, independent study, internships, off-campus study, part-time degree program, services for LD students, study abroad, summer session for credit. *Unusual degree programs:* 3-2 computer science with Polytechnic University.

Computers on Campus 175 computers/terminals are available on campus for general student use. Students can access the following: computer help desk, free student e-mail accounts, online (class) grades, online (class) registration, online (class) schedules. Campuswide network is available. 100% of college-owned or -operated housing units are wired for high-speed Internet access. Wireless service is available via classrooms, computer centers, computer labs, libraries.

Student Life *Housing options:* coed. Campus housing is university owned and leased by the school. Freshman applicants given priority for college housing. *Activities and organizations:* drama/theater group, student-run newspaper, radio station, Education Club, African-American Heritage Club, Asian-American Heritage Club, Latino Heritage Club, Business Club. *Campus security:* 24-hour emergency response devices and patrols, student patrols, 24-hour security in residence halls. *Student services:* personal/psychological counseling.

Athletics *Intramural sports:* softball M/W.

Standardized Tests *Required:* SAT or ACT (for admission).

Costs (2007–08) *Comprehensive fee:* $32,850 includes full-time tuition ($19,666), mandatory fees ($934), and room and board ($12,250). Part-time tuition: $628 per credit. *Required fees:* $334 per term part-time. *College room only:* $10,250. *Payment plan:* installment.

Financial Aid In 2004, 301 non-need-based awards were made. *Average non-need-based aid:* $5044. *Average indebtedness upon graduation:* $16,903.

Applying *Options:* electronic application, deferred entrance. *Application fee:* $60. *Required:* essay or personal statement, high school transcript, minimum 2.0 GPA, 2 letters of recommendation. *Required for some:* audition for dance and theater programs. *Recommended:* interview. *Application deadlines:* rolling (freshmen), rolling (transfers). *Notification:* continuous (freshmen), continuous (transfers).

Freshman Application Contact Mr. James Rogers, Dean of Admissions, Marymount Manhattan College, 221 East 71st Street, New York, NY 10021. *Phone:* 212-517-0430. *Toll-free phone:* 800-MARYMOUNT. *Fax:* 212-517-0448. *E-mail:* admissions@mmm.edu.

See page 1782 for the College Close-Up.

MEDAILLE COLLEGE

Buffalo, New York www.medaille.edu/

- **Independent** comprehensive, founded 1875
- **Urban** 13-acre campus
- **Endowment** $492,107
- **Coed** 1,665 undergraduate students, 95% full-time, 63% women, 37% men
- **Moderately difficult** entrance level, 79% of applicants were admitted

Undergraduates 1,589 full-time, 76 part-time. Students come from 4 states and territories, 2 other countries, 4% are from out of state, 13% African American, 0.5% Asian American or Pacific Islander, 2% Hispanic American, 0.5% Native American, 11% transferred in, 26% live on campus. *Retention:* 64% of 2006 full-time freshmen returned.

Freshmen *Admission:* 1,079 applied, 857 admitted, 420 enrolled. *Average high school GPA:* 2.9. *Test scores:* SAT critical reading scores over 500: 37%; SAT math scores over 500: 37%; ACT scores over 18: 75%; SAT critical reading scores over 600: 5%; SAT math scores over 600: 5%; ACT scores over 24: 25%; SAT critical reading scores over 700: 1%; SAT math scores over 700: 1%.

Faculty *Total:* 383, 24% full-time, 21% with terminal degrees. *Student/faculty ratio:* 15:1.

Majors Accounting; biology/biological sciences; business administration and management; criminal justice/safety; elementary education; English; financial planning and services; liberal arts and sciences/liberal studies; mass communication/media; middle school education; physiological psychology/psychobiology; pre-law studies; psychology; sport and fitness administration/management; veterinary/animal health technology; web page, digital/multimedia and information resources design.

Academics *Calendar:* semesters (modular courses available for evening studies and weekend college program). *Degrees:* certificates, associate, bachelor's, master's, and post-master's certificates. *Special study options:* academic remediation for entering students, accelerated degree program, adult/continuing education programs, advanced placement credit, double majors, honors programs, independent study, internships, off-campus study, part-time degree program, services for LD students, student-designed majors, summer session for credit. *ROTC:* Army (c). *Unusual degree programs:* 3-2 business administration; sports management.

Computers on Campus 120 computers/terminals are available on campus for general student use. Students can access the following: campus intranet, computer help desk, free student e-mail accounts, online (class) grades, online (class) registration, online (class) schedules. Campuswide network is available. 100% of college-owned or -operated housing units are wired for high-speed Internet access. Wireless service is available via classrooms, computer centers, computer labs, dorm rooms, learning centers, libraries, student centers.

Student Life *Housing options:* coed, men-only, women-only, disabled students. Campus housing is university owned. *Activities and organizations:* drama/theater group, student-run newspaper, radio and television station, student government, radio station, ASRA (admissions club), Student Activities Board, Teach. *Campus security:* 24-hour emergency response devices and patrols, late-night transport/escort service, controlled dormitory access. *Student services:* health clinic, personal/psychological counseling.

Athletics Member NCAA. All Division III. *Intercollegiate sports:* baseball M, basketball M/W, bowling W, cross-country running W, golf M, lacrosse M/W, soccer M/W, softball W, volleyball M/W. *Intramural sports:* basketball M/W, soccer M/W, softball M/W, table tennis M/W, tennis M/W, volleyball M/W, weight lifting M/W.

Standardized Tests *Required:* SAT or ACT (for admission). *Recommended:* SAT (for admission).

Costs (2007–08) *Comprehensive fee:* $25,014 includes full-time tuition ($16,590) and room and board ($8424). Full-time tuition and fees vary according to location. Part-time tuition: $588 per credit hour. Part-time tuition and fees vary according to course load. *Room and board:* Room and board charges vary according to housing facility. *Payment plan:* installment. *Waivers:* adult students, senior citizens, and employees or children of employees.

Financial Aid Of all full-time matriculated undergraduates who enrolled in 2006, 1,500 applied for aid, 1,500 were judged to have need, 50 had their need fully met. 150 Federal Work-Study jobs (averaging $1500). In 2006, 50 non-need-based awards were made. *Average percent of need met:* 70%. *Average financial aid package:* $14,000. *Average need-based loan:* $5500. *Average need-based gift aid:* $3000. *Average non-need-based aid:* $2000. *Average indebtedness upon graduation:* $23,000.

Applying *Options:* electronic application, early admission, deferred entrance. *Application fee:* $25. *Required:* high school transcript, interview. *Required for some:* essay or personal statement, 2.5 high school GPA for veterinary technology and elementary teacher education majors. *Recommended:* essay or personal statement, minimum 2.0 GPA, 1 letter of recommendation. *Application deadlines:* 8/1 (freshmen), rolling (transfers). *Notification:* continuous (freshmen), continuous (transfers).

Freshman Application Contact Mr. Greg Florczak, Director of Undergraduate Admissions, Medaille College, Medaille College, Office of Admissions, Buffalo, NY 14214. *Phone:* 716-880-2200. *Toll-free phone:* 800-292-1582. *Fax:* 716-880-2007. *E-mail:* admissionsug@medaille.edu.

Medgar Evers College of the City University of New York

Brooklyn, New York **www.mec.cuny.edu/**

- **State and locally supported** 4-year, founded 1969, part of City University of New York System
- **Urban** 1-acre campus
- **Coed** 5,551 undergraduate students, 64% full-time, 75% women, 25% men
- **Noncompetitive** entrance level, 100% of applicants were admitted

Undergraduates 3,532 full-time, 2,019 part-time. Students come from 4 states and territories, 50 other countries, 1% are from out of state, 89% African American, 0.9% Asian American or Pacific Islander, 4% Hispanic American, 0.1% Native American, 2% international, 10% transferred in. *Retention:* 59% of 2006 full-time freshmen returned.

Freshmen *Admission:* 4,267 applied, 4,267 admitted, 892 enrolled. *Average high school GPA:* 1.98. *Test scores:* SAT critical reading scores over 500: 12%; SAT math scores over 500: 15%; SAT critical reading scores over 600: 1%.

Faculty *Total:* 444, 39% full-time, 23% with terminal degrees. *Student/faculty ratio:* 16:1.

Majors Accounting; biology/biological sciences; business administration and management; business/commerce; computer programming; ecology; elementary education; information science/studies; liberal arts and sciences/liberal studies; nursing (licensed practical/vocational nurse training); nursing (registered nurse training); psychology; special education.

Academics *Calendar:* semesters. *Degrees:* certificates, associate, and bachelor's. *Special study options:* academic remediation for entering students, adult/continuing education programs, advanced placement credit, cooperative education, English as a second language, external degree program, honors programs, independent study, internships, off-campus study, part-time degree program, services for LD students, study abroad, summer session for credit.

Computers on Campus 120 computers/terminals are available on campus for general student use. Students can access the following: free student e-mail accounts, online (class) grades, online (class) registration, online (class) schedules. Campuswide network is available. Wireless service is available via entire campus.

Student Life *Housing:* college housing not available. *Activities and organizations:* drama/theater group, student-run newspaper, radio and television station, choral group, American Marketing Association, Drama Students Association, Rising Stars, Medgar Evers College Society of Public Administrators, National Society of Black Accountants. *Campus security:* 24-hour patrols. *Student services:* women's center, legal services.

Athletics Member NCAA. All Division III. *Intercollegiate sports:* basketball M/W, cross-country running M/W, soccer M/W, tennis W, track and field M/W, volleyball M/W. *Intramural sports:* basketball M/W, tennis W.

Standardized Tests *Recommended:* SAT and SAT Subject Tests or ACT (for admission).

Costs (2007–08) *Tuition:* state resident $4000 full-time, $170 per credit part-time; nonresident $8640 full-time, $360 per credit part-time. *Required fees:* $126 full-time, $89 per term part-time. *Room and board:* $1500. *Payment plans:* installment, deferred payment.

Financial Aid *Average financial aid package:* $3270. *Average need-based loan:* $1528. *Average need-based gift aid:* $2914.

Applying *Options:* electronic application, deferred entrance. *Application fee:* $65. *Required:* high school transcript. *Application deadlines;* rolling (freshmen), rolling (transfers). *Notification:* continuous (freshmen), continuous (transfers).

Freshman Application Contact Ms. Rose Banton, Director of Admissions, Medgar Evers College of the City University of New York, 1665 Bedford Avenue, Brooklyn, NY 11225. *Phone:* 718-270-6030. *Fax:* 718-270-6411. *E-mail:* rosebanton@mec.cuny.edu.

Mercy College

Dobbs Ferry, New York **www.mercy.edu/**

- **Independent** comprehensive, founded 1951
- **Suburban** 60-acre campus with easy access to New York City
- **Endowment** $30.5 million
- **Coed** 5,124 undergraduate students, 66% full-time, 70% women, 30% men
- **Minimally difficult** entrance level, 39% of applicants were admitted

Undergraduates 3,402 full-time, 1,722 part-time. Students come from 25 states and territories, 6% are from out of state, 24% African American, 3% Asian American or Pacific Islander, 26% Hispanic American, 0.7% Native American, 1% international, 16% transferred in, 3% live on campus. *Retention:* 62% of 2006 full-time freshmen returned.

Freshmen *Admission:* 2,313 applied, 892 admitted, 594 enrolled.

Faculty *Total:* 780, 23% full-time. *Student/faculty ratio:* 16:1.

Majors Accounting; animal sciences; banking and financial support services; behavioral sciences; biology/biological sciences; business administration and management; business/corporate communications; business/managerial economics; commercial and advertising art; communication and journalism related; communication disorders; computer and information sciences; computer/information technology services administration related; computer science; criminal justice/law enforcement administration; English; English as a second/foreign language (teaching); English/language arts teacher education; health professions related; history; human services; information science/studies; legal professions and studies related; liberal arts and sciences/liberal studies; mathematics; nursing (registered nurse training); occupational therapist assistant; psychology; public administration and social service professions related; social sciences; social studies teacher education; social work; sociology; Spanish; Spanish language teacher education; special education; therapeutic recreation.

Academics *Calendar:* semesters. *Degrees:* certificates, associate, bachelor's, master's, and doctoral. *Special study options:* academic remediation for entering students, accelerated degree program, adult/continuing education programs, advanced placement credit, cooperative education, distance learning, double majors, English as a second language, honors programs, independent study, internships, off-campus study, part-time degree program, services for LD students, student-designed majors, study abroad, summer session for credit. *ROTC:* Air Force (c).

Computers on Campus 588 computers/terminals are available on campus for general student use. Students can access the following: campus intranet, computer help desk, free student e-mail accounts, online (class) grades, online (class) registration, online (class) schedules. Campuswide network is available. Wireless service is available via classrooms, computer labs, dorm rooms, learning centers, libraries, student centers.

Student Life *Housing options:* coed. Campus housing is university owned. *Activities and organizations:* student-run newspaper, radio station, Latin American Student Association, African Descendants of One Mind, Veterinarian Technology Club, The Reporters Impact, Resident Student Association. *Campus security:* 24-hour patrols. *Student services:* personal/psychological counseling.

Athletics Member NCAA. All Division II. *Intercollegiate sports:* baseball M (s), basketball M (s)/W (s), cross-country running M (s)/W (s), golf M (s), soccer M (s)/W (s), softball W (s), tennis M (s), track and field M (s)/W (s), volleyball W (s). *Intramural sports:* basketball M/W, volleyball M/W.

Costs (2007–08) *Comprehensive fee:* $23,990 includes full-time tuition ($13,730), mandatory fees ($440), and room and board ($9820). Part-time tuition: $575 per credit. *Required fees:* $110 per term part-time. *Room and board:* Room and board charges vary according to housing facility. *Payment plans:* installment, deferred payment. *Waivers:* senior citizens and employees or children of employees.

Applying *Options:* electronic application, deferred entrance. *Application fee:* $37. *Required:* high school transcript. *Recommended:* letters of recommendation, interview. *Application deadlines:* rolling (freshmen), rolling (transfers). *Notification:* continuous (freshmen), continuous (transfers).

Freshman Application Contact Ms. Kathleen Jackson, Director of Admissions, Mercy College, 555 Broadway, Dobbs Ferry, NY 10522-1189. *Toll-free phone:* 800-MERCY-GO. *Toll-free phone:* 800-MERCY-NY. *Fax:* 914-674-7382. *E-mail:* admissions@mercy.edu.

Mesivta of Eastern Parkway Rabbinical Seminary

Brooklyn, New York

Director of Admissions Rabbi Joseph Halberstadt, Dean, Mesivta of Eastern Parkway Rabbinical Seminary, 510 Dahill Road, Brooklyn, NY 11218-5559. *Phone:* 718-438-1002.

Mesivta Tifereth Jerusalem of America

New York, New York

Director of Admissions Rabbi Fishellis, Director of Admissions, Mesivta Tifereth Jerusalem of America, 141 East Broadway, New York, NY 10002-6301. *Phone:* 212-964-2830.

Mesivta Torah Vodaath Rabbinical Seminary

Brooklyn, New York

Director of Admissions Rabbi Issac Braun, Administrator, Mesivta Torah Vodaath Rabbinical Seminary, 425 East Ninth Street, Brooklyn, NY 11218-5209. *Phone:* 718-941-8000.

Metropolitan College of New York

New York, New York www.metropolitan.edu/

- **Independent** comprehensive, founded 1964
- **Urban** campus
- **Endowment** $5.9 million
- **Coed, primarily women** 651 undergraduate students, 91% full-time, 73% women, 27% men
- **Moderately difficult** entrance level, 37% of applicants were admitted

Undergraduates 592 full-time, 59 part-time. Students come from 3 states and territories, 71% are from out of state, 53% African American, 0.8% Asian American or Pacific Islander, 14% Hispanic American, 2% international. *Retention:* 32% of 2006 full-time freshmen returned.

Freshmen *Admission:* 282 applied, 103 admitted.

Faculty *Total:* 224, 16% full-time. *Student/faculty ratio:* 11:1.

Majors Business administration and management; business/commerce; urban studies/affairs.

Academics *Calendar:* 3 15-week semesters. *Degrees:* certificates, associate, bachelor's, and master's. *Special study options:* academic remediation for entering students, accelerated degree program, adult/continuing education programs, cooperative education, distance learning, English as a second language, internships, part-time degree program, services for LD students, study abroad, summer session for credit.

Computers on Campus 150 computers/terminals are available on campus for general student use. Students can access the following: free student e-mail accounts, online (class) grades. Campuswide network is available. Wireless service is available via entire campus.

Student Life *Housing:* college housing not available. *Activities and organizations:* student-run newspaper, student government, student newsletter, honor societies, Networking Club, yearbook committee. *Campus security:* 24-hour patrols. *Student services:* personal/psychological counseling.

Standardized Tests *Required for some:* Accuplacer. *Recommended:* SAT or ACT (for admission).

Costs (2007–08) *Tuition:* $16,320 full-time, $544 per credit part-time. Full-time tuition and fees vary according to degree level and program. Part-time tuition and fees vary according to degree level and program. No tuition increase for student's term of enrollment. *Required fees:* $400 full-time, $200 per term part-time. *Payment plans:* installment, deferred payment. *Waivers:* employees or children of employees.

Financial Aid Of all full-time matriculated undergraduates who enrolled in 2000, 1,066 applied for aid, 1,062 were judged to have need. 52 Federal Work-Study jobs (averaging $1969). 30 state and other part-time jobs (averaging $1920). *Average financial aid package:* $6337. *Average need-based loan:* $3377. *Average need-based gift aid:* $3650. *Average indebtedness upon graduation:* $20,130.

Applying *Options:* electronic application, deferred entrance. *Application fee:* $30. *Required:* essay or personal statement, high school transcript, 2 letters of recommendation, interview. *Required for some:* college entrance exam. *Recommended:* minimum 3.0 GPA. *Application deadlines:* 8/15 (freshmen), 8/15 (transfers). *Notification:* continuous until 8/31 (freshmen), continuous until 8/31 (transfers).

Freshman Application Contact Metropolitan College of New York, 75 Varick Street, 12th Floor, New York, NY 10013. *Phone:* 212-343-1234 Ext. 2700. *Toll-free phone:* 800-33-THINK Ext. 5001. *Fax:* 212-343-8470.

Mirrer Yeshiva

Brooklyn, New York

Director of Admissions Director of Admissions, Mirrer Yeshiva, 1795 Ocean Parkway, Brooklyn, NY 11223-2010. *Phone:* 718-645-0536.

Molloy College

Rockville Centre, New York www.molloy.edu/

- **Independent** comprehensive, founded 1955
- **Suburban** 30-acre campus with easy access to New York City
- **Endowment** $23.0 million
- **Coed** 2,962 undergraduate students, 72% full-time, 79% women, 21% men
- **Moderately difficult** entrance level, 63% of applicants were admitted

Undergraduates 2,127 full-time, 835 part-time. Students come from 7 states and territories, 9 other countries, 21% African American, 7% Asian American or Pacific Islander, 10% Hispanic American, 0.3% Native American, 0.3% international, 11% transferred in. *Retention:* 80% of 2006 full-time freshmen returned.

Freshmen *Admission:* 1,483 applied, 928 admitted, 372 enrolled. *Average high school GPA:* 3.0. *Test scores:* SAT critical reading scores over 500: 44%; SAT math scores over 500: 60%; SAT critical reading scores over 600: 13%; SAT math scores over 600: 13%; SAT critical reading scores over 700: 1%; SAT math scores over 700: 1%.

Faculty *Total:* 483, 32% full-time, 41% with terminal degrees. *Student/faculty ratio:* 11:1.

Majors Accounting; art; audiology and speech-language pathology; biology/biological sciences; biology teacher education; business administration and management; cardiovascular technology; communication/speech communication and rhetoric; computer science; criminal justice/safety; education; elementary education; English; English/language arts teacher education; environmental studies; French; French language teacher education; health information/medical records technology; history; interdisciplinary studies; liberal arts and sciences/liberal studies; mathematics; mathematics teacher education; music; music therapy; nuclear medical technology; nursing (registered nurse training); peace studies and conflict resolution; philosophy; political science and government; pre-dentistry studies; pre-law studies; pre-medical studies; pre-veterinary studies; psychology; religious studies; respiratory care therapy; secondary education; social studies teacher education; social work; sociology; Spanish; Spanish language teacher education; special education.

Academics *Calendar:* 4-1-4. *Degrees:* associate, bachelor's, master's, and post-master's certificates. *Special study options:* academic remediation for entering students, adult/continuing education programs, advanced placement credit, cooperative education, double majors, English as a second language, honors programs, internships, part-time degree program, services for LD students, study abroad, summer session for credit. *ROTC:* Army (c), Navy (c), Air Force (c).

Computers on Campus 357 computers/terminals are available on campus for general student use. Campuswide network is available. Wireless service is available via entire campus.

Student Life *Housing:* college housing not available. *Activities and organizations:* drama/theater group, student-run newspaper, choral group, Nursing Student Association, African-American Caribbean Organization, Gaelic Society, Education Club, International Society. *Campus security:* 24-hour emergency response devices and patrols, late-night transport/escort service. *Student services:* health clinic, personal/psychological counseling, women's center.

Athletics Member NCAA. All Division II. *Intercollegiate sports:* baseball M (s), basketball M (s)/W (s), cross-country running M (s)/W (s), equestrian sports W, lacrosse M (s)/W (s), rugby M/W, soccer M (s)/W (s), softball W (s), tennis W (s), volleyball W (s).

Standardized Tests *Required:* SAT or ACT (for admission).

Costs (2007–08) *Tuition:* $17,640 full-time, $585 per credit part-time. *Required fees:* $930 full-time. *Payment plan:* installment. *Waivers:* employees or children of employees.

Financial Aid Of all full-time matriculated undergraduates who enrolled in 2007, 1,719 applied for aid, 1,453 were judged to have need, 234 had their need fully met. 501 Federal Work-Study jobs (averaging $2467). In 2007, 250 non-need-based awards were made. *Average percent of need met:* 59%. *Average financial aid package:* $12,611. *Average need-based loan:* $5841. *Average need-based gift aid:* $7388. *Average non-need-based aid:* $12,779. *Average indebtedness upon graduation:* $27,000. *Financial aid deadline:* 5/1.

Applying *Options:* electronic application, early admission, early action, deferred entrance. *Application fee:* $30. *Required:* essay or personal statement, high school transcript. *Required for some:* 1 letter of recommendation. *Recommended:* interview. *Application deadlines:* rolling (freshmen), rolling (transfers). *Early decision deadline:* 11/1. *Notification:* continuous (freshmen), continuous (transfers), 12/1 (early decision).

Freshman Application Contact Ms. Marguerite Lane, Director of Admissions, Molloy College, 1000 Hempstead Avenue, PO Box 5002, Rockville Centre,

NY 11571-5002. *Phone:* 516-678-5000 Ext. 6240. *Toll-free phone:* 888-4MOLLOY. *Fax:* 516-256-2247. *E-mail:* admissions@molloy.edu.

See page 1784 for the College Close-Up.

Monroe College

Bronx, New York **www.monroecollege.edu/**

- **Proprietary** comprehensive, founded 1933
- **Urban** campus
- **Coed** 4,502 undergraduate students, 83% full-time, 73% women, 27% men
- **Moderately difficult** entrance level, 58% of applicants were admitted

Undergraduates 3,718 full-time, 784 part-time. Students come from 8 states and territories, 14 other countries, 1% are from out of state, 14% transferred in, 1% live on campus. *Retention:* 70% of 2006 full-time freshmen returned.

Freshmen *Admission:* 1,531 applied, 885 admitted, 796 enrolled.

Faculty *Total:* 251, 24% full-time, 15% with terminal degrees. *Student/faculty ratio:* 21:1.

Majors Accounting; baking and pastry arts; business administration and management; computer science; criminal justice/law enforcement administration; criminal justice/police science; culinary arts; health services administration; hospitality administration; information science/studies; information technology; medical administrative assistant and medical secretary; medical/clinical assistant; nursing (licensed practical/vocational nurse training); public health.

Academics *Calendar:* trimesters. *Degrees:* associate, bachelor's, and master's. *Special study options:* academic remediation for entering students, adult/continuing education programs, cooperative education, distance learning, English as a second language, internships, part-time degree program, summer session for credit.

Computers on Campus 541 computers/terminals are available on campus for general student use. Students can access the following: campus intranet, computer help desk, free student e-mail accounts, online (class) grades, online (class) registration, online (class) schedules. Campuswide network is available. 100% of college-owned or -operated housing units are wired for high-speed Internet access. Wireless service is available via entire campus.

Student Life *Housing options:* coed. Campus housing is university owned and leased by the school. Freshman applicants given priority for college housing. *Activities and organizations:* drama/theater group, student-run newspaper, choral group, Students in Free Enterprise (SIFE), Creative Campus Club, Multicultural Student Association, Criminal Justice Club, Poetry is Truth. *Campus security:* late-night transport/escort service. *Student services:* personal/psychological counseling.

Athletics Member NJCAA. *Intercollegiate sports:* baseball M, basketball M/W, soccer M, softball W, track and field M/W, volleyball W. *Intramural sports:* basketball M/W, bowling M/W, cheerleading W.

Standardized Tests *Recommended:* SAT or ACT (for admission).

Costs (2007–08) *Comprehensive fee:* $21,342 includes full-time tuition ($9984), mandatory fees ($700), and room and board ($10,658). Full-time tuition and fees vary according to degree level and program. Part-time tuition: $416 per credit hour. Part-time tuition and fees vary according to degree level and program. *Required fees:* $175 per term part-time. *Room and board:* Room and board charges vary according to board plan. *Payment plan:* installment. *Waivers:* employees or children of employees.

Financial Aid Of all full-time matriculated undergraduates who enrolled in 2006, 3,453 applied for aid, 3,332 were judged to have need, 733 had their need fully met. 234 Federal Work-Study jobs (averaging $4000). *Average percent of need met:* 91%. *Average financial aid package:* $9915. *Average need-based loan:* $4150. *Average need-based gift aid:* $6215. *Average indebtedness upon graduation:* $7400.

Applying *Options:* electronic application, early admission, early decision, early action, deferred entrance. *Application fee:* $35. *Required:* essay or personal statement, high school transcript, interview. *Required for some:* letters of recommendation. *Application deadlines:* 8/26 (freshmen), 8/26 (transfers). *Notification:* continuous until 9/3 (freshmen), continuous until 9/3 (transfers).

Freshman Application Contact Monroe College, Monroe College Way, 2501 Jerome Avenue, Bronx, NY 10468. *Phone:* 718-933-6700 Ext. 8246. *Toll-free phone:* 800-55MONROE.

See page 1786 for the College Close-Up.

Monroe College

New Rochelle, New York **www.monroecollege.edu/**

- **Proprietary** 4-year, founded 1983
- **Suburban** campus with easy access to New York City
- **Coed** 1,935 undergraduate students, 89% full-time, 66% women, 34% men
- **Moderately difficult** entrance level, 58% of applicants were admitted

Undergraduates 1,721 full-time, 214 part-time. Students come from 9 states and territories, 16 other countries, 2% are from out of state, 56% African American, 0.7% Asian American or Pacific Islander, 19% Hispanic American, 0.1% Native American, 18% international, 9% transferred in, 20% live on campus. *Retention:* 74% of 2006 full-time freshmen returned.

Freshmen *Admission:* 912 applied, 533 admitted, 468 enrolled.

Faculty *Total:* 93, 26% full-time, 9% with terminal degrees. *Student/faculty ratio:* 20:1.

Majors Business administration and management; computer science; criminal justice/police science; health services/allied health/health sciences; hospitality administration; medical administrative assistant and medical secretary.

Academics *Calendar:* trimesters. *Degrees:* associate, bachelor's, and master's. *Special study options:* academic remediation for entering students, adult/continuing education programs, cooperative education, distance learning, English as a second language, external degree program, internships, part-time degree program, summer session for credit.

Computers on Campus 370 computers/terminals are available on campus for general student use. Students can access the following: campus intranet, computer help desk, free student e-mail accounts, online (class) grades, online (class) registration, online (class) schedules. Campuswide network is available. Wireless service is available via entire campus.

Student Life *Housing options:* coed. Campus housing is university owned and leased by the school. Freshman applicants given priority for college housing. *Activities and organizations:* drama/theater group, student-run newspaper. *Campus security:* late-night transport/escort service. *Student services:* personal/psychological counseling.

Athletics Member NJCAA. *Intercollegiate sports:* baseball M, basketball M/W, soccer M, softball W, volleyball W. *Intramural sports:* basketball M/W, bowling M/W, cheerleading W, soccer M, volleyball M/W.

Costs (2007–08) *Comprehensive fee:* $18,784 includes full-time tuition ($9984), mandatory fees ($700), and room and board ($8100). Part-time tuition: $416 per credit. *Required fees:* $175 per term part-time. *College room only:* $6700.

Financial Aid Of all full-time matriculated undergraduates who enrolled in 2006, 1,189 applied for aid, 1,060 were judged to have need, 494 had their need fully met. 69 Federal Work-Study jobs (averaging $4845). *Average percent of need met:* 92%. *Average financial aid package:* $11,450. *Average need-based loan:* $4300. *Average need-based gift aid:* $6325. *Average indebtedness upon graduation:* $15,000.

Applying *Options:* electronic application, early admission, deferred entrance. *Application fee:* $35. *Required:* high school transcript, interview. *Application deadlines:* 8/26 (freshmen), 8/26 (transfers). *Notification:* 9/3 (freshmen), 9/3 (transfers).

Freshman Application Contact Ms. Lisa Scorca, High School Admissions, Monroe College, 434 Main Street, New Rochelle, NY 10801. *Phone:* 914-654-3200. *Toll-free phone:* 800-55MONROE. *E-mail:* lscora@monroecollege.edu.

Mount Saint Mary College

Newburgh, New York **www.msmc.edu/**

- **Independent** comprehensive, founded 1960
- **Suburban** 72-acre campus with easy access to New York City
- **Endowment** $5.0 million
- **Coed** 2,086 undergraduate students, 81% full-time, 72% women, 28% men
- **Moderately difficult** entrance level, 77% of applicants were admitted

Undergraduates 1,700 full-time, 386 part-time. Students come from 13 states and territories, 2 other countries, 12% are from out of state, 10% African American, 3% Asian American or Pacific Islander, 9% Hispanic American, 0.1% Native American, 10% transferred in, 38% live on campus. *Retention:* 72% of 2006 full-time freshmen returned.

Freshmen *Admission:* 1,600 applied, 1,231 admitted, 366 enrolled. *Average high school GPA:* 3.1. *Test scores:* SAT critical reading scores over 500: 53%; SAT math scores over 500: 54%; SAT writing scores over 500: 47%; ACT scores over

18: 87%; SAT critical reading scores over 600: 8%; SAT math scores over 600: 11%; SAT writing scores over 600: 6%; ACT scores over 24: 17%; SAT math scores over 700: 1%.

Faculty *Total:* 219, 34% full-time, 46% with terminal degrees. *Student/faculty ratio:* 17:1.

Majors Accounting; biology/biological sciences; business administration and management; chemistry; clinical laboratory science/medical technology; clinical/medical laboratory technology; computer and information sciences; computer science; criminal justice/safety; education; education (K-12); elementary education; English; history; human services; information technology; interdisciplinary studies; international business/trade/commerce; international relations and affairs; liberal arts and sciences/liberal studies; marketing related; mass communication/media; mathematics; nursing (registered nurse training); physical therapy; political science and government; pre-law studies; psychology; public relations/image management; secondary education; social sciences; social work; sociology; special education; special education related; speech-language pathology.

Academics *Calendar:* semesters. *Degrees:* certificates, bachelor's, master's, and postbachelor's certificates. *Special study options:* academic remediation for entering students, accelerated degree program, adult/continuing education programs, advanced placement credit, cooperative education, distance learning, double majors, freshman honors college, honors programs, independent study, internships, off-campus study, part-time degree program, services for LD students, student-designed majors, study abroad, summer session for credit. *Unusual degree programs:* 3-2 social work with Fordham University; publishing with Pace University, counseling with Pace University.

Computers on Campus 570 computers/terminals are available on campus for general student use. Students can access the following: computer help desk, free student e-mail accounts, online (class) grades, online (class) registration, online (class) schedules, intranet. Campuswide network is available. 100% of college-owned or -operated housing units are wired for high-speed Internet access. Wireless service is available via entire campus.

Student Life *Housing options:* coed, men-only, women-only. Campus housing is university owned. Freshman applicants given priority for college housing. *Activities and organizations:* drama/theater group, student-run newspaper, radio station, choral group, Student Government Association, Different Stages, Big Brothers/Big Sisters, Black and Latin Student Unions, Habitat for Humanity. *Campus security:* 24-hour emergency response devices and patrols, student patrols, late-night transport/escort service, controlled dormitory access, monitored surveillance cameras in all residence halls. *Student services:* health clinic, personal/psychological counseling.

Athletics Member NCAA. All Division III. *Intercollegiate sports:* baseball M, basketball M/W, cross-country running M/W, soccer M/W, softball W, swimming and diving M/W, tennis M/W, volleyball W. *Intramural sports:* basketball M/W, bowling M/W, cheerleading W (c), football M, golf M/W, lacrosse M (c), soccer M/W, softball M/W, swimming and diving M/W, table tennis M/W, volleyball M/W.

Standardized Tests *Required:* SAT or ACT (for admission).

Costs (2007–08) *Comprehensive fee:* $29,920 includes full-time tuition ($18,900), mandatory fees ($620), and room and board ($10,400). Full-time tuition and fees vary according to degree level. Part-time tuition: $630 per credit hour. Part-time tuition and fees vary according to degree level. *Required fees:* $45 per term part-time. *College room only:* $6090. Room and board charges vary according to board plan, housing facility, and student level. *Payment plan:* installment. *Waivers:* employees or children of employees.

Financial Aid Of all full-time matriculated undergraduates who enrolled in 2007, 1,415 applied for aid, 1,221 were judged to have need, 250 had their need fully met. 263 Federal Work-Study jobs (averaging $1002). 24 state and other part-time jobs (averaging $1396). In 2007, 224 non-need-based awards were made. *Average percent of need met:* 56%. *Average financial aid package:* $12,284. *Average need-based loan:* $5572. *Average need-based gift aid:* $7680. *Average non-need-based aid:* $13,885. *Average indebtedness upon graduation:* $36,625.

Applying *Options:* electronic application, early admission, deferred entrance. *Application fee:* $40. *Required:* high school transcript. *Required for some:* essay or personal statement, 3 letters of recommendation, interview. *Recommended:* essay or personal statement, minimum 3.0 GPA, 3 letters of recommendation, interview. *Application deadlines:* rolling (freshmen), rolling (transfers). *Notification:* continuous (freshmen), continuous (transfers).

Freshman Application Contact Mr. J. Ognibene, Director of Admissions, Mount Saint Mary College, 330 Powell Avenue, Newburgh, NY 12550. *Phone:* 845-569-3248. *Toll-free phone:* 888-937-6762. *Fax:* 845-562-6762. *E-mail:* admissions@msmc.edu.

See page 1788 for the College Close-Up.

NAZARETH COLLEGE OF ROCHESTER

Rochester, New York **www.naz.edu/**

- **Independent** comprehensive, founded 1924
- **Suburban** 150-acre campus
- **Endowment** $61.5 million
- **Coed** 2,167 undergraduate students, 92% full-time, 75% women, 25% men
- **Moderately difficult** entrance level, 74% of applicants were admitted

Undergraduates 1,996 full-time, 171 part-time. Students come from 24 states and territories, 26 other countries, 5% are from out of state, 5% African American, 2% Asian American or Pacific Islander, 3% Hispanic American, 0.4% Native American, 0.9% international, 7% transferred in, 55% live on campus. *Retention:* 83% of 2006 full-time freshmen returned.

Freshmen *Admission:* 2,076 applied, 1,545 admitted, 458 enrolled. *Average high school GPA:* 3.31.

Faculty *Total:* 369, 41% full-time, 50% with terminal degrees. *Student/faculty ratio:* 12:1.

Majors Accounting; American studies; anthropology; art; art history, criticism and conservation; art teacher education; art therapy; audiology and speech-language pathology; biochemistry; biology/biological sciences; biology teacher education; business administration and management; business teacher education; ceramic arts and ceramics; chemistry; chemistry teacher education; commercial and advertising art; communication/speech communication and rhetoric; creative writing; dramatic/theater arts; drawing; economics; education; elementary education; English; English/language arts teacher education; environmental science; environmental studies; fine/studio arts; foreign language teacher education; French; German; gerontology; history; history teacher education; human resources management; information science/studies; information technology; interdisciplinary studies; international relations and affairs; Italian; literature; management information systems; marketing/marketing management; mathematics; mathematics teacher education; modern languages; music; music history, literature, and theory; music teacher education; music therapy; nursing (registered nurse training); peace studies and conflict resolution; philosophy; photography; physical therapy; political science and government; pre-dentistry studies; pre-law studies; pre-medical studies; pre-veterinary studies; psychology; religious studies; science teacher education; secondary education; social sciences; social studies teacher education; social work; sociology; Spanish; special education; women's studies.

Academics *Calendar:* semesters. *Degrees:* bachelor's, master's, doctoral, and post-master's certificates. *Special study options:* academic remediation for entering students, adult/continuing education programs, advanced placement credit, cooperative education, double majors, honors programs, independent study, internships, off-campus study, part-time degree program, services for LD students, study abroad, summer session for credit. *ROTC:* Army (c), Air Force (c).

Computers on Campus 150 computers/terminals are available on campus for general student use. Students can access the following: computer help desk, free student e-mail accounts, online (class) grades, online (class) registration, online (class) schedules. Campuswide network is available. 100% of college-owned or -operated housing units are wired for high-speed Internet access. Wireless service is available via classrooms, libraries, student centers.

Student Life *Housing options:* coed, women-only, disabled students. Campus housing is university owned. Freshman campus housing is guaranteed. *Activities and organizations:* drama/theater group, student-run newspaper, radio station, choral group, Student Activities Council, French Club, Theater Club, Campus Ministry Council, Coffeehouse, Arts, Lecture, Entertainment Board (CALEB). *Campus security:* 24-hour emergency response devices and patrols, student patrols, late-night transport/escort service, controlled dormitory access, alarm system, security beeper, lighted pathways. *Student services:* health clinic, personal/psychological counseling.

Athletics Member NCAA. All Division III. *Intercollegiate sports:* basketball M/W, cheerleading W, cross-country running M/W, equestrian sports M/W, field hockey W, golf M/W, lacrosse M/W, soccer M/W, softball W, swimming and diving M/W, tennis M/W, track and field M/W, volleyball M/W. *Intramural sports:* basketball M/W, golf M/W, soccer M/W, swimming and diving M/W, tennis M/W, track and field M/W, ultimate Frisbee M/W, volleyball M/W.

Costs (2007–08) *Comprehensive fee:* $32,380 includes full-time tuition ($21,900), mandatory fees ($980), and room and board ($9500). Part-time tuition: $520 per credit hour. *College room only:* $5230. Room and board charges vary according to board plan and housing facility. *Payment plan:* installment. *Waivers:* minority students, children of alumni, and employees or children of employees.

Financial Aid Of all full-time matriculated undergraduates who enrolled in 2006, 1,731 applied for aid, 1,517 were judged to have need, 302 had their need fully met. 1,093 Federal Work-Study jobs (averaging $959). In 2006, 368 non-need-based awards were made. *Average percent of need met:* 73%. *Average financial aid package:* $15,214. *Average need-based loan:* $4502. *Average* *need-based gift aid:* $10,701. *Average non-need-based aid:* $9213. *Average indebtedness upon graduation:* $26,795. *Financial aid deadline:* 5/1.

Applying *Options:* electronic application, early admission, early decision, early action, deferred entrance. *Application fee:* $40. *Required:* essay or personal statement, high school transcript, 1 letter of recommendation. *Required for some:* audition/portfolio review. *Recommended:* 2 letters of recommendation, interview. *Application deadlines:* 2/15 (freshmen), 2/15 (out-of-state freshmen), 5/15 (transfers), 12/15 (early action). *Early decision deadline:* 11/15. *Notification:* continuous (freshmen), continuous (out-of-state freshmen), 2/15 (transfers), 12/15 (early decision), 1/15 (early action).

Freshman Application Contact Thomas DaRin, Vice President for Enrollment Management, Nazareth College of Rochester, 4245 East Avenue, Rochester, NY 14618-3790. *Phone:* 585-389-2860. *Toll-free phone:* 800-462-3944. *Fax:* 585-389-2826. *E-mail:* admissions@naz.edu.

See page 1790 for the College Close-Up.

THE NEW SCHOOL FOR GENERAL STUDIES

New York, New York **www.nsu.newschool.edu/**

- **Independent** upper-level, founded 1919, part of The New School
- **Urban** campus
- **Coed** 726 undergraduate students, 50% full-time, 64% women, 36% men
- **Moderately difficult** entrance level

Undergraduates 362 full-time, 364 part-time. Students come from 37 states and territories, 22 other countries, 37% are from out of state, 11% African American, 2% Asian American or Pacific Islander, 7% Hispanic American, 0.3% Native American, 4% international, 27% transferred in.

Faculty *Total:* 437, 10% full-time.

Majors Liberal arts and sciences/liberal studies.

Academics *Calendar:* semesters. *Degrees:* bachelor's, master's, and postbachelor's certificates. *Special study options:* accelerated degree program, adult/continuing education programs, advanced placement credit, distance learning, English as a second language, independent study, internships, part-time degree program, student-designed majors, summer session for credit.

Computers on Campus 1,200 computers/terminals are available on campus for general student use. Students can access the following: computer help desk, free student e-mail accounts, online (class) grades, online (class) registration, online (class) schedules, online portal. Campuswide network is available. 94% of college-owned or -operated housing units are wired for high-speed Internet access. Wireless service is available via entire campus.

Student Life *Housing options:* coed, disabled students. Campus housing is university owned and leased by the school. Freshman applicants given priority for college housing. *Activities and organizations:* student-run newspaper, choral group. *Campus security:* 24-hour emergency response devices, controlled dormitory access, trained security personnel in central buildings. *Student services:* health clinic, personal/psychological counseling.

Standardized Tests *Recommended:* SAT or ACT (for admission).

Costs (2007–08) *Comprehensive fee:* $34,322 includes full-time tuition ($22,032), mandatory fees ($540), and room and board ($11,750). Part-time tuition: $918 per credit. *College room only:* $8750. Room and board charges vary according to board plan. *Waivers:* employees or children of employees.

Financial Aid Of all full-time matriculated undergraduates who enrolled in 2003, 180 applied for aid, 171 were judged to have need, 22 had their need fully met. In 2003, 2 non-need-based awards were made. *Average percent of need met:* 58%. *Average financial aid package:* $9046. *Average need-based loan:* $3978. *Average need-based gift aid:* $5264. *Average non-need-based aid:* $3125. *Average indebtedness upon graduation:* $18,407.

Applying *Options:* deferred entrance. *Application fee:* $50. *Application deadline:* 7/1 (transfers). *Notification:* continuous (transfers).

Application Contact Ms. Cory Meyers, Assistant Director of Admissions, The New School for General Studies, 66 West 12th Street, New York, NY 10011-8603. *Phone:* 212-229-5630. *Toll-free phone:* 800-862-5039. *Fax:* 212-989-3887. *E-mail:* nsadmissions@newschool.edu.

THE NEW SCHOOL FOR JAZZ AND CONTEMPORARY MUSIC

New York, New York **www.jazz.newschool.edu**

- **Independent** 4-year, founded 1986, part of The New School
- **Urban** campus
- **Coed** 245 undergraduate students, 93% full-time, 20% women, 80% men
- **Very difficult** entrance level, 60% of applicants were admitted

Undergraduates 227 full-time, 18 part-time. Students come from 37 states and territories, 24 other countries, 73% are from out of state, 8% African American, 1% Asian American or Pacific Islander, 4% Hispanic American, 22% international, 12% transferred in, 22% live on campus. *Retention:* 80% of 2006 full-time freshmen returned.

Freshmen *Admission:* 236 applied, 142 admitted, 33 enrolled. *Average high school GPA:* 3.18.

Faculty *Total:* 64, 3% full-time. *Student/faculty ratio:* 10:1.

Majors Jazz; jazz/jazz studies; music; musical instrument technology; musicology and ethnomusicology; music pedagogy; music performance; music theory and composition; piano and organ; violin, viola, guitar and other stringed instruments.

Academics *Calendar:* semesters. *Degree:* bachelor's.

Computers on Campus Students can access the following: computer help desk, free student e-mail accounts, online (class) grades, online (class) registration, online (class) schedules, online portal. Campuswide network is available. 94% of college-owned or -operated housing units are wired for high-speed Internet access. Wireless service is available via entire campus.

Student Life *Housing options:* coed, disabled students. Campus housing is university owned and leased by the school. Freshman applicants given priority for college housing. *Activities and organizations:* student-run newspaper, choral group. *Student services:* health clinic, personal/psychological counseling.

Costs (2007–08) *Comprehensive fee:* $42,200 includes full-time tuition ($29,800), mandatory fees ($650), and room and board ($11,750). Part-time tuition: $972 per credit. *College room only:* $8750. Room and board charges vary according to board plan. *Payment plan:* installment. *Waivers:* employees or children of employees.

Financial Aid Of all full-time matriculated undergraduates who enrolled in 2006, 127 applied for aid, 127 were judged to have need, 13 had their need fully met. In 2006, 103 non-need-based awards were made. *Average percent of need met:* 71%. *Average financial aid package:* $11,713. *Average need-based loan:* $3482. *Average need-based gift aid:* $5191. *Average non-need-based aid:* $9104. *Average indebtedness upon graduation:* $28,106.

Applying *Options:* deferred entrance. *Application fee:* $40. *Required:* essay or personal statement, high school transcript, 1 letter of recommendation, Audition. *Recommended:* interview. *Application deadlines:* 3/15 (freshmen), 3/15 (transfers). *Notification:* continuous (freshmen).

Freshman Application Contact Ms. Terri Lucas, Jazz Admissions, The New School for Jazz and Contemporary Music, 55 West 13th Street, 5th Floor, New York, NY 10011. *Phone:* 212-229-5896 Ext. 4589. *Fax:* 212-229-8936. *E-mail:* jazzadm@newschool.edu.

See page 1792 for the College Close-Up.

NEW YORK CITY COLLEGE OF TECHNOLOGY OF THE CITY UNIVERSITY OF NEW YORK

Brooklyn, New York **www.citytech.cuny.edu/**

- **State and locally supported** primarily 2-year, founded 1946, part of City University of New York System
- **Urban** campus
- **Endowment** $11.7 million
- **Coed**
- **Noncompetitive** entrance level

Faculty *Student/faculty ratio:* 18:1.

Academics *Calendar:* semesters. *Degrees:* certificates, associate, and bachelor's.

Student Life *Campus security:* 24-hour emergency response devices and patrols.

Athletics Member NCAA. All Division III.

Standardized Tests *Required for some:* SAT (for admission), ACT (for admission), SAT or ACT (for admission).
Costs (2007–08) *Tuition:* state resident $4000 full-time, $170 per credit part-time; nonresident $10,800 full-time, $360 per credit part-time. *Required fees:* $289 full-time.
Applying *Application fee:* $65. *Required:* high school transcript.
Freshman Application Contact Alexis Chaconis, Director of Admissions, New York City College of Technology of the City University of New York, 300 Jay Street, Brooklyn, NY 11201-2983. *Phone:* 718-260-5500. *E-mail:* achaconis@citytech.cuny.edu.

NEW YORK COLLEGE OF HEALTH PROFESSIONS

Syosset, New York **www.nycollege.edu/**

- **Independent** founded 1981
- **Suburban** campus with easy access to New York City
- **Coed**
- **Moderately difficult** entrance level

Faculty *Student/faculty ratio:* 19:1.
Academics *Calendar:* trimesters. *Degrees:* associate, incidental bachelor's, and master's.
Student Life *Campus security:* 24-hour emergency response devices and patrols, security guard evening and weekend hours.
Costs (2007–08) *Tuition:* $9900 full-time, $275 per credit part-time. *Required fees:* $1000 full-time.
Financial Aid Of all full-time matriculated undergraduates who enrolled in 2006, 15 Federal Work-Study jobs.
Applying *Options:* electronic application, deferred entrance. *Application fee:* $85. *Required:* essay or personal statement, high school transcript, minimum 2.0 GPA, interview.
Director of Admissions Ms. Mary Rodas, Associate Director of Admissions, New York College of Health Professions, 6801 Jericho Turnpike, Syosset, NY 11791. *Toll-free phone:* 800-922-7337 Ext. 351. *E-mail:* rdodas@nycollege.edu.

NEW YORK INSTITUTE OF TECHNOLOGY

Old Westbury, New York **www.nyit.edu/**

- **Independent** university, founded 1955
- **Suburban** 1050-acre campus with easy access to New York City
- **Endowment** $40.4 million
- **Coed** 6,884 undergraduate students, 75% full-time, 37% women, 63% men
- **Moderately difficult** entrance level, 69% of applicants were admitted

Undergraduates 5,138 full-time, 1,746 part-time. Students come from 48 states and territories, 82 other countries, 19% are from out of state, 8% African American, 9% Asian American or Pacific Islander, 7% Hispanic American, 0.1% Native American, 6% international, 7% transferred in, 9% live on campus. *Retention:* 72% of 2006 full-time freshmen returned.
Freshmen *Admission:* 4,073 applied, 2,797 admitted, 1,441 enrolled. *Average high school GPA:* 3.1. *Test scores:* SAT critical reading scores over 500: 68%; SAT math scores over 500: 88%; SAT critical reading scores over 600: 21%; SAT math scores over 600: 45%; SAT critical reading scores over 700: 3%; SAT math scores over 700: 10%.
Faculty *Total:* 849, 33% full-time. *Student/faculty ratio:* 16:1.
Majors Accounting; accounting technology and bookkeeping; administrative assistant and secretarial science; advertising; aeronautical/aerospace engineering technology; architecture related; art teacher education; biology/biological sciences; biology teacher education; biomedical technology; business teacher education; chemistry; chemistry teacher education; commercial and advertising art; community psychology; computer and information sciences; criminal justice/law enforcement administration; culinary arts related; data processing and data processing technology; design and applied arts related; economics; education; electrical, electronic and communications engineering technology; electrical, electronics and communications engineering; elementary education; environmental control technologies related; finance; fine/studio arts; health occupations teacher education; hotel/motel administration; human resources management; industrial engineering; information science/studies; interior design; international business/trade/commerce; management information systems; marketing/marketing management; mathematics teacher education; mechanical engineering; mechanical engineering technologies related; multi-/interdisciplinary studies related; nursing (registered nurse training); nursing related; nutrition sciences; occupational therapy; physical therapy; physician assistant; physics; physics teacher education; political science and government; pre-medical studies; psychology; radio and television; radio and television broadcasting technology; sales and marketing/marketing and distribution teacher education; social sciences; social studies teacher education; sociology; technical and business writing; technical teacher education; telecommunications; trade and industrial teacher education.
Academics *Calendar:* semesters. *Degrees:* certificates, associate, bachelor's, master's, doctoral, first professional, post-master's, and postbachelor's certificates. *Special study options:* academic remediation for entering students, accelerated degree program, adult/continuing education programs, advanced placement credit, cooperative education, distance learning, double majors, English as a second language, external degree program, honors programs, independent study, internships, off-campus study, part-time degree program, services for LD students, student-designed majors, study abroad, summer session for credit. *ROTC:* Army (b), Air Force (b). *Unusual degree programs:* 3-2 occupational therapy, physical therapy, communication arts, architectural technology/energy management, architectural technology/MBA, mechanical engineering/energy management.
Computers on Campus 815 computers/terminals are available on campus for general student use. Students can access the following: e-mail. Campuswide network is available.
Student Life *Housing options:* coed. Campus housing is university owned and is provided by a third party. Freshman campus housing is guaranteed. *Activities and organizations:* drama/theater group, student-run newspaper, radio and television station, choral group, Physical Therapy Society, Occupational Therapy Association, ASHRAM, Bio-Medical Society, National Society of Black Engineers, national fraternities, national sororities. *Campus security:* 24-hour emergency response devices and patrols, late-night transport/escort service, controlled dormitory access. *Student services:* health clinic, personal/psychological counseling, women's center.
Athletics Member NCAA. All Division II except baseball (Division I). *Intercollegiate sports:* baseball M (s), basketball M (s)/W (s), cross-country running M (s)/W (s), lacrosse M (s), soccer M (s)/W (s), softball W (s), track and field M (s)/W (s), volleyball W (s). *Intramural sports:* basketball M/W, football M/W, golf M/W, soccer M/W, softball W, swimming and diving M/W, tennis M/W, volleyball M/W, weight lifting M/W.
Standardized Tests *Required:* SAT or ACT (for admission).
Costs (2007–08) *Comprehensive fee:* $31,512 includes full-time tuition ($20,908), mandatory fees ($590), and room and board ($10,014). Full-time tuition and fees vary according to course load and program. Part-time tuition: $705 per credit. Part-time tuition and fees vary according to course load. *Required fees:* $250 per term part-time. *Room and board:* Room and board charges vary according to board plan, housing facility, and location. *Payment plan:* installment. *Waivers:* senior citizens and employees or children of employees.
Financial Aid Of all full-time matriculated undergraduates who enrolled in 2006, 3,418 applied for aid, 2,942 were judged to have need. In 2006, 528 non-need-based awards were made. *Average financial aid package:* $15,876. *Average need-based loan:* $4978. *Average need-based gift aid:* $4727. *Average non-need-based aid:* $9660. *Average indebtedness upon graduation:* $17,125.
Applying *Options:* electronic application, deferred entrance. *Application fee:* $50. *Required:* essay or personal statement, high school transcript. *Required for some:* letters of recommendation, interview, proof of volunteer or work experience required for physical therapy, physician assistant and occupational therapy programs; portfolio for fine arts programs. *Application deadlines:* rolling (freshmen), rolling (transfers). *Notification:* continuous (freshmen), continuous (transfers).
Freshman Application Contact Ms. Doreen Meyer, Director of Financial Aid, New York Institute of Technology, PO Box 8000, Old Westbury, NY 11568. *Phone:* 516-686-1083. *Toll-free phone:* 800-345-NYIT. *Fax:* 516-686-7613. *E-mail:* admissions@nyit.edu.

NEW YORK SCHOOL OF INTERIOR DESIGN

New York, New York **www.nysid.edu/**

- **Independent** comprehensive, founded 1916
- **Urban** 1-acre campus
- **Endowment** $2.7 million
- **Coed, primarily women** 685 undergraduate students, 25% full-time, 92% women, 8% men
- **Moderately difficult** entrance level, 48% of applicants were admitted

The New York School of Interior Design is a private, not-for-profit college that is focused exclusively on interior design education and accredited by the National

Association of Schools of Art and Design (NASAD). The Bachelor of Fine Arts degree program is accredited by CIDA, the Council for Interior Design Accreditation (formerly FIDER). Located on Manhattan's Upper East Side, the School is surrounded by world-famous museums, showrooms, and architectural landmarks.

Undergraduates 170 full-time, 515 part-time. Students come from 26 other countries, 32% are from out of state, 4% African American, 9% Asian American or Pacific Islander, 8% Hispanic American, 0.1% Native American, 13% transferred in. *Retention:* 20% of 2006 full-time freshmen returned.

Freshmen *Admission:* 122 applied, 58 admitted, 24 enrolled. *Average high school GPA:* 3.1. *Test scores:* SAT critical reading scores over 500: 20%; SAT math scores over 500: 39%; SAT writing scores over 500: 19%; ACT scores over 18: 33%; SAT math scores over 600: 4%.

Faculty *Total:* 79, 3% full-time, 33% with terminal degrees. *Student/faculty ratio:* 10:1.

Majors Interior design.

Academics *Calendar:* semesters. *Degrees:* certificates, associate, bachelor's, and master's. *Special study options:* advanced placement credit, English as a second language, independent study, internships, part-time degree program, services for LD students, study abroad, summer session for credit.

Computers on Campus 135 computers/terminals are available on campus for general student use. Campuswide network is available.

Student Life *Housing:* college housing not available. *Activities and organizations:* American Society of Interior Designers. *Campus security:* security during school hours.

Standardized Tests *Required for some:* SAT or ACT (for admission).

Costs (2008–09) *Tuition:* $19,500 full-time, $650 per credit part-time. *Required fees:* $290 full-time, $145 per term part-time.

Financial Aid Of all full-time matriculated undergraduates who enrolled in 2006, 66 applied for aid, 56 were judged to have need, 5 had their need fully met. *Average percent of need met:* 50%. *Average financial aid package:* $6500. *Average need-based loan:* $3000. *Average need-based gift aid:* $2384. *Average indebtedness upon graduation:* $30,000.

Applying *Options:* electronic application, deferred entrance. *Application fee:* $50. *Required:* essay or personal statement, high school transcript, minimum 2.8 GPA, 2 letters of recommendation, portfolio. *Application deadlines:* 3/1 (freshmen), 3/1 (transfers). *Notification:* 4/1 (freshmen), 4/1 (transfers).

Freshman Application Contact Cassandra Ramirez, Admissions Associate, New York School of Interior Design, 170 East 70th Street, New York, NY 10021-5110. *Phone:* 212-472-1500 Ext. 204. *Toll-free phone:* 800-336-9743 Ext. 204. *Fax:* 212-472-1867. *E-mail:* admissions@nysid.edu.

See page 1794 for the College Close-Up.

NEW YORK UNIVERSITY

New York, New York — www.nyu.edu/

- **Independent** university, founded 1831
- **Urban** campus
- **Endowment** $1.8 billion
- **Coed** 21,327 undergraduate students, 93% full-time, 62% women, 38% men
- **Most difficult** entrance level, 37% of applicants were admitted

Undergraduates 19,914 full-time, 1,413 part-time. Students come from 52 states and territories, 93 other countries, 64% are from out of state, 4% African American, 19% Asian American or Pacific Islander, 8% Hispanic American, 0.2% Native American, 6% international, 3% transferred in, 52% live on campus. *Retention:* 92% of 2006 full-time freshmen returned.

Freshmen *Admission:* 34,389 applied, 12,842 admitted, 4,927 enrolled. *Average high school GPA:* 3.6. *Test scores:* SAT critical reading scores over 500: 99%; SAT math scores over 500: 99%; SAT writing scores over 500: 99%; ACT scores over 18: 100%; SAT critical reading scores over 600: 84%; SAT math scores over 600: 84%; SAT writing scores over 600: 85%; ACT scores over 24: 99%; SAT critical reading scores over 700: 32%; SAT math scores over 700: 35%; SAT writing scores over 700: 33%; ACT scores over 30: 45%.

Faculty *Total:* 4,260, 50% full-time. *Student/faculty ratio:* 12:1.

Majors Accounting; actuarial science; African-American/Black studies; anthropology; archeology; area, ethnic, cultural, and gender studies related; art; art history, criticism and conservation; Asian studies (East); biochemistry; biology/biological sciences; biology teacher education; business administration and management; business, management, and marketing related; business/managerial economics; chemistry; chemistry teacher education; cinematography and film/video production; city/urban, community and regional planning; classics and languages, literatures and linguistics; communication/speech communication and rhetoric; comparative literature; computer and information sciences; computer programming; computer science; dance; dental hygiene; diagnostic medical sonography and ultrasound technology; digital communication and media/multimedia; dramatic/theater arts; economics; education; elementary education; engineering related; English; English/language arts teacher education; European studies; film/cinema studies; finance; fine/studio arts; foods, nutrition, and wellness; foreign language teacher education; French; French language teacher education; general studies; German; graphic communications; health/health care administration; health information/medical records technology; Hebrew; history; hospitality administration; hotel/motel administration; humanities; human services; information science/studies; interdisciplinary studies; international business/trade/commerce; international relations and affairs; Italian; Jewish/Judaic studies; journalism; kindergarten/preschool education; Latin; Latin American studies; liberal arts and sciences/liberal studies; linguistics; management information systems; marketing/marketing management; mass communication/media; mathematics; mathematics and statistics related; mathematics teacher education; medieval and Renaissance studies; middle school education; modern Greek; music; music management and merchandising; music performance; music teacher education; music theory and composition; Near and Middle Eastern studies; neuroscience; nursing (registered nurse training); operations research; philosophy; photography; physical therapist assistant; physics; physics teacher education; piano and organ; playwriting and screenwriting; political science and government; Portuguese; pre-dentistry studies; pre-medical studies; psychology; radio and television; real estate; religious studies; Romance languages; Russian; secondary education; social sciences; social studies teacher education; social work; sociology; Spanish; special education; special education (speech or language impaired); sport and fitness administration/management; statistics; theater literature, history and criticism; tourism and travel services management; urban studies/affairs; voice and opera.

Academics *Calendar:* semesters. *Degrees:* certificates, associate, bachelor's, master's, doctoral, first professional, post-master's, postbachelor's, and first professional certificates. *Special study options:* adult/continuing education programs, advanced placement credit, cooperative education, distance learning, double majors, English as a second language, honors programs, independent study, internships, off-campus study, part-time degree program, services for LD students, student-designed majors, study abroad, summer session for credit. *ROTC:* Army (c), Navy (c). *Unusual degree programs:* 3-2 engineering with Stevens Institute of Technology.

Computers on Campus 4,500 computers/terminals are available on campus for general student use. Students can access the following: computer help desk, free student e-mail accounts, online (class) registration, online (class) schedules. Campuswide network is available. 100% of college-owned or -operated housing units are wired for high-speed Internet access. Wireless service is available via computer labs, learning centers, libraries, student centers.

Student Life *Housing options:* coed, disabled students. Campus housing is university owned and leased by the school. Freshman campus housing is guaranteed. *Activities and organizations:* drama/theater group, student-run newspaper, radio and television station, choral group, marching band, Inter-Varsity Christian Fellowship, Asian Cultural Union, Hillel, Latinos Unidos Con Honor y Amistad (LUCHA), South Asian Student Association (SHRUTI), national fraternities, national sororities. *Campus security:* 24-hour emergency response devices and patrols, student patrols, late-night transport/escort service, controlled dormitory access, 24-hour security in residence halls. *Student services:* health clinic, personal/psychological counseling, women's center.

Athletics Member NCAA. All Division III. *Intercollegiate sports:* baseball M (c)/W (c), basketball M/W, cheerleading M/W, crew M (c)/W (c), cross-country running M/W, equestrian sports M (c)/W (c), fencing M/W, golf M, ice hockey M (c), lacrosse M (c)/W (c), soccer M/W, softball W (c), swimming and diving M/W, tennis M/W, track and field M/W, ultimate Frisbee M (c)/W (c), volleyball M/W, wrestling M. *Intramural sports:* badminton M/W, baseball M, basketball M/W, bowling M/W, football M/W, golf M/W, ice hockey M (c), lacrosse M (c)/W (c), racquetball M/W, rock climbing M/W, softball M (c)/W (c), squash M/W, table tennis M (c)/W (c), tennis M/W, volleyball M/W, water polo M/W (c), weight lifting M/W.

Standardized Tests *Required:* SAT or ACT (for admission), SAT Subject Tests (for admission).

Costs (2007–08) *Comprehensive fee:* $47,490 includes full-time tuition ($33,268), mandatory fees ($2022), and room and board ($12,200). Full-time tuition and fees vary according to course load and program. Part-time tuition: $980 per credit. Part-time tuition and fees vary according to program. *Required fees:* $57 per credit part-time, $347 per term part-time. *Room and board:* Room and board charges vary according to board plan and housing facility. *Payment plans:* installment, deferred payment. *Waivers:* employees or children of employees.

Financial Aid Of all full-time matriculated undergraduates who enrolled in 2007, 11,740 applied for aid, 10,131 were judged to have need. 2,423 Federal Work-Study jobs (averaging $1451). In 2007, 1784 non-need-based awards were made. *Average percent of need met:* 65%. *Average financial aid package:* $22,207. *Average need-based loan:* $5712. *Average need-based gift aid:* $15,231. *Average non-need-based aid:* $7924. *Average indebtedness upon graduation:* $33,637.

Applying *Options:* electronic application, early decision, deferred entrance. *Application fee:* $65. *Required:* essay or personal statement, high school transcript, 2 letters of recommendation. *Required for some:* audition, portfolio. *Application deadlines:* 1/15 (freshmen), 4/1 (transfers). *Early decision deadline:* 11/1. *Notification:* 4/1 (freshmen), 5/1 (transfers), 12/15 (early decision).

Freshman Application Contact Ms. Barbara Hall, Associate Provost for Admissions and Financial Aid, New York University, 22 Washington Square North, New York, NY 10011. *Phone:* 212-998-4500. *Fax:* 212-995-4902. *E-mail:* nyuadmit@uccvm.nyu.edu.

See page 1796 for the College Close-Up.

NIAGARA UNIVERSITY

Niagara Falls, New York **www.niagara.edu/**

- **Independent** comprehensive, founded 1856, affiliated with Roman Catholic Church
- **Suburban** 160-acre campus with easy access to Buffalo and Toronto
- **Endowment** $74.8 million
- **Coed** 3,259 undergraduate students, 96% full-time, 62% women, 38% men
- **Moderately difficult** entrance level, 77% of applicants were admitted

Niagara University (NU) offers an extensive merit scholarship and grant program. Students, regardless of need, may be eligible to receive an academic award ranging from $5500 to full tuition. These merit-based grants, awards, and scholarships are renewable. To be considered, students must meet certain academic criteria and other NU guidelines.

Undergraduates 3,126 full-time, 133 part-time. Students come from 31 states and territories, 12 other countries, 7% are from out of state, 4% African American, 1% Asian American or Pacific Islander, 2% Hispanic American, 0.4% Native American, 12% international, 6% transferred in, 55% live on campus. *Retention:* 81% of 2006 full-time freshmen returned.

Freshmen *Admission:* 3,078 applied, 2,358 admitted, 739 enrolled. *Average high school GPA:* 3.3. *Test scores:* SAT critical reading scores over 500: 55%; SAT math scores over 500: 64%; ACT scores over 18: 91%; SAT critical reading scores over 600: 11%; SAT math scores over 600: 15%; ACT scores over 24: 30%; SAT critical reading scores over 700: 1%; SAT math scores over 700: 1%; ACT scores over 30: 4%.

Faculty *Total:* 377, 40% full-time, 36% with terminal degrees. *Student/faculty ratio:* 14:1.

Majors Accounting; biochemistry; biology/biological sciences; biology/biotechnology laboratory technician; biology teacher education; business administration and management; business/commerce; business/managerial economics; business teacher education; chemistry; chemistry teacher education; computer science; criminal justice/law enforcement administration; criminology; dramatic/theater arts; economics; education; elementary education; English; English as a second/foreign language (teaching); French; French language teacher education; history; hospitality administration related; hotel/motel administration; human resources management; human resources management and services related; information science/studies; international business/trade/commerce; international relations and affairs; liberal arts and sciences/liberal studies; logistics and materials management; marketing/marketing management; mass communication/media; mathematics; mathematics teacher education; nursing (registered nurse training); philosophy; political science and government; pre-dentistry studies; pre-engineering; pre-law studies; pre-medical studies; pre-veterinary studies; psychology; religious studies; restaurant/food services management; science teacher education; secondary education; social sciences; social studies teacher education; social work; sociology; Spanish; Spanish language teacher education; special education; sport and fitness administration/management; tourism and travel services management; transportation technology.

Academics *Calendar:* semesters. *Degrees:* associate, bachelor's, master's, post-master's, and postbachelor's certificates. *Special study options:* academic remediation for entering students, accelerated degree program, adult/continuing education programs, advanced placement credit, cooperative education, double majors, English as a second language, freshman honors college, honors programs, internships, off-campus study, part-time degree program, services for LD students, study abroad, summer session for credit. *ROTC:* Army (b).

Computers on Campus 175 computers/terminals are available on campus for general student use. Students can access the following: campus intranet, computer help desk, free student e-mail accounts, online (class) grades, online (class) registration, online (class) schedules. Campuswide network is available. 100% of college-owned or -operated housing units are wired for high-speed Internet access. Wireless service is available via classrooms, computer centers, computer labs, libraries, student centers.

Student Life *Housing:* on-campus residence required through sophomore year. *Options:* coed, women-only. Campus housing is university owned. Freshman campus housing is guaranteed. *Activities and organizations:* drama/theater group, student-run newspaper, radio station, choral group, Niagara University Community Action Program, student government, Programming Board, national fraternities. *Campus security:* 24-hour emergency response devices and patrols, late-night transport/escort service, controlled dormitory access, 24-hour escort service. *Student services:* health clinic, personal/psychological counseling.

Athletics Member NCAA. All Division I. *Intercollegiate sports:* baseball M (s), basketball M (s)/W (s), cross-country running M (s)/W (s), golf M (s), ice hockey M (s)/W (s), lacrosse M/W (s), soccer M (s)/W (s), softball W (s), swimming and diving M (s)/W (s), tennis M (s)/W (s), volleyball W (s). *Intramural sports:* basketball M/W, ice hockey M/W, lacrosse M/W, racquetball M/W, rugby M (c)/W (c), skiing (downhill) M (c)/W (c), soccer M/W, softball M/W, volleyball M/W, water polo M/W.

Standardized Tests *Required:* SAT or ACT (for admission).

Costs (2007–08) *Comprehensive fee:* $31,600 includes full-time tuition ($21,400), mandatory fees ($900), and room and board ($9300). Part-time tuition: $715 per credit. *Payment plans:* installment, deferred payment. *Waivers:* senior citizens and employees or children of employees.

Financial Aid Of all full-time matriculated undergraduates who enrolled in 2007, 2,621 applied for aid, 2,238 were judged to have need, 806 had their need fully met. 425 Federal Work-Study jobs (averaging $2784). 47 state and other part-time jobs (averaging $3981). In 2007, 547 non-need-based awards were made. *Average percent of need met:* 79%. *Average financial aid package:* $17,544. *Average need-based loan:* $4792. *Average need-based gift aid:* $11,811. *Average non-need-based aid:* $8678. *Average indebtedness upon graduation:* $23,267.

Applying *Options:* electronic application, early admission, deferred entrance. *Application fee:* $30. *Required:* high school transcript. *Recommended:* minimum 3.0 GPA, 3 letters of recommendation, interview. *Application deadlines:* 8/1 (freshmen), 8/15 (transfers).

Freshman Application Contact Ms. Christine M. McDermott, Associate Director of Admissions, Niagara University, Office of Admissions, Niagara, NY 14109. *Phone:* 716-286-8700 Ext. 8715. *Toll-free phone:* 800-462-2111. *Fax:* 716-286-8733. *E-mail:* admissions@niagara.edu.

See page 1798 for the College Close-Up.

NYACK COLLEGE

Nyack, New York **www.nyack.edu**

- **Independent** 4-year, founded 1882, affiliated with The Christian and Missionary Alliance
- **Suburban** 102-acre campus with easy access to New York City
- **Coed** 2,043 undergraduate students, 83% full-time, 57% women, 43% men
- **Moderately difficult** entrance level

Undergraduates 1,690 full-time, 353 part-time. 35% African American, 7% Asian American or Pacific Islander, 21% Hispanic American, 0.6% Native American, 4% international.

Freshmen *Admission:* 512 enrolled. *Test scores:* SAT critical reading scores over 500: 37%; SAT math scores over 500: 35%; ACT scores over 18: 60%; SAT critical reading scores over 600: 8%; SAT math scores over 600: 7%; ACT scores over 24: 24%; SAT critical reading scores over 700: 1%; ACT scores over 30: 3%.

Faculty *Total:* 290, 35% full-time, 34% with terminal degrees. *Student/faculty ratio:* 20:1.

Majors Accounting; biblical studies; business administration and management; communication/speech communication and rhetoric; computer science; elementary education; English; English as a second/foreign language (teaching); general studies; history; interdisciplinary studies; liberal arts and sciences/liberal studies; mathematics; missionary studies and missiology; music teacher education; music theory and composition; pastoral studies/counseling; philosophy; piano and organ; psychology; religious education; religious/sacred music; religious studies; secondary education; social sciences; social work; theology; voice and opera.

Academics *Calendar:* semesters. *Degrees:* certificates, bachelor's, master's, and first professional. *Special study options:* academic remediation for entering students, accelerated degree program, adult/continuing education programs, advanced placement credit, distance learning, double majors, English as a second language, honors programs, independent study, internships, off-campus study, part-time degree program, study abroad, summer session for credit.

Computers on Campus 180 computers/terminals are available on campus for general student use. Students can access the following: computer help desk, free student e-mail accounts, online (class) grades, online (class) registration, online (class) schedules. Campuswide network is available.

Student Life *Housing options:* Campus housing is university owned. *Activities and organizations:* student-run newspaper, choral group, gospel teams, Drama Club. *Campus security:* 24-hour emergency response devices and patrols, student patrols, late-night transport/escort service.

Athletics Member NCAA. All Division II.

Standardized Tests *Required for some:* SAT or ACT (for admission).

Costs (2008–09) *One-time required fee:* $100. *Comprehensive fee:* $20,925 includes full-time tuition ($16,500), mandatory fees ($625), and room and board ($3800). *College room only:* $3400.

Financial Aid Of all full-time matriculated undergraduates who enrolled in 2005, 1,200 applied for aid, 1,130 were judged to have need, 229 had their need fully met. 221 Federal Work-Study jobs (averaging $1284). 46 state and other part-time jobs (averaging $1332). In 2005, 191 non-need-based awards were made. *Average percent of need met:* 65%. *Average financial aid package:* $14,285. *Average need-based loan:* $5096. *Average need-based gift aid:* $8910. *Average non-need-based aid:* $7356. *Average indebtedness upon graduation:* $19,351.

Applying *Options:* electronic application, early admission, deferred entrance. *Required:* essay or personal statement, high school transcript, letters of recommendation, interview. *Application deadlines:* 9/1 (freshmen), 9/1 (out-of-state freshmen), 9/1 (transfers).

Freshman Application Contact Ms. Andrea Hennessey, Director of Admissions, Nyack College, 1 South Boulevard, Nyack, NY 10960-3698. *Phone:* 845-675-4415. *Toll-free phone:* 800-33-NYACK. *Fax:* 845-353-1297. *E-mail:* admissions@nyack.edu.

OHR HAMEIR THEOLOGICAL SEMINARY

Peekskill, New York

Director of Admissions Rabbi M. Z. Weisverg, Director of Admissions, Ohr Hameir Theological Seminary, Furnace Woods Road, Peekskill, NY 10566. *Phone:* 914-736-1500.

OHR SOMAYACH/JOSEPH TANENBAUM EDUCATIONAL CENTER

Monsey, New York www.ohrsomayach.edu/

- **Independent Jewish** 5-year, founded 1979
- **Small-town** 7-acre campus with easy access to New York City
- **Coed, primarily men** 88 undergraduate students, 100% full-time, 100% men
- **Moderately difficult** entrance level, 65% of applicants were admitted

Undergraduates 88 full-time. Students come from 10 states and territories, 8 other countries, 39% are from out of state, 40% international, 6% transferred in.

Freshmen *Admission:* 100 applied, 65 admitted, 18 enrolled.

Faculty *Total:* 18, 44% full-time.

Majors Rabbinical studies.

Academics *Calendar:* semesters. *Degrees:* bachelor's and first professional. *Special study options:* academic remediation for entering students, adult/continuing education programs, honors programs, internships, part-time degree program, services for LD students, summer session for credit.

Student Life *Housing:* on-campus residence required through senior year. *Options:* men-only. Campus housing is university owned. *Campus security:* 24-hour emergency response devices and patrols, controlled dormitory access. *Student services:* personal/psychological counseling.

Costs (2007–08) *Tuition:* $13,500 full-time.

Applying *Options:* early admission. *Required:* letters of recommendation, interview. *Required for some:* essay or personal statement. *Recommended:* high school transcript. *Application deadlines:* rolling (freshmen), rolling (transfers).

Director of Admissions Rabbi Avrohom Braun, Dean of Students, Ohr Somayach/Joseph Tanenbaum Educational Center, PO Box 334, Monsey, NY 10952-0334. *Phone:* 845-425-1370 Ext. 22. *E-mail:* ohr@os.edu.

PACE UNIVERSITY

New York, New York www.pace.edu/

- **Independent** university, founded 1906
- **Urban** campus
- **Endowment** $112.4 million
- **Coed** 7,716 undergraduate students, 78% full-time, 60% women, 40% men
- **Moderately difficult** entrance level, 78% of applicants were admitted

Undergraduates 6,027 full-time, 1,689 part-time. Students come from 41 states and territories, 30 other countries, 35% are from out of state, 10% African American, 9% Asian American or Pacific Islander, 11% Hispanic American, 0.3% Native American, 3% international, 7% transferred in, 34% live on campus. *Retention:* 75% of 2006 full-time freshmen returned.

Freshmen *Admission:* 7,444 applied, 5,772 admitted, 1,551 enrolled. *Average high school GPA:* 3.3. *Test scores:* SAT critical reading scores over 500: 70%; SAT math scores over 500: 70%; ACT scores over 18: 97%; SAT critical reading scores over 600: 20%; SAT math scores over 600: 21%; ACT scores over 24: 37%; SAT critical reading scores over 700: 2%; SAT math scores over 700: 2%; ACT scores over 30: 2%.

Faculty *Total:* 1,122, 39% full-time, 48% with terminal degrees. *Student/faculty ratio:* 9:1.

Majors Accounting; advertising; art; art history, criticism and conservation; biochemistry; biology/biological sciences; biology teacher education; business administration and management; business/commerce; business teacher education; chemistry; chemistry teacher education; clinical laboratory science/medical technology; commercial and advertising art; communication disorders; communication/speech communication and rhetoric; community organization and advocacy; computer and information sciences; computer science; computer systems analysis; computer teacher education; criminal justice/law enforcement administration; data processing and data processing technology; dramatic/theater arts; early childhood education; economics; elementary education; English; English/language arts teacher education; entrepreneurship; environmental studies; finance; fine/studio arts; foreign languages and literatures; forensic science and technology; French; French language teacher education; geology/earth science; history; history teacher education; hotel/motel administration; human resources management; information science/studies; international business/trade/commerce; international marketing; liberal arts and sciences/liberal studies; management science; marketing/marketing management; mass communication/media; mathematics; mathematics teacher education; non-profit management; nursing (registered nurse training); philosophy and religious studies related; physician assistant; physics; physics teacher education; political science and government; psychology; science teacher education; social sciences; social science teacher education; social studies teacher education; Spanish; Spanish language teacher education; special education (speech or language impaired); speech and rhetoric; speech-language pathology; telecommunications; women's studies.

Academics *Calendar:* semesters. *Degrees:* certificates, diplomas, associate, bachelor's, master's, doctoral, first professional, post-master's, postbachelor's, and first professional certificates. *Special study options:* academic remediation for entering students, accelerated degree program, adult/continuing education programs, advanced placement credit, cooperative education, distance learning, double majors, English as a second language, freshman honors college, honors programs, independent study, internships, part-time degree program, study abroad, summer session for credit. *ROTC:* Army (c), Air Force (c). *Unusual degree programs:* 3-2 engineering with Manhattan College, Rensselaer Polytechnic Institute; occupational therapy with Columbia University College of Physicians and Surgeons.

Computers on Campus 247 computers/terminals are available on campus for general student use. Students can access the following: computer help desk, free student e-mail accounts, online (class) registration, online (class) schedules. Campuswide network is available.

Student Life *Housing options:* coed. Campus housing is university owned and leased by the school. *Activities and organizations:* drama/theater group, student-run newspaper, radio and television station, choral group, AALANA-African American Latino Asian and Native American Mentorship Program, BSU-Black Student Union, Accounting Society, Student Association, PIPE- Pace Inspirational Ensemble, national fraternities, national sororities. *Campus security:* 24-hour emergency response devices and patrols, late-night transport/escort service, controlled dormitory access. *Student services:* health clinic, personal/psychological counseling.

Athletics Member NCAA. All Division II except baseball (Division I). *Intercollegiate sports:* baseball M (s), basketball M (s)/W (s), cross-country running M (s)/W (s), equestrian sports W, football M, golf M (s), lacrosse M (s), soccer W (s), softball W (s), swimming and diving M/W, tennis M (s)/W (s), track and field M (s)/W (s), volleyball W (s). *Intramural sports:* basketball M/W, football M, soccer M/W, softball M/W, volleyball M/W.

Standardized Tests *Required:* SAT or ACT (for admission).

Costs (2007–08) *Comprehensive fee:* $40,478 includes full-time tuition ($29,454), mandatory fees ($704), and room and board ($10,320). Part-time tuition: $845 per credit. Part-time tuition and fees vary according to course load. *Room and board:* Room and board charges vary according to board plan and housing facility. *Payment plan:* installment. *Waivers:* senior citizens and employees or children of employees.

Financial Aid Of all full-time matriculated undergraduates who enrolled in 2003, 6,248 applied for aid, 5,798 were judged to have need, 382 had their need fully met. 1,018 Federal Work-Study jobs (averaging $3585). In 2003, 345 non-need-based awards were made. *Average percent of need met:* 87%. *Average financial aid package:* $12,919. *Average need-based loan:* $4120. *Average need-based gift aid:* $4780. *Average non-need-based aid:* $5644. *Average indebtedness upon graduation:* $20,670.

Applying *Options:* electronic application, early action, deferred entrance. *Application fee:* $45. *Required:* essay or personal statement, high school transcript, 2 letters of recommendation. *Recommended:* minimum 3.0 GPA, interview. *Application deadlines:* 3/1 (freshmen), rolling (transfers), 11/1 (early action). *Notification:* continuous (freshmen), continuous (transfers), 12/15 (early action).

Freshman Application Contact Ms. Joanna Broda, Director of Admission, NY and Westchester, Pace University, One Pace Plaza, New York, NY 10038. *Phone:* 212-346-1323. *Toll-free phone:* 800-874-7223. *Fax:* 212-346-1040. *E-mail:* infoctr@pace.edu.

See page 1800 for the College Close-Up.

PARSONS THE NEW SCHOOL FOR DESIGN

New York, New York — www.parsons.newschool.edu/

- **Independent** comprehensive, founded 1896, part of New School University
- **Urban** 2-acre campus
- **Coed** 3,537 undergraduate students, 93% full-time, 79% women, 21% men
- **Very difficult** entrance level, 50% of applicants were admitted

Undergraduates 3,285 full-time, 252 part-time. Students come from 52 states and territories, 62 other countries, 67% are from out of state, 4% African American, 17% Asian American or Pacific Islander, 7% Hispanic American, 0.2% Native American, 33% international, 20% transferred in, 22% live on campus. *Retention:* 86% of 2006 full-time freshmen returned.

Freshmen *Admission:* 2,559 applied, 1,284 admitted, 595 enrolled. *Average high school GPA:* 3.33. *Test scores:* SAT critical reading scores over 500: 68%; SAT math scores over 500: 72%; SAT writing scores over 500: 72%; ACT scores over 18: 95%; SAT critical reading scores over 600: 26%; SAT math scores over 600: 29%; SAT writing scores over 600: 23%; ACT scores over 24: 48%; SAT critical reading scores over 700: 3%; SAT math scores over 700: 4%; SAT writing scores over 700: 2%; ACT scores over 30: 5%.

Faculty *Total:* 992, 13% full-time. *Student/faculty ratio:* 9:1.

Majors Architecture; art; arts management; design and visual communications; fashion/apparel design; fashion merchandising; fine/studio arts; graphic design; illustration; industrial design; interior design; photography.

Academics *Calendar:* semesters. *Degrees:* certificates, associate, bachelor's, and master's. *Special study options:* accelerated degree program, adult/continuing education programs, advanced placement credit, cooperative education, distance learning, English as a second language, honors programs, independent study, internships, off-campus study, services for LD students, student-designed majors, study abroad, summer session for credit.

Computers on Campus 1,200 computers/terminals are available on campus for general student use. Students can access the following: computer help desk, free student e-mail accounts, online (class) grades, online (class) registration, online (class) schedules, online portal. Campuswide network is available. 94% of college-owned or -operated housing units are wired for high-speed Internet access. Wireless service is available via entire campus.

Student Life *Housing options:* coed, disabled students. Campus housing is university owned and leased by the school. Freshman applicants given priority for college housing. *Activities and organizations:* student-run newspaper, choral group. *Campus security:* 24-hour emergency response devices, controlled dormitory access. *Student services:* health clinic, personal/psychological counseling.

Standardized Tests *Required:* SAT or ACT (for admission).

Costs (2007–08) *Comprehensive fee:* $44,390 includes full-time tuition ($31,940), mandatory fees ($700), and room and board ($11,750). Part-time tuition: $1090 per credit. *College room only:* $8750. Room and board charges vary according to board plan and housing facility. *Waivers:* employees or children of employees.

Financial Aid Of all full-time matriculated undergraduates who enrolled in 2006, 1,590 applied for aid, 1,411 were judged to have need, 190 had their need fully met. In 2006, 940 non-need-based awards were made. *Average percent of need met:* 53%. *Average financial aid package:* $9940. *Average need-based loan:* $3389. *Average need-based gift aid:* $9708. *Average non-need-based aid:* $4436. *Average indebtedness upon graduation:* $42,784.

Applying *Options:* early admission, deferred entrance. *Application fee:* $50. *Required:* high school transcript, portfolio, home examination. *Required for some:* essay or personal statement, interview. *Recommended:* minimum 3.0 GPA. *Application deadlines:* 2/1 (freshmen), 2/1 (transfers). *Notification:* continuous (freshmen), continuous (transfers).

Freshman Application Contact Director of Admissions, Parsons The New School for Design, 66 Fifth Avenue, New York, NY 10011-8878. *Phone:* 212-229-8989. *Toll-free phone:* 877-528-3321. *Fax:* 212-229-8975. *E-mail:* parsadm@newschool.edu.

See page 1802 for the College Close-Up.

PAUL SMITH'S COLLEGE

Paul Smiths, New York — www.paulsmiths.edu/

- **Independent** 4-year, founded 1937
- **Rural** 14,200-acre campus
- **Endowment** $18.7 million
- **Coed, primarily men** 910 undergraduate students
- **Minimally difficult** entrance level, 86% of applicants were admitted

Undergraduates 85% live on campus.

Freshmen *Admission:* 831 applied, 715 admitted. *Average high school GPA:* 2.8. *Test scores:* SAT critical reading scores over 500: 36%; SAT math scores over 500: 47%; ACT scores over 18: 68%; SAT critical reading scores over 600: 9%; SAT math scores over 600: 11%; ACT scores over 24: 17%; SAT math scores over 700: 1%; ACT scores over 30: 1%.

Faculty *Total:* 83, 69% full-time, 25% with terminal degrees. *Student/faculty ratio:* 14:1.

Majors Business administration and management; culinary arts; ecology; environmental studies; forestry; forestry technology; hospitality administration; hotel/motel administration; liberal arts and sciences/liberal studies; natural resources management and policy; parks, recreation and leisure facilities management; survey technology.

Academics *Calendar:* semesters. *Degrees:* certificates, associate, and bachelor's. *Special study options:* academic remediation for entering students, adult/continuing education programs, advanced placement credit, cooperative education, double majors, honors programs, internships, services for LD students, study abroad, summer session for credit. *Unusual degree programs:* 3-2 forestry with Duke University.

Computers on Campus 300 computers/terminals and 200 ports are available on campus for general student use. Students can access the following: campus intranet, computer help desk, free student e-mail accounts, online (class) grades, online (class) registration, online (class) schedules. Campuswide network is available. 100% of college-owned or -operated housing units are wired for high-speed Internet access. Wireless service is available via classrooms, computer labs, learning centers, libraries, student centers.

Student Life *Housing:* on-campus residence required through sophomore year. *Options:* coed, men-only, women-only. Campus housing is university owned. Freshman campus housing is guaranteed. *Activities and organizations:* student-run newspaper, radio station, Forestry Club, Junior American Culinary, Wildlife Society, Fish & Game Club, Koinonia. *Campus security:* 24-hour emergency response devices and patrols, controlled dormitory access. *Student services:* health clinic, personal/psychological counseling.

Athletics Member NAIA. *Intercollegiate sports:* basketball M/W, cross-country running M/W, skiing (cross-country) M/W, soccer M/W, volleyball W. *Intramural sports:* basketball M/W, cross-country running M/W, ice hockey M/W, rock climbing M/W, rugby M (c)/W (c), soccer M/W, softball M/W, ultimate Frisbee M/W, volleyball M/W.

Standardized Tests *Required for some:* SAT or ACT (for admission). *Recommended:* SAT or ACT (for admission).

Costs (2008–09) *Comprehensive fee:* $28,600 includes full-time tuition ($18,460), mandatory fees ($1790), and room and board ($8350). Part-time tuition: $520 per credit hour.

Financial Aid Of all full-time matriculated undergraduates who enrolled in 2007, 890 applied for aid, 854 were judged to have need, 41 had their need fully met. 632 Federal Work-Study jobs (averaging $2000). In 2007, 43 non-need-based awards were made. *Average percent of need met:* 45%. *Average financial aid package:* $13,964. *Average need-based loan:* $3795. *Average need-based gift aid:* $4750. *Average non-need-based aid:* $3178. *Average indebtedness upon graduation:* $6625.

Applying *Options:* electronic application, deferred entrance. *Application fee:* $30. *Required:* high school transcript. *Required for some:* interview. *Recommended:* essay or personal statement, 2 letters of recommendation, interview. *Application deadlines:* rolling (freshmen), rolling (transfers).

Freshman Application Contact Admissions Office, Paul Smith's College, PO Box 265, Paul Smiths, NY 12970-0265. *Phone:* 518-327-6227. *Toll-free phone:* 800-421-2605. *Fax:* 518-327-6016. *E-mail:* admissions@paulsmiths.edu.

See page 1804 for the College Close-Up.

PLAZA COLLEGE

Jackson Heights, New York **www.plazacollege.edu/**

Freshman Application Contact Rose Ann Black, Dean of Admissions, Plaza College, 7409 37th Avenue, Jackson Heights, NY 11372-6300. *Phone:* 718-779-1430. *Toll-free phone:* 877-752-9233. *E-mail:* info@plazacollege.edu.

POLYTECHNIC UNIVERSITY, BROOKLYN CAMPUS

Brooklyn, New York **www.poly.edu/**

- **Independent** university, founded 1854
- **Urban** 3-acre campus
- **Endowment** $145.3 million
- **Coed** 1,495 undergraduate students, 96% full-time, 19% women, 81% men
- **Very difficult** entrance level, 22% of applicants were admitted

Undergraduates 1,430 full-time, 65 part-time. Students come from 14 states and territories, 43 other countries, 7% are from out of state, 12% African American, 30% Asian American or Pacific Islander, 12% Hispanic American, 0.2% Native American, 13% international, 5% transferred in, 20% live on campus. *Retention:* 84% of 2006 full-time freshmen returned.

Freshmen *Admission:* 1,482 applied, 331 admitted, 331 enrolled. *Average high school GPA:* 3.3. *Test scores:* SAT critical reading scores over 500: 67%; SAT math scores over 500: 92%; SAT critical reading scores over 600: 26%; SAT math scores over 600: 58%; SAT critical reading scores over 700: 3%; SAT math scores over 700: 20%.

Faculty *Total:* 297, 47% full-time, 70% with terminal degrees. *Student/faculty ratio:* 14:1.

Majors Agricultural/biological engineering and bioengineering; bioinformatics; chemistry; civil engineering; computer engineering; computer science; construction management; electrical, electronics and communications engineering; journalism; liberal arts and sciences/liberal studies; management information systems; mathematics; mechanical engineering; molecular biochemistry; physics.

Academics *Calendar:* semesters. *Degrees:* certificates, bachelor's, master's, doctoral, and postbachelor's certificates. *Special study options:* academic remediation for entering students, accelerated degree program, advanced placement credit, cooperative education, double majors, English as a second language, honors programs, internships, part-time degree program, summer session for credit. *ROTC:* Army (c), Air Force (c).

Computers on Campus 1,334 computers/terminals are available on campus for general student use. Students can access the following: campus intranet, computer help desk, free student e-mail accounts, online (class) grades, online (class) registration, online (class) schedules. Campuswide network is available. Wireless service is available via entire campus.

Student Life *Housing options:* coed. Campus housing is university owned. Freshman applicants given priority for college housing. *Activities and organizations:* student-run newspaper, National Society of Black Engineers, Society of Hispanic Professional Engineers, Association for Computing Machinery, Alpha Phi Omega, Chinese Student Society, national fraternities, national sororities. *Campus security:* 24-hour patrols, controlled dormitory access. *Student services:* health clinic, personal/psychological counseling, women's center.

Athletics Member NCAA. All Division III. *Intercollegiate sports:* baseball M, basketball M/W, cross-country running M/W, soccer M/W, softball W, tennis M/W, track and field M/W, volleyball M/W. *Intramural sports:* badminton M/W, basketball M/W, bowling M/W, football M/W, golf M (c)/W (c), soccer M/W, table tennis M (c)/W (c), track and field M (c)/W (c), volleyball M/W, weight lifting M (c)/W (c).

Standardized Tests *Required:* SAT or ACT (for admission). *Recommended:* SAT Subject Tests (for admission).

Costs (2007–08) *Comprehensive fee:* $39,472 includes full-time tuition ($29,894), mandatory fees ($1078), and room and board ($8500). Full-time tuition and fees vary according to course load. Part-time tuition: $951 per credit. Part-time tuition and fees vary according to course load. No tuition increase for student's term of enrollment. *Required fees:* $394 per year part-time. *College room only:* $6500. Room and board charges vary according to housing facility. *Payment plans:* installment, deferred payment. *Waivers:* employees or children of employees.

Financial Aid Of all full-time matriculated undergraduates who enrolled in 2006, 1,367 applied for aid, 1,100 were judged to have need, 698 had their need fully met. 211 Federal Work-Study jobs (averaging $1797). In 2006, 250 non-need-based awards were made. *Average percent of need met:* 91%. *Average financial aid package:* $22,221. *Average need-based loan:* $4133. *Average need-based gift aid:* $8027. *Average non-need-based aid:* $16,342. *Average indebtedness upon graduation:* $25,012.

Applying *Options:* electronic application, deferred entrance. *Application fee:* $50. *Required:* essay or personal statement, high school transcript, 2 letters of recommendation. *Recommended:* interview. *Application deadlines:* 2/1 (freshmen), rolling (transfers).

Freshman Application Contact Joy Colelli, Dean of Admissions and New Students, Polytechnic University, Brooklyn Campus, Six Metrotech Center, Brooklyn, NY 11201-2990. *Phone:* 718-260-5917. *Toll-free phone:* 800-POLYTECH. *Fax:* 718-260-3446. *E-mail:* uadmit@poly.edu.

See page 1806 for the College Close-Up.

PRATT INSTITUTE

Brooklyn, New York **www.pratt.edu/**

- **Independent** comprehensive, founded 1887
- **Urban** 25-acre campus
- **Endowment** $74.0 million
- **Coed** 3,066 undergraduate students, 95% full-time, 60% women, 40% men
- **Very difficult** entrance level, 43% of applicants were admitted

Pratt Institute, one of the premier art, design, writing, and architecture schools nationwide, is located in the historic Clinton Hill section of Brooklyn, 25 minutes from downtown Manhattan. Most freshmen live on the Institute's 25-acre enclosed, tree-lined campus. Pratt offers accredited four-year, two-year, and master's degrees, as well as a five-year bachelor's degree in architecture.

Undergraduates 2,903 full-time, 163 part-time. Students come from 48 states and territories, 36 other countries, 60% are from out of state, 7% African American, 13% Asian American or Pacific Islander, 8% Hispanic American, 0.5% Native American, 10% international, 7% transferred in, 48% live on campus.

Freshmen *Admission:* 4,341 applied, 1,881 admitted, 586 enrolled. *Average high school GPA:* 3.47. *Test scores:* SAT critical reading scores over 500: 80%; SAT math scores over 500: 83%; ACT scores over 18: 91%; SAT critical reading scores over 600: 41%; SAT math scores over 600: 36%; ACT scores over 24: 61%; SAT critical reading scores over 700: 7%; SAT math scores over 700: 6%; ACT scores over 30: 11%.

Faculty *Total:* 939, 13% full-time. *Student/faculty ratio:* 11:1.

Majors Applied art; architecture; art; art history, criticism and conservation; art teacher education; ceramic arts and ceramics; cinematography and film/video production; commercial and advertising art; computer graphics; construction management; creative writing; design and applied arts related; drawing; fashion/apparel design; film/video and photographic arts related; fine arts related; fine/studio arts; graphic design; illustration; industrial design; interior design; metal and jewelry arts; painting; photography; printmaking; sculpture.

Academics *Calendar:* semesters plus optional May term and summer session. *Degrees:* associate, bachelor's, master's, and post-master's certificates (Associate). *Special study options:* advanced placement credit, cooperative education, double majors, English as a second language, independent study, internships, off-campus study, part-time degree program, services for LD students, study abroad, summer session for credit.

Computers on Campus 250 computers/terminals are available on campus for general student use. Students can access the following: online (class) registration. Campuswide network is available.

Student Life *Housing options:* coed. Campus housing is university owned. Freshman campus housing is guaranteed. *Activities and organizations:* student-run newspaper, radio and television station, travel and recreation, student newspaper, athletic clubs, Performing Arts Committee, national fraternities. *Campus security:* 24-hour emergency response devices and patrols, late-night transport/escort service. *Student services:* health clinic, personal/psychological counseling.

Athletics Member NCAA. All Division III. *Intercollegiate sports:* basketball M, cross-country running M/W, soccer M/W, tennis M/W, track and field M/W, volleyball W. *Intramural sports:* badminton M/W, basketball M, field hockey M, football M, golf M, lacrosse M/W, volleyball M, weight lifting M/W.

Standardized Tests *Required:* SAT or ACT (for admission).

Costs (2008–09) *Comprehensive fee:* $42,466 includes full-time tuition ($31,700), mandatory fees ($1290), and room and board ($9476). Part-time tuition: $1026 per credit. *College room only:* $5976.

Financial Aid Of all full-time matriculated undergraduates who enrolled in 2006, 2,552 applied for aid, 1,907 were judged to have need. In 2006, 185 non-need-based awards were made. *Average percent of need met:* 59%. *Average financial aid package:* $15,092. *Average need-based loan:* $5301. *Average need-based gift aid:* $7531. *Average non-need-based aid:* $8114. *Average indebtedness upon graduation:* $18,731.

Applying *Options:* electronic application, early action, deferred entrance. *Application fee:* $50. *Required:* essay or personal statement, high school transcript, 1 letter of recommendation. *Required for some:* portfolio. *Recommended:* minimum 3.0 GPA. *Application deadlines:* 1/5 (freshmen), 2/1 (transfers), 11/1 (early action). *Notification:* continuous until 4/1 (freshmen), 4/1 (transfers), 12/22 (early action).

Freshman Application Contact Ms. Olga Burger, Visit Coordinator, Pratt Institute, DeKalb Hall, 200 Willoughby Avenue, Brooklyn, NY 11205-3899. *Phone:* 718-636-3779. *Toll-free phone:* 800-331-0834. *Fax:* 718-636-3670. *E-mail:* admissions@pratt.edu.

See page 1808 for the College Close-Up.

PURCHASE COLLEGE, STATE UNIVERSITY OF NEW YORK

Purchase, New York **www.purchase.edu/**

- **State-supported** comprehensive, founded 1967, part of State University of New York System
- **Small-town** 500-acre campus with easy access to New York City
- **Endowment** $42.0 million
- **Coed** 4,106 undergraduate students, 89% full-time, 55% women, 45% men
- **Moderately difficult** entrance level, 37% of applicants were admitted

Purchase College, State University of New York, combines selective liberal arts and sciences programs with professional conservatory programs in the visual and performing arts. Purchase offers undergraduate degree programs in arts management, biochemistry, cinema studies, creative writing, journalism, stage design/technology (including costume design), and visual arts. Programs in cinema studies, creative writing, journalism, and new media are very popular. Purchase is a small college community that offers students the opportunity to enter into apprentice relationships with artists, performers, scholars, and scientists who are making significant contributions to their fields. Residential learning communities are provided for select students. Purchase is committed to fostering educational creativity, individual achievement, and personal and intellectual exploration.

Undergraduates 3,654 full-time, 452 part-time. Students come from 45 states and territories, 36 other countries, 19% are from out of state, 7% African American, 3% Asian American or Pacific Islander, 9% Hispanic American, 0.4% Native American, 2% international, 9% transferred in, 63% live on campus. *Retention:* 82% of 2006 full-time freshmen returned.

Freshmen *Admission:* 5,986 applied, 2,228 admitted, 785 enrolled. *Average high school GPA:* 3.1. *Test scores:* SAT critical reading scores over 500: 78%; SAT math scores over 500: 68%; SAT writing scores over 500: 68%; ACT scores over 18: 95%; SAT critical reading scores over 600: 34%; SAT math scores over 600: 21%; SAT writing scores over 600: 25%; ACT scores over 24: 47%; SAT critical reading scores over 700: 5%; SAT math scores over 700: 2%; SAT writing scores over 700: 3%; ACT scores over 30: 5%.

Faculty *Total:* 370, 40% full-time. *Student/faculty ratio:* 17:1.

Majors Anthropology; art; art history, criticism and conservation; biology/biological sciences; chemistry; cinematography and film/video production; commercial and advertising art; communication/speech communication and rhetoric; creative writing; dance; dramatic/theater arts; economics; environmental studies; film/cinema studies; fine arts related; French; history; humanities; journalism; liberal arts and sciences/liberal studies; literature; mathematics; mathematics and statistics related; modern languages; philosophy; photography; physics; playwriting and screenwriting; political science and government; printmaking; psychology; sociology; Spanish; theater design and technology; visual and performing arts; visual and performing arts related; women's studies.

Academics *Calendar:* semesters. *Degrees:* certificates, bachelor's, master's, and post-master's certificates. *Special study options:* academic remediation for entering students, adult/continuing education programs, advanced placement credit, distance learning, double majors, English as a second language, independent study, internships, off-campus study, part-time degree program, student-designed majors, study abroad, summer session for credit.

Computers on Campus 600 computers/terminals and 3,500 ports are available on campus for general student use. Students can access the following: campus intranet, computer help desk, free student e-mail accounts, online (class) grades, online (class) registration, online (class) schedules. Campuswide network is available. 100% of college-owned or -operated housing units are wired for high-speed Internet access. Wireless service is available via classrooms, computer centers, computer labs, learning centers, libraries, student centers.

Student Life *Housing options:* coed. Campus housing is university owned. *Activities and organizations:* drama/theater group, student-run newspaper, radio and television station, choral group, Student Union, WPUR radio station, Latinos Unidos, Gay/Lesbian/Bi-Sexual/Transgender Union, Organization of African People in America. *Campus security:* 24-hour emergency response devices and patrols, late-night transport/escort service, controlled dormitory access, 24-hour patrols by police officers. *Student services:* health clinic, personal/psychological counseling, women's center, legal services.

Athletics Member NCAA. All Division III. *Intercollegiate sports:* baseball M/W, basketball M/W, cross-country running M/W, soccer M/W, softball M/W, volleyball M/W. *Intramural sports:* badminton M/W, basketball M/W, bowling M/W, cross-country running M/W, fencing M/W, football M/W, golf M/W, racquetball M/W, skiing (cross-country) M/W, skiing (downhill) M/W, soccer M/W, softball M/W, squash M/W, swimming and diving M/W, table tennis M/W, tennis M/W, volleyball M/W, water polo M/W, weight lifting M/W.

Standardized Tests *Required:* SAT or ACT (for admission). *Recommended:* SAT (for admission).

Costs (2008–09) *Tuition:* state resident $4350 full-time, $181 per credit part-time; nonresident $10,610 full-time, $442 per credit part-time. *Required fees:* $1647 full-time. *Room and board:* $9484; room only: $5886.

Financial Aid Of all full-time matriculated undergraduates who enrolled in 2007, 2,408 applied for aid, 1,793 were judged to have need, 308 had their need fully met. 199 Federal Work-Study jobs (averaging $937). 250 state and other part-time jobs (averaging $1100). In 2007, 815 non-need-based awards were made. *Average percent of need met:* 70%. *Average financial aid package:* $10,664. *Average need-based loan:* $4196. *Average need-based gift aid:* $4536. *Average non-need-based aid:* $2158. *Average indebtedness upon graduation:* $19,247.

Applying *Options:* electronic application, early admission, early decision, deferred entrance. *Application fee:* $40. *Required:* high school transcript, minimum 3.0 GPA. *Required for some:* essay or personal statement, 1 letter of recommendation, interview, audition, portfolio. *Application deadlines:* 7/15 (freshmen), rolling (transfers). *Early decision deadline:* 11/1. *Notification:* 5/1 (freshmen), continuous (transfers), 12/5 (early decision).

Freshman Application Contact Stephanie McCaine, Director of Admissions, Purchase College, State University of New York, 735 Anderson Hill Road, Purchase, NY 10577-1400. *Phone:* 914-251-6300. *Fax:* 914-251-6314. *E-mail:* admission@purchase.edu.

See page 1810 for the College Close-Up.

QUEENS COLLEGE OF THE CITY UNIVERSITY OF NEW YORK

Flushing, New York **www.qc.cuny.edu/**

- **State and locally supported** comprehensive, founded 1937, part of City University of New York System
- **Urban** 77-acre campus
- **Endowment** $750,000
- **Coed** 14,618 undergraduate students, 70% full-time, 61% women, 39% men
- **Very difficult** entrance level, 40% of applicants were admitted

Queens College of the City University of New York offers students a rigorous education in the liberal arts and sciences under the guidance of faculty members who are dedicated to teaching and research. Students graduate with a real competitive advantage—the ability to think critically, explore cultures, and use modern technologies. With a student population that reflects the diversity of New York City, Queens College provides an unusually rich education.

Undergraduates 10,271 full-time, 4,347 part-time. Students come from 15 states and territories, 130 other countries, 1% are from out of state, 9% African American, 20% Asian American or Pacific Islander, 18% Hispanic American, 0.1% Native American, 6% international, 13% transferred in. *Retention:* 84% of 2006 full-time freshmen returned.

Freshmen *Admission:* 14,436 applied, 5,835 admitted, 1,777 enrolled. *Average high school GPA:* 3.2. *Test scores:* SAT critical reading scores over 500: 51%; SAT math scores over 500: 68%; SAT writing scores over 500: 50%; SAT critical reading scores over 600: 13%; SAT math scores over 600: 20%; SAT writing scores over 600: 12%; SAT critical reading scores over 700: 2%; SAT math scores over 700: 3%; SAT writing scores over 700: 2%.

Faculty *Total:* 1,321, 48% full-time, 60% with terminal degrees. *Student/faculty ratio:* 17:1.

Majors Accounting; actuarial science; African studies; American studies; ancient/classical Greek; anthropology; area, ethnic, cultural, and gender studies related; art history, criticism and conservation; art teacher education; Asian studies (East); audiology and speech-language pathology; biology/biological sciences; biology teacher education; chemistry; commercial and advertising art; comparative literature; computer and information sciences; dramatic/theater arts; economics; elementary education; English; English as a second/foreign language (teaching); environmental science; environmental studies; family and consumer sciences/home economics teacher education; family and consumer sciences/human sciences; film/cinema studies; finance; fine/studio arts; French; geology/earth science; German; Hebrew; history; interdisciplinary studies; international business/trade/commerce; Italian; Jewish/Judaic studies; kinesiology and exercise science; labor studies; Latin; Latin American studies; liberal arts and sciences/liberal studies; linguistics; mass communication/media; mathematics; music performance; music teacher education; philosophy; physical education teaching and coaching; physics; physics teacher education; political science and government; psychology; religious studies; Russian; social sciences related; social studies teacher education; sociology; Spanish; urban studies/affairs; visual and performing arts related; women's studies.

Academics *Calendar:* semesters. *Degrees:* bachelor's, master's, post-master's, and postbachelor's certificates. *Special study options:* accelerated degree program, adult/continuing education programs, advanced placement credit, cooperative education, distance learning, double majors, English as a second language, freshman honors college, honors programs, independent study, internships, off-campus study, part-time degree program, services for LD students, student-designed majors, study abroad, summer session for credit. *ROTC:* Army (c), Navy (c). *Unusual degree programs:* 3-2 engineering with Columbia University; chemistry, biochemistry, computer science, physics, political science, music, philosophy.

Computers on Campus 2,300 computers/terminals are available on campus for general student use. Students can access the following: campus intranet, computer help desk, free student e-mail accounts, online (class) grades, online (class) registration, online (class) schedules. Campuswide network is available. Wireless service is available via classrooms, computer centers, computer labs, learning centers, libraries, student centers.

Student Life *Housing:* college housing not available. *Activities and organizations:* drama/theater group, student-run newspaper, radio station, choral group, Alliance of Latin American Students, Black Student Union, Caribbean Student Association, Hillel-Jewish Student Organization, India Cultural Exchange, national fraternities, national sororities. *Campus security:* 24-hour emergency response devices and patrols. *Student services:* health clinic, personal/psychological counseling.

Athletics Member NCAA. All Division II. *Intercollegiate sports:* baseball M (s), basketball M (s)/W (s), cross-country running M (s)/W (s), fencing W (s), golf M (s), soccer M (s)/W (s), softball W (s), swimming and diving M (s)/W (s), tennis M (s)/W (s), track and field M (s)/W (s), volleyball M (s), water polo M (s)/W (s). *Intramural sports:* baseball M, basketball M/W, cross-country running M/W, football M/W, ice hockey M, racquetball M/W, soccer M/W, softball M/W, tennis M/W, track and field M/W, volleyball M/W, water polo M/W.

Standardized Tests *Required:* SAT or ACT (for admission). *Required for some:* SAT Subject Tests (for admission). *Recommended:* SAT Subject Tests (for admission).

Costs (2008–09) *Tuition:* state resident $4000 full-time, $170 per credit part-time; nonresident $8640 full-time, $360 per credit part-time. *Required fees:* $377 full-time, $120 per term part-time.

Financial Aid Of all full-time matriculated undergraduates who enrolled in 2003, 4,993 applied for aid, 3,744 were judged to have need, 2,700 had their need fully met. 1,253 Federal Work-Study jobs (averaging $1300). In 2003, 292 non-need-based awards were made. *Average percent of need met:* 90%. *Average financial aid package:* $5000. *Average need-based gift aid:* $3400. *Average indebtedness upon graduation:* $12,000.

Applying *Options:* electronic application, deferred entrance. *Application fee:* $65. *Required:* high school transcript, minimum 3.0 GPA. *Application deadlines:* rolling (freshmen), rolling (transfers). *Notification:* continuous (freshmen), continuous (transfers).

Freshman Application Contact Mr. Vincent Angrisani, Executive Director of Enrollment Management and Admissions, Queens College of the City University of New York, Undergraduate Admissions, Kiely Hall 217, 65-30 Kissena Boulevard, Flushing, NY 11367. *Phone:* 718-997-5600. *Fax:* 718-997-5617. *E-mail:* vincent.angrisani@qc.edu.

See page 1812 for the College Close-Up.

RABBINICAL ACADEMY MESIVTA RABBI CHAIM BERLIN

Brooklyn, New York

Director of Admissions Mr. Mayer Weinberger, Executive Administrator, Office of Admissions, Rabbinical Academy Mesivta Rabbi Chaim Berlin, 1605 Coney Island Avenue, Brooklyn, NY 11230-4715. *Phone:* 718-377-0777. *Fax:* 718-338-5578.

RABBINICAL COLLEGE BETH SHRAGA

Monsey, New York

Director of Admissions Rabbi Schiff, Director of Admissions, Rabbinical College Beth Shraga, 28 Saddle River Road, Monsey, NY 10952-3035.

RABBINICAL COLLEGE BOBOVER YESHIVA B'NEI ZION

Brooklyn, New York

Director of Admissions Mr. Israel Licht, Director of Admissions, Rabbinical College Bobover Yeshiva B'nei Zion, 1577 Forty-eighth Street, Brooklyn, NY 11219. *Phone:* 718-438-2018.

RABBINICAL COLLEGE CH'SAN SOFER

Brooklyn, New York

Director of Admissions Director of Admissions, Rabbinical College Ch'san Sofer, 1876 Fiftieth Street, Brooklyn, NY 11204. *Phone:* 718-236-1171.

RABBINICAL COLLEGE OF LONG ISLAND

Long Beach, New York

Director of Admissions Director of Admissions, Rabbinical College of Long Island, 201 Magnolia Boulevard, Long Beach, NY 11561-3305. *Phone:* 516-431-7414.

RABBINICAL COLLEGE OF OHR SHIMON YISROEL

Brooklyn, New York

RABBINICAL SEMINARY ADAS YEREIM

Brooklyn, New York

Director of Admissions Mr. Hersch Greenschweig, Director of Admissions, Rabbinical Seminary Adas Yereim, 185 Wilson Street, Brooklyn, NY 11211-7206. *Phone:* 718-388-1751.

RABBINICAL SEMINARY M'KOR CHAIM

Brooklyn, New York

Director of Admissions Rabbi Benjamin Paler, Director of Admissions, Rabbinical Seminary M'kor Chaim, 1571 Fifty-fifth Street, Brooklyn, NY 11219. *Phone:* 718-851-0183.

RABBINICAL SEMINARY OF AMERICA

Flushing, New York

Director of Admissions Rabbi Abraham Semmel, Director of Admissions, Rabbinical Seminary of America, 76-01 147th Street, Flushing, NY 11367. *Phone:* 718-268-4700.

RENSSELAER POLYTECHNIC INSTITUTE

Troy, New York www.rpi.edu/

- **Independent** university, founded 1824
- **Suburban** 284-acre campus with easy access to Albany
- **Endowment** $812.3 million
- **Coed** 5,167 undergraduate students, 99% full-time, 27% women, 73% men
- **Very difficult** entrance level, 49% of applicants were admitted

A world-class technological university with global reach and global impact, today's Rensselaer Polytechnic Institute is combining its legacy of leadership in technology-based education with an expanding emphasis on the pursuit of discovery. Students conduct research alongside renowned faculty members in biotechnology, nanotechnology, information technology, energy and the environment, and the experimental media arts.

Undergraduates 5,136 full-time, 31 part-time. Students come from 49 states and territories, 34 other countries, 57% are from out of state, 4% African American, 10% Asian American or Pacific Islander, 6% Hispanic American, 0.4% Native American, 2% international, 2% transferred in, 53% live on campus. *Retention:* 92% of 2006 full-time freshmen returned.

Freshmen *Admission:* 10,162 applied, 5,021 admitted, 1,288 enrolled. *Test scores:* SAT critical reading scores over 500: 98%; SAT math scores over 500: 99%; SAT writing scores over 500: 96%; ACT scores over 18: 100%; SAT critical reading scores over 600: 77%; SAT math scores over 600: 94%; SAT writing scores over 600: 66%; ACT scores over 24: 85%; SAT critical reading scores over 700: 24%; SAT math scores over 700: 46%; SAT writing scores over 700: 15%; ACT scores over 30: 17%.

Faculty *Total:* 470, 85% full-time, 83% with terminal degrees. *Student/faculty ratio:* 14:1.

Majors Aerospace, aeronautical and astronautical engineering; Air Force R.O.T.C./air science; applied mathematics; architecture; architecture related; Army R.O.T.C./military science; biochemistry; bioinformatics; biological and biomedical sciences related; biological and physical sciences; biology/biological sciences; biomedical/medical engineering; biophysics; building/construction finishing, management, and inspection related; business administration and management; chemical engineering; chemistry; civil engineering; communication/speech communication and rhetoric; computer and information sciences; computer engineering; computer science; economics; electrical, electronics and communications engineering; engineering; engineering physics; engineering science; environmental/environmental health engineering; finance; geology/earth science; hydrology and water resources science; industrial engineering; information technology; interdisciplinary studies; management information systems; management information systems and services related; manufacturing engineering; marketing/marketing management; materials engineering; mathematics; mechanical engineering; Navy/Marine Corps R.O.T.C./naval science; nuclear engineering; philosophy; pre-law studies; pre-medical studies; psychology; science, technology and society; social sciences; systems engineering; visual and performing arts related.

Academics *Calendar:* semesters. *Degrees:* bachelor's, master's, and doctoral. *Special study options:* accelerated degree program, adult/continuing education programs, advanced placement credit, cooperative education, distance learning, double majors, English as a second language, honors programs, independent study, internships, off-campus study, part-time degree program, services for LD students, student-designed majors, study abroad, summer session for credit. *ROTC:* Army (c), Navy (b), Air Force (b). *Unusual degree programs:* 3-2 engineering.

Computers on Campus 5,639 computers/terminals and 10,000 ports are available on campus for general student use. Students can access the following: campus intranet, computer help desk, free student e-mail accounts, online (class) registration, online (class) schedules, billing. Campuswide network is available. 100% of college-owned or -operated housing units are wired for high-speed Internet access. Wireless service is available via classrooms, computer centers, computer labs, dorm rooms, learning centers, libraries, student centers.

Student Life *Housing:* on-campus residence required for freshman year. *Options:* coed, disabled students. Campus housing is university owned. Freshman campus housing is guaranteed. *Activities and organizations:* drama/theater group, student-run newspaper, radio and television station, choral group, Red Army Spirit Club, Outing Club, Indian Student Association, Chinese American Student Association, Pep Band, national fraternities, national sororities. *Campus security:* 24-hour emergency response devices and patrols, late-night transport/escort service, controlled dormitory access, campus foot patrols at night. *Student services:* health clinic, personal/psychological counseling, women's center, legal services.

Athletics Member NCAA. All Division III except men's and women's ice hockey (Division I). *Intercollegiate sports:* archery M (c)/W (c), badminton M (c)/W (c), baseball M, basketball M/W, cheerleading M (c)/W (c), crew M (c)/W (c), cross-country running M/W, equestrian sports M (c)/W (c), fencing M (c)/W (c), field hockey W, football M, golf M, gymnastics M (c)/W (c), ice hockey M (s)/W (s), lacrosse M/W, racquetball M (c)/W (c), riflery M (c)/W (c), rugby M (c)/W (c), sailing M (c)/W (c), skiing (cross-country) M (c)/W (c), skiing (downhill) M (c)/W (c), soccer M/W, softball W, squash M (c)/W (c), swimming and diving M/W, table tennis M (c)/W (c), tennis M/W, track and field M/W, volleyball M (c)/W, water polo M (c)/W (c), weight lifting M (c)/W (c). *Intramural sports:* badminton M/W, basketball M/W, bowling M/W, cheerleading M/W, football M/W, golf M/W, ice hockey M/W, soccer M/W, softball M/W, swimming and diving M/W, table tennis M/W, tennis M/W, track and field M/W, ultimate Frisbee M/W, volleyball M/W, water polo M/W, wrestling M.

Standardized Tests *Required:* SAT or ACT (for admission). *Required for some:* SAT and SAT Subject Tests or ACT (for admission).

Costs (2008–09) *Comprehensive fee:* $48,720 includes full-time tuition ($36,950), mandatory fees ($1040), and room and board ($10,730). Part-time tuition: $1155 per credit hour. *College room only:* $6025.

Financial Aid Of all full-time matriculated undergraduates who enrolled in 2007, 3,492 applied for aid, 3,065 were judged to have need, 1,656 had their need fully met. 996 Federal Work-Study jobs (averaging $1971). In 2007, 1403 non-need-based awards were made. *Average percent of need met:* 87%. *Average financial aid package:* $27,810. *Average need-based loan:* $7482. *Average need-based gift aid:* $20,188. *Average non-need-based aid:* $14,621. *Average indebtedness upon graduation:* $27,125.

Applying *Options:* electronic application, early admission, early decision, deferred entrance. *Application fee:* $70. *Required:* essay or personal statement, high school transcript, 1 letter of recommendation. *Required for some:* portfolio for Electronic Arts is required; portfolio for Architecture highly recommended. *Application deadline:* 1/15 (freshmen). *Early decision deadline:* 11/1 (for plan 1), 1/1 (for plan 2). *Notification:* 3/14 (freshmen), continuous (transfers), 12/7 (early decision plan 1), 2/1 (early decision plan 2).

Freshman Application Contact Mr. James Nondorf, Vice President for Enrollment, Rensselaer Polytechnic Institute, 110 8th Street, Troy, NY 12180-3590. *Phone:* 518-276-6216. *Toll-free phone:* 800-448-6562. *Fax:* 518-276-4072. *E-mail:* admissions@rpi.edu.

See page 1814 for the College Close-Up.

ROBERTS WESLEYAN COLLEGE

Rochester, New York www.roberts.edu/

- **Independent** comprehensive, founded 1866, affiliated with Free Methodist Church of North America
- **Suburban** 75-acre campus
- **Endowment** $16.3 million
- **Coed** 1,312 undergraduate students, 90% full-time, 69% women, 31% men
- **Moderately difficult** entrance level, 63% of applicants were admitted

Founded in 1866 by B. T. Roberts, Roberts Wesleyan is an independent, coeducational Christian liberal arts college that is committed to integrating a Christian worldview with academic study. Roberts Wesleyan College is accredited by the Middle States Association of Colleges and Schools and is a member of the Council for Christian Colleges & Universities.

Undergraduates 1,186 full-time, 126 part-time. Students come from 24 states and territories, 22 other countries, 13% are from out of state, 8% African American, 1% Asian American or Pacific Islander, 3% Hispanic American, 0.4% Native American, 2% international, 8% transferred in, 65% live on campus. *Retention:* 80% of 2006 full-time freshmen returned.

Freshmen *Admission:* 1,531 applied, 957 admitted, 250 enrolled. *Average high school GPA:* 3.2. *Test scores:* SAT critical reading scores over 500: 77%; SAT math scores over 500: 60%; ACT scores over 18: 96%; SAT critical reading scores over 600: 41%; SAT math scores over 600: 24%; ACT scores over 24: 45%; SAT critical reading scores over 700: 5%; SAT math scores over 700: 3%; ACT scores over 30: 7%.

Faculty *Total:* 246, 46% full-time, 40% with terminal degrees. *Student/faculty ratio:* 14:1.

Majors Accounting; art; art teacher education; biochemistry; biological and physical sciences; biology/biological sciences; biology teacher education; business administration and management; chemistry; chemistry teacher education; clinical laboratory science/medical technology; communication/speech communication and rhetoric; computer and information sciences and support services related; computer science; criminal justice/law enforcement administration; divinity/ministry; education; elementary education; English; English/language arts teacher education; fine/studio arts; history; humanities; human resources management; management information systems; marketing/marketing management; mathematics; mathematics teacher education; music; music teacher education; natural sciences; nursing (registered nurse training); nursing related; pastoral studies/counseling; philosophy; philosophy and religious studies related; physical sciences; physics; physics teacher education; piano and organ; pre-dentistry studies; pre-engineering; pre-law studies; pre-medical studies; pre-pharmacy studies; pre-theology/pre-ministerial studies; pre-veterinary studies; psychology; science teacher education; secondary education; social studies teacher education; social work; sociology; special education; voice and opera.

Academics *Calendar:* semesters. *Degrees:* associate, bachelor's, and master's. *Special study options:* academic remediation for entering students, adult/continuing education programs, advanced placement credit, cooperative education, double majors, English as a second language, freshman honors college, honors programs, independent study, internships, off-campus study, services for LD students, study abroad, summer session for credit. *ROTC:* Army (c), Air Force (c). *Unusual degree programs:* 3-2 engineering with Clarkson University, Rensselaer Polytechnic Institute, Rochester Institute of Technology.

Computers on Campus 250 computers/terminals are available on campus for general student use. Students can access the following: campus intranet, computer help desk, free student e-mail accounts, online (class) grades, online (class) registration, online (class) schedules, Wireless. Campuswide network is available. 100% of college-owned or -operated housing units are wired for high-speed Internet access. Wireless service is available via classrooms, computer centers, computer labs, learning centers, libraries, student centers.

Student Life *Housing:* on-campus residence required through senior year. *Options:* men-only, women-only. Campus housing is university owned. Freshman campus housing is guaranteed. *Activities and organizations:* drama/theater group, student-run newspaper, radio station, choral group, Habitat for Humanity, Foot of the Cross, Radiant Light, Nursing Club, Drama Club. *Campus security:* 24-hour emergency response devices and patrols, late-night transport/escort service, controlled dormitory access, 24-hour Resident Life staff on-call. *Student services:* health clinic, personal/psychological counseling.

Athletics Member NCAA, NAIA, NCCAA. All NCAA Division II. *Intercollegiate sports:* basketball M (s)/W (s), cross-country running M (s)/W (s), golf M (s)/W (s), soccer M (s)/W (s), tennis M (s)/W (s), track and field M (s)/W (s), volleyball W (s). *Intramural sports:* archery M, basketball M/W, racquetball M/W, soccer M/W, softball M/W, table tennis M/W, tennis M/W, ultimate Frisbee M/W, volleyball M/W, water polo M/W.

Standardized Tests *Required:* SAT or ACT (for admission).

Costs (2008–09) *Comprehensive fee:* $31,150 includes full-time tuition ($21,766), mandatory fees ($1156), and room and board ($8228). *College room only:* $5702.

Financial Aid Of all full-time matriculated undergraduates who enrolled in 2007, 928 applied for aid, 864 were judged to have need, 169 had their need fully met. 686 Federal Work-Study jobs (averaging $1711). 26 state and other part-time jobs (averaging $1923). In 2007, 126 non-need-based awards were made. *Average percent of need met:* 76%. *Average financial aid package:* $18,180. *Average need-based loan:* $6382. *Average need-based gift aid:* $11,366. *Average non-need-based aid:* $10,572. *Average indebtedness upon graduation:* $22,574.

Applying *Options:* electronic application, early admission, deferred entrance. *Application fee:* $35. *Required:* essay or personal statement, high school transcript, 2 letters of recommendation. *Recommended:* minimum 2.5 GPA, interview. *Application deadlines:* 2/1 (freshmen), rolling (transfers).

Freshman Application Contact Ms. Linda Kurtz Hoffman, Vice President for Admissions and Marketing, Roberts Wesleyan College, 2301 Westside Drive, Rochester, NY 14624. *Phone:* 585-594-6400. *Toll-free phone:* 800-777-4RWC. *Fax:* 585-594-6371. *E-mail:* admissions@roberts.edu.

See page 1816 for the College Close-Up.

ROCHESTER INSTITUTE OF TECHNOLOGY

Rochester, New York **www.rit.edu/**

- **Independent** comprehensive, founded 1829
- **Suburban** 1300-acre campus with easy access to Buffalo
- **Endowment** $661.5 million
- **Coed** 13,476 undergraduate students, 88% full-time, 32% women, 68% men
- **Moderately difficult** entrance level, 65% of applicants were admitted

Undergraduates 11,901 full-time, 1,575 part-time. Students come from 54 states and territories, 95 other countries, 42% are from out of state, 4% African American, 5% Asian American or Pacific Islander, 4% Hispanic American, 0.4% Native American, 11% international, 6% transferred in, 65% live on campus. *Retention:* 89% of 2006 full-time freshmen returned.

Freshmen *Admission:* 11,012 applied, 7,112 admitted, 2,514 enrolled. *Average high school GPA:* 3.7. *Test scores:* SAT critical reading scores over 500: 86%; SAT math scores over 500: 94%; ACT scores over 18: 100%; SAT critical reading scores over 600: 42%; SAT math scores over 600: 59%; ACT scores over 24: 78%; SAT critical reading scores over 700: 8%; SAT math scores over 700: 13%; ACT scores over 30: 15%.

Faculty *Total:* 1,233, 66% full-time. *Student/faculty ratio:* 14:1.

Majors Accounting; advertising; aerospace, aeronautical and astronautical engineering; animation, interactive technology, video graphics and special effects; biochemistry; bioinformatics; biological and biomedical sciences related; biomedical/medical engineering; biopsychology; biotechnology; cardiovascular technology; civil engineering technology; clinical laboratory science/medical technology; commercial photography; communication and media related; computer and information sciences; computer and information systems security; computer engineering; computer engineering technology; computer graphics; computer software engineering; computer systems analysis; computer systems networking and telecommunications; crafts, folk art and artisanry; criminal justice/law enforcement administration; criminal justice/safety; data modeling/warehousing and database administration; design and visual communications; economics; electrical and electronic engineering technologies related; electrical, electronics and communications engineering; electromechanical technology; engineering; engineering related; engineering-related technologies; engineering science; environmental science; finance; foodservice systems administration; graphic communications; hazardous materials management and waste technology; hospitality administration; hospitality and recreation marketing; human nutrition; illustration; industrial engineering; industrial safety technology; information technology; interdisciplinary studies; international business/trade/commerce; international relations and affairs; management information systems; manufacturing technology; marketing/marketing management; mathematics; mathematics and computer science; mechanical engineering; medical illustration; natural resources management and policy; occupational safety and health technology; ophthalmic laboratory technology; photographic and film/video technology; photojournalism; physician assistant; polymer chemistry; pre-dentistry studies; pre-law studies; pre-medical studies; pre-veterinary studies; psychology; public policy analysis; public relations, advertising, and applied communication related; public relations/image management; publishing; quality control and safety technologies related; sculpture; special products marketing; statistics; system administration; system, networking, and LAN/WAN management; systems engineering; telecommunications; telecommunications technology; tourism and travel services marketing; web/multimedia management and webmaster; web page, digital/multimedia and information resources design.

Academics *Calendar:* quarters. *Degrees:* certificates, diplomas, associate, bachelor's, master's, doctoral, post-master's, and postbachelor's certificates. *Special study options:* accelerated degree program, adult/continuing education programs, advanced placement credit, cooperative education, distance learning, double majors, English as a second language, honors programs, independent study, internships, off-campus study, part-time degree program, services for LD students, student-designed majors, study abroad, summer session for credit. *ROTC:* Army (b), Navy (c), Air Force (b).

Computers on Campus 2,500 computers/terminals are available on campus for general student use. Students can access the following: campus intranet, computer help desk, free student e-mail accounts, online (class) grades, online (class) registration, student account information. Campuswide network is available. Wireless service is available via classrooms, computer centers, computer labs, libraries, student centers.

Student Life *Housing:* on-campus residence required for freshman year. *Options:* coed, men-only, women-only, disabled students. Campus housing is university owned. Freshman campus housing is guaranteed. *Activities and organizations:* drama/theater group, student-run newspaper, radio station, choral group, campus radio station, campus weekly magazine, student government, Off-Campus Student Association, Music Association, national fraternities, national sororities. *Campus security:* 24-hour emergency response devices and patrols, student patrols, late-night transport/escort service. *Student services:* health clinic, personal/psychological counseling, women's center, legal services.

Athletics Member NCAA. All Division III except ice hockey (Division I). *Intercollegiate sports:* baseball M, basketball M/W, bowling M (c)/W (c), cheerleading M (c)/W (c), crew M/W, cross-country running M/W, equestrian sports M (c)/W (c), fencing M (c)/W (c), field hockey W (c), ice hockey M/W, lacrosse M/W, rugby M (c)/W (c), skiing (downhill) M (c)/W (c), soccer M/W, softball W, swimming and diving M/W, tennis M/W, track and field M/W, ultimate Frisbee M (c)/W (c), volleyball M (c)/W, water polo M (c)/W (c), wrestling M. *Intramural sports:* badminton M/W, basketball M/W, bowling M/W, football M, golf M/W, ice hockey M/W, lacrosse M (c), racquetball M/W, rock climbing M (c)/W (c), soccer M/W, softball M/W, table tennis M/W, tennis M/W, volleyball M/W.

Standardized Tests *Required:* SAT or ACT (for admission).

Costs (2007–08) *Comprehensive fee:* $35,535 includes full-time tuition ($26,085), mandatory fees ($396), and room and board ($9054). Full-time tuition and fees vary according to course load. Part-time tuition: $564 per credit hour. Part-time tuition and fees vary according to class time and course load. *Required fees:* $34 per term part-time. *College room only:* $5211. Room and board charges vary according to board plan and housing facility. *Payment plans:* tuition prepayment, installment, deferred payment. *Waivers:* employees or children of employees.

Financial Aid Of all full-time matriculated undergraduates who enrolled in 2006, 8,148 applied for aid, 7,226 were judged to have need, 5,980 had their need fully met. 2,100 Federal Work-Study jobs (averaging $1400). 4,700 state and other part-time jobs (averaging $1780). In 2006, 1000 non-need-based awards were made. *Average percent of need met:* 88%. *Average financial aid package:* $18,600. *Average need-based loan:* $5400. *Average need-based gift aid:* $12,500. *Average non-need-based aid:* $6500.

Applying *Options:* electronic application, early admission, early decision, deferred entrance. *Application fee:* $50. *Required:* essay or personal statement, high school transcript. *Required for some:* portfolio. *Recommended:* minimum 3.0 GPA, 1 letter of recommendation, interview. *Application deadline:* 2/1 (freshmen). *Early decision deadline:* 12/1. *Notification:* continuous (freshmen), continuous (transfers), 1/15 (early decision).

Freshman Application Contact Dr. Daniel Shelley, Assistant Vice President, Rochester Institute of Technology, 60 Lomb Memorial Drive, Rochester, NY 14623-5604. *Phone:* 585-475-6631. *Fax:* 585-475-7424. *E-mail:* admissions@rit.edu.

See page 1818 for the College Close-Up.

RUSSELL SAGE COLLEGE

Troy, New York **www.sage.edu/rsc/index.php**

- **Independent** 4-year, founded 1916, part of The Sage Colleges
- **Urban** 8-acre campus
- **Endowment** $32.1 million
- **Undergraduate: women only; graduate: coed** 682 undergraduate students, 93% full-time, 100% women
- **Moderately difficult** entrance level, 76% of applicants were admitted

Russell Sage College is a comprehensive, undergraduate college that is devoted to women of influence—where individuals count and are consistently challenged to think differently and ultimately succeed. The College offers a wide selection of academic opportunities in the liberal arts in addition to the latest professional degree programs in fields such as the health sciences, humanities, natural sciences and mathematics, and social and professional sciences. To schedule a visit to its beautiful Victorian campus in the heart of New York's "Tech Valley" and capital region, students should call 518-244-2217 or 888-VERY-SAGE (toll-free). E-mail: rscadm@sage.edu; Web site: http://www.sage.edu.

Undergraduates 633 full-time, 49 part-time. Students come from 18 states and territories, 9% are from out of state, 5% African American, 4% Asian American or Pacific Islander, 3% Hispanic American, 0.6% Native American, 14% transferred in, 38% live on campus. *Retention:* 69% of 2006 full-time freshmen returned.

Freshmen *Admission:* 340 applied, 259 admitted, 82 enrolled. *Average high school GPA:* 3.40. *Test scores:* SAT critical reading scores over 500: 65%; SAT math scores over 500: 63%; ACT scores over 18: 94%; SAT critical reading scores over 600: 28%; SAT math scores over 600: 21%; ACT scores over 24: 44%; SAT critical reading scores over 700: 8%; SAT math scores over 700: 3%.

Faculty *Total:* 90, 61% full-time, 73% with terminal degrees. *Student/faculty ratio:* 10:1.

Majors Art therapy; biochemistry; biology/biological sciences; biopsychology; business administration and management; chemistry; corrections and criminal justice related; dramatic/theater arts; elementary education; engineering; English; forensic science and technology; history; interdisciplinary studies; international/global studies; mass communication/media; mathematics; nursing (registered nurse training); nutrition sciences; occupational therapy; physical therapy; political science and government; psychology; sociology; Spanish.

Academics *Calendar:* semesters. *Degree:* bachelor's. *Special study options:* academic remediation for entering students, accelerated degree program, adult/continuing education programs, advanced placement credit, cooperative education, distance learning, double majors, external degree program, freshman honors college, honors programs, independent study, internships, off-campus study, part-time degree program, services for LD students, student-designed majors, study abroad, summer session for credit. *ROTC:* Army (c), Air Force (c). *Unusual degree programs:* 3-2 business administration with Sage Graduate School; engineering with Rensselaer Polytechnic Institute; nursing with Sage Graduate School; occupational therapy, physical therapy, public administration with Sage Graduate School, 3+3 BA/JD with Albany Law School; BA/MS Accelerated Physician Assistant Program with Albany Medical College.

Computers on Campus 157 computers/terminals are available on campus for general student use. Students can access the following: campus intranet, computer help desk, free student e-mail accounts, online (class) grades, online (class) registration, online (class) schedules. Campuswide network is available. 100% of college-owned or -operated housing units are wired for high-speed Internet access. Wireless service is available via classrooms, computer labs, dorm rooms, learning centers, libraries.

Student Life *Housing options:* women-only. Campus housing is university owned. Freshman campus housing is guaranteed. *Activities and organizations:* drama/theater group, student-run newspaper, choral group, student government, Sage Recreation Association, Physical Therapy Club, Crew Club, Black-Latin Student Alliance. *Campus security:* 24-hour emergency response devices and patrols, late-night transport/escort service, controlled dormitory access. *Student services:* health clinic, personal/psychological counseling, women's center.

Athletics Member NCAA. All Division III. *Intercollegiate sports:* basketball W, soccer W, softball W, tennis W, volleyball W. *Intramural sports:* basketball W, cheerleading W (c), crew W (c), equestrian sports W (c), field hockey W (c), football W, lacrosse W (c), soccer W, softball W, tennis W, track and field W (c), volleyball W.

Standardized Tests *Required for some:* SAT or ACT (for admission).

Costs (2007–08) *Comprehensive fee:* $34,790 includes full-time tuition ($25,000), mandatory fees ($990), and room and board ($8800). Part-time tuition: $835 per credit hour. *College room only:* $4500. *Payment plans:* installment, deferred payment. *Waivers:* employees or children of employees.

Financial Aid Of all full-time matriculated undergraduates who enrolled in 2006, 750 applied for aid, 661 were judged to have need, 2 had their need fully met. 432 Federal Work-Study jobs (averaging $1500). 91 state and other part-time jobs (averaging $1200). In 2006, 31 non-need-based awards were made. *Average non-need-based aid:* $9451. *Average indebtedness upon graduation:* $26,000.

Applying *Options:* electronic application, early admission, early decision, deferred entrance. *Application fee:* $30. *Required:* high school transcript, minimum 2.0 GPA, 2 letters of recommendation. *Recommended:* essay or personal statement, interview. *Application deadlines:* rolling (freshmen), rolling (transfers). *Early decision deadline:* 12/1. *Notification:* continuous (freshmen), continuous (transfers), 12/15 (early decision).

Freshman Application Contact Ms. Kathy Rusch, Director of Admission, Russell Sage College, 45 Ferry Street, Troy, NY 12180. *Phone:* 518-244-2444. *Toll-free phone:* 888-VERY-SAGE (in-state); 888-VERY SAGE (out-of-state). *Fax:* 518-244-6880. *E-mail:* ruschk@sage.edu.

SAGE COLLEGE OF ALBANY

Albany, New York **www.sage.edu/sca/index.php**

- **Independent** 4-year, founded 1957, part of The Sage Colleges
- **Urban** 15-acre campus
- **Endowment** $32.1 million
- **Coed** 989 undergraduate students, 57% full-time, 71% women, 29% men
- **Minimally difficult** entrance level, 67% of applicants were admitted

At Sage College of Albany, a student's future is unlimited. Students can combine two unique academic disciplines by beginning professional studies early in their college career and adding an internship as early as their second year. Students can pursue multiple areas of interest, change directions easily if needed, and develop interdisciplinary competencies important in today's workplace. Prospective students should check out the bachelor's degrees Sage offers and the secondary disciplines with which students can combine them. In addition, adult learners can finish their bachelor's degree by studying weekends, evenings, and online through Sage After Work. Prospective students may schedule a visit (phone: 518-292-1730 or 888-VERY-SAGE (toll-free); e-mail: scaadm@sage.edu; Web site: http://www.sage.edu/admission).

Undergraduates 566 full-time, 423 part-time. Students come from 9 states and territories, 2 other countries, 4% are from out of state, 9% African American, 2% Asian American or Pacific Islander, 3% Hispanic American, 0.1% Native American, 0.2% international, 16% transferred in, 28% live on campus. *Retention:* 69% of 2006 full-time freshmen returned.

Freshmen *Admission:* 322 applied, 215 admitted, 80 enrolled. *Average high school GPA:* 2.96. *Test scores:* SAT critical reading scores over 500: 38%; SAT

math scores over 500: 36%; ACT scores over 18: 85%; SAT critical reading scores over 600: 8%; SAT math scores over 600: 6%; ACT scores over 24: 19%.

Faculty *Total:* 88, 47% full-time, 42% with terminal degrees. *Student/faculty ratio:* 13:1.

Majors Accounting; biological and biomedical sciences related; clinical laboratory science/medical technology; computer science; criminology; fine/studio arts; graphic design; health and physical education; humanities; information science/studies; marketing/marketing management; mass communication/media; multi-/interdisciplinary studies related; parks, recreation, and leisure related; photography; psychology; social sciences.

Academics *Calendar:* semesters. *Degrees:* certificates, associate, and bachelor's. *Special study options:* academic remediation for entering students, adult/continuing education programs, advanced placement credit, cooperative education, distance learning, external degree program, freshman honors college, honors programs, independent study, internships, off-campus study, part-time degree program, services for LD students, student-designed majors, summer session for credit. *Unusual degree programs:* 3-2 business administration with Sage Graduate School; clinical biology and cytotechnology with Albany College of Pharmacy.

Computers on Campus 183 computers/terminals are available on campus for general student use. Students can access the following: campus intranet, computer help desk, free student e-mail accounts, online (class) grades, online (class) registration, online (class) schedules. Campuswide network is available. 100% of college-owned or -operated housing units are wired for high-speed Internet access. Wireless service is available via classrooms, computer labs, learning centers, libraries.

Student Life *Housing options:* coed, women-only. Campus housing is university owned. Freshman applicants given priority for college housing. *Activities and organizations:* student government, Phi Theta Kappa, Psychology Club, Ski Club, "Vernacular" (art and literary publication). *Campus security:* 24-hour emergency response devices and patrols, late-night transport/escort service, controlled dormitory access, 24-hour security cameras. *Student services:* health clinic, personal/psychological counseling.

Athletics *Intramural sports:* basketball M/W, cheerleading W (c), football M/W, ice hockey M (c)/W (c), soccer M/W.

Standardized Tests *Required for some:* SAT or ACT (for admission).

Costs (2007–08) *Comprehensive fee:* $27,590 includes full-time tuition ($17,650), mandatory fees ($990), and room and board ($8950). Part-time tuition: $585 per credit hour. *College room only:* $4650. *Payment plans:* installment, deferred payment. *Waivers:* employees or children of employees.

Financial Aid Of all full-time matriculated undergraduates who enrolled in 2006, 521 applied for aid, 444 were judged to have need. 210 Federal Work-Study jobs (averaging $1500). 19 state and other part-time jobs (averaging $1200). In 2006, 31 non-need-based awards were made. *Average non-need-based aid:* $5450. *Average indebtedness upon graduation:* $18,000.

Applying *Options:* electronic application, deferred entrance. *Application fee:* $30. *Required:* high school transcript, 1 letter of recommendation, portfolio for fine arts program. *Recommended:* essay or personal statement, interview. *Application deadlines:* rolling (freshmen), 8/1 (transfers). *Notification:* continuous until 8/15 (freshmen), continuous until 8/15 (transfers).

Freshman Application Contact Ms. Amy Sullivan, Director of Admission, Sage College of Albany, 140 New Scotland Avenue, Albany, NY 12208. *Phone:* 518-292-1730. *Toll-free phone:* 888-VERY-SAGE. *Fax:* 518-292-1912. *E-mail:* scaadm@sage.edu.

St. Bonaventure University

St. Bonaventure, New York **www.sbu.edu/**

Offering more than fifty academic programs, a five-year M.B.A. program, and dual-admission programs in medicine, dentistry, and pharmacy, St. Bonaventure University attracts exceptional students from thirty-four states and twelve countries. Adding to the Bonaventure experience are broadcast journalism and modern language laboratories, an expanded fiber-optic computer network, a regional arts center, Division I athletics, a new $6.2-million recreation center, and a new, 5,500-square-foot coffee café flanking a renovated dining hall. *U.S. News & World Report* repeatedly ranks St. Bonaventure in its top tier of regional universities.

Freshman Application Contact Mr. James M. DiRisio, Director of Admissions, St. Bonaventure University, PO Box D, St. Bonaventure, NY 14778. *Phone:* 716-375-2400. *Toll-free phone:* 800-462-5050. *Fax:* 716-375-4005. *E-mail:* jdirisio@sbu.edu.

See page 1820 for the College Close-Up.

St. Francis College

Brooklyn Heights, New York **www.stfranciscollege.edu/**

- **Independent Roman Catholic** 4-year, founded 1884
- **Urban** 1-acre campus with easy access to New York City
- **Endowment** $75,811
- **Coed**
- **Moderately difficult** entrance level

Faculty *Student/faculty ratio:* 17:1.

Academics *Calendar:* semesters. *Degrees:* associate, bachelor's, and master's.

Student Life *Campus security:* ID checks, crime awareness workshops, pamphlets, posters, films.

Athletics Member NCAA. All Division I.

Standardized Tests *Required:* SAT (for admission).

Costs (2007–08) *Tuition:* $14,400 full-time, $480 per credit part-time. Full-time tuition and fees vary according to course level, course load, degree level, program, and student level. Part-time tuition and fees vary according to course level, course load, degree level, program, and student level. *Required fees:* $520 full-time, $140 per term part-time. *Payment plans:* installment, deferred payment.

Financial Aid Of all full-time matriculated undergraduates who enrolled in 2006, 1,747 applied for aid, 1,683 were judged to have need, 443 had their need fully met. 161 Federal Work-Study jobs (averaging $2200). *Average percent of need met:* 64. *Average financial aid package:* $9300. *Average need-based loan:* $7700. *Average need-based gift aid:* $6640.

Applying *Options:* electronic application, deferred entrance. *Application fee:* $35. *Required:* essay or personal statement, high school transcript, minimum 2.0 GPA, 1 letter of recommendation. *Recommended:* interview.

Freshman Application Contact Ms. Monica Michalski, St. Francis College, Brooklyn Heights, NY 11201. *Phone:* 718-489-5472. *Fax:* 718-522-1274. *E-mail:* mmichalski@stfranciscollege.edu.

St. John Fisher College

Rochester, New York **www.sjfc.edu/**

- **Independent** comprehensive, founded 1948, affiliated with Roman Catholic Church
- **Suburban** 136-acre campus
- **Endowment** $41.5 million
- **Coed** 2,856 undergraduate students, 92% full-time, 60% women, 40% men
- **Moderately difficult** entrance level, 61% of applicants were admitted

In 2005, St. John Fisher College established a School of Pharmacy to help alleviate the projected shortfall of qualified pharmacists nationwide. Fisher's program offers a 2-4 pharmacy curriculum leading to the Pharm.D. degree. Similarly, in 2006, the College announced the creation of a School of Nursing to address the critical shortage of nurses. Fisher's program offers a fully accredited B.S. in nursing; an RN-B.S. completion program; an M.S. in advanced practice nursing for family nurse practitioners, clinical nurse specialists, and nurse educators; and post-master's certificates in nursing education and advanced practice nursing/family nurse practitioner studies.

Undergraduates 2,632 full-time, 224 part-time. Students come from 20 states and territories, 6 other countries, 2% are from out of state, 5% African American, 2% Asian American or Pacific Islander, 3% Hispanic American, 0.5% Native American, 0.4% international, 10% transferred in, 53% live on campus. *Retention:* 86% of 2006 full-time freshmen returned.

Freshmen *Admission:* 3,209 applied, 1,944 admitted, 548 enrolled. *Average high school GPA:* 3.5. *Test scores:* SAT critical reading scores over 500: 66%; SAT math scores over 500: 80%; SAT writing scores over 500: 63%; SAT critical reading scores over 600: 16%; SAT math scores over 600: 28%; SAT writing scores over 600: 15%; SAT critical reading scores over 700: 1%; SAT math scores over 700: 2%; SAT writing scores over 700: 1%.

Faculty *Total:* 371, 49% full-time, 41% with terminal degrees. *Student/faculty ratio:* 13:1.

Majors Accounting; American studies; anthropology; biochemistry; biology/biological sciences; business administration and management; chemistry; computer science; economics; elementary education; English; finance; French; German; health and physical education related; history; human resources management; international business/trade/commerce; international relations and affairs; Italian; management information systems; marketing/marketing management; mass communication/media; mathematics; mathematics teacher education; multi-/interdisciplinary studies related; nursing (registered nurse training); philosophy;

physics; political science and government; psychology; religious studies; science teacher education; sociology; Spanish; special education; technology/industrial arts teacher education.

Academics *Calendar:* semesters. *Degrees:* bachelor's, master's, doctoral, first professional, post-master's, postbachelor's, and first professional certificates. *Special study options:* academic remediation for entering students, accelerated degree program, adult/continuing education programs, advanced placement credit, double majors, honors programs, independent study, internships, off-campus study, part-time degree program, services for LD students, student-designed majors, study abroad, summer session for credit. *ROTC:* Army (c), Air Force (c). *Unusual degree programs:* 3-2 engineering with Clarkson University, Manhattan College, State University of New York at Buffalo, Columbia University, University of Detroit Mercy.

Computers on Campus 525 computers/terminals and 1,875 ports are available on campus for general student use. Students can access the following: online (class) registration. Campuswide network is available. 100% of college-owned or -operated housing units are wired for high-speed Internet access. Wireless service is available via learning centers, libraries.

Student Life *Housing options:* coed, women-only. Campus housing is university owned. Freshman campus housing is guaranteed. *Activities and organizations:* drama/theater group, student-run newspaper, radio and television station, choral group, Student government, Student Activities Board, Commuter Council, Resident Student Association. *Campus security:* 24-hour emergency response devices and patrols, late-night transport/escort service, controlled dormitory access. *Student services:* health clinic, personal/psychological counseling.

Athletics Member NCAA. All Division III. *Intercollegiate sports:* baseball M, basketball M/W, cheerleading W, football M, golf M/W, lacrosse M/W, soccer M/W, softball W, tennis M/W, volleyball W. *Intramural sports:* basketball M/W, cheerleading W (c), ice hockey M (c)/W (c), racquetball M/W, rugby M (c)/W (c), skiing (cross-country) M (c)/W (c), skiing (downhill) M (c)/W (c), soccer M/W, softball M, volleyball M/W.

Standardized Tests *Required:* SAT or ACT (for admission).

Costs (2008–09) *Comprehensive fee:* $33,000 includes full-time tuition ($22,960) and room and board ($10,040). Part-time tuition: $625 per credit. *College room only:* $6420.

Financial Aid Of all full-time matriculated undergraduates who enrolled in 2007, 2,167 applied for aid, 1,885 were judged to have need, 1,190 had their need fully met. 1,619 Federal Work-Study jobs (averaging $1500). In 2007, 586 non-need-based awards were made. *Average percent of need met:* 83%. *Average financial aid package:* $18,210. *Average need-based loan:* $7382. *Average need-based gift aid:* $10,644. *Average non-need-based aid:* $5872. *Average indebtedness upon graduation:* $35,987.

Applying *Options:* electronic application, early admission, early decision, early action, deferred entrance. *Application fee:* $30. *Required:* high school transcript, minimum 2.0 GPA, 1 letter of recommendation. *Recommended:* essay or personal statement, interview. *Application deadlines:* rolling (freshmen), rolling (transfers). *Early decision deadline:* 12/1. *Notification:* continuous until 9/1 (freshmen), continuous until 9/1 (transfers), 12/15 (early decision).

Freshman Application Contact Mrs. Stacy A. Ledermann, Director of Freshmen Admissions, St. John Fisher College, 3690 East Avenue, Rochester, NY 14618. *Phone:* 585-385-8064. *Toll-free phone:* 800-444-4640. *Fax:* 585-385-8386. *E-mail:* admissions@sjfc.edu.

See page 1822 for the College Close-Up.

ST. JOHN'S UNIVERSITY

Queens, New York **www.stjohns.edu/**

- **Independent** university, founded 1870, affiliated with Roman Catholic Church
- **Urban** 98-acre campus with easy access to New York City
- **Endowment** $367.0 million
- **Coed** 14,798 undergraduate students, 79% full-time, 56% women, 44% men
- **Moderately difficult** entrance level, 56% of applicants were admitted

Undergraduates 11,763 full-time, 3,035 part-time. Students come from 45 states and territories, 108 other countries, 15% are from out of state, 3% transferred in, 19% live on campus. *Retention:* 79% of 2006 full-time freshmen returned.

Freshmen *Admission:* 27,754 applied, 15,410 admitted, 3,162 enrolled. *Average high school GPA:* 3.2. *Test scores:* SAT critical reading scores over 500: 66%; SAT math scores over 500: 69%; SAT critical reading scores over 600: 20%; SAT math scores over 600: 26%; SAT critical reading scores over 700: 3%; SAT math scores over 700: 5%.

Faculty *Total:* 1,479, 45% full-time, 58% with terminal degrees. *Student/faculty ratio:* 17:1.

Majors Accounting; actuarial science; advertising; anthropology; Asian studies; audiology and speech-language pathology; biology/biological sciences; biology teacher education; business administration and management; chemistry; clinical child psychology; clinical laboratory science/medical technology; communication/speech communication and rhetoric; computer and information sciences; computer and information systems security; criminal justice/law enforcement administration; criminology; economics; elementary education; English; English/language arts teacher education; environmental studies; finance; fine arts related; French; funeral service and mortuary science; graphic design; health/health care administration; history; hospitality administration; human services; illustration; information science/studies; insurance; Italian; journalism; legal studies; liberal arts and sciences/liberal studies; management information systems; marketing/marketing management; mathematics; mathematics teacher education; pastoral counseling and specialized ministries related; pathologist assistant; pharmacy; philosophy; photographic and film/video technology; photography; physical sciences; physician assistant; physics; physics teacher education; political science and government; psychology; public relations/image management; secondary education; securities services administration; social sciences; social studies teacher education; sociology; Spanish; Spanish language teacher education; special education; speech and rhetoric; sport and fitness administration/management; teacher assistant/aide; telecommunications technology; theology; toxicology.

Academics *Calendar:* semesters. *Degrees:* certificates, diplomas, associate, bachelor's, master's, doctoral, first professional, post-master's, and postbachelor's certificates. *Special study options:* accelerated degree program, adult/continuing education programs, advanced placement credit, distance learning, double majors, English as a second language, honors programs, independent study, internships, off-campus study, part-time degree program, services for LD students, study abroad, summer session for credit. *ROTC:* Army (b). *Unusual degree programs:* 3-2 engineering with Manhattan College; dentistry-Columbia University, optometry-SUNY Optometry.

Computers on Campus 9,900 computers/terminals and 100 ports are available on campus for general student use. Students can access the following: campus intranet, computer help desk, free student e-mail accounts, online (class) grades, online (class) registration, online (class) schedules, various software packages. Campuswide network is available. 100% of college-owned or -operated housing units are wired for high-speed Internet access. Wireless service is available via entire campus.

Student Life *Housing options:* coed. Campus housing is university owned. Freshman applicants given priority for college housing. *Activities and organizations:* drama/theater group, student-run newspaper, radio and television station, choral group, Student Government, Incorporated, Student Programming Board, Haraya, American Pharmaceutical Association, Latin American Student Organization/Muslim Student Organization, national fraternities, national sororities. *Campus security:* 24-hour emergency response devices and patrols, student patrols, late-night transport/escort service, controlled dormitory access. *Student services:* health clinic, personal/psychological counseling.

Athletics Member NCAA. All Division I. *Intercollegiate sports:* baseball M (s), basketball M (s)/W (s), cross-country running W (s), fencing M (s)/W (s), golf M (s)/W (s), lacrosse M (s), soccer M (s)/W (s), softball W (s), tennis M (s)/W (s), track and field W, volleyball W (s). *Intramural sports:* badminton M/W, basketball M/W, bowling M (c), cheerleading M/W, fencing M/W, football M/W, racquetball M/W, soccer M/W, softball M/W, table tennis M/W, tennis M/W, volleyball M (c)/W (c), weight lifting M/W.

Standardized Tests *Required:* SAT or ACT (for admission).

Costs (2007–08) *Comprehensive fee:* $38,960 includes full-time tuition ($26,200), mandatory fees ($690), and room and board ($12,070). Full-time tuition and fees vary according to class time, course load, program, and student level. Part-time tuition: $873 per credit. Part-time tuition and fees vary according to class time, course load, program, and student level. No tuition increase for student's term of enrollment. *Required fees:* $173 per term part-time. *College room only:* $7600. Room and board charges vary according to board plan and housing facility. *Payment plans:* installment, deferred payment. *Waivers:* senior citizens and employees or children of employees.

Financial Aid Of all full-time matriculated undergraduates who enrolled in 2006, 9,998 applied for aid, 9,169 were judged to have need, 1,079 had their need fully met. 872 Federal Work-Study jobs (averaging $2618). In 2006, 555 non-need-based awards were made. *Average percent of need met:* 62%. *Average financial aid package:* $17,371. *Average need-based loan:* $4325. *Average need-based gift aid:* $7527. *Average non-need-based aid:* $8630. *Average indebtedness upon graduation:* $28,010.

Applying *Options:* electronic application, early admission, deferred entrance. *Application fee:* $50. *Required:* high school transcript. *Recommended:* essay or personal statement, letters of recommendation, interview. *Application deadlines:* rolling (freshmen), rolling (transfers). *Notification:* continuous (freshmen), continuous (transfers).

Freshman Application Contact Mrs. Karem Vahey, Admission Director, St. John's University, 8000 Utopia Parkway, Queens, NY 11439. *Phone:* 718-990-2000. *Toll-free phone:* 888-9STJOHNS (in-state); 888-9ST JOHNS (out-of-state). *Fax:* 718-990-2160. *E-mail:* admhelp@stjohns.edu.

St. Joseph's College, New York

Brooklyn, New York **www.sjcny.edu/**

- **Independent** comprehensive, founded 1916
- **Urban** campus
- **Endowment** $23.4 million
- **Coed** 1,065 undergraduate students, 68% full-time, 77% women, 23% men
- **Moderately difficult** entrance level, 75% of applicants were admitted

Since 1916, St. Joseph's College has been inspiring students to transform their lives. Here, young men and women find academic excellence, a vibrant community, and an unrivaled degree of personal attention. Students can choose from a variety of four-year programs leading to B.A. and B.S. degrees, accelerate their careers through fast-track master's degree programs, or choose from career-oriented, preprofessional programs such as law, medicine, and criminal justice. One of the most affordable private colleges in the country, St. Joseph's offers a values-oriented education, inspiring students to lead lives characterized by integrity, a commitment to upholding intellectual and spiritual values, social responsibility, and service to others.

Undergraduates 726 full-time, 339 part-time. Students come from 3 states and territories, 10 other countries, 2% are from out of state, 37% African American, 7% Asian American or Pacific Islander, 12% Hispanic American, 0.2% Native American, 0.7% international, 14% transferred in, 3% live on campus. *Retention:* 73% of 2006 full-time freshmen returned.

Freshmen *Admission:* 874 applied, 655 admitted, 171 enrolled. *Average high school GPA:* 3.1. *Test scores:* SAT critical reading scores over 500: 48%; SAT math scores over 500: 51%; ACT scores over 18: 100%; SAT critical reading scores over 600: 7%; SAT math scores over 600: 11%; SAT critical reading scores over 700: 1%; SAT math scores over 700: 1%.

Faculty *Total:* 137, 38% full-time. *Student/faculty ratio:* 15:1.

Majors Accounting; biology/biological sciences; business administration and management; chemistry; child guidance; developmental and child psychology; education; English; general studies; health/health care administration; history; human resources management; human services; mathematics; mathematics and computer science; nursing (registered nurse training); pre-law studies; psychology; public health; social sciences; Spanish; speech and rhetoric.

Academics *Calendar:* semesters. *Degrees:* bachelor's and master's. *Special study options:* adult/continuing education programs, advanced placement credit, distance learning, honors programs, independent study, internships, part-time degree program, summer session for credit. *Unusual degree programs:* 3-2 podiatry with New York College of Podiatric Medicine.

Computers on Campus 90 computers/terminals are available on campus for general student use. Students can access the following: online (class) registration.

Student Life *Housing options:* coed. Campus housing is leased by the school. *Activities and organizations:* drama/theater group, student-run newspaper, choral group, Admissions Club, Science Club, dramatics, Shild Study Club, Dance Team. *Campus security:* late-night transport/escort service. *Student services:* personal/psychological counseling.

Athletics *Intercollegiate sports:* basketball M/W, cross-country running M/W, softball W, volleyball M/W. *Intramural sports:* basketball M/W, bowling M/W, table tennis M/W, volleyball M/W.

Standardized Tests *Required:* SAT or ACT (for admission).

Costs (2007–08) *Tuition:* $14,000 full-time, $460 per credit part-time. *Required fees:* $382 full-time, $13 per credit part-time, $77 per term part-time. *Payment plan:* installment. *Waivers:* employees or children of employees.

Financial Aid Of all full-time matriculated undergraduates who enrolled in 2006, 660 applied for aid, 575 were judged to have need, 350 had their need fully met. 75 Federal Work-Study jobs (averaging $1700). 6 state and other part-time jobs (averaging $1700). In 2006, 120 non-need-based awards were made. *Average percent of need met:* 74%. *Average financial aid package:* $10,500. *Average need-based loan:* $3750. *Average need-based gift aid:* $6200. *Average non-need-based aid:* $4800. *Average indebtedness upon graduation:* $17,978.

Applying *Options:* electronic application, early admission, deferred entrance. *Application fee:* $25. *Required:* high school transcript, minimum 2.5 GPA. *Required for some:* interview. *Recommended:* essay or personal statement, 2 letters of recommendation. *Application deadlines:* 8/15 (freshmen), 8/15 (transfers). *Notification:* continuous until 8/30 (freshmen), continuous until 8/30 (transfers).

Freshman Application Contact Ms. Theresa LaRocca Meyer, Director of Admissions, St. Joseph's College, New York, 245 Clinton Avenue, Brooklyn, NY 11205-3688. *Phone:* 718-636-6868. *E-mail:* asinfob@sjcny.edu.

See page 1824 for the College Close-Up.

St. Joseph's College, Suffolk Campus

Patchogue, New York **www.sjcny.edu/**

- **Independent** comprehensive, founded 1916, administratively affiliated with St. Joseph's College, Brooklyn Campus
- **Small-town** 28-acre campus with easy access to New York City
- **Coed** 3,453 undergraduate students, 79% full-time, 74% women, 26% men
- **Moderately difficult** entrance level, 79% of applicants were admitted

Undergraduates 2,733 full-time, 720 part-time. Students come from 13 states and territories, 1 other country, 1% are from out of state, 4% African American, 2% Asian American or Pacific Islander, 7% Hispanic American, 11% transferred in. *Retention:* 81% of 2006 full-time freshmen returned.

Freshmen *Admission:* 1,393 applied, 1,100 admitted, 495 enrolled. *Average high school GPA:* 3.6. *Test scores:* SAT critical reading scores over 500: 71%; SAT math scores over 500: 76%; SAT writing scores over 500: 57%; SAT critical reading scores over 600: 11%; SAT math scores over 600: 23%; SAT writing scores over 600: 10%; SAT critical reading scores over 700: 1%; SAT math scores over 700: 2%; SAT writing scores over 700: 1%.

Faculty *Total:* 376, 29% full-time, 34% with terminal degrees. *Student/faculty ratio:* 17:1.

Majors Accounting; adult and continuing education; behavioral sciences; biology/biological sciences; biology teacher education; business administration and management; communication/speech communication and rhetoric; computer science; developmental and child psychology; early childhood education; economics; education; elementary education; English; English/language arts teacher education; health/health care administration; history; history teacher education; human resources management; information technology; kindergarten/preschool education; liberal arts and sciences/liberal studies; mathematics; mathematics teacher education; middle school education; nursing (registered nurse training); parks, recreation and leisure; political science and government; pre-dentistry studies; pre-law studies; pre-medical studies; pre-veterinary studies; psychology; science teacher education; secondary education; social sciences; sociology; Spanish; Spanish language teacher education; special education; special education (developmentally delayed); special education (early childhood); speech and rhetoric; therapeutic recreation.

Academics *Calendar:* 4-1-4. *Degrees:* certificates, bachelor's, and master's. *Special study options:* adult/continuing education programs, advanced placement credit, cooperative education, distance learning, double majors, honors programs, independent study, internships, off-campus study, part-time degree program, services for LD students, study abroad, summer session for credit. *ROTC:* Army (c), Air Force (c). *Unusual degree programs:* business administration; biology with New York College of Podiatric Medicine; computer science with Polytechnic University, Farmingdale Campus.

Computers on Campus 238 computers/terminals and 9 ports are available on campus for general student use. Students can access the following: computer help desk, free student e-mail accounts, online (class) grades, online (class) registration. Campuswide network is available. Wireless service is available via entire campus.

Student Life *Housing:* college housing not available. *Activities and organizations:* drama/theater group, student-run newspaper, choral group, STARS (Students Taking an Active Role in Society), Dance Chiild, Keep A Child Alive, Diversity Union, Drama Society. *Campus security:* 24-hour patrols, late-night transport/escort service. *Student services:* personal/psychological counseling.

Athletics Member NCAA. All Division III. *Intercollegiate sports:* baseball M, basketball M/W, cross-country running M/W, equestrian sports M/W, golf M, soccer M/W, softball W, swimming and diving W, tennis M/W, track and field M/W, volleyball W. *Intramural sports:* lacrosse M (c).

Standardized Tests *Required:* SAT or ACT (for admission).

Costs (2007–08) *Tuition:* $14,000 full-time, $460 per credit part-time. Part-time tuition and fees vary according to course load. *Required fees:* $532 full-time, $13 per credit part-time, $120 per term part-time. *Payment plan:* installment. *Waivers:* employees or children of employees.

Financial Aid Of all full-time matriculated undergraduates who enrolled in 2006, 2,383 applied for aid, 2,147 were judged to have need, 1,426 had their need fully met. 61 Federal Work-Study jobs (averaging $2409). 106 state and other part-time jobs (averaging $2750). In 2006, 573 non-need-based awards were made. *Average percent of need met:* 32%. *Average financial aid package:* $5829. *Average need-based loan:* $4095. *Average need-based gift aid:* $3645. *Average non-need-based aid:* $5380. *Average indebtedness upon graduation:* $17,806.

Applying *Options:* early admission, deferred entrance. *Application fee:* $25. *Required:* high school transcript, minimum 3.0 GPA. *Required for some:* essay or personal statement, 2 letters of recommendation. *Recommended:* interview. *Application deadlines:* rolling (freshmen), rolling (transfers). *Notification:* continuous (freshmen), continuous (transfers).

Freshman Application Contact St. Joseph's College, Suffolk Campus, 155 West Roe Boulevard, Patchogue, NY 11772. *Phone:* 631-447-3219. *Toll-free phone:* 866-AT ST JOE. *Fax:* 631-447-3601. *E-mail:* longislandas@sjcny.edu.

ST. LAWRENCE UNIVERSITY

Canton, New York **www.stlawu.edu/**

- **Independent** comprehensive, founded 1856
- **Small-town** 1000-acre campus with easy access to Ottawa
- **Endowment** $269.2 million
- **Coed** 2,198 undergraduate students, 99% full-time, 55% women, 45% men
- **Very difficult** entrance level, 44% of applicants were admitted

Undergraduates 2,167 full-time, 31 part-time. Students come from 43 states and territories, 46 other countries, 48% are from out of state, 3% African American, 2% Asian American or Pacific Islander, 3% Hispanic American, 0.7% Native American, 6% international, 0.7% transferred in, 100% live on campus. *Retention:* 88% of 2006 full-time freshmen returned.

Freshmen *Admission:* 4,645 applied, 2,030 admitted, 627 enrolled. *Average high school GPA:* 3.5. *Test scores:* SAT critical reading scores over 500: 95%; SAT math scores over 500: 96%; SAT writing scores over 500: 94%; ACT scores over 18: 99%; SAT critical reading scores over 600: 54%; SAT math scores over 600: 63%; SAT writing scores over 600: 55%; ACT scores over 24: 91%; SAT critical reading scores over 700: 5%; SAT math scores over 700: 6%; SAT writing scores over 700: 8%; ACT scores over 30: 17%.

Faculty *Total:* 190, 90% full-time, 92% with terminal degrees. *Student/faculty ratio:* 11:1.

Majors African studies; agriculture; American literature; anthropology; art; art history, criticism and conservation; Asian studies; biochemistry; biology/biological sciences; biophysics; Canadian studies; chemistry; computer science; creative writing; dramatic/theater arts; economics; English; English literature (British and Commonwealth); environmental studies; fine/studio arts; foreign languages and literatures; French; geology/earth science; geophysics and seismology; German; history; international/global studies; mathematics; mathematics and computer science; modern languages; music; neurobiology and neurophysiology; neuroscience; philosophy; physics; political science and government; psychology; religious studies; sociology; Spanish.

Academics *Calendar:* semesters. *Degrees:* bachelor's, master's, and post-master's certificates. *Special study options:* advanced placement credit, double majors, independent study, internships, off-campus study, part-time degree program, services for LD students, student-designed majors, study abroad, summer session for credit. *ROTC:* Army (c), Air Force (c). *Unusual degree programs:* 3-2 business administration with Clarkson University, Union College; engineering with Columbia University, Clarkson University, Rensselaer Polytechnic Institute, University of Rochester, University of Southern California, Washington University in St. Louis, Worcester Polytechnic Institute.

Computers on Campus 569 computers/terminals are available on campus for general student use. Students can access the following: computer help desk, free student e-mail accounts, online (class) grades, online (class) registration, online (class) schedules. Campuswide network is available. 100% of college-owned or -operated housing units are wired for high-speed Internet access. Wireless service is available via classrooms, computer centers, computer labs, learning centers, libraries, student centers.

Student Life *Housing:* on-campus residence required through senior year. *Options:* coed. Campus housing is university owned. Freshman campus housing is guaranteed. *Activities and organizations:* drama/theater group, student-run newspaper, radio and television station, choral group, Outing Club, student newspaper, student government, Circle K, Habitat for Humanity, national fraternities, national sororities. *Campus security:* 24-hour emergency response devices and patrols, student patrols, late-night transport/escort service, controlled dormitory access. *Student services:* health clinic, personal/psychological counseling, women's center.

Athletics Member NCAA. All Division III except men's and women's ice hockey (Division I). *Intercollegiate sports:* baseball M, basketball M/W, crew M/W, cross-country running M/W, equestrian sports M/W, field hockey W, football M, golf M/W, ice hockey M (s)/W (s), lacrosse M/W, skiing (cross-country) M/W, skiing (downhill) M/W, soccer M/W, softball W, squash M/W, swimming and diving M/W, tennis M/W, track and field M/W, volleyball W. *Intramural sports:* basketball M/W, football M, ice hockey M/W, rugby M/W, skiing (cross-country) M/W, soccer M/W, softball W, volleyball M/W.

Costs (2007–08) *Comprehensive fee:* $44,660 includes full-time tuition ($35,375), mandatory fees ($225), and room and board ($9060). Part-time tuition: $4420 per course. *College room only:* $4870. Room and board charges vary according to board plan. *Payment plans:* installment, deferred payment. *Waivers:* employees or children of employees.

Financial Aid Of all full-time matriculated undergraduates who enrolled in 2006, 1,648 applied for aid, 1,482 were judged to have need, 747 had their need fully met. 883 Federal Work-Study jobs (averaging $1360). 445 state and other part-time jobs (averaging $1365). In 2006, 274 non-need-based awards were made. *Average percent of need met:* 94%. *Average financial aid package:* $32,471. *Average need-based loan:* $3770. *Average need-based gift aid:* $22,070. *Average non-need-based aid:* $9897. *Average indebtedness upon graduation:* $28,611. *Financial aid deadline:* 2/15.

Applying *Options:* electronic application, early admission, early decision, deferred entrance. *Application fee:* $60. *Required:* essay or personal statement, high school transcript, 2 letters of recommendation. *Recommended:* minimum 2.0 GPA, interview. *Application deadlines:* 2/1 (freshmen), 4/1 (transfers). *Early decision deadline:* 11/15 (for plan 1), 1/15 (for plan 2). *Notification:* 3/31 (freshmen), 5/1 (transfers), 12/15 (early decision plan 1), 2/15 (early decision plan 2).

Freshman Application Contact Ms. Terry Cowdrey, Dean of Admissions and Financial Aid, St. Lawrence University, Payson Hall, Canton, NY 13617-1455. *Phone:* 315-229-5261. *Toll-free phone:* 800-285-1856. *Fax:* 315-229-5818. *E-mail:* admissions@stlawu.edu.

See page 1826 for the College Close-Up.

ST. THOMAS AQUINAS COLLEGE

Sparkill, New York **www.stac.edu/**

- **Independent** comprehensive, founded 1952
- **Suburban** 46-acre campus with easy access to New York City
- **Endowment** $25.7 million
- **Coed** 2,022 undergraduate students, 67% full-time, 54% women, 46% men
- **Moderately difficult** entrance level, 80% of applicants were admitted

Undergraduates 1,359 full-time, 663 part-time. Students come from 13 states and territories, 6 other countries, 27% are from out of state, 6% African American, 3% Asian American or Pacific Islander, 15% Hispanic American, 0.1% Native American, 1% international, 5% transferred in, 41% live on campus. *Retention:* 72% of 2006 full-time freshmen returned.

Freshmen *Admission:* 1,331 applied, 1,067 admitted, 326 enrolled. *Average high school GPA:* 2.64. *Test scores:* SAT critical reading scores over 500: 31%; SAT math scores over 500: 39%; SAT writing scores over 500: 34%; ACT scores over 18: 74%; SAT critical reading scores over 600: 8%; SAT math scores over 600: 11%; SAT writing scores over 600: 7%; ACT scores over 24: 19%; SAT critical reading scores over 700: 1%; SAT math scores over 700: 1%; SAT writing scores over 700: 1%; ACT scores over 30: 2%.

Faculty *Total:* 151, 42% full-time, 50% with terminal degrees. *Student/faculty ratio:* 16:1.

Majors Accounting; applied mathematics; art; art therapy; biology/biological sciences; business administration and management; clinical laboratory science/medical technology; clinical/medical laboratory technology; commercial and advertising art; criminal justice/law enforcement administration; education; elementary education; engineering science; English; finance; fine/studio arts; history; humanities; information science/studies; journalism; kindergarten/preschool education; liberal arts and sciences/liberal studies; marketing/marketing management; mass communication/media; mathematics; modern languages; natural sciences; parks, recreation and leisure; philosophy; pre-medical studies; psychology; religious studies; Romance languages; secondary education; social sciences; Spanish; special education.

Academics *Calendar:* semesters. *Degrees:* associate, bachelor's, master's, and postbachelor's certificates. *Special study options:* academic remediation for entering students, accelerated degree program, adult/continuing education programs, advanced placement credit, double majors, freshman honors college, honors programs, independent study, internships, off-campus study, part-time degree program, services for LD students, study abroad, summer session for credit. *ROTC:* Air Force (c). *Unusual degree programs:* 3-2 engineering with George Washington University, Manhattan College; physical therapy with New York Medical College.

Computers on Campus 200 computers/terminals are available on campus for general student use. Students can access the following: campus intranet, computer help desk, free student e-mail accounts, online (class) grades, online (class) registration, online (class) schedules. Campuswide network is available. Wireless service is available via entire campus.

Student Life *Housing options:* men-only, women-only, disabled students. Campus housing is university owned. Freshman campus housing is guaranteed. *Activities and organizations:* drama/theater group, student-run newspaper, radio station, choral group, Spartan Volunteers, Campus Activities Board, WSTK campus radio, Bowling Club, Laetare Players, national fraternities. *Campus security:* 24-hour emergency response devices and patrols, student patrols, late-night transport/escort service, controlled dormitory access. *Student services:* health clinic, personal/psychological counseling.

Athletics Member NAIA. *Intercollegiate sports:* baseball M (s), basketball M (s)/W (s), cross-country running M (s)/W (s), golf M/W, lacrosse W, soccer M (s)/W (s), softball W (s), tennis M/W, volleyball W (s). *Intramural sports:* basketball M/W, volleyball M/W.

Standardized Tests *Required:* SAT or ACT (for admission). *Required for some:* ACT (for admission).

Costs (2008–09) *Comprehensive fee:* $29,730 includes full-time tuition ($19,500), mandatory fees ($500), and room and board ($9730). Part-time tuition: $630 per credit. *Required fees:* $125 per term part-time. *College room only:* $5260.

Applying *Options:* electronic application, early action, deferred entrance. *Application fee:* $30. *Required:* high school transcript, minimum 2.0 GPA. *Required for some:* 3 letters of recommendation. *Recommended:* essay or personal statement, 2 letters of recommendation, interview. *Application deadlines:* rolling (freshmen), rolling (transfers), 12/15 (early action). *Early decision deadline:* 12/1. *Notification:* 10/1 (freshmen), continuous (transfers), 1/15 (early decision), 1/15 (early action).

Freshman Application Contact Mr. Vincent Crapanzano, Dean of Enrollment Management and Marketing, St. Thomas Aquinas College, 125 Route 340, Sparkill, NY 10976. *Phone:* 845-398-4100. *Toll-free phone:* 800-999-STAC. *Fax:* 845-398-4114. *E-mail:* vcrapanz@stac.edu.

See page 1828 for the College Close-Up.

SARAH LAWRENCE COLLEGE

Bronxville, New York **www.sarahlawrence.edu/**

- **Independent** comprehensive, founded 1926
- **Suburban** 40-acre campus with easy access to New York City
- **Endowment** $72.2 million
- **Coed** 1,383 undergraduate students, 96% full-time, 74% women, 26% men
- **Very difficult** entrance level, 44% of applicants were admitted

At the heart of the Sarah Lawrence learning experience is the seminar and conference system. Every course has two parts: a seminar limited to 15 students and an individual meeting held every two weeks between student and teacher, during which they create a project that extends the seminar material and connects it to the student's academic goals and aspirations. Through dialogue, reading, and research, students work with their teachers to create an individualized education.

Undergraduates 1,328 full-time, 55 part-time. Students come from 47 states and territories, 34 other countries, 77% are from out of state, 4% African American, 5% Asian American or Pacific Islander, 5% Hispanic American, 0.6% Native American, 3% international, 3% transferred in, 86% live on campus. *Retention:* 86% of 2006 full-time freshmen returned.

Freshmen *Admission:* 2,801 applied, 1,236 admitted, 363 enrolled. *Average high school GPA:* 3.6.

Faculty *Total:* 243, 80% full-time. *Student/faculty ratio:* 6:1.

Majors Acting; African-American/Black studies; African studies; American history; American literature; American studies; animal genetics; anthropology; archeology; architectural history and criticism; art; art history, criticism and conservation; Asian history; Asian studies; Asian studies (East); Asian studies (South); astronomy; biological and physical sciences; biology/biological sciences; chemistry; Chinese studies; cinematography and film/video production; classics and languages, literatures and linguistics; comparative literature; computer science; creative writing; dance; dance related; developmental and child psychology; directing and theatrical production; dramatic/theater arts; drawing; early childhood education; ecology; economics; education; elementary education; English; English language and literature related; English literature (British and Commonwealth); environmental studies; European history; European studies; European studies (Central and Eastern); film/cinema studies; fine/studio arts; foreign languages and literatures; French; gay/lesbian studies; geology/earth science; German; history; history and philosophy of science and technology; history related; human development and family studies; humanities; human/medical genetics; interdisciplinary studies; international relations and affairs; Italian; Japanese; jazz/jazz studies; kindergarten/preschool education; Latin; Latin American studies; liberal arts and sciences and humanities related; liberal arts and sciences/liberal studies; literature; marine biology and biological oceanography; mathematics; Middle/Near Eastern and Semitic languages related; modern languages; molecular biology; music; music history, literature, and theory; music performance; music theory and composition; natural sciences; Near and Middle Eastern studies; organic chemistry; painting; philosophy; philosophy and religious studies related; photography; physics; piano and organ; playwriting and screenwriting; political science and government; pre-dentistry studies; pre-law studies; pre-medical studies; pre-veterinary studies; printmaking; psychology; public policy analysis; religious studies; religious studies related; Romance languages; Russian; sculpture; social sciences; social sciences related; sociology; Spanish; urban studies/affairs; violin, viola, guitar and other stringed instruments; visual and performing arts; visual and performing arts related; voice and opera; western civilization; wind/percussion instruments; women's studies.

Academics *Calendar:* semesters. *Degrees:* bachelor's and master's. *Special study options:* adult/continuing education programs, advanced placement credit, double majors, independent study, internships, off-campus study, part-time degree program, services for LD students, student-designed majors, study abroad. *Unusual degree programs:* 3-2 engineering with Columbia University; education.

Computers on Campus 110 computers/terminals and 30 ports are available on campus for general student use. Students can access the following: campus intranet, computer help desk, free student e-mail accounts. Campuswide network is available. 100% of college-owned or -operated housing units are wired for high-speed Internet access. Wireless service is available via classrooms, computer centers, computer labs, libraries, student centers.

Student Life *Housing:* on-campus residence required for freshman year. *Options:* coed, men-only, women-only, cooperative. Campus housing is university owned. Freshman campus housing is guaranteed. *Activities and organizations:* drama/theater group, student-run newspaper, radio station, choral group, APICAD (Asian Pacific Islander Coalition), New Kids on the Block (transfer student group), Harmabe (African Americans), Sarah Lawrence Christian Union, Hillel. *Campus security:* 24-hour emergency response devices and patrols, late-night transport/escort service, controlled dormitory access. *Student services:* health clinic, personal/psychological counseling.

Athletics *Intercollegiate sports:* basketball M, crew M/W, equestrian sports M/W, softball W, swimming and diving W, tennis M/W, volleyball W. *Intramural sports:* cross-country running M, fencing M, softball M/W, squash M/W, tennis M/W, water polo M/W.

Costs (2007–08) *Comprehensive fee:* $50,810 includes full-time tuition ($37,230), mandatory fees ($860), and room and board ($12,720). Full-time tuition and fees vary according to course load. Part-time tuition: $1241 per credit. Part-time tuition and fees vary according to course load. *Required fees:* $430 per term part-time. *College room only:* $8500. Room and board charges vary according to board plan. *Payment plan:* installment. *Waivers:* employees or children of employees.

Financial Aid Of all full-time matriculated undergraduates who enrolled in 2006, 775 applied for aid, 678 were judged to have need, 591 had their need fully met. 550 Federal Work-Study jobs (averaging $1625). 30 state and other part-time jobs (averaging $1519). In 2006, 3 non-need-based awards were made. *Average percent of need met:* 88%. *Average financial aid package:* $27,282. *Average need-based loan:* $3363. *Average need-based gift aid:* $25,400. *Average non-need-based aid:* $13,117. *Average indebtedness upon graduation:* $16,332. *Financial aid deadline:* 2/1.

Applying *Options:* electronic application, early admission, early decision, deferred entrance. *Application fee:* $60. *Required:* essay or personal statement, high school transcript, 3 letters of recommendation. *Recommended:* minimum 3.0 GPA, interview. *Application deadlines:* 1/1 (freshmen), 3/1 (transfers). *Early decision deadline:* 11/15. *Notification:* 4/1 (freshmen), 4/1 (transfers), 12/15 (early decision plan 1), 2/15 (early decision plan 2).

Freshman Application Contact Mr. Stephen M. Schierloh, Acting Dean of Admission, Sarah Lawrence College, 1 Mead Way, Bronxville, NY 10708-5999. *Phone:* 914-395-2510. *Toll-free phone:* 800-888-2858. *Fax:* 914-395-2515. *E-mail:* slcadmit@sarahlawrence.edu.

See page 1830 for the College Close-Up.

SCHOOL OF VISUAL ARTS

New York, New York **www.schoolofvisualarts.edu/**

- **Proprietary** comprehensive, founded 1947
- **Urban** 1-acre campus
- **Endowment** $21.8 million

- **Coed** 3,522 undergraduate students, 93% full-time, 54% women, 46% men
- **Moderately difficult** entrance level, 72% of applicants were admitted

Undergraduates 3,266 full-time, 256 part-time. Students come from 47 states and territories, 45 other countries, 52% are from out of state, 4% African American, 13% Asian American or Pacific Islander, 10% Hispanic American, 0.5% Native American, 13% international, 10% transferred in, 33% live on campus. *Retention:* 84% of 2006 full-time freshmen returned.

Freshmen *Admission:* 2,565 applied, 1,851 admitted, 664 enrolled. *Average high school GPA:* 3.00. *Test scores:* SAT critical reading scores over 500: 61%; SAT math scores over 500: 55%; SAT writing scores over 500: 58%; ACT scores over 18: 88%; SAT critical reading scores over 600: 20%; SAT math scores over 600: 17%; SAT writing scores over 600: 15%; ACT scores over 24: 40%; SAT critical reading scores over 700: 3%; SAT math scores over 700: 2%; SAT writing scores over 700: 2%.

Faculty *Total:* 830, 12% full-time, 45% with terminal degrees. *Student/faculty ratio:* 4:1.

Majors Cinematography and film/video production; commercial and advertising art; commercial photography; design and applied arts related; drawing; film/cinema studies; film/video and photographic arts related; fine/studio arts; graphic design; illustration; interior design; painting; photography; printmaking; sculpture.

Academics *Calendar:* semesters. *Degrees:* bachelor's and master's. *Special study options:* academic remediation for entering students, adult/continuing education programs, advanced placement credit, English as a second language, freshman honors college, honors programs, independent study, internships, services for LD students, study abroad, summer session for credit.

Computers on Campus 600 computers/terminals are available on campus for general student use. Students can access the following: campus intranet, computer help desk, free student e-mail accounts, online (class) grades, online (class) schedules. Campuswide network is available. 100% of college-owned or -operated housing units are wired for high-speed Internet access. Wireless service is available via classrooms, computer centers, computer labs, dorm rooms, libraries, student centers.

Student Life *Housing options:* coed, women-only. Campus housing is university owned, leased by the school and is provided by a third party. Freshman applicants given priority for college housing. *Activities and organizations:* student-run newspaper, radio station, Visual Arts Student Association, Film Club, Korean Christian Organization, Asian Association, Bible study. *Campus security:* 24-hour patrols. *Student services:* health clinic, personal/psychological counseling.

Athletics *Intramural sports:* baseball M/W, softball M/W.

Standardized Tests *Required:* SAT or ACT (for admission).

Costs (2007–08) *Tuition:* $23,520 full-time, $785 per credit part-time. Full-time tuition and fees vary according to program. *Room only:* $11,350. Room and board charges vary according to board plan, gender, housing facility, and location. *Payment plan:* installment. *Waivers:* employees or children of employees.

Financial Aid Of all full-time matriculated undergraduates who enrolled in 2006, 1,881 applied for aid, 1,682 were judged to have need, 40 had their need fully met. 186 Federal Work-Study jobs (averaging $3490). In 2006, 156 non-need-based awards were made. *Average percent of need met:* 42%. *Average financial aid package:* $12,498. *Average need-based loan:* $4031. *Average non-need-based aid:* $6238. *Average indebtedness upon graduation:* $30,600. *Financial aid deadline:* 3/1.

Applying *Options:* electronic application, early action, deferred entrance. *Application fee:* $50. *Required:* essay or personal statement, high school transcript, minimum 2.5 GPA, portfolio. *Recommended:* letters of recommendation, interview. *Application deadlines:* rolling (freshmen), rolling (transfers), 12/1 (early action). *Notification:* continuous (freshmen), continuous (transfers), 1/15 (early action).

Freshman Application Contact Admissions Office, School of Visual Arts, 209 East 23rd Street, New York, NY 10010. *Phone:* 212-592-2100. *Toll-free phone:* 800-436-4204. *Fax:* 212-592-2116. *E-mail:* admissions@sva.edu.

See page 1832 for the College Close-Up.

SH'OR YOSHUV RABBINICAL COLLEGE

Lawrence, New York **www.shoryoshuv.org/**

Director of Admissions Rabbi Avrohom Halpern, Executive Director, Sh'or Yoshuv Rabbinical College, 1284 Central Avenue, Far Rockaway, NY 11691-4002. *Phone:* 718-327-7244.

SIENA COLLEGE

Loudonville, New York **www.siena.edu/**

- **Independent Roman Catholic** 4-year, founded 1937
- **Suburban** 164-acre campus
- **Endowment** $122.0 million
- **Coed** 3,217 undergraduate students, 94% full-time, 55% women, 45% men
- **Moderately difficult** entrance level, 54% of applicants were admitted

Siena develops leaders capable of extraordinary achievement. Siena offers a broad, time-tested liberal arts curriculum. The College's approach is to involve each student as part of its unique community of scholars who are devoted to teaching and empowering the students with competence, compassion, and confidence. The curriculum includes twenty-eight bachelor's degree programs and forty-six minors and certificate programs in business, liberal arts, and sciences. Siena's 166-acre campus is located in Loudonville, New York, minutes from Albany, the state capital.

Undergraduates 3,019 full-time, 198 part-time. Students come from 30 states and territories, 6 other countries, 13% are from out of state, 2% African American, 4% Asian American or Pacific Islander, 4% Hispanic American, 0.1% Native American, 0.5% international, 5% transferred in, 74% live on campus. *Retention:* 87% of 2006 full-time freshmen returned.

Freshmen *Admission:* 5,792 applied, 3,138 admitted, 781 enrolled. *Test scores:* SAT critical reading scores over 500: 81%; SAT math scores over 500: 88%; SAT writing scores over 500: 75%; ACT scores over 18: 99%; SAT critical reading scores over 600: 24%; SAT math scores over 600: 40%; SAT writing scores over 600: 24%; ACT scores over 24: 38%; SAT critical reading scores over 700: 2%; SAT math scores over 700: 5%; SAT writing scores over 700: 3%; ACT scores over 30: 2%.

Faculty *Total:* 317, 59% full-time, 73% with terminal degrees. *Student/faculty ratio:* 13:1.

Majors Accounting; American studies; biology/biological sciences; chemistry; classics and languages, literatures and linguistics; computer and information sciences; ecology; economics; English; finance; fine/studio arts; French; history; marketing/marketing management; mathematics; philosophy; physics; political science and government; pre-dentistry studies; pre-law studies; pre-medical studies; psychology; religious studies; secondary education; social work; sociology; Spanish.

Academics *Calendar:* semesters. *Degree:* certificates and bachelor's. *Special study options:* academic remediation for entering students, accelerated degree program, adult/continuing education programs, advanced placement credit, double majors, English as a second language, external degree program, honors programs, independent study, internships, off-campus study, part-time degree program, services for LD students, study abroad, summer session for credit. *ROTC:* Army (b), Air Force (c). *Unusual degree programs:* 3-2 engineering with Clarkson University, Manhattan College, Catholic University of America, Western New England College, Rensselaer Polytechnic Institute, State University of New York at Binghamton; forestry with State University of New York College of Environmental Science and Forestry; Pace University Law School, Western New England College of Law.

Computers on Campus 462 computers/terminals are available on campus for general student use. Students can access the following: online (class) registration. Campuswide network is available. 100% of college-owned or -operated housing units are wired for high-speed Internet access. Wireless service is available via classrooms, computer labs, dorm rooms, libraries.

Student Life *Housing:* on-campus residence required through senior year. *Options:* coed, disabled students. Campus housing is university owned. Freshman applicants given priority for college housing. *Activities and organizations:* drama/theater group, student-run newspaper, radio and television station, Student Senate, Student Events Board, Big Brothers/Big Sisters, Gaelic Society, Outing Club. *Campus security:* 24-hour emergency response devices and patrols, late-night transport/escort service, controlled dormitory access, call boxes in parking lots and on roadways. *Student services:* health clinic, personal/psychological counseling, women's center.

Athletics Member NCAA. All Division I. *Intercollegiate sports:* baseball M (s), basketball M (s)/W (s), cheerleading W (c), crew M (c)/W (c), cross-country running M/W, equestrian sports M (c)/W (c), field hockey W, golf M/W, ice hockey M (c), lacrosse M/W, rugby M (c)/W (c), soccer M (s)/W (s), softball W (s), swimming and diving W (s), tennis M (s)/W (s), track and field M (c)/W (c), volleyball M (c)/W (s), water polo W (s). *Intramural sports:* basketball M/W, bowling M/W, cheerleading W, golf M/W, racquetball M/W, soccer M/W, softball M/W, volleyball M/W.

Standardized Tests *Required:* SAT or ACT (for admission).

Costs (2007–08) *Comprehensive fee:* $31,560 includes full-time tuition ($22,510), mandatory fees ($175), and room and board ($8875). Part-time tuition: $450 per credit hour. *Required fees:* $60 per term part-time. *College room only:* $5500. Room and board charges vary according to board plan and housing facility. *Payment plan:* installment. *Waivers:* senior citizens and employees or children of employees.

Financial Aid Of all full-time matriculated undergraduates who enrolled in 2002, 2,359 applied for aid, 1,960 were judged to have need, 328 had their need fully met. 391 Federal Work-Study jobs (averaging $675). In 2002, 365 non-need-based awards were made. *Average percent of need met:* 80%. *Average financial aid package:* $12,655. *Average need-based loan:* $4192. *Average need-based gift aid:* $9030. *Average non-need-based aid:* $5581. *Average indebtedness upon graduation:* $12,700.

Applying *Options:* electronic application, early admission, early decision, early action, deferred entrance. *Application fee:* $50. *Required:* essay or personal statement, high school transcript, 1 letter of recommendation. *Required for some:* interview. *Recommended:* interview. *Application deadlines:* 3/1 (freshmen), 8/15 (transfers), 12/1 (early action). *Early decision deadline:* 12/1. *Notification:* 3/15 (freshmen), continuous (transfers), 12/15 (early decision), 1/1 (early action).

Freshman Application Contact Ms. Heather Renault, Director of Admissions, Siena College, 515 Loudon Road, Loudonville, NY 12211-1462. *Phone:* 518-783-2426. *Toll-free phone:* 888-AT-SIENA. *Fax:* 518-783-2436. *E-mail:* admit@siena.edu.

See page 1834 for the College Close-Up.

SKIDMORE COLLEGE

Saratoga Springs, New York — www.skidmore.edu/

- **Independent** comprehensive, founded 1903
- **Small-town** 800-acre campus with easy access to Albany
- **Endowment** $287.0 million
- **Coed** 2,809 undergraduate students, 93% full-time, 60% women, 40% men
- **Very difficult** entrance level, 37% of applicants were admitted

Undergraduates 2,612 full-time, 197 part-time. Students come from 44 states and territories, 41 other countries, 65% are from out of state, 4% African American, 7% Asian American or Pacific Islander, 5% Hispanic American, 0.5% Native American, 3% international, 1% transferred in, 85% live on campus. *Retention:* 94% of 2006 full-time freshmen returned.

Freshmen *Admission:* 6,768 applied, 2,479 admitted, 682 enrolled. *Average high school GPA:* 3.33. *Test scores:* SAT critical reading scores over 500: 93%; SAT math scores over 500: 96%; SAT writing scores over 500: 94%; ACT scores over 18: 100%; SAT critical reading scores over 600: 68%; SAT math scores over 600: 65%; SAT writing scores over 600: 71%; ACT scores over 24: 89%; SAT critical reading scores over 700: 19%; SAT math scores over 700: 14%; SAT writing scores over 700: 21%; ACT scores over 30: 26%.

Faculty *Total:* 344, 67% full-time, 68% with terminal degrees. *Student/faculty ratio:* 9:1.

Majors American studies; anthropology; area, ethnic, cultural, and gender studies related; art; art history, criticism and conservation; Asian studies; biology/biological sciences; business/commerce; business, management, and marketing related; chemistry; classics and languages, literatures and linguistics; computer and information sciences; dance; dramatic/theater arts; economics; elementary education; English; English language and literature related; environmental studies; fine arts related; French; French studies; geology/earth science; German; history; international relations and affairs; kinesiology and exercise science; Latin American studies; law and legal studies related; liberal arts and sciences/liberal studies; mathematics; music history, literature, and theory; neuroscience; philosophy; physics; political science and government; psychology; religious studies; social sciences related; social work; sociology; Spanish; women's studies.

Academics *Calendar:* semesters plus optional 6-week internship period. *Degrees:* bachelor's and master's. *Special study options:* accelerated degree program, adult/continuing education programs, advanced placement credit, distance learning, double majors, external degree program, honors programs, independent study, internships, off-campus study, student-designed majors, study abroad, summer session for credit. *ROTC:* Army (c), Air Force (c). *Unusual degree programs:* 3-2 business administration with Clarkson University; engineering with Dartmouth College, Clarkson University.

Computers on Campus 230 computers/terminals and 600 ports are available on campus for general student use. Students can access the following: campus intranet, computer help desk, free student e-mail accounts, online (class) grades, online (class) registration, online (class) schedules. Campuswide network is available. 100% of college-owned or -operated housing units are wired for high-speed Internet access. Wireless service is available via classrooms, computer centers, computer labs, learning centers, libraries, student centers.

Student Life *Housing:* on-campus residence required through sophomore year. *Options:* coed, men-only, women-only, disabled students. Campus housing is university owned. Freshman campus housing is guaranteed. *Activities and organizations:* drama/theater group, student-run newspaper, radio and television station, choral group, Student Government Association, student radio station, Student Volunteer Bureau, Outing Club, Skidmore News. *Campus security:* 24-hour emergency response devices and patrols, late-night transport/escort service, controlled dormitory access, well-lit campus. *Student services:* health clinic, personal/psychological counseling.

Athletics Member NCAA. All Division III. *Intercollegiate sports:* baseball M, basketball M/W, crew M/W, equestrian sports W, field hockey W, golf M, ice hockey M, lacrosse M/W, soccer M/W, softball W, swimming and diving M/W, tennis M/W, volleyball W. *Intramural sports:* basketball M/W, football M, ice hockey M (c)/W (c), racquetball M/W, skiing (downhill) M (c)/W (c), soccer M/W, tennis M/W, ultimate Frisbee M (c)/W (c), volleyball M/W.

Standardized Tests *Required:* SAT or ACT (for admission). *Recommended:* SAT Subject Tests (for admission).

Costs (2007–08) *Comprehensive fee:* $46,696 includes full-time tuition ($36,126), mandatory fees ($734), and room and board ($9836). Full-time tuition and fees vary according to course load. Part-time tuition: $1205 per credit hour. Part-time tuition and fees vary according to course load. *Required fees:* $25 per term part-time. *College room only:* $5816. Room and board charges vary according to board plan and housing facility. *Payment plans:* tuition prepayment, installment. *Waivers:* senior citizens and employees or children of employees.

Financial Aid Of all full-time matriculated undergraduates who enrolled in 2007, 1,182 applied for aid, 1,050 were judged to have need, 900 had their need fully met. 500 Federal Work-Study jobs (averaging $1080). 650 state and other part-time jobs (averaging $800). In 2007, 9 non-need-based awards were made. *Average percent of need met:* 94%. *Average financial aid package:* $27,280. *Average need-based loan:* $3531. *Average need-based gift aid:* $22,810. *Average non-need-based aid:* $10,000. *Average indebtedness upon graduation:* $16,078. *Financial aid deadline:* 1/15.

Applying *Options:* electronic application, early admission, early decision, deferred entrance. *Application fee:* $60. *Required:* essay or personal statement, high school transcript, 2 letters of recommendation. *Recommended:* interview. *Application deadlines:* 1/15 (freshmen), 4/1 (transfers). *Early decision deadline:* 11/15 (for plan 1), 1/15 (for plan 2). *Notification:* 4/1 (freshmen), 12/15 (early decision plan 1), 2/15 (early decision plan 2).

Freshman Application Contact Ms. Mary Lou Bates, Dean of Admissions and Financial Aid, Skidmore College, 815 North Broadway, Saratoga Springs, NY 12866-1632. *Phone:* 518-580-5570. *Toll-free phone:* 800-867-6007. *Fax:* 518-580-5584. *E-mail:* admissions@skidmore.edu.

See page 1836 for the College Close-Up.

STATE UNIVERSITY OF NEW YORK AT BINGHAMTON

Binghamton, New York — www.binghamton.edu/

- **State-supported** university, founded 1946, part of State University of New York System
- **Suburban** 930-acre campus
- **Endowment** $39.5 million
- **Coed** 11,515 undergraduate students, 96% full-time, 48% women, 52% men
- **Very difficult** entrance level, 39% of applicants were admitted

Undergraduates 11,042 full-time, 473 part-time. Students come from 41 states and territories, 66 other countries, 7% are from out of state, 5% African American, 13% Asian American or Pacific Islander, 7% Hispanic American, 0.2% Native American, 8% international, 7% transferred in, 57% live on campus. *Retention:* 90% of 2006 full-time freshmen returned.

Freshmen *Admission:* 25,242 applied, 9,799 admitted, 2,304 enrolled. *Average high school GPA:* 3.7. *Test scores:* SAT critical reading scores over 500: 97%; SAT math scores over 500: 100%; ACT scores over 18: 100%; SAT critical reading scores over 600: 63%; SAT math scores over 600: 80%; ACT scores over 24: 89%; SAT critical reading scores over 700: 13%; SAT math scores over 700: 24%; ACT scores over 30: 23%.

Faculty *Total:* 848, 68% full-time. *Student/faculty ratio:* 20:1.

Majors Accounting; African-American/Black studies; ancient/classical Greek; anthropology; Arabic; art; art history, criticism and conservation; Asian-American studies; biochemistry; biology/biological sciences; biomedical/medical engineering; business administration and management; business/commerce; cell and molecular biology; chemistry; cinematography and film/video production; classics and classical languages related; classics and languages, literatures and linguistics; comparative literature; computer and information sciences; computer engineering; computer science; creative writing; dance; design and visual communications; directing and theatrical production; dramatic/theater arts; ecology; economics; electrical, electronics and communications engineering; engineering; English; environmental studies; evolutionary biology; fine/studio arts; French; geography; geology/earth science; geophysics and seismology; German; Hebrew; history; human development and family studies related; industrial engineering; information science/studies; international business/trade/commerce; international/global studies; international relations and affairs; Italian; Jewish/Judaic studies; Latin; Latin American studies; linguistics; management information systems; management science; marketing/marketing management; mathematics; mechanical engineering; medieval and Renaissance studies; multi-/interdisciplinary studies related; music; music history, literature, and theory; music performance; nursing (registered nurse training); philosophy; philosophy related; physics; physics related; physiological psychology/psychobiology; political science and government; pre-law studies; pre-medical studies; psychology; sculpture; social sciences; sociology; Spanish; systems engineering; theater design and technology; visual and performing arts.

Academics *Calendar:* semesters. *Degrees:* bachelor's, master's, doctoral, and post-master's certificates. *Special study options:* academic remediation for entering students, accelerated degree program, adult/continuing education programs, advanced placement credit, distance learning, double majors, English as a second language, honors programs, independent study, internships, off-campus study, part-time degree program, services for LD students, student-designed majors, study abroad, summer session for credit. *ROTC:* Air Force (c). *Unusual degree programs:* 3-2 business administration with Harpur College, SUNY Oneonta, SUNY Fredonia; engineering; management, engineering and physics with Columbia University, Clarkson University, Rochester Institute of Technology, State University of New York at Buffalo, State University of New York at Stony Brook, University of Rochester, chemistry and materials science, biology, computer science.

Computers on Campus 650 computers/terminals are available on campus for general student use. Students can access the following: campus intranet, computer help desk, free student e-mail accounts, online (class) grades, online (class) registration, online (class) schedules, course management system, personal Web space. Campuswide network is available. 100% of college-owned or -operated housing units are wired for high-speed Internet access. Wireless service is available via entire campus.

Student Life *Housing:* on-campus residence required for freshman year. *Options:* coed, disabled students. Campus housing is university owned and is provided by a third party. Freshman campus housing is guaranteed. *Activities and organizations:* drama/theater group, student-run newspaper, radio and television station, choral group, Intramurals, Club sports, Student Association, Cultural organizations, Peer Counseling/Mentoring/Volunteering Program, national fraternities, national sororities. *Campus security:* 24-hour emergency response devices and patrols, student patrols, late-night transport/escort service, controlled dormitory access, safety awareness programs, well-lit campus, self-defense education, secured campus entrance 12 a.m. to 5 a.m. emergency telephones. *Student services:* health clinic, personal/psychological counseling, women's center, legal services.

Athletics Member NCAA. All Division I. *Intercollegiate sports:* baseball M (s), basketball M (s)/W (s), cheerleading M/W, cross-country running M (s)/W (s), golf M (s), lacrosse M (s)/W (s), soccer M (s)/W (s), softball W (s), swimming and diving M (s)/W (s), tennis M (s)/W (s), track and field M (s)/W (s), volleyball W (s), wrestling M (s). *Intramural sports:* badminton M (c)/W (c), baseball M (c), basketball M/W, bowling M/W, crew M (c)/W (c), equestrian sports M (c)/W (c), fencing M (c)/W (c), field hockey M (c)/W (c), golf M (c)/W (c), gymnastics M (c)/W (c), ice hockey M (c)/W (c), lacrosse M (c)/W (c), racquetball M/W, rugby M (c)/W (c), skiing (downhill) M (c)/W (c), soccer M/W, softball M/W, swimming and diving M (c)/W (c), table tennis M/W, tennis M/W, ultimate Frisbee M (c)/W (c), volleyball M/W, water polo M (c)/W (c).

Standardized Tests *Required:* SAT or ACT (for admission).

Costs (2007–08) *Tuition:* state resident $4350 full-time, $181 per credit hour part-time; nonresident $10,610 full-time, $442 per credit hour part-time. *Required fees:* $1662 full-time, $53 per credit hour part-time, $87 per term part-time. *Room and board:* $9188; room only: $5662. Room and board charges vary according to board plan and housing facility. *Payment plan:* installment. *Waivers:* employees or children of employees.

Financial Aid Of all full-time matriculated undergraduates who enrolled in 2007, 7,240 applied for aid, 4,972 were judged to have need, 3,520 had their need fully met. 1,442 Federal Work-Study jobs (averaging $1408). In 2007, 443 non-need-based awards were made. *Average percent of need met:* 79%. *Average financial aid package:* $12,403. *Average need-based loan:* $4583. *Average need-based gift aid:* $5250. *Average non-need-based aid:* $3277. *Average indebtedness upon graduation:* $14,530.

Applying *Options:* electronic application, early admission, early action, deferred entrance. *Application fee:* $40. *Required:* essay or personal statement, high school transcript, letters of recommendation. *Required for some:* 1 letter of recommendation, portfolio, audition. *Application deadlines:* rolling (freshmen), rolling (out-of-state freshmen), rolling (transfers), 11/15 (early action). *Notification:* continuous until 4/1 (freshmen), continuous until 4/1 (out-of-state freshmen), continuous (transfers), 1/1 (early action).

Freshman Application Contact Ms. Cheryl S. Brown, Director of Admissions, State University of New York at Binghamton, PO Box 6001, Binghamton, NY 13902-6001. *Phone:* 607-777-2171. *Fax:* 607-777-4445. *E-mail:* admit@binghamton.edu.

STATE UNIVERSITY OF NEW YORK AT FREDONIA

Fredonia, New York **www.fredonia.edu/**

- **State-supported** comprehensive, founded 1826, part of State University of New York System
- **Small-town** 249-acre campus with easy access to Buffalo
- **Endowment** $17.4 million
- **Coed** 5,085 undergraduate students, 96% full-time, 56% women, 44% men
- **Moderately difficult** entrance level, 56% of applicants were admitted

Undergraduates 4,898 full-time, 187 part-time. Students come from 21 states and territories, 9 other countries, 2% are from out of state, 3% African American, 2% Asian American or Pacific Islander, 3% Hispanic American, 0.7% Native American, 0.1% international, 9% transferred in, 53% live on campus. *Retention:* 85% of 2006 full-time freshmen returned.

Freshmen *Admission:* 5,893 applied, 3,322 admitted, 1,061 enrolled. *Average high school GPA:* 3.4. *Test scores:* SAT critical reading scores over 500: 68%; SAT math scores over 500: 75%; ACT scores over 18: 98%; SAT critical reading scores over 600: 19%; SAT math scores over 600: 22%; ACT scores over 24: 47%; SAT critical reading scores over 700: 1%; SAT math scores over 700: 1%; ACT scores over 30: 4%.

Faculty *Total:* 446, 53% full-time, 49% with terminal degrees. *Student/faculty ratio:* 16:1.

Majors Accounting; American studies; applied art; art; art history, criticism and conservation; arts management; audio engineering; audiology and speech-language pathology; biochemistry; biological and physical sciences; biology/biological sciences; biology/biotechnology laboratory technician; biomedical sciences; broadcast journalism; business administration and management; chemistry; clinical laboratory science/medical technology; commercial and advertising art; communication disorders; computer graphics; computer science; criminal justice/law enforcement administration; dance; dramatic/theater arts; drawing; economics; education; elementary education; English; environmental studies; film/cinema studies; finance; fine/studio arts; French; geochemistry; geology/earth science; geophysics and seismology; gerontology; health/health care administration; history; information science/studies; interdisciplinary studies; intermedia/multimedia; kindergarten/preschool education; labor and industrial relations; legal studies; liberal arts and sciences/liberal studies; marketing/marketing management; mass communication/media; mathematics; music; music history, literature, and theory; music management and merchandising; music teacher education; music therapy; philosophy; physics; piano and organ; political science and government; pre-law studies; pre-medical studies; pre-veterinary studies; psychology; radio and television; science teacher education; secondary education; social work; sociology; Spanish; speech therapy; violin, viola, guitar and other stringed instruments; voice and opera; wind/percussion instruments; women's studies.

Academics *Calendar:* semesters. *Degrees:* bachelor's and master's. *Special study options:* accelerated degree program, adult/continuing education programs, advanced placement credit, distance learning, double majors, honors programs, independent study, internships, off-campus study, part-time degree program, services for LD students, student-designed majors, study abroad, summer session for credit. *Unusual degree programs:* 3-2 business administration with Clarkson University, State University of New York at Buffalo, University of Pittsburgh; engineering with Clarkson University, State University of New York at Buffalo, Case Western Reserve, Columbia University, Cornell University, Louisiana Technical University, New York State College of Ceramics at Alfred, Ohio State University.

Computers on Campus 500 computers/terminals are available on campus for general student use. Students can access the following: campus intranet, computer help desk, free student e-mail accounts, online (class) registration. Campuswide network is available. 100% of college-owned or -operated housing units are wired for high-speed Internet access. Wireless service is available via classrooms, computer centers, computer labs, learning centers, libraries, student centers.

Student Life *Housing:* on-campus residence required through sophomore year. *Options:* coed, men-only, women-only. Campus housing is university owned.

Freshman campus housing is guaranteed. *Activities and organizations:* drama/theater group, student-run newspaper, radio and television station, choral group, Student Association, Undergraduate Alumni Council, Communication Club, Ethnic Organizations, national fraternities, national sororities. *Campus security:* 24-hour emergency response devices and patrols, late-night transport/escort service, controlled dormitory access. *Student services:* health clinic, personal/psychological counseling, legal services.

Athletics Member NCAA. All Division III. *Intercollegiate sports:* baseball M, basketball M/W, cheerleading M/W, cross-country running M/W, field hockey M (c)/W (c), ice hockey M, lacrosse W, soccer M/W, softball W, swimming and diving M/W, tennis M/W, track and field M/W, volleyball M/W. *Intramural sports:* basketball M/W, cross-country running M/W, field hockey W, football M, golf M, lacrosse M, racquetball M/W, rock climbing M/W, rugby M (c)/W (c), skiing (cross-country) M/W, skiing (downhill) M/W, soccer M/W, softball W, squash M/W, table tennis M/W, tennis M/W, ultimate Frisbee M/W, volleyball M (c)/W, water polo M/W.

Standardized Tests *Required:* SAT or ACT (for admission).

Costs (2007–08) *Tuition:* state resident $4350 full-time, $228 per credit hour part-time; nonresident $10,610 full-time, $489 per credit hour part-time. *Required fees:* $1192 full-time, $47 per credit hour part-time. *Room and board:* $8380; room only: $5050. Room and board charges vary according to board plan and housing facility. *Payment plan:* installment.

Financial Aid Of all full-time matriculated undergraduates who enrolled in 2006, 4,091 applied for aid, 3,006 were judged to have need, 892 had their need fully met. In 2006, 266 non-need-based awards were made. *Average percent of need met:* 70%. *Average financial aid package:* $7346. *Average need-based loan:* $4284. *Average need-based gift aid:* $2978. *Average non-need-based aid:* $5236. *Average indebtedness upon graduation:* $23,435.

Applying *Options:* electronic application, early admission, early decision, deferred entrance. *Application fee:* $40. *Required:* high school transcript, minimum 2.5 GPA. *Required for some:* essay or personal statement, interview, audition for music and theater programs, portfolio for art and media arts program. *Recommended:* letters of recommendation. *Application deadlines:* rolling (freshmen), rolling (transfers). *Early decision deadline:* 11/1. *Notification:* continuous (freshmen), continuous (transfers), 12/1 (early decision).

Freshman Application Contact Office of Admissions, State University of New York at Fredonia, Fredonia, NY 14063-1136. *Phone:* 716-673-3251. *Toll-free phone:* 800-252-1212. *Fax:* 716-673-3249. *E-mail:* admissions.office@fredonia.edu.

See page 1838 for the College Close-Up.

STATE UNIVERSITY OF NEW YORK AT NEW PALTZ

New Paltz, New York **www.newpaltz.edu/**

- **State-supported** comprehensive, founded 1828, part of State University of New York System
- **Small-town** 216-acre campus
- **Endowment** $7.4 million
- **Coed** 6,224 undergraduate students, 86% full-time, 68% women, 32% men
- **Very difficult** entrance level, 36% of applicants were admitted

Undergraduates 5,364 full-time, 860 part-time. Students come from 32 states and territories, 36 other countries, 4% are from out of state, 7% African American, 3% Asian American or Pacific Islander, 10% Hispanic American, 0.3% Native American, 2% international, 14% transferred in, 48% live on campus. *Retention:* 83% of 2006 full-time freshmen returned.

Freshmen *Admission:* 12,543 applied, 4,526 admitted, 943 enrolled. *Average high school GPA:* 3.3. *Test scores:* SAT critical reading scores over 500: 83%; SAT math scores over 500: 79%; SAT critical reading scores over 600: 26%; SAT math scores over 600: 29%; SAT critical reading scores over 700: 2%; SAT math scores over 700: 2%.

Faculty *Total:* 712, 45% full-time, 40% with terminal degrees. *Student/faculty ratio:* 14:1.

Majors Accounting; African-American/Black studies; anthropology; art; art history, criticism and conservation; art teacher education; Asian studies; biology/biological sciences; business administration and management; business/managerial economics; ceramic arts and ceramics; chemistry; commercial and advertising art; communication/speech communication and rhetoric; computer and information sciences; computer engineering; creative writing; dramatic/theater arts; economics; education; electrical, electronics and communications engineering; elementary education; engineering physics; English; environmental studies; finance; French; geography; geology/earth science; German; history; international business/trade/commerce; international economics; international relations and affairs; journalism; Latin American studies; marketing/marketing management; mathematics; metal and jewelry arts; music; music therapy; nursing (registered nurse training); painting; philosophy; photography; physics; political science and government; printmaking; psychology; sculpture; secondary education; sociology; Spanish; special education; special education (specific learning disabilities); speech and rhetoric; theater design and technology; women's studies.

Academics *Calendar:* semesters. *Degrees:* bachelor's, master's, and post-master's certificates. *Special study options:* academic remediation for entering students, adult/continuing education programs, advanced placement credit, cooperative education, distance learning, double majors, English as a second language, honors programs, independent study, internships, off-campus study, part-time degree program, services for LD students, student-designed majors, study abroad, summer session for credit. *Unusual degree programs:* 3-2 forestry with State University of New York College of Environmental Science and Forestry.

Computers on Campus 600 computers/terminals are available on campus for general student use. Students can access the following: campus intranet, computer help desk, free student e-mail accounts, online (class) grades, online (class) registration, online (class) schedules. Campuswide network is available. 100% of college-owned or -operated housing units are wired for high-speed Internet access. Wireless service is available via classrooms, libraries, student centers.

Student Life *Housing:* on-campus residence required for freshman year. *Options:* disabled students. Campus housing is university owned. Freshman campus housing is guaranteed. *Activities and organizations:* drama/theater group, student-run newspaper, radio and television station, choral group, Outing Club, intramurals, Residence Hall Student Association, Student Art Alliance, national fraternities, national sororities. *Campus security:* 24-hour emergency response devices and patrols, late-night transport/escort service, controlled dormitory access, safety seminars, RAD Women's Self Defense. *Student services:* health clinic, personal/psychological counseling, legal services.

Athletics Member NCAA. All Division III. *Intercollegiate sports:* baseball M, basketball M/W, cheerleading W (c), cross-country running M/W, equestrian sports W (c), fencing M (c)/W (c), field hockey W, ice hockey M (c), lacrosse M (c)/W, rugby M (c)/W (c), soccer M/W, softball W, swimming and diving M/W, tennis W, volleyball M/W. *Intramural sports:* basketball M/W, golf M/W, racquetball M/W, softball M/W, tennis M/W, track and field M/W, ultimate Frisbee M/W, volleyball M/W.

Standardized Tests *Required:* SAT or ACT (for admission).

Costs (2007–08) *Tuition:* state resident $4350 full-time, $181 per credit part-time; nonresident $10,610 full-time, $442 per credit part-time. *Required fees:* $1040 full-time, $30 per credit part-time, $153 per term part-time. *Room and board:* $8070; room only: $5200. Room and board charges vary according to board plan. *Payment plan:* installment.

Financial Aid Of all full-time matriculated undergraduates who enrolled in 2006, 4,234 applied for aid, 2,910 were judged to have need, 656 had their need fully met. 1,250 Federal Work-Study jobs (averaging $900). 500 state and other part-time jobs (averaging $1250). In 2006, 162 non-need-based awards were made. *Average percent of need met:* 66%. *Average financial aid package:* $2419. *Average need-based loan:* $956. *Average need-based gift aid:* $2360. *Average non-need-based aid:* $1744. *Average indebtedness upon graduation:* $19,500.

Applying *Options:* electronic application, early admission, early action, deferred entrance. *Application fee:* $40. *Required:* high school transcript. *Required for some:* portfolio for art program, audition for music and theater programs. *Recommended:* minimum 3.4 GPA. *Application deadlines:* 4/1 (freshmen), 4/1 (transfers), 11/15 (early action). *Notification:* continuous (freshmen), 12/15 (early action).

Freshman Application Contact Ms. Kimberly A. Strano, Director of Freshmen Admissions, State University of New York at New Paltz, 75 South Manheim Boulevard, Suite 1, New Paltz, NY 12561-2499. *Phone:* 845-257-3200. *Toll-free phone:* 888-639-7589. *Fax:* 845-257-3209. *E-mail:* admissions@newpaltz.edu.

STATE UNIVERSITY OF NEW YORK AT OSWEGO

Oswego, New York **www.oswego.edu/**

- **State-supported** comprehensive, founded 1861, part of State University of New York System
- **Small-town** 696-acre campus with easy access to Syracuse
- **Endowment** $8.7 million
- **Coed** 7,680 undergraduate students, 86% full-time, 55% women, 45% men
- **Moderately difficult** entrance level, 50% of applicants were admitted

Undergraduates 6,570 full-time, 1,110 part-time. Students come from 28 states and territories, 12 other countries, 2% are from out of state, 4% African American, 2% Asian American or Pacific Islander, 4% Hispanic American, 0.5%

Native American, 1% international, 9% transferred in, 58% live on campus. *Retention:* 78% of 2006 full-time freshmen returned.

Freshmen *Admission:* 9,400 applied, 4,700 admitted, 1,400 enrolled. *Average high school GPA:* 3.29. *Test scores:* SAT critical reading scores over 500: 76%; SAT math scores over 500: 83%; ACT scores over 18: 100%; SAT critical reading scores over 600: 18%; SAT math scores over 600: 21%; ACT scores over 24: 40%; SAT critical reading scores over 700: 2%; SAT math scores over 700: 1%; ACT scores over 30: 3%.

Faculty *Total:* 509, 61% full-time, 56% with terminal degrees. *Student/faculty ratio:* 18:1.

Majors Accounting; accounting related; agricultural teacher education; American studies; anthropology; applied mathematics; art; atmospheric sciences and meteorology; biology/biological sciences; broadcast journalism; business administration and management; chemistry; cognitive psychology and psycholinguistics; cognitive science; commercial and advertising art; computer science; creative writing; criminal justice/law enforcement administration; dramatic/theater arts; econometrics and quantitative economics; economics; education; elementary education; English; finance; French; geochemistry; geology/earth science; German; health teacher education; history; human development and family studies; human resources management; information science/studies; international economics; international relations and affairs; journalism; linguistics; management science; marketing/marketing management; mass communication/media; mathematics; music; philosophy; philosophy and religious studies related; physics; political science and government; pre-dentistry studies; pre-law studies; premedical studies; pre-veterinary studies; psychology; psychology related; public relations/image management; sales and marketing/marketing and distribution teacher education; science teacher education; secondary education; sociology; Spanish; sport and fitness administration/management; technology/industrial arts teacher education; trade and industrial teacher education; women's studies; zoology/animal biology.

Academics *Calendar:* semesters. *Degrees:* bachelor's, master's, and post-master's certificates. *Special study options:* accelerated degree program, adult/continuing education programs, advanced placement credit, cooperative education, distance learning, double majors, English as a second language, freshman honors college, honors programs, independent study, internships, off-campus study, part-time degree program, services for LD students, student-designed majors, study abroad, summer session for credit. *ROTC:* Army (c). *Unusual degree programs:* 3-2 engineering with Clarkson University, Case Western Reserve University, State University of New York at Binghamton.

Computers on Campus 750 computers/terminals are available on campus for general student use. Students can access the following: campus intranet, computer help desk, free student e-mail accounts, online (class) grades, online (class) registration, online (class) schedules. Campuswide network is available. 100% of college-owned or -operated housing units are wired for high-speed Internet access. Wireless service is available via classrooms, computer centers, computer labs, learning centers, libraries, student centers.

Student Life *Housing:* on-campus residence required through sophomore year. *Options:* coed, disabled students. Campus housing is university owned. Freshman campus housing is guaranteed. *Activities and organizations:* drama/theater group, student-run newspaper, radio and television station, choral group, club/intramural sports, student radio/television stations, Outing/Recreation Club, student government, programming boards, national fraternities, national sororities. *Campus security:* 24-hour emergency response devices and patrols, controlled dormitory access. *Student services:* health clinic, personal/psychological counseling, women's center, legal services.

Athletics Member NCAA. All Division III. *Intercollegiate sports:* baseball M, basketball M/W, crew M (c)/W (c), cross-country running M/W, field hockey W, golf M, ice hockey M, lacrosse M/W, soccer M/W, softball W, swimming and diving M/W, tennis M/W, track and field M/W, volleyball W, wrestling M. *Intramural sports:* basketball M/W, cheerleading W (c), equestrian sports M (c)/W (c), fencing M (c)/W (c), field hockey W (c), football M/W, golf M/W, ice hockey M (c)/W (c), lacrosse M/W, racquetball M/W, rock climbing M (c)/W (c), sailing M (c)/W (c), skiing (cross-country) M (c)/W (c), skiing (downhill) M (c)/W (c), soccer M/W, softball M/W, swimming and diving M/W, tennis M/W, volleyball M (c)/W, weight lifting M, wrestling M.

Standardized Tests *Required:* SAT or ACT (for admission).

Costs (2008–09) *Tuition:* state resident $4350 full-time, $181 per credit hour part-time; nonresident $10,610 full-time, $442 per credit hour part-time. *Required fees:* $1130 full-time. *Room and board:* $9470; room only: $5890.

Financial Aid Of all full-time matriculated undergraduates who enrolled in 2006, 5,644 applied for aid, 4,240 were judged to have need, 1,802 had their need fully met. 393 Federal Work-Study jobs (averaging $1025). 1,349 state and other part-time jobs (averaging $1084). In 2006, 1246 non-need-based awards were made. *Average percent of need met:* 80%. *Average financial aid package:* $8594. *Average need-based loan:* $4549. *Average need-based gift aid:* $4021. *Average non-need-based aid:* $6120. *Average indebtedness upon graduation:* $21,845.

Applying *Options:* electronic application, early admission, early decision, deferred entrance. *Application fee:* $40. *Required:* high school transcript. *Required for some:* letters of recommendation. *Recommended:* essay or personal statement, interview. *Application deadlines:* rolling (freshmen), rolling (transfers). *Early decision deadline:* 11/15. *Notification:* 1/15 (freshmen), 1/15 (transfers), 12/15 (early decision).

Freshman Application Contact Dr. Joseph Grant, Vice President for Student Affairs and Enrollment, State University of New York at Oswego, 7060 State Route 104, Oswego, NY 13126. *Phone:* 315-312-2250. *Fax:* 315-312-3260. *E-mail:* admiss@oswego.edu.

See page 1840 for the College Close-Up.

STATE UNIVERSITY OF NEW YORK AT PLATTSBURGH

Plattsburgh, New York **www.plattsburgh.edu/**

- **State-supported** comprehensive, founded 1889, part of State University of New York System
- **Small-town** 265-acre campus with easy access to Montreal
- **Endowment** $12.7 million
- **Coed** 5,634 undergraduate students, 94% full-time, 56% women, 44% men
- **Very difficult** entrance level, 46% of applicants were admitted

Undergraduates 5,293 full-time, 341 part-time. Students come from 34 states and territories, 50 other countries, 4% are from out of state, 5% African American, 2% Asian American or Pacific Islander, 4% Hispanic American, 0.5% Native American, 7% international, 11% transferred in, 49% live on campus. *Retention:* 80% of 2006 full-time freshmen returned.

Freshmen *Admission:* 7,136 applied, 3,318 admitted, 975 enrolled. *Average high school GPA:* 3.2. *Test scores:* SAT critical reading scores over 500: 69%; SAT math scores over 500: 76%; ACT scores over 18: 99%; SAT critical reading scores over 600: 19%; SAT math scores over 600: 21%; ACT scores over 24: 39%; SAT critical reading scores over 700: 3%; SAT math scores over 700: 2%; ACT scores over 30: 2%.

Faculty *Total:* 503, 53% full-time, 55% with terminal degrees. *Student/faculty ratio:* 17:1.

Majors Accounting; anthropology; art; art history, criticism and conservation; biochemistry; biology/biological sciences; biology teacher education; broadcast journalism; business administration and management; business, management, and marketing related; business/managerial economics; Canadian studies; chemistry; chemistry teacher education; clinical laboratory science/medical technology; communication disorders; computer science; criminal justice/safety; cytotechnology; dramatic/theater arts; ecology; economics; education; elementary education; English; English/language arts teacher education; entrepreneurship; environmental studies; finance; fine/studio arts; foods, nutrition, and wellness; French; French language teacher education; geography; geology/earth science; history; hotel/motel administration; human development and family studies; international business/trade/commerce; journalism; Latin American studies; liberal arts and sciences/liberal studies; marketing/marketing management; mass communication/media; mathematics; music; nursing (registered nurse training); parks, recreation and leisure; philosophy; physical education teaching and coaching; physics; political science and government; psychology; public relations; radio and television; social work; sociology; Spanish; Spanish language teacher education; special education; women's studies.

Academics *Calendar:* semesters plus 2 5-week summer sessions and 1 winter session. *Degrees:* bachelor's, master's, and post-master's certificates. *Special study options:* academic remediation for entering students, accelerated degree program, adult/continuing education programs, advanced placement credit, cooperative education, distance learning, double majors, English as a second language, honors programs, independent study, internships, off-campus study, part-time degree program, services for LD students, student-designed majors, study abroad, summer session for credit. *Unusual degree programs:* 3-2 engineering with Clarkson University, State University of New York at Stony Brook, Syracuse University, University of Vermont, McGill University, State University of New York at Binghamton; international policy studies with Monterey Institute of International Studies in French and Spanish.

Computers on Campus 308 computers/terminals and 8 ports are available on campus for general student use. Students can access the following: campus intranet, computer help desk, free student e-mail accounts, online (class) grades, online (class) registration, online (class) schedules, online library databases. Campuswide network is available. 100% of college-owned or -operated housing units are wired for high-speed Internet access. Wireless service is available via computer labs, learning centers, libraries, student centers.

Student Life *Housing:* on-campus residence required through sophomore year. *Options:* coed, disabled students. Campus housing is university owned. Freshman campus housing is guaranteed. *Activities and organizations:* drama/theater group, student-run newspaper, radio and television station, choral group, Student Association, Honor societies, Student media organizations, Service/leadership organizations, Intramural and recreational sports, national fraternities, national sororities. *Campus security:* 24-hour emergency response devices and patrols, late-night transport/escort service, controlled dormitory access, enhanced 911 system. *Student services:* health clinic, personal/psychological counseling, women's center, legal services.

Athletics Member NCAA. All Division III. *Intercollegiate sports:* baseball M, basketball M/W, cross-country running M/W, ice hockey M/W, lacrosse M, soccer M/W, softball W, swimming and diving M/W, tennis W, track and field M/W, volleyball W. *Intramural sports:* basketball M/W, ice hockey M (c)/W (c), racquetball M/W, rock climbing M (c)/W (c), softball M/W, tennis W, ultimate Frisbee M (c)/W (c), volleyball M/W.

Standardized Tests *Required:* SAT or ACT (for admission).

Costs (2007–08) *Tuition:* state resident $4350 full-time, $181 per credit hour part-time; nonresident $10,610 full-time, $442 per credit hour part-time. Part-time tuition and fees vary according to course load. *Required fees:* $1066 full-time. *Room and board:* $7970. Room and board charges vary according to board plan. *Payment plans:* installment, deferred payment. *Waivers:* employees or children of employees.

Financial Aid Of all full-time matriculated undergraduates who enrolled in 2007, 4,091 applied for aid, 3,052 were judged to have need, 894 had their need fully met. 300 Federal Work-Study jobs (averaging $2200). In 2007, 1523 non-need-based awards were made. *Average percent of need met:* 87%. *Average financial aid package:* $9985. *Average need-based loan:* $6514. *Average need-based gift aid:* $4543. *Average non-need-based aid:* $5779. *Average indebtedness upon graduation:* $21,855.

Applying *Options:* electronic application, early admission, early decision, deferred entrance. *Application fee:* $40. *Required:* high school transcript, minimum 2.5 GPA. *Required for some:* minimum 3.4 GPA. *Recommended:* essay or personal statement, minimum 3.0 GPA, letters of recommendation, interview. *Application deadlines:* 3/1 (freshmen), rolling (transfers). *Early decision deadline:* 11/15. *Notification:* continuous (freshmen), continuous (transfers), 12/15 (early decision).

Freshman Application Contact Mr. Richard Higgins, Director of Admissions, State University of New York at Plattsburgh, 101 Broad Street, Plattsburgh, NY 12901-2681. *Phone:* 518-564-2040. *Toll-free phone:* 888-673-0012. *Fax:* 518-564-2045. *E-mail:* admissions@plattsburgh.edu.

STATE UNIVERSITY OF NEW YORK COLLEGE AT CORTLAND

Cortland, New York **www.cortland.edu/**

- **State-supported** comprehensive, founded 1868, part of State University of New York System
- **Small-town** 191-acre campus with easy access to Syracuse
- **Endowment** $8.2 million
- **Coed**
- **Moderately difficult** entrance level

Faculty *Student/faculty ratio:* 15:1.

Academics *Calendar:* semesters. *Degrees:* bachelor's, master's, post-master's, and postbachelor's certificates.

Student Life *Campus security:* 24-hour emergency response devices and patrols, late-night transport/escort service.

Athletics Member NCAA. All Division III.

Standardized Tests *Required:* SAT or ACT (for admission).

Costs (2008–09) *Tuition:* state resident $4350 full-time, $181 per credit hour part-time; nonresident $10,610 full-time, $442 per credit hour part-time. *Required fees:* $1089 full-time. *Room and board:* $8760; room only: $5170.

Financial Aid Of all full-time matriculated undergraduates who enrolled in 2004, 4,841 applied for aid, 3,732 were judged to have need, 742 had their need fully met. 609 Federal Work-Study jobs. In 2004, 946 non-need-based awards were made. *Average percent of need met:* 75. *Average financial aid package:* $9372. *Average need-based loan:* $3784. *Average need-based gift aid:* $3550. *Average non-need-based aid:* $6724. *Financial aid deadline:* 3/31.

Applying *Options:* electronic application, early admission, early decision, deferred entrance. *Application fee:* $40. *Required:* essay or personal statement, high school transcript, minimum 2.3 GPA, 1 letter of recommendation. *Recommended:* minimum 3.0 GPA, 3 letters of recommendation, interview.

Freshman Application Contact Mr. Mark Yacavone, Director of Admission, State University of New York College at Cortland, PO Box 2000, Cortland, NY 13045. *Phone:* 607-753-4711. *Fax:* 607-753-5998. *E-mail:* admissions@cortland.edu.

See page 1842 for the College Close-Up.

STATE UNIVERSITY OF NEW YORK COLLEGE AT GENESEO

Geneseo, New York **www.geneseo.edu/**

- **State-supported** comprehensive, founded 1871, part of State University of New York System
- **Small-town** 220-acre campus with easy access to Rochester
- **Endowment** $9.7 million
- **Coed** 5,395 undergraduate students, 98% full-time, 58% women, 42% men
- **Very difficult** entrance level, 36% of applicants were admitted

Undergraduates 5,273 full-time, 122 part-time. Students come from 24 states and territories, 27 other countries, 1% are from out of state, 2% African American, 6% Asian American or Pacific Islander, 3% Hispanic American, 0.4% Native American, 2% international, 7% transferred in, 56% live on campus. *Retention:* 89% of 2006 full-time freshmen returned.

Freshmen *Admission:* 10,274 applied, 3,744 admitted, 1,035 enrolled. *Average high school GPA:* 3.8. *Test scores:* SAT critical reading scores over 500: 99%; SAT math scores over 500: 100%; ACT scores over 18: 100%; SAT critical reading scores over 600: 86%; SAT math scores over 600: 89%; ACT scores over 24: 98%; SAT critical reading scores over 700: 26%; SAT math scores over 700: 22%; ACT scores over 30: 31%.

Faculty *Total:* 329, 74% full-time, 72% with terminal degrees. *Student/faculty ratio:* 19:1.

Majors Accounting; African-American/Black studies; American studies; anthropology; art; art history, criticism and conservation; biochemistry; biology/biological sciences; biophysics; business administration and management; chemistry; communication/speech communication and rhetoric; comparative literature; computer science; dramatic/theater arts; early childhood education; economics; education; elementary education; English; fine/studio arts; French; geochemistry; geography; geology/earth science; geophysics and seismology; history; international relations and affairs; mathematics; music; natural sciences; philosophy; physics; political science and government; pre-dentistry studies; pre-law studies; pre-medical studies; pre-veterinary studies; psychology; sociology; Spanish; special education; special education (early childhood); speech therapy; visual and performing arts related.

Academics *Calendar:* semesters. *Degrees:* bachelor's and master's. *Special study options:* advanced placement credit, double majors, English as a second language, honors programs, independent study, internships, off-campus study, part-time degree program, services for LD students, study abroad, summer session for credit. *ROTC:* Army (c), Air Force (c). *Unusual degree programs:* 3-2 business administration with Pace University, Syracuse University, State University of New York at Buffalo; engineering with Columbia University, Case Western Reserve University, Alfred University, Clarkson University, Syracuse University, The Pennsylvania State University, University of Rochester, SUNY Binghamton, SUNY Buffalo, Rochester Institute of Technology.

Computers on Campus 900 computers/terminals are available on campus for general student use. Students can access the following: online (class) registration. Campuswide network is available. 100% of college-owned or -operated housing units are wired for high-speed Internet access. Wireless service is available via entire campus.

Student Life *Housing:* on-campus residence required through sophomore year. *Options:* coed. Campus housing is university owned. Freshman campus housing is guaranteed. *Activities and organizations:* drama/theater group, student-run newspaper, radio and television station, choral group, national fraternities, national sororities. *Campus security:* 24-hour emergency response devices and patrols, student patrols, late-night transport/escort service, controlled dormitory access. *Student services:* health clinic, personal/psychological counseling, women's center, legal services.

Athletics Member NCAA. All Division III. *Intercollegiate sports:* basketball M/W, cheerleading M (c)/W (c), crew M (c)/W (c), cross-country running M/W, equestrian sports M/W, field hockey W, ice hockey M, lacrosse M/W, rugby M (c)/W (c), skiing (downhill) M (c)/W (c), soccer M/W, softball W, swimming and diving M/W, tennis W, track and field M/W, ultimate Frisbee M (c)/W (c), volleyball M (c)/W. *Intramural sports:* badminton M/W, basketball M/W, football M/W, golf M/W, racquetball M/W, rock climbing M/W, skiing (downhill) M/W, soccer M/W, softball M/W, squash M/W, table tennis M/W, tennis M/W, ultimate Frisbee M/W, volleyball M/W.

Standardized Tests *Required:* SAT or ACT (for admission).

Costs (2007–08) *Tuition:* state resident $4350 full-time, $181 per credit hour part-time; nonresident $10,610 full-time, $442 per credit hour part-time. Part-time tuition and fees vary according to course load. *Required fees:* $1266 full-time, $53 per credit hour part-time. *Room and board:* $8550. Room and board charges vary according to board plan and housing facility. *Payment plans:* installment, deferred payment.

Financial Aid Of all full-time matriculated undergraduates who enrolled in 2007, 3,851 applied for aid, 2,257 were judged to have need, 1,920 had their need fully met. 372 Federal Work-Study jobs (averaging $1381). In 2007, 231 non-need-based awards were made. *Average percent of need met:* 85%. *Average financial aid package:* $7786. *Average need-based loan:* $4687. *Average need-based gift aid:* $3436. *Average non-need-based aid:* $2203. *Average indebtedness upon graduation:* $18,300. *Financial aid deadline:* 2/15.

Applying *Options:* electronic application, early admission, early decision, deferred entrance. *Application fee:* $40. *Required:* essay or personal statement, high school transcript. *Recommended:* minimum 3.5 GPA, letters of recommendation, interview. *Application deadlines:* 1/1 (freshmen), 1/1 (transfers). *Early decision deadline:* 11/15. *Notification:* continuous until 3/1 (freshmen), 3/1 (transfers), 12/15 (early decision).

Freshman Application Contact Kris Shay, Director of Admissions, State University of New York College at Geneseo, 1 College Circle, Geneseo, NY 14454-1401. *Phone:* 585-245-5571. *Toll-free phone:* 866-245-5211. *Fax:* 585-245-5550. *E-mail:* admissions@geneseo.edu.

STATE UNIVERSITY OF NEW YORK COLLEGE AT OLD WESTBURY

Old Westbury, New York — www.oldwestbury.edu/

- **State-supported** comprehensive, founded 1965, part of State University of New York System
- **Suburban** 605-acre campus with easy access to New York City
- **Coed** 3,512 undergraduate students, 83% full-time, 57% women, 43% men
- **Moderately difficult** entrance level, 55% of applicants were admitted

Undergraduates 2,920 full-time, 592 part-time. Students come from 11 states and territories, 24 other countries, 1% are from out of state, 30% African American, 6% Asian American or Pacific Islander, 19% Hispanic American, 0.2% Native American, 1% international, 16% transferred in, 28% live on campus. *Retention:* 73% of 2006 full-time freshmen returned.

Freshmen *Admission:* 3,976 applied, 2,185 admitted, 434 enrolled. *Average high school GPA:* 2.7. *Test scores:* SAT critical reading scores over 500: 35%; SAT math scores over 500: 43%; SAT writing scores over 500: 31%; ACT scores over 18: 100%; SAT critical reading scores over 600: 5%; SAT math scores over 600: 7%; SAT writing scores over 600: 4%; ACT scores over 24: 9%; SAT math scores over 700: 1%.

Faculty *Total:* 270, 48% full-time, 49% with terminal degrees. *Student/faculty ratio:* 18:1.

Majors Accounting; American studies; art; bilingual and multilingual education; biochemistry; biology/biological sciences; biology teacher education; business administration and management; chemistry; chemistry teacher education; communication/speech communication and rhetoric; computer and information sciences; computer science; criminology; early childhood education; economics; elementary education; finance; foreign languages and literatures; foreign language teacher education; humanities; information science/studies; labor and industrial relations; literature; management information systems; marketing/marketing management; mathematics; mathematics teacher education; middle school education; philosophy; psychology; public health; religious studies; science teacher education; secondary education; social sciences; social studies teacher education; sociology; Spanish; Spanish language teacher education; special education; visual and performing arts.

Academics *Calendar:* semesters. *Degrees:* certificates, bachelor's, and master's. *Special study options:* academic remediation for entering students, advanced placement credit, distance learning, double majors, English as a second language, honors programs, independent study, internships, off-campus study, part-time degree program, services for LD students, study abroad, summer session for credit. *ROTC:* Army (c), Air Force (c). *Unusual degree programs:* 3-2 engineering with State University of New York at Stony Brook.

Computers on Campus 400 computers/terminals and 700 ports are available on campus for general student use. Students can access the following: online (class) grades, online (class) registration, financial aid, billing information. Campuswide network is available. 100% of college-owned or -operated housing units are wired for high-speed Internet access. Wireless service is available via entire campus.

Student Life *Housing options:* coed. Campus housing is university owned. Freshman campus housing is guaranteed. *Activities and organizations:* drama/theater group, student-run newspaper, radio station, choral group, All the Right Moves, Caribbean Student Association, Aspiring Leaders of Tomorrow, Step Tunes, Peer Counseling, national fraternities, national sororities. *Campus security:* 24-hour emergency response devices and patrols, student patrols, late-night transport/escort service, controlled dormitory access. *Student services:* health clinic, personal/psychological counseling, women's center.

Athletics Member NCAA. All Division III. *Intercollegiate sports:* baseball M, basketball M/W, cross-country running M/W, soccer M, softball W, swimming and diving M/W, volleyball W. *Intramural sports:* badminton M/W, cheerleading W, equestrian sports M/W, football M/W, racquetball M/W, soccer M/W, softball M/W, swimming and diving M/W, tennis M/W, volleyball M/W, weight lifting M/W.

Standardized Tests *Required:* SAT or ACT (for admission).

Costs (2007–08) *Tuition:* state resident $4350 full-time, $181 per credit part-time; nonresident $10,610 full-time, $442 per credit part-time. Part-time tuition and fees vary according to course load. *Required fees:* $827 full-time. *Room and board:* $8800; room only: $6100. Room and board charges vary according to board plan and housing facility. *Payment plan:* installment. *Waivers:* senior citizens.

Financial Aid Of all full-time matriculated undergraduates who enrolled in 2006, 2,105 applied for aid, 2,095 were judged to have need, 2,095 had their need fully met. 245 Federal Work-Study jobs (averaging $751). In 2006, 1 non-need-based awards were made. *Average percent of need met:* 45%. *Average financial aid package:* $6438. *Average need-based loan:* $2294. *Average need-based gift aid:* $4791. *Average non-need-based aid:* $2600. *Average indebtedness upon graduation:* $15,533.

Applying *Options:* electronic application, early admission, early decision, deferred entrance. *Application fee:* $40. *Required:* essay or personal statement, high school transcript. *Required for some:* 2 letters of recommendation, interview. *Application deadlines:* rolling (freshmen), 12/15 (transfers). *Early decision deadline:* 11/1. *Notification:* continuous (freshmen), continuous (transfers), 12/15 (early decision).

Freshman Application Contact State University of New York College at Old Westbury, PO Box 307, Old Westbury, NY 11568. *Phone:* 516-876-3073. *Fax:* 516-876-3307. *E-mail:* enroll@oldwestbury.edu.

STATE UNIVERSITY OF NEW YORK COLLEGE AT ONEONTA

Oneonta, New York — www.oneonta.edu/

- **State-supported** comprehensive, founded 1889, part of State University of New York System
- **Small-town** 250-acre campus
- **Endowment** $32.6 million
- **Coed** 5,688 undergraduate students, 97% full-time, 57% women, 43% men
- **Very difficult** entrance level, 38% of applicants were admitted

The College at Oneonta is a comprehensive public college with studies that include the arts and sciences, elementary and secondary education, business, criminal justice, computer science, music industry, computer art, and prelaw as well as premedicine. An exceptional library, outstanding campuswide computing facilities, and a distinctive student center for volunteering enhance students' intellectual and personal development in a safe, scenic, and convenient campus environment.

Undergraduates 5,541 full-time, 147 part-time. Students come from 18 states and territories, 20 other countries, 2% are from out of state, 3% African American, 2% Asian American or Pacific Islander, 5% Hispanic American, 0.2% Native American, 2% international, 8% transferred in, 57% live on campus. *Retention:* 81% of 2006 full-time freshmen returned.

Freshmen *Admission:* 12,540 applied, 4,767 admitted, 1,194 enrolled. *Average high school GPA:* 3.50. *Test scores:* SAT critical reading scores over 500: 88%; SAT math scores over 500: 93%; ACT scores over 18: 97%; SAT critical reading scores over 600: 23%; SAT math scores over 600: 29%; ACT scores over 24: 74%; SAT critical reading scores over 700: 2%; SAT math scores over 700: 2%; ACT scores over 30: 9%.

Faculty *Total:* 485, 54% full-time, 50% with terminal degrees. *Student/faculty ratio:* 17:1.

Majors Accounting; African-American/Black studies; anthropology; art; art history, criticism and conservation; atmospheric sciences and meteorology; biochemistry; biology/biological sciences; biology/biotechnology laboratory technician; biology teacher education; business/managerial economics; cartography;

chemistry; chemistry teacher education; child development; computer graphics; computer science; consumer services and advocacy; criminal justice/safety; dietetics; dramatic/theater arts; early childhood education; economics; education; elementary education; engineering science; English; English/language arts teacher education; environmental studies; family and consumer sciences/home economics teacher education; family and consumer sciences/human sciences; fashion merchandising; fine/studio arts; foodservice systems administration; French; French language teacher education; geography; geology/earth science; gerontology; Hispanic-American, Puerto Rican, and Mexican-American/Chicano studies; history; human ecology; hydrology and water resources science; interdisciplinary studies; international relations and affairs; liberal arts and sciences/liberal studies; mass communication/media; mathematics; mathematics teacher education; middle school education; music; music management and merchandising; ophthalmic/optometric services; philosophy; physics; physics teacher education; political science and government; pre-dentistry studies; pre-law studies; pre-medical studies; pre-veterinary studies; psychology; reading teacher education; science teacher education; secondary education; social science teacher education; sociology; Spanish; Spanish language teacher education; speech and rhetoric; statistics.

Academics *Calendar:* semesters. *Degrees:* bachelor's, master's, post-master's, and postbachelor's certificates. *Special study options:* academic remediation for entering students, adult/continuing education programs, advanced placement credit, distance learning, double majors, English as a second language, honors programs, independent study, internships, off-campus study, part-time degree program, services for LD students, study abroad, summer session for credit. *Unusual degree programs:* 3-2 business administration with State University of New York at Binghamton, Rochester Institute of Technology, University of Rochester; engineering with Georgia Institute of Technology, State University of New York at Buffalo, Clarkson University; forestry with State University of New York College of Environmental Science and Forestry; nursing with Johns Hopkins University; accounting with State University of New York at Binghamton, fashion with American Intercontinental University in London.

Computers on Campus 700 computers/terminals are available on campus for general student use. Students can access the following: campus intranet, computer help desk, free student e-mail accounts, online (class) grades, online (class) registration, online (class) schedules. Campuswide network is available. 100% of college-owned or -operated housing units are wired for high-speed Internet access. Wireless service is available via entire campus.

Student Life *Housing:* on-campus residence required through sophomore year. *Options:* coed. Campus housing is university owned. Freshman campus housing is guaranteed. *Activities and organizations:* drama/theater group, student-run newspaper, radio and television station, choral group, Center for Social Responsibility and Community, Mask and Hammer, Terpsichorean, student government, WONY radio station, national fraternities, national sororities. *Campus security:* 24-hour emergency response devices and patrols, late-night transport/escort service, controlled dormitory access. *Student services:* health clinic, personal/psychological counseling, women's center.

Athletics Member NCAA. All Division III. *Intercollegiate sports:* baseball M, basketball M/W, cheerleading W (c), cross-country running M/W, fencing M (c)/W (c), field hockey W, ice hockey M (c), lacrosse M/W, rugby M (c)/W (c), soccer M/W, softball W, swimming and diving M/W, tennis M/W, track and field M/W, volleyball M (c)/W, wrestling M. *Intramural sports:* basketball M/W, football M, lacrosse M, skiing (downhill) M/W, soccer M/W, softball M/W, ultimate Frisbee M/W, volleyball M/W.

Standardized Tests *Required:* SAT or ACT (for admission).

Costs (2007–08) *Tuition:* state resident $4350 full-time, $181 per semester hour part-time; nonresident $10,610 full-time, $442 per semester hour part-time. Part-time tuition and fees vary according to course load. *Required fees:* $1100 full-time, $35 per semester hour part-time. *Room and board:* $8306; room only: $4866. Room and board charges vary according to board plan and housing facility. *Payment plan:* installment. *Waivers:* employees or children of employees.

Financial Aid Of all full-time matriculated undergraduates who enrolled in 2007, 4,311 applied for aid, 3,096 were judged to have need, 569 had their need fully met. 351 Federal Work-Study jobs (averaging $1200). In 2007, 1231 non-need-based awards were made. *Average percent of need met:* 63%. *Average financial aid package:* $9856. *Average need-based loan:* $4571. *Average need-based gift aid:* $3840. *Average non-need-based aid:* $5424. *Average indebtedness upon graduation:* $19,967.

Applying *Options:* electronic application, early admission, early action, deferred entrance. *Application fee:* $40. *Required:* essay or personal statement, high school transcript. *Recommended:* minimum 3.0 GPA, 3 letters of recommendation. *Application deadlines:* rolling (freshmen), rolling (transfers), 11/15 (early action). *Notification:* continuous (freshmen), continuous (transfers), 12/15 (early action).

Freshman Application Contact Ms. Karen Brown, Director of Admissions, State University of New York College at Oneonta, Alumni Hall 116, Oneonta, NY 13820-4015. *Phone:* 607-436-2524. *Toll-free phone:* 800-SUNY-123. *Fax:* 607-436-3074. *E-mail:* admissions@oneonta.edu.

See page 1844 for the College Close-Up.

STATE UNIVERSITY OF NEW YORK COLLEGE AT POTSDAM

Potsdam, New York **www.potsdam.edu/**

- **State-supported** comprehensive, founded 1816, part of State University of New York System
- **Small-town** 240-acre campus
- **Endowment** $17.4 million
- **Coed** 3,614 undergraduate students, 96% full-time, 56% women, 44% men
- **Moderately difficult** entrance level, 66% of applicants were admitted

Undergraduates 3,481 full-time, 133 part-time. Students come from 22 states and territories, 31 other countries, 3% are from out of state, 2% African American, 1% Asian American or Pacific Islander, 3% Hispanic American, 1% Native American, 4% international, 9% transferred in, 57% live on campus. *Retention:* 72% of 2006 full-time freshmen returned.

Freshmen *Admission:* 4,112 applied, 2,734 admitted, 841 enrolled. *Average high school GPA:* 3.2. *Test scores:* SAT critical reading scores over 500: 64%; SAT math scores over 500: 68%; ACT scores over 18: 92%; SAT critical reading scores over 600: 20%; SAT math scores over 600: 24%; ACT scores over 24: 28%; SAT critical reading scores over 700: 2%; SAT math scores over 700: 2%; ACT scores over 30: 2%.

Faculty *Total:* 377, 71% full-time, 71% with terminal degrees. *Student/faculty ratio:* 14:1.

Majors Anthropology; archeology; art; art history, criticism and conservation; biochemistry; biology/biological sciences; biology teacher education; business administration and management; business/managerial economics; chemistry; chemistry teacher education; computer and information sciences; criminal justice/safety; dance; dramatic/theater arts; economics; education related; education (specific subject areas) related; elementary education; English; English/language arts teacher education; environmental studies; foreign language teacher education; French; French language teacher education; geology/earth science; health professions related; history; labor and industrial relations; mathematics; mathematics teacher education; multi-/interdisciplinary studies related; music; music management and merchandising; music performance; music teacher education; music theory and composition; philosophy; physics; physics teacher education; political science and government; psychology; science teacher education; social studies teacher education; sociology; Spanish; Spanish language teacher education; speech and rhetoric; visual and performing arts; women's studies.

Academics *Calendar:* semesters. *Degrees:* bachelor's and master's. *Special study options:* advanced placement credit, distance learning, double majors, honors programs, independent study, internships, off-campus study, part-time degree program, services for LD students, student-designed majors, study abroad, summer session for credit. *ROTC:* Army (c), Air Force (c). *Unusual degree programs:* 3-2 engineering with Clarkson University, State University of New York at Binghamton; management, accounting with State University of New York Institute of Technology at Utica/Rome, applied science with State University of New York College of Technology at Canton.

Computers on Campus 690 computers/terminals and 100 ports are available on campus for general student use. Students can access the following: campus intranet, computer help desk, free student e-mail accounts, online (class) grades, online (class) registration, online (class) schedules, online access to financial aid status, unofficial transcripts, billing, meal plan and housing sign ups. Campuswide network is available. 100% of college-owned or -operated housing units are wired for high-speed Internet access. Wireless service is available via classrooms, computer centers, computer labs, learning centers, libraries, student centers.

Student Life *Housing:* on-campus residence required through sophomore year. *Options:* coed, disabled students. Campus housing is university owned. Freshman campus housing is guaranteed. *Activities and organizations:* drama/theater group, student-run newspaper, radio station, choral group, Student Government Association, Crane Student Association, Student Entertainment Services (Programming Board), Black Student Alliance, The Racquette Student Newspaper, national fraternities, national sororities. *Campus security:* 24-hour emergency response devices and patrols, late-night transport/escort service, controlled dormitory access, safety and educational programs, crime prevention program, vehicle jump start, vehicle lock outs. *Student services:* health clinic, personal/psychological counseling, women's center, legal services.

Athletics Member NCAA. All Division III. *Intercollegiate sports:* basketball M/W, cheerleading M/W, cross-country running M/W, equestrian sports W, golf M, ice hockey M/W, lacrosse M/W, rugby W (c), soccer M/W, softball W, swimming and diving M/W, tennis W, track and field M (c)/W (c), volleyball W. *Intramural sports:* archery M (c)/W (c), basketball M/W, cheerleading M (c)/W (c), cross-country running M (c)/W (c), football M, racquetball M/W, soccer M/W, softball M/W, tennis M/W, volleyball M/W, water polo M/W, weight lifting M/W.

Standardized Tests *Required:* SAT or ACT (for admission).

Costs (2007–08) *Tuition:* state resident $4350 full-time, $181 per credit hour part-time; nonresident $10,610 full-time, $442 per credit hour part-time. *Required fees:* $1056 full-time, $48 per credit hour part-time. *Room and board:* $8420; room only: $4920. Room and board charges vary according to board plan and housing facility. *Payment plan:* installment. *Waivers:* minority students and employees or children of employees.

Financial Aid Of all full-time matriculated undergraduates who enrolled in 2007, 2,937 applied for aid, 2,245 were judged to have need, 1,846 had their need fully met. 263 Federal Work-Study jobs (averaging $1200). In 2007, 360 non-need-based awards were made. *Average percent of need met:* 83%. *Average financial aid package:* $12,637. *Average need-based loan:* $4588. *Average need-based gift aid:* $5098. *Average non-need-based aid:* $5391. *Average indebtedness upon graduation:* $18,272. *Financial aid deadline:* 5/1.

Applying *Options:* electronic application, early admission, deferred entrance. *Application fee:* $40. *Required:* high school transcript, minimum 2.5 GPA, audition for music program. *Required for some:* essay or personal statement, letters of recommendation. *Recommended:* interview. *Application deadlines:* rolling (freshmen), rolling (transfers). *Notification:* continuous (freshmen), continuous (transfers).

Freshman Application Contact Mr. Thomas Nesbitt, Director of Admissions, State University of New York College at Potsdam, 44 Pierrepont Avenue, Potsdam, NY 13676. *Phone:* 315-267-2180. *Toll-free phone:* 877-POTSDAM. *Fax:* 315-267-2163. *E-mail:* admissions@potsdam.edu.

STATE UNIVERSITY OF NEW YORK COLLEGE OF AGRICULTURE AND TECHNOLOGY AT COBLESKILL

Cobleskill, New York **www.cobleskill.edu/**

- **State-supported** 4-year, founded 1916, part of State University of New York System
- **Rural** 750-acre campus
- **Endowment** $3.8 million
- **Coed** 2,601 undergraduate students, 95% full-time, 47% women, 53% men
- **Minimally difficult** entrance level, 81% of applicants were admitted

Undergraduates 2,466 full-time, 135 part-time. Students come from 16 states and territories, 16 other countries, 10% are from out of state, 7% African American, 0.9% Asian American or Pacific Islander, 5% Hispanic American, 0.2% Native American, 3% international, 10% transferred in, 76% live on campus. *Retention:* 74% of 2006 full-time freshmen returned.

Freshmen *Admission:* 3,045 applied, 2,478 admitted, 983 enrolled. *Average high school GPA:* 2.3. *Test scores:* SAT critical reading scores over 500: 27%; SAT math scores over 500: 33%; ACT scores over 18: 64%; SAT critical reading scores over 600: 5%; SAT math scores over 600: 5%; ACT scores over 24: 10%; ACT scores over 30: 2%.

Faculty *Total:* 200, 55% full-time, 19% with terminal degrees. *Student/faculty ratio:* 18:1.

Majors Accounting; agribusiness; agricultural animal breeding; agricultural business and management; agricultural mechanization; agriculture; agronomy and crop science; animal sciences; biological and physical sciences; biology/biotechnology laboratory technician; business administration and management; business, management, and marketing related; chemical technology; child care and support services management; clinical/medical laboratory technology; commercial and advertising art; communication/speech communication and rhetoric; computer and information sciences and support services related; computer programming; computer science; computer technology/computer systems technology; culinary arts; dairy science; data processing and data processing technology; diesel mechanics technology; emergency medical technology (EMT paramedic); engineering technology; environmental studies; equestrian studies; family and community services; fish/game management; fishing and fisheries sciences and management; food services technology; horticultural science; hotel/motel administration; humanities; information science/studies; institutional food workers; international business/trade/commerce; kindergarten/preschool education; landscape architecture; landscaping and groundskeeping; liberal arts and sciences/liberal studies; ornamental horticulture; parks, recreation and leisure facilities management; plant nursery management; plant sciences; poultry science; pre-medical studies; social work; telecommunications; tourism and travel services marketing; turf and turfgrass management; wildlife and wildlands science and management.

Academics *Calendar:* semesters. *Degrees:* certificates, associate, and bachelor's. *Special study options:* academic remediation for entering students, adult/continuing education programs, advanced placement credit, cooperative education, distance learning, English as a second language, honors programs, independent study, internships, off-campus study, part-time degree program, services for LD students, study abroad, summer session for credit.

Computers on Campus 255 computers/terminals and 255 ports are available on campus for general student use. Students can access the following: campus intranet, computer help desk, free student e-mail accounts, online (class) grades, online (class) registration, online (class) schedules. Campuswide network is available. 100% of college-owned or -operated housing units are wired for high-speed Internet access. Wireless service is available via classrooms, computer labs, dorm rooms, learning centers, libraries, student centers.

Student Life *Housing:* on-campus residence required for freshman year. *Options:* coed, men-only, women-only, disabled students. Campus housing is university owned. Freshman campus housing is guaranteed. *Activities and organizations:* drama/theater group, student-run newspaper, Orange Key, Post-Secondary Agricultural Students, Xpressions of Kolor, Student Government, Council for Student Activities. *Campus security:* 24-hour emergency response devices and patrols, student patrols, late-night transport/escort service, controlled dormitory access, bicycle patrols. *Student services:* health clinic, personal/psychological counseling.

Athletics Member NJCAA. *Intercollegiate sports:* baseball M, basketball M/W, cross-country running M/W, golf M/W, lacrosse M, soccer M/W, softball W, swimming and diving M/W, tennis M/W, track and field M/W, volleyball W. *Intramural sports:* bowling M/W, football M/W, soccer M/W, softball M/W, volleyball M/W.

Standardized Tests *Required for some:* SAT or ACT (for admission). *Recommended:* SAT or ACT (for admission).

Costs (2007–08) *Tuition:* state resident $4350 full-time, $181 per credit hour part-time; nonresident $10,610 full-time, $442 per credit hour part-time. *Required fees:* $1064 full-time, $12 per credit hour part-time. *Room and board:* $8650; room only: $5160. Room and board charges vary according to board plan. *Payment plan:* installment. *Waivers:* employees or children of employees.

Financial Aid Of all full-time matriculated undergraduates who enrolled in 2006, 2,251 applied for aid, 1,824 were judged to have need, 175 had their need fully met. 190 Federal Work-Study jobs (averaging $1150). *Average percent of need met:* 53%. *Average financial aid package:* $6952. *Average need-based loan:* $3481. *Average need-based gift aid:* $4226. *Average indebtedness upon graduation:* $21,353. *Financial aid deadline:* 3/1.

Applying *Options:* electronic application, early admission, deferred entrance. *Application fee:* $40. *Required:* high school transcript. *Required for some:* essay or personal statement, minimum 2.0 GPA, 3 letters of recommendation, interview. *Recommended:* minimum 1.8 GPA. *Application deadlines:* rolling (freshmen), rolling (transfers). *Notification:* continuous (freshmen), continuous (transfers).

Freshman Application Contact Christopher Tacea, Director of Admissions, State University of New York College of Agriculture and Technology at Cobleskill, Office of Admissions, Cobleskill, NY 12043. *Phone:* 518-255-5525. *Toll-free phone:* 800-295-8988. *Fax:* 518-255-6769. *E-mail:* admissions@cobleskill.edu.

STATE UNIVERSITY OF NEW YORK COLLEGE OF AGRICULTURE AND TECHNOLOGY AT MORRISVILLE

Morrisville, New York **www.morrisville.edu/**

- **State-supported** primarily 2-year, founded 1908, part of State University of New York System
- **Rural** 185-acre campus with easy access to Syracuse
- **Endowment** $1.1 million
- **Coed**
- **Minimally difficult** entrance level

Faculty *Student/faculty ratio:* 13:1.

Academics *Calendar:* semesters. *Degrees:* certificates, associate, and bachelor's.

Student Life *Campus security:* 24-hour emergency response devices and patrols, late-night transport/escort service, controlled dormitory access.

Athletics Member NJCAA.

Standardized Tests *Required for some:* SAT (for admission), SAT or ACT (for admission), TOEFL.

Costs (2007–08) *Tuition:* state resident $4350 full-time, $181 per credit part-time; nonresident $7210 full-time, $300 per credit part-time. *Required fees:* $1303 full-time, $42 per credit part-time. *Room and board:* $7740; room only: $4160.

Financial Aid Of all full-time matriculated undergraduates who enrolled in 2006, 300 Federal Work-Study jobs (averaging $1500).

Applying *Options:* electronic application, early admission, deferred entrance. *Application fee:* $40. *Required:* high school transcript. *Required for some:* essay or personal statement, letters of recommendation. *Recommended:* minimum 2.0 GPA, 2 letters of recommendation, interview.

Director of Admissions Mr. Timothy Williams, Dean of Enrollment Management, State University of New York College of Agriculture and Technology at Morrisville, Box 901, Morrisville, NY 13408. *Phone:* 315-684-6046. *Toll-free phone:* 800-258-0111.

STATE UNIVERSITY OF NEW YORK COLLEGE OF ENVIRONMENTAL SCIENCE AND FORESTRY

Syracuse, New York **www.esf.edu/**

- **State-supported** university, founded 1911, part of State University of New York System
- **Urban** 12-acre campus
- **Endowment** $9.6 million
- **Coed** 1,545 undergraduate students, 91% full-time, 38% women, 62% men
- **Moderately difficult** entrance level, 51% of applicants were admitted

Undergraduates 1,413 full-time, 132 part-time. Students come from 24 states and territories, 6 other countries, 10% are from out of state, 0.8% African American, 3% Asian American or Pacific Islander, 4% Hispanic American, 0.7% Native American, 0.8% international, 13% transferred in, 40% live on campus. *Retention:* 84% of 2006 full-time freshmen returned.

Freshmen *Admission:* 1,349 applied, 685 admitted, 250 enrolled. *Average high school GPA:* 3.75. *Test scores:* SAT critical reading scores over 500: 82%; SAT math scores over 500: 90%; ACT scores over 18: 98%; SAT critical reading scores over 600: 34%; SAT math scores over 600: 41%; ACT scores over 24: 58%; SAT critical reading scores over 700: 4%; SAT math scores over 700: 6%; ACT scores over 30: 5%.

Faculty *Total:* 170, 84% full-time, 89% with terminal degrees. *Student/faculty ratio:* 12:1.

Majors Agricultural/biological engineering and bioengineering; biochemistry; biological and physical sciences; biology/biological sciences; biology teacher education; biotechnology; botany/plant biology; chemical engineering; chemistry; chemistry teacher education; city/urban, community and regional planning; construction engineering; construction management; ecology; entomology; environmental biology; environmental design/architecture; environmental education; environmental/environmental health engineering; environmental studies; fish/game management; fishing and fisheries sciences and management; forest engineering; forest/forest resources management; forestry; forest sciences and biology; hydrology and water resources science; landscape architecture; land use planning and management; natural resources/conservation; natural resources management and policy; parks, recreation and leisure; physical therapy; plant pathology/phytopathology; plant physiology; plant protection and integrated pest management; plant sciences; polymer chemistry; pre-dentistry studies; pre-law studies; pre-medical studies; pre-veterinary studies; science teacher education; water resources engineering; wildlife and wildlands science and management; wildlife biology; wood science and wood products/pulp and paper technology; zoology/animal biology.

Academics *Calendar:* semesters. *Degrees:* associate, bachelor's, master's, doctoral, and postbachelor's certificates. *Special study options:* academic remediation for entering students, accelerated degree program, adult/continuing education programs, advanced placement credit, cooperative education, distance learning, double majors, English as a second language, freshman honors college, honors programs, independent study, internships, off-campus study, part-time degree program, services for LD students, study abroad. *ROTC:* Army (c), Air Force (c). *Unusual degree programs:* 3-2 social work; landscape architecture.

Computers on Campus 150 computers/terminals are available on campus for general student use. Students can access the following: campus intranet, computer help desk, free student e-mail accounts, online (class) grades, online (class) registration, online (class) schedules. Campuswide network is available. 100% of college-owned or -operated housing units are wired for high-speed Internet access. Wireless service is available via classrooms, computer labs, dorm rooms, libraries.

Student Life *Housing:* on-campus residence required for freshman year. *Options:* coed, men-only, women-only, disabled students. Campus housing is university owned and is provided by a third party. Freshman campus housing is guaranteed. *Activities and organizations:* drama/theater group, student-run newspaper, radio station, choral group, marching band, Bob Marshall/Outing Club, Forestry Club, Student Environmental Action Coalition, national fraternities, national sororities. *Campus security:* 24-hour emergency response devices and patrols, late-night transport/escort service, controlled dormitory access. *Student services:* health clinic, personal/psychological counseling, women's center, legal services.

Athletics *Intramural sports:* archery M/W, badminton M/W, baseball M/W, basketball M/W, bowling M/W, crew M/W, cross-country running M/W, equestrian sports M/W, fencing M/W, field hockey W, football M, golf M/W, gymnastics M/W, ice hockey M/W, lacrosse M/W, racquetball M/W, riflery M, rugby M/W, sailing M/W, skiing (cross-country) M/W, skiing (downhill) M/W, soccer M/W, softball M/W, squash M/W, swimming and diving M/W, table tennis M/W, tennis M/W, track and field M/W, ultimate Frisbee M/W, volleyball M/W, weight lifting M/W.

Standardized Tests *Required:* SAT or ACT (for admission).

Costs (2008–09) *Tuition:* state resident $4350 full-time, $181 per credit hour part-time; nonresident $10,610 full-time, $442 per credit hour part-time. *Required fees:* $1325 full-time. *Room and board:* $11,320; room only: $5660.

Financial Aid Of all full-time matriculated undergraduates who enrolled in 2007, 1,182 applied for aid, 868 were judged to have need, 800 had their need fully met. 310 Federal Work-Study jobs (averaging $1129). 120 state and other part-time jobs (averaging $1667). In 2007, 96 non-need-based awards were made. *Average percent of need met:* 100%. *Average financial aid package:* $12,800. *Average need-based loan:* $6500. *Average need-based gift aid:* $5200. *Average non-need-based aid:* $2500. *Average indebtedness upon graduation:* $19,000.

Applying *Options:* electronic application, early admission, early action, deferred entrance. *Application fee:* $40. *Required:* essay or personal statement, high school transcript, minimum 3.3 GPA, supplemental application. *Recommended:* 3 letters of recommendation, interview. *Application deadlines:* 12/1 (freshmen), rolling (transfers), 12/1 (early action). *Notification:* continuous (freshmen), continuous (transfers), 1/2 (early action).

Freshman Application Contact Ms. Susan Sanford, Director of Admissions, State University of New York College of Environmental Science and Forestry, Office of Undergraduate Admissions, 106 Bray Hall, 1 Forestry Lane, Syracuse, NY 13210-2779. *Phone:* 315-470-6600. *Toll-free phone:* 800-777-7373. *Fax:* 315-470-6933. *E-mail:* esfinfo@esf.edu.

See page 1846 for the College Close-Up.

STATE UNIVERSITY OF NEW YORK COLLEGE OF TECHNOLOGY AT ALFRED

Alfred, New York **www.alfredstate.edu/**

- **State-supported** primarily 2-year, founded 1908, part of State University of New York System
- **Rural** 175-acre campus
- **Endowment** $2.6 million
- **Coed**
- **Moderately difficult** entrance level

Faculty *Student/faculty ratio:* 20:1.

Academics *Calendar:* semesters. *Degrees:* certificates, associate, and bachelor's.

Student Life *Campus security:* 24-hour emergency response devices and patrols, late-night transport/escort service, residence hall entrance guards.

Athletics Member NJCAA.

Standardized Tests *Required for some:* SAT or ACT (for admission). *Recommended:* SAT or ACT (for admission).

Costs (2007–08) *Tuition:* state resident $4350 full-time; nonresident $7210 full-time. Full-time tuition and fees vary according to degree level. additional tuition of $3400 for Bachelor's degree. *Required fees:* $1109 full-time. *Room and board:* $8040; room only: $4570. Room and board charges vary according to board plan and housing facility.

Financial Aid Of all full-time matriculated undergraduates who enrolled in 2006, 350 Federal Work-Study jobs (averaging $1100).

Applying *Options:* electronic application, deferred entrance. *Application fee:* $40. *Required:* high school transcript. *Required for some:* minimum 2.0 GPA. *Recommended:* essay or personal statement, letters of recommendation, interview.

Freshman Application Contact Ms. Deborah Goodrich, Director of Admissions, State University of New York College of Technology at Alfred, Huntington Administration Building, 10 Upper College Drive, Alfred, NY 14802. *Phone:*

607-587-4215. *Toll-free phone:* 800-4-ALFRED. *Fax:* 607-587-4299. *E-mail:* admissions@alfredstate.edu.

State University of New York College of Technology at Canton

Canton, New York www.canton.edu/

- **State-supported** primarily 2-year, founded 1906, part of State University of New York System
- **Small-town** 555-acre campus
- **Endowment** $310,031
- **Coed**
- **Minimally difficult** entrance level

Faculty *Student/faculty ratio:* 23:1.

Academics *Calendar:* semesters. *Degrees:* certificates, associate, and bachelor's.

Student Life *Campus security:* 24-hour emergency response devices and patrols, late-night transport/escort service, controlled dormitory access.

Athletics Member NJCAA.

Standardized Tests *Required:* SAT or ACT (for admission). *Recommended:* SAT or ACT (for admission).

Costs (2007–08) *One-time required fee:* $80. *Tuition:* state resident $4350 full-time, $181 per credit hour part-time; nonresident $7210 full-time, $442 per credit hour part-time. Full-time tuition and fees vary according to degree level, location, and program. Part-time tuition and fees vary according to degree level, location, and program. *Required fees:* $1175 full-time, $0 per credit hour part-time, $5 per term part-time. *Room and board:* $8370; room only: $4750. Room and board charges vary according to housing facility. *Payment plans:* installment, deferred payment.

Financial Aid Of all full-time matriculated undergraduates who enrolled in 2006, 200 Federal Work-Study jobs (averaging $1250). 10 state and other part-time jobs (averaging $1000).

Applying *Options:* electronic application, early admission, deferred entrance. *Application fee:* $40. *Required:* high school transcript. *Required for some:* interview. *Recommended:* minimum 2.0 GPA.

Freshman Application Contact Mr. Jonathan Kent, Director of Admissions, State University of New York College of Technology at Canton, 34 Cornell Drive, Canton, NY 13617. *Phone:* 315-386-7123. *Toll-free phone:* 800-388-7123. *Fax:* 315-386-7929. *E-mail:* admissions@canton.edu.

State University of New York College of Technology at Delhi

Delhi, New York www.delhi.edu/

Director of Admissions Mr. Larry Barrett, Dean of Enrollment, State University of New York College of Technology at Delhi, 2 Main Street, Delhi, NY 13753. *Phone:* 607-746-4000 Ext. 4856. *Toll-free phone:* 800-96-DELHI.

State University of New York Downstate Medical Center

Brooklyn, New York www.downstate.edu/

- **State-supported** upper-level, founded 1858, part of State University of New York System
- **Urban** campus
- **Coed** 309 undergraduate students, 63% full-time, 83% women, 17% men
- **Moderately difficult** entrance level

Undergraduates 196 full-time, 113 part-time. 1% are from out of state, 41% African American, 11% Asian American or Pacific Islander, 6% Hispanic American, 50% transferred in.

Faculty *Total:* 981, 85% full-time.

Majors Diagnostic medical sonography and ultrasound technology; health information/medical records administration; nursing (registered nurse training); occupational therapy; physical therapy; physician assistant.

Academics *Calendar:* semesters. *Degrees:* bachelor's, master's, doctoral, first professional, post-master's, and postbachelor's certificates. *Special study options:* accelerated degree program, adult/continuing education programs, advanced placement credit, independent study, internships, off-campus study, part-time degree program, services for LD students, summer session for credit. *Unusual degree programs:* 3-2 nursing.

Computers on Campus 183 computers/terminals are available on campus for general student use. Campuswide network is available.

Student Life *Housing options:* coed. Campus housing is university owned. *Campus security:* late-night transport/escort service. *Student services:* health clinic, personal/psychological counseling.

Costs (2007–08) *Tuition:* state resident $4745 full-time, $181 per credit part-time; nonresident $11,005 full-time, $442 per credit part-time. *Required fees:* $2603 full-time. *Room and board:* $12,816; room only: $8748.

Financial Aid Of all full-time matriculated undergraduates who enrolled in 2005, 302 applied for aid, 302 were judged to have need. 40 Federal Work-Study jobs (averaging $1000). *Average percent of need met:* 50%. *Average financial aid package:* $12,500. *Average need-based loan:* $4186. *Average need-based gift aid:* $2729.

Applying *Application fee:* $30. *Application deadline:* 5/1 (transfers). *Notification:* continuous until 8/31 (transfers).

Application Contact SUNY Downstate Admissions Office, State University of New York Downstate Medical Center, 450 Clarkson Avenue, Box 60, Brooklyn, NY 11203. *Phone:* 718-270-2446. *Fax:* 718-270-7592. *E-mail:* admissions@downstate.edu.

State University of New York Empire State College

Saratoga Springs, New York www.esc.edu/

- **State-supported** comprehensive, founded 1971, part of State University of New York System
- **Small-town** campus
- **Endowment** $13.6 million
- **Coed** 12,197 undergraduate students, 34% full-time, 60% women, 40% men
- **Minimally difficult** entrance level, 77% of applicants were admitted

Empire State College is an international leader in adult higher education. Students design their own individualized associate, bachelor's, and master's degree programs based on their academic and professional goals. Students benefit from flexible, guided independent study; credit earned for learning gained in work and life; and low SUNY tuition. Empire State College, which is accredited by the Middle States Association of Colleges and Schools, has thirty-five locations throughout New York State as well as online and blended learning options.

Undergraduates 4,175 full-time, 8,022 part-time. Students come from 23 states and territories, 10 other countries, 7% are from out of state, 12% African American, 1% Asian American or Pacific Islander, 7% Hispanic American, 0.5% Native American, 6% international, 25% transferred in. *Retention:* 49% of 2006 full-time freshmen returned.

Freshmen *Admission:* 1,749 applied, 1,344 admitted, 733 enrolled.

Faculty *Total:* 1,270, 12% full-time. *Student/faculty ratio:* 10:1.

Majors Art; biological and physical sciences; business administration and management; community organization and advocacy; economics; education; history; human development and family studies; humanities; human services; interdisciplinary studies; labor and industrial relations; mathematics; social sciences.

Academics *Calendar:* continuous. *Degrees:* associate, bachelor's, and master's (branch locations at 7 regional centers with 35 auxiliary units). *Special study options:* adult/continuing education programs, advanced placement credit, cooperative education, distance learning, external degree program, independent study, off-campus study, part-time degree program, services for LD students, student-designed majors.

Computers on Campus 100 computers/terminals are available on campus for general student use. Students can access the following: online (class) registration. Campuswide network is available.

Student Life *Housing:* college housing not available.

Costs (2007–08) *One-time required fee:* $350. *Tuition:* state resident $4350 full-time, $181 per credit part-time; nonresident $10,610 full-time, $442 per credit part-time. Full-time tuition and fees vary according to location and program. Part-time tuition and fees vary according to location and program. *Required fees:* $225 full-time, $7 per credit part-time, $75 per term part-time. *Payment plan:* installment. *Waivers:* adult students.

Applying *Options:* electronic application, early admission. *Required:* essay or personal statement, high school transcript. *Required for some:* interview. *Application deadlines:* rolling (freshmen), rolling (transfers). *Notification:* continuous (transfers).

Freshman Application Contact Ms. Jennifer Riley, Director of Admissions, State University of New York Empire State College, One Union Avenue, Saratoga Springs, NY 12866. *Phone:* 518-587-2100 Ext. 2214. *Toll-free phone:* 800-847-3000. *Fax:* 518-587-9759. *E-mail:* jennifer.riley@esc.edu.

See page 1848 for the College Close-Up.

STATE UNIVERSITY OF NEW YORK INSTITUTE OF TECHNOLOGY

Utica, New York **www.sunyit.edu/**

- **State-supported** comprehensive, founded 1966, part of State University of New York System
- **Suburban** 850-acre campus
- **Endowment** $2.2 million
- **Coed** 2,210 undergraduate students, 64% full-time, 49% women, 51% men
- **Moderately difficult** entrance level, 39% of applicants were admitted

State University of New York Institute of Technology (SUNYIT) offers undergraduate and graduate degree programs in professional studies, technology, and the liberal arts. Distinctive programs include business, computer science, health-related disciplines, psychology and sociology, and the engineering technologies. Highly rated town-house-style residence halls are conducive to living and learning.

Undergraduates 1,412 full-time, 798 part-time. Students come from 17 states and territories, 11 other countries, 2% are from out of state, 8% African American, 3% Asian American or Pacific Islander, 3% Hispanic American, 0.3% Native American, 0.6% international, 30% transferred in, 21% live on campus. *Retention:* 64% of 2006 full-time freshmen returned.

Freshmen *Admission:* 1,610 applied, 628 admitted, 204 enrolled. *Average high school GPA:* 3.3. *Test scores:* SAT critical reading scores over 500: 67%; SAT math scores over 500: 85%; ACT scores over 18: 100%; SAT critical reading scores over 600: 17%; SAT math scores over 600: 29%; ACT scores over 24: 44%; SAT critical reading scores over 700: 1%; SAT math scores over 700: 2%.

Faculty *Total:* 183, 48% full-time, 51% with terminal degrees. *Student/faculty ratio:* 19:1.

Majors Accounting; applied mathematics; business administration and management; civil engineering technology; communication and journalism related; computer and information sciences; computer engineering technology; computer science; criminal justice/safety; electrical, electronic and communications engineering technology; finance; general studies; health/health care administration; health information/medical records administration; industrial technology; information science/studies; mechanical engineering/mechanical technology; nursing (registered nurse training); psychology; sociology.

Academics *Calendar:* semesters. *Degrees:* bachelor's, master's, and post-master's certificates. *Special study options:* academic remediation for entering students, accelerated degree program, advanced placement credit, distance learning, double majors, English as a second language, independent study, internships, part-time degree program, services for LD students, study abroad, summer session for credit. *ROTC:* Army (c), Air Force (c).

Computers on Campus 244 computers/terminals and 144 ports are available on campus for general student use. Students can access the following: campus intranet, computer help desk, free student e-mail accounts, online (class) grades, online (class) registration, online (class) schedules, various other software applications. Campuswide network is available. 100% of college-owned or -operated housing units are wired for high-speed Internet access.

Student Life *Housing:* on-campus residence required for freshman year. *Options:* coed. Campus housing is university owned. Freshman campus housing is guaranteed. *Activities and organizations:* student-run newspaper, radio and television station, SUNYIT Gamers Club, Telecommunications Club, Black & Latino Student Union, American Society of Civil Engineers, Japanese Anime Club. *Campus security:* 24-hour emergency response devices and patrols, student patrols, late-night transport/escort service, controlled dormitory access, closed-circuit TV monitors. *Student services:* health clinic, personal/psychological counseling, legal services.

Athletics Member NCAA. All Division III. *Intercollegiate sports:* baseball M, basketball M/W, bowling M/W, cross-country running W, golf M/W, lacrosse M, soccer M/W, softball W, volleyball W. *Intramural sports:* badminton M/W, basketball M/W, bowling M/W, golf M/W, racquetball M/W, soccer M/W, softball M/W, tennis M/W, volleyball M/W.

Standardized Tests *Required:* SAT or ACT (for admission).

Costs (2007–08) *Tuition:* state resident $4350 full-time, $181 per credit hour part-time; nonresident $10,610 full-time, $442 per credit hour part-time. Full-time tuition and fees vary according to course load. Part-time tuition and fees vary according to course load. *Required fees:* $1055 full-time, $43 per credit hour part-time. *Room and board:* $7950. Room and board charges vary according to board plan. *Payment plans:* installment, deferred payment.

Financial Aid Of all full-time matriculated undergraduates who enrolled in 2006, 1,190 applied for aid, 879 were judged to have need. 99 Federal Work-Study jobs (averaging $1239). In 2006, 249 non-need-based awards were made. *Average need-based loan:* $1808. *Average need-based gift aid:* $2452. *Average non-need-based aid:* $1141.

Applying *Options:* electronic application, early admission, early decision, deferred entrance. *Application fee:* $40. *Required:* essay or personal statement, high school transcript. *Recommended:* letters of recommendation, interview. *Application deadlines:* rolling (freshmen), rolling (transfers). *Early decision deadline:* 11/1. *Notification:* continuous until 1/15 (freshmen), 12/1 (transfers), 12/15 (early decision).

Freshman Application Contact Amy stokes, State University of New York Institute of Technology, PO Box 3050, Utica, NY 13504-3050. *Phone:* 315-792-7500. *Toll-free phone:* 800-SUNYTEC. *Fax:* 315-792-7837. *E-mail:* admissions@sunyit.edu.

See page 1850 for the College Close-Up.

STATE UNIVERSITY OF NEW YORK MARITIME COLLEGE

Throggs Neck, New York **www.sunymaritime.edu/**

- **State-supported** comprehensive, founded 1874, part of State University of New York System
- **Suburban** 56-acre campus
- **Endowment** $1.2 million
- **Coed, primarily men**
- **Moderately difficult** entrance level

Faculty *Student/faculty ratio:* 17:1.

Academics *Calendar:* semesters plus 2-month summer sea term. *Degrees:* associate, bachelor's, and master's.

Student Life *Campus security:* 24-hour emergency response devices and patrols, student patrols, late-night transport/escort service, controlled dormitory access.

Athletics Member NCAA. All Division III.

Standardized Tests *Required:* SAT or ACT (for admission). *Recommended:* SAT Subject Tests (for admission).

Costs (2007–08) *Tuition:* state resident $4350 full-time, $181 per credit part-time; nonresident $10,610 full-time, $442 per credit part-time. *Required fees:* $2200 full-time. *Room and board:* $8919; room only: $5570.

Applying *Options:* electronic application, early admission, early decision, deferred entrance. *Application fee:* $40. *Required:* high school transcript, minimum 2.5 GPA, medical history. *Recommended:* essay or personal statement, 1 letter of recommendation, interview.

Freshman Application Contact Ms. Deirdre Whitman, Vice President of Enrollment and Campus Life, State University of New York Maritime College, 6 Pennyfield Avenue, Throggs Neck, NY 10465. *Phone:* 718-409-7220. *Toll-free phone:* 800-654-1874 (in-state); 800-642-1874 (out-of-state). *Fax:* 718-409-7465. *E-mail:* admissions@sunymaritime.edu.

See page 1852 for the College Close-Up.

STATE UNIVERSITY OF NEW YORK UPSTATE MEDICAL UNIVERSITY

Syracuse, New York **www.upstate.edu/**

- **State-supported** upper-level, founded 1950, part of State University of New York System
- **Urban** 25-acre campus
- **Coed** 264 undergraduate students, 62% full-time, 73% women, 27% men
- **Moderately difficult** entrance level, 25% of applicants were admitted

Undergraduates 163 full-time, 101 part-time. Students come from 11 states and territories, 4 other countries, 7% are from out of state, 6% African American,

4% Asian American or Pacific Islander, 2% Hispanic American, 0.4% Native American, 0.8% international, 100% transferred in, 50% live on campus.

Freshmen *Admission:* 443 applied, 112 admitted.

Faculty *Total:* 633, 69% full-time. *Student/faculty ratio:* 2:1.

Majors Cardiovascular technology; clinical laboratory science/medical technology; cytotechnology; medical radiologic technology; nursing science; perfusion technology; radiologic technology/science; respiratory care therapy.

Academics *Calendar:* semesters. *Degrees:* bachelor's, master's, doctoral, first professional, and post-master's certificates. *Special study options:* advanced placement credit, internships, off-campus study, part-time degree program, services for LD students, summer session for credit.

Computers on Campus 150 computers/terminals are available on campus for general student use. Students can access the following: campus intranet, computer help desk, free student e-mail accounts. Campuswide network is available. 100% of college-owned or -operated housing units are wired for high-speed Internet access. Wireless service is available via classrooms, dorm rooms, libraries.

Student Life *Housing options:* coed. Campus housing is university owned. *Activities and organizations:* Undergraduate Student Council, Diversity in Allied Health. *Campus security:* 24-hour emergency response devices, late-night transport/escort service, controlled dormitory access. *Student services:* health clinic, personal/psychological counseling.

Athletics *Intramural sports:* basketball M/W, football M, golf M/W, racquetball M/W, skiing (cross-country) M/W, skiing (downhill) M/W, softball M, squash M/W, swimming and diving M/W, table tennis M/W, tennis M/W, volleyball M/W, water polo M/W, weight lifting M/W.

Costs (2007–08) *Tuition:* state resident $8700 full-time, $181 per credit part-time; nonresident $21,200 full-time, $422 per credit part-time. *Required fees:* $536 full-time. *Room and board:* $8800; room only: $3200.

Financial Aid Of all full-time matriculated undergraduates who enrolled in 2004, 170 applied for aid, 170 were judged to have need, 167 had their need fully met. *Average percent of need met:* 100%. *Average financial aid package:* $19,250. *Average need-based loan:* $8400. *Average need-based gift aid:* $3200. *Average indebtedness upon graduation:* $9970. *Financial aid deadline:* 4/1.

Applying *Options:* early admission, deferred entrance. *Application fee:* $40. *Application deadline:* rolling (transfers). *Early decision deadline:* 3/15.

Application Contact Ms. Donna L. Vavonese, Associate Director of Admissions, State University of New York Upstate Medical University, Weiskotten Hall, 766 Irving Avenue, Syracuse, NY 13210. *Phone:* 315-464-4570. *Toll-free phone:* 800-736-2171. *Fax:* 315-464-8867. *E-mail:* admiss@upstate.edu.

STONY BROOK UNIVERSITY, STATE UNIVERSITY OF NEW YORK

Stony Brook, New York **www.sunysb.edu/**

- **State-supported** university, founded 1957, part of State University of New York System
- **Small-town** 1100-acre campus with easy access to New York City
- **Endowment** $104.6 million
- **Coed** 15,519 undergraduate students, 92% full-time, 50% women, 50% men
- **Very difficult** entrance level, 43% of applicants were admitted

Since its founding in 1957, Stony Brook University has grown tremendously and is now recognized as one of the world's leading centers of learning and scholarship. With both students and faculty members excited about making new discoveries, Stony Brook is at the forefront of integrating research and education at the undergraduate level and prides itself on the high quality of its academic programs and distinguished faculty.

Undergraduates 14,339 full-time, 1,180 part-time. Students come from 47 states and territories, 87 other countries, 5% are from out of state, 9% African American, 22% Asian American or Pacific Islander, 8% Hispanic American, 0.2% Native American, 6% international, 10% transferred in, 55% live on campus. *Retention:* 89% of 2006 full-time freshmen returned.

Freshmen *Admission:* 24,060 applied, 10,382 admitted, 2,768 enrolled. *Average high school GPA:* 3.6. *Test scores:* SAT critical reading scores over 500: 84%; SAT math scores over 500: 95%; SAT writing scores over 500: 78%; SAT critical reading scores over 600: 37%; SAT math scores over 600: 59%; SAT writing scores over 600: 32%; SAT critical reading scores over 700: 6%; SAT math scores over 700: 13%; SAT writing scores over 700: 4%.

Faculty *Total:* 1,505, 61% full-time. *Student/faculty ratio:* 18:1.

Majors African-American/Black studies; American studies; anthropology; applied mathematics; art history, criticism and conservation; Asian-American studies; astronomy; athletic training; atmospheric sciences and meteorology; biochemistry; biology/biological sciences; biomedical/medical engineering; business administration and management; chemistry; chemistry related; clinical laboratory science/medical technology; comparative literature; computer hardware engineering; computer science; cytotechnology; dramatic/theater arts; economics; electrical, electronics and communications engineering; engineering; English; environmental studies; European studies; fine/studio arts; French; geology/earth science; German; health professions related; history; humanities; information science/studies; Italian; journalism; linguistics; marine biology; mathematics; mechanical engineering; multi-/interdisciplinary studies related; music; nursing (registered nurse training); pharmacology; philosophy; physical sciences related; physics; political science and government; psychology; religious studies; respiratory care therapy; Russian; social sciences; social work; sociology; Spanish; women's studies.

Academics *Calendar:* semesters. *Degrees:* bachelor's, master's, doctoral, first professional, post-master's, postbachelor's, and first professional certificates. *Special study options:* academic remediation for entering students, adult/continuing education programs, advanced placement credit, distance learning, double majors, English as a second language, freshman honors college, honors programs, independent study, internships, off-campus study, part-time degree program, services for LD students, student-designed majors, study abroad, summer session for credit. *ROTC:* Army (c), Air Force (c).

Computers on Campus 2,600 computers/terminals are available on campus for general student use. Students can access the following: campus intranet, computer help desk, free student e-mail accounts, online (class) grades, online (class) registration, online (class) schedules. Campuswide network is available. Wireless service is available via computer labs, libraries, student centers.

Student Life *Housing options:* coed. Campus housing is university owned. Freshman campus housing is guaranteed. *Activities and organizations:* drama/theater group, student-run newspaper, radio and television station, choral group, marching band, Caribbean Student Organization, Muslim Student Association, Commuter Student Association, Student Activities Board, national fraternities, national sororities. *Campus security:* 24-hour emergency response devices and patrols, late-night transport/escort service, controlled dormitory access. *Student services:* health clinic, personal/psychological counseling, women's center, legal services.

Athletics Member NCAA, NAIA. All NCAA Division I. *Intercollegiate sports:* baseball M (s), basketball M (s)/W (s), cross-country running M (s)/W (s), football M (s), lacrosse M (s)/W (s), soccer M (s)/W (s), softball W (s), swimming and diving M (s)/W (s), tennis M (s)/W (s), track and field M (s)/W (s), volleyball W (s). *Intramural sports:* badminton M/W, basketball M/W, bowling M/W, cheerleading W, crew M (c)/W (c), equestrian sports M (c)/W (c), golf M, ice hockey M (c), racquetball M/W, rugby M (c)/W (c), soccer M/W, softball M/W, table tennis M/W, tennis M/W, ultimate Frisbee M (c)/W (c), volleyball M/W.

Standardized Tests *Required:* SAT or ACT (for admission). *Recommended:* SAT Subject Tests (for admission).

Costs (2007–08) *Tuition:* state resident $4350 full-time, $181 per credit part-time; nonresident $10,610 full-time, $442 per credit part-time. *Required fees:* $1410 full-time, $69 per credit part-time. *Room and board:* $8734. Room and board charges vary according to board plan and housing facility. *Payment plan:* installment.

Financial Aid Of all full-time matriculated undergraduates who enrolled in 2006, 9,883 applied for aid, 7,685 were judged to have need, 1,153 had their need fully met. 346 Federal Work-Study jobs (averaging $1599). 1,793 state and other part-time jobs (averaging $2014). In 2006, 827 non-need-based awards were made. *Average percent of need met:* 64%. *Average financial aid package:* $8335. *Average need-based loan:* $4041. *Average need-based gift aid:* $5539. *Average non-need-based aid:* $3274. *Average indebtedness upon graduation:* $16,096.

Applying *Options:* electronic application, early action, deferred entrance. *Application fee:* $40. *Required:* essay or personal statement, high school transcript, minimum 3.0 GPA. *Required for some:* audition. *Recommended:* 2 letters of recommendation, interview. *Application deadlines:* 3/1 (freshmen), 4/15 (transfers), 11/15 (early action). *Notification:* continuous (freshmen), continuous (transfers), 1/1 (early action).

Freshman Application Contact Ms. Judith Burke-Berhanan, Stony Brook University, State University of New York, Stony Brook, NY 11794. *Phone:* 631-632-6868. *Toll-free phone:* 800-872-7869. *Fax:* 631-632-9898. *E-mail:* ugadmissions@notes.cc.sunysb.edu.

See page 1854 for the College Close-Up.

Swedish Institute, College of Health Sciences

New York, New York **www.swedishinstitute.org/**

- **Proprietary** comprehensive, founded 1916
- **Urban** campus
- **Coed**
- **Moderately difficult** entrance level

Faculty *Student/faculty ratio:* 11:1.

Academics *Calendar:* trimesters.

Student Life *Campus security:* 24-hour emergency response devices and patrols.

Standardized Tests *Required:* Nelson-Denny; TOEFL is required for some (for admission).

Applying *Application fee:* $50. *Required:* essay or personal statement, 2 letters of recommendation, interview. *Required for some:* high school transcript.

Freshman Application Contact Admissions Advisor, Swedish Institute, College of Health Sciences, 226 West 26th Street, New York, NY 10001-6700. *Phone:* 212-914-5900 Ext. 125. *E-mail:* admissions@swedishinstitute.edu.

Syracuse University

Syracuse, New York **www.syracuse.edu/**

- **Independent** university, founded 1870
- **Urban** 200-acre campus
- **Endowment** $1.1 billion
- **Coed** 11,796 undergraduate students, 99% full-time, 55% women, 45% men
- **Very difficult** entrance level, 51% of applicants were admitted

Undergraduates 11,731 full-time, 65 part-time. Students come from 50 states and territories, 63 other countries, 56% are from out of state, 7% African American, 9% Asian American or Pacific Islander, 6% Hispanic American, 0.8% Native American, 4% international, 2% transferred in, 75% live on campus. *Retention:* 91% of 2006 full-time freshmen returned.

Freshmen *Admission:* 21,219 applied, 10,744 admitted, 3,096 enrolled. *Average high school GPA:* 3.6. *Test scores:* SAT critical reading scores over 500: 91%; SAT math scores over 500: 94%; SAT critical reading scores over 600: 43%; SAT math scores over 600: 55%; SAT critical reading scores over 700: 7%; SAT math scores over 700: 12%.

Faculty *Total:* 1,458, 62% full-time. *Student/faculty ratio:* 15:1.

Majors Accounting; advertising; aerospace, aeronautical and astronautical engineering; African-American/Black studies; American studies; anthropology; apparel and textiles; architecture; area, ethnic, cultural, and gender studies related; art; art history, criticism and conservation; art teacher education; audiology and speech-language pathology; biochemistry; biological and biomedical sciences related; biology/biological sciences; biomedical/medical engineering; business administration and management; business, management, and marketing related; chemical engineering; chemistry; chemistry teacher education; cinematography and film/video production; civil engineering; classics and languages, literatures and linguistics; commercial and advertising art; communication and journalism related; communication/speech communication and rhetoric; computer and information sciences; computer and information sciences and support services related; computer engineering; creative writing; dramatic/theater arts; economics; education related; education (specific subject areas) related; electrical, electronics and communications engineering; engineering physics; English/language arts teacher education; English literature (British and Commonwealth); entrepreneurship; environmental/environmental health engineering; family and consumer sciences/home economics teacher education; finance; fine arts related; fine/studio arts; foodservice systems administration; foods, nutrition, and wellness; foreign languages and literatures; French; geography; geology/earth science; German; health professions related; history; human development and family studies; information science/studies; interior architecture; international relations and affairs; Italian; journalism; Latin American studies; legal professions and studies related; liberal arts and sciences/liberal studies; library science; linguistics; marketing/marketing management; mathematics; mathematics teacher education; mechanical engineering; mechanical engineering/mechanical technology; music; music history, literature, and theory; music performance; music teacher education; music theory and composition; operations research; philosophy; philosophy and religious studies related; photography; physical education teaching and coaching; physics; physics teacher education; political science and government; psychology; public administration; radio and television; religious studies; Russian; Russian studies; sales, distribution and marketing; social sciences; social studies teacher education; social work; sociology; Spanish; special education; special education (hearing impaired); speech and rhetoric; transportation and materials moving related; visual and performing arts related; women's studies.

Academics *Calendar:* semesters. *Degrees:* associate, bachelor's, master's, doctoral, first professional, post-master's, and postbachelor's certificates. *Special study options:* accelerated degree program, adult/continuing education programs, advanced placement credit, cooperative education, distance learning, double majors, English as a second language, external degree program, honors programs, independent study, internships, off-campus study, part-time degree program, services for LD students, student-designed majors, study abroad, summer session for credit. *ROTC:* Army (b), Air Force (b).

Computers on Campus 2,715 computers/terminals and 650 ports are available on campus for general student use. Students can access the following: campus intranet, computer help desk, free student e-mail accounts, online (class) registration, online (class) schedules, online services, networked client and server computing. Campuswide network is available. 100% of college-owned or -operated housing units are wired for high-speed Internet access. Wireless service is available via classrooms, computer centers, computer labs, dorm rooms, libraries, student centers.

Student Life *Housing:* on-campus residence required through sophomore year. *Options:* coed, disabled students. Campus housing is university owned. Freshman campus housing is guaranteed. *Activities and organizations:* drama/theater group, student-run newspaper, radio and television station, choral group, marching band, Student Government Association, Programming Council, First Year Players, Student African-American Society, national fraternities, national sororities. *Campus security:* 24-hour emergency response devices and patrols, late-night transport/escort service, controlled dormitory access, crime prevention and neighborhood outreach programs. *Student services:* health clinic, personal/psychological counseling, women's center, legal services.

Athletics Member NCAA. All Division I except football (Division I-A). *Intercollegiate sports:* badminton M (c)/W (c), baseball M (c)/W (c), basketball M (s)/W (s), bowling M (c)/W (c), cheerleading M/W, crew M (s)/W (s), cross-country running M (s)/W (s), equestrian sports M (c)/W (c), fencing M (c)/W (c), field hockey W (s), gymnastics M (c)/W (c), ice hockey M (c)/W (c), lacrosse M (s)/W (s), riflery M (c)/W (c), rugby M (c)/W (c), sailing M (c)/W (c), skiing (downhill) M (c)/W (c), soccer M (s)/W (s), softball M (c)/W (s), squash M (c)/W (c), swimming and diving M (s)/W (s), tennis M (c)/W (s), track and field M (s)/W (s), volleyball M (c)/W (s), water polo M (c)/W (c), wrestling M (c). *Intramural sports:* basketball M/W, field hockey M (c)/W (c), football M/W, golf M (c)/W (c), lacrosse M (c)/W (c), racquetball M/W, soccer M/W, softball M/W, swimming and diving M/W, tennis M/W, ultimate Frisbee M (c)/W (c), volleyball M/W.

Standardized Tests *Required:* SAT or ACT (for admission).

Costs (2007–08) *Comprehensive fee:* $42,626 includes full-time tuition ($30,470), mandatory fees ($1216), and room and board ($10,940). Part-time tuition: $1327 per credit hour. *College room only:* $5660. Room and board charges vary according to board plan and housing facility. *Payment plan:* installment. *Waivers:* employees or children of employees.

Financial Aid Of all full-time matriculated undergraduates who enrolled in 2007, 8,036 applied for aid, 7,094 were judged to have need, 4,620 had their need fully met. In 2007, 1660 non-need-based awards were made. *Average percent of need met:* 82%. *Average financial aid package:* $24,200. *Average need-based loan:* $5450. *Average need-based gift aid:* $17,750. *Average non-need-based aid:* $9300. *Average indebtedness upon graduation:* $27,152. *Financial aid deadline:* 2/1.

Applying *Options:* electronic application, early admission, early decision, deferred entrance. *Application fee:* $70. *Required:* essay or personal statement, high school transcript, letters of recommendation, audition for drama and music programs, portfolio for art and architecture programs. *Recommended:* interview. *Application deadlines:* 1/1 (freshmen), 1/1 (transfers). *Early decision deadline:* 11/15. *Notification:* 3/15 (freshmen), continuous (transfers), 12/15 (early decision).

Freshman Application Contact Office of Admissions, Syracuse University, 201 Tolley Administration Building, Syracuse, NY 13244-1100. *Phone:* 315-443-3611. *E-mail:* orange@syr.edu.

See page 1856 for the College Close-Up.

Talmudical Institute of Upstate New York

Rochester, New York **www.tiuny.org/**

Director of Admissions Rabbi Menachem Davidowitz, Director of Admissions, Talmudical Institute of Upstate New York, 769 Park Avenue, Rochester, NY 14607-3046. *Phone:* 716-473-2810. *E-mail:* tiuny@frontiernet.net.

TALMUDICAL SEMINARY OHOLEI TORAH

Brooklyn, New York

Director of Admissions Rabbi E. Piekarski, Director of Academic Affairs, Talmudical Seminary Oholei Torah, 667 Eastern Parkway, Brooklyn, NY 11213-3310. *Phone:* 718-363-2034.

TORAH TEMIMAH TALMUDICAL SEMINARY

Brooklyn, New York

Director of Admissions Rabbi I. Hisiger, Principal, Torah Temimah Talmudical Seminary, 555 Ocean Parkway, Brooklyn, NY 11218-5913. *Phone:* 718-853-8500.

TOURO COLLEGE

New York, New York **www.touro.edu/**

Director of Admissions Mr. Andre Baron, Director of Admissions, Touro College, 27-33 West 23rd Street, New York, NY 10010. *Phone:* 212-463-0400 Ext. 665.

UNION COLLEGE

Schenectady, New York **www.union.edu/**

- **Independent** 4-year, founded 1795
- **Urban** 120-acre campus
- **Endowment** $378.7 million
- **Coed** 2,177 undergraduate students, 99% full-time, 48% women, 52% men
- **Very difficult** entrance level, 43% of applicants were admitted

Undergraduates 2,149 full-time, 28 part-time. Students come from 37 states and territories, 26 other countries, 60% are from out of state, 3% African American, 6% Asian American or Pacific Islander, 4% Hispanic American, 0.2% Native American, 2% international, 0.7% transferred in, 89% live on campus. *Retention:* 91% of 2006 full-time freshmen returned.

Freshmen *Admission:* 4,837 applied, 2,093 admitted, 560 enrolled. *Average high school GPA:* 3.5. *Test scores:* SAT critical reading scores over 500: 94%; SAT math scores over 500: 97%; SAT writing scores over 500: 95%; ACT scores over 18: 100%; SAT critical reading scores over 600: 60%; SAT math scores over 600: 75%; SAT writing scores over 600: 63%; ACT scores over 24: 93%; SAT critical reading scores over 700: 12%; SAT math scores over 700: 15%; SAT writing scores over 700: 11%; ACT scores over 30: 23%.

Faculty *Total:* 236, 82% full-time, 91% with terminal degrees. *Student/faculty ratio:* 10:1.

Majors American studies; anthropology; astronomy; biochemistry; biological and biomedical sciences related; biological and physical sciences; biology/biological sciences; chemistry; classics and languages, literatures and linguistics; computer and information sciences; economics; electrical, electronics and communications engineering; English; fine/studio arts; foreign languages and literatures; geology/earth science; history; humanities; liberal arts and sciences/liberal studies; mathematics; mechanical engineering; neuroscience; philosophy; physics; political science and government; psychology; social sciences; sociology.

Academics *Calendar:* trimesters. *Degree:* bachelor's. *Special study options:* accelerated degree program, advanced placement credit, double majors, honors programs, independent study, internships, off-campus study, part-time degree program, student-designed majors, study abroad, summer session for credit. *ROTC:* Army (c), Navy (c), Air Force (c).

Computers on Campus 482 computers/terminals and 3,032 ports are available on campus for general student use. Students can access the following: campus intranet, computer help desk, free student e-mail accounts, online (class) grades, online (class) registration, online (class) schedules, multimedia lab. Campuswide network is available. 100% of college-owned or -operated housing units are wired for high-speed Internet access. Wireless service is available via classrooms, computer centers, computer labs, learning centers, libraries, student centers.

Student Life *Housing:* on-campus residence required through senior year. *Options:* coed. Campus housing is university owned. Freshman campus housing is guaranteed. *Activities and organizations:* drama/theater group, student-run newspaper, radio station, choral group, U-Program (Programming Board), student radio station, student newspaper, Concert Committee, Ski Club, national fraternities, national sororities. *Campus security:* 24-hour emergency response devices and patrols, late-night transport/escort service, controlled dormitory access, awareness programs, bicycle patrol, shuttle service. *Student services:* health clinic, personal/psychological counseling, women's center.

Athletics Member NCAA. All Division III except men's and women's ice hockey (Division I). *Intercollegiate sports:* baseball M, basketball M/W, bowling M (c)/W (c), cheerleading M (c)/W (c), crew M/W, cross-country running M/W, fencing M (c)/W (c), field hockey W, football M, golf M (c)/W (c), ice hockey M/W, lacrosse M/W, rock climbing M (c)/W (c), rugby M (c)/W (c), skiing (downhill) M (c)/W (c), soccer M/W, softball W, swimming and diving M/W, tennis M/W, track and field M/W, ultimate Frisbee M (c)/W (c), volleyball W, water polo M (c)/W (c). *Intramural sports:* basketball M/W, football M/W, ice hockey M (c)/W (c), lacrosse M/W, soccer M/W, softball M/W, volleyball M/W.

Standardized Tests *Required for some:* SAT and SAT Subject Tests or ACT (for admission).

Costs (2007–08) *Comprehensive fee:* $46,245. *Payment plan:* installment. *Waivers:* senior citizens and employees or children of employees.

Financial Aid Of all full-time matriculated undergraduates who enrolled in 2006, 1,222 applied for aid, 1,073 were judged to have need, 911 had their need fully met. 480 Federal Work-Study jobs (averaging $1595). 44 state and other part-time jobs (averaging $1830). In 2006, 222 non-need-based awards were made. *Average percent of need met:* 97%. *Average financial aid package:* $28,800. *Average need-based loan:* $4600. *Average need-based gift aid:* $23,600. *Average non-need-based aid:* $10,500. *Average indebtedness upon graduation:* $24,100. *Financial aid deadline:* 2/1.

Applying *Options:* electronic application, early admission, early decision, deferred entrance. *Application fee:* $50. *Required:* essay or personal statement, high school transcript, 2 letters of recommendation. *Recommended:* interview. *Application deadlines:* 1/15 (freshmen), 5/1 (transfers). *Early decision deadline:* 11/15 (for plan 1), 1/15 (for plan 2). *Notification:* 4/1 (freshmen), continuous (transfers), 12/15 (early decision plan 1), 2/1 (early decision plan 2).

Freshman Application Contact Dean of Admissions, Union College, Grant Hall, Union College, 807 Union Street, Schenectady, NY 12308. *Phone:* 518-388-6112. *Toll-free phone:* 888-843-6688. *Fax:* 518-388-6986. *E-mail:* admissions@union.edu.

See page 1858 for the College Close-Up.

UNITED STATES MERCHANT MARINE ACADEMY

Kings Point, New York **www.usmma.edu/**

- **Federally supported** 4-year, founded 1943
- **Suburban** 82-acre campus with easy access to New York City
- **Coed** 925 undergraduate students, 100% full-time, 13% women, 87% men
- **Very difficult** entrance level, 16% of applicants were admitted

Undergraduates 925 full-time. Students come from 50 states and territories, 5 other countries, 90% are from out of state, 2% African American, 4% Asian American or Pacific Islander, 3% Hispanic American, 0.6% Native American, 2% international, 100% live on campus. *Retention:* 92% of 2006 full-time freshmen returned.

Freshmen *Admission:* 1,754 applied, 279 admitted, 279 enrolled. *Average high school GPA:* 3.6. *Test scores:* SAT critical reading scores over 500: 99%; SAT math scores over 500: 100%; ACT scores over 18: 100%; SAT critical reading scores over 600: 37%; SAT math scores over 600: 68%; ACT scores over 24: 99%; SAT critical reading scores over 700: 7%; SAT math scores over 700: 12%; ACT scores over 30: 10%.

Faculty *Total:* 97, 90% full-time. *Student/faculty ratio:* 11:1.

Majors Engineering/industrial management; engineering-related technologies; marine science/merchant marine officer; marine transportation related; maritime science; naval architecture and marine engineering; nuclear engineering technology; transportation and materials moving related.

Academics *Calendar:* trimesters. *Degrees:* bachelor's and master's. *Special study options:* honors programs, internships.

Computers on Campus 1,200 computers/terminals are available on campus for general student use. Students can access the following: campus intranet, computer help desk, free student e-mail accounts, engineering and economics software. Campuswide network is available.

Student Life *Housing:* on-campus residence required through senior year. *Options:* coed. Campus housing is university owned. Freshman campus housing is guaranteed. *Activities and organizations:* drama/theater group, student-run newspaper, choral group, marching band, Regimental Band, CFC, Neuman Club, Honor Guard. *Campus security:* 24-hour patrols. *Student services:* health clinic, personal/psychological counseling.

Athletics Member NCAA. All Division III. *Intercollegiate sports:* baseball M, basketball M/W, crew M/W, cross-country running M/W, football M, golf M/W, ice hockey M (c), lacrosse M, rugby M (c), sailing M/W, soccer M, softball W, swimming and diving M/W, tennis M/W, track and field M/W, volleyball W, wrestling M. *Intramural sports:* basketball M/W, bowling M/W, crew M/W, cross-country running M/W, football M, golf M/W, lacrosse M, racquetball M/W, riflery M/W, rugby M, sailing M/W, skiing (cross-country) M/W, skiing (downhill) M/W, soccer M/W, softball M/W, swimming and diving M/W, tennis M/W, track and field M/W, volleyball M/W, water polo M, wrestling M.

Standardized Tests *Required:* SAT or ACT (for admission).

Costs (2007–08) *Tuition:* Full-time tuition and fees vary according to program and student level. tuition, room and board, and medical and dental care are provided by the U.S. government. Each midshipman receives a monthly salary while assigned aboard ship for training. Entering freshmen are required to deposit $6250 to defray the initial cost of computer equipment and activities fees. *Required fees:* $3888 full-time.

Applying *Options:* electronic application, early decision. *Required:* essay or personal statement, high school transcript, 3 letters of recommendation. *Recommended:* interview. *Application deadlines:* 3/1 (freshmen), 3/1 (transfers). *Notification:* continuous until 4/1 (freshmen), continuous until 4/1 (transfers).

Freshman Application Contact Capt. Robert E. Johnson, Director of Admissions and Financial Aid, United States Merchant Marine Academy, 300 Steamboat Road, Kings Point, NY 11024-1699. *Phone:* 516-773-5391. *Toll-free phone:* 866-546-4778. *Fax:* 516-773-5390. *E-mail:* admissions@usmma.edu.

See page 1860 for the College Close-Up.

UNITED STATES MILITARY ACADEMY

West Point, New York **www.usma.edu/**

West Point is all about leadership. For more than 200 years, West Point has developed many of the nation's finest leaders. The Academy offers a premier undergraduate education, develops strong leadership skills, and provides unique and unforgettable life experiences. West Point builds the foundation for an Army officer's career success, enabling him or her to motivate, guide, and protect the nation's young, promising soldiers. West Point is tough, but it's well worth the challenge. As one West Point cadet said, "The person I have become is so much better than the person who first came here."

Freshman Application Contact Col. Michael Jones, Director of Admissions, United States Military Academy, Building 606, West Point, NY 10996. *Phone:* 845-938-4041. *E-mail:* 8dad@sunams.usma.army.mil.

See page 1862 for the College Close-Up.

UNITED TALMUDICAL SEMINARY

Brooklyn, New York

Director of Admissions Director of Admissions, United Talmudical Seminary, 82 Lee Avenue, Brooklyn, NY 11211-7900. *Phone:* 718-963-9770.

UNIVERSITY AT ALBANY, STATE UNIVERSITY OF NEW YORK

Albany, New York **www.albany.edu/**

- **State-supported** university, founded 1844, part of State University of New York System
- **Suburban** 560-acre campus
- **Endowment** $26.7 million
- **Coed** 12,748 undergraduate students, 94% full-time, 50% women, 50% men
- **Moderately difficult** entrance level, 52% of applicants were admitted

Undergraduates 11,959 full-time, 789 part-time. Students come from 41 states and territories, 43 other countries, 5% are from out of state, 9% African American, 6% Asian American or Pacific Islander, 7% Hispanic American, 0.2% Native American, 2% international, 11% transferred in, 57% live on campus. *Retention:* 84% of 2006 full-time freshmen returned.

Freshmen *Admission:* 20,249 applied, 10,432 admitted, 2,519 enrolled. *Average high school GPA:* 3.4. *Test scores:* SAT critical reading scores over 500: 88%; SAT math scores over 500: 94%; ACT scores over 18: 100%; SAT critical reading scores over 600: 28%; SAT math scores over 600: 38%; ACT scores over 24: 8%; SAT critical reading scores over 700: 4%; SAT math scores over 700: 4%; ACT scores over 30: 5%.

Faculty *Total:* 1,312, 51% full-time. *Student/faculty ratio:* 19:1.

Majors Accounting; actuarial science; African-American/Black studies; anthropology; applied mathematics; art; art history, criticism and conservation; Asian studies; Asian studies (East); atmospheric sciences and meteorology; biochemistry; biology/biological sciences; business administration and management; chemistry; Chinese; classics and languages, literatures and linguistics; computer and information sciences; computer science; criminal justice/law enforcement administration; dramatic/theater arts; economics; English; environmental science; European studies (Central and Eastern); French; geography; geology/earth science; Hispanic-American, Puerto Rican, and Mexican-American/Chicano studies; history; information science/studies; interdisciplinary studies; Italian; Japanese studies; Jewish/Judaic studies; Latin; Latin American studies; linguistics; mass communication/media; mathematics; mathematics and computer science; medieval and Renaissance studies; molecular biology; music; philosophy; physics; political science and government; psychology; public administration; public policy analysis; religious studies; Romance languages; Russian; Russian studies; Slavic languages; social work; sociology; Spanish; speech and rhetoric; urban studies/affairs; women's studies.

Academics *Calendar:* semesters. *Degrees:* bachelor's, master's, doctoral, post-master's, and postbachelor's certificates. *Special study options:* accelerated degree program, advanced placement credit, distance learning, double majors, English as a second language, freshman honors college, honors programs, independent study, internships, off-campus study, services for LD students, student-designed majors, study abroad, summer session for credit. *ROTC:* Army (b), Air Force (c). *Unusual degree programs:* 3-2 business administration; engineering with Rensselaer Polytechnic Institute, State University of New York at Binghamton, State University of New York at New Paltz, Clarkson University.

Computers on Campus 500 computers/terminals are available on campus for general student use. Students can access the following: computer help desk, free student e-mail accounts, online (class) grades, online (class) registration, online (class) schedules. Campuswide network is available. 100% of college-owned or -operated housing units are wired for high-speed Internet access. Wireless service is available via dorm rooms, libraries, student centers.

Student Life *Housing:* on-campus residence required through sophomore year. *Options:* coed. Campus housing is university owned. Freshman campus housing is guaranteed. *Activities and organizations:* drama/theater group, student-run newspaper, radio station, choral group, intramural athletics, cultural organizations, political organizations, community service, national fraternities, national sororities. *Campus security:* 24-hour emergency response devices and patrols, late-night transport/escort service, controlled dormitory access, Five Quad Ambulance Service; On-Campus Dead Car Battery Assistance. *Student services:* health clinic, personal/psychological counseling, legal services.

Athletics Member NCAA. All Division I. *Intercollegiate sports:* baseball M (s), basketball M (s)/W (s), crew M/W, cross-country running M (s)/W (s), field hockey W (s), football M (s), golf W (s), lacrosse M (s)/W (s), rock climbing M/W, soccer M (s)/W (s), softball W (s), tennis W (s), track and field M (s)/W (s), volleyball W (s). *Intramural sports:* badminton M/W, baseball M, basketball M/W, equestrian sports M/W, fencing M/W, ice hockey M, lacrosse M, racquetball M/W, skiing (cross-country) M/W, skiing (downhill) M/W, soccer M/W, softball M/W, tennis M/W, track and field M/W, ultimate Frisbee M/W, volleyball M/W, wrestling M.

Standardized Tests *Required:* SAT or ACT (for admission).

Costs (2007–08) *Tuition:* state resident $4350 full-time, $181 per credit part-time; nonresident $10,610 full-time, $442 per credit part-time. Part-time tuition and fees vary according to course load. *Required fees:* $1668 full-time. *Room and board:* $9032; room only: $5532. Room and board charges vary according to board plan and housing facility. *Payment plan:* installment. *Waivers:* senior citizens.

Financial Aid Of all full-time matriculated undergraduates who enrolled in 2006, 8,729 applied for aid, 6,331 were judged to have need, 1,851 had their need fully met. 1,223 Federal Work-Study jobs (averaging $1474). 255 state and other part-time jobs (averaging $4898). In 2006, 641 non-need-based awards were made. *Average percent of need met:* 79%. *Average financial aid package:* $8399. *Average need-based loan:* $4225. *Average need-based gift aid:* $4767. *Average non-need-based aid:* $3107. *Average indebtedness upon graduation:* $11,856. *Financial aid deadline:* 4/15.

Applying *Options:* electronic application, early admission, early action, deferred entrance. *Application fee:* $40. *Required:* high school transcript. *Required for some:* portfolio, audition. *Recommended:* essay or personal statement, letters of recommendation. *Application deadlines:* 3/1 (freshmen), 8/1 (transfers), 11/15 (early action). *Notification:* continuous (freshmen), continuous (transfers), 1/1 (early action).

Freshman Application Contact Mr. Robert Andrea, Director of Undergraduate Admissions, University at Albany, State University of New York, 1400 Washington Avenue, University Administration Building 101, Albany, NY 12222. *Phone:* 518-442-5435. *Toll-free phone:* 800-293-7869. *Fax:* 518-442-5383. *E-mail:* ugadmissions@albany.edu.

See page 1864 for the College Close-Up.

UNIVERSITY AT BUFFALO, THE STATE UNIVERSITY OF NEW YORK

Buffalo, New York **www.buffalo.edu/**

- **State-supported** university, founded 1846, part of State University of New York System
- **Suburban** 1350-acre campus
- **Endowment** $566.4 million
- **Coed** 18,779 undergraduate students, 93% full-time, 46% women, 54% men
- **Moderately difficult** entrance level, 52% of applicants were admitted

The University at Buffalo (UB) attracts exceptional students with its collaborative and experiential learning programs, more than 100 undergraduate degree programs, and growing number of combined bachelor's and master's programs. The University is dedicated to providing undergraduates the opportunity to work with its award-winning faculty on advanced research projects. In one of the nation's most up-to-date campus environments, students have access to cutting-edge facilities and technological resources. UB is committed to enhancing student life by offering new on-campus apartment housing options, NCAA Division I men's and women's athletics, and hundreds of cultural, athletic, and special interest clubs and organizations.

Undergraduates 17,517 full-time, 1,262 part-time. Students come from 45 states and territories, 84 other countries, 4% are from out of state, 7% African American, 9% Asian American or Pacific Islander, 3% Hispanic American, 0.4% Native American, 10% international, 9% transferred in, 36% live on campus. *Retention:* 87% of 2006 full-time freshmen returned.

Freshmen *Admission:* 19,831 applied, 10,245 admitted, 3,272 enrolled. *Average high school GPA:* 3.2. *Test scores:* SAT critical reading scores over 500: 78%; SAT math scores over 500: 91%; ACT scores over 18: 96%; SAT critical reading scores over 600: 30%; SAT math scores over 600: 50%; ACT scores over 24: 67%; SAT critical reading scores over 700: 5%; SAT math scores over 700: 9%; ACT scores over 30: 11%.

Faculty *Total:* 1,827, 65% full-time, 97% with terminal degrees. *Student/faculty ratio:* 16:1.

Majors Aerospace, aeronautical and astronautical engineering; African-American/Black studies; American studies; anthropology; architecture; art; art history, criticism and conservation; Asian studies; audiology and speech-language pathology; biochemistry; bioinformatics; biological and biomedical sciences related; biology/biological sciences; biophysics; biostatistics; biotechnology; business administration and management; chemical engineering; chemistry; chemistry related; civil engineering; classics and languages, literatures and linguistics; clinical laboratory science/medical technology; communication/speech communication and rhetoric; computer engineering; computer science; dance; dramatic/theater arts; dramatic/theater arts and stagecraft related; economics; electrical, electronics and communications engineering; engineering; engineering physics; engineering science; English; environmental design/architecture; environmental/environmental health engineering; film/cinema studies; fine/studio arts; French; geography; geology/earth science; German; history; humanities; industrial engineering; information science/studies; Italian; kinesiology and exercise science; liberal arts and sciences/liberal studies; linguistics; mass communication/media; maternal/child health and neonatal nursing; mathematics; mathematics related; mechanical engineering; multi-/interdisciplinary studies related; music; music performance; nuclear medical technology; nursing (registered nurse training); nursing related; nutrition sciences; occupational therapy; pediatric nursing; pharmacology; pharmacology and toxicology; pharmacy administration/pharmaceutics; pharmacy, pharmaceutical sciences, and administration related; philosophy; physics; physics related; political science and government; psychology; sociology; Spanish; structural engineering; theoretical and mathematical physics; women's studies.

Academics *Calendar:* semesters. *Degrees:* bachelor's, master's, doctoral, first professional, post-master's, and first professional certificates. *Special study options:* academic remediation for entering students, accelerated degree program, adult/continuing education programs, advanced placement credit, cooperative education, distance learning, double majors, English as a second language, freshman honors college, honors programs, independent study, internships, off-campus study, part-time degree program, services for LD students, student-designed majors, study abroad, summer session for credit. *ROTC:* Army (c). *Unusual degree programs:* 3-2 business administration; engineering; nursing; social work; law.

Computers on Campus 2,435 computers/terminals are available on campus for general student use. Students can access the following: campus intranet, computer help desk, free student e-mail accounts, online (class) grades, online (class) registration, online (class) schedules. Campuswide network is available. 100% of college-owned or -operated housing units are wired for high-speed Internet access.

Student Life *Housing options:* coed, disabled students. Campus housing is university owned. Freshman campus housing is guaranteed. *Activities and organizations:* drama/theater group, student-run newspaper, radio and television station, choral group, marching band, national fraternities, national sororities. *Campus security:* 24-hour emergency response devices and patrols, student patrols, late-night transport/escort service, controlled dormitory access, self-defense and awareness programs. *Student services:* health clinic, personal/psychological counseling, women's center, legal services.

Athletics Member NCAA. All Division I except football (Division I-A). *Intercollegiate sports:* baseball M (s), basketball M (s)/W (s), crew W (s), cross-country running M (s)/W (s), soccer M (s)/W (s), softball W (s), swimming and diving M (s)/W (s), tennis M (s)/W (s), track and field M (s)/W (s), volleyball W (s), wrestling M (s). *Intramural sports:* badminton M/W, baseball M (c), basketball M/W, bowling M/W, crew M (c), cross-country running M/W, equestrian sports M (c)/W (c), field hockey M (c)/W (c), gymnastics M (c)/W (c), ice hockey M (c)/W (c), lacrosse M (c)/W (c), racquetball M/W, rugby M (c)/W (c), skiing (downhill) M (c)/W (c), soccer M/W, softball M/W, tennis M (c)/W (c), ultimate Frisbee M (c)/W (c), volleyball M (c)/W, wrestling M (c)/W (c).

Standardized Tests *Required:* SAT or ACT (for admission).

Costs (2007–08) *Tuition:* state resident $4350 full-time, $181 per credit hour part-time; nonresident $10,610 full-time, $442 per credit hour part-time. Part-time tuition and fees vary according to course load. *Required fees:* $1867 full-time, $82 per credit hour part-time. *Room and board:* $8620; room only: $5360. Room and board charges vary according to board plan and housing facility. *Payment plan:* installment. *Waivers:* minority students.

Financial Aid Of all full-time matriculated undergraduates who enrolled in 2006, 13,023 applied for aid, 9,533 were judged to have need, 2,676 had their need fully met. 840 Federal Work-Study jobs (averaging $1626). 1,096 state and other part-time jobs (averaging $5424). In 2006, 1089 non-need-based awards were made. *Average percent of need met:* 69%. *Average financial aid package:* $6079. *Average need-based loan:* $3878. *Average need-based gift aid:* $2311. *Average non-need-based aid:* $2728. *Average indebtedness upon graduation:* $19,062.

Applying *Options:* electronic application, early admission, early decision. *Application fee:* $40. *Required:* high school transcript. *Required for some:* letters of recommendation, portfolio, audition. *Recommended:* essay or personal statement. *Early decision deadline:* 11/1. *Notification:* continuous (freshmen), continuous (transfers), 12/15 (early decision).

Freshman Application Contact Ms. Patricia Armstrong, Director of Admissions, University at Buffalo, the State University of New York, Capen Hall, Room 15, North Campus, Buffalo, NY 14260-1660. *Phone:* 716-645-6900. *Toll-free phone:* 888-UB-ADMIT. *Fax:* 716-645-6411. *E-mail:* ub-admissions@buffalo.edu.

See page 1866 for the College Close-Up.

UNIVERSITY OF ROCHESTER

Rochester, New York **www.rochester.edu/**

- **Independent** university, founded 1850
- **Suburban** 534-acre campus
- **Endowment** $1.7 billion
- **Coed** 5,131 undergraduate students, 94% full-time, 51% women, 49% men
- **Very difficult** entrance level, 41% of applicants were admitted

Dedicated in spring 2007, Goergen Hall is the new home of both the Institute of Optics and biomedical engineering—one of the College's newest and fastest-growing departments. Financial economics and international business are two new majors, and literary translation studies is the latest certificate program option for undergraduates.

Undergraduates 4,839 full-time, 292 part-time. Students come from 52 states and territories, 52 other countries, 54% are from out of state, 4% African American, 10% Asian American or Pacific Islander, 4% Hispanic American, 0.2% Native American, 6% international, 2% transferred in, 86% live on campus. *Retention:* 93% of 2006 full-time freshmen returned.

Freshmen *Admission:* 11,676 applied, 4,815 admitted, 1,182 enrolled. *Average high school GPA:* 3.72. *Test scores:* SAT critical reading scores over 500: 97%; SAT math scores over 500: 97%; ACT scores over 18: 100%; SAT critical reading

scores over 600: 75%; SAT math scores over 600: 84%; ACT scores over 24: 94%; SAT critical reading scores over 700: 26%; SAT math scores over 700: 34%; ACT scores over 30: 45%.

Faculty *Total:* 763, 67% full-time. *Student/faculty ratio:* 9:1.

Majors African-American/Black studies; American Sign Language (ASL); anthropology; applied mathematics; art history, criticism and conservation; biological and physical sciences; biology/biological sciences; biomedical/medical engineering; chemical engineering; chemistry; classics and languages, literatures and linguistics; cognitive science; comparative literature; computer science; economics; electrical, electronics and communications engineering; engineering science; English; environmental science; environmental studies; film/cinema studies; fine/studio arts; French; geological/geophysical engineering; geology/earth science; German; history; Japanese; jazz/jazz studies; linguistics; mathematics; mathematics and statistics related; mechanical engineering; music; music teacher education; music theory and composition; nursing (registered nurse training); optical sciences; philosophy; physics; physics related; political science and government; psychology; religious studies; Russian; Russian studies; social sciences related; Spanish; statistics; women's studies.

Academics *Calendar:* semesters plus optional summer term. *Degrees:* bachelor's, master's, doctoral, first professional, post-master's, postbachelor's, and first professional certificates. *Special study options:* accelerated degree program, advanced placement credit, double majors, English as a second language, honors programs, independent study, internships, off-campus study, part-time degree program, services for LD students, student-designed majors, study abroad, summer session for credit. *ROTC:* Army (c), Navy (b), Air Force (c). *Unusual degree programs:* 3-2 business administration; engineering; nursing; public health, optics, public policy, human development, computer science, medical statistics, applied mathematics, elementary teacher education, music education, materials science.

Computers on Campus 450 computers/terminals and 4,000 ports are available on campus for general student use. Students can access the following: computer help desk, free student e-mail accounts, online (class) grades, online (class) registration, online (class) schedules. Campuswide network is available. 100% of college-owned or -operated housing units are wired for high-speed Internet access. Wireless service is available via classrooms, computer centers, computer labs, learning centers, libraries, student centers.

Student Life *Housing:* on-campus residence required through sophomore year. *Options:* coed. Campus housing is university owned. Freshman campus housing is guaranteed. *Activities and organizations:* drama/theater group, student-run newspaper, radio and television station, choral group, Campus Activities Board, Student Government, Greek System, Hillel, Catholic Newman Community, national fraternities, national sororities. *Campus security:* 24-hour emergency response devices and patrols, late-night transport/escort service, controlled dormitory access. *Student services:* health clinic, personal/psychological counseling, women's center, legal services.

Athletics Member NCAA. All Division III. *Intercollegiate sports:* badminton M (c)/W (c), baseball M, basketball M/W, crew M (c)/W (c), cross-country running M/W, equestrian sports M (c)/W (c), field hockey W, football M, golf M, ice hockey M (c)/W (c), lacrosse M (c)/W, rugby M (c)/W (c), skiing (downhill) M (c)/W (c), soccer M/W, softball W, squash M, swimming and diving M/W, tennis M/W, track and field M/W, ultimate Frisbee M (c)/W (c), volleyball M (c)/W, water polo M (c)/W (c). *Intramural sports:* archery M (c)/W (c), basketball M/W, cheerleading M (c)/W (c), fencing M (c)/W (c), football M/W, gymnastics M (c)/W (c), sailing M (c)/W (c), soccer M/W, softball M/W, tennis M/W, ultimate Frisbee M/W, volleyball M/W.

Standardized Tests *Required:* SAT or ACT (for admission). *Required for some:* SAT and SAT Subject Tests or ACT (for admission). *Recommended:* SAT Subject Tests (for admission).

Costs (2007–08) *Comprehensive fee:* $45,830 includes full-time tuition ($34,380), mandatory fees ($810), and room and board ($10,640). Part-time tuition: $1075 per credit hour. Part-time tuition and fees vary according to course load. *College room only:* $6200. Room and board charges vary according to board plan. *Payment plan:* installment. *Waivers:* employees or children of employees.

Financial Aid Of all full-time matriculated undergraduates who enrolled in 2007, 2,776 applied for aid, 2,236 were judged to have need, 756 had their need fully met. 1,474 Federal Work-Study jobs (averaging $2033). In 2007, 1402 non-need-based awards were made. *Average percent of need met:* 86%. *Average financial aid package:* $28,668. *Average need-based loan:* $5550. *Average need-based gift aid:* $23,475. *Average non-need-based aid:* $9086. *Average indebtedness upon graduation:* $29,800.

Applying *Options:* electronic application, early admission, early decision, deferred entrance. *Application fee:* $50. *Required:* essay or personal statement, high school transcript, 1 letter of recommendation. *Required for some:* audition, portfolio. *Recommended:* 2 letters of recommendation, interview. *Application deadlines:* 1/1 (freshmen), 1/1 (out-of-state freshmen), 6/1 (transfers). *Early decision deadline:* 11/1. *Notification:* 4/1 (freshmen), 4/1 (out-of-state freshmen), continuous until 7/1 (transfers), 12/15 (early decision).

Freshman Application Contact Admissions Office, University of Rochester, PO Box 270251, 300 Wilson Boulevard, Rochester, NY 14627-0251. *Phone:* 585-275-3221. *Toll-free phone:* 888-822-2256. *Fax:* 585-461-4595. *E-mail:* admit@admissions.rochester.edu.

See page 1868 for the College Close-Up.

U.T.A. Mesivta of Kiryas Joel

Monroe, New York

Utica College

Utica, New York **www.utica.edu/**

- **Independent** comprehensive, founded 1946
- **Suburban** 128-acre campus
- **Endowment** $19.9 million
- **Coed** 2,431 undergraduate students, 81% full-time, 60% women, 40% men
- **Moderately difficult** entrance level, 76% of applicants were admitted

Utica College offers a warm, friendly atmosphere with small classes and a dedicated faculty. Students choose from thirty-two majors in both the liberal arts and professional career programs. Extensive cooperative education and internship opportunities provide students with valuable experience in the workplace. Upon graduation, Utica College students receive the internationally recognized Syracuse University undergraduate degree.

Undergraduates 1,975 full-time, 456 part-time. Students come from 40 states and territories, 15 other countries, 17% are from out of state, 10% African American, 2% Asian American or Pacific Islander, 3% Hispanic American, 0.6% Native American, 2% international, 7% transferred in, 46% live on campus. *Retention:* 67% of 2006 full-time freshmen returned.

Freshmen *Admission:* 2,541 applied, 1,936 admitted, 494 enrolled. *Average high school GPA:* 2.99. *Test scores:* SAT critical reading scores over 500: 34%; SAT math scores over 500: 40%; SAT writing scores over 500: 33%; ACT scores over 18: 83%; SAT critical reading scores over 600: 7%; SAT math scores over 600: 11%; SAT writing scores over 600: 7%; ACT scores over 24: 18%; SAT math scores over 700: 1%; SAT writing scores over 700: 1%; ACT scores over 30: 1%.

Faculty *Total:* 323, 40% full-time. *Student/faculty ratio:* 12:1.

Majors Accounting; biology/biological sciences; biology teacher education; business administration and management; business, management, and marketing related; business/managerial economics; business teacher education; chemistry; chemistry teacher education; communication/speech communication and rhetoric; computer and information sciences; computer teacher education; criminal justice/law enforcement administration; developmental and child psychology; economics; elementary education; English; English/language arts teacher education; foreign languages and literatures; health/medical preparatory programs related; history; history teacher education; international business/trade/commerce; international relations and affairs; journalism; liberal arts and sciences/liberal studies; mathematics; mathematics teacher education; nursing (registered nurse training); philosophy; physics; physics teacher education; political science and government; pre-dentistry studies; pre-law studies; pre-medical studies; pre-veterinary studies; psychology; public relations/image management; secondary education; social sciences; social science teacher education; social studies teacher education; sociology; therapeutic recreation.

Academics *Calendar:* semesters. *Degrees:* bachelor's, master's, first professional, and postbachelor's certificates. *Special study options:* academic remediation for entering students, accelerated degree program, adult/continuing education programs, advanced placement credit, cooperative education, distance learning, double majors, honors programs, independent study, internships, off-campus study, part-time degree program, services for LD students, study abroad, summer session for credit. *ROTC:* Army (b), Air Force (c). *Unusual degree programs:* 3-2 engineering with Syracuse University (or any other university).

Computers on Campus 242 computers/terminals are available on campus for general student use. Students can access the following: computer help desk, free student e-mail accounts, online (class) grades, online (class) registration, online (class) schedules. Campuswide network is available.

Student Life *Housing:* on-campus residence required through sophomore year. *Options:* coed, disabled students. Campus housing is university owned. Freshman campus housing is guaranteed. *Activities and organizations:* drama/theater group, student-run newspaper, radio station, choral group, Student Nurses Association, Economic Crime Investigation Student Association, Student Senate, Asa Gray

Biological Society, Latin American Student Union, national fraternities, national sororities. *Campus security:* 24-hour emergency response devices and patrols, late-night transport/escort service, controlled dormitory access. *Student services:* health clinic, personal/psychological counseling, women's center.

Athletics Member NCAA. All Division III. *Intercollegiate sports:* baseball M, basketball M/W, field hockey W, football M, golf M/W, ice hockey M/W, lacrosse M/W, soccer M/W, softball W, swimming and diving M/W, tennis M/W, volleyball W, water polo W. *Intramural sports:* basketball M/W, bowling M/W, cheerleading M (c)/W (c), fencing M (c)/W (c), racquetball M/W, soccer M/W, softball M/W, tennis M/W, volleyball M/W, water polo M/W.

Standardized Tests *Required for some:* SAT or ACT (for admission). *Recommended:* SAT or ACT (for admission).

Costs (2007–08) *Comprehensive fee:* $34,878 includes full-time tuition ($24,264), mandatory fees ($320), and room and board ($10,294). Full-time tuition and fees vary according to class time and course load. Part-time tuition: $818 per hour. Part-time tuition and fees vary according to class time and course load. *Room and board:* Room and board charges vary according to board plan and housing facility. *Payment plans:* installment, deferred payment. *Waivers:* senior citizens and employees or children of employees.

Financial Aid Of all full-time matriculated undergraduates who enrolled in 2005, 1,859 applied for aid, 1,736 were judged to have need, 319 had their need fully met. 872 Federal Work-Study jobs (averaging $1512). 367 state and other part-time jobs (averaging $1540). In 2005, 129 non-need-based awards were made. *Average percent of need met:* 73%. *Average financial aid package:* $18,190. *Average need-based loan:* $4447. *Average need-based gift aid:* $7451. *Average non-need-based aid:* $6004. *Average indebtedness upon graduation:* $25,565.

Applying *Options:* electronic application, early admission, deferred entrance. *Application fee:* $40. *Required:* essay or personal statement, high school transcript, minimum 2.0 GPA, 1 letter of recommendation. *Required for some:* minimum 3.0 GPA. *Recommended:* interview. *Application deadlines:* rolling (freshmen), rolling (transfers). *Notification:* 9/1 (freshmen), continuous (transfers).

Freshman Application Contact Mr. Patrick Quinn, Vice President for Enrollment Management, Utica College, 1600 Burrstone Road, Utica, NY 13502. *Phone:* 315-792-3006. *Toll-free phone:* 800-782-8884. *Fax:* 315-792-3003. *E-mail:* admiss@utica.edu.

See page 1870 for the College Close-Up.

VASSAR COLLEGE

Poughkeepsie, New York **www.vassar.edu/**

- **Independent** comprehensive, founded 1861
- **Suburban** 1000-acre campus with easy access to New York City
- **Endowment** $869.1 million
- **Coed** 2,450 undergraduate students, 98% full-time, 61% women, 39% men
- **Very difficult** entrance level, 29% of applicants were admitted

Undergraduates 2,407 full-time, 43 part-time. Students come from 51 states and territories, 50 other countries, 74% are from out of state, 5% African American, 10% Asian American or Pacific Islander, 7% Hispanic American, 0.2% Native American, 6% international, 0.4% transferred in, 95% live on campus. *Retention:* 96% of 2006 full-time freshmen returned.

Freshmen *Admission:* 6,393 applied, 1,830 admitted, 678 enrolled. *Average high school GPA:* 3.7. *Test scores:* SAT critical reading scores over 500: 100%; SAT math scores over 500: 100%; SAT writing scores over 500: 100%; SAT critical reading scores over 600: 96%; SAT math scores over 600: 93%; SAT writing scores over 600: 96%; SAT critical reading scores over 700: 58%; SAT math scores over 700: 38%; SAT writing scores over 700: 53%.

Faculty *Total:* 346, 85% full-time, 83% with terminal degrees. *Student/faculty ratio:* 8:1.

Majors African studies; American studies; ancient/classical Greek; anthropology; art history, criticism and conservation; Asian studies; astronomy; biochemistry; biology/biological sciences; chemistry; Chinese; classics and languages, literatures and linguistics; cognitive psychology and psycholinguistics; computer and information sciences; dramatic/theater arts; economics; English; environmental science; environmental studies; film/cinema studies; fine/studio arts; French; geography; geology/earth science; German; history; interdisciplinary studies; international relations and affairs; Italian; Japanese; Jewish/Judaic studies; Latin; Latin American studies; liberal arts and sciences and humanities related; mass communication/media; mathematics; medieval and Renaissance studies; multi-/interdisciplinary studies related; music; philosophy; physics; physiological psychology/psychobiology; political science and government; psychology; religious studies; Russian; science, technology and society; sociology; Spanish; urban studies/affairs; visual and performing arts; women's studies.

Academics *Calendar:* semesters. *Degrees:* bachelor's and master's. *Special study options:* advanced placement credit, cooperative education, double majors, independent study, internships, off-campus study, part-time degree program, services for LD students, student-designed majors, study abroad. *Unusual degree programs:* 3-2 engineering with Dartmouth College.

Computers on Campus 300 computers/terminals are available on campus for general student use. Students can access the following: campus intranet, computer help desk, free student e-mail accounts, online (class) grades, online (class) registration, online (class) schedules, Ethernet. Campuswide network is available. 100% of college-owned or -operated housing units are wired for high-speed Internet access. Wireless service is available via entire campus.

Student Life *Housing:* on-campus residence required through senior year. *Options:* coed, women-only, cooperative. Campus housing is university owned. Freshman campus housing is guaranteed. *Activities and organizations:* drama/theater group, student-run newspaper, radio and television station, choral group, Student Association, WVKR Radio Station, VICE (programming social events), Vassar Greens, Ultimate Frisbee. *Campus security:* 24-hour emergency response devices and patrols, student patrols, late-night transport/escort service, controlled dormitory access. *Student services:* health clinic, personal/psychological counseling, women's center.

Athletics Member NCAA. All Division III. *Intercollegiate sports:* baseball M, basketball M/W, crew M/W, cross-country running M/W, fencing M/W, field hockey W, golf W, lacrosse M/W, rugby M (c)/W (c), soccer M/W, squash M/W, swimming and diving M/W, tennis M/W, track and field M (c)/W (c), ultimate Frisbee M (c)/W (c), volleyball M/W. *Intramural sports:* badminton M (c)/W (c), basketball M/W, bowling M/W, equestrian sports M (c)/W (c), golf M/W, sailing M (c)/W (c), skiing (cross-country) M (c)/W (c), skiing (downhill) M (c)/W (c), soccer M/W, softball M/W, squash M/W, tennis M/W, volleyball M/W, water polo M/W.

Standardized Tests *Required:* SAT and SAT Subject Tests or ACT (for admission).

Costs (2007–08) *Comprehensive fee:* $46,685 includes full-time tuition ($37,570), mandatory fees ($545), and room and board ($8570). Part-time tuition and fees vary according to course load. *College room only:* $4570. Room and board charges vary according to board plan and housing facility. *Payment plan:* installment. *Waivers:* employees or children of employees.

Financial Aid Of all full-time matriculated undergraduates who enrolled in 2006, 1,482 applied for aid, 1,254 were judged to have need, 1,254 had their need fully met. 827 Federal Work-Study jobs (averaging $1850). 389 state and other part-time jobs (averaging $1847). *Average percent of need met:* 100%. *Average financial aid package:* $31,747. *Average need-based loan:* $3163. *Average need-based gift aid:* $26,350. *Average indebtedness upon graduation:* $20,589. *Financial aid deadline:* 2/1.

Applying *Options:* electronic application, early decision, deferred entrance. *Application fee:* $60. *Required:* essay or personal statement, high school transcript, 2 letters of recommendation. *Application deadlines:* 1/1 (freshmen), 4/1 (transfers). *Early decision deadline:* 11/15. *Notification:* 4/1 (freshmen), 5/10 (transfers), 12/15 (early decision).

Freshman Application Contact Dr. David M. Borus, Dean of Admission and Financial Aid, Vassar College, 124 Raymond Avenue, Poughkeepsie, NY 12604. *Phone:* 845-437-7300. *Toll-free phone:* 800-827-7270. *Fax:* 845-437-7063. *E-mail:* admissions@vassar.edu.

VAUGHN COLLEGE OF AERONAUTICS AND TECHNOLOGY

Flushing, New York **www.vaughn.edu/**

- **Independent** comprehensive, founded 1932
- **Urban** 6-acre campus
- **Endowment** $22.0 million
- **Coed, primarily men**
- **Minimally difficult** entrance level

Faculty *Student/faculty ratio:* 11:1.

Academics *Calendar:* semesters. *Degrees:* associate and bachelor's.

Student Life *Campus security:* 24-hour emergency response devices and patrols.

Standardized Tests *Required:* SAT or ACT (for admission).

Costs (2007–08) *Comprehensive fee:* $24,280 includes full-time tuition ($14,000), mandatory fees ($280), and room and board ($10,000). Part-time tuition: $475 per credit.

Financial Aid Of all full-time matriculated undergraduates who enrolled in 2005, 798 applied for aid, 772 were judged to have need, 80 had their need fully met. In 2005, 20 non-need-based awards were made. *Average percent of need met:*

80. *Average financial aid package:* $4900. *Average need-based loan:* $1750. *Average need-based gift aid:* $1000. *Average non-need-based aid:* $500. *Average indebtedness upon graduation:* $17,125.

Applying *Options:* deferred entrance. *Application fee:* $45. *Required:* essay or personal statement, high school transcript. *Required for some:* interview. *Recommended:* interview.

Freshman Application Contact Mr. Vincent Papandrea, Director, Admissions, Vaughn College of Aeronautics and Technology, La Guardia Airport, 86-01 23rd Avenue, Flushing, NY 11369. *Phone:* 718-429-6600. *Toll-free phone:* 800-776-2376 Ext. 145. *Fax:* 718-779-2231. *E-mail:* admitme@vaughn.edu.

See page 1872 for the College Close-Up.

VILLA MARIA COLLEGE OF BUFFALO

Buffalo, New York **www.villa.edu/**

- **Independent** primarily 2-year, founded 1960, affiliated with Roman Catholic Church
- **Suburban** 9-acre campus
- **Endowment** $523,318
- **Coed**
- **Minimally difficult** entrance level

Faculty *Student/faculty ratio:* 10:1.

Academics *Calendar:* semesters. *Degrees:* associate and bachelor's.

Student Life *Campus security:* late-night transport/escort service.

Costs (2007–08) *Tuition:* $11,840 full-time, $400 per credit hour part-time. Full-time tuition and fees vary according to course level, course load, degree level, program, and student level. Part-time tuition and fees vary according to course level, degree level, program, and student level. *Required fees:* $435 full-time, $85 per term part-time.

Financial Aid Of all full-time matriculated undergraduates who enrolled in 2006, 159 Federal Work-Study jobs (averaging $320).

Applying *Options:* electronic application, deferred entrance. *Required:* essay or personal statement, high school transcript, interview, writing sample.

Freshman Application Contact Mr. Kevin Donovan, Director of Admissions, Villa Maria College of Buffalo, 240 Pine Ridge Road, Buffalo, NY 14225-3999. *Phone:* 716-896-0700 Ext. 1802. *Fax:* 716-896-0705. *E-mail:* admmissions@villa.edu.

WAGNER COLLEGE

Staten Island, New York **www.wagner.edu/**

- **Independent** comprehensive, founded 1883
- **Urban** 105-acre campus with easy access to New York City
- **Coed** 1,935 undergraduate students, 98% full-time, 63% women, 37% men
- **Moderately difficult** entrance level, 60% of applicants were admitted

Undergraduates 1,889 full-time, 46 part-time. Students come from 38 states and territories, 14 other countries, 52% are from out of state, 5% African American, 2% Asian American or Pacific Islander, 5% Hispanic American, 0.5% Native American, 0.8% international, 3% transferred in, 72% live on campus. *Retention:* 81% of 2006 full-time freshmen returned.

Freshmen *Admission:* 2,842 applied, 1,716 admitted, 524 enrolled. *Average high school GPA:* 3.56. *Test scores:* SAT critical reading scores over 500: 89%; SAT math scores over 500: 94%; SAT writing scores over 500: 88%; ACT scores over 18: 100%; SAT critical reading scores over 600: 48%; SAT math scores over 600: 51%; SAT writing scores over 600: 44%; ACT scores over 24: 90%; SAT critical reading scores over 700: 6%; SAT math scores over 700: 8%; SAT writing scores over 700: 4%; ACT scores over 30: 8%.

Faculty *Total:* 249, 40% full-time. *Student/faculty ratio:* 13:1.

Majors Accounting; anthropology; art; arts management; biology/biological sciences; business administration and management; chemistry; computer and information sciences related; computer science; dramatic/theater arts; economics; education; elementary education; English; finance; history; international relations and affairs; kindergarten/preschool education; mathematics; medical microbiology and bacteriology; music; nursing (registered nurse training); physician assistant; physics; political science and government; pre-dentistry studies; pre-engineering; pre-law studies; pre-medical studies; pre-theology/pre-ministerial studies; psychology; public administration; secondary education; sociology; Spanish.

Academics *Calendar:* semesters. *Degrees:* bachelor's, master's, and post-bachelor's certificates. *Special study options:* double majors, honors programs, internships, off-campus study, part-time degree program, services for LD students, study abroad, summer session for credit. *ROTC:* Army (c).

Computers on Campus 150 computers/terminals are available on campus for general student use. Campuswide network is available.

Student Life *Housing options:* coed. Campus housing is university owned and leased by the school. Freshman campus housing is guaranteed. *Activities and organizations:* drama/theater group, student-run newspaper, radio station, choral group, Student Government Association, Student Activities Board, Wagner College Theatre, Wagner College Choir, student newspaper, national fraternities, national sororities. *Campus security:* 24-hour emergency response devices and patrols, late-night transport/escort service, controlled dormitory access. *Student services:* health clinic, personal/psychological counseling.

Athletics Member NCAA. All Division I except football (Division I-AA). *Intercollegiate sports:* baseball M (s), basketball M (s)/W (s), cross-country running M (s)/W (s), golf M (s)/W (s), ice hockey M (c), lacrosse M (s)/W (s), soccer W (s), softball W (s), swimming and diving W (s), tennis M (s)/W (s), track and field M (s)/W (s), volleyball W (s), water polo W (s), wrestling M (s). *Intramural sports:* basketball M/W, bowling M/W, football M, soccer M/W, softball M/W, table tennis M/W, tennis M/W, volleyball M/W.

Standardized Tests *Required:* SAT or ACT (for admission).

Costs (2007–08) *Comprehensive fee:* $38,400 includes full-time tuition ($29,400), mandatory fees ($100), and room and board ($8900). Part-time tuition: $3675 per unit. *Waivers:* employees or children of employees.

Financial Aid Of all full-time matriculated undergraduates who enrolled in 2006, 1,274 applied for aid, 990 were judged to have need, 538 had their need fully met. 670 Federal Work-Study jobs (averaging $1176). In 2006, 642 non-need-based awards were made. *Average percent of need met:* 78%. *Average financial aid package:* $14,734. *Average need-based loan:* $4464. *Average need-based gift aid:* $10,759. *Average non-need-based aid:* $8670.

Applying *Options:* electronic application, early decision, deferred entrance. *Application fee:* $50. *Required:* essay or personal statement, high school transcript, minimum 2.7 GPA, 2 letters of recommendation. *Required for some:* interview. *Recommended:* minimum 3.0 GPA, interview. *Application deadlines:* 2/15 (freshmen), 5/1 (transfers). *Early decision deadline:* 12/1. *Notification:* continuous until 3/1 (freshmen), continuous until 5/15 (transfers), 12/15 (early decision).

Freshman Application Contact Ms. Leigh-Ann DePascale, Director of Admissions, Wagner College, One Campus Road, Staten Island, NY 10301. *Phone:* 718-390-3411 Ext. 3412. *Toll-free phone:* 800-221-1010. *Fax:* 718-390-3105. *E-mail:* adm@wagner.edu.

See page 1874 for the College Close-Up.

WEBB INSTITUTE

Glen Cove, New York **www.webb-institute.edu/**

- **Independent** 4-year, founded 1889
- **Suburban** 26-acre campus with easy access to New York City
- **Endowment** $59.9 million
- **Coed** 91 undergraduate students, 100% full-time, 22% women, 78% men
- **Most difficult** entrance level, 31% of applicants were admitted

Webb Institute is a private engineering college, where all undergraduate students receive a full-tuition scholarship. Bachelor of Science degrees in naval architecture and marine engineering are offered. There is a cooperative work term in each year and a 100 percent employment record. Competitive selection of students is based on academic record, standardized test scores, and motivation for the program. The Institute's programs are fully accredited.

Undergraduates 91 full-time. Students come from 22 states and territories, 78% are from out of state, 2% Asian American or Pacific Islander, 2% Hispanic American, 3% transferred in, 100% live on campus. *Retention:* 96% of 2006 full-time freshmen returned.

Freshmen *Admission:* 95 applied, 29 admitted, 23 enrolled. *Average high school GPA:* 3.9. *Test scores:* SAT critical reading scores over 500: 100%; SAT math scores over 500: 100%; SAT writing scores over 500: 100%; SAT critical reading scores over 600: 74%; SAT math scores over 600: 100%; SAT writing scores over 600: 82%; SAT critical reading scores over 700: 35%; SAT math scores over 700: 52%; SAT writing scores over 700: 30%.

Faculty *Total:* 16, 69% full-time, 63% with terminal degrees. *Student/faculty ratio:* 12:1.

Majors Naval architecture and marine engineering.

Academics *Calendar:* semesters. *Degree:* bachelor's. *Special study options:* cooperative education, double majors, independent study, internships, off-campus study.

Computers on Campus 110 computers/terminals are available on campus for general student use. Students can access the following: campus intranet, computer help desk, free student e-mail accounts. Campuswide network is available. 100% of college-owned or -operated housing units are wired for high-speed Internet access. Wireless service is available via entire campus.

Student Life *Housing:* on-campus residence required through senior year. *Options:* coed, men-only, women-only. Campus housing is university owned. Freshman campus housing is guaranteed. *Activities and organizations:* drama/theater group, choral group, Student Organization, Society of Naval Architects and Marine Engineers, American Society of Naval Engineers, Society of Women Engineers. *Campus security:* 24-hour emergency response devices and patrols, controlled dormitory access. *Student services:* personal/psychological counseling.

Athletics *Intercollegiate sports:* basketball M/W, cross-country running M/W, sailing M/W, soccer M/W, tennis M/W, volleyball M/W. *Intramural sports:* ultimate Frisbee M/W, volleyball M/W.

Standardized Tests *Required:* SAT (for admission), SAT Subject Tests in math and either physics or chemistry (for admission).

Costs (2008–09) *Comprehensive fee:* includes room and board ($9500).

Financial Aid Of all full-time matriculated undergraduates who enrolled in 2005, 16 applied for aid, 9 were judged to have need, 4 had their need fully met. In 2005, 6 non-need-based awards were made. *Average percent of need met:* 85%. *Average financial aid package:* $2797. *Average need-based loan:* $2769. *Average need-based gift aid:* $2225. *Average non-need-based aid:* $1160. *Average indebtedness upon graduation:* $11,612.

Applying *Options:* early decision. *Application fee:* $25. *Required:* high school transcript, minimum 3.5 GPA, 2 letters of recommendation, interview, proof of US citizenship or permanent residency status. *Application deadlines:* 2/15 (freshmen), 2/15 (transfers). *Early decision deadline:* 10/15. *Notification:* continuous until 4/30 (freshmen), continuous until 4/30 (transfers), 12/15 (early decision).

Freshman Application Contact Webb Institute, Crescent Beach Road, Glen Cove, NY 11542-1398. *Phone:* 516-671-2213. *Fax:* 516-674-9838. *E-mail:* admissions@webb-institute.edu.

See page 1876 for the College Close-Up.

WELLS COLLEGE

Aurora, New York **www.wells.edu/**

- **Independent** 4-year, founded 1868
- **Rural** 365-acre campus with easy access to Syracuse
- **Endowment** $47.4 million
- **Coed, primarily women** 557 undergraduate students, 97% full-time, 77% women, 23% men
- **Moderately difficult** entrance level, 64% of applicants were admitted

Undergraduates 541 full-time, 16 part-time. Students come from 31 states and territories, 14 other countries, 30% are from out of state, 5% African American, 2% Asian American or Pacific Islander, 4% Hispanic American, 0.6% Native American, 2% international, 7% transferred in, 75% live on campus. *Retention:* 76% of 2006 full-time freshmen returned.

Freshmen *Admission:* 1,148 applied, 740 admitted, 174 enrolled. *Average high school GPA:* 3.5. *Test scores:* SAT critical reading scores over 500: 81%; SAT math scores over 500: 71%; ACT scores over 18: 91%; SAT critical reading scores over 600: 44%; SAT math scores over 600: 22%; ACT scores over 24: 62%; SAT critical reading scores over 700: 10%; SAT math scores over 700: 3%; ACT scores over 30: 7%.

Faculty *Total:* 84, 57% full-time, 70% with terminal degrees. *Student/faculty ratio:* 9:1.

Majors African-American/Black studies; American studies; anthropology; art; art history, criticism and conservation; biochemistry; biology/biological sciences; business administration and management; chemistry; computer science; creative writing; dance; dramatic/theater arts; economics; education; elementary education; engineering; English; environmental studies; fine/studio arts; French; history; international relations and affairs; mathematics; molecular biology; music; philosophy; physics; political science and government; pre-dentistry studies; pre-law studies; pre-medical studies; pre-veterinary studies; psychology; public policy analysis; religious studies; secondary education; sociology; Spanish; women's studies.

Academics *Calendar:* semesters. *Degree:* bachelor's. *Special study options:* accelerated degree program, adult/continuing education programs, advanced placement credit, double majors, English as a second language, independent study, internships, off-campus study, part-time degree program, services for LD students, student-designed majors, study abroad. *ROTC:* Army (c), Air Force (c). *Unusual degree programs:* 3-2 business administration with University of Rochester; engineering with Columbia University, Clarkson University, Cornell University, Case Western Reserve University; community health with University of Rochester.

Computers on Campus 96 computers/terminals and 1,224 ports are available on campus for general student use. Students can access the following: computer help desk, free student e-mail accounts. Campuswide network is available. 100% of college-owned or -operated housing units are wired for high-speed Internet access.

Student Life *Housing:* on-campus residence required through senior year. *Options:* coed, women-only. Campus housing is university owned. Freshman campus housing is guaranteed. *Activities and organizations:* drama/theater group, student-run newspaper, choral group, creative and performing arts groups, POWER, Amnesty International, Athletic Association, choral groups. *Campus security:* 24-hour emergency response devices and patrols, late-night transport/escort service, controlled dormitory access. *Student services:* health clinic, personal/psychological counseling, women's center.

Athletics Member NCAA. All Division III. *Intercollegiate sports:* cross-country running M/W, field hockey W, lacrosse M/W, soccer M/W, softball W, swimming and diving W, tennis W. *Intramural sports:* basketball M/W, field hockey W, football W, golf W, rugby W, sailing W, skiing (cross-country) W, skiing (downhill) W, soccer M/W, swimming and diving M, tennis W, volleyball W.

Standardized Tests *Required:* SAT or ACT (for admission).

Costs (2008–09) *Comprehensive fee:* $27,830 includes full-time tuition ($17,510), mandatory fees ($1900), and room and board ($8420). Part-time tuition: $730 per credit hour. *College room only:* $4210.

Financial Aid Of all full-time matriculated undergraduates who enrolled in 2007, 479 applied for aid, 414 were judged to have need, 120 had their need fully met. 69 Federal Work-Study jobs (averaging $1600). 362 state and other part-time jobs (averaging $1600). In 2007, 71 non-need-based awards were made. *Average percent of need met:* 91%. *Average financial aid package:* $18,890. *Average need-based loan:* $4685. *Average need-based gift aid:* $13,185. *Average non-need-based aid:* $6475. *Average indebtedness upon graduation:* $20,355.

Applying *Options:* electronic application, early admission, early decision, early action, deferred entrance. *Application fee:* $40. *Required:* essay or personal statement, high school transcript, 2 letters of recommendation. *Recommended:* interview. *Application deadlines:* 3/1 (freshmen), rolling (transfers), 12/15 (early action). *Early decision deadline:* 12/15. *Notification:* 4/1 (freshmen), continuous (transfers), 1/15 (early decision), 2/1 (early action).

Freshman Application Contact Ms. Susan Raith Sloan, Wells College, 170 Main Street, Aurora, NY 13026. *Phone:* 315-364-3264. *Toll-free phone:* 800-952-9355. *Fax:* 315-364-3227. *E-mail:* admissions@wells.edu.

See page 1878 for the College Close-Up.

YESHIVA AND KOLEL BAIS MEDRASH ELYON

Monsey, New York

YESHIVA AND KOLLEL HARBOTZAS TORAH

Brooklyn, New York

YESHIVA DERECH CHAIM

Brooklyn, New York

Director of Admissions Mr. Y. Borchardt, Administrator, Yeshiva Derech Chaim, 4907 18th Avenue, Brooklyn, NY 11218. *Phone:* 718-438-5476.

YESHIVA D'MONSEY RABBINICAL COLLEGE

Monsey, New York

YESHIVA GEDOLAH IMREI YOSEF D'SPINKA
Brooklyn, New York

YESHIVA KARLIN STOLIN RABBINICAL INSTITUTE
Brooklyn, New York

Director of Admissions Mr. Aryeh L. Wolpin, Director of Admissions, Yeshiva Karlin Stolin Rabbinical Institute, 1818 Fifty-fourth Street, Brooklyn, NY 11204. *Phone:* 718-232-7800 Ext. 26.

YESHIVA OF NITRA RABBINICAL COLLEGE
Mount Kisco, New York

Director of Admissions Mr. Ernest Schwartz, Administrator, Yeshiva of Nitra Rabbinical College, Pines Bridge Road, Mount Kisco, NY 10549. *Phone:* 718-384-5460. *Fax:* 718-387-9400.

YESHIVA OF THE TELSHE ALUMNI
Riverdale, New York

YESHIVA SHAAREI TORAH OF ROCKLAND
Suffern, New York

YESHIVA SHAAR HATORAH TALMUDIC RESEARCH INSTITUTE
Kew Gardens, New York

Director of Admissions Rabbi Kalman Epstein, Assistant Dean, Yeshiva Shaar Hatorah Talmudic Research Institute, 83-96 117th Street, Kew Gardens, NY 11418-1469. *Phone:* 718-846-1940.

YESHIVAS NOVOMINSK
Brooklyn, New York

YESHIVATH VIZNITZ
Monsey, New York

Director of Admissions Rabbi Bernard Rosenfeld, Registrar, Yeshivath Viznitz, Phyllis Terrace, PO Box 446, Monsey, NY 10952. *Phone:* 914-356-1010.

YESHIVATH ZICHRON MOSHE
South Fallsburg, New York

Director of Admissions Rabbi Abba Gorelick, Dean, Yeshivath Zichron Moshe, Laurel Park Road, South Fallsburg, NY 12779. *Phone:* 914-434-5240.

YESHIVAT MIKDASH MELECH
Brooklyn, New York

Director of Admissions Rabbi S. Churba, Director of Admissions, Yeshivat Mikdash Melech, 1326 Ocean Parkway, Brooklyn, NY 11230-5601. *Phone:* 718-339-1090.

YESHIVA UNIVERSITY
New York, New York **www.yu.edu/**

Director of Admissions Mr. Michael Kranzler, Director of Undergraduate Admissions, Yeshiva University, 500 West 185th Street, New York, NY 10033-3201. *Phone:* 212-960-5277.

YORK COLLEGE OF THE CITY UNIVERSITY OF NEW YORK
Jamaica, New York **www.york.cuny.edu/**

- **State and locally supported** 4-year, founded 1967, part of City University of New York System
- **Urban** 50-acre campus with easy access to New York City
- **Endowment** $438,007
- **Coed** 6,682 undergraduate students, 62% full-time, 67% women, 33% men
- **Moderately difficult** entrance level, 60% of applicants were admitted

Undergraduates 4,137 full-time, 2,545 part-time. Students come from 7 states and territories, 0.2% are from out of state, 45% African American, 11% Asian American or Pacific Islander, 17% Hispanic American, 0.3% Native American, 10% transferred in. *Retention:* 70% of 2006 full-time freshmen returned.

Freshmen *Admission:* 8,329 applied, 5,022 admitted, 1,017 enrolled. *Test scores:* SAT critical reading scores over 500: 11%; SAT math scores over 500: 15%; SAT critical reading scores over 600: 1%; SAT math scores over 600: 2%.

Faculty *Total:* 470, 39% full-time. *Student/faculty ratio:* 17:1.

Majors Accounting; African-American/Black studies; anthropology; art; biology/biological sciences; biology/biotechnology laboratory technician; business administration and management; chemistry; clinical laboratory science/medical technology; computer management; dramatic/theater arts; economics; English; environmental health; French; geology/earth science; gerontology; health teacher education; history; information science/studies; Italian; liberal arts and sciences/liberal studies; marketing/marketing management; mathematics; music; nursing (registered nurse training); occupational therapy; philosophy; physical education teaching and coaching; physics; political science and government; psychology; social work; sociology; Spanish; speech and rhetoric.

Academics *Calendar:* semesters. *Degrees:* bachelor's and master's. *Special study options:* adult/continuing education programs, advanced placement credit, cooperative education, double majors, English as a second language, honors programs, independent study, internships, off-campus study, part-time degree program, services for LD students, summer session for credit. *ROTC:* Army (c), Air Force (c).

Computers on Campus 530 computers/terminals and 844 ports are available on campus for general student use. Students can access the following: computer help desk, free student e-mail accounts, online (class) grades, online (class) registration, online (class) schedules. Campuswide network is available. Wireless service is available via entire campus.

Student Life *Housing:* college housing not available. *Activities and organizations:* drama/theater group, student-run newspaper, television station, choral group, Haitian Students Association, Caribbean Students Association, Haitian Cultural Association, Latin Caucus. *Campus security:* 24-hour emergency response devices and patrols, late-night transport/escort service. *Student services:* health clinic, personal/psychological counseling, women's center.

Athletics Member NCAA. All Division III. *Intercollegiate sports:* baseball M/W, basketball M/W, cross-country running M/W, soccer M, softball W, swimming and diving M/W, tennis M, track and field M/W, volleyball M/W. *Intramural sports:* basketball M/W, cross-country running M/W, soccer M, softball W, swimming and diving M/W, table tennis M/W, tennis M, track and field M/W, volleyball M/W.

Standardized Tests *Required:* SAT or ACT (for admission).

Costs (2007–08) *Tuition:* state resident $4000 full-time, $170 per credit hour part-time; nonresident $8640 full-time, $360 per credit hour part-time. No tuition increase for student's term of enrollment. *Required fees:* $180 full-time. *Payment plan:* installment. *Waivers:* senior citizens and employees or children of employees.

Financial Aid Of all full-time matriculated undergraduates who enrolled in 2007, 3,203 applied for aid, 3,083 were judged to have need, 209 had their need fully met. In 2007, 219 non-need-based awards were made. *Average percent of need met:* 39%. *Average financial aid package:* $4956. *Average need-based loan:* $2899. *Average need-based gift aid:* $4381. *Average non-need-based aid:* $870. *Average indebtedness upon graduation:* $8899.

Applying *Options:* electronic application, deferred entrance. *Application fee:* $65. *Required:* high school transcript, minimum 2.0 GPA. *Required for some:* minimum 2.5 GPA. *Recommended:* minimum 3.0 GPA. *Application deadlines:* rolling (freshmen), rolling (transfers). *Notification:* continuous (freshmen), continuous (transfers).

Freshman Application Contact Ms. Diane Warmsley, Director of Admissions, York College of the City University of New York, 94-20 Guy R. Brewer Boulevard, Jamaica, NY 11451. *Phone:* 718-262-2188. *Fax:* 718-262-2601. *E-mail:* warmsley@york.cuny.edu.

See page 1880 for the College Close-Up.

ADELPHI UNIVERSITY

GARDEN CITY, NEW YORK

The University

Adelphi University, founded in 1896, is Long Island's first private coeducational institution of higher learning. A nonsectarian, independent university, Adelphi welcomes men and women of all backgrounds who display intellectual inquisitiveness, academic commitment, and a desire for achievement and purpose in life. The University enrolls 4,930 undergraduates and 3,403 graduate students. Thirty-seven states and forty-five countries are represented in its diverse student body. The campus is located on 75 landscaped acres in Garden City, New York, 20 miles east of New York City and easily accessible by public transportation. The University also has three off-campus centers: the Manhattan Center in New York City, the Hauppauge Center on Long Island, and the Hudson Valley Center in Poughkeepsie, New York.

Adelphi University's schools and programs include the College of Arts and Sciences; the Honors College; the Schools of Business, Nursing, and Social Work; the Ruth S. Ammon School of Education; the Gordon F. Derner Institute of Advanced Psychological Studies; and adult academic programs in University College.

The University's six residence halls accommodate more than 1,100 students. The Residential Life staff at Adelphi is committed to bringing education to the residence halls. A lecture and discussion series brings faculty members together with students to examine events of the day and issues related to the classroom. In addition, about 200 seminars, workshops, and events are offered each year. Faculty and guest lecturers lead discussions on such topics as American politics, ethnic diversity, legal affairs, job interviewing, sexual conduct, and AIDS.

Opportunities for enhancing life beyond the classroom abound at Adelphi. Students participate in intramural and intercollegiate athletics (including nationally ranked men's and women's soccer, women's softball, and men's baseball, basketball, and lacrosse), drama productions, and more than seventy student clubs, community-service groups, and organizations. The University gymnasium houses a swimming pool; basketball court; weight-training and exercise rooms; and dance studios. Other physical education facilities include a large indoor running track, and separate fields for baseball, lacrosse, soccer, and softball. In addition, a vast array of activities such as movies, exhibits, cabarets, symposia, and field trips are scheduled every semester.

The Adelphi student newspaper (*Delphian*), the yearbook (*Oracle*), and the student literary and arts magazine, *Magnum Opus*, welcome writers and photographers.

In the Ruth S. Harley University Center (UC)—the central meeting place on campus—Adelphi students browse in the full-service bookstore, refresh themselves and relax in one of the center's lounges (commuter students have a special lounge equipped with lockers), eat in the UC Cafeteria, and enjoy a vast array of activities including movies, comedy shows, lectures, dance parties, and musical events. Cultural trips are also offered. The University Center also houses Adelphi's numerous student organizations.

Location

Adelphi's main campus is located in the picturesque and architecturally distinctive suburban community of Garden City, New York, a village of stately homes, historic buildings, and parks. The cultural and commercial resources of New York City and the recreation and entertainment of Long Island are only a short distance away by public or private transit.

Majors and Degrees

Undergraduate studies leading to the degrees of Bachelor of Arts (B.A.), Bachelor of Business Administration (B.B.A.), Bachelor of Fine Arts (B.F.A.), Bachelor of Science (B.S.), and Bachelor of Social Work (B.S.W.) are offered at Adelphi University. Programs of study at Adelphi include: accounting; African American and ethnic studies; anthropology/forensic anthropology; art, with specializations in art education*, art history, fine arts* (ceramics, painting, photography, printmaking, and sculpture), and graphic design*; Asian studies; biochemistry; biology; chemistry; communication sciences and disorders; communications; computer and management information systems; computer science; criminal justice; economics; education studies, with plans of study in childhood education (STEP) and adolescence education (STEP); English; environmental studies; exercise physiology; finance; foreign language studies; French; history; interdisciplinary studies; international studies; Italian; journalism; Latin American studies; management, with specializations in finance, human resource management, management information systems, and marketing; mathematics; music; nursing; performing arts: dance and theater arts (with specializations in acting and design/technical); philosophy; physical education; physical education/health education; physics; political science; psychology; public service; social work; sociology; Spanish; sport management; and women's studies. (A * indicates that an art portfolio is required.)

Five-year bachelor's/master's programs are offered in Scholars Teacher Education Program (STEP), childhood education, adolescence education, and social work.

Opportunities for preprofessional studies are available in predental, pre-engineering, prelaw, premedicine, preoptometry, and pre-physical therapy/allied health.

Academic Programs

The goal of the academic programs at Adelphi is to provide higher education that cultivates the intellect and prepares students for the future. Consistent with the University's approach to liberal learning, students take part in the University's general education distribution requirements.

A minimum of 120 credits is required for a baccalaureate degree, with a specified number in the chosen major. Double majors and various minors may be elected. Seniors of superior academic ability may be admitted to graduate courses in their major field.

Off-Campus Programs

Adelphi University offers study-abroad programs that can last several weeks or span up to an academic year. Students can participate in Adelphi-run programs in Florence, London, Mexico, Greece, and the Bahamas, or join programs run by other educational institutions.

Academic Facilities

The University Libraries are composed of the Swirbul Library, the Archives and Special Collections, and the libraries at the Manhattan, Hauppauge, and Hudson Valley centers. These libraries contain 667,383 volumes and 805,179 items in microformat, plus 23,230 audiovisual items, 1,635 periodical subscriptions, and access to over 27,000 electronic titles. The University Libraries are fully automated with holdings accessible through ALICAT (the Adelphi Libraries Catalog Online). As an enhancement of the traditional reference services, online access is provided to 233 research databases.

The Swirbul Library is also the center of information technology on campus. Its amenities include a battery of personal computers that are fully networked for student use, a faculty development lab, and a technology infrastructure that reaches into every classroom and every part of the curriculum to provide Web-based learning and other applications of communication and information media.

The new 18,000-square-foot Adele and Herbert J. Klapper Center for Fine Arts has greatly expanded Adelphi's art studio and classroom space and offers greater opportunity for nonmajors to take art courses. This is in addition to the current state-of-the-art digital graphics design studio and faculty offices and the expansion of drawing studios in Blodgett Hall.

In 2006, Adelphi broke ground on an ambitious construction project to expand and enhance academic, cultural, and athletic facilities. Adelphi's plans for expansion include a new performing arts complex, a new recreation and sports complex, and a new Early Learning Center.

Costs

The 2007–08 tuition and fees for full-time undergraduates was $23,000. For students living on campus, additional costs include room ($6700 for a typical double room without air conditioning) and board ($2200 for a basic meal plan).

Financial Aid

The Office of Student Financial Services administers federal and New York State programs that provide funds to assist students in pursuing their academic goals. In addition to grants based on need, Adelphi annually offers almost 1,000 of its own scholarships based on merit, talent, and extracurricular excellence. Eighty-six percent of Adelphi undergraduates receive some form of financial aid each year. The average financial aid package award for a full-time freshman is approximately $14,500.

Faculty

At Adelphi, the quality of education is entrusted to its distinguished faculty members, who are noted for their serious commitment to students, as well as for their research and professional contributions. Here, professors, not graduate assistants, teach undergraduate courses, and students learn in small, intimate environments.

Student Government

The Student Government Association is the elected student group that represents the opinions of the full-time undergraduate body to the administration and other groups. The Student Government Association hosts speakers, sponsors awareness days, and serves as a voice for student concerns and interests.

Admission Requirements

Recommended admission qualifications include graduation from a four-year public or private high school or equivalent credentials, 4 years of English, 3 years of science, 3 years of mathematics, 2–3 years of a foreign language or languages, and 4 additional units chosen from the fields mentioned or from history and social studies. Official test results from the SAT or ACT are required.

Personal interviews and campus tours are strongly recommended for all applicants. Arrangements can be made by contacting the Office of Admissions.

Application and Information

The following admission credentials should be submitted by applicants: a completed application for admission, the $35 application fee, an official high school transcript or graduate equivalency diploma, official results of the SAT or ACT, and letters of recommendation. Transfer students must submit official transcripts from all colleges previously attended.

Adelphi accepts applications on a rolling basis, with admission twice each year for the semesters beginning in September and January. Freshman filing dates are December 1 for early action, March 1 for regular admission to the fall semester (applications received later are reviewed on a rolling basis), and November 1 for regular admission for the spring semester (applications received later are reviewed on a rolling basis). The nonbinding early-action plan is available only for the September term. An early-action decision means that applicants who submit their applications by December 1 receive an admissions decision by December 31 and that they are considered for scholarships and financial aid.

For more information, students should contact:

University Admissions
Adelphi University
Garden City, New York 11530
Phone: 800-ADELPHI (toll-free)
E-mail: admissions@adelphi.edu
Web site: http://www.adelphi.edu

BARNARD COLLEGE

NEW YORK, NEW YORK

The College

Barnard College was among the pioneers in the late nineteenth-century crusade to make higher education available to young women. Founded in 1889, it became affiliated with the Columbia University system in 1900 and today serves 2,360 students who come from nearly every state and almost forty countries. It remains a partner of the university, and students at the two schools may cross-register for courses at either institution. Barnard students have access to Columbia University libraries, and graduates receive their degree from the university. Despite this close connection, Barnard College remains a small, independent liberal arts college, devoted solely to the undergraduate education of women. The College maintains its own Board of Trustees, faculty, and administrative staff; its own endowment; an independent admissions process; and sole ownership of its property and physical plant. It offers the intimacy of a small college with all the added advantages of a major university.

The self-contained Barnard campus occupies 4 acres of urban property along Broadway between 116th and 120th streets. Barnard Hall, with its newly renovated Ethel S. LeFrak '41 and Samuel J. LeFrak Gymnasium and Julius S. Held Lecture Hall, stands opposite the main gates of the College, while the south end of the campus contains the Brooks, Reid, Hewitt, and Sulzberger residence halls complex. Additional housing is located nearby, and some options for coed housing with Columbia are available. Students are guaranteed housing for all four years at Barnard. The College is currently building a new state-of-the-art student center called the Nexus, which is scheduled to open fall 2009. The Nexus will house student leadership offices, a coffee house, a theater, and lounges.

Location

Barnard is located in the safe and quiet Morningside Heights neighborhood of New York City, directly across from Columbia University. Abounding with cultural, educational, internship, and professional opportunities, New York is Barnard's laboratory.

Majors and Degrees

Students can earn a Bachelor of Arts in the following subjects: Africana studies, American studies, ancient studies, anthropology, architecture, art history, Asian and Middle Eastern cultures, astronomy, biochemistry, biological sciences, chemistry, classics (Greek and Latin), comparative literature, computer science, dance, economics, education, English, environmental biology, environmental science, film studies, foreign area studies, French, German, history, human rights studies, Italian, Jewish studies, mathematics and applied mathematics, medieval and Renaissance studies, music, neuroscience, philosophy, physics, political science, psychology, religion, Russian and Slavic studies, sociology, Spanish and Latin American cultures, statistics, theater, urban studies, and women's studies.

Barnard College also offers double- and joint-degree programs in cooperation with other schools within the Columbia University community. These include a five-year (3-2) program offered in conjunction with the School of International Affairs, in which a student earns both an A.B. degree and a Master in International Affairs (M.I.A.) or a Master of Public Administration (M.P.A). In cooperation with the School of Law, Barnard offers an accelerated program in interdisciplinary legal education, whereby selected students can begin their legal studies after three years of undergraduate course work. Through the School of Engineering and Applied Science, Barnard students can pursue a five-year (3-2) program in all branches of engineering, including aerospace, civil, and electrical engineering, leading to both an A.B. and a B.S. degree. In cooperation with the School of Dentistry, a limited number of students may enter the Columbia University School of Dental and Oral Surgery after three years of undergraduate work at Barnard. Outside the university, a student can earn both an A.B. degree and a Master of Music (M.M.) in a five-year (3-2) program with the Juilliard School. Through an agreement with List College of the Jewish Theological Seminary, students can earn an A.B. degree from Barnard and a bachelor's degree in Hebrew literature.

Academic Programs

Two required courses, First-Year Seminar and First-Year English, set the foundation for a Barnard education with small classes limited to 16 students. General education requirements are organized around nine Ways of Knowing that reflect the breadth and depth of a true liberal arts education while building the skills of analysis, independent thought, and self-expression. The Ways of Knowing offer a flexible structure and a wide array of courses under the following categories: reason and values, social analysis, cultures in comparison, language, laboratory science, quantitative and deductive reasoning, historical studies, literature, and visual and performing arts.

Advanced placement and I.B. credit are available. Barnard operates on a two-semester calendar, with classes beginning in early September. The fall semester ends in mid-December; classes resume for the spring semester in mid-January and end in mid-May.

Off-Campus Programs

As independent affiliates of Columbia University, Barnard students have open access to the courses, libraries, and other facilities of Columbia. With special permission, students may also register for selected classes in Columbia's graduate and professional schools. A program offered in cooperation with the Jewish Theological Seminary, located two blocks north of Barnard, allows qualified students to take courses for credit. In a similar exchange with both the Juilliard School and the nearby Manhattan School of Music, qualified Barnard students may take music lessons in a conservatory setting.

Under the auspices of Reid Hall in Paris, a Barnard-Columbia facility, several semester-long and full-year programs are offered. Students of classics are eligible to study at the Intercollegiate Center for Classical Studies in Rome. Qualified students may also study at Oxford (Somerville College), Cambridge (Newnham College), the University of London (University College, London School of Economics, King's College, or Queen Mary College), or the University of Warwick. Qualified students are also eligible to study in Germany, Italy, Japan, and more than 300 programs in sixty countries worldwide. Students may also participate in exchange programs with Spelman College in Atlanta and Howard University in Washington, D.C.

Barnard's metropolitan location offers its students a variety of work experiences through its extensive program of more than 2,500 internships. More than two thirds of Barnard students participate in internships throughout the academic year and summer; approximately one third of these internship opportunities receive stipends.

Academic Facilities

Milbank Hall, the oldest building on the campus, houses administrative and faculty offices, classrooms, the Arthur Ross Greenhouse, and the Minor Latham Playhouse. Fourteen-story Altschul Hall, devoted mainly to the sciences, has classrooms, department offices, and modern laboratory equipment.

Wollman Library offers three floors of reading areas and more than 170,000 volumes in open stacks. Students also have access to the 8 million volumes within the Columbia University library system.

Currently under construction, the Nexus, a 70,000-square-foot state-of-the-art facility, will expand and increase the space available for teaching, for learning, for student activities, for dining, and for large lectures and theatrical productions.

Costs

Tuition and fees for 2008–09 are yet to be announced. Room and board costs have not yet been determined.

Financial Aid

All financial aid supplied or administered by Barnard is awarded on the basis of demonstrated need as determined by federal regulations and the College's Office of Financial Aid. Barnard gives no merit or athletic scholarships. College aid is supplementary to family resources. Once need has been established, Barnard is committed to covering 100 percent of demonstrated need for U.S. citizens and permanent residents through a combination of grants, loans, and work-study. Approximately 55 percent of the students at Barnard receive some form of financial aid. A limited number of scholarships are available to international citizens.

Barnard College has a need-blind admission policy in which all applications are judged on merit without reference to the applicant's financial circumstances.

Faculty

Barnard College employs 319 teaching faculty members. The student-faculty ratio is 10:1. The faculty includes editors of leading scholarly journals, prize-winning novelists and translators, and frequent winners of awards from respected foundations, corporations, and government agencies. They are actively engaged in research and publication in their respective fields, but they regard teaching as their primary commitment. All students have faculty advisers who assist them in selecting courses and designing individual academic programs.

Student Government

Every Barnard student is a member of the Student Government Association, which sponsors numerous extracurricular activities. These include the College newspaper, the literary magazine, dramatic groups, political and religious organizations, and preprofessional and departmental clubs. Cooperation between Barnard and Columbia groups is common and seamless. Students, faculty members, and administrators serve on tripartite committees and share responsibility for policy recommendations on curriculum, housing, financial aid, orientation, and the library.

Admission Requirements

The Committee on Admissions selects young women of proven academic strength who exhibit the potential for further intellectual growth. Careful consideration is given to candidates' high school records, recommendations, writing skills, standardized test scores, and special abilities and interests. While admission is highly selective, no one criterion determines acceptance. Each applicant is considered in terms of her individual qualities of mind and spirit and her potential for successfully completing her program of study at Barnard.

Candidates for admission to the first-year class must have taken a college-preparatory program at an approved secondary school or have an equivalent level of education. A recommended program comprises 4 years of work in English, 3 or more years in mathematics, 3 or more years in a foreign language, 3 or more years in science (with laboratory), and 3 or more years in history. Barnard also requires candidates to submit scores from the SAT Reasoning Test, along with two SAT Subject Tests. Alternatively, students may submit scores from the ACT with writing in place of the SAT and subject tests. Students educated in a non-English-speaking setting or who have studied in English for less than five years should take the TOEFL exam as well. An interview is recommended but not required.

Application and Information

Applicants for first-year admission should apply to Barnard in the fall of their senior year of high school. Applications must be received by January 1 and should be accompanied by a nonrefundable fee of $55. Students are notified of the admission decision in early April. Well-qualified high school seniors who have selected Barnard as their first-choice college may apply under the binding Early Decision Plan. Early Decision applications must be submitted by November 15. Barnard accepts transfer students to the sophomore and junior classes. Transfer applications must be submitted by April 1 for consideration for September enrollment and by November 1 for consideration for January enrollment.

For more information about Barnard College, students should contact:

Jennifer Gill Fondiller
Dean of Admissions
Barnard College
3009 Broadway
New York, New York 10027
Phone: 212-854-2014
Fax: 212-854-6220
E-mail: admissions@barnard.edu
Web site: http://www.barnard.edu

A view of Milbank Hall from McIntosh Plaza at Barnard College.

BERNARD M. BARUCH COLLEGE OF THE CITY UNIVERSITY OF NEW YORK

NEW YORK, NEW YORK

The City University of New York

The College

Baruch College, one of the best academic resources in the New York City area, has earned a reputation for excellence that extends to all parts of the world, attracting students from New York State, neighboring states, and abroad. A senior institution of the City University of New York (CUNY), Baruch offers students a broad array of undergraduate and graduate programs through its three schools: the Zicklin School of Business, the Weissman School of Arts and Sciences, and the School of Public Affairs.

Baruch is accredited by the Middle States Association of Colleges and Schools. All baccalaureate and master's programs in business offered by the Zicklin School of Business are accredited by AACSB International–The Association to Advance Collegiate Schools of Business. In addition to the business accreditation, both the undergraduate and graduate accounting curriculums have been awarded the accounting accreditation from AACSB International.

The student body is remarkably diverse, reflecting the extraordinary ethnic spectrum of the city. Baruch currently enrolls more than 15,000 students, including 2,900 graduate students. There are more than 170 student clubs and organizations representing a wide range of interests: academic, artistic, cultural, ethnic, professional, and athletic. Intercollegiate sports include, among others, basketball, tennis, and volleyball. The Sidney Mishkin Gallery mounts notable exhibitions of photographs, drawings, prints, and paintings. Several music and theater groups are in residence at the College, including the Alexander String Quartet. Plays, concerts, dance performances, readings, and other events are scheduled throughout the year at the Baruch Performing Arts Center, which draws upon the vast cultural offerings of New York City.

In addition to its extensive array of undergraduate majors, Baruch offers graduate programs leading to the M.B.A., M.P.A., M.S., M.S.Ed., and M.S.I.L.R. An M.B.A. in health-care administration is offered jointly with the Mount Sinai School of Medicine; a J.D./M.B.A. is offered jointly with Brooklyn Law School and New York Law School.

U.S. News & World Report ranks Baruch's undergraduate business programs among the top fifty in the nation, and it consistently ranks Baruch's part-time M.B.A. program among the top twenty-five in the nation.

Location

Situated at 24th Street and Lexington Avenue in the Flatiron/Gramercy Park neighborhood of Manhattan, Baruch is in the heart of one of the world's most dynamic financial and cultural centers, within easy reach of Wall Street, Midtown, and the global headquarters of major companies, firms, and organizations. This prime location offers Baruch students unparalleled access to top career and internship opportunities. The College is convenient to public transportation from other boroughs, surrounding counties, and New Jersey and Connecticut.

Majors and Degrees

The Zicklin School of Business, the largest collegiate business school in the country, awards the Bachelor of Business Administration (B.B.A.) degree with majors in accountancy, computer information systems, economics, finance and investments, industrial/organizational psychology, management, marketing, operations research, quantitative methods and modeling, and real estate. In addition, a five-year combined bachelor's and master's program in accounting is offered.

The Weissman School of Arts and Sciences awards the Bachelor of Arts (B.A.) degree in thirteen major fields: actuarial science, communication (business, corporate, and graphic arts), economics, English, history, mathematics, music, philosophy, political science, psychology, sociology, Spanish, and statistics. It also offers interdisciplinary specializations in arts administration, business journalism, and management of musical enterprises. Students can work with faculty advisers to design other specialized programs that combine two or more areas of interest.

The School of Public Affairs offers a Bachelor of Science (B.S.) degree in public affairs.

Academic Programs

Baruch College requires that all students take general liberal arts courses as the necessary preparation and framework within which specialized knowledge can be most effectively used.

Baruch's degree programs in business require 124 credits. Candidates for the B.B.A. are required to take at least half of their credits in the liberal arts and sciences. The business base is made up of 29 required credits, and students must take a minimum of 24 credits in the major field. The degree programs in the arts and sciences and public affairs require 120 credits. Candidates for the B.A. degree are expected to complete the base curriculum (at least 54 credits) in their freshman and sophomore years, select a major field of study by their junior year, and complete at least 90 credits in the arts and sciences. All students must maintain an overall C average or better and a C average or better in their major. Students are required to complete a minor consisting of three courses of study in one discipline of the humanities, natural sciences, or social sciences. At least 60 percent of the credits in the major must be taken at Baruch.

Entering freshmen may receive a maximum of 21 credits for Advanced Placement (AP) examinations on which appropriate grades have been earned and for work completed in recognized prefreshman programs.

Baruch College participates in the Macaulay Honors College at CUNY. This is a select group of high-achieving students. These students have available to them the combined resources of the country's largest urban university and the world's most exciting city. Special funding provides a package that includes full-tuition coverage. A Cultural Passport provides an entrée to the riches of the city, including concerts, theater, museums, and other cultural institutions. University Scholars participate in challenging honors programs through the Honors College Seminar, where they take part in a wide range of activities and common projects with honors college students from other CUNY campuses.

Off-Campus Programs

Students may study abroad for credit for a semester or a year through exchange programs with the University of Paris, Ecole Supérieure de Commerce of Rouen (France), Middlesex University (England), Tel Aviv University (Israel), Mannheim University (Germany), and Universidad Iberoamericana (Mexico).

Academic Facilities

Baruch's Information and Technology Building houses the William and Anita Newman Library, one of the most technologically advanced facilities in New York. Recently, the library won the prestigious Excellence in Academic Libraries Award for the best college library in the nation from the Association of Colleges and Research Libraries. The 1,450-seat library provides access to extensive print and electronic information resources, including several hundred online databases, many of which are available to students via remote access from off-campus locations. A Web-based reference service is available 24 hours a day, seven days a week. Students and faculty members also have access to the 4.5 million volumes in the CUNY library system.

Also housed in the Information and Technology Building is the Baruch Computing and Technology Center, which provides computer access to 250 students at a time. It is the largest student computing center in New York City.

Baruch's award-winning Computer Center for Visually Impaired People provides access to specialized computer equipment and to data in such forms as Braille, large print, and synthetic speech. Staff members are available to translate class material to Braille. In addition, the center has a Kurzweil Reading Machine.

Baruch's College's seventeen-floor, 800,000-square-foot William and Anita Newman Vertical Campus features high-technology classrooms, over 1,500 student-access computers, computer labs, and research facilities as well as a three-level Athletics and Recreation Complex and the state-of-the-art Baruch Performing Arts Center.

Costs

For a New York State resident, the current undergraduate tuition for full-time attendance (a minimum of 12 credits or the equivalent) is $2000 per semester; for part-time study, tuition is $170 per credit. For nonresidents, tuition is $360 per credit. In addition, full-time students pay an $85 activity fee; part-time students pay a $55 activity fee. More information about tuition and fees is available on the Baruch Web site (http://www.baruch.cuny.edu/tuition). Tuition and fees are subject to change without notice.

Financial Aid

Financial aid is available for eligible students through various state and federal programs, which include the New York State Tuition Assistance Program (TAP), Federal Pell Grant, Federal Supplemental Educational Opportunity Grant (FSEOG), Federal Perkins Loan, and Federal Work-Study Program. To apply for aid, students must complete the Free Application for Federal Student Aid (FAFSA). Applications are processed as long as funds are available.

Baruch rewards academic excellence with generous scholarships to entering freshmen each year. The Presidential Scholarship, the Isabelle and William Brunman Scholarship, the Joseph Drown Scholarship, the Paul Odess Scholarship award, the Abraham Rosenberg Scholarship, and the Henry and Lucy Moses Scholarship are the most selective. The Baruch Incentive Grant offers awards ranging from $500 to $1000 per year for four years.

Faculty

Baruch faculty members are among the most distinguished and most widely known in their fields. They combine outstanding academic credentials with significant real-world experience. Approximately 500 teach full time, with about 95 percent holding a Ph.D. or other terminal degree. Full-time faculty members teach both entry-level and advanced courses and serve as advisers to student organizations and preprofessional programs.

Student Government

Undergraduate Student Government (USG) represents undergraduate students and the Graduate Student Assembly (GSA) represents graduate students. The two organizations oversee the granting of club charters and the allocation of student activity fees and participation in campus educational and community affairs.

Admission Requirements

Freshman applicants are screened initially to select those with a minimum of 3 units of both high school English and math and a minimum of two lab sciences. Students who meet these criteria are admitted based on their overall high school performance and their performance on these index subjects. Students with a GED score of at least 3000 are considered, provided that they have satisfactorily completed the required high school units of English and math. Freshmen are required to submit SAT or ACT scores.

The best preparation for success at Baruch College is a full program of college-preparatory courses in high school completed with high grades. The College strongly recommends a minimum of 4 years of English, 4 years of social studies, 3 years of mathematics, 2 years of a foreign language, 2 years of lab sciences, and 1 year of performing or visual arts. Mathematics courses are especially important for Baruch's degree programs, and elementary algebra and geometry should be completed prior to enrollment. For students interested in majoring in business, mathematics, or science, 4 units of mathematics, including trigonometry and precalculus, are recommended.

Students who have attended a college or postsecondary institution must meet admission requirements based on the number of credits they have completed.

Application and Information

General freshman applications with all official documentation and fees that are received on or before October 15 for spring admission or December 15 for fall admission are processed first. Complete transfer applications received on or before October 15 for spring admission or March 1 for fall admission are processed first. Any freshman or transfer applications received after the dates indicated above are processed on a space-available basis.

Requests to schedule an appointment with an admissions counselor, to join a campus tour, or for application materials and additional information should be made to:

Office of Undergraduate Admissions
Baruch College of the City University of New York
One Bernard Baruch Way, Box H-0720
New York, New York 10010-5585
Phone: 646-312-1400
Fax: 646-312-1363
E-mail: admissions@baruch.cuny.edu
Web site: http://www.baruch.cuny.edu

BROOKLYN COLLEGE OF THE CITY UNIVERSITY OF NEW YORK

BROOKLYN COLLEGE IS CUNY

BROOKLYN, NEW YORK

The College

Founded in 1930, Brooklyn College is a premier, four-year liberal arts college where students are given the knowledge, awareness, and experience to succeed. The College is situated on a 26-acre campus in the most dynamic New York City borough.

Brooklyn College enrolls nearly 16,000 undergraduate and graduate students, offering more than 130 programs in the humanities, education, the arts, business, sciences, and social sciences leading to bachelor's and master's degrees and advanced certificates. As one of the eleven senior colleges of the City University of New York, it shares the mission of the University, whose primary goals are access and excellence. Emblematic of the College's student success is 2006 Truman Scholarship winner Ryan Merola, one of only 2 students in New York State to win the award. Merola, '07, who graduated with a double major in political science and philosophy, was also a recipient of a 2007–08 New York City Urban Fellowship. He plans to attend law school and pursue a career in public service. Moses Feaster, '06, won a 2006 National Science Foundation fellowship to pursue a Ph.D. in developmental biology at Rockefeller University. And the 2005 Rhodes Scholar winner, Eugene Shenderov, is now studying immunology at England's Oxford University.

The tradition of academics is reflected in the accomplishments of the College's graduates and faculty members. Brooklyn College ranks nineteenth nationally in the number of undergraduates who have gone on to receive Ph.D. degrees, and it has a faculty distinguished by master teaching and scholarly achievement. Ninety percent of the full-time faculty members hold the highest degree in their field. Among them are Fulbright, Guggenheim, and MacArthur Foundation fellows, an Obie Award–winning playwright, Pulitzer Prize and National Book Award–winning authors, and award-winning scientists and musicians.

The College has an ambitious program of expansion and renewal. In 2002 the College completed an extensive renovation and expansion of its library, now the most technologically advanced facility in the CUNY system. The College's West Quad Building, which will create a second verdant quadrangle on the campus, is currently under construction and is scheduled to open its doors in 2008. The building is designed to consolidate under one roof all student services—admissions, financial aid, scholarships, registration, and the bursar. Its plans also include state-of-the-art physical education and athletic facilities, including a swimming pool, competition and practice gymnasiums, racquetball courts, a fitness center, and teaching and research labs.

Brooklyn College's students participate in more than 140 chartered campus groups, including academic clubs, service and honor societies, athletics groups, special interest groups, and performing arts organizations. Special lectures, concerts, and events are scheduled throughout the year. On the campus quad and in the Student Center, fraternities and sororities provide social and community service activities. The Hillel Foundation, Intervarsity Christian Fellowship, and Newman Center are among the many special interest clubs on campus. Student publications include newspapers, magazines, and journals. Students also operate WBCR, the Brooklyn College radio station. The staff of experienced career professionals at the Magner Center for Career Development and Internships assists Brooklyn College students and alumni to develop the skills necessary to attain their lifelong career goals.

The Morton and Angela Topfer Library Café is the only CUNY facility that is available to assist students with their academic needs 24 hours a day, seven days a week. It is equipped with computers with Internet access and data management programs.

The newly redesigned Center for Student Disability Services provides counseling and assistance to students with disabilities to ensure that they have complete access to College programs and facilities. College and departmental counseling programs provide students with academic and personal counseling. Career, preprofessional, veterans', and psychological counseling services are also available. Other services include child care for students and a health clinic.

Location

Brooklyn College is located in the residential Midwood section of Brooklyn. The many different cultures of Brooklyn contribute to the wide ethnic diversity of the College's student and teacher population. The availability of a wide variety of New York City cultural events and institutions enriches students' educational experience. Subway and bus transportation to all points inside and outside the borough is easily accessible from the College.

Majors and Degrees

Brooklyn College awards the Bachelor of Arts (B.A.), Bachelor of Science (B.S.), Bachelor of Music (B.M.), Bachelor of Fine Arts (B.F.A.), and Bachelor of Business Administration (B.B.A.) degrees.

Majors are available in the following areas: accounting; Africana studies; American studies; anthropology; art; art history; art studio; biology; broadcast journalism; business administration; business, finance, and management; Caribbean studies; chemistry; classics; comparative literature; computer and information science; creative writing; economics; education (childhood education, early childhood education, secondary education with certification in twelve subject areas); English; environmental studies; film; French; geology; health and nutrition sciences; Italian; journalism; Judaic studies; linguistics; mathematics; mathematics-computational; music; music composition; music performance; philosophy; physical education; physics; political science; psychology; Puerto Rican and Latino studies; religion studies; Russian; sociology; Spanish; speech; speech and language disabilities; speech-language pathology, audiology, speech and hearing science; television and radio; theater; and women's studies.

Certificate programs are offered in accounting, computers and programming, and film; credits earned in these programs are also applicable toward a baccalaureate degree.

Students interested in economics and computer applications may apply to enter a 4½-year program that leads to the Bachelor of Science and the Master of Professional Studies (M.P.S.) degrees.

Brooklyn College and the State University of New York Health Science Center at Brooklyn offer a coordinated eight-year honors program that leads to B.A. and M.D. degrees. The program is limited each year to 15 qualified students who are admitted only in the fall following their graduation from high school.

Professional options include the opportunity for qualified students to earn a B.A. or B.S. degree from Brooklyn College by satisfactorily completing all requirements for graduation (except 30 elective credits) and by also satisfactorily completing at least one year's work in an accredited dental, engineering, law, medical, optometry, podiatry, or veterinary school. Students interested in pursuing an engineering degree may participate in Brooklyn College's approved two-year coordinated engineering program. Students attend Brooklyn College for two years of pre-engineering studies and then transfer to Polytechnic University, City College, or the College of Staten Island for an additional two years of study to fulfill the B.S. degree requirements in a specific engineering field.

Academic Programs

The liberal arts education at Brooklyn College consists of three kinds of study: the College-wide core curriculum, which provides a diverse educational experience in the liberal arts for all students; major studies, which comprise specialized, intensive study in one discipline or an interdisciplinary program; and elective courses, selected from more than seventy-five areas. The undergraduate curriculum aims to prepare students to make rational career and personal choices by developing their critical and independent thinking skills, their ability to acquire and organize knowledge, and their proficiency with both verbal and written communication. Students pursuing a bachelor's degree must successfully complete a minimum of 120 credits.

The Honors Academy comprises eight units: the Scholars Program, which offers students who combine academic excellence with initiative and inquisitiveness the opportunity to take classes and special courses that are open only to members of the program; the Coordinated B.A./M.D. Program; the William E. Macaulay Honors College Program, which consists of a challenging honors curriculum and cultural experiences as well as a full-tuition scholarship, internship opportunities, and an academic expense account; the Mellon Mays Undergraduate Fellowship, a two-year program for members of minority groups who are considering scholarly study in the humanities; the Honors Academy Research Colloquium; the Dean's List Honors Research Program; the Engineering Honors Program; and the Special Baccalaureate Degree Program. Applications for all eight programs are available in the Office of Admissions.

Students who have completed college-level courses in high school may be considered for exemption, with or without credit, from equivalent college courses on the basis of Advanced Placement tests given by the College Board. Brooklyn College gives exemption examinations in subjects not offered by the College Board. Students completing three years of foreign language in high school are exempt from the College's language requirement.

TOCA (The On-Course Advantage) offers eligible second-semester freshmen the opportunity to graduate in four years with priority registration and guaranteed availability of required courses.

The academic calendar consists of a fall and a spring semester. Two summer sessions and a January intersession are available. Classes are offered in day, evening, and weekend sessions.

Academic Facilities

The newly expanded and renovated Brooklyn College Library serves as the crossroads of the campus. Much more than a traditional academic library, it is a comprehensive and complex information center that includes substantial physical and digital collections, the College archives, the New Media Center, and both academic and administrative computing, all brought together in a single state-of-the-art building that doubles as the College's information hub. The library's physical collections total more than 1.3 million volumes and about 25,000 audiovisual units (sound recordings, videotapes, and DVDs). The library's digital collections include 15,000 electronic subscriptions and works of reference, as well as several thousand electronic books. The new library has seating capacity for 2,317 students, twenty-two group-study rooms, five computer classrooms, and more than 600 computers for student and faculty access. Four of every ten seats include either a fixed computer or a net tap to which readers may attach their own laptops.

The Brooklyn Center for the Performing Arts at Brooklyn College, presents music, dance, and theater productions. The current facilities include a 2,500-seat auditorium, a theater, a recital hall, and a workshop theater. Plans are underway for the on-campus construction of a new $50-million center for the performing arts, which will serve the Conservatory of Music, the Department of Theater, and related disciplines.

The Public Computing Lab is a state-of-the-art facility that supports student course requirements as well as research. Other special facilities include microcomputer learning centers, a language laboratory, art studios, an advanced color-television studio, an early childhood education center, a speech and hearing center, psychology laboratories, laser laboratories, an astronomical observatory, an optical mineralogy laboratory, a greenhouse, an aquatic research center, and a nuclear physics laboratory.

Costs

In 2006–07, New York State residents paid tuition of $2000 per semester for full-time students, $170 per credit for part-time students, and $250 per credit for non-degree resident students. Non–New York State residents and international students paid tuition of $360 per credit for both full-time and part-time students, and $530 per credit for non-degree students. (Students pay per credit for all summer session and intersession courses.) The College is a commuter institution and does not have on-campus housing.

Financial Aid

Admission decisions and financial aid and scholarship decisions are made independently of each other, and an application for aid does not hinder a student's opportunity for admission. Financial assistance is available for eligible students through state and federal grant, loan, and work-study programs.

New students, especially those with strong high school or college academic records and SAT scores, are encouraged to apply for annual scholarships. Continuing students may qualify for one of the more than 400 scholarships, prizes, and awards that are given each year to Brooklyn College students. The requirements vary for each award, but recipients are chosen based on academic performance, financial need, and various other criteria that may be stipulated by the donors. Scholarships range from $100 to $4000 per year.

For more information, students should contact the Office of Financial Aid at 718-951-5051 and the Office of Scholarships at 718-951-4796. Both offices have Web pages that are accessible online at http://www.brooklyn.cuny.edu.

Faculty

The College has an outstanding faculty (534 full-time and 722 part-time) whose members have demonstrated excellence in teaching and scholarly research. Faculty members assist in the academic advisement of entering students and provide counseling to students majoring in their department. They also hold regular office hours and are generally available to support student activities.

Student Government

Student governments are active in the day, evening, and graduate divisions. By participating in the student government organizations, members gain valuable political, civic, and social experiences. Student government is expected to advocate for the interests of the student body, provide a venue for making decisions that can shape students' academic futures, and help improve campus life by creating and maintaining student services. Students also serve on the Policy Council, the major college-wide governing body. Student government is primarily funded by the collected student activity fee. Elections are held annually and all civic-minded students in good standing are encouraged to seek office.

Admission Requirements

High school students, students who want to transfer from other institutions, and adults returning to school are encouraged to apply. Freshman admission criteria involve a combination of a student's GPA, academic units, and SAT/ACT scores. Senior high school students applying as freshman applicants scoring 1100 or better on the SAT (composite math and verbal scores) are automatically admitted. Freshman students should demonstrate successful completion of at least 12 or more high school academic units (of which at least 5 units must include 2 or more years of English and 2 or more years of math). The recommended high school preparation for the College's curriculum is 4 years of English, 4 years of social studies, 3 years of mathematics, 3 years of science, and 3 years of a foreign language. Students seeking admission to the Scholars Program, Macaulay Honors College Program, or the B.A./M.D. Program must present a high school average of 90 or better, exceptional SAT or ACT scores, letters of recommendation, and an autobiographical essay and must also complete a personal interview. Qualified high school juniors may apply for early admission. Students with special educational needs may qualify for admission into the Search for Education, Elevation, and Knowledge (SEEK) program.

Application and Information

Application for admission to the undergraduate program for the fall or spring semester should be made on a standard CUNY application form, available from the Office of Admissions at any CUNY college. At http://www.brooklyn.cuny.edu, students may access online forms to apply for either freshman, transfer, or honors admission. For some honors programs, fellowships, and coordinated programs, as well as for summer and intersession courses, applications are available only through the Brooklyn College Office of Admissions. Although applications for admission are processed by the City University on a rolling basis, applicants who apply before January 15 for fall admission and before October 15 for spring admission receive prompt notification of their admission status and have the best opportunity for comprehensive advisement and course registration. The CUNY Honors College Program applicants are required to apply by November 1 (early decision) and December 15 (regular decision) for fall admission.

For an application form, additional financial aid information, scholarship information, and brochures, students should contact:

Office of Admissions
1103 James Hall
Brooklyn College
The City University of New York
2900 Bedford Avenue
Brooklyn, New York 11210
Phone: 718-951-5001
E-mail: adminqry@brooklyn.cuny.edu
Web site: http://www.brooklyn.cuny.edu

BUFFALO STATE COLLEGE, STATE UNIVERSITY OF NEW YORK

BUFFALO, NEW YORK

Buffalo State
State University of New York

The College

Buffalo State is the college of choice for high-achieving students who want to develop close relationships with professors—a major contributor to college success. Most classes have fewer than 40 students; major courses average 12 to 16. And professors, not graduate students, teach even introductory courses. Buffalo State offers more than 130 majors for undergraduate students on a safe, convenient metropolitan campus.

Buffalo State graduates are highly sought after by employers. Internships provide students with the real-world experience necessary for success in the marketplace. Buffalo State students gain experience in such places as museums, hospitals, political offices, schools, wildlife rehabilitation centers, police laboratories, banks and investment firms, advertising agencies, and engineering firms.

Of a total enrollment of about 11,000 students, approximately 9,000 are undergraduates. Most students come from New York State, but the College has a growing number of out-of-state and international students.

Buffalo State is known for its excellent teacher training programs. Its professional education programs have been continuously accredited by the National Council for Accreditation of Teacher Education (NCATE) since 1954. NCATE is a national, professional organization that evaluates teacher preparation programs to ensure that they meet rigid standards of excellence. Graduates from Buffalo State are recruited by school districts throughout the United States.

With roots as a normal school, about one third of Buffalo State's undergraduate majors prepare students for careers in teaching. (The College has been continuously accredited by NCATE since 1954.) Buffalo State also offers a healthy mix of traditional and unusual majors. The College has one of the largest and most diverse arts programs in the state, from design (jewelry, furniture, interior, and more) to performing arts to fashion and textile technology. Buffalo State's science, technology, engineering, and mathematics (STEM) programs have received millions of dollars in support in recent years; demand for Buffalo State graduates is 100 percent in some majors. Two new undergraduate degree programs—the B.A. in television arts and the B.A. in writing—are designed to provide graduates with a unique blend of a liberal arts worldview and hands-on skills.

The Sports Arena, housing Buffalo's only college ice hockey rink, is home to the NCAA Division III Bengals varsity teams, which include nineteen men's and women's teams. In addition, club and intramural teams involve students in friendly competition in sports such as basketball, dodge ball, racquetball, softball, and more. The Sports Complex also includes outdoor fields, an indoor arena, a pool, dance studios, weight rooms, and a new student fitness center.

A variety of living and learning options are available on campus, including suite- and apartment-style housing and special floors for honors and international students. Attractive off-campus housing is readily available in surrounding residential neighborhoods.

More than 100 student organizations—from the radio station and volunteer groups to sororities and fraternities—allow students to meet new people, take breaks from classes, and develop leadership skills.

Location

Buffalo State is definitely not the place for students wishing to attend a school surrounded by cow pastures. Buffalo State is the only SUNY comprehensive college located in a major city. The College is situated in the Elmwood Museum District adjacent to Delaware Park, the world-famous Albright-Knox Art Gallery, the Buffalo and Erie County Historical Society, Hoyt Lake, and the Buffalo Zoo. Students find trendy restaurants, shops, cyber cafés, and coffee bars within walking distance of campus. Outdoor sports, from windsurfing and beach volleyball to downhill skiing, are minutes away. Buffalo is minutes from Niagara Falls, less than 2 hours from Toronto, and a day's drive—or an hour's flight—from New York City and Boston. The Buffalo Niagara International Airport is 15 minutes from campus, with daily service to major metropolitan areas.

Majors and Degrees

The Bachelor of Arts degree is available with majors in anthropology, art, art history, the arts, biology, chemistry, communication studies, economics, English, French language and literature, geography, geology, history, humanities, journalism, mathematics, media production, music, philosophy, physics, political science, psychology, public communication, sociology, Spanish language and literature, television arts, theater, and writing.

The Bachelor of Science degree is awarded in the following programs: applied mathematics, applied sociology, art education, biology education, business administration, business and marketing education, career and technical education, chemistry education, childhood education, computer information systems, criminal justice, design, dietetics: coordinated, dietetics: didactic, early childhood and childhood education, earth science education, earth sciences, economics, electrical engineering technology (electronics or power and machines), English education, fashion and textile technology, forensic chemistry, French education, health and wellness, hospitality administration, individualized studies, industrial technology, mathematics education, mechanical engineering technology, physics, physics education, physics-engineering (3-2 cooperative program), psychology, social studies education, social work, sociology, Spanish education, speech language pathology, technology education, and urban and regional analysis and planning.

The Bachelor of Fine Arts degree is awarded in design, painting, photography, printmaking, and sculpture.

The Bachelor of Music degree is offered in music education.

The Bachelor of Science in Education degree is awarded in exceptional education.

Fifty-eight departmental minors are available.

The College offers advisement programs for an increasing number of prelaw and prehealth students who are preparing for graduate study in dentistry, law, medicine, or veterinary science.

Academic Programs

All Buffalo State undergraduate students must complete a minimum of 120 credit hours to qualify for a bachelor's degree. In 2006 the College implemented a "required courses" program called Intellectual Foundations. It is designed to provide broad knowledge, analytical skills, and "the tools to unlock the wisdom and insights to be found across the spectrum of human knowledge." This ambitious effort will provide the College's students with a signature Buffalo State undergraduate education.

The Foundations of Inquiry course (BSC 101) is the cornerstone of the Intellectual Foundations program. Each course, which is limited to no more than 25 students, is taught by full-time professors or exceptional adjuncts or emeriti. The Foundations of Inquiry course is designed to help students understand the connections between individual subjects and the larger "cognate areas"—the arts, the humanities, the natural sciences, and the social sciences. The professors hope to demonstrate to students that the required curriculum is not a disjointed smorgasbord of unrelated courses but a well-thought-out introduction to all the liberal arts, including math and science.

Buffalo State offers an All-College Honors Program as well as honors sequences in eleven majors. Learning communities—open to all freshmen—involve small groups of students who take the same block of thematically related classes, taught by teams of faculty members. These students have access to special gathering places on campus, equipped with computers and kitchens, where they can meet and study with other students in the program and their professors.

The College operates on a semester basis, with a three-week intersemester term in January. A summer program of three 4-week sessions is also offered.

Off-Campus Programs

Several off-campus educational opportunities provide flexibility to broaden intellectual horizons and tailor learning to individual interests and career goals. These opportunities include internships, independent study projects, clinical practice, workshops, exchange opportunities at 177 other U.S. colleges and universities, study-abroad programs at more than 300 institutions around the world, credit for experiential learning, and the ability to cross-register or complete degrees at other schools through special arrangement. All options carry college credit.

Academic Facilities

The 125-acre campus is built for academic excellence, beginning with E. H. Butler Library. Its holdings include more than 525,000 volumes (including bound periodicals); 950,000 microforms; 20,000 audiovisual and nonbook items, including CD-ROMs and DVDs; and 7,500 periodical subscriptions, all easily accessed through the user-friendly online catalog.

Students have access to 875 computer workstations in sixty labs and classrooms throughout campus. Every student has a personal computer account with continuous e-mail and Internet access, as well as individual network accounts for file storage and Web pages. Residence halls are wired with high-speed Internet ports.

The Burchfield-Penney Art Center, accredited by the American Association of Museums, houses the world's largest collection of works by watercolorist Charles E. Burchfield. An impressive, $30-million art center is under construction and expected to open in 2008. Completion of a $7.3-million renovation of the Campbell Student Union dining services is expected in January 2008. Other planned construction includes a $100-million renovation of the Science and Mathematics Complex and a new $43-million technology building. A new stadium and athletic complex are under consideration. An 856-seat auditorium in stately Rockwell Hall houses the Performing Arts Center. Broadcast majors gain hands-on experience through the College's television studio and radio station (WBNY-FM 91.3). The Warren Enters Theater is a $2.6-million state-of-the-art learning laboratory. The campus also offers several other "learning lab" opportunities for students: the Buckham Campus School (a K–8 Buffalo public school), Campus House (a private faculty-staff club operated by hospitality administration students), the Speech-Language-Hearing Clinic, and the Whitworth Ferguson Planetarium. Buffalo State's Great Lakes Center for Environmental Research and Education, located 1 mile from campus on Buffalo's waterfront, features a fleet of research vessels and an on-shore field station.

Costs

For academic year 2007–08, full-time tuition for in-state students was $4350; fees were $1025. Out-of-state students paid $10,610 per year in tuition and $1025 in fees. On-campus housing costs ranged from $2514 to $4102 per semester, and meal plans from $1075 to $1766 per semester are offered. Books, supplies, and personal expenses, including transportation, were estimated at $2900 per year. Costs are subject to change.

Financial Aid

About 75 percent of Buffalo State undergraduates receive financial assistance through grants, scholarships, loans, and employment averaging $8340 per year. The Financial Aid Office helps students find ways to pay for their college education. The office oversees distribution of more than $32.5 million in federal and state grants, loans, and student employment annually. In addition, more than 125 scholarship funds are managed by the Scholarship Office.

For information on financial aid or scholarships, students may visit http://www.fafsa.ed.gov or Buffalo State's Web site, listed in the Application and Information section. The recommended filing date for submission of aid applications for fall semester is March 15. Applications received after published deadlines are processed on a first-come, first-served basis, with awards subject to availability of funds.

Faculty

Buffalo State's faculty consists of 416 full-time and 339 part-time members. Eighty percent of the full-time faculty members have earned doctorates or terminal degrees in their fields. Faculty members are scholars, actively involved in research, publishing, and the arts. Buffalo State does not rely on teaching assistants or graduate students for classroom instruction. The College is especially proud of its 45 recipients of the SUNY Chancellor's Award for Excellence in Teaching, its 4 distinguished professors, 13 distinguished service professors, and 6 distinguished teaching professors. Faculty members provide academic advisement for majors. Professional staff members provide academic advisement for undeclared students, tutoring, personal and career counseling, and health care.

Student Government

United Students Government (USG) represents the interests of all students and encourages their participation in educational, recreational, cultural, and social activities. USG offers a variety of services and programs, including concerts, a campus newspaper, the Whispering Pines college camp, and a dental clinic funded through the mandatory student activity fee.

Admission Requirements

Buffalo State accepts both proven and promising students who demonstrate the ability to complete college-level work. Admission counselors look for a broad, balanced high school education that includes study in English, foreign language(s), mathematics, science, and social studies.

Admission decisions are based on a variety of factors, including performance in rigorous college-preparatory course work, standardized test scores (SAT or ACT), rank in class, and recommendations from teachers and school counselors. Satisfactory results on the General Educational Development (GED) test are also acceptable. For transfer students, a minimum grade point average of 2.0 out of 4.0 is required for consideration, although some programs require a higher grade point average.

Buffalo State welcomes applications from international students (contact: International Student Affairs Office, telephone: 716-878-5331, http://www.buffalostate.edu/offices/isa).

Application and Information

Candidates must complete the State University of New York application, available from the Buffalo State Admissions Office, high school guidance offices, college transfer offices, or online at http://www.suny.edu/student. Decisions are made on a rolling basis beginning in mid-September for spring applicants, and in mid-December for fall applicants. Processing of applications continues until new-student enrollment goals have been met. On-campus interviews are encouraged.

Admissions Office
Moot Hall 110
Buffalo State College
1300 Elmwood Avenue
Buffalo, New York 14222-1095

Phone: 716-878-4017
Fax: 716-878-6100
E-mail: admissions@buffalostate.edu
Internet: http://www.buffalostate.edu

CANISIUS COLLEGE

BUFFALO, NEW YORK

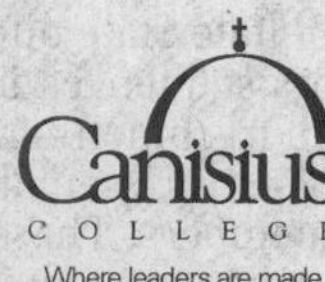

The College

Canisius College offers the best in high-quality academic programs and facilities as well as outstanding faculty members who are leaders in their fields. With more than seventy distinct majors, minors, and special programs and an exciting urban location to support internships and out-of-class experiences, Canisius College prepares students for success. Canisius is a place where leaders are made.

Canisius College offers a state-of-the-art campus with enhanced technology in academic and living facilities. Canisius housing is like a home away from home, not just a temporary living accommodation. Bosch and Frisch Residence Halls, which were recently renovated, and Dugan Hall, which opened in 2005, are the primary residences for first-year students at Canisius. Apartment-style living is available to sophomores, juniors, and seniors in one of the Delevan Townhouses or other town-house complexes and apartment buildings on campus. Specialty house options include George Martin Honors Hall, available to students in the All-College Honors Program, and the Intercultural Living Center, a learning community residence for international and U.S. students. All campus housing is equipped with high-speed Internet access and cable television.

Students have opportunities to develop leadership skills through involvement in student clubs and organizations, research, and service learning. There is something for everyone at Canisius. There are more than 100 college-sponsored student clubs and organizations and a wide range of athletic teams from which to choose. The students are not only leaders in the classroom but also on the NCAA Division I athletic field. Most of the sixteen Golden Griffin teams compete in the Metro Atlantic Athletic Conference (MAAC), in which a majority of the champions receive an entry into their respective NCAA tournaments. Since joining the MAAC in 1989, men's basketball, baseball, women's cross-country, men's soccer, and softball have claimed conference titles.

Location

Canisius College's urban setting is a significant advantage for students who are seeking internship, research, and service learning opportunities because of the proximity to a wide range of businesses and organizations.

Canisius is located on 58 acres in a residential neighborhood in north-central Buffalo. Buffalo is a great college town that has it all: professional sports teams, a world-renowned art gallery, historic architecture, and scenic parks and waterways all within minutes from campus.

The internationally known Albright-Knox Art Gallery holds one of the world's finest collections of nineteenth- and twentieth-century American and European works of art. Buffalo is also home to the Buffalo Philharmonic Orchestra and the Studio Arena Theatre, which provides a wide variety of theater experiences.

The Metro Rail rapid transit system connects the College with some of Buffalo's most exciting venues, including HSBC Arena, home of the National Hockey League's Buffalo Sabres. The arena also hosts college basketball with Canisius' Golden Griffins as well as major popular and rock music concerts. During the summer, students can catch Buffalo Bisons Triple-A baseball games at Dunn Tire Park. At Ralph Wilson Stadium, in Orchard Park, the Buffalo Bills are a focal point throughout the football season.

The Buffalo Zoo and Delaware Park, a 350-acre park with a lake and a golf course, are located less than a mile from the campus.

Majors and Degrees

The College of Arts and Sciences is the largest and most diverse of Canisius' three academic divisions, with majors in the natural and social sciences, humanities, and preprofessional studies. It also houses the core curriculum, which strengthens fundamental critical thinking, oral, and written communication skills and helps enhance students' understanding of other cultures. The College of Arts and Sciences offers programs leading to bachelor's degrees in anthropology, art history, biochemistry, bioinformatics, biology, chemistry, clinical laboratory science, communication studies, computer science, criminal justice, digital media arts, economics, English, environmental science, European studies, history, international relations, mathematics and statistics, modern languages (French, German, and Spanish), music, philosophy, physics, political science, psychology, religious studies and theology, sociology, and urban studies.

The Richard J. Wehle School of Business offers a well-rounded business curriculum to complement the liberal arts courses in the major, which gives the student an understanding of the broad and interrelated nature of business issues. There are programs leading to the B.S. degree in accounting, accounting information systems, business economics, entrepreneurship, finance, information systems, international business, management, and marketing. All the business programs are accredited by the AACSB International–The Association to Advance Collegiate Schools of Business.

The School of Education and Human Services offers degrees that lead to teacher certification at the early childhood, childhood, middle childhood, or adolescent level, such as adolescence education, athletic training/sports medicine, childhood education, early childhood education, physical education, and special education. All programs are accredited by the National Council for Accreditation of Teacher Education (NCATE).

Canisius also offers diverse and flexible academic programs, such as fashion merchandising (in conjunction with the Fashion Institute of Technology), fine arts, and military science, and certification programs in gerontology and women's studies. Preprofessional programs are available in dentistry, engineering, environmental science, and forestry (in conjunction with the State University of New York (SUNY) College of Environmental Science and Forestry at Syracuse), law, medicine, pharmacy, and veterinary medicine. Canisius also has an early assurance of admission agreement for New York State residents, with the Schools of Medicine and Dental Medicine of SUNY at Buffalo and SUNY Medical School at Syracuse. Seven-year joint-degree programs exist between Canisius and the SUNY Buffalo School of Dental Medicine, the Ohio College of Podiatric Medicine, the New York College of Podiatric Medicine, and the SUNY College of Optometry. Joint-degree programs offered with Lake Erie College of Osteopathic Medicine include a seven-year program in osteopathic medicine and a five-year program in pharmacy. A five-year combined-degree program leads to the B.A. in a major in one of the liberal arts disciplines and a Master of Business Administration degree.

Academic Programs

To earn a bachelor's degree from Canisius College, students must complete forty courses and a minimum of 120 credit hours. Within each curriculum, the courses are distributed into three areas: core curriculum, major field requirements, and free electives. The College requires that students complete a rounded program of humanistic studies embracing literature, the physical and social sciences, oral and written communication, philosophy, history, religious studies, and language.

The All-College Honors Program is available for qualified students. This program includes rigorous exploration of the arts and sciences in an enriched curriculum with close faculty supervision and small classes. Students may also obtain college credit through the Advanced Placement Program of the College Board. Students with scores of 4 or better on Advanced Placement tests are considered for credit and advanced standing.

Off-Campus Programs

Many Canisius students choose to spend a semester or a year studying abroad, improving their fluency in another language and opening the doors to exciting personal and professional opportunities. Canisius administers semester-abroad programs in London, England; Oviedo, Spain; Lille, France; Dortmund, Germany; Morelia, Mexico; and Galway, Ireland. Canisius also works with other U.S. colleges and universities to make it possible for students to spend a semester or a year studying in Italy, Australia, Japan, Canada, and other countries. Some Canisius-sponsored programs also enable students to work as volunteers or interns in countries overseas. The Office of International Student Programs assists students in selecting a study-abroad program, organizes a predeparture orientation, and assists students upon their return to the United States.

Students majoring in international relations and political science may participate in programs in Washington, D.C., or Albany, New York, which have been designed to give students practical experience in their fields.

Academic Facilities

Canisius has invested nearly $120 million over the last thirteen years to create state-of-the-art technology classrooms, residence halls, and cultural and recreational spaces. In addition, the campus provides wireless access in every building and residence hall. Instructional computing facilities include duel-platform computers located in general-purpose labs and teaching labs. The College offers fifty laptops students can check out for use within the library as well as e-mail and Internet stations at various convenient locations on campus.

Costs

For the academic year 2007–08, tuition was $25,370, room and board were $9770, and fees were $1007. Books and supplies were estimated to cost $700. An additional $1130 per year was recommended for travel and personal expenses.

Financial Aid

Of the class of 2011, 98 percent receive some form of financial aid, and the average award is $23,936. This aid includes Canisius College scholarships and grants, state grants, state and federal loans, federal grants, and Federal Work-Study Program awards. Applications for financial aid should be completed by February 15. The Free Application for Federal Student Aid (FAFSA) and the TAP application (New York State residents only) must be filed before consideration can be given to applicants.

Faculty

The Canisius College faculty consists of 217 full-time teachers, including Jesuits and lay men and women. More than 93 percent hold doctorates or other terminal degrees. The primary emphasis of the faculty members is teaching, and many also serve as academic advisers. The student-faculty ratio is 12:1.

Student Government

The Undergraduate Student Association comprises the entire undergraduate student body and is represented by elected officers who serve on the Student Senate. The senate assists and supervises student activities and advocates on behalf of the students, presenting their views to the College administration. In addition, students serve on many College committees.

Admission Requirements

Students' applications for admission are evaluated on a combination of factors, including a student's academic ability, strength of character, high school record, rank in class, an essay, aptitude tests (SAT or ACT), extracurricular activities, and recommendations. An applicant to the College is encouraged to pursue a challenging college-preparatory program in high school. This program of studies should include a minimum of 16 units of credit in the academic subjects of English, foreign language, mathematics, science, and social studies. Recommendations from teachers or guidance counselors are not required but are encouraged, and they are considered in reviewing applications for admission. Campus interviews are strongly recommended and in some cases may be required.

Transfer students are welcome and are admitted to Canisius in the fall and spring semesters. In addition to meeting the academic standards required of all entering students, transfer students are considered for admission if they have a minimum 2.0 cumulative quality point average when transferring from either a two-year or a four-year accredited institution.

Canisius College does not discriminate on the basis of age, race, religion or creed, color, sex, national or ethnic origin, sexual orientation, marital status, veteran's status, genetic predisposition or carrier status, or disability in administration of its educational policies, employment practices, admissions policies, scholarship and loan programs, and athletic and other school-administered programs.

Application and Information

Students are encouraged to submit their applications for admission in the fall of their senior year in high school. Application forms are available from the Office of Admissions, or fee-waived applications can be found on the Web at http://www.canisius.edu/admissions. The completed application form should be presented to the high school guidance counselor, to be forwarded to the director of admissions with an official high school transcript, SAT or ACT scores, and any letters of recommendation. Arrangements for interviews may be made by contacting the Office of Admissions at least one week in advance of the desired date for a visit.

Canisius considers applications under a rolling admission policy. Students applying by November 15 are notified of admission decision by December 15, along with scholarship notification. Students are encouraged to apply no later than March 1 for full and equal consideration.

For application forms and additional information, students should contact:

Admissions Office
Canisius College
2001 Main Street
Buffalo, New York 14208
Phone: 716-888-2200
800-843-1517 (toll-free)
Fax: 716-888-3230
E-mail: admissions@canisius.edu
Web site: http://www.canisius.edu/admissions

Canisius College is the ideal size for each individual to be an important part of campus life.

CAZENOVIA COLLEGE

CAZENOVIA, NEW YORK

The College

Cazenovia College, founded in 1824, is a small, private undergraduate college located in the lakeside community of Cazenovia, in central New York. The College was founded as a seminary. It later became a two-year women's college and finally became the four-year coeducational institution that it is today. One of the thirty oldest continuously operating independent colleges in the United States, the College offers innovative baccalaureate degree programs.

Cazenovia College is a residential institution drawing primarily traditional-age, full-time college students. The undergraduate student body is 70 percent women and 30 percent men. The majority of students live on campus. Freshmen are assigned housing based on an interest questionnaire; upperclass housing assignments are selected by lottery. Student dining facilities are open seven days a week and continuously provide students with meals or snacks.

The main campus is located in the heart of the village of Cazenovia. All residence halls are fully wired for fiber-optic communications, including full Internet and e-mail capability. Nearby, the College's athletic complex, home to its NCAA Division III teams, features two gymnasiums, a swimming pool, outdoor playing fields, and tennis courts. A short drive from the main campus, the 250-acre Equine Education Center is home to the College's nationally known equestrian program and champion riding teams.

Cazenovia students enjoy the advantages of small-town life combined with nearby opportunities for urban cultural, athletic, and recreational activities. Social life focuses on activities sponsored by individual residence halls and campus clubs, as well as dances, professional and student performances, sports events, and intramurals. The College's health and counseling center offers a wide range of medical and counseling services.

Cazenovia College has always been committed to helping students prepare for real-life situations. Students combine career and liberal arts course work throughout their studies. Internships are a part of most academic programs. Students develop the skills and knowledge necessary to pursue a career or go on to further academic study. Cazenovia College is fully accredited by the Middle States Association of Colleges and Schools.

Location

Cazenovia College is situated in the picturesque lakeside village of Cazenovia, New York, a quiet village of 4,000 in central New York. Many structures in the village are listed on the National Register of Historic Places. The village retains much of its nineteenth-century charm with unique specialty shops, fine inns, and restaurants that cater to a variety of tastes. Cazenovia Lake is enjoyed for its beauty and for the opportunities it provides for summer and winter sports. Students have the opportunity to attend many cultural events on campus. In the city of Syracuse, a half-hour drive from Cazenovia, cultural attractions include a symphony orchestra, an opera company, several widely acclaimed regional theaters, museums, fine restaurants, and recreational events, among other social and cultural offerings. The Cazenovia area offers a wonderful living and learning environment.

Majors and Degrees

Cazenovia College offers the Bachelor of Arts degree in communication studies, English, liberal studies, and social science, with specializations in history and government, theater arts, interdisciplinary social science, and literature and culture.

The Bachelor of Fine Arts degree is offered in interior design; studio art, with specializations in studio art and photography; fashion design; and visual communications, with courses in advertising design, graphic design, and Web design.

The Bachelor of Science degree is offered in business management; criminal justice; early childhood education and program administration; early childhood teacher education; inclusive elementary education; environmental studies; English; human services (specializations in alcohol and substance abuse, counseling and mental health, generalist studies, and social services for children and youth); psychology; social science (specialization in history and government); and liberal studies (in communications, interdisciplinary social science, literature and culture, and theater arts).

The Bachelor of Professional Studies degree is offered in management, with specializations in accounting, business management, equine business management, fashion merchandising, and sport management.

Academic Programs

Part of what distinguishes Cazenovia College is the diversity and flexibility of its degree programs. Cazenovia offers a wide range of programs in art, business, early childhood education, equine studies, and human services as well as in interdisciplinary liberal and professional studies. All students complete a common core grounded in liberal arts. The general education core includes required course work in literacy and effective communication. Students select a major field of study and conclude their work by demonstrating the ability to integrate and apply their knowledge in a culminating senior capstone experience.

All programs feature small classes and personal attention from faculty members. Interdisciplinary studies, the use of computer technology, and innovative instructional methods are hallmarks of College course work. Opportunities for internships and course work in Great Britain and Washington, D.C., are offered through Canterbury Christ Church University, the American Intercontinental University (London), and the Institute for Experiential Learning (Washington, D.C.). The College continues to develop additional opportunities for study abroad and internships across the United States. Students also have the opportunity to earn honors at graduation through the College honors program.

The Cazenovia College Center for Teaching and Learning staff provides workshops and individualized tutoring to help students improve their math, reading, writing, and study skills. The center's programs have been cited by the *National Directory of Exemplary Programs*, and it offers support services to all students. The center includes the Higher Education Opportunity Program, Collegiate Science and Technology Entry Program, Office of Special Services, and Title IV: Student Support Services. An excellent job placement program is also available on campus.

To earn a bachelor's degree, a student must complete 120 credits (except where otherwise specified) with a grade point average of at least 2.0 and must satisfy all additional program requirements. Sixty credits must be completed prior to the junior year. Arts and sciences credit requirements vary according to the degree sought. Advanced placement and credit by examination are offered to qualified students, and honors courses are available in selected areas. An independent study arrangement is possible for full-time students. The academic year is divided into two 15-week terms and one 6-week summer semester offering both academic course work and internships.

Off-Campus Programs

An increasing focus of the College is experiential education through internships offered in conjunction with classes and co-curricular service learning projects offered by the Office of Student Leadership. Students are able to integrate academic study and career development through these learning experiences. Each student learns the practical side of a career and develops the versatility to adapt to the competitive marketplace. Students gain valuable experience off campus in major corporations, banks, newspapers, hospitals, local businesses, government agencies, and radio and television.

Academic Facilities

The main campus consists of twenty-four buildings on 20 acres in the heart of the village. Classrooms, residence halls, and administrative buildings surround a centrally located quad that is a popular gathering place for students to study, relax, or join in a tag football game. A modern art and design building featuring advanced computer technology opened in 2004.

The Witherill Library has holdings totaling more than 86,000 pieces, including bound volumes, extensive microfilm and video libraries, and subscriptions to hundreds of journals, newspapers, and index/abstract publications. Approximately 3,000 pieces are acquired annually. The library is a member of the national/international Online Computer Library Center (OCLC) Interlibrary Loan Network, which allows loans to and from libraries all over the United States and the world. In addition, the library's Web page includes subscriptions to 11 online databases, which include more than 2,600 full-text journals, indexes, and abstracts to be called up at a moment's notice. The library's professional staff is available for assistance to groups or on an individual basis.

The College's computer resources rival the best-wired facilities in the nation. Two main campus computer classrooms and one open lab host seventy-six Pentium III–based Windows NT systems. Labs dedicated to art and design host more than fifty G3 and G4 Macintosh workstations and an up-to-date AutoCAD/3-D Studio Viz Lab. All facilities support laser printers and scanners and (where appropriate) wide-bed printers and other specialized peripherals.

The College has extensive art studios and regularly hosts major art exhibits. The Cazenovia College Theatre is a resource for both the College and the community. Students produce plays and other entertainment, and the theater is also used for film showings and large-group lectures. The College's 250-acre Equine Education Center, just a 5-minute drive from the campus, is one of the premier collegiate equestrian facilities in the nation.

Costs

For academic year 2007–08, tuition was $21,280 per year, room was $4900, and board was $4072. Books and supplies were about $1000, and personal and travel expenses averaged $1400.

Financial Aid

Financial aid resources exist at Cazenovia College to bridge the gap between the amount the student's family can pay and the cost of attending the College. Ninety percent of students receive some form of financial assistance, either merit- or need-based. About 30 percent of the students are recipients of academic achievement scholarships designed to recognize and reward students for their scholastic achievements. These awards range from $12,000 to full tuition. Need-based federal, state, and institutional sources include grants, loans, and on-campus work-study arrangements.

Faculty

Cazenovia has 141 faculty positions. All full-time faculty members must possess a Ph.D. or other appropriate professional degree, and all faculty members must demonstrate proficiency in the discipline in which they teach. The faculty is more strongly committed to teaching than to research. In addition, many of the part-time faculty members pursue careers outside the College; their professional experiences enrich the College's programs. Faculty members also function as student advisers and academic counselors. The student-faculty ratio is 15:1.

Student Government

The Student Government Association (SGA) is elected and empowered to represent the student body in various aspects of their educational experience at the College. While all students are members of this association, voting membership consists of executive officers, class officers, representatives of the residential communities, commuter representatives, and the student chair of the Community Judicial Board. Responsibilities include allocation of funds to student clubs and organizations, representation of students in the campus governance structure, planning and sponsoring of campus events, and student contribution to the campus disciplinary process.

Admission Requirements

Cazenovia College seeks students whose high school and college records, standardized test scores, official recommendations, and qualities of mind and character promise success in college. Prospective students should send in a completed application, a transcript, teacher recommendation, test scores (where applicable), and a resume of extracurricular activities. A campus interview is strongly recommended. For freshman applicants, the SAT or ACT is not required but is recommended. Students may be admitted for deferred entrance or to advanced standing. Transfer applicants must have a minimum overall GPA of 2.0.

Application and Information

The College has no application deadlines. Students are accepted on a rolling basis and are notified of a decision within thirty days of receipt of the application and all supporting documents. The College advises candidates to submit all materials before March 1 for admission in September. Cazenovia is a member of the Common Application group and also accepts the Common Application.

Robert A. Croot
Dean for Enrollment Management
Cazenovia College
Cazenovia, New York 13035
Phone: 315-655-7208
800-654-3210 (toll-free)
Fax: 315-655-4860
E-mail: admission@cazenovia.edu
Web site: http://www.cazenovia.edu/

On the campus of Cazenovia College.

CITY COLLEGE OF THE CITY UNIVERSITY OF NEW YORK

NEW YORK, NEW YORK

The College

Since its founding in 1847, the City College of New York (CCNY) has stressed the dual goals of offering access to higher education combined with academic excellence. That policy has had remarkable results, making CCNY one of America's greatest educational success stories. For example, 9 Nobel Prize winners are City College graduates, as is former Secretary of State Colin Powell and INTEL cofounder Andrew Grove, placing CCNY's graduates among the nation's leaders. The College ranks among the top dozen in the number of alumni who are members of the prestigious National Academy of Engineering and in producing graduates who have become America's leading business executives. Reflecting the College's commitment to equal educational opportunity, CCNY is also one of the nation's leaders in producing minority engineering graduates and in the number of black graduates who gain admission to medical school.

Overall, CCNY graduates exceed the national average in obtaining admission to medical school. The College has more full-time doctoral students in campus-based programs than all of the other City University of New York (CUNY) colleges combined. CCNY houses several major centers and institutes, including the CUNY Institute for Transportation Systems, the Colin Powell Center for Policy Studies, and the New York State Structural Biology Center, and offers the largest undergraduate research program in the metropolitan area.

The College offers students a wide variety of social activities; more than 100 clubs are organized on campus. Students can also participate in numerous intercollegiate and intramural sports. There are thirteen varsity teams for men and women.

In fall 2006, the first residence hall at City College, The Towers, opened on South Campus. The campus is a hub of construction activity, with the new School of Architecture and two new science buildings scheduled to open in the next five years.

Location

The City College campus occupies 36 acres in Manhattan along Convent Avenue from 131st to 141st Streets in the area known as Hamilton Heights. The surrounding neighborhoods are predominantly residential, although there are shopping areas west of the campus along Broadway and south toward 125th Street.

Majors and Degrees

The College of Liberal Arts and Science offers the Bachelor of Arts (B.A.), the Bachelor of Science (B.S.), and the Bachelor of Fine Arts (B.F.A.) degrees in the following majors: advertising, American studies, anthropology, area studies, art, art history, biochemistry, biology, chemistry, communication, comparative literature, creative writing, earth systems sciences, economics, electronic art and graphic design, English, environmental science, film and video production, foreign languages and literature, history, international studies, management and administration, mathematics, music (performance, sonic arts technology, theory), optometry (combined B.S./O.D.), philosophy, physics, political science, prelaw, premedical studies, psychology, public policy and public affairs, public relations, sociology, theater, and women's studies.

The School of Architecture, Urban Design, and Landscape Architecture offers a B.S. in architecture and the five-year Bachelor of Architecture.

The Sophie Davis School of Biomedical Education provides a seven-year B.S./M.D. curriculum for highly qualified high school graduates who reside in New York State. The Physician's Assistant Program, also part of the School of Biomedical Education, offers a B.S. degree and is a joint program between City College and Harlem Hospital. This is an upper-division (junior and senior years) program.

The School of Education offers programs that lead to the Bachelor of Science in Education (B.S.Ed.) in the following majors: bilingual education, early childhood education, and elementary education. In addition, students are prepared to teach a wide variety of subjects in secondary schools. City College is one of seven colleges participating in the new CUNY Teacher Academy to train mathematics and science teachers.

The Grove School of Engineering offers the Bachelor of Engineering (B.E.) degree in the fields of biomedical, chemical, civil, computer, electrical, environmental, and mechanical engineering and the B.S. in computer science.

The Center for Worker Education is an off-site program that helps adults return to college while continuing their full-time employment. Students can complete a bachelor's degree program in the evening.

Academic Programs

City College includes the College of Liberal Arts and Science and the largest complex of professional schools in the City University. These include the Schools of Architecture and Education, the Sophie Davis School of Biomedical Education, and the Grove School of Engineering. Accelerated five-year combined undergraduate/graduate degree programs are available in economics, English, history, mathematics, and psychology.

A Freshman Honors Program is available for qualified students who are interested in advanced research work and independent study. City College is one of seven campuses that form the consortium in the Macaulay Honors College program. The Macaulay Honors College program is designed to provide an outstanding educational opportunity to academically gifted students by offering a challenging undergraduate experience shaped by the combined resources of CUNY and New York City.

Cooperative education internships are also provided for interested applicants. Such programs as Minority Access to Research Careers (MARC), Minority Biomedical Research Support (MBRS), and City College Research Scholars (CRS) provide paid and volunteer opportunities to do research at various institutions.

City College has a core curriculum that is founded on a strong liberal arts base and is designed to ensure the continued quality and relevance of its academic programs. The core curriculum reflects a global vision of human achievement in an increasingly interdependent world and is designed to provide City College students with superior academic preparation while enhancing their capacity to think critically and creatively. The College has a long history of encouraging independent thought and initiative and continues to foster an educational atmosphere in which students can explore and develop their interests and talents.

For most bachelor's degree programs, the total number of credits necessary to earn a degree is 120; a bachelor's degree in engineering requires up to 136 credits. The College works on a semester calendar and offers three summer sessions (one 7½-week session and two 4-week sessions) and a winter session.

Off-Campus Programs

City College has exchange programs in Austria, China, England, Germany, and Morocco as well as a summer program in the Dominican Republic. Students are able to spend a semester, a full academic year, or a summer term at one of the cooperating schools.

Through a cooperative arrangement, students are also able to take courses at the various branches of the City University.

Academic Facilities

New facilities add a modern tone to the original neo-Gothic buildings, which have been designated state and national landmarks. In addition, a $200-million renovation of the neo-Gothic buildings is nearing completion. The thirteen-story Robert E. Marshak Science Building houses more than 200 teaching and research laboratories, a planetarium, a weather station, an electron microscope, laser research facilities, a science and engineering library, and a major physical education complex. The Grove School of Engineering has more than forty research laboratories. Aaron Davis Hall contains a 750-seat proscenium theater, a 200-seat experimental theater, and a seventy-five-seat studio workshop for rehearsals. The North Academic Center occupies three full city blocks and has 2,000 classrooms, laboratories, lecture halls, offices, and dining and student activity areas. It includes the Morris Raphael Cohen Library, which houses more than 1.3 million volumes, the largest collection in the City University.

Computer facilities are extensive at City College. The Computation Center provides services to meet instructional, administrative, and research needs. Numerous computer labs are located throughout the College, utilizing microcomputers and minicomputers to provide research and academic services to students and faculty and staff members.

Costs

In 2007–08 for students who were residents of New York State, the tuition for full-time attendance (12 or more credits or the equivalent) was $2000 per semester, or $4000 per year. Part-time students who were residents of New York State paid $170 per credit. Tuition for out-of-state and international students was $360 per credit. Tuition and fees are subject to change. Books, supplies, and commuting and personal expenses average $5905 a year for full-time students who live with their parents and $12,916 for students who live on their own, excluding tuition and moderate activity fees. The cost for housing in the recently constructed Towers residence hall is from $7980 to $11,250 per academic year.

Financial Aid

Financial assistance is available for eligible City College students through state and federal programs. Students who wish to apply for financial aid must file the Free Application for Federal Student Aid (FAFSA) and the TAP/APTS Application and CUNY Supplement. Among the forms of financial aid available are Federal Supplemental Educational Opportunity Grants, Federal Perkins Loans, and Federal Work-Study Program awards. A large percentage of City College students receive some type of aid. For information, students should contact the Financial Aid Office at City College at 212-650-5819.

The City College of New York Scholarship Program offers a variety of scholarships to entering freshman and transfer students. Freshman applicants should have a minimum combined score of 1100 on the critical reading and math section of the SAT (or the equivalent on the ACT) and a high school average of 85, while transfer students should have a minimum GPA of 3.0. For information about the many scholarships available, including deadlines, eligibility, and credentials, students should contact the City College Office of Admissions or visit the Web site at http://www.ccny.cuny.edu/admissions.

Faculty

City College's outstanding faculty represents a broad range of disciplines, and many members have earned the nation's highest forms of recognition—Guggenheim and Fulbright awards as well as grants that amount to millions of dollars annually in support of their research and scholarship. Eighty-five percent of the faculty members hold Ph.D. degrees. The student-teacher ratio is 14:1.

Student Government

Students have traditionally played an active role in campus government. Each year, two different senates are elected at the undergraduate level: one each for the day and evening divisions. Student government funds pay for the activities of student organizations, which send representatives to a student-faculty administrative committee that advises the College president on matters of an extracurricular nature. Through their representatives, students are given a voice on departmental committees, and they vote on matters of educational policy, budget, and faculty appointments and reappointments.

Admission Requirements

In determining admission to City College, the following factors are considered: a student's overall high school academic average from grades 9 through 12, the total number of academic units completed (New York State Regents courses), and the combined SAT score obtained on the Critical Reading and Mathematics sections of the exam. These factors are weighted together to determine eligibility. The College recommends that students preparing to apply to programs at City College complete 4 years of English, 4 years of social studies, 3 years of sequential math (or its equivalent), 2 years of laboratory science, 2 years of a foreign language, and 1 year of performing or visual arts in high school as the academic preparation needed for success and admission to the College. Qualified high school juniors may apply for early admission. Students who take the General Educational Development test (GED) and receive a score of at least 3250 (325 old scoring) are accepted to the City College. Students with special educational and financial needs may qualify for admission to the Search for Education, Elevation, and Knowledge (SEEK) Program. City College accepts students who wish to transfer from other postsecondary institutions. Requirements for admission vary according to the program and the number of credits completed. Applicants should contact the College for information about admission as a transfer student.

Application and Information

Applications to City College are processed through the City University of New York Processing Center. Although applications are processed on a rolling basis, students who wish a prompt response should adhere to the initial deadline dates of October 1 (spring admission) and March 15 (fall admission). Applications from qualified students that are received after these deadlines are processed on a space-available basis. Further information and application materials can be obtained from either:

Office of Admissions
The City College of the City University of New York
160 Convent Avenue, A-101
New York, New York 10031
Phone: 212-650-6977
E-mail: admissions@ccny.cuny.edu
Web site: http://www.ccny.cuny.edu/admissions

Office of Admission Services (O.A.S.)
City University of New York
1114 Avenue of the Americas
New York, New York 10036
Phone: 212-997-2869
Web site: http://www.cuny.edu

CLARKSON UNIVERSITY

POTSDAM, NEW YORK

The University

Founded in 1896, Clarkson stands out among America's private, nationally ranked research institutions because of its dynamic collaborative learning environment, innovative degree and research programs, and unmatched track record for producing leaders and innovators.

The University attracts 3,000 enterprising students from diverse backgrounds (including some 400 graduate students) who thrive in rigorous programs in engineering, arts, sciences, business, and health sciences and in the University's close-knit, residential learning/living community. Clarkson defies convention in the classroom, in its laboratories, and by the impact its graduates have in the world. The University is New York State's highest-ranked small research institution. However, size is Clarkson's advantage—fostering leadership and problem-solving skills and readily affording students and faculty members the flexibility to span the boundaries of traditional academic areas.

Clarkson students also enjoy extraordinary opportunities to pursue faculty-mentored research. They gain professional experience through internships and co-ops with corporations and government organizations and can broaden their perspectives through a wide range of study-abroad opportunities.

Top graduate schools welcome Clarkson graduates to study medicine, law, and other professions. Johns Hopkins, MIT, Princeton, Yale, Caltech, Rice, and Stanford are just some of the schools chosen by Clarkson students.

Clarkson's 98 percent placement rate is among the nation's highest, with the most recent starting salaries averaging more than $50,000. Clarkson is a key recruitment source for many of America's industry leaders, including General Electric, Alcoa, Xerox, Accenture, IBM, and Procter & Gamble. In fact, 1 in 7 Clarkson alumni is already a CEO, president, vice president, or company owner.

Clarkson's active campus also offers a wide variety of extracurricular activities, including more than eighty clubs and interest groups. Students publish a lively campus newspaper and run campus radio and television stations. Active professional and honor societies enrich the campus experience.

There are Division I men's and women's hockey teams as well as seventeen Division III intercollegiate athletic teams for women and men. Recreational facilities include a field house and gym with racquetball, basketball, and indoor tennis courts; a state-of-the-art fitness center; and a swimming pool.

Location

Clarkson is located in Potsdam, the quintessential "college town," nestled in the foothills of the northern Adirondack region of New York. The beautiful northeast corner of the state is the home of the 6-million-acre Adirondack Park. Within 2 hours of the campus are Lake Placid and the cosmopolitan Canadian cities of Montreal and Ottawa.

Majors and Degrees

Undergraduate degree programs offered are aeronautical engineering, American studies, applied mathematics and statistics, Areté (liberal arts/business), biology, biomolecular engineering, biomolecular science, business and technology management, chemical engineering, chemistry, civil engineering, communication, computer engineering, computer science, digital arts and sciences, e-business, electrical engineering, engineering and management, environmental engineering, environmental health science, environmental science and policy, financial information and analysis, history, humanities, information systems and business processes, liberal studies, mathematics, mechanical engineering, physical therapy (pre–physical therapy leading to a doctorate), physics, political science, psychology, social sciences, and software engineering.

First-year students who are still deciding on a major may begin in a general program in business studies, engineering studies, science studies, or university studies.

Clarkson offers a University honors program, a three-year bachelor's degree option, a five-year B.S./M.S. in chemistry/biochemistry, a five-year B.S./M.B.A., and preprofessional programs in dentistry, law, medicine, physical therapy, and veterinary science.

Academic Programs

Clarkson's historic strengths in business, engineering, liberal arts, and science remain at the core of the curriculum. These programs have also been combined into cutting-edge, cross-disciplinary majors: biomolecular science, digital arts and sciences, environmental science and policy, information technology, interdisciplinary engineering and management, and software engineering.

A dynamic, hands-on approach to learning is one of the hallmarks of a Clarkson education. Clarkson students learn about business by actually starting a business. They conduct scientific research alongside distinguished faculty mentors in state-of-the-art laboratories. The University's undergraduate research program has produced 13 Goldwater Scholars in eight years.

National rankings and honors include the following: among the 125 "Best National Universities–Doctoral," *U.S. News & World Report*, 2008; among the "Best Undergraduate Engineering Programs," *U.S. News & World Report*, 2008; among the "Top 20 Wired Campuses," in *PC Magazine* and the *Princeton Review* 2007; the Supply Chain Management Program ranks eleventh in the nation, *U.S. News & World Report*, 2008; and among the best business schools in the nation, the *Princeton Review's Best 282 Business Schools*, 2007 edition. The undergraduate program in innovation and entrepreneurship is ranked number twenty-two among 700 U.S. higher educational institutions by the *Princeton Review* and *Entrepreneur* magazine, 2006.

Clarkson was also ranked among the top 100 graduate schools in environmental engineering (23) and civil engineering (54) by *U.S. News & World Report's* "Best Graduate Programs," 2006.

In addition, Clarkson's award-winning Student Projects for Engineering Experience and Design (SPEED) program promotes multidisciplinary, project-based extracurricular learning opportunities for more than 400 undergraduates annually. Some fifteen design teams compete in national and regional collegiate competitions that involve design and analysis, teamwork, and communication skills.

Off-Campus Programs

Students benefit from the resources of the Associated Colleges of the St. Lawrence Valley, which comprises Clarkson University, St. Lawrence University, SUNY Canton, and SUNY Potsdam. Benefits for students include opportunities to participate in activities ranging from clubs to concerts, interlibrary exchange, and cross-registration that allows students to pursue two courses per year at member colleges at no extra cost.

Academic Facilities

The University's 640-acre wooded campus is the site of forty-six buildings that comprise more than 1.2-million square feet of assignable space. Dedicated exclusively to instructional programs are more than 375,000 square feet, including some 54,000 square feet of traditional classrooms and more than 168,000 square feet assigned as laboratory areas. In the Center for Advanced Materials Processing (a New York State Center for Advanced Technology), there are seventy state-of-the-art research labs, including many related to nanotechnology and environmental research. Others include a multidisciplinary engineering and project laboratory for team-based projects, such as the mini-Baja and Formulae SAE racers, a robotics laboratory, a high-voltage lab, electron microscopy, a Class 10 clean room, a polymer fabrication lab, crystal growth labs, and a structural testing lab. School of Arts and Sciences facilities include a virtual-reality laboratory, the Clarkson Open Source Institute, a molecular design laboratory, a human brain electrophysiology laboratory, and other specialized facilities.

Bertrand H. Snell Hall houses the School of Business and the School of Arts and Sciences administrative offices as well as fully networked classrooms and study spaces and collaborative centers that feature wireless network access and videoconferencing capabilities. The facility includes three academic centers, which are available to all students: the Shipley Center for Leadership and Entrepreneurship, the Center for Global Competitiveness, and the Eastman Kodak Center for Excellence in Communication. The Center for Health Sciences at Clarkson is a regional center of excellence for education, treatment, and research in physical rehabilitation and other health sciences.

Costs

Tuition was $28,470 for the 2007–08 year, room (2-person) was $5320, and the meal plan was $4810. Student fees totaled $690. In addition, students usually spend about $2000 annually on books, supplies, travel, and personal expenses.

Financial Aid

The University offers a variety of scholarships and loans, including state and federal student loans, state scholarships and awards, individual scholarships, federal grants, and federal work-study programs.

Faculty

Clarkson's 190 full-time faculty members teach undergraduate and graduate classes, with graduate students assisting only in undergraduate lab sciences. With an excellent student-faculty ratio of 15:1, undergraduates benefit from regular interaction with the school's faculty members and small class sizes (especially at the upper levels). The University attracts teacher/scholars who are also highly regarded scholars in their fields. Ninety-six percent hold a doctorate.

Student Government

The Student Senate and the Interfraternity Council combine to form the student government at Clarkson University. The former supervises all extracurricular activities (except athletics) and has responsibility for the allocation of student activity funds and for other appropriate business. The latter prescribes standards and rules for fraternities. Students are involved in the formation of University policies through membership, with faculty and staff representatives, on all important committees.

Admission Requirements

Clarkson recommends that prospective students follow a challenging secondary school curriculum that includes mathematics, science, and English. Candidates for entrance to the Wallace H. Coulter School of Engineering or students pursuing a degree in the sciences or an interdisciplinary engineering and management degree should have successfully completed secondary school courses in physics and chemistry. All candidates for admission are required to take the SAT or ACT. SAT Subject Tests are optional. The high school record is the most important factor in an admission decision. International students for whom English is a second language must submit a minimum TOEFL score of 550 (paper-based) or 212 (computer-based). All applicants must include a personal statement of 250 to 500 words describing a special interest, experience, or achievement.

Students achieving scores of 4 or better on the College Board's Advanced Placement examinations are considered for advanced placement and credit in virtually all academic areas. Advanced standing is most common in English, mathematics, and science.

An early decision plan is offered on a "first-choice" basis; this plan does not prohibit the student from making other applications, but it does commit the student to withdrawing other applications if accepted at Clarkson.

Although not required, a personal interview with a member of the Office of Admission is highly recommended, especially for early decision candidates. Interviews on campus should be arranged by letter or telephone at least one week prior to the intended visit. The Office of Admission is open Monday through Friday, from 8 a.m. to 4:30 p.m., and Saturday by appointment. The University welcomes visitors to the campus and makes arrangements, as requested, for families to tour and meet with academic and other departments on campus.

Application and Information

Office of Undergraduate Admission
Holcroft House
Clarkson University
P.O. Box 5605
Potsdam, New York 13699-5605
Phone: 315-268-6480
800-527-6577 (toll-free)
Fax: 315-268-7647
E-mail: admission@clarkson.edu
Web site: http://www.clarkson.edu

Clarkson is a leader in project-based learning, providing students with strong communication skills, leadership ability, and technological skill in their fields.

COLLEGE OF MOUNT SAINT VINCENT

RIVERDALE, NEW YORK

The College

The College of Mount Saint Vincent is a four-year, coeducational, liberal arts college offering both undergraduate and graduate programs. Founded by the Sisters of Charity of New York in 1847, the College currently enrolls students from twenty-two states and five countries. About 55 percent of full-time undergraduates live on campus. The current full-time undergraduate student enrollment is more than 1,300 men and women.

Career, academic, and personal counseling; academic support; and health services are available to all students. Cahill Lounge is the site of many student social events and features regular live entertainment.

The College recognizes more than twenty campus clubs and organizations, and these groups sponsor a full calendar of events, including dances, readings, dinners, and frequent social and educational trips to Manhattan. Some of the larger groups on campus include SAMAHAN (Filipino awareness), La Casa Latina (Latino culture), MSV Players (repertory company), and FLAVA (dance club). Students interested in broadcasting can gain valuable experience in the state-of-the-art TV and radio stations on campus. Student writers have a host of College publications to choose from, including the *Moun Times* (student newspaper), *Fonthill Dial* (literary journal), and *Parapet* (yearbook). Fifteen academic honor societies have chapters on campus.

Athletic facilities include a gymnasium, a state-of-the-art Fitness Center and Health Lounge, a 60-foot swimming pool, tennis courts, weight room, and a dance studio. A fall 2008 groundbreaking for the expansion of the Athletics Center is scheduled.

Varsity sports include women's and men's basketball, cross-country, lacrosse, soccer, tennis, and volleyball; men's baseball; and women's softball and swimming. The College also supports a popular intramural sports program. Mount Saint Vincent is an active member of the National Collegiate Athletic Association (NCAA), the Eastern College Athletic Conference (ECAC), the Hudson Valley Men's and Women's Athletic Conference, and the Skyline Conference on the Division III level.

Community service is a large part of students' lives, and the Campus Ministry team offers many opportunities for students to give back to the community. Students participate in Habitat for Humanity, Midnight Run (delivery of food and clothing to the homeless), POTS Soup Kitchen, Appalachia Spring Break, Pasta Suppas, clothing drives, and much more.

The College offers two graduate degree programs: nursing and teacher education.

The graduate nursing program offers four areas of study: adult nurse practitioner, clinical nurse specialist for adults and the aged, family nurse practitioner, and nursing administration. These programs prepare nurses for the complex decision-making process necessary in today's health-care environment. A registered nurse license and baccalaureate degree in nursing are required for application.

The graduate program in teacher education results in a Master of Science in urban and multicultural education. It is a values-centered program reflecting the belief that learning and culture are inseparable, as are relationships among learner, teacher, environment, and purpose for learning. A bachelor's degree and a provisional or initial teaching certificate are required for application.

Location

Located on the Hudson River, the 70-acre campus of Mount Saint Vincent encompasses rolling lawns, stone walls, wooded fields, and several buildings designated as historic landmarks of the city of New York. The campus is only 12 miles from midtown Manhattan. This proximity offers to students all the cultural, social, and academic opportunities of New York City, all within a short bus or subway ride.

Majors and Degrees

The College offers majors in biochemistry, biology, business, business administration, chemistry, communication, economics, English, French, history, liberal arts, mathematics, modern foreign languages, philosophy, psychology, religious studies, sociology, and Spanish. Students can pursue minors in biochemistry, biology, business, chemistry, communication, economics, English, fine arts, French, history, mathematics, performing arts, philosophy, psychology, religious studies, sociology, Spanish, and writing.

The Department of Teacher Education offers programs for prospective teachers in elementary, secondary, and special education. In addition, there are dual certification programs, a five-year B.A./M.S., and the master's program in urban and multicultural education. Students may specialize in areas such as early childhood, childhood, or adolescence education. Students pursuing adolescence education may obtain certification in one of seven fields: biology, chemistry, English, French, history, mathematics, or Spanish. A five-year combined B.A./M.S. program in urban and multicultural education is also available.

Certificate programs are offered in a variety of programs.

Academic Programs

The regular academic year is divided into two semesters, with intersessions in January and three summer sessions.

A core curriculum allows all Mount Saint Vincent students to participate in a common intellectual experience and a core of shared learning. The core extends over a full four years, pairing classes from a range of disciplines to provide all students with a solid foundation of knowledge, an appreciation of values, and a wide range of skills such as analysis, problem solving, and communication.

Candidates for the B.A. must earn 120 credits, and candidates for the B.S. must earn 126 credits, distributed in accordance with the requirements of the curriculum pursued. The selection of elective courses is planned with guidance from the student's academic adviser, according to the student's aims and interests. Students who are preparing to teach after graduation follow a program outlined by the Department of Teacher Education.

Students may prepare for careers in dentistry, law, medicine, physical and occupational therapy, optometry, and podiatry through the Mount's pre-professional programs. The College also supports an honors program for talented and dedicated students. The honors program provides a supportive community that encourages critical thinking and independent scholarship so that participants can realize their scholarly potential.

The College has an extensive internship program that enables students to combine course work with practical, job-related experience. There are more than 500 organizations currently participating in the College's internship program throughout the tristate area.

Off-Campus Programs

The College of Mount Saint Vincent encourages students to participate in study-abroad programs. The College participates in numerous study-abroad programs, including those offered by the Lower Hudson Valley Catholic College and University Consortium.

Academic Facilities

The library contains more than 170,000 volumes, 616 current periodical subscriptions, 9,850 microfilms, 6,150 audiovisual units (recordings, films, and cassettes), and numerous electronic databases. The ground floor of the library contains the Stephen J. Maloney Computer Center, with digital and general computer labs, lounges for individual and group study, and a cybercafe.

The newly renovated and expanded Maryvale Hall houses the Communication and Fine Arts Departments and includes two art studios, a radio station, and a state-of-the art TV production studio. The three-story Science Hall contains recently renovated laboratories, a lecture hall, classrooms, darkrooms, and environmental research facilities in addition to classrooms. The Administration Building is the main building on campus, housing most of the administrative and faculty offices, classrooms, general computer labs, and Academic Counseling and Educational Services (ACES), which includes the Center for Academic Excellence, the Office of Career Development and Internships, TRIO Student Support Services, and Academic Advisement.

Costs

Tuition for the 2006–07 year was $22,150; room and board were $8925. Fees were $600.

Financial Aid

The College awards Academic Merit Scholarships, Distinguished Scholarships, and federal, state, and institutional financial aid. Among the full-tuition scholarships are the Corazon C. Aquino Scholarship and the Fonthill Writing Award.

To be eligible for any merit or distinguished scholarship, freshman applicants must have a completed application for admission on file with the Admissions Office by March 1. In addition to providing College scholarships, Mount Saint Vincent participates in all available federal and state programs of financial assistance, including Federal Pell Grants, Federal Supplemental Educational Opportunity Grants, Federal Work-Study awards, federal and New York State student loans, and New York State Tuition Assistance Program (TAP) awards.

To be eligible for all forms of financial aid, freshman applicants must submit the Free Application for Federal Student Aid (FAFSA) by March 15; transfer applicants should submit the FAFSA by June 15. Eligibility for these programs is based on need. More than 90 percent of the students at Mount Saint Vincent receive aid from government or private agencies.

Faculty

The faculty is composed of 75 full-time and 89 part-time members who, in addition to their teaching responsibilities, act as academic advisers and moderate student activities. The student-faculty ratio is 13:1. Of the full-time faculty members, 78 percent hold terminal degrees in their fields.

Student Government

Students participate in College governance through a strong Student Government with elected representatives on most major governing bodies of the College, including the College Senate, the Undergraduate and Graduate Committees, the Policies and Procedures Council, the Orientation Committee, and the Commencement Committee. Student Government leaders meet regularly with members of the Board of Trustees and make most decisions regarding the disbursement of student activities fees and budgeted funds for clubs and organizations. Students also play a central role in discipline through an elected Student Judicial Council. This constitutionally ensured involvement guarantees that students have direct access to information and multiple opportunities to present student views and articulate student needs to both faculty and administrators.

Admission Requirements

Applicants to the College of Mount Saint Vincent must have graduated from an accredited secondary school, should rank in the upper half of their class, and must achieve satisfactory scores on the SAT, ACT, or TOEFL. International students who qualify for admission are welcome. Students attending a community college or another four-year college may apply for admission with advanced standing. It is recommended that prospective students telephone or e-mail for an interview and tour.

Students may apply online by visiting the College's Web site (http://www.mountsaintvincent.edu/application.htm) or by using the Common Application (http://www.commonapp.org). The College hosts an annual open house in the fall and is regularly open on the weekends for interviews and information sessions.

Application and Information

In order to be evaluated for admission, a candidate must present the following: an application fee of $35 (waived if the student applies online); a completed application; scores on the SAT, ACT, or TOEFL; an essay; a letter of recommendation; and a high school transcript. Transfer applicants should submit all college transcripts.

The Admission Committee operates on a rolling admission basis. Starting December 1, candidates are notified within four weeks of completing their application. The deadline is April 1, after which admission is considered on the basis of space availability. Early action—a nonbinding, flexible admission program—is also offered. The deadline for applying early action is November 1, and notifications arrive by December 1. Scholarship award letters are mailed simultaneously with acceptance letters. Recommended transfer application guidelines are June 1 for fall and December 1 for spring.

Information, brochures, and application forms for admission and financial aid may be obtained by contacting:

Timothy P. Nash
Vice President/Dean of Admission and Financial Aid
College of Mount Saint Vincent
6301 Riverdale Avenue
Riverdale, New York 10471-1093
Phone: 718-405-3267
800-665-CMSV (toll-free)
E-mail: admissions.office@mountsaintvincent.edu
Web site: http://www.mountsaintvincent.edu

THE COLLEGE OF NEW ROCHELLE

NEW ROCHELLE, NEW YORK

The College

The College of New Rochelle (CNR), founded in 1904 by the Ursuline Order, is an independent college that is Catholic in origin and heritage. Its primary purpose is the intellectual development of students through the maintenance of high standards of academic excellence. The College is composed of four separate schools. The School of Arts and Sciences (women only) enrolls approximately 500 young women between the ages of 18 and 22 and offers baccalaureate degree programs in the liberal arts and sciences and in a number of professionally oriented fields. The School of Nursing (coeducational), founded in 1976 and accredited by the Commission on Collegiate Nursing Education (CCNE), offers baccalaureate and graduate-level professional nursing programs that combine clinical experience with a liberal arts background. A Master of Science (M.S.) degree program in nursing is available. About 400 women and men are enrolled in the nursing programs. The School of New Resources, which maintains six campuses in New Rochelle and New York City, offers a nontraditional baccalaureate program designed specifically for adults. The Graduate School offers professional degree programs in education, art, community/school psychology, gerontology, communication studies, career development, and guidance and counseling. The main campus includes four residence halls that provide guaranteed housing for all undergraduates. Other students live in Westchester County, and some commute from the Greater New York metropolitan area. Students come to CNR from twenty states and eight countries.

Location

The College of New Rochelle is located on a 20-acre historic campus in New Rochelle, New York, a suburban community in southern Westchester County, half an hour away from New York City and easily accessible by commuter trains. The area contains numerous parks and recreational areas, and the Long Island Sound, with its many beaches, is within walking distance of the campus. Four airports—Kennedy, LaGuardia, Newark, and Westchester—are all within an hour of the College, and Amtrak makes daily stops at New Rochelle. New York City provides countless opportunities, including shopping expeditions, museums, and Broadway plays. Manhattan and the four other boroughs of New York City also contribute immeasurably to the education of the College's students through various internship, honors, and cooperative education programs, which are conducted by CNR in New York City.

Majors and Degrees

The School of Arts and Sciences at The College of New Rochelle confers the Bachelor of Arts (B.A.) degree in art (studio), art history, biology, chemistry, classics, communication arts, economics, English, environmental studies, history, mathematics, modern and classical languages, philosophy, political science, psychology, religious studies, and sociology; the Bachelor of Science (B.S.) degree in art education, biology, business, chemistry, mathematics, and social work; the Bachelor of Fine Arts (B.F.A.) degree in art education, art therapy, and studio art; and a Bachelor of Arts in interdisciplinary studies, which offers the student the viewpoints of several disciplines, including American studies, comparative literature, international studies, and women's studies. A series of field experiences and competency-based learning activities lead to certification in childhood education (grades 1–6) and adolescence education (grades 7–12). Childhood education allows for dual certification in early childhood (birth–grade 2), middle childhood (grades 5–9), and students with disabilities (grades 1–6). Adolescence education allows for dual certification in middle childhood and students with disabilities (grades 7–12). Certification is also available in art education (K–12). The School of Nursing offers a Bachelor of Science in Nursing (B.S.N.) degree program. Preprofessional programs are available in art therapy, health professions, law, and medicine.

Academic Programs

The College emphasizes the importance of a liberal arts background. Each undergraduate in the Schools of Arts and Sciences and Nursing must complete a variety of courses focusing on philosophy and religious studies, social analysis, literature and the arts, foreign languages, and scientific inquiry. To earn a B.A., B.S., or B.F.A., students must complete 120 credits. Typically, a B.A. degree requires 90 credits in liberal arts and 30 credits in a major area; B.S. and B.F.A. degrees require 60 credits in liberal arts and 60 credits in major and elective courses. To earn a B.S.N. degree, students must complete 120 credits. Students who earn successful scores of 3 or higher on the College Board's Advanced Placement examinations may qualify for credit and course exemption.

Interdisciplinary studies and dual-degree programs are available. Independent study options and seminars play important roles in undergraduate programs as well. The honors program, which provides an alternative structure for the liberal arts curriculum, fosters the growth of intellectual independence and initiative, offers the opportunity for independent study and research, and encourages the pursuit of scholarly interests in a broad variety of disciplines. The Learning Support Services staff offers tutoring programs, quiet study areas, professional tutors, and student-peer tutors to help students.

The academic calendar consists of two 15-week semesters; during each semester, students generally take five courses. The fall semester is in session from September through December; the spring semester runs from late January through May. Courses are offered during the January intersession but are not required. Two 5-week summer sessions are also offered.

Off-Campus Programs

The College of New Rochelle offers an extensive internship program. Art students have opportunities to gain hands-on experience in art galleries and museums around the New York metropolitan area, such as the Metropolitan Museum of Art and the Guggenheim Museum, while continuing to develop their artistic talents. Communication arts majors participate in internships at numerous radio stations, newspapers, film companies, advertising and public relations firms, and national and cable broadcasting networks. Social science majors are offered opportunities with government agencies in Washington, D.C.; Albany; New York City; and Westchester, New York. Social work majors complete their fieldwork at a variety of human services agencies, and education majors gain experience through fieldwork and student teaching in local school districts and institutions. Business majors put theory into practice at companies such as Merrill Lynch and IBM, as well as at the New York Stock Exchange.

Clinical experiences for School of Nursing students take place in some of the most modern and sophisticated health-care institutions in the world, including Blythdale Children's Hospital, Hospital for Special Surgery, and Montefiore Medical Center.

Students in all academic areas are encouraged to study and travel abroad. The College works with the American Institute for Foreign Study and the Institute for European Studies. Scholarships for study abroad are also available.

Academic Facilities

The New Rochelle campus contains twenty buildings, including classroom and laboratory facilities, student residences, and centers for academic support services. In addition, the newly expanded wireless network allows Internet access from almost anywhere on campus. Each full-time, matriculating freshman or transfer student in the School of Arts and Sciences and the School of Nursing receives a laptop computer.

The recently renovated Mother Irene Gill Memorial Library holds more than 200,000 volumes in open stacks. About 3,000 new volumes are purchased each year. Holdings in education, psychology, health sciences, gerontology, and art are extensive. Renovations to the library included the addition of approximately 200 data ports and forty computer stations offering a variety of computer capabilities, including access to Gill Library's extensive online databases as well as the Internet. Gill Library is a member of an international network of libraries.

The Mooney Center provides technology and programs to assist students in the development of academic, professional, and personal lifetime goals. Facilities include state-of-the-art computer laboratories and classrooms, a computer graphics studio and desktop publishing facilities, a photography laboratory, a television studio, the Romita Auditorium, art studios and gallery space, a model classroom for student teachers, and the H. W. Taylor Institute for Entrepreneurial Studies. More than a dozen laboratories are housed in Rogick Life Science Center and Science Hall. Facilities include a research microscope room, a radiation laboratory and counting room, a plant/animal tissue-culture room, a computer room, a darkroom, a greenhouse, and laboratories set aside entirely for student research.

The Learning Center for Nursing is composed of a nursing laboratory, which simulates a hospital setting, and a multimedia laboratory equipped with four mobile television centers and a media library. The computer room in the nursing center contains computers and printers and COMMES, an artificial intelligence system that simulates a professional nursing consultant. The system supports clinical decision making by students and professional nurses.

The Student Campus Center houses the food service operation, featuring a variety of hot and cold food choices and an attractive, comfortable seating area; a completely renovated bookstore; centralized mailboxes for all students on campus; student activity rooms; and meeting rooms and lounge areas designed to hold large groups of people for lectures and special events.

A state-of-the-art Wellness Center is scheduled to open in spring 2008. Housed within the 55,000-square-foot facility will be a gymnasium with basketball and volleyball courts, interior running track, NCAA competition swimming pool, dance and aerobics studio, and fitness and weight room.

Costs

Tuition for the 2007–08 academic year was $23,200. Room and board costs were $8700. Total estimated annual costs, including travel, books, fees, and personal expenses, were $34,900.

Financial Aid

Approximately 90 percent of all freshmen receive some kind of financial aid through Pell Grants, Supplemental Educational Opportunity Grants, Federal Work-Study Program awards, institutional awards, and student loans. New York State residents are encouraged to apply for Tuition Assistance Program (TAP) awards. The College of New Rochelle also has numerous grants and scholarships available. The scholarships are all based on academic achievement, community service, and leadership qualities. Amounts vary from $3000 per year to full tuition. All students applying for financial aid are required to fill out a College of New Rochelle Financial Aid Application and to complete the Free Application for Federal Student Aid (FAFSA).

Faculty

In no small measure, the College owes its growth and success to a highly committed faculty and administration. The faculty consists of dedicated scholars and teachers who have been recognized for excellence in teaching. Ninety percent of the faculty members hold doctoral degrees or the highest degree available in their field. No graduate students or teaching assistants teach undergraduates. Faculty advisers are available to students for consultation and guidance in academic and career planning. To supplement and complement its faculty, the College invites adjunct professors, artists, business executives, and social workers to teach courses in their areas of expertise. The student-faculty ratio is 10:1.

Student Government

The Office of Student Development and Programs oversees undergraduate extracurricular activities. The Student Government Association is comprised of elected officials and club and organization leaders.

Admission Requirements

The College is selective in its admission process and evaluates each candidate's secondary school record, class rank, grade point average, extracurricular activities, SAT (critical reading and math sections only) or ACT scores, essay, and a counselor's recommendation. The secondary school curriculum should include 16 academic units in English, mathematics, foreign language, social science, and natural science. Applicants to the School of Nursing should complete biology and chemistry lab courses plus one other science course and three years of high school mathematics, including algebra I, algebra II, and geometry. While an admission interview is not required, it is recommended. First-time and transfer students may apply for either the September or January term. Students interested in transferring to the School of Arts and Sciences must have maintained at least a 2.0 GPA at their previous institution. Students interested in transferring to the School of Nursing must have maintained at least a 3.0 GPA and earned at least a C+ in all prerequisite courses. International students are welcome and must submit scores on the Test of English as a Foreign Language (TOEFL), when necessary. A minimum TOEFL score of 550 (paper-based test) is required for admission.

Application and Information

Interested students should begin the admission process early in their senior year. The College accepts applications and renders decisions on a rolling basis. Students particularly interested in the College may apply for early decision; all credentials must arrive in the Office of Admission by November 1. Early decision candidates are notified by December 1. Applications for regular admission are accepted until all class spaces are filled. On-campus housing is guaranteed. Enrollment deferrals are available.

For additional information about the School of Arts and Sciences and the School of Nursing, students should contact:

Stephanie Decker
Director of Admission
The College of New Rochelle
New Rochelle, New York 10805
Phone: 800-933-5923 (toll-free)
E-mail: admission@cnr.edu
Web site: http://www.cnr.edu

The College of New Rochelle students catch up on some studying while enjoying the beautiful weather and scenery.

THE COLLEGE OF SAINT ROSE

ALBANY, NEW YORK

The College

The College of Saint Rose is an independent, residential, coeducational institution where academics and career preparation are top priorities. The College's progressive liberal education core prepares students to dive into one of the College's fifty-eight undergraduate fields of study, most of which incorporate a field experience or internship component. The College offers small class sizes, with a student-faculty ratio of 15:1 and an experienced, mentoring faculty. *Money* magazine and *U.S. News & World Report* have ranked Saint Rose as one of the top colleges in the Northeast and the nation, based on such factors as affordability and high academic quality. With the capital of New York as its convenient location and a distinctly friendly atmosphere on campus, the College of Saint Rose is a place where students realize they will be challenged intellectually and have the ability to change the world.

Saint Rose was founded in 1920 by the Sisters of Saint Joseph of Carondelet and is a distinguished college interwoven within a remarkable city. The campus is part of the fabric of the city and the students and faculty members the threads that make it whole. The College is located in an area that gives it a distinct educational advantage and a college dedicated to cultivating intellectual dynamic leaders appreciative of diversity and active citizenship. The College encompasses eighty buildings, including the new Thelma P. Lally School of Education, a state-of-the-art Science Center, a high-tech music studio, and the Hubbard Interfaith Sanctuary.

Saint Rose students make up a community of leaders. Most of the 3,000 undergraduates at Saint Rose come from twenty-two states and sixteen different countries. The College of Saint Rose actively seeks to enroll students of all backgrounds who can contribute to and benefit from the experience of shared learning and academic success.

Campus housing includes traditional and suite-style residence halls and town houses as well as more than thirty Victorian homes. Each house has its own history and character, with unique wraparound porches and stained-glass windows.

Students participate in organized social activities as well as ten associations related to academic majors. The College of Saint Rose is a member of the National Collegiate Athletic Association (NCAA) Division II and the Northeast-10 Conference. Intercollegiate teams include men's baseball and golf; men's and women's basketball, cross-country, soccer, swimming, tennis, and track and field, and women's softball and volleyball.

Although students ultimately attend Saint Rose to receive a superior education, they also participate in organized social activities that enhance the Saint Rose experience. Saint Rose students belong to more than thirty groups that include academic-related clubs as well as special-interest clubs. They also play in ten to fifteen intramural programs and produce three publications—the award-winning *Chronicle* weekly student newspaper, the *Sphere* literary magazine, and *Reflections*, the College's yearbook.

Location

Saint Rose is located in the historic Pine Hills neighborhood of Albany. With more than 60,000 college students in the area, there are always things to do and people to meet. A wide variety of restaurants, shops, museums, malls, and theaters are within walking distance or are easily accessible by buses that stop at Saint Rose.

Majors and Degrees

The College of Saint Rose offers programs of study in the fields of accounting, American studies, art education (K–12), biochemistry, biology, biology education (7–12), biology/cytotechnology, business administration, chemistry, chemistry education (7–12), childhood education, childhood education/special education, communication disorders, communications, computer information systems, computer science, criminal justice, early childhood education, early childhood/special education, earth science (7–12), English, English education (7–12), environmental affairs, exploratory, graphic design, history, history/political science, mathematics, mathematics education (7–12), medical technology, music education (K–12), music industry, prelaw, premedicine, pre–veterinary studies, psychology, religious studies, social studies education (7–12), social work, sociology, Spanish, Spanish education (7–12), sport management, studio art, technology education, and women's studies.

Academic Programs

In addition to several Express Master programs that allow students to complete both bachelor's and master's degrees in four to five years, the College offers qualified students the opportunity to pursue an accelerated bachelor's/master's degree program that can be completed in approximately five years of study. The College offers these options in accounting, business, communications disorders (speech therapy), computer information systems, computer science, English, and history. It also offers those who wish to enroll as early admission students the option to complete their senior year of high school and freshman year of college simultaneously.

Qualified students may also participate in other special programs: a 3+3 option with Albany Law School, a 3+1 medical technology option with Albany College of Pharmacy or Rochester, and a 3+2 engineering option with Union College, Clarkson University, Rensselaer Polytechnic Institute, or Alfred University. Students in these programs complete selected bachelor's degree programs at Saint Rose in three years and transfer to the cooperating institution to finish the professional program.

Students are provided with assistance in planning their programs of study by faculty advisers in their major areas and by the Office of Academic Advisement. They may elect double majors or minors or may design their own programs within the guidelines set by the interdepartmental studies major.

To earn a bachelor's degree, a student must complete a minimum of 122 credits, including, for most majors, the liberal education curriculum requirement of 42 credits, two courses in physical education, and the major requirements as specified. A minimum of 60 credits must be earned on the Saint Rose campus or at one of the colleges in the Hudson-Mohawk Association of Colleges and Universities through cross-registration.

The College's participation in the Hudson-Mohawk Association of Colleges and Universities provides an opportunity for students to enroll in classes at twenty participating colleges and universities in the Capital Region on a space-available basis.

The College operates on a semester calendar, with a fall term extending from August to December and a spring term from January to May. Two summer session programs offer undergraduate and graduate evening courses.

Off-Campus Programs

Saint Rose students can study in one of more than thirty countries, which is made possible by the school's affiliations with the College Consortium for International Studies, Regent's College in London, and the Center for Cross-Cultural Study. All study-abroad opportunities are offered at the same price as Saint Rose tuition (plus airfare and personal expenses), including the Saint Rose financial aid package. All credits count toward the student's degree.

Academic Facilities

A recent partnership with IBM and a $7-million technology upgrade greatly enhanced the speed and performance of the College's network, providing the infrastructure for wireless networking, videoconferencing, streaming media, and Blackboard, the Web-based instruction tool. The campuswide network provides access to the College's Neil Hellman Library and all campus computer laboratories and residence hall rooms.

The Center for Art and Design houses the Saint Rose Art Gallery as well as extensive photography labs, graphic design computers, and one of the largest screen-printing facilities in the state of New York. The College's Music Center features the Saints and Sinners Sound Studio, a music library, a performance hall, and practice rooms. Science and mathematics majors have access to the latest equipment and research facilities in the College's 27,000-square-foot Science Center.

The newest facility at the College is the Thelma P. Lally School of Education. This new $15-million, 56,000-square-foot building features a multimedia education forum, classrooms, computer labs, offices, an education and curriculum library, a laboratory nursery school, and a multidisciplinary services clinic. The school provides a learning and teaching environment in which technology plays a critical role and where teachers, parents, and students exchange ideas on how to make the American education system second to none.

The most recent transformation project at the College is the construction of a $7.5-million Events and Athletics Center. With the creation of this facility, the College of Saint Rose plans to provide an on-campus venue worthy of welcoming best-selling authors, Nobel Prize winners, and world-famous performers. This space is also designed to serve as a unique collegiate basketball venue in the Capital Region, large enough to accommodate the Golden Knights' loyal fan base. In addition, Saint Joseph's Hall, one of Saint Rose's original buildings, received a $5.5-million renovation, turning the building into a student service hub centralized around the College's Student Solution Center.

Costs

Tuition for 2007–08 was $19,960. Room and board costs averaged $8558 per year, depending on the meal plan chosen by the student. Estimated annual costs for books and personal expenses are $1000 and $1400, respectively.

Financial Aid

More than 95 percent of the students receive scholarships and financial assistance. The College of Saint Rose participates in the Federal Pell Grant, FSEOG, TAP, and Federal Work-Study programs and in the Federal Perkins Loan and Federal Stafford Loan Programs. The College provides ample aid in the form of grants, service awards, and scholarships for need or academic achievement. Candidates for financial assistance must file the Free Application for Federal Student Aid. ISIR and SAR forms should be on file in the Financial Aid Office by March 1. Students interested in being considered for academic scholarships must apply to the College by February 1.

Faculty

Saint Rose has a full-time faculty of 174 members, with a student-faculty ratio of 15:1. The average class size is 20–25 students, with more than 55 percent of classes having less than 20 students.

Student Government

The Student Association (SA) consists of elected students who want to make life at the College as enjoyable, interesting, and meaningful as possible. It budgets student funds, appoints representatives to College policymaking committees, and assists individual students and clubs in planning and carrying out projects. It also provides an organ of self-government, promotes an exchange of ideas within the College community, fosters opportunities beyond those offered in the formal curriculum, and advances the welfare of the entire College community. SA also oversees the College's thirty clubs and organizations.

Admission Requirements

The College wishes to admit students who show evidence of strong academic motivation and the ability to benefit from a challenging liberal and professional education. Admission decisions are made after careful study of all the data available for each candidate. Interviews are strongly recommended but not required. Freshman applicants should submit a high school transcript, a letter of recommendation from a teacher or guidance counselor, and scores on the SAT or ACT.

Transfer applicants must submit high school and college transcripts, a letter of recommendation from a college instructor, and a written statement of the reasons for transfer.

Application and Information

The College has an early action (nonbinding) application deadline of December 1. Students are accepted for admission for the fall and spring semesters on a rolling admissions basis. Interested students must apply by February 1 to be considered for academic scholarships ranging from $3000 to full tuition for each undergraduate year. New students who are accepted for admission are asked to submit a $300 enrollment deposit to secure their place in the new class. Information on all aspects of the campus and the academic programs can be obtained by contacting the Office of Admissions; this office also can arrange personal interviews, campus tours, classroom visits, and overnight accommodations.

Office of Undergraduate Admissions
The College of Saint Rose
432 Western Avenue
Albany, New York 12203
Phone: 518-454-5150
800-637-8556 (toll-free)
Fax: 518-454-2013
E-mail: admit@strose.edu (admissions)
finaid@strose.edu (financial aid)
Web site: http://www.strose.edu

Located in the historic Pine Hills neighborhood of Albany, New York, the Saint Rose campus features a mix of classic brick buildings and new stone and glass structures, with the Campus Green at its center. The border of the campus is outlined by more than thirty restored historic Victorian houses featuring wraparound porches and stained-glass windows.

COLLEGE OF STATEN ISLAND OF THE CITY UNIVERSITY OF NEW YORK

STATEN ISLAND, NEW YORK

The College and The University

The College of Staten Island (CSI) is part of the City University of New York, the largest urban university in the country. The College, like the University, is committed to both access and excellence. CSI's superb campus serves the pivotal endeavors of teaching and research that promote discovery and dissemination of knowledge while developing human minds and spirits. CSI was founded in 1976 by the union of two existing colleges within the City University of New York: Staten Island Community College and Richmond College. Staten Island Community College, the first community college in the University system, opened in 1955. Richmond College, the University's first upper-division college, was founded in 1965. CSI's current undergraduate enrollment is slightly more than 12,000 men and women.

A general education is assured through requirements that allow students to explore a range of knowledge and acquire educational breadth in the arts and humanities, mathematics, science, and social sciences. Requirements for the associate degree provide a curriculum based on study in a specific area that is often directed toward a career. Requirements for the bachelor's degree provide a disciplined and cumulative program of study in a major field of inquiry.

CSI awards the Master of Arts degree in cinema and media studies, English, environmental science, history, and liberal studies; the Master of Science degree in biology, computer science, neuroscience, mental retardation and developmental disabilities, and nursing; the Master of Science in Education degree in childhood (elementary) education, adolescence (secondary education), and special education; and post-master's advanced certificates in leadership in education (supervision and administration) and nursing. CSI participates with the CUNY Graduate School and University Center and Brooklyn College in a doctoral program in polymer chemistry and with the Graduate School and University Center in doctoral programs in computer science, physical therapy, and physics. With the Center for Developmental Neurosciences and Developmental Disabilities, the College participates in CUNY doctoral subprograms in neuroscience (biology) and learning processes (psychology).

Study-abroad opportunities are available through three Culture and Commerce programs, emphasizing the study of Italian, French, or Spanish, and through the Center for International Service.

The Campus Center incorporates facilities for a complete program of student activities. It contains the main dining facilities, the College health services, a bookstore, offices for student organizations, study lounges, a small performance/cafe space, game rooms, and the studios of WSIA, the student-operated FM radio station. The two-story rotunda space at the heart of the structure contains the dining areas and information services.

Location

The College occupies a 204-acre campus located near the center of Staten Island. The campus is the largest site for a college (public or private) within New York City. Set in a parklike landscape, the grounds and facilities create a rural oasis in an urban setting. In this attractive learning environment, classrooms and academic offices are located in ten buildings that form two quadrangles connected by the campus walk, which extends between the library building and the campus center. Five newly built and equipped buildings—the library building, the campus center, the biological sciences/chemical sciences building, the center for the arts, and the sports and recreation center—provide outstanding facilities for College and community activities.

The College's location offers students the best of two worlds. While Staten Island provides a suburban environment with some of the most interesting landscape in the metropolitan area, Manhattan, the center of cultural and social life of the city, is only 25 minutes from the island by ferry. The Verrazano-Narrows Bridge provides direct access to the island from Brooklyn.

Majors and Degrees

The Associate in Arts degree is offered in liberal arts and sciences. The Associate in Science degree is offered in engineering science, liberal arts and sciences, and liberal arts and sciences with a prearchitecture concentration. The Associate in Applied Science degree is offered in business, civil engineering technology, computer technology, electrical engineering technology, medical laboratory technology, and nursing.

The Bachelor of Arts degree is conferred in African-American studies; American studies; art; art with a photography concentration; cinema studies; economics; English; English with a dramatic literature concentration; history; international studies; music; philosophy; political science; psychology; science, letters, and society; sociology/anthropology; social work; Spanish; and women's studies.

The Bachelor of Science degree is offered in accounting; art; art with a photography concentration; biochemistry; bioinformatics; biology; business; business with a finance concentration, an international business concentration, a management concentration, or a marketing concentration; chemistry; communications; computer science; computer science/mathematics; dramatic arts; economics; economics with a business specialization or a finance specialization; engineering science; information systems; international studies; mathematics; medical technology; music; music with an electronics concentration; nursing (upper-division program); physician assistant studies; and physics.

The teacher education program prepares students for teaching at the early childhood, elementary, and secondary levels. The academic work and field experience meet the requirements for the certification and licensing examinations given by the state and city of New York.

Academic Programs

A four-year senior college, CSI offers two-year programs in career areas and in liberal arts and sciences and four-year programs with majors in the traditional fields of study. General education requirements have been established for all degrees. The associate degree programs require 60–64 credits, depending on the field; the bachelor's degree programs require 120 credits, with a few exceptions. Credit may be awarded for experiential learning, internships, and independent study, and credit may be earned by examination. Minors may be taken in several fields, and double majors are permitted. Students may graduate with honors in their field of study in most bachelor's degree majors.

The College follows a semester calendar, with classes scheduled both day and evening; a summer session is also held. The Weekend College, which was established to provide an opportunity for students with weekday commitments to pursue a college education, offers a variety of course combinations leading to associate and bachelor's degrees.

Off-Campus Programs

The College gives a number of courses for credit at off-campus locations throughout the city. These include employee-development programs for major corporations and other programs, supported by grants and by participating employers and unions, that provide courses for city and state employees at agency or institutional locations.

Academic Facilities

The academic buildings are designed to house approximately 200 modern laboratories and classrooms. Each also houses a study lounge for students, department and program offices, and offices for faculty members. Academic and research programs are served by a computer network that allows students and faculty members full access to specialized software, the Internet, online library resources, and e-mail. All major computer languages and software packages are supported. The College is a wireless campus, and its network is available to all students.

The Center for the Arts complex provides facilities for teaching in the instructional wing and areas of public assembly in the public wing. The complex of public facilities includes a 900-seat auditorium, a 450-seat fully equipped theater, a recital hall, an experimental theater, an art gallery, and a conference center. Classrooms, lecture halls, studios, and offices for faculty members are located in the instructional wing fronting the campus walk.

The CSI Library is staffed with 14 full-time faculty librarians and 7 adjunct librarians who also hold faculty status and rank. The library also has 40 support staff members. The library's total collection consists of approximately 219,000 books; 900 print journal subscriptions; 77 electronic databases with more than 15,000 full-text journals; 5,000 videos and films; and more than 4,000 sound recordings. The library's online catalog, CUNY+Plus, provides complete access to the collections, including access to holdings of other CUNY libraries. In addition, the library maintains a collection of current textbooks donated by the CSI Student Government. These and other course materials are available at the Reserve Desk. Wireless laptops are loaned to students for use throughout the library. The library building also houses Instructional Support Services and the Cybercafé.

The laboratory science building provides facilities for teaching and for two research centers: the Center for Environmental Science and the Center for Developmental Neuroscience and Developmental Disabilities. It consists of a research wing and an instructional wing. State-of-the-art laboratories serve students and faculty members in their teaching and research.

The 77,000-gross-square-foot Sports and Recreation Center is a multipurpose facility providing basketball, handball/paddleball, racquetball, and volleyball courts; locker rooms; instructional areas; an indoor 25-meter swimming pool; and offices for faculty members. Recreational fields occupy the meadows in the northwest quadrant of the campus, providing a green and landscaped open area at the main approach to the campus that includes a running track, indoor and outdoor tennis courts, a soccer field, handball/paddleball courts, softball fields, and a semiprofessional baseball field (original home field to Staten Island's minor-league baseball team).

Costs

For 2007–08, costs for first-time freshmen or non-CUNY transfer students were $170 per credit (part-time matriculated) or $2000 per semester (full-time matriculated) for New York State (NYS) residents and $360 per credit for out-of-state students..

Financial Aid

Financial aid is available through state and federal programs and includes the New York State Tuition Assistance Program (TAP) awards, Federal Pell Grants, Federal Supplemental Educational Opportunity Grants (FSEOG), Search for Elevation and Education through Knowledge (SEEK) awards, scholarships, Federal Work-Study Program awards, and student loan programs. Information about programs, application procedures, and deadlines is available from the Financial Aid Office.

CSI Presidential Scholarships are awarded annually to full-time students on the basis of academic proficiency and service. In addition, endowments have been established for scholarships in a number of fields. Further information about scholarships is available from the Career and Scholarship Center.

Faculty

The College has a full-time faculty of 300, of whom approximately 80 percent hold a doctoral degree or the equivalent. The faculty members have made significant contributions in many areas of scholarship, creativity, and public service. Numerous faculty members have received prestigious grants and awards, and more than 30 serve as members of the City University doctoral faculty.

Student Government

The Student Government is composed of 20 elected representatives, and it is through this structure that students are represented in the College's governance.

Admission Requirements

A freshman applicant for admission to a bachelor's degree program must pass the three CUNY Freshman Skills Assessment Tests unless he or she qualifies for exemption based on a satisfactory performance on the SAT or ACT standardized tests or Regents Examinations. Admission to a bachelor's degree program is determined by an applicant's score on the College's admissions index. The index is based on the applicant's high school courses and academic average and the combined verbal and mathematics SAT scores. An applicant whose score reaches or exceeds the College's minimum index number is admitted to a bachelor's degree program. A faculty admissions committee may consider the admission of applicants whose scores approach the College's minimum index number. Transfer students to baccalaureate programs who have fewer than 25 credits must have a GPA of at least 2.0 and must meet freshman entrance criteria. Students must have passed the CUNY Freshman Skills Assessment Tests in mathematics, writing, and reading prior to enrolling in a bachelor's degree program or if they are transferring from another college in the City University.

Entering first-year students may be admitted to two-year programs if they have graduated from an accredited high school or have earned an equivalency diploma (GED) with a satisfactory score.

As a general rule, the College requires a grade point average equivalent to at least a C for transfer as a matriculated student into a two-year degree program.

Application and Information

Requests for further information and application materials should be directed to:

Office of Recruitment and Admissions
North Administration Building (2A-103)
College of Staten Island
City University of New York
2800 Victory Boulevard
Staten Island, New York 10314
Phone: 718-982-2010
E-mail: admissions@mail.csi.cuny.edu
Web site: http://www.csi.cuny.edu

COLUMBIA UNIVERSITY
Columbia College/The Fu Foundation School of Engineering and Applied Science

NEW YORK, NEW YORK

The University

In 1754 King George II granted a charter to a group of New York citizens to found King's College, dedicated to instruction in "the Learned Languages and the Liberal Arts and Sciences." In its early days, King's College taught such students as Alexander Hamilton, John Jay, Robert Livingston, and Gouverneur Morris. After the Revolution, New York State issued the college a new charter with a more patriotic name—Columbia. In 1897 Columbia moved to a new site on Morningside Heights on the Upper West Side of Manhattan. The architectural firm of McKim, Mead and White, the preeminent architects of their day, designed an open central enclave six blocks long, with a majestic domed and colonnaded library at the center. To this day, it remains one of New York's most impressive settings.

Today, Columbia College and The Fu Foundation School of Engineering and Applied Science (Columbia Engineering) offer their students unique advantages; they are at the same time small, selective colleges and integral components of a major research-oriented university.

The College enrolls approximately 4,100 students; the Columbia Engineering student body is roughly 1,400. Students come from all fifty states and several dozen countries. They represent a dazzling array of ethnic, social, economic, cultural, religious, and geographic backgrounds. The diversity of Columbia's student body reflects the diversity of New York City, the world's most international city.

Columbia guarantees four years of on-campus housing to all entering first-year students. Nearly all undergraduates remain in residence halls for all four years.

Columbia students take part in extracurricular groups of all kinds: artistic (theater, musical, and dance), athletic (twenty-nine varsity sports and dozens of club and intramural sports), communications (the *Columbia Daily Spectator,* the *Columbian* yearbook, many other publications, WKCR-FM, a campus television station, and others), community service (Amnesty International, Big Brother/Big Sister programs, tutoring programs, a volunteer ambulance squad, and hospitals, soup kitchens, and homeless shelters), and preprofessional (the Charles Hamilton Houston Pre-Law Association and the National Society of Black Engineers). Other groups represent students' ethnic, religious, political, and gender identities. There are twenty-nine fraternities and sororities. Alfred Lerner Hall houses office and meeting space for student organizations, a theater, a cinema, and many dining options.

Location

Columbia shares its Morningside Heights neighborhood with a number of other famous institutions: Barnard College, the Cathedral of St. John the Divine, Union Theological Seminary, Jewish Theological Seminary, and the Manhattan School of Music, to name a few. Most of the faculty members from Columbia and the other surrounding schools make their homes in the neighborhood. Morningside Heights is an area known for bookstores, wonderfully varied restaurants, and merchants that cater to student tastes, student budgets, and student hours.

Students are encouraged and assisted in making full use of New York's breathtaking variety of cultural, recreational, and professional resources. Columbia students can be found any day of the week exploring the Metropolitan Museum of Art, the Museum of Modern Art, the Guggenheim Museum, the Museum of African Art, the Museo del Barrio, the Asia Society, or any other of the city's hundreds of museums and galleries. Any evening, they might be discovering the theatrical offerings on, off, or "off-off" Broadway (or on campus); attending the opera, ballet, or symphony at Lincoln Center; taking in a movie on campus or in one of New York's 400-plus cinemas; enjoying jazz in Greenwich Village or blues at the Apollo; sampling *pai gwat* in Chinatown; or biking or boating in Central Park. Columbia's internship programs offer students opportunities to explore a career possibility in depth; nowhere else in the world does the concentration of industries allow such a range of possibilities. New York's public transportation system puts the entire city within easy reach of Columbia students; the campus is directly served by a subway line and five bus routes.

Majors and Degrees

Columbia College grants the B.A. degree in approximately ninety programs of study in the humanities, social sciences, and pure sciences, including many interdisciplinary majors. Columbia Engineering grants the B.S. degree in about fifteen engineering fields. A five-year program that begins in either school allows students to receive both a B.A. from Columbia College and a B.S. from Columbia Engineering.

Joint degree programs offer selected students the opportunity to combine their undergraduate work with study in Columbia University's schools of law and international affairs and with the Juilliard School.

Academic Programs

Unlike many other colleges that are attempting to restore structure to their course offerings, Columbia has maintained a coherent and relevant curriculum since the time of the First World War, when it introduced the renowned Core Curriculum, a program of general education that has served as a model for hundreds of colleges around the country. One of the two oldest courses in the core is Contemporary Civilization, a year-long historical survey of western civilization's religious, political, and moral philosophies; the other is Literature Humanities, a year-long introduction to western culture's most seminal and meaningful literary works. A second year of humanities offers a semester each of music and art appreciation, encouraging students to experience the cultural treasures of New York City. The Major Cultures core courses enlarge the scope of inquiry beyond the Western focus in order to promote learning and thought about the variety of cultures and the diversity of traditions that interact in the United States and the world today. The Frontiers of Science course outlines the approaches that scientists take to answer interesting problems in the natural world and introduces students to scientific research methods. The Core Curriculum exposes Columbia's multicultural student body to a variety of disciplines, preparing them for the complex questions and issues of modern society.

One hallmark that distinguishes a Columbia Engineering education from that of other prestigious engineering schools is the number of nonengineering courses that every Columbia Engineering undergraduate takes; almost a quarter of a student's program is in the humanities and social sciences and includes components of the Core Curriculum. Alumni often cite this feature of their Columbia Engineering education as the most important reason for success in their careers. Within the first year, all engineering students also take the Gateway class, which requires engineering design work with a New York City nonprofit agency. For example, students worked at the Apollo Theater in Harlem to design their intranet system and at Downtown Little League to design a safer dugout.

Off-Campus Programs

Columbia students may, with the help of a dean, choose from 150 study-abroad programs on every continent, many of which are Columbia's own programs.

Columbia maintains at Reid Hall, its Paris campus, several undergraduate programs. Courses at Reid Hall are quite varied, permitting students to work not only in the areas of French language, literature, and culture but also in several other fields throughout the range of the humanities and social sciences. In addition, there is a year-long program that includes course work in the French university system.

Columbia was the first U.S. college to offer an integrated year-abroad program with the Universities of Oxford and Cambridge. Other programs allow students to work at the University of Kyoto in Japan or at the Free University of Berlin in Germany.

Academic Facilities

Columbia has the eighth-largest research library system in North America, consisting of 8.6 million volumes and 26 million manuscripts within 3,000 collections. Included in Columbia's twenty-five libraries are collections of particular significance, including those of the Avery Architectural and Fine Arts Library, the Starr East Asian Library, the Rare Book and Manuscript Library, and the Burke Library of Union Theological Seminary. All divisions are open to Columbia undergraduates. The Columbia Computer Center has five mainframe computers used for academic research and instruction as well as clusters of microcomputers, terminals, and printers; it has remote units and terminals all over campus, including in residence halls, to guarantee accessibility. The chemistry building, Havemeyer Hall, houses modern laboratory facilities for research and undergraduate instruction. Students may also make use of outstanding facilities throughout the University, including an electronic music lab, a cyclotron, an oral history collection, the facilities and programs of the Lamont-Doherty Earth Observatory, and oceanographic research ships.

Costs

Tuition for the 2007–08 academic year was $35,516. Room and board for all first-year students were $9937. With typical fees, books, and supplies, the total cost of a year at Columbia was approximately $49,625.

Financial Aid

All first-year candidates who are U.S., Canadian, or Mexican citizens or who have U.S. permanent resident or political refugee status are considered for admission without regard to their financial need, and if admitted they receive financial aid packages to meet their full demonstrated need for the cost of a Columbia education. Financial aid deadlines are November 15 for early decision candidates and March 1 for regular decision candidates. Prospective students should go to http://www.studentaffairs.columbia.edu/finaid/ for information on specific requirements and deadlines. Financial aid packages may include a loan and a job (self-help); need not met by the self-help component is met by grant aid. All financial aid at Columbia is based on need; no aid is given in the form of academic, athletic, artistic, or other merit awards. About 50 percent of Columbia students are receiving some form of financial assistance, and 80 percent of first-year students who applied for financial aid received a need-based award. The Office of Financial Aid and Educational Financing believes that cost should not be a barrier to students pursuing their educational dreams. Students who are not U.S., Canadian, or Mexican citizens and do not have U.S. permanent resident or political refugee status should be aware that their admissions process is not need-blind and that their applications are read in a more selective process than are other students'.

Faculty

The student-to-faculty ratio is 7:1. Core curriculum classes are capped at 22 students, and 70 percent of classes have 20 students or less. The Columbia faculty is committed to both teaching and research, and students are taught by the most eminent professors as well as young assistant professors. All faculty members maintain office hours, and each student receives a faculty adviser from the department that he or she chooses as a major.

Student Government

Each undergraduate division has its own student council and elects representatives to the Columbia University Senate.

Admission Requirements

The Columbia first-year class of 1,332 students is selected from a much larger pool of applicants through a holistic, committee-based review process. Candidates for admission are expected to demonstrate the necessary ability and interest to do successful college work in a variety of disciplines as required for the Columbia degree. The following secondary school preparation is recommended: 4 years of English, including meaningful work in literature and writing; 3 (preferably 4) years of mathematics, including precalculus and calculus where offered; 3 (preferably 4) years of history and social studies; 3 or more years of the same foreign language; and 2 or more years of laboratory science (including chemistry and physics where available). The Admissions Committee recognizes that secondary schools vary in offerings and standards; consideration is given to applicants whose preparations differ from the recommended course of study but have taken advantage of what their schools offer.

Standardized tests are required for admission, according to the following guidelines. Students may take the SAT, which consists of three sections, each graded on an 800-point scale. Students who take the test more than once are evaluated on the highest score they receive in any individual section. Applicants may alternately take the ACT, which is graded on a 36-point scale. Students taking the test more than once are evaluated on the highest composite score they receive. The writing component of the ACT is mandatory for candidates for Columbia.

In addition to either the SAT or ACT, students must also take two SAT Subject Tests. For Columbia College, they may take any two tests; for The Fu Foundation School of Engineering and Applied Science, they must take any mathematics test and either the physics or the chemistry test.

Students who attend a school that does not give conventional grades or who are homeschooled must take two additional SAT Subject Tests in addition to all requirements outlined above for Columbia College or The Fu Foundation School of Engineering and Applied Science.

It is absolutely imperative that applicants have the testing service report their standardized test scores directly to either Columbia College (SAT code 2116, ACT code 2717) or The Fu Foundation School of Engineering and Applied Science (SAT code 2111, ACT code 2719), as appropriate.

Transfer students may enter Columbia in September only.

The College has a Visiting Students Program, which allows students to attend for one or both semesters of their sophomore, junior, or senior year.

Application and Information

The postmark deadline for applications is the first business day after January 1. Candidates are notified of the Admissions Committee's decisions on or about April 1. Admitted candidates must respond to Columbia's offer of admission by May 1. Candidates for whom Columbia is their definite first choice may apply under the early decision plan; the deadline is November 1 for all application material, and a decision is rendered by December 15. Candidates admitted to Columbia under early decision are required to withdraw applications at any other colleges. The application fee is $70. The fee may be waived if a school official testifies that the fee would cause the candidate's family financial hardship. The application materials are available online. For further information or for applications, interested students should contact:

Office of Undergraduate Admissions
Columbia University
1130 Amsterdam Avenue, MC2807
New York, New York 10027

Phone: 212-854-2522
Fax: 212-854-1209
Web site: http://www.studentaffairs.columbia.edu/admissions
E-mail: ugrad-ask@columbia.edu

COLUMBIA UNIVERSITY, SCHOOL OF GENERAL STUDIES

NEW YORK, NEW YORK

The University and The School

The School of General Studies (GS) of Columbia University is one of the finest liberal arts colleges in the country dedicated specifically to students with nontraditional backgrounds seeking a traditional education at an Ivy League university. Most students at GS have, for personal or professional reasons, interrupted their education, never attended college, or are only able to attend part-time. GS is unique among colleges of its type, because its students are fully integrated into the Columbia undergraduate curriculum: they take the same courses with the same faculty members and earn the same degree as all other Columbia undergraduates.

GS students come from varied backgrounds and all walks of life. They have the option to study either full- or part-time. Many students work full-time while pursuing a degree, and many have family responsibilities; others attend classes full-time and experience Columbia's more traditional college life. In the classroom, the diversity and varied personal experience of the student body promote discussion and debate, fostering an environment of academic rigor and intellectual development. GS has approximately 1,200 undergraduate degree candidates and close to 400 postbaccalaureate premedical students. The average age of a GS student is 29. More than 60 percent of GS students attend classes full-time.

In addition to its bachelor's degree program, GS offers combined undergraduate/graduate degree programs with Columbia's Schools of Social Work, International and Public Affairs, Law, Business, Dental Medicine, Teachers College, and the College of Physicians and Surgeons. Between 80 and 85 percent of the School's students continue on to graduate and professional study after graduation. The acceptance rate for GS postbaccalaureate premedical students applying to U.S. medical schools is more than 90 percent.

Location

Columbia University is located in Morningside Heights, on the Upper West Side of Manhattan. The University's neighbors include the Union Theological Seminary, the Jewish Theological Seminary, the Manhattan School of Music, St. Luke's Hospital, Riverside Church, and the Cathedral of St. John the Divine. The diversity of intellectual and social activities offered by these institutions is one of Columbia's great assets as a university; another is New York City itself, which offers Columbia students a rich and almost boundless variety of social, cultural, and recreational opportunities that are themselves an education.

Majors and Degrees

The School of General Studies grants the B.A. and B.S. degrees and offers the following majors: African studies; African American studies; American studies; ancient studies; anthropology; applied mathematics; archaeology; architecture; architecture, history and theory; art history; art history–visual arts; Asian American studies; astronomy; astrophysics; biochemistry; biology; biophysics; chemistry; classical studies; classics; comparative ethnic studies; comparative literature and society; computer science; creative writing; dance; drama and theater arts; earth and environmental sciences; East Asian languages and cultures; economics; economics–mathematics; economics–operations research; economics–philosophy; economics–political science; economics–statistics; English and comparative literature; environmental biology; evolutionary biology of the human species; film studies; French; French and Francophone studies; German literature and cultural history; Hispanic studies; history; human rights; Italian cultural studies; Italian literature; Latino studies; mathematics; mathematics–statistics; Middle East and Asian languages and cultures; music; neuroscience and behavior; philosophy; physics; political science; political science-statistics; psychology; regional studies; religion; Russian; sociology; statistics; urban studies; visual arts; women's and gender studies; and Yiddish studies. Individually designed majors are also available. In addition, the School offers two undergraduate dual-degree programs: one in conjunction with Columbia's School of Engineering and Applied Science and the other in conjunction with the Jewish Theological Seminary.

Academic Programs

The School of General Studies offers a traditional liberal arts education designed to provide students with the broad knowledge and intellectual skills that foster continued education and growth in the years after college as well as providing a sound foundation for positions of responsibility in the professional world.

Requirements for the bachelor's degree comprise three elements: (1) core requirements, intended to develop in students the ability to write and communicate clearly; to understand the modes of thought that characterize the humanities, social sciences, and sciences; to gain familiarity with central cultural ideas through literature, fine arts, and music; and to acquire a working proficiency in a foreign language; (2) major requirements, designed to give students sustained and coherent exposure to a particular discipline in an area of strong intellectual interest; and (3) elective courses, in which students pursue particular interests and skills for their own personal growth or for their relationship to future professional or personal objectives. Students are required to complete a minimum of 124 credits for the bachelor's degree; 60 of these may be in transfer credit, but at least 64 credits (including the last 30 credits) must be completed at Columbia. In addition to the usual graduation honors (cum laude, magna cum laude, and summa cum laude), honors programs for superior students are available in a majority of the University's departments.

Off-Campus Programs

Columbia students may enhance their academic experiences through various study-abroad programs around the world. For example, students may spend a term at the Reid Hall Program in the Montparnasse district of Paris, the Berlin Consortium for German Studies, the Kyoto Consortium for Japanese Studies, or the Language Program in Beijing, China. In addition, students may apply to participate in one of the Columbia-approved study-abroad programs located in countries around the world.

Academic Facilities

The Columbia University libraries constitute the nation's sixth-largest academic library system, with a collection of more than 9.8 million volumes, more than 5 million microform pieces, and 26 million manuscript items in 850 separate collections. Of the twenty-five libraries in the system, five are designated Distinctive Collections because of their unusual depth and nationally recognized excellence. All library divisions are available to GS students. The University's Computer Center is one of the largest and most powerful university installations in the world and has remote units and terminals in several parts of the campus to enhance its accessibility. The Fairchild Life Sciences Building houses research facilities, laboratories, electron microscopes, and a vast amount of biochemical equipment used for teaching and research. The University's physics building has been the scene of many important developments in the recent history of physics, including the invention of the laser and the first U.S. demonstration of nuclear fission.

Costs

For the 2007–08 academic year, tuition was $1146 per credit, monthly living expenses (including rent) were about $1600, fees were approximately $1400, and books were $1000 to $1300.

Financial Aid

The School of General Studies awards financial aid based upon need and academic ability. Approximately 70 percent of GS degree candidates receive some form of financial aid, including Federal Pell Grants, New York State TAP Grants, Federal Stafford and unsubsidized Stafford Loans, Federal Perkins Loans, General Studies Scholarships, and Federal Work-Study Program awards. Priority application deadlines for new students are June 1 for the fall semester and October 15 for the spring semester.

Faculty

The faculty of the School of General Studies, which is shared with Columbia College, the Graduate School of Arts and Sciences, and the School of International and Public Affairs, includes distinguished scholars in virtually every discipline. Of the School's more than 1,000 faculty members, over 99 percent hold a Ph.D. Students, whether full-time or part-time, have many opportunities to work closely with faculty members, both in small classes and in research projects. Faculty members also serve as advisers to students majoring in their area of study and maintain regular office hours to see students.

Student Government

One student of the School represents GS students in the University Senate, a decision-making body comprising students, faculty members, and administrative staff members from each division of the University. In addition, 2 GS students sit as voting members on the Committee on Instruction, which oversees the curriculum of the School. The General Studies Student Council elects officers each year and sponsors activities for students. *The Observer*, the School's student-run magazine, is published several times each year. The Premedical Association (PMA) sponsors events related to the medical school admissions process.

Admission Requirements

The GS admission policy is geared to the maturity and varied backgrounds of its students. Aptitude and motivation are considered along with past academic performance, standardized test scores, and employment history. The School's admission decisions are based on a careful review of each application and reflect the Admissions Committee's considered judgment of the applicant's maturity, academic potential, and present ability to undertake course work at Columbia.

Admission requirements include a completed application form; a 1,500- to 2,000-word autobiographical statement describing the applicant's past educational history and work experience, present situation, and future plans; two letters of recommendation from academic or professional evaluators; an official high school transcript; official transcripts from all colleges and universities attended; official SAT or ACT scores (applicants may take the General Studies Admissions Examination); and a nonrefundable application fee of $65.

Students from outside the United States may apply to the School of General Studies to start or complete a baccalaureate degree. In addition to the materials described above, international applicants must submit official TOEFL scores.

Application and Information

Application deadlines are March 1 for early action (nonbinding), June 1 for the fall semester, and October 15 for the spring semester. Applicants from countries outside the U.S. are urged to apply by August 15 for the spring semester and April 1 for the fall semester. Applications are reviewed as they are completed, and applicants are notified of decisions shortly thereafter.

For more information, students should contact:

Curtis M. Rodgers, Dean of Admissions
Office of Admissions and Financial Aid
School of General Studies
408 Lewisohn Hall
2970 Broadway
Columbia University, Mail Code 4101
New York, New York 10027
Phone: 212-854-2772
E-mail: gsdegree@columbia.edu
Web site: http://www.gs.columbia.edu

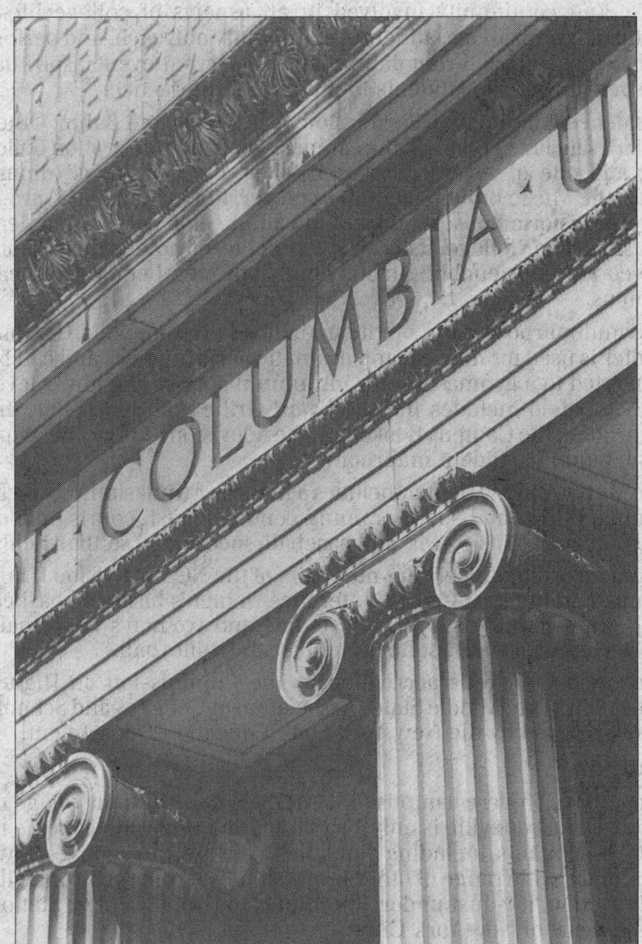

The Low Memorial Library/Visitors Center.

CONCORDIA COLLEGE–NEW YORK

BRONXVILLE, NEW YORK

The College

Founded in 1881, Concordia College–New York is a four-year, coeducational institution offering a Christ-centered, value-oriented liberal arts education for lives of service to church and community. Part of the Concordia University System, Concordia is affiliated with the Lutheran Church–Missouri Synod.

Students come from twenty-seven states and thirty-four countries worldwide; 60 percent are women. As members of a close-knit community, Concordia students are mentored by a dedicated faculty and staff, most of whom live within a 10-minute walk of the campus. Students develop lifelong relationships as they prepare for fulfilling lives and careers. During their time at Concordia, students are encouraged to reach their full academic, spiritual, athletic, and artistic potential.

Two-thirds of the students live on campus, forming an active, close-knit community involved in all aspects of college life—student organizations, athletics, community outreach, and performance ensembles. From daily chapel to servant events, spiritual life activities invite students to put faith into practice.

Residence halls include Sieker, Romoser, Rippe, and Bohm. Other facilities include Feth Hall, the campus's main administration building and one of several classroom sites, the Commons (dining hall), the Music Building, and Ressmeyer, Koepchen, and Ward—several historic houses adjacent to campus that serve as student housing. The College also owns a number of homes throughout the community, enabling faculty and staff members to live near campus.

The multipurpose room on the main level of Schoenfeld Campus Center is used for musical and dramatic performances and can be converted to a gymnasium for intramural sports. The lower level of Schoenfeld includes the Brickyard Grille and Snack Bar, the Coop Store, the Campus Bookstore, the television lounge, the game room, and the student mailroom.

The Meyer Athletic Center includes a full-size gymnasium, a weight room, a fitness and sports training center, squash courts, indoor and outdoor tennis courts, and baseball, soccer, and softball fields.

The Concordia Clippers are members of the NCAA Division II and compete in the East Coast Conference in men's baseball, basketball, cross-country, soccer, and tennis and women's basketball, cross-country, soccer, softball, tennis, and volleyball.

Concordia College is accredited by the Commission on Higher Education of the Middle States Association of Colleges and Schools and registered by the New York State Education Department.

Location

Concordia's 33-acre campus is set in the small, affluent village of Bronxville. Bronxville is only 1 square mile in size and is home to 7,000 inhabitants, including diplomats, corporate executives, lawyers, and a wide range of other professionals. From the Bronxville train station, it is just under 30 minutes to Grand Central Station in the heart of New York City.

Concordia is the right place for students who participate in their education, want to be involved in lots of activities, seek a broad-based education, want to be part of a Christian community, and want to be near New York City.

Majors and Degrees

Concordia offers Bachelor of Arts (B.A.) and Bachelor of Science (B.S.) degrees. The B.A. is offered in biology (with tracks in health, environmental, and research), education (NCATE-accredited, with tracks in early childhood, childhood, and middle childhood generalist), English (with tracks in literature and writing), liberal studies (with tracks in art, biblical languages, English, history, math, music, new media, psychology, religion, and sociology), and social sciences (with tracks in history, international studies, psychology, and sociology).

The B.S. is offered in business (with tracks in international management and Certified Financial Planning®) and social work (with a track in family life ministry). The social work program is CSWE-accredited and allows for advanced standing in the Master of Social Work graduate degree program.

The College also offers a Fellows Program (honors); Lutheran Teaching Diploma; the Concordia Connection, a support program for students with a diagnosed learning disability; and an English as a second language program. The College also offers preprofessional studies programs (deaconess, law, medicine, and seminary).

Academic Programs

At Concordia, students are immersed in a learning environment that sparks the imagination and provides the skills to build a future. The curriculum emphasizes an interdisciplinary, hands-on approach to academics grounded by a strong foundation of the liberal arts. What students learn in the classroom is connected to the real world through exciting experiential learning opportunities.

To graduate, students must complete the Concordia Distinctive (the College's highly regarded core curriculum), the program of study, and general studies requirements, integrated with field experience and internships in Westchester County and the New York area. All these components together are known as The Concordia Experience.

Concordia operates on a two-semester calendar. A minimum of 122 completed semester hours is required to earn the bachelor's degree.

The Concordia Fellows Program (honors) is open via application to all students who demonstrate high academic achievement. Fellows are enriched through a variety of unique academic experiences, seminars, and travel.

Concordia offers an intensive English as a second language (ESL) program, serving students at a variety of proficiency levels. The ESL program is housed on campus and serves both matriculated and nonmatriculated students.

The Concordia Connection Program is for students with diagnosed learning differences. Support services are provided to qualified students who meet regular admission requirements but need specific assistance in order to maximize their academic success. Space in this program is quite limited and additional fees are assessed.

Concordia also offers an Adult Education Program with Accelerated Degree Programs for adult students over age 25. Degrees are offered in behavioral sciences (B.A.), business administration (B.S.), and liberal studies (A.A.).

Off-Campus Programs

Study abroad and international travel experiences are available. Students may study abroad for a semester (through AHA International) or join a Concordia faculty-led tour during the month of May.

Concordia is part of the national Concordia University System, which is made up of ten colleges and universities affiliated with the Lutheran Church–Missouri Synod. Students may enroll for up to one year at any of these sister institutions.

Academic Facilities

Concordia's quintessential college campus is designed around the work of the College's first campus architect, Edward L. Tilton—an award-winning architect of Ellis Island. Inside these historical buildings, students have access to some of the finest technology and performing arts resources around. A perfect blend of old and new, Concordia's facilities reflect its history and its future. Students and faculty and staff members alike take pride in a safe, clean, and inviting campus. Simply put, Concordia College's facilities help nourish students' minds, bodies, and spirits.

The Donald A. Krenz Academic Center on the top floor of the library contains technology-enhanced classrooms, including the eighty-two-seat Pietruski Auditorium, a forty-eight-seat classroom overlooking the quad, a twenty-station computer teaching room, and the Darlene Hedin Krenz New Media Center designed for electronic and digital media instruction. Fully handicapped accessible, the center is also home to the OSilas Art Gallery, the Yeager Collection of original autographs of American financial leaders, a spacious student lounge, and the campus Information Technology Services department.

Sommer Center for Worship and the Performing Arts includes a recital/lecture hall with tiered seating for 315 and the College's Chapel. Private rehearsal rooms for individual and ensemble, vocal, instrumental, and organ practice adjoin the recital hall. The recital hall has hosted recording sessions for artists such as Itzhak Perlman, Yehudi Menuhin, and Harry Connick Jr., as well as the Concordia Choir.

Scheele Memorial Library offers support and assistance in the academic pursuits of the Concordia College community. The library provides an online catalog to search its own resources as well as those of forty-two other colleges. In addition, the library subscribes to over 20 databases, which are available for both on- and off-campus use. The library also houses the Curriculum Materials Center for education students; the Information Commons, complete with computer Internet access; a computerized writing center; and group study rooms.

Brunn-Maier Science Hall contains a full range of science laboratories and general classrooms.

Stein Hall houses individual practice studios and an electric piano laboratory. Stein Hall is home to the Concordia Conservatory—the College's music conservatory serving both students and the surrounding community.

Costs

Tuition and fees for the 2008–09 academic year are $22,930. Room and board charges are $8745. Costs are the same for in-state, out-of-state, and transfer students.

Financial Aid

Awards, merit scholarships, Lutheran grants and scholarships, need-based financial aid, and more make Concordia a valuable and affordable investment. Ninety-three percent of the students receive some form of financial aid, totaling over $8.25 million. To be considered, students must file the Free Application for Federal Student Aid (FAFSA). Concordia's FAFSA code is 002709.

Faculty

Concordia College's faculty members are dedicated and talented; over 75 percent hold the highest degrees in their respective fields of study. The 16:1 student-faculty ratio enables students and faculty members to interact on a very personal level. In classes and labs, students see professors up front, not teaching assistants.

Student Government

All full-time students are members of the Student Government Association (SGA) and elect its representatives each spring. The SGA organizes and supports a host of campus events and provides a voice for all student concerns.

Admission Requirements

Concordia College–New York is proud to be a member of the Common Application. Applications are evaluated using a holistic selection process. Admission to the College is based upon a wide range of criteria designed to identify a student body with integrity, high academic standards, and serious educational and personal goals. Applicants are considered on the basis of academic record, class rank, test scores, essay, and recommendations. In order to be considered for first-year admission, students should submit the $50 application fee ($100 for international students), application for admission (available at http://www.commonapp.org), official high school transcripts, SAT or ACT scores, school report form (part of the application), supplemental application (part of the application), a written personal statement, and an optional activity/volunteer resume. In addition, transfer students must submit official transcripts from all colleges and universities attended plus SAT or ACT scores (if they have earned fewer than 28 college credits).

Prospective students are encouraged to visit the campus and meet with a faculty member in their area of interest. Open house preview day events are regularly scheduled; Concordia is also happy to arrange individual visits. Campus visit scholarships of $500 are awarded upon enrollment after an official campus visit.

Application and Information

The application priority deadline is March 15, with a rolling/space-available policy thereafter. The transfer application deadline is July 15. Requests for information and applications should be addressed to:

Office of Admission
Concordia College
171 White Plains Road
Bronxville, New York 10708
Phone: 914-337-9300 Ext. 2155
800-YES-COLLEGE (937-2655; toll-free)
Fax: 914-395-4636
E-mail: admission@concordia-ny.edu
Web site: http://www.concordia-ny.edu

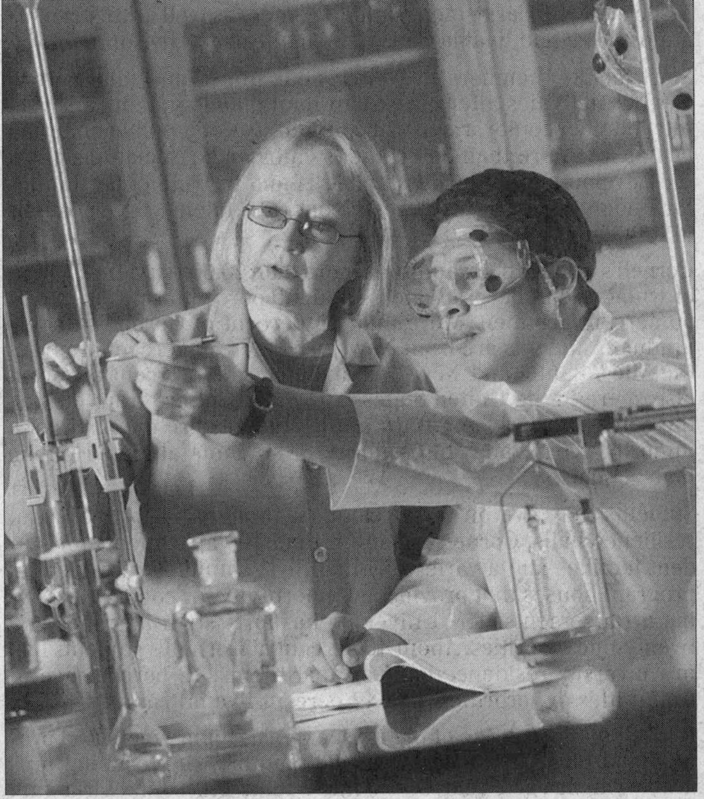

At Concordia College, students benefit from the 16:1 student-faculty ratio and the dedication of the faculty members.

CORNELL UNIVERSITY

ITHACA, NEW YORK

The University

Cornell University is unique in American higher education. At once the largest, most comprehensive school in the Ivy League and the public land-grant university for New York State, Cornell is distinct in its combination of privately funded and state-assisted colleges. As a result, Cornell students benefit from outstanding educational programs and are nurtured by the prestigious intellectual tradition of the Ivy League. At the same time, they tap into the democratic spirit and sense of public service that energize the nation's great public universities.

Cornell's seven undergraduate colleges and schools offer instruction in virtually every field, and the University's numerous interdisciplinary programs provide wide-ranging opportunities for study that cuts across traditional department boundaries. Students at Cornell arguably are exposed to the widest arrays of subjects and approaches to learning available anywhere. Moreover, they share the excitement of intellectual discovery with faculty members who are Nobel laureates, Pulitzer Prize winners, and researchers at the forefront of their fields—clear evidence of the University's commitment to undergraduate education. It is not uncommon to find prominent scholars teaching introductory classes and offering courses for general enrollment.

Cornell comprises people of all races, many nationalities, and every social and economic background, and the interplay of differences finds full expression throughout the University and in the surrounding Ithaca community. To put it simply, Cornell offers students the cultural diversity and intellectual vigor often associated with large metropolitan centers as well as the friendly atmosphere and livable pace of a smaller city environment.

Most faculty members live in or near Ithaca and take part in campus activities after classroom hours, and students and faculty members enjoy a sense of community not possible on urban campuses. More than 800 campus clubs and associations allow the development of leadership skills and provide opportunities for students who share interests, concerns, talents, or avocations to find each other.

Cornell's student body numbers more than 20,000 students, 13,500 of whom are undergraduates. About 50 percent are women and 50 percent are men. More than 35 percent of Cornell's undergraduate students are from New York State, 30 percent are from the Mid-Atlantic and New England states, 27 percent are from elsewhere in the United States, and 8 percent are from outside the country. Nearly one third of the students are members of a minority group, and the majority of students attended public high schools.

Students may live on or off campus. In addition to traditional residence halls, Cornell has more than 400 apartments for student families and a variety of small living units and residential program houses that provide an opportunity for cooperative living arrangements. The University has forty-six fraternities and twenty-one sororities. About 46 percent of Cornell's students live in University residence halls or apartments, 12 percent live in fraternities or sororities, and 42 percent live off campus.

Cornell maintains one of the most extensive and diversified programs of physical education in the country. The teaching program, which each year offers more than 150 courses ranging from ballroom dancing to rock climbing, emphasizes recreational activities that students can continue to enjoy after they leave the University. The intramural athletics program—the largest in the Ivy League—provides opportunities for members of the University community to compete in more than thirty sports. Cornell also supports eighteen varsity sports for men and eighteen varsity sports for women.

Location

Cornell is on a hillside at the southern tip of Cayuga Lake, in the Finger Lakes region of New York State. Within easy walking distance of the campus is the Cornell Plantations—a living laboratory of natural resources comprising 2,800 acres of woodlands, trails, streams, and gorges. Several ski areas, an extensive system of hiking trails, and three unusually scenic state parks with facilities for hiking, boating, swimming, and camping are a short drive away.

Majors and Degrees

Cornell University offers degrees at the baccalaureate level in seven undergraduate colleges (Agriculture and Life Sciences; Architecture, Art, and Planning; Arts and Sciences; Engineering; Hotel Administration; Human Ecology; and Industrial and Labor Relations). Undergraduates may choose from an impressive range of programs in fields such as agricultural sciences, animal science, architecture, art, behavioral sciences, biological sciences, business management, communications, design and environmental analysis, engineering, environmental studies, food science, government, history, hotel administration, human development, humanities, industrial and labor relations, languages and linguistics, mathematics and computer science, nutritional sciences, physical sciences, plant sciences, policy analysis and management, preprofessional studies, and social sciences.

Academic Programs

Although degree requirements vary among the undergraduate units, students are encouraged to take courses in other divisions. This interdisciplinary approach is exemplified by Cornell's nationally recognized ethnic studies programs: Africana studies, Asian studies, Asian American studies, Latino studies, Latin American studies, and Native American studies. In addition to offering courses, these programs promote multicultural understanding on campus by supporting lectures, conferences, seminars, exhibits, publications, and research projects. Honors programs, independent majors, double majors, and dual-degree programs are available in most areas of study. Entering freshmen may qualify for advanced placement or credit on the recommendation of the appropriate departments of instruction at Cornell.

The academic year is divided into two semesters, which run from late August to mid-December and from January to mid-May. There also are three consecutive summer sessions.

Off-Campus Programs

Students in many areas participate in fieldwork programs, internships, engineering cooperative programs, and research projects. They study in Albany; Washington, D.C.; New York City; and other places where they can best learn about the work of government, community organizations, businesses, and industry. Undergraduates participate in Cornell Abroad programs in many countries, including Australia, China, Denmark, Egypt, England, France, Germany, Greece, Indonesia, Israel, Italy, Japan, Kenya, Korea, Mexico, Nepal, Nigeria, Russia, Sweden, and Vietnam.

Academic Facilities

Cornell's library system is one of the ten largest academic research libraries in the United States. Two central libraries and an extensive system of libraries in the undergraduate colleges contain more than 7.1 million volumes, subscribe to 65,000 periodicals, and add about 130,000 volumes to their collections each year.

The University's computer resources are important to students in almost every area of study. Cornell Information Technologies operates public terminals and microcomputers, produces documentation, and offers a variety of user education programs. In addition, all of Cornell's undergraduate residence hall rooms have direct Internet connections, enabling residents to log on around the clock.

Costs

Tuition and fees for the 2007–08 academic year for students enrolled in Cornell's state-assisted units (Agriculture and Life Sciences, Human Ecology, and Industrial and Labor Relations) were $19,291 for New York residents and $33,681 for nonresidents. Tuition and fees for those in the University's privately funded units (Architecture, Art, and Planning; Arts and Sciences; Engineering; and Hotel Administration) were $34,781. Typical room and board costs amount to $11,190 per academic year, and personal expenses, including books, are about $2180.

Financial Aid

Admission decisions are not affected by a prospective student's need for financial assistance, and the University's comprehensive financial aid program offers a wide array of financial support options to students and their families. More than 65 percent of all Cornell undergraduates receive some form of financial aid from University, state, federal, or other sources, and about 50 percent receive Cornell-allocated scholarships, jobs, and/or loans. All financial assistance is awarded on the basis of need, according to the standards of the College Scholarship Service.

Of particular importance to prospective students is Cornell's nationally recognized program of financial assistance known as the Cornell Commitment, which consists of three programs: the Cornell Tradition, which rewards students who demonstrate a commitment to working and funding a portion of their own education; the Meinig Family National Scholars, which rewards outstanding leaders in high school; and the Presidential Research Scholars, which recognizes students who have a strong interest in research.

Faculty

The Cornell faculty, numbering more than 2,600 members worldwide, include many men and women who are recognized internationally as leaders in their fields. Among them are Nobel laureates, Pulitzer Prize winners, and scores of individuals who are members of the National Academy of Sciences, the National Academy of Engineering, or the National Academy of Education. Twenty-three members of the faculty have received Guggenheim Fellowships in recent years, and 3 members of the faculty have received MacArthur Foundation genius awards.

Nearly all teaching faculty members are involved in research, scholarship, or public service. Maintaining the quality of undergraduate programs is one of Cornell's highest priorities, and there is no distinction between the graduate and undergraduate faculty. Professors act as advisers and keep regular office hours to ensure their availability to students. The University community also enjoys a constant succession of visiting lecturers and professors from other institutions.

Student Government

Cornell students participate in governing the University through the Student Assembly, which has legislative authority over the policies of several campus life departments. Students may also be members of policymaking committees within each undergraduate college, and students sit as voting members on the University's Board of Trustees.

Admission Requirements

Cornell is among the most selective universities in the nation. There were more than 30,000 applications for the 2007–08 freshman class.

Each undergraduate unit has its own selection committee, and applicants compete only with other students seeking admission to the same division. Intellectual preparedness and evidence of the applicant's abilities in nonacademic areas are important considerations in admission decisions, as are work experience and other activities related to educational or professional objectives. The University seeks individuals with outstanding personal qualities, such as initiative and leadership. A few of Cornell's divisions also require or recommend interviews.

All seven undergraduate colleges offer an early decision plan to highly qualified high school seniors whose first preference is Cornell. A few students may be approved for early admission after only three years of secondary school.

Application and Information

For freshman admission, Cornell University uses the Common Application exclusively and requires a Cornell-specific supplement and a financial aid form for students applying for aid. The application deadline for early decision is November 1; the application deadline for regular decision is January 1. For transfer students, Cornell also uses the Common Application exclusively and requires a Cornell-specific transfer supplement that can be found online and in the Guide for Transfer Students. The application deadline for fall transfer admission is March 15; for spring transfer, the application deadline is November 1.

For additional information and application forms, students should contact:

Undergraduate Admissions Office
Cornell University
Ithaca, New York 14850-2488
Phone: 607-255-5241
E-mail: admissions@cornell.edu
Internet: http://admissions.cornell.edu

A student studies in one of the libraries.

THE CULINARY INSTITUTE OF AMERICA

HYDE PARK, NEW YORK

The Institute

The Culinary Institute of America (CIA) is a private, not-for-profit college dedicated to providing the world's best undergraduate education in culinary arts and baking and pastry arts. Guided by its core values of excellence, leadership, professionalism, ethics, and respect for diversity, the CIA strives to foster an atmosphere where students can develop both professionally and personally. At the CIA, aspiring culinarians gain the general knowledge and specific skills they need to grow into positions of leadership in the foodservice and hospitality industry, the largest private employer in the United States.

Founded in 1946, The Culinary Institute of America today enrolls more than 2,800 students from virtually every state and thirty countries around the world, all united by their shared passion for food. The CIA student body has an equal balance of recent high school graduates and adults returning to higher education.

As the world's premier culinary college, the CIA is renowned for its degree programs, extraordinary faculty, and outstanding educational facilities. All CIA degree programs emphasize professional, hands-on learning in the college's kitchens, bakeshops, and restaurants. CIA classes span the culinary globe, exploring great cultures, cooking techniques, and cuisines to prepare students for the diversity and creativity of the foodservice industry. Classes are taken in a progressive sequence optimized to build skills, food knowledge, and production experience. These studies culminate in operating courses that give students both kitchen and front-of-the-house experiences in the college's famous restaurants. Bachelor's degree students also focus on foodservice management development, with a broad range of business management and liberal arts courses.

CIA students enjoy an active campus life, with a variety of year-round fitness programs, intramural and club sports, student clubs, and extracurricular activities such as ski and camping trips, on-campus live entertainment events, presentations by leading chefs and industry executives, and cook-offs. The college's Student Recreation Center includes a six-lane pool, a gymnasium, racquetball courts, an aerobics studio, a fitness center and free-weight room, a game room, outdoor tennis courts, and the Courtside Café and Pub. Four coed residence halls and six Adirondack-style lodges house approximately 1,700 students on campus. The college's dining plan provides students with two meals per instructional day.

The Culinary Institute of America is accredited by the Middle States Commission on Higher Education, 3624 Market Street, Philadelphia, Pennsylvania 19104 (telephone: 215-662-5000). The Middle States Commission on Higher Education is an institutional accrediting agency recognized by the U.S. Secretary of Education and the Council for Higher Education Accreditation.

The CIA is also accredited by the Accrediting Commission of Career Schools and Colleges of Technology (ACCSCT). The certificate of accreditation is available for viewing on the wall of the President's Wing on the second floor of Roth Hall at the college's Hyde Park, New York, campus. Supporting documentation can be reviewed in the office of the Associate Vice President of Planning, Research, and Accreditation, located on the third floor of Roth Hall. Information related to tuition charges, fees, and length of comparable programs at other institutions may be obtained from the ACCSCT at 2101 Wilson Boulevard, Suite 302, Arlington, Virginia 22201 (telephone: 703-247-4212).

Location

The CIA's scenic 170-acre campus is set along the east bank of the Hudson River in Hyde Park, New York, conveniently located 1½–2 hours from New York City and Albany.

The Mid-Hudson region's attractions and recreational opportunities offer something for everyone in both rural and urban settings. There are a number of state parks and historic sites throughout the area. Students can taste wines at local vineyards, visit farmer's markets, and pick apples at nearby orchards. To the west lie the Catskill and Shawangunk Mountains, with many opportunities for hiking, skiing, rock climbing, mountain biking, and sightseeing. Concerts, plays, films, and other cultural and special events are offered regularly at the many colleges, theaters, and community facilities throughout the Hudson Valley and Catskill regions. In addition, students can take advantage of the campus's proximity to New York City to experience the culture, arts, and nightlife of this exciting city and food mecca.

Majors and Degrees

The Culinary Institute of America awards the degree of Bachelor of Professional Studies (B.P.S.) in baking and pastry arts management and in culinary arts management, as well as the degree of Associate in Occupational Studies (A.O.S.) in baking and pastry arts and in culinary arts.

Academic Programs

At the core of The Culinary Institute of America's curriculum lies more than 1,300 hours of hands-on instruction in its kitchens and bakeshops as well as classes developing the managerial skills and creative thinking that today's culinary professional requires. Students learn about foods, cooking and baking techniques, cuisines, and business fundamentals while advancing through skills and production kitchens. They also gain invaluable experience in a paid externship program and by cooking and serving in the college's bakery café or in some of the four fine-dining public restaurants on campus. Bachelor's degree students also take courses in marketing, communications, psychology, foreign languages and cultures, accounting and the use of computers in the food business, and financial and human resources management.

Students must earn 132 total credits in culinary arts management or in baking and pastry arts management to graduate with a bachelor's degree. Students must earn 69 total credits in culinary arts or in baking and pastry arts to graduate with an associate degree.

Off-Campus Programs

All students work in externships for a minimum of eighteen weeks (600 hours). These externships provide students with valuable on-the-job experience at one of more than 1,200 top foodservice and hospitality properties—such as hotels, restaurants, and resorts—around the world. B.P.S. students also travel to California for a wine and food seminar, where they can learn from local purveyors and visit area wineries and vineyards.

Academic Facilities

CIA students learn the fundamentals of the culinary and baking and pastry arts in the college's forty-one professionally equipped production kitchens and bakeshops and five student-staffed public restaurants on campus—the American Bounty Restaurant, Escoffier Restaurant, Ristorante Caterina de' Medici, St. Andrew's Café, and Apple Pie Bakery Café, sponsored by Rich Products Corporation. Classes are centered in the college's main building, Roth Hall, as well as in the Shunsuke Takaki School of Baking and Pastry, General Foods Nutrition Center, and Colavita Center for Italian Food and Wine. The Culinary regularly hosts world-renowned chefs for lectures, cooking demonstrations, and discussions with students in its Danny Kaye Theatre and Anheuser-Busch Theatre. Other valuable academic resources include the 76,000-volume Conrad N. Hilton Library, which contains the largest culinary collection of any culinary school; audiovisual programs to supplement course work; computer labs and workstations; and a wireless network that allows students to access online resources from almost anywhere on campus.

Costs

Freshman tuition for academic year 2007–08 is $21,280. Board is $1120 per semester, which includes two meals per instructional day. Housing costs range from $1190 to $3170 per semester, depending on the room to which the student is assigned.

Additional required fees for the freshman year include a confirmation fee of $100, equipment fees of $1180 for culinary supplies or $995 for baking and pastry supplies, and a general fee of $495 per semester, which includes student activity and exam fees, as well as secondary accident insurance. The CIA offers students a tuition installment plan. Details are available from the college's Bursar's Office.

Financial Aid

More than 90 percent of the CIA's students receive financial aid in the form of scholarships, grants, loans, and work-study. Federal programs offered at the college include the Federal Pell Grant, Federal Supplemental Educational Opportunity Grant (FSEOG), Federal Stafford Loan, Unsubsidized Federal Stafford Loan, Federal Perkins Loan, Federal Work-Study Program (which provides a variety of on-campus and community service jobs to eligible students), Federal PLUS Program, and Veterans Administration benefits. Students should also investigate their own state's programs and apply if those grants or scholarships can be used in New York State.

Students who have applied for admission or who are currently enrolled at the CIA may apply for scholarships offered by various organizations in the foodservice industry. A list of these scholarships, which are administered by the college, is available from the Financial Aid Office.

Faculty

The college's faculty is composed of more than 130 chefs and instructors from sixteen countries whose credentials and industry experience are unmatched in culinary education. The faculty also includes the largest concentration of American Culinary Federation–Certified Master Chefs anywhere. The 18:1 student-faculty ratio in hands-on classes provides student support and mentoring, while giving students the opportunity to work in an environment closely representative of the foodservice industry.

Student Government

All students in good standing are members of the Student Government Association (SGA). The association's Executive Board acts as a liaison between students and the administration. The SGA helps support student activities and funds all student clubs and committees.

Admission Requirements

The Admissions Committee seeks candidates who have demonstrated a commitment to a culinary career and who have the personal initiative, confidence, and motivation to succeed. The basic requirements are successful completion of a secondary school education or its equivalent and some experience in the foodservice and hospitality industry. The applicant's educational record is evaluated on the basis of overall performance and the type of program taken. Academics and leadership ability are key requirements for the B.P.S. programs. SATs or ACTs are strongly recommended but not required.

Preference is given to candidates who have worked in foodservice, particularly in a kitchen that offers a varied menu. Before entering the program, students should have had about six months of hands-on food preparation in a non-fast-food environment.

Applicants must submit a formal application for admission, a nonrefundable $50 application fee, an official secondary school transcript (not a student copy), an essay of between 400 and 500 words, and an official college transcript, if applicable. Students applying directly from high school may include an optional secondary school report. In addition, A.O.S. candidates must provide one recommendation, and B.P.S. applicants must provide two. Bachelor's degree candidates must also participate in an on-campus or telephone interview.

Application and Information

Students may apply for admission to the CIA year-round, as the college offers multiple enrollment seasons from which to choose. Applicants should submit their materials according to the enrollment schedule (available at the Web site listed below) that corresponds to the season they are interested in beginning the degree program. Students are notified of an admission decision according to that schedule. For information, to schedule a tour, or to participate in an Open House program, students should contact:

Admissions Office
The Culinary Institute of America
1946 Campus Drive
Hyde Park, New York 12538-1499
Phone: 800-CULINARY (toll-free)
E-mail: admissions@culinary.edu
Web site: http://www.ciachef.edu

Set along the banks of the Hudson River, the Culinary Institute of America's campus lies on 170 scenic acres in historic Hyde Park, New York.

DAEMEN COLLEGE

AMHERST, NEW YORK

The College

Daemen College is a private, career-oriented liberal arts college serving approximately 2,500 students in Amherst, New York.

The mission of Daemen College is to prepare students for life and leadership in an increasingly complex world. Founded on the principle that education should elevate human dignity and foster civic responsibility and compassion, the College seeks to integrate the intellectual qualities acquired through study of the liberal arts with the education necessary for professional accomplishment. This integration, which recognizes equal value in liberal studies and professional programs, aims at preparing graduates who are dedicated to the health and well-being of both their local and global communities.

With a Daemen education, students acquire the skills to solve problems creatively and think critically. They are comfortable with diversity and recognize the importance of a global perspective. They are able to work with others and be invigorated by environments that present challenges and demand innovation. Daemen students are expected to be active participants in their own education and informed citizens who understand that learning is a lifelong journey.

At the heart of Daemen's integrated learning experience is the relationship that can develop between the College's faculty members and its students. Daemen prides itself on maintaining a student-centered atmosphere and a close professional and collaborative association among all members of the College community. Assisted by a supportive faculty, Daemen students are encouraged to pursue goals beyond their initial expectations, to respond to academic challenges, and to develop habits of mind that enrich their lives and their community.

Freshmen spend a year at Canavan Hall, to make friends and learn about life. By sophomore year, students move to Daemen's garden-style apartments, featuring private bedrooms with free Internet access and phone lines. These 4-person suites include eat-in kitchens and living rooms. With over fifty student organizations, themed dinners, movie nights, and other activities available, students can find many choices on campus.

Location

Daemen is located on a 39-acre campus in Amherst, New York. The campus is easily accessible by the major rail, plane, and motor routes that serve the city of Buffalo, just minutes away. Buffalo has theater, music, art, restaurants, major league sports, and a first-rate zoo. Scenic Niagara Falls is nearby.

Majors and Degrees

Daemen's Division of Arts and Sciences is designed to provide broad exposure to multiple disciplines that aid students in developing the intellectual and civic competencies that prepare them for life in an increasingly complex society. The career possibilities are nearly endless, as many graduates have gone on to successful leadership in corporations, human service agencies, government, the arts, educational organizations, religious institutions, environmental organizations, medicine, law, veterinary medicine, and research-related fields. Preparation for advanced health-related careers is a strength of the natural science department at Daemen College. The faculty is committed to each student's success, and the College has considerable expertise in teaching the basic sciences that are prerequisites for medical studies.

Daemen's Division of Health and Human Services is designed to provide students with the unique opportunity to work with and learn from both scholars and practitioners—an experience that is critical to understanding the relationship between academic course work and practical application. Experienced and dedicated faculty members provide students with a balanced education through innovative and contemporary courses, exceptional professional internships, field placements, clinical experiences, and pioneering research opportunities. Daemen is dedicated to providing a broad-based education to prepare individuals for the demands of professional and scholarly roles in the health and human services fields. Daemen's liberal arts core and professional curricula ensure that its students integrate liberal studies with their professional education to prepare them for life and leadership.

Academic Programs

Daemen's competency-based core curriculum (sometimes referred to as general education requirements) places the College among the national leaders in innovation and creativity. The core is composed of 45 hours or fifteen courses that help students master the seven core competencies. The core relies on several innovative features, including linked course work taught within the framework of learning communities, a progressive composition program, interdisciplinary courses that break down barriers among majors, and opportunities for extended research and public presentation.

The Honors Program provides an enriched curriculum for students that examines complex issues from multiple perspectives, uses primary sources rather than textbooks, and presents special opportunities for research. Honors Program students enjoy special residential accommodations and opportunities for domestic and international travel, as well as unique offerings such as field trips and access to campus speakers and presenters. Students also have a chance to publish their works.

Off-Campus Programs

Alongside the outstanding and innovative courses that provide the academic foundation at Daemen, there are many other opportunities to enhance a student's education.

Cross-registration arrangements with other colleges and universities enable students to take courses for credit at twenty nearby colleges.

Daemen offers opportunities for students of every major to study abroad after completing their first year of college. The Center for Cross-Cultural Studies in Seville, Spain, and Havana, Cuba, provide a full range of opportunities to study language, art, history, political science, business, and literature in these culturally rich areas of the world. Daemen students from all departments are eligible to travel with the Students Without Borders program to work alongside physician assistant majors who offer their services in a health clinic in the Dominican Republic.

In the Consortium for North American Sustainability (CNAS), students spend one or two semesters earning college credits at one of Daemen's partner institutions. They develop a broad understanding of what civic society and sustainable communities mean to people throughout North America. The program emphasizes special research opportunities for both students and faculty members. Partner institutions include the University of Northern British Columbia; St. Francis Xavier University, Nova Scotia; Universidad LaSalle, Mexico; and Universidad de Guanajuato, Mexico.

Service learning is part of Daemen's core curriculum. In order to graduate, all students are required to take part in course work that links learning to service, with hundreds of organizations, agencies, and groups to choose from. Students are assigned the task of working in a wide variety of locales including hospitals; urban public schools; nursing homes; underprivileged community centers/churches; homeless shelters; agencies for the physically, mentally, and emotionally challenged; and environmental organizations.

Academic Facilities

The College's modern library has more than 139,000 volumes, more than 950 periodical subscriptions, a wide selection of musical scores and records, and a complete collection of American Enterprise Institute monographs. A learning resources center augments the library. Art department facilities include ten large studios and one of the largest bronze-casting foundries of any college in the country. Students of French and Spanish find a well-equipped language laboratory in the main classroom building. The beautiful and modern Business Building houses all of the business classrooms, including breakout rooms, which are used for smaller discussion groups. There is also a computer lab, which has fifty Pentium (IBM compatible) computers.

Costs

For the 2007–08 academic year, tuition and fees were $18,750, and room and board were $8610.

Financial Aid

Daemen makes a conscious effort to award financial assistance based upon academic achievement and financial need. In the 2006–07 academic year, 85 percent of full-time Daemen undergraduates received some kind of financial aid. Seventy-eight percent of full-time Daemen undergraduates received need-based (TAP, PELL, Federal Work-Study, etc.) financial aid. The average award made to full-time undergraduates was approximately $13,000. The average need-based award made to full-time undergraduates was approximately $6000. Daemen College participates in all federal and state financial aid programs and has private sources of scholarship monies to award to eligible students.

Faculty

Class size ranges from about 15 to 25 students, enabling faculty members to get to know the interests and goals of each student. There are 151 full- and part-time faculty members, 98 percent of whom hold terminal degrees.

Student Government

Through the elected Student Governing Board, students are responsible for all nonacademic matters that affect their life at the College. Students serve on advisory committees to the president, the academic dean, and others within the College community.

Admission Requirements

The Admissions Committee places particular emphasis on a student's overall academic achievement. The committee evaluates the high school grade point average and standardized test scores (SAT or ACT). Students admitted last year had an average GPA of 90 percent. Daemen College considers this as the single best predictor of academic success. The College also considers a student's SAT or ACT test scores—the average scores for Daemen freshmen were 1050 SAT (composite math and verbal scores) and 22 ACT. Students interested in attending Daemen College should contact the Office of Admissions to arrange an appointment for an interview and campus tour.

Application and Information

For application forms, a catalog, or further information, students should contact:

Daemen College
4380 Main Street
Amherst, New York 14226
Phone: 716-839-8225
800-462-7652 (toll-free)
E-mail: admissions@daemen.edu
Web site: http://www.daemen.edu/admissions

While Daemen College is small enough so that all students receive individual attention, it still offers a broad range of programs and facilities.

No person shall, on the basis of sex, race, color, ethnic and national origin, handicap, religion, or age, be denied admission or be subjected to discrimination in admission to Daemen College.

DOMINICAN COLLEGE

ORANGEBURG, NEW YORK

The College

Dominican College reflects the traditions of its founding Dominican order in its emphasis on a value-centered, liberal arts–based education. Dominican College celebrated its fiftieth anniversary in 2002–03. Its 1,800 students represent a diverse ethnic population and include both campus residents and commuters. The College offers undergraduate and graduate programs. Graduate programs include a five-year Bachelor of Science/Master of Science degree in occupational therapy; a Family Nurse Practitioner Program leading to a Master of Science (M.S.) degree; a Master of Science in Education (M.S.Ed.) degree leading to certification as teachers of students with disabilities, including those with multiple and severe disabilities; a Master of Science in Education (M.S.Ed.) degree for teachers of the blind and visually impaired; and a new Doctor of Physical Therapy (D.P.T.).

Dominican's campus is growing. The Hennessy Student Center contains a 1,000-seat gymnasium, a physical fitness room, a suspended running track, athletic training facilities, athletic offices, and all-purpose meeting rooms. Hertel Hall and Rosary Hall, the residence centers, contain social areas, computer-equipped study lounges, student meeting rooms, and computer- and cable-equipped dorm rooms. The residence halls have round-the-clock security. The Granito Center houses the main dining hall, health center, bookstore, and Global Communications Center. Eight other buildings make up the campus: Cooke Hall houses administration offices; the Admissions Office is in De Porres Hall; the library is located in Pius X Hall; and Casey, Forke, Jarius, and Rosary Halls contain classrooms and offices. Casey Hall also houses the deans' offices and the offices of the arts and sciences, business administration, social sciences, and allied health faculties. The brand-new Pruzmack Center for Health and Science Education provides state-of-the-art labs and communication centers for all students.

The College offers a variety of activities for students. They include clubs, community service, internships, honor societies, student government, a choral group, and intramural sports. Activities are organized to take advantage of the opportunities offered by Rockland County, the mid–Hudson Valley region, and New York City.

Dominican College has a strong and successful athletic program. Varsity sports include men's baseball, basketball, cross-country, golf, lacrosse, and soccer and women's basketball, cross-country, lacrosse, soccer, softball, and volleyball. Dominican College is a member of the National Collegiate Athletic Association (NCAA) Division II and the Central Atlantic Collegiate Conference (CACC).

In order to serve adult and nontraditional students, the College offers an Accelerated Evening Program (eight-week terms), a Weekend College, and evening courses. Students who are enrolled in these programs may pursue full-time study while maintaining full-time employment. Academic support services, career counseling, internships, and placement opportunities are provided for all students.

Location

Dominican College is located in Rockland County, New York, 17 miles north of New York City and approximately 3 miles north of Bergen County, New Jersey. This convenient suburban location offers easy access to the outstanding cultural and educational resources of New York City.

Majors and Degrees

Dominican College undergraduate programs award B.A., B.S., B.S.Ed., B.S./M.S., B.S.N., and B.S.W. degrees. The College offers programs in athletic training, biology (which includes a premedicine track and pre–physical therapy studies), business administration (areas of concentration include accounting, computer information systems, economics, health service administration, and management), English, history, humanities, mathematics, natural sciences, nursing, occupational therapy (B.S./M.S.), psychology, social sciences, social work, and teacher education (areas of concentration are adolescence education, childhood education, special education/adolescence education, and special education/childhood education). A five-year integrated program in engineering offers a Bachelor of Arts degree in mathematics from Dominican and a Bachelor of Engineering degree from Manhattan College.

Academic Programs

The degree programs at Dominican College have been designed to give students the benefit of study in the liberal arts disciplines and in professional preparation. The baccalaureate degree accommodates varied learning styles, previous academic backgrounds, divergent learning and career goals, and prior experience.

To receive a degree, students must complete a minimum of 120 semester hours, at least 30 of which must be earned at Dominican College. The College grants up to 60 hours for achievement on proficiency examinations administered by American College Testing, Inc.; the New York State Regents' External Degree Program; and the College-Level Examination Program (CLEP). Learning acquired through experience may also be validated by the submission of a portfolio demonstrating that the student has acquired knowledge that corresponds to courses required at Dominican College.

Placement testing and a coordinated advisement process provide students with information and guidance for the selection of courses that best suit their individual needs and program. Support for the ongoing development of academic skills is provided through the Learning Resources and Writing Center, which offers tutoring in basic mathematics, writing, and other subjects. Opportunities for elective internships enable students to pursue a wide range of career and academic interests. An Honors Program provides innovative learning opportunities for students with superior academic preparation.

Academic Facilities

The College library provides more than 104,000 volumes and approximately 490 periodical titles, with more than 17,000 volumes of additional back files on microfilm and 10,377 full-text journals online. The Pruzmack Center contains science laboratories and a nursing practicum lab. Casey Hall houses the Learning Resources and Writing Center. Students may use computer labs in Casey and Rosary Halls; the residence centers are also equipped with computers.

Costs

The tuition for 2006–07 was $8965 per semester. Room and board costs were $4490 per semester. For part-time and weekend students, the undergraduate tuition was $515 per semester hour.

Financial Aid

Dominican College offers extensive academic and athletic scholarships and need-based aid programs. In addition, the College participates in federal and state grants, loans, and work-study programs. Students applying for aid should file the Free Application for Federal Student Aid (FAFSA) by February 15. Supplementary aid opportunities are available through the New York State Tuition Assistance Program (TAP), the Federal Pell Grant Program, the Federal Family Education Loan Program, the Federal Supplemental Educational Opportunity Grant (FSEOG) Program, Nursing Student Loans, Nursing Scholarships, the Federal Perkins Loan Program, the Federal Work-Study Program, and veterans' benefits.

Faculty

The Dominican faculty has approximately 170 members, and the present student-faculty ratio is 14:1. Faculty members hold degrees from thirty different universities and colleges located in fourteen states and three other countries. Many have had varied experiences prior to teaching at the college level. Faculty members work with students as academic advisers and as advisers for nonacademic activities.

Student Government

The Dominican College Student Government Association is the official representative of the students. It approves charters for clubs and organizations, helps to plan the cultural and social calendar, aids in directing and coordinating social activities, and manages the student activity budget.

Admission Requirements

Entering freshmen are expected to have completed a secondary school program or its equivalent. The recommended preparation includes 16 academic units distributed among English, mathematics, natural sciences, social sciences, and foreign languages. All applicants for admission as freshmen should submit scores from the SAT or the ACT. TOEFL scores are required for international applicants. A cumulative GPA of at least 2.0 is required for transfer students, with a maximum of 70 credits accepted from accredited two-year colleges and 90 credits from four-year colleges.

A personal interview is recommended in order to allow the applicant to become better acquainted with the College and to exchange information with an admissions counselor. Dominican College does not discriminate on the basis of sex, race, color, age, national origin, religious affiliation, or physical limitation and is an Equal Opportunity/Affirmative Action employer.

Application and Information

Applicants should submit the completed Dominican College application form to the Office of Admissions.

For more information and application forms, students may contact:

Joyce Elbe
Director of Admissions
Dominican College
470 Western Highway
Orangeburg, New York 10962
Phone: 866-4DC-INFO (toll-free)
E-mail: admissions@dc.edu
Web site: http://www.dc.edu

Dominican College fosters relationships between students and faculty members through small, personal classes.

D'YOUVILLE COLLEGE

BUFFALO, NEW YORK

The College

D'Youville College is a private, coeducational, liberal arts and professional college that has offered students an education of high quality since 1908. The College was the first in western New York to offer baccalaureate degrees to women. Its current enrollment is 3,000 men and women. Students may choose from thirty undergraduate and graduate degree programs that are enhanced by a 14:1 student-faculty ratio. The College is committed to helping its students to grow not only in academics but in the social and personal areas of their college experience as well.

The multiple-option Nursing Degree Program is one of the largest four-year private-college nursing programs in the country. Available nursing programs include B.S.N., B.S.N./M.S. (five years), and RN to B.S.N. Of D'Youville's 2005 graduates, 94 percent are employed in their field or are in graduate school.

Students residing in Marguerite Hall have a scenic view of the Niagara River and Lake Erie, which separate the U.S. and Canadian shorelines. The Koessler Administration Building contains the Offices of Admissions, Financial Aid, the President, Student Accounts, and the Registrar; the Learning Center; and the Kavinoky Theatre. The Student Center, the focal point of leisure and extracurricular activities, has a new gymnasium, a swimming pool, a weight-training room, a dance studio, a general recreation center, a pub, and dining facilities. Student organizations and regularly scheduled activities, including intramural sports, NCAA Division III intercollegiate sports (baseball, basketball, crew, volleyball, golf, cross-country, soccer, and softball), a ski club, the College newspaper, the yearbook, and social organizations, as well as academic programs, all help to make up an active campus life.

Location

D'Youville is situated on Buffalo's residential west side. The College is within minutes of many local attractions, including the downtown shopping center, the Kleinhans Music Hall, the Albright-Knox Art Gallery, two museums, and several theaters that offer stage productions. Seasonal changes in the area offer a variety of recreational opportunities. Buffalo is only 90 miles from Toronto and 25 minutes from Niagara Falls, making it a gateway to recreation areas in western New York and Ontario. Holiday Valley, a skier's paradise, is an hour's drive away. The city is served by the New York State Thruway, Amtrak, Greyhound and Trailways bus lines, and most major airlines.

D'Youville enjoys a diversified interchange with the community due to its affiliations with schools, hospitals, and social agencies in the area. College students in the Buffalo area number more than 60,000.

Majors and Degrees

D'Youville offers the degrees of Bachelor of Arts (B.A.), Bachelor of Science (B.S.), and Bachelor of Science in Nursing (B.S.N.). Majors include accounting, biology, business management, chemistry, chiropractic, dietetics, education (elementary, secondary, and special), English, exercise and sports studies, global studies, health services, history, information technology, international business, mathematics, nursing, occupational therapy, philosophy, physical therapy, physician assistant studies, preprofessional studies (dental, law, medicine, pharmacy, and veterinary studies), psychology, and sociology. Five-year combined bachelor's/master's (B.S./M.S.) programs are offered in accounting, dietetics, education, information technology (B.S.)/international business (M.S.), international business, nursing, occupational therapy, and physician assistant studies. A six-year B.S./D.P.T. program is offered in physical therapy. A seven-year B.S./D.C. program is offered in chiropractic.

Academic Programs

The area of concentration recognizes individual differences and varying interests but still provides sufficient specialization in one discipline to form a foundation for graduate studies and professional careers. Students attending D'Youville are expected to complete the requirements of their chosen concentration while earning a minimum of 120 credit hours. Core requirements include humanities, 24 hours; social science, 12 hours; science, 7 hours; mathematics/computer science, 6 hours; and electives, 9 hours. A cumulative average of at least 2.0 must be maintained to meet graduation requirements. Sixteen credit hours, or five or six courses per semester, are considered a normal workload. Internships to meet specific career goals may be arranged in any major.

The College offers a Career Discovery Program that was purposely designed for the undecided student. This program, which can last for two years, offers credit courses and internships meeting two years of study in any major.

The academic year is composed of two semesters, each lasting approximately fifteen weeks. The first semester, including final examinations, ends before the Christmas holidays. During the eight-week summer sessions, programs of selected courses are given at all levels on a daily basis.

Off-Campus Programs

The baccalaureate program in nursing is affiliated with thirteen area hospitals and public health agencies. The education program is affiliated with local elementary, junior high, and secondary schools and with special education centers in the area for purposes of student teaching. The occupational therapy, physical therapy, and physician assistant programs are affiliated with appropriate clinical settings throughout the United States.

Academic Facilities

D'Youville's modern Library Resources Center, which was completed in fall 1999, contains 154,000 volumes, including microtext and software, and subscriptions to 870 periodicals and newspapers. The multimillion-dollar Health Science Building houses laboratories, including those for anatomy, organic chemistry, and gross anatomy; activity and daily living labs for the health professions; and additional laboratories for physics, chemistry, quantitative analysis, and computer science. It also houses classrooms, faculty member offices, and development centers, including one for career development. This is augmented by a modern academic center, which opened in 2001.

Costs

For 2007–08, tuition was $8800 per semester, and room and board cost $4375 per semester. A general College fee is required and is based on credit hours taken; a Student Association fee of $40 per semester is applied toward concerts, yearbooks, activities, and guest lectures. A $100 deposit ($150 for dietetics, physician assistant studies, occupational therapy, and physical therapy programs), credited toward tuition, must be submitted by all candidates who accept an offer of admission.

Financial Aid

D'Youville attempts to provide financial aid for students who would not otherwise be able to attend. Determination of aid is based on the Free Application for Federal Student Aid. Aid is available in the form of grants, loans, and employment on campus. In addition, D'Youville offers scholarships for academic achievement to incoming students.

All students may qualify for D'Youville's Instant Scholarship Program, which offers scholarships with total values up to $55,000. Students who apply, are accepted, and meet the criteria instantly qualify for one of these scholarships, all of which are renewable annually. These scholarships are not based on need. The three scholarship programs are the Honors Scholarship, the Academic Initiative Scholarship, and the Achievement Scholarship. The Honors Scholarship requires a minimum SAT score of 1100 (math and verbal) or an ACT score of at least 24 and awards 50 percent of tuition and 25 percent of room and board costs. The Academic Initiative Scholarship requires SAT scores of at least 1000 (math and verbal) or ACT scores of 21 to 23 and an academic average of at least 85. It awards 25 percent of tuition and 50 percent of room and board costs. The Achievement Scholarship criteria include SAT scores of 900 to 1090 (math and verbal) or ACT scores of 19 to 23 and an academic average of 80 to 84. This scholarship awards $1000–$5000. The Transfer Scholarship is based on a starting GPA of 2.75. This scholarship's award ranges from $1000 to $5000.

Faculty

The ratio of faculty members to students is 1:14. All members of the full-time instructional staff hold a doctorate or another advanced degree. Faculty members act as advisers and are available for consultation with students.

Student Government

The Student Association (SA), a representative form of student self-government, seeks to inspire in its members dedication to the intellectual, social, and moral ideals of the College and works closely with the administration and faculty. All students of D'Youville are considered members of the SA and may be elected to the executive council and the student senate. There are seventeen academic and social clubs affiliated with the SA.

Admission Requirements

An applicant must be a high school graduate or have a high school equivalency diploma before matriculating. The applicant should have a college-preparatory background, including required English and history courses and a sequence in either mathematics or science. Scores on the SAT or the ACT are also required for admission. High school advanced placement credit is acceptable and transferable. The admission decision is based on high school grade point average, rank in class, and scores on the SAT or ACT. Students who have difficulty meeting normal admission standards may be admitted with a reduced academic load.

The College Learning Center offers academic assistance to students whose education has been interrupted or has not prepared them adequately for college courses. The Tutor Bank, a system of peer tutoring, offers the assistance of qualified students to those who need help in specific academic disciplines.

Application and Information

D'Youville admits students on a rolling admission basis; therefore, applications are reviewed as they are received by the admissions office. Transfer students who have a quality point average of at least 2.0 are encouraged to apply by December 1 for the spring semester and by July 1 for the fall semester. A brochure listing course offerings and giving details about costs and room and board is available upon request.

R. H. Dannecker
Director of Admissions
D'Youville College
One D'Youville Square
320 Porter Avenue
Buffalo, New York 14201-1084
Phone: 716-829-7600
800-777-3921 (toll-free)
Fax: 716-829-7900
E-mail: admissions@dyc.edu
Web site: http://www.dyc.edu

ELMIRA COLLEGE

ELMIRA, NEW YORK

The College

Elmira College is a small, private, coeducational college that is recognized for its emphasis on education of high quality in the liberal arts and preprofessional programs. One of the oldest colleges in the United States, Elmira was founded in 1855. The College has always produced graduates interested in both community service and successful careers. Friendliness, personal attention, strong college spirit, and support for learning beyond the classroom help to make Elmira a special place. Elmira College is one of only 270 colleges in the nation to be granted a chapter of the prestigious Phi Beta Kappa honor society.

The full-time undergraduate enrollment is about 1,200 men and women. The students at Elmira represent more than thirty-five states, primarily those in the Northeast, with the highest representation coming from New York, New Jersey, Massachusetts, Connecticut, Maine, and Pennsylvania. International students from more than thirty countries were enrolled in 2007. Ninety percent of the full-time undergraduates live in College residence halls, and dormitory rooms are equipped to provide direct access to the Internet. Wireless access is also available in the Library and Campus Center.

The intercollegiate sports program includes men's and women's basketball, golf, ice hockey, lacrosse, soccer, and tennis and women's cheerleading, field hockey, softball, and volleyball. An intramural program is also available. Emerson Hall houses the student fitness center, a pool, and a gym capable of seating 1,000, as well as the Gibson Theatre, which has a state-of-the-art sound and lighting system. Professional societies; clubs; music, dance, and drama groups; a student-operated FM radio station; and the student newspaper, yearbook, and literary magazine also provide numerous opportunities for extracurricular activity.

Location

Elmira College is located in the city of Elmira, which has a population of 35,000, in the Finger Lakes region of New York. The campus is a 10-minute walk from downtown Elmira. The relationship between the College and the local community is excellent, and numerous community activities and facilities are open to students, including the Elmira Symphony and Choral Society, the Elmira Little Theatre, clubs and civic groups, museums, movies, and a performing arts center. Excellent recreational areas are available in upstate New York and nearby Pennsylvania.

Majors and Degrees

Elmira College offers programs leading to the bachelor's degree in more than thirty-five majors, including accounting, American studies, art, art education, biology, biology-chemistry, business administration, chemistry, classical studies, criminal justice, economics, elementary education, English literature, environmental studies, French, history, human services, individualized studies, international business, international studies, mathematics, medical technology, music, nursing, philosophy and religion, political science, psychology, public affairs, secondary education, social studies, sociology and anthropology, Spanish, speech and hearing, and theater. Secondary teaching certification is offered in several areas. A 3-2 program in chemical engineering with Clarkson University is available, and 4-1 M.B.A. programs are available at Alfred University, Clarkson University, and Union College. Army and Air Force ROTC are available through respective units at Cornell University.

Preprofessional preparation is offered in education, medical technology, nursing, and speech pathology and audiology. Faculty advisers assist those who seek preparation for graduate study in dentistry, law, or medicine in choosing appropriate course work. Nearly 50 percent of Elmira graduates pursue graduate study.

Academic Programs

The College's calendar is composed of two 12-week terms followed by a six-week spring term. Students enroll for four subjects during the twelve-week terms, completing the first term by mid-December and the second during the first week of April. The six-week term, from mid-April through May, may be devoted to a particular project involving travel, internship, research, or independent study. Students are required to participate in internships in order to gain practical and meaningful experience related to their program of study. Credit is awarded for these projects. Forty percent of Elmira College students study abroad at some point during their four years of study.

Special opportunities for outstanding students include participation in thirteen national honorary societies on campus and a chance to assist faculty members in teaching and research. The College also offers an accelerated three-year graduation option for outstanding students, and an Advanced Placement Program is available.

Army ROTC and Air Force ROTC are available.

Off-Campus Programs

Through the study-abroad programs, students may study in the United Kingdom, France, Spain, and Japan, as well as in other countries throughout Europe and Asia. Elmira students may study at the Washington Center for Learning Alternatives. Students from Elmira may spend the third term studying marine biology or doing sociological research on the island of San Salvador in the Bahamas. The six-week Term III permits students in any major to study abroad, and students are able to participate in this program starting in their freshman year.

Academic Facilities

The Elmira campus offers exceptional academic facilities in a beautiful setting. The modern Gannett-Tripp Library houses more than 391,000 volumes, receives 2,500 periodicals, and includes a special Mark Twain collection room and photography and audiovisual facilities.

The College Computer Center offers PC and Apple Macintosh microcomputers for student use.

A Center for Mark Twain Studies has been established at Quarry Farm, the author's summer home, which is located a few miles from campus. The College also operates a Speech and Hearing Clinic on campus, which serves the public and provides valuable internship experience for students. Excellent facilities for drama and music are available.

Costs

Tuition for 2007–08 was $30,500, room is $5500, board is $4000, and fees are $1200.

Financial Aid

Financial aid is available for both freshmen and transfer students. Awards are based upon the Free Application for Federal Student Aid (FAFSA) as well as the student's past academic performance. Types of aid include grants, scholarships, loans, and work opportunities. Sources of aid include college, federal, state, and private dollars. In addition, superior students may qualify for non-need Elmira College Honors Scholarships, which are available to both freshmen and transfer students and range from $4000 to full tuition per year. For 2006–07, the average freshman aid package (including all types of aid) amounted to more than $23,500. About 76 percent of the full-time undergraduates receive need-based financial aid. Twenty-one percent of students receive non-need merit aid.

Faculty

Members of the faculty are chosen for their ability in and dedication to teaching. All full-time faculty members serve as advisers. Currently, the full-time faculty consists of 10 full professors, 28 associate professors, 30 assistant professors, and 12 instructors. Ninety-eight percent of the faculty hold the Ph.D. or highest degree necessary to teach undergraduate students in their field.

Student Government

Student government, an important part of the educational system at Elmira College, prepares students for active and responsible citizenship in society. Student government organizations include the Student Senate, the Judicial Board, and the Student Activities Board.

Admission Requirements

The Office of Admissions at Elmira College uses a rolling admission system. Each applicant is evaluated individually on the basis of his or her total application, including academic record, rank in class, SAT or ACT scores, essay, activities, references, and goals. The College strongly advises a personal interview. The recommendations of teachers and guidance counselors are also important. Special consideration is given to applicants from distant states and other countries, applicants with special skills, and applicants who are prepared to become actively involved in designing their own programs.

Elmira has early decision and early admission programs.

Application and Information

For further information, applicants should contact:

Dean of Admissions
Elmira College
Elmira, New York 14901
Phone: 800-935-6472 (toll-free)
E-mail: admissions@elmira.edu
Web site: http://www.elmira.edu

The Mark Twain Study is one of the most famous literary landmarks in America.

COLLEGE DATA CENTER • NEW YORK

EUGENE LANG COLLEGE THE NEW SCHOOL FOR LIBERAL ARTS

THE NEW SCHOOL
A UNIVERSITY

NEW YORK, NEW YORK

The College

Eugene Lang College is the distinctive liberal arts division of The New School, a leading urban university with a tradition of innovative learning. Eugene Lang College offers all the benefits of a small and supportive college as well as the full range of opportunities found in a university setting. At Lang, rigorous academic programs are closely connected with all that New York City has to offer: its wealth of music, theater, and arts; its vibrant international community; its history; and its energy.

Eugene Lang students are encouraged to participate in the creation and direction of their education. The desire to explore and the freedom to imagine shared by students and faculty members contribute to a distinctive academic community.

Eugene Lang College students currently come from forty-five states and thirteen countries. The ratio of men to women is approximately 2:3. About 45 percent of the College's 985 students come from outside the New York metropolitan area; 4 percent hold foreign citizenship and 23 percent are members of minority groups. The student body is composed of both residential and day students. The university operates residence halls within walking distance of classes; incoming freshmen and transfer students are given housing priority within these facilities, and housing is guaranteed for the first year for new students. Great diversity in interests and aspirations is found among the students. Through the Office of Student Services, students produce a student newspaper and an award-winning literary magazine. They organize and participate in dramatic, musical, and artistic events through the "Lang in the City Program," as well as numerous political, social, and cultural organizations at the university and throughout New York City.

The New School was founded in 1919 by such notable scholars and intellectuals as John Dewey, Alvin Johnson, and Thorstein Veblen. It has long been a home for leading artists, educators, and public figures. For example, the university was the first institution of higher learning to offer college-level courses in such "new" fields as black culture and race, taught by W. E. B. DuBois, and psychoanalysis, taught by Freud's disciple Sandor Ferenczi. Among the world-famous artists and performers who have taught at The New School are Martha Graham, Aaron Copland, and Thomas Hart Benton. Today, such noted scholars as Robert Heilbroner, Eric Hobsbawm, Jerome Bruner, and Rayna Rapp are among the hundreds of university faculty members accessible to Eugene Lang College students.

The other divisions of the university are The New School for General Studies, which offers nearly 1,000 credit and noncredit courses to students each semester and awards the B.A., B.S., M.A., M.S., and M.F.A. degrees; The New School for Social Research, which grants M.A. and Ph.D. degrees; Milano The New School for Management and Urban Policy, which awards the M.S. and Ph.D. degrees; Parsons The New School for Design, one of the oldest and most influential art schools in the country; Mannes College The New School for Music, a renowned classical conservatory; The New School for Jazz and Contemporary Music; and The New School for Drama. The total university enrollment in 2006–07 was approximately 8,800 degree-seeking students.

Location

The university is located in New York City's Greenwich Village, which historically has been a center for intellectual and artistic life. This legendary New York City neighborhood of town houses and tree-lined streets offers students a friendly and stimulating environment. Over and above the resources of Greenwich Village, New York City offers virtually unlimited cultural, artistic, recreational, and intellectual resources that make it one of the world's great cities.

Majors and Degrees

Eugene Lang College awards the Bachelor of Arts degree. Students are encouraged to design their own program of study in consultation with their faculty adviser. They must choose from twelve paths of study: the arts; cultural studies and media; education studies; history; literature; philosophy; psychology; religious studies; science, technology, and society; social and historical inquiry; urban studies; and writing. Pending New York State approval, Lang plans to begin offering a B.A. in environmental studies in fall 2008. A student's concentration consists of eight to ten courses (32–40 credits) leading to relatively advanced and specialized knowledge of an area of study. In addition, students are encouraged to pursue an internship, where appropriate.

Students may also apply to a five-year, dual-degree B.A./B.F.A. program in conjunction with Parsons The New School for Design or The New School for Jazz and Contemporary Music, and advanced students may apply for the accelerated B.A./M.A. option offered in conjunction with the university's graduate divisions.

Academic Programs

When planning a program of study, Eugene Lang College students are encouraged to reflect on what their education means to them. Their program should parallel their own academic and personal development. By actively participating in the process of their education, students gain the knowledge to make informed choices about the direction of their studies with the help of their advisers and peers.

Small seminar classes serve as the focus of the academic program at the College. The maximum class size is 20 students. Classes are in-depth, interdisciplinary inquiries into topics or issues selected each semester by the College's outstanding faculty. Most important, the classes engage participants in the study of primary texts, rather than textbooks, and emphasize dialogue between teacher and student as a mode of learning. Here, not only is intellectual curiosity fostered by the small classes, but a genuine sense of community develops as well.

Although the College does not emphasize course requirements outside the path of study, freshmen are required to take one writing course and three other seminars of their choice in each of their first two semesters at the College. Upper-level students create their programs by selecting seminars from the College's curriculum, or they may combine offerings of the College with courses and workshops offered by The New School for General Study, The New School for Social Research, Milano The New School for Management and Urban Policy, and Parsons The New School for Design.

The College operates on a semester calendar; the first semester runs from September through mid-December, and the second runs from late January through mid-May. Students generally earn 16 credits per semester; a minimum of 120 credits is required for graduation.

Off-Campus Programs

Eugene Lang College recognizes the immense value of work undertaken beyond the classroom. The College arranges appropriate projects—internships with private and nonprofit organizations—which serve to strengthen the connection between theoretical work in the classroom and practical work on the job. Sophomores and juniors have the option of spending a year on a sponsored exchange with Sarah Lawrence College and the University of Amsterdam. Other exchanges, both in the United States and abroad, are available.

Academic Facilities

Eugene Lang College is located on 11th Street between Fifth and Sixth Avenues in Greenwich Village. The university includes twelve academic buildings, including a student center, the University Computing Center with IBM and Macintosh stations, a 500-seat auditorium, art galleries, studios for the fine arts, classrooms, a writing center, and faculty offices. Eugene Lang College students have full and easy access to the Raymond Fogelman Library and the Adam and Sophie Gimbel Design Library. In addition, the university participates in the South Manhattan Library Consortium. Together, the libraries in the consortium house approximately 3 million volumes covering all the traditional liberal arts disciplines and the fine arts.

Costs

Tuition and fees for the 2007–08 academic year were $30,995. Room and board cost approximately $11,000, depending upon the student's choice of specific meal plan and dormitory accommodations.

Financial Aid

Students are encouraged to apply for aid by filing the Free Application for Federal Student Aid (FAFSA) and requesting that a copy of the need analysis report be sent to The New School (FAFSA code number 002780). Qualified College students are eligible for all federal and state financial aid programs in addition to university gift aid. University aid is awarded on the basis of need and merit and is part of a package consisting of both gift aid (grants and/or scholarships) and a self-help component (loans and Federal Work-Study Program awards). Aid is renewable each year as long as need continues and students maintain satisfactory academic standing at the College. Special attention is given to continuing students who have done exceptionally well.

Faculty

At Eugene Lang College, the faculty-student ratio is 1:10. Class size ranges from 10 to 20 students. Faculty members are graduates of outstanding colleges and universities and represent a wide variety of academic disciplines; 95 percent hold Ph.D.'s. College faculty members also serve as academic advisers, who are selected carefully in order to ensure thoughtful supervision of students' programs and academic progress.

Well-known faculty members from other divisions of the university teach at the College on a regular basis. In addition, every semester, the College hosts distinguished scholars and writers as visiting faculty and guest lecturers who further enrich the academic program of the College and the university.

Student Government

There is a student union at the College, which is an organized vehicle for student expression and action as well as a means of funding student projects and events. Students are encouraged to express their views and concerns about academic policies and community life through regular student-faculty member meetings.

Admission Requirements

Eugene Lang College welcomes admission applications from students of diverse racial, ethnic, religious, and political backgrounds whose past performance and academic and personal promise make them likely to gain from and give much to the College community. The College seeks students who combine inquisitiveness and seriousness of purpose with the ability to engage in a distinctive, rigorous liberal arts program. Each applicant to the College is judged individually; the Admissions Committee, which renders all admission decisions, considers both academic qualifications and the personal, creative, and intellectual qualities of each applicant. A strong academic background, including a college-preparatory program, is recommended. An applicant's transcript; teacher and counselor recommendations; SAT, ACT, or SAT Subject Test scores; and personal essays are all taken into consideration. In addition, an interview, a tour of university facilities, and a visit to Eugene Lang College seminars are optional but highly recommended.

High school students for whom the College is their first choice are strongly encouraged to apply as early decision candidates and are notified early of an admission decision. Early entrance is an option for qualified high school juniors who wish to enter college prior to high school graduation. Candidates for early entrance must submit two teacher recommendations.

Students who have successfully completed one full year or more at another accredited institution may apply as transfer candidates. If accepted, transfer students may enter upper-level seminars and pursue advanced work. International students may apply for admission as freshmen or transfers by submitting a regular application to the College. If English is spoken as a second language, TOEFL scores are required. The New York Connection Program invites students from other colleges to Eugene Lang College for a semester and incorporates an internship into their studies.

Students interested in applying for the combined B.A./B.F.A. degree program in fine arts or jazz studies are encouraged to apply for admission as freshmen to these special five-year programs. In addition to the admission requirements outlined above, a home exam and a portfolio are required for fine arts, and an audition is required for jazz studies.

Application and Information

Freshmen, transfers, and visiting students may apply for either the September (fall) or January (spring) semester. To apply for admission to the College, students must request an application packet and submit the required credentials and a $50 application fee by the appropriate deadline. The application fee may be waived in accordance with the College Board's Fee Waiver Service. For the semester beginning in January, the required credentials must be submitted by November 15, with notification by December 15. For the September semester, early decision candidates must submit the required credentials by November 15, with notification by December 15. For freshman candidates applying for general admission and freshman early entrants, the deadline is February 1, with notification by April 1. For transfers and visiting students, the deadline is rolling to May 15, with notification rolling until July 1.

For further information, students should contact:

Nicole Curvin
Director of Admissions
Eugene Lang College The New School for Liberal Arts
65 West 11th Street, Third Floor
New York, New York 10011

Phone: 212-229-5665
Fax: 212-229-5355
E-mail: lang@newschool.edu
Web site: http://www.lang.newschool.edu

EXCELSIOR COLLEGE

ALBANY, NEW YORK

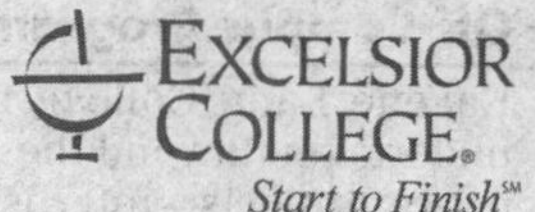

The College

In 1971, Regents College was founded to make college degrees more accessible to busy, working adults. The college focused on what students knew rather than where or how they learned it. It was a radical concept in its day because it recognized that college-level knowledge can be attained in many ways—and students should receive credit for what they know. Today, Regents College is known as Excelsior College®, a name that means "ever upward" and more accurately describes what the College does—propels students ever upward toward reaching their lifetime goals.

As a world leader in distance education, Excelsior College does not insist that learning can take place only in the classroom. Students have access to more avenues than are available at most traditional colleges and universities, because it is not realistic to expect active adults with family and career commitments to drop out of life to earn a degree. Each student's journey upward is begun with Excelsior College acknowledging college credits already earned, so students can earn a respected degree in business, technology, the liberal arts, nursing, or the health sciences. Students advance with a customized degree-completion plan and choose from many credit-earning options—distance courses from Excelsior College and other regionally accredited institutions; traditional courses at a local campus; credit-bearing exams, including Excelsior College® Examinations (ECE); or a portfolio assessment, which can allow students to earn credit through work, community, or volunteer experiences. More than fifty associate, bachelor's, master's, and certificate programs, as well as military and professional development programs, are available. Alumni advance ever upward to graduate schools and better jobs in business, government, and health care.

Approximately 13 percent of students come from New York State; the remaining 87 percent come from all other states and many countries. Nearly 125,000 graduates have earned degrees from Excelsior College. Many indicate that they expect to earn an advanced degree at some point in the future, and a large percentage of baccalaureate graduates pursue postgraduate studies immediately after earning their degrees at Excelsior. Continuing its national winning streak, Excelsior College, one of the nation's oldest distance learning schools, topped the *U.S. News & World Report*'s "America's Best Colleges 2008" report in two key categories—the number of transfer students enrolled and the highest percentage of students older than 25.

Location

Located in Albany, New York, the College is in the heart of New York State's Capital Region. The population of the metropolitan area, which includes Troy, Schenectady, and Saratoga Springs, is approximately 850,000. New York City, Boston, and Montreal are within a 3-hour drive from Albany.

Majors and Degrees

Excelsior College offers the Associate in Applied Science (A.A.S.), Associate in Occupational Science (A.O.S.), and Associate in Science (A.S.), with majors in administrative/management studies, business, computer software, electronics technology, liberal arts, military specialties, nuclear technology, nursing, and technology with specialty. Bachelor's degrees are offered in accounting (general or New York State CPA track), computer technology, electronics engineering technology, finance, general business, global business, health sciences, hospitality management, information technology, liberal arts, management information systems, management of human resources, marketing, nuclear engineering technology, nursing, operations management, risk management and insurance, and technology. Certificate programs are available in end-of-life care, entrepreneurship, health-care informatics, health-care management, and homeland security.

Academic Programs

Excelsior College is a thriving, dynamic institution that is committed to serving the diverse needs of its students. Academic programs are continuously reviewed for currency and relevancy to ensure that each degree represents the best in academic rigor and includes the most up-to-date thinking in related career areas. In addition, the College continues to develop new programs and services to meet student needs.

Excelsior College accepts undergraduate credits from a wide variety of sources, generally from those colleges and universities that are regionally accredited, that are recognized by the New York State Education Department, and that have been evaluated by the Excelsior College faculty. Credit by exam is a tool many adult learners use to help meet their educational goals. Every year, thousands of Excelsior students take one or more proficiency exams. Excelsior College Examinations include about fifty undergraduate-level tests. The majority are multiple-choice tests, but the series also includes extended-response (essay) and mixed-format (multiple-choice and free-response) exams.

Excelsior College offers a number of professional development and training programs completely online. These noncredit programs are geared toward those looking for professional development, continuing education, and lifelong learning. Many can be completed in three to six months and open new opportunities for job growth or career change.

The Associate in Science degree requires a total of 60 semester hours, at least 30 of which must be earned in the arts and sciences; the remaining 30 semester hours may be earned in applied professional courses, additional arts and sciences credits, or a combination of both. The Associate in Arts degree requires a total of 60 semester hours; a minimum of 48 semester hours must be earned in the arts and sciences, with the remaining 12 in applied professional courses, additional arts and sciences courses, or a combination of both. Bachelor's degree programs require a minimum of 120 semester hours, with the Bachelor of Arts requiring more arts and science credits (a minimum of 90 semester hours). Students who have taken or intend to take a large number of applied professional credits find the Bachelor of Science degree to be a more flexible option for them.

Academic Facilities

Excelsior College students have access to the Excelsior College Virtual Library (ECVL). The library is full of carefully selected and annotated sources pertinent to each program and provides a reliable and trustworthy place to start research. ECVL is continuously growing and offers a wide range of library sources and services, including help with getting started on research or with general search strategies, finding material online or in print, or locating material in a local library. There are interlibrary loan services for books and photocopies of articles. Resource collections specific to every degree program, such as databases, electronic journals, handbooks, and reports, are available. Students have access to carefully selected and annotated electronic reference material, including general and specialized dictionaries, almanacs, and directories; bibliographic databases such as nursing resources like Medline and Health Source: Nursing/Academic Edition, liberal arts resources like Academic Search Premier, business and technology resources such as Business Source Premier and Regional Business News, and general resources like WorldCat; tutorials related to using databases and finding and evaluating information; and a virtual reading room with full-text books, newspapers, and governmental and nongovernmental reports.

Costs

To enroll officially, students must pay an enrollment fee, which is currently $895 for associate and bachelor's programs and $495 for the A.O.S. in aviation and the A.A.S. in administration/management, aviation studies, and technical studies. For every year a student is enrolled following the first year, the Student Service Annual Fee (SSAF), now $440, is assessed. Tuition is $290 per credit.

Financial Aid

Excelsior College participates in a variety of financial aid programs to help students meet educational expenses. The College is a Title IV eligible educational institution, offering federal financial assistance (Federal Pell Grants, Federal Stafford Student Loans, and Federal PLUS loans) to qualified students. (The College's federal code number is 014251.)

Some students may qualify for the Hope Scholarship or Lifetime Learning tax credit. In addition, Excelsior participates in New York State financial aid programs, the Veterans Affairs Educational Benefits Program, and several private educational loan programs and offers a select number of scholarships. For more information, students should contact the financial aid office at 888-647-2388 Ext. 143 (toll-free).

Faculty

Students' high-quality academic experience at Excelsior College is due, in large part, to the faculty. Drawn from many colleges and universities as well as from industry and the professions, faculty members are subject-matter experts who are strongly grounded in scholarship and research. The highly credentialed faculty also teaches at other prestigious colleges and universities, such as Rensselaer Polytechnic Institute, Skidmore College, and Northeastern University, and includes members of the Fellows in the American Academy of Nursing. Faculty members establish and monitor academic policies and standards, determine degree requirements and the ways in which credit can be earned, develop the content for all examinations, teach courses, review student records to verify degree-requirement completion, and recommend degree conferral to the Board of Trustees.

Student Government

Excelsior College has no student government.

Admission Requirements

Applicants must be self-directed and committed to completing a college degree, and they should have previous college credit, the time and motivation to study, and computer skills. Students must submit the completed application, the $75 application fee, and official transcripts. In addition, there are program-specific requirements, which can be found at http://www.excelsior.edu/apply.

Application and Information

Admissions Office
Excelsior College
7 Columbia Circle
Albany, New York 12203-5159
Phone: 518-464-8500
888-647-2388 (toll-free)
Fax: 518-464-8777
E-mail: admissions@excelsior.edu
Web site: http://www.excelsior.edu

FASHION INSTITUTE OF TECHNOLOGY
State University of New York
NEW YORK, NEW YORK

The Institute

The Fashion Institute of Technology (FIT) is New York City's celebrated urban college for creative and business talent. A selective State University of New York (SUNY) college of art and design, business, and technology, FIT is a creative axis for a rich mix of innovative achievers, original thinkers, and industry pioneers, with nearly forty programs of study leading to the A.A.S., B.F.A., and B.S. degrees. The School of Graduate Studies offers six programs leading to either a Master of Arts (M.A.) or Master of Professional Studies (M.P.S.) degree. The college is accredited by the Middle States Association of Colleges and Schools, National Association of Schools of Art and Design, and Council for Interior Design Accreditation.

FIT serves approximately 10,000 students from the Greater New York metropolitan area, across the country, and around the world, offering full- and part-time study options, evening/weekend programs, and online studies. The college provides a singular approach to higher education—balancing a real-world-based curriculum and hands-on instruction with a rigorous liberal arts foundation, marrying design and business, supporting individual creativity in a collaborative environment, and encouraging faculty members to match pedagogy with professional experience. It offers a complete college experience with a vibrant student life.

FIT's mission is to produce well-rounded graduates: doers and thinkers who raise the professional bar to become the next generation of business pacesetters and creative icons.

All full-time, matriculated students are eligible for FIT housing. Four residence halls house 2,300 in fully furnished single-, double-, triple-, and quad-occupancy rooms. Each residence hall has centrally located lounges and laundry facilities; George and Marianna Kaufman Residence Hall also provides an on-site fitness center. Students have the option of either traditional (meal plan included) or apartment-style accommodations. Counselors and student staff members live in the halls, helping students adjust to college life and living in New York City.

Throughout the David Dubinsky Student Center are lounges, a game room, a student radio station, the Style Shop (the FIT student-run boutique), student government and club offices, a comprehensive health center, two gyms, a dance studio, a weight room, and a counseling center.

Location

FIT's extraordinary location at the center of New York City—world capital of the arts, business, and media—allows it to maintain close ties with the professions it serves. The campus comprises an entire city block in Manhattan's Chelsea neighborhood, and the college makes extensive use of the city's vast resources, providing students with unrivaled internship opportunities and valuable professional connections. A wide range of cultural and entertainment options—from art galleries to theater to world-class dining—are available within a short walking distance of campus, as is easy and convenient access to several subway and bus routes and the city's major rail and bus transportation hubs.

Majors and Degrees

FIT offers fifteen Associate in Applied Science (A.A.S.) and twenty-two baccalaureate programs. All students complete a two-year A.A.S. program in their major area of study and the liberal arts and then typically continue in a related, two-year Bachelor of Fine Arts (B.F.A.) or Bachelor of Science (B.S.) program. If students choose, they may begin their careers with the A.A.S. degree, which qualifies them for entry-level positions in a wide range of creative and/or business professions.

The School of Art and Design offers eleven A.A.S. and thirteen B.F.A. degree programs, the Jay and Patty Baker School of Business and Technology offers four A.A.S. and eight B.S. degree programs, and the School of Liberal Arts offers one B.S. degree program.

The fifteen A.A.S. degree programs, all of which provide the foundation for one or more corresponding baccalaureate-level programs, are accessories design*; advertising and marketing communications*; communication design*; fashion design*; fashion merchandising management*; fine arts (with a career-exploration component); illustration; interior design; jewelry design*; menswear; photography; production management: fashion and related industries; textile development and marketing*; textile/surface design*; and visual presentation and exhibition design. Programs with an * are also available in a one-year format for students with acceptable transferable credits.

The thirteen B.F.A. degree programs are accessories design and fabrication; advertising design; computer animation and interactive media; fabric styling; fashion design (with specializations in children's wear, fashion design, intimate apparel, and knitwear); fine arts; graphic design; illustration; interior design; packaging design; photography and the digital image; textile/surface design; and toy design.

The nine B.S. degree programs are advertising and marketing communications; cosmetics and fragrance marketing; direct and interactive marketing; fashion merchandising management; home products development; international trade and marketing for the fashion industries; production management: fashion and related industries; textile development and marketing; and visual art management.

For those students looking to balance the demands of career or family with their education, FIT offers nine degree programs available through evening/weekend study that include advertising and marketing communications (A.A.S. and B.S.), communication design (A.A.S.), fashion design (A.A.S.), fashion merchandising management (A.A.S. and B.S.), graphic design (B.F.A.), illustration (B.F.A.), and international trade and marketing for the fashion industries (B.S.).

Academic Programs

Each undergraduate program builds upon a core of traditional liberal arts courses, providing students with a global perspective, critical-thinking skills, and the ability to communicate effectively.

All degree programs are designed to prepare students for creative and business careers—the college's Career Services, which offers lifetime placement, reports a graduate employment rate of 90 percent—and to provide them with the necessary prerequisite studies so that they may go on to graduate degree programs. Internships are a required element of most programs and are available to all students. More than one third of FIT student internships result in employment offers by the sponsoring organization.

The Presidential Scholars Program, available to academically exceptional students in all disciplines, offers special liberal arts courses, projects, colloquiums, extracurricular activities, and off-campus visits designed to broaden horizons and stimulate discourse. Past areas of study have included cultural studies, Greek mythology, theories of public space, and urban archeology. Presidential Scholars are also awarded priority course registration and an annual merit stipend.

Precollege programs (Saturday/Summer Live) are available to high school students during the fall, spring, and summer. More than forty-five courses provide the chance to learn in an innovative environment, to develop art and design portfolios, to explore the business and technological sides of a wide range of creative careers, and to discover natural talents and abilities. Courses designed for middle school students are available in the summer.

The School of Continuing Education and Professional Studies provides convenient evening and weekend credit and noncredit classes to students and working professionals alike who are interested in pursuing a degree or certificate or furthering their knowledge and expertise in a particular industry.

Off-Campus Programs

The study-abroad experience offers students the opportunity to immerse themselves in diverse cultures and prepares them to live and work in a global community. Through its international program offerings, FIT provides students, chosen on a competitive basis, the option of studying abroad for a year, a semester, or in the summer or winter sessions in countries such as Australia, China, England, France, Israel, Italy, and Mexico.

Academic Facilities

FIT provides its students with an urban campus of classrooms, laboratories, and studios that reflects the most advanced educational and professional practices. The Fred P. Pomerantz Art and Design Center houses photography studios; drawing, painting, and sculpture studios; a printmaking room; display and exhibit design rooms; a model-making workshop; and a graphics printing service bureau. The Peter G. Scotese Computer-Aided Design and Communications Facility provides students with the opportunity to explore the latest advancements in technology and their integration in the design of textiles, toys, interiors, fashion, and advertising, as well as photography and computer graphics and animation. The Annette Green/Fragrance Foundation Studio, a professionally equipped fragrance development laboratory, is the only one of its kind on a college campus. Cutting and sewing laboratories for the production management: fashion and related industries program students offer the most advanced design and cutting machinery among educational facilities in the U.S. The Design/Research Lighting Laboratory, an educational and professional development facility for interior design and other disciplines, features more than 400 commercially available lighting fixtures. Other college facilities include a broadcasting studio, knitting and weaving labs, a multimedia foreign language laboratory, and twenty-three computer labs containing nearly 700 Mac and PC workstations, in addition to several additional labs with computers reserved for students in specific programs.

The renowned Museum at FIT is New York City's only museum dedicated to the art of fashion, and it is used by students, designers, and historians alike for research and inspiration. The museum operates year-round, and its exhibitions are free and open to the public. Recent exhibitions of note include She's Like a Rainbow: Colors in Fashion; Exoticism; and Madame Grès: Sphinx of Fashion. The Gladys Marcus Library provides more than 300,000 volumes of print, nonprint, and electronic materials. The newspaper and periodical collection includes 500 current subscriptions, with a specialization in international design and trade publications; online resources include more than 90 searchable databases. The library also offers specialized resources, such as clipping files, fashion and trend forecasting services, sketch collections, and runway show DVDs.

Also on campus are three multimedia venues—the Katie Murphy Amphitheatre, the Morris W. and Fannie B. Haft Auditorium, and the John E. Reeves Great Hall—used for student presentations, industry panels, conferences, and special events.

Costs

The 2007–08 associate-level tuition per semester for New York State residents was $1646; for nonresidents, it was $4938. Baccalaureate-level tuition per semester was $2283.50 for residents and $5570 for nonresidents. For fall 2007, per-semester housing rates were $3051–$3190 for traditional residence hall accommodations and $3981.50–$7412.50 for apartment-style accommodations. Meal plans (mandatory for traditional residence hall residents) ranged from $1395 to $1795 per semester. A $325 annual fee for technology services and the Student Resident Association was required of all residence hall students. Textbook costs and other nominal fees, such as locker rental or laboratory use, vary per program of study. All costs are subject to change.

Financial Aid

FIT attempts to remove financial barriers to college entrance by providing scholarships, grants, loans, and work-study employment for students in financial need. Nearly all full-time, matriculated students who apply for financial aid receive some type of assistance. The college directly administers its own institutional grants and scholarships, which are provided by the Educational Foundation for the Fashion Industries.

College-administered federal funding includes Federal Pell Grants, Federal Perkins Loans, Federal Supplemental Educational Opportunity Grants, Federal Work-Study awards, and Federal Family Educational Loans, which include student and parent loans. New York State residents who meet state guidelines for eligibility may also receive Tuition Assistance Program (TAP) and/or Educational Opportunity Program (EOP) grants. Financial aid applicants must file the Free Application for Federal Student Aid (FAFSA), through which they apply for the Federal Pell Grant. They should also apply for all available outside sources of aid. Other documentation may be requested by the Financial Aid Office. Applications for financial aid should be completed prior to February 15 for fall admission or prior to November 1 for spring admission.

Faculty

FIT's faculty is drawn equally from top professionals in academia, art, and business who bring their experience to the classroom and introduce students to the real-life opportunities and challenges of their disciplines through field trips, guest lectures, and sponsored competitions. Academic departments consult with industry advisory boards of noted experts in their fields, who ensure that the course work and classroom technology adapt to mirror evolving industry practices. Student-instructor interaction is encouraged, with a maximum class size of 25, and courses are structured to foster participation, independent thinking, and self-expression.

Student Government

The Student Council, the governing body of the Student Association, gives all students the privileges and responsibilities of citizens in a self-governing college community. Many faculty committees include student representatives, and the president of the student government sits on FIT's Board of Trustees.

Admission Requirements

Applicants for admission must be either candidates for or recipients of a high school diploma or the General Educational Development (GED) certificate. Candidates are judged on class rank, grades in college-preparatory course work, and the student essay. Letters of recommendation are not required. A portfolio evaluation is required for art and design majors. Specific portfolio requirements are explained on FIT's Web site.

Transfer students from regionally accredited colleges must submit official transcripts for credit evaluation. Students may qualify for the one-year A.A.S. option if they hold a baccalaureate degree from an accredited college or if they have a minimum of 30 transferable credits from an accredited college, including 24 credits that are equivalent to FIT's liberal arts requirements and at least one semester of physical education.

Students seeking admission to a B.F.A. or B.S. program must hold an A.A.S. degree from FIT or an equivalent degree from an accredited and approved college. They must also meet the appropriate prerequisites as required by the major and have completed FIT's liberal arts requirements. Further requirements may include an individual interview with a departmental committee, review of academic standing, and a portfolio review (for applicants to B.F.A. programs). Any student who applies for transfer to FIT from a four-year program must have completed a minimum of 60 credits, including the requisite art or technical courses and the liberal arts requirements.

Application and Information

Students wishing to visit FIT are encouraged to attend a group information session, held at noon throughout the year on Tuesday, Wednesday, and Friday, except on major holidays. Sessions are held in the Marvin Feldman Center, Room C205, and run approximately 90 minutes.

Interested candidates may apply online at http://www.fitnyc.edu/admissions. For more information, students should contact:

Admissions
Fashion Institute of Technology
Seventh Avenue at 27th Street
New York, New York 10001-5992
Phone: 212-217-3760
800-GO-TO-FIT (toll-free)
E-mail: fitinfo@fitnyc.edu
Web site: http://www.fitnyc.edu

FIVE TOWNS COLLEGE

DIX HILLS, NEW YORK

The College

Located on Long Island's North Shore, Five Towns College offers students the opportunity to study in a suburban environment that is close to New York City. Founded in 1972, Five Towns College is an independent, nonsectarian, coeducational institution that places its emphasis on the student as an individual. Many students are drawn to the College because of its strong reputation in music, media, and the performing arts. The College offers associate, bachelor's, master's, and doctoral degrees. The College also offers programs leading to the Master of Music (M.M.) degree in jazz/commercial music and in music education as well as a master's in elementary education (M.S.Ed.) and a doctorate in musical arts (D.M.A.).

From as far away as England and Japan and from as close as Long Island and New York City, the 1,000 full-time students reflect a rich cultural diversity. The College's enrollment is 60 percent men and 40 percent women, with a minority population of approximately 30 percent. The College's music programs are contemporary jazz in nature, although classical musicians are also part of this creative community. The most popular programs are audio recording technology, broadcasting, journalism, music performance, music business, music and elementary teacher education, theater, and film/video production.

Coeducational living accommodations are available on campus. The Five Towns College Living/Learning Center is a brand-new complex containing modern dormitories. Each residence hall contains single- and double-occupancy rooms equipped with private bathrooms, broadband Internet access, cable television, and other amenities.

Location

The College's beautiful 40-acre campus, located in the wooded countryside of Dix Hills, New York, provides students with a park-like refuge where they can pursue their studies. Just off campus is Long Island's bustling Route 110 corridor, home to numerous national and multinational corporations. New York City, with everything from Lincoln Center to Broadway, is just a train ride away and provides students with some of the best cultural advantages in the world.

Closer to the campus, the many communities of Long Island abound with cultural and recreational opportunities. The College is located within the historic town of Huntington, which is home to the Cinema Arts Center, InterMedia Arts Center, Hecksher Museum, Vanderbilt Museum, and numerous restaurants, coffeehouses, and quaint shops. The nearby shores of Jones Beach State Park and the Fire Island National Seashore are world renowned for their white, sandy beaches.

Majors and Degrees

Five Towns College offers the Associate in Arts (A.A.) degree in liberal arts, with concentrations in teaching assistant studies and theater arts; the Associate in Science (A.S.) degree in business administration; and the Associate in Applied Science (A.A.S.) degree in business management and in jazz commercial music, with concentrations in accounting, audio recording technology, computer business applications, and music business.

The College offers the Bachelor of Music (Mus.B.) degree in music education and in jazz/commercial music, with concentrations in audio recording technology, composition/songwriting, music business, musical theater, and performance; the Bachelor of Fine Arts (B.F.A.) degree in theater or film/video arts; the Bachelor of Professional Studies (B.P.S.) degree in business management, with concentrations in audio recording technology and music business; the Bachelor of Science (B.S.) degree in childhood education; and the B.S. in mass communication, which features broadcasting and journalism concentrations.

Academic Programs

The following describes some of the more popular programs at Five Towns College. For a complete description of the College's academic program, students should visit the Five Towns College Web site at http://www.ftc.edu.

The music education program is designed for students interested in a career as a teacher of music in a public or private school. The undergraduate program leads to New York State provisional certification. The course work provides professional training and includes a student-teaching experience. The audio recording technology concentration is designed to provide students with the tools needed to succeed as professional studio engineers and producers in the music industry. The music business concentration is designed for students interested in a career in entertainment-related business fields. The course work includes the technical, legal, production, management, and merchandising aspects of the music business. The composition/songwriting concentration provides intensive instruction in a core of technical studies in harmony, orchestration, counterpoint, MIDI, songwriting, form and analysis, arranging, and composition for those who intend to pursue careers as composers, arrangers, and songwriters. The performance concentration includes a common core of technical studies and a foundation of specialized courses, such as music history, harmony, counterpoint, improvisation, ensemble performance, and private instruction. The theater arts program is designed for students interested in careers as actors, entertainers, scenic designers, directors, stage managers, and lighting or sound directors. The film/video program includes extensive technical preparation in videography, filmmaking, linear and nonlinear editing, storyboarding, scriptwriting, producing, and directing for filmmakers and videographers. Elementary education students are prepared as teachers for grades 1–6, while those interested in journalism and broadcasting are prepared for careers in radio, television, newspaper, and editorial writing.

To earn a bachelor's degree, students must accumulate between 122 and 130 credits, depending on the program of study, with a proper distribution of courses and a GPA of at least 2.0. To earn an associate degree, students must accumulate between 62 and 66 credits.

Off-Campus Programs

Off-campus internship opportunities are available to Five Towns College students who have fulfilled the necessary prerequisites, including a cumulative grade point average of at least 2.5, with a 3.0 in their major. In recent semesters, students have interned for major corporations such as MTV, Atlantic Records, Polygram Records, CBS, ABC, EMI Records, MCA Records, Sony Records, The Power Station, Pyramid Recording Studios, Channel 12 News, and many others.

Academic Facilities

Five Towns College occupies a multiwinged facility that comprises approximately 120,000 square feet and includes a 500-seat auditorium, production studios, athletic and dining facilities, classrooms, PC and Mac computer labs, and a student center. T-3 lines connect the College's completely fiber-optic computer network to the Internet. All students have access to this network and are provided with an e-mail account.

The Five Towns College Library has more than 35,000 print and nonprint materials. These include nearly 30,000 books and print items, 500 periodical subscriptions, and approximately 5,000 records, 2,500 videos and DVDs, and more than 2,000 CDs. Through its membership in the Long Island Library Resource Council (LILRC), students have access to other libraries around the country.

The Technical Wing at Five Towns College consists of eleven studio/control rooms. These facilities house the College's state-of-the-art 72-channel SL9000J audio board, 48-track SSL and 24-track digital recording studios, and the Electronic Music-MIDI Studio. The Film/Video Studio utilizes Beta Sp, SVHS video formats, and the 16mm film format. Nonlinear edit suites utilize the Media 100 XS and XR operating systems on Macintosh G4 platforms. Students utilize these facilities to develop their skills while creating professional-quality productions, both in the studio and on location, under the supervision of industry professionals. Student productions include CDs, music videos, documentaries, sitcoms, public service announcements, commercials, and talk shows, among many others.

The Dix Hills Center for Performing Arts at Five Towns College is an acoustically "perfect" venue, with digital lighting systems, digital sound reinforcement for concert production, and a Barco 6300 digital projection system for multimedia productions. The professional stage is 60 feet wide, with a proscenium opening of 16 feet and 32 feet of fly space. Students utilize this facility to produce live concerts, plays, musicals, and other performances and special presentations.

Costs

The tuition for 2007–08 was $16,400 per year. Miscellaneous fees cost approximately $400, and books cost about $700. Private instruction fees for performing music students were $675 per semester.

Financial Aid

The annual tuition at Five Towns College is among the lowest of all the private colleges in the region. Nevertheless, approximately 72 percent of all students receive some form of financial assistance. Need-based and/or merit-based grants, scholarships, loans, and work-study programs are available to qualified recipients, including transfer students. Prospective students are urged to contact the Financial Aid Office as early as possible.

Faculty

The College's growing faculty consists of 110 full- and part-time members. The student-faculty ratio is 14:1. While the faculty is more strongly committed to teaching than to research, many members continue to be active in their respective areas of expertise.

Student Government

The Student Council (SC) serves as the representative governance body for all students. The SC consists of an elected president and vice president and 9 elected at-large representatives, who select from among themselves a secretary and a treasurer. The Student Council charters clubs and organizations, allocates student activity fees, and recommends policies that affect student life. There is also a Dormitory Council.

Admission Requirements

The College encourages applications from students who will engage themselves in its creative community and who will contribute to the academic debate with honor and integrity. Students seeking a seat in the entering class of students should have attained a minimum high school average grade of 80 percent. The SAT or ACT exam is required for all freshmen. Transfer students must also submit official transcripts of all college-level work attempted. International students from non-English-speaking countries must submit a paper-based TOEFL score of at least 550 or its equivalent. Students may be admitted for deferred entrance or with advanced standing. The College does not accept students on an early admissions basis, although early decision is available. Candidates for admission must submit a completed Application for Undergraduate Admission, official high school transcripts, at least two letters of recommendation, and a personal statement. International students must submit additional information and should contact the Foreign Student Advisor.

Application and Information

Admission into any music program is contingent upon passing an audition demonstrating skill in performance on a major instrument or vocally. Admission into any theater program is also contingent upon passing an audition. In some cases, the Admissions Committee may request an on-campus interview with an applicant. Music, theater, and film/video students are encouraged to submit a portfolio tape or reel, if available.

Except for applicants applying on an early decision basis, new students are accepted on a rolling basis, with decisions for the fall and spring semesters mailed starting February 15 and October 15, respectively. There is an application fee of $35.

For further information, students should contact:

Director of Admissions
Five Towns College
305 North Service Road
Dix Hills, New York 11746-5871
Phone: 631-424-7000 Ext. 2110
Fax: 631-656-2172
E-mail: admissions@ftc.edu
Web site: http://www.ftc.edu

Five Towns College Studio A.

FORDHAM UNIVERSITY

NEW YORK, NEW YORK

The University

Fordham, the Jesuit University of New York, offers a distinctive educational experience that is rooted in the 450-year-old Jesuit tradition of intellectual rigor and personal respect for the individual. The University enrolls approximately 14,700 students, of whom 7,652 are undergraduates.

Fordham has four undergraduate colleges and six graduate schools. In addition to its full-time undergraduate programs, the University offers part-time undergraduate study at Fordham College of Liberal Studies and during two summer sessions.

Fordham College at Rose Hill and the College of Business Administration, located on the Rose Hill campus, are adjacent to the New York Botanical Garden and the Bronx Zoo. Rose Hill is a self-contained 85-acre campus with residential facilities for more than 3,100 students and ample parking for commuters. It is easily accessible by public and private transportation. Fordham also provides an intercampus van service to transport students to and from Manhattan. Fordham College at Lincoln Center is located on Manhattan's Upper West Side, overlooking the famous Lincoln Center for the Performing Arts complex. The Lincoln Center campus has an 850-bed apartment-style residence, McMahon Hall, and is accessible via the West Side Highway and major subway lines.

The University has an extensive athletics program consisting of twenty-three varsity sports and numerous club and intramural sports. The recently renovated Murphy Field is the heart of intramural and recreational sports at Fordham, hosting softball, soccer, and flag football games. The Vincent T. Lombardi Memorial Center provides facilities for basketball, squash, swimming and diving, tennis, track, and water polo.

Location

As the Jesuit University of New York, Fordham offers its students the unparalleled cultural, recreational, and academic advantages of one of the world's great cities. More than 2,600 corporations and organizations offer valuable work experience to Fordham interns. The University also provides unusual opportunities for participating in activities of direct service to the city, ranging from small-group community initiatives to large government-sponsored projects.

Majors and Degrees

Fordham offers undergraduates more than sixty-five majors. Fordham College at Rose Hill offers programs of study leading to the B.A. or B.S. in African and African American studies, American studies, anthropology, art history, biological sciences, chemistry, classical civilization, classical languages (Latin and Greek), communication and media studies, comparative literature, computer and information sciences, economics, engineering physics, English, French, French studies, general science, German, history, international political economy, Italian, Italian studies, Latin American and Latino studies, mathematics, mathematics/economics, medieval studies, Middle East studies, music, philosophy, physics, political science, psychology, religious studies, sociology, Spanish, Spanish studies, theology, urban studies, visual arts, and women's studies.

Also at the Rose Hill campus, the College of Business Administration offers programs leading to the B.S. in accounting, accounting information services, applied accounting and finance, business administration, business economics, communication and media management, e-business, entrepreneurship, finance, human resource management, information and communication systems, legal and ethical studies, management of information and communication systems, management systems, marketing, and public accountancy. The G.L.O.B.E. Program provides business students with an international study option that incorporates course offerings in language, culture, and history with business.

Special programs at Rose Hill include a cooperative engineering program, double majors or individualized majors, interdisciplinary studies, a B.S./M.B.A. program, and honors programs. Preprofessional programs are offered in architecture, dentistry, law, medicine, and veterinary medicine, and a program for teacher certification is offered in elementary and secondary education.

Fordham College at Lincoln Center offers the B.A. in African and African American studies, anthropology, art history, classical civilization, classical languages (Latin and Greek), communication and media studies, comparative literature, computer science, dance, economics, English, French, French studies, history, information science, international studies, Italian, Italian studies, Latin American and Latino studies, mathematics, mathematics/economics, medieval studies, Middle East studies, music, natural science, philosophy, political science, psychology, religious studies, social science, social work, sociology, Spanish, Spanish studies, theater, theology, urban studies, visual arts, and women's studies. Special programs at Fordham College at Lincoln Center include extensive offerings in the performing arts (including a B.F.A. in dance with the Ailey School), creative writing, double majors or individualized majors, independent study, an honors program, and interdisciplinary studies. Preprofessional studies are offered in dentistry, health, and law. A teacher certification program is offered in elementary and secondary education.

Academic Programs

Students in all undergraduate colleges pursue a common core curriculum designed to provide them with the breadth of knowledge that marks the educated person. Drawn from nine disciplines, the core includes the study of philosophy, English composition and literature, history, theology, mathematical reasoning, natural science, social sciences, the fine arts, and foreign language. Business students benefit from the core curriculum as well as from required business core courses.

Off-Campus Programs

Fordham participates in a study-abroad program with other major U.S. universities and offers opportunities to study in Australia, China, El Salvador, England, Ireland, Italy, Korea, Mexico, Spain, and many other countries. More than 350 Fordham students study abroad each year. Fordham also offers international community service trips through its global outreach program.

Academic Facilities

The outstanding libraries on the two campuses have combined holdings of more than 2.1 million volumes and more than 49,920 electronic and print periodicals. On the Rose Hill campus, the William D. Walsh Family Library, which serves the entire Fordham community, has seating for more than 1,500 and a state-of-the-art Electronic Information Center, as well as media production laboratories, studios, and auditoriums. Students also have access to the vast library facilities of New York City, neighboring universities, and the various specialized collections maintained by numerous local museums and other institutions. Among laboratory facilities utilized by undergraduates are Mulcahy Hall (chemistry), Larkin Hall (biology), and Freeman Hall (physics and biology). The University has more than forty buildings that provide ample space for smart classrooms, science laboratories, theaters, and athletic facilities.

Costs

At the Rose Hill and Lincoln Center campuses, undergraduate costs for the 2007–08 academic year were $32,720 for tuition and fees and averaged $12,300 for room and board. Residence halls are available at each campus. Chemistry, physics, and biology fees were approximately $50 per laboratory course. Nominally priced meals are available in cafeterias on each campus. Such incidentals as transportation and laundry vary in cost. There is no difference in fees for out-of-state students.

Financial Aid

More than 85 percent of the entering students enroll with aid from Fordham as well as from outside sources. Among the major aid programs are Federal Pell Grants, Federal Supplemental Educational Opportunity Grants, Federal Perkins Loans, work grants sponsored by both the government and the University, and University grants-in-aid. Outside sources of aid include state scholarships, the New York State Tuition Assistance Program (TAP), privately sponsored scholarships, state government loan programs, and deferred-payment programs. The University also offers academic scholarships ranging from $10,000 to the full cost of tuition and room.

Applicants for aid must submit the Free Application for Federal Student Aid (FAFSA) and the College Scholarship Service (CSS) PROFILE. Inquiries should be directed to Fordham's Office of Undergraduate Admission or Office of Student Financial Services.

Faculty

The University has a full-time faculty of 667 and a student-faculty ratio of 12:1. Most members of the undergraduate faculty also teach at the graduate level, and 94 percent of the full-time faculty members hold doctoral or other terminal degrees.

Student Government

The traditional student governing body at Fordham has been the United Student Government, composed of undergraduates attending the University.

Admission Requirements

Admission is based on academic performance, class rank (if available), secondary school recommendation, and SAT or ACT scores. Extracurricular activities and essays are also factors in the evaluation process. Religious preference, physical handicap, race, or ethnic origin are not considered. Out-of-state students are encouraged to apply. More than 85 percent of the students accepted for the freshman class ranked in the top quarter of their secondary school class. The middle 50 percent combined SAT score for students entering in fall 2007 was 1200–1330. Recommended are 22 high school units, including 4 in English, 3 in mathematics, 3 in science, 2 in social studies, 2 in foreign language, 2 in history, and 6 electives. For regular admission, the SAT or the ACT should be taken no later than the January preceding entrance. Candidates for early action should complete the examinations by October of their senior year. The University participates in the College Board's Advanced Placement Program. Personal interviews are not required.

Application and Information

Application may be made for either September or January enrollment. The application deadline is January 15 for fall admission. The completed application, the secondary school report, the results of the SAT or ACT, all financial aid forms, and an application fee of $50 (check or money order made payable to Fordham University) should be submitted by this date. Students are notified on or about April 1. Candidates for Early Action should apply by November 1 and receive notification by December 25. Transfer students must apply by December 1 for spring admission or by July 1 for fall admission.

For additional details and application forms, students should contact:

Peter Farrell
Director of Admission
Duane Library
Fordham University
441 East Fordham Road
Bronx, New York 10458
Phone: 800-FORDHAM (367-3426) (toll-free)
E-mail: enroll@fordham.edu
Web site: http://www.fordham.edu

Members of the class of 2007 join Fordham's distinguished alumni family of more than 120,000.

COLLEGE DATA CENTER • NEW YORK

GLOBE INSTITUTE OF TECHNOLOGY

NEW YORK, NEW YORK

The Institute

Globe Institute of Technology is a dynamic and personalized four-year college located in the heart of New York City's financial district. Under new and committed leadership, it has a small-college environment with large-college resources and provides students with a challenging and broad-based education. Globe Institute of Technology offers a flexible curriculum and degree programs at an affordable cost. Students may choose any number of options in bachelor's and associate degrees and certificate programs from more than 120 subject areas, including accounting, health care, finance, information technology, computer programming, and sports, hospitality, legal, medical, or business management.

No matter when or where a student begins course work—summer, fall, or spring; day or evening; on campus or online—Globe Institute of Technology is geared to accommodate flexible course needs and work schedules. Yet the campus has a full range of athletics, activities, and housing, which helps to make it a cohesive college community and allows students to have a complete college life experience. The college is a member of the NJCAA Division I, with athletic teams in basketball, bowling, cross-country, soccer, track and field, men's baseball and football, and women's volleyball. Many other clubs and associations are available, including a newsletter, Chess Club, Dance Club, Ski Club, hiking, Ping-Pong, Chinese Club, Latino Club, and African American Club.

Globe Institute of Technology provides a broad range of services to enhance students' educational experiences and help make them more competitive in the marketplace. These services include career planning and job search, counseling, internship notices, graduate advisement, financial aid assistance, and faculty mentor opportunities.

Location

Globe Institute of Technology is located in the Tribeca neighborhood in the heart of lower Manhattan. The campus location puts students just blocks from Chinatown, Little Italy, City Hall, the Seaport, and Wall Street. Nearby access to the New York subway system links students with the rest of the world right from their own back door. New York City has limitless possibilities for recreation, culture, and nightlife, with 18,000 restaurants, 150 museums, theater on and off Broadway, arenas and stadiums for sporting events, world-renowned shopping, neighborhoods to explore, and gardens and parks. New York City is the main center of world trade and finance, a center for educational excellence, a creative outlet for the arts, and an international hub for advertising, publishing, entertainment, and fashion.

Majors and Degrees

Globe Institute of Technology offers the following degrees: Associate in Applied Science (A.A.S.), with majors in banking and finance with computer applications, business management and computer applications, computer information systems, health-care management, hospitality management, information technology, legal office management, management information systems, and sports science management; Associate in Occupational Studies (A.O.S.), with a major in computer programming and systems design; Bachelor of Business Administration (B.B.A.), with majors in accounting, business management and finance; and Bachelor of Technology (B.Tech.), with a major in computer information systems, including Web development and video game design, computer programming, and information technology. Certificate programs include banking and finance with computer applications, business management with computer applications, computer programming and design, health-care management, hospitality management, information systems, legal office management, microcomputer programming for business, and sports science management.

Academic Programs

The A.A.S. degree at Globe Institute of Technology requires completion of 63 to 66 credits; major course requirements, including sciences, general education courses, math and computer science, social and behavioral sciences, and humanities; and elective courses.

The A.O.S. degree in computer programming and system design requires 63 credits of study, including 28 credits from major core courses.

The B.B.A. and B.Tech. degrees require 123–150 credits, and the certificate program requires 36–51 credits. Every baccalaureate program includes a required senior project, which serves as a capstone to the four years of study, integrating intellectual, critical, analytical, organizational, and oral and written communication skills from across the curriculum.

Academic Facilities

The Globe Institute of Technology library maintains a collection of more than 17,00 books on topics that are pertinent to study at the Institute, including computer science, mathematics, business, finance, psychology, social sciences, health care, and literature. In addition, students find current job information to help them make career choices that parallel their course of study. The library subscribes to dozens of print and online journals and newspaper indexes. The library's computer room gives students free access not only to the Internet but also to Microsoft Excel, PowerPoint, and Word to help them prepare projects and research papers.

The Business & Company Resources Center database supplies global business information, securities data, and company profiles. The Health Reference Center academic database provides information for health research and consumer/patient education information. The National Newspaper Index contains nearly twenty years of the top 5 national newspapers in its database; the Custom Newspapers index provides an additional 150 full-text newspapers. Spanish-speaking students can use the ?Informe! database to access forty full-text Spanish-language magazine articles and reports.

Another unique facility for students is the Globe Institute Gallery. Founded in 2002, the gallery focuses on many art forms to promote students' understanding of contemporary visual works. Its walls display samples of painting, drawing, photography, video and sculpture. Student may use the gallery in their art studies and research, and most specifically, in the contemporary component of art history.

Costs

Full-time tuition at Globe is $5475 per semester. Books and supplies are approximately $800, and dormitory housing is $3500.

Financial Aid

Scholarships based on academic merit, financial need, and athletic ability are available to Globe students. More than 85 percent of students receive some form of need-based financial aid.

Faculty

The student-faculty ratio is about 10:1, so students enjoy many opportunities for mentoring relationships. The diverse faculty at Globe Institute of Technology has members from all over the United States and many hold multiple degrees.

Student Government

Globe's Student Government is composed of leaders elected by the student body. These representatives organize events, coordinate activities, and act as spokespersons for the student body.

Admission Requirements

U.S. citizens must submit a high school diploma or its equivalent, recommendations from their college adviser and a teacher, a transcript, SAT or ACT scores, AP results, an admission application, and an immunization form. International applicants must submit an essay, a notarized copy of a high school diploma and English translation or its equivalent, high school and college transcripts, TOEFL scores, and other supporting data required for obtaining a visa. Every applicant must have an admissions interview and placement testing. Placement testing may be required to measure an incoming student's level of proficiency for basic skills work. Students may be accepted with advanced standing status through credit by examination or through transfer of credits from course work completed at another college.

Applicants for admission are accepted without regard to race, color, religion, gender, sexual orientation, age, national or ethnic origin, handicap, or marital, parental, or veteran status.

Application and Information

Applications for all the Globe Institute of Technology's degree and certification programs may be found on the Institute Web site or may be obtained by contacting the school or visiting the campus in person. An application fee of $50 is required. Upon acceptance, there is a $20 registration fee that may be waived for students who apply and register for classes on the same visit to the campus. For more information, students should contact Globe Institute of Technology.

Office of Admissions
Globe Institute of Technology
291 Broadway
New York, New York 10007
Phone: 212-349-4330
877-EZ-GLOBE (toll-free)
E-mail: admissions@globe.edu
Web site: http://www.globe.edu

HILBERT COLLEGE

HAMBURG, NEW YORK

The College

Since its founding in 1957, Hilbert College has provided challenging academic programs and close personal attention to its students. The College is an independent, Catholic four-year institution that grants degrees on both the baccalaureate and associate levels. There is a strong commitment to the philosophy of a liberal arts education being the cornerstone of any Hilbert graduate's success. In harmony with its Franciscan spirit, the College provides individual counseling and support services for students whose diversified needs are best met in this small-college setting. Hilbert's campus currently consists of the following buildings: Bogel Hall, which is the academic building; the Francis J. and Marie McGrath Library; the Campus Center; five on-campus residence halls, one traditional-style and four apartment-style facilities; a grounds and maintenance building; the Hafner Recreation Center, which hosts several athletic events and where the fitness center is located; and Franciscan Hall, which is the student services and administration building. Hilbert's newest buildings opened in fall 2006. Paczesny Hall and the William E. Swan Auditorium are joined in a building that houses classrooms, faculty offices, and a communications lab and serves the region by hosting a number of cultural events. Hilbert is also the home of the Institute for Law and Justice, a local, regional, and national resource for law enforcement, crime prevention, and community well-being.

Hilbert College has a student body of approximately 1,100 students. There is an on-campus residential population of 160 students. Hilbert College offers students both a traditional-style residence hall and four apartment-style facilities. All students are offered myriad social activities, ranging from academic and student clubs to NCAA Division III athletics. Student government takes an active role in the planning and operation of most campus events. Hilbert also offers a select comprehensive Leadership Development Program as well as an honors program.

The College's Division III athletics program offers intercollegiate competition in men's baseball, basketball, cross-country, golf, soccer, and volleyball. Women's sports include basketball, cross-country, soccer, softball, and volleyball. Hilbert College competes as a member of the Allegheny Mountain Collegiate Conference. In addition, bowling, cheerleading, hockey, and lacrosse all compete as club-level sports.

Location

Hilbert College's nearly 50-acre campus is located in the town of Hamburg in western New York State, on the shore of Lake Erie. The campus is approximately 15 miles south of Buffalo, a city of 350,000 people. Hilbert's proximity to Buffalo makes many cultural and recreational resources easily accessible to its students. Downtown attractions include Kleinhans Music Hall, Studio Arena Theatre, the Albright-Knox Art Gallery, the Museum of Science, and the Buffalo Zoo. The historic Shea's Theatre is also located downtown and is Buffalo's home to many concerts, operas, and Broadway shows. Niagara Falls, one of the nation's greatest natural attractions, is just a 35-minute drive from the campus. Buffalo also provides professional sports in football, hockey, lacrosse, and triple-A baseball. Hamburg also is located a short distance from several cross-country and downhill ski resorts.

Majors and Degrees

Hilbert College offers programs of study leading to a Bachelor of Arts (B.A.) degree in digital media and communication, English, and psychology. The Bachelor of Science (B.S.) degree is offered in accounting, business administration, criminal justice, economic crime investigation, forensic science/crime scene investigation, human services, liberal studies (law and government), paralegal studies, political science, and rehabilitation studies. The College also offers associate degree programs (A.A. and A.A.S.) in accounting, banking, business administration, criminal justice, human services, liberal arts, and paralegal studies.

Academic Programs

The Bachelor of Arts and Bachelor of Science degrees are granted upon completion of 120 credit hours.

The Associate in Arts, the Associate in Applied Science, and the Associate in Science degrees are all granted upon successful completion of 60 credit hours.

Common to all programs is the completion of the Liberal Learning Core Curriculum. All students must fulfill the following graduation requirements: advanced communication skills, intercultural awareness, responsible local and global citizenship, an array of inquiry strategies, advanced research skills, the capacity for integrative learning, and a commitment to lifelong learning. The purpose of the Liberal Learning Core Curriculum is to provide students with a cumulative, holistic liberal arts education to complement and strengthen their professional training. The curriculum is designed to develop habits of critical examination, methods of critical investigation, and ethical perspectives that enable students to make sound judgments and increase their capacity for leading fuller lives. By studying the various liberal arts disciplines, students should achieve a greater awareness of their cultural and social identity while cultivating the intellectual skills and competence that allow them to perform successfully in their chosen careers.

Hilbert has developed a series of transfer articulation agreements with most two-year colleges in New York State. These agreements allow two-year college graduates to move directly into related four-year programs at Hilbert College as full juniors and with no course duplication. In addition, Hilbert is accredited by the Commission on Higher Education of the Middle States Association of Colleges and Schools. Therefore, its credits are readily transferable nationwide to other four-year colleges and universities.

Academic Facilities

Bogel Hall, the original academic building, underwent a massive expansion and renovation in 2007. It contains the Palisano Lecture Hall, faculty offices, computer labs, a hands-on economic crime investigation computer lab, a newly designed forensic science wing with labs, the Academic Services Center, the chapel, and classroom space.

McGrath Library, an expansive building consisting of a two-level core housing the library collection, a seminar wing, and a conference wing, maintains a collection approaching 45,000 volumes, more than 340 periodicals, and a large selection of microforms and audio and video materials. In addition, the McGrath Library supports a law collection for its criminal justice, paralegal studies, and law and government programs on the campus. This collection ranks as one of the largest academic law collections open to the public in western New York State. The library's seminar wing has video-equipped classrooms and a legal research lab. Ample study space is available throughout the library, with both private carrels and group-study tables available for student use.

Paczesny Hall, which opened in 2006, is an academic building that holds faculty offices, high-tech computer labs, smart classrooms, a digital media lab for digital media and communication, and the 435-seat William E. Swan Auditorium.

Costs

For 2007–08, tuition and fees are $16,600, and room and board are $6600. The approximate cost for books and supplies is $700 and for travel and miscellaneous expenses, $1000.

Financial Aid

Ninety-two percent of the members of the current freshman class receive financial aid. Financial aid packages consist of loans, scholarships, grants, and jobs. Most awards are provided on the basis of need, as established by the Free Application for Federal Student Aid (FAFSA), and as funds are available. There are several merit-based scholarships for academic and leadership talents as well as transfer articulation and minority scholarships.

Faculty

Hilbert has a faculty of 91 men and women. Sixty-four percent of the full-time faculty members hold doctoral or terminal degrees. Faculty members play a primary role in the advisement of all students at Hilbert College. The student-faculty ratio is 14:1, with an average class size of 25.

Student Government

The largest student organization on campus is the Student Government Association (SGA). Headed by student-elected officers, this representative organization acts on the behalf of the entire student body. The SGA administers student funds to sponsor on-campus activities and events that range from intimate concerts to larger campuswide festivities. The SGA is composed of two bodies, the association and the student senate. The association comprises elected students who represent the needs of different classes, residents, and commuters. The student senate is a smaller group that consists of student government–elected officers and individual class representatives. The senate is responsible for the disbursement of funds to student-run clubs and organizations.

Admission Requirements

Hilbert College is open to men and women regardless of faith, race, age, physical handicap, or national origin. All students have an equal opportunity to pursue their educational goals through programs available at the College.

The College considers for admission to regular degree study those applicants who have been awarded a high school diploma or a New York State High School Equivalency Diploma.

Application and Information

The closing date for the receipt of applications is September 1. Admission decisions are made on a rolling basis.

For a catalog or an application, students should contact:

Office of Admissions
Hilbert College
5200 South Park Avenue
Hamburg, New York 14075
Phone: 716-649-7900
800-649-8003 (toll-free)
E-mail: admissions@hilbert.edu
Web site: http://www.hilbert.edu

Franciscan Hall, the Student Services Center.

COLLEGE DATA CENTER • NEW YORK

HOBART AND WILLIAM SMITH COLLEGES

GENEVA, NEW YORK

The Colleges

Hobart and William Smith are independent, coordinate liberal arts colleges in Geneva, New York. Hobart College for men was founded in 1822; William Smith College for women, in 1908. The two colleges have the same faculty; men and women attend all classes together and share one campus. Each college, however, awards its own degrees, has its own dean's office, and maintains its own student government and athletic programs. More than forty residential options include both coeducational and single-sex housing, small houses, cooperatives, and theme houses. Last year, two new residence halls were opened, housing an additional 175 students.

Location

Geneva, New York, a city of 15,000 people, is located on the northern shore of Seneca Lake, the largest of the scenic Finger Lakes. Rochester, Syracuse, and Ithaca are all less than an hour's drive. Twenty-seven other colleges and universities are located in the Finger Lakes area.

Majors and Degrees

Hobart and William Smith Colleges offer Bachelor of Arts and Bachelor of Science degrees. Programs leading to provisional certification in elementary, secondary, and special education are offered. Departmental majors include anthropology, art (history and studio), biology, chemistry, classics, comparative literature, computer science, dance, economics, English, French, geoscience, history, international relations, mathematics, modern languages, music, philosophy, physics, political science, psychology, religious studies, sociology, and Spanish. Interdisciplinary and individualized majors have been developed in Africana studies; American studies; architectural studies; arts and education; Asian studies; biochemistry; critical social studies dialogues; environmental studies; European studies; Latin American studies; lesbian, gay, and bisexual studies; media and society; public policy studies; Russian area studies; urban studies; and women's studies.

The Colleges offer dual-degree programs in engineering in cooperation with Columbia University, Dartmouth College, Rensselaer Polytechnic Institute, and the University of Rochester. A 4-1 M.B.A. program is offered in conjunction with Clarkson University and the Rochester Institute of Technology. In addition, the Colleges offer a 3-4 degree in architecture with Washington University in Saint Louis, and a five-year M.A.T. program is offered. The Blackwell Medical Scholars program, in cooperation with SUNY Upstate Medical University College of Medicine at Syracuse, offers students who meet the standards of the program a guaranteed seat in medical school.

Academic Programs

At the heart of a Hobart and William Smith education is the requirement that each student complete a major and a minor or two majors, one of which must be disciplinary and the other interdisciplinary. The first option gives a student depth of knowledge; the latter gives breadth by reaching across traditional disciplines. Each student must also address the Colleges' educational goals and objectives, which represent an understanding of the skills, areas of knowledge, and qualities of mind and character that identify a liberally educated man or woman. Students must demonstrate the following abilities: critical reading and listening; effective speaking and writing; skills for critical thinking and argumentation; experience with scientific inquiry; quantitative reasoning; an appreciation of artistic expression based in experience; an intellectually grounded understanding of race, gender, and class; critical knowledge of the multiplicity of world cultures; and an intellectually grounded foundation for ethical judgment and action.

The academic year is divided into two 14-week semesters. Students normally take four courses each semester.

Off-Campus Programs

There are a number of opportunities for off-campus study. Hobart and William Smith offer terms abroad on six continents, with programs in Australia, Brazil, Central Europe, China, Denmark, the Dominican Republic, Ecuador, England, France, Germany, India, Ireland, Israel, Italy, Japan, Korea, New Zealand, Peru, Russia, Senegal, South Africa, Spain, Switzerland, Taiwan, and Vietnam. Many off-campus programs include internships. Hobart and William Smith participate in cooperative programs in architecture and engineering and in a 4-1 M.B.A. program.

Academic Facilities

Among the major academic and administrative buildings on the campus is the Warren Hunting Smith Library. The library contains more than 380,400 volumes, 2,469 periodicals, and 77,510 microform titles as well as classrooms, study areas, and audiovisual facilities. As a member of the Rochester Regional Resources Library Council, the library provides students with access to holdings in excess of 5 million volumes in other library collections through the interlibrary loan system. Included among the Colleges' academic facilities are three of the newest buildings on campus: Rosenberg Hall, described as "one of the best-designed undergraduate science teaching/learning, research facilities"; Stern Hall, housing the departments of economics, anthropology, sociology, political science, and Asian studies; and the Colleges' newest academic building, the Elliot Studio Arts Center. The Colleges also own a 110-acre research preserve and maintain a 65-foot research vessel that is used for studies on Seneca Lake.

Costs

For 2007–08, tuition was $35,720 and room and board totaled $9250. Total costs of $45,968 included $998 in student fees.

Financial Aid

More than 70 percent of Hobart and William Smith students receive financial aid. Hobart and William Smith Colleges' Scholarships, Federal Pell Grants, Federal Supplemental Educational Opportunity Grants, Federal Perkins Loans, Federal Work-Study Program awards, loans through the Federal Family Education Loan programs, and part-time employment are the most frequent sources of financial aid. New York State residents may be eligible for the New York State Tuition Assistance Program.

To determine financial need, the Colleges rely on an evaluation of the Free Application for Federal Student Aid (FAFSA) and the College Scholarship Service's Financial Aid PROFILE. Both forms should be filed before February 15. Financial aid awards are adjusted annually to meet changing needs.

Faculty

The full-time teaching faculty numbers 178 members, of whom more than 95 percent hold Ph.D. degrees. The student-faculty ratio is 11:1.

Student Government

There are two student governments at Hobart and William Smith. All Hobart students are members of the Hobart Student Government. All William Smith students are members of the William Smith Congress. The students each maintain legislative, judicial, and committee functions that provide for student self-determination at the Colleges. The student governments are also responsible for appropriating student financial resources to support the numerous cultural and social activities on campus.

Admission Requirements

Admission to the Colleges is based on demonstrated potential to undertake college-level work and to contribute to life on campus. The Committee on Admission is most interested in students with comprehensive high school programs. Applicants are expected to have had a minimum of 4 years of English, 3 years of math, 3 years of science (2 laboratory), and at least 2 years of a modern or classical language (3 years preferred). Other units could come from social studies and from additional work in mathematics, science, literature, and languages. One academic recommendation is required. Standardized test scores (SAT or ACT) are optional. Campus tours and personal interviews are available throughout the year and may be arranged by contacting the admissions office.

Application and Information

Application should be made early in the senior year of high school and not later than February 1. A nonrefundable $45 fee must accompany each application. A campus visit, which may include an interview, is strongly recommended. First-year candidates are notified of their application results in late March and must respond by the candidates reply date of May 1. Two early decision plans are offered to students who name Hobart or William Smith as their first-choice college. Under these plans, students must apply before November 15 of their senior year in high school and are notified of the admission decision by December 15; students applying before January 1 are notified by February 1.

For more information, students should contact:

John W. Young
Director of Admissions
Hobart and William Smith Colleges
629 South Main Street
Geneva, New York 14456
Phone: 800-852-2256 (toll-free)
E-mail: admissions@hws.edu
Web site: http://www.hws.edu

Coxe Hall, on the campus of Hobart and William Smith Colleges.

COLLEGE DATA CENTER • NEW YORK

HOFSTRA UNIVERSITY

HEMPSTEAD, NEW YORK

The University

Hofstra University is a dynamic, private University where students find their edge to succeed in 145 undergraduate and 155 graduate programs of study. With an outstanding faculty, advanced technological resources, and state-of-the-art facilities, Hofstra has a growing national reputation. Yet the average class size is just 22, and the student-to-faculty ratio is 14:1. Professors teach small classes that emphasize interaction, critical thinking, and analysis.

Six undergraduate colleges at Hofstra offer students a broad array of academic offerings. Major University divisions are the Hofstra College of Liberal Arts and Sciences, the School of Communication, the Frank G. Zarb School of Business, the School of Education and Allied Human Services, Honors College, and New College.

Hofstra's student body is diverse, with students on the main campus representing fifty-one states and territories and sixty-five countries. Total enrollment at Hofstra is about 12,600, with 7,718 full-time undergraduates.

Residential facilities accommodate more than 4,000 students in thirty-seven modern residence halls. Hofstra is 100 percent program accessible to persons with disabilities. Necessary services are provided for students with physical, learning, and/or psychological disabilities who meet all academic requirements for admission.

Hofstra has a vibrant campus life, with more than 150 clubs and organizations, about thirty local and national fraternities and sororities, eighteen NCAA Division I athletic teams for men and women, and more than 500 cultural events on campus each year.

Recreational and athletic facilities include a 15,000-seat stadium, a 5,000-seat arena, a 1,600-seat field turf soccer stadium, and a new field hockey stadium. Students can also take advantage of a physical fitness center, a swim center with an indoor Olympic-size swimming pool and high-dive area, a softball stadium, a recreation center offering a multipurpose gymnasium, an indoor track, a fully equipped weight room, spacious locker rooms, a cardio area, and mirrored aerobics/martial arts room. Extensive recreational and intramural sports are also available.

Location

A nationally recognized arboretum, Hofstra's distinctive 240-acre campus is situated just 25 miles east of New York City. Students have easy access by train or car to the incredible cultural resources of New York City as well as the corporate headquarters of some of the world's leading companies, where many students find internships that lead to careers. The surrounding Long Island area offers world-class beaches and parks, golf courses, fine dining, and theaters. Long Island's Nassau Coliseum is just minutes from Hofstra's campus and features the NHL's Islanders and numerous concerts and cultural events each year.

Majors and Degrees

The Bachelor of Arts (B.A.) is awarded in Africana studies, American studies, anthropology, art education, art history, Asian studies, audio/radio, audio/video/film, biology, broadcast journalism, chemistry, Chinese, Chinese studies, classics, comparative literature, computer science, computer science and mathematics, creative arts, creative studies, dance, drama, early childhood and childhood education (with dual major in another discipline), early childhood education (with dual major in another discipline), economics, elementary education (with dual major in another discipline), engineering science, English, English education, film studies and production, fine arts, foreign language education (French, German, Italian, Russian, Spanish), French, geography, geology, German, Hebrew, history, humanities, Ibero-American studies, interdisciplinary studies, Italian, Jewish studies, labor studies, Latin, Latin American and Caribbean studies, liberal arts, linguistics, mass media studies, math education, mathematical economics, mathematics, music, natural sciences, philosophy, physics, political science, print journalism, psychology, public relations, religion, Russian, science education, social sciences, social studies, sociology, Spanish, speech communication and rhetorical studies, speech-language-hearing sciences, University Without Walls, video/television, and women's studies.

The Bachelor of Business Administration (B.B.A.) is awarded in accounting, business, business education, entrepreneurship, finance, information technology, international business, legal studies in business, management, and marketing.

The Bachelor of Science (B.S.) is offered in applied physics, athletic training, biochemistry, biology, business economics, chemistry, community health, computer engineering, computer science, computer science and mathematics, electrical engineering, environmental resources, exercise specialist studies, fine arts, forensic science, geology, health education, industrial engineering, mathematical business economics, mathematics, mechanical engineering, music, physician assistant studies, physics, pre–physician assistant studies, school health education, University Without Walls, video/television, video/television and business, and video/television and film.

The Bachelor of Science in Education (B.S.Ed.) is offered with specializations in fine arts, music, and physical education.

The Bachelor of Engineering (B.E.) is offered in engineering science with specializations in biomedical engineering, civil engineering, and environmental engineering.

The Bachelor of Fine Arts (B.F.A.) is awarded in theater arts with specializations in performance and production.

Academic Programs

Requirements for graduation vary among schools and majors. A liberal arts core curriculum is an integral part of all areas of concentration. The University calendar is organized on a traditional semester system, including one January session and three summer sessions. Some divisions offer part-time programs during the day and evening and on weekends.

Hofstra offers many innovative programs designed to meet the needs of its diverse student body. These include Honors College, New College, Legal Education Accelerated Program, and First Year Connections.

Honors College provides a rich academic and social experience for students who show both the potential and the desire to excel. Honors students can elect to study in any of the University's 145 undergraduate programs; these students are involved in all fields of advanced study, including premedicine, prelaw, engineering, business, communication and media arts, humanities, and social sciences.

New College offers interdisciplinary study and innovative block scheduling. The Legal Education Accelerated Program allows students to earn both a B.A. and a J.D. in just six years. First Year Connections, an integrated academic and social program, helps first-year students connect to all of the resources and opportunities of the University.

Off-Campus Programs

Hofstra extends learning beyond the classroom through an active internship program and many study-abroad opportunities. The internship program takes advantage of the proximity of New York City, allowing students to gain on-the-job experience in areas such as finance, business, media, advertising, and entertainment.

Hofstra sponsors study-abroad programs in such places in Europe as Athens, London, France, Ireland, Spain, Prague, and Venice and Sorrento, Italy; as well as in Japan, Jamaica, Ecuador, and Mexico. Previous locales have included Australia, Austria, Belgium, China, Germany, the Netherlands, Russia, Singapore, South Korea, Taiwan, Ukraine, and the West Indies. Students wishing to pursue such study should contact the program director or the Office of International Off-Campus Education. Other overseas courses are organized by faculty members as part of credit-bearing courses. Recent courses have been held in Greece, Mexico, Egypt, and China.

Academic Facilities

Hofstra's libraries contain more than 1.4 million print volumes and provide 24/7 electronic access to more than 50,000 journals and electronic books. There are special units for periodicals, reserve books, documents, curriculum materials, special collections, and microfilm.

Hofstra University's Student Computing Services provides students with a multitude of resources and learning opportunities. The Hofstra computer network provides individual accounts for all students for Internet, e-mail, and about 200 networked software programs. Almost 1,600 PC, Macintosh, and UNIX workstations are available to students in the various labs and classrooms on campus. The labs are staffed, and one computer lab is open 24 hours a day, seven days a week. All campus workstations have high-speed Internet access, and numerous wireless hotspots provide Internet access to students with wireless capability. All resident students are provided with Internet and e-mail access from their residence hall rooms.

Other facilities include an art gallery, an arboretum, an accredited museum, bird sanctuary, writing center, career center, cultural center, language lab, technology lab, six theaters, dance studios and performing arts classrooms, and a rooftop observatory with powerful telescopes. The state-of-the-art facilities in Hofstra's School of Communication house a 24-hour student-operated radio station, one of the largest noncommercial television broadcast facilities in the Northeast; audio production studios; a film/video screening room; film editing rooms; and a cutting-edge converged newsroom and multimedia classroom. C.V. Starr Hall, home to the Zarb School of Business, features one of the most advanced academic trading rooms in the nation, complete with Bloomberg terminals and Internet access at every student seat. The innovative School of Education and Allied Health Services building, Hagedorn Hall, is a completely wireless environment featuring assessment centers for child observation and mock counseling and interactive Smart Boards in many classrooms.

Costs

The annual cost of tuition and fees at Hofstra University for 2007–08 for a full-time undergraduate student was $26,730. The average housing and meal plan was $9616. Books and supplies cost approximately $1000; personal expenses and transportation generally amount to $2640. For the full tuition and fees schedule, students should visit http://www.hofstra.edu/tuition.

Financial Aid

To help students achieve their education goals, Hofstra University offers several financial aid options. Hofstra awarded more than $55 million in financial assistance in 2007–08, and 81 percent of all Hofstra students received some type of financial aid. For more detailed information, students should visit http://www.hofstra.edu/FinancialAid.

Faculty

Hofstra has 1,193 faculty members, including 544 full-time members; 90 percent of the full-time faculty members hold the highest degree in their fields. The faculty members are dedicated to excellence in teaching, scholarship, and research, and many have been recognized with the nation's highest academic honors, including membership in the American Academy of Arts and Sciences, Fulbright and Guggenheim Fellowships, Emmy Awards, and a Pulitzer Prize. The student-faculty ratio is 14:1. The average class size is 22. All classes are taught by faculty members who make it a point to be accessible to their students outside the classroom; no courses are taught by graduate assistants.

Student Government

The chief instrument of government is the Student Government Association, a student-run governing body that supervises and coordinates all student activities and serves as a liaison with the faculty and administration. The Student Government Association sends representatives to the committees of the University Senate. The Judiciary Panel has responsibility for promoting justice in the conduct of student affairs.

Admission Requirements

Hofstra is a competitive institution that seeks to enroll students who demonstrate academic ability, intellectual curiosity, and the motivation to be successful and to be a contributing member of the campus community. Careful consideration is given to a student's high school record, types of courses taken, SAT or ACT scores, letters of recommendation, extracurricular involvement, and the personal essay. Typical applicants rank in the top 25 percent of their graduating class and present 16 academic units, including 4 of English, 3 of history and social studies, 2 of foreign language, 3 of mathematics, and 3 of science. Prospective engineering majors need at least 4 years of mathematics, 1 year of chemistry, and 1 year of physics. Campus visits are strongly recommended. Hofstra accepts applications from freshmen, transfers, and international students.

The University offers an early action plan for students whose first choice is Hofstra. The completed application must be received either by November 15 or by December 15. Students applying for regular decision are considered on a rolling basis.

Freshman applicants must submit an application, a $50 application fee, their high school transcript, SAT or ACT scores, a personal essay and a letter of recommendation. Hofstra accepts applications via mail or online and participates in the Common Application; the online application fee is $30.

Application and Information

Hofstra University
100 Hofstra University
Hempstead, New York 11549-1000
Phone: 516-463-6700
800-HOFSTRA Ext. 618 (toll-free)
Fax: 516-463-5100
Web site: http://www.hofstra.edu

HUNTER COLLEGE
OF THE CITY UNIVERSITY OF NEW YORK

NEW YORK, NEW YORK

The College

In 1870, Thomas Hunter founded Hunter College to train young women to become school teachers. Their contributions helped make New York City's schools among the most highly regarded public school systems in the world. Today, Hunter College is a coeducational liberal arts college serving 21,000 undergraduate and graduate students of all racial, ethnic, and cultural backgrounds. Wide offerings in the liberal arts and sciences and three professional schools—education, health sciences, and social work—meet the highest academic standards. A distinguished faculty encourages intellectual and personal growth in each student.

Location

Hunter students study in the heart of Manhattan. Many of the world's finest museums, libraries, concert halls, cultural centers, and theaters are just a quick walk away.

Majors and Degrees

Hunter College offers bachelor's and master's degrees in the arts and sciences, education, health professions, nursing, and social work, along with several combined (B.A./M.A. or B.A./M.S.) degrees. The following programs of study are available: accounting, Africana and Puerto Rican/Latino studies, anthropology, archaeology, art history, biological sciences, chemistry, Chinese language and literature, classical studies, community health education, comparative literature, computer science, dance, economics, elementary education, environmental studies, English, English language arts, film, French, geography, German, Greek, Hebrew, history, honors curriculum, Italian, Jewish social studies, Latin, Latin American and Caribbean Studies, Latin and Greek, mathematics, media studies, medical laboratory sciences, music, nursing, nutrition and food science, philosophy, physics, political science, psychology, religion, Romance languages, Russian, secondary education, sociology, Spanish, statistics, studio art, theater, urban studies, and women's studies. Secondary education programs are for grades 7–12 unless otherwise noted and include biology, chemistry, Chinese, dance (pre-K–12), English, French, German, Hebrew, Italian, mathematics, music (pre-K–12, accelerated B.A./M.A. program only), physics, Russian, social studies, and Spanish.

Special programs in anthropology, biological sciences/environmental and occupational health sciences, biopharmacology, biotechnology, economics, English, history, mathematics, music, physics, sociology/social research, and statistics and applied mathematics lead to the combined bachelor's/master's degree, enabling highly qualified students to earn both degrees more quickly.

Hunter College also provides preprofessional advisement and preparation for advanced study in chiropractic, dentistry, engineering, law, medicine, optometry, osteopathy, pharmacy, podiatry, and veterinary medicine.

Academic Programs

Hunter instills a rich and informed sense of the possibilities of humanity in its students and expects them to carry their liberal arts education forward in their careers, their public responsibilities, and their personal lives.

The College trains its students in the sciences, the humanities, and a number of professional fields. As they strive to achieve their career goals, students are expected to perceive their chosen fields of study as only a part of a wider realm of knowledge. Undergraduate programs of study at Hunter consist of five parts, totaling 120 credits: a general education requirement, a pluralism and diversity requirement, a concentration of in-depth study (major), elective courses, and a minor.

Undergraduate students at Hunter who exhibit intellectual curiosity and exceptional ability may apply to the Thomas Hunter Scholars Program, an interdisciplinary program that individualizes study according to needs and interests and grants a Bachelor of Arts degree.

Students may earn sophomore standing (up to 30 credits) if they score well on the College-Level Examination Program (CLEP) subject tests, the Advanced Placement examinations of the College Board, and the Regents College Examination (RCE) Program of New York State.

Off-Campus Programs

Hunter College taps Manhattan to allow innumerable internships. Hosts have included Atlantic Records, CNN, the Council on Foreign Relations, DreamWorks SKG, Madison Square Garden, Metropolitan Museum of Art, New York City Council, Simon & Schuster, and many more. Interns perform curatorial and administrative work in museums, research and production work on TV news shows and newspapers, design work in commercial graphics, and booking, managing, and technical work in theaters.

Academic Facilities

The College is made up of five sites in Manhattan. The largest, a modern complex of buildings connected by skywalks at 68th Street and Lexington Avenue, sits above a convenient subway stop. This campus offers programs in the arts and sciences and in teacher education.

Downtown, the Brookdale Campus on East 25th Street houses the Division of the Schools of the Health Professions, which includes the Hunter-Bellevue School of Nursing, one of the nation's largest nursing programs, and the School of Health Sciences.

Uptown on East 79th Street is the Hunter College School of Social Work, which was recently listed among the top ten schools of its kind in the nation by *U.S. News & World Report*.

On Manhattan's West Side, Hunter's Studio Art Building houses an 8,000-square-foot gallery and provides M.F.A. students with individual studios that are among the best in the city.

At East 94th Street, the Campus Schools house an elementary school and a high school for the intellectually gifted that are renowned, as is the College itself, for a long tradition of academic excellence.

All locations are minutes from Grand Central Terminal, Penn Station, and the New York/New Jersey Port Authority Bus Terminal, making Hunter easily accessible from Connecticut, Westchester, New Jersey, and Long Island.

The collections of the Hunter College libraries are housed in the Jacqueline Grennan Wexler Library and the Art Slide Library (located at the main campus), as well as at the branch libraries at the Brookdale Campus and the School of Social Work. The libraries hold 750,000 volumes, 2,300 periodicals, a nonprint collection of more than 1 million microforms, and 250,000 art slides in addition to records, tapes, scores, music CDs, and videos. Recently, Hunter installed new computer, multimedia, and Internet labs and its first CD-ROM network. The CD-ROM network provides access to indexes, abstracts, and complete texts and multimedia resources, and Internet labs make the World Wide Web accessible.

Costs

Hunter College is affordable. In 2007–08, New York State residents enrolled as full-time, matriculated students paid $2000 per semester ($170 per credit part-time). Nonresidents enrolled as full-time, matriculated students paid $360 per credit. All students paid a Student Activity Fee ($84.50 per semester for full-time students and $54.45 per semester for part-time students) and a $15-per-semester Consolidated Fee.

Financial Aid

Hunter College participates in all state and federal financial aid programs. Financial aid is available to matriculated students in the form of grants, loans, and work-study. Grants provide funds that do not have to be repaid. Loans must be repaid in regular installments over a prescribed period of time. Work-study consists of part-time employment, either on campus or in an outside agency. More information is available from the Office of Financial Aid at 212-772-4820.

Entering freshmen whose high school records indicate a high level of academic achievement may apply to the Macaulay Honors College at Hunter College. This prestigious program offers a generous financial aid package, including a full academic scholarship, as well as extensive benefits, including a free room at the Hunter College Residence Hall. In addition, Hunter College offers a wide array of other scholarships.

Faculty

Thanks to its location in the heart of New York City, Hunter College attracts a special kind of faculty member. Some are well-known scholars and researchers in their fields, such as biologists involved in advanced research on genetic structure. Others are professionals with active careers in the city, including well-known painters, sculptors, architects, and urban design experts. Hunter's faculty also includes environmental health scientists who work on occupational health and safety issues, nursing administrators who work in the country's leading hospitals, and film directors, theater critics, and musicians who are engaged in New York City's cultural milieu. Many members of the faculty are nationally renowned; they maintain Hunter's reputation for academic excellence through outstanding teaching and cutting-edge publications and by securing millions of dollars in annual grants for research.

Student Government

Several governing assemblies involve students in Hunter's governance. The College Senate, the legislative body of the College, includes faculty members, students, and administrators. Two Student Governments (undergraduate and graduate) also play essential roles in the life of the College. Students with voting power sit on faculty and administrative committees.

Admission Requirements

Candidates for freshman admission are considered based on the overall strength of their academic preparation, cumulative high school averages, and SAT or ACT scores. The College recommends 4 years of English, 4 years of social studies, 3 years of mathematics, 2 years of a foreign language, 2 years of laboratory sciences, and 1 year of performing or visual arts as the minimum academic preparation for success in college.

Transfer applicants with fewer than 24 credits must have a cumulative grade point average (GPA) of at least 2.3 and must meet the freshman criteria previously outlined. Those with 14 to 23.9 credits and a GPA of at least 2.5 as well as those with 24 or more credits and a GPA of at least 2.3 are eligible, regardless of high school average. For more information, applicants should visit Hunter College's Web site.

Application and Information

Applicants are considered for fall (September) and spring (February) admission. Applications for the fall must be filed no later than October 1 and for spring, no later than March 1. Applications can be filed from the CUNY Web site at http://www.cuny.edu. Requests for further information should be sent to:

Welcome Center
Hunter College
695 Park Avenue, Room 100N
New York, New York 10065
Phone: 212-772-4490
Fax: 212-650-3336
E-mail: WelcomeCenter@hunter.cuny.edu
Web site: http://www.hunter.cuny.edu

Students at Hunter College enjoy the convenience of skywalks that connect all four buildings at the 68th Street campus. Hunter's Upper East Side location provides easy access to some of New York's finest offerings; Central Park and the Metropolitan Museum of Art are just blocks away.

IONA COLLEGE

NEW ROCHELLE, NEW YORK

The College

Iona College is a four-year, coed, comprehensive college in the suburbs of New York City. It is a medium-sized college with an average class size of 15 students. Iona offers more than forty majors. The most popular undergraduate majors are business, mass communication, education, biology, and criminal justice. Iona is a Catholic college, founded by the Congregation of Christian Brothers, where learning ethical decisions and a commitment of service to others are part of the mission.

Iona's overall enrollment is about 4,500 students, of whom 3,000 are traditional undergraduate students. The student body is talented and diverse, with students coming from thirty-five states and fifty-four countries. Thirty-three percent of the students are members of minority groups, and contribute to a college environment that values diversity.

Students are active and involved on campus. More than sixty clubs and activities are available for student participation, including student government, nine fraternities and sororities, intramural sports, community service organizations, an award-winning newspaper, radio and television stations, the yearbook, theater groups, a pipe band, ethnic-affinity groups, various honor societies, music groups, and many other possibilities.

Iona offers twenty-one NCAA Division I sports. Men's sports include baseball, basketball, cross-country, football, rowing, soccer, swimming and diving, track (indoor and outdoor), and water polo. Women's sports include basketball, cross-country, lacrosse, rowing, soccer, softball, swimming and diving, track (indoor and outdoor), and water polo.

The Office of Student Development operates two student clubs: the Gael Club, a nightclub; and the Iona coffeehouse in the new LaPenta Student Union. Student Development also organizes many activities for students to participate in each week. The activities include trips to New York City for theater, sports, and museums; movie nights; parties and dances; karaoke nights; wellness workshops; and other activities.

Iona offers five different residence facilities, and 67 percent of freshmen live on campus. The College's board plan includes the normal campus dining hall, but also can be used at nine local restaurants.

Location

Iona's campus is located in New Rochelle, New York, one of the oldest cities in the U.S. Founded in 1654, New Rochelle is a city of 70,000 on the shore of the Long Island Sound. It is a suburban community that borders New York City. Public transportation allows students to easily travel to Manhattan via commuter train in less than 30 minutes.

Majors and Degrees

Iona College offers the Bachelor of Arts, Bachelor of Science, and Bachelor of Business Administration degrees in majors including accounting, biochemistry, biology (general, predental, pre–physical therapy, preprofessional, and premedicine), business administration, chemistry, computer science, criminal justice, economics, education (early childhood, childhood, and adolescence), English, environmental science, finance, foreign languages (French, Italian, and Spanish), health professions preparation, history, information systems, interdisciplinary science, international business, international studies, management, marketing, mass communication (advertising, journalism, public relations, and television and video), mathematics, mathematics–applied, medical technology, philosophy, physical therapy (joint B.S./M.S. program with New York Medical College), physics, political science, psychology, religious studies, social work, sociology, speech communication studies (humanistic communication and speech arts), and speech/language pathology and audiology. Five-year combined bachelor's and master's degree programs are offered in computer science, English, history, and psychology.

There are also minors available in accounting, biology, business, chemistry, classical humanities, computer science, criminal justice, economics, English, film studies, finance, fine arts, French, German, gerontology, history, information systems, international business, Italian, management, marketing, mass communication, mathematics, peace and justice studies, philosophy, physics, political science, psychology, religious studies, sociology, Spanish, speech communication, women's studies, and writing. A number of programs offer a business minor in combination with a major or concentration.

Academic Programs

The College offers the B.A., B.S., and B.B.A. degrees to undergraduate students. The B.A. and B.S. degrees require a total of 120 credits for completion; for B.B.A. degrees, a total of 126 credits are required. As a general rule, the core curriculum fills one third of the student's credit total; a major fills the second third; and elective courses, a minor, or a second major fill the final third. During the fall and spring semesters, most students take five 3-credit courses. Classes are also offered during an intensive winter session and during two summer sessions.

An honors program is available for top students who want additional enhancement to their academic program. Special courses, seminars, mentoring, advising, and off-campus opportunities are part of the honors students' curriculum.

Off-Campus Programs

Iona College encourages students to broaden their educational experience through study and travel abroad. Iona sponsors summer, semester, and intersession programs in Australia, England, France, Ireland, Italy, and Spain. The College also offers a wide range of internships in most majors. In recent years, students have held internships at some of the best-known corporate names in New York City and the surrounding area.

Academic Facilities

During the past few years, every major facility on campus has been renovated. Iona College has two new state-of-the-art facilities, the Robert V. LaPenta Student Union and the Hynes Athletics Center. Future projects include an expansion of the Ryan Library that will enhance its technological infrastructure while increasing study and research space.

The Robert V. LaPenta Student Union is a 41,000 square foot Georgian-brick facility that features a bookstore, commons/lounge areas, a food court, a bistro, a state-of-the-art media center, and offices for student services and campus organizations. Situated centrally on campus, the Robert V. LaPenta Student Union will provide Iona students expanded and enhanced dining and social opportunities and will broaden their perspectives through increased participation in clubs and organizations.

The Hynes Athletics Center includes a multipurpose arena, an Olympic-size swimming pool, a Nautilus center, training facilities, and coaching offices. Featuring a state-of-the-art cardiovascular center, three multipurpose courts, a rowing tank, and an aerobics/dance studio, the Hynes Center will enable Iona's nonathletes to participate in an intramural program that includes many various sports. Classes in Pilates, yoga, salsa dancing, and more are also be offered by qualified instructors at a very reasonable cost.

Another addition to Iona's campus is the new Iona College Arts Center, which provides space for the study of art, dance, and theater and includes the Brother Kenneth Chapman Gallery. Some of the major academic buildings, including John G. Hagan Hall, Myles B. Amend Hall, and Doorley Hall, have been renovated recently to include seminar rooms and computer presentation facilities. Cornelia Hall, home of Iona's science programs, was completely renovated in 2000 and features state-of-the-art equipment for the study of biology and chemistry. Mazzella Field is centrally located on Iona's campus and has an artificial turf surface for football, lacrosse, soccer, and other intercollegiate and intramural sports. The Murphy Science and Technology Center is a modern facility complete with communication and computer labs, classrooms, and a technological library. Overall, the College's computer labs have more than 800 computer stations available for student use.

The two campus libraries, Ryan Library and the Helen T. Arrigoni Library/Technology Center, house extensive collections and offer computer access to collections worldwide. The on-site collections, including more than 261,000 volumes, 687 periodical titles, audiovisual materials, and microforms, have been developed to support Iona's curriculum and special interests. Students can access these resources from on and off campus, as well as from the libraries' eighty networked public computers and laptops.

In 2001, Iona launched one of the nation's first wireless Internet campuses. Students benefit from 24-hour access to the College's network, extensive library databases, and the Internet. Iona is committed to providing students an environment constantly adapting to the innovations of our changing world.

Costs

For the 2007–08 academic year, tuition and fees are $24,724; room and board costs are $10,500.

Financial Aid

Financial aid is critical to a student's decision to attend any college, and Iona College is no exception. Iona uses a system of academic scholarships in combination with need-based financial aid to help students enroll. For the 2006–07 academic year, 89 percent of Iona students received aid, with the average financial aid award near $18,371. To apply for financial aid, students should file the Free Application for Federal Student Aid (FAFSA) and the Iona College Financial Aid Application forms by February 15.

Faculty

Iona College has approximately 170 full-time and 80 part-time faculty members; 92 percent possess the terminal degree in their field. Faculty members conduct research and write books and articles, but their primary responsibility is teaching undergraduate students. All classes are taught by faculty members—there are no teaching assistants.

The student-faculty ratio is 15:1. Faculty members are readily available to meet for individual conferences. In addition, because of the College's proximity to New York City, many faculty members include regular trips to Manhattan as part of their classes and invite guest speakers to lecture about special topics.

Student Government

The Student Government Association (SGA) is a service organization that coordinates, supervises, and promotes student activities. The office of student activities hosts hundreds of on- and off-campus events throughout the year, and students participate in more than sixty student-run organizations.

Admission Requirements

Admission decisions at Iona are based on a wide range of criteria. Most important is an applicant's academic record, including the level of curriculum taken and grades earned. Also considered are SAT or ACT scores, grade trends, a writing sample, activities, and recommendations.

For the class entering in September 2007, the average grade point average was 3.4 (89 percent), and the middle 50 percent on the SAT ranged from 1050 to 1250. About 6,000 applications were submitted for 850 spaces, and about 60 percent of the applicants were offered admission.

Application and Information

The Office of Admissions at Iona College works with each applicant on an individual basis. While the outcome of the admission decision may not be what every applicant hopes, Iona tries to ensure that each applicant is treated with courtesy and dignity. In order to considered for admission, Iona requires students to submit an application (paper or online), a $50 application fee, an official transcript, SAT or ACT scores, a counselor recommendation, and an essay. Transfer students must also submit official transcripts from all colleges and universities previously attended.

The deadline for submitting applications for regular admission is February 15; for early action, it is December 1. Decisions are mailed by April 1 for regular admission and on December 21 for early action. Deposits for all accepted students are due on May 1.

Campus visits are available on most weekdays that school is in session and on selected Saturdays; appointments are recommended. A visit can be scheduled by calling the Campus Visit Center at 914-633-2622 or by e-mail at eenglish@iona.edu.

For more information, students should contact:

Office of Admissions
Iona College
715 North Avenue
New Rochelle, New York 10801
Phone: 914-633-2502
800-231-IONA (toll-free)
Fax: 914-637-2778
E-mail: admissions@iona.edu
Web site: http://www.iona.edu

ITHACA COLLEGE
ITHACA, NEW YORK

The College

Coeducational and nonsectarian since its founding in 1892, Ithaca College enrolls approximately 6,400 students. The College community is a diverse one; virtually every state is represented in the student population, as are sixty-one other countries. Students come to Ithaca College to get active, hands-on learning that brings together the best of liberal arts and professional studies. Academic programs are offered in five schools—the School of Humanities and Sciences (2,350 students), School of Business (600 students), Roy H. Park School of Communications (1,250 students), School of Health Sciences and Human Performance (1,200 students), and School of Music (500 students)—and the Division of Interdisciplinary and International Studies (100 students). There are approximately 400 graduate students.

Freshmen and most upperclassmen (with some exceptions) are expected to live on campus. There are fifty-two residence halls, which range from garden apartments to fourteen-story towers. Extracurricular life abounds at Ithaca. There are approximately 150 student organizations, a strong Division III intercollegiate athletic program (twenty-five teams), extensive intramural and club sports programs, and dramatic and musical ensembles. A wide range of services is available, beginning with summer orientation for new students and including career planning and placement assistance, a counseling center, and a health center that is staffed by 4 physicians as well as numerous physician assistants, nurses, and lab technologists.

According to College surveys completed in the past three years, 97 percent of first-year graduates are employed and/or are full-time graduate students.

Location

Ithaca College is in Ithaca, New York. More than 90,000 people live in the city and surrounding county, more than a quarter of whom are Ithaca College or Cornell University students. The city combines the cultural and commercial features of a diverse, multicultural, mostly youthful population with the spectacular scenery of central New York's Finger Lakes.

Majors and Degrees

Ithaca awards the Bachelor of Arts, Bachelor of Fine Arts, Bachelor of Music, Bachelor of Science, and the Master of Arts in Teaching, Master of Business Administration, Master of Music, Master of Science, and Doctor of Physical Therapy degrees. More than 100 academic programs are offered through its five schools and Division of Interdisciplinary and International Studies.

The School of Business, accredited by AACSB International—The Association to Advance Collegiate Schools of Business, offers a B.S. in business administration, with concentrations in corporate accounting, finance, international business, management, and marketing as well as a B.S./M.B.A. degree in accounting for those pursuing CPA licensure. In addition, the School of Business offers a one-year M.B.A. program.

The Roy H. Park School of Communications offers a B.A. in journalism. Also offered are a B.S. in cinema and photography; communication management and design; integrated marketing communications; and television-radio and a B.F.A. in film, photography, and visual arts.

Through the School of Health Sciences and Human Performance, students can earn a B.A. in health policy studies or sport studies or a B.S. in athletic training, clinical exercise science, community health education, exercise science, health-care management, health education,* health and physical education,* health sciences, outdoor adventure leadership, physical education,* recreation management, speech-language pathology, sport management, sport media, and therapeutic recreation. They may also enroll in the six-year B.S./D.P.T. clinical health studies/physical therapy program or five-year occupational science/occupational therapy program.

The School of Humanities and Sciences offers a B.A. in anthropology, art, art history, biology,* chemistry,* computer science, drama, economics, English,* environmental science, environmental studies, French,* German area studies,* history, Italian studies, mathematics,* mathematics–computer science,* mathematics-economics, mathematics-physics, philosophy, philosophy-religion, physics,* planned studies, politics, psychology, social studies,* sociology, Spanish,* speech communication, and writing; the B.S. is offered in applied economics, applied psychology, biology, chemistry,* computer information systems, computer science, mathematics–computer science,* planned studies, and theater arts management; a B.F.A. is offered in acting, art, musical theater, and theatrical production arts.

Students in the School of Music can earn a B.A. in music and a B.M. in composition, jazz studies, music education, music in combination with an outside field, performance, performance/music education,* sound recording technology, and theory.

Special programs offered by Ithaca include the Exploratory Program and HSHP Preprofessional Program for undecided majors; accelerated programs with the Pennsylvania College of Optometry and the State University of New York College of Optometry; and 3-2 programs in chemistry-engineering and in physics-engineering, offered in cooperation with Cornell University, Rensselaer Polytechnic Institute, and other schools.

The Division of Interdisciplinary and International Studies offers a B.A. in aging studies, culture and communication, and legal studies; a B.S. is also offered in aging studies.

The asterisk (*) indicates areas that offer programs that lead to initial New York State teacher certification. Students may also pursue a Master of Arts in Teaching (M.A.T.) in adolescence education program through the Department of Education.

Academic Programs

Undergraduate programs of study address two primary needs: the need for rigorous academic preparation in highly specialized professional fields and the need for students to prepare for the complex demands of society by acquiring an intellectual breadth that extends beyond their chosen profession. Each degree offered requires a minimum of 120 credit hours and a specified number of liberal arts credits. Minors, academic concentrations, and numerous teacher certification programs are available. Exceptionally qualified applicants to the School of Humanities and Sciences will be invited to apply to the honors program, an intensive four-year program of interdisciplinary seminars. The Writing Center offers assistance to students at any stage of the writing process, and Information Technology Services aids students in the use of personal and College computers. The Center for the Study of Culture, Race, and Ethnicity serves as a multidisciplinary clearinghouse for studying the experiences of groups that traditionally have been marginalized, underrepresented, or misrepresented in the United States as well as in college curricula. The Gerontology Institute provides opportunities for students to work with the elderly in a variety of community settings. The Department of Education coordinates the courses of study leading to a teaching certificate.

ROTC programs are offered in conjunction with Cornell University.

The academic year comprises two 15-week semesters, from late August to mid-December and from mid-January to mid-May.

Off-Campus Programs

The College maintains a center in London, England, and offers courses in the business, communications, liberal arts, music, and theater arts. Study-abroad options include programs in Australia, the Czech Republic, Japan, Singapore, Spain, and Sweden or in about fifty other countries through affiliate arrangements with the Center for Cross-Cultural Study, the Institute for the International Education of Students, and the Institute for American Universities. Selected juniors and seniors in communications may study at the Ithaca College James B. Pendleton Center in Los Angeles, which offers outstanding internship opportunities. Students from all disciplines may participate in an internship semester in Washington, D.C.

Academic Facilities

All academic facilities have been built since 1960; the most recent buildings include a 69,000-square-foot addition to the music building and a fitness center, and construction has begun on a highly energy- and resource-efficient building for the School of Business. The Roy H. Park School of Communications contains television and radio studios, a film and photography complex, and a variety of digital laboratories. The College's two science buildings house state-of-the-art physics, biology, chemistry, mathematics, computer, and psychology laboratories. Additional campus facilities include theaters, auditoriums, concert halls, an observatory, and research laboratories. Computing facilities include hundreds of computers in labs and classrooms across campus, allowing easy access to e-mail and the Internet. The library contains approximately 400,000 materials in various formats in addition to access to a vast array of scholarly journals and databases via the Web.

Costs

For 2007–08, tuition is $28,670, room is $5604, board is $5124, and the optional health and accident insurance fee is $400.

Financial Aid

Financial aid totaling more than $125 million from all sources is extended to approximately 85 percent of Ithaca students. To apply for financial aid, students should check the proper space on the Common Application, and if seeking federal aid, complete the Free Application for Federal Student Aid (FAFSA) online by February 1. All accepted applicants are considered for merit aid in recognition of their academic and personal achievement. Federal aid programs include Stafford, Perkins, and PLUS loans; work-study funds; Pell grants; and Supplemental Educational Opportunity Grants.

Faculty

There are 460 full-time and 210 part-time faculty members; the overall student-faculty ratio is 11:1. More than 90 percent of the full-time faculty members have a Ph.D. or a terminal degree in their field. While the faculty is principally devoted to teaching at all levels, they also regularly invite undergraduate students to join them in their research and publishing projects. Faculty members serve as academic advisers to students and are active in the community.

Student Government

The student government is composed of the student senate, all-College committee representatives, executive officers and assistants, and the student government executive board. Students administer a budget of nearly $400,000. The student senate includes representatives from each residence hall and school as well as students who live off campus. There is a student member of the Ithaca College Board of Trustees, and the student government appoints representatives to several standing all-College committees, including the Academic Policies Committee. The College encourages and expects student participation in governance.

Admission Requirements

Admission is based on the high school record, personal recommendations, SAT or ACT scores, and, for some programs, auditions or portfolios. Campus visits and personal appointments are recommended but not required. Admission is selective and competitive; individual talents and circumstances are always given serious consideration. Transfer students must also submit official transcripts from each college or university they have attended. Applicants whose native language is not English must take the Test of English as a Foreign Language. Typically, there are about 12,500 applicants for 1,550 places in the freshman class.

Application and Information

For fall enrollment, prospective students should apply early in their senior year and no later than February 1; applicants are notified of a decision on a rolling basis no later than April 15 and must confirm their enrollment by May 1. Freshman applicants seeking institutional and federal aid should file the FAFSA by February 1 with the federal processor.

Students who want to transfer into Ithaca College should apply by March 1 for fall admission and by November 1 for spring admission. Applicants seeking institutional and federal financial aid should file the FAFSA by February 1.

Ithaca accepts the Common Application. An overview of the application process, a list of special requirements, and Ithaca's Common Application supplement form may be found online at http://www.ithaca.edu/admission/apply.php. For additional information and application forms, students should contact:

Gerard Turbide
Director of Admission
Office of Admission
Ithaca College
100 Job Hall
Ithaca, New York 14850-7020
Phone: 607-274-3124
800-429-4274 (toll-free)
Fax: 607-274-1900
E-mail: admission@ithaca.edu
Web site: http://www.ithaca.edu/admission

The Ithaca College campus.

JOHN JAY COLLEGE OF CRIMINAL JUSTICE OF THE CITY UNIVERSITY OF NEW YORK

NEW YORK, NEW YORK

The College

An international leader in educating for justice, John Jay offers a rich liberal arts and professional studies curriculum to a diverse student body in a vibrant urban setting. In teaching and research, the College defines justice both narrowly, with an eye to the needs of criminal justice and public service agencies, and broadly and humanistically, in terms of enduring questions about fairness, equality, and the rule of law. John Jay College is accredited by the Middle States Association of Colleges and Schools.

John Jay enrolls students from more than 130 nations around the world. Although approximately 20 percent of the College's 14,000 students are members of the uniformed criminal justice and fire service agencies, the majority of John Jay students are civilian preprofessionals, many of whom plan to pursue careers in public service.

Most John Jay students are residents of New York City or surrounding communities in New York, New Jersey, and Connecticut. All students commute to their classes directly from their homes or from their places of employment.

John Jay College of Criminal Justice offers master's degrees in six fields of study: criminal justice, forensic computing, forensic psychology, forensic science, protection management, and public administration, including the Public Administration–Inspector General Program. These master's programs complement a baccalaureate program as well as enhance the academic and professional body of knowledge in the criminal justice field and the public service field. Each program is intended to meet the special needs of precareer, in-career, and second-career students.

The doctoral programs in criminal justice and forensic psychology are considered premier Ph.D. programs in the nation. They are awarded through the Graduate School and University Center of the City University of New York and John Jay College of Criminal Justice.

Location

John Jay College occupies four buildings on the west side of Manhattan. The main location is Haaren Hall, at 899 Tenth Avenue. This building houses classrooms, a state-of-the-art theater, the country's leading criminal justice library, administrative offices, and an extensive athletics facility.

The campus is close to Lincoln Center for the Performing Arts, the theater district, Carnegie Hall, and numerous other cultural and entertainment landmarks. In addition to its proximity to many of New York City's greatest cultural institutions, the College's location provides easy access to major criminal justice agencies.

Majors and Degrees

Undergraduate degrees are offered in nineteen criminal justice–related majors: computer information systems in criminal justice and public administration, correctional studies, criminal justice, criminal justice administration and planning, criminology, deviant behavior and social control, fire science, fire and emergency service, forensic psychology, forensic science, government, international criminal justice, judicial studies, justice studies, legal studies, police studies, public administration, and security management.

The Baccalaureate/Master's Degree Program (B.A./M.A.) provides academically advanced students the opportunity to pursue simultaneously the baccalaureate and master's degrees. It is available to students studying criminal justice, forensic psychology, and public administration. The number of undergraduate electives and courses in the major are reduced for B.A./M.A. candidates, thus enabling them to begin graduate courses once they have fulfilled the general education requirements and some of the requirements of their major. Graduate courses then fulfill certain undergraduate requirements.

The A.S. degree is granted in correction administration, criminal justice, police science, and security management.

Academic Programs

Although John Jay's unique mission emphasizes programs in law enforcement and fire science, every program offered by the College includes a strong liberal arts component. Students investigate both practical and theoretical aspects of the humanities, the physical sciences, and the social sciences, especially to the extent that these are related to public service fields. This interdisciplinary approach broadens the students' intellectual horizons and makes them more effective professionals.

Candidates for the baccalaureate degree at John Jay College must complete 43–60 credits in general education. They are encouraged to complete the English, mathematics, and speech requirements within the first 30 credits of course work. In addition, all candidates must complete a major field of study of at least 36 credits. A minimum of 30 of the candidate's total credits and at least 50 percent of the selected major must be completed in residence. The associate degree at John Jay requires completion of basic distribution requirements and a specialization program (60 credits).

The Interdisciplinary Studies Program offers an alternate way of meeting basic course requirements and of completing the liberal arts portion of the baccalaureate and associate degree programs. Students who enroll in Interdisciplinary Studies take a package of classes related to a specific theme, combining literature, sociology, psychology, ethnic studies, history, writing, philosophy, government, and criminal justice. Each course centers on a broad topic or theme to which all classwork and projects are related. These interdisciplinary courses are taught by teams of 6 to 8 professors. Students undertake individual or group projects, supplementary lectures, readings, discussions, and papers.

Students may be awarded credit for successful scores on the College-Level Examination Program (CLEP) subject tests, the Regents External Degree Examinations (REDE), and College Board Advanced Placement (AP) tests. Students may apply for and may be granted up to 30 credits for external and/or equivalent learning experiences.

John Jay offers certificate programs to individuals who are seeking career advancement in the following areas: dispute resolution, EMT-D, emergency psychology technician, New York City police studies, and terrorism studies.

Off-Campus Programs

The College's location in midtown Manhattan and its special focus on criminal justice and related fields offer unparalleled opportunities for students to earn academic credits while gaining experience. Internship courses, which provide 3 credits each, combine classes and supervision with practical experience in criminal justice and government agencies, cultural organizations, private businesses, and health, research, and nonprofit institutions. Internships are available in such places as legislators' offices, hospitals, courts, New York City agencies, district attorneys' offices, juvenile-diversion programs, museums, legal societies, fire and police departments, social service agencies, and federal agencies.

The cooperative education program provides alternating periods of paid employment and college work. Juniors and seniors with satisfactory college records may enter into this program with such employers as IBM, the U.S. Customs Service, the U.S. Marshals Service of the Department of Justice, and the Inspector General's Office of the Department of Health and Human Services. No College credit is offered for this off-campus employment.

Academic Facilities

John Jay's Lloyd Sealy Library houses one of the world's premier criminal justice libraries. With unique holdings of 440,000 books, periodicals, microforms, and digital collections, the library supports the general education and curricular aims of the College and provides opportunities for extensive research in the social sciences, criminal justice, forensic psychology, forensic science, and related fields.

Five specially equipped laboratories are used to educate students in the professionally oriented forensic science program. In addition, research rooms are available for use by forensic science majors and faculty members.

The Security Management Lab provides hands-on training in computer security and other modern security systems and techniques that are applicable in the field.

The Microcomputer Laboratory consists of four separate labs for classroom instruction and individual assignments. The labs are staffed with supervisors and consultants who assist students in their individual projects.

In addition, John Jay College houses thirteen centers and institutes that concentrate on specialties within criminal justice and public affairs. These centers include the Center for Crime Prevention and Control, the Prisoner Reentry Institute, the Criminal Justice Research Center, and the Center on Race, Crime, and Justice.

Costs

For New York State residents, tuition costs for 2007–08 were $170 per credit hour, or a maximum of $2000 per term. Tuition costs for out-of-state residents were $360 per credit hour. Tuition and fee charges are subject to change without prior notice by action of the Board of Trustees of the City University of New York.

Financial Aid

John Jay College makes every effort to help students finance their education. It offers students both government-funded and private sources of financial assistance, such as Federal Pell Grants, Federal Work-Study Program employment, Tuition Assistance Program (TAP) awards, Federal Stafford Student Loans, Federal Perkins Loans, Federal Supplemental Educational Opportunity Grants (FSEOG), and veterans' benefits. The College also awards scholarships in a variety of categories based on academic merit.

Faculty

John Jay's 350 full-time and 750 part-time faculty members bring together at one college men and women who are among the most renowned and internationally recognized experts in the criminal justice field. The College's tradition of academic excellence affords students the opportunity to learn from scholars whose work and dedication win coveted prizes, but who put teaching first.

All faculty members teach undergraduate courses as well as graduate courses.

Student Government

The student government consists of an executive board of elected representatives from each class, including graduate students. Among the chief functions of the student government are the allocation of student fees, the chartering of campus clubs and monitoring of their activities and expenditures, and the selection of students to serve on College Council committees. Members also serve as student advocates before faculty members and administrators.

The College Council is composed of faculty members, students, and administrators. Students are also voting members of College committees on personnel and budget, curriculum, retention, and other areas of College governance.

Admission Requirements

Admission to John Jay is competitive. To be eligible for freshman admission to a baccalaureate (four-year) program, students must have a high school average of at least 80 with a minimum of 14 academic units (based on a three-year high school record) or achieve an SAT score of at least 1020 and present evidence of having received either a high school diploma from an accredited institution or a General Educational Development (GED) certificate with a score of at least 3000 (300 if taken before 2002). Students may be admitted to a four-year program with a lower academic average, dependent upon the strength of the high school academic program.

All new students are required to meet minimal standards in three skills areas (reading, writing, and mathematics) before enrolling in a CUNY senior college. Students can demonstrate that they meet the University's skills requirement based on SAT, ACT, or New York State Regents test scores or through the CUNY Skills Assessment Test.

Applicants who do not meet the baccalaureate criteria may be accepted into the associate degree program if they present evidence of having received either a high school diploma from an accredited institution, a General Educational Development (GED) certificate with a minimum score of 2850 (285 if taken before 2002), or an SAT score of at least 900.

Students who have attended a college or postsecondary institution must have a minimum cumulative GPA of 2.0 based on the total number of credits attempted and completed. Prospective transfer students with fewer than 12 credits must have a minimum GPA of 2.0, along with the prerequisite high school average and academic units for admission to the baccalaureate program.

Applicants who have attended college since graduation from high school may apply for admission with advanced standing.

Application and Information

For application materials and additional information, requests should be made to:

Office of Undergraduate Admissions
John Jay College of Criminal Justice
445 West 59th Street, Room 4205
New York, New York 10019
Phone: 212-ONE-STOP
877-JOHNJAY (toll-free)
Web site: http://www.jjay.cuny.edu

THE KING'S COLLEGE

NEW YORK, NEW YORK

The University

The King's College, which was founded in 1938, has been providing high-quality undergraduate education for more than sixty years. King's seeks ambitious students who want to make a difference in the world. The College aims to contribute to American society by producing graduates who have a command of the important intellectual traditions, who think lucidly about the social and political issues that confront them today, who write with force and flair, who speak with eloquence, and who are eager to exchange ideas in open debate with those who espouse different views.

The King's College educates students to lead with principle as they aspire to make America better. To the King's College, leadership requires facility in complex ideas and the sophistication to guide the strategic institutions of society—government, commerce, law, the media, civil society, education, the arts, and the church. The College teaches a compelling worldview rooted in the Bible and informed by close study of great works of philosophy, political theory, and economics. With a demanding curriculum and a campus in the heart of New York City, King's is not for the timid soul.

King's places a high value on helping students develop their spiritual lives. Students entering the College are at various places in their spiritual journeys, but they grow in significant ways during their time at King's. To that end, King's provides a number of opportunities designed for Christian spiritual growth. Small-group Bible studies and discipleship groups occur on campus weekly and are designed to help students meet, encourage, and challenge one another. In addition, King's students are invited to participate in retreats, conferences, and missions projects in New York City, in the United States, and around the world.

The King's College has more than 240 undergraduates, 64 percent of whom are women. Seven percent are international students representing nineteen countries.

New Student Orientation (NSO) is held each year during the week before fall classes start. NSO delivers a first installment of the College's mission. Students connect with their classmates and King's faculty and staff members. Important College policies and systems are explained. Attendance at NSO is required.

The King's College leases nearby apartments, in which about 90 percent of students live. Studios and one- and two-bedroom apartments are offered to King's students on an as-available basis. First priority is given to returning and full-time students. Housing contracts are for one school year unless otherwise stipulated.

The King's College is institutionally accredited by the New York State Board of Regents and the Commissioner of Education, a nationally recognized accrediting agency.

Location

Located in the Empire State Building in midtown Manhattan, the King's College is strategically positioned to take advantage of all New York City has to offer. Home to more than 8 million people, the city has some of the nation's most influential institutions and significant landmarks, including Wall Street, the United Nations, Times Square, Broadway, Madison Square Garden, all four of the major American broadcast television networks (ABC, CBS, Fox, and NBC), the Statue of Liberty, Ellis Island, and Lincoln Center. In fact, the city is often referred to as the "capital of the world." Some have described New York City as one of the global economy's three "command centers" (along with London and Tokyo). A diverse collection of world-class museums, art galleries, music groups, and performing arts venues converge to make New York City one of the world's most popular tourist destinations. The Metropolitan Museum of Art is one such attraction, with more than 2 million works of art from around the world, representing 5,000 years of history. Just down the street are the iconic Museum of Modern Art (MoMA) and the Guggenheim Museum. Across town, the Lincoln Center of the Performing Arts offers a myriad of artistic expressions, ranging from ballet to jazz to opera. Employment opportunities in New York City are numerous. Because of its ideal location in the heart of midtown Manhattan, the King's College offers proximity to many work environments, which makes combining employment with furthering one's education possible. It is no coincidence that the King's College chose New York City as its campus. The city influences and shapes culture not just in the United States but also in the entire world.

Majors and Degrees

The King's College offers two degree programs—the Bachelor of Arts in politics, philosophy, and economics (PPE) and the Bachelor of Science in business management. Students are required to declare a major in one of these two degree programs before registering for their third semester. PPE concentrations are available in literature, media, propaedeutics, or theology.

Academic Programs

The King's College was created to prepare students for a particular kind of cultural, political, and economic leadership. Students who aspire to change the key institutions of society for the better need to know the best ideas, the most important arguments, and the most influential traditions. Students must also achieve excellence in the written and the spoken word. The Common Core is a classical answer to these challenges—it recognizes that some subjects are more fundamental than others, that subjects are best learned in a specific sequence, and that truly advanced courses must be built on secure foundations. The core consists of twenty courses in a particular sequence. Students are required to take the first ten during the freshman year. Altogether, the Common Core accounts for half the courses a student needs to graduate from King's.

Every spring semester, the King's College takes time out from regular classes to spend time on a single intellectual theme of both philosophical depth and current pubic importance. In 2002–03, the College focused on the topic of God, War, and Terrorism, exploring the issues surrounding the war with Iraq from political, social, theological, and ethical perspectives. The following academic year focused on the topics Building a Christian Worldview and How to Win Elections. The 2004–05 series took students into the strategic institution of New York City (the New York Stock Exchange, the United Nations, the New York City Bar, the FBI, and the Second Circuit Federal Court). In fall 2005, the interregnum focused on secularism and included guest speakers Peter Berger and Christian Smith, as well as debates and presentations by students. In spring 2006, the interregnum focused on trust, engaging both the secular and the religious world.

The PPE program weaves together the academic disciplines that examine the nature of human communities. Politics deals with the question of how people should govern themselves, philosophy wonders what they can know through reason, and economics asks how the community can prosper within the constraints of the material world. The business management program prepares students for careers in commerce, teaching not just the techniques of management, such as accounting and marketing, but also how to understand the social, political, and economic foundations of free markets. The program centers on the Christian concept of stewardship, preparing students to be wise in their prosperity and employ their wealth for the betterment of society.

Off-Campus Programs

King's wants all full-time students to be a part of at least one cross-cultural trip during their time in college. By taking advantage of such trips, students are better prepared for Christian leadership in today's world, wherever they live. New York City has incredible opportunities for ministry and service. King's has created strategic opportunities with key partners to provide avenues for students to have an impact. A listing of current opportunities can be found in the Student Handbook.

Academic Facilities

The Rosezella Battles Library, with its distinctive lighting and beautiful furniture, provides a quiet setting conducive to study. The library's collection is particularly strong in a biblical worldview and the integration of faith and learning. The library also houses hundreds of educational videos and dozens of academic journals. Through its catalog on the student Web page, the library provides 24-hour access to virtual study halls, reference desks, and reading lounges. The Battles Library also offers such helpful services as reference assistance, classroom instruction in academic research methods, group tours of nearby public libraries, access to the Internet, and borrowing privileges from other libraries. Students have access to millions of books housed in three New York Public Libraries, all within walking distance of the College. The computer lab contains a number of desktop computers for student and faculty use. All computers contain DVD players and CD-RW drives. A black-and-white laser printer is also available for student use.

Costs

Tuition, fees, room, and board are $14,595 per semester in 2007–08.

Financial Aid

Nearly all students receive some form of financial aid. In 2006, award packages ranged between $1500 and $23,750. Assistance is available in the form of scholarships, grants, and loans. Scholarships are awarded based on academic abilities, leadership potential, and character. Grants and loans are awarded based on both merit and financial need. Institutional financial aid awards are made on a yearly basis. All students who receive financial aid from the King's College are expected to have a part-time job to help meet the cost of their education. The College does not participate in any federal financial aid programs; therefore, students do not need to file the FAFSA.

Faculty

More than half of the College's faculty members are full-time, and 92 percent hold the terminal degree in their field. The student-faculty ratio is 14:1. Business management classes are taught by both full-time faculty members and people currently working in the fields they teach. Faculty members include a venture capitalist, a former bank executive, and a Wall Street investment specialist.

Student Government

The goal of the student government is to enable, advance, and serve the College's community, primarily through responsibly distributing available funds to student-led organizations and planning events consistent with the College's vision and goals.

Admission Requirements

Admission to the King's College is based primarily upon previous academic success. Students should have earned a high school diploma, with a minimum of 16 academic units, including 4 of standard English courses, 3 each of mathematics and science, and 2 each in foreign language and social studies. Students who have successfully completed a college-preparatory curriculum that includes at least two years of a modern language are given preference. Those who have attained a GED certificate should contact the admissions office directly regarding admission. Applicants must submit the completed application, the $30 application fee, official high school transcripts, and official SAT or ACT scores. An interview is required.

Application and Information

The deadlines for early and regular admission are November 15 and February 1, respectively. Students who complete their admission and financial aid application by November 15 receive an admission decision and estimated financial aid package by December 15. For students who matriculate by January 15, a special one-time $1500 early-action scholarship is awarded.

Brian Parker, Vice President of Admissions
The King's College
Empire State Building
350 Fifth Avenue, Lower Lobby
New York, New York 10118
Phone: 212-659-7200
888-969-7200 Ext. 3610 (toll-free)
Fax: 212-659-3611
E-mail: info@tkc.edu
Web site: http://www.tkc.edu

King's College students explore New York City.

LABORATORY INSTITUTE OF MERCHANDISING (LIM COLLEGE)

NEW YORK, NEW YORK

LIM
LABORATORY INSTITUTE OF MERCHANDISING

The College

With its flagship location situated in a lovely town house in the center of the fashion capital of the world, the Laboratory Institute of Merchandising (LIM College) has been a major force in fashion and business education for almost seven decades. Its graduates can be found throughout all aspects of the industry, and its high standards of education have earned LIM accreditation from the Middle States Association of Colleges and Schools.

LIM is a highly personal college where students learn about the business of fashion, with an emphasis on academic and professional study. Lifelong friends are made at LIM, as well as lifelong careers. Although most students come to the College directly from high school or transfer from other colleges, there are also those of nontraditional college age who enter LIM. Students come to LIM from many parts of the country and the world. The current enrollment at LIM is approximately 1,100.

LIM prides itself on its placement record. Prior to graduation, the Career Services Office undertakes the important task of counseling each student with regard to her or his career. The office has had outstanding success in helping both four-year and two-year graduates obtain positions relevant to their studies. More than 90 percent of the graduates available for placement have been placed in positions related to their studies within six months of graduation.

The unique nature of LIM's curriculum provides students with a foundation of core courses in liberal arts and business while offering diverse and intensive hands-on preparation in the fashion industry. This affords graduates the opportunity to accept executive training, merchandising, management, marketing, and communications positions in a wide variety of areas within the fashion and business worlds.

Support services are important at LIM. In addition to academic and career advising, personal counseling is available. Because of the College's small size and the close relationships between students and staff members, any faculty member or administrator, including the president, is readily accessible to help and advise all students. LIM's Advisory Board members, all successful fashion industry executives, may also serve as mentors to students, offering additional guidance and advice.

Aside from the student government and the Fashion Club, other clubs are formed according to student interest. Students have responsibility for *LIMLIGHT*, which is the College yearbook, and fashion shows and other social and cultural events.

LIM currently offers three housing facilities. The de Hirsch Residence is located at the 92nd Street Y, on the corner of 92nd Street and Lexington Avenue. Residents at the de Hirsch are primarily freshmen. Two other facilities house sophomore- to senior-level students as well as all male students. The New Yorker Residence is located in the heart of Herald Square, at 481 Eighth Avenue (at 34th Street). The Clark Residence is located in Brooklyn Heights. The facility is just one stop from lower Manhattan and provides easy access to the subway. Each residence hall is staffed with 24-hour security and equipped with a communal kitchen and fitness center. Upon acceptance, students receive a housing application by mail. Rooms are limited and are assigned on a first-come, first-served basis.

LIM's unique Open-House Program offers to students and their families the opportunity to tour the College and learn not only of LIM's unique academic programs, but also of the vast array of careers found in the fashion industry. The day also includes a special presentation on financial aid information on a group or individual level. Current LIM students assist in hosting the event and are available to answer questions. In addition, students are invited to stay for a personal interview, which is a requirement for admission.

Location

LIM is situated in four buildings—on East 53rd, East 54th, and East 45th Streets, and on Fifth Avenue, one of the most fashionable locales in the world. A whole world of fashion is at the College's doorstep and includes such famous stores as Saks Fifth Avenue, Bloomingdale's, Henri Bendel, Armani, and Ralph Lauren. New York City is the headquarters for the garment, cosmetics, advertising, publishing, and textile industries, all of which are essential to the fashion industry and are visited regularly by LIM students. The College incorporates all of these resources into the curriculum. For example, the Fashion Magazines course includes trips to photography studios and modeling agencies as well as tours of magazine offices and advertising firms. New York City offers LIM students an unparalleled learning experience.

Majors and Degrees

LIM offers four-year programs in fashion merchandising, management, marketing, and visual merchandising, leading to a Bachelor of Business Administration (B.B.A.) or a Bachelor of Professional Studies (B.P.S.) degree, and a two-year program in fashion merchandising leading to the Associate in Applied Sciences (A.A.S.) degree. Qualified students with a bachelor's degree may also apply to a one-year program (ACCESS) leading to the associate degree.

Academic Programs

LIM offers a combination of classroom education and supervised practical fieldwork that has been designed to prepare students for executive training programs and other entry-level executive positions in various areas of the fashion industry. Classroom study is supplemented by weekly field trips into the heart of the fashion industry and guest lectures by luminaries from the fashion world.

Work experience is an integral part of an LIM student's education. During the four-year bachelor's degree program, a student enters the fashion industry three times. Each of the first two years of study contains a five-week, 3-credit work project. During Work Project I, freshmen are placed in paid, full-time positions in order to learn the basics of retailing. Work Project II, sophomore year, continues the retailing experience, or qualified sophomores may choose an internship in more specialized areas, such as cosmetics, magazines, designer showrooms, and fashion forecasting companies.

The third and most significant work experience is the Senior Co-op. Students spend one semester working full-time in the fashion industry in an area relevant to their career goals and ambitions. This is required for graduation from the bachelor's degree program. The responsibility, challenge, and fun of this semester prepare students for their next step—the business world.

Students who are applying to the associate degree program follow the first two years of the bachelor's degree program, including the required Work Projects.

To graduate, students must complete 126 credits for the bachelor's degree or 65 credits for the associate degree (33 for one-year ACCESS students), achieve a grade point average of at least 2.0, and satisfactorily complete the cooperative work assignments.

LIM accepts qualified students as transfers throughout the four years. Those with an associate degree in fashion merchandising or related field or with 65 acceptable college credits from a regionally accredited college are usually eligible for junior-year status. Transfer students must complete a minimum of 33 semester hours in addition to the co-op semester at LIM.

LIM's calendar runs on a traditional semester format, offering both fall and spring start dates. Also offered are summer and Saturday programs for high school students. The specially selected courses, such as Fashion Buying and Fashion Magazines, blend academics with hands-on experience.

Off-Campus Programs

Study-abroad options are available, including study in places such as London, Paris, Milan, Barcelona, and China.

Academic Facilities

The 5,000-square-foot library contains 9,000 volumes pertaining to fashion, management, marketing, and the liberal arts, as well as 110 professional and academic journals. The library has more than forty computer terminals that connect to the Internet and provide access to online databases through the library's subscriptions. DVDs and VHS cassettes useful for fashion-related studies are also at students' disposal. Personal computers are available for use in the library, lounges, and classrooms. The student-to-computer ratio is 4:1. The Math Center and Writing Centers offer one-on-one tutoring and thirty-eight computer stations.

LIM's brand-new facility on Fifth Avenue is equipped with two fashion merchandising studios, one of which has a laboratory area for cosmetics. There are also two new 1,100-square-foot visual merchandising studios, as well as a state-of-the-art Color and Materials Laboratory at the new location.

Costs

In 2007–08, tuition was $18,100 and additional mandatory fees were $425. Other expenses vary, depending on residence. In 2007–08, off-campus rooms cost about $11,000–$15,000. Students who commute spend from $700 to $2000 for transportation, depending on distance. Books and supplies average between $750 and $1000 per year. The personal expense allowance is approximately $2000 a year.

Financial Aid

LIM believes that lack of funds should not keep students from attending college; thus, admissions decisions and financial aid are totally separate, and a request for aid has no effect on admissions. About 80 percent of LIM's students receive some form of financial aid. Institutional scholarships, Federal Pell Grants, Federal Supplemental Educational Opportunity Grants, and New York State TAP grants are all available for eligible students. In addition, LIM participates in the Federal Stafford Loan program for students and Federal PLUS Loan program for parents. The College also works with several private lenders to offer alternative education loans for students to supplement their federal loans. International students are eligible to apply for alternative loans with a credit-worthy U.S.-based co-signer. The Free Application for Federal Student Aid (FAFSA) should be filed by all applicants by April 1 for priority consideration. Aid is granted on the basis of financial need and scholarships are merit based, although some awards take need into consideration. Details of the financial aid programs are available on the LIM Web site or are available directly from the Office of Student Financial Services.

LIM features a Merit Scholarship Program for incoming freshmen and transfer students. These scholarship monies are awarded for academic achievement in high school or college. Students can remain eligible for their scholarship throughout their stay at LIM by maintaining a GPA of 3.0 or above. LIM's nonprofit Fashion Education Foundation also administers a number of merit scholarships (both need and nonneed based) other than direct institutional awards.

Faculty

LIM prides itself on its faculty members. More than a third of the teaching staff, including all members of the liberal arts faculty, have advanced degrees; all professional subject faculty members have wide business and professional experience. Many, through their business contacts, bring guests to class to share in the lectures and discussions. The student-faculty ratio is 8:1.

Each student is assigned an academic adviser. Work-study and career guidance is given to students by the Career Services Office, with conferences held before, during, and after the cooperative work assignments and prior to permanent placement interviews. Students are always welcome to discuss career options at any other time as well.

Student Government

The Office of Student Life is the center of all student activities at LIM. This department supports student government and approves other student organizations and establishes their operating budgets.

Admission Requirements

Applicants must hold a high school or equivalency (GED) diploma and submit SAT or ACT scores. International students must achieve a TOEFL score of at least 550. Great emphasis is placed on the required personal interview, which the College conducts on campus. Transfer students' records are evaluated individually with liberal interpretation placed on course equivalencies. Transfer students may enter LIM in either semester and with any amount of credits accumulated. Students applying for junior year status must hold either an associate degree or have at least 65 acceptable semester hours of credit. LIM's Admissions Committee recognizes that many intangibles go into the making of a successful fashion merchandising student, and it evaluates each application individually.

Application and Information

The application should be accompanied by the $40 fee, an official high school transcript, an official college transcript (if applicable), SAT or ACT scores, two letters of recommendation, a one-page essay, and TOEFL scores (if applicable). Applicants must also make an appointment for a personal interview. The College uses a rolling admission policy. Applicants are informed of the admission decision within approximately four to six weeks after all admission requirements have been fulfilled. An application may be obtained from the LIM Web site or by contacting the Director of Admissions.

Kristina Gibson
Assistant Dean of Admissions
LIM College
12 East 53rd Street
New York, New York 10022-5268
Phone: 212-752-1530
800-677-1323 (toll-free outside New York City)
Fax: 212-750-3432
E-mail: admissions@limcollege.edu
Web site: http://www.limcollege.edu

LEHMAN COLLEGE OF THE CITY UNIVERSITY OF NEW YORK

BRONX, NEW YORK

The College

Established in 1968 as a senior college of the City University of New York (CUNY), Lehman offers more than ninety undergraduate and graduate degree programs and specializations in business administration, computer graphics and imaging, liberal arts, natural and social sciences, education, nursing and health professions, social work, and the fine and performing arts. Many programs provide training for particular careers and lead to professional degrees, preparing students for positions in private, nonprofit, and government organizations as well as for graduate study.

Lehman offers more than thirty master's degree programs, including those in art; biological sciences; early childhood and childhood education; economics, accounting, and business administration; English; health sciences; history; mathematics; middle and high school education; music; nursing; plant sciences (Ph.D.); sociology and social work; specialized services in education; and speech-language-hearing sciences. In addition, there are several advanced certificate programs and two new programs, the Master of Social Work (M.S.W.) and Master of Public Health (M.P.H.).

Lehman offers an active, diversified, and supportive campus life. Organized around various cultural, religious, political, academic, and personal interests, more than sixty clubs are housed in a Student Life Building that also features computer, conference, kitchen, and recreation areas. Many of these activities give students valuable experiences both for careers and for life. Through counseling and additional support services, students find the answers to academic and career questions, while a Child Care Center, a Student Health Center, and an Office of Disability Services help meet a variety of other needs.

Lehman serves as a regional center for the arts and recreation. The campus has a 2,300-seat concert hall, a 500-seat theater, a 150-seat recital hall, and an art gallery. In addition, the campus publishes several newspapers and hosts a radio station and a cable television station. The APEX, a sports and recreation facility, includes a fully equipped fitness center; a free-weight room; two full-size gymnasiums; four racquetball courts; a two-lane, 1/14-mile indoor track; an aerobics/dance studio; a ballet studio; an Olympic-size indoor swimming pool; and five outdoor tennis courts.

Location

Lehman College is located in a quiet residential neighborhood in the northwest Bronx. Convenient to major highways and multiple bus and subway lines, this location offers students easy access to the cultural, social, and academic resources of a city that is world renowned for its opportunities in every field of endeavor.

Majors and Degrees

Lehman offers both bachelor's and master's degrees. Undergraduate majors at Lehman College include accounting; African and African American studies; American studies; anthropology; anthropology (physical), biology, and chemistry; art (specialties in art history and studio art in ceramics, computer imaging, painting, photography, printmaking, and sculpture); biology; business administration; chemistry (specialty in biochemistry); comparative literature; computer graphics and imaging; computer science; computing and management; dance-theater; dietetics, foods, and nutrition; economics; English (specialties in creative writing, literature, and professional writing); French; geography; geology; Greek; Greek and Latin studies; health education and promotion (options in community health and community health and nutrition); health N–12 teacher studies; health services administration; Hebraic and Judaic studies; Hebrew; history; Italian; Italian-American studies; Latin; Latin American and Caribbean studies; linguistics; mass communication; mathematics; multilingual journalism; music; nursing; philosophy (specialties in ethics and public policy); physics; political science; psychology; Puerto Rican studies; recreation education; Russian; social work; sociology; Spanish; speech pathology and audiology; and theater.

Academic Programs

Lehman College offers 120-credit Bachelor of Arts, Bachelor of Science, and Bachelor of Business Administration degrees and a dual Bachelor of Arts/Master of Arts in mathematics. Many of these programs include course work and fieldwork that lead to professional certification. These programs include the B.S. in accounting–certified public accountant; dietetics, foods, and nutrition–dietitian; education (elementary)–elementary school teacher (N–6); education (secondary)–secondary school teacher in academic subjects; health education and promotion–health education specialist and health N–12 teacher; health services administration–nursing home administrator; professional nursing–registered nurse; recreation education–therapeutic recreation specialist and certified leisure professional; and speech education–teacher of the speech and hearing handicapped. Lehman also offers courses that lead to graduate programs for professional certification, including predentistry, prelaw, premedicine, prepharmacy, preveterinary science, and social work; these Lehman programs include a professional option that allows students to complete the undergraduate degree at an accredited professional school in their senior year. In addition, a pre-engineering transfer program is offered in cooperation with the School of Engineering at City College.

The baccalaureate programs include courses in English composition, natural sciences, mathematics, and foreign language. Students must also complete distribution courses in seven major areas of study, two upper-division interdisciplinary courses, and a set of writing-intensive classes. In addition to fulfilling the requirements of a major, most students are also required to select a minor field of study. All students also must be in compliance with CUNY testing requirements.

Lehman offers an array of exciting programs designed to challenge its students and meet their intellectual needs. The Freshman Year Initiative (FYI) is an award-winning, nationally recognized program offering first-year students a supportive and carefully structured college experience. All first-year students participate in the program, which promotes an interdisciplinary curriculum, faculty collaboration, and peer support. Behind FYI is the idea that people learn better, and benefit from reinforced social and academic support, when they are integrated into learning communities. During their first and second semesters, students take a set of integrated courses with the same group of fellow students. Faculty members teaching the courses meet regularly to collaborate on assignments and lesson plans in order to ensure thematic and conceptual linkages across the curriculum. The learning communities also foster connections between students and faculty members and promote the development of peer support networks during the first college year. Students interested in premed, teacher education, and the performing arts, as well as prospective majors in accounting, business administration, nursing, psychology, or sociology, may request placement in a learning community targeted to their planned field of study. Students who qualify, based on combined SAT scores, may be placed in honors blocks.

The Macaulay Honors College at Lehman challenges students to continue their record of high achievement and prepares them for top graduate and professional programs. Honors College students are chosen from a highly competitive field of applicants who demonstrate exceptional academic skills. They are rewarded for their hard work and achievements with a complete package of financial benefits, including a full-tuition scholarship for four years of study; up to $3000 a year for living expenses, transportation, and other indirect college-related expenses; an option of residential housing; an expense account for study abroad or other academically enriching experiences; a free laptop computer; and a "cultural passport" for special entree to concerts, theaters, museums, and other cultural events and institutions in New York City. For more information, students should visit http://www.lehman.edu/lehman/honorscollege/.

The new Teacher Academy at Lehman is geared toward training and rewarding the mathematics and science teachers of tomorrow. Students are selected from a highly competitive pool of applicants with exceptional academic skills and a passion for mathematics or science. The academy offers four years of free tuition and no fees for students who graduate and teach at least two years in New York City public schools, paid internships ($1600 each year) to work with high school or middle school students, opportunities to study and do research in math or science with exceptional CUNY faculty members, hands-on experiences in New York City public middle schools or high schools, a full-time teaching position in a New York City middle school or high school after successful completion of the program, and, for a select group of academy graduates, support for a master's degree in their field at a CUNY college. Students in the Teacher Academy are challenged and inspired to make a difference in their own lives and in the lives of others by helping the next generation of students discover the wonder of science and the power of mathematics. For more information, students should visit http://www.lehman.edu/lehman/services/teacheracademy.html.

The Lehman Scholars Program (LSP), for capable and highly motivated students possessing the desire and ability to pursue a somewhat more traditional liberal arts course of study, offers the advantages of a small, intimate college: special courses, seminars, and individual counseling. Students are exempt from Lehman general education requirements; they must, however, pass the CUNY Skills Assessment Tests to be admitted to the program and meet all course prerequisites and major requirements. Students take a one-semester honors course in English composition; two years of a foreign language at the college level or its equivalent; four honors seminars, three at the 100 level and one at the 300 level, from the four different academic areas—fine and performing arts, humanities, natural science, and social science; and a senior honors essay. Each student entering the program is assigned to a faculty mentor, who advises the student in the areas of program planning and academic and career goals.

The Adult Degree Program at Lehman, designed to meet the special needs of mature men and women with family and work responsibilities, schedules classes for days, evenings, and weekends. Faculty counselors help students choose a course of study toward their individual career goal. College credits may be awarded for life experience, including current paid or volunteer work. Courses are offered to refresh writing, reading, and math skills and prepare the students for college-level work.

The academic calendar is divided into fall and spring semesters, with two summer sessions. There is also a new winter session.

Off-Campus Programs

Through a cooperative arrangement, students may take courses at other colleges within the City University of New York, one of the nation's most distinguished and extensive university systems. Off-campus internships are available through the academic departments and the Career Services Office. Opportunities for overseas study are available for an intersession, a semester, or an academic year through sponsored trips and the Study-Abroad and Paris/CUNY Exchange Programs.

Academic Facilities

Lehman's 37-acre campus is dominated by Gothic towers and tree-lined walks, where a blend of traditional and modern design helps reinforce the College's sense of community. This sense of community is further enhanced by the computers (including personal and multiuser systems) available for student use in the Information Technology Center, the library, and departmental facilities that provide access to general-purpose and specialized-application software, local and regional networks, and the Internet. Audio/video reception/distribution capability via satellite and other means is available in many classrooms, as are specialized facilities to support multimedia, distance learning, and high-end graphics capabilities. The library offers an open-stack book collection of 572,000 volumes that is supplemented by 713,500 microforms and a growing collection of 5,391 films and videotapes. The library also subscribes to 1,535 print periodicals and more than 13,000 electronic journals.

Costs

Eligible New York State residents who are matriculated students pay $2000 per semester for full-time study, which is at least 12 credits or credit equivalents; $170 per credit for matriculated part-time study; or $250 per credit for nonmatriculated study. Nonresidents and international students pay $360 per credit for full-time and part-time matriculated study and $530 per credit for nonmatriculated study. Each semester, all students must pay a student activity fee. The fee is $55 for full-time students, $35 for part-time students for the fall and spring semesters, and $30 during the summer sessions. Each semester, students pay a $15 consolidated service fee and a technology fee. The technology fee is $75 for full-time students and $37.50 for part-time students.

Financial Aid

Lehman College participates in federal and New York State financial aid programs. Students may request aid by filing a Free Application for Federal Student Aid (FAFSA) for consideration for the Federal Pell Grant, Federal Supplemental Educational Opportunity Grant (FSEOG), SEEK, Federal Work-Study Program, and federal student loans. New York State residents may also apply for the Tuition Assistance Program (TAP). Lehman recommends filing for aid electronically at http://www.fafsa.ed.gov. The College also offers various scholarships. Other scholarships and awards are tied to specific areas of study; students in eligible fields of study are given assistance in pursuing federal scholarship programs.

Faculty

The College has more than 300 full-time faculty members, of whom 83 percent hold doctoral degrees or their equivalent. Many have been recognized nationally and internationally for their scholarship and research through grants and awards; a significant number serve as faculty members at CUNY's graduate center. Most important, faculty members work closely with students outside the classroom in individual and group settings to support their academic, professional, and personal growth. The faculty-student ratio is 1:15.

Student Government

Lehman's student government is divided into the Campus Association for Student Activities (CASA), the programming arm of the student government, and the Student Conference, the legislative arm of the student government. CASA officers are responsible for the appropriation and management of student funds for clubs, cultural programs, entertainment, and other activities. The Student Conference makes up approximately one third of the Lehman College Senate, the decision-making body on matters of academic policy.

Admission Requirements

Candidates for freshman admission are considered based on the overall strength of their academic preparation, grades in individual subjects, cumulative high school averages, and SAT or ACT scores. The College recommends completion of 4 years of English, 4 years of social studies, 3 years of mathematics, 2 years of a foreign language, 2 years of laboratory sciences, and 1 year of performing or visual arts as the minimum academic preparation for success in college. Applicants who do not meet these freshman admission requirements but who satisfy particular academic and economic criteria may be eligible for admission through the SEEK program, the City University's opportunity program for senior colleges.

Transfer students who have earned at least 13 credits must have an overall cumulative average of at least 2.0 in all previous college work. Students transferring with fewer than 13 credits must have an overall cumulative average of at least 2.5 and meet the requirements for freshman admission.

Applicants with student or other nonimmigrant visas who were not educated in an English-speaking system are required to score a minimum of 500 on the paper-based or 173 on the computer-based TOEFL.

Application and Information

Students must apply online at http://www.cuny.edu. Applicants are encouraged to submit all official documentation and fees by March 15 for fall admission or by October 1 for spring admission.

The staff of the admissions office is available to answer questions and provide assistance with the admissions process. Students may speak with an Admissions Counselor or schedule a campus tour by contacting:

Office of Admissions
Shuster Hall, Room 161
Lehman College
250 Bedford Park Boulevard West
Bronx, New York 10468-1589
Phone: 718-960-8713
877-LEHMAN-1 (toll-free)
Web site: http://www.lehman.edu

LE MOYNE COLLEGE

SYRACUSE, NEW YORK

The College

Le Moyne College is a four-year, coeducational Jesuit college of approximately 2,500 undergraduate students that uniquely balances a comprehensive liberal arts education with preparation for specific career paths or graduate study. Founded by the Society of Jesus in 1946, Le Moyne is the second youngest of the twenty-eight Jesuit colleges and universities in the United States. Its emphasis is on the education of the whole person and on the search for meaning and value as integral parts of an intellectual life. Le Moyne's personal approach to education is reflected in the quality of contact between students and faculty members. A wide range of student-directed activities, athletics, clubs, and service organizations complement the academic experience. Intramural sports are very popular with Le Moyne students; nearly 85 percent of the students participate. Le Moyne also has sixteen NCAA intercollegiate teams (eight for men and eight for women). Athletic facilities include soccer/lacrosse, softball, and baseball fields; tennis, basketball, and racquetball courts; a weight-training and fitness center; practice fields; and two gymnasiums. A recreation center houses an Olympic-size indoor swimming pool, jogging track, indoor tennis and volleyball courts, and additional basketball, racquetball, and fitness areas. More than 80 percent of students live in residence halls, apartments, and town houses on campus. The Residence Hall Councils and the Le Moyne Student Programming Board organize a variety of campus activities, including concerts, dances, a weekly film series, student talent programs, and special lectures as well as off-campus trips and skiing excursions.

Location

Le Moyne's 160-acre, tree-lined campus is located in a residential setting 10 minutes from downtown Syracuse, the heart of New York State, whose metropolitan population is about 700,000. Syracuse is convenient to most major cities throughout the Northeast, New England, and Canada and offers a wide array of shopping centers and restaurants, many near Le Moyne. Syracuse offers year-round entertainment in the form of rock concerts at the Landmark Theatre, professional baseball and hockey, Bristol Omnitheatre, the Syracuse Symphony Orchestra, Syracuse Stage, Everson Museum of Art, and the Armory Square district downtown, which offers one-of-a-kind eateries, pubs, and coffeehouses in addition to a wide variety of social and cultural events. All are easily accessible via the excellent public transportation service, which schedules regular stops on Le Moyne's campus. Just a few miles outside the city are the rolling hills, picturesque lakes, and miles of open country for which central New York is renowned. An extensive network of state and county parks, recreational areas, and other facilities offer an abundance of recreational opportunities, including swimming, boating, hiking, downhill and cross-country skiing, snowboarding, and golf.

Majors and Degrees

Le Moyne College awards the Bachelor of Arts degree in biological sciences, communication (advertising, media and film studies, print journalism, public relations, television/radio), computer science, criminology and crime and justice studies (forensic science, human services, international affairs, law enforcement, research), economics, English (creative writing, literature), French, history, mathematics (actuarial science, operations research, pure mathematics, statistics), peace and global studies, philosophy, physics, political science, psychology, religious studies, sociology (anthropology, criminology and criminal justice, human services, research and theory), Spanish, and theater arts. The Bachelor of Science degree is awarded in biochemistry, biological sciences (health professions, molecular biology, neurobiology), chemistry, economics, general science, natural systems science, physics, and psychology. The Bachelor of Science in business is awarded in accounting, applied management analysis, finance, industrial relations and human resource management, information systems, management and leadership, and marketing. A Bachelor of Science in Nursing is also offered.

Students may minor in Catholic studies, classical humanities, computer science, film, gender and women's studies, Irish literature, Italian, Japanese, Latin, management information systems, music, urban and regional studies, or visual arts as well as most of the major fields of study offered. Preprofessional programs are offered in dentistry, law, medicine, optometry, physical therapy, physician assistant studies, podiatry, and veterinary science. Students may prepare for teaching careers through certification programs in adolescent education, dual adolescent/special education, dual childhood/special education, middle childhood specialist studies, and TESOL.

Le Moyne College and the L. C. Smith College of Engineering and Computer Science at Syracuse University are finalizing an agreement to establish a dual-degree program in which students may earn a bachelor's degree from Le Moyne and a master's degree in engineering from Syracuse University in as few as five years. It is anticipated that concentrations in aerospace, chemical, electrical, and mechanical engineering as well as computer science and other fields of engineering will be available.

Formal accelerated 3-4 programs are offered in dentistry, optometry, and podiatry in cooperation with the State University of New York at Buffalo School of Dental Medicine, Pennsylvania College of Optometry, and the New York College of Podiatric Medicine. Predental students may also participate in an early assurance program with the State University of New York at Buffalo School of Dental Medicine. Cooperative 3-2 dual-degree programs in engineering are available with Clarkson University, Manhattan College, and University of Detroit Mercy.

SUNY Upstate Medical University in Syracuse offers students pursuing careers in the health-related professions an accelerated 3-3 doctoral-level transfer program in physical therapy as well as two-year cooperative transfer programs in cytotechnology, medical technology, and respiratory care. Premedical students at Le Moyne are also offered the opportunity to participate in a medical school early assurance program. An early assurance program for premedical students is also available through the State University of New York at Buffalo School of Medicine.

Academic Programs

While each major department has its own sequence requirements for the minimum 120 credit hours needed for the Le Moyne degree, the College is convinced that there is a fundamental intellectual discipline that should characterize the graduate of a superior liberal arts college. Le Moyne's core curriculum provides this foundation by including studies of English language and literature, philosophy, history, religious studies, natural sciences, and social sciences.

For exceptional students, Le Moyne offers an integral honors program that includes an interdisciplinary humanities sequence as well as departmental honors courses. Le Moyne also offers a part-time course of study during evening hours through its Center for Continuous Education.

Le Moyne students may enroll in Army and Air Force ROTC programs in conjunction with Syracuse University.

Off-Campus Programs

The study-abroad program allows qualified students to spend a semester or year in almost any country throughout the world. Le Moyne College has study-abroad programs or affiliations in China, Czech Republic, Dominican Republic, Germany, Italy, Spain, and the United Kingdom. Students can also use partner programs to study in locations such as Australia, Costa Rica, Egypt, France, Ireland, Japan, and South Africa. Le Moyne is a participant in the sixty-member New York State Visiting Student Program. As part of the mission of preparing future leaders, Le Moyne College places a strong emphasis on career preparation through internships and other forms of experiential education. Academic departments and the Office of Career Services both provide programs and services for students interested in interning part-time and full-time, both locally and in major cities such as New York and Washington, D.C. The Offices of Service Learning and the Academic Deans are also involved in experiential education to promote learning outside the classroom. In the sciences, students take part in campus research with mentor faculty members. Others re-

COLLEGE DATA CENTER • NEW YORK

ceive assistance in pursuing outstanding opportunities off campus in leading research laboratories and health-care settings. The College has maintained a long-standing relationship with the "Washington center" internship programs, where students from all majors complete full-time semester-long internships in Washington, D.C., with government, business, or major nonprofit organizations. Faculty members in the Political Science Department assist students interested in opportunities in Albany, New York State's seat of government, with either the New York State Senate or Assembly. Finally, the education programs at Le Moyne put students into school classrooms starting immediately as freshmen and continuing each year until graduation.

Academic Facilities

Le Moyne students benefit from an ongoing commitment to technological excellence. The College's thirty-four buildings are equipped with accounting, biology, chemistry, computer science, physics, psychology, and statistics laboratories. The W. Carroll Coyne Center for the Performing Arts houses generous production, performance, and classroom space; the latest light and sound technology; scene and costume shops; an aerobics and dance studio; and rehearsal rooms for instrumental and choral music. Academic facilities also include an extensively renovated color television studio; a radio/recording studio; a receiver-antenna satellite dish; transmission and scanning electron microscopes; a nuclear magnetic resonance spectrometer; a gas chromatograph/mass spectrophotometer; a 230,000-volume, open-stack library; and extensive on-site computer facilities. A fiber-optic network enables students to access the library system, the campus network, and the Internet from several computer labs around the campus or from their personal computers in their rooms. All classrooms have been converted to smart classrooms, with multimedia capabilities that expand and enrich the learning process. Le Moyne students have access to other libraries through the Central New York Library Resources Council, and the campus Academic Support Center is available to students for instructional support.

Costs

For 2007–08, Le Moyne's tuition was $23,040. Room and board charges were $9030. Additional fees amounted to approximately $720, and books and supplies cost approximately $700.

Financial Aid

Financial aid is offered to a large percentage of Le Moyne's students through scholarships, grants, loans, and work-study assignments. Le Moyne offers a generous program of merit-based academic and athletic scholarships as well as financial aid based on a student's need and academic promise. Federal funds are available through the Federal Pell Grant, Federal Work-Study, Federal Supplemental Educational Opportunity Grant, and Federal Perkins Loan programs. A student's eligibility for need-based financial aid is determined from both the Free Application for Federal Student Aid (FAFSA) and the Le Moyne Financial Aid Application Form. It is recommended that these forms be mailed by February 1.

Faculty

The Le Moyne full-time faculty numbers 161 men and women; 92 percent have earned the highest degree in their field. With an average class size of 21, a student-faculty ratio of 13:1, and private offices for all full-time faculty members, the College promotes a personal as well as an academic relationship between students and faculty members. All classroom instruction is done by faculty members, and they are happy to assist and encourage students who wish to pursue undergraduate research through tutorials or senior research projects. These projects are carried out in an atmosphere free of competition from graduate students for books, laboratories, or professors' time. Le Moyne emphasizes advising and academic counseling for students throughout their four years.

Student Government

The College encourages student leadership in all activities. Positions of leadership are open to students in all class years. Students are represented by a Student Senate and have formal representation through the senate on most College-wide committees involved in decision making and policy formation.

Admission Requirements

Le Moyne seeks qualified students who are well prepared for serious academic study. Secondary school preparation must have included at least 17 college-preparatory high school units, 4 of which must be in English, 4 in social studies, 3–4 in mathematics, 3–4 in foreign language, and 3–4 in science. It is also recommended that prospective science and mathematics majors complete 4 units of mathematics and science. The SAT or ACT is required and should be taken by December or January of the senior year in high school. Campus visits are strongly recommended, as the admission process is a personal one. As bases for selection, academic achievement and secondary school recommendations are of primary importance; SAT or ACT scores are important as they relate to the record of achievement and to recommendations. Out-of-state students are encouraged to apply.

Application and Information

The Admission Committee reviews applications and mails decisions on a rolling admission cycle beginning January 1. The priority deadline for applications is February 1; all students who wish to be considered for academic merit scholarships should have a completed application on file in the Office of Admission before this date. Students who wish to be considered under the early-decision program must have a completed application submitted by December 1. Early-decision applicants are notified by December 15. Transfer students are encouraged to apply before June 1 for the fall semester and December 1 for the spring semester. Orientation programs for incoming freshmen and transfer students take place in midsummer.

Dennis J. Nicholson
Director of Admission
Le Moyne College
Syracuse, New York 13214-1399
Phone: 315-445-4300
800-333-4733 (toll-free)
E-mail: admission@lemoyne.edu
Web site: http://www.lemoyne.edu

Grewen Hall, the oldest building on campus, overlooks Le Moyne's beautiful 160-acre campus.

LONG ISLAND UNIVERSITY, BROOKLYN CAMPUS

BROOKLYN, NEW YORK

The Campus

Located in convenient downtown Brooklyn, Long Island University's Brooklyn Campus is the perfect choice for students who wish to be in a metropolitan setting while in college. The proximity of many cultural, commercial, educational, and governmental institutions is reflected in the University's curricula and activities. The more than 13,000 students represent every region of the United States and many other countries. Many students live on campus, while a large number commute from the surrounding New York City region. There are two residence halls: the sixteen-story Conolly Residence Hall and the new Hoyt Street Residence, which houses seniors and graduate students. Both residence halls have wireless access and access to basic cable TV and the Internet.

An integrative approach to undergraduate education known as The Long Island University Plan (The LIU Plan) includes the Freshman Year Program, comprehensive academic advisement, cooperative education and career development, and an innovative, integrative curriculum in the University Honors Program. Through workplace experiences, workshops, development of technological skills, consultation services, integrative seminars, and tools for self-assessment and exploration, The LIU Plan enables students to develop skills and talents that can lead to coherent, well-informed, and successful lives. Cornerstones of The LIU Plan are: (1) expanded academic and personal counseling from application to graduation; (2) enhanced academic and career opportunities—to give students decisive advantages in career fields of their choice by providing an option for well-paid, professional-level work or other types of special semesters that build professional connections, credentials, and experience; and (3) essential literacies—to hone students' analytic and writing skills and to familiarize them with the fundamental languages of culture and science. For further information about The LIU Plan, students should contact the Brooklyn Campus Office of Admissions.

In addition to its eighty-three undergraduate degree programs, the Brooklyn Campus also offers ninety-three master's-level programs leading to the M.A., M.S., M.S.Ed., M.F.A., M.B.A., and M.P.A. degrees as well as doctoral programs in clinical psychology, pharmacy, pharmaceutics, and physical therapy.

Location

The 11-acre campus is located in downtown Brooklyn, 10 minutes from midtown Manhattan and convenient to public transportation that serves all parts of the metropolitan area. Excellent sightseeing, restaurants, and entertainment are within walking distance.

Majors and Degrees

The Bachelor of Arts degree is granted in the following areas: economics, English, history, humanities, jazz studies, journalism, media arts, modern languages (French, Italian, Spanish), music (applied), music theory, philosophy, political science, psychology, social work, sociology-anthropology, speech communications, and visual arts. The Bachelor of Science degree is granted in the following areas: accounting, adolescence urban education (7–12), bilingual teacher of special education studies, bilingual teacher of students with speech and language disabilities studies, biochemistry, biology, business finance, business management, chemistry, childhood urban education (1–6), communication sciences and disorders, computer science, cytotechnology, dance, health science, humanities, inclusive childhood education, integrated information systems, marketing, mathematics, mathematics teacher studies (7–12), medical technology, middle childhood and adolescence urban education (5–12), molecular biology, music education, nuclear medicine technology, nursing, physical education teacher studies, physician assistant studies, social science, sports science, and teacher of students with speech and language disabilities studies. The Bachelor of Fine Arts degree is granted in the following areas: art education, computer art, dance, music (jazz studies), and studio art. The Associate of Applied Science degree is offered in business administration; the Associate of Arts degree is offered in humanities, science, and social science. Five-year dual B.S./M.S. degree programs are offered in accounting, adult nurse practitioner studies, athletic training and sports sciences, communication sciences and disorders/speech-language pathology, nursing (executive program for nursing and health-care management), and occupational therapy. The Arnold & Marie Schwartz College of Pharmacy offers a six-year Pharm.D. program.

Academic Programs

All undergraduate students are required to complete a core curriculum in the liberal arts and sciences in order to acquire a general background of ideas and knowledge. The core curriculum consists of courses in the humanities, the natural sciences, mathematics, and the social sciences. Specific requirements may vary depending on the major. Of the 128 credits required for graduation, a student must take 24 or more credits of advanced work in the major and have at least 48 credits in upper-division work. The minimum number of credits required in the liberal arts and sciences varies from 64 to 96, depending on the degree awarded. Qualified students in any major may arrange for independent studies and honors work.

The University Honors Program, open to all majors, offers academically qualified students core courses, designed for cross-disciplinary inquiry, and advanced seminars, which are theme-oriented and field-based. The program also allows for creative or research projects for independent study. Members of the program are eligible for Distinction in Honors when they write a thesis. All members may extend independent study beyond the stated limits through the Honors Program.

All students may enroll in the Cooperative Education Program, gaining valuable field experience and pay for employment related to their major field of study.

In the Arnold & Marie Schwartz College of Pharmacy and Health Sciences, degree requirements vary according to the individual program.

The commitment of the University to the support of each student's individual learning needs is reflected in the number of counseling and academic support services it offers. Instructional resources include the Academic Reinforcement Center, Achievement Studies, and Guided Studies, all of which are designed to provide one-on-one counseling and advisement for students who need additional academic resources, as well as the Academic Advisement Center, which provides free tutoring for nearly all undergraduate disciplines. Other academic support services include the Writing Center, the Mathematics Center, the Academic Computing Center, and the Apple Macintosh Computer Skills Lab. Special programs include the Higher Education Opportunity Program (HEOP) and the Special Educational Services Program for Disabled and Academically High Risk Students. For academic majors, faculty advisers and/or professional academic counselors are provided. The Freshman Orientation Seminar familiarizes incoming students with the academic and cultural resources of the University and the community.

Off-Campus Programs

The Brooklyn Campus offers an innovative study-abroad bachelor's degree program through its one-of-a-kind Global College (formerly Friends World Program).

Academic Facilities

In 2005, the Brooklyn Campus celebrated the opening of a new performing arts complex, which includes the 320-seat Kumble Theater for the Performing Arts that provides a sophisticated venue for student, community, and professional productions; space for rehearsals and smaller programs; music practice rooms; and classrooms. In 2006, the campus opened a $40-million Wellness, Recreation, and Athletic Center with facilities to support the clinical education of students in nursing and other health profession programs. The center also offers students extensive athletic training and recreation facilities, including a 25-yard swimming pool, exercise equipment, a track, tennis courts, and a 2,800-seat arena for the school's NCAA Division I teams. In 2007, the Brooklyn Campus opened a Cyber Café that provides technology resources and support to the campus community.

The Salena Library Learning Center combines traditional library resources with modern educational technology. Cooperative agreements make the collections of the Academic Libraries of Brooklyn (ALB) as well as the riches of libraries in New York City available to Long Island University students. The Brooklyn Campus of Long Island University is part of a University-wide electronically linked library/resource network of more than 2.7 million volumes. Students have remote access to online library resources. Special library collections are in law, transportation, pharmacy, the LIU Artists' Book Collection, The Polk Awards Archives, and the Weinberg Archives of Architecture and City Planning. The library includes a Media Center and a Library Cyber Lab.

The Department of Information Technology serves both the administrative and academic needs of the institution and is responsible for introducing new technologies into the everyday educational life of the University. The IT department supports students and faculty and staff members in all computer issues through a wide range of services, including hardware repairs, software problem resolution, and e-mail, telephone, network, wireless network, and other software-related issues. On campus, students have free access to more than 600 computers and thirty computer labs, including special labs for writing, science, and other disciplines.

The state-of-the-art Health Sciences Center houses programs in nursing, occupational therapy, pharmacy, physical therapy, physician assistant studies, respiratory care, and sports sciences.

Costs

Tuition for 2007–08 was $771 per credit hour plus University and Student Activity fees, which vary with the number of courses for which the student is enrolled each semester. The 2006–07 cost for a residence hall room ranged from $2010 to $4000 per semester, apartments ranged from $3450 to $5300 per semester, suites ranged from $2900 to $4100 per semester, and board costs ranged from $935 to $1690 per semester. Apartments, suites, and standard rooms are available on a first-come, first-served basis. The Conolly Residence Hall has a 24-hour study lounge, an IBM computer lab, and an on-site dining hall.

Financial Aid

Long Island University has a no-need-test scholarship program, which awards scholarships on the basis of academic qualifications or talent and skills. State and federal financial aid is awarded on the basis of need and includes combinations of grants, loans, and work-study programs. Cooperative education placements are available to all students and serve as a valuable resource in meeting the cost of tuition. The entitlement programs of New York State's Tuition Assistance Program (TAP) and the Federal Pell Grant Program form the foundation of a student's financial aid package. Applicants must complete a Free Application for Federal Student Aid (FAFSA), available on the Internet at http://www.fafsa.ed.gov. Students are assisted in securing part-time employment by the Office of Career Services.

Faculty

Most faculty members teach both graduate and undergraduate courses. Students have the opportunity to work with senior faculty members early in their college career. Although engaged in research projects of varying types, the faculty's primary focus is on student academic development.

Student Government

The Student Government Association, the Campus's governing body of student life and its functions, consists of all registered students. The executive council includes president, vice president, treasurer, secretary, and 4 representatives from each academic class. Graduate, evening, and part-time students are represented on the council. The council's prime responsibility is to allocate funds to the various student organizations, thus assuring a full range of student activities.

Admission Requirements

Admission requirements vary depending on the academic program. Freshmen applicants must submit official high school transcripts, and it is recommended that they submit SAT or ACT scores, two letters of recommendation, and an essay. Transfer applicants must submit official copies of all college/university transcripts. High school transcripts are also required if the applicant has not yet earned a minimum of 24 college credits. Students should present 16 units of high school work, including 4 years of English, 3 of social studies, and 2 of mathematics (including geometry). GED (high school equivalency) scores can be accepted in lieu of a high school diploma for older students or service veterans. Credit for life experience may be awarded to qualified applicants.

Long Island University does not discriminate on the basis of sex, handicap, race, national origin, religion, political belief, or sexual preference in any of its educational programs and activities, including employment practices and policies relating to recruitment and admission of students.

Application and Information

Admission applications should be completed by August 15. Late applications are considered.

Forms may be requested from:

Undergraduate Admissions Office
Long Island University, Brooklyn Campus
1 University Plaza
Brooklyn, New York 11201
Phone: 718-488-1011
800-LIU-PLAN (toll-free)
Fax: 718-797-2399
E-mail: admissions@brooklyn.liu.edu
Web site: http://www.brooklyn.liu.edu/apply

Long Island University's Brooklyn Campus.

LONG ISLAND UNIVERSITY, C.W. POST CAMPUS

BROOKVILLE, NEW YORK

The Campus

C.W. Post Campus is a campus of Long Island University (LIU), one of the most comprehensive private universities in the U.S. Founded in 1954, the campus is situated on the North Shore of Long Island, approximately 25 miles from mid-Manhattan, on the former estate of cereal heiress Marjorie Merriweather Post.

Most of the more than 4,900 undergraduates are from New York, but students also attend from all parts of the United States and forty-eight other countries. More than 1,900 students live in residence halls. On-campus organizations are numerous and include the traditional interest-oriented activities. Students also frequently take an active part in local or national public affairs. Two percent of the students join fraternities and sororities. Intercollegiate and intramural sports for men and women include basketball, football, baseball, horseback riding, and more. More than 1,000 cultural and entertainment activities are offered on campus throughout the year, and most are open to the general public. The Hillwood Commons campus center has an outstanding art museum and film theater. Musical and dramatic presentations are offered in the Little Theater, Great Hall, and Tilles Center for the Performing Arts. The campus features a state-of-the-art recreation center with an eight-lane swimming pool, indoor track, basketball and racquetball courts, and weight and fitness rooms.

Location

C.W. Post's attractive 307-acre campus is nestled in the quiet, safe suburban community of Brookville, New York. Bus transportation is available to the Long Island Rail Road's stations in Greenvale and Hicksville and to nearby communities. Two major shopping centers in the immediate area include popular restaurants, movie theaters, and department stores. The cultural opportunities in New York City, only 50 minutes away, are also easily accessible to students.

Majors and Degrees

The major areas of study are accountancy, acting, anthropology, applied mathematics (with computer science), art, art education, art history and theory, arts management, art therapy, biology, biology education, biomedical technology, business administration, chemistry, chemistry education, clinical laboratory sciences (medical biology), comparative languages, computer science, criminal justice, dance studies, digital art and design, earth science education, earth system science, economics, education, electronic media (broadcasting), English, English education, environmental science, film, finance, forensic science, French, French education, geography, geology, graphic design, health and physical education, health-care administration, health education, health information management, history, information management and technology, information systems, interdisciplinary studies, international business, international studies, Italian, Italian education, journalism (print and electronic), management, management information systems, marketing, mathematics, mathematics education, mathematics/physics, music, music education, nursing (for RNs only), nutrition, painting, philosophy, photography, physical education, physics, political science, pre-engineering math, pre-engineering physics, prelaw, premedicine, prepharmacy, pre-respiratory therapy, psychology, public administration, public relations, radiologic technology, social studies education, social work, sociology, Spanish, Spanish education, speech-language pathology and audiology, and theater arts.

There are also accelerated five-year dual-degree programs: B.S./M.S. in accountancy, B.S./M.B.A. in accountancy, B.S./M.S. in biology, B.A./M.S. in criminal justice, B.A./M.B.A. in international studies/business administration, B.S./M.S. in nutrition, B.A./M.A. in political science, B.S./M.P.A. in health-care administration, B.S./M.P.A. in public administration, and B.A./M.P.A. in political science/public administration. C.W. Post also offers thirty-six dual bachelor's/master's degree programs in education, which cover infancy, preschool, and elementary, middle, and high school.

Academic Programs

To be eligible for a bachelor's degree, a student must complete at least 129 credits, 44 of which must be taken in general core courses. The B.F.A. degree programs require between 134 and 136 credits. All students in good academic standing, including freshmen, may take two elective courses per academic year (including summer school sessions) on a pass/fail basis for regular credit. A total of 24 credits may be taken on this basis.

The Long Island University Plan (LIU Plan) offers students a complete counseling network that ties together all academic, career, and financial counseling for students, beginning before enrollment and extending throughout the undergraduate years. Freshmen meet with faculty mentors and peer counselors in a 1-credit freshman seminar, College 101. The plan also provides opportunities to earn income while gaining hands-on career experience. Through C.W. Post's award-winning, nationally recognized program in cooperative education, students may build a resume, explore potential careers, establish contacts through networking, and earn money to defray the cost of a college education. C.W. Post places more than 250 students in paid cooperative education positions each year.

C.W. Post is liberal arts based, and all undergraduates, regardless of major, are exposed to different ways of thinking through courses in a broad range of subject areas, such as math, English, fine arts, history, and sociology. The C.W. Post Access program provides academic and career counseling to students who are undecided about their majors. The campus's Writing Across the Curriculum program offers courses in all majors to help students improve their writing skills.

An outstanding Honors and Merit Fellowship Program provides talented students with an academic environment designed to help them achieve their greatest potential. Approximately 9 percent of undergraduates who have demonstrated outstanding intellectual potential and academic achievement are selected to participate in this nationally respected program. Classes are usually limited to 20 students and run as discussion-style seminars in which the approach to the material is more sophisticated than in regular classes. Honors students also work independently with professors on tutorial and thesis projects and enhance their study with field trips to New York City, participation in national conferences, and lectures with noted guest speakers.

Off-Campus Programs

In today's global community, technology, business, and culture are critically intertwined. To address this integration, C.W. Post offers a variety of study-abroad opportunities. Students can deepen their perspectives on the world, gain invaluable cross-cultural experience, and earn credit toward their degrees. C.W. Post is affiliated with more than ten foreign study programs. Students may receive direct credit for courses and apply their financial aid and tuition toward program costs. C.W. Post students have studied abroad at Regent's College in London and Foreign Affairs College in Beijing. C.W. Post also has study-abroad opportunities with institutions in Australia, Cyprus, Egypt, France, Japan, and Korea.

Academic Facilities

This high-tech campus includes more than 500 computers for student use as well as wireless Internet connectivity in classrooms, study lounges, dining halls, and even outdoors on the campus's Great Lawn. The Student Technology Center offers free printing services, software assistance, and laptop rentals. The campus features several major-specific computer labs in journalism, public relations, computer science, and art. The B. Davis Schwartz Memorial Library is one of the largest research libraries in New York and houses more than 2.8 million volumes as part of the Long Island University System. The multilevel library is a digital powerhouse, with high-speed Web connections, online subscriptions, and more than 100 database services. The library features the nationally respected Center for Business and Information Research, Media Center, Rare Books Collection, and Government Information Department. Other campus facilities include an interfaith center, two modern student centers, and a world-famous concert hall that seats 2,200.

Costs

For 2007–08, tuition was $24,700, room and board averaged $4800 per semester, and student activity/University fees were $600 per semester.

Financial Aid

C.W. Post participates in all major federal and New York State financial aid programs. Aid includes Federal Pell Grants, Federal Supplemental Educational Opportunity Grants, Federal Perkins Loans, Federal Direct Loans, Federal Work-Study Program awards, and institutional grants and scholarships. C.W. Post students receive $90 million in financial aid each year. Students should consult the admissions office for criteria and deadlines.

The LIU Plan combines scholarships and cooperative education to provide a high-quality education at an affordable cost. All C.W. Post students are strongly encouraged to participate in paid professional internships (also known as cooperative education). Students gain work experience related to their major, begin to build a resume, and help reduce their costs by supplementing financial aid with co-op earnings.

The C.W. Post Campus requires all applicants for financial aid to submit the Free Application for Federal Student Aid (FAFSA) and New York State TAP Application (New York State applicants only) in addition to the application for admission. All applicants seeking financial assistance are strongly urged to apply early in order to be assured of full exposure to the funding possibilities. The recommended submission date for application is March 1 in order to meet the University's deadline of May 15 each year. Financial aid is granted only after a student has been offered admission. All aid is granted for one year but is renewable, based on published criteria and federal and state eligibility guidelines.

Faculty

C.W. Post has more than 320 full-time faculty members. Most full-time faculty members have the highest degrees in their fields.

Student Government

The Student Government Association is the representative body of all students and is composed of three branches: the executive, the legislative, and the judicial. The Student Government Association works closely with the administration on many student-life issues such as recognition and funding of student clubs and organizations, special events, faculty evaluations, and campus issues that affect the academic life of the C.W. Post student.

Admission Requirements

Undergraduates apply from all parts of the United States and from more than forty-five other countries. Last year, 7,300 applicants from both public and private schools competed for 1,000 places in the freshman class and 700 in the transfer class. Each year, the Admissions Committee seeks a diverse group of students who are academically prepared for the college experience. The committee considers not only academic achievement but also a student's talent and potential to contribute to the C.W. Post community. Applicants should complete an admission application and present a high school or previous college transcript, SAT or ACT scores, and a personal statement. The credentials of all applicants are considered carefully by the Admissions Committee, and attention is given to each candidate's individual strengths. On-campus interviews with admissions counselors are highly recommended.

Application and Information

Classes are offered year-round. Students may begin studies in the fall, winter, spring, or summer semesters. Campus tours are available Monday through Saturday and by appointment. Summer and holiday schedules vary. Admission decisions are made on a rolling basis, but those wishing to be considered for scholarships should consult with the admissions office for application deadlines. The Office of Admissions is open Monday through Thursday, 9 a.m. to 8 p.m.; Friday, 9 a.m. to 5 p.m.; and Saturday, 10 a.m. to 2 p.m. For additional information and to schedule interviews and campus visits, students are encouraged to contact:

Office of Admissions
Long Island University, C.W. Post Campus
720 Northern Boulevard
Brookville, New York 11548-1300

Phone: 516-299-2900
800-LIU-PLAN (toll-free)
Fax: 516-299-2137
E-mail: enroll@cwpost.liu.edu
Web site: http://www.liu.edu/cwpost

A view of the C.W. Post Campus.

COLLEGE DATA CENTER • NEW YORK

MANHATTAN COLLEGE

RIVERDALE, NEW YORK

The College

Manhattan College surpassed a historic anniversary milestone in 2003 when it celebrated 150 years of its commitment to excellence in Lasallian education. But making history does not end here. Since its inception in 1853, Manhattan College has never wavered from its principal goal—to deliver today the high quality of education necessary for the leaders of tomorrow.

The College has an enrollment of some 3,200 students, of whom 2,700 are undergraduates. Approximately 70 percent of Manhattan's students come from New York State; the remaining 30 percent represent thirty-nine other states and fifty other countries. Approximately 1,800 housing units are available, consisting of on-campus residence halls and off-campus apartments. More than half of the student population resides on campus. Manhattan offers seventy extracurricular organizations and five student publications and fields twenty varsity and club sports teams. Of Manhattan's 40,000 living alumni, a large number are prominent leaders in business, government, education, the arts, the sciences, and engineering.

Location

The main campus of the College is located 10 miles north of midtown Manhattan in the suburban Riverdale section of the Bronx, about a mile from Westchester County. Riverdale is an upper-middle-class community, the home of many New York business, political, and education leaders. The area offers the calm and quiet of a residential, suburban setting as well as easy access to the many advantages of New York City. The College is easily accessible by subway, bus, or highway.

Majors and Degrees

The liberal arts curriculum of the School of Arts provides programs that lead to a Bachelor of Arts or Bachelor of Science with majors in the humanities and the social sciences, including communications, economics, English, French, government, history, modern foreign languages, philosophy, psychology, religious studies, and sociology. Interdisciplinary majors include international studies, peace studies, and urban affairs. In the School of Science, programs lead to a Bachelor of Science or Bachelor of Arts with majors in biochemistry, biology, chemistry, computer science, mathematics, and physics. Premedical, predental, and preveterinary programs are also available.

The School of Engineering has programs leading to a Bachelor of Science in chemical, civil, computer, electrical, environmental, and mechanical engineering.

The School of Business has programs leading to a Bachelor of Science in Business Administration with majors in accounting, computer information systems, economics, finance, global business studies, management, and marketing.

The School of Education offers a curriculum leading to a Bachelor of Arts in childhood education, childhood/special education (dual program), and adolescent education. The physical education curriculum leads to a Bachelor of Science in physical education and exercise science. The health education curriculum leads to a Bachelor of Science in allied health, with a concentration in health-care administration, health counseling, or scientific foundations. Curricula in radiological and health sciences lead to a Bachelor of Science in radiation therapy or nuclear medicine technology.

Academic Programs

The core curriculum shared by the School of Arts and the School of Science studies some of the vital works of humankind, explores new ideas, examines the meaning of scientific experimentation, and encourages a student to develop his or her thinking and leadership abilities. The major programs offer advanced work in specific humanistic and scientific disciplines and opportunities to work on research projects in collaboration with faculty scholars.

In the School of Engineering, all engineering students follow a common core curriculum during the first two years and choose a major at the beginning of the junior year. Each curriculum includes a generous selection of courses in basic sciences, the engineering sciences, humanistic studies, and mathematics.

The School of Business prepares students for positions of executive responsibility in business, government, and nonprofit organizations. The business curriculum is based on a strong commitment to liberal education and is well balanced between professional business courses, humanities, sciences, and social sciences. This is a reflection of the school's belief that executives should be broadly educated and should involve themselves, as well as their organizations, in efforts to solve social problems.

The School of Education prepares students for teaching, counseling, and health professions. Students complete the College's core curriculum in liberal arts and sciences and then complete a major in various programs in the school's three departments: Education, Physical Education and Exercise Science, and Radiological and Health Professions. All programs include internships/practicums in schools, hospitals, or other institutions. Graduates of the school's teacher-preparation programs receive New York State provisional teaching certification. The school also offers a five-year B.A./M.S. program in childhood/special education and special education.

Off-Campus Programs

Students in the liberal arts curricula who have demonstrated superior achievement in their first two years are encouraged to spend their junior year studying abroad. Manhattan College offers study-abroad programs; arrangements can be made to study in a country of choice. Students in the School of Business may participate in the International Field Studies Seminar. As participants in the seminar, students spend time in another country studying the effect of that environment on international firms. Career services and co-op education integrate classroom theory with the practical experience of a job in industry, business, the social services, the arts, or government. Portions of the education courses are conducted in New York City schools, in order that student teachers may gain experience in urban education at an early stage.

Academic Facilities

There are more than forty scientific and engineering laboratories at Manhattan, including the Research and Learning Center, as well as a modern language laboratory and a computer information systems laboratory. Manhattan's newly built O'Malley Library is a state-of-the-art facility featuring modern accommodations for study and research. It is connected to the renovated and updated Cardinal Hayes Pavilion (formerly the Cardinal Hayes Library). The library combines Hayes' traditional neo-Georgian accents with strong contemporary lines. The five-story addition to the original building doubles the original square footage and connects the current library to the upper campus. Students and faculty members are able to enter directly from a brick walkway that starts at the Quadrangle.

Costs

For 2006–07, the tuition for Manhattan College was $20,350 per year plus program fees. The cost of room and board for the year was $9325.

Financial Aid

Manhattan grants or administers financial assistance in the form of tuition awards to students on the basis of need and/or ability. Need is evaluated through the FAFSA. In addition to a general scholarship fund, Manhattan offers endowed scholarships, special-category scholarships and grants, student athletic grants, Federal Pell Grants, Federal Supplemental Educational Opportunity Grants, student loans, Federal Work-Study Program awards, and New York State financial assistance. A total of 1,650 students receive financial aid from Manhattan College, and approximately 87 percent receive financial aid from government or private agencies.

Faculty

Manhattan's faculty has about 185 full-time and about 100 part-time teachers. The faculty-student ratio is approximately 1:13. Nearly 95 percent of the faculty members hold doctorates. The maximum teaching load on the undergraduate level is 9 credit hours per semester. Faculty members serve on the College Senate, the Council for Faculty Affairs, and numerous faculty and campus committees. In addition, they are available to students for informal guidance and counseling and also serve as official moderators of many campus organizations.

Student Government

The Manhattan Student Government is composed of students elected annually by their peers to fill posts outlined in the Student Government Constitution. The Student Government allocates funds to all student organizations. Members of the Student Government are also full voting members of the College Senate.

Admission Requirements

Manhattan has a long-standing policy of nondiscrimination. No applicant is refused admission because of race, color, religion, age, national origin, sex, or disability. All applicants must present an academic diploma from an accredited high school and must offer a minimum of 16 credits in academic subjects. Liberal arts candidates must be proficient in at least one foreign language. At the discretion of the Committee on Admissions, quantitative requirements may be modified for applicants with especially strong records who show promise of doing well in college. In the selection process, attention is given to scholastic ability, as indicated by grades and rank in class, as well as to standardized test scores and recommendations from principals and counselors. All candidates must submit either SAT or ACT results. An interview with a member of the admission staff is recommended. Applicants may submit scores on the General Educational Development test in lieu of a formal high school diploma; however, all such applicants must submit the results of the appropriate College Board tests. Manhattan College offers early acceptance for high school seniors, admission to advanced standing, advanced placement, and credit by examination. Junior college or other transfer students are welcome. Manhattan College requires applicants whose native language is not English to take the Test of English as a Foreign Language (TOEFL) as well as the SAT. The average SAT scores of entering freshmen in 2006 were 575 in mathematics and 557 in the verbal portion.

Application and Information

Application forms are furnished by the Admission Office on request. The Common Application Form, which is available in many high school guidance offices, may also be used. After supplying the information required, students must send the application for admission to the Admission Office at Manhattan College. The high school report and the student evaluation and transcript must be submitted by the high school guidance counselor. This should be done after six terms of high school or right after the seventh term. There is a rolling admissions policy and a March 1 deadline for financial aid applications. A nonrefundable application fee of $50 is required.

William J. Bisset
Vice President for Enrollment Management
Manhattan College
Riverdale, New York 10471
Phone: 718-862-7200
800-MC2-XCEL (toll-free)
E-mail: admit@manhattan.edu
Web site: http://www.manhattan.edu

Students walking in the Quadrangle of the Manhattan College campus.

MANHATTAN SCHOOL OF MUSIC

NEW YORK, NEW YORK

The School

Since 1917, Manhattan School of Music (MSM) has been preparing gifted young musicians to assume places on the great stages of the world. When they select Manhattan School of Music, students choose to work with faculty members who are themselves performers with international reputations. In addition, they choose to be with exceptional students from around the world who come together to create an environment remarkable not only for its intensity, but also for its genuine friendliness and sincere cooperation. When students choose Manhattan School of Music, they also choose New York itself, the very heart of music and art in America.

While all music conservatories of the first rank are acknowledged for their ability to develop talents and refine skills, Manhattan School of Music has a particular combination of strengths that makes it something more—an unrivaled place from which to launch a career.

Performance is the vital expression of a musician's life. At Manhattan School of Music, performance is not simply the goal for students, it is at the center of their lives. With extensive performance opportunities on campus and the chance to freelance and begin to develop a network of professional contacts, students undergo remarkable changes; they start to think and function as professional musicians while they are still in school. It is this powerful convergence of unmatched opportunity and rigorous training that gives these students the best chance to go as far as their talent, their intelligence, and their courage can take them.

Manhattan School of Music enrolls 825 students, approximately 48 percent of whom are undergraduates. They come from more than forty-one states and more than thirty countries. Nineteen percent are students of color and 32 percent are international.

Students must live in residence housing for the first and second years of their study and may apply to stay longer. The School opened a residence facility in 2001. The G. Chris and Sungeun Han-Andersen Residence Hall is a 380-bed facility that is attached to the main building. Double and single rooms are available, as well as approximately sixty practice rooms, an exercise room, a computer lounge, a multipurpose lounge, and a laundry facility for resident students.

Location

For musicians and other artists of great ability and ambition, New York is universally acknowledged as the best place to be. Around the corner and down every street there are opportunities to see and hear the best music in the world every night of the year. With Broadway and off-Broadway theaters, world-famous jazz clubs, and countless museums, New York remains what it has always been—one of the most extraordinary cities on earth. The names of the legendary places and performers that make New York what it is are the very definition of excellence. Carnegie Hall, Lincoln Center, the Blue Note, the Metropolitan Opera, the New York Philharmonic, the American Ballet Theater, the New York City Ballet, the New York City Opera, the Alvin Ailey American Dance Theater, and the Metropolitan Museum of Art are all accessible from the campus.

As part of New York's "Academic Acropolis," Manhattan School of Music shares its student-oriented, Upper West Side location with Columbia University, Barnard College, Union Theological Seminary, Jewish Theological Seminary, Bank Street College, the Cathedral of St. John the Divine, and Riverside Church.

Majors and Degrees

Manhattan School of Music offers Bachelor of Music degrees in classical composition, classical performance (guitar, orchestral instruments, piano, and voice), jazz composition, and jazz performance (no jazz voice at the undergraduate level).

Academic Programs

The degree requires completion of a four-year program of study, with a required humanities core sequence, a music history and music theory core sequence, required courses relevant to each instrument/major, and large and small performance ensembles. Faculty members provide weekly, private, one-on-one instruction in each major. The number of credits required to graduate depends on the instrument/major but is no fewer than 120.

Because the School is dedicated to training outstanding performing artists, performance is at the core of most courses. Appropriate assignments to symphony orchestras, opera studios and workshops, jazz ensembles, and chamber music ensembles evolve into more than 400 public performances per academic year by students. Performance opportunities include Symphony Orchestra, Philharmonia Orchestra, Chamber Sinfonia, Opera Theater, American Musical Theater Ensemble, Percussion Ensemble, Guitar Ensemble, Baroque Aria Ensemble, Jazz Orchestra, Concert Jazz Band, Afro-Cuban Ensemble, and more than seventy-five jazz combos and chamber music groups.

A cross-registration program between Manhattan School of Music and Barnard College of Columbia University enables qualified undergraduates to have access to a wide variety of academic courses. Musically qualified Barnard students may enroll in lessons with Manhattan School of Music faculty members.

Academic Facilities

Performance spaces at Manhattan School of Music include the 846-seat John C. Borden Auditorium for symphony, opera, and jazz performances; the Gordon K. and Harriet Greenfield Hall, a 281-seat recital hall; the 153-seat William R. and Irene D. Miller Recital Hall; the multiuse Alan M. and Joan Taub Ades Performance Space; Carl and Lilly Pforzheimer Hall, a 50-seat recital hall; and the Charles Myers Recital Hall, a 35-seat recital hall/recording studio.

Four excellent electronic music studios provide students with state-of-the-art computers, software, keyboards, and other equipment for composition, recording, editing, sound design, and performance.

The Peter Jay Sharpe Library (opened fall 2004), has a collection that includes more than 29,000 recordings, 50,000 scores, 18,000 books, 2500 DVDs, and 107 periodicals. Additional services include WiFi and data ports, streaming audio, online subscriptions, Finale and Sibelius software, and catalog, interlibrary loan, and reference services. PCs, listening and viewing equipment, a microform reader, exhibits, study carrels, and photocopiers are also available, creating an environment focused on serving students' musical and academic interests and needs.

MSM also has a campus store that carries a wide variety of inventory to appeal to students, parents, and faculty and staff members. The store maintains required textbooks and a selection of orchestral scores, chamber music, piano music, violin solos, and music for voice.

Costs

Tuition for the 2008–09 academic year (12–18 credits per semester) is $29,975. Annual fees required of all students total $500 plus a health insurance fee estimated to be $2250. Housing costs are $8750 to $13,400 per year, and food costs are approximately $4400 per year.

Financial Aid

Manhattan School of Music offers federal and state financial assistance as well as its own institutional resources in the form of scholarships and grants. Federal and state aid is administered in accordance with federal and state laws and regulations. The majority of institutional scholarships are awarded on the basis of audition results, financial need, previous academic work, and the School's need for particular instruments/majors. Each year the School also awards some of its resources on the basis of merit alone. Forty percent of the School's students receive scholarships. The financial aid deadline is March 1 for both government and institutional aid.

Faculty

The faculty forms the essential core of any school, but at a conservatory, faculty members take on an additional importance, for it is not simply what they know but what they do that helps to transform their students.

Manhattan School of Music's 250 faculty members are soloists and chamber and jazz artists as well as members of the New York Philharmonic, the Metropolitan Opera Company, the Chamber Music Society of Lincoln Center, New York City Opera, and the Orpheus Chamber Orchestra. Artists-in-residence include American String Quartet and Windscape.

Regular faculty members teach 98 percent of all courses and 100 percent of private lesson instruction.

Each year, Manhattan School of Music brings more than 50 internationally renowned conductors and performing artists to the School. Selected conductors during 2006–08 were Pierre Boulez, Joanna Carniero, Mei-Ann Chen, Philippe Entremont, JoAnn Falletta, David Gilbert, Marc Gould, Sidney Harth, Kenneth Kiesler, Raymond Leppard, George Manahan, Robert Mann, Kurt Masur, Rossen Milanov, Alisdair Neale, Steven Osgood, Lawrence Leighton Smith, Jean-Philippe Tremblay, Claudio Vandelli, and Pinchas Zukerman.

Each season a number of internationally renowned artists are invited to present master classes at Manhattan School of Music. Some of the artists who have recently worked with MSM students are Yuri Bashmet, Isidore Cohen, Glenn Dicterow, Mignon Dunn, Eliot Fisk, Philip Glass, Richard Goode, Thomas Hampson, Marilyn Horne, Martin Katz, Ani Kavafian, David Liebman, Yo-Yo Ma, Marian McPartland, Zara Nelsova, Ursula Oppens, Emanuel Pahlud, Hermann Prey, Ned Rorem, Mstislav Rostropovich, Janos Starker, Richard Stoltzman, Billy Taylor, Michael Tree, Dawn Upshaw, Benita Valente, Andre Watts, and Pinchas Zukerman.

Artists who have conducted concert programs or held readings with the MSM orchestras include Roberto Abaddo, Marin Alsop, Pierre Boulez, Leon Fleisher, Kurt Masur, David Robertson, Gunther Schuller, Jerzy Semkow, Leonard Slatkin, Yuri Temerakonov, JoAnn Faletta, and Phillipe Entremont.

Student Government

The Manhattan School of Music Student Council serves as the voice of the student body. Made up of both undergraduate and graduate students, the council voluntarily serves a one-year renewable term and serves as an advisory body to the administration. The council also sponsors various social activities at the School.

Admission Requirements

Manhattan School of Music requires an in-person audition in New York City during the annual March audition period. Many instruments have a prescreening requirement. Cellists, bassists, and tubists may submit a DVD in lieu of a live audition. A high school transcript or an official high school equivalency diploma is required of all applicants.

International applicants residing outside of North America may submit a DVD (U.S. format only) in lieu of a live audition. Applicants whose first language is not English must take the TOEFL and submit their scores before consideration for admission.

Additional admission requirements can be found on the application and on the Web site.

Manhattan School of Music is a highly selective college and admitted only 30 percent of the freshman applicants for admission for the 2006–07 academic year. Manhattan School of Music seeks a geographically and ethnically diverse student body.

Recognition of transfer credits from other institutions of higher education in theory, sight singing, dictation, keyboard harmony, required piano, and music history is determined by placement tests given during new student orientation before the first semester. Credit for other courses completed with a minimum grade of C or its equivalent depends on the extent to which these subjects satisfy the curricular requirements of the School.

Application and Information

Applications for both freshmen and transfer students must be received by December 1. The online application can be found at http://www.unifiedapps.org. Notification of admission status is sent by mail two to four weeks after the audition period.

For more information, students should contact:

Amy A. Anderson
Associate Dean for Enrollment Management
Manhattan School of Music
120 Claremont Avenue
New York, New York 10027
Phone: 212-749-2802 Ext. 2
Fax: 212-749-3025
E-mail: admission@msmnyc.edu
Web site: http://www.msmnyc.edu

The Manhattan School of Music building and the Andersen Residence Hall as viewed from across Broadway.

MANHATTANVILLE COLLEGE

PURCHASE, NEW YORK

The College

On its 100-acre campus 30 minutes north of New York City, Manhattanville College has created a small global village. The private coeducational college founded in 1841 draws its 1,600 students from seventy-six different countries and forty states. This richly diverse community embodies the College's mission: to educate ethically and socially responsible leaders for the global community.

Manhattanville's proximity to New York City creates a constant flow of opportunity that brings learning to life. Many students choose to spend a "semester abroad" living, interning, and studying in the city. Manhattanville students know how to have fun, but they also have a sense of purpose. The College's social conscience is informed by a commitment to serving the community—whether it is defined as the surrounding geographic area, where undergraduates logged 23,000 hours of service in a year, or as the global community. Manhattanville students actively seek opportunities to serve humanitarian causes in the developing world.

Manhattanville's global perspective is enriched by its role as a Non-Government Organization of the United Nations. Select students have an opportunity to intern at the UN and to study with an ambassador on Manhattanville's faculty. In addition, the College offers a Meet the Ambassadors Series on campus, where students attend lectures by leading ambassadors, followed by dinner at the home of the College's president.

Location

Manhattanville's campus lies in the heart of Westchester County, bordered on the east by Long Island Sound and on the west by the Hudson River. From the roof of the castle that serves as the campus' main hall, the skyline of Manhattan is clearly visible. This proximity to the city that calls itself the "Capital of the World" is one of Manhattanville's many assets. The College provides transportation to the city on weekends and to Manhattan-bound commuter trains during the week so students can take advantage of all New York City has to offer.

Majors and Degrees

Manhattanville College offers undergraduate degrees in more than fifty academic concentrations in the arts and sciences, including Bachelor of Arts (B.A.), Bachelor of Science (B.S.), Bachelor of Fine Arts (B.F.A.), and Bachelor of Music (B.Mus.) degrees; a self-designed major; a double major with teacher certification; and preparation for professional and graduate study (prelaw, premed, prehealth, and predentistry).

Students may choose from the following areas of study: African studies, American literature, American studies, art history, art (studio), Asian studies, biochemistry, biology, British literature, chemistry, communications studies, computer science, creative writing, criminal justice, dance and theater, dance therapy, economics, education (five-year M.A.T. program offered), English, environmental studies, film studies, finance, French, German, history, Holocaust and genocide studies, human resource management, international management, international studies, Irish studies, Italian, Latin American studies, legal studies, management, mathematics, music, music management, musical theater, neuroscience, philosophy, physics, political science, psychology, Romance languages, self-designed major, social justice, sociology and anthropology, Spanish, theater education, women's studies, world literature, and world religions.

Manhattanville also offers undergraduate certification programs in computer science, finance management, and teaching.

Academic Programs

Manhattanville College offers full-time, part-time, and accelerated opportunities for study as well as dual-degree programs. The Manhattanville curriculum nurtures intellectual curiosity and independent thinking. Students and professors form close collaborative relationships beginning with the Preceptorial, an interdisciplinary survey of the liberal arts that is required of all freshmen.

The core of the Manhattanville curriculum is the Portfolio System, which provides for a level of flexibility that is unusual in traditional liberal arts education. Under the guidance of a faculty adviser, the student maps an academic and cocurricular program, establishing a major and minor from different branches of the liberal arts. The student may begin studies in the chosen field as early as the freshman year. Over the course of four years of study, the student assembles a portfolio consisting of study plans, evidence of academic proficiency in written critical analysis and qualitative research, annual evaluations, transcripts, and examples of the student's best work. A College-wide review board evaluates the portfolio.

A special option for B.A. candidates is the self-designed major. If a student's interests direct them beyond existing departmental majors, they may propose a program of study to the Board of Academic Standards. Manhattanville students also have the opportunity to earn academic credit for internships in New York City.

Manhattanville College offers college credit for A-level exams, International Baccalaureates, and Advanced Placement examinations.

Off-Campus Programs

Manhattanville offers more than two dozen study-abroad opportunities at various levels of language proficiency, including Argentina, Belgium (internship at the European Union), Chile, Czech Republic, England, France, Germany, Ireland, Italy, Japan, Kenya, and Spain, among others, as well as a semester in New York City or a semester at sea.

Academic Facilities

Manhattanville has been named one of the "Top 100 Wired Colleges in the U.S." The Manhattanville Library capitalizes on the power of the Internet to connect students with information and analysis found in powerful subscription databases, electronic journals, and electronic books. Manhattanville is one of the first colleges in the U.S. to outsource a service that enables students to interact online with experienced reference librarians at any time of the day or night from anywhere in the world. The virtual research service, "Ask a Librarian 24/7," uses cobrowsing to connect students with professional librarians who can answer questions about research and help students navigate the College's extensive array of subscription databases and other library resources. Manhattanville's teaching library, which supports the School of Education, ranks among the foremost undergraduate teaching libraries in the country. The Menendez Language Laboratory includes tapes and record libraries that provide materials for class instruction and individual practice in French, Spanish, Russian, Italian, German, Chinese, Japanese, Hindi, Marathi, modern Hebrew, and English as a second language. The College provides a writing clinic, a reading clinic, audiovisual facilities, and a bibliographic instruction program. The library building is open 24 hours a day, seven days a week through most of the fall and spring semesters, and it has computer labs, quiet study areas, group-study rooms, and a café where students and faculty members can meet informally.

The College has state-of-the-art computers, computer labs, and campus networking for student use and instruction. In addition, advanced music technology systems offer performing arts students limitless opportunities for creativity.

Costs

For the 2007–08 academic year, tuition and fees were $29,680. Average room and board costs were $12,240.

Financial Aid

Manhattanville College offers both merit scholarships and need-based financial aid. Nearly 80 percent of students receive financial awards. The institutional form and the Free Application for Federal Student Aid (FAFSA) are required. The types of awards available are honors, merit, arts, and community service scholarships; Manhattanville grants and scholarships; Federal Perkins Loans; Federal Stafford Student Loans; Federal Pell Grants; Federal Supplemental Educational Opportunity Grants; Federal Work-Study Program awards; and Tuition Assistance Program awards.

Faculty

Nearly 90 percent of faculty members have Ph.D. or terminal degrees in their fields, and the vast majority serve full-time. Many faculty members live on the campus. The Manhattanville curriculum nurtures intellectual curiosity and independent thinking. The student-faculty ratio of 12:1 promotes close and collaborative relationships between faculty members and students, aided by the structure of the curriculum and the Portfolio System, which fosters collaboration between student and faculty adviser. Faculty members, not teaching assistants, teach all Manhattanville classes, and 80 percent of the classes have 20 or fewer students.

Student Government

Students in large measure shape the quality of life on the Manhattanville campus. Elected representatives of the student body run the student government, which serves as a principal means of communication among the administration, faculty members, and students. Its board of directors is responsible for formulating policy on student life and for implementing this policy through various committees. Student government members also serve on the College's policymaking and ad hoc committees.

Admission Requirements

Manhattanville College admits men and women as candidates for undergraduate degrees if their academic records indicate a competence to engage in a challenging liberal arts curriculum. Admission to the College is selective, and the most important consideration is the student's secondary school performance. When weighing this aspect, the admissions committee evaluates the quality of the school, the strength of the student's program, and success in those studies. Next, the committee considers the various recommendations that are submitted on behalf of the student, along with scores on required standardized tests and the student's personal statement. The SAT or the ACT is required. A campus interview is strongly recommended. Students who plan to specialize in music or musical theater should come to Manhattanville for an audition or should secure permission to submit a tape. Students who plan to apply for the B.F.A. degree program should present portfolios to the art department for evaluation. The portfolios are not required for admission to the College. Students who plan to study dance and theater may audition for scholarships.

Application and Information

The deadline for early decision applications is December 1, 2007, and the deadline for rolling admission is March 1, 2008. The College subscribes to the Candidates Reply Date. Applications should be submitted as early in the senior year as possible. The application fee of $60 is waived for online applications. All application decisions are made without regard to race, religion, sex, national or ethnic origin, or handicap. Candidates may apply online at http://www.manhattanville.edu.

For further information, students should contact:

Office of Undergraduate Admissions
Manhattanville College
2900 Purchase Street
Purchase, New York 10577
Phone: 914-323-5464
800-32-VILLE (toll-free)
Web site: http://www.manhattanville.edu

Reid Hall ("The Castle") is the centerpiece of the Manhattanville College campus.

COLLEGE DATA CENTER • NEW YORK

MANNES COLLEGE THE NEW SCHOOL FOR MUSIC

THE NEW SCHOOL
A UNIVERSITY

NEW YORK, NEW YORK

The College

Mannes College The New School for Music in New York City is one of the world's preeminent conservatories of classical music. The Mannes community is made up of students and a faculty of professional musicians from every corner of the world. Here, aspiring artists learn and play music with scholars, composers, conductors, and performing artists from some of the world's most revered orchestras, ensembles, and opera companies. Most of the more than 400 concerts produced by the School each year at its two concert halls or at venues throughout the New York metropolitan region feature Mannes students. With only 300 college students, Mannes provides an intimate, supportive atmosphere that allows for close and constructive relationships among students, faculty members, and administrators.

Part of The New School, a leading urban university, Mannes offers its own undergraduate academic curriculum focused on areas most pertinent to classical music. Students may choose to supplement this curriculum by taking courses at the other divisions of The New School. In addition, throughout their studies, students follow a program of instruction in the techniques of music. This program includes studies in ear training, sight singing, keyboard skills, theory, analysis, and dictation that are among the best in the world, all helping to train students to meet the unique challenges faced by musicians in the twenty-first century.

Graduate degrees offered include the Master of Music (M.M.), a two-year degree program offered in all orchestral instruments (violin, viola, cello, bass, flute, oboe, clarinet, bassoon, saxophone, horn, trumpet, trombone, tuba, harp, and percussion), piano, harpsichord, guitar, voice, composition, conducting, and theory. Students receive private lessons in their major field and take performance classes (such as orchestra, opera, and chamber music), courses in the techniques of music, and chosen electives that focus on specialized topics of the student's interest.

Mannes also offers the Professional Studies Diploma (PSD), an advanced course of study designed to enhance performance or compositional skills. The PSD is generally pursued following a master's degree or the equivalent. Individual programs are designed in coordination with the associate/assistant dean. Orchestral instrument majors participate in orchestra during each semester of residency. Additionally, chamber music is a curricular component of some instrumental majors. All Mannes and some New School courses are available to qualified students; however, only graduate-level courses apply toward the Professional Studies Diploma.

Total enrollment is 277, 49 percent of whom are international students. There are 156 faculty members, and the student-teacher ratio is less than 2:1. The average class size is 10–12 students.

Through The New School, Mannes is proud to offer housing facilities that include apartment-style dormitory suites equipped with full kitchens, full bathrooms, air conditioning, Internet service, and other amenities. Residences available to Mannes students are located in Chelsea, Greenwich Village, Union Square, and lower Manhattan. All dormitories are equipped with a 24-hour security guard and resident advisers on every floor. All incoming freshman are offered on-campus housing, but it is not a requirement for admission. The housing office offers assistance with off-campus housing.

Location

Mannes is located in Manhattan's Upper West Side, one of the finest residential areas of New York City. It is within walking distance of the Museum of Natural History and Lincoln Center for the Performing Arts (home to the New York Philharmonic, the Metropolitan Opera, and other world-renowned orchestras and ballet companies). Mannes students also benefit from and contribute to New York City's rich musical and cultural life.

Majors and Degrees

Undergraduate degrees offered include the Bachelor of Music (B.M.) in all orchestral instruments (bass, bassoon, cello, clarinet, flute, harp, horn, oboe, percussion, saxophone, trombone, trumpet, tuba, viola, and violin), composition, conducting, guitar, harpsichord, piano, theory, and voice. Students receive private lessons in their major field and take performance classes (such as chamber music, orchestra, or opera) and courses in the techniques of music and liberal arts, as well as electives.

A Bachelor of Science (B.S.) is offered in all majors by completing the Bachelor of Music curriculum and taking or transferring from another institution an additional 30 academic credits.

The Undergraduate Diploma (UDPL) is offered in all majors and is equivalent to the Bachelor of Music degree minus the liberal arts courses.

Academic Programs

Some outstanding performance opportunities include the Mannes Orchestra, led by David Hayes; the Mannes Opera Program, led by Joseph Colaneri; the Mannes Chorus; the Mannes Baroque Chamber Players; the Percussion Ensemble; NewMusicMannes; and numerous chamber music ensembles that perform year-round.

The Mannes Community Services Office employs students to perform in the widest range of New York settings, such as official receptions, galas, and public and private settings, and also encourages them to perform with many of New York's orchestras, choruses, and opera companies.

Mannes also offers concerto competitions for all performance majors, an audio recording facility, and career development advisement.

Academic Facilities

Degree candidates have access to the university's broad liberal arts curriculum, with offerings in the humanities, fine arts, and the social sciences. Mannes students share resources with The New School's other divisions, which include Parsons The New School for Design, Eugene Lang College The New School for Liberal Arts, The New School for General Studies, The New School for Drama, The New School for Social Research, Milano The New School for Management and Urban Policy, and The New School for Jazz and Contemporary Music.

Mannes' home is a Federal-style building on Manhattan's Upper West Side. The building houses classrooms, practice rooms, a state-of-the art computer lab, and the Harry Sherman Library, which offers access to more than 3 million books, 25,000 journals, a complete music and listening library, and study carrels. The New School also offers the facilities of the Bobst Library at New York University through a consortium known as the Research Library Association of South Manhattan. The consortium's online catalog, Bobcat, is accessible over the Internet.

Mannes' two concert halls, seating 250 and 75 people, are the venues for hundreds of performances each year by students, faculty members, and artists-in-residence, as well as for master classes. The John Goldmark Practice Center, adjacent to Lincoln Center, provides additional practice rooms and an opera rehearsal room.

Costs

Tuition for the 2007–08 school year was as follows: for the B.M., B.S., M.M., and UDPL programs, $29,800; for the Professional Studies Diploma, $21,130; and for the ESL course work program, $3500. University fees are $1928. Estimated living expenses are $18,135, which includes room, board, books, and supplies. A small percentage increase in costs is expected for the 2008–09 school year.

Financial Aid

Scholarships are available on the basis of merit and are determined at the time of the audition. Approximately 75 percent of Mannes students receive some form of scholarship. The average award ranges from 25 percent to 50 percent of tuition. In certain majors, opportunities exist for further assistance up to full tuition. Loans, grants, and work-study programs are available to students who fill out the Free Application for Federal Student Aid, the filing of which is required for U.S. citizens and permanent residents seeking financial aid of any type. A package of loans and information is sent along with the acceptance letter.

Faculty

Mannes is committed to providing broad and rigorous musical training in a friendly and supportive community that encourages artistic growth. The distinguished faculty includes some of New York City's most prominent musicians, as well as internationally known artists and ensembles. All students receive private lessons and participate in ensembles, and the 2:1 student-faculty ratio ensures personalized instruction and close interaction among, students, faculty and staff members, and administrators.

Admission Requirements

An application for admission to Mannes College The New School for Music consists of a completed Unified Application for Conservatory Admission–Mannes Edition (available online at http://www.unifiedapps.org), a $100 nonrefundable application fee, official high school or college academic transcripts for all schools attended (graduate degree applicants need only send college transcripts), and one letter of recommendation from a recent music teacher or an evaluation from a professional musician. International students must submit a recent TOEFL score. Mannes' school code is 2398. A minimum computer-based TOEFL score of 213 and a successful English test taken at the audition is required. A minimum computer-based TOEFL score of 250 is required for all graduate theory, composition, and conducting majors.

Audition requirements vary by field of study and program sought, outlines of which can be found in the Mannes College catalog. During the audition period, musicianship skills are tested for all degree and UDPL applicants. These tests in dictation, ear training, piano, and theory are required in order to complete the application for entrance to the undergraduate and master's degree programs. English language testing is required of applicants whose first language is not English.

Application and Information

The application deadline for the main March entrance auditions is December 1. The application deadline for the late auditions in May is April 1.

For more information, students should contact:

Office of Admissions
Mannes College The New School for Music
150 West 85th Street
New York, New York 10024
Phone: 212-580-0210 Ext. 4862
800-292-3040 (toll-free)
E-mail: mannesadmissions@newschool.edu
Web site: http://www.mannes.newschool.edu/

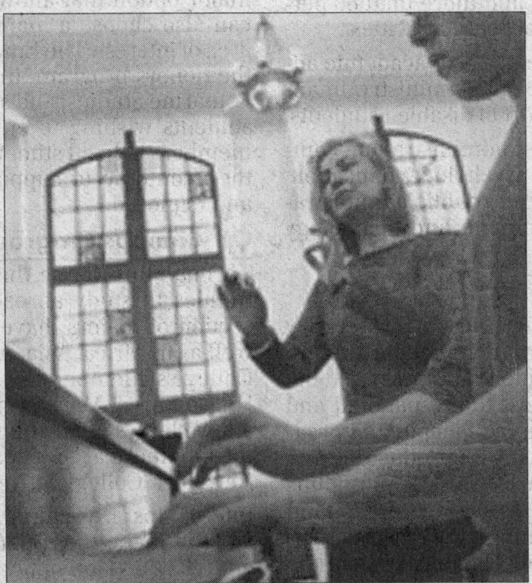

Mannes College The New School for Music.

MARIST COLLEGE

POUGHKEEPSIE, NEW YORK

The College

Marist College is located in the Hudson River Valley, midway between New York City and Albany. The 180-acre riverside campus comfortably accommodates 4,193 full-time undergraduates. The campus has twenty-eight buildings, including eleven residence halls, five major classroom buildings, the James A. Cannavino Library, and a student center that includes a bookstore, music rooms, a theater, and a cafeteria. Town-house residences and garden-style apartments are also available for upperclass students. There are three major athletics fields and a boathouse with waterfront facilities for sailing and crew. The James J. McCann Recreation Center, one of the largest collegiate sports complexes in the Mid-Hudson Valley, houses a 4,000-seat field house and a natatorium with a diving well and spectator space for 700 as well as an indoor track, handball and racquetball courts, a weight room, a dance studio, and other facilities for recreation and competition.

Campus life accommodates a wide range of interests and talents. The student-administered Student Programming Council annually presents a full schedule of films, concerts, and social activities. More than eighty clubs and organizations are available in many areas, including theater, music, debate, TV and radio stations, and volunteer programs, such as Habitat for Humanity. Varsity sports for men include baseball, basketball, crew, cross-country, diving, football, lacrosse, soccer, swimming, tennis, and track. Varsity sports for women are offered in basketball, crew, cross-country, diving, lacrosse, soccer, softball, swimming, tennis, track, volleyball, and water polo. Cheerleading, field hockey, ice hockey, rugby, skiing, and soccer are available as club sports. An equestrian team is also available. The Marist Red Foxes compete in NCAA Division I in the Metro-Atlantic Athletic Conference (MAAC). An extensive intramural program encourages all students to participate in athletic recreation, and more than 80 percent of Marist students take part in club or team activities.

Special student services are offered in the areas of academic advising, counseling, career development, campus ministry, financial aid, health, residence living, and support of disabled students.

Graduate degrees are available in business administration, communication, counseling and community psychology, education, educational psychology, information systems, public administration, school psychology, software development, and technology management.

Location

Marist's location in the historic and scenic Hudson River Valley provides access to many cultural and recreational opportunities. The Franklin D. Roosevelt Home and Presidential Library and the original plant of the IBM Corporation attest to the national and international significance of the region and its people and organizations. The river also serves as a focus for the College's Environmental Studies Program, while the nearby Catskill Mountains provide areas for such outdoor activities as hiking, skiing, and rock climbing. A short distance from the campus, the city of Poughkeepsie offers a major civic center that consolidates many of the area's cultural programs and expands leisure-time choices. With Amtrak and Metro North railroad stations only minutes from the campus, students also have convenient access to New York City, Albany, Boston, and other major metropolitan areas.

Majors and Degrees

The College is organized into the academic areas of the School of Communication and the Arts, the School of Computer Science and Math, the School of Liberal Arts, the School of Management, the School of Science, and the School of Social and Behavioral Sciences.

The Bachelor of Arts is awarded in American studies, communication arts, computer mathematics, economics, English, fine arts, French, history, integrative studies, mathematics, philosophy, political science, psychology, psychology/special childhood education, and Spanish. The Bachelor of Science is offered in accounting, athletic training, biology, business administration, chemistry, computer science, criminal justice, digital media, environmental science, information systems, information technology, integrative studies, medical technology, and social work. The Bachelor of Professional Studies is offered in fashion design and fashion merchandising. Concentrations are offered in Jewish studies, Latin American studies, paralegal studies, and public administration, among others. In order to provide greater academic opportunities for students, the College offers two combined B.A./M.A. programs (one in psychology and one in teacher education) and two combined B.S./M.S. programs (one in computer science and one in information systems). These accelerated programs allow students to graduate with both degrees in five years.

Preprofessional programs in dentistry, law, medicine, veterinary medicine, and other allied health professions are available. Marist's teacher education program qualifies students for adolescence education teacher certification in biology, chemistry, English, French, history, mathematics, and Spanish and for certification to teach grades 1–6 in special-childhood education.

Academic Programs

Central to academic planning at Marist is the core curriculum, a program that provides all students with a solid educational foundation in the liberal arts. Students can take advantage of the double-major option that allows equal study in two subject areas. They can also choose a major in one subject and a minor in another area of interest. The Emerging Leaders Program, the Dean's Circle, the honors program, the Marist Abroad Program, the Center for Estuarine Studies, and special academic advising are available for students wishing to enhance the academic experience. Faculty members help all students identify areas of academic interest and then continue to support students as that interest is developed and explored.

Off-Campus Programs

Through the Marist Abroad Program, students have many opportunities to study abroad. Marist students, representing a cross section of majors, have studied in many countries in Europe as well as in Africa, Asia, Australia, and Latin America. Through the College's membership in the Associated Colleges of the Mid-Hudson Area, Marist students have the opportunity to register for a few classes at any one of four other institutions: Culinary Institute of America, Dutchess Community College, State University of New York College at New Paltz, and Ulster Community College.

Internships are offered in all majors, and students are encouraged to make them part of their educational experience. Cooperative education opportunities (paid work experiences) are currently available in several majors.

Academic Facilities

Marist College is consistently recognized for excellence in the use of digital technology in the classroom and was listed in *Yahoo! Internet Life*'s "100 Most Wired Colleges." A partnership with IBM has provided the College with more than $30 million in computer technology, and the 6-year-old James A. Cannavino Library has been hailed by the *New York Times* as a model for digital libraries of the twenty-first century. This three-story landmark facility allows students and faculty members to access material stored on the College's powerful IBM S/390 mainframe as well as online sources of information from around the world. The $25-million library houses book stacks on its ground floor; research materials, periodicals, and an "e-scriptorium" on its main floor; and four state-of-the-art digital classrooms, a Center for Collaborative Learning, and the Weiss Language Center on its top floor. The Cannavino Library also offers more ports per student than any other college or university library in the United States; at any of the 860 seats—ranging from individual study carrels to soft-cushioned easy chairs overlooking the Hudson River—students and faculty members can plug in laptops and connect to sources of information from around the world. (In addition to the more than 200 desktop systems in place, IBM ThinkPad laptops are available for loan at the circulation desk.) Recently, the library became a wireless location on campus. Collaborative study rooms allow group discussions on projects, while quiet study areas with scenic vistas offer space from which to read and research. The Cannavino Library's two-story atrium entrance also features a coffee bar and is a popular gathering place for students, faculty members, and staff members.

Donnelly Hall houses classrooms, lecture halls, the School of Science, the Department of Fashion Design and Merchandising, the College's information technology facilities, a computer lab, and the Offices of Safety and Security, Human Resources, Financial Aid, and the Registrar.

The College's newest academic facility, Fontaine Hall, replaced a building of the same name that had been located on the site of the Cannavino Library. Named for the founding president of modern-day Marist College, Fontaine Hall houses multimedia classrooms, a black-box theater, a conference room overlooking the Hudson River, the School of Liberal Arts, the Marist College Institute for Public Opinion, and the Office of College Advancement, including the Offices of Alumni Relations and Public Affairs. Historic photographs documenting the life of President Franklin Delano Roosevelt are displayed on the first floor of Fontaine Hall, reminding the Marist community and visitors of the close affiliation between the College and the FDR Presidential Library in neighboring Hyde Park.

The Department of Art and Art History is housed in the open, spacious, and newly renovated Steel Plant Studios, a former steel-fabrication facility. The building is home to the digital media, 2-D/graphic design, 3-D/sculpture, and photography studios. The art gallery is also located in Steel Plant Studios. In addition, a complete photography lab and darkroom is housed in nearby Donnelly Hall.

The Lowell Thomas Communications Center links the study of communications with computer technology. It features two sets of television and radio broadcast studios, computer-equipped classrooms, and print journalism areas as well as a public gallery displaying memorabilia of the late Lowell Thomas, the legendary broadcaster and explorer.

The Instructional Media Center's functions include consultation on media methods; production of films, slides, and videotapes; dispensing of audiovisual hardware; and distribution of video programming to classrooms. Group work and individual study in Arabic, Chinese, French, German, Italian, Japanese, and Spanish, as well as in English for non-English-speaking students, are available.

The Margaret M. and Charles H. Dyson Center incorporates some of the most advanced technologies in education and houses the College's undergraduate and graduate programs in business, social and behavioral sciences, public administration, and public policy. The center is also used for innovative computer simulations and computer-assisted group learning and problem solving. In addition, it houses the School of Adult Education and the Office of Graduate Admissions.

Costs

Tuition and fees for 2006–07 were $22,066 for a full year. Room and board for a full year were $9790. The additional costs of transportation, clothes, and spending money usually amount to several hundred dollars. Students should plan on books and supplies costing an estimated $1200 per year.

Financial Aid

Approximately 80 percent of the College's full-time students receive aid from Marist and outside sources, including New York State Tuition Assistance Program (TAP) grants, Federal Pell Grants, Federal Supplemental Educational Opportunity Grants, Federal Perkins Loans, Federal Stafford Student Loans (Subsidized and Unsubsidized), and Federal Work-Study Program awards. Marist also has merit awards for outstanding students that are not based on financial need. Overall, Marist annually awards more than $20 million in grants and scholarships from its own funds. For a student to be considered for assistance, the Free Application for Federal Student Aid (FAFSA) should be filed as soon as possible after January 1. The financial aid staff is available to discuss financial aid possibilities with all prospective students.

Faculty

The College has 199 full-time faculty members, approximately 85 percent of whom either hold doctorates or are doctoral candidates. A strong working relationship between students and faculty members is an important aspect of the learning process at Marist. The student-faculty ratio is currently 15:1.

Student Government

Student representation in decisions affecting the College is a tradition at Marist. Through Student Government committees, the student body is given a role in both administrative and academic policy making.

Admission Requirements

Applicants must have graduated from an accredited high school. Rigor of high school curriculum, grade point average, and rank in class are primary considerations; admission is based on a review of the high school transcript, scores on the SAT or ACT, a personal essay, and the recommendation of the guidance counselor or college adviser.

Application and Information

Application may be made for either September or January enrollment, depending on the choice of the applicant. Students applying to Marist have several options: prospective students are able to complete the online Marist application, submit the Common Application and Marist supplement, or fill out the Marist paper application. The College notifies regular decision candidates of the admission decision in mid-March. The completed application form, secondary school transcript, essay, SAT or ACT test results, recommendation of the guidance counselor or college adviser, teacher recommendation, and application fee of $50 must be submitted before a decision on admission can be made. Candidates for early decision should apply by November 15 and for early action, by December 1. Candidates for regular admission should apply by February 15.

Additional details and application forms are available by contacting:

Admission Office
Marist College
3399 North Road
Poughkeepsie, New York 12601
Phone: 845-575-3226
800-436-5483 (toll-free)
E-mail: admission@marist.edu
Web site: http://www.marist.edu

MARYMOUNT MANHATTAN COLLEGE

MarymountManhattan
a college of the liberal arts

NEW YORK, NEW YORK

The College

Marymount Manhattan College (MMC) is an urban, independent, coeducational, undergraduate liberal arts college. The mission of the College is to educate a socially and economically diverse population by fostering intellectual achievement and personal growth and by providing opportunities for career development. Inherent in this mission is the intent to develop an awareness of social, political, cultural, and ethical issues in the belief that this awareness will lead to concern for, participation in, and the improvement of society. To accomplish this mission, the College offers a strong program in the arts and sciences to students of all ages—as well as substantial preprofessional preparation. Central to these efforts is the particular attention given to the individual student. Marymount Manhattan College also seeks to be a resource and learning center for the metropolitan community.

The social and extracurricular life of the student body of approximately 2,000 students centers on more than forty clubs and organizations sponsored through the Student Affairs Office, including the International Students Club, Psychology Club, French Club, Philosophy Club, Science Society, Black and Latino Student Organization, the student newspaper and yearbook, WMMC Radio, Student Government Association, intramural sports, and other special interest organizations. Students attend musical events, and MMC's own off-Broadway theater, the only one on the Upper East Side of Manhattan, offers students an opportunity to participate in student productions.

The Residence Life Office at Marymount Manhattan College is committed to providing residents with numerous opportunities and experiences that foster intellectual achievement and social and personal growth. Students are encouraged to become involved in the many activities that are sponsored by Residence Life and are assisted with assuming responsibility for their own lives and living environment. The College provides housing for approximately 750 students at various locations in Manhattan. The buildings offer suite-style, traditional dormitories, or apartment-style living, with classrooms, lounges, a laundry room, and rehearsal space. Additional off-campus facilities are obtained as needed.

The Office of Career Development and Internships serves the entire College community by providing an integrated program of academic and career counseling. The office helps students by offering internship opportunities and workshops in job placement, resume writing, and graduate school preparation. For the past five years, 90 percent of biology majors who apply are accepted to advanced professional schools, including Mt. Sinai School of Medicine and Cornell Medical College. Other College services include personal and financial aid counseling and campus ministry.

Location

Marymount Manhattan College is centrally located on Manhattan's Upper East Side at 221 East 71st Street between Second and Third avenues. Within walking distance of the campus are the Frick, Metropolitan, Whitney, and Guggenheim museums; the Asian Society, French Institute, and National Audubon Society; Central Park; New York Hospital and Sloan-Kettering Research Center; and public libraries. All forms of public transportation are easily accessible. Within minutes of the College are shops, restaurants, and movie theaters. This location gives students the opportunity to take advantage of New York City's rich culture and to explore a variety of neighborhoods.

Majors and Degrees

Marymount Manhattan College offers programs leading to the Bachelor of Arts, Bachelor of Science, and Bachelor of Fine Arts degrees. Majors are offered in accounting, acting, art, biology, business management, communication arts, dance, English, history, humanities, international studies, philosophy and religious studies, political science, psychology, sociology, speech-language pathology and audiology, and theater arts (B.A., B.S., and B.F.A. degrees). Some of the minors offered are business, creative writing, education, French, Hispanic studies, media studies, neuroscience, religious studies, and Spanish. Certificate programs are offered in industrial organizational psychology and teacher certification.

Academic Programs

Marymount Manhattan College has designed its programs to enable students to meet the challenges of contemporary society. MMC is committed to the belief that a liberal arts education provides students with the ability and the flexibility to manage change and with broad understanding and the communication and problem-solving skills that are essential for success in any career and in life. To accomplish its goals, the College offers a liberal arts education, integrated with preprofessional training opportunities and individualized attention. The curricula are organized into five divisions: humanities, fine and performing arts, sciences, social sciences, and business management. Also offered are special-interest sequences that complement the student's major and minor, with added concentration in such areas as art history, creative writing, finance and investments, international business, marketing, photography, predentistry, prelaw, premedicine, preveterinary science, and social work. The College's small size provides students with an individually planned academic career, reflects students' academic needs and interests, and supports their career goals.

Candidates for the Bachelor of Arts, Bachelor of Science, and Bachelor of Fine Arts degrees must complete 120 credits. To qualify for a degree, a student must maintain an overall scholastic average of at least 2.0. Requirements for certificate programs vary.

The College recognizes various types of nontraditional credit, including credit for acceptable scores on the Advanced Placement (AP), International Baccalaureate (IB), College-Level Examination Program (CLEP), and New York State College Proficiency Examination (CPE) tests and credit for life experience.

MMC encourages its students to participate in internship programs in New York City that range from work at hospitals, financial institutions, magazines, publishing houses, and off-Broadway theaters to HBO and CBS.

Off-Campus Programs

The College's Academic Year Abroad offers an opportunity for students to broaden their educational experience and to gain cultural perspectives through study at other colleges in the Americas and overseas. Students may spend one or both semesters of their junior year in this program. MMC summer sessions and January inter-sessions also offer students opportunities in travel/study-abroad courses in Egypt, France, Great Britain, Greece, Eastern Europe, Ireland, Italy, Russia, and Spain.

Academic Facilities

The Thomas J. Shanahan Library at MMC is a library/learning center. It contains more than 100,000 volumes in open stacks and maintains an extensive periodical collection. The media center, on the main library floor, houses nonprint materials, microfiche, microfilm, filmstrips, slides, tapes, videotapes, DVDs, and records. Through the library's affiliation with the New York Metropolitan Reference and Research Library Agency, MMC faculty members and students have access to the materials of the member libraries. The library also participates in the Online Computer Library Center (OCLC), a computerized database of the holdings of some 4,000 libraries that is currently being used for cataloging and reference purposes.

The modern 250-seat Theresa Lang Theatre is equipped with an orchestra pit capable of accommodating 40 musicians. The theater has a special acoustical design, a sprung dance floor, a full technical balcony with equipment for lighting and sound, thirty-five counterweighted-line sets in the fly system, dressing rooms with showers, and a scene shop. Students benefit from exposure to the numerous professional dance, opera, and theatrical groups that perform at the College.

Recently, two completely remodeled laboratory facilities were opened to strengthen education in two areas in which MMC has always excelled—science and communication arts.

MMC's science facilities in biology, chemistry, and physics underwent a total reconstruction valued at close to $1 million, thanks to the generosity of the Samuel Freeman Charitable Trust and the Ira De Camp Foundation. The Samuel Freeman Science Center opens many new doors of opportunity to students who are biology/premedicine majors or who are interested in pursuing careers in other science or health-related fields.

The College's Theresa Lang Center for Producing features the latest in digital computer technology and is one of the most advanced facilities of its kind in New York City. With digital multimedia capability, a decor inspired by top television postproduction houses, and access to the public library's B. Altman Advanced Learning Superblock, the center further enhances students' skills in traditional video and television production and allows them to develop, design, and evaluate cutting-edge multimedia projects. In conjunction with the Communication Arts Department, the College offers students the Media Library, where many videos and screening computers are available to students.

The Writing Center at MMC provides a range of services and activities, including career-based courses, personal critiques and one-on-one assistance, lectures, workshops, and special events such as the Best-Selling Author Series and Annual Writers' Conference, as well as a minor in creative writing. This enables students to be a part of the highly respected New York City writing community.

Costs

For the 2007–08 academic year, full-time tuition and fees were $20,133. Room and board costs were $12,250 per year. For part-time students, tuition was $628 per credit. Additional fees are applicable for various laboratory and studio classes.

Financial Aid

The College administers a variety of financial aid programs, including scholarships sponsored by the College. Some of the awards are based on academic achievement; others are based on financial need. Students are also eligible for aid through a wide variety of state and federal programs. In addition, a number of jobs are available for students on campus, and the Offices of Financial Aid and Academic and Career Advisement can help students locate part-time off-campus jobs to help finance their education. More than 85 percent of MMC students receive some form of financial assistance. Therefore, limited finances alone need not prevent any student from attending the College. Priority consideration for merit- and need-based financial aid is November 15 for spring admission and March 15 for fall admission.

Faculty

Marymount Manhattan College's student-faculty ratio is 11:1. In addition to the staff of the advisement office, faculty members act as advisers to students. Full-time faculty members teach in all sessions and divisions (days, evenings, and some weekends). Part-time instructors, who are drawn from the wealth of experienced teaching professionals in New York City, supplement the full-time faculty.

Student Government

The Student Government Association responds to three areas of concern at MMC. The association primarily serves the needs of its constituents by managing the student government budget, planning and publicizing events, and establishing organizations that reflect the interests of the students. In addition, the association assists faculty and administrative groups and committees in their policy and procedural tasks and communicates the results of committee work to the student body. Finally, the Student Government Association provides special representatives for students' rights and freedoms through established and clearly defined channels of authority.

Admission Requirements

Marymount Manhattan College seeks candidates with qualities that indicate potential for success in higher education and the ability to contribute to the College community. Admission is based on a combination of factors: the student's academic program, including scholastic average; two recommendations from teachers, counselors, or employers; an essay; and SAT or ACT scores. TOEFL scores are required for international student applicants.

Each year the College enrolls an increasing number of transfer students. Transfer students may receive up to 90 credits for course work completed at a regionally accredited postsecondary institution with a grade of C- or better. Transcripts are evaluated on a course-by-course basis.

Prior to registering, some students are required to take placement examinations in the basic subject areas of English composition, reading, algebra, and mathematics.

Application and Information

The admissions application must be received by March 15 for priority consideration for MMC scholarships. Students may apply online. For application forms and for more information about Marymount Manhattan College, students should contact:

Office of Admissions
Marymount Manhattan College
221 East 71st Street
New York, New York 10021
Phone: 212-517-0430
800-MARYMOUNT (toll-free)
Fax: 212-517-0448
E-mail: admissions@mmm.edu
Web site: http://www.mmm.edu

Marymount Manhattan College, in the heart of Manhattan.

MOLLOY COLLEGE

ROCKVILLE CENTRE, NEW YORK

The College

In 1955, 44 students became part of an exciting new tradition in higher education on Long Island. As the first freshman class of Molloy College, these young students made a commitment to academic excellence. So did the College, which had a distinguished faculty of 15 and a library containing 5,000 books.

Today, Molloy College has become one of the most respected four-year private coeducational institutions of higher learning in the area. It provides academic programs in both day and evening divisions. The Molloy population consists of recent high school graduates, transfer students, and graduate students. Molloy College is accredited by the Board of Regents of the University of the State of New York and the Middle States Association of Colleges and Schools, and its programs in nursing, social work, and education are accredited by the National League for Nursing Accrediting Commission, the Council on Social Work Education, and NCATE.

Molloy College provides an intimate and personal atmosphere; it encourages the 3,700 students to develop close working relationships with the faculty. The student body represents many ethnic and socioeconomic groups; to meet their varied needs, the College offers more than fifty undergraduate majors and programs.

The key word at the College is involvement. Student-run clubs and organizations offer a variety of planned activities. Student publications, which include the yearbook, a literary magazine, and a newspaper, provide an outlet for students who want to share their literary and journalistic talents.

Molloy College offers opportunities for students to exercise their leadership abilities, contribute their special talents, utilize their initiative, and expand their social horizons through the variety of activities made conveniently available to them. Athletics, an integral part of student life, are represented at Molloy College on the varsity level. Women's teams are offered in basketball, lacrosse, soccer, softball, tennis, and volleyball. Men's teams include baseball, basketball, lacrosse, and soccer. Cross-country is offered for men and women. These teams compete in the NCAA Division II, the ECAC, and the NYCAC. The equestrian team holds membership in the Intercollegiate Horse Show Association.

Student services include the Career and Counseling Center, Campus Ministry, the Siena Women's Center, and health services.

On the graduate level, Molloy College offers a Master of Science degree in nursing and education and post-master's certification in nursing and education. M.B.A. programs are available in business, accounting, and personal financial planning. A Master of Social Work is offered through Molloy's partnership with Fordham University.

Location

Located on a 30-acre campus in Rockville Centre, Long Island, Molloy College is close to metropolitan New York and all its diverse and rich resources. The College is easily accessible from all parts of Nassau, Suffolk, and Queens counties.

Majors and Degrees

Molloy College offers the A.A. degree in liberal arts; the A.A.S. degree in nuclear medicine technology, respiratory therapy, and cardiovascular technology; and B.A., B.S., B.F.A., or B.S.W. degrees in accounting, art, biology, business management, communication arts, computer information systems, computer science, criminal justice, English, environmental studies, history, interdisciplinary studies, international peace and justice studies, mathematics, modern languages, music, music therapy, nursing, philosophy, political science, psychology, social work, sociology, speech-language pathology/audiology, theater arts, and theology. Teacher certification programs are available in childhood (1–6), adolescence (7–12), special education, and TESOL.

Special advisement is offered for students interested in predental, prelaw, premedical, or preveterinary programs.

The internship program at the College offers students the opportunity for on-the-job experience along with the classroom exposure so essential to the completely educated person. Internships are available in all areas of study.

Academic Programs

Molloy College, dedicated to the total development of the student, offers a strong liberal arts core curriculum as an integral part of all major fields of study. A minimum of 128 credits is required for a baccalaureate degree. Double majors can be chosen, and numerous minors are available.

Advanced placement credit is granted for a score of 3 or better on the AP exam. CLEP and CPE credit is also given. Qualified full-time students may participate in the Army ROTC program at Hofstra University or St. John's University on a cross-enrolled basis. Molloy students may also elect Air Force ROTC on a cross-enrolled basis with New York Institute of Technology.

Molloy has a 4-1-4 academic calendar.

Academic Facilities

The James E. Tobin Library houses a collection of 110,000 volumes. There are 675 subscriptions to print journals and periodicals. The Main Reference Room of the library has twelve computers, which students can use to access the Internet and more than 50 subject-specific online databases. Students and faculty members have access to the library's databases on campus and off campus as well as through the College's Web site. The library also houses a library instruction room, where librarians meet with professors and individual classes for instruction on the use of the databases and related research methods. The Tobin Library is a wireless facility.

In the Media Center there are 750 DVDs and 2,300 VHS tapes that support the curriculum. There are twenty-four media-enhanced classrooms in the College, fourteen PowerPoint packages, and laptop computers for student and faculty member use. Students have access to PC and Macintosh computers.

The College's computer labs house 357 microcomputers. In addition, many academic departments have their own computer labs. For example, the International Business Center has twenty-five state-of-the-art microcomputers that allow students to communicate internationally. Laptop computers are available on loan to students, and nearly the entire campus has wireless capability.

The Wilbur Arts Center features numerous art studios, music studios, a cable television studio, and the Lucille B. Hays Theatre.

Kellenberg Hall houses six science labs, a language lab, and the education resource center. The Casey Center houses two nursing labs, and the behavioral sciences research facility is located in Siena Hall.

Costs

For 2006–07, tuition and fees were $16,000. The cost per credit for part-time students was $550.

Financial Aid

More than 85 percent of the student body of Molloy College is awarded financial aid in the form of scholarships, grants, loans, and Federal Work-Study Program employment. Financial aid awards are based on academic achievement and financial need. Completion of the Molloy College Application for Financial Aid/Scholarship and the Free Application for Federal Student Aid (FAFSA) is required. No-need scholarships and grants are also available.

Students who have attained a 95 percent or better high school average and a minimum combined score of 1250 on the SAT (composite math and verbal scores) are considered for the Molloy Scholars' Program, which awards full-tuition scholarships. Partial scholarships are available under Dominican, Community Service, and Performing Arts Scholarships. The Transfer Scholarship Program grants partial-tuition scholarships to students transferring into Molloy College with at least a 3.0 cumulative average. Athletic grants (Division II only) are awarded to full-time students based on athletic ability in baseball, basketball, cross-country, equestrian, lacrosse, soccer, softball, tennis, and volleyball. The Community Service Award is awarded to full-time freshmen demonstrating a commitment to their community and their school.

Faculty

The 307 full-time and part-time faculty members at Molloy are dedicated as much to the students as to their respective fields. The 11:1 student-faculty ratio allows for small classes where students can receive the individual attention they deserve.

In addition to their teaching responsibilities, faculty members advise students in their fields to help them select courses that both satisfy major course requirements and lead to the attainment of career goals.

Student Government

Every member of the Molloy College student body belongs to the Molloy Student Association, whose elected leaders form the Molloy Student Government. This group of students provides the leadership necessary to keep extracurricular life at Molloy College alive, productive, and practical.

Admission Requirements

Recommended admission qualifications include graduation from a four-year public or private high school or equivalent (GED test) with a minimum of 18.5 units, including 4 in English, 4 in social studies, 3 in a foreign language, 3 in mathematics, and 3 in science. Nursing applicants must have taken courses in biology and chemistry. Mathematics applicants must have taken 4 units of math and 3 of science (including chemistry or physics). Biology applicants must have credits in biology, chemistry, and physics and 4 units of math. A portfolio is required of art applicants, and music students must audition. Social work applicants must file a special application with the director of the social work program.

The admissions committee bases its selection of candidates on the secondary school record, SAT or ACT scores, class rank, and the school's recommendation. A particular talent or ability can be important. Character and personality, extracurricular participation, and alumni relationships are all considered. On-campus interviews are recommended but not required.

The St. Thomas Aquinas Program, which houses both HEOP and the Albertus Magnus Program, may be an option for students not normally eligible for admission.

Molloy College offers an honors program, and an early admission plan is available.

Application and Information

To apply to Molloy College, students should submit the following credentials to the Admissions Office: a completed application for admission, a nonrefundable $30 application fee, an official high school transcript or GED score report, official results of the SAT or ACT, and official college transcripts (transfer students only).

The College uses a rolling admission system. Students are advised of an admission decision within a few weeks after the application filing process is complete.

For further information, prospective students should contact:

Director of Admissions
Molloy College
1000 Hempstead Avenue
P.O. Box 5002
Rockville Centre, New York 11571-5002
Phone: 888-4-MOLLOY (toll-free)
Web site: http://www.molloy.edu

On the campus of Molloy College.

COLLEGE DATA CENTER • NEW YORK

MONROE COLLEGE

BRONX, NEW YORK
NEW ROCHELLE, NEW YORK

The College

Monroe College is a private, four year college located in New York State. It offers a master's degree program in business management and undergraduate programs in accounting, baking and pastry, business management, business technologies, criminal justice, culinary arts, health services administration, hospitality management, information technology, medical administration, medical assisting, nursing, and public health. Monroe College is committed to providing a high-quality education and individualized attention to serious-minded students. Students have the opportunity to gain academic and professional competency through comprehensive curricula and are also offered a support system that provides services that are essential for academic and professional success. Monroe, which has campuses in both the Bronx and New Rochelle, is accredited by the Commission on Higher Education of the Middle States Association of Colleges and Schools.

Monroe enrolls nearly 7,000 students at its two campuses and through online learning. The diverse student population includes recent high school graduates as well as adult students who are returning to the educational forum. This diverse student population is made up of students from New York and abroad. About 30 percent of the New Rochelle campus is composed of international students. Many New Rochelle students are commuters, but a variety of housing facilities are available at this campus, including new modern dormitories.

Social activities are centered on the Student Activities Committee (SAC) and the athletic program. Monroe's activities provide an opportunity for the development of the whole student within the college experience. There are a variety of clubs and activities for students, such as intramural sports, student publications, drama club, cheerleading, and cultural organizations. In addition, each academic major offers students an opportunity to participate in a professional organization. Intercollegiate sports include baseball, basketball, soccer, softball, track and field, and volleyball teams.

Location

Monroe is part of the New York City metropolitan area, with an urban campus in the Fordham section of the Bronx, which is easily accessible by car or public transportation. It is located in the vicinity of Yankee Stadium, the Bronx Zoo, and the New York Botanical Garden. A short train ride away is Manhattan, famous for Central Park, Broadway, Wall Street and the Financial District, many museums, the Statue of Liberty, the Empire State Building, the Staten Island Ferry, and South Street Seaport.

The suburban New Rochelle campus is located in the heart of the Sound Shore Corridor in bustling Westchester County. The campus offers convenient and spacious housing located in downtown New Rochelle and also serves commuter students. Within a short distance is the Long Island Sound, with abundant opportunities for recreation and leisure-time activities. Students can make use of a multitude of cultural facilities in New Rochelle and the surrounding communities, or they can be in New York City in just a few minutes.

Majors and Degrees

Monroe College confers the Bachelor of Business Administration (B.B.A.) degree in accounting, business management, general business, health services administration, hospitality management, and information technology and the Bachelor of Science (B.S.) degree in criminal justice and public health. Monroe also offers a practical nursing program as well as an associate degree program in registered nursing.

Academic Programs

Monroe College's programs immerse students into each academic major as well as emphasize the study of the liberal arts. Students entering a bachelor's degree program are required to complete 120 credits. Students may apply for direct admission to the bachelor degree and forgo earning an associate degree. Monroe operates on a three-semester calendar. The fifteen-week semesters begin in early September, early January, and late April.

This calendar offers students the ability to earn their degree in less time than a traditional two-semester schedule. In addition, there are online learning opportunities through Internet courses.

Advanced placement is available for CLEP, transfer credit, prior learning experience (life experience evaluation), and proficiency examinations. Students can receive advanced-standing placement for up to 50 percent of the required credits for their chosen degree program.

Off-Campus Programs

Internships are conducted by the College in cooperation with businesses, industries, government agencies, and nonprofit organizations. They integrate on-campus study with off-campus work-study experience. The programs complement and reinforce the professional curriculum studied in the class, providing a broader comprehension of the context in which the student will be employed.

Academic Facilities

Both campuses have complete libraries with Online Computer Library Center (OCLC) access to other metropolitan New York and Westchester libraries. The Learning Resource Centers, which are available to all students from early in the morning to late at night, are equipped with computers and academic enrichment programs and videos. Staff tutors are available on a daily basis to reinforce classroom lectures in all subjects.

The Monroe College culinary arts program is taught in the new Culinary Arts Center on the New Rochelle campus. This facility, which may be the most state-of-the-art culinary instructional facility in metropolitan New York, provides students with four kitchen/labs.

Student Services provides close educational advisement as well as health clinics and primary-level psychological counseling. Students are also urged to take advantage of the Lifetime Career Resource Center. This program evaluates the academic performance and personal attributes of the student in order to identify skills and career goals so they may obtain a position in their field of study upon graduation. The Office of Career Advancement also assists students in obtaining part-time employment during their college careers in a co-op program. Workshops are provided on self-assessment, resume preparation, interview skills, and job search strategies.

Costs

Tuition for the 2008–09 academic year is $10,512 per year (nursing is $13,320 per year), and individual courses cost $1314 plus an administrative fee of $175 for up to 6 credits and $350 for more than 6 credits. Students choosing to reside in campus housing pay $5700 per year (double room), with a nonrefundable $150 application fee. Books cost approximately $300 per semester.

Financial Aid

Financial assistance is determined by the need of the student along with the availability of funds from federal, state, and institutional sources. More than 90 percent of the students receive some type of financial aid. The College takes into account the objective facts and the financial circumstances of the student and family, recognizing the differences of each family situation. Available assistance includes Federal Pell Grants, Federal Supplemental Educational Opportunity Grants, Federal Stafford Student Loans (subsidized and unsubsidized), Federal PLUS loans, and the Federal Work-Study Program. For those students who have been New York State residents for one year or more, TAP may also be available. In addition, the College offers institutional aid (grant-in-aid), scholarships, loans, and employment to students, as well as funding for the purchase of some special equipment and services for disabled students.

Faculty

Monroe has more than 250 full-time faculty members and adjunct faculty members who are experts in their fields as well as excellent teachers. They work closely with their students, both inside and outside the classroom, to help them make the most of their talents, interests, and dreams. The undergraduate student-faculty ratio is 15:1.

Admission Requirements

Monroe College seeks serious individuals who demonstrate that they have the interest, ability, and potential to successfully complete appropriate requirements for the course of study selected. Graduation from an accredited high school, or the equivalent, and a personal interview are the basic requirements for admission to Monroe College. Submission of SAT scores is required if a student wants to be considered for a scholarship.

Application and Information

Submission of the following credentials is required: a completed application, a transcript of all prior formal education, and an essay on a topic provided to all applicants.

Applications are accepted on a rolling basis. Students are informed of the decision by the Admission Committee within two weeks of submission of all required documentation.

Students interested in applying to the College should contact:

Evan Jerome
Director of Admissions
Monroe College–Bronx Campus
2501 Jerome Avenue
Bronx, New York 10468
Phone: 718-933-6700
800-55-MONROE (toll-free)
E-mail: ejerome@monroecollege.edu
Web site: http://www.monroecollege.edu

Gersom Lopez
Director of Admissions
Monroe College–New Rochelle Campus
434 Main Street
New Rochelle, New York 10801
Phone: 914-632-5400
800-55-MONROE (toll-free)
E-mail: glopez@monroecollege.edu

Gersom Lopez
Director of International Student Admissions
Monroe College–New Rochelle Campus
434 Main Street
New Rochelle, New York 10801
Phone: 914-632-5400 Ext. 6406
800-55-MONROE (toll-free)
E-mail: glopez@monroecollege.edu
Web site: http://www.monroecollege.edu

Alexis Safonoff
Assistant Director of Bachelor's Degree Admissions
Monroe College–Bronx Campus
2468 Jerome Avenue
Bronx, New York 10468
Phone: 718-933-6700
E-mail: asafonoff@monroecollege.edu

MOUNT SAINT MARY COLLEGE

NEWBURGH, NEW YORK

The College

Mount Saint Mary College is a private, four-year liberal arts college for men and women founded in 1960 by the Dominican Sisters of Newburgh.

The College has set the goal of preparing its students, within the environment of a small, independent, undergraduate college, to assume, by choice and preparation, their roles in an ever-changing cultural, intellectual, psychological, and social climate. According to the plan of its founders and the aims of the total college community, Mount Saint Mary College strives to produce alumni marked by intellectual acuity and professional competence who possess constructive attitudes toward the challenges of living in the world of their times. With its favorable student-faculty ratio of 18:1, the Mount provides an atmosphere that is warm and personal, and it also gives students an educational experience that will prove valuable throughout their lifetime. Mount Saint Mary College is a young, vibrant, growing school where group commitment is made to the individual student.

The current enrollment is more than 2,600 men and women. Students at Mount Saint Mary College come to the campus with various backgrounds and educational objectives. They are able to express individual desires and find an avenue for special talents not only in the academic environment but also through participation in extracurricular activities. A wide variety of choices make it possible for all students to find activities that fit their own interests. Intercollegiate athletics programs include baseball, basketball, cross-country, soccer, softball, swimming, tennis, and volleyball. The newly renovated, 47,000-square-foot recreational facility features two NCAA basketball/volleyball courts, a cardiovascular fitness center, a weight room, an aerobics/dance studio, a swimming pool, a raised running track, training rooms, study lounges, a TV lounge, a snack bar, a game room, and four classrooms. Social programs, such as dances and other intercollegiate events, are held frequently in conjunction with neighboring colleges and the Military Academy at West Point. Students and their guests attend such social activities as Oktoberfest and Siblings' Weekend. Traditional College events include Parents' Weekend, Freshman Investiture, and One Hundredth Night.

The Mount has two new freshman residence halls, along with twenty-eight town-house residence halls for upperclass students. The residence areas are equipped with full kitchen facilities, lounges, laundry facilities, computer centers, workout areas, and private study rooms.

In addition to its undergraduate curricula, the Mount offers graduate programs leading to the Master of Science degree in elementary education, elementary/special education, secondary education, and special education; the Master of Business Administration; and the Master of Science in Nursing.

Location

Mount Saint Mary College is located in a residential section of Newburgh, New York, about 60 miles north of New York City and 15 minutes north of the United States Military Academy at West Point. The accessibility of New York City makes it possible for students to take advantage of a variety of cultural and social activities as well as the many attractions of the Mid-Hudson Valley. Recreational areas nearby provide facilities for skiing, boating, hiking, golfing, riding, and swimming. Shopping facilities are near the College. Many students are involved in some aspect of community service, often combining their academic interests with a community activity.

Majors and Degrees

Mount Saint Mary College awards Bachelor of Arts (B.A.) and Bachelor of Science (B.S.) degrees in such programs as accounting, biology, business management, chemistry, computer information technology, English, Hispanic studies, history, history/political science, human services, information technology, interdisciplinary studies, mathematics, media studies, medical technology, nursing, psychology, public relations, social science, sociology, and undeclared. Concentrations include criminology, cytotechnology, finance, general concentration in human services, general science concentration (for students enrolled in childhood education), human resource management, international business, management information systems, marketing, networking, social and community services, systems analyst and project management, and Web technologies.

Certification programs are available in childhood education and childhood education and teaching students with disabilities (grades 1–6), childhood education with middle school extension and adolescence education with middle school extension (grades 5–6), adolescence education and adolescence education and teaching students with disabilities (grades 7–12).

Preprofessional studies are available in dentistry, law, medicine, and veterinary medicine. Mount Saint Mary College offers a 3-3 optometry program with SUNY College of Optometry, a 3-4 program with New York College of Podiatric Medicine, and a 4-3 physical therapy program and 4-2 speech-language pathology program with New York Medical College. The Mount also offers a 3-2 publishing/English or media studies program with Pace University and a 3-2 social work degree program with Fordham University.

Academic Programs

The Mount is dedicated to providing a diversity of programs to accommodate people with individual needs and specific objectives while developing a total learning environment for all students. Each individualized program is geared to the complex and varied needs of each student seeking to become a whole person, ready for a rewarding career and ready to make full use of his or her leisure hours. A minimum of 120 credit hours is required for degrees granted by the Mount, including 90 credit hours in the liberal arts and sciences for the Bachelor of Arts degree and 60 credit hours in the liberal arts and sciences for the Bachelor of Science degree. A core curriculum of 39 credit hours is also required. Major requirements consist of 28 to 40 credit hours.

Advanced placement, credit for life experience, accelerated courses, and an honors program are available. Students are encouraged to take part in the Mount's study-abroad program. All students have the opportunity to gain practical experience within their major through cooperative education and internships.

Academic Facilities

Aquinas Hall, the main College building, has laptop-friendly smart classrooms with LCD projection and stereo sound systems; science, nursing, language, and state-of-the-art computer science laboratories; an art studio; administrative and faculty offices; the library; a theater; a multimedia digital production center; a video production studio; a photography lab; and the music department's facilities. The fully automated Curtain Memorial Library, a tri-level wing at the southern end of Aquinas Hall, houses 120,000 volumes plus subscriptions to 1,129 current journals and periodicals. The Media Center contains recordings, cassettes, filmstrips, and tapes, along with individual listening areas and carrels to augment innovative courses and independent study. Internet access is available to all students in the Academic Computing Lab and throughout the campus via the Wireless Academic Network. The Curriculum Library has been designed to meet the many needs of education students, and the Bishop Dunn Memorial School, an elementary and junior high school on campus, provides a place where education students can participate in observing and teaching. Individually guided instruction is conducted here, as are a modified Montessori program and classes in special education. The on-campus Office of Academic Assessment and Developmental Instruction assists students in academic endeavors through tutorial services and skills development at no additional cost.

Costs

Tuition for the 2007–08 academic year was $18,900 for most full-time students. Room and board costs were $10,400, including a room and a full weekly meal plan. Additional fees totaled approximately $820 annually.

Financial Aid

About 80 percent of the College's students receive financial aid from one or more sources. Scholarships, grants, loans, and work-study programs constitute most awards. The College provides aid from all federal aid programs, such as the Federal Pell Grant, Federal Supplemental Educational Opportunity Grant, Federal Perkins Loan, Nursing Scholarship and/or Loan, and Federal Work-Study programs. New York State residents may be eligible for Tuition Assistance Program (TAP) awards. The Mount also offers its own scholarship and grant programs. On-campus jobs are plentiful. All students are encouraged to apply for financial aid. Application may be made by filing the Free Application for Federal Student Aid (FAFSA) and the Mount Saint Mary College Supplemental Form (New York State residents should file the TAP Form) by March 15. For further information about financial aid, students should contact the director of financial aid. All students who apply for admission are eligible for consideration for half-tuition Presidential Scholarships, Merit Grant Awards, and Mount Saint Mary College Scholarships.

Faculty

Mount Saint Mary College offers its students an environment that fosters close student-teacher interaction with the aid of a very committed faculty. The student-teacher ratio is 18:1, which allows for individualized advisement and instruction. The average class size is 25, and classes emphasize seminar and discussion-based learning.

Student Government

Students at Mount Saint Mary College participate in a very active system of student governance. Student representatives are members of every College committee. The Resident Living Council governs and represents the resident students of the College, while the Commuter Council focuses on the commuting population. Most student activities are generated by Student Government organizations, and the Student Government plays a leading role in the development of College policy; it is the main outlet for student participation in the College's decision-making process and in the planning of events. The Student Government manages its own student activities budget.

Admission Requirements

Mount Saint Mary College welcomes students whose potential for academic and social success is in keeping with the objectives of the College. Applicants are evaluated primarily on their past academic performance. SAT or ACT scores and class rank are also considered. Transfer applicants should be in good academic standing at their previous college. Campus visits and interviews are strongly recommended. Early admission to the College is available.

Application and Information

Students who wish to apply to the Mount should submit a completed application and a $40 application fee to the Admissions Office. Students should also make arrangements for their high school transcript and SAT or ACT scores to be forwarded to the same office. Letters of recommendation, while not required, are strongly advised. Mount Saint Mary College operates on a rolling admission policy. Once a student's file is complete, he or she is usually notified of the admission decision within two to four weeks.

For further information, students should contact:

Director of Admissions
Mount Saint Mary College
330 Powell Avenue
Newburgh, New York 12550
Phone: 845-569-3248
888-YES-MSMC (toll-free)
E-mail: admissions@msmc.edu
Web site: http://www.msmc.edu

Mount Saint Mary College, with the Hudson River in the background.

NAZARETH COLLEGE OF ROCHESTER

ROCHESTER, NEW YORK

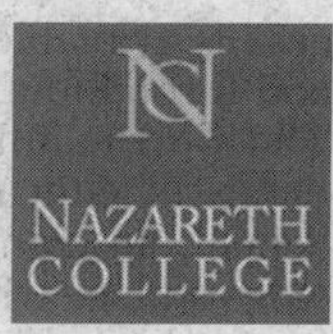

The College

Nazareth College is an independent, coeducational, comprehensive college that offers career programs solidly based in the liberal arts. Its suburban campus is located in Pittsford in western upstate New York, approximately 7 miles from the city of Rochester. Founded in 1924, the College has conferred more than 27,000 baccalaureate and master's degrees. Of the more than 3,200 men and women enrolled at Nazareth, more than 2,000 are undergraduates.

Twenty-two buildings of traditional and contemporary design are conveniently situated on the College's 150-acre campus. The Otto A. Shults Community Center, housing a 20,000-square-foot gymnasium, the student union, a multifaith religious center, a 25-meter swimming pool, the fitness center, and student personnel offices, is the hub of on-campus student life. The resident students, constituting two-thirds of the undergraduate population, are housed in eleven separate residence halls. As an alternative to traditional campus housing, foreign language majors may live in La Maison Française, which is maintained by the language department. The Casa Italiana, Casa Hispana, and German Cultural Center serve as facilities for social, cultural, and academic programs reflecting Italian, Spanish, and German heritages, respectively.

Intercollegiate athletics are available in the areas of men's and women's basketball, equestrian, golf, lacrosse, soccer, swimming and diving, tennis, track and field and cross-country, volleyball, and women's field hockey and softball.

Location

Rochester, a city of more than 300,000 people, is the third-largest city in New York State and the site of cultural, educational, and industrial centers. Located on the shore of Lake Ontario, the city is noted for the Eastman Theatre, the Strasenburg Planetarium, and the International Museum of Photography at the George Eastman House. Rochester is the world headquarters of Eastman Kodak and Bausch & Lomb and the site of a major Xerox facility. It is only 20 minutes from beautiful mountains, lakes, and recreational areas, where students can enjoy various outdoor activities, including skiing, hiking, water sports, and camping. The city supports professional sports teams in baseball, hockey, lacrosse, and soccer.

Majors and Degrees

Nazareth College awards the Bachelor of Music degree and Bachelor of Arts and Bachelor of Science degrees in accounting, American studies, anthropology, art (studio), art education, art history, biochemistry, biology, business administration, business and marketing education, chemistry, communication and rhetoric, communication sciences and disorders, economics, English, environmental science, foreign languages (French, German, Italian, Spanish, and modern foreign languages), health science/physical therapy, history, information technology, international studies, mathematics, music, music business, music education, music performance, music theater, music theory, music therapy, nursing, peace and justice studies, philosophy, political science, psychology, religious studies, social science, social work, sociology, and theater arts.

Preprofessional programs are available in dentistry, law, and medicine. Teacher certification (grades 1–9 and 7–12) is offered with many majors. Certification in learning disabilities is available through an undergraduate program in inclusive education (grades 1–9 and 7–12). Certification for birth–12 is offered in art education, business education, music education, and speech pathology (communication sciences and disorders).

Academic Programs

To qualify for a degree, a candidate must fulfill the core curriculum requirements of the College as well as those of the major department or area of concentration. The candidate must also earn a minimum of 120 semester credits and satisfy a comprehensive test requirement in the major field during the senior year.

Off-Campus Programs

Nazareth College offers Junior Year Abroad programs in affiliation with the Université de Haute Bretagne in Rennes, France; the Institute of Spanish Students in Valencia, Spain; and the Universita degli G. D'Annunzio in Pescara, Italy. Students need not be language majors to take advantage of this exceptional program. Language students taking German or Japanese have the opportunity to study at the Studienforum in Berlin and Osaka University in Japan, respectively.

Nazareth College is a member of the Rochester Area Colleges, a consortium that includes Rochester Institute of Technology, the State University of New York College at Geneseo, and the University of Rochester, among others. Through this consortium, Nazareth College students can cross-register for credit in up to two courses per semester at any of the member institutions on a space-available basis.

Academic Facilities

Nazareth's classrooms, laboratories, and studios are located in Smyth Hall, Carroll Hall, the Golisano Academic Center, and the award-winning Arts Center, which houses art, music, and theater facilities as well as a 1,200-seat auditorium. The Golisano Academic Center and Carroll Hall houses speech pathology, physical therapy, counseling, and health services. Lorette Wilmot Library houses 248,000 volumes and has extensive resources in such areas as women's studies, education, minority issues, and religions in America. The library subscribes to approximately 1,900 periodicals and other serials. The building has seating for 450 students and includes a large number of individual carrels. The library also has a fine collection of lecture tapes and a growing collection of musical and spoken-word disks and tapes. The Rare Book Room is distinguished by special collections of works by Maurice Baring, Hilaire Belloc, Gilbert Keith Chesterton, and the Sitwells. The library is currently enlarging its resources and services in the nonprint media. In addition, the College's membership in the regional consortium and the Online Computer Library Center provides students with access to the resources of 1,300 other academic and research libraries.

Costs

Total costs for 2007–08 were $32,375. This included $21,900 for tuition, $9500 for room and board, and $975 for the required fees. The total does not include books, personal expenses, or transportation (if applicable). All fees are subject to change; up-to-date information can be obtained from the Admissions Office.

Financial Aid

Nazareth College endeavors to meet financial need as demonstrated on the Free Application for Federal Student Aid (FAFSA). The FAFSA should be submitted by February 15 of the year in which the student intends to enroll. The CSS PROFILE is required of early decision applicants only and should be submitted by November 15. Financial assistance is available through grants, loans, employment, and scholarships. Sources of aid include the Federal Pell Grant, New York Tuition Assistance Program, Federal Perkins Loan, and Federal Work-Study programs; the New York State Higher Education Services Corporation; and Nazareth College merit scholarships and grants.

Faculty

The full-time faculty members in the various academic departments hold advanced degrees from more than 100 institutions throughout the United States and abroad. Ninety-four percent of the faculty members hold the highest degree offered in their field of study. The student-faculty ratio of approximately 12:1 and an average class size of 19 ensure that students receive the individual attention that only a small college can offer.

Student Government

The Undergraduate Association of Nazareth College is the vehicle through which students can express the need for and initiate change within the College community. It is also responsible for the disbursement of funds, generated from the undergraduate activities fee, to various activities and social/cultural clubs.

Admission Requirements

Nazareth College welcomes applicants of all ages and educational backgrounds. Students of any race, color, sex, or national or ethnic origin are admitted to all of the rights, privileges, programs, and activities generally accorded or made available to students at the College. Nazareth College does not discriminate on the basis of race, color, sex, or national or ethnic origin in the administration of its educational policies, scholarship and loan programs, and sports and other school-administered programs.

Recommended academic preparation includes courses in English, college-preparatory mathematics, social studies, a foreign language, and science. Although the Admissions Committee gives primary consideration to academic achievement and potential for collegiate success, it also considers talent in art, drama, or music and involvement in cocurricular activities. A personal interview, although not required, is strongly recommended, as it allows the applicant to view the campus and facilities, talk with students and faculty members, and meet with an admissions counselor.

Nazareth College is pleased to consider applications from students in good standing at accredited two- and four-year colleges and universities. A minimum GPA of 2.5 or better is expected. Transfer applicants who hold, or will hold prior to registration, the Associate in Arts (A.A.) or the Associate in Science (A.S.) degree from a fully accredited college may transfer a maximum of 60 semester hours of credit and enter with full junior status. Transfer applicants who hold, or will hold prior to registration, the Associate in Applied Science (A.A.S.) degree or the Associate of Occupational Studies (A.O.S.) degree from a fully accredited college or institute will have these credits evaluated on a course-by-course basis. Careful advisement on tailoring programs for holders of these degrees is offered by Nazareth College.

Application and Information

Regular decision applicants for the fall semester should submit the application form, transcripts, standardized test scores, an essay, recommendations, and a $40 application fee by February 15 (November 15 for early decision and December 15 for early action). Notification for regular decision begins March 1 (December 15 for early decision and January 15 for early action). For more information regarding the different application options, students should contact the Admissions Office.

For an application packet or information about a campus tour and interview, applicants should contact:

Vice President for Enrollment Management
Nazareth College
4245 East Avenue
Rochester, New York 14618-3790
Phone: 585-389-2860
800-462-3944 (toll-free)

THE NEW SCHOOL FOR JAZZ AND CONTEMPORARY MUSIC

NEW YORK, NEW YORK

THE NEW SCHOOL
A UNIVERSITY

The School

Part of The New School, a leading university in New York City, The New School for Jazz and Contemporary Music offers a unique course of study in which a passionately engaged faculty of professional artists, drawn from New York's renowned jazz community, guides serious, talented students toward high standards of achievement and the ongoing development of the individual creative voice. The School's curriculum is based on the respected tradition of artist-as-mentor and is taught by accomplished, active musicians with significant links to the history and evolution of jazz, blues, pop, and new genres. Students combine the expertise traditionally linked to classical conservatory training with the generative spirit and vigor of jazz.

The School sees its mission as "respecting tradition, embracing innovation." The widely varied backgrounds of both students and instructors combined with curricular depth has resulted in The New School for Jazz and Contemporary Music receiving international recognition as a leading center of arts education today. Students do their core work in classrooms and private studios with exceptional musician-educators, gaining direct exposure to modern music's traditions and practices in an intellectual context that encourages exploration and innovation. Students have numerous opportunities for cross-registration in classes ranging from classical theory, composition, counterpoint, and musicology to music therapy, management, and liberal arts. The opportunity to take courses at Mannes College The New School for Music adds greater depth and provides an additional standard of professionalism against which students can measure their achievements and progress.

The School's primary goal is to provide students with a thorough technical, conceptual, and historical grasp of jazz and contemporary music, employing a comprehensive curricular structure in which teaching takes place in three environments: in the classroom, where students are instructed in ensemble playing, instrumental music, music history, and related topics; in traditional, tutorial instrumental study, where students meet one-on-one with great jazz and classical performers who live, work, and teach in New York City; and in master classes. These scheduled lectures/performances/workshops have featured such artists as Jon Faddis, Jim Hall, Barry Harris, Lee Konitz, Wynton Marsalis, and Jimmy McGriff.

There are a variety of activities in which students can become involved at New School Jazz and throughout the university. Interested students may serve on most New School committees, including Student Life, Libraries, Diversity, Food Services, and the Student Advisory Council. Jazz students have opportunities for involvement on the Executive Committee, the Curriculum Committee, the Student Advisory Council, and in the Pan-African Cultural Organization. The New School is also home to a wide variety of student organizations and clubs. Students are encouraged to form new student groups by contacting the Office of Student Life.

All first-time freshmen are guaranteed dormitory housing for their first year. The New School maintains several residence halls as well as university-leased apartments, most located within six blocks of the Greenwich Village campus. Through the enthusiasm and creativity of the resident advisers, students are exposed to diverse programs that take advantage of the rich traditions of The New School and the cultural opportunities of New York City. For additional information, students should contact the Office of University Housing at universityhousing@newschool.edu or 212-229-5459 or visit the Web site at http://www.newschool.edu/studentaffairs/housing/.

Location

The New School is located in Greenwich Village, a historic neighborhood with a style and atmosphere found nowhere else in New York City. The area is home to design and art studios, galleries, shops, and restaurants as well as avant-garde artists, musicians, and writers. With its rich cultural resources, international sophistication, and cutting-edge attitude, New York City is a vibrant environment that has inspired and challenged artists throughout its history.

Majors and Degrees

The New School for Jazz and Contemporary Music offers the Bachelor of Fine Arts (B.F.A.) for instrumentalists and for vocalists. A five-year combined Bachelor of Arts/Bachelor of Fine Arts (B.A./B.F.A.) program is also available in conjunction with Eugene Lang College The New School for Liberal Arts. Instrumentalists enrolled in this program can major in music composition.

Academic Programs

The B.F.A. degree is granted upon completion of at least 134 credits and must include 90 credits of applied music, along with the required liberal studies and music history distribution. The B.A./B.F.A. degrees are granted upon completion of at least 90 credits of applied music, along with 90 credits of liberal arts, which includes the required Lang seminars and senior work and can also include music history or other liberal arts credits.

Student progress is monitored on the basis of entrance evaluations, ensemble work, student juries (normally in the second half of the sophomore year), successful completion of the core curriculum, and the normal accumulation of course credits. Composition majors begin with courses in jazz theory, ear training, rhythmic analysis, classical theory and counterpoint, piano, and basic compositional skills. In addition to course work within The New School for Jazz and Contemporary Music, students take some classes at Mannes College. Once this foundation is acquired, students experiment with a large number of theory and performance electives to define personal goals.

Off-Campus Programs

The New School's proximity to several major jazz record labels and performance venues offers significant opportunities for students. Music industry internships, such as those at Blue Note Records, Verve Records, BMG Records, Jazz at Lincoln Center, the Blue Note Jazz Club, and the Knitting Factory, provide hands-on experience, develop networking skills, and create potential job opportunities.

The New School for Jazz and Contemporary Music and Veneto Jazz offer a two-week workshop in Bassano del Grappa, Italy. The workshop is taught by 8 of the finest New York musicians and faculty members from The New School. Courses are divided into various levels and include master classes, theory, arranging, combos, and Big Band, and public performances take place in the city theaters. This workshop is part of the Veneto Jazz Festival, one of the most important European jazz festivals.

Academic Facilities

The New School for Jazz and Contemporary Music is located on the fifth and sixth floors of 55 West 13th Street, the university's primary building for technology services. The School's 20,000-square-foot, state-of-the-art facility was designed specifically to help young artists realize their goal of becoming effective music professionals. The facility offers administrative, classroom, practice, and rehearsal space, all constructed with the highest quality and attention to acoustics, soundproofing, and aesthetics. All classrooms are fully dedicated with Yamaha grand pianos, drum kits, amplifiers, vocal PA systems, and full-component stereo systems. Specialized instrumental practice and teaching rooms are offered, as well as a listening library and piano/MIDI labs.

Performance and recording needs are served in an intimate and beautiful 120-seat performance space, with full capacity for professional sound, lighting, and recording. A second recording studio is used for additional recording and engineering, with both studios connected to the university's server and Internet sites, with the possibility for both posted archival recordings and live streaming performance. Additional university performance facilities within a two-block radius of the Greenwich Village campus include a 170-seat performance auditorium and an excellent and acoustically balanced concert hall with an audience capacity of 500.

The New School's 188,000-volume Raymond Fogelman Library is complemented by the Adam and Sophie Gimbel Library at Parsons The New School for Design and the Harry Scherman Library at Mannes College The New School for Music. A library consortium links the libraries at The New School with those at New York University and Cooper Union, making library privileges available reciprocally to matriculated students. This constitutes a resource of more than 3 million volumes and includes the Avery Fisher Center for Music and Media, which provides access to the most up-to-date electronic media, records, tapes, video, and a library of music materials. In addition, New School students have access to a wealth of public library resources throughout the five boroughs of New York City, including the New York City Public Library for the Performing Arts in Manhattan.

The Office of Academic Computing operates three general-access laboratories; each offers a wide variety of software, including word processing, spreadsheets, databases, e-mail, music notation, and graphics and statistical packages. Students using the centers are supported by a full-time staff and assisted by lab aides. Training seminars and documentation are available on supported software and hardware. The Knowledge Union is a state-of-the-art film, video, and multimedia production facility located on the eighth and ninth floors of 55 West 13th Street. Among its studios is a dedicated music lab where many New School Jazz music technology courses are held.

Costs

Tuition for all full-time (12–18 credits) students was $14,900 each semester for 2007–08 ($29,800 for the year). B.A./B.F.A. students paid $15,330 (12–21 credits) per term ($30,660 for the year). Fees totaled $325 per semester (University Services $100, Health Services $210, divisional fee $15). Although housing costs vary depending on accommodations and meal plan selected, room and board average about $12,000 per year.

Financial Aid

Students may receive a merit scholarship award, which is determined at the initial audition as part of the acceptance package. Students are encouraged to apply during Audition Period 1, as scholarships are available on a limited basis to students auditioning during Audition Period 2 (late auditions). Students are encouraged to file the FAFSA form (online at http://www.fafsa.ed.gov) to determine eligibility for federal grants and loans. Almost 75 percent of students receive some kind of financial aid, awarded on the basis of financial need and merit. The university's financial aid office is open year-round to assist students and their families with the task of meeting educational costs. For information on specific kinds of assistance, amounts of funding, loan repayment, and scholarships for students meeting certain criteria, students should contact the financial aid office at 212-229-8930 or financialaid@newschool.edu.

Faculty

The faculty members of The New School for Jazz and Contemporary Music are drawn from the top ranks of professional musicians in the New York area. This unique artist-as-faculty concept offers extraordinary resources for weekly classes, individual private lessons, special performance events, and master classes. The key to the success of the School lies in its use of experienced professionals to guide the intense involvement of students in the challenges of small-group playing. Students work with the creators, not just the interpreters, of jazz and its offshoots.

Admission Requirements

An applicant must submit the completed application, the nonrefundable $100 application fee, a personal statement, official high school/secondary school transcript or school records, and one letter of recommendation from a teacher, counselor, or professional who can comment on the applicant's qualifications for study at The New School for Jazz and Contemporary Music. International applicants should supply official English translations of all documents and credentials and scores from the TOEFL (minimum 550 on the paper-based exam is preferred).

A performance audition is required of all students. A prescreen tape or CD is required for all applicants on drums, guitar, and voice. Vocalists who pass the prescreen must audition live; drummers and guitarists may audition live or online or submit an audition tape or CD. In lieu of a performance audition, composition majors must submit clearly notated scores and/or lead sheets of their work. The pieces submitted should include at least three works of varying character and demonstrate at minimum an elementary competence in arranging. Live auditions are held in February, March, and April.

Prospective students and their parents are welcome to tour the facilities of The New School for Jazz and Contemporary Music. Tours are offered Tuesday, Wednesday, and Thursday at 3 p.m. while school is in session. Students also have the opportunity to observe one of the improvisation ensembles. Students interested in scheduling a tour should call the Jazz office at 212-229-5896 Ext. 4589 or schedule online at http://www.jazz.newschool.edu at least one week in advance.

Application and Information

Applications are available online at http://www.jazz.newschool.edu. The deadline for fall admission is January 1; the deadline for spring is November 1. Applicants are notified by April 1 and November 15, respectively. For more information, students should contact:

Teri Lucas, Director of Admissions
The New School for Jazz and Contemporary Music
55 West 13th Street, 5th floor
New York, New York 10011
Phone: 212-229-5896 Ext. 4584
Fax: 212-229-8936
E-mail: lucast@newschool.edu
Web site: http://www.jazz.newschool.edu

NEW YORK SCHOOL OF INTERIOR DESIGN

NEW YORK, NEW YORK

The School

The New York School of Interior Design (NYSID) is an independent, coeducational, nonprofit college accredited by National Association of Schools of Art and Design. It was established in 1916 by architect Sherrill Whiton and chartered by the Board of Regents of the University of the State of New York in 1924. Throughout its history, the School has devoted all of its resources to a single field of study—interior design—and has played a significant role in the development of the interior design profession. Enrollment is approximately 750.

NYSID continually updates its curriculum to reflect the many changes taking place in interior design. Today's students learn not only the colors and materials appropriate to period residential interiors, but also how to design hospitals, offices, and restaurants with barrier-free access. Whether learning the importance of historic preservation or the latest programs in computer-aided design, NYSID students learn a wide range of skills and techniques taught by faculty members who work in the field. The area's art and antique shops, museums, professional design studios, and showrooms, are all an exciting part of the college's "campus."

The atmosphere of the college is cosmopolitan, not only because of its excellent location but also because it attracts students from all areas of the United States and abroad. International students make up approximately 10 percent of the student population. Students also transfer from other colleges in order to obtain a more professional, career-directed education.

Because of its select faculty and established reputation, the School continues to maintain a close relationship with the interior design industry. This provides an excellent means for students to develop associations that offer opportunities to move into the profession after completing their degree program at NYSID.

In addition to the three programs in interior design listed below, NYSID also offers a postprofessional Master of Fine Arts (M.F.A.) degree in interior design.

Location

The New York School of Interior Design is located on Manhattan's Upper East Side, where many of the major interior design studios are located. Many of the world's most important galleries, museums, and showrooms are close by, most within walking distance. The city is world-renowned for its architecture, cosmopolitan urban experience, cultural activities, and historic districts. The college can be reached easily by bus, car, subway, and train.

Majors and Degrees

The New York School of Interior Design offers three programs in interior design: a four-year Bachelor of Fine Arts (B.F.A.) degree accredited by the Council for Interior Design Accreditation (CIDA, formerly FIDER), a two-year Associate in Applied Science (A.A.S.) degree, and a 24-credit nondegree Basic Interior Design Program.

Academic Programs

The New York School of Interior Design is a single-major college. It devotes all of its resources to providing a comprehensive education in interior design, and the carefully organized curriculum is constantly evaluated by professionals in the field. The various academic programs compose an integrated curriculum covering interior design concepts; history of art, architecture, furniture, and interiors; technical and communication skills, materials and methods, philosophy and theory; and professional design procedures and design problem solving.

The Basic Interior Design Program consists of a 24-credit required sequence of foundation courses in which all students enroll. These courses provide a cultural, general, and professional introduction to the field of interior design. Although completion of the Basic Interior Design Program may be the major goal for some, for most students it serves as the foundation for matriculation into the degree programs.

The A.A.S. degree program provides the minimum educational requirement to become a certified interior designer in New York State. The 66-credit program includes design, liberal arts, and professional courses.

The 132-credit Bachelor of Fine Arts degree program provides the education that, with practical experience, enables the graduate to take qualifying exams for interior design certification in many states and to join national and local professional associations. Studies focus on the development of a broad array of conceptual analysis, creative problem solving, relevant cultural developments, and technical skills. Students are required to take 32 credits of liberal arts courses in addition to 100 credits of professional design-related courses.

The program planning is flexible and permits students to take courses on a full-time or part-time basis during the day, evening, and on weekends. The School maintains an active job placement service. Students may be placed in a wide variety of positions that reflect the full spectrum of job opportunities in the interior design profession.

Academic Facilities

The NYSID campus occupies two buildings on Manhattan's Upper East Side. The college has a first-rate physical plant with light-filled studios; a unique lighting laboratory; a centralized computer facility for computer-aided design (CAD); a large atelier for independent work furnished with drafting tables, computers, and a materials collection for use in projects; a lecture hall and seminar rooms; a well-stocked bookstore; and a handsome auditorium. The library contains more than 12,000 volumes devoted to design, 100 periodical subscriptions, a product literature collection, and a select collection of 35 mm slides illustrating the history of interior design and decorative arts.

Costs

Tuition for 2008–09 will be $650 per credit, plus a $145 registration/technology fee each semester. Typical expenses for the first year are projected to be $21,450 for tuition and $290 in registration fees.

Financial Aid

The New York School of Interior Design makes every effort to provide assistance to students with financial need. Several institutional scholarships are available for students who meet the criteria. Students are encouraged to apply for the New York State Tuition Assistance Program (TAP—for New York State residents only), the Federal Pell Grant, and Federal Education Loans. The college also participates in the Federal College Work-Study Program, which offers opportunities for on-campus employment.

Faculty

The college's programs are supported by an excellent and dedicated faculty of 85. In addition to teaching, faculty members have active professional careers in appraising, architecture, decorative arts, fine arts, furniture and fabric design, history, interior design, law, lighting design, and psychology.

Student Government

The college has an active student chapter of the American Society of Interior Designers (ASID). ASID organizes lectures, tours, workshops, and other events throughout the school year, providing an inside view of the interior design industry.

Admission Requirements

All applicants must submit an application, an official secondary school transcript, SAT or ACT scores, and two letters of recommendation. Applicants to degree programs must meet the visual requirements by providing a portfolio or sketchbook described in the catalog; transfer students must also submit college transcripts.

International applicants should contact the college's International Student Adviser for assistance in applying.

Application and Information

Admission decisions are made on a rolling basis. However, for processing purposes, it is recommended that the Admissions Office receive an application for fall admission by March 1. An application for spring admission should be received by October 1. Applicants are notified of the Admission Committee's decision by mail shortly after all required documents have been received and visual requirements fulfilled.

Inquiries and applications should be directed to:

Director of Admissions
New York School of Interior Design
170 East 70th Street
New York, New York 10021-5110
Phone: 212-472-1500 Ext. 204
800-33NYSID (toll-free)
Fax: 212-472-1867
E-mail: admissions@nysid.edu
Web site: http://www.nysid.edu

The campus of the New York School of Interior Design is centered on its building at 170 East 70th Street in the Upper East Side Historic District.

COLLEGE DATA CENTER • NEW YORK

NEW YORK UNIVERSITY

NEW YORK, NEW YORK

The University

New York University (NYU) was founded in 1831 by Albert Gallatin, Secretary of the Treasury under Thomas Jefferson; he believed that the place for a university was not in "the seclusion of cloistered halls but in the throbbing heart of a great city." NYU draws top students from every state and more than 133 other countries. The distinguished academic atmosphere attracts the teachers, and the teachers and the atmosphere together attract students who are capable of benefiting from both. Eighty-seven percent of recent NYU graduates say they are either enrolled in a postbaccalaureate program or are planning to do so within the next five years. The faculty includes world-famous scholars, researchers, and artists, among them Nobel laureates, Pulitzer Prize winners, and National Science Foundation members. NYU is a member of the prestigious Association of American Universities. Full professors teach on both the graduate and undergraduate levels. Eight undergraduate schools and colleges provide extensive offerings in a wide range of subjects: more than 2,500 courses in more than 160 major fields are available to NYU's full-time undergraduates. The average class size is under 30, and the faculty-student ratio is 1:11—benefits generally associated with a much smaller institution.

NYU's residence hall program is an important aspect of the total educational experience. Approximately 12,500 undergraduate students live in twenty-one University residence halls, seven of which are reserved exclusively for freshmen. All freshmen who request housing on their admission application and meet all deadlines are guaranteed housing accommodations during all their years of undergraduate study. Freshmen are not required to live on campus, and many students live in private apartments off campus.

The traditions of campus life—nearly 400 clubs, fourteen fraternities and six sororities, and athletics and other activities—are very much a part of the University. Students have the opportunity to write for the campus newspaper and to work with the University's radio station, WNYU-FM. The Jerome S. Coles Sports and Recreation Center and the Palladium Athletic Facility serve the recreational needs of all students. Coles provides the setting for seventy-five intramural sports teams and is the home of NYU's twenty intercollegiate teams. NYU and eight other private, urban research universities have formed a varsity league, the University Athletic Association. The athletic program includes men's basketball, fencing, golf, soccer, swimming and diving, tennis, track and cross-country, volleyball, and wrestling and women's basketball, cross-country, fencing, golf, soccer, swimming and diving, tennis, track, and volleyball.

Location

NYU's undergraduate center is located in historic Greenwich Village, which is virtually an extension of the University. Greenwich Village, traditionally a community of artists and intellectuals, is famous for its contributions to the fine arts, literature, and drama and for its small-scale, European style of living. NYU's campus is within minutes of off-Broadway drama and dance, boutiques, art galleries, coffeehouses, restaurants, clubs, bookstores, record stores, SoHo, Little Italy, Chinatown, and world-renowned museums and libraries. Intellectual stimulation abounds.

Through course work and outside activities, students can enjoy all of the advantages of New York City. As an international center of finance, culture, and communications, New York City offers unmatched educational, internship, and social opportunities. NYU's campus is perhaps one campus in America that could not be mistaken for any other.

Majors and Degrees

The College of Arts and Science awards B.A. and B.S. degrees in Africana studies, anthropology, anthropology-linguistics, art history, biochemistry, biology, chemistry, cinema studies (in conjunction with Tisch School of the Arts), classical civilization and Hellenic studies, classical civilization-anthropology, classics, classics-art history, comparative literature, computer science, dramatic literature, East Asian studies, economics, economics and computer science, economics and mathematics, engineering (biomedical, chemical, civil, computer, electrical, environmental, and mechanical, in conjunction with Stevens Institute of Technology), English, English and American literature, environmental studies, European and Mediterranean studies, French, French and linguistics, gender and sexuality studies, German, German and linguistics, Greek, Hebrew language and literature, Hellenic studies, history, international relations, Italian, Italian and linguistics, Jewish history and civilization, journalism, language and mind, Latin, Latin American studies, Latino studies, linguistics, Luso-Brazilian language and literature, mathematics, mathematics and computer science, medieval and Renaissance studies, metropolitan studies, Middle Eastern and Islamic studies, music, neural science, philosophy, physics, politics, psychology, religious studies, Romance languages, Russian and Slavic studies, self-designed honors major, social and cultural analysis, sociology, South Asian studies, Spanish, Spanish and linguistics, and urban design and architecture studies. Preprofessional programs are available in dentistry, law, medicine, optometry, and podiatry. A B.S./B.E. program in engineering in a dual-degree program with the Stevens Institute of Technology and a seven-year B.A./D.D.S. program are available.

The Leonard N. Stern School of Business awards the B.S. degree in accounting, actuarial science, economics, finance, information systems, management and organizational behavior, marketing, and statistics.

The Steinhardt School of Culture, Education, and Human Development awards the B.S. degree in applied psychology, communication (with a major in media, culture, and communications), education (with majors in childhood education/childhood special education, early childhood education/early childhood special education, and secondary education, with a teaching specialization in English, foreign languages, mathematics, science, or social studies), health (with a major in nutrition and food studies with specializations in food and restaurant management, food studies, and nutrition and dietetics), and speech pathology. In the area of arts professions, Steinhardt offers the B.F.A. degree in studio art and teaching art (all grades), the B.S. in educational theater, and the B.Mus. in instrumental, music business, music education, music technology, music theory and composition, piano (classical and jazz), and voice (classical voice and music theater).

Tisch School of the Arts awards the B.A. degree in cinema studies (film history, theory, and criticism) and the B.F.A. in dance, dramatic writing, film and television (animation, film, television, and video), photography and imaging, recorded music, and theater (acting, directing, musical theater, and technical management).

The Silver School of Social Work awards the B.S. degree in social work.

At the Gallatin School of Individualized Study, students under the mentorship of faculty advisers create and refine their own plans of study by combining Gallatin courses with courses at other schools within NYU, independent studies, and internships and, upon completion, receive a B.A. degree.

The School of Continuing and Professional Studies offers the B.S. degree in sports management and leisure studies, the B.S. degree in hotel and tourism management, and the B.A. degree for adults.

The College of Nursing awards the B.S. degree in nursing.

The General Studies Program is an interdisciplinary liberal arts program offered to a select group of students chosen by the NYU Admissions Committee. After successful completion of this program, students move on as juniors into the school or college to which they originally applied.

Academic Programs

Requirements for graduation vary among departments and schools. A liberal arts core curriculum is an integral part of all areas of concentration. The baccalaureate degree requires completion of at least 128 credits. The University calendar is organized on the traditional semester system, including two 6-week summer sessions. Some divisions offer part-time programs during the day and evening and on weekends.

Off-Campus Programs

Through its eight undergraduate schools and colleges, the University administers a number of programs abroad, including those at NYU sites in Argentina, China, the Czech Republic, England, France, Germany, Ghana, Italy, and Spain, with a future site planned in Tel Aviv, Israel. Exchange programs with several historically black colleges in the U.S. and thirty exchange programs with urban universities around the world are also offered.

Academic Facilities

NYU's Bobst Library, one of the largest open-stack research libraries in the world, has more than 40 miles of open stacks housing over 3.6 million volumes. Among the collections in Bobst are the Avery R. Fisher Center for Music and Media, the Microfilm Center, and the largest official depository of United Nations records and publications outside of the UN itself. Bobst is one of eight NYU libraries that together hold more than 4.9 million volumes. La Maison Française, the Deutsches Haus, the Lewis L. and Loretta Brennen Glucksman Ireland House, the Hagop Kervorkian Center for Near Eastern Studies, the Casa Italiana, the King Juan Carlos I of Spain Center, and the Lillian Vernon Center for International Affairs broaden the range of international programs on campus. The Grey Art Gallery and Study Center, the University's fine arts museum, presents six or seven innovative exhibitions each year that encompass all aspects of the visual arts.

Costs

For 2007–08, tuition and fees were $35,290, and average room and board costs were $11,780. Books and supplies cost about $700, and personal expenses total between $500 and $1000.

Financial Aid

Financial aid at NYU comes from many sources. All students are encouraged to apply for financial assistance or one of NYU's innovative financing plans. Seventy-seven percent of NYU's full-time undergraduates receive financial assistance. Each year, approximately 2,500 entering freshmen are awarded scholarships based on academic promise and/or financial need. The University may offer a package of aid that includes scholarships or grants, loans, or work-study programs. NYU requires the submission of the Free Application for Federal Student Aid (FAFSA). The deadline for filing this financial aid form is February 15 for the fall semester and November 1 for the spring semester. An estimated financial aid package is available to early decision admitted students. The early decision financial aid application is included in the admissions packet or online at http://www.nyu.edu/financial.aid.

Faculty

NYU employs 3,363 full-time faculty members. The faculty-student ratio is 1:11. The faculty devotes equal time to teaching and research. All faculty members keep office hours, and each student meets regularly with a faculty adviser. More than 1,000 faculty members reside on campus. Faculty honors include 147 Guggenheim Fellowships, 4 Nobel and Crafoord prizes, 12 MacArthur Foundation Awards, 4 Pulitzer Prizes, 7 Lasker Awards, 21 elected to the National Academy of Sciences, 68 elected to the American Academy of Arts and Sciences, and numerous Tony, Obie, and Academy awards.

Student Government

Each of NYU's schools and colleges has a student council, organized by its respective students, that represents those students. The University Senate, the major policymaking body for all matters relating to academic concerns not delegated to the separate schools and colleges, has 22 student members.

Admission Requirements

Admission to the undergraduate colleges of New York University is highly selective. The admission process involves a comprehensive review of the applicant's academic background, standardized test scores, extracurricular activities, essay, and letters of recommendation. Several programs also require the applicant to audition or submit creative materials. The Admissions Committee pays particular attention to the number of honors, AP, and I.B. courses the applicant has completed in high school. Applicants must submit scores from the SAT or the ACT (with the Writing Test). Scores from the TOEFL examination are also required if English is not the applicant's native language. The Admissions Committee also requires that applicants submit scores from two SAT Subject Tests (with the exception of applicants to the Steinhardt School of Culture, Education, and Human Development music and arts programs and the Tisch School of the Arts). The committee carefully considers the applicant's special talents, alumni affiliation, socioeconomic background, geographic location, and race or ethnicity. It is also interested in applicants who have an active and sustained level of involvement in school and/or community activities and who have taken on the responsibility of leadership.

Application and Information

For entrance in the fall term, the application for admission—including all supporting credentials—must be received by November 1 (early decision freshman candidates), January 15 (freshmen), or April 1 (transfer students). For entrance in the spring term (transfer students only), the application materials must be received by November 1. For entrance in the summer (transfer students only), the application materials should be received by April 1. Applications for admission received after these dates are considered only if space remains. Official notification of fall admission is made on April 1 and on a rolling basis thereafter. A campus tour or an appointment for an information session can be arranged online at http://admissions.nyu.edu or by calling 212-998-4524.

Office of Undergraduate Admissions
New York University
22 Washington Square North
New York, New York 10011
Phone: 212-998-4500
Internet: http://admissions.nyu.edu

NIAGARA UNIVERSITY

NIAGARA UNIVERSITY, NEW YORK

The University

Niagara University (NU), founded in 1856, is a private, independent university rooted in a Catholic and Vincentian tradition. The suburban 160-acre campus combines the old and new; both ivy-covered buildings and modern architectural structures are among its thirty-three buildings. The University is easily accessible from every major city in the eastern and midwestern United States via the New York State Thruway, Buffalo International Airport, and rail and bus service.

There are 2,900 undergraduate and 900 graduate students enrolled at Niagara. A large percentage of these students take advantage of the more than eighty extracurricular and cocurricular activities offered. Volunteer work in the community is popular among the students and enhances community relations. Students work with numerous organizations, including Habitat for Humanity, Big Brothers/Big Sisters, and the Skating Association for the Blind and Handicapped.

University teams compete on the Division I level and are members of the NCAA, the Eastern College Athletic Conference, and the Metro Atlantic Athletic Conference. Intercollegiate sports for men include baseball, basketball, cross-country, golf, ice hockey, soccer, swimming and diving, and tennis. Intercollegiate sports for women include basketball, cross-country, ice hockey, lacrosse, soccer, softball, swimming and diving, tennis, and volleyball. Club sports include cheerleading, crew, danceline, hockey, martial arts, rugby, and skiing. The Kiernan Center offers a variety of sports and recreational facilities, including a multipurpose gymnasium, a swimming and diving pool, an indoor track, racquetball courts, free-weight and Nautilus rooms, and aerobics rooms. There are several outdoor athletic fields and basketball and tennis courts.

Special student services include the Health Center, which provides inpatient and outpatient care during the day; the Learning Center, which provides free tutoring services; and the Career Development Office, which offers professional and career counseling. Other services include counseling, orientation, academic planning, career planning, and job placement.

Niagara University's housing accommodations include five residence halls, a grouping of five small cottages, and a student apartment complex. Both coed and single-gender accommodations are available.

The University offers graduate studies in business, counseling, criminal justice, education, and interdisciplinary studies.

Location

Niagara University is situated on Monteagle Ridge overlooking the lower Niagara River, which connects the two Great Lakes of Erie and Ontario. Niagara's suburban campus setting is just a few miles from the world-famous Niagara Falls. Millions of visitors view the scenic majesty of the Falls every year. NU is located 20 minutes from Buffalo, which offers a variety of cultural events, sports, and entertainment opportunities. Toronto, Canada's largest metropolitan area, is just 90 minutes north of Niagara's campus and offers an even wider variety of experiences for NU students. In addition, the University is minutes away from the quaint village of Lewiston, New York, and the city of Niagara Falls, New York.

Majors and Degrees

The College of Arts and Sciences offers the Bachelor of Arts degree in chemistry, communication studies, English, French, history, international studies, liberal arts, life sciences, mathematics, philosophy, political science, psychology, religious studies, social sciences, sociology, and Spanish. The Bachelor of Science degree is awarded in biochemistry (with a concentration in bioinformatics), biology (with concentrations in bioinformatics and biotechnology), chemistry (with a concentration in computational chemistry), computer and information sciences, criminal justice and criminology, mathematics, nursing (completion program for students who are registered nurses), and social work. This division also offers the Bachelor of Fine Arts degree in theater studies (with concentrations in design technology, general theater, and performance). Preprofessional programs are offered in dentistry, law, medicine, pharmacy, veterinary medicine, and Army-ROTC. An Associate of Arts degree is available in general studies. In addition, Niagara offers an environmental studies concentration to supplement a degree in biology, chemistry, or political science. Enrichment courses in fine arts and languages are also available.

In addition to the programs listed above NU offers a number of preprofessional partnerships. These include a 3+4 partnership in pharmacy with the State University of New York at Buffalo (SUNY), a 2+3 partnership in pharmacy with Lake Erie College of Osteopathic Medicine (LECOM), a 3+4 partnership in medicine with LECOM, and a 3+4 partnership in dentistry with SUNY at Buffalo. Qualified premedical Niagara students are eligible to apply for the early assurance program sponsored by the SUNY at Buffalo.

Niagara University's College of Business Administration is accredited by AACSB International—The Association to Advance Collegiate Schools of Business and offers a B.B.A. and a combination B.B.A./M.B.A. degree (five-year program) in accounting. This division offers a B.S. degree in commerce with concentrations in economics and finance, general business, human resources, international business, management, marketing, and supply chain management. In addition, an A.A.S. degree can be earned in business. The College of Business Administration follows a project-based model, which means students gain substantive experience that is the equivalent to the work of a consultant. More real-world learning occurs through internships, study abroad, and cooperative education programs as well as research being conducted in several business-focused campus centers. These centers include the Family Business Center, the Center for Supply Chain Management, and the Center for International Accounting.

Holding the highest accreditations possible in both the United States and Canada—the United States National Council for Teacher Education (NCATE) and Canada's Ontario College of Teachers—Niagara University's College of Education provides students with an option of earning dual certification to teach in both countries. The College of Education offers bachelor's degree programs leading to New York State initial certification in early childhood (birth–grade 6), childhood (grades 1–6), childhood and middle childhood (grades 1–9), middle childhood and adolescence (grades 5–12), adolescence (grades 7–12), certification for teaching students with disabilities (grades 1–6 childhood and grades 7–12 adolescence), and in Teaching English to Speakers of Other Languages (TESOL). All education majors pursue an academic concentration to establish expertise in one of the following subject areas: biology, business, chemistry, English, French, liberal arts, mathematics, social studies, and Spanish. Business education is offered only at grades 5–12. The academic concentration in liberal arts can only be pursued in the early childhood and childhood (birth–grade 6), special education and childhood (grades 1–6), and TESOL programs. Most other states, and Puerto Rico, have reciprocity agreements with New York, meaning that an NU education would qualify education majors to teach in those states as well. In addition, the Canadian province of Ontario recognizes Niagara graduates as qualified for the Letter of Eligibility to teach in that province.

The College of Hospitality and Tourism Management provides a career-oriented curriculum leading to a B.S. degree in three specific areas: hotel and restaurant management (with concentrations in hotel and restaurant planning and control, foodservice management, and hotel entrepreneurship), sport management (with a concentration in sport operations), and tourism and recreation management (with concentrations in special events and conference management and tourism destination management). The College of Hospitality and Tourism Management offered the world's first bachelor's degree in tourism. NU's hotel and restaurant program, the second oldest in New York State, has the distinction of being the seventh program nationally to be accredited by the Accreditation Commission for Programs in Hospitality Administration by the Council of Hotel, Restaurant, and Institutional Education. The College introduces students to a comprehensive body of knowledge about the hotel, restaurant, tourism, and recreational areas and applies this knowledge to current industry challenges. The College requires that its students accumulate 800 hours of industry-related experience. These and other practical experiences offer NU students the knowledge necessary to advance in the field. Students work with industry leaders in classroom projects, join academic clubs and professional organizations, and participate in special field trips to trade shows and conventions and specially designed study-abroad experiences, making NU a national leader in the area.

For students who are undecided about which major to choose, Niagara University offers an award-winning Academic Exploration Program (AEP). AEP provides a structured opportunity for students to participate in a thorough, organized process of selecting a major that meets their academic talents and career goals.

Academic Programs

Niagara University's curricula enable students to pursue their academic preferences and to complete courses that lead to proficiency in other academic areas. Courses that have been considered upper-division courses are available to all students. This provides students with the opportunity to avoid introductory and survey courses and permits motivated students to take advantage of more challenging courses early in their collegiate career. The honors program provides special academic opportunities that stimulate, encourage, and challenge participants. In addition, an accelerated three-year degree program is offered to qualified students.

Students pursuing a bachelor's degree must complete a total of 40 or 42 course units (120 or 126 hours) to meet graduation requirements. Niagara grants credit for successful scores on the Advanced Placement and College-Level Examination Program tests.

Internships, research, independent study, and cooperative education are available in many academic programs. An Army ROTC program is also offered.

The University operates on a two-semester plan (fall and spring). A comprehensive summer session offers a variety of courses.

NU is fully accredited by the Middle States Association of Colleges and Schools. Its programs in the respective areas are accredited by the National Council for Accreditation of Teacher Education, AACSB International–The Association to Advance Collegiate Schools of Business, and the Council on Social Work Education, and the chemistry department has the approval of the American Chemical Society. The travel, hotel, and restaurant administration program is accredited by the Commission for Programs in Hospitality Administration.

Off-Campus Programs

For those students who wish to study abroad, the University offers semester and summer programs in Chile, England, France, Mexico, Netherlands, Spain, Switzerland, Thailand, and many other countries. Upon request, programs may be offered in other countries. NU is also affiliated with Western New York Consortium. Through this program, students may take courses at other colleges and universities and apply the credits to Niagara's graduation requirements.

Academic Facilities

The University's open-stack library exceeds 200,000 books and has more than 15,000 periodical titles as well as reference databases accessible through the Web. The library is housed in a modern facility that includes seating for 500 people, including individual study carrels. The library is affiliated with the Online Computer Library Center (OCLC) network.

The Academic Complex, the new home to the College of Education and the College of Business Administration (Bisgrove Hall), is a state-of-the-art learning facility. Dunleavy Hall, outstanding both educationally and architecturally, includes a behavioral science laboratory, a computerized lecture hall, and TV production rooms. The University's facilities also include the Computer Center; DePaul Hall of Science; St. Vincent's Hall; the Kiernan Center, NU's athletic and recreation center; the Leary Theatre; the Castellani Art Museum; Bailo Hall, which houses the Office of Admissions; and the Dwyer Arena, a dual-rink ice hockey complex.

Costs

Tuition for 2007–08 was $21,400. Room and board (with a choice of meal plans) cost an additional $9300 per year. Fees were estimated at $900 per year. Niagara estimates that an additional $2600 per year is adequate for books, laundry, and other essentials, such as travel to and from home.

Financial Aid

Ninety-eight percent of the incoming students who enrolled at NU received a financial aid package averaging $17,510 per year. They receive assistance in the form of merit scholarships, loans, grants, or campus employment. Students seeking financial aid should file the Free Application for Federal Student Aid (FAFSA). New York State residents should also file a Tuition Assistance Program (TAP) application.

Faculty

Niagara University has a dedicated, accessible faculty who genuinely cares about the academic and personal growth of their students. Their commitment to teaching is their primary concern. A student-faculty ratio of 14:1 and an average class size of 25 allow personal attention and classroom interaction.

Student Government

The Student Government represents all parts of the student body equally. It coordinates and legislates all student activities, serving as both liaison to and a participating member of the University. In addition, students serve on all major departmental committees and on the University Senate, which is the major advisory committee to the president and Board of Trustees.

Admission Requirements

The University welcomes men and women who have demonstrated aptitude and academic achievement at the high school level. Either SAT or ACT test scores are required. International students are required to submit the results of their TOEFL examination. Interviews are recommended. Transfer students are accepted in any semester. (Transfer credit is evaluated individually by the dean of each division.) Students who complete high school in less than four years are eligible for early admission. Students may also apply under an early action program. Economically and educationally disadvantaged students from New York State are eligible to apply for admission through the Higher Educational Opportunity Program (HEOP).

Application and Information

Niagara operates on a rolling admission basis and adheres to the College Board Candidates Reply Date. A visit to the campus is encouraged, and overnight accommodations in a residence hall are available through the Niagara Nights program.

Information on all aspects of the University can be obtained by contacting the Office of Admissions.

Harry Gong
Director of Admissions
630 Bailo Hall
Niagara University
Niagara University, New York 14109-2011
Phone: 716-286-8700
800-462-2111 (toll-free)
Fax: 716-286-8710
E-mail: admissions@niagara.edu
Web site: http://www.niagara.edu

The main campus of Niagara University.

PACE UNIVERSITY

NEW YORK CITY AND PLEASANTVILLE, NEW YORK

The University

Pace University was founded by two brothers, Homer and Charles Pace, in 1906. Their vision is reflected in Pace's motto "Opportunitas." A comprehensive, diversified, coeducational institution, Pace provides an array of opportunities for learning, living, and working at two distinct campus locations: metropolitan New York City and suburban Pleasantville, New York. More than eighty majors and 3,000 courses of study are offered through five undergraduate schools and colleges: the Lubin School of Business, the Dyson College of Arts and Sciences, the School of Computer Science and Information Systems, the School of Education, and the Lienhard School of Nursing. Pace University is chartered by the New York State Board of Regents and is accredited by the Middle States Association of Colleges and Schools.

Many student-led clubs and organizations are active on the campus, including the Model United Nations, Black Students Organization, the Chinese Club, the Caribbean Students Association, and the Collegiate Italian American Organization. Pace also offers many campus activities, including student government associations, fraternities, sororities, two campus newspapers, two literary magazines, two yearbooks, and two campus broadcasting systems. Athletic facilities are available for students, and intercollegiate sports include baseball, basketball, cross-country, equestrian, football, golf, lacrosse, women's soccer, softball, swimming and diving, tennis, track and field, and volleyball.

In 2007–08, approximately 8,500 undergraduate students enrolled at Pace University. The student body is diverse, representing forty-eight states, five U.S. territories, and more than 100 countries.

Location

Pace University is a multicampus institution with campuses in both New York City and Pleasantville, New York. Both locations are within reach of cultural, business, and social resources and opportunities. The New York City campus is located in the heart of downtown Manhattan, adjacent to the financial district and City Hall and within a short walking distance of Wall Street and the South Street Seaport. Lincoln Center, Broadway theaters, museums, and many world-famous attractions are minutes away by public transportation. Located 35 miles north of New York City, the Pleasantville campus is located in suburban New York and includes an environmental center, riding stables, and a new athletic center. The town of Pleasantville houses gifted resident artisans and local musical and theater groups, and museums surround the campus. The campus is within easy reach of the resort and ski areas of the Catskills, Berkshires, and Poconos as well as all that the New York City area has to offer. Both campuses are accessible by car and public transportation.

Students can take courses at either campus, and housing is available in both New York City and Pleasantville. Residence facilities feature Internet connectivity, voicemail, and cable TV access.

Majors and Degrees

The following programs are offered at both the New York City and Pleasantville campuses. The Bachelor of Business Administration (B.B.A.) is offered with majors in finance, accounting-general, accounting-public, information systems, international management, management (with concentrations in business, entrepreneurship, hotel management, and human resources), and marketing (with concentrations in advertising and promotion, database marketing, e-business and interactive media, international marketing, and management). In addition, five-year combined B.B.A./M.B.A and B.B.A./M.S. programs in public accounting are available for qualified students. The Bachelor of Arts (B.A.) degree is granted in art history; childhood education; communication; computer science; earth science; economics; English; English language and literature; environmental studies; French; history; language and cognition/childhood education; liberal studies; philosophy and religious studies; political science; psychology; social science; sociology/anthropology; and Spanish. The Bachelor of Science (B.S.) degree is offered in biochemistry, biology, chemistry, computer science, criminal justice, early childhood development, information systems, mathematics, medical technology, nursing, professional communication studies, professional computer studies, teaching adolescents, and technology systems.

Certain programs are available only on one campus. The B.S. programs in speech communication and forensic science and the B.F.A. program in theater are offered only at the New York City campus. The B.A. programs in biological sciences, communications, English and communications, global studies, human services, Italian, and teaching adolescents Italian and the B.S. programs in art, physics, and teaching adolescents physics are available at the Pleasantville campus only.

Pace University offers two 5-year engineering programs in cooperation with Manhattan College and Rensselaer Polytechnic Institute. In one program, students attend Pace for three years and Manhattan College for two years, leading to a B.S. degree in science with a concentration in physics from Pace and a B.S. degree in electrical engineering from Manhattan. In the other program, students attend Pace for three years and either Manhattan College or Rensselaer for two years. Upon successful completion, students receive a B.S. degree in chemistry from Pace and either a Bachelor of Chemical Engineering (B.C.E.) in chemical engineering from Manhattan or a B.S. degree in engineering from Rensselaer.

Academic Programs

At Pace University, the core curriculum emphasizes educational breadth and civic engagement. Students enroll in prerequisite courses in the first two years and major courses and electives in the junior and senior years. Selective academic programs in the University are preparatory for professional training in dentistry, law, medicine, and veterinary science.

The Pforzheimer Honors College is a highly esteemed opportunity at Pace—a community of talented undergraduate scholars studying under the distinguished faculty of the University's five undergraduate schools and colleges. It is a place to excel and realize potential.

The Cooperative Education Program is nationally recognized and offers qualified students the opportunity to gain experience in their field of study while earning a four-year degree. Students can choose full-time, part-time, or summer positions working in an area directly related to their major course of study.

Academic Facilities

The Pace University Library is a comprehensive teaching library and student learning center, a virtual library that combines strong core collections with ubiquitous access to global Internet resources to support broad and diversified curricula. Reciprocal borrowing and access accords, traditional interlibrary loan services, and commercial document delivery options supplement the aggregate library. Pace offers Instructional Services librarians, a state-of-the-art electronic classroom, digital reference services, and multimedia applications. Pace's computer resource centers are linked to high-speed data networks and feature sophisticated hardware and software to facilitate active learning. Pace supports high-speed Internet and Internet2 access on every campus—residence facilities are wired, and most public areas are enabled for wireless connectivity. Full-motion videoconference facilities enable remote delivery of instruction between campus sites for synchronous learning applications.

Costs

For the 2008–09 academic year, undergraduate tuition is $30,632 per year for full-time study. The cost for an on-campus double-occupancy room is $8000–$10,000, with different housing options available. The cost of the meal plan is approximately $3600. Additional fees are approximately $700, and books and supplies average $1000 per year.

Financial Aid

Pace University strives to provide opportunities to students of diverse backgrounds and varied circumstances and is committed to offering financial aid to students to the fullest extent of its resources. Scholarships are awarded to students in recognition of superior academic achievement and are available for full-time and part-time study. Pace's comprehensive student financial aid assistance program includes scholarships, student loans (federal and alternative plans), and tuition payment plans. Pace participates in all federal financial aid programs and the New York State Tuition Assistance Program (TAP) and honors awards from other states' incentive grant programs.

Students should submit the Free Application for Federal Student Aid (FAFSA) by February 15 for priority consideration for the fall semester. Further information about any financial aid programs can be obtained by contacting the Office of Financial Aid at any campus location.

Faculty

The undergraduate faculty at Pace is outstanding. Senior staff members, including department heads, teach freshman- and sophomore-level courses as well as upper-division classes. Approximately 90 percent of full-time faculty members hold a doctoral degree; many act as professional consultants to other educational institutions, businesses, and governments. Adjunct faculty members pursue professional careers while teaching their specialty part-time. Undergraduate classes are not taught by teaching assistants.

Admission Requirements

A minimum of 16 units from an accredited secondary school, or equivalent, are required. Academic subjects in high school should be distributed as follows: 4 units of English, 3–4 units of college-preparatory mathematics, 2 units of foreign language, 4 units of history/social science, 2 units of laboratory science, and 4–5 units of academic electives. It is recommended that students applying to the Lubin School of Business complete 4 units of preparatory mathematics. Applicants to the Lienhard School of Nursing should complete 3–4 units of science (2 of which should be laboratory science) and 3–4 units of college-preparatory mathematics. All applicants are required to take either the SAT or ACT examination and have results forwarded to the University. International students are required to take the TOEFL.

Application and Information

The freshman application deadline is March 1. Transfer applications are reviewed on a rolling basis. Requests for application forms and information for both the New York City and Pleasantville campuses should be addressed to:

Enrollment Information Center
Pace University
1 Pace Plaza
New York, New York 10038
Phone: 800-874-7223 (toll-free)
E-mail: infoctr@pace.edu
Web site: http://www.pace.edu

PARSONS THE NEW SCHOOL FOR DESIGN

THE NEW SCHOOL
A UNIVERSITY

NEW YORK, NEW YORK

The University

Part of The New School, a leading university in New York City, Parsons The New School for Design is one of the premier degree-granting colleges of art and design in the nation. Founded in 1896 by the American impressionist painter William Merritt Chase, Parsons focuses on creating engaged citizens and outstanding artists, designers, scholars, and business leaders through a design-based professional and liberal education. Parsons students learn to rise to the challenges of living, working, and creative decision making in a world where human experience is increasingly designed. The school embraces curricular innovation, pioneering uses of technology, collaborative methods, and global perspectives on the future of design. Parsons graduates and faculty members appear on the short list of outstanding practitioners in every realm of art and design—creative, management, and scholarly. Responsive to societal needs and predictive of cultural trends, Parsons makes tangible, usable, and beautiful The New School's mission of bringing positive, innovative change to the world.

Approximately 2,400 undergraduate students and more than 400 graduate students are enrolled in Parsons The New School for Design. Nearly a third of all degree-seeking students are international, coming from sixty-eight countries. Some 2,000 continuing education students take individual courses or are enrolled in certificate programs. More than 700 children and young people attend weekend and summer precollege programs.

More than 1,100 students live in the seven different residence halls in the Greenwich Village and Wall Street areas and take part in the social and educational programs and activities provided there. Through the enthusiasm and creativity of the resident advisers, students are exposed to diverse programs that take advantage of the rich traditions of The New School and the cultural opportunities of New York City. Through programming that addresses students' intellectual, artistic, and creative efforts, the residence life program fosters the development of the whole student. The University endeavors to provide comfortable and inclusive communities where students and staff members promote cultural awareness and academic success and develop new ideas and diverse experiences. For more information, students should contact the Office of University Housing at universityhousing@newschool.edu or 212-229-5459 or visit the Web site at http://www.newschool.edu/studentaffairs/housing/.

Parsons and The New School are fully accredited by the Commission on Higher Education of the Middle States Association of Colleges and Schools. Its credits and degrees are recognized and accepted by other accredited colleges, universities, and professional schools throughout the United States. The New School, a privately supported institution, is chartered as a university by the Regents of the State of New York.

Location

Parsons' main campus is located downtown in Greenwich Village, a historic neighborhood with a style and atmosphere found nowhere else in New York City. The area is home to design and art studios, galleries, shops, and restaurants as well as avant-garde artists, musicians, and writers. With its rich cultural resources, international sophistication, and cutting-edge attitude, New York City is a vibrant environment that has inspired and challenged artists and designers throughout its history. The city offers more than eighty museums, such as the Metropolitan Museum of Art, the Museum of Modern Art, and Cooper-Hewitt, National Design Museum. Parsons faculty members teach the architecture of the city, the fabric of its populations, and the language of its commercial and private communication. In short, the faculty uses New York City as an urban design laboratory to teach students to look, learn, and feel the world around them.

Majors and Degrees

Undergraduate degrees offered are an Associate in Applied Science (A.A.S.), a Bachelor of Business Administration (B.B.A.), and a Bachelor of Fine Arts (B.F.A.). Students may also earn a Bachelor of Arts and a Bachelor of Fine Arts (B.A./B.F.A.) through a five-year, dual-degree program offered in conjunction with Eugene Lang College The New School for Liberal Arts, with classes and studios located conveniently on one campus. Pending New York State approval, Parsons plans to begin offering a Bachelor of Science (B.S.) in environmental studies in fall 2008.

Associate degrees are available in fashion marketing, fashion studies, graphic design, and interior design. Bachelor's degrees are offered in administration, architectural design, communication design, design and management, design and technology, fashion design, fine arts, illustration, integrated design, interior design, photography, product design, and, pending New York State approval, environmental studies.

Academic Programs

The degree programs at Parsons are academically challenging, demanding, and, ultimately, professionally rewarding for emerging designers. On average, students register for 16 to 18 credits (six classes) per semester. Most students are in class for 20 to 30 hours per week and spend an equivalent amount of time in preparation. Studio critique sessions and critical studies seminars depend on thoughtful student input and discussion. All courses require active attendance and regular participation.

The A.A.S. degree requires 65 credits; the B.B.A. and B.F.A., 134 credits each; and the B.A./B.F.A., 180 credits. The five-year B.A./B.F.A. program (BAFA), is offered in conjunction with Eugene Lang College The New School for Liberal Arts.

Off-Campus Programs

In 1920, Parsons School of Design, as it was known then, was the first art and design school in America to found a campus abroad. Today, the school offers its students the possibility to expand their horizons by studying at art and design schools around the world. During their junior year, bachelor's degree students may enroll for one or two semesters in another school in the United States or abroad. Several departments assist students in securing noncredit internships that provide valuable work experience and professional contacts. Current and past internships include Marc Jacobs, Polo-Ralph Lauren, HBO, MTV, the *New York Times, Rolling Stone* magazine, Marvel Comics, and the Museum of Modern Art.

Academic Facilities

The Sheila C. Johnson Design Center is a new campus center for Parsons that combines learning and public program spaces with exhibition galleries, creating an important and new destination for art and design programming in Greenwich Village. The center features the Anna-Maria and Stephen Kellen Gallery and Auditorium and the Arnold and Sheila Aronson Galleries. These spaces present exhibitions and public programs exploring key issues within contemporary culture through the work of architects, artists, and designers. The center also provides a new home for the Anna-Maria and Stephen Kellen Archives, a significant collection of drawings, photographs, letters, and objects documenting twentieth-century design. In addition, several learning and meeting spaces are incorporated into the design, including an innovative student critique area located in the highly visible intersection of

Fifth Avenue and 13th Street, which will enable the public to observe the design dialogue that is central to a Parsons education.

The Angelo Donghia Materials Library and Study Center, funded by the Angelo Donghia Foundation, comprises a library, a gallery, a computer lab, and a lecture hall. The library allows students and faculty members to review and check out state-of-the-art resources, putting the latest and most exclusive materials at their fingertips. Regular exhibitions at the gallery run by a full-time curator are open to the public, creating an open forum and dialogue with the larger interior design community. The heart of the architecture program is the large, open studio loft where students develop design projects in interaction with faculty members and peers. The 5,000-square-foot space is supported by wireless digital technology, allowing for direct access for printing and plotting from students' desks to the adjacent twenty-five-station computer laboratories. In addition, a consortium membership gives Parsons students access to the libraries of Cooper Union and New York University.

Over the past several years, The New School has invested more than $30 million in a series of extensive labs. The Knowledge Union consists of state-of-the-art technology spread over four floors; the 600 networked workstations include all relevant platforms. Servers support work that ranges from traditional print output to online projects using webcasting and secure transaction technology. Specialty work—whether audio or video production, MIDI, recording, or physical computing installation—takes place in private studios spread across the campus. Portable production equipment, including digital still, video, and audio, is readily available. Digital projectors, surround sound, and active white boards feed into equipment racks that enable presentation of all media types.

The University Computing Center, on the third and fourth floors at 55 West 13th Street, is a central hub of technologies. Computers and hands-on classrooms support multimedia, Web design, and desktop publishing as well as word processing and research. The Fashion Computing Center at 560 Seventh Avenue provides computing support for the Parsons B.F.A. program in fashion design. It has more than forty UNIX, Macintosh, and Windows workstations and color and black-and-white printers. Software includes high-end graphic and three-dimensional modeling applications.

Costs

For 2007–08, full-time (12–19 credits) undergraduate students paid $15,970 in tuition and $140 in fees per term. Although housing costs vary depending on accommodations and meal plan selected, room and board averaged about $11,800 per year. Additional fees may apply.

Financial Aid

Almost 75 percent of Parsons students receive some kind of financial aid, awarded on the basis of financial need and merit. The University's financial aid office is open year-round to assist students and their families with the task of meeting educational costs. For information on specific kinds of assistance, amounts of funding, loan repayment, and scholarships for students meeting certain criteria, students should visit Student Financial Services' Web site at http://www.newschool.edu/studentservices/financialaid/.

Faculty

More than 700 full- and part-time faculty members teach at Parsons. All of them are successful professionals in the design, art, and business fields. The student-faculty ratio is 9:1. Faculty members and visiting critics—such as installation artist Brian Tolle, architect David Lewis, communication designer Charles Nix, and interior designer Shashi Caan—are principals in their own design firms, hold key positions in the art and design community, and frequently have their work published. Parsons' strong ties to industry bring numerous guest lecturers and critics into forums and classrooms. Visiting critics include Richard Meier, Donna Karan, Mayer Rus, Arthur Corwin, and Paula Scher.

Admission Requirements

Parsons seeks serious, responsible, and highly motivated applicants. Each applicant is reviewed individually with regard to experience, achievements, and potential for artistic growth. While Parsons recognizes the benefits of strong artistic preparation, some applicants are admitted based on their academic strengths more than their visual material. For B.F.A. applicants, a large part of the Admissions Committee's decision is based on portfolio evaluations and the Parsons Challenge, as well as academic achievement. For B.B.A. applicants, academic achievement is weighted heavily along with the Parsons Challenge. The A.A.S. program is best suited to students who have had some prior college experience, are clear about their interests within the world of design, and are prepared for rapid immersion in a professional course of study.

All applicants must submit the completed application, the nonrefundable $50 application fee, and original copies of official high school and/or college transcripts. Bachelor's applicants who are residents of the United States must also submit SAT or ACT scores; international students must send in their TOEFL scores (minimum of 580 on the paper-based exam or 237 on the computerized exam). All applicants must submit the multipart Parsons Challenge exercise. A portfolio is required of all B.F.A. applicants (except those applying to study design and management). This must consist of eight to twelve pieces of work, including, but not limited to, drawings, paintings, photographs, digital media, or design. A personal interview is recommended for all applicants.

Application and Information

The admission and financial aid deadline for the fall semester is February 1, and the deadline for spring admission is October 15. The Admissions Committee reviews applications and sends students its decision a few weeks after all materials are received.

Admissions Office
Parsons The New School for Design
65 Fifth Avenue
New York, New York 10011
Phone: 212-229-8989
Fax: 212-229-8975
E-mail: parsadm@newschool.edu
Web site: http://www.parsons.newschool.edu/

Part of the Parsons experience—taking part in critiquing student assignments.

PAUL SMITH'S COLLEGE

PAUL SMITHS, NEW YORK

The College

Paul Smith's College is named for an entrepreneur whose famous resort on Lower St. Regis Lake was synonymous with Adirondack hospitality. Many of the rich and famous of the late nineteenth and early twentieth centuries gathered at the resort to enjoy the mountain wilderness and the comfortable accommodations provided by Paul Smith and his wife, Lydia. Vast land holdings acquired over the years were passed on to Smith's son Phelps, who, upon his death in 1937, bequeathed the bulk of the estate to the establishment of a college in his father's name. Paul Smith's College was chartered as a college of the arts and sciences; in the tradition of Paul Smith, who believed in "learning by doing," the school provides students with the opportunity to gain practical experience in a chosen field, while obtaining the academic background necessary for a well-rounded education. The immense expanse of woodlands, lakes, and streams surrounding the campus offers vast research opportunities to students of forestry, ecology, and environmental studies. Such a hands-on approach is shared by other programs as well. Students of hotel, resort, and culinary management, for example, train in the student-operated St. Regis Café, a bistro-style experience, as well as the Ganzi Training Restaurant, a fine-dining operation; both facilities are located on campus. This experiential approach has attracted students from across the country and throughout the world to Paul Smith's.

Student activities are an important part of life at Paul Smith's. Popular organizations include the Forestry Club, Ski and Snowboard Club, Fish and Game Club, Wildlife Society, Junior American Culinary Federation, B-GLAD, and Koinonia.

For those interested in athletics, Paul Smith's has a swimming pool, basketball courts, a fitness center with cardio machines and weights, a rock-climbing wall, a dance room, and a multiple-use court for badminton, volleyball, and other indoor sports. Outside, the College has tennis, volleyball, and basketball courts, a horseshoe pit, and miles of wooded trails for the cross-country runner or mountain-biking enthusiast. Canoes, snowshoes, and cross-country skis are all available free of charge. Paul Smith's participates at the intercollegiate level in men's and women's basketball, cross-country running, cross-country skiing, soccer, and woodsmen's competitions and in women's volleyball; the College recently joined the National Association of Intercollegiate Athletics (NAIA). Cross-country snowshoeing, men's rugby, and woodsmen's competitions are offered as club sports.

Paul Smith's College of Arts and Sciences is approved and chartered by the Regents of the University of the State of New York and the Commissioner of Education of New York State. The College is accredited by the Commission on Higher Education of the Middle States Association of Colleges and Schools. Individual majors at Paul Smith's are accredited additionally by the Society of American Foresters (forest recreation and forest technician); the Technology Accreditation Commission of the Accreditation Board for Engineering and Technology (surveying technology); and the American Culinary Federation Educational Institute Accrediting Commission (culinary arts).

Location

The College's more than 14,000-acre campus is on the shore of the Lower St. Regis Lake in the Adirondack Mountains of northern New York State. Students have access to 23 miles of navigable water for boating and fishing, while nearby forests and mountains provide opportunities for hiking, climbing, and more. The campus is located 22 miles from Lake Placid, site of the 1932 and 1980 Winter Olympics. Students frequently go to the resort community to shop, dine, and watch athletes train in luge, bobsled, ski jumping, and other winter sports. Whiteface Mountain, Mount Pisgah, and Titus Mountain provide skiing venues for the beginner as well as the expert.

Majors and Degrees

Paul Smith's College awards Bachelor of Science (B.S.), Bachelor of Professional Studies (B.P.S.), Bachelor of Arts (B.A.), Associate in Science (A.S.), Associate in Arts (A.A.), and Associate in Applied Science (A.A.S.) degrees. Bachelor's degree programs of study include biology (general and environmental science); business and entrepreneurial studies; culinary arts and service management; fisheries and wildlife sciences; forestry (ecological forest management, forest biology, industrial forest operations, recreation resource management, vegetation management); hotel, resort, and tourism management; natural resources management and policy; nature and culture; and recreation, adventure travel, and ecotourism.

Associate degree programs of study include culinary arts, culinary arts baking track, forest recreation, forest technician studies, hotel and restaurant management, liberal arts, surveying technology, and urban tree management. Paul Smith's also offers certificate programs in baking and geographic information systems (GIS).

Academic Programs

The real value of a Paul Smith's College education comes from the emphasis on not just learning something from a book, but actually doing it. Paul Smith's College provides a dynamic educational environment that encourages students to be actively engaged in their own learning experiences through the integration of traditional and experiential learning. This approach, when coupled with its setting in the world-renowned Adirondack Park, leads to discovery, discipline, and creativity. In addition, the College's commitment to sustainable development fosters a sense of environmental stewardship and hospitality among the students.

The College runs on a two-semester schedule (fall and spring). The number of credit hours required for graduation is dependent on the field of study chosen. Students must complete general education core requirements as well as courses specific to their program.

The role of general education requirements at Paul Smith's College goes beyond just the acquisition of skills and knowledge. General education helps students to appreciate multiple perspectives that come from interacting with people outside their disciplines. By expecting students to collaborate productively with a diverse group of people, general education strengthens interpersonal skills useful in the workplace and the community and in life. Through reinforcement across the more focused curriculum, general education enriches students with the practical skills needed by every adult: analytical skills, effective communication, practical intelligence, ethical judgment, and social responsibility.

Off-Campus Programs

Cooperative work experiences are encouraged for all students and are required in the following programs: baking, business and entrepreneurial studies, culinary arts, hotel and restaurant management, recreation, surveying technology, and urban tree management. Students in these programs have the opportunity to practice what they have learned at locations throughout the country as well as internationally.

Academic Facilities

Thousands of acres of College-owned lands and waterways in the Adirondack Mountains provide natural laboratories for students in the forestry and environmental programs. The College also manages International Paper John Dillon Park, a 200-acre park designed for people with disabilities. The College's more traditional classroom buildings include state-of-the-art smart classrooms and computer labs as well as laboratories for biology, chemistry, culinary arts, GIS, and mechanical drawing. They also feature the student-operated A. P. Smith's Bakery, student-run St. Regis Café, and Ganzi Restaurant Training Center, a kitchen and dining room modeled after the famed Palm steakhouses. The Forestry Division's resources are augmented by a permanent Lane sawmill complex, a mechanical skidder, and a sugar bush. The Joan Weill Adirondack Library houses 50,000 volumes, 700 periodicals, access to more than 17,000 online periodicals, two computer labs, more than 600 data ports, fifty computer stations, Wi-Fi access, audiovisual equipment, and eight study rooms. The Weill Student Center accommodates the Lakeside Dining Hall, Student Health Center, Packbasket campus store, St. Regis Café, student mailboxes, recreation and programming rooms, Wi-Fi access, and outdoor deck seating providing beautiful lake views. Paul Smith's also provides 24-hour computer access, 24-hour campus security, a Career Center, personal counseling, and campus ministry.

Costs

In 2008–09, yearly tuition is approximately $18,460, and room and board are approximately $8340. Summer sessions are required for some programs. Additional fees to cover lab charges, student activities, and other costs vary from $510 to $1620 per year, depending on the program. The cost of books and supplies is estimated at $1000 per year.

Financial Aid

Federal programs available at the College include the Federal Pell Grant, Federal Supplemental Educational Opportunity Grant (FSEOG), SMART Grant, Academic Competitiveness Grant (ACG), Federal Stafford Student Loan, Federal Perkins Loan, and Federal Work-Study programs. The Federal Work-Study awards provide work for more than 80 percent of the student body, and more than 98 percent of the students receive some form of financial aid. The Financial Aid Office encourages students to apply for aid with the Free Application for Federal Student Aid (FAFSA) by March. State programs processed through the College include the New York State Tuition Assistance Program (TAP), Vermont Student Assistance Corporation (VSAC) Program, and Rhode Island Educational Assistance Program. Merit Scholarships are awarded based on SAT/ACT scores and high school GPA.

Faculty

Paul Smith's College faculty is composed of 57 full-time and 26 part-time members. Most faculty members live near the campus and participate in all phases of academic life. The student-faculty ratio is approximately 14:1, and the average class size is 15.

Student Government

The Student Government represents the needs of the student body and acts as a liaison with faculty and staff members. It oversees all active campus clubs and organizations, handles student appeals, and holds weekly meetings with food service, maintenance, campus safety, student activities, and other departments on campus that directly impact student life.

Admission Requirements

Admission requirements vary by program. Each candidate is evaluated individually based on the requirements of the program applied for. Assuming all course prerequisites have been fulfilled, admissions decisions are based on academic performance, overall GPA, rigor of course work, and test scores.

Application and Information

Applicants for either the associate or bachelor's degree programs must submit a formal application for admission, a $30 application fee, and an official high school transcript. All bachelor's degree students as well as associate degree students who want to be considered for scholarships must submit SAT or ACT test scores. Letters of recommendation, a personal interview, and an essay are strongly recommended. Transfer students must submit an official copy of their college transcript from all colleges attended; letters of recommendation and an essay are recommended. Nonnative English-speaking international students are required to submit TOEFL scores. International students are also required to submit transcripts in English and a confidential financial statement. Applications are reviewed on a rolling basis; reviews begin September 1 for the following fall. Prospective students typically receive a decision within two weeks of receipt of all application materials.

For more information, students should contact:

Admissions Office
Paul Smith's College
Paul Smiths, New York 12970
Phone: 518-327-6227
800-421-2605 (toll-free; 8 a.m. to 4:30 p.m.)
Fax: 518-327-6016
E-mail: admiss@paulsmiths.edu
Web site: http://www.paulsmiths.edu

Paul Smith's College sits on the shore of Lower St. Regis Lake.

POLYTECHNIC UNIVERSITY

BROOKLYN, NEW YORK

The University

Long recognized as a leading technological university, research center, and center for innovation, entrepreneurship, and invention, Polytechnic University offers degrees in computer science, digital media, engineering, humanities, the sciences, and technology management. Founded in 1854 as Polytechnic Institute of Brooklyn (Brooklyn Poly), it is the second-oldest independent technological university in the United States. Polytechnic has a main campus in the MetroTech Center in downtown Brooklyn, New York, and graduate centers in Long Island, Manhattan, and Westchester. Polytechnic has an undergraduate student body of approximately 1,500 students.

Polytechnic University is a microcosm of greater New York. Undergraduates come from twenty-five states and forty-seven countries. The students represent a mosaic of racial, ethnic, religious, and cultural backgrounds, all working together to achieve common goals. A student-faculty ratio of 14:1 enables students to work closely with professors in both the classroom and the research lab. Located at Polytechnic are a variety of research centers where students and world-renowned faculty members are involved in innovative fields of study and research, including telecommunications, electronics, robotics, aerospace, digital systems, wireless communications, and integrative digital media, among others. Although it emphasizes science and engineering, the University has long recognized the importance of tempering technology with humanistic understanding.

The University offers a wide variety of student activities, as it ranks among the top 5 universities in the nation in social diversity. The Student Council and a school newspaper are just two of the many options available. A number of academic organizations, many with national affiliations, host programs, lectures, and discussion groups for students majoring in the various disciplines. Athletics for both men and women—from basketball to lacrosse to volleyball—are popular and widely available at Polytechnic on both intercollegiate and intramural levels.

The University offers on-campus housing in the Othmer Residence Hall. The residence hall is located across the street from the MetroTech campus in downtown Brooklyn. It features 4-student, two-bedroom suites for underclassmen and two-bedroom apartments for upperclassmen. Amenities include rooms that are fully wired for personal computers, laptops, cable TV, and telephone access; study rooms; student lounges; 24-hour security; a laundry room; and a modern dining hall.

Students can use the central computer labs and various specialized labs, connect wirelessly with a laptop, or dial in from home. The University was voted among the "100 Most Wired Colleges" by *Yahoo! Internet Life.*

Location

Polytechnic is located in the heart of historic downtown Brooklyn and in the middle of MetroTech Center, a 16-acre, $1-billion academic/professional park in New York City. Situated at the foot of the famous Brooklyn Bridge, just across from the tip of Manhattan, the campus is the gateway to such places as Wall Street, Broadway, and the South Street Seaport on one side of the river and the Brooklyn Museum and Prospect Park on the other. All of these attractions are readily accessible via public transportation and a network of modern highways. The University is just a 10-minute subway ride from Manhattan.

Exceptional careers begin with exceptional locations, and Polytechnic has an unrivaled one in the greater New York area. Serving students with a dynamic range of experiences and powerful examples of excellence, New York City gives a unique context to their studies. In addition, it places them in the middle of an international capital with diverse surroundings, unique perspectives, vibrant cultures, and thriving enterprises. The career opportunities are virtually everywhere—from Wall Street to New York's new media industry, affectionately dubbed "Silicon Alley."

Majors and Degrees

Polytechnic University offers the Bachelor of Science degree. The undergraduate majors include biomolecular science (premed), chemical and biological engineering, civil engineering, computer engineering, computer science, construction management, digital media studies, electrical engineering, liberal studies, mathematics, mechanical/aerospace engineering, physics, technical and professional communications, and technology management. Five-year B.S./M.S. programs are also available.

Academic Programs

While requirements vary according to the major, students must complete an average of 128 credits with an average of at least 2.0 (on a 4.0 scale) to earn the Bachelor of Science degree. Science and engineering students begin fundamental courses in their specialties during their second year and concentrate on advanced courses in their last two years.

Recent academic initiatives include an Honors College and an admission assurance program with the State University of New York Health Science Center at Brooklyn for outstanding premed students.

Academic Facilities

The Bern Dibner Library of Science and Technology houses one of the finest collections of technical and scientific literature in the metropolitan area. In addition, the library hosts a massive collection of online reference databases to assist in classwork and scholarly research. A $130-million upgrade to the MetroTech campus is reflected in an academic building, a modern residence hall, an athletic facility, labs, and a state-of-the-art computing infrastructure. Wireless networking is available, allowing students to connect to the University network and the Internet from virtually anywhere on campus. Computer labs feature high-end workstations for research, 3-D modeling, and dynamic simulation.

Well-known for scientific and technological discovery, Polytechnic sponsors a number of important research centers that typically involve multidisciplinary teams of Polytechnic faculty members, research staff members, and students. Included among these centers are the Institute for Mathematics and Advanced Supercomputing, the Transportation Research Institute, the Othmer Institute for Interdisciplinary Studies, and the Polymer Research Institute, the oldest academic center of polymer (plastics) investigation in the United States. In 1983, the University was designated a Center for Advanced Technology in Telecommunications in New York State.

Costs

Tuition for 2008–09 is $31,239. Estimates of other expenses are $1105 for fees, $1000 for books, $2500 for personal expenses, and $8500 for room and board.

Financial Aid

Scholarships and loans are the principal sources of financial aid for full-time undergraduates. Federal sources of funds include Federal Pell Grants, Federal Supplemental Educational Opportunity Grants, Federal Stafford Student Loans, Federal Perkins Loans, and Federal Work-Study Program awards. New York State residents may be eligible for assistance under the New York State Tuition Assistance Program. In addition to the usual financial aid programs, Polytechnic offers a large number of scholarships, including several full-tuition, four-year scholarships that are awarded to students admitted to the Honors College. Approximately 98 percent of all undergraduates at the University receive some financial aid. Opportunities for student employment are good. Students desiring financial assistance should submit the Free Application for Federal Student Aid. For more detailed information about financial aid, students should contact the Office of Financial Aid at Polytechnic or visit http://www.poly.edu/admissions.

Faculty

Polytechnic has 160 full-time faculty members, 90 percent of whom have doctoral degrees. Most of the faculty members teach both graduate and undergraduate courses. The University's faculty is world renowned for the research, inventions, and scholarly publications of its members. Several are members of the National Academy of Engineering, and many are frequent recipients of both national and international awards for excellence. Recent examples include the Institute of Electrical and Electronics Engineers' Educational Medal for Excellence, the President's Medal of Sciences, and the prestigious Humboldt Award. The American Society for Engineering Education recently ranked the graduate electrical engineering faculty among the top 10 in the nation for scholarly activity; many of its members also teach on the undergraduate level.

Student Government

The Student Council is important on the Polytechnic campus. In working with the Student Leadership Office and administration, it directs the activities of the undergraduate student body and represents student interests. As the administrating agency for student fees, the council allocates money to student organizations, publications, and activities. Student representatives also serve on many faculty and administrative committees dealing with all phases of academic and student life.

Admission Requirements

Admission to Polytechnic is competitive. Candidates must submit a formal application for admission, a secondary school transcript, an essay, two academic recommendations, and standardized test scores (SAT or ACT). The Committee on Admissions evaluates each applicant on an individual basis regardless of financial need and seeks students who rank in the top 25 percent of their graduating class, have taken 3 to 4 years of college-preparatory math and science, and have achieved a grade average of B+ or higher.

Students whose first language is not English are advised to submit scores on the Test of English as a Foreign Language (TOEFL). This test must be taken by all international applicants whose native language is not English regardless of whether or not their previous education was conducted in English. Advanced placement is awarded to students whose scores on the Advanced Placement tests indicate proficiency in a given subject.

Application and Information

A completed application form, $55 application fee, and supporting documents are required for evaluation of prospective students. Applications should be submitted as early as possible, preferably by January 15 for admission in the fall and December 1 for admission in the spring. Admission decisions are made on a rolling basis. For application forms and additional information, students should contact:

Ms. Joy Colelli
Dean of Undergraduate Admissions
Wunsch Building
Polytechnic University
6 MetroTech Center
Brooklyn, New York 11201
Phone: 718-260-3589
800-POLY-TECH (toll-free)
Web site: http://www.poly.edu/admit

A view of the campus at Polytechnic University.

COLLEGE DATA CENTER • NEW YORK

PRATT INSTITUTE

BROOKLYN, NEW YORK

The Institute

Founded in 1887 on its present site in Brooklyn by industrialist and philanthropist Charles Pratt, Pratt Institute educated on nonbaccalaureate levels for its first half-century. As the educational preparation necessary for various professions expanded, Pratt Institute moved with the times. It granted its first baccalaureate degree in 1938 and started its first graduate program in 1950. With a wide variety of programs in art, design, and architecture, Pratt has continued to add programs at all educational levels, including undergraduate programs in creative writing and critical and visual studies, undergraduate and graduate programs in art history, and graduate programs in art education, arts and cultural management, historic preservation, and design management. Although the characteristics and educational requirements of the professions for which Pratt prepares people have changed over the course of a century, the Institute has succeeded in pursuing its abiding purpose—to blend theoretical learning with professional and humanistic development.

Pratt offers four-year bachelor's, two-year associate, and master's degrees. In educating more than four generations of students to be creative, technically skilled, and adaptable professionals as well as responsible citizens, Pratt has gained a national and international reputation that attracts undergraduate and graduate students from more than forty-six states, the District of Columbia, Puerto Rico, the Virgin Islands, and seventy countries. Unlike the typical American college student, most of those who choose Pratt already have career objectives, or at least they know they want to study art, design, architecture, or creative writing.

A short bus or subway ride from the museum, gallery, and design centers of both Manhattan and Brooklyn, Pratt Institute has twenty-four buildings of differing architectural styles spread about a 25-acre campus. Eighteen of the buildings house studios, classrooms, laboratories, administrative offices, auditoria, sports facilities, food services, and student centers. Six buildings are student residences, including the new Stabile Hall freshman residence, which provides studio space on each floor. There are adequate parking facilities for residents and commuters. Student services include career planning and placement, health and counseling, and student development. The more than sixty student organizations include fraternities and sororities, honorary societies, professional societies, and clubs.

Location

Pratt Institute, the country's premier college of art, design, writing, and architecture, is located in the Clinton Hill section of Brooklyn, just minutes from downtown Manhattan. The majority of Pratt's freshmen and half of its undergraduates live on the school's 25-acre, tree-lined campus.

Majors and Degrees

Pratt Institute offers the Bachelor of Architecture, Bachelor of Fine Arts, Bachelor of Art, Bachelor of Industrial Design, Bachelor of Professional Studies, Bachelor of Science, Associate of Occupational Studies, and Associate of Applied Science degrees.

The Bachelor of Architecture degree program is a five-year accredited program. For the Bachelor of Fine Arts degree, a candidate may choose to major in art and design education, art history, communications design (advertising, graphic design, illustration), computer graphics and interactive media, fashion design, film/video, fine arts (ceramics, drawing, jewelry, painting, printmaking, sculpture), interior design, photography, or writing for publication, performance, and media. The Bachelor of Arts is offered in critical and visual studies and art history. The Bachelor of Industrial Design is offered for students interested in car, product, and furniture design. In the Bachelor of Professional Studies degree program, the major is in construction management. Students seeking the Bachelor of Science degree can major in construction management.

The two-year Associate of Occupational Studies degree is offered in digital design and interactive media, graphic design, and illustration. The Associate of Applied Science is offered in painting/drawing and graphic design/illustration. The two-year A.A.S. degree is transferable to a four-year program.

Students may also earn combined bachelor's/master's degrees. Programs include the B.F.A./M.S. in art and design education.

Academic Programs

Educating artists and creative professionals to be responsible contributors to society has been the mission of Pratt Institute since it assembled its first group of students in 1887. Within the structure of that professional education, Pratt students are encouraged to acquire the diverse knowledge that is necessary for them to succeed in their chosen fields. In addition to the professional studies, the curriculum in each of Pratt's schools includes a broad range of liberal arts courses. Students from all schools take these courses together and have the opportunity to examine the interrelationships of art, science, technology, and human need.

At the time of graduation, students in the associate degree programs have completed 67 credit hours of course work. In the bachelor's programs, credit-hour requirements range from 132 to 135 credits, depending on the particular program. For the Bachelor of Architecture degree, 170 credits are required.

Pratt's academic calendar consists of two semesters plus optional summer terms that allows students to choose alternative courses or various options usually not offered during the fall or spring semester. Two summer sessions are offered.

Off-Campus Programs

Pratt Institute offers credit for a wide variety of off-campus study programs. The Internship Program offers qualified students challenging on-the-job experience related to their major fields of interest; this extension of the classroom and laboratory into the professional world adds a practical dimension to periods of on-campus study.

International programs, available during all academic sessions, have included art and design offerings in the cities of Copenhagen and Rome and in the countries of England, France, and Italy. Architecture programs have been held in Venice, Italy, and in Finland and Japan. New programs are developed regularly in these and other countries. A semester-long program is offered in Rome each year.

Academic Facilities

Founded as the first free library in Brooklyn, the Pratt Institute Library now has more than 186,589 bound volumes, serial backfiles, and other material, including government documents; 251,603 audiovisual materials; and 3,996 microforms and subscribes to 925 periodicals. Its the largest collection of any independent art school. Through the use of their ID cards, Pratt students also have access to numerous college libraries in the metropolitan area. The Multi-Media Center has been developed to facilitate and improve the educational communication process by providing materials in multimedia formats to support and enrich the Institute's curricula. These include slides, ¾-inch videotapes, 16-mm films, audiocassettes, and other formats appropriate for group use.

Extensive studio and state-of-the-art computer lab facilities are provided for all Pratt students. In the School of Art and Design, these include studio, shop, and technical facilities for work in all media, from the traditional to the most experimental. Graphics labs include color Macintosh IIs, Macintosh SEs, Cubicomps, Targa TIPS PCs with digitizer tablets, ALIAS labs, and a Quantel graphics system. Within the School of Architecture, students benefit not only from the design studios but also from the collective research facilities of the Institute. The School of Architecture uses SKOK CAD, Sun, and IRIS workstations. The School of Liberal Arts and Sciences maintains laboratory facilities for all science courses. Apple, AT&T, IBM, LSI-11, and TI microcomputers; a Burroughs batch-processing system; and an HP 100 computer are available to students in all majors. Pratt also has a DEC VAX 6210 minicomputer for Institute-wide integration of computer graphics and computer-aided design capabilities as well as AT&T 386 PCs and an extensive telecommunications laboratory. Gallery space, both on campus and at Pratt Manhattan, is extensive, showing the work of students, alumni, faculty members, staff members, and other well-known artists, architects, and designers. The Pratt Institute Center for Community and Environmental Development functions as a laboratory for the study of planning and advocacy issues in real-world situations.

Costs

Tuition for the 2007–08 academic year was $29,900. Room charges are approximately $5700 per academic year. A meal plan is available and costs about $3200 per year. The fees are approximately $1180. The estimated cost of books and supplies is $3000 per academic year. Students should allow an additional $650 for transportation and personal expenses. For an updated list of tuition and fees, prospective students should visit http://www.pratt.edu/financial_aid/general_information.

Financial Aid

Pratt Institute offers a large number of grants, scholarships, loans, and awards on the basis of academic achievement, talent, financial need, or all three. More than 75 percent of Pratt students receive aid in one or more of these kinds of aid. Through funds from the federal and state governments, contributions from Pratt alumni, and industry scholarships, Pratt is able to maintain an effective aid program in a time of escalating costs. Pratt attempts to ensure that no student is prevented by lack of funds from completing his or her education.

Faculty

The faculty at Pratt Institute is exceptional in that a large number of practicing professionals augment the regular full-time faculty. There are 119 full-time and 820 part-time faculty members; there are no graduate teaching assistants. In small classes and studios, students have easy access to professors whose natural environment is the design studio, the architectural office, or the industrial research department.

Student Government

The Student Government Association (SGA) maintains primary responsibility for all student interests and involvement at Pratt. The SGA structure includes the Executive Committee, Senate, Finance Committee, Buildings and Grounds Committee, Academic and Administrative Affairs Committee, and Program Board. Student representatives serve on the Board of Trustees and on its various committees. All undergraduate students are encouraged to become involved in the SGA, whose main functions are allocating and administering funds collected through the student activities fee, scheduling student activities, and representing the student viewpoint to the rest of the Pratt community.

Admission Requirements

Pratt Institute attracts and enrolls highly motivated and talented students from diverse backgrounds. Applications are welcome from all qualified students, regardless of age, sex, race, color, religion, national origin, or handicap. Admission standards at Pratt are high. One of the major components for admission consideration in art, design, or architecture is the evaluation of a student's art or writing portfolio, which must be submitted along with the other required documents.

All applicants must submit transcripts and letters of recommendation from any high schools and colleges attended. Additional professional requirements are specific to each school or major. Instructions can be found at http://www.pratt.edu/admiss/apply.

The admission committee bases its decisions on careful reviews of all credentials submitted by applicants in relation to the requirements of the program to which students seek admission. The SAT or ACT and a strong college-preparatory background are required of all applicants for four-year programs. International students must submit the TOEFL or IELTS instead, if available, or the SAT, but not both. In certain cases, an extraordinary talent may offset a low grade or a test score.

Application and Information

Pratt has two admissions deadlines: November 1 for early action and January 15 for regular admissions. To receive full consideration, students must submit applications by January 15 for anticipated entrance in the fall semester and by October 1 for anticipated entrance in the spring semester.

For more information about Pratt Institute, students should contact:

Office of Admissions
Pratt Institute
200 Willoughby Avenue
Brooklyn, New York 11205
Phone: 718-636-3514
800-331-0834 (toll-free)
E-mail: admissions@pratt.edu
Web site: http://www.pratt.edu
http://www.pratt.edu/admiss/request (to request a catalog)

PURCHASE COLLEGE, STATE UNIVERSITY OF NEW YORK

PURCHASE, NEW YORK

The College

Enrolling just over 4,000 students, Purchase College is a selective public coeducational college that serves both residential and commuter students. A Purchase College education is founded upon a unique vision that combines the energy and excitement of professional training in the performing and the visual arts with the intellectual traditions and spirit of discovery of the sciences and the humanities. The College emphasizes creativity, individual accomplishment, openness, and exploration of the world. A student's education at Purchase College culminates in a senior project that serves as an excellent springboard to a career or advanced academic study.

Purchase students come from around the world, and nearly all of them share a love of imagination, originality, and new experiences. The mix of students in the liberal arts and sciences and the performing and visual arts contributes to a campus that is wide open to diversity in perspectives and ambitions. The intersection of the arts and liberal arts and sciences also fosters an appreciation of the contributions of both scholarly and artistic achievement to make a humane culture.

The youngest of the SUNY system's sixty-four campuses, Purchase College has rapidly emerged and is increasingly recognized as a distinguished, imaginative, and dynamic institution for the study of the liberal arts and sciences and the visual and performing arts and for its service to the region and the state.

Purchase is primarily a full-time undergraduate institution, but as a public institution, Purchase College also promotes lifelong learning for students of all ages, backgrounds, and incomes through its School of Liberal Studies and Continuing Education, which offers a Bachelor of Arts in liberal studies as well as various credit and noncredit courses, certificate programs, and part-time degree programs.

In addition to its baccalaureate degrees, Purchase College also offers an M.F.A. in theater arts/stage design, visual arts, and dance and an M.A. in art history. The College also offers three postgraduate programs in music: Music Performance Certificate (one to two years of postbaccalaureate study), Master of Music, and Music Artist Diploma (one to two years of post-master's study).

Location

Built in the early 1970s on the 500-acre estate that was settled in 1734 by Judge Thomas Thomas, the Purchase campus combines the advantages of a semirural setting with proximity to the educational and cultural opportunities of Westchester County and New York City. As the only four-year public institution in Westchester, Purchase College is a cultural resource for the entire community. Approximately 250,000 people visit the campus each year to take advantage of its many programs and activities, including exhibits at the Neuberger Museum of Art, world-class performances at the Performing Arts Center, and public programs and lectures, such as the Royal and Shirley Durst Chair Lecture Series.

Majors and Degrees

Purchase College's liberal arts and sciences programs lead to Bachelor of Arts (B.A.) and Bachelor of Science (B.S.) degrees. The College offers a full range of disciplines through its two liberal arts schools: Humanities (art history, cinema studies, creative writing, drama studies, history, journalism, language and culture, literature, and philosophy) and Natural and Social Sciences (anthropology; biochemistry; biology; chemistry; economics; environmental studies; mathematics/computer science; media, society, and the arts; political science; psychology; and sociology). Students may also pursue premedicine or prelaw tracks. There are interdisciplinary programs in Asian studies, global black studies, Latin American studies, lesbian and gay studies, new media, and women's studies.

Purchase College offers professional conservatory training that leads to a Bachelor of Music degree; a Bachelor of Fine Arts (B.F.A.) degree in acting, dance, dramatic writing, film, stage design/technology, or visual arts; and a B.A. in arts management.

Academic Programs

Purchase College operates on a semester calendar. Students typically take 16 credits per semester in order to fulfill the minimum requirement of 120 hours for a bachelor's degree as well as the SUNY-mandated general education requirements. Most courses in liberal arts are 4 credits, as the College specializes in intensive study within the majors, and many courses include scheduled classwork in the arts, fieldwork, plenary sessions, and intensive tutorials.

Students in the liberal arts and sciences declare their major concentrations by the junior year, electing intensive course work that builds toward their senior projects. The senior project represents a culmination of their four years at Purchase and can take the form of a research paper, presentation, or original expression of thought and research (e.g., a work of fiction, poetry, or art or a multimedia presentation). The curriculum in each major is organized to build on disciplinary expertise, research, and writing skills, starting with the freshman year and culminating in the senior project. Senior projects in natural sciences are often published or copublished with a faculty member.

The senior project is a solid foundation for graduate study, professional school, or a career. For many Purchase students, internships in agencies, businesses, and corporations are also an important part of their educational experience that often leads to full-time employment.

Purchase College has some of the few conservatory training programs for the arts within the State University of New York System. Much of this training is provided by instructors who are also practicing professionals. Proximity to New York City gives access to these professionals and their respective art worlds, establishing a valuable network of contacts for undergraduate students. Professional job placement begins at an early stage, with special assistance from the active career development office. For example, some students occasionally interrupt their study program to work with a professional dance company or with a professional filmmaker.

Academic Facilities

The College's extraordinary facilities include the first building in the United States designed exclusively for the study and performance of dance; a large science research center; The Performing Arts Center and its five theaters; and the Neuberger Museum, which has an outstanding collection of modern American art. Both the center and the museum play central roles in the curriculum and the student experience. There is also an exceptionally well-equipped physical education building; an increasing number of multimedia and computer classrooms; and a 160,000-square-foot visual arts building.

Costs

For 2007–08, tuition for undergraduate in-state residents was $4350 for the academic year; it was $10,610 for out-of-state students. Room and board (dormitory double room and full meal plan) cost $8496. Books and supplies were estimated at $1100. There was also an applied music fee of $2128 per year for music majors. Costs are subject to change for 2008–09.

Financial Aid

Purchase College participates in all federal and state financial aid programs. All students who complete the Free Application for Federal Student Aid (FAFSA) receive some form of financial assistance, which may include low-interest student loans. It is strongly recommended that students file the FAFSA prior to April 1 in order to receive the maximum amount of financial aid for which they are eligible. Approximately 70 percent of all Purchase College undergraduates receive some type of financial assistance.

Scholarships based on merit only and scholarships based on both merit and need are available to qualified students.

Faculty

The Purchase College faculty is distinguished by depth of specialized knowledge as well as broad interdisciplinary interests, scholarly and professional activity, and dedication to undergraduate teaching. The liberal arts and sciences faculty includes prominent scholars in a variety of fields. More than 95 percent hold doctorates from prestigious schools, and several have won Guggenheim, Fulbright, NEH, and NEA awards, among others. The visual and performance arts faculty consists of leading teachers and practicing professionals in dance, film, music, theater, and visual arts.

Student Government

The Student Government Association, a campuswide organization, is made up of students elected by their peers. The organization is responsible for campus activities, sends representatives to faculty and administrative councils, and administers its own budget.

Admission Requirements

Applicants are considered by the Office of Admissions on an individual basis without regard to race, religion, geographic origin, or handicap. Major factors for admission consideration in the liberal arts and sciences programs are the high school and the academic records, including subjects studied, proficiency in English, test scores (SAT or ACT), and recommendations. All students write an application essay to demonstrate an appropriate fit with Purchase. The liberal arts program has become increasingly selective, and early application is encouraged. A rolling admission system is used, with selective deadlines in some programs.

In the visual and performing arts, students must demonstrate talent by means of an audition, interview, or portfolio review in addition to an assessment of their academic credentials. Because these programs are very competitive, early application is encouraged for both freshmen and transfers. Typically, auditions of conservatory candidates are completed by the end of March.

Application and Information

Students are urged to visit the campus for information sessions and open houses. For further information, students should contact:

Ms. Stephanie McCaine
Director of Admissions
Purchase College, State University of New York
735 Anderson Hill Road
Purchase, New York 10577-1400
Phone: 914-251-6300
Fax: 914-251-6314
E-mail: admission@purchase.edu
Web site: http://www.purchase.edu

A reason to cheer—graduation day at Purchase College.

QUEENS COLLEGE OF THE CITY UNIVERSITY OF NEW YORK

FLUSHING, NEW YORK

The College

Queens College, with more than 13,000 undergraduates, is one of the largest of the four-year colleges in the City University of New York (CUNY) system. The College opened its doors in 1937 with the goal of offering a first-rate education to talented people of all backgrounds and financial means. Often referred to as "the jewel of the CUNY system," Queens College enjoys a national reputation for its liberal arts and sciences and preprofessional programs. Students come from 140 different nations; the result is an unusually rich education that gives Queens College graduates a competitive edge in today's global society. Like other CUNY colleges, Queens is a commuter school, but it plans to open its first residence hall in the fall of 2009.

The 77-acre campus is lined with trees surrounding grassy open spaces and a traditional quad. Some of the original Spanish-style stucco-and-tile buildings from the early 1900s still stand, including Jefferson Hall, which houses the beautiful Welcome Center. The completely renovated Powdermaker Hall, the major classroom building, reopened in fall 2003 with state-of-the-art technology throughout. The College is also expanding its wireless capability, undertaking a $30-million renovation of its science labs, opening new cafés and dining areas, updating the spacious Student Union and several other buildings, and embarking on a variety of campus beautification projects.

The administration is dedicated to making students feel that the College is their home away from home. A Child Development Center, staffed by professionals, offers inexpensive child-care services to students with children. There are more than seventy clubs on the campus, from the Accounting Honors Society and Alliance of Latin American Students to clubs for theater, fencing, environmental science, science fiction, and the fine arts. Queens, the only CUNY college that participates in Division II sports, sponsors twenty men's and women's teams and has some of the finest athletics facilities in the metropolitan area. Ongoing cultural events include readings by renowned authors such as Toni Morrison, Frank McCourt, and Norman Mailer; concerts by world-famous artists; and theater and dance performances. The College is home to the Godwin-Ternbach Museum, the only comprehensive museum in the borough of Queens, with art from antiquity to the present.

The College's centers and institutes also serve students and the larger urban community by addressing society's most important challenges, including cancer, AIDS, pollution, and racism; the changing workplace and workforce; and the heritages of the borough's many ethnic communities, including Asians, Greeks, Italians, and Jews.

Queens College has had a chapter of Phi Beta Kappa since 1950 (less than 10 percent of the nation's liberal arts colleges are members of Phi Beta Kappa, the nation's oldest and most respected undergraduate honors organization). In 1968, Queens College became a member of Sigma Xi, the national science honor society. The American Association of University Women includes Queens College in its list of approved colleges for membership.

Location

Queens College, located off Exit 24 of the Long Island Expressway, is in a residential area of Flushing. It is easily accessible by public transportation. The College is only 20 minutes from Manhattan, whose magnificent skyline overlooks the campus quad.

Majors and Degrees

The Bachelor of Arts degree is awarded in accounting, Africana studies, American studies, anthropology, art, art history, biology, Byzantine and modern Greek studies, chemistry, communication arts and media, communication sciences and disorders, comparative literature, computer science, drama and theater, East Asian studies, economics, education (early childhood and elementary), English, environmental sciences, environmental studies, film studies, French, geology, German, Greek, Hebrew, history, home economics, Italian, Jewish studies, labor studies, Latin, Latin American area studies, linguistics, mathematics, music, neuroscience, philosophy, physics, political science and government, psychology, Russian, sociology, Spanish, studio art, theater-dance, urban studies, and women's studies.

The Bachelor of Arts program in secondary school teaching includes the following subject areas: Africana studies, anthropology, biology, chemistry, economics, English, French, geology, German, history, Italian, Latin American area studies, mathematics, physics, political science and government, sociology, Spanish, and urban studies.

The College also awards the Bachelor of Arts in interdisciplinary studies; an individualized Bachelor of Arts program; the Bachelor of Business Administration; the Bachelor of Fine Arts in studio art; the Bachelor of Music in instrumental or vocal performance studies; and the Bachelor of Science in applied social science, computer science, environmental sciences, geology, graphic design, nutrition and exercise sciences, and physical education.

The Departments of Chemistry, Computer Science, Philosophy, Physics, and Political Science and the Aaron Copland School of Music offer qualified undergraduates the opportunity to take combined bachelor's and master's degree programs.

Special interdisciplinary programs include Africana studies, American studies, business and liberal arts, business administration, Byzantine and modern Greek studies, Honors in Mathematics and Natural Sciences, Honors in the Humanities, Honors in the Social Sciences, Irish studies, Italian American studies, journalism, Latin American and Latino studies, and religious studies. Special programs and advisement are also available in accounting, pre-engineering, prelaw, and the pre–health professions.

Academic Programs

Queens College prepares students to become leaders of today's global society by offering a rigorous education in the liberal arts and sciences under the guidance of a faculty dedicated to both teaching and research. Students graduate with the ability to think critically, address complex problems, explore various cultures, and use modern technologies and information resources.

The wide range of majors and interdisciplinary studies, combined with the award-winning Freshman Year Initiative program, encourages students to explore their interests and abilities to the fullest. In most cases, degree programs require the completion of 120 credits.

The Bachelor of Business Administration (B.B.A.) degree provides a solid business education that responds to the demand of employers for specific quantitative and technological skills. Students may choose from three majors: finance, international business, and actuarial studies. The B.B.A. also has an investments/chartered financial analyst track to prepare students for the CFA examination, the only such undergraduate program in New York.

The Business and Liberal Arts program is designed for students who want to study the theory and practice of business in a liberal arts context. Internships are sponsored by participating corporations.

The William E. Macaulay Honors College of the City University of New York includes unique interdisciplinary seminars, access to instructional technology, mentors, internships, and study-abroad programs as well as a Cultural Passport that provides entry to the vast resources of New York City. Financial awards include full tuition and fees, a grant of $7500 over four years, a textbook allowance, and a free laptop computer. The current profile for a Queens College honor student is a 94 average and 1365 combined SAT score (critical reading and math).

Honors in the Humanities includes a challenging curriculum based on the Great Books. Its facilities provide a quiet place for scholarly work and original research.

Honors in Mathematics and Natural Sciences is for students who have demonstrated exceptional ability in mathematics and science at the high school level.

The Honors in the Social Sciences program encourages students to gain an in-depth understanding of the traditions and methods of the social sciences.

The Adult Collegiate Education program, offered to students 25 and older, includes the option of obtaining college credit for life achievement. The Weekend College allows busy students to pursue their degrees by taking classes on Saturdays and Sundays.

Academic Facilities

Among the many centers where research and creativity are joined in the pursuit of knowledge are the Kupferberg Center for the Visual and Performing Arts, which brings together the College's academic departments in the arts (Music, Drama, Art, and Media Studies), its museums (the Godwin-Ternbach, the Queens College Art Center, and the Louis Armstrong House Museum), and the celebrated Evening Reading Series. The center's facilities include the 2,200-seat Colden Auditorium; the Goldstein Theatre, designed especially for the staging of experimental student productions; and the Aaron Copland School of Music facility, which includes thirty-five practice rooms and the 491-seat LeFrak Concert Hall. The College is also home to the Institute for Low-Temperature Physics; and the Speech and Hearing Center, which investigates communication disabilities and provides clinical experience for students of speech and hearing therapy.

The College administers the historic Louis Armstrong House Museum in Corona. The Benjamin Rosenthal Library, with its soaring, light-filled atrium and art center, has more than 1 million print and electronic volumes. The Louis Armstrong Archives in the library, home to a vast personal collection of Armstrong's photographs, papers, recordings, and memorabilia, draws scholars and jazz fans alike from around the world.

Costs

For New York State residents, undergraduate tuition for 2007–08 was $4000. For out-of-state and international students, undergraduate tuition was $360 per credit. In addition to tuition, there are various expenses each semester, such as student activity and technology fees.

Financial Aid

More than 50 percent of Queens College students receive need-based financial aid. The aid may include state and federal loans and grants, Tuition Assistance Program awards, Regents Scholarships, Federal Direct Student Loans, Federal Pell Grants, State Aid for Native Americans, and Federal Work-Study Program awards.

The Queens College Scholars Program offers a variety of merit-based scholarships to full-time freshmen, with awards ranging from $2000 to $4500 per year. Selection is competitive, and scholarships are awarded on the basis of the high school record, test scores (SAT and SAT Subject Tests), writing ability, letters of recommendation, and extracurricular activities. Scholarships are renewable with continued high academic achievement. Applicants who rank in or near the top 10 percent of their class and have a rigorous academic program, excellent grades, and minimum combined SAT (critical reading and math) scores of 1250 are encouraged to apply. The application deadline is February 1.

Faculty

The College's faculty consists of top scholars who are dedicated to teaching. There are 545 full-time faculty members; 86 percent have the terminal degree in their field and 66 percent have tenure. Many also teach in the doctoral programs at the CUNY Graduate Center. Faculty members have received numerous fellowships, awards, and research grants from such prestigious organizations as the National Science Foundation and the National Institutes of Health. In recent years, faculty members received two Guggenheim awards and two Fulbright grants. CUNY has recognized the excellence of the faculty by honoring 9 members with the title of Distinguished Professor in fields as diverse as chemistry, economics, English, history, and physics. Among the more widely known faculty members are scientist Steven Markowitz; poets Jeffrey Renard Allen, Nicole Cooley, and Kimiko Hahn; and Distinguished Professor Gregory Rabassa, who was awarded the 2006 National Medal of Arts as one of the world's leading translators of Latin American literature.

Student Government

Through the Student Association, students at Queens are able to run many services and activities that influence the daily operations of the College. Its elected officers and senators poll students regularly about relevant topics and sponsor such services as free legal advice, a typing center, apartment and tutor referral, and voter registration. In addition, students constitute one third of the College's Academic Senate.

Admission Requirements

Queens College seeks to admit freshmen who have completed a strong college-preparatory program in high school with at least a B+ average. Admission is based on a variety of factors, including the applicant's high school grades, academic program, and SAT or ACT scores. Successful candidates have chosen a well-rounded program of study that includes academic course work in English (4 years), foreign language (3 years), math (3 years), lab science (2 years), and social studies (4 years).

The Search for Education, Elevation & Knowledge Program (SEEK) offers academic support, counseling, and financial assistance to motivated students who would not otherwise qualify for admission. The SEEK Program has its own admissions criteria, including financial need.

For earliest consideration, students should apply by January 1 for fall admission and by October 15 for spring admission.

Application and Information

The staff of the Undergraduate Office of Admissions is available to answer questions and give more information. To make an appointment for a tour or to meet with a counselor, students should contact:

Office of Admissions
Jefferson Hall
Queens College of the City University of New York
65-30 Kissena Boulevard
Flushing, New York 11367-1597
Phone: 718-997-5600
E-mail: admissions@qc.cuny.edu
Web site: http://www.qc.cuny.edu

A view of the Queens College quad, part of a 77-acre campus in New York City, where students from 140 nations receive a solid education for today's global society.

RENSSELAER POLYTECHNIC INSTITUTE

Rensselaer

TROY, NEW YORK

The Institute

The oldest degree-granting technological university in North America, Rensselaer Polytechnic Institute (RPI) was founded in 1824 "for the purpose of instructing persons in the application of science to the common purposes of life." Rensselaer has become one of the world's premier technological research universities, offering more than 144 programs and 1,000 courses that lead to bachelor's, master's, and doctoral degrees. Undergraduates pursue their studies in the Schools of Architecture, Engineering, Humanities and Social Sciences, Management and Technology, and Science and in the multidisciplinary area of information technology (IT). As a pioneer in interactive learning, Rensselaer has a long tradition of providing real-world, hands-on educational experiences to its students. Many of the courses cut across academic disciplines. Students have ready access to laboratories and often work in teams on research projects. Classes involve lively discussion, problem solving, and faculty mentoring, which encourages students to formulate new ideas and new discoveries. Rensselaer's approach to education has created generations of graduates who are known for their ability to solve some of the world's most challenging technical problems.

Rensselaer's 5,000 undergraduate and 1,200 graduate students are a bright, ambitious, and technologically savvy group who come from forty-eight states, the District of Columbia, Puerto Rico, the Virgin Islands, and sixty-seven other countries. A wide variety of nonacademic activities, virtually all of which are run by the students, is available. There are thirty-three fraternities and sororities, a weekly newspaper, a progressive 10,000-watt FM stereo station, dramatics groups, musical ensembles, and more than 160 clubs, special-interest groups, professional societies, sports, and organizations. More than 5,000 students participate in twenty-four intramural sports. Rensselaer is a member of the NCAA. Varsity sports include Division I men's and women's ice-hockey teams and twenty-one Division III men's and women's teams in twelve sports. Recreational facilities include the Mueller Fitness Center, an indoor track, all-weather track and field facilities, handball and squash courts, weight rooms, several indoor tennis courts, and two swimming pools. The Student Union, Chapel and Cultural Center, and Houston Field House bring many forms of entertainment and nationally known performing groups and lecturers to the campus.

The Office of the First-Year Experience offers a comprehensive array of programs and initiatives for both students and their primary support team that begins before students arrive on campus and continues well beyond their first year. This office sponsors the Navigating Rensselaer & Beyond orientation program, family programs, community service, and the Information and Personal Assistance Center (IPAC), along with many other programming initiatives for students and families.

Rensselaer continually upgrades residence halls and dining facilities across the campus. The Institute also is pursuing the development of several new athletic facilities, including a new field house, basketball arena, and natatorium as well as new administrative space, locker rooms, and weight rooms.

Location

Rensselaer is located in the northeastern United States in the heart of New York's Capital Region. The region, which includes the cities of Albany, Schenectady, and Troy and their suburbs, has a combined population of approximately 870,000 and is an important business, government, industrial, and academic hub. There are more than 40,000 college students at fourteen colleges and universities in the immediate area. Overlooking the city of Troy and the historic Hudson River, Rensselaer's 275-acre campus blends recently constructed facilities with a cluster of classical-style, ivy-covered brick buildings dating from the turn of the century. A program of extensive renovation has equipped the campus with ultramodern teaching facilities while preserving the traditional elegance of its historic buildings. Rensselaer retains the quiet and natural beauty of a parklike setting while offering many conveniences of an urban campus. Students enjoy easy access to Boston (3 hours away), New York City (2½ hours away), and Montreal (4 hours away). The Adirondacks, the Berkshires, and the Catskills, all within an hour of Troy, offer hundreds of areas for camping, hiking, and skiing. Many student clubs take full advantage of these natural resources.

Majors and Degrees

The Bachelor of Science is offered in aeronautical engineering; applied physics; biochemistry/biophysics; bioinformatics and molecular biology; biology; biomedical engineering; chemical engineering; chemistry; civil engineering; communication; computer and systems engineering; computer science; economics; electrical engineering; electric power engineering; electronic arts; electronic media, arts, and communication; engineering physics; environmental engineering; environmental science; geology; hydrogeology; industrial and management engineering; information technology; interdisciplinary science; management; materials engineering; mathematics; mechanical engineering; nuclear engineering; philosophy; physics; psychology; and science, technology, and society.

Professionally accredited degree programs are offered in the fields of architecture and engineering. Architecture students may earn the Bachelor of Architecture after five years or the Master of Architecture after six. A five-year professional engineering curriculum can be accelerated to allow completion of both the Bachelor of Science and Master of Engineering degrees in four years. Rensselaer's professional program in engineering is one of the first of its type in the nation.

Accelerated physician-scientist students earn a B.S. degree in biology and an M.D. (from Albany Medical College) in seven years. Accelerated law programs allow management or science, technology, and society majors to earn a B.S. degree from Rensselaer and a J.D. from Albany Law School in six years. Other programs allow students to earn a B.S. in three years and a B.S./M.S. in four or five years.

Undergraduates at more than forty-four liberal arts colleges may transfer to Rensselaer and earn a B.A. from the first college and a B.S. or a master's degree from Rensselaer.

Academic Programs

While each of Rensselaer's schools has its own sequence requirements, the following minimums apply to all students: 124 credit hours and a 1.8 quality point average in all courses; 24 credit hours in physical, life, and engineering sciences; 24 in humanities and social sciences; 30 in a selected discipline; and 24 in electives. Students are strongly encouraged to learn outside the classroom through independent projects, study abroad, cooperative education, internships, and partnering with faculty members on specific research projects. The Undergraduate Research Program offers hands-on experience to students in hundreds of areas where a full-time undergraduate may participate for credit or pay during the academic year or the summer. Co-op assignments give students the opportunity to add practical experience to their academic study. Air Force, Army, and Naval/Marine ROTC programs are available on an elective basis. Computing is integrated into the curriculum at Rensselaer, and all incoming undergraduates are required to have a laptop computer. Rensselaer's Mobile Computing Program provides students with the latest computing technology choices. Students may bring their own laptops to the campus, but they must comply with Rensselaer's computing requirements.

Off-Campus Programs

Rensselaer has study-abroad programs in Australia, China, Denmark, England, France, Germany, India, Italy, Japan, Spain, Switzerland, and Turkey. Cooperative programs with fifteen 2- and 4-year area institutions allow Rensselaer students to take courses for credit at no additional cost. More than 200 Rensselaer students use this cross-registration program each year. Rensselaer has transfer agreements with more than ninety institutions, including the 107 campuses of the California community college system.

Academic Facilities

Studio classrooms and laboratories across the campus use the latest educational technologies and encourage collaboration and team learning among students, with extensive wireless computing capabilities as well as more than 8,000 data ports available on campus, along with specialized systems such as the visualization laboratory for high-performance computing.

Student research projects are supported by excellent facilities such as the Low Center for Industrial Innovation, the Darrin Fresh Water Institute at Lake George, the Center for Integrated Electronics, and the Lighting Research Center. One of the newest facilities, the Social Behavioral Research Lab (SBRL) provides a platform for research on the social, cognitive, and behavioral impact of IT on society. The Center for Biotechnology and Interdisciplinary Studies provides a fertile environment for student research and learning at the intersection of science and engineering. The Experimental Media and Performing Arts Center (EMPAC) plans to showcase Rensselaer's distinctive programs in the electronic arts while providing facilities to broaden campus discourse and allow students and artists-in-residence to fully engage the larger community in the performing arts.

The entrepreneurial spirit is infused throughout the curriculum at Rensselaer and supported by one of the first university-sponsored business incubators in the country. The Rensselaer Incubator Program harnesses academic, research, and community resources to assist technology-based start-up enterprises. Many Rensselaer students have created new companies, nurtured them in the incubator, and then moved them to Rensselaer Technology Park, which is owned and operated by the university.

Costs

Tuition for 2008–09 is $36,950. Fees are $1040. Room and board costs average $10,730. Books and miscellaneous personal expenses are $1815. A required laptop, offered through Rensselaer, costs $2000. All incoming undergraduate students are required to have a laptop computer that meets Rensselaer's specifications.

Financial Aid

Nearly all freshmen who have financial need are offered assistance under a comprehensive program of scholarships, loans, and part-time employment that provides annual assistance ranging from $100 up to full tuition, room, and board. Available federal funds include student loans, Federal Work-Study Program awards, and ROTC scholarships.

Faculty

Rensselaer has embarked on a program to hire the brightest faculty "stars" in selected fields and cluster them into constellations, where they engage in innovative research to the benefit of the Institute's students as well as society. To date, Rensselaer's "constellation" initiative has met with great success in the areas of nanotechnology, biotechnology, and information technology. During the past seven years, Rensselaer has welcomed 180 new faculty members, 73 into entirely new positions. Approximately 450 tenured and tenure-track faculty members call Rensselaer home. Indicative of the talent of Rensselaer's young faculty members, more than 40 of them have won the prestigious National Science Foundation (NSF) Early Career Development (CAREER) Award. Faculty members are highly accessible to students, due to the university's internationally recognized studio-style classes, faculty-undergraduate research opportunities, and academic advising programs. While graduate students assist in some laboratory and recitation sessions, it is Rensselaer's policy to have professors teach undergraduate courses. Ninety-six percent of the faculty members have earned a Ph.D., first professional, or other terminal degree in their field.

Student Government

Students have an active voice in major university decisions through involvement in student government, a vital and influential force at Rensselaer. Elected student leaders include a Grand Marshal (student government president) and the President of the Student Union. The President of the Union and the Executive Board manage an $8.7-million budget to oversee more than 165 student clubs, intramural sports, and organizations.

Admission Requirements

All applications are reviewed individually by the admissions committee. It is important to note that some differences in preparation and academic background may be considered. The applicants who are best suited for Rensselaer have completed four years of English, four years of mathematics through precalculus, three years of science, and two years of social studies and/or history. In addition, the admissions committee pays particular attention to candidates who demonstrate qualities and talents that will contribute to the richness of the Rensselaer community.

Students must submit official scores for the SAT (critical reading, math, and writing); the ACT, which must include the optional writing component, may be substituted for the SAT. Applicants for accelerated programs must also submit scores for SAT Subject Tests in a math and a science; ACT scores, which must include the optional writing component, may be submitted in lieu of the SAT and SAT Subject Tests.

Portfolios are part of the application process for some students. Electronic arts applicants are required to submit a creative portfolio by November 1 (early decision I), January 1 (early decision II), or January 15 (regular admission). Architecture applicants should submit a creative portfolio by November 1 (early decision I), January 1 (early decision II), or January 15 (regular admission). Students with unusually strong academic profiles may be reviewed without the portfolio. Students expressing interest in product design and innovation who have completed design projects should submit a portfolio or documentation describing program-related work.

International applicants' official transcripts must be translated into English, and the international financial statement should be completed and mailed with the application. International applicants who do not achieve a minimum SAT verbal score of 580 must take the TOEFL. Rensselaer expects a TOEFL score of at least 230 on the computer-based test, 88 on the Internet-based test, or 580 on the paper-based test.

The early decision application deadlines are November 1 for early decision I and January 1 for early decision II, and the regular admission application deadline for September admission is January 15 of the student's senior year. Rensselaer admits qualified students without regard to race, color, sexual orientation, national or ethnic origin, religion, gender, age, or disability.

Application and Information

Rensselaer Admissions
Undergraduate Programs
Rensselaer Polytechnic Institute
Troy, New York 12180-3590
Phone: 518-276-6216
Fax: 518-276-4072
E-mail: admissions@rpi.edu
Web site: http://admissions.rpi.edu

Many of Rensselaer's turn-of-the-century buildings house ultramodern classrooms and laboratories.

ROBERTS WESLEYAN COLLEGE

ROCHESTER, NEW YORK

The College

Roberts Wesleyan College (RWC) is characterized by its mission: scholarship, spiritual formation, and service. RWC was founded in 1866 as the first Free Methodist academic institution in North America. Since then, the institution has continually adapted its programs to meet the current academic, professional, and personal needs of its students. The integration of broad-based intellectual thought with the Judeo-Christian heritage is and always has been the motivation for Roberts Wesleyan's existence. The College fosters wholesome principles by setting standards for student life, requiring regular chapel attendance, and maintaining a perspective rich in values within the classroom.

The current enrollment is 1,871: 1,346 women and 525 men. Although students come primarily from New York State, twenty-one other states and twenty-two other countries are represented. The majority of students are between 18 and 25 years of age, but there is a growing population of married and older students. The traditional undergraduate population is primarily residential, with approximately 70 percent of students living on campus.

RWC offers a broad selection of student activities. Student leaders, in cooperation with the Assistant Dean for Student Programming, plan a calendar of numerous events each year, including social, cultural, and religious programs. The College's suburban Rochester location also allows students to take advantage of cultural and academic opportunities within the community. The College's intramural program complements the intercollegiate sports program. There are six varsity sports for men: basketball, cross-country, golf, soccer, tennis, and track and field; there are seven varsity sports for women: basketball, cross-country, golf, soccer, tennis, track and field, and volleyball. Students may take advantage of the Voller Athletic Center, which includes a pool, four basketball courts, an indoor track, racquetball courts, a weight room, saunas, a student center, BT's Café, and a bookstore. The Career Services Office provides numerous services for students. Other College services available to students include academic advisement, counseling, and assistance from the Learning Center.

The College is a member of the Middle States Association of Colleges and Schools, the Association of Colleges and Universities of the State of New York, Rochester Area Colleges, the Association of Free Methodist Educational Institutions, the Council of Independent Colleges and Universities, and the Council for Christian Colleges & Universities. The programs in accounting, art, business, education, management, marketing, music, nursing, and social work are professionally accredited. The Art Department is accredited by the National Association of Schools of Art and Design. The Music Department is an accredited member of the National Association of Schools of Music. The Division of Nursing is accredited by the National League for Nursing Accrediting Commission. The Division of Social Work is accredited by the Council on Social Work Education. The Division of Business and Management is accredited by the International Assembly for Collegiate Business Education. The Division of Teacher Education is accredited by New York State Regents Accreditation of Teacher Education.

In addition to its undergraduate programs, Roberts Wesleyan offers the Master of Arts in Counseling in Ministry, Master of Education, Master of Music in Education, Master of Science in Health Administration, Master of Science in Nursing Administration, Master of Science in Nursing Education, Master of Science in School Counseling, Master of Science in School Psychology, Master of Science in Strategic Leadership, Master of Science in Strategic Marketing, and Master of Social Work degree programs. Northeastern Seminary at Roberts Wesleyan College offers the Master of Divinity, Master of Arts in Theological Studies, Master of Divinity/Master of Social Work, and Doctor of Ministry degree programs.

Location

Roberts Wesleyan College is located 8 miles southwest of Rochester, New York, in the suburb of North Chili. Rochester, with a metropolitan-area population of more than 1 million, is a thriving cultural and corporate area. Eastman School of Music, the Rochester Philharmonic Orchestra, and several of America's leading corporations, such as Eastman Kodak, Xerox, Paychex, Bausch & Lomb, and PAETEC make their home there.

The College continues to develop a strong relationship with the community, and the resulting internships and opportunities for practical work are particularly advantageous for Roberts Wesleyan students. Current students and graduates enjoy the extensive employment opportunities that result from Rochester's healthy economy. Lake Ontario, Niagara Falls, Watkins Glen, Letchworth Park, and the Finger Lakes are all nearby.

Majors and Degrees

Baccalaureate degrees are offered in accounting and information management, adolescence education (biology, chemistry, English, mathematics, physics, social studies, and Spanish), art, art education, art–graphic design, biblical studies, biochemistry, biology, business administration, chemistry, childhood education and special education (elementary education), communication, comprehensive science, comprehensive social studies, computer science, contemporary ministries, criminal justice, early childhood education and special education, economic crime investigation, elementary education (see childhood education), English, fine arts–art, fine arts–music, forensic science, health administration, history, humanities, information systems management, management, marketing, mathematics, middle childhood education and special education, music, music education, music performance (instrument, piano, and voice), nursing, organizational management, physics, psychology, public safety administration, religion/philosophy, religious studies, secondary education (see adolescence education), social work, Spanish, time-based media, and visual art education.

A 3-2 program in engineering is offered in cooperation with Clarkson University, Rensselaer Polytechnic Institute, and Rochester Institute of Technology (RIT). The program leads to a B.S. in mathematics, chemistry, or physics from RWC and a B.S. in engineering from Clarkson, Rensselaer, or RIT. A B.S./M.S. program is also available with RIT.

Secondary (grades 5–12) teaching certification may be earned in biology, chemistry, English, mathematics, physics, social studies, and Spanish. Preprofessional programs include dentistry, law, medicine, pharmacy, and veterinary medicine.

Academic Programs

RWC endeavors to involve each student in learning experiences that promote commitment to Christian stewardship and service to society. Approximately 45 semester hours of core courses are required of each baccalaureate degree candidate. These liberal arts survey courses introduce four main fields of knowledge: biological science, physical science, and mathematics; history and the behavioral sciences; language, literature, and the fine arts; and biblical studies and philosophy. A minimum of 124 semester hours is required for graduation with a baccalaureate degree, including a minimum of 30 to 81 semester hours within the student's major discipline.

Many academic programs at Roberts Wesleyan include internships or practical work experiences. Independent study and cross-cultural study opportunities are also available. Students may receive credit through the Advanced Placement Program, the International Baccalaureate Program, or the College-Level Examination Program. The Learning Center provides assistance for students possessing exceptional skills or a deficiency in any area.

The College calendar consists of two 15-week semesters scheduled from September to December and from January to May. Three sessions are held in the summer.

Off-Campus Programs

Various off-campus opportunities exist for which credit is awarded. These include the Appalachian Semester in Kentucky, Focus on the Family Institute in Colorado, Spanish language studies at the University of Murcia in Spain, EDUVenture in Irian Jaya, and a semester or full year of study at Richmond College in London, England. Under the direction of an RWC professor, students may also participate in a short-term exchange study program with Osaka Christian College and Seminary in Osaka, Japan. Opportunities for off-campus experiences also exist for Roberts Wesleyan students through the Council for Christian Colleges & Universities. These include the American Studies Program, Australia Studies Centre, China Studies Program, Contemporary Music Center, Latin American Studies Program, Los Angeles Film Studies Center, Middle East Studies Program, Programmes in Oxford, Russian Studies Program, Uganda Studies Program, and Washington Journalism Center. The January Experience Program offers transcultural and enrichment courses in this country or abroad. In addition, through RWC's membership in the Rochester Area Colleges consortium, RWC students may cross-register to take courses at any of the other member institutions.

Academic Facilities

The new 43,000-square-foot B. Thomas Golisano Library is a LEEDS-certified building, with a geothermal heating and cooling system. The Golisano Library includes a 24-hour computer lab and study café, two smart classrooms for bibliographic instruction (including forty computer stations), two fireplaces for comfortable study areas, 375 student stations, and a graduate study room. The library holds 132,000 volumes (with room for 300,000), 1,100 periodicals, more than 100 online databases (most with full text, including JSTOR), Internet access, and 171,000 microforms, recordings, and filmstrips. Also included in the library are the Learning Center, the Historical Center, and Archives. Through its participation in the Rochester Regional Research Library Council, the library provides access to extensive interlibrary loan resources.

Well-equipped science laboratories, a lecture auditorium, and computer laboratories connected to the campus network are included in the Merlin G. Smith Science Center. Other facilities are the newly renovated music studios, practice rooms, and recital auditorium of Cox Hall; the educational curriculum laboratory in Carpenter Hall; the Cultural Life Center, which houses Shewan Recital Hall, Hale Auditorium, and Davison Art Gallery; the Rinker Community Service Center; and the soccer stadium and Mondo track. High-speed Internet connections for each student are available in all residence halls. The academic areas of campus are wireless.

Costs

Tuition for full-time study for the 2007–08 academic year was $20,564. Costs vary if a student's course load is fewer than 12 or more than 18 hours. Additional fees are charged for music and laboratory courses. Room and board costs were $7,774. Miscellaneous fees were $788. Book costs and personal expenses vary, depending on individual needs.

Financial Aid

Roberts Wesleyan College offers a complete financial aid program, consisting of grants, scholarships, loans, and employment. Filing the Free Application for Federal Student Aid (FAFSA) is a prerequisite for determining eligibility for most financial aid programs. Sources of aid include Federal Pell Grants, Federal Supplemental Educational Opportunity Grants, Federal Perkins Loans, and Federal Stafford Student Loans; New York State Tuition Assistance Program awards; and institutional resources. Numerous on-campus employment opportunities are available. Institutional aid is also available in recognition of academic, athletic, artistic, and musical achievement. More than 94 percent of the student body receives financial aid each year. In 2007 Roberts Wesleyan College was ranked number 3 in the Princeton Review's Top 10 Best Value Colleges.

Faculty

The primary concern of the faculty at RWC is to provide an educational experience of high-quality. Sixty-four percent of the professors hold the doctoral or terminal degree, and all are well respected within their specific discipline. The 112 full-time and 134 part-time faculty members are committed to Christian higher education and are genuinely interested in each student's development. A 11:1 student-faculty ratio allows for much individualized attention, and most professors go well beyond their tasks of teaching and advising to participate in campus activities.

Student Government

All students belong to the Student Association and have the freedom to express their opinions to the staff, faculty, and administration. There are also elected senators and officers, under the direction of the Office of Student Services, who act as liaisons between the student body and the administration in areas concerning academics and student activities.

Admission Requirements

Because the type of student a college enrolls significantly determines the personality of the institution, Roberts Wesleyan seeks students whose personal lives are characterized by honesty, integrity, and devotion to high moral and ethical standards. Admission consideration is given to applicants who rank in the upper third of their graduating class and have earned a minimum of 12 academic units of high school credit, with no fewer than 4 units in English, 2 units in algebra (or 1 in algebra and 1 in geometry), and 1 unit in biology, chemistry, or physics. Three years each of social studies, a foreign language, and science are strongly recommended. Further preparation in mathematics and science is required of applicants who wish to enter degree programs in nursing, mathematics, or science. Scores on the SAT or ACT and a formal recommendation are required. Special talents are considered an asset for applicants but are not required. An on-campus admission interview is strongly recommended. In admitting students, the College does not discriminate on the basis of race, age, color, sex, handicap, creed, or national or ethnic origin. Children of alumni and staff members are considered for admission on the same basis as all other applicants.

Transfer students must fulfill the same admission requirements as first-time students and must also have transcripts forwarded to the College from all the institutions they have attended. Credit is usually accepted for any course in which a grade of C– or above has been earned if the course parallels a course given at RWC.

Application and Information

Applicants should submit an application form (or apply online), the $35 application fee, a completed recommendation form, SAT or ACT scores, and transcripts from all schools previously attended. Art students should prepare a portfolio for review by the art faculty, and music students should schedule an audition with the Music Department. Students are encouraged to submit an application prior to the February 1 priority deadline. Admission decisions are made on a rolling basis, and students are notified of the admission decision as soon as all of their credentials have been received and evaluated.

For additional information and application forms, students should contact:

Kirk Kettinger
Director of Admissions
Roberts Wesleyan College
2301 Westside Drive
Rochester, New York 14624-1997
Phone: 585-594-6400
800-777-4RWC (toll-free)
Fax: 585-594-6371
E-mail: admissions@roberts.edu
Web site: http://www.roberts.edu

The New B. Thomas Golisano Library.

ROCHESTER INSTITUTE OF TECHNOLOGY

R·I·T

ROCHESTER, NEW YORK

The Institute

Rochester Institute of Technology (RIT) is one of the world's leading career-oriented, technological universities. RIT's eight colleges offer more than ninety undergraduate programs in areas such as engineering, computing, information technology, engineering technology, business, hospitality, science, art, design, photography, biomedical sciences, game design and development, and the liberal arts including psychology, advertising and public relations, and public policy. Students may choose from more than seventy different minors to develop personal and professional interests that complement their academic program. Experiential education is integrated into many programs through cooperative education, internships, study abroad, and undergraduate research. As home to the National Technical Institute for the Deaf (NTID), RIT is a leader in providing access services for deaf and hard-of-hearing students. The university enrolls students from every state and more than ninety foreign countries.

Close to 70 percent of RIT's approximately 11,000 full-time undergraduate students live on the campus in residence halls or campus apartments. The residence halls have eight special-interest houses where students with shared interests live and learn together. Park Point, scheduled to open in summer 2008, is located on the northeast corner of the campus, and will consist of approximately 80,000 square feet of retail spaces and more than 100 residential units. The retail spaces will consist of a mix of restaurants and retail shops.

Because RIT's student body is so diverse, there are many different activities, clubs, organizations, and sports in which students may participate. There are seventeen fraternities and twelve sororities, representing approximately 5 percent of the student population. A radio station and a biweekly student magazine allow those interested in media to gain experience on campus. A number of special interest clubs and career organizations are also available, and RIT offers twenty-three varsity sports, including Division I men's hockey. Recreational facilities include an ice rink, an aquatics center, a field house with an indoor track, and fitness facilities.

Location

The greater Rochester area has a population of about 745,000. Per-capita income is among the highest in the nation for metropolitan centers. The area's many internationally known industries employ a high proportion of scientists, technologists, and skilled workers. Rochester is the world center of photography, the largest producer of optical goods in the United States, and among the leaders in graphic arts and reproduction and in production of electronic equipment and precision instruments. Rochester's industries have always been closely associated with RIT's programs and progress.

Majors and Degrees

The College of Applied Science and Technology offers the Bachelor of Science in civil engineering technology, computer engineering technology, electrical engineering technology, electrical/mechanical engineering technology, manufacturing engineering technology, mechanical engineering technology, and telecommunications engineering technology. It also grants the Bachelor of Science in environmental management and technology, hospitality and service management, nutrition management, packaging science, and safety technology. Undeclared options allowing freshmen to delay the selection of their major for up to one year are available in both the School of Hospitality and Service Management and in Engineering Technology.

The E. Philip Saunders College of Business offers the Bachelor of Science in accounting, consumer finance, finance, graphic media marketing, international business, management, management information systems, and marketing. An accelerated B.S./M.B.A. option is available, as is a minor in entrepreneurship. An undeclared option allowing freshmen to delay the selection of their major for up to one year is also available.

The B. Thomas Golisano College of Computing and Information Sciences offers the Bachelor of Science degree in applied networking and systems administration, computer science, game design and development, information technology, medical informatics, new media interactive development, and software engineering.

The Kate Gleason College of Engineering grants the Bachelor of Science in computer engineering, electrical engineering, industrial and systems engineering, mechanical engineering, and microelectronic engineering. Degree options in aerospace, automotive, bioengineering, biomedical, energy and environment, ergonomics, information systems, manufacturing, and software engineering are also offered within the college. Accelerated B.S./M.S. options are available. The Engineering Exploration Program, which allows freshmen to delay the selection of their major for up to one year, is also available.

The College of Imaging Arts and Sciences offers the Bachelor of Fine Arts in advertising photography; ceramics and ceramic sculpture; film, video, and animation; fine art photography; fine arts studio, glass and glass sculpture; graphic design; illustration; industrial design; interior design; medical illustration; metals and jewelry design; new media design and imaging; photojournalism; visual media; and woodworking and furniture design. The college also offers the Bachelor of Science in biomedical photographic communications, digital media, graphic media, imaging and photographic technology, and new media/publishing. An undeclared option allowing freshmen to delay the selection of their major for up to one year is also available in the School of Art, the School of Design, and the School for American Crafts.

The College of Liberal Arts confers the Bachelor of Science in advertising and public relations, criminal justice, economics, international studies, professional and technical communication, psychology, public policy, and urban and community studies. The RIT Exploration Program is designed to help undecided students formulate education and career plans. Students may spend up to one year sampling courses in each of RIT's colleges (except NTID) before selecting a major.

The College of Science offers the Bachelor of Science in applied mathematics, applied statistics, biology, biochemistry, bioinformatics, biomedical sciences, biotechnology, chemistry, computational mathematics, diagnostic medical sonography (ultrasound), environmental chemistry, environmental science, imaging science, physician assistant studies, physics, and polymer chemistry. Special options are available in premedical studies (medicine, dentistry, veterinary medicine). Minors are available in astronomy, exercise science, imaging science, mathematics, physics, and statistics. Accelerated B.S./M.S. and B.S./M.B.A. programs are available. The General Science Exploration Program, which allows freshmen to delay the selection of their major for up to one year, is also available.

As home of the National Technical Institute for the Deaf, RIT is a leader in providing educational opportunities and access services for deaf and hard-of-hearing students. NTID awards associate degree programs and offers a prebaccalaureate studies program for the deaf and hard-of-hearing. The associate degree programs prepare students for immediate employment after graduation or transfer into one of RIT's bachelor's degree programs. The prebaccalaureate studies program prepares students, who may not qualify initially, for entry into a bachelor's degree program. Nearly 50 percent of the 1,100 deaf and hard-of-hearing students at RIT are enrolled directly into one of the bachelor's degree programs in the other seven colleges.

Academic Programs

Students entering RIT enroll directly in the college and academic program of their choice; specialization is spread over the duration of their study. Approximately one third of the program of each professional curriculum consists of general education courses in the humanities, math and science, and social sciences. Students may choose from more than seventy different minors to develop personal and professional interests that complement their academic program. Double-major and accelerated dual-degree (combined bachelor's/masters) options are available. Experiential education is integrated into many programs through cooperative education, internships, study abroad, and undergraduate research are also available. An honors program admits approximately 100 students each year, representing the top 5 percent of students admitted to each of the colleges. Air

Force and Army ROTC programs are available on the campus. A Naval ROTC program is offered jointly with the University of Rochester.

Every academic program at RIT offers some form of experiential education opportunity. Experiential education takes many forms, including cooperative education, internships, study abroad, undergraduate research, and industry-sponsored project work. Notable among these programs at RIT is cooperative education (co-op). The College of Applied Science and Technology, the E. Philip Saunders College of Business, the B. Thomas Golisano College of Computing and Information Sciences, and the Kate Gleason College of Engineering all require co-op for undergraduate students. It is available on an optional basis in other RIT colleges. Co-op students alternate periods of full-time study with periods of full-time paid work experience in business and industry directly related to their field of study and career interests. Last year more than 3,500 students completed work assignments with nearly 1,900 employers, earning collectively in excess of $30 million.

Off-Campus Programs

RIT has two international branch campuses. The American College of Management and Technology is a branch campus located in Croatia. The college offers an associate degree and a Bachelor of Science degree in hospitality and service management, a Master of Science degree in service management, and several certificate programs to serve the local tourism industries. The American University of Kosovo provides a career-oriented education that fosters the links between the university, industry, and government necessary to support the workforce development needs of Kosovo. RIT has a growing study-abroad program. Through affiliations with other institutions, RIT offers study-abroad programs in twenty countries around the world. RIT students may choose from more than 150 affiliated programs.

Academic Facilities

Excellent facilities add to the quality of academic life. Students have access to a laser-optics laboratory, an observatory, an animal-care facility, more than 100 color and black-and-white photography darkrooms, electronic prepress and publishing equipment, ceramic kilns, glass furnaces, a blacksmithing area, a student-operated restaurant, computer graphics and robotic labs, and some of the most up-to-date microelectronic, telecommunications, and computer engineering facilities in the U.S. Wallace Memorial Library is a true multimedia learning center. Its collections are exceptionally extensive in the areas of art and design, education for the deaf, photography, and printing.

RIT is a leader in academic computing, and students work with state-of-the-art computer equipment regardless of their major. Central computer systems can be accessed via a high-speed data network connecting the library, academic facilities, residence hall rooms, and on-campus apartments. There are more than sixty locations campuswide, with wireless networking connectivity utilizing 802.11b technology. The RIT campus network is served by two OC3 connections, each operating at a data rate of 155 Mbps, and one T3 connection operating at 45 Mbps. RIT is among a select group of institutions with access to the Internet2 research network. Internet2 is a collaborative research and development effort led by more than 170 U.S. universities working in partnership with industry and government. Its goal is to develop a new family of advanced Internet applications and technologies.

Costs

For 2007–08, tuition for the normal academic year (three academic quarters) was $26,085. Students on the cooperative education plan pay tuition only for the quarters they are at RIT. Fees, including the activities and health fees, are $396 for the academic year. Room and board (twenty meals per week) cost $9054.

Financial Aid

Approximately 77 percent of the full-time undergraduates receive some form of financial aid that includes RIT scholarships, alumni or industry-supported scholarships, and state and federal government grants. A variety of loans and part-time work positions are also available. The FAFSA must be submitted by March 1. Giving full recognition to scholarship apart from financial need, RIT awards a number of academic scholarships based on grades, test scores, and activities. Freshmen applying by February 1 and transfers applying as juniors by April 1 are considered for these scholarships.

Faculty

There are 798 full-time faculty members, 406 part-time faculty members, and an administrative and supporting staff of more than 1,800. Approximately 80 percent of the faculty members have earned a Ph.D. or the terminal degree in their field.

Student Government

The Student Government is the representative body for students. It works with RIT administration and faculty and staff members to communicate the needs and desires of the student body and to communicate the decisions of the administration to the students. Fraternity and sorority members, off-campus and hearing-impaired students, and students from minority groups elect special representative bodies. All full-time and part-time undergraduate and graduate students become members of the Student Government when they pay the student activities fee.

Admission Requirements

The general requirements for freshman entrance are a high school diploma (an equivalency diploma is considered), high school grades that give evidence of the ability to complete college work successfully, satisfactory scores on the SAT or ACT, and completion of prerequisite high school–level math and science courses indicated in the college catalog. An important factor for admission is the record of academic achievement in high school (or in another college in the case of transfer students). The results of standardized tests, while important, are supplementary. Students applying for programs in the fine and applied arts must submit a portfolio of original artwork.

Rochester Institute of Technology admits qualified men and women of any race, color, national or ethnic origin, religion, sexual orientation, gender identity, gender expression, or marital status. RIT does not discriminate on the basis of handicap in the recruitment or admission of students or in the operation of any of its programs or activities, as specified by federal laws and regulations.

Application and Information

An application, a nonrefundable processing fee of $50, official transcripts of all high school or college records, and SAT or ACT scores (for prospective freshmen) should be forwarded to RIT. Freshman applicants who provide all required materials for entry in the fall quarter by February 1 receive admission notification by March 15. Prospective freshmen who apply after February 1 and all transfer students are notified of the admission decision by mail on a rolling basis four to six weeks after their application is complete. RIT also offers an early decision plan, whereby prospective freshmen must have their completed application with all supporting credentials on file in the Admissions Office by December 1 to receive notification by January 15.

For application forms, students should contact:

Director of Undergraduate Admissions
Rochester Institute of Technology
60 Lomb Memorial Drive
Rochester, New York 14623-5604
Phone: 585-475-6631
Fax: 585-475-7424
E-mail: admissions@rit.edu
Web site: http://www.rit.edu

A view of the campus.

ST. BONAVENTURE UNIVERSITY

ST. BONAVENTURE, NEW YORK

The University

St. Bonaventure University provides a values-based, Franciscan liberal arts education with individual attention from professors, a beautiful residential setting, and a friendly, close-knit atmosphere. Of the 2,600 students enrolled, 2,000 are undergraduates. More than 74 percent of the undergraduates are full-time residents. Complementing St. Bonaventure's traditions are innovative degree programs, computerized career placement aids, comprehensive student life activities, and modern academic facilities. Among major campus events during the academic year are concerts and coffeehouse acts, indoor and outdoor recreational programs, current and classic film offerings, and dramatic and musical plays. Aspiring writers and broadcasters from all academic majors—Bonaventure has produced 5 Pulitzer Prize winners—find challenging and plentiful opportunities working with one of the four University media: WSBU-88.3 FM-The Buzz, the nationally ranked campus radio station; *The Bona Venture*, the award-winning weekly newspaper; *The Bonadieu*, the yearbook; and *The Laurel*, the nation's oldest student literary publication, which marked its 100th anniversary in 1999. Other organizations on campus include academic fraternities, academic honor societies, a variety of club and intramural sports, and arts organizations that include choral, instrumental, dance, and drama ensembles. The Thomas Merton Ministry Center is open 24 hours a day and aims to foster a community of friendship and mutual service. Many students take the opportunity to serve as Bona Buddies to area children or senior citizens; help with the national award–winning soup kitchen The Warming House, which is the oldest student-run soup kitchen in the nation; or volunteer in other service organizations. Volunteer opportunities expanded with the opening of St. Bonaventure's Franciscan Center for Social Concern, which offers immersion experiences and service opportunities with the poor.

St. Bonaventure University students enjoy two athletic facilities: the new $6.2-million Richter Center, which is open 24 hours a day, features three basketball courts, a running/walking track, racquetball/squash/wallyball courts, an aerobics room, a recreational area for roller hockey, a weight room, a cardiovascular fitness room, locker rooms, an equipment check-out, a reception area, and a climbing wall; and the Reilly Center, housing a 6,000-seat sports arena, swimming pool, and weight room. Also available are outdoor tennis and basketball courts and a nine-hole golf course. NCAA Division I athletics for men are baseball, basketball, cross-country, golf, soccer, swimming, and tennis. Division I competition for women includes basketball, cross-country, lacrosse, soccer, softball, swimming, and tennis.

In addition to its undergraduate programs, St. Bonaventure offers the Master of Arts degree in English and in Franciscan studies. A Master of Science is offered in professional leadership, while a Master of Science in Education program includes adolescence education, advanced inclusive processes, counselor education, differentiated instruction, educational leadership, literacy, school building leader, school district leader, and supervision and curriculum. A Master of Business Administration degree program is available with concentrations in accounting/finance, general business, international business, and management/marketing, and a Master of Arts degree in integrated marketing communications was added in 2003.

Location

St. Bonaventure is located on Route 417 between Olean, a city of approximately 17,000 residents, and Allegany, a village with about 2,000 residents. Shops, restaurants, and movie theaters are all within walking distance. The campus is spread over 500 acres in a valley surrounded by the Allegheny Mountains. The free Bona Bus connects the campus with Olean and Allegany, carrying students to and from the area attractions. The region around St. Bonaventure provides a beautiful setting for many outdoor activities. A ski resort, ice rink, and snow-tubing resort attract students, and nearby Allegany State Park offers excellent facilities for swimming, boating, and hiking. St. Bonaventure is accessible by car, bus, and commercial air transportation, with Buffalo/Niagara International the nearest major airport.

Majors and Degrees

St. Bonaventure University grants the Bachelor of Arts degree with majors in classical languages, English, history, interdisciplinary studies, journalism and mass communication, modern languages (French and Spanish), music, philosophy, political science, psychology, social sciences, sociology, theology, visual arts, and women's studies. The Bachelor of Science is granted with majors in biochemistry, biology, chemistry, computer science, early childhood education, economics, elementary/special education (dual certification), environmental science, interdisciplinary studies, mathematics, physical education, physics, and psychology. The Bachelor of Business Administration is granted with majors in accounting, finance, management sciences, and marketing. Popular five-year programs are also available in business, English, physics, and psychology, and dual-admission programs offer unique opportunities for students pursuing careers in medicine, dentistry, and pharmacy.

Academic Programs

Students in all majors begin their intellectual journey in Clare College, St. Bonaventure's nationally acclaimed core curriculum, which offers a values-based education grounded in the vision of St. Francis and St. Bonaventure.

A candidate for a bachelor's degree must complete at least 120 credit hours, with a cumulative index of 2.0 or better in the major field and the overall program. A pass/fail grade option, available to all upperclass students, may be elected for one course per semester, but not for courses in a student's major field.

Advanced credit is granted for grades of C or better on either the College Proficiency Examination or the College-Level Examination Program (CLEP) tests. Advanced placement is granted on the basis of scores obtained on the College Board's Advanced Placement (AP) examinations.

Men and women may also elect to participate in the University's Army ROTC program, MacArthur Award winner as best small unit in the nation in 1998.

Off-Campus Programs

Through St. Bonaventure's membership in the College Consortium for International Studies (CCIS), St. Bonaventure students have access to six continents. More than sixty semester-long international study programs, including St. Bonaventure–sponsored study in Spain, Ireland, and Australia, are available to students in good academic standing in their junior year. Faculty-directed, short-term opportunities include a three-week intersession in China, the Francis E. Kelly Oxford summer program, and a three-week travel study program to Mexico. For further information, students should contact the Office of International Studies. Fieldwork or internships are available in several major programs.

Academic Facilities

Friedsam Memorial Library houses more than 250,000 volumes and includes a trilevel resource center with a curriculum center,

COLLEGE DATA CENTER • NEW YORK

the University archives, and digital media and conferencing centers, as well as world-class special collections. An automated online card catalog greatly improves research capabilities.

A $13-million science center addition is planned for DeLaRoche Hall in 2008; it currently houses equipment for instruction and research in a variety of fields, including chemistry, geology, mathematics, microbiology, physics, and psychology. Research facilities include an atomic absorption spectrophotometer, a tissue-culture laboratory, a greenhouse, a radioactivity laboratory, equipment for research in the growth of microorganisms, and an extensive mammal collection.

The John J. Murphy Professional Building provides the most up-to-date equipment for the School of Business and the School of Journalism and Mass Communication. The Bob Koop Broadcast Journalism Laboratory features a television studio with an anchor desk, digital and videotape editing bays, while the building also houses offices, classrooms, and a 432-seat auditorium. A fiber-optic network connects microcomputers in academic and administrative areas. There are seven labs for student use containing more than 100 DOS and Macintosh systems. St. Bonaventure students also have access to the Internet via every residence hall.

An annex to Plassmann Hall houses computer-adaptable education classrooms, seminar rooms, and offices for the education faculty. An observatory allows students access to three compact telescopes, two 8-inch Celestron telescopes, and one 11-inch Schmidt-Cassegrain telescope, along with a heated classroom.

The Regina A. Quick Center for the Arts provides acoustically designed classroom space for music courses and painting and drawing studios for students enrolled in visual arts classes. The center also includes a musical instrument digital interface lab, a 325-seat theater, and an atrium that is often used for poetry readings and impromptu musical performances. The F. Donald Kenney Museum and Art Study Wing includes four climate-controlled galleries offering nationally acclaimed traveling exhibits, works from the University's permanent collections, and student exhibits.

St. Bonaventure is in the midst of the most dramatic renovation in school history. Historic Hickey Dining Hall received a spectacular makeover in 2006, and a 5,500-square-foot coffee café flanking Hickey opened in spring 2007. Some residence halls were overhauled in 2006, work continues on the $13-million science center, and ground will soon be broken on a $2.2-million library addition.

Costs

For 2006–07, the annual costs were $21,650 for tuition and $865 for fees. Room and meal plans averaged $7760 per year.

Financial Aid

Students who qualify for financial aid normally receive a package consisting of a combination of scholarships, grants, loans, and work-study awards. Athletic Grants-in-Aid are available for men in baseball, basketball, golf, soccer, swimming, and tennis and for women in basketball, lacrosse, soccer, softball, swimming, and tennis. Music scholarships are also available. Students must file the Free Application for Federal Student Aid (FAFSA) in order to be considered for financial assistance. For more complete details, a student should contact the director of financial aid at the University.

Faculty

Like the student body, the 160 full-time and 67 part-time faculty members at St. Bonaventure come from a wide range of geographic, ethnic, and religious backgrounds. The student-faculty ratio of 15:1 allows faculty members the time to help each student to understand different modes of thinking, develop as a person, and lay a foundation for lifelong learning. Eighty-four percent of the faculty members hold the terminal degree in their field. Friars, many of whom teach, add to the unique atmosphere of St. Bonaventure.

Student Government

Life at St. Bonaventure is centered on the residence halls, and the foundation of student government begins in the dormitories with the Residence Hall Councils. The elected council members determine the norms by which the residents are guided in their daily lives. The Student Government, whose members are elected from the student body, serves as the general student-governing unit, and its members serve on every major University board and committee.

Admission Requirements

St. Bonaventure University welcomes applications for admission from all serious candidates from a variety of backgrounds. St. Bonaventure University provides equal opportunity without regard to race, creed, color, gender, age, national or ethnic origin, marital status, veteran status, or disability in admission, employment, and in all of its educational programs and activities. Applicants, who are welcome to apply online, must show evidence of academic achievement to be selected for admission. The criteria used in making admission decisions, in order of importance, are quality of the high school curriculum, grade point average in college-preparatory courses, ACT (preferred) or SAT scores, class rank, recommendations from high school teachers and counselors, and extracurricular activities.

Application and Information

For more information about St. Bonaventure University, prospective students should contact:

Director of Admissions
St. Bonaventure University
P.O. Box D
St. Bonaventure, New York 14778
Phone: 716-375-2400
800-462-5050 (toll-free)
E-mail: admissions@sbu.edu
Web site: http://www.sbu.edu

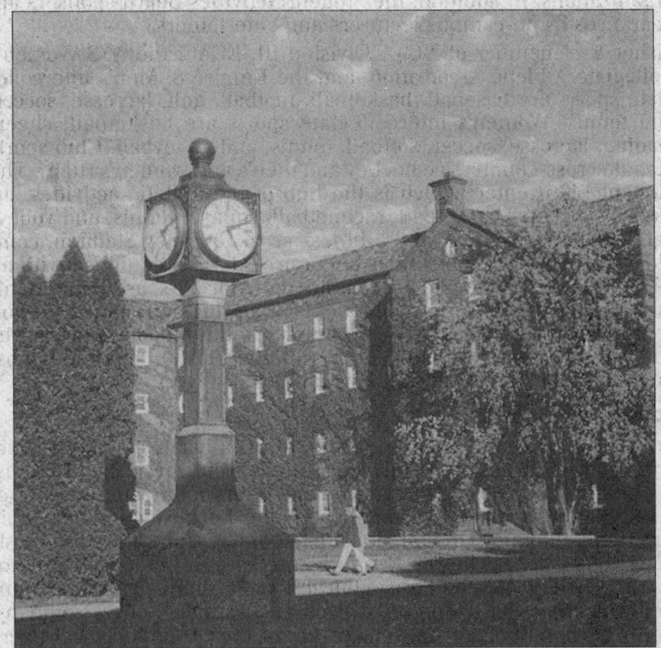

Built in 1928 and renovated in 1999, Devereux Hall is an example of the beautiful Florentine architecture found at St. Bonaventure University.

ST. JOHN FISHER COLLEGE

ROCHESTER, NEW YORK

The College

Founded in 1948 by the Basilian fathers, St. John Fisher College is dedicated to serving the individual needs of its students. Originally a Catholic college for men, Fisher is now an independent, coeducational college with 58 percent women and 55 percent resident students. The College offers thirty-one undergraduate programs in business, the humanities, nursing, sciences, and social sciences and is accredited by the Middle States Association of Colleges and Schools. The College also offers eleven master's programs and two doctoral programs leading to the Master of Business Administration, the Master of Science, the Master of Science in Education, the Doctor of Education, and the Doctor of Pharmacy.

Fisher's unique First-Year Program reaches beyond the transition to college to focus on developing responsible campus citizens with independent learning skills, who fully explore educational and career aspirations. The Learning Community Program gives first-year students the opportunity to take courses in clusters that focus on a central theme. Through this approach to learning, students and faculty members examine a complex topic from multiple perspectives and discover connections among various disciplines. Fisher's Learning Communities also enable students to learn cooperatively and develop close working relationships with other students and faculty members.

All of the residence halls have been renovated, giving all students access to the Internet and cable TV in their rooms. Keough Hall, the College's newest residence, opened in September 2005 and added more than 200 beds.

Fisher offers a full range of extracurricular activities designed to cater to the diverse interests of the 2,625 full-time and 225 part-time undergraduate students, 770 master's students, and 170 doctoral students. Such activities include a student newspaper, a campus radio station, a complete intramural program, and more than sixty student organizations. In addition, the Student Activities Board sponsors appearances by on-campus lecturers and entertainers.

Fisher is a member of NCAA Division III, ECAC, the NYS Women's Collegiate Athletic Association, and the Empire 8. Men's intercollegiate sports are baseball, basketball, football, golf, lacrosse, soccer, and tennis. Women's intercollegiate sports are basketball, cheerleading, lacrosse, soccer, softball, tennis, and volleyball. Club sports include cross-country, ice hockey and men's and women's rugby. The Student Life Center, which is the hub of the athletic activities, includes courts for basketball, racquetball, squash, tennis, and volleyball; a sauna; a lounge; and a fitness area. Growney Stadium, complete with 2,100 bleacher seats and a press box, is equipped with an all-weather synthetic playing field to allow for all-season and nighttime play. Other on-campus athletics facilities include a nine-hole golf course, a softball field, a baseball complex, four outdoor tennis courts, and two grass practice fields. In the summer, Fisher is proud to host the Buffalo Bills training camp on campus.

Location

Located on 154 parklike acres, Fisher offers a balance of city activity and suburban tranquility. Just 10 minutes from the Fisher campus, Rochester, the "World's Image Center," offers many cultural attractions, including the Eastman Theater, the Rochester Philharmonic Orchestra, the International Museum of Photography at George Eastman House, the Rochester Museum and Science Center, the Memorial Art Gallery, and the Strasenburgh Planetarium. Home to a number of Fortune 500 companies, such as Eastman Kodak Company, Xerox Corporation, and Bausch and Lomb, the city of Rochester offers Fisher students opportunities for internships and employment after graduation.

Majors and Degrees

St. John Fisher College offers courses leading to the Bachelor of Arts and Bachelor of Science degrees. Undergraduate majors are offered in accounting, adolescence education, American studies, anthropology, applied information technology, biology, chemistry, childhood education, communication/journalism, computer science, corporate finance, economics, English, French, history, interdisciplinary studies, international studies, management, mathematics, nursing, philosophy, physics, political science, psychology, religious studies, sociology, Spanish, special education, sport management, and statistics. The areas of concentration available in the management major include corporate finance, financial planning, general business management, human resource management, and marketing.

Fisher offers a fast track to the B.S./M.S. in advanced practice nursing. The College also offers a cooperative 3+4 program with the Pennsylvania College of Optometry and a cooperative engineering program with the University of Detroit, Clarkson University, Manhattan College, Columbia University, and the University at Buffalo, the State University of New York.

Academic Programs

The bachelor's degree is conferred upon those who complete a minimum of 120 semester hours of credit with a cumulative GPA of at least 2.0. Thirty hours of credit and half of the requirements for the major must be earned at St. John Fisher College. Graduates of the accounting program are eligible to sit for the CPA exam in New York State.

Off-Campus Programs

Fisher offers a multitude of special programs that are designed to complement its academic programs. Students in various disciplines can take advantage of an internship program, Albany and Washington Semesters, and cross-registration with fourteen member colleges of the Rochester Area College Consortium. Study-abroad opportunities throughout the world are also available to students.

Academic Facilities

Over the last ten years, most of the academic and athletic facilities on campus have been upgraded and enhanced. Classrooms have been modernized and outfitted with state-of-the-art media facilities. Laboratory space has been upgraded with state-of-the-market educational technology. The Golisano Academic Gateway, complete with the Frontier Cyber Café and the learning resource center, opened in January 2001. The Ralph C. Wilson, Jr. Building opened in September 2003, expanding classroom capacity by 20 percent and providing additional faculty offices, seminar rooms, and meeting spaces.

The Campus Center opened in fall 2005 and serves as the hub and central gathering place of student activity on campus. This two-story facility supports general student gathering spaces, which include a performance space, recreational area, offices for student clubs and organizations, and the College Store (bookstore), all located on the first floor. The second floor of the Campus Center houses the Offices of the Dean of Students, Residential Life, Campus Life, and Campus Ministry, as well as additional student organization offices and meeting spaces.

The Charles J. Lavery Library meets the information needs of twenty-first-century students. A blend of traditional and electronic resources covering a broad range of subjects is available to the Fisher community. The library's print collection is supplemented by an extensive offering of online scholarly resources. Information resources include 190,000 volumes, 28,000 audiovisual items, 882 print periodical subscriptions, and access to over 9,000 electronic periodical titles.

Professional librarians welcome students to the library reference desk during day and evening hours. There is also a 24/7 online-chat reference service. The librarians are information specialists committed to the academic success of all students. Individual research guidance is available by appointment. Librarians also teach classes in information literacy and subject-specific research to all levels of students.

Lavery Library is a member of the Rochester Regional Library Council, representing a regional collection of more than 3,400,000 titles. Interlibrary loan staff members can obtain resources not owned by Lavery Library from regional, national, and international libraries.

Costs

Tuition for 2007–08 was $21,670. Room and board costs were $9410 with a meal plan and a room in one of Fisher's residence halls.

Financial Aid

Committed to helping students meet the cost of their education, Fisher works to assess each individual's financial need. Financial aid is provided through scholarships, grants, loans, and work-study arrangements and is awarded by Fisher, the state, and the federal government. In 2007–08, the average financial aid package for incoming Fisher students was $16,000.

St. John Fisher College offers a generous academic scholarship program that is based on high school average, strength of curriculum, and SAT or ACT scores. Students eligible for academic scholarships are automatically notified by the Office of Freshman Admissions. Scholarship award amounts are $8500 to $11,000 per year. The College also offers an honors program and a science scholars program. The award in each of these programs is $3000, in addition to any academic scholarships for which the student qualifies.

Twelve years ago, the College introduced the Service Scholars Program. This program is designed to recognize and reward high school seniors who demonstrate an ongoing interest in serving the needs of others through a commitment to community service. Scholarship awards equal one third of the total yearly cost of tuition, fees, room, and board for four years. In 2002, the Service Scholars Program won the President's Community Volunteer Award—the highest national honor for volunteering. The College was honored, along with 19 other winners from across the country, at a White House ceremony. Fisher was the only college or university and the only organization in New York State to be honored that year.

In 1998, the College announced the creation of the Fannie and Sam Constantino First Generation Scholarship Program, designed to provide financial assistance to students whose parents did not graduate from a postsecondary institution—much like the pioneer classes of St. John Fisher College. Recipients receive annual scholarships ranging from $3000 to one third of the total yearly cost of Fisher's tuition, fees, room, and board for four years.

Faculty

Fisher's 182 full-time faculty members are dedicated to helping students, both in and out of the classroom, as they strive to achieve their goals. Eighty-three percent of full-time faculty members hold doctoral or terminal degrees. The student-teacher ratio of 14:1 offers a personal approach to education; 75 percent of all classes have fewer than 30 students. Fisher's Office of Academic Affairs and an outstanding faculty share responsibility for academic advising, helping students to explore the thirty-one majors that are available to them.

Student Government

Student leadership skills are developed through the Student Government Association, which is responsible for the social, cultural, and judicial areas of student life. Resident students elect a Resident Student Association, while commuting students elect a Commuter Council to represent them in planning special activities. The Student Activities Board is responsible for social activities and cultural events throughout the academic year.

Admission Requirements

Admission to St. John Fisher College is based primarily on the following: grade point average, strength of curriculum, scores on standardized tests (SAT/ACT), extracurricular activities and/or work experience, and the counselor/teacher recommendation. Interviews are also considered and strongly encouraged.

A candidate for admission to the freshman class must be a graduate of an approved secondary school and present a minimum of 16 units of college-preparatory course work in English, foreign languages, mathematics, and natural and social sciences. An applicant should present a secondary school average of 85 percent or above in these academic subjects.

Fisher welcomes qualified transfer students from two- and four-year colleges for both the fall and spring terms. To be considered for admission, transfer students must have a cumulative grade point average of 2.0 or better. If the student has obtained an A.A., A.S., or A.A.S. degree, 60 to 66 credit hours are transferred. All transfer applicants should consult the Undergraduate Bulletin for details.

The College has various special admission programs, including early decision, abbreviated procedures for veterans and other military personnel, and admission for part-time study.

The College offers the Arthur O. Eve Higher Education Opportunity Program (HEOP) for students who need special academic and financial assistance. The program provides academic support services, counseling, and financial aid for qualified students to help them achieve academic success.

Fisher grants college credit for satisfactory grades on the Advanced Placement test, the International Baccalaureate (IB) Program exams, and the College-Level Examination Program (CLEP). Only students who receive a 3 or higher in all AP subjects and a 4 or higher on the AP science and language exams are granted Advanced Placement credit. CLEP and IB scoring guidelines are available through the Office of Freshman Admissions. Credit is only granted for subject-specific CLEP exams.

Application and Information

Applications are accepted on a rolling basis. Early-decision applications are due December 1. The admissions application deadline for merit scholarship consideration is February 1.

Although a personal interview is not required for admission, all applicants are encouraged to visit the College. Interviews and campus tours are available weekdays from 8:30 to 4:30 and on specific Saturdays throughout the academic year.

For additional information or an application, students should contact:

Office of Freshman Admissions
St. John Fisher College
3690 East Avenue
Rochester, New York 14618
Phone: 585-385-8064
800-444-4640 (toll-free)
Fax: 585-385-8386
E-mail: admissions@sjfc.edu
Web site: http://www.sjfc.edu/admissions

Kearney Hall, Fisher's main administration building.

ST. JOSEPH'S COLLEGE

BROOKLYN AND PATCHOGUE, NEW YORK

The College

Since 1916, St. Joseph's College has been inspiring students to transform their lives. A private coeducational institution with campuses in Brooklyn and Patchogue, Long Island, the College enrolls 4,885 undergraduates and 508 graduate students in its School of Arts and Sciences and School of Professional and Graduate Studies.

St. Joseph's helps students turn aspirations into accomplishments. In addition to offering a liberal arts education of the highest quality, St. Joseph's offers students an unrivaled degree of personal attention, encouraging them to lead lives characterized by integrity, a commitment to upholding intellectual and spiritual values, social responsibility, and service to others.

St. Joseph's students immerse themselves in learning in ways that go far beyond the classroom, through independent projects, team-building assignments, internships, community service opportunities, and study-abroad programs designed to suit every schedule. And, with just 15 students for every professor on campus, St. Joseph's students easily find mentors to guide them in everything from academics to focusing on future career and life goals.

Although most of St. Joseph's students live off campus, the Brooklyn campus offers student housing through Educational Housing Services at the nearby St. George Residence. Each of the campuses offers a lively atmosphere enriched by social events, athletic competitions, and a Common Hour to encourage students to explore new possibilities for fun, leadership, and connections. On any given day at St. Joseph's, students might come to campus to hear a Pulitzer Prize–winning author, enjoy a jazz concert, join a community service effort, view an art exhibit, attend an athletic event, or engage in a political debate over dinner with other students and professors. Each campus supports over thirty student clubs and activities, including intercollegiate basketball; women's softball, tennis, and volleyball; men's basketball; and coed cross-country. The Long Island campus also offers men's soccer, a women's swim team, and a coed equestrian team.

For undergraduates, St. Joseph's offers fast tracks to advanced degrees through special affiliated programs in accounting, podiatry, and computer science. The School of Professional and Graduate Studies at St. Joseph's College offers a wide range of graduate programs in education, management, and nursing, including the Executive M.B.A., an M.B.A. in accounting, an M.B.A. in health-care management, and the M.S. in nursing.

Location

The Brooklyn campus is located in the Clinton Hill Historic District, a neighborhood where so many of New York's wealthiest citizens once lived that it was dubbed Brooklyn's "Gold Coast" in the 1920s. Today this area is home to several prestigious schools, including the Pratt Institute of Art and the Brooklyn Academy of Music, and serves as a hub of cultural and intellectual activity. This convenient location allows students to enjoy the freedom of a safe, well-landscaped campus easily accessible to New York City by car or public transportation.

St. Joseph's Long Island campus is located in the village of Patchogue on Great South Bay, about 50 miles from Manhattan and 60 miles from Montauk Point. Patchogue offers plenty to do, with fine harbors, shops, restaurants, athletic fields, and tennis courts right in the village. There are lovely parks nearby as well as museums, golf courses, hiking and ski trails, and beaches. Patchogue is easily accessible via Long Island Rail Road, bus service, or ferry. A major regional airport, McArthur Airport, is just minutes away.

Majors and Degrees

Through individual attention, interactive teaching, and intensive advising, St. Joseph's meets students where they are academically, then guides them through the essential next steps to help them stretch intellectually, personally, and professionally. St. Joseph's offers four-year programs leading to B.A. and B.S. degrees at both the Brooklyn and Patchogue campuses, with majors in accounting/business administration, biology, chemistry, child study, computer information science, computer science, criminal justice, economics, English, gerontology, history, human relations, information technology, management, marketing, mathematics, political science, recreation, religious studies, social sciences, Spanish, and speech communication.

No matter what major students choose, they can also earn additional certificates designed to help them delve deeper into specific interests and give them a head start when entering the workforce. Certificate programs include criminology/criminal justice; gerontology; information technology; leadership and supervision; management, marketing, advertising, and public relations; and religious studies.

For students interested in a fast track to an advanced degree after completing their undergraduate studies, St. Joseph's offers special affiliated programs. Through a partnership between St. Joseph's College and Polytechnic University, students at the Brooklyn campus can pursue a bachelor's degree in any field and a master's degree in computer science in a combined B.A./B.S. plus M.S. program. The Brooklyn campus also offers an accelerated biomedical program in cooperation with the New York College of Podiatric Medicine. This program allows students to receive a B.S. in biology and a doctorate in podiatric medicine within six years. Students at both the Brooklyn and Patchogue campuses can earn B.S./M.B.A. degrees in accounting within five years or can choose to pursue preprofessional programs in law, teaching, and numerous health fields, including dentistry, medicine, and optometry.

Those with nontraditional academic backgrounds or with professional training and experience can pursue degrees in community health, general studies, health administration, nursing, and organizational management through St. Joseph's School of Professional and Graduate Studies at either campus.

Academic Programs

The School of Arts and Sciences at each campus operates on the semester system, with additional courses offered in January and during the summer. St. Joseph's students take a core curriculum of 128 credits to graduate; a wide range of choices allows students to tailor their academic programs to their personal and professional needs. The College recognizes the Advanced Placement (AP) Program and offers credit and placement for scores of 3 or above on AP tests. In each case, the score is reviewed by the registrar and/or department chairperson to determine credit and placement.

The School of Professional and Graduate Studies on each campus offers flexible schedules, summer programs, and online courses to meet the needs of working students. Courses may meet for a semester or for six- or twelve-week sessions.

Academic Facilities

The Brooklyn campus is composed of eight buildings, including historic landmark buildings. Students majoring in the widely recognized child-study program use the Dillon Child Study Center, which is a laboratory preschool enrolling approximately 100 hundred students and a teaching and observation resource right on campus. McEntegart Hall, a modern five-level structure, houses the library, audiovisual resource center, curriculum library, archives, and computer labs. Other academic facilities include top-notch biology, chemistry, computer, physics, and psychology research laboratories.

At the Long Island campus, students enjoy 28 acres of well-landscaped grounds and athletic fields. The main building houses administrative and faculty offices; laboratories for biology, chemistry, physics, and psychology; the computer center; art and music studios; the Local History Center; and the Office of Counseling. The library building houses a curriculum library, seminar rooms, administrative offices, and classrooms. This campus also features the John A. Danzi Recreation/Fitness Center, which includes a competition-sized swimming pool, fitness rooms, and a full-sized gym with an elevated track. The 33,000-square-foot Business and Technology Center allows St. Joseph's students to integrate technology into their studies. The Clare Rose Playhouse serves as a cultural center where students and local communities can explore theater production and performance.

A high-speed fiber-optic network connects all offices, institutional facilities, computer laboratories, and libraries on both the Brooklyn and Long Island campuses. Direct Internet access is available to all students and faculty and staff members through the College's server. The integrated online library system enables students to locate and check out books at either campus and also provides links to online databases and other electronic information sources.

Costs

The annual full-time tuition rate for undergraduates is $15,400, or $505 per credit.

Financial Aid

St. Joseph's offers scholarships and grants-in-aid. Students who wish to apply for either form of assistance must file the Free Application for Federal Student Aid (FAFSA) and a state aid form. After a student has been accepted to the College and all financial aid forms are processed, the Financial Aid Office prepares aid packages that usually consist of federal, state, and College funds. St. Joseph's is fully approved for veterans. Campus work-study programs are also available.

Faculty

With more than 400 faculty members who are widely respected scholars in their fields and a student-faculty ratio of 15:1, St. Joseph's students benefit from close professional and personal working relationships with their professors. Faculty members serve as academic advisers, are active on student affairs committees, and act as moderators in student organizations.

Admission Requirements

St. Joseph's College seeks a diverse student body and welcomes applications from high school students, transfer students, and those students who may have a nontraditional academic background. The College offers programs to serve all of these groups.

Students who wish to enter as freshmen are expected to have completed at least 18 units of college-preparatory work by the end of their senior year. This should include the following distribution: 4 years of English, 2 years of foreign language, 3 years of mathematics, 2 years of science, and 4 years of social studies. Applicants interested in accounting, allied health fields, biology, business administration, chemistry, or mathematics should have more extensive backgrounds in mathematics and science. In addition, the College requires the submission of official results from the critical reading and math sections of the SAT.

St. Joseph's College accepts a block transfer of credits from students holding an A.A. or A.S. degree in certain majors from an accredited junior or community college. All other transfers are considered on an individual basis.

Application and Information

Admission is offered on a rolling basis. Applications and supporting documents should be submitted online or to the appropriate school. The College reviews each application carefully and usually sends a decision one month after receiving all necessary credentials. For more information and an online application, students can access the Web site at http://www.sjcny.edu.

Brooklyn Campus:
Director of Admissions
St. Joseph's College
245 Clinton Avenue
Brooklyn, New York 11205
Phone: 718-636-6868

Long Island Campus:
Director of Admissions
St. Joseph's College
155 West Roe Boulevard
Patchogue, New York 11772
Phone: 631-447-3219
Web site: http://www.sjcny.edu

Both campuses of St. Joseph's College provide up-to-date science, computer, and psychology laboratories.

ST. LAWRENCE UNIVERSITY

CANTON, NEW YORK

The University

St. Lawrence University invites students to learn new ways of seeing the world, voicing ideas, and connecting with others. Graduates have the tools with which to think clearly, express themselves persuasively, and step into the world community with an understanding of their responsibility to all people and to the planet.

Founded in 1856, St. Lawrence is the oldest continuously coeducational degree-granting institution of higher learning in New York State. Initially established as a theology school for the Universalist Church, it quickly evolved into the liberal arts college that it is today. St. Lawrence is a private, nonsectarian university of approximately 2,100 undergraduate men and women, with a small graduate program in education. St. Lawrence is known for its residential/academic First-Year Program, its international study opportunities and area studies programs, its students' strong interest in the environment and the outdoors, and its friendliness.

St. Lawrence students are self-starters. The self-designed major is popular, intramural sports leagues are always full, and more than 100 student organizations serve broad interests from communication to community service and creativity to social action. The University routinely hosts well-known speakers, and concerts, plays, and films are regulars on the weekly events calendar. A 60,000-square-foot Student Center opened in winter 2004.

St. Lawrence students have historically placed high value on athletic activity, and a large number participate in varsity, intramural, or club sports. The thirty-two varsity men's and women's teams compete at the Division III level of the NCAA, with the exception of men's and women's ice hockey, which compete in Division I. Recreational facilities include cross-country ski and running trails, indoor and outdoor tennis courts, an athletic complex with a gymnasium, two field houses, a 133-station fitness center, a three-story climbing wall, a pool, an ice rink, an equestrian center, a boathouse, a golf course, a nine-lane all-weather track, an artificial turf field for lacrosse and field hockey, nine squash courts, and newly renovated performance fields for soccer, football, baseball, and softball.

Residential life is an important aspect of the St. Lawrence experience. The University's innovative and highly regarded First-Year Program creates communities where groups of approximately 30–35 first-year students live and learn together. In the upperclass years, students can choose from traditional dormitories, Greek chapter houses, and suites and theme cottages that focus on student interests such as low-impact living and community service. Seniors may also choose townhouses. St. Lawrence sponsors a full range of student services, from counseling to career planning.

Location

St. Lawrence is situated on a 1,000-acre campus on the edge of the village of Canton, New York (population 6,400), the seat of St. Lawrence County. Canton, with its Victorian homes, tree-lined streets, village green, and small shops, is typical of college towns throughout the Northeast. Students and residents often mix in stores, at athletic events, and in community projects. Ottawa, Canada's capital, is 75 minutes to the north, while Lake Placid, one of America's hiking and skiing meccas, is 90 minutes to the southeast.

Majors and Degrees

St. Lawrence offers the Bachelor of Arts and Bachelor of Science degrees; students can choose from thirty-five majors and have the option of picking one of thirty-six minors. Combined five-year programs with other institutions are in place in engineering and management, and specialized advising is offered in preparation for postgraduate work in dentistry, law, medicine, and veterinary medicine.

Academic Programs

St. Lawrence's foremost mission is to provide its students with a liberal arts education. Students complete requirements in six areas and concentrated work in a major field as well as demonstrating competence in writing. Close faculty-student interaction is a hallmark of a St. Lawrence education, and every semester many students engage in independent or honors projects, often working with professors on joint research projects that lead to publication in leading scholarly journals. A senior project is required in most majors.

Off-Campus Programs

Nearly 50 percent of St. Lawrence students study in one of the University's international programs during their collegiate careers. St. Lawrence operates programs in Australia, Austria, Canada, China, Costa Rica, Denmark, England, France, India, Italy, Japan, Kenya, Spain, and Trinidad and Tobago. In addition, the University's membership in the International Student Exchange Program permits students to directly enroll in universities in more than thirty-five additional countries. St. Lawrence also operates programs at two other campuses in the U.S.: Fisk University in Nashville, Tennessee, and American University in Washington, D.C. St. Lawrence also administers its own Adirondack Semester Program.

Academic Facilities

Owen D. Young Library and Launders Science Library contain more than half a million volumes as well as electronic resources and ample space for reading and research. Griffiths Arts Center is the home of the University's fine arts and performance and communication studies programs, as well as two theaters and an art gallery in which selections from St. Lawrence's 7,000-piece collection are frequently shown. Facilities for the arts have undergone expansion into the building that was formerly the student center, and the Newell Center for Arts Technology opened in spring 2007. A unified science complex houses the Departments of Biology, Chemistry, Physics, Psychology, Geology, and Mathematics, Computer Science and Statistics and is connected via a covered hallway to the science library and computing center. A new 120,000-square-foot Hall of Science opened in fall 2007. Richardson Hall, St. Lawrence's oldest building and on the National Register of Historic Places, is home to the English and religious studies departments. Other departments can be found in academic buildings clustered on one part of the campus so classrooms are not a long walk apart.

Costs

The comprehensive fee for 2007–08 was $44,660, including tuition, fees, and average room and board. Students should allow approximately $1450 for books and personal expenses.

Financial Aid

St. Lawrence awards both merit scholarships and need-based financial aid. More than 80 percent of the University's students receive some form of financial assistance, including scholarships, grants, student loans, and campus jobs. St. Lawrence is committed to assisting as many students as possible and will recognize academic and personal achievement in making financial aid decisions. To apply for need-based financial aid, students must file the Free Application for Federal Student Aid (FAFSA) between January 1 and February 1 and request that the results be sent directly to St. Lawrence. Submission of the Financial Aid PROFILE form is encouraged; completion of the St. Lawrence supplemental form is an acceptable alternative to the PROFILE.

Faculty

The 190 members of St. Lawrence's faculty are teachers and scholars. While teaching and advising are their primary responsibilities, they are also active researchers, artists, performers, and regular contributors in their academic disciplines. Faculty members teach all courses at St. Lawrence; no undergraduate courses are taught by graduate students. Active teaching assistant and tutoring programs, involving qualified upperclass students, are closely supervised by faculty members. The student-faculty ratio is about 11:1. Faculty members hold regular office hours, serve as academic advisers to students, and frequently take part in extracurricular activities on campus.

Student Government

The Thelomathesian Society, comprising all students on campus, is governed by a senate of elected representatives. The senate distributes funds in support of student activities and provides two student delegates to the University's Board of Trustees.

Admission Requirements

St. Lawrence seeks students who can be successful in a demanding academic program and who can contribute to the quality of life of the community. The University is committed to enrolling students who represent the widest possible diversity of economic, social, ethnic, and geographic backgrounds. Academic preparation and ability are the most important criteria, but demonstrated ability in the creative arts, athletics, or social service is also a measure of a student's potential to benefit St. Lawrence. Candidates may choose whether or not they submit standardized test scores (SAT or ACT). A campus visit is strongly encouraged, and interviews may be scheduled on campus or off campus in certain areas.

Although there is no set distribution of required high school courses, successful applicants typically show strong preparation in the humanities, the social sciences, mathematics, and the natural sciences. Honors work, Advanced Placement, and International Baccalaureate courses are opportunities for applicants to demonstrate intellectual maturity and curiosity, qualities highly valued in the admission process.

Application and Information

St. Lawrence uses the Common Application, with the St. Lawrence Supplement, as its sole application form. The application is available on the University's Web site. The application processing fee is $60. Regular decision applications should be submitted by February 1, with notification by late March. Students who decide that St. Lawrence is their first choice may apply under one of the early decision deadlines: November 15 or January 15. In each case, notification is one month after the deadline. Transfer candidates should submit applications no later than November 1 for the spring semester or March 1 for the fall semester.

To request an application or for more information, students should contact:

Office of Admissions and Financial Aid
St. Lawrence University
Canton, New York 13617
Phone: 315-229-5261
800-285-1856 (toll-free)
E-mail: admissions@stlawu.edu
Web site: http://www.stlawu.edu

The St. Lawrence University Student Center.

ST. THOMAS AQUINAS COLLEGE

SPARKILL, NEW YORK

The College

St. Thomas Aquinas College (STAC) was founded in 1952 as a three-year teacher-training college with 30 students. Today, the College offers over sixty majors, minors, and specializations and has a total student body of 2,700 in all programs, on and off campus. Much growth and development has taken place over the College's history. The College offers a Master of Science in Education, with concentrations in literacy education, special education, and educational leadership as well as postgraduate certificate programs in literacy and special education. The College also offers a quarterly weekend Master of Business Administration (M.B.A.) program with concentrations in finance, management, and marketing. St. Thomas offers a Master of Science in Teaching program for individuals without a background in teacher education who are seeking a career change. Certification is offered in childhood education, grades 1–6; childhood education and special education, grades 1–6; and adolescence education, grades 7–12. The College is home to New York University's Master in Social Work program, and St. John's University's Master in Library Science program is also offered through the College's campus.

The College's most dramatic growth has occurred to meet the challenges of the twenty-first century. Capital improvements were made and new facilities added, so that the main campus now consists of twenty-one buildings on 48 acres. The suburban campus includes two residential complexes: Aquinas Village, which consists of self-contained town-house units that house 250 students, and the McNelis Commons, which consists of town-house residential units that house 400 students and a common dining hall and laundry building. Approximately 40 percent of the College's full-time student population resides on campus.

Extracurricular activities are provided through some thirty-five different organizations, including the Spartan Volunteers, a community service program; a student-run radio station (WSTK); and the student-edited campus newspaper and yearbook. The College has excellent sports facilities, and several of its athletic teams have competed in national championships. The College fields NCAA Division II teams in men's and women's cross-country, golf, indoor track and field, and tennis; women's basketball, lacrosse, soccer, and softball; and men's baseball, basketball, and soccer. Intramural athletics are also available.

The College has a campus ministry office, a health office, and residence life, career placement, and counseling services.

Location

The College is located in Sparkill, a hamlet in southern Rockland County, New York, 16 miles north of New York City and adjacent to Bergen County, New Jersey. Rockland County, a sprawling suburban area of about 300,000 people, is rich in history and convenient to the vast cultural and educational resources of New York City.

Majors and Degrees

St. Thomas Aquinas College's business administration division awards Bachelor of Science (B.S.) degrees in accounting (and accounting as a dual degree with a Master of Business Administration degree), business administration, finance, and marketing. Minors are offered in business administration, international business, and management information systems. Specializations are offered in management relations/industrial and organizational psychology. The humanities division awards Bachelor of Arts (B.A.) degrees in art therapy and fine arts and a B.S. in graphic design, which are all also offered as minors. B.A. degrees include communication arts, English, philosophy and religious studies, Romance languages, and Spanish. A journalism minor is also offered. The natural sciences and mathematics division offers B.S. degrees in applied mathematics, computer and information sciences, and mathematics. B.S. degrees are offered in biology, medical technology, and natural sciences and, beginning in fall 2008, forensic science. There are specializations in biology, chemistry, and physics. Dual-degree options are also offered and are described below. The social sciences division awards B.S. degrees in criminal justice, psychology, recreation and leisure studies, and social science and a B.A. in history. The division of teacher education offers programs in grades 1–6 childhood education, the same plus special education, and grades 7–12 adolescence education, the latter offering certification in biology, English, mathematics, natural science with either biology or chemistry, social sciences, and Spanish.

The College offers a five-year dual-degree program in mathematics/engineering with the George Washington University (GWU) or Manhattan College. Students study at St. Thomas for three years. After completion of their final two years at either GWU or Manhattan, they earn a B.S. in mathematics from STAC and a B.S. in engineering from one of the latter two institutions. The College also offers several dual-degree options in biology: a dual degree in biology (B.S. from STAC) and biomedical engineering (M.S. from Polytechnic University), a dual degree in biology (B.S. from STAC) and physical therapy (D.P.T. from New York Medical College), a dual degree in biology (B.S. from STAC) and chiropractic (D.C. from New York Chiropractic College), and a dual degree in biology (B.S. from STAC) and podiatry (D.P.M. from New York College of Podiatric Medicine). St. Thomas offers a 63-credit prepharmacy program that enables a qualified student to transfer into the Arnold and Marie Schwartz College of Pharmacy and Health Sciences of Long Island University. There are several other strategic alliances, such as a guaranteed slot at the St. John's University School of Law in New York and a similar program with Barry University School of Law in Florida that includes scholarship funds. St. Thomas seeks out additional strategic opportunities for its undergraduate and graduate students on a regular basis; students should contact the College for information about new alliances.

Academic Programs

The College maintains academic flexibility and is committed to responding to the needs of individual students. The College strives to develop students who are not only generally educated but also possess advanced knowledge in specialized areas, are prepared for further study, and have the background to undertake fulfilling careers. To earn a bachelor's degree, students must complete a total of 120 semester hours, including a minimum of 51 credits in a core curriculum; complete all requirements for the specific major; and complete the final 30 hours at St. Thomas. The College awards up to 30 credits for life experience and up to 30 credits for achievement on the College-Level Examination Program (CLEP). The College operates on a semester calendar (trimester on the M.B.A. level). Students may enroll in classes in the fall, winter (a one-month session), spring, and summer (three separate sessions). Classes are scheduled during the day and evening, and students are permitted considerable academic flexibility in planning their programs.

Students can pursue independent study and internships, and many majors require a field practicum. The College maintains an active Center for Academic Excellence as a resource for developmental skills, and students are encouraged to meet regularly with faculty advisers for academic guidance and career direction.

Several unusual programs supplement the traditional academic areas. The College has a widely recognized program for college-age learning-disabled students, called the Pathways Program (at an additional cost). The College also participates in the New York State Higher Education Opportunity Program for economically and academically disadvantaged students and provides an Honors Program for exceptionally qualified students. The full-tuition-scholarship Honors Program provides a summer of study at Oxford University.

Off-Campus Programs

The College offers a campus interchange program involving three other fully accredited colleges (Barry University in Miami Shores, Florida; Dominican College of San Rafael in San Rafael, California; and Aquinas College in Grand Rapids, Michigan) through which a student may attend a semester at one of the participating colleges during the junior year.

The College offers courses at local businesses and industries and an associate degree program at West Point for eligible students at the United States Military Academy and Stewart Army Subpost.

A study-abroad program is offered through the College, providing students with the opportunity to study at colleges and universities in such places as Brazil, Canada, England, Hungary, Ireland, Italy, and Morocco. Several other locations are available.

Academic Facilities

The College's most dramatic growth occurred during the last decade as it modernized to meet the challenges of the twenty-first century. Costello Hall houses the science laboratories, technology theaters, and Azarian-McCullough Art Gallery. Spellman Hall houses a multiroom technology corridor with state-of-the-art technology and language labs. Lougheed Library provides a variety of online research opportunities for students. Aquinas Hall houses athletic facilities and a new fitness center. Maguire Hall is home to classrooms, art studios, and the newly renovated Sullivan Theater, and Marian Hall houses accounting labs and a communications studio. Additional meeting areas are provided in the Romano Student-Alumni Center and in the two residence complexes, McNelis Commons and Aquinas Village.

Costs

For 2007–08, the tuition for full-time study (12 to 16 credits per semester) was $18,400. Room and board at the College Commons cost $9400. Certain studio, laboratory, and computer courses carry fees.

Financial Aid

In 2006–07, 75 percent of the student body received financial aid. The College is committed to providing competent but needy students with the resources necessary to continue their education. Students who lack adequate financial resources should submit the Financial Aid Form to the College Scholarship Service and to the College. Financial aid is usually granted in a package of awards. Financial aid programs include Presidential Grants, special scholarships, athletic grants, Federal Pell Grants, Federal Supplemental Educational Opportunity Grants, New York State Tuition Assistance Program (TAP) grants, Federal Perkins Loans, Federal Stafford Student Loans, Federal PLUS loans, and Federal Work-Study Program awards.

Faculty

The faculty has 75 full-time and 55 part-time members; 75 percent have earned doctorates. The student-faculty ratio is 17:1. All faculty members participate in the academic advising of students and serve on College committees. Many serve as advisers to extracurricular activities.

Student Government

The Student Government consists of elected members who officially represent the student body, are responsible for planning and implementing student-originated programs, and coordinate and oversee all extracurricular organizations. Through its various offices, students play a vital part in offering consultation on new policies, planning social and cultural events, managing student funds, and operating the judicial system. In addition, the All-College Forum, which is composed of elected students, faculty members, alumni, administrators, and trustees, meets regularly to discuss policies, procedures, long-range plans, and any problems affecting the College.

Admission Requirements

All applicants must have successfully completed an approved secondary school program or the equivalent, including four years in English, two years in college-preparatory mathematics, at least two years in science, one year in a single foreign language, and at least one year in American history. Applicants whose high school background varies from the recommended pattern are considered if they demonstrate interest and ability. Freshman applicants must submit the application for admission, including an essay, high school transcripts, SAT or ACT scores, and their guidance counselor's recommendation. Transfer students must submit the application and official transcripts of all previous college work. All students are encouraged to visit the campus for an interview. An academic evaluation is prepared for every matriculant.

Application and Information

Candidates should submit completed application forms to the Admissions and Financial Aid Office and must request that their official transcripts be sent to the Admissions Office from their school. Students are notified of the admission decision on a rolling basis upon receipt of all the necessary credentials.

The College does not discriminate against students, faculty and staff members, and other beneficiaries on the basis of race, color, national origin, gender, age, sexual orientation, disability, marital status, genetic predisposition, carrier status, veteran status, or religious affiliation in admission to or in the provision of its programs and services. The Section 504 Coordinator, the Title IX Coordinator, and the Age Act Coordinator is the Executive Director of Human Resources, Marian Hall, 845-398-4038.

For more information or an application, students should contact:

Admissions and Financial Aid Office
St. Thomas Aquinas College
125 Route 340
Sparkill, New York 10976-1050
Phone: 800-999-STAC (toll-free)
Web site: http://www.stac.edu

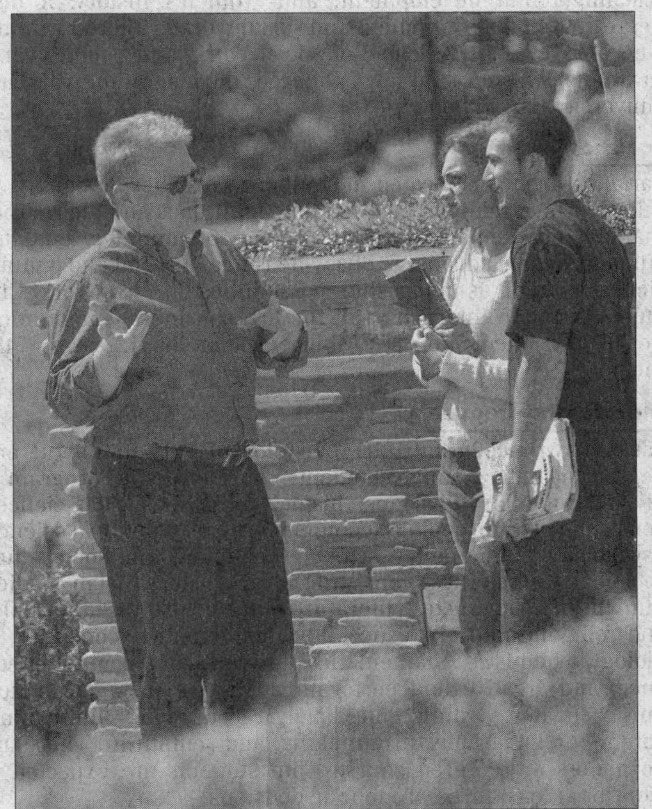

A view of the campus at St. Thomas Aquinas College.

SARAH LAWRENCE COLLEGE

BRONXVILLE, NEW YORK

The College

Sarah Lawrence College is a model for individualized education among liberal arts colleges. It offers an innovative program of study that encourages students to take intellectual risks and explore highly challenging topics as they take an active role in the planning and pursuit of their education.

The College's forty-six buildings are set on a 41-acre campus combining the charm of a rural English village with award-winning contemporary buildings. There are 1,391 undergraduates and 318 graduate students. Approximately 40 students attend the Center for Continuing Education, which is a flexible, supportive program for returning adult students. The College draws its students from across the country and around the world. Nearly 90 percent live on campus. Sarah Lawrence has an active campus, offering opportunities for involvement in clubs, student organizations, dramatic productions, musical performances, literary societies, student publications, student government, and athletics. There are no sororities or fraternities.

The College is accredited by the Middle States Association of Colleges and Schools and approved by the New York State Education Department.

On the graduate level, the College offers programs in writing, theater, dance, human genetics, health advocacy, art of teaching, child development, and women's history. A dual degree in child development and social work is offered with the New York University School of Social Work, and a joint degree in women's history and law is offered in cooperation with Pace University Law School.

Location

Sarah Lawrence is located in southern Westchester County, 15 miles north of midtown Manhattan. Main roads and the railroad make it possible to reach the city in 30 minutes, enabling students to take advantage of a wide range of social and cultural riches as well as internship possibilities in New York City. Students obtain internships in the arts, business, communications, law, medicine, publishing, social services, and the theater.

Majors and Degrees

Sarah Lawrence grants the Bachelor of Arts in liberal arts degree to undergraduate students. The academic program is divided into four divisions: history and the social sciences, consisting of anthropology, economics, history, political science, psychology, public policy, science technology and society, and sociology; humanities, consisting of art history, Asian studies, film history, languages, literature, music history, philosophy, and religion; natural sciences and mathematics, consisting of biology, chemistry, mathematics, physics, and computer science; and creative and performing arts, consisting of dance, music, theater, writing, and visual arts (drawing, filmmaking, painting, photography, printmaking, and sculpture). There are no majors or required courses, but students are expected to work in at least three of the four divisions.

Academic Programs

Each student works with his or her faculty adviser, called a don in the Oxford and Cambridge tradition, to plan a course of study. Most courses consist of two parts: the seminar, limited to 15 students, and the conference, a private, biweekly meeting with the seminar professor. In conference, students create individual projects that extend the material assigned in the seminar and connect it to their academic and career goals. In the performing arts—dance, music, and theater—students' work makes up several components that together constitute a full course. Although transcripts of official grades are available, written evaluations that more clearly define strengths, weaknesses, and progress are provided to each student.

The College operates on the semester system, with terms beginning in early September and late January.

Off-Campus Programs

Within the U.S., Sarah Lawrence College has established exchange programs with Reed College in Portland, Oregon, and Eugene Lang College, the undergraduate division of New School University in New York City's historic Greenwich Village. Outside the United States, the College sponsors academic programs in Florence, Catania (Sicily), Havana, Oxford, and Paris as well as a program in cooperation with the British American Drama Academy in London. Students may also study in other countries around the world. Students can combine on-campus study with off-campus fieldwork and internships at a variety of places, including art museums, theaters, and hospitals and with orchestras, dance companies, publications, social action programs, government agencies, and businesses.

Academic Facilities

The College's facilities include classrooms, laboratories, and computer centers; a college-wide academic network to which all students' rooms are fully wired; a 90MB connection via two access points to the Internet; a library with 283,000 volumes and 916 periodicals, which is linked by computer to more than 6,000 other libraries; the Performing Arts Center, consisting of four theaters, a dance studio, and a concert hall; a music building, including a music library; a Sports Center with a competition pool, basketball and squash courts, a fitness center, an aerobics room, and a rowing tank; a laboratory preschool; a science center; and the Center for Continuing Education. A 60,000-square-foot visual arts center includes a 200-seat lecture hall/film theater, a café, new media facilities, a sound stage, darkrooms, workshops, printmaking facilities, and eight studios—each with individual work areas for sculpture, painting, and visual fundamentals.

Costs

Tuition for the 2007–08 academic year was $37,230. The costs of a room and the average meal plan were $12,720. The College fee was $860.

Financial Aid

All applicants with financial need are considered for Sarah Lawrence College aid programs and all federal campus-based programs. About half of the students receive financial aid. The awarding of institutional funds is based on a determination of the student's financial need. Students are expected to apply for financial aid from the Federal Pell Grant Program and from their state scholarship and grant programs. Students must submit the Financial Aid PROFILE and the Free Application for Federal Student Aid (FAFSA) by February 1.

Faculty

Sarah Lawrence's student-faculty ratio is 6:1, one of the lowest in the country. Students work closely with an exceptional faculty of respected scholars, writers, artists, scientists, historians, and social scientists. Each faculty member is a committed teacher who attaches great importance to individual work with students. Ninety percent of Sarah Lawrence's faculty members in the sciences, social sciences, and the humanities hold a Ph.D. or terminal degree. Faculty members in the arts have achieved demonstrable excellence in the fields of music, dance, theater, the visual arts, and writing.

Student Government

The Sarah Lawrence College student body is self-governed by the Student Senate and the Student Life Committee. The Student Senate is the principal policymaking and legislative body for matters concerning student affairs.

Admission Requirements

Sarah Lawrence College accepts first-year students for the fall semester and transfer applicants for both the fall and spring semesters. The College recognizes that intelligence and creative power can be expressed in many different ways and is willing to look at both traditional and nontraditional criteria in assessing applicants. The completion of 16 units of secondary school work or the equivalent is the standard academic requirement for first-year admission. The College specifies these units as follows: 4 units required of English; a minimum of 2 units required (3–4 units recommended) each of mathematics, science, foreign language, and history; and 3–4 units recommended of social studies.

High school seniors who consider Sarah Lawrence their first-choice college and who wish to be informed of an admission decision early in their senior year may apply as early decision candidates. The Admission Committee also considers as early admission applicants those students with very strong academic qualifications and personal maturity who have completed three years of high school and who wish to apply after their junior year of high school.

The College welcomes transfer applications from students who have completed at least one full year of college and from students who expect, in qualifying for the Bachelor of Arts degree, to spend at least two consecutive years at Sarah Lawrence College. (Students with less than one full year of credits who have matriculated at another college may apply for first-year admission with possible advanced standing.) Approximately 50 transfers matriculate each year from a wide range of postsecondary institutions.

Sophomores, juniors, and seniors enrolled at other institutions may apply to the Sarah Lawrence Guest Year Program for one semester or a complete year of full-time study at the College. Guests attend Sarah Lawrence to concentrate in a particular discipline not offered at their home institution, work with respected master teachers one-on-one in conferences, and take advantage of the facilities of New York City in conjunction with rigorous academic study. Students who have not matriculated elsewhere but wish to enroll in one or two specific courses for credit may apply as nonmatriculated students.

Sarah Lawrence does not consider the SAT or ACT scores in the application process. The Test of English as a Foreign Language (TOEFL) must be taken by students who speak English as a second language and who have not been educated in an English-language medium. A personal interview on campus or with a local alumna/alumnus is strongly recommended for all applicants.

Sarah Lawrence College admits students regardless of race, color, sex, sexual orientation, disability, or national origin and thereafter accords them all the rights and privileges generally made available to students at the College. The College is strongly committed to basing judgments about individuals upon their qualifications and abilities and to protecting individual rights of privacy, association, belief, and expression.

Application and Information

Students interested in attending Sarah Lawrence College should request application materials from the Office of Admission. The application deadline for first-year students for the fall semester is January 1. The notification date is early April, and the reply date is May 1. The College has two early decision programs. The fall early decision deadline is November 15, and notification is made on December 15. The winter early decision deadline is January 1, and notification is made on February 15.

The application deadline for transfer students for fall semester is March 1. Notification is in April and reply is in May. The application deadline for transfer students for spring semester is November 1. Notification and reply are in late November or early December.

Office of Admission
Sarah Lawrence College
Bronxville, New York 10708
Phone: 914-395-2510
800-888-2858 (toll-free)
Fax: 914-395-2515
E-mail: slcadmit@sarahlawrence.edu
Web site: http://www.sarahlawrence.edu

Students relax on Westland's lawn.

COLLEGE DATA CENTER • NEW YORK

SCHOOL OF VISUAL ARTS

NEW YORK, NEW YORK

The School

The School of Visual Arts (SVA) is currently the largest independent college of art in the country, with a full-time enrollment of approximately 3,000. Students who choose SVA are often attracted by the breadth and professional standing of the faculty members, the passion of the student body, the rigors of the curriculum, the industry standards within the studio facilities, and the energy and excitement that is New York City.

Location

Located in the heart of New York City, SVA offers students the opportunity to become involved in one of America's largest and most vibrant cities, the art capital of the world. The energy, the spirit, and the desire to be the best—three characteristics of New York City—constantly challenge and inspire the students. The unparalleled leadership and accomplishment of the city's arts and design communities demand excellence, and the School of Visual Arts prepares students to compete successfully in this environment.

Majors and Degrees

SVA offers Bachelor of Fine Arts (B.F.A.) degrees in advertising, animation, cartooning, computer art, film and video, fine arts, graphic design, illustration, interior design, photography, and visual and critical studies.

Academic Programs

The curriculum has been designed to prepare students to graduate as working professionals in the arts. Consequently, the four-year curriculum is designed to allow students greater freedom of choice in electives and requirements with each succeeding year. The first year of the program, a foundation year, ensures the mastery of basic skills in the chosen discipline as well as in writing and art history. After the first year, students choose their own area of concentration and, under the guidance of the academic advisers and faculty members, pursue their own individual goals. The B.F.A. degree programs require the completion of 120 credits, including 72 studio credits, 12 in art history, 6 in electives, and 30 in humanities and sciences.

Off-Campus Programs

Students have the opportunity to participate in art programs abroad during the summer semester in Barcelona, Florence, and Toulouse. SVA also offers third-year students in photography, graphic design, illustration, interior design, film and video, and fine arts the opportunity to study abroad at an AIAS (Association of Independent Art Schools) affiliate in Europe.

Academic Facilities

The Animation Department has fully equipped animation studios, a Stop Motion Control Studio, digital pencil test facilities, a Motion Control Pencil test stand and control tables, and a new, state-of-the-art Digital Compositing Ink and Paint facility. Film students use Bolex cameras, Arriflex S camera packages, and Arriflex BL camera packages. The department also houses a large inventory of lighting and grip equipment.

Sound inventory includes Fostex digital time code recorders, Sony D-10 Pro II DAT recorders, Nagra recorders, an audio transfer facility, and a large collection of specialized microphones and mixers. There is also a film library that houses more than 1,500 titles from a variety of film, video, DVD, laser, and tape formats. A 100-seat film theater is available for cinema studies classes.

Students utilize a variety of digital cameras: VX-1000, VX-2000, PD-100, and PD-150 digital video cameras and more than thirty Sony digital handycams. Thesis and third-year students have access to ENG-style professional camcorders, including UVW-100, DSR-370, and DXC-537 cameras and support accessories, including production monitors, remotes, follow focus units, and matte boxes.

Postproduction facilities include a state-of-the-art Avid nonlinear editing center containing Avid X-press DVs, a newly created Final Cut Pro facility, and a new digital postproduction audio facility complete with Pro Tools Mix24 suites. The department also supports multiplatform dub rooms with Beta SP, DVCAM, DVCPRO, S-VHS, DAT decks, and a telecine projection system.

In the Fine Arts Department, there are eleven large, well-ventilated studios with slop sinks and storage closets for foundation and second- and third-year drawing and painting workshops. Fourth-year students have their own studio spaces.

Printmaking studios are fully equipped for etching, lithography, silkscreen, papermaking, and woodcut/lino and mono print. The litho room has five lithography presses and a graining sink; etching has four etching presses, a rosin box, and hot plates; and silkscreen has a 48-inch by 48-inch exposure unit and screen darkroom and reclaiming facilities. There is a complete platemaking darkroom containing a flip top Nu Arc exposing unit for making photo lithography and etching plates, a developing sink, and a plate cutter. In addition to traditional hand-drawn separations, students can create digital color separations in the printmaking output facilities. The facilities contain four Macintosh G5 computers and one 7200 Macintosh used as a scanning station (8.5-inch by 14-inch maximum scanning area). Each computer has a Zip drive and Adobe Photoshop, Adobe Illustrator, and QuarkXPress installed. A large output laser printer (12-inch by 36-inch maximum) and a Toshiba photocopier (11-inch by 17-inch maximum) are available for creating separations.

The Sculpture Center has facilities for welding, woodworking, stone carving, ceramics, and performance and video art. The wood, metal, stone, and ceramic facilities are equipped with everything artists need for the physical construction of their work. The woodshop has a table saw, a sliding compound miter saw, a panel saw, a table sander, four band saws, and two drill presses. In the metalshop are three MIG welders, two ARC welders, one TIG welder, two plasma cutters, a horizontal and a vertical band saw, a sand blaster, and OXY-ACE torches. Stone facilities have air hammers and stone chisels. The ceramic studio has two electric kilns that fire up to cone 7, a clay extruder, six potter's wheels, and a slab roller. In addition to these facilities, there is a toolroom stocked with power hand tools and safety equipment. The Sculpture Center also has a performance area, a live-model area, and a slide room for presentations. The video computer lab has seven digital video cameras, three video projectors, and a postproduction facility consisting of three G3 and G4 iMacs and two G4 iMacs with Photoshop, Illustrator, Flash, Final Cut Pro, and DVD Pro software, which allows for professional editing and special effects. The center also manages an audiovisual facility with slide and video projectors, VCRs, DVDs, monitors, and audio equipment.

Fine Arts majors can choose to concentrate in traditional mediums of painting, drawing, sculpture, or printmaking; in recent trends in installation, computer art, or time-based media in computer, video, or performance art; in alternative media; or any combination of the above.

Graphic design and advertising students use the Digital Imaging Center, which houses 140 Macintosh G5 computers with CD/DVD burners. Peripheral drives include floppy drives, Zip drives, and Compact Flash/Smart Media card readers. There are sixteen high-definition flatbed scanners, a Polaroid film recorder, and a Polaroid slide scanner as well as nine high-quality laser printers, including two HP color printers and three Fuji dye-sub printers. The Broadcast Media room has Sony DV decks, JVC S-VHS VCRs, and Sony NTSC monitors. Students have access to Nikon digital cameras and Sony DV video cameras. Software includes Adobe Photoshop, Adobe Illustrator, Adobe Premiere, Adobe After Effects, QuarkXPress, Macromedia Director, Macromedia Dreamweaver, Macromedia Flash, Apple Final Cut Pro, Cleaner, and other print media, Web design, and broadcast design applications. The equipment and software enables the students to produce and output work at a superior and highly professional quality. In addition, the Digital Imaging Center's workshop has twenty-two drafting tables for drawing, cutting, and mounting artwork for presentations. The workshop also provides the students with color copiers.

SVA's Computer Art Department continues to feature the finest and most powerful digital tools available. Currently, there are twenty-one SGI, twenty-one Intergraph, twenty-one Boxx, and 171 Apple Macintosh computers in fifteen instructional labs and DV editing facilities. The department features the latest software applications, including AliasWavefront Maya, SoftImage, Discreet Logic Flint, 3D Studio Max, Adobe AfterEffects, Adobe Photoshop, MacroMedia Director, and QuarkXPress. Computer art majors can choose to concentrate their studies in the fields of computer animation, interactive media, or dynamic media.

The Photography Department's black-and-white darkrooms are equipped with ninety omega D5XL enlargers for printing everything from Minox to 4-inch by 5-inch negatives. There is also an enlarger specifically designed to handle 8-inch by 10-inch negatives. Twenty-seven of these enlargers are equipped with dichroic color heads for making RA-4 prints. SVA also houses nine black-and-white film-processing workstations and two 30-inch Kreonite Promate RA4 processors. The color print viewing area is equipped with GTI 5000K viewing booths. The BFA Photo Department's two state-of-the-art digital labs contain a total of forty-three Macintosh G5 student workstations, and two instructor's G5s with projectors. All of these computers are loaded with digital-imaging software, including Photoshop 7, Illustrator 10, and Final Cut Pro and all of the necessary hardware and software to download images and video from digital cameras. All of the G5s are equipped with DVD/CD burners.

In addition, the labs contain six Nikon Coolscan film scanners capable of scanning 120mm and 35mm transparencies, four Epson Perfection flatbed scanners for reflective material up to 11-inch by 17-inch, and eight Epson Stylus Photo 870 printers. All of these workstations are networked together and provide Internet access for students. The seven shooting studios are included in the Photography Department's computer network, and each studio is set up with an iMac equipped with a CD burner, a Zip 250, and a Smart Card reader to allow the students to download and save digital images. Digital cameras available for student use include seventeen Canon D30 digital camera kits, twenty Nikon Coolpix 950, 990, and 4500 digital cameras, and thirty Sony digital video cameras. Students have access to a wide range of studio equipment, including Profoto strobes; Vivitar, Quantum, and Lumidyne portable flashes; Lowel quartz lights; Ari quartz lights; and an assortment of lighting accessories. SVA also provides large- and medium-format cameras for the students to use. SVA's stock includes twelve Hasselblad kits, seven Mamiya RZ67 kits, ten Mamiya 645 kits, six Mamiya M7 kits, four Contax 645 AF kits, Toyo 4x5 view and field cameras, a variety of Polaroid cameras, and 8x10 studio and field cameras.

The Interior Design program is FIDER-accredited. The curriculum integrates well-known professional faculty members and state-of-the-art technology with the traditions of drawing and drafting, with an emphasis on design. Classes are held in a studio environment. Each student has a personal 3-foot by 5-foot fully equipped drafting station and unlimited use of computers. Architectural Desktop, Form Z Radiosity, and 3D Studio VIZ software are in a 3D AutoCAD lab for exclusive use by interior design students. Output options include a large-format Hewlett Packard Designjet ColorPro CAD, a Hewlett-Packard Designjet 1055CM plotter, and an Epson Stylus Photo 2200.

SVA's library holdings include distinctive multimedia collections, more than 65,000 books, more than 260 current periodical subscriptions, and special collections of pictures, color slides, film scripts, comics, videotapes, exhibition catalogs, CD-ROMs, and recordings. The college has three campus galleries as well as a gallery at 601 West 26th Street, in the heart of Chelsea.

Costs

Tuition for the 2007–08 academic year is $23,520. SVA offers housing at costs that range from $8500 to $14,500 per academic year. Other annual costs vary greatly, but it is estimated that supplies cost up to $3150 each year, depending on the department.

Financial Aid

During the 2006–07 academic year, 74 percent of incoming students received financial aid. Students interested in financial aid are required to file the Free Application for Federal Student Aid (FAFSA). There are also scholarships available to both first-time freshman and transfer applicants.

Faculty

The faculty at SVA is composed of more than 700 practicing artists and designers who represent an array of fields in the fine and applied arts. Each faculty member has chosen to commit to the professional art world as well as to teaching the next generation of artists. As a result of the college's policy of using working professionals to teach, the college has been able to attract to the faculty some of the most prominent artists in New York.

Student Government

The Visual Arts Student Association (VASA), the student government organization, represents the student point of view at SVA. The three officers elected to VASA each year serve as the liaisons between students and the administrators. VASA also funds and supports a number of clubs that are organized by students.

Admission Requirements

Admissions requirements are as follows: application for undergraduate admission form, nonrefundable $50 application fee ($80 for international applicants), official transcripts from all high schools and colleges attended, results of the SAT or ACT, statement of intent, and portfolio (two-part essay for film and video applicants). Applicants whose primary language is not English are required to demonstrate their English proficiency, and international applicants must submit a declaration of finances (DOF) form, a verification of finances (VOF), and a copy of their Alien Registration Card.

Application and Information

Applications are reviewed on a rolling-admission basis. First-time freshman applicants seeking scholarships must complete the application process by February 1. Transfer applicants seeking scholarships must complete the application process by March 1. Spring admission is also an option for some departments. The recommended deadline for spring admission is December 1. Interested students should contact the Office of Admissions for more information regarding spring admission.

For more information about SVA, students should contact:

Office of Admissions
School of Visual Arts
209 East 23rd Street
New York, New York 10010
Phone: 212-592-2100
Fax: 212-592-2116
E-mail: admissions@sva.edu
Web site: http://www.sva.edu

SIENA COLLEGE
LOUDONVILLE, NEW YORK

SIENA*college*

The College

Siena College is a four-year, coeducational, independent liberal arts college with a Franciscan and Catholic tradition. It is a community of 2,900 full-time students that offers undergraduate degrees in business, liberal arts, and sciences. Student-focused professors are at the heart of a supportive and challenging learning community that allows students to realize their potential and prepares them for careers and an active leadership role in their communities. Founded by the Franciscan Friars in 1937, Siena seeks to develop the potential for extraordinary achievement. It welcomes all races and creeds and prides itself on the care and concern for the intellectual, spiritual, ethical, and social growth of all students.

Approximately 80 percent of the College's students live on campus. Siena offers traditional residence halls, suites, and town-house units. When Siena students are not in class, they have plenty to do. More than sixty clubs and organizations are active each year. The Franciscan Center for Service and Advocacy is the College's primary vehicle for service with and among the poor and marginalized and offers service to Habitat for Humanity, soup kitchens, and teaching in religious education programs. More than 70 percent of the student body is involved in some type of athletic program. The College offers eighteen Division I intercollegiate sports, club teams, and intramurals. Siena also provides numerous student support services, including counseling, tutoring, health services, peer counseling, and a career center. Popular activities include the Stage III Theatre, the student newspaper, the radio station, the yearbook, the Rugby Club, the Black and Latino Student Union, and Model United Nations.

Siena College's Marcelle Athletic Complex features a field house with an elevated running track, racquetball and squash courts, an aerobics/dance studio, and an area with exercise and other weight-training equipment. Serra Hall, the dining hall on campus, underwent a $4.5-million renovation during the summer of 2006.

Siena provides additional learning and cultural experiences outside of its academic programs to its students and the wider community. Examples of these efforts include the Martin Luther King Jr. Lecture Series, the Niebuhr Institute of Religion and Culture, and the Sister Thea Bowman Center for Women.

Siena has developed a number of cooperative and special programs. In addition to the college-wide honors program, Siena offers a premed program with Albany Medical College; a five-year M.B.A. program with Clarkson University, Union University, and Pace University; a seven-year accelerated predental program with Boston University; a 3-2 engineering program in cooperation with Clarkson University, Catholic University, Rensselaer Polytechnic Institute, Manhattan College, SUNY at Binghamton, and Western New England College; and the Washington Semester at American University.

Location

Siena's 166-acre campus is ideally located in Loudonville, a residential community 2 miles north of Albany, the capital of New York. With eighteen colleges in the area, there is a wide variety of activities off campus. The Times Union Center hosts performances by major concert artists and professional sporting events. Within 50 miles are the Adirondacks, the Berkshires, and the Catskill Mountains, providing outdoor recreation throughout the year. Montreal, New York City, and Boston are less than 3 hours away. With all of the professional, cultural, and recreational opportunities the Capital Region offers, many Siena graduates choose to begin their careers here.

Majors and Degrees

The College offers bachelor's degrees in the following areas: accounting, American studies, biochemistry, biology, chemistry, classics, computational science, computer science, creative arts, economics, English, environmental studies, finance, French, history, marketing and management, mathematics, philosophy, physics, political science, psychology, religious studies, social work, sociology, and Spanish. In addition, the College offers forty-six minors and certificate programs.

Academic Programs

A strong liberal arts core forms the basis for all of Siena's programs. All students take courses within a broad core requirement: 30 hours in the humanities and social sciences (including a 6-credit freshman foundations course), 9 hours in mathematics and science (with 3 of these in a natural science), and 3 hours in creative arts. Students must also maintain a minimum cumulative index of 2.0 and earn at least a C in every major field concentration course. Within the major, students must take a minimum of 30 credits, with no more than 39 credits counting toward the degree requirements. A total of 120 hours is required to qualify for a bachelor's degree.

Students may get credit for prior work by taking standardized college proficiency exams with the approval of the head of the department in the discipline to be examined. A total of 18 credits may be obtained this way. Siena offers honors courses in English, history, philosophy, and political science. ROTC affiliation is available at Siena in a U.S. Army unit, and an Air Force ROTC unit is available at a nearby college through cross-registration.

Off-Campus Programs

Siena students have the opportunity to spend a semester or a year studying abroad. Programs directly affiliated with the College include Siena at Regent's College, London; the Siena in London Internship Experience; the Siena semester at the Centre d'Études Franco-Américain de Management in Lyon, France; and the Center for Cross-Cultural Studies in Seville, Spain. In addition, programs are available for all majors everywhere on the globe. International study is typically pursued during the junior year.

Locally, internships are available through government, business, and nonprofit organizations on a two- or three-day-a-week basis, enabling students to continue with their course work at the same time. Many students are offered jobs by their internship organization upon graduation.

In addition, through the Hudson Mohawk Association of Colleges and Universities (which comprises the eighteen colleges in the area), cross-registration is possible at such institutions as the College of Saint Rose, Rensselaer Polytechnic Institute, Skidmore College, Union College, and the University at Albany, State University of New York.

Academic Facilities

The Standish Library collection of more than 321,000 volumes consists of books, journals, microforms, compact discs, videocassettes, and a growing number of electronic information sources. More than 6,000 volumes are added annually, and 1,600 serial subscriptions are currently maintained, with electronic access to thousands of additional journals. In 2004, Siena completed the renovation of Siena Hall, a high-technology teaching and learning center. It is also home to Siena's Hickey Financial Technology Center. The Hickey Center provides Siena's students the opportunity to trade stocks, bonds, cash, and currency in a virtual environment and provides students with access to leading sources of financial data.

All academic and residential buildings are interconnected with a high-speed Ethernet network connected via fiber optics. This network backbone runs at 10 and 100 Mbps. Every student residence space includes a 10 Mbps connection point to access the College's network and the Internet. The network includes more than 2,500 ports. The computer facilities are accessible 24 hours a day, seven days a week. Numerous computers are available throughout the campus for student use.

Costs

Tuition at Siena remains reasonable, helping the College to provide an education of fine quality at moderate cost. For 2007–08, tuition was $22,510 and room and board were $8875. There are lab fees for accounting, natural sciences, languages, and some fine arts and psychology courses. Miscellaneous fees may account for about $600 per year.

Financial Aid

Siena is committed to providing personal attention to every student's financial needs, recognizing that each situation is different. More than 86 percent of students receive financial aid. Federal programs that Siena students may qualify for include Federal Pell Grants, Federal Supplemental Educational Opportunity Grants, Federal Perkins Loans, Federal Stafford Student Loans, and Federal PLUS loans. Residents of New York State may receive Tuition Assistance Program and Aid for Part-time Work-Study awards. Financial need is determined by the Free Application for Federal Student Aid and, where applicable, the state version of the supplemental Financial Aid Form. Aid is usually awarded in a package combining scholarships or grants, loans, and a job. Students who remain in good academic standing have their aid renewed.

Faculty

Siena's faculty members are committed to teaching. Student concerns and development are at the heart of the curriculum. Nine out of every 10 full-time faculty members hold the highest degree awarded in their field. The student-faculty ratio of 14:1 helps to develop interaction with students, as does the fact that Siena professors teach labs. Students are assigned a faculty adviser to help in the planning of their course of study.

Student Government

The Student Senate oversees student involvement in academic and social life and interprets students' attitudes, opinions, and rights for the faculty and administration. It charters all student organizations and provides funds for many through fees collected by the College. The governing board is made up of officers and representatives of all four classes and of the commuting students. Elections are held in April for the following year, except for freshmen, who are elected in September.

Admission Requirements

Siena seeks bright, articulate people who will take advantage of the opportunities available at the College. Academic standards are demanding but not threatening. The average SAT score of accepted students is 1125. The high school curriculum, activities, recommendations, and campus visit all affect the final decision. Students seeking degrees in the science or business division should be well versed in mathematics. Those interested in American studies, English, history, or philosophy are likely to find a working knowledge of a foreign language very helpful.

Application and Information

The deadline for the submission of a regular application is March 1 of a student's senior year in high school. Decisions are sent starting in mid-March. Siena also offers an early decision and an early action program. Early applications should be submitted before December 1. Candidates are notified by January 1. Presidential Scholar candidates must apply by January 15.

Transfer students must apply by December 1 for the spring semester or by June 1 for the fall semester. Generally, transfers are expected to have a cumulative average of at least 2.5. A minimum of 30 semester hours and half of the credits for the major must be earned at Siena. A maximum of 66 credits may be transferred from accredited two-year institutions. Credit is given only for courses that are similar in content, level, and scope to those at Siena.

For more information, students should contact:

Admissions Office
Siena College
515 Loudon Road
Loudonville, New York 12211
Phone: 518-783-2423
888-AT-SIENA (toll-free)
E-mail: admit@siena.edu
Web site: http://www.siena.edu

SKIDMORE COLLEGE

SARATOGA SPRINGS, NEW YORK

The College

Skidmore College is an independent liberal arts college of 2,300 men and women with a creative spirit that has been evident since its beginnings. Founded by Lucy Skidmore Scribner as the Skidmore School of Arts in 1911, it became Skidmore College in 1922. In addition to being accredited by the Middle States Association of Colleges and Schools, the College has a chapter of Phi Beta Kappa and has program accreditation with the Council on Social Work Education and the National Association of Schools of Art and Design.

Throughout its history, Skidmore has steadily reflected a spirit of innovation and imagination in response to need. In the 1960s, the College built an entirely new campus; in 1971, it became coeducational; in 1983, it completely revised its curriculum to emphasize interdisciplinarity through a comprehensive liberal studies program; and in 1993, it installed the Master of Arts in Liberal Studies program. Skidmore has embraced change, seeing in it the opportunity to serve the needs and realize the potential of its students. By expanding and refining its programs, the College has broadened its educational mission to reflect the evolving opportunities and challenges of a global society.

Students enjoy a full schedule of cultural, intellectual, and social activities, including lectures, art exhibits, concerts, opera, dance, and theater. There are more than 100 student organizations, such as a weekly newspaper, a radio station, an Asian cultural association, an art and literary journal, and a student-volunteer network. There are no fraternities or sororities. A strong intercollegiate sports program for men and women—nineteen teams in all—includes baseball, basketball, field hockey, golf, ice hockey, lacrosse, riding, rowing, soccer, softball, swimming and diving, tennis, and volleyball. The College has a vigorous intramural program, supports team activities of club status, and provides a growing health, fitness, and wellness program.

Skidmore's campus includes forty-nine buildings. The sports and recreation complex includes a pool, racquet-sport courts, basketball and volleyball courts, a small stadium with artificial turf field and a 400-meter all-weather track, three dance studios, a weight room, a fitness center, a human performance laboratory, and other recreational and competitive sport facilities. The $11-million Frances Young Tang Teaching Museum and Art Gallery, unique in its interdisciplinary approach, opened in fall 2000, and recent renovations to the student center include a cyber café and an intercultural center.

September 2006 saw two major additions to the campus. The Northwoods Apartments opened with 380 single-room units across ten new buildings. A brand new dining hall also opened, offering extensive vegetarian options, fresh-made pasta, locally grown organic items, and a broad range of daily choices. A new music building with a 700-seat auditorium is scheduled to open in early 2009.

Location

Set on 850 acres in the historic destination city of Saratoga Springs, New York, the College offers students the advantage of a beautiful, wooded campus setting and the benefits of a city of 30,000 residents that balloons in size during the summer months. Saratoga Springs has long been famous as a resort and as a horse-racing and cultural center. The city is located 30 miles north of Albany, the capital of New York State, and is cosmopolitan in character. Skidmore is within an hour of major ski areas, state parks, large lakes, and mountainous regions of eastern New York, Vermont, and western Massachusetts. During the summer, groups such as the New York City Ballet and the Philadelphia Orchestra are in residence at the Saratoga Performing Arts Center as are top jazz and rock performers.

Bus service is available from Saratoga Springs to New York City, Montreal, Boston, and other major cities. There are daily trains to and from New York City and Montreal. Rental cars are available at the Albany International Airport, which is served by major airlines. The College is located near Exit 15 of I-87 (the Northway).

Majors and Degrees

Skidmore College grants a Bachelor of Arts degree in the following liberal arts subjects: American studies, anthropology, Asian studies, biology, chemistry, classical studies, computer science, economics, English, environmental studies, foreign languages and literatures (French, German, and Spanish), geosciences, government, history, history of art, international affairs, mathematics, music, neuroscience, philosophy, physics, political economy, psychology, religious studies, sociology, and women's studies. The Bachelor of Science degree is granted in areas of a more professional nature, including business, dance, education studies, exercise science, social work, studio art, and theater. There are twenty-seven interdepartmental majors, biology-philosophy major being just one example. Self-determined majors, double majors, and minors are also available. Almost half of Skidmore students choose a second major or minor.

The College offers 3-2 programs in engineering with Dartmouth College and Clarkson University. Also available is a 4-1 M.B.A. program offered with Clarkson and a 4+1 Master of Arts in Teaching program with Union College. Through a cooperative program with the Cardozo Law School of Yeshiva University, Skidmore students may obtain a bachelor's degree and a law degree in six years. In addition, Skidmore has certification programs in teaching and social work and preprofessional programs in law and medicine.

Academic Programs

Skidmore College is known for its unusual blend of courses in the traditional liberal arts with opportunities in preprofessional disciplines, the combination of which often creates interesting and unexpected courses of study and career directions. It is also recognized for its interdisciplinary approach, which starts with a required first-year seminar. Students choose from a myriad of topics. Faculty seminar leaders function as their students' first-year advisers. Additional core requirements include one lab course in science, one in the social sciences, one in the humanities, one in the arts, one in a foreign language, and one in non-Western culture. All students choose a major at the end of their sophomore year from among sixty-four options, some of which include interdepartmental concentrations, self-determined majors, and minors.

The College operates on a two-semester system with opportunities for internships directly following the end of the second semester in May. Students normally carry four or five courses during each semester.

The College offers a six-week residential academic summer program (PASS) enabling high school students to take two courses for college credit.

University Without Walls (UWW) is Skidmore's nontraditional, nonresidential baccalaureate degree program. Students admitted to the program work individually with a faculty adviser to define the specific content of their degree programs. Skidmore UWW also encourages and helps the student to identify and use nontraditional means to acquire the requisite knowledge, including independent and self-directed study, as well as experiences gained in paid volunteer work. A similarly designed Master of Arts in Liberal Studies program was implemented in 1993.

Off-Campus Programs

Skidmore's membership in the Hudson-Mohawk Association of Colleges and Universities enables students to cross-register at any of fourteen other colleges and universities in the area. The Washington Semester, conducted through American University in Washington, D.C., offers an intensive, twelve-week workshop experience through course work, seminars, research projects, and internships with government committees. Skidmore's Office of International Programs enables students to study in China, England, France, India, and Spain. Skidmore is also affiliated with other study-abroad programs, facilitating study for a semester or a year in many locations in Asia, Australia, Europe, and Latin America. Approximately 55 percent of Skidmore students study abroad for a year or a semester.

Arrangements for credit-bearing internships are made through academic departments or through the Office of Career Services. Internships are available in such diverse fields as government, social work, the arts (dance, theater, and museum work), business, scientific research, and medicine.

Academic Facilities

Scribner Library, housing approximately 400,000 volumes, numerous online publications, and advanced information technology, has been designated a depository for U.S. government documents. Students have access to forty libraries in the region through the College's membership in an area council. Skidmore also participates in the Lockheed/Dialog system for information search and retrieval. Dana Science Center has laboratories and sophisticated university-like equipment for the biology, chemistry, environmental studies, physics, and geology departments/programs.

The Filene Music Building contains a large recital hall, practice and listening rooms, and an electronic and a music library. Other special facilities include a language laboratory in Bolton Hall; the Saisselin Art Building, with drawing, painting, ceramics, sculpture, weaving, and jewelry-making studios—in addition to a state-of-the art digital photography lab and the Schick Art Gallery; the Skidmore Theatre; dance studios; and an $11-million museum at the center of the campus.

Students have access to ample computer resources, including 350 MAC and Windows PCs in general-purpose rooms, eight Linux workstations, twelve Silicon Graphics workstations, network connections in all residence hall rooms, and nearly 650 computers in public areas and academic departments.

Costs

In 2007–08, tuition for all students was $36,860; room and board cost $9836; and the student general activity fees totaled $734.

Financial Aid

Skidmore awards financial aid based on demonstrated need. The Free Application for Federal Student Aid (FAFSA), a copy of the federal income tax form, and the CSS PROFILE must be filed each year. The application date is January 15 for entering freshmen. The College hosts an annual Filene Music Scholarship Competition to award four $40,000 ($10,000 per year) scholarships on the basis of musical ability without regard to financial need. Five $10,000 scholarships in math and science are also awarded annually. Other grants are available for superior math and science students. Detailed information concerning scholarships, grants, loans, and/or work awards can be obtained through the Office of Student Aid and Family Finance.

Faculty

Skidmore College has 229 full-time teaching faculty members and 68 part-time members, including those with special appointments. Ninety-four percent of the liberal arts and sciences faculty members hold the doctoral degree or the highest degree in their field. The student-to-faculty ratio is about 9:1, and the average class size is 16. Although actively engaged in research and publication in their individual fields, the Skidmore faculty members regard teaching as their primary commitment. All students have faculty advisers who assist them in selecting courses and in designing individual academic programs.

Student Government

Students at Skidmore play an active role in College governance. Through the Student Government Association (SGA) and by membership on a number of major College committees, they participate in all phases of academic and social life. The SGA operates under the authority granted by the Board of Trustees and is dedicated to the principles of democratic self-government and responsible citizenship. Within the association, elected faculty members and student representatives serve on the All-College Council, the Academic Integrity Board, and the Social Integrity Board. The broad concerns of the SGA include educational policy, elections, social and student events, freshman orientation, student publications, and student clubs and organizations.

Admission Requirements

Applicants for admission to the freshman class are expected to complete a secondary school program with a minimum of 16 college-preparatory credits. The Admissions Committee also considers applications from qualified high school juniors who plan to accelerate and enter college early. Typical preparation for entrance includes 4 years of English, 4 years of a foreign language, 4 years of mathematics, 4 years of social studies, and 3–4 years of laboratory science. Among the required credentials are a secondary school transcript, a report from the school guidance counselor, and assessments from 2 teachers. Skidmore also requires applicants to take the SAT or ACT (with writing test) examination and recommends that two SAT Subject Tests be taken. A campus interview is strongly recommended.

Through the Higher Education Opportunity Program (HEOP) and the Academic Opportunity Program (AOP), Skidmore enrolls talented, energetic, and motivated students who have been economically and educationally disadvantaged and who otherwise would be unable to attend the College.

Application and Information

An applicant for admission registers by completing the Common Application and submitting it with a $60 fee. All information should be postmarked by January 15. Applications from early decision candidates may be submitted by November 15 for the Round I early decision plan or by January 15 for the Round II early decision plan. Transfer candidates are urged to apply by April 1 for the next fall term and by November 15 for the next spring term. Interested freshmen and transfer students are strongly urged to visit the campus for interviews and guided tours.

Mary Lou W. Bates
Dean of Admissions and Financial Aid
Skidmore College
Saratoga Springs, New York 12866
Phone: 518-580-5570
800-867-6007 (toll-free)
E-mail: admissions@skidmore.edu
Web site: http://www.skidmore.edu

Aerial view of the Skidmore College campus.

STATE UNIVERSITY OF NEW YORK AT FREDONIA

FREDONIA, NEW YORK

The University

SUNY Fredonia is a selective, public, comprehensive, liberal arts university located near Lake Erie in beautiful Western New York. Founded in 1826, Fredonia is a highly respected liberal arts institution with recognized programs in business, communications, education, the fine and performing arts, science, and the social sciences. The University maintains a traditional small-college atmosphere, and students enjoy a variety of cultural and social activities. Many of the 5,085 undergraduate students participate actively in clubs, organizations, athletics, and intramural sports.

Fredonia's 240-acre campus has twenty-nine buildings. A modern field house provides facilities for ice hockey, swimming, diving, and indoor track and includes a large gymnasium. A second facility contains a fitness center, a dance studio, and two intramural gymnasiums. Fourteen residence halls house 2,600 students and offer accommodations to suit a variety of lifestyles, including traditional, coed, and apartment-style residence halls. On-campus housing is guaranteed for all undergraduates. University Commons is a state-of-the-art facility that includes a dining center, bookstore, Starbucks, and residence hall.

Location

The village of Fredonia is located 45 miles south of Buffalo near Lake Erie and is home to 11,000 residents. The village has preserved its traditional small-town atmosphere. Tree-lined streets lead to a spacious downtown common surrounded by outstanding examples of nineteenth-century village architecture. Fredonia is surrounded by orchards and vineyards leading south to the Allegheny foothills. Summer and winter recreational facilities abound. The University benefits from its relative proximity to Buffalo, Toronto, Cleveland, and Pittsburgh.

Majors and Degrees

SUNY Fredonia degrees and program offerings include the Bachelor of Arts (B.A.) degree in applied music, art history, ceramics, communication disorders, criminal justice, drawing, earth science, economics, English, French, graphic design, history, illustration, interdisciplinary studies, painting, philosophy, photography, political science, psychology, sculpture, sociology, Spanish, and theater. A Bachelor of Fine Arts (B.F.A.) degree is offered in acting, animation and illustration, ceramics, dance, drawing, graphic design, media arts, musical theater, painting, photography, production design, and sculpture. The Bachelor of Music (Mus.B.) degree is available in composition, music education, and performance. The Bachelor of Science (B.S.) degree is awarded in accounting, audio/radio production, biochemistry, biology, business administration, chemistry, communication disorders, computer and information sciences, finance, geochemistry, geology, geophysics, industrial management, interdisciplinary studies, management, management information systems, marketing, mathematics, mathematics-physics, media management, medical technology, molecular genetics, music therapy, physics, public relations, social work, sound recording technology, and TV/digital film production. A Bachelor of Science in Education (B.S.Ed.) degree is offered with majors in childhood education, early childhood education, and inclusive education. Adolescent education certification is available in biology, chemistry, earth science, English, French, mathematics, physics, social studies, and Spanish.

The Interdisciplinary Studies degree gives students the opportunity to design an individualized interdisciplinary major with guidance from experienced faculty members. Students in these programs work toward a Bachelor of Arts or Bachelor of Science degree. The Interdisciplinary Studies option also offers model majors and minors in such areas as African American studies, American studies, arts administration, environmental sciences, exercise studies, geographic information systems, legal studies, multiethnic studies, music business, sport management and exercise science, and women's studies.

Fredonia takes part in a cooperative 3-2 engineering program with the following institutions: Alfred University, Case Western Reserve, Clarkson, Columbia, Cornell, Louisiana Tech, Ohio State, Penn State Behrend, Rensselaer Polytechnic Institute, Rochester Institute of Technology, SUNY Binghamton, SUNY Buffalo, Syracuse, and Tri-State University. The Department of Business Administration offers an accelerated M.B.A. program, including a 3-2 program with SUNY at Binghamton and SUNY at Buffalo and a 4-1 program with Clarkson and the University of Pittsburgh. A complete listing of offerings is available online at http://www.fredonia.edu.

Academic Programs

The bachelor's degree requires 120 credit hours, including a general education component, and there are opportunities for double majors, minors, and concentrations. The University offers an honors program for academically talented students. Up to 30 credits may be awarded through Advanced Placement, CLEP, and International Baccalaureate examinations.

Fredonia operates on a semester system with the fall term beginning in late August and ending in mid-December. The spring term begins the third week of January and continues into May. A summer program of two 5-week sessions is available.

Retention and graduation rates of entering freshmen at Fredonia are among the highest in the nation. To ensure continued success, the University has implemented "Fredonia in 4," a program for first-time freshmen that stipulates that the University pledges to adhere to an agreement wherein it provides the necessary courses and academic advising to ensure that a student graduates in four years provided that the student successfully completes the courses recommended by his or her adviser.

Off-Campus Programs

Fredonia students enjoy opportunities to study abroad through SUNY's expansive overseas education program. Students may take part in opportunities throughout the world in virtually every discipline. The University offers internships in courts and government agencies as well as in the areas of public relations, psychology, journalism, television production, radio, business, and the health sciences.

Academic Facilities

Fredonia's academic buildings host an array of up-to-date teaching and research facilities. Students have wireless connections throughout campus and Ethernet connections in their residence hall rooms. A 1,200-seat concert hall and a new 500-seat recital hall support excellent performing arts programs. The Rockefeller Arts Center provides outstanding facilities for concert and theatrical productions and houses art galleries, art studios, and classrooms.

Costs

Tuition and fees for 2007–08 are estimated at $5532 per year for New York State residents and $11,792 for non–New York State residents. Students living in residence halls pay an additional fee of $5050 for room, and meal plans range from $2800 to $3400.

Financial Aid

More than 84 percent of Fredonia's undergraduates received financial assistance in 2006–07. The average award, consisting of grants, scholarships, loans, and campus jobs, was $9200. Students who are interested in applying for aid are encouraged to submit the Free Application for Federal Student Aid (FAFSA) by February 1. Sources of aid include Federal Pell Grants, Federal Supplemental Educational Opportunity Grants, New York State Tuition Assistance Program awards, Educational Opportunity Grants, Federal Academic Competitive Grants, Federal Smart Grants, Federal Perkins Loans, Federal Stafford Student Loans, Federal Work-Study Program awards, on- and off-campus jobs, and Fredonia University Scholarships, including a freshman merit scholarship program.

Faculty

Fredonia's faculty includes 245 full-time and 160 part-time instructional staff members. Ninety percent of faculty members have earned doctorates or terminal degrees in their field. All professors have weekly office hours during which they are available to students. Faculty members are involved in instruction, research, publication, and academic advising. Small class size contributes to excellent faculty-student interaction; the average class size is 22 students.

Student Government

All students are members of the Student Association, which functions through elected officers and elected senators from the various University groups and organizations. Student representatives are voting members of the Faculty Council and are represented on most committees of the University. The Student Association provides funding for 120 campus organizations and clubs.

Admission Requirements

Admission to Fredonia is competitive. Particular attention is given to the quality of the academic program and the high school average. Other factors considered in the admissions process include SAT or ACT scores, recommendations, rank in class, and extracurricular activities. Applicants should have completed at least 16 units in core academic subjects. Those seeking admission to math- or science-related majors should include 4 units each of mathematics and science; those seeking admission to programs in business administration and accounting should include 4 units of college-preparatory mathematics. An audition is required for admission to programs in acting, dance, music, musical theater, and production design. A portfolio is required for admission to visual arts and new media majors. A campus visit is recommended; a personal interview is not required.

Application and Information

The SUNY Fredonia undergraduate application is available online at http://www.fredonia.edu/admissions/applying.html. New York State residents may obtain paper applications from their high school guidance offices or any SUNY campus. Nonresidents should contact the Office of Admissions. Application review and notification are made on a rolling basis. Applicants may seek admission through the Early Decision Program. A deposit of $100, due May 1, is required to reserve a space in the entering class. Students interested in visiting the campus may obtain a visiting schedule and an appointment by calling the Office of Admissions.

For further information, students should contact:

Office of Admissions
Fenner House
State University of New York at Fredonia
Fredonia, New York 14063
Phone: 716-673-3251
800-252-1212 (toll-free)
E-mail: admissions.office@fredonia.edu
Web site: http://www.fredonia.edu

On the campus at SUNY Fredonia.

STATE UNIVERSITY OF NEW YORK AT OSWEGO

OSWEGO, NEW YORK

The University

Founded in 1861, SUNY Oswego is well into its second century of meeting the needs of today's students. Although its origins were in teacher education, the University expanded its curriculum in 1962 to include the arts and sciences and professional studies. Today, Oswego is a comprehensive college with an excellent academic reputation and commitment to undergraduate education. Approximately 3,060 men and 3,560 women are currently enrolled as full-time undergraduates. More than 110 liberal arts and career-oriented programs are offered through the College of Arts and Sciences, the School of Business, and the School of Education. The School of Education is nationally accredited by the National Council for the Accreditation of Teacher Education (NCATE), and the School of Business is accredited by AACSB International–The Association to Advance Collegiate Schools of Business. Individual programs within the College of Arts and Sciences are accredited by specific discipline-oriented accrediting organizations.

Located on 696 acres on the southern shore of Lake Ontario, the spacious tree-lined campus consists of forty-five buildings. Eleven residence halls offer a variety of on-campus housing opportunities to all degree-seeking students. The campus is alive with more than 125 extracurricular organizations covering a wide range of social, academic, cultural, and intellectual interests. Theater, art, film, music, dance, and discussion events fill the campus cultural calendar. SUNY Oswego also offers a full slate of twenty-four NCAA Division III intercollegiate sports for men and women, along with a full complement of club sports and intramural athletics for men and women.

Traditionally, Oswego receives among the largest number of applications of any similar-size college in the Northeast. It is accredited by the Middle States Association of Colleges and Schools and has been recognized by a number of authoritative guides as a college with outstanding academic opportunities and high academic standards. In addition, Oswego is among a select few colleges or universities in New York State to offer both nationally accredited schools of business and education. During the last several years, SUNY Oswego has been cited for excellence and selectivity in *The Princeton Review's Best Northeastern Colleges* and *U.S. News & World Report's Best Colleges Guide.*

Oswego is taking part in a comprehensive renewal project involving more than $250 million of investments for the future. This includes the opening in fall 2007 of the $56-million Campus Center, a state-of-the-art facility integrating a campus convocation and ice arena, food courts, public meeting areas, student service areas, academic departments, and academic support services; renovation of several academic buildings and residence halls; and a coming investment in new and renovated spaces for its science facilities.

Location

With a population of nearly 20,000, the city of Oswego is a modest-sized, friendly upstate New York community. It is the country's oldest freshwater port and one of the leading ports on the Great Lakes and St. Lawrence Seaway. The city and its surrounding area are well known for all kinds of summer and winter recreation, including camping, boating, sailing, fishing, tennis, and golf and, in the winter months, ice skating, cross-country skiing, and sledding. It is at the heart of the booming sports fishing industry, with a thriving tourism scene. The campus is conveniently located 35 miles northwest of Syracuse and 65 miles east of Rochester. Students traveling by rail or air may utilize bus service to Oswego through the Regional Transportation Center located adjacent to the Carousel Mall in Syracuse.

Majors and Degrees

SUNY Oswego awards the Bachelor of Arts (B.A.), Bachelor of Science (B.S.), and Bachelor of Fine Arts (B.F.A.) degrees through its College of Arts and Sciences, School of Business, and School of Education.

Through the College of Arts and Sciences, students can earn a baccalaureate degree in American studies, anthropology, applied mathematical economics, art, biochemistry, biology, broadcasting, chemistry, cinema and screen studies, cognitive science, communication studies, computer science, creative writing, economics, English, French, geochemistry, geology, German, global and international studies, graphic design, history, human development, information science, journalism, language and international trade, linguistics, mathematics, meteorology, music, philosophy, philosophy-psychology, physics, political science, psychology, public justice, public relations, sociology, Spanish, theater, women's studies, and zoology.

The School of Business offers Bachelor of Science degree programs in accounting, business administration, finance, human resource management, management accounting, marketing, and operations management and information systems.

The School of Education offers Bachelor of Science degree programs in adolescence education, childhood education, teaching English to speakers of other languages (TESOL), technology education, technology management, vocational-teacher preparation, and wellness management.

In addition, a pair of innovative five-year combined bachelor's and master's programs are available. One offers a bachelor's degree in accounting joined with a master's in business administration; the other provides a bachelor's in psychology with an M.B.A.

Cooperative programs include a 3+2 zoo technology program, resulting in a bachelor's degree in zoology at Oswego and an associate degree in zoo technology from Santa Fe Community College (Florida) or Niagara Community College; 3+2 engineering programs leading to a bachelor's degree from Oswego in chemistry or physics and a B.S. in engineering from the cooperating universities (Case Western Reserve, Clarkson, or SUNY Binghamton); 2+2 programs leading to a B.S. in cardiovascular perfusion, cytotechnology, medical imaging sciences, medical technology, radiation therapy, or respiratory care from SUNY Upstate Medical University (formerly SUNY Health Science Center) in Syracuse; a 3+3 program leading to a B.S./D.P.S. in physical therapy from SUNY Upstate Medical University; a 3+4 preoptometry program leading to a bachelor's in chemistry from Oswego and an O.D. in optometry from SUNY College of Optometry; and a 3+4 prepharmacy program leading to a B.A. in chemistry from Oswego and a pharmaceutical doctorate from SUNY Buffalo.

Academic Programs

Because interest in obtaining marketable skills continues to increase, SUNY Oswego offers students a broad range of courses in the liberal arts and in preprofessional and professional studies.

In addition to core courses within a major, all students must satisfy general education requirements designed to strengthen basic writing and analytical proficiency, give students awareness of their cultural heritage, and provide a level of literacy in the social and behavioral sciences, natural sciences, and humanities. By completing these general education requirements during their first two years of study, Oswego students are able to select a major with a sense of confidence and purpose. However, students who are certain of their academic interest may begin working on their major program in the first year.

Before arriving on campus, students are assigned an adviser from either their major area or the college's Student Advisement Center. Advisers assist students who have not declared a major; help with academic, personal, and career concerns; and collaborate in scheduling courses needed for graduation. In addition, most students are matched with a first-year peer adviser, an older student, to help them face the challenges of the first year. Even for those who have not chosen a career path coming into college, Oswego is a popular destination; the college has more than 500 undeclared students, many drawn by Oswego's reputation for helping learners find their way in education and life.

Students may consider applying for the college's Honors Program, which provides a challenging academic experience for high achievers regardless of major. Students also have the option of receiving credit through proficiency CLEP and Advanced Placement examinations.

Off-Campus Programs

Opportunities exist for students to broaden their knowledge of other countries by participating in one of more than 300 overseas academic programs offered. Programs are available throughout the world, and costs are held as close as possible to the cost of an average semester on the Oswego campus. A newer option is short study-abroad quarter courses offering an intensive curriculum with about ten days' immersion in a foreign culture. Through cooperative arrangements, Oswego also participates in semester programs in Albany and Washington.

Internships and other field experiences are available for students from all disciplines through the Experience-Based Education Office. Each year, more than 1,000 Oswego students participate in internships and career-awareness activities on the Oswego campus, in the local area, and throughout the Northeast, the country, and the world.

Academic Facilities

Penfield Library is a high-tech information center supporting the curriculum, teaching, and research of SUNY Oswego. The library houses a collection of over 475,000 bound volumes, including partial U.S. and New York State government documents depositories, and provides access to nearly 26,000 print and/or electronic journals, magazines, and newspapers. Through InterLibrary Loan, Penfield can provide additional materials from libraries all over the world. The library's listening area has more than 12,000 recordings, cassettes, and CDs, ranging from classical to rock. Additional facilities include the Lake Effect Café, an online catalog, a 24-hour study room, study carrels, wireless Internet access, and computer labs with word processing.

Campuswide computer technology services for student use include instructional and administrative technologies as well as network and telecommunications. The campus maintains several Sun servers, providing e-mail and Web publishing support. In addition, the campus has hundreds of Macintosh and Windows-based computers in several public-access labs. Students also have access to more than 500 computers and numerous Sun workstations in forty specialized departmental labs. Students receive an account that can be activated online to use the time-sharing computers and to access e-mail, the Web, and other Internet services. Internet service is available from all residence hall rooms via Ethernet (fee required) or modem (free) connections. Wireless network access is available in an ever-increasing number of locations throughout the campus, including many academic buildings, the Campus Center complex, Hewitt Union, Penfield Library, and all resident dining centers.

Adjacent to the campus, the college maintains Rice Creek Field Station, including the 26-acre Rice Pond, surrounded by almost 300 acres of natural habitat. The facility contains two lab/classrooms, a lecture room, and exhibit areas with an indoor viewing gallery, providing a unique vista of the creek and pond. College classes and community education programs are regularly held at the field station, which ranks among the five most extensively used facilities of its kind in the country.

Tyler Hall, Oswego's fine arts center, hosts two art galleries that feature annual traveling exhibitions, locally produced theme exhibitions, and the best work of students and faculty members. Tyler Hall's Waterman Theatre hosts a variety of student plays, musical performances, and productions by internationally renowned traveling artists.

The WRVO Stations, the college's 50,000-watt public radio outlet, provides outstanding on-campus internship opportunities. Communication department facilities also include two new all-digital television studios, a modern radio lab, and two new journalism labs in Lanigan Hall. Student-run TV and radio stations and the college newspaper are located in new Campus Center facilities.

Costs

Tuition for 2007–08 was $2175 per semester for New York State residents and $5305 per semester for nonresidents. Room and board charges are approximately $4700 per semester for entering students, depending on the meal plan selected. SUNY Oswego guarantees that a student's initial first-year costs for room and board will be frozen for up to four consecutive years. Books and supplies cost approximately $400 per semester, depending on the student's choice of major program. Although many activities on campus are free of charge, students need to budget for personal expenses.

Financial Aid

Financial assistance, granted according to student need, consists of grants, loans, and part-time employment. Oswego offers an annual total of nearly $65 million in aid to its student body. Students interested in financial aid must file a Free Application for Federal Student Aid (FAFSA). New York State residents also need to file an application for the state's Tuition Assistance Program. Priority is given to those applications on file by April 1 for the fall term and November 15 for the spring term.

Oswego offers a very generous merit scholarship program, with more than 35 percent of the entering freshman class receiving an Oswego merit scholarship. In total, Oswego students receive over $2.5 million annually in merit scholarships; the average four-year renewable scholarship is approximately $2300 per year. For scholarship qualifications and details, students should visit http://www.oswego.edu/admissions/costs/financial/scholarships/merit.html.

Faculty

Oswego's faculty, consisting of more than 300 full-time educators, is dedicated to teaching undergraduate students. With 83 percent of teachers holding doctoral or other terminal degrees from many of the finest institutions in the country, students can be assured of the opportunity for an outstanding undergraduate education. The student-faculty ratio is approximately 18:1. While the Oswego faculty is first and foremost dedicated to teaching, faculty members are also actively engaged in research—often in partnership with undergraduate students—as well as publications and public service.

Student Government

Students at SUNY Oswego are represented by the Student Association, which has as its aim the efficient and intelligent governance of a democratic student body. The functions of the Student Association are divided among various committees that allocate funds to student organizations, intercollegiate and intramural athletics, the student newspaper, and the student literary magazine, along with various campus social, cultural, and intellectual activities.

Admission Requirements

Admission to Oswego is competitive, with high school average, academic program, and standardized test scores the most important criteria for applicants. Special talents such as artistic, musical, athletic, and creative writing skills are also considered. The Committee on Admissions accepts results on either the ACT or the SAT. Although not required, a campus admissions visit is encouraged.

Transfer students in good standing are encouraged to apply for admission to a specific major. The average GPA for entering transfer students is 3.0.

Application and Information

Application forms are available from New York State high school guidance offices and college transfer offices. Oswego evaluates applications as they are completed and as space remains available. Those applications completed by January 15 for the fall term or October 15 for the spring term are ensured equal consideration. Applications received after those dates are considered as space remains available.

Prospective students and their parents are encouraged to visit the campus to participate in a student-guided tour and speak with an admissions counselor. Visits can be scheduled online through the college's Web site (http://www.oswego.edu). Interested candidates can also call the Office of Admissions at least one or two weeks in advance to schedule a visit. For further information, students should contact:

Office of Admissions
229 Sheldon Hall
SUNY Oswego
Oswego, New York 13126
Phone: 315-312-2250
Fax: 315-312-3260
E-mail: admiss@oswego.edu
Web site: http://www.oswego.edu

SUNY Oswego is located on 696 acres on the southern shore of Lake Ontario.

STATE UNIVERSITY OF NEW YORK COLLEGE AT CORTLAND

COURTLAND, NEW YORK

Cortland
State University of New York College at Cortland

The University

State University of New York (SUNY) College at Cortland students study on a beautiful hillside campus in Central New York. They are inspired by friendly and supportive faculty members to attain their full potential, dig deeper, reach higher, and achieve more than they thought possible. Students at Cortland have the opportunity to take their abilities to the highest level. They can excel in the classroom, conduct one-on-one research with faculty, earn a spot on a nationally ranked athletic team, provide valuable community service, perform in a musical production, or take classes around the world. With guidance from faculty and staff members, they discover their unique role in the global society and match their interests with Cortland's rewarding internship and volunteer opportunities close to campus or across the nation.

SUNY Cortland traces its beginnings to 1868 and today offers programs leading to degrees in the arts and sciences, education, and professional studies. SUNY Cortland is a moderate-size institution with approximately 6,000 undergraduate and 1,300 graduate students. State assisted, Cortland is a charter member of the State University of New York. The College now has more than 57,000 living alumni; Cortland graduates can be found in each of the fifty states, the District of Columbia, and more than forty foreign countries.

The College campus covers 191 acres located within walking distance of the City of Cortland's business district. The main campus is divided into three distinct areas. Most of the classroom buildings, the Memorial Library, the Miller Building, Brockway Hall, and Cheney and DeGroat residence halls are found on the upper campus. The remaining residence halls, Neubig Hall and Corey Union, are at the center of the campus. Studio West, Park Center, Lusk Field House, the Stadium Complex, athletic fields, and tracks are located on the lower campus. A shuttle bus service is operated between the lower and upper campuses when classes are in session.

SUNY Cortland offers more than 100 groups and activities and is the home of the Center for International Education, the Center for Multicultural and Gender Studies, and the Cortland Urban Recruitment of Educators Program. An honors program is offered as well as Army and Air Force ROTC programs. Cortland also offers graduate programs leading to certificates and the M.A., M.A.T., M.S., M.S.Ed., and M.S.T.

State University of New York College at Cortland is accredited by the Middle States Association of Colleges and Secondary Schools. The teacher preparation programs are accredited by the National Council for Accreditation of Teacher Education, and national accreditation is maintained for many other programs offered on campus.

Location

SUNY Cortland is located in the beautiful Finger Lakes region of Central New York, just off I-81, a major north-south interstate highway. Cortland, in the geographic center of New York State, is a small city of about 20,000 offering a quaint downtown business district with shops and restaurants, as well as easy access to major ski areas, biking trails, and rivers and lakes. Ithaca, Binghamton, and Syracuse are just a short drive away.

Majors and Degrees

With fifty-nine majors and forty-four minors available through the Schools of Arts and Sciences, Education, and Professional Studies, SUNY Cortland offers an outstanding array of programs leading to Bachelor of Arts (B.A.), Bachelor of Fine Arts (B.F.A.), Bachelor of Science (B.S.), and Bachelor of Science in Education (B.S.Ed.). Programs are available in adolescence education (7–12): biology, chemistry, English, French, French/Spanish, Earth science, math, physics, physics and mathematics, social studies, and Spanish; African American studies; anthropology; art: art, art studio, and new media design; athletic training; biomedical sciences; business economics; conservation biology; chemistry; chemistry/engineering (3+2); communication studies; computer applications; criminology; economics; education: childhood education (1–6), early childhood and childhood education (birth–6), early childhood education (birth–2), and inclusive special education (certification, 1–6); English; English as a second language: teaching (certification, K–12) and noncertification; environmental studies; French; geography: geography, geographic information systems, tourism development; geographic information systems; geology; health: health education (certification, K–12), college health promotion and prevention services, and health science; history; human service studies; individualized degree; international studies; kinesiology: kinesiology, fitness development; mathematics; musical theater; new communication media; physical education (certification, K–12); physics; physics and engineering (3+2); political science; professional writing; psychology; recreation: recreation, outdoor recreation, recreation management, and therapeutic recreation; social philosophy; social studies; sociology; Spanish; speech pathology and audiology: speech and hearing science (noncertification) and speech and language disabilities; and sport management.

Preprofessional studies are offered in medical/dental, law, and engineering.

Academic Programs

The bachelor's degree requires a minimum of 124 credit hours for all majors. Programs that are externally accredited may require more than 124 credit hours.

All students must successfully complete, with a minimum grade of C-, 6 to 8 credit hours in English composition. In addition, at least 6 credit hours of work in writing-intensive courses must be completed.

All students must demonstrate proficiency in a foreign language through the 101 level. In addition, students in teacher education programs leading to a B.S. (other than speech and language disabilities) must demonstrate proficiency in a foreign language through the 102 level. All students earning a B.A. (including those in teacher education programs and those earning a B.S. in speech and language disabilities) must demonstrate proficiency through the 202 level.

At least 45 credit hours for a student's degree must be completed at SUNY Cortland. In addition, one half of the credits for the major, minor, and/or concentration must be completed at SUNY Cortland.

All students must complete a minimum of 90 credit hours of liberal arts and sciences courses in B.A. and B.F.A. programs, or a minimum of 60 credit hours in B.A. or B.S.Ed. programs.

Cortland students must earn a minimum of a 2.0 GPA both overall and in the major, minor, and concentrations. Some degree programs may require a higher GPA.

Off-Campus Programs

SUNY Cortland strives to emphasize an international dimension in every field of study, principally through the International Programs Office. Internships are available in some locations. Students are also eligible to participate in more than 400 other international study programs offered by other SUNY campuses. Credits earned during foreign study are transferred automatically toward meeting Cortland's graduation requirements. Participants usually are juniors and seniors, although qualified freshmen and sophomores may be accepted into certain programs. Study-abroad programs are available in such countries as Australia, Belize, China, Costa Rica, Egypt, England, France, Germany, Ireland, Kenya, Mexico, Spain, and Venezuela. A number of scholarships are available for summer study-abroad programs. For more information about Cortland's study abroad opportunities, students should visit http://www.cortlandabroad.com.

Costs

Residents of New York who live on campus should expect to pay about $17,300 per year ($5450 for tuition and fees, $8750 for room and meals, $800 for books and supplies, $800 for transportation, and $1500 for personal expenses). State residents who commute should budget about $14,500 per year ($5450 for tuition and fees, $5550 for room and meals, $800 for books and supplies, $1200 for transportation, and $1500 for personal expenses). Nonresidents living on campus have total costs of about $23,250 ($11,400 for tuition and fees, $8750 for room and meals, $800 for books and supplies, $800 for transportation, and $1500 for personal expenses).

Financial Aid

Each student at SUNY Cortland has their very own financial aid adviser to work with and guide them through the financial aid process. The adviser helps students having difficulties with financial aid forms or those who have questions on a more personal level. Before a student or parent can be considered eligible for any government programs, including government loans, they must complete and submit a Free Application for Federal Student Aid (or FAFSA). The information provided on the FAFSA determines how much financial aid a student is eligible to receive. The fastest and most accurate way of submitting the FAFSA application is the online process at http://www.fafsa.ed.gov. To make the process easier, Cortland has available printable step-by-step instructions for the entire online process. For those without computer access, a limited number of paper applications are still available annually from any college financial aid office, many high school guidance offices, public libraries, or by telephone at 800-433-3243 (toll-free).

The most common types of federal student aid include grants, government loans, and work-study. Federal student aid programs are regulated by the government and are usually the first resources students turn to when looking for financial aid. Private loans, on the other hand, are most often used to cover education costs that cannot be met by federal aid.

Faculty

At SUNY Cortland, professors are at the top of their game because they teach teachers. No college or university in New York State or the northeastern United States has more students pursuing majors leading to teacher certification. SUNY Cortland is the largest and among the most successful in preparing its students, with more than 99 percent annually passing New York State teaching certification exams.

Student Government

The Student Government Association is the voice of the student body at SUNY Cortland. Its dedicated staff and elected officers act as liaisons to the administration in order to address student concerns. The SGA Executive Board consists of 9 students; 3 elected by the student body in late April and 6 who are appointed by the elected officers in early fall. The primary duty of these student leaders is to persistently work on improving the SUNY Cortland campus. SGA funding for clubs and organizations that exist to educate and create programming to enhance the campus community comes from the Mandatory Activity Fee (MAF).

Admission Requirements

SUNY Cortland participates in the common application program of the State University of New York. Applications are available in secondary school guidance offices in New York State, in the admissions offices of SUNY-affiliated colleges, or directly from the SUNY Cortland Admissions Office. Completed applications should be mailed to: SUNY Application Processing Center, Albany, New York 12246. The application will be forwarded to the SUNY Cortland Admissions Office.

Candidates for admission must graduate from a secondary school program or present a General Educational Development (GED) certificate. For freshmen candidates, preparation should include 4 units of English, 4 of social studies, 3–4 of mathematics, 3–4 of science, and 3–4 of foreign language. (If less than three units are taken in math or science, a minimum of four units is required in the other.) All applicants are expected to be enrolled in a college preparatory track according to their state requirements (Regents level or higher in New York State).

SUNY Cortland is committed to a strong liberal arts foundation in all of its academic programs. All applications are individually reviewed and admission decisions are based on a variety of factors. Results from the ACT or the SAT, class rank, extracurricular activities, essays, and recommendations enter into the admission decision. However, primary consideration is given to course selection and performance in English, social studies, mathematics, science, and foreign language. A challenging college preparatory program with significant achievements both in and out of the classroom helps ensure that an application is competitive.

A complete application includes the following: official secondary school transcript or official GED results, official results from the ACT or SAT sent directly from the testing agency, the required online Supplemental Application, a personal statement or essay, and one letter of recommendation submitted directly to the SUNY Cortland Admissions Office. Students with prior military service must also provide a copy of their discharge papers (DD214). Students will receive acknowledgement of SUNY Cortland's receipt of their applications. The fee for applying to a State University of New York college is $40.

Application and Information

For spring semester consideration, completed applications should be received by November 15 for both freshmen and transfers. For fall semester consideration, freshmen and transfers should apply by February 15. Candidates are encouraged to apply as early as possible in order to receive the fullest possible consideration. For additional information, students should contact:

Admissions Office
SUNY Cortland
P.O. Box 2000
Cortland, New York 13045
Phone: 607-753-4711
E-mail: admissions@cortland.edu
Web site: http://www.cortland.edu/

STATE UNIVERSITY OF NEW YORK COLLEGE AT ONEONTA

ONEONTA, NEW YORK

The College

A comprehensive college of arts and sciences in the SUNY system, the College at Oneonta strives to develop students to their full potential both academically and personally. Ranked by *Kiplinger's* as one of the "100 Best Values in Public Colleges" and by *U.S. News & World Report* in the top tier of universities in "America's Best Colleges 2008," Oneonta was named to the 2007 *President's Higher Education Community Service Honor Roll* and twice named to the Templeton Foundation *Honor Roll of Character-Building Colleges.* Emphasizing excellence in classroom instruction, Oneonta's curriculum includes courses that broaden students' understanding of the human experience; sharpen writing, reasoning, and analytical skills; and offer in-depth, career-focused work in a broad range of major fields. With an outstanding library collection of print and electronic resources, excellent computer facilities, and strong advisement and support programs, Oneonta provides students a solid academic foundation for careers or graduate study. Varied residence life programs and outstanding volunteer service and internship arrangements offer students vast opportunities for personal development. The College's Center for Social Responsibility and Community actively develops and coordinates community service opportunities. Career planning and placement services assist students in preparing for careers and securing employment after graduation. A recent survey of graduates indicated that more than 80 percent were employed or enrolled in graduate study within six months.

Established as a state normal school in 1889, Oneonta was a founding college of the SUNY system in 1948. Now one of SUNY's highly selective colleges, Oneonta is accredited by the Middle States Association of Colleges and Schools. Its programs in chemistry are accredited by the American Chemical Society, programs in human ecology are accredited by the American Association of Family and Consumer Sciences, the dietetics program is accredited by the American Dietetic Association, the music industry program is accredited by the National Association of Schools of Music, and programs in education are accredited by the National Council for Accreditation of Teacher Education. The 250-acre campus is supplemented by 284 acres at the nearby College Camp. Off-campus facilities include the 600-acre Biological Field Station and research area on Otsego Lake and a history museum studies graduate program in nearby Cooperstown.

Though more than 90 percent of Oneonta students are state residents, the College attracts many out-of-state and international students. The College's 5,600 undergraduates represent a medley of cultures, backgrounds, ages, and experiences. More than half of Oneonta's students live in one of the fifteen on-campus residence halls, which have full-time professional directors and staffs of resident advisers. Residence life options include special interest areas. In addition to campuswide wireless network access, residence halls are wired for telephone and cable television. With card-key entry to residence halls, a campuswide emergency phone system, and other security measures, Oneonta has been cited as one of the safest campus settings in New York State. The Counseling, Health, and Wellness Center furnishes on-campus health care and confidential counseling. Three dining halls, a food court, a quick-serve restaurant, a coffeehouse, and a convenience store offer various dining options from early morning to late evening. Off-campus apartments and rooms are available in the community. A regular bus service, funded through activity fees, is provided free to all students.

More than seventy student organizations provide extracurricular cultural, social, athletic, and intellectual activities. A gymnasium, fitness center, field house, athletic fields and courts, and a lighted, all-weather track and field provide recreational facilities. Ten varsity men's teams and eleven women's teams compete in Division III intercollegiate sports, and the women's soccer team won the 2003 NCAA Division III national championship. Nearby state parks, ski resorts, museums, and theaters enhance on-campus recreational and cultural opportunities.

Location

Located in the scenic, historic Susquehanna Valley in the western foothills of the Catskills, Oneonta (population 15,000) is midway between Albany and Binghamton on Interstate 88. A convenient 3-hour drive from the New York City area and accessible from anywhere in the state, the city provides an exceptional setting for college life. Downtown Oneonta, a short walk from the campus, offers many restaurants and shops. The campus bus service provides transportation to and from downtown businesses, malls, and recreational facilities. Students are heavily involved in volunteer service and employment in the Oneonta community.

Majors and Degrees

The SUNY College at Oneonta offers a wide range of undergraduate programs leading to Bachelor of Arts and Bachelor of Science degrees. In the Division of Behavioral and Applied Science, majors are offered in accounting; business economics; child and family studies; dietetics; economics; family and consumer science education; food service and restaurant administration; gerontology; human ecology, with options in child and family studies, consumer studies, fashion merchandising and design, and general human ecology; international studies; psychology; and sociology, with options in criminal justice, general sociology, and human services.

In the Division of Education, majors are offered in adolescence education (biology, chemistry, earth science, English, family and consumer sciences (K–12), French, math, physics, social studies, and Spanish), childhood education (1–6), early childhood education (B–2), and early childhood/childhood education (B–6).

In the Division of Humanities and Fine Arts, majors are offered in art history, art studio, computer art, English, French, interdisciplinary studies, mass communication, music, music industry, philosophy, Spanish, speech communication, studio art, and theater.

In the Division of Science and Social Science, majors are offered in Africana and Latino studies; anthropology; biology, with options in biochemistry, biotechnology, ecological science, general biology, and human biology; chemistry; computer science; earth science; environmental sciences, with options in biology, earth science, general environmental sciences, and planning; geography, with options in cartography, general geography, and urban and regional planning; geology; history; mathematics; meteorology; physics; political science; statistics; and water resources.

Preprofessional programs prepare students for advanced study in dentistry, law, medicine, and veterinary science.

Oneonta offers a variety of programs in conjunction with other institutions: 3+2 dual majors in accounting, management, and business economics; a 4+1 M.B.A. program; cooperative programs in engineering; 3+1 programs in advertising and communications, advertising design, fashion buying and merchandising, and fashion design; programs in cytotechnology, medical technology, physical therapy, and respiratory care; and programs in pre-environmental science and forestry.

Academic Programs

Oneonta's academic program has three primary components: a general education requirement, specialized in-depth study in a

COLLEGE DATA CENTER • NEW YORK

major, and free electives. This combination helps students understand a plurality of perspectives, enables them to clarify their thought processes, and enhances their abilities to communicate effectively. The 36-hour general education requirement includes courses in American history, the arts, foreign language, humanities, mathematics, natural sciences, other world civilizations, social sciences, and Western civilization, as well as courses that develop thinking, problem-solving, and communication skills. In their major, students complete 30–60 hours of course work on their way to the 122 hours required for graduation. Transfer applications are encouraged, and students may transfer up to 66 credits from two-year colleges or 77 credits from four-year institutions. Degree credits may be earned through proficiency examinations, course challenges, and assessment of prior learning. Students must declare a major by their junior year. A strong academic advisement program provides assistance in choosing curricula and in planning the academic year, which is divided into two 15-week semesters with optional summer sessions.

The Oneonta honors program is designed for students with demonstrated high academic ability, a desire to succeed, and a willingness to seek out new challenges and experiences. It offers scholars the benefits of an enriched undergraduate experience while emphasizing flexibility and choice.

Off-Campus Programs

Oneonta offers many opportunities to earn degree credits while studying abroad and to gain valuable employment experience through internships. The SUNY Study Abroad Program enables students to study throughout the world in nearly 300 programs. Oneonta offers programs with the University of Würzburg in Germany, the American Intercontinental University in London, and the University of Wales intersession programs in Europe; semester or academic-year programs in Ireland and England; direct exchange programs with Seinan Gakuin University in Japan and with the Siberian Aerospace Academy, the Higher Business Academy, and other academic institutions in Krasnoyarsk, Russia; the Learn and Serve in India intersession program; and summer programs in Israel. Credit-bearing internships are available through many academic departments and agencies. The Center for Social Responsibility and Community provides opportunities for noncredit community service, often in a field related to the student's major.

Academic Facilities

An exceptional library, excellent computer equipment, and several specialized facilities provide outstanding academic resources for students. The Milne Library houses more than 550,000 volumes of print material, offers an online catalog and computers with access to specialized CD-ROMs and the Internet, and provides study space for 900 students. The College's forty computer labs, many of which are open seven days a week, provide more than 700 computers. Students have free access to a powerful campuswide network and the Internet, with wireless connections all throughout the College. Unique computer facilities include the Chemistry and Physics Multimedia Lab, the Computer Art Lab, and the Geographic Information Systems Lab. Enhanced classrooms enable faculty members to incorporate multimedia presentations into their classes. Recently upgraded television, music, and video production equipment enables the campus to broadcast live events and the students to produce videos. The hands-on Science Discovery Center and the observatory and planetarium offer unique resources. Academic support services provide individualized self-instructional programs, tutorials, and skill-building classes.

Costs

Tuition for 2007–08 was $4350 per year for state residents and $10,610 for nonresidents. Fees were $1100. Room and board were $8306. Costs for books, supplies, and personal expenses vary.

Financial Aid

Nearly 80 percent of Oneonta's full-time undergraduate students receive financial aid through federal, state, and local programs, including the Federal Pell Grant Program, Federal Supplemental Educational Opportunity Grants, Federal Perkins Loans, the Federal Family Educational Loan Program, the Federal Work-Study Program, on-campus part-time employment, and College scholarships. To be eligible for financial assistance, students must submit the Free Application for Federal Student Aid to the College as early as possible. Through a concerted effort to expand scholarship opportunities, the College now offers more than $1.5 million in scholarship awards. Information about scholarships is available through the Admissions or Financial Aid Offices.

Faculty

Oneonta's 263 full-time instructional faculty members, nearly all of whom hold doctoral degrees, are responsible for the development and implementation of the undergraduate programs. While many undertake research, their primary focus is on instruction, advisement, and counseling. A genuine sense of concern for the individual student's intellectual and personal development is the hallmark of Oneonta's faculty.

Student Government

Oneonta's Student Association, of which all registered students are members, is managed through democratically elected executive, legislative, and judicial branches. The Student Senate, which is composed of representatives of residence halls and off-campus residents, administers the student activity budget, which funds the campus organizations, athletics, entertainment activities, bus service, campus radio station, and student newspaper. Students are represented on the College Council, Alumni Association, College Senate, and many College-wide committees.

Admission Requirements

The College is strongly committed to academic excellence and the development of students to their full potential. Oneonta receives many more applications than there are available spaces, so admission is competitive. Applicants are evaluated on academic records, including their program of studies and results of standardized tests (ACT or SAT), and on personal experiences, achievements, and talents. Each fall, the College enrolls more than 1,000 freshmen and 400 transfer students. Approximately 200 additional students enter in the spring. The College welcomes applications from all candidates, including out-of-state and international students. On-campus interviews, tours, and information sessions are available but not required. Oneonta offers early action, admission through the Educational Opportunity Program, and admission to qualified high school students who graduate early. Freshman candidates should present a solid college-preparatory academic program, with at least 8 units of mathematics, science, and foreign language in addition to required social science and English courses. Accepted candidates generally rank in the top third of their class and have above-average test scores. Transfer students must present a minimum GPA of 2.5; education majors must have a GPA of 2.8 or better.

Application and Information

The College at Oneonta uses the standard SUNY application, which is available online, in most New York State high school guidance offices, or from the College's Admissions Office. Applications are accepted year-round and are evaluated on a rolling basis. For fall semester admission, freshman applicants should submit all materials by February 1; transfer applicants should submit materials by April 1. For more information, students should contact:

Director of Admissions
State University of New York College at Oneonta
Oneonta, New York 13820
Phone: 607-436-2524
800-SUNY-123 (toll-free)
Fax: 607-436-3074
E-mail: admissions@oneonta.edu
Qs4Oneonta (instant message)
Web site: http://www.oneonta.edu

STATE UNIVERSITY OF NEW YORK COLLEGE OF ENVIRONMENTAL SCIENCE AND FORESTRY

SYRACUSE, NEW YORK

The College

Since it was founded in 1911 as the New York State College of Forestry, the SUNY College of Environmental Science and Forestry (ESF) has expanded both its role in education and its physical boundaries. The College has expanded its initial emphasis on forestry to include professional education in environmental science, landscape architecture, environmental studies, and engineering in addition to distinguished programs in the biological and physical sciences. Throughout its history, the College has focused on the environmental issues of the time in each of its three mission areas—instruction, research, and public service. The College is dedicated to educating future scientists and managers who, through specialized skills, will be able to use a holistic approach to solving the environmental and resource problems facing society.

A leader in its field, ESF is one of the doctoral degree–granting colleges in the State University of New York System. The College currently supports undergraduate and graduate degree programs in several disciplinary areas and in its broad program in environmental science. (Undergraduate programs are described in the Majors and Degrees section below.) Graduate programs lead to the Master of Science (M.S.), Master of Landscape Architecture (M.L.A.), Master of Professional Studies (M.P.S.), and Doctor of Philosophy (Ph.D.) degrees. ESF's research program has attracted a worldwide clientele, and support currently amounts to $5.5 million a year.

ESF's main campus is located on 12 acres adjacent to Syracuse University and the SUNY Upstate Medical University in an urban residential setting. There are 1,500 undergraduates enrolled (40 percent are women); the College's traditional affiliation with Syracuse University offers ESF students the opportunity for academic diversity and depth, as well as participation in cultural events, honorary societies, social fraternities and sororities, and professional and academic organizations.

Location

Syracuse, a metropolitan area of nearly 654,000 people, is a leader in the manufacture of china, air-conditioning equipment, medical diagnostic equipment, drugs, automotive parts, and lighting equipment. It offers many cultural, recreational, and educational opportunities, including a symphony orchestra, museums, live theater, and historic points of interest. Syracuse is one of the few cities in the nation situated at the crossing point of two superhighways. The driving time to Syracuse from New York City, Philadelphia, Boston, Toronto, and Montreal is about 5 hours; from Buffalo and Albany, about 3 hours. The city is served by a modern international airport and major bus and rail lines.

Majors and Degrees

The SUNY College of Environmental Science and Forestry offers three undergraduate degrees: the Bachelor of Science (B.S.), the Bachelor of Landscape Architecture (B.L.A.), and the Associate in Applied Science (A.A.S.). The B.S. degree is awarded in aquatic and fisheries science, bioprocess engineering, biotechnology, chemistry, conservation biology, construction management, environmental biology, environmental resources and forest engineering, environmental science, environmental studies, forest health, forest resources management, natural history and interpretation, natural resources management, paper engineering, paper science, wildlife science, wood products engineering, and an undeclared option. A dual option in forest resources management and environmental forest biology is also offered, as are a number of options and concentrations within specific curricula. The B.L.A. degree, which requires an additional year of study, is awarded in landscape architecture. A.A.S. degrees are awarded in forest technology and land surveying technology at the Ranger School campus in Wanakena, New York.

Academic Programs

Students at ESF all have opportunities for additional specialized study, as well as research and field experience. The Department of Environmental and Forest Biology is the largest department on campus and encompasses seven different majors, including studies in biotechnology, conservation, wildlife, aquatic and fisheries science, forest health, and natural history and interpretation. With the exception of biotechnology students, biology students are required to take a four-week period of summer field study, usually at ESF's Cranberry Lake Biological Station, after the junior year. Options for specialization within the chemistry program include biochemistry and natural products chemistry, environmental chemistry, and natural and synthetic polymer chemistry. Biology and chemistry students can also earn their secondary science teacher certification through Syracuse University.

The construction management program teaches management, analysis, and design of the construction process, with an emphasis on environmental and engineering issues. Wood products engineering students focus on marketing and production of forest products, wood science and technology, and building construction and renovation.

Environmental resources and forest engineering students learn skills in such areas as biological, environmental, and water resources engineering, mapping science, and geographic information systems. The closely related environmental science program also deals with mapping and engineering science, along with areas of focus in watershed science, health and the environment, earth and atmospheric systems science, and environmental analysis.

Bioprocess engineering students focus on the engineering, biology, and chemistry of ecologically sound industrial technologies and processes, giving students career opportunities in areas such as resource and bioengineering, pharmaceuticals, renewable energy, and environmental engineering. The forest resources management curriculum offers areas of focus in forest management, measurement, and policy, along with forest ecology and biology. The program also includes a minor in management in conjunction with Syracuse University. Natural resources management students can concentrate in either recreation or water resources management. Forest and natural resources management students are required to participate in a four-week period of summer field study, which is usually taken at ESF's Wanakena campus prior to the junior year.

Environmental studies offers specializations in environmental communication and culture, policy and management, and biological science applications. The landscape architecture program is a five-year bachelor's degree with options in site design, urban and regional planning, historic preservation, community and environmental design, and computer applications. During the first semester of the fifth year, the landscape architecture curriculum requires participation in off-campus independent study. Paper engineering students can study process and product design and environmental engineering applied to pulp, paper, and other related chemical industries, while paper science students have the flexibility to focus on a variety of areas, including management and computer systems. In addition, ESF offers preprofessional advisement in the areas of dentistry, law, veterinary science, and medicine, including a transfer articulation agreement with the College of Health Professions at SUNY Upstate Medical University.

Academic Facilities

Specialized facilities and equipment include electron microscopes, plant-growth chambers, climate-controlled greenhouses, an animal environmental simulation chamber, a bioacoustical laboratory, a radioisotope laboratory, a computer center, nuclear magnetic resonance spectrometers, gas chromatography apparatus, a mass spectrometer, ultracentrifuges, and X-ray and infrared spectrophotometers. The photogrammetric and geodetic facilities of the environmental resources and forest engineering department are among the most extensive available in the United States. The paper science and engineering laboratory has a semi-commercial paper mill with accessory equipment. The construction management and wood products engineering faculty has a complete strength-of-materials laboratory, a pilot-scale plywood laboratory, and a machining laboratory. The landscape architecture faculty has a one-of-a-kind environmental simulation laboratory with a visual simulator. The greenhouses and forest insectary are used to produce plant and insect materials for the classroom and laboratory. Extensive collections are available, including wood samples from all over the world, botanical materials, insects, birds, mammals, and fishes. The Theodore Roosevelt Wildlife Collection contains more than 10,000 species of well-preserved vertebrate and invertebrate animals.

A complete renovation to the F. Franklin Moon Library was completed in 2007 with the addition of an Academic Success Center for tutorial support in mathematics and other SUNY ESF courses. A Writing Center is also located in Moon Library. Moon Library contains 106,000 cataloged items, and more than 1,800 journals and their corresponding indexes are currently received. The library also provides comprehensive abstract and indexing services that are relevant to the College's programs. These facilities and services are supplemented by the collections of Syracuse University and the SUNY Upstate Medical University, both of which are within easy walking distance. Students should visit http://www.esf.edu/communications/news/2007/06.25.moon.htm to read more about the improvements to the F. Franklin Moon Library.

ESF's regional campuses in Tully, Warrensburg, Cranberry Lake, Newcomb, and Wanakena, New York, have a great diversity of forest sites that are used as outdoor teaching laboratories and for intensive research. ESF also operates several field stations to support its instruction, research, and public service programs.

Costs

Estimated costs for the 2007–08 academic year included resident tuition and fees of $5100 and out-of-state tuition and fees of $11,360. Room and board, which are provided for ESF students by Syracuse University, were $11,320. Books, personal expenses, and travel are estimated at $2250.

Financial Aid

A wide variety of financial aid is available for ESF students, and more than 90 percent of the students receive some type of support. The forms of financial aid include merit- and need-based scholarships, grants, low-interest student loans, and student employment programs. All students are encouraged to apply for financial aid by completing the Free Application for Federal Student Aid (FAFSA).

Faculty

The members of the faculty at ESF are highly trained and are dedicated to the College's teaching, research, and public-service missions. There are 117 regular faculty members, 10 research associates, and 46 adjunct members. Many are nationally and internationally recognized for their expertise in specialized fields. Nearly all regular faculty members serve full-time, and most hold twelve-month appointments. Just over 80 percent are tenured, and more than half are full professors, of whom 93 percent have earned doctorates. There is no distinction between the undergraduate and graduate faculty. Faculty members teach at both levels, and no courses are taught by teaching assistants. Faculty members serve as advisers to students and student groups and encourage excellence in scholarship and research. The student-faculty ratio is about 12:1.

Student Government

The College has a representative Undergraduate Student Association, and student representatives also participate in a counterpart association at Syracuse University. The ESF student government body organizes and presents student social activities, and its representatives attend College administrative meetings, communicate students' concerns and ideas to the administration, and serve as a conduit of information back to the student body. A formal set of student rules and regulations has been established. In addition, ESF students are obligated to abide by Syracuse University's general rules and regulations.

Admission Requirements

Students who are interested in the academic programs offered at ESF have four enrollment options: Early Action, Regular Freshman Entry, Guaranteed Transfer Admissions, and Transfer Admissions.

Outstanding high school seniors who have selected SUNY-ESF as a top choice may apply for Early Action, a nonbinding early application/early notification program for fall-entry freshmen. Early Action allows students to apply to as many institutions as they wish and, if admitted, make their final college choice no later than May 1. Students filing an application for Early Action must meet the SUNY application filing deadline date of November 15 and have supporting credentials to SUNY-ESF by December 1. Students applying for Early Action are notified by January 1.

Regular Freshman Entry is for applicants who want to enroll immediately following high school. These candidates should demonstrate strong academic performance in a college-preparatory program, with emphasis on mathematics and science preparation. Freshman candidates must apply to their intended programs of study.

Guarantee Transfer Admission (GTA) candidates apply to ESF as high school seniors but are offered admission to either their sophomore or junior year. Students who plan to attend another college prior to transferring to ESF select this option to ensure a place at ESF for their chosen entry date. This option may also be offered to students who do not meet the freshman admissions criteria. Those who are accepted for guaranteed transfer admission receive a letter of acceptance for their sophomore or junior year of college, contingent upon the successful completion of all the prerequisite courses required for the curriculum they have selected. The prerequisite courses are outlined and described in an enclosure with the student's acceptance letter and can also be found on the College's Web site at http://www.esf.edu.

Students not applying or not accepted under these programs are considered for admission to ESF on the basis of their previous college course work, overall academic aptitude, and interest in the College's programs. Consideration is given to both the quality and the appropriateness of each student's prior academic experience. Students may spend one or two years at any accredited college of their choice. The College has developed Cooperative Transfer Programs with other four-year and two-year colleges in New York, Connecticut, Maryland, Massachusetts, New Jersey, and Pennsylvania. All admission acceptances are conditional upon satisfactory completion of course work in progress.

Application and Information

Students may apply for fall or spring admission. Admission decisions are made on a rolling basis until the class is filled. Decisions for the fall semester are made beginning on or around December 15, and decisions for the spring semester are made beginning on or around October 15. Application forms are available for New York State residents at New York State high schools and at all SUNY two- and four-year colleges. Out-of-state students should request an application form directly from the Office of Undergraduate Admissions at ESF. Both parts of the application can also be found online at the College Web site. Requests for more information should be directed to:

Office of Undergraduate Admissions
106 Bray Hall
State University of New York College of Environmental Science and Forestry
1 Forestry Drive
Syracuse, New York 13210-2779
Phone: 315-470-6600
800-777-7373 (toll-free)
Fax: 315-470-6933
E-mail: esfinfo@esf.edu
Web site: http://www.esf.edu

STATE UNIVERSITY OF NEW YORK EMPIRE STATE COLLEGE

SARATOGA SPRINGS, NEW YORK

The College

Empire State College, of the State University of New York (SUNY), was founded in 1971 to enable motivated adults, regardless of geography of life circumstance, to design a rigorous, individualized academic program and earn a college degree. The College offers degree programs in the arts and sciences through independent study, online courses, and study groups as well as credit earned through college-level life learning on the undergraduate and graduate levels. The College continues to expand to meet the needs of working adults at thirty-five locations in New York State as well as nationally and internationally through its Center for Distance Learning. In addition, the College's Center for International Programs brings an accredited SUNY degree to international students in several locations across the globe. Empire State College now serves more than 17,000 students and has over 50,000 alumni.

In addition to its undergraduate degrees, Empire State College offers five graduate degree programs, including two Master of Arts in policy (labor and policy studies and social policy), a Master of Arts in Liberal Studies, a Master of Business Administration, and a Master of Arts in Teaching.

Location

From the first locations established in Albany and New York City in 1971, Empire State College has continued to grow. Today it has thirty-five locations from the Canadian border to Long Island's eastern shore. In New York State, its seven regional learning centers are located in Albany, Cheektowaga (Buffalo region), Hartsdale, New York City, Rochester, Syracuse, and Old Westbury on Long Island, with smaller units located in the surrounding communities. Through its Center for Distance Learning, the College serves students online throughout the state, across the nation, and around the world. The coordinating center is located in historic Saratoga Springs, New York.

Majors and Degrees

Five undergraduate degrees are offered in eleven areas of study, from the arts to business, management, and economics. When students select the area of study they are interested in, they then choose a concentration—similar to a major—within this area. With the guidance of their professor—called a faculty mentor—students have the opportunity to design their own degree program based on their goals and objectives. The faculty mentor is there to advise and assist every step of the way.

Degrees offered include the Associate in Arts (A.A.), Associate in Science (A.S.), Bachelor of Arts (B.A.), Bachelor of Science (B.S.), and Bachelor of Professional Studies (B.P.S.).

There is no hard and fast time frame for how long it takes to earn a degree, since that depends upon how many courses a student takes at a time and how much credit they can include from other sources. However, approximately 40 percent of the students who enter at an advanced level complete their degrees within two to four years on a part-time basis; many take as little as a year. Students design individually tailored concentrations and earn degrees in the following areas of study: the arts; business, management, and economics; community and human services; cultural studies; educational studies; historical studies; human development; interdisciplinary studies; labor studies; science, mathematics, and technology; and social theory, social structure, and change.

Empire State College provides students with choices regarding how best to pursue their degree and offers a number of flexible education options. Guided independent study, where students complete course requirements on their own schedule and at times convenient to them, is one option. Instead of taking classes, a student and his or her mentor develop "a learning contract" specifying what he or she is expected to learn during a given term. After enrolling at an Empire State College location, a student works with a mentor to define a schedule to meet and evaluate progress.

If students need even more flexibility or live far from one of the College's learning locations, they may study online. With courses for all areas of study available online, most students who choose to can complete their entire degree program via the Web. Students who take online courses enjoy the opportunity to interact through course discussion areas and e-mail, not only with their professor, but with other students taking the same course. The College's Center for Distance Learning also offers onsite and online degree programs through a number of corporate and organizational partnerships. For other students, blended learning, a combination of face-to-face and online courses, is best.

Study groups are for students who study independently yet want to delve deeper into a subject through face-to-face interaction with others. Study groups allow students to discuss topics and assignments and share insights with other students.

Academic Programs

The College has a five-term academic calendar. In keeping with the College's interest in providing adults with flexible start dates, the calendar features four 15-week terms that begin in September, November, January, and March. The fifth term, beginning in May, includes the option of an eight-week (Term A) or fifteen-week term (Term B).

Empire State College recognizes the value of lifelong learning. Whether a student has attended other colleges, built a career, or simply pursued personal interests, odds are they've spent much of their life learning. Provided the life-learning experience is college level and relevant to their degree program, students can earn credits based on transcripts and evaluation.

The Harry Van Arsdale Jr. Center for Labor Studies offers members of unions and others interested in labor-related careers one of the most comprehensive labor programs in the nation. Although it specializes in labor issues, students can enroll in any of the areas of study offered by Empire State College. Many of the most prominent labor leaders across New York State can be counted among the center's graduates.

The College also offers a number of specialized programs to serve various adult learners, such as the FORUM Management Education Program, a bachelor's degree program designed for experienced business professionals looking for a way to earn a college degree while they work.

Off-Campus Programs

Empire State College students may cross register at other institutions to expand their course options, to get hands-on experience not readily available through independent study, or because a subject lends itself to classroom study. Empire State College grants credit toward a degree program for classes completed at other accredited institutions.

Academic Facilities

Empire State College is a college designed with the adult learner in mind, and students have access to many public and private library collections. As part of the State University system, the College participates in the SUNY Open Access library program, which allows students to use most services at participating SUNY libraries. Residents of the New York City metropolitan region benefit from a similar arrangement with the City of New York (CUNY) libraries.

Costs

Tuition and fees for the 2006–07 academic year were $4555 for in-state residents and $10,815 for out-of-state students. Books and supplies cost approximately $500 per semester.

Financial Aid

Empire State College's Financial Aid Office administers funds from a variety of federal and state sources to students based on need. More than 50 percent of the students receive some kind of financial aid. There are three types of aid available at Empire State College: grants/scholarships, loans, and work-study. Other sources of financial assistance may be available from a wide variety of organizations, civic and cultural groups, and employers. Students are urged to explore these possibilities. In order to be considered for financial aid, students must complete the Free Application for Federal Student Aid (FAFSA). A time payment plan is also available whereby tuition and fees may be paid in three installments. For more specific information, students should visit http://www.esc.edu/financialservices.

Faculty

The 1,118 full-time, part-time, and adjunct members of Empire State College's faculty come from a variety of backgrounds, including business, the arts, and traditional four-year colleges. Ninety-six percent hold doctoral degrees or other terminal degrees in their area of expertise. What they all have in common is a passion for teaching adult students. Faculty members are called mentors because they are both partners and guides in students' education. They respect the years of experience and knowledge that adults bring to an academic program and are glad to share their own expertise. Students meet with their mentors on a regular basis to receive advice and to develop plans for carrying out their learning contracts. Students maintain contact with their mentors on an agreed-upon schedule, either face-to-face or by phone, mail, or e-mail. Most students value the personal attention, and when Empire State College students graduate, often it is their mentor whom they celebrate when they look back on their college years.

Admission Requirements

Decisions on admission to the College are made without regard to the race, sex, disability, religion, or national origin of the applicant. The two principal requirements for admission are the possession of a high school diploma or its equivalent or the ability to benefit from college study as demonstrated through means required by the College and the ability of an Empire State College learning location to meet the applicant's educational needs and objectives. Although the majority of applicants to the College are admitted, the College reserves the right to deny admission based on its ability to meet a student's needs. Standardized test scores are not used as part of the application process for admission.

Application and Information

Because the College's mode of education is unique, it is strongly recommended that students attend an information session at the nearest Empire State College location. Details regarding times and places of the information sessions are available on the College's Web site or by calling the phone number listed below.

Administrative Offices
Empire State College
One Union Avenue
Saratoga Springs, New York 12866
Phone: 518-587-2100
Web site: http://www.esc.edu

STATE UNIVERSITY OF NEW YORK INSTITUTE OF TECHNOLOGY

UTICA, NEW YORK

The College

The State University of New York Institute of Technology (SUNYIT) offers undergraduate degree programs in technology, professional studies, and the liberal arts. SUNYIT's broad curriculum embraces the humanities, communications, math, and science. Students enjoy close contact with faculty members in small classes, many with fewer than 20 students.

Founded as an upper-division and graduate institution in 1966, SUNYIT offers twenty bachelor's degree programs for freshmen and undergraduate transfer students and thirteen graduate degrees, including the Master of Business Administration in technology management.

SUNYIT enrolled 2,069 undergraduate and 518 graduate students on both a full-time and part-time basis in fall 2006. The men-women ratio was approximately 1:1. Approximately 4 percent were international students, and 10 percent of students were members of minority groups.

In addition to its academic facilities, SUNYIT provides student services through the Campus Life, Career Services, Health, and Counseling Center Offices. Town-house-style residence halls provide on-campus housing to 584 students. The Campus Center provides health, physical education, and recreation facilities as well as a dining hall and student services offices. In addition to providing a wide variety of intramural sports for students, SUNYIT has competitive intercollegiate teams in men's and women's basketball, bowling, cross-country, golf, and soccer; men's baseball; and women's softball and volleyball.

Location

SUNYIT is located in Marcy, New York, a few minutes from Utica. The city of Utica, which has a population of 60,000, is situated in the geographic center of New York State, approximately 220 miles from New York City and 190 miles from Buffalo on the New York State Thruway. Utica, a cultural and recreational center for this area of New York State, has a variety of recreational and educational opportunities. Museums, theaters, restaurants, and professional sports events are available either within walking distance of the campus or a short bus ride away. As a natural gateway to the Adirondack Mountains, Utica provides its residents with access to hiking, boating, skiing, and other outdoor activities. Served by buses, Amtrak, and airlines, the city is easily reached from locations throughout the eastern United States.

Majors and Degrees

SUNYIT awards the following baccalaureate degrees: Bachelor of Professional Studies (B.P.S.), Bachelor of Science (B.S.), Bachelor of Arts (B.A.), and Bachelor of Business Administration (B.B.A.).

Academic majors available to undergraduate students include accounting, applied mathematics, business administration, civil engineering technology, communication and information design, computer and information science, computer engineering technology, computer information systems, electrical engineering, electrical engineering technology, finance, general studies, health-information management, health services management, industrial engineering technology, mechanical engineering technology, nursing, psychology, sociology, and telecommunications.

A number of options and concentrations within specific curricula are also available, as are minors in accounting; anthropology; communication and information design; computer science; economics; finance; gerontology; health services management; manufacturing/quality assurance technology; mathematics; physics; psychology; science, technology, and society; and sociology.

Academic Programs

SUNYIT's academic year is divided into two semesters and runs from September through May. Summer sessions are also available.

Baccalaureate degree requirements vary from program to program but usually consist of a combination of specific major courses and liberal arts studies. Specializations and other options exist within the Schools of Arts and Sciences, Business, Information Systems and Engineering Technology, and Nursing and Health Systems. Specializations are developed through the use of electives and individual advisement.

Off-Campus Programs

Internship and cooperative education experiences are integral to effective career planning and job search strategies. These experiences can influence career plans by providing an opportunity for occupational exploration, developing marketable career-related skills and characteristics, and establishing a network of contacts that can provide relevant and timely information critical to the career decision-making process. In addition, employers are increasingly using internships and cooperative education programs as training opportunities leading to full-time permanent employment. All students, regardless of major, are encouraged to consider gaining experience in their chosen field that complements classroom learning. For additional information, students should contact the academic department or the Office of Career Services.

Academic Facilities

SUNYIT's academic facilities are located on its scenic 800-acre campus just north of the city of Utica, easily accessible by municipal bus service. The campus consists of four building complexes, a facilities building, and residence halls. Construction is planned for two new buildings: a $20-million sports complex and a $13-million student center.

Dedicated in 2003, the $14-million Peter J. Cayan Library comprises 68,000 square feet of space, group and individual study rooms, and an advanced computerized library instruction room.

Kunsela Hall contains administrative offices, classrooms, a bookstore, and laboratories for the telecommunications, electrical engineering, electrical engineering technology, and computer science programs. Donovan Hall—the academic complex—houses classrooms, faculty offices, and laboratory facilities for all other programs, including business, industrial engineering technology, mechanical engineering technology, health services management, nursing, and arts and sciences. The Campus

Center contains a cafeteria, gymnasium, recreational facilities, student services offices, a swimming pool, and meeting rooms for clubs, special activities, and student government.

Costs

Costs for the 2006–07 academic year included state resident tuition and fees of $5317 and out-of-state tuition and fees of $11,577. Room and board costs were $7600, and personal expenses, books, supplies, and travel cost approximately $2890. The total expenses were about $15,807 for New York State residents and $22,067 for out-of-state students. Costs may be subject to change.

Financial Aid

A wide variety of financial aid is available to students at SUNYIT. All financial aid is awarded on the basis of need, as determined by an assessment of the Free Application for Federal Student Aid. At present, approximately 85 percent of the students receive financial assistance. The forms of financial aid available include Tuition Assistance Program awards (for New York State residents only), Federal Supplemental Educational Opportunity Grants, Federal Pell Grants, Federal Work-Study Program employment, Federal Perkins Loans, federal Nursing Student Loans, Federal Direct Student Loans, a variety of state-sponsored loans, and a broad range of private scholarships and grants. Students with a GPA of 3.25 or better or a high school average of 90 are automatically considered for merit scholarships at the time of their application.

Faculty

SUNYIT faculty members come from all over the world and are committed to teaching, research, and service to the community. Among the faculty members are a Distinguished Service Professor, a Fulbright Scholar, and numerous recipients of the Chancellor's Award for Excellence in Teaching. More than 80 percent of SUNYIT's full-time faculty members have doctoral or terminal degrees. The faculty members are fully engaged in academic orientation and advisement, individualized instruction, cooperative faculty-student efforts in research projects, and concern for students as individuals. In the classroom, the average student-faculty ratio is 17:1.

Student Government

All full-time undergraduates are members of the SUNYIT Student Association. Its primary functions are to develop and monitor the student-activity-fee budget, to approve and oversee all student organizations, to debate issues of concern to students and take action as needed, and to develop programs of interest to all students. Student government consists of a 7-person executive committee and 11 senators. Students are encouraged to take an active role in the governance process, and many opportunities for involvement, in addition to those listed above, are available for interested students.

Admission Requirements

Generally, freshman applicants should carry a B/B+ average in a college-preparatory program and have achieved an SAT score in the 1000–1100 range (or approximately 22–24 composite ACT score). Admission is based on high school average, SAT or ACT scores, strength of course work, and other relevant information.

For transfer students, most programs require a minimum GPA of 2.5 for guaranteed admission. Transfer students below a 2.5 GPA but above a 2.0 GPA may be required to participate in an interview. Transfer students are required to furnish an official transcript from all previous colleges they attended.

Students with a cumulative GPA of at least 3.25 are automatically considered for merit and residential scholarships; no separate application is required.

Application and Information

All applications are reviewed on an individual basis. All EOP applicants are also required to complete a supplemental application and are encouraged to apply for fall semester by November 23. The recommended application deadline for EOP and regular admission is February 15. However, applications received after that date will be considered on a rolling basis. Notification of admissions decisions begins on December 16. Acceptances are mailed beginning December 16.

SUNYIT participates in the SUNY Early Decision program. Early Decision students must submit their application by November 1; applications are reviewed and students are notified of admission by December 15. Students admitted under Early Decision are required to submit a deposit by January 15 and withdraw applications to other campuses.

Transfer applications are accepted on a rolling admissions basis. Prospective students are urged to apply early.

Students who wish to apply should obtain a copy of the State University of New York application booklet from a two-year college, a local high school, or the Admissions Office. In addition, students may apply online through the SUNYIT Web site. Application forms for international students may also be obtained through the Admissions Office.

SUNYIT adheres to the principle that all persons should have equal opportunity and access to its educational facilities without regard to race, creed, sex, or national origin.

Official transcripts from all previously attended high schools and colleges should be sent to the Director of Admissions. All communications and requests for additional information should also be directed to:

Director of Admissions
SUNY Institute of Technology
P.O. Box 3050
Utica, New York 13504-3050
Phone: 315-792-7500
866-2SUNYIT (toll-free)
Fax: 315-792-7837
E-mail: admissions@sunyit.edu
Web site: http://www.sunyit.edu

Town-house-style residence halls afford students the opportunity to live and learn in a convenient, safe, and comfortable environment.

STATE UNIVERSITY OF NEW YORK MARITIME COLLEGE

FORT SCHUYLER, THROGGS NECK, NEW YORK

The College

Founded in 1874, the State University of New York Maritime College is the original, federally approved, commercial nautical institution in the United States. Maritime College has as its primary mission the preparation of men and women for a full spectrum of professional careers by providing high-quality undergraduate and graduate programs in international business, engineering, science, and technology, with particular emphasis on the marine industry. Most of the degree programs may be completed while concurrently preparing for the U.S. Merchant Marine officer's license as a third mate or third assistant engineer.

Maritime College graduates receive a well-rounded education that enables them to pursue career options in engineering or business, in private industry or government service, or at sea as civilian officers of merchant ships, research ships, and other U.S. vessels. In addition, while there is no military obligation, commissioning options exist for those seeking careers as officers in the U.S. Navy, Marine Corps, Coast Guard, or Air Force or in the National Oceanographic and Atmospheric Administration (NOAA). Maritime College is the only college that hosts a Naval ROTC program in the greater New York metropolitan area. The College has a consistent record of 100 percent career placement upon graduation.

Maritime College fields twenty-one varsity sports and is nationally known for its sailing and crew teams.

Location

The scenic 56-acre campus is located at historic Fort Schuyler on the Throggs Neck peninsula, where the East River meets Long Island Sound. The College campus has a suburban setting yet is a short bus ride from midtown Manhattan. The peninsula offers panoramic views of the East River and Long Island Sound, with impressive sights of coastal Connecticut, the North Shore of Long Island, and the Manhattan skyline.

The College's extensive waterfront property allows berthing of the College training ship, *Empire State VI;* several research craft; and a training coastal tanker and includes a waterfront activities center/boathouse. The waterfront is home for its fleet of 420s, Lasers, FJ's, and offshore racing yachts.

Majors and Degrees

The College offers Bachelor of Engineering degrees in electrical, facilities, marine, and mechanical engineering; marine electrical and electronic systems; and naval architecture. It offers the Bachelor of Science degree in business administration/marine transportation, general business and commerce (with a humanities concentration), general engineering, international transportation and trade, marine environmental science (with a marine biology, meteorology, or oceanography concentration), marine operations, and maritime studies. All degree programs may be combined with preparation for the professional license as a U.S. Merchant Marine Officer, except international transportation and trade.

Business administration/marine transportation couples the nautical education and training required of a ship's deck officer with the business administration academic core (liberal arts and sciences, accounting, economics, and marketing and management). Students may concentrate in the areas of management, logistics, international business, or vessel operations.

Graduates enrolled in this degree/license program are qualified to sail as third mates aboard oceangoing ships, on the Great Lakes, and on all types of inland and near-coastal vessels. In addition to careers at sea, the federal license enhances graduates' opportunities to find exciting positions in virtually all aspects of global transportation, from marine insurance to management of import/export industries and terminal operations. A related program, international transportation and trade, does not require license preparation. Also available is a major in general business and commerce, which includes deck license preparation and a humanities study area concentration.

The College offers Accreditation Board for Engineering and Technology (ABET)–accredited programs in engineering and naval architecture. The marine engineering program at Maritime College provides graduates with a broad understanding of the energy and power industries and includes preparation for a third-assistant engineer's license. Electrical, facilities, and mechanical engineering programs offer specialization within some of the areas covered by the marine engineering discipline and may be pursued as license-option or intern-option students. Naval architecture, offered with a deck- or engine-license option or intern option, is a challenging enterprise, demanding imagination and technical expertise in the design of seaborne structures from ultralarge tankers to high-speed recreational craft. Engine-license candidates experience operating a live power plant aboard the training ship, while intern-option students utilize an industrial co-op experience to gain the hands-on component for which Maritime graduates are renown. A Bachelor of Science degree in marine operations combines a deck license with a technical background and a limited horsepower engineering license, and general engineering qualifies students for an engine license and offers a humanities study area concentration.

The marine environmental science (MES) program offers undergraduate study in the ocean and atmospheric sciences, including environmental chemistry, environmental protection, marine biology and ecology, and physical oceanography and meteorology. MES students have deck, engine, and nonlicense options.

A two-year associate degree program in marine technology/small-vessel operations qualifies graduates for a 200-ton U.S. Coast Guard mate's license.

Academic Programs

Academic programs at the Maritime College lead to the Bachelor of Science or Bachelor of Engineering degree, and most include licensure as a commercial ship's officer (mate or engineer) as an option (license qualification is a requirement in some programs). These licenses, issued by the Coast Guard, qualify graduates to sail on oceangoing vessels engaged in international commerce or coastal, Great Lakes, or inland waterway shipping. License candidates are required to be members of the Regiment of Cadets. All programs include a hands-on, professional experience, either during Summer Sea Terms aboard the training ship *Empire State VI* or through industrial co-ops/internships.

The annual Summer Sea Term, which is an important part of all Maritime College curricula, takes place aboard the 565-foot training ship *Empire State VI,* the largest and best-equipped training ship in the United States. Summer Sea Term provides a leadership laboratory in which cadets assume responsibility for the operation of the ship under the supervision of licensed officers and staff. The *Empire State VI* visits nine European ports by the time the students graduate. Recent ports of call include the Bahamas, Bermuda, Ireland, Italy, London, and Spain.

Academic Facilities

Pre–Civil War Fort Schuyler houses the Stephen B. Luce Library with its more than 80,000 volumes and 375 periodical subscriptions, accessed through an online catalog. Full-text CD-ROM databases and online searches are also available. A $1.5-million Center for Simulation and Marine Operations also resides in the fort. It contains a state-of-the-art full bridge simulator, a liquid cargo simulator, an electronic navigation simulator, ten Automatic Radar Plotting Aid (ARPA)–equipped radar simulators, and Global Maritime Distress and Safety System (GMDSS) simulators.

The Science and Engineering Building contains a marine diesel simulator, a ship model basin (towing tank), and five computer classroom/laboratories as well as advanced electrical and mechanical engineering labs; physics, chemistry, and meteorology laboratories; and smart classrooms.

Floating laboratories include the training ship *Empire State VI*, a coastal tanker used for liquid cargo training, and several marine research craft, including a 147-foot buoy tender.

Costs

For 2007–08, tuition for New York State residents was $4350. Since the Maritime College has been designated as a regional maritime college, students from East and Gulf Coast states (Alabama, Connecticut, Delaware, Florida, Georgia, Louisiana, Maryland, Mississippi, New Jersey, North Carolina, Pennsylvania, Rhode Island, South Carolina, and Virginia) and the District of Columbia also pay the New York State tuition rate of $4350 per year. In addition, students from any state who apply for and are qualified to enroll in the federally funded Student Incentive Program (SIP) are charged New York State tuition.

For students who did not participate in SIP and were not residents of New York or any of the regional states, tuition was $10,610 per year in 2007–08. This rate also applied to international students.

Additional costs in the 2007–08 school year totaled approximately $17,000. This fee includes room and board, Summer Sea Term, uniform fees, and other costs.

Financial Aid

Maritime College students have access to several special forms of aid. Cadets who apply for and are selected for the federal Student Incentive Program receive $3000 per year. SIP participants pay New York State tuition rates regardless of residence and agree to complete one of the license programs at the College and serve in the U.S. Naval Reserve (inactive duty, including the Merchant Marine Reserve). Full-tuition scholarships are also available through Naval ROTC. Four-year NROTC scholarship winners are also offered free room at the College, and the Maritime Academy Reserve Training Program (MARTP), a Coast Guard Commissioning Program, provides generous compensation to select Maritime College cadets beginning their sophomore year.

A variety of privately funded scholarships, including a number of full-tuition Cadet Appointment Program Scholarships, are available to qualified students. Need-based aid, including Federal Pell Grants, TAP grants, Federal Perkins Loans, Federal Stafford Student Loans, and Federal Work-Study awards, is available and requires the Free Application for Federal Student Aid (FAFSA) as well as the Maritime College institutional form.

New York State residents who are in great financial need and who have not been able to achieve up to their academic potential because of factors beyond their control may apply for assistance through the Educational Opportunity Program when they apply for admission.

Faculty

Maritime College prides itself on an innovative, hands-on approach to instruction that is directed by a dedicated faculty composed of experts in their fields. The faculty members involved with license preparation course work have the appropriate United States Coast Guard licenses and professional credentials. Faculty members teaching in traditional academic disciplines possess appropriate credentials, with 35 holding the doctorate or other terminal degree in their field. Many faculty members, recognized as experts within the maritime industry, are involved with consulting work. A student-faculty ratio of 13:1 is maintained.

Student Government

The College has an active government association. It oversees College-wide activities, clubs and organizations, and a diverse athletic program. Students are also represented on various faculty committees.

Admission Requirements

Admission is competitive and is based strictly on the applicant's abilities. Political nomination is not required. Decisions are based on strength of academic preparation; grades, rank in class, and test scores; outside activities and achievements; and trends in performance. Transfer students are welcome. Math, through at least intermediate algebra and trigonometry, and a year of either chemistry or physics are required.

Application and Information

Applications (the SUNY Common Application for Admission form and College forms), catalogs, and additional information are available from the Office of Admissions. Prospective students are encouraged to schedule an interview and a student-guided tour (arranged with the admissions office). Students may apply online through the College's Web page.

Office of Admissions
State University of New York Maritime College
6 Pennyfield Avenue
Throggs Neck, New York 10465
Phone: 718-409-7220
E-mail: admissions@sunymaritime.edu
Web site: http://www.sunymaritime.edu

Maritime College—a degree and more!

STONY BROOK UNIVERSITY, STATE UNIVERSITY OF NEW YORK

STONY BROOK, LONG ISLAND, NEW YORK

The University

Since its founding in 1957, Stony Brook University has grown tremendously and is now recognized as one of the nation's leading centers of learning and scholarship, fulfilling the mandate given by the State Board of Regents in 1960 to become a university that would "stand with the finest in the country."

Stony Brook, at the forefront of integrating research and education at the undergraduate level, was selected by the National Science Foundation as one of only ten universities in the nation to receive special recognition for this based on educational vision, a significant record of accomplishments, and leadership in the field of higher education. A member of the highly selective Association of American Universities, Stony Brook is one of only ninety-four research universities nationwide identified by the Carnegie Foundation as having very high research activity. Stony Brook faculty members have been responsible for more than 1,000 inventions and more than 500 patents. With seventy academic departments, Stony Brook is among the top twenty-five institutions funded by the National Science Foundation, and external support for research has grown to an annual sum of more than $125 million.

Stony Brook has exceptional strength in the sciences, mathematics, humanities, fine arts, social sciences, engineering, and health professions. Major academic units of the University include the College of Arts and Sciences, the College of Engineering and Applied Sciences, the College of Business, the School of Journalism, the School of Marine and Atmospheric Sciences, and the Health Sciences Center, which is made up of the Schools of Medicine, Health Technology and Management, Dental Medicine, Nursing, and Social Welfare.

Stony Brook enrolls 23,351 full- and part-time students—15,523 undergraduates and 7,828 graduate and professional students. Students hail from all fifty states and 110 other countries. Nearly 19,000 students are enrolled full-time. More than half of Stony Brook's undergraduates live in campus residence halls, which are organized as small residential colleges in order to foster social, intellectual, and cultural interaction.

Stony Brook Southampton, the University's newest acquisition, comprises 81 acres in the Hamptons and opened its doors in spring 2007. With a focus on sustainability, three majors are currently available: environmental studies (B.A.), marine sciences (B.S.), and marine vertebrate biology (B.S.). The fast-track M.B.A. combined degree program is also available to students enrolled at Stony Brook Southampton.

The Stony Brook Seawolves' twenty varsity teams compete in NCAA Division I and include men's baseball and football; women's softball and volleyball; and men's and women's basketball, cross-country, lacrosse, soccer, swimming, tennis, and indoor and outdoor track and field. Athletic facilities are extensive and include the Indoor Sports Complex, which seats up to 5,000; a multipurpose outdoor stadium with seating for 8,500; and several outdoor athletic fields, tennis courts, bicycle and jogging paths, handball courts, and a track.

Location

Situated on 1,100 wooded acres, Stony Brook is located midway between New York City and the resort area of the Hamptons on Long Island's East End, a setting rich in both natural and architectural beauty. Students find large wooded areas on and around campus, sandy beaches are a comfortable bicycle ride away, a working harbor and tourist area are nearby, and a historic hamlet that was once home to George Washington's Revolutionary War spy ring is within walking distance. A train station on the University's perimeter offers students easy access to New York City.

Majors and Degrees

The University offers undergraduate majors leading to Bachelor of Arts (B.A.), Bachelor of Science (B.S.), and Bachelor of Engineering (B.E.) degrees in Africana studies, American studies, anthropology, applied mathematics and statistics, art history and criticism, Asian and Asian American studies, astronomy and planetary sciences, athletic training, atmospheric and oceanic sciences, biochemistry, biology, biomedical engineering, business management, chemical and molecular engineering, chemistry, cinema and cultural studies, clinical laboratory sciences, comparative literature, computer engineering, computer science, cytotechnology, earth and space sciences, economics, electrical engineering, engineering chemistry, engineering science, English, environmental studies, European studies, French, geology, German, health science, history, humanities, information systems, Italian, journalism, linguistics, marine sciences, marine vertebrate biology, mathematics, mechanical engineering, multidisciplinary studies, music, nursing, pharmacology, philosophy, physics, political science, psychology, religious studies, respiratory care, social work, sociology, Spanish, studio art, technological systems management, theater arts, and women's studies. The University also offers more than sixty minors.

Students may earn New York State provisional certification for secondary school teaching in biology, chemistry, earth science, English, French, German, Italian, mathematics, physics, Russian, social studies, Spanish, and K–12 in teaching English as a second language. A combined-degree program is available in which students earn an M.B.A. along with their choice of nearly any undergraduate major (B.A. or B.S.). Dual bachelor's/master's degree programs are available in all of the engineering departments, applied mathematics and statistics, computer science, health sciences/occupational therapy, nursing, and political science/public affairs. Stony Brook's Scholars for Medicine Program, an integrated eight-year bachelor's/M.D. course of study offered to exceptional high school students, enables students to participate in medical school classes and activities as undergraduates.

Academic Programs

All freshmen belong to one of six undergraduate colleges: Science and Society; Leadership and Service; Arts, Culture, and Humanities; Human Development; Global Studies; and Information and Technology Studies. The undergraduate college program at Stony Brook is unique among SUNY schools and offers students academic and residential advising, 1-credit classes in small-group settings, and informal gatherings with faculty members.

Stony Brook's Honors College is unusual among such programs in that it has a special curriculum just for honors students. High-achieving students in the program enjoy small seminar courses and the opportunity to work closely with faculty members. A mentoring program, small study groups, and special classes are highlights of Stony Brook's Women in Science and Engineering (WISE) program, for women talented in math, science, or engineering. There are also Living-Learning Centers, which are designed to enable students with common interests to live and learn together.

Stony Brook accepts up to 30 credits by examination toward the bachelor's degree, through such means as AP, CLEP, CPE, higher-level International Baccalaureate subjects, and Stony Brook's own Challenge Program. Students need a minimum of 120 credits for the B.A. or B.S. degree and 128 credits for the B.E. degree; 39 of these credits must be earned at the upper-division level. All students must satisfy general education requirements and maintain at least a 2.0 cumulative grade point average. Grading is traditional; a pass/no-credit option is available for some elective courses. Stony Brook's academic year starts in early September and ends in mid-May, with the exception of some Health Sciences Center programs that begin in June or July.

Off-Campus Programs

Students have the opportunity to enrich their education by pursuing their academic interests in an overseas location for a summer, semester, or academic year. Stony Brook sponsors programs in France, India, Italy, Jamaica, Japan, Korea, Madagascar, Poland, Russia, Spain, and Tanzania; students may also participate in programs sponsored by the State University of New York system in Western Europe, the Middle East, the Far East, Canada, and Latin America.

Statewide and national exchanges enable students to study for up to a year at one of more than fifty colleges and universities in New York and eight institutions elsewhere in the United States.

Opportunities also exist for students to earn academic credit and gain valuable experience while participating in internships and field research. Placements include government agencies and laboratories, hospitals and clinics, businesses and industries, and legal and social agencies on Long Island and in New York City, Albany, and Washington, D.C.

Academic Facilities

Stony Brook's major academic facilities include the Frank Melville Jr. Memorial Library, Stony Brook University Medical Center, and the five-theater Staller Center for the Arts. Stony Brook is also home to myriad centers, laboratories, and institutes. Some of these include the Institute for Theoretical Physics, Institute for Mathematical Sciences, Institute for Pattern Recognition, Institute for Terrestrial and Planetary Atmospheres, Center for High Pressure Geophysics, Center for Biotechnology, Howard Hughes Medical Institute, and Center for Regional Policy Studies.

Costs

For 2007–08, the annual tuition and fees for New York State residents were $5760. Nonresident tuition and fees were $12,020. Room and board cost $8920. Books and supplies are estimated at $900.

Financial Aid

The Office of Financial Aid and Student Employment administers several federal and state programs, including the Federal Perkins Loan, Federal Supplemental Educational Opportunity Grant, Federal Work-Study Program, New York State Higher Education Tuition Assistance Program (TAP), and Federal Stafford Student Loan. To apply for these programs, a student must complete the Free Application for Federal Student Aid (FAFSA). The FAFSA is available at all high schools and colleges. The University's scholarship program includes more than $5 million in scholarship offers to new students each year, based on meritorious academic performance.

Faculty

Stony Brook's faculty members are intellectual leaders in their disciplines and include a Nobel laureate; a Pulitzer Prize winner; 5 MacArthur Fellows; a Fields prize winner; recipients of the National Medal of Technology, the National Medal of Science, and the Benjamin Franklin Medal; 17 members of the National Academy of Sciences; 2 members of the Institute of Medicine; 14 members of the American Academy of Arts and Sciences; 4 Fellows of the Royal Society; and 4 members of the National Academy of Engineering. They are also dedicated teachers and include more than 100 recipients of the Chancellor's Awards for Excellence in Teaching.

With nearly 2,000 faculty members, the faculty-student ratio is about 1:17. All of Stony Brook's full-time faculty members hold either doctoral or terminal degrees in their fields, and more than 90 percent are engaged in active research that leads to publication. In fact, Stony Brook's faculty is ranked second in the nation in articles published in prestigious journals.

Student Government

Undergraduates are represented by the Undergraduate Student Government (USG), whose members are elected by the students. Student representatives help shape University policy and advise fellow students as members of the University Senate and other organizations. USG administers an annual budget of more than $2 million, which it uses to sponsor more than 200 student interest clubs and organizations. Varied student interests are represented by groups as diverse as the Pre-Med Society, the Commuter Student Association, Stony Brook at Law, the Cycling Club, the Committee on Cinematic Arts (COCA), the Chess Masters, the Science Fiction Forum, and several cultural clubs that include the Caribbean Students Organization, Asian Students' Alliance, Club India, African Student Union, and Latin American Student Organization.

Admission Requirements

Stony Brook is a selective institution and evaluates applicants on an individual basis. There is no automatic cutoff in the admission process, either in grade point average, rank, or test scores. The Admissions Committee seeks to enroll the strongest and most diverse class possible. Stony Brook welcomes applications from those with special talent or exceptional ability in a particular area. Freshman admission is based primarily upon the strength and breadth of the student's academic preparatory program, grade point average, and standardized test scores. Additional criteria include class rank, extracurricular activities, and letters of recommendation, if requested. The University accepts a limited number of high school students for early admission. Students who have attended college or university after graduating from high school are eligible to apply as transfers. Transfer applicants are expected to have performed well in a strong academic program. Transfer students applying to the upper-division programs in the Health Sciences Center must have completed at least 57 credits in liberal arts and sciences and some specific course requirements. If fewer than 24 credits were earned, the student's high school record and standardized test scores are requested for review.

Application and Information

Students are encouraged to submit applications for admission by December 1. Although interviews are not mandatory, they are recommended as a useful part of the application process. Admission counselors are available to meet with prospective students and their families by appointment throughout the year. Campus tours with knowledgeable student guides are also available throughout the year; interested students should call ahead for a schedule. To request an application form, schedule an interview, sign up for a campus tour, or obtain additional information, students should contact:

Office of Undergraduate Admissions
Stony Brook University
Stony Brook, New York 11794-1901
Phone: 631-632-6868
631-632-6859 (TDD)
Fax: 631-632-9898
E-mail: enroll@stonybrook.edu
Web site: http://www.stonybrook.edu/admissions

Stony Brook combines a small-college environment with all the advantages of a major research university.

SYRACUSE UNIVERSITY

SYRACUSE, NEW YORK

The University

Syracuse University (SU), which was founded in 1870, is an independent, privately endowed university with an international reputation. Students attend from all over the United States and from more than 100 other countries. There are about 16,500 students enrolled; 11,500 are undergraduates. Approximately 65 percent of the students live in University housing, which includes modern residence halls, apartments, and town houses. The 200-acre campus features a main grassy quadrangle surrounded by academic buildings, with residential facilities nearby. The campus is situated on a hill overlooking the downtown area of Syracuse. Social life is centered on the campus, and there are innumerable recreational, athletic, and academic activities. The 50,000-seat Carrier Dome is the site of concerts, sports events, and Commencement. All of campus is connected to the University's high-speed wired or wireless networks.

Location

The city of Syracuse (metropolitan-area population of 700,000) is the business, educational, and cultural hub of central New York. The city offers professional theater and opera, as well as visiting artists and performers. Highlights of the downtown area include the Everson Museum of Art, the impressive Civic Center, and the Armory Square shopping area. Central New York has many lakes, parks, mountains, and outstanding recreational opportunities.

Majors and Degrees

Syracuse University awards B.A., B.S., B.Arch., B.I.D., B.Mus., and B.F.A. degrees.

The School of Architecture offers a five-year baccalaureate program leading to the first professional degree of B.Arch.

Departmental and interdisciplinary majors in the College of Arts and Sciences are African-American studies, American studies, anthropology, art, art history, biochemistry, biology, biophysical science, chemistry, classical civilization, classics (Greek and Latin), communication sciences and disorders, economics, English and textual studies, European literature, fine arts, French, geography, geology (Earth sciences), German, Greek, history, history of architecture, international relations, Italian, Latin, Latino–Latin American studies, linguistic studies, mathematics, modern foreign languages, music, music history and cultures, philosophy, physics, policy studies (public affairs), political philosophy, political science, psychology, religion, religion and society, Russian, Russian and Central European studies, sociology, Spanish, and women's studies.

The College of Ecology majors include child and family studies, health and wellness, hospitality and food service management, nutrition/dietetics, nutrition science, social work, and sport management.

The School of Education offers majors in art education, elementary education (inclusive with special education), health and exercise science (including pre–physical therapy and 3+3 D.P.T.), music education, physical education, secondary education, selected studies in education, and special education (inclusive with elementary education).

The L. C. Smith College of Engineering and Computer Science majors include aerospace, chemical, civil, computer, electrical, environmental, and mechanical engineering; bioengineering; and computer science.

The School of Information Studies offers a four-year bachelor's degree program in information management and technology.

The Martin J. Whitman School of Management majors include accounting, entrepreneurship and emerging enterprises, finance, general studies in management, marketing management, retail management, and supply chain management.

The S. I. Newhouse School of Public Communications majors are in the following areas: advertising, broadcast journalism, graphic arts, magazine, newspaper, photography, public relations, and television/radio/film.

The College of Visual and Performing Arts majors are in the following areas: art and design, communication and rhetorical studies, drama, music, and transmedia. Art majors offered are advertising design, ceramics, communications design, environmental design (interiors), fashion design, fiber arts/material studies, history of art, illustration, industrial and interaction design, interior design, jewelry and metalsmithing, painting, printmaking, sculpture, surface pattern design, and textile design. Transmedia majors include art photography, art video, computer art, and film. Drama majors include design/technical theater, drama (acting), musical theater, and stage management. Music majors include the Bandier Program for Music and the Entertainment Industries, music composition, music industry, performance organ, performance percussion, performance piano, performance strings, performance voice, and performance wind instruments. The Department of Communication and Rhetorical Studies offers a Bachelor of Science degree.

Academic Programs

The University operates on a two-semester calendar with two 6-week summer sessions. Students generally take five 3-credit-hour courses each semester. A minimum of 120 credit hours is required for graduation. Special programs include dual and combined enrollment, selected studies, internships, an honors program, ROTC, and preprofessional advising for students going on to study dentistry, law, medicine, or veterinary science.

Off-Campus Programs

The Syracuse University Abroad program operates campuses in London, Madrid, Hong Kong, Beijing, Florence, Santiago (Chile), and Strasbourg. SU Abroad also offers opportunities at thirty universities in many other countries, including Australia, Costa Rica, Ecuador, Egypt, India, Ireland, Japan, Korea, Poland, and Russia.

Academic Facilities

The academic buildings at Syracuse University span the century, with fifteen listed in the National Register of Historic Places and others representative of some of the most modern and technologically sophisticated architecture in the country. The Ernest Stevenson Bird Library houses approximately 3.1 million printed volumes, more than 16,000 online and print journals, and extensive collections of microforms, maps, images, music scores, sound recordings, video, rare books, and manuscripts. The University has computer facilities with laboratories and a data communications network that links computers to hundreds of terminals. The Newhouse Communications Center has some of the finest facilities available for journalism and telecommunications. The Center for Science and Technology is a state-of-the-art facility uniting research and academic programs in computer science and technology. It also houses the CASE Center for research in computer applications and software engineering. The high-tech Melvin A. Eggers Hall offers superior facilities for the University's social science programs. The new multimillion-dollar Whitman School of Management building provides students with access to the latest educational technologies.

Costs

Tuition for 2007–08 was $30,470. The costs for housing and meals averaged $10,940, and fees were $1216. Books and supplies averaged $1230; travel expenses, $558; and personal expenses, $866. Therefore, the total cost of attendance was approximately $45,280.

Financial Aid

About 80 percent of all entering first-year and transfer students receive some form of financial aid. By filing the Free Application for Federal Student Aid (FAFSA) and the CSS Financial Aid PROFILE, students are automatically considered for all financial aid programs administered by Syracuse University, including federal financial aid, Syracuse University Grants, and Federal Work-Study Program awards. Merit-based scholarships are available to both first-year and transfer students, based solely on their academic record. Syracuse University evaluates candidates for admission without respect to financial need. Information on financial aid policies, procedures, and deadlines can be obtained from the Office of Financial Aid and Scholarship Programs.

Faculty

The majority of faculty members hold the highest degree in their professional field. There are nearly 900 full-time faculty members, including recognized experts in their fields who teach at both the graduate and undergraduate levels.

Student Government

The Syracuse University Student Association works to protect students' rights and offers services through its three branches—the executive, the legislative, and the judicial.

Admission Requirements

Syracuse University seeks a diverse student body from all social, cultural, and educational backgrounds. Each candidate is evaluated individually, based on the requirements of the college of the University to which he or she has applied. Emphasis is placed on students' high school performance, standardized test scores (SAT or ACT), an essay, recommendations, extracurricular activities and community service, and portfolios or auditions, when required. Special admission requirements and deadlines for some programs are described on the University's Web site and in the Undergraduate Application for Admission.

Syracuse University is an Equal Opportunity/Affirmative Action institution and does not discriminate on the basis of race, creed, color, gender, national origin, religion, marital status, age, disability, sexual orientation, or gender identity or expression.

Application and Information

Regular Decision applicants for the fall semester should submit their completed application along with transcripts, standardized test scores, the essay, teacher recommendations, and the counselor evaluation by January 1 (postmarked deadline). Notification begins in mid-March. Completed applications for Early Decision applicants must be postmarked by November 15. Notification begins in mid-December.

Detailed information may be obtained by contacting:

Office of Admissions
100 Crouse-Hinds Hall
900 South Crouse Avenue
Syracuse University
Syracuse, New York 13244-2130
Phone: 315-443-3611
Web site: http://admissions.syr.edu

The historic buildings that make up the SU campus stand in testimony to the many years of distinction that are at the foundation of Syracuse University.

UNION COLLEGE
SCHENECTADY, NEW YORK

The College

Union College is an independent, undergraduate, residential college for men and women of high academic promise and strong personal motivation. Founded in 1795, it was the first college chartered by the Regents of the State of New York and is one of the oldest nondenominational colleges in the country. The first college in America with a unified campus plan, Union was the first liberal arts college to offer engineering (in 1845). It has more than 20,000 alumni and an endowment of approximately $378 million. The College seeks a geographically and socially diverse student body; at this time, the 2,128 undergraduates represent thirty-seven states and twenty-six countries. Approximately one third of each graduating class continues directly on to graduate or professional school, and Union has earned an excellent reputation for the placement of its graduates in medical, law, and business schools.

Union believes that a student's life outside the classroom is a vital part of his or her total education and therefore encourages a variety of student organizations—approximately 100 at last count—and a rich cultural and social life. Union also offers an extensive program of intercollegiate, intramural, club, and recreational sports. Among the athletic facilities are the Alumni Gymnasium, with an eight-lane swimming/diving pool and squash and racquetball courts; a 3,000-seat ice rink; a state-of-the-art hardwood-floor venue for basketball and volleyball; Astroturf fields; and an all-weather track. The Reamer Campus Center provides space for social and community activities and services for the entire campus. Dining facilities, a pub, an auditorium, a radio station, and multiple student activities spaces are important parts of the building. The historic Nott Memorial has been renovated into a discussion and display center for students and alumni.

Students are expected to live on campus during their undergraduate years. Union's innovative new Minerva Houses are designed to provide additional social, academic, and residential opportunities for students; they join a residence life program that includes student-initiated theme houses, traditional residence halls, apartments, and fraternities and sororities.

Location

Union is located in the small upstate New York city of Schenectady, part of a metropolitan area based on Albany, the capital of New York. The Capital District's population of nearly 900,000 includes more than 55,000 college and university students. Schenectady is 3 hours from New York City and Boston and 4 hours from Montreal. Wilderness camping, white-water canoeing, skiing, and cross-country ski touring are available in the nearby Catskills, Adirondacks, Green Mountains, and Massachusetts Berkshires. A great number of volunteer opportunities are available within the Schenectady community.

Majors and Degrees

Union offers the Bachelor of Arts (B.A.) degree in anthropology, art (art history, music, theater arts, and visual arts), astronomy, classics, economics, English, history, modern languages, philosophy, political science, and sociology. The Bachelor of Science (B.S.) degree is awarded in biology, chemistry, computer engineering, computer science, electrical engineering, geology, mathematics, mechanical engineering, physics, and psychology. Formal interdepartmental work is offered in Africana studies; American studies; biochemistry; East Asian studies; environmental studies; Latin American and Caribbean studies; managerial economics; neuroscience; Russia and Eastern European studies; science, medicine, and technology in culture; and women's and gender studies. Transdisciplinary studies, individually designed majors, and concentrations within departments are also available. Programs in which a student may earn two baccalaureate degrees are available in the following combinations: engineering and Bachelor of Science or Bachelor of Arts or two engineering degrees. Students may also declare up to two academic minors in any of fifty-two disciplines. In addition, Union offers programs that lead to a B.A. degree from Union and a law degree from Albany Law School or to a B.S. from Union and an M.S. or M.B.A. from Union Graduate College and an M.D. from Albany Medical College. Union also offers a variety of programs that combine a Union College degree with an advanced degree from Union Graduate College.

Academic Programs

As a college committed to the liberal arts ideal, Union prepares students for roles as useful, informed citizens and leaders as well as jobholders. Students are encouraged to strive for a breadth of learning to complement the expertise acquired through studies in their major. In its General Education program, for example, Union ensures that its students are exposed to important areas of knowledge in history, literature, science, mathematics, and social science and offers strong incentives to study other cultures. In its Converging Technologies programs, faculty members from engineering and the liberal arts work together to create courses that cross traditional disciplinary boundaries. Students may explore such areas as bioengineering, mechatronics, nanotechnology, neuroscience, and pervasive computing. Independent study and undergraduate research are strongly encouraged. To foster initiative in educational programs and individual academic exploration, Union's own Internal Education Foundation makes grants for special projects to students, faculty members, and administrators. The College annually sends one of the largest delegations to the National Conference on Undergraduate Research. Degree requirements include successful completion of a minimum of 36 term courses in all programs except engineering, which may require up to 40, and the successful completion of the requirements in the major and the general education program. Students who pass examinations taken under the College Board's Advanced Placement Program with a score of 4 or higher (except in calculus, for which a score of 3 is acceptable) are typically given college course credit and are exempted from any requirement to take the equivalent college courses. Union's calendar consists of three 10-week terms, and students normally take three courses each term. The academic year begins in early September and ends in early June.

Off-Campus Programs

Union participates in programs of cross-registration that enable students to take courses at fourteen consortium colleges and universities in the Capital District, including Reserve Officers' Training Corps (ROTC). Union's own international resident-study programs are among the most extensive of any American college. Terms abroad are available in China, England, Fiji, France, Germany, Greece, Italy, Japan, Mexico, Spain, and Tasmania. There is a term of marine studies in Bermuda and Newfoundland and at the Woods Hole Oceanographic Institution in Massachusetts as well as a summer program in which students examine the national health programs of Canada, England, and Holland. Union, in conjunction with Hobart and William Smith Colleges, also offers programs in Australia, Brazil, Ireland, Vietnam, and Central Europe (Germany, Hungary, and Romania). The College has seven formal exchange programs: full-year exchanges in Japan and Wales and one-term exchanges in Barbados, Belgium, the Czech Republic, India, and Korea. Political science internships are available in the New York State legislature and in Washington, D.C.

Academic Facilities

The F. W. Olin Center, a high-technology classroom and laboratory building, contains a multimedia auditorium, collaborative computer classrooms, and a 20-inch remote-controlled telescope. Available for student use in the nearby Science and Engineering Center are such research tools as a nuclear magnetic resonance spectrometer, a Pelletron accelerator, X-ray diffraction equipment, a centrifuge, and a scanning electron microscope. A state-of-the-art music center and the Yulman Theatre greatly enhance the arts program.

Housed in the Stanley G. Peschel Center for Computer Science and Information Systems, Union's central computer facility consists of several multiuser servers on a campuswide fiber-optic-based network. Included in the network are UNIX, Windows, and Apple Macintosh servers. Connected to the network are more than 1,500 College-owned personal computers and workstations. More than thirty-five electronic classrooms are used to enhance the integration of technology and academic studies through the use of the Internet and multimedia materials. Each residence hall room is wired with one Ethernet network connection per resident, providing access to the College's computing resources and the Internet. Wireless network connectivity is available in all academic buildings, study and common areas in all residence halls, and the library. Personal computer laboratories with Windows, Apple Macintosh, and UNIX workstations are available for student use. Departmental computer labs provide access to specialized computing needs. Access to the Internet, personal Web page space, and e-mail is provided for all Union students and faculty and staff members. Scanners, digital cameras, video capture and editing resources, and other equipment are also available for student use.

Schaffer Library houses more than 600,000 volumes and approximately 6,200 periodicals, a periodicals reading room, faculty studies, and more than 500 individual study spaces. The library operates on the open-stack plan and offers bibliographic instruction, interlibrary loans, online bibliographic retrieval services, electronic document delivery, and Internet workstations for access to indexes, abstracts, full-text journals online, automated circulation of books, and other library materials as well as the online catalog. Professional reference service is offered during nearly all the hours that the library is open.

Costs

Charges for 2007–08 included a comprehensive fee of $46,245.

Financial Aid

Union has a strong philosophical and financial commitment to ensure the affordability of a high-quality education for its students and recognizes students' outstanding academic performance with scholarship assistance. Scholarship awards are based on academic performance and financial need. In 2007–08, Union's total financial aid program amounted to approximately $39 million; about $28 million came from the College itself and the rest from federal, state, and private sources. More than 60 percent of Union's students receive some form of aid each year (e.g., scholarships, guaranteed loans, and job opportunities), and the average aid package is $30,000. Union strives to keep students' total debt as low as possible. Candidates for aid should complete the Free Application for Federal Student Aid (FAFSA) and the College Scholarship Service's PROFILE form and mail them directly to the appropriate agencies by February 1.

Faculty

Union believes that the close relationship between its students and faculty members motivates students to learn through inquiry and discourse. Faculty members are chosen with specific reference to their capabilities as teachers. Excluding the library staff, 95 percent of the faculty members hold the doctorate, first professional, or terminal degree, and faculty salaries are above the national averages for colleges of comparable size. Union does not determine the functions of faculty members on the basis of rank; full professors often teach introductory courses. Class size generally is small; many upper-level courses function as seminars.

Student Government

Students have full voting rights on the two councils that recommend educational policy and student life policy to the president. Students also have seats in groups that advise the president on such matters as budgetary planning and long-range needs.

Admission Requirements

In evaluating each application, the College considers the secondary school record, including rank in class and the quality of courses taken; the recommendations of secondary school teachers; and the personal qualities and extracurricular record of the applicant. Scores on the tests given by the College Board (SAT) or ACT are optional except for accelerated programs. Those interested in accelerated programs must submit the SAT and two SAT Subject Tests. Normally, 16 units of secondary school preparation are required for admission. These should include credits in certain fundamental subjects, such as English, a foreign language, mathematics, social studies, and science. It is strongly recommended that students visit Union for an admission interview and a student-guided tour. Alumni interviews may be arranged for students by calling the Admissions Office.

Application and Information

Early decision candidates have two options. The application deadline for Option I is November 15, with notification by December 15. Option II has a January 15 deadline and February 1 notification. All supporting credentials are due November 15 for Option I and January 15 for Option II. Applications for regular admission should be filed by January 15, with the exception of the accelerated programs. Applications to the eight-year leadership in medicine program must be filed no later than December 15, and applications for the six-year law and public policy and the five-year B.A./B.S. and Master of Business Administration programs must be filed no later than January 1. Those deferred under early decision and all regular applicants are given a final decision by early April. Union adheres to the Candidates Reply Date of May 1.

Office of Admissions
Grant Hall
Union College
Schenectady, New York 12308
Phone: 518-388-6112
888-843-6688 (toll-free)
Fax: 518-388-6986
E-mail: admissions@union.edu
Web site: http://www.union.edu

The sixteen-sided Nott Memorial is Union College's centerpiece.

UNITED STATES MERCHANT MARINE ACADEMY

KINGS POINT, NEW YORK

The Academy

The United States Merchant Marine Academy is a four-year, tuition-free federal service academy that was founded in 1943 to educate and train merchant marine officers, officers on active duty in the armed forces, and leaders in the maritime and intermodal transportation industry. It is an accredited, degree-granting college whose students are commissioned as Ensigns in the Navy Reserve upon graduation. The Academy is one of the world's foremost institutions in the field of maritime education and is operated under the Maritime Administration (MARAD) of the Department of Transportation.

There are approximately 975 men and women enrolled as midshipmen at the Academy. Their daily routine at Kings Point is very demanding. The academic day begins at 8 a.m. and concludes at 4 p.m. After classes, midshipmen are free to participate in recreational activities until dinnertime. After dinner, they are required to devote their time to study and academic preparation.

The extracurricular program is broad and varied. In addition to varsity athletics in twenty-five intercollegiate sports, the Academy has an extensive intramural program that permits all students to enjoy physical activity and competition.

The nonathletic activities are also wide ranging and abundant, falling into as many categories as there are individual interests. Publications and the Drill Team, Glee Club, Regimental Band, Scuba-Diving Club, Eagle Scouts Association, International Relations Club, and Fencing Club are but a few of the pursuits available to the midshipmen. Regimental and class dances and informal mixers provide the midshipmen with an interesting social program.

Midshipmen are granted liberty on weekends and leave at Thanksgiving, Winter Holidays (December), and fall and spring trimester breaks as well as annual leave during July. Perhaps the most unusual and exciting part of the Academy curriculum is the Shipboard Training Program. Each midshipman, during three trimesters of the sophomore and junior years, serves 300–360 days at sea aboard commercially operated American-flag merchant ships. This exceptional work-study program takes the midshipmen to many parts of the world and provides them with practical experience on several different types of vessels. It can be said that the world is their campus during their three trimesters of sea service.

Location

The Academy is located on 80.5 acres of land at Kings Point, on the North Shore of Long Island. Kings Point is a suburban residential community only 20 miles east of midtown New York City, close to various cultural and recreational facilities.

Majors and Degrees

A graduate of the U.S. Merchant Marine Academy receives a Bachelor of Science degree, a merchant marine license as a third mate or third assistant engineer, and a commission as an Ensign in the U.S. Navy Reserve. Graduates may apply to the Army, Navy, Air Force, Marine Corps, Coast Guard, or National Oceanic and Atmospheric Administration (NOAA) to serve on active duty. Six major programs are offered: marine transportation for the preparation of deck officers; maritime operations and technology (a marine transportation program enhanced with marine engineering studies); marine engineering for students interested in becoming engineering officers; marine engineering systems, which, in addition to leading to a license as a third assistant engineer, is accredited by the Accreditation Board for Engineering and Technology (ABET) and includes a curriculum with greater depth in mathematics and a significant component of engineering design, as compared to the marine engineering curriculum; shipyard and engineering management, which is also accredited by ABET; and logistics and intermodal transportation, a marine transportation program focusing on logistics and intermodal systems management.

Academic Programs

During the first trimester of the plebe (or freshman) year, all students take a common program of mathematics, science, English, and professional courses. This background enables midshipmen to determine intelligently the area of their special interest. After the first trimester, midshipmen select their major and from then on concentrate on a program aligned with their career choice. The professional majors each consist of required core courses in technical and general education areas as well as selected electives. The option program consists of six courses for marine transportation and marine engineering majors, who have a choice of taking a series of related elective courses in a specific area of concentration or any individual elective course for which they qualify. These courses include such specialized fields as nuclear engineering, management science, computer science, mathematics, chemistry, and naval architecture. By choosing to take the series of related courses, midshipmen can develop a proficiency in a subspecialty, supplementing their major field of study. Students in the marine engineering systems majors are not offered the choice of electives because of the required course load in their programs. General education courses make up about one third of each of the professional curriculums, and all midshipmen are required to take naval science courses prescribed by the Department of the Navy.

Thus, the Academy provides a balanced program of theoretical and practical study designed to provide the undergraduate with technical competence, leadership skills, and the well-rounded general education so essential for responsible citizenship in contemporary society.

Exemption credit may be awarded for college-level work completed at an accredited college if the course is equivalent to a course offered at the Academy.

Academic Facilities

With the exception of Wiley Hall, the former residence of Walter P. Chrysler and now the Administration Building, all the buildings of the Academy have been constructed since 1942. The Inter-Faith Chapel was dedicated in 1961, a three-story library was completed in 1968, and an indoor swimming pool and an engineering and science wing have been added since 1972. A modernization of all other academic buildings was completed in 1982. The Dean ('45) & Barbara White Admissions Center was dedicated in 2004. Upgrades to the dormitories and other facilities are currently under way.

Costs

Tuition, room and board, and medical and dental care are provided by the U.S. government. In addition, the government pays for books and the initial issue of uniforms. Each midshipman also receives $820 per month during periods when they are assigned aboard ship for training. Entering plebes are required to pay a little more than $7000 to cover the initial cost of a laptop computer as well as lab fees, equipment, and service, license, and activity fees. Upperclass members are also charged for service, license, and activity fees for the trimesters they are on campus (when they are not at sea).

Financial Aid

In effect, each midshipman receives a four-year scholarship from the U.S. government. Financial assistance is also available through the Federal Pell Grant Program, the Federal Stafford Student Loan Program, the Federal PLUS Program, the Federal Academic Competitiveness Grant, and the National Science and Mathematics Access to Retain Talent (SMART) Grant. A very limited number of need-based scholarships are also offered, and students may use outside scholarships to defray their costs.

Faculty

The Academy has 84 full-time faculty members and a student-faculty ratio of approximately 11:1. One third of the faculty members are licensed deck or engineering officers. Most hold advanced degrees in an academic discipline: 90 percent of the total faculty members hold master's degrees or higher; 50 percent have earned doctorates.

Student Government

The student body at the Academy is organized along military lines as a regiment, consisting of two battalions. Regimental life at the Academy is a form of student government and is an important part of the midshipman's total educational experience. The first classmen, or seniors, under the direction of the Commandant of Midshipmen, are responsible for exercising military command of the regiment and for administering the daily routine of the midshipmen. The military program is designed to develop leadership ability, self-discipline, and a sense of responsibility—attributes that are essential for effective citizenship as well as for a successful career as an officer.

Admission Requirements

Candidates for admission must be American citizens, be at least 17 years of age and must not have passed their twenty-fifth birthday by July 1 of the year of entry into the Academy, and be of good moral character. Candidates must be nominated by a U.S. representative or senator and must compete for vacancies allocated to their state in proportion to its representation in Congress. Candidates must achieve qualifying scores on the standard administration (timed) SAT or ACT. Candidates must have successfully completed chemistry or physics (including lab), as well as mathematics up to and including one semester of trigonometry or precalculus. Candidates' competitive standing is determined by their College Board score, their high school academic record and extracurricular participation, and their overall leadership potential. All candidates must meet the physical requirements for appointment as a midshipman in the Navy Reserve. Although not required, all applicants are strongly encouraged to perform a day or overnight visit to learn firsthand about midshipman life and academics. Visits are arranged through the Admissions Office when classes are in session, which is from mid-August to May.

Application and Information

Prospective candidates should write to the Admissions Office. They are sent detailed information on the nomination procedure, required tests, application procedures, and specific requirements. It is advisable to apply for a nomination during the late spring of the junior year in high school. The deadline for applications is March 1 of the year of desired entry.

Further information may be obtained by contacting:

Director of Admissions
U.S. Merchant Marine Academy
300 Steamboat Road
Kings Point, New York 11024-1699
Phone: 516-773-5391
866-546-4778 (toll-free)
Fax: 516-773-5390
E-mail: admissions@usmma.edu
Web site: http://www.usmma.edu

An aerial view of the 80.5-acre "sea campus" of the U.S. Merchant Marine Academy at Kings Point, Long Island, on the shores of Long Island Sound.

UNITED STATES MILITARY ACADEMY

WEST POINT, NEW YORK

The Academy

The United States Military Academy (USMA) at West Point, the nation's oldest service academy, offers young men and women the nation's premier education and leadership development programs. West Point advocates the "whole person" concept and provides a broadly structured undergraduate curriculum that balances the physical sciences and engineering with the behavioral and social sciences.

West Point's mission is to educate, train, and inspire the Corps of Cadets so that each graduate is a commissioned leader of character who is committed to the values of duty, honor, and country and prepared for a career of professional excellence and service to the nation as an officer in the United States Army. West Point provides its graduates with a solid foundation for intellectual and moral/ethical growth that is essential for successfully handling high-level responsibilities in national service. When students enter West Point, they are also entering the profession of arms. Upon graduation, cadets are commissioned as second lieutenants in the U.S. Army and are normally required to serve on active duty for at least five years.

There are more than 4,100 men and women enrolled at West Point. Cadets compete for Rhodes, Fulbright, Marshall, Olmsted, Gates Cambridge, George Mitchell, Hertz, National Science Foundation, Rotary Foundation, Truman, and East-West Center Scholarships. West Pointers who remain in the Army are normally selected to attend civilian graduate schools in the United States or abroad between their fourth and tenth years of service.

The Academy develops the nation's future Army leaders by immersing cadets in programs of academic, military, and physical development. Each of these programs is rooted in principles of ethical-moral development, epitomized by the Academy motto, "Duty, Honor, Country." The Academy provides cadets with opportunities to observe and practice leadership and to develop vital intellectual and interpersonal skills through formal instruction. The honor code simply states: "A cadet will not lie, cheat, steal, or tolerate those who do." The code is a source of pride and mutual trust that are essential in the profession of arms.

In addition to academic and military education, cadets participate in athletic and extracurricular activities. Cadets have distinguished themselves in twenty-six intercollegiate varsity sports: baseball, basketball, cross-country, football, golf, gymnastics, hockey, indoor track, lacrosse, outdoor track, rifle, soccer, sprint football, swimming, tennis, and wrestling for men and basketball, cross-country, indoor track, outdoor track, rifle, soccer, softball, swimming, tennis, and volleyball for women.

West Point's modern academic facilities are matched by its athletic facilities. Michie Stadium, home of Army football, attracts crowds in excess of 39,000 during picturesque fall football weekends. Kimsey Athletic Center is a four-story, state-of-the-art facility that includes a strength-development center, an athletic training center, locker rooms, football coaches' offices, and meeting rooms, as well as the Blaik Gallery and the Kenna Hall of Army Sports. Randolph Hall is the new home for Army men's and women's basketball teams. It also provides four skybox seating areas overlooking Michie Stadium. The Gross Center is a gymnastics and multisport practice and competition facility. Adjacent to Michie Stadium is the Holleder Athletic Center, a multisport complex housing a hockey rink with seating for 2,746 and a basketball arena with a 5,045-seat capacity. The huge state-of-the-art Arvin Cadet Physical Development Center renovation was recently completed. West Point has a track stadium, a new softball complex, a baseball stadium, an indoor tennis facility, numerous athletic fields, outdoor tennis courts, and outdoor swimming facilities. Victor Constant Ski Slope is used for instructional and recreational skiing. An eighteen-hole golf course is also located on the Academy grounds.

There are more than 100 organized extracurricular activities, including mountaineering, hunting, fishing, scuba diving, archery, team handball, and orienteering clubs as well as clubs that compete on a national or intercollegiate level in crew, orienteering, powerlifting, handball, rugby, sport parachuting, triathlon, horseback riding, sailing, judo, karate, bowling, and marathon running. There are academic clubs, including mathematics, language, and electronics clubs; the Cadet Fine Arts Forum; Model United Nations; and the Debate Council. The Student Conference on United States Affairs has met for more than thirty years.

Location

The military reservation, consisting of more than 16,000 acres, is in New York's scenic Hudson Valley, overlooking the Hudson River, 50 miles north of New York City.

Majors and Degrees

Cadets may choose an academic concentration from more than forty majors. A cadet may study art, philosophy, and literature; basic sciences; behavioral sciences; chemistry and life science; civil and electrical engineering; computer science; economics; electronic and information technology systems engineering management; engineering psychology; environmental engineering; environmental geography; environmental science; foreign area studies (Latin American, Western Europe, Middle East, Eastern Europe, and East Asia); foreign languages (Arabic, Chinese, French, German, Portuguese, Russian, or Spanish); geospatial information science; history; human geography; law and legal studies; leadership; life science; management; mathematical sciences; mechanical engineering; military art and science; nuclear engineering; operations research; physics; political science; psychology; sociology; systems engineering; systems management; and others.

Academic Programs

The academic program at the United States Military Academy provides cadets with a broad background in the arts and sciences and prepares them for future graduate study. The total curriculum is designed to develop essential character, competence, and intellectual ability in an officer. The core curriculum is the cornerstone of the academic program and provides a foundation in mathematics, basic sciences, engineering sciences, information technology, humanities, behavior sciences, and social sciences. The core curriculum, including twenty-six to thirty courses, depending upon the major, represents the essential broad base of knowledge that is necessary for success as a commissioned officer while also supporting each cadet's choice of academic specialization.

Classes at West Point are small, averaging 12 to 18 cadets per section. Cadets receive individual attention, and tutorial sessions are available upon request. Advanced and honors courses are available to cadets having exceptional ability.

All cadets study military science and receive classroom instruction in the principles of small-unit tactics and leadership in eight semester-long courses. Concentrated summer field training provides each cadet with the opportunity to learn and practice individual military skills and to apply the principles of tactics and leadership studied in the classroom.

Off-Campus Programs

During the summer before their first (freshman) academic year, students are initiated into the United States Corps of Cadets through the Cadet Basic Training (CBT) program. Uniforms, room inspections, military drill, parades, and physical exercise become part of everyday life, and extensive demands are made upon new cadets to foster maturity, perseverance, and ability to succeed when challenged. All cadets complete Cadet Field Training (CFT) during their second summer at West Point. The emphasis in CFT is on advanced individual skills and small-unit tactics in order to create competent, confident leaders for the Army. Extensive training in infantry operations, artillery firing, weapons training, Army aviation, military engineering, and land navigation make up most of this training experience. CFT also provides a powerful leadership experience that develops the leadership skills and abilities of the first- and second-class (senior and junior) cadets. Operation Highland Warrior, a ten-day tactical field exercise that focuses on the combined-arms-close-fight, is the capstone event of CFT. During Operation Highland Warrior, cadets execute air assault raids and lead fire ambushes and defensive operations. Cadets are also exposed to the heavy forces of the Army (armor, artillery, air defense, and aviation) when they deploy to Fort Knox, Kentucky, for a week of Mounted Maneuver Training. The highlights of this training event are a Combined Arms Live Fire Exercise, which allows the cadets to see all of the Army's most lethal fighting systems operating as a team on the battlefield, and Operation Thunderbolt Strike, a mounted "force-on-force" battle, where cadet companies engage each other in M1A2 tanks.

All cadets complete Cadet Advanced Training during their last two summers at West Point. Cadet Advanced Training consists of three parts: attending a military school, serving in a field Army unit, and serving in a leadership position at West Point during CBT or CFT. Cadets can attend one of many United States Army military schools, which include Airborne School, Air Assault School, the Sapper Leader's Course, and the Combat Diver Qualification Course. First-class cadets also participate in Cadet Troop Leading Training (CTLT). CTLT is a thirty-day troop-leading experience, during which cadets go to a field Army unit and perform the day-to-day functions of a platoon leader. Each summer, more than 1,000 cadets participate in CTLT at more than twenty-seven locations worldwide. Selected second-class cadets may participate in the Drill Cadet Leader Training (DCLT) instead of CTLT. During DCLT, second-class cadets serve as company executive officers and platoon trainers in basic training units. DCLT is conducted at major training installations such as Fort Benning, Georgia; Fort Sill, Oklahoma; Fort Leonard Wood, Missouri; and Fort Jackson, South Carolina. Each summer, approximately 40 second-class cadets participate in DCLT. During one of their last two summers at West Point, second- and first-class cadets are also required to serve in various leadership positions, from platoon leader to regimental commander, in Cadet Basic Training or Cadet Field Training. The training allows second- and first-class cadets to further develop their leadership skills while teaching, training, and leading new cadets or third-class cadets in demanding, fast-paced environments.

Academic Facilities

West Point maintains some of the finest facilities and equipment in the world. Every cadet is issued a laptop computer, and everyone is connected to a large array of powerful academic computing services at West Point, with unlimited access to the Internet. West Point has carefully crafted an electronic environment in which virtually every course offered has integrated computer use. This developmental "computer thread" fosters cadet use of personal computers in the barracks. Computer-aided math, design, and simulation; dynamic news sources; worldwide e-mail; spreadsheets; statistical analyses; database access; library bibliographic research; electronic bulletin boards; and document preparation and printing, among other resources, all contribute to an academic environment that is rich with information resources and electronic media tools. Among the research facilities are general and physical chemistry laboratories and engineering, analog computer, digital computer, electromagnetic energy, electronics, physics, solid-state, hydraulic turbine, thermodynamics, fluid mechanics, nuclear science, free flight, rocket testing, land locomotion, and wind tunnel laboratories. The modern 600,000-volume library contains reading rooms, seminar rooms, and microfilm and audiovisual facilities.

Costs

The cost of the four-year West Point experience, including tuition, room, board, and medical and dental expenses, is paid by the U.S. government. Cadets, as members of the Army, receive an annual salary of almost $10,000, which helps to pay for uniforms, books, a laptop computer, supplies, and incidental living expenses. A deposit of about $3000 is required to cover initial uniform costs, a personal computer, and other incidental services (haircuts, laundry, etc.) during the first year.

Financial Aid

There are no financial aid programs because expenses are paid by the U.S. government. Scholarship awards that are not earmarked specifically for tuition may be used by candidates to offset the cost of the initial deposit.

Faculty

Most faculty members are Army officers who hold advanced degrees from civilian colleges and universities; approximately 30 percent have earned doctorates. The teaching faculty numbers nearly 500 and includes civilian professors and several visiting professors from civilian academic institutions. Because many of the faculty members are Academy alumni and most are Army officers, the faculty has an exceptional rapport with the cadets. The student-faculty ratio is 8:1. Typical class size is 16.

Student Government

All cadets are strongly encouraged to serve in positions of student leadership and to seek responsibility as a means of enhancing their effectiveness as leaders. Cadets manage the social program, the Cadet Honor System, the intramural athletic program, and a wide range of extracurricular activities.

Admission Requirements

Admission is open to all unmarried U.S. citizens who are at least 17 and have not yet had their 23rd birthday by July 1 of the year of admission. They must have no legal responsibility to support a dependent (e.g., a child or family member). The United States Military Academy offers equal admission opportunities for all qualified candidates. Candidates must seek a nomination from a legal authority (usually a member of Congress), preferably in the winter of the junior year in high school. All candidates must take either the standardized timed ACT or the SAT. Applicants must also pass a Qualifying Medical Examination and a Candidate Fitness Assessment.

The Directorate of Admissions has a rolling admissions process. As soon as the candidate's file is complete, it is evaluated by the Admissions Committee. All applicants must complete their admissions file by the last working day in February.

Application and Information

First, prospective candidates should visit the Directorate of Admissions Web site at http://admissions.usma.edu and read through the Prospectus prior to completing the Candidate Questionnaire, because it outlines the West Point entrance requirements. They should then complete the Candidate Questionnaire, which opens a candidate's admissions file, to begin the application process. All applicants are encouraged to start a candidate file at West Point during the spring semester of their junior year or as soon thereafter as possible. This allows for early completion of all candidate file requirements. The Directorate of Admissions Web site also contains forms, sample letters, frequently asked questions, and additional information on the admissions process.

Director of Admissions
United States Military Academy
606 Thayer Road
West Point, New York 10996-1797
Phone: 845-938-4041
E-mail: admissions@usma.edu
Web site: http://admissions.usma.edu

Every class at USMA has integrated computer use, and all cadets have unlimited access to the Internet.

UNIVERSITY AT ALBANY, STATE UNIVERSITY OF NEW YORK

ALBANY, NEW YORK

The University

A University Center of the State University of New York (SUNY), the University at Albany offers a broad spectrum of academic programs for undergraduate and graduate students while fulfilling the missions of research and service. More than 17,000 students, including 12,000 undergraduates, are enrolled in the University's ten schools and colleges: arts and sciences, business, education, criminal justice, public affairs, computing and information, social welfare, public health, and nanoscale science and engineering, one of the first schools of its kind in the country. The University has also established an Honors College for academically talented and motivated students.

Albany is distinguished by the high quality of its academic programs, many of which are consistently ranked among the best in the nation. These include atmospheric science, management information systems, criminal justice, public administration and policy, social welfare, psychology, and sociology. More than 900 faculty members jointly offer Albany's graduate and undergraduate programs, thus giving all students access to leading researchers in an environment that emphasizes active learning, inquiry, and discovery. Throughout their undergraduate education, students are encouraged to pursue the intellectual goals of breadth and coherence while acquiring the skills of critical inquiry and public responsibility.

Freshmen are invited to participate in Project Renaissance, a distinctive general education program. Project Renaissance offers an integrated introduction to the University through a yearlong 12-credit interdisciplinary course that is team taught by several faculty members. The course includes inquiry projects, which grow out of students' community action work and require them to become researchers, inquiring into the meaning of events that surround them. Thus, students learn how the larger issues of research are often tied to everyday life and how systematic inquiry helps address these questions. Students create a true living-learning community by also sharing a residence hall.

Since the University is located in New York State's capital, Albany students have access to a wide range of internship opportunities, including a full-semester, 15-credit internship with the New York State Legislature.

The University at Albany offers many opportunities for ambitious students to challenge themselves further through rich, supportive, intellectual programs and honor societies. The Honors College at the University at Albany was established to create a vibrant community of scholars where students and faculty members work together in a challenging environment to stimulate the highest levels of academic achievement. The Honors College offers a challenging curriculum, exposes students to the very best and most passionate teachers at the University, and mentors students to compete strongly for professional school placement, top jobs in industry, and competitive national scholarships such as Rhodes, Truman, Marshall, or Goldwater. The University recognizes incoming freshmen for their outstanding academic achievements in high school with merit awards ranging from $1000 to $6500. Honors opportunities in the major are currently available in thirty-four majors at the University. They are designed to provide opportunities for talented and motivated students to work closely with each other and with faculty members. There are many academic and honors organizations at the University at Albany for students, including Phi Beta Kappa.

About 40 percent of Albany graduates go directly on to graduate or professional school. More than 52 percent of the qualified medical school applicants educated at Albany are accepted, while almost 60 percent of law school applicants from Albany are accepted. Albany's graduation rate is 10 points higher than the national average. A network of more than 140,000 Albany alumni throughout the nation and the world provide an important link to business, education, law, medicine, and state, national, and international government as well as other related fields.

Six residential quadrangles uptown and one quad downtown house 7,000 Albany students. Most residential facilities are organized in suite arrangements, and each resident student has access to phone, voice mail, and cable television hookup. All residential facilities on the uptown campus are wireless. In fall 2002, Empire Commons opened, providing single-room apartment-style living for 1,200 students.

Campus life is sustained by the activities of the nearly 200 University-recognized social and professional clubs, which offer numerous opportunities for leadership development. The University competes at the Division I level and is affiliated with the America East Conference and the Northeast Conference in football. In 2006, the University's men's basketball team became the first public institution in New York to qualify for the NCAA Division I tournament. Men's varsity sports are baseball, basketball, cross-country, football, indoor track, lacrosse, outdoor track, and soccer. Women's varsity sports are basketball, cross-country, field hockey, golf, indoor track, lacrosse, outdoor track, soccer, softball, tennis, and volleyball. In addition, Albany offers a wide range of intramural opportunities, and more than 5,000 Albany students participate each year. The S.E.F.C.U. arena, a 4,800-seat recreational facility, offers students the latest in sports facilities, including three full basketball courts, racquetball and squash courts, a main arena with an indoor track, and a fitness center with Nautilus equipment. The arena is also used for concerts and other events.

Location

Albany, the hub of the lively Capital Region, offers students a host of internship and work opportunities in government, finance, education, high technology, business, and the arts as well as the cultural and social environment of a major city. The climate is milder than elsewhere in upstate New York and New England, with stunning natural beauty. Albany's historic Hudson Valley location is convenient to recreation areas in Vermont's Green Mountains, the Berkshires of Massachusetts, the Catskills, and the Adirondacks, site of two Winter Olympics. Boston, Hartford, New York City, Montreal, and Philadelphia are also within a convenient distance. Two major interstates, I-87 and I-90, serve the campus, and airline, train, and bus terminals are just minutes away.

Majors and Degrees

Undergraduates may choose from more than 100 degree programs. SUNY at Albany offers the bachelor's degree in accounting, actuarial and mathematical sciences, Africana studies, anthropology, art, atmospheric science, biology, business administration, chemistry, Chinese studies, computer science, computer science and applied mathematics, criminal justice, earth and atmospheric science, economics, English, environmental science, French, geography, Greek and Roman civilization, history, information science, Italian, journalism, Judaic studies, Latin American studies, linguistics, mathematics, music, philosophy, physics, political science, psychology, public policy, Puerto Rican studies, rhetoric and communication, Russian, Russian and East European studies, social welfare, sociology, Spanish, theater, urban studies and planning, and women's studies.

Interdisciplinary majors are offered in art history, Asian studies, biochemistry and molecular biology, documentary studies, East Asian studies, globalization studies, human biology, Japanese studies, medieval and Renaissance studies, public health, and religious studies. Student-designed interdisciplinary majors are available with the guidance of a faculty member.

Academic Programs

To earn the bachelor's degree, a student must complete a minimum of 120 credits (including general education requirements), satisfy major requirements, and complete a minor or a second major. Students are admitted to the University as open majors and are encouraged to use their general education requirements to explore a variety of disciplinary interests. Students may elect a double major or create their own interdisciplinary major if no existing program suits their particular interests. Prehealth, predental, and prelaw preparation is available through selected course work with any of the major programs. Special advisement for these programs is also available. Admission to most programs occurs at the end of the student's sophomore year.

The University also offers many combined bachelor's/master's degree programs that allow students to complete the requirements of both degrees at an accelerated pace. A host of combined degree options is available, including the option of combining a bachelor's degree in an area of the liberal arts and sciences with the M.B.A. degree. Albany's 3-3 program with Albany Law School allows students to earn a bachelor's degree and a law degree in a total of six years rather than seven. Students apply for this program as freshmen. The 3-2 engineering program allows Albany students to study physics on the Albany campus for three years and then complete an engineering degree through Clarkson University, Rensselaer Polytechnic Institute, SUNY at Binghamton, or SUNY at New Paltz.

Albany also offers special admissions programs for prehealth students: the Early Assurance of Admission Programs to Albany Medical College and SUNY Upstate Medical College; the Joint Seven-Year Biology/Optometry Program, in conjunction with the SUNY College of Optometry in New York City; the seven-year dental program with Boston University's Goldman School of Dental Medicine; and the agreements with Sage Graduate School in Occupational Therapy and Physical Therapy.

Off-Campus Programs

For juniors and seniors, Albany offers study-abroad programs in Brazil, China, Costa Rica, Denmark, Dominican Republic, Finland, France, Germany, Ghana, Ireland, Israel, Japan, Korea, the Netherlands, Norway, Puerto Rico, Russia, Singapore, South Africa, Spain, Sweden, Tanzania, Thailand, United Arab Emirates, and the United Kingdom. Albany students may also participate in any of the more than 300 study-abroad programs offered through the State University of New York system. The University also offers summer archaeological dig programs, performance experiences in music and theater, and opportunities for independent study and projects.

The school's location in the state's capital has created exciting career-preparation opportunities for students. A wide range of internships are available, including those in agencies, accounting firms, high-technology facilities, a major medical facility, local and national television stations, and various corporations. In addition, students may participate in an internship through the Washington Center or elect the Washington Semester at American University in Washington, D.C. They can also earn academic credit for approved volunteer work through the Community and Public Service Program.

Academic Facilities

SUNY at Albany's main campus, designed by the noted architect Edward Durrell Stone, is a unique architectural structure. Its thirteen academic buildings rest on a common "Academic Podium" of classrooms, laboratories, and offices. The University also has a large computing center, a nuclear-particle accelerator, a new Life Sciences facility, a sculpture studio, and the largest fine arts museum in the SUNY system. The University maintains three libraries that contain more than 2 million volumes. They include the University Library and the new Science Library located on the main campus and the Dewey Graduate Library located on the downtown campus.

Costs

For 2007–08, the annual undergraduate tuition was $4350 for New York State residents and $10,610 for out-of-state students. Mandatory fees totaled $1668. Room cost $5532 and board cost $3500.

Financial Aid

Merit scholarships are available to high-achieving students. The Office of Financial Aid administers all undergraduate need-based financial assistance, including Federal Work-Study Program employment, Federal Perkins Loans, Federal Supplemental Educational Opportunity Grants, New York Equality of Opportunity Grants, Alumni Scholarships, Federal Pell Grants, Federal Stafford Student Loans, New York Tuition Assistance Program awards, and New York Regents Scholarships. General part-time employment is available both on and off the campus. Aid awarded to students through the Office of Financial Aid is based on demonstrated financial need as determined by the Free Application for Federal Student Aid (FAFSA).

Faculty

At SUNY at Albany, the faculty is fully engaged in teaching undergraduates. There are 635 full-time faculty members, 95 percent of whom have earned a Ph.D or terminal degree. Undergraduates have the opportunity to conduct supervised research with Albany faculty members, who are known for their expertise in a wide variety of fields. The University is also the home of the New York State Writers Institute, which affords students access to lectures and readings by acclaimed authors and poets. Residential quads include a faculty member in residence. The student-faculty ratio is 20:1.

Student Government

Students are represented on the University Senate and its committees and have their own governing organization, the Student Association (SA). The Central Council, the SA's legislative body, deals with internal policy and administers more than $1 million from student activity fees.

Admission Requirements

Applicants are evaluated on the basis of their three-year high school average, class ranking, and SAT and/or ACT scores. Students should generally have grades of at least B and rank within the top third of their class in order to be competitive. All applicants must complete a minimum of 18 credits in high school, including 2 units of academic mathematics, 1 unit of which must be in elementary algebra. The University also actively seeks transfer students; competition for admission varies, depending on the program sought. The average grade point average for an admitted transfer student is 3.1. (Applicants for the Schools of Business, Criminal Justice, and Social Welfare are expected to achieve a cumulative average above 3.1.) The University also welcomes applications from educationally and financially disadvantaged students (Educational Opportunity Program), multicultural students, and international students. Recommendations are welcome, especially when they can help the University to assess the validity of the credentials being reviewed. Interviews are generally not required. The Admissions Office conducts information sessions, and student-led tours are available during the week throughout the school year as well as many weekends when the University is in session. Students should call for an appointment.

Application and Information

Students may apply for fall, spring, or summer admission. SUNY Application forms are available in New York State high schools and all SUNY two- and four-year colleges. The University at Albany is also a member of the Common Application, Inc. To receive full consideration, students should apply by March 1 for the fall term and by December 1 for the spring. Transfer students are encouraged to apply as early as possible and no later than July 1 for fall admission and December 15 for spring admission. Notification is on a rolling basis.

For further information, students should contact:

Director of Admissions
University at Albany, State University of New York
1400 Washington Avenue
Albany, New York 12222
Phone: 518-442-5435
E-mail: ugadmissions@albany.edu
Web site: http://www.albany.edu/

UNIVERSITY AT BUFFALO, THE STATE UNIVERSITY OF NEW YORK

BUFFALO, NEW YORK

The University

The University at Buffalo (UB) is a major public research university where undergraduate education is enriched and intensified by its close association with graduate programs and cutting-edge scholarship. With more than 100 bachelor's degree programs and more than fifty undergraduate minors, 184 master's and ninety doctoral degree programs, and more than 3,000 courses, UB offers more academic choices than any other public university in New York and New England. In addition to twenty-nine departments in the College of Arts and Sciences, the University has schools of architecture and planning, dental medicine, education (graduate, with a provisional teacher certification program for undergraduates), engineering and applied sciences, law, management, medicine and biomedical sciences, nursing, pharmacy, public health and health professions, and social work.

Because the University at Buffalo is a research-intensive university, undergraduates study and work with faculty members who are leaders in their fields in academic and research facilities that support work at the most advanced levels of knowledge. Through the University's Center for Undergraduate Research and Creative Activities, Discovery Seminars for first- and second-year students, and the new Undergraduate Academies, UB undergraduates have the opportunity to collaborate with faculty members on groundbreaking research and creative projects. This environment immerses students in the discovery process and encourages them to develop the kind of critical thinking required in the creation of new knowledge. UB's undergraduates have an opportunity to combine elements from several fields of knowledge or to design their own bachelor's degree programs. UB's Honors College enrolls more than 200 freshmen every year with SAT scores ranging from 1300 to 1600 (combined critical reading and math). Graduates of the honors program have won Fulbright, Marshall, Guggenheim, and other distinguished awards.

As a large university with more than 27,000 students, of whom more than 18,000 are undergraduates, the University at Buffalo can sustain a rich and varied student life. UB is home to a culturally diverse student body and ranks among the nation's leaders in international enrollment, with more than 3,600 students from 109 countries. The University has men's and women's sports programs at both the intramural and NCAA Division I levels, extensive recreational and entertainment facilities, more than 200 student organizations, and a busy calendar of general interest lectures, concerts, and films.

UB's North Campus, the seat of most of the undergraduate academic programs, occupies 2 square miles in suburban Amherst. It is one of the most modern university campuses in the nation, with more than 5 million square feet of academic space, laboratories, libraries, residence halls, and recreation facilities. An expanded athletics stadium, a natural sciences complex, a mathematics building, and a state-of-the-art earthquake engineering simulation laboratory were completed in recent years. The University's commitment to adding apartment-style living space has resulted in five apartment complexes on or adjacent to campus, providing attractive living options for more than 1,900 students. Creekside, Flickinger Court, Flint Village, Hadley Village, and South Lake Village apartments have opened during the past decade.

The South Campus, 3 miles away in the residential northeast corner of Buffalo, is largely devoted to the health sciences and architecture. Buffalo's rapid transit line connects that campus with the city center and the waterfront. The South Campus also has residence halls for undergraduates. Many students who live off campus find apartments in the surrounding area.

UB also collaborates with two local partners on a major research center, the New York State Center of Excellence in Bioinformatics and Life Sciences, located in downtown Buffalo. The Center of Excellence, Roswell Park's Center for Genetics and Pharmacology, and the Hauptman-Woodward Medical Research Institute make up the Buffalo Life Sciences Complex on the Buffalo Niagara Medical Campus.

Location

Buffalo is a Great Lakes city on an international border with a metropolitan area population of more than 1 million. It is a city of friendly neighborhoods with big-city recreation for all tastes: professional sports teams, the Buffalo Philharmonic Orchestra, the renowned twentieth-century art collection in the Albright-Knox Art Gallery, and a lively club scene. It also has a dramatic setting on Lake Erie and the Niagara River. Buffalo has abundant outdoor recreation in all four seasons. Skiing, hiking, camping, Lake Erie beaches, and the natural wonder of Niagara Falls are all nearby.

Majors and Degrees

The University is organized into one college and seven schools that serve undergraduates. The College of Arts and Sciences offers academic majors in African American studies, American studies, anthropology, art, art history, Asian studies, bioinformatics and computational biology, biological sciences, chemistry, classics, communication, computational physics, dance, economics, English, film studies, fine arts, geography, geological sciences, history, informatics, linguistics, mathematical physics, mathematics, mathematics-economics, media study, medicinal chemistry, modern languages and literatures (French, German, Italian, and Spanish), music, music performance, music theater, philosophy, physics, political science, psychology, sociology, speech and hearing science, studio art, theater, and women's studies. An interdisciplinary degree program in the social sciences, with concentrations in cognitive science, environmental studies, health and human services, international studies, legal studies, and urban and public policy studies, is also offered. The School of Architecture and Planning offers majors in architecture and environmental design. The School of Engineering and Applied Sciences offers academic majors in computer science and engineering physics and in aerospace, chemical, civil, computer, electrical, environmental, industrial, and mechanical engineering. The School of Management offers a major in business administration, with concentrations in accounting, financial analysis, human resources management, internal auditing, international business, management information systems, and marketing. The School of Medicine and Biomedical Sciences offers academic majors in biochemistry, biomedical sciences, biophysics, biotechnology, medical technology, nuclear medicine technology, and pharmacology and toxicology,. The School of Nursing offers an academic major in nursing. The School of Pharmacy and Pharmaceutical Sciences offers academic majors in pharmaceutical sciences and a six-year Pharm.D. pharmacy program. The School of Public Health and Health Professions offers academic majors in exercise science and occupational therapy. Physical therapy is offered as a six-year doctorate; undergraduates major in exercise science. UB also offers an undergraduate certification program for secondary education. The University has approximately thirty combined-degree programs (B.A./M.A. and B.S./M.B.A., for example) that can be completed in five years. Students whose objectives cannot be met through existing programs can formulate their own degree programs through double-degree or double-, joint-, or special-major options and an extensive minors program.

Academic Programs

Candidates for a baccalaureate degree are required to complete a minimum of 120 semester hours, 30 of which must be completed in residence, and earn a minimum grade point average of 2.0. Students have great flexibility in planning their academic programs. All students must fulfill a University general education requirement. They must also complete an academic major, which is selected, with the advice of an academic adviser, usually by the end of the sophomore year. Students also have ample opportunity for independent study under departmental or faculty auspices. Placement and credit are granted on the basis of Advanced Placement or College-Level Examination Program scores. The academic year has two semesters, one beginning in late August, and the other in mid-January. An extensive summer session is also offered.

Off-Campus Programs

Full-time undergraduates may cross-register for a maximum of two courses per term at other colleges in Western New York. Many students take advantage of study-abroad programs. The University administers overseas programs in thirty countries for full academic years or fall, spring, or summer sessions. Students who wish to study abroad in locations not offered by the University may take advantage of nearly 300 programs offered by other colleges in the SUNY system.

Academic Facilities

The University at Buffalo's academic library collections are the largest in the SUNY system; in addition to more than 3.6 million bound volumes, they include more than 30,000 serials and periodicals, 5.4 million microforms, specialized holdings including the world's largest collection of James Joyce manuscripts, and a renowned collection of twentieth-century poetry in manuscript. All library holdings are digitally cataloged and accessible from terminals and computers on and off campus. The University is among the first to have software that makes the entire SUNY library system—more than 18 million volumes—available to students. State-of-the-art computer workstations for student use are located at public sites in the University's libraries.

Costs

In 2007–08, tuition for New York State residents is $4350 and for out-of-state residents, $10,610. For all students, fees are $1867, and room and board costs are $9132. Students should expect additional expenses for books and supplies, transportation, and personal expenses. Costs are subject to change.

Financial Aid

The University participates in all New York State and federal financial aid programs, including the Tuition Assistance Program (available only to New York State residents) and the Federal Pell Grant, Federal Work-Study, Federal Direct Student Loan, and Federal Perkins Loan programs. The recommended deadline for completing the Free Application for Federal Student Aid is February 1 for fall semester entry. All inquiries concerning financial aid should be addressed to the Student Response Center, 232 Capen Hall (telephone: 866-838-7257 (toll-free)). The University awards more merit-based scholarships than any other public university in New York State. In fall 2007, UB awarded more than $4 million in merit scholarship support to incoming freshmen. UB's top incoming freshmen receive the Presidential Scholarship, which covers the full cost of attendance, for all four years, and are invited to join the Honors College. Provost Scholarships range from $2500 to the full cost of tuition, depending on academic achievement, talent in the creative or performing arts, and the cost of attendance. The Daniel Acker Scholarship is for talented students who are traditionally underrepresented in higher education. Acker Scholars receive full tuition aid and participate in a comprehensive program of support services and activities. Athletic grants-in-aid are awarded to students recruited to participate in the University's NCAA Division I athletics program.

Faculty

The University's nationally renowned faculty includes winners of the National Medal of Science, the Nobel Prize, the Pulitzer Prize, and other awards. Of the 1,901 faculty members, 97 percent hold the doctorate or other terminal degree. A large number have published books or scholarly articles. Many have held major national or international fellowships; conducted research funded by government agencies or national foundations; served as consultants to business, education, and government; or otherwise demonstrated professional expertise. More than 100 have won the SUNY Chancellor's Award for Excellence in Teaching, the largest number of recipients on any SUNY campus.

Student Government

All daytime undergraduate students are members of the Student Association and are entitled to participate in its activities. The Student Association is involved at every level of student life, from freshman orientation to commencement. By their membership on many University-wide policy committees, representatives of the association are given a legitimate, permanent voice in the policies and direction of the University.

Admission Requirements

Applicants are required to submit their high school record and the results of the ACT or SAT critical reading and math sections. Applicants should plan to take the SAT or ACT no later than November. Application review and notification begins in early February and continues until the freshman class is filled. Most freshmen admitted to the University make application to the major of their choice during the sophomore year. However, architecture, business administration, engineering and applied sciences, exercise science, nuclear medicine technology, nursing, and occupational therapy may offer departmental admission to freshman applicants.

Admission to programs in dance, music, music theater, and theater requires an audition.

Admission is competitive. Most successful students at the University have come with a strong level of academic preparation in basic academic areas. Among accepted freshmen in fall 2007, the mean high school average was 92 percent, 87 percent were in the top third of their high school class, and 81 percent scored at or above 1100 on the SAT (critical reading and math).

The University enrolls and provides specialized advisement and support to a limited number of freshmen who demonstrate academic potential through means other than quantitative measures. Creative talent, athletics, special academic achievement, demonstrated leadership, community service, and personal circumstances are examples of areas that the University may consider. These non-academic factors must be documented by submission of a supplemental application, which includes an essay section.

Transfer applicants must have completed a minimum of 12 semester hours at a regionally accredited college prior to application. Students with fewer than 24 semester hours are evaluated on the basis of their college and high school credentials in combination with standardized test score results. Admission of transfer students is based on the quality of previous academic performance and space availability. In order to receive consideration for transfer admission to SUNY at Buffalo it is recommended that students present a strong record of college study, earning a minimum cumulative grade point average of 2.5 on a 4.0 scale. It should be noted, however, that requirements may vary depending on the academic program.

Admission to an academic department may occur concurrently with University admission if the applicant has fulfilled prerequisite requirements. These requirements include completed courses, but may also comprise essay, portfolio, exam, or audition requirements. Some departments have significantly higher GPA standards and early deadlines for application.

Application and Information

Students can apply online at http://www.admissions.buffalo.edu/apply. Paper applications are available in New York State high schools or by contacting:

Office of Admissions
12 Capen Hall
University at Buffalo, the State University of New York
Buffalo, New York 14260-1660
Phone: 716-645-6900
888-UB-ADMIT (toll-free)
E-mail: ub-admissions@buffalo.edu
Web site: http://www.admissions.buffalo.edu

UNIVERSITY OF ROCHESTER

ROCHESTER, NEW YORK

The University

Founded in 1850, Rochester is one of the leading private universities in the country, one of sixty-two members of the prestigious Association of American Universities, and one of eight national private research institutions in the premier University Athletic Association. Including the Eastman School of Music, the University has a full-time enrollment of 4,608 undergraduates and 2,900 graduate students. Rochester's personal scale and the breadth of its research and academic programs permit both attention to the individual and unusual flexibility in planning undergraduate studies.

Along with the distinctive Rochester Curriculum to help make the most of the undergraduate years, students in the College of Arts, Sciences, and Engineering (the College) also have access to resources at the Eastman School of Music, the William E. Simon Graduate School of Business Administration, the Margaret Warner Graduate School of Education and Human Development, the School of Medicine and Dentistry, and the School of Nursing. Special opportunities include the Take Five program, which allows selected undergraduates a tuition-free fifth year or semester of academic study; Rochester Early Medical Scholars (REMS), an eight-year combined B.A. or B.S./M.D. program; Rochester Early Business Scholars (REBS), a six-year combined B.A. or B.S./M.B.A program; Guaranteed Rochester Accelerated Degree in Education (GRADE), a five-year B.A. or B.S./M.S. program; study abroad; Quest courses, first-year classes designed to allow collaborative research between faculty and students; seven certificate programs; Senior Scholars Program; and employment opportunities that include a national summer jobs program and paid internship experiences.

Located on a bend in the Genesee River, the River Campus is home to almost all undergraduates who live in a variety of residence halls, fraternity houses, and special-interest housing. Most of the campus is built in a consistent neoclassical architecture, yet all academic buildings are wireless, and all residence halls are wired for the Internet and cable television. Among the facilities are Wilson Commons, the student union; the multipurpose Athletic Center; and a brand-new research facility, the Goergen Hall of Biomedical Engineering and Optics.

Rochester students participate in more than 220 student organizations, including twenty-two varsity teams, thirty-six intramural and club sports, eighteen fraternities and thirteen sororities, performing arts groups, musical ensembles, WRUR radio, URTV, and various campus publications.

Location

With Lake Ontario on its northern border, the scenic Finger Lakes to the south, and more than a million people, Rochester has been rated among the most livable cities in the United States. It offers a wide range of cultural and recreational opportunities through its museums, parks, orchestras, planetarium, theater companies, and professional sports teams.

Majors and Degrees

The University of Rochester offers a Bachelor of Arts program through the College, with majors in African and African-American studies, American Sign Language, anthropology, art history, astronomy, biology, brain and cognitive sciences, economics, chemistry, classics, comparative literature, computer science, economics, English, environmental studies, film and media studies, financial economics, French, geological sciences, German, health and society, history, interdepartmental studies, international relations, Japanese, linguistics, mathematics, mathematics/statistics, music, philosophy, physics, political science, psychology, religion, Russian, Russian studies, Spanish, statistics, studio arts, and women's studies.

Bachelor of Science programs are offered in the College, with majors in applied mathematics, biological sciences (biochemistry, cell and developmental biology, ecology and evolutionary biology, microbiology, molecular genetics, or neuroscience), brain and cognitive sciences, chemistry, computer science, environmental science, geological sciences, geomechanics, physics, and physics and astronomy.

The College also offers certificate programs in actuarial studies, Asian studies, biotechnology, international relations, literary translation studies, management studies, mathematical modeling in political science and economics, and Polish and Central European studies.

The School of Engineering and Applied Sciences—part of the College—offers Bachelor of Science programs in biomedical, chemical, electrical and computer, and mechanical engineering; geomechanics; optics; and engineering and applied science, an interdepartmental program with specializations in a variety of areas. A B.A. program in engineering science is also offered.

In addition to the College's Bachelor of Arts in Music, a Bachelor of Music degree is offered through the Eastman School, with majors in applied music, composition, jazz studies and contemporary media, music education, musical arts, and music theory. Students may pursue a double-degree in Eastman and the College.

A Bachelor of Science degree is offered through the School of Nursing for those who already have their RN certification.

Additional opportunities include 3-2 or guaranteed 4-2 admissions programs offered through the William E. Simon Graduate School of Business Administration, in which students earn both a B.A. or B.S. from the College and an M.B.A. from the Simon School; 3-2 B.S./M.S. programs in biological sciences—biomedical engineering, chemical engineering, electrical and computer engineering, mechanical engineering, neuroscience, and optics; a program leading to a B.A. or B.S. and a master's in public health; a 3-2 program leading to a B.A. in music and an M.A. in music education; and a guaranteed admission program leading to a B.A. or B.S. in an undergraduate major and an M.S. from the Margaret Warner Graduate School of Education and Human Development. Transfer students can pursue a 3-2 program that combines a B.A. and a B.S. in an engineering concentration.

Academic Programs

The University's calendar includes two regular semesters. The distinctive Rochester Curriculum allows students to select their major from one of the three branches of learning (the humanities, the natural sciences, and the social sciences). In each of the two branches outside their major, students choose a "cluster" of three courses that allows them to dig deeply in an area that particularly interests them. For most students, there are no other distribution requirements, except choosing one of seventy freshman writing classes.

The Take Five program offers selected students the opportunity to take a tuition-free fifth year or semester in order to pursue their varied interests.

The Quest program offers first-year students the advantages of small classes, student/teacher collaboration, and original research. As a result, Quest courses teach students how to learn, both as undergraduates and beyond.

Students may arrange independent study courses or pursue research in all departments. Those whose interests may not be fully realized through a traditional major, double major, or major/minor, may work with faculty advisers to design an interdepartmental concentration.

Undergraduates from any academic discipline may devote their senior year to a self-designed creative project in the form of scholarly research, a scientific experiment, or a literary or artistic work through the Senior Scholars Program.

Undergraduates enrolled in the College may take private instruction at the Eastman School of Music. A double-degree program leading to the Bachelor of Music degree from Eastman and a bachelor's degree from the College is also available.

The Rochester Early Medical Scholars program is an eight-year B.A. or B.S./M.D. program for exceptionally talented undergraduates. Students enrolled in this program enter the University of Rochester with assurance of admission to the University's medical school upon successful completion of their undergraduate degree program.

The University's research centers include the Frederick Douglass Institute for African and African-American Studies, the Susan B. Anthony Institute for Gender and Women's Studies, the Gandhi Institute for Nonviolence, the Center for Future Health, the Center for Judaic Studies, the W. Allen Wallis Institute of Political Economy, the Center for Visual Science, the Sign Language Research Center, the Skalny Center for Polish and Central European Studies, the Center for Optics Manufacturing, the Laboratory of Laser Energetics, the Center for Electronic Imaging Systems, and the Center for Biomedical Ultrasound, and many others in the School of Medicine and Dentistry and Strong Medicine.

Off-Campus Programs

Rochester offers full-year and semester-long study-abroad opportunities, as well as special summer and winter trips, through sixty different study-abroad programs. Semester and full-year destinations include Argentina, Australia, Austria, Belgium, Chile, China, Czech Republic, Egypt, England, France, Germany, Ghana, Hungary, Ireland, Israel, Italy, Japan, Jordan, Mexico, Netherlands, New Zealand, Peru, Poland, Russia, Senegal, Spain, Sweden, and Taiwan. International internships are offered in Berlin, Bonn, Brussels, London, Madrid, and Paris.

Academic Facilities

As one of the smallest of the 151 American universities classified by the Carnegie Foundation for the Advancement of Teaching as offering an extensive range of doctoral programs, Rochester offers an environment that combines the vast learning resources of a national university with the intensive personalized attention of a private college. Research opportunities for undergraduates are available in every field. Major research facilities include a comprehensive Medical Center; an extensive on-campus computer system; direct access to the CYBER 205 Supercomputer in Princeton, New Jersey; fifteen electron microscopes; a 12-trillion watt, 24-beam laser fusion laboratory; and a 3-million-volume library system, including the Eastman School's Sibley Music Library, the largest collection of any music school in the Western Hemisphere. The University is widely known as the nation's premier institution for the study of optics and is home to the Omega, the world's most powerful ultraviolet laser.

Costs

In 2007–08, tuition and fees cost $35,190, room and board averaged $10,640, and books, transportation, and other expenses averaged $2320. Part-time study is offered on a per-course basis.

Financial Aid

The University offers a strong program of financial assistance, including academic merit scholarships, grants, loans, tuition payment plans, and part-time jobs. Applicants for financial aid should submit the CSS PROFILE application and the Free Application for Federal Student Aid (FAFSA). Special awards include full-tuition Renaissance Scholarships, Bausch & Lomb Honorary Science Scholarships, the Frederick Douglass and Susan B. Anthony Scholarships, George Eastman Young Leaders Scholarships, Xerox Scholarships for Innovation and Information Technology, International Baccalaureate Scholarships, Seventh Generation Scholarships, FIRST Scholarships, National Merit Scholarships, National Achievement Scholarships, Urban League Scholarships, AHORA Scholarships, and other merit-based awards. The University also awards room and board grants to selected Naval ROTC scholars and Phi Theta Kappa Scholarships for transfer students. Special applications are not required for merit scholarship consideration.

Faculty

Students work closely with a stimulating faculty of internationally renowned scholars, all of whom engage both in advanced research and in teaching at the undergraduate level. The University's faculty is held in particularly high regard by colleagues at sister institutions, and many of its departments are widely recognized as among the best in the country.

Student Government

All undergraduates are members of the Students' Association, which has an annually elected president and a student Senate; there is also a Judicial Council, whose members are appointed by the Senate. The Students' Association in the College strives to coordinate student activities; protect academic freedom; improve students' cultural, social, and physical welfare; develop educational standards and facilities; and provide a forum for the expression of student views and interests.

Admission Requirements

The University of Rochester seeks to admit students who will take advantage of its resources, be strongly motivated to do their best, and contribute to the life of the University community. An applicant's character, extracurricular activities, job experience, academic accomplishments, and career goals are considered. More than three quarters of last year's enrolled students ranked in the top tenth of their secondary school classes. The middle 50 percent of enrolled freshmen scored between 600 and 700 on the SAT verbal exam and 630 and 720 on the SAT math and between 27 and 31 on the ACT.

The recommended application filing date for freshman applicants is January 1 for fall admission and October 1 for spring admission. An early decision plan is available. Transfer students are welcome for entrance in the fall and spring semesters. Transfer applications are due by June 1 for fall enrollment and November 1 for spring. The University accepts the Common Application. An electronic online application is available from the University's Web site. Applicants for freshman admission are required to submit scores from either the SAT or the ACT. SAT Subject Test results are reviewed but are not required. An interview is recommended. Candidates for admission from lower-income groups are encouraged to investigate the Higher Education Opportunity Program (New York State residents only), which provides supportive services and financial aid.

The University of Rochester provides equal opportunity in admissions and student aid regardless of sex, age, race, color, creed, disability, sexual orientation, and national or ethnic origin. Further, the University complies with all applicable nondiscrimination laws. Questions on compliance should be directed to the particular school or department and/or to the University's Intercessor at University of Rochester, P.O. Box 270039, Rochester, New York 14627-0039; 585-275-9125.

Application and Information

To obtain application forms and further information on admission and financial aid, students should contact:

Dean of Admissions and Financial Aid
University of Rochester
P.O. Box 270251
Rochester, New York 14627-0251
Phone: 585-275-3221
888-822-2256 (toll-free)
Web site: http://www.enrollment.rochester.edu/admissions

Director of Admissions
Eastman School of Music
26 Gibbs Street
Rochester, New York 14604
Phone: 585-274-1060
800-388-9695 (toll-free)
Web site: http://www.rochester.edu/eastman

Rush Rhees Library on the University of Rochester's Eastman Quadrangle.

UTICA COLLEGE

UTICA, NEW YORK

The College

Founded by Syracuse University in 1946, Utica College (UC) is known for its excellent academic programs, outstanding faculty members, personal attention, and diversity among students. The hallmarks of Utica College's academic programs are the integration of liberal and professional studies and a strong emphasis on internships, research, and other experiential learning opportunities, but UC is best known for the close, personal relationship students have with both faculty and staff members. Approximately 2,952 undergraduate and graduate students attend UC, including men and women from a wide variety of socioeconomic and cultural backgrounds as well as older students, veterans, and students with disabilities. While most students come from New York, New England, and the Middle Atlantic States, students are drawn to UC from all parts of the United States, and there is a growing international student population.

Academic programs of note include accounting-CPA, economic crime investigation, education, the health sciences, journalism, management, psych–child life, and public relations. Utica College also offers a robust study-abroad program as well as an honors program. Although a private, independent institution, Utica College maintains an academic relationship with Syracuse University and offers the Syracuse undergraduate degree.

Utica College is located on a modern, 128-acre campus on the southwestern edge of Utica, New York. Its facilities include an academic complex where most classes are held, the Frank E. Gannett Memorial Library, seven residence halls, an athletic center, a 1,200 seat stadium, and numerous athletic fields.

Half of UC's students live on campus in residence halls that feature a variety of housing options, modern amenities, and lounges for studying or relaxing with friends. Freshmen primarily live in North and South Halls, which offer mostly double-occupancy rooms. Campus dining services provide a wide variety of options, including American and international cuisines, vegetarian meals, a large salad bar, and lighter fare such as burgers and pizza.

Whether students live on or off campus, they can take advantage of more than eighty student organizations—all devoted to such interests as community service, fraternities and sororities, music, theater, and politics as well as major-related clubs that provide opportunities for students to organize career-related events. Students can write for the student newspaper, work at the College's radio station, submit entries for the College's literary magazine, or work on the yearbook. Events throughout the year give students opportunities to enjoy lectures, concerts, poetry readings, art exhibits, plays, and nationally recognized speakers.

Utica College offers twenty-one NCAA Division III varsity sports, including men's baseball, basketball, cross-country, football, ice hockey, lacrosse, soccer, swimming and diving, and tennis; women's basketball, cross-country, field hockey, ice hockey, lacrosse, soccer, softball, swimming and diving, tennis, volleyball, and water polo; and coed golf. UC also offers club sports and a wide variety of intramural opportunities. Utica College is a member of the Empire 8 Athletic Conference, the Eastern College Athletic Conference, and the New York State Women's Collegiate Athletic Association. Nearly 30 percent of all UC students participate in at least one Division III intercollegiate sport, and more than 45 percent are active in intramural or nonvarsity club sports.

Athletic facilities include a 1,200-seat multisport stadium with a state-of-the-art Field Turf synthetic grass playing surface; the Clark Athletic Center, which contains a large gymnasium, racquetball courts, a swimming pool, saunas, a recently renovated 6,400-square-foot free-weight room and fully equipped fitness facility, and numerous outdoor fields and courts. Ice hockey games are played at the downtown Utica Memorial Auditorium, which features pro-style hockey locker rooms and training facilities.

Graduate degrees are available in business administration, economic crime management, education, liberal studies, occupational therapy, and physical therapy.

Location

The city of Utica, with a population of 300,000, is located in the heart of the historic Mohawk Valley. Just 90 miles west of Albany and 50 miles east of Syracuse, Utica has a thriving arts community, beautiful parks, and expanding shopping centers featuring national retailers. There are numerous recreational facilities, including a municipal ski slope and a world-class golf course less than a mile from the Utica College campus. Other nearby recreational opportunities include tennis, swimming, boating, fishing, hiking, and camping.

Majors and Degrees

Utica College offers undergraduate degree programs in accounting, accounting-CPA, biology, business economics, chemistry, communication arts, computer science, criminal justice, criminal justice–economic crime investigation, cybersecurity and information assurance, economics, English, foreign language, government and politics, health studies, health studies–human behavior, health studies–management, history, international studies, journalism studies, liberal studies, management, mathematics, nursing, occupational therapy, philosophy, physical therapy, physics, psychology, psychology–child life, public relations, public relations/journalism studies, sociology and anthropology, and therapeutic recreation.

Students interested in the occupational therapy or physical therapy major earn a bachelor's degree in health studies with direct entry into UC's graduate programs, as long as academic requirements are met. Utica College offers a master's degree in occupational therapy and a doctorate in physical therapy (D.P.T.).

Students may minor in anthropology, chemistry, communication arts, computer science, economics, English language, film studies, French, gender studies, geoscience, gerontology, government, history, human rights advocacy, literature, management, mathematics, philosophy, psychology, recreation leadership, sociology, Spanish, theater, and writing.

Preprofessional programs include dentistry, law, medicine, optometry, podiatry, and veterinary medicine. Special programs are available in teacher education, gerontology, engineering, and joint health professions.

Academic Programs

Students may choose from thirty-two undergraduate majors and twenty-six minors in a wide variety of fields as well as accelerated programs, independent study, cooperative education, field placements, and internships. Utica College also offers a rapidly growing education program; students wishing to pursue a career in teaching choose either a liberal arts major (to teach elementary education) or a major in their intended field (to teach at the secondary level).

For those students who are undecided, the Academic Support Services Center provides academic advising and career counseling, and Career Services offers students opportunities to explore career options.

To earn a bachelor's degree, students must complete a minimum of 120 to 128 credits, satisfy major and major-related requirements, and complete any special program requirements. In addition, all Utica College students, regardless of their major, must complete a liberal arts core program as part of the degree requirements.

Utica College operates on a semester system, with the fall term beginning in late August and ending shortly before Christmas, and the spring term beginning in late January and ending in early May. Summer and winter sessions offer students opportunities to accelerate their studies or take classes for which they have no time during the regular academic year.

First-Year Seminar offers freshmen and transfer students opportunities to earn academic credit while learning how to make the transition to college. Utica College offers the Higher Education Opportunity Program (HEOP), the Collegiate Science and Technology Entry Program (CSTEP), and a Summer Institute, which serves as an academic bridge between high school and college.

Off-Campus Programs

Studying abroad gives students opportunities to widen their global perspectives. Utica College is proud to participate in exchange programs with universities in Spain, Italy, Poland, Finland, Hungary, Peru, Scotland, and Wales. Students may also study at American College in Dublin in Ireland. UC students are also eligible to participate in Syracuse University's Division of International Programs Abroad. This arrangement allows students to study in Madrid, Strasbourg, Florence, London, and Hong Kong.

Students are encouraged to complete internships and field placements to gain professional experience with businesses and organizations while they are earning college credit. Utica College's cooperative education program allows students to earn money while gaining professional experience.

Academic Facilities

The Frank E. Gannett Memorial Library collection includes 200,000 volumes, 1,200 serial subscriptions, hundreds of online journals, and a microform collection of more than 60,000 journals, newspapers, and books. The library is fully automated and shares a local system with Mid-York Library System. It also is a member of OCLC, a bibliographic database through which it is possible to locate and borrow interlibrary loan items from local, regional, national, and international libraries. Located on the lower level of the library are the Media Center, computer labs, the Edith Langley Barrett Fine Arts Gallery, and a large concourse—the site of special events, such as musical recitals, receptions, and guest lectures.

Classes, laboratories, and faculty offices are primarily located in an academic complex composed of five buildings: Hubbard Hall, White Hall, Gordon Science Center, F. Eugene Romano Hall, and the Faculty Center. Other offices are located in DePerno Hall.

F. Eugene Romano Hall, the first phase of Utica College's new science and technology complex, opened in summer 2007 and provides classroom, laboratory, and clinical space in addition to modern technology for students majoring in physical therapy, occupational therapy, and nursing. Subsequent phases of the science and technology complex will provide modern facilities for programs in economic crime, cybersecurity, and the traditional sciences.

Utica College maintains eight academic computer laboratories with both IBM-compatible and Macintosh computers, including two portable wireless laptop laboratories. Students have additional Internet access in the Pioneer Café and in all student residence hall rooms. Other resources include the Academic Support Services Center, the Math/Science Center, and the Writing Center.

Costs

For 2007–08, tuition was $24,264. Room and board costs were $10,030. Student activity and technology fees cost $320. Books and supplies average $900 per year.

Financial Aid

The College is recognized as a best buy in education and works to control costs and keep its education affordable. The average financial aid package for 2006–07 freshmen was $21,390. About two thirds of that aid came from grants and a third from loans and/or jobs. Approximately 90 percent of the freshmen received a financial aid package. At the same time, UC awarded numerous merit scholarships to students with outstanding grades and test scores.

Almost every federal and state financial aid program is available through Utica College. Students apply for institutional and governmental financial aid by filing the Free Application for Federal Student Aid (FAFSA) by February 15. In addition, UC offers three different deferred-payment programs that spread payments over the academic year.

Faculty

Utica College's faculty is diverse, energetic, accomplished, and devoted to their students. The vast majority—95 percent—have earned their Ph.D. or other terminal degree, and while many are involved in research, the primary focus of faculty members is teaching. The typical class size is 20 students, the student-faculty ratio is 15:1, and all faculty members are involved in assisting students with their academic planning.

Student Government

One of Utica College's strongest traditions is student participation in the College's governance structure. Students may serve on a number of student governing bodies, and students also serve on all standing committees of the College.

Admission Requirements

Utica College admits students who can best benefit from the educational opportunities the College offers. The Admission Committee gives each application individual attention, and the potential for a student's success at UC is measured primarily by an evaluation of past academic performance, scholastic ability, and personal characteristics. Freshman applicants must have completed 16 academic units, including 4 years of English. Students should follow a college-preparatory program, including 3 units of mathematics, 3 units of science, 2 units of foreign language, and 3 units of social studies.

Application and Information

Students may apply for fall, spring, or summer admission. Materials required include a completed Utica College application form, official high school or college transcripts, and a $40 application fee. Utica College prefers, but does not require, SAT or ACT scores, with the exception of the programs listed below. A personal interview for all applications is strongly suggested.

Occupational therapy, physical therapy, nursing, and joint health professions program applicants must submit SAT or ACT scores, a preferred letter of clinical recommendation if applicable, and a personal statement. International students must complete the international student application form. The application fee is waived for students who apply to HEOP or CSTEP; however, SAT or ACT scores are required to be considered for either program.

The College conducts a rolling admissions program; however certain programs do have application deadlines. For students applying to the occupational therapy or physical therapy programs, the joint health professions program, or for academic achievement awards, the application deadline is January 15. For students applying to the nursing program, the preferred application deadline is February 1. The application deadline for the HEOP program is January 15. Students should note that a tuition deposit of $200 is required by April 1 to secure a place in the HEOP program.

Additional admissions information can be found online at http://www.utica.edu/enrollment/admission/international.htm or http://www.utica.edu/enrollment/admission/transfer/htm or http://www.utica.edu/academic/honorsprogram.htm.

Inquiries should be sent to:

Director of Admissions
Utica College
1600 Burrstone Road
Utica, New York 13502-4892
Phone: 315-792-3006
800-782-8884 (toll-free)
E-mail: admiss@utica.edu
Web site: http://www.utica.edu

The Addison Miller White Hall Plaza.

VAUGHN COLLEGE OF AERONAUTICS AND TECHNOLOGY

FLUSHING, NEW YORK

The College

Vaughn College of Aeronautics and Technology is a private, four-year college committed to providing its students with the excellent education and skills needed to achieve professional success in engineering, technology, management, and aviation. Founded in 1932, the College, adjacent to LaGuardia Airport, is a small, high-quality institution where students can experience personal attention as they progress through their academic course work. The College fosters a culture of excellence in which rigorous degree, professional, technical, and certification programs are offered. These programs, built upon the College's aeronautical heritage, incorporate the latest technology and meet the universal needs of the industries they serve. The result is well-educated graduates who are successful in their fields. The College's student body of nearly 1,200 and its low 11:1 student-faculty ratio ensure a highly personalized learning environment. More than 93 percent of Vaughn College graduates are employed within six months of obtaining their degrees, and they work in twenty countries and in all fifty states.

On September 1, 2004, the College of Aeronautics became Vaughn College of Aeronautics and Technology. The name reflects the College's aviation heritage as well as its future as a greatly expanded academic institution, with new programs to include a Bachelor of Science in mechatronic engineering in fall 2006 and a master's-level management offering in fall 2007. The name change is part of the College's five-year strategic plan and includes plans for a new library, a residence hall, additional degree programs, and other improvements to the campus.

Location

Located in New York City, the College offers numerous internship opportunities with a vast array of technology, manufacturing, and aviation companies. The cultural, spiritual, and physical needs of the students are met by the outstanding facilities of New York City. Restaurants are easily accessible, and hospitals and other medical facilities are among the best in the world. Various museums focus on arts, natural history, science, and world civilization.

Majors and Degrees

The College awards the Associate of Applied Science (A.A.S.) degree in aeronautical engineering technology, airport management, aviation maintenance, computerized design and animated graphics, electronic engineering technology–avionics, and flight.

The Bachelor of Science (B.S.) degree is available general management, airline management, airport management, aviation maintenance, aviation maintenance management, electronic engineering technology–avionics, electronic technology–general electronics, electronic technology–optical communications (fiber optics), flight, mechatronics engineering, mechanical engineering technology–aeronautical option, and mechanical engineering technology–computer-aided design option. A nondegree course of study in air traffic control, a Federal Aviation Administration Collegiate Training Initiative program, is also available. The College is one of thirteen institutions nationwide to offer this program.

Academic Programs

All students in associate and baccalaureate degree programs complete a core curriculum as part of their degree requirements. The core curriculum is derived from the mission of the College and reflects what the institution believes is important and elemental to students' education and development. In general, the core instills in students critical-thinking skills, values appropriate to an educated person, and the ability to communicate, and the curriculum provides context for advanced learning. The baccalaureate core consists of three components—academic skills (13 credits, including a year of English composition, a course in oral communication, and precalculus), the liberal arts (12 credits, including a year of world and American literature), and math and science (15 credits).

Off-Campus Programs

Internships are an important part of a student's learning experience at Vaughn College, and they often lead to job offers upon graduation. The Office of Career Development and faculty chair members arrange for internships with top U.S. corporations. As a Hispanic-serving institution, the College participates with the Hispanic Association of Colleges and Universities (HACU) to place students in internships with various federal agencies year-round. Some of the other active internships and cooperatives include the Boeing Company, Federal Aviation Administration (FAA), Federal Express, Global Air Dispatch, HACU, jetBlue, Lockheed Martin, the Metropolitan Transportation Authority (MTA), the National Broadcasting Company, the Northrop Grumman Corporation, Northwest Airlines, ORBIS, the Port Authority of New York and New Jersey, and Teterboro Airport.

Academic Facilities

Each laboratory provides the work/study environment suited to the requirements of each program. Students experience the technology that they will ultimately use once employed. This practical, hands-on experience helps qualify students for immediate employment upon graduation. From the new photonics laboratory to the CATIA/NASTRAN computer center, the College's faculty members are committed to providing students with the knowledge and tools they are likely to find in today's businesses. The FRASCA 142 flight simulator is a major component of the flight students on campus.

Over the last several years, the College has installed a $1-million computer network, which allows a common interface for a number of operating systems, including Novell and Microsoft Windows. The system also supports other operating systems, including Windows NT, Windows 2000, Windows 2003, Windows XP, Macintosh OSX, and UNIX as well as all of the previous server versions of Windows Operating Systems. More than 200 computers are connected through fiber-optic cables to allow sharing of more than thirty of the most up-to-date applications, including desktop publishing, CATIA, Autocad, Mechanical Desktop, mathematics, word processing, spread sheets, databases, shared print services, and file and scanning services. Two T1 lines give each workstation access to the Internet and full e-mail and messaging services on and off campus. In addition to the T1 lines, the College also has added wireless Internet access that is available across the campus. More information can be found on the College's Web site at http://www.vaughn.edu.

The College's library offers extensive general, technical, resource, and periodical material totaling more than 42,000 volumes. The real and virtual resources include books, periodicals, videos, and research databases. There are more than 150 periodical titles in the library's collection. The video collection consists of subject videos to support the College's curriculum, general interest videos, and movies. The library houses almost 2,000 VHS tapes and DVDs. In addition, there are research databases available that contain more than 8,000 full-text periodicals and newspapers. Ten personal computers are available for student use in the reference area. The library, which occupies more than 4,500 square feet, offers seating for 100 students and has an attached computer lab with twenty computer stations.

Costs

In 2007–08, full-time tuition (12 to 18 credits per semester) was $7350. Students taking fewer than 11 credits paid $500 per credit. The semester fee, which covers the cost of orientation courses, Internet and computer usage, and student-support services, activities, and leadership programs, was $140.

For the 2007–08 academic year, rooms in Vaughn's new residence hall were $3750 for a double room and $4300 for a single room, per semester. A $250 housing deposit is required. Residents live in either a two-person or four-person suite with a semi-private bath. The residence hall has laundry, study, and kitchen facilities in a common area within the building. Residence hall rooms are supplied with a bed, dresser, closet, desk, chair, and wastebasket for each student. Each room is also equipped with a phone, cable TV hookup, and computer port.

Financial Aid

Vaughn College of Aeronautics and Technology offers federal, state, and institutional funds to help students pay for their education. More than 85 percent of students are eligible for some type of financial aid. The first step is to file the Free Application for Federal Student Aid (FAFSA) and, if appropriate, the New York State Tuition Assistance Program (TAP) application. Applications for the fall semester should be filed by March 1. The College recognizes academic excellence by awarding scholarships to high-achieving students pursuing Bachelor of Science degree programs. In order to be eligible, all applicants must file the FAFSA.

Awards for new students include Founders' Scholarships, which are merit-based and range between $500 to $6000 per year; the Vaughn College financial grants, which are awarded based on need and range from $250 to $2200; and the National Science Foundation's Computer Science, Engineering, and Mathematics Scholarships (CSEMS), which provide up to $3125 per academic year for students majoring in mechanical or electronic engineering technology.

Faculty

What separates Vaughn College of Aeronautics and Technology from other institutions is its uniquely committed faculty, whose members come to the classroom with extensive experience in such fields as engineering, manufacturing, management, and communications. Working closely with industry, the College has developed rigorous curricula that incorporate the latest technology and the knowledge students need for that all-important first professional position. The small student-faculty ratio of 11:1 enables students to work closely with faculty members in the classroom and laboratory settings.

Student Government

The Student Government Association (SGA) is primarily concerned with the quality of student life on campus. SGA carries the concerns of its constituency, the student body, to the administration and is the voice of the student body. Serving students as the liaison to the administration, SGA coordinates social programming and provides a system for cocurricular involvement through many clubs and organizations. SGA meets on a regular basis and encourages all students to attend meetings and become involved.

Admission Requirements

High school graduates must submit the completed application; the $40 application fee; SAT or ACT scores; an official copy of the high school transcript and any college transcripts (if applicable); a copy of the high school diploma (or GED), complete with scores; and immunizations records. Some students may need to take a placement exam, while flight operations applicants must pass the FAA Class II physical examination. An interview with an admissions counselor and a financial aid counselor is required for all flight operations applicants and recommended for all others.

Students who have lived in the United States for less than three years and for whom English is a second language, or international applicants from countries where English is not an official language, may substitute results of the TOEFL exam. Students who have completed 24 or more college credits are exempt from the SAT/ACT requirement.

Application and Information

The admissions office reviews applications on a rolling basis. All applicants are encouraged to file by March 1 for the fall semester and November 15 for the spring semester in order to take advantage of scholarship opportunities.

Vaughn College of Aeronautics and Technology
86-01 23rd Avenue
Flushing, New York 11369
Phone: 718-429-6600
866-6VAUGHN (toll-free)
Fax: 718-779-2231
E-mail: admitme@vaughn.edu
Web site: http://www.vaughn.edu

WAGNER COLLEGE

STATEN ISLAND, NEW YORK

The College

Founded in 1883, Wagner College is a four-year, private residential college with a strong tradition in the liberal arts. Located in New York City's borough of Staten Island, the campus is situated atop Grymes Hill on the nineteenth-century estate of the Cunard family, founders of the famous shipping line. Wagner's 105-acre campus provides a setting that feels far away from the city; yet, Manhattan is just a free 25-minute ferry ride away. Recently, the College received attention for its nationally recognized curriculum, the Wagner Plan for the Practical Liberal Arts, which integrates courses across disciplines and directly connects course work to field experiences and internships. Wagner College is ranked among the national leaders in first-year programs and learning communities in the "Programs to Look for" section of the *U.S. News & World Report*'s "America's Best Colleges" 2006 annual guide. The College also received the 2005 TIAA-CREF Theodore M. Hesburgh Award in recognition of the first-year program. Wagner College is a member of the Associated New American Colleges, Project Pericles, and Colleges of Distinction.

Wagner enrolls approximately 1,950 undergraduate and 350 graduate students. About 80 percent of Wagner undergraduates live on campus in three residence halls that offer spectacular views of the New York Harbor, Manhattan, and the Atlantic Ocean. Students come from thirty-eight states and several other countries. Students choose Wagner because it offers excellent academic preparation, superb access to professional and cultural opportunities, and a traditional college campus setting. Students gain access to exceptional professional opportunities within the curriculum and through the College's large and supportive alumni base in the New York City area and beyond. Wagner strongly believes that career development is an integral part of a student's education—one that begins in a student's first year at Wagner and culminates in a senior year practicum in a specific field of study.

Student life is active on the campus with more than sixty different clubs and organizations, including both national and local fraternities and sororities. Wagner offers a full array of activities and social events, many of which are planned by the student life staff. Wagner expands students' experiences beyond the campus with trips around New York City to museums, concerts, professional sporting events, Broadway shows, and many other attractions.

The College offers outstanding athletics programs, which include NCAA Division I standing in twenty areas, many intramurals, and an excellent coaching staff. Athletic teams offered are men's baseball, basketball, football (I-AA), golf, lacrosse, tennis, track/cross-country, and wrestling and women's basketball, golf, lacrosse, soccer, softball, swimming, tennis, track/cross-country, volleyball, and water polo; club sports are cheerleading and men's ice hockey.

In addition to undergraduate programs, Wagner offers master's degree programs in business administration (M.B.A.), education, microbiology, nursing, and physician assistant studies.

Location

Wagner's location offers students the best of both worlds. Living on a wooded campus 35 minutes from Manhattan has distinct advantages. The 105-acre campus overlooks New York Harbor and Manhattan. Students enjoy living in the beautiful Grymes Hill section of Staten Island and the proximity to the resources of Manhattan, which are easily accessible by bus, ferry, or car. Wagner has much to offer students who want the benefits of an education in New York City but who also wish to pursue their studies in a classic suburban college setting.

Majors and Degrees

Wagner College offers the Bachelor of Arts, Bachelor of Science, and Bachelor of Science in Education. Undergraduate majors and fields of concentration are in accounting (five-year program), anthropology, art, art history, arts administration, biology, biopsychology, business administration, chemistry, computer science, dance, economics, education, English, environmental studies, film/media studies, foreign languages, gender studies, government and politics, history, information systems, international affairs, journalism, mathematics, microbiology, music, nursing, philosophy, physician assistant studies (five-year program), physics, psychology, public policy and administration, religious studies, sociology, and theater. Preprofessional programs and a seven-year dentistry program with NYU are also offered.

Academic Programs

Wagner's undergraduate program, the Wagner Plan, is designed to provide a broad education in the liberal arts and in-depth study in a major. Wagner also believes that students learn best by "reading, writing, and doing" and, therefore, incorporates field experiences directly into the curriculum. As part of the graduation requirements, students must complete three Learning Communities (LCs)—one in the first year, one in either sophomore or junior year, and one in the senior year in the major area of study. At Wagner, LCs consist of three courses that are linked by a single theme and share a common set of students. They are also directly connected to field experience based on the theme of the LC. Throughout the first semester, first-year students spend time at the designated site observing the organization, its practices, and its dynamics. Seniors are involved in a practicum connected to their major field of study.

Each candidate is required to complete 36 units for the baccalaureate degree. Students must elect a major as part of their studies and may select from more than sixty different majors, minors, and/or concentrations. Majors must be selected by the end of the sophomore year, with the exception of physician assistant studies and theater students, who must apply directly to the respective program. The academic year is divided into the fall semester (September–December) and spring semester (January–May). Students may also enroll in one of several summer sessions.

Off-Campus Programs

Wagner College is a member of the prestigious Institute for the International Education of Students (IES) program, which is the nation's oldest and most selective study-abroad program. Interested and qualified Wagner students may choose among semester, summer, and vacation study-abroad programs in such diverse urban-based centers as Beijing, Berlin, Canberra, Dublin, LaPlata, London, Madrid, Paris, Tokyo, and Vienna. Classes are taught through a combination approach in which U.S. students take classes designed expressly for them as well as classes run by universities located within the host city, thereby integrating the U.S. students with students from that nation. Wagner College also sponsors an exchange program with California Lutheran University.

Academic Facilities

College facilities include twenty-three buildings for academic, recreational, and residential use. Wagner's recently updated science buildings house two electron microscopes and a fully functioning planetarium. Other facilities include a theater, a studio theater, an art gallery, a sports and fitness facility, an indoor pool, and a football stadium.

Computer facilities at Wagner are abundant and accessible. The Spiro Computer Technology Center features Pentium III PCs, while Novell network servers provide numerous application software programs for word processing, spreadsheet, graphics, statistical analysis, and programming languages. In addition, Wagner provides a Mac lab for graphics applications and a UNIX lab. The three residence halls are fully wired for free Internet and e-mail access in each room, along with a new voice-mail system and free cable. Students also have wireless Internet access in certain campus locations.

The Horrmann Library houses approximately 300,000 volumes as well as 1,000 titles in its periodical collection. The library is a member of the New York Metropolitan Reference and Research Agency, which provides access to more than 25 million volumes in the area.

Costs

Tuition for the 2007–08 academic year is $29,400. Room and board for the academic year are $8900.

Financial Aid

More than 70 percent of Wagner students receive some kind of financial aid. In addition to the availability of state and federal aid programs, the College itself is a source of more than $9 million in student aid each year. Counselors are available to assist in completing the Financial Aid Form.

Faculty

Because of its commitment to academic excellence, Wagner has always drawn a gifted faculty. Ninety-five percent of the 100 full-time faculty members hold a doctoral degree or the equivalent in their field. Many have published books and articles, and a large number have a combination of in-depth experience and academic qualifications. Wagner is strongly committed to keeping classes small and maintaining close relationships between faculty members and students; the student-faculty ratio is 16:1. Teaching is the first priority at Wagner, and all classes are taught by professors. Because faculty members are concerned about their students' intellectual and personal growth, they participate in all areas of College life. Faculty members regard New York City as an incomparable resource for course work and field experience.

Student Government

The Wagner College Student Government is democratically elected by the student body. The government has legislative and judicial responsibilities. Students have numerous opportunities for involvement in organizations, special interest groups, and committees. Activities and events are planned by students with the assistance of the director of cocurricular programs.

Admission Requirements

Admission to Wagner is based primarily on academic ability. The admission committee also considers personal qualities that, in the College's view, enable a student to take maximum advantage of what Wagner has to offer and to contribute to the quality of campus life.

The applicant is assessed on the basis of high school achievement, class rank, recommendations of the guidance counselor or academic teacher, standardized test scores (SAT or ACT), and an essay. In addition, the student's citizenship record (participation in extracurricular, community, or religious activities) and character record (including information derived from the recommendations) are reviewed. A personal interview is optional but recommended. Scores on the SAT or ACT are required, and SAT Subject Tests are recommended. None of these factors is considered in isolation; all are weighed together so that a clear picture of the applicant and his or her chances for success at Wagner emerge.

Students considering Wagner should have completed a minimum of 18 units in the following academic areas: English, 4; history, 3; mathematics, 3; foreign language, 2; and science, 2. Four additional units from the following list of electives are recommended: art, 1; computer science, 1; foreign language, 2–4; history, 1–3; mathematics, 1–3; music, 1–2; natural sciences, 1–3; religion, 1; and social studies, 1–2.

Application and Information

Application should be made early in the senior year of high school. In addition to the completed application form and the nonrefundable fee, students are responsible for forwarding a secondary school transcript, two letters of recommendation, their personal essay, and SAT or ACT scores to the Admissions Office. The early decision application deadline is January 1. The deadline for the theater program is December 1, and it is December 15 for physician assistant studies. The general application deadline is February 15, and there is a final application deadline of March 15.

Candidates are urged, whenever possible, to make an appointment with the Admissions Office to visit the campus and discuss their plans and goals with a member of the admission staff. They are also encouraged to talk with currently enrolled Wagner students. Arrangements can be made for candidates to meet with faculty members in departments of particular interest.

Further information may be obtained by contacting:

Admissions Office
Wagner College
1 Campus Road
Staten Island, New York 10301
Phone: 718-390-3411
800-221-1010 (toll-free outside New York)
Fax: 718-390-3105
E-mail: admissions@wagner.edu
Web site: http://www.wagner.edu

Wagner students in front of Main Hall.

WEBB INSTITUTE

GLEN COVE, NEW YORK

The Institute

Webb Institute was founded in 1889 to provide an opportunity for worthy young students to obtain an education in the "art and science of designing ships and their propulsion systems." The Institute has followed this basic objective to the present, and its graduates are active throughout the United States in the ship design, ship construction, yacht design, and marine operations industries and in appropriate government offices.

The 26-acre campus is the former estate of Herbert L. Pratt and is located on Long Island Sound. Because of the Institute's small size and intensive academic program, varsity sports are limited. However, Webb participates in intercollegiate basketball, cross-country, sailing, soccer, tennis, and volleyball, for which ample facilities are provided. The campus has a gymnasium, tennis courts, playing fields, and a beach. Golf and swimming facilities are available nearby.

Webb Institute maintains an enrollment that ranges from 70 to 90 students, all of whom live on campus. Webb students must be U.S. citizens or permanent residents with a green card.

Location

Glen Cove is a city of more than 25,000 residents and is located on Long Island's North Shore, which is nearly an hour from New York City. Convenient train service from Glen Cove to New York brings the variety of cultural, educational, and recreational activities available in the city within easy reach of Webb students.

Majors and Degrees

Webb Institute offers an engineering program in ship design, which involves both naval architecture and marine engineering. The undergraduate degree awarded is the Bachelor of Science in naval architecture and marine engineering.

Academic Programs

The engineering program in ship design consists of fundamental foundation courses in mathematics, science, and engineering sciences, capped by extensive professional design courses. A coherent program in humanities supplements the technical program to round out undergraduate education.

In addition, students have a two-month, cooperative job experience each year in the U.S. marine and maritime industry. During this period, freshmen work as helper mechanics in shipyards, sophomores obtain seagoing experience aboard ship, and juniors and seniors work as engineering assistants in design and technical offices of various marine firms. This important part of the program provides excellent articulation of the educational and career experiences. Innovative engineering ideas are encouraged in the thesis required during the last year. The program is fully accredited. Graduates are well equipped to pursue postgraduate studies.

Semesters run from late August to mid-December and from late February to late June. January and February are winter work periods, and the period from late June to late August is designated for vacation.

Academic Facilities

Full laboratory support is provided for chemistry, physics, metallurgy, and various engineering courses. A ship-model testing tank is available for ship and boat hull studies. Computer facilities are provided on campus. The Livingston Library contains extensive holdings in naval architecture, marine engineering, and general engineering, as well as collections in literature, arts, social sciences, and music.

Costs

All students admitted to Webb are accepted on a tuition- and fee-free basis (full scholarship). Room and board costs were approximately $9000 in 2007–08. Nearly $800 per year is required for books and supplies. A $150 room deposit fee is payable on entry and refunded, less any breakage costs, on departure. The Student Organization requires a $100 deposit on entry, also refundable on departure.

Financial Aid

As stated, a full scholarship that covers tuition and fees is awarded to all accepted candidates. The winter work co-op in industry provides income for students that significantly assists in other expenses. Supplementary aid opportunities are available through the Federal Pell Grant, Federal Stafford Student Loans, and in-house grant programs. Students requiring financial assistance must submit the Free Application for Federal Student Aid (FAFSA) after March 31 but not later than July 1 of the year of entry.

Faculty

Webb Institute has a highly qualified faculty. Many members possess engineering licenses and engage in sponsored research programs, consult for commercial firms, and research and write technical papers. Classes are limited to 25 students, and the student-faculty ratio is 8:1. Each student is assigned a faculty adviser, and consultation with individual faculty members is encouraged.

Student Government

The Student Organization is highly active in student administrative, social, and educational affairs. It is supplemented by an Honor Council and honor system. Together, these entities

COLLEGE DATA CENTER • NEW YORK

provide students with a high degree of responsibility for ordering and conducting student life.

Admission Requirements

Admission to Webb is highly competitive. The qualifying requirements for admission are graduation from high school with a B+ (87) or better average in 16 credits of basic high school subjects. Admission selections are based on high school standing (generally in the upper 10 percent) and scores on the College Board's SAT and Subject Tests in Mathematics (Level 1 or 2), and Physics or Chemistry. The final selection follows a personal interview conducted at Webb or at a location convenient to the applicant. The entering class is usually restricted to 25 freshmen.

All application papers must be submitted by February 15, and all required College Board tests must be taken before that date. Advanced placement is not given in any of the course offerings. Campus visits by interested students are strongly recommended; prior appointments must be made. An early decision plan is available for qualified candidates.

Webb Institute does not discriminate in admission in the areas of gender, race, or religion. Academic qualities and career motivation are the only criteria.

Application and Information

For a catalog and application forms, students may contact:

Office of Admissions
Webb Institute
Glen Cove, New York 11542
Phone: 516-671-2213
E-mail: admissions@webb-institute.edu
Web site: http://www.webb-institute.edu

The academic facilities of Webb Institute are located on Long Island Sound in the former residence of Herbert L. Pratt.

WELLS COLLEGE

AURORA, NEW YORK

The College

Wells College is consistently ranked among the nation's top liberal arts colleges that offer high-quality education at an affordable price and has one of the most beautiful campuses in the United States. The College was established in 1868 by Henry Wells, who also founded the Wells Fargo and American Express companies.

At Wells, professors are dedicated to teaching, and because of the intimate nature of the campus community (the student body is 550), they get to know their students as individuals in and outside the classroom. Students frequently collaborate with their professors on original research and creative projects. At most other schools, these opportunities are only available to graduate students. Because faculty members at Wells know their students so well, they are especially effective advisers and mentors. Students have a competitive edge entering careers and top graduate and professional schools.

Another aspect of the Wells tradition is hands-on learning. In addition to dynamic classroom teaching, Wells students have a variety of other experiential opportunities: internships, service, study abroad, and off-campus study. Professors encourage students to apply theory in practical settings and to discover what they want to do in life through involvement.

Wells currently fields intercollegiate teams at the NCAA Division III level in cross-country, field hockey, men's and women's lacrosse, men's and women's soccer, softball, men's and women's swimming, and women's tennis. Men's and women's basketball teams are planned to be added during the 2008–09 academic year. There are also a number of intramural opportunities, including basketball, soccer, swimming, tennis, and volleyball. Athletic facilities include indoor and outdoor tennis courts, a gymnasium, a newly renovated fitness center, a nine-hole golf course, and a campus boathouse and dock used in teaching sailing, canoeing, and lifeguarding.

Wells has a full range of active student organizations, including a literary magazine and newspaper, music and drama groups, environmental and political organizations, and abundant opportunities for community service, among others. A busy calendar of cultural events, symposia, and lectures enhances the academic and social life of the College.

Location

Wells is located in the village of Aurora on the eastern shore of Cayuga Lake—part of New York's scenic Finger Lakes region. The area is well known for its high concentration of prestigious colleges and universities, including Cornell University, Ithaca College, Hobart and William Smith Colleges, Colgate University, Hamilton College, and Syracuse University. Aurora is 25 miles from Ithaca and 60 miles from both Rochester and Syracuse. Students have abundant opportunities for outdoor recreation and sports, including sailing, swimming, horseback riding, skiing, and hiking.

Majors and Degrees

Wells offers majors and concentrations in African American studies, American cultures, American studies, anthropology/cross-cultural sociology, art history, biochemistry and molecular biology, biology, chemistry, computer science, creative writing, economics, English, environmental policies and values, environmental studies, ethics and philosophy, French, German, government and politics, historical and comparative studies, history, human nature and values, international studies, literature, management, mathematics, music, performing arts, physics, psychology, public affairs, religion, sociology, Spanish, studio art, theater and dance, visual arts, and women's studies. Students also have the option of a self-designed major. In addition, they can choose minors from a list of more than thirty programs.

The College has preprofessional programs in dentistry, education, engineering, law, medicine, teaching, and veterinary medicine. Wells has a cross-registration agreement with nearby Cornell University and affiliations with Cornell's engineering and veterinary medicine schools.

Wells awards the Bachelor of Arts degree and has a number of programs through which students can earn their bachelor's degree at Wells and a graduate or professional degree from an affiliated university. Participating schools are Clarkson University, Columbia University, and Cornell University (engineering) and the University of Rochester (business, community health, education).

Academic Programs

All Wells students benefit from an academic environment similar to honors programs available to only a small number of students at other schools. The College has a tradition of preparing students for leadership in their chosen fields, and the breadth of knowledge they gain and the range of life experiences they encounter enable them to achieve their career goals and establish a foundation for a rich and fulfilling life.

All students entering Wells to pursue a four-year course of study leading to a bachelor's degree are required to take the First-Year Experience (WLLS 101) and the New Student Experience (WLLS 111). Distribution requirements are a foreign language (two courses or exemption by exam), formal reasoning (one course), arts and humanities (three courses), natural and social sciences (three courses), and physical education (four courses). Team sports and dance technique can partially satisfy requirements.

Approximately sixteen courses must be taken in the student's major, and at least six must be taken at Wells. Eighteen credit hours must be taken at the 300 level or above. A senior project or thesis and a comprehensive evaluation are required for graduation.

A student must successfully complete 120 semester hours (60 of which must be taken at Wells and through affiliated programs, such as study abroad) to be recommended by the faculty for a degree. To learn more about the academic program and requirements for transfer students, prospective students should visit the Wells College Web site.

Off-Campus Programs

Students can spend January term, a semester, or even a year in another college or university abroad or in the United States. Typically, Wells students choose to study off campus for a semester during the junior year, but many different possibilities are available depending on a student's academic program and interests.

The College offers affiliated study-abroad experiences in Denmark, the Dominican Republic, France, Germany, Great Britain, India, Ireland, Italy, Japan, Mexico, Senegal, Spain, and Sweden. Currently, the three most popular programs are study abroad in Florence, Italy; Paris, France; and Seville, Spain. These off-campus study experiences are flexible as well as financially and academically accessible. After at least one semester at Wells, a student's financial aid applies to one semester of off-campus study.

Wells provides off-campus study options in the United States through its affiliations with American University, serving a wide range of academic and internship interests in Washington, D.C.; the Salt Center, offering documentary field studies in Portland, Maine; and the Public Leadership Education Network (PLEN), providing leadership development through seminars and internships in Washington, D.C. As part of the PLEN affiliation, students can spend a semester studying at the London School of Economics and Political Science and hold an internship in the British government. Through the School for Field Studies, Wells offers semester-long study-abroad experiences in Africa, Australia, the Caribbean, and other locations. The College also offers credit-bearing courses during the January term that take students to a single destination in the U.S. or abroad for intensive study that requires travel in a region or country with a faculty member.

Academic Facilities

From the contemporary elegance of Weld House to the nineteenth-century Glen Park mansion, the former home of College founder Henry Wells, the residence halls encompass enough variety to satisfy every taste. Students eat their meals together in the majestic Tudor-style dining hall in Main Building.

The Louis Jefferson Long Library has received numerous awards for its architectural design. Facilities include an online computer center, individual study carrels, seminar and group-study rooms, and an art gallery. There are department libraries in art, economics, English, mathematics, music, philosophy, and the sciences located across the campus.

The Barler Hall of Music houses a recital hall with superb acoustics, vocal and instrumental practice rooms, a music library, and a listening laboratory. Facilities for printmaking, painting, ceramics, sculpture, and photography are located in the Campbell Arts Building. The Cleveland Hall of Languages contains state-of-the-art equipment for learning foreign languages. Stratton Science Hall, completed in 2007, houses state-of-the-art laboratories for chemistry, biology, environmental science, and physics as well as a computer laboratory. Morgan Hall houses the Book Arts Center and the Wells College Press. Macmillan Hall has classrooms, faculty and administrative offices, several computer laboratories, and department libraries. The east wing of Macmillan contains the Margaret Phipps Auditorium, a theater facility used for teaching, concerts, lectures, and dramatic productions.

Costs

Wells has a long-term commitment to providing talented students with access to the best education, which requires offering excellence at an affordable price. Wells is ranked among the best liberal arts colleges in the nation, yet the cost of a Wells education is, in many cases, about half the price charged by other comparable schools.

Wells students today still benefit from a 30 percent tuition reduction policy that brought the College national acclaim several years ago. The cost of a Wells education for the 2007–08 year was $16,510 for tuition, $8100 for room and board, and $1300 for fees.

Financial Aid

Approximately 90 percent of Wells students receive financial aid packaged in the form of grants, scholarships, loans, and work-study opportunities. The College works closely with students and their families to design a financial aid package that meets their needs and their budgets.

Award determinations are made on a rolling basis following acceptance. College financial aid is complex; however, Wells College's well-informed financial aid and admissions professionals are always pleased to answer questions and discuss methods of financing higher education with prospective students.

Faculty

At Wells, learning takes place in small, seminar-style classes where students are partners with faculty members in the learning process. Starting immediately in their first semester, students take classes with scholars who are recognized experts in their fields, not teaching assistants.

All Wells professors hold terminal degrees in their areas of expertise. They have been educated at the world's leading research universities, including Harvard, Yale, Columbia, Cornell, Brown, and Stanford. What students discover in Wells' classes is the importance of exploring ideas with others.

Wells is student centered, and academic programs focus on collaborative learning and teaching that meets the needs of students' different learning styles. As one would expect at a nationally recognized liberal arts college, professors are also engaged in research and a full range of scholarly activities. Their books are published by leading academic presses, their articles appear in top journals, and they are a presence at national and international conferences. Due to close faculty-student interaction, students have numerous opportunities to collaborate with faculty members on research, publications, and presentations.

Student Government

The student body is self-governing through the Collegiate Association. The three main governing bodies of the association are the Student-Faculty Administration Board, the Collegiate Council, and the Community Court. Students serve on faculty committees that make decisions concerning administrative and curricular matters.

Leadership development is an inherent part of the Wells experience, and students are encouraged to take an active role in student government and in the life of the campus community.

Admission Requirements

Wells admits students on the basis of the strength of their academic preparation. A student is expected to possess intellectual curiosity, motivation, and maturity to profit from the experience. In all cases, the College seeks students who have followed a solid college-preparatory program throughout high school.

Wells seeks students from varied backgrounds with diverse interests and talents in order to promote a stimulating learning community. Every admissions decision is made on an individual basis.

Wells students share an enthusiasm for academic pursuits and a serious intent to use their education in the future to enhance both their lives and the communities in which they choose to live.

Application and Information

Applications should be received early in the senior year of high school and not later than March 1 of the year in which entrance is desired. Applications from early decision and early action candidates must be received by December 15.

Transfer applications are reviewed on a rolling basis. Transfer students are eligible for merit scholarships and financial aid.

A campus visit is highly recommended for prospective students. For more information about Wells College or to schedule a campus visit, students should contact:

Admissions Office
Wells College
Aurora, New York 13026
Phone: 800-952-9355 (toll-free)
E-mail: admissions@wells.edu
Web site: http://www.wells.edu

The newly renovated Schwartz Athletic Center.

COLLEGE DATA CENTER • NEW YORK

YORK COLLEGE OF THE CITY UNIVERSITY OF NEW YORK

YORK COLLEGE
The City University of New York

JAMAICA, NEW YORK

The College

York College is one of New York's premiere public institutions of higher learning. It offers a distinctive educational experience within the City University of New York (CUNY) system. This comparatively small institution embodies the essential qualities of a major university: a strong liberal arts foundation, a distinguished faculty, and career planning. At the same time, students are offered the intimate learning environment, individualized attention, and sense of community that are usually absent at larger universities.

More than fifty student organizations, representing various academic and ethnic interests and an award-winning student publication, welcome student participation. Students participate in intercollegiate and intramural athletics and a variety of recreational activities.

Founded in 1966, York opened its architecturally-forward, state-of-the-art permanent home in Queens, New York, twenty years later in 1986. The structure—which includes an interior mall that covers four levels and is topped by a glass skylight—houses up-to-date laboratory, computer, and library facilities. It provides an excellent academic and social environment for York College students. The 50-acre campus also features an athletic and physical education complex, a performing arts center with a 1,500-seat theater, and a state-of-the-art regional office of the Food and Drug Administration.

York College also has a master's program in occupational therapy.

Location

Centrally located in Queens, New York, York College is accessible by car, bus, subway, and the Long Island Rail Road. Easy access to the rest of Queens and New York City enables York College students to engage in extensive community service as a part of their curriculum. The College is 4 miles from John F. Kennedy International Airport.

Majors and Degrees

York College awards Bachelor of Arts and Bachelor of Science degrees in the following liberal arts and career-oriented majors: accounting; adolescence education for mathematics (7–12); adolescence education in biology, chemistry, or earth science (7–12); adolescence education for Spanish (7–12); African American studies; anthropology; art (studio); art history; aviation management; biology; biotechnology; business administration; chemistry; childhood education (1–6); communications technology; community health education; computer science; economics; English; environmental health science; French; geology; gerontological studies and services; health education (K–12); health-promotion management; history; information systems management; liberal studies; marketing; mathematics; medical technology; movement science (nonteaching physical education); music; nursing; occupational therapy; philosophy; physical education (K–12); physician assistant studies; physics; political science; psychology; social work; sociology; Spanish; and speech/communication and theater arts. York College also offers certificate programs in aviation management, child and youth workers, mortgage finance, Spanish for professional purposes, and survey research.

Academic Programs

The curriculum at York College is designed to give students a firm and broad base in the liberal arts as well as to permit specialization in a career or professional area. The required liberal arts core includes courses in the humanities, social sciences, and natural sciences, and selections may be made from a range of courses. At least 120 credits are required to earn a bachelor's degree. Students should refer to the College's current catalog for the credit requirements for each major.

Many majors have an integral cooperative education component that enables students in the junior and senior years to alternate semesters between school and paid internships. Cooperative education is designed to give students practical work experience to supplement the theoretical work in the classroom. Three job placements are made, giving students a range of opportunities. Upon graduation, students are better prepared for the labor market, have significant job experience and references, and are well equipped to seek employment in their field.

York College, which, at 40, is proud of a broad spectrum of distinguished alumni excelling in the fields of publishing, contemporary literature, medicine, law, academia, and business, has an ongoing commitment to its community, and community service is an integral part of many of the academic programs. Students in the areas of community health, education, gerontology, health science, occupational therapy, physical education, physician assistant studies, political science, psychology, and social work have the opportunity to become involved in community service fieldwork and internships. They gain valuable experience while making a contribution to the community.

Academic Facilities

York College's modern facility on Guy R. Brewer Boulevard and Liberty Avenue provides extensive science and computer laboratories, a large library, and up-to-date education technology. Music majors studying electronic music and jazz have access to a computer music studio that has microcomputers, digital synthesizers, MIDI interfaces, sound sampling systems, and multitrack tape recorders. The Computer Graphics Lab of York College is the most modern graphics lab in the City University system. In this advanced facility, students can display three-dimensional scientific figures, create graphic business charts and presentations, develop desktop publishing skills, or utilize computer-aided design in other disciplines and fields of study. Students interested in media and the communication arts have access to a fully equipped television production studio, including audio production. There are also a theater complex and a physical education facility that includes an Olympic-size swimming pool, an athletic field, tennis and handball courts, a health promotion center, a health promotion lab, and biofeedback facilities.

Costs

For 2006–07, the cost of tuition for newly enrolled full-time students was $4000 per year for in-state residents and $360 per credit for newly enrolled out-of-state residents. The student activity fee was $81.70, and the educational technology fee was $150. Room and board are not available at York College. Tuition and fees are subject to change.

Financial Aid

Financial aid is available for qualified students on the basis of need through state and federal aid programs. For full consideration, applicants should file the City University of New York Application for Federal State Student Aid (CUNY AFSSA). Applications for the fall semester should be submitted by the preceding June. Merit scholarships are available to qualified freshmen and transfer students with awards ranging from $1000 to $8000 per year.

Faculty

More than 85 percent of the full-time faculty members hold a doctoral degree. The faculty is dedicated to scholarship, research, and high-quality teaching. Faculty members work closely with students to provide the academic and intellectual support necessary for the students' successful development.

Student Government

The student government, composed of elected student representatives, is responsible for the allocation of money for student activities. Members of the student government serve on College-wide committees that decide College policy.

Admission Requirements

Admission is based upon the applicant's academic average, academic units, and SAT or ACT scores, which are required for recent high school graduates. Admission is centrally processed by the City University of New York and directly at the Admissions Office of York College. Students are expected to present at least a 75 average to qualify for general admission. Students who score below 75 and can demonstrate significant financial need are encouraged to apply for the SEEK Program.

Application and Information

Applicants to the freshman class are admitted on a monthly basis starting in January for the fall semester; transfer applicants are admitted starting in March. The application fee for freshmen is $65 and for transfer students, $70. Application forms may be obtained by contacting the Admissions Office.

For further information, students should contact:

Admissions Office 1B07
York College of the City University of New York
Jamaica, New York 11451
Phone: 718-262-2165
Fax: 718-262-2601
E-mail: admissions@york.cuny.edu
Web site: http://www.york.cuny.edu

On the campus of York College of the City University of New York.

COLLEGE DATA CENTER • NEW YORK

NORTH CAROLINA

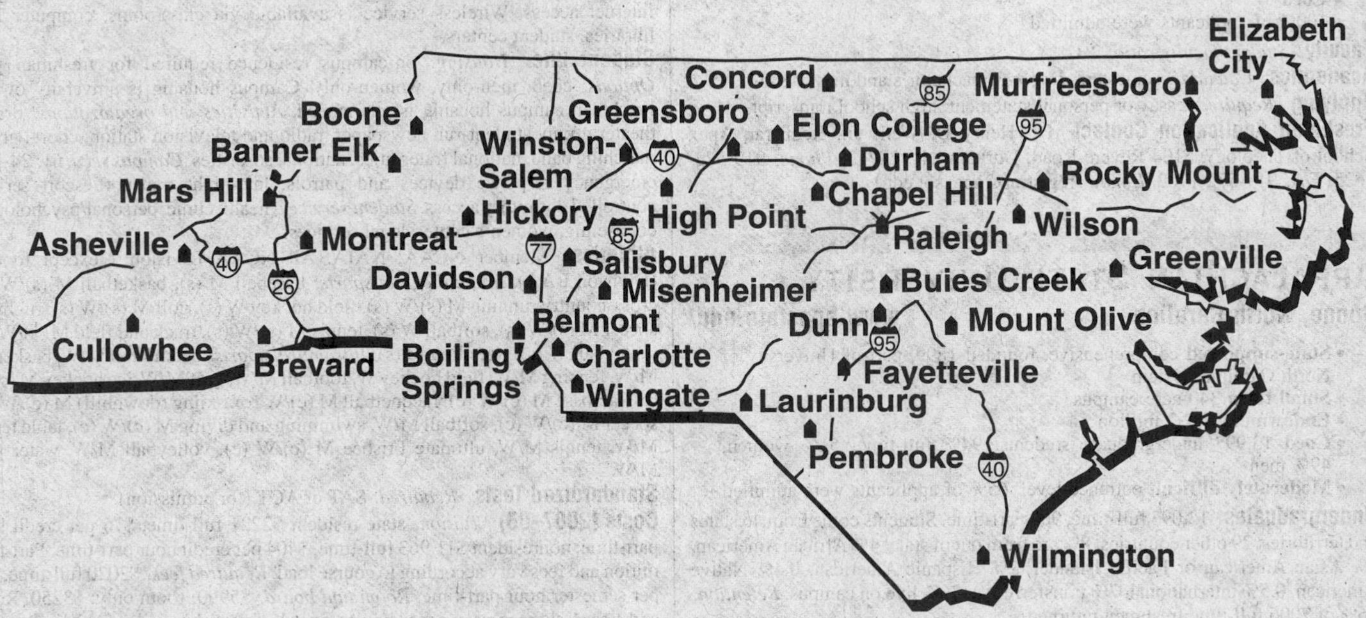

APEX SCHOOL OF THEOLOGY

Durham, North Carolina **www.apexsot.edu/**

- **Independent interdenominational** comprehensive, founded 1995
- **Suburban** campus
- **Coed**
- 100% of applicants were admitted

Faculty *Student/faculty ratio:* 2:1.

Academics *Calendar:* semesters. *Degrees:* bachelor's and master's.

Applying *Required:* essay or personal statement, high school transcript.

Freshman Application Contact Dr. Henry D. Wells Jr., Registrar, Apex School of Theology, 5104 Revere Road, Durham, NC 27713. *Phone:* 919-572-1625. *Fax:* 919-572-1762. *E-mail:* registrar@apexsot.edu.

APPALACHIAN STATE UNIVERSITY

Boone, North Carolina **www.appstate.edu/**

- **State-supported** comprehensive, founded 1899, part of University of North Carolina System
- **Small-town** 340-acre campus
- **Endowment** $62.2 million
- **Coed** 13,997 undergraduate students, 94% full-time, 51% women, 49% men
- **Moderately difficult** entrance level, 65% of applicants were admitted

Undergraduates 13,093 full-time, 904 part-time. Students come from 46 states and territories, 29 other countries, 8% are from out of state, 4% African American, 1% Asian American or Pacific Islander, 2% Hispanic American, 0.4% Native American, 0.5% international, 7% transferred in, 36% live on campus. *Retention:* 86% of 2006 full-time freshmen returned.

Freshmen *Admission:* 11,468 applied, 7,397 admitted, 2,737 enrolled. *Average high school GPA:* 3.68. *Test scores:* SAT critical reading scores over 500: 81%; SAT math scores over 500: 87%; SAT writing scores over 500: 74%; ACT scores over 18: 95%; SAT critical reading scores over 600: 29%; SAT math scores over 600: 34%; SAT writing scores over 600: 22%; ACT scores over 24: 47%; SAT critical reading scores over 700: 3%; SAT math scores over 700: 2%; SAT writing scores over 700: 2%; ACT scores over 30: 4%.

Faculty *Total:* 1,108, 67% full-time, 59% with terminal degrees. *Student/faculty ratio:* 17:1.

Majors Accounting; actuarial science; advertising; anthropology; apparel and textiles; art; arts management; art teacher education; athletic training; biology/biological sciences; biology teacher education; business administration and management; business teacher education; chemistry; chemistry teacher education; child development; city/urban, community and regional planning; clinical laboratory science/medical technology; communication disorders; computer science; construction management; criminal justice/safety; dance; drama and dance teacher education; dramatic/theater arts; ecology; economics; education (specific subject areas) related; elementary education; English; English/language arts teacher education; family and consumer sciences/home economics teacher education; finance; fine/studio arts; foods, nutrition, and wellness; French; French language teacher education; geography; geology/earth science; graphic and printing equipment operation/production; graphic design; health/health care administration; health teacher education; history; history teacher education; hospitality administration; industrial design; industrial production technologies related; industrial technology; insurance; interior design; international business/trade/commerce; journalism; kindergarten/preschool education; kinesiology and exercise science; liberal arts and sciences/liberal studies; management information systems; marketing/marketing management; mathematics; mathematics teacher education; middle school education; music management and merchandising; music performance; music teacher education; music therapy; nursing (registered nurse training); parks, recreation and leisure facilities management; philosophy; philosophy and religious studies related; physical education teaching and coaching; physics; physics teacher education; political science and government; psychology; public health education and promotion; public relations/image management; radio and television; religious studies; social studies teacher education; social work; sociology; solar energy technology; Spanish; Spanish language teacher education; special education (specific learning disabilities); statistics; technology/industrial arts teacher education.

Academics *Calendar:* semesters. *Degrees:* bachelor's, master's, doctoral, post-master's, and postbachelor's certificates. *Special study options:* academic remediation for entering students, adult/continuing education programs, advanced placement credit, distance learning, double majors, English as a second language, honors programs, independent study, internships, off-campus study, part-time degree program, services for LD students, student-designed majors, study abroad, summer session for credit. *ROTC:* Army (b). *Unusual degree programs:* 3-2 engineering with Auburn University, Clemson University.

Computers on Campus 2,500 computers/terminals are available on campus for general student use. Students can access the following: campus intranet, computer help desk, free student e-mail accounts, online (class) grades, online (class) registration, online (class) schedules. Campuswide network is available. 100% of college-owned or -operated housing units are wired for high-speed Internet access. Wireless service is available via classrooms, computer labs, libraries, student centers.

Student Life *Housing:* on-campus residence required for freshman year. *Options:* coed, men-only, women-only. Campus housing is university owned. Freshman campus housing is guaranteed. *Activities and organizations:* drama/theater group, student-run newspaper, radio and television station, choral group, marching band, national fraternities, national sororities. *Campus security:* 24-hour emergency response devices and patrols, late-night transport/escort service, controlled dormitory access. *Student services:* health clinic, personal/psychological counseling, women's center, legal services.

Athletics Member NCAA, NAIA. All NCAA Division I except football (Division I-AA). *Intercollegiate sports:* baseball M (s), basketball M (s)/W (s), cross-country running M (s)/W (s), field hockey W (s), golf M (s)/W (s), rugby W, soccer M (s)/W (s), softball W (s), tennis M (s)/W (s), track and field M (s)/W (s), volleyball W (s), wrestling M (s). *Intramural sports:* badminton M/W, basketball M/W, fencing M/W, field hockey W, football M/W, golf M/W, ice hockey M (c)/W (c), lacrosse M (c)/W (c), racquetball M (c)/W (c), skiing (downhill) M (c)/W (c), soccer M (c)/W (c), softball M/W, swimming and diving M (c)/W (c), table tennis M/W, tennis M/W, ultimate Frisbee M (c)/W (c), volleyball M/W, water polo M/W.

Standardized Tests *Required:* SAT or ACT (for admission).

Costs (2007–08) *Tuition:* state resident $2221 full-time, $75 per credit hour part-time; nonresident $11,963 full-time, $404 per credit hour part-time. Part-time tuition and fees vary according to course load. *Required fees:* $2020 full-time, $12 per semester hour part-time. *Room and board:* $5990; room only: $3250. Room and board charges vary according to board plan and housing facility. *Payment plans:* installment, deferred payment. *Waivers:* senior citizens and employees or children of employees.

Financial Aid Of all full-time matriculated undergraduates who enrolled in 2006, 7,977 applied for aid, 4,717 were judged to have need, 1,082 had their need fully met. 340 Federal Work-Study jobs (averaging $1648). 2,859 state and other part-time jobs (averaging $1236). In 2006, 777 non-need-based awards were made. *Average percent of need met:* 76%. *Average financial aid package:* $5844. *Average need-based loan:* $3381. *Average need-based gift aid:* $4711. *Average non-need-based aid:* $3016. *Average indebtedness upon graduation:* $14,838.

Applying *Options:* electronic application, early admission, deferred entrance. *Application fee:* $50. *Required:* high school transcript. *Application deadlines:* rolling (freshmen), rolling (transfers). *Notification:* continuous (freshmen), continuous (transfers).

Freshman Application Contact Appalachian State University, Admissions, Appalachian State University, Boone, NC 28608. *Phone:* 828-262-2120.

THE ART INSTITUTE OF CHARLOTTE

Charlotte, North Carolina **www.aich.artinstitutes.edu/**

- **Proprietary** 4-year, founded 1973, part of Education Management Corporation
- **Suburban** campus
- **Coed**
- **Minimally difficult** entrance level

Faculty *Student/faculty ratio:* 19:1.

Academics *Calendar:* quarters. *Degrees:* certificates, associate, and bachelor's.

Student Life *Campus security:* 24-hour emergency response devices, late-night transport/escort service.

Standardized Tests *Required for some:* SAT (for admission). *Recommended:* SAT (for admission).

Costs (2007–08) *Tuition:* $18,576 full-time, $387 per credit part-time. *Room only:* $5780.

Applying *Options:* electronic application, deferred entrance. *Application fee:* $50. *Required:* essay or personal statement, high school transcript. *Required for some:* interview.

Director of Admissions Ms. Pamela Notemyer Rogers, Director of Admissions, The Art Institute of Charlotte, 2110 Water Ridge Parkway, Charlotte, NC 28217. *Phone:* 704-357-8020. *Fax:* 704-357-1133. *E-mail:* pnotemyer@aii.edu.

See page 1914 for the College Close-Up.

BARTON COLLEGE

Wilson, North Carolina www.barton.edu/

- **Independent** 4-year, founded 1902, affiliated with Christian Church (Disciples of Christ)
- **Small-town** 76-acre campus with easy access to Raleigh-Durham, NC
- **Endowment** $28.4 million
- **Coed** 1,130 undergraduate students, 78% full-time, 71% women, 29% men
- **Minimally difficult** entrance level, 63% of applicants were admitted

Undergraduates 883 full-time, 247 part-time. Students come from 25 states and territories, 8 other countries, 19% are from out of state, 23% African American, 0.9% Asian American or Pacific Islander, 3% Hispanic American, 0.5% Native American, 2% international, 13% transferred in, 41% live on campus. *Retention:* 68% of 2006 full-time freshmen returned.

Freshmen *Admission:* 1,409 applied, 882 admitted, 218 enrolled. *Average high school GPA:* 3.09. *Test scores:* SAT critical reading scores over 500: 32%; SAT math scores over 500: 38%; SAT writing scores over 500: 29%; ACT scores over 18: 61%; SAT critical reading scores over 600: 2%; SAT math scores over 600: 5%; SAT writing scores over 600: 3%; ACT scores over 24: 7%; SAT math scores over 700: 1%; SAT writing scores over 700: 1%; ACT scores over 30: 2%.

Faculty *Total:* 112, 65% full-time, 44% with terminal degrees. *Student/faculty ratio:* 11:1.

Majors Accounting; art teacher education; athletic training; biology/biological sciences; business administration and management; chemistry; computer and information sciences; criminal justice/law enforcement administration; dramatic/theater arts; economics; elementary education; English; environmental studies; fine/studio arts; history; human resources management; liberal arts and sciences and humanities related; marketing/marketing management; mass communication/media; mathematics; middle school education; musical instrument fabrication and repair; nursing (registered nurse training); philosophy and religious studies related; physical education teaching and coaching; political science and government; psychology; social work; Spanish; special education; special education (hearing impaired); sport and fitness administration/management.

Academics *Calendar:* 4-1-4. *Degree:* bachelor's. *Special study options:* academic remediation for entering students, adult/continuing education programs, advanced placement credit, cooperative education, double majors, English as a second language, honors programs, independent study, internships, part-time degree program, services for LD students, study abroad, summer session for credit. *Unusual degree programs:* 3-2 engineering with North Carolina State University, North Carolina Agricultural and Technical State University, UNC-Charlotte.

Computers on Campus 125 computers/terminals are available on campus for general student use. Students can access the following: campus intranet, computer help desk, free student e-mail accounts, online (class) schedules, student picture directory. Campuswide network is available. 100% of college-owned or -operated housing units are wired for high-speed Internet access. Wireless service is available via classrooms, computer labs, libraries, student centers.

Student Life *Housing:* on-campus residence required through sophomore year. *Options:* coed, women-only. Campus housing is university owned. Freshman campus housing is guaranteed. *Activities and organizations:* drama/theater group, student-run newspaper, television station, choral group, Barton College Association of Nurses, Students in Free Enterprise, Stage and Script, Campus Activities Board, College Habitat for Humanity, national fraternities, national sororities. *Campus security:* 24-hour emergency response devices, late-night transport/escort service, controlled dormitory access, city police substation on campus. *Student services:* health clinic, personal/psychological counseling.

Athletics Member NCAA. All Division II. *Intercollegiate sports:* baseball M (s), basketball M (s)/W (s), cross-country running M (s)/W (s), golf M (s), soccer M (s)/W (s), softball W (s), tennis M (s)/W (s), volleyball W (s). *Intramural sports:* archery M/W, badminton M/W, baseball M/W, basketball M/W, cheerleading M/W, football M/W, golf M/W, soccer M/W, softball M/W, swimming and diving M/W, tennis M/W, volleyball M/W, weight lifting M/W.

Standardized Tests *Required:* SAT or ACT (for admission).

Costs (2008–09) *Comprehensive fee:* $26,720 includes full-time tuition ($18,460), mandatory fees ($1478), and room and board ($6782). Part-time tuition: $785 per credit hour. *College room only:* $3178.

Financial Aid Of all full-time matriculated undergraduates who enrolled in 2006, 711 applied for aid, 662 were judged to have need, 106 had their need fully met. 438 Federal Work-Study jobs (averaging $1138). In 2006, 196 non-need-based awards were made. *Average percent of need met:* 69%. *Average financial aid package:* $15,760. *Average need-based loan:* $4748. *Average need-based gift aid:* $4536. *Average non-need-based aid:* $5324. *Average indebtedness upon graduation:* $22,809.

Applying *Options:* electronic application, deferred entrance. *Application fee:* $25. *Required:* high school transcript. *Recommended:* interview. *Application deadlines:* rolling (freshmen), rolling (transfers). *Notification:* continuous (freshmen), continuous (transfers).

Freshman Application Contact Ms. Amanda Humphrey, Director of Admissions, Barton College, Box 5000, College Station, Wilson, NC 27893. *Phone:* 252-399-6315. *Toll-free phone:* 800-345-4973. *Fax:* 252-399-6572. *E-mail:* enroll@barton.edu.

See page 1916 for the College Close-Up.

BELMONT ABBEY COLLEGE

Belmont, North Carolina www.belmontabbeycollege.edu/

- **Independent Roman Catholic** 4-year, founded 1876
- **Small-town** 650-acre campus with easy access to Charlotte
- **Endowment** $14.0 million
- **Coed** 1,337 undergraduate students, 92% full-time, 61% women, 39% men
- **Moderately difficult** entrance level, 70% of applicants were admitted

Undergraduates 1,235 full-time, 102 part-time. Students come from 36 states and territories, 15 other countries, 31% are from out of state, 21% African American, 1% Asian American or Pacific Islander, 4% Hispanic American, 0.4% Native American, 3% international, 19% transferred in, 48% live on campus. *Retention:* 64% of 2006 full-time freshmen returned.

Freshmen *Admission:* 1,034 applied, 721 admitted, 210 enrolled. *Average high school GPA:* 3.06. *Test scores:* SAT critical reading scores over 500: 56%; SAT math scores over 500: 55%; SAT critical reading scores over 600: 20%; SAT math scores over 600: 14%; SAT critical reading scores over 700: 5%.

Faculty *Total:* 120, 47% full-time, 42% with terminal degrees. *Student/faculty ratio:* 16:1.

Majors Accounting; biology/biological sciences; business administration and management; clinical laboratory science/medical technology; economics; education; elementary education; English; history; information science/studies; international business/trade/commerce; philosophy; political science and government; pre-dentistry studies; pre-law studies; pre-medical studies; pre-pharmacy studies; pre-veterinary studies; psychology; secondary education; sociology; theology; therapeutic recreation.

Academics *Calendar:* semesters. *Degree:* bachelor's. *Special study options:* accelerated degree program, adult/continuing education programs, advanced placement credit, cooperative education, double majors, external degree program, freshman honors college, honors programs, independent study, internships, off-campus study, part-time degree program, services for LD students, study abroad, summer session for credit. *ROTC:* Army (c), Air Force (c).

Computers on Campus 125 computers/terminals are available on campus for general student use. Students can access the following: computer help desk, free student e-mail accounts, online (class) grades, online (class) registration, online (class) schedules. Campuswide network is available. Wireless service is available via student centers.

Student Life *Housing:* on-campus residence required through senior year. *Options:* coed, men-only. Campus housing is university owned. Freshman campus housing is guaranteed. *Activities and organizations:* drama/theater group, student-run newspaper, radio station, choral group, College Union, WABY (student radio station), Abbey Players, national fraternities, national sororities. *Campus security:* 24-hour emergency response devices and patrols, late-night transport/escort service. *Student services:* health clinic, personal/psychological counseling.

Athletics Member NCAA. All Division II. *Intercollegiate sports:* baseball M (s), basketball M (s)/W (s), cheerleading M/W, cross-country running M (s)/W (s), golf M (s)/W (s), lacrosse M (s)/W (s), soccer M (s)/W (s), softball W (s), tennis M (s)/W (s), volleyball W, wrestling M. *Intramural sports:* badminton M/W, basketball M/W, crew M/W, cross-country running M/W, football M/W, rugby M (c), soccer M/W, softball M/W, table tennis M/W, tennis M/W, ultimate Frisbee M/W, volleyball M/W, weight lifting M, wrestling M.

Standardized Tests *Required:* SAT or ACT (for admission).

Costs (2007–08) *One-time required fee:* $884. *Comprehensive fee:* $28,509 includes full-time tuition ($17,880), mandatory fees ($916), and room and board ($9713). Full-time tuition and fees vary according to class time, course level, course load, location, program, reciprocity agreements, and student level. Part-time tuition: $596 per credit hour. Part-time tuition and fees vary according to class time, course level, course load, location, reciprocity agreements, and student level. *Required fees:* $31 per credit hour part-time. *College room only:* $5613. Room and board charges vary according to board plan, housing facility, location, and student level. *Payment plans:* installment, deferred payment. *Waivers:* senior citizens and employees or children of employees.

Financial Aid Of all full-time matriculated undergraduates who enrolled in 2007, 1,082 applied for aid, 980 were judged to have need, 133 had their need fully met. 104 Federal Work-Study jobs (averaging $1733). In 2007, 298 non-need-based awards were made. *Average percent of need met:* 55%. *Average financial aid package:* $12,168. *Average need-based loan:* $3910. *Average need-based gift aid:* $8501. *Average non-need-based aid:* $14,521. *Average indebtedness upon graduation:* $18,575.

Applying *Options:* electronic application, deferred entrance. *Application fee:* $35. *Required:* high school transcript, minimum 2.25 GPA. *Required for some:* essay or personal statement, 2 letters of recommendation. *Recommended:* interview. *Application deadlines:* 8/1 (freshmen), 8/15 (transfers). *Notification:* continuous (freshmen), continuous (transfers).

Freshman Application Contact Roger L. Jones, Director of Admission, Belmont Abbey College, 100 Belmont-Mt. Holly Road, Belmont, NC 28012-1802. *Phone:* 704-825-6214. *Toll-free phone:* 888-BAC-0110. *Fax:* 704-825-6220. *E-mail:* admissions@bac.edu.

BENNETT COLLEGE FOR WOMEN

Greensboro, North Carolina **www.bennett.edu/**

- **Independent United Methodist** 4-year, founded 1873
- **Urban** 55-acre campus
- **Endowment** $10.3 million
- **Women only**
- **Moderately difficult** entrance level

Faculty *Student/faculty ratio:* 12:1.

Academics *Calendar:* semesters. *Degree:* bachelor's.

Student Life *Campus security:* 24-hour patrols, late-night transport/escort service.

Athletics Member NCAA. All Division III.

Standardized Tests *Recommended:* SAT or ACT (for admission).

Costs (2007–08) *Comprehensive fee:* $21,126 includes full-time tuition ($12,748), mandatory fees ($1900), and room and board ($6478). Part-time tuition: $531 per credit hour. *Required fees:* $785 per term part-time. *College room only:* $3226.

Financial Aid Of all full-time matriculated undergraduates who enrolled in 2005, 526 applied for aid, 492 were judged to have need, 24 had their need fully met. 82 Federal Work-Study jobs (averaging $1800). In 2005, 46 non-need-based awards were made. *Average percent of need met:* 45. *Average financial aid package:* $9393. *Average need-based loan:* $3043. *Average need-based gift aid:* $7196. *Average non-need-based aid:* $16,857. *Average indebtedness upon graduation:* $15,531. *Financial aid deadline:* 3/15.

Applying *Options:* deferred entrance. *Application fee:* $30. *Required:* essay or personal statement, high school transcript, minimum 2.0 GPA, letters of recommendation. *Required for some:* interview.

Freshman Application Contact Ms. Ulisa Bowles, Director of Admissions, Bennett College For Women, Campus Box H, Greensboro, NC 27401. *Phone:* 336-517-8624. *E-mail:* admiss@bennett.edu.

BREVARD COLLEGE

Brevard, North Carolina **www.brevard.edu/**

- **Independent United Methodist** 4-year, founded 1853
- **Small-town** 120-acre campus
- **Endowment** $24.2 million
- **Coed** 675 undergraduate students, 96% full-time, 42% women, 58% men
- **Minimally difficult** entrance level, 63% of applicants were admitted

Undergraduates 648 full-time, 27 part-time. Students come from 33 states and territories, 11 other countries, 47% are from out of state, 7% African American, 0.3% Asian American or Pacific Islander, 1% Hispanic American, 0.9% Native American, 5% international, 10% transferred in, 74% live on campus. *Retention:* 56% of 2006 full-time freshmen returned.

Freshmen *Admission:* 1,050 applied, 663 admitted, 169 enrolled. *Average high school GPA:* 3.14. *Test scores:* SAT critical reading scores over 500: 54%; SAT math scores over 500: 54%; ACT scores over 18: 87%; SAT critical reading scores over 600: 20%; SAT math scores over 600: 9%; ACT scores over 24: 33%; SAT critical reading scores over 700: 1%; ACT scores over 30: 7%.

Faculty *Total:* 93, 61% full-time, 56% with terminal degrees. *Student/faculty ratio:* 11:1.

Majors Biological and physical sciences; criminal justice/law enforcement administration; dramatic/theater arts; ecology; elementary education; English; environmental science; fine/studio arts; health services/allied health/health sciences; history; kinesiology and exercise science; mathematics; multi-/interdisciplinary studies related; music; music teacher education; parks, recreation and leisure; psychology; religious studies.

Academics *Calendar:* semesters. *Degree:* bachelor's. *Special study options:* academic remediation for entering students, adult/continuing education programs, advanced placement credit, double majors, external degree program, honors programs, independent study, internships, part-time degree program, services for LD students, student-designed majors, study abroad.

Computers on Campus 100 computers/terminals are available on campus for general student use. Students can access the following: campus intranet, computer help desk, free student e-mail accounts, online (class) grades, online (class) schedules. Campuswide network is available. 100% of college-owned or -operated housing units are wired for high-speed Internet access. Wireless service is available via learning centers, libraries, student centers.

Student Life *Housing:* on-campus residence required through senior year. *Options:* coed, men-only, women-only, disabled students. Campus housing is university owned. Freshman campus housing is guaranteed. *Activities and organizations:* drama/theater group, student-run newspaper, choral group, Fine Arts Organizations, Omicron Delta Kappa, Fellowship of Christian Athletes, BC Recycles, Acting Club. *Campus security:* 24-hour emergency response devices and patrols. *Student services:* health clinic, personal/psychological counseling, women's center.

Athletics Member NCAA. All Division II. *Intercollegiate sports:* baseball M (s), basketball M (s)/W (s), cheerleading W (s), cross-country running M (s)/W (s), football M (s), golf M (s), soccer M (s)/W (s), softball W (s), tennis M (s)/W (s), track and field M (s)/W (s), volleyball W (s). *Intramural sports:* badminton M/W, basketball M/W, bowling M/W, fencing M (c)/W (c), football M/W, soccer M/W, softball M/W, tennis M/W, track and field M/W, ultimate Frisbee M/W, volleyball M/W, weight lifting M/W.

Standardized Tests *Required:* SAT or ACT (for admission).

Costs (2007–08) *Comprehensive fee:* $25,800 includes full-time tuition ($18,700), mandatory fees ($50), and room and board ($7050). Full-time tuition and fees vary according to course load. Part-time tuition: $700 per credit hour. Part-time tuition and fees vary according to course load. *Required fees:* $25 per term part-time. *Room and board:* Room and board charges vary according to board plan and housing facility. *Payment plan:* installment. *Waivers:* senior citizens and employees or children of employees.

Financial Aid Of all full-time matriculated undergraduates who enrolled in 2007, 489 applied for aid, 422 were judged to have need, 137 had their need fully met. 35 Federal Work-Study jobs (averaging $1350). 100 state and other part-time jobs (averaging $1300). In 2007, 174 non-need-based awards were made. *Average percent of need met:* 82%. *Average financial aid package:* $16,800. *Average need-based loan:* $4570. *Average need-based gift aid:* $11,380. *Average non-need-based aid:* $6760. *Average indebtedness upon graduation:* $16,996.

Applying *Options:* electronic application, deferred entrance. *Application fee:* $30. *Required:* essay or personal statement, high school transcript, minimum 2.0 GPA. *Required for some:* letters of recommendation, interview, students in music-auditions, music tests; students in art-portfolio. *Application deadlines:* rolling (freshmen), rolling (out-of-state freshmen), rolling (transfers). *Notification:* continuous (freshmen), continuous (out-of-state freshmen), continuous (transfers).

Freshman Application Contact Mr. Ken Sigler, Vice President for Enrollment Management, Brevard College, 400 North Broad Street, Brevard, NC 28712. *Phone:* 828-884-8300. *Toll-free phone:* 800-527-9090. *Fax:* 828-884-3790. *E-mail:* admissions@brevard.edu.

See page 1918 for the College Close-Up.

CABARRUS COLLEGE OF HEALTH SCIENCES

Concord, North Carolina **www.cabarruscollege.edu/**

- **Independent** 4-year, founded 1942
- **Suburban** 5-acre campus with easy access to Charlotte
- **Coed, primarily women** 358 undergraduate students, 63% full-time, 88% women, 12% men
- **Moderately difficult** entrance level, 62% of applicants were admitted

Undergraduates 225 full-time, 133 part-time. Students come from 2 states and territories, 6% African American, 1% Asian American or Pacific Islander, 2% Hispanic American, 21% transferred in.

Freshmen *Admission:* 66 applied, 41 admitted, 38 enrolled. *Average high school GPA:* 3.62. *Test scores:* SAT critical reading scores over 500: 62%; SAT math scores over 500: 59%; ACT scores over 18: 100%; SAT critical reading scores over 600: 17%; SAT math scores over 600: 10%; ACT scores over 24: 29%.

Faculty *Total:* 50, 48% full-time, 10% with terminal degrees. *Student/faculty ratio:* 7:1.
Majors Health/health care administration; medical/clinical assistant; nursing assistant/aide and patient care assistant; nursing (registered nurse training); occupational therapist assistant; surgical technology.
Academics *Calendar:* semesters. *Degrees:* certificates, diplomas, associate, and bachelor's. *Special study options:* advanced placement credit, distance learning, double majors, independent study, part-time degree program.
Computers on Campus 44 computers/terminals are available on campus for general student use. Students can access the following: campus intranet, free student e-mail accounts, online (class) grades, online (class) registration, online (class) schedules. Campuswide network is available. Wireless service is available via student centers.
Student Life *Housing:* college housing not available. *Activities and organizations:* student-run newspaper, Student Nurse Association, Christian Student Union, student government, Honor Society, Allied Health Student Association. *Campus security:* 24-hour emergency response devices and patrols. *Student services:* health clinic, personal/psychological counseling.
Standardized Tests *Required:* SAT or ACT (for admission).
Costs (2007–08) *Tuition:* $8500 full-time, $275 per hour part-time. Full-time tuition and fees vary according to course load. *Required fees:* $250 full-time. *Payment plan:* installment.
Financial Aid Of all full-time matriculated undergraduates who enrolled in 2006, 12 Federal Work-Study jobs.
Applying *Options:* electronic application. *Application fee:* $35. *Required:* essay or personal statement, high school transcript, minimum 2.0 GPA, 2 letters of recommendation. *Required for some:* interview. *Recommended:* minimum 3.0 GPA. *Application deadlines:* 3/1 (freshmen), 3/1 (transfers). *Notification:* 4/15 (freshmen), 4/15 (transfers).
Freshman Application Contact Mr. Mark Ellison, Director of Admissions, Cabarrus College of Health Sciences, 401 Medical Park Drive, Concord, NC 28025-2405. *Phone:* 704-403-1616. *Fax:* 704-403-2077. *E-mail:* mellison@cabarruscollege.edu.

CAMPBELL UNIVERSITY

Buies Creek, North Carolina **www.campbell.edu/**

- **Independent** university, founded 1887, affiliated with North Carolina Baptist State Convention
- **Rural** 850-acre campus with easy access to Raleigh
- **Endowment** $104.7 million
- **Coed**
- **Moderately difficult** entrance level

Faculty *Student/faculty ratio:* 14:1.
Academics *Calendar:* semesters. *Degrees:* associate, bachelor's, master's, doctoral, and first professional.
Student Life *Campus security:* 24-hour emergency response devices and patrols, late-night transport/escort service, controlled dormitory access.
Athletics Member NCAA. All Division I.
Standardized Tests *Required:* SAT or ACT (for admission).
Costs (2008–09) *One-time required fee:* $350. *Comprehensive fee:* $26,880 includes full-time tuition ($19,650), mandatory fees ($400), and room and board ($6830). Part-time tuition: $325 per credit hour.
Financial Aid Of all full-time matriculated undergraduates who enrolled in 2006, 2,636 applied for aid, 2,237 were judged to have need, 2,237 had their need fully met. 841 Federal Work-Study jobs (averaging $1361). 559 state and other part-time jobs (averaging $791). In 2006, 579 non-need-based awards were made. *Average percent of need met:* 100. *Average financial aid package:* $23,850. *Average need-based loan:* $3957. *Average need-based gift aid:* $4432. *Average non-need-based aid:* $6127. *Average indebtedness upon graduation:* $21,703.
Applying *Options:* electronic application, early admission, deferred entrance. *Application fee:* $35. *Required:* high school transcript. *Required for some:* 3 letters of recommendation. *Recommended:* essay or personal statement, interview.
Freshman Application Contact Ms. Peggy Mason, Director of Admissions, Campbell University, PO Box 546, 56 Main Street, Buies Creek, NC 27506. *Phone:* 910-893-1290. *Toll-free phone:* 800-334-4111. *Fax:* 910-893-1288. *E-mail:* adm@mailcenter.campbell.edu.

See page 1920 for the College Close-Up.

CAROLINA CHRISTIAN COLLEGE

Winston-Salem, North Carolina **www.wsbc.edu/**

Director of Admissions Admissions Office, Carolina Christian College, 4117 Northampton Drive, PO Box 777, Winston-Salem, NC 27102-0777. *Phone:* 336-744-0900.

CATAWBA COLLEGE

Salisbury, North Carolina **www.catawba.edu/**

- **Independent** comprehensive, founded 1851, affiliated with United Church of Christ
- **Small-town** 210-acre campus with easy access to Charlotte
- **Endowment** $37.3 million
- **Coed** 1,291 undergraduate students, 95% full-time, 50% women, 50% men
- **Moderately difficult** entrance level, 75% of applicants were admitted

Undergraduates 1,222 full-time, 69 part-time. Students come from 32 states and territories, 15 other countries, 30% are from out of state, 16% African American, 0.9% Asian American or Pacific Islander, 1% Hispanic American, 0.5% Native American, 1% international, 11% transferred in, 67% live on campus. *Retention:* 71% of 2006 full-time freshmen returned.
Freshmen *Admission:* 822 applied, 620 admitted, 266 enrolled. *Average high school GPA:* 3.36. *Test scores:* SAT critical reading scores over 500: 57%; SAT math scores over 500: 60%; ACT scores over 18: 75%; SAT critical reading scores over 600: 19%; SAT math scores over 600: 22%; ACT scores over 24: 40%; SAT critical reading scores over 700: 1%; SAT math scores over 700: 2%; ACT scores over 30: 5%.
Faculty *Total:* 105, 67% full-time, 69% with terminal degrees. *Student/faculty ratio:* 15:1.
Majors Athletic training; biology/biological sciences; business administration and management; business/managerial economics; chemistry; clinical laboratory science/medical technology; computer science; dramatic/theater arts; education; elementary education; English; environmental studies; French; history; humanities; information science/studies; interdisciplinary studies; international relations and affairs; marketing/marketing management; mass communication/media; mathematics; middle school education; music; music teacher education; parks, recreation and leisure; philosophy; physical education teaching and coaching; physician assistant; piano and organ; political science and government; pre-dentistry studies; pre-law studies; pre-medical studies; pre-veterinary studies; psychology; reading teacher education; religious studies; secondary education; sociology; Spanish; therapeutic recreation; voice and opera.
Academics *Calendar:* semesters. *Degrees:* bachelor's and master's. *Special study options:* adult/continuing education programs, advanced placement credit, double majors, honors programs, independent study, internships, part-time degree program, services for LD students, student-designed majors, study abroad, summer session for credit. *ROTC:* Army (c).
Computers on Campus 97 computers/terminals are available on campus for general student use. Students can access the following: campus intranet, computer help desk, free student e-mail accounts, online (class) grades, online (class) schedules. Campuswide network is available. 100% of college-owned or -operated housing units are wired for high-speed Internet access. Wireless service is available via classrooms, computer centers, learning centers, libraries, student centers.
Student Life *Housing:* on-campus residence required through senior year. *Options:* coed, men-only, women-only. Campus housing is university owned. Freshman campus housing is guaranteed. *Activities and organizations:* drama/theater group, student-run newspaper, choral group, Volunteer Catawba, Catawba Ambassadors (admissions guides), Blue Masque (drama), L'il Chiefs, Wigwam Productions (student activities board). *Campus security:* 24-hour emergency response devices and patrols, late-night transport/escort service, controlled dormitory access. *Student services:* health clinic, personal/psychological counseling.
Athletics Member NCAA. All Division II. *Intercollegiate sports:* baseball M (s), basketball M (s)/W (s), cross-country running M (s)/W (s), field hockey W (s), football M (s), golf M (s), lacrosse M, soccer M (s)/W (s), softball W (s), swimming and diving W (s), tennis M (s)/W (s), volleyball W (s). *Intramural sports:* archery M/W, basketball M/W, football M/W, golf M, ice hockey M, lacrosse M, racquetball M/W, soccer M/W, swimming and diving M/W, table tennis M/W, tennis M/W, volleyball M/W, weight lifting M/W.
Standardized Tests *Required:* SAT or ACT (for admission).
Costs (2007–08) *Comprehensive fee:* $29,990 includes full-time tuition ($22,290) and room and board ($7700). Full-time tuition and fees vary according to class time. Part-time tuition: $590 per credit hour. Part-time tuition and fees

vary according to class time, course load, and degree level. *Payment plan:* installment. *Waivers:* employees or children of employees.

Financial Aid Of all full-time matriculated undergraduates who enrolled in 2007, 1,004 applied for aid, 857 were judged to have need, 252 had their need fully met. 227 Federal Work-Study jobs (averaging $1707). 235 state and other part-time jobs (averaging $1567). In 2007, 158 non-need-based awards were made. *Average percent of need met:* 84%. *Average financial aid package:* $16,338. *Average need-based loan:* $4479. *Average need-based gift aid:* $4846. *Average non-need-based aid:* $9090. *Average indebtedness upon graduation:* $21,726.

Applying *Options:* electronic application, early admission, deferred entrance. *Application fee:* $30. *Required:* essay or personal statement, high school transcript, minimum 2.0 GPA, 2 letters of recommendation. *Recommended:* interview. *Application deadlines:* rolling (freshmen), rolling (transfers). *Notification:* continuous (freshmen), continuous (transfers).

Freshman Application Contact Dr. Michael Bitzer, Dean of Admissions, Catawba College, 2300 West Innes Street, Salisbury, NC 28144-2488. *Toll-free phone:* 800-CATAWBA. *Fax:* 704-637-4222. *E-mail:* admission@catawba.edu.

See page 1922 for the College Close-Up.

CHOWAN UNIVERSITY

Murfreesboro, North Carolina **www.chowan.edu**

Freshman Application Contact Mr. Jonathan Wirt, Vice President for Enrollment Management, Chowan University, 200 Jones Drive, Murfreesboro, NC 27855. *Phone:* 252-398-6314. *Toll-free phone:* 800-488-4101. *Fax:* 252-398-1190. *E-mail:* admissions@chowan.edu.

DAVIDSON COLLEGE

Davidson, North Carolina **www.davidson.edu/**

- **Independent Presbyterian** 4-year, founded 1837
- **Small-town** 556-acre campus with easy access to Charlotte
- **Endowment** $489.5 million
- **Coed** 1,674 undergraduate students, 100% full-time, 51% women, 49% men
- **Very difficult** entrance level, 28% of applicants were admitted

Undergraduates 1,674 full-time. Students come from 49 states and territories, 36 other countries, 80% are from out of state, 7% African American, 3% Asian American or Pacific Islander, 4% Hispanic American, 0.6% Native American, 4% international, 0.6% transferred in, 91% live on campus. *Retention:* 96% of 2006 full-time freshmen returned.

Freshmen *Admission:* 3,992 applied, 1,127 admitted, 465 enrolled. *Average high school GPA:* 4.0. *Test scores:* SAT critical reading scores over 500: 100%; SAT math scores over 500: 99%; ACT scores over 18: 100%; SAT critical reading scores over 600: 87%; SAT math scores over 600: 88%; ACT scores over 24: 97%; SAT critical reading scores over 700: 41%; SAT math scores over 700: 40%; ACT scores over 30: 56%.

Faculty *Total:* 178, 94% full-time, 96% with terminal degrees. *Student/faculty ratio:* 10:1.

Majors Anthropology; art; biology/biological sciences; chemistry; classics and languages, literatures and linguistics; dramatic/theater arts; economics; English; French; German; history; mathematics; multi-/interdisciplinary studies related; music; philosophy; physics; political science and government; psychology; religious studies; sociology; Spanish.

Academics *Calendar:* semesters. *Degree:* bachelor's. *Special study options:* advanced placement credit, double majors, honors programs, independent study, off-campus study, services for LD students, student-designed majors, study abroad. *ROTC:* Army (b), Air Force (c). *Unusual degree programs:* 3-2 engineering with Columbia University, Washington University in St. Louis, North Carolina State University, Georgia Institute of Technology, Duke University.

Computers on Campus 142 computers/terminals are available on campus for general student use. Students can access the following: campus intranet, computer help desk, free student e-mail accounts, online (class) registration, online (class) schedules. Campuswide network is available. 100% of college-owned or -operated housing units are wired for high-speed Internet access. Wireless service is available via entire campus.

Student Life *Housing:* on-campus residence required through senior year. *Options:* coed, men-only, women-only. Campus housing is university owned. Freshman campus housing is guaranteed. *Activities and organizations:* drama/theater group, student-run newspaper, radio station, choral group, Inter-Varsity Christian Fellowship, Dean Rusk Program Student Advisory Council, music organizations, Community Service Council, Student Government Association, national fraternities. *Campus security:* 24-hour emergency response devices and patrols, late-night transport/escort service, controlled dormitory access. *Student services:* health clinic, personal/psychological counseling, women's center.

Athletics Member NCAA. All Division I except football (Division I-AA). *Intercollegiate sports:* baseball M (s), basketball M (s)/W (s), crew M (c)/W (c), cross-country running M (s)/W (s), fencing M (c)/W (c), field hockey W (s), golf M (s), lacrosse W (s), rugby M (c), sailing M (c)/W (c), soccer M (s)/W (s), swimming and diving M (s)/W (s), tennis M (s)/W (s), track and field M (s)/W (s), ultimate Frisbee M (c)/W (c), volleyball W (s), weight lifting M (c)/W (c), wrestling M (s). *Intramural sports:* basketball M/W, field hockey M (c)/W (c), football M/W, lacrosse M (c)/W (c), soccer M (c)/W (c), softball M/W, swimming and diving M (c)/W (c), tennis M (c)/W (c), volleyball M/W (c).

Standardized Tests *Required:* SAT or ACT (for admission). *Recommended:* SAT Subject Tests (for admission).

Costs (2007–08) *Comprehensive fee:* $40,814 includes full-time tuition ($31,794) and room and board ($9020).

Financial Aid Of all full-time matriculated undergraduates who enrolled in 2005, 684 applied for aid, 574 were judged to have need, 565 had their need fully met. 200 Federal Work-Study jobs (averaging $1635). 150 state and other part-time jobs (averaging $1766). In 2005, 335 non-need-based awards were made. *Average percent of need met:* 100%. *Average financial aid package:* $19,548. *Average need-based loan:* $3365. *Average need-based gift aid:* $18,209. *Average non-need-based aid:* $14,498. *Average indebtedness upon graduation:* $28,100.

Applying *Options:* early admission, early decision, deferred entrance. *Application fee:* $50. *Required:* essay or personal statement, high school transcript, 3 letters of recommendation. *Recommended:* interview. *Application deadlines:* 1/2 (freshmen), 3/15 (transfers). *Early decision deadline:* 11/15. *Notification:* 4/1 (freshmen), 5/15 (transfers), 12/15 (early decision).

Freshman Application Contact Mr. Christopher J. Gruber, Vice President and Dean of Admission and Financial Aid, Davidson College, Box 7156, Davidson, NC 28035-7156. *Phone:* 704-894-2230. *Toll-free phone:* 800-768-0380. *Fax:* 704-894-2016. *E-mail:* admission@davidson.edu.

See page 1924 for the College Close-Up.

DEVRY UNIVERSITY

Charlotte, North Carolina **www.devry.edu/**

- **Proprietary** comprehensive, part of DeVry University
- **Coed** 111 undergraduate students, 47% full-time, 55% women, 45% men
- **Minimally difficult** entrance level

Undergraduates 52 full-time, 59 part-time. 17% are from out of state, 61% African American, 3% Asian American or Pacific Islander, 7% Hispanic American, 31% transferred in. *Retention:* 44% of 2006 full-time freshmen returned.

Freshmen *Admission:* 21 enrolled.

Faculty *Total:* 12, 25% full-time. *Student/faculty ratio:* 21:1.

Majors Business administration and management; business administration, management and operations related; computer systems analysis.

Academics *Calendar:* semesters. *Degrees:* bachelor's, master's, and post-bachelor's certificates. *Special study options:* academic remediation for entering students, accelerated degree program, adult/continuing education programs, advanced placement credit, distance learning, part-time degree program, summer session for credit.

Student Life *Housing:* college housing not available.

Costs (2008–09) *Tuition:* $13,810 full-time, $515 per credit part-time. *Required fees:* $80 full-time.

Applying *Options:* electronic application, early admission, deferred entrance. *Application fee:* $50. *Required:* high school transcript, interview. *Application deadlines:* rolling (freshmen), rolling (transfers). *Notification:* continuous (freshmen), continuous (transfers).

Director of Admissions Admissions Office, DeVry University, 4521 Sharon Road, Suite 145, Charlotte, NC 28211-3627.

DUKE UNIVERSITY

Durham, North Carolina **www.duke.edu/**

- **Independent** university, founded 1838, affiliated with United Methodist Church
- **Suburban** 8500-acre campus
- **Endowment** $5.3 billion

- **Coed** 6,394 undergraduate students, 99% full-time, 49% women, 51% men
- **Most difficult** entrance level, 23% of applicants were admitted

Undergraduates 6,361 full-time, 33 part-time. Students come from 53 states and territories, 89 other countries, 87% are from out of state, 10% African American, 19% Asian American or Pacific Islander, 6% Hispanic American, 0.2% Native American, 6% international, 0.3% transferred in, 83% live on campus. *Retention:* 97% of 2006 full-time freshmen returned.

Freshmen *Admission:* 17,748 applied, 4,077 admitted, 1,700 enrolled. *Test scores:* SAT critical reading scores over 500: 99%; SAT math scores over 500: 100%; SAT writing scores over 500: 99%; ACT scores over 18: 100%; SAT critical reading scores over 600: 92%; SAT math scores over 600: 94%; SAT writing scores over 600: 91%; ACT scores over 24: 96%; SAT critical reading scores over 700: 60%; SAT math scores over 700: 68%; SAT writing scores over 700: 57%; ACT scores over 30: 72%.

Faculty *Total:* 990. *Student/faculty ratio:* 8:1.

Majors African-American/Black studies; anatomy; ancient/classical Greek; anthropology; art; art history, criticism and conservation; Asian studies; biology/biological sciences; biomedical/medical engineering; Canadian studies; chemistry; civil engineering; classics and languages, literatures and linguistics; computer science; design and visual communications; dramatic/theater arts; economics; electrical, electronics and communications engineering; English; environmental studies; French; geology/earth science; German; history; international relations and affairs; Italian; Latin; linguistics; literature; materials science; mathematics; mechanical engineering; medieval and Renaissance studies; music; philosophy; physics; political science and government; psychology; public policy analysis; religious studies; Russian; Slavic languages; sociology; Spanish; women's studies.

Academics *Calendar:* semesters. *Degrees:* bachelor's, master's, doctoral, first professional, post-master's, and postbachelor's certificates. *Special study options:* accelerated degree program, adult/continuing education programs, advanced placement credit, distance learning, double majors, English as a second language, honors programs, independent study, internships, off-campus study, part-time degree program, services for LD students, student-designed majors, study abroad, summer session for credit. *ROTC:* Army (b), Navy (b), Air Force (b). *Unusual degree programs:* 3-2 law.

Computers on Campus 450 computers/terminals are available on campus for general student use. Students can access the following: campus intranet, computer help desk, free student e-mail accounts, online (class) registration. Campuswide network is available. 100% of college-owned or -operated housing units are wired for high-speed Internet access. Wireless service is available via entire campus.

Student Life *Housing:* on-campus residence required through junior year. *Options:* coed, men-only, women-only. Campus housing is university owned. Freshman campus housing is guaranteed. *Activities and organizations:* drama/theater group, student-run newspaper, radio and television station, choral group, marching band, national fraternities, national sororities. *Campus security:* 24-hour emergency response devices and patrols, late-night transport/escort service, controlled dormitory access. *Student services:* health clinic, personal/psychological counseling, women's center, legal services.

Athletics Member NCAA. All Division I except football (Division I-A). *Intercollegiate sports:* badminton M (c)/W (c), baseball M (s), basketball M (s)/W (s), crew M (c)/W (s), cross-country running M/W, equestrian sports M (c)/W (c), fencing M/W, field hockey M (c)/W (s), football M (s)/W (c), golf M (s)/W (s), ice hockey M (c)/W (c), lacrosse M (s)/W (s), racquetball M (c)/W (c), rugby M (c)/W (c), sailing M (c)/W (c), skiing (cross-country) M (c)/W (c), skiing (downhill) M (c)/W (c), soccer M (s)/W (s), softball M (c)/W (c), squash M (c)/W (c), swimming and diving M/W, table tennis M (c)/W (c), tennis M (s)/W (s), track and field M/W, ultimate Frisbee M (c)/W (c), volleyball M (c)/W (s), water polo M (c)/W (c), wrestling M. *Intramural sports:* badminton M/W, baseball M/W, basketball M/W, football M, golf M/W, soccer M/W, softball M/W, squash M/W, swimming and diving M/W, table tennis M/W, tennis M/W, volleyball M/W.

Standardized Tests *Required:* SAT and SAT Subject Tests or ACT (for admission).

Costs (2007–08) *Comprehensive fee:* $45,121 includes full-time tuition ($34,335), mandatory fees ($1177), and room and board ($9609). Part-time tuition: $4292 per course. Part-time tuition and fees vary according to course load. *College room only:* $5150. Room and board charges vary according to board plan and housing facility. *Payment plans:* tuition prepayment, installment, deferred payment. *Waivers:* employees or children of employees.

Financial Aid Of all full-time matriculated undergraduates who enrolled in 2007, 2,806 applied for aid, 2,535 were judged to have need, 2,535 had their need fully met. 1,757 Federal Work-Study jobs (averaging $1798). 473 state and other part-time jobs (averaging $1639). In 2007, 257 non-need-based awards were made. *Average percent of need met:* 100%. *Average financial aid package:* $31,014. *Average need-based loan:* $4373. *Average need-based gift aid:* $26,505. *Average non-need-based aid:* $25,161. *Average indebtedness upon graduation:* $23,392. *Financial aid deadline:* 2/1.

Applying *Options:* electronic application, early admission, early decision, deferred entrance. *Application fee:* $75. *Required:* essay or personal statement, high school transcript, letters of recommendation. *Required for some:* audition tape for dance, drama, or music; slides of work for art. *Recommended:* interview. *Application deadlines:* 1/2 (freshmen), 3/15 (transfers). *Early decision deadline:* 11/1. *Notification:* 4/1 (freshmen), 5/1 (transfers), 12/15 (early decision).

Freshman Application Contact Mr. Christoph Guttentag, Director of Admissions, Duke University, 2138 Campus Drive, Durham, NC 27708. *Phone:* 919-684-3214. *E-mail:* askduke@admiss.duke.edu.

See page 1926 for the College Close-Up.

East Carolina University

Greenville, North Carolina — www.ecu.edu/

- **State-supported** university, founded 1907, part of The University of North Carolina
- **Urban** 1377-acre campus
- **Endowment** $90.4 million
- **Coed** 19,767 undergraduate students, 88% full-time, 59% women, 41% men
- **Moderately difficult** entrance level, 84% of applicants were admitted

Undergraduates 17,309 full-time, 2,458 part-time. Students come from 41 states and territories, 10% are from out of state, 16% African American, 2% Asian American or Pacific Islander, 2% Hispanic American, 0.7% Native American, 0.5% international, 8% transferred in, 18% live on campus. *Retention:* 77% of 2006 full-time freshmen returned.

Freshmen *Admission:* 14,653 applied, 12,328 admitted, 4,222 enrolled. *Average high school GPA:* 3.45. *Test scores:* SAT critical reading scores over 500: 60%; SAT math scores over 500: 48%; SAT writing scores over 500: 43%; ACT scores over 18: 86%; SAT critical reading scores over 600: 12%; SAT math scores over 600: 8%; SAT writing scores over 600: 6%; ACT scores over 24: 15%.

Faculty *Total:* 1,162, 91% full-time, 81% with terminal degrees. *Student/faculty ratio:* 20:1.

Majors Accounting; African-American/Black studies; anthropology; art; art history, criticism and conservation; art teacher education; athletic training; biochemistry; biology/biological sciences; broadcast journalism; business administration and management; business teacher education; chemistry; child development; city/urban, community and regional planning; clinical laboratory science/medical technology; communication/speech communication and rhetoric; computer engineering technology; computer science; criminal justice/safety; dance; dietetics; drama and dance teacher education; dramatic/theater arts; economics; elementary education; engineering; engineering technologies related; English; English/language arts teacher education; environmental engineering technology; environmental health; exercise physiology; family and community services; family and consumer sciences/home economics teacher education; finance; fine/studio arts; French; French language teacher education; geography; geology/earth science; German; German language teacher education; health and physical education related; health/health care administration; health information/medical records administration; history; hospitality administration; hotel/motel administration; human development and family studies; industrial production technologies related; industrial technology; information technology; interior design; kinesiology and exercise science; liberal arts and sciences/liberal studies; management information systems; manufacturing technology; marketing/marketing management; mathematics; mathematics teacher education; middle school education; music performance; music teacher education; music theory and composition; music therapy; nursing (registered nurse training); parks, recreation and leisure facilities management; philosophy; physical education teaching and coaching; physics; political science and government; psychology; public/applied history and archival administration; public health education and promotion; sales and marketing/marketing and distribution teacher education; science teacher education; social studies teacher education; social work; sociology; Spanish; Spanish language teacher education; special education; special education (emotionally disturbed); special education (mentally retarded); special education related; special education (specific learning disabilities); therapeutic recreation; vocational rehabilitation counseling; women's studies.

Academics *Calendar:* semesters. *Degrees:* bachelor's, master's, doctoral, first professional, and post-master's certificates. *Special study options:* adult/continuing education programs, advanced placement credit, distance learning, double majors, honors programs, independent study, internships, off-campus study, part-time degree program, services for LD students, study abroad, summer session for credit. *ROTC:* Army (b), Air Force (b). *Unusual degree programs:* 3-2 accounting.

Computers on Campus 1,886 computers/terminals and 5,500 ports are available on campus for general student use. Students can access the following: campus intranet, computer help desk, free student e-mail accounts, online (class) grades, online (class) registration, online (class) schedules. Campuswide network is available. 100% of college-owned or -operated housing units are wired for high-speed Internet access. Wireless service is available via classrooms, computer centers, computer labs, learning centers, libraries, student centers.

Student Life *Housing options:* coed, men-only, women-only. Campus housing is university owned. *Activities and organizations:* drama/theater group, student-run newspaper, radio station, choral group, marching band, Student Government Association, Student Union, Residence Hall Association, Student Pirate Club, Black Student Union, national fraternities, national sororities. *Campus security:* 24-hour emergency response devices and patrols, student patrols, late-night transport/escort service, controlled dormitory access, Operation ID, Staff and Faculty Eyes, Campus Community Watch program. *Student services:* health clinic, personal/psychological counseling, legal services.

Athletics Member NCAA. All Division I except football (Division I-A). *Intercollegiate sports:* baseball M (s), basketball M (s)/W (s), cross-country running M (s)/W (s), golf M (s)/W (s), soccer M (s)/W (s), softball W (s), swimming and diving M (s)/W (s), tennis M (s)/W (s), track and field M (s)/W (s), volleyball W (s). *Intramural sports:* badminton M/W, baseball M (c), basketball M (c)/W (c), bowling M (c)/W (c), cross-country running M/W, equestrian sports M (c)/W (c), fencing M (c)/W (c), field hockey W (c), football M/W, golf M/W, ice hockey M (c), lacrosse M (c)/W (c), racquetball M/W, rugby M (c)/W (c), skiing (downhill) M (c)/W (c), soccer M (c)/W (c), softball M/W (c), swimming and diving M (c)/W (c), table tennis M/W, tennis M/W (c), ultimate Frisbee M (c)/W (c), volleyball M/W (c), water polo M (c)/W (c), wrestling M (c).

Standardized Tests *Required:* SAT or ACT (for admission).

Costs (2007–08) *Tuition:* state resident $2431 full-time, $304 per course part-time; nonresident $12,945 full-time, $1618 per course part-time. Part-time tuition and fees vary according to course load. *Required fees:* $1937 full-time, $196 per term part-time. *Room and board:* $7150; room only: $4150. Room and board charges vary according to board plan and housing facility. *Payment plans:* installment, deferred payment. *Waivers:* senior citizens and employees or children of employees.

Financial Aid Of all full-time matriculated undergraduates who enrolled in 2006, 10,926 applied for aid, 8,022 were judged to have need, 1,004 had their need fully met. In 2006, 366 non-need-based awards were made. *Average percent of need met:* 8%. *Average financial aid package:* $4570. *Average need-based loan:* $7367. *Average need-based gift aid:* $8923. *Average non-need-based aid:* $2990.

Applying *Options:* electronic application, early admission, deferred entrance. *Application fee:* $60. *Required:* high school transcript, minimum 2.0 GPA. *Application deadline:* 3/15 (freshmen). *Notification:* continuous (freshmen), continuous (transfers).

Freshman Application Contact East Carolina University, Undergraduate Admission, Whichard Building 106, East 5th Street, Greenville, NC 27858-4353. *Phone:* 252-328-6640.

ELIZABETH CITY STATE UNIVERSITY

Elizabeth City, North Carolina **www.ecsu.edu/**

Director of Admissions Mr. Grady Deese, Director of Admissions, Elizabeth City State University, Campus Box 901, Elizabeth City, NC 27909-7806. *Phone:* 252-335-3305. *Toll-free phone:* 800-347-3278.

ELON UNIVERSITY

Elon, North Carolina **www.elon.edu/**

- **Independent** comprehensive, founded 1889, affiliated with United Church of Christ
- **Suburban** 580-acre campus with easy access to Raleigh
- **Endowment** $78.5 million
- **Coed** 4,939 undergraduate students, 98% full-time, 59% women, 41% men
- **Moderately difficult** entrance level, 41% of applicants were admitted

Undergraduates 4,832 full-time, 107 part-time. Students come from 46 states and territories, 45 other countries, 72% are from out of state, 6% African American, 1% Asian American or Pacific Islander, 2% Hispanic American, 0.2% Native American, 2% international, 2% transferred in, 58% live on campus. *Retention:* 90% of 2006 full-time freshmen returned.

Freshmen *Admission:* 9,380 applied, 3,870 admitted, 1,286 enrolled. *Average high school GPA:* 3.9. *Test scores:* SAT critical reading scores over 500: 93%; SAT math scores over 500: 95%; SAT writing scores over 500: 94%; ACT scores over 18: 99%; SAT critical reading scores over 600: 59%; SAT math scores over 600: 61%; SAT writing scores over 600: 58%; ACT scores over 24: 83%; SAT critical reading scores over 700: 9%; SAT math scores over 700: 11%; SAT writing scores over 700: 11%; ACT scores over 30: 13%.

Faculty *Total:* 430, 72% full-time, 75% with terminal degrees. *Student/faculty ratio:* 14:1.

Majors Accounting; anthropology; art; art history, criticism and conservation; athletic training; biology/biological sciences; broadcast journalism; business administration and management; business/corporate communications; chemical engineering; chemistry; clinical laboratory science/medical technology; communication/speech communication and rhetoric; computer and information sciences; computer science; dance; dramatic/theater arts; economics; education; elementary education; engineering; English; environmental studies; foreign languages and literatures; French; health teacher education; history; human services; journalism; mathematics; middle school education; music; music performance; music teacher education; parks, recreation and leisure; philosophy; physical education teaching and coaching; physics; political science and government; pre-dentistry studies; pre-law studies; pre-medical studies; pre-veterinary studies; psychology; public administration; religious studies; science teacher education; secondary education; social science teacher education; social studies teacher education; sociology; Spanish; special education; sport and fitness administration/management; theater design and technology.

Academics *Calendar:* 4-1-4. *Degrees:* bachelor's, master's, doctoral, and first professional. *Special study options:* accelerated degree program, advanced placement credit, double majors, English as a second language, honors programs, independent study, internships, off-campus study, part-time degree program, services for LD students, student-designed majors, study abroad, summer session for credit. *ROTC:* Army (b), Air Force (c). *Unusual degree programs:* 3-2 engineering with North Carolina State University, North Carolina Agricultural and Technical State University, Virginia Polytechnic Institute and State University, Washington University, Columbia University.

Computers on Campus 540 computers/terminals are available on campus for general student use. Students can access the following: free student e-mail accounts, online (class) grades, online (class) registration, online (class) schedules. Campuswide network is available. Wireless service is available via entire campus.

Student Life *Housing:* on-campus residence required through sophomore year. *Options:* coed, men-only, women-only. Campus housing is university owned and leased by the school. Freshman campus housing is guaranteed. *Activities and organizations:* drama/theater group, student-run newspaper, radio and television station, choral group, marching band, Elon volunteers, student media, intramural athletics, religious life, Habitat for Humanity, national fraternities, national sororities. *Campus security:* 24-hour emergency response devices and patrols, late-night transport/escort service, controlled dormitory access. *Student services:* health clinic, personal/psychological counseling, women's center.

Athletics Member NCAA. All Division I except football (Division I-AA). *Intercollegiate sports:* baseball M (s), basketball M (s)/W (s), cheerleading M/W, cross-country running M (s)/W (s), equestrian sports M (c)/W (c), field hockey W (c), golf M (s)/W (s), lacrosse M (c)/W (c), rugby M (c)/W (c), soccer M (s)/W (s), softball W (s), swimming and diving M (c)/W (c), tennis M (s)/W (s), track and field W (s), ultimate Frisbee M (c)/W (c), volleyball W (s). *Intramural sports:* basketball M/W, bowling M/W, football M/W, golf M/W, racquetball M/W, soccer M/W, softball M/W, table tennis M/W, tennis M/W, volleyball M/W.

Standardized Tests *Required:* SAT or ACT (for admission).

Costs (2007–08) *Comprehensive fee:* $29,462 includes full-time tuition ($21,886), mandatory fees ($280), and room and board ($7296). Part-time tuition: $688 per hour. Part-time tuition and fees vary according to course load. *College room only:* $3536. Room and board charges vary according to board plan and housing facility. *Payment plan:* installment. *Waivers:* employees or children of employees.

Financial Aid Of all full-time matriculated undergraduates who enrolled in 2007, 2,165 applied for aid, 1,583 were judged to have need. 817 Federal Work-Study jobs (averaging $2324). In 2007, 981 non-need-based awards were made. *Average percent of need met:* 68%. *Average financial aid package:* $13,400. *Average need-based loan:* $4607. *Average need-based gift aid:* $7619. *Average non-need-based aid:* $4370. *Average indebtedness upon graduation:* $21,268.

Applying *Options:* electronic application, early admission, early decision, early action, deferred entrance. *Application fee:* $50. *Required:* essay or personal statement, high school transcript, minimum 2.7 GPA. *Required for some:* interview. *Application deadlines:* 1/10 (freshmen), rolling (transfers), 11/10 (early action). *Early decision deadline:* 11/1. *Notification:* 3/15 (freshmen), continuous (transfers), 12/1 (early decision), 12/20 (early action).

Freshman Application Contact Ms. Melinda Wood, Associate Director of Admissions and Director of Application Review, Elon University, 100 Campus Drive, Elon, NC 27244. *Phone:* 336-278-3566. *Toll-free phone:* 800-334-8448. *Fax:* 336-278-7699. *E-mail:* admissions@elon.edu.

FAYETTEVILLE STATE UNIVERSITY

Fayetteville, North Carolina www.uncfsu.edu/

- **State-supported** comprehensive, founded 1867, part of University of North Carolina System
- **Urban** 156-acre campus with easy access to Raleigh
- **Endowment** $11.3 million
- **Coed** 6,068 undergraduate students, 74% full-time, 69% women, 31% men
- **Minimally difficult** entrance level, 78% of applicants were admitted

Undergraduates 4,471 full-time, 1,597 part-time. Students come from 31 states and territories, 3 other countries, 5% are from out of state, 74% African American, 1% Asian American or Pacific Islander, 4% Hispanic American, 0.9% Native American, 0.3% international, 12% transferred in, 19% live on campus. *Retention:* 73% of 2006 full-time freshmen returned.

Freshmen *Admission:* 2,454 applied, 1,914 admitted, 942 enrolled. *Average high school GPA:* 2.77. *Test scores:* SAT critical reading scores over 500: 12%; SAT math scores over 500: 15%; SAT writing scores over 500: 15%; SAT critical reading scores over 600: 1%; SAT math scores over 600: 1%; SAT writing scores over 600: 6%.

Faculty *Total:* 321, 93% full-time. *Student/faculty ratio:* 21:1.

Majors Accounting; art; art teacher education; biology/biological sciences; biology teacher education; biotechnology; business administration and management; business teacher education; chemistry; communication/speech communication and rhetoric; computer science; criminal justice/law enforcement administration; dramatic/theater arts and stagecraft related; early childhood education; elementary education; English; English/language arts teacher education; finance; fire services administration; forensic science and technology; geography; health teacher education; history; management information systems; marketing/marketing management; mathematics; mathematics teacher education; middle school education; music; music teacher education; nursing (registered nurse training); physical education teaching and coaching; political science and government; psychology; sales and marketing/marketing and distribution teacher education; social science teacher education; sociology; Spanish; Spanish language teacher education.

Academics *Calendar:* semesters. *Degrees:* bachelor's, master's, and doctoral. *Special study options:* academic remediation for entering students, accelerated degree program, adult/continuing education programs, advanced placement credit, cooperative education, distance learning, double majors, honors programs, independent study, internships, part-time degree program, services for LD students, study abroad, summer session for credit. *ROTC:* Army (c), Air Force (b). *Unusual degree programs:* 3-2 engineering with North Carolina State University.

Computers on Campus 600 computers/terminals and 1,800 ports are available on campus for general student use. Students can access the following: campus intranet, computer help desk, free student e-mail accounts, online (class) grades, online (class) registration, online (class) schedules. Campuswide network is available. 100% of college-owned or -operated housing units are wired for high-speed Internet access. Wireless service is available via classrooms, computer centers, computer labs, learning centers, libraries, student centers.

Student Life *Housing options:* coed, men-only, women-only, disabled students. Campus housing is university owned. Freshman applicants given priority for college housing. *Activities and organizations:* drama/theater group, student-run newspaper, choral group, marching band, Student Government Association, Student Activities Council, Pan Hellenic Council, Residence Hall Association, Illusions & Black Millennium Modeling Clubs, national fraternities, national sororities. *Campus security:* 24-hour emergency response devices and patrols, late-night transport/escort service, controlled dormitory access. *Student services:* health clinic, personal/psychological counseling.

Athletics Member NCAA. All Division II. *Intercollegiate sports:* basketball M (s)/W (s), bowling W (s), cheerleading M/W, cross-country running M/W, football M (s)/W (s), golf M (s), softball W (s), tennis W (s), track and field M/W, volleyball M (s)/W (s). *Intramural sports:* basketball M/W, football M/W, soccer M/W, softball M/W, volleyball M/W.

Standardized Tests *Required:* SAT or ACT (for admission).

Costs (2007–08) *One-time required fee:* $50. *Tuition:* state resident $1826 full-time; nonresident $12,008 full-time. *Required fees:* $1556 full-time. *Room and board:* $4870; room only: $2870.

Financial Aid Of all full-time matriculated undergraduates who enrolled in 2001, 2,508 applied for aid, 2,174 were judged to have need, 1,423 had their need fully met. In 2001, 247 non-need-based awards were made. *Average percent of need met:* 69%. *Average financial aid package:* $6690. *Average need-based loan:* $9341. *Average need-based gift aid:* $7976. *Average non-need-based aid:* $4106. *Average indebtedness upon graduation:* $9225. *Financial aid deadline:* 3/1.

Applying *Options:* electronic application, early admission, early decision, early action, deferred entrance. *Application fee:* $25. *Required:* high school transcript, minimum 2.0 GPA. *Recommended:* essay or personal statement, letters of recommendation. *Application deadlines:* 7/1 (freshmen), 7/1 (transfers). *Notification:* continuous (freshmen), continuous (transfers).

Freshman Application Contact Ms. Rozie Shabazz, Associate Vice Chancellor for Enrollment Management, Fayetteville State University, 1200 Murchison Road, Fayetteville, NC 28301. *Phone:* 910-486-1784. *Toll-free phone:* 800-222-2594. *Fax:* 910-672-2209. *E-mail:* rshabzz@uncfsu.edu.

GARDNER-WEBB UNIVERSITY

Boiling Springs, North Carolina www.gardner-webb.edu/

- **Independent Baptist** comprehensive, founded 1905
- **Small-town** 250-acre campus with easy access to Charlotte
- **Endowment** $42.9 million
- **Coed** 2,659 undergraduate students, 84% full-time, 67% women, 33% men
- **Moderately difficult** entrance level, 70% of applicants were admitted

Undergraduates 2,225 full-time, 434 part-time. Students come from 32 states and territories, 30 other countries, 22% are from out of state, 18% African American, 1% Asian American or Pacific Islander, 2% Hispanic American, 0.6% Native American, 0.1% international, 21% transferred in, 38% live on campus. *Retention:* 68% of 2006 full-time freshmen returned.

Freshmen *Admission:* 1,973 applied, 1,382 admitted, 405 enrolled. *Average high school GPA:* 3.51. *Test scores:* SAT critical reading scores over 500: 53%; SAT math scores over 500: 45%; SAT critical reading scores over 600: 18%; SAT math scores over 600: 15%; SAT critical reading scores over 700: 2%; SAT math scores over 700: 2%.

Faculty *Total:* 339, 40% full-time. *Student/faculty ratio:* 15:1.

Majors Accounting; American Sign Language (ASL); art; athletic training; biology/biological sciences; business administration and management; chemistry; clinical laboratory science/medical technology; clinical/medical laboratory technology; computer science; dramatic/theater arts; early childhood education; education; elementary education; English; English/language arts teacher education; fine/studio arts; foreign language teacher education; French; French language teacher education; health and physical education; health teacher education; history; journalism; kindergarten/preschool education; management information systems; mass communication/media; mathematics; mathematics teacher education; missionary studies and missiology; music performance; music teacher education; nursing (registered nurse training); pastoral studies/counseling; physical education teaching and coaching; physician assistant; political science and government; pre-dentistry studies; pre-law studies; pre-medical studies; pre-pharmacy studies; pre-veterinary studies; psychology; radio and television broadcasting technology; religious education; religious/sacred music; religious studies; secondary education; social sciences; sociology; Spanish; sport and fitness administration/management; youth ministry.

Academics *Calendar:* semesters. *Degrees:* associate, bachelor's, master's, doctoral, and first professional. *Special study options:* academic remediation for entering students, accelerated degree program, adult/continuing education programs, advanced placement credit, cooperative education, distance learning, double majors, English as a second language, honors programs, internships, off-campus study, part-time degree program, services for LD students, study abroad, summer session for credit. *ROTC:* Army (b). *Unusual degree programs:* 3-2 engineering with Auburn University, University of North Carolina at Charlotte; music/business.

Computers on Campus 150 computers/terminals are available on campus for general student use. Students can access the following: free student e-mail accounts, online (class) grades, online (class) registration, online (class) schedules. Campuswide network is available. 100% of college-owned or -operated housing units are wired for high-speed Internet access. Wireless service is available via entire campus.

Student Life *Housing:* on-campus residence required through junior year. *Options:* men-only, women-only, disabled students. Campus housing is university owned. Freshman campus housing is guaranteed. *Activities and organizations:* drama/theater group, student-run newspaper, choral group, marching band, Campus Ministries United (houses FCA, small groups, student led worship, service and ministry groups, etc.), Community Service Organizations (student YMCA, ministry clubs, campus volunteerism office, mission trips), Student Government Association, Student Alumni Council. *Campus security:* 24-hour emergency response devices and patrols, student patrols, late-night transport/escort service, controlled dormitory access. *Student services:* personal/psychological counseling.

Athletics Member NCAA. All Division I except football (Division I-AA). *Intercollegiate sports:* baseball M (s), basketball M (s)/W (s), cheerleading M (s)/W (s), cross-country running M (s)/W (s), golf M (s)/W (s), soccer M (s)/W (s), softball W (s), swimming and diving M (s)/W (s), tennis M (s)/W (s), track and field M (s)/W (s), volleyball W (s), wrestling M (s). *Intramural sports:* basketball M/W, football M/W, racquetball M/W, soccer M/W, softball M/W, table tennis M/W, tennis M/W, ultimate Frisbee M/W, volleyball M/W.

Standardized Tests *Required:* SAT or ACT (for admission).

Costs (2007–08) *Comprehensive fee:* $24,740 includes full-time tuition ($18,310), mandatory fees ($370), and room and board ($6060). Part-time tuition: $315 per semester hour. Part-time tuition and fees vary according to course load. *Room and board:* Room and board charges vary according to board plan and housing facility. *Payment plan:* installment. *Waivers:* senior citizens and employees or children of employees.

Financial Aid Of all full-time matriculated undergraduates who enrolled in 2006, 1,103 applied for aid, 986 were judged to have need, 236 had their need fully met. In 2006, 216 non-need-based awards were made. *Average percent of need met:* 68%. *Average financial aid package:* $14,100. *Average need-based loan:* $3916. *Average need-based gift aid:* $5436. *Average non-need-based aid:* $4843.

Applying *Options:* electronic application. *Application fee:* $40. *Required:* essay or personal statement, high school transcript, minimum 2.4 GPA. *Required for some:* interview. *Recommended:* 2 letters of recommendation. *Application deadlines:* rolling (freshmen), rolling (transfers).

Freshman Application Contact Mr. Nathan Alexander, Assistant Vice President of Admissions, Gardner-Webb University, PO Box 817, 110 South Main Street, Boiling Springs, NC 28017. *Phone:* 704-406-4491. *Toll-free phone:* 800-253-6472. *Fax:* 704-406-4488. *E-mail:* admissions@gardner-webb.edu.

See page 1928 for the College Close-Up.

GREENSBORO COLLEGE

Greensboro, North Carolina **www.gborocollege.edu/**

- **Independent United Methodist** comprehensive, founded 1838
- **Urban** 75-acre campus with easy access to Charlotte
- **Endowment** $32.7 million
- **Coed** 1,135 undergraduate students, 83% full-time, 51% women, 49% men
- **Moderately difficult** entrance level, 64% of applicants were admitted

Undergraduates 947 full-time, 188 part-time. Students come from 32 states and territories, 12 other countries, 28% are from out of state, 9% African American, 0.3% Asian American or Pacific Islander, 2% Hispanic American, 0.1% Native American, 0.7% international, 12% transferred in, 65% live on campus. *Retention:* 53% of 2006 full-time freshmen returned.

Freshmen *Admission:* 1,425 applied, 919 admitted, 217 enrolled. *Average high school GPA:* 2.98. *Test scores:* SAT critical reading scores over 500: 36%; SAT math scores over 500: 42%; SAT writing scores over 500: 33%; ACT scores over 18: 68%; SAT critical reading scores over 600: 7%; SAT math scores over 600: 11%; SAT writing scores over 600: 7%; ACT scores over 24: 25%; SAT critical reading scores over 700: 1%; SAT writing scores over 700: 2%; ACT scores over 30: 3%.

Faculty *Total:* 125, 49% full-time, 59% with terminal degrees. *Student/faculty ratio:* 13:1.

Majors Accounting; acting; art; art teacher education; athletic training; biology/biological sciences; biology teacher education; business administration and management; business/managerial economics; chemistry; clinical laboratory science/medical technology; communication/speech communication and rhetoric; drama and dance teacher education; dramatic/theater arts; early childhood education; education; elementary education; English; English/language arts teacher education; foreign language teacher education; French; health and physical education related; history; interdisciplinary studies; kindergarten/preschool education; kinesiology and exercise science; mathematics; mathematics teacher education; middle school education; music; music performance; music teacher education; physical education teaching and coaching; political science and government; psychology; religious studies; science teacher education; secondary education; social studies teacher education; sociology; Spanish; Spanish language teacher education; special education; special education (emotionally disturbed); special education (mentally retarded); special education (specific learning disabilities); sport and fitness administration/management; theater design and technology.

Academics *Calendar:* semesters. *Degrees:* certificates, bachelor's, master's, and postbachelor's certificates. *Special study options:* academic remediation for entering students, accelerated degree program, adult/continuing education programs, advanced placement credit, double majors, English as a second language, freshman honors college, honors programs, independent study, internships, off-campus study, part-time degree program, services for LD students, student-designed majors, study abroad, summer session for credit. *ROTC:* Army (c), Air Force (c).

Computers on Campus 180 computers/terminals and 325 ports are available on campus for general student use. Students can access the following: campus intranet, computer help desk, free student e-mail accounts, online (class) grades, online (class) schedules. Campuswide network is available. 100% of college-owned or -operated housing units are wired for high-speed Internet access. Wireless service is available via entire campus.

Student Life *Housing:* on-campus residence required through sophomore year. *Options:* coed, men-only, women-only. Campus housing is university owned. Freshman campus housing is guaranteed. *Activities and organizations:* drama/theater group, student-run newspaper, choral group, marching band, Pheta VI, Alpha Z Delta, Student Athletic Advisor Counsel, Pride Productions, United African American Society, national fraternities, national sororities. *Campus security:* 24-hour patrols, late-night transport/escort service, controlled dormitory access. *Student services:* health clinic, personal/psychological counseling.

Athletics Member NCAA. All Division III. *Intercollegiate sports:* baseball M, basketball M/W, cheerleading M/W, cross-country running M/W, football M, golf M, lacrosse M/W, soccer M/W, softball W, swimming and diving W, tennis M/W, volleyball W. *Intramural sports:* basketball M/W, bowling M/W, football M/W, racquetball M/W, skiing (downhill) M/W, ultimate Frisbee M/W.

Standardized Tests *Required:* SAT or ACT (for admission).

Costs (2008–09) *Comprehensive fee:* $30,668 includes full-time tuition ($21,978), mandatory fees ($270), and room and board ($8420). Part-time tuition: $605 per credit hour. *College room only:* $4020.

Financial Aid Of all full-time matriculated undergraduates who enrolled in 2002, 718 applied for aid, 574 were judged to have need, 234 had their need fully met. 162 Federal Work-Study jobs (averaging $1100). 23 state and other part-time jobs (averaging $1100). In 2002, 238 non-need-based awards were made. *Average percent of need met:* 71%. *Average financial aid package:* $9395. *Average need-based loan:* $4011. *Average need-based gift aid:* $3824. *Average non-need-based aid:* $4473. *Average indebtedness upon graduation:* $11,802.

Applying *Options:* electronic application, early admission, early action, deferred entrance. *Application fee:* $35. *Required:* high school transcript. *Required for some:* 2 letters of recommendation, interview. *Recommended:* essay or personal statement, interview. *Application deadlines:* rolling (freshmen), rolling (transfers), 12/15 (early action). *Notification:* continuous (freshmen), continuous (transfers), 1/15 (early action).

Freshman Application Contact Mr. Timothy L. Jackson, Dean of Enrollment Management, Greensboro College, 815 West Market Street, Greensboro, NC 27401. *Phone:* 336-272-7102. *Toll-free phone:* 800-346-8226. *Fax:* 336-378-0154. *E-mail:* admissions@gborocollege.edu.

See page 1930 for the College Close-Up.

GUILFORD COLLEGE

Greensboro, North Carolina **www.guilford.edu/**

- **Independent** 4-year, founded 1837, affiliated with Society of Friends
- **Suburban** 340-acre campus
- **Endowment** $69.1 million
- **Coed** 2,688 undergraduate students, 84% full-time, 61% women, 39% men
- **Moderately difficult** entrance level, 58% of applicants were admitted

Undergraduates 2,268 full-time, 420 part-time. Students come from 45 states and territories, 16 other countries, 66% are from out of state, 22% African American, 2% Asian American or Pacific Islander, 2% Hispanic American, 0.7% Native American, 1% international, 2% transferred in, 73% live on campus. *Retention:* 72% of 2006 full-time freshmen returned.

Freshmen *Admission:* 3,486 applied, 2,015 admitted, 491 enrolled. *Average high school GPA:* 3.12. *Test scores:* SAT critical reading scores over 500: 74%; SAT math scores over 500: 75%; ACT scores over 18: 80%; SAT critical reading scores over 600: 38%; SAT math scores over 600: 29%; ACT scores over 24: 54%; SAT critical reading scores over 700: 9%; SAT math scores over 700: 4%; ACT scores over 30: 14%.

Faculty *Total:* 218, 62% full-time, 55% with terminal degrees. *Student/faculty ratio:* 16:1.

Majors Accounting; African-American/Black studies; art; athletic training; biological and biomedical sciences related; biology/biological sciences; business administration and management; chemistry; computer and information sciences; criminal justice/safety; dramatic/theater arts; economics; elementary education; English; environmental studies; French; geology/earth science; German; health and physical education; health/medical preparatory programs related; history; information science/studies; interdisciplinary studies; international relations and affairs; mathematics; music; peace studies and conflict resolution; philosophy;

physics; political science and government; psychology; religious studies; secondary education; sociology; Spanish; sport and fitness administration/management; women's studies.

Academics *Calendar:* semesters. *Degree:* certificates and bachelor's. *Special study options:* academic remediation for entering students, accelerated degree program, adult/continuing education programs, advanced placement credit, cooperative education, double majors, English as a second language, honors programs, independent study, internships, off-campus study, part-time degree program, services for LD students, student-designed majors, study abroad, summer session for credit. *ROTC:* Army (c), Navy (c), Air Force (c).

Computers on Campus 275 computers/terminals are available on campus for general student use. Students can access the following: computer help desk, free student e-mail accounts, online (class) grades, online (class) registration, online (class) schedules, network storage. Campuswide network is available. 100% of college-owned or -operated housing units are wired for high-speed Internet access. Wireless service is available via libraries, student centers.

Student Life *Housing:* on-campus residence required through junior year. *Options:* coed, men-only, women-only, cooperative, disabled students. Campus housing is university owned. Freshman campus housing is guaranteed. *Activities and organizations:* drama/theater group, student-run newspaper, radio station, choral group, student government, student radio station, student newspaper, Project Community, African-American Cultural Society. *Campus security:* 24-hour emergency response devices and patrols, student patrols, late-night transport/escort service, controlled dormitory access. *Student services:* health clinic, personal/psychological counseling, women's center.

Athletics Member NCAA. All Division III. *Intercollegiate sports:* baseball M/W, basketball M/W, cross-country running M/W, football M, golf M, lacrosse M/W, rugby M (c)/W (c), soccer M/W, softball W, swimming and diving W, tennis M/W, volleyball W. *Intramural sports:* baseball M (c)/W (c), basketball M (c)/W (c), bowling M (c)/W (c), cheerleading W (c), rugby M (c)/W (c), soccer M (c)/W (c), softball M (c)/W (c), table tennis M (c)/W (c), tennis M (c)/W (c), ultimate Frisbee M (c)/W (c), volleyball M (c)/W (c).

Standardized Tests *Recommended:* SAT or ACT (for admission).

Costs (2008–09) *Comprehensive fee:* $33,240 includes full-time tuition ($26,100) and room and board ($7140).

Financial Aid Of all full-time matriculated undergraduates who enrolled in 2007, 1,631 applied for aid, 1,454 were judged to have need, 525 had their need fully met. 160 Federal Work-Study jobs (averaging $1378). 195 state and other part-time jobs (averaging $1285). In 2007, 718 non-need-based awards were made. *Average financial aid package:* $15,596. *Average need-based loan:* $5066. *Average need-based gift aid:* $9296. *Average non-need-based aid:* $6534. *Average indebtedness upon graduation:* $22,780.

Applying *Options:* electronic application, early admission, early action, deferred entrance. *Application fee:* $25. *Required:* essay or personal statement, high school transcript, minimum 2.0 GPA. *Recommended:* minimum 3.0 GPA, 2 letters of recommendation, interview. *Application deadlines:* 2/15 (freshmen), 4/1 (transfers), 1/15 (early action). *Notification:* continuous until 4/1 (freshmen), continuous until 5/1 (transfers), 2/15 (early action).

Freshman Application Contact Ms. Tania Johnson, Associate Director of Admissions, Guilford College, 5800 West Friendly Avenue, Greensboro, NC 27410. *Phone:* 336-316-2100. *Toll-free phone:* 800-992-7759. *Fax:* 336-316-2954. *E-mail:* admission@guilford.edu.

See page 1932 for the College Close-Up.

HERITAGE BIBLE COLLEGE

Dunn, North Carolina **www.heritagebiblecollege.org/**

- **Independent Pentecostal Free Will Baptist** 4-year, founded 1971
- **Small-town** 82-acre campus with easy access to Raleigh-Durham
- **Endowment** $27,000
- **Coed** 84 undergraduate students, 73% full-time, 48% women, 52% men
- **Minimally difficult** entrance level, 83% of applicants were admitted

Undergraduates 61 full-time, 23 part-time. 7% are from out of state, 32% African American, 4% Hispanic American, 4% Native American, 11% transferred in, 23% live on campus. *Retention:* 52% of 2006 full-time freshmen returned.

Freshmen *Admission:* 46 applied, 38 admitted, 11 enrolled.

Faculty *Total:* 17, 24% full-time, 24% with terminal degrees. *Student/faculty ratio:* 20:1.

Majors Christian studies; religious education.

Academics *Calendar:* semesters. *Degrees:* associate and bachelor's. *Special study options:* academic remediation for entering students, adult/continuing education programs, external degree program, independent study, internships, off-campus study, summer session for credit.

Computers on Campus 25 computers/terminals are available on campus for general student use. Students can access the following: free student e-mail accounts, online (class) schedules.

Student Life *Housing options:* coed. Campus housing is university owned. *Activities and organizations:* drama/theater group, choral group. *Campus security:* controlled dormitory access.

Costs (2008–09) *Comprehensive fee:* $7800 includes full-time tuition ($4800), mandatory fees ($600), and room and board ($2400). Part-time tuition: $200 per hour. *Required fees:* $150 per hour part-time. *College room only:* $1440.

Financial Aid Of all full-time matriculated undergraduates who enrolled in 2006, 114 applied for aid, 85 were judged to have need, 85 had their need fully met. 3 Federal Work-Study jobs (averaging $300). In 2006, 10 non-need-based awards were made. *Average percent of need met:* 90%. *Average financial aid package:* $4250. *Average need-based loan:* $3500. *Average need-based gift aid:* $250. *Average non-need-based aid:* $300. *Average indebtedness upon graduation:* $14,554. *Financial aid deadline:* 7/1.

Applying *Application fee:* $25. *Required:* essay or personal statement, high school transcript, letters of recommendation. *Application deadlines:* rolling (freshmen), rolling (transfers).

Freshman Application Contact Mr. Jeff Nichols, Director of Admissions, Heritage Bible College, PO Box 1628, Dunn, NC 28335. *Phone:* 910-892-3178 Ext. 223. *Toll-free phone:* 800-297-6351 Ext. 230. *Fax:* 910-892-1809. *E-mail:* jnichols@heritagebiblecollege.edu.

HIGH POINT UNIVERSITY

High Point, North Carolina **www.highpoint.edu/**

- **Independent United Methodist** comprehensive, founded 1924
- **Suburban** 130-acre campus with easy access to Charlotte
- **Endowment** $47.1 million
- **Coed** 2,746 undergraduate students, 90% full-time, 62% women, 38% men
- **Moderately difficult** entrance level, 73% of applicants were admitted

Undergraduates 2,479 full-time, 267 part-time. Students come from 44 states and territories, 40 other countries, 42% are from out of state, 17% African American, 3% Asian American or Pacific Islander, 3% Hispanic American, 0.6% Native American, 4% international, 5% transferred in, 71% live on campus. *Retention:* 79% of 2006 full-time freshmen returned.

Freshmen *Admission:* 2,546 applied, 1,857 admitted, 685 enrolled. *Average high school GPA:* 3.18. *Test scores:* SAT critical reading scores over 500: 57%; SAT math scores over 500: 61%; ACT scores over 18: 88%; SAT critical reading scores over 600: 14%; SAT math scores over 600: 16%; ACT scores over 24: 26%; SAT critical reading scores over 700: 1%; SAT math scores over 700: 1%; ACT scores over 30: 3%.

Faculty *Total:* 265, 48% full-time, 46% with terminal degrees. *Student/faculty ratio:* 15:1.

Majors Accounting; American studies; art teacher education; athletic training; biology/biological sciences; business administration and management; chemistry; clinical laboratory science/medical technology; community organization and advocacy; computer and information sciences; computer science; creative writing; criminal justice/safety; dramatic/theater arts; education; elementary education; English; fine/studio arts; French; history; human services; information science/studies; interior design; international business/trade/commerce; international relations and affairs; kindergarten/preschool education; kinesiology and exercise science; literature; marketing/marketing management; mass communication/media; mathematics; middle school education; parks, recreation and leisure; parks, recreation and leisure facilities management; philosophy; physical education teaching and coaching; physician assistant; political science and government; pre-dentistry studies; pre-law studies; pre-medical studies; pre-veterinary studies; psychology; religious studies; secondary education; sociology; Spanish; special education; sport and fitness administration/management.

Academics *Calendar:* semesters. *Degrees:* bachelor's, master's, and post-bachelor's certificates. *Special study options:* academic remediation for entering students, accelerated degree program, adult/continuing education programs, advanced placement credit, cooperative education, double majors, English as a second language, honors programs, independent study, internships, off-campus study, part-time degree program, student-designed majors, study abroad, summer session for credit. *ROTC:* Army (c), Air Force (c). *Unusual degree programs:* 3-2 forestry with Duke University; medical technology with Wake Forest University.

Computers on Campus 950 computers/terminals and 950 ports are available on campus for general student use. Students can access the following: campus intranet, computer help desk, free student e-mail accounts, online (class) registration, online (class) schedules. Campuswide network is available. 100% of college-owned or -operated housing units are wired for high-speed Internet access. Wireless service is available via entire campus.

Student Life *Housing:* on-campus residence required through sophomore year. *Options:* coed, men-only, women-only, cooperative, disabled students. Campus housing is university owned and leased by the school. Freshman campus housing is guaranteed. *Activities and organizations:* drama/theater group, student-run newspaper, radio and television station, choral group, student government, Habitat for Humanity, International Club, Student Activities Board, Honors Club, national fraternities, national sororities. *Campus security:* 24-hour emergency response devices and patrols, student patrols, late-night transport/escort service, controlled dormitory access. *Student services:* health clinic, personal/psychological counseling.

Athletics Member NCAA. All Division I. *Intercollegiate sports:* baseball M (s), basketball M (s)/W (s), cross-country running M (s)/W (s), golf M (s), soccer M (s)/W (s), tennis M (s)/W (s), track and field M (s)/W (s), volleyball W (s). *Intramural sports:* basketball M/W, bowling M/W, football M/W, racquetball M/W, soccer M/W, softball M/W, swimming and diving M/W, table tennis W, tennis M/W, track and field M/W, volleyball M/W, water polo M.

Standardized Tests *Required:* SAT or ACT (for admission). *Recommended:* SAT or ACT (for admission), SAT Subject Tests (for admission).

Costs (2008–09) *Comprehensive fee:* $31,000.

Financial Aid Of all full-time matriculated undergraduates who enrolled in 2006, 1,864 applied for aid, 1,292 were judged to have need, 388 had their need fully met. 111 Federal Work-Study jobs (averaging $1500). In 2006, 214 non-need-based awards were made. *Average percent of need met:* 76%. *Average financial aid package:* $15,001. *Average need-based loan:* $4833. *Average need-based gift aid:* $3811. *Average non-need-based aid:* $10,471. *Average indebtedness upon graduation:* $16,850.

Applying *Options:* electronic application, early decision, early action, deferred entrance. *Application fee:* $40. *Required:* high school transcript, minimum 2.0 GPA, 2 letters of recommendation. *Recommended:* essay or personal statement, minimum 3.0 GPA, interview. *Application deadlines:* 8/15 (freshmen), 8/15 (transfers), 11/16 (early action). *Early decision deadline:* 11/6. *Notification:* continuous until 8/15 (freshmen), continuous (transfers), 11/27 (early decision), 12/17 (early action).

Freshman Application Contact Ms. Jessie McIlrath-Carter, Director of Admissions, High Point University, University Station 3187, High Point, NC 27262-3598. *Phone:* 336-841-9148. *Toll-free phone:* 800-345-6993. *Fax:* 336-888-6382. *E-mail:* jmcilrat@highpoint.edu.

See page 1934 for the College Close-Up.

JOHNSON & WALES UNIVERSITY

Charlotte, North Carolina **www.jwucharlotte.org/**

- **Independent** 4-year, founded 2004
- **Coed**
- **Minimally difficult** entrance level

Faculty *Student/faculty ratio:* 28:1.

Academics *Calendar:* quarters. *Degrees:* associate and bachelor's.

Student Life *Campus security:* 24-hour emergency response devices and patrols, late-night transport/escort service, controlled dormitory access.

Standardized Tests *Required for some:* SAT or ACT (for admission). *Recommended:* SAT or ACT (for admission).

Costs (2008–09) *Comprehensive fee:* $31,477 includes full-time tuition ($21,297), mandatory fees ($1288), and room and board ($8892). Part-time tuition: $394 per quarter hour.

Financial Aid Of all full-time matriculated undergraduates who enrolled in 2005, 1,960 applied for aid, 1,760 were judged to have need, 48 had their need fully met. In 2005, 250 non-need-based awards were made. *Average percent of need met:* 64. *Average financial aid package:* $13,109. *Average need-based loan:* $5857. *Average need-based gift aid:* $5178. *Average non-need-based aid:* $4348.

Applying *Options:* electronic application, deferred entrance. *Required:* high school transcript. *Required for some:* letters of recommendation, interview. *Recommended:* minimum 2.0 GPA.

Freshman Application Contact Director of Admissions, Johnson & Wales University, 901 West Trade Street, Suite 175, Charlotte, NC 28202. *Phone:* 866-598-2427. *Toll-free phone:* 866-598-2427. *Fax:* 980-598-1111. *E-mail:* admissions.clt@jwu.edu.

JOHNSON C. SMITH UNIVERSITY

Charlotte, North Carolina **www.jcsu.edu/**

- **Independent** 4-year, founded 1867
- **Urban** 100-acre campus
- **Coed** 1,463 undergraduate students, 97% full-time, 58% women, 42% men
- **Moderately difficult** entrance level, 46% of applicants were admitted

Undergraduates 1,426 full-time, 37 part-time. Students come from 34 states and territories, 74% are from out of state, 99% African American, 0.1% Hispanic American, 0.1% Native American, 0.1% international, 2% transferred in, 74% live on campus. *Retention:* 64% of 2006 full-time freshmen returned.

Freshmen *Admission:* 5,299 applied, 2,436 admitted, 502 enrolled. *Average high school GPA:* 2.80. *Test scores:* SAT critical reading scores over 500: 13%; SAT math scores over 500: 18%.

Faculty *Total:* 120, 84% full-time, 65% with terminal degrees. *Student/faculty ratio:* 14:1.

Majors Biological and physical sciences; biology/biological sciences; business administration and management; chemistry; computer and information sciences; computer engineering; criminology; economics; elementary education; English; French; health and physical education related; health teacher education; history; information technology; liberal arts and sciences/liberal studies; mass communication/media; mathematics; mathematics teacher education; music; music management and merchandising; natural sciences; physical education teaching and coaching; political science and government; psychology; social sciences; social studies teacher education; social work; Spanish; sport and fitness administration/management.

Academics *Calendar:* semesters. *Degree:* bachelor's. *Special study options:* adult/continuing education programs, advanced placement credit, cooperative education, double majors, freshman honors college, honors programs, independent study, internships, off-campus study, part-time degree program, services for LD students, study abroad, summer session for credit. *ROTC:* Army (b), Air Force (c). *Unusual degree programs:* 3-2 engineering with University of North Carolina at Charlotte, Florida Agricultural and Mechanical University.

Computers on Campus 335 computers/terminals are available on campus for general student use. Students can access the following: campus intranet, computer help desk, free student e-mail accounts, online (class) grades, online (class) registration, online (class) schedules. Campuswide network is available. 100% of college-owned or -operated housing units are wired for high-speed Internet access. Wireless service is available via entire campus.

Student Life *Housing:* on-campus residence required for freshman year. *Options:* coed, men-only, women-only. Campus housing is university owned. Freshman campus housing is guaranteed. *Activities and organizations:* drama/theater group, student-run newspaper, choral group, marching band, Religious Life Programs, Communication Arts Student Association, Golden Bull Activities Committee, National Pan-Hellenic Council, Student Ambassadors, national fraternities, national sororities. *Campus security:* 24-hour emergency response devices and patrols, late-night transport/escort service. *Student services:* health clinic, personal/psychological counseling.

Athletics Member NCAA. All Division II. *Intercollegiate sports:* basketball M (s)/W (s), bowling W (s), cheerleading W, cross-country running M (s)/W (s), football M (s), golf M (s)/W (s), softball W (s), tennis M (s)/W (s), track and field M (s)/W (s), volleyball W (s). *Intramural sports:* basketball M/W, table tennis M/W, track and field M/W.

Standardized Tests *Required:* SAT or ACT (for admission).

Costs (2007–08) *Comprehensive fee:* $21,886 includes full-time tuition ($13,361), mandatory fees ($2393), and room and board ($6132). Full-time tuition and fees vary according to course load. Part-time tuition: $361 per credit hour. Part-time tuition and fees vary according to course load. *Required fees:* $253 per term part-time. *College room only:* $3529. Room and board charges vary according to board plan and housing facility. *Payment plan:* installment. *Waivers:* employees or children of employees.

Financial Aid Of all full-time matriculated undergraduates who enrolled in 2006, 1,239 applied for aid, 954 were judged to have need, 30 had their need fully met. *Average percent of need met:* 60%. *Average financial aid package:* $9725. *Average need-based loan:* $5500. *Average need-based gift aid:* $3000. *Average indebtedness upon graduation:* $25,000.

Applying *Options:* electronic application, early admission, deferred entrance. *Application fee:* $25. *Required:* high school transcript, minimum 2.2 GPA. *Required for some:* letters of recommendation. *Recommended:* essay or personal statement, interview. *Notification:* continuous (freshmen), continuous (transfers).

Freshman Application Contact Ms. Jocelyn Biggs, Director of Admissions, Johnson C. Smith University, 100 Beatties Ford Road, Charlotte, NC 28216. *Phone:* 704-378-1010. *Toll-free phone:* 800-782-7303. *Fax:* 704-378-1242. *E-mail:* admissions@jcsu.edu.

JOHN WESLEY COLLEGE

High Point, North Carolina **www.johnwesley.edu/**

- **Independent interdenominational** 4-year, founded 1932
- **Urban** 24-acre campus
- **Coed** 107 undergraduate students, 70% full-time, 33% women, 67% men
- **Minimally difficult** entrance level, 100% of applicants were admitted

Undergraduates 75 full-time, 32 part-time. Students come from 10 states and territories, 9% are from out of state, 25% African American, 2% Asian American or Pacific Islander, 3% Hispanic American, 0.9% Native American, 94% transferred in, 14% live on campus. *Retention:* 57% of 2006 full-time freshmen returned.

Freshmen *Admission:* 15 applied, 15 admitted, 6 enrolled. *Average high school GPA:* 2.5.

Faculty *Total:* 21, 48% full-time, 38% with terminal degrees. *Student/faculty ratio:* 12:1.

Majors Biblical studies; business administration and management; divinity/ministry; elementary education; liberal arts and sciences/liberal studies; pastoral studies/counseling; psychology; religious education; religious studies; theology.

Academics *Calendar:* semesters. *Degrees:* certificates, associate, and bachelor's. *Special study options:* academic remediation for entering students, adult/continuing education programs, advanced placement credit, distance learning, double majors, external degree program, independent study, internships, off-campus study, part-time degree program, summer session for credit.

Computers on Campus 7 computers/terminals are available on campus for general student use.

Student Life *Housing options:* men-only, women-only. *Activities and organizations:* student-run newspaper, choral group, Student Government, Travel Team, Praise Band.

Costs (2007–08) *Tuition:* $10,114 full-time, $465 per semester hour part-time. Full-time tuition and fees vary according to course load. Part-time tuition and fees vary according to course load. *Required fees:* $730 full-time, $365 per term part-time. *Room only:* $2344. Room and board charges vary according to housing facility. *Payment plan:* installment. *Waivers:* employees or children of employees.

Financial Aid Of all full-time matriculated undergraduates who enrolled in 2007, 125 applied for aid. 5 Federal Work-Study jobs (averaging $3500). In 2007, 2 non-need-based awards were made. *Average percent of need met:* 53%. *Average financial aid package:* $8600. *Average need-based loan:* $4000. *Average need-based gift aid:* $2050. *Average non-need-based aid:* $1000. *Average indebtedness upon graduation:* $15,000.

Applying *Options:* electronic application, early admission, deferred entrance. *Application fee:* $35. *Required:* high school transcript, 2 letters of recommendation, interview. *Recommended:* minimum 2.0 GPA. *Application deadlines:* 8/1 (freshmen), 8/1 (transfers). *Notification:* continuous until 8/10 (freshmen), continuous until 8/10 (transfers).

Freshman Application Contact Amanda Ziemba, Admissions Officer, John Wesley College, 2314 North Centennial Street, High Point, NC 27265-3197. *Phone:* 336-889-2262 Ext. 127. *Fax:* 336-889-2261. *E-mail:* admissions@johnwesley.edu.

LEES-MCRAE COLLEGE

Banner Elk, North Carolina **www.lmc.edu/**

- **Independent** 4-year, founded 1900, affiliated with Presbyterian Church (U.S.A.)
- **Rural** 400-acre campus
- **Endowment** $19.3 million
- **Coed** 882 undergraduate students, 98% full-time, 60% women, 40% men
- **Minimally difficult** entrance level, 74% of applicants were admitted

Undergraduates 863 full-time, 19 part-time. Students come from 31 states and territories, 20 other countries, 35% are from out of state, 5% African American, 0.7% Asian American or Pacific Islander, 3% Hispanic American, 0.2% Native American, 3% international, 17% transferred in, 54% live on campus. *Retention:* 63% of 2006 full-time freshmen returned.

Freshmen *Admission:* 821 applied, 606 admitted, 203 enrolled. *Average high school GPA:* 3.14. *Test scores:* SAT critical reading scores over 500: 42%; SAT math scores over 500: 53%; ACT scores over 18: 79%; SAT critical reading scores over 600: 10%; SAT math scores over 600: 13%; ACT scores over 24: 19%; SAT critical reading scores over 700: 2%.

Faculty *Total:* 52, 100% full-time, 56% with terminal degrees.

Majors Athletic training; biological and physical sciences; biology/biological sciences; business administration and management; criminal justice/law enforcement administration; dramatic/theater arts; education; elementary education; English; entrepreneurship; environmental studies; history; humanities; information science/studies; interdisciplinary studies; international relations and affairs; liberal arts and sciences/liberal studies; mass communication/media; mathematics; natural sciences; physical education teaching and coaching; pre-law studies; pre-medical studies; pre-veterinary studies; psychology; religious studies; social sciences; sociology; wildlife biology.

Academics *Calendar:* semesters. *Degree:* bachelor's. *Special study options:* academic remediation for entering students, adult/continuing education programs, advanced placement credit, double majors, external degree program, honors programs, independent study, internships, off-campus study, part-time degree program, services for LD students, student-designed majors, study abroad, summer session for credit. *ROTC:* Army (c). *Unusual degree programs:* 3-2 forestry with Duke University.

Computers on Campus 60 computers/terminals are available on campus for general student use. Campuswide network is available.

Student Life *Housing:* on-campus residence required through sophomore year. *Options:* coed, men-only, women-only, disabled students. Campus housing is university owned. *Activities and organizations:* drama/theater group, Student Government Association, Students Against a Vanishing Environment, CATCH, Order of the Tower, Student Ambassadors. *Campus security:* 24-hour patrols. *Student services:* health clinic, personal/psychological counseling.

Athletics Member NCAA. All Division II. *Intercollegiate sports:* basketball M (s)/W (s), cross-country running M (s)/W (s), golf M (s), lacrosse M (s)/W (s), soccer M (s)/W (s), softball W (s), tennis M (s)/W (s), track and field M (s)/W (s), volleyball M (s)/W (s). *Intramural sports:* basketball M/W, cross-country running M/W, fencing M/W, football M, golf M, lacrosse M (c), skiing (downhill) M/W, soccer M/W, softball M/W, swimming and diving M/W, table tennis M/W, tennis M/W, track and field M/W, volleyball M/W, weight lifting M.

Costs (2007–08) *Comprehensive fee:* $26,000 includes full-time tuition ($19,500) and room and board ($6500). *Payment plan:* installment. *Waivers:* employees or children of employees.

Financial Aid Of all full-time matriculated undergraduates who enrolled in 2002, 826 applied for aid, 508 were judged to have need, 90 had their need fully met. 240 Federal Work-Study jobs (averaging $1400). 200 state and other part-time jobs (averaging $1400). In 2002, 366 non-need-based awards were made. *Average percent of need met:* 91%. *Average financial aid package:* $9871. *Average need-based loan:* $3574. *Average need-based gift aid:* $4185. *Average non-need-based aid:* $4500. *Average indebtedness upon graduation:* $9234.

Applying *Options:* electronic application, deferred entrance. *Required:* high school transcript, minimum 2.0 GPA. *Required for some:* interview. *Recommended:* essay or personal statement, letters of recommendation. *Application deadlines:* rolling (freshmen), rolling (transfers). *Notification:* continuous (freshmen), continuous (transfers).

Freshman Application Contact Mr. Bill Sliwa, Lees-McRae College, PO Box 128, Banner Elk, NC 28604-0128. *Phone:* 828-898-8723. *Toll-free phone:* 800-280-4562. *Fax:* 828-898-8707. *E-mail:* admissions@lmc.edu.

See page 1936 for the College Close-Up.

LENOIR-RHYNE COLLEGE

Hickory, North Carolina **www.lrc.edu/**

- **Independent Lutheran** comprehensive, founded 1891
- **Small-town** 100-acre campus with easy access to Charlotte
- **Endowment** $58.9 million
- **Coed** 1,472 undergraduate students, 89% full-time, 63% women, 37% men
- **Moderately difficult** entrance level, 84% of applicants were admitted

Undergraduates 1,303 full-time, 169 part-time. Students come from 38 states and territories, 8 other countries, 20% are from out of state, 8% African American, 3% Asian American or Pacific Islander, 1% Hispanic American, 0.3% Native American, 0.8% international, 8% transferred in, 58% live on campus. *Retention:* 72% of 2006 full-time freshmen returned.

Freshmen *Admission:* 1,770 applied, 1,478 admitted, 367 enrolled. *Average high school GPA:* 3.71. *Test scores:* SAT critical reading scores over 500: 54%; SAT math scores over 500: 68%; ACT scores over 18: 91%; SAT critical reading

scores over 600: 15%; SAT math scores over 600: 22%; ACT scores over 24: 29%; SAT critical reading scores over 700: 2%; SAT math scores over 700: 3%; ACT scores over 30: 2%.

Faculty *Total:* 163, 57% full-time. *Student/faculty ratio:* 13:1.

Majors Accounting; adult and continuing education; arts management; art teacher education; athletic training; biology/biological sciences; biology teacher education; business administration and management; business teacher education; chemical technology; chemistry; chemistry teacher education; child development; clinical laboratory science/medical technology; communication/speech communication and rhetoric; computer and information sciences; counselor education/school counseling and guidance; dramatic/theater arts; economics; education; elementary education; engineering technology; English; English as a second/foreign language (teaching); English/language arts teacher education; environmental studies; finance; forestry; French; German; graphic design; history; history teacher education; human services; information science/studies; international business/trade/commerce; international relations and affairs; kindergarten/preschool education; kinesiology and exercise science; Latin; liberal arts and sciences/liberal studies; management information systems; management science; marketing/marketing management; mathematics; mathematics teacher education; middle school education; music; music performance; music teacher education; nursing (registered nurse training); occupational therapy; philosophy; physical education teaching and coaching; physician assistant; physics; political science and government; pre-law studies; pre-medical studies; psychology; psychology teacher education; religious education; religious/sacred music; religious studies; science teacher education; secondary education; social science teacher education; social studies teacher education; sociology; Spanish; special education (hearing impaired); sport and fitness administration/management.

Academics *Calendar:* semesters. *Degrees:* bachelor's and master's. *Special study options:* academic remediation for entering students, accelerated degree program, adult/continuing education programs, advanced placement credit, cooperative education, distance learning, double majors, English as a second language, honors programs, independent study, internships, part-time degree program, services for LD students, student-designed majors, study abroad, summer session for credit. *ROTC:* Army (c). *Unusual degree programs:* 3-2 engineering with North Carolina State University, University of North Carolina at Charlotte, Clemson University, North Carolina Agricultural and Technical State University; forestry with Duke University.

Computers on Campus 112 computers/terminals and 45 ports are available on campus for general student use. Students can access the following: campus intranet, computer help desk, free student e-mail accounts. Campuswide network is available. 100% of college-owned or -operated housing units are wired for high-speed Internet access. Wireless service is available via entire campus.

Student Life *Housing:* on-campus residence required through junior year. *Options:* coed, men-only, women-only, disabled students. Campus housing is university owned. Freshman campus housing is guaranteed. *Activities and organizations:* drama/theater group, student-run newspaper, radio station, choral group, Student Government Association, religious clubs, Outdoors and Service Club, Playmakers, Music clubs, national fraternities, national sororities. *Campus security:* 24-hour emergency response devices and patrols, late-night transport/escort service, controlled dormitory access. *Student services:* health clinic, personal/psychological counseling.

Athletics Member NCAA. All Division II. *Intercollegiate sports:* baseball M (s), basketball M (s)/W (s), cheerleading M (s)/W (s), cross-country running M (s)/W (s), football M (s), golf M (s)/W (s), soccer M (s)/W (s), softball W (s), swimming and diving W (s), tennis M (s)/W (s), track and field M (s)/W (s), volleyball W (s). *Intramural sports:* basketball M/W, football M/W, lacrosse M, soccer M/W, softball M/W, ultimate Frisbee M/W.

Standardized Tests *Required:* SAT or ACT (for admission).

Costs (2008–09) *Comprehensive fee:* $31,220 includes full-time tuition ($23,070) and room and board ($8150). Part-time tuition: $960 per credit hour.

Financial Aid Of all full-time matriculated undergraduates who enrolled in 2006, 1,406 applied for aid, 1,361 were judged to have need, 281 had their need fully met. 151 Federal Work-Study jobs (averaging $682). 166 state and other part-time jobs (averaging $728). In 2006, 58 non-need-based awards were made. *Average percent of need met:* 41%. *Average financial aid package:* $14,193. *Average need-based loan:* $3747. *Average need-based gift aid:* $11,550. *Average non-need-based aid:* $7076. *Average indebtedness upon graduation:* $27,562.

Applying *Options:* electronic application, early admission, early action, deferred entrance. *Application fee:* $35. *Required:* high school transcript, minimum 2.5 GPA. *Recommended:* interview. *Application deadlines:* 8/15 (freshmen), 8/15 (transfers), 8/1 (early action). *Notification:* continuous (freshmen), continuous (transfers).

Director of Admissions Karen Feezor, Lenoir-Rhyne College, PO Box 7227, Hickory, NC 28603. *Phone:* 828-328-7300. *Toll-free phone:* 800-277-5721. *Fax:* 828-328-7378. *E-mail:* admission@lrc.edu.

LIVINGSTONE COLLEGE

Salisbury, North Carolina **www.livingstone.edu/**

- **Independent** 4-year, founded 1879, affiliated with African Methodist Episcopal Zion Church
- **Small-town** 45-acre campus
- **Endowment** $1.1 million
- **Coed** 960 undergraduate students, 99% full-time, 44% women, 56% men
- **Minimally difficult** entrance level, 98% of applicants were admitted

Undergraduates 947 full-time, 13 part-time. Students come from 34 states and territories, 3 other countries, 43% are from out of state, 94% African American, 0.2% Asian American or Pacific Islander, 0.3% Hispanic American, 0.2% Native American, 0.8% international, 60% live on campus.

Freshmen *Admission:* 2,093 applied, 2,051 admitted, 331 enrolled. *Average high school GPA:* 2.32. *Test scores:* SAT critical reading scores over 500: 1%; SAT math scores over 500: 16%; SAT writing scores over 500: 7%; ACT scores over 18: 21%; ACT scores over 24: 3%.

Faculty *Total:* 73, 70% full-time, 27% with terminal degrees. *Student/faculty ratio:* 16:1.

Majors Accounting; biology/biological sciences; business administration and management; chemistry; computer science; education; elementary education; English; history; human services; information science/studies; kindergarten/preschool education; mathematics; music; music teacher education; physical education teaching and coaching; political science and government; psychology; social sciences; social work; sociology; sport and fitness administration/management.

Academics *Calendar:* semesters. *Degree:* bachelor's. *Special study options:* academic remediation for entering students, adult/continuing education programs, advanced placement credit, cooperative education, double majors, honors programs, internships, part-time degree program. *ROTC:* Army (c). *Unusual degree programs:* 3-2 engineering with North Carolina Agricultural and Technical State University; law, history, political science with St. John's University.

Computers on Campus 100 computers/terminals are available on campus for general student use. Students can access the following: free student e-mail accounts, online (class) grades, online (class) schedules. Campuswide network is available. 100% of college-owned or -operated housing units are wired for high-speed Internet access. Wireless service is available via computer centers, computer labs, libraries.

Student Life *Housing:* on-campus residence required for freshman year. *Options:* men-only, women-only. Campus housing is university owned. Freshman applicants given priority for college housing. *Activities and organizations:* drama/theater group, choral group, marching band, Greek Organizations, Modeling Troups, Choirs, Band, Rotary and Optimist Clubs (Community), national fraternities, national sororities. *Campus security:* 24-hour emergency response devices and patrols, late-night transport/escort service, controlled dormitory access. *Student services:* health clinic, personal/psychological counseling.

Athletics Member NCAA. All Division II. *Intercollegiate sports:* basketball M (s)/W (s), bowling W, cross-country running M/W, football M (s), softball W (s), tennis W (s), track and field M (s)/W (s), volleyball W (s).

Standardized Tests *Required:* SAT or ACT (for admission).

Costs (2007–08) *Comprehensive fee:* $18,115 includes full-time tuition ($10,279), mandatory fees ($2195), and room and board ($5641). Part-time tuition: $428 per credit hour. *Required fees:* $79 per credit hour part-time. *College room only:* $2501. *Payment plan:* installment. *Waivers:* employees or children of employees.

Applying *Options:* deferred entrance. *Application fee:* $25. *Required:* high school transcript, minimum 2.0 GPA. *Application deadlines:* rolling (freshmen), rolling (transfers). *Notification:* continuous (freshmen), continuous (transfers).

Freshman Application Contact Livingstone College, 701 West Monroe Street, Salisbury, NC 28144. *Phone:* 704-216-6001. *Toll-free phone:* 800-835-3435. *Fax:* 704-216-6215. *E-mail:* admissions@livingstone.edu.

MARS HILL COLLEGE

Mars Hill, North Carolina **www.mhc.edu/**

- **Independent Baptist** 4-year, founded 1856
- **Small-town** 194-acre campus
- **Endowment** $34.0 million
- **Coed**
- **Moderately difficult** entrance level

Faculty *Student/faculty ratio:* 12:1.

Academics *Calendar:* semesters. *Degree:* bachelor's.
Student Life *Campus security:* 24-hour emergency response devices and patrols, late-night transport/escort service, controlled dormitory access.
Athletics Member NCAA. All Division II.
Standardized Tests *Required:* SAT or ACT (for admission).
Costs (2007–08) *Comprehensive fee:* $25,274 includes full-time tuition ($17,024), mandatory fees ($1788), and room and board ($6462). Part-time tuition: $624 per hour. *College room only:* $3150.
Financial Aid Of all full-time matriculated undergraduates who enrolled in 2006, 938 applied for aid, 859 were judged to have need, 171 had their need fully met. 225 Federal Work-Study jobs (averaging $1095). 3 state and other part-time jobs (averaging $1250). In 2006, 65 non-need-based awards were made. *Average percent of need met:* 70. *Average financial aid package:* $11,536. *Average need-based loan:* $3448. *Average need-based gift aid:* $8813. *Average non-need-based aid:* $11,141. *Average indebtedness upon graduation:* $9518.
Applying *Options:* early admission, deferred entrance. *Application fee:* $25. *Required:* high school transcript, minimum 2.0 GPA. *Required for some:* interview. *Recommended:* minimum 3.0 GPA.
Freshman Application Contact Mr. Bob McLendon, Vice President of Administration, Mars Hill College, PO Box 370, Mars Hill, NC 28754. *Phone:* 828-689-1201. *Toll-free phone:* 866-MHC-4-YOU. *Fax:* 828-689-1473. *E-mail:* admissions@mhc.edu.

MEREDITH COLLEGE
Raleigh, North Carolina www.meredith.edu/

- **Independent** comprehensive, founded 1891
- **Urban** 225-acre campus
- **Endowment** $85.6 million
- **Undergraduate: women only; graduate: coed** 2,039 undergraduate students, 87% full-time, 100% women, 0% men
- **Moderately difficult** entrance level, 88% of applicants were admitted

Undergraduates 1,767 full-time, 272 part-time. Students come from 29 states and territories, 12 other countries, 9% are from out of state, 11% African American, 2% Asian American or Pacific Islander, 2% Hispanic American, 0.3% Native American, 0.9% international, 7% transferred in, 50% live on campus. *Retention:* 74% of 2006 full-time freshmen returned.
Freshmen *Admission:* 1,205 applied, 1,056 admitted, 464 enrolled. *Average high school GPA:* 3.25. *Test scores:* SAT critical reading scores over 500: 61%; SAT math scores over 500: 60%; ACT scores over 18: 91%; SAT critical reading scores over 600: 19%; SAT math scores over 600: 15%; ACT scores over 24: 23%; SAT critical reading scores over 700: 3%; SAT math scores over 700: 1%; ACT scores over 30: 4%.
Faculty *Total:* 292, 48% full-time, 59% with terminal degrees. *Student/faculty ratio:* 10:1.
Majors Accounting; art teacher education; biology/biological sciences; business administration and management; chemistry; child development; communication/speech communication and rhetoric; computer and information sciences; computer science; dance; dietetics; drama and dance teacher education; dramatic/theater arts; dramatic/theater arts and stagecraft related; economics; English; environmental science; environmental studies; family and consumer sciences/human sciences; fashion/apparel design; fashion merchandising; fine/studio arts; French; graphic design; health/medical preparatory programs related; history; interior design; international/global studies; international relations and affairs; kinesiology and exercise science; mass communication/media; mathematics; molecular biology; multi-/interdisciplinary studies related; music; music pedagogy; music performance; music teacher education; music theory and composition; physical education teaching and coaching; political science and government; psychology; public/applied history and archival administration; religious studies; social work; sociology; Spanish; women's studies.
Academics *Calendar:* semesters. *Degrees:* bachelor's, master's, and post-bachelor's certificates. *Special study options:* academic remediation for entering students, accelerated degree program, adult/continuing education programs, advanced placement credit, cooperative education, double majors, honors programs, independent study, internships, off-campus study, part-time degree program, services for LD students, student-designed majors, study abroad, summer session for credit. *ROTC:* Army (c), Air Force (c). *Unusual degree programs:* 3-2 engineering with North Carolina State University (Meredith 1st 3 years, NCSU last 2 years).
Computers on Campus 140 computers/terminals are available on campus for general student use. Students can access the following: computer help desk, online (class) registration, laptop computers for full-time students. Campuswide network is available. 100% of college-owned or -operated housing units are wired for high-speed Internet access. Wireless service is available via classrooms, computer labs, dorm rooms, learning centers, libraries, student centers.
Student Life *Housing:* on-campus residence required through sophomore year. *Options:* women-only. Campus housing is university owned. Freshman campus housing is guaranteed. *Activities and organizations:* drama/theater group, student-run newspaper, choral group, Student Government Association, Entertainment Association, Recreation Association, Class Organizations, choral groups. *Campus security:* 24-hour emergency response devices and patrols, late-night transport/escort service, controlled dormitory access, self-defense instruction. *Student services:* health clinic, personal/psychological counseling.
Athletics Member NCAA. All Division III. *Intercollegiate sports:* basketball W, cross-country running W, soccer W, softball W, tennis W, volleyball W. *Intramural sports:* swimming and diving W (c).
Standardized Tests *Required:* SAT or ACT (for admission). *Required for some:* SAT Subject Tests (for admission).
Costs (2008–09) *Comprehensive fee:* $30,290 includes full-time tuition ($23,500), mandatory fees ($50), and room and board ($6740). Part-time tuition: $615 per credit hour. *Required fees:* $25 per term part-time. *College room only:* $3370.
Financial Aid Of all full-time matriculated undergraduates who enrolled in 2006, 1,280 applied for aid, 1,096 were judged to have need, 167 had their need fully met. 132 Federal Work-Study jobs (averaging $1284). 316 state and other part-time jobs (averaging $1292). In 2006, 110 non-need-based awards were made. *Average percent of need met:* 73%. *Average financial aid package:* $15,027. *Average need-based loan:* $3909. *Average need-based gift aid:* $11,150. *Average non-need-based aid:* $5564. *Average indebtedness upon graduation:* $18,962.
Applying *Options:* electronic application, early admission, early decision, deferred entrance. *Application fee:* $40. *Required:* high school transcript, minimum 2.0 GPA, 2 letters of recommendation. *Required for some:* essay or personal statement, interview. *Application deadlines:* 2/15 (freshmen), 2/15 (transfers). *Early decision deadline:* 10/15. *Notification:* continuous (freshmen), continuous (transfers), 11/1 (early decision).
Freshman Application Contact Ms. Heidi Fletcher, Director of Admissions, Meredith College, 3800 Hillsborough Street, Raleigh, NC 27607-5298. *Phone:* 919-760-8581. *Toll-free phone:* 800-MEREDITH. *Fax:* 919-760-2348. *E-mail:* admissions@meredith.edu.

See page 1938 for the College Close-Up.

METHODIST UNIVERSITY
Fayetteville, North Carolina www.methodist.edu/

- **Independent United Methodist** comprehensive, founded 1956
- **Suburban** 600-acre campus with easy access to Raleigh-Durham
- **Endowment** $15.6 million
- **Coed** 1,996 undergraduate students, 85% full-time, 46% women, 54% men
- **Moderately difficult** entrance level, 73% of applicants were admitted

Undergraduates 1,701 full-time, 295 part-time. Students come from 44 states and territories, 31 other countries, 48% are from out of state, 19% African American, 2% Asian American or Pacific Islander, 5% Hispanic American, 1% Native American, 4% international, 10% transferred in, 57% live on campus. *Retention:* 67% of 2006 full-time freshmen returned.
Freshmen *Admission:* 2,484 applied, 1,820 admitted, 437 enrolled. *Average high school GPA:* 3.25. *Test scores:* SAT critical reading scores over 500: 41%; SAT math scores over 500: 54%; SAT writing scores over 500: 39%; ACT scores over 18: 84%; SAT critical reading scores over 600: 7%; SAT math scores over 600: 15%; SAT writing scores over 600: 6%; ACT scores over 24: 20%; SAT critical reading scores over 700: 1%; SAT math scores over 700: 1%; ACT scores over 30: 3%.
Faculty *Total:* 213, 60% full-time, 83% with terminal degrees. *Student/faculty ratio:* 12:1.
Majors Accounting; Army R.O.T.C./military science; art; art teacher education; athletic training; behavioral sciences; biblical studies; biological and physical sciences; biology/biological sciences; business administration and management; chemistry; computer science; creative writing; criminal justice/law enforcement administration; dramatic/theater arts; economics; education; education (K-12); elementary education; English; finance; French; German; health/health care administration; history; hospitality and recreation marketing; international relations and affairs; kindergarten/preschool education; legal studies; liberal arts and sciences/liberal studies; marketing research; mass communication/media; mathematics; music; music management and merchandising; music teacher education; parks, recreation and leisure facilities management; philosophy; physical education teaching and coaching; physician assistant; political science and government;

pre-dentistry studies; pre-engineering; pre-law studies; pre-medical studies; pre-veterinary studies; psychology; religious education; religious studies; science teacher education; secondary education; social work; sociology; Spanish; special education; sport and fitness administration/management.

Academics *Calendar:* semesters. *Degrees:* associate, bachelor's, and master's. *Special study options:* academic remediation for entering students, accelerated degree program, adult/continuing education programs, advanced placement credit, cooperative education, distance learning, double majors, English as a second language, honors programs, independent study, internships, part-time degree program, services for LD students, study abroad, summer session for credit. *ROTC:* Army (b), Air Force (c).

Computers on Campus 200 computers/terminals are available on campus for general student use. Students can access the following: campus intranet, free student e-mail accounts, online (class) schedules. Campuswide network is available. 100% of college-owned or -operated housing units are wired for high-speed Internet access. Wireless service is available via classrooms, computer labs, libraries, student centers.

Student Life *Housing:* on-campus residence required through sophomore year. *Options:* coed, men-only, women-only. Campus housing is university owned. Freshman campus housing is guaranteed. *Activities and organizations:* drama/theater group, student-run newspaper, choral group, marching band, Student Activities Committee, Student Government Association, Student Education Association, Fellowship of Christian Athletes, Residence Hall Association, national fraternities, national sororities. *Campus security:* 24-hour emergency response devices and patrols, student patrols, late-night transport/escort service, controlled dormitory access, regular patrol by county sheriff department. *Student services:* health clinic, personal/psychological counseling.

Athletics Member NCAA. All Division III. *Intercollegiate sports:* baseball M, basketball M/W, cheerleading M/W, cross-country running M/W, football M, golf M/W, ice hockey M (c), lacrosse M (c)/W, soccer M/W, softball W, tennis M/W, track and field M/W, volleyball W. *Intramural sports:* basketball M/W, bowling M/W, football M/W, golf M/W, racquetball M/W, soccer M/W, softball M/W, table tennis M/W, tennis M/W, volleyball M/W, weight lifting M/W.

Standardized Tests *Required:* SAT or ACT (for admission).

Costs (2008–09) *Comprehensive fee:* $29,594 includes full-time tuition ($21,520), mandatory fees ($424), and room and board ($7650). Part-time tuition: $650 per semester hour. *College room only:* $4086.

Financial Aid Of all full-time matriculated undergraduates who enrolled in 2006, 1,699 applied for aid, 1,220 were judged to have need, 197 had their need fully met. 779 Federal Work-Study jobs (averaging $625). 124 state and other part-time jobs (averaging $625). In 2006, 160 non-need-based awards were made. *Average percent of need met:* 74%. *Average financial aid package:* $13,170. *Average need-based loan:* $3373. *Average need-based gift aid:* $7133. *Average non-need-based aid:* $4153. *Average indebtedness upon graduation:* $24,716.

Applying *Options:* deferred entrance. *Application fee:* $25. *Required:* high school transcript. *Required for some:* essay or personal statement, letters of recommendation, interview. *Recommended:* interview. *Application deadlines:* rolling (freshmen), rolling (out-of-state freshmen), rolling (transfers). *Notification:* continuous until 8/15 (freshmen), continuous until 8/15 (transfers).

Freshman Application Contact Mr. Jamie Legg, Director of Admissions, Methodist University, 5400 Ramsey Street, Fayetteville, NC 28311. *Phone:* 910-630-7027. *Toll-free phone:* 800-488-7110 Ext. 7027. *Fax:* 910-630-7285. *E-mail:* admissions@methodist.edu.

MONTREAT COLLEGE

Montreat, North Carolina — www.montreat.edu/

- **Independent** comprehensive, founded 1916, affiliated with Presbyterian Church (U.S.A.)
- **Small-town** 112-acre campus
- **Endowment** $9.7 million
- **Coed**
- **Moderately difficult** entrance level

Faculty *Student/faculty ratio:* 17:1.

Academics *Calendar:* semesters. *Degrees:* associate, bachelor's, and master's.

Student Life *Campus security:* 24-hour emergency response devices and patrols, controlled dormitory access.

Athletics Member NAIA.

Standardized Tests *Required:* SAT or ACT (for admission).

Costs (2007–08) *Comprehensive fee:* $23,467 includes full-time tuition ($17,316), mandatory fees ($365), and room and board ($5786). Full-time tuition and fees vary according to course load, program, and reciprocity agreements. Part-time tuition: $480 per credit hour. Part-time tuition and fees vary according to course load, program, and reciprocity agreements. *Required fees:* $100 per year part-time. *Room and board:* Room and board charges vary according to board plan.

Financial Aid Of all full-time matriculated undergraduates who enrolled in 2006, 427 applied for aid, 252 were judged to have need. 76 Federal Work-Study jobs (averaging $1431). 35 state and other part-time jobs (averaging $1518). In 2006, 456 non-need-based awards were made. *Average percent of need met:* 81. *Average financial aid package:* $14,051. *Average need-based loan:* $3071. *Average need-based gift aid:* $5310. *Average non-need-based aid:* $5276. *Average indebtedness upon graduation:* $17,682.

Applying *Options:* early admission, deferred entrance. *Application fee:* $30. *Required:* essay or personal statement, high school transcript, minimum 2.75 GPA, 1 letter of recommendation. *Required for some:* interview.

Freshman Application Contact Kate Rogers, Director of Admissions, Montreat College, PO Box 1267, 310 Gaither Circle, Montreat, NC 28757-1267. *Phone:* 828-669-8012. *Toll-free phone:* 800-622-6968. *Fax:* 828-669-0120. *E-mail:* admissions@montreat.edu.

MOUNT OLIVE COLLEGE

Mount Olive, North Carolina — www.moc.edu/

- **Independent Free Will Baptist** 4-year, founded 1951
- **Small-town** 123-acre campus with easy access to Raleigh
- **Endowment** $7.3 million
- **Coed** 3,277 undergraduate students, 77% full-time, 66% women, 34% men
- **Minimally difficult** entrance level, 67% of applicants were admitted

Undergraduates 2,523 full-time, 754 part-time. Students come from 21 states and territories, 5% are from out of state, 17% transferred in, 10% live on campus. *Retention:* 64% of 2006 full-time freshmen returned.

Freshmen *Admission:* 975 applied, 654 admitted, 357 enrolled. *Average high school GPA:* 3.08. *Test scores:* SAT critical reading scores over 500: 28%; SAT math scores over 500: 37%; ACT scores over 18: 52%; SAT critical reading scores over 600: 5%; SAT math scores over 600: 7%; ACT scores over 24: 13%.

Faculty *Total:* 303, 28% full-time, 39% with terminal degrees. *Student/faculty ratio:* 17:1.

Majors Accounting; art; athletic training; biological and physical sciences; biology/biological sciences; business administration and management; commercial and advertising art; criminal justice/law enforcement administration; divinity/ministry; English; environmental studies; health science; history; human services; information science/studies; liberal arts and sciences/liberal studies; mathematics; middle school education; music; parks, recreation and leisure; psychology; religious studies.

Academics *Calendar:* semester or continuous accelerated programs. *Degrees:* associate and bachelor's. *Special study options:* academic remediation for entering students, accelerated degree program, adult/continuing education programs, advanced placement credit, cooperative education, double majors, external degree program, freshman honors college, honors programs, independent study, internships, off-campus study, part-time degree program, summer session for credit.

Computers on Campus 50 computers/terminals are available on campus for general student use. Students can access the following: Web site. Campuswide network is available.

Student Life *Housing:* on-campus residence required for freshman year. *Options:* men-only, women-only. Campus housing is university owned. *Activities and organizations:* student-run newspaper, choral group, Student Government Association, Phi Beta Lambda, commuters organization, Christian Student Fellowship, English Society. *Campus security:* overnight security patrols; weekend patrols. *Student services:* health clinic, personal/psychological counseling.

Athletics Member NCAA. All Division II. *Intercollegiate sports:* baseball M (s), basketball M (s)/W (s), cheerleading W, cross-country running M (s)/W (s), golf M (s), soccer M (s)/W (s), softball W (s), tennis M (s)/W (s), volleyball M (s)/W (s). *Intramural sports:* basketball M/W, football M/W, racquetball M/W, soccer M/W, softball W, table tennis M/W, tennis M/W, volleyball M/W.

Standardized Tests *Required:* SAT or ACT (for admission).

Costs (2007–08) *Comprehensive fee:* $18,426 includes full-time tuition ($13,126) and room and board ($5300). Part-time tuition: $250 per credit hour. *College room only:* $2200.

Financial Aid Of all full-time matriculated undergraduates who enrolled in 2005, 1,941 applied for aid, 1,525 were judged to have need, 302 had their need fully met. 120 Federal Work-Study jobs (averaging $719). In 2005, 321 non-need-based awards were made. *Average percent of need met:* 67%. *Average financial aid package:* $7296. *Average need-based loan:* $2833. *Average need-based gift aid:* $4972. *Average non-need-based aid:* $4602. *Average indebtedness upon graduation:* $9786.

Applying *Options:* deferred entrance. *Application fee:* $20. *Required:* high school transcript, minimum 2.0 GPA. *Recommended:* 2 letters of recommendation, interview. *Application deadlines:* rolling (freshmen), rolling (transfers). *Notification:* continuous (freshmen), continuous (transfers).

Director of Admissions Mr. Tim Woodard, Director of Admissions, Mount Olive College, 634 Henderson Street, Mount Olive, NC 28365. *Phone:* 919-658-2502 Ext. 3009. *Toll-free phone:* 800-653-0854. *Fax:* 919-658-9816. *E-mail:* admissions@moc.edu.

NEW LIFE THEOLOGICAL SEMINARY
Charlotte, North Carolina

NORTH CAROLINA AGRICULTURAL AND TECHNICAL STATE UNIVERSITY
Greensboro, North Carolina **www.ncat.edu/**

- **State-supported** university, founded 1891, part of University of North Carolina System
- **Urban** 800-acre campus
- **Coed** 9,687 undergraduate students, 89% full-time, 53% women, 47% men
- **Moderately difficult** entrance level, 77% of applicants were admitted

Undergraduates 8,666 full-time, 1,021 part-time. Students come from 43 states and territories, 23% are from out of state, 92% African American, 0.9% Asian American or Pacific Islander, 0.8% Hispanic American, 0.2% Native American, 0.4% international, 6% transferred in, 20% live on campus.

Freshmen *Admission:* 6,016 applied, 4,611 admitted, 2,094 enrolled. *Average high school GPA:* 2.94. *Test scores:* SAT critical reading scores over 500: 16%; SAT math scores over 500: 23%; SAT critical reading scores over 600: 1%; SAT math scores over 600: 3%.

Majors Accounting; administrative assistant and secretarial science; agricultural business and management; agricultural economics; agricultural mechanization; agricultural teacher education; agriculture; animal sciences; applied mathematics; architectural engineering; art teacher education; biology/biological sciences; business administration and management; business teacher education; chemical engineering; chemistry; child development; civil engineering; clothing/textiles; computer science; construction management; dietetics; dramatic/theater arts; economics; education; electrical, electronics and communications engineering; elementary education; engineering physics; English; family and consumer sciences/home economics teacher education; family and consumer sciences/human sciences; food science; foods, nutrition, and wellness; French; health teacher education; history; industrial arts; industrial engineering; industrial technology; kindergarten/preschool education; landscape architecture; mass communication/media; mathematics; mechanical engineering; music teacher education; nursing (registered nurse training); occupational safety and health technology; parks, recreation and leisure; physical education teaching and coaching; physics; political science and government; psychology; social sciences; social work; sociology; special education; speech and rhetoric; trade and industrial teacher education; transportation technology.

Academics *Calendar:* semesters. *Degrees:* bachelor's, master's, and doctoral. *Special study options:* academic remediation for entering students, adult/continuing education programs, advanced placement credit, cooperative education, honors programs, internships, off-campus study, part-time degree program, services for LD students, study abroad, summer session for credit. *ROTC:* Army (b), Air Force (b).

Computers on Campus 250 computers/terminals are available on campus for general student use. Students can access the following: online (class) registration. Campuswide network is available.

Student Life *Housing options:* coed, men-only, women-only. Campus housing is university owned. *Activities and organizations:* drama/theater group, student-run newspaper, radio and television station, choral group, marching band, student government, national fraternities, national sororities. *Campus security:* 24-hour emergency response devices and patrols, late-night transport/escort service, controlled dormitory access. *Student services:* health clinic, personal/psychological counseling.

Athletics Member NCAA. All Division I except football (Division I-AA). *Intercollegiate sports:* baseball M (s), basketball M (s)/W (s), cross-country running M (s)/W (s), softball W, swimming and diving W (s), tennis M (s)/W (s), track and field M (s)/W (s), volleyball W (s). *Intramural sports:* baseball M/W, basketball M/W, bowling W, cross-country running M/W, football M, golf M/W, racquetball M/W, soccer M/W, softball M/W, swimming and diving M/W, table tennis M/W, tennis M/W, track and field M/W, volleyball M/W, weight lifting M/W.

Standardized Tests *Required:* SAT or ACT (for admission).

Costs (2007–08) *Tuition:* state resident $1994 full-time; nonresident $11,436 full-time. Full-time tuition and fees vary according to student level. Part-time tuition and fees vary according to student level. *Required fees:* $1506 full-time. *Room only:* $2956. Room and board charges vary according to board plan and housing facility. *Payment plan:* installment. *Waivers:* senior citizens and employees or children of employees.

Financial Aid Of all full-time matriculated undergraduates who enrolled in 2005, 7,873 applied for aid, 6,818 were judged to have need, 480 had their need fully met. In 2005, 257 non-need-based awards were made. *Average percent of need met:* 50%. *Average financial aid package:* $5898. *Average need-based loan:* $7202. *Average need-based gift aid:* $4028. *Average non-need-based aid:* $4466. *Average indebtedness upon graduation:* $20,052.

Applying *Options:* early admission, deferred entrance. *Application fee:* $45. *Required:* high school transcript, minimum 2.0 GPA. *Application deadlines:* 6/1 (freshmen), rolling (transfers). *Notification:* continuous until 8/1 (freshmen), continuous (transfers).

Freshman Application Contact Mr. Lee Young, Director of Admissions, North Carolina Agricultural and Technical State University, 1601 East Market Street, Webb Hall, Greensboro, NC 27411. *Phone:* 336-334-7946. *Toll-free phone:* 800-443-8964. *Fax:* 336-334-7478. *E-mail:* uadmit@ncat.edu.

NORTH CAROLINA CENTRAL UNIVERSITY
Durham, North Carolina **www.nccu.edu/**

- **State-supported** comprehensive, founded 1910, part of University of North Carolina System
- **Urban** 103-acre campus
- **Endowment** $17.8 million
- **Coed** 6,326 undergraduate students, 82% full-time, 65% women, 35% men
- **Minimally difficult** entrance level, 74% of applicants were admitted

A historically black constituent institution of the UNC System, North Carolina Central University (NCCU) is located in Durham, near Research Triangle, North Carolina. Raleigh, Durham, and Chapel Hill are a hotbed of academic institutions. Both major private grant and federal funding support opportunities for undergraduate involvement in meaningful research activity under the guidance of a faculty mentor.

Undergraduates 5,191 full-time, 1,135 part-time. Students come from 38 states and territories, 20 other countries, 13% are from out of state, 88% African American, 0.8% Asian American or Pacific Islander, 0.8% Hispanic American, 0.3% Native American, 0.5% international, 4% transferred in, 43% live on campus. *Retention:* 77% of 2006 full-time freshmen returned.

Freshmen *Admission:* 3,513 applied, 2,585 admitted, 1,265 enrolled. *Average high school GPA:* 2.74. *Test scores:* SAT critical reading scores over 500: 14%; SAT math scores over 500: 15%; SAT writing scores over 500: 9%; ACT scores over 18: 29%; SAT critical reading scores over 600: 3%; SAT math scores over 600: 3%; SAT writing scores over 600: 2%; ACT scores over 24: 2%; SAT critical reading scores over 700: 1%; SAT math scores over 700: 1%.

Faculty *Total:* 649, 60% full-time, 55% with terminal degrees. *Student/faculty ratio:* 15:1.

Majors Accounting; art; art teacher education; athletic training; biology/biological sciences; biology teacher education; biomedical sciences; business administration and management; chemistry; chemistry teacher education; computer science; criminal justice/safety; drama and dance teacher education; dramatic/theater arts; elementary education; English; English/language arts teacher education; environmental science; family and consumer sciences/human sciences; French; French language teacher education; geography; health and physical education; health teacher education; history; history teacher education; hospitality administration; information science/studies; jazz/jazz studies; kindergarten/preschool education; mass communication/media; mathematics; mathematics teacher education; middle school education; music; music teacher education; nursing (registered nurse training); parks, recreation and leisure facilities management; physical education teaching and coaching; physics; physics teacher education; political science and government; psychology; public health education and promotion; religious/sacred music; social work; sociology; Spanish; Spanish language teacher education.

Academics *Calendar:* semesters. *Degrees:* bachelor's, master's, and first professional. *Special study options:* academic remediation for entering students, adult/continuing education programs, advanced placement credit, cooperative education, distance learning, double majors, English as a second language, external degree program, honors programs, independent study, internships, off-campus study, part-time degree program, services for LD students, study abroad, summer session for credit. *ROTC:* Army (c), Air Force (c).

Computers on Campus 175 computers/terminals and 3,135 ports are available on campus for general student use. Students can access the following: campus intranet, computer help desk, free student e-mail accounts, online (class) grades, online (class) registration, online (class) schedules. Campuswide network is available. 100% of college-owned or -operated housing units are wired for high-speed Internet access. Wireless service is available via entire campus.

Student Life *Housing options:* coed, women-only. Campus housing is university owned, leased by the school and is provided by a third party. Freshman applicants given priority for college housing. *Activities and organizations:* drama/theater group, student-run newspaper, choral group, marching band, national fraternities, national sororities. *Campus security:* 24-hour emergency response devices and patrols, student patrols, late-night transport/escort service, controlled dormitory access. *Student services:* health clinic, personal/psychological counseling, women's center.

Athletics Member NCAA, NAIA. All NCAA Division II. *Intercollegiate sports:* basketball M (s)/W (s), bowling M/W, cross-country running M (s)/W (s), football M (s), golf M (s)/W (s), softball W (s), tennis M (s)/W (s), track and field M (s)/W (s), volleyball W (s).

Standardized Tests *Required:* SAT or ACT (for admission).

Costs (2008–09) *Tuition:* state resident $2218 full-time, $277 per course part-time; nonresident $11,962 full-time, $1495 per course part-time. *Required fees:* $1452 full-time. *Room and board:* $6015; room only: $3433.

Financial Aid Of all full-time matriculated undergraduates who enrolled in 2001, 2,894 applied for aid, 2,429 were judged to have need, 862 had their need fully met. In 2001, 410 non-need-based awards were made. *Average percent of need met:* 72%. *Average financial aid package:* $6621. *Average need-based loan:* $3487. *Average need-based gift aid:* $3348. *Average non-need-based aid:* $7144.

Applying *Options:* electronic application, deferred entrance. *Application fee:* $30. *Required:* high school transcript, minimum 2.0 GPA. *Application deadlines:* 8/1 (freshmen), 8/1 (transfers). *Notification:* continuous until 10/15 (freshmen), continuous until 10/15 (transfers).

Freshman Application Contact Ms. Jocelyn Foy, Undergraduate Director of Admissions, North Carolina Central University, PO Box 19717, Durham, NC 27707. *Phone:* 919-530-6298. *Toll-free phone:* 877-667-7533. *Fax:* 919-530-7625. *E-mail:* admissions@nccu.edu.

See page 1940 for the College Close-Up.

NORTH CAROLINA SCHOOL OF THE ARTS

Winston-Salem, North Carolina **www.ncarts.edu/**

- **State-supported** comprehensive, founded 1963, part of University of North Carolina System
- **Urban** 57-acre campus
- **Endowment** $16.8 million
- **Coed** 743 undergraduate students, 99% full-time, 40% women, 60% men
- **Very difficult** entrance level, 51% of applicants were admitted

Undergraduates 739 full-time, 4 part-time. Students come from 38 states and territories, 11 other countries, 54% are from out of state, 10% African American, 2% Asian American or Pacific Islander, 5% Hispanic American, 1% Native American, 0.5% international, 5% transferred in, 55% live on campus. *Retention:* 74% of 2006 full-time freshmen returned.

Freshmen *Admission:* 679 applied, 346 admitted, 186 enrolled.

Faculty *Total:* 183, 79% full-time, 33% with terminal degrees. *Student/faculty ratio:* 8:1.

Majors Cinematography and film/video production; dance; dramatic/theater arts; film/cinema studies; music performance; piano and organ; theater design and technology; visual and performing arts; voice and opera.

Academics *Calendar:* trimesters. *Degrees:* diplomas, bachelor's, master's, and post-master's certificates. *Special study options:* academic remediation for entering students, advanced placement credit, freshman honors college, services for LD students.

Computers on Campus 60 computers/terminals are available on campus for general student use. Students can access the following: computer help desk, free student e-mail accounts, online (class) grades. Campuswide network is available. Wireless service is available via entire campus.

Student Life *Housing:* on-campus residence required through sophomore year. *Options:* coed. Campus housing is university owned and is provided by a third party. Freshman campus housing is guaranteed. *Activities and organizations:* drama/theater group, student-run newspaper, choral group, Pride (gay/lesbian organization), Appreciation of Black Artists. *Campus security:* 24-hour emergency response devices and patrols, controlled dormitory access. *Student services:* health clinic, personal/psychological counseling.

Standardized Tests *Recommended:* SAT or ACT (for admission).

Costs (2007–08) *Tuition:* state resident $3224 full-time; nonresident $14,654 full-time. Full-time tuition and fees vary according to program. Part-time tuition and fees vary according to course load. *Required fees:* $1837 full-time. *Room and board:* $6431; room only: $3289. Room and board charges vary according to board plan and housing facility. *Payment plan:* installment.

Financial Aid Of all full-time matriculated undergraduates who enrolled in 2006, 475 applied for aid, 367 were judged to have need, 48 had their need fully met. 98 Federal Work-Study jobs (averaging $434). In 2006, 114 non-need-based awards were made. *Average percent of need met:* 81%. *Average financial aid package:* $12,271. *Average need-based loan:* $3759. *Average need-based gift aid:* $5932. *Average non-need-based aid:* $2970. *Average indebtedness upon graduation:* $18,131.

Applying *Options:* electronic application. *Application fee:* $50. *Required:* high school transcript, 2 letters of recommendation, audition. *Required for some:* essay or personal statement, interview. *Application deadlines:* 3/1 (freshmen), rolling (transfers). *Notification:* continuous (freshmen), continuous (transfers).

Freshman Application Contact Ms. Sheeler Lawson, Director of Admissions, North Carolina School of the Arts, 1533 South Main Street, PO Box 12189, Winston-Salem, NC 27127-2188. *Phone:* 336-770-3290. *Fax:* 336-770-3370. *E-mail:* admissions@ncarts.edu.

NORTH CAROLINA STATE UNIVERSITY

Raleigh, North Carolina **www.ncsu.edu/**

- **State-supported** university, founded 1887, part of University of North Carolina System
- **Urban** 2110-acre campus
- **Endowment** $534.0 million
- **Coed** 24,145 undergraduate students, 86% full-time, 44% women, 56% men
- **Very difficult** entrance level, 60% of applicants were admitted

Undergraduates 20,724 full-time, 3,421 part-time. Students come from 52 states and territories, 64 other countries, 7% are from out of state, 9% African American, 5% Asian American or Pacific Islander, 3% Hispanic American, 0.6% Native American, 1% international, 4% transferred in, 34% live on campus. *Retention:* 89% of 2006 full-time freshmen returned.

Freshmen *Admission:* 16,437 applied, 9,869 admitted, 4,907 enrolled. *Average high school GPA:* 4.0. *Test scores:* SAT critical reading scores over 500: 85%; SAT math scores over 500: 94%; SAT writing scores over 500: 81%; ACT scores over 18: 97%; SAT critical reading scores over 600: 35%; SAT math scores over 600: 55%; SAT writing scores over 600: 30%; ACT scores over 24: 60%; SAT critical reading scores over 700: 5%; SAT math scores over 700: 11%; SAT writing scores over 700: 3%; ACT scores over 30: 9%.

Faculty *Total:* 1,939, 89% full-time, 87% with terminal degrees. *Student/faculty ratio:* 16:1.

Majors Accounting; aerospace, aeronautical and astronautical engineering; agribusiness; agricultural and extension education; agricultural and food products processing; agricultural/biological engineering and bioengineering; agricultural business and management; agricultural economics; agricultural teacher education; agriculture; agronomy and crop science; American government and politics; animal sciences; anthropology; apparel and textile manufacturing; apparel and textile marketing management; applied mathematics; architecture; arts management; biochemistry; biology/biological sciences; biology teacher education; biomedical/medical engineering; botany/plant biology; business administration and management; chemical engineering; chemistry; chemistry teacher education; civil engineering; communication/speech communication and rhetoric; computer engineering; computer science; construction engineering; construction management; creative writing; criminology; design and applied arts related; design and visual communications; ecology; economics; education; electrical, electronics and communications engineering; engineering; English; English/language arts teacher education; environmental design/architecture; environmental/environmental health engineering; environmental science; environmental studies; film/cinema studies; finance; fishing and fisheries sciences and management; food science; foreign language teacher education; forest/forest resources management; French; French language teacher education; geology/earth science; graphic design; health occupations teacher education; history; history teacher education; horticultural science; human resources management; hydrology and water resources science; industrial design; industrial engineering; information technology; landscape architecture; landscaping and groundskeeping; liberal arts and sciences/liberal studies;

marketing/marketing management; mass communication/media; materials engineering; materials science; mathematics; mathematics teacher education; mechanical engineering; meteorology; microbiology; middle school education; natural resources/conservation; natural resources management and policy; nuclear engineering; oceanography (chemical and physical); paleontology; parks, recreation and leisure facilities management; parks, recreation, and leisure related; philosophy; physics; physics related; physics teacher education; plant protection and integrated pest management; political science and government; political science and government related; poultry science; psychology; psychology related; public policy analysis; public relations/image management; religious studies; sales and marketing/marketing and distribution teacher education; science teacher education; science, technology and society; secondary education; social studies teacher education; social work; sociology; soil science and agronomy; Spanish; Spanish language teacher education; sport and fitness administration/management; statistics; technology/industrial arts teacher education; textile science; textile sciences and engineering; tourism and travel services management; turf and turfgrass management; wildlife and wildlands science and management; wood science and wood products/pulp and paper technology; zoology/animal biology.

Academics *Calendar:* semesters. *Degrees:* certificates, associate, bachelor's, master's, doctoral, first professional, postbachelor's, and first professional certificates. *Special study options:* academic remediation for entering students, accelerated degree program, adult/continuing education programs, advanced placement credit, cooperative education, distance learning, double majors, honors programs, independent study, internships, off-campus study, part-time degree program, services for LD students, student-designed majors, study abroad, summer session for credit. *ROTC:* Army (b), Navy (b), Air Force (b).

Computers on Campus 3,000 computers/terminals and 500 ports are available on campus for general student use. Students can access the following: campus intranet, computer help desk, free student e-mail accounts, online (class) grades, online (class) registration, online (class) schedules, course materials, online homework submission, online testing/quizzes, financial aid/cashier's office account balances, wiki space, blogging service, Web space, online storage space, on-site OS and virus removal, online/hybrid courses. Campuswide network is available. 100% of college-owned or -operated housing units are wired for high-speed Internet access. Wireless service is available via classrooms, computer centers, computer labs, dorm rooms, learning centers, libraries, student centers.

Student Life *Housing options:* coed, men-only, women-only, disabled students. Campus housing is university owned. Freshman applicants given priority for college housing. *Activities and organizations:* drama/theater group, student-run newspaper, radio and television station, choral group, marching band, student government, student media, student musical groups, intramural sports, national fraternities, national sororities. *Campus security:* 24-hour emergency response devices and patrols, student patrols, late-night transport/escort service, controlled dormitory access. *Student services:* health clinic, personal/psychological counseling, women's center, legal services.

Athletics Member NCAA. All Division I except football (Division I-A). *Intercollegiate sports:* badminton M (c)/W (c), baseball M (s), basketball M (s)/W (s), bowling M (c)/W (c), cheerleading M/W, crew M (c)/W (c), cross-country running M (s)/W (s), equestrian sports M (c)/W (c), fencing M/W, field hockey M (c)/W (c), golf M (s)/W, gymnastics W (s), ice hockey M (c)/W (c), lacrosse M (c)/W (c), racquetball M (c)/W (c), riflery M/W, rugby M (c)/W (c), sailing M (c)/W (c), skiing (downhill) M (c)/W (c), soccer M (s)/W (s), softball W (s), swimming and diving M (s)/W (s), table tennis M (c)/W (c), tennis M (s)/W (s), track and field M (s)/W (s), ultimate Frisbee M (c)/W (c), volleyball M (c)/W (s), water polo M (c)/W (c), wrestling M (s). *Intramural sports:* badminton M/W, baseball M, basketball M/W, bowling M/W, cheerleading W (c), crew M/W, cross-country running M/W, equestrian sports M/W, fencing M/W, field hockey W, football M/W, golf M/W, gymnastics W, ice hockey M, lacrosse M/W, racquetball M/W, rugby M/W, sailing M/W, skiing (downhill) M/W, soccer M/W, softball M/W, swimming and diving M/W, table tennis M/W, tennis M/W, track and field M/W, volleyball M/W, water polo M/W, wrestling M.

Standardized Tests *Required:* SAT or ACT (for admission). *Recommended:* SAT Subject Tests (for admission).

Costs (2007–08) *Tuition:* state resident $3760 full-time; nonresident $15,958 full-time. Full-time tuition and fees vary according to program. Part-time tuition and fees vary according to course load and program. *Required fees:* $1357 full-time. *Room and board:* $7373; room only: $4460. Room and board charges vary according to board plan and housing facility. *Payment plan:* installment. *Waivers:* senior citizens and employees or children of employees.

Financial Aid Of all full-time matriculated undergraduates who enrolled in 2006, 11,645 applied for aid, 8,355 were judged to have need, 4,075 had their need fully met. 705 Federal Work-Study jobs (averaging $1403). 198 state and other part-time jobs (averaging $7370). In 2006, 4102 non-need-based awards were made. *Average percent of need met:* 81%. *Average financial aid package:* $9540. *Average need-based loan:* $2886. *Average need-based gift aid:* $7682. *Average non-need-based aid:* $7314. *Average indebtedness upon graduation:* $14,930.

Applying *Options:* electronic application, early action, deferred entrance. *Application fee:* $60. *Required:* high school transcript. *Required for some:* interview. *Recommended:* essay or personal statement. *Application deadlines:* 2/1 (freshmen), 4/1 (transfers), 11/1 (early action). *Notification:* continuous (freshmen), continuous (transfers), 1/15 (early action).

Freshman Application Contact Mr. Thomas Griffin, Director of Undergraduate Admissions, North Carolina State University, Box 7103, 112 Peele Hall, Raleigh, NC 27695. *Phone:* 919-515-2434. *Fax:* 919-515-5039. *E-mail:* undergrad_admissions@ncsu.edu.

NORTH CAROLINA WESLEYAN COLLEGE

Rocky Mount, North Carolina **www.ncwc.edu/**

- **Independent** 4-year, founded 1956, affiliated with United Methodist Church
- **Suburban** 200-acre campus
- **Endowment** $7.5 million
- **Coed** 1,510 undergraduate students, 77% full-time, 58% women, 42% men
- **Moderately difficult** entrance level, 63% of applicants were admitted

Undergraduates 1,160 full-time, 350 part-time. Students come from 23 states and territories, 9 other countries, 16% are from out of state, 47% African American, 1% Asian American or Pacific Islander, 2% Hispanic American, 1% Native American, 1% international, 7% transferred in, 32% live on campus. *Retention:* 47% of 2006 full-time freshmen returned.

Freshmen *Admission:* 1,245 applied, 781 admitted, 221 enrolled. *Average high school GPA:* 2.96. *Test scores:* SAT critical reading scores over 500: 8%; SAT math scores over 500: 13%; SAT critical reading scores over 600: 5%; SAT math scores over 600: 4%; SAT critical reading scores over 700: 1%; SAT math scores over 700: 1%.

Faculty *Total:* 169, 33% full-time, 50% with terminal degrees. *Student/faculty ratio:* 18:1.

Majors Accounting; anthropology; biology/biological sciences; business administration and management; chemistry; criminal justice/law enforcement administration; dramatic/theater arts; education; elementary education; English; environmental studies; history; hotel/motel administration; information science/studies; legal studies; mathematics; middle school education; philosophy; physical education teaching and coaching; political science and government; pre-medical studies; psychology; religious studies; secondary education; sociology; special products marketing.

Academics *Calendar:* semesters. *Degrees:* bachelor's (also offers adult part-time degree program with significant enrollment not reflected in profile). *Special study options:* academic remediation for entering students, accelerated degree program, adult/continuing education programs, advanced placement credit, cooperative education, distance learning, double majors, honors programs, independent study, internships, part-time degree program, services for LD students, summer session for credit.

Computers on Campus 43 computers/terminals are available on campus for general student use. Campuswide network is available.

Student Life *Housing:* on-campus residence required through sophomore year. *Options:* coed, men-only, women-only, disabled students. Campus housing is university owned. Freshman campus housing is guaranteed. *Activities and organizations:* drama/theater group, student-run newspaper, choral group, Club Dramatica, Student Government Association, gospel choir, Wesleyan Singers, pep band, national fraternities, national sororities. *Campus security:* 24-hour emergency response devices and patrols, late-night transport/escort service, controlled dormitory access. *Student services:* health clinic, personal/psychological counseling.

Athletics Member NCAA. All Division III. *Intercollegiate sports:* baseball M, basketball M/W, football M, golf M, soccer M/W, softball W, tennis M/W, volleyball W. *Intramural sports:* basketball M/W, football M/W, lacrosse M/W, softball M/W, table tennis M/W, tennis M/W, volleyball M/W.

Standardized Tests *Required:* SAT or ACT (for admission).

Costs (2007–08) *Comprehensive fee:* $26,000 includes full-time tuition ($18,900) and room and board ($7100). Full-time tuition and fees vary according to location. Part-time tuition: $258 per semester hour. Part-time tuition and fees vary according to location. *College room only:* $3400. Room and board charges vary according to housing facility. *Payment plan:* installment. *Waivers:* employees or children of employees.

Financial Aid Of all full-time matriculated undergraduates who enrolled in 2007, 926 applied for aid, 714 were judged to have need, 221 had their need fully met. 627 Federal Work-Study jobs (averaging $1127). 34 state and other part-time jobs (averaging $755). In 2007, 54 non-need-based awards were made. *Average percent of need met:* 69%. *Average financial aid package:* $12,213. *Average* *need-based loan:* $3880. *Average need-based gift aid:* $3841. *Average non-need-based aid:* $8027. *Average indebtedness upon graduation:* $7090.

Applying *Options:* electronic application. *Application fee:* $25. *Required:* high school transcript. *Required for some:* essay or personal statement, interview. *Recommended:* minimum 2.0 GPA, 2 letters of recommendation, interview. *Application deadlines:* rolling (freshmen), 7/15 (transfers). *Notification:* continuous (freshmen), continuous (transfers).

Freshman Application Contact Ms. Cecelia Summers, Associate Director of Admissions, North Carolina Wesleyan College, 3400 North Wesleyan Boulevard, Rocky Mount, NC 27804. *Phone:* 252-985-5200. *Toll-free phone:* 800-488-6292. *Fax:* 252-985-5295. *E-mail:* adm@ncwc.edu.

PEACE COLLEGE

Raleigh, North Carolina — www.peace.edu/

- **Independent** 4-year, founded 1857, affiliated with Presbyterian Church (U.S.A.)
- **Urban** 19-acre campus
- **Endowment** $46.1 million
- **Women only** 692 undergraduate students, 93% full-time
- **Moderately difficult** entrance level, 75% of applicants were admitted

Undergraduates 642 full-time, 50 part-time. 11% are from out of state, 15% African American, 2% Asian American or Pacific Islander, 3% Hispanic American, 1% Native American, 6% transferred in, 82% live on campus. *Retention:* 65% of 2006 full-time freshmen returned.

Freshmen *Admission:* 743 applied, 555 admitted, 185 enrolled. *Average high school GPA:* 3.2. *Test scores:* SAT critical reading scores over 500: 31%; SAT math scores over 500: 38%; ACT scores over 18: 49%; SAT critical reading scores over 600: 6%; SAT math scores over 600: 7%; ACT scores over 24: 9%.

Faculty *Total:* 78, 53% full-time, 58% with terminal degrees. *Student/faculty ratio:* 11:1.

Majors Biology/biological sciences; business administration and management; communication/speech communication and rhetoric; design and visual communications; English; graphic design; human resources management; music performance; political science and government related; psychology; Spanish.

Academics *Calendar:* semesters. *Degree:* bachelor's. *Special study options:* academic remediation for entering students, adult/continuing education programs, advanced placement credit, double majors, English as a second language, freshman honors college, honors programs, independent study, internships, off-campus study, part-time degree program, services for LD students, study abroad, summer session for credit. *ROTC:* Army (c), Navy (c), Air Force (c).

Computers on Campus 45 computers/terminals are available on campus for general student use. Students can access the following: campus intranet, computer help desk, free student e-mail accounts, online (class) registration, online (class) schedules. Campuswide network is available.

Student Life *Housing:* on-campus residence required through sophomore year. *Options:* women-only. Campus housing is university owned. Freshman campus housing is guaranteed. *Activities and organizations:* drama/theater group, student-run newspaper, choral group, Student Government Association, Peace Student Christian Association, Human Resources Society, Psychology Club, Student Newspaper. *Campus security:* 24-hour emergency response devices and patrols, late-night transport/escort service, controlled dormitory access. *Student services:* health clinic, personal/psychological counseling.

Athletics Member NCAA. All Division III. *Intercollegiate sports:* basketball W, cross-country running W, soccer W, softball W, tennis W, volleyball W. *Intramural sports:* badminton W, basketball W, equestrian sports W, soccer W, softball W, swimming and diving W, table tennis W, tennis W, volleyball W.

Standardized Tests *Required:* SAT or ACT (for admission).

Costs (2007–08) *One-time required fee:* $150. *Comprehensive fee:* $29,490 includes full-time tuition ($21,628), mandatory fees ($344), and room and board ($7518). Full-time tuition and fees vary according to course load. Part-time tuition: $409 per credit hour. *College room only:* $5323. Room and board charges vary according to board plan and housing facility. *Payment plan:* installment. *Waivers:* senior citizens and employees or children of employees.

Financial Aid Of all full-time matriculated undergraduates who enrolled in 2007, 519 applied for aid, 466 were judged to have need, 61 had their need fully met. 231 Federal Work-Study jobs (averaging $1833). 31 state and other part-time jobs (averaging $1691). In 2007, 155 non-need-based awards were made. *Average percent of need met:* 72%. *Average financial aid package:* $17,027. *Average need-based loan:* $3993. *Average need-based gift aid:* $12,950. *Average non-need-based aid:* $11,543. *Average indebtedness upon graduation:* $18,396.

Applying *Options:* electronic application, early admission, deferred entrance. *Application fee:* $25. *Required:* high school transcript, minimum 2.0 GPA. *Recommended:* essay or personal statement, 2 letters of recommendation, interview. *Application deadlines:* rolling (freshmen), rolling (transfers). *Notification:* continuous (freshmen), continuous (transfers).

Freshman Application Contact Mr. Matt Green, Dean of Enrollment, Peace College, 15 East Peace Street, Raleigh, NC 27604-1194. *Phone:* 919-509-2016. *Toll-free phone:* 800-PEACE-47. *Fax:* 919-508-2326. *E-mail:* mtgreen@peace.edu.

PFEIFFER UNIVERSITY

Misenheimer, North Carolina — www.pfeiffer.edu/

- **Independent United Methodist** comprehensive, founded 1885
- **Rural** 300-acre campus with easy access to Charlotte
- **Endowment** $14.0 million
- **Coed** 1,082 undergraduate students, 89% full-time, 57% women, 43% men
- **Moderately difficult** entrance level, 74% of applicants were admitted

Undergraduates 963 full-time, 119 part-time. Students come from 41 states and territories, 8 other countries, 17% are from out of state, 21% African American, 1% Asian American or Pacific Islander, 3% Hispanic American, 0.5% Native American, 4% international, 7% transferred in, 65% live on campus. *Retention:* 65% of 2006 full-time freshmen returned.

Freshmen *Admission:* 726 applied, 535 admitted, 189 enrolled. *Average high school GPA:* 3.20. *Test scores:* SAT critical reading scores over 500: 41%; SAT math scores over 500: 57%; SAT writing scores over 500: 39%; ACT scores over 18: 81%; SAT critical reading scores over 600: 10%; SAT math scores over 600: 17%; SAT writing scores over 600: 7%; ACT scores over 24: 31%; SAT math scores over 700: 1%; ACT scores over 30: 3%.

Faculty *Total:* 153, 50% full-time, 61% with terminal degrees. *Student/faculty ratio:* 14:1.

Majors Accounting; arts management; athletic training; biology/biological sciences; business administration and management; business/managerial economics; chemistry; communication/speech communication and rhetoric; criminal justice/law enforcement administration; economics; education; elementary education; engineering; English; environmental science; environmental studies; exercise physiology; finance; history; human services; international business/trade/commerce; journalism; management information systems; marketing/marketing management; mathematics; mathematics and computer science; music; music teacher education; organizational communication; physical education teaching and coaching; political science and government; pre-law studies; pre-medical studies; psychology; public relations/image management; religious education; religious/sacred music; religious studies; science teacher education; social sciences; social studies teacher education; sociology; special education; sport and fitness administration/management; youth ministry.

Academics *Calendar:* semesters. *Degrees:* bachelor's and master's. *Special study options:* academic remediation for entering students, accelerated degree program, advanced placement credit, cooperative education, double majors, English as a second language, honors programs, independent study, internships, part-time degree program, services for LD students, study abroad, summer session for credit. *ROTC:* Army (c). *Unusual degree programs:* 3-2 business administration; engineering with Auburn University.

Computers on Campus 90 computers/terminals and 576 ports are available on campus for general student use. Students can access the following: computer help desk, free student e-mail accounts, online (class) grades, online (class) schedules. Campuswide network is available. 100% of college-owned or -operated housing units are wired for high-speed Internet access.

Student Life *Housing:* on-campus residence required through senior year. *Options:* coed, men-only, women-only. Campus housing is university owned. Freshman applicants given priority for college housing. *Activities and organizations:* drama/theater group, student-run newspaper, choral group, Student Government Association, Religious Life Council, Commuter Student Association, Programming Activities Council, Residence Hall Association. *Campus security:* 24-hour emergency response devices and patrols, late-night transport/escort service, controlled dormitory access. *Student services:* health clinic, personal/psychological counseling, women's center.

Athletics Member NCAA. All Division II. *Intercollegiate sports:* baseball M (s), basketball M (s)/W (s), cheerleading M (s)/W (s), cross-country running M (s)/W (s), golf M (s)/W (s), lacrosse M (s)/W (s), soccer M (s)/W (s), softball W (s), swimming and diving M (s)/W (s), tennis M (s)/W (s), volleyball W (s). *Intramural sports:* badminton M/W, basketball M/W, football M/W, soccer M/W, softball M/W, tennis M/W, ultimate Frisbee M/W, volleyball M/W, water polo M/W.

Standardized Tests *Required:* SAT or ACT (for admission).

Costs (2008–09) *Comprehensive fee:* $25,930 includes full-time tuition ($18,570) and room and board ($7360). Part-time tuition: $425 per credit hour. *College room only:* $4410.

met. 20 Federal Work-Study jobs (averaging $645). In 2006, 12 non-need-based awards were made. *Average percent of need met:* 73%. *Average financial aid package:* $7612. *Average need-based loan:* $3661. *Average need-based gift aid:* $4111. *Average non-need-based aid:* $3848. *Average indebtedness upon graduation:* $25,371.

Applying *Options:* electronic application, early admission, deferred entrance. *Application fee:* $50. *Required:* essay or personal statement, high school transcript, minimum 2.0 GPA, letters of recommendation, reference from church. *Required for some:* interview. *Application deadlines:* 8/1 (freshmen), 8/1 (transfers). *Notification:* continuous (freshmen), continuous (transfers).

Freshman Application Contact Mrs. Julie Fields, Roanoke Bible College, 715 North Poindexter Street, Elizabeth City, NC 27909-4054. *Phone:* 252-334-2028. *Toll-free phone:* 800-RBC-8980. *Fax:* 252-334-2064. *E-mail:* admissions@roanokebible.edu.

ST. ANDREWS PRESBYTERIAN COLLEGE

Laurinburg, North Carolina **www.sapc.edu/**

- **Independent Presbyterian** 4-year, founded 1958
- **Small-town** 600-acre campus
- **Endowment** $14.8 million
- **Coed** 747 undergraduate students, 94% full-time, 60% women, 40% men
- **Moderately difficult** entrance level, 73% of applicants were admitted

Undergraduates 705 full-time, 42 part-time. Students come from 41 states and territories, 8 other countries, 53% are from out of state, 9% African American, 0.7% Asian American or Pacific Islander, 3% Hispanic American, 0.8% Native American, 2% international, 5% transferred in, 76% live on campus. *Retention:* 55% of 2006 full-time freshmen returned.

Freshmen *Admission:* 918 applied, 669 admitted, 216 enrolled. *Average high school GPA:* 3.0. *Test scores:* SAT critical reading scores over 500: 54%; SAT math scores over 500: 49%; SAT writing scores over 500: 44%; ACT scores over 18: 74%; SAT critical reading scores over 600: 13%; SAT math scores over 600: 15%; SAT writing scores over 600: 9%; ACT scores over 24: 21%; SAT critical reading scores over 700: 1%; SAT math scores over 700: 1%; SAT writing scores over 700: 1%; ACT scores over 30: 3%.

Faculty *Total:* 88, 48% full-time, 49% with terminal degrees. *Student/faculty ratio:* 12:1.

Majors Art; biology/biological sciences; business administration and management; chemistry; creative writing; elementary education; English; equestrian studies; fine/studio arts; history; interdisciplinary studies; liberal arts and sciences/liberal studies; mass communication/media; mathematics; philosophy; physical education teaching and coaching; political science and government; pre-law studies; pre-medical studies; pre-veterinary studies; psychology; religious studies; therapeutic recreation.

Academics *Calendar:* semesters. *Degree:* bachelor's. *Special study options:* accelerated degree program, adult/continuing education programs, advanced placement credit, double majors, honors programs, independent study, internships, part-time degree program, services for LD students, student-designed majors, study abroad, summer session for credit. *Unusual degree programs:* 3-2 engineering with North Carolina State University; accounting with University of Georgia.

Computers on Campus 100 computers/terminals are available on campus for general student use. Campuswide network is available.

Student Life *Housing:* on-campus residence required through senior year. *Options:* coed, men-only, women-only, disabled students. Campus housing is university owned. *Activities and organizations:* drama/theater group, student-run newspaper, choral group, Riding Council, Student Activities Union, Writer's Forum, Christian Student Union, Lion's Club. *Campus security:* 24-hour emergency response devices and patrols, late-night transport/escort service. *Student services:* health clinic, personal/psychological counseling, women's center.

Athletics Member NCAA. All Division II. *Intercollegiate sports:* baseball M (s), basketball M (s)/W (s), cross-country running M (s)/W (s), equestrian sports M (s)/W (s), golf M (s)/W (s), lacrosse M (s)/W (s), rugby M (c)/W (c), soccer M (s)/W (s), softball W (s), tennis M (s)/W (s), volleyball W (s), wrestling M. *Intramural sports:* basketball M/W, football M/W, rugby M (c)/W (c), softball M/W, table tennis M/W, tennis M/W, volleyball M/W.

Standardized Tests *Required:* SAT or ACT (for admission).

Costs (2007–08) *One-time required fee:* $100. *Comprehensive fee:* $26,184 includes full-time tuition ($18,192) and room and board ($7992). Full-time tuition and fees vary according to course load and location. Part-time tuition: $420 per credit. Part-time tuition and fees vary according to location. room, board, and fees are no longer listed separately; all are included in the room and board costs. *Room and board:* Room and board charges vary according to housing facility. *Payment plan:* installment. *Waivers:* adult students, senior citizens, and employees or children of employees.

Financial Aid Of all full-time matriculated undergraduates who enrolled in 2007, 551 applied for aid, 464 were judged to have need, 137 had their need fully met. 274 Federal Work-Study jobs (averaging $1800). 30 state and other part-time jobs (averaging $1800). In 2007, 238 non-need-based awards were made. *Average percent of need met:* 78%. *Average financial aid package:* $14,558. *Average need-based loan:* $4415. *Average need-based gift aid:* $10,507. *Average non-need-based aid:* $9480. *Average indebtedness upon graduation:* $15,786.

Applying *Options:* electronic application, early decision, deferred entrance. *Application fee:* $30. *Required:* high school transcript. *Required for some:* essay or personal statement, letters of recommendation, interview. *Recommended:* minimum 2.0 GPA. *Application deadlines:* rolling (freshmen), rolling (transfers). *Notification:* continuous (freshmen), continuous (transfers).

Freshman Application Contact Rev. Glenn Batten, Dean for Student Affairs and Enrollment, St. Andrews Presbyterian College, 1700 Dogwood Mile, Laurinburg, NC 28352. *Phone:* 910-277-5555. *Toll-free phone:* 800-763-0198. *Fax:* 910-277-5087. *E-mail:* admission@sapc.edu.

SAINT AUGUSTINE'S COLLEGE

Raleigh, North Carolina **www.st-aug.edu/**

Freshman Application Contact Mrs. Charlotte McKenzie-Hunter, Assistant Director, Admissions, Saint Augustine's College, 1315 Oakwood Avenue, Raleigh, NC 27610-2298. *Phone:* 919-516-4016. *Toll-free phone:* 800-948-1126. *Fax:* 919-516-5805. *E-mail:* admissions@es.st-aug.edu.

See page 1942 for the College Close-Up.

SALEM COLLEGE

Winston-Salem, North Carolina **www.salem.edu/**

- **Independent Moravian** comprehensive, founded 1772
- **Urban** 57-acre campus
- **Endowment** $51.6 million
- **Undergraduate: women only; graduate: coed** 768 undergraduate students, 82% full-time, 97% women, 3% men
- **Moderately difficult** entrance level, 62% of applicants were admitted

Undergraduates 626 full-time, 142 part-time. Students come from 29 states and territories, 18 other countries, 23% are from out of state, 19% African American, 1% Asian American or Pacific Islander, 3% Hispanic American, 0.1% Native American, 13% international, 9% transferred in, 86% live on campus. *Retention:* 76% of 2006 full-time freshmen returned.

Freshmen *Admission:* 420 applied, 260 admitted, 121 enrolled. *Average high school GPA:* 3.7. *Test scores:* SAT critical reading scores over 500: 70%; SAT math scores over 500: 64%; ACT scores over 18: 100%; SAT critical reading scores over 600: 35%; SAT math scores over 600: 33%; ACT scores over 24: 22%; SAT critical reading scores over 700: 8%; SAT math scores over 700: 2%; ACT scores over 30: 11%.

Faculty *Total:* 106, 54% full-time, 63% with terminal degrees. *Student/faculty ratio:* 12:1.

Majors Accounting; American studies; art history, criticism and conservation; arts management; biology/biological sciences; business administration and management; chemistry; clinical laboratory science/medical technology; creative writing; economics; education; English; fine/studio arts; French; German; history; interdisciplinary studies; interior design; international business/trade/commerce; international relations and affairs; mass communication/media; mathematics; music; music performance; non-profit management; philosophy; physician assistant; psychology; religious studies; sociology; Spanish.

Academics *Calendar:* 4-1-4. *Degrees:* bachelor's and master's (only students age 23 or over are eligible to enroll part-time; men may attend evening program only). *Special study options:* adult/continuing education programs, advanced placement credit, double majors, honors programs, independent study, internships, off-campus study, part-time degree program, student-designed majors, study abroad, summer session for credit. *Unusual degree programs:* 3-2 engineering with Duke University, Vanderbilt University.

Computers on Campus 54 computers/terminals are available on campus for general student use. Students can access the following: campus intranet, computer help desk, free student e-mail accounts, online (class) grades, online (class) schedules. Campuswide network is available. 100% of college-owned or -operated housing units are wired for high-speed Internet access. Wireless service is available via entire campus.

Financial Aid Of all full-time matriculated undergraduates who enrolled in 2005, 918 applied for aid, 803 were judged to have need, 158 had their need fully met. 233 Federal Work-Study jobs (averaging $668). In 2005, 113 non-need-based awards were made. *Average percent of need met:* 76%. *Average financial aid package:* $11,351. *Average need-based loan:* $3462. *Average need-based gift aid:* $8498. *Average non-need-based aid:* $10,102. *Average indebtedness upon graduation:* $17,350.

Applying *Options:* electronic application, early admission, deferred entrance. *Application fee:* $25. *Required:* high school transcript. *Required for some:* 2 letters of recommendation. *Recommended:* minimum 2.0 GPA, interview. *Application deadlines:* rolling (freshmen), rolling (transfers). *Notification:* continuous (freshmen), continuous (transfers).

Freshman Application Contact Ms. Jennifer Pate, Assistant Director of Admissions, Pfeiffer University, PO Box 960, Highway 52 North, Misenheimer, NC 28109. *Phone:* 704-463-1360 Ext. 3054. *Toll-free phone:* 800-338-2060. *Fax:* 704-463-1363. *E-mail:* admiss@pfeiffer.edu.

PIEDMONT BAPTIST COLLEGE AND GRADUATE SCHOOL

Winston-Salem, North Carolina **www.pbc.edu/**

Freshman Application Contact Piedmont Baptist College and Graduate School, 716 Franklin Street, Winston-Salem, NC 27101-5197. *Phone:* 336-725-8344 Ext. 2322. *Toll-free phone:* 800-937-5097.

QUEENS UNIVERSITY OF CHARLOTTE

Charlotte, North Carolina **www.queens.edu/**

- **Independent Presbyterian** comprehensive, founded 1857
- **Suburban** 30-acre campus
- **Endowment** $65.3 million
- **Coed** 1,715 undergraduate students, 64% full-time, 76% women, 24% men
- **Moderately difficult** entrance level, 79% of applicants were admitted

Undergraduates 1,106 full-time, 609 part-time. Students come from 34 states and territories, 18 other countries, 18% African American, 2% Asian American or Pacific Islander, 4% Hispanic American, 0.6% Native American, 5% international, 5% transferred in, 72% live on campus. *Retention:* 67% of 2006 full-time freshmen returned.

Freshmen *Admission:* 1,189 applied, 939 admitted, 303 enrolled. *Average high school GPA:* 3.42. *Test scores:* SAT critical reading scores over 500: 63%; SAT math scores over 500: 55%; SAT writing scores over 500: 56%; ACT scores over 18: 89%; SAT critical reading scores over 600: 19%; SAT math scores over 600: 12%; SAT writing scores over 600: 14%; ACT scores over 24: 33%; SAT critical reading scores over 700: 4%; SAT writing scores over 700: 2%; ACT scores over 30: 2%.

Faculty *Total:* 192, 51% full-time, 48% with terminal degrees. *Student/faculty ratio:* 12:1.

Majors American literature; American studies; applied mathematics; art; biochemistry; biology/biological sciences; business administration and management; chemistry; computer/information technology services administration related; dramatic/theater arts; education; elementary education; English; English/language arts teacher education; environmental science; fine/studio arts; foreign languages and literatures; history; information science/studies; international relations and affairs; journalism; mass communication/media; mathematics; mathematics teacher education; music; music therapy; nursing (registered nurse training); nursing science; philosophy; piano and organ; political science and government; pre-dentistry studies; pre-law studies; pre-medical studies; pre-veterinary studies; psychology; religious studies; secondary education; voice and opera.

Academics *Calendar:* semesters. *Degrees:* associate, bachelor's, master's, and postbachelor's certificates. *Special study options:* adult/continuing education programs, advanced placement credit, double majors, honors programs, independent study, internships, off-campus study, part-time degree program, study abroad, summer session for credit. *ROTC:* Army (c), Air Force (c).

Computers on Campus 125 computers/terminals are available on campus for general student use. Students can access the following: campus intranet, free student e-mail accounts, online (class) grades, online (class) schedules. Campuswide network is available. 100% of college-owned or -operated housing units are wired for high-speed Internet access. Wireless service is available via student centers.

Student Life *Housing:* on-campus residence required through sophomore year. *Options:* coed. Campus housing is university owned. Freshman campus housing is guaranteed. *Activities and organizations:* drama/theater group, student-run newspaper, choral group, Senate, College Union Board, Admissions Ambassadors, Students for Black Awareness, International Club, national fraternities, national sororities. *Campus security:* 24-hour emergency response devices and patrols, late-night transport/escort service, controlled dormitory access. *Student services:* health clinic, personal/psychological counseling.

Athletics Member NCAA. All Division II. *Intercollegiate sports:* basketball M (s)/W (s), cross-country running M (s)/W (s), golf M (s)/W (s), lacrosse M (s)/W (s), soccer M (s)/W (s), softball W (s), tennis M (s)/W (s), volleyball W (s). *Intramural sports:* basketball M/W, soccer M/W, softball M/W, tennis M/W, volleyball M/W.

Standardized Tests *Required:* SAT or ACT (for admission).

Costs (2008–09) *Comprehensive fee:* $29,950 includes full-time tuition ($22,068) and room and board ($7882).

Financial Aid Of all full-time matriculated undergraduates who enrolled in 2002, 510 applied for aid, 382 were judged to have need, 110 had their need fully met. 134 Federal Work-Study jobs (averaging $879). 4 state and other part-time jobs (averaging $999). In 2002, 266 non-need-based awards were made. *Average percent of need met:* 74%. *Average financial aid package:* $10,198. *Average need-based loan:* $2962. *Average need-based gift aid:* $7790. *Average non-need-based aid:* $7426. *Average indebtedness upon graduation:* $15,874.

Applying *Options:* electronic application, deferred entrance. *Application fee:* $40. *Required:* high school transcript, minimum 2.5 GPA. *Required for some:* essay or personal statement, letters of recommendation. *Recommended:* interview. *Application deadlines:* rolling (freshmen), rolling (transfers). *Notification:* continuous (freshmen), continuous (transfers).

Freshman Application Contact Queens University of Charlotte, 1900 Selwyn Avenue, Charlotte, NC 28274. *Phone:* 704-337-2212. *Toll-free phone:* 800-849-0202. *Fax:* 704-337-2403. *E-mail:* admissions@queens.edu.

ROANOKE BIBLE COLLEGE

Elizabeth City, North Carolina **www.roanokebible.edu/**

- **Independent Christian** 4-year, founded 1948
- **Small-town** 19-acre campus with easy access to Norfolk
- **Endowment** $2.9 million
- **Coed** 146 undergraduate students, 77% full-time, 45% women, 55% men
- **Minimally difficult** entrance level, 55% of applicants were admitted

Undergraduates 112 full-time, 34 part-time. Students come from 11 states and territories, 60% are from out of state, 11% African American, 3% Hispanic American, 17% transferred in, 63% live on campus. *Retention:* 60% of 2006 full-time freshmen returned.

Freshmen *Admission:* 94 applied, 52 admitted, 30 enrolled. *Average high school GPA:* 2.96. *Test scores:* SAT critical reading scores over 500: 32%; SAT math scores over 500: 54%; ACT scores over 18: 100%; SAT critical reading scores over 600: 14%; SAT math scores over 600: 14%; ACT scores over 24: 40%.

Faculty *Total:* 27, 44% full-time, 44% with terminal degrees. *Student/faculty ratio:* 7:1.

Majors Biblical studies; religious studies; theology.

Academics *Calendar:* semesters. *Degrees:* certificates, associate, and bachelor's. *Special study options:* academic remediation for entering students, advanced placement credit, internships, part-time degree program.

Computers on Campus 24 computers/terminals are available on campus for general student use. Students can access the following: free student e-mail accounts. Campuswide network is available. Wireless service is available via classrooms, learning centers, libraries.

Student Life *Housing:* on-campus residence required through senior year. *Options:* men-only, women-only. Campus housing is university owned. *Activities and organizations:* choral group, Student Advisory Council, Counseling Club, Drama Club, choral group. *Campus security:* 24-hour emergency response devices, controlled dormitory access. *Student services:* personal/psychological counseling.

Athletics *Intercollegiate sports:* basketball M/W, volleyball W. *Intramural sports:* basketball M/W, golf M/W, softball M/W, table tennis M/W, tennis M/W, volleyball M/W, weight lifting M.

Standardized Tests *Required:* SAT or ACT (for admission), SAT or ACT (for placement).

Costs (2007–08) *Comprehensive fee:* $15,635 includes full-time tuition ($9440), mandatory fees ($475), and room and board ($5720). Part-time tuition: $295 per credit hour. *Required fees:* $12 per credit hour part-time. *College room only:* $3120.

Financial Aid Of all full-time matriculated undergraduates who enrolled in 2006, 117 applied for aid, 105 were judged to have need, 9 had their need fully

over 18: 95%; SAT critical reading scores over 600: 47%; SAT math scores over 600: 35%; SAT writing scores over 600: 36%; ACT scores over 24: 57%; SAT critical reading scores over 700: 9%; SAT math scores over 700: 5%; SAT writing scores over 700: 4%; ACT scores over 30: 4%.

Faculty *Total:* 324, 64% full-time, 66% with terminal degrees. *Student/faculty ratio:* 13:1.

Majors Accounting; art; atmospheric sciences and meteorology; biology/biological sciences; business administration and management; chemistry; classics and languages, literatures and linguistics; computer science; dramatic/theater arts; economics; engineering; English; environmental studies; fine/studio arts; French; German; history; liberal arts and sciences/liberal studies; mass communication/media; mathematics; music; music related; operations management; philosophy; physics; political science and government; psychology; religious studies; sociology; Spanish; web page, digital/multimedia and information resources design; women's studies.

Academics *Calendar:* semesters. *Degrees:* certificates, bachelor's, master's, and postbachelor's certificates. *Special study options:* academic remediation for entering students, adult/continuing education programs, advanced placement credit, distance learning, double majors, honors programs, independent study, internships, off-campus study, part-time degree program, services for LD students, student-designed majors, study abroad, summer session for credit. *Unusual degree programs:* 3-2 chemistry and textile chemistry with North Carolina State University.

Computers on Campus 390 computers/terminals are available on campus for general student use. Students can access the following: online (class) registration, online grade reports. Campuswide network is available. 100% of college-owned or -operated housing units are wired for high-speed Internet access. Wireless service is available via classrooms, libraries, student centers.

Student Life *Housing:* on-campus residence required for freshman year. *Options:* coed, men-only, women-only, disabled students. Campus housing is university owned and leased by the school. Freshman campus housing is guaranteed. *Activities and organizations:* drama/theater group, student-run newspaper, radio station, choral group, Student Government Association, Underdog Productions, Residence Hall Association, African-American Association, International Student Association, national fraternities, national sororities. *Campus security:* 24-hour emergency response devices and patrols, late-night transport/escort service, dorm entrances secured at night. *Student services:* health clinic, personal/psychological counseling, women's center.

Athletics Member NCAA. All Division I. *Intercollegiate sports:* baseball M (s), basketball M (s)/W (s), cheerleading M/W, cross-country running M (s)/W (s), soccer M (s)/W (s), tennis M (s)/W (s), track and field M (s)/W (s), volleyball W (s). *Intramural sports:* badminton M/W, basketball M/W, football M, golf M/W, racquetball M/W, soccer M/W, softball M/W, table tennis M/W, tennis M/W, ultimate Frisbee M/W, volleyball M/W, water polo M/W.

Standardized Tests *Required:* SAT or ACT (for admission).

Costs (2007–08) *Tuition:* state resident $2307 full-time; nonresident $13,297 full-time. Full-time tuition and fees vary according to course load. Part-time tuition and fees vary according to course load. *Required fees:* $1857 full-time. *Room and board:* $6230; room only: $3450. Room and board charges vary according to housing facility. *Waivers:* senior citizens and employees or children of employees.

Financial Aid Of all full-time matriculated undergraduates who enrolled in 2006, 1,793 applied for aid, 1,164 were judged to have need, 512 had their need fully met. 70 Federal Work-Study jobs (averaging $1297). In 2006, 186 non-need-based awards were made. *Average percent of need met:* 83%. *Average financial aid package:* $8703. *Average need-based loan:* $3847. *Average need-based gift aid:* $4595. *Average non-need-based aid:* $3586. *Average indebtedness upon graduation:* $15,972.

Applying *Options:* electronic application, early action, deferred entrance. *Application fee:* $50. *Required:* essay or personal statement, high school transcript, letters of recommendation, Minimum Course Requirement. *Required for some:* interview. *Application deadlines:* 2/15 (freshmen), 3/15 (transfers), 11/10 (early action). *Notification:* 4/1 (freshmen), 5/1 (transfers), 12/23 (early action).

Freshman Application Contact Ms. Leigh McBride, Associate Director of Admissions, The University of North Carolina at Asheville, 117 Lipinsky Hall, CPO 2210, One University Heights, Asheville, NC 28804-8510. *Phone:* 828-251-6481. *Toll-free phone:* 800-531-9842. *Fax:* 828-251-6482. *E-mail:* admissions@unca.edu.

See page 1946 for the College Close-Up.

THE UNIVERSITY OF NORTH CAROLINA AT CHAPEL HILL

Chapel Hill, North Carolina **www.unc.edu/**

- **State-supported** university, founded 1789, part of University of North Carolina System
- **Suburban** 729-acre campus with easy access to Raleigh-Durham
- **Endowment** $2.2 billion
- **Coed** 17,628 undergraduate students, 95% full-time, 59% women, 41% men
- **Very difficult** entrance level, 35% of applicants were admitted

Undergraduates 16,722 full-time, 906 part-time. Students come from 50 states and territories, 103 other countries, 17% are from out of state, 11% African American, 7% Asian American or Pacific Islander, 4% Hispanic American, 0.8% Native American, 1% international, 4% transferred in, 46% live on campus. *Retention:* 97% of 2006 full-time freshmen returned.

Freshmen *Admission:* 20,090 applied, 6,999 admitted, 3,893 enrolled. *Test scores:* SAT critical reading scores over 500: 97%; SAT math scores over 500: 98%; SAT writing scores over 500: 96%; ACT scores over 18: 99%; SAT critical reading scores over 600: 75%; SAT math scores over 600: 80%; SAT writing scores over 600: 71%; ACT scores over 24: 89%; SAT critical reading scores over 700: 27%; SAT math scores over 700: 29%; SAT writing scores over 700: 22%; ACT scores over 30: 35%.

Faculty *Total:* 1,621, 93% full-time, 88% with terminal degrees.

Majors African-American/Black studies; American studies; anthropology; applied mathematics; area, ethnic, cultural, and gender studies related; art history, criticism and conservation; Asian studies; astronomy; biology/biological sciences; biostatistics; business administration and management; chemistry; classics and languages, literatures and linguistics; clinical laboratory science/medical technology; communication/speech communication and rhetoric; comparative literature; computer science; dental hygiene; dramatic/theater arts; early childhood education; economics; elementary education; English; environmental health; environmental science; environmental studies; fine/studio arts; foods, nutrition, and wellness; geography; geology/earth science; German; health and physical education; health/health care administration; history; human resources management; information science/studies; Latin American studies; liberal arts and sciences/liberal studies; mass communication/media; mathematics; medical radiologic technology; middle school education; music; music performance; nursing (registered nurse training); parks, recreation and leisure facilities management; pathology/experimental pathology; peace studies and conflict resolution; pharmacy, pharmaceutical sciences, and administration related; philosophy; physical sciences related; physics; political science and government; psychology; public policy analysis; religious studies; Romance languages; Romance languages related; Russian studies; Slavic, Baltic, and Albanian languages related; sociology; women's studies.

Academics *Calendar:* semesters. *Degrees:* certificates, bachelor's, master's, doctoral, first professional, post-master's, postbachelor's, and first professional certificates. *Special study options:* advanced placement credit, distance learning, double majors, freshman honors college, honors programs, independent study, internships, off-campus study, services for LD students, student-designed majors, study abroad, summer session for credit. *ROTC:* Army (b), Navy (b), Air Force (b).

Computers on Campus 600 computers/terminals are available on campus for general student use. Students can access the following: computer help desk, free student e-mail accounts, online (class) grades, online (class) registration, online (class) schedules. Campuswide network is available. 100% of college-owned or -operated housing units are wired for high-speed Internet access. Wireless service is available via entire campus.

Student Life *Housing options:* coed, men-only, women-only, disabled students. Campus housing is university owned. Freshman applicants given priority for college housing. *Activities and organizations:* drama/theater group, student-run newspaper, radio and television station, choral group, marching band, Campus Y, Newman Catholic Student Center Parish, Friendship Association of Chinese Students and Scholars, Residence Hall Association, North Carolina Hillel, national fraternities, national sororities. *Campus security:* 24-hour emergency response devices and patrols, student patrols, late-night transport/escort service, controlled dormitory access, crime prevention programs. *Student services:* health clinic, personal/psychological counseling, women's center, legal services.

Athletics Member NCAA. All Division I except football (Division I-A). *Intercollegiate sports:* baseball M (s), basketball M (s)/W (s), crew M (c)/W (s), cross-country running M (s)/W (s), equestrian sports M (c)/W (c), fencing M/W, field hockey W (s), golf M (s)/W (s), gymnastics W (s), lacrosse M (s)/W (s), racquetball M (c)/W (c), rock climbing M (c)/W (c), sailing M (c)/W (c), soccer M (s)/W (s), softball W (s), swimming and diving M (s)/W (s), tennis M (s)/W (s),

Student Life *Housing:* on-campus residence required through senior year. *Options:* women-only. Campus housing is university owned. Freshman campus housing is guaranteed. *Activities and organizations:* drama/theater group, student-run newspaper, choral group, marching band, Student Government Association, Onua, Campus Activities Council, International Club, Ambassadors. *Campus security:* 24-hour emergency response devices and patrols, late-night transport/escort service, controlled dormitory access. *Student services:* health clinic, personal/psychological counseling.

Athletics *Intercollegiate sports:* basketball W, cross-country running W, field hockey W, soccer W, swimming and diving W, tennis W, volleyball W.

Standardized Tests *Required:* SAT or ACT (for admission).

Costs (2007–08) *Comprehensive fee:* $29,240 includes full-time tuition ($18,850), mandatory fees ($340), and room and board ($10,050). Part-time tuition: $965 per course. *Payment plan:* installment. *Waivers:* employees or children of employees.

Financial Aid Of all full-time matriculated undergraduates who enrolled in 2006, 514 applied for aid, 474 were judged to have need, 474 had their need fully met. 105 Federal Work-Study jobs (averaging $1011). In 2006, 43 non-need-based awards were made. *Average percent of need met:* 100%. *Average financial aid package:* $15,340. *Average need-based loan:* $3664. *Average need-based gift aid:* $6954. *Average non-need-based aid:* $10,966. *Average indebtedness upon graduation:* $22,414.

Applying *Options:* electronic application, early admission, deferred entrance. *Application fee:* $30. *Required:* essay or personal statement, high school transcript, 2 letters of recommendation. *Recommended:* interview. *Application deadlines:* rolling (freshmen), rolling (transfers). *Notification:* continuous (freshmen), continuous (transfers).

Freshman Application Contact Katherine Knapp Watts, Chief Admissions Officer, Salem College, PO Box 10548, Shober House, Winston-Salem, NC 27108. *Phone:* 336-721-2621. *Toll-free phone:* 800-327-2536. *Fax:* 336-724-7102. *E-mail:* admissions@salem.edu.

See page 1944 for the College Close-Up.

SHAW UNIVERSITY

Raleigh, North Carolina **www.shawuniversity.edu/**

- **Independent Baptist** comprehensive, founded 1865
- **Urban** 30-acre campus
- **Endowment** $7.1 million
- **Coed** 2,656 undergraduate students, 89% full-time, 64% women, 36% men
- **Minimally difficult** entrance level, 45% of applicants were admitted

Undergraduates 2,369 full-time, 287 part-time. Students come from 37 states and territories, 19 other countries, 37% are from out of state, 85% African American, 0.3% Hispanic American, 0.1% Native American, 1% international, 7% transferred in, 31% live on campus. *Retention:* 55% of 2006 full-time freshmen returned.

Freshmen *Admission:* 5,632 applied, 2,535 admitted, 606 enrolled. *Average high school GPA:* 2.48. *Test scores:* SAT critical reading scores over 500: 7%; SAT math scores over 500: 8%; SAT writing scores over 500: 6%; ACT scores over 18: 18%; SAT math scores over 600: 1%; SAT writing scores over 600: 1%; ACT scores over 24: 1%.

Faculty *Total:* 272, 43% full-time, 50% with terminal degrees. *Student/faculty ratio:* 16:1.

Majors Accounting; athletic training; audiology and speech-language pathology; biology/biological sciences; business administration and management; chemistry; computer and information sciences; computer science; criminal justice/safety; dramatic/theater arts; elementary education; English; English/language arts teacher education; entrepreneurship; environmental studies; international business/trade/commerce; international relations and affairs; kindergarten/preschool education; kinesiology and exercise science; liberal arts and sciences/liberal studies; mass communication/media; mathematics; mathematics teacher education; music; parks, recreation and leisure; philosophy; physics; political science and government; psychology; public administration; religious studies; social work; sociology; Spanish; special education (mentally retarded); therapeutic recreation.

Academics *Calendar:* semesters. *Degrees:* certificates, associate, bachelor's, master's, and first professional. *Special study options:* academic remediation for entering students, accelerated degree program, adult/continuing education programs, advanced placement credit, distance learning, double majors, honors programs, independent study, internships, off-campus study, part-time degree program, services for LD students, student-designed majors, study abroad, summer session for credit. *ROTC:* Army (c), Air Force (c). *Unusual degree programs:* 3-2 engineering with North Carolina State University, North Carolina Agricultural and Technical State University.

Computers on Campus 280 computers/terminals and 4,000 ports are available on campus for general student use. Students can access the following: computer help desk, free student e-mail accounts, online (class) grades, online (class) registration, online (class) schedules. Campuswide network is available. 100% of college-owned or -operated housing units are wired for high-speed Internet access. Wireless service is available via classrooms, computer centers, computer labs, learning centers, libraries, student centers.

Student Life *Housing:* on-campus residence required for freshman year. *Options:* men-only, women-only. Campus housing is university owned. *Activities and organizations:* drama/theater group, student-run newspaper, radio station, choral group, marching band, Student Government Association, choir, University band, Shaw Players, academic clubs, national fraternities, national sororities. *Campus security:* 24-hour emergency response devices and patrols, late-night transport/escort service, 24-hour electronic surveillance cameras. *Student services:* health clinic, personal/psychological counseling.

Athletics Member NCAA. All Division II. *Intercollegiate sports:* baseball M (s), basketball M (s)/W (s), bowling W (s), cross-country running M (s)/W (s), football M (s), golf M, softball W (s), tennis M (s)/W (s), track and field M (s)/W (s), volleyball W (s). *Intramural sports:* basketball M/W, football M, tennis M/W, volleyball M/W.

Standardized Tests *Required:* SAT or ACT (for admission).

Costs (2007–08) *Comprehensive fee:* $17,640 includes full-time tuition ($8800), mandatory fees ($2040), and room and board ($6800). Part-time tuition: $367 per semester hour. *Required fees:* $43 per semester hour part-time, $300 per term part-time. *College room only:* $3200. *Payment plans:* installment, deferred payment. *Waivers:* employees or children of employees.

Financial Aid Of all full-time matriculated undergraduates who enrolled in 2005, 2,197 applied for aid, 2,068 were judged to have need, 201 had their need fully met. 347 Federal Work-Study jobs (averaging $1120). In 2005, 117 non-need-based awards were made. *Average percent of need met:* 63%. *Average financial aid package:* $8992. *Average need-based loan:* $3394. *Average need-based gift aid:* $5898. *Average non-need-based aid:* $9333. *Average indebtedness upon graduation:* $15,982. *Financial aid deadline:* 6/1.

Applying *Options:* electronic application, early admission, deferred entrance. *Application fee:* $25. *Required:* essay or personal statement, high school transcript, minimum 2.0 GPA. *Application deadlines:* 7/30 (freshmen), 7/30 (transfers). *Notification:* continuous (freshmen).

Freshman Application Contact Ms. Sandy Clifton, Interim Director of Admissions and Recruitment, Shaw University, 118 East South Street, Raleigh, NC 27601-2399. *Phone:* 919-546-8275. *Toll-free phone:* 800-214-6683. *Fax:* 919-546-8271. *E-mail:* sclifton@shawu.edu.

SOUTHEASTERN BAPTIST THEOLOGICAL SEMINARY

Wake Forest, North Carolina **www.sebts.edu/**

Director of Admissions Mr. Jason Hall, Director of Admissions, Southeastern Baptist Theological Seminary, PO Box 1889, Wake Forest, NC 27588. *Phone:* 919-761-2280. *Toll-free phone:* 800-284-6317.

THE UNIVERSITY OF NORTH CAROLINA AT ASHEVILLE

Asheville, North Carolina **www.unca.edu/**

- **State-supported** comprehensive, founded 1927, part of University of North Carolina System
- **Suburban** 265-acre campus
- **Endowment** $23.6 million
- **Coed** 3,663 undergraduate students, 80% full-time, 58% women, 42% men
- **Moderately difficult** entrance level, 76% of applicants were admitted

Undergraduates 2,942 full-time, 721 part-time. Students come from 45 states and territories, 16 other countries, 14% are from out of state, 3% African American, 1% Asian American or Pacific Islander, 2% Hispanic American, 0.3% Native American, 0.8% international, 8% transferred in, 33% live on campus. *Retention:* 76% of 2006 full-time freshmen returned.

Freshmen *Admission:* 2,653 applied, 2,014 admitted, 577 enrolled. *Average high school GPA:* 3.84. *Test scores:* SAT critical reading scores over 500: 87%; SAT math scores over 500: 83%; SAT writing scores over 500: 81%; ACT scores

track and field M (s)/W (s), ultimate Frisbee M (c)/W (c), volleyball M (c)/W (s), wrestling M (s). *Intramural sports:* badminton M/W, baseball M (c), basketball M/W, bowling M/W, cheerleading W (c), cross-country running M/W, field hockey M (c)/W (c), football M/W, golf M (c)/W (c), gymnastics W (c), ice hockey M (c), lacrosse M (c)/W (c), racquetball M/W, soccer M/W, softball M/W, squash M (c)/W (c), swimming and diving M/W, table tennis M/W, tennis M/W, track and field M/W, ultimate Frisbee M/W, volleyball M/W, water polo M/W, weight lifting M/W, wrestling M (c).

Standardized Tests *Required:* SAT or ACT (for admission).

Costs (2007–08) *Tuition:* state resident $3705 full-time; nonresident $19,353 full-time. Full-time tuition and fees vary according to program. Part-time tuition and fees vary according to course load and program. *Required fees:* $1635 full-time. *Room and board:* $7696; room only: $4830. Room and board charges vary according to board plan, housing facility, and location. *Payment plans:* installment, deferred payment. *Waivers:* senior citizens and employees or children of employees.

Financial Aid Of all full-time matriculated undergraduates who enrolled in 2006, 10,498 applied for aid, 5,349 were judged to have need, 5,070 had their need fully met. 1,024 Federal Work-Study jobs (averaging $1839). In 2006, 2351 non-need-based awards were made. *Average percent of need met:* 100%. *Average financial aid package:* $11,394. *Average need-based loan:* $4070. *Average need-based gift aid:* $8771. *Average non-need-based aid:* $5217.

Applying *Options:* electronic application, early action, deferred entrance. *Application fee:* $70. *Required:* essay or personal statement, high school transcript, 1 letter of recommendation, counselor's statement. *Application deadlines:* 1/15 (freshmen), 3/1 (transfers), 11/1 (early action). *Notification:* 3/31 (freshmen), 4/21 (transfers), 1/15 (early action).

Freshman Application Contact Stephen Farmer, Assistant Provost and Director of Undergraduate Admissions, The University of North Carolina at Chapel Hill, Campus Box # 2200, Jackson Hall, Chapel Hill, NC 27599-2200. *Phone:* 919-966-3621. *Fax:* 919-962-3045. *E-mail:* uadm@email.unc.edu.

THE UNIVERSITY OF NORTH CAROLINA AT CHARLOTTE

Charlotte, North Carolina — www.uncc.edu/

- **State-supported** university, founded 1946, part of University of North Carolina System
- **Suburban** 1000-acre campus
- **Endowment** $159.1 million
- **Coed** 17,598 undergraduate students, 84% full-time, 52% women, 48% men
- **Moderately difficult** entrance level, 75% of applicants were admitted

Undergraduates 14,826 full-time, 2,772 part-time. Students come from 48 states and territories, 92 other countries, 10% are from out of state, 14% African American, 5% Asian American or Pacific Islander, 4% Hispanic American, 0.5% Native American, 2% international, 12% transferred in, 32% live on campus. *Retention:* 77% of 2006 full-time freshmen returned.

Freshmen *Admission:* 9,911 applied, 7,477 admitted, 2,955 enrolled. *Average high school GPA:* 3.55. *Test scores:* SAT critical reading scores over 500: 62%; SAT math scores over 500: 74%; ACT scores over 18: 89%; SAT critical reading scores over 600: 13%; SAT math scores over 600: 21%; ACT scores over 24: 37%; ACT scores over 30: 3%.

Faculty *Total:* 1,344, 70% full-time, 67% with terminal degrees. *Student/faculty ratio:* 15:1.

Majors Accounting; African-American/Black studies; anthropology; architecture; area, ethnic, cultural, and gender studies related; art; art teacher education; athletic training/sports medicine; biology/biological sciences; business administration and management; business/managerial economics; chemistry; chemistry teacher education; child guidance; civil engineering; civil engineering technology; clinical laboratory science/medical technology; communication/speech communication and rhetoric; computer engineering; computer science; criminal justice/safety; dance; drama and dance teacher education; dramatic/theater arts; earth sciences; economics; electrical, electronics and communications engineering; elementary education; English; English/language arts teacher education; family living/parenthood; finance; fine/studio arts; fire services administration; French; French language teacher education; geography; geological and earth sciences/geosciences related; geology/earth science; German; German language teacher education; health and physical education; history; history teacher education; human development and family studies; industrial technology; international business/trade/commerce; kindergarten/preschool education; Latin American studies; management information systems; mathematics; mathematics teacher education; mechanical engineering; mechanical engineering/mechanical technology; meteorology; middle school education; music; music performance; music teacher education; nursing (registered nurse training); operations management; philosophy; physics; political science and government; psychology; religious studies; social work; sociology; Spanish; Spanish language teacher education; special education (mentally retarded).

Academics *Calendar:* semesters. *Degrees:* bachelor's, master's, doctoral, and post-master's certificates. *Special study options:* adult/continuing education programs, advanced placement credit, cooperative education, distance learning, double majors, English as a second language, freshman honors college, honors programs, internships, off-campus study, part-time degree program, services for LD students, study abroad, summer session for credit. *ROTC:* Army (b), Air Force (b).

Computers on Campus 1,400 computers/terminals and 4,921 ports are available on campus for general student use. Students can access the following: computer help desk, free student e-mail accounts, online (class) grades, online (class) registration, online (class) schedules. Campuswide network is available. 100% of college-owned or -operated housing units are wired for high-speed Internet access. Wireless service is available via classrooms, dorm rooms, learning centers, libraries, student centers.

Student Life *Housing options:* coed, men-only, women-only, disabled students. Campus housing is university owned. *Activities and organizations:* drama/theater group, student-run newspaper, choral group, University Program Board, Student Government Association, Resident Student Association, Black Student Union, national fraternities, national sororities. *Campus security:* 24-hour emergency response devices and patrols, late-night transport/escort service, controlled dormitory access. *Student services:* health clinic, personal/psychological counseling.

Athletics Member NCAA. All Division I. *Intercollegiate sports:* baseball M (s), basketball M (s)/W (s), cross-country running M (s)/W (s), golf M (s), soccer M (s)/W (s), softball W (s), tennis M (s)/W (s), track and field M (s)/W (s), volleyball W (s). *Intramural sports:* archery M (c)/W (c), badminton M (c)/W (c), baseball M (c)/W (c), basketball M/W, bowling M (c)/W (c), fencing M (c)/W (c), football M/W, golf M/W, ice hockey M (c)/W (c), lacrosse M (c)/W (c), racquetball M (c)/W (c), rock climbing M/W, rugby M (c)/W (c), soccer M (c)/W (c), softball M (c)/W (c), swimming and diving M (c)/W (c), table tennis M/W, tennis M (c)/W (c), track and field M/W, volleyball M (c)/W (c), water polo M/W, wrestling M (c)/W (c).

Standardized Tests *Required:* SAT or ACT (for admission).

Costs (2007–08) *Tuition:* state resident $2460 full-time, $173 per credit hour part-time; nonresident $12,873 full-time, $607 per credit hour part-time. Full-time tuition and fees vary according to course load. Part-time tuition and fees vary according to course load. *Required fees:* $1692 full-time. *Room and board:* $6034; room only: $3064. Room and board charges vary according to board plan and housing facility. *Payment plan:* installment. *Waivers:* senior citizens.

Financial Aid Of all full-time matriculated undergraduates who enrolled in 2006, 8,978 applied for aid, 6,727 were judged to have need, 591 had their need fully met. 541 Federal Work-Study jobs (averaging $1630). 1,833 state and other part-time jobs (averaging $2090). In 2006, 212 non-need-based awards were made. *Average percent of need met:* 62%. *Average financial aid package:* $7267. *Average need-based loan:* $3725. *Average need-based gift aid:* $4006. *Average non-need-based aid:* $3363. *Average indebtedness upon graduation:* $17,730.

Applying *Options:* electronic application, early admission, deferred entrance. *Application fee:* $50. *Required:* high school transcript, minimum 2.0 GPA, medical history, no criminal record. *Required for some:* interview. *Application deadlines:* 7/1 (freshmen), 7/1 (transfers). *Notification:* continuous (freshmen), continuous (transfers).

Freshman Application Contact Tina McEntire, Director of Admissions, The University of North Carolina at Charlotte, 9201 University City Boulevard, 1st Floor, Cato Hall, Charlotte, NC 28223-0001. *Phone:* 704-687-2213. *Fax:* 704-687-6483. *E-mail:* unccadm@uncc.edu.

THE UNIVERSITY OF NORTH CAROLINA AT GREENSBORO

Greensboro, North Carolina — www.uncg.edu/

- **State-supported** university, founded 1891, part of University of North Carolina System
- **Urban** 210-acre campus
- **Endowment** $156.0 million
- **Coed** 13,408 undergraduate students, 86% full-time, 68% women, 32% men
- **Moderately difficult** entrance level, 71% of applicants were admitted

Undergraduates 11,550 full-time, 1,858 part-time. Students come from 51 states and territories, 12 other countries, 7% are from out of state, 21% African American, 3% Asian American or Pacific Islander, 3% Hispanic American, 0.5%

Native American, 1% international, 11% transferred in, 31% live on campus. *Retention:* 76% of 2006 full-time freshmen returned.

Freshmen *Admission:* 8,856 applied, 6,285 admitted, 2,446 enrolled. *Average high school GPA:* 3.57. *Test scores:* SAT critical reading scores over 500: 57%; SAT math scores over 500: 62%; SAT writing scores over 500: 54%; SAT critical reading scores over 600: 15%; SAT math scores over 600: 15%; SAT writing scores over 600: 11%; SAT critical reading scores over 700: 2%; SAT math scores over 700: 1%; SAT writing scores over 700: 1%.

Faculty *Total:* 1,080, 75% full-time, 71% with terminal degrees. *Student/faculty ratio:* 16:1.

Majors Accounting; African-American/Black studies; anthropology; apparel and textiles; applied mathematics; archeology; art; art teacher education; audiology and speech-language pathology; biochemistry; biology/biological sciences; biology teacher education; business administration and management; business/managerial economics; business teacher education; chemistry; child development; classics; classics and languages, literatures and linguistics; clinical laboratory science/medical technology; computer and information sciences; computer systems networking and telecommunications; dance; drama and dance teacher education; dramatic/theater arts; early childhood education; economics; education; elementary education; English; English/language arts teacher education; family and consumer sciences/human sciences; finance; fine/studio arts; foodservice systems administration; French; French language teacher education; geography; German; German language teacher education; health teacher education; history; hospitality administration; human development and family studies; interdisciplinary studies; interior design; international business/trade/commerce; jazz/jazz studies; kinesiology and exercise science; liberal arts and sciences/liberal studies; management information systems; mass communication/media; mass communications; mathematics; mathematics teacher education; middle school education; music; music history, literature, and theory; music performance; music teacher education; music theory and composition; nursing (registered nurse training); nutrition sciences; parks, recreation and leisure; parks, recreation and leisure facilities management; philosophy; physical education teaching and coaching; physics; political science and government; psychology; public health education and promotion; religious studies; social science teacher education; social studies teacher education; social work; sociology; Spanish; Spanish language teacher education; special education; special education (hearing impaired); speech and rhetoric; speech teacher education; statistics; women's studies.

Academics *Calendar:* semesters. *Degrees:* bachelor's, master's, doctoral, post-master's, and postbachelor's certificates. *Special study options:* academic remediation for entering students, accelerated degree program, adult/continuing education programs, advanced placement credit, distance learning, double majors, freshman honors college, honors programs, independent study, internships, off-campus study, part-time degree program, services for LD students, study abroad, summer session for credit. *ROTC:* Army (c), Air Force (c). *Unusual degree programs:* 3-2 business administration with North Carolina State University, University of North Carolina at Charlotte.

Computers on Campus 500 computers/terminals are available on campus for general student use. Students can access the following: computer help desk, free student e-mail accounts, online (class) grades, online (class) registration, online (class) schedules. Campuswide network is available. Wireless service is available via computer labs, libraries.

Student Life *Housing options:* coed, women-only. Campus housing is university owned. Freshman applicants given priority for college housing. *Activities and organizations:* drama/theater group, student-run newspaper, radio station, choral group, marching band, Campus Activities Board, Neo-Black Society, religious organizations, International Students Association, national fraternities, national sororities. *Campus security:* 24-hour emergency response devices and patrols, late-night transport/escort service, controlled dormitory access. *Student services:* health clinic, personal/psychological counseling, women's center.

Athletics Member NCAA. All Division I. *Intercollegiate sports:* baseball M (s), basketball M (s)/W (s), cross-country running M (s)/W (s), golf M (s)/W (s), soccer M (s)/W (s), softball W (s), tennis M (s)/W (s), volleyball W (s), wrestling M (s). *Intramural sports:* badminton M/W, basketball M/W, bowling M/W, equestrian sports M (c)/W (c), fencing M (c)/W (c), football M/W, golf M/W, ice hockey M (c), lacrosse M (c)/W (c), racquetball M/W, rugby M (c)/W (c), soccer M/W, softball M/W, swimming and diving M/W, table tennis M/W, tennis M/W, track and field M/W, ultimate Frisbee M/W, volleyball M/W.

Standardized Tests *Required:* SAT or ACT (for admission).

Costs (2007–08) *Tuition:* state resident $2458 full-time, $307 per credit hour part-time; nonresident $13,726 full-time, $1716 per credit hour part-time. *Required fees:* $1571 full-time. *Room and board:* $6051; room only: $3427.

Financial Aid Of all full-time matriculated undergraduates who enrolled in 2007, 8,057 applied for aid, 7,869 were judged to have need, 2,289 had their need fully met. 627 Federal Work-Study jobs (averaging $936). In 2007, 488 non-need-based awards were made. *Average percent of need met:* 56%. *Average financial aid package:* $8989. *Average need-based loan:* $4189. *Average need-based gift aid:* $4852. *Average non-need-based aid:* $4187. *Average indebtedness upon graduation:* $16,708.

Applying *Options:* electronic application, early admission. *Application fee:* $45. *Required:* high school transcript, minimum 2.0 GPA. *Application deadlines:* 3/1 (freshmen), 8/1 (transfers). *Notification:* continuous (freshmen), continuous (transfers).

Freshman Application Contact Ms. Lise Keller, Director of Admissions, The University of North Carolina at Greensboro, 123 Mossman, PO Box 26170, Greensboro, NC 27402. *Phone:* 336-334-5243. *Fax:* 336-334-4180. *E-mail:* undergrad_admissions@uncg.edu.

THE UNIVERSITY OF NORTH CAROLINA AT PEMBROKE

Pembroke, North Carolina **www.uncp.edu/**

- **State-supported** comprehensive, founded 1887, part of University of North Carolina System
- **Rural** 152-acre campus
- **Endowment** $8.2 million
- **Coed** 5,237 undergraduate students, 79% full-time, 63% women, 37% men
- **Moderately difficult** entrance level, 86% of applicants were admitted

Undergraduates 4,126 full-time, 1,111 part-time. Students come from 28 states and territories, 11 other countries, 5% are from out of state, 28% African American, 2% Asian American or Pacific Islander, 4% Hispanic American, 18% Native American, 0.8% international, 9% transferred in, 32% live on campus. *Retention:* 72% of 2006 full-time freshmen returned.

Freshmen *Admission:* 2,750 applied, 2,375 admitted, 1,119 enrolled. *Average high school GPA:* 3.03. *Test scores:* SAT critical reading scores over 500: 28%; SAT math scores over 500: 38%; SAT writing scores over 500: 22%; ACT scores over 18: 62%; SAT critical reading scores over 600: 4%; SAT math scores over 600: 7%; SAT writing scores over 600: 3%; ACT scores over 24: 11%; ACT scores over 30: 1%.

Faculty *Total:* 435, 64% full-time, 57% with terminal degrees. *Student/faculty ratio:* 14:1.

Majors Accounting; American Indian/Native American studies; American studies; art teacher education; athletic training; athletic training/sports medicine; biology/biological sciences; biology teacher education; biotechnology; business administration and management; chemistry; college student counseling and personnel services; computer science; counselor education/school counseling and guidance; criminal justice/safety; dramatic/theater arts; early childhood education; education (specific levels and methods) related; elementary education; English; English/language arts teacher education; environmental science; fine/studio arts; health and physical education; history; information technology; kindergarten/preschool education; mass communications; mathematics; mathematics teacher education; middle school education; multi-/interdisciplinary studies related; music; music performance; music teacher education; nursing (registered nurse training); parks, recreation and leisure facilities management; philosophy and religious studies related; physical education teaching and coaching; physics; political science and government; psychology; public administration; public health education and promotion; reading teacher education; science teacher education; secondary school administration/principalship; social studies teacher education; social work; sociology; Spanish; special education (mentally retarded); special education (specific learning disabilities).

Academics *Calendar:* semesters. *Degrees:* bachelor's and master's. *Special study options:* academic remediation for entering students, accelerated degree program, adult/continuing education programs, advanced placement credit, cooperative education, distance learning, double majors, English as a second language, honors programs, independent study, internships, off-campus study, part-time degree program, services for LD students, study abroad, summer session for credit. *ROTC:* Army (b), Air Force (b).

Computers on Campus 650 computers/terminals are available on campus for general student use. Students can access the following: computer help desk, free student e-mail accounts, online (class) grades, online (class) registration, online (class) schedules. Campuswide network is available. 100% of college-owned or -operated housing units are wired for high-speed Internet access. Wireless service is available via classrooms, computer centers, computer labs, dorm rooms, learning centers, libraries, student centers.

Student Life *Housing options:* coed, men-only, women-only. Campus housing is university owned and is provided by a third party. Freshman campus housing is guaranteed. *Activities and organizations:* drama/theater group, student-run newspaper, television station, choral group, NAACP, African Student Organization, English Club, International Student Organization, Voices of Serenity and Disabled

Student Organization, national fraternities, national sororities. *Campus security:* 24-hour emergency response devices and patrols, late-night transport/escort service, controlled dormitory access. *Student services:* health clinic, personal/psychological counseling.

Athletics Member NCAA. All Division II. *Intercollegiate sports:* baseball M (s), basketball M (s)/W (s), cross-country running M (s)/W (s), football M (s), golf M (s), soccer M (s)/W (s), softball W (s), tennis W (s), track and field M (s), volleyball W (s), wrestling M (s). *Intramural sports:* basketball M/W, bowling M/W, football M/W, golf M/W, soccer M/W, softball M/W, tennis M/W, ultimate Frisbee M/W, volleyball M/W, wrestling M/W.

Standardized Tests *Required:* SAT or ACT (for admission).

Costs (2008–09) *Tuition:* state resident $2046 full-time, $256 per credit hour part-time; nonresident $11,769 full-time, $1471 per credit hour part-time. *Required fees:* $1589 full-time, $66 per credit hour part-time. *Room and board:* $6190; room only: $3250.

Financial Aid Of all full-time matriculated undergraduates who enrolled in 2006, 3,456 applied for aid, 2,910 were judged to have need, 238 had their need fully met. 269 Federal Work-Study jobs (averaging $1227). 29 state and other part-time jobs (averaging $1500). In 2006, 20 non-need-based awards were made. *Average percent of need met:* 73%. *Average financial aid package:* $8235. *Average need-based loan:* $3756. *Average need-based gift aid:* $5288. *Average non-need-based aid:* $1205. *Average indebtedness upon graduation:* $16,296.

Applying *Options:* deferred entrance. *Application fee:* $40. *Required:* high school transcript. *Required for some:* letters of recommendation, interview. *Recommended:* essay or personal statement, minimum 2.0 GPA. *Application deadlines:* rolling (freshmen), rolling (transfers). *Notification:* continuous (freshmen), continuous (transfers).

Freshman Application Contact Mrs. Natayla Freeman Locklear, Associate Director of Admissions, The University of North Carolina at Pembroke, PO Box 1510, Pembroke, NC 28372-1510. *Phone:* 910-521-6507. *Toll-free phone:* 800-949-UNCP. *Fax:* 910-521-6497.

See page 1948 for the College Close-Up.

THE UNIVERSITY OF NORTH CAROLINA WILMINGTON

Wilmington, North Carolina **www.uncw.edu/**

- **State-supported** comprehensive, founded 1947, part of University of North Carolina System
- **Urban** 650-acre campus
- **Endowment** $49.8 million
- **Coed** 10,753 undergraduate students, 91% full-time, 58% women, 42% men
- **Moderately difficult** entrance level, 58% of applicants were admitted

Undergraduates 9,818 full-time, 935 part-time. Students come from 48 states and territories, 41 other countries, 15% are from out of state, 5% African American, 2% Asian American or Pacific Islander, 3% Hispanic American, 0.8% Native American, 0.4% international, 11% transferred in, 22% live on campus. *Retention:* 85% of 2006 full-time freshmen returned.

Freshmen *Admission:* 8,740 applied, 5,098 admitted, 1,920 enrolled. *Average high school GPA:* 3.74. *Test scores:* SAT critical reading scores over 500: 87%; SAT math scores over 500: 91%; SAT writing scores over 500: 79%; ACT scores over 18: 98%; SAT critical reading scores over 600: 27%; SAT math scores over 600: 37%; SAT writing scores over 600: 24%; ACT scores over 24: 49%; SAT critical reading scores over 700: 2%; SAT math scores over 700: 3%; SAT writing scores over 700: 1%; ACT scores over 30: 5%.

Faculty *Total:* 850, 64% full-time, 67% with terminal degrees. *Student/faculty ratio:* 17:1.

Majors Accounting; anthropology; art history, criticism and conservation; athletic training; biology/biological sciences; biology teacher education; business administration and management; business/managerial economics; chemistry; chemistry teacher education; cinematography and film/video production; communication/speech communication and rhetoric; computer science; creative writing; criminal justice/safety; dramatic/theater arts; economics; education (specific subject areas) related; elementary education; English; English/language arts teacher education; environmental science; environmental studies; finance; fine/studio arts; French; French language teacher education; geography; geology/earth science; German; health and physical education; health professions related; history; history teacher education; kindergarten/preschool education; management information systems; marine biology and biological oceanography; marketing/marketing management; mathematics; mathematics teacher education; middle school education; music; music performance; music teacher education; nursing (registered nurse training); parks, recreation and leisure facilities management; philosophy and religious studies related; physical education teaching and coaching; physics; political science and government; psychology; social work; sociology; Spanish; Spanish language teacher education; special education; special education (emotionally disturbed); special education (mentally retarded); special education (multiply disabled); special education (specific learning disabilities); statistics; therapeutic recreation.

Academics *Calendar:* semesters. *Degrees:* bachelor's, master's, doctoral, post-master's, and postbachelor's certificates. *Special study options:* academic remediation for entering students, accelerated degree program, adult/continuing education programs, advanced placement credit, cooperative education, distance learning, double majors, English as a second language, honors programs, independent study, internships, part-time degree program, services for LD students, study abroad, summer session for credit.

Computers on Campus 1,170 computers/terminals are available on campus for general student use. Students can access the following: campus intranet, computer help desk, free student e-mail accounts, online (class) grades, online (class) registration, online (class) schedules. Campuswide network is available. 100% of college-owned or -operated housing units are wired for high-speed Internet access. Wireless service is available via entire campus.

Student Life *Housing options:* coed, women-only. Campus housing is university owned. Freshman applicants given priority for college housing. *Activities and organizations:* drama/theater group, student-run newspaper, radio and television station, choral group, Student Government Association, Association of Campus Entertainment, Residence Hall Association, Sailing Club, national fraternities, national sororities. *Campus security:* 24-hour emergency response devices and patrols, late-night transport/escort service, controlled dormitory access, escort service. *Student services:* health clinic, personal/psychological counseling, legal services.

Athletics Member NCAA. All Division I. *Intercollegiate sports:* baseball M (s), basketball M (s)/W (s), cheerleading M/W (s), cross-country running M (s)/W (s), golf M (s)/W (s), soccer M (s)/W (s), softball W (s), swimming and diving M (s)/W (s), tennis M (s)/W (s), track and field M (s)/W (s), volleyball W (s). *Intramural sports:* baseball M (c), basketball M/W, crew M (c)/W (c), cross-country running M/W, field hockey W (c), golf M (c)/W, gymnastics W (c), lacrosse M (c)/W (c), rugby M (c), sailing M (c)/W (c), soccer M (c)/W (c), softball M/W (c), swimming and diving M (c)/W (c), tennis M (c)/W (c), ultimate Frisbee M (c)/W (c), volleyball M (c)/W.

Standardized Tests *Required:* SAT or ACT (for admission).

Costs (2007–08) *Tuition:* state resident $2413 full-time; nonresident $12,376 full-time. Full-time tuition and fees vary according to course load. Part-time tuition and fees vary according to course load. *Required fees:* $1985 full-time. *Room and board:* $6998. Room and board charges vary according to board plan and housing facility. *Payment plan:* installment. *Waivers:* senior citizens and employees or children of employees.

Financial Aid Of all full-time matriculated undergraduates who enrolled in 2007, 5,591 applied for aid, 2,963 were judged to have need, 2,114 had their need fully met. 244 Federal Work-Study jobs (averaging $2500). In 2007, 148 non-need-based awards were made. *Average percent of need met:* 88%. *Average financial aid package:* $6476. *Average need-based loan:* $3807. *Average need-based gift aid:* $4278. *Average non-need-based aid:* $1626. *Average indebtedness upon graduation:* $16,350.

Applying *Options:* electronic application, early admission, early action, deferred entrance. *Application fee:* $45. *Required:* essay or personal statement, high school transcript. *Recommended:* letters of recommendation. *Application deadlines:* 2/1 (freshmen), 3/1 (transfers), 11/1 (early action). *Notification:* 4/1 (freshmen), continuous (transfers), 1/20 (early action).

Freshman Application Contact Dr. Terrence M. Curran, Associate Provost, The University of North Carolina Wilmington, 601 South College Road, Wilmington, NC 28403-3297. *Phone:* 910-962-3876. *Toll-free phone:* 800-228-5571. *Fax:* 910-962-3038. *E-mail:* admissions@uncw.edu.

See page 1950 for the College Close-Up.

UNIVERSITY OF PHOENIX–CHARLOTTE CAMPUS

Charlotte, North Carolina **www.phoenix.edu/**

- **Proprietary** comprehensive, founded 2003
- **Urban** campus
- **Coed**
- **Noncompetitive** entrance level

Faculty *Student/faculty ratio:* 9:1.

Academics *Calendar:* continuous. *Degrees:* bachelor's and master's.

Student Life *Campus security:* late-night transport/escort service.

Costs (2007–08) *Tuition:* $11,100 full-time, $370 per credit part-time. Full-time tuition and fees vary according to course level.

Financial Aid *Average financial aid package:* $4289. *Average need-based gift aid:* $2238.
Applying *Options:* deferred entrance. *Application fee:* $45. *Required:* 1 letter of recommendation. *Required for some:* high school transcript.
Freshman Application Contact Ms. Beth Barilla, Associate Vice President, Student Admissions and Services, University of Phoenix–Charlotte Campus, 4615 East Elwood Street, Mail Stop AA-K101, Phoenix, AZ 58040-1958. *Phone:* 480-317-6000. *Toll-free phone:* 800-776-4867 (in-state); 800-228-7240 (out-of-state). *Fax:* 480-894-1758. *E-mail:* beth.barilla@phoenix.edu.

UNIVERSITY OF PHOENIX–RALEIGH CAMPUS

Raleigh, North Carolina **www.phoenix.edu/**

- **Proprietary** comprehensive
- **Urban** campus
- **Coed**
- **Noncompetitive** entrance level

Faculty *Student/faculty ratio:* 7:1.
Academics *Degrees:* bachelor's and master's.
Student Life *Campus security:* late-night transport/escort service.
Costs (2007–08) *Tuition:* $11,100 full-time, $370 per credit part-time. Full-time tuition and fees vary according to course level.
Financial Aid *Average financial aid package:* $4157. *Average need-based gift aid:* $2266.
Applying *Options:* deferred entrance. *Application fee:* $45. *Required:* 1 letter of recommendation. *Required for some:* high school transcript.
Freshman Application Contact Ms. Beth Barilla, Associate Vice President, Student Admissions and Services, University of Phoenix–Raleigh Campus, 4615 East Elwood Street, Mail Stop AA-K101, Phoenix, AZ 85040-1958. *Phone:* 480-317-6000. *Toll-free phone:* 800-776-4867 (in-state); 800-228-7240 (out-of-state). *Fax:* 480-894-1758. *E-mail:* beth.barilla@phoenix.edu.

WAKE FOREST UNIVERSITY

Winston-Salem, North Carolina **www.wfu.edu/**

- **Independent** university, founded 1834
- **Suburban** 340-acre campus
- **Endowment** $1.2 billion
- **Coed** 4,412 undergraduate students, 99% full-time, 51% women, 49% men
- **Very difficult** entrance level, 42% of applicants were admitted

Undergraduates 4,350 full-time, 62 part-time. Students come from 50 states and territories, 25 other countries, 75% are from out of state, 7% African American, 5% Asian American or Pacific Islander, 2% Hispanic American, 0.6% Native American, 1% international, 1% transferred in, 69% live on campus. *Retention:* 94% of 2006 full-time freshmen returned.
Freshmen *Admission:* 7,177 applied, 3,041 admitted, 1,124 enrolled. *Test scores:* SAT critical reading scores over 500: 98%; SAT math scores over 500: 98%; SAT critical reading scores over 600: 83%; SAT math scores over 600: 86%; SAT critical reading scores over 700: 26%; SAT math scores over 700: 32%.
Faculty *Total:* 666, 70% full-time, 75% with terminal degrees. *Student/faculty ratio:* 10:1.
Majors Accounting; ancient/classical Greek; anthropology; art history, criticism and conservation; biology/biological sciences; business/commerce; chemistry; Chinese; classics and languages, literatures and linguistics; clinical laboratory science/medical technology; communication/speech communication and rhetoric; computer and information sciences; dramatic/theater arts; econometrics and quantitative economics; economics; education (multiple levels); engineering; English; finance; fine/studio arts; French; German; history; Japanese; kinesiology and exercise science; Latin; management information systems; management science; mathematics; music; philosophy; physician assistant; physics; political science and government; psychology; religious studies; Russian; sociology; Spanish.
Academics *Calendar:* semesters. *Degrees:* bachelor's, master's, doctoral, and first professional. *Special study options:* advanced placement credit, double majors, honors programs, independent study, internships, off-campus study, part-time degree program, services for LD students, study abroad, summer session for credit. *ROTC:* Army (b). *Unusual degree programs:* 3-2 engineering with North Carolina State University; forestry with Duke University; dentistry with University of North Carolina at Chapel Hill; physician's assistant, accounting, medical technology, Latin American studies with Georgetown University.
Computers on Campus 150 computers/terminals and 3,500 ports are available on campus for general student use. Students can access the following: campus intranet, computer help desk, free student e-mail accounts, online (class) grades, online (class) registration, online (class) schedules, financial information online, drop-add, transcript requests. Campuswide network is available. 100% of college-owned or -operated housing units are wired for high-speed Internet access. Wireless service is available via entire campus.
Student Life *Housing:* on-campus residence required through sophomore year. *Options:* coed. Campus housing is university owned. Freshman campus housing is guaranteed. *Activities and organizations:* drama/theater group, student-run newspaper, radio and television station, choral group, marching band, Student Union Network, Volunteer Service Corps, Screamin' Demons, student government, national fraternities, national sororities. *Campus security:* 24-hour emergency response devices and patrols, late-night transport/escort service, controlled dormitory access. *Student services:* health clinic, personal/psychological counseling.
Athletics Member NCAA. All Division I except football (Division I-A). *Intercollegiate sports:* baseball M (s), basketball M (s)/W (s), cross-country running M (s)/W (s), field hockey W (s), golf M (s)/W (s), soccer M (s)/W (s), tennis M (s)/W (s), track and field M (s)/W (s), volleyball W (s). *Intramural sports:* baseball M (c), basketball M/W, bowling M/W, cheerleading M (c)/W (c), crew M (c)/W (c), cross-country running M (c)/W (c), equestrian sports M (c)/W (c), fencing M (c)/W (c), field hockey W (c), football M, golf M (c)/W (c), ice hockey M (c)/W (c), lacrosse M (c)/W (c), racquetball M/W, rugby M (c), skiing (cross-country) M (c)/W (c), skiing (downhill) M (c)/W (c), soccer M (c)/W (c), softball M/W (c), swimming and diving M/W, table tennis M/W, tennis M/W, ultimate Frisbee M/W, volleyball M/W, wrestling M (c).
Standardized Tests *Required:* SAT or ACT (for admission).
Costs (2008–09) *Comprehensive fee:* $46,842 includes full-time tuition ($36,560), mandatory fees ($415), and room and board ($9867). Part-time tuition: $1517 per credit hour. *College room only:* $6186.
Financial Aid Of all full-time matriculated undergraduates who enrolled in 2007, 1,765 applied for aid, 1,561 were judged to have need, 956 had their need fully met. 983 Federal Work-Study jobs (averaging $1818). In 2007, 345 non-need-based awards were made. *Average percent of need met:* 97%. *Average financial aid package:* $27,709. *Average need-based loan:* $8626. *Average need-based gift aid:* $23,138. *Average non-need-based aid:* $11,071. *Average indebtedness upon graduation:* $23,397. *Financial aid deadline:* 3/1.
Applying *Options:* electronic application, early admission, early decision, deferred entrance. *Application fee:* $50. *Required:* essay or personal statement, high school transcript, 1 letter of recommendation. *Application deadline:* 1/15 (freshmen). *Early decision deadline:* 11/15. *Notification:* 4/1 (freshmen), 12/15 (early decision).
Director of Admissions Ms. Martha Allman, Director of Admissions, Wake Forest University, PO Box 7305, Winston-Salem, NC 27109. *Phone:* 336-758-5201.

WARREN WILSON COLLEGE

Swannanoa, North Carolina **www.warren-wilson.edu/**

- **Independent** comprehensive, founded 1894, affiliated with Presbyterian Church (U.S.A.)
- **Small-town** 1135-acre campus
- **Endowment** $38.4 million
- **Coed** 873 undergraduate students, 99% full-time, 62% women, 38% men
- **Moderately difficult** entrance level, 81% of applicants were admitted

Undergraduates 865 full-time, 8 part-time. Students come from 48 states and territories, 16 other countries, 88% are from out of state, 1% African American, 1% Asian American or Pacific Islander, 2% Hispanic American, 0.3% Native American, 3% international, 6% transferred in, 89% live on campus. *Retention:* 71% of 2006 full-time freshmen returned.
Freshmen *Admission:* 808 applied, 651 admitted, 235 enrolled. *Average high school GPA:* 3.30. *Test scores:* SAT critical reading scores over 500: 93%; SAT math scores over 500: 77%; SAT writing scores over 500: 88%; SAT critical reading scores over 600: 56%; SAT math scores over 600: 32%; SAT writing scores over 600: 45%; SAT critical reading scores over 700: 20%; SAT math scores over 700: 5%; SAT writing scores over 700: 8%.
Faculty *Total:* 79, 81% full-time, 86% with terminal degrees. *Student/faculty ratio:* 13:1.
Majors Art; Asian studies; biology/biological sciences; business administration and management; chemistry; creative writing; economics; education; elementary education; English; entrepreneurial and small business related; environmental studies; history; humanities; interdisciplinary studies; international business/trade/

commerce; international/global studies; Latin American studies; mathematics; non-profit management; philosophy; psychology; secondary education; social work; sociology; Spanish; women's studies.

Academics *Calendar:* semesters. *Degrees:* bachelor's and master's. *Special study options:* advanced placement credit, cooperative education, double majors, English as a second language, honors programs, independent study, internships, off-campus study, part-time degree program, services for LD students, student-designed majors, study abroad. *Unusual degree programs:* 3-2 engineering with Washington University in St. Louis; forestry with Duke University.

Computers on Campus 92 computers/terminals are available on campus for general student use. Students can access the following: computer help desk, free student e-mail accounts, online (class) grades, online (class) registration, online (class) schedules, word processing, GIS, Statistical Analysis, Graphica. Campuswide network is available. 100% of college-owned or -operated housing units are wired for high-speed Internet access. Wireless service is available via classrooms, dorm rooms, student centers.

Student Life *Housing:* on-campus residence required for freshman year. *Options:* coed, men-only, women-only. Campus housing is university owned. Freshman campus housing is guaranteed. *Activities and organizations:* drama/theater group, student-run newspaper, radio station, choral group, Collective Conscience/Social Justice/Student Caucus, Resistance and Peacemaking (RAP), yoga, Outing Club, African Dance Club. *Campus security:* 24-hour emergency response devices and patrols, student patrols, late-night transport/escort service, controlled dormitory access. *Student services:* health clinic, personal/psychological counseling.

Athletics Member NSCAA. *Intercollegiate sports:* basketball M/W, cross-country running M/W, soccer M/W, swimming and diving M/W. *Intramural sports:* crew M/W, fencing M/W, golf M/W, lacrosse M/W, rock climbing M/W, soccer M/W, softball M/W, table tennis M/W, tennis M/W, ultimate Frisbee M/W, volleyball M/W, weight lifting M/W.

Standardized Tests *Required:* SAT or ACT (for admission).

Costs (2008–09) *Comprehensive fee:* $29,782 includes full-time tuition ($22,366), mandatory fees ($300), and room and board ($7116). Part-time tuition: $932 per credit.

Financial Aid Of all full-time matriculated undergraduates who enrolled in 2006, 623 applied for aid, 509 were judged to have need, 76 had their need fully met. 410 Federal Work-Study jobs (averaging $2645). 400 state and other part-time jobs (averaging $2559). In 2006, 149 non-need-based awards were made. *Average percent of need met:* 71%. *Average financial aid package:* $15,730. *Average need-based loan:* $3084. *Average need-based gift aid:* $11,307. *Average non-need-based aid:* $3795. *Average indebtedness upon graduation:* $20,554.

Applying *Options:* electronic application, early admission, early decision, deferred entrance. *Required:* essay or personal statement, high school transcript, minimum 2.5 GPA, 2 letters of recommendation. *Recommended:* interview. *Application deadlines:* 3/15 (freshmen), 3/15 (transfers). *Early decision deadline:* 11/15. *Notification:* continuous (freshmen), continuous until 4/1 (transfers), 12/1 (early decision).

Freshman Application Contact Mr. Richard Blomgren, Dean of Admission, Warren Wilson College, PO Box 9000, Asheville, NC 28815-9000. *Phone:* 828-771-2073. *Toll-free phone:* 800-934-3536. *Fax:* 828-298-1440. *E-mail:* admit@warren-wilson.edu.

See page 1952 for the College Close-Up.

WESTERN CAROLINA UNIVERSITY

Cullowhee, North Carolina **www.wcu.edu/**

- **State-supported** comprehensive, founded 1889, part of University of North Carolina System
- **Rural** 260-acre campus
- **Endowment** $32.5 million
- **Coed** 7,120 undergraduate students, 85% full-time, 53% women, 47% men
- **Moderately difficult** entrance level, 68% of applicants were admitted

Undergraduates 6,022 full-time, 1,098 part-time. Students come from 36 states and territories, 18 other countries, 7% are from out of state, 5% African American, 0.8% Asian American or Pacific Islander, 1% Hispanic American, 1% Native American, 1% international, 11% transferred in, 45% live on campus. *Retention:* 67% of 2006 full-time freshmen returned.

Freshmen *Admission:* 4,792 applied, 3,254 admitted, 1,259 enrolled. *Average high school GPA:* 3.35. *Test scores:* SAT critical reading scores over 500: 48%; SAT math scores over 500: 61%; SAT writing scores over 500: 40%; ACT scores over 18: 79%; SAT critical reading scores over 600: 12%; SAT math scores over 600: 15%; SAT writing scores over 600: 9%; ACT scores over 24: 17%; SAT critical reading scores over 700: 1%; SAT math scores over 700: 1%; SAT writing scores over 700: 1%; ACT scores over 30: 1%.

Faculty *Total:* 698, 71% full-time, 59% with terminal degrees. *Student/faculty ratio:* 13:1.

Majors Accounting; anthropology; art; art teacher education; biology/biological sciences; business administration and management; chemistry; clinical laboratory science/medical technology; communication disorders; communication/speech communication and rhetoric; computer science; construction management; criminal justice/safety; dietetics; dramatic/theater arts; electrical and electronic engineering technologies related; electrical, electronic and communications engineering technology; electrical, electronics and communications engineering; elementary education; emergency medical technology (EMT paramedic); engineering technology; English; English/language arts teacher education; entrepreneurship; environmental health; environmental science; finance; fine/studio arts; forensic science and technology; French language teacher education; geography; geology/earth science; German; German language teacher education; health/health care administration; health information/medical records administration; history; hospitality administration; industrial technology; interior design; international business/trade/commerce; liberal arts and sciences/liberal studies; management information systems; manufacturing technology; marketing/marketing management; marketing related; mathematics; mathematics teacher education; middle school education; music; music performance; music teacher education; natural resources management and policy; nursing (registered nurse training); parks, recreation and leisure facilities management; philosophy; physical education teaching and coaching; political science and government; psychology; public administration; radio, television, and digital communication related; science teacher education; social sciences; social studies teacher education; social work; sociology; Spanish; Spanish language teacher education; special education; sport and fitness administration/management; therapeutic recreation.

Academics *Calendar:* semesters. *Degrees:* bachelor's, master's, doctoral, post-master's, and postbachelor's certificates. *Special study options:* academic remediation for entering students, accelerated degree program, adult/continuing education programs, advanced placement credit, cooperative education, distance learning, double majors, English as a second language, honors programs, independent study, internships, part-time degree program, services for LD students, student-designed majors, study abroad, summer session for credit.

Computers on Campus 226 computers/terminals and 6,550 ports are available on campus for general student use. Students can access the following: campus intranet, computer help desk, free student e-mail accounts, online (class) grades, online (class) registration, online (class) schedules, student Web pages, online music services. Campuswide network is available. 100% of college-owned or -operated housing units are wired for high-speed Internet access. Wireless service is available via entire campus.

Student Life *Housing:* on-campus residence required for freshman year. *Options:* coed, men-only, women-only, disabled students. Campus housing is university owned, leased by the school and is provided by a third party. Freshman campus housing is guaranteed. *Activities and organizations:* drama/theater group, student-run newspaper, radio and television station, choral group, marching band, College Panhellenic Council, Inter-Fraternity Council, Physical Therapy Club, Online Gaming Club, UNITY, national fraternities, national sororities. *Campus security:* 24-hour emergency response devices and patrols, controlled dormitory access. *Student services:* health clinic, personal/psychological counseling, women's center.

Athletics Member NCAA. All Division I except football (Division I-AA). *Intercollegiate sports:* baseball M (s), basketball M (s)/W (s), cheerleading M (c)/W (c), cross-country running M (s)/W (s), equestrian sports M (c)/W (c), fencing M (c)/W (c), field hockey M (c)/W (c), golf M (s)/W (s), lacrosse M (c)/W (c), racquetball M (c)/W (c), rugby M (c)/W (c), soccer W (s), softball W (s), swimming and diving M (c)/W (c), tennis W (s), track and field M (s)/W (s), ultimate Frisbee M (c)/W (c), volleyball W (s), weight lifting W (c). *Intramural sports:* badminton M/W, basketball M/W, bowling M/W, cross-country running M/W, football M/W, soccer M/W, softball M/W, swimming and diving M/W, table tennis M/W, tennis M/W, track and field M/W, ultimate Frisbee M/W, volleyball M/W, water polo M/W, weight lifting M/W, wrestling M/W.

Standardized Tests *Required:* SAT or ACT (for admission).

Costs (2008–09) *Tuition:* state resident $2078 full-time; nonresident $11,661 full-time. *Required fees:* $2337 full-time. *Room and board:* $5626; room only: $2916.

Financial Aid Of all full-time matriculated undergraduates who enrolled in 2007, 4,185 applied for aid, 3,057 were judged to have need, 1,451 had their need fully met. 444 Federal Work-Study jobs (averaging $1599). In 2007, 401 non-need-based awards were made. *Average percent of need met:* 83%. *Average financial aid package:* $7696. *Average need-based loan:* $3373. *Average need-based gift aid:* $5252. *Average non-need-based aid:* $1399. *Average indebtedness upon graduation:* $11,285.

Applying *Options:* electronic application, early admission, early decision, early action. *Application fee:* $40. *Required:* high school transcript, minimum 2.5 GPA. *Application deadlines:* 4/1 (freshmen), 6/1 (transfers). *Notification:* continuous (freshmen), continuous (transfers).

Freshman Application Contact Mr. Alan Kines, Director of Admissions, Western Carolina University, Cullowhee, NC 28723. *Phone:* 828-227-7317. *Toll-free phone:* 877-WCU4YOU. *Fax:* 828-277-7319. *E-mail:* admiss@email.wcu.edu.

See page 1954 for the College Close-Up.

WINGATE UNIVERSITY

Wingate, North Carolina **www.wingate.edu/**

- **Independent Baptist** comprehensive, founded 1896
- **Small-town** 330-acre campus with easy access to Charlotte
- **Endowment** $29.1 million
- **Coed** 1,471 undergraduate students, 96% full-time, 53% women, 47% men
- **Moderately difficult** entrance level, 50% of applicants were admitted

Undergraduates 1,407 full-time, 64 part-time. Students come from 32 states and territories, 13 other countries, 32% are from out of state, 14% African American, 2% Asian American or Pacific Islander, 2% Hispanic American, 0.8% Native American, 3% international, 6% transferred in, 89% live on campus. *Retention:* 68% of 2006 full-time freshmen returned.

Freshmen *Admission:* 3,437 applied, 1,719 admitted, 426 enrolled. *Average high school GPA:* 3.5. *Test scores:* SAT critical reading scores over 500: 46%; SAT math scores over 500: 53%; ACT scores over 18: 86%; SAT critical reading scores over 600: 11%; SAT math scores over 600: 18%; ACT scores over 24: 24%; SAT critical reading scores over 700: 1%; SAT math scores over 700: 2%; ACT scores over 30: 3%.

Faculty *Total:* 109. *Student/faculty ratio:* 13:1.

Majors Accounting; American studies; art; art teacher education; athletic training; biology/biological sciences; biology teacher education; business administration and management; chemistry; computer graphics; economics; elementary education; English; environmental biology; finance; fine/studio arts; French; health and physical education; history; human services; liberal arts and sciences/liberal studies; management information systems; marketing/marketing management; mass communication/media; mathematics; middle school education; music; music teacher education; parks, recreation and leisure; philosophy; pre-law studies; pre-medical studies; pre-pharmacy studies; pre-veterinary studies; psychology; reading teacher education; religious studies; social studies teacher education; sociology; Spanish; sport and fitness administration/management.

Academics *Calendar:* semesters. *Degrees:* bachelor's, master's, and first professional. *Special study options:* adult/continuing education programs, advanced placement credit, double majors, honors programs, independent study, internships, off-campus study, part-time degree program, services for LD students, study abroad, summer session for credit. *ROTC:* Army (c), Air Force (c).

Computers on Campus 75 computers/terminals are available on campus for general student use. Students can access the following: free student e-mail accounts, online (class) grades, online (class) registration, online (class) schedules. Campuswide network is available. 100% of college-owned or -operated housing units are wired for high-speed Internet access. Wireless service is available via classrooms, computer centers, libraries, student centers.

Student Life *Housing:* on-campus residence required through senior year. *Options:* men-only, women-only. Campus housing is university owned. Freshman campus housing is guaranteed. *Activities and organizations:* drama/theater group, student-run newspaper, television station, choral group, Student Community Service Organization, Fellowship of Christian Athletes, Student Government Association, Christian Student Union, Bulldogs Running Club, national fraternities, national sororities. *Campus security:* 24-hour emergency response devices and patrols, late-night transport/escort service, controlled dormitory access. *Student services:* health clinic, personal/psychological counseling.

Athletics Member NCAA. All Division II. *Intercollegiate sports:* baseball M (s), basketball M (s)/W (s), cross-country running M (s)/W, football M (s), golf M (s)/W (s), lacrosse M (s), soccer M (s)/W, softball W (s), swimming and diving M (s)/W (s), tennis M (s)/W (s), volleyball W (s). *Intramural sports:* basketball M/W, bowling M/W, cross-country running M, football M/W, golf M/W, racquetball M/W, swimming and diving M/W, table tennis M/W, tennis M/W, track and field M/W, volleyball M/W, water polo M/W, weight lifting M/W.

Standardized Tests *Recommended:* SAT or ACT (for admission).

Costs (2007–08) *Comprehensive fee:* $25,580 includes full-time tuition ($17,430), mandatory fees ($1050), and room and board ($7100). Part-time tuition: $580 per credit hour. Part-time tuition and fees vary according to course load. *Required fees:* $175 per term part-time. *Room and board:* Room and board charges vary according to board plan. *Payment plan:* installment. *Waivers:* employees or children of employees.

Financial Aid Of all full-time matriculated undergraduates who enrolled in 2006, 1,131 applied for aid, 830 were judged to have need, 234 had their need fully met. 164 Federal Work-Study jobs (averaging $786). 373 state and other part-time jobs (averaging $560). In 2006, 405 non-need-based awards were made. *Average percent of need met:* 80%. *Average financial aid package:* $15,049. *Average need-based loan:* $3619. *Average need-based gift aid:* $5240. *Average non-need-based aid:* $4623. *Average indebtedness upon graduation:* $2424.

Applying *Options:* electronic application, early admission, early decision, deferred entrance. *Application fee:* $30. *Required:* high school transcript, minimum 2.0 GPA. *Recommended:* minimum 3.0 GPA, letters of recommendation, interview. *Application deadlines:* rolling (freshmen), rolling (transfers). *Notification:* continuous (freshmen), continuous (transfers).

Freshman Application Contact Mr. Rhett Brown, Dean of Enrollment Management, Wingate University, PO Box 159, Wingate, NC 28174. *Phone:* 704-233-8000. *Toll-free phone:* 800-755-5550. *Fax:* 704-233-8110. *E-mail:* admit@wingate.edu.

WINSTON-SALEM STATE UNIVERSITY

Winston-Salem, North Carolina **www.wssu.edu/**

- **State-supported** comprehensive, founded 1892, part of University of North Carolina System
- **Urban** 94-acre campus
- **Endowment** $17.3 million
- **Coed**
- **Minimally difficult** entrance level

Faculty *Student/faculty ratio:* 15:1.

Academics *Calendar:* semesters. *Degrees:* certificates, bachelor's, master's, and postbachelor's certificates.

Student Life *Campus security:* 24-hour emergency response devices and patrols.

Athletics Member NCAA. All Division I.

Standardized Tests *Required:* SAT or ACT (for admission).

Costs (2007–08) *Tuition:* state resident $1700 full-time; nonresident $10,341 full-time. Full-time tuition and fees vary according to degree level. Part-time tuition and fees vary according to course load and location. *Required fees:* $1599 full-time. *Room and board:* $5670; room only: $3434. Room and board charges vary according to board plan and housing facility.

Financial Aid Of all full-time matriculated undergraduates who enrolled in 2006, 4,644 applied for aid, 4,095 were judged to have need, 354 had their need fully met. 258 Federal Work-Study jobs (averaging $1361). 26 state and other part-time jobs (averaging $2755). In 2006, 54 non-need-based awards were made. *Average percent of need met:* 71. *Average financial aid package:* $5602. *Average need-based loan:* $2926. *Average need-based gift aid:* $2350. *Average non-need-based aid:* $4414. *Average indebtedness upon graduation:* $10,200. *Financial aid deadline:* 4/1.

Applying *Options:* deferred entrance. *Application fee:* $40. *Required:* high school transcript. *Recommended:* 1 letter of recommendation.

Freshman Application Contact Ms. Tomikia LeGrande, Director of Admissions, Winston-Salem State University, 601 Martin Luther King Jr Drive, Thompson Center, Winston-Salem, NC 27110-0003. *Phone:* 336-750-2070. *Toll-free phone:* 800-257-4052. *Fax:* 336-750-2079. *E-mail:* admissions@wssu.edu.

THE ART INSTITUTE OF CHARLOTTE

CHARLOTTE, NORTH CAROLINA

The Institute

The Art Institute of Charlotte prepares students for entry-level employment in the creative arts. Students learn through programs of study that reflect the needs of a changing job market. Courses are taught by faculty members who have professional experience in their fields of expertise. The school offers seven bachelor's degree programs, five associate degree programs, and four certificate programs.

Students come to The Art Institute of Charlotte from throughout the southeastern United States and abroad. The student population includes recent high school graduates, transfer students, and those who have left a previous employment situation to study and train for a new career. Students are creative, competitive, and open to new ideas. They place great value on an education that prepares them for an exciting entry-level position in the arts.

Student housing options include apartments that comfortably accommodate 4 students in two-bedroom, two-bath units complete with living room, dining area, and full kitchen. Students submit a roommate preference form and are assigned to apartments by the housing staff. The apartments are located close to The Art Institute of Charlotte and shopping, dining, and entertainment venues.

Students enrolled in The Art Institute of Charlotte can get involved in student-led activities through the Student Affairs Department. Activities stimulate cultural awareness, creativity, and social and professional development. Students enrolled in the Interior Design Program may join the Interior Design Student Association. In addition, academic departments regularly organize trips to the International Home Furnishing Market in High Point, North Carolina, as well as to local museums and galleries.

Services are available to assist students with resume writing, networking, and keeping aware of what employers are looking for in job applicants.

The Art Institute of Charlotte is accredited by the Accrediting Council for Independent Colleges and Schools (ACICS) to award bachelor's degrees, associate degrees, and certificates. ACICS is listed as a nationally recognized accrediting agency by the U.S. Department of Education. Its accreditation of degree-granting institutions is recognized by the Council for Higher Education Accreditation. ACICS can be contacted at 750 First Street NE, Suite 980, Washington, D.C. 20002; telephone: 202-336-6780.

Location

Charlotte mixes the characteristics of a large urban center with the charm of suburban life. With a mild climate and central location, Charlotte residents are only 2 hours from the Blue Ridge Mountains and 3 hours from the Atlantic coast. Charlotte is known for its arts community, sports, shopping, and restaurants. More than 300 Fortune 500 companies have offices in Charlotte, the nation's second-largest banking center. The city is the nation's fifth-largest urban region, with 6.3 million people living within a 100-mile radius.

Majors and Degrees

Bachelor's degree programs are available in culinary arts management, digital filmmaking and video production, fashion marketing and management, graphic design, interior design, photography, and Web design and interactive media.

Associate degree programs are offered in culinary arts, fashion marketing, graphic design, interior design, and Web design and interactive media.

Certificate programs are available in digital design, residential design, the art of cooking, and Web design.

Academic Programs

The Art Institute of Charlotte operates on a year-round, four-quarter system.

Academic Facilities

The Art Institute of Charlotte facility has computer labs for student use. Additional computers are available in the library. Studios, classrooms, and meetings rooms are available for students and faculty members.

Costs

Tuition cost varies by program. Prospective students should contact the school for current tuition costs. Other charges include a starting kit for all first quarter students. Kits vary in price depending on the program of study.

Financial Aid

Financial aid is available for those who qualify. Students who require financial assistance should first complete and submit a Free Application for Federal Student Aid (FAFSA) and meet with a financial aid officer. The officer determines the level of need based on a required federal formula, the cost of education, and other factors. Gift aid is available in the form of Federal Pell Grants, Federal Supplemental Educational Opportunity Grants, and veterans' benefits. Loans include Federal Stafford Loans, Federal PLUS Loans, and alternative loans. Other scholarships are available from the school and private sources. Application deadlines and eligibility requirements vary by program.

Faculty

Faculty members at The Art Institute of Charlotte are experienced instructors, many of whom have professional experience outside of the classroom. There are full- and part-time faculty members at the school.

Admission Requirements

Applicants must be high school graduates or have a General Educational Development (GED) certificate. A 150-word written essay is required, as are high school transcripts and any records from other academic institutions attended. All interested students are interviewed in person or over the phone. Following this interview, prospective students complete an application for admission and submit the enrollment fee. Applicants who have taken the SAT or ACT are encouraged to submit their scores to the Admissions Office for evaluation. There is a $50 application fee.

Application and Information

To obtain an application or make arrangements for an interview or tour of the school, prospective students should contact:

The Art Institute of Charlotte
Three LakePointe Plaza
2110 Water Ridge Parkway
Charlotte, North Carolina 28217-4536

Phone: 704-357-8020
800-872-4417 (toll-free)
Fax: 704-357-1133
Web site: http://www.artinstitutes.edu/charlotte

The Art Institute of Atlanta®, GA; The Art Institute of Atlanta®–Decatur, GA; The Art Institute of Austin℠, TX; The Art Institute of California℠–Inland Empire; The Art Institute of California℠–Los Angeles; The Art Institute of California℠–Orange County; The Art Institute of California℠–Sacramento; The Art Institute of California℠–San Diego; The Art Institute of California℠–San Francisco; The Art Institute of California℠–Sunnyvale; The Art Institute of Charleston℠, SC, A branch of The Art Institute of Atlanta, GA; The Art Institute of Charlotte®, NC; The Art Institute of Colorado® (Denver); The Art Institute of Dallas®, TX; The Art Institute of Fort Lauderdale®, FL; The Art Institute of Houston®, TX; The Art Institute of Indianapolis℠, IN*; The Art Institute of Jacksonville℠, FL, A branch of Miami International University of Art & Design; The Art Institute of Las Vegas®, NV; The Art Institute of Michigan℠ (Detroit); The Art Institute of New York City®, NY; The Art Institute of Ohio℠–Cincinnati**; The Art Institute of Philadelphia®, PA; The Art Institute of Phoenix®, AZ; The Art Institute of Pittsburgh®, PA; The Art Institute of Pittsburgh®–Online Division; The Art Institute of Portland®, OR; The Art Institute of Salt Lake City℠, UT; The Art Institute of Seattle®, WA; The Art Institute of Tampa℠, FL, A branch of Miami International University of Art & Design; The Art Institute of Tennessee℠–Nashville, A branch of The Art Institute of Atlanta, GA; The Art Institute of Tucson℠, AZ; The Art Institute of Washington® (Arlington, VA), A branch of The Art Institute of Atlanta, GA; The Art Institute of York–Pennsylvania℠; The Art Institutes International Minnesota℠ (Minneapolis); California Design College℠ (Los Angeles–Wilshire Blvd.); The Illinois Institute of Art®–Chicago; The Illinois Institute of Art®–Schaumburg; Miami International University of Art & Design℠, FL; The New England Institute of Art® (Boston, MA).

*The Art Institute of Indianapolis is licensed by the Indiana Commission on Proprietary Education, 302 W. Washington St., Rm. E201, Indianapolis, IN 46204, AC-0080.

**The Art Institute of Ohio–Cincinnati, 8845 Governors Hill Drive, Suite 100, Cincinnati, OH 45249-3317, OH Reg. #04-01-1698B.

BARTON COLLEGE

WILSON, NORTH CAROLINA

The College

Founded in 1902 as the first degree-granting institution in eastern North Carolina, Barton College opened its doors to 107 students with one building on 5 acres of campus. Today, Barton welcomes approximately 1,200 students from thirty-one states and sixteen countries to a campus of twenty-six buildings on 65 acres.

The College offers several avenues of assistance for students, especially during the freshman year, including an innovative freshman advising program designed to assist students in making the transition from home and high school to college and residence hall life. All freshmen meet with their adviser three times a week in a classroom seminar setting. Outside the classroom experience, the First-Year Seminar program also offers exposure to a variety of cultural and social events, including concerts, lectures, art exhibits, drama productions, and sports events. Inside the classroom, Barton's student-centered core curriculum enhances academic success and provides students with an outstanding foundation from which the total liberal arts experience is achieved.

Barton's Student Affairs Program includes residence life programs, special activities, fellowship programs, and counseling services that provide for the students' cultural, social, spiritual, and emotional development. In addition, Barton has fifty clubs and organizations in which students can be involved, including academic organizations, specialty clubs, fraternities, and sororities. Another vital component of student life is the Career Services Center. The center provides a vigorous on-campus recruiting program that brings approximately 100 recruiters to Barton's campus annually, representing corporations, government, and educational areas. In addition, several hundred other employers seek to hire Barton students each year. Barton's graduates rank exceptionally well in obtaining employment in their chosen field of study, and their salaries are competitive with those of students from other North Carolina colleges and universities.

On-campus housing is provided in five residence halls: East Campus Suites, Hilley, Hackney, Waters, and Wenger. All five facilities feature cable television and information technology access in each room. East Campus Suites is Barton's newest residence hall for juniors and seniors and offers additional amenities and more independence.

Offering a strong, competitive sports program, Barton College's Bulldogs compete in the NCAA Division II and the Conference Carolinas. The intercollegiate sports program includes women's basketball, cross-country, fast-pitch softball, soccer, tennis, and volleyball and men's baseball, basketball, cross-country, golf, soccer, and tennis. In 2007, the Barton College men's basketball team won the NCAA Division II National Championship. In recent years, Barton has won the Joby Hawn Award three years in a row, recognizing the College as having the best overall athletics program within the Conference Carolinas. A wide variety of intramural sports are also offered to the entire campus community. All students and especially those involved in Barton's intramural, physical education, and athletic programs benefit from the Kennedy Recreation and Intramural Center that features an indoor swimming pool, walking/jogging areas, an auxiliary gym, and a weight/fitness room. Barton also has a twelve-court tennis complex to add to its outstanding facilities package.

The 30-acre Barton College Athletic Complex includes the award-winning Nixon Baseball Field, the Jeffries Softball Field, and a newly lighted soccer field, in addition to several practice fields and the Scott Davis Field House.

Location

Wilson is in the coastal plain region of eastern North Carolina. The city provides an excellent home for the College and is within easy driving distance of several metropolitan areas and scenic attractions. The state capital of Raleigh is a 45-minute drive to the west; to the north, Richmond is 2 hours away and Washington, D.C., is 4 hours away. The beautiful Atlantic coast of North Carolina is 100 miles from the campus, and the scenic Blue Ridge Mountains are easily accessible. Located on Interstate 95, Wilson is also accessible by U.S. Routes 264, 117, and 301 and North Carolina Routes 42 and 58. Wilson is 1 hour from Raleigh/Durham International Airport. Amtrak has daily service with one northbound and one southbound departure.

The College's historic neighborhood is just a few minutes from busy downtown Wilson. Banks, theaters, shopping centers, and restaurants are close by. Many of Wilson's arts and cultural events take place on the College campus. The Wilson community (population 48,000) enjoys a mild climate that has an average annual temperature of 65 degrees.

Majors and Degrees

Barton College offers six baccalaureate degrees: Bachelor of Arts, Bachelor of Science, Bachelor of Fine Arts, Bachelor of Nursing, Bachelor of Social Work, and Bachelor of Liberal Studies. These degrees are administered by five schools.

The School of Arts and Sciences offers programs in art education (K–12), art and design (with concentrations in ceramics, design, painting, and photography), athletic training, biology, (preprofessional programs in dentistry, medical technology, medicine, physical therapy, and veterinary medicine), chemistry (preprofessional program in pharmacy), English*, environmental science, fitness management, history, mass communications (concentrations include audio recording technology, broadcast/video production, print and electronic journalism), mathematics (preprofessional program in engineering), physical education (with teacher licensure), political science (concentrations include business and prelaw), psychology, religion and philosophy, social studies (with teacher licensure), Spanish*, sport management, and theater (concentrations include design, management, and performance).

The School of Behavioral Sciences offers programs in criminology and criminal justice, gerontology, and social work.

The School of Business offers programs in accounting, business management, computer information systems, and management of human resources.

The School of Education offers programs in education of the deaf and hard of hearing (K–12), elementary education (K–6), middle school education (6–9), and special education: general curriculum.

The School of Nursing offers a program in nursing.

*Programs indicated with an asterisk (*) are available with or without a teacher licensure program.

Minors can be earned in accounting, American studies, art and design, biology, business administration, chemistry, communications, computer information systems, criminal justice and criminology, economics, English, finance, geography, gerontology, history, international business, management, marketing, mathematics, physical education, political science, psychology, religion and philosophy, Spanish, strength and conditioning, theater, and writing.

Academic Programs

Barton College offers a strong liberal arts tradition, and students follow a core curriculum during their freshman and sophomore years. Through a carefully guided advising program they declare a major area of study at the end of their freshman year or at the beginning of their sophomore year. At that point, they begin an intense and challenging program of study in their chosen field while completing general college requirements.

Expanded travel opportunities and concentrated study are enhanced by Barton's 4-1-4 semester system featuring the January Term.

Barton College's athletic training education, nursing, education, and social work programs are nationally accredited programs. The School of Business majors continue to be popular areas of study. Barton is one of the few colleges on the East Coast to offer a program for the education of the deaf and the hard of hearing. Also unique is the recording technology program, which features a 32-track digital recording studio. The School of Behavioral Sciences offers a social work degree program, a gerontology major, and a criminology and criminal justice major with law enforcement certification available to students choosing that track.

Off-Campus Programs

Each year students participate in faculty-led trips to different areas of the world. Students recognize this travel as an excellent opportunity to enrich their college experience. Depending on the nature and destination of the travel, students may obtain college credit for their participation. Barton also has exchange agreements with colleges in Europe and Asia for extended overseas study offered in conjunction with a global focus emphasis.

Academic Facilities

Barton College has a fiber-optic underground network that includes an infrastructure of data, voice, and video wiring across campus. The Willis N. Hackney Library is open 86.5 hours per week to serve the College community. BARTON LINC, the College's library information network center, offers a variety of services for users, including library information (hours, services, etc.), library online catalog, connection to other databases, connection to other libraries, and connection to subject-related Internet sites. The library's collection includes 173,464 total volumes, including more than 23,905 electronic books, and U.S. government documents, as well as a substantial collection of microfilm, maps, filmstrips, and pamphlets. It also subscribes to 355 periodicals and newspapers and 14,546 electronic subscriptions. The Media Center, located on the basement level of Harper Hall, provides checkout service for audiovisual equipment.

Located on the first floor of J. W. Hines Hall are two computer labs for classes and individual student use. Computer labs are also available for student use in the Nixon Nursing Building, the Belk Education Building, Hamlin Student Center, and Moye Science Hall. The Nixon Nursing Building also has a multimedia center with a state-of-the-art projection system, installed for a broad range of lecture and teaching purposes, and the Belk Education Building houses the state-of-the-art Merck Science and Mathematics Instructional Lab. The Sam and Marjorie Ragan Writing Center supplements Barton's commitment to language and writing as vital components of the liberal arts curriculum. Students have access to more than 125 computer terminals on campus.

WEDT-TV, a local cable television station operated by Barton College and staffed by Barton students, is located in the Roma Hackney Music Building. The TV studio offers up-to-date equipment and facilities for study and use in television, videotape, and audiotape production. The Hackney Music Building also houses classrooms, the College's library for recordings and musical scores, and the Sara Lynn Kennedy Recording Studio. Moye Science Hall provides classrooms, laboratories, a greenhouse, and research-related study areas for students. The Nixon Nursing Building houses classrooms and a laboratory for the nursing program. Case Art Building provides classrooms, private and class studios, and two art galleries for Barton's permanent art collection and for visiting exhibits. The art building also houses state-of-the-art computer graphics and darkroom labs.

Costs

Expenses for the 2007–08 year included tuition, $17,490; room, $3100; board plan, $3420; and combined fees, $1396. These totaled $25,406 for the year. The estimated cost of books per semester was $600. Rates for East Campus Suites are not listed because of limited availability; this facility is reserved for juniors and seniors.

Financial Aid

The objective of the financial aid program at Barton College is to provide financial assistance to qualified students who would not otherwise be able to begin or continue their college education. Financial aid is awarded on the basis of need. (Financial need exists when the total cost of education exceeds the amount of money a student and family can reasonably make available from income and assets.) Barton College requires that all applicants for financial aid complete the Free Application for Federal Student Aid (FAFSA) as a means of determining financial need. Approximately 84 percent of Barton students receive financial aid. Aid comes from federal, state, and institutional resources and may be awarded as scholarships, grants, loans, or work-study. In addition, many students apply for part-time jobs on campus or in the community through the Career Services Center.

Students are encouraged to apply early for financial aid and should have their completed application in the Financial Aid Office by June 1 in order to ensure receipt of awards by the beginning of the fall semester. Every effort is made to process completed applications received after this date; however, earlier applications receive top priority in the awards process.

Faculty

Faculty members at Barton College recognize the importance of personalized attention for the students' learning experience. Because of the 11:1 student-faculty ratio, professors at Barton are able to teach small classes and have the opportunity to meet and to get to know their students as individuals. Faculty members make every effort to be accessible to students between classes and during regularly scheduled office hours. Professors at Barton are committed to the success of their students.

Student Government

The Student Government Association (SGA) of Barton College provides students with opportunities to express themselves on issues of concern. Student government also provides a setting for studying the democratic process. The officers of the SGA are elected by the members of the student body, and the president of the SGA serves as an ex officio member of the College Board of Trustees.

Admission Requirements

To be considered for admission to Barton College, a student must have a high school diploma or its equivalent with a minimum total of 13 college-preparatory units. The following courses are recommended: English, 4 units; mathematics, 3 or more units (algebra I, geometry, and algebra II are required); natural sciences, 2 or more units (one lab science is required); social sciences, 2 or more units; and foreign language, 2 or more units (encouraged, but not required). A student applying for admission must also take the SAT or ACT and achieve a score that, when considered along with the high school record, predicts probable success in college.

Application and Information

To apply for admission to the College, a student must submit a completed application, a nonrefundable $25 application fee ($50 for international students), and an official transcript of high school credits. A copy of SAT or ACT scores should be sent to the Office of Admissions by the testing agency. International applicants whose native language is not English must also submit the results of the Test of English as a Foreign Language (TOEFL). Students are encouraged to apply early and are usually notified of a decision within two weeks of the admission office's receipt of the completed application and information.

For further information, students may contact:

Office of Admissions
Barton College
Box 5000
Wilson, North Carolina 27893-7000
Phone: 252-399-6317
800-345-4973 (toll-free)
Fax: 252-399-6572
E-mail: enroll@barton.edu
Web site: http://www.barton.edu

BREVARD COLLEGE

BREVARD, NORTH CAROLINA

The College

Brevard College (BC) offers a range of distinctive baccalaureate degree programs on a beautiful residential campus in Brevard, North Carolina.

With more than forty majors and minors, preprofessional studies, and teacher's education, Brevard College offers an engaging education for just about everyone. Whether a student is leaning toward a more traditional degree or would like to do something that is a little out-of-the-box, BC accommodates the individual and the experiential learner. Brevard offers everything from business and organizational leadership and religion studies to a wilderness leadership and experiential education program that shows students how to turn mountain climbing and kayaking into a career. The College's music and fine arts program remains one of the finest in the region.

Brevard offers an education that is supportive, flexible, and challenging. Every Brevard College student takes part in a one-semester course called the First-Year Forum (FYF). FYF allows students to learn about traditions, service opportunities, academic resources, and clubs and gives students a chance to meet weekly with a faculty mentor and other first-year students. Brevard's unique orientation program is ranked as one of the best freshman-year experience programs in the country by *U.S. News & World Report.*

The College's low 10:1 student-faculty ratio allows professors to design their classes based on student interest and to forge bonds with students that last the entire four years—if not a lifetime. Brevard also offers an honors program for students seeking greater challenges in the classroom as well as a recently renovated Academic Enrichment Center that provides one-on-one academic support, career exploration and counseling services, and weekly tutoring sessions under one roof.

Brevard has an active student government association and approximately twenty student-run clubs and organizations, including Omicron Delta Kappa, the national leadership honor society; Campus Crusade for Christ, a nondenominational fellowship group; and the Outing Club, which sponsors the Banff Mountain World Tour, an outdoor adventure film festival, each year. Service to others is a big part of the Brevard College experience; in fact, every student club and organization is involved in volunteer work in the surrounding forests or at local schools, churches, and hospitals.

The residence halls are the center of student life at Brevard College. Most have all of the amenities of home: high-speed Internet access, free washers and dryers, and kitchens. All are located near the recently updated Myers Dining Hall and the new food court, which is housed within the student commons. The Annabel Jones women's residence hall recently completed a $1.9-million renovation. In addition to an updated heating and cooling system, residents enjoy new windows, carpets, and furniture as well as modern bathrooms, a new student lounge, and vending areas. The College completed a renovation of its Beam freshmen residence hall in 2005.

The College has been recognized as a Champion of Character Institution by the National Association of Intercollegiate Athletics (NAIA). The Brevard Tornadoes offer some of the best varsity sports teams in the region. More than half of the College's sixteen varsity teams have placed in the top twenty in the NAIA. In 2006, the College fielded its first football team in more than fifty years and added cycling as a varsity sport. It is in its final provisional year in the NCAA Division II. The College recently completed renovations to its gymnasium, creating a new fitness, weight, and recreation area, and also offers a state-of-the-art tennis facility, which is one of the finest in the Southeast. Students enjoy a variety of intramural sports, including basketball, beach volleyball, bowling, flag football, floor hockey, softball, Ultimate Frisbee, volleyball, and other sport-of-the-month activities.

Location

Brevard College is located in the beautiful Blue Ridge Mountains of western North Carolina, next to the 157,000-acre Pisgah National Forest and right in the middle of a vibrant region known for its arts, music, and culture. Once students arrive on campus, they are surrounded by the forests and rivers of the Blue Ridge Mountains. Nearby Pisgah National Forest offers hiking and mountain-biking trails, white water, pristine trout waters, and some of the most challenging rock-climbing sites east of the Rockies. In fact, *Outside* magazine calls Brevard one of the forty Best College Towns in the United States. The College is less than 30 minutes from the Asheville airport and 45 minutes from Asheville; 2 hours from Charlotte, North Carolina; and 3 hours from Atlanta, Georgia.

Majors and Degrees

At Brevard, students can explore many fields of study, including majors in art, business and organizational leadership, criminal justice, ecology (B.S.), English/interdisciplinary studies, environmental science (B.S.), environmental studies, exercise science, general science, health sciences studies, history, integrated studies, mathematics, music (B.A. or B.M.), psychology, religious studies, theater studies, and wilderness leadership and experiential education. Minors are available in art, biology, chemistry, coaching, criminal justice, ecology, English, environmental studies, fitness leadership, geology, history, information technology, management and organizational leadership, mathematics, music, natural history, personal fitness, prelaw, psychology, religious studies, social sciences, sport and event management, theater, and wilderness leadership and experiential education. Preprofessional studies are offered in dentistry, law, medicine, nursing, and veterinary studies. Brevard College has also instituted a teacher education program that enables students to earn teacher licensure in a number of academic disciplines at both the elementary and secondary levels.

Academic Programs

Brevard College education is partially characterized by its distinctive, sometimes individually designed, combination of the newly revised general education program and a strong academic major program. Neither the general education program nor a major can fully define a Brevard College education. Brevard College uses a semester calendar and offers Bachelor of Arts degrees. In addition to traditional disciplines, Brevard incorporates the surrounding natural resources into course work, taking students to study in the Pisgah National Forest, the Davidson and French Broad River ecosystems, the Great Smoky Mountain National Park, and the Cradle of Forestry in America. A special, selective academic program called Voice of the Rivers blends wilderness leadership skills with environmental studies. The College also offers strong programs in music and art, in which students benefit from on- and off-campus performance and exhibition opportunities at the Paul Porter Center for the Performing Arts at Brevard College, the Brevard Music Center, and the Asheville Art Museum. In fall 2008, Brevard is scheduled to launch its Institute for Women in Leadership (IWIL) program. IWIL fosters the development of female students through academic, social, and personal programs in a residential and cocurricular experience. Other opportunities for students include internships, study-abroad programs, and the honor societies Alpha Chi, Beta Beta Beta, and Omicron Delta Kappa. Brevard College incorporates community service into the academic curriculum through a variety of service-oriented classes.

Academic Facilities

Brevard College's 120-acre campus reflects the beauty of its mountain setting, the balance of tradition, and the energy of change. Major buildings on campus include the McLarty-Goodson Building for the humanities and social sciences, the Moore Science Building, the Paul Porter Center for the Performing Arts, the Dunham Music Building, the Sims Art Center, and the Beam Administration Building.

The College's new Moore Science Building annex offers additional classroom spaces, including an ecology/environmental studies lab and a state-of-the-art chemistry/biochemistry laboratory. The expansion was necessitated by the growth of the College's programs in ecology, environmental studies, and the sciences.

Brevard's Lyday Natural Science Lab, an outdoor laboratory on the banks of the French Broad River, supports eighteen field research courses and provides boat access for College field trips.

The Porter Center, which houses a 700-seat auditorium, a magnificent 3,500-pipe organ, and an experimental black-box theater, offers students their first chance to stage their own theater and music productions and to perform with nationally recognized artists. The Porter Center is a world-class performance hall, hosting the finest in jazz, classical, bluegrass, opera, and pop—from Peru Negro to Pat Metheny to Edgar Meyer musically and from the Second City comedy troupe to writer and humorist David Sedaris.

The Sims Art Building is the home of the College's Spiers Gallery, which hosts exhibitions by visiting artists, students, faculty members, and community artists throughout the year.

The James A. Jones Library provides access to diverse information resources, including more than 57,000 volumes, 540,000 e-books, 250 print subscriptions, access to 19,000 electronic journals, and 3,900 audiovisual materials, such as compact discs and videos. Internet-access databases containing indexes, abstracts, and thousands of full-text resources are available from a variety of online vendors. The library also offers wireless Internet access to students.

In addition to its regular academic buildings and facilities, the College maintains state-of-the-art computer labs on campus. The College also has several specialty labs, including a Macintosh-based lab for graphic design and a Macintosh-based music lab.

Costs

The College makes every effort to offer high-quality educational programs while keeping costs as reasonable as possible. At Brevard College, students are able to obtain an education for less than the actual cost of instruction and other student services. The difference, which averages about 35 percent of the total cost, is provided through the support of earnings on endowment investments and gifts from friends of the College.

For 2007–08, tuition was $18,700 and room and board cost $7050. For North Carolina residents, total costs were reduced by the North Carolina Legislative Tuition Grant, which covered $1950 for the 2007–08 academic year.

Financial Aid

Brevard College's Office of Financial Aid is committed to assisting students in meeting their financial obligations to the College through need-based or merit-based grants, scholarships, loans, and work-study to the maximum extent possible, based on eligibility and available funds. Every student requiring financial assistance must file the Free Application for Federal Student Aid (FAFSA). Opportunities for student financial aid are available to every student who can show financial need, superior academic achievement, significant leadership and community service experience, or talent in athletics, art, drama, or music. Brevard College does not discriminate on the basis of sex, race, color, handicap, religion, or national or ethnic origin in the administration of its financial aid resources.

Faculty

Brevard College's faculty is an exceptional group of 56 full-time instructors characterized by their accomplishments and strong personal character. The faculty members are dedicated to undergraduate teaching and take pride in all aspects of their jobs, from instruction and lecturing to advising and mentoring. This dedication, along with the 10:1 student-faculty ratio, gives students an opportunity to form lasting and meaningful student-teacher relationships. The College's faculty members pride themselves on being as devoted to the teaching of freshmen and sophomores as to the mentoring of juniors and seniors.

Student Government

Brevard College makes a special commitment to experiential learning opportunities through the Student Government Association (SGA). SGA seeks broad representation from students so they can work together to make a difference in academic and campus life. This organization gives students invaluable experience in leadership and governance. SGA leaders meet regularly with the administration, faculty members, and trustees and are actively engaged in the shared governance of the institution, holding places on all campus committees.

Admission Requirements

Brevard College seeks to admit students who distinguish themselves by their talents, creativity, leadership, adventurous spirit, motivation, and concern for others. At Brevard, students have every opportunity to take advantage of educational programs, small classes, and caring faculty members in order to realize their potential as students and as leaders among their peers. The College is interested in enrolling students who give proof of academic curiosity, creativity, and community concern and actively seeks those who add diversity to the student body, welcoming students of any race, national origin, religious belief, gender, or physical ability. The College seeks students who display a willingness to exhibit personal initiative and leadership and are likely to contribute their energies to the campus community. An admissions staff of energetic and caring people invites all interested students to visit and learn about Brevard's special community. The application process is candidate oriented; the admissions staff serves as the applicant's advocate.

When the applicant's file is complete, it is reviewed by an Admissions Counselor and/or Committee. The Admissions Counselor notifies the candidate of the decision. Decisions are made on a rolling basis, every week. A completed applicant file comprises a completed application; a nonrefundable $30 application fee; official transcript(s) showing all high school work, grades, and test scores; and official SAT or ACT scores. Transfer applicants must also include transcripts of all college work attempted. International students for whom English is a second language must also submit Test of English as a Foreign Language (TOEFL) scores.

For students wishing to be considered for degree programs in music or studio art, an audition with a Brevard College music faculty member or submission of a ten-slide portfolio of the student's artwork is required. For freshmen who have not successfully completed at least a semester of collegiate work, the high school transcript should show successful completion of college-preparatory work, including 4 units of English, 3 units of mathematics, and courses in social studies, laboratory sciences, and the arts. The program at Brevard College requires completion of core requirements that include studies in the above fields.

Specific guidelines for freshman, transfer, and international students can be found on the admissions Web site at http://www.brevard.edu/admissions.

Application and Information

For more information, students should contact:

Office of Admissions
Brevard College
400 North Broad Street
Brevard, North Carolina 28712
Phone: 800-527-9090 (toll-free)
E-mail: admissions@brevard.edu
Web site: http://www.brevard.edu

CAMPBELL UNIVERSITY

BUIES CREEK, NORTH CAROLINA

The University

Founded in 1887, Campbell University has had the distinction of being North Carolina's second-largest private undergraduate institution. In 1979, the name of the institution was changed from Campbell College to Campbell University. Its current enrollment is about 6,500 students at all campuses. There are more than 4,200 students at the main campus in Buies Creek. In an average year, the student body comes from all 100 North Carolina counties, all fifty states, and fifty countries. Seventy-five percent of the students come from North Carolina. Members of minority groups make up 25 percent of the student body.

Campbell University is nonsectarian. Approximately 48 percent of its students are Baptist, but young people of twenty-two other faiths complete its student body. It is concerned with maintaining, for living and learning, an environment consistent with Christian ideals. Among the extracurricular activities available at Campbell are band, choir, and drama groups; religious, political, professional, social, and academic groups; and intercollegiate and intramural sports organizations.

In athletics, the University is a member of NCAA Division I (Sun Athletic Conference) for men and women (with the exception of wrestling, which is in the Colonial Conference). Men's sports include baseball, basketball, cross-country, golf, soccer, tennis, track, wrestling, and NCAA Division II football. Women's sports include basketball, cheerleading, cross-country, golf, soccer, softball, swimming, tennis, track, and volleyball.

A $30-million convocation center is scheduled to be completed in 2008. The facility will house 3,000 spectators for athletic events and up to 5,000 for special concerts. A stadium to accommodate the return of football to Campbell University is also scheduled for completion in 2008. The stadium seating will hold an estimated 1,200 students and visitors.

A number of activities are available on campus during the summer for juniors and seniors in high school. Campbell University hosts an array of camps, such as band, basketball, golf, and volleyball, just to mention a few. During the ten-week period, Campbell accommodates more than 5,000 students.

The University also has campuses offering a variety of undergraduate and graduate courses at Fort Bragg, Raleigh/Morrisville, Rocky Mount, and Jacksonville, North Carolina.

Location

Buies Creek is a small, well-kept residential community in Harnett County, where North Carolina's coastal plain and Piedmont meet just east of the center of the state. The region is one of the most progressive for education and research in the Southeast. Raleigh, the capital, and Fayetteville are 30 miles from the campus; within about an hour's drive are the Research Triangle Park and the city of Durham.

Majors and Degrees

Campbell University confers seven undergraduate degrees: Bachelor of Arts, Bachelor of Science, Bachelor of Applied Science, Bachelor of Business Administration, Bachelor of Health Science, and Bachelor of Social Work and an Associate in Arts degree. The major and/or the concentration may be in any one of the following fields: accounting, advertising, art, athletic training, biochemistry, biological sciences, birth–kindergarten, business administration, chemistry, child development, church music, clinical research, composition of music, comprehensive music, criminal justice administration, drama and Christian ministries, economics, education, educational studies (no licensure), electronic media, elementary education, English, exercise and sport science, family/consumer science, family studies, fitness/wellness management, French, government, graphic design, history, information technology and security, international business, international studies, K–12 education, journalism, kinesiology, language arts, mass communication, mathematics, middle grades education, military science, music, music education, pharmaceutical sciences, physical education, piano pedagogy, predentistry, pre-engineering, prelaw, premedicine, prepharmacy, pre-physical therapy, pre-physician's assistant studies, preveterinary, professional golf management, psychology, public administration, public relations, religion (with concentrations in biblical studies, Christian history, and theology), science education, secondary education, social science, social studies education, social work, Spanish, sport management, studio art, theater arts, trust and wealth management, U.S. Army ROTC, and vocational education.

Academic Programs

The curriculum of Campbell University is designed to meet individual needs and interests. During the first two years, students follow a general course of study, the General College Curriculum, to broaden their backgrounds in the basic fields of knowledge. By the end of the sophomore year, they should have selected a major subject for specialized study during the final two years. Basic curriculum requirements for the first two years in semester hours are math, 6; English, 12; social studies, 6; natural science, 8; religion, 6; music, art appreciation, or drama, 3; foreign language, up to 9, depending on high school credits and the program of study; and health and physical education, 3. Candidates for a bachelor's degree must earn a minimum of 128 semester hours, including the 3 in health and physical education, while maintaining at least a C average in academic course work; must complete a minimum of 32 semester hours in the departmental major at Campbell; and must average C or better in all courses required for the major. Candidates for the Associate in Arts degree must complete 64 semester hours of work and have at least a 2.0 GPA on all work required for graduation and at least a 2.0 GPA on 80 percent of all work attempted. The University calendar enables students to complete first-semester course work and examinations before Christmas vacation and end the spring session by the middle of May.

Campbell offers a complete curriculum of evening courses on its main campus and at its nearby Fort Bragg campus. The Fort Bragg campus is primarily a service for military personnel on active duty, but classes are open to civilian students.

Campbell offers the nation's first undergraduate program in trust and wealth management and since 1968 has been training prospective trust officers for the banks and trust companies of the region. Campbell also sponsors the Southeastern Trust School, a summer institute for trust officers.

Campbell's School of Pharmacy has served the health-care needs of North Carolina and beyond for more than twenty years, paving the path for minority student recruitment and education enhancement through the Advancement for Underrepresented Minority Pharmacists Program. The school's curriculum is designed to focus on Pharmacy College Admission Test preparation, educational seminars, and a mentoring program in order to better prepare students for a career in pharmacy. Campbell's pharmacy students have maintained a 99 percent passage rate on the national board exams and 99 percent on state board exams.

Campbell's School of Education was established in 1985 in response to the need for fully qualified educators for the educational system of North Carolina and the country. School of Education students continue their history of academic excellence, posting a passage rate for the Praxis II exam of 96 percent in 2007. The School of Education has also been selected to participate in the North Carolina Teaching Fellows, joining thirteen public and four private institutions across the state.

The Military Science Department offers Army Reserve Officer Training Corps (ROTC) classes, leading to a commission as an officer in the Active, Reserve, or National Guard component of the United States Army. Campbell's ROTC program is one of the best in the nation, earning the MacArthur Award seven times since 1989 as the premier leadership-training program in the nation. This annual award is given jointly by the MacArthur Foundation and the Commander, U.S. Army Cadet Command. The Campbell training program is one of the best preparations possible for the nation's future leaders.

Off-Campus Programs

Credit may be earned in off-campus settings through apprenticeships or internships in communications, government, public education, religious education, psychology, social work, and trust management. Campbell's philosophy on internships is department based. Departmental inquiries are welcomed. The American Studies Program in Washington, D.C.; the Los Angeles Film Studies Center in Hollywood, California; and the Summer Institute of Journalism, also in Washington, D.C., each offer a semester-long internship program. New study-abroad opportunities allow students to study in Australia, China, Costa Rica, Egypt, England (Oxford), and Russia.

Academic Facilities

The $11-million Lundy Fetterman School of Business building provides 76,000 square feet of space for state-of-the-art classrooms, a computer lab, breakout rooms, and a library. The Leslie H. Campbell Hall of Science provides the individual student with facilities for research projects, which the University encourages in four sciences. Campbell's own computer center is supplemented by more than twenty departmental labs offering both PC and Macintosh computers. It is linked with the Triangle Universities Computation Center of the North Carolina Educational Computer Service. Campbell's Carrie Rich Library houses a collection of more than 218,000 volumes, breakout rooms for group study, and laptops that may be checked out by students. The D. Rich Memorial Building, housing Turner Auditorium, and the four-story Fred L. Taylor Hall of Religion contain classrooms, laboratories, and faculty offices. The Taylor Bott Rogers Fine Arts Complex, containing 48,820 square feet of space, is well equipped for the wide range of events staged by active music, drama, and art groups. The closed-circuit television equipment of the school's audiovisual center enhances teacher training. A 7,000-square-foot, $4-million research facility supports the Master of Science programs in pharmaceutical sciences and clinical research. Maddox Hall, a new $7.7-million School of Pharmacy teaching facility, offers 42,000 square feet dedicated to Doctor of Pharmacy students. Keith Hills housing development and golf course provides a 36-hole course for students and the community.

Costs

The 2008–09 comprehensive fee for tuition and general fees is $19,650. On-campus students are provided with board and room at a minimum of $6830.

Financial Aid

Campbell University has private and institutional scholarships, federal grants, loans, and Federal Work-Study Program awards. Loans are available through the Federal Stafford Student Loan Program and the Federal Perkins Loan Program. Needs analysis forms (Free Application for Federal Student Aid) are available January 1 and are due in the Financial Aid Office by March 15 if the applicant wishes to be considered for a maximum award. Ninety-one percent of the student body received financial assistance in 2007–08. All assistance is offered without regard to race, creed, or national origin.

Faculty

The faculty consists of 305 teachers, of whom approximately 91 percent have earned the doctorate or the highest degree in their field. Ninety-three percent of classes have fewer than 50 students.

Student Government

Through the Student Government Association (SGA), the student body has an opportunity for self-government and a means to channel ideas and wishes to the proper administrative personnel. The SGA is composed of executive, judicial, and legislative branches. The executive officers are the president, vice president, secretary, treasurer, advancement officer, parliamentarian, executive officer of the Disciplinary Committee, and presidents of the women's campus, the men's campus, and the day students. The legislative branch includes the Student Congress, made up of representatives from each of the four classes elected by popular vote.

Admission Requirements

The minimum requirements for admission to Campbell include graduation from high school or equivalent credentials, with at least 13 nonvocational units, which must include 4 in English, 3 in college-preparatory mathematics (including 2 of algebra and 1 of geometry), 2 in foreign language, 2 in social sciences (1 must be in United States history), and 2 in natural sciences (1 must be a laboratory science). Two units of a foreign language are highly desirable. Acceptable scores must be earned on the SAT or the ACT.

Application and Information

An application for admission, accompanied by a $35 nonrefundable application fee, must be filed. Students may also apply online. When all records are on file, the Admissions Committee notifies the student of its decision. Application forms and further information may be requested from:

Office of Admissions
Campbell University
P.O. Box 546
Buies Creek, North Carolina 27506
Phone: 910-893-1320
910-893-1417 (international)
800-334-4111 (toll-free)
E-mail: adm@mailcenter.campbell.edu
Web site: http://www.campbell.edu/

Students on the Mall in front of D. Rich Memorial Hall on the Academic Circle.

CATAWBA COLLEGE

SALISBURY, NORTH CAROLINA

The College

Established in 1851, Catawba College is the sixth-oldest college in North Carolina. It is a private, coeducational college affiliated with the United Church of Christ. It has chosen to remain a four-year institution rooted in the liberal arts tradition. Its purpose is to enrich the educational experiences of students and to prepare these students for productive and meaningful lives of purpose following their graduation. Catawba provides an education that integrates the liberal arts and career preparation. This education is marked by academic challenges and a strong emphasis on enhancing leadership and character.

The College is situated on 276 wooded acres. The campus consists of thirty-five buildings and a 189-acre ecological preserve. The student body consists of 1,300 students from thirty-three states and nineteen other countries. About 85 percent of Catawba's students are from the Eastern Seaboard. Seventy percent of the traditional-age students reside on the campus in one of thirteen residence halls.

Students can choose from a wide variety of campus activities, including theater productions, athletic events in eighteen intercollegiate sports, multiple choral and instrumental groups, academic clubs, community service organizations, the student government association, religious groups, and intramural activities. Excellent exercise facilities are available in the Lerner Wellness Center, and most campus organizations offer a variety of social activities both on campus and in the homes of faculty and staff members. Religious services organized by students and the campus minister are offered in the Omwake-Dearborn Chapel and are open to all faiths.

Location

Catawba is located in Salisbury, a historic Southern city of 30,000. The city is situated in the Piedmont section of North Carolina near Interstate 85. The Catawba campus is located on the western edge of Salisbury in a residential section within 5 minutes of downtown. The city has movie theaters, malls, restaurants, parks, and golf courses; other entertainment facilities are available in the immediate area.

Salisbury is centrally located one hour from the greater Charlotte area, one of the fastest-growing areas in the country, and an hour from the cities of Greensboro and Winston-Salem. These cities provide Catawba students with a wealth of cultural experiences and internship opportunities, plus opportunities to attend professional athletic events. Salisbury is a 4-hour drive from some of the best beaches on the Atlantic Coast and about a 2-hour drive from the scenic Appalachian Mountains and ski resorts.

Majors and Degrees

Catawba College offers a variety of different majors; three undergraduate degrees, including the Bachelor of Arts, Bachelor of Fine Arts, and Bachelor of Science; and a graduate Master of Education degree. While course work is demanding, Catawba also effectively prepares students to both ponder the meaning of vocation within a liberal arts context and to ultimately pursue meaningful careers or graduate studies.

Catawba's academic majors include athletic training, biology, business administration (concentrations in accounting, economics, general management, information systems, and marketing), chemistry, communication arts, education–elementary K–6, education–middle school 6–9 (specializations in language arts, mathematics, science, and social studies), English (concentrations in literature and writing), environmental education, environmental science, environmental studies, French, history, mathematics, medical technology, music (concentrations in music business, music education, music performance, and sacred music), musical theater, physical education, political science (emphases in American political experience, international relations, prelaw, and public administration), psychology, recreation, religion and philosophy (concentrations in Christian education, outdoor ministries, and religion and philosophy), sociology, Spanish, sports management, sustainable business and community development, theater arts, theater arts administration, and therapeutic recreation.

Catawba also offers preprofessional advising programs in health (dentistry, medicine, nursing, and veterinary medicine), law, ministerial, and pharmacy.

Academic Programs

The College operates on the semester calendar and stresses rigorous academic courses, close contact between students and faculty members, and a supportive educational environment. The academic program allows the student opportunities to study in a wide range of fields while concentrating in one (the major).

All freshmen at Catawba enroll in an annual First-Year Experience designed to facilitate their academic transition from high school to college. Although the topics for these courses vary according to the academic specialties and interests of the faculty members teaching them, they share some common features. Each course unites students with a core group of fellow students whom they come to know and with whom they study. Each course also orients students to effective study strategies and helps them to develop critical communications skills and appropriate attitudes to ensure success on campus.

The College offers a strong Honors Program, challenging able students with opportunities to participate in research and study with engaging faculty members. Honors courses may feature travel components, and foreign study is available for those students seeking unique cultural and academic challenges. Recently Catawba's honors students have traveled to Ireland, Belize, the Galapagos Islands, Costa Rica, Italy, and England.

Catawba encourages students to actively pursue internship opportunities in their majors that will enrich and supplement their classroom experiences. These internships range from semester-long positions with area businesses, corporations, or governmental agencies to paid summer positions in various industries, including entertainment, medicine, travel, and tourism.

Academic Facilities

Catawba College's Center for the Environment is a 20,000-square-foot classroom building that overlooks the College's 189-acre ecological preserve. This award-winning model of sustainable design opened in 2001 and is a teaching tool in itself. The College also owns a 300-acre wildlife refuge that is located 7 miles from the main campus. This building and these natural resources offer Catawba students endless opportunities for research and nature education.

The Shuford Science Building offers state-of-the-art laboratories and classrooms for chemistry and biology students. Atop this building sits the Montgomery Observatory, which houses a 15-inch Fecker reflecting telescope.

Ketner Hall serves as a primary classroom area and houses the College's School of Business, its nationally accredited teacher education program, and the Peeler Academy for Teaching. This facility is also equipped with computer laboratories that are available to students.

The Robertson College–Community Center includes the 1,500-seat Keppel Auditorium and the 250-seat Hedrick Theatre. The College's theater arts department uses both of these venues in staging its annual performances. In addition, the Florence Busby Corriher Theatre, located adjacent to the community center, offers an intimate venue for student performances. Brodbeck Music Building offers individual practice rooms, recital halls, classrooms, and a music library.

The Corriher-Linn-Black Library's resources include more than 300,000 volume equivalents. Library services include online database searching, individualized reference assistance, group library instruction, photocopying, and a document delivery system (including interlibrary loan service). The library, completely renovated in 2007, is connected to the Internet and provides access to library and information sources around the world. The library also participates in the North Carolina Information Network (NCIN) for statewide library and information resources and the Online Computer Library Center (OCLC) via the Southeastern Library Network (SOLINET) for international online access to cataloging and reference services. All students have access to the Internet on the campus.

The Abernethy Physical Education Center houses three basketball courts, an indoor swimming pool, an athletic training room, racquetball courts, a weight room, and locker rooms for the indoor athletic programs. The College's Hayes Athletic Field House is equipped with a weight room, an athletic training room, and locker rooms for the outdoor athletic programs. This facility is adjacent to the Shuford Stadium (football stadium). A 20-acre athletic complex consists of two soccer fields, a hockey field, a softball field, a lacrosse field, and a football practice field. Six tennis courts, with lighting and spectator seating, are also available on the campus. These facilities and fields are available for extracurricular activities, as are training areas for the eighteen NCAA Division II varsity athletic teams (men's and women's).

Costs

For the 2007–08 academic year, tuition and fees were $20,836. Room and board cost $7190.

Financial Aid

Ninety-five percent of Catawba College students receive some sort of financial assistance and 98 percent of freshmen students do. Thirty-six percent of all students work on campus. Various academic scholarships are available to students who have demonstrated high levels of academic achievement, leadership, and character, including the College's prestigious First Family Scholarships and the Presidential Scholarships. Performance scholarships are offered in the fields of music and theater, and Catawba also awards athletic scholarships to selected student-athletes in eighteen varsity sports. Other scholarships and access grants are also available.

Students applying for financial assistance must be accepted by the Admissions Office and must submit the Free Application for Federal Student Aid (FAFSA). Financial assistance includes federal and state grants, Federal Work-Study programs, campus employment, and a variety of student loans.

Catawba College is committed to making a high-quality college education affordable and will assist families in tailoring financial aid packages that meet the needs of their students. For complete details on all types of financial assistance available at the institution, prospective students should visit http://www.catawba.edu/administrative/financialaid.

Faculty

The faculty members serve as advisers to students during registration periods and throughout a student's four years at Catawba. Faculty members are readily accessible to students and participate with them in activities on and off campus. More than 70 percent of the faculty members have doctorates.

Admission Requirements

Students seeking admission to Catawba must present evidence of outstanding educational achievement and be a graduate of an accredited public or private secondary school.

Candidates must submit the following items directly to the Office of Admissions: the completed application for admission; either an official copy of their high school transcript (a notarized English translation is required when records are in another language), an official General Educational Development (GED) certificate, or a certified Adult High School Diploma; a completed essay, following guidelines provided on the application for admission; two letters of recommendation from their high school teacher; a nonrefundable $25 processing fee; and an official copy of their scores on either the SAT or ACT.

All freshmen applicants taking the SAT after March 2005 are required to submit the results of the writing test as well as the math and critical reading (formerly known as verbal) tests.

All freshmen applicants taking the ACT after February 2005 are required to submit the results of the ACT standard test and writing test.

Students may also submit performance scores on other achievement tests or scales, such as the CEEB's Advanced Placement (AP) exams, the College-Level Examination Program (CLEP), or the International Baccalaureate (I.B.) Program if they so desire

International students who are able to provide evidence of suitable academic preparation and adequate financial resources are encouraged to apply at least three months prior to the term in which they intend to begin their studies. Acceptable scores are a minimum of 525 for the TOEFL (computer equivalent of 197). For more details regarding international student admissions, students should visit http://www.catawba.edu/catalog/.

Application and Information

For fall admission, the application deadline is March 15. All applications received after March 15 will be reviewed on a space-available basis only. For spring admission, the application deadline is January 5. For summer sessions, the application deadline is the first day of each intended semester.

Qualified applicants are encouraged to complete the application process early in their high school senior year. Applicants are encouraged to contact the Office of Admissions at 800-CATAWBA (toll-free) to determine their admission status. Denied applications may be appealed to the Student Appeals Committee.

Dean of Admissions
Catawba College
Salisbury, North Carolina 28144
Phone: 704-637-4402
800-228-2922 (toll-free)
E-mail: admission@catawba.edu
Web site: http://www.catawba.edu

Ralph W. Ketner Hall.

DAVIDSON COLLEGE

DAVIDSON, NORTH CAROLINA

The College

Founded in 1837, Davidson College consistently ranks as one of the most competitive liberal arts and sciences colleges in the United States. Davidson's student body is made up of 1,700 students from forty-six states and thirty-nine other countries, chosen not only for their academic promise but also for their character and leadership.

The liberal arts curriculum at Davidson is designed to give students knowledge and skills that they can put to use throughout their lives. Davidson offers more than 850 courses in twenty major fields and in special interdisciplinary programs. Students benefit from the careful attention of 162 full-time faculty members, who are dedicated to teaching and guiding undergraduates. Close relationships between faculty members and students are a hallmark of the Davidson experience.

The Honor System serves as a foundation for life at Davidson. The Honor Code represents a declaration by the entire College community—students, faculty and staff members, and alumni—that an honorable course is the most just and, therefore, the best.

Student life at Davidson is active and varied. Davidson students participate in a wide range of organizations of special interest and attend cultural and social events offered on campus. From the Student Government Association to Amnesty International, from the United Community Action service organization to the Black Student Coalition, Davidson's more than 180 campus organizations provide students with opportunities to develop leadership skills, share their talents, and explore new interests. As one of the only colleges of its size competing in Division I of the NCAA, Davidson supports true scholar-athletes in twenty-one varsity sports. Approximately 25 percent of the student body play on varsity teams and 80 percent participate in intramural and club sports.

Location

Davidson's 450-acre campus is located in Davidson, North Carolina. Davidson students tutor children at the area elementary school, build houses for Davidson's chapter of Habitat for Humanity, bike and jog throughout the residential neighborhoods, and gather with friends at the local coffeehouse. Davidson also owns 106 acres of waterfront property on Lake Norman, the largest lake in North Carolina, where students participate in a variety of water sports and other recreational activities.

Charlotte, one of America's fastest-growing cities, the nation's second-largest banking center, and home to nearly 400 multinational corporations, is located 19 miles south of Davidson. From community service to internships, from cultural events to professional sports teams, Davidson students draw on Charlotte's advantages.

Majors and Degrees

Davidson grants the Bachelor of Arts and the Bachelor of Science degrees in twenty major fields: anthropology, art, biology, chemistry, classical studies, economics, English, French, German, history, mathematics, music, philosophy, physics, political science, psychology, religion, sociology, Spanish, and theater. Minors are available in anthropology, chemistry, economics, education, French, German, mathematics, music, philosophy, religion, Russian, Spanish, and theater. Students may double major or choose to complement their majors with an interdisciplinary concentration in applied mathematics, Asian studies, computer science, education, ethnic studies, film and media studies, gender studies, genomics, international studies, medical humanities, neuroscience, or Southern studies. Each year, a number of students choose to design their own majors through Davidson's Center for Interdisciplinary Studies. Recent self-designed majors have included visual communications, bioethics, peace studies, and environmental economics.

Academic Programs

The liberal arts curriculum at Davidson gives students a broad-based and rich education, exposing them to many different academic areas. Davidson requires a total of thirty-two courses to graduate. Through core distribution requirements, every Davidson student takes courses in six areas: the fine arts, natural sciences and mathematics, philosophy and religion, literature, history, and the social sciences. Additional courses are taken in composition, foreign language, cultural diversity, and physical education. In addition to the core curriculum, students choose a major by the end of their sophomore year. A major normally requires up to twelve courses, including at least five upper-level courses. The academic year at Davidson consists of two 15-week semesters. Notably, 90 percent of those who enroll at Davidson graduate within four academic years.

Off-Campus Programs

Davidson supports a vigorous program of international education and opportunity for all students. More than 80 percent of all Davidson students have an abroad experience during their Davidson tenure, 65 percent for academic credit. Options include study abroad in England, France, Ghana, India, Italy, Mexico, Nepal, Peru, Russia, Spain, and the Mediterranean region; internship programs in Washington, D.C., and Philadelphia; environmental research with the School for Field Studies in the Virgin Islands, Australia, or Kenya; Biosphere 2 Center in Phoenix, Arizona; marine biology off the coast of North Carolina; psychology study at Broughton Hospital in Morganton, North Carolina; exchange programs with Morehouse College and Howard University; and independently arranged programs elsewhere. Davidson's Dean Rusk International Studies Program provides more than $100,000 in grants each year to fund students in exploring their international interests.

In addition to off-campus programs, the Career Services Office helps students find internships in Charlotte, across the nation, and worldwide. Recent internship sites include the Carolinas Medical Center, the *Charlotte Observer*, Bank of America, the Philadelphia Museum of Art, and the Overseas Private Investment Corporation in Washington, D.C., among many others.

Academic Facilities

Davidson's campus features seventy-five academic and residential buildings. Chambers Building, the central academic building built in 1929, has recently undergone a $21-million renovation. The E. H. Little Library houses nearly 600,000 volumes, all listed in the online catalog, and provides access to countless journals and databases online. The Baker-Watt Science Complex includes the 32,000-square-foot Watson Life Sciences Building (with state-of-the-art biology and psychology laboratories) and the Dana Physics Building (housing physics and additional biology laboratories). A 7,000-volume chemistry library, laboratories, and classrooms may be found in the Martin Chemical Laboratories. The Belk Visual Arts Center contains two galleries, a computerized slide library, a lecture hall, and private studios for sculpting, painting, and drawing. The Duke Family Performance Hall provides professional space for the performing arts. Sloan Music Building, renovated in 2002, provides performance, class, and rehearsal space as well as an extensive library, a keyboard laboratory, and a recording studio. Cunningham Fine Arts Building houses performance and rehearsal space, a scene shop, and a script library for the Theatre Department. The campus computer network provides wired access from all campus locations and ample wireless hot zones on campus. All residence halls provide network and telephone ports for each student.

Costs

Required student charges (tuition, student activity fee, and laundry) for the 2007–08 academic year are $31,794. A room costs $4763, and full board costs $4257.

Financial Aid

Davidson is committed to being affordable, adhering to a need-blind admission policy and meeting 100 percent of students' demonstrated financial need with grants and student employment. All admitted students are considered for an array of merit-based scholarships. Students' demonstrated need is met without loans so that all students, independent of their financial situation, can have the opportunity to attend Davidson College and graduate debt-free. Through a combination of state, federal, and private sources, Davidson administers in excess of $26 million in student financial assistance each year. The instructions for applying for need-based aid are included with Davidson's application for admission. Students with financial need are assisted through a combination of Davidson, federal, and state grants and student employment.

Davidson awards merit scholarships to approximately 20 percent of each entering first-year class. These awards recognize students' academic promise, special talents, and personal qualities. Recipients are selected based on the strength of their admission application. For some scholarships, selection may also be based on the outcome of an audition, interview, portfolio review, or writing sample. Merit scholarships range from $1000 to full costs and include the following awards: the John Montgomery Belk Scholarship (ten awarded, comprehensive fee), the Thomas S. and Sarah B. Baker Scholarship (two awarded, comprehensive fee), the William Holt Terry Scholarship (two awarded to students with exceptional leadership qualities, full tuition), the Bryan Scholarship (two awarded to students who contribute in a superlative manner to their sport as well as to the academic and cocurricular life at Davidson), and the Missy and John Kuykendall Scholarship (three awarded to students who provide service leadership).

Faculty

Davidson's 162 full-time faculty members choose to teach at Davidson because they gain their greatest professional satisfaction from working with undergraduates. All classes are taught by full professors, and 100 percent of faculty members have a terminal degree. With a student-faculty ratio of 10:1, classes are small (the average class size is 15 students), and individual attention is the norm. Professors' ongoing involvement with students takes many forms: encouraging lively class discussion, including students in their research projects, inviting students to their homes for dinner, and participating in many facets of student life outside of the classroom. Each student is assigned a faculty adviser, who provides guidance on academic choices throughout the student's four years.

Student Government

Davidson students have the opportunity to develop valuable interpersonal skills through leadership roles in the Student Government Association, the College Union Board, the Honor Council, United Community Action, and many special interest organizations. The Honor System governs Davidson's social and academic life, demanding the highest personal and community values and engendering an atmosphere of openness, mutual trust, and integrity among the entire Davidson community.

Admission Requirements

Davidson seeks students of outstanding academic ability and strong character who show promise of leadership. To be considered for admission, a student must have completed at least 16 high school academic units, including 4 units of English, 3 units of mathematics, 2 units of the same foreign language, and 2 units of history. Electives should include 3 or 4 years of science and additional courses in mathematics, history, and the same foreign language. In addition to the SAT or the ACT, the Davidson application requires three essay responses, an official transcript, and recommendations from 2 teachers, a peer, and a high school counselor. SAT Subject Tests are recommended but not required. Davidson accepts the Common Application along with required supplemental information.

Admission to Davidson is highly selective. The selection process is composed of three major elements: the evaluation of academic performance and potential, the assessment of individual characteristics, and the recognition of outstanding interests, achievements, and activities. These three elements are used to gain an understanding of each student's academic and personal strengths and give an overall impression of the individual's eligibility for admission. As a college that welcomes students and faculty and staff members from a variety of nationalities, ethnic groups, and traditions, Davidson seeks students who are likely to bring diverse and unique talents and strengths to the College community.

Application and Information

Early decision—round one—has an application deadline of November 15, with notification by December 15. Early decision—round two—has an application deadline of January 2, with notification by February 1. Regular decision has an application deadline of January 2, with notification by April 1. Students are encouraged to visit Davidson for a campus tour and an information session with a member of the Admission Office staff. For additional information about Davidson, students should contact the Office of Admission and Financial Aid:

Christopher J. Gruber
Vice President and Dean of Admission and Financial Aid
Davidson College
Box 7156
Davidson, North Carolina 28035-7156
Phone: 704-894-2230
800-768-0380 (toll-free)
E-mail: admission@davidson.edu
Web site: http://www.davidson.edu

Graduation Day in front of Chambers, Davidson's signature academic building.

DUKE UNIVERSITY

DURHAM, NORTH CAROLINA

The University

Duke University is an independent, comprehensive, coeducational research university that traces its roots to 1838, when it was established as Union Institute in Randolph County, North Carolina. Renamed Trinity College twenty-one years later, the school moved to Durham in 1892. In recognition of its primary benefactors, the Duke family, Trinity College became Duke University in 1924.

Duke offers a variety of outstanding undergraduate programs in two schools—Trinity College of Arts and Sciences and the Pratt School of Engineering. At the graduate level, the master's and doctoral programs in these schools (as well as the University's professional schools in business administration, divinity, the environment, law, medicine, and nursing) consistently rank at or near the top of their fields.

With a limited enrollment of 13,088 full-time students, Duke is among the smallest of the nation's major universities. Of these, 6,244 are undergraduates—5,225 in arts and sciences and 1,019 in engineering. Because of its size and the emphasis on meeting the needs of a diverse student body, the University maintains a commitment to individual education. At Duke, learning is a priority and teaching is personal. As a result, the student body, as a whole, reflects a quality of creativity and mental restlessness that goes far beyond excellent grades and testing. The University attracts students from all fifty states as well as eighty-five other countries, and about 85 percent of Duke's undergraduates come from states other than North and South Carolina.

Duke believes that to build a strong community students must live together. For this reason, all undergraduates are guaranteed housing as long as space remains available and are required to live on campus for their first three years. To accommodate students' widely varying interests, the residence halls provide diverse living styles, including single-sex or coed dorms, unique academic environments, and theme houses or other selective living groups. About 85 percent of undergraduates live on campus. All first-year students live on East Campus in a community designed to support the academic, residential, and recreational needs and interests of new students, and all sophomores live on West Campus. About 36 percent of undergraduates belong to fraternities or sororities. In addition to a rich campus living environment, students can enjoy a full calendar of activities through the University Union, the University-sponsored Artists Series, the Broadway at Duke Series, and nearly 400 clubs and organizations based on diverse political, cultural, social, arts, health, recreational, service, academic, and religious interests as well as intramural sports.

Location

Durham, located about 450 miles from Atlanta and 250 miles from Washington, D.C., is a city of about 234,000 with active research, medical, and arts communities. Together, Durham and nearby Raleigh and Chapel Hill, with a combined population of around 1 million, compose the Research Triangle, one of the nation's foremost centers for research and high-tech industry. The Research Triangle has one of the highest concentrations of Ph.D.'s and M.D.'s in the world. Two interstates and the Raleigh-Durham International Airport, only 20 minutes from campus, make Durham easily accessible.

Majors and Degrees

Duke offers both a rigorous academic program and considerable flexibility in course selection and degree programs. Undergraduates can choose courses in nearly 100 different programs in the humanities, social sciences and natural sciences, mathematics, and engineering. Thirty-seven majors are offered in Trinity College of Arts and Sciences, and students with interests that cannot be met within an established major are able to design their own curriculum with the help of a faculty adviser. In addition, students may pursue dual degrees, minors in most fields, and any of the University's twenty certificate programs.

Trinity College of Arts and Sciences offers programs leading to the A.B. degree or the B.S. degree in African and African American studies, art, art history and visual studies, Asian and African languages and literature, biological anthropology and anatomy, biology, Canadian studies, chemistry, classical studies, computer science, cultural anthropology, dance, earth and ocean sciences, economics, English, environmental sciences, environmental sciences and policy, French studies, Germanic languages and literature, history, international comparative studies, Italian and European studies, linguistics, literature, mathematics, medieval and Renaissance studies, music, philosophy, physics, political science, psychology, public policy studies, religion, Slavic and Eurasian studies, sociology, Spanish, theater studies, and women's studies.

Interdisciplinary nonmajor certificate programs are available in architectural engineering; arts management and cultural policy; children in contemporary society; documentary studies; early childhood education studies; film/video/digital; global health; health policy; human development; information sciences and information studies; Islamic studies; Jewish studies; Latin American studies; markets and management studies; Marxism and society; neurosciences; philosophy, politics, and economics; policy journalism and media studies; primatology; and the study of ethics.

The Pratt School of Engineering offers accredited four-year programs leading to the B.S.E. in biomedical engineering, civil engineering, electrical and computer engineering, and mechanical engineering.

Academic Programs

The year is divided into two semesters with two optional summer terms; first-semester exams fall before the winter break. Students in the liberal arts plan their own courses of study, with the help of an adviser, according to guidelines rather than specific course requirements. Academic Writing, a one-semester class in expository writing, is the only course required of undergraduates. The Trinity College liberal arts curriculum of approximately 15 semester courses encompasses five areas of knowledge: arts, literatures, and performance; civilizations; social sciences; natural sciences; and quantitative studies. As students take courses in these areas, the curriculum provides significant exposure to cross-cultural and ethical inquiry, methods of analysis and reasoning, foreign language, writing, research, and the relationships between science, technology, and society. Thirty-four courses are required for graduation.

First-year students are encouraged to participate in the Focus Program, consisting of about a dozen clusters of interrelated seminars spanning topics such as The Global Americas, Engineering Frontiers: Living Systems for a Living Planet, Exploring the Mind, the Genome Revolution and its Impact on Society, Humanitarian Challenges, and Visions of Freedom. Students in each Focus Cluster live together to expand the opportunities for discussion and learning. Also, in more than forty-five first-year seminars, offered in nearly every department, professors chosen for their outstanding undergraduate teaching lead classes of 15 or fewer students. In general, other than the occasional large lecture hall, classes at Duke contain between 16 and 35 students.

When students declare a major—no later than the end of the sophomore year in Trinity College and the end of the first year in the Pratt School of Engineering—a faculty member from the major department becomes their adviser. Students who plan to continue their study in a professional school also work with career-specific advisers to plan a program of study that provides the appropriate foundation for advanced work and meets their unique interests.

Off-Campus Programs

Through internships and study-abroad programs, students are encouraged to take advantage of nearly 120 Duke-affiliated off-campus study opportunities. These range from oceanographic studies at the Duke Marine Laboratory in Beaufort, North Carolina, and arts programs in New York or Los Angeles to a variety of overseas programs. Through the Office of Study Abroad, students can choose international programs from four weeks to a full year in length. In most cases, scholarship aid can be applied to study abroad. Approximately 40 percent of each graduating class studies away from campus on nearly every continent in the world. Duke has recently announced a new program, DukeEngage, that will provide funding and faculty support for any undergraduate student who wishes to pursue a summer or semester-long service project.

Academic Facilities

With more than 5.0 million volumes, 16 million manuscripts, 1.4 million public documents, 3.9 million microforms, and tens of thousands of films, video recordings, and serials, Duke University's library holdings are among the most extensive in the nation. The University's most sophisticated teaching and research facilities—including the Fitzpatrick Center for Interdisciplinary Engineering, Medicine, and Applied Sciences and the Bostock Library—are available to undergraduates as they work with faculty mentors on various research projects.

All students have access to extensive computing facilities and services supported by the Office of Information Technology. Services include free accounts on Duke's main computer system, which provide access to high-speed Internet and e-mail as well as access to the twenty campus computer labs, which provide computers, printers, and access to DukeNet, the campuswide fiber-optic network. All undergraduate residence hall rooms are wired for DukeNet access.

Costs

For 2007–08, a year in Trinity College or the Pratt School of Engineering cost $48,327, with $35,856 allotted for tuition and fees and an average of $9780 for room and board (although costs vary with accommodations). The total yearly estimate included $2604 for books and miscellaneous expenses. All fees are subject to change, and up-to-date information is available through the Office of Undergraduate Financial Aid.

Financial Aid

Duke University believes that access to a high-quality private education should depend on a student's qualifications, not his or her family's financial strength. The University meets 100 percent of the demonstrated need for all admitted U.S. citizens and permanent residents, and applying for financial aid has no bearing on the admissions decision for these students. The University also makes need-based financial aid available for a limited number of international students who are not U.S. citizens or permanent residents. Duke meets the full demonstrated financial need for these students, as it does for admitted U.S. citizens and permanent residents, but financial aid is a factor in the admissions decision for these students. Citizens of other nations who apply for financial aid must apply under the regular decision plan.

The aid program includes honorary and need-based scholarships, grants, federal and institutional college work-study program awards, Federal Perkins Loans and Stafford Student Loans, and University-sponsored internships. Limited merit, ROTC, and athletic scholarships are available, and all admitted students are automatically considered for all appropriate scholarships.

U.S. citizens and permanent residents applying for financial aid should submit the PROFILE application provided by the College Scholarship Service, the Free Application for Federal Student Aid (FAFSA), and a copy of their family's most recently filed tax forms. Financial aid applicants who are citizens of other countries should submit the College Board's International Student Financial Aid Application along with a copy of their family's most recent national tax forms. Also, their parents' employers must provide, in English, statements that outline annual income and benefits received in connection with their current employment. Further information is available through the Office of Undergraduate Financial Aid.

Faculty

Duke has a faculty of 2,664 full-time and part-time members in its undergraduate, graduate, and professional schools, 991 of whom teach undergraduates, making the student-faculty ratio 18:1. More importantly, people of national or international prominence, members of major academic societies, state and national advisers, and faculty chairs honoring professors of extraordinary ability are found in every department or division. About 90 percent of tenured or tenure-track faculty members teach undergraduates, and many serve as first-year student and departmental advisers.

Student Government

Students at Duke are considered mature individuals capable of governing their own actions, while furthering the best interests of the broader University community. The Duke Student Government and various student-faculty-administration committees provide diverse avenues for student interaction with professors and administrators. In addition, the Duke Student Government supports students who want to start their own campus organizations. Undergraduates also serve as voting members of the University's Board of Trustees.

Admission Requirements

The Committee on Admissions selects students on the basis of their academic record and quality of their secondary school program, recommendations from teachers and counselors, extracurricular activities and accomplishments, the application essay, and standardized test scores. The University does not discriminate on the basis of race, color, national or ethnic origin, gender, handicap, or sexual orientation or preference in its admission policies. No geographic quotas are imposed. Applicants should have at least four years of English and at least three of mathematics, natural science, foreign language, and social studies. Most engineering applicants have four years of mathematics and four years of science, including physics and chemistry. Engineering applicants must have taken calculus before they enroll. Students are encouraged to enroll in advanced-level work as preparation for the Duke curriculum.

Duke accepts both ACT and SAT scores. Students should take either the ACT including writing or the three-part SAT Reasoning and SAT Subject Tests in two areas. Engineering applicants who submit SAT scores must take the SAT Subject Test in mathematics. Personal interviews in the applicants' local areas by members of the Alumni Admissions Advisory Committee are recommended but not required.

Application and Information

Application deadlines for first-year students are November 1 for early decision and January 2 for regular decision. Duke accepts the Common Application or the Universal College Application plus the Student Supplement (Form A). Students who want to arrange an alumni interview should file the Student Supplement (Form A) of their application by October 19 for early decision or by December 10 for regular decision. For transfer students, the application deadline for fall admission is March 15. Students must apply either to Trinity College of Arts and Sciences or the Pratt School of Engineering at the time of application. Required tests should be taken by January of the senior year or by October for early decision applicants. For additional information, students should contact:

Office of Undergraduate Admissions
Duke University
2138 Campus Drive, Box 90586
Durham, North Carolina 27708-0586

Phone: 919-684-3214
Fax: 919-681-8941
Web site: http://www.admissions.duke.edu/

GARDNER-WEBB UNIVERSITY

BOILING SPRINGS, NORTH CAROLINA

The University

Gardner-Webb University was founded in 1905 as a private high school by a group of Baptist associations. It became a junior college in 1928, was renamed Gardner-Webb College in 1942 in honor of former governor O. Max Gardner, and became a fully accredited senior college in 1971. Gardner-Webb moved to university status in 1993. Gardner-Webb's mission is to provide a high-quality liberal arts education in a Christian environment with the personal touch. The most outstanding characteristics of the University are its Christian environment, sense of community, and proven record of academic distinction. Its origins are obviously deep in Christian tradition, which is exemplified in the lives of staff and faculty members. Because the University is small, students can be well known by a large percentage of the faculty and administration members. The cosmopolitan student body (more than 3,800 men and women, of whom nearly 2,700 are undergraduates) represents thirty states and thirty other countries and gives an added, valuable dimension to a student's educational experience.

The heritage of the University is reflected in its beautiful landscape and stately brick buildings. However, the University is constantly forging ahead with advanced technology and state-of-the-art facilities. There are several social and service clubs on campus, including the Drama Club, Fellowship of Christian Athletes (FCA), Campus Ministries United, student government, and various University and student committees. There are many extracurricular activities for those who are interested. An Army ROTC program; the Gardner-Webb Student YMCA (GWSY), which trains students for leadership positions at YMCAs; and the GWU Marching Band provide strong outlets for student involvement on campus. The Student Entertainment Association offers a full program of social events and entertainment. The Gardner-Webb Theatre offers a full season of plays. There are a student newspaper, a literary magazine, a television studio, and a campus radio station. Students may also participate in community projects or in various kinds of off-campus ministries, including those to the deaf and to prison inmates.

The Master of Arts degree is awarded in elementary education, English, English education, mental health counseling, middle school education, school administration, school counseling, and sport and science pedagogy. Gardner-Webb also offers the following degrees: a Master of Business Administration, International Master of Business Administration, Master of Accounting, Master of Science in Nursing, Master of Divinity, Doctor of Ministry, and Doctor of Education.

There are over 20 intramural sports, in which all students are urged to participate, including basketball, racquetball, softball, tennis, touch football, and volleyball among others. Intercollegiate sports include baseball, basketball, cross-country running, football, golf, soccer, softball, swimming, tennis, track and field, volleyball, and wrestling. A modern physical education building, an indoor heated pool, and an athletic field amply accommodate these programs. A new wellness center and an Alpine Tower are available for student use.

The Program for the Blind at Gardner-Webb University has been developed to allow students with visual handicaps to receive a liberal arts education. Special support services and job opportunities are provided for every entering student who is visually impaired.

The Degree Program for the Deaf provides interpreters, note takers, and tutors who are skilled in sign language so that hearing-impaired students have full access to all University programs.

Location

The University is located at the foot of the beautiful Blue Ridge Mountains in Boiling Springs, North Carolina, a university town of about 3,000 people. The campus comprises 250 acres of land in an area of gently rolling, wooded hills. Nine miles away is Shelby, a town of about 30,000 people. There are a Greater Shelby Community Theatre and a Community Concert Series, and restaurants abound in the area. Charlotte, an area of about 400,000 people only 50 miles away, offers many other opportunities for cultural, social, and recreational activities. Several nearby lakes and Asheville and Beech Mountain, an hour and a half away in the heart of the mountains, provide facilities for summer and winter sports. Greenville, South Carolina, is 55 miles away and Spartanburg, 36 miles. Shelby is served by Greyhound-Trailways bus lines, and the Charlotte airport is served by major airlines. Interstate 85 is only 15 miles away, and Highway 74 runs through Shelby.

Majors and Degrees

The degrees of Bachelor of Arts, Bachelor of Music, Bachelor of Science, and Associate in Arts are offered. Fields of concentration are available in the following subjects: accounting, American sign language, athletic training, biology, business administration, chemistry, communications, computer science, elementary education, English, environmental science, finance, French, health/wellness, history, international business, interpreter training, management information systems, mathematics, middle grades education, music, nursing, physical education, physician assistant studies, political science, psychology, public relations, religion, sacred music, social sciences, sociology, Spanish, sports management, and theater arts.

Preprofessional programs are available in dentistry, law, medicine, ministry, pharmacy, and veterinary medicine.

Academic Programs

The total program is marked by flexibility for the student but encourages, through active faculty advisement, choosing a substantial course of study. Elements of the humanities, the social and physical sciences, and mathematics or related disciplines must be taken. A typical bachelor's degree program requires 128 semester hours for graduation: 59 to 63 in the core (humanities and social and physical sciences), 30 in the major, and 39 to 42 in supporting subjects and free electives. Requirements for science curricula vary somewhat. The associate degree requires the completion of 64 semester hours. A cumulative average of C (2.0 on a 4.0 scale) or better is required for graduation.

Gardner-Webb grants advanced placement and credit on the basis of the College-Level Examination Program (CLEP), the Advanced Placement (AP) tests of the College Board, and the International Baccalaureate Program.

Off-Campus Programs

Students in the Departments of Business, Fine Arts, Foreign Languages and Literature, and Religious Studies and Philosophy are given the opportunity to enrich their educational experiences through travel and study in Europe, Latin America, and the Holy Land.

Academic Facilities

The University's library currently holds 250,000 volumes. There are fully equipped biology, chemistry, and physics laboratories as well as computer and learning-assistance laboratories. A special-events/convocation center houses a theater and an athletics arena. The University also has a 50,000-watt FM stereo radio station.

Costs

Costs for the 2007–08 academic year are $18,310 for tuition and $6060 for room and board. Part-time tuition is $315 per semester hour for 1 to 9 hours. Books and supplies average $800 to $1000 per year.

Financial Aid

Gardner-Webb University makes available to its students a variety of scholarships, loans, grants-in-aid, and work-study awards. Prospective applicants with financial need should contact the financial aid director early in their senior year of high school for a financial need estimate. Applications received after April 1 can be considered only in terms of available funds. An applicant must be accepted for admission before being awarded aid. Students must file the Free Application for Federal Student Aid (FAFSA). Scholarships and other types of aid include academic awards, Christian service awards, endowed scholarships, and annual scholarships. There are several Gardner-Webb loan funds. The University also administers aid from the full range of federal programs: Federal Pell Grants, Federal Work-Study Program awards, Federal Perkins Loans, and federally guaranteed Federal Stafford Student Loans and Federal PLUS loans. North Carolina students have access to state grant funds administered by the University. Scholarships based on academic promise are also granted each year. Of all students, 90 percent receive aid in some form. The two criteria for receiving financial aid are financial need and academic promise.

Faculty

The faculty-student ratio is 1:15. Faculty members engage both formally and informally in student advising and counseling. A staff of professional counselors is also available. Faculty members teach at all class levels without regard to academic rank or length of service. Graduate assistants are not used to teach classes.

Student Government

The University has a student government whose members are elected by the student body. This organization, which is set up with executive, legislative, and judicial branches, is very influential in campus affairs. In addition, students have voting positions on all standing committees of the University.

Admission Requirements

Although a fixed pattern of high school credits is not prescribed, the following minimum course distribution is recommended: 4 units in English, 2 in a foreign language, 2 in social science, 2 in algebra, 1 in geometry, and 2 in natural science, plus electives. The University requires each applicant to submit an application form, a high school transcript, and SAT scores. ACT scores are also acceptable. Acceptance to Gardner-Webb is based on the applicant's high school record, rank in class, SAT or ACT scores, and extracurricular activities. Transfer students' course credits are evaluated on courses as credit only, not on grade point average. An interview is recommended but not mandatory.

Gardner-Webb admits students of any race, color, and national or ethnic origin to all the rights, privileges, programs, and activities generally accorded or made available to students at the University.

Application and Information

Applications, together with a nonrefundable $40 application fee, may be submitted for either semester. Students may also apply online at http://www.gardner-webb.edu. Early application is advised. Notification of the admission decision is given on a rolling basis upon receipt of all application data. A $150 room deposit for boarding students is due thirty days after acceptance and is refundable until May 1. A $50 deposit is required of commuting students.

For further information, students should contact:

Director of Undergraduate Admissions and Enrollment Management
Gardner-Webb University
Boiling Springs, North Carolina 28017
Phone: 704-406-4GWU
800-253-6472 (toll-free)
Web site: http://www.gardner-webb.edu

Gardner-Webb University seeks a higher ground in education—one that embraces faith and intellectual freedom, balances conviction with compassion, and inspires in students a love of learning, service, and leadership. Gardner-Webb University has great things in mind—for its students and the world.

GREENSBORO COLLEGE

GREENSBORO, NORTH CAROLINA

The College

Established in 1838, Greensboro College is a four-year coeducational liberal arts college affiliated with the United Methodist Church. It is located in the College Hill Historic District of Greensboro, North Carolina. With an enrollment of approximately 1,250 men and women, the College enjoys a small-community atmosphere and maintains a student-faculty ratio of 11:1.

The College has completed an exciting $40-million building and renovation program that provides new classrooms and laboratories and transforms the gardens and grounds to preserve and enhance the special character of the 60-acre campus. Its architecture is in the traditional Georgian style. The buildings include an indoor athletic center, four residential halls, classroom buildings, a chapel, a performing arts center, a library, and a main administrative building.

At the Royce Reynolds Family Student Life Center, students enjoy squash, racquetball, and basketball courts; a fitness facility; an indoor pool; an aerobics room; a Jacuzzi; a steam room; and a sauna. Intercollegiate sports include baseball, basketball, cross-country, football, golf, lacrosse, soccer, and tennis for men as well as basketball, cross-country, lacrosse, soccer, softball, swimming, tennis, and volleyball for women. Greensboro College is a member of the NCAA Division III and competes in the U.S.A. South Athletic Conference. An intramural program is also offered for students.

There is cultural, religious, and ethnic diversity at Greensboro College, where students come from more than thirty states and twenty-four nations. Many graduates have earned distinction in graduate and professional schools in all parts of the United States and abroad. Recent Greensboro College graduates have been accepted into the graduate schools of the College of William and Mary as well as Duke, Emory, Georgetown, Johns Hopkins, North Carolina State, Princeton, St. Andrews (Scotland), Temple, Vanderbilt, and Wake Forest Universities and the Eastman School of Music. Most graduates pursue careers in business, education, health care, and the arts.

Extracurricular activities are designed to supplement and reinforce academic study at the College. More than 100 student leadership positions are available in more than sixty different student organizations, enabling most students to be as active in campus life as they wish.

In addition to its undergraduate programs, Greensboro College offers the Master of Education degree.

Location

The city of Greensboro, which is located near the center of North Carolina, offers major industries, including insurance companies and textile manufacturers, and many cultural, social, and athletic opportunities. With a population of more than 1 million people in the Triad region, the city is a thriving business center that offers excellent internship opportunities. More than 40,000 college students study at the six colleges and universities within the city. Greensboro College is at the heart of this community.

Majors and Degrees

Greensboro College awards the Bachelor of Arts (B.A.), Bachelor of Science (B.S.), and Bachelor of Business Administration degrees. Students can major in the following areas: accounting, art, athletic training, biology, birth-through-kindergarten teacher education, business administration and economics, chemistry, criminal justice, education or special education, English and communications, exercise and sport studies, French, history, history and political science, mathematics, middle school education, music, physical education, political science, psychology, religion and philosophy, secondary education, sociology, Spanish, and theater. Minors are available in child and family studies, Christian education, computer information systems, computer science, dance, ethics, interdisciplinary studies, international studies, legal administration, women's studies, and other areas in which majors are offered. Combined-degree programs are offered in medical technology and radiological technology.

Academic Programs

All students are required to take courses in the humanities, the natural sciences, the social sciences, and the arts. The general education requirements for both the B.A. and B.S. degrees total 52 semester hours. Graduation requires the completion of 124 semester hours.

Greensboro College offers an honors program for superior students who qualify on the basis of SAT or ACT scores, high school grade point averages, or AP examination results. Students enrolled in the program must complete requirements in addition to those expected of students in the regular B.A. and B.S. degree programs.

Because Greensboro College recognizes that people must learn not only how to live but also how to make a living, the liberal arts curriculum and setting provide the context for a variety of professional programs, including accounting, business, and legal administration, as well as preprofessional programs in law, medicine, and theology. Besides providing career and academic counseling, the College seeks to ensure that its graduates acquire the basic intellectual and communications capabilities to cope with the changing demands of any career. An internship program during the junior and senior years places students in business and agency settings that are related to their major and career aspirations. The College also seeks to develop in its graduates a philosophy of life and an appreciation of Judeo-Christian values that transcend particular vocational skills.

Off-Campus Programs

Greensboro College is a member of the Greater Greensboro Consortium and the Piedmont Independent Colleges Association, which provide for arrangements with Bennett College, Elon University, Guilford College, Guilford Technical Community College, High Point University, North Carolina Agricultural and Technical State University, Salem College, and the University of North Carolina at Greensboro. With permission from the academic dean, students at Greensboro College may take courses offered at any of the other campuses. Library resources are shared.

Academic Facilities

The James Addison Jones Library has approximately 110,000 volumes, periodicals, CD-ROMs, and microfilm reels. The computerized card catalog system allows students to access the holdings of other area colleges. Interlibrary loan among the colleges is permitted. There are reading rooms, periodical and browsing rooms, and a multipurpose meeting room.

One of the College's goals is to ensure that every student develops a broad range of technical skills in order to flourish in the twenty-first century. State-of-the-art computer labs are available for all students, and students can access the Internet and World

Wide Web from most points on campus. All dorm rooms provide high-speed access to the Internet.

Other facilities include a computerized writing laboratory, natural science laboratories, the Annie Sellars Jordan Parlor Theater, and the Gail Brower Huggins Performance Center, one of the most elegant and state-of-the-art performance facilities in the area. Music facilities include a computerized music laboratory, practice rooms, two recital areas, thirty-nine pianos (including a 9-foot concert grand), and a concert stage. In addition, Greensboro College is one of only three colleges in the state to have a Fisk organ. There are two large art studios, one for the teaching of two-dimensional media and one for the teaching of three-dimensional media. Students in the education department are served by the Curriculum Materials Center, which contains audiovisual equipment, books, teaching kits, and a variety of other special supplies.

Costs

For 2007–08, the total cost of tuition, fees, room, and board was $28,740. A private room cost an additional $3080. Greensboro College estimates that $800 to $1600 is adequate for books, clothing, entertainment, and other incidental expenses.

Financial Aid

Greensboro College participates in many federal programs of student aid, including the Federal Pell Grant, Federal Work-Study, Federal Perkins Loan, Federal Supplemental Educational Opportunity Grant, Federal Parent Loan for Undergraduate Students, and Federal Stafford Student Loan programs. Authorized state programs include North Carolina Legislative Tuition Grants, the State Contractual Scholarship Fund, North Carolina Prospective Teacher's Scholarships/Loans, and North Carolina Student Incentive Grants. Institutional programs funded by Greensboro College include the College work-study program, grants, scholarships, and loans. Full- and partial-tuition scholarships are awarded to students based on merit. United Methodist Church scholarships and grants, which are based on both financial need and merit, are available. Full Tuition Presidential Scholarships, valued at more than $80,000 each, are available. Approximately 90 percent of the students at Greensboro College receive some form of financial assistance. All students are encouraged to apply for financial aid, and the College accepts the Free Application for Federal Student Aid (FAFSA). Applications for United Methodist Church scholarships and grants are available from the financial planning office. A career-development office on campus is available to aid all students seeking a part-time job, regardless of their financial need.

Faculty

Greensboro College has 105 full- and part-time faculty members. All of the full-time faculty members hold the highest degree in their areas of study. Although some faculty members have distinguished themselves by their research, scholarship, and creativity, all are deeply and primarily committed to undergraduate teaching and the personal welfare of the students. Every student has a faculty adviser; the average class size is 16, and there is a favorable student-faculty ratio of 11:1.

Student Government

The College's Student Government Association (SGA), acting within the policies and regulations of the College, is the main representative voice of the students. The SGA addresses various policy decisions that affect the students and acts as a sounding board for student opinions. The SGA is the communication link between student organizations, the student body, the administration, the staff, and the faculty. The Campus Activities Board plans and executes student events on campus.

Admission Requirements

Admission decisions are based on all available information. Although applicants are asked to submit scores from the SAT and/or ACT, the high school record is actually the most important single factor. No exact formula can be applied to all applications, but acceptable scores on the SAT or ACT, rank in class, grade point average, and high school program form the basis for evaluation. Candidates for admission should demonstrate academic achievement in a select academic program in high school, although completion of a given program of study is not as important as evidence of intellectual curiosity and emotional and social maturity. A curriculum that provides good preparation for Greensboro College might include 4 units of English, 3 units of college-preparatory math (algebra I and II and geometry), 2 units of science (including one laboratory science), 2 units of history, 2 units of the same foreign language, and electives chosen from art, music, physical education, and social science. An interview on campus is very helpful to the student and to the College. Arrangements may be made for the interview at the student's convenience.

Greensboro College accepts transfer credits on a case-by-case basis. Credit is given for courses that have been successfully completed at accredited universities, senior colleges, junior colleges, community colleges, and technical colleges.

Application and Information

Students should submit an application for admission and immediately ask high schools and any colleges they have attended to forward official transcripts to Greensboro College. SAT or ACT scores should be forwarded to the College by the testing agency or the student's high school. Reference letters may be requested by the Admissions Committee, which reviews all applications on a rolling basis. As soon as a decision is reached, the student is notified. Greensboro College has no closing date for applications, but those received before March 31 are given priority.

For inquiries and application materials, students should contact:

Office of Admissions
Greensboro College
815 West Market Street
Greensboro, North Carolina 27401-1875
Phone: 800-346-8226 (toll-free)
Fax: 336-378-0154
E-mail: admissions@gborocollege.edu
Web site: http://www.gborocollege.edu

Greensboro College students frequently gather near the historic Main Building.

GUILFORD COLLEGE

GREENSBORO, NORTH CAROLINA

The College

Founded in 1837 as the Quaker New Garden Boarding School, Guilford College, with its Georgian buildings set on 340 wooded acres on the western edge of Greensboro, North Carolina, retains a sense of tranquility and tradition. Guilford is among the oldest coeducational colleges in the nation and has a long-standing history of commitment to the individual student and to Quaker values. Guilford College draws on Quaker and liberal arts traditions to prepare men and women for a lifetime of learning, work, and constructive action dedicated to the betterment of the world.

Guilford's 2,688 students come from more than forty states and eighteen other countries. Guilford College is the home of 1,452 traditional-aged students (ages 17–22, 80 percent of whom live on campus), 1,141 adult students (23 and older, all living off campus), and 95 "early college" students (eleventh and twelfth graders, all living off campus). The College's size ensures the academic community's commitment to personalized education without giving up academic diversity. Students are encouraged to take an active part in extracurricular activities on campus, including seminars and lecture series, interest and service clubs, wide-ranging cultural opportunities as well as a program of intercollegiate athletics for both men and women. The Student Union, a student organization, sponsors many of the social, recreational, and cultural programs offered at the College. Many students participate in a variety of community service projects and volunteer programs.

There are frequent exhibitions featuring distinguished artists as well as College faculty members and students. Dramatic presentations range from *Romeo and Juliet* to *Waiting for Godot*. A touring choir and opportunities for individual lessons complement the music program. Each summer, Guilford is the home of the famous Eastern Music Festival. Orchestra, drama, opera, and ballet performances are also available in the city of Greensboro. The Bryan Distinguished Visiting Professorship in the Arts, Humanities, and Public Affairs at Guilford College brings individuals to campus who are widely regarded as experts in their field. Past professors include Cokie Roberts, Archbishop Desmond Tutu, Mikhail Gorbachev, Sidney Portier, and Madeleine Albright. Guilford College students are able to attend Bryan Series lectures free of charge.

Guilford's intercollegiate athletic teams compete at the NCAA Division III level and in the Old Dominion Athletic Conference (ODAC). The sports include women's basketball, cross-country, lacrosse, soccer, softball, swimming, tennis, and volleyball and men's baseball, basketball, cross-country, football, golf, lacrosse, soccer, and tennis. Sports programs are coupled with special academic opportunities in sports medicine, sport management, and physical education. Guilford's athletic facilities include basketball courts, a swimming pool, racquetball courts, and additional multipurpose courts.

Location

Greensboro, North Carolina, is a city of 234,000 people, located midway between Washington, D.C., and Atlanta, Georgia. The greater metropolitan area has a population of approximately 1.3 million. Greensboro is the home of six colleges and universities, with a total student enrollment of approximately 40,000. The city is served by two interstate highways, and the Piedmont Triad International Airport is less than 5 miles from campus. Numerous historic sites as well as local, state, and national parks are within day-trip distance of the College. Greensboro's central location in the state allows easy access both to the coast and to several major ski areas in the mountains. The amenities of life in the Southeast—climate, pace, and friendliness—coupled with rich cultural opportunities and sound economic growth make the Sun Belt an attractive area in which to study and to live.

Majors and Degrees

Guilford College offers B.A. or B.S. degrees in accounting, African-American studies, art, biology, business management, chemistry, community and justice studies, computer information systems, computing and information technology, criminal justice, economics, education studies, English, environmental studies, exercise and sports studies, forensic biology, French, geology and earth sciences, German, German studies, health sciences, history, integrative studies, international studies, life sciences, mathematics, music, peace and conflict studies, philosophy, physics, political science, psychology, religious studies, sociology/anthropology, Spanish, sport management, sports medicine, theater studies, and women's studies. The B.F.A. is offered in art.

Concentrations are available in accounting, African-American studies, African studies, anthropology, applied ethics, astronomy, business, business law, chemistry, communications, community studies, computing and information technology, criminal justice, dance, earth science, East Asian studies, economics, education studies, English, environmental studies, field biology, forensic science, French language and society, German language and society, history, human resource management, integrated science, international business management, international political economy, interpersonal communication, Japanese language and society, Latin American studies, mathematics for the sciences, medieval/early modern studies, money and finance, music, nonprofit management, organizational communication, peace and conflict studies, philosophy, philosophy of mathematics, physics, political science, psychology, Quaker studies, religious studies, sociology, Spanish language and society, sport administration, sport marketing, theater studies, visual arts, and women's studies.

A cooperative program with Duke University is available leading to graduate study in natural resources and the environment. Most recently, Guilford College has entered into an agreement with University of North Carolina at Greensboro to be able to offer an accelerated Masters of Business Administration (M.B.A.). Preprofessional programs are offered in dentistry, law, medicine, ministry, and veterinary science.

Academic Programs

Each student works closely with a faculty adviser to select courses that meet his or her individual educational and career goals. Thirty-two semester courses are required for graduation, eight of which are generally in the major field of study. Required courses are few but represent a distribution over the principal fields of the arts and sciences. Flexible requirements allow for interdisciplinary and double majors.

Incoming first-year students and transfer students participate in CHAOS (Community, Health, Advising, Orientation, Services), an orientation program that includes computer training, learning skills, academic advising, self-awareness workshops, and outdoor experiences.

Independent study, off-campus internships, and off-campus seminars are open to all students. An expanded honors program includes a variety of honors courses for students with exceptional academic credentials and motivation. One pass/fail elective course may be taken each semester.

Entering students may waive courses through Advanced Placement (AP) examinations in English, history, laboratory science, mathematics, and foreign languages. Advanced placement requires an AP score of 3 or better or a general CLEP score of 500 or better; credit requires an AP score of 4 or better or a general CLEP score of 550 or better. Subject CLEP scores must be at least 50 for advanced placement and at least 55 for credit.

Guilford College has a two-semester calendar. The first semester ends before winter break; the second semester ends in early May.

Off-Campus Programs

Semester abroad programs enable students to study in Africa, China, England, France, Germany, Ireland, Italy, Japan, Mexico, the Netherlands, Scotland, Spain, and Wales. Students may also participate in programs sponsored by other American colleges and universities. A full year of academic credit for study in Japan is available through a cooperative program with International Christian University in Tokyo.

Guilford participates in two consortia that allow open registration in seven area colleges and universities without additional fees. Other member schools are Bennett College, Elon University, Greensboro College, Guilford Technical Community College, High Point University, North Carolina A&T State University, and the University of North Carolina at Greensboro.

An on-campus programs director assists students who wish to study abroad. An internship director helps to place students who wish to study elsewhere in the United States. Course credit is given for all approved off-campus study. The Washington Semester in Washington, D.C., supplements the academic program and helps students develop professional skills and career potential through internships with the federal government, lobbying organizations, or public agencies.

Internships may be done in any discipline. Locally, students may pursue internships as part of their academic and career development in business, education, government, health services, law, medicine, scientific research, and social services. In addition, the Career and Community Learning Center sponsors a variety of community service activities, such as the Student Literacy Corps and Project Community.

Academic Facilities

Stately Georgian-style buildings in excellent condition house classrooms, a spacious auditorium, the library, a well-appointed student center, administrative offices, and residence halls. The 65,000-square-foot Frank Family Science Center opened in August 2000 and features fourteen laboratories (with twenty-four workstations each), 1,600 computer connections, a rooftop observatory with a computer-driven telescope, and a 150-seat multipurpose auditorium/planetarium. Multiple studio space is available to students in the fine arts.

Guilford's Hege Library is one of the three largest private libraries in North Carolina. The library contains 250,000 volumes and includes an art gallery, a media center, and the only Friends Historical Collection in the Southeast. Hege Library is fully automated and is linked to buildings across the entire campus. Students also have library privileges at six colleges within 20 miles that have an additional 1.3 million volumes.

The state-of-the-art Bauman Telecommunications Center houses two computer-equipped classrooms, faculty offices, and three computer labs with ninety-one personal computers. In addition, there are 200 public terminals in the Center and other terminals in academic buildings around the campus. Fiber-optic hookups link Bauman Telecommunications Center to most academic buildings on campus, and all students living on campus can access the facility from their residence hall rooms. In addition, satellite connections make it possible to bring in foreign language programming from around the world. Guilford offers state-of-the-art computers in its multimedia learning center for cultures and languages. Most residential students have PCs in their rooms connected to the College network, and the College has full Internet access. Wireless access is available in Hege Library, Founders Hall Terrace, and Community Center Terrace. All students have e-mail accounts, and, through an interdisciplinary course, students play an active role in developing the College's Web site.

Costs

Basic expenses for the 2007–08 academic year were $24,140 for tuition, $6860 for room and board, and $435 for fees. Personal expenses, book costs, and transportation expenses vary according to individual need.

Financial Aid

Guilford College tries to meet the demonstrated financial need of all students, as determined by the Free Application for Federal Student Aid (FAFSA). More than $22 million in scholarships, loans, grants, and work-study opportunities was awarded to students last year. Academic scholarships are awarded on a competitive basis. Guilford offers six merit-based and special-interest scholarship programs. Approximately 86 percent of last year's student body received some form of merit-based or need-based assistance. The average need-based award was more than $19,052 a year per recipient. The average merit-based award was $6286.

Faculty

Guilford has 136 full-time faculty members. The College seeks faculty members who value the sense of community and concern for individuals that are part of Guilford's heritage. The student-faculty ratio is currently 16:1. The average class size is 19.

Student Government

Guilford entrusts its students with responsibility for governing their own actions and furthering the best interests of the entire College community. The student Community Senate is composed of representatives from residence halls and the day-student organization, a member of the administration, and 2 faculty members. Students serve on all faculty and administrative committees and on the College's Board of Trustees and Alumni Board.

Admission Requirements

As one of the oldest coeducational institutions in the nation, Guilford takes the commitment to academics and the liberal arts seriously. To that end, the Admission Committee uses a holistic method of application evaluation. Each applicant is considered on an individual basis. Students are encouraged to challenge themselves within their high school environment, both in and out of the classroom. While the majority of applicants submit some form of standardized test scores (ACT or SAT), students have the option of submitting a portfolio of written work in lieu of standardized test scores. The Guilford College community is full of active and involved citizens. The evaluation process seeks to continue to admit students that bring a diverse variety of backgrounds and interests to the College. Interviews, although not required, are available so that the applicant can become better acquainted with Guilford and so that the admission staff can better evaluate the candidate. Guilford is competitive with respect to admissions.

Application and Information

Admission plans include early action and regular decision. Early action applicants must apply by January 15 and are notified by February 15. The regular decision priority deadline is February 15, and applicants are notified by April 1. After February 15, applications are considered on a space-available basis. Candidates admitted for regular decision must reply to their offers of admission by May 1.

Early entrance applicants are considered after their junior year of high school. They must have an outstanding academic record and must be sufficiently mature socially to adjust to college life.

Transfer candidates should apply for admission by December 1 for the spring semester and by June 1 for the fall semester.

The priority deadline for applying for financial aid is March 1.

The Admission Office is open for visits Monday through Friday and Saturdays during the academic year. During the summer, the Admission Office is open for visits Monday through Friday. Guilford College encourages students to visit for a campus tour. More than a classroom education, the Guilford experience is designed to stimulate the whole person and provide the critical thinking that will help today's students take their place as leaders who will guide tomorrow.

For further information and application forms for admission and financial aid, students should contact:

Admission Office
Guilford College
5800 West Friendly Avenue
Greensboro, North Carolina 27410
Phone: 336-316-2100
800-992-7759 (toll-free)
E-mail: admission@guilford.edu
Web site: http://www.guilford.edu

HIGH POINT UNIVERSITY

HIGH POINT, NORTH CAROLINA

The University

High Point University is a private university related to the United Methodist Church. At High Point, every student receives an extraordinary education in a fun environment with caring people. With 3,000 students, the University is large enough to guarantee high quality and diversity in programs and services yet small enough to enable community among students and faculty and staff members. Approximately 2,500 students are enrolled at the High Point campus, and about 500 students are enrolled at the Madison Park campus in Winston-Salem, North Carolina. In a typical year, students come from forty-two states and fifty countries, making the campus a microcosm of the nation and the world, thereby creating an ideal learning environment.

The University fully recognizes its responsibility to provide the best liberal arts education possible, but faculty and staff members recognize that education, as often defined, is not sufficient. Therefore, the University intentionally seeks to develop character by encouraging personal responsibility and by inculcating values through curricular and cocurricular programs and services, including a required ethics course, the President's Seminar on Life Skills, and the University chapel, where services are offered each week. Although attendance is voluntary, chapel services are packed each Wednesday.

In addition to the bachelor's degrees described below, the University offers five master's degrees: the Master of Business Administration (M.B.A.); the Master of Education (M.Ed.) in elementary education and educational leadership; the Master of Science (M.S.) in international management, management, and sport studies; the Master of Public Administration (M.P.A.) in nonprofit organizations; and the Master of Arts (M.A.) in history.

Location

Together, High Point, Greensboro, and Winston-Salem form the Piedmont Triad of North Carolina, a metropolitan area of approximately 1.4 million people, more than 90,000 of whom live within the city of High Point. Both Winston-Salem and Greensboro are 20 minutes from the campus, as is the Piedmont Triad (Greensboro–High Point) International Airport. Both Raleigh and Charlotte are 1½ hours away, the Appalachian Mountains are 2 hours away, and the Atlantic Ocean and beaches are 4 hours away.

The region is known nationally and internationally for the quality of its institutions of higher education. Within a 60-mile radius are Duke University, the University of North Carolina at Chapel Hill, and Wake Forest University, along with twenty-eight other colleges and universities. Obviously, such an area is replete with athletic, cultural, recreational, and social activities for young adults.

Majors and Degrees

High Point University awards the Bachelor of Arts degree in art, art education, criminal justice, elementary education, English: literature, English: writing, French, history, human relations, international studies, middle grades education, music: general studies, music: organ or piano, music: voice, North American studies, philosophy, political science, religion, sociology, Spanish, special education, theater: performance, and theater: technical. The University awards the Bachelor of Science degree in accounting, athletic training, biology, business administration (accounting, economics, finance, information security and privacy, international management, management, and marketing), chemistry, chemistry: business, communications, computer information systems, computer science, entrepreneurship, exercise science, forestry, home furnishings marketing, interior design, international business, management information systems, mathematics, medical technology, physical education, psychology, recreation, and sport management. Within the liberal arts major, students can complete the requirements for admission to professional schools, including dentistry, engineering, forestry, law, medicine, pharmacy, physician assistant studies, and veterinary medicine.

Academic Programs

The academic program includes sixty-eight majors administered through the College of Arts and Science, the Phillips School of Business, and the Brayton School of Education. In addition, the University allows students with well-defined objectives that cannot be satisfied within the regular curriculum to design their own individualized majors. An honors program recognizes and encourages creativity and academic achievement.

The curriculum emphasizes the study of the liberal arts in the belief that there is no better way to encourage communication skills, critical thinking, and personal integrity and in the belief that in the process of acquiring these skills, students become self-learners who are equipped to succeed in life and work. Within the liberal arts framework, the University provides several professional programs, including athletic training, business administration, computer information systems, computer science, exercise science, home furnishings marketing, human relations (a program affiliated with American Humanics, Inc.), information security and privacy, international business, management information systems, and sport management. Cooperative baccalaureate programs are offered in engineering, environmental management, forestry, and medical technology.

The curriculum prepares students to pursue graduate programs consistent with the majors listed above and professional programs beyond the baccalaureate degree in areas that include, but are not limited to, business, dentistry, law, medicine, ministry, pharmacy, physical therapy, physician assistant studies, and sports medicine.

Through the Student Career Intern Program, juniors and seniors at High Point University are able to explore career opportunities outside the classroom. The program enables a student to assume the responsibilities of a regular employee in a local business or agency before graduating from High Point, thereby enabling the student to evaluate a career choice prior to graduation.

Students who have completed Advanced Placement courses in high school and who have achieved a score of 3, 4, or 5 on the Advanced Placement tests administered by the College Board may receive credit at High Point University. Applicants may also receive credit for university-parallel courses successfully completed prior to enrollment at High Point, including courses completed while in high school through dual enrollment or international baccalaureate programs.

Off-Campus Programs

Students may choose to study abroad for a year, a semester, or a summer through the High Point University in England program, which is offered in cooperation with the University of Leeds, or through the University's program at Oxford/Brookes. The University's affiliation with international-study programs administered by other institutions also makes it possible for students to study in Canada, France, Germany, Scotland, Spain, and Mexico. In addition, the University is now offering new venues in Swansea, Wales; Florence, Italy; and London, England. In spring 2007, students took advantage of the opportunity to choose from many of these study-abroad locations in a concentrated three- to four-week "Maymester" program. In addition to the countries listed above, Australia, China, Ireland, and Japan have been added to the "Maymester" program. Subject to prior approval, transfer credit may be awarded for university-parallel work offered by institutions other than those with which the University has formal affiliation.

Students enrolled at High Point University may cross-register on the campus of any other member institution in the Greater Greensboro Consortium, including two state institutions and a women's college.

Academic Facilities

Smith Library, a fully electronically integrated library system, supports sixty-eight undergraduate majors and seven graduate programs. The library contains more than 290,000 print volumes, including more than 50,000 electronic books, and more than 20,000 electronic journals. All electronic resources are accessible online by students and other patrons, both on and off campus.

The Learning Assistance Center, which is located in the library, provides tutoring and other programs designed to facilitate learning. Although 80 percent of enrolled students own personal computers, more than 400 computers are available for student use in classrooms, laboratories, the library, the University Center, and other locations. A roaming profile enables students to save and access their personal documents from any campus PC, including their personal computers and those provided by the University. Computer laboratories in computer science and mathematics are equipped with Linux-based PCs connected to a Linux computing cluster.

Phillips Hall, opened in August 2007, houses a state-of-the-art School of Business designed after the Harvard School of Business. The Congdon Hall of Science provides science laboratories and modern equipment. The James H. and Jesse E. Millis Athletic and Convocation Center houses a state-of-the-art sports medicine center, along with facilities for physical education that include, but are not limited to, the Aerobic Center, an Olympic-size pool, racquetball courts, and tennis courts. The Charles E. and Pauline Lewis Hayworth Fine Arts Center includes the Pauline Theatre, the Sechrest Art Gallery, galleries for student exhibits, a laboratory for computer graphics, and studios for design, drawing, music, painting, photography, printmaking, and theater. Norton Hall, which was built on campus by the international furnishings industry, is a state-of-the-art facility that houses the Knabusch-Shoemaker International School of Furnishings and Design. Currently under construction, and scheduled to open in January 2009, are the Qubein School of Communication, with $2 million in television, radio, and video gaming studios, and the Plato Wilson School of Commerce that will include a Wall Street-style ticker tape trading room and other state-of-the-art amenities.

Costs

For 2008–09, High Point University's comprehensive fee (including tuition, room, board, and general fees) for full-time boarding students range from $31,000 to $32,600 for a private room.

Financial Aid

Students who require financial assistance should complete the Free Application for Federal Student Aid (FAFSA). The FAFSA provides an estimate of how much the student and the parents/guardians of dependent students can contribute toward the cost of attending High Point University. The University's Office of Student Financial Services uses the results of the FAFSA to determine the types of assistance available to students. Scholarships, grants, loans, and college work-study are possible sources of support.

Presidential Fellowships, ranging from $12,000 to $22,100 per year, are awarded on a competitive basis to entering freshmen. The University awards up to fifty $7000 Presidential Scholarships to entering freshmen annually, also on a competitive basis.

Faculty

High Point University has a student-faculty ratio of 14:1 and an average class size of fewer than 20 students. More than 82 percent of faculty members have earned either the Ph.D. or another terminal degree. All classes are taught by full faculty members, and one of the professors in each student's major will be his or her adviser. High Point University does not use any graduate students or assistants to teach class. Faculty members routinely interact with students outside of class.

Student Government

High Point University intentionally seeks to involve students in campus life through Student Government, service on University-wide committees, and student activities, including sixteen NCAA Division I athletic teams, nine Greek organizations, and more than seventy other campus organizations. In addition, High Point University students provide more than 25,000 hours of voluntary service to the community of High Point.

Admission Requirements

Freshman applicants must be graduates of an accredited secondary school and must exhibit satisfactory performance in a college-preparatory curriculum of 18 units, distributed as follows: English, 4; foreign language, 2; mathematics, 3; history, 3; laboratory science, 3; and electives, 3. Every freshman applicant must submit scores on the SAT or the ACT. International applicants may submit TOEFL scores as an alternative to the SAT or ACT; however, students who wish to play on an athletic team must take the SAT. Campus visits and personal interviews are strongly recommended.

Application and Information

Application forms must be completed by the student and sent to the Office of Admissions, along with a nonrefundable $40 processing fee. Official transcripts (high school and college, where applicable) must be sent directly to the University by the appropriate school official. Students should request that a copy of their SAT, ACT, or TOEFL scores be sent to the Office of Admissions at High Point University by the testing agency. High Point University operates under a deadline admission plan, including early decision and early action. Because enrollment is limited by available residential spaces, early application is encouraged. All requests for application materials and information should be directed to:

Office of Undergraduate Admissions
High Point University
833 Montlieu Avenue
High Point, North Carolina 27262-3598
Phone: 336-841-9216
800-345-6993 (toll-free)
E-mail: admiss@highpoint.edu
Web site: http://www.highpoint.edu

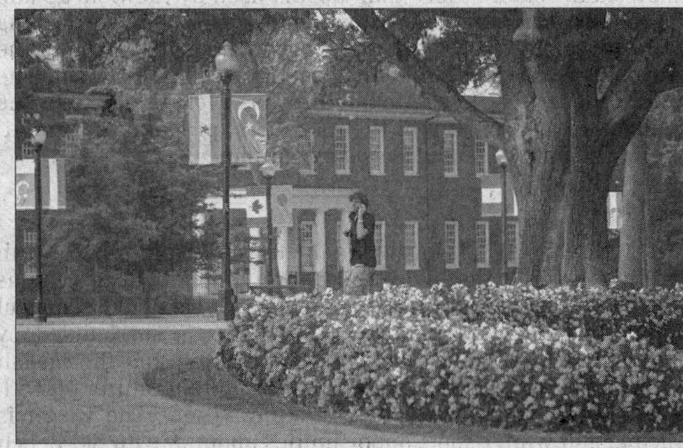

High Point University, which is located on a 140-acre campus, enrolls 3,000 students from forty-four states and fifty countries.

LEES-McRAE COLLEGE

BANNER ELK, NORTH CAROLINA

The College

Lees-McRae College, a small, private, coeducational liberal arts college affiliated with the Presbyterian Church (USA), was founded in 1900 and offers a stimulating and caring academic environment. Primarily a residential campus, Lees-McRae enrolls approximately 900 students from more than thirty states and twenty-five other countries. The 400-acre campus provides twelve residence halls to house on-campus students.

Service to others is a big part of Lees-McRae College. Students and staff and faculty members take advantage of many opportunities throughout the year to make the community a better place. They become engaged in meaningful outreach projects in the immediate communities, as well as fartherreaching destinations, through mission trips and alternative semester breaks. Participants become involved, explore social issues, and learn many lessons outside the classroom. Social life centers on activities planned by members of the Student Government Association and the Student Development staff and includes a variety of intramural sports, films, comedians, lectures, and concerts.

Lees-McRae College is a member of the Carolinas-Virginia Athletics Conference (CVAC) of NCAA Division II and participates in men's intercollegiate basketball, cross-country, cycling, golf, lacrosse, skiing, soccer, tennis, track and field, and volleyball. Women participate in basketball, cross-country, cycling, lacrosse, skiing, soccer, softball, tennis, track and field, and volleyball. The athletic facilities include indoor and outdoor tennis courts, lacrosse and soccer fields, volleyball and basketball courts, athletic training facilities, a large, heated indoor pool, and fitness facilities. The Cannon Student Center, comprising more than 22,000 square feet, provides ample lounge space, Wily's Snack Bar, health services, a Nautilus workout room, and an art exhibit area as well as student support offices. In addition, Evans Auditorium serves as a forum for presentations and the weekly chapel service. Hayes Auditorium, seating more than 800, is used by the College and community for cultural activities. The Lees-McRae Performing Arts Department has numerous productions throughout the year, and, during the summer, three musicals are shown. The Performing Arts at Lees-McRae also has a clogging team, the Highlanders choral group; their dancers' preparations culminate in the annual *Kaleidoscope* performance.

Location

Lees-McRae College is located in the town of Banner Elk, North Carolina, and has the highest elevation of any college campus east of the Rocky Mountains. Situated 4,000 feet above sea level in the Blue Ridge Mountains, the campus is surrounded by Grandfather Mountain, the Appalachian Trail, and the Pisgah National Forest. The average summer temperature of 65°F makes Banner Elk an excellent summer resort. The winter is bracing, and winter sport opportunities abound, with Ski Beech and Sugar Mountain ski resorts just minutes from the campus. A ski team and ski/snowboarding classes bring this type of adventure within reach of the students. Ample opportunities exist in the areas for natural recreational activities such as hiking, whitewater rafting, canoeing, fishing, mountain biking, and camping.

Majors and Degrees

Lees-McRae College awards the Bachelor of Arts (B.A.) and Bachelor of Sciences (B.S.) degrees. Majors currently offered are athletic training; biology, with concentrations in wildlife biology, pre–health science, preveterinary, and wildlife rehabilitation; business administration, with concentrations in accounting, computer information systems, management, and small business development/entrepreneurship; communication arts; criminal justice; elementary education (K–6); history; humanities; interdisciplinary studies; international studies; literature; mathematics; performing arts studies; physical education (K–12); psychology; religious studies; sociology; sport management; and theater arts education (K–12).

Academic Programs

At Lees-McRae College, all students complete the general education core of courses, which are distributed among the various academic fields. In addition, students must successfully complete the requirements of their specific major. Students may also select a minor to complement their program-of-study concentration. Advanced Placement and College-Level Examination Program credits are accepted. The College is on a semester system and also offers two 5-week summer sessions. The Honors Program at Lees-McRae College exposes academically strong students to courses that offer innovative and creative approaches to learning. Study-abroad opportunities are coordinated by the faculty; past destinations include Australia, England, France, Italy, Ireland, Kenya, Nicaragua, Russia, and Scotland.

Academic Facilities

Because Lees-McRae is a very dynamic and diverse institution, the types of academic settings vary greatly. These include classrooms equipped with the latest technology; science labs and a greenhouse; the Blue Ridge Wildlife Institute; the Elk Valley Biology Field Station; 400 acres of the outdoors; the Carson Library, housing the Sterling Collection and curriculum center; computer labs, including a Communication Arts Mac Lab; as well as a photo lab and performing arts auditoriums.

The College recently installed a campuswide wireless computer network system that includes all classrooms and residence halls, and even the green spaces on campus, and provides high speed Internet access to all students.

Costs

The cost to attend Lees-McRae College for the 2007–08 academic year was $26,000 for students living on campus and $19,500 for commuting students. This comprehensive cost included room, board, tuition, and all required fees. As a private institution, the College does not require additional fees for out-of-state students.

Financial Aid

Over ninety percent of Lees-McRae students receive financial assistance. Students may apply by filing the FAFSA (Free Application for Federal Student Aid) in the year that they plan to enroll. Financial aid sources include Federal Pell Grants, Federal Supplemental Educational Opportunity Grants, North Carolina Contract Grants, the North Carolina Legislative Tuition Grant, the Federal Perkins Loan Program, and Federal

Stafford Loans. In addition, the Federal Parental Loan for Undergraduate Students (FPLUS) and loans for international students may be available.

Many merit-based academic scholarships and grants, as well as athletic and performing arts scholarships, are also readily available to qualified students and are based on talent and achievement, not on financial need. The Lees-McRae Grant serves as an additional funding source to meet students' financial need as fully as possible.

Faculty

Lees-McRae has a well-credentialed and experienced faculty that is devoted to effective, individualized teaching by using current and well-developed methodology. Nearly eighty-five percent have earned the highest degree awarded in their field. The student-faculty ratio is less than 12:1, allowing for mentoring as well as close relationships. Seventy-four percent of the classes have fewer than 20 students, and all courses are taught by experienced faculty members, not graduate students.

Student Government

Students are actively involved in institutional government, and Student Government Association (SGA) members are chosen in campuswide elections. Class representatives' responsibilities include creating an atmosphere of free discussion, inquiry, and self-expression; fostering meaningful traditions of the College; and striving to strengthen cooperation among students, faculty members, and the administration. The SGA members also play an active role in planning campus activities and entertainment with the help of the Campus After the Classroom Hours (CATCH).

Admission Requirements

Graduation from an accredited high school is required; however, students with a high school equivalency diploma (GED) are considered. Applicants are required to take the SAT or ACT, and the high school curriculum should include 4 units of English, 3 in math, 2 in science, 1 in history, and other units that meet requirements for graduation from high school. Lees-McRae College carefully considers each applicant on an individual basis to determine their admissibility.

Transfer students are encouraged to apply to Lees-McRae College. To be favorably considered for admission, they must be in good social and academic standing at their previous institution and be eligible to return.

All interested students should contact the Admissions Office to schedule a visit to experience the unique mountain setting of the Lees-McRae campus. Open houses are offered throughout the year and are excellent times to visit and learn about the outstanding educational opportunities available at Lees-McRae College.

Application and Information

To be considered for admission, all applicants should complete the Lees-McRae application and provide the additional required documentation. Lees-McRae does not require an application fee from applicants. Applications for freshman admission should be sent in as early as possible during the senior year in high school. Lees-McRae uses a rolling-admissions policy and informs students of the admissions decision promptly once the student file is complete. Lees-McRae College follows a policy of nondiscrimination in its admission procedures and welcomes applications from all qualified students.

Application materials should be sent to:

Director of Admissions
Lees-McRae College
P.O. Box 128
Banner Elk, North Carolina 28604-0128
Phone: 828-898-8723
800-280-4562 (toll-free)
Fax: 828-898-8707
E-mail: admissions@lmc.edu
Web site: http://www.lmc.edu
http://www.lmc.edu/applyonline

Tufts Tower, like most buildings on the Lees-McRae College campus, is made of native river rock.

MEREDITH COLLEGE

RALEIGH, NORTH CAROLINA

The College

Meredith College, chartered in 1891, is today the largest private women's college in the Southeast. Even as the College has grown to more than 2,100 undergraduate degree candidates, the student-faculty ratio of 10:1 offers students individualized attention in all aspects of their experience at Meredith College. With a focus on the liberal arts, students are encouraged in all areas from career preparation to personal development. Degree candidates choose from more than fifty fields, including preprofessional studies.

The faculty is dedicated to teaching, advising, and challenging the students to meet their academic and personal goals. Undergraduate students pursue programs leading to Bachelor of Arts, Science, Music, and Social Work degrees; the College also offers Master of Business Administration, Master of Education, and Master of Science in nutrition degrees. College programs are accredited by the Southern Association of Colleges and Schools, the National Council for the Accreditation of Teacher Education, the Council on Social Work Education, the Council for Interior Design Accreditation (formerly FIDER), and the National Association of Schools of Music. The College has an approved American Dietetic Association Plan V Program.

The College focuses heavily on leadership development for women. Students are encouraged to participate in a wide variety of campus activities, including performing groups, sports, publications, academic and personal interest clubs, and student government. More than 500 leadership positions are available for women to fill. Rich with diversity with students from thirty states and sixteen countries, Meredith celebrates its students' uniqueness and potential to return to their communities as active participants in whatever capacity that they choose. A member of NCAA Division III, Meredith fields intercollegiate teams in six sports: basketball, cross-country, softball, soccer, tennis, and volleyball. The College joined the USA South Athletic Conference in 2007.

Location

Meredith's beautiful 225-acre campus is on the western edge of Raleigh, North Carolina's capital city, and is adjacent to the booming Research Triangle area of Raleigh, Durham, and Chapel Hill. A total of eleven colleges and universities that serve approximately 108,000 students can be found here. Raleigh, a city of 286,000 people, is centrally located between the North Carolina coast and the mountain ranges of the western part of the state. Two interstates and the Raleigh-Durham International Airport (15 minutes from the campus) make Raleigh easily accessible.

Majors and Degrees

Meredith confers four baccalaureate degrees. A candidate for the Bachelor of Arts degree can select her major from American civilization, art, biology, chemistry, communication, dance, economics, English, environmental studies, French, history, international studies, mathematics, music, political science, psychology, public history, religion, social work, sociology, Spanish, theater, and women's studies. The Bachelor of Science degree is available in accounting, biology, business administration, chemistry, child development, computer information systems, computer science, exercise and sports science, family and consumer science, fashion merchandising and design, foods and nutrition, interior design, and mathematics. The Bachelor of Music degree candidate can major in music education or performance. The Bachelor of Social Work degree is available in social work. In addition, a student may work with the faculty to create a self-designed major.

Licensure programs taken in addition to a major are offered in birth to kindergarten (B–K), elementary (K–6), middle grades (6–9), secondary (9–12), and special subject areas (K–12).

Preprofessional preparation is available in dentistry, law, medicine, pharmacy, physical therapy, physician assistant studies, and veterinary medicine. Minors are offered in most major fields and in some other areas, such as communication, criminal justice, ethics, philosophy, and physical education. Concentrations are also available within most departments. A five-year dual-degree program with North Carolina State University is available in engineering.

Academic Programs

Meredith's academic program blends a strong liberal arts foundation with opportunities for career and preprofessional preparation. To achieve breadth in her education, each student must fulfill general education requirements in humanities and arts, social and behavioral sciences, mathematics and natural sciences, and health and physical education. By the end of her sophomore year, she declares a major and begins to study her chosen field in depth. She may round out her program by completing options such as a second major, a minor or a concentration, a teacher education program, an experiential learning component (an internship, co-op, or fieldwork), or a study-abroad program.

There are opportunities for advanced placement with credit for those who show by examination (AP, I.B., CLEP, and/or departmental examinations) that they have mastered the material for any college-level course. Each year approximately 25 entering students are invited to participate in the Honors Program. Nearly 30 entering students participate in the Teaching Fellows Program, which provides special seminars, mentors, honors classes, and cultural opportunities for the winners of the prestigious North Carolina Teaching Fellows Scholarship/Loan.

Off-Campus Programs

Through the Cooperating Raleigh Colleges consortium, students may take courses with typically no extra cost at North Carolina State and Shaw Universities and at Peace and St. Augustine's Colleges.

Women who are interested in expanding their international horizons can participate in either summer or academic-year intercultural programs in almost any country. Every summer, students and faculty members travel to England, Italy, and Switzerland for five or eleven weeks of study. It is possible to earn an entire semester of credit through this summer study at approximately the same price as a regular semester on campus in Raleigh. Art students above the freshman level may study in Florence, Italy. Students of French may study at the Université Catholique de l'Ouest in Angers, France, and students of Spanish may study at Universitas Nebrissensis in Madrid, Spain. Students of almost any major can study in Australia, Hong Kong, and the United Kingdom. Those seeking a less traditional venue can study at Meredith affiliates in the People's Republic of China or can work with the Office of Study Abroad to find a program appropriate to their academic or travel interests.

Students may take advantage of opportunities within the United States by completing a United Nations Semester at Drew University, a federal government semester through the Washington Semester program at American University, a semester at Marymount College in New York City, and a capital city semester in state government through Meredith's own program in Raleigh.

Academic Facilities

The Carlyle Campbell Library contains more than 150,000 volumes, 6,100 videos, and 7,200 musical scores. Online, full-text versions of articles from thousands of academic periodicals are also available. As part of its academic department facilities, the campus also houses a music library, art galleries, a research greenhouse, music practice rooms, a state-of-the-art language lab, an autism lab, computer labs, a child-care lab, an indoor swimming pool, lighted outdoor tennis courts, a putting green, and a soccer field. The campus is also cabled to provide network and e-mail access in classrooms, computer labs, and residence halls as well as wireless Internet access throughout much of the campus.

Costs

For 2007–08, tuition and fees were $22,400 and room and board were $6300.

Financial Aid

Meredith's financial aid program is designed to meet a high percentage of the analyzed need of the student. Approximately 50 percent of undergraduate students receive need-based assistance; when competitive scholarships and state entitlement grants are added, approximately 70 percent of Meredith students receive some form of financial assistance. The Free Application for Federal Student Aid (FAFSA) is used to determine eligibility for need-based federal, state, and institutional funds that include grants and scholarships, loans, and work-study. A freshman candidate may also file special application forms for the competitive scholarships that recognize students for superior academic ability and talent in art, music, or interior design. A North Carolina Teaching Fellow who is selected for Meredith's program may use her scholarship at the College and will have other gift assistance coordinated to match the stipend provided by the state.

Faculty

The College has 250 full-time and part-time faculty members. Eighty-nine percent of the full-time faculty members have earned terminal degrees. The student-faculty ratio is 10:1, and the average class size is 16. Sixty-six percent of the full-time faculty members are women.

Student Government

Meredith has one of the oldest student government associations in the South and has an honor code that is a key ingredient of the Meredith community. All students assume primary responsibility for making and enforcing regulations; therefore, every student is a member of the Student Government Association (SGA). As members, students are encouraged to actively participate in branches of the SGA, such as the Association for Meredith Commuters, Elections Board, Honor Council, Residence Hall Board, Senate, Student Life, and Women in New Goal Settings.

Admission Requirements

Along with academic achievement, Meredith values individuality, integrity, and diversity. Each application is evaluated to determine how the student's academic preparation and ability match Meredith's requirements and challenges and to assess motivation, special talents, and commitment to learning. A freshman candidate is expected to have at least 16 units of credit earned in grades 9–12, with at least 15 in the academic subjects. Her program should include English (4 units), history/social studies (3 units), mathematics (3 units in algebra I, algebra II, and geometry or a higher level course), science (3 units), foreign language (2 units), and electives (1 unit from the academic subjects). Careful attention is given to an unweighted grade average on the academic subjects and to class rank; test scores (SAT preferred, or ACT) are reviewed in relation to the high school record; recommendations from a school official and a teacher are also required. An interview may be requested in some instances, and students are encouraged to visit for an admissions conference and campus tour.

For transfer admission from an accredited college or university, the student needs at least an overall C average in transferable courses, must be eligible to return to the last institution regularly attended, and must be recommended by college officials. If the student has fewer than 30 semester hours of transferable work, she must also meet Meredith's freshman admission requirements. Nontraditional students and international students should contact the Office of Admissions.

Application and Information

An application for admission should be sent to the Office of Admissions along with a nonrefundable $40 processing fee (or acceptable fee-waiver request). Electronic filing is available. The student is responsible for requesting that her official high school transcript, SAT or ACT scores, and recommendations be sent to the admissions office. A transfer student must file an official transcript from each postsecondary institution attended.

Meredith has two freshman admission plans: early decision and rolling admissions. An early decision candidate must apply by October 15; this "first choice" plan means that if accepted under early decision, the student fully expects to enroll and will withdraw any other pending applications. The student is notified by November 1. A candidate under the rolling plan is encouraged to file early in the senior year, with February 15 as the recommended deadline. Notifications under this plan begin in mid-November. The candidates' reply dates are December 1 for early decision and May 1 for rolling admission candidates.

Transfer applicants are encouraged to apply by February 15. Notifications begin in late January, and May 1 is the candidates' reply date. For admission to the spring semester, a freshman or transfer student should apply by December 1.

For additional information and for planning a campus visit, students should contact the College by e-mail at admissions@meredith.edu or by phone at 800-MEREDITH (toll-free).

Office of Admissions
Meredith College
3800 Hillsborough Street
Raleigh, North Carolina 27607-5298
Phone: 919-760-8581
800-MEREDITH (toll-free)
Fax: 919-760-2348
E-mail: admissions@meredith.edu
Web site: http://www.meredith.edu

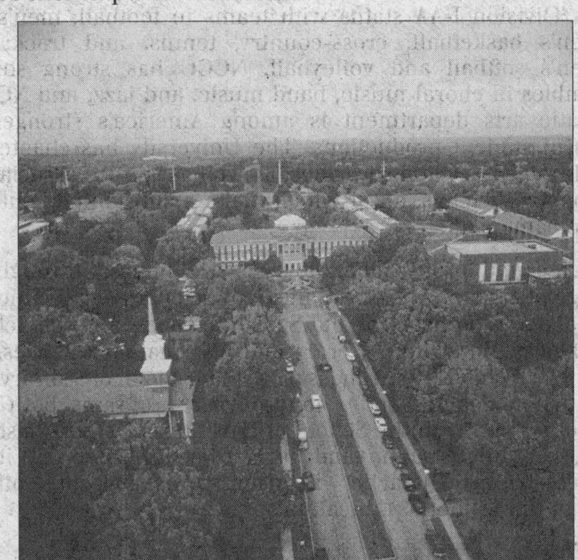

Meredith College's beautiful 225-acre campus is located on the edge of North Carolina's capital city near urban activity and eleven other colleges and universities.

NORTH CAROLINA CENTRAL UNIVERSITY

DURHAM, NORTH CAROLINA

The University

North Carolina Central University (NCCU) is a comprehensive public university, a constituent institution of the seventeen-campus University of North Carolina System. NCCU was founded in 1910 by Dr. James Edward Shepard, a pharmacist and political leader. In 1925, the institution became America's first state-supported liberal arts college for African Americans. Today, NCCU enrolls 8,384 students in undergraduate, graduate, and professional programs. Predominantly black (14 percent of the students are Caucasian), NCCU enrolls slightly more than 2 women to every 1 man. The average age of full-time undergraduate students is 23 years. Only 17 percent of freshmen are from outside the state of North Carolina, the percentage that prevails at almost every one of the sixteen state institutions. Approximately 50 of these students are from outside the United States. About 46 percent of the students are from Durham, Wake, and Mecklenburg Counties, and most of these are commuting students. On-campus housing is available for approximately 2,300 students.

NCCU's motto is "Truth and Service," and over the years, the University's alumni have taken leadership roles in political life and the law. The governor holds a degree from NCCU, as does the former chair of the Board of Governors for the University of North Carolina and the U.S. Ambassador to the Central African Republic. NCCU graduates have served as district attorneys in the federal and state courts and as judges of state appellate courts, including a state supreme court. Other NCCU graduates are outstanding teachers at all levels of academic life, lawyers of national reputation, corporate vice presidents and executives, and school and university administrators.

NCCU is a former member of the Central Intercollegiate Athletic Association. In 2007, the University transitioned to NCAA Division I-AA status with teams in football; men's and women's basketball, cross-country, tennis, and track; and women's softball and volleyball. NCCU has strong student ensembles in choral music, band music, and jazz, and NCCU's dramatic arts department is among America's strongest in terms of student productions. The University has chapters of social fraternities and sororities, as well as service associations and honor societies, all of which make a substantial contribution to campus life.

Graduate and professional degrees are offered through the College of Liberal Arts, the College of Science and Technology, the College of Behavioral and Social Sciences, and the Schools of Business, Education, Library and Information Sciences, and Law. The School of Business and the School of Library and Information Sciences offer joint-degree programs both with each other and with the School of Law (Juris Doctor/Master of Business Administration and Juris Doctor/Master of Library Science). Several teacher licensure programs are offered through the School of Education.

Location

Durham is at the center of North Carolina's Research Triangle, which incorporates three major research universities in addition to NCCU, as well as three senior liberal arts colleges, two private junior colleges, and two state-funded technical community colleges. Several major corporations, particularly electronics and pharmaceutical operations, have large facilities in the Research Triangle area, whose total population is approximately 500,000. Durham itself is called the City of Medicine, with a quarter of the population employed in the field of health care.

Majors and Degrees

NCCU offers the following degrees and their respective majors: the Bachelor of Arts in art (general), art education, dramatic arts, dramatic arts (secondary education), early childhood education, economics, elementary education, English, English (concentrations in media journalism and secondary education), fine arts, French, French (secondary education), history, history (secondary education), middle grades education, music, music education, political science, political science (concentrations in criminal justice and public administration), psychology, social sciences, sociology, Spanish, Spanish (secondary education), theater arts, theater arts education (K–12), and visual communications; the Bachelor of Business Administration in accounting, business administration, computer information systems, finance, management, and marketing; the Bachelor of Music in jazz; the Bachelor of Science in biology, biology (secondary education), chemistry, chemistry (secondary education), community health education, computer science, family and consumer sciences, family and consumer science education (birth through kindergarten), geography, health education, mathematics, mathematics (secondary education), physical education, physics, physics (secondary education), and recreation administration; and the Bachelor of Science in Nursing.

NCCU has a cooperative arrangement with Georgia Institute of Technology and Duke University that enables a student, over a period of approximately five years, to earn a bachelor's degree in physics from NCCU and a bachelor's degree in engineering from Georgia Tech or Duke University.

There are organized preprofessional programs in dentistry, law, and medicine. The English department offers a substantial curriculum in media journalism as an alternative route to the Bachelor of Arts degree in English. A concentration in public administration leads to the bachelor's degree in political science.

Academic Programs

NCCU's undergraduate program is designed to stimulate intellectual curiosity and the habit of disciplined learning, to give students a strong background in both general Western culture and African-American culture, and to equip students with marketable intellectual and professional skills. Credit hours required to earn a degree may range between 124 and 128, depending on the student's choice of major or concentration and desire to earn teaching certification.

NCCU offers a variety of Web-enhanced distance education courses in the areas of business administration, criminal justice, education, hospitality and tourism, human sciences, and social work. Internet courses are offered through the Schools of Library and Information Sciences, Nursing, and Recreation. Several new Internet courses and programs are being developed to meet student demand.

Special honors seminars are open to qualified freshmen and sophomores. ROTC is available by cooperative arrangement with neighboring institutions.

Academic Facilities

NCCU's James E. Shepard Memorial Library has a collection of some 6 million volumes, not including serials; microforms; manuscripts; or graphics, audio, film, or video materials. A Learning Resources Center provides technical assistance and support for academic programs, including the production of audiovisual materials. The University's academic facilities include a variety of laboratories and 147 classrooms.

Costs

In 2007–08, the cost per semester, including tuition and fees, for in-state students living in a residence hall was $6928; out-of-state students living in a residence hall paid $11,800. In-state students not living in a residence hall paid $2556; out-of-state students not living in a residence hall paid $7428. There was a residence hall security deposit of $100. Costs are subject to change by the state legislature.

Financial Aid

NCCU's financial aid program has the primary purpose of helping families find resources to cover the cost of tuition, fees, housing, meals, and books. The burden of financing a college education has been eased due to the availability of grants, scholarships, work assistance, and loans. While most families initially seek funds that are free, such as grants and scholarships, low-interest student and parent loans are also available to help cover the cost of education. Some students are also afforded the opportunity to work and earn funds for personal expenses. Regardless of income, there are funds available at NCCU to assist students with college expenses. The most widely distributed federal and state grants and loans are Pell, FSEOG, NCCU, Eagle, Federal Work-Study, Perkins, Direct Stafford, and Federal PLUS. Generally, the financial aid process begins when the Free Application for Federal Student Aid (FAFSA) is filed. Students should file the FAFSA as early as possible after January 1. Awards to new students are typically made after April 1 for the ensuing fall semester.

Faculty

NCCU's teaching faculty members number approximately 565, of whom about 280 are full-time teachers. (Specific numbers vary from semester to semester.) Of the full-time faculty members, 65 percent hold a doctorate. An additional 6 percent hold degrees considered to be the terminal degree in their discipline or specialty. Departments and schools offering undergraduate programs assign all of their faculty members to teach undergraduate courses.

Student Government

Undergraduate students elect class representatives to the Student Congress and the president and vice president of the Student Government Association. Also elected by student vote are Miss NCCU and officers of the four undergraduate classes. The Student Government Association recommends policies and regulations governing student life to the vice chancellor for student affairs. From the vice chancellor the recommendations go to the chancellor and the institutional Board of Trustees, to which the general authority to set regulations and policies affecting student life and discipline has been delegated by the Board of Governors of the University of North Carolina System. The president of the Student Government Association is a voting member of the Board of Trustees. The Student Government Association has substantial authority in managing the expenditure of student activity fees collected from undergraduates.

Admission Requirements

North Carolina Central University practices rolling admissions. Applications are accepted before the beginning of the semester in which a prospective student wishes to enroll. Applicants for entry as freshmen must provide evidence (a complete transcript) of graduation from an approved or accredited high school and a satisfactory score on the SAT or ACT. Students who graduated from high school after spring 1990 must present in their high school transcripts 4 course units in English, emphasizing grammar, composition, and literature; 4 course units in mathematics, including algebra I, algebra II, and geometry or a higher-level mathematics course for which algebra II is a prerequisite; 3 course units in science, including at least 1 unit in a life science, at least 1 unit in a physical science, and at least one laboratory course in science; and 2 course units in social studies, including 1 unit in U.S. history. Two units of the same foreign language are required, and students are encouraged to take a math class and a foreign language class during the senior year. NCCU and other North Carolina state universities are required to limit out-of-state freshman enrollment. In practice, out-of-state students admitted have higher SAT scores and higher class standing.

For a transfer student at the undergraduate level seeking admission to the University, several standards are considered. The transfer applicant must not presently be on probation at the last or current school of attendance and must submit the required confidential statement form. The transfer applicant must not have been suspended or dropped from the last or current institution attended. The transfer applicant must have a cumulative average of at least a 2.0 grade point average at the institution from which they are transferring. Evidence of the applicant's participation in scholastic, community, and civic organizations, including leadership participation, is also considered. Transfer students who have attended another college or university but have earned fewer than 30 semester hours of specific acceptable credit must meet all freshman requirements.

Application and Information

Students should submit applications for the fall semester by July 1 (March 1 for out-of-state students and for students seeking on-campus housing or financial aid) and for the semester beginning in January by November 1. Early application with partial transcripts is encouraged, but final admission is deferred until all required documents are received and reviewed. International applicants must submit applications and other required materials at least ninety days before registration for each semester.

Application forms and additional information are available from:

Director of Undergraduate Admissions
North Carolina Central University
P.O. Box 19717
Durham, North Carolina 27707
Phone: 919-530-6298
877-667-7533 (toll-free)
Fax: 919-530-7625
E-mail: admissions@nccu.edu
Web site: http://www.nccu.edu

SAINT AUGUSTINE'S COLLEGE

RALEIGH, NORTH CAROLINA

The College

Saint Augustine's College, founded in 1867 in Raleigh, North Carolina, is a private, urban, coeducational, undergraduate liberal arts institution with a core curriculum that includes rigorous, in-depth programs in adult education; business; communications; computer science; forensic science; mathematics; military science (a required course for all members of the College's notable Army ROTC battalion); behavioral, premedical, and social and sciences; teacher education; and theater and film. Accredited by the Commission on Colleges of the Southern Association of Colleges and Schools, the College awards the Bachelor of Arts and the Bachelor of Science.

With a student-faculty ratio of 14:1, Saint Augustine's provides an intimate educational setting where faculty members know students by name. The College enrolls more than 1,300 students; nearly half come from North Carolina, with the remainder from twenty-eight states, the District of Columbia, the U.S. Virgin Islands, Jamaica, and eighteen other countries. Its faculty consists of more than 100 dedicated members who are all skilled teachers and scholars.

Saint Augustine's College was the nation's first historically black college to have its own on-campus commercial radio and television stations (WAUG-AM 750, WAUG-TV 68, and Time Warner cable channel 10) and is the only school in the Raleigh/Durham area to offer a degree in film production.

Saint Augustine's College competes in NCAA Division II competitions within the Central Intercollegiate Athletic Association (CIAA). In addition, the College's intercollegiate athletic program is the home of its award winning track and field program that competes and wins awards nationally and internationally. The program is coached by the 2005 U.S. Olympic men's and field coach, George "Pup" Williams, and has had several students win during Olympic competitions. Its football program was regionally and nationally ranked during the fall 2005 season for its defensive line performance.

Location

Located in the state's capital, Raleigh, Saint Augustine's College has a beautiful 105-acre campus. The campus's thirty-seven historic and contemporary buildings are just minutes from downtown Raleigh's commercial, education, government, and entertainment centers. Located just 3 hours from the mountains and 2 hours from the coast, Raleigh has something for everyone. Its rich history and cultural sophistication are evident through an array of museums, art galleries, professional sports, and entertainment facilities.

With a comfortable climate, a great location, and a variety of resources, Raleigh is among the best places to live in the nation.

Majors and Degrees

The mission of Academic Affairs at Saint Augustine's College is to promote an educational environment that is conducive to lifelong learning across the broad spectrum of liberal arts. An important element of this mission is to prepare students for graduate and professional studies or employment in a complex, diverse, and rapidly changing world. The most popular majors at Saint Augustine's College are business administration, computer information systems, criminal justice, organizational management, and computer science.

Saint Augustine's College offers the Bachelor of Arts degree in communication, elementary education, English, history, music, political science, religion and community service, sociology, theater/film production, and the visual arts.

The Bachelor of Science degree is offered in accounting, biology, business administration, biomedical and scientific communications, chemistry, computer information systems, computer science, criminal justice, engineering mathematics, forensic science, human performance and wellness, industrial hygiene and safety, industrial mathematics, international business, mathematics, organizational management, premedical sciences, psychology, sociology, and sports management.

Academic Programs

The College is a member of the Cooperating Raleigh Colleges (CRC) consortium that enables students to cross-enroll in five colleges in the city of Raleigh.

A recently implemented program referred to as the Three-Tiered Approach to Learning (the TTAL Plan) applies a three-tier approach to education, allowing students to enroll in either a three-, four-, or five-year plan of study. Transitional students are those who fall short of the College's entrance standards but have demonstrated potential to succeed, both by attitude and by hard work. These students, enrolled in a five-year plan of study, spend their entire first year developing the skills and knowledge base to successfully transition into a regular four-year program. The unique aspect of this program is that it allows financial aid for participating students. The traditional four-year plan is targeted toward the college student who has the requisite skills to compete on the college level. This plan encompasses the majority of the student body. The accelerated three-year plan recruits high-achieving high school students who excel both academically and on the SAT and/or ACT examination. These students carry a minimum of 18 credit hours per semester and attend both summer sessions in order to complete their degree program in three years.

Some students may qualify for advanced placement (AP) or degree credits for certain college-level courses through the College Examination Board Advanced Placement Examinations. In addition, qualified high school students may dually enroll at Saint Augustine's for college credit. Other programs offered by the College for nontraditional students are the Gateway Adult Learner Program and the Second Chance Alternative Teacher's Certification Program, which allow professionals who are changing careers or teachers currently in the field to enhance their skills or to prepare for teacher certification.

The College also offers a First Year Experience (FYE), which is a freshman-year academic advising and first-year enhancement program offered exclusively to first-time freshman enrollees. The Honors Program allows academically gifted students to pursue advanced-level courses in addition to participating in opportunities that enhance the student's educational experience.

The Office of Career Services provides career services, workshops, internship opportunities, counseling, and job fair participation opportunities.

Academic Facilities

An Army ROTC program is housed in the Tuttle Building on the campus. The Prezell R. Robinson Library is a depository for African-American historical collections as well as the Delany sisters' (*Having Our Say*) papers and artifacts. The Seby B. Jones Fine Arts Center is home to art works produced by student art majors. The campus is home to radio and TV stations (WAUG) that offer internship opportunities to the College's communication majors. The College manages a Community Development Facility, a small-business incubator sponsor. Equipped with an exercise and training room for its student athletes, Emery Gymnasium is the site of a variety of athletic competitions and also provides for noncompetitive student leisure sporting activities.

The Martin Luther King, Jr. Student Union serves as the hub of campus life, housing student activities, campus dining, and the campus bookstore. Students also have access to campus track-and-field facilities and a state-of-the-art Wellness Center.

Costs

For 2006–07, tuition, fees, room, and board totaled $18,828. Residence hall charges vary, depending on the facility.

Financial Aid

Saint Augustine's College offers financial aid through various federal and private programs. Students must complete the Free Application for Federal Student Aid (FAFSA) in order for the Department of Education to determine their expected family contribution (EFC), which is the amount the student and parents/spouse are expected to pay toward their estimated cost of attendance (COA). The cost of attendance at Saint Augustine's College consists of tuition and fees, room and board, books and supplies, transportation, and personal expenses. Ninety-five percent of Saint Augustine's College students are receiving some form of financial assistance to help defray the cost of their education. Financial aid packages consist of federal and state grants, loans, institutional scholarships (Presidential, Falcon-Incentive Grant, Scholarship of Excellence, and Meritorious Achievement), United Negro College Fund (UNCF) scholarships, outside scholarships, and College work-study opportunities.

Two forms are required in order to apply for aid at Saint Augustine's College. Students must submit the Financial Aid Institutional Application and the FASFA to the Financial Aid Office no later than March 1 each year.

Faculty

The College has 112 faculty members, approximately 60 percent of whom hold terminal degrees. The student-faculty ratio is 14:1.

Student Government

The campus has a vibrant Student Government Association that is open to all students. There is also an at-large student representative to the Board of Trustees. Other opportunities for campus leadership include the Panhellenic Council and close to sixty student clubs and organizations.

Admission Requirements

Candidates for admission should be scheduled to graduate from an accredited high school. Students should have completed 20 units, consisting of at least 4 English, 2 math (1 must be algebra), 2 science, 2 social science, and 10 electives. The recommendations and reputation of the high school, the student's record in extracurricular activities and athletics, and International Baccalaureate program credit and Advanced Placement (AP) or honors courses are all factors that affect the admissions decision. Students are required to submit an official high school transcript (GED certificate and test scores, limited, are accepted), SAT or ACT scores, class rank, and two letters of recommendation. There is a $25 nonrefundable application fee.

Application and Information

The College adheres to a rolling admissions schedule, with priority given to those enrolling by June 1 for the fall semester and November 1 for the spring semester. The application deadline for international students is June 1 for fall and November 1 for the spring. A $150 nonrefundable room reservation fee is required for those living in campus housing. The deadline for payment is May 15 for the fall term and December 1 for the spring term.

For questions or assistance, students should contact:

Office of Admission
Saint Augustine's College
1315 Oakwood Avenue
Raleigh, North Carolina 27610
Phone: 919-516-4016
800-948-1126 (toll-free)
E-mail: admissions@st-aug.edu
Web site: http://www.st-aug.edu/

Students on the campus of Saint Augustine's College.

SALEM COLLEGE

WINSTON-SALEM, NORTH CAROLINA

The College

Since its founding in 1772, Salem College has been committed to preparing young women for productive lives and careers, increasing and adjusting its programs to educate women for roles in a continuously changing society. Of special interest to the 1,100 women at Salem today are the services of the Career Development Office, which aids students in formulating career goals.

Students are encouraged to take advantage of the broad selection of extracurricular activities on campus, including intercollegiate and intramural athletics, publications, performing groups in the arts, academic organizations related to specific subjects, and social organizations.

The Center for Student Life and Fitness provides space for athletic, fitness, and recreational activities in the gymnasium and 25-yard competition indoor swimming pool. The Salem Commons is a four-level student center with lounges for dances and large social gatherings, the student grill and coffee house, meeting rooms, a dance studio, and performance space. Students enjoy the use of twelve tennis courts and newly expanded playing fields for team sports such as soccer and field hockey.

Fully wired for cable and computers, seven residence halls blend well with their surroundings in atmosphere and style. For juniors and seniors, Fogle Flats offers apartment-style living on campus.

Location

The College's 67-acre campus is located in the nationally recognized Old Salem restoration area of Winston-Salem, only a 10-minute walk from the downtown area. Winston-Salem (population 187,500) is a recognized cultural center of the Southeast.

Winston-Salem is served by major airlines at Piedmont Triad International Airport near Greensboro and at Smith Reynolds Airport in Winston-Salem.

Majors and Degrees

The B.A., B.S., and B.M. degrees are conferred, with majors in accounting, American studies, art history, arts management, biology, business administration, chemistry, communication, creative writing, economics, education, English, French, German, history, interior design, international business, international relations, mathematics, medical technology, music, music education, music performance, not-for-profit management, philosophy, psychology, religion, sociology, Spanish, and studio art.

A careful selection of courses provides a foundation for a wide variety of professional careers, including business, communication, law, library work, medicine, and social service. Students may earn teacher licensure in elementary education, secondary school subjects, special education (general curriculum), and TESOL (teaching English to speakers of other languages).

Salem also offers a 3-2 program in engineering in cooperation with Duke University and Vanderbilt University.

Academic Programs

Each degree program includes certain basic distribution requirements, the completion of a major, and a varying number of elective courses. The distribution requirements offer considerable latitude in the planning of individual programs. Independent study, planned jointly by students and faculty members, is encouraged. Minors in twenty-three areas may be taken in addition to a major to enhance and expand a student's academic experience. Minors are available in most majors as well as in creative writing, dance, music theater, political science, and women's studies. All students participate in the unique Salem Signature, a four-year leadership/development program. As part of the Salem Signature, each student completes 30 hours of community service and an internship in her field of interest before graduating.

Salem's 4-1-4 calendar gives students opportunities for preprofessional internships, in-depth courses, travel programs, and independent studies during the January term, either on campus or abroad.

Salem's Center for Women Writers provides opportunities for students who are interested in writing and in publishing their work. Through lectures and readings by acclaimed women writers as well as workshops and courses taught by experienced professionals, Salem students derive firsthand knowledge of the creative process, writing techniques, and the publication process.

The Women in Science and Mathematics program provides academic and career support for women planning to enter traditionally male-dominated fields. The program sponsors seminars, trips to conferences, and a mentoring program.

Off-Campus Programs

A qualifying full-time student may register at Wake Forest University for any course unavailable at Salem. Salem is affiliated with the Bowman Gray School of Medicine and Forsyth Memorial Hospital for professional training in medical technology.

Salem offers a variety of options for off-campus study. The College also participates in the American University Washington Semester and the Drew University United Nations Semester and has two summer study programs with St. Peter's College, University of Oxford, England. The six-week program in science and humanities allows students to study in the traditional tutorial setting. A three-week business program consists of in-depth study of cultural, ethical, and gender issues facing international business. Salem also offers study-travel opportunities to twenty locations in seventeen countries through Brethren Colleges Abroad.

Salem students have the opportunity to work closely with social and health agencies, public schools, the police department, business firms, and churches in Winston-Salem. Internships also provide opportunities in other cities nationwide and even abroad.

Academic Facilities

The Salem College libraries contain more than 128,000 print volumes and 10,000 sound recordings. The libraries are fully automated and share an online catalog with four other area colleges. An online request feature enables students to borrow circulating materials (exceeding 750,000 volumes) from all five institutions.

The Salem libraries offer users access to more than 100 databases, including LexisNexis Academic Universe, Historical Newspapers, and the full range of NC LIVE databases—providing full-text articles published in thousands of scholarly journals, magazines, and reference resources. Salem faculty members and students have remote access to most of the databases accessible on campus. Public computers in the libraries, including wireless laptops, provide access to word processing, spreadsheet, and graphics software as well as to the Internet, catalog, and database services.

The Fine Arts Center houses a large auditorium, a smaller recital hall, a workshop theater, extensive gallery space, music teaching rooms, practice rooms, a library, four listening rooms, classrooms, a rehearsal-lecture hall, a videoconferencing room, and large art studios. The four-story Science Building has modern, fully equipped classrooms and laboratories for the teaching of biology, chemistry, physics, psychology, and mathematics.

Computer labs in the science building and learning center provide students with access to word processing, spreadsheet, database, graphics, and other software that is course specific. All campus computers and data ports in campus residence halls allow access to the Internet and the campus network for e-mail and an online library catalog.

Costs

The comprehensive fee in 2008–09 for traditional-age students who reside on campus is $30,780 (traditional-age students must reside on campus unless they reside with family in the immediate vicinity). Tuition is $20,075 and room and board cost $10,705. Books and supplies are estimated at $800 per year. The student government fee of approximately $215 covers class dues, the yearbook, other student publications, and organizational dues. Students enrolled in the Adult Degree Program pay $890 per course.

Financial Aid

The College makes every effort to assist as many qualified students as funds permit. Approximately 70 percent of students receive assistance through scholarships, loans, employment, and grants-in-aid. The Free Application for Federal Student Aid and the Salem College application form are required.

Salem participates in the Federal Perkins Loan Program, the Federal Pell Grant Program, and the Federal Work-Study Program. The Federal Family Education Loan Programs, which include Federal Stafford Student Loans and Federal PLUS loans for parents, are also available. Competitive scholarships based on general academic excellence and leadership experience, as well as on talent in music and art, are available. Special application must be made for these Honor Awards.

Faculty

The Salem faculty numbers 93. Approximately 89 percent of the full-time faculty members hold Ph.D.'s or the equivalent. Sixty-one percent are women. The emphasis at Salem is on teaching, and full professors teach freshmen and upperclass students. The student-faculty ratio is 13:1.

Student Government

The primary goals of the Student Government Association are to build a spirit of community and unity among students and to set and maintain standards for achievement and behavior in keeping with Salem's honor tradition. Students serve as consultants or voting members of faculty committees and the Board of Trustees.

Admission Requirements

Salem welcomes applicants whose school records give evidence of academic ability, personal integrity, and a desire for continuing growth and achievement. Students from all social, religious, geographical, racial, and ethnic backgrounds are encouraged to apply. The Admissions Committee requires a minimum of 16 academic units (4 in English; 3 in mathematics: algebra I, algebra II, and geometry; 2 to 4 in foreign languages; 2 in history; 3 in science; and 3 recommended in academic electives), scores on the SAT or ACT, and two teacher recommendations. Applications are evaluated on the basis of individual merit; the selection of courses, grade point average, test scores, and recommendations receive major emphasis, and participation in extracurricular and community activities is also noted. Auditions are required of all prospective music majors. Interviews are recommended.

Application and Information

All students are urged to submit their applications in the fall of the year preceding proposed college entrance. The evaluation of applications is done on a rolling basis, beginning in the fall. Students may apply online at the College's Web site or by using the Common Application. There is no deadline for transfer applicants, but it is suggested that their credentials be submitted by March 1. The College subscribes to the College Board's Candidates Reply Date of May 1.

Arrangements for an interview, a campus tour, or class visits may be made through the Admissions Office. An application form, a College catalog, and other informational brochures may be obtained by writing to:

Dean of Admissions
Salem College
Winston-Salem, North Carolina 27108
Phone: 336-721-2621
800-32-SALEM (toll-free)
E-mail: admissions@salem.edu
Web site: http://www.salem.edu

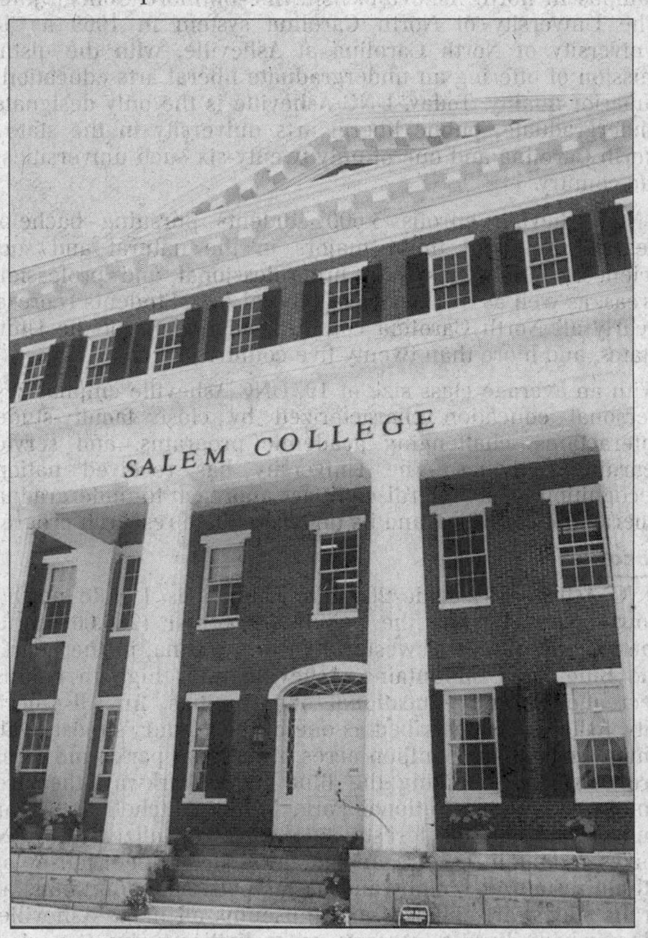

Main Hall of Salem College.

THE UNIVERSITY OF NORTH CAROLINA AT ASHEVILLE

ASHEVILLE, NORTH CAROLINA

The University

An outstanding learning community, The University of North Carolina at Asheville (UNC Asheville) focuses on undergraduates, with a core curriculum covering humanities, language and culture, arts and ideas, and health and wellness. Students thrive in small classes with faculty members dedicated to teaching. The liberal arts emphasis develops discriminating thinkers and expert and creative communicators with a passion for learning. These are qualities needed for today's challenges and the changes of tomorrow. UNC Asheville is advancing as the premier public liberal arts university in the country and is pursuing new initiatives that emphasize academic excellence, service-learning, diversity, and community partnerships.

UNC Asheville opened in 1927 as Buncombe County Junior College for area residents interested in pursuing higher education. The school underwent several name changes, mergers, and moves before relocating in 1961 to its present campus in north Asheville. Asheville-Biltmore College joined The University of North Carolina system in 1969 as The University of North Carolina at Asheville, with the distinct mission of offering an undergraduate liberal arts education of superior quality. Today, UNC Asheville is the only designated, undergraduate, public liberal arts university in the state of North Carolina and one of only twenty-six such universities in the country.

UNC Asheville enrolls 3,600 students pursuing bachelor's degrees in about thirty majors in the natural and social sciences, humanities, and preprofessional and professional areas, as well as the Master of Liberal Arts. Students represent nearly all North Carolina counties, all regions of the United States, and more than twenty-five countries.

With an average class size of 19, UNC Asheville emphasizes a personal education characterized by close faculty-student interactions, challenging academic programs, and service-learning activities. The University has received national recognition for its interdisciplinary approach to undergraduate liberal arts education and its undergraduate research program.

Location

UNC Asheville's scenic 265-acre campus is 1 mile north of downtown Asheville, the population center (286,000 in the metropolitan area) of western North Carolina, in the heart of the Blue Ridge Mountains. Asheville rates high in cultural, recreational, and educational opportunities. An All-America city, Asheville is described as one of the country's most livable cities. More than 1 million acres of national parks and forests are close by, including the Blue Ridge Parkway, the Great Smoky Mountains National Park, Mount Mitchell State Park, and several national forests. Asheville's revitalized downtown mixes mountain culture and modern life. Coffee houses and ethnic restaurants, clubs and night spots, shopping malls and crafts shops, art galleries and museums all make Asheville a place where diverse interests and activities thrive. A regional airport is minutes away, and the campus is 2 to 4 hours from Atlanta, Chapel Hill, Charlotte, Raleigh, and Knoxville, Tennessee.

Majors and Degrees

UNC Asheville grants the Bachelor of Arts in art, chemistry, classics, drama, economics, French, German, health and wellness, history, interdisciplinary studies, literature, mass communication, mathematics, multimedia arts and sciences, music, philosophy, political science, psychology, sociology, Spanish, and women's studies. A joint Bachelor of Science in Engineering in mechatronics is offered with North Carolina State University. A Bachelor of Fine Arts is offered. UNC Asheville also grants the Bachelor of Science in accounting, atmospheric sciences, biology, chemistry, computer science, environmental studies, industrial and engineering management, management, music technology, and physics. Teacher licensure is available for Birth–12 in a variety of subject areas.

Minors are offered in all major departments as well as in Africana studies, art history, creative writing, dance, humanities, international studies, and religious studies.

A 2+2 program in engineering with North Carolina State University is also available. Preprofessional programs in dentistry, law, medicine, pharmacy, and veterinary medicine further expand UNC Asheville's offerings.

Academic Programs

The University is committed to a liberating education emphasizing the central role of human values in thought and action, the free and rigorous pursuit of truth, and a respect for differing points of view and heritage. It aims to develop men and women of broad perspective who think critically and creatively and who communicate effectively. All students must complete a minimum of 120 semester hours of credit, which includes Integrative Liberal Studies (ILS), the University's core curriculum. The ILS program emphasizes the integration and synthesis of knowledge across traditional disciplinary boundaries and invites students to deepen their understanding of complex contemporary issues through interdisciplinary topics and courses.

The University operates on a semester schedule, with a fall (August until December) and spring (January until May) semester, plus summer terms.

Off-Campus Programs

Students may participate in numerous study-abroad opportunities. Summer programs are offered in England, France, Bolivia, Honduras, Spain, Greece, Ireland, and Italy. Semester or yearlong programs are available in some thirty-five countries through various UNC Asheville–sponsored or affiliated programs. Academic credit may be earned, allowing students to progress toward their liberal arts degree. In addition, UNC Asheville is a member of the National Student Exchange, which allows a student to study at more than 175 other U.S. institutions for either a semester or year exchange.

Academic Facilities

UNC Asheville's campus comprises about thirty buildings for classrooms, administration, residence, and recreation. The newest buildings on the campus, employing "green" building methods and energy-conservation features, are a state-of-the-art science building, a facilities management complex, and a classroom building.

All academic buildings and residence halls have Macintosh and PC computer lab facilities. Each student has access to these labs, some open 24 hours, as well as to high-speed Internet connections in each residence hall room.

Ramsey Library and the Media Center house 3,334 current journal subscriptions; 378,000 books, bound periodicals, and government documents; and 9,300 audiovisuals, in addition to a special archives collection. The online library system connects students to the combined holdings of the libraries at UNC Asheville, Western Carolina University, and Appalachian State University. The Media Center includes the Square D Teleconference Center, allowing for distance learning; the Writing Center is also located in the library.

Robinson and Rhoades Halls house several laboratories, a mathematics assistance center, a computer center, Steelcase Teleconference Center, a meteorology lab, and other research facilities. Carol Belk Theatre is a 200-seat arena theater that hosts the four main-stage productions each year in addition to student-directed forum plays. Owen Hall is home to a conference center, art gallery, and numerous indoor and outdoor art studios. Karpen Hall is home to the Honors Program.

Other buildings include Lipinsky Hall, New Hall, Phillips Hall, Weizenblatt Hall, and Zageir and Carmichael Halls.

Costs

For 2008–09, estimated tuition and fees for North Carolina residents are $4325 per year. For out-of-state students, tuition and fees are $15,655 annually. Room and board costs for all on-campus students are $6620 per year. Books average $850 per year.

Financial Aid

Both merit- and need-based financial assistance are available to students. Nearly all merit-based scholarships for incoming freshmen are part of the University Laurels Scholarship Program. In order to be considered for the Laurels Scholarship Program, students must apply by the early action deadline in November. North Carolina Teaching Fellowships are also available to North Carolina students interested in teaching.

Need-based assistance is available and may include grants, loans, Federal Work-Study, and/or scholarships. The Free Application for Federal Student Aid should be filed by March 1 for the upcoming academic year. Applications received after March 1 are given consideration on a fund-available basis.

In addition, numerous on-campus jobs are available to students, permitting flexible scheduling around classes and providing competitive wages.

Faculty

UNC Asheville is focused on undergraduate education. Its 210 faculty members, 88 percent with the highest degrees in their fields, make excellence in teaching their highest priority. All courses are taught by faculty members, including introductory courses. The student-faculty ratio is 13:1. Students attending UNC Asheville work one-on-one with faculty members in both classes and collaborative research projects. Faculty members serve as general academic advisers and as advisers in specific departments in addition to serving as mentors to students engaged in research.

Student Government

Students may participate in more than eighty student organizations, spanning a wide variety of interest areas, from religious to academic to social. Greek fraternities and sororities, honor societies, a student newspaper, academic clubs, activist groups, religious organizations, student activities, and ethnic and cultural groups are just a few. An extensive outdoor program sponsors activities ranging from white-water rafting and kayaking to backpacking and rock climbing. Intramural and club sports are also popular. Volunteer and community service, a part of UNC Asheville's service-learning curriculum, are popular with students outside the classroom, and an active Student Government Association is elected annually by the student body.

Admission Requirements

Admission to UNC Asheville is competitive. Applicants are reviewed individually to evaluate how well their goals and strengths match the University's educational mission. UNC Asheville does not discriminate based on race, color, national origin, religion, gender, age, sexual orientation, gender expression, or disability. The majority of the decision is based on the high school record. Close attention is paid to college-preparatory course work, including honors and other advanced work, grade trend, overall grade point average, and rank in class. SAT (Critical Reading with Writing) and/or ACT with Writing scores, extracurricular activities, and special interests and talents are also considered. Financial need is not a factor in the admission decision. TOEFL scores are required of students whose native language is not English.

Students must complete the Minimum Course Requirements for the UNC system, which include a high school diploma from an accredited secondary school; 4 units of English; 4 units of math (including algebra I and II, geometry, and a fourth math having algebra II as a prerequisite); 3 units of science (including physical science, biological science, and a laboratory science); 2 units of social studies, including U.S. history; and 2 units of the same foreign language. Additional math and science courses are strongly recommended. A maximum of 18 percent of the incoming class is from out-of-state (including international students).

Transfer student applications are accepted for both fall and spring semesters and must include both high school and college transcripts. In order to be considered for admission, applicants must be eligible to reenroll at their previous institutions and have a cumulative GPA of at least 2.0; however, offers of admission are based on the strength of the academic course work and overall academic performance. Applicants from the North Carolina Community College system are encouraged to complete their associate degree prior to their anticipated enrollment term at UNC Asheville.

Application and Information

Freshman applications and required credentials for early action are due by November 10, with notification by the week of December 22, and by February 15 for regular admission, with notification by the week of March 24. Transfer students should submit applications and required credentials by March 23 for the fall semester, with notification mailed by the week of April 14, and by October 15 for the spring semester, with notification by the week of November 17. Applications and all credentials should be submitted along with the $50 application fee to:

Office of Admissions
University Hall, CPO #1320
The University of North Carolina at Asheville
One University Heights
Asheville, North Carolina 28804-8502
Phone: 828-251-6481
800-531-9842 (toll-free)
Fax: 828-251-6482
E-mail: admissions@unca.edu
Web site: http://www.unca.edu

THE UNIVERSITY OF NORTH CAROLINA AT PEMBROKE

PEMBROKE, NORTH CAROLINA

The University

The University of North Carolina at Pembroke (UNCP), a constituent institution of the University of North Carolina, serves as a comprehensive university committed to academic excellence in a balanced program of teaching, research, and service. Combining the opportunities available at a large university with the personal attention characteristic of a small college, the University provides an intellectually challenging environment created by a faculty that is dedicated to effective teaching, to interactions with students, and to scholarship. Graduates are academically and personally prepared for rewarding careers, postgraduate education, and community leadership.

UNC Pembroke is a coeducational institution that enrolls approximately 5,800 students in undergraduate and graduate programs. Class size ranges from 25 to 40, and the student-faculty ratio is 16:1. Freshmen are guaranteed housing and are allowed to have cars. UNC Pembroke offers more than 100 clubs and organizations, including fraternities and sororities, professional honor societies, and ethnic and religious groups. UNCP offers special programs, such as the North Carolina Teaching Fellows, Esther Maynor Honors College, and North Carolina Health Careers Access Program, as well as various research and internship opportunities. UNC Pembroke also has strong student ensembles in the performing and dramatic arts.

UNCP is a member of the Peach Belt Athletic Conference of the National Collegiate Athletic Association Division II and fields teams in men's and women's basketball, cross-country, soccer, and track; men's baseball, football, golf, and wrestling; and women's golf, softball, tennis, and volleyball. The University also offers a full range of intramural sports programs.

Founded in 1887 to educate Native Americans, the University now serves a student body reflective of the rich cultural diversity of American society. *U.S. News & World Report* ranks UNCP second in campus diversity among Southern regional universities. According to *The Princeton Review*, the University of North Carolina at Pembroke is one of the nation's "best value" undergraduate institutions. As it stimulates interaction within and among its cultural groups, the University enables students to become informed, principled, and tolerant citizens with a global perspective. Drawing strength from its heritage, UNCP continues to expand its leadership role in enriching the intellectual, economic, social, and cultural life of the region, the state, and the nation.

Location

UNCP is located in the sandhills of North Carolina, an area famous for its temperate climate, natural scenic beauty, golf resorts, and Southern hospitality, in the historic town of Pembroke. Easily accessible from Interstate 95 and U.S. 74, North and South Carolina beaches are within a 1½-hour drive, and campus is within a 2-hour drive of the cities of the Research Triangle Park, Fayetteville, and Charlotte.

Majors and Degrees

UNC Pembroke offers a broad range of degrees and nationally accredited professional programs at the bachelor's and master's levels. The University is organized into the College of Arts and Sciences, School of Mass Communications and Business, School of Education, and School of Graduate Studies. UNCP confers five undergraduate degrees: the Bachelor of Arts, Bachelor of Music, Bachelor of Science, Bachelor of Science in Nursing, and Bachelor of Social Work.

Majors, minors, and/or concentrations are offered in African American studies; American Indian studies; art (art education, arts management, studio art—ceramics, digital arts, painting, print making, and sculpture); biology (biology education, biomedical emphasis, biotechnology, botany, environmental biology, environmental science, medical technology, molecular biology, premed, zoology); business administration (accounting, applied science, economics, finance, information technology management, international business, management, marketing); chemistry and physics (applied physics; chemistry—biomedical emphasis, environmental chemistry, forensic chemistry, medical technology, molecular biotechnology, prepharmacy, professional emphasis, premed, and science education); education (birth–kindergarten, elementary, middle grades (language arts, mathematics, science, social science), special education–learning disabilities and mental retardation); English, theater, and languages (English, English education, Spanish, theater arts); health, physical education, and recreation (athletic training, community health education, exercise and sports management, health and physical education, health promotion, physical education, recreational management/administration); history (American studies, social studies education); mass communications (broadcasting, journalism, public relations); mathematics and computer science (computer science, mathematics—mathematics education); music (elective studies in business/music industry option, music education (instrumental emphasis, keyboard emphasis/instrumental, keyboard emphasis/vocal, and vocal emphasis), music theater); nursing (B.S.N. and RN to B.S.N. programs); philosophy and religion; political science (international studies, prelaw, public policy and administration); psychology; social work and criminal justice; and sociology (medical sociology).

Preprofessional programs are offered in dentistry, law, medicine, optometry, pharmacy, public health, and veterinary medicine. A candidate for a degree in medical technology completes a three-year program at UNC Pembroke and an additional year at one of several cooperating hospitals. The student receives a Bachelor of Science in either biology or chemistry upon completion of the year's hospital work.

Academic Programs

UNC Pembroke seeks to produce graduates with broad vision, who are sensitive to values, who recognize the complexity of social problems, and who will be contributing citizens with an international perspective and an appreciation for the achievements of diverse civilizations. To earn a degree, students must earn at least 120 to 128 semester hours of credit in a program of study. In addition to meeting all major program requirements, students seeking baccalaureate degrees are required to complete a 44-hour General Education program, which provides students with an understanding of the fundamental principles and contributions of a variety of disciplines. Moreover, the program fosters the ability to analyze and weigh evidence, exercise quantitative and scientific skills, make informed decisions, write and speak clearly, and think critically and creatively.

Academic Facilities

The Sampson-Livermore Library houses more than 200,000 books, 1,300 periodicals, and local historical materials and serves as the depository for selected state and federal documents. The School of Education's Education Center maintains a curriculum laboratory and test review resource center. The Department of English, Theatre, and Languages maintains a library of books, journals, and media resources for English education and foreign languages. Moreover, the Department of Music's library is home to various recordings and music scores by regional artists.

The Native American Resource Center offers a rich collection of authentic American Indian artifacts, handicrafts, and art as well as books, cassettes, record albums, and filmstrips about Native Americans, with emphasis on the Lumbee Indians of Robeson County. The center's exhibits include prehistoric tools and weapons, nineteenth-century household and farm equipment, and contemporary Indian art. Artifacts from Indian cultures of Canada and Central and South America as well as from other sections of the United States are also on display.

Each academic building houses at least one microcomputer laboratory. Additional computers are located in the Computer Center, the D. F. Lowry Building, and the Sampson-Livermore Library. The University's computer network is connected to LINC NET, a statewide data network, and the Internet, which provides worldwide computer access.

Costs

The 2007–08 cost, including tuition and fees, for in-state students residing on campus was $9217, and out-of-state students residing on campus paid $18,477.

Financial Aid

U.S. News & World Report listed UNC Pembroke as one of the most affordable universities in the South. UNC Pembroke makes every effort to assist students in securing the financial means necessary to attend the University. Aid is available to eligible students through scholarships, state and federal grants, loans, and college work-study. To apply for financial aid, students must complete the Free Application for Federal Student Aid (FAFSA), which is available from high school guidance offices. A variety of scholarships are available to students who demonstrate superior academic ability. Scholarships are awarded on the basis of personal and academic merit; some, however, are also based on financial need. The deadline for scholarship applications is March 1 for fall admission. Students applying for financial aid should complete the FAFSA by March 15.

Faculty

UNC Pembroke's teaching faculty numbers 238 full-time members, 80 percent of whom have doctoral or terminal degrees. The University has long valued personal attention within the classroom. With that in mind, all classes are taught by faculty members, not graduate assistants.

Student Government

The Student Government Association represents and safeguards the interests of the student body. Once a student enrolls at UNCP, he or she becomes a member of the SGA. Officers and class representatives are elected by the student body each spring. The Student Senate is the legislative branch and policymaking body of the SGA. The senate recommends policies and regulations necessary for the general welfare of the student body.

Admission Requirements

Applicants for freshman admission must provide evidence (high school transcript) of graduation from high school, satisfactory class rank and GPA, and scores from either the SAT or the ACT (with the writing component). First-year students are expected to have completed: 4 course units in English (the courses should emphasize grammar, composition, and literature); 4 course units in mathematics, including algebra I, algebra II, geometry, and a higher-level mathematics course for which algebra II is a prerequisite; 3 course units in science, including a life or biological science, a physical science, and a laboratory science; 2 course units in social studies, including 1 unit in United States history; and 2 years of the same foreign language. It is recommended that students take mathematics in their senior year. Transfer students are evaluated for admission based on college work. For those students who have fewer than 24 semester credit hours, admissions decisions may be based on freshman criteria.

Application and Information

Applications should be submitted by December 1 for the spring semester and by July 15 for the fall semester. Students are encouraged to apply earlier if they wish to be considered for financial aid and scholarships. In addition, applications are accepted for both summer sessions. The priority deadlines are May 15 for summer session I and June 15 for summer session II. Applications and additional information are available from:

Director of Admissions
The University of North Carolina at Pembroke
One University Drive
P.O. Box 1510
Pembroke, North Carolina 28372-1510
Phone: 910-521-6262
800-949-UNCP (toll-free)
Fax: 910-521-6497
E-mail: admissions@uncp.edu
Web site: http://www.uncp.edu/admissions

THE UNIVERSITY OF NORTH CAROLINA WILMINGTON

WILMINGTON, NORTH CAROLINA

The University

The University of North Carolina Wilmington (UNCW) is a public comprehensive university dedicated to excellence in teaching, scholarship and artistic achievement, and service. The University provides an intimate learning environment that integrates teaching and mentoring with research and service, and promotes cultural diversity, community engagement, and individual growth and development. The school is ranked seventh in the 2007 *U.S. News & World Report* list of the top public regional undergraduate universities in the South, and it is one of the top three Best Values according to *Kiplinger's* in 2006. UNCW also offers 27 graduate degree programs and two doctoral degrees. The University is accredited by the Commission on Colleges of the Southern Association of Colleges and Schools.

Chartered in 1789, the University of North Carolina (UNC) became the first public university in the United States. The first class was admitted in 1795, making the university the only one to graduate students in the eighteenth century. For more than 130 years, there was only one campus, in Chapel Hill. In 1931, the University added three state-supported institutions, located in Chapel Hill, Raleigh, and Greensboro. By 1969, three additional campuses, including UNC Wilmington, had joined the university. In 1971, ten other campuses were added. Today, 16 wholly independent universities comprise the public university system in the state of North Carolina.

UNCW enrolls 11,700 students in seventy-three bachelor's degree and twenty-seven graduate degree programs. Of the nearly 2,000 freshman students, approximately three fourths surveyed said the school was their first choice. Moreover, the University has the fourth-highest freshman SAT (critical reading and math only) average (1150), the third-highest freshman retention rate (85.7 percent), and the third-highest six-year graduation rate (61.2 percent) in the UNC system. With an average GPA of 3.68, incoming students have already demonstrated their motivation and ability to succeed in an academic setting.

One of UNCW's strengths is its close ties to the region. The internationally respected marine biology programs have created promising research and development opportunities for pharmaceutical companies and food-service firms. The School of Education works closely with nearly 100 area schools and agencies to improve the quality of public schools in the region. The rapidly growing School of Nursing has developed collaborative partnerships with area health-care providers to give students a wide range of clinical-practice experiences and to assist in improving community health-care services.

Campus life is a vibrant part of the UNCW experience. Students can live in one of eight residence halls, twenty-six apartment buildings, or seven suite buildings, and enjoy a variety of cutting-edge cuisines at the University's eleven dining locations. Students may participate in over 170 student organizations, including political, academic, professional, sports, service, ethnic, religious, and student media groups. As a member of NCAA Division I, UNCW fields nineteen varsity teams, including men's and women's baseball, basketball, cross-country, golf, soccer, softball, swimming, tennis, and track and field.

Several facilities serve as hubs for the entire campus community. The Fisher Student Center includes a two-story bookstore, a 360-seat movie theater, offices for student organizations, student lounges, a large game room, a lighted water feature, a student art exhibition, and a dining area. The Campus Commons features a lake with lighted fountains, a network of sidewalks, and an open-air amphitheater. Monthly exhibitions of paintings, sculptures, and graphic arts are held in a variety of spaces on campus, including Claude Howell Gallery, Randall Library, Cultural Arts Building, Warwick Center, and the Ann Flack Boseman Gallery.

The Campus Recreation Department provides facilities where students and faculty members can participate in sports and other recreational activities. Facilities include the Gazebo Complex, which features four tennis courts, three basketball courts, two volleyball courts, and a softball field; a natatorium, which features an eight-lane swimming pool and adjacent diving tank; and a fitness center, complete with treadmills, stair climbers, and stationary bicycles as well as a rock climbing wall and an elevated track.

Location

The campus occupies 660 acres in the southeastern part of North Carolina, midway between the Cape Fear River and the Atlantic Ocean. The city of Wilmington is situated on the east bank of the Cape Fear River, about 15 miles from Carolina Beach and 10 miles from Wrightsville Beach. Several main highways lead into the city, and a nearby airport provides easy access from the city to other destinations.

Wilmington combines historical beauty and modern convenience. Visitors can visit many art galleries, museums, and historical landmarks; enjoy an evening of theater, music, and nightlife; or visit the city's many shops and restaurants. Ocean breezes and the nearness of the Gulf Stream give Wilmington a delightful year-round climate. Nature lovers can go biking, hiking, or bird watching in one of Wilmington's parks or play golf on one of the city's six courses. Wilmington's proximity to the river and the ocean makes it an ideal haven for water lovers, whether they prefer taking a riverboat cruise or spending the day surfing and swimming at the beach.

Majors and Degrees

Bachelor of Arts degree programs are available in: anthropology, art history, athletic training, biology, chemistry, communication studies, criminal justice, economics, education of young children, elementary education, English, environmental studies, film studies, French, geography, geology, German studies, history, mathematics, middle grades education, music, parks and recreation management, philosophy and religion, physical education and health, physics, political science, psychology, sociology, Spanish, special education, studio art, theater, and therapeutic recreation.

Bachelor of Science degrees are available in biology, business administration, chemistry, clinical research, computer science, environmental science, geology, marine biology, mathematics, nursing, physics, and statistics. Also available are a Bachelor of Fine Arts degree in creative writing and a Bachelor of Social Work. Bachelor of Music degrees are available in music education and music performance.

Academic Programs

To earn a bachelor's degree, students must complete a minimum of 124 semester hours with a minimum GPA of 2.0. All students must complete a minimum of 45 semester hours in general education courses that include 6 hours in composition courses; 2 hours in physical education; 12–18 hours in humanities courses (including at least 3 hours each in literature, history, philosophy, and language courses; 3–9 hours in fine arts courses; 10–16 hours in natural science and mathematics courses, with at least 7 hours (including at least one laboratory science course) in the life and physical sciences and at least 3 hours in mathematics; 6–12 hours in social and behavioral sciences; and up to 6 hours in interdisciplinary courses. Some requirements may be satisfied by passing Advanced Placement or CLEP examinations.

The academic year consists of three semesters. The fall semester begins in late August and ends in early December. Following a winter break, the spring semester extends from early January to early May. The summer semester consists of two sessions, one from mid-May to mid-June and the other from mid-June to mid-July.

Off-Campus Programs

Several foreign language programs and other academic departments sponsor study-abroad programs that are designed to strengthen relationships between the University and the international community, including international students and institutions in other countries. These programs, which are coordinated by the Office of International Programs, may last a few weeks, a semester, or an entire academic year; several occur during the summer. The University has developed programs in over forty countries, including Argentina, Ghana, Israel, Thailand, and the United Kingdom.

The University also coordinates study-abroad experiences that include more than study—or do not include study at all. Internships may consist of a combination of course work and/or supervised work experience in a government agency, profit or nonprofit agency, or company. Students and recent graduates may work abroad as family caretakers or English-language teachers, either in exchange for room and board or for a salary. Volunteer opportunities in other countries may involve health-care, agriculture, community development, language training, youth camps, or house-building projects.

Academic Facilities

The William Madison Randall Library holds nearly 2 million items, including 800,000 books, journals, and government documents; 920,000 microform pieces; and more than 22,000 multimedia items. In addition, the library provides extensive indexes and full texts for thousands of journals and books, including NC LIVE, Lexis-Nexis, Science Direct, and JSTOR. The library's specialized collections include the Rare Book Collection and the Southeastern North Carolina Collection, devoted to publications about or written by residents of the Lower Cape Fear region. In addition, the library is a selective depository for United States government publications and a full depository for North Carolina documents.

Costs

In 2007–08, full-time undergraduate tuition and fees cost a total of $4398 per year for in-state residents and $14,361 for non-residents. Students living on campus can also expect to spend approximately $7000 per academic year on room and board, $934 on books and supplies, $1378 on transportation, and $1053 on miscellaneous costs. Room, board, and transportation costs for commuters vary. Students enrolled part-time pay according to the number of credit hours earned each semester; costs range from $550.15 to $1897.59 for in-state students and $1795.53 to $5633.71 for non-residents.

Financial Aid

In order to be considered for the maximum amount of financial assistance, prospective students should submit the Free Application for Federal Student Aid (FAFSA) by March 1 of their senior year. In an average year, the University awards a total of $57 million to assist students. Most of this aid is need-based, but a limited number of merit-based scholarships are available for the most outstanding students.

The University offers a limited number of scholarships—including scholarships specifically for incoming freshmen and student enrolled in specific programs—that have been generously donated in honor of individuals or organizations. Award amounts and eligibility criteria vary, but most of these scholarships are renewable as long as the student is enrolled in a degree program and continues to meet the eligibility requirements. For students with exceptional financial need, the University participates in the Federal Pell Grant Program and the Federal Supplemental Educational Opportunity Grant (FSEOG) Program.

Several federal loan programs are available for students who require additional assistance. The Federal Perkins Loan allows students to borrow up to $20,000 for undergraduate study. The Federal Stafford Loan allows borrowing of up to $5500 per year in loans. The Federal Parent Loan for Undergraduate Students (PLUS) allows students to borrow the cost of attendance minus all other aid awarded. Some students also participate in federal work-study, which awards money to students who work up to 20 hours per week on campus.

Faculty

The University seeks to attract and maintain a faculty of outstanding individuals who are capable of contributing to the enrichment of its diverse and comprehensive instructional and research programs. The University employs nearly 800 faculty members, approximately half of whom are full-time professors. Faculty members come from all geographic sections of the United States and several foreign countries, bringing a rich variety of educational experiences, training, and scholarship. Of the more than 515 instructional and research faculty members, more than 86 percent hold doctoral degrees.

Student Government

The Student Government Association is devoted to the best interest of the University and committed to upholding a high standard of morals and conduct. Student activity fees support the Student Government Association in its objectives and activities. The student body president and class representatives are elected by the student body, and the president appoints an executive board, which includes a chief of staff, treasurer, and secretary.

Admission Requirements

All prospective students must meet the following minimum course requirements for enrollment: 6 course units in language (including 4 units in English grammar, composition, and literature, and 2 units of a foreign language); 4 units of mathematics (one for which algebra II is a prerequisite); 3 units in science (including at least 1 unit in biology, 1 unit in the physical sciences, and one laboratory course); and 2 units in social science (including 1 unit in United States history).

Prospective students are required to submit the following materials: a completed application for admission, official transcripts from all high schools attended, answers to the essay questions on the application, official SAT or ACT scores, and a $45 application fee. When reviewing a freshman application, the admissions committee looks carefully at the applicant's academic achievements, test scores, and personal qualities, including difficulty of course work, grade point average, and extracurricular activities. Most students admitted to the University had a minimum SAT score between 1110 and 1240 and/or an ACT composite (with the writing portion) of at least 24.

Application and Information

Students applying for early action should have their applications postmarked November 1 or earlier and are notified on or around January 20. Applications must be postmarked by February 1; students are notified of the University's decision on or around April 1.

Transfer applicants may apply for fall, summer session I, and summer session II. Applications must be postmarked by March 1. Decision letters are mailed on a rolling basis.

To request application materials or receive additional information, interested students may contact:

Office of Admissions
University of North Carolina Wilmington
601 South College Road
Wilmington, North Carolina 28403-5904
Phone: 910-962-3243
Fax: 910-962-3038
E-mail: admissions@uncw.edu
Web site: http://www.uncw.edu/

The Fisher Student Center.

COLLEGE DATA CENTER • NORTH CAROLINA

WARREN WILSON COLLEGE

ASHEVILLE, NORTH CAROLINA

The College

Since its founding in 1894, Warren Wilson College has educated students with a unique triad of a strong liberal arts program, work for the College, and service to those in need, which makes Warren Wilson unlike any other college. Its 800 students come from forty-two states and twenty-five countries, creating a diverse and vibrant academic community.

The academic program features a first-rate faculty that does all of the teaching and frequently participates in research with students. The average class size is small, and discussion is an important part of teaching. Twenty-one majors are offered, with a commitment to quality in each program. Art, English, creative writing, economics and business administration, education, biology, the nationally recognized environmental studies program, and outdoor leadership are the most popular majors.

Students at Warren Wilson are integral to the day-to-day operation of the College. Each student works 15 hours a week at a job that is essential to running the school. This experience helps build student confidence (students learn that there is no job they cannot learn to do) and a strong sense of community at the College. Many juniors and seniors have work assignments that coincide with their majors. Students receive a work fellowship in the amount of $2952 each year for the work they do.

Service is also integral to the College's way of thinking. Warren Wilson is one of only a few colleges in the country that require student participation in community service for graduation. Service is offered to a wide range of individuals and agencies, nationally and abroad. Students must provide at least 20 hours of service each year to someone off campus.

The 1,100-acre campus includes a 300-acre working farm, 600 acres of forest, 25 miles of hiking trails, and a white-water kayaking course. The campus and the area are havens for outdoor activities, such as white-water sports, hiking, camping, mountain biking, and rock climbing.

Ninety percent of the students and 50 percent of the faculty and staff members live on campus. The College offers intercollegiate basketball, cross-country, soccer, and swimming for men and women. White-water sports, softball, and cross-country are offered as club sports. The College also offers intramural sports, a wellness program, and a wide range of other activities.

Location

Warren Wilson, on the edge of the city of Asheville, North Carolina, is in the heart of the Blue Ridge Mountains. Asheville, a city of nearly 100,000 people, is considered one of the most livable cities in the United States and was selected by the National League of Cities as the All-America City for 1998.

Surrounded by more than 1 million acres of national forest, Asheville is located in an ideal setting, presenting views of outstanding beauty throughout all four seasons. In the spring and summer, variations in altitude together with warm southern sun favor native vegetation: dogwood, wildflowers, rhododendron, mountain laurel, and azaleas cover the mountains. The arresting beauty of the autumn colors attracts photographers, artists, and sports enthusiasts from the world over. During the winter, natural snow is enhanced by machine-made snow, producing excellent downhill skiing.

A short drive from the Warren Wilson College campus are Great Smoky Mountains National Park, Pisgah National Forest, and the Blue Ridge Parkway, offering panoramic views, excellent camping facilities, and a perfect setting for class field trips.

Majors and Degrees

The bachelor's degree is awarded in art, biology, chemistry, creative writing, economics and business administration, English, environmental studies, history and political science, humanities, global studies, integrative studies, mathematics and computer science, outdoor leadership, psychology, religion, social work, and sociology/anthropology.

Academic Programs

The goal of the degree program at Warren Wilson College is the completion of three well-designed areas of study. First, students are expected to complete a core of required courses based on the theme "ways of knowing." A student earns 4 credits in each of the ten core areas. Second, students must develop a strength in one or more disciplines. A minimum of 128 semester hours is required for the baccalaureate degree, including the core plus major hours. Finally, a student must demonstrate the ability to work effectively with others by participation in a work-and-service program.

There is a required freshman seminar designed to provide new students the opportunity to explore various fields. A senior seminar, designed as a capstone experience, is required, as is a senior letter to evaluate the student's college experiences.

All Warren Wilson students must demonstrate competence in writing and mathematics either through testing or by completing core courses.

Each semester in the academic calendar is broken into two 8-week terms. A student traditionally takes only two courses per term (3 or 4 credit hours per course).

There are two honors programs at Warren Wilson. One is in English and the other is in the Division of Natural Sciences, where honors can be earned in biology, chemistry, environmental studies, and mathematics.

Off-Campus Programs

In addition to academics, work, and service, all qualified students are afforded the opportunity to study abroad. The College heavily subsidizes the cost for a cross-cultural international experience taken during the junior year or summer.

Academic Facilities

The Martha Ellison Library houses a collection of 100,000 books and 450 periodicals. It provides written records in all areas of the College curriculum and contributes to the cultural enrichment of students. The library is open and served by librarians and student assistants 75 hours each week. The building provides open access to books and periodicals during these hours. Individual carrels, lounge areas, and microfilm readers and printers are available, and there are Windows and Macintosh computers that students may use as word processors or for other prescribed purposes, including access to the Internet.

Computerized literature searching is available. The Martha Ellison Library is a teaching library, providing extensive and continuing bibliographic services, including courses, for the entire student body. Any resource materials not owned by the library may be acquired through interlibrary loan.

The campus arts complex includes the modern Kittredge Theatre; the Kittredge Music Wing, housing classrooms, studios, and a performance area; the Holden Arts Center, with a gallery, classrooms, studios, and a lecture hall; and an outdoor amphitheater. Instruction and performance events also take place in the chapel and the Craftshop/Ceramics Studio.

Costs

Total costs for the 2007–08 school year were $28,084. From this amount, the student's Work Program Fellowship of $2952 was deducted, leaving an actual cost of $25,132 for each student before any other aid.

Financial Aid

Warren Wilson offers a comprehensive financial aid program that seeks to enroll students from all economic backgrounds. This is accomplished through a combination of work, loans, grants, entitlements, and scholarships to students who complete their file prior to May. Students and their families should file the FAFSA and the Warren Wilson Financial Aid Application to be considered for all possible funds.

Faculty

The teaching faculty consists of 64 full-time members. Of these, 93 percent hold doctoral degrees. All classes and labs are taught by faculty members, not graduate students. Faculty members—1 for every 11 students—are available after class, during regular office hours, and in their homes.

Student Government

The student body is involved in the democratic decision-making process of the College. A wide variety of leadership positions, elected and appointed, are open to students. Campuswide elections provide opportunities for student involvement in Student Caucus, Judicial Board, Social Regulations Committee, other College advisory committees, and the Cabinet. Student Caucus, the representative voice of the student body, is also responsible for appointing students to positions on approximately fifteen other campus committees ranging from Admission to Library to Buildings and Grounds.

Admission Requirements

Admission to Warren Wilson College is based on both the personal and the academic qualifications of the applicant.

The selection criteria are devised to choose a student body with high standards of scholarship and personal goals and a willingness to provide community service.

Each candidate for admission must present an academic transcript from a secondary school. The transcript must show at least 12 academic units (a unit is one year's study in one subject). At least 4 years of English, 2 years of algebra, 1 year of geometry, 2 years of laboratory science, and 1 year of history are recommended for admission. Performance during high school is the best predictor of success in college. Therefore, great emphasis is placed upon the high school record. Grade trends can be very important.

Applicants must submit a recommendation from their high school counselor and scores from the SAT or ACT. Students are also required to submit a personal essay.

Transfer students must present both high school and college transcripts. Transfer applicants must be in good standing with the college last attended and should also have a minimum 2.75 cumulative grade point average. At least one school year in residence at Warren Wilson is required for a transfer student to be eligible for a degree from Warren Wilson College.

There is no fee to apply for admission to Warren Wilson College.

Application and Information

An application form and further information may be obtained by contacting:

Office of Admission
Warren Wilson College
701 Warren Wilson Road
Asheville, North Carolina 28815-9000
Phone: 800-934-3536 (toll-free)
E-mail: admit@warren-wilson.edu
Web site: http://www.warren-wilson.edu

Warren Wilson College's Valley Home.

WESTERN CAROLINA UNIVERSITY
CULLOWHEE, NORTH CAROLINA

The University

Western Carolina University (WCU) is a dynamic and fast-growing campus of the University of North Carolina. The University is attracting more and better students than ever before—students who thrive in a challenging learning environment where academic standards are going up and professors combine their academic credentials with years of professional experiences to create an effective connection between the classroom and the world beyond. With a strong emphasis on teaching, learning, and service, WCU is preparing students to lead and succeed in their communities and careers.

Academically, WCU offers a wide range of programs for students who plan to start their professional lives immediately after graduation and for those who intend to go on to graduate school. To a long tradition of excellence in teacher education, nursing, and business, WCU has added exciting new studies in forensic anthropology, construction management, TV and motion picture production, musical theater, electrical engineering, entrepreneurship, and more. On a national survey, students give WCU high marks for having a supportive environment with professors who get to know their students and are committed to their success.

Founded in 1889 to educate the people of the mountains, WCU has expanded its mission to serve the state and the nation. The University's main campus is located in Cullowhee, with programs in Asheville and Cherokee, at various community colleges, and online. The University offers degrees at the bachelor's and master's levels with a doctorate in educational leadership and an educational specialist degree.

WCU's 600-acre campus offers all the amenities of a small town, including academic and administrative buildings, fourteen residence halls, two full-service cafeterias, two food courts with fast-food outlets, health services and counseling, a bookstore, a library, two indoor swimming pools, tennis courts, a movie theater, jogging trail and quarter-mile track, intramural fields, and ample parking so that students can bring their cars to campus. A new $17-million student recreation center, scheduled for completion in 2008, features two multipurpose courts, a three-lane indoor track, and an indoor climbing wall. Still ahead are new residence halls, a new dining hall, and development of the 300-acre Millennial Campus with a mix of academic buildings, research facilities, business, industry, and housing.

Location

WCU is located in Cullowhee, North Carolina, 52 miles west of Asheville in a beautiful valley between the Blue Ridge and Great Smoky mountains. With abundant rivers and forests and the mild climate of Southern Appalachia, the region offers endless opportunities for outdoor activities such as climbing, hiking, biking, rafting, kayaking, and camping. Cities within a 2- to 3-hour drive of campus include Atlanta, Georgia; Charlotte, North Carolina; Knoxville, Tennessee; and Greenville/Spartanburg, South Carolina.

Majors and Degrees

WCU offers 120 majors and areas of concentration to undergraduates through five colleges—Arts and Sciences, Business, Education and Allied Professions, Fine and Performing Arts, and Health and Human Sciences—as well as programs offered through the Kimmel School of Construction Management and Technology. The Honors College offers extra academic challenge and social opportunities in an optional residential setting for high-achieving, qualified students. For undergraduates, WCU offers the Bachelor of Arts (B.A.), Bachelor of Science (B.S.), Bachelor of Science in Education, Bachelor of Fine Arts (B.F.A.), Bachelor of Science in Business Administration, and Bachelor of Science in Nursing (B.S.N.) degrees in the following majors: accounting, anthropology, art, art education, athletic training, biology, birth-kindergarten, business administration and law, chemistry, clinical laboratory sciences, communication, communication science and disorders, computer information systems, computer science, construction management, criminal justice, electrical and computer engineering technology, electrical engineering, elementary education, emergency medical care, engineering technology, English, English education, entrepreneurship, environmental health, environmental sciences, finance, forensic science, geology, German, health information administration, history, hospitality and tourism management, humanities, interior design, international business, management, marketing, mathematics, mathematics education, middle grades education, motion picture and television production, music, music education, natural resources management, nursing, nursing: RN to B.S.N., nutrition and dietetics, parks and recreation management, philosophy, physical education, political science, psychology, public safety and security management, recreational therapy, science education, social sciences, social sciences education, social work, sociology, Spanish, Spanish education, special education, special studies, sport management, telecommunications engineering technology, and theater. WCU's preprofessional programs (dental, engineering, law, medicine, optometry, pharmacy, physical therapy, physician's assistant, and veterinary medicine) prepare students well for admission to professional schools with tailor-made academic programs, small classes, undergraduate research, internships, and individual counseling. Students who participate in the International Baccalaureate (I.B.) or Advanced Placement (AP) programs in high school may receive college credit from WCU in as many as thirty areas.

Academic Programs

WCU grants scholarships to students who qualify as National Merit Finalists. The Western Meritorious Award for Finalists provides a four-year scholarship, which covers the equivalent amount of in-state tuition, fees, room, and board, to National Merit Finalists, who also receive a computer. The Honors College offers extra academic and social opportunities for qualified students who want to make the best of their college experience. One of the few honors programs in the state to offer students a residential option, the college is among the few nationwide to award graduates with a special honors diploma. Each spring, students are invited to present research findings in the WCU Undergraduate Research Symposium. The best projects proceed to national conventions, where WCU students consistently win top honors. At Western Carolina University, all bachelor's degree programs include courses in liberal studies designed to provide each student with the knowledge, skills, and attitudes of an educated person. These include the ability to think critically, to communicate effectively, to identify and solve problems reflectively, to use information and technology responsibly, to appreciate the creative and performing arts, and to seek personal development and lifelong learning. To earn a bachelor's degree, students must successfully complete between 120 and 128 semester hours of credit, or about forty courses. Students are encouraged to select a major—an academic area of focus—by their second year, which determines course selections for the junior and senior years and often a career path. Students who are undecided about a major can get help from a variety of sources, including professors, personal academic advisers, and career counselors.

Off-Campus Programs

WCU offers a wide array of study-abroad experiences. Students take advantage of opportunities such as studying the criminal justice and education systems in England, construction management in Ireland, international business law in the Netherlands, hospitality management in China, and language and culture in Mexico. Closer to home, WCU students in natural resources management and the sciences routinely conduct field work at off-campus field stations in the nearby Pisgah and Nantahala National Forests and in the Great Smoky Mountains National Park, where WCU students are participating in a vast scientific inventory of all the park's living organisms. Education, nursing, geography, and other fields offer off-campus internships and opportunities for hands-on learning as well.

Academic Facilities

WCU lends its resources—cultural, financial, and informational—to the western North Carolina region, sustaining and enhancing the lives and livelihoods of businesses, families, individuals, schools, and local governments. WCU fulfills part of this commitment through galleries, museums, theaters, music halls, and centers such as the Center for Mathematics and Science Education, Computer Center, Coulter Faculty Center, Highlands Biological Station, International Programs and Services, Mountain Heritage Museum, North Carolina Center for the Advancement of Teaching, Hunter Library's Special Collections, Reading Center, Southern Appalachian Biodiversity and Ecology Center, Speech and Hearing Center, and Distance Learning and Teleconference Center. WCU is home to two of the largest facilities in western North Carolina. The 8,000-seat Ramsey Regional Activity Center attracts nationally known speakers, major concerts, theater and television productions, banquets, receptions, and conferences, as well as WCU athletic events. A major research facility, Hunter Library contains more than 700,000 books and bound periodicals and provides access to 23,000 e-books, 3,330 serial subscriptions, an interlibrary loan exchange system, and the Internet.

Costs

The projected undergraduate costs for the 2008–09 academic year (fall and spring semesters), including tuition and fees, room, the standard meal option, and a cost-saving book rental program, are $10,277 for North Carolina residents and $19,860 for out-of-state residents and international students. All undergraduate students are required to have an appropriate, networkable laptop computer.

Financial Aid

Nearly two thirds of Western's freshmen receive some form of financial assistance, which includes grants, loans, scholarships, and student employment. Entering students who are interested in applying for financial aid must complete the Free Application for Federal Student Aid (FAFSA) as soon as possible after January 1. Since the most attractive sources of assistance are limited, applicants are encouraged by the University to complete the FAFSA by Western's priority deadline of March 31. WCU awards three types of financial aid: scholarships and grants, which do not have to be repaid; long-term and low-interest loans; and employment. University and departmental merit scholarships, such as the Chancellor's Award, Distinguished Scholar's Award, Founder's Scholarship, Computer Scholarship, WCU Meritorious Award, and Valedictorian Scholarship, are also available to qualified students. The North Carolina Teaching Fellows Program at WCU provides full tuition and other expenses for eight semesters to qualified North Carolina residents who agree to teach in the state for a specified period upon graduation. Students who complete the application for admission, submit supporting documentation, and gain admittance receive automatic consideration for University merit-based awards for which they may be eligible.

Faculty

There are approximately 450 full-time faculty members, who hold degrees from major colleges and universities. Eighty percent have doctoral or terminal degrees. The student-faculty ratio is 14:1. As a result, WCU faculty members know their students as well as they do their subjects. They spend time with students outside of class, meeting for informal study groups, organized trips, and individual counseling sessions. While they conduct research, write books, publish in professional journals, and belong to state and national professional organizations, WCU faculty members love to teach.

Student Government

WCU strongly supports active student participation in campus leadership through groups such as the Student Government Association (SGA), Resident Student Association, Student Media Board, fraternities and sororities, and student advisory councils. The SGA promotes students' interests while serving as a liaison between students and the administration. The SGA governs through the executive, legislative, and judicial branches. The SGA president is an ex officio member of the WCU Board of Trustees and a member of the Association of Student Governments, which serves the sixteen campuses of the University of North Carolina. The SGA coordinates the disbursement of student activity fees to some sixty campus organizations. Each year, WCU students receive a copy of the Student Handbook, which lists student organizations and includes the Student Bill of Rights and Code of Conduct.

Admission Requirements

Western Carolina University seeks students with proven academic performance and solid academic potential. National Merit Finalists, high school valedictorians, and students taking rigorous courses who have earned a solid A average are strongly encouraged to apply for admission so that they may be considered for merit scholarships. Admission decisions for incoming freshmen are based on the strength of the applicants' credentials, including high school course work, grades, class rank, and standardized test scores (SAT or ACT). Required courses include 4 units of English; algebra I, algebra II, geometry or an advanced math course for which algebra II is a prerequisite, and an additional mathematics course above algebra II; one physical science, one biological science, and a third laboratory science; U.S. history and one additional social science course; and two units of one foreign language. On-campus interviews and letters of recommendation are not required but are useful for students who wish to appeal an admission decision. College courses and grades are used to determine the eligibility of transfer students and freshmen with dual enrollment credit.

Application and Information

Western accepts students on a modified rolling admission basis. Western offers students the option of the Early Action Deadline of October 15. This means students who apply by this date and submit all required admission materials have their decision mailed out around December 15. This is a nonbinding decision. Students who apply after this deadline are notified on a rolling basis starting in mid to late January. Students are usually notified of a decision within three to four weeks of submitting all required admissions materials. All required materials must be received no later than thirty days prior to the term for which a student is making application. The application for admission and supporting documentation also serve as a student's merit-based scholarship application. For more information, application forms, and additional information, students may contact:

Alan Kines, Director of Admissions
Office of Admissions
102 Camp Building
Western Carolina University
Cullowhee, North Carolina 28723
Phone: 828-227-7317
877-WCU4YOU (toll-free)
Fax: 828-227-7319
E-mail: admission@wcu.edu
Web site: http://www.wcu.edu

An opening celebration welcomes students each fall to Western Carolina University, in the Great Smoky Mountains of North Carolina.

NORTH DAKOTA

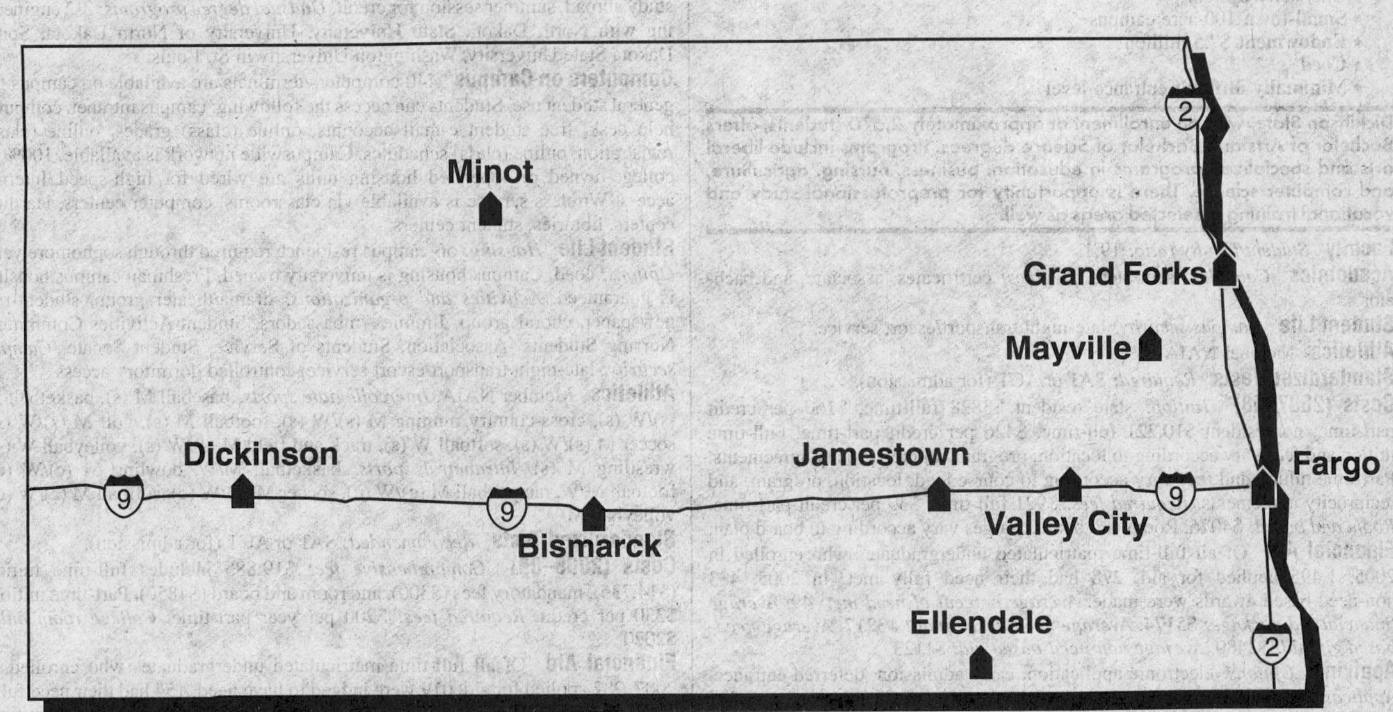

DICKINSON STATE UNIVERSITY

Dickinson, North Dakota **www.dsu.nodak.edu/**

- **State-supported** 4-year, founded 1918, part of North Dakota University System
- **Small-town** 100-acre campus
- **Endowment** $7.5 million
- **Coed**
- **Minimally difficult** entrance level

Dickinson State, with an enrollment of approximately 2,670 students, offers Bachelor of Arts and Bachelor of Science degrees. Programs include liberal arts and specialized programs in education, business, nursing, agriculture, and computer science. There is opportunity for preprofessional study and vocational training in selected areas as well.

Faculty *Student/faculty ratio:* 19:1.

Academics *Calendar:* semesters. *Degrees:* certificates, associate, and bachelor's.

Student Life *Campus security:* late-night transport/escort service.

Athletics Member NAIA.

Standardized Tests *Required:* SAT or ACT (for admission).

Costs (2007–08) *Tuition:* state resident $3828 full-time, $160 per credit part-time; nonresident $10,221 full-time, $426 per credit part-time. Full-time tuition and fees vary according to location, program, and reciprocity agreements. Part-time tuition and fees vary according to course load, location, program, and reciprocity agreements. *Required fees:* $921 full-time, $39 per credit part-time. *Room and board:* $4076. Room and board charges vary according to board plan.

Financial Aid Of all full-time matriculated undergraduates who enrolled in 2005, 1,495 applied for aid, 278 had their need fully met. In 2005, 483 non-need-based awards were made. *Average percent of need met:* 49. *Average financial aid package:* $5174. *Average need-based loan:* $3217. *Average need-based gift aid:* $2480. *Average non-need-based aid:* $1123.

Applying *Options:* electronic application, early admission, deferred entrance. *Application fee:* $35. *Required:* high school transcript, medical history, proof of measles-rubella shot.

Freshman Application Contact Mr. Steve Glasser, Director of Enrollment Services, Dickinson State University, Campus Box 169, Dickinson, ND 58601. *Phone:* 701-483-2175. *Toll-free phone:* 800-279-4295. *Fax:* 701-483-2409. *E-mail:* dsu.hawks@dsu.nodak.edu.

See page 1964 for the College Close-Up.

JAMESTOWN COLLEGE

Jamestown, North Dakota **www.jc.edu/**

- **Independent Presbyterian** 4-year, founded 1883
- **Small-town** campus
- **Endowment** $26.0 million
- **Coed** 1,024 undergraduate students, 92% full-time, 53% women, 47% men
- **Minimally difficult** entrance level, 79% of applicants were admitted

Undergraduates 940 full-time, 84 part-time. Students come from 27 states and territories, 8 other countries, 42% are from out of state, 1% African American, 1% Asian American or Pacific Islander, 1% Hispanic American, 1% Native American, 5% international, 5% transferred in, 59% live on campus. *Retention:* 74% of 2006 full-time freshmen returned.

Freshmen *Admission:* 1,183 applied, 930 admitted, 272 enrolled. *Average high school GPA:* 3.39. *Test scores:* ACT scores over 18: 91%; ACT scores over 24: 39%; ACT scores over 30: 3%.

Faculty *Total:* 79, 72% full-time, 43% with terminal degrees. *Student/faculty ratio:* 15:1.

Majors Accounting; actuarial science; applied mathematics; art; biochemistry; biology/biological sciences; biology teacher education; business administration and management; business/managerial economics; chemistry; clinical laboratory science/medical technology; communication/speech communication and rhetoric; computer science; counseling psychology; criminal justice/safety; dramatic/theater arts; educational leadership and administration; education (K-12); elementary education; English; English composition; English/language arts teacher education; financial planning and services; fine/studio arts; history; history teacher education; industrial radiologic technology; international business/trade/commerce; management information systems; marketing/marketing management; mathematics; mathematics teacher education; music; music performance; music teacher education; nursing (registered nurse training); philosophy; physical education teaching and coaching; political science and government; psychology; radiologic technology/science; religious studies; secondary education.

Academics *Calendar:* semesters. *Degree:* bachelor's. *Special study options:* advanced placement credit, cooperative education, distance learning, double majors, honors programs, independent study, internships, off-campus study, part-time degree program, services for LD students, student-designed majors, study abroad, summer session for credit. *Unusual degree programs:* 3-2 engineering with North Dakota State University, University of North Dakota, South Dakota State University, Washington University in St. Louis.

Computers on Campus 440 computers/terminals are available on campus for general student use. Students can access the following: campus intranet, computer help desk, free student e-mail accounts, online (class) grades, online (class) registration, online (class) schedules. Campuswide network is available. 100% of college-owned or -operated housing units are wired for high-speed Internet access. Wireless service is available via classrooms, computer centers, learning centers, libraries, student centers.

Student Life *Housing:* on-campus residence required through sophomore year. *Options:* coed. Campus housing is university owned. Freshman campus housing is guaranteed. *Activities and organizations:* drama/theater group, student-run newspaper, choral group, Jimmie Ambassadors, Student Activities Committee, Nursing Students' Association, Students of Service, Student Senate. *Campus security:* late-night transport/escort service, controlled dormitory access.

Athletics Member NAIA. *Intercollegiate sports:* baseball M (s), basketball M (s)/W (s), cross-country running M (s)/W (s), football M (s), golf M (s)/W (s), soccer M (s)/W (s), softball W (s), track and field M (s)/W (s), volleyball W (s), wrestling M (s). *Intramural sports:* basketball M/W, bowling M (c)/W (c), football M/W, racquetball M (c)/W (c), soccer M (c)/W (c), softball M (c)/W (c), volleyball M/W.

Standardized Tests *Recommended:* SAT or ACT (for admission).

Costs (2008–09) *Comprehensive fee:* $19,885 includes full-time tuition ($14,735), mandatory fees ($300), and room and board ($4850). Part-time tuition: $330 per credit. *Required fees:* $200 per year part-time. *College room only:* $2070.

Financial Aid Of all full-time matriculated undergraduates who enrolled in 2007, 782 applied for aid, 619 were judged to have need, 154 had their need fully met. 240 Federal Work-Study jobs (averaging $978). 42 state and other part-time jobs (averaging $909). In 2007, 304 non-need-based awards were made. *Average percent of need met:* 76%. *Average financial aid package:* $9431. *Average need-based loan:* $4018. *Average need-based gift aid:* $5847. *Average non-need-based aid:* $7261. *Average indebtedness upon graduation:* $22,097.

Applying *Options:* electronic application, deferred entrance. *Application fee:* $20. *Required:* high school transcript. *Required for some:* letters of recommendation, minimum ACT score of 18 or minimum SAT score of 850. *Recommended:* minimum 2.5 GPA, minimum ACT score of 18 or minimum SAT score of 850. *Application deadlines:* rolling (freshmen), rolling (transfers).

Freshman Application Contact Jamestown College, 6081 College Lane, Jamestown, ND 58405. *Phone:* 701-252-3467 Ext. 5512. *Toll-free phone:* 800-336-2554.

MAYVILLE STATE UNIVERSITY

Mayville, North Dakota **www.mayvillestate.edu/**

- **State-supported** 4-year, founded 1889, part of North Dakota University System
- **Rural** 60-acre campus
- **Coed** 769 undergraduate students, 62% full-time, 58% women, 42% men
- **Noncompetitive** entrance level, 70% of applicants were admitted

Undergraduates 478 full-time, 291 part-time. Students come from 32 states and territories, 4 other countries, 31% are from out of state, 5% African American, 1% Asian American or Pacific Islander, 1% Hispanic American, 4% Native American, 4% international, 9% transferred in, 40% live on campus. *Retention:* 59% of 2006 full-time freshmen returned.

Freshmen *Admission:* 204 applied, 142 admitted, 90 enrolled. *Test scores:* ACT scores over 18: 68%; ACT scores over 24: 19%; ACT scores over 30: 3%.

Faculty *Total:* 64, 55% full-time, 38% with terminal degrees. *Student/faculty ratio:* 14:1.

Majors Administrative assistant and secretarial science; biology/biological sciences; biology teacher education; business administration and management; business administration, management and operations related; business/commerce; chemistry; chemistry teacher education; child care provision; computer and information sciences; computer and information sciences and support services related; early childhood education; education; elementary education; English; English/language arts teacher education; general studies; geography teacher education; health and physical education; health and physical education related; health teacher education; history teacher education; kinesiology and exercise science; mathematics; mathematics teacher education; office management; physical education teaching and coaching; physical sciences; physics teacher education; pre-dentistry studies; pre-law studies; pre-medical studies; pre-pharmacy studies; pre-veterinary studies; psychology related; social sciences; social science teacher education.

Academics *Calendar:* semesters. *Degrees:* associate and bachelor's. *Special study options:* academic remediation for entering students, accelerated degree program, adult/continuing education programs, advanced placement credit, cooperative education, distance learning, double majors, honors programs, internships, part-time degree program, services for LD students, student-designed majors, summer session for credit. *ROTC:* Army (c), Air Force (c).

Computers on Campus Students can access the following: campus intranet, computer help desk, free student e-mail accounts, online (class) grades, online (class) registration, online (class) schedules. Campuswide network is available. 100% of college-owned or -operated housing units are wired for high-speed Internet access. Wireless service is available via entire campus.

Student Life *Housing:* on-campus residence required through sophomore year. *Options:* coed, men-only, women-only. Campus housing is university owned and is provided by a third party. Freshman campus housing is guaranteed. *Activities and organizations:* drama/theater group, choral group, Student Activities Council, Student Education Association, Health and Physical Education Club, Campus Crusade, Student Ambassadors. *Campus security:* controlled dormitory access. *Student services:* health clinic, personal/psychological counseling.

Athletics Member NAIA. *Intercollegiate sports:* baseball M (s), basketball M (s)/W (s), football M (s), softball W (s), volleyball W (s). *Intramural sports:* basketball M/W, bowling M/W, football M/W, golf M/W, ice hockey M, racquetball M/W, softball M/W, table tennis M/W, tennis M/W, track and field M/W, volleyball M/W.

Standardized Tests *Required:* SAT or ACT (for admission).

Costs (2007–08) *Tuition:* state resident $3795 full-time, $158 per credit hour part-time; nonresident $5692 full-time, $237 per credit hour part-time. Full-time tuition and fees vary according to course load and reciprocity agreements. Part-time tuition and fees vary according to course load and reciprocity agreements. *Required fees:* $1643 full-time, $68 per hour part-time. *Room and board:* $4072; room only: $1650. Room and board charges vary according to board plan and housing facility. *Payment plan:* installment. *Waivers:* minority students and senior citizens.

Financial Aid Of all full-time matriculated undergraduates who enrolled in 2006, 469 applied for aid, 371 were judged to have need, 151 had their need fully met. 50 Federal Work-Study jobs (averaging $1200). In 2006, 163 non-need-based awards were made. *Average percent of need met:* 46%. *Average financial aid package:* $4622. *Average need-based loan:* $3246. *Average need-based gift aid:* $2243. *Average non-need-based aid:* $653. *Average indebtedness upon graduation:* $15,758.

Applying *Options:* electronic application, deferred entrance. *Application fee:* $35. *Required:* high school transcript, minimum 2.0 GPA. *Recommended:* interview. *Application deadlines:* rolling (freshmen), rolling (transfers). *Notification:* 1/1 (freshmen), 1/1 (transfers).

Freshman Application Contact Dr. Ray Gerszewski, Vice President, Student Affairs and International Research, Mayville State University, 330 3rd Street, NE, Mayville, ND 58257-1299. *Phone:* 701-788-4842. *Toll-free phone:* 800-437-4104. *Fax:* 701-788-4748. *E-mail:* admit@mayvillestate.edu.

MEDCENTER ONE COLLEGE OF NURSING

Bismarck, North Dakota

medcenterone.com/college/nursing.htm

- **Independent** upper-level, founded 1988, administratively affiliated with Medcenter One Health Systems
- **Small-town** 15-acre campus
- **Endowment** $1.1 million
- **Coed, primarily women** 89 undergraduate students, 98% full-time, 89% women, 11% men
- **Moderately difficult** entrance level, 59% of applicants were admitted

Undergraduates 87 full-time, 2 part-time. Students come from 7 states and territories, 7% are from out of state, 1% Hispanic American, 53% transferred in.

Freshmen *Admission:* 86 applied, 51 admitted.

Faculty *Total:* 12, 83% full-time, 8% with terminal degrees. *Student/faculty ratio:* 9:1.

Majors Nursing (registered nurse training).

Academics *Calendar:* semesters. *Degree:* bachelor's. *Special study options:* independent study, internships.

Computers on Campus 17 computers/terminals are available on campus for general student use. Students can access the following: free student e-mail accounts.

Student Life *Housing:* college housing not available. *Activities and organizations:* Student Body Organization, Student Nurses Association. *Campus security:* late-night transport/escort service. *Student services:* health clinic, personal/psychological counseling.

Costs (2007–08) *Tuition:* $9258 full-time, $386 per credit part-time. *Required fees:* $759 full-time, $15 per credit part-time, $200 per term part-time.

Financial Aid Of all full-time matriculated undergraduates who enrolled in 2006, 78 applied for aid, 69 were judged to have need, 59 had their need fully met. 6 Federal Work-Study jobs (averaging $900). In 2006, 5 non-need-based awards were made. *Average percent of need met:* 97%. *Average financial aid package:* $13,095. *Average need-based loan:* $3488. *Average need-based gift aid:* $2790. *Average non-need-based aid:* $340. *Average indebtedness upon graduation:* $25,921.

Applying *Options:* early admission. *Application fee:* $40. *Application deadline:* 11/7 (transfers). *Notification:* continuous (transfers).

Application Contact Ms. Mary Smith, Director of Student Services, Medcenter One College of Nursing, 512 North 7th Street, Bismarck, ND 58501-4494. *Phone:* 701-323-6271. *Fax:* 701-323-6289. *E-mail:* msmith@mohs.org.

MINOT STATE UNIVERSITY

Minot, North Dakota

www.minotstateu.edu/

- **State-supported** comprehensive, founded 1913, part of North Dakota University System
- **Small-town** 103-acre campus
- **Endowment** $14.1 million
- **Coed** 3,140 undergraduate students, 71% full-time, 63% women, 37% men
- **Minimally difficult** entrance level, 80% of applicants were admitted

Undergraduates 2,227 full-time, 913 part-time. Students come from 36 states and territories, 20 other countries, 12% are from out of state, 3% African American, 1% Asian American or Pacific Islander, 2% Hispanic American, 4% Native American, 7% international, 9% transferred in, 9% live on campus. *Retention:* 60% of 2006 full-time freshmen returned.

Freshmen *Admission:* 670 applied, 536 admitted, 445 enrolled. *Average high school GPA:* 3.82.

Faculty *Total:* 259, 73% full-time, 39% with terminal degrees. *Student/faculty ratio:* 12:1.

Majors Accounting; art; art teacher education; biology/biological sciences; biology teacher education; business administration and management; business teacher education; chemistry; chemistry teacher education; clinical laboratory science/medical technology; communication disorders; computer science; criminal justice/safety; digital communication and media/multimedia; economics; education (specific subject areas) related; elementary education; English; English/language arts teacher education; finance; French; French language teacher education; general studies; geology/earth science; German; German language teacher education; history; history teacher education; humanities; international business/trade/commerce; management information systems; marketing/marketing management; mathematics; mathematics teacher education; medical radiologic technology; music; music teacher education; nursing (registered nurse training); nursing related; physical education teaching and coaching; physical sciences; physics; physics teacher education; psychology; radio and television; science teacher education; social sciences; social science teacher education; social work; sociology; Spanish; Spanish language teacher education; special education (hearing impaired); special education (mentally retarded); special education related; special education (speech or language impaired); speech and rhetoric; sport and fitness administration/management; substance abuse/addiction counseling.

Academics *Calendar:* semesters. *Degrees:* certificates, associate, bachelor's, master's, and post-master's certificates. *Special study options:* academic remediation for entering students, accelerated degree program, adult/continuing education programs, advanced placement credit, cooperative education, distance learning, double majors, honors programs, independent study, internships, part-time degree program, services for LD students, student-designed majors, study abroad, summer session for credit.

Computers on Campus 460 computers/terminals are available on campus for general student use. Students can access the following: online (class) registration. Campuswide network is available.

Student Life *Housing:* on-campus residence required for freshman year. *Options:* coed, men-only, women-only. Campus housing is university owned.

Freshman campus housing is guaranteed. *Activities and organizations:* drama/theater group, student-run newspaper, radio and television station, choral group, Student ND Education Association, Minot State Club of Physical Education, Inter-Varsity Christian Fellowship, Residence Hall Association, National Student Speech and Hearing Association. *Campus security:* controlled dormitory access, patrols by trained security personnel. *Student services:* health clinic, personal/psychological counseling, women's center.

Athletics Member NAIA. *Intercollegiate sports:* baseball M (s), basketball M (s)/W (s), cheerleading W, cross-country running M (s)/W (s), football M (s), golf M/W, ice hockey M (c), softball W (s), track and field M (s)/W (s), volleyball W (s). *Intramural sports:* basketball M/W, racquetball M/W, softball M/W, volleyball M/W.

Standardized Tests *Required:* SAT or ACT (for admission).

Costs (2007–08) *Tuition:* area resident $3984 full-time, $252 per credit hour part-time; state resident $4973 full-time, $252 per credit hour part-time; nonresident $10,622 full-time, $619 per credit hour part-time. Full-time tuition and fees vary according to class time, course load, location, program, and reciprocity agreements. Part-time tuition and fees vary according to class time, location, program, and reciprocity agreements. *Required fees:* $793 full-time, $33 per credit hour part-time. *Room and board:* $3914. Room and board charges vary according to board plan and housing facility. *Payment plan:* installment. *Waivers:* minority students, children of alumni, and employees or children of employees.

Financial Aid Of all full-time matriculated undergraduates who enrolled in 2005, 1,833 applied for aid, 1,524 were judged to have need, 364 had their need fully met. 142 Federal Work-Study jobs (averaging $1779). In 2005, 449 non-need-based awards were made. *Average financial aid package:* $4931. *Average need-based loan:* $3523. *Average need-based gift aid:* $3022. *Average non-need-based aid:* $927. *Average indebtedness upon graduation:* $16,354.

Applying *Options:* electronic application, deferred entrance. *Application fee:* $35. *Required:* high school transcript. *Required for some:* minimum 2.75 GPA, ACT composite score of 16 or higher or comparative SAT score (under age of 25). *Application deadlines:* rolling (freshmen), rolling (transfers). *Notification:* continuous (freshmen), continuous (transfers).

Freshman Application Contact Dr. John Girard, Director of Enrollment, Minot State University, 500 University Avenue West, Minot, ND 58707-0002. *Phone:* 701-858-3126. *Toll-free phone:* 800-777-0750 Ext. 3350. *Fax:* 701-858-3825. *E-mail:* askmsu@minotstateu.edu.

NORTH DAKOTA STATE UNIVERSITY

Fargo, North Dakota **www.ndsu.edu/**

- **State-supported** university, founded 1890, part of North Dakota University System
- **Urban** 2,100-acre campus
- **Coed** 10,403 undergraduate students, 90% full-time, 45% women, 55% men
- **Moderately difficult** entrance level, 85% of applicants were admitted

Undergraduates 9,397 full-time, 1,006 part-time. Students come from 45 states and territories, 58 other countries, 46% are from out of state, 1% African American, 1% Asian American or Pacific Islander, 0.7% Hispanic American, 1% Native American, 3% international, 7% transferred in, 30% live on campus. *Retention:* 82% of 2006 full-time freshmen returned.

Freshmen *Admission:* 4,381 applied, 3,719 admitted, 2,166 enrolled. *Average high school GPA:* 3.39. *Test scores:* SAT critical reading scores over 500: 66%; SAT math scores over 500: 76%; ACT scores over 18: 95%; SAT critical reading scores over 600: 28%; SAT math scores over 600: 42%; ACT scores over 24: 45%; SAT critical reading scores over 700: 3%; SAT math scores over 700: 8%; ACT scores over 30: 7%.

Faculty *Total:* 655, 85% full-time, 75% with terminal degrees. *Student/faculty ratio:* 19:1.

Majors Accounting; agribusiness; agricultural/biological engineering and bioengineering; agricultural business and management; agricultural economics; agricultural mechanization; agricultural teacher education; agriculture; animal sciences; apparel and textiles; architecture; art; athletic training; biochemistry/biophysics and molecular biology; biology/biological sciences; biology teacher education; biotechnology; botany/plant biology; business administration and management; chemistry; chemistry teacher education; civil engineering; classics and languages, literatures and linguistics; clinical laboratory science/medical technology; computer engineering; computer science; construction engineering; construction management; corrections and criminal justice related; crop production; dietetics; dramatic/theater arts; electrical, electronics and communications engineering; elementary education; engineering; English; English/language arts teacher education; environmental design/architecture; equestrian studies; facilities planning and management; family and consumer sciences/home economics teacher education; food science; French; French language teacher education; geology/earth science; health teacher education; history; history teacher education; horticultural science; hospitality administration; human development and family studies; humanities; industrial engineering; interior design; international/global studies; landscape architecture; manufacturing engineering; mass communication/media; mathematics; mathematics teacher education; mechanical engineering; microbiology; multi-/interdisciplinary studies related; music; music teacher education; natural resources management and policy; nursing (registered nurse training); parks, recreation and leisure; pharmacy; philosophy; physical education teaching and coaching; physics; physics teacher education; plant protection and integrated pest management; political science and government; polymer/plastics engineering; psychology; psychometrics and quantitative psychology; radiologic technology/science; respiratory care therapy; science teacher education; security and protective services related; social sciences; social science teacher education; sociology; soil science and agronomy; Spanish; Spanish language teacher education; speech and rhetoric; speech teacher education; sport and fitness administration/management; statistics; turf and turfgrass management; veterinary/animal health technology; zoology/animal biology.

Academics *Calendar:* semesters. *Degrees:* certificates, bachelor's, master's, doctoral, first professional, and post-master's certificates. *Special study options:* academic remediation for entering students, advanced placement credit, cooperative education, distance learning, double majors, English as a second language, honors programs, independent study, internships, off-campus study, part-time degree program, services for LD students, student-designed majors, study abroad, summer session for credit. *ROTC:* Army (b), Air Force (b).

Computers on Campus 500 computers/terminals are available on campus for general student use. Students can access the following: computer help desk, free student e-mail accounts, online (class) grades, online (class) registration, online (class) schedules. Campuswide network is available. Wireless service is available via classrooms, computer centers, computer labs, libraries, student centers.

Student Life *Housing:* on-campus residence required for freshman year. *Options:* coed, men-only, women-only, disabled students. Campus housing is university owned. Freshman campus housing is guaranteed. *Activities and organizations:* drama/theater group, student-run newspaper, radio station, choral group, marching band, Saddle and Sirloin, Habitat for Humanity, Residence Hall Association, Juggling Club, national fraternities, national sororities. *Campus security:* 24-hour emergency response devices and patrols, student patrols, late-night transport/escort service, controlled dormitory access. *Student services:* health clinic, personal/psychological counseling.

Athletics Member NCAA. All Division I. *Intercollegiate sports:* archery M (c)/W (c), baseball M (s), basketball M (s)/W (s), bowling M (c)/W (c), cheerleading M (c)/W (c), cross-country running M (s)/W (s), football M (s), golf M/W (s), ice hockey M (c), lacrosse M (c), riflery M (c)/W (c), rugby M (c)/W (c), soccer M (c)/W (s), softball W (s), track and field M (s)/W (s), volleyball M (c)/W (s), wrestling M (s). *Intramural sports:* basketball M/W, football M/W, softball M/W, volleyball M/W, wrestling M.

Standardized Tests *Required:* SAT or ACT (for admission).

Costs (2007–08) *One-time required fee:* $45. *Tuition:* state resident $5013 full-time, $209 per credit part-time; nonresident $13,384 full-time, $558 per credit part-time. Full-time tuition and fees vary according to reciprocity agreements. Part-time tuition and fees vary according to course load and reciprocity agreements. *Required fees:* $962 full-time, $40 per credit part-time. *Room and board:* $5820; room only: $2460. Room and board charges vary according to board plan and housing facility. *Payment plan:* installment. *Waivers:* minority students, children of alumni, senior citizens, and employees or children of employees.

Financial Aid Of all full-time matriculated undergraduates who enrolled in 2006, 7,256 applied for aid, 5,398 were judged to have need, 1,012 had their need fully met. 648 Federal Work-Study jobs (averaging $1323). In 2006, 2127 non-need-based awards were made. *Average percent of need met:* 32%. *Average financial aid package:* $6438. *Average need-based loan:* $4302. *Average need-based gift aid:* $3218. *Average non-need-based aid:* $1600. *Average indebtedness upon graduation:* $24,001.

Applying *Options:* electronic application. *Application fee:* $35. *Required:* high school transcript, minimum 2.5 GPA. *Application deadlines:* 8/15 (freshmen), 8/15 (transfers). *Notification:* continuous (freshmen), continuous (transfers).

Freshman Application Contact Jobey Lichtblau, Director of Admission, North Dakota State University, PO Box 5454, Fargo, ND 58105-5454. *Phone:* 701-231-8643. *Toll-free phone:* 800-488-NDSU. *Fax:* 701-231-8802. *E-mail:* ndsu.admission@ndsu.edu.

RASMUSSEN COLLEGE FARGO

Fargo, North Dakota **www.rasmussen.edu/**

- **Proprietary** primarily 2-year, founded 1902
- **Coed**
- **Minimally difficult** entrance level

Faculty *Student/faculty ratio:* 13:1.
Academics *Calendar:* quarters. *Degrees:* diplomas, associate, and bachelor's.
Costs (2007–08) *Tuition:* $11,700 full-time, $1025 per course part-time. Part-time tuition and fees vary according to course level, course load, degree level, and program.
Applying *Application fee:* $60. *Required:* high school transcript.
Freshman Application Contact Ms. Elizabeth Largent, Director, Rasmussen College Fargo, 4012 19th Avenue, SW, Fargo, ND 58103. *Phone:* 701-277-3889. *Toll-free phone:* 800-817-0009. *Fax:* 701-277-5604.

TRINITY BIBLE COLLEGE

Ellendale, North Dakota **www.trinitybiblecollege.edu/**

Director of Admissions Rev. Steve Tvedt, Vice President of College Relations, Trinity Bible College, 50 South Sixth Avenue, Ellendale, ND 58436. *Phone:* 701-349-3621 Ext. 2045. *Toll-free phone:* 888-TBC-2DAY.

UNIVERSITY OF MARY

Bismarck, North Dakota **www.umary.edu/**

- **Independent Roman Catholic** comprehensive, founded 1959
- **Suburban** 107-acre campus
- **Endowment** $29.3 million
- **Coed** 2,060 undergraduate students, 80% full-time, 60% women, 40% men
- **Moderately difficult** entrance level, 85% of applicants were admitted

Undergraduates 1,645 full-time, 415 part-time. Students come from 33 states and territories, 23 other countries, 30% are from out of state, 3% African American, 0.6% Asian American or Pacific Islander, 2% Hispanic American, 5% Native American, 2% international, 13% transferred in, 31% live on campus. *Retention:* 74% of 2006 full-time freshmen returned.
Freshmen *Admission:* 1,008 applied, 855 admitted, 353 enrolled. *Average high school GPA:* 3.36. *Test scores:* ACT scores over 18: 94%; ACT scores over 24: 40%; ACT scores over 30: 3%.
Faculty *Total:* 288, 36% full-time, 28% with terminal degrees. *Student/faculty ratio:* 17:1.
Majors Accounting; athletic training; biology/biological sciences; biology teacher education; business administration and management; business/corporate communications; business teacher education; clinical laboratory science/medical technology; computer and information sciences; criminal justice/police science; criminal justice/safety; divinity/ministry; early childhood education; elementary education; engineering science; English; English/language arts teacher education; general studies; health and physical education; history teacher education; information science/studies; kinesiology and exercise science; management information systems; management science; mass communication/media; mathematics; mathematics teacher education; music performance; music teacher education; nursing (registered nurse training); physical education teaching and coaching; psychology; public relations/image management; radiologic technology/science; religious studies; respiratory care therapy; social sciences; social science teacher education; social work; special education (mentally retarded); sport and fitness administration/management; substance abuse/addiction counseling; theology.
Academics *Calendar:* 4-4-1. *Degrees:* associate, bachelor's, master's, and doctoral. *Special study options:* academic remediation for entering students, accelerated degree program, adult/continuing education programs, advanced placement credit, cooperative education, distance learning, double majors, external degree program, independent study, internships, off-campus study, part-time degree program, services for LD students, study abroad, summer session for credit. *Unusual degree programs:* 3-2 engineering with University of Minnesota; pharmacy with North Dakota State University.
Computers on Campus 235 computers/terminals and 1,000 ports are available on campus for general student use. Students can access the following: campus intranet, computer help desk, free student e-mail accounts, online (class) grades, online (class) registration, online (class) schedules. Campuswide network is available. 100% of college-owned or -operated housing units are wired for high-speed Internet access. Wireless service is available via libraries, student centers.
Student Life *Housing:* on-campus residence required through sophomore year. *Options:* men-only, women-only. Campus housing is university owned. Freshman campus housing is guaranteed. *Activities and organizations:* drama/theater group, student-run newspaper, choral group, Student Senate, Lion's Club, Circle K, HealthPro, Spurs. *Campus security:* late-night transport/escort service. *Student services:* health clinic, personal/psychological counseling.
Athletics Member NCAA. All Division II. *Intercollegiate sports:* baseball M (s), basketball M (s)/W (s), cross-country running M (s)/W (s), football M (s), golf M (s)/W (s), soccer M (s)/W (s), softball W (s), tennis M (s)/W (s), track and field M (s)/W (s), volleyball W (s), wrestling M (s). *Intramural sports:* badminton M/W, basketball M/W, bowling M/W, cheerleading M/W, football M/W, golf M/W, racquetball M/W, soccer M/W, softball M/W, swimming and diving M/W, table tennis M/W, tennis M/W, volleyball M/W, water polo M/W, weight lifting M/W.
Standardized Tests *Required:* SAT or ACT (for admission).
Costs (2007–08) *Comprehensive fee:* $16,984 includes full-time tuition ($11,940), mandatory fees ($224), and room and board ($4820). Full-time tuition and fees vary according to course load and program. Part-time tuition: $375 per credit. Part-time tuition and fees vary according to course load and degree level. *Required fees:* $7 per credit part-time. *College room only:* $2200. Room and board charges vary according to board plan, housing facility, and location. *Payment plan:* installment. *Waivers:* senior citizens and employees or children of employees.
Financial Aid Of all full-time matriculated undergraduates who enrolled in 2006, 291 Federal Work-Study jobs (averaging $879). 74 state and other part-time jobs (averaging $1223).
Applying *Options:* electronic application, early admission, deferred entrance. *Application fee:* $25. *Required:* high school transcript, 1 letter of recommendation. *Required for some:* essay or personal statement, interview. *Recommended:* minimum 2.5 GPA. *Application deadlines:* rolling (freshmen), rolling (transfers).
Freshman Application Contact Dr. Dave Heringer, Vice President for Enrollment Services, University of Mary, 7500 University Drive; Bismarck, ND 58504-9652. *Phone:* 701-355-8191. *Toll-free phone:* 800-288-6279. *Fax:* 701-255-7687. *E-mail:* marauder@umary.edu.

UNIVERSITY OF NORTH DAKOTA

Grand Forks, North Dakota **www.und.nodak.edu/**

- **State-supported** university, founded 1883, part of North Dakota University System, administratively affiliated with University of North Dakota
- **Urban** 550-acre campus
- **Endowment** $11.3 million
- **Coed** 10,085 undergraduate students, 87% full-time, 45% women, 55% men
- **Minimally difficult** entrance level, 70% of applicants were admitted

Undergraduates 8,798 full-time, 1,287 part-time. Students come from 57 states and territories, 29 other countries, 48% are from out of state, 1% African American, 1% Asian American or Pacific Islander, 1% Hispanic American, 3% Native American, 3% international, 7% transferred in, 28% live on campus. *Retention:* 74% of 2006 full-time freshmen returned.
Freshmen *Admission:* 3,783 applied, 2,649 admitted, 1,855 enrolled. *Average high school GPA:* 3.36. *Test scores:* ACT scores over 18: 96%; ACT scores over 24: 41%; ACT scores over 30: 5%.
Faculty *Total:* 629, 90% full-time, 75% with terminal degrees. *Student/faculty ratio:* 19:1.
Majors Accounting; accounting and finance; airline pilot and flight crew; air traffic control; American Indian/Native American studies; anthropology; art; athletic training; atmospheric sciences and meteorology; aviation/airway management; biological and biomedical sciences related; biology/biological sciences; business administration and management; business/managerial economics; business teacher education; chemical engineering; chemistry; civil engineering; classics and languages, literatures and linguistics; clinical laboratory science/medical technology; clinical nutrition; communication disorders; communication/speech communication and rhetoric; computer and information sciences; computer systems analysis; criminal justice/safety; cytotechnology; dietetics; drafting/design technology; dramatic/theater arts; early childhood education; economics; electrical, electronics and communications engineering; elementary education; English; entrepreneurship; environmental/environmental health engineering; finance; flight instruction; foreign languages and literatures; forensic science and technology; French; general studies; geography; geological/geophysical engineering; geology/earth science; German; graphic communications; graphic design; history; industrial technology; international/global studies; marketing/marketing management; mathematics; mathematics teacher education; mechanical engineering; middle school education; multi-/interdisciplinary studies related; music; music performance; music teacher education; music therapy; nursing (registered nurse training); occupational safety and health technology; parks, recreation and leisure facilities management; philosophy; physical education teaching and coaching; physical sciences; physical therapy; physics; political science and government; psychology; public administration; religious studies; sales and marketing/marketing and distribution teacher education; Scandinavian languages; science

teacher education; social sciences; social science teacher education; social work; sociology; Spanish; vocational rehabilitation counseling; wildlife biology.

Academics *Calendar:* semesters. *Degrees:* diplomas, bachelor's, master's, doctoral, first professional, and post-master's certificates. *Special study options:* accelerated degree program, adult/continuing education programs, advanced placement credit, cooperative education, distance learning, double majors, English as a second language, honors programs, independent study, internships, off-campus study, part-time degree program, services for LD students, student-designed majors, study abroad, summer session for credit. *ROTC:* Army (b), Air Force (b). *Unusual degree programs:* 3-2 applied economics, counseling, chemistry, public administration.

Computers on Campus 1,100 computers/terminals and 400 ports are available on campus for general student use. Students can access the following: campus intranet, computer help desk, free student e-mail accounts, online (class) registration. Campuswide network is available. 100% of college-owned or -operated housing units are wired for high-speed Internet access. Wireless service is available via classrooms, computer centers, computer labs, dorm rooms, learning centers, libraries, student centers.

Student Life *Housing options:* coed, men-only, women-only, disabled students. Campus housing is university owned. Freshman campus housing is guaranteed. *Activities and organizations:* drama/theater group, student-run newspaper, radio and television station, choral group, marching band, student government, National Society of Collegiate Scholars, Association of Residence Halls, University of North Dakota Indian Association, Sioux Crew, national fraternities, national sororities. *Campus security:* 24-hour emergency response devices and patrols, student patrols, late-night transport/escort service, controlled dormitory access, emergency telephones. *Student services:* health clinic, personal/psychological counseling, women's center, legal services.

Athletics Member NCAA. All Division II. *Intercollegiate sports:* baseball M (s), basketball M (s)/W (s), cross-country running M/W, football M (s), golf M/W, ice hockey M (s)/W (s), soccer W, softball W (s), swimming and diving M/W (s), tennis W, track and field M (s)/W (s), volleyball W (s). *Intramural sports:* badminton M/W, baseball M, basketball M/W, cross-country running M/W, football M, golf M/W, ice hockey M/W, racquetball M/W, soccer M/W, softball M/W, swimming and diving M/W, table tennis M/W, tennis M/W, track and field M/W, ultimate Frisbee M/W, volleyball M/W.

Standardized Tests *Required:* SAT or ACT (for admission). *Recommended:* ACT (for admission).

Costs (2007–08) *Tuition:* state resident $5025 full-time; nonresident $13,418 full-time. Full-time tuition and fees vary according to degree level, program, and reciprocity agreements. Part-time tuition and fees vary according to course load, degree level, program, and reciprocity agreements. *Required fees:* $1105 full-time. *Room and board:* $5203; room only: $2137. Room and board charges vary according to board plan and housing facility. *Payment plan:* deferred payment. *Waivers:* minority students, senior citizens, and employees or children of employees.

Financial Aid Of all full-time matriculated undergraduates who enrolled in 2007, 6,888 applied for aid, 5,175 were judged to have need, 1,201 had their need fully met. 1,902 Federal Work-Study jobs (averaging $1749). In 2007, 1,757 non-need-based awards were made. *Average percent of need met:* 31%. *Average financial aid package:* $7375. *Average need-based loan:* $5375. *Average need-based gift aid:* $3203. *Average non-need-based aid:* $1103. *Average indebtedness upon graduation:* $21,330.

Applying *Options:* electronic application, deferred entrance. *Application fee:* $35. *Required:* high school transcript. *Recommended:* minimum 2.5 GPA. *Application deadline:* rolling (transfers). *Notification:* continuous (transfers).

Freshman Application Contact Deborah Melby, Director of Admissions, University of North Dakota, PO Box 8135, Grand Forks, ND 58202. *Phone:* 701-777-3821. *Toll-free phone:* 800-CALL UND. *Fax:* 701-777-2721. *E-mail:* enrollmentservices@mail.und.nodak.edu.

VALLEY CITY STATE UNIVERSITY

Valley City, North Dakota **www.vcsu.edu/**

- **State-supported** 4-year, founded 1890, part of North Dakota University System
- **Small-town** 55-acre campus
- **Endowment** $5.8 million
- **Coed** 899 undergraduate students, 75% full-time, 55% women, 45% men
- **Noncompetitive** entrance level, 93% of applicants were admitted

Undergraduates 675 full-time, 224 part-time. Students come from 15 states and territories, 6 other countries, 30% are from out of state, 4% African American, 0.3% Asian American or Pacific Islander, 1% Hispanic American, 2% Native American, 5% international, 6% transferred in, 40% live on campus. *Retention:* 62% of 2006 full-time freshmen returned.

Freshmen *Admission:* 271 applied, 251 admitted, 184 enrolled. *Average high school GPA:* 3.14. *Test scores:* SAT critical reading scores over 500: 44%; SAT math scores over 500: 39%; ACT scores over 18: 85%; SAT critical reading scores over 600: 13%; SAT math scores over 600: 13%; ACT scores over 24: 21%.

Faculty *Total:* 91, 62% full-time, 40% with terminal degrees. *Student/faculty ratio:* 11:1.

Majors Art; art teacher education; biology/biological sciences; biology teacher education; business administration and management; business teacher education; chemistry; chemistry teacher education; computer and information sciences; computer and information sciences and support services related; education; elementary education; English; English/language arts teacher education; health teacher education; history; history teacher education; human resources management; mass communication/media; mathematics; mathematics teacher education; music; music teacher education; office management; physical education teaching and coaching; pre-dentistry studies; pre-engineering; pre-law studies; pre-medical studies; pre-pharmacy studies; pre-veterinary studies; psychology; science teacher education; secondary education; social sciences; social science teacher education; Spanish; Spanish language teacher education; technical teacher education; technology/industrial arts teacher education.

Academics *Calendar:* semesters. *Degree:* bachelor's. *Special study options:* academic remediation for entering students, cooperative education, distance learning, double majors, internships, off-campus study, part-time degree program, services for LD students, student-designed majors, summer session for credit.

Computers on Campus 925 computers/terminals are available on campus for general student use. Students can access the following: campus intranet, computer help desk, free student e-mail accounts, online (class) grades, online (class) registration, online (class) schedules. Campuswide network is available. 100% of college-owned or -operated housing units are wired for high-speed Internet access. Wireless service is available via entire campus.

Student Life *Housing:* on-campus residence required for freshman year. *Options:* coed, men-only, women-only. Campus housing is university owned. Freshman campus housing is guaranteed. *Activities and organizations:* drama/theater group, student-run newspaper, choral group, departmental clubs, Fellowship of Christian Athletes, intramural sports, VCAB, Viking Ambassadors. *Campus security:* controlled dormitory access. *Student services:* health clinic, personal/psychological counseling.

Athletics Member NAIA. *Intercollegiate sports:* baseball M (s), basketball M (s)/W (s), football M (s), softball W (s), volleyball W (s). *Intramural sports:* basketball M/W, bowling M/W, football M/W, golf M/W, ice hockey M/W, racquetball M/W, skiing (cross-country) M/W, soccer M/W, softball M/W, tennis M/W, track and field M/W, volleyball M/W.

Standardized Tests *Required for some:* SAT or ACT (for admission).

Costs (2007–08) *Tuition:* state resident $3941 full-time, $131 per semester hour part-time; nonresident $10,522 full-time, $351 per semester hour part-time. Full-time tuition and fees vary according to course load, location, program, and reciprocity agreements. Part-time tuition and fees vary according to course load, location, program, and reciprocity agreements. *Required fees:* $1643 full-time, $68 per semester hour part-time. *Room and board:* $3880; room only: $1510. Room and board charges vary according to board plan and housing facility. *Waivers:* children of alumni and employees or children of employees.

Financial Aid Of all full-time matriculated undergraduates who enrolled in 2007, 599 applied for aid, 397 were judged to have need, 107 had their need fully met. 63 Federal Work-Study jobs (averaging $1725). 245 state and other part-time jobs (averaging $1850). In 2007, 201 non-need-based awards were made. *Average percent of need met:* 50%. *Average financial aid package:* $7967. *Average need-based loan:* $3860. *Average need-based gift aid:* $3911. *Average non-need-based aid:* $1524. *Average indebtedness upon graduation:* $19,722.

Applying *Options:* electronic application, early admission, deferred entrance. *Application fee:* $35. *Required:* high school transcript. *Application deadlines:* rolling (freshmen), rolling (transfers). *Notification:* continuous (freshmen), continuous (transfers).

Freshman Application Contact Ms. Charlene Stenson, Admission Counselor, Valley City State University, 101 College Street Southwest, Valley City, ND 58072. *Phone:* 701-845-7105. *Toll-free phone:* 800-532-8641 Ext. 37101. *Fax:* 701-845-7299. *E-mail:* c.stenson@vcsu.edu.

DICKINSON STATE UNIVERSITY

DICKINSON, NORTH DAKOTA

The University

Student success, both inside and outside the classroom, has been the focus of Dickinson State University since 1918, when the University was established as Dickinson Normal School and Model High. The tradition continues today, allowing easy access to and meaningful relationships with qualified professors, supportive and comfortable living arrangements on campus, and student activities that provide something for everyone.

Dickinson State, with an enrollment of approximately 2,670 students, is the only comprehensive, four-year public university in West River North Dakota. The University is proud of its safe campus. Its location offers students a secure environment in which to pursue their educational and social interests.

The University's mission is to provide high-quality, accessible programs; to promote excellence in teaching and learning; to support scholarly and creative activities; and to provide service that is relevant to the economy, health, and quality of life of the citizens of North Dakota. With a wide range of academic programs, Dickinson State University prepares students to live, learn, and lead in the twenty-first century.

Dickinson State University is accredited by the Higher Learning Commission of the North Central Association of Colleges and Schools (NCA), the National Council for Accreditation of Teacher Education (NCATE), and the National League for Nursing Accrediting Commission (NLNAC).

At Dickinson State, there are approximately forty-five different organizations to help every student find a niche. Students choose from intramural sports, band, chorus, drama, art, student government, honorary societies, academic clubs, and cheerleading, to name just a few.

Living in a residence hall at Dickinson State offers many conveniences and countless opportunities to build friendships in an exciting environment that is close to classes and University activities. Meal plans are available on campus for five or seven days per week. For added ease, students can also opt to purchase meals at the snack bar. Rooms have free access to the campus computer network and cable television. Features in each hall include a game room, exercise equipment, computer stations, free laundry facilities, and a kitchenette. Students can select to live in women's, men's, or coed halls or student apartments. Family student housing complexes provide apartments at reasonable housing rates to nontraditional students.

Location

Dickinson State is located in Dickinson, North Dakota, near the rugged and beautiful Badlands. With a population of more than 17,000, Dickinson is the intellectual, social, economic, and cultural hub of the West River Region of North Dakota. The community lies only 30 miles from Theodore Roosevelt National Park, and it is just 1 hour's drive south of Lake Sakakawea. Dickinson is served by commercial air transportation.

Dickinson's location provides abundant opportunities for people to enjoy outdoor recreational activities year-round. The area's picturesque rivers, lakes, and Badlands are ideal for hiking, fishing, boating, hunting, cross-country skiing, and much more.

As the state's fifth-largest community, Dickinson offers a wide array of restaurants, shopping malls, specialty stores, historic landmarks, museums, movie theaters, and other entertainment outlets. The region offers abundant dinosaur fossils and geological phenomena for explorers of all ages. Many of these treasures are displayed in Dickinson's impressive Dakota Dinosaur Museum.

Health-care services are provided by a 109-bed acute-care hospital, two major clinics, and numerous specialty clinics. The University's Student Health Service provides prompt care on campus for routine health concerns.

Majors and Degrees

Programs offered at Dickinson State University include liberal arts along with specialized programs in education, business, health services, agriculture, and computer science. There are opportunities for preprofessional study in selected areas as well.

Dickinson State offers Bachelor of Arts and Bachelor of Science degrees in eleven departments, including majors and/or minors (indicated with a *) in accounting, agriculture (with options in business/marketing, equine studies, integrated ranch management, natural resource management, and range management), applied science in technology, art, biology, business administration (with minors in accounting, agribusiness, banking and finance, entrepreneurship, human resource management, management, management information systems, manufacturing technology, marketing, and office administration), business education, chemistry, coaching*, communications, computer science, dance*, earth science*, elementary education, English, entrepreneurship*, environmental health, finance*, forensic accounting*, geography*, graphic design*, history, human resource management*, journalism*, leadership studies*, mathematics, music, music education, nursing, physical education, political science, psychology, science composite, secondary education, social science composite, social science (elementary education)*, sociology*, social work (linked with University of North Dakota), Spanish, technology education, theater, university studies, and writing.

Associate degree and certificate programs include agriculture, with specialty areas in agriculture sales and service (with options in agriculture business management, equine management, and technology in agriculture) or farm and ranch management; nursing; office administration (with concentrations in accounting, agribusiness, computer science, graphic design, legal studies, management, and medical studies); and university studies.

Preprofessional programs include athletic training, chiropractic, criminal justice, dentistry, dental hygiene, dietetics, law, medicine, medical/lab technology, mortuary science, occupational therapy, optometry, pharmacy, physical therapy, veterinary studies, and wildlife management.

Academic Programs

While many of the majors that Dickinson State University offers have unique academic requirements, the basic baccalaureate degree academic curriculum consists of approximately 39 semester hours of general education courses from the areas of communications, scientific inquiry, expression of human civilization, understanding human civilization, multicultural studies, and physical education; a specific major core curriculum of 32 to 60 or more semester hours; approximately 24 semester hours of credit in a minor field of study (when a minor is required); and professional education course work for those students entering the teaching profession. Students seeking a Bachelor of Arts degree must also complete a minimum of 16 semester hours of a foreign language. A minimum of 128 semester hours is required for graduation in a baccalaureate degree program. Associate degree programs require 64 credit hours for graduation.

Academic Facilities

The commitment to technology at Dickinson State is evident in the number of cutting-edge computers that are provided for student use. There is an outstanding student–personal computer ratio, resulting in easy access to the type of technology students need to excel. Computer labs are located in academic areas, the library, and all residence halls. Students also have free access to e-mail and the Internet.

Stoxen Library is proud of its highly sophisticated automated library. The Online Dakota Information Network allows students to access resources from across the United States.

Murphy Hall, which houses the Department of Natural Sciences, has recently been renovated and expanded in a $9-million project. The new-look Murphy Hall includes classrooms, state-of-the-art laboratories, faculty offices, and John Thompson Auditorium, making it the premiere science teaching and learning center in the region.

Costs

In 2007–08, tuition and fees were $2386 per semester for North Dakota residents; $2510 per semester for Minnesota residents; $2865 per semester for residents of Montana, South Dakota, Manitoba (Canada), and Saskatchewan (Canada); and $3344 per semester for residents of Alaska, Arizona, California, Colorado, Hawaii, Idaho, Kansas, Michigan, Missouri, Nebraska, Nevada, New Mexico, Oregon, Utah, Washington, and Wyoming. For residents of other states, tuition and fees were $5583 per semester. Room and board costs averaged $2038 per semester. Books were approximately $450 per semester. These figures are subject to change.

Financial Aid

College is a valuable investment in the future, and Dickinson State realizes financing it can be challenging. One of the best college buys in the region, Dickinson State's tuition and housing rates are among the lowest in the upper Midwest. In addition, attractive tuition rates are offered for students living in states and provinces bordering on North Dakota. Special rates also exist for students who live in those states participating in the Western Undergraduate Exchange (WUE) and the Midwest Student Exchange Program (MSEP). These include Alaska, Arizona, California, Colorado, Hawaii, Idaho, Kansas, Michigan, Missouri, Nebraska, Nevada, New Mexico, Oregon, Utah, Washington, and Wyoming.

The Office of Financial Aid is ready to help ease the cost of a college education through a number of financial aid programs, including scholarships, grants, loans, student employment opportunities, cultural diversity awards, and international awards. Approximately 80 percent of Dickinson State's students received financial assistance last year.

Faculty

Dickinson State University has 93 full-time and 70 part-time faculty members. Students develop close relationships with their teachers since three fourths of the classes have fewer than 30 students.

Student Government

The Student Senate is the governing body and official voice of Dickinson State University students. The Senate is composed of a cross-section of students who have been elected by the campus community. The Campus Activity Board (CAB) offers a broad range of social and recreational activities, including dances, films, comedians, and other special events. The Campus Programming Committee (CPC) provides a variety of educational, instructional, and cultural programs. Residence Hall Councils are made up of elected student residents and deal with matters relating to campus housing. The Student Policies Council is composed of students and faculty and staff members. The council recommends policies and programs related to student affairs.

Admission Requirements

Dickinson State's admission policy allows students to enroll if they are high school graduates or have successfully completed the GED examination, along with completion of the ACT or SAT. The completion of a high school college-preparatory course core curriculum is also required for admission into a baccalaureate program.

The nursing program has special enrollment and admission requirements. Students should apply early for this program.

All students under the age of 21 who have not completed 60 semester hours are required to live on campus. Exceptions to this policy include married students; students living locally with parents, grandparents, or a legal guardian; students who live with a brother or sister who is a head of a household; and single parents with one or more dependents.

Application and Information

The enrollment services staff is anxious to discuss the variety of programs the University has to offer and give a tour of the beautiful campus and its classrooms, facilities, and residence halls. When students are on campus, they should meet with the financial aid staff to discuss concerns about financing an education. Enrollment counselors are available Monday through Friday, 8 a.m. to 4:30 p.m., Mountain Time. Students should contact:

Office of Enrollment Services
Dickinson State University
Dickinson, North Dakota 58601-4896
Phone: 701-483-2175
800-279-HAWK Ext. 2175 (toll-free)
E-mail: dsu.hawks@dickinsonstate.edu
Web site: http://www.dickinsonstate.edu

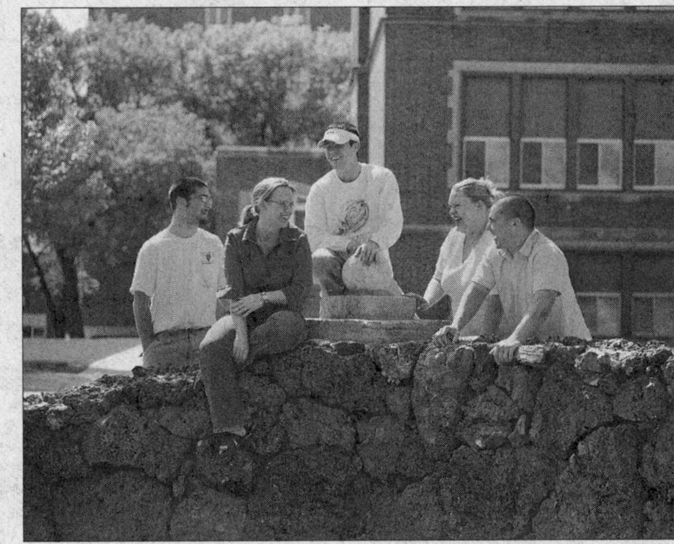

Dickinson State University ensures student success with flexible schedules and by providing numerous group activities, allowing students to live, learn, and lead as they grow together.

NORTHERN MARIANA ISLANDS

NORTHERN MARIANAS COLLEGE

Saipan, Northern Mariana Islands **www.nmcnet.edu/**

- **Territory-supported** primarily 2-year, founded 1981
- **Rural** 14-acre campus
- **Coed**
- **Noncompetitive** entrance level

Academics *Calendar:* semesters. *Degrees:* certificates, diplomas, associate, and bachelor's.

Student Life *Campus security:* patrols by trained security personnel.

Applying *Options:* early admission, deferred entrance. *Application fee:* $25. *Required:* high school transcript.

Freshman Application Contact Ms. Leilani M. Basa-Alam, Admission Specialist, Northern Marianas College, PO Box 501250, Saipan, MP 96950-1250. *Phone:* 670-234-3690 Ext. 1539. *Fax:* 670-235-4967. *E-mail:* leilanib@nmcnet.edu.

OHIO

The Cleveland area includes the towns of Beachwood, South Euclid, University Heights, and Pepper Pike.

The Columbus area includes the town of Westerville.

The Akron area includes the town of Kent.

The Canton area includes the town of North Canton.

The Newark area includes the town of Granville.

ALLEGHENY WESLEYAN COLLEGE

Salem, Ohio **www.awc.edu/**

Director of Admissions Admissions Office, Allegheny Wesleyan College, 2161 Woodsdale Road, Salem, OH 44460. *Phone:* 330-337-6403. *Toll-free phone:* 800-292-3153.

ANTIOCH COLLEGE

Yellow Springs, Ohio **www.antioch-college.edu/**

- **Independent** 4-year, founded 1852, part of Antioch University
- **Small-town** 100-acre campus with easy access to Dayton
- **Endowment** $28.4 million
- **Coed**
- **Moderately difficult** entrance level

Faculty *Student/faculty ratio:* 8:1.

Academics *Calendar:* trimesters. *Degree:* bachelor's.

Student Life *Campus security:* 24-hour emergency response devices and patrols, late-night transport/escort service.

Costs (2007–08) *Comprehensive fee:* $35,904 includes full-time tuition ($27,800), mandatory fees ($750), and room and board ($7354). Part-time tuition: $458 per credit hour. *College room only:* $3597.

Financial Aid Of all full-time matriculated undergraduates who enrolled in 2006, 279 applied for aid, 254 were judged to have need, 120 had their need fully met. 263 Federal Work-Study jobs (averaging $2500). In 2006, 55 non-need-based awards were made. *Average percent of need met:* 94. *Average financial aid package:* $30,640. *Average need-based loan:* $3656. *Average need-based gift aid:* $11,076. *Average non-need-based aid:* $23,327. *Average indebtedness upon graduation:* $17,112.

Applying *Options:* electronic application, early action, deferred entrance. *Required:* essay or personal statement, high school transcript, minimum 2.5 GPA, 2 letters of recommendation. *Recommended:* interview.

Freshman Application Contact Ms. Cathy Paige, Information Manager, Antioch College, 795 Livermore Street, Yellow Springs, OH 45387. *Phone:* 937-769-1100 Ext. 1119. *Toll-free phone:* 800-543-9436. *E-mail:* admissions@college.antioch.edu.

ANTIOCH UNIVERSITY MCGREGOR

Yellow Springs, Ohio **www.mcgregor.edu/**

- **Independent** upper-level, founded 1988, part of Antioch University
- **Small-town** 100-acre campus with easy access to Dayton
- **Coed** 169 undergraduate students, 39% full-time, 72% women, 28% men
- **Noncompetitive** entrance level

Undergraduates 66 full-time, 103 part-time. Students come from 1 other state, 21% African American, 0.6% Asian American or Pacific Islander, 4% Hispanic American, 2% Native American, 17% transferred in.

Faculty *Total:* 77, 23% full-time, 36% with terminal degrees. *Student/faculty ratio:* 8:1.

Majors Business administration and management; human development and family studies; humanities; human resources management; human services; liberal arts and sciences/liberal studies.

Academics *Calendar:* quarters. *Degrees:* certificates, bachelor's, master's, and post-master's certificates. *Special study options:* accelerated degree program, adult/continuing education programs, advanced placement credit, cooperative education, distance learning, double majors, independent study, internships, part-time degree program, summer session for credit.

Computers on Campus 49 computers/terminals are available on campus for general student use. Students can access the following: campus intranet, computer help desk, free student e-mail accounts, online (class) grades, online (class) registration, online (class) schedules. Campuswide network is available. Wireless service is available via entire campus.

Student Life *Housing:* college housing not available. *Campus security:* 24-hour emergency response devices and patrols. *Student services:* personal/psychological counseling.

Costs (2007–08) *Tuition:* $13,584 full-time, $283 per credit hour part-time. *Required fees:* $450 full-time, $150 per term part-time.

Financial Aid Of all full-time matriculated undergraduates who enrolled in 2006, 98 applied for aid, 94 were judged to have need. *Average percent of need met:* 22%. *Average financial aid package:* $6300. *Average need-based loan:* $4000. *Average need-based gift aid:* $1000. *Average indebtedness upon graduation:* $20,625.

Applying *Options:* electronic application, deferred entrance. *Application fee:* $45. *Application deadline:* rolling (transfers).

Application Contact Mr. Oscar Robinson, Director of Admissions, Antioch University McGregor, Student and Alumni Services Division, Enrollment Services, 800 Livermore Street, Yellow Springs, OH 45387. *Phone:* 937-769-1823. *Toll-free phone:* 937-769-1818. *Fax:* 937-769-1804. *E-mail:* sas@mcgregor.edu.

ART ACADEMY OF CINCINNATI

Cincinnati, Ohio **www.artacademy.edu/**

- **Independent** comprehensive, founded 1887
- **Urban** 184-acre campus
- **Endowment** $12.5 million
- **Coed** 137 undergraduate students, 93% full-time, 65% women, 35% men
- **Moderately difficult** entrance level, 24% of applicants were admitted

Undergraduates 128 full-time, 9 part-time. Students come from 15 states and territories, 16% are from out of state, 6% African American, 3% Asian American or Pacific Islander, 3% Hispanic American, 0.7% Native American, 7% transferred in, 15% live on campus. *Retention:* 80% of 2006 full-time freshmen returned.

Freshmen *Admission:* 416 applied, 101 admitted, 38 enrolled. *Average high school GPA:* 2.9. *Test scores:* SAT critical reading scores over 500: 67%; SAT math scores over 500: 31%; ACT scores over 18: 79%; SAT critical reading scores over 600: 17%; SAT math scores over 600: 5%; ACT scores over 24: 22%; SAT critical reading scores over 700: 11%; ACT scores over 30: 4%.

Faculty *Total:* 45, 33% full-time. *Student/faculty ratio:* 9:1.

Majors Art history, criticism and conservation; drawing; graphic design; illustration; intermedia/multimedia; painting; photography; printmaking; sculpture.

Academics *Calendar:* semesters. *Degrees:* associate, bachelor's, and master's. *Special study options:* adult/continuing education programs, advanced placement credit, cooperative education, double majors, honors programs, independent study, internships, off-campus study, part-time degree program, services for LD students, student-designed majors, study abroad, summer session for credit.

Computers on Campus 40 computers/terminals are available on campus for general student use. Students can access the following: campus intranet, computer help desk, free student e-mail accounts. Campuswide network is available. 100% of college-owned or -operated housing units are wired for high-speed Internet access.

Student Life *Housing:* on-campus residence required for freshman year. *Options:* coed. Campus housing is university owned. Freshman applicants given priority for college housing. *Campus security:* 24-hour emergency response devices and patrols. *Student services:* personal/psychological counseling.

Athletics *Intramural sports:* soccer M/W.

Standardized Tests *Required:* SAT or ACT (for admission).

Costs (2008–09) *Tuition:* $20,950 full-time, $875 per hour part-time. *Required fees:* $350 full-time, $175 per term part-time. *Room only:* $5800.

Financial Aid Of all full-time matriculated undergraduates who enrolled in 2003, 145 applied for aid, 126 were judged to have need, 28 had their need fully met. 47 Federal Work-Study jobs. In 2003, 46 non-need-based awards were made. *Average percent of need met:* 69%. *Average financial aid package:* $12,020. *Average need-based loan:* $5322. *Average need-based gift aid:* $7439. *Average non-need-based aid:* $7762. *Average indebtedness upon graduation:* $25,030.

Applying *Options:* electronic application, deferred entrance. *Required:* essay or personal statement, high school transcript, minimum 2.0 GPA, 1 letter of recommendation, portfolio. *Recommended:* interview. *Application deadlines:* 6/30 (freshmen), 6/30 (transfers). *Notification:* continuous (freshmen), continuous (transfers).

Freshman Application Contact Mr. John J. Wadell, Director of Admissions, Art Academy of Cincinnati, 1212 Jackson Street, Cincinnati, OH 45202. *Phone:* 513-562-8744. *Toll-free phone:* 800-323-5692. *Fax:* 513-562-8778. *E-mail:* admissions@artacademy.edu.

ASHLAND UNIVERSITY

Ashland, Ohio **www.exploreashland.com/**

- **Independent** comprehensive, founded 1878, affiliated with Brethren Church
- **Small-town** 98-acre campus with easy access to Cleveland
- **Endowment** $50.4 million

- **Coed** 2,772 undergraduate students, 90% full-time, 54% women, 46% men
- **Moderately difficult** entrance level, 83% of applicants were admitted

Ashland University's (AU's) academic experience includes individual attention to each student; a unique blend of liberal arts with professional curricula; practical internships, field experiences, and service-learning opportunities; and a holistic approach to educating the student. AU's commitment to the future is evident in the construction of an $18-million Sport Sciences/Recreation Center, an $11-million renovation and addition to the Kettering Science Center, and a $10-million College of Education, all of which opened in 2006.

Undergraduates 2,497 full-time, 275 part-time. Students come from 31 states and territories, 23 other countries, 6% are from out of state, 8% African American, 0.7% Asian American or Pacific Islander, 3% Hispanic American, 0.4% Native American, 2% international, 5% transferred in, 72% live on campus. *Retention:* 72% of 2006 full-time freshmen returned.

Freshmen *Admission:* 2,904 applied, 2,422 admitted, 637 enrolled. *Average high school GPA:* 3.35. *Test scores:* SAT critical reading scores over 500: 56%; SAT math scores over 500: 63%; ACT scores over 18: 92%; SAT critical reading scores over 600: 15%; SAT math scores over 600: 18%; ACT scores over 24: 38%; SAT critical reading scores over 700: 1%; SAT math scores over 700: 2%; ACT scores over 30: 3%.

Faculty *Total:* 581, 40% full-time, 54% with terminal degrees. *Student/faculty ratio:* 16:1.

Majors Accounting; American studies; art teacher education; athletic training; biology/biological sciences; business administration and management; chemistry; child development; commercial and advertising art; computer science; creative writing; dietetics; dramatic/theater arts; economics; education; elementary education; English; environmental studies; family and consumer economics related; family and consumer sciences/home economics teacher education; family and consumer sciences/human sciences; fashion merchandising; finance; fine/studio arts; foods, nutrition, and wellness; French; geology/earth science; health teacher education; history; hotel/motel administration; human development and family studies; information science/studies; international relations and affairs; journalism; kindergarten/preschool education; liberal arts and sciences/liberal studies; marketing/marketing management; marketing research; mass communication/media; mathematics; middle school education; music; music teacher education; parks, recreation and leisure; philosophy; physical education teaching and coaching; physics; political science and government; pre-dentistry studies; pre-law studies; pre-medical studies; pre-pharmacy studies; pre-theology/pre-ministerial studies; pre-veterinary studies; psychology; religious education; religious studies; science teacher education; secondary education; social sciences; social work; sociology; Spanish; special education; speech and rhetoric; therapeutic recreation; toxicology.

Academics *Calendar:* semesters. *Degrees:* associate, bachelor's, master's, doctoral, and first professional. *Special study options:* academic remediation for entering students, adult/continuing education programs, advanced placement credit, double majors, English as a second language, honors programs, independent study, internships, off-campus study, part-time degree program, services for LD students, student-designed majors, study abroad, summer session for credit.

Computers on Campus 760 computers/terminals are available on campus for general student use. Students can access the following: campus intranet, computer help desk, free student e-mail accounts, online (class) grades, online (class) registration, online (class) schedules. Campuswide network is available. 100% of college-owned or -operated housing units are wired for high-speed Internet access. Wireless service is available via classrooms, computer centers, computer labs, learning centers, libraries, student centers.

Student Life *Housing:* on-campus residence required through junior year. *Options:* coed, men-only, women-only, disabled students. Campus housing is university owned. Freshman campus housing is guaranteed. *Activities and organizations:* drama/theater group, student-run newspaper, radio and television station, choral group, marching band, Campus Activity Board, Fellowship of Christian Athletes, Hope Fellowship, intramurals, Community Care, national fraternities, national sororities. *Campus security:* 24-hour emergency response devices and patrols, student patrols, late-night transport/escort service, controlled dormitory access. *Student services:* health clinic, personal/psychological counseling, women's center.

Athletics Member NCAA. All Division II. *Intercollegiate sports:* baseball M (s), basketball M (s)/W (s), cross-country running M (s)/W (s), football M (s), golf M (s)/W (s), soccer M (s)/W (s), softball M/W (s), swimming and diving M (s)/W (s), tennis M/W, track and field M (s)/W (s), volleyball W (s), wrestling M (s). *Intramural sports:* badminton M/W, baseball M (c), basketball M/W, bowling M/W, cross-country running M/W, field hockey M/W, football M, golf M/W, racquetball M/W, rugby M (c)/W (c), skiing (downhill) M (c)/W (c), soccer M/W, softball M (c)/W (c), swimming and diving M/W, table tennis M/W, tennis M/W, track and field M/W, ultimate Frisbee M/W, volleyball M (c)/W (c), wrestling M.

Standardized Tests *Required:* SAT or ACT (for admission).

Costs (2008–09) *Comprehensive fee:* $33,216 includes full-time tuition ($23,550), mandatory fees ($790), and room and board ($8876). Part-time tuition: $723 per semester hour. *College room only:* $4768.

Financial Aid Of all full-time matriculated undergraduates who enrolled in 2005, 2,252 applied for aid, 1,758 were judged to have need. 1,155 Federal Work-Study jobs (averaging $1841). In 2005, 361 non-need-based awards were made. *Average percent of need met:* 90%. *Average need-based loan:* $4183. *Average need-based gift aid:* $11,409. *Average non-need-based aid:* $6206. *Average indebtedness upon graduation:* $18,250.

Applying *Options:* electronic application, deferred entrance. *Required:* high school transcript, minimum 2.5 GPA. *Required for some:* letters of recommendation, interview. *Recommended:* interview. *Application deadlines:* rolling (freshmen), rolling (transfers). *Notification:* continuous (freshmen), continuous (transfers).

Freshman Application Contact Mr. Thomas Mansperger, Director of Admission, Ashland University, 401 College Avenue, Ashland, OH 44805. *Phone:* 419-289-5052. *Toll-free phone:* 800-882-1548. *Fax:* 419-289-5999. *E-mail:* enrollme@ashland.edu.

See page 2010 for the College Close-Up.

BALDWIN-WALLACE COLLEGE

Berea, Ohio **www.bw.edu/**

- **Independent Methodist** comprehensive, founded 1845
- **Suburban** 100-acre campus with easy access to Cleveland
- **Endowment** $142.6 million
- **Coed** 3,638 undergraduate students, 83% full-time, 57% women, 43% men
- **Moderately difficult** entrance level, 66% of applicants were admitted

Undergraduates 3,037 full-time, 601 part-time. Students come from 35 states and territories, 15 other countries, 11% are from out of state, 7% African American, 1% Asian American or Pacific Islander, 2% Hispanic American, 0.1% Native American, 1% international, 4% transferred in, 59% live on campus. *Retention:* 83% of 2006 full-time freshmen returned.

Freshmen *Admission:* 3,126 applied, 2,058 admitted, 740 enrolled. *Average high school GPA:* 3.5. *Test scores:* SAT critical reading scores over 500: 76%; SAT math scores over 500: 72%; SAT writing scores over 500: 66%; ACT scores over 18: 95%; SAT critical reading scores over 600: 32%; SAT math scores over 600: 27%; SAT writing scores over 600: 21%; ACT scores over 24: 52%; SAT critical reading scores over 700: 5%; SAT math scores over 700: 2%; SAT writing scores over 700: 2%; ACT scores over 30: 7%.

Faculty *Total:* 390, 43% full-time, 47% with terminal degrees. *Student/faculty ratio:* 15:1.

Majors Accounting; art; art history, criticism and conservation; athletic training; biology/biological sciences; broadcast journalism; business administration and management; chemistry; communication disorders; communication/speech communication and rhetoric; computer science; computer software and media applications related; computer systems analysis; computer systems networking and telecommunications; creative writing; criminal justice/safety; dramatic/theater arts and stagecraft related; early childhood education; econometrics and quantitative economics; economics; English; exercise physiology; film/cinema studies; finance; fine/studio arts; French; German; health and physical education; health professions related; history; human resources management; international/global studies; marketing/marketing management; mass communication/media; mathematics; middle school education; multi-/interdisciplinary studies related; music; music history, literature, and theory; musicology and ethnomusicology; music performance; music teacher education; music theory and composition; music therapy; neuroscience; philosophy; physical sciences related; physics; piano and organ; political science and government; psychology; public relations/image management; religious studies; sociology; Spanish; special education (specific learning disabilities); sport and fitness administration/management; visual and performing arts related.

Academics *Calendar:* semesters. *Degrees:* certificates, bachelor's, and master's. *Special study options:* academic remediation for entering students, accelerated degree program, adult/continuing education programs, advanced placement credit, distance learning, double majors, English as a second language, honors programs, independent study, internships, off-campus study, part-time degree program, services for LD students, student-designed majors, study abroad, summer session for credit. *ROTC:* Air Force (c). *Unusual degree programs:* 3-2 engineering with Case Western Reserve University, Columbia University, Washington University in St. Louis; social work with Case Western Reserve University; biology with Case Western Reserve University, MBA programs in Accounting and Human Resources.

Computers on Campus 465 computers/terminals and 100 ports are available on campus for general student use. Students can access the following: campus intranet, computer help desk, free student e-mail accounts, online (class) grades, online (class) registration, online (class) schedules. Campuswide network is available. 100% of college-owned or -operated housing units are wired for high-speed Internet access. Wireless service is available via entire campus.

Student Life *Housing:* on-campus residence required through sophomore year. *Options:* coed, women-only, disabled students. Campus housing is university owned. Freshman campus housing is guaranteed. *Activities and organizations:* drama/theater group, student-run newspaper, radio and television station, choral group, marching band, campus entertainment productions, Student Senate, Dance Marathon, Campus Crusade, Black Student Alliance, national fraternities, national sororities. *Campus security:* 24-hour emergency response devices and patrols, student patrols, late-night transport/escort service, controlled dormitory access. *Student services:* health clinic, personal/psychological counseling, women's center.

Athletics Member NCAA. All Division III. *Intercollegiate sports:* baseball M, basketball M/W, cross-country running M/W, football M, golf M/W, soccer M/W, softball W, swimming and diving M/W, tennis M/W, track and field M/W, volleyball W, wrestling M. *Intramural sports:* archery M (c)/W (c), badminton M/W, basketball M/W, bowling M/W, cheerleading W (c), crew M (c)/W (c), football M/W, golf M/W, gymnastics W (c), ice hockey M (c), lacrosse M (c), racquetball M/W, skiing (cross-country) M (c)/W (c), skiing (downhill) M (c)/W (c), soccer M/W, softball M/W, tennis M/W, volleyball M/W, water polo M (c)/W (c), wrestling M.

Standardized Tests *Required:* SAT or ACT (for admission).

Costs (2008–09) *Comprehensive fee:* $31,252 includes full-time tuition ($23,524) and room and board ($7728). Part-time tuition: $748 per semester hour. *College room only:* $3776.

Financial Aid Of all full-time matriculated undergraduates who enrolled in 2004, 2,730 applied for aid, 2,353 were judged to have need, 1,716 had their need fully met. 775 Federal Work-Study jobs (averaging $601). 775 state and other part-time jobs (averaging $605). In 2004, 449 non-need-based awards were made. *Average percent of need met:* 91%. *Average financial aid package:* $18,444. *Average need-based loan:* $4508. *Average need-based gift aid:* $13,437. *Average non-need-based aid:* $9007. *Average indebtedness upon graduation:* $17,849. *Financial aid deadline:* 9/1.

Applying *Options:* electronic application, deferred entrance. *Application fee:* $25. *Required:* essay or personal statement, high school transcript, minimum 2.75 GPA, 1 letter of recommendation. *Recommended:* minimum 3.2 GPA, interview. *Application deadlines:* rolling (freshmen), rolling (transfers). *Notification:* continuous until 3/1 (freshmen), 6/1 (transfers).

Freshman Application Contact Ms. Grace B. Chalker, Interim Associate Director of Admissions, Baldwin-Wallace College, 275 Eastland Road, Berea, OH 44017-2088. *Phone:* 440-826-2222. *Toll-free phone:* 877-BWAPPLY. *Fax:* 440-826-3830. *E-mail:* admission@baldwinw.edu.

See page 2012 for the College Close-Up.

BLUFFTON UNIVERSITY

Bluffton, Ohio **www.bluffton.edu/**

- **Independent Mennonite** comprehensive, founded 1899
- **Small-town** 65-acre campus with easy access to Toledo
- **Endowment** $22.6 million
- **Coed** 1,000 undergraduate students, 91% full-time, 57% women, 43% men
- **Moderately difficult** entrance level, 61% of applicants were admitted

Undergraduates 913 full-time, 87 part-time. Students come from 21 states and territories, 10 other countries, 11% are from out of state, 4% African American, 0.7% Asian American or Pacific Islander, 2% Hispanic American, 0.2% Native American, 2% international, 2% transferred in, 81% live on campus. *Retention:* 68% of 2006 full-time freshmen returned.

Freshmen *Admission:* 1,343 applied, 817 admitted, 208 enrolled. *Average high school GPA:* 3.39. *Test scores:* SAT critical reading scores over 500: 43%; SAT math scores over 500: 53%; ACT scores over 18: 95%; SAT critical reading scores over 600: 16%; SAT math scores over 600: 14%; ACT scores over 24: 44%; SAT critical reading scores over 700: 4%; ACT scores over 30: 3%.

Faculty *Total:* 116, 57% full-time, 43% with terminal degrees. *Student/faculty ratio:* 13:1.

Majors Accounting; apparel and accessories marketing; art; biology/biological sciences; business administration and management; chemistry; clothing/textiles; communication/speech communication and rhetoric; computer science; creative writing; criminal justice/safety; economics; elementary education; English; family and consumer sciences/home economics teacher education; family and consumer sciences/human sciences; foods, nutrition, and wellness; health and physical education; history; information science/studies; information technology; kindergarten/preschool education; mathematics; middle school education; multi-/interdisciplinary studies related; music; music teacher education; organizational behavior; parks, recreation and leisure; physics; pre-medical studies; psychology; religious studies; social sciences; social work; sociology; Spanish; sport and fitness administration/management; youth ministry.

Academics *Calendar:* semesters. *Degrees:* bachelor's and master's. *Special study options:* academic remediation for entering students, adult/continuing education programs, advanced placement credit, double majors, honors programs, independent study, internships, off-campus study, part-time degree program, student-designed majors, study abroad, summer session for credit.

Computers on Campus 170 computers/terminals and 1,600 ports are available on campus for general student use. Students can access the following: campus intranet, computer help desk, free student e-mail accounts, online (class) grades, online (class) registration, online (class) schedules. Campuswide network is available. 100% of college-owned or -operated housing units are wired for high-speed Internet access. Wireless service is available via computer labs, libraries, student centers.

Student Life *Housing:* on-campus residence required through senior year. *Options:* coed, men-only, women-only. Campus housing is university owned. Freshman campus housing is guaranteed. *Activities and organizations:* drama/theater group, student-run newspaper, radio station, choral group, Brothers and Sisters in Christ, Campus Government, Student Union Board, music groups/chorale, chapel service. *Campus security:* 24-hour emergency response devices, late-night transport/escort service, controlled dormitory access, night security guards. *Student services:* health clinic, personal/psychological counseling.

Athletics Member NCAA. All Division III. *Intercollegiate sports:* baseball M, basketball M/W, cross-country running M/W, football M, soccer M/W, softball W, tennis M/W, track and field M/W, volleyball W. *Intramural sports:* basketball M/W, bowling M/W, football M/W, softball M/W, volleyball M/W.

Standardized Tests *Required:* SAT or ACT (for admission).

Costs (2007–08) *Comprehensive fee:* $29,074 includes full-time tuition ($21,380), mandatory fees ($400), and room and board ($7294). Full-time tuition and fees vary according to course load and program. Part-time tuition: $890 per credit hour. Part-time tuition and fees vary according to course load and program. *College room only:* $3358. Room and board charges vary according to board plan and housing facility. *Payment plan:* installment. *Waivers:* employees or children of employees.

Financial Aid Of all full-time matriculated undergraduates who enrolled in 2007, 701 applied for aid, 648 were judged to have need, 265 had their need fully met. 548 Federal Work-Study jobs (averaging $1956). 263 state and other part-time jobs (averaging $2088). In 2007, 119 non-need-based awards were made. *Average percent of need met:* 90%. *Average financial aid package:* $20,341. *Average need-based loan:* $5132. *Average need-based gift aid:* $13,550. *Average non-need-based aid:* $8321. *Average indebtedness upon graduation:* $27,584. *Financial aid deadline:* 10/1.

Applying *Options:* electronic application, deferred entrance. *Application fee:* $20. *Required:* high school transcript, 2 letters of recommendation, rank in upper 50% of high school class or 2.3 high school GPA. *Required for some:* essay or personal statement. *Recommended:* interview. *Application deadlines:* 8/15 (freshmen), rolling (transfers). *Notification:* continuous (freshmen), continuous (transfers).

Freshman Application Contact Mr. Chris Jebsen, Director of Admissions, Bluffton University, 1 University Drive, Bluffton, OH 45817. *Phone:* 419-358-3254. *Toll-free phone:* 800-488-3257. *Fax:* 419-358-3081. *E-mail:* admissions@bluffton.edu.

BOWLING GREEN STATE UNIVERSITY

Bowling Green, Ohio **www.bgsu.edu/**

- **State-supported** university, founded 1910
- **Small-town** 1230-acre campus with easy access to Toledo
- **Endowment** $140.8 million
- **Coed** 15,638 undergraduate students, 93% full-time, 54% women, 46% men
- **Moderately difficult** entrance level, 88% of applicants were admitted

Undergraduates 14,538 full-time, 1,100 part-time. Students come from 52 states and territories, 53 other countries, 10% are from out of state, 10% African American, 0.8% Asian American or Pacific Islander, 4% Hispanic American, 0.7% Native American, 1% international, 5% transferred in, 42% live on campus. *Retention:* 76% of 2006 full-time freshmen returned.

Freshmen *Admission:* 11,343 applied, 9,927 admitted, 3,241 enrolled. *Average high school GPA:* 3.2. *Test scores:* SAT critical reading scores over 500: 64%; SAT math scores over 500: 56%; ACT scores over 18: 89%; SAT critical reading scores over 600: 24%; SAT math scores over 600: 20%; ACT scores over 24: 31%; SAT critical reading scores over 700: 3%; SAT math scores over 700: 1%; ACT scores over 30: 5%.

Faculty *Total:* 1,112, 79% full-time. *Student/faculty ratio:* 18:1.

Majors Accounting; acting; adult development and aging; aeronautical/aerospace engineering technology; African studies; American studies; applied mathematics; art; art history, criticism and conservation; art teacher education; Asian studies; athletic training; aviation/airway management; biology/biological sciences; biology teacher education; broadcast journalism; business/commerce; business, management, and marketing related; business/managerial economics; business teacher education; chemistry; child development; cinematography and film/video production; classics and languages, literatures and linguistics; clinical laboratory science/medical technology; communication and journalism related; communication disorders; communication/speech communication and rhetoric; computer and information sciences; construction engineering technology; creative writing; criminal justice/safety; design and visual communications; dietetics; drama and dance teacher education; dramatic/theater arts; dramatic/theater arts and stagecraft related; ecology; economics; education; education related; education (specific subject areas) related; electrical, electronic and communications engineering technology; electromechanical technology; English; English/language arts teacher education; environmental design/architecture; environmental health; ethnic, cultural minority, and gender studies related; fashion merchandising; film/cinema studies; finance; fine arts related; fine/studio arts; foods, nutrition, and wellness; foreign language teacher education; French; geography; geology/earth science; German; gerontology; health and physical education related; health/health care administration; health professions related; health teacher education; history; hospitality administration; human development and family studies; human resources management; industrial technology; interior architecture; international business/trade/commerce; international relations and affairs; journalism; kindergarten/preschool education; Latin; liberal arts and sciences/liberal studies; logistics and materials management; management information systems and services related; marketing related; mathematics; mathematics teacher education; mechanical engineering/mechanical technology; medical microbiology and bacteriology; middle school education; multi-/interdisciplinary studies related; music; music history, literature, and theory; music performance; music related; music teacher education; music theory and composition; natural resources management and policy; neuroscience; nursing (registered nurse training); parks, recreation and leisure; philosophy; physical education teaching and coaching; physics; piano and organ; political science and government; pre-law studies; psychology; public administration; public relations/image management; quality control technology; Russian; sales and marketing/marketing and distribution teacher education; science teacher education; social studies teacher education; social work; sociology; Spanish; special education; special education (hearing impaired); speech and rhetoric; sport and fitness administration/management; statistics; technical and business writing; technical teacher education; theater design and technology; tourism and travel services management; tourism promotion; voice and opera; women's studies.

Academics *Calendar:* semesters. *Degrees:* certificates, bachelor's, master's, doctoral, and post-master's certificates. *Special study options:* academic remediation for entering students, accelerated degree program, adult/continuing education programs, advanced placement credit, cooperative education, distance learning, double majors, English as a second language, honors programs, independent study, internships, off-campus study, part-time degree program, services for LD students, student-designed majors, study abroad, summer session for credit. *ROTC:* Army (b), Air Force (b).

Computers on Campus 1,563 computers/terminals and 500 ports are available on campus for general student use. Students can access the following: computer help desk, free student e-mail accounts, online (class) grades, online (class) registration, online (class) schedules. Campuswide network is available. 100% of college-owned or -operated housing units are wired for high-speed Internet access. Wireless service is available via classrooms, computer centers, computer labs, dorm rooms, learning centers, libraries, student centers.

Student Life *Housing:* on-campus residence required through sophomore year. *Options:* coed, disabled students. Campus housing is university owned. Freshman campus housing is guaranteed. *Activities and organizations:* drama/theater group, student-run newspaper, radio station, choral group, marching band, University Activities Organization, Undergraduate Student Government, Latino Student Union, Religious/Spiritual Group, national fraternities, national sororities. *Campus security:* 24-hour emergency response devices and patrols, student patrols, late-night transport/escort service, controlled dormitory access. *Student services:* health clinic, personal/psychological counseling, women's center, legal services.

Athletics Member NCAA. All Division I except football (Division I-A). *Intercollegiate sports:* baseball M (s), basketball M (s)/W (s), crew M (c), cross-country running M (s)/W (s), golf M (s)/W (s), gymnastics W (s), ice hockey M (s), soccer M (s), softball W (s), swimming and diving M (s)/W (s), tennis M (s)/W (s), track and field M (s)/W (s), volleyball M (c)/W (s), water polo M (c)/W (c), weight lifting M (c)/W (c). *Intramural sports:* basketball M/W, bowling M/W, cross-country running M/W, football M/W, golf M/W, ice hockey M/W, lacrosse M (c)/W (c), racquetball M/W, rugby M (c)/W (c), skiing (cross-country) M (c)/W (c), skiing (downhill) M (c)/W (c), soccer M/W, softball M/W, tennis M/W, track and field M/W, volleyball M/W, water polo M (c)/W (c).

Standardized Tests *Required:* SAT and SAT Subject Tests or ACT (for admission).

Costs (2007–08) *Tuition:* state resident $7778 full-time, $380 per credit hour part-time; nonresident $15,086 full-time, $729 per credit hour part-time. Part-time tuition and fees vary according to course load. *Required fees:* $1282 full-time, $64 per credit hour part-time. *Room and board:* $6878; room only: $4200. Room and board charges vary according to board plan and housing facility. *Payment plan:* installment. *Waivers:* senior citizens and employees or children of employees.

Financial Aid Of all full-time matriculated undergraduates who enrolled in 2006, 10,655 applied for aid, 8,850 were judged to have need, 1,264 had their need fully met. 900 Federal Work-Study jobs (averaging $1143). In 2006, 1,703 non-need-based awards were made. *Average percent of need met:* 78%. *Average financial aid package:* $11,717. *Average need-based loan:* $6939. *Average need-based gift aid:* $6191. *Average non-need-based aid:* $5718. *Average indebtedness upon graduation:* $24,075.

Applying *Options:* electronic application, deferred entrance. *Application fee:* $40. *Required:* high school transcript, minimum 2.5 GPA. *Recommended:* interview. *Application deadlines:* 7/15 (freshmen), 7/15 (transfers). *Notification:* continuous (freshmen), continuous (transfers).

Freshman Application Contact Mr. Gary Swegan, Assistant Vice Provost/Director of Admissions, Bowling Green State University, 110 McFall, Bowling Green, OH 43403. *Phone:* 419-372-BGSU. *Fax:* 419-372-6955. *E-mail:* admissions@bgsu.edu.

See page 2014 for the College Close-Up.

BOWLING GREEN STATE UNIVERSITY–FIRELANDS COLLEGE

Huron, Ohio **www.firelands.bgsu.edu/**

- **State-supported** primarily 2-year, founded 1968, part of Bowling Green State University System
- **Rural** 216-acre campus with easy access to Cleveland and Toledo
- **Endowment** $2.3 million
- **Coed**
- **Noncompetitive** entrance level

Faculty *Student/faculty ratio:* 19:1.

Academics *Calendar:* semesters. *Degrees:* certificates, associate, and bachelor's (also offers some upper-level and graduate courses).

Student Life *Campus security:* 24-hour emergency response devices, late-night transport/escort service, patrols by trained security personnel.

Costs (2007–08) *Tuition:* state resident $4022 full-time, $196 per credit part-time; nonresident $11,330 full-time, $545 per credit part-time. Full-time tuition and fees vary according to course load and location. Part-time tuition and fees vary according to course load and location. *Required fees:* $206 full-time, $10 per credit part-time, $8 per term part-time. *Payment plans:* tuition prepayment, installment.

Applying *Options:* electronic application, early admission, deferred entrance. *Application fee:* $35. *Required:* high school transcript.

Freshman Application Contact Ms. Debralee Divers, Director of Admissions and Financial Aid, Bowling Green State University–Firelands College, One University Drive, Huron, OH 44839. *Phone:* 419-433-5560. *Toll-free phone:* 800-322-4787. *Fax:* 419-372-0604. *E-mail:* divers@bgsu.edu.

BRYANT AND STRATTON COLLEGE

Cleveland, Ohio **www.bryantstratton.edu/**

- **Proprietary** 4-year, founded 1929, part of Bryant and Stratton Business Institute, Inc
- **Urban** campus
- **Coed**
- **Minimally difficult** entrance level

Faculty *Student/faculty ratio:* 10:1.

Academics *Calendar:* semesters. *Degrees:* associate and bachelor's.

Student Life *Campus security:* controlled dormitory access.

Standardized Tests *Required:* TABE (for admission). *Recommended:* SAT or ACT (for admission).

Costs (2007–08) *Tuition:* $13,080 full-time, $436 per credit hour part-time. Full-time tuition and fees vary according to class time, course load, degree level, and program. Part-time tuition and fees vary according to course load and degree level.

Financial Aid Of all full-time matriculated undergraduates who enrolled in 2001, 110 applied for aid, 108 were judged to have need, 90 had their need fully met. 8 Federal Work-Study jobs (averaging $3000). *Average percent of need met:* 89. *Average financial aid package:* $6200. *Average need-based loan:* $3065. *Average need-based gift aid:* $1500. *Average indebtedness upon graduation:* $12,000.

Applying *Options:* deferred entrance. *Required:* high school transcript, interview, entrance evaluation and placement evaluation.

Freshman Application Contact Ted Hanson, Director of Admissions, Bryant and Stratton College, 1700 East 13th Street, Cleveland, OH 44114-3203. *Phone:* 216-771-1700. *Fax:* 216-771-7787. *E-mail:* thanson@bryantstratton.edu.

BRYANT AND STRATTON COLLEGE

Parma, Ohio **www.bryantstratton.edu/**

Freshman Application Contact Mr. F. Lee Nelly, Director of Admissions, Bryant and Stratton College, 12955 Snow Road, Parma, OH 44130. *Phone:* 216-265-3151 Ext. 229. *Toll-free phone:* 800-327-3151. *Fax:* 216-265-0325. *E-mail:* finelly@bryantstratton.edu.

CAPITAL UNIVERSITY

Columbus, Ohio **www.capital.edu/**

- **Independent** comprehensive, founded 1830, affiliated with Evangelical Lutheran Church in America
- **Suburban** 48-acre campus
- **Endowment** $58.2 million
- **Coed** 2,737 undergraduate students, 86% full-time, 62% women, 38% men
- **Moderately difficult** entrance level, 75% of applicants were admitted

Recognition as one of the top Universities–Master's in *U.S. News & World Report*; the Center for Excellence in Learning and Teaching, which helps each student succeed academically; and the Capital Center, a state-of-the-art recreational, educational, and athletic complex, are just a few reasons Capital University is a leader in the Midwest.

Undergraduates 2,344 full-time, 393 part-time. Students come from 28 states and territories, 19 other countries, 5% are from out of state, 9% African American, 1% Asian American or Pacific Islander, 2% Hispanic American, 0.2% Native American, 1% international, 4% transferred in, 43% live on campus. *Retention:* 76% of 2006 full-time freshmen returned.

Freshmen *Admission:* 3,394 applied, 2,539 admitted, 631 enrolled. *Average high school GPA:* 3.40. *Test scores:* SAT critical reading scores over 500: 65%; SAT math scores over 500: 67%; ACT scores over 18: 97%; SAT critical reading scores over 600: 24%; SAT math scores over 600: 23%; ACT scores over 24: 48%; SAT critical reading scores over 700: 2%; SAT math scores over 700: 4%; ACT scores over 30: 4%.

Faculty *Total:* 401, 54% full-time, 46% with terminal degrees. *Student/faculty ratio:* 9:1.

Majors Accounting; agricultural business and management; art; art teacher education; art therapy; athletic training; biochemistry; biological and biomedical sciences related; biology/biological sciences; biology teacher education; business administration and management; business administration, management and operations related; business/commerce; business/managerial economics; chemistry; chemistry teacher education; communication/speech communication and rhetoric; computer engineering; computer science; computer teacher education; creative writing; criminal justice/safety; criminology; drama and dance teacher education; dramatic/theater arts; early childhood education; economics; education; educational/instructional media design; elementary education; English; English/language arts teacher education; environmental science; finance; fine/studio arts; French; health and physical education; health and physical education related; health teacher education; history; human resources management; interdisciplinary studies; international relations and affairs; jazz/jazz studies; kinesiology and exercise science; liberal arts and sciences/liberal studies; literature; marketing/marketing management; mathematics; mathematics teacher education; middle school education; multi-/interdisciplinary studies related; music; music management and merchandising; music performance; music related; music teacher education; music theory and composition; nursing (registered nurse training); nursing related; organizational communication; philosophy; philosophy and religious studies related; physical education teaching and coaching; piano and organ; political science and government; political science and government related; pre-dentistry studies; pre-medical studies; pre-veterinary studies; psychology; public administration; public health/community nursing; public relations/image management; radio, television, and digital communication related; religious education; religious studies; science teacher education; secondary education; social studies teacher education; social work; sociology; Spanish; special education; speech and rhetoric; speech teacher education; taxation; violin, viola, guitar and other stringed instruments; voice and opera; wind/percussion instruments.

Academics *Calendar:* semesters. *Degrees:* bachelor's, master's, and first professional. *Special study options:* accelerated degree program, adult/continuing education programs, advanced placement credit, cooperative education, double majors, English as a second language, freshman honors college, honors programs, independent study, internships, off-campus study, part-time degree program, services for LD students, student-designed majors, study abroad, summer session for credit. *ROTC:* Army (b), Air Force (c). *Unusual degree programs:* 3-2 engineering with Washington University in St. Louis, Case Western Reserve University; occupational therapy with Washington University in St. Louis, University of Indianapolis.

Computers on Campus 100 computers/terminals are available on campus for general student use. Students can access the following: campus intranet, computer help desk, free student e-mail accounts, online (class) grades, online (class) registration, online (class) schedules. Campuswide network is available. 100% of college-owned or -operated housing units are wired for high-speed Internet access. Wireless service is available via entire campus.

Student Life *Housing:* on-campus residence required through sophomore year. *Options:* coed, disabled students. Campus housing is university owned. Freshman campus housing is guaranteed. *Activities and organizations:* drama/theater group, student-run newspaper, radio and television station, choral group, Campus Crusade for Christ, Student Government, University Programming, College Republicans, American Marketing Association, national fraternities, national sororities. *Campus security:* 24-hour emergency response devices and patrols, late-night transport/escort service, controlled dormitory access. *Student services:* health clinic, personal/psychological counseling.

Athletics Member NCAA. All Division III. *Intercollegiate sports:* baseball M, basketball M/W, cross-country running M/W, football M, golf M/W, soccer M/W, softball W, tennis M/W, track and field M/W, volleyball W. *Intramural sports:* basketball M/W, bowling M/W, football M/W, soccer M/W, softball M/W, table tennis M/W, tennis M/W, track and field M/W, volleyball M/W.

Standardized Tests *Required:* SAT or ACT (for admission).

Costs (2007–08) *Comprehensive fee:* $33,180 includes full-time tuition ($26,360) and room and board ($6820). Full-time tuition and fees vary according to course load, degree level, program, and student level. Part-time tuition: $880 per credit hour. Part-time tuition and fees vary according to course load, degree level, program, and student level. *Room and board:* Room and board charges vary according to board plan and housing facility. *Payment plan:* installment. *Waivers:* senior citizens and employees or children of employees.

Financial Aid Of all full-time matriculated undergraduates who enrolled in 2006, 1,979 applied for aid, 1,806 were judged to have need, 372 had their need fully met. In 2006, 482 non-need-based awards were made. *Average percent of need met:* 80%. *Average financial aid package:* $17,938. *Average need-based loan:* $4249. *Average need-based gift aid:* $10,604. *Average non-need-based aid:* $8927. *Average indebtedness upon graduation:* $25,171.

Applying *Options:* electronic application, deferred entrance. *Application fee:* $25. *Required:* high school transcript, minimum 2.6 GPA. *Required for some:* 1 letter of recommendation, audition. *Recommended:* interview. *Application deadlines:* 4/1 (freshmen), rolling (transfers). *Notification:* 9/15 (freshmen), continuous (transfers).

Freshman Application Contact Dr. Amy Adams, Director of Institutional Research and Assessment, Capital University, 2199 East Main Street, Columbus, OH 43209. *Phone:* 614-236-6101. *Toll-free phone:* 800-289-6289. *Fax:* 614-236-6926. *E-mail:* admissions@capital.edu.

See page 2016 for the College Close-Up.

CASE WESTERN RESERVE UNIVERSITY

Cleveland, Ohio **www.case.edu/**

- **Independent** university, founded 1826
- **Urban** 150-acre campus
- **Endowment** $1.9 billion
- **Coed** 4,207 undergraduate students, 95% full-time, 42% women, 58% men
- **Very difficult** entrance level, 75% of applicants were admitted

Undergraduates 3,996 full-time, 211 part-time. Students come from 52 states and territories, 26 other countries, 45% are from out of state, 5% African

American, 16% Asian American or Pacific Islander, 2% Hispanic American, 0.2% Native American, 3% international, 1% transferred in, 82% live on campus. *Retention:* 91% of 2006 full-time freshmen returned.

Freshmen *Admission:* 7,297 applied, 5,452 admitted, 1,133 enrolled. *Test scores:* SAT critical reading scores over 500: 94%; SAT math scores over 500: 97%; SAT writing scores over 500: 94%; ACT scores over 18: 100%; SAT critical reading scores over 600: 70%; SAT math scores over 600: 82%; SAT writing scores over 600: 67%; ACT scores over 24: 90%; SAT critical reading scores over 700: 25%; SAT math scores over 700: 38%; SAT writing scores over 700: 21%; ACT scores over 30: 46%.

Faculty *Total:* 923, 79% full-time, 85% with terminal degrees. *Student/faculty ratio:* 9:1.

Majors Accounting; aerospace, aeronautical and astronautical engineering; American studies; anthropology; applied mathematics; art history, criticism and conservation; art teacher education; Asian studies; astronomy; biochemistry; biology/biological sciences; biomathematics and bioinformatics related; biomedical/medical engineering; business administration and management; chemical engineering; chemistry; civil engineering; classics and languages, literatures and linguistics; cognitive science; communication disorders; comparative literature; computer engineering; computer science; dietetics; dramatic/theater arts; economics; electrical, electronics and communications engineering; engineering; engineering physics; engineering science; English; environmental studies; evolutionary biology; French; French studies; geology/earth science; German; German studies; gerontology; history; history and philosophy of science and technology; human nutrition; international/global studies; international relations and affairs; Japanese studies; materials engineering; materials science; mathematics; mechanical engineering; music; music teacher education; natural sciences; nursing (registered nurse training); nutrition sciences; philosophy; political science and government; polymer/plastics engineering; psychology; religious studies; sociology; Spanish; statistics; systems engineering; women's studies.

Academics *Calendar:* semesters. *Degrees:* bachelor's, master's, doctoral, first professional, and postbachelor's certificates. *Special study options:* accelerated degree program, adult/continuing education programs, advanced placement credit, cooperative education, double majors, English as a second language, honors programs, independent study, internships, off-campus study, part-time degree program, services for LD students, student-designed majors, study abroad, summer session for credit. *ROTC:* Army (c), Air Force (c). *Unusual degree programs:* 3-2 engineering; astronomy, biochemistry.

Computers on Campus 415 computers/terminals and 1,000 ports are available on campus for general student use. Students can access the following: campus intranet, computer help desk, free student e-mail accounts, online (class) grades, online (class) registration, online (class) schedules, software library, online reference databases, electronic books and journals. Campuswide network is available. 100% of college-owned or -operated housing units are wired for high-speed Internet access. Wireless service is available via entire campus.

Student Life *Housing:* on-campus residence required through sophomore year. *Options:* coed. Campus housing is university owned. Freshman campus housing is guaranteed. *Activities and organizations:* drama/theater group, student-run newspaper, radio station, choral group, marching band, Student Government, Student Radio Station, Habitat for Humanity and service organizations, International Student Groups, Music/Dance Groups, national fraternities, national sororities. *Campus security:* 24-hour emergency response devices and patrols, student patrols, late-night transport/escort service, controlled dormitory access, crime prevention programs. *Student services:* health clinic, personal/psychological counseling, women's center, legal services.

Athletics Member NCAA. All Division III. *Intercollegiate sports:* archery M (c)/W (c), baseball M, basketball M/W, cheerleading M (c)/W (c), crew M (c)/W (c), cross-country running M/W, fencing M (c)/W (c), football M, ice hockey M (c)/W (c), soccer M/W, softball W, swimming and diving M/W, tennis M/W, track and field M/W, ultimate Frisbee M (c)/W (c), volleyball M (c)/W, wrestling M. *Intramural sports:* badminton M/W, basketball M/W, bowling M/W, cross-country running M/W, football M/W, golf M/W, racquetball M/W, soccer M/W, softball M/W, squash M/W, swimming and diving M/W, table tennis M/W, tennis M/W, track and field M/W, ultimate Frisbee M/W, volleyball M/W, water polo M/W, weight lifting M/W, wrestling M.

Standardized Tests *Required:* SAT or ACT (for admission).

Costs (2007–08) *Comprehensive fee:* $43,476 includes full-time tuition ($32,800), mandatory fees ($738), and room and board ($9938). Full-time tuition and fees vary according to student level. Part-time tuition: $1367 per credit hour. Part-time tuition and fees vary according to course load. *College room only:* $5790. Room and board charges vary according to board plan, housing facility, and student level. *Payment plan:* installment. *Waivers:* employees or children of employees.

Financial Aid Of all full-time matriculated undergraduates who enrolled in 2007, 2,799 applied for aid, 2,498 were judged to have need, 2,234 had their need fully met. 2,053 Federal Work-Study jobs (averaging $2537). In 2007, 889 non-need-based awards were made. *Average percent of need met:* 90%. *Average financial aid package:* $33,565. *Average need-based loan:* $6135. *Average need-based gift aid:* $20,998. *Average non-need-based aid:* $18,140. *Average indebtedness upon graduation:* $32,195.

Applying *Options:* electronic application, early admission, early action, deferred entrance. *Required:* essay or personal statement, high school transcript, 1 letter of recommendation. *Recommended:* interview. *Application deadlines:* 1/15 (freshmen), 5/15 (transfers), 11/1 (early action). *Notification:* 4/1 (freshmen), continuous until 6/15 (transfers), 1/1 (early action).

Freshman Application Contact Ms. Elizabeth Woyczynski, Director of Undergraduate Admission, Case Western Reserve University, 10900 Euclid Avenue, Cleveland, OH 44106. *Phone:* 216-368-4450. *Fax:* 216-368-5111. *E-mail:* admission@case.edu.

See page 2018 for the College Close-Up.

CEDARVILLE UNIVERSITY

Cedarville, Ohio **www.cedarville.edu/**

- **Independent Baptist** comprehensive, founded 1887
- **Rural** 400-acre campus with easy access to Columbus and Dayton
- **Endowment** $19.1 million
- **Coed** 3,006 undergraduate students, 96% full-time, 55% women, 45% men
- **Moderately difficult** entrance level, 76% of applicants were admitted

Undergraduates 2,878 full-time, 128 part-time. Students come from 49 states and territories, 14 other countries, 64% are from out of state, 1% African American, 1% Asian American or Pacific Islander, 2% Hispanic American, 0.3% Native American, 0.5% international, 4% transferred in, 100% live on campus. *Retention:* 85% of 2006 full-time freshmen returned.

Freshmen *Admission:* 2,654 applied, 2,014 admitted, 762 enrolled. *Average high school GPA:* 3.62. *Test scores:* SAT critical reading scores over 500: 91%; SAT math scores over 500: 85%; SAT writing scores over 500: 87%; ACT scores over 18: 99%; SAT critical reading scores over 600: 52%; SAT math scores over 600: 48%; SAT writing scores over 600: 42%; ACT scores over 24: 72%; SAT critical reading scores over 700: 15%; SAT math scores over 700: 8%; SAT writing scores over 700: 8%; ACT scores over 30: 23%.

Faculty *Total:* 238, 78% full-time, 50% with terminal degrees. *Student/faculty ratio:* 16:1.

Majors Accounting; administrative assistant and secretarial science; American studies; athletic training; biblical studies; biological and physical sciences; biology/biological sciences; biology teacher education; broadcast journalism; business administration and management; chemistry; clinical laboratory science/medical technology; communication/speech communication and rhetoric; communications technology; computer and information sciences; computer engineering; computer science; criminal justice/law enforcement administration; dramatic/theater arts; early childhood education; electrical, electronics and communications engineering; English; English/language arts teacher education; environmental biology; finance; fine/studio arts; forensic science and technology; graphic design; health and physical education; health teacher education; history; information science/studies; interdisciplinary studies; international business/trade/commerce; international/global studies; international relations and affairs; kinesiology and exercise science; management information systems; marketing/marketing management; mathematics; mathematics teacher education; mechanical engineering; middle school education; missionary studies and missiology; music; music pedagogy; music performance; music teacher education; music theory and composition; nursing (registered nurse training); pastoral counseling and specialized ministries related; pastoral studies/counseling; philosophy; physical education teaching and coaching; physics; physics teacher education; piano and organ; political science and government; pre-dentistry studies; pre-law studies; pre-medical studies; pre-veterinary studies; psychology; public administration; radio and television; religious education; religious/sacred music; religious studies; science teacher education; secondary education; social studies teacher education; social work; sociology; Spanish; Spanish language teacher education; special education; speech and rhetoric; sport and fitness administration/management; technical and business writing; theology; voice and opera; youth ministry.

Academics *Calendar:* semesters. *Degrees:* certificates, bachelor's, and master's. *Special study options:* academic remediation for entering students, accelerated degree program, advanced placement credit, distance learning, double majors, honors programs, independent study, internships, off-campus study, part-time degree program, services for LD students, study abroad, summer session for credit. *ROTC:* Army (c), Air Force (c).

Computers on Campus 2,600 computers/terminals are available on campus for general student use. Students can access the following: campus intranet,

computer help desk, free student e-mail accounts, online (class) registration, online (class) schedules, over 150 software packages. Campuswide network is available. 100% of college-owned or -operated housing units are wired for high-speed Internet access. Wireless service is available via classrooms, computer centers, computer labs, dorm rooms, learning centers, libraries, student centers.

Student Life *Housing:* on-campus residence required through senior year. *Options:* men-only, women-only, disabled students. Campus housing is university owned. Freshman campus housing is guaranteed. *Activities and organizations:* drama/theater group, student-run newspaper, radio station, choral group, Student Government Association, College Republicans, ASME, Chi Theta Pi, MENC. *Campus security:* 24-hour emergency response devices and patrols, student patrols, late-night transport/escort service, controlled dormitory access. *Student services:* health clinic, personal/psychological counseling.

Athletics Member NAIA, NCCAA. *Intercollegiate sports:* baseball M (s), basketball M (s)/W (s), cross-country running M (s)/W (s), golf M (s), soccer M (s)/W (s), softball W (s), tennis M (s)/W (s), track and field M (s)/W (s), volleyball W (s). *Intramural sports:* badminton M/W, basketball M/W, bowling M/W, cross-country running M/W, football M/W, golf M/W, racquetball M/W, rock climbing M/W, skiing (downhill) M/W, soccer M/W, softball M/W, table tennis M/W, tennis M/W, ultimate Frisbee M/W, volleyball M/W.

Standardized Tests *Required:* SAT or ACT (for admission). *Recommended:* SAT and SAT Subject Tests or ACT (for admission).

Costs (2007–08) *Comprehensive fee:* $26,140 includes full-time tuition ($19,680), mandatory fees ($1450), and room and board ($5010). Part-time tuition: $615 per credit hour. Part-time tuition and fees vary according to course load. *College room only:* $2684. Room and board charges vary according to board plan. *Payment plan:* installment. *Waivers:* senior citizens and employees or children of employees.

Financial Aid Of all full-time matriculated undergraduates who enrolled in 2006, 2,119 applied for aid, 1,746 were judged to have need, 1,001 had their need fully met. 271 Federal Work-Study jobs (averaging $1188). 1,413 state and other part-time jobs (averaging $1096). In 2006, 680 non-need-based awards were made. *Average percent of need met:* 41%. *Average financial aid package:* $18,834. *Average need-based loan:* $4047. *Average need-based gift aid:* $3167. *Average non-need-based aid:* $7324. *Average indebtedness upon graduation:* $24,890.

Applying *Options:* electronic application, early admission, deferred entrance. *Application fee:* $30. *Required:* essay or personal statement, high school transcript, minimum 3.0 GPA, 2 letters of recommendation, clear testimony of faith in Jesus Christ and evidence of consistent Christian lifestyle. *Required for some:* interview. *Application deadlines:* rolling (freshmen), rolling (transfers). *Notification:* continuous (freshmen), continuous (transfers).

Freshman Application Contact Mr. Roscoe Smith, Director of Admissions, Cedarville University, 251 North Main Street, Cedarville, OH 45314-0601. *Phone:* 937-766-7700. *Toll-free phone:* 800-CEDARVILLE. *Fax:* 937-766-7575. *E-mail:* admiss@cedarville.edu.

CENTRAL STATE UNIVERSITY

Wilberforce, Ohio **www.centralstate.edu/**

- **State-supported** comprehensive, founded 1887, part of Ohio Board of Regents
- **Rural** 60-acre campus with easy access to Dayton
- **Endowment** $3.9 million
- **Coed** 1,997 undergraduate students, 91% full-time, 50% women, 50% men
- **Minimally difficult** entrance level, 38% of applicants were admitted

Undergraduates 1,818 full-time, 179 part-time. Students come from 35 states and territories, 7 other countries, 36% are from out of state, 92% African American, 0.2% Asian American or Pacific Islander, 1% Hispanic American, 0.2% Native American, 0.3% international, 6% transferred in, 63% live on campus. *Retention:* 54% of 2006 full-time freshmen returned.

Freshmen *Admission:* 5,717 applied, 2,159 admitted, 571 enrolled. *Average high school GPA:* 2.43. *Test scores:* SAT critical reading scores over 500: 15%; SAT math scores over 500: 11%; ACT scores over 18: 29%; SAT critical reading scores over 600: 1%; SAT math scores over 600: 8%; ACT scores over 24: 1%.

Faculty *Total:* 184, 58% full-time, 49% with terminal degrees. *Student/faculty ratio:* 14:1.

Majors Accounting; art; biology/biological sciences; broadcast journalism; business administration and management; chemistry; computer and information sciences; criminal justice/safety; economics; education (multiple levels); education related; English; geology/earth science; history; industrial technology; jazz/jazz studies; journalism related; mathematics; middle school education; music performance; parks, recreation and leisure; political science and government; psychology; radio and television; secondary education; social work; sociology; special education; water resources engineering.

Academics *Calendar:* semesters. *Degrees:* bachelor's and master's. *Special study options:* adult/continuing education programs, cooperative education, double majors, honors programs, independent study, internships, off-campus study, part-time degree program, services for LD students, study abroad, summer session for credit. *ROTC:* Army (b).

Computers on Campus 400 computers/terminals are available on campus for general student use. Students can access the following: campus intranet, free student e-mail accounts, online (class) grades, online (class) registration, online (class) schedules. Campuswide network is available. 98% of college-owned or -operated housing units are wired for high-speed Internet access. Wireless service is available via classrooms, computer centers, computer labs, dorm rooms, learning centers, libraries, student centers.

Student Life *Housing:* on-campus residence required for freshman year. *Options:* coed, men-only, women-only. Campus housing is university owned. Freshman campus housing is guaranteed. *Activities and organizations:* drama/theater group, student-run newspaper, radio and television station, choral group, marching band, Student Ambassadors, student government, national fraternities, national sororities. *Campus security:* 24-hour emergency response devices and patrols, controlled dormitory access. *Student services:* health clinic, personal/psychological counseling.

Athletics Member NCAA. All Division II. *Intercollegiate sports:* basketball M (s)/W (s), cheerleading M (s)/W (s), cross-country running M (s)/W (s), golf M (s)/W (s), tennis M (s)/W (s), track and field M (s)/W (s), volleyball W (s). *Intramural sports:* basketball M/W, bowling M/W, softball M/W, tennis M/W.

Standardized Tests *Required:* SAT or ACT (for admission). *Recommended:* ACT (for admission).

Costs (2007–08) *Tuition:* state resident $5294 full-time, $218 per credit hour part-time; nonresident $11,462 full-time, $496 per credit hour part-time. Full-time tuition and fees vary according to course load. *Room and board:* $7402; room only: $3978. Room and board charges vary according to board plan. *Payment plans:* installment, deferred payment. *Waivers:* senior citizens and employees or children of employees.

Financial Aid Of all full-time matriculated undergraduates who enrolled in 2006, 1,470 applied for aid, 1,405 were judged to have need. *Average percent of need met:* 93%.

Applying *Options:* electronic application. *Application fee:* $20. *Required:* high school transcript. *Required for some:* essay or personal statement, minimum 2.0 GPA, 2 letters of recommendation, 2.5 high school GPA for nonresidents. *Recommended:* interview. *Application deadlines:* 6/15 (freshmen), 6/15 (transfers). *Notification:* continuous (freshmen), continuous (transfers).

Freshman Application Contact Ms. Robin Rucker, Interim Associate Director, Admissions, Central State University, PO Box 1004, 1400 Blush Row Road, Wilberforce, OH 45384. *Phone:* 937-376-6580. *Toll-free phone:* 800-388-CSU1. *Fax:* 937-376-6648. *E-mail:* admissions@centralstate.edu.

CINCINNATI CHRISTIAN UNIVERSITY

Cincinnati, Ohio **www.ccuniversity.edu/**

- **Independent** comprehensive, founded 1924, affiliated with Church of Christ
- **Urban** 40-acre campus
- **Coed**
- **Minimally difficult** entrance level

Faculty *Student/faculty ratio:* 19:1.

Academics *Calendar:* semesters. *Degrees:* associate, bachelor's, master's, and first professional.

Student Life *Campus security:* 24-hour emergency response devices and patrols, student patrols, late-night transport/escort service, controlled dormitory access.

Athletics Member NCCAA.

Standardized Tests *Required:* SAT or ACT (for admission).

Costs (2007–08) *Comprehensive fee:* $17,580 includes full-time tuition ($10,720), mandatory fees ($600), and room and board ($6260). Full-time tuition and fees vary according to course load and student level. Part-time tuition: $335 per credit hour. Part-time tuition and fees vary according to course load and student level. *Required fees:* $105 per term part-time. *College room only:* $1500. Room and board charges vary according to board plan and student level.

Financial Aid Of all full-time matriculated undergraduates who enrolled in 2004, 529 applied for aid, 460 were judged to have need, 64 had their need fully met. 197 Federal Work-Study jobs (averaging $429). In 2004, 69 non-need-based awards were made. *Average percent of need met:* 56. *Average financial aid* *package:* $7707. *Average need-based gift aid:* $4484. *Average non-need-based aid:* $10,808. *Average indebtedness upon graduation:* $13,891.

Applying *Options:* early admission, deferred entrance. *Application fee:* $40. *Required:* essay or personal statement, high school transcript, 3 letters of recommendation. *Recommended:* minimum 2.0 GPA, interview.

Director of Admissions Ms. Rachel Kitterman, Office Manager of Undergraduate Admissions, Cincinnati Christian University, 2700 Glenway Avenue, Cincinnati, OH 45204-1799. *Phone:* 800-949-4222 Ext. 8610. *Toll-free phone:* 800-949-4228.

CINCINNATI COLLEGE OF MORTUARY SCIENCE

Cincinnati, Ohio **www.ccms.edu/**

Freshman Application Contact Ms. Pat Leon, Director of Financial Aid, Cincinnati College of Mortuary Science, 645 West North Bend Road, Cincinnati, OH 45224-1462. *Phone:* 513-761-2020. *Fax:* 513-761-3333.

THE CLEVELAND INSTITUTE OF ART

Cleveland, Ohio **www.cia.edu/**

- **Independent** comprehensive, founded 1882
- **Urban** 488-acre campus
- **Endowment** $34.0 million
- **Coed** 482 undergraduate students, 96% full-time, 53% women, 47% men
- **Moderately difficult** entrance level, 71% of applicants were admitted

Undergraduates 464 full-time, 18 part-time. Students come from 29 states and territories, 10 other countries, 32% are from out of state, 5% African American, 5% Asian American or Pacific Islander, 4% Hispanic American, 0.2% Native American, 3% international, 8% transferred in, 21% live on campus. *Retention:* 80% of 2006 full-time freshmen returned.

Freshmen *Admission:* 407 applied, 291 admitted, 97 enrolled. *Average high school GPA:* 3.09. *Test scores:* SAT critical reading scores over 500: 72%; SAT math scores over 500: 76%; ACT scores over 18: 87%; SAT critical reading scores over 600: 29%; SAT math scores over 600: 19%; ACT scores over 24: 23%; SAT critical reading scores over 700: 10%; ACT scores over 30: 2%.

Faculty *Total:* 89, 48% full-time, 73% with terminal degrees. *Student/faculty ratio:* 8:1.

Majors Ceramic arts and ceramics; commercial and advertising art; crafts, folk art and artisanry; drawing; fiber, textile and weaving arts; graphic design; illustration; industrial design; interior design; intermedia/multimedia; medical illustration; metal and jewelry arts; painting; photography; printmaking; sculpture; web page, digital/multimedia and information resources design.

Academics *Calendar:* semesters. *Degrees:* bachelor's and master's. *Special study options:* academic remediation for entering students, advanced placement credit, honors programs, independent study, internships, off-campus study, part-time degree program, services for LD students, study abroad.

Computers on Campus 80 computers/terminals are available on campus for general student use. Students can access the following: campus intranet, free student e-mail accounts, online (class) grades, online (class) registration, online (class) schedules. Campuswide network is available. 100% of college-owned or -operated housing units are wired for high-speed Internet access. Wireless service is available via classrooms.

Student Life *Housing:* on-campus residence required for freshman year. *Options:* coed. Campus housing is leased by the school. Freshman applicants given priority for college housing. *Activities and organizations:* student-run newspaper, Photo Club, Paint Club, Artist for Christ, Student Leadership Council, Student Artist Association, national fraternities, national sororities. *Campus security:* 24-hour emergency response devices and patrols, late-night transport/escort service, controlled dormitory access. *Student services:* health clinic, personal/psychological counseling, women's center, legal services.

Athletics *Intramural sports:* basketball M/W, bowling M/W, cross-country running M/W, football M/W, golf M/W, ice hockey M/W, racquetball M/W, soccer M/W, softball M/W, swimming and diving M/W, tennis M/W, track and field M/W, ultimate Frisbee M/W, volleyball M/W.

Standardized Tests *Required:* SAT or ACT (for admission).

Costs (2007–08) *Comprehensive fee:* $38,859 includes full-time tuition ($28,100), mandatory fees ($1990), and room and board ($8769). Full-time tuition and fees vary according to program. Part-time tuition: $1175 per credit hour. Part-time tuition and fees vary according to course load and program. *Required fees:* $110 per credit hour part-time. *Room and board:* Room and board charges vary according to board plan. *Waivers:* employees or children of employees.

Financial Aid Of all full-time matriculated undergraduates who enrolled in 2007, 410 applied for aid, 376 were judged to have need, 26 had their need fully met. 332 Federal Work-Study jobs (averaging $2125). In 2007, 81 non-need-based awards were made. *Average percent of need met:* 55%. *Average financial aid package:* $18,775. *Average need-based loan:* $5004. *Average need-based gift aid:* $12,706. *Average non-need-based aid:* $15,461. *Average indebtedness upon graduation:* $57,968.

Applying *Options:* electronic application, deferred entrance. *Application fee:* $30. *Required:* essay or personal statement, high school transcript, minimum 2.0 GPA, 1 letter of recommendation, portfolio. *Recommended:* interview. *Application deadlines:* rolling (freshmen), rolling (transfers). *Notification:* continuous (freshmen), continuous (transfers).

Freshman Application Contact Office of Admissions, The Cleveland Institute of Art, 11141 East Boulevard, Cleveland, OH 44106. *Phone:* 216-421-7418. *Toll-free phone:* 800-223-4700. *Fax:* 216-754-3634. *E-mail:* admissions@cia.edu.

See page 2020 for the College Close-Up.

CLEVELAND INSTITUTE OF MUSIC

Cleveland, Ohio **www.cim.edu/**

- **Independent** comprehensive, founded 1920
- **Urban** 488-acre campus
- **Endowment** $33.1 million
- **Coed**
- **Very difficult** entrance level

Ranked as one of the foremost schools of music in the United States, Cleveland Institute of Music (CIM) provides exceptionally talented students from all over the world an outstanding, thoroughly professional education in the art of music. Graduates are routinely admitted to leading graduate schools, win major competitions, and occupy important performance and teaching positions throughout the world.

Faculty *Student/faculty ratio:* 7:1.

Academics *Calendar:* semesters. *Degrees:* certificates, bachelor's, master's, doctoral, and postbachelor's certificates.

Student Life *Campus security:* 24-hour emergency response devices and patrols, late-night transport/escort service, controlled dormitory access.

Standardized Tests *Required for some:* SAT or ACT (for admission).

Financial Aid Of all full-time matriculated undergraduates who enrolled in 2007, 187 applied for aid, 147 were judged to have need, 36 had their need fully met. 86 Federal Work-Study jobs (averaging $1689). 30 state and other part-time jobs (averaging $1792). In 2007, 87 non-need-based awards were made. *Average percent of need met:* 73. *Average financial aid package:* $20,588. *Average need-based loan:* $6395. *Average need-based gift aid:* $14,466. *Average non-need-based aid:* $15,486. *Average indebtedness upon graduation:* $23,657. *Financial aid deadline:* 2/15.

Applying *Options:* early admission, deferred entrance. *Application fee:* $100. *Required:* essay or personal statement, high school transcript, 2 letters of recommendation, audition. *Recommended:* interview.

Freshman Application Contact Mr. William Fay, Director of Admission, Cleveland Institute of Music, 11021 East Boulevard, Cleveland, OH 44106-1776. *Phone:* 216-795-3107. *Fax:* 216-791-1530. *E-mail:* cimadmission@po.cwru.edu.

See page 2022 for the College Close-Up.

CLEVELAND STATE UNIVERSITY

Cleveland, Ohio **www.csuohio.edu/**

- **State-supported** university, founded 1964
- **Urban** 70-acre campus with easy access to Akron
- **Endowment** $26.4 million
- **Coed** 9,798 undergraduate students, 71% full-time, 56% women, 44% men
- **Moderately difficult** entrance level, 73% of applicants were admitted

Undergraduates 6,973 full-time, 2,825 part-time. Students come from 23 states and territories, 75 other countries, 2% are from out of state, 22% African American, 3% Asian American or Pacific Islander, 3% Hispanic American, 0.3% Native American, 2% international, 14% transferred in, 6% live on campus.

Freshmen *Admission:* 3,752 applied, 2,742 admitted, 1,141 enrolled. *Average high school GPA:* 2.0. *Test scores:* SAT critical reading scores over 500: 40%; SAT math scores over 500: 44%; ACT scores over 18: 66%; SAT critical reading scores over 600: 11%; SAT math scores over 600: 13%; ACT scores over 24: 19%; SAT critical reading scores over 700: 2%; SAT math scores over 700: 2%; ACT scores over 30: 1%.

Faculty *Total:* 1,035, 55% full-time, 66% with terminal degrees. *Student/faculty ratio:* 16:1.

Majors Accounting; anthropology; applied art; art; audiology and hearing sciences; bioethics/medical ethics; biology/biological sciences; biology/biotechnology laboratory technician; business administration and management; business administration, management and operations related; business/managerial economics; business statistics; chemical engineering; chemistry; civil engineering; communication/speech communication and rhetoric; community health services counseling; community organization and advocacy; computer and information sciences; computer engineering; computer science; dance; dramatic/theater arts; early childhood education; economics; education; educational leadership and administration; education related; electrical, electronic and communications engineering technology; electrical, electronics and communications engineering; elementary education; engineering; engineering mechanics; engineering related; engineering science; engineering technology; English; environmental studies; finance; French; general studies; geology/earth science; Germanic languages; gerontology; health professions related; industrial engineering; industrial technology; information science/studies; interdisciplinary studies; international relations and affairs; kinesiology and exercise science; labor and industrial relations; liberal arts and sciences/liberal studies; linguistics; marketing/marketing management; mathematics; mechanical engineering; mechanical engineering technologies related; metallurgical engineering; middle school education; multi-/interdisciplinary studies related; music; nursing (registered nurse training); occupational therapy; philosophy; physical education teaching and coaching; physical therapy; physics; political science and government; pre-nursing studies; psychology; public administration; public relations/image management; religious studies; science, technology and society; social sciences; social sciences related; social work; sociology; Spanish; special education; sport and fitness administration/management; urban studies/affairs.

Academics *Calendar:* semesters. *Degrees:* certificates, bachelor's, master's, doctoral, first professional, post-master's, postbachelor's, and first professional certificates. *Special study options:* academic remediation for entering students, accelerated degree program, adult/continuing education programs, advanced placement credit, cooperative education, English as a second language, freshman honors college, honors programs, independent study, internships, off-campus study, part-time degree program, student-designed majors, study abroad, summer session for credit. *ROTC:* Army (c), Navy (c), Air Force (c).

Computers on Campus 600 computers/terminals are available on campus for general student use. Students can access the following: online (class) registration. Campuswide network is available.

Student Life *Housing options:* coed. Campus housing is university owned. Freshman campus housing is guaranteed. *Activities and organizations:* drama/theater group, student-run newspaper, radio station, choral group, honor societies, International Student Association, Chinese Student Association, national fraternities, national sororities. *Campus security:* 24-hour emergency response devices and patrols, student patrols, late-night transport/escort service, controlled dormitory access. *Student services:* health clinic, personal/psychological counseling, women's center.

Athletics Member NCAA. All Division I. *Intercollegiate sports:* baseball M (s), basketball M (s)/W (s), cross-country running W (s), fencing M (s)/W (s), golf M (s), soccer M (s), softball W (s), swimming and diving M (s)/W (s), tennis W (s), track and field W (s), volleyball W (s), wrestling M (s). *Intramural sports:* badminton M/W, basketball M/W, bowling M/W, cross-country running M/W, fencing M/W, field hockey M/W, football M, golf M/W, racquetball M/W, sailing M/W, soccer M/W, swimming and diving M/W, tennis M/W, track and field M/W, volleyball M/W, water polo M/W, weight lifting M (c)/W (c), wrestling M.

Standardized Tests *Required:* SAT or ACT (for admission).

Costs (2007–08) *Tuition:* state resident $7920 full-time, $330 per credit hour part-time; nonresident $10,664 full-time, $444 per credit hour part-time. Full-time tuition and fees vary according to program. Part-time tuition and fees vary according to program. *Room and board:* $8100; room only: $5200. Room and board charges vary according to board plan and housing facility. *Payment plan:* installment. *Waivers:* senior citizens and employees or children of employees.

Financial Aid Of all full-time matriculated undergraduates who enrolled in 2007, 5,860 applied for aid, 5,298 were judged to have need, 523 had their need fully met. In 2007, 837 non-need-based awards were made. *Average percent of need met:* 47%. *Average financial aid package:* $8050. *Average need-based loan:* $4359. *Average need-based gift aid:* $5363. *Average non-need-based aid:* $9555.

Applying *Options:* electronic application, early action, deferred entrance. *Application fee:* $30. *Required:* high school transcript. *Application deadlines:* 8/15 (freshmen), 7/15 (transfers), 5/1 (early action). *Notification:* continuous (freshmen), continuous (transfers).

Freshman Application Contact Undergraduate Admissions Office, Cleveland State University, Rhodes Tower West, Room 204, 1806 East 22nd Street, Cleveland, OH 44114. *Phone:* 216-687-2100. *Toll-free phone:* 888-CSU-OHIO. *Fax:* 216-687-9210. *E-mail:* admissions@csuohio.edu.

COLLEGE OF MOUNT ST. JOSEPH

Cincinnati, Ohio **www.msj.edu/**

- **Independent Roman Catholic** comprehensive, founded 1920
- **Suburban** 92-acre campus
- **Endowment** $24.5 million
- **Coed** 1,938 undergraduate students, 70% full-time, 68% women, 32% men
- **Moderately difficult** entrance level, 72% of applicants were admitted

Undergraduates 1,351 full-time, 587 part-time. Students come from 25 states and territories, 4 other countries, 14% are from out of state, 9% African American, 0.6% Asian American or Pacific Islander, 0.9% Hispanic American, 0.4% Native American, 0.2% international, 9% transferred in, 22% live on campus. *Retention:* 76% of 2006 full-time freshmen returned.

Freshmen *Admission:* 1,153 applied, 835 admitted, 345 enrolled. *Average high school GPA:* 3.21. *Test scores:* SAT critical reading scores over 500: 43%; SAT math scores over 500: 48%; ACT scores over 18: 88%; SAT critical reading scores over 600: 9%; SAT math scores over 600: 12%; ACT scores over 24: 30%; SAT critical reading scores over 700: 1%; SAT math scores over 700: 1%; ACT scores over 30: 2%.

Faculty *Total:* 244, 48% full-time, 50% with terminal degrees. *Student/faculty ratio:* 11:1.

Majors Accounting; adult development and aging; art; art teacher education; athletic training; biochemistry; biology/biological sciences; business administration and management; chemistry; communication/speech communication and rhetoric; computer and information sciences; criminology; early childhood education; English; fine/studio arts; graphic design; history; interior design; legal assistant/paralegal; liberal arts and sciences/liberal studies; mathematics; middle school education; music; natural sciences; nursing (registered nurse training); pastoral studies/counseling; psychology; religious education; religious studies; social work; sociology; special education; sport and fitness administration/management.

Academics *Calendar:* semesters. *Degrees:* certificates, associate, bachelor's, master's, doctoral, and postbachelor's certificates. *Special study options:* academic remediation for entering students, accelerated degree program, adult/continuing education programs, advanced placement credit, cooperative education, distance learning, double majors, honors programs, independent study, internships, off-campus study, part-time degree program, services for LD students, study abroad, summer session for credit. *ROTC:* Army (c), Air Force (c).

Computers on Campus 278 computers/terminals are available on campus for general student use. Students can access the following: computer help desk, free student e-mail accounts, online (class) grades, online (class) registration, online (class) schedules, computer-aided instruction. Campuswide network is available. 100% of college-owned or -operated housing units are wired for high-speed Internet access. Wireless service is available via entire campus.

Student Life *Housing:* on-campus residence required through sophomore year. *Options:* coed. Campus housing is university owned. Freshman applicants given priority for college housing. *Activities and organizations:* drama/theater group, student-run newspaper, radio station, choral group, marching band, Student Government Association, Black Student Union, Residence Hall Council, Campus Activities Board, Campus Ambassadors. *Campus security:* 24-hour emergency response devices and patrols, late-night transport/escort service. *Student services:* health clinic, personal/psychological counseling, women's center.

Athletics Member NCAA. All Division III. *Intercollegiate sports:* baseball M, basketball M/W, cheerleading W, cross-country running M/W, football M, golf M/W, lacrosse M, soccer M/W, softball W, tennis M/W, track and field M/W, volleyball W, wrestling M. *Intramural sports:* basketball M/W, racquetball M/W, soccer M/W, softball M/W, table tennis M/W, tennis M/W, volleyball M/W.

Standardized Tests *Required:* SAT or ACT (for admission).

Costs (2007–08) *Comprehensive fee:* $27,700 includes full-time tuition ($20,400), mandatory fees ($800), and room and board ($6500). Part-time tuition: $450 per semester hour. *Required fees:* $200 per semester part-time. *College room only:* $3200.

Financial Aid Of all full-time matriculated undergraduates who enrolled in 2005, 1,278 applied for aid, 909 were judged to have need, 485 had their need fully met. 188 Federal Work-Study jobs (averaging $1431). 71 state and other part-time jobs (averaging $1397). In 2005, 163 non-need-based awards were made. *Average* *percent of need met:* 90%. *Average financial aid package:* $15,832. *Average need-based loan:* $4737. *Average need-based gift aid:* $6998. *Average non-need-based aid:* $6990. *Average indebtedness upon graduation:* $13,400.

Applying *Options:* electronic application, deferred entrance. *Application fee:* $25. *Required:* high school transcript. *Required for some:* 1 letter of recommendation, interview. *Recommended:* minimum 2.5 GPA, minimum SAT score of 1028 or ACT score of 21. *Application deadlines:* 8/15 (freshmen), 8/1 (transfers). *Notification:* continuous (freshmen), continuous (transfers).

Freshman Application Contact Ms. Peggy Minnich, Director of Admission, College of Mount St. Joseph, 5701 Delhi Road, Cincinnati, OH 45233-1672. *Phone:* 513-244-4531. *Toll-free phone:* 800-654-9314. *Fax:* 513-244-4629. *E-mail:* admissions@mail.msj.edu.

See page 2024 for the College Close-Up.

THE COLLEGE OF WOOSTER

Wooster, Ohio **www.wooster.edu/**

- **Independent** 4-year, founded 1866, affiliated with Presbyterian Church (U.S.A.)
- **Small-town** 240-acre campus with easy access to Cleveland
- **Endowment** $227.1 million
- **Coed**
- **Moderately difficult** entrance level

The College of Wooster acts on this conviction: everyone, not only "honors" students, can benefit from an honors education. At Wooster, that philosophy enhances the entire college experience. Small classes and accessible faculty members who are committed to teaching ensure individual attention for every student—from First-Year Seminar to senior year, when students work one-on-one with a faculty adviser on an Independent Study project that pulls together everything they have learned in their first three years at Wooster.

Faculty *Student/faculty ratio:* 12:1.

Academics *Calendar:* semesters. *Degree:* bachelor's.

Student Life *Campus security:* 24-hour emergency response devices and patrols, student patrols, late-night transport/escort service, controlled dormitory access.

Athletics Member NCAA. All Division III.

Standardized Tests *Required:* SAT or ACT (for admission).

Costs (2008–09) *Comprehensive fee:* $42,420 includes full-time tuition ($33,770) and room and board ($8650). *College room only:* $3860.

Financial Aid Of all full-time matriculated undergraduates who enrolled in 2006, 1,167 applied for aid, 1,013 were judged to have need, 892 had their need fully met. In 2006, 760 non-need-based awards were made. *Average percent of need met:* 95. *Average financial aid package:* $24,981. *Average need-based loan:* $4364. *Average need-based gift aid:* $18,821. *Average non-need-based aid:* $13,017. *Average indebtedness upon graduation:* $23,527. *Financial aid deadline:* 9/1.

Applying *Options:* electronic application, early admission, early decision, deferred entrance. *Application fee:* $40. *Required:* essay or personal statement, high school transcript, 2 letters of recommendation. *Recommended:* interview.

Freshman Application Contact Mary Karen Vellines, Vice President for Enrollment, The College of Wooster, 847 College Avenue, Wooster, OH 44691. *Phone:* 330-263-2270 Ext. 2118. *Toll-free phone:* 800-877-9905. *Fax:* 330-263-2621. *E-mail:* admissions@wooster.edu.

See page 2026 for the College Close-Up.

COLUMBUS COLLEGE OF ART & DESIGN

Columbus, Ohio **www.ccad.edu/**

- **Independent** 4-year, founded 1879
- **Urban** 10-acre campus
- **Endowment** $9.7 million
- **Coed** 1,623 undergraduate students, 81% full-time, 59% women, 41% men
- **Moderately difficult** entrance level, 76% of applicants were admitted

Undergraduates 1,308 full-time, 315 part-time. Students come from 36 states and territories, 18 other countries, 21% are from out of state, 8% African American, 2% Asian American or Pacific Islander, 3% Hispanic American, 0.5% Native American, 5% international, 4% transferred in, 23% live on campus. *Retention:* 77% of 2006 full-time freshmen returned.

Freshmen *Admission:* 805 applied, 613 admitted, 319 enrolled. *Average high school GPA:* 2.8. *Test scores:* SAT critical reading scores over 500: 48%; SAT math scores over 500: 43%; SAT writing scores over 500: 47%; ACT scores over 18: 72%; SAT critical reading scores over 600: 18%; SAT math scores over 600: 11%; SAT writing scores over 600: 13%; ACT scores over 24: 19%; SAT math scores over 700: 2%; SAT writing scores over 700: 1%.

Faculty *Total:* 187, 43% full-time, 41% with terminal degrees. *Student/faculty ratio:* 12:1.

Majors Commercial and advertising art; fashion/apparel design; film/video and photographic arts related; fine arts related; illustration; industrial design; interior design.

Academics *Calendar:* semesters. *Degree:* bachelor's. *Special study options:* academic remediation for entering students, advanced placement credit, double majors, English as a second language, independent study, internships, off-campus study, part-time degree program, services for LD students, summer session for credit.

Computers on Campus 238 computers/terminals are available on campus for general student use. Students can access the following: campus intranet, computer help desk, free student e-mail accounts, online (class) grades, online (class) schedules, online library. Campuswide network is available. 100% of college-owned or -operated housing units are wired for high-speed Internet access. Wireless service is available via classrooms, computer centers, computer labs, dorm rooms, learning centers, libraries, student centers.

Student Life *Housing:* on-campus residence required for freshman year. *Options:* coed. Campus housing is university owned and leased by the school. Freshman applicants given priority for college housing. *Activities and organizations:* Student Government Association, Gay Straight Student Alliance, Sanctuary, African Cultural Association, Environmental Awareness Society. *Campus security:* 24-hour emergency response devices and patrols, late-night transport/escort service, controlled dormitory access. *Student services:* personal/psychological counseling, legal services.

Athletics *Intramural sports:* basketball M/W, soccer M/W, volleyball M/W.

Standardized Tests *Required:* SAT or ACT (for admission).

Costs (2007–08) *Comprehensive fee:* $29,062 includes full-time tuition ($21,768), mandatory fees ($644), and room and board ($6650). Part-time tuition: $907 per credit. Part-time tuition and fees vary according to course load. *Required fees:* $322 per term part-time. *Room and board:* Room and board charges vary according to housing facility and student level. *Payment plans:* installment, deferred payment. *Waivers:* employees or children of employees.

Financial Aid Of all full-time matriculated undergraduates who enrolled in 2006, 1,216 applied for aid, 1,066 were judged to have need, 212 had their need fully met. 148 Federal Work-Study jobs (averaging $3250). 337 state and other part-time jobs (averaging $3000). In 2006, 254 non-need-based awards were made. *Average percent of need met:* 67%. *Average financial aid package:* $14,881. *Average need-based loan:* $5539. *Average need-based gift aid:* $10,080. *Average non-need-based aid:* $10,629. *Average indebtedness upon graduation:* $31,349.

Applying *Options:* deferred entrance. *Application fee:* $25. *Required:* essay or personal statement, high school transcript, minimum 2.0 GPA, 1 letter of recommendation, portfolio. *Recommended:* interview. *Application deadlines:* rolling (freshmen), rolling (transfers). *Notification:* continuous (freshmen), continuous (transfers).

Freshman Application Contact Columbus College of Art & Design, 107 North Ninth Street, Columbus, OH 43215-1758. *Phone:* 614-224-9101. *Toll-free phone:* 877-997-2223. *Fax:* 614-232-8344. *E-mail:* admissions@ccad.edu.

DEFIANCE COLLEGE

Defiance, Ohio **www.defiance.edu/**

- **Independent** comprehensive, founded 1850, affiliated with United Church of Christ
- **Small-town** 150-acre campus with easy access to Toledo
- **Endowment** $12.9 million
- **Coed** 893 undergraduate students, 81% full-time, 53% women, 47% men
- **Moderately difficult** entrance level, 80% of applicants were admitted

Undergraduates 724 full-time, 169 part-time. Students come from 14 states and territories, 3 other countries, 16% are from out of state, 7% African American, 0.1% Asian American or Pacific Islander, 4% Hispanic American, 0.2% Native American, 0.3% international, 5% transferred in, 55% live on campus. *Retention:* 64% of 2006 full-time freshmen returned.

Freshmen *Admission:* 922 applied, 740 admitted, 231 enrolled. *Average high school GPA:* 3.11. *Test scores:* SAT critical reading scores over 500: 43%; SAT math scores over 500: 38%; SAT writing scores over 500: 43%; ACT scores over 18: 80%; SAT critical reading scores over 600: 14%; SAT math scores over 600:

9%; SAT writing scores over 600: 14%; ACT scores over 24: 18%; SAT critical reading scores over 700: 2%; SAT math scores over 700: 2%; ACT scores over 30: 1%.

Faculty *Total:* 98, 45% full-time, 39% with terminal degrees. *Student/faculty ratio:* 12:1.

Majors Accounting; art; art teacher education; athletic training; biology/biological sciences; business administration and management; business teacher education; clinical laboratory science/medical technology; computer science; criminal justice/law enforcement administration; criminal justice/police science; ecology; education; elementary education; English; environmental studies; forensic science and technology; health teacher education; history; kinesiology and exercise science; liberal arts and sciences/liberal studies; mass communication/media; mathematics; natural sciences; physical education teaching and coaching; physical sciences; pre-dentistry studies; pre-law studies; pre-medical studies; pre-veterinary studies; psychology; religious education; religious studies; science teacher education; secondary education; social sciences; social work; sport and fitness administration/management.

Academics *Calendar:* semesters. *Degrees:* associate, bachelor's, and master's. *Special study options:* academic remediation for entering students, adult/continuing education programs, advanced placement credit, cooperative education, distance learning, double majors, external degree program, honors programs, independent study, internships, off-campus study, part-time degree program, student-designed majors, study abroad, summer session for credit.

Computers on Campus 16 computers/terminals are available on campus for general student use. Students can access the following: computer help desk, free student e-mail accounts, online (class) grades, online (class) schedules. Campuswide network is available. Wireless service is available via entire campus.

Student Life *Housing:* on-campus residence required through junior year. *Options:* coed. Campus housing is university owned. Freshman campus housing is guaranteed. *Activities and organizations:* drama/theater group, student-run newspaper, choral group, Campus Activities Board, Criminal Justice Society, Student Senate, Black Action Student Association, DC Players, national fraternities, national sororities. *Campus security:* late-night transport/escort service, controlled dormitory access. *Student services:* health clinic, personal/psychological counseling.

Athletics Member NCAA. All Division III. *Intercollegiate sports:* baseball M, basketball M/W, cross-country running M/W, football M, golf M/W, soccer M/W, softball W, tennis M/W, track and field M/W, volleyball W. *Intramural sports:* baseball M, basketball M/W, bowling M/W, field hockey M/W, football M/W, racquetball M/W, soccer M/W, softball M/W, table tennis M/W, volleyball M/W, weight lifting M.

Standardized Tests *Required:* SAT or ACT (for admission).

Costs (2008–09) *One-time required fee:* $75. *Comprehensive fee:* $28,980 includes full-time tuition ($21,310), mandatory fees ($520), and room and board ($7150). Part-time tuition: $345 per credit hour. *Required fees:* $70 per term part-time. *College room only:* $3850.

Financial Aid Of all full-time matriculated undergraduates who enrolled in 2007, 697 applied for aid, 658 were judged to have need, 137 had their need fully met. 340 Federal Work-Study jobs (averaging $1809). 116 state and other part-time jobs (averaging $1733). In 2007, 52 non-need-based awards were made. *Average percent of need met:* 76%. *Average financial aid package:* $16,219. *Average need-based loan:* $4435. *Average need-based gift aid:* $5319. *Average non-need-based aid:* $7979. *Average indebtedness upon graduation:* $25,814.

Applying *Options:* electronic application, deferred entrance. *Application fee:* $25. *Required:* high school transcript, minimum 2.25 GPA. *Required for some:* essay or personal statement, interview. *Recommended:* letters of recommendation, interview. *Application deadlines:* 8/15 (freshmen), 8/15 (transfers). *Notification:* continuous (freshmen), continuous (transfers).

Freshman Application Contact Defiance College, 701 North Clinton Street, Defiance, OH 43512-1610. *Phone:* 419-783-2365. *Toll-free phone:* 800-520-4632 Ext. 2359.

DENISON UNIVERSITY

Granville, Ohio

www.denison.edu/

- **Independent** 4-year, founded 1831
- **Small-town** 900-acre campus with easy access to Columbus
- **Endowment** $533.2 million
- **Coed** 2,242 undergraduate students, 99% full-time, 57% women, 43% men
- **Very difficult** entrance level, 39% of applicants were admitted

Denison University attracts intellectually serious, well-rounded students from throughout the U.S. and twenty-seven other countries. Its model honors program, unique Summer Scholars Program that provides exceptional collaborative research opportunities with faculty members, state-of-the-art science facilities, and leadership training through 150 campus organizations provide its students with a challenging and enriching college experience.

Undergraduates 2,211 full-time, 31 part-time. Students come from 50 states and territories, 27 other countries, 64% are from out of state, 5% African American, 3% Asian American or Pacific Islander, 2% Hispanic American, 0.4% Native American, 4% international, 1% transferred in, 99% live on campus. *Retention:* 93% of 2006 full-time freshmen returned.

Freshmen *Admission:* 5,196 applied, 2,033 admitted, 586 enrolled. *Average high school GPA:* 3.6. *Test scores:* SAT critical reading scores over 500: 98%; SAT math scores over 500: 97%; ACT scores over 18: 100%; SAT critical reading scores over 600: 70%; SAT math scores over 600: 68%; ACT scores over 24: 92%; SAT critical reading scores over 700: 23%; SAT math scores over 700: 16%; ACT scores over 30: 35%.

Faculty *Total:* 212, 91% full-time, 93% with terminal degrees. *Student/faculty ratio:* 10:1.

Majors African-American/Black studies; anthropology; area studies; art; art history, criticism and conservation; Asian studies (East); biochemistry; biology/biological sciences; chemistry; classics and languages, literatures and linguistics; computer science; creative writing; dance; dramatic/theater arts; economics; English; environmental studies; film/cinema studies; fine/studio arts; French; geology/earth science; German; history; international relations and affairs; Latin American studies; mass communication/media; mathematics; music; organizational behavior; philosophy; physical education teaching and coaching; physics; political science and government; psychology; religious studies; sociology; Spanish; speech and rhetoric; women's studies.

Academics *Calendar:* semesters plus optional May term. *Degree:* bachelor's. *Special study options:* advanced placement credit, cooperative education, double majors, honors programs, independent study, internships, off-campus study, part-time degree program, services for LD students, student-designed majors, study abroad. *ROTC:* Army (c). *Unusual degree programs:* 3-2 engineering with Case Western Reserve University, Columbia University, Rensselaer Polytechnic Institute, Washington University in St. Louis; forestry with Duke University; natural resources with University of Michigan; occupational therapy with Washington University in St. Louis; environmental management, dentistry with Case Western Reserve University; medical technology with Rochester General Hospital.

Computers on Campus 587 computers/terminals are available on campus for general student use. Campuswide network is available.

Student Life *Housing:* on-campus residence required through senior year. *Options:* coed, men-only, women-only. Campus housing is university owned. Freshman campus housing is guaranteed. *Activities and organizations:* drama/theater group, student-run newspaper, radio and television station, choral group, Community Association, Black Student Union, International Student Association, Student Activities Committee, national fraternities, national sororities. *Campus security:* 24-hour emergency response devices and patrols, student patrols, late-night transport/escort service, controlled dormitory access, security lighting, escort service. *Student services:* health clinic, personal/psychological counseling, women's center.

Athletics Member NCAA. All Division III. *Intercollegiate sports:* baseball M, basketball M/W, crew M (c), cross-country running M/W, equestrian sports M (c)/W (c), field hockey W, football M, golf M, ice hockey M (c), lacrosse M/W, riflery M (c)/W (c), rugby M (c)/W (c), sailing M (c)/W (c), skiing (downhill) M (c)/W (c), soccer M/W, softball W, squash M (c)/W (c), swimming and diving M/W, tennis M/W, track and field M/W, volleyball W. *Intramural sports:* badminton M (c)/W (c), basketball M/W, cheerleading M/W, crew W (c), fencing M (c)/W (c), football M/W, golf M/W, lacrosse M (c), racquetball M/W, soccer M/W, softball M/W, squash M/W, table tennis M/W, tennis M/W, ultimate Frisbee M/W, volleyball M (c)/W, water polo M/W, weight lifting M/W.

Standardized Tests *Required for some:* SAT or ACT (for admission).

Costs (2007–08) *Comprehensive fee:* $41,580 includes full-time tuition ($32,160), mandatory fees ($850), and room and board ($8570). Part-time tuition: $1000 per semester hour. Part-time tuition and fees vary according to course load. *College room only:* $4750. Room and board charges vary according to housing facility. *Payment plan:* installment. *Waivers:* employees or children of employees.

Financial Aid Of all full-time matriculated undergraduates who enrolled in 2007, 1,162 applied for aid, 941 were judged to have need, 375 had their need fully met. 391 Federal Work-Study jobs (averaging $944). 1,308 state and other part-time jobs (averaging $2150). In 2007, 1,129 non-need-based awards were made. *Average percent of need met:* 98%. *Average financial aid package:* $27,693. *Average need-based loan:* $4742. *Average need-based gift aid:* $21,895. *Average non-need-based aid:* $13,502.

Applying *Options:* early admission, early decision, deferred entrance. *Application fee:* $40. *Required:* essay or personal statement, high school transcript, 2 letters of recommendation. *Recommended:* interview. *Application deadlines:* 1/15 (freshmen), 7/1 (transfers). *Early decision deadline:* 11/1. *Notification:* 4/1 (freshmen), continuous (transfers), 11/15 (early decision).

Freshman Application Contact Mr. Perry Robinson, Director of Admissions, Denison University, Box H, Granville, OH 43023. *Phone:* 740-587-6276. *Toll-free phone:* 800-DENISON. *E-mail:* admissions@denison.edu.

See page 2028 for the College Close-Up.

DeVry University
Cleveland, Ohio

DeVry University
Columbus, Ohio www.devry.edu/

- **Proprietary** comprehensive, founded 1952, part of DeVry University
- **Urban** 21-acre campus
- **Coed** 2,406 undergraduate students, 61% full-time, 38% women, 62% men
- **Minimally difficult** entrance level

Undergraduates 1,472 full-time, 934 part-time. 2% are from out of state, 24% African American, 2% Asian American or Pacific Islander, 1% Hispanic American, 0.3% Native American, 0.1% international, 13% transferred in. *Retention:* 52% of 2006 full-time freshmen returned.

Freshmen *Admission:* 509 enrolled.

Faculty *Total:* 100, 50% full-time. *Student/faculty ratio:* 28:1.

Majors Biomedical technology; business administration and management; business administration, management and operations related; computer engineering technology; computer systems analysis; computer systems networking and telecommunications; electrical, electronic and communications engineering technology; health information/medical records technology.

Academics *Calendar:* semesters. *Degrees:* associate, bachelor's, and master's. *Special study options:* academic remediation for entering students, accelerated degree program, adult/continuing education programs, advanced placement credit, distance learning, part-time degree program, services for LD students, summer session for credit. *ROTC:* Army (c).

Computers on Campus 408 computers/terminals are available on campus for general student use. Students can access the following: online (class) registration. Campuswide network is available.

Student Life *Housing:* college housing not available. *Activities and organizations:* Institute for Electrical and Electronic Engineers, American Production and Inventory Control Society, Association of Information Technology Professionals, Tau Alpha Pi, Asian-American Association or Prism. *Campus security:* late-night transport/escort service, security at evening activities.

Costs (2008–09) *Tuition:* $13,810 full-time, $515 per credit part-time. *Required fees:* $180 full-time.

Financial Aid Of all full-time matriculated undergraduates who enrolled in 2002, 2,500 applied for aid, 2,392 were judged to have need, 99 had their need fully met. In 2002, 230 non-need-based awards were made. *Average percent of need met:* 45%. *Average financial aid package:* $9184. *Average need-based loan:* $5820. *Average need-based gift aid:* $4181. *Average non-need-based aid:* $6932.

Applying *Options:* electronic application, early admission, deferred entrance. *Application fee:* $50. *Required:* high school transcript, interview. *Application deadlines:* rolling (freshmen), rolling (transfers). *Notification:* continuous (freshmen), continuous (transfers).

Freshman Application Contact DeVry University, 1350 Alum Creek Drive, Columbus, OH 43209-2705.

DeVry University
Seven Hills, Ohio

Franciscan University of Steubenville
Steubenville, Ohio www.franciscan.edu/

- **Independent Roman Catholic** comprehensive, founded 1946
- **Suburban** 124-acre campus with easy access to Pittsburgh
- **Endowment** $32.6 million
- **Coed** 2,033 undergraduate students, 93% full-time, 60% women, 40% men
- **Moderately difficult** entrance level, 81% of applicants were admitted

Undergraduates 1,889 full-time, 144 part-time. Students come from 51 states and territories, 13 other countries, 78% are from out of state, 0.5% African American, 1% Asian American or Pacific Islander, 1% Hispanic American, 0.5% Native American, 1% international, 9% transferred in, 70% live on campus. *Retention:* 88% of 2006 full-time freshmen returned.

Freshmen *Admission:* 1,273 applied, 1,027 admitted, 442 enrolled. *Average high school GPA:* 3.60. *Test scores:* SAT critical reading scores over 500: 89%; SAT math scores over 500: 84%; ACT scores over 18: 99%; SAT critical reading scores over 600: 50%; SAT math scores over 600: 41%; ACT scores over 24: 54%; SAT critical reading scores over 700: 14%; SAT math scores over 700: 6%; ACT scores over 30: 14%.

Faculty *Total:* 199, 58% full-time, 47% with terminal degrees. *Student/faculty ratio:* 15:1.

Majors Accounting; anthropology; biology/biological sciences; business administration and management; chemistry; child development; classics and languages, literatures and linguistics; communication/speech communication and rhetoric; computer and information sciences; computer science; dramatic/theater arts; economics; elementary education; English; French; general studies; German; history; humanities; legal studies; mathematics; nursing (registered nurse training); philosophy; political science and government; psychiatric/mental health services technology; psychology; religious education; religious/sacred music; social work; sociology; Spanish; theology.

Academics *Calendar:* semesters. *Degrees:* associate, bachelor's, and master's. *Special study options:* accelerated degree program, adult/continuing education programs, advanced placement credit, distance learning, double majors, honors programs, independent study, internships, part-time degree program, services for LD students, study abroad, summer session for credit. *ROTC:* Army (c). *Unusual degree programs:* 3-2 business administration.

Computers on Campus 126 computers/terminals are available on campus for general student use. Students can access the following: campus intranet, computer help desk, free student e-mail accounts, online (class) grades, online (class) registration, online (class) schedules. Campuswide network is available.

Student Life *Housing:* on-campus residence required through junior year. *Options:* men-only, women-only. Campus housing is university owned and leased by the school. Freshman campus housing is guaranteed. *Activities and organizations:* drama/theater group, student-run newspaper, radio station, choral group, Franciscan University Student Association, Student Activities Board, Human Life Concerns, Works of Mercy, Troubadour (student newspaper), national sororities. *Campus security:* 24-hour emergency response devices and patrols, student patrols, late-night transport/escort service. *Student services:* health clinic, personal/psychological counseling.

Athletics Member NCAA. *Intercollegiate sports:* baseball M, basketball M/W, cross-country running M/W, rugby M, soccer M/W, softball W, track and field M/W, volleyball W. *Intramural sports:* basketball M/W, racquetball M/W, soccer M/W, softball M/W, tennis M/W, ultimate Frisbee M/W, volleyball M/W, weight lifting M/W, wrestling M.

Standardized Tests *Required:* SAT or ACT (for admission).

Costs (2007–08) *Comprehensive fee:* $24,480 includes full-time tuition ($17,800), mandatory fees ($380), and room and board ($6300). Part-time tuition: $595 per credit hour. Part-time tuition and fees vary according to class time and course load. *Required fees:* $15 per credit hour part-time. *Room and board:* Room and board charges vary according to board plan. *Payment plan:* installment. *Waivers:* employees or children of employees.

Financial Aid Of all full-time matriculated undergraduates who enrolled in 2007, 1,503 applied for aid, 1,251 were judged to have need, 155 had their need fully met. 320 Federal Work-Study jobs (averaging $568). 665 state and other part-time jobs (averaging $1095). In 2007, 446 non-need-based awards were made. *Average percent of need met:* 59%. *Average financial aid package:* $11,511. *Average need-based loan:* $4728. *Average need-based gift aid:* $6676. *Average non-need-based aid:* $8460. *Average indebtedness upon graduation:* $29,341.

Applying *Options:* early admission, deferred entrance. *Application fee:* $20. *Required:* essay or personal statement, high school transcript, minimum 2.4 GPA. *Required for some:* letters of recommendation. *Recommended:* interview. *Application deadlines:* rolling (freshmen), rolling (transfers). *Notification:* continuous (freshmen), continuous (transfers).

Freshman Application Contact Mrs. Margaret Weber, Director of Admissions, Franciscan University of Steubenville, 1235 University Boulevard, Steubenville, OH 43952-1763. *Phone:* 740-283-6226. *Toll-free phone:* 800-783-6220. *Fax:* 740-284-5456. *E-mail:* admissions@franciscan.edu.

See page 2030 for the College Close-Up.

FRANKLIN UNIVERSITY

Columbus, Ohio **www.franklin.edu/**

Freshman Application Contact Mr. Tracy Austin, Chief Student Officer, Franklin University, 201 South Grant Avenue, Columbus, OH 43215. *Phone:* 614-797-4700. *Toll-free phone:* 877-341-6300. *Fax:* 614-224-8027. *E-mail:* info@franklin.edu.

GOD'S BIBLE SCHOOL AND COLLEGE

Cincinnati, Ohio **www.gbs.edu/**

- **Independent interdenominational** 4-year, founded 1900
- **Urban** 14-acre campus
- **Coed**
- 88% of applicants were admitted

Faculty *Student/faculty ratio:* 13:1.
Academics *Calendar:* semesters. *Degrees:* associate and bachelor's.
Student Life *Campus security:* 24-hour patrols.
Standardized Tests *Required:* SAT or ACT (for admission). *Recommended:* SAT (for admission).
Costs (2007–08) *Comprehensive fee:* $8280 includes full-time tuition ($4200), mandatory fees ($780), and room and board ($3300). Part-time tuition: $162 per credit hour. *Required fees:* $28 per credit hour part-time.
Applying *Application fee:* $25. *Required:* high school transcript, 3 letters of recommendation, interview.
Freshman Application Contact Mrs. Lisa Profitt, Director of Admissions, God's Bible School and College, 1810 Young Street, Cincinnati, OH 45202-6838. *Phone:* 513-721-7944 Ext. 205. *Toll-free phone:* 800-486-4637. *Fax:* 513-721-3971. *E-mail:* lprofitt@gbs.edu.

HEIDELBERG COLLEGE

Tiffin, Ohio **www.heidelberg.edu/**

- **Independent** comprehensive, founded 1850, affiliated with United Church of Christ
- **Small-town** 115-acre campus
- **Endowment** $35.5 million
- **Coed** 1,397 undergraduate students, 84% full-time, 50% women, 50% men
- **Moderately difficult** entrance level, 73% of applicants were admitted

Undergraduates 1,168 full-time, 229 part-time. Students come from 25 states and territories, 12 other countries, 8% are from out of state, 7% African American, 0.5% Asian American or Pacific Islander, 2% Hispanic American, 2% international, 3% transferred in, 87% live on campus. *Retention:* 68% of 2006 full-time freshmen returned.
Freshmen *Admission:* 1,860 applied, 1,366 admitted, 373 enrolled. *Average high school GPA:* 3.22. *Test scores:* SAT critical reading scores over 500: 43%; SAT math scores over 500: 56%; SAT writing scores over 500: 43%; ACT scores over 18: 88%; SAT critical reading scores over 600: 15%; SAT math scores over 600: 18%; SAT writing scores over 600: 15%; ACT scores over 24: 30%; SAT critical reading scores over 700: 3%; SAT math scores over 700: 3%; SAT writing scores over 700: 3%; ACT scores over 30: 3%.
Faculty *Total:* 148, 36% full-time, 45% with terminal degrees. *Student/faculty ratio:* 14:1.
Majors Accounting; anthropology; athletic training; biology/biological sciences; business administration and management; chemistry; computer science; dramatic/theater arts; economics; education; elementary education; English; environmental biology; environmental science; environmental studies; German; health/health care administration; health teacher education; history; hydrology and water resources science; information science/studies; international relations and affairs; mass communication/media; mathematics; music; music management and merchandising; music teacher education; philosophy; physical education teaching and coaching; physics; piano and organ; political science and government; pre-dentistry studies; pre-law studies; pre-medical studies; pre-veterinary studies; psychology; public administration; public relations/image management; religious studies; science teacher education; secondary education; Spanish; special education; violin, viola, guitar and other stringed instruments; voice and opera.
Academics *Calendar:* semesters. *Degrees:* bachelor's and master's. *Special study options:* academic remediation for entering students, accelerated degree program, adult/continuing education programs, advanced placement credit, double majors, English as a second language, honors programs, internships, off-campus study, part-time degree program, services for LD students, study abroad, summer session for credit. *ROTC:* Army (c), Air Force (c). *Unusual degree programs:* 3-2 nursing with Case Western Reserve University; environmental management with Duke University.
Computers on Campus 125 computers/terminals are available on campus for general student use. Students can access the following: computer help desk, free student e-mail accounts, online (class) grades, online (class) registration, online (class) schedules. Campuswide network is available. 100% of college-owned or -operated housing units are wired for high-speed Internet access. Wireless service is available via entire campus.
Student Life *Housing:* on-campus residence required through junior year. *Options:* coed, women-only, cooperative. Campus housing is university owned. Freshman campus housing is guaranteed. *Activities and organizations:* drama/theater group, student-run newspaper, radio and television station, choral group, Alpha Phi Omega, BERG Events Council, Student Senate, Campus Fellowship, Black Student Union/World Student Union. *Campus security:* 24-hour emergency response devices and patrols, student patrols, late-night transport/escort service. *Student services:* health clinic, personal/psychological counseling.
Athletics Member NCAA. All Division III. *Intercollegiate sports:* baseball M, basketball M/W, cross-country running M/W, football M, golf M/W, soccer M/W, softball W, tennis M/W, track and field M/W, volleyball M/W, wrestling M. *Intramural sports:* archery M/W, badminton M/W, cheerleading M/W, football M, golf M/W, racquetball M/W, skiing (cross-country) M/W, softball W, table tennis M/W.
Standardized Tests *Required:* SAT or ACT (for admission).
Costs (2008–09) *Comprehensive fee:* $28,060 includes full-time tuition ($19,464), mandatory fees ($458), and room and board ($8138). *College room only:* $3852.
Financial Aid Of all full-time matriculated undergraduates who enrolled in 2007, 1,106 applied for aid, 976 were judged to have need, 199 had their need fully met. 650 Federal Work-Study jobs (averaging $1560). 80 state and other part-time jobs (averaging $1335). In 2007, 109 non-need-based awards were made. *Average percent of need met:* 87%. *Average financial aid package:* $15,849. *Average need-based loan:* $4797. *Average need-based gift aid:* $10,575. *Average non-need-based aid:* $6217. *Average indebtedness upon graduation:* $30,589.
Applying *Options:* electronic application, deferred entrance. *Application fee:* $25. *Required:* high school transcript, minimum 2.5 GPA. *Required for some:* letters of recommendation. *Recommended:* essay or personal statement, interview. *Application deadlines:* 8/15 (freshmen), 8/15 (out-of-state freshmen), 8/15 (transfers). *Notification:* continuous until 8/15 (freshmen), 8/15 (transfers).
Freshman Application Contact Ms. Lindsay Sooy, Director of Admission, Heidelberg College, 310 East Market Street, Tiffin, OH 44883. *Phone:* 419-448-2330. *Toll-free phone:* 800-434-3352. *Fax:* 419-448-2334. *E-mail:* adminfo@heidelberg.edu.

HIRAM COLLEGE

Hiram, Ohio **www.hiram.edu/**

- **Independent** 4-year, founded 1850, affiliated with Christian Church (Disciples of Christ)
- **Rural** 110-acre campus with easy access to Cleveland
- **Endowment** $62.7 million
- **Coed**
- **Moderately difficult** entrance level

Faculty *Student/faculty ratio:* 12:1.
Academics *Calendar:* semesters. *Degrees:* bachelor's and master's.
Student Life *Campus security:* 24-hour emergency response devices and patrols, late-night transport/escort service, controlled dormitory access.
Athletics Member NCAA. All Division III.
Standardized Tests *Required:* SAT or ACT (for admission).
Costs (2008–09) *Comprehensive fee:* $33,540 includes full-time tuition ($24,490), mandatory fees ($670), and room and board ($8380). *College room only:* $4190.
Financial Aid Of all full-time matriculated undergraduates who enrolled in 2002, 790 applied for aid, 736 were judged to have need, 699 had their need fully met. 587 Federal Work-Study jobs (averaging $1600). 18 state and other part-time jobs (averaging $1580). In 2002, 114 non-need-based awards were made. *Average percent of need met:* 95. *Average financial aid package:* $21,218. *Average need-based loan:* $6960. *Average need-based gift aid:* $8163. *Average non-need-based aid:* $8635. *Average indebtedness upon graduation:* $17,125.
Applying *Options:* electronic application, early admission, deferred entrance. *Application fee:* $35. *Required:* essay or personal statement, high school tran-

script, 2 letters of recommendation. *Required for some:* interview. *Recommended:* 3 letters of recommendation, interview.

Freshman Application Contact Mr. Sherman C. Dean II, Director of Admission, Hiram College, PO Box 96, Hiram, OH 44234. *Phone:* 330-569-5169. *Toll-free phone:* 800-362-5280. *Fax:* 330-569-5944. *E-mail:* admission@hiram.edu.

JOHN CARROLL UNIVERSITY

University Heights, Ohio **www.jcu.edu/**

- **Independent Roman Catholic (Jesuit)** comprehensive, founded 1886
- **Suburban** 60-acre campus with easy access to Cleveland
- **Endowment** $179.5 million
- **Coed** 3,075 undergraduate students, 96% full-time, 54% women, 46% men
- **Moderately difficult** entrance level, 86% of applicants were admitted

Undergraduates 2,948 full-time, 127 part-time. Students come from 38 states and territories, 28% are from out of state, 5% African American, 2% Asian American or Pacific Islander, 3% Hispanic American, 0.3% Native American, 5% transferred in, 44% live on campus. *Retention:* 84% of 2006 full-time freshmen returned.

Freshmen *Admission:* 3,309 applied, 2,830 admitted, 720 enrolled. *Average high school GPA:* 3.36. *Test scores:* SAT critical reading scores over 500: 71%; SAT math scores over 500: 72%; SAT writing scores over 500: 71%; ACT scores over 18: 97%; SAT critical reading scores over 600: 26%; SAT math scores over 600: 29%; SAT writing scores over 600: 24%; ACT scores over 24: 51%; SAT critical reading scores over 700: 3%; SAT math scores over 700: 3%; SAT writing scores over 700: 4%; ACT scores over 30: 6%.

Faculty *Total:* 393, 52% full-time, 66% with terminal degrees. *Student/faculty ratio:* 14:1.

Majors Accounting; art history, criticism and conservation; Asian studies; Asian studies (East); biological and physical sciences; biology/biological sciences; business administration and management; chemistry; classics and languages, literatures and linguistics; computer science; economics; education; education (K-12); elementary education; engineering physics; English; environmental studies; finance; French; German; gerontology; history; humanities; interdisciplinary studies; international economics; international relations and affairs; kindergarten/preschool education; Latin; literature; marketing/marketing management; mass communication/media; mathematics; modern Greek; neuroscience; philosophy; physical education teaching and coaching; physics; political science and government; pre-dentistry studies; pre-law studies; pre-medical studies; pre-veterinary studies; psychology; public administration; religious education; religious studies; secondary education; sociology; Spanish; special education.

Academics *Calendar:* semesters. *Degrees:* bachelor's and master's. *Special study options:* accelerated degree program, adult/continuing education programs, advanced placement credit, cooperative education, double majors, honors programs, independent study, internships, off-campus study, part-time degree program, student-designed majors, study abroad, summer session for credit. *ROTC:* Army (b). *Unusual degree programs:* 3-2 engineering with Case Western Reserve University, University of Detroit Mercy; nursing with Case Western Reserve University.

Computers on Campus 210 computers/terminals are available on campus for general student use. Students can access the following: campus intranet, computer help desk, free student e-mail accounts, online (class) grades, online (class) registration, online (class) schedules. Campuswide network is available. 100% of college-owned or -operated housing units are wired for high-speed Internet access. Wireless service is available via entire campus.

Student Life *Housing options:* coed, men-only, women-only. Campus housing is university owned. Freshman campus housing is guaranteed. *Activities and organizations:* drama/theater group, student-run newspaper, radio and television station, choral group, Volunteer Service Organization, Student Union, Carroll News, band, University Concert Choir, national fraternities, national sororities. *Campus security:* 24-hour emergency response devices and patrols, late-night transport/escort service. *Student services:* health clinic, personal/psychological counseling.

Athletics Member NCAA. All Division III. *Intercollegiate sports:* baseball M, basketball M/W, cheerleading W (c), crew M (c)/W (c), cross-country running M/W, football M, golf M/W, ice hockey M (c), lacrosse M (c)/W (c), rock climbing M (c)/W (c), sailing M (c)/W (c), skiing (downhill) M (c)/W (c), soccer M/W, softball W, swimming and diving M/W, tennis M/W, track and field M/W, volleyball M (c)/W, wrestling M. *Intramural sports:* basketball M/W, football M/W, racquetball M/W, softball M/W, swimming and diving M/W, tennis M/W, volleyball M/W, water polo M/W.

Standardized Tests *Required:* SAT or ACT (for admission).

Costs (2008–09) *One-time required fee:* $325. *Comprehensive fee:* $36,024 includes full-time tuition ($27,190), mandatory fees ($900), and room and board ($7934). Part-time tuition: $823 per credit hour. *College room only:* $4206.

Financial Aid *Average financial aid package:* $14,104. *Average indebtedness upon graduation:* $12,695.

Applying *Options:* electronic application, deferred entrance. *Required:* high school transcript, 1 letter of recommendation. *Required for some:* interview. *Recommended:* essay or personal statement, interview. *Application deadlines:* 2/1 (freshmen), rolling (transfers). *Notification:* continuous (freshmen).

Freshman Application Contact Mr. Thomas P. Fanning, Director of Admission, John Carroll University, 20700 North Park Boulevard, University Heights, OH 44118. *Phone:* 216-397-4246. *Fax:* 216-397-4981. *E-mail:* tfanning@jcu.edu.

See page 2032 for the College Close-Up.

KENT STATE UNIVERSITY

Kent, Ohio **www.kent.edu/**

- **State-supported** university, founded 1910, part of Kent State University System
- **Suburban** 1347-acre campus with easy access to Cleveland
- **Endowment** $87.8 million
- **Coed** 18,090 undergraduate students, 85% full-time, 59% women, 41% men
- **Moderately difficult** entrance level, 80% of applicants were admitted

Undergraduates 15,425 full-time, 2,665 part-time. Students come from 47 states and territories, 57 other countries, 10% are from out of state, 8% African American, 1% Asian American or Pacific Islander, 1% Hispanic American, 0.4% Native American, 1% international, 5% transferred in, 35% live on campus. *Retention:* 73% of 2006 full-time freshmen returned.

Freshmen *Admission:* 12,364 applied, 9,854 admitted, 3,800 enrolled. *Average high school GPA:* 3.15. *Test scores:* SAT critical reading scores over 500: 56%; SAT math scores over 500: 53%; ACT scores over 18: 88%; SAT critical reading scores over 600: 15%; SAT math scores over 600: 16%; ACT scores over 24: 29%; SAT critical reading scores over 700: 2%; SAT math scores over 700: 2%; ACT scores over 30: 3%.

Faculty *Total:* 1,476, 60% full-time. *Student/faculty ratio:* 17:1.

Majors Accounting; acting; advertising; aeronautics/aviation/aerospace science and technology; African-American/Black studies; American studies; anthropology; applied mathematics; architecture; area, ethnic, cultural, and gender studies related; area studies related; art history, criticism and conservation; art teacher education; athletic training; audiology and speech-language pathology; aviation/airway management; biological and biomedical sciences related; biology/biological sciences; biotechnology; botany/plant biology; business administration and management; business/managerial economics; business teacher education; ceramic arts and ceramics; chemistry; chemistry teacher education; classics and languages, literatures and linguistics; clinical laboratory science/medical technology; commercial and advertising art; computer programming; computer programming (specific applications); computer science; computer systems analysis; crafts, folk art and artisanry; cultural studies; dance; digital communication and media/multimedia; dramatic/theater arts; ecology; economics; education; English; English/language arts teacher education; environmental design/architecture; European studies (Central and Eastern); family and consumer sciences/home economics teacher education; family and consumer sciences/human sciences; fashion/apparel design; fashion merchandising; finance; fine/studio arts; foods and nutrition related; foods, nutrition, and wellness; foreign language teacher education; French; French language teacher education; general studies; geography; geology/earth science; German; health and medical administrative services related; health services/allied health/health sciences; health teacher education; history; hospitality administration related; human development and family studies; human development and family studies related; human nutrition; industrial engineering; industrial technology; interior design; international relations and affairs; journalism; journalism related; kindergarten/preschool education; kinesiology and exercise science; Latin; Latin American studies; Latin teacher education; liberal arts and sciences/liberal studies; linguistics of ASL and other sign languages; marketing/marketing management; mass communication/media; mathematics; metal and jewelry arts; middle school education; multi-/interdisciplinary studies related; music; music performance; music teacher education; natural resources/conservation; nursing (registered nurse training); operations management; parks, recreation and leisure facilities management; peace studies and conflict resolution; philosophy; photographic and film/video technology; physical education teaching and coaching; physics; piano and organ; political science and government; pre-dentistry studies; pre-medical studies; printmaking; professional studies; psychology; public relations/image management; radio and television;

radiologic technology/science; Russian; Russian studies; sales and marketing/marketing and distribution teacher education; science teacher education; sculpture; social sciences; social studies teacher education; social work; sociology; Spanish; Spanish language teacher education; special education; speech and rhetoric; technology/industrial arts teacher education; trade and industrial teacher education; zoology/animal biology.

Academics *Calendar:* semesters. *Degrees:* certificates, bachelor's, master's, doctoral, post-master's, and postbachelor's certificates. *Special study options:* academic remediation for entering students, accelerated degree program, adult/continuing education programs, advanced placement credit, cooperative education, distance learning, double majors, English as a second language, external degree program, freshman honors college, honors programs, independent study, internships, off-campus study, part-time degree program, services for LD students, student-designed majors, study abroad, summer session for credit. *ROTC:* Army (b), Air Force (b).

Computers on Campus 1,690 computers/terminals and 5,500 ports are available on campus for general student use. Students can access the following: computer help desk, free student e-mail accounts, online (class) grades, online (class) registration, online (class) schedules. Campuswide network is available. 100% of college-owned or -operated housing units are wired for high-speed Internet access. Wireless service is available via entire campus.

Student Life *Housing:* on-campus residence required through sophomore year. *Options:* coed, men-only, women-only, disabled students. Campus housing is university owned. Freshman campus housing is guaranteed. *Activities and organizations:* drama/theater group, student-run newspaper, radio and television station, choral group, marching band, Kent Interhall Council, Black United Students, All Campus Programming Board, Delta Sigma PI, Late Night Christian Fellowship, national fraternities, national sororities. *Campus security:* 24-hour emergency response devices and patrols, student patrols, late-night transport/escort service, controlled dormitory access, campus police and fire department, electronic locks on computer labs, studios and laboratory research areas. *Student services:* health clinic, personal/psychological counseling, women's center, legal services.

Athletics Member NCAA. All Division I. *Intercollegiate sports:* baseball M (s), basketball M (s)/W (s), cross-country running M (s)/W (s), field hockey W (s), football M (s), golf M (s)/W (s), gymnastics W (s), soccer W (s), softball W (s), track and field M (s)/W (s), volleyball W (s), wrestling M (s). *Intramural sports:* badminton M (c)/W (c), baseball M (c), basketball M/W, bowling M (c)/W (c), equestrian sports M (c)/W (c), fencing M (c)/W (c), field hockey W (c), football M/W, golf M (c)/W (c), ice hockey M (c), lacrosse M (c), racquetball M (c)/W (c), rugby M (c)/W (c), sailing M (c)/W (c), skiing (downhill) M (c)/W (c), soccer M (c)/W (c), softball M/W, swimming and diving M (c)/W (c), table tennis M/W, tennis M/W, ultimate Frisbee M/W, volleyball M (c)/W (c), water polo M/W, wrestling M.

Standardized Tests *Required:* SAT or ACT (for admission).

Costs (2008–09) *Tuition:* state resident $8430 full-time, $384 per credit hour part-time; nonresident $15,862 full-time, $722 per credit hour part-time. *Room and board:* $7200; room only: $4410.

Financial Aid Of all full-time matriculated undergraduates who enrolled in 2006, 10,787 applied for aid, 9,013 were judged to have need, 1,221 had their need fully met. 1,042 Federal Work-Study jobs (averaging $2316). In 2006, 1,503 non-need-based awards were made. *Average percent of need met:* 58%. *Average financial aid package:* $7685. *Average need-based loan:* $4075. *Average need-based gift aid:* $5051. *Average non-need-based aid:* $3874. *Average indebtedness upon graduation:* $22,230.

Applying *Options:* electronic application, early admission. *Application fee:* $30. *Required:* high school transcript, minimum 2.5 GPA. *Application deadline:* 5/1 (freshmen). *Notification:* continuous (transfers).

Freshman Application Contact Mr. Christopher Buttenschon, Assistant Director of Admissions, Kent State University, 161 Michael Schwartz Center, Kent, OH 44242-0001. *Phone:* 330-672-2444. *Toll-free phone:* 800-988-KENT. *Fax:* 330-672-2499. *E-mail:* admissions@kent.edu.

See page 2034 for the College Close-Up.

Kent State University, Ashtabula Campus

Ashtabula, Ohio **www.ashtabula.kent.edu/**

- **State-supported** primarily 2-year, founded 1958, part of Kent State University System
- **Small-town** 120-acre campus with easy access to Cleveland
- **Coed**
- **Noncompetitive** entrance level

Academics *Calendar:* semesters. *Degrees:* certificates, associate, and bachelor's (also offers some upper-level and graduate courses).

Student Life *Campus security:* 24-hour emergency response devices.

Standardized Tests *Recommended:* SAT or ACT (for placement).

Costs (2007–08) *Tuition:* state resident $4770 full-time, $217 per credit hour part-time; nonresident $12,202 full-time, $555 per credit hour part-time.

Financial Aid Of all full-time matriculated undergraduates who enrolled in 2006, 1,042 Federal Work-Study jobs (averaging $2316).

Applying *Options:* early admission, deferred entrance. *Application fee:* $30.

Director of Admissions Ms. Kelly Sanford, Director, Enrollment Management and Student Services, Kent State University, Ashtabula Campus, 3300 Lake Road West, Ashtabula, OH 44004-2299. *Phone:* 440-964-4217. *E-mail:* sanford@ashtabula.kent.edu.

Kent State University, Geauga Campus

Burton, Ohio **www.geauga.kent.edu/**

- **State-supported** founded 1964, part of Kent State University System
- **Rural** 87-acre campus with easy access to Cleveland
- **Coed**
- **Noncompetitive** entrance level

Faculty *Student/faculty ratio:* 15:1.

Academics *Calendar:* semesters. *Degrees:* certificates, diplomas, associate, and bachelor's.

Student Life *Campus security:* 24-hour emergency response devices.

Standardized Tests *Required for some:* SAT or ACT (for admission). *Recommended:* SAT or ACT (for admission).

Costs (2007–08) *Tuition:* state resident $4770 full-time, $217 per credit hour part-time; nonresident $12,202 full-time, $555 per credit hour part-time. Full-time tuition and fees vary according to course level. Part-time tuition and fees vary according to course level. *Payment plans:* installment, deferred payment.

Financial Aid Of all full-time matriculated undergraduates who enrolled in 2006, 257 applied for aid, 224 were judged to have need, 11 had their need fully met. 11 Federal Work-Study jobs (averaging $1554). In 2006, 2 non-need-based awards were made. *Average percent of need met:* 50. *Average financial aid package:* $5960. *Average need-based loan:* $3380. *Average need-based gift aid:* $3519. *Average non-need-based aid:* $180. *Average indebtedness upon graduation:* $18,289.

Applying *Options:* early admission, deferred entrance. *Application fee:* $30. *Required:* high school transcript.

Freshman Application Contact Ms. Betty Landrus, Kent State University, Geauga Campus, 14111 Claridon-Troy Road, Burton, OH 44021. *Phone:* 440-834-4187. *Fax:* 440-834-8846. *E-mail:* blandrus@kent.edu.

Kent State University, Salem Campus

Salem, Ohio **www.salem.kent.edu/**

Freshman Application Contact Mrs. Judy Heisler, Admissions Secretary, Kent State University, Salem Campus, 2491 State Route 45 South, Salem, OH 44460-9412. *Phone:* 330-332-0361 Ext. 74201. *E-mail:* ask-us@salem.kent.edu.

Kent State University, Stark Campus

Canton, Ohio **www.stark.kent.edu/**

Freshman Application Contact Ms. Deborah Ann Speck, Director of Admissions, Kent State University, Stark Campus, 6000 Frank Avenue NW, Canton, OH 44720-7599. *Phone:* 330-499-9600 Ext. 53259.

Kent State University, Trumbull Campus

Warren, Ohio **www.trumbull.kent.edu/**

- **State-supported** primarily 2-year, founded 1954, part of Kent State University System
- **Suburban** 200-acre campus with easy access to Cleveland
- **Coed**
- **Noncompetitive** entrance level

Faculty *Student/faculty ratio:* 16:1.

Academics *Calendar:* semesters. *Degrees:* certificates, associate, and bachelor's (also offers some upper-level and graduate courses).

Student Life *Campus security:* 24-hour emergency response devices, late-night transport/escort service, patrols by trained security personnel during open hours.

Standardized Tests *Required for some:* SAT or ACT (for admission). *Recommended:* SAT or ACT (for admission).

Costs (2007–08) *Tuition:* state resident $4770 full-time, $217 per credit hour part-time; nonresident $12,202 full-time, $555 per credit hour part-time. Full-time tuition and fees vary according to course level. Part-time tuition and fees vary according to course level. *Payment plans:* installment, deferred payment.

Financial Aid Of all full-time matriculated undergraduates who enrolled in 2006, 31 Federal Work-Study jobs (averaging $2708).

Applying *Options:* early admission, deferred entrance. *Application fee:* $30. *Required:* high school transcript.

Freshman Application Contact Ms. Patricia Davis, Clerical Specialist, Kent State University, Trumbull Campus, 4314 Mahoning Avenue, NW, Warren, OH 44483-1998. *Phone:* 330-675-888. *Fax:* 330-847-6571. *E-mail:* pdavis1@kent.edu.

Kent State University, Tuscarawas Campus

New Philadelphia, Ohio **www.tusc.kent.edu/**

- **State-supported** primarily 2-year, founded 1962, part of Kent State University System
- **Small-town** 172-acre campus with easy access to Cleveland
- **Endowment** $1.6 million
- **Coed**
- **Noncompetitive** entrance level

Faculty *Student/faculty ratio:* 19:1.

Academics *Calendar:* semesters. *Degrees:* certificates, diplomas, associate, bachelor's, and master's (also offers some upper-level and graduate courses).

Standardized Tests *Recommended:* SAT or ACT (for admission).

Costs (2007–08) *Tuition:* state resident $5590 full-time, $217 per credit hour part-time; nonresident $12,202 full-time, $555 per credit hour part-time.

Financial Aid Of all full-time matriculated undergraduates who enrolled in 2006, 26 Federal Work-Study jobs (averaging $2699).

Applying *Options:* early admission, deferred entrance. *Application fee:* $30. *Required:* high school transcript.

Freshman Application Contact Director of Admissions, Kent State University, Tuscarawas Campus, 330 University Drive NE, New Philadelphia, OH 44663-9403. *Phone:* 330-339-3391 Ext. 47425. *Fax:* 330-339-3321.

Kenyon College

Gambier, Ohio **www.kenyon.edu/**

- **Independent** 4-year, founded 1824
- **Rural** 1,200-acre campus with easy access to Columbus
- **Endowment** $192.9 million
- **Coed** 1,663 undergraduate students, 99% full-time, 52% women, 48% men
- **Very difficult** entrance level, 29% of applicants were admitted

Undergraduates 1,653 full-time, 10 part-time. Students come from 46 states and territories, 29 other countries, 80% are from out of state, 4% African American, 5% Asian American or Pacific Islander, 3% Hispanic American, 0.5% Native American, 3% international, 0.6% transferred in, 98% live on campus. *Retention:* 95% of 2006 full-time freshmen returned.

Freshmen *Admission:* 4,626 applied, 1,352 admitted, 458 enrolled. *Average high school GPA:* 3.86. *Test scores:* SAT critical reading scores over 500: 99%; SAT math scores over 500: 99%; SAT writing scores over 500: 99%; ACT scores over 18: 100%; SAT critical reading scores over 600: 88%; SAT math scores over 600: 79%; SAT writing scores over 600: 87%; ACT scores over 24: 95%; SAT critical reading scores over 700: 44%; SAT math scores over 700: 22%; SAT writing scores over 700: 37%; ACT scores over 30: 53%.

Faculty *Total:* 190, 80% full-time, 91% with terminal degrees. *Student/faculty ratio:* 10:1.

Majors African-American/Black studies; African studies; American studies; ancient/classical Greek; anthropology; art; art history, criticism and conservation; Asian studies; biochemistry; biology/biological sciences; chemistry; classics and languages, literatures and linguistics; creative writing; dance; dramatic/theater arts; economics; English; environmental studies; ethnic, cultural minority, and gender studies related; fine/studio arts; foreign languages and literatures; French; German; history; humanities; interdisciplinary studies; international/global studies; international relations and affairs; Latin; legal studies; literature; mathematics; modern Greek; modern languages; molecular biology; multi-/interdisciplinary studies related; music; natural sciences; neuroscience; philosophy; physics; political science and government; pre-dentistry studies; pre-law studies; premedical studies; pre-veterinary studies; psychology; public policy analysis; religious studies; Romance languages; sociology; Spanish; statistics; women's studies.

Academics *Calendar:* semesters. *Degree:* bachelor's. *Special study options:* accelerated degree program, advanced placement credit, double majors, honors programs, independent study, internships, off-campus study, services for LD students, student-designed majors, study abroad. *Unusual degree programs:* 3-2 engineering with Washington University in St. Louis, Case Western Reserve University, Rensselaer Polytechnic Institute; environmental science with Duke University, education with The Bank Street College of Education.

Computers on Campus 300 computers/terminals are available on campus for general student use. Students can access the following: campus intranet, computer help desk, free student e-mail accounts, online (class) grades, online (class) registration, online (class) schedules, commercial databases. Campuswide network is available. 99% of college-owned or -operated housing units are wired for high-speed Internet access. Wireless service is available via entire campus.

Student Life *Housing:* on-campus residence required through senior year. *Options:* coed, women-only, disabled students. Campus housing is university owned. Freshman campus housing is guaranteed. *Activities and organizations:* drama/theater group, student-run newspaper, radio station, choral group, music groups, Student Theater Organization, writing organizations, student radio station, Ballroom Dance Club, national fraternities. *Campus security:* 24-hour emergency response devices and patrols, student patrols, late-night transport/escort service. *Student services:* health clinic, personal/psychological counseling, women's center.

Athletics Member NCAA. All Division III. *Intercollegiate sports:* archery M (c)/W (c), baseball M, basketball M/W, cross-country running M/W, equestrian sports M (c)/W (c), fencing M (c)/W (c), field hockey W, football M, golf M, ice hockey M (c)/W (c), lacrosse M/W, rugby M (c)/W (c), sailing M (c)/W (c), soccer M/W, softball W, squash M (c)/W (c), swimming and diving M/W, tennis M/W, track and field M/W, ultimate Frisbee M (c)/W (c), volleyball M (c)/W. *Intramural sports:* basketball M/W, football M, racquetball M/W, soccer M/W, softball M/W, squash M/W, tennis M/W, volleyball M/W, water polo M/W.

Standardized Tests *Required:* SAT or ACT (for admission).

Costs (2008–09) *Comprehensive fee:* $46,830 includes full-time tuition ($39,080), mandatory fees ($1160), and room and board ($6590). *College room only:* $3100.

Financial Aid Of all full-time matriculated undergraduates who enrolled in 2007, 882 applied for aid, 746 were judged to have need, 335 had their need fully met. 282 Federal Work-Study jobs (averaging $617). 198 state and other part-time jobs (averaging $587). In 2007, 366 non-need-based awards were made. *Average percent of need met:* 98%. *Average financial aid package:* $28,589. *Average need-based loan:* $4386. *Average need-based gift aid:* $25,260. *Average non-need-based aid:* $11,581. *Average indebtedness upon graduation:* $19,489.

Applying *Options:* electronic application, early admission, early decision, deferred entrance. *Application fee:* $50. *Required:* essay or personal statement, high school transcript, 1 letter of recommendation, counselor recommendation. *Recommended:* minimum 3.5 GPA, 2 letters of recommendation, interview. *Application deadlines:* 1/15 (freshmen), 1/15 (out-of-state freshmen), 4/1 (transfers). *Early decision deadline:* 11/15 (for plan 1), 1/15 (for plan 2). *Notification:* 4/1 (freshmen), 4/1 (out-of-state freshmen), 5/1 (transfers), 12/15 (early decision plan 1), 2/1 (early decision plan 2).

Freshman Application Contact Ms. Jennifer Delahunty, Dean of Admissions, Kenyon College, Ransom Hall, Gambier, OH 43022. *Phone:* 740-427-5778. *Toll-free phone:* 800-848-2468. *Fax:* 740-427-5770. *E-mail:* admissions@kenyon.edu.

Kettering College of Medical Arts

Kettering, Ohio **www.kcma.edu/**

- **Independent Seventh-day Adventist** 4-year, founded 1967, administratively affiliated with Kettering Health Network
- **Suburban** 35-acre campus
- **Coed, primarily women** 741 undergraduate students, 53% full-time, 81% women, 19% men
- **Moderately difficult** entrance level, 50% of applicants were admitted

Undergraduates 394 full-time, 347 part-time. Students come from 24 states and territories, 3 other countries, 7% are from out of state, 9% African American, 2% Asian American or Pacific Islander, 2% Hispanic American, 0.1% Native American, 0.3% international, 16% transferred in, 15% live on campus. *Retention:* 78% of 2006 full-time freshmen returned.

Freshmen *Admission:* 204 applied, 101 admitted, 67 enrolled. *Average high school GPA:* 3.41. *Test scores:* ACT scores over 18: 100%; ACT scores over 24: 26%.

Faculty *Total:* 70, 79% full-time, 31% with terminal degrees. *Student/faculty ratio:* 10:1.

Majors General studies; health science; nuclear medical technology; nursing (registered nurse training); physician assistant; pre-medical studies; radiologic technology/science; respiratory care therapy.

Academics *Calendar:* semesters. *Degrees:* certificates, associate, bachelor's, and master's. *Special study options:* advanced placement credit, distance learning, honors programs, independent study, off-campus study, part-time degree program, study abroad, summer session for credit.

Computers on Campus 30 computers/terminals are available on campus for general student use. Students can access the following: campus intranet, computer help desk, free student e-mail accounts, online (class) grades, online (class) registration, online (class) schedules. Campuswide network is available. 100% of college-owned or -operated housing units are wired for high-speed Internet access. Wireless service is available via entire campus.

Student Life *Housing options:* coed. Campus housing is university owned. *Activities and organizations:* drama/theater group, choral group, Student association/student life, Campus ministries. *Campus security:* 24-hour emergency response devices and patrols, late-night transport/escort service. *Student services:* health clinic, personal/psychological counseling.

Athletics *Intramural sports:* basketball M/W, volleyball M/W.

Standardized Tests *Required:* ACT (for admission). *Recommended:* SAT (for admission).

Costs (2008–09) *Comprehensive fee:* $13,930 includes full-time tuition ($7560), mandatory fees ($570), and room and board ($5800). Part-time tuition: $315 per credit hour. *Required fees:* $220 per term part-time. *College room only:* $2800.

Applying *Options:* early admission. *Application fee:* $25. *Required:* essay or personal statement, high school transcript, minimum 2.0 GPA. *Recommended:* minimum 3.0 GPA, interview. *Application deadlines:* rolling (freshmen), rolling (transfers). *Notification:* continuous (freshmen), continuous (transfers).

Freshman Application Contact Mrs. Becky McDonald, Director of Enrollment Services, Kettering College of Medical Arts, 3737 Southern Boulevard, Kettering, OH 45429-1299. *Phone:* 937-395-8628. *Toll-free phone:* 800-433-5262. *Fax:* 937-296-4238.

Lake Erie College

Painesville, Ohio **www.lec.edu/**

Freshman Application Contact Mr. Eric Felver, Director of Admissions, Lake Erie College, 391 West Washington Street, Painesville, OH 44077-3389. *Phone:* 440-375-7050. *Toll-free phone:* 800-916-0904. *Fax:* 440-375-7005. *E-mail:* admissions@lec.edu.

See page 2036 for the College Close-Up.

Laura and Alvin Siegal College of Judaic Studies

Beachwood, Ohio **www.siegalcollege.edu/**

Freshman Application Contact Ms. Ruth Kronick, Director of Student Services, Laura and Alvin Siegal College of Judaic Studies, 26500 Shaker Boulevard, Beachwood, OH 44122-7116. *Phone:* 216-464-4050. *Toll-free phone:* 888-336-2257. *Fax:* 216-464-5827. *E-mail:* admissions@siegalcollege.edu.

Lourdes College

Sylvania, Ohio **www.lourdes.edu/**

- **Independent Roman Catholic** comprehensive, founded 1958
- **Suburban** 90-acre campus with easy access to Toledo
- **Endowment** $6.8 million
- **Coed** 1,826 undergraduate students, 53% full-time, 82% women, 18% men
- 80% of applicants were admitted

Undergraduates 974 full-time, 852 part-time. Students come from 6 states and territories, 9% are from out of state, 13% African American, 0.7% Asian American or Pacific Islander, 3% Hispanic American, 0.5% Native American, 17% transferred in. *Retention:* 70% of 2006 full-time freshmen returned.

Freshmen *Admission:* 405 applied, 326 admitted, 120 enrolled. *Average high school GPA:* 2.89.

Faculty *Total:* 204, 38% full-time, 27% with terminal degrees. *Student/faculty ratio:* 11:1.

Majors Accounting; adult and continuing education; art; art history, criticism and conservation; biology/biological sciences; business administration and management; chemistry; criminal justice/law enforcement administration; criminal justice/safety; early childhood education; English; environmental science; health/health care administration; history; human resources management; kindergarten/preschool education; liberal arts and sciences/liberal studies; management science; marketing/marketing management; middle school education; multi-/interdisciplinary studies related; music; natural sciences; nursing (registered nurse training); pre-medical studies; psychology; religious studies; secondary education; social work; sociology.

Academics *Calendar:* semesters. *Degrees:* certificates, associate, bachelor's, master's, and postbachelor's certificates. *Special study options:* academic remediation for entering students, adult/continuing education programs, advanced placement credit, cooperative education, distance learning, double majors, independent study, internships, part-time degree program, services for LD students, student-designed majors, study abroad, summer session for credit. *ROTC:* Army (c), Air Force (c).

Computers on Campus 173 computers/terminals are available on campus for general student use. Students can access the following: computer help desk, free student e-mail accounts, online (class) grades, online (class) schedules. Campuswide network is available. Wireless service is available via entire campus.

Student Life *Housing:* college housing not available. *Activities and organizations:* drama/theater group, choral group, Student Government Association, Sigma Alpha Pi (Society for Leadership and Success), Student Nurses Association, Prism, Phi Beta Lambda (Business Fraternity). *Campus security:* 24-hour emergency response devices, late-night transport/escort service, evening patrols by trained security personnel. *Student services:* personal/psychological counseling.

Costs (2007–08) *Tuition:* $12,390 full-time, $413 per credit hour part-time. Full-time tuition and fees vary according to course load and location. Part-time tuition and fees vary according to course load and location. *Required fees:* $1650 full-time, $55 per credit hour part-time. *Payment plans:* installment, deferred payment. *Waivers:* senior citizens and employees or children of employees.

Financial Aid Of all full-time matriculated undergraduates who enrolled in 2006, 800 applied for aid, 656 were judged to have need. 62 Federal Work-Study jobs (averaging $1523). 35 state and other part-time jobs (averaging $2444). *Average financial aid package:* $9820. *Average need-based loan:* $3752. *Average need-based gift aid:* $5727.

Applying *Options:* electronic application, early admission, deferred entrance. *Application fee:* $25. *Required:* high school transcript. *Application deadlines:* rolling (freshmen), rolling (transfers). *Notification:* continuous (freshmen), continuous (transfers).

Freshman Application Contact Ms. Amy Mergen, Office of Admissions, Lourdes College, 6832 Convent Boulevard, Sylvania, OH 43560. *Phone:* 419-885-5291. *Toll-free phone:* 800-878-3210 Ext. 1299. *Fax:* 419-882-3987. *E-mail:* lcadmits@lourdes.edu.

Malone College

Canton, Ohio **www.malone.edu/**

- **Independent** comprehensive, founded 1892, affiliated with Evangelical Friends Church–Eastern Region
- **Suburban** 78-acre campus with easy access to Cleveland
- **Endowment** $20.0 million
- **Coed** 2,021 undergraduate students, 88% full-time, 61% women, 39% men

• **Moderately difficult** entrance level, 76% of applicants were admitted

Malone College is a Christian college that is committed to offering an education of the highest quality in a setting that encourages a solid devotion to God. The combination of strong academics, great location, and spiritual development makes Malone an attractive and challenging opportunity for students.

Undergraduates 1,776 full-time, 245 part-time. Students come from 30 states and territories, 14 other countries, 13% are from out of state, 6% African American, 0.6% Asian American or Pacific Islander, 1% Hispanic American, 0.2% Native American, 1% international, 6% transferred in, 56% live on campus. *Retention:* 78% of 2006 full-time freshmen returned.

Freshmen *Admission:* 1,484 applied, 1,127 admitted, 392 enrolled. *Average high school GPA:* 3.38. *Test scores:* SAT critical reading scores over 500: 65%; SAT math scores over 500: 68%; SAT writing scores over 500: 69%; ACT scores over 18: 93%; SAT critical reading scores over 600: 22%; SAT math scores over 600: 14%; SAT writing scores over 600: 22%; ACT scores over 24: 41%; SAT critical reading scores over 700: 2%; SAT writing scores over 700: 1%; ACT scores over 30: 4%.

Faculty *Total:* 209, 52% full-time, 45% with terminal degrees. *Student/faculty ratio:* 14:1.

Majors Accounting; art teacher education; biblical studies; biology/biological sciences; business administration and management; business administration, management and operations related; chemistry; clinical laboratory science/medical technology; communication and journalism related; computer science; early childhood education; English; English/language arts teacher education; fine/studio arts; health and physical education; health teacher education; history; kinesiology and exercise science; liberal arts and sciences and humanities related; mathematics; middle school education; music; music teacher education; nursing (registered nurse training); parks, recreation, and leisure related; pastoral counseling and specialized ministries related; physical education teaching and coaching; political science and government; psychology; public health education and promotion; public health related; recording arts technology; religious education; religious/sacred music; science teacher education; social studies teacher education; social work; Spanish; Spanish language teacher education; special education (specific learning disabilities); sport and fitness administration/management; youth ministry; zoology/animal biology.

Academics *Calendar:* semesters. *Degrees:* bachelor's, master's, and post-bachelor's certificates. *Special study options:* academic remediation for entering students, accelerated degree program, adult/continuing education programs, advanced placement credit, distance learning, double majors, honors programs, independent study, internships, off-campus study, part-time degree program, services for LD students, student-designed majors, study abroad, summer session for credit. *ROTC:* Army (c), Air Force (c).

Computers on Campus 212 computers/terminals and 240 ports are available on campus for general student use. Students can access the following: campus intranet, computer help desk, free student e-mail accounts, online (class) grades, online (class) registration, online (class) schedules, online advising, online financial aid information, and online credit card payments. Campuswide network is available. 100% of college-owned or -operated housing units are wired for high-speed Internet access. Wireless service is available via classrooms, computer centers, computer labs, dorm rooms, libraries, student centers.

Student Life *Housing:* on-campus residence required through junior year. *Options:* men-only, women-only. Campus housing is university owned. Freshman applicants given priority for college housing. *Activities and organizations:* drama/theater group, student-run newspaper, radio and television station, choral group, marching band, Spiritual Life Committee, Student Activities Council, Student Senate, Woolman-Whittier-Fox Hall Council, Intramural athletics. *Campus security:* 24-hour emergency response devices and patrols, late-night transport/escort service, controlled dormitory access. *Student services:* health clinic, personal/psychological counseling.

Athletics Member NAIA, NCCAA. *Intercollegiate sports:* baseball M (s), basketball M (s)/W (s), cheerleading M/W, cross-country running M (s)/W (s), football M (s), golf M (s)/W (s), soccer M (s)/W (s), softball W (s), tennis M (s)/W (s), track and field M (s)/W (s), volleyball W (s). *Intramural sports:* basketball M/W, bowling M/W, cross-country running M/W, football M/W, soccer M/W, softball M/W, table tennis M/W, ultimate Frisbee M/W, volleyball M/W, weight lifting M/W.

Standardized Tests *Required:* SAT or ACT (for admission).

Costs (2007–08) *Comprehensive fee:* $25,470 includes full-time tuition ($18,600), mandatory fees ($270), and room and board ($6600). Part-time tuition: $330 per semester hour. Part-time tuition and fees vary according to course load. *Required fees:* $68 per term part-time. *College room only:* $3400. Room and board charges vary according to board plan. *Payment plan:* installment. *Waivers:* senior citizens and employees or children of employees.

Financial Aid Of all full-time matriculated undergraduates who enrolled in 2006, 1,407 applied for aid, 1,242 were judged to have need, 213 had their need fully met. 300 Federal Work-Study jobs (averaging $1953). 66 state and other part-time jobs (averaging $2553). In 2006, 188 non-need-based awards were made. *Average percent of need met:* 70%. *Average financial aid package:* $12,794. *Average need-based loan:* $4309. *Average need-based gift aid:* $8846. *Average non-need-based aid:* $4894. *Average indebtedness upon graduation:* $20,505. *Financial aid deadline:* 7/31.

Applying *Options:* electronic application, early admission, deferred entrance. *Application fee:* $20. *Required:* essay or personal statement, high school transcript, minimum 2.5 GPA. *Recommended:* interview. *Application deadlines:* 7/1 (freshmen), 7/1 (transfers). *Notification:* continuous (freshmen), continuous (transfers).

Freshman Application Contact Mr. John Russell, Director of Admissions, Malone College, 515 25th Street, NW, Canton, OH 44709-3897. *Phone:* 330-471-8145. *Toll-free phone:* 800-521-1146. *Fax:* 330-471-8149. *E-mail:* admissions@malone.edu.

See page 2038 for the College Close-Up.

MARIETTA COLLEGE

Marietta, Ohio — www.marietta.edu/

• **Independent** comprehensive, founded 1835
• **Small-town** 120-acre campus
• **Endowment** $70.0 million
• **Coed** 1,502 undergraduate students, 95% full-time, 51% women, 49% men
• **Moderately difficult** entrance level, 75% of applicants were admitted

Undergraduates 1,434 full-time, 68 part-time. Students come from 35 states and territories, 20 other countries, 42% are from out of state, 4% African American, 2% Asian American or Pacific Islander, 1% Hispanic American, 0.3% Native American, 6% international, 3% transferred in, 75% live on campus. *Retention:* 80% of 2006 full-time freshmen returned.

Freshmen *Admission:* 2,320 applied, 1,751 admitted, 416 enrolled. *Average high school GPA:* 3.41. *Test scores:* SAT critical reading scores over 500: 66%; SAT math scores over 500: 73%; ACT scores over 18: 95%; SAT critical reading scores over 600: 26%; SAT math scores over 600: 28%; ACT scores over 24: 48%; SAT critical reading scores over 700: 6%; SAT math scores over 700: 2%; ACT scores over 30: 6%.

Faculty *Total:* 139, 69% full-time, 66% with terminal degrees. *Student/faculty ratio:* 12:1.

Majors Accounting; art; athletic training; biochemistry; biology/biological sciences; business administration and management; business/corporate communications; chemistry; commercial and advertising art; communication/speech communication and rhetoric; computer science; dramatic/theater arts; economics; education; elementary education; English; environmental science; environmental studies; fine/studio arts; geology/earth science; graphic design; history; human resources management; information science/studies; international business/trade/commerce; journalism; liberal arts and sciences/liberal studies; marketing/marketing management; mathematics; music; petroleum engineering; philosophy; physics; political science and government; psychology; public relations, advertising, and applied communication related; radio and television; secondary education; Spanish; speech and rhetoric.

Academics *Calendar:* semesters. *Degrees:* certificates, associate, bachelor's, and master's. *Special study options:* academic remediation for entering students, accelerated degree program, adult/continuing education programs, advanced placement credit, double majors, English as a second language, honors programs, independent study, internships, off-campus study, part-time degree program, services for LD students, student-designed majors, study abroad, summer session for credit. *Unusual degree programs:* 3-2 engineering with University of Pennsylvania, Columbia University, Case Western Reserve University, Washington University in St. Louis.

Computers on Campus 350 computers/terminals are available on campus for general student use. Students can access the following: campus intranet, computer help desk, free student e-mail accounts, online (class) grades, online (class) registration, online (class) schedules. Campuswide network is available. 100% of college-owned or -operated housing units are wired for high-speed Internet access. Wireless service is available via classrooms, computer centers, computer labs, dorm rooms, learning centers, libraries, student centers.

Student Life *Housing:* on-campus residence required through senior year. *Options:* coed, men-only, women-only, disabled students. Campus housing is university owned, leased by the school and is provided by a third party. Freshman campus housing is guaranteed. *Activities and organizations:* drama/theater group, student-run newspaper, radio and television station, choral group, Student Programming Board, student government, Great Outdoors Club, Inter-Varsity Christian Fellowship, Arts and Humanities Council, national fraternities, national sororities. *Campus security:* 24-hour emergency response devices and patrols, student patrols, late-night transport/escort service, controlled dormitory access. *Student services:* health clinic, personal/psychological counseling.

Athletics Member NCAA. All Division III. *Intercollegiate sports:* baseball M, basketball M/W, cheerleading W (c), crew M/W, cross-country running M/W, football M, lacrosse M (c), soccer M/W, softball W, tennis M/W, track and field M/W, volleyball W. *Intramural sports:* badminton M/W, basketball M/W, bowling M/W, cross-country running M/W, football M/W, racquetball M/W, rock climbing M/W, rugby M (c)/W (c), soccer M/W, softball M/W, swimming and diving M/W, tennis M/W, ultimate Frisbee M/W, volleyball M/W, weight lifting M.

Standardized Tests *Required:* SAT or ACT (for admission). *Recommended:* SAT Subject Tests (for admission).

Costs (2007–08) *Comprehensive fee:* $32,232 includes full-time tuition ($24,220), mandatory fees ($622), and room and board ($7390). Full-time tuition and fees vary according to course load. Part-time tuition: $805 per credit. Part-time tuition and fees vary according to course load. *College room only:* $4070. Room and board charges vary according to board plan and housing facility. *Payment plan:* installment. *Waivers:* employees or children of employees.

Financial Aid Of all full-time matriculated undergraduates who enrolled in 2007, 1,367 applied for aid, 1,123 were judged to have need, 574 had their need fully met. 928 Federal Work-Study jobs (averaging $1884). In 2007, 244 non-need-based awards were made. *Average percent of need met:* 93%. *Average financial aid package:* $22,222. *Average need-based loan:* $4926. *Average need-based gift aid:* $17,418. *Average non-need-based aid:* $8887. *Average indebtedness upon graduation:* $19,181.

Applying *Options:* electronic application, early admission, deferred entrance. *Application fee:* $25. *Required:* essay or personal statement, high school transcript, minimum 2.0 GPA, 1 letter of recommendation. *Recommended:* minimum 3.0 GPA, interview. *Application deadlines:* 5/1 (freshmen), rolling (transfers). *Notification:* continuous until 5/1 (freshmen), continuous (transfers).

Freshman Application Contact Mr. Jason Turley, Director of Admission, Marietta College, 215 Fifth Street, Marietta, OH 45750. *Phone:* 740-376-4600. *Toll-free phone:* 800-331-7896. *Fax:* 740-376-8888. *E-mail:* admit@marietta.edu.

See page 2040 for the College Close-Up.

MedCentral College of Nursing

Mansfield, Ohio **www.medcentral.edu/**

Freshman Application Contact Mrs. Wendi Snyder, Admissions Counselor, MedCentral College of Nursing, 335 Glessner Avenue, Mansfield, OH 44903. *Toll-free phone:* 877-656-4360.

Mercy College of Northwest Ohio

Toledo, Ohio **www.mercycollege.edu/**

- **Independent** 4-year, founded 1993, affiliated with Roman Catholic Church
- **Urban** campus with easy access to Detroit
- **Endowment** $5.6 million
- **Coed, primarily women**
- **Moderately difficult** entrance level

Faculty *Student/faculty ratio:* 12:1.

Academics *Calendar:* semesters. *Degrees:* certificates, associate, and bachelor's.

Student Life *Campus security:* 24-hour patrols, late-night transport/escort service, controlled dormitory access.

Standardized Tests *Required for some:* SAT or ACT (for admission). *Recommended:* SAT or ACT (for admission).

Costs (2008–09) *One-time required fee:* $15. *Tuition:* $8896 full-time, $308 per credit hour part-time. *Required fees:* $650 full-time, $5 per credit hour part-time.

Financial Aid Of all full-time matriculated undergraduates who enrolled in 2006, 18 Federal Work-Study jobs (averaging $1900).

Applying *Application fee:* $25. *Required:* high school transcript.

Freshman Application Contact Admissions Counselor, Mercy College of Northwest Ohio, 2221 Madison Avenue, Toledo, OH 43624-1197. *Phone:* 419-251-1313. *Toll-free phone:* 888-80-Mercy. *Fax:* 419-251-1462. *E-mail:* admissions@mercycollege.edu.

Miami University

Oxford, Ohio **www.muohio.edu/**

- **State-related** university, founded 1809, part of Miami University System
- **Small-town** 2,000-acre campus with easy access to Cincinnati
- **Endowment** $409.3 million
- **Coed** 14,555 undergraduate students, 98% full-time, 54% women, 46% men
- **Moderately difficult** entrance level, 75% of applicants were admitted

Undergraduates 14,264 full-time, 291 part-time. Students come from 50 states and territories, 38 other countries, 30% are from out of state, 3% African American, 3% Asian American or Pacific Islander, 2% Hispanic American, 0.6% Native American, 1% international, 2% transferred in, 48% live on campus. *Retention:* 89% of 2006 full-time freshmen returned.

Freshmen *Admission:* 15,925 applied, 12,012 admitted, 3,404 enrolled. *Average high school GPA:* 3.7. *Test scores:* SAT critical reading scores over 500: 90%; SAT math scores over 500: 94%; ACT scores over 18: 99%; SAT critical reading scores over 600: 49%; SAT math scores over 600: 61%; ACT scores over 24: 79%; SAT critical reading scores over 700: 9%; SAT math scores over 700: 11%; ACT scores over 30: 15%.

Faculty *Total:* 1,256, 66% full-time, 71% with terminal degrees. *Student/faculty ratio:* 15:1.

Majors Accounting; accounting technology and bookkeeping; administrative assistant and secretarial science; aerospace, aeronautical and astronautical engineering; African-American/Black studies; American studies; ancient/classical Greek; anthropology; architecture; art; art history, criticism and conservation; art teacher education; Asian studies (East); athletic training; audiology and speech-language pathology; biochemistry; biology/biological sciences; biology teacher education; botany/plant biology; business administration and management; business/commerce; business/managerial economics; chemical engineering; chemical technology; chemistry; child development; city/urban, community and regional planning; classics and languages, literatures and linguistics; clinical laboratory science/medical technology; computer and information sciences; computer engineering; computer systems analysis; creative writing; data processing and data processing technology; dietetics; dramatic/theater arts; early childhood education; economics; electrical, electronic and communications engineering technology; electrical, electronics and communications engineering; elementary education; engineering/industrial management; engineering physics; engineering technology; English; English/language arts teacher education; environmental design/architecture; family and consumer economics related; family and consumer sciences/home economics teacher education; family and consumer sciences/human sciences; finance; fine/studio arts; French; geography; geology/earth science; German; graphic design; health and physical education; health teacher education; history; human development and family studies; human resources management; industrial engineering; interdisciplinary studies; interior design; international relations and affairs; Italian studies; journalism; kindergarten/preschool education; kinesiology and exercise science; Latin; liberal arts and sciences/liberal studies; linguistics; management information systems; management science; marketing/marketing management; mass communication/media; mathematics; mechanical engineering; mechanical engineering/mechanical technology; medical microbiology and bacteriology; middle school education; modern Greek; multi-/interdisciplinary studies related; music; music performance; music teacher education; nursing (registered nurse training); office management; operations management; operations research; organizational behavior; philosophy; physical education teaching and coaching; physics; political science and government; pre-dentistry studies; pre-law studies; pre-medical studies; pre-veterinary studies; psychology; public administration; purchasing, procurement/acquisitions and contracts management; religious studies; Russian; science teacher education; secondary education; social studies teacher education; social work; sociology; Spanish; special education; speech and rhetoric; speech-language pathology; sport and fitness administration/management; statistics; systems science and theory; technical and business writing; women's studies; wood science and wood products/pulp and paper technology; zoology/animal biology.

Academics *Calendar:* semesters. *Degrees:* certificates, associate, bachelor's, master's, doctoral, and post-master's certificates. *Special study options:* adult/continuing education programs, advanced placement credit, cooperative education, double majors, honors programs, independent study, internships, off-campus study, services for LD students, student-designed majors, study abroad, summer session for credit. *ROTC:* Army (c), Navy (b), Air Force (b). *Unusual degree programs:* 3-2 engineering with Case Western Reserve University, Columbia University; forestry with Duke University.

Computers on Campus 1,000 computers/terminals are available on campus for general student use. Students can access the following: campus intranet,

computer help desk, free student e-mail accounts, online (class) grades, online (class) registration. Campuswide network is available. Wireless service is available via entire campus.

Student Life *Housing:* on-campus residence required for freshman year. *Options:* coed, men-only, women-only, disabled students. Campus housing is university owned. Freshman campus housing is guaranteed. *Activities and organizations:* drama/theater group, student-run newspaper, radio and television station, choral group, marching band, Student Government, Alpha Phi Omega, Miami Marketing Enterprises, Campus Crusade for Christ, national fraternities, national sororities. *Campus security:* 24-hour emergency response devices and patrols, student patrols, late-night transport/escort service, controlled dormitory access. *Student services:* health clinic, personal/psychological counseling, women's center.

Athletics Member NCAA. All Division I except football (Division I-A). *Intercollegiate sports:* archery M (c)/W (c), baseball M (s), basketball M (s)/W (s), cross-country running M (s)/W (s), equestrian sports M (c)/W (c), fencing M (c)/W (c), field hockey W (s), golf M (s), gymnastics M (c)/W (c), ice hockey M (s), lacrosse M (c), racquetball M (c)/W (c), rugby M (c), sailing M (c)/W (c), soccer M (c)/W (s), softball W (s), swimming and diving M (s)/W (s), tennis M (c)/W (s), track and field M (s)/W (s), volleyball M (c)/W (s), wrestling M (c). *Intramural sports:* archery M/W, badminton M (c)/W (c), basketball M/W, cheerleading M (c)/W (c), crew M (c)/W (c), cross-country running M (c)/W (c), equestrian sports M (c)/W (c), fencing M (c)/W (c), field hockey W, football M/W, golf M (c)/W (c), gymnastics M (c)/W (c), ice hockey M (c)/W (c), lacrosse M (c)/W (c), racquetball M (c)/W (c), rugby M (c), sailing M/W, skiing (cross-country) M/W, skiing (downhill) M (c)/W (c), soccer M (c)/W (c), softball M/W, squash M (c)/W (c), swimming and diving M/W, table tennis M (c)/W (c), tennis M (c)/W (c), track and field M/W, ultimate Frisbee M (c)/W (c), volleyball M (c)/W (c), water polo M (c)/W (c), weight lifting M (c)/W (c), wrestling M (c).

Standardized Tests *Required:* SAT or ACT (for admission).

Costs (2007–08) *Tuition:* state resident $9910 full-time, $350 per credit hour part-time; nonresident $22,362 full-time, $875 per credit hour part-time. *Required fees:* $2015 full-time, $43 per credit hour part-time. *Room and board:* $8600; room only: $4410. Room and board charges vary according to board plan and housing facility. *Payment plan:* installment. *Waivers:* employees or children of employees.

Financial Aid Of all full-time matriculated undergraduates who enrolled in 2007, 7,586 applied for aid, 5,344 were judged to have need, 1,186 had their need fully met. 1,421 Federal Work-Study jobs (averaging $2113). In 2007, 2,308 non-need-based awards were made. *Average percent of need met:* 66%. *Average financial aid package:* $10,299. *Average need-based loan:* $4360. *Average need-based gift aid:* $5272. *Average non-need-based aid:* $4292. *Average indebtedness upon graduation:* $26,378.

Applying *Options:* electronic application, early decision, early action, deferred entrance. *Application fee:* $45. *Required:* high school transcript. *Recommended:* essay or personal statement, 1 letter of recommendation. *Application deadlines:* 1/31 (freshmen), 5/1 (transfers), 12/1 (early action). *Early decision deadline:* 11/1. *Notification:* 3/15 (freshmen), continuous (transfers), 12/15 (early decision), 2/1 (early action).

Freshman Application Contact Laurie Koehler, Interim Director of Undergraduate Admissions, Miami University, 301 South Campus Avenue, Oxford, OH 45056. *Phone:* 513-529-2531. *Fax:* 513-529-1550. *E-mail:* admissions@muohio.edu.

MIAMI UNIVERSITY HAMILTON

Hamilton, Ohio **www.ham.muohio.edu/**

- **State-supported** 4-year, founded 1968, part of Miami University System
- **Suburban** 78-acre campus with easy access to Cincinnati
- **Coed** 3,349 undergraduate students, 75% full-time, 55% women, 45% men
- **Noncompetitive** entrance level

Undergraduates 2,496 full-time, 853 part-time. 6% African American, 2% Asian American or Pacific Islander, 2% Hispanic American, 0.5% Native American, 5% transferred in.

Freshmen *Admission:* 659 enrolled.

Faculty *Total:* 221, 37% full-time. *Student/faculty ratio:* 21:1.

Majors Accounting; American studies; anthropology; architectural history and criticism; architecture; art; art teacher education; athletic training; audiology and speech-language pathology; biochemistry; botany/plant biology related; business administration and management; business administration, management and operations related; business/commerce; business/managerial economics; chemistry; chemistry teacher education; city/urban, community and regional planning; classics and languages, literatures and linguistics; clinical laboratory science/medical technology; communication/speech communication and rhetoric; computer and information sciences related; computer engineering; computer science; computer systems analysis; computer technology/computer systems technology; creative writing; dietetics; early childhood education; econometrics and quantitative economics; economics; education (multiple levels); electrical and electronic engineering technologies related; electromechanical technology; engineering/industrial management; engineering physics; engineering technology; English; English composition; English/language arts teacher education; environmental science; environmental studies; ethnic, cultural minority, and gender studies related; exercise physiology; finance; French; French language teacher education; general studies; geography; geology/earth science; German; German language teacher education; gerontology; graphic design; health teacher education; history; human resources management and services related; interior design; international/global studies; journalism; Latin; Latin teacher education; linguistics; management information systems; marketing/marketing management; marketing related; mass communication/media; mathematics; mathematics and statistics related; mathematics teacher education; mechanical engineering/mechanical technology; microbiology; multi-/interdisciplinary studies related; music; music teacher education; office management; philosophy; physical education teaching and coaching; physics; physics teacher education; political science and government; psychology; public administration; purchasing, procurement/acquisitions and contracts management; real estate; Russian; science teacher education; social studies teacher education; social work related; sociology; Spanish; Spanish language teacher education; special education; speech-language pathology; statistics; technical and business writing; theater/theater arts management; work and family studies; zoology/animal biology.

Academics *Calendar:* semesters plus summer sessions. *Degrees:* certificates, associate, bachelor's, and master's (degrees awarded by Miami University main campus). *Special study options:* academic remediation for entering students, adult/continuing education programs, advanced placement credit, cooperative education, distance learning, double majors, English as a second language, honors programs, internships, part-time degree program, services for LD students, student-designed majors, study abroad, summer session for credit. *ROTC:* Navy (c), Air Force (c).

Computers on Campus 300 computers/terminals are available on campus for general student use. Students can access the following: campus intranet, computer help desk, free student e-mail accounts, online (class) grades, online (class) registration, online (class) schedules. Campuswide network is available.

Student Life *Housing:* college housing not available. *Activities and organizations:* drama/theater group, choral group, student government, Campus Activities Committee, Ski Club, Student Nursing Association, Minority Action Committee. *Campus security:* 24-hour emergency response devices and patrols, late-night transport/escort service. *Student services:* personal/psychological counseling.

Athletics *Intercollegiate sports:* baseball M (c), basketball M (c)/W (c), cheerleading W, golf M (c), softball W (c), tennis M (c)/W (c), volleyball W (c). *Intramural sports:* basketball M/W, bowling M/W, skiing (cross-country) M/W, soccer M/W, softball M/W, tennis M/W, volleyball M/W, weight lifting M/W.

Costs (2007–08) *Tuition:* state resident $3948 full-time, $165 per credit part-time; nonresident $16,808 full-time, $700 per credit part-time. *Required fees:* $402 full-time, $15 per credit part-time, $18 per term part-time. *Payment plan:* installment. *Waivers:* employees or children of employees.

Applying *Options:* electronic application. *Application fee:* $35. *Required:* high school transcript. *Application deadline:* rolling (freshmen). *Notification:* continuous (freshmen), continuous (transfers).

Freshman Application Contact Mr. Archie Nelson, Director of Admission and Financial Aid, Miami University Hamilton, 1601 University Boulevard, Hamilton, OH 45011-3399. *Phone:* 513-785-3111. *Fax:* 513-785-1807. *E-mail:* nelsona3@muohio.edu.

MIAMI UNIVERSITY–MIDDLETOWN CAMPUS

Middletown, Ohio **www.mid.muohio.edu/**

- **State-supported** primarily 2-year, founded 1966, part of Miami University System
- **Small-town** 141-acre campus with easy access to Cincinnati and Dayton
- **Endowment** $779,742
- **Coed**
- **Noncompetitive** entrance level

Faculty *Student/faculty ratio:* 13:1.

Academics *Calendar:* semesters. *Degrees:* certificates, diplomas, associate, and bachelor's (also offers up to 2 years of most bachelor's degree programs offered at Miami University main campus).
Student Life *Campus security:* 24-hour patrols, late-night transport/escort service.
Standardized Tests *Recommended:* SAT or ACT (for placement).
Costs (2007–08) *Tuition:* state resident $4350 full-time; nonresident $17,210 full-time. *Required fees:* $402 full-time.
Applying *Options:* electronic application, early admission, deferred entrance. *Application fee:* $25. *Required:* high school transcript.
Freshman Application Contact Mrs. Mary Lou Flynn, Director of Enrollment Services, Miami University–Middletown Campus, 4200 East University Boulevard, Middletown, OH 45042. *Phone:* 513-727-3346. *Toll-free phone:* 866-426-4643. *Fax:* 513-727-3223. *E-mail:* flynnml@muohio.edu.

MOUNT CARMEL COLLEGE OF NURSING
Columbus, Ohio **www.mccn.edu/**

- **Independent** comprehensive, founded 1903
- **Urban** campus
- **Endowment** $599,825
- **Coed, primarily women** 642 undergraduate students, 82% full-time, 91% women, 9% men
- **Moderately difficult** entrance level, 60% of applicants were admitted

Undergraduates 525 full-time, 117 part-time. Students come from 6 states and territories, 11 other countries, 1% are from out of state, 13% transferred in, 12% live on campus. *Retention:* 81% of 2006 full-time freshmen returned.
Freshmen *Admission:* 144 applied, 87 admitted, 87 enrolled. *Average high school GPA:* 3.37. *Test scores:* ACT scores over 18: 90%; ACT scores over 24: 11%.
Faculty *Total:* 59, 63% full-time, 15% with terminal degrees. *Student/faculty ratio:* 13:1.
Majors Nursing (registered nurse training).
Academics *Calendar:* semesters. *Degrees:* bachelor's, master's, and post-master's certificates.
Computers on Campus 51 computers/terminals are available on campus for general student use. Students can access the following: campus intranet, computer help desk, free student e-mail accounts, online (class) grades, online (class) schedules. Campuswide network is available. 100% of college-owned or -operated housing units are wired for high-speed Internet access. Wireless service is available via classrooms, computer centers, computer labs, libraries, student centers.
Student Life *Housing:* on-campus residence required for freshman year. *Options:* coed. Campus housing is provided by a third party. Freshman applicants given priority for college housing. *Activities and organizations:* Student Nurses Association, Campus Ministry, Sigma Theta Tau. *Student services:* personal/psychological counseling.
Athletics *Intramural sports:* basketball W (c), softball W (c), volleyball M (c)/W (c).
Costs (2007–08) *One-time required fee:* $225. *Tuition:* $15,450 full-time, $296 per semester hour part-time. *Required fees:* $312 full-time, $312 per term part-time. *Payment plan:* installment. *Waivers:* employees or children of employees.
Financial Aid Of all full-time matriculated undergraduates who enrolled in 2003, 380 applied for aid, 365 were judged to have need, 100 had their need fully met. 27 state and other part-time jobs (averaging $1930). In 2003, 20 non-need-based awards were made. *Average percent of need met:* 70%. *Average financial aid package:* $9000. *Average need-based loan:* $7500. *Average need-based gift aid:* $1500. *Average non-need-based aid:* $2000. *Average indebtedness upon graduation:* $25,000.
Applying *Application fee:* $30. *Required:* essay or personal statement, high school transcript, 3 letters of recommendation, activities/interests resume. *Required for some:* interview. *Application deadlines:* rolling (freshmen), rolling (transfers).
Freshman Application Contact Mount Carmel College of Nursing, 127 South Davis Avenue, Columbus, OH 43222. *Phone:* 614-234-1085.

MOUNT UNION COLLEGE
Alliance, Ohio **www.muc.edu/**

- **Independent United Methodist** 4-year, founded 1846
- **Suburban** 115-acre campus with easy access to Cleveland
- **Endowment** $130.0 million
- **Coed**
- **Moderately difficult** entrance level

One of the nation's first coeducational institutions, Mount Union College is a private liberal arts college affiliated with the United Methodist Church. The College affirms the importance of reason, open inquiry, living faith, and individual worth. Mount Union's mission is to prepare students for meaningful work, fulfilling lives, and responsible citizenship.

Faculty *Student/faculty ratio:* 13:1.
Academics *Calendar:* semesters. *Degree:* bachelor's.
Student Life *Campus security:* 24-hour emergency response devices and patrols, late-night transport/escort service, controlled dormitory access, 24-hour locked residence hall entrances, outside phones.
Athletics Member NCAA. All Division III.
Standardized Tests *Required:* SAT or ACT (for admission).
Costs (2007–08) *Comprehensive fee:* $28,750 includes full-time tuition ($21,800), mandatory fees ($250), and room and board ($6700). Part-time tuition: $920 per semester hour. *Required fees:* $50 per term part-time. *Room and board:* Room and board charges vary according to board plan and housing facility. *Payment plans:* tuition prepayment, installment.
Financial Aid Of all full-time matriculated undergraduates who enrolled in 2006, 1,825 applied for aid, 1,630 were judged to have need, 355 had their need fully met. 1,100 Federal Work-Study jobs (averaging $261). 472 state and other part-time jobs (averaging $1057). In 2006, 365 non-need-based awards were made. *Average percent of need met:* 80. *Average financial aid package:* $16,645. *Average need-based loan:* $5097. *Average need-based gift aid:* $11,796. *Average non-need-based aid:* $11,337. *Average indebtedness upon graduation:* $19,590.
Applying *Options:* electronic application, early admission, deferred entrance. *Required:* essay or personal statement, high school transcript, minimum 2.0 GPA, 1 letter of recommendation. *Recommended:* interview.
Freshman Application Contact Mr. Vincent Heslop, Director of Enrollment Technology, Mount Union College, 1972 Clark Avenue, Alliance, OH 44601. *Phone:* 330-823-2590. *Toll-free phone:* 800-334-6682 (in-state); 800-992-6682 (out-of-state). *Fax:* 330-823-5097. *E-mail:* admission@muc.edu.

See page 2042 for the College Close-Up.

MOUNT VERNON NAZARENE UNIVERSITY
Mount Vernon, Ohio **www.mvnu.edu/**

- **Independent Nazarene** comprehensive, founded 1964
- **Small-town** 401-acre campus with easy access to Columbus
- **Endowment** $12.4 million
- **Coed** 2,169 undergraduate students, 88% full-time, 58% women, 42% men
- **Moderately difficult** entrance level, 77% of applicants were admitted

Undergraduates 1,912 full-time, 257 part-time. Students come from 28 states and territories, 5 other countries, 10% are from out of state, 5% African American, 0.6% Asian American or Pacific Islander, 2% Hispanic American, 0.1% Native American, 0.5% international, 4% transferred in, 78% live on campus. *Retention:* 71% of 2006 full-time freshmen returned.
Freshmen *Admission:* 837 applied, 646 admitted, 351 enrolled. *Average high school GPA:* 3.37. *Test scores:* SAT critical reading scores over 500: 50%; SAT math scores over 500: 55%; ACT scores over 18: 94%; SAT critical reading scores over 600: 17%; SAT math scores over 600: 19%; ACT scores over 24: 38%; SAT critical reading scores over 700: 2%; SAT math scores over 700: 2%; ACT scores over 30: 3%.
Faculty *Total:* 255, 45% full-time, 40% with terminal degrees. *Student/faculty ratio:* 13:1.
Majors Accounting; art; art teacher education; biblical studies; biological and physical sciences; biology/biological sciences; broadcast journalism; business/commerce; business, management, and marketing related; business teacher education; chemistry; child care and support services management; clinical laboratory science/medical technology; communication/speech communication and rhetoric; computer and information sciences; computer science; criminal justice/law enforcement administration; data processing and data processing technology; design and visual communications; dramatic/theater arts; early childhood education; education; elementary education; English; English/language arts teacher education; family and consumer sciences/home economics teacher education; family and consumer sciences/human sciences; finance; general studies; graphic design; health and physical education; health teacher education; history; history teacher education; human services; international business/trade/commerce; journalism; kindergarten/preschool education; kinesiology and exercise science;

marketing/marketing management; mathematics; mathematics teacher education; medical staff services technology; middle school education; music; music performance; music teacher education; natural resources/conservation; nursing (registered nurse training); office management; philosophy; physical education teaching and coaching; physical therapy; physics; physics teacher education; pre-dentistry studies; pre-law studies; pre-medical studies; pre-pharmacy studies; pre-veterinary studies; psychology; religious education; religious/sacred music; science teacher education; secondary education; social sciences; social studies teacher education; social work; sociology; Spanish; Spanish language teacher education; special education; sport and fitness administration/management; theology; youth ministry.

Academics *Calendar:* 4-1-4. *Degrees:* associate, bachelor's, and master's. *Special study options:* academic remediation for entering students, adult/continuing education programs, advanced placement credit, distance learning, double majors, honors programs, independent study, internships, off-campus study, part-time degree program, services for LD students, study abroad, summer session for credit. *Unusual degree programs:* 3-2 engineering with Olivet Nazarene University; pre-occupational therapy/physician assistant with Chatham College.

Computers on Campus 196 computers/terminals and 1,200 ports are available on campus for general student use. Students can access the following: campus intranet, computer help desk, free student e-mail accounts, online (class) grades, online (class) schedules. Campuswide network is available. 100% of college-owned or -operated housing units are wired for high-speed Internet access. Wireless service is available via computer centers, learning centers, libraries, student centers.

Student Life *Housing:* on-campus residence required through senior year. *Options:* men-only, women-only, disabled students. Campus housing is university owned. Freshman campus housing is guaranteed. *Activities and organizations:* drama/theater group, student-run newspaper, radio station, choral group, campus ministry groups, Student Government Association, Student Education Association, Drama Club, music department ensembles. *Campus security:* 24-hour emergency response devices and patrols, late-night transport/escort service, controlled dormitory access. *Student services:* health clinic, personal/psychological counseling.

Athletics Member NAIA, NCCAA. *Intercollegiate sports:* baseball M (s), basketball M (s)/W (s), cross-country running M (s)/W (s), golf M (s), soccer M (s)/W (s), softball W (s), volleyball W (s). *Intramural sports:* basketball M/W, bowling M/W, cheerleading M/W, football M/W, soccer M/W, softball M/W, table tennis M/W, volleyball M/W.

Standardized Tests *Required:* SAT or ACT (for admission).

Costs (2008–09) *Comprehensive fee:* $24,880 includes full-time tuition ($18,770), mandatory fees ($560), and room and board ($5550). Part-time tuition: $670 per semester hour. *Required fees:* $19 per semester hour part-time. *College room only:* $3100.

Financial Aid Of all full-time matriculated undergraduates who enrolled in 2006, 1,354 applied for aid, 1,016 were judged to have need, 169 had their need fully met. 176 Federal Work-Study jobs (averaging $1450). 380 state and other part-time jobs (averaging $1529). In 2006, 140 non-need-based awards were made. *Average percent of need met:* 84%. *Average financial aid package:* $13,283. *Average need-based loan:* $4140. *Average need-based gift aid:* $7434. *Average non-need-based aid:* $2886. *Average indebtedness upon graduation:* $21,719.

Applying *Options:* electronic application, deferred entrance. *Application fee:* $25. *Required:* essay or personal statement, high school transcript, minimum 2.5 GPA, 2 letters of recommendation. *Application deadline:* 8/1 (freshmen). *Notification:* continuous until 9/1 (freshmen), continuous (transfers).

Freshman Application Contact Mr. Jay Mahan, Director of Traditional Undergraduate Admissions, Mount Vernon Nazarene University, 800 Martinsburg Road, Mount Vernon, OH 43050. *Phone:* 740-392-6868 Ext. 4516. *Toll-free phone:* 866-462-6868. *Fax:* 740-393-0511. *E-mail:* admissions@mvnu.edu.

MUSKINGUM COLLEGE

New Concord, Ohio **www.muskingum.edu/**

Freshman Application Contact Mrs. Beth DaLonzo, Director of Admission, Muskingum College, 163 Stormont Street, New Concord, OH 43762. *Phone:* 740-826-8137. *Toll-free phone:* 800-752-6082. *Fax:* 740-826-8100. *E-mail:* adminfo@muskingum.edu.

See page 2044 for the College Close-Up.

MYERS UNIVERSITY

Cleveland, Ohio **www.myers.edu/**

Director of Admissions Christina Johnson, Vice President for Enrollment Management, Myers University, 3921 Chester Avenue, Cleveland, OH 44114-4624. *Phone:* 216-523-3806 Ext. 805. *Toll-free phone:* 877-366-9377. *E-mail:* rgbrown@myers.edu.

NOTRE DAME COLLEGE

South Euclid, Ohio **www.notredamecollege.edu/**

- **Independent Roman Catholic** comprehensive, founded 1922
- **Suburban** 53-acre campus with easy access to Cleveland
- **Endowment** $7.7 million
- **Coed**
- **Moderately difficult** entrance level

Notre Dame College, a Catholic institution in the tradition of the Sisters of Notre Dame, educates a diverse population in the liberal arts for personal, professional, and global responsibility. The coeducational, career-focused College provides a small class size and personalized attention. The College offers nearly thirty majors and eighteen scholarship athletic teams.

Faculty *Student/faculty ratio:* 13:1.

Academics *Calendar:* semesters. *Degrees:* certificates, associate, bachelor's, master's, and postbachelor's certificates.

Student Life *Campus security:* 24-hour emergency response devices and patrols, late-night transport/escort service, controlled dormitory access.

Athletics Member NAIA.

Standardized Tests *Required:* SAT or ACT (for admission).

Costs (2007–08) *Comprehensive fee:* $28,144 includes full-time tuition ($20,540), mandatory fees ($550), and room and board ($7054). Full-time tuition and fees vary according to course load and degree level. Part-time tuition: $425 per credit. Part-time tuition and fees vary according to course load and degree level. *Room and board:* Room and board charges vary according to board plan and housing facility.

Financial Aid Of all full-time matriculated undergraduates who enrolled in 2007, 473 applied for aid, 430 were judged to have need, 97 had their need fully met. 81 Federal Work-Study jobs (averaging $1042). In 2007, 86 non-need-based awards were made. *Average percent of need met:* 7. *Average financial aid package:* $18,558. *Average need-based loan:* $4520. *Average need-based gift aid:* $13,961. *Average non-need-based aid:* $11,488. *Average indebtedness upon graduation:* $22,178.

Applying *Options:* electronic application, deferred entrance. *Application fee:* $30. *Required:* essay or personal statement, high school transcript, minimum 2.0 GPA, interview. *Recommended:* minimum 2.5 GPA.

Freshman Application Contact Mr. David Armstrong, Dean of Admissions, Notre Dame College, 4545 College Road, South Euclid, OH 44121-4293. *Phone:* 216-373-5214. *Toll-free phone:* 800-632-1680. *Fax:* 216-381-3802. *E-mail:* admissinos@ndc.edu.

See page 2046 for the College Close-Up.

OBERLIN COLLEGE

Oberlin, Ohio **www.oberlin.edu/**

- **Independent** comprehensive, founded 1833
- **Small-town** 440-acre campus with easy access to Cleveland
- **Endowment** $797.0 million
- **Coed** 2,762 undergraduate students, 98% full-time, 55% women, 45% men
- **Very difficult** entrance level, 31% of applicants were admitted

Oberlin is a community of thinkers, scholars, scientists, musicians, athletes, activists, and artists—all of whom seek to make the world a better place. Oberlin's 2,800 students pursue studies in the College of Arts and Sciences, the Conservatory of Music, or both divisions through a distinctive five-year double-degree program.

Undergraduates 2,718 full-time, 44 part-time. Students come from 50 states and territories, 44 other countries, 91% are from out of state, 6% African American, 8% Asian American or Pacific Islander, 5% Hispanic American, 0.6% Native American, 6% international, 2% transferred in, 86% live on campus. *Retention:* 92% of 2006 full-time freshmen returned.

Freshmen *Admission:* 7,014 applied, 2,193 admitted, 742 enrolled. *Average high school GPA:* 3.6. *Test scores:* SAT critical reading scores over 500: 99%; SAT math scores over 500: 98%; ACT scores over 18: 99%; SAT critical reading scores over 600: 87%; SAT math scores over 600: 81%; ACT scores over 24: 89%; SAT critical reading scores over 700: 53%; SAT math scores over 700: 33%; ACT scores over 30: 46%.

Faculty *Total:* 325, 85% full-time. *Student/faculty ratio:* 9:1.

Majors African-American/Black studies; anthropology; archeology; art; art history, criticism and conservation; Asian studies (East); biochemistry; biology/biological sciences; chemistry; classics and languages, literatures and linguistics; comparative literature; computer science; creative writing; dance; dramatic/theater arts; ecology; economics; English; environmental studies; fine/studio arts; French; geology/earth science; German; history; interdisciplinary studies; jazz/jazz studies; Jewish/Judaic studies; Latin; Latin American studies; legal studies; mathematics; modern Greek; music; music history, literature, and theory; music teacher education; music theory and composition; Near and Middle Eastern studies; neuroscience; philosophy; physics; physiological psychology/psychobiology; piano and organ; political science and government; psychology; religious studies; Romance languages; Russian; Russian studies; sociology; Spanish; violin, viola, guitar and other stringed instruments; voice and opera; wind/percussion instruments; women's studies.

Academics *Calendar:* 4-1-4. *Degrees:* diplomas, bachelor's, master's, and postbachelor's certificates. *Special study options:* advanced placement credit, double majors, English as a second language, honors programs, independent study, internships, off-campus study, part-time degree program, services for LD students, student-designed majors, study abroad. *Unusual degree programs:* 3-2 engineering with Washington University in St. Louis, Case Western Reserve University, California Institute of Technology.

Computers on Campus 340 computers/terminals are available on campus for general student use. Students can access the following: campus intranet, computer help desk, free student e-mail accounts, online (class) registration, online (class) schedules. Campuswide network is available. 100% of college-owned or -operated housing units are wired for high-speed Internet access. Wireless service is available via classrooms, computer centers, computer labs, dorm rooms, learning centers, libraries, student centers.

Student Life *Housing:* on-campus residence required through sophomore year. *Options:* coed, women-only, cooperative, disabled students. Campus housing is university owned. Freshman campus housing is guaranteed. *Activities and organizations:* drama/theater group, student-run newspaper, radio station, choral group, marching band, Experimental College, Community Outreach, Black Students Organization, Students Cooperative Association, student radio station. *Campus security:* 24-hour emergency response devices and patrols, student patrols, late-night transport/escort service, controlled dormitory access, crime prevention programs. *Student services:* health clinic, personal/psychological counseling, women's center.

Athletics Member NCAA. All Division III. *Intercollegiate sports:* baseball M, basketball M/W, cheerleading W (c), cross-country running M/W, equestrian sports M (c)/W (c), fencing M (c)/W (c), field hockey W, football M, golf M/W, ice hockey M (c)/W (c), lacrosse M/W, rugby M (c)/W (c), soccer M/W, softball W (c), swimming and diving M/W, tennis M/W, track and field M/W, ultimate Frisbee M (c)/W (c), volleyball M (c)/W, water polo M (c)/W (c). *Intramural sports:* baseball M, basketball M/W, bowling M/W, cross-country running M/W, football M, golf M/W, racquetball M/W, rock climbing M/W, soccer M/W, softball M/W, squash M/W, table tennis M/W, tennis M/W, track and field M/W, volleyball M/W, water polo M/W, weight lifting M/W.

Standardized Tests *Required:* SAT or ACT (for admission). *Recommended:* SAT Subject Tests (for admission).

Costs (2007–08) *Comprehensive fee:* $46,362 includes full-time tuition ($36,064), mandatory fees ($218), and room and board ($10,080). Full-time tuition and fees vary according to course load. Part-time tuition: $1500 per credit. Part-time tuition and fees vary according to course load. *College room only:* $4850. Room and board charges vary according to board plan and housing facility. *Payment plan:* installment. *Waivers:* employees or children of employees.

Financial Aid Of all full-time matriculated undergraduates who enrolled in 2006, 1,752 applied for aid, 1,546 were judged to have need, 1,546 had their need fully met. In 2006, 350 non-need-based awards were made. *Average percent of need met:* 100%. *Average financial aid package:* $24,255. *Average need-based loan:* $4423. *Average need-based gift aid:* $18,807. *Average non-need-based aid:* $10,409. *Average indebtedness upon graduation:* $16,922.

Applying *Options:* electronic application, early admission, early decision, deferred entrance. *Application fee:* $35. *Required:* essay or personal statement, high school transcript, 2 letters of recommendation. *Required for some:* interview. *Application deadlines:* 1/15 (freshmen), 3/15 (transfers). *Early decision deadline:* 11/15 (for plan 1), 1/2 (for plan 2). *Notification:* 4/1 (freshmen), 5/1 (transfers), 12/10 (early decision plan 1), 2/1 (early decision plan 2).

Freshman Application Contact Ms. Debra Chermonte, Dean of Admissions and Financial Aid, Oberlin College, Admissions Office, Carnegie Building, Oberlin, OH 44074-1090. *Phone:* 440-775-8411. *Toll-free phone:* 800-622-OBIE. *Fax:* 440-775-6905. *E-mail:* college.admissions@oberlin.edu.

See page 2048 for the College Close-Up.

OHIO CHRISTIAN UNIVERSITY

Circleville, Ohio **www.ohiochristian.edu/**

Director of Admissions Mr. Scott Faughn, Acting Director of Enrollment, Ohio Christian University, PO Box 458, Circleville, OH 43113-9487. *Phone:* 740-477-7741. *Toll-free phone:* 800-701-0222. *E-mail:* sfaughn@biblecollege.edu.

OHIO DOMINICAN UNIVERSITY

Columbus, Ohio **www.ohiodominican.edu/**

- **Independent Roman Catholic** comprehensive, founded 1911
- **Urban** 62-acre campus
- **Endowment** $20.9 million
- **Coed** 2,560 undergraduate students, 69% full-time, 61% women, 39% men
- **Moderately difficult** entrance level, 69% of applicants were admitted

Undergraduates 1,754 full-time, 806 part-time. Students come from 18 states and territories, 12 other countries, 3% are from out of state, 21% African American, 1% Asian American or Pacific Islander, 2% Hispanic American, 0.4% Native American, 0.5% international, 5% transferred in, 38% live on campus. *Retention:* 59% of 2006 full-time freshmen returned.

Freshmen *Admission:* 2,442 applied, 1,680 admitted, 399 enrolled. *Average high school GPA:* 3.04. *Test scores:* ACT scores over 18: 88%; ACT scores over 24: 18%; ACT scores over 30: 1%.

Faculty *Total:* 217, 31% full-time, 42% with terminal degrees. *Student/faculty ratio:* 14:1.

Majors Accounting; art teacher education; biology/biological sciences; business administration and management; business/corporate communications; chemistry; chemistry teacher education; communication/speech communication and rhetoric; criminal justice/law enforcement administration; early childhood education; economics; education (K-12); English; finance; fine/studio arts; foreign language teacher education; general studies; gerontology; graphic design; history; information science/studies; international business/trade/commerce; kindergarten/preschool education; liberal arts and sciences/liberal studies; mathematics; mathematics teacher education; middle school education; peace studies and conflict resolution; philosophy; physics teacher education; political science and government; psychology; public relations/image management; science teacher education; secondary education; social studies teacher education; social work; sociology; special education; sport and fitness administration/management; theology.

Academics *Calendar:* semesters. *Degrees:* certificates, associate, bachelor's, and master's. *Special study options:* academic remediation for entering students, adult/continuing education programs, advanced placement credit, distance learning, English as a second language, honors programs, independent study, internships, off-campus study, part-time degree program, student-designed majors, study abroad, summer session for credit. *ROTC:* Army (c). *Unusual degree programs:* 3-2 business administration.

Computers on Campus 198 computers/terminals and 1,900 ports are available on campus for general student use. Students can access the following: campus intranet, computer help desk, free student e-mail accounts, online (class) grades, online (class) registration, online (class) schedules. Campuswide network is available. 100% of college-owned or -operated housing units are wired for high-speed Internet access.

Student Life *Housing:* on-campus residence required through junior year. *Options:* coed. Campus housing is university owned. *Activities and organizations:* drama/theater group, student-run newspaper, radio station, choral group, Delta Sigma Pi, Student Government, Panther Activities Council, Black Student Union, Panther Players. *Campus security:* 24-hour emergency response devices and patrols, late-night transport/escort service, controlled dormitory access. *Student services:* health clinic, personal/psychological counseling.

Athletics Member NAIA. *Intercollegiate sports:* baseball M (s), basketball M (s)/W (s), cheerleading M/W, cross-country running M/W, football M (s), golf M (s)/W (s), soccer M (s)/W (s), softball W (s), tennis M (s)/W (s), volleyball W (s). *Intramural sports:* badminton M/W, basketball M/W, bowling M/W, golf M/W, lacrosse M/W, soccer M/W, table tennis M/W, tennis M/W, volleyball M/W.

Standardized Tests *Required:* SAT or ACT (for admission).

Costs (2007–08) *One-time required fee:* $125. *Comprehensive fee:* $28,994 includes full-time tuition ($21,720), mandatory fees ($74), and room and board ($7200). Part-time tuition: $440 per credit hour. *Required fees:* $135 per term part-time. *Room and board:* Room and board charges vary according to board plan and housing facility. *Payment plan:* installment. *Waivers:* senior citizens and employees or children of employees.

Financial Aid Of all full-time matriculated undergraduates who enrolled in 2006, 200 Federal Work-Study jobs (averaging $2000). *Average percent of need met:* 92%. *Average financial aid package:* $12,467. *Average indebtedness upon graduation:* $13,500.

Applying *Options:* electronic application, deferred entrance. *Application fee:* $25. *Required:* high school transcript, minimum 2.0 GPA, interview. *Required for some:* essay or personal statement, letters of recommendation. *Application deadlines:* rolling (freshmen), rolling (transfers). *Notification:* continuous (freshmen), continuous (transfers).

Freshman Application Contact Ms. Nicole A. Evans, Director of Admissions, Ohio Dominican University, 1216 Sunbury Road, Columbus, OH 43219. *Phone:* 614-251-4500. *Toll-free phone:* 800-854-2670. *Fax:* 614-251-0156. *E-mail:* admissions@ohiodominican.edu.

OHIO NORTHERN UNIVERSITY

Ada, Ohio **www.onu.edu/**

- **Independent** comprehensive, founded 1871, affiliated with United Methodist Church
- **Small-town** 300-acre campus
- **Coed** 2,605 undergraduate students, 96% full-time, 46% women, 54% men
- **Moderately difficult** entrance level, 88% of applicants were admitted

Undergraduates 2,511 full-time, 94 part-time. Students come from 47 states and territories, 16 other countries, 15% are from out of state, 3% African American, 1% Asian American or Pacific Islander, 1% Hispanic American, 0.3% Native American, 2% international, 2% transferred in, 71% live on campus. *Retention:* 81% of 2006 full-time freshmen returned.

Freshmen *Admission:* 3,308 applied, 2,903 admitted, 722 enrolled. *Average high school GPA:* 3.64. *Test scores:* SAT critical reading scores over 500: 80%; SAT math scores over 500: 87%; SAT writing scores over 500: 81%; ACT scores over 18: 99%; SAT critical reading scores over 600: 40%; SAT math scores over 600: 57%; SAT writing scores over 600: 42%; ACT scores over 24: 72%; SAT critical reading scores over 700: 6%; SAT math scores over 700: 13%; SAT writing scores over 700: 8%; ACT scores over 30: 20%.

Faculty *Total:* 307, 74% full-time, 65% with terminal degrees. *Student/faculty ratio:* 13:1.

Majors Accounting; art; art teacher education; athletic training; biochemistry; biology/biological sciences; biology teacher education; business administration and management; business/commerce; ceramic arts and ceramics; chemistry; chemistry related; chemistry teacher education; civil engineering; civil engineering related; clinical laboratory science/medical technology; commercial and advertising art; communication and journalism related; communication/speech communication and rhetoric; computer engineering; computer engineering related; computer science; creative writing; criminal justice/law enforcement administration; criminal justice/police science; criminal justice/safety; design and visual communications; dramatic/theater arts; early childhood education; education; education (multiple levels); education related; electrical, electronics and communications engineering; elementary education; engineering; engineering related; English; English/language arts teacher education; environmental studies; fine/studio arts; foreign language teacher education; French; French language teacher education; general studies; Germanic languages related; German language teacher education; graphic design; health and physical education; health and physical education related; health teacher education; history; history teacher education; industrial arts; industrial technology; international business/trade/commerce; international relations and affairs; journalism; kindergarten/preschool education; kinesiology and exercise science; management science; management sciences and quantitative methods related; mass communication/media; mathematics; mathematics related; mathematics teacher education; mechanical engineering; medicinal and pharmaceutical chemistry; middle school education; molecular biology; music; music management and merchandising; music performance; music related; music teacher education; organizational communication; painting; pharmacy; pharmacy, pharmaceutical sciences, and administration related; philosophy; philosophy related; physical education teaching and coaching; physics; physics related; physics teacher education; political science and government; pre-dentistry studies; pre-law studies; pre-medical studies; pre-theology/pre-ministerial studies; pre-veterinary studies; printmaking; psychology; psychology related; public relations/image management; radio and television; religious studies; religious studies related; science teacher education; sculpture; secondary education; social studies teacher education; sociology; Spanish; Spanish language teacher education; sport and fitness administration/management; statistics; statistics related; technical and business writing; theater/theater arts management; visual and performing arts; visual and performing arts related.

Academics *Calendar:* quarters. *Degrees:* bachelor's, master's, first professional, and postbachelor's certificates. *Special study options:* academic remediation for entering students, advanced placement credit, cooperative education, distance learning, double majors, English as a second language, honors programs, independent study, internships, off-campus study, part-time degree program, services for LD students, study abroad, summer session for credit. *ROTC:* Army (c), Air Force (c).

Computers on Campus 533 computers/terminals and 3,000 ports are available on campus for general student use. Students can access the following: campus intranet, computer help desk, free student e-mail accounts, online (class) grades, online (class) registration, online (class) schedules. Campuswide network is available. 100% of college-owned or -operated housing units are wired for high-speed Internet access. Wireless service is available via classrooms, computer centers, computer labs, dorm rooms, libraries, student centers.

Student Life *Housing:* on-campus residence required through junior year. *Options:* coed, men-only, women-only, disabled students. Campus housing is university owned. Freshman campus housing is guaranteed. *Activities and organizations:* drama/theater group, student-run newspaper, radio and television station, choral group, marching band, Habitat for Humanity, Student Planning Committee, Student Senate, Northern Christian Fellowship, Marching Band, national fraternities, national sororities. *Campus security:* 24-hour emergency response devices and patrols, late-night transport/escort service, controlled dormitory access. *Student services:* health clinic, personal/psychological counseling, legal services.

Athletics Member NCAA. All Division III. *Intercollegiate sports:* baseball M, basketball M/W, cross-country running M/W, football M, golf M/W, soccer M/W, softball W, swimming and diving M/W, tennis M/W, track and field M/W, volleyball W, wrestling M. *Intramural sports:* badminton M/W, basketball M/W, bowling M/W, cheerleading M (c)/W (c), racquetball M/W, rock climbing M (c)/W (c), skiing (downhill) M (c)/W (c), soccer M/W, softball M/W, swimming and diving M/W, table tennis M/W, tennis M/W, ultimate Frisbee M (c)/W (c), volleyball M (c)/W, water polo M (c)/W (c).

Standardized Tests *Required:* SAT or ACT (for admission).

Costs (2008–09) *Comprehensive fee:* $38,655 includes full-time tuition ($30,555), mandatory fees ($210), and room and board ($7890). Part-time tuition: $850 per quarter hour. *Required fees:* $70 per quarter part-time. *College room only:* $3945.

Financial Aid Of all full-time matriculated undergraduates who enrolled in 2007, 2,202 applied for aid, 2,018 were judged to have need, 464 had their need fully met. 1,357 Federal Work-Study jobs (averaging $1792). 249 state and other part-time jobs (averaging $1585). In 2007, 264 non-need-based awards were made. *Average percent of need met:* 87%. *Average financial aid package:* $23,919. *Average need-based loan:* $4155. *Average need-based gift aid:* $18,960. *Average non-need-based aid:* $15,266. *Average indebtedness upon graduation:* $39,349.

Applying *Options:* electronic application, deferred entrance. *Application fee:* $30. *Required:* high school transcript. *Required for some:* 2 letters of recommendation. *Recommended:* essay or personal statement, minimum 2.5 GPA, interview. *Application deadlines:* 8/15 (freshmen), 9/1 (transfers). *Notification:* continuous (freshmen), continuous (transfers).

Freshman Application Contact Ms. Deborah Miller, Director of Admission, Ohio Northern University, 525 South Main, Ada, OH 45810-1599. *Phone:* 419-772-2260. *Toll-free phone:* 888-408-4ONU. *Fax:* 419-772-2821. *E-mail:* admissions-ug@onu.edu.

See page 2050 for the College Close-Up.

THE OHIO STATE UNIVERSITY

Columbus, Ohio **www.osu.edu/**

- **State-supported** university, founded 1870
- **Urban** 6191-acre campus
- **Endowment** $2.0 billion
- **Coed**
- **Moderately difficult** entrance level

Faculty *Student/faculty ratio:* 13:1.

Academics *Calendar:* quarters. *Degrees:* associate, bachelor's, master's, doctoral, first professional, post-master's, and post-bachelor's certificates.

Student Life *Campus security:* 24-hour emergency response devices and patrols, student patrols, late-night transport/escort service; controlled dormitory access, dorm entrances locked after 9 p.m., lighted pathways and sidewalks, self-defense education.

Athletics Member NCAA. All Division I except football (Division I-A).

Standardized Tests *Required:* SAT or ACT (for admission).

Costs (2007–08) *Tuition:* state resident $8406 full-time; nonresident $21,015 full-time. Full-time tuition and fees vary according to course load, program, reciprocity agreements, and student level. Part-time tuition and fees vary according to course load, program, reciprocity agreements, and student level. *Required fees:* $270 full-time. *Room and board:* $7365; room only: $4605. Room and board charges vary according to board plan and housing facility.

Financial Aid Of all full-time matriculated undergraduates who enrolled in 2007, 23,900 applied for aid, 18,994 were judged to have need, 3,653 had their need fully met. 3,164 Federal Work-Study jobs (averaging $2963). In 2007, 6809 non-need-based awards were made. *Average percent of need met:* 65. *Average financial aid package:* $10,225. *Average need-based loan:* $4781. *Average need-based gift aid:* $6480. *Average non-need-based aid:* $4384. *Average indebtedness upon graduation:* $19,978.

Applying *Options:* electronic application. *Application fee:* $40. *Required:* essay or personal statement, high school transcript.

Freshman Application Contact Dr. Mabel G. Freeman, Assistant Vice President for Undergraduate Admissions and First Year Experience, The Ohio State University, Enarson Hall, 154 West 12th Avenue, Columbus, OH 43210. *Phone:* 614-247-6281. *Fax:* 614-292-4818. *E-mail:* askabuckeye@osu.edu.

THE OHIO STATE UNIVERSITY AT LIMA

Lima, Ohio **www.lima.osu.edu/**

- **State-supported** comprehensive, founded 1960, part of Ohio State University
- **Small-town** 565-acre campus
- **Coed**
- **Noncompetitive** entrance level

Faculty *Student/faculty ratio:* 21:1.

Academics *Calendar:* quarters. *Degrees:* associate, bachelor's, and master's.

Student Life *Campus security:* 24-hour emergency response devices and patrols, late-night transport/escort service.

Standardized Tests *Required for some:* SAT or ACT (for admission).

Costs (2007–08) *Tuition:* state resident $5664 full-time; nonresident $18,273 full-time. Full-time tuition and fees vary according to course load and student level. Part-time tuition and fees vary according to course load and student level.

Applying *Options:* early admission. *Application fee:* $40. *Required:* essay or personal statement, high school transcript.

Freshman Application Contact Ms. Beth Keehn, Director of Admissions, The Ohio State University at Lima, 4240 Campus Drive, Lima, OH 45804. *Phone:* 419-995-8434. *Fax:* 419-995-8483. *E-mail:* admissions@lima.ohio-state.edu.

THE OHIO STATE UNIVERSITY AT MARION

Marion, Ohio **www.marion.ohio-state.edu/**

- **State-supported** comprehensive, founded 1958, part of Ohio State University
- **Small-town** 180-acre campus with easy access to Columbus
- **Coed**
- **Noncompetitive** entrance level

Faculty *Student/faculty ratio:* 22:1.

Academics *Calendar:* quarters. *Degrees:* associate, bachelor's, and master's.

Student Life *Campus security:* 24-hour emergency response devices.

Costs (2007–08) *Tuition:* state resident $5664 full-time; nonresident $18,273 full-time. Full-time tuition and fees vary according to course load and student level. Part-time tuition and fees vary according to course load and student level.

Applying *Options:* early admission. *Application fee:* $40. *Required:* essay or personal statement, high school transcript.

Freshman Application Contact Mr. Matthew Moreau, Admissions and Financial Aid Coordinator, The Ohio State University at Marion, 1465 Mount Vernon Avenue, Marion, OH 43302. *Phone:* 740-725-6337. *Fax:* 740-386-2439. *E-mail:* moreau.1@osu.edu.

THE OHIO STATE UNIVERSITY–MANSFIELD CAMPUS

Mansfield, Ohio **www.mansfield.osu.edu/**

- **State-supported** comprehensive, founded 1958, part of The Ohio State University
- **Small-town** 644-acre campus with easy access to Columbus and Cleveland
- **Coed**
- **Noncompetitive** entrance level

Faculty *Student/faculty ratio:* 19:1.

Academics *Calendar:* quarters. *Degrees:* associate, bachelor's, and master's.

Student Life *Campus security:* 24-hour emergency response devices and patrols, late-night transport/escort service.

Standardized Tests *Required for some:* SAT or ACT (for admission).

Costs (2007–08) *Tuition:* state resident $5664 full-time; nonresident $18,273 full-time. Full-time tuition and fees vary according to course load and student level. Part-time tuition and fees vary according to course load and student level. *Room and board:* $4275. Room and board charges vary according to housing facility.

Applying *Options:* early admission. *Application fee:* $40. *Required:* essay or personal statement, high school transcript.

Freshman Application Contact Mr. Henry D. Thomas, Coordinator of Admissions and Financial Aid, The Ohio State University–Mansfield Campus, 1680 University Drive, Mansfield, OH 44906. *Phone:* 419-755-4225. *Fax:* 419-755-4241. *E-mail:* admissions@mansfield.ohio-state.edu.

THE OHIO STATE UNIVERSITY–NEWARK CAMPUS

Newark, Ohio **www.newark.osu.edu/**

- **State-supported** comprehensive, founded 1957, part of Ohio State University
- **Small-town** 106-acre campus with easy access to Columbus
- **Coed**
- **Noncompetitive** entrance level

Faculty *Student/faculty ratio:* 26:1.

Academics *Calendar:* quarters. *Degrees:* associate, bachelor's, and master's.

Student Life *Campus security:* 24-hour emergency response devices and patrols, late-night transport/escort service, self-defense education.

Costs (2007–08) *Tuition:* state resident $5664 full-time; nonresident $18,273 full-time. Full-time tuition and fees vary according to course load and student level. Part-time tuition and fees vary according to course load and student level. *Room only:* $5265. Room and board charges vary according to housing facility.

Applying *Options:* early admission. *Application fee:* $40. *Required:* essay or personal statement, high school transcript.

Freshman Application Contact Mr. Claude R. Barclay, Admissions Counselor/Staff Assistant, The Ohio State University–Newark Campus, 1179 University Drive, Newark, OH 43055. *Phone:* 614-366-9396. *Fax:* 740-364-9645. *E-mail:* barclay.3@osu.edu.

OHIO UNIVERSITY

Athens, Ohio **www.ohio.edu/**

- **State-supported** university, founded 1804, part of Ohio Board of Regents, University System of Ohio
- **Small-town** 1,700-acre campus
- **Endowment** $242.8 million
- **Coed** 17,054 undergraduate students, 94% full-time, 51% women, 49% men
- **Moderately difficult** entrance level, 82% of applicants were admitted

Undergraduates 16,009 full-time, 1,045 part-time. Students come from 50 states and territories, 126 other countries, 8% are from out of state, 4% African American, 0.9% Asian American or Pacific Islander, 2% Hispanic American, 0.3% Native American, 2% international, 3% transferred in, 44% live on campus. *Retention:* 78% of 2006 full-time freshmen returned.

Freshmen *Admission:* 13,020 applied, 10,679 admitted, 4,005 enrolled. *Average high school GPA:* 3.34. *Test scores:* SAT critical reading scores over 500: 70%; SAT math scores over 500: 71%; SAT writing scores over 500: 67%; ACT scores over 18: 99%; SAT critical reading scores over 600: 26%; SAT math scores over 600: 26%; SAT writing scores over 600: 21%; ACT scores over 24: 47%; SAT critical reading scores over 700: 5%; SAT math scores over 700: 4%; SAT writing scores over 700: 3%; ACT scores over 30: 7%.

Faculty *Total:* 1,173, 73% full-time, 80% with terminal degrees. *Student/faculty ratio:* 19:1.

Majors Accounting technology and bookkeeping; acting; administrative assistant and secretarial science; advertising; aeronautical/aerospace engineering technology; aeronautics/aviation/aerospace science and technology; African-American/Black studies; African languages; African studies; ancient/classical Greek; anthropology; apparel and textiles; applied mathematics; art history, criticism and conservation; art teacher education; Asian studies; Asian studies (Southeast); astrophysics; atmospheric sciences and meteorology; atomic/molecular physics; audiology and hearing sciences; audiology and speech-language pathology; aviation/airway management; biological and physical sciences; biology/biological sciences; biology teacher education; botany/plant biology; broadcast journalism; business administration and management; business/commerce; business, management, and marketing related; cell biology and histology; ceramic arts and ceramics; chemical engineering; chemistry; child development; cinematography and film/video production; civil engineering; classics and languages, literatures and linguistics; commercial and advertising art; communication and journalism related; communication disorders sciences and services related; communication/speech communication and rhetoric; computer engineering; computer science; conducting; creative writing; criminal justice/law enforcement administration; criminal justice/police science; criminal justice/safety; criminology; curriculum and instruction; dance; design and applied arts related; design and visual communications; directing and theatrical production; dramatic/theater arts; dramatic/theater arts and stagecraft related; drawing; early childhood education; economics; education; educational leadership and administration; education (specific subject areas) related; electrical, electronic and communications engineering technology; electrical, electronics and communications engineering; elementary and middle school administration/principalship; elementary education; engineering; engineering related; engineering technologies related; English; English as a second/foreign language (teaching); environmental biology; environmental engineering technology; environmental/environmental health engineering; equestrian studies; European studies; family and consumer sciences/human sciences; family resource management; film/cinema studies; fine/studio arts; foods, nutrition, and wellness; French; French language teacher education; general studies; geography; geological and earth sciences/geosciences related; geology/earth science; German; German language teacher education; hazardous materials information systems technology; hazardous materials management and waste technology; health and physical education; housing and human environments; human development and family studies; humanities; human services; industrial engineering; industrial technology; interdisciplinary studies; international economics; international relations and affairs; journalism; journalism related; kindergarten/preschool education; kinesiology and exercise science; Latin; Latin American studies; liberal arts and sciences and humanities related; liberal arts and sciences/liberal studies; linguistics; mathematics; mathematics teacher education; mechanical engineering; mechanical engineering/mechanical technology; medical/clinical assistant; medical microbiology and bacteriology; middle school education; multi-/interdisciplinary studies related; music; music history, literature, and theory; music management and merchandising; music performance; music teacher education; music theory and composition; painting; parks, recreation and leisure; parks, recreation and leisure facilities management; philosophy; photographic and film/video technology; physical education teaching and coaching; physical sciences related; physics; physics related; piano and organ; playwriting and screenwriting; political science and government; pre-law studies; printmaking; psychology; public administration and social service professions related; public relations/image management; radio and television; radio and television broadcasting technology; reading teacher education; Russian; safety/security technology; science teacher education; sculpture; secondary education; security and protective services related; social sciences; social studies teacher education; social work; sociology; Spanish; Spanish language teacher education; special education; special education (multiply disabled); speech and rhetoric; sport and fitness administration/management; systems engineering; telecommunications; theater design and technology; theater literature, history and criticism; theater/theater arts management; tourism and travel services management; tourism and travel services marketing; visual and performing arts; voice and opera; wildlife biology; zoology/animal biology.

Academics *Calendar:* quarters. *Degrees:* associate, bachelor's, master's, doctoral, and first professional. *Special study options:* academic remediation for entering students, accelerated degree program, adult/continuing education programs, advanced placement credit, cooperative education, distance learning, double majors, English as a second language, external degree program, honors programs, independent study, internships, off-campus study, part-time degree program, services for LD students, student-designed majors, study abroad, summer session for credit. *ROTC:* Army (b), Air Force (b).

Computers on Campus 1,500 computers/terminals and 22,000 ports are available on campus for general student use. Students can access the following: computer help desk, free student e-mail accounts, online (class) grades, online (class) registration. Campuswide network is available. 100% of college-owned or -operated housing units are wired for high-speed Internet access. Wireless service is available via entire campus.

Student Life *Housing:* on-campus residence required through sophomore year. *Options:* coed, men-only, women-only, cooperative, disabled students. Campus housing is university owned. *Activities and organizations:* drama/theater group, student-run newspaper, radio and television station, choral group, marching band, Gamma Pi Delta, Golden Key, International Student Union, Chinese Students and Visiting Scholars Club, Campus Crusade for Christ, national fraternities, national sororities. *Campus security:* 24-hour emergency response devices and patrols, late-night transport/escort service, controlled dormitory access, security lighting. *Student services:* health clinic, personal/psychological counseling, women's center, legal services.

Athletics Member NCAA. All Division I except football (Division I-A). *Intercollegiate sports:* baseball M (s), basketball M (s)/W (s), cheerleading M/W, cross-country running M (s)/W (s), equestrian sports M (c)/W (c), field hockey W (s), golf M (s)/W (s), ice hockey M (c), lacrosse W (c), rock climbing M (c)/W (c), soccer M (c)/W (s), softball W (s), swimming and diving W (s), track and field W (s), volleyball M (c)/W (s), water polo M (c)/W (c), weight lifting M (c), wrestling M (s). *Intramural sports:* baseball M, basketball M/W, bowling M/W, cross-country running M/W, football M, racquetball M/W, soccer M/W, softball M/W, swimming and diving W, tennis M/W, track and field W, volleyball M/W.

Standardized Tests *Required:* SAT or ACT (for admission).

Costs (2007–08) *Tuition:* state resident $8907 full-time, $283 per quarter hour part-time; nonresident $17,871 full-time, $578 per quarter hour part-time. *Room and board:* $8427; room only: $4476. Room and board charges vary according to board plan. *Payment plan:* installment. *Waivers:* employees or children of employees.

Financial Aid Of all full-time matriculated undergraduates who enrolled in 2007, 11,582 applied for aid, 8,167 were judged to have need, 1,334 had their need fully met. 599 Federal Work-Study jobs (averaging $1900). In 2007, 1,809 non-need-based awards were made. *Average percent of need met:* 58%. *Average financial aid package:* $7712. *Average need-based loan:* $4257. *Average need-based gift aid:* $4829. *Average non-need-based aid:* $3906. *Average indebtedness upon graduation:* $20,880.

Applying *Options:* early admission, deferred entrance. *Application fee:* $45. *Required:* high school transcript. *Required for some:* essay or personal statement, interview. *Recommended:* 2 letters of recommendation. *Application deadlines:* 2/1 (freshmen), 2/1 (out-of-state freshmen), 5/15 (transfers). *Notification:* continuous (freshmen), 2/1 (out-of-state freshmen), continuous (transfers).

Freshman Application Contact Undergraduate Admissions, Ohio University, Athens, OH 45701-2979. *Phone:* 740-593-4100. *Fax:* 740-593-0560. *E-mail:* admissions@ohio.edu.

OHIO UNIVERSITY–CHILLICOTHE

Chillicothe, Ohio **www.chillicothe.ohiou.edu/**

Freshman Application Contact TJ Eveland, Coordinator of Student Enrollment, Ohio University–Chillicothe, 571 West Fifth Street, Chillicothe, OH 45601. *Phone:* 740-774-7200 Ext. 242. *Toll-free phone:* 877-462-6824. *Fax:* 740-774-7295.

OHIO UNIVERSITY–EASTERN

St. Clairsville, Ohio **www.eastern.ohiou.edu/**

Director of Admissions Assistant Vice President for Enrollment Services/Director of Admissions, Ohio University–Eastern, 45425 National Road, St. Clairsville, OH 43950-9724. *Phone:* 740-593-4120. *Toll-free phone:* 800-648-3331. *E-mail:* howardn@ohio.edu.

OHIO UNIVERSITY–LANCASTER

Lancaster, Ohio **www.ohiou.edu/lancaster/**

Director of Admissions Mr. Nathan Thomas, Admissions Officer, Ohio University–Lancaster, 1570 Granville Pike, Lancaster, OH 43130-1097. *Phone:* 740-654-6711 Ext. 215. *Toll-free phone:* 888-446-4468 Ext. 215. *E-mail:* shepherd@ohiou.edu.

OHIO UNIVERSITY–SOUTHERN CAMPUS

Ironton, Ohio **www.ohiou.edu/**

Director of Admissions Dr. Kim K. Lawson, Coordinator of Admissions, Ohio University–Southern Campus, 1804 Liberty Avenue, Ironton, OH 45638. *Phone:* 740-533-4612. *Toll-free phone:* 800-626-0513.

OHIO UNIVERSITY–ZANESVILLE

Zanesville, Ohio **www.zanesville.ohiou.edu/**

- **State-supported** comprehensive, founded 1946, part of Ohio Board of Regents
- **Rural** 179-acre campus with easy access to Columbus
- **Coed** 1,805 undergraduate students, 60% full-time, 73% women, 27% men
- **Noncompetitive** entrance level, 92% of applicants were admitted

Undergraduates 1,089 full-time, 716 part-time. Students come from 2 states and territories, 1 other country, 1% are from out of state, 3% African American, 0.3% Asian American or Pacific Islander, 0.8% Hispanic American, 0.6% Native American, 0.3% international. *Retention:* 62% of 2006 full-time freshmen returned.

Freshmen *Admission:* 510 applied, 470 admitted, 300 enrolled. *Test scores:* ACT scores over 18: 74%; ACT scores over 24: 21%.

Faculty *Total:* 130, 24% full-time, 25% with terminal degrees. *Student/faculty ratio:* 23:1.

Majors Biological and physical sciences; broadcast journalism; criminal justice/law enforcement administration; elementary education; public relations/image management; radio and television; social sciences.

Academics *Calendar:* quarters. *Degrees:* associate, bachelor's, and master's (offers first 2 years of most bachelor's degree programs available at the main campus in Athens; also offers several bachelor's degree programs that can be completed at this campus; also offers some graduate courses). *Special study options:* academic remediation for entering students, adult/continuing education programs, advanced placement credit, external degree program, off-campus study, part-time degree program, services for LD students, student-designed majors, summer session for credit.

Computers on Campus 42 computers/terminals are available on campus for general student use. Campuswide network is available.

Student Life *Housing:* college housing not available. *Activities and organizations:* drama/theater group, student-run newspaper, radio station, Student Senate, Student Nurses Association, Drama Club, Chess Club. *Campus security:* night security.

Athletics *Intercollegiate sports:* baseball M, basketball M/W, golf M/W, softball W, tennis M/W, ultimate Frisbee M (s)/W (s), volleyball M (s)/W (s). *Intramural sports:* basketball M/W, bowling M/W, football M, golf M/W, skiing (downhill) M/W, soccer M/W, softball M/W, table tennis M/W, tennis M/W, ultimate Frisbee M/W, volleyball M/W.

Standardized Tests *Required for some:* SAT or ACT (for admission).

Costs (2007–08) *Tuition:* state resident $4515 full-time, $137 per credit hour part-time; nonresident $8838 full-time, $268 per credit hour part-time. *Required fees:* $81 full-time, $2 per credit hour part-time, $5 per term part-time. *Room and board:* $8067.

Financial Aid Of all full-time matriculated undergraduates who enrolled in 2007, 995 applied for aid, 868 were judged to have need, 105 had their need fully met. 30 Federal Work-Study jobs (averaging $1820). In 2007, 67 non-need-based awards were made. *Average percent of need met:* 63%. *Average financial aid package:* $7604. *Average need-based loan:* $4143. *Average need-based gift aid:* $4553. *Average non-need-based aid:* $1829. *Average indebtedness upon graduation:* $20,880.

Applying *Options:* early admission, deferred entrance. *Application fee:* $20. *Required:* high school transcript. *Application deadlines:* rolling (freshmen), rolling (transfers).

Freshman Application Contact Mrs. Karen Ragsdale, Student Services Secretary, Ohio University–Zanesville, Office of Student Services, 1425 Newark Road, Zanesville, OH 43701. *Phone:* 740-588-1440. *Fax:* 740-588-1444. *E-mail:* ouzservices@ohio.edu.

OHIO WESLEYAN UNIVERSITY

Delaware, Ohio **www.owu.edu/**

- **Independent United Methodist** 4-year, founded 1842
- **Small-town** 200-acre campus with easy access to Columbus
- **Endowment** $158.4 million
- **Coed** 1,967 undergraduate students, 99% full-time, 52% women, 48% men
- **Very difficult** entrance level, 66% of applicants were admitted

Ohio Wesleyan is a liberal arts university that transforms lives. Students form lifelong relationships with each other and their professors as they pursue a rigorous academic program. Internships, research, service learning, and mission trips encourage students to push personal boundaries and develop a wider perspective. Ohio Wesleyan helps students discover and follow their passions and prepares them to change the world.

Undergraduates 1,949 full-time, 18 part-time. Students come from 45 states and territories, 45 other countries, 46% are from out of state, 5% African American, 2% Asian American or Pacific Islander, 1% Hispanic American, 0.4% Native American, 9% international, 1% transferred in, 82% live on campus. *Retention:* 84% of 2006 full-time freshmen returned.

Freshmen *Admission:* 3,815 applied, 2,499 admitted, 576 enrolled. *Average high school GPA:* 3.27. *Test scores:* SAT critical reading scores over 500: 88%; SAT math scores over 500: 87%; ACT scores over 18: 100%; SAT critical reading scores over 600: 51%; SAT math scores over 600: 52%; ACT scores over 24: 76%; SAT critical reading scores over 700: 11%; SAT math scores over 700: 11%; ACT scores over 30: 20%.

Faculty *Total:* 188, 72% full-time, 84% with terminal degrees. *Student/faculty ratio:* 12:1.

Majors Accounting; African-American/Black studies; ancient studies; animal genetics; anthropology; art history, criticism and conservation; art teacher education; art therapy; Asian studies (East); astronomy; astrophysics; biology/biological sciences; biology teacher education; botany/plant biology; broadcast journalism; business administration and management; business/managerial economics; business teacher education; chemistry; chemistry teacher education; classics and languages, literatures and linguistics; computer science; creative writing; cultural studies; drama and dance teacher education; dramatic/theater arts; early childhood education; economics; education; education (K-12); education (multiple levels); elementary education; engineering related; engineering science; English; environmental studies; fine/studio arts; foreign language teacher education; French; French language teacher education; general studies; genetics; geography; geology/earth science; German; German language teacher education; health teacher education; history; history teacher education; humanities; international business/trade/commerce; international relations and affairs; journalism; kindergarten/preschool education; Latin American studies; Latin teacher education; literature; mathematics; mathematics teacher education; medical microbiology and bacteriology; medieval and Renaissance studies; middle school education; multi-/interdisciplinary studies related; music; music performance; music teacher education; neuroscience; philosophy; physical education teaching and coaching; physics; physics teacher education; political science and government; pre-dentistry studies; pre-law studies; pre-medical studies; pre-theology/pre-ministerial studies; pre-veterinary studies; psychology; psychology teacher education; public administration; religious studies; secondary education; social studies teacher education; sociology; Spanish; Spanish language teacher education; statistics; urban studies/affairs; women's studies; zoology/animal biology.

Academics *Calendar:* semesters. *Degree:* bachelor's. *Special study options:* advanced placement credit, double majors, freshman honors college, honors programs, independent study, internships, off-campus study, part-time degree program, services for LD students, student-designed majors, study abroad, summer session for credit. *ROTC:* Army (c), Air Force (c). *Unusual degree programs:* 3-2 engineering with Rensselaer Polytechnic Institute, California Institute of Technology, Case Western Reserve University, New York State College of Ceramics at Alfred University, Polytechnic Institute of New York, Washington University in St. Louis; medical technology, optometry, physical therapy.

Computers on Campus 320 computers/terminals are available on campus for general student use. Campuswide network is available.

Student Life *Housing:* on-campus residence required through senior year. *Options:* coed, women-only. Campus housing is university owned. Freshman campus housing is guaranteed. *Activities and organizations:* drama/theater group, student-run newspaper, radio station, choral group, community services, student government, Campus Programming Board, religious organizations, ethnic organizations, national fraternities, national sororities. *Campus security:* 24-hour emergency response devices and patrols, late-night transport/escort service, controlled dormitory access. *Student services:* health clinic, personal/psychological counseling, women's center.

Athletics Member NCAA. All Division III. *Intercollegiate sports:* baseball M, basketball M/W, cross-country running M/W, equestrian sports M (c)/W (c), field hockey W, football M, golf M, ice hockey M (c)/W (c), lacrosse M/W, rugby M (c)/W (c), sailing M (c)/W (c), soccer M/W, softball W, swimming and diving M/W, tennis M/W, track and field M/W, ultimate Frisbee M (c)/W (c), volleyball M (c)/W. *Intramural sports:* badminton M/W, basketball M/W, football M/W, golf M/W, lacrosse M/W, racquetball M/W, skiing (cross-country) M/W, skiing (downhill) M/W, soccer M/W, softball M/W, squash M/W, swimming and diving M/W, tennis M/W, track and field M/W, volleyball M/W, water polo M/W.

Standardized Tests *Required:* SAT or ACT (for admission).

Costs (2007–08) *Comprehensive fee:* $39,960 includes full-time tuition ($31,510), mandatory fees ($420), and room and board ($8030). Part-time tuition: $3400 per course. *College room only:* $4000. Room and board charges vary according to board plan. *Payment plan:* installment. *Waivers:* children of alumni and employees or children of employees.

Financial Aid Of all full-time matriculated undergraduates who enrolled in 2007, 1,236 applied for aid, 1,089 were judged to have need, 273 had their need fully met. In 2007, 775 non-need-based awards were made. *Average percent of need met:* 83%. *Average financial aid package:* $25,579. *Average need-based loan:* $5290. *Average need-based gift aid:* $18,892. *Average non-need-based aid:* $13,794. *Average indebtedness upon graduation:* $25,627. *Financial aid deadline:* 5/1.

Applying *Options:* electronic application, early admission, early decision, early action, deferred entrance. *Application fee:* $35. *Required:* essay or personal statement, high school transcript, minimum 2.5 GPA, 1 letter of recommendation. *Recommended:* 2 letters of recommendation, interview. *Application deadlines:* 3/1 (freshmen), 5/15 (transfers), 12/15 (early action). *Early decision deadline:* 12/1. *Notification:* 10/1 (freshmen), continuous (transfers), 12/30 (early decision), 1/15 (early action).

Freshman Application Contact Ms. Carol DelPropost, Assistant Vice President of Admission and Financial Aid, Ohio Wesleyan University, 61 South Sandusky Street, Delaware, OH 43015. *Phone:* 740-368-3059. *Toll-free phone:* 800-922-8953. *Fax:* 740-368-3314. *E-mail:* cjdelpro@owu.edu.

See page 2052 for the College Close-Up.

OTTERBEIN COLLEGE

Westerville, Ohio **www.otterbein.edu/**

- **Independent United Methodist** comprehensive, founded 1847
- **Suburban** 142-acre campus with easy access to Columbus
- **Endowment** $80.0 million
- **Coed** 2,715 undergraduate students, 84% full-time, 65% women, 35% men
- **Moderately difficult** entrance level, 81% of applicants were admitted

Undergraduates 2,285 full-time, 430 part-time. Students come from 29 states and territories, 12 other countries, 9% are from out of state, 5% African American, 1% Asian American or Pacific Islander, 2% Hispanic American, 0.1% Native American, 3% transferred in, 53% live on campus. *Retention:* 92% of 2006 full-time freshmen returned.

Freshmen *Admission:* 3,360 applied, 2,729 admitted, 647 enrolled. *Average high school GPA:* 3.39. *Test scores:* SAT critical reading scores over 500: 65%; SAT math scores over 500: 67%; ACT scores over 18: 94%; SAT critical reading scores over 600: 24%; SAT math scores over 600: 24%; ACT scores over 24: 45%; SAT critical reading scores over 700: 2%; SAT math scores over 700: 2%; ACT scores over 30: 5%.

Faculty *Total:* 275, 58% full-time. *Student/faculty ratio:* 12:1.

Majors Accounting; art; art teacher education; athletic training; audiology and speech-language pathology; biochemistry; biology/biological sciences; business administration and management; business/managerial economics; chemistry; computer science; dramatic/theater arts; economics; education; elementary education; English; environmental biology; environmental science; equestrian studies; finance; French; health teacher education; history; international business/trade/commerce; international relations and affairs; journalism; literature; marketing/marketing management; mathematics; middle school education; molecular biology; multi-/interdisciplinary studies related; music; music history, literature, and theory; music management and merchandising; music performance; music teacher education; nursing (registered nurse training); philosophy; physical education teaching and coaching; physical sciences; physics; piano and organ; political science and government; pre-dentistry studies; pre-law studies; pre-medical studies; pre-veterinary studies; psychology; public relations/image management; radio and television; religious studies; science teacher education; secondary education; sociology; Spanish; sport and fitness administration/management; violin, viola, guitar and other stringed instruments; voice and opera; wind/percussion instruments.

Academics *Calendar:* quarters. *Degrees:* bachelor's and master's. *Special study options:* academic remediation for entering students, adult/continuing education programs, advanced placement credit, double majors, honors programs, internships, off-campus study, part-time degree program, services for LD students, student-designed majors, study abroad, summer session for credit. *ROTC:* Army (c), Air Force (c). *Unusual degree programs:* 3-2 engineering with Case Western Reserve University, Washington University in St. Louis.

Computers on Campus 146 computers/terminals are available on campus for general student use. Students can access the following: campus intranet, computer help desk, free student e-mail accounts, online (class) grades, online (class) registration, online (class) schedules. Campuswide network is available. 100% of college-owned or -operated housing units are wired for high-speed Internet access. Wireless service is available via classrooms, computer centers, computer labs, dorm rooms, libraries, student centers.

Student Life *Housing:* on-campus residence required through sophomore year. *Options:* coed, men-only, women-only. Campus housing is university owned. Freshman campus housing is guaranteed. *Activities and organizations:* drama/theater group, student-run newspaper, radio and television station, choral group, marching band, Musical groups, Honoraries, Academic interest clubs, Governance, national fraternities. *Campus security:* 24-hour emergency response devices and patrols, student patrols, late-night transport/escort service, controlled dormitory access, 24-hour locked residence hall entrances. *Student services:* health clinic, personal/psychological counseling.

Athletics Member NCAA. All Division III. *Intercollegiate sports:* baseball M, basketball M/W, cheerleading M/W, cross-country running M/W, equestrian sports M/W, football M, golf M/W, soccer M/W, softball W, tennis M/W, track and field M/W, volleyball W. *Intramural sports:* basketball M/W, football M, racquetball M/W, soccer M/W, softball M/W, volleyball M/W.

Standardized Tests *Required:* SAT or ACT (for admission).

Costs (2007–08) *Comprehensive fee:* $32,214 includes full-time tuition ($25,065) and room and board ($7149). Full-time tuition and fees vary according to course load and program. Part-time tuition: $300 per credit. Part-time tuition and fees vary according to course load and program. *College room only:* $3399. Room and board charges vary according to housing facility. *Payment plan:* installment. *Waivers:* employees or children of employees.

Applying *Options:* electronic application, deferred entrance. *Application fee:* $25. *Required:* high school transcript. *Recommended:* minimum 2.5 GPA, interview. *Application deadlines:* 3/1 (freshmen), rolling (transfers). *Notification:* continuous (freshmen), continuous (transfers).

Freshman Application Contact Dr. Cass Johnson, Director of Admissions, Otterbein College, One Otterbein College, Westerville, OH 43081-9924. *Phone:* 614-823-1500. *Toll-free phone:* 800-488-8144. *Fax:* 614-823-1200. *E-mail:* uotterb@otterbein.edu.

See page 2054 for the College Close-Up.

PONTIFICAL COLLEGE JOSEPHINUM

Columbus, Ohio **www.pcj.edu/**

- **Independent Roman Catholic** comprehensive, founded 1888
- **Suburban** 100-acre campus
- **Endowment** $41.8 million
- **Coed, primarily men** 119 undergraduate students, 100% full-time, 100% men
- **Minimally difficult** entrance level, 93% of applicants were admitted

Undergraduates 119 full-time. Students come from 20 states and territories, 3 other countries, 73% are from out of state, 2% Asian American or Pacific Islander, 9% Hispanic American, 6% international, 14% transferred in, 100% live on campus. *Retention:* 80% of 2006 full-time freshmen returned.

Freshmen *Admission:* 27 applied, 25 admitted, 22 enrolled. *Test scores:* ACT scores over 18: 75%; ACT scores over 24: 50%; ACT scores over 30: 25%.

Faculty *Total:* 31, 35% full-time, 39% with terminal degrees. *Student/faculty ratio:* 7:1.

Majors Classics; English; history; humanities; Latin American studies; philosophy.

Academics *Calendar:* semesters. *Degrees:* bachelor's, master's, and first professional. *Special study options:* academic remediation for entering students, advanced placement credit, double majors, English as a second language, honors programs, internships, off-campus study, services for LD students.

Computers on Campus 10 computers/terminals are available on campus for general student use. Students can access the following: campus intranet, free student e-mail accounts. Campuswide network is available. 100% of college-owned or -operated housing units are wired for high-speed Internet access. Wireless service is available via classrooms, libraries.

Student Life *Housing:* on-campus residence required through senior year. *Options:* men-only. Campus housing is university owned. Freshman campus housing is guaranteed. *Activities and organizations:* drama/theater group, choral group. *Campus security:* 24-hour emergency response devices, controlled dormitory access. *Student services:* health clinic, personal/psychological counseling.

Athletics *Intramural sports:* basketball M, bowling M, football M, golf M, soccer M, softball M, swimming and diving M, table tennis M, tennis M, volleyball M, weight lifting M.

Standardized Tests *Required:* SAT or ACT (for admission), SAT and SAT Subject Tests or ACT (for admission).

Costs (2007–08) *Comprehensive fee:* $23,178 includes full-time tuition ($14,997), mandatory fees ($683), and room and board ($7498). Part-time tuition: $606 per credit hour. *Payment plan:* installment.

Financial Aid Of all full-time matriculated undergraduates who enrolled in 2003, 44 applied for aid, 36 were judged to have need, 17 had their need fully met. 4 Federal Work-Study jobs (averaging $507). In 2003, 5 non-need-based awards were made. *Average percent of need met:* 82%. *Average financial aid package:* $14,762. *Average need-based loan:* $4157. *Average need-based gift aid:* $3148. *Average non-need-based aid:* $2000. *Average indebtedness upon graduation:* $13,698.

Applying *Application fee:* $25. *Required:* essay or personal statement, high school transcript, 3 letters of recommendation, interview. *Application deadlines:* 7/31 (freshmen), rolling (transfers).

Freshman Application Contact Mrs. Arminda Crawford, Secretary for Admissions, Pontifical College Josephinum, Columbus, OH 43235. *Phone:* 614-985-2241. *Toll-free phone:* 888-252-5812. *Fax:* 614-885-2307. *E-mail:* acrawford@pcj.edu.

RABBINICAL COLLEGE OF TELSHE
Wickliffe, Ohio

SHAWNEE STATE UNIVERSITY
Portsmouth, Ohio **www.shawnee.edu/**

- **State-supported** 4-year, founded 1986, part of Ohio Board of Regents
- **Small-town** 52-acre campus
- **Endowment** $13.4 million
- **Coed** 3,674 undergraduate students, 81% full-time, 60% women, 40% men
- **Noncompetitive** entrance level, 100% of applicants were admitted

Undergraduates 2,992 full-time, 682 part-time. Students come from 13 states and territories, 13 other countries, 9% are from out of state, 3% African American, 0.3% Asian American or Pacific Islander, 0.4% Hispanic American, 1% Native American, 0.7% international, 4% transferred in, 16% live on campus. *Retention:* 56% of 2006 full-time freshmen returned.

Freshmen *Admission:* 2,939 applied, 2,939 admitted, 417 enrolled. *Test scores:* ACT scores over 18: 76%; ACT scores over 24: 17%; ACT scores over 30: 1%.

Faculty *Total:* 289, 51% full-time. *Student/faculty ratio:* 17:1.

Majors Accounting; applied mathematics; art; art teacher education; athletic training; biological and physical sciences; biology/biological sciences; business administration and management; CAD/CADD drafting/design technology; ceramic arts and ceramics; chemistry; clinical/medical laboratory technology; computer engineering technology; dental hygiene; dramatic/theater arts; drawing; early childhood education; education; education (multiple levels); electromechanical technology; elementary education; emergency medical technology (EMT paramedic); English; English/language arts teacher education; environmental engineering technology; fine/studio arts; general studies; geography teacher education; graphic design; history; history teacher education; humanities; international relations and affairs; kindergarten/preschool education; legal administrative assistant/secretary; legal assistant/paralegal; management information systems; mathematics; mathematics teacher education; medical radiologic technology; middle school education; music; natural sciences; nursing (registered nurse training); occupational therapy; office management; painting; photography; physical sciences; physical therapy; physics teacher education; plastics engineering technology; pre-engineering; pre-law studies; pre-medical studies; pre-veterinary studies; psychology; psychology teacher education; respiratory care therapy; science teacher education; secondary education; social sciences; social studies teacher education; sociology; special education; sport and fitness administration/management.

Academics *Calendar:* quarters. *Degrees:* certificates, associate, bachelor's, and master's. *Special study options:* academic remediation for entering students, adult/continuing education programs, advanced placement credit, distance learning, double majors, honors programs, independent study, internships, off-campus study, part-time degree program, services for LD students, study abroad, summer session for credit.

Computers on Campus 620 computers/terminals are available on campus for general student use. Students can access the following: campus intranet, computer help desk, free student e-mail accounts, online (class) grades, online (class) registration, online (class) schedules, financial aid, student billing, courses, student service portal. Campuswide network is available. 100% of college-owned or -operated housing units are wired for high-speed Internet access. Wireless service is available via entire campus.

Student Life *Housing:* on-campus residence required for freshman year. *Options:* coed. Campus housing is university owned. Freshman applicants given priority for college housing. *Activities and organizations:* drama/theater group, student-run newspaper, choral group, campus ministry, Health Executives and Administrators Learning Society, Student Programming Board, SGA, national fraternities. *Campus security:* 24-hour emergency response devices and patrols. *Student services:* health clinic, personal/psychological counseling, women's center.

Athletics Member NAIA. *Intercollegiate sports:* baseball M, basketball M/W, cross-country running M/W, golf M, soccer M/W, softball W, tennis W, volleyball W. *Intramural sports:* basketball M/W, bowling M/W, golf M/W, racquetball M/W, softball M, swimming and diving M/W, table tennis M/W, tennis M/W, volleyball M/W.

Standardized Tests *Required for some:* ACT (for admission). *Recommended:* ACT (for admission).

Costs (2007–08) *Tuition:* state resident $5184 full-time, $216 per credit hour part-time; nonresident $9324 full-time, $389 per credit hour part-time. Full-time tuition and fees vary according to course load, reciprocity agreements, and student level. Part-time tuition and fees vary according to course load, reciprocity agreements, and student level. *Required fees:* $648 full-time, $23 per credit hour part-time. *Room and board:* $7234; room only: $4692. *Payment plan:* installment. *Waivers:* senior citizens and employees or children of employees.

Financial Aid Of all full-time matriculated undergraduates who enrolled in 2006, 2,591 applied for aid, 1,806 were judged to have need, 1,751 had their need fully met. 104 Federal Work-Study jobs (averaging $2018). *Average percent of need met:* 70%. *Average financial aid package:* $3972. *Average need-based gift aid:* $2620. *Average indebtedness upon graduation:* $10,944.

Applying *Options:* electronic application, deferred entrance. *Required:* high school transcript. *Required for some:* letters of recommendation, interview. *Application deadlines:* rolling (freshmen), rolling (transfers). *Notification:* continuous (freshmen), continuous (transfers).

Freshman Application Contact Mr. Bob Trusz, Director of Admission, Shawnee State University, 940 Second Street, Commons Building, Portsmouth, OH 45662. *Phone:* 740-351-3610 Ext. 610. *Toll-free phone:* 800-959-2SSU. *Fax:* 740-351-3111. *E-mail:* to_ssu@shawnee.edu.

TEMPLE BAPTIST COLLEGE
Cincinnati, Ohio

TIFFIN UNIVERSITY
Tiffin, Ohio **www.tiffin.edu/**

- **Independent** comprehensive, founded 1888
- **Small-town** 110-acre campus with easy access to Toledo
- **Endowment** $4.9 million
- **Coed** 1,638 undergraduate students, 90% full-time, 54% women, 46% men
- **Minimally difficult** entrance level, 71% of applicants were admitted

Undergraduates 1,475 full-time, 163 part-time. Students come from 21 states and territories, 16 other countries, 12% are from out of state, 16% African American, 0.4% Asian American or Pacific Islander, 2% Hispanic American, 0.1% Native American, 4% international, 4% transferred in, 39% live on campus. *Retention:* 63% of 2006 full-time freshmen returned.

Freshmen *Admission:* 1,852 applied, 1,324 admitted, 325 enrolled. *Average high school GPA:* 2.98.

Faculty *Total:* 150, 32% full-time, 23% with terminal degrees. *Student/faculty ratio:* 19:1.

Majors Accounting; arts management; business administration and management; communication/speech communication and rhetoric; computer and information sciences and support services related; computer programming; corrections; criminal justice/law enforcement administration; criminal justice/police science; criminal justice/safety; English; finance; forensic psychology; forensic science and technology; history; human services; information science/studies; international relations and affairs; marketing/marketing management; pre-law studies; psychology.

Academics *Calendar:* semesters. *Degrees:* associate, bachelor's, and master's. *Special study options:* accelerated degree program, adult/continuing education programs, advanced placement credit, distance learning, double majors, English as a second language, external degree program, honors programs, independent study, internships, study abroad, summer session for credit. *ROTC:* Army (c), Air Force (c).

Computers on Campus 60 computers/terminals are available on campus for general student use. Students can access the following: campus intranet, computer help desk, free student e-mail accounts, online (class) grades, online (class) registration, online (class) schedules. Campuswide network is available. Wireless service is available via computer labs, learning centers, libraries, student centers.

Student Life *Housing:* on-campus residence required through sophomore year. *Options:* coed, men-only, women-only, disabled students. Campus housing is university owned. Freshman campus housing is guaranteed. *Activities and organizations:* drama/theater group, student-run newspaper, choral group, marching band, Student Government Association, Black United Students, International Student Association, Gay, Lesbian and Straight Supporters (GLASS), national fraternities, national sororities. *Campus security:* student patrols, late-night transport/escort service. *Student services:* health clinic, personal/psychological counseling.

Athletics Member NCAA, NAIA. All NCAA Division II. *Intercollegiate sports:* baseball M (s), basketball M (s)/W (s), cheerleading M (s)/W (s), cross-country running M (s)/W (s), equestrian sports M (s)/W (s), football M (s), golf M (s)/W (s), soccer M (s)/W (s), softball W (s), tennis M (s)/W (s), track and field M (s)/W (s), volleyball W (s). *Intramural sports:* basketball M/W, bowling M/W, football M, rugby M (c), soccer M/W, softball M/W, table tennis M/W, tennis M/W, volleyball M/W, weight lifting M/W.

Standardized Tests *Required:* SAT or ACT (for admission).

Costs (2008–09) *Comprehensive fee:* $24,800 includes full-time tuition ($17,220) and room and board ($7580). Part-time tuition: $574 per credit hour. *College room only:* $3830.

Financial Aid Of all full-time matriculated undergraduates who enrolled in 2006, 1,222 applied for aid, 1,104 were judged to have need, 153 had their need fully met. In 2006, 140 non-need-based awards were made. *Average percent of need met:* 14%. *Average financial aid package:* $13,044. *Average need-based loan:* $3833. *Average need-based gift aid:* $5041. *Average non-need-based aid:* $7123. *Average indebtedness upon graduation:* $19,624.

Applying *Options:* electronic application. *Application fee:* $20. *Required:* high school transcript. *Required for some:* essay or personal statement, letters of recommendation, interview. *Recommended:* essay or personal statement, minimum 3.0 GPA, interview, minimum score of 19 on ACT or 890 on SAT. *Application deadline:* rolling (freshmen). *Notification:* continuous (transfers).

Freshman Application Contact Mr. Jeremy Marinis, Director of Undergraduate Admissions, Tiffin University, 155 Miami Street, Tiffin, OH 44883. *Phone:* 419-448-3301. *Toll-free phone:* 800-968-6446. *Fax:* 419-443-5006. *E-mail:* marinisjj@tiffin.edu.

See page 2056 for the College Close-Up.

Tri-State Bible College

South Point, Ohio **www.tsbc.edu/**

Director of Admissions Mr. Dale Cook, Admissions Director, Tri-State Bible College, 506 Margaret Street, PO Box 445, South Point, OH 45680-8402. *Phone:* 740-377-2520. *Fax:* 740-377-0001. *E-mail:* tsbc@zoomnet.net.

Union Institute & University

Cincinnati, Ohio **www.tui.edu/**

Freshman Application Contact Dr. Emily Harbold, Associate Vice President, Academic Affairs, Union Institute & University, 440 East McMillan Street, Cincinnati, OH 45206. *Toll-free phone:* 800-486-3116. *E-mail:* admissions@tui.edu.

The University of Akron

Akron, Ohio **www.uakron.edu/**

- **State-supported** university, founded 1870
- **Urban** 218-acre campus with easy access to Cleveland
- **Endowment** $212.0 million
- **Coed** 18,974 undergraduate students, 77% full-time, 50% women, 50% men
- **Moderately difficult** entrance level, 82% of applicants were admitted

Undergraduates 14,590 full-time, 4,384 part-time. Students come from 37 states and territories, 43 other countries, 2% are from out of state, 14% African American, 2% Asian American or Pacific Islander, 1% Hispanic American, 0.3% Native American, 0.9% international, 5% transferred in, 16% live on campus. *Retention:* 67% of 2006 full-time freshmen returned.

Freshmen *Admission:* 11,410 applied, 9,314 admitted, 4,109 enrolled. *Average high school GPA:* 2.99. *Test scores:* SAT critical reading scores over 500: 50%; SAT math scores over 500: 54%; ACT scores over 18: 78%; SAT critical reading scores over 600: 14%; SAT math scores over 600: 19%; ACT scores over 24: 27%; SAT critical reading scores over 700: 1%; SAT math scores over 700: 3%; ACT scores over 30: 3%.

Faculty *Total:* 1,565, 47% full-time, 55% with terminal degrees. *Student/faculty ratio:* 19:1.

Majors Accounting; accounting technology and bookkeeping; administrative assistant and secretarial science; American government and politics; animal physiology; apparel and textiles; applied mathematics; art history, criticism and conservation; art teacher education; athletic training; audiology and speech-language pathology; biochemistry; biology/biological sciences; biomedical/medical engineering; botany/plant biology; business administration and management; cartography; ceramic arts and ceramics; chemical engineering; chemistry; child development; city/urban, community and regional planning; civil engineering; classics and languages, literatures and linguistics; communication disorders; communication/speech communication and rhetoric; computer engineering; computer science; computer systems analysis; computer systems networking and telecommunications; construction engineering technology; criminal justice/police science; criminal justice/safety; criminology; culinary arts; dance; data entry/microcomputer applications; drafting and design technology; drama and dance teacher education; dramatic/theater arts; early childhood education; ecology; e-commerce; economics; economics related; education related; education (specific subject areas) related; electrical, electronic and communications engineering technology; electrical, electronics and communications engineering; engineering; English; English/language arts teacher education; family and consumer economics related; family and consumer sciences/home economics teacher education; family systems; finance and financial management services related; financial planning and services; fine arts related; fine/studio arts; fire protection and safety technology; fire protection related; French; French language teacher education; geography; geological and earth sciences/geosciences related; geology/earth science; geophysics and seismology; graphic design; health/medical preparatory programs related; histologic technician; history; hospitality administration; hotel/motel administration; housing and human environments; humanities; human resources management; international business/trade/commerce; international relations and affairs; jazz/jazz studies; journalism related; kinesiology and exercise science; legal assistant/paralegal; liberal arts and sciences and humanities related; liberal arts and sciences/liberal studies; logistics and materials management; management information systems; manufacturing technology; marketing/marketing management; marketing related; mathematics; mathematics teacher education; mechanical engineering; mechanical engineering/mechanical technology; medical/clinical assistant; medical office management; medical radiologic technology; merchandising; metal and jewelry arts; microbiology; middle school education; multi-/interdisciplinary studies related; music; music history, literature, and theory; music performance; music related; music teacher education; music theory and composition; nursing (licensed practical/vocational nurse training); nursing (registered nurse training); nursing related; operations management; organizational communication; philosophy; photography; physical education teaching and coaching; physics; piano and organ; polymer chemistry; polymer/plastics engineering; printmaking; psychology; public administration and social service professions related; public relations/image management; radio and television; radio, television, and digital communication related; respiratory care therapy; restaurant/food services management; sales, distribution and marketing; science teacher education; sculpture; selling skills and sales; small business administration; social sciences; social sciences related; social studies teacher education; social work; social work related; sociology; Spanish; Spanish language teacher education; special education; special education (early childhood); sport and fitness administration/management; statistics; substance abuse/addiction counseling; surgical technology; survey technology; technical teacher education; therapeutic recreation; tourism and travel services management; violin, viola, guitar and other stringed instruments; voice and opera; zoology/animal biology.

Academics *Calendar:* semesters. *Degrees:* certificates, associate, bachelor's, master's, doctoral, first professional, post-master's, postbachelor's, and first professional certificates (associate). *Special study options:* academic remediation for entering students, accelerated degree program, adult/continuing education programs, advanced placement credit, cooperative education, distance learning, double majors, English as a second language, external degree program, freshman honors college, honors programs, independent study, internships, part-time degree program, services for LD students, student-designed majors, study abroad, summer session for credit. *ROTC:* Army (b), Air Force (c). *Unusual degree programs:* 3-2 accounting, BSMD (NEOUCOM), mathematics.

Computers on Campus 3,100 computers/terminals and 16,000 ports are available on campus for general student use. Students can access the following: campus intranet, computer help desk, free student e-mail accounts, online (class) grades, online (class) registration, online (class) schedules, library laptops for student checkout. Campuswide network is available. 100% of college-owned or -operated housing units are wired for high-speed Internet access. Wireless service is available via entire campus.

Student Life *Housing:* on-campus residence required for freshman year. *Options:* coed, men-only, women-only. Campus housing is university owned. Freshman applicants given priority for college housing. *Activities and organizations:* drama/theater group, student-run newspaper, radio and television station, choral group, marching band, Associated Student Government, Residence Hall Program Board, American Society of Mechanical Engineers, national fraternities, national sororities. *Campus security:* 24-hour emergency response devices and patrols, student patrols, late-night transport/escort service, controlled dormitory access. *Student services:* health clinic, personal/psychological counseling, women's center, legal services.

Athletics Member NCAA. All Division I except football (Division I-A). *Intercollegiate sports:* baseball M (s), basketball M (s)/W (s), cheerleading M/W, cross-country running M (s)/W (s), golf M (s)/W (s), riflery M/W (s), soccer M (s)/W (s), softball W (s), swimming and diving W (s), tennis W (s), track and field M (s)/W (s), volleyball W (s). *Intramural sports:* badminton M/W, basketball M/W, bowling M/W, cross-country running M/W, golf M/W, racquetball M/W, skiing (cross-country) M/W, skiing (downhill) M/W, soccer M/W, softball M/W, swimming and diving M/W, table tennis M/W, track and field M/W, volleyball W, wrestling M.

Standardized Tests *Required:* SAT or ACT (for admission).

Costs (2007–08) *Tuition:* state resident $7218 full-time, $301 per credit part-time; nonresident $16,467 full-time, $609 per credit part-time. Full-time tuition and fees vary according to course load, degree level, and location. Part-time tuition and fees vary according to course load, degree level, and location. *Required fees:* $1164 full-time, $49 per credit part-time. *Room and board:* $8003; room only: $4955. Room and board charges vary according to board plan and housing facility. *Payment plan:* installment. *Waivers:* senior citizens and employees or children of employees.

Financial Aid Of all full-time matriculated undergraduates who enrolled in 2006, 10,627 applied for aid, 8,529 were judged to have need, 659 had their need fully met. 769 Federal Work-Study jobs (averaging $1398). 2,776 state and other part-time jobs (averaging $1513). In 2006, 687 non-need-based awards were made. *Average percent of need met:* 48%. *Average financial aid package:* $6437. *Average need-based loan:* $3453. *Average need-based gift aid:* $4394. *Average non-need-based aid:* $3652. *Average indebtedness upon graduation:* $17,450.

Applying *Options:* electronic application, early action, deferred entrance. *Application fee:* $30. *Required:* high school transcript. *Required for some:* essay or personal statement, 3 letters of recommendation, interview. *Application deadlines:* 8/11 (freshmen), rolling (transfers), 11/1 (early action). *Notification:* continuous until 9/15 (freshmen), continuous (transfers).

Freshman Application Contact Ms. Diane Raybuck, Director of Admissions, The University of Akron, Simone Hall, 277 East Buchtel Avenue, Akron, OH 44325-2001. *Phone:* 330-972-6427. *Toll-free phone:* 800-655-4884. *Fax:* 330-972-7022. *E-mail:* admissions@uakron.edu.

UNIVERSITY OF CINCINNATI

Cincinnati, Ohio **www.uc.edu/**

- **State-supported** university, founded 1819
- **Urban** 137-acre campus
- **Endowment** $1.1 billion
- **Coed** 20,501 undergraduate students, 83% full-time, 51% women, 49% men
- **Moderately difficult** entrance level, 75% of applicants were admitted

Undergraduates 16,949 full-time, 3,552 part-time. Students come from 54 states and territories, 94 other countries, 10% are from out of state, 11% African American, 3% Asian American or Pacific Islander, 2% Hispanic American, 0.3% Native American, 1% international, 6% transferred in, 21% live on campus. *Retention:* 82% of 2006 full-time freshmen returned.

Freshmen *Admission:* 11,876 applied, 8,902 admitted, 4,059 enrolled. *Average high school GPA:* 3.38. *Test scores:* SAT critical reading scores over 500: 72%; SAT math scores over 500: 76%; SAT writing scores over 500: 66%; ACT scores over 18: 98%; SAT critical reading scores over 600: 30%; SAT math scores over 600: 37%; SAT writing scores over 600: 23%; ACT scores over 24: 54%; SAT critical reading scores over 700: 5%; SAT math scores over 700: 7%; SAT writing scores over 700: 3%; ACT scores over 30: 9%.

Faculty *Total:* 1,248, 97% full-time, 59% with terminal degrees. *Student/faculty ratio:* 14:1.

Majors Accounting; administrative assistant and secretarial science; aerospace, aeronautical and astronautical engineering; African-American/Black studies; anthropology; architectural engineering; architectural engineering technology; architecture; art; art history, criticism and conservation; artificial intelligence and robotics; art teacher education; Asian studies; audiology and speech-language pathology; biochemistry; biological and physical sciences; biology/biological sciences; broadcast journalism; business administration and management; chemical engineering; chemistry; child development; city/urban, community and regional planning; civil engineering; civil engineering technology; classics and languages, literatures and linguistics; clinical laboratory science/medical technology; clinical/medical laboratory technology; commercial and advertising art; comparative literature; computer and information sciences; computer engineering; computer engineering technology; computer management; computer programming; computer science; construction engineering; construction engineering technology; construction management; court reporting; criminal justice/law enforcement administration; criminal justice/police science; dance; data processing and data processing technology; drafting and design technology; dramatic/theater arts; early childhood education; economics; education; electrical, electronic and communications engineering technology; elementary education; energy management and systems technology; engineering; engineering mechanics; engineering science; English; environmental engineering technology; environmental studies; fashion/apparel design; finance; fire protection and safety technology; fire science; foods, nutrition, and wellness; French; geography; geology/earth science; German; health/health care administration; health information/medical records administration; health teacher education; heating, air conditioning and refrigeration technology; heating, air conditioning, ventilation and refrigeration maintenance technology; history; humanities; human services; industrial arts; industrial design; industrial engineering; industrial radiologic technology; industrial technology; information science/studies; insurance; interior design; international relations and affairs; jazz/jazz studies; Jewish/Judaic studies; kindergarten/preschool education; Latin American studies; legal administrative assistant/secretary; legal assistant/paralegal; liberal arts and sciences/liberal studies; linguistics; literature; management information systems; marketing/marketing management; mass communication/media; mathematics; mechanical engineering; mechanical engineering/mechanical technology; medical administrative assistant and medical secretary; medical microbiology and bacteriology; metallurgical engineering; metallurgical technology; music; music history, literature, and theory; music teacher education; natural sciences; nuclear engineering; nuclear medical technology; nursing (registered nurse training); occupational safety and health technology; operations research; pharmacology; pharmacy; philosophy; physical education teaching and coaching; physical therapy; physics; piano and organ; political science and government; pre-law studies; pre-medical studies; pre-veterinary studies; psychology; public health; public policy analysis; quality control technology; radio and television; real estate; Romance languages; safety/security technology; science teacher education; secondary education; social sciences; social work; sociology; Spanish; special education; transportation technology; urban studies/affairs; violin, viola, guitar and other stringed instruments; voice and opera; wind/percussion instruments.

Academics *Calendar:* quarters. *Degrees:* certificates, associate, bachelor's, master's, doctoral, first professional, and postbachelor's certificates. *Special study options:* academic remediation for entering students, accelerated degree program, adult/continuing education programs, advanced placement credit, cooperative education, distance learning, double majors, English as a second language, honors programs, independent study, internships, off-campus study, part-time degree program, services for LD students, study abroad, summer session for credit. *ROTC:* Army (b), Air Force (b).

Computers on Campus Students can access the following: campus intranet, computer help desk, free student e-mail accounts, online (class) grades, online (class) registration, online (class) schedules. Campuswide network is available. 100% of college-owned or -operated housing units are wired for high-speed Internet access. Wireless service is available via entire campus.

Student Life *Housing:* on-campus residence required for freshman year. *Options:* coed, men-only, women-only. Campus housing is university owned and is provided by a third party. Freshman campus housing is guaranteed. *Activities and organizations:* drama/theater group, student-run newspaper, radio station, choral group, marching band, national fraternities, national sororities. *Campus security:* 24-hour emergency response devices and patrols, late-night transport/escort service, controlled dormitory access. *Student services:* health clinic, personal/psychological counseling, women's center, legal services.

Athletics Member NCAA. All Division I except football (Division I-A). *Intercollegiate sports:* baseball M, basketball M (s)/W (s), cheerleading M/W, crew M (c)/W (c), cross-country running M (s)/W (s), golf M (s), ice hockey M (c), lacrosse W (s), rugby M (c), soccer M (s)/W (s), swimming and diving M (s)/W (s), tennis M (s)/W (s), track and field M (s)/W, ultimate Frisbee M (c), volleyball W (s), wrestling M (c). *Intramural sports:* archery W, badminton M/W, baseball M, basketball M/W, bowling M/W, crew M (c)/W (c), football M, golf M/W, gymnastics W, racquetball M/W, soccer M/W, softball M/W, squash M/W, swimming and diving M/W, tennis M/W, track and field M/W, ultimate Frisbee M/W, volleyball M/W, weight lifting M, wrestling M.

Standardized Tests *Required:* SAT or ACT (for admission).

Costs (2007–08) *Tuition:* state resident $7896 full-time, $220 per credit hour part-time; nonresident $22,419 full-time, $623 per credit hour part-time. Full-time tuition and fees vary according to course load, degree level, location, program, and reciprocity agreements. Part-time tuition and fees vary according to course load, degree level, location, program, and reciprocity agreements. *Required fees:* $1503 full-time, $42 per credit hour part-time. *Room and board:* $8799; room only: $5259. Room and board charges vary according to board plan and housing facility. *Payment plan:* installment. *Waivers:* employees or children of employees.

Financial Aid Of all full-time matriculated undergraduates who enrolled in 2007, 11,299 applied for aid, 9,255 were judged to have need, 649 had their need fully met. In 2007, 3,141 non-need-based awards were made. *Average percent of need met:* 59%. *Average financial aid package:* $8304. *Average need-based loan:* $4742. *Average need-based gift aid:* $5432. *Average non-need-based aid:* $4670. *Average indebtedness upon graduation:* $21,302.

Applying *Options:* electronic application, deferred entrance. *Application fee:* $40. *Required:* high school transcript. *Required for some:* 2 letters of recommendation, audition. *Recommended:* interview. *Application deadlines:* 9/1 (freshmen), rolling (transfers). *Notification:* continuous (freshmen), continuous (transfers).

Freshman Application Contact Mr. Thomas Canepa, Assistant Vice President, Admissions, University of Cincinnati, 340 University Pavillion, Cincinnati, OH 45221-0091. *Phone:* 513-556-1100. *Fax:* 513-556-1105. *E-mail:* admissions@uc.edu.

UNIVERSITY OF DAYTON

Dayton, Ohio **www.udayton.edu/**

- **Independent Roman Catholic** university, founded 1850
- **Suburban** 259-acre campus with easy access to Cincinnati
- **Endowment** $410.4 million
- **Coed** 7,434 undergraduate students, 92% full-time, 50% women, 50% men
- **Moderately difficult** entrance level, 82% of applicants were admitted

As one of the preeminent Catholic universities in the nation, the University of Dayton offers the resources and diversity of a comprehensive university and the attention and accessibility of a small college. The impressive campus, challenging academic programs, advanced research facilities, NCAA Division I athletic programs, technology-enhanced learning opportunities, and access to the Dayton metropolitan community are big-school advantages. The small classes, undergraduate emphasis, student-centered faculty and staff members, residential campus, and friendliness are small-school qualities.

Undergraduates 6,845 full-time, 589 part-time. Students come from 51 states and territories, 50 other countries, 35% are from out of state, 3% African American, 1% Asian American or Pacific Islander, 2% Hispanic American, 0.3% Native American, 1% international, 2% transferred in, 74% live on campus. *Retention:* 87% of 2006 full-time freshmen returned.

Freshmen *Admission:* 8,742 applied, 7,156 admitted, 1,762 enrolled. *Average high school GPA:* 3.46. *Test scores:* SAT critical reading scores over 500: 85%; SAT math scores over 500: 86%; ACT scores over 18: 99%; SAT critical reading scores over 600: 38%; SAT math scores over 600: 46%; ACT scores over 24: 68%; SAT critical reading scores over 700: 6%; SAT math scores over 700: 10%; ACT scores over 30: 15%.

Faculty *Total:* 798, 57% full-time. *Student/faculty ratio:* 16:1.

Majors Accounting; American studies; applied art; applied mathematics related; art history, criticism and conservation; art teacher education; biochemistry; biology/biological sciences; broadcast journalism; business administration and management; business/managerial economics; chemical engineering; chemistry; civil engineering; commercial and advertising art; computer engineering; computer engineering technology; computer science; criminal justice/law enforcement administration; dietetics; dramatic/theater arts; economics; education; electrical, electronic and communications engineering technology; electrical, electronics and communications engineering; elementary education; English; environmental biology; environmental studies; finance; fine/studio arts; foods, nutrition, and wellness; French; general studies; geology/earth science; German; health teacher education; history; industrial technology; information science/studies; international business/trade/commerce; international relations and affairs; journalism; kindergarten/preschool education; kinesiology and exercise science; management information systems; marketing/marketing management; mass communication/media; mathematics; mechanical engineering; mechanical engineering/mechanical technology; music; music teacher education; music therapy; philosophy; photography; physical education teaching and coaching; physical sciences; physics; political science and government; pre-dentistry studies; pre-law studies; pre-medical studies; psychology; public relations/image management; radio and television; religious education; religious studies; science teacher education; secondary education; sociology; Spanish; special education; sport and fitness administration/management.

Academics *Calendar:* semesters plus 2 6-week summer terms. *Degrees:* bachelor's, master's, doctoral, first professional, and post-master's certificates. *Special study options:* academic remediation for entering students, accelerated degree program, adult/continuing education programs, advanced placement credit, cooperative education, distance learning, double majors, English as a second language, honors programs, independent study, internships, off-campus study, part-time degree program, services for LD students, student-designed majors, study abroad, summer session for credit. *ROTC:* Army (b), Air Force (c). *Unusual degree programs:* 3-2 business administration; engineering.

Computers on Campus 250 computers/terminals and 100 ports are available on campus for general student use. Students can access the following: campus intranet, computer help desk, free student e-mail accounts, online (class) grades, online (class) registration, online (class) schedules, applications, admission/enrollment status, virtual orientation, online digital resources, online courses, assistive technology, learning management system, multimedia labs, payment, cyber cafes, centrally-licensed, downloadable software and training. Campuswide network is available. 100% of college-owned or -operated housing units are wired for high-speed Internet access. Wireless service is available via entire campus.

Student Life *Housing:* on-campus residence required through sophomore year. *Options:* coed, men-only, women-only, disabled students. Campus housing is university owned. Freshman campus housing is guaranteed. *Activities and organizations:* drama/theater group, student-run newspaper, radio and television station, choral group, marching band, Student Government Association, marching band, Red Scare (basketball student cheering section), Campus Connection, Habitat Humanity, national fraternities, national sororities. *Campus security:* 24-hour emergency response devices and patrols, student patrols, late-night transport/escort service, controlled dormitory access. *Student services:* health clinic, personal/psychological counseling, women's center.

Athletics Member NCAA. All Division I except football (Division I-AA). *Intercollegiate sports:* baseball M (s), basketball M (s)/W (s), cheerleading M/W, crew W, cross-country running M (s)/W (s), golf M (s)/W (s), soccer M (s)/W (s), softball W (s), tennis M (s)/W (s), track and field W (s), volleyball W (s). *Intramural sports:* badminton M/W, baseball M (c), basketball M/W, bowling M (c)/W (c), crew M (c), fencing M (c)/W (c), field hockey W (c), football M/W, gymnastics M (c)/W (c), ice hockey M (c), lacrosse M (c)/W (c), racquetball M/W, rugby M (c)/W (c), soccer M (c)/W (c), softball M/W, tennis M/W, track and field M (c), ultimate Frisbee M (c)/W (c), volleyball M (c)/W (c), water polo M (c)/W (c), wrestling M (c)/W (c).

Standardized Tests *Required:* SAT or ACT (for admission).

Costs (2007–08) *Comprehensive fee:* $33,670 includes full-time tuition ($24,880), mandatory fees ($1070), and room and board ($7720). Full-time tuition and fees vary according to program. Part-time tuition: $829 per credit hour. Part-time tuition and fees vary according to course load and program. *Required fees:* $25 per term part-time. *College room only:* $4550. Room and board charges vary according to board plan, housing facility, and student level. *Payment plan:* deferred payment. *Waivers:* senior citizens and employees or children of employees.

Financial Aid Of all full-time matriculated undergraduates who enrolled in 2006, 5,106 applied for aid, 4,038 were judged to have need, 1,892 had their need fully met. 823 Federal Work-Study jobs (averaging $1421). 2,765 state and other part-time jobs (averaging $1915). In 2006, 2,769 non-need-based awards were made. *Average percent of need met:* 96%. *Average financial aid package:* $17,980. *Average need-based loan:* $7335. *Average need-based gift aid:* $10,646. *Average non-need-based aid:* $6549. *Average indebtedness upon graduation:* $20,438.

Applying *Options:* electronic application, deferred entrance. *Application fee:* $50. *Required:* essay or personal statement, high school transcript, 1 letter of recommendation. *Required for some:* audition required for music, music therapy, music education programs. *Recommended:* interview. *Application deadlines:* rolling (freshmen), 6/15 (transfers). *Notification:* continuous (freshmen), continuous (transfers).

Freshman Application Contact Mr. Robert Durkle, Director of Admission, University of Dayton, 300 College Park, Dayton, OH 45469-1300. *Phone:* 937-229-4411. *Toll-free phone:* 800-837-7433. *Fax:* 937-229-4729. *E-mail:* admission@udayton.edu.

See page 2058 for the College Close-Up.

THE UNIVERSITY OF FINDLAY

Findlay, Ohio **www.findlay.edu/**

- **Independent** comprehensive, founded 1882, affiliated with Church of God
- **Small-town** 200-acre campus with easy access to Toledo
- **Endowment** $19.8 million
- **Coed** 4,004 undergraduate students, 72% full-time, 61% women, 39% men
- **Moderately difficult** entrance level, 70% of applicants were admitted

Neither a mega-university nor a small college, the University of Findlay (UF) is just the right size. It offers students options and opportunities without sacrificing personal attention. Total enrollment is more than 4,500. Some of UF's more innovative degree programs include eleven majors in the health professions, equestrian studies, pre–veterinary medicine, business, and education.

Undergraduates 2,875 full-time, 1,129 part-time. Students come from 45 states and territories, 34 other countries, 18% are from out of state, 3% African American, 1% Asian American or Pacific Islander, 1% Hispanic American, 0.3% Native American, 7% international, 2% transferred in, 40% live on campus. *Retention:* 77% of 2006 full-time freshmen returned.

Freshmen *Admission:* 2,948 applied, 2,052 admitted, 662 enrolled. *Average high school GPA:* 3.39. *Test scores:* SAT critical reading scores over 500: 63%; SAT math scores over 500: 69%; SAT writing scores over 500: 64%; ACT scores over 18: 93%; SAT critical reading scores over 600: 18%; SAT math scores over 600: 23%; SAT writing scores over 600: 23%; ACT scores over 24: 43%; SAT critical reading scores over 700: 2%; SAT math scores over 700: 2%; SAT writing scores over 700: 4%; ACT scores over 30: 5%.

Faculty *Total:* 363, 52% full-time, 34% with terminal degrees. *Student/faculty ratio:* 17:1.

Majors Accounting; administrative assistant and secretarial science; art; art teacher education; athletic training; bilingual and multilingual education; biological and physical sciences; biology/biological sciences; broadcast journalism; business administration and management; business/corporate communications; business teacher education; clinical laboratory science/medical technology; community organization and advocacy; computer science; computer systems networking and telecommunications; creative writing; criminal justice/law enforcement administration; dramatic/theater arts; economics; education; elementary education; English; English as a second/foreign language (teaching); environmental studies; equestrian studies; farm and ranch management; history; hotel/motel administration; humanities; human resources management; international business/trade/commerce; Japanese; journalism; logistics and materials management; marketing/marketing management; mathematics; nuclear medical technology; occupational therapy; philosophy; physical education teaching and coaching; physical therapy; physician assistant; political science and government; pre-law studies; pre-medical studies; pre-veterinary studies; psychology; public relations/image management; religious studies; sales, distribution and marketing; science teacher education; secondary education; social sciences; social work; sociology; Spanish; special education.

Academics *Calendar:* semesters. *Degrees:* associate, bachelor's, master's, and first professional. *Special study options:* academic remediation for entering students, accelerated degree program, adult/continuing education programs, advanced placement credit, cooperative education, distance learning, double majors, English as a second language, honors programs, independent study, internships, off-campus study, part-time degree program, services for LD students, student-designed majors, study abroad, summer session for credit. *ROTC:* Army (c), Air Force (c). *Unusual degree programs:* 3-2 nursing with Mount Carmel College of Nursing.

Computers on Campus 200 computers/terminals are available on campus for general student use. Students can access the following: online (class) registration. Campuswide network is available.

Student Life *Housing:* on-campus residence required through junior year. *Options:* coed, men-only, women-only, disabled students. Campus housing is university owned. Freshman campus housing is guaranteed. *Activities and organizations:* drama/theater group, student-run newspaper, radio and television station, choral group, marching band, Campus Program Board, Pre-Vet Club, Horse Club, Circle K, International Club, national fraternities, national sororities. *Campus security:* 24-hour emergency response devices and patrols, late-night transport/escort service. *Student services:* health clinic, personal/psychological counseling, women's center.

Athletics Member NCAA. All Division II. *Intercollegiate sports:* baseball M (s), basketball M (s)/W (s), cross-country running M (s)/W (s), football M (s), golf M (s)/W (s), ice hockey M (c)/W (c), soccer M (s)/W (s), softball W (s), swimming and diving M (s)/W (s), tennis M (s)/W (s), track and field M (s)/W (s), volleyball W (s), water polo M (c)/W (c), wrestling M (s). *Intramural sports:* basketball M/W, volleyball M/W.

Standardized Tests *Required:* SAT or ACT (for admission).

Costs (2007–08) *Comprehensive fee:* $31,916 includes full-time tuition ($22,906), mandatory fees ($984), and room and board ($8026). Full-time tuition and fees vary according to location and program. Part-time tuition and fees vary according to location and program. *College room only:* $4024. *Payment plan:* installment. *Waivers:* children of alumni, senior citizens, and employees or children of employees.

Financial Aid Of all full-time matriculated undergraduates who enrolled in 2006, 2,511 applied for aid, 1,999 were judged to have need, 391 had their need fully met. 420 Federal Work-Study jobs (averaging $830). 300 state and other part-time jobs (averaging $850). In 2006, 505 non-need-based awards were made. *Average percent of need met:* 77%. *Average financial aid package:* $14,900. *Average need-based loan:* $4000. *Average need-based gift aid:* $9300. *Average non-need-based aid:* $7500. *Average indebtedness upon graduation:* $19,500. *Financial aid deadline:* 3/1.

Applying *Options:* electronic application, deferred entrance. *Required:* essay or personal statement, high school transcript, minimum 2.3 GPA, letters of recommendation. *Required for some:* interview. *Application deadlines:* 6/1 (freshmen), rolling (transfers). *Notification:* continuous (freshmen), continuous (transfers).

Freshman Application Contact Mr. Randall Langston, Executive Director of Enrollment Services, The University of Findlay, 1000 North Main Street, Findlay, OH 45840-3653. *Phone:* 419-434-4732. *Toll-free phone:* 800-548-0932. *Fax:* 419-434-4898. *E-mail:* admissions@findlay.edu.

See page 2060 for the College Close-Up.

UNIVERSITY OF NORTHWESTERN OHIO

Lima, Ohio **www.unoh.edu/**

Freshman Application Contact Mr. Dan Klopp, Vice President for Enrollment Management, University of Northwestern Ohio, 1441 North Cable Road, Lima, OH 45805-1498. *Phone:* 419-227-3141. *Fax:* 419-229-6926. *E-mail:* klopp_d@unoh.edu.

UNIVERSITY OF PHOENIX–CINCINNATI CAMPUS

West Chester, Ohio **www.phoenix.edu/**

- **Proprietary** comprehensive, founded 2003
- **Urban** campus
- **Coed**
- **Noncompetitive** entrance level

Faculty *Student/faculty ratio:* 6:1.

Academics *Calendar:* continuous. *Degrees:* bachelor's and master's.

Student Life *Campus security:* late-night transport/escort service.

Costs (2007–08) *Tuition:* $12,180 full-time, $406 per credit part-time. Full-time tuition and fees vary according to course level.

Financial Aid *Average financial aid package:* $3974. *Average need-based gift aid:* $1862.

Applying *Options:* deferred entrance. *Application fee:* $45. *Required:* 1 letter of recommendation. *Required for some:* high school transcript.

Freshman Application Contact Ms. Beth Barilla, Associate Vice President, Student Admissions and Services, University of Phoenix–Cincinnati Campus, 4615 East Elwood Street, Mail Stop AA-K101, Phoenix, AZ 85040-1958. *Phone:* 480-317-6000. *Toll-free phone:* 800-776-4867 (in-state); 800-228-7240 (out-of-state). *Fax:* 480-894-1758. *E-mail:* beth.barilla@phoenix.edu.

UNIVERSITY OF PHOENIX–CLEVELAND CAMPUS

Independence, Ohio **www.phoenix.edu/**

- **Proprietary** comprehensive, founded 2000
- **Urban** campus
- **Coed**
- **Noncompetitive** entrance level

Faculty *Student/faculty ratio:* 6:1.

Academics *Calendar:* continuous. *Degrees:* bachelor's and master's.

Costs (2007–08) *Tuition:* $12,180 full-time, $406 per credit part-time. Full-time tuition and fees vary according to course level.

Financial Aid *Average financial aid package:* $4211. *Average need-based gift aid:* $2270.

Applying *Options:* deferred entrance. *Application fee:* $45. *Required:* 1 letter of recommendation. *Required for some:* high school transcript.

Freshman Application Contact Ms. Beth Barilla, Associate Vice President, Student Admissions and Services, University of Phoenix–Cleveland Campus, 4615 East Elwood Street, Mail Stop AA-K101, Phoenix, AZ 85040-1958. *Phone:* 480-317-6000. *Toll-free phone:* 800-776-4867 (in-state); 800-228-7240 (out-of-state). *Fax:* 480-594-1758. *E-mail:* beth.barilla@phoenix.edu.

UNIVERSITY OF PHOENIX–COLUMBUS OHIO CAMPUS

Columbus, Ohio **www.phoenix.edu/**

- **Proprietary** comprehensive, founded 2003
- **Urban** campus
- **Coed**
- **Noncompetitive** entrance level

Faculty *Student/faculty ratio:* 7:1.

Academics *Calendar:* continuous. *Degrees:* bachelor's and master's.

Student Life *Campus security:* late-night transport/escort service.

Costs (2007–08) *Tuition:* $12,180 full-time, $406 per credit part-time. Full-time tuition and fees vary according to course level.

Financial Aid *Average financial aid package:* $3460. *Average need-based gift aid:* $1757.

Applying *Options:* deferred entrance. *Application fee:* $45. *Required:* 1 letter of recommendation. *Required for some:* high school transcript.

Freshman Application Contact Ms. Beth Barilla, Associate Vice President, Student Admissions and Services, University of Phoenix–Columbus Ohio Campus, 8415 Pulsar Place, Columbus, OH 43240-4032. *Phone:* 480-317-6000. *Toll-free phone:* 800-776-4867 (in-state); 800-228-7240 (out-of-state). *Fax:* 480-894-1758. *E-mail:* beth.barilla@phoenix.edu.

UNIVERSITY OF RIO GRANDE

Rio Grande, Ohio **www.rio.edu/**

- **Independent** comprehensive, founded 1876
- **Rural** 170-acre campus
- **Endowment** $19.5 million
- **Coed** 2,107 undergraduate students, 78% full-time, 59% women, 41% men
- **Noncompetitive** entrance level, 63% of applicants were admitted

Undergraduates 1,638 full-time, 469 part-time. Students come from 7 states and territories, 7 other countries, 5% are from out of state, 3% African American, 0.4% Asian American or Pacific Islander, 0.6% Hispanic American, 0.4% Native American, 0.3% international, 9% transferred in, 27% live on campus. *Retention:* 58% of 2006 full-time freshmen returned.

Freshmen *Admission:* 3,056 applied, 1,936 admitted, 408 enrolled. *Average high school GPA:* 3.06. *Test scores:* ACT scores over 18: 77%; ACT scores over 24: 15%; ACT scores over 30: 1%.

Faculty *Total:* 308, 30% full-time, 14% with terminal degrees. *Student/faculty ratio:* 18:1.

Majors Accounting; accounting technology and bookkeeping; administrative assistant and secretarial science; American studies; art; art teacher education; biology/biological sciences; biology teacher education; business administration and management; business automation/technology/data entry; business/corporate communications; business teacher education; chemistry; clinical laboratory science/medical technology; clinical/medical laboratory technology; communication/speech communication and rhetoric; computer science; drafting and design technology; ecology; economics; education; education (multiple levels); elementary education; energy management and systems technology; English; English/language arts teacher education; general studies; graphic design; health and physical education; health teacher education; history; history teacher education; humanities; industrial technology; information technology; international business/trade/commerce; kindergarten/preschool education; legal administrative assistant/secretary; marketing/marketing management; mass communication/media; mathematics; mathematics teacher education; mechanical engineering/mechanical technology; medical administrative assistant and medical secretary; music; music teacher education; nursing (registered nurse training); physical education teaching and coaching; physical sciences; physics teacher education; political science and government; pre-dentistry studies; pre-law studies; pre-medical studies; pre-theology/pre-ministerial studies; pre-veterinary studies; psychology; public relations/image management; radiologic technology/science; robotics technology; science teacher education; secondary education; social sciences; social science teacher education; social work; sociology; special education (mentally retarded); special education (specific learning disabilities); speech teacher education; theater design and technology; visual and performing arts.

Academics *Calendar:* semesters. *Degrees:* associate, bachelor's, and master's. *Special study options:* academic remediation for entering students, accelerated degree program, adult/continuing education programs, advanced placement credit, cooperative education, distance learning, double majors, English as a second language, freshman honors college, honors programs, independent study, internships, part-time degree program, services for LD students, student-designed majors, study abroad, summer session for credit. *ROTC:* Army (c).

Computers on Campus 300 computers/terminals are available on campus for general student use. Students can access the following: online (class) registration. Campuswide network is available.

Student Life *Housing options:* coed, men-only, women-only. Campus housing is university owned. *Activities and organizations:* drama/theater group, student-run newspaper, radio and television station, choral group, student government, Honoraries, Bible studies, Students in Free Enterprise, national fraternities. *Campus security:* 24-hour emergency response devices and patrols, late-night transport/escort service, controlled dormitory access. *Student services:* health clinic, personal/psychological counseling.

Athletics Member NAIA. *Intercollegiate sports:* baseball M (s), basketball M (s)/W (s), cross-country running M (s)/W (s), soccer M (s)/W, softball W (s), track and field M (s)/W (s), volleyball W (s). *Intramural sports:* basketball M/W, football M, golf M, gymnastics W, racquetball M/W, soccer M/W, table tennis M/W, tennis M/W, volleyball M/W.

Standardized Tests *Recommended:* ACT (for admission).

Costs (2007–08) *Tuition:* $110 per credit hour part-time; state resident $129 per credit hour part-time; nonresident $16,600 full-time, $695 per credit hour part-time. Full-time tuition and fees vary according to course load, degree level, and program. Part-time tuition and fees vary according to course load, degree level, and program. *Required fees:* $106 per term part-time. *Room and board:* $6820. Room and board charges vary according to board plan, housing facility, and student level. *Waivers:* senior citizens.

Financial Aid Of all full-time matriculated undergraduates who enrolled in 2003, 1,511 applied for aid, 1,326 were judged to have need, 707 had their need fully met. In 2003, 366 non-need-based awards were made. *Average percent of need met:* 73%. *Average financial aid package:* $9651. *Average need-based loan:* $3733. *Average need-based gift aid:* $4765. *Average indebtedness upon graduation:* $13,750.

Applying *Options:* electronic application. *Application fee:* $25. *Required:* high school transcript, medical history. *Application deadlines:* rolling (freshmen), rolling (transfers). *Notification:* continuous (freshmen), continuous (transfers).

Freshman Application Contact Ms. Tammy McCain, Admissions Officer, University of Rio Grande, PO Box 500, Rio Grande, OH 45674. *Phone:* 740-245-7208. *Toll-free phone:* 800-282-7201. *Fax:* 740-245-7260. *E-mail:* admissions@rio.edu.

THE UNIVERSITY OF TOLEDO

Toledo, Ohio **www.utoledo.edu/**

- **State-supported** university, founded 1872, part of University System of Ohio
- **Suburban** 407-acre campus with easy access to Detroit
- **Endowment** $49.6 million
- **Coed** 16,527 undergraduate students, 81% full-time, 49% women, 51% men
- **Noncompetitive** entrance level, 93% of applicants were admitted

Undergraduates 13,394 full-time, 3,133 part-time. Students come from 40 states and territories, 91 other countries, 10% are from out of state, 14% African American, 2% Asian American or Pacific Islander, 3% Hispanic American, 0.3% Native American, 2% international, 7% transferred in, 22% live on campus. *Retention:* 68% of 2006 full-time freshmen returned.

Freshmen *Admission:* 11,156 applied, 10,348 admitted, 3,595 enrolled. *Average high school GPA:* 3.13. *Test scores:* SAT critical reading scores over 500: 53%; SAT math scores over 500: 63%; SAT writing scores over 500: 49%; ACT scores over 18: 81%; SAT critical reading scores over 600: 16%; SAT math scores over 600: 26%; SAT writing scores over 600: 14%; ACT scores over 24: 33%; SAT critical reading scores over 700: 2%; SAT math scores over 700: 3%; SAT writing scores over 700: 1%; ACT scores over 30: 5%.

Faculty *Total:* 1,204, 71% full-time. *Student/faculty ratio:* 17:1.

Majors Accounting; administrative assistant and secretarial science; adult and continuing education; adult development and aging; African-American/Black studies; allied health diagnostic, intervention, and treatment professions related; American studies; anthropology; applied art; architectural drafting and CAD/CADD; art; art history, criticism and conservation; art teacher education; Asian studies; astronomy; audiology and speech-language pathology; biological and physical sciences; biology/biological sciences; biomedical/medical engineering; business administration and management; business administration, management and operations related; business automation/technology/data entry; business/commerce; business, management, and marketing related; business/managerial economics; business teacher education; cardiovascular technology; chemical engineering; chemical technology; chemistry; civil engineering; civil engineering technology; classics and languages, literatures and linguistics; clinical laboratory science/medical technology; communication/speech communication and rhetoric; community organization and advocacy; computer engineering; computer programming; computer programming (specific applications); computer science; computer systems analysis; computer typography and composition equipment operation; construction engineering technology; consumer merchandising/retailing management; corrections; criminal justice/police science; criminal justice/safety; data processing and data processing technology; developmental and child psychology; drafting and design technology; dramatic/theater arts; drawing; economics; education; educational/instructional media design; education (specific levels and methods) related; education (specific subject areas) related; electrical, electronic and communications engineering technology; electrical, electronics and communications engineering; electromechanical technology; elementary education; emergency medical technology (EMT paramedic); engineering; engineering physics; English; English/language arts teacher education; entrepreneurship; environmental engineering technology; environmental studies; European studies; experimental psychology; film/cinema studies; finance; fine/studio arts; fire protection and safety technology; French; French language teacher education; general studies; geography; geology/earth science; German; German language teacher education; gerontology; health information/medical records administration; health teacher education; history; hospital and health care facilities administration; human development and family studies related; humanities; human resources management; industrial engineering; industrial technology; information science/studies; international business/trade/commerce; international relations and affairs; journalism; kindergarten/preschool education; kinesiology and exercise science; Latin American studies; legal administrative assistant/secretary; legal assistant/paralegal; liberal arts and sciences/liberal studies; linguistics; literature; logistics and materials management; management information systems; management sciences and quantitative methods related; marketing/marketing management; marketing research; mass communication/media; mathematics; mathematics teacher education; mechanical engineering; mechanical engineering/mechanical technology; medical/clinical assistant; medieval and Renaissance studies; mental and social health services and allied professions related; mental health/rehabilitation; multi-/interdisciplinary studies related; music; music teacher education; natural sciences; Near and Middle Eastern studies; nursing (registered nurse training); nursing related; operations management; organizational behavior; parks, recreation and leisure; parks, recreation, and leisure related; pharmacy; pharmacy, pharmaceutical sciences, and administration related; philosophy; physical education teaching and coaching; physical sciences; physical therapy; physics; political science and government; pre-dentistry studies; pre-law studies; premedical studies; pre-veterinary studies; psychiatric/mental health services technology; psychology; psychology related; public health education and promotion; public policy analysis; religious studies; respiratory care therapy; science teacher education; secondary education; social sciences; social studies teacher education; social work; sociology; Spanish; Spanish language teacher education; special education; special education (emotionally disturbed); special education (hearing impaired); special education (multiply disabled); special education related; special education (specific learning disabilities); special education (speech or language impaired); special education (vision impaired); speech-language pathology; speech therapy; structural engineering; substance abuse/addiction counseling; trade and industrial teacher education; transportation technology; urban studies/affairs; welding technology; women's studies.

Academics *Calendar:* semesters. *Degrees:* certificates, associate, bachelor's, master's, doctoral, first professional, post-master's, and postbachelor's certificates. *Special study options:* academic remediation for entering students, adult/continuing education programs, advanced placement credit, cooperative education, distance learning, double majors, English as a second language, honors programs, independent study, internships, off-campus study, part-time degree program, services for LD students, student-designed majors, study abroad, summer session for credit. *ROTC:* Army (b), Air Force (c).

Computers on Campus 2,800 computers/terminals and 5,000 ports are available on campus for general student use. Students can access the following: campus intranet, computer help desk, free student e-mail accounts, online (class) grades, online (class) registration, online (class) schedules, online transcripts, student account. Campuswide network is available. 100% of college-owned or -operated housing units are wired for high-speed Internet access. Wireless service is available via classrooms, libraries, student centers.

Student Life *Housing:* on-campus residence required for freshman year. *Options:* coed, disabled students. Campus housing is university owned. *Activities and organizations:* drama/theater group, student-run newspaper, radio station, choral group, marching band, student government, University YMCA, Newman Club, International Student Association, Campus Activities and Programming, national fraternities, national sororities. *Campus security:* 24-hour emergency response devices and patrols, student patrols, late-night transport/escort service, controlled dormitory access, bicycle patrols by security staff, crime prevention officer. *Student services:* health clinic, personal/psychological counseling, women's center, legal services.

Athletics Member NCAA. All Division I. *Intercollegiate sports:* baseball M (s), basketball M (s)/W (s), cross-country running M (s)/W (s), football M (s), golf M (s)/W (s), ice hockey M (s)/W (s), soccer W (s), softball W (s), swimming and diving W (s), tennis M (s)/W (s), track and field W (s), volleyball W (s). *Intramural sports:* badminton M/W, basketball M/W, bowling M/W, crew M (c)/W (c), fencing M (c)/W (c), football M/W, golf M/W, lacrosse M/W, racquetball M/W, sailing M (c)/W (c), skiing (cross-country) M (c)/W (c), skiing (downhill) M (c)/W (c), soccer M (c)/W (c), softball M/W, swimming and diving M/W, table tennis M/W, tennis M/W, track and field M/W, volleyball M/W, water polo M/W, weight lifting M/W, wrestling M.

Standardized Tests *Required:* SAT or ACT (for admission).

Costs (2008–09) *Tuition:* state resident $6816 full-time, $284 per semester hour part-time; nonresident $15,627 full-time, $651 per semester hour part-time. *Required fees:* $1111 full-time, $46 per semester hour part-time. *Room and board:* $8446; room only: $5496.

Financial Aid Of all full-time matriculated undergraduates who enrolled in 2005, 9,788 applied for aid, 7,685 were judged to have need, 768 had their need fully met. 470 Federal Work-Study jobs (averaging $1705). In 2005, 1,933 non-need-based awards were made. *Average percent of need met:* 54%. *Average financial aid package:* $6979. *Average need-based loan:* $3434. *Average need-based gift aid:* $4746. *Average non-need-based aid:* $3120. *Average indebtedness upon graduation:* $21,531.

Applying *Options:* electronic application, deferred entrance. *Application fee:* $40. *Required:* high school transcript. *Required for some:* minimum 2.0 GPA, CORE high school curriculum. *Application deadlines:* rolling (freshmen), rolling (transfers). *Notification:* continuous (freshmen), continuous (transfers).

Freshman Application Contact Mr. William Pierce, Director of Undergraduate Admissions, The University of Toledo, 2801 West Bancroft, Toledo, OH 43606-3398. *Phone:* 419-530-5705. *Toll-free phone:* 800-5TOLEDO. *Fax:* 419-530-5713. *E-mail:* william.pierce@utoledo.edu.

URBANA UNIVERSITY

Urbana, Ohio **www.urbana.edu/**

Founded in 1850, Urbana University is located on 128 acres in Urbana, Ohio. Urbana offers a liberal arts education in a small-university environment, while emphasizing individual attention in the academic and social aspects of campus life. Degrees are awarded within four academic colleges at the associate, bachelor's, and master's levels. Scholarships are available for academics, athletics, and special interest activities.

Freshman Application Contact Ms. Paula Brown, Director of Admissions, Urbana University, 579 College Way, Urbana, OH 43078. *Phone:* 937-484-1356. *Toll-free phone:* 800-7-URBANA. *Fax:* 937-652-6871. *E-mail:* admiss@urbana.edu.

URSULINE COLLEGE

Pepper Pike, Ohio **www.ursuline.edu/**

- **Independent Roman Catholic** comprehensive, founded 1871
- **Suburban** 112-acre campus with easy access to Cleveland
- **Endowment** $27.4 million
- **Undergraduate: women only; graduate: coed** 1,169 undergraduate students, 68% full-time, 93% women, 7% men
- **Minimally difficult** entrance level, 66% of applicants were admitted

Undergraduates 796 full-time, 373 part-time. Students come from 8 states and territories, 8 other countries, 1% are from out of state, 25% African American, 3% Asian American or Pacific Islander, 2% Hispanic American, 0.3% Native American, 0.4% international, 22% transferred in, 16% live on campus. *Retention:* 73% of 2006 full-time freshmen returned.

Freshmen *Admission:* 436 applied, 287 admitted, 113 enrolled. *Average high school GPA:* 3.28. *Test scores:* SAT critical reading scores over 500: 47%; SAT math scores over 500: 53%; ACT scores over 18: 86%; SAT critical reading scores over 600: 15%; SAT math scores over 600: 18%; ACT scores over 24: 17%; SAT critical reading scores over 700: 3%; SAT math scores over 700: 3%; ACT scores over 30: 3%.

Faculty *Total:* 201, 38% full-time, 29% with terminal degrees. *Student/faculty ratio:* 9:1.

Majors Accounting; American studies; art history, criticism and conservation; art teacher education; biological and biomedical sciences related; biology/biological sciences; biotechnology; business administration and management; business administration, management and operations related; Christian studies; early childhood education; English; English/language arts teacher education; fashion/apparel design; fashion merchandising; fine/studio arts; graphic design; health and medical administrative services related; health/health care administration; health services administration; health services/allied health/health sciences; historic preservation and conservation; history; hospital and health care facilities administration; humanities; human resources management; interior design; legal assistant/paralegal; management information systems; marketing/marketing management; mathematics; mathematics teacher education; middle school education; multi-/interdisciplinary studies related; nursing (registered nurse training); philosophy; psychology; public relations/image management; religious studies related; science teacher education; social studies teacher education; social work; sociology; special education; work and family studies.

Academics *Calendar:* semesters. *Degrees:* certificates, bachelor's, master's, and post-master's certificates (applications from men are also accepted). *Special study options:* academic remediation for entering students, accelerated degree program, adult/continuing education programs, advanced placement credit, cooperative education, distance learning, double majors, independent study, internships, off-campus study, part-time degree program, services for LD students, summer session for credit. *ROTC:* Army (c). *Unusual degree programs:* 3-2 pharmacy-University of Toledo.

Computers on Campus 72 computers/terminals are available on campus for general student use. Campuswide network is available. 100% of college-owned or -operated housing units are wired for high-speed Internet access. Wireless service is available via classrooms, computer centers, computer labs, libraries.

Student Life *Housing options:* coed, women-only. Campus housing is university owned. *Activities and organizations:* drama/theater group, choral group, Student Government Association, Student Nurses of Ursuline College, Fashion Focus, Students United for Black Awareness, Drama Club. *Campus security:* 24-hour emergency response devices and patrols, late-night transport/escort service, controlled dormitory access. *Student services:* personal/psychological counseling.

Athletics Member NAIA. *Intercollegiate sports:* basketball W (s), cross-country running W (s), golf W (s), soccer W (s), softball W (s), tennis W (s), track and field W (s), volleyball W (s).

Standardized Tests *Required:* SAT or ACT (for admission).

Costs (2007–08) *Comprehensive fee:* $28,176 includes full-time tuition ($20,910), mandatory fees ($230), and room and board ($7036). Full-time tuition and fees vary according to location. Part-time tuition: $697 per credit hour. Part-time tuition and fees vary according to location. *Required fees:* $150 per term part-time. *College room only:* $3594. Room and board charges vary according to board plan and housing facility. *Payment plan:* installment. *Waivers:* employees or children of employees.

Financial Aid Of all full-time matriculated undergraduates who enrolled in 2006, 621 applied for aid, 589 were judged to have need, 132 had their need fully met. In 2006, 111 non-need-based awards were made. *Average percent of need met:* 76%. *Average financial aid package:* $15,511. *Average need-based loan:* $4200. *Average non-need-based aid:* $4124. *Average indebtedness upon graduation:* $21,680.

Applying *Options:* electronic application, early action, deferred entrance. *Application fee:* $25. *Required:* essay or personal statement, high school transcript. *Recommended:* minimum 2.0 GPA, letters of recommendation, interview. *Application deadlines:* rolling (freshmen), rolling (transfers), 11/15 (early action). *Notification:* continuous (freshmen), continuous (transfers), 2/15 (early action).

Freshman Application Contact Director of Admissions, Ursuline College, 2550 Lander Road, Pepper Pike, OH 44124. *Phone:* 440-449-4203. *Toll-free phone:* 888-URSULINE. *Fax:* 440-684-6138. *E-mail:* admission@ursuline.edu.

WALSH UNIVERSITY

North Canton, Ohio **www.walsh.edu/**

- **Independent Roman Catholic** comprehensive, founded 1958
- **Small-town** 134-acre campus with easy access to Cleveland
- **Endowment** $8.3 million
- **Coed** 2,146 undergraduate students, 80% full-time, 65% women, 35% men
- **Moderately difficult** entrance level, 79% of applicants were admitted

Undergraduates 1,710 full-time, 436 part-time. Students come from 18 states and territories, 24 other countries, 3% are from out of state, 5% African American, 0.7% Asian American or Pacific Islander, 0.9% Hispanic American, 0.3% Native American, 0.7% international, 11% transferred in, 50% live on campus. *Retention:* 80% of 2006 full-time freshmen returned.

Freshmen *Admission:* 1,313 applied, 1,035 admitted, 453 enrolled. *Average high school GPA:* 3.34. *Test scores:* SAT critical reading scores over 500: 42%; SAT math scores over 500: 53%; ACT scores over 18: 93%; SAT critical reading scores over 600: 14%; SAT math scores over 600: 17%; ACT scores over 24: 34%; SAT critical reading scores over 700: 2%; SAT math scores over 700: 2%; ACT scores over 30: 2%.

Faculty *Total:* 243, 40% full-time, 37% with terminal degrees. *Student/faculty ratio:* 14:1.

Majors Accounting; behavioral sciences; biological and physical sciences; biology/biological sciences; business administration and management; chemistry; communication and media related; computer science; early childhood education; education; English; finance; French; health and physical education; history; human services; kindergarten/preschool education; liberal arts and sciences and humanities related; liberal arts and sciences/liberal studies; management information systems; marketing/marketing management; mathematics; mathematics teacher education; middle school education; modern languages; nursing (registered nurse training); pastoral studies/counseling; philosophy; physical education teaching and coaching; political science and government; pre-dentistry studies; premedical studies; pre-veterinary studies; psychology; religious studies; science teacher education; secondary education; sociology; Spanish; special education; theology.

Academics *Calendar:* semesters. *Degrees:* associate, bachelor's, master's, and first professional. *Special study options:* academic remediation for entering students, accelerated degree program, adult/continuing education programs, advanced placement credit, double majors, English as a second language, honors programs, independent study, internships, off-campus study, part-time degree program, services for LD students, study abroad, summer session for credit. *Unusual degree programs:* 3-2 behavioral science/counseling; biology/physical therapy.

Computers on Campus 344 computers/terminals are available on campus for general student use. Students can access the following: computer help desk, free student e-mail accounts, online (class) grades, online (class) registration, online (class) schedules. Campuswide network is available. 100% of college-owned or -operated housing units are wired for high-speed Internet access.

Student Life *Housing:* on-campus residence required through senior year. *Options:* coed, men-only, women-only, disabled students. Campus housing is university owned. Freshman campus housing is guaranteed. *Activities and organizations:* drama/theater group, student-run newspaper, radio station, choral group, Walsh University Student Government, University Programming Board, Business and Communication Club, Behavioral Science Club, Education Club. *Campus security:* 24-hour emergency response devices and patrols, late-night transport/escort service, controlled dormitory access. *Student services:* health clinic, personal/psychological counseling.

Athletics Member NAIA. *Intercollegiate sports:* baseball M (s), basketball M (s)/W (s), cheerleading W, cross-country running M (s)/W (s), football M (s), golf M (s)/W (s), soccer M (s)/W (s), softball W (s), tennis M (s)/W (s), track and field M (s)/W (s), volleyball W (s). *Intramural sports:* basketball M/W, bowling M/W, football M/W, skiing (downhill) M (c)/W (c), soccer M/W, softball M/W, table tennis M/W, tennis M/W, ultimate Frisbee M (c)/W (c), volleyball M/W.

Standardized Tests *Required:* SAT or ACT (for admission).

Costs (2008–09) *One-time required fee:* $215. *Comprehensive fee:* $27,810 includes full-time tuition ($19,390), mandatory fees ($660), and room and board ($7760). *College room only:* $5100.

Financial Aid Of all full-time matriculated undergraduates who enrolled in 2006, 1,202 applied for aid, 1,044 were judged to have need, 544 had their need fully met. 182 Federal Work-Study jobs (averaging $1480). 30 state and other part-time jobs (averaging $1418). In 2006, 188 non-need-based awards were made. *Average percent of need met:* 83%. *Average financial aid package:* $11,262. *Average need-based loan:* $4220. *Average need-based gift aid:* $5827. *Average non-need-based aid:* $4834. *Average indebtedness upon graduation:* $18,775.

Applying *Options:* electronic application, early admission, deferred entrance. *Application fee:* $25. *Required:* high school transcript, minimum 2.3 GPA. *Required for some:* essay or personal statement, minimum 3.0 GPA, 2 letters of recommendation. *Recommended:* interview. *Application deadlines:* rolling (freshmen), rolling (transfers). *Notification:* continuous (freshmen), continuous (transfers).

Freshman Application Contact Mr. Brett Freshour, Vice President for Enrollment Management, Walsh University, 2020 East Maple, North Canton, OH 44720. *Phone:* 330-490-7171. *Toll-free phone:* 800-362-9846 (in-state); 800-362-8846 (out-of-state). *Fax:* 330-490-7165. *E-mail:* admissions@walsh.edu.

See page 2062 for the College Close-Up.

WILBERFORCE UNIVERSITY

Wilberforce, Ohio **www.wilberforce.edu/**

Director of Admissions Ms. Kenya LeNoir Messer, Vice President for Student Development and Enrollment Management/Dean of Admissions, Wilberforce University, PO Box 1001, Wilberforce, OH 45384-1001. *Phone:* 937-708-5721. *Toll-free phone:* 800-367-8568. *Fax:* 937-376-4751. *E-mail:* kmesser@wilberforce.edu.

WILMINGTON COLLEGE

Wilmington, Ohio **www.wilmington.edu/**

- **Independent Friends** comprehensive, founded 1870
- **Small-town** 1465-acre campus with easy access to Cincinnati and Columbus
- **Endowment** $19.0 million
- **Coed** 1,562 undergraduate students, 83% full-time, 54% women, 46% men
- **Moderately difficult** entrance level, 98% of applicants were admitted

Undergraduates 1,296 full-time, 266 part-time. Students come from 15 states and territories, 6 other countries, 3% are from out of state, 4% transferred in, 70% live on campus. *Retention:* 68% of 2006 full-time freshmen returned.

Freshmen *Admission:* 1,409 applied, 1,381 admitted, 374 enrolled. *Average high school GPA:* 3.17. *Test scores:* SAT critical reading scores over 500: 39%; SAT math scores over 500: 51%; ACT scores over 18: 80%; SAT critical reading scores over 600: 11%; SAT math scores over 600: 16%; ACT scores over 24: 21%; SAT critical reading scores over 700: 1%; ACT scores over 30: 1%.

Faculty *Total:* 122, 59% full-time, 41% with terminal degrees. *Student/faculty ratio:* 14:1.

Majors Accounting; agricultural business and management; agricultural teacher education; agriculture; art teacher education; athletic training; biological and physical sciences; biology/biological sciences; business administration and management; business/managerial economics; business teacher education; chemistry; computer science; criminal justice/law enforcement administration; dramatic/theater arts; economics; education; elementary education; English; health teacher education; history; liberal arts and sciences/liberal studies; marketing/marketing management; mass communication/media; mathematics; modern languages; music teacher education; philosophy; physical education teaching and coaching; political science and government; pre-dentistry studies; pre-law studies; pre-medical studies; pre-veterinary studies; psychology; religious studies; science teacher education; secondary education; social sciences; social work; Spanish; sport and fitness administration/management.

Academics *Calendar:* semesters. *Degrees:* bachelor's and master's. *Special study options:* academic remediation for entering students, accelerated degree program, adult/continuing education programs, advanced placement credit, double majors, honors programs, internships, off-campus study, part-time degree program, services for LD students, student-designed majors, study abroad, summer session for credit.

Computers on Campus 80 computers/terminals are available on campus for general student use. Students can access the following: online (class) registration, OhioLink. Campuswide network is available.

Student Life *Housing:* on-campus residence required through senior year. *Options:* coed, women-only. Campus housing is university owned. *Activities and organizations:* drama/theater group, student-run newspaper, choral group, Aggie Club, Quest, student publications, Commuter Concerns, national fraternities. *Campus security:* 24-hour emergency response devices and patrols, late-night transport/escort service, controlled dormitory access. *Student services:* health clinic, personal/psychological counseling.

Athletics Member NCAA. All Division III. *Intercollegiate sports:* baseball M, basketball M/W, cross-country running M/W, football M, golf M/W, soccer M/W, softball W, swimming and diving M/W, tennis M/W, track and field M/W, volleyball W, wrestling M. *Intramural sports:* basketball M/W, football M, racquetball M/W, soccer M/W, softball M/W, squash M/W, swimming and diving M/W, table tennis M/W, volleyball M/W.

Standardized Tests *Required:* SAT or ACT (for admission).

Costs (2007–08) *Comprehensive fee:* $29,784 includes full-time tuition ($21,578), mandatory fees ($500), and room and board ($7706). Part-time tuition: $880 per credit. Part-time tuition and fees vary according to course load. *College room only:* $3498. Room and board charges vary according to board plan and housing facility. *Payment plan:* installment. *Waivers:* employees or children of employees.

Financial Aid Of all full-time matriculated undergraduates who enrolled in 2003, 1,067 applied for aid, 1,001 were judged to have need, 542 had their need fully met. 518 Federal Work-Study jobs (averaging $1342). In 2003, 158 non-need-based awards were made. *Average percent of need met:* 92%. *Average financial aid package:* $17,080. *Average need-based loan:* $5630. *Average need-based gift aid:* $11,159. *Average non-need-based aid:* $5729. *Average indebtedness upon graduation:* $21,932.

Applying *Options:* deferred entrance. *Application fee:* $25. *Required:* high school transcript. *Recommended:* minimum 2.5 GPA, 1 letter of recommendation, interview. *Application deadlines:* rolling (freshmen), rolling (transfers). *Notification:* continuous (freshmen), continuous (transfers).

Freshman Application Contact Ms. Tina Garland, Director of Admission and Financial Aid, Wilmington College, Pyle Center Box 1325, 251 Ludovic Street, Wilmington, OH 45177. *Phone:* 937-382-6661 Ext. 426. *Toll-free phone:* 800-341-9318. *Fax:* 937-383-8542. *E-mail:* admissions@wilmington.edu.

WITTENBERG UNIVERSITY

Springfield, Ohio **www.wittenberg.edu/**

- **Independent** comprehensive, founded 1845, affiliated with Evangelical Lutheran Church
- **Suburban** 71-acre campus with easy access to Columbus and Dayton
- **Coed** 2,066 undergraduate students, 94% full-time, 55% women, 45% men
- **Moderately difficult** entrance level, 73% of applicants were admitted

Undergraduates 1,943 full-time, 123 part-time. Students come from 36 states and territories, 16 other countries, 24% are from out of state, 5% African American, 0.6% Asian American or Pacific Islander, 1% Hispanic American, 0.2% Native American, 2% international, 2% transferred in, 82% live on campus. *Retention:* 80% of 2006 full-time freshmen returned.

Freshmen *Admission:* 2,887 applied, 2,096 admitted, 551 enrolled. *Average high school GPA:* 3.41. *Test scores:* SAT critical reading scores over 500: 73%; SAT math scores over 500: 78%; ACT scores over 18: 97%; SAT critical reading scores over 600: 32%; SAT math scores over 600: 32%; ACT scores over 24: 58%; SAT critical reading scores over 700: 5%; SAT math scores over 700: 5%; ACT scores over 30: 11%.

Faculty *Total:* 195, 73% full-time, 74% with terminal degrees. *Student/faculty ratio:* 12:1.

Majors American studies; art; Asian studies (East); biochemistry/biophysics and molecular biology; biology/biological sciences; business administration and management; chemistry; communication/speech communication and rhetoric; computer science; dramatic/theater arts; economics; education; English; French; geography; geological and earth sciences/geosciences related; geology/earth science; German; history; liberal arts and sciences/liberal studies; mathematics; music; philosophy; physics; political science and government; psychology; religious/sacred music; religious studies; Russian studies; sociology; Spanish.

Academics *Calendar:* semesters. *Degrees:* bachelor's and master's. *Special study options:* academic remediation for entering students, adult/continuing education programs, advanced placement credit, cooperative education, double majors, English as a second language, freshman honors college, honors programs, independent study, internships, off-campus study, part-time degree program, student-designed majors, study abroad, summer session for credit. *ROTC:* Army (c), Air Force (c). *Unusual degree programs:* 3-2 engineering with Georgia Institute of Technology, Washington University in St. Louis, Case Western Reserve University; forestry with Duke University; nursing with Case Western Reserve University, Johns Hopkins University; occupational therapy with Washington University in St. Louis.

Computers on Campus Students can access the following: computer help desk, free student e-mail accounts, online (class) grades, online (class) registration, online (class) schedules. Campuswide network is available.

Student Life *Housing:* on-campus residence required through sophomore year. *Options:* coed, women-only. Campus housing is university owned, leased by the school and is provided by a third party. Freshman campus housing is guaranteed. *Activities and organizations:* drama/theater group, student-run newspaper, radio station, choral group, Student Senate, Union Board, choirs, Weaver Chapel Association, national fraternities, national sororities. *Campus security:* 24-hour emergency response devices and patrols, student patrols, late-night transport/escort service, controlled dormitory access, crime prevention programs. *Student services:* health clinic, personal/psychological counseling, women's center.

Athletics Member NCAA. All Division III. *Intercollegiate sports:* baseball M, basketball M/W, crew M (c)/W (c), cross-country running M/W, field hockey W, football M, golf M/W, lacrosse M/W, rugby M (c)/W (c), soccer M/W, softball W, swimming and diving M/W, tennis M/W, track and field M/W, volleyball M (c)/W. *Intramural sports:* basketball M/W, football M, golf M/W, sailing M/W, soccer M/W, softball M/W, swimming and diving M/W, tennis M/W, track and field M/W, volleyball M/W.

Costs (2008–09) *Comprehensive fee:* $41,550 includes full-time tuition ($32,936), mandatory fees ($300), and room and board ($8314). Part-time tuition: $1098 per credit hour. *College room only:* $4316.

Financial Aid Of all full-time matriculated undergraduates who enrolled in 2006, 1,612 applied for aid, 1,401 were judged to have need. 586 Federal Work-Study jobs (averaging $1723). 761 state and other part-time jobs (averaging $1826). In 2006, 512 non-need-based awards were made. *Average percent of need met:* 85%. *Average financial aid package:* $23,022. *Average need-based loan:* $3424. *Average need-based gift aid:* $17,843. *Average non-need-based aid:* $10,747. *Average indebtedness upon graduation:* $25,568.

Applying *Options:* electronic application, early admission, early decision, early action, deferred entrance. *Application fee:* $40. *Required:* essay or personal statement, high school transcript, letters of recommendation, interview. *Application deadlines:* rolling (transfers), 12/1 (early action). *Early decision deadline:* 11/15. *Notification:* continuous (freshmen), continuous (transfers), 1/1 (early decision), 2/1 (early action).

Freshman Application Contact Mr. Brad Pochard, Director of Admission, Wittenberg University, PO Box 720, Springfield, OH 45501-0720. *Phone:* 877-206-0332 Ext. 6377. *Toll-free phone:* 800-677-7558 Ext. 6314. *Fax:* 937-327-6379. *E-mail:* admission@wittenberg.edu.

See page 2064 for the College Close-Up.

WRIGHT STATE UNIVERSITY

Dayton, Ohio **www.wright.edu/**

- **State-supported** university, founded 1964
- **Suburban** 557-acre campus with easy access to Cincinnati
- **Endowment** $73.9 million
- **Coed** 12,279 undergraduate students, 85% full-time, 55% women, 45% men
- **Minimally difficult** entrance level, 83% of applicants were admitted

Undergraduates 10,497 full-time, 1,782 part-time. Students come from 47 states and territories, 66 other countries, 4% are from out of state, 13% African American, 3% Asian American or Pacific Islander, 2% Hispanic American, 0.4% Native American, 1% international, 8% transferred in, 22% live on campus. *Retention:* 69% of 2006 full-time freshmen returned.

Freshmen *Admission:* 5,866 applied, 4,898 admitted, 2,385 enrolled. *Average high school GPA:* 3.10. *Test scores:* SAT critical reading scores over 500: 51%; SAT math scores over 500: 51%; ACT scores over 18: 80%; SAT critical reading scores over 600: 11%; SAT math scores over 600: 13%; ACT scores over 24: 26%; SAT critical reading scores over 700: 1%; SAT math scores over 700: 1%; ACT scores over 30: 3%.

Faculty *Total:* 655, 100% full-time. *Student/faculty ratio:* 25:1.

Majors Accounting; accounting technology and bookkeeping; administrative assistant and secretarial science; adult health nursing; African-American/Black studies; anatomy; anthropology; applied mathematics; area studies related; art; art history, criticism and conservation; arts management; art teacher education; art therapy; biochemistry; biological and physical sciences; biology/biological sciences; biomedical/medical engineering; biomedical technology; business administration and management; business/commerce; business/managerial economics; business teacher education; chemistry; city/urban, community and regional planning; classics and languages, literatures and linguistics; clinical laboratory science/medical technology; communication/speech communication and rhetoric; community psychology; computer and information sciences; computer engineering; computer science; computer teacher education; construction engineering technology; counselor education/school counseling and guidance; criminal justice/police science; criminology; curriculum and instruction; dance; data processing and data processing technology; drafting and design technology; dramatic/theater arts; drawing; economics; economics related; education; educational, instructional, and curriculum supervision; educational leadership and administration; education (multiple levels); education related; education (specific levels and methods) related; education (specific subject areas) related; electrical, electronic and communications engineering technology; electrical, electronics and communications engineering; electromechanical technology; elementary education; engineering; engineering physics; engineering related; engineering science; English; English as a second/foreign language (teaching); English/language arts teacher education; environmental engineering technology; environmental health; environmental science; film/cinema studies; finance; foreign languages and literatures; foreign language teacher education; French; geography; geology/earth science; geophysics and seismology; German; health/health care administration; health/medical preparatory programs related; health teacher education; higher education/higher education administration; history; humanities; human resources management; hydrology and water resources science; industrial and organizational psychology; industrial technology; information science/studies; international relations and affairs; kindergarten/preschool education; legal administrative assistant/secretary; liberal arts and sciences and humanities related; liberal arts and sciences/liberal studies; linguistics; logistics and materials management; management information systems; management science; marketing/marketing management; mass communication/media; materials engineering; mathematics; mathematics teacher education; mechanical engineering; medical administrative assistant and medical secretary; mental and social health services and allied professions related; microbiological sciences and immunology related; middle school education; military technologies; modern Greek; modern languages; multi-/interdisciplinary studies related; music; music history, literature, and theory; music performance; music teacher education; music theory and composition; nursing (registered nurse training); nursing related; occupational safety and health technology; office management; office occupations and clerical services; operations management; organizational communication; pharmacology and toxicology; philosophy; photography; physical education teaching and coaching; physics related; political science and government; pre-dentistry studies; pre-law studies; pre-medical studies; pre-pharmacy studies; pre-veterinary studies; psychology; public administration; public health/community nursing; purchasing, procurement/acquisitions and contracts management; reading teacher education; religious studies; sales and marketing/marketing and distribution teacher education; science teacher education; secondary education; social studies teacher education; social work; sociology; Spanish; special education (administration); special education (emotionally disturbed); special education (gifted and talented); special education (mentally retarded); special education (multiply disabled); special education (orthopedic and other physical health impairments); special education related; special education (specific learning disabilities); statistics; systems engineering; systems science and theory; technical teacher education; theater design and technology; trade and industrial teacher education; urban studies/affairs; vocational rehabilitation counseling; water quality and wastewater treatment management and recycling technology; women's studies.

Academics *Calendar:* quarters. *Degrees:* certificates, associate, bachelor's, master's, doctoral, first professional, and post-master's certificates. *Special study options:* academic remediation for entering students, adult/continuing education programs, advanced placement credit, cooperative education, English as a second language, honors programs, internships, off-campus study, part-time degree program, services for LD students, student-designed majors, study abroad, summer session for credit. *ROTC:* Army (b), Air Force (b).

Computers on Campus 450 computers/terminals are available on campus for general student use. Students can access the following: campus intranet, computer help desk, free student e-mail accounts, online (class) grades, online (class) registration, online (class) schedules. Campuswide network is available. Wireless service is available via entire campus.

Student Life *Housing options:* coed, disabled students. Campus housing is university owned and leased by the school. *Activities and organizations:* drama/theater group, student-run newspaper, radio and television station, choral group, national fraternities, national sororities. *Campus security:* 24-hour emergency response devices and patrols, student patrols, late-night transport/escort service, controlled dormitory access. *Student services:* health clinic, personal/psychological counseling, women's center, legal services.

Athletics Member NCAA. All Division I. *Intercollegiate sports:* baseball M (s), basketball M (s)/W (s), cross-country running M (s)/W (s), golf M (s), soccer M (s)/W (s), softball W (s), swimming and diving M (s)/W (s), tennis M (s)/W (s), track and field W (s), volleyball W (s). *Intramural sports:* baseball M, basketball M/W, cheerleading M/W, cross-country running M/W, football M/W, golf M/W, racquetball M (c)/W (c), rugby M (c)/W (c), skiing (downhill) M (c)/W (c), soccer M/W, softball M/W, squash M/W, table tennis M (c)/W (c), tennis M/W, volleyball M (c)/W.

Standardized Tests *Required:* SAT or ACT (for admission).

Costs (2007–08) *Tuition:* state resident $7278 full-time, $219 per hour part-time; nonresident $14,004 full-time, $425 per hour part-time. *Room and board:* $7180.

Financial Aid In 2002, 4,027 non-need-based awards were made. *Average financial aid package:* $7857.

Applying *Options:* electronic application, early admission, deferred entrance. *Application fee:* $30. *Required:* high school transcript. *Recommended:* minimum 2.0 GPA. *Application deadlines:* rolling (freshmen), rolling (transfers). *Notification:* continuous (freshmen), continuous (transfers).

Freshman Application Contact Ms. Cathy Davis, Director of Undergraduate Admissions, Wright State University, 3640 Colonel Glenn Highway, Dayton, OH 45435. *Phone:* 937-775-5700. *Toll-free phone:* 800-247-1770. *Fax:* 937-775-5795. *E-mail:* admissions@wright.edu.

See page 2066 for the College Close-Up.

XAVIER UNIVERSITY

Cincinnati, Ohio **www.xu.edu/**

- **Independent Roman Catholic** comprehensive, founded 1831
- **Urban** 140-acre campus
- **Endowment** $125.0 million
- **Coed** 3,961 undergraduate students, 87% full-time, 56% women, 44% men
- **Moderately difficult** entrance level, 73% of applicants were admitted

Founded in 1831, Xavier University is a Jesuit university that seeks to educate the whole person. The Jesuit tradition is evident in Xavier's love of ideas and rigorous intellectual inquiry, respect for life, passion for justice, sense of community, and working together for the common good. With seventy-four majors and forty-four minors, numerous scholarships, and opportunities for leadership and service, Xavier is more than a degree—it's an education for life.

Undergraduates 3,459 full-time, 502 part-time. Students come from 45 states and territories, 34 other countries, 40% are from out of state, 11% African American, 3% Asian American or Pacific Islander, 3% Hispanic American, 0.4% Native American, 2% international, 2% transferred in, 46% live on campus. *Retention:* 88% of 2006 full-time freshmen returned.

Freshmen *Admission:* 5,649 applied, 4,147 admitted, 858 enrolled. *Average high school GPA:* 3.56. *Test scores:* SAT critical reading scores over 500: 85%; SAT math scores over 500: 83%; SAT writing scores over 500: 77%; ACT scores over 18: 99%; SAT critical reading scores over 600: 44%; SAT math scores over 600: 45%; SAT writing scores over 600: 35%; ACT scores over 24: 68%; SAT critical reading scores over 700: 8%; SAT math scores over 700: 7%; SAT writing scores over 700: 6%; ACT scores over 30: 19%.

Faculty *Total:* 623, 50% full-time, 49% with terminal degrees. *Student/faculty ratio:* 12:1.

Majors Accounting; advertising; art; athletic training; biological and physical sciences; biology/biological sciences; biology teacher education; business administration and management; business/managerial economics; chemical engineering; chemistry; chemistry teacher education; classics and languages, literatures and linguistics; clinical laboratory science/medical technology; computer science; corrections; criminal justice/safety; economics; education; education (specific levels and methods) related; elementary education; English; entrepreneurship; finance; fine/studio arts; French; German; history; human resources management; international business/trade/commerce; international relations and affairs; liberal arts and sciences/liberal studies; management information systems; marketing/marketing management; mathematics; middle school education; Montessori teacher education; music; music teacher education; natural sciences; nursing science; occupational therapy; philosophy; physics; physics teacher education; political science and government; psychology; public relations/image management; radio and television; science teacher education; social work; sociology; Spanish; special education; sport and fitness administration/management; theology.

Academics *Calendar:* semesters. *Degrees:* certificates, associate, bachelor's, master's, doctoral, post-master's, and postbachelor's certificates. *Special study options:* academic remediation for entering students, adult/continuing education programs, advanced placement credit, cooperative education, double majors, English as a second language, honors programs, independent study, internships, off-campus study, part-time degree program, services for LD students, study abroad, summer session for credit. *ROTC:* Army (b), Air Force (c). *Unusual degree programs:* 3-2 forestry with Duke University; environmental management, accounting.

Computers on Campus 204 computers/terminals are available on campus for general student use. Students can access the following: computer help desk, free student e-mail accounts, online (class) grades, online (class) registration, online (class) schedules. Campuswide network is available. 99% of college-owned or -operated housing units are wired for high-speed Internet access. Wireless service is available via entire campus.

Student Life *Housing:* on-campus residence required through sophomore year. *Options:* coed. Campus housing is university owned. Freshman campus housing is guaranteed. *Activities and organizations:* drama/theater group, student-run newspaper, radio and television station, choral group, Student Government Association, Performing Arts Group, Alternative Breaks, Club Sports, Extreme Fans. *Campus security:* 24-hour emergency response devices and patrols, late-night transport/escort service, campus-wide shuttle service. *Student services:* health clinic, personal/psychological counseling, women's center.

Athletics Member NCAA. All Division I. *Intercollegiate sports:* baseball M (s), basketball M (s)/W (s), cheerleading M (c)/W (c), crew M (c)/W (c), cross-country running M (s)/W (s), equestrian sports M (c)/W (c), fencing M (c)/W (c), football M (c)/W (c), golf M (s)/W (s), lacrosse M (c)/W (c), riflery M (s)/W (s), rock climbing M (c)/W (c), soccer M (s)/W (s), softball M (c)/W (c), swimming and diving M (s)/W (s), tennis M (s)/W (s), track and field M (s) (c)/W (s) (c), volleyball M (c)/W (s), water polo M (c), wrestling M (c). *Intramural sports:* baseball M (c), basketball M/W, bowling M/W, football M/W, soccer M (c)/W (c), tennis M/W, volleyball M/W.

Standardized Tests *Required:* SAT or ACT (for admission).

Costs (2008–09) *One-time required fee:* $175. *Comprehensive fee:* $36,130 includes full-time tuition ($26,250), mandatory fees ($610), and room and board ($9270). Part-time tuition: $483 per credit hour. *College room only:* $5100.

Financial Aid Of all full-time matriculated undergraduates who enrolled in 2007, 2,305 applied for aid, 1,866 were judged to have need, 435 had their need fully met. 815 Federal Work-Study jobs (averaging $1277). 64 state and other part-time jobs (averaging $1787). In 2007, 1,044 non-need-based awards were made. *Average percent of need met:* 75%. *Average financial aid package:* $15,759. *Average need-based loan:* $4849. *Average need-based gift aid:* $10,683. *Average non-need-based aid:* $9535. *Average indebtedness upon graduation:* $23,988.

Applying *Options:* electronic application, early action, deferred entrance. *Application fee:* $35. *Required:* essay or personal statement, high school transcript, 1 letter of recommendation. *Recommended:* interview. *Application deadlines:* 2/1 (freshmen), rolling (transfers), 12/1 (early action). *Notification:* 3/15 (freshmen), continuous (transfers), 1/15 (early action).

Freshman Application Contact Ms. Marianne Borgmann, Interim Director of Admission, Xavier University, 3800 Victory Parkway, Cincinnati, OH 45207-5311. *Phone:* 513-745-3301. *Toll-free phone:* 800-344-4698. *Fax:* 513-745-4319. *E-mail:* xuadmit@xavier.edu.

See page 2068 for the College Close-Up.

YOUNGSTOWN STATE UNIVERSITY

Youngstown, Ohio **www.ysu.edu/**

- **State-supported** comprehensive, founded 1908
- **Urban** 200-acre campus with easy access to Cleveland and Pittsburgh
- **Endowment** $170.2 million
- **Coed** 12,267 undergraduate students, 79% full-time, 54% women, 46% men
- **Noncompetitive** entrance level, 81% of applicants were admitted

Undergraduates 9,665 full-time, 2,602 part-time. Students come from 38 states and territories, 48 other countries, 9% are from out of state, 14% African American, 0.9% Asian American or Pacific Islander, 2% Hispanic American, 0.4% Native American, 0.5% international, 5% transferred in, 10% live on campus. *Retention:* 73% of 2006 full-time freshmen returned.

Freshmen *Admission:* 4,582 applied, 3,731 admitted, 2,388 enrolled. *Average high school GPA:* 2.84. *Test scores:* SAT critical reading scores over 500: 38%; SAT math scores over 500: 43%; ACT scores over 18: 69%; SAT critical reading scores over 600: 14%; SAT math scores over 600: 14%; ACT scores over 24: 20%; SAT critical reading scores over 700: 3%; SAT math scores over 700: 3%; ACT scores over 30: 2%.

Faculty *Total:* 1,004, 43% full-time. *Student/faculty ratio:* 17:1.

Majors Accounting; advertising; African-American/Black studies; American studies; anthropology; art; art history, criticism and conservation; art teacher education; astronomy; athletic training; biology/biological sciences; business administration and management; business/commerce; business/managerial economics; business teacher education; chemical engineering; chemistry; child care and support services management; child development; civil engineering; civil engineering technology; clinical laboratory science/medical technology; clinical/medical laboratory science and allied professions related; clinical/medical laboratory technology; community health services counseling; computer programming; computer science; criminal justice/safety; data processing and data processing technology; dental hygiene; dietetics; dietetic technician; dietitian assistant; drafting and design technology; drama and dance teacher education; early childhood education; economics; education; electrical and electronic engineering technologies related; electrical, electronic and communications engineering technology; electrical, electronics and communications engineering; elementary education; emergency medical technology (EMT paramedic); engineering; engineering technology; English; English/language arts teacher education; environmental science; family and community services; family and consumer sciences/home economics teacher education; family and consumer sciences/human sciences; fashion merchandising; finance; fine/studio arts; foods, nutrition, and wellness; foreign languages and literatures; foreign language teacher education; forensic science and technology; French; French language teacher education; general studies; geography; geology/earth science; German; graphic design; health and physical education; health professions related; health science; health teacher education; history; hospital and health care facilities administration; hospitality administration; human development and family studies; human resources management; industrial engineering; information technology; Italian; journalism; kinesiology and exercise science; labor and industrial relations; legal administrative assistant/secretary; liberal arts and sciences/liberal studies; management information systems; marketing/marketing management; mathematics; mathematics teacher education; mechanical engineering; mechanical engineering/mechanical technology; medical/clinical assistant; middle school education; music; music history, literature, and theory; music performance; music teacher education; music theory and composition; nursing (registered nurse training); philosophy; photography; physical education teaching and coaching; physics; political science and government; pre-dentistry studies; pre-law studies; pre-medical studies; pre-pharmacy studies; pre-veterinary studies; psychology; radio and television; religious studies; respiratory care therapy; science teacher education; secondary education; social sciences; social science teacher education; social studies teacher education; social work; sociology; Spanish; Spanish language teacher education; special education; speech and rhetoric; technical and business writing.

Academics *Calendar:* semesters. *Degrees:* diplomas, associate, bachelor's, master's, doctoral, and postbachelor's certificates. *Special study options:* academic remediation for entering students, accelerated degree program, adult/continuing education programs, advanced placement credit, cooperative education, distance learning, double majors, English as a second language, honors programs, internships, off-campus study, part-time degree program, services for LD students, student-designed majors, study abroad, summer session for credit. *ROTC:* Army (b), Air Force (c). *Unusual degree programs:* 3-2 chemistry.

Computers on Campus 1,619 computers/terminals are available on campus for general student use. Students can access the following: campus intranet, computer help desk, free student e-mail accounts, online (class) grades, online (class) registration, online (class) schedules. Campuswide network is available. 100% of college-owned or -operated housing units are wired for high-speed Internet access. Wireless service is available via entire campus.

Student Life *Housing options:* coed, women-only. Campus housing is university owned and is provided by a third party. *Activities and organizations:* drama/theater group, student-run newspaper, choral group, marching band, student government, Omicron Delta Kappa, Golden Key Society, national fraternities, national sororities. *Campus security:* 24-hour emergency response devices and patrols, student patrols, late-night transport/escort service, controlled dormitory access, residence hall patrols. *Student services:* health clinic, personal/psychological counseling, women's center.

Athletics Member NCAA. All Division I except football (Division I-AA). *Intercollegiate sports:* baseball M (s), basketball M (s)/W (s), cross-country running M (s)/W (s), golf M (s)/W, soccer W, softball W (s), swimming and diving W, tennis M (s)/W (s), track and field M (s)/W (s), volleyball W (s). *Intramural sports:* badminton M/W, basketball M/W, bowling M/W, golf M/W, ice hockey M/W, lacrosse M/W, racquetball M/W, soccer M/W, softball M/W, swimming and diving M/W, table tennis M/W, tennis M/W, ultimate Frisbee M/W, volleyball M/W, water polo M/W.

Standardized Tests *Required:* SAT or ACT (for admission).

Costs (2007–08) *Tuition:* state resident $6492 full-time, $280 per credit part-time; nonresident $12,165 full-time, $516 per credit part-time. Full-time tuition and fees vary according to course load. Part-time tuition and fees vary according to course load. *Required fees:* $229 full-time. *Room and board:* $6740. Room and board charges vary according to board plan and housing facility. *Payment plan:* installment. *Waivers:* senior citizens and employees or children of employees.

Financial Aid Of all full-time matriculated undergraduates who enrolled in 2006, 286 Federal Work-Study jobs (averaging $2314).

Applying *Options:* electronic application, early admission, deferred entrance. *Application fee:* $30. *Required:* high school transcript. *Required for some:* interview. *Application deadlines:* 8/15 (freshmen), 8/15 (transfers), 2/15 (early action). *Notification:* continuous (freshmen), continuous (transfers), 2/15 (early action).

Freshman Application Contact Ms. Sue Davis, Director of Undergraduate Admissions, Youngstown State University, One University Plaza, Youngstown, OH 44555-0001. *Phone:* 330-941-2000. *Toll-free phone:* 877-468-6978. *Fax:* 330-941-3674. *E-mail:* enroll@ysu.edu.

ASHLAND UNIVERSITY

ASHLAND, OHIO

The University

Education at Ashland University (AU) goes beyond small classes, low student-faculty ratios, and personal attention. The campuswide philosophy of "Accent on the Individual" means that students are challenged to grow and change in a community of respect where they can find their perfect balance.

"Perfect balance" is a phrase that AU students, faculty members, and alumni recently developed to describe the environment and experience of Ashland University. Characteristics that are seemingly opposite coexist at Ashland and make it distinct. For example, Ashland University is rich in its heritage, yet always moving forward. AU students are challenged academically, yet nurtured along the way. While Ashland provides the benefits of a small school (such as individual attention and small classes), there are incredibly big opportunities in every field, including the Ashbrook Center for Public Affairs, NCAA Division II athletics, research opportunities, and internships. Ashland's mission is to serve the educational needs of all students—undergraduate and graduate, traditional and nontraditional, full- and part-time—by providing educational programs of high quality in an environment that is both challenging and supportive.

The result of the balanced environment is balanced graduates—people who are whole, who think deeply and communicate clearly. Graduates are successful and productive, yet are team players. They are prepared and confident enough to take risks and at the same time are caring friends and good citizens. They are balanced.

Ashland University is home to 2,200 full-time undergraduate students, 85 percent of whom are from Ohio. Students also come from twenty-seven other states and twenty-three other countries. The University's total enrollment of nearly 6,500 includes students in graduate programs in business, education, and theology; and thirteen off-campus degree-granting program centers throughout Ohio. Students of minority groups account for 6 percent of the student population; 25 percent of the incoming class is made up of transfer students.

Ashland University is a residential campus, with men's and women's residence halls and options for coed divided housing, three-room suites, sorority suites, and residential fraternity houses, as well as the Servant Leadership House and the Ashbrook Scholar Floor. Fully furnished, 1,400-square-foot, two-bedroom apartments are available for seniors.

AU is a many-time recipient of an award for having the best student dining and the best student programming in the nation. More than 100 student organizations are available on campus, ranging from Orientation Team to intramurals and from the Campus Activities Board to community service. HOPE Christian Fellowship and the Fellowship of Christian Athletes are among the largest on campus. Ten men's teams and ten women's teams compete at the NCAA Division II level, several of which are in contention for national titles each year.

The University's ever-increasing wireless system currently includes all academic buildings, the student center, the recreation center, the quadrangle, and several residence halls, and laptop computers are available to students. Patterson Instructional Center features a large computer lab, teleconferencing, distance learning classrooms, multimedia classrooms, and an instructional media center.

In 2006, the $18-million Recreation and Rybolt Sport Sciences Center opened, with the recreation portion housing a competition swimming pool and diving well, a 5,000-square-foot electronic fitness center, two multiuse basketball courts, an indoor soccer area, an aerobic dance and exercise room, two racquetball courts, an indoor running track, a gold simulator, a game room, and a climbing wall.

The beautiful 55,000-square-foot student center features several student lounges, a unique bookstore, a grill and snack bar, and many meeting rooms. The 60,000-square-foot Dauch College of Business and Economics opened in 2004 and features an executive education center, two conference areas, a state-of-the-art trading room, three computer labs, a tiered lecture hall, a product development lab, a student lounge, a parent lounge, and M.B.A. and undergraduate staff offices.

To learn more about Ashland University, prospective students should go directly to http://www.exploreashland.com, where they can learn more about the University's programs, but more importantly, its people. Personal weekday visits, some Saturday group visits, and several open houses provide ways for prospective students to explore Ashland for real. Students may register for them online by clicking on "Visit Campus."

Location

Ashland is an attractive community of 22,000, midway between Cleveland and Columbus. Recent FBI statistics show Ashland as having the lowest violent crime rate in the state for cities with populations between 10,000 and 24,999. *The Rating Guide to Life in America's Small Cities* lists the Ashland, Ohio, area as having the lowest crime rate of micropolitan areas in the U.S.

Majors and Degrees

Ashland University confers seven baccalaureate degrees: the Bachelor of Arts, Bachelor of Music, Bachelor of Science, and Bachelor of Science in Business Administration, Education, and Social Work. Undergraduate programs of study include accounting; American studies; art*; athletic training; biochemistry, biology*; business administration; business management; chemistry*; child and family studies; commercial art; computer art and graphics programming; computer science*; creative writing; criminal justice; economics; education: early childhood (preK–3), middle grades (4–9), grades 7–12, multiage (preK–12), vocational, intervention specialist (special education), Christian education, and physical education; electronic media production: radio/audio production, television production and programming, and professional video production; English; environmental science; exercise science; fashion merchandising; finance; fine art; foods and nutrition; French*; geology; history; hospitality administration; integrated language arts*; integrated mathematics*; integrated science*; integrated social studies*; international business; international studies; journalism*; management information systems; marketing; mathematics; music*; philosophy; physics; political science; predentistry; prelaw; premedical technology; premedicine; pre-optometry; prepharmacy; pre-physical therapy; preseminary; pre–veterinary medicine; psychology; recreation; religion; social studies*; social work; sociology; Spanish*; speech communication; sport management; sports communication; theater*; and toxicology. (Programs marked with an asterisk are education licensure areas.) The University also awards the Associate in Arts degree in art, criminal justice, office administration, and radio-TV and in a two-year curriculum in general education.

Academic Programs

At Ashland, learning involves understanding new ideas, solving problems, and pushing limits. Through small classes, which allow individual instruction, field experiences in every academic area, academic support services, and an honors program for students with a minimum GPA of 3.5, AU's goal of helping students excel is achieved.

Institutional requirements are designed to allow for interdisciplinary opportunities in the students' programs. Basic degree requirements include English composition (6 hours), contemporary issues (4 hours), communications (3 hours), religion (3 hours), and physical education (2 hours). Distribution requirements in humanities (6 hours), social science (6 hours), science/mathematics (6 hours), fine/performing arts (6 hours), and business/economics (3 hours), or interdisciplinary seminars substituted for distribution requirements, complete the degree requirements.

There are two semesters in the University's academic year. Classification of students is based on progress toward meeting degree requirements in terms of semester hours earned, as follows: freshman, 1–29 semester hours; sophomore, 30–59; junior, 60–89; senior, 90 or more. A total of 128 semester hours of credit is needed for graduation.

Off-Campus Programs

Study semesters are available at both foreign and domestic universities. Commercial art and fashion merchandising students have the option of spending their junior year at one of the art institutes in

Pittsburgh, Atlanta, Dallas, Fort Lauderdale, Houston, Philadelphia, Seattle, or Denver. Some art majors spend a semester in New York City through an affiliate program with Hunter College or Drew University, and fashion merchandising students may attend the Fashion Institute of Technology in New York City. In cooperation with the Ohio Agricultural Research Center in Wooster, Ohio, selected science majors may spend one semester or more participating in the agriscience program. Ashland's classrooms extend around the world, with overseas student teaching opportunities, summer language classes, faculty-sponsored student tours, mission trips, and other special programs. Numerous study-abroad opportunities are available.

Academic Facilities

Three new facilities opened in 2006. The two-story, 52,000-square-foot Dwight Schar College of Education is home to the undergraduate teacher education program as well as the Master of Education program and Doctor of Education program. The building provides twelve classrooms, four seminar rooms, sixty faculty and staff offices, several commons or meeting areas, a state-of-the-art media center, a peer teaching studio with a one-way viewing mirror, and a ninety-seat lecture hall. The building's state-of-the-art technology has moved Ashland University to a new level of instructional capability and academic recognition. The two-way interactive, distance learning capability allows the College to do live broadcasts from several locations inside the facility.

The Rybolt Sport Sciences Center includes five technology-enhanced classrooms, a 5,000-square-foot athletic training room that made possible the accreditation of the athletic training program, a human performance laboratory, fifteen faculty offices, and a student lounge area. The newly renovated Kettering Science Center now includes twenty-seven laboratories with state-of-the-art equipment, numerous classrooms, and meeting rooms.

Ashland's other facilities include nine computer labs, modern science laboratories, fully equipped radio/TV studios, music studios and practice rooms, art studios and a gallery, and a 750-seat theater. The Ashbrook Center, a nationally known institute for the study of public affairs, publishes scholarly books, hosts academic forums, and sponsors lectures by famous political speakers.

Costs

Tuition for the 2007–08 school year was $22,216, fees totaled $790, a double room was $4498, and board was $3876. The total cost of tuition, fees, room, and board was $31,380.

Financial Aid

Approximately 98 percent of Ashland University's students receive financial assistance, enabling them to receive the benefits of a private college education. Awards are based on outstanding scholarship, accomplishment, talent, and/or financial need.

To apply for financial assistance, students must file the Free Application for Federal Student Aid (FAFSA) with the federal government and submit the Ashland University Financial Aid Application to the AU Financial Aid Office.

Faculty

Ashland's teaching faculty includes 250 full-time members, 80 percent of whom hold doctoral degrees. The faculty's first priority is teaching, placing emphasis on individual instruction and helping students achieve. They listen, advise, coordinate internship and research opportunities, write letters of recommendation, and introduce professional perspectives into every class.

Student Government

Ashland University allows its students a role of major importance and responsibility in the conduct of all affairs relating to their lives as members of the University community. The Student Senate acts as the principal governing body and serves as a liaison between students and the faculty and administration.

Admission Requirements

Ashland strongly recommends that applicants have 16 units of college-preparatory high school credit to ensure that they have sufficient background for college work. Freshman applicants must present an official transcript of courses and grades from secondary school and scores on either the SAT or ACT examination (the writing section is not required). Each applicant is encouraged to visit the campus for an interview with an admission counselor. A visit provides the applicant with an opportunity to see the campus and ask questions of students and faculty members.

Transfer students from accredited institutions are considered for admission to Ashland provided that they are in good standing socially and academically (having at least a C average or a 2.0 GPA) at any institutions attended previously.

Applicants who complete their secondary education through an alternative program (e.g., homeschooling) must present evidence that they have been adequately prepared for university work to be considered for admission to AU. Such evidence may include appropriate scores on ACT or SAT tests, a high school equivalency diploma (GED test), satisfactory achievement on state or nationally normed tests that evaluate achievement level in high school academic subjects, and adequate performance on AU placement tests.

Application and Information

Freshman applicants are encouraged to submit applications early in the senior year of high school. To be considered for admission, a student must submit a completed application form; a secondary school transcript listing rank in class and all courses and grades, beginning with the ninth grade; and scores on the SAT or ACT. Transfer students are considered for admission after they have submitted the application form and official college transcripts from all colleges previously attended. The preferred method of applying is online at the University Web site. An enrollment deposit of $200 is requested thirty days after acceptance and is nonrefundable after May 1.

Additional information may be obtained by contacting:

Director of Admission
Ashland University
Ashland, Ohio 44805
Phone: 419-289-5052
800-882-1548 (toll-free)
Fax: 419-289-5999
E-mail: enrollme@ashland.edu
Web site: http://www.exploreashland.com

Ashland University's fabulous Recreation and Sport Sciences Center opened in March 2006.

COLLEGE DATA CENTER • OHIO

BALDWIN-WALLACE COLLEGE

BEREA, OHIO

The College

Founded in 1845, Baldwin-Wallace College (B-W) in Berea, Ohio, is an accredited institution affiliated with the United Methodist Church that blends the hallmarks of a traditional liberal arts education with an emphasis on professional preparation. Baldwin-Wallace celebrates a long history of diversity and prides itself as being one of the first colleges in Ohio to admit students without regard to race or gender. That spirit of inclusiveness has flourished and evolved into a personalized approach to education—one that stresses individual growth as students learn to learn, respond to new ideas, adapt to new situations, and prepare for the certainty of change.

B-W's reputation as one of the most respected independent colleges in Ohio has led to consistent growth over the past decade and enrollment of approximately 3,000 full-time undergraduate students. The student profile shows that 27 percent of incoming freshmen come from the top 10 percent of their high school classes, with more than 60 percent in the top quarter. In addition to the traditional-aged college student, Baldwin-Wallace has helped adult learners for more than fifty years to develop skills, redirect careers, and enhance lives. Today, 600 adult learners of all ages participate in evening and weekend classes in a variety of programs that are designed to accommodate the varying learning styles and schedules of busy adult learners. Another 800 students are enrolled in part-time graduate programs in education and business administration.

Baldwin-Wallace College is an academic community committed to the liberal arts and sciences as the foundation for lifelong learning. The College fulfills this mission through a rigorous academic program that is characterized by excellence in teaching and learning within a challenging, supportive environment that enhances students' intellectual and personal growth. Baldwin-Wallace College is committed to the success of its students. In addition to receiving a top-notch liberal arts education, students also enjoy numerous opportunities for internships, faculty-directed research, and service-learning programs. Moreover, students work with their faculty adviser to develop personal action plans that are designed to help each individual student prepare fully for life after college. These programs and approaches are enhanced by B-W's student-focused faculty, close-knit community, and rich college traditions. In all, Baldwin-Wallace College provides a truly unique place to study and prepare for future success.

More than 90 percent of Baldwin-Wallace graduates find employment or enter graduate or professional school within nine months of graduation. Recent Baldwin-Wallace graduates have been accepted at some of the finest graduate schools in the world, including Boston College, Boston University, Carnegie Mellon University, Case Western Reserve University, University of Leeds (England), Manhattan School of Music, University of North Carolina, University of Virginia, Vanderbilt University, and Washington University.

Location

B-W students enjoy the best of both worlds. Berea, Ohio, with its tree-lined streets, picturesque homes, and population of 19,000, is an ideal college town. At the same time, students are only 20 minutes from the heart of Cleveland, which is home to Fortune 500 companies as well as unique recreational and cultural opportunities. Cleveland is home to outstanding museums and galleries, professional sporting events, a world-class orchestra, exciting nightlife, and an extensive park system.

Majors and Degrees

Baldwin-Wallace offers the Bachelor of Arts (B.A.), Bachelor of Science (B.S.), Bachelor of Science in Education (B.S.E.), Bachelor of Music (B.M.), and Bachelor of Music in Education (B.M.E.) degrees. Majors include accounting, art history, art studio, athletic training, biology, broadcasting and mass communications, business, chemistry, communication disorders, communication studies, computer information systems, computer science, criminal justice, economics, education, English, English creative writing, exercise science, film studies, finance, French, German, health promotion and education, history, human resource management, international business, international studies, management, marketing, mathematical economics, mathematics, medical technology, neuroscience, philosophy, physical education, physics, political science, pre-engineering, pre–physical therapy, psychology, public relations, religion, sociology, Spanish, sport management, and theater. The Conservatory of Music offers majors in arts management, music composition, music education, music history and literature, music in the liberal arts, music management, music performance, music theater, music theory, and music therapy.

Academic Programs

More than fifty majors and several 3-2 cooperative and preprofessional programs are available to traditional B-W undergraduates. Evening and weekend programs include thirteen majors and six certificate programs.

Off-Campus Programs

Baldwin-Wallace College has institutional partnerships with several other universities around the globe, some of which include Edge Hill College (England), University of the Sunshine Coast (Australia), Ewha University (Korea), Bohme Jesus (Brazil), University of Osnabrück (Germany), Kansai Gaidai University (Japan), Hong Kong Baptist University (China), University of Hull (England), Athlone Institute of Technology (Ireland), Galway Mayo Institute of Technology (Ireland), American Business School in Paris, York St John University (England), Washington Center, New York Media Institute at Marist College, Christ College (India), and American University (Washington, D.C.).

In addition to traditional study-abroad programs, with students studying and living on a particular campus for the semester, B-W features a series of focused-study tours that are led by B-W faculty and staff members and examine specific topics or geographic regions. Some programs involve homestays, while others use hostels and hotels. Quite literally, students learn while on the road. Study tours are offered in alternating academic years.

B-W often sponsors faculty-led two- to three-week seminars for credit in May, which is perfect for students who seek an international experience but do not want to be away for extended periods. Destinations have included Vienna, Prague, and Budapest. Spring trips in 2008 included India and Italy, and there was a Seminar in Europe as well as an environmental excursion to Ecuador. Most locations for study-abroad programs offered during the academic year—such as Australia, China, England, Korea, and Spain—are also offered during the summer term. The Semester at Sea program sends students to ten different countries—such as Brazil, Egypt, India, Japan, and Vietnam—aboard a 23,000-ton ship with 600 other college undergraduates.

Academic Facilities

The Ritter Library offers special programs, including instruction on how to use the library and a reference service to help students find specific information quickly. The library's 250 convenient online databases, 45 million OhioLINK books, and 20,000 electronic and print periodicals offer a wealth of information. The Jones Music Library is located on the lower level of Merner-Pfeiffer Hall. Jones is the only lending music library on campus, and its collection of nearly 40,000 items composes a significant portion of Baldwin-Wallace College's music holdings. The Riemenschneider Bach Institute, located on the floor above the Jones Music Library, is the other music library at B-W and functions primarily as a research library. The institute is a world-renowned Bach center—the guardian of priceless Bach-related manuscripts and first editions and the publisher of *BACH: Journal of the Riemenschneider Bach Institute,* an international journal. The institute's facilities include a research library and a vault for manuscripts and rare books. Other resources include twenty campus computer labs; a 4,000-watt campus radio station; a multimedia lab for video digitizing and editing, Web site development, computer animation, and more; an on-campus gallery showcasing the work of student, faculty, and area artists; and the Burrell Memorial Observatory. The neuroscience lab includes a two-room vivarium, a small-animal surgery room, a neurophysical laboratory, and several rooms dedicated to behavioral observation and computer analysis.

Costs

In 2008–09, full-time (12–18 credit hours) liberal arts students pay $31,252 per academic year in tuition, room, board, and fees. Conservatory students pay $33,212 per academic year.

Financial Aid

Baldwin-Wallace's tuition ranks among the lowest and most affordable of private colleges in Ohio. To help students and their families meet the cost of a high-quality education, B-W awards more than $50 million annually to students in the form of scholarships, grants, loans, and work-study opportunities. B-W is committed to working with students and their families to offer financial support in terms of scholarships, grants, loans from government and private sources, and an array of campus employment opportunities. More than 90 percent of Baldwin-Wallace students receive some sort of financial assistance.

Merit scholarships are offered in the amounts of $6500, $9500, and $12,000 to academically exceptional incoming freshmen. The College also offers competitive awards, ranging from $1000 to $4000. Baldwin-Wallace provides scholarships for transfer students. More information is available from the Office of Financial Aid.

Faculty

Close relationships are at the heart of the B-W experience. Most classes average only 18 students, and the student-faculty ratio is 15:1. Professors share their wisdom and experience on a one-to-one basis, helping students choose classes or assisting students in their search for the perfect internship. Faculty members regularly give out their home phone numbers. From corporate executives and lifelong educators to environmentalists and practicing psychologists, B-W's more than 300 full-time and part-time faculty members bring impressive credentials from their fields. Nearly 80 percent have earned the highest degrees in their field. They are dedicated and talented teachers who want to provide an educational experience that goes well beyond the textbook.

Student Government

Student Government consists of three branches—the legislative, the executive, and the judicial. The Student Senate is the official representative body of the students of Baldwin-Wallace College. All meetings are open, and all students are welcome to participate. Senators meet with College administrators and faculty members to express the opinions of the student body in matters affecting student life and to establish and fund official student organizations. The president and vice president of the student body lead the executive branch of Student Government and work closely with the Senate to express student body views to the College faculty and administration. The judicial branch of the Student Government consists of the supreme court of the student body, which hears cases pertaining to Student Government and the clubs it funds. Elections for student body government occur each February. All class officers are elected by the student body and help in planning various events on campus, including Homecoming, April Reign, and senior class events.

Admission Requirements

Applicants must submit the completed application (electronic or paper), a high school transcript, a teacher recommendation, the Secondary School Record Request Form, and the $25 application fee (waived if applying online). SAT and ACT results are optional. Transfer applicants also must submit college or university transcripts. Candidates applying to the Conservatory of Music also must complete the Conservatory Audition Portfolio.

Application and Information

The deadline for undergraduate admission is May 1. Priority admission is March 1. Applicants are notified on a rolling basis within four to six weeks of receipt of a completed application.

Office of Admission
Baldwin-Wallace College
275 Eastland Road
Berea, Ohio 44017-2088
Phone: 440-826-2222
877-BW-APPLY (toll-free)
Fax: 440-826-3830
E-mail: info@bw.edu
Web site: http://www.bw.edu/admission

BOWLING GREEN STATE UNIVERSITY

BOWLING GREEN, OHIO

The University

Bowling Green State University (BGSU) offers a transformational educational experience. At BGSU, academic learning is paired with a campuswide commitment to values exploration and prepares graduates to go out into the world as critical thinkers, skilled communicators, and ethical leaders in all areas of study. This vision distinguishes BGSU as a public university with a unified purpose and one that inspires students to explore and achieve their dreams.

BGSU has approximately 21,000 students who are challenged to stay curious, think critically, and keep learning. With more than 200 undergraduate majors and programs, BGSU's learning community provides high-quality faculty members who care about their students, an appreciation for diversity, and the latest in information technology. About 7,000 students live on campus. BGSU attracts students who balance academic excellence with involvement in more than 300 student organizations. Committed to ensuring that every student succeeds, Bowling Green challenges and supports students, both in and out of the classroom. Integral to campus life are five core values: respect for one another, cooperation, intellectual and spiritual growth, creative imaginings, and pride in a job well done.

BGSU enjoys a physically compact campus located within the Bowling Green community. Most restaurants and businesses are within walking or biking distance of residence halls. All students are permitted to have cars.

Combined enrollment at Bowling Green's main campus and the BGSU–Firelands regional campus is approximately 21,000 students, including 3,000 graduate students. The total University population includes students from forty-nine states and eighty-two nations. In addition, the University's diverse population includes 19 percent who are students of color. Students are actively involved outside of class, participating in student organizations, service learning opportunities, and the more than 400 cultural and special events that are offered each year.

Residence halls reinforce the learning environment with a computer laboratory for each residence complex and one personal computer available for every 23 resident students. Every residence hall room has high-speed Ethernet connections to the University's computing backbone.

BGSU's Graduate College offers a broad range of doctoral and master's degree programs and specialist and certificate programs. BGSU Firelands also has an array of programs, from one-year certificate and two-year associate degree programs to bachelor's and master's degree programs.

The University is fully accredited by the Higher Learning Commission and is a member of the North Central Association of Schools and Colleges (30 LaSalle Street, Suite 3400, Chicago, Illinois 60602-2504; telephone: 800-621-7440, toll-free).

Location

The city of Bowling Green, Ohio, population 29,600, is located in northwest Ohio about 20 miles south of Toledo. It is within comfortable driving distance of all major cities in Ohio and is an easy commute from nearby towns.

Majors and Degrees

BGSU offers more than 200 undergraduate majors and programs in seven undergraduate colleges: Arts and Sciences, Business Administration, Education and Human Development, Health and Human Services, Musical Arts, Technology, and BGSU–Firelands, the regional campus in Huron, Ohio. Numerous programs within these colleges are accredited by their respective national accrediting agencies.

Majors (and specializations) within the Bachelor of Arts degree include Africana studies, American culture studies, art, art history, Asian studies, classical civilization, computer science (business systems, geographic information systems), economics, English, environmental policy and analysis, ethnic studies, film (film production, film studies), French, geography, geology, German, history, international studies, interpersonal communication, Latin, mathematics (actuarial science), music, philosophy, political science, popular culture, preprofessional programs, psychology, Russian, scientific and technical communication, sociology, Spanish (Latin American culture studies), statistics, theater, and women's studies.

Within the Bachelor of Arts in Communications, students can choose majors (and specializations) in interpersonal communication, telecommunications, and theater (acting/directing, design/technical theater, musical theater, performance studies, youth theater/puppetry).

Majors (and specializations) within the Bachelor of Fine Arts include art education (three-dimensional studies, two-dimensional studies), creative writing, digital arts, graphic design, three-dimensional studies, and two-dimensional studies.

Within the Bachelor of Science degree, students can choose majors (and specializations) in biology, chemistry (biochemistry), computer science (business systems, geographic information systems), environmental science, geology (geochemistry, geophysics), gerontology (long-term-care administration), mathematics (actuarial science, applied mathematics), microbiology, neuroscience, physics (applied physics), psychology, scientific and technical communication, and statistics.

Students can choose from among three specializations in the Bachelor of Science degree in journalism: broadcast journalism, print journalism, and public relations.

The Bachelor of Science in Business Administration degree offers the following specializations: accounting, business prelaw, economics, finance, financial economics, general business, information systems auditing and control, international business, management information systems, marketing, public policy and administration, and supply chain management.

The Bachelor of Science in Education offers majors (and specializations) that include the teaching areas of adolescent/young adult education (secondary education), including integrated language arts, mathematics, and social studies; single and double field sciences in earth sciences, life sciences, and physical sciences in chemistry and physics; foreign language (French, German, Latin, Russian, and Spanish); intervention specialist (deaf/hard of hearing, dual mild/moderate and moderate/intensive, mild/moderate and moderate/intensive); middle childhood studies; physical education teacher education; and marketing education. The human development programs include apparel merchandising, athletic training and clinic management, human development and family studies, dance, developmental disabilities and habilitation, dietetics, exercise specialist, human movement science, interior design, nutrition science, recreation, sport management (marketing, enterprise, and communication), and tourism (industry administration and tourism studies).

The Bachelor of Applied Health Science offers specializations in allied health, applied microbiology, health science, and pre–physical therapy.

The Bachelor of Music offers majors (and specializations) in jazz studies, music composition, music education (choral, classroom/general music, instrumental), music history and literature, music performance (church music, guitar: jazz and classical emphasis, harpsichord, instrumental, keyboard/accompanying, keyboard/literature, keyboard/pedagogy, organ, vocal pedagogy, voice, voice/musical theater, woodwind specialist), and world music.

The Bachelor of Science in Technology offers majors (and specializations) in advanced technological education, architectural/environmental design studies, aviation studies (aviation management and operations, aviation technical management, flight technology and operations), construction management and technology, electronics and computer technology, mechanical design, technology education, and visual communication technology.

The following degrees are offered without separately identified majors within the degree: Bachelor of Liberal Studies, Bachelor of Science in apparel merchandising and product development, Bachelor of Science in communication disorders, Bachelor of Science in criminal justice, Bachelor of Science in dietetics, Bachelor of Science in economics, Bachelor of Science in environmental health, Bachelor of Science in interior design, Bachelor of Science in medical technology,

Bachelor of Science in nursing, Bachelor of Science in nutrition sciences, and Bachelor of Science in social work.

BGSU–Firelands offers fourteen programs that lead to associate degrees in applied business, applied sciences, nursing, science, and technical study, plus eight bachelor's degree programs.

Every entering student has the option of enrolling in an undergraduate college with a declared major or enrolling as an undecided student. Students who are undecided about a college begin their studies in premajor advising.

Academic Programs

The academic program at BGSU is designed to help students achieve their full potential. All students, regardless of their major, take a core group of general education courses.

Classroom work is closely integrated with out-of-class experiences in the residence halls and off campus. Students can choose one of fourteen smaller residential learning or theme communities. *U.S. News & World Report*'s "America's Best Colleges for 2008" includes BGSU's residential learning communities and first-year programs in "Programs to Look For," a section on programs that lead to student success. In the University's academically based communities, professors teach classes and have offices in the residence halls and extend experiential and service learning beyond the classroom. Community interests include the arts, music, health sciences, Hispanic and French language and culture, middle childhood and secondary education, international culture, and wellness. The Chapman Community at Kohl and IMPACT (integrating moral principles and critical thinking) are open to all majors.

Bowling Green offers a challenging honors program, honors housing, and the opportunity to complete a senior honors project for graduation with University or departmental honors. All students receive academic advising, and tutoring services are available. Bowling Green has Army and Air Force ROTC programs.

Off-Campus Programs

Education-abroad programs range from a full academic year to a few weeks and are available at thirty sites in twenty countries. BGSU participates in the National Student Exchange Program with 170 other colleges and universities in the U.S.

Every Bowling Green student can take advantage of at least one opportunity to gain practical experience related to his or her major. Cooperative education, an "earn-while-you-learn" program, allowed 700 students from approximately seventy majors to earn more than $3.5 million during 2006–07. Co-op participants earn an average of $12.58 per hour. The University's co-op program ranks in the top 10 percent in the country for number of placements and is open to all students in all majors.

Academic Facilities

Extensive state-of-the-art facilities support the work of faculty members and students at Bowling Green. BGSU Libraries provide a gateway to several million items on site and online, including resources of the Music Library and Sound Recordings Archives, Popular Culture Library, Curriculum Resource Center, and Center for Archival Collections. The libraries are linked to the resources of all major colleges and universities in Ohio and can locate materials worldwide.

Far-reaching access to information and the latest technological learning and teaching resources are a staple of the BGSU campus, from digital media, digital textbooks, and satellite links to high-speed Internet access in every residence hall room, online courses, and numerous labs with highly specialized hardware and software for individual disciplines.

Olscamp Hall, a classroom building with seating for 2,000, is equipped for teleteaching/distance learning. BGSU has a modern physical sciences laboratory building and planetarium, a renovated fine arts center, and outstanding music facilities.

Costs

A full-time first-year student from Ohio living on campus in standard housing and with the limited meal plan paid $16,018 in 2007–08. Out-of-state students paid a surcharge of $7308, for a total of $23,326. Students are encouraged to budget about $800 to $1100 a year for books and supplies and an additional $2400 for other expenses, such as entertainment, clothing, transportation, and laundry.

Financial Aid

About 73 percent of all BGSU undergraduates receive an average financial aid package of $9000. In addition, BGSU awards more than $20 million in scholarships each year. BGSU offers automatic and renewable scholarships (from $1000 to $5000) to students who have a minimum 3.0 grade point average and a minimum 20 ACT or 920 SAT score; credentials must be submitted to the Office of Admissions by January 15. Students who qualify for the $5000 award may also be considered for a scholarship of up to full in-state fees, currently $9140. All awards are renewable for three additional years, provided the student maintains a 2.75 minimum cumulative grade point average. Academically qualified nonresidents are eligible for the BG Success Scholarship, which covers half of the nonresident surcharge, currently $3654. Student employment, grants, and loans are other options available. BGSU employs about 4,500 students annually. Students apply for aid by completing the Free Application for Federal Student Aid (FAFSA). Prospective students should contact the Office of Admissions for additional information.

Faculty

At the heart of Bowling Green State University are 921 full-time faculty members who devote their energies to teaching, research, and working closely with students; 75 percent have the highest degree in their field. Their reputations as scholars, authors, and teachers complement the faculty's role as people who care about students and the future of the University. The personal attention students receive from the faculty and support staff contributes to the small-college atmosphere that is distinctive at BGSU.

Student Government

The Undergraduate Student Government (USG) is the representative body for Bowling Green's undergraduate students. Leaders and delegates are elected by the entire student body and carry the students' voice to both the University Board of Trustees and the Faculty Senate. Each year, the governor appoints an undergraduate and a graduate student to the University Board of Trustees.

Admission Requirements

High school seniors can apply to BGSU beginning August 1 before their senior year. Admission to the fall semester is competitive. Nonresidents of Ohio are considered for admission on the same basis as in-state students. To be admitted, a freshman applicant must be a graduate of a high school approved or accredited by the state or have earned a high school equivalency diploma. Results of either the ACT or SAT are required (ACT preferred). An applicant is considered on the basis of high school course work, cumulative GPA, official ACT or SAT results, and class rank. The University also considers the diversity of the student body and applicants' special abilities, talents, and achievements in making admission decisions.

Admission to the University for transfer students is determined by their college academic credentials. Several academic majors and programs have specific requirements for transfer students, but, in general, a minimum 2.0 GPA is required for students who have earned at least 60 semester hours; a minimum 2.5 GPA is required for students who have earned fewer than 60 semester (90 quarter) hours.

Application and Information

Prospective students are encouraged to have all admission credentials complete before February 1 of the year they intend to enroll. Notification of admission decisions begins on October 1 for those who have submitted all credentials and continues on a rolling basis. Bowling Green does not discriminate in admission on the basis of race, sex, sexual orientation, color, national origin, religion, creed, age, marital status, mental or physical disability, or veteran status. Students are encouraged to apply online at BGSU's Web site or obtain an application for admission by contacting:

Gary D. Swegan
Assistant Vice Provost and Director of Admissions
110 McFall Center
Bowling Green State University
Bowling Green, Ohio 43403-0085
Phone: 419-372-BGSU
866-CHOOSE-BGSU (toll-free)
Fax: 419-372-6955
E-mail: choosebgsu@bgsu.edu
Web site: http://www.bgsu.edu

CAPITAL UNIVERSITY

COLUMBUS, OHIO

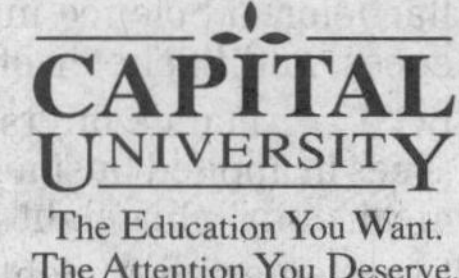

CAPITAL
UNIVERSITY
The Education You Want.
The Attention You Deserve.

The University

Since its founding in 1830 by the Lutheran Church, Capital has earned a reputation for academic excellence and affordability, an accomplishment that earned Capital recognition as one of the top regional universities by *U.S. News & World Report.* The University's undergraduate and graduate programs combine personal attention with a balanced liberal arts and professional studies education to prepare students for lifelong learning, leadership, and service. Students also benefit from the attention faculty and staff members pay to their moral, social, and ethical development. Students at Capital are part of the "CAP Family," a family that cares about the total growth and well-being of each of its members.

Capital University is composed of the College of Arts and Sciences; Conservatory of Music; School of Nursing; School of Management; and the Law School. Capital serves its adult learners through the Center for Lifelong Learning, providing bachelor's degree completion opportunities. Capital offers five undergraduate degrees and nine graduate degrees, with sixty majors and forty minors. Of the approximately 3,800 students enrolled at Capital, more than 1,800 are traditional undergraduates. Approximately 65 percent of these students reside on campus in the University's six residence halls, including suite-style housing and apartments for upperclass students.

There are more than seventy student organizations, including a number of musical groups that are open to music and nonmusic majors alike. Other opportunities for involvement include preprofessional groups, theater, the student newspaper, departmental organizations, and the debate team. Numerous opportunities for volunteerism and service projects also exist. Approximately 20 percent of Capital's undergraduates are members of the nine social fraternities and sororities on campus.

There is an active and influential student government on the Capital campus. Students are elected in campuswide elections each spring. Through this organization, students have the opportunity to gain leadership experiences.

As a university affiliated with the Evangelical Lutheran Church in America, Capital believes that the religious, social, racial, and ethnic diversity found on campus enhances each student's development. In this spirit, worship, study, and extracurricular opportunities are offered in a cooperative, ecumenical way.

Varsity and intramural athletics are offered for men and women. The eight varsity sports for men are baseball, basketball, cross-country, football, golf, soccer, tennis, and track. Women's varsity sports are basketball, cross-country, golf, soccer, softball, tennis, track, and volleyball. Capital's sports teams are sanctioned by the National Collegiate Athletic Association Division III, and the University is a member of the Ohio Athletic Conference. Intramural sports are also a big part of campus life. In addition, Capital's fitness rooms and activities such as aerobics provide options for students who want to develop their own individual fitness programs.

Location

Capital is located in the Columbus suburb of Bexley, which is primarily a residential community with a number of small shops and restaurants. Downtown Columbus is just 3 miles from campus and easily reached by city buses. As the fifteenth-largest city in the country and part of a major metropolitan area, Columbus offers a wide variety of social and cultural opportunities. Students can enjoy performances by the Columbus Symphony Orchestra, BalletMet, Opera Columbus, or the Columbus Jazz Orchestra, or they may visit the more than fifty art galleries in the area. Students may follow professional sports by attending the games of the Columbus Crew (Major League Soccer), the Columbus Blue Jackets (National Hockey League), or the Columbus Clippers (AAA franchise of the Washington Nationals). There is also an expansive network of parks and recreation facilities, bike trails, and the Columbus Zoo. Many of the city's attractions are free or offer substantial student discounts. In addition, as Ohio's capital and largest city, Columbus is the home of many national and international corporations. These companies offer Capital students unlimited opportunities for internships and employment after graduation.

Majors and Degrees

Capital University offers the Bachelor of Arts degree in art, art therapy, athletic training, biochemistry, biology, business (accounting, financial economics, leadership and management, and marketing), chemistry (major approved by the American Chemical Society), communication, computer science, criminology, economics, education, English (literature and professional writing), environmental science, exercise science, health and fitness management, history, international studies, mathematics, modern languages (French and Spanish), organizational communication, philosophy, political science, professional studies, psychology, public administration, public relations, radio-television, religion, sociology, and theater studies. Preparation for professional programs is available in dentistry, medicine, optometry, pharmacy, physical therapy, physician assistant studies, and veterinary medicine. Prelaw and pre-seminary studies help prepare students for graduate studies in religion and the legal profession.

Capital also offers the Bachelor of Fine Arts, Bachelor of Science in Nursing (approved by the National League for Nursing Accrediting Commission), and Bachelor of Social Work (approved by the Council on Social Work Education). For music students, Capital offers a Bachelor of Music in composition, jazz studies, keyboard pedagogy (church music, organ, and piano), music education (vocal and instrumental), music industry, music media, music merchandising, music technology, and performance (instrumental, organ, piano, and vocal). The Bachelor of Arts in music is also offered.

A program in engineering, which leads to dual degrees, is offered in cooperation with Washington University in St. Louis and Case Western Reserve University in Cleveland. A similar dual-degree program in pre–occupational therapy is also offered in conjunction with Washington University and the University of Indianapolis.

Academic Programs

The academic year consists of two semesters, the first of which begins in late August and ends in December. The second semester begins in early January and ends in early May. Summer classes are available.

In addition to taking courses related to their field of study, all undergraduate students take courses that fulfill a set of general education goals and bring together the University's academic, scientific, religious, and artistic disciplines.

Learning is not confined to the classroom at Capital. All undergraduate students, regardless of their major, may participate in an internship that allows them to apply newly learned skills to on-the-job situations.

Faculty advisers help students select a major, choose appropriate classes, and suggest career options. In addition, staff members in Capital's Career Services Office help students plan careers, provide instruction in resume writing and interviewing, and share information about graduate schools. On-campus recruiting sessions and a job-referral service also enhance employment opportunities.

Off-Campus Programs

At Capital, one way students learn more about other cultures and countries is through international study.

Capital is the only school in the country that offers a semester of undergraduate study at the Zoltán Kodály Pedagogical Institute of Music in Hungary for students in the Conservatory of Music.

In addition, Capital's Office of International Education offers overseas study opportunities in countries around the world, including China, Ecuador, France, Germany, Israel, the Netherlands, Spain, and Tanzania.

Closer to home, students may participate in a semester internship in one of thousands of organizations in the nation's capital through an arrangement with the Washington Center. In addition, cross-registration for enrolled students is available with Columbus College of Art and Design, Columbus State Community College, Ohio Dominican University, The Ohio State University, Otterbein College, and other area colleges and universities.

Academic Facilities

Capital's campus consists of twenty-four buildings. Through CAP-Net, Capital's campuswide voice, data, and video network, every residence hall room, classroom, and office is connected to the Internet and the Web. Through the library's connection to OhioLINK, students have access to more than 10 million items held by fifty libraries throughout the state. Information Technology provides a television studio and computer labs for student use. The Advanced Computational Studies Laboratory includes an array of computer hardware that allows students to access an extensive collection of scientific software and to simulate a parallel computing environment. A newly created state-of-the-art technology classroom and language lab enhance teaching and learning. Nursing students may also use the microcomputers and instructional software contained in the School of Nursing's Helene Fuld Health Trust Learning Resources Laboratory. For the art lover, Chagall, Picasso, and Warhol are as close as Capital's Blackmore Library, which houses the University's Schumacher Gallery and its 2,500-piece collection.

Costs

In 2007–08, tuition and fees were $26,360. Room and board fees were $6820.

Financial Aid

Approximately 99 percent of Capital's undergraduate students receive some form of financial assistance. To apply, a student must file the Free Application for Federal Student Aid (FAFSA).

University scholarships are awarded to incoming freshmen and transfer students on the basis of academic achievement (and standardized test scores for freshmen). Full-tuition scholarships (Collegiate Fellowships) are awarded to incoming freshmen based on academic achievement and an on-campus competition. Music scholarships and participation awards are granted based on music ability as demonstrated during an audition. Additional grants are available for leadership, underrepresented or disadvantaged students, and out-of-state residents.

Faculty

The University has 230 full- and part-time faculty members for its undergraduate programs. Student-faculty ratios are 10:1 in the College of Arts and Sciences and the School of Management, 4:1 in the Conservatory of Music, and 10:1 in the School of Nursing.

Admission Requirements

Capital University admits qualified students regardless of race, color, religion, gender, age, disability, or national or ethnic origin to all the rights, privileges, programs, and activities generally accorded or made available to the students at the University.

To be considered for admission to any of the undergraduate programs, students must submit copies of their high school transcript, ACT or SAT scores, and a counselor recommendation. Applicants to the Conservatory of Music must also arrange for an audition, either in person or by videotape. There are special admission requirements for the School of Nursing, and students should contact the Admission Office for details. Scores on Advanced Placement tests and College-Level Examination Program subject examinations are accepted as additional indicators of an applicant's ability, and course credit may be awarded for satisfactory scores on these examinations. Campus visits are encouraged. Arrangements for a tour of the campus and an interview, class visits, and appointments with professors may be made through the Admission Office. When an admission representative visits high schools, interested students in the area are notified and encouraged to meet with the representative. Transfer applicants must be in good social and academic standing and have a minimum grade point average of 2.25 at the institutions they attended previously. International applicants must submit official secondary school transcripts and photocopies of school-leaving certificates, TOEFL scores, SAT scores if available, and recommendation letters from a guidance counselor or headmaster and from a teacher.

Application and Information

Applications for admission may be submitted starting September 1 for the following year. Applicants are notified of their status as soon as their application is complete. The priority application deadline for the fall semester is April 15. Applications received after April 15 are reviewed on a space-available basis.

Director of Admission
Capital University
1 College and Main
Columbus, Ohio 43209-2394
Phone: 614-236-6101
866-544-6175 (toll-free)
Fax: 614-236-6926
E-mail: admissions@capital.edu
Web site: http://www.capital.edu

Capital students have the best of both worlds—a campus located in a residential neighborhood combined with all the business, cultural, and educational benefits just minutes away in downtown Columbus, the state capital and fifteenth-largest city in the country.

CASE WESTERN RESERVE UNIVERSITY

CLEVELAND, OHIO

The University

Ranking consistently among the top private universities in the United States, Case Western Reserve University (Case) offers unlimited opportunities for motivated students. Its faculty members challenge and support students to help them flourish, and its partnerships with world-class cultural, educational, and scientific institutions ensure that undergraduate education extends beyond the classroom.

Challenging and innovative academic programs and experiential learning opportunities are at the core of the Case experience. Case's 9:1 student-faculty ratio allows students to have close interaction with professors. Co-ops, internships, study abroad, and other experiential opportunities bring theory to life in amazing settings, and 66 percent of students participate in research and independent study.

Although Case was formed in 1967 by the merger of Western Reserve University and Case Institute of Technology, it traces its roots back to the 1826 founding of Western Reserve College, making Case both a young university and one of the oldest private colleges in the nation. Currently, more than 4,300 undergraduates are enrolled in programs in engineering, science, management, nursing, the arts, the humanities, and the social and behavioral sciences. Students access Case's graduate and professional schools in applied social sciences, dental medicine, graduate studies, law, management, medicine, and nursing. Several undergraduate programs and majors combine undergraduate and graduate and professional degrees and resources. Examples are five-year B.A./M.A. or B.S./M.S. degrees, including a five-year B.S./M.S. degree in engineering and management, and dual admission to undergraduate and professional school. In addition, collaborative arrangements with neighboring cultural and health-care institutions enable the University to provide special opportunities in other fields, such as art history, offered in conjunction with the renowned Cleveland Museum of Art.

Nearly every type of student interest group, from political organizations to multiethnic student unions, is represented on campus. Campus Greek life consists of sixteen national fraternities and seven sororities, with approximately 27 percent of undergraduate students participating. Residence halls are coeducational, and 80 percent of the students reside on campus.

A charter member of the University Athletic Association, an NCAA Division III conference, Case has won championships in cross-country, football, softball, track and field, and wrestling. Twenty percent of undergraduates wear the blue-and-white varsity uniform, and 70 percent join an intramural team. Nonvarsity club sports include fencing, golf, ice hockey, skiing, and Ultimate Frisbee.

Location

Case is located in University Circle, a unique cultural district comprising 550 acres of parks, gardens, museums, schools, hospitals, churches, and human service institutions. The Cleveland Museum of Art, the Cleveland Museum of Natural History, and Severance Hall, home of the Cleveland Orchestra, are within walking distance; downtown Cleveland is 10 minutes away by car or public transportation. Partnerships in education and research among University Circle institutions enable students to make full use of resources beyond those of the University itself, and students receive free access to these and other local institutions, including the downtown Rock and Roll Hall of Fame and Museum.

Majors and Degrees

Case has a single-door admission policy—once students are admitted, they can pursue any major(s) they wish. Programs of study leading to the Bachelor of Arts degree include anthropology, art history (joint program with the Cleveland Museum of Art), Asian studies, astronomy, biochemistry, biology, chemistry, classics, cognitive science, communication sciences (collaborative program with the Cleveland Hearing and Speech Center), computer science, dance, economics, English, environmental geology, environmental studies, French, French and Francophone studies, geological sciences, German, German studies, history, history and philosophy of science, international studies, Japanese studies, mathematics, music (joint program with the Cleveland Institute of Music), nutrition, nutritional biochemistry and metabolism, philosophy, physics, political science, psychology, religious studies, sociology, Spanish, statistics, theater, and world literature. The following B.A. programs are available as a second major only: American studies, evolutionary biology, gerontological studies, natural sciences, prearchitecture, teacher education, and women's studies.

Bachelor of Science degrees are offered in the following fields: accounting, aerospace engineering, applied mathematics, art education (joint program with the Cleveland Institute of Art), astronomy, biochemistry, biology, biomedical engineering, chemical engineering, chemistry, civil engineering, computer engineering, computer science, electrical engineering, engineering physics, geological sciences, management (business), materials science and engineering, mathematics, mathematics and physics (combined major), mechanical engineering, music education, nursing, nutrition, nutritional biochemistry and metabolism, physics, polymer science and engineering, statistics, systems and control engineering, systems biology, and an undesignated engineering major.

Minor areas of concentration include artificial intelligence, art studio, childhood studies, Chinese, electronics, entrepreneurship, ethnic studies, finance, history of science and technology, Italian, Japanese, Judaic studies, management information and decision systems, marketing, photography, public policy, Russian, sports medicine, and teacher licensure. In addition, most major subjects are available as minors. A minor in electrical engineering is available to students pursuing any other engineering major.

Students may work toward a combined B.A./B.S. degree or integrate undergraduate and graduate studies to complete both the bachelor's and master's degrees in five years or less. Students who are interested in both the liberal arts and engineering can benefit from the Binary Program. Students spend three years at one of forty participating liberal arts colleges and then spend two years at Case studying engineering or a related field. Graduates of this program receive both a B.A. and a B.S. degree.

Academic Programs

Students in all majors participate in SAGES, the Seminar Approach to General Education and Scholarship program. SAGES consists of four innovative and engaging seminars that emphasize written and verbal communication skills and concludes with a Senior Capstone project. As a result, all Case students benefit from building on these important skills throughout their undergraduate education. Through a combination of core curricula, major requirements, and minors or approved course sequences, all undergraduates receive a broad educational base as well as specialized knowledge in their chosen fields.

The University offers students opportunities for independent research and internships in business, health care, government, and the arts. A co-op option providing two 7-month work periods in industry or government is available for majors in engineering, science, management, accounting, and computer science.

The Senior Year in Professional Studies option allows B.A. candidates who are admitted during their junior year to Case's Schools of Applied Social Sciences, Dental Medicine, Management, Medicine, or Nursing to substitute the first year of professional school for their senior year.

High school seniors who are exceptionally well qualified in specific fields are eligible for the Pre-professional Scholars Program (PPSP), which is offered in association with the Schools of Applied Social Sciences, Dental Medicine, Law, and Medicine. Each PPSP student is awarded admission to Case as an undergraduate and conditional admission to the appropriate professional school upon completion of the entrance requirements set by each school.

The University has two 4-month semesters and one 4- to 8-week summer session.

Off-Campus Programs

Selected students may enroll as juniors and seniors in the Washington Semester program, which is conducted each spring at American University. Students with a B average or higher may participate in the Junior Year Abroad program. Up to 36 hours of credit may be granted for study at an international university. Engineering students can participate in a Global Exchange with universities such as Waseda in Tokyo, Japan. Students may also cross-register at other Cleveland-area colleges and universities for one course per semester.

Academic Facilities

The $30-million Kelvin Smith Library is located in the heart of the campus. Through reciprocal borrowing arrangements, Case students have access to the holdings of the Cleveland Public Library as well as the libraries of five University Circle institutions; the members of OhioLINK, a network that includes state colleges and universities; the State Library of Ohio; and several private institutions. Case is classified by the Carnegie Foundation as a university with very high research activity (RU/VH), and its lab facilities are state of the art. The University operates two astronomical observatories, a biological field station, a $6-million undergraduate engineering lab, and nearly 100 other designated research centers and laboratories. The University's high-speed communications network links every residence hall room with computing centers, libraries, and databases on and off campus. Case's wireless network is one of the largest in the U.S. Other computer facilities on campus offer various models of computers and a wide variety of software programs, available free of charge to Case students.

The University Farm, located in nearby Hunting Valley, Ohio, offers educational opportunities in natural settings. Its 389 acres encompass a variety of deciduous forests, ravines, waterfalls, meadows, ponds, and a self-contained natural watershed.

Costs

For 2007–08, tuition and compulsory health and laboratory fees totaled $32,800. Room and board cost an average of $9938. Required fees totaled $1108.

Financial Aid

Financial aid consisting of grants, loans, and work assistance is awarded on the basis of a student's need. Last year, 93 percent of incoming students received some type of financial aid, and 61 percent received merit-based scholarships. Applicants must file the Free Application for Federal Student Aid (FAFSA) as well as Case's own financial aid application. A signed copy of the most recent federal tax return (Form 1040) is also required. Students are automatically considered for merit-based scholarships when they apply to the University; these awards range from $500 to 80 percent of tuition.

Faculty

The undergraduate student-faculty ratio at Case is 9:1. Ninety-six percent of credit hours are taught by faculty members, not graduate students. Each college provides counselors who are available for both academic and personal advice. Once a major has been chosen, a member of the department in which the student is majoring acts as his or her academic adviser.

Case counts 14 Nobel laureates among its alumni and current and former faculty members, including the first American scientist ever to receive the prize. Undergraduate students have several opportunities to partner with faculty members on research or special projects, allowing for valuable learning opportunities, mentoring, networking, and personal development.

Student Government

Case's Undergraduate Student Government represents all undergraduate students. The assembly acts as a liaison between undergraduate students and the faculty, administration, and other groups; grants recognition to undergraduate organizations; and has the responsibility and authority to allocate funds from student activity fees to student organizations. The Residence Hall Association is a governing body for on-campus living, the University Program Board plans special events, and the Interfraternity Congress and Panhellenic Council govern the Greek community.

Admission Requirements

It is recommended that students pursue 4 units of English, 3 units of math, 3 units of science (2 of which must be laboratory science), 3 units of social studies, and 2 units of foreign language. The University recommends that applicants interested in engineering and the sciences have an additional unit of math and laboratory science. For students interested in the liberal arts, it is recommended that students take an additional unit of social studies and foreign language. An interview is not a required part of the admission process, but it is strongly recommended as the best way to learn about the University. To receive full consideration for admission and scholarships, students must take the SAT or ACT prior to their selected application deadline.

Application and Information

Students who wish to receive early notification of their admission status may apply for early action by November 15; they are notified by January 1. The final application deadline is January 15 for notification by April 1. Application deadlines for transfer students are May 15 for fall admission and October 15 for spring admission. The application deadline for the Pre-professional Scholars Program (medicine, dentistry, law, or social work) is December 1. Students can apply to Case via the free online Common Application. The fall semester begins in late August.

Live chats with admission counselors, campus visits, group information sessions, and other resources are available to all prospective students. For more information, students should contact:

Office of Undergraduate Admission
Case Western Reserve University
10900 Euclid Avenue
Cleveland, Ohio 44106-7055
Phone: 216-368-4450
E-mail: admission@case.edu
Internet: http://admission.case.edu

Case Western Reserve University students meet on the lawn of the Kelvin Smith Library to discuss an assignment for their civil engineering class.

THE CLEVELAND INSTITUTE OF ART

CLEVELAND, OHIO

The Institute

Established in 1882, the Cleveland Institute of Art has earned a reputation for being one of the finest fully accredited independent professional colleges of art and design in the country. Students seeking an intellectually stimulating and artistically challenging campus atmosphere are drawn to the Institute's location in the heart of University Circle, Cleveland's dynamic cultural and educational hub. The college's fundamental mission is to provide students pursuing professional careers in art and design with the most comprehensive visual arts education available. As an accredited founding member of the National Association of Schools of Art and Design (NASAD), the school's educational objectives include encouraging student artists to think originally and inventively within the creative possibilities of their chosen media, to achieve excellence in visual art techniques, and to experience increased powers of visual awareness and observation. The Institute also strives to provide a nurturing learning environment dedicated to the mission of the visual artist and designer, mindful of the societal and cultural roles of the visual artist and the responsibility that lies therein, and to foster discernment in judgment and in values, in both art and life.

The Institute's consistent realization of these goals is the result of outstanding interaction among the students, faculty members, and administration. An undergraduate enrollment of about 550 students ensures intimate class sizes (students enjoy a 9:1 student-faculty ratio); a contemporary mentoring style of instruction ensures a higher level of collaboration between students and faculty members. The students at the Institute are guided on a daily basis by a faculty composed of some of the nation's most capable artists and designers. In addition, the college's small population allows students to develop a productive and amicable rapport with administrators.

While sensitive to the student artist's need for individual experimentation, the Institute is built upon solid fundamentals. The Institute's Foundation program develops skills in drawing, design, color, and visual arts computer software while allowing students to explore potential career paths through an elective class. The three years of major study that follow incorporate a professional practices curriculum that prepares the student for a smooth transition from college to a professional setting. The Institute also offers the studio courses necessary to earn a master's degree in art education from neighboring Case Western Reserve University (CWRU).

Location

The Institute's campus is nestled amidst 488 acres of parks and buildings known as University Circle, an educational, civic, and cultural complex located 4 miles east of downtown Cleveland. The Cleveland Museum of Art is directly across the street from the Institute, Case Western Reserve University is next door, and the world-famous Cleveland Orchestra performs a block away in the internationally renowned Severance Hall. Within walking distance and offering a variety of cultural and social experiences are the Cleveland Museum of Natural History, Cleveland Botanical Garden, Western Reserve Historical Society, Cleveland Institute of Music, and twenty-two other institutions.

Majors and Degrees

The Cleveland Institute of Art offers a program leading to a Bachelor of Fine Arts degree. A major may be chosen from one of sixteen studio areas: biomedical art, ceramics, drawing, enameling, fiber and material studies, glass, graphic/communication design, illustration, industrial design, interior design, jewelry and metals, painting, photography, printmaking, sculpture, and TIME–digital arts, which explores digital and time-based art and is the college's newest major. The Institute also participates in a four-year Bachelor of Science degree program in art education granted through Case Western Reserve University. The biomedical art program is offered in conjunction with Case's School of Medicine.

Academic Programs

A comprehensive liberal arts program is an integral part of the academic curriculum at the Institute. The Foundation program includes art history and world literature along with accompanying studio work in drawing, color, and two- and three-dimensional design. The remaining liberal arts requirements are distributed over the following three years, with study available in sociology, economics, philosophy, aesthetics, anthropology, music, psychology, and additional art history and literature courses. With the beginning of study in a major art field, the student has increased opportunities to pursue personal artistic objectives. In addition to their chosen major, students may also pursue an emphasis in art history, criticism, and theory. By the final year, studio work is essentially independent in nature, under the guidance of a faculty adviser.

Requirements for graduation are 126–135 credits, varying by major.

Off-Campus Programs

As a member of the Association of Independent Colleges of Art and Design (AICAD), a consortium of the nation's principal private colleges of art and design, the Cleveland Institute of Art is able to provide a variety of unique opportunities to students. One such opportunity, the Student Mobility Program, allows a student to spend up to two semesters at any of the other member schools. The foreign study program gives students the opportunity to study at a number of colleges, including Studio Art Centers International (SACI) in Florence, Italy; Edinburgh College of Art in Scotland; University of Newcastle, England; and Strate College in France.

Academic Facilities

The Institute has two main buildings, the George Gund Building and the Joseph McCullough Center for the Visual Arts. The McCullough Center formerly housed Ford Motor Company's Model T assembly line and is on Ohio's list of historical buildings. The facility has been renovated into studios and features large loft-like areas that provide excellent space and light. The campus offers approximately fifty studios, shops, and technical facilities supporting a full industrial-design studio, a sculpture foundry, ceramics and metalworking studios, fiber study in weaving and textiles, and graphic design facilities with state-of-the-art printing equipment, as well as film, video and photography, printmaking, drawing, and painting studio areas. Spaces for glassblowing and papermaking are also available. The Institute makes every effort to ensure that its students have access to the latest technology used by professional artists and designers. To that end, the student-computer ratio is 3:1. Computer facilities include fourteen separate student labs supported by the following hardware: 145 G5 Macintosh computers running OS 10.4, 164 Dell Dimension 4700s and 9200s running Windows XP, flatbed and slide/film scanning stations, instructor projection capabilities for each lab, black-and-white and color laser printing provided by Epson and/or HP printers in all labs, two Epson Stylus Photo 2200 printers, three HP color plotters, and three Axis milling machines. The software is continually upgraded to reflect professional standards. Currently, computer labs have the following programs available: Adobe CS3 Suite of Illustrator, Photoshop, InDesign, After Effects, Premier Pro, Flash Pro, Dreamweaver, and Fireworks. Microsoft Office is available in all labs, as are a variety of specialized software titles that are native to each department. Selected labs also have Alias Studio Tools, AutoCAD, Maya, Rhino 3D, FormZ, and Final Cut Studio. Computer labs and student dorms are connected to the Internet using Internet1 and Internet2 technologies. Most of the Institute's majors take advantage of the technology available. For example, a computerized loom is used in the fiber major, and a computerized lathe is used in metals.

The Jessica Gund Memorial Library contains more than 44,000 books, exhibition catalogs, and CD-ROMs; 150,000 art and architecture slides and access to more than 500,000 digital images; 160 current print and online periodical subscriptions; 2,000 sound recordings; 600 videotapes, DVDs, and films; online databases and full-text resources; an extensive collection of books made by artists ("artists' books"); and AV and digital equipment. The library's Web page and online catalog can be found at http://www.cia.edu/library. Library patrons may borrow materials directly from area libraries as well as most Ohio public and private academic libraries.

Costs

Tuition and fees for academic year 2007–08 were $28,100 and $2200, respectively; room and board were $8768. (These costs are subject to change.)

Financial Aid

The Institute participates in all of the federal assistance programs, including the Federal Pell Grant, Federal Work-Study, Federal Supplemental Educational Opportunity Grant, and Federal Perkins Loan programs. In addition, the Institute has its own grant program for new and returning students. The Institute makes every effort to offer financial assistance to students whenever possible. All aid is granted on the basis of financial need, as demonstrated through the Free Application for Federal Student Aid (FAFSA). A certified copy of the most recent federal tax return (Form 1040) and the Cleveland Institute of Art financial aid form are also required.

Merit scholarships, currently ranging from $4000 to full tuition, are awarded in a scholarship competition for high school seniors based on outstanding portfolios and strong academic preparation.

Faculty

The Institute has 44 full-time and 46 part-time faculty members, of whom 18 teach in liberal arts and 72 in the studio areas. The latter are all practicing professionals in their respective fields who add the dimension of experience to the classroom.

Student Government

The Student Leadership Council is a volunteer organization designed to facilitate interaction and cooperation among the students, faculty members, and administration. It is made up of students from each major and representatives from recognized student organizations. The council plans and coordinates student activities and officially represents the views of students to the faculty members and administration. One of its responsibilities is the sponsorship of the annual Student Independent Exhibition in the Reinberger Galleries. Other sponsored activities include managing display cases that exhibit student work, planning holiday parties and a spring picnic, and organizing intramural sports teams and out-of-town trips to museums and galleries. Recognized organizations include the Student Artists Association, United Nations Club, Nature and Hiking Club, Community Service Association, Gay and Lesbian Student Association, Student Activities Program Board, and Student Independent Exhibition Committee.

Admission Requirements

At the Cleveland Institute of Art, admission officers counsel prospective students on an individual basis. If a student wants to attend, the Institute wishes to help; it also helps students find alternatives to this college. Any student who wants assistance is encouraged to contact the Admissions Office.

Applicants must be high school graduates or must pass the high school equivalency examination. A high school transcript and transcripts of any subsequent college study must be filed in the Admissions Office. No credentials received for admission are released after the Institute receives them. A slide or digital portfolio of at least twelve and no more than twenty of the applicant's most recent works must also be submitted for review. A personal interview is not a requirement, although it is recommended.

Application and Information

Applications for the fall term are accepted until classes are filled. The priority scholarship application deadline for the fall term is March 1.

Admissions Office
The Cleveland Institute of Art
11141 East Boulevard
Cleveland, Ohio 44106
Phone: 216-421-7418
800-223-4700 (toll-free)
Fax: 216-754-3634
E-mail: admissions@cia.edu
Web site: http://www.cia.edu

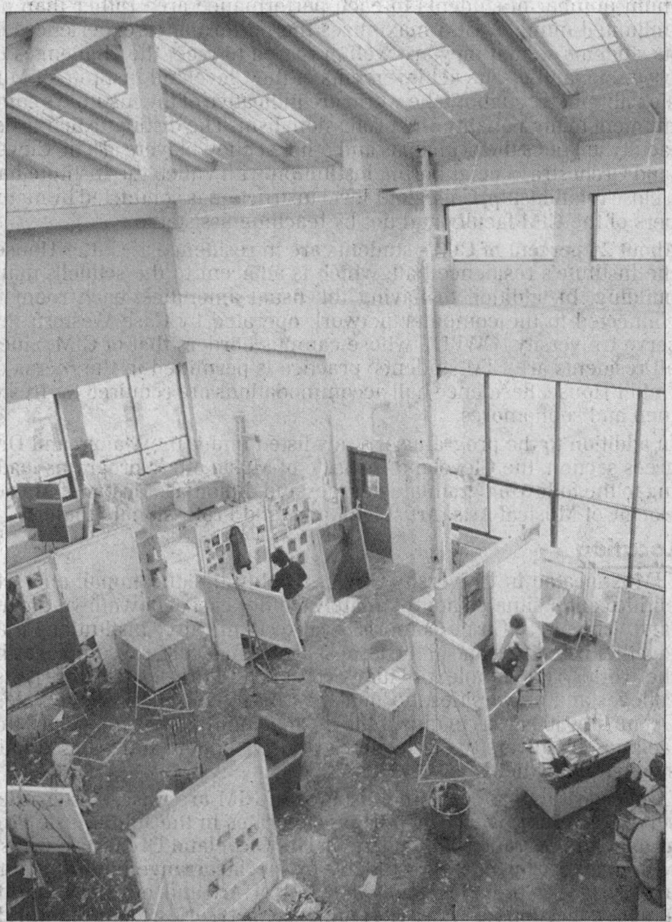

Student studios in McCullough Center.

CLEVELAND INSTITUTE OF MUSIC

CLEVELAND, OHIO

The Institute

The mission of the Cleveland Institute of Music (CIM) is to provide exceptionally talented students from around the world an outstanding, thoroughly professional education in the art of music performance and related musical disciplines. The Institute embraces the legacy of the past and promotes the continuing evolution of music within a supportive and nurturing environment. The Institute also provides rigorous training in programs for gifted precollege musicians and serves as a resource for the community, with training for individuals of all ages and abilities.

A guiding principle at the Institute maintains that a liberal arts education contributes to a broad, humanistic perspective and is a vital component of the undergraduate curriculum. Equally important is the faculty's commitment to incorporating new technologies to complement and enhance the educational program.

The distinguished faculty of the Institute aims to develop the full artistic potential of all of its students. Through performance and teaching, the faculty and administration are dedicated to passing along their knowledge and love for this great art and to providing the bridge to an exciting and fulfilling career.

Founded in 1920, the Cleveland Institute of Music maintains its current size of approximately 400 undergraduate and graduate students and 90 full- and part-time faculty members by controlling the enrollment through carefully balanced admission policies, thus ensuring personal, individual attention for each student. In admitting the optimum number of students to each performance area rather than an unlimited number, CIM maximizes the performance experiences of its students so that they are well prepared to meet the challenges of professional life. The achievements of the Cleveland Institute of Music's alumni throughout the world are indicative of the Institute's commitment to high quality and professionalism. The distinguished-artist faculty includes the principals and other section players of The Cleveland Orchestra, a neighboring institution with which the Institute has a close relationship. Collegiate-level instruction is conducted by members of the CIM faculty and not by teaching assistants.

About 25 percent of CIM's students are in residence at Cutter House, the Institute's residence hall, which is adjacent to the school's main building. In addition to having the usual amenities, each room is connected to the computer network operated by Case Western Reserve University (CWRU), whose campus borders that of CIM. Since all residents are CIM students, practice is permitted in the rooms of Cutter House. Residence hall accommodations are required for freshmen and sophomores.

In addition to the programs of study listed under the Majors and Degrees section, the Cleveland Institute of Music offers programs leading to the following graduate degrees and diplomas: Master of Music, Doctor of Musical Arts, Artist Diploma, and Professional Studies.

Location

CIM is located in University Circle, a cultural, educational, and scientific center situated approximately 3 miles east of downtown Cleveland. University Circle comprises more than thirty institutions that together constitute one of the largest diversified cultural complexes in the world. The complex includes museums, libraries, concert halls, colleges and universities, hospitals, gardens, churches, and temples. Occupying 500 acres in one of the most beautiful areas in the city, the facilities of University Circle offer extensive opportunities for serious study in many fields.

Located within easy walking distance of CIM are Case Western Reserve University, with which CIM cooperates in the Joint Music Program, and Severance Hall, home of The Cleveland Orchestra, whose rehearsals are open to CIM students by special arrangement. Students may also visit the Cleveland Museum of Art and enjoy its world-famous collections as well as its annual concert series, featuring world-renowned performers. Easily accessible to Institute students are numerous other University Circle institutions, such as the Cleveland Institute of Art, the Cleveland Play House, the Cleveland Museum of Natural History, the Western Reserve Historical Society, the Crawford Auto-Aviation Museum, and the Cleveland Botanical Garden.

Majors and Degrees

Students may major in audio recording, bassoon, bass trombone, cello, clarinet, collaborative piano, composition, double bass, eurhythmics, flute, guitar, harp, harpsichord, horn, oboe, orchestral conducting, organ, piano, Suzuki violin pedagogy, timpani and percussion, trombone, trumpet, tuba, viola, violin, and voice.

Through the Joint Music Program with Case Western Reserve University, five-year double-degree programs are available to CIM students. Of the two degrees earned by students in these programs, the Bachelor of Music is one component. Both B.M./B.A. and B.M./B.S. programs may be structured within music or with the CWRU component in a nonmusic field.

Academic Programs

CIM programs offer intensive and comprehensive preparation for professional careers in music. All courses at the school revolve around a core of studies in theory, music history, and literature; the core is designed to provide a thorough musical education. At the undergraduate level, additional educational breadth is provided by required liberal arts courses.

An unusually intense performance environment involves students in a wide repertoire, including solo, chamber, orchestral, and operatic literature.

The development of the disciplines and skills required of a solo performer is an integral part of a student's training at CIM. This training, involving access to faculty members and visiting artists who are practicing professionals, is augmented by the many master classes, repertoire classes, and recitals offered annually. A concerto competition is held each semester, and approximately 6 to 8 students are selected for either public performances or readings with orchestra.

The orchestral training programs are designed to develop and maintain the disciplines and skills essential in making the smoothest possible transition from school to professional life. Sectional rehearsals and orchestral repertoire classes are conducted by principals of The Cleveland Orchestra. CIM's two symphony orchestras present approximately twenty concerts during the academic year, including multiple performances of fully staged operas. The orchestras also provide a vehicle by which students in the Composition Department may hear and record readings of their works.

The sequence of opera courses is devoted to the principles of theory and practice of the various arts that combine to create an operatic performance. Emphasis is placed on vocal, musical, stylistic, linguistic, and dramatic techniques. Study stresses the application of these elements to role preparation for operas of different historical periods.

Started in 1969, the Joint Music Program between CWRU and CIM represents one of the strongest and most successful academic alliances in the U.S. It is a formal agreement for degree study at both the undergraduate and graduate levels. Each institution focuses on its strengths, which complement those of the partner institution. CIM concentrates on the education and training of professionals skilled in the art of performance, composition, and other related disciplines. CWRU concentrates on the fields of music history, musicology, music education, and early music performance.

Campuses for each institution are adjacent, allowing for easy access to classes and lessons and providing opportunities for regular exchanges of ideas for joint projects.

At its simplest level, the Joint Music Program provides CWRU music majors with instrumental, vocal, and composition lessons, as well as theory classes at CIM. It provides CIM students with music history and general education classes at CWRU. The program also provides a shared Audio Recording Degree Program; a partnership between CIM's library and CWRU's Kulas Music Library, with each collection complementing the other; academic advisement for D.M.A. candidates; and distance learning partnerships, with CIM adding an arts focus to CWRU's advanced Internet2 network.

CIM operates on a two-semester calendar, with fall examinations preceding the Christmas holiday recess.

Academic Facilities

CIM recently completed a $40-million expansion project that adds practice, teaching, and performance space to its facility. The project provides two major additions, including a new state-of-the-art recital hall and new façade at its main entrance. The recital hall seats 250 in an acoustically outstanding space for recitals and chamber music. Another addition at the rear of the main building includes practice rooms, teaching studios, audio recording and distance learning studios, administrative space, a new student lounge, and an outdoor patio.

Cleveland Institute of Music's main building includes a concert hall, classrooms, teaching studios, practice rooms, a library, a eurhythmics studio, an orchestra library, an opera theater workshop and studio, and a music store. Through connection of the entire facility to Case Western Reserve University's computer network, CIM also provides wireless Internet access as well as a Technology Learning Center that enables students to become aware of and accustomed to the ways in which music and technology go hand in hand.

CIM's Robinson Music Library contains 52,309 books and scores, 110 periodical subscriptions, and an audiovisual collection of 26,813 items in the Library Media Center. Through the Institute's relationship with CWRU, CIM students have access to additional library resources, especially those at the CWRU Music Department. CWRU holdings include more than 2,471,504 volumes, 2,548,156 microforms, and 20,265 current serial subscriptions. A shared online system with Case Western Reserve permits the viewing of CWRU library holdings from online public catalogs in the CIM library. There is also wireless computer access in the library.

The residence hall, Cutter House, is adjacent to CIM's main building. In addition to the usual amenities, each room has fiber-optic computer access. Also adjacent to CIM's main building is the Hazel Road Annex, an additional facility for individual practice, chamber music, rehearsal and coaching, master classes, and class recitals.

Costs

A comprehensive catalog, including information on costs as well as other areas of vital interest, is available upon request.

Financial Aid

The Cleveland Institute of Music offers outstanding professional training for talented musicians. While such training can be costly, CIM provides many forms of financial assistance, including scholarships, fellowships, work-study awards, and loans. Awards are available to full-time students and are based upon both musical capability and financial need. Entrance auditions as well as financial need serve as the basis for determining the eligibility of new students. More than 95 percent of CIM students receive some form of financial assistance. Further information is available by contacting the Institute's director of financial aid.

Faculty

The distinguished faculty of performers, composers, and teachers includes more than 40 members of the renowned Cleveland Orchestra and many other outstanding musicians. All liberal arts course offerings are taught by members of the faculty of Case Western Reserve University.

Student Government

The Student Government is the representative organization of the student body. Members are elected annually by the students. The organization carries on an active dialogue with the administration and addresses the daily and long-term needs of currently enrolled students.

Admission Requirements

Acceptance for study at the Cleveland Institute of Music is determined by musical talent, achievement, and academic performance. The Institute expects applicants to have achieved a sufficient musical and academic background demonstrating their potential for successful completion of the intended course of study. Audition appointments are scheduled through the Admission Office upon receipt of the application. Candidates are required to submit two letters of recommendation from appropriate musically qualified individuals as well as all appropriate academic transcripts. Freshman applicants who are U.S. citizens or permanent residents must also submit scores on either the SAT or American College Testing's ACT Assessment. International applicants for whom English is a second language must submit scores on the Test of English as a Foreign Language (TOEFL).

CIM does not discriminate on the basis of race, color, national or ethnic origin, citizenship, religion, age, sex, sexual orientation, or disability in its admission and scholarship policies, in the educational programs or activities it operates, or in employment.

Application and Information

The application deadline is December 1. An appointment for an entrance audition and the required admission examinations is scheduled by the Admission Office upon receipt of the application. The application process should be completed online at the Web address below. There is an application fee of $100.

Director of Admission
Cleveland Institute of Music
11021 East Boulevard
Cleveland, Ohio 44106-1705
Phone: 216-795-3107
Web site: http://www.cim.edu/colAdmission.php

CIM production of Mozart's *The Magic Flute.*

COLLEGE DATA CENTER • OHIO

THE COLLEGE OF MOUNT ST. JOSEPH

CINCINNATI, OHIO

The College

The College of Mount St. Joseph offers a variety of academic programs, a faculty known for high standards of excellence and innovation, and student activities that include twenty NCAA Division III sports teams. Small class sizes and individual attention, as well as opportunities for leadership and service learning, contribute to a positive college experience and student success. A campus-wide wireless network enables students to e-mail faculty members, check grades, complete research, and register for classes anytime, from anywhere.

Specialized services are also part of a Mount education and include renewable scholarships, financial aid, cooperative education, multicultural programs, the Wellness Center, child-care services for students with children, and on-campus housing.

Spacious rooms are available in the newly renovated Seton Center Residence Hall, with some offering private bedrooms, a bath, and a shared living area for studying and socializing. Resident students may keep cars on the campus. The close-knit campus community is part of a living and learning environment that encourages and nurtures the personal and academic growth of each student.

The undergraduate student body consists of students from twenty-five states and five countries. Seventy-nine percent of students are women, and 10 percent are members of minority groups. The average freshman has an ACT score of 21 and/or a combined SAT score of 1011 and a high school GPA of 3.25. Seventy percent of all freshman students attended a public high school. Seventy-four percent of freshman applicants are accepted.

There are more than forty clubs and organizations at the College. These include student government, the student newspaper, academic honor societies, environmental clubs, social clubs, marching and concert band, chamber singers, and intramural athletics. Events and activities include Homecoming, spring-break service trips, Exam Jam, and Little Sibs Weekend.

The Mount offers a full intercollegiate athletic program for men and women. Women's programs include basketball, cheerleading, cross-country, dance, golf, soccer, softball, tennis, track and field, and volleyball. Lacrosse is planned for 2008. Programs for men include baseball, basketball, cross-country, football, golf, lacrosse, soccer, tennis, track and field, and wrestling. The Mount Lions compete in the NCAA Division III as a member of the Heartland Collegiate Athletic Conference.

The College offers both graduate and undergraduate programs and receives its regional accreditation from the Higher Learning Commission of the North Central Association of Colleges and Schools. Catholic in tradition, the Mount emphasizes a value-centered education, academic excellence, diversity, respect for others, and service.

Location

Located 15 minutes from downtown Cincinnati, the College is situated on a 92-acre suburban campus overlooking the Ohio River and is easily accessible from the airport, bus terminal, railway station, and interstate. Well known for its scenic and rolling hills, greater Cincinnati offers numerous parks, cultural and arts events, museums, theaters, professional athletics, shopping areas, and a wide assortment of fine restaurants. Mount students often join other students attending colleges and universities in and around Cincinnati to participate in social and service activities.

Majors and Degrees

The Mount awards bachelor's degrees in the following areas: accounting, art, art education, athletic training, biochemistry, biology, business administration, chemistry, communication studies, criminology/sociology, English, fine arts, graphic design, history, inclusive early childhood education, interior design, liberal studies, mathematics, middle childhood education, music, natural science, nursing, paralegal studies, psychology, religious education, religious pastoral ministry, religious studies, social work, sociology, special education, and sport management.

Associate degrees are offered in accounting, art, business administration, communication studies, computer information systems, graphic design, interior design, liberal studies, and paralegal studies.

Certificate programs in iDesign and paralegal studies are available, as are teacher licensure programs.

For the state of Ohio licensure in education, the Mount offers programs in adolescent and young adults, inclusive early childhood, middle childhood, multiage, and intervention specialist/special education. Licensure programs for other states are also available.

Preprofessional programs are offered in a number of areas, including allied health professions, law, and medicine.

Academic Programs

To help students explore options in choosing a major, the Academic Exploration Program provides advising, career counseling, and the opportunity to attend linked courses with classmates who are also undecided.

In recognition of its commitment to provide cooperative education experiences in all baccalaureate majors, the Mount's program has received top honors from the Ohio Cooperative Education Association. Students may participate as early as the second semester of their sophomore year and gain paid work experience in their field of study. More than 100 local corporations, businesses, health-care facilities, schools, and nonprofits hire co-ops from the Mount. Other opportunities for practical experience and career development are available through the Career and Experiential Learning Center, on-campus recruiting programs, networking opportunities, and resume services.

All majors are backed by a strong liberal arts curriculum that encourages students to develop skills in analytical thinking, problem solving, decision making, and communication. Students must earn 128 credit hours for a bachelor's degree, with 52 of those credits from the liberal arts and science core. For an associate degree, students must earn 64 credit hours, with 27 to 28 of those credits from the liberal arts and science core.

The academic year consists of fall and spring semesters and two summer terms. Classes are held in day, evening, or weekend time frames.

For students with specific learning disabilities, Project EXCEL assists in the transition from a secondary program to a college curriculum. Project EXCEL promotes the development of learning strategies and compensatory skills and provides support services and accommodations to meet individual needs. There is a fee for testing and services while in the program. Interested students must apply for admission through Project EXCEL.

Off-Campus Programs

Study-abroad programs are available in London, England. Travel study programs to Rome, Egypt, Ireland, Berlin, and Japan are also offered. Immersion courses introduce students to the cultures and histories of Pine Ridge Indian Reservation, South Dakota; Tierra Madre Mission, New Mexico; and Appalachia.

Academic Facilities

The Mount's campus features a totally wireless environment as well as up-to-date facilities, including electronic classrooms. The Computer Learning Center offers all students access to IBM and Macintosh systems that support more than 500 different software packages. Students in health sciences learn in laboratories on the campus and benefit from the College's partnerships with nearby hospitals and clinics.

The Mount's Learning Center, which includes a math center and a writing center, offers peer and professional tutoring as well as diagnostic testing.

The library is home to more than 96,000 volumes of books, journals, videotapes, DVDs, and CDs. Patrons have access to more than 140 databases, thousands of electronic books, and hundreds of Web sites specifically chosen for students, faculty, and staff. Through its wide variety of services, the library plays an active role in the College's educational process. Some of these services include interlibrary loan, in-person and online research help, traditional and electronic course reserves, instructional sessions designed for specific courses, a group study room, and full Internet access.

Costs

For the 2007–08 academic year, full-time tuition was $20,400. Part-time tuition (less than 12 hours) was $450 per hour. Room costs ranged from $3200 to $5200 a year, and costs for board ranged from $3100 to $3300 a year. The College offers private and semi-private housing accommodations and a variety of meal plans. A general fee of $800 a year covers student activities, technology, counseling, student and academic support services, and logistical services. The orientation fee for new students is $150. These costs do not include the purchase of a required laptop. The cost of books varies, depending on course load and major.

Financial Aid

The Mount offers academic scholarship programs in the areas of scholastic achievement and leadership, based on merit or on a combination of merit and need. Many scholarships are renewable each year. Approximately 83 percent of full-time undergraduate students receive some form of financial aid, and the average financial aid package is $15,000. The most common are federal, state, or College grants; work-study awards; and loans. Part-time employment may be available on the campus or in the metropolitan area. Interested students should inquire early in their senior year of high school.

Students needing financial support must submit the Free Application for Federal Student Aid (FAFSA) no later than April 15 prior to the fall semester. Most College-sponsored scholarships are awarded on a rolling basis.

Faculty

There are 103 full-time professors at the College. Faculty members have been recognized regionally and nationally for their research and expertise outside the classroom as well as for their contributions as teachers, particularly in the fields of art, science, math, sociology, and education. The student-faculty ratio of 11:1 encourages personal interaction between students and professors.

Student Government

All matriculated students at the Mount are members of the Student Government Association (SGA). Its purpose is to help students understand their rights, privileges, and responsibilities and maintain effective communication with the faculty, staff, and administration.

The SGA encourages students to participate in College governance through active membership on College committees and by assisting in the development of policies that affect student life. Programs and activities sponsored by SGA include Campus Fair, community service projects, fund-raising events, and social activities such as movies and dances.

Admission Requirements

The Mount reviews every candidate's request for admission. Credentials should include evidence of a college-preparatory high school curriculum, grade point average, standardized test scores, leadership, and extracurricular activities. In addition, personal background and attributes as well as life circumstances are taken into consideration.

Application and Information

Decisions on offers of admission are generally made within two weeks of the date the application process is completed. The application fee is $25, which is not refundable and does not apply toward tuition. Students who want to learn more about the Mount may arrange a visit by contacting the Office of Admission. In addition to individual appointments, the College schedules Get Acquainted Days throughout the year, giving students and their parents the opportunity to visit the campus, explore academic programs, and take a tour.

Office of Admission
College of Mount St. Joseph
5701 Delhi Road
Cincinnati, Ohio 45233-1672
Phone: 513-244-4531
800-654-9314 (toll-free)
Web site: http://www.msj.edu/admission

The College of Mount St. Joseph provides a liberal arts and professional education that integrates learning and life through academic excellence, respect for others, and service.

THE COLLEGE OF WOOSTER

WOOSTER, OHIO

The College

The College of Wooster engages every student in a process of learning that places the student at its center. This ability to democratize excellence—and to infuse students with self-reliance—gives Wooster incomparable value. Some colleges reserve that heightened experience for honors students; Wooster honors every student with personal attention and the tools to develop his or her own vision. The College of Wooster acts on the conviction that everyone can benefit from an honors education. At Wooster, that philosophy enhances the entire college experience. Small classes and an accessible faculty committed to teaching ensure individual attention for every student, from First-Year Seminar to senior year, when students work one-on-one with a faculty adviser on an Independent Study project that pulls together everything they have learned in their first three years at Wooster.

Founded as a Presbyterian college in 1866, Wooster has been an independent, residential college of the liberal arts and sciences since 1969. With small classes (70 percent have fewer than 20 students) and an 11:1 student-faculty ratio, students receive close attention both in and out of the classroom.

Wooster's 1,800 students come from forty-six states and thirty countries from all backgrounds and life experiences. They are serious about their academic lives, but they are just as intense about exploring their other interests—and having fun.

Ninety-nine percent of Wooster students live on campus. First-year students can choose to live with their First-Year Seminar classmates or a mix of students from all years. After the first year, the options multiply. Wooster's thirty program houses allow students to live with a group of 7 to 14 others who share their interests. Together, they might work on a service project in the community throughout the year, from Habitat for Humanity to the Humane Society.

Close to a third of Wooster students follow their passion for making music through three choirs, a symphony orchestra, symphonic and marching bands, a jazz ensemble, four a cappella groups, and other ensembles. Three in 10 participate in intercollegiate athletics and regularly earn All-American and Academic All-American honors. In the past dozen years, 10 Wooster athletes have won the prestigious NCAA Postgraduate Scholarship.

From the improv group Don't Throw Shoes to the student-run investment club (managing a $1-million portfolio for the College's endowment) and the equestrian team to the radio station, there is something for just about every interest.

Location

The College is located in Wooster, Ohio, a city of approximately 26,000. Wooster is 55 miles southwest of Cleveland and 30 miles west of Akron. An unusually close relationship exists between the College and the community. College-community activities include the Wooster Symphony, the Ambassador Program, and a variety of volunteer and internship experiences.

Majors and Degrees

The College of Wooster offers the degrees of Bachelor of Arts, Bachelor of Music, and Bachelor of Music Education. A student may choose from more than fifty majors and programs of study, including Africana studies, anthropology, archaeology, art history, art–studio, biochemistry and molecular biology, biology, business economics, chemical physics, chemistry, classical studies (Greek, Latin, classical civilization), communication sciences and disorders, communication studies, comparative literature, computer science, cultural area studies (African studies; Latin American studies; modern Western Europe, Russia, and East Europe studies; South Asia studies), economics, English, French, geology, German (language, literature, culture), history, international relations, mathematics, music, music education, music history and literature, music performance, music theory–composition, music therapy, philosophy, physics, political science, psychology, religious studies, Russian studies, sociology, Spanish, student-designed major (e.g., journalism, neuroscience, sports medicine), theater and dance, urban studies, and women's studies. In addition, minors are available in most areas as well as Chinese, education (with licensure in elementary or secondary teaching), film studies, international business, and physical education.

Wooster offers dual-degree programs in cooperation with other institutions; such programs lead to either two bachelor's degrees (one from each institution) or a bachelor's degree from Wooster and a master's from the cooperating institution. The dual-degree programs are in the areas of architecture, dentistry, engineering, forestry and environmental studies, nursing, and social work.

The College also offers a preprofessional advising program to support those students who want to combine the study of liberal arts with preparation for a specific profession. The preprofessional advising programs provide students with advice on the development of an appropriate academic program, cocurricular and volunteer experiences, guidance on summer research opportunities, lectures by leaders in the various professions, and information about the process of selecting and applying to graduate and professional schools. Wooster's preprofessional programs are in the areas of business, medicine, veterinary medicine, law, and seminary studies.

Academic Programs

A student's academic journey begins with First-Year Seminar, a writing-intensive course that exercises their intellect and sharpens their critical faculties. In a class of no more than 15, with a professor who is also their academic adviser, students approach a wide range of texts, questioning and analyzing them to tease out meaning and then formulating arguments through extensive writing and discussion.

To ensure that they are conversant with forms of inquiry and discourse in a range of disciplines, students select courses in each of three areas: arts and humanities, history and social sciences, and mathematical and natural sciences. They also gain insight into other cultures through a course in global and cultural perspectives and another in religious perspectives.

Once a major is selected, students engage with the scholarship of that field, master its particular methodologies, and prepare to participate in the creation of knowledge themselves. There are numerous opportunities to work with faculty members on research projects (as early as the second semester of the first year), participate in internships, or study abroad.

It all culminates in the senior Independent Study (I.S.) project. Working one-on-one with a faculty adviser over the course of a year, students conduct research, create art, or shape a performance that demonstrates their understanding of a discipline and their ability to communicate that knowledge to others. It is called Independent Study, but it is a journey that the student and the faculty adviser take together. In weekly, hour-long, one-on-one meetings, the adviser helps refine and focus the topic, suggests areas for exploration, asks questions that provoke thought and creativity, and evaluates progress. Students, in turn, review and synthesize literature related to the subject, plan and conduct research in the lab, or work to realize a creative vision in the studio, recital hall, or theater. Students present drafts of their work to their advisers, who offer extensive thoughtful feedback as close collaborators.

If the I.S. project requires travel or special equipment or supplies, the College's Henry J. Copeland Fund for Independent Study can help. In a typical year, the fund disburses more than $90,000 to support a diverse array of student projects, from studying the lives of West African immigrants in Paris or producing a documentary on survivors of Hiroshima to researching ways to purify methane gas to permit its use as a renewable energy source. When the I.S. is complete, students may find themselves presenting the results at a national conference in their discipline or coauthoring papers with their advisers. (Geology professor Mark Wilson has published articles with more than 40 student coauthors.)

Throughout the I.S. project, students learn not just about a specific topic but also about how to break down any complex project into manageable pieces, develop a plan of action, and follow it through. Students learn how to analyze a problem, gather and evaluate information, propose a solution, test its validity, and communicate the results clearly and persuasively. The completed I.S. gives employers tangible proof of resourcefulness, creativity, and communication skills. It also marks the student as an independent scholar who is ready to take on graduate-level research wherever his or her interests lead.

To get a full sense of the range of possibilities, students should check out the I.S. database or read student I.S. profiles at http://academics.wooster.edu/is/.

Off-Campus Programs

Students who wish to enrich their undergraduate experience by overseas study may choose from a variety of fully accredited programs. Wooster sponsors a number of off-campus programs in the United States and abroad, and, as a member of the Great Lakes Colleges Association, offers off-campus study opportunities in more than fifty countries spanning the globe.

A variety of off-campus opportunities within the United States provide both academic and internship experiences. The Washington Semester and the Semester at the United Nations offer extensive possibilities in national and international government. Urban studies centers in Philadelphia and Portland provide many different experiential options. There is also a fine-arts semester in New York City. Other internship possibilities exist in business, the humanities, the natural sciences, and psychology.

Academic Facilities

The College libraries consist of the Andrews Library, the adjacent Flo K. Gault Library for Independent Study, and the nearby Timken Science Library in Frick Hall. Together, they contain more than 1 million books, periodicals, microforms, electronic journals, videotapes, and audio recordings. As a member of CONSORT and OhioLINK, the libraries can provide almost any book from Ohio's academic libraries within two to three days. The libraries subscribe to a wide variety of electronic databases and to some 5,000 periodicals in electronic form, all available campuswide via the computing network. The libraries house more than 300 study carrels, each of which is equipped with electrical and data connections.

Computing is an important part of Wooster's academic environment. All academic buildings and residence hall rooms are connected to the campus network. The Taylor Hall computer center houses fifty-two terminals for student use while the Wired Scot, a cyber café, features twenty-two PC workstations with Internet access, two large plasma-screen TVs, and wireless Internet access throughout the building.

The College's science facilities contain the most up-to-date laboratory equipment, libraries, computer terminals, and instrumentation, including ultraviolet, visible, fluorescence, and infrared spectrometers; a scanning electron microscope; an atomic force microscope; a nuclear magnetic resonance spectrometer; a mass spectrometer; an X-ray diffractometer; and various chromatographs.

Wooster's Learning Center provides academic support for students, and priority is given to students with identified learning disabilities. Adult tutors work with individual students on time management, organization skills, and effective study strategies. Wooster's Writing Center provides writing assistance through one-to-one tutorial sessions and group workshops covering all aspects of the writing process.

The Freedlander Theatre complex contains excellent technical equipment and a separate theater for students' experimental productions. The speech facility houses a radio station and a speech and hearing clinic that also serves the community.

The Scheide Music Center, a 35,000-square-foot complex, contains five classrooms, eleven teaching studios, twenty-three soundproof practice rooms, a music library, and a listening lab. The Timken Rehearsal Hall and the acoustically balanced Gault Recital Hall are "tunable" so that the halls can be rendered "live" to greater or lesser degrees.

The Ebert Art Center has expansive space for studio art and art history. The building includes classrooms, individual studios for senior studio art majors, and the Sussel Art Gallery.

Costs

The comprehensive fee (room, board, tuition, and fees) for 2007–08 is $40,022.

Financial Aid

Financial assistance is awarded on merit and/or need. Need-based aid is determined by the Free Application for Federal Student Aid (FAFSA). Aid is allocated when students are admitted to the College. Applications for need-based aid should be submitted by February 15.

The College of Wooster believes in recognizing individual talent and hard work. Thus, Wooster offers merit-based scholarships that range from $2500 to $23,500 in a number of academic, performance, and leadership areas. All scholarship awards are applicable only toward tuition and are renewable for four years. Each year the College awards about $17 million in competitive scholarship funds. Students should call the Office of Admissions to request detailed information about scholarship opportunities.

Faculty

The faculty, 97 percent of whom hold a doctoral degree or terminal degree in their field, are dedicated to meeting the educational needs of individual students; they strive to help them realize their inherent potential. The student-faculty ratio is 11:1.

Student Government

The Campus Council, which consists of representatives from the student body, faculty, and administration, is the main legislative body in the areas of student life and cocurricular affairs. The Student Government Association, the Black Students Association, and the International Student Association also contribute to policymaking at Wooster. Students may attend open meetings of the faculty and are represented on virtually all faculty committees.

Admission Requirements

A candidate for admission to the College should have earned a minimum of 16 academic units in high school, with emphases in English, foreign language, mathematics, natural science, and social studies. The student must present satisfactory scores on either the SAT or the ACT. No College Board Subject Test scores are required.

The deadline for regular admission is February 15. Students are notified of the decision by April 1 and must reply by May 1. Early Decision I applicants must apply by December 1 and are notified on December 15. Early Decision II candidates must apply by January 15 and are notified by February 1. Students are encouraged to visit the campus and have a personal interview.

The College of Wooster does not discriminate on the basis of age, sex, race, creed, national origin, handicap, sexual orientation, or political affiliation in the admission of students or in their participation in College educational programs, activities, financial aid, or employment.

Application and Information

Dean of Admissions
The College of Wooster
Wooster, Ohio 44691
Phone: 330-263-2000 Ext. 2270 or 2322
800-877-9905 (toll-free)
Fax: 330-263-2621
E-mail: admissions@wooster.edu
Web site: http://www.wooster.edu

COLLEGE DATA CENTER • OHIO

DENISON UNIVERSITY

GRANVILLE, OHIO

The University

Denison University (DU) is a private, four-year, residential liberal arts college that provides a rigorous and challenging education while preparing students for lives of leadership and service. The University was founded in 1831, when the Ohio Baptist Education Society established the Granville Literary and Theological Institution. The University was given its present name and moved to its current location in the 1850s. Denison has more than 28,000 alumni, and, as of June 2007, an endowment of $640 million. The Denison Annual Fund received nearly $5 million in gifts from alumni, parents, and friends during fiscal year 2006–07. Historic Cleveland Hall, built in 1904 and home to the Art Department, is undergoing a major renovation that includes a glass plaza and sculpture pavilion. Completion of the Samson Talbot Hall of Biological Science and the Burton D. Morgan Center for student, faculty, and alumni-related activities further enhances the beautiful campus. Other newer buildings are the F. W. Olin Science Hall, Mitchell Recreation and Athletics Center, McPhail Center for Environmental Studies, and eight suite-style residence halls. The University is proud of the 590 outstanding members of the class of 2011, 52 percent of whom were in the top 10 percent of their graduating class.

Denison has achieved a national reputation based upon its lengthy cultural heritage, the vitality of its intellectual and ethical concerns, and the performance of its graduates. Extensive personal, career, and professional school counseling is available to students. Approximately 40 percent of Denison students take part in at least one of the University's summer internship programs by the time they graduate. More than half of Denison's graduates enroll in graduate or professional schools within ten years of graduation. Denison students are consistent finalists for a number of postgraduate awards, including the Rhodes and Marshal scholarships. The University has had 10 National Science Foundation Fellows, 8 Goldwater Science scholars, 2 Truman Scholars, 1 Udall Fellow, 1 Charles B. Rangel International Affairs Fellowship, and 37 Fulbright Scholarship winners in the last sixteen years. This year, 23 Denison students have applied for Fulbright Scholarships.

As a residential college, Denison requires its students to live in University housing all four years and offers a variety of housing options in its thirty-six residence halls. A full slate of social and cultural events is scheduled each semester. Thirty percent of the approximately 2,100 students join the seventeen fraternities and sororities present on campus. The Denison International Student Association, the Black Student Union, the Asian American Association, and La Fuerza Latina help to enrich the campus community.

Twenty-three intercollegiate sports for men and women and a wide variety of club sports are available. The Mitchell Recreation and Athletics Center and the Physical Education Center serve as the focal point for intercollegiate sports for men and women, all student athletic recreation, physical education classes, and club sports. The Mitchell Center includes a six-lane, 200-meter indoor track, four state-of-the-art indoor tennis courts, a spacious strength room, a modern fitness apparatus room, a large multipurpose and aerobics room, and international squash courts. The Physical Education Center is home to the Alumni Memorial Field House with its recreational track and three hardwood basketball/volleyball courts; Livingston Gym, home of varsity basketball and volleyball with seating for 3,000; Gregory Pool, a six-lane, 25-yard competition and recreation facility; and five racquetball/handball courts. More than 75 percent of Denison students participate in athletics or recreational activities. DU's varsity teams won nine consecutive North Coast Athletic Conference All-Sports titles between 1997 and 2006 and have captured ninety-four conference championships since 1984.

Location

The 1,000-acre Denison campus is located on a ridge overlooking the village of Granville, in central Ohio. Founded in 1805 by settlers from Massachusetts, Granville bears a marked resemblance to a New England village. Columbus, the state capital, 27 miles to the west, is the nearest large city and is served by numerous national airlines. Newark, 7 miles to the east, is an industrial city of 50,000 people. Granville has several fine restaurants and some shopping facilities, but those seeking the larger department stores go to nearby Easton Town Center or downtown Columbus. The University is a cultural and recreational center for the local community, and the Denison Community Association encourages student participation in community service activities, providing more than 18,000 hours of volunteer fieldwork each year. State parks, lakes, bike trails, and ski areas are nearby.

Majors and Degrees

Denison offers the degrees of Bachelor of Arts, Bachelor of Science, and Bachelor of Fine Arts. Departmental, interdepartmental, and individually designed majors, as well as concentrations within departments, are available within the degree programs. The B.A. can be earned through departmental programs in art (history or studio), biology, chemistry, cinema, communication, computer science, dance, economics, English (literature or writing), environmental studies, geosciences, history, international studies (as a double major), Latin, mathematics, modern languages (French, German, and Spanish), music, philosophy, physics, political science, psychology, religion, sociology/anthropology, and theater. The B.A. can also be earned through interdepartmental programs in black studies; East Asian studies; educational studies; philosophy, politics, and economics (PPE); and women's studies. The B.S. is offered in biochemistry, biology, chemistry, computer science, geosciences, mathematics, physics, and psychology. The B.F.A. major is art (studio). Concentrations can be arranged in geophysics, the Lugar Program, queer studies, and neuroscience. Certification is available in organizational studies.

Preprofessional preparation is available in business, dentistry, engineering, environmental management, forestry, law, medical technology, medicine, natural resources, nursing, occupational therapy, and veterinary science. Denison offers 3-2 programs in engineering with Rensselaer Polytechnic Institute, Washington University in St. Louis, Case Western Reserve University, and Columbia University; in forestry and environmental management with Duke University; in natural resources management with the University of Michigan; and in medical technology with Rochester General Hospital. A 3-4 program in dentistry with Case Western Reserve Dental School is also available along with a cooperative program with Case Western's Weatherhead School of Management for entrance into a year-long M.S. program followed by an additional year for an M.B.A.

Academic Programs

Denison expects its students to benefit from exposure to a broad liberal arts education and to achieve proficiency in a major field. Its selective Honors Program has matriculated more than 3,000 students in the last twenty-one years. University degree requirements include successful completion of approximately thirty-five courses (127 semester hours) with a 2.0 or better average, both overall and in the major and minor fields; fulfillment of all general education requirements; passing comprehensive examinations if required in the major; and fulfillment of minimum residence requirements. Approximately one third of a student's course work (thirteen courses) must be chosen from core course offerings in the humanities, sciences, social sciences, and fine arts. Another third is in the major field of study, and the remainder is in electives. There are opportunities for directed and independent study. Students may receive advanced placement or credit through College Board Advanced Placement (AP) tests or International Baccalaureate higher level examinations. Credit is given for an AP score of 4 or 5. Denison's academic calendar consists of two semesters and an optional summer internship program, which includes internships and travel seminars. The academic year begins in late August and ends in early May.

Off-Campus Programs

Denison cooperates in off-campus study programs approved by recognized American colleges and universities and by the Great Lakes Colleges Association. Qualified students may participate for a semester or a year of international study in Africa, Asia, the Caribbean, Europe, Latin America, the Middle East, or Oceania. Domestic programs, offered on a one- or two-semester basis, include the Washington Semester; the Philadelphia Semester; the New York Arts Program; the Oak Ridge, Tennessee Science Semester; the Newberry Library Program in Chicago; the Border Studies Program; and linkages with historically black universities. Close to 45 percent of the student body participates in an off-campus program by the time of graduation.

Academic Facilities

As a member of the Five Colleges of Ohio consortium, Denison offers access through a combined online catalog to a collection of 1.2 million volumes that can be accessed from computers anywhere on campus via the campus network. As a member of the OhioLINK statewide academic library consortium, library users also have ready access to more than 45.3 million titles from Ohio's library holdings. The William Howard Doane Library, one of thirteen academic and administrative buildings on the academic and science quadrangles, has on-campus collections of nearly 419,000 volumes, 358,000 government documents, 2,245 periodical subscriptions, 24,430 sound recordings, and 6,465 videocassettes. More than 650 Macintosh and Dell personal computers are available for student use in forty-three public and departmental labs and student clusters. A network outlet is available to every student living in a residence hall and wireless network zones are campuswide. Network services include central multiuser computers and servers, personal and departmental Web server space, free laser printing, hundreds of software packages, student and staff Web portals and e-mail. Approximately 95 percent of Denison's students own computers. For more information, students should refer to the library or computing links on the home page of the Denison Web site, listed in this description.

Samson Talbott Hall of Biological Science features flexible teaching labs and interactive lecture and seminar rooms crowned by a spectacular greenhouse. The Chemistry Center contains well-equipped laboratories and a 292-seat circular auditorium. Features of the $7.2-million F. W. Olin Science Hall include a forty-two-seat planetarium with a Zeiss Skymaster projector, a laser spectrometer, and computer-based learning centers for physics and astronomy, geology and geography, and mathematics and computer science. The fine arts quadrangle on the lower campus is made up of six buildings with classrooms and performance facilities for art, music, theater and cinema, and dance. Burke Hall features a recital hall, a theater workshop, and the Denison Museum. Other buildings are the Theatre Arts Building; the Doane Dance Building; Burton Hall, which houses the Department of Music; Cleveland Hall, for studio art courses; the Art Annex; and the Cinema Annex, the center of Denison's nationally recognized cinematography program.

Costs

Annual charges for the 2007–08 academic year were as follows: tuition, $32,160; room and board, $8570; and student fees, $850. An estimated $1800 for books, travel, and personal expenses brings the total annual cost to $43,380.

Financial Aid

In 2006–07, Denison students received more than $50 million in financial assistance. More than 65 percent was awarded from Denison funds. Financial aid packages based on need are composed of grants, loans, and employment on campus. Applicants for both federal and Denison grant aid must complete a Free Application for Federal Student Aid (FAFSA) as early as possible after January 1 and request that the information be sent to Denison. In addition to the institutional need-based grants, Denison offers more than 1,000 merit-based scholarships, including the Paschal Carter Scholarship, which range from $2000 to $34,000. Denison awards up to thirty Paschal Carter Scholarships for selected first-year applicants who earn National Merit Finalist status as determined by the National Merit Scholarship Corporation. It approximates full tuition, and the amount of the award stays constant during a student's enrollment at Denison. Alumni Awards in the amounts of $13,000 and $8000, recognizing academic achievement, leadership, and talent, are also offered. The financial aid decision is entirely separate from the admission decision. For more information, students should write to Denison's Office of Financial Aid and ask for the financial aid brochure.

Faculty

Denison's 199 full-time faculty members are deeply committed to teaching and to students. Many have national reputations in their fields; each year faculty members win national awards for teaching excellence. Ninety-seven percent of faculty members have an earned doctorate or terminal degree in their fields. The faculty-student ratio is 1:10. Small classes (average class size is 19) and unique opportunities for one-on-one research with a faculty member encourage active learning. In 2007, about 120 summer scholars did research with their professors on campus. All incoming first-year students are assigned a faculty adviser to assist with course selection and to ease the transition to college life.

Student Government

Through the Denison Campus Government Association, students budget and direct such campus organizations as the Student Senate, FM radio station, Denison Film Society, and campus newspaper. Students are strongly represented on the governance councils of the University.

Admission Requirements

Entering first-year students must have earned at least 16 academic credits in secondary school, including 4 years of college-preparatory English. Strongly recommended are 3 years each of mathematics, science, foreign language, and social studies. A candidate for admission must file a formal application and an essay. Submission of the results of the SAT or the ACT is optional. SAT Subject Tests are not required, although students may provide these scores as additional information in support of their application for admission. International applicants must submit the results of the Test of English as a Foreign Language (TOEFL) or the results of the SAT. The Admissions Committee is particularly interested in the rigor of the academic program and the grade point average. Other selection criteria are written references from a college adviser and an academic teacher, extracurricular and personal accomplishments, and the student's essay on the application. An interview is strongly encouraged. It is Denison's goal to enroll academically talented students. Denison University admits students of any race, color, religion, age, personal handicap, sex, sexual orientation, veteran status, and national or ethnic origin.

Application and Information

First-Choice Early Decision candidates should apply by December 1, with rolling notification through the middle of January. All admitted early decision candidates must send an enrollment deposit within two weeks of notification. Students interested in applying for admission under regular status and for merit-based scholarship consideration must apply by January 15. Those deferred under early decision and all regular applicants are given a final decision by mid-March. Admitted candidates must respond to the admission offer by May 1.

Director of Admissions
Denison University
Box 740
Granville, Ohio 43023-0740
Phone: 740-587-6276
800-336-4766 (toll-free)
E-mail: admissions@denison.edu
Web site: http://www.denison.edu

Denison—preparing students for a lifetime of leadership and learning.

FRANCISCAN UNIVERSITY OF STEUBENVILLE

STEUBENVILLE, OHIO

The University

From unassuming beginnings as a college for World War II veterans, Franciscan University of Steubenville today is a prominent example of the renaissance underway in Catholic higher education. Operated by the Franciscan Friars of the Third Order Regular, the University attracts students from all fifty states and twelve countries. The University is listed in every edition of Barron's *Best Buys in College Education* and ranked in the top tier in its division in *U.S. News & World Report*'s 2008 list of America's Best Colleges. The school offers thirty-six undergraduate majors; seven preprofessional programs, including predentistry and premedicine; and seven graduate programs. Despite the recent enrollment growth to more than 2,400, the University maintains a low 15:1 student-faculty ratio, allowing for plenty of personal attention and direction.

The newest academic building on campus, Saints Cosmas and Damian Science Hall, has been a boon to science and math majors, while expanded facilities for the Nursing Program and a new legal studies major open doors to careers in the medical and legal professions. In addition, new concentrations in international business and multimedia prepare students for careers in two emerging fields. And, as they have since 1991, up to 150 students per semester eagerly sign up to study and live in a renovated fourteenth-century monastery in the foothills of the Austrian Alps.

The heart of the Franciscan University experience, however, is found in its mission to prepare the next generation of Catholic leaders—for business, society, home, and Church life. Toward this goal, the University offers a wide range of programs within and outside the classroom.

Franciscan University sponsors the nation's only human life studies minor, which teaches students to think, speak, and act intelligently on human life issues. It also offers a unique humanities and Catholic culture major and a challenging Great Books Honors Program that introduces students to the most important writings of Western civilization. The combined catechetics and theology programs are the largest in the country, allowing students to learn from professors whose writings and presentations on the Catholic faith are known worldwide.

Faith households, small groups of students whose members support, recreate, and pray with one another, break through the isolation that frequently permeates dorm life. Up to 600 students join households that foster Christian values through mutual encouragement and development of positive peer support. The campus is also known for its vibrant liturgies and strong turnout for retreats and spiritual talks. Hundreds make a weekly commitment to Eucharistic adoration, and most Masses have standing room only, even on weekdays.

The popular Works of Mercy Program places students shoulder-to-shoulder with the poor and marginalized in inner city and rural communities. Over summer, winter, and spring breaks, Missions of Peace offers students the chance to help others and share the Gospel in the United States and in countries such as Ecuador, Haiti, Jamaica, and Thailand. Many students join the pro-life group, Students for Life, while others sign up for evangelization and Christian outreach activities spearheaded by the Student Life Office, households, and other campus groups. A wide range of student-run academic clubs and a thriving athletic program that offers varsity sports, intramural sports, recreational sports, and outdoor adventures for every athletic ability round out a Franciscan education.

This combination of demanding academics, Christ-centered social activities, and dynamic spirituality has earned Franciscan University high praise from Church leaders and educators. The Templeton Foundation, for example, describes Franciscan University as "a liberal arts school where faith and reason are allies, not enemies."

In addition to its undergraduate programs, the University also offers a Master of Arts in Counseling, Master of Arts in Philosophy, Master of Arts in Theology and Christian Ministry, Master of Business Administration (M.B.A.), Master of Science in Education, Master of Science in Educational Administration, and Master of Science in Nursing. The Master of Arts in Theology and Christian Ministry can be earned almost entirely through the Distance Learning Program, with most courses available via audiotaped lectures.

Location

Located on 206 acres of rolling hills overlooking the Ohio River, Franciscan University is an hour's drive west of Pittsburgh and 2½ hours south of Cleveland. Steubenville is a small urban community of 20,000. Because of the town's proximity to metropolitan areas, students have the advantages of a large city as well as the atmosphere of a small community.

Majors and Degrees

Franciscan University of Steubenville grants the Bachelor of Arts degree in biology, chemistry, classics, communication arts (journalism, multimedia, and TV/radio), drama, economics, English (drama, British and American literature, Western and world literature, and writing), French, German, history, humanities and Catholic culture, legal studies, philosophy, political science, psychology, religious education, sacred music, sociology, Spanish, and theology.

The Bachelor of Science degree is granted in accounting, anthropology, biology, business administration (economics, finance, international business, management, and marketing), computer information science, computer science, education (with twenty different licensure programs), mathematical science, mental health and human services, nursing, and social work.

Associate degrees are awarded in accounting, business administration, child development, general studies, and theology.

Minors are offered in Franciscan studies, human life studies, and film studies. The special honors program in the Great Books of Western Civilization is offered to highly qualified candidates.

For undergraduate business majors, a 4+1 program allows for accelerated completion of an M.B.A.

The University offers the following preprofessional programs: dentistry, law, medicine, optometry, pharmacy, physical therapy, and veterinary medicine. In addition, the University's Pre-Theologate Program is one of the few of its kind in the nation, offering a community of prayer, support, and study for men discerning the priesthood.

Academic Programs

The academic curriculum is divided into three main categories: The Major Program, the student's area of specialization, consists of introductory courses and a minimum of 24 credit hours in upper-level courses. Grounded in the teachings of the Catholic Church and drawing upon important Franciscan themes and values, the Core Program exposes students to different points of view; challenges them to rethink their positions on questions of values, religion, society, nature, and self; and enables them to communicate their thoughts, beliefs, questions, and opinions effectively. Elective courses, the third main category, permit students to sample courses of their own interests that may complement their major or prepare them for alternative careers.

Students need a minimum of 124 credits for graduation. The number of electives varies with each major program. The University operates on the semester system. Three summer sessions also are available.

Many students select courses that fulfill requirements in a second field for a minor or double major. Internships in many majors provide hands-on field experience and give students a distinct advantage when seeking employment. Franciscan University of Steubenville participates in the Advanced Placement (AP) Program, the College-Level Examination Program (CLEP), and International Baccalaureate (IB) and gives credit by examination in a number of subjects.

Off-Campus Programs

A highlight of the Franciscan University experience for many is the "life-changing" semester spent at the University's program in Gaming, Austria. Located in a renovated fourteenth-century monastery in the foothills of the Austrian Alps, the Austrian Program features a four-day class schedule, so students may spend extended time visiting religious shrines and cultural and historical sites throughout Europe. The program also includes a ten-day pilgrimage to Rome and Assisi.

Academic Facilities

With its inviting design and spacious views, the John Paul II Library is the center of academic life on campus. The library's collection includes more than 230,000 books and bound periodicals, and more than 390 current periodicals. The OPAL Catalog and OhioLINK Network provide access to countless Web sites and databases and more than 7 million books and journals.

Egan Hall houses classrooms; a theater; television and radio studios; special laboratories for the education, computer science, and psychology departments; and computer workstations on each floor. In the newly remodeled nursing wing, a simulated clinic gives nursing students the opportunity to practice their skills.

Franciscan University opened Saints Cosmas and Damian Science Hall, an $11-million state-of-the-art science building, in 2000. This 43,000-square-foot, four-story campus addition contains extensive classroom and laboratory space for the departments of biology, chemistry, physics, and computer science and mathematical science. It has enormously enhanced the University's ability to give students the first-class education they need to thrive in the highly sophisticated and increasingly complex scientific fields.

Costs

For the 2007–08 academic year, tuition and fees for full-time students were $18,180. Room and board costs were $6300.

Financial Aid

Through a combination of grants, scholarships, loans, and student-work opportunities, 80 percent of the students receive financial aid. Aid is offered to needy students as well as to students with high academic achievements. The goal is to provide maximum financial aid from federal, state, private, and institutional sources.

Faculty

Franciscan's full-time and part-time faculty members, both lay and religious, make personal attention the rule rather than the exception. The student-faculty ratio is 15:1. Professors—not teaching assistants—teach at all class levels. Professors of all disciplines are committed to presenting Christian truths based on the teachings of the Roman Catholic Church and often present their material within a Catholic perspective.

Student Government

The heart of student participation in the decision-making process of the University is in the Franciscan University Student Association. Excite, the Office of Student Activities, along with related groups, provides social and cultural activities. Chapel Ministry addresses pastoral concerns involved in meeting students' spiritual needs.

Admission Requirements

The University has a rolling admission policy. The recommended application deadline for fall resident student enrollment is February 1. No single factor determines admission. The decision is based on a satisfactory high school record and recommendation and satisfactory entrance examination scores (SAT or ACT), all in relation to the student's proposed major.

A student must present a minimum of 15 high school units, with at least 10 units in four of the following fields: English, foreign language, social science, mathematics, and natural sciences. The remaining 5 units may be in other subjects counted toward graduation. Students applying for admission with a major in chemistry or mathematical sciences should have 2 units in algebra and 2 units in geometry and trigonometry combined.

Transfer students must also submit a transcript from every college previously attended; once accepted, they may request preliminary evaluations of these transcripts. Full credit is given for courses transferred from an approved institution, provided the grade for each course is a C or better. No correspondence courses are accepted, but a maximum of 30 credits is allowed for extension work from an approved institution.

Application and Information

Prospective students are encouraged to apply as early as possible. Applicants must submit a completed application with the $20 application fee (fee waived for applications submitted online), official high school (and previous college) transcripts, and scores on the SAT or ACT (which may be included on the high school transcript).

More information about Franciscan University of Steubenville is available by contacting:

Director of Admissions
Franciscan University of Steubenville
1235 University Boulevard
Steubenville, Ohio 43952
Phone: 740-283-6226
800-783-6220 (toll-free)
E-mail: admissions@franciscan.edu
Web site: http://www.franciscan.edu/admissions

Franciscan University of Steubenville.

JOHN CARROLL UNIVERSITY

UNIVERSITY HEIGHTS, OHIO

The University

In the Jesuit tradition of leadership, faith, and service, John Carroll University provides its students with a rigorous education, rooted in the liberal arts and focused on questions of moral and ethical value. The University wants its graduates to make a difference in their chosen careers and in bettering their communities. One of twenty-eight Jesuit colleges and universities in the United States, John Carroll offers degree programs at the undergraduate and graduate levels in fifty-four arts and sciences, business, and preprofessional fields.

John Carroll was founded in 1886 as St. Ignatius College. In 1923, its name was briefly changed to Cleveland College. Later it became John Carroll University, named after the first Catholic bishop of the United States. In 1934, the University moved from its original location on Cleveland's near west side to its current location in University Heights. Originally a men's college, the University and all its programs officially became coeducational in 1968.

In 2006–07, the enrollment was 3,826, with 3,008 students enrolled in full-time undergraduate programs and 697 in graduate programs. Students come from thirty-six states, the Virgin Islands, Puerto Rico, and fifteen other countries. The student body, including graduate students, is 45 percent men, 55 percent women, and 8.8 percent minority group members. The University's eight residence halls house 1,900 students.

A well-rounded education includes learning and leadership activities outside the classroom. The University owns Thorn Acres, a 30-acre recreational facility used for fishing, canoeing, retreats, and student-group meetings. John Carroll offers more than eighty student organizations and clubs, as well as community volunteer-service opportunities, men's and women's varsity and intramural sports, and academic honor societies. A natatorium, racquetball and tennis courts, two gymnasiums, and weight-training and fitness facilities are located in the Student Center. Office space is set aside for a host of student activities, including the newspaper, radio station, yearbook, Student Union, fraternities and sororities, and various student organizations. University Counseling Services provides free personal and psychological counseling, therapy, in-depth analysis of academic and vocational concerns, and testing.

Students at John Carroll, in the Jesuit spirit of "making a difference," volunteer to help improve the local community. Each year, students paint the homes of the elderly or underprivileged, feed the homeless, and aid the dying. Student-organized Project Gold, a community service program, has supplemented University-run community service projects, such as Christmas in April and Meals on Wheels.

The Graduate School at John Carroll offers Master of Science degree programs in accountancy, biology, and mathematics; Master of Arts degree programs in biology, communications management, community counseling, education, English, history, humanities, integrated science, mathematics, nonprofit administration, and religious studies; the Master of Education; and Master of Business Administration degree programs. In addition, Economics America (the Cleveland Center for Economic Education), a nonprofit educational organization located on John Carroll's campus, provides advanced course work in economics for educators.

Location

Just 20 minutes from downtown Cleveland, John Carroll is located in the quiet, residential Heights neighborhood; it is surrounded by Shaker Heights, University Heights, and Cleveland Heights. The graceful walkways, rich landscape, and Gothic and contemporary architecture of the campus complement the surrounding community beautifully. The campus is easily accessible by bus, rapid transit, and car. Three shopping centers are within walking distance, so restaurants, theaters, banks, department stores, grocery stores, and specialty shops are all nearby. University Circle, 10 minutes from the campus, is the home of the Cleveland Symphony Orchestra; Cleveland Museums of Art, Natural History, and Health Education; and Garden Center of Greater Cleveland. Downtown Cleveland offers comedy clubs; world-class shopping; theater at the Cleveland Play House; the Warehouse District, an extensive entertainment district located near the Cuyahoga River; the Rock and Roll Hall of Fame; the Great Lakes Science Center; Jacobs Field, home to the Cleveland Indians; Quicken Loans Arena, home to the Cleveland Cavaliers; and Cleveland Browns Stadium.

Majors and Degrees

The Bachelor of Arts degree is awarded in art history, communication and theater arts, economics, education and allied studies, English, French, German, history, humanities, mathematics teaching, philosophy, physical education and exercise science, political science, religious studies, sociology, and Spanish.

The Bachelor of Arts in Classics degree is awarded in classical languages (Greek and Latin).

The Bachelor of Science degree is awarded in biology, chemistry, computer information systems, computer science, engineering physics, mathematics, physics, and psychology.

The Bachelor of Science in Business Administration degree is granted from John Carroll's Boler School of Business in accounting, business information systems, business logistics, finance, management, and marketing. A Bachelor of Science in Economics is awarded in economics.

Optional minors are offered in art history, biology, business, chemistry, classical studies, communication and theater arts, computer science, creative writing, economics, engineering physics, English, foreign affairs, French, German, Greek, history, humanities, Latin, mathematics, philosophy, physical education and exercise science, physics, political science, probability and statistics, psychology, religious studies, sociology, Spanish, and U.S. politics.

The University is well known for its preprofessional programs, including dentistry, engineering, law, and medicine. Interdisciplinary concentrations for students interested in exploring selected topics in several academic disciplines are available. These include Africana studies, aging studies, biochemistry/molecular biology, Catholic studies, East Asian studies, economics and mathematics, environmental studies, honors program, international business, international economics and modern language, international studies, Italian studies, Latin American studies, military science (Army ROTC), modern European studies, neuroscience, perspectives on sex and gender, political communication, and public administration and policy studies.

Academic Programs

In keeping with the Jesuit tradition of liberal arts education, every undergraduate takes a core curriculum that includes a single-theme first-year seminar course, three courses in humanities, three in science and mathematics, three in philosophy, two in social sciences, two in religious studies, one in English composition and rhetoric, and one in speech communication. Therefore, all students enroll in the College of Arts and Sciences for their first two years. After the first two years, students select a major and are admitted to their respective degree programs.

To earn a degree, a student must complete a minimum of 128 credit hours with a grade point average of at least 2.0 (C) for all course work. The last 30 hours of instruction must be completed at John Carroll. Candidates for graduation must complete all the courses and proficiency requirements for the degree, and they must complete all the major requirements with an average of at least 2.0. All course work required for a declared minor or concentration must be completed with a GPA of at least 2.0.

The University operates on a semester calendar, with three 5-week summer sessions offered between academic years.

Off-Campus Programs

John Carroll offers many special educational opportunities. Exchange programs are available with two universities in Japan; the Center for Global Education works with students who hope to study abroad.

John Carroll University is a member of the Northeast Ohio Commission on Higher Education and offers students the opportunity to take one course per semester at one of the other sixteen area universities while enrolled full-time at John Carroll. There is no additional charge for tuition; the only stipulation is that the course may not be offered at the home institution. Students often take courses in the performance-based arts or in specific engineering fields through this cross-registration program.

Academic Facilities

The Dolan Center for Science and Technology, a $66.4-million, 265,000-square-foot building, opened with a grand celebration on September 6, 2003. This facility houses the biology, chemistry, psychology, physics, mathematics, and computer science departments. With the Dolan Center, the University has advanced its science and mathematics curriculum, upgraded instructional technology, and expanded partnerships with area schools and employers. A number of years ago, a $6.8-million expansion of the Grasselli Library doubled the capacity of the building and has enhanced accessibility of electronic databases. The O'Malley Center for Communications and Language Arts features a television studio and an electronic newsroom, computer-assisted and audio language laboratories, and a center for writing instruction.

Costs

Tuition and fees were $26,434 for the 2007–08 academic year. Room and board were $7790. The average cost for books and supplies is $800 per year.

Financial Aid

In 2006–07, 75 percent of the student body received some type of need-based financial assistance. Qualified students may be awarded scholarships, honor awards, grants, work-study employment, and loans or a combination of these to help offset the cost of their education. Merit-based scholarships are awarded to approximately half of the freshman class. Most students apply for need-based aid by completing the Free Application for Federal Student Aid (FAFSA). The financial aid application deadline is March 1.

Faculty

The majority of John Carroll's 215 faculty members teach undergraduate classes, although some teach graduate programs as well. Of the full-time faculty, 94 percent hold doctorates or the appropriate terminal degree in their field, and 72 percent are tenured. The faculty's primary focus is teaching and scholarship. Counseling of students, research and publication, and community service are also important pursuits. John Carroll's faculty includes 8 resident Jesuit priests. The student-faculty ratio is 14:1.

Student Government

The John Carroll student body is self-governed, with the elected Student Union officers actively representing all students—undergraduate, graduate, full- and part-time, and day and evening—in all academic, social, religious, and disciplinary matters. Fifty-six men and women are elected to Student Union service for one-year terms.

Admission Requirements

Applications for admission from all serious candidates are welcome. John Carroll attracts students of diverse geographic, economic, racial, and religious backgrounds. Admission criteria, in descending order of importance, are the quality of the high school curriculum, grade point average, test scores on either the SAT or ACT, extracurricular activities, and the recommendation of a high school counselor or teacher.

The deadline for applications to John Carroll is February 1. Admission decisions are mailed to candidates approximately twice a month, starting in December.

Application and Information

There is no application fee to apply to John Carroll. John Carroll is a member of the Common Application and also offers its own online application at http://www.jcu.edu/apply. John Carroll subscribes to the Candidates Reply Date of May 1. Accepted students who wish to reserve their place in the freshman class must submit their enrollment reservation form and $300 enrollment deposit by May 1 to ensure their place in the class. All deposits are refundable by written request up to the May 1 deadline.

To request more information, students are encouraged to contact:

Thomas P. Fanning
Director of Admission and Retention
John Carroll University
University Heights, Ohio 44118-4581
Phone: 216-397-4294
E-mail: admission@jcu.edu
Web site: http://www.jcu.edu/admission

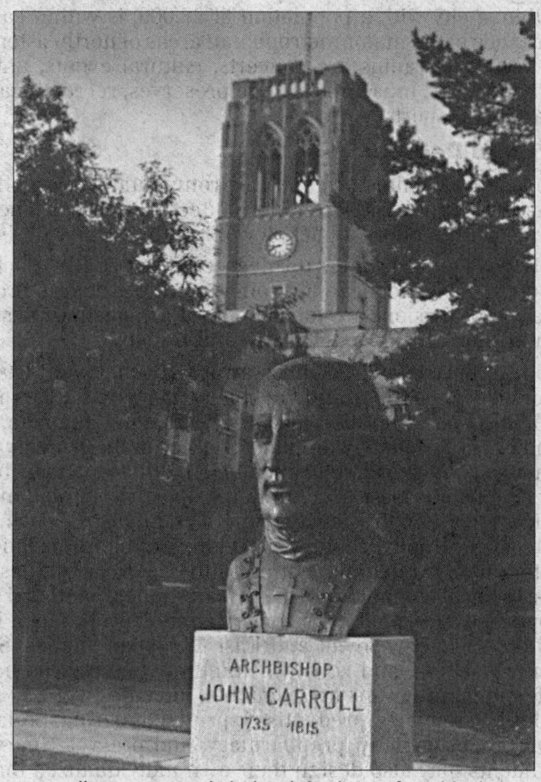

Grasselli Tower stands behind the bust of Archbishop John Carroll, the University's namesake, along the main quadrangle.

COLLEGE DATA CENTER • OHIO

KENT STATE UNIVERSITY

KENT, OHIO

The University

Kent State University has experienced tremendous growth since its founding in 1910. Today, Kent State is a multicampus network serving more than 34,000 students at eight locations throughout northeastern Ohio. The eight-campus network is anchored by a classic residential campus in Kent, Ohio. Throughout the network, students can pursue certificate, associate, bachelor's, master's, and doctoral degrees. The Kent Campus, serving 18,163 undergraduates and 4,561 graduates, offers 281 undergraduate study areas and numerous graduate degrees. Kent State's seven regional campuses are located in Ashtabula, Geauga, Stark, Trumbull, and Tuscarawas counties and the cities of Salem and East Liverpool.

As a residential campus, Kent State requires students to reside in more than thirty residence halls until junior academic standing is achieved. Exceptions include commuting and nontraditional students. Students can easily walk to any of the more than 100 academic, residential, administrative, and recreational buildings. The University has an eighteen-hole golf course, a 291-acre airport, a two-rink indoor ice arena, three on-campus theaters, and a student recreation and wellness center. There are more than 230 student organizations, nineteen fraternities, ten sororities, and eighteen varsity sports. The Career Service Center provides career counseling and job placement assistance for students and alumni.

Location

Kent, Ohio, a city with a population of 28,000, is within easy traveling distance of the major metropolitan areas of northeastern Ohio. Within a 20-mile radius are concerts, cultural events, numerous amusement parks, museums, nature preserves, recreational areas, and year-round sports.

Majors and Degrees

The College of Architecture and Environmental Design offers the Bachelor of Science and Master of Architecture degrees. The School of Interior Design offers a Bachelor of Arts in interior design.

The College of the Arts offers the degrees of B.A., B.F.A., Bachelor of Music, and B.S. The college also offers multiple-degree programs. The academic divisions are the Schools of Art, Fashion Design and Merchandising, Music, and Theatre and Dance.

The College of Arts and Sciences awards Bachelor of Arts (B.A.), Bachelor of Science (B.S.), and Bachelor of General Studies degrees. Major fields of concentration are American Sign Language, American studies, anthropology, applied conflict management, applied mathematics, biology, biological chemistry, biology, biotechnology, botany, chemistry, classics, computer science, conservation, criminal justice studies, earth science, economics, English, French, French translation, geography, geology, German, German translation, history, international relations, Latin, Latin American studies, mathematics, medical technology, Pan-African studies, paralegal studies, philosophy, physics, political science, psychology, Russian, Russian translation, sociology, Soviet and East European studies, Spanish, Spanish translation, and zoology. Numerous interdisciplinary and preprofessional programs are available, including general studies, integrated life sciences, predentistry, pre-engineering, prelaw, premedicine, preosteopathy, prepharmacy, and pre–veterinary medicine. Students may also design their own individualized major.

The College of Business Administration awards the Bachelor of Business Administration degree. Major fields of concentration are accounting, business management, computer information systems, economics, finance, marketing, and operations management. Students can choose a minor in any of these programs as well as international business.

The College of Communication and Information offers the B.A., Bachelor of Fine Arts (B.F.A.), and the B.S. degrees. Major fields of concentration are advertising, communication studies, electronic media, news, photo illustration, public relations, radio-television, visual communication design, and visual journalism.

The College of Education, Health, and Human Services offers the Bachelor of Science in Education, B.A. and B.S. degrees, and Master of Arts degrees, with licensure programs available in adolescence/young adult education, early childhood education, intervention specialist studies (majors include deaf education, educational interpreter studies, gifted education, mild/moderate educational needs, and moderate/intensive educational needs), middle childhood education, multi-age education, and career technical teacher education (vocational education). In addition, separate degree programs are offered in the Schools of Exercise, Leisure, and Sport; Family and Consumer Studies; Integrated Health Studies; and Speech Pathology and Audiology.

The College of Nursing awards the Bachelor of Science in Nursing degree. The four-year program includes clinical practicums in the Cleveland-Akron-Warren-Youngstown areas.

The College of Technology offers associate, bachelor's, and master's degree programs throughout Kent State's eight-campus system. Students can select from a number of specialized academic programs in aeronautics, industrial, electrical, manufacturing, or educational technologies.

Academic Programs

Kent State's colleges and schools all maintain separate academic programs; completion of 36 to 37 credits of liberal education course work is a University requirement for all students. The number of credit hours required for graduation varies but is generally 121 semester hours. Credits can be transferred from previous college work satisfactorily completed or earned through courses taken at one of Kent State's regional campuses. Credit by examination is available. Generally, to earn a degree, students must earn at least 30 semester hours in residence.

The Honors College provides opportunities for students and faculty members to develop and implement special learning experiences. It offers four-year programs of undergraduate study with concurrent enrollment in one of the University's degree-granting programs. In addition, the Honors College awards Advanced Placement and International Baccalaureate credit, early admission to high school students, and specialized academic advising. Its Experimental and Integrative Studies Division offers nontraditional learning experiences for students and faculty members of the entire University community.

Support services are available for students needing assistance to ensure a successful college experience. The Academic Success Center program offers tutoring, and Student Accessibility Services provides assistance to students with various physical disabilities and specific learning disabilities.

Army and Air Force ROTC programs are offered on campus.

Off-Campus Programs

Through the Office of International Affairs, Kent State offers students a variety of overseas academic programs that provide a balance of academic, linguistic, and cross-cultural experiences and learning opportunities. Credit is granted toward degrees.

Academic Facilities

The collections of the University libraries total more than 2.7 million bound volumes, 14,560 periodicals, and 1.36 million microform pieces. The Honors Center is a living-learning residential complex that houses undergraduate students as well as staff offices, a library-seminar room, a student computer facility, and an audiovisual center. The Center for Applied Conflict Management is an academic unit offering programs of study, research, and service activities that focus on the dynamics of change in human systems. The Instructional Television Service operates a closed-circuit, campuswide network and a production center for NETO, Inc., Channels 45 and 49, northeastern Ohio's public television stations. Audiovisual services support regularly scheduled classes with films and other educational materials. The Instructional Resources Center assists students in the production of educational media materials. The Language Laboratory provides tapes and other tools to assist students in foreign language studies. The Academic Testing Services Office offers test administration, test scoring, and research activities. The School of Fashion Design and Merchandising sponsors a working museum of fashion for students and the general public. This school houses classrooms, labs, a library, and a collection of costumes donated from the Silverman-Rogers estate for hands-on study.

As a recognized leader in liquid crystal technology, Kent State's Glenn H. Brown Liquid Crystal Institute is the nation's only center devoted solely to liquid crystal research. With a recent grant from the National Science Foundation, Kent State became the home of Ohio's first Science and Technology Research Center for the Study of Advanced Liquid Crystalline Optical Materials.

Costs

Instructional and other fees for Ohio residents for 2007–08 were $8430 per year. For students residing outside Ohio, instructional and other fees were $15,862 per year. Although room rates vary, costs for board and a double room averaged $7200 per year. The average student spends $1030 per year for books and supplies and should budget extra money for personal needs and expenses. All fees and charges are subject to change.

Financial Aid

More than 80 percent of Kent State's freshmen receive assistance through scholarships, grants, loans, or employment opportunities. To be considered for financial aid awards, students must be admitted to the University and must submit the Free Application for Federal Student Aid (FAFSA). Ohio students should also check the Ohio College Opportunity Grant (OCOG) box on the FAFSA if they are interested in being considered. Students planning to attend the fall semester as freshmen should apply for financial aid after January 1 and before March 1 of the same year. In order to meet the March 1 priority deadline, it is recommended that all financial aid forms be completed and mailed no later than February 1. Applications received after March 1 are considered, but sufficient funds to assist all late applicants may be lacking. Additional information is available from the Student Financial Aid Office at http://www.sfa.kent.edu.

First-time freshmen and incoming transfer students from forty-nine states outside of Ohio are eligible for a $3700 University Award. For eligibility requirements, students should visit http://www.sfa.kent.edu.

Kent State's Honors College awards merit scholarships to selected individuals who have the potential for superior scholarly and creative work at the University as determined by academic performance and creative artist competitions. For additional information, students should visit the Honors College Web site at http://www.kent.edu/honors.

The Student Financial Aid Office also administers numerous private scholarships, including the Founder's Scholarship, the Oscar Ritchie Memorial Scholarship, the President's Scholarship for out-of-state students, the President's Grant for out-of-state students who are children of alumni, and various departmental scholarships.

To be considered for freshman scholarships at the Kent Campus, students must complete an application for admission by January 15 for priority consideration. Scholarships range from $1000 to full tuition and fees. Freshmen applying after this date are considered for scholarships if funds are available.

Faculty

The University's commitment to scholarship and teaching excellence is enhanced by a full-time faculty of approximately 2,100 members. Some of the faculty members are research oriented, and others publish widely.

Student Government

Students have leadership opportunities through residence hall and Greek organizations and the Undergraduate Student Senate. The senate is responsible for allocating student activity fees to registered undergraduate organizations, appointing undergraduates to all University committees and to other positions, conducting elections, and polling student opinion. Two students serve on Kent State's Board of Trustees.

Admission Requirements

Kent State's freshman admission policy differs for students with varying degrees of preparation for college studies. The students most likely to be admitted and to succeed at the Kent campus are those who have graduated with at least 16 units of the recommended college-preparatory curriculum in high school, achieved a high school grade point average of 2.5 or higher, and acquired an ACT score of 21 or better (or a combined SAT critical reading and math score of 980 or better).

For freshmen, selective admission requirements apply to aeronautics flight technology, architecture, dance, education, fashion design and merchandising, interior design, journalism and mass communication, music, nursing, sports administration, theater, and the six-year B.S./M.D. medical program with the Northeastern Ohio Universities College of Medicine (NEOUCOM). For transfer students, selective requirements apply to all of the preceding and to art and business. Students should refer to http://www.admissions.kent.edu for information.

Application and Information

Students are strongly encouraged to apply for admission online at http://www.admissions.kent.edu/apply. A $30 nonrefundable application fee is required. Application early in the senior year helps ensure priority consideration for fall registration, residence hall preference, and financial aid. Applications are processed on a rolling basis.

Nancy J. DellaVecchia
Director, Admissions Office
Kent State University
P.O. Box 5190
Kent, Ohio 44242-0001
Phone: 330-672-2444
800-988-KENT (toll-free)
E-mail: kentadm@kent.edu
Web site: http://www.kent.edu
http://www.admissions.kent.edu

LAKE ERIE COLLEGE

PAINESVILLE, OHIO

LAKE ERIE COLLEGE

The College

Lake Erie College, founded in 1856, is an independent, coeducational institution located in the city of Painesville in northeastern Ohio. Instruction is provided at the baccalaureate and master's degree levels to academically qualified individuals. Programs of study, founded in the liberal arts, are offered in the following areas: education, equine studies, fine arts, languages and communication, management studies, social sciences, and science and math. Lake Erie College accommodates both residential and commuting students of various ages on a full-time and part-time basis. Local, national, and international students benefit from the College's traditional emphasis on intercultural programs.

Intercollegiate sports play an important role in student life. Athletic teams compete at the NCAA Division II level. Men compete in baseball, basketball, cross-country, football, golf, lacrosse, soccer, and track and field. Women compete in basketball, cross-country, soccer, softball, track and field, and volleyball. The College also sponsors an intercollegiate equestrian team.

Lake Erie College invites students to feel at home in one of four residence halls. Each spacious room is equipped with high-speed Internet access, individual phone lines, cable access, and furniture (desks, beds, and chairs). The College's residence halls have laundry facilities, community lounges, and kitchen areas. Upperclassmen have the opportunity to experience apartment-style living in a College-owned complex adjacent to the campus. Since many students bring their cars to the campus, convenient parking is available near each residence hall.

Location

Lake Erie College is located on 57 acres of naturally wooded land in Painesville, Ohio. Painesville is an attractive community in northeast Ohio, 28 miles east of Cleveland and 3 miles south of Lake Erie. The Cleveland Museum of Art; Playhouse Square; Lake Metro Parks; Holden Arboretum; professional baseball, football, and basketball teams; theaters; comedy clubs; and other recreational attractions are located nearby. The area is served by two national highways, U.S. 90 and 20, and state routes 2 and 44.

Majors and Degrees

At the undergraduate level, Lake Erie College offers the Bachelor of Arts, Bachelor of Science, and Bachelor of Fine Arts degrees. Majors are available in accounting, arts management, biology, business administration, chemistry, communications, criminal justice, dance, early childhood education, English, environmental science, equine facilities management, equestrian teacher/trainer studies, fine arts (multidisciplinary), fine arts (with concentrations in art, dance, music, and theater), forensic psychology, international business, legal studies, management, marketing, mathematics, middle childhood education, modern foreign language (French, German, Italian, and Spanish), music, psychology, preprofessional studies (dentistry, law, medicine, pharmacy, and veterinary science), secondary/young adult education, social sciences (history and sociology), sports management, and therapeutic horsemanship. Students may also pursue an individualized academic major.

Academic Programs

The philosophy of Lake Erie College is that the well-being and enrichment of society are dependent upon the abilities of individuals to think both creatively and critically, to make reasoned and informed decisions, and to assume responsibility for their personal actions and continuing education.

Education at Lake Erie College promotes the knowledge and understanding of various cultures and the growth of personal and social responsibilities associated with the acquisition of knowledge and the mastery of skills. The liberal arts and career-oriented disciplines the College offers are not mutually exclusive bodies of knowledge, and the best education is one that promotes the integration of both types of disciplines. The process of education is as vital as the subject matter communicated. It is through intercultural awareness, directed practice in discerning relationships among disciplines, and making informed judgments that a person becomes educated and acquires the flexibility necessary to meet the rapidly changing demands of the marketplace and the world.

One hundred twenty-eight semester hours are required to earn a bachelor's degree.

Off-Campus Programs

Through the College's Academic Program Abroad, students live and study at one of many international colleges or universities while earning Lake Erie College credits. This affords students the opportunity to study within the special educational experience that is part of living in another country, speaking another language, and learning another culture. Academic experiences abroad range in duration from one semester to an entire year, depending upon individual schedules. Following the fourth semester of full-time study, students may have the opportunity to participate in a shorter study trip abroad.

Academic Facilities

The scenic Lake Erie College campus provides the ideal setting to pursue an academic career; it reflects the College's commitment to provide a high-quality education in a personalized environment. The focal point of the campus is College Hall, which was completed in 1859. College Hall is a center for classroom and student administrative activities.

The Arthur S. Holden Center houses a telecommunications center, a computer center, computerized classrooms, conference rooms, and faculty offices. In the Holden Center, students also find the bookstore, Storm Café, a cafeteria, student life offices, student government offices, Lake Erie College security, and student mailboxes. Since its dedication in 1997, this facility has been Lake Erie College's premier student center.

The Fine Arts Building houses the 200-seat C. K. Rickel Theatre, the B. K. Smith Gallery, art studios, the dance studio, photography laboratories, faculty offices, and classrooms. The Austin Hall of Science includes laboratories, classrooms, and offices and will be completely renovated in 2009 to include added laboratory spaces, smart classrooms, and improved study areas for students. The new Athletic, Recreation, and Wellness Center, completed in August 2004, includes two full-size gymnasiums, an indoor track, a complete fitness center, multiple locker rooms, an athletic training room, classrooms, a team conference room, and coaches' offices. Adjacent to the center is Jack Slattery Field, with fields for soccer and softball. Kilcawley Hall houses the President's Office, the Institutional Advancement Office, Human Resources, and College Relations.

The Lincoln Library/Learning Resource Center maintains a collection of more than 90,000 books and subscribes to more than 750 periodicals. Audiovisual services, educational media and media production centers, two computerized indexes, and two computer laboratories are also located in the library.

The 85-acre George M. Humphrey Equestrian Center is located just 5 miles from the campus. Served daily by the College van, the equestrian center includes an indoor arena of 100 feet by 225 feet, with seating for 1,000 spectators, and an indoor warm-up area of 75 feet by 130 feet. The Clarence T. Reinberger Equestrian Work Center has an additional indoor ring of 80 feet by 96 feet. Other facilities include the Equine Stud Farm Laboratory and breeding facilities as well as stabling for 100 horses. The equestrian center also features outdoor riding rings with all-weather footing and a hunt field with several cross-country obstacles.

Costs

Tuition per year for 2008–09 is $23,950 for full-time students (12–18 credit hours) and $655 per credit hour for part-time students. The room charges per year are $3860 based on double occupancy. Residential students may choose from three meal plans, with the fourteen-meal-per-week plan equaling $3540 per year. Yearly fees (student activity, library, and computer) are $1120 for full-time students and $47 per credit hour for part-time students. At the established sites, the fees for the Academic Program Abroad are comparable to a semester's costs on the Lake Erie campus.

Financial Aid

Lake Erie College offers a number of competitive scholarship programs that are not based on need. Most incoming freshman students receive a renewable scholarship ranging from $3000 to $14,000 per academic year based on cumulative high school grade point average, standardized test scores, letters of recommendation, and an essay.

Five Presidential Honors Scholarships, which cover 90 percent of tuition, are awarded to incoming students ranking in the top 5 percent of their graduating high school class and achieving a minimum ACT score of 27 or minimum SAT score of 1800 (minimum combination of the three section scores). The award is competitive, with an essay required after the initial GPA and ACT/SAT test score requirements are met. The essay, admissions application, and transcripts are reviewed by a selection committee, and 5 winners are selected. Recipients of the scholarship must live on campus, maintain at least a 3.5 GPA, and take part in the Honors Scholars Program.

Other forms of financial aid, all based on need, include scholarships, grants (federal, state, local, and College), loans (federal and state), and work-study programs; the priority date for need-based aid is March 1. Approximately 98 percent of full-time undergraduate students receive financial aid. Estimates of the expected family contribution are available from the Office of Financial Aid. To apply for aid, students must submit a Free Application for Federal Student Aid (FAFSA), Form 1040, and other documents required by Lake Erie. The deadline for priority consideration is March 1.

Faculty

The Lake Erie College faculty members are well qualified, capable, and eager to teach. Eighty-five percent of the faculty members hold doctoral or terminal degrees in their field. Many bring firsthand experiences in their disciplines to the classroom. They remain active in their respective academic disciplines and are able to provide students with information on current research, new trends, and career opportunities. The average class size is 15, and the student-faculty ratio is 13:1.

Student Government

Students at Lake Erie College play an important role in decision making in many aspects of campus life. Students retain membership on most faculty and administrative committees. The Student Government Association provides a means for students to govern their nonacademic lives and to maintain channels of communication with the faculty and administration.

Admission Requirements

A composite evaluation is made of each applicant, with special attention given to high school credentials. A college-preparatory background is highly recommended and should include 4 units of English, 3 units of mathematics, 3 units of science, 3 units of social studies, and 6 additional units from other academic areas; 2 units of foreign language are advised. ACT and/or SAT scores are required. Lake Erie College welcomes students of all races and backgrounds.

Application and Information

Lake Erie College operates with a rolling admission policy; however, it is recommended that students complete their application and financial aid processes by May 1 in order to maximize their academic and financial aid opportunities. Applicants are notified of the admission decision within two weeks of receipt of all materials.

For further information, students may contact:

Office of Admissions
Lake Erie College
391 West Washington Street
Painesville, Ohio 44077
Phone: 440-375-7050
800-916-0904 (toll-free)
E-mail: admissions@lec.edu
Web site: http://www.lec.edu

The Arthur S. Holden Center.

MALONE COLLEGE

CANTON, OHIO

The College

Malone College is a Christian college committed to offering a high-quality education in a setting that encourages a solid devotion to God. The College was founded and established in 1892 by Walter and Emma Malone as the Cleveland Bible College. Later renamed Malone College to honor its founders, the school moved to Canton, Ohio, in 1957 and began expanding its liberal arts offerings. Today, Malone is one of four Christian colleges in Ohio that is a member of the Council for Christian Colleges and Universities (CCCU). Malone also belongs to the thirteen-member Christian College Consortium.

At Malone College, students are challenged to grow in three vital aspects of life. Spiritually, students are placed in an environment that lends itself to cultivating a deeper relationship with God. Academically, students encounter rigorous challenges offered by a strong faculty, of whom 68 percent hold doctoral, first professional, or terminal degrees. Socially, Malone offers students a chance to experience the real world through on-campus and off-campus activities in which they are exposed to almost every kind of social influence. This requires them to make vital personal decisions and to formulate their own ideas and moral values.

Malone's total enrollment (undergraduate, adult degree-completion, and graduate students) for fall 2007 was 2,379 students. More than 1,670 of these students are traditional undergraduates who represent thirty states and fourteen other countries. The average class size is 22 students. More than 980 students live on campus in nine residence halls.

Students can participate in a variety of clubs and activities, including Christian organizations and fourteen intramural sports. Malone also offers strong varsity programs, including nine men's sports: baseball, basketball, cross-country, football, golf, indoor track, outdoor track, soccer, and tennis and nine women's sports: basketball, cross-country, golf, indoor track, outdoor track, soccer, softball, tennis, and volleyball. Students may also participate in the campus radio station, campus TV station, newspaper, yearbook, student government, marching band, symphonic band, chorale, and forensics and debate.

Malone offers the following graduate programs: Master of Arts in Christian ministries (core areas: leadership in the Christian church and Christian leadership in sports ministry), Master of Arts in education (core areas in counselor education: clinical counseling and school counseling; core areas in graduate education: curriculum and instruction; curriculum, instruction, and professional development; instructional technology; intervention specialist studies; and reading), Master of Science in Nursing (tracks: family nurse practitioner studies and clinical nurse specialist studies), and Master of Business Administration.

Location

Malone College sits on an 87-acre campus in a quiet, residential area of Canton, Ohio. This setting lends itself to a variety of cultural experiences, including the Professional Football Hall of Fame; the ballet, symphony, and theater; museums; and professional sports teams. There is also easy interstate access to the metropolitan areas of Cleveland, Akron, and Youngstown.

Majors and Degrees

The Bachelor of Arts is offered in accounting, adult fitness, art, Bible/theology, biology, biology–clinical laboratory science, business administration, chemistry, commercial music technology, communication arts, community health education, computer science, educational ministries, English, exercise science, history, integrated language arts, integrated science, integrated social studies, liberal arts, life science/chemistry education, mathematics, music, music ministry, outdoor leadership, philosophy, physical science, political science, psychology, social work, Spanish, sport management, sports ministry, youth ministry, and zoo biology. Combination majors in sports/educational ministries, youth/educational ministries, and youth/sports ministries are available. An individualized (student-designed) major is also an option.

Many of these majors and several other fields are available as secondary education fields.

The Bachelor of Science is offered in early childhood education, health education, intervention specialist education, middle childhood education, music education, nursing, physical education, Spanish education, and visual arts education.

Malone also offers adult degree-completion programs in nursing and management.

Academic Programs

Since Malone is a college for the arts, sciences, and professions, there is a comprehensive general education requirement regardless of the chosen course of study. Students must meet requirements in each of Malone's academic areas, including communications, science, English, Bible/theology, and social science.

Malone students must complete a total of 50 to 56 semester credit hours in the aforementioned areas. A minimum of 124 credit hours is required to graduate. This is an accumulation of the major requirements, general education curriculum, and, in most cases, a series of electives. Malone offers forty-nine undergraduate degree opportunities, the most popular of which are early childhood education, nursing, and business administration.

Malone's academic calendar is based on two semesters, with a summer school that includes three sessions.

Off-Campus Programs

Malone students are given the opportunity to spend a semester on another Christian college campus through the Christian College Consortium Visitor Program. Other off-campus opportunities include the following programs sponsored by the CCCU: American Studies Program and Washington Journalism Center (Washington, D.C.), Australia Studies Centre (Sydney), China Studies (Shanghai), Latin American Studies (San Jose, Costa Rica), Middle East Studies (Cairo, Egypt), Russian Studies (Moscow, Nizhni Novgorod, and St. Petersburg), Uganda Studies Program (Mukono), Los Angeles Film Studies (Los Angeles, California), the Scholars' Semester in Oxford (Oxford, England), and studies at the Contemporary Music Center (Martha's Vineyard). In addition, numerous other programs are endorsed by or affiliated with the CCCU. Malone also provides international study opportunities in Guatemala (for teacher education) and Kenya (at Daystar University).

Academic Facilities

The Everett L. Cattell Library, built in 1972 with seating for 299 students, has more than 173,000 book and periodical volumes, 1,025 current periodical subscriptions, 684,500 microform units (including complete ERIC document microfiche from 1989 to 2004), about 3,000 music CDs, and various multimedia materials. Communication majors also have a television studio on campus. There are approximately 200 computers available for general student use in the library, residence halls, and the three computer labs.

Costs

The cost for the 2007–08 year at Malone is $25,470, which includes $18,600 for tuition and $6870 in room, board, and fees.

Financial Aid

A college education is a family investment that requires realistic support. Malone College is committed to assisting with that support. More than 95 percent of traditional Malone students receive some form of financial assistance. This is offered through federal grants and loans, state grants, work opportunities both on and off campus, or Malone College scholarships. These scholarships are awarded on the basis of one or more of the following: need; academic, musical, or athletic talent; or Christian perspective and leadership ability. Malone requires the completion of the Free Application for Federal Student Aid (FAFSA). The average financial aid package amounts to approximately $15,230 per year.

Faculty

Sixty-eight percent of Malone College faculty members hold doctoral, first professional, or terminal degrees. The undergraduate student-faculty ratio is 14:1. This allows students to learn and achieve in a comfortable setting and gives them easy access to assistance from professors.

Student Government

Malone's student organizations are directed by the Student Senate, which in turn is guided by a president and a vice president. The Senate is represented at nearly all of the institution's committee meetings, including the Board of Trustees' meetings. Working through committees, the Senate plays a significant role in shaping the total academic, spiritual, and social life of the Malone community. In addition, positions on the Senate are paid positions.

Admission Requirements

Malone welcomes applications for admission from bright, qualified high school graduates who want to attend college in an atmosphere of high academic standards and evangelical Christianity. Admission is based on objective evaluation of an applicant's motivation, maturity, and other personal qualifications and the applicant's academic credentials, with an emphasis on high school grade point average (2.5 or higher), ACT composite results equal to or above the national mean, class rank, standardized test scores, and depth of high school courses. Other applicants may be accepted by committee approval. A personal interview and campus visit are required in such instances. Malone admits students of any race, color, religion, sex, and national or ethnic origin who meet the academic requirements.

Application and Information

Applications for admission to Malone College are accepted until July 1, and there is a $20 fee required with the application. The Malone Admissions Center is open for campus visitation Monday through Friday from 8:30 a.m. to 5 p.m. The visitation includes a one-on-one interview with an admissions counselor and an individual tour of Malone's campus.

For more information about Malone College, students should contact:

John C. Russell
Director of Admissions
Admissions Center
Malone College
515 25th Street, NW
Canton, Ohio 44709
Phone: 330-471-8145
800-521-1146 (toll-free)
E-mail: admissions@malone.edu
Web site: http://www.malone.edu

Mitchell Hall is home to the classrooms and faculty offices for the School of Business and the School of Education and the 138-seat Silk Auditorium.

MARIETTA COLLEGE

MARIETTA, OHIO

The College

Founded in 1835, Marietta College traces its roots to the Muskingum Academy, which was founded in 1797 as the first institution of higher learning in the Northwest Territory. Marietta's chapter of Phi Beta Kappa was the sixteenth in the nation, showing the College's early dedication to scholarship. Women were first admitted in 1897. About half of Marietta's 1,400 students come from a variety of states along the Eastern Seaboard, the South, and the Midwest; the rest come primarily from Ohio, the surrounding states, and twelve other countries. More than forty states are represented in the Marietta student body. Situated on 120 acres within a block of downtown Marietta, the College has a number of academic and extracurricular facilities. Highlights of the campus include the McDonough Leadership Center, home to the most comprehensive program in leadership studies in the country; the McKinney Media Center, which houses two radio stations, a cable television station, and an award-winning student newspaper; and a pedestrian mall that enhances the central campus. A new recreation center features a 200-meter competition track, performance gymnasium, indoor rowing training room, and more. The new Rickey Science Center opened in spring 2003, and it offers state-of-the-art science labs to house biology, chemistry, biochemistry, environmental science, math, computer science, and physics.

Marietta is one of the few colleges in Ohio with intercollegiate crew, a sport in which it has excelled. In 2006, Marietta crew captured the Dad Vail national title in Philadelphia. Marietta's premier men's baseball program has earned twenty-eight conference championships, nineteen world series appearances, and four world series titles for NCAA Division III. Students become involved with the campus radio and television stations, the student newspaper, the literary magazine, the yearbook, drama productions, and musical groups, plus service and special interest clubs. National invitational art exhibits are sponsored annually by the College for the educational and cultural enrichment of students.

Location

Historic Marietta, Ohio, was the first permanent settlement in the Northwest Territory, settled by New Englanders in 1787. The city of 17,000 people retains a New England flavor with its wide, tree-lined brick streets, Colonial architecture, and large parks. Marietta is readily accessible by car via Interstate 77 (2 miles from campus) or by air from Wood County/Parkersburg Airport in West Virginia (6 miles from campus). The Ohio and Muskingum Rivers meet in Marietta, contributing to the economic, cultural, and recreational vitality of the area.

Majors and Degrees

Marietta offers all students foundation study in the liberal arts and sciences and the opportunity to gain concentrated study in either the traditional liberal arts disciplines or a number of preprofessional programs. Among the liberal arts are strong programs in biochemistry, biology, chemistry, English, physics, and psychology. Preprofessional programs include accounting, computer science, education, environmental science, graphic design, journalism, musical theater, petroleum engineering, radio/television studies, and a nationally renowned program in sports medicine.

Marietta College grants four baccalaureate degrees: the Bachelor of Arts, the Bachelor of Fine Arts, the Bachelor of Science, and the Bachelor of Science in Petroleum Engineering. Marietta is the only liberal arts college in the nation offering the petroleum engineering degree, which is accredited by the Accreditation Board for Engineering and Technology. Marietta also offers a major in athletic training, the first such program at a small college to be accredited by the National Athletic Trainers Association. Students have the opportunity to be involved in the Bernard McDonough Leadership Program. The program, known as "the Marietta Model," allows students to study leadership through a multidisciplinary liberal arts perspective. Students involved in the McDonough Leadership Program have the option of completing a minor in leadership or receiving a certificate. In addition, students have the opportunity to major in international leadership studies—the only undergraduate program in the nation. Along with the core courses of problem solving, critical thinking, and leadership, the program also requires an internship and community service involvement at one of the many organizations in the Marietta area or throughout the world.

"Binary" programs—cooperative study programs with other institutions—enable qualified Marietta students to earn two degrees in such fields as engineering, forestry, and natural resources. Preprofessional programs are offered in dentistry, law, medicine, physical therapy, and veterinary medicine.

The College's Education Department is accredited by NCATE and the state of Ohio Department of Education and offers programs leading to licensure in early childhood, middle childhood, and secondary school education. Ohio has reciprocity with many other states. In addition, the College's programs are accredited by the North Central Association of Colleges and Schools.

Academic Programs

Marietta students are known for both their breadth and depth of study. Freshmen take a special first-year program that begins with the College Experience Seminar and includes courses in composition (English 101), oral presentation (Speech 101), and mathematics. Every student also completes a liberal arts core of sequence courses in the humanities, social sciences, science, and the fine arts. There is an honors program for students who are prepared for and desire an extra challenge and who wish to graduate with honors.

Off-Campus Programs

Students seeking international study experience may make use of Marietta's association with the Institute for the International Education of Students (IES), the international study program of Central College of Iowa, or the programs of the East Central College Exchange. The programs have centers in Austria, the British Isles, France, Germany, Mexico, and Spain and in Asia. Students may also choose other accredited international-study programs. Finally, the College has numerous exchange programs with the People's Republic of China and annually has both faculty members and students teaching and studying in China.

Students whose interests range from economics to government and politics may take advantage of programs offered through the College's affiliation with two institutions located in the nation's capital. Courses are offered through the Washington Semester program of American University, and internships are available through the Washington Center for Learning Alternatives.

Academic Facilities

A new learning and library/resource center is expected to open in January 2009. The $20-million project will house 250,000 volumes, 6,700 periodicals, and an online card catalog. As a member of OhioLINK, the Library provides access to a substantial number of books, materials, and databases. Among the special collections are the Rodney M. Stimson Collection of Americana, a collection of rare fifteenth- through nineteenth-century books, and an extraordinary collection of historic documents pertaining to the Northwest Territory and early Ohio. The card catalog and database are computerized through OCLC (Online Computer Library Center). The Hermann Fine Arts Center includes a laboratory theater, providing study and performance facilities for the College's art, drama, and music departments. Modern computing facilities include 200 personal computers connected by campus network. The campuswide network provides e-mail, Internet, and World Wide Web access. Students can work in computer labs, the library, and the student center, as well as in five academic buildings. The College has well-equipped science labs and its own astronomical observatory and a state-of-the-art computer lab for graphic design students. For instructional and communications purposes, the College operates a media center with a 9,200-watt stereo FM station, a 10-watt FM station, and a television station that reaches more than 12,000 homes via a community cable system. All programs are run by students.

Costs

The total two-semester cost for 2007–08 for a student residing on campus was $32,232. This figure includes $4070 for room, $3320 for board, and $622 for fees, but does not include the cost of books (approximately $500 per year) and personal expenses.

Financial Aid

About 90 percent of current Marietta students receive financial aid based on need. The average award for 2007–08 was $20,000. A number of merit-based scholarships are available in addition to funds allocated through College grants and federal and state sources. Qualified students can also compete in the annual Pioneer Scholars Competition. Pioneer Scholars are a select cadre of students who rank among the best college bound seniors in the nation based on their high school academic record and test scores. Base scholarships begin at $6000 with the opportunity to increase the value of the scholarship up to full tuition. Fine Arts Scholarships are awarded annually to winners of an art, music, and drama competition. Numerous work-study jobs are available to students in many campus departments. Grants are available for children and grandchildren of alumni.

Faculty

Close personal contact between students and professors is one of Marietta's primary features. All departmental faculty members, regardless of rank, teach courses. Full professors teach freshman courses. Ninety-two percent of the College's full-time faculty members hold doctorates or other terminal degrees. Professors share their homes, outside interests, and hobbies with students. A 12:1 student-faculty ratio makes this possible.

Student Government

Through the Student Senate and its committee system, students have responsibility for the cocurricular aspects of College life. Students hold memberships on most faculty and trustee committees, as well as on various departmental committees. Housing boards in both men's and women's residence halls provide programming and dormitory governance. In addition, there are more than 100 active clubs and organizations on campus.

Admission Requirements

Admission decisions are based upon the high school record, scores on national exams (SAT or ACT), an essay, extracurricular involvement, and recommendations from guidance counselors or teachers. While admission is selective and competitive, individual consideration is given to each application. The admission committee seeks a cross section of students whose ability and past performance indicate that they can compete successfully. Credit is granted for Advanced Placement and International Baccalaureate higher-level 1B exams.

Application and Information

Students should apply late in their junior year or early in their senior year of high school to guarantee a place in the fall. Marietta operates on a rolling admission plan, and students are notified of acceptance within one month after all application materials are complete. Students applying for financial aid should apply before March 1 of their senior year to be considered for merit scholarships.

To receive information about Marietta or to apply for admission, students should contact:

Office of Admission
Marietta College
Marietta, Ohio 45750-4005
Phone: 800-331-7896 (toll-free)
E-mail: admit@marietta.edu
Web site: http://www.marietta.edu

Erwin Hall (1850), the oldest building on the Marietta campus, is listed on the National Register of Historic Places.

MOUNT UNION COLLEGE

ALLIANCE, OHIO

The College

Mount Union College was established in 1846 as a select school to meet the educational demands of a small community. Mount Union College offers a liberal arts education grounded in the Judeo-Christian tradition. The College affirms the importance of reason, open inquiry, living faith, and individual worth. Mount Union's mission is to prepare students for meaningful work, fulfilling lives, and responsible citizenship.

Mount Union is primarily a residential campus, and its residence halls mirror the variety of lifestyles and diversity of interests of the students. Students have the opportunity to select from large residence halls housing from 70 to 175, suite-style halls, small houses, or fraternity houses. New apartment-style residences opened on campus in fall 2007. Upperclass students in good academic standing may be permitted to live off campus.

Student activities are an important complement to the academic program. From clubs allied with academic interests to those that are purely social, Mount Union has more than eighty student organizations in its cocurricular program, including chapters of three national sororities and four national fraternities. Nearly 85 percent of Mount Union students participate in the cocurricular program either on or off campus. There are facilities on campus for basketball, dance, racquetball, swimming, tennis, track, volleyball, and wrestling. The College also has a physical education complex, which includes the McPherson Wellness Center, the Peterson Field House, and the Timken Physical Education Building. Nearly 65 percent of Mount Union students participate in organized intramural or intercollegiate sports. Mount Union competes in twenty-one intercollegiate sports: baseball, basketball, cross-country, football, golf, indoor track, outdoor track, soccer, swimming, tennis, and wrestling for men and basketball, cross-country, golf, indoor track, outdoor track, soccer, softball, swimming, tennis, and volleyball for women.

Location

Mount Union College is located in Alliance, Ohio, a town of approximately 25,000 people. Alliance is situated 55 miles southeast of Cleveland, 75 miles northwest of Pittsburgh, 35 miles southeast of Akron, 40 miles west of Youngstown, and 15 miles northeast of Canton.

Majors and Degrees

The Bachelor of Arts is offered in accounting, American studies, art, business administration, cognitive and behavioral neuroscience, communication studies, early childhood education, economics, English, French, German, health, history, international business and economics, international studies, intervention specialist (special education), Japanese, media computing, media studies, middle childhood education, music, non-Western studies, philosophy, physical education, political science, psychology, religious studies, sociology, Spanish, sport management, theater, and writing.

The Bachelor of Science is offered in athletic training, biochemistry, biology, chemistry, computer science, environmental science, exercise science, geology, information systems, mathematics, medical technology, and physics-astronomy.

Mount Union offers three degrees in music: the Bachelor of Music in performance, which is a professional degree; the Bachelor of Music Education, which is a professional degree; and the Bachelor of Arts in music, which is a liberal arts degree.

Preprofessional programs are available in engineering, health professions (including premedicine), law, and the ministry.

Academic Programs

The Mount Union education program is based on an academic year divided into two semesters of fifteen weeks each. The regular academic load is 12 to 19 semester hours per semester.

The Mount Union curriculum is designed with considerable flexibility to meet the needs of students who enter with widely varying educational backgrounds and objectives. The College has five basic educational plans: (1) a program geared toward specialization, with the student taking as many as sixteen courses in one department; (2) a program with a lesser degree of specialization, in which the student takes the minimum number of courses required for a major; (3) a program that permits concentration in interdepartmental areas, such as American studies, and non-Western studies; (4) a preprofessional program that prepares students for entry into professional degree programs in engineering, health professions (including premedicine), law, and the ministry; and (5) an interdisciplinary, individualized program, which students design in conjunction with a committee of faculty advisers to meet particular interests. While students have considerable latitude in determining their individual programs, the all-College comprehensive requirements ensure exposure to the fine arts, the humanities, the social sciences, the physical sciences, and mathematics. In addition, each student must complete a major requirement and a senior-year culminating experience.

Advanced placement, involving the awarding of credit or the waiving of certain prerequisites or requirements, is based on high school records, scores on College Board examinations or similar tests, scores and school reports on College Board Advanced Placement Program examinations, and tests devised and administered by departments within the College. Entering students are encouraged to take placement tests in applicable areas in order to begin course work at the proper level.

Academic Facilities

The library contains more than 230,000 volumes, receives more than 900 periodicals, and provides seating for 350 persons. The computer center, housed in the library, is equipped with the latest in computer and communications technology. The Kolenbrander-Harter Information Center houses two PC computer labs, a Macintosh computer lab, a language lab, several multimedia classrooms, and 24-hour access to study space. There also is a PC lab with thirty-six stations in Tolerton and Hood Hall and a twenty-station PC lab in the Hoover-Price Campus Center. All residence halls are wired for computers and closed-circuit television.

The Fine Arts Complex includes a 290-seat theater, an art gallery, a music library, an outdoor Greek theater, a large rehearsal hall, and a recital hall with a three-manual organ. The Eells Art Center contains classrooms, a printmaking area, a drawing and design studio, a kiln room, a sculpture and woodworking area, and a drama rehearsal hall.

Bracy Hall, a natural sciences facility that opened in 2003, houses the departments of biology, chemistry, geology, and physics and astronomy. The 87,000-square-foot, $23-million structure has four floors and includes twenty-two laboratories of various types and sizes, three lecture halls, two classrooms, and twenty-one faculty offices.

The Clarke Astronomical Observatory is located on the roof of Bracy Hall, and a nearby private observatory is also used by the College. Mount Union also has a 126-acre nature center, located 6 miles from the campus, for biology, chemistry, and ecology studies.

Costs

For 2007–08, the cost of a year at Mount Union College was $28,750, including $22,050 for tuition and fees and $6700 for room and board. This figure may vary slightly, depending upon the type of on-campus housing selected by the student. An additional $1000 should cover such expenses as books and transportation.

Financial Aid

Mount Union College believes that no student should fail to apply for admission to the College purely for financial reasons. Approximately 78 percent of students receive some financial assistance based on demonstrated need. The College also offers allocated institutional dollars to students as merit-based awards. In 2007–08, Mount Union students received financial aid in excess of $39 million. More than $18.6 million of that total was awarded in the form of institutional grants and scholarships.

Faculty

Mount Union employs 125 full-time faculty members, nearly 84 percent of whom hold a terminal degree. The student-faculty ratio is 13:1.

Student Government

Student government is a significant part of Mount Union's decision-making process. Students are represented on all major campus committees that discuss matters affecting student life, and they serve as representatives at meetings of the administration, faculty, and trustees.

Admission Requirements

It is the policy of Mount Union College not to discriminate on the basis of race, sex, sexual orientation, religion, age, color, creed, national or ethnic origin, marital or parental status, or disability in student admissions, financial aid, educational or athletic programs, or employment as now or may hereafter be required by Title VII of the Civil Rights Act of 1964, Title IX of the Educational Amendments of 1972, Section 504 of the Rehabilitation Act of 1973, the Americans with Disabilities Act of 1990, regulations of the Internal Revenue Service, and all other applicable federal, state, and local statutes, ordinances, and regulations.

The qualifications of each candidate are evaluated on the basis of academic background, class rank, references, a required essay, recommendations, and entrance examinations. Applicants should have pursued a strong college-preparatory course in high school. All candidates are required to submit either SAT or ACT scores.

Mount Union welcomes applications from students wishing to transfer from other institutions.

Application and Information

Admission decisions are made on a rolling basis throughout the year. The first admission decisions are made in October. Students can apply for admission for free using either the online application on the College's Web site at http://www.muc.edu, or by submitting a paper application. The admission packet contains instructions, an application form, a secondary school transcript form, and a reference request form.

The Office of Admission is located in Beeghly Hall and is open throughout the year from 8 a.m. until 4:30 p.m. on weekdays and from 9 a.m. until noon on Saturdays throughout the academic year. Candidates who find it possible to visit the campus are encouraged to schedule an interview, although this is not a requirement.

Applicants may obtain further information by contacting:

Director of Admission
Mount Union College
1972 Clark Avenue
Alliance, Ohio 44601
Phone: 330-823-2590
800-334-6682 (toll-free)
E-mail: admission@muc.edu
Web site: http://www.muc.edu

Chapman Hall, built in 1864, serves as one of the main classroom buildings at Mount Union College.

MUSKINGUM COLLEGE
NEW CONCORD, OHIO

The College

Since its founding in 1837, Muskingum has been a community of people learning from and with each other. Its mission is to offer high-quality academic programs in the liberal arts and sciences that educate the whole person intellectually, spiritually, socially, and physically. Muskingum's programs foster critical thinking, positive action, ethical sensitivity, and spiritual growth so that students may lead vocationally productive, personally satisfying, and socially responsible lives. Muskingum College is accredited by the North Central Association of Colleges and Schools and receives periodic reauthorization from the Ohio Board of Regents.

The College's proud heritage reaches back to the first half of the nineteenth century, when settlers were traveling westward over the newly completed National Road. During its first half-century, Muskingum adhered to the educational patterns of the classical college of the period. In 1877, Muskingum became associated with the Synod of Ohio of the United Presbyterian Church. Today, approximately 1,700 undergraduate students are enrolled at Muskingum; 90 percent of these students live on campus, representing twenty-eight states and fifteen other countries.

One of Muskingum's longest traditions is its affiliation with the Presbyterian Church. The Center for Church Life—a joint venture of Muskingum College, the Presbyterian Church Bicentennial Fund, and the Presbytery of Muskingum Valley—provides programs and services to support the ministries and missions of local congregations. On campus, the Office of the College Minister has created a multidimensional, unified campus ministry that allows students to worship and celebrate their faith.

While worship is important at Muskingum, students participate in other activities as well. More than ninety campus groups operate at the College, including varsity athletics, honor societies, music and religious organizations, and FM radio and cable TV stations. The residence halls are another center of student activity; living options range from traditional residence halls and sorority/fraternity houses to special program houses and College-owned apartments. Each residence hall provides lounges, computer labs, and television, kitchen, and laundry facilities.

Location

The village of New Concord, one of the many attractions along National Road, is a 1-hour drive from Columbus and a 2-hour drive from Pittsburgh and Cleveland. New Concord is surrounded by venues for boating, golfing, trail biking, skiing, hiking, camping, and rock climbing, all of which can be enjoyed in the town's temperate climate. New Concord is perhaps best known for its most famous resident—former astronaut and senator (and Muskingum alumnus) John Glenn, whose childhood home has become a museum.

Majors and Degrees

Bachelor's degrees are offered in the following areas: accounting, anthropology, art, biology, business, chemistry, Christian education, computer science, earth science, economics, early childhood education, English, French, geology, German, health education, history, mathematics, middle childhood education, music, philosophy, physical education, physics, political science, psychology, religion, religion and philosophy, sociology, Spanish, special education, speech communication, and theater. Interdisciplinary majors include American studies, child and family studies, conservation science, criminal justice, environmental science, humanities, international affairs, international business, journalism, molecular biology, neuroscience, and public affairs. Students may also design their own interdisciplinary program. Preprofessional programs are available in Christian ministry, dentistry, engineering, law, medical technology, medicine, physical therapy, and veterinary medicine. Teacher licensure programs are available in the following areas: adolescent/young adult, art, early childhood, foreign language (French, German, or Spanish), middle childhood, music, physical education, and special education. A nursing major is anticipated for fall 2008.

Academic Programs

Undergraduate programs combine solid classroom curricula with a level of field work and independent study that is rarely encountered in an undergraduate setting. The bachelor's degree requires completion of at least 124 credit hours with a minimum GPA of 2.0. The curriculum includes Liberal Arts Essentials, a series of courses that ensure the breadth that is inherent in a liberal arts education. This core requires 21–24 hours in core courses, including one English course, two writing courses, one speech course, one mathematics course, one art and humanities course, and one physical education course. Another 35–37 hours are completed in area requirements such as religious understanding, moral inquiry, Western civilization, foreign languages, social sciences, global studies, and other subjects. Students are also required to complete 15 credits in their major area of study, 12 of which must be completed at the College. Credit by examination allows students to earn credit for a course by passing a proficiency examination. A student earns credit for the course by scoring a C or better on the exam.

Off-Campus Programs

Selected students may spend one semester at American University in Washington, D.C., studying the American governmental system in action. Assignments may include the State Department, lobbying groups, or Capitol Hill. Students majoring in art may be able to spend their junior year studying at one of seventeen Art Institutes locations. Commercial art programs are available in the areas of fashion merchandising, industrial design technology, interior design, photography/multimedia, and visual communications. United Nations Semester is a program under which Muskingum students may apply for one semester of study at Drew University, during which time they take two courses involving on-site study at the United Nations headquarters in New York. International study provides the opportunity for sophomores, juniors, and seniors to study for one or two semesters at an international university in Asia, Canada, Europe, Latin America, or Puerto Rico.

Academic Facilities

The library contains 215,000 volumes, 574 print journals, and an extensive microfilm collection, plus access to more than 16,500 online journals, 17,000 electronic books, 1,200 electronic videos, and 110 research databases. The library is a member of the OPAL and OhioLINK consortia, thus giving students and faculty and staff members borrowing privileges at eighty-four academic libraries throughout the state. Brown Chapel serves as church, chapel, and auditorium for the College. Its main auditorium seats nearly 500, and the basement contains a lounge area, music practice rooms, and a small chapel. The John Glenn Physical Education Building houses two gymnasiums, a swimming pool, recreation and intramural equipment, and coaches' offices, while the Physical Education and Recreation Center holds a 2,800-seat gymnasium, four handball/racquetball courts, a baseball/softball hitting area, a weight room, and an athletic training room.

Costs

In the 2007–08 academic year, tuition was $8750 per semester. Other costs per semester included a student activity fee of $110 and a technology fee of $125. Students living on campus can expect to pay $3500 per semester for room and board, as well as $30 for telephone service and $50 for laundry services. Books and supplies, transportation, and other miscellaneous costs vary according to the student's specific needs.

Financial Aid

A small number of entering students receive the John Glenn Scholarship, a full-tuition award, while other students may receive academic scholarships ranging from $1000 to $12,000 per year. These awards are renewable with a GPA of 3.0 or higher. Other scholarships are available in the performing arts. These awards range from $500 to $2000 per year and are renewable with a satisfactory GPA. The College also offers Awards of Circumstance to students who meet the eligibility requirements. These awards range from $500 to $5000 per year. The limit on non-need assistance is $13,500 for recipients of Presidential Scholarships and $12,000 for all other students. Students may also be eligible for federal and state grants, including Federal Pell Grants of up to $4050, Federal Supplemental Educational Opportunity Grants of up to $2000 per year, Ohio College Opportunity Grants of up to $4992 per year, and Federal PLUS loans of up to $2000 annually.

Federal Stafford Student Loans are available to all students who are enrolled at least half-time at a 6.8 percent interest rate. Federal Perkins Loans are available at an interest rate of 5 percent and are repayable after completion of studies. Federal PLUS loans are loans to parents of dependent students. The interest rate is 8.5 percent, and repayment begins within sixty days of disbursement. The College has a limited amount of funding available to be used as loan assistance to students. Repayment with 8 percent interest begins upon the student's departure from Muskingum. Students may also borrow from other lenders. Campus job opportunities are available to students under the Federal Work-Study Program or the Muskingum Work Program. Most students are paid minimum wage and work 5–10 hours per week; students are limited to a total of 20 hours per week for all jobs combined.

Faculty

Of the more than 100 faculty members at the College, more than 90 percent hold a doctorate or the highest degree in their fields; 25 percent of them are full professors, while another 70 percent are associate and assistant professors. A student-faculty ratio of 16:1 allows for greater classroom participation.

Student Government

The Student Senate includes members elected from classes, social clubs, and residence areas. The Executive Board includes a president, vice president, secretary, and treasurer, all of whom are elected each spring, and four independent representatives. In addition, the sophomore, junior, and senior classes each elect a president, vice president, secretary, and treasurer. Student Senate meetings are held biweekly and are open to all members of the College community.

Admission Requirements

Prospective students must submit an application form, a Secondary School Report Form that has been completed and signed by a guidance counselor, official high school transcripts, official ACT or SAT scores, and, optionally, letters of recommendation, a personal written statement, and a recent photo. The admission decision is based on an evaluation of the student's overall background, including extracurricular activities, community service, and volunteerism. However, students who have completed a college-preparatory curriculum with a C+ average or better and scored 18 or higher on the ACT (860 or higher on the SAT) may be qualified for admission. The college-preparatory curriculum includes 4 years of English, 3 years of college-prep math, and at least 2 years each of laboratory science, social sciences, and foreign language.

Application and Information

Admission is made on a rolling basis, so prospective students may apply any time after the end of their senior year. After all application materials are received, the Admission Committee notifies the applicant of their decision within a few weeks. Interested students may request applications from:

Office of Admission
Muskingum College
163 Stormont Street
New Concord, Ohio 43762
Phone: 740-826-8137
800-752-6082 (toll-free)
Fax: 740-826-8100
E-mail: adminfo@muskingum.edu
Web site: http://muskingum.edu/home/index.html

NOTRE DAME COLLEGE

SOUTH EUCLID, OHIO

The College

Notre Dame College was established in 1922. The College believes that truly progressive education selectively blends traditional values with new ideas that represent real growth. Within the scope of a career-oriented liberal arts education, students can grow to meet the challenges of the present and the future. The College is accredited by the North Central Association of Colleges and Schools. It is registered for the awarding of State Teachers' Licenses by the State of Ohio Department of Education.

A variety of clubs and activities enrich the educational experiences of the College's 1,300 students. Campus Ministry promotes the spiritual growth of the Notre Dame College community. The Campus Ministry program facilitates service in the community, retreats, liturgy, and more. The Masquers promote talent in the performing arts and provide entertainment for the College community and general public. Campus publications include the *Notre Dame News* and *PIVOT,* the literary magazine. Faculty members and students schedule and coordinate lectures, plays, performances, and concerts. Most on-campus events are free, and students may purchase tickets at reduced rates for off-campus programs such as performances of the world-famous Cleveland Orchestra, the Cleveland Opera, and road shows of Broadway productions at the Palace Theatre, State Theatre, and Ohio Theatre at Playhouse Square. Performances at the Cleveland Play House are also available.

Notre Dame College is a member of the National Association of Intercollegiate Athletics and competes in the American Mideast Conference. Notre Dame College fields seventeen scholarship athletic teams, including men's and women's intercollegiate basketball, cross-country, golf, soccer, and track; men's baseball, tennis, and wrestling; and women's lacrosse, softball, swimming and diving, and volleyball.

A Master of Education degree, which is designed for classroom teachers, is offered, with concentrations available in special education, reading, and critical and creative thinking.

Location

The College is located in South Euclid, 25 minutes from downtown Cleveland and only 5 minutes from Legacy Village, Cleveland's new lifestyle retail center. The area combines the excitement and cultural wealth of a major urban and educational center with the relaxed atmosphere of a suburban setting. University Circle in Cleveland, a 500-acre complex containing an unusual blend of cultural, educational, medical, religious, and social service institutions, is easily accessible from the College.

Situated on the shores of Lake Erie, Cleveland is the home of the Rock and Roll Hall of Fame and several professional sports teams. The Cleveland Metroparks offer a variety of activities and recreational opportunities. Snowy winters provide abundant opportunities for skiing and tobogganing, and popular ski areas are located a short distance from the city.

The beautiful 53-acre wooded campus provides the perfect setting for the Clara Fritzsche Library; the Administration Building, housing all of the classrooms and offices; Connelly Center, the cafeteria and student center; the Keller Center, the recreational and fitness facility; and three residence halls.

Majors and Degrees

The College awards the Bachelor of Arts degree in accounting (business administration); biology; chemistry; communication; education, including early childhood (pre-K–3), middle childhood (4–9), and young adult education and mild-moderate intervention specialist studies; English; graphic design; history/political science; information systems; management; marketing; mathematics; political science; psychology; public administration; sports management; studio art; and theology. The Bachelor of Science is awarded in biology, chemistry, and mathematics. A student can also design his or her own major that leads to a Bachelor of Arts or Bachelor of Science degree by combining two or three academic areas, such as graphic design, human resource management, and public relations.

Notre Dame College also offers a Bachelor of Science in Nursing program. An RN to B.S.N. completion program is also available.

Teacher licensure is available in early childhood education, middle childhood education, adolescent/young adult education, and multiage for mild/moderate intervention specialist studies.

The Associate in Arts degree is awarded at the completion of two-year programs in business management, education paraprofessional studies, and pastoral ministry.

The Center for Pastoral Theology and Ministry grants a two-year catechetical diploma and the Bachelor of Arts degree.

Academic Programs

All students pursue a career-oriented liberal arts education. For the bachelor's degree, students must earn 128 semester hours of credit, with a minimum cumulative grade point average of 2.0. From 36 to 68 semester hours of credit are required in the major field of study.

Through a cooperative education program, students can earn a maximum of 6 credit hours for paid or volunteer work experience related to their academic field of study.

Advanced Placement credit is awarded to students who have demonstrated the ability to pursue course work beyond the level of entering freshmen, as indicated by their scores on the Advanced Placement (AP) or College-Level Examination Program (CLEP) tests of the College Board. College credit is given on the basis of a decision made jointly by the academic dean and the department involved.

Academic Facilities

The Clara Fritzsche Library, housing the modern Media Center, has a capacity for 100,000 volumes. As a member of Ohiolink, the College also has online access to members throughout the state, with access to more than 31 million library items and more than 90 research databases. The library also houses the smart classroom, a state-of-the-art classroom equipped with laptops for each student and two SMARTBoards.

The Dwyer Learning Center consists of an electronic classroom, a student computer lab, a writing lab, and a tutoring room. The writing lab and tutoring room are available for students to work one-on-one with peer tutors in specific areas.

The Academic Support Center for Students with Learning Differences (ASC) was designed to support students with disabilities such as Attention Deficit Disorder (ADD), Attention Deficit Hyperactivity Disorder (ADHD), and dyslexia. In order to be accepted into the Learning Differences Program, students must meet the admission requirements of Notre Dame College. To participate in the Academic Support Center, students must submit documentation of a learning disability. Among its services, ASC provides professional tutoring, advising, and lessons on adaptive equipment.

The Multi-Media Lab for graphic design majors offers PC and Macintosh technology for advanced multimedia production capabilities.

The Center for Professional Development offers course work for working adults on a variety of topics. The center offers seminars and short, flexibly scheduled courses for professionals throughout the year, along with certificate programs in athletic coaching, business intelligence, and intelligence for homeland security.

Costs

For the 2007–08 academic year, tuition charges were $20,540. Room and board costs were $7156 for double occupancy. Student fees were $550.

Financial Aid

A comprehensive financial assistance program of approximately $16.4 million assists nearly 93 percent of all full-time students. Students applying for aid must submit the Free Application for Federal Student Aid (FAFSA).

Faculty

The faculty has 40 full-time and 70 part-time members. The faculty is augmented by highly qualified instructors in special areas. Faculty members hold advanced degrees from more than thirty universities in the United States, Canada, and Europe.

Student Government

The Undergraduate Student Government (USG) is the central coordinating group for all student organizations. In addition, students have representation on various College committees.

Admission Requirements

In fulfilling its mission, Notre Dame College seeks to attract students of diverse religious, racial, and economic backgrounds. Candidates for admission as first-time, full-time freshmen are reviewed on an individual basis, and decisions are based on a broad range of criteria. The most important consideration is the candidate's high school performance, as demonstrated by her/his overall grade average, class rank, grade trends, and level of courses completed. Aptitude for verbal and mathematical reasoning, as measured by performance on standardized tests, is also considered. In addition, counselor and teacher recommendations are reviewed.

Notre Dame College recommends that students complete at least 16 units of high school credit in academic subjects as a prerequisite for matriculation in the College. The distribution of these subject areas and the units are as follows: English, 4; mathematics, 3 (to include algebra I, geometry, and algebra II); science, 3 (with laboratory experience); social studies, 3; foreign language, 2 (from the same language); and fine arts, 1. Applicants should generally rank in the upper half of their high school graduating class and have a minimum average of C+. Either ACT or SAT scores are accepted.

Students wishing to transfer from other regionally accredited colleges and universities are admitted to advanced standing upon presentation of satisfactory evidence of scholarship and character.

Special consideration may be granted to an applicant whose academic preparation is not consistent with the requirements stated above.

Notre Dame College strongly recommends that prospective students schedule an appointment to visit the campus and talk with an admissions counselor.

Application and Information

The College maintains a rolling admission policy. To apply, students should submit the completed application for undergraduate admission, an official transcript of their high school record, results of the ACT or SAT, and a nonrefundable $30 application fee to:

Office of Admissions
Notre Dame College
4545 College Road
South Euclid, Ohio 44121
Phone: 216-373-5355
877-NDC-OHIO Ext. 5355 (toll-free)
Fax: 216-373-5278
E-mail: admissions@ndc.edu
Web site: http://www.NotreDameCollege.edu

OBERLIN COLLEGE

OBERLIN, OHIO

The College

Oberlin College, which was founded in 1833, is an independent, coeducational liberal arts college dedicated to recruiting students from diverse backgrounds. Oberlin comprises two divisions: the College of Arts and Sciences, with roughly 2,200 students, and the Conservatory of Music, with about 600 students. Students in both divisions share one campus; they also share residence and dining halls as part of one academic community. Many students take courses in both divisions. Oberlin awards the Bachelor of Arts (B.A.) and the Bachelor of Music (B.Mus.) degrees. In Oberlin's distinctive double-degree program, students pursue the B.A. and the B.Mus. degrees in a unified, five-year program. Selected master's degrees are offered in the conservatory.

Oberlin made interracial education central to its mission in 1835; by 1900, nearly half of all the black college graduates in the country—128 to be exact—had graduated from Oberlin. This core of Oberlin-educated men and women formed the first black professional class in the country. In 1837, Oberlin became the first consistently coeducational school in the United States.

Today, Oberlin is a community of thinkers, scholars, scientists, musicians, athletes, activists, and artists—all of whom seek to make the world a better place. Students are united by a commitment to social justice and a willingness to confront social issues that many would prefer to ignore. As the *New York Times* noted in an article marking Oberlin's 150th anniversary, "In its century and a half, while Harvard worried about the classics and Yale about God, Oberlin worried about the state of America and the world beyond."

Recognizing that interaction with others of widely different backgrounds and experiences fosters the effective and concerned participation in the larger society so characteristic of Oberlin graduates, Oberlin is dedicated to recruiting a culturally, economically, geographically, and racially diverse group of students. Diverse students from every walk of life and from around the world seek pathways of individual expression inside Oberlin's tight-knit community of learners, doers, and volunteers. More Oberlin graduates have gone on to earn Ph.D.'s than at any other American college. Its alumni, who include 3 Nobel laureates and 6 MacArthur "Genius" award recipients, are leaders in law, scientific and scholarly research, medicine, the arts, theology, communications, business, and government.

Oberlin has several distinctive academic programs. During the four-week Winter Term, students focus on career aspirations or explore new interests on or off campus. Past projects have taken students to every corner of the globe, from a geology department expedition to Java to a group of students working in a Russian orphanage. Oberlin's Experimental College, a student-run program, offers courses for limited academic credit taught by Oberlin students, townspeople, administrators, and faculty members. Oberlin's First Year Seminar Program is a series of small discussion-based seminars designed to hone students' writing and critical-thinking skills while establishing a context and direction for their personal development.

Oberlin offers a small-town atmosphere and is located not far from Cleveland. There is never a lack of something to do. More than 400 concerts and recitals take place on campus annually, from ticketed events like the Cleveland Orchestra to free student and faculty recitals. Each year, the conservatory stages two operas, and the theater and dance programs present more than fifty productions. Numerous lectures and readings feature guests prominent in a variety of disciplines.

Location

Oberlin College is an integral part of the city of Oberlin, a town of about 8,100 residents located 35 miles southwest of Cleveland. The town is primarily residential, with tree-lined streets and fine old clapboard houses. The College is located in the center of town, close to the business district, and virtually everything a student needs is within walking or biking distance.

Majors and Degrees

Oberlin offers the Bachelor of Arts degree (awarded by the College of Arts and Sciences) and the Bachelor of Music degree (awarded by the Conservatory of Music). Oberlin also offers a distinctive double-degree program, a five-year course of study leading to the B.A. and B.Mus. degrees. Students wishing to enter the double-degree program must be accepted by both the College of Arts and Sciences and the Conservatory of Music.

The B.A. is awarded in African American studies, anthropology, archaeological studies, art (history and studio), biology, chemistry, cinema studies, classics (Greek, Latin, and classical civilization), comparative American studies, comparative literature, computer science, creative writing, dance, East Asian studies, economics, English, environmental studies, French, geology, German, Hispanic studies, history, Jewish studies, Latin American studies, law and society, mathematics, music, neuroscience, philosophy, physics, politics, psychology, religion, Russian, Russian and East European studies, sociology, theater, Third World studies, 3/2 engineering, and women's studies. In addition, many students pursue interdisciplinary individual majors as well as preprofessional studies in law and medicine.

The B.Mus. is awarded in composition, electronic and computer music, historical performance, jazz studies (performance or composition), music history, and performance (baroque cello/viola da gamba, baroque flute, baroque oboe, baroque violin, bassoon, clarinet, classical guitar, double bass, flute, harp, harpsichord, horn, lute, oboe, organ, percussion, piano, recorder, saxophone, trombone, trumpet, tuba, viola, violin, violoncello, and voice). A major in music theory is only offered as part of a double major.

The Conservatory of Music also offers combined five-year B.Mus. and M.Mus. degrees in opera theater, conducting, and music education and teaching, as well as an M.Mus. in historical performance and a four-semester Artist Diploma.

Academic Programs

To receive the B.A. or the B.Mus. degree, students must complete a major; 9 credit hours in each of Oberlin's three divisions: humanities, natural sciences, and social sciences, as well as 9 hours in courses dealing with cultural diversity; and three Winter Term projects. Students must also demonstrate quantitative proficiency and writing proficiency. For the B.A., 112 credit hours are required for graduation; for the B.Mus., 124 hours are required. The recommended semester course load is

14 credit hours for students in the College of Arts and Sciences and 15 or 16 credit hours for students in the Conservatory of Music.

Academic Facilities

Oberlin's four libraries contain more than 1.75 million items, including 1.1 million catalogued volumes—an unusually large collection for a college of Oberlin's size. Other features include an online catalog, connections to several networks, and access to numerous online and CD-ROM databases. The College's Allen Memorial Art Museum is considered one of the top college or university art museums in the nation. Seventeenth-century Dutch and Flemish painting, European art of the late nineteenth and twentieth centuries, and contemporary art are especially well represented among the more than 14,000 objects spanning the range of art history in the museum. The one-of-a-kind art-rental program allows students to rent original works of art each semester, including works by such artists as Picasso, Rembrandt, and Toulouse-Lautrec.

The Conservatory of Music contains 153 practice rooms—all with windows—and houses 168 Steinway grand pianos and eighteen uprights. The conservatory also has two concert halls, numerous instrument collections, state-of-the-art electronic music studios, and recording facilities. A state-of-the-art jazz studies facility will soon be constructed, the result of what is believed to be the largest private gift in support of jazz education at a U.S. college.

Oberlin's Irvin E. Houck Computing Center provides more than 250 Macintosh and Dell computers for student use in several locations on campus. In all of the residence hall rooms, students have direct access to the Internet and the campus network from their personal computers. Computer accounts are automatically given to all students at no charge. Although it is becoming more wireless, Oberlin is considered to be one of the most wired colleges in the country.

Oberlin's Science Center was designed to accommodate contemporary methods in science education. Everything is interconnected, promoting communication across disciplines and the collaborative research relationships for which Oberlin is so well known. The strength of Oberlin's science program and its supercomputer capability make Oberlin one of the leading undergraduate colleges in computational modeling. The Science Center complex is a testament to Oberlin's long-held belief that the best liberal arts education has a strong science component and that the best science education occurs in a liberal arts environment.

The Adam Joseph Lewis Center for Environmental Studies is the largest photovoltaic-run building among colleges and universities in the country. The Lewis Center is a living laboratory for the emerging field of ecological design. The center is a classroom, a case study, and a stunning example of how environmental commitment, the latest technologies, and life-cycle thinking can come together to create living and working spaces that minimize the negative impact on the world.

Costs

Tuition for the 2007–08 academic year was $36,064. Double-room and board fees were an additional $9280. The student activity fee was $218.

Financial Aid

In an average year, Oberlin commits more than $39 million, more than one fifth of the College budget, to financial aid. The Office of Financial Aid works to develop financial aid packages that meet the demonstrated financial need of all regularly admitted students who comply with the filing deadlines. Canadian citizens are treated as U.S. citizens for financial aid purposes. Limited financial aid is also available for other international students.

To apply for assistance, students must submit the Financial Aid PROFILE of the College Scholarship Service and the Free Application for Federal Student Aid (FAFSA).

Faculty

Of Oberlin's 339 faculty members, 253 teach in the College of Arts and Sciences and 86 teach in the Conservatory of Music. They are eminently qualified for their positions, with more than 97 percent having earned doctoral or terminal degrees in their field, many from the world's finest graduate institutions. The student-faculty ratio is 11:1 in the College and 8:1 in the conservatory.

Student Government

By serving on Oberlin's Student Senate and in other ways, Oberlin College students have the opportunity to influence College policy on academic and student-life issues. Student representatives sit on nearly every faculty committee, and allocation of the student activity fee is determined by a committee composed solely of students.

Admission Requirements

Admission to both the College of Arts and Sciences and the Conservatory of Music is highly selective. Candidates for admission must submit the results of the SAT or ACT with writing. The College also recommends that two SAT Subject Tests be taken. For the class of 2011, the median 50 percent of SAT scores were 660–750 verbal, 650–710 math, and 650–740 writing. The median 50 percent of ACT scores was 27–32. Of those students who attend high schools that rank their students, 78 percent were in the top tenth percentile of their high school class, and 96 percent were in the top fifth percentile. For admission to the Conservatory of Music, the most important factor is the performance audition or, in the case of composition and electronic and computer music applicants, the compositions, tapes, and supporting materials submitted.

Application and Information

For more information or to request an application, students should write to:

Office of Admissions, College of Arts and Sciences
Oberlin College
Oberlin, Ohio 44074
Phone: 440-775-8411
800-622-OBIE (toll-free)
E-mail: college.admissions@oberlin.edu

Office of Admissions, Conservatory of Music
Oberlin College
Oberlin, Ohio 44074
Phone: 440-775-8413
E-mail: conservatory.admissions@oberlin.edu
Web site: http://www.oberlin.edu

Office of Financial Aid
Carnegie Building
Oberlin College
52 West Lorain Street
Oberlin, Ohio 44074
Phone: 440-775-8142
800-693-3173 (toll-free)
E-mail: financial.aid@oberlin.edu

OHIO NORTHERN UNIVERSITY

ADA, OHIO

The University

Founded in 1871, Ohio Northern University (ONU) offers a dynamic learning environment with its four undergraduate colleges, the College of Law, and a combination of professional and liberal arts programs. The University is related to the United Methodist Church and is committed to promoting spiritual as well as intellectual values. With a student population of more than 3,600, ONU is small enough to provide a personalized atmosphere but large enough to attract students with many different educational goals. Students attending Ohio Northern are presented with many opportunities to explore a wide range of activities—academic, social, spiritual, and physical.

Residence hall living is considered to be an integral part of the educational program, and the residence halls' professional staff, facilities, and programs contribute to students' personal development. The residence halls serve as key places for study sessions and student activities. There are ten residence halls on campus as well as seven campus apartment complexes and an Affinity Housing complex, which typically houses juniors and seniors. The dining hall is located in the student union. There are also six national fraternities and four national sororities as well as thirty-nine honorary societies that recognize scholastic achievement or service.

The University is a member of the Ohio Athletic Conference and fields intercollegiate teams in men's baseball, basketball, cross-country, football, golf, soccer, swimming and diving, tennis, indoor and outdoor track, and wrestling and in women's basketball, cross-country, fastpitch softball, golf, soccer, swimming and diving, tennis, indoor and outdoor track, and volleyball.

In addition to the undergraduate programs, the University offers a Juris Doctor, a Doctor of Pharmacy (Pharm.D.), and a Doctor of Pharmacy/Law.

Location

Surrounding the campus is the town of Ada, a small, quiet, friendly community of 5,000 residents. Located in northwestern Ohio, ONU and Ada are easily accessible by major highways. Students have convenient access to Columbus, Dayton, and Toledo while enjoying the hospitality and comfort of Ada's hometown atmosphere.

Majors and Degrees

Ohio Northern University offers the undergraduate degrees of Bachelor of Arts, Bachelor of Fine Arts, Bachelor of Music, Bachelor of Science, Bachelor of Science in Business Administration, Bachelor of Science in Civil Engineering, Bachelor of Science in Clinical Laboratory Science, Bachelor of Science in Computer Engineering, Bachelor of Science in Electrical Engineering, Bachelor of Science in Mechanical Engineering, and Bachelor of Science in Nursing. Majors are offered in accounting, art (advertising design, graphic design, studio arts), athletic training, biochemistry, biology, chemistry, civil engineering, clinical laboratory science, communication arts (broadcasting and electronic media, international theater production, musical theater, professional and organizational communication, public relations, theater), computer engineering, computer science, creative writing, criminal justice (administration of justice, behavioral science), early childhood education, electrical engineering, environmental studies, exercise physiology, finance, forensic biology, French, German, health education, history, international business and economics, international studies, journalism, language arts education, literature, management, marketing, mathematics, mathematics/statistics, mechanical engineering, medicinal chemistry, middle childhood education, molecular biology, music, music composition, music education, music performance, music with elective studies in business, nursing, pharmaceutical business (economics, management, marketing), pharmacy, philosophy, philosophy/religion, physical education, physics, political science, professional writing, psychology, religion, social studies, sociology, Spanish, sport management, technology, technology education, and youth ministry.

Special preprofessional programs are available in dentistry, law, medicine, occupational therapy, physical therapy, physician assistant studies, seminary, and veterinary medicine. Interdisciplinary degree programs are available in arts/engineering and arts–business/pharmacy. Additional programs are offered in athletic coaching certification. Teacher licensure programs are offered at the adolescent, early childhood, middle childhood, and multiage levels and in sixteen program areas.

Academic Programs

In the College of Arts and Sciences, the first two years of study are usually devoted to a program of general education. Work in a major is usually taken at the advanced level during the junior and senior years. To graduate with a Bachelor of Arts, Bachelor of Fine Arts, or Bachelor of Science degree, students are required to complete a minimum of 182 quarter hours, which includes appropriate general education courses, completion of an approved major, and a cumulative grade point average of at least 2.0. To graduate with a Bachelor of Music degree, students are required to complete a minimum of 182 quarter hours in music education, performance, composition, or music with elective studies in business. To fulfill the minimum residence requirements, all students must spend the last three quarters of their program in residence and complete 45 quarter hours with at least 90 quality points in courses elected mainly from junior- and senior-level courses. The Bachelor of Science in Clinical Laboratory Science and the Bachelor of Science in Nursing have different requirements.

In the College of Business Administration, the first two years of study are devoted to general education courses plus introductory courses in several of the business disciplines. To graduate, a student must satisfactorily complete a minimum of 182 quarter hours of appropriate course work for the specific major(s) and maintain at least a 2.0 grade point average. Students in all four majors are encouraged to participate in an internship program in either the junior or senior year.

The College of Engineering offers degrees in civil engineering, computer engineering, computer science, electrical engineering, and mechanical engineering. The courses for the first academic year are essentially the same for each degree program, offering students an easy track to move from one program to another if they are initially uncertain which disciplines they prefer to study. Students are required to maintain a minimum cumulative grade point average of 2.0 as well as a minimum GPA of 2.0 computed for all engineering and computer science courses. An optional five-year co-op program is available for students in each engineering program provided they maintain a minimum 2.5 GPA. A minor in computer science and options in environmental studies and business administration are available to engineering students provided they maintain at least a 2.5 GPA.

The College of Pharmacy offers the six-year, direct-entry Doctor of Pharmacy program (0-6), and admission may be granted to students directly out of their high school programs. After three years of course work in the physical sciences, social sciences, humanities, and professional areas, students spend two years studying the practice of pharmacy through a patient-care-oriented curriculum that utilizes body system and disease-based modules as well as modules with an administrative and practice-based focus. The last year is experiential and takes place in a variety of clinical settings throughout the country. Resident students have available a strong undergraduate research program and may pursue minors or dual majors in biochemistry and medicinal chemistry. The College of Pharmacy operates on a November 1 application review deadline.

The University offers a special prelaw program, which guarantees Ohio Northern graduates admission to the Pettit College of Law if they complete the specially designed program with a grade point average of at least 3.4 in any of ONU's undergraduate colleges, score in at least the 75th percentile on the LSAT, pass the character and fitness review by the admissions committee of the College of Law, and are deemed by the law school admissions committee to appear capable of satisfactorily completing its program and being admitted to the bar. To take advantage of an automatic admission, a student must enroll in the College of Law in the fall semester immediately following the date that the student receives an undergraduate degree from Ohio Northern.

Off-Campus Programs

Many majors may take part in study-abroad programs developed in consultation with faculty members. Field experiences and internships are available in most majors. Externships are required of all pharmacy majors and place students in retail and clinical experiences. Teacher licensure requires one quarter of primary or secondary classroom teaching experience under the supervision of practicing teachers. Additional opportunities include computer science and mathematics co-op programs (professional practice), engineering co-op programs (professional practice, domestic and international), an honors program, and a nontraditional pharmacy doctorate program. All of these off-campus learning experiences carry credit.

Academic Facilities

ONU's Heterick Memorial Library and the Taggart Law Library provide information resources and services to support course offerings and foster independent study. In addition to books and periodicals, the library houses microforms, CD-ROM services, state and federal documents, records, audiotapes, videocassette tapes, DVDs, films, filmstrips, and slides. Facilities include individual study carrels, study rooms, microform reading and printing equipment, copy services, audiovisual equipment, personal computers, and access to the University's computer network. An online catalog system, compact disc indexing, and abstract services are readily available in the library and through the campus computer network.

The Freed Center for the Performing Arts features a 551-seat theater/concert hall, a 120-seat studio theater, and television and radio production facilities. WONB-FM is the commercial-free 3,000-watt voice of ONU. The facility accommodates the entire Communication Arts Department in state-of-the-art style. The University is among the leaders in offering the creative and efficient application of information technology in support of teaching, learning, administrative, and student services. Information technologies are integrated into all aspects of University life, enhancing classroom, laboratory, research, and living experiences as well as recreation and communications.

The University provides a heterogeneous environment of computer equipment integrated by local area networks. The campus network is attached to the Internet and Internet2 through high-speed fiber-optic connection. The campus network is available in every academic building and residence hall room. In addition, wireless networking is available in most academic and administrative buildings. More than 580 computers are available to students in academic areas.

Costs

Charges for the 2007–08 year were $37,080 for tuition, room, and board for the Colleges of Arts and Sciences and Business Administration; $39,090 for the College of Engineering; and $40,740 for the College of Pharmacy. The cost of books and supplies is approximately $1500 per year.

Financial Aid

Ohio Northern University makes every effort to ensure that no qualified applicant is denied admission because of inability to pay the total cost. More than 90 percent of the student body receive some type of financial assistance. To be considered for financial assistance, the student should submit the FAFSA and the ONU financial aid application to the University along with the admission application. Both merit and need-based aid are available to students.

Faculty

Students are served by 215 full-time and 69 part-time faculty members whose full responsibilities are to the undergraduate students. The primary interest of the faculty is teaching, although research as an adjunct to good teaching is pursued by many faculty members in order to maintain current professional awareness. Most of the faculty members live near the campus and participate in some area of cocurricular student activities. Emphasis is placed on careful advising of students in academic and personal matters. The student-faculty ratio is 14:1.

Student Government

The Student Senate provides self-government in many areas of student life and seeks to further ideals of character and service to the University. Officers of the Student Senate are elected by the students, and the group meets on a weekly basis. The Student Senate serves as the official representative group of the student body to the University administration and agencies in matters pertaining to the student body.

Admission Requirements

High school students applying for admission to the University should present an official transcript indicating at least 16 total units, including work in the academic areas indicated by each college, as follows: College of Arts and Sciences, 12 units—4 in English, 2 in mathematics (algebra and geometry), and 6 in history, social studies, language, or natural science; College of Business Administration, 13 units—4 in English, 3 in mathematics (including algebra and geometry), and 6 in history, social studies, language, or natural sciences; College of Engineering, 16 units—4 in English, 4 in mathematics (including geometry, trigonometry, and 2 of algebra), 2 in science (including physics and, preferably, chemistry), and 6 in history, social studies, language, or natural sciences; and College of Pharmacy, 20 units—4 in English, 4 in mathematics (algebra I and II, plane geometry, trigonometry, precalculus, or calculus), 4 in science (including biology, chemistry, and physics), and 6 of history, social studies, languages, or any combination thereof. Applicants are also required to submit scores on the ACT. (Scores on the SAT of the College Board may be substituted for the ACT.) Ohio Northern University recommends that students take the writing section of the ACT. For scholarship purposes, the traditional sections of the ACT and the SAT are considered. An interview on campus is recommended.

Application and Information

Completed applications should be sent along with a $30 nonrefundable application fee. It is recommended that students apply for admission at the end of their junior year in high school or early in the senior year. Students are encouraged to apply no later than December 1 of their senior year for maximum scholarship consideration (November 1 for Pharmacy).

The Colleges of Arts and Sciences, Business Administration, and Engineering operate on a rolling admission basis, and applications are processed immediately upon receipt of all necessary information (application, application fee, high school transcript, and ACT and/or SAT scores).

The College of Pharmacy application deadline is November 1 for entering freshmen. A student file is considered complete when it contains the application, application fee, high school transcript, ACT and/or SAT scores, Pharmacy addendum (including both essays), and two letters of reference. A campus visit is strongly encouraged for consideration for admittance into the College of Pharmacy.

Requests for catalogs, application forms, or additional information should be directed to:

Office of Admissions
Ohio Northern University
Ada, Ohio 45810
Phone: 888-408-4668 (toll-free)
Fax: 419-772-2313
E-mail: admissions-ug@onu.edu
Web site: http://www.onu.edu

Students outside the Dukes Memorial building.

OHIO WESLEYAN UNIVERSITY

DELAWARE, OHIO

The University

"We inspire you. You change the world." That is Ohio Wesleyan's charge to its students, and the University provides the tools to help its students achieve that goal. A unique blend of liberal arts learning and preprofessional preparation sets Ohio Wesleyan University (OWU) apart. Founded by the United Methodist Church in 1842, the University is strongly committed to education for leadership and service, to fusing theory and practice, and to confronting specific issues of long-range public importance.

A selective, residential institution, Ohio Wesleyan is home to approximately 1,850 undergraduates, with a nearly equal number of men and women. Students come to Ohio Wesleyan from forty states and forty-five countries and live on the attractive 200-acre campus. Housing options include six large residence halls; several small living units (SLUs), such as the Creative Arts House, the Modern Foreign Languages House, and the Peace and Justice House; and eleven fraternity houses, nine of which offer housing. The five sorority houses are nonresidential.

There is a wide range of cocurricular activities. Students initiate discussion groups, service projects, and intramural athletics. Other activities include the nation's oldest independent student newspaper; cultural- and ethnic-interest groups such as the Student Union on Black Awareness (SUBA) and SANGAM and VIVA (which promote an understanding of the cultures of South Asia and Latin America, respectively); the College Republicans and College Democrats; and prelaw and premed clubs. In the course of a year, students may enjoy more than 100 concerts, plays, dance programs, films, exhibits, and speakers. The Department of Theatre and Dance stages four major productions and much additional studio work each year, while the Music Department sponsors four large performance groups and other small ensembles. The impressive Hamilton-Williams Campus Center is the hub of cocurricular life on campus.

There are twenty-three Division III varsity athletic teams—eleven for men and eleven for women; sailing is a coed sport. In 2006–07, the University won the North Coast Athletic Conference (NACA) All-Sports Trophy, posting top-two finishes in ten sports and bringing home NCAC championships in six: baseball, golf, men's soccer and lacrosse, and women's indoor and outdoor track and field. Sixty Battling Bishops representing nearly every sport were named to All-NCAC teams

Both soccer player Josh Warren and basketball player Ben Chojnacki received NCAA Postgraduate Scholarships. Warren also was voted Academic All-America® Team Member of the Year of the 2006 *ESPN The Magazine* Academic All-America® teams and was a first-team Academic All-America® selection. The men's and women's cross-country teams received All-Academic team honors from the U.S. Track & Field and Cross Country Coaches Association.

Men's soccer coach Jay Martin received the National Soccer Association of America Honor Award in 2007 and men's basketball coach Mike DeWitt was NCAC Coach of the Year in 2006.

Intramural programs are extensive, and all students have access to racquet sports, swimming, and weight-lifting facilities in the Branch Rickey Physical Education Center. Fitness equipment and health services are housed in the 7,000–square-foot Health and Wellness Center, conveniently located in Stuyvesant Hall. Off-campus opportunities for backpacking, boating, camping, golf, skiing, and swimming are abundant.

Location

Delaware combines the small-town pace and maple-lined streets of the county seat (population 26,000) with easy access to the state capital, Columbus, the fifteenth-largest city in America. Thirty minutes south of the campus, Columbus provides rich internship opportunities, international research centers, fine dining and shopping, and cultural events that complement campus life.

Majors and Degrees

Ohio Wesleyan offers the Bachelor of Arts degree in accounting; ancient, medieval, and Renaissance studies; astronomy; biological sciences (botany, genetics, microbiology, and zoology); chemistry; computer science; economics (including accounting, international business, and management); education (elementary and secondary licensing in seventeen areas); English literature and writing; fine arts; French; geography; geology; German; history; humanities-classics; journalism; mathematics; music (applied or history/literature); philosophy; physical education; physics; politics and government; psychology; religion; sociology/anthropology; Spanish; and theater and dance. Interdisciplinary majors include Black world studies, East Asian studies, environmental studies, international studies, Latin American studies, neuroscience, urban studies, and women's and gender studies, as well as prelaw and premedicine. Students may also design majors in topical, period, or regional studies.

Two professional degrees are awarded: the Bachelor of Fine Arts in art history, arts education, and studio art, and the Bachelor of Music in music education and performance. Combined-degree (generally 3-2) programs are offered in engineering, medical technology, optometry, and physical therapy.

Academic Programs

Ohio Wesleyan provides opportunities for students to acquire not only depth in a major area but also knowledge about their cultural past through the insight provided by a broad liberal arts curriculum. At Ohio Wesleyan, education is placed in a context of values, and students are encouraged to develop the intellectual skills of effective communication, independent and logical thought, and creative problem solving. To these ends, students are required to demonstrate competence in English composition and a foreign language (often through placement testing) and to complete distributional study in the natural and social sciences, the humanities, and the arts. With few exceptions, the major requires the completion of eight to fifteen courses. Many students double major or take more than one minor in addition to their major. Thirty-four courses are required for graduation.

Advanced placement is available with or without credit. Under the four-year honors program, even first-year students may be named Merit Scholars and work individually with faculty mentors on research, directed readings, or original creative work. Upperclass students also are encouraged to participate in independent study. Phi Beta Kappa is only one of the twenty-six scholastic honorary societies with chapters on campus.

The objectives of an Ohio Wesleyan education are crystallized in the distinctive Sagan National Colloquium, a program focused annually on one issue of compelling public importance, such as "Cities and Suburbs: Life in a Metropolitan World." Through weekly speakers and semester-long seminars, the colloquium stimulates campuswide dialogue and encourages students to integrate knowledge from many different disciplines and apply what is studied to life. Participants discover not only what they think about the issue, but also why they think as they do and how to make important decisions based on their beliefs.

Off-Campus Programs

Full-semester internships and apprenticeships, as well as programs of advanced research, are actively developed through most departments. Many are approved by the Great Lakes Colleges Association, Inc. (GLCA), a highly regarded academic consortium of twelve independent institutions. Programs include the Philadelphia Center, the GLCA New York Arts Program, and the Oak Ridge Science Semester. Other cooperative arrangements include the Newberry Library Program, Wesleyan in Washington, and the Drew University United Nations Semester. Research is done locally at the U.S. Department of Agriculture (USDA) Laboratories in Delaware, the nearby Columbus Zoo, The Wilds, and several other sites.

Ohio Wesleyan has been long committed to education for a global society. The curriculum has an international perspective, a significant portion of the student body is drawn from other countries, and a wide variety of opportunities are offered overseas. Students can arrange individual projects, but formal programs are offered in more than twenty countries. These include Ohio Wesleyan's affiliation with the University of Salamanca in Spain as well as programs in Mexico, Ireland, Central Europe, Turkey, Africa, China, England, India/Nepal, Japan, Russia, and others.

Academic Facilities

The Beeghly Library houses more than 550,000 holdings, one of the largest collections in the country for a private university of Ohio Wesleyan's size. The library's federal documents depository is among the nation's oldest and largest, providing an additional 200,000 reference publications. Beeghly Library also offers the Online Computer Library Center's most advanced cataloging system. The collection is enhanced by OhioLINK and CONSORT membership. An Internet Café within the Beeghly Library provides students with a 24-hour study area. The café has eight computer workstations and wireless capabilities and serves Starbucks coffee and other assorted sandwiches and snacks.

The comprehensive academic computing system is accessible to students 24 hours per day, and all residence hall rooms are wired for campus network and global Internet access.

The Conrades-Wetherell Science Center includes a 145,000-square-foot three-level building that houses a wide variety of state-of-the-art instrumentation, including a scanning electron microscope and scanning and transmission electron microscopes, all for undergraduate use. Located in the Science Center is the Hobson Science Library, which consolidates all of OWU's science holdings.

The Woltemade Center for Economics, Business, and Entrepreneurship; the Department of Economics; the Sagan Academic Resource Center, which houses the Writing Resource Center, the Academic Skills Center, and the Quantitative Skills Center; and Information Systems are located in the R. W. Corns Building. The University has a state-of-the-art Geographic Information Systems Computer Laboratory.

Perkins Observatory features a 32-inch reflecting telescope and two smaller instruments, while an on-campus student observatory includes a 9.5-in refracting telescope. Two University wilderness preserves cover a total of 100 acres. Other special facilities are the multistage Chappelear Drama Center; Sanborn Hall, home to the Music Department, Jemison Auditorium, and the Kinnison Music Library; and the 1,100-seat Gray Chapel, which houses the largest of only six Klais concert organs in the United States.

Costs

The general fee for 2007–08 is $39,960. This amount covers tuition and fees ($31,930) and room and board ($8030). Books and personal expenses average $1100. Nominal fees are charged for some studio art courses, off-campus study, private music lessons for students who are not majoring in music, and student teaching.

Financial Aid

Nearly all first-year students who demonstrate need have been awarded an aid package. Packages include grant, loan, and employment assistance from Ohio Wesleyan and the standard federal and state programs (such as Federal Pell Grant, Federal Stafford Student Loan, Federal Perkins Loan, and Federal Work-Study). More than two thirds of the student body receive some form of need-based aid, and another quarter receive merit- or non-need-based aid. More than 75 percent of all aid is provided by grants and scholarships. On the average, students on financial aid at Ohio Wesleyan receive more scholarship and grant assistance and rely less on loan support than do students at most other institutions.

Several merit scholarship programs worth as much as $31,510 per year, private loan programs, and flexible payment plans are available without regard to financial need. This year, more than 140 enrolling first-year students received merit awards.

Faculty

The full-time faculty numbers 138, providing a student-faculty ratio of approximately 13:1. Nearly 100 percent of the full-time faculty members hold the highest degree in their fields. Although committed first to teaching and advising, most faculty members maintain active research programs and publish important articles and books. Some members of the faculty are practicing artists whose contributions include the creation and exhibition of original works of art and theater.

Student Government

Students have a significant voice in the government of campus life. The Wesleyan Council on Student Affairs formulates basic policy. Students also sit on judicial boards and nine faculty committees and are represented at all meetings of the Board of Trustees.

Admission Requirements

The admission process is competitive. Each application is carefully studied on an individual basis. Although the applicant's academic record is most important, followed closely by teacher and counselor evaluations and SAT or ACT scores, many other factors are considered, such as evidence of creativity, community service, and leadership. A sixteen-course preparatory program is required. Four units of English and 3 each of mathematics, social studies, science, and foreign language are recommended, but variations of this program are considered. SAT Subject Tests are not required but may qualify students for advanced placement. Candidates for the Bachelor of Music degree must audition (tapes are accepted). Early action, early decision, and transfer admission are offered. Campus interviews are strongly recommended but not required. For the 2007–08 school year, approximately 3,800 applications were received; about 65 percent of the applicants gained admission.

Application and Information

Students are urged to complete the application process as early as possible in the senior year of secondary school, especially if they are applying for financial aid. Once complete credentials (application, transcript, recommendations, and SAT or ACT scores) are received, decisions are made on a rolling basis after January 1. The student's response is required by May 1. The deadline for early decision application is December 1; the deadline for early action application is December 15. Notification is given within four weeks. After April 1, students are admitted on a space-available, rolling admission basis.

For further information, students should contact:

Office of Admission
Ohio Wesleyan University
Delaware, Ohio 43015
Phone: 740-368-3020
800-922-8953 (toll-free)
Fax: 740-368-3314
E-mail: owuadmit@owu.edu
Web site: http://www.owu.edu

The Hamilton-Williams Campus Center is a magnificent meeting place for the campus community.

COLLEGE DATA CENTER • OHIO

OTTERBEIN COLLEGE

WESTERVILLE, OHIO

The College

Otterbein College, a private, coeducational institution affiliated with the United Methodist Church, blends the traditional and contemporary and continues to pride itself on offering a comprehensive liberal arts education. Its 2,357 full-time and 750 part-time students come from all over the United States and several countries, but most, including 392 graduate students, are from Ohio. Founded in 1847 with only two buildings on 8 acres of land, Otterbein has since grown to fifty buildings on 140 acres in the heart of historic Westerville, Ohio, a suburb of Columbus.

The College offers a wide range of extracurricular activities. They include theater productions, vocal and instrumental ensembles, religious programming activities, the *Tan and Cardinal* weekly student newspaper, the campus radio station (WOBN), the Otterbein-Westerville television station (WOCC), and intramural and intercollegiate athletics. Otterbein men and women compete in the Ohio Athletic Conference, NCAA Division III. There are eight varsity sports for men and eight for women. The Rike Physical Education–Recreation Center is the home for men's and women's athletics and physical education facilities and includes racquetball and tennis courts, an indoor track, a weight room, and seating for 3,000. The Clements Recreation Center allows students to participate in a wide range of personal wellness opportunities. Seven local fraternities and six local sororities attract approximately 22 percent of Otterbein's students. Roush Hall, a multipurpose, handicapped-accessible building, houses academic departments, multimedia classrooms, contemporary conference rooms, a gallery, and a computer center. In fall 2006, the College dedicated a new facility for the Department of Art and, in fall 2007, a new facility for the Department of Communication. The state-of-the-art facility is designed to house all art and communication majors.

A Master of Science in Nursing program is offered for students who have completed a four-year baccalaureate program. Majors are offered in adult health care, adult nurse practitioner studies, family nurse practitioner studies, and nursing service administration.

A Master of Arts in Teaching (M.A.T.) degree program is available to qualified liberal arts graduates to prepare for teacher certification in elementary education or secondary education—biology (life science), computer science, English, and mathematics. A Master of Arts in Education (M.A.E.) degree program is available to certified teachers. Majors are offered in curriculum and instruction, reading, and teacher leadership and supervision. Otterbein also offers an M.B.A. program.

Location

Otterbein is located in Westerville, Ohio, 20 minutes from downtown Columbus, one of the fastest-growing cities in the Midwest and Northeast. The College's proximity to Columbus means more than access to entertainment and recreation; as a thriving business center, the city provides many internship opportunities for students that often lead to full-time employment after graduation. The College is easily accessible from Interstates 71 and 270 and is close to the Port Columbus International Airport.

Majors and Degrees

The Bachelor of Arts degree is offered in accounting, allied health, art, athletic training, broadcasting, business administration, chemistry, computer science, economics, English, environmental science, equine science, French, health education, health promotion and fitness, history, individualized, international studies, journalism, life science, mathematics, music, music and business, organizational communication, philosophy, physical education, physics, political science, psychology, public accounting, public relations, religion, secondary education, sociology, Spanish, speech communication, sports management, and theater.

The Bachelor of Science degree is offered in accounting, actuarial science, athletic training, biochemistry, business administration, chemistry, computer science, cooperative engineering, economics, environmental science, equine science, life science, mathematics, molecular biology, physics, physical science, psychology, and public accounting. The Bachelor of Science in Education is awarded in early childhood education and middle childhood education. The Bachelor of Science in Nursing degree is also offered.

The Bachelor of Fine Arts is available in acting, musical theater, musical theater with a concentration in dance, and theater design and technology. The Bachelor of Music Education prepares students for teaching careers in music. The Bachelor of Music degree is offered for students interested in performance careers.

Preprofessional programs are offered in dentistry, law, medicine, optometry, physical therapy, and veterinary medicine.

A dual degree in engineering is offered in conjunction with Washington University in St. Louis and Case Western Reserve University in Cleveland.

Minors are offered in accounting, arts administration, athletic training, black studies, broadcasting, business, chemistry, coaching, computer science, dance, economics, English, French, geology, health sciences, history, mathematics, music, philosophy, physical education, physics, political science, psychology, public relations, religion, sign language, sociology, sound production, Spanish, speech communication, visual art, and women's studies.

Academic Programs

Otterbein College offers a program of liberal arts education in the Christian tradition. The College encourages serious dialogue so that students develop to serve within the community. The fulfillment of this purpose requires students to read well, write well, think clearly, and identify ideas; know how to discuss, listen, and seek data; and have the abilities of synthesis and creativity.

Graduation with a bachelor's degree from the College requires successful completion of 180 quarter hours, of which 50 quarter hours are in core requirements offered under the title of Integrative Studies in Human Nature. The College's quarter calendar lends itself to the wide variety of internships and other off-campus educational opportunities offered by the College. The academic year begins in mid-September and ends in early June.

Through other academic opportunities, students may design an individualized major as well as receive advanced placement by examination and credit through CLEP examinations in some academic areas.

Off-Campus Programs

A variety of off-campus programs are available, including foreign language study in Dijon, France. Study opportunities also exist with the Washington Semester Plan, operated through the American University in Washington, D.C., and with the Philadelphia Center. The Roehampton Exchange, located in the Wimbledon area of London, England, consists of a federation of four institutions, providing students with many cultural opportunities.

Academic Facilities

Roush Hall houses state-of-the-art computer labs, classrooms, a multimedia room, a two-story art gallery, and faculty and administrative offices. The Courtright Memorial Library houses 400,000 books, periodicals, microforms, federal government publications, videotapes, DVDs, CDs, CD-ROMs, and other instructional materials. The McFadden-Schear Science Hall has modern laboratories and classrooms and a renovated planetarium and observatory. Cowan Hall houses modern facilities for speech and theater. The Battelle Fine Arts Center is the home for programs in music and dance and also houses an electronic music laboratory. Historic Towers Hall, a campus landmark since 1870, had an $8.5-million renovation in 1999–2000 and houses classrooms, faculty offices, and updated math and computer science labs. The new art and communication facility houses classrooms; state-of-the-art studio space; an art gallery; the studios of the Otterbein-Westerville television station, WOCC; and the campus radio station, WOBN-FM.

Costs

For 2007–08, Otterbein's tuition and fees were $25,065. Room and board cost $7149 per year. Books and supplies amount to approximately $600–$700 per year.

Financial Aid

Otterbein offers a wide variety of scholarships and grants, including Presidential Scholar Awards, Otterbein Scholar Awards, Endowed Scholarships, Dean's Scholarships, Community Service Awards, Talent Awards, Federal Pell Grants, Ohio Instructional Grants, and Ammons-Thomas minority scholarships. In addition, Federal Perkins Loans, Federal Stafford Student Loans, and United Methodist Student Loans are available. To be considered for need-based College financial aid, students must file the Free Application for Federal Student Aid (FAFSA). Otterbein's financial aid policy is to attempt to meet the financial need of each full-time dependent and independent student offered admission who files financial aid forms by April 1. Approximately 95 percent of Otterbein's students receive some form of financial aid. In addition to its need-based awards, the College offers scholarships to students on the basis of academic ability and proven talent.

Faculty

Otterbein has a faculty of 287 members (giving a student-faculty ratio of 12:1). Ninety-five percent of the full-time faculty members hold a doctorate or appropriate terminal degree. Faculty members are actively involved in campus governance, committees, and activities. The extensive sabbatical plan at Otterbein helps ensure that the faculty members constantly update and improve their classroom teaching.

Student Government

Otterbein's governance program gives students a voting voice, along with faculty members and administrators, on all campus policymaking and decision-making bodies. Students are elected to the College Senate, all governance committees, and the College's Board of Trustees.

Admission Requirements

To be considered for admission to Otterbein College, students must complete and sign an admission application, submit an official copy of their high school transcript, and provide the College with their scores on either the ACT or SAT. Applicants should have a solid high school academic record with at least 16 college-preparatory units. Otterbein does not discriminate on the basis of sex, race, gender, sexual orientation, age, political affiliation, national origin, or disabling condition in the admission of students, educational policies, financial aid and scholarships, housing, athletics, employment, and other activities. Inquiries regarding compliance with federal nondiscrimination regulations may be directed to the chairperson of the Affirmative Action Committee, the vice president for academic affairs, or the vice president for business affairs.

Students can gain a fuller understanding of student life at Otterbein by spending a day on campus. Prospective students are welcome to visit classes, eat in the Campus Center, and talk informally with Otterbein students and should simply notify the Office of Admission in advance so arrangements can be made.

Application and Information

Students are urged to begin the application process early in their senior year of high school. Applicants are notified of their admission status as soon as their application file is completed. Otterbein College's application is available on the Web at http://www.otterbein.edu/admission/applying/application.asp.

For further information, students should contact:

Office of Admission
Otterbein College
One Otterbein College
Westerville, Ohio 43081
Phone: 614-823-1500
800-488-8144 or 877-OTTERBEIN (toll-free)
E-mail: uotterb@otterbein.edu
Web site: http://www.otterbein.edu

Students on the campus of Otterbein College.

TIFFIN UNIVERSITY

TIFFIN, OHIO

The University

Tiffin University (TU), established in 1888, is an independent, coeducational institution of higher learning that enrolls approximately 2,300 students in undergraduate and graduate degree programs. TU is set on a 108-acre campus in Tiffin, Ohio.

Because part of the college experience takes place outside the classroom, Tiffin University students are strongly encouraged to get involved. TU offers students a variety of opportunities, including social clubs, entertainment events, academic organizations, and community service. Some of the clubs or organizations that students can join are academic clubs, band, campus newspaper, NightWatch, the residence hall council, theater, and vocal music.

TU is a member of the National Collegiate Athletic Association, Great Lakes Intercollegiate Athletic Conference, and NCAA Division II. TU participates in intercollegiate athletics for men in baseball, basketball, cross-country, equestrian, football, golf, soccer, tennis, and track and field. Women's intercollegiate athletics are available in basketball, cross-country, equestrian, golf, soccer, softball, tennis, track and field, and volleyball.

TU also sponsors coed club and recreational sports, such as bowling, cheerleading, dance, equestrian, inline hockey, martial arts, men's volleyball, and outdoor adventure.

TU also offers three graduate programs: the Master of Business Administration, Master of Humanities, and Master of Science in Criminal Justice, which includes concentrations in crime analysis, criminal behavior, forensic psychology, homeland security administration, and justice administration.

The University is accredited by the Commission on Institutions of Higher Education of the North Central Association of Colleges and Schools. The Bachelor of Business Administration and Master of Business Administration degrees offered by TU are accredited by the Association of Collegiate Business Schools and Programs.

Location

Tiffin University is located on State Route 53 in Tiffin, Ohio, 50 miles south of Toledo, 90 miles southwest of Cleveland, and 90 miles north of Columbus. With a population of approximately 20,000, Tiffin offers residents and visitors a variety of restaurants, historic sites, and shopping and recreational opportunities. Tiffin is also the home of the historic Ritz Theatre, which offers a wide selection of cultural events throughout the year.

Majors and Degrees

Tiffin University has created a strong academic tradition and offers undergraduate degree programs in three schools: arts and sciences, business, and criminal justice and social sciences.

The Bachelor of Arts degree is offered in arts administration, communication, education, English, government and national security, history, law and society, and psychology. Tiffin also offers an Associate of Arts degree in general studies.

The Bachelor of Business Administration degree is awarded in accounting, computer and information technology, equine management, finance, management, marketing, organizational management, and sports and recreation management. Tiffin also offers an Associate of Business Administration degree, which is conferred in accounting, business, and information technology.

The Bachelor of Criminal Justice degree is offered in corrections, forensic psychology, forensic science, homeland security/terrorism, and law enforcement, and the Associate of Criminal Justice degree is granted in law enforcement.

Teacher education programs are offered through a partnership with Lourdes College, and the Associate of Arts in paraprofessional education is offered as a joint program with Heidelberg College.

Academic Programs

Along with their regular course work, students must also participate in TU's cocurricular program. This program provides students with the opportunity to develop an interest in such areas as health and personal fitness, recreation, the arts, and community service. Students are required to participate in 26 clock hours (2 units) of cocurricular activity in order to graduate.

Off-Campus Programs

Education at TU is more than classrooms and textbooks. Students can also choose to study abroad or complete an internship in exciting places like Washington, D.C. TU participates in several semester-abroad programs, with campuses located in Geneva, Leiden, London, Shanghai, and Vienna. All courses are taught in English and are accredited in the United States.

TU also encourages students to gain practical work experience by participating in an internship. Internships provide students with the opportunity to receive extensive training, responsibility, and hands-on experience in addition to their academic study at TU.

Academic Facilities

The Tiffin campus is a blend of traditional historic and modern buildings that create a vibrant and warm home for an educational community. The focal point of the campus is Main Classroom Building, which was built in 1884 and is now listed on the National Register of Historic Places. The building houses classrooms, faculty and administrative offices, and a computer center.

The Richard C. Pfeiffer Library has an extensive collection of books, subscriptions to magazines and newspapers, microfiche units, and computers for online searching. The library is a member of OhioLINK and Online Computer Library Center (OCLC).

The Hayes Center for the Arts and the Hertzer Technology Center were two additions to the campus in 2004. The Hayes Center for the Arts includes an art gallery, two art studios, music rehearsal rooms, and faculty offices. The Hertzer Technology Center features faculty offices, the Information Technology Services Department, and classrooms with up-to-date technology.

Costs

Tuition for 2008–09 is $17,220 for full-time students and $574 per credit hour for part-time students. The average room and board charges are $7580. Books and supplies are approximately $1000.

Financial Aid

More than 90 percent of all students at Tiffin University receive some type of financial aid. The average financial aid package for 2006–07 was $14,000. Aid is available in the form of scholarships, grants, and loans. A complete Free Application for Federal Student Aid (FAFSA) is required for financial aid consideration. Some scholarships and grants require special applications, tests, or recommendations from counselors, teachers, and coaches. Additional information can be obtained from the Financial Aid Office.

Faculty

The low student-faculty ratio and small class size create a close and personal atmosphere at Tiffin University. The TU faculty members are accessible to students and show genuine interest in their academic and personal concerns.

The TU faculty consists of 133 dedicated individuals serving in either a full-time or adjunct capacity. More than 80 percent of the full-time faculty members hold doctorates or the highest certification in their field. Many faculty members are involved in the business community or other organizations in either a research or consulting capacity and many are actively involved in regional and national academic organizations.

Admission Requirements

Individuals wishing to further their education are invited to apply to Tiffin University. Applicants must have earned a diploma from an accredited high school in a college-preparatory course of study or a GED certificate. It is also required that the applicant's high school curriculum include 4 units of English, 3 units of math, 3 units of science, and 3 units of social studies. Students with a minimum 3.0 grade point average on a 4.0 scale in college-preparatory classes and an ACT score of at least 20 or an SAT score of at least 890 receive priority in the admission process.

Application and Information

Students must submit a completed application, an official copy of their high school transcript, their ACT or SAT scores, and the $20 application fee to Tiffin University's Office of Undergraduate Admissions. The application fee is waived for students who apply online at the University's Web site (http://www.tiffin.edu).

For further information, students should contact:

Jeremy Marinis, Director of Admissions
Tiffin University
155 Miami Street
Tiffin, Ohio 44883
Phone: 419-448-3423
800-968-OHIO (toll-free)
Fax: 419-443-5006
E-mail: admiss@tiffin.edu
Web site: http://www.tiffin.edu

Franks Hall, on the campus of Tiffin University.

COLLEGE DATA CENTER • OHIO

UNIVERSITY OF DAYTON

DAYTON, OHIO

The University

Established in 1850 by the Marianists, the University of Dayton (UD) is a top-10 national Catholic university, committed to educating students as value-centered leaders in their chosen professions and in society. More than 10,000 students attend UD, including 6,900 full-time undergraduate students. Students attracted to the University come from most states and many countries. UD offers a vibrant campus life, as more than 90 percent of undergraduates live in residence halls and the student neighborhood. The technology-enhanced learning and student computer initiative provides every student living in a UD residence with high-speed data access to learning resources and collaboration tools. Extensive programs of study are offered in the College of Arts and Sciences and in the Schools of Business Administration, Education and Allied Professions, Engineering, and Law.

The residential nature of the campus encourages active extracurricular involvement. More than 180 clubs and organizations exist on campus, including more than thirty service organizations, forty academic/professional clubs, fifteen honor societies, recreation/sports clubs, theatrical and musical performance groups, and fraternities and sororities. A variety of special events include everything from symposia and concerts to parents' weekends and a huge Christmas on Campus celebration each December 8.

Whether they're on the field or in the stands, UD students show their spirit. UD's intercollegiate sports teams compete at the NCAA Division I level, and 70 percent of students participate in intramural activities. Men's intercollegiate teams include baseball, basketball, cross-country, football, golf, soccer, and tennis. Women's intercollegiate sports include basketball, crew, cross-country, golf, indoor and outdoor track, soccer, softball, tennis, and volleyball. Club sports such as lacrosse, rugby, and soccer are also popular.

The John F. Kennedy Memorial Student Union offers a variety of services for the University community, including numerous cultural, educational, recreational, and social activities. The facility includes a theater; a food court containing a pizzeria, bakery, grill, and delicatessen; Flyer TV, a student-run television station; The Galley, a student-operated snack shop; and The Hangar, a games room providing bowling lanes, billiards, a cyber café, video games, and lounge and performance spaces.

Location

The campus is located on 259 acres, 2 miles from the city of Dayton. The Dayton metropolitan area is a vibrant, growing community of approximately 950,000 people in southwestern Ohio. Top cultural, recreational, and entertainment programs are available during the year. Varied business, industrial, research, and educational enterprises provide students with extensive work opportunities related to their academic disciplines.

Majors and Degrees

The College of Arts and Sciences offers the Bachelor of Arts degree in American studies, art history, chemistry, communication (communication management, electronic media, journalism, public relations, and theater), criminal justice studies, economics, English, fine arts, history, international studies and human rights, languages (French, German, and Spanish), mathematics, music, philosophy, photography, political science, psychology, religious studies, sociology, theater, visual communication design, and women's and gender studies.

The Bachelor of Science is awarded in applied mathematical economics, biochemistry, biology, chemistry, computer information systems, computer science, environmental biology, environmental geology, geology, mathematics, physical science, physics, physics–computer science, predentistry, premedicine, and psychology.

The School of Business Administration offers the Bachelor of Science degree in accounting, business economics, entrepreneurship (available sophomore year), finance, international business, management information systems, management (leadership), marketing, and operations management.

The Bachelor of Science in Education is awarded in the ADA didactic program in dietetics, exercise science/fitness management, exercise science/fitness and nutrition, exercise science/pre–physical therapy, physical education, and sport management through the Department of Health and Sport Science. Through the Department of Teacher Education, a Bachelor of Science degree is awarded in adolescence to young adult education, art education, early childhood education, foreign language education, intervention specialist (special education), middle childhood education, and special secondary Catholic religious education.

The School of Engineering awards the Bachelor of Chemical Engineering, Bachelor of Civil Engineering, Bachelor of Science in Computer Engineering, Bachelor of Electrical Engineering, and Bachelor of Mechanical Engineering. The School of Engineering also offers a Bachelor of Science in engineering technology, one of the few four-year programs available in the country. Programs include computer engineering technology, electronic engineering technology, industrial engineering technology, manufacturing engineering technology, and mechanical engineering technology. The Integrated Arts and Technology Program is available to students who wish to combine their interests in arts and engineering technology.

The University also offers the Bachelor of Fine Arts (art education, fine arts, photography, and visual communication design), Bachelor of Music (music composition, music education, music performance, and music therapy), and Bachelor of General Studies. Undeclared admission options are offered in the College of Arts and Sciences and the Schools of Business Administration, Education and Allied Professions, and Engineering. A prelaw program (including advising and assistance in course selection) is available to students in all degree programs.

Academic Programs

The academic year consists of two semesters, with two 6-week sessions available during the summer. While graduation requirements vary according to academic majors, a minimum of 120 semester credit hours is required of all bachelor's degree programs. Students following four-year programs must successfully complete requirements in communication, English, and mathematics. Likewise, the University has instituted a program of study for all students that provides a general education in the humanities, arts, and social and natural sciences. This program develops students' abilities to integrate their knowledge and express themselves effectively. Students are also encouraged to integrate traditional academic studies with experiential innovative programs, such as education abroad, cooperative education, and internship programs; a bachelor's degree and teacher certification; and multidisciplinary programs.

The University offers two distinct programs for its most academically accomplished students—the University Honors Program and the John W. Berry Sr. Scholars Program. The programs' academic benefits and privileges are numerous and multifaceted, but both offer UD students an enhanced undergraduate education through research, international experiences, and service and leadership opportunities.

Academic Facilities

In recent years, there have been several new additions to the University of Dayton's campus. ArtStreet, an innovative living and learning complex, combines student residence quarters with performance and visual arts spaces, a recording studio, a radio station, and a café. The Arena Sports Complex is home to athletic venues used by UD intercollegiate teams. Recent construction added a practice track and football practice field, a baseball facility, an area for long jumping and pole vault, a softball field, and track throwing fields. UD's newest residence hall, Marianist Hall, includes student housing, a bookstore, a post office, a credit union, a food emporium, worship space, and a learning center. The student housing component consists of three 4-story residential wings with a total of 400 beds.

The RecPlex, a fitness and recreation complex containing state-of-the-art equipment and facilities, opened in 2006. The RecPlex houses four courts for basketball and volleyball; three racquetball courts; two courts for aerobics, basketball, floor hockey, inline hockey, lacrosse, soccer, tennis, and volleyball; two aerobics/multipurpose rooms; sixty cardiovascular machines; selectorized weight machines; a free-weight area; a ⅛-mile track; administrative offices; classrooms; a climbing wall; a juice bar; a lounge; men's and women's locker rooms; an eight-lane natatorium; an outdoor deck; a sand volleyball court; and a whirlpool.

Other recently completed campus construction projects include Kettering Laboratories, home to the School of Engineering and part of the University of Dayton Research Institute. Recent renovations added a five-story tower for classroom space and a lounge, updated classroom and laboratory spaces, an Innovation Center, and new exterior walkways and lawn seating.

The Science Center, a 44,000-square-foot facility that connects Sherman and Wohlleben Halls, provides laboratories, classrooms, offices, and gathering spaces. In summer 2007, UD completed renovations to Marycrest Complex, which houses 900 students. In addition, University-owned houses in the student neighborhood have been and continue to be rebuilt or renovated.

Existing campus facilities include the recently renovated Miriam Hall, home of the School of Business Administration, the Davis Center for Portfolio Management, and the Crotty Center for Entrepreneurial Leadership. Opened in 2000, the Ryan C. Harris Learning-Teaching Center is a high-tech experimental learning space that includes a meeting room with groupware capability and an adaptive computer lab to help students with physical or learning disabilities. Roesch Library, an eight-story facility with more than 1.3 million volumes, provides exceptional resources for research and scholarship. The Anderson Information Sciences Center, a $3.5-million complex donated to the University by NCR Corporation, contains state-of-the-art undergraduate computer laboratories and classrooms. The University's nationally famous general education program is housed in the Jesse Philips Center for the Humanities, which opened in fall 1993. The $4.3-million Donoher Basketball Center, a 23,000-square-foot, NBA-quality facility, opened in fall 1998.

Costs

Tuition, including the University fee, for 2007–08 is $12,975 per semester. The cost of a double room in a residence hall is $2275 per semester. Private and University-owned accommodations are available in the student neighborhood for upperclass students. Five types of meal plan contracts are available, ranging from $1525 to $1780 per term. To cover weekend meals and other food expenses, students may open a debit account, Flyer Express, which is accepted at most on-campus locations as well as select off-campus vendors.

Financial Aid

The University of Dayton is one of the most affordable private Catholic schools in the country. In 2006, more than 97 percent of incoming first-year UD students received some form of institutional aid (scholarships and grants). Last year, the University of Dayton provided $42 million in institutional aid to students.

UD's extensive academic scholarship program recognizes the academic excellence of high school seniors. Students interested in majoring in any academic program are considered for these awards based on their ACT or SAT scores. To be considered for an academic scholarship, students must submit either UD's Application for Undergraduate Admission and Scholarship or the Common Application. Although the University prefers early submission, the application priority date is December 15.

Athletic scholarships are available in men's intercollegiate baseball, basketball, cross-country, golf, soccer, and tennis as well as women's intercollegiate basketball, cross-country, indoor/outdoor track, soccer, softball, tennis, and volleyball. Athletic scholarship eligibility is determined by the Department of Intercollegiate Athletics.

Music awards are available for both music majors and nonmajors who distinguish themselves as outstanding performers at their admission audition. Scholarships for musical or visual art talents are determined by the faculties of the appropriate academic departments.

UD offers additional financial assistance in the form of nonrepayable grants, educational loans, and part-time employment. A parent loan program and a University-sponsored payment plan are available. Students applying for federal, state, and University-sponsored financial aid must complete the Free Application for Federal Student Aid (FAFSA). Priority is given to applications received by March 31.

A financial aid counselor is available to meet with interested students and their parents to review information pertaining to financial aid eligibility. High school seniors and their parents who are interested in receiving an estimate of financial aid eligibility are encouraged to request an appointment when scheduling a campus visit and should bring a copy of their completed FAFSA so their eligibility for aid can be discussed in detail.

Faculty

There are 458 full-time faculty members, 91 percent of whom hold a Ph.D. or terminal degree. UD faculty members have been recognized for their excellence by several organizations, including General Motors Corporation, the National Institute of Education, and the National Endowment for the Humanities. Professors are actively engaged in research and scholarship, often involving undergraduate students, but their primary focus is teaching. With an average class size of 27, faculty members are able to create an interactive learning environment and offer personal attention to each student. Faculty members act as advisers to students and are frequently accessible in and out of the classroom.

Student Government

The Student Government Association (SGA) is an autonomous association that concerns itself with the academic, recreational, and cultural welfare of UD students. SGA support prompted the opening of UD's first student-owned and -operated convenience store. The organization's efforts were instrumental in creating the National Association for Students at Catholic Colleges and Universities, which addresses the specific concerns of Catholic campuses.

Admission Requirements

The University of Dayton admits qualified students regardless of sex, race, color, creed, national or ethnic origin, age, or handicap. Students possessing the aptitude and motivation to succeed at UD are encouraged to apply for admission. Balanced consideration is given to all aspects of students' demonstrated preparation, including selection of college-preparatory courses, grade point average and grade pattern throughout high school, class rank, standardized test scores (ACT or SAT), and record of leadership and service. A personal statement and guidance counselor recommendation are required. In recent years, more than 80 percent of entering students graduated in the top half of their high school class.

Applicants should present 16 core units from an accredited high school. The minimum core includes 4 units in English, 4 electives, 3 in math, 3 in social studies, and 2 in science. Some programs may require more extensive preparation in specific subject areas. Two units of a foreign language are required for admission to the College of Arts and Sciences. Students who plan to major in a natural science, mathematics, computer science, engineering, or business will find a strong mathematics background necessary.

Application and Information

To apply to the University of Dayton, students can submit either UD's online Application for Undergraduate Admission and Scholarship or the Common Application. Applicants must also submit a satisfactory high school record, results of the ACT or SAT examination, and a guidance counselor recommendation. The University operates on a rolling admission policy; however, the priority application date is December 15. The first notifications of acceptance are mailed in October. Some academic programs close new student enrollment before others, so it is recommended that students apply as early as possible.

The UD admission Web site allows students to apply for admission and scholarship, check the status of their application, and take a virtual tour.

Office of Admission
University of Dayton
300 College Park
Dayton, Ohio 45469-1300
Phone: 800-UD PRIDE (800-837-7433) (toll-free)
E-mail: admission@udayton.edu
Internet: http://admission.udayton.edu

THE UNIVERSITY OF FINDLAY

FINDLAY, OHIO

The University

The University of Findlay (UF) is a private coeducational institution with more than 4,500 full- and part-time students. Founded in 1882 by the Churches of God, General Conference, it emphasizes preparation for careers and professions in an educational program that blends liberal arts and career education. Students of many denominations attend Findlay, and religious participation is a matter of personal choice.

Bachelor's degree programs are available in more than sixty different majors. Master's degrees are offered in athletic training; business administration; education; environmental, safety, and health management; liberal studies; occupational therapy; physical therapy; and teaching English to speakers of other languages (TESOL). A new Doctor of Pharmacy (Pharm.D.) degree program is expected to graduate its first class in 2010.

The largest programs at Findlay are business, education, equestrian studies, pharmacy, and pre–veterinary medicine. Majors in the sciences and health professions include athletic training, chemistry, computer science, equestrian studies (English, Western, and equine management), nuclear medicine, occupational therapy, physical therapy, physician assistant studies, premedicine, and pre–veterinary medicine. Business degrees are founded in a comprehensive core program with eleven different majors.

Opportunities for internships and work-related experiences are available in most major fields through the Professional Experience Program (PEP).

Most of Findlay's students come from Ohio and the surrounding states of Michigan, Indiana, and Pennsylvania. More than thirty other states are also represented. UF also has a strong international-student population, with more than 800 international students from thirty countries.

Resident students live in eight modern residence halls and several town-house-style apartments. Social life at Findlay centers on student organizations, fraternities, and sororities. Findlay has three officially recognized fraternities: Alpha Sigma Phi, Tau Kappa Epsilon, and Theta Chi; there are two sororities: Phi Sigma Sigma and Sigma Kappa. Organizations include department and special interest clubs, the newspaper, musical groups, a radio and TV station, Circle K, and Aristos Eklektos (honors).

Athletic programs are affiliated with NCAA Division II and the Great Lakes Intercollegiate Athletic Conference, with the exception of the equestrian teams, which have won national championships in the Intercollegiate Horse Show Association. Findlay offers twelve intercollegiate sports for men: baseball, basketball, cross-country, equestrian, football, golf, indoor track and field, outdoor track and field, soccer, swimming and diving, tennis, and wrestling. It has eleven varsity sports for women: basketball, cross-country, equestrian, golf, indoor track and field, outdoor track and field, soccer, softball, swimming and diving, tennis, and volleyball. Athletic scholarships are available.

Croy Physical Education Center has a 25-meter swimming pool, exercise areas, a gymnasium, offices, and classrooms. The Gardner Fitness Center is a state-of-the-art facility. The 130,000-square-foot Koehler Recreation and Fitness Complex, opened in 1999, contains the Malcolm Athletic Center, with a six-lane, NCAA regulation track and four multipurpose courts; the Clauss Ice Arena; locker rooms; and offices for the athletic department.

Student services include career and placement counseling, the Cosiano Health Center, academic tutoring and personal counseling, and study skills assistance through the Academic Support Center.

Location

Findlay was voted the most livable micropolitan city in Ohio and scored among the top twelve in the United States. It is within easy driving distance of Toledo, Columbus, Detroit, and Fort Wayne. Interstate 75 and the Ohio Turnpike (Interstates 80 and 90) are major highways serving the area. Airports in Toledo, Columbus, and Detroit are convenient. The town of Findlay has more than 39,000 residents and is home to Marathon Oil Corporation and Cooper Tire and Rubber Company. The Findlay campus consists of more than 200 acres on several sites. A 72-acre campus-owned farm houses the pre–veterinary medicine and Western equestrian studies programs. A second 32-acre facility houses the English riding program. Many opportunities exist for students who want business-related and social service agency experience. The University has established strong relationships with the community, which supports athletic and cultural events on the campus. Besides the full program of on-campus activities, off-campus trips to cultural and entertainment events are scheduled. The city of Findlay, which has an excellent business climate, offers part-time job opportunities, volunteer service organizations, and the chance to be involved with the larger civic community. Findlay's campus is attractive, safe, comfortable, and friendly.

Majors and Degrees

The Bachelor of Arts (B.A.) degree is awarded in the following majors: adolescent/young adult/integrated English/language arts, adolescent/young adult/integrated social studies, art, children's book illustration, criminal justice administration, digital media, English, English as an international language, graphic communication, health communication, history, interpersonal communication, Japanese, journalism, law and the liberal arts, middle childhood/language arts and social studies, multiage/drama/theater, multiage/Japanese, multiage/Spanish, multiage/visual arts, philosophy/applied philosophy, political science, psychology, public relations, religious studies, social work, sociology, Spanish, studio art, teaching English to speakers of other languages, and theater. Minors are offered in numerous areas.

The Bachelor of Science (B.S.) degree is granted in accounting; adolescent/young adult/earth science; adolescent/young adult/integrated mathematics; adolescent/young adult/life science; animal science; biology; business administration; business management; chemistry; computer science; early childhood; economics; entrepreneurship; environmental, safety, and occupational health management; equestrian studies (English and Western emphases); equine business management; finance; forensic science; health education; health studies; hospitality management; human resource management; international business; intervention specialist/mild to moderate disabilities; marketing; mathematics; medical technology; middle childhood/language arts/math; middle childhood/language arts/science; middle childhood/math/science; middle childhood/math/social studies; middle childhood/science/social studies; multiage/health education; multiage/physical education; nuclear medicine technology; occupational therapy; operations and logistics; physical education; physician assistant; physical therapy; premedicine; pre–veterinary medicine; recreation therapy; and strength and conditioning.

The Associate of Arts degree is available in accounting, computer science, criminal justice administration (corrections or law enforcement emphases), English as an international language, equestrian studies (English and Western riding), financial management, general social studies, human resource management, humanities, management information systems, massage therapy, nuclear medicine technology, personal training, religious studies, sales/retail management, and small business/entrepreneurship. Certificate programs are available in a variety of areas.

Academic Programs

Findlay operates on the semester system. Students must complete at least 124 semester hours with a minimum overall grade point average of 2.0 to earn a bachelor's degree. General education requirements and competency requirements in English, computer literacy, and speech must be fulfilled. The Oiler Experience is intended to introduce all freshmen to college life at UF. The course is designed and taught by a cadre of student services professionals whose educational backgrounds and specialized training are focused on assisting students to succeed, both in and out of the classroom. The Foundations Program offers students the chance to develop those skills in writing, reading, and thinking needed for their success as college students. Study skills, time management, and academic advising are included. Students are selected for this program at the time of admission. The Honors Program provides additional challenge to those students who qualify on the basis of academic credentials. Study- and travel-abroad programs are offered by various departments. Credit and/or placement can be earned through Advanced Placement (AP) exams.

The Equestrian Program is a well-recognized program of its kind and serves approximately 250 students from throughout the United States and abroad. Majors in equine business management and in English and Western riding are offered. The instruction, both in the classroom and on horseback, makes use of the expertise of recognized national equestrian champions. The pre–veterinary medicine program, using the farm facilities, offers the advantages of hands-on experience with livestock and an internship program in a distinctive curriculum. Graduates of the pre–veterinary program have been accepted to twenty-seven of twenty-eight veterinary schools in the United States, and several internationally.

The Nuclear Medicine Institute provides the training necessary to qualify students for careers in nuclear medicine technology, a growing health-related career field.

Academic Facilities

The focal point of the Findlay campus is Old Main, which houses classrooms, faculty and administrative offices, the computer center, facilities for various student activities, and the Ritz Auditorium. Shafer Library is a member of a consortium that provides extensive resources to students. The Gardner Fine Arts Pavilion, dedicated in 1994, houses the Mazza Museum of International Art from Children's Books, which is expanding its literacy programming through a 9,000-square-foot addition completed this year. The University has numerous computer labs. Other academic buildings include the Frost Science Center, with a greenhouse and the Newhard Planetarium, and the Egner Center for the Performing Arts, which houses a 200-seat theater and the student-operated radio and television stations. A 101,000-square-foot athletic complex was completed in 1999. This facility houses a six-lane indoor track, sand pits for long jump, a state-of-the-art timing system, and a wrestling room. Also under the same roof is an ice arena with a seating capacity of 1,200. Approximately 450 horses are stabled and trained at the equestrian facilities, which offer barns and indoor and outdoor riding arenas.

Costs

Tuition for the 2007–08 academic year totaled $22,906 for most programs. Room and board cost $8026. The estimated cost for transportation, books, and supplies was $3700. There are additional program surcharges for equestrian studies and pre–veterinary medicine.

Financial Aid

Ninety-nine percent of Findlay students receive financial aid. Assistance is based on need as well as scholastic achievement. In 2006, UF students received approximately $25.1 million in institutional financial aid from the University. The average freshman in 2006 was awarded $11,096 in institutional aid. Merit scholarships at UF range from $7500 to $12,000 a year. Notification of aid awards is made on a rolling basis. Work-study jobs are available. Scholarships for high-achieving students and student athletes are offered.

Faculty

The 16:1 student-faculty ratio results in small classes—usually fewer than 30 students. Professors know their students, and every student has a faculty adviser.

Student Government

The Student Government Association (SGA) and the Campus Program Board are involved in planning and implementing student activities. SGA provides leadership experience for students and enhances cooperation among faculty members, the administration, and students. A representative from SGA sits on the Board of Trustees. The Campus Program Board plans activities for recreation and cultural enrichment.

Admission Requirements

The University of Findlay considers each applicant on an individualized basis. The University accepts applications on a rolling basis, but it encourages students to complete applications by January 15, as the class fills rapidly. Application deadlines are August 1 for the fall semester and December 15 for the spring semester. Major factors associated with rendering a decision include GPA, standardized test scores, and strength of curriculum. Although it is not required, a campus admission visit is encouraged. Applicants to Findlay should have a college-preparatory high school background, including 4 years of English, 3 to 4 years of mathematics, 2 to 3 years of social studies, and 2 years of sciences. A foreign language is recommended but not required. Results of the ACT or SAT should be submitted with the application for admission. Transfer students must be eligible to return to the institution last attended and must submit transcripts of all college work. For students not meeting regular minimum admission requirements, Findlay has a Foundations Program, which provides skill building and academic support during the first semester of the freshman year. Findlay is an equal opportunity institution in admission and employment.

Application and Information

For application forms and other information, students may contact:

Office of Undergraduate Admissions
The University of Findlay
1000 North Main Street
Findlay, Ohio 45840
Phone: 419-434-4732
800-548-0932 (toll-free)
E-mail: admissions@findlay.edu
Web site: http://www.findlay.edu

Old Main.

WALSH UNIVERSITY

NORTH CANTON, OHIO

The University

Walsh University is a fully accredited, liberal arts and sciences Catholic university in North Canton, Ohio, offering fifty majors, five graduate programs, and an accelerated-degree program for working adults. With 2,700 students and a 15:1 student-faculty ratio, the University offers a very friendly, personable, and safe campus and a unique broad-based curriculum with close student-faculty interaction. Most residence halls and academic buildings on Walsh's 136-acre campus are new or have been renovated within the last several years, providing state-of-the-art facilities for students. Walsh also offers generous financial aid packages to 95 percent of full-time students.

Active and involved in campus and community life, more than 60 percent of Walsh students participate in extracurricular programs. Students also enjoy intramural and intercollegiate sports programs that include football, baseball, soccer, and volleyball to name a few. Walsh's Division II NAIA athletic teams have won national championships.

Walsh University welcomes students from around the world of all faiths and backgrounds. The University currently has students from numerous countries and looks forward to continued growth.

Walsh University was founded in 1958 by the Brothers of Christian Instruction and is accredited by the North Central Association of Colleges and Schools, the National League for Nursing Accrediting Commission, and the Commission on Accreditation in Physical Therapy Education. Walsh is a member of the Ohio College Association, the National Association of Independent Colleges and Universities, and the Association of Catholic Colleges and Universities.

In addition to its undergraduate degree programs, Walsh offers five graduate degree programs in business (M.B.A.), counseling and human development, education, physical therapy, and theology.

Location

Walsh University has a beautiful, tree-lined campus located just 3 miles east of I-77 in North Canton, a safe, pleasant residential suburban community. Canton, which is about 5 miles south of the Walsh campus, is a city of 84,000 that offers a wide array of cultural, recreational, and athletic activities. Home of the Professional Football Hall of Fame, the President McKinley National Memorial, and the National First Ladies Library, the city also hosts a symphony orchestra, an art museum, and a civic opera, theater guild, and ballet. A number of major companies are headquartered in Stark County, including the Hoover Company, the Timken Company, and Diebold, Inc.

Majors and Degrees

Bachelor of Arts and Bachelor of Science degrees are offered in the following majors: accounting (general and specialized CPA tracks), bioinformatics, biology, chemistry, clinical laboratory science, communication, computer science, corporate communication, education (early childhood, middle childhood, adolescence to young adulthood, integrated language arts, integrated mathematics teacher licensure, integrated science teacher licensure, integrated social studies teacher, intervention specialist, life science/biology teacher licensure, life science/biology and chemistry teacher licensure, and multiage physical education), English, finance, French, general business, history, international studies, management, management information systems, marketing, mathematics, nursing, philosophy/theology, physical education, political science, psychology, sociology, and Spanish.

Walsh offers preprofessional programs in dentistry, law, medicine, natural resources, optometry, physical therapy, podiatry, and veterinary science. Each is developed within the context of a regular academic major. Walsh's physical therapy graduates have the option to continue their studies by entering Walsh's newly accredited Doctor of Physical Therapy degree program. Students enrolled in the University's B.A./M.A. program can earn a bachelor's degree in behavioral science and a master's degree in counseling and human development in 5½ years. An affiliation with Case Western Reserve University's (CWRU) program in dentistry leads to a B.S. from Walsh and ultimately a D.D.S. from CWRU.

In addition, Walsh offers the Associate of Arts degree in accounting, finance, human services, liberal arts management, and marketing.

Academic Programs

The student's academic program comprises courses within the liberal arts, a major field of study, and elective courses. Major course work, constituting one fourth or more of a student's program of studies, is designed to help students prepare for their careers. Forty percent of a student's program of studies is within the liberal arts. Elective courses, which constitute the remaining portion of a student's program of studies, enable students to develop personal interests, take more courses within their major field, or enroll in additional core courses. The University encourages students to give careful thought to selecting a program of study and a major. While many students select double majors as a way to improve their career opportunities, the design of individual programs requires consultation with a faculty adviser and a division chair. To earn a bachelor's degree, students must successfully complete 130 semester hours.

Designed for the academically gifted, the honors program offers challenges that lead students to achieve academic excellence. Honors students take advantage of such offerings as special seminars, independent studies, internships, and research projects.

The University's School for Professional Studies Program is for working adults who have earned college credits and who wish to earn their bachelor's degree in an accelerated format. Classes are scheduled on nights and weekends to accommodate busy schedules.

Academic Facilities

The Walsh Library contains 130,000 volumes, 630 current periodical subscriptions on paper, thousands of online periodicals, a curriculum library, and an audiovisual collection. Databases bring many full-text articles immediately for download or print, and information technology systems enable online requests for physical delivery of material, often via rapid courier. Library staff members give introductory lectures on research techniques. The library has a quiet study room, a snack lounge, and a mini-theater.

Faculty

Walsh University fosters close working relationships between faculty members and students. Beyond classroom teaching, faculty members serve as student counselors and tutors and take on roles as advisers for student organizations. The Walsh faculty is composed of full-time, part-time, and adjunct members. The student-faculty ratio is 15:1. The majority of full-time faculty members hold Ph.D.'s or terminal degrees in their respective fields.

Student Government

Walsh University Student Government provides capable, responsible student governance. Through its executive, legislative, and judicial branches, it fosters student involvement in the governance of the University, serves as a forum for student opinion, and functions as a liaison between students, faculty and staff members, and the administration. Along with the Student Affairs staff, it plans student activities and community projects.

Costs

Tuition and fees for the 2007–08 academic year were $18,300 plus an $18 per-credit-hour general fee. Room and board charges were approximately $6900 per year and varied by residence hall. Books and personal expenses cost an estimated $700–$900 for the year. The University reserves the right to change the cost structure without notice.

Financial Aid

Walsh is dedicated to providing outstanding liberal arts education at an affordable price. The primary purpose of Walsh University's financial aid program is to assist deserving students who cannot otherwise meet the costs of a college education. Financial aid takes the form of scholarships, work-study awards, grants, or loans, depending upon the resources available. The University offers a number of scholarships in amounts from $1500 to full tuition, in addition to institutional need-based grants. The Alumni Association offers scholarships as well. State and federal grants and loans are available to students along with the University's work-study program that provides work compatible with a student's academic schedule. Financial aid is awarded for one year and is renewable in subsequent years if the student shows a continuing need and maintains an appropriate academic record.

Applicants for admission may apply for financial aid by submitting the Free Application for Federal Student Aid (FAFSA) and the University's financial aid form. To allow for timely notification of financial awards, the University recommends that the FAFSA be mailed by March 15 in order to receive full analysis by May 1. Prospective students may obtain a FAFSA from their high school guidance counselor or from the University's financial aid office. The Walsh financial aid form is available from the financial aid and admissions offices of the University.

Admission Requirements

Every student seeking admission to Walsh University is reviewed individually to asses the student's ability to meet the rigors of the University's curriculum. The average academic credentials of the fall of 2006 freshman class were a cumulative grade point average of 3.28 and a composite ACT score of 21.6. The composition of high school classes, grades achieved, class rank, and standardized test scores are all taken into consideration before an admission decision is rendered. Essays and interviews are highly recommended but not required.

Walsh grants credit for college-level work completed in high school and for credits earned through the College Level Examination Program. Qualified high school juniors and seniors may enroll for college credit under the University's postsecondary enrollment program. The University seeks a diverse student body.

Application and Information

Early application is recommended. Walsh University operates under a rolling admissions policy. The completed admission application, $25 application fee, ACT or SAT scores, and a high school transcript are required for a student's application to be considered for admission. Transfer students must also submit transcripts from all colleges and universities attended.

Interested students are encouraged to contact:

Brett Freshour
Dean of Enrollment Management
Walsh University
2020 East Maple Street NW
North Canton, Ohio 44720-3336
Phone: 330-492-7172
800-362-9846 (toll-free)
Fax: 330-490-7165
E-mail: admissions@walsh.edu
Web site: http://www.walsh.edu

On the campus of Walsh University.

WITTENBERG UNIVERSITY

SPRINGFIELD, OHIO

The University

For more than 160 years, students at Wittenberg University have not only discovered their light, they have passed it on to others—on campus, in the classroom, in their communities, and around the world. Founded in 1845, Wittenberg, a four-year comprehensive liberal arts and sciences college, is affiliated with the Evangelical Lutheran Church in America (ELCA), a connection that helps the University preserve its commitment to producing graduates who have considered their own personal values and take an active interest in the health of their communities.

Wittenberg University provides a liberal arts education dedicated to intellectual inquiry and wholeness of person within a diverse residential community. Reflecting its Lutheran heritage, Wittenberg challenges students to become responsible global citizens, to discover their callings, and to lead personal, professional, and civic lives of creativity, service, compassion, and integrity. Wittenberg's primary purpose is to provide a close, supportive, caring learning environment and a superior teaching faculty committed to the liberal arts and willing to impart knowledge, inspire inquiry, and encourage independent thought.

In keeping with its motto "Having light we pass it on to others," Wittenberg also empowers students to find their light through numerous collaborative research opportunities, a strong commitment to global engagement, and a passion for service both at home and abroad.

Wittenberg is distinguished by its strong interdisciplinary programs, such as the East Asian Studies Program and the Russian Area Studies Program. Although Wittenberg's traditional strengths have been in the liberal arts, the sciences, management, communication, and education have also developed into popular majors for students. One in 4 students chooses a science major designed to emphasize collaborative problem solving among students and collaborative research among students and faculty members. Wittenberg is one of only a handful of colleges in the country to include community service as a graduation requirement. Also, Phi Beta Kappa is one of the many academic honoraries to grace the campus.

The University is accredited by the Higher Learning Commission of the North Central Association of Colleges and Schools and by the American Association of University Women.

Of Wittenberg's 2,000 students, 60 percent come from Ohio. Wittenberg hosts approximately 30 to 40 new international students each year from twenty to thirty countries. Deliberate efforts to maintain cultural, ethnic, social, and economic diversity avoid the homogeneity of many small private colleges and allow Wittenberg's student body to reflect the broader society.

Wittenberg's residential program is based on a philosophy of progressive responsibility. First- and second-year students live in the residence halls. After the second year, students have the opportunity to live in Greek housing or one of the many University-owned rental units in the University district and other theme housing. A modern, 195-bed residence hall designed for new students opened in summer 2006. The award-winning food service catered by Sodexho serves food in the Central Dining Room, a cafeteria-style eatery, and in Post 95, a café-style eatery.

Location

Wittenberg's 95-acre parklike campus is as functional as it is attractive, with beautiful rolling hills, lush green spaces, and numerous mature trees. Its twenty-seven buildings include outstanding facilities for the sciences, arts, and music, as well as comfortable residence halls and excellent recreational and athletics facilities. The school is located in Springfield, Ohio, which is a small city with a population of 65,000 that provides easy access to big-city excitement in nearby Columbus and Dayton.

While Wittenberg plays a major role in the lives of Springfield residents, the community also offers unique opportunities to the University's students. Wittenberg is a major leader in the community's cultural, academic, and athletic life, yet the University sees a great benefit to being in Springfield. The community provides an area rich in cultural opportunities and recreational activities, with lakes, public parkland, nature preserves, bike trails, and public golf courses.

Majors and Degrees

Wittenberg offers the degrees of Bachelor of Arts, Bachelor of Fine Arts, Bachelor of Music, Bachelor of Music Education, and Bachelor of Science. Many students increase the power of their education degree by double majoring or adding a minor. The Bachelor of Arts degree may be earned in American studies, art, biochemistry/molecular biology, chemistry, communication, computer science, East Asian studies, economics, education (early childhood, elementary, and middle childhood licensing), English, geography, geology, history, languages (French, Spanish, and German), management (with concentrations in accounting, finance, human resources, international business, and marketing), mathematics, music, philosophy, physics, political science, psychology, religion, Russian area studies, sociology, and theater. The Bachelor of Science degree is offered in biology, chemistry, computer science, geology, mathematics, physics, and psychology. Minors may be completed in all the above majors and the following: Africana studies, computational science, creative writing, dance, environmental studies, global studies, marine science, music composition, premodern and ancient world studies, urban studies, and women's studies.

Special areas of study include forestry and environmental studies, international education, languages (Chinese, Japanese, and Russian), and marine biology/freshwater ecology. Through one of the comprehensive preprofessional programs, Wittenberg students can prepare for law school, medical school (including dental, optometry, or veterinary school), physical therapy, theology, nursing, or another postgraduate program. Wittenberg also offers 3-2 programs in computer engineering, engineering, environmental studies, nursing, and occupational therapy. Advanced study during the two years is completed at schools such as Case Western Reserve, Columbia, Duke, Georgia Tech, Johns Hopkins, and Washington (St. Louis).

Academic Programs

Wittenberg graduates are critical thinkers who are equipped for a lifetime of success in a changing world. A Wittenberg education exposes students to a broad range of ideas and inquiries, from scientific investigations to philosophical explorations. Developing excellent communication, writing, and critical-thinking skills, as well as engaging diverse subjects, improves students as scholars and global citizens.

Wittenberg students must complete a course of study in two broad categories: comprehensive education in the liberal arts and sciences and a major program of study. Each of these categories makes up one third of the total credits required for graduation. To make up the remaining one third of the credits, students may choose either elective courses from across the curriculum or courses required for a minor within one or more particular areas. The comprehensive program is based upon general education learning goals. These goals reflect Wittenberg's emphasis on teaching and student learning.

All candidates for the Bachelor of Arts, Music, Science, and Fine Arts degrees must complete 130 semester hours of credit. Generally, a major consists of 32 to 42 semester hours of credit, and a minor consists of 20 to 22 semester hours of credit.

Off-Campus Programs

Every year, around 100 students from Wittenberg study abroad in more than twenty countries. Some programs last for only a few weeks during semester break or take place over the summer for one to two months; other programs last for a semester or an entire academic year. In addition, some students choose to study off campus with cooperative programs in such places as Washington, D.C., and Duke University.

Academic Facilities

Wittenberg's twenty-seven buildings combine the best of tradition (Myers Hall and Recitation Hall are on the National Register of Historic Places) and the best of tomorrow. Hollenbeck Hall, a state-of-the-art academic building, opened in 2000, and the Barbara Deer Kuss Science Center was dedicated in 2003. The new science center is equipped with the latest technology in its laboratories and classrooms. The Wittenberg Department of Music is housed in Krieg Hall, a spacious structure specially designed to provide the best instruction in music. The music building houses a sixteen-unit electronic keyboard laboratory that students use for advanced music composition.

All of the residence halls have computer labs open to the students around the clock. In Hollenbeck Hall, the computer lab is open 24 hours a day. Departmental labs set their own hours, and the computer lab in the Thomas Library is available during open hours. A fiber-optic network connects classroom and administration buildings, the library, and residence halls. All students are given a network account and an e-mail account. Thomas Library has 367,000 volumes and access to millions more through the statewide electronic library catalog OhioLINK.

Costs

Total annual charges for the 2007–08 academic year were $39,280. This amount included tuition ($31,400), room ($4110), and board ($3770). Estimated costs for books, travel, miscellaneous expenses, and entertainment are $2400 for in-state students. Wittenberg estimates a total of $3400 for out-of-state students to account for additional travel expenses.

Financial Aid

Two features that keep Wittenberg affordable for many families are that more than 80 percent of Wittenberg students receive nearly $25 million each year in scholarships and financial assistance and that Wittenberg's four-year graduation guarantee states that with proper planning, students should be able to graduate in four years rather than the five- to six-year average of many universities. Students are not charged additional tuition or fees if they have met minimum criteria. Financial aid packages are made up of scholarships, grants, loans, and employment on campus. In order to be considered for financial aid, students must complete the Free Application for Federal Student Aid (FAFSA). Academic and talent-based scholarships are available from $1000 per year to full tuition regardless of financial need.

Faculty

Since its founding, personal attention from Wittenberg's award-winning faculty has defined the University's innovative approach to educating young people. From providing encouraging words in one-on-one conversations or assisting with career preparation to engaging in intellectual debate or sharing some laughs after class, Wittenberg faculty members are outstanding classroom instructors and true mentors who consider students their top priority and have a genuine interest in teaching undergraduates. Many of the faculty members are also renowned experts in their fields. Robert P. Welker, an education professor, was named Ohio Professor of the Year in 2001. He is the fourth professor from Wittenberg in fifteen years to win this prestigious award. Ninety-seven percent of the faculty members have the highest degree in their field; full-time faculty members number 156, and part-time faculty members number 67. The faculty-student ratio is 1:12, which allows for the average class size of 19 students.

Student Government

The student government for the undergraduate student body is the Student Senate. The Student Senate operates primarily as a legislative body. The senate is elected/selected each spring. Through its committees this body addresses each aspect of student life.

Admission Requirements

Admission to Wittenberg is selective and is based on the following information: high school record, including the strength of the high school and its curriculum and trends in the student's academic work; cocurricular activities and community participation; recommendations; and an essay. International students and transfer students are encouraged to apply. Applicants have the option of submitting their ACT or SAT scores for review for admission and scholarships. An on-campus interview is not required but is highly recommended. Students may apply using the regular application or online at the University's Web site.

Application and Information

The deadlines for applying are as follows for incoming freshmen: early decision is November 15, early action I is December 1, early action II is January 15, and regular action is March 15. For full consideration for the Smith or Provost scholarship, a complete application for admission must be received by December 1. Students must apply by February 15 to be considered for merit-based scholarships. Transfer student application deadlines are December 1 for the spring semester and July 1 for the fall semester. The international student application deadline is March 15. More information may be obtained by contacting:

Office of Admission
Wittenberg University
Ward Street at North Wittenberg Avenue
Post Office Box 720
Springfield, Ohio 45501-0720
Phone: 937-327-6314
877-206-0332 (toll-free)
E-mail: admission@wittenberg.edu
Web site: http://www.wittenberg.edu

On the campus of Wittenberg University.

WRIGHT STATE UNIVERSITY

DAYTON, OHIO

The University

Wright State University (WSU) is a comprehensive doctoral, research institution of approximately 17,000 students and 2,200 faculty and staff members. Through its eleven colleges and schools, Wright State offers over 100 undergraduate majors as well as more than fifty graduate and professional degree programs. Currently celebrating its fortieth anniversary, the University continues to grow and mature as an institution, while striving to maintain an innovative spirit between its faculty members and students and programs and research.

The growing reputation of Wright State has attracted students from throughout Ohio as well as nearly every state in the nation and sixty-nine other countries. The building of additional on-campus student housing has increased the opportunity for students from across the state and the world to attend Wright State. From traditional residence-hall-style dorms to modern apartment-style housing, Wright State offers a variety of campus housing options to fit the needs of today's college student. As a matter of fact, the majority of first-year students choose to be one of the nearly 3,500 students who live on-campus. Wright State also offers a variety of living-learning communities that are designed to allow students with similar goals and interests to share living arrangements and the chance to extend their studies beyond the classroom and into their daily experience. C.H.O.I.C.E./ Substance Free Living-learning Community, Honors Living-learning Community, International House, and the Engineering and Computer Science Living-learning Community are some of the more popular living-learning community choices.

Wright State takes pride in keeping up with new technology. State-of-the-art computer labs are located in every academic building and the University library. Each residence hall facility also offers wireless Internet access and 24-hour computer labs. Many classrooms have advanced audiovisual equipment, which has increased the use of technology for instructional purposes by faculty members.

Wright State offers a variety of recreational and social outlets for the campus community. The newly renovated Student Union is the main hub of recreational activity on campus. The new state-of-the-art fitness center offers over fifty pieces of cardio equipment, LCD flat screen displays, cardio theater, group exercise studios, and more. The Student Union also features a new wellness center, which houses Counseling and Wellness Services, Student Health Services, and the WSU Pharmacy; a student-organization suite that is home to more than 150 student clubs and organizations; and a brand new rock-climbing wall. Also adding excitement and energy to campus life, Wright State University's sixteen varsity athletics teams compete in the NCAA Division I level through the Horizon League. Wright State athletics is home to champion basketball, baseball, swim, and softball teams.

Nationally-recognized for its active and extensive disability services program, Wright State encourages disabled students to participate in every aspect of the university experience. To meet the needs of disabled students, Wright State facilities have been designed to remove architectural barriers and permit more effective and independent use of the campus. Also, the majority of Wright State buildings are connected by a series of tunnels at the basement level. Students can navigate much of the campus without having to go outside. Applicants who require supportive services should arrange for an interview with the Office of Disability Services at least three months prior to enrollment.

Location

The 557-acre main campus, surrounded by a lush biological preserve, is located in a Miami Valley suburban community 12 miles northeast of Dayton, Ohio. The Miami Valley area has a tradition of innovation and is rich in industry and research, including nearby Wright-Patterson Air Force Base. The University has convenient highway access and is less than a 2-hour drive from Cincinnati and Columbus. Wright State University Lake Campus, located in Celina, Ohio, is approximately 70 miles northwest of Dayton. The Lake Campus is on the shore of beautiful Grand Lake St. Mary's.

Majors and Degrees

Fully accredited by the North Central Association of Colleges and Schools, Wright State's main campus grants the following degrees: Bachelor of Arts, Bachelor of Arts in Computer Science, Bachelor of Fine Arts, Bachelor of Music, Bachelor of Science, Bachelor of Science in Biomedical Engineering, Bachelor of Science in Business, Bachelor of Science in Clinical Laboratory Science, Bachelor of Science in Computer Engineering, Bachelor of Science in Computer Science, Bachelor of Science in Education, Bachelor of Science in Electrical Engineering, Bachelor of Science in Engineering Physics, Bachelor of Science in Industrial and Systems Engineering, Bachelor of Science in Materials Science and Engineering, Bachelor of Science in Mechanical Engineering, and Bachelor of Science in Nursing.

Raj Soin College of Business majors and programs are accountancy, business economics, finance, financial services, human resource management, international business, management, management information systems, marketing, and operations management.

College of Education and Human Services majors and programs are athletic training, early childhood education, health education, integrated business education, marketing education, middle childhood education, organizational leadership, physical education, rehabilitation services, sign language interpreter, and career and technical education.

College of Engineering and Computer Science majors and programs are biomedical engineering, computer engineering, computer science, electrical engineering, engineering physics, industrial and systems engineering, materials science and engineering, and mechanical engineering.

College of Liberal Arts majors and programs are acting, acting-musical theater, African and African American studies, anthropology, art, art education, art history, classical humanities, communication studies, criminal justice, dance, economics, English, English: integrated language arts, French, geography, German, Greek, history, international studies, Latin, liberal studies, mass communications, modern languages, motion picture history: theory and criticism, motion picture production, music, music education, music history and literature, music performance, organizational communication, philosophy, political science, religion, selected studies, social science education, social work, sociology, Spanish, theater design/technology/stage management, theater studies, urban affairs, and women's studies.

College of Science and Mathematics majors and programs are biological sciences, biological sciences education, chemistry, chemistry education, clinical laboratory science, earth and environmental sciences, earth and environmental sciences education, environmental health sciences, integrated science education, mathematics, mathematics education, physics, physics education, and psychology.

The College of Nursing and Health offers the Bachelor of Science in Nursing.

Wright State University Lake Campus offers the Associate of Arts and Associate of Science degrees, as well as a variety of two-year Associate of Applied Business, Associate of Applied Science, and Associate of Technical Study degree programs. Selected Bachelor of Science and master's degree programs are also offered. The associate degrees are offered with course work in: associate of technical study, biological sciences, business and administration, chemistry, communication, computer-aided drafting design technology, earth and environmental sciences, financial management technology, information technology: graphic communication and design, history, liberal studies, psychology, social work, sociology, and office information systems (administrative assistant studies, legal administrative assistant studies, and medical administrative assistant studies options).

Academic Programs

University College serves as the academic home of many first-year students. It can help students determine and achieve their academic and career goals. Academic advisers in University College provide students with assistance in scheduling courses and meeting entry

COLLEGE DATA CENTER • OHIO

requirements for their major. All students, regardless of their intended major, must complete a core group of general education requirements.

Students who complete Advanced Placement (AP) or International Baccalaureate (IB) course work while in high school may be granted University credit based on their examination scores. Wright State also accepts credits from accredited institutions earned through dual-enrollment programs, such as Ohio's Post Secondary Enrollment Program.

The University honors program creates a learning environment that students would expect to find at a small liberal arts college rather than within a large university. For over 30 years, the program has provided a challenging and unique living-learning environment where students can develop a strong sense of community, engage in critical analysis, experience diversity, and realize their full potential. In addition, the program also provides an opportunity for independent research working one-on-one with faculty members and features a student lounge and study area, special advising, a strong peer group, honors housing, and opportunities for travel, leadership development, and community service. Admission to the honors program is based on ACT and SAT scores, high school grade point average, and class rank. Upon admission to the University, eligible students will be sent an application for the honors program.

Other academic programs of note include Air Force and Army ROTC.

Off-Campus Programs

Wright State's membership in the Southwestern Ohio Council for Higher Education enables full-time students to take courses at many area colleges and universities at Wright State's tuition rates. Students can also apply their knowledge while gaining hands-on experience through cooperative education and internships. Students who have attained sophomore status can work with the Office of Career Services and faculty members in their major to find co-op and internship opportunities. In addition, many majors include courses that require students to work with community agencies, businesses, and industries to solve real-world problems.

Wright State students who desire an international experience can spend a quarter or more overseas in one of more than twenty countries or travel with a group of Wright State students and faculty members to Ireland, Italy, France, Spain, or Japan during the summer.

Academic Facilities

Major academic buildings on the main campus include the Creative Arts Center, the Paul Lawrence Dunbar Library, the Television Center, four main classroom buildings, the Brehm Laboratory, the Biological Sciences Building, the Joshi Research Center, the Russ Engineering Center, the Mathematical and Microbiological Sciences Building, the Health Sciences Building, the medical sciences building, the Rike Hall Raj Soin Business Building, and the new Matthew O. Diggs III Laboratory for Life Sciences Research Building. Other facilities are available in downtown Dayton and Celina. Wright State students also have access to the libraries of all of the institutions in the Southwestern Ohio Council for Higher Education. The combined library holdings total more than 1 million volumes.

Costs

To support the Ohio legislature and Governor Ted Strickland's plan to encourage more Ohioians to attend college, earn their degrees, and achieve their dreams, the Wright State University Board of Trustees has frozen the current tuition costs for undergraduate students for the 2007–08 and 2008–09 academic years. The 2007–08 cost for tuition and fees for Ohio residents was $2426 per quarter. Tuition and fees for out-of-state students were $4668 per quarter. Room and board fees were $2474 per quarter, and additional expenses, including books and supplies, cost approximately $1500 per year.

Financial Aid

Three forms of financial aid are available: grants and scholarships, which do not require repayment; long-term and short-term loans, which must be repaid; and part-time student employment. Students applying for financial aid must complete the Free Application for Federal Student Aid (FAFSA). Seventy-nine percent of Wright State's students receive some type of financial aid. University scholarships, based solely on academic ability, are awarded each fall. A special scholarship application must be filled out and additional credentials such as letters of recommendation may be required. Further details concerning financial aid and scholarship programs are available through the Office of Financial Aid.

Faculty

The Wright State faculty has approximately 830 members, of which approximately 80 percent hold the highest degrees in their fields. More than 75 percent of classes have fewer than 50 students.

Student Government

The Student Government Association is the representative body for Wright State students. Leaders and representatives are elected by the entire student body and members participate in the University Senate, which is composed of faculty members, administration, and student representatives. The Student Government Association deals with academic regulations, curriculum changes, and other matters of University-wide policy.

Admission Requirements

Ohio students who have graduated from an accredited high school with a college-preparatory curriculum, a 2.0 or higher high school grade point average, and at least an 18 ACT composite score or 840 SAT (math and critical reading only) score are eligible for admission at Wright State. Applications from students not meeting these requirements, or from students who hold a state-approved high school equivalency certificate, are reviewed on an individual basis.

Out-of-state students must present evidence of an above-average ability to do college-level work, which is generally illustrated by having a 2.5 or higher high school grade point average, completing a college preparatory curriculum, and scoring at least a 20 ACT composite score or 960 SAT(math and critical reading) score.

Students applying as freshmen should submit a WSU application form, a non-refundable $30 application fee, a copy of their high school transcript, a College Preparatory Curriculum Completion form and official ACT or SAT scores.

The transfer policies among the University's academic divisions vary and depend on the number of transfer hours that applicants have acquired and their cumulative GPA. The Office of Admissions can provide specific requirements for each college at WSU. Transfer applicants must submit official transcripts from each college or university previously attended and must have at least a 2.0 GPA for admission to the University. The appropriate college of the University determines how a student's credit is to be applied to the Wright State academic credit requirements.

Application and Information

Application deadlines vary depending on the quarter for which a student is applying. In general, students should submit the completed application and appropriate fee, transcripts, and test scores (where applicable) as soon as possible to ensure a good selection of courses. International students and others with questions about exceptional circumstances should contact the Office of Admissions.

Cathy Davis, Director of Admissions
E148 Student Union
Wright State University
3640 Colonel Glenn Highway
Dayton, Ohio 45435
Phone: 937-775-5700
800-247-1770 (toll-free)
E-mail: admissions@wright.edu
Web site: http://www.wright.edu/admissions

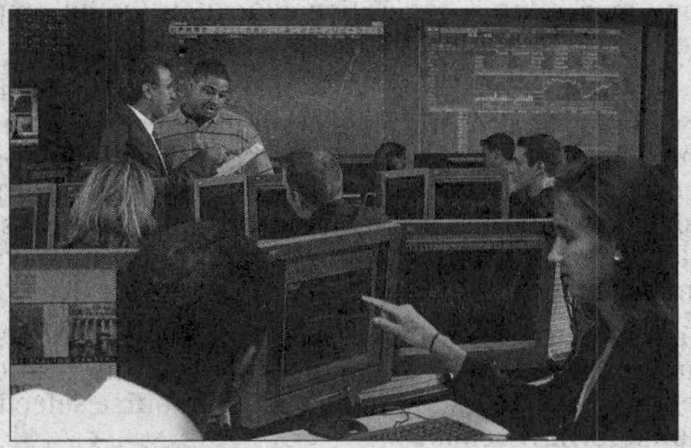

The MTC Technologies Trading Center was selected by *BusinessWeek* as one of the top ten trading rooms in the nation.

XAVIER UNIVERSITY
CINCINNATI, OHIO

The University

Founded in 1831, Xavier University is the fourth-oldest of the twenty-eight Jesuit colleges and universities in the United States. There are approximately 4,000 undergraduate students attending Xavier during the day, and the total University enrollment is 6,600. Coeducational in all divisions, the University has students from forty-four states and forty-four countries. Students may choose from seventy-six undergraduate majors in three colleges and can later pursue graduate degrees in twenty areas. Xavier is nationally recognized for providing a high-quality, personalized education rooted in the Catholic Jesuit tradition. Major University divisions include the College of Arts and Sciences; the Williams College of Business; the College of Social Sciences, Health, and Education; the Center for Adult and Part-Time Students; and the graduate programs.

Location

Xavier University's 160-acre campus is located in a residential neighborhood that is a short drive from downtown Cincinnati, in the nation's twenty-fifth-largest region. Cincinnati is one of America's most livable cities, according to *Places Rated Almanac* and "Partners for Livable Communities." Greater Cincinnati is home to 2 million people, two major-league sports teams, and sixteen Fortune 1,000 companies. Cincinnati is located on the banks of the Ohio River and at the convergence of three states—Ohio, Kentucky, and Indiana.

Majors and Degrees

Xavier's College of Arts and Sciences awards the Bachelor of Arts or Bachelor of Science degree in applied science (biology, chemistry, or physics), art, biology, chemical science, chemistry, classical humanities, classics, communication arts, computer science, English, history, mathematics, medical technology, modern languages (French, German, or Spanish), music, music education, natural science (preprofessional programs in dentistry, medicine, and veterinary studies), philosophy, physics, and theology. Students studying the preprofessional programs in the natural sciences are assisted with entrance into a health career or medical school by the preprofessional health advising office. Xavier also offers an associate degree in radiologic technology.

The Williams College of Business awards the Bachelor of Science in Business Administration degree in accounting, economics, entrepreneurial studies, finance, general business, human resources, information systems, international business, management, and marketing. Cooperative education (co-op) opportunities are offered to qualified students.

Majors and areas of study offered through Xavier's College of Social Sciences, Health, and Education include athletic training, criminal justice, economics, education (early childhood, middle childhood, Montessori, secondary, and special education), international affairs, nursing, occupational therapy, political science, psychology, social work, sociology, and sports management/ sports marketing.

Xavier offers a preprofessional program in law. Students in the program are free to select any major that is of interest to them. The prelaw adviser assists students in their course selection and preparation for law school.

A two-year preprofessional program in pharmacy is also offered, preparing students for entrance into a school of pharmacy. Students who decide not to go on in pharmacy may continue at Xavier for a four-year degree in science.

Xavier offers pre-engineering programs in conjunction with the University of Cincinnati. In addition, an environmental management program is offered in conjunction with Duke University. After spending three years at Xavier in biology and two years at Duke in environmental management, students graduate with a Bachelor of Science in applied biology from Xavier and either a Master of Environmental Management or a Master of Forestry from Duke.

Students may choose from forty-three different minor areas of study, including art history, biology, business, chemistry, classical studies, communication arts, computer science, corrections, criminal justice, economics, education (Montessori and secondary), English, environmental studies, French, German, Greek, history, information technology, international affairs, international business, international studies, jazz, Latin, Latin American studies, mathematics, music, natural sciences, peace studies, performance studies, philosophy, physics, political science, psychology, Spanish, studio art, theology, and women's and minorities' studies. The Center for Adult and Part-Time Students serves those individuals age 22 and older who wish to continue their education but are not in a position to attend regular daytime classes. In addition to the bachelor's degrees, the division offers two-year associate degree programs in a number of fields.

Academic Programs

The academic year consists of two semesters, and summer courses are available. While the number of semester hours required for graduation varies with the program chosen, a minimum of 120 hours are required for a degree. A student must fulfill the required semester hours in a major as well as the basic requirements of the core curriculum. With an emphasis on liberal arts education, the curriculum serves to prepare the individual for a full and purposeful life as well as for a career. The student must complete a designated number of hours in the humanities, mathematics, philosophy, sciences, social sciences, and theology, and considerable freedom is permitted in the selection of courses in these areas.

Special programs include three challenging honors programs: the Honors Bachelor of Arts, University Scholars, and the newest program, Philosophy, Politics and the Public (PPP). The PPP includes a rich academic curriculum in a multidisciplinary study of the many meanings of "public." Students earn an honors degree and are well prepared for graduate study or careers in many professions, including business, law, economics, and public policy. Other special programs include programs in peace and justice and the gender and diversity studies minor.

Off-Campus Programs

Fifteen area colleges, including Xavier, have formed the Greater Cincinnati Consortium of Colleges and Universities, through which all students at member colleges may take courses that are not available at their home institution. Xavier encourages full-time students to take advantage of this opportunity for curriculum enrichment through cross-registration. In addition, students who wish to spend a semester or year abroad as part of their undergraduate education have a number of possibilities open to them through the Xavier Study-Abroad Programs and Service Learning.

Academic Facilities

The McDonald Memorial Library supports all of the University's programs and offers a wireless computer environment with laptops available for checkout. McDonald Memorial Library also offers extensive computerized research, including online and CD-ROM resources. XPLORE, the library's computerized catalog, allows students to search online for books, periodicals, articles, and videos. XPLORE can be reached from any terminal on the campus or from home. Students also have access to a variety of university and public libraries through a consortium and a computer program called OhioLINK. The Cintas Center is a multipurpose facility with a 10,250-seat arena, a conference center, banquet space, and a student dining center. The Gallagher Student Center has a wireless computer environment with laptops available for checkout. The center also houses a state-of-the-art 350-seat theater, where students can attend a variety of performances, including the University's drama group, the Xavier Players. The Science Center provides a modern science facility that serves the needs of today's students. The center comprises three departments: biology, chemistry, and physics.

Costs

Annual tuition for full-time undergraduates for 2007–08 was $24,660. Room and board costs averaged $8950 per year, depending on accommodations. Costs are subject to change.

Financial Aid

Xavier is committed to helping students afford to attend Xavier University. Each year, more than 95 percent of undergraduates receive some type of financial assistance, with nearly 60 percent receiving need-based aid; approximately half of all freshmen receive an academic scholarship. All applicants are automatically considered for academic scholarships, and decisions are typically sent with admission decisions. To compete for Xavier's highest academic awards, students must submit a scholarship application by December 1. Ten 4-year, non-need, full-tuition St. Francis Xavier Scholarships are awarded annually to students of superior academic ability. The Xavier Service Fellowships are awarded based on high academic ability and a demonstration of exemplary involvement in voluntary service. These awards pay full tuition, room, and board. In addition, Xavier offers departmental scholarships, music and art scholarships, performing arts grants, athletic scholarships, minority awards, and ROTC scholarships. The University also participates in the following federally sponsored aid programs: the Federal Perkins Loan, Federal Pell Grant, Federal Supplemental Educational Opportunity Grant, Federal Work-Study, and Federal Stafford Student Loan programs. Residents of Ohio may qualify for assistance under the Ohio Instructional Grant Program. In order to be considered for financial aid, students must complete the Free Application for Federal Student Aid (FAFSA).

Faculty

The faculty for all divisions numbers 598 members, of whom 308 are full-time. There are no teaching assistants, and graduate students do not teach. Eighty percent of the full-time faculty members hold doctoral degrees. The student-faculty ratio is 13:1, and the average class size is 20 students. Academic, vocational, and personal counseling and counseling for veterans are readily available. The University has always enjoyed a reputation for good rapport and excellent personal relationships between faculty members and students.

Student Government

The Student Government is the principal agency of student participation in University governance and is devoted to improving the quality of student life. Students choose from more than 100 different academic clubs, social organizations, and intramural group teams. The Student Senate, the main governing organization of the student body, is composed of 16 elected members. Xavier students sit on numerous University committees.

Admission Requirements

Xavier is open to qualified men and women regardless of age, race, religion, handicap, or national origin. Undergraduate students may apply to commence their studies at Xavier for either the fall or spring semester. Students are encouraged to apply by the appropriate deadlines. Each student who applies to Xavier is given a thorough, individual evaluation. Factors considered in making admission decisions include, but are not limited to, the following: the candidate's previous academic performance, including the rigor of the curriculum pursued and the grades achieved; results from the SAT and/or ACT exams; the candidate's rank in class (when available); the application essay; letters of recommendation; the candidate's extracurricular profile; life or work experience; and any other factors that help to determine the candidate's potential to be successful academically at Xavier and to contribute positively to the Xavier community as a whole.

Transfer applicants with fewer than 30 transferable semester hours must follow the instructions for freshman applicants. Transfer applicants with 30 or more hours do not need to submit the application essay, the counselor recommendation, or SAT/ACT results. In addition to the application, transfer candidates must submit official copies of academic and financial aid transcripts from all colleges previously attended, as well as a list of any courses in progress.

Application and Information

To be considered for admission, a student must submit the application form with the $35 application fee, the official high school transcript sent by the school with a counselor recommendation, and scores on the SAT or ACT, which may be included on the high school record. Students may also apply online, where the application fee is waived. For freshman applicants, Xavier has a single-notification admission process with two options: Early Action and Regular Decision. Students should check with the University for application deadlines.

An application and additional information may be obtained by contacting:

Office of Admission
Xavier University
3800 Victory Parkway
Cincinnati, Ohio 45207-5311
Phone: 513-745-3301
877-XUADMIT (982-3648) (toll-free)
E-mail: xuadmit@xavier.edu
xuglobal@xavier.edu (international students)
Web site: http://www.xavier.edu

Xavier University's academic mall.

Admission Requirements

Xavier is open to qualified men and women regardless of age, race, religion, handicap, or national origin. Undergraduate students may apply to commence their studies at Xavier for either the fall or spring semester. Students are encouraged to apply by the appropriate deadlines. Each student who applies to Xavier is given a thorough individual evaluation. Factors considered in making admission decisions include, but are not limited to, the following: the candidate's previous academic performance, including the rigor of the curriculum pursued and the grades achieved; results from the SAT and/or ACT exams; the candidate's rank in class (when available); the application essay; letters of recommendation; the candidate's extracurricular profile or work experience; and any other factors that help to determine the candidate's potential to be successful academically at Xavier and to contribute positively to the Xavier community as a whole.

Transfer applicants with fewer than 30 transferable semester hours must follow the instructions for freshman applicants. Transfer applicants with 30 or more hours do not need to submit the application essay, the counselor recommendation, or SAT/ACT results. In addition to the application, transfer candidates must submit official copies of academic and financial aid transcripts from all colleges previously attended, as well as a list of any courses in progress.

Application and Information

To be considered for admission, a student must submit the application form with the $35 application fee, the official high school transcript sent by the school with a counselor recommendation, and scores on the SAT or ACT, which may be included on the high school record. Students may also apply online, where the application fee is waived. For freshman applicants, Xavier has a single-notification admission process with two options: Early Action and Regular Decision. Students should check with the University for application deadlines.

An application and additional information may be obtained by contacting:

Office of Admission
Xavier University
3800 Victory Parkway
Cincinnati, Ohio 45207-5311
Phone: 513-745-3301
877-XAVIERU (982-8378) (toll-free)
E-mail: xuadmit@xavier.edu
[illegible]@xavier.edu (international students)
Web site: http://www.xavier.edu

Xavier University's academic mall.

[illegible] McDonald Memorial Library also [illegible] computerized research [illegible] and [illegible] resources. [illegible], the library's computerized catalog, allows students to search online for books, periodicals, and [illegible]. [illegible] can be reached from any terminal on [illegible]. Students also have access to a variety [illegible] public libraries through a consortium [illegible] computer program called OhioLINK. The [illegible] Center is a multipurpose facility with a [illegible]-seat arena, a conference center, meeting space, and a student dining center. The Gallagher Student Center has a wireless computer environment with [illegible] available for student use. The center also houses a state-of-the-art [illegible]-seat theater where students can attend a variety of performances, including the University's drama group, the Xavier Players. The science center provides a modern science facility that serves the needs of today's students. The center comprises three departments: biology, chemistry, and physics.

Costs

Annual tuition for full-time undergraduates for 2007–08 was $24,[illegible]. Room and board costs averaged $8,[illegible] per year, depending on accommodations. Costs are subject to change.

Financial Aid

Xavier is committed to helping students afford to attend Xavier University. Each year, more than 95 percent of undergraduates receive some type of financial assistance, with nearly 60 percent receiving need-based aid. Approximately half of all freshmen receive an academic scholarship. All applicants are automatically considered for academic scholarships, and decisions are made after an admission decision. To compete for Xavier's highest academic awards, students must submit a scholarship application. The number of [illegible] awards [illegible] full-tuition [illegible] are awarded annually to [illegible] students. The Xavier Service Fellowship is an award based on high academic ability and a demonstrated commitment to community service. These awards [illegible] tuition, room, and board. In addition, Xavier offers [illegible] scholarships, music and art scholarships, matching [illegible] grants, athletic scholarships, tuition awards, and ROTC scholarships. The University also participates in the following federal programs: the Federal Perkins Loan, Federal Pell Grant, Federal Supplemental Educational Opportunity Grant, Federal Work-Study, and Federal Stafford Student Loan programs. Residents of Ohio may qualify for assistance under the Ohio Instructional Grant Program. In order to be considered for financial aid, students must complete the Free Application for Federal Student Aid (FAFSA).

Faculty

The faculty for all divisions numbers 598 members, of whom 308 are full-time. There are no teaching assistants, and graduate students do not teach. Eighty percent of the full-time faculty members hold doctoral degrees. The student-faculty ratio is 13:1, and the average class size is 20 students. Academic, vocational, and personal counseling and counseling for careers are readily available. The University has always enjoyed a reputation for good rapport and excellent personal relationships between faculty members and students.

Student Government

The Student Government is the principal agency of student participation in University governance and is dedicated to improving the quality of campus life. Students choose from more than 100 [illegible] academic clubs, honor organizations, and intramural sports teams. The Student Senate, the main governing organization of the student body, is composed of 16 elected members. Xavier students sit on various University committees.

OKLAHOMA

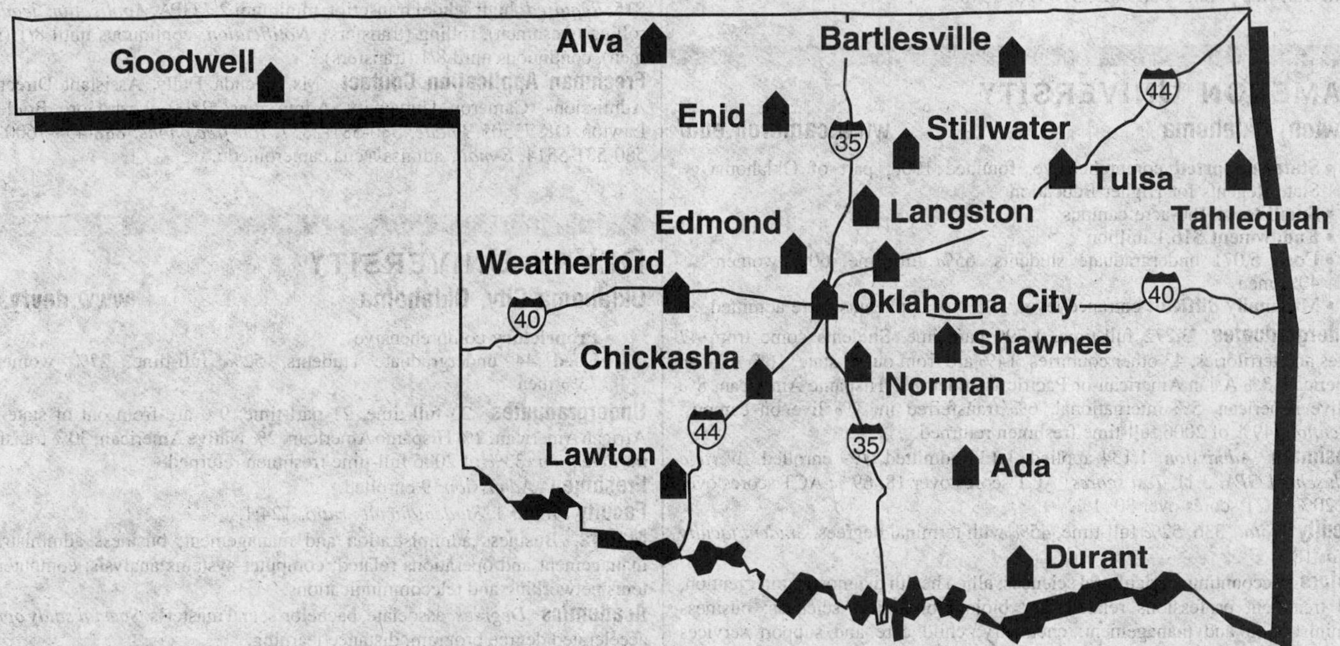

The Oklahoma City area includes the towns of Bethany and Moore.

BACONE COLLEGE

Muskogee, Oklahoma **www.bacone.edu/**

Freshman Application Contact Ms. Tina Sorick, Admissions Counselor, Bacone College, 2299 Old Bacone Road, Muskogee, OK 74403. *Phone:* 918-781-7340. *Toll-free phone:* 888-682-5514 Ext. 7340.

CAMERON UNIVERSITY

Lawton, Oklahoma **www.cameron.edu/**

- **State-supported** comprehensive, founded 1908, part of Oklahoma State Regents for Higher Education
- **Small-town** 160-acre campus
- **Endowment** $16.1 million
- **Coed** 5,071 undergraduate students, 65% full-time, 60% women, 40% men
- **Minimally difficult** entrance level, 100% of applicants were admitted

Undergraduates 3,272 full-time, 1,799 part-time. Students come from 47 states and territories, 43 other countries, 14% are from out of state, 16% African American, 3% Asian American or Pacific Islander, 8% Hispanic American, 8% Native American, 5% international, 6% transferred in, 7% live on campus. *Retention:* 49% of 2006 full-time freshmen returned.

Freshmen *Admission:* 1,134 applied, 1,133 admitted, 799 enrolled. *Average high school GPA:* 3.11. *Test scores:* ACT scores over 18: 69%; ACT scores over 24: 20%; ACT scores over 30: 1%.

Faculty *Total:* 336, 52% full-time, 45% with terminal degrees. *Student/faculty ratio:* 18:1.

Majors Accounting; agricultural sciences; allied health diagnostic, intervention, and treatment professions related; art; biology/biological sciences; business administration and management; chemistry; child care and support services management; child care services management; clinical laboratory science/ medical technology; clinical/medical laboratory technology; computer and information sciences; computer science; digital communication and media/multimedia; drafting and design technology; education; education (specific subject areas) related; electrical, electronic and communications engineering technology; elementary education; English; family and consumer sciences/human sciences; health and physical education; history; industrial technology; management information systems; mathematics; mechanical drafting; mechanical drafting and CAD/ CADD; music; natural sciences; physics; political science and government; psychology; respiratory care therapy; Romance languages; secondary education; sociology; visual and performing arts.

Academics *Calendar:* semesters. *Degrees:* associate, bachelor's, master's, and postbachelor's certificates. *Special study options:* academic remediation for entering students, accelerated degree program, adult/continuing education programs, advanced placement credit, distance learning, double majors, English as a second language, honors programs, independent study, internships, off-campus study, part-time degree program, services for LD students, summer session for credit. *ROTC:* Army (b).

Computers on Campus 319 computers/terminals are available on campus for general student use. Students can access the following: computer help desk, free student e-mail accounts, online (class) grades, online (class) schedules, online courses, student information system. Campuswide network is available. 100% of college-owned or -operated housing units are wired for high-speed Internet access. Wireless service is available via classrooms, computer centers, computer labs, dorm rooms, learning centers, libraries, student centers.

Student Life *Housing options:* coed, men-only, women-only. Campus housing is university owned. *Activities and organizations:* drama/theater group, student-run newspaper, radio and television station, choral group, Student Government Association, Programming Activities Council, Student Housing Association, International Club, Greek Life, national fraternities, national sororities. *Campus security:* 24-hour emergency response devices and patrols, late-night transport/ escort service, controlled dormitory access. *Student services:* personal/ psychological counseling.

Athletics Member NCAA. All Division II. *Intercollegiate sports:* baseball M (s), basketball M (s)/W (s), cross-country running M (s), golf M (s)/W (s), softball W (s), tennis M (s)/W (s), volleyball W (s). *Intramural sports:* badminton M/W, basketball M/W, bowling M/W, golf M/W, racquetball M/W, softball M/W, tennis M/W, volleyball M/W.

Standardized Tests *Required:* SAT or ACT (for admission).

Costs (2007–08) *Tuition:* state resident $2571 full-time, $86 per hour part-time; nonresident $7920 full-time, $264 per hour part-time. Full-time tuition and fees vary according to course load. Part-time tuition and fees vary according to course load. *Required fees:* $1185 full-time, $40 per hour part-time. *Room and board:* $3970. Room and board charges vary according to board plan. *Payment plan:* installment. *Waivers:* senior citizens and employees or children of employees.

Financial Aid Of all full-time matriculated undergraduates who enrolled in 2003, 150 Federal Work-Study jobs (averaging $1215). 286 state and other part-time jobs (averaging $1542). *Average indebtedness upon graduation:* $6300.

Applying *Options:* electronic application, deferred entrance. *Application fee:* $15. *Required:* high school transcript, minimum 2.7 GPA. *Application deadlines:* rolling (freshmen), rolling (transfers). *Notification:* continuous until 8/1 (freshmen), continuous until 8/1 (transfers).

Freshman Application Contact Ms. Brenda Dally, Assistant Director of Admissions, Cameron University, Admissions, 2800 West Gore Boulevard, Lawton, OK 73505. *Phone:* 580-581-2837. *Toll-free phone:* 888-454-7600. *Fax:* 580-581-5514. *E-mail:* admiss@cua.cameron.edu.

DEVRY UNIVERSITY

Oklahoma City, Oklahoma **www.devry.edu/**

- **Proprietary** comprehensive
- **Coed** 44 undergraduate students, 52% full-time, 27% women, 73% men

Undergraduates 23 full-time, 21 part-time. 9% are from out of state, 18% African American, 2% Hispanic American, 2% Native American, 30% transferred in. *Retention:* 33% of 2006 full-time freshmen returned.

Freshmen *Admission:* 9 enrolled.

Faculty *Total:* 1. *Student/faculty ratio:* 124:1.

Majors Business administration and management; business administration, management and operations related; computer systems analysis; computer systems networking and telecommunications.

Academics *Degrees:* associate, bachelor's, and master's. *Special study options:* accelerated degree program, distance learning.

Costs (2008–09) *Tuition:* $13,810 full-time, $515 per credit part-time. *Required fees:* $80 full-time.

Applying *Options:* electronic application, early admission, deferred entrance. *Application fee:* $50. *Application deadlines:* rolling (freshmen), rolling (transfers). *Notification:* continuous (freshmen), continuous (transfers).

Director of Admissions Admissions Office, DeVry University, 4013 NW Expressway Street, Suite 100, Oklahoma City, OK 73116.

EAST CENTRAL UNIVERSITY

Ada, Oklahoma **www.ecok.edu/**

- **State-supported** comprehensive, founded 1909, part of Oklahoma State Regents for Higher Education
- **Small-town** 140-acre campus with easy access to Oklahoma City
- **Endowment** $4.1 million
- **Coed** 3,665 undergraduate students, 81% full-time, 59% women, 41% men
- **Minimally difficult** entrance level, 96% of applicants were admitted

Undergraduates 2,956 full-time, 709 part-time. Students come from 32 states and territories, 27 other countries, 7% are from out of state, 4% African American, 0.5% Asian American or Pacific Islander, 3% Hispanic American, 21% Native American, 2% international, 40% transferred in, 21% live on campus. *Retention:* 64% of 2006 full-time freshmen returned.

Freshmen *Admission:* 745 applied, 717 admitted, 552 enrolled. *Average high school GPA:* 3.32. *Test scores:* ACT scores over 18: 83%; ACT scores over 24: 20%; ACT scores over 30: 3%.

Faculty *Total:* 253, 64% full-time, 51% with terminal degrees. *Student/faculty ratio:* 18:1.

Majors Accounting; advertising; art; art teacher education; biology/biological sciences; biology teacher education; business administration and management; business automation/technology/data entry; business/managerial economics; business teacher education; cartography; chemistry; chemistry teacher education; clinical/medical laboratory technology; computer science; consumer merchandising/ retailing management; corrections; counselor education/school counseling and guidance; criminal justice/law enforcement administration; criminal justice/ police science; drafting and design technology; early childhood education; ecology; education; electrical, electronic and communications engineering technology; elementary education; English; English/language arts teacher education; entrepreneurship; environmental health; environmental science; environmental studies; family and consumer sciences/home economics teacher education; family and consumer sciences/human sciences; fashion merchandising; finance; general studies; health information/medical records administration; health teacher education; history; history teacher education; human resources management; human services; hydrology and water resources science; juvenile corrections; kindergarten/preschool education; legal studies; literature; management information systems; marketing/marketing management; mass communication/media; mass communications; mathematics; mathematics teacher education; medical staff services technology; music; music teacher education; nursing (registered nurse training); physical education teaching and coaching; physics; physics teacher education; piano and organ; political science and government; pre-dentistry studies; pre-law studies; pre-medical studies; pre-pharmacy studies; pre-veterinary studies; psychology; public relations, advertising, and applied communication related; public relations/image management; radio and television; science teacher education; secondary education; social work; sociology; special education; speech and rhetoric; speech teacher education; theater/theater arts management; voice and opera.

Academics *Calendar:* semesters. *Degrees:* bachelor's and master's. *Special study options:* academic remediation for entering students, adult/continuing education programs, advanced placement credit, distance learning, double majors, honors programs, independent study, internships, off-campus study, part-time degree program, services for LD students, summer session for credit.

Computers on Campus 500 computers/terminals are available on campus for general student use. Campuswide network is available.

Student Life *Housing:* on-campus residence required for freshman year. *Options:* coed, women-only, disabled students. Campus housing is university owned. *Activities and organizations:* drama/theater group, student-run newspaper, choral group, marching band, BACCHUS, Fellowship of Christian Athletes, Human Resources, national fraternities, national sororities. *Campus security:* 24-hour emergency response devices and patrols, student patrols, late-night transport/escort service, agreements with all local, state, federal, and tribal police departments for added crime and violation prevention. *Student services:* health clinic, personal/psychological counseling.

Athletics Member NCAA, NAIA. All NCAA Division II. *Intercollegiate sports:* baseball M (s), basketball M (s)/W (s), cheerleading M/W, cross-country running M (s)/W (s), football M (s), golf M (s)/W, soccer W (s), softball W (s), tennis M (s)/W (s), track and field M/W, volleyball W (s). *Intramural sports:* basketball M/W, football M/W, racquetball M/W, soccer M/W, softball M/W, tennis M/W, volleyball M/W.

Standardized Tests *Required:* SAT or ACT (for admission). *Recommended:* ACT (for admission).

Costs (2007–08) *Tuition:* state resident $2662 full-time, $89 per semester hour part-time; nonresident $8135 full-time, $271 per semester hour part-time. Full-time tuition and fees vary according to course load. Part-time tuition and fees vary according to course load. *Required fees:* $1134 full-time, $38 per semester hour part-time, $48 per term part-time. *Room and board:* $3860; room only: $1500. Room and board charges vary according to board plan and housing facility. *Waivers:* senior citizens and employees or children of employees.

Financial Aid Of all full-time matriculated undergraduates who enrolled in 2006, 2,396 applied for aid, 2,085 were judged to have need, 756 had their need fully met. 175 Federal Work-Study jobs (averaging $2349). 232 state and other part-time jobs (averaging $572). In 2006, 542 non-need-based awards were made. *Average percent of need met:* 70%. *Average financial aid package:* $7597. *Average need-based loan:* $3835. *Average need-based gift aid:* $3420. *Average non-need-based aid:* $1567. *Average indebtedness upon graduation:* $19,190.

Applying *Options:* early admission. *Application fee:* $20. *Required:* high school transcript. *Required for some:* minimum 2.7 GPA, rank in upper 50% of high school class. *Notification:* continuous (freshmen), continuous (transfers).

Freshman Application Contact Ms. Pam Denny, Freshman Admissions Officer, East Central University, PMBJ8, 1100 East 14th Street, Ada, OK 74820-6999. *Phone:* 580-310-5233 Ext. 233. *Fax:* 580-310-5432. *E-mail:* pdenny@ecok.edu.

HILLSDALE FREE WILL BAPTIST COLLEGE

Moore, Oklahoma — www.hc.edu/

- **Independent Free Will Baptist** comprehensive, founded 1959
- **Suburban** 41-acre campus with easy access to Oklahoma City
- **Coed** 248 undergraduate students, 88% full-time, 37% women, 63% men
- **Noncompetitive** entrance level

Undergraduates 218 full-time, 30 part-time. Students come from 11 states and territories, 4 other countries, 19% are from out of state, 10% African American, 4% Hispanic American, 10% Native American, 1% international, 10% transferred in.

Freshmen *Admission:* 84 enrolled. *Test scores:* ACT scores over 18: 65%; ACT scores over 24: 11%; ACT scores over 30: 1%.

Majors Biblical studies; business/commerce; communication/speech communication and rhetoric; elementary education; English; general studies; interdisciplinary studies; liberal arts and sciences/liberal studies; missionary studies and missiology; music; music performance; pastoral studies/counseling; physical education teaching and coaching; physical sciences; piano and organ; psychology; religious education; religious/sacred music; secondary education; social sciences; theology; youth ministry.

Academics *Calendar:* semesters. *Degrees:* associate, bachelor's, and master's. *Special study options:* academic remediation for entering students, accelerated degree program, adult/continuing education programs, advanced placement credit, English as a second language, independent study, internships, part-time degree program, summer session for credit.

Computers on Campus 22 computers/terminals are available on campus for general student use. Students can access the following: campus intranet, free student e-mail accounts. Campuswide network is available.

Student Life *Housing:* on-campus residence required through sophomore year. *Options:* men-only, women-only. Campus housing is university owned. *Activities and organizations:* drama/theater group, choral group. *Campus security:* 24-hour emergency response devices, controlled dormitory access. *Student services:* personal/psychological counseling.

Athletics Member NCCAA. *Intercollegiate sports:* baseball M, basketball M/W, soccer M, softball W, volleyball W. *Intramural sports:* basketball M/W, volleyball M/W.

Standardized Tests *Required:* SAT or ACT (for admission).

Costs (2008–09) *Comprehensive fee:* $13,960 includes full-time tuition ($7700), mandatory fees ($1560), and room and board ($4700). Part-time tuition: $280 per credit hour. *Required fees:* $17 per credit hour part-time, $170 per term part-time.

Applying *Options:* electronic application, early admission, deferred entrance. *Application fee:* $20. *Required:* high school transcript. *Required for some:* interview. *Recommended:* minimum 2.0 GPA.

Freshman Application Contact Hillsdale Free Will Baptist College, PO Box 7208, Moore, OK 73153-1208. *Phone:* 405-912-9007. *Fax:* 405-912-9050. *E-mail:* recruitment@hc.edu.

ITT TECHNICAL INSTITUTE

Oklahoma City, Oklahoma — www2.itt-tech.edu/dnm/campus/

- **Proprietary** 4-year, founded 2006
- **Coed**

Academics *Calendar:* quarters. *Degrees:* associate and bachelor's.

Freshman Application Contact Mr. Ron Gross, Director of Recruitment, ITT Technical Institute, 50 Penn Place—Suite 305, Oklahoma City, OK 73118. *Phone:* 405-810-4100. *Toll-free phone:* 800-518-1612.

ITT TECHNICAL INSTITUTE

Tulsa, Oklahoma — www.itt-tech.edu/

- **Proprietary** primarily 2-year, founded 2005
- **Coed**

Academics *Calendar:* quarters. *Degrees:* associate and bachelor's.

Standardized Tests *Required:* Wonderlic aptitude test (for admission).

Applying *Application fee:* $100. *Required:* high school transcript, interview. *Recommended:* letters of recommendation.

Freshman Application Contact Gigi Braecklein, Director of Recruitment, ITT Technical Institute, 4943 South 78th East Avenue, Tulsa, OK 74145. *Phone:* 918-619-8700.

LANGSTON UNIVERSITY

Langston, Oklahoma — www.lunet.edu/

- **State-supported** comprehensive, founded 1897, part of Oklahoma State Regents for Higher Education
- **Rural** 40-acre campus with easy access to Oklahoma City
- **Coed**

- **Minimally difficult** entrance level

Faculty *Student/faculty ratio:* 30:1.

Academics *Calendar:* semesters. *Degrees:* associate, bachelor's, and master's.

Athletics Member NAIA.

Standardized Tests *Required:* SAT or ACT (for admission), SAT or ACT (for placement).

Costs (2007–08) *Tuition:* contact university directly for tuition costs.

Financial Aid Of all full-time matriculated undergraduates who enrolled in 2006, 2,574 applied for aid, 1,919 were judged to have need, 875 had their need fully met. In 2006, 893 non-need-based awards were made. *Average percent of need met:* 65. *Average financial aid package:* $8496. *Average need-based loan:* $4614. *Average need-based gift aid:* $897. *Average non-need-based aid:* $2328. *Average indebtedness upon graduation:* $16,650.

Applying *Options:* electronic application. *Required:* high school transcript, minimum 2.7 GPA. *Required for some:* letters of recommendation.

Freshman Application Contact Maurice Osborne, Assistant Director of Admission, Langston University, Langston University, PO Box 728, Langston, OK 73120. *Phone:* 405-466-2984. *Toll-free phone:* 405-466-3428.

MID-AMERICA CHRISTIAN UNIVERSITY

Oklahoma City, Oklahoma **www.macu.edu/**

Freshman Application Contact Ms. Dani Brunet, Admissions Office Manager, Mid-America Christian University, 3500 Southwest 119th Street, Oklahoma City, OK 73170. *Phone:* 405-692-3180. *Fax:* 405-692-3165. *E-mail:* mbcinfo@mabc.edu.

NORTHEASTERN STATE UNIVERSITY

Tahlequah, Oklahoma **www.nsuok.edu/**

- **State-supported** comprehensive, founded 1846, part of Regional University System of Oklahoma
- **Small-town** 160-acre campus with easy access to Tulsa
- **Endowment** $85,590
- **Coed** 8,191 undergraduate students, 75% full-time, 62% women, 38% men
- **Moderately difficult** entrance level, 71% of applicants were admitted

Undergraduates 6,134 full-time, 2,057 part-time. Students come from 26 states and territories, 51 other countries, 4% are from out of state, 5% African American, 1% Asian American or Pacific Islander, 2% Hispanic American, 30% Native American, 3% international, 12% transferred in, 19% live on campus. *Retention:* 63% of 2006 full-time freshmen returned.

Freshmen *Admission:* 2,273 applied, 1,609 admitted, 1,017 enrolled. *Average high school GPA:* 3.20. *Test scores:* ACT scores over 18: 77%; ACT scores over 24: 19%; ACT scores over 30: 2%.

Faculty *Total:* 470, 65% full-time, 59% with terminal degrees. *Student/faculty ratio:* 22:1.

Majors Accounting; advertising; American Indian/Native American studies; American native/native American education; art; art teacher education; audiology and speech-language pathology; biology/biological sciences; biology teacher education; business administration and management; business/commerce; business teacher education; cell biology and histology; chemistry; chemistry teacher education; clinical laboratory science/medical technology; commercial and advertising art; computer science; criminal justice/law enforcement administration; design and visual communications; developmental and child psychology; dramatic/theater arts; early childhood education; education; electrical, electronic and communications engineering technology; elementary education; engineering technology; English; English/language arts teacher education; entrepreneurship; environmental/environmental health engineering; environmental science; family and consumer sciences/home economics teacher education; family and consumer sciences/human sciences; finance; fine/studio arts; foods, nutrition, and wellness; general studies; geography; health/health care administration; health professions related; health teacher education; history; human resources management; industrial safety technology; international business/trade/commerce; journalism; kindergarten/preschool education; kinesiology and exercise science; logistics and materials management; management information systems; marketing/marketing management; mathematics; mathematics teacher education; multi-/interdisciplinary studies related; music; music teacher education; nursing (registered nurse training); operations management; physical education teaching and coaching; physics teacher education; political science and government; psychology; public relations/image management; science teacher education; secondary education; social studies teacher education; social work; sociology; Spanish; Spanish language teacher education; special education; special education (specific learning disabilities); speech and rhetoric; speech teacher education; tourism and travel services management; wildlife biology.

Academics *Calendar:* semesters. *Degrees:* bachelor's, master's, first professional, post-master's, and postbachelor's certificates. *Special study options:* academic remediation for entering students, adult/continuing education programs, advanced placement credit, cooperative education, distance learning, double majors, honors programs, independent study, internships, part-time degree program, services for LD students, student-designed majors, summer session for credit. *ROTC:* Army (b).

Computers on Campus 897 computers/terminals and 900 ports are available on campus for general student use. Students can access the following: campus intranet, computer help desk, free student e-mail accounts, online (class) grades, online (class) schedules. Campuswide network is available. 100% of college-owned or -operated housing units are wired for high-speed Internet access. Wireless service is available via computer centers, computer labs, libraries, student centers.

Student Life *Housing:* on-campus residence required for freshman year. *Options:* coed, disabled students. Campus housing is university owned. Freshman applicants given priority for college housing. *Activities and organizations:* drama/theater group, student-run newspaper, television station, choral group, marching band, national fraternities, national sororities. *Campus security:* 24-hour emergency response devices and patrols, late-night transport/escort service, controlled dormitory access. *Student services:* health clinic, personal/psychological counseling.

Athletics Member NCAA. All Division II. *Intercollegiate sports:* baseball M (s), basketball M (s)/W (s), football M (s), golf M (s)/W (s), rock climbing M (c)/W (c), soccer M (s)/W (s), softball W (s), tennis W (s). *Intramural sports:* basketball M/W, bowling M/W, football M/W, golf M/W, racquetball M/W, soccer M/W, softball M/W, swimming and diving M/W, tennis M/W, volleyball M/W.

Standardized Tests *Required:* ACT (for admission).

Costs (2007–08) *Tuition:* state resident $2895 full-time, $97 per credit hour part-time; nonresident $8415 full-time, $281 per credit hour part-time. Full-time tuition and fees vary according to course level, course load, and location. Part-time tuition and fees vary according to course level and course load. *Required fees:* $903 full-time, $30 per credit hour part-time. *Room and board:* $4544. Room and board charges vary according to board plan and housing facility. *Waivers:* senior citizens and employees or children of employees.

Financial Aid Of all full-time matriculated undergraduates who enrolled in 2006, 4,477 applied for aid, 3,793 were judged to have need, 2,497 had their need fully met. 243 Federal Work-Study jobs (averaging $1536). 825 state and other part-time jobs (averaging $2111). In 2006, 241 non-need-based awards were made. *Average percent of need met:* 68%. *Average financial aid package:* $7393. *Average need-based loan:* $3665. *Average need-based gift aid:* $4106. *Average non-need-based aid:* $1861. *Average indebtedness upon graduation:* $19,971.

Applying *Options:* deferred entrance. *Required:* high school transcript, minimum 2.7 GPA, rank in upper 50% of high school class or minimum ACT composite score of 20. *Application deadlines:* 8/1 (freshmen), 8/1 (transfers). *Notification:* continuous (freshmen), continuous (transfers).

Freshman Application Contact Ms. Dawn Cain, Director of Admissions, Northeastern State University, 601 North Grand, Tahlequah, OK 74464. *Phone:* 918-444-2211. *Toll-free phone:* 800-722-9614. *Fax:* 918-458-2342. *E-mail:* cain@nsuok.edu.

NORTHWESTERN OKLAHOMA STATE UNIVERSITY

Alva, Oklahoma **www.nwosu.edu/**

- **State-supported** comprehensive, founded 1897, part of Oklahoma State Regents for Higher Education
- **Small-town** 70-acre campus
- **Endowment** $18.1 million
- **Coed** 1,787 undergraduate students, 78% full-time, 59% women, 41% men
- **Moderately difficult** entrance level, 100% of applicants were admitted

Undergraduates 1,385 full-time, 402 part-time. Students come from 35 states and territories, 25 other countries, 20% are from out of state, 5% African American, 0.6% Asian American or Pacific Islander, 4% Hispanic American, 5% Native American, 2% international, 20% transferred in, 20% live on campus. *Retention:* 68% of 2006 full-time freshmen returned.

Freshmen *Admission:* 541 applied, 541 admitted, 340 enrolled. *Average high school GPA:* 3.22. *Test scores:* ACT scores over 18: 70%; ACT scores over 24: 12%; ACT scores over 30: 1%.

Faculty *Total:* 133, 56% full-time, 34% with terminal degrees. *Student/faculty ratio:* 16:1.

Majors Accounting; agricultural business and management; agriculture; biology/biological sciences; business administration and management; business teacher education; chemistry; computer science; computer systems networking and telecommunications; criminal justice/police science; early childhood education; e-commerce; elementary education; English; English/language arts teacher education; general studies; health teacher education; history; information science/studies; kindergarten/preschool education; mass communication/media; mathematics; mathematics teacher education; multi-/interdisciplinary studies related; music; music teacher education; nursing (registered nurse training); physical education teaching and coaching; physics; political science and government; pre-dentistry studies; pre-law studies; pre-medical studies; psychology; science teacher education; secondary education; security and protective services related; social sciences; social work; sociology; Spanish; special education; speech and rhetoric; speech teacher education.

Academics *Calendar:* semesters. *Degrees:* bachelor's, master's, post-master's, and postbachelor's certificates. *Special study options:* academic remediation for entering students, adult/continuing education programs, advanced placement credit, distance learning, double majors, independent study, internships, off-campus study, part-time degree program, services for LD students, study abroad, summer session for credit.

Computers on Campus 172 computers/terminals are available on campus for general student use. Students can access the following: campus intranet, computer help desk, free student e-mail accounts, online (class) grades, online (class) registration, online (class) schedules. Campuswide network is available. 100% of college-owned or -operated housing units are wired for high-speed Internet access. Wireless service is available via classrooms, computer centers, computer labs, learning centers, libraries, student centers.

Student Life *Housing:* on-campus residence required for freshman year. *Options:* men-only, women-only. Campus housing is university owned. Freshman campus housing is guaranteed. *Activities and organizations:* drama/theater group, student-run newspaper, radio and television station, choral group, marching band, Student Government Association, Aggie Club, Phi Beta Lambda, Baptist Student Union. *Campus security:* 24-hour emergency response devices and patrols, late-night transport/escort service. *Student services:* personal/psychological counseling.

Athletics Member NAIA. *Intercollegiate sports:* baseball M (s), basketball M (s)/W (s), cheerleading M (s)/W (s), cross-country running M (s)/W (s), football M (s), golf M (s)/W (s), soccer W (s), softball W (s). *Intramural sports:* basketball M/W, football M, racquetball M/W, softball M/W, ultimate Frisbee M/W, volleyball M/W.

Standardized Tests *Required:* SAT or ACT (for admission), SAT or ACT (for placement).

Costs (2007–08) *Tuition:* state resident $3750 full-time, $125 per credit hour part-time; nonresident $9300 full-time, $310 per credit hour part-time. Full-time tuition and fees vary according to course load, location, and program. Part-time tuition and fees vary according to course load, location, and program. *Room and board:* $3400; room only: $1250. Room and board charges vary according to board plan. *Payment plan:* installment. *Waivers:* senior citizens and employees or children of employees.

Financial Aid Of all full-time matriculated undergraduates who enrolled in 2006, 901 applied for aid, 703 were judged to have need, 342 had their need fully met. 138 Federal Work-Study jobs (averaging $1087). 168 state and other part-time jobs (averaging $1068). In 2006, 203 non-need-based awards were made. *Average percent of need met:* 70%. *Average financial aid package:* $5872. *Average need-based loan:* $3273. *Average need-based gift aid:* $4148. *Average non-need-based aid:* $1263. *Average indebtedness upon graduation:* $13,808.

Applying *Options:* electronic application, early admission. *Application fee:* $15. *Required:* high school transcript. *Required for some:* essay or personal statement, minimum 2.7 GPA, 3 letters of recommendation. *Application deadlines:* rolling (freshmen), rolling (transfers). *Notification:* continuous (freshmen), continuous (transfers).

Freshman Application Contact Mr. Matt Adair, Director of Recruitment, Northwestern Oklahoma State University, 709 Oklahoma Boulevard, Alva, OK 73717-2799. *Phone:* 580-327-8545. *Fax:* 580-327-8699. *E-mail:* wmadair@nwosu.edu.

OKLAHOMA BAPTIST UNIVERSITY

Shawnee, Oklahoma **www.okbu.edu/**

Director of Admissions Mr. Trent Argo, Dean of Enrollment Management, Oklahoma Baptist University, Box 61174, Shawnee, OK 74804. *Phone:* 405-878-2033. *Toll-free phone:* 800-654-3285. *E-mail:* admissions@mail.okbu.edu.

OKLAHOMA CHRISTIAN UNIVERSITY

Oklahoma City, Oklahoma **www.oc.edu/**

- **Independent** comprehensive, founded 1950, affiliated with Church of Christ
- **Suburban** 200-acre campus
- **Endowment** $45.0 million
- **Coed** 1,998 undergraduate students, 97% full-time, 51% women, 49% men
- **Noncompetitive** entrance level, 74% of applicants were admitted

Undergraduates 1,944 full-time, 54 part-time. Students come from 29 other countries, 64% are from out of state, 5% African American, 2% Asian American or Pacific Islander, 3% Hispanic American, 4% Native American, 1% international, 5% transferred in, 72% live on campus. *Retention:* 73% of 2006 full-time freshmen returned.

Freshmen *Admission:* 1,602 applied, 1,192 admitted, 544 enrolled. *Average high school GPA:* 3.16. *Test scores:* ACT scores over 18: 92%; ACT scores over 24: 46%; ACT scores over 30: 8%.

Faculty *Total:* 213, 49% full-time, 48% with terminal degrees. *Student/faculty ratio:* 14:1.

Majors Accounting; advertising; American government and politics; art; biblical studies; biochemistry; biology/biological sciences; broadcast journalism; business administration and management; business/commerce; chemistry; child development; clinical laboratory science/medical technology; commercial and advertising art; computer engineering; computer science; creative writing; dramatic/theater arts; early childhood education; electrical, electronics and communications engineering; elementary education; engineering; English; English as a second/foreign language (teaching); English/language arts teacher education; family and community services; history; information science/studies; interior design; journalism; kindergarten/preschool education; liberal arts and sciences/liberal studies; marketing/marketing management; mass communication/media; mathematics; mathematics teacher education; mechanical engineering; missionary studies and missiology; music; music teacher education; physical education teaching and coaching; pre-law studies; psychology; public relations/image management; radio and television; religious education; religious studies; science teacher education; secondary education; social studies teacher education; Spanish; speech and rhetoric; voice and opera; wind/percussion instruments.

Academics *Calendar:* semesters. *Degrees:* bachelor's and master's. *Special study options:* academic remediation for entering students, accelerated degree program, advanced placement credit, distance learning, double majors, English as a second language, honors programs, independent study, internships, off-campus study, services for LD students, study abroad, summer session for credit. *ROTC:* Army (c), Air Force (c).

Computers on Campus 101 computers/terminals and 450 ports are available on campus for general student use. Students can access the following: campus intranet, computer help desk, free student e-mail accounts, online (class) grades, online (class) registration, online (class) schedules. Campuswide network is available. 100% of college-owned or -operated housing units are wired for high-speed Internet access. Wireless service is available via entire campus.

Student Life *Housing:* on-campus residence required through senior year. *Options:* men-only, women-only, disabled students. Campus housing is university owned. Freshman campus housing is guaranteed. *Activities and organizations:* drama/theater group, student-run newspaper, radio station, choral group, Outreach, Agape, College Women for Christ, Young Republicans, College Democrats. *Campus security:* 24-hour emergency response devices and patrols, late-night transport/escort service, controlled dormitory access. *Student services:* health clinic, personal/psychological counseling.

Athletics Member NAIA. *Intercollegiate sports:* baseball M (s), basketball M (s)/W (s), cross-country running M (s)/W (s), golf M (s), soccer M (s)/W (s), softball W (s), tennis M (s)/W (s), track and field M (s)/W (s). *Intramural sports:* basketball M/W, bowling M/W, cheerleading M/W, cross-country running M/W, football M/W, golf M/W, soccer M/W, softball M/W, swimming and diving M/W, table tennis M/W, tennis M/W, track and field M/W, volleyball M/W.

Standardized Tests *Required:* SAT or ACT (for admission).

Costs (2008–09) *Comprehensive fee:* $22,956 includes full-time tuition ($14,690), mandatory fees ($1876), and room and board ($6390). Part-time tuition: $612 per credit hour. *Required fees:* $925 per term part-time. *College room only:* $3190.

Financial Aid Of all full-time matriculated undergraduates who enrolled in 2003, 1,546 applied for aid, 1,049 were judged to have need, 237 had their need fully met. 200 Federal Work-Study jobs (averaging $1500). In 2003, 347 non-need-based awards were made. *Average percent of need met:* 57%. *Average financial aid package:* $11,748. *Average need-based loan:* $3841. *Average need-based gift aid:* $1737. *Average non-need-based aid:* $2233. *Average indebtedness upon graduation:* $25,100. *Financial aid deadline:* 8/31.

Applying *Options:* electronic application, early admission, deferred entrance. *Application fee:* $25. *Required:* high school transcript. *Application deadlines:* rolling (freshmen), rolling (transfers). *Notification:* continuous (freshmen), continuous (transfers).

Freshman Application Contact Ms. Risa Forrester, Dean of Admissions and Marketing, Oklahoma Christian University, Box 11000, Oklahoma City, OK 73136-1100. *Phone:* 405-425-5050. *Toll-free phone:* 800-877-5010. *Fax:* 405-425-5208. *E-mail:* info@oc.edu.

OKLAHOMA CITY UNIVERSITY

Oklahoma City, Oklahoma www.okcu.edu/

- **Independent United Methodist** comprehensive, founded 1904
- **Urban** 75-acre campus
- **Endowment** $87.6 million
- **Coed** 2,146 undergraduate students, 84% full-time, 62% women, 38% men
- **Moderately difficult** entrance level, 81% of applicants were admitted

Undergraduates 1,800 full-time, 346 part-time. Students come from 47 states and territories, 58 other countries, 39% are from out of state, 8% African American, 4% Asian American or Pacific Islander, 5% Hispanic American, 5% Native American, 17% international, 8% transferred in, 51% live on campus. *Retention:* 81% of 2006 full-time freshmen returned.

Freshmen *Admission:* 998 applied, 808 admitted, 400 enrolled. *Average high school GPA:* 3.52. *Test scores:* SAT critical reading scores over 500: 80%; SAT math scores over 500: 88%; ACT scores over 18: 99%; SAT critical reading scores over 600: 38%; SAT math scores over 600: 39%; ACT scores over 24: 62%; SAT critical reading scores over 700: 13%; SAT math scores over 700: 6%; ACT scores over 30: 9%.

Faculty *Total:* 340, 56% full-time. *Student/faculty ratio:* 11:1.

Majors Accounting; advertising; American studies; art history, criticism and conservation; arts management; art teacher education; biochemistry; biological and physical sciences; biology/biological sciences; biophysics; broadcast journalism; business administration and management; business/commerce; business/managerial economics; chemistry; cinematography and film/video production; commercial and advertising art; computer science; corrections; criminal justice/law enforcement administration; criminal justice/police science; dance; dramatic/theater arts; education; elementary education; English; finance; fine/studio arts; French; German; history; humanities; international business/trade/commerce; journalism; kindergarten/preschool education; kinesiology and exercise science; liberal arts and sciences/liberal studies; management information systems; marketing/marketing management; mass communication/media; mathematics; Montessori teacher education; music; music management and merchandising; music teacher education; music theory and composition; nursing (registered nurse training); philosophy; physical education teaching and coaching; physics; piano and organ; political science and government; pre-dentistry studies; pre-law studies; pre-medical studies; pre-nursing studies; pre-pharmacy studies; pre-veterinary studies; psychology; public relations/image management; radio and television; religious education; religious/sacred music; religious studies; science teacher education; secondary education; sociology; Spanish; speech and rhetoric; speech/theater education; theater design and technology; violin, viola, guitar and other stringed instruments; voice and opera; wind/percussion instruments.

Academics *Calendar:* semesters. *Degrees:* bachelor's, master's, and first professional. *Special study options:* academic remediation for entering students, accelerated degree program, adult/continuing education programs, advanced placement credit, cooperative education, double majors, English as a second language, external degree program, honors programs, independent study, internships, off-campus study, part-time degree program, services for LD students, student-designed majors, study abroad, summer session for credit. *ROTC:* Army (c), Air Force (c). *Unusual degree programs:* 3-2 Logan College of Chiropractic.

Computers on Campus 257 computers/terminals are available on campus for general student use. Students can access the following: campus intranet, computer help desk, free student e-mail accounts, online (class) grades, online (class) registration, online (class) schedules. Campuswide network is available. 100% of college-owned or -operated housing units are wired for high-speed Internet access. Wireless service is available via entire campus.

Student Life *Housing:* on-campus residence required through senior year. *Options:* men-only, women-only. Campus housing is university owned and is provided by a third party. Freshman applicants given priority for college housing. *Activities and organizations:* drama/theater group, student-run newspaper, television station, choral group, Residence Hall Association, STAR, Fellowship of Christian Athletes, Multicultural Student Association, A B Association, national fraternities, national sororities. *Campus security:* 24-hour emergency response devices and patrols, student patrols, late-night transport/escort service, Operation ID. *Student services:* health clinic, personal/psychological counseling.

Athletics Member NAIA. *Intercollegiate sports:* baseball M (s), basketball M (s)/W (s), cheerleading M (s)/W (s), crew M/W, golf M (s)/W (s), soccer M (s)/W (s), softball W (s), wrestling M (s)/W (s). *Intramural sports:* badminton M/W, basketball M/W, bowling M/W, crew M/W, fencing M/W, football M, golf M/W, softball M/W, table tennis M/W, volleyball M/W.

Standardized Tests *Required:* SAT or ACT (for admission).

Costs (2007–08) *Comprehensive fee:* $29,400 includes full-time tuition ($19,600), mandatory fees ($1400), and room and board ($8400). Full-time tuition and fees vary according to program. Part-time tuition: $670 per semester hour. Part-time tuition and fees vary according to program. *Required fees:* $120 per term part-time. *College room only:* $4650. Room and board charges vary according to board plan and housing facility. *Payment plans:* installment, deferred payment. *Waivers:* employees or children of employees.

Financial Aid Of all full-time matriculated undergraduates who enrolled in 2003, 868 applied for aid, 705 were judged to have need, 123 had their need fully met. 190 Federal Work-Study jobs (averaging $1842). 55 state and other part-time jobs (averaging $2214). In 2003, 130 non-need-based awards were made. *Average percent of need met:* 79%. *Average financial aid package:* $11,702. *Average need-based loan:* $3547. *Average need-based gift aid:* $8155. *Average non-need-based aid:* $7046. *Average indebtedness upon graduation:* $20,584.

Applying *Options:* electronic application, deferred entrance. *Application fee:* $30. *Required:* essay or personal statement, high school transcript, minimum 3.0 GPA. *Required for some:* interview, audition for music and dance programs. *Recommended:* interview. *Application deadlines:* 8/20 (freshmen), rolling (transfers). *Notification:* continuous (freshmen), continuous until 8/15 (transfers).

Freshman Application Contact Ms. Michelle Lockhart, Associate Director, Undergraduate Admissions, Oklahoma City University, 2501 North Blackwelder, Oklahoma City, OK 73106. *Phone:* 405-208-5340. *Toll-free phone:* 800-633-7242. *Fax:* 405-208-5916. *E-mail:* mlockhart@okcu.edu.

OKLAHOMA PANHANDLE STATE UNIVERSITY

Goodwell, Oklahoma www.opsu.edu/

- **State-supported** 4-year, founded 1909, part of Oklahoma State Regents for Higher Education
- **Rural** 40-acre campus
- **Coed** 1,152 undergraduate students, 83% full-time, 51% women, 49% men
- **Noncompetitive** entrance level, 96% of applicants were admitted

Undergraduates 954 full-time, 198 part-time. Students come from 35 states and territories, 17 other countries, 46% are from out of state, 7% African American, 0.6% Asian American or Pacific Islander, 13% Hispanic American, 3% Native American, 4% international, 18% transferred in, 17% live on campus.

Freshmen *Admission:* 313 applied, 301 admitted, 275 enrolled. *Average high school GPA:* 3.16. *Test scores:* SAT math scores over 500: 46%; SAT writing scores over 500: 24%; ACT scores over 18: 61%; SAT math scores over 600: 14%; SAT writing scores over 600: 8%; ACT scores over 24: 10%; SAT math scores over 700: 4%; ACT scores over 30: 1%.

Faculty *Total:* 82, 70% full-time, 26% with terminal degrees. *Student/faculty ratio:* 14:1.

Majors Accounting; agricultural business and management; agricultural teacher education; agriculture; agronomy and crop science; animal sciences; art; biological and physical sciences; biology/biological sciences; business administration and management; business teacher education; chemistry; clinical laboratory science/medical technology; computer and information sciences; elementary education; English; farm and ranch management; general studies; health and physical education; history; horse husbandry/equine science and management; industrial technology; mathematics; music; psychology; social sciences; Spanish.

Academics *Calendar:* semesters. *Degrees:* associate and bachelor's. *Special study options:* academic remediation for entering students, advanced placement credit, distance learning, double majors, English as a second language, internships, summer session for credit.

Computers on Campus Students can access the following: free student e-mail accounts, online (class) registration, online (class) schedules. Campuswide network is available. 85% of college-owned or -operated housing units are wired for high-speed Internet access. Wireless service is available via entire campus.

Student Life *Housing:* on-campus residence required for freshman year. *Options:* coed, men-only, women-only. Campus housing is university owned. Freshman campus housing is guaranteed. *Activities and organizations:* drama/theater group, student-run newspaper, radio station, choral group, marching band. *Campus security:* safety bars over door latches. *Student services:* health clinic, personal/psychological counseling.

Athletics Member NCAA. except baseball (Division II), men's and women's basketball (Division II), men's and women's cross-country running (Division II), football (Division II), men's and women's golf (Division II), softball (Division II), volleyball (Division II) *Intercollegiate sports:* baseball M (s), basketball M (s)/W (s), cheerleading W (s) (c), cross-country running M (s)/W (s), equestrian sports W (s) (c), football M (s), golf M (s)/W (s), soccer M (c)/W (c), softball W (s), volleyball W (s). *Intramural sports:* basketball M/W, football M/W, golf M/W, softball M/W, table tennis M/W, volleyball M/W.

Standardized Tests *Recommended:* SAT or ACT (for admission).

Costs (2007–08) *Tuition:* state resident $2490 full-time, $83 per hour part-time; nonresident $4890 full-time, $163 per hour part-time. Full-time tuition and fees vary according to course level and program. Part-time tuition and fees vary according to course level. *Required fees:* $1330 full-time, $40 per hour part-time, $65 per term part-time. *Room and board:* $3300; room only: $900. Room and board charges vary according to board plan and housing facility. *Payment plan:* installment. *Waivers:* senior citizens and employees or children of employees.

Financial Aid Of all full-time matriculated undergraduates who enrolled in 2006, 34 Federal Work-Study jobs (averaging $1207). 189 state and other part-time jobs (averaging $1604).

Applying *Options:* electronic application. *Required:* high school transcript. *Application deadlines:* rolling (freshmen), rolling (transfers).

Freshman Application Contact Mr. Bobby Jenkins, Registrar and Director of Admissions, Oklahoma Panhandle State University, PO Box 430, 323 Eagle Boulevard, Goodwell, OK 73939-0430. *Phone:* 580-349-1376. *Toll-free phone:* 800-664-6778. *Fax:* 580-349-1371. *E-mail:* opsu@opsu.edu.

OKLAHOMA STATE UNIVERSITY

Stillwater, Oklahoma **osu.okstate.edu/**

- **State-supported** university, founded 1890, part of Oklahoma State University
- **Small-town** 840-acre campus with easy access to Oklahoma City and Tulsa
- **Endowment** $302.5 million
- **Coed** 18,368 undergraduate students, 87% full-time, 49% women, 51% men
- **Moderately difficult** entrance level, 88% of applicants were admitted

Undergraduates 15,979 full-time, 2,389 part-time. Students come from 49 states and territories, 81 other countries, 16% are from out of state, 4% African American, 2% Asian American or Pacific Islander, 2% Hispanic American, 10% Native American, 3% international, 9% transferred in, 39% live on campus. *Retention:* 80% of 2006 full-time freshmen returned.

Freshmen *Admission:* 6,415 applied, 5,651 admitted, 3,209 enrolled. *Average high school GPA:* 3.54. *Test scores:* SAT critical reading scores over 500: 73%; SAT math scores over 500: 81%; ACT scores over 18: 98%; SAT critical reading scores over 600: 31%; SAT math scores over 600: 38%; ACT scores over 24: 60%; SAT critical reading scores over 700: 6%; SAT math scores over 700: 8%; ACT scores over 30: 12%.

Faculty *Total:* 1,216, 81% full-time, 79% with terminal degrees. *Student/faculty ratio:* 19:1.

Majors Accounting; aeronautics/aviation/aerospace science and technology; aerospace, aeronautical and astronautical engineering; agricultural business and management; agricultural communication/journalism; agricultural economics; agricultural teacher education; agriculture; American studies; animal sciences; architectural engineering; architecture; art; athletic training; biochemistry; biochemistry, biophysics and molecular biology related; biology/biological sciences; biomedical/medical engineering; botany/plant biology; broadcast journalism; business/commerce; business/managerial economics; cell and molecular biology; chemical engineering; chemistry; civil engineering; communication disorders; computer management; computer science; construction management; dramatic/theater arts; ecology; economics; education; electrical, electronic and communications engineering technology; electrical, electronics and communications engineering; elementary education; engineering; engineering technology; English; entomology; environmental science; environmental studies; finance; fire protection and safety technology; food science; forestry; French; general studies; geography; geology/earth science; German; health science; history; horticultural science; hotel/motel administration; human development and family studies; industrial engineering; interior design; international business/trade/commerce; journalism; landscape architecture; liberal arts and sciences/liberal studies; management information systems; management science; marketing/marketing management; mathematics; mechanical engineering; mechanical engineering/mechanical technology; microbiology; music; music teacher education; nutritional sciences; philosophy; physical education teaching and coaching; physics; physiology; plant sciences; political science and government; pre-veterinary studies; psychology; public health education and promotion; Russian; secondary education; sociology; Spanish; speech and rhetoric; statistics; technical teacher education; zoology/animal biology.

Academics *Calendar:* semesters. *Degrees:* bachelor's, master's, doctoral, first professional, post-master's, and postbachelor's certificates. *Special study options:* academic remediation for entering students, accelerated degree program, adult/continuing education programs, advanced placement credit, distance learning, double majors, English as a second language, freshman honors college, honors programs, independent study, internships, off-campus study, part-time degree program, services for LD students, student-designed majors, study abroad, summer session for credit. *ROTC:* Army (b), Air Force (b). *Unusual degree programs:* 3-2 accounting.

Computers on Campus Students can access the following: campus intranet, computer help desk, free student e-mail accounts, online (class) grades, online (class) registration, online (class) schedules. Campuswide network is available. 100% of college-owned or -operated housing units are wired for high-speed Internet access. Wireless service is available via computer centers, libraries, student centers.

Student Life *Housing:* on-campus residence required for freshman year. *Options:* coed, men-only, women-only, disabled students. Campus housing is university owned. Freshman campus housing is guaranteed. *Activities and organizations:* drama/theater group, student-run newspaper, radio and television station, choral group, marching band, Student Government Association, Campus Crusade for Christ, Flying Aggies, Block and Bridle Club, OSU Ski Club, national fraternities, national sororities. *Campus security:* 24-hour emergency response devices and patrols, student patrols, controlled dormitory access. *Student services:* health clinic, personal/psychological counseling, women's center, legal services.

Athletics Member NCAA. All Division I. *Intercollegiate sports:* baseball M (s), basketball M (s)/W (s), cross-country running M (s)/W (s), equestrian sports W (s), football M (s), golf M (s)/W (s), soccer W (s), softball W (s), tennis M (s)/W (s), track and field M (s)/W (s), wrestling M (s). *Intramural sports:* archery M/W, badminton M/W, basketball M/W, bowling M/W, crew M (c)/W (c), cross-country running M/W, football M/W, golf M/W, ice hockey M (c)/W (c), lacrosse M (c)/W (c), racquetball M/W, riflery M (c)/W (c), rugby M (c)/W (c), sailing M (c)/W (c), soccer M (c)/W (c), softball M/W, squash M/W, swimming and diving M/W, table tennis M/W, tennis M/W, track and field M/W, ultimate Frisbee M (c)/W (c), volleyball M/W, water polo M/W, weight lifting M/W, wrestling M.

Standardized Tests *Required:* SAT or ACT (for admission).

Costs (2007–08) *One-time required fee:* $70. *Tuition:* state resident $3585 full-time, $120 per credit hour part-time; nonresident $13,010 full-time, $434 per credit hour part-time. Full-time tuition and fees vary according to program and student level. Part-time tuition and fees vary according to program and student level. *Required fees:* $1906 full-time, $64 per credit hour part-time. *Room and board:* $6267; room only: $3267. Room and board charges vary according to board plan and housing facility. *Payment plan:* installment. *Waivers:* children of alumni.

Financial Aid Of all full-time matriculated undergraduates who enrolled in 2006, 10,643 applied for aid, 8,505 were judged to have need, 1,585 had their need fully met. 328 Federal Work-Study jobs (averaging $1796). 3,746 state and other part-time jobs (averaging $2091). In 2006, 3919 non-need-based awards were made. *Average percent of need met:* 73%. *Average financial aid package:* $9650. *Average need-based loan:* $4109. *Average need-based gift aid:* $4188. *Average non-need-based aid:* $3281. *Average indebtedness upon graduation:* $18,044.

Applying *Options:* electronic application. *Application fee:* $40. *Required:* high school transcript, minimum 3.0 GPA, class rank. *Required for some:* interview. *Application deadlines:* rolling (freshmen), rolling (out-of-state freshmen), rolling (transfers). *Notification:* continuous (freshmen), continuous (out-of-state freshmen), continuous (transfers).

Freshman Application Contact Oklahoma State University, 219 Student Union, Stillwater, OK 74078. *Phone:* 405-744-5358. *Toll-free phone:* 800-233-5019 Ext. 1 (in-state); 800-852-1255 (out-of-state). *Fax:* 405-744-7092. *E-mail:* admissions@okstate.edu.

OKLAHOMA WESLEYAN UNIVERSITY

Bartlesville, Oklahoma **www.okwu.edu/**

- **Independent** comprehensive, founded 1909, affiliated with Wesleyan Church
- **Small-town** 127-acre campus with easy access to Tulsa
- **Endowment** $2.5 million
- **Coed** 1,001 undergraduate students
- **Minimally difficult** entrance level, 48% of applicants were admitted

Undergraduates Students come from 33 states and territories, 9 other countries, 60% are from out of state, 5% African American, 0.5% Asian American or

Pacific Islander, 2% Hispanic American, 11% Native American, 2% international, 27% live on campus. *Retention:* 65% of 2006 full-time freshmen returned.

Freshmen *Admission:* 613 applied, 295 admitted. *Average high school GPA:* 3.43. *Test scores:* ACT scores over 18: 92%; ACT scores over 24: 34%; ACT scores over 30: 3%.

Faculty *Total:* 34, 91% full-time, 50% with terminal degrees. *Student/faculty ratio:* 14:1.

Majors Accounting; athletic training; behavioral sciences; biological and physical sciences; biology/biological sciences; business administration and management; business teacher education; chemistry; divinity/ministry; education; elementary education; English; English as a second/foreign language (teaching); history; information science/studies; kinesiology and exercise science; liberal arts and sciences/liberal studies; linguistics; mass communication/media; mathematics; music; music performance; natural sciences; nursing (registered nurse training); physical education teaching and coaching; physical therapy; political science and government; pre-dentistry studies; pre-law studies; pre-medical studies; pre-veterinary studies; religious studies; science teacher education; secondary education; social sciences; theology.

Academics *Calendar:* semesters. *Degrees:* certificates, diplomas, associate, bachelor's, and master's. *Special study options:* academic remediation for entering students, accelerated degree program, adult/continuing education programs, advanced placement credit, cooperative education, distance learning, double majors, English as a second language, external degree program, independent study, internships, off-campus study, part-time degree program, student-designed majors, study abroad, summer session for credit.

Computers on Campus 30 computers/terminals are available on campus for general student use. Students can access the following: computer help desk, free student e-mail accounts, online (class) grades, online (class) schedules. Campuswide network is available. 100% of college-owned or -operated housing units are wired for high-speed Internet access. Wireless service is available via entire campus.

Student Life *Housing:* on-campus residence required through junior year. *Options:* men-only, women-only. Campus housing is university owned. Freshman campus housing is guaranteed. *Activities and organizations:* student-run newspaper, choral group, Operation Saturation (Community Service Opportunities), Fellowship of Christian Athletes, Missions Support Groups, Intramurals, Student Government groups. *Campus security:* 24-hour emergency response devices and patrols, controlled dormitory access. *Student services:* health clinic, personal/psychological counseling.

Athletics Member NAIA, NCCAA. *Intercollegiate sports:* baseball M (s), basketball M (s)/W (s), golf M (s), soccer M (s)/W (s), tennis M (s)/W (s), volleyball W (s). *Intramural sports:* basketball M/W, football M/W, softball M/W, volleyball M/W.

Standardized Tests *Required:* SAT or ACT (for admission).

Costs (2008–09) *Comprehensive fee:* $22,635 includes full-time tuition ($15,685), mandatory fees ($900), and room and board ($6050). Part-time tuition: $650 per credit hour. *Required fees:* $55 per credit hour part-time. *College room only:* $3200.

Financial Aid Of all full-time matriculated undergraduates who enrolled in 2007, 449 applied for aid, 392 were judged to have need, 94 had their need fully met. 176 Federal Work-Study jobs (averaging $1484). 25 state and other part-time jobs (averaging $1425). In 2007, 57 non-need-based awards were made. *Average percent of need met:* 64%. *Average financial aid package:* $13,011. *Average need-based loan:* $4281. *Average need-based gift aid:* $10,910. *Average non-need-based aid:* $3741. *Average indebtedness upon graduation:* $21,473.

Applying *Options:* electronic application. *Application fee:* $25. *Required:* high school transcript, minimum ACT of 18 or SAT 860. *Recommended:* minimum 2.0 GPA. *Application deadlines:* rolling (freshmen), rolling (transfers).

Freshman Application Contact Mark Molder, Assistant Director of Enrollment Services, Oklahoma Wesleyan University, 2201 Silver Lake Road, Bartlesville, OK 74006-6299. *Phone:* 866-222-8226. *Toll-free phone:* 866-222-8226. *Fax:* 918-335-6229. *E-mail:* admissions@okwu.edu.

ORAL ROBERTS UNIVERSITY

Tulsa, Oklahoma **www.oru.edu/**

- **Independent interdenominational** comprehensive, founded 1963
- **Urban** 263-acre campus
- **Endowment** $66.4 million
- **Coed** 2,714 undergraduate students, 91% full-time, 59% women, 41% men
- **Moderately difficult** entrance level, 75% of applicants were admitted

Undergraduates 2,468 full-time, 246 part-time. Students come from 41 other countries, 61% are from out of state, 17% African American, 2% Asian American or Pacific Islander, 6% Hispanic American, 2% Native American, 7% international, 8% transferred in, 75% live on campus. *Retention:* 77% of 2006 full-time freshmen returned.

Freshmen *Admission:* 1,201 applied, 904 admitted, 627 enrolled. *Test scores:* SAT critical reading scores over 500: 68%; SAT math scores over 500: 56%; ACT scores over 18: 86%; SAT critical reading scores over 600: 25%; SAT math scores over 600: 23%; ACT scores over 24: 31%; SAT critical reading scores over 700: 7%; SAT math scores over 700: 5%; ACT scores over 30: 4%.

Faculty *Total:* 292, 65% full-time, 43% with terminal degrees. *Student/faculty ratio:* 13:1.

Majors Accounting; acting; art teacher education; biblical studies; biology/biological sciences; biomedical/medical engineering; business administration and management; business teacher education; chemistry; clinical laboratory science/medical technology; commercial and advertising art; communication/speech communication and rhetoric; computer and information sciences; computer engineering; computer science; dance; design and visual communications; dramatic/theater arts; early childhood education; education; educational leadership and administration; electrical, electronics and communications engineering; elementary education; engineering; engineering physics; English composition; English/language arts teacher education; finance; fine/studio arts; foreign language teacher education; French; German; health and physical education; health teacher education; history; international business/trade/commerce; international relations and affairs; kinesiology and exercise science; liberal arts and sciences/liberal studies; management information systems; management science; marketing/marketing management; mathematics; mathematics teacher education; mechanical engineering; missionary studies and missiology; music; music performance; music teacher education; music theory and composition; nursing (registered nurse training); organizational behavior; parks, recreation and leisure facilities management; pastoral studies/counseling; physical education teaching and coaching; physics; piano and organ; political science and government; psychology; religious education; religious/sacred music; science teacher education; social studies teacher education; social work; Spanish; Spanish language teacher education; special education; theater design and technology; theology; voice and opera.

Academics *Calendar:* semesters. *Degrees:* bachelor's, master's, doctoral, and first professional. *Special study options:* academic remediation for entering students, adult/continuing education programs, advanced placement credit, distance learning, double majors, English as a second language, external degree program, freshman honors college, honors programs, independent study, internships, off-campus study, part-time degree program, services for LD students, student-designed majors, study abroad, summer session for credit. *ROTC:* Air Force (c). *Unusual degree programs:* 3-2 education.

Computers on Campus 382 computers/terminals are available on campus for general student use. Students can access the following: free student e-mail accounts, online (class) registration. Campuswide network is available.

Student Life *Housing:* on-campus residence required through senior year. *Options:* men-only, women-only, disabled students. *Activities and organizations:* drama/theater group, student-run newspaper, radio and television station, choral group, missions, Student Nurse Association, American Management Society, Accounting Society. *Campus security:* 24-hour emergency response devices and patrols, late-night transport/escort service. *Student services:* health clinic, personal/psychological counseling.

Athletics Member NCAA. All Division I. *Intercollegiate sports:* baseball M (s), basketball M (s)/W (s), cross-country running M (s)/W (s), golf M (s)/W (s), soccer M (s)/W (s), tennis M (s)/W (s), track and field M (s)/W (s), volleyball W (s), wrestling M. *Intramural sports:* badminton M/W, basketball M/W, bowling M/W, football M/W, golf M/W, racquetball M/W, softball M/W, swimming and diving M/W, table tennis M/W, tennis M/W, volleyball M/W.

Standardized Tests *Required:* SAT or ACT (for admission).

Costs (2007–08) *Comprehensive fee:* $24,750 includes full-time tuition ($17,000), mandatory fees ($400), and room and board ($7350). Part-time tuition: $710 per credit hour.

Financial Aid Of all full-time matriculated undergraduates who enrolled in 2006, 2,338 applied for aid, 1,675 were judged to have need, 681 had their need fully met. 313 Federal Work-Study jobs (averaging $1590). 750 state and other part-time jobs (averaging $1500). In 2006, 466 non-need-based awards were made. *Average percent of need met:* 90%. *Average financial aid package:* $18,732. *Average need-based loan:* $10,999. *Average need-based gift aid:* $8802. *Average non-need-based aid:* $6885. *Average indebtedness upon graduation:* $35,200.

Applying *Options:* early action, deferred entrance. *Application fee:* $35. *Required:* essay or personal statement, high school transcript, minimum 2.0 GPA, 1 letter of recommendation, proof of immunization. *Required for some:* interview. *Recommended:* interview. *Application deadlines:* rolling (freshmen), rolling (transfers), 11/15 (early action). *Notification:* continuous (freshmen), continuous (transfers), 11/15 (early action).

Freshman Application Contact Chris Belcher, Director of Admissions, Oral Roberts University, 7777 South Lewis Avenue, Tulsa, OK 74171. *Phone:* 918-495-6529. *Toll-free phone:* 800-678-8876. *Fax:* 918-495-6222. *E-mail:* cbelcher@oru.edu.

ROGERS STATE UNIVERSITY

Claremore, Oklahoma www.rsu.edu/

- **State-supported** 4-year, founded 1909, part of Oklahoma State Regents for Higher Education
- **Small-town** 40-acre campus with easy access to Tulsa
- **Endowment** $8.1 million
- **Coed** 3,855 undergraduate students, 58% full-time, 64% women, 36% men
- **Noncompetitive** entrance level, 64% of applicants were admitted

Undergraduates 2,217 full-time, 1,638 part-time. Students come from 31 states and territories, 11 other countries, 4% are from out of state, 3% African American, 0.9% Asian American or Pacific Islander, 3% Hispanic American, 28% Native American, 0.5% international, 11% transferred in, 6% live on campus. *Retention:* 53% of 2006 full-time freshmen returned.

Freshmen *Admission:* 1,589 applied, 1,017 admitted, 799 enrolled. *Average high school GPA:* 3.08. *Test scores:* ACT scores over 18: 71%; ACT scores over 24: 16%; ACT scores over 30: 1%.

Faculty *Total:* 218, 44% full-time, 34% with terminal degrees. *Student/faculty ratio:* 20:1.

Majors Accounting; biology/biological sciences; business administration and management; community psychology; computer and information sciences; computer graphics; criminal justice/law enforcement administration; elementary education; emergency medical technology (EMT paramedic); engineering technologies related; fine arts related; history; legal assistant/paralegal; liberal arts and sciences/liberal studies; management information systems and services related; multi-/interdisciplinary studies related; nursing (registered nurse training); physics; radio, television, and digital communication related; secondary education; social sciences; sport and fitness administration/management.

Academics *Calendar:* semesters. *Degrees:* associate and bachelor's. *Special study options:* academic remediation for entering students, adult/continuing education programs, advanced placement credit, cooperative education, distance learning, double majors, external degree program, honors programs, independent study, internships, off-campus study, part-time degree program, services for LD students, summer session for credit. *ROTC:* Air Force (c).

Computers on Campus 327 computers/terminals are available on campus for general student use. Students can access the following: computer help desk, free student e-mail accounts, online (class) grades, online (class) registration, online (class) schedules, software to support courses. Campuswide network is available. 100% of college-owned or -operated housing units are wired for high-speed Internet access. Wireless service is available via libraries.

Student Life *Housing options:* coed. Campus housing is university owned. *Activities and organizations:* drama/theater group, student-run radio station, Student Government Association, Campus Crusade for Christ, Campus RiOT, Students in Free Enterprise (SIFE), Biology Club, national fraternities, national sororities. *Campus security:* 24-hour emergency response devices and patrols, student patrols, late-night transport/escort service. *Student services:* health clinic, personal/psychological counseling.

Athletics Member NAIA. *Intercollegiate sports:* basketball M/W, soccer M/W, softball W. *Intramural sports:* basketball M/W, football M/W, soccer M/W, softball M/W, table tennis M/W, volleyball M/W.

Standardized Tests *Required:* SAT or ACT (for admission). *Required for some:* ACT COMPASS (for students over 21). *Recommended:* ACT (for admission).

Costs (2007–08) *Tuition:* area resident $2483 full-time, $83 per credit hour part-time; nonresident $7448 full-time, $248 per credit hour part-time. Full-time tuition and fees vary according to course load, location, and program. Part-time tuition and fees vary according to course load, location, and program. *Required fees:* $1410 full-time, $46 per credit hour part-time, $15 per term part-time. *Room and board:* $6615; room only: $4455. Room and board charges vary according to board plan and housing facility. *Payment plan:* installment. *Waivers:* senior citizens and employees or children of employees.

Financial Aid Of all full-time matriculated undergraduates who enrolled in 2007, 4,004 applied for aid, 2,274 were judged to have need, 20 had their need fully met. 73 Federal Work-Study jobs (averaging $1331). 233 state and other part-time jobs (averaging $2043). In 2007, 80 non-need-based awards were made. *Average percent of need met:* 66%. *Average financial aid package:* $5408. *Average need-based loan:* $1624. *Average need-based gift aid:* $4092. *Average non-need-based aid:* $812. *Average indebtedness upon graduation:* $12,250.

Applying *Options:* electronic application. *Required:* high school transcript. *Required for some:* minimum 2.7 GPA. *Application deadlines:* rolling (freshmen), rolling (transfers).

Freshman Application Contact Ms. Lindsay Fields, Director of Enrollment Management, Roger's State University, Office of Admissions, 1701 West Will Rogers Boulevard, Claremore, OK 74017. *Phone:* 918-343-7545. *Toll-free phone:* 800-256-7511. *Fax:* 918-343-7595. *E-mail:* info@rsu.edu.

ST. GREGORY'S UNIVERSITY

Shawnee, Oklahoma www.stgregorys.edu/

- **Independent Roman Catholic** 4-year, founded 1875
- **Small-town** 640-acre campus with easy access to Oklahoma City
- **Endowment** $10.7 million
- **Coed** 755 undergraduate students, 53% full-time, 63% women, 37% men
- **Minimally difficult** entrance level, 72% of applicants were admitted

Undergraduates 398 full-time, 357 part-time. Students come from 17 states and territories, 15 other countries, 10% are from out of state, 7% African American, 0.4% Asian American or Pacific Islander, 7% Hispanic American, 8% Native American, 6% international, 16% transferred in, 65% live on campus. *Retention:* 65% of 2006 full-time freshmen returned.

Freshmen *Admission:* 271 applied, 195 admitted, 107 enrolled. *Average high school GPA:* 3.4. *Test scores:* ACT scores over 18: 78%; ACT scores over 24: 22%.

Faculty *Total:* 111, 31% full-time, 36% with terminal degrees. *Student/faculty ratio:* 10:1.

Majors Art; biology/biological sciences; business administration and management; criminal justice/police science; dance; English; English language and literature related; English/language arts teacher education; fine/studio arts; history; humanities; journalism; liberal arts and sciences/liberal studies; management science; marketing/marketing management; mathematics; mathematics teacher education; natural resources and conservation related; pastoral studies/counseling; philosophy; political science and government; pre-dentistry studies; pre-law studies; pre-medical studies; pre-nursing studies; pre-pharmacy studies; psychology; social sciences; social studies teacher education; sociology; theology; visual and performing arts.

Academics *Calendar:* semesters. *Degrees:* associate and bachelor's. *Special study options:* accelerated degree program, adult/continuing education programs, advanced placement credit, distance learning, double majors, English as a second language, external degree program, honors programs, independent study, internships, off-campus study, part-time degree program, services for LD students, student-designed majors, study abroad, summer session for credit. *ROTC:* Air Force (c).

Computers on Campus 60 computers/terminals and 100 ports are available on campus for general student use. Students can access the following: campus intranet, computer help desk, free student e-mail accounts, online (class) grades, online (class) registration, online (class) schedules. Campuswide network is available. 100% of college-owned or -operated housing units are wired for high-speed Internet access. Wireless service is available via entire campus.

Student Life *Housing:* on-campus residence required through senior year. *Options:* men-only, women-only, disabled students. Campus housing is university owned. Freshman campus housing is guaranteed. *Activities and organizations:* drama/theater group, choral group, Student Government Association, Delta Epsilon Sigma Homer Society, Campus Ministry, Institute for Theological Encounter with Science and Technology, Drama Club. *Campus security:* 24-hour emergency response devices and patrols, late-night transport/escort service, controlled dormitory access. *Student services:* personal/psychological counseling.

Athletics Member NAIA. *Intercollegiate sports:* baseball M (s), basketball M (s)/W (s), soccer M (s)/W (s), softball W (s), volleyball W (s). *Intramural sports:* basketball M/W, cheerleading M/W, football M/W, racquetball M/W, soccer M/W, softball M/W, swimming and diving M/W, table tennis M/W, tennis M/W, volleyball M/W.

Standardized Tests *Required:* SAT or ACT (for admission).

Costs (2008–09) *Comprehensive fee:* $21,554 includes full-time tuition ($14,660), mandatory fees ($900), and room and board ($5994). Part-time tuition: $490 per hour. *Required fees:* $38 per hour part-time. *College room only:* $3400.

Financial Aid Of all full-time matriculated undergraduates who enrolled in 2005, 555 applied for aid, 521 were judged to have need, 60 had their need fully met. 38 Federal Work-Study jobs (averaging $867). 24 state and other part-time jobs (averaging $2551). In 2005, 61 non-need-based awards were made. *Average percent of need met:* 69%. *Average financial aid package:* $10,686. *Average need-based loan:* $3720. *Average need-based gift aid:* $6883. *Average non-need-based aid:* $1500. *Average indebtedness upon graduation:* $10,160.

Applying *Options:* electronic application, deferred entrance. *Application fee:* $25. *Required:* high school transcript, minimum 2.75 GPA. *Required for some:* essay or personal statement, letters of recommendation, interview. *Application deadlines:* rolling (freshmen), rolling (transfers). *Notification:* continuous (freshmen), continuous (transfers).

Freshman Application Contact Mr. Bill Halbach, Director of Admissions, St. Gregory's University, 1900 West MacArthur Drive, Shawnee, OK 74804. *Phone:* 405-878-5447. *Toll-free phone:* 888-STGREGS. *Fax:* 405-878-5198. *E-mail:* admissions@stgregorys.edu.

SOUTHEASTERN OKLAHOMA STATE UNIVERSITY

Durant, Oklahoma **www.sosu.edu/**

- **State-supported** comprehensive, founded 1909, part of Oklahoma State Regents for Higher Education
- **Small-town** 177-acre campus
- **Endowment** $13.0 million
- **Coed** 3,615 undergraduate students, 78% full-time, 56% women, 44% men
- **Moderately difficult** entrance level, 72% of applicants were admitted

Undergraduates 2,824 full-time, 791 part-time. Students come from 33 states and territories, 24 other countries, 22% are from out of state, 6% African American, 0.8% Asian American or Pacific Islander, 3% Hispanic American, 30% Native American, 0.9% international, 11% transferred in, 9% live on campus.

Freshmen *Admission:* 1,130 applied, 810 admitted, 663 enrolled. *Average high school GPA:* 3.29. *Test scores:* ACT scores over 18: 82%; ACT scores over 24: 20%; ACT scores over 30: 1%.

Faculty *Total:* 238, 60% full-time, 52% with terminal degrees. *Student/faculty ratio:* 19:1.

Majors Accounting; airline pilot and flight crew; art; art teacher education; aviation/airway management; biology/biological sciences; biotechnology; botany/plant biology; business administration and management; chemistry; communication and journalism related; communication/speech communication and rhetoric; computer and information sciences; criminal justice/safety; dramatic/theater arts; economics; education; elementary education; English; English/language arts teacher education; environmental science; finance; fish/game management; general studies; health teacher education; history; industrial technology; information science/studies; kindergarten/preschool education; management information systems and services related; management science; marketing/marketing management; mathematics; mathematics teacher education; medical laboratory technology; music; music performance; music teacher education; natural resources/conservation; occupational safety and health technology; office management; parks, recreation and leisure; physical education teaching and coaching; political science and government; psychology; science teacher education; secondary education; social studies teacher education; sociology; Spanish; Spanish language teacher education; special education related; wildlife and wildlands science and management; zoology/animal biology.

Academics *Calendar:* semesters. *Degrees:* bachelor's, master's, and post-master's certificates. *Special study options:* academic remediation for entering students, accelerated degree program, adult/continuing education programs, advanced placement credit, distance learning, double majors, honors programs, independent study, internships, off-campus study, part-time degree program, services for LD students, summer session for credit.

Computers on Campus 472 computers/terminals and 472 ports are available on campus for general student use. Students can access the following: campus intranet, computer help desk, free student e-mail accounts, online (class) grades, online (class) registration, online (class) schedules, campus Blackboard classes. Campuswide network is available. 100% of college-owned or -operated housing units are wired for high-speed Internet access. Wireless service is available via classrooms, computer labs, dorm rooms, learning centers, libraries, student centers.

Student Life *Housing:* on-campus residence required for freshman year. *Options:* coed, men-only, women-only, disabled students. Campus housing is university owned. Freshman campus housing is guaranteed. *Activities and organizations:* drama/theater group, student-run newspaper, radio station, choral group, marching band, Baptist Collegiate Ministries, Fellowship of Christian Athletes, Wesley Foundation, Resident Hall Association, national fraternities, national sororities. *Campus security:* 24-hour patrols, late-night transport/escort service. *Student services:* health clinic, personal/psychological counseling.

Athletics Member NCAA. All Division II. *Intercollegiate sports:* baseball M (s), basketball M (s)/W (s), cross-country running W (s), football M (s), softball W (s), tennis M (s)/W (s), volleyball W (s). *Intramural sports:* basketball M/W, football M.

Standardized Tests *Required:* SAT or ACT (for admission).

Costs (2007–08) *Tuition:* state resident $3249 full-time, $108 per credit hour part-time; nonresident $9044 full-time, $301 per credit hour part-time. Full-time tuition and fees vary according to course level. Part-time tuition and fees vary according to course level and course load. *Required fees:* $677 full-time, $23 per credit hour part-time. *Room and board:* $4284; room only: $1730. Room and board charges vary according to board plan and housing facility. *Waivers:* minority students, children of alumni, senior citizens, and employees or children of employees.

Financial Aid Of all full-time matriculated undergraduates who enrolled in 2006, 1,525 applied for aid, 1,462 were judged to have need, 938 had their need fully met. 143 Federal Work-Study jobs (averaging $1179). 576 state and other part-time jobs (averaging $1011). In 2006, 24 non-need-based awards were made. *Average percent of need met:* 67%. *Average financial aid package:* $1190. *Average need-based loan:* $2022. *Average need-based gift aid:* $1202. *Average non-need-based aid:* $633. *Average indebtedness upon graduation:* $6852.

Applying *Application fee:* $20. *Required:* high school transcript. *Required for some:* interview. *Application deadlines:* rolling (freshmen), rolling (transfers). *Notification:* continuous (freshmen), continuous (transfers).

Director of Admissions Ms. Kristie Luke, Associate Dean of Admissions and Records/Registrar, Southeastern Oklahoma State University, 1405 North 4th Avenue PMB 4225, Durant, OK 74701-0609. *Phone:* 580-745-2060. *Toll-free phone:* 800-435-1327. *Fax:* 580-745-7502. *E-mail:* kluke@sosu.edu.

SOUTHERN NAZARENE UNIVERSITY

Bethany, Oklahoma **www.snu.edu/**

Freshman Application Contact Mr. Warren W. Rogers III, Director of Admissions, Southern Nazarene University, 6729 Northwest 39th Expressway, Bethany, OK 73008. *Phone:* 405-491-6324. *Toll-free phone:* 800-648-9899. *Fax:* 405-491-6320. *E-mail:* admiss@snu.edu.

SOUTHWESTERN CHRISTIAN UNIVERSITY

Bethany, Oklahoma **www.swcu.edu/**

Freshman Application Contact Megan Miles, Director of Admissions, Southwestern Christian University, PO Box 340, Bethany, OK 73008-0340. *Phone:* 405-789-7661. *Fax:* 405-495-0078. *E-mail:* admissions@swcu.edu.

SOUTHWESTERN OKLAHOMA STATE UNIVERSITY

Weatherford, Oklahoma **www.swosu.edu/**

- **State-supported** comprehensive, founded 1901, part of Southwestern Oklahoma State University
- **Small-town** 73-acre campus with easy access to Oklahoma City
- **Endowment** $9.1 million
- **Coed** 4,279 undergraduate students, 85% full-time, 59% women, 41% men
- **Minimally difficult** entrance level, 90% of applicants were admitted

Undergraduates 3,653 full-time, 626 part-time. Students come from 32 states and territories, 32 other countries, 12% are from out of state, 5% African American, 1% Asian American or Pacific Islander, 5% Hispanic American, 7% Native American, 3% international, 7% transferred in, 25% live on campus. *Retention:* 64% of 2006 full-time freshmen returned.

Freshmen *Admission:* 1,425 applied, 1,284 admitted, 899 enrolled. *Average high school GPA:* 3.35. *Test scores:* ACT scores over 18: 79%; ACT scores over 24: 29%; ACT scores over 30: 4%.

Faculty *Total:* 230, 93% full-time. *Student/faculty ratio:* 20:1.

Majors Accounting; art teacher education; biology/biological sciences; biophysics; business administration and management; chemistry; clinical laboratory science/medical technology; commercial and advertising art; computer and information sciences; computer science; criminal justice/law enforcement administration; education; elementary education; engineering physics; engineering technology; English; English/language arts teacher education; finance; health/health care administration; health information/medical records administration; history; history teacher education; industrial arts; industrial technology; marketing/marketing management; mass communication/media; mathematics; music; music management and merchandising; music teacher education; music therapy; nursing (registered nurse training); parks, recreation and leisure; pharmacy; physical education teaching and coaching; physics; piano and organ; political science and government; pre-dentistry studies; pre-law studies; pre-medical studies; pre-veterinary studies; psychology; religious/sacred music; science teacher education; secondary education; social science teacher education; social work; special education; technology/industrial arts teacher education; therapeutic recreation; voice and opera; wind/percussion instruments.

Academics *Calendar:* semesters. *Degrees:* associate, bachelor's, master's, and first professional. *Special study options:* academic remediation for entering students, accelerated degree program, adult/continuing education programs, advanced placement credit, cooperative education, distance learning, double majors, independent study, internships, off-campus study, part-time degree program, services for LD students, student-designed majors, summer session for credit.

Computers on Campus 270 computers/terminals are available on campus for general student use. Campuswide network is available.

Student Life *Housing options:* men-only, women-only. Campus housing is university owned. Freshman campus housing is guaranteed. *Activities and organizations:* drama/theater group, student-run newspaper, choral group, marching band, Student Education Association, Baptist Student Union, Southwestern Pharmaceutical Association, Gamma Delta Kappa, Bible Chair Student Union, national fraternities. *Campus security:* late-night transport/escort service, controlled dormitory access, 20-hour campus emergency security. *Student services:* health clinic, personal/psychological counseling.

Athletics Member NCAA. All Division II. *Intercollegiate sports:* baseball M (s), basketball M (s)/W (s), cheerleading M/W, cross-country running W (s), equestrian sports M (s)/W (s), football M (s), golf M (s)/W (s), soccer W (s), softball W (s). *Intramural sports:* basketball M/W, bowling M/W, football M/W, softball M/W, volleyball M/W, weight lifting M.

Standardized Tests *Required:* SAT (for admission).

Costs (2007–08) *Tuition:* state resident $3000 full-time, $100 per credit hour part-time; nonresident $7800 full-time, $260 per credit hour part-time. Full-time tuition and fees vary according to program. Part-time tuition and fees vary according to program. *Required fees:* $750 full-time, $25 per credit hour part-time. *Room and board:* $3800; room only: $1500. Room and board charges vary according to board plan. *Payment plan:* installment. *Waivers:* senior citizens and employees or children of employees.

Applying *Options:* deferred entrance. *Application fee:* $15. *Required:* high school transcript, minimum 2.0 GPA. *Application deadlines:* rolling (freshmen), rolling (transfers). *Notification:* continuous (freshmen), continuous (transfers).

Freshman Application Contact Ms. Connie Phillips, Admission Counselor, Southwestern Oklahoma State University, 100 Campus Drive, Weatherford, OK 73096. *Phone:* 580-774-3009. *Fax:* 580-774-3795. *E-mail:* ropers@swosu.edu.

SPARTAN COLLEGE OF AERONAUTICS AND TECHNOLOGY

Tulsa, Oklahoma **www.spartan.edu/**

Freshman Application Contact Mr. Mark Fowler, Vice President of Student Records and Finance, Spartan College of Aeronautics and Technology, 8820 East Pine Street, PO Box 582833, Tulsa, OK 74158-2833. *Phone:* 918-836-6886.

UNIVERSITY OF CENTRAL OKLAHOMA

Edmond, Oklahoma **www.ucok.edu/**

- **State-supported** comprehensive, founded 1890, part of Oklahoma State Regents for Higher Education
- **Suburban** 200-acre campus with easy access to Oklahoma City
- **Endowment** $8.6 million
- **Coed** 14,339 undergraduate students, 70% full-time, 58% women, 42% men
- **Minimally difficult** entrance level, 72% of applicants were admitted

Undergraduates 9,973 full-time, 4,366 part-time. Students come from 47 states and territories, 76 other countries, 4% are from out of state, 10% African American, 3% Asian American or Pacific Islander, 4% Hispanic American, 5% Native American, 6% international, 11% transferred in, 12% live on campus.

Freshmen *Admission:* 4,450 applied, 3,219 admitted, 2,179 enrolled. *Average high school GPA:* 3.28. *Test scores:* ACT scores over 18: 89%; ACT scores over 24: 24%; ACT scores over 30: 2%.

Faculty *Total:* 834, 52% full-time. *Student/faculty ratio:* 22:1.

Majors Accounting; actuarial science; adult and continuing education; advertising; applied mathematics; art; art teacher education; audiology and speech-language pathology; biology/biological sciences; biomedical/medical engineering; broadcast journalism; business administration and management; business/commerce; business/managerial economics; business teacher education; chemistry; child development; child guidance; clinical laboratory science/medical technology; clothing/textiles; commercial and advertising art; communication/speech communication and rhetoric; computer science; consumer merchandising/retailing management; counselor education/school counseling and guidance; criminal justice/law enforcement administration; criminal justice/safety; dance; dietetics; dramatic/theater arts; economics; educational/instructional media design; educational leadership and administration; education (specific subject areas) related; elementary education; English; English/language arts teacher education; family and consumer sciences/home economics teacher education; family and consumer sciences/human sciences; fashion merchandising; finance; foods, nutrition, and wellness; forensic science and technology; French; funeral service and mortuary science; geography; German; health and physical education related; health occupations teacher education; history; history teacher education; hotel/motel administration; human resources management; interior design; journalism; kindergarten/preschool education; liberal arts and sciences/liberal studies; marketing/marketing management; mathematics; mathematics teacher education; music; music teacher education; nursing (registered nurse training); occupational safety and health technology; philosophy; photography; physical education teaching and coaching; physics; piano and organ; political science and government; psychology; public relations/image management; radio and television; reading teacher education; real estate; retailing; safety/security technology; sales, distribution and marketing; science teacher education; secondary education; social studies teacher education; sociology; Spanish; special education; trade and industrial teacher education; violin, viola, guitar and other stringed instruments; voice and opera; wind/percussion instruments.

Academics *Calendar:* semesters. *Degrees:* certificates, bachelor's, and master's. *Special study options:* accelerated degree program, adult/continuing education programs, advanced placement credit, distance learning, double majors, English as a second language, honors programs, independent study, internships, part-time degree program, services for LD students, summer session for credit. *ROTC:* Army (b).

Computers on Campus 400 computers/terminals are available on campus for general student use. Campuswide network is available.

Student Life *Housing options:* coed, men-only, women-only. Campus housing is university owned and leased by the school. *Activities and organizations:* drama/theater group, student-run newspaper, radio and television station, choral group, marching band, Malaysian Student Association, Baptist Student Union, Student Government Association, Association of Women Students, University Center Activities Board, national fraternities, national sororities. *Campus security:* 24-hour emergency response devices and patrols, late-night transport/escort service. *Student services:* health clinic, personal/psychological counseling.

Athletics Member NCAA. All Division II. *Intercollegiate sports:* baseball M (s), basketball M (s)/W (s), cross-country running M (s)/W (s), football M (s), golf M (s)/W (s), soccer W (s), softball W (s), tennis M (s)/W (s), volleyball W (s), wrestling M (s). *Intramural sports:* baseball M, basketball M/W, bowling M/W, football M/W, golf M/W, soccer M/W, softball M/W, swimming and diving M/W, table tennis M/W, tennis M/W, track and field M/W, volleyball M/W, wrestling M.

Standardized Tests *Required:* SAT or ACT (for admission).

Costs (2007–08) *Tuition:* state resident $3315 full-time, $111 per semester hour part-time; nonresident $9188 full-time, $306 per semester hour part-time. Full-time tuition and fees vary according to course load, degree level, and program. Part-time tuition and fees vary according to course load, degree level, and program. *Required fees:* $542 full-time, $18 per semester hour part-time. *Room and board:* $6380; room only: $3930. Room and board charges vary according to board plan and housing facility. *Payment plans:* installment, deferred payment. *Waivers:* employees or children of employees.

Financial Aid Of all full-time matriculated undergraduates who enrolled in 2006, 6,042 applied for aid, 4,861 were judged to have need, 515 had their need fully met. 204 Federal Work-Study jobs (averaging $2012). In 2006, 823 non-need-based awards were made. *Average percent of need met:* 67%. *Average financial aid package:* $6291. *Average need-based loan:* $3840. *Average need-based gift aid:* $6422. *Average non-need-based aid:* $2523. *Average indebtedness upon graduation:* $15,785.

Applying *Options:* electronic application, deferred entrance. *Application fee:* $25. *Required:* high school transcript, minimum 2.7 GPA, rank in upper 50% of high school class. *Application deadlines:* rolling (freshmen), rolling (transfers). *Notification:* continuous (freshmen), continuous (transfers).

Freshman Application Contact Ms. Linda Lofton, Director, Admissions and Records Processing, University of Central Oklahoma, Office of Enrollment Services, 100 North University Drive, Box 151, Edmond, OK 73034-5209.

Phone: 405-974-2338 Ext. 2338. *Toll-free phone:* 800-254-4215. *Fax:* 405-341-4964. *E-mail:* admituco@ucok.edu.

UNIVERSITY OF OKLAHOMA

Norman, Oklahoma **www.ou.edu/**

- **State-supported** university, founded 1890
- **Suburban** 3762-acre campus with easy access to Oklahoma City
- **Endowment** $783.3 million
- **Coed** 19,693 undergraduate students, 86% full-time, 49% women, 51% men
- **Moderately difficult** entrance level, 89% of applicants were admitted

Undergraduates 17,013 full-time, 2,680 part-time. Students come from 52 states and territories, 75 other countries, 25% are from out of state, 6% African American, 6% Asian American or Pacific Islander, 4% Hispanic American, 8% Native American, 2% international, 8% transferred in, 29% live on campus. *Retention:* 84% of 2006 full-time freshmen returned.

Freshmen *Admission:* 8,767 applied, 7,788 admitted, 3,883 enrolled. *Average high school GPA:* 3.59. *Test scores:* SAT critical reading scores over 500: 82%; SAT math scores over 500: 87%; ACT scores over 18: 98%; SAT critical reading scores over 600: 41%; SAT math scores over 600: 47%; ACT scores over 24: 73%; SAT critical reading scores over 700: 12%; SAT math scores over 700: 12%; ACT scores over 30: 25%.

Faculty *Total:* 1,370, 81% full-time, 77% with terminal degrees. *Student/faculty ratio:* 19:1.

Majors Accounting; advertising; aeronautics/aviation/aerospace science and technology; aerospace, aeronautical and astronautical engineering; African-American/Black studies; American Indian/Native American studies; anthropology; architecture; architecture related; area studies; area studies related; art; art history, criticism and conservation; astronomy; astrophysics; atmospheric sciences and meteorology; biomedical/medical engineering; botany/plant biology; broadcast journalism; business administration and management; business/managerial economics; chemical engineering; chemistry; Chinese; cinematography and film/video production; civil engineering; classics and languages, literatures and linguistics; clinical/medical laboratory technology; communication and journalism related; communication/speech communication and rhetoric; computer and information sciences; computer engineering; criminology; dance; design and visual communications; dramatic/theater arts; early childhood education; economics; education (specific subject areas) related; electrical, electronics and communications engineering; elementary education; engineering; engineering physics; English; English language and literature related; English/language arts teacher education; entrepreneurship; environmental design/architecture; environmental/environmental health engineering; environmental science; finance; fine/studio arts; foreign language teacher education; French; geography; geological and earth sciences/geosciences related; geology/earth science; geophysics and seismology; German; health and physical education; history; human resources management and services related; industrial engineering; interior design; international business/trade/commerce; journalism; liberal arts and sciences/liberal studies; library science; linguistics; management information systems; marketing/marketing management; mathematics; mathematics teacher education; mechanical engineering; medical laboratory technology; microbiology; multi-/interdisciplinary studies related; music; music performance; music theory and composition; petroleum engineering; philosophy; photography; physics; piano and organ; political science and government; professional studies; psychology; public administration; public relations/image management; religious studies; Russian; science teacher education; social studies teacher education; social work; sociology; Spanish; special education; violin, viola, guitar and other stringed instruments; visual and performing arts related; voice and opera; wind/percussion instruments; women's studies; zoology/animal biology.

Academics *Calendar:* semesters. *Degrees:* certificates, bachelor's, master's, doctoral, first professional, and post-master's certificates. *Special study options:* academic remediation for entering students, accelerated degree program, adult/continuing education programs, advanced placement credit, cooperative education, distance learning, double majors, English as a second language, external degree program, freshman honors college, honors programs, independent study, internships, off-campus study, part-time degree program, services for LD students, student-designed majors, study abroad, summer session for credit. *ROTC:* Army (b), Navy (b), Air Force (b). *Unusual degree programs:* 3-2 business administration; engineering; English, mathematics/biostatistics, computer science.

Computers on Campus 1,200 computers/terminals and 500 ports are available on campus for general student use. Students can access the following: campus intranet, computer help desk, free student e-mail accounts, online (class) grades, online (class) registration, online (class) schedules. Campuswide network is available. 100% of college-owned or -operated housing units are wired for high-speed Internet access. Wireless service is available via classrooms, computer centers, computer labs, learning centers, libraries, student centers.

Student Life *Housing:* on-campus residence required for freshman year. *Options:* coed, men-only, women-only, disabled students. Campus housing is university owned. Freshman campus housing is guaranteed. *Activities and organizations:* drama/theater group, student-run newspaper, radio and television station, choral group, marching band, Campus Activities Council, University of Oklahoma Student Association, OU Cousins, fraternities/sororities, cultural student organizations, national fraternities, national sororities. *Campus security:* 24-hour emergency response devices and patrols, student patrols, late-night transport/escort service, controlled dormitory access, crime prevention programs, police bicycle patrols, self-defense classes. *Student services:* health clinic, personal/psychological counseling, women's center, legal services.

Athletics Member NCAA. All Division I except football (Division I-A). *Intercollegiate sports:* baseball M (s), basketball M (s)/W (s), cross-country running M (s)/W (s), golf M (s)/W (s), gymnastics M (s)/W (s), soccer W (s), softball W (s), tennis M (s)/W (s), track and field M (s)/W (s), volleyball W (s), wrestling M (s). *Intramural sports:* badminton M/W, basketball M/W, crew M (c)/W (c), cross-country running M/W, equestrian sports M (c)/W (c), football M/W, golf M/W, ice hockey M (c), lacrosse M (c), racquetball M/W, rock climbing M/W, rugby M (c)/W (c), sailing M (c)/W (c), soccer M/W, softball M/W, swimming and diving M/W, table tennis M/W, tennis M/W, ultimate Frisbee M (c)/W (c), volleyball M/W, water polo M (c)/W (c).

Standardized Tests *Required:* SAT or ACT (for admission).

Costs (2007–08) *Tuition:* state resident $2609 full-time, $109 per credit hour part-time; nonresident $9900 full-time, $413 per credit hour part-time. Full-time tuition and fees vary according to course load, location, program, and reciprocity agreements. Part-time tuition and fees vary according to course load, location, program, and reciprocity agreements. *Required fees:* $1925 full-time, $70 per credit hour part-time, $122 per term part-time. *Room and board:* $7058; room only: $3854. Room and board charges vary according to board plan and housing facility. *Payment plan:* installment. *Waivers:* children of alumni, senior citizens, and employees or children of employees.

Financial Aid Of all full-time matriculated undergraduates who enrolled in 2006, 8,863 applied for aid, 7,939 were judged to have need, 3,731 had their need fully met. 603 Federal Work-Study jobs (averaging $2267). In 2006, 1,580 non-need-based awards were made. *Average percent of need met:* 85%. *Average financial aid package:* $9811. *Average need-based loan:* $4362. *Average need-based gift aid:* $4032. *Average non-need-based aid:* $1267. *Average indebtedness upon graduation:* $19,454.

Applying *Options:* electronic application. *Application fee:* $40. *Required:* high school transcript, minimum 3.0 GPA, 15 specified curricular units. *Required for some:* essay or personal statement. *Application deadlines:* 4/1 (freshmen), 4/1 (transfers). *Notification:* continuous (freshmen), continuous (transfers).

Freshman Application Contact Mr. Craig Hayes, Executive Director of Recruitment Services, University of Oklahoma, 1000 Asp Avenue, Norman, OK 73019. *Phone:* 405-325-2151. *Toll-free phone:* 800-234-6868. *Fax:* 405-325-7478. *E-mail:* ou-pss@ou.edu.

UNIVERSITY OF OKLAHOMA HEALTH SCIENCES CENTER

Oklahoma City, Oklahoma **www.ouhsc.edu/**

- **State-supported** upper-level, founded 1890, part of University of Oklahoma
- **Urban** 200-acre campus with easy access to Oklahoma City
- **Endowment** $318.3 million
- **Coed** 1,016 undergraduate students, 90% full-time, 88% women, 12% men

Undergraduates 912 full-time, 104 part-time. Students come from 25 states and territories, 16 other countries, 14% are from out of state, 4% African American, 7% Asian American or Pacific Islander, 3% Hispanic American, 9% Native American, 1% international.

Faculty *Total:* 447, 67% full-time, 69% with terminal degrees. *Student/faculty ratio:* 8:1.

Majors Audiology and hearing sciences; audiology and speech-language pathology; communication disorders sciences and services related; dental hygiene; dietetics; nuclear medical technology; nursing (registered nurse training); radiologic technology/science; speech-language pathology; speech therapy.

Academics *Calendar:* semesters. *Degrees:* bachelor's, master's, doctoral, first professional, post-master's, and postbachelor's certificates. *Special study options:* advanced placement credit, distance learning, honors programs, internships, part-time degree program, summer session for credit. *ROTC:* Army (c), Air Force (c).

Computers on Campus 120 computers/terminals are available on campus for general student use. Students can access the following: campus intranet, computer help desk, free student e-mail accounts, online (class) grades, online (class) registration, online (class) schedules. Campuswide network is available. Wireless service is available via learning centers, libraries, student centers.

Student Life *Housing:* college housing not available. *Activities and organizations:* student-run newspaper, Student Government Association, Public Health Student Association, Student National Medical Association, Graduate Student Council, Student Medical Association. *Campus security:* 24-hour emergency response devices and patrols, late-night transport/escort service. *Student services:* health clinic, personal/psychological counseling.

Costs (2007–08) *Tuition:* state resident $3261 full-time, $109 per credit hour part-time; nonresident $12,375 full-time, $413 per credit hour part-time. Full-time tuition and fees vary according to program. Part-time tuition and fees vary according to program. *Required fees:* $1504 full-time, $42 per credit hour part-time, $124 per term part-time. *Payment plan:* installment. *Waivers:* employees or children of employees.

Applying *Options:* electronic application, deferred entrance. *Application deadline:* rolling (transfers). *Notification:* continuous (transfers).

Application Contact Mr. Heath Burge, Director of Admissions, University of Oklahoma Health Sciences Center, BSE-200, PO Box 26901, 941 S. L. Young Boulevard, Oklahoma City, OK 73190. *Phone:* 405-271-2359 Ext. 48902. *Fax:* 405-271-2480. *E-mail:* admissions@ouhsc.edu.

UNIVERSITY OF PHOENIX–OKLAHOMA CITY CAMPUS

Oklahoma City, Oklahoma **www.phoenix.edu/**

- **Proprietary** comprehensive, founded 1976
- **Urban** campus
- **Coed**
- **Noncompetitive** entrance level

Faculty *Student/faculty ratio:* 7:1.

Academics *Calendar:* continuous. *Degrees:* bachelor's and master's.

Student Life *Campus security:* late-night transport/escort service.

Costs (2007–08) *Tuition:* $10,140 full-time, $338 per credit part-time. Full-time tuition and fees vary according to course level.

Financial Aid *Average financial aid package:* $4443. *Average need-based gift aid:* $2337.

Applying *Options:* deferred entrance. *Application fee:* $45. *Required:* 1 letter of recommendation. *Required for some:* high school transcript.

Freshman Application Contact Ms. Beth Barilla, Associate Vice President, Student Admissions and Services, University of Phoenix–Oklahoma City Campus, 4615 East Elwood Street, Mail Stop AA-K101, Phoenix, AZ 85040-1958. *Phone:* 480-317-6000. *Toll-free phone:* 800-776-4867 (in-state); 800-228-7240 (out-of-state). *Fax:* 480-894-1758. *E-mail:* beth.barilla@phoenix.edu.

UNIVERSITY OF PHOENIX–TULSA CAMPUS

Tulsa, Oklahoma **www.phoenix.edu/**

- **Proprietary** comprehensive, founded 1998
- **Urban** campus
- **Coed**
- **Noncompetitive** entrance level

Faculty *Student/faculty ratio:* 6:1.

Academics *Calendar:* continuous. *Degrees:* certificates, bachelor's, and master's.

Student Life *Campus security:* late-night transport/escort service.

Costs (2007–08) *Tuition:* $10,140 full-time, $338 per credit part-time. Full-time tuition and fees vary according to course level.

Financial Aid *Average financial aid package:* $4528. *Average need-based gift aid:* $2296.

Applying *Options:* deferred entrance. *Application fee:* $45. *Required:* 1 letter of recommendation. *Required for some:* high school transcript.

Freshman Application Contact Ms. Beth Barilla, Associate Vice President, Student Admissions and Services, University of Phoenix–Tulsa Campus, 4615 East Elwood Street, Mail Stop AA-K101, Phoenix, AZ 85040-1958. *Phone:* 480-317-6000. *Toll-free phone:* 800-776-4867 (in-state); 800-228-7240 (out-of-state). *Fax:* 480-894-1758. *E-mail:* beth.barilla@phoenix.edu.

UNIVERSITY OF SCIENCE AND ARTS OF OKLAHOMA

Chickasha, Oklahoma **www.usao.edu/**

- **State-supported** 4-year, founded 1908, part of Oklahoma State Regents for Higher Education
- **Small-town** 75-acre campus with easy access to Oklahoma City
- **Endowment** $4.2 million
- **Coed** 1,254 undergraduate students, 77% full-time, 63% women, 37% men
- **Moderately difficult** entrance level, 94% of applicants were admitted

Undergraduates 966 full-time, 288 part-time. Students come from 22 states and territories, 12 other countries, 6% are from out of state, 4% African American, 1% Asian American or Pacific Islander, 4% Hispanic American, 13% Native American, 4% international, 8% transferred in, 40% live on campus. *Retention:* 69% of 2006 full-time freshmen returned.

Freshmen *Admission:* 348 applied, 326 admitted, 222 enrolled. *Average high school GPA:* 3.37. *Test scores:* ACT scores over 18: 85%; ACT scores over 24: 36%; ACT scores over 30: 5%.

Faculty *Total:* 91, 59% full-time, 59% with terminal degrees. *Student/faculty ratio:* 14:1.

Majors American Indian/Native American studies; art; biology/biological sciences; business/commerce; chemistry; clinical/medical laboratory technology; communication/speech communication and rhetoric; computer and information sciences; dramatic/theater arts; early childhood education; economics; elementary education; English; fine/studio arts; health and physical education; history; mathematics; music; natural sciences; physics; political science and government; psychology; sociology; special education (hearing impaired); speech-language pathology.

Academics *Calendar:* trimesters. *Degree:* bachelor's. *Special study options:* academic remediation for entering students, accelerated degree program, adult/continuing education programs, advanced placement credit, double majors, independent study, internships, off-campus study, part-time degree program, services for LD students, student-designed majors, summer session for credit.

Computers on Campus 125 computers/terminals are available on campus for general student use. Students can access the following: computer help desk, free student e-mail accounts, personal Web space. Campuswide network is available. 100% of college-owned or -operated housing units are wired for high-speed Internet access. Wireless service is available via entire campus.

Student Life *Housing:* on-campus residence required for freshman year. *Options:* coed. Campus housing is university owned and is provided by a third party. Freshman campus housing is guaranteed. *Activities and organizations:* drama/theater group, student-run newspaper, television station, choral group, Student Activities Council, Volunteer Action Council, Baptist Student Union, Intertribal Heritage Club, Psychology Club, national fraternities. *Campus security:* 24-hour emergency response devices and patrols, controlled dormitory access. *Student services:* health clinic, personal/psychological counseling.

Athletics Member NAIA. *Intercollegiate sports:* baseball M (s), basketball M (s)/W (s), cheerleading M (s)/W (s), soccer M (s)/W (s), softball W (s). *Intramural sports:* basketball M/W, football M/W, golf M/W, softball M/W, volleyball M/W.

Standardized Tests *Required:* SAT or ACT (for admission).

Costs (2007–08) *Tuition:* state resident $2880 full-time, $96 per hour part-time; nonresident $8460 full-time, $282 per hour part-time. *Required fees:* $1170 full-time, $39 per hour part-time. *Room and board:* $4540; room only: $2380. Room and board charges vary according to board plan and housing facility. *Payment plan:* installment. *Waivers:* senior citizens and employees or children of employees.

Financial Aid Of all full-time matriculated undergraduates who enrolled in 2006, 727 applied for aid, 611 were judged to have need, 128 had their need fully met. 151 Federal Work-Study jobs (averaging $1335). In 2006, 193 non-need-based awards were made. *Average percent of need met:* 68%. *Average financial aid package:* $7543. *Average need-based loan:* $3069. *Average need-based gift aid:* $5649. *Average non-need-based aid:* $4296. *Average indebtedness upon graduation:* $16,623.

Applying *Options:* deferred entrance. *Application fee:* $15. *Required for some:* high school transcript, minimum 3.0 GPA, graduated in top half of high school class. *Recommended:* graduated in top half of high school class. *Application deadlines:* 8/31 (freshmen), 8/31 (transfers). *Notification:* 2/10 (freshmen).

Freshman Application Contact Office of Admissions, University of Science and Arts of Oklahoma, 1727 West Alabama, Chickasha, OK 73018-5322. *Phone:* 405-574-1357. *Toll-free phone:* 800-933-8726 Ext. 1212. *Fax:* 405-574-1220. *E-mail:* usao-admissions@usao.edu.

UNIVERSITY OF TULSA

Tulsa, Oklahoma **www.utulsa.edu/**

- **Independent** university, founded 1894, affiliated with Presbyterian Church (U.S.A.)
- **Urban** 2,090-acre campus with easy access to Tulsa
- **Endowment** $918.0 million
- **Coed** 2,987 undergraduate students, 94% full-time, 48% women, 52% men
- **Very difficult** entrance level, 51% of applicants were admitted

Undergraduates 2,812 full-time, 175 part-time. Students come from 44 states and territories, 46 other countries, 38% are from out of state, 6% African American, 3% Asian American or Pacific Islander, 4% Hispanic American, 3% Native American, 11% international, 5% transferred in, 68% live on campus. *Retention:* 88% of 2006 full-time freshmen returned.

Freshmen *Admission:* 3,804 applied, 1,944 admitted, 656 enrolled. *Average high school GPA:* 3.8. *Test scores:* SAT critical reading scores over 500: 91%; SAT math scores over 500: 96%; ACT scores over 18: 100%; SAT critical reading scores over 600: 61%; SAT math scores over 600: 68%; ACT scores over 24: 77%; SAT critical reading scores over 700: 26%; SAT math scores over 700: 28%; ACT scores over 30: 28%.

Faculty *Total:* 380, 81% full-time, 96% with terminal degrees. *Student/faculty ratio:* 10:1.

Majors Accounting; anthropology; applied mathematics; art history, criticism and conservation; arts management; athletic training; audiology and speech-language pathology; biochemistry; biology/biological sciences; business administration and management; business/commerce; chemical engineering; chemistry; communication/speech communication and rhetoric; computer science; dramatic/theater arts; early childhood education; economics; education; electrical, electronics and communications engineering; elementary education; engineering physics; English; environmental studies; film/cinema studies; finance; fine/studio arts; French; geology/earth science; geophysics and seismology; German; history; information science/studies; information technology; international business/trade/commerce; kinesiology and exercise science; legal professions and studies related; liberal arts and sciences/liberal studies; management information systems; marketing/marketing management; mathematics; mathematics teacher education; mechanical engineering; music; music performance; music related; music teacher education; music theory and composition; nursing (registered nurse training); organizational behavior; petroleum engineering; philosophy; physics; piano and organ; political science and government; psychology; religious studies; Russian studies; sociology; Spanish; special education (hearing impaired); sport and fitness administration/management; voice and opera.

Academics *Calendar:* semesters. *Degrees:* bachelor's, master's, doctoral, first professional, postbachelor's, and first professional certificates. *Special study options:* accelerated degree program, adult/continuing education programs, advanced placement credit, double majors, English as a second language, honors programs, independent study, internships, part-time degree program, services for LD students, student-designed majors, study abroad, summer session for credit. *ROTC:* Air Force (c). *Unusual degree programs:* 3-2 business administration; law (3 year bachelor's and 3 year Law School).

Computers on Campus 900 computers/terminals are available on campus for general student use. Students can access the following: campus intranet, computer help desk, free student e-mail accounts, online (class) grades, online (class) registration, online (class) schedules. Campuswide network is available. 100% of college-owned or -operated housing units are wired for high-speed Internet access. Wireless service is available via entire campus.

Student Life *Housing:* on-campus residence required through sophomore year. *Options:* coed, men-only, women-only, disabled students. Campus housing is university owned. Freshman campus housing is guaranteed. *Activities and organizations:* drama/theater group, student-run newspaper, radio and television station, choral group, marching band, Student Association, Residence Hall Association, honor societies, intramural sports, pre-professional clubs, national fraternities, national sororities. *Campus security:* 24-hour emergency response devices and patrols, late-night transport/escort service, controlled dormitory access. *Student services:* health clinic, personal/psychological counseling, women's center.

Athletics Member NCAA. All Division I except football (Division I-A). *Intercollegiate sports:* basketball M (s)/W (s), crew W (s), cross-country running M (s)/W (s), golf M (s)/W (s), soccer M (s)/W (s), softball W (s), tennis M (s)/W (s), track and field M (s)/W (s), volleyball W (s). *Intramural sports:* badminton M/W, basketball M/W, bowling M/W, crew M (c), cross-country running M/W, fencing M (c)/W (c), football M/W, golf M/W, racquetball M/W, rugby M (c), soccer M/W, softball M/W, squash M/W, swimming and diving M/W, table tennis M/W, tennis M/W, track and field M/W, volleyball M/W, water polo M/W, weight lifting M/W.

Standardized Tests *Required:* SAT or ACT (for admission).

Costs (2007–08) *One-time required fee:* $425. *Comprehensive fee:* $29,184 includes full-time tuition ($21,690), mandatory fees ($90), and room and board ($7404). Part-time tuition: $778 per credit hour. *Required fees:* $3 per credit hour part-time. *College room only:* $4090. Room and board charges vary according to board plan and housing facility. *Payment plans:* tuition prepayment, installment. *Waivers:* employees or children of employees.

Financial Aid Of all full-time matriculated undergraduates who enrolled in 2005, 2,410 applied for aid, 1,192 were judged to have need, 582 had their need fully met. 643 Federal Work-Study jobs (averaging $2700). 8 state and other part-time jobs (averaging $2200). In 2005, 962 non-need-based awards were made. *Average percent of need met:* 87%. *Average financial aid package:* $22,586. *Average need-based loan:* $5918. *Average need-based gift aid:* $4716. *Average non-need-based aid:* $11,342. *Average indebtedness upon graduation:* $12,411.

Applying *Options:* electronic application, early admission, deferred entrance. *Application fee:* $35. *Required:* essay or personal statement, high school transcript, 1 letter of recommendation, interview. *Recommended:* minimum 3.0 GPA. *Application deadlines:* rolling (freshmen), rolling (transfers). *Notification:* continuous (freshmen), continuous (transfers).

Freshman Application Contact Mr. Earl Johnson, Dean of Admission, University of Tulsa, 600 South College Avenue, Tulsa, OK 74104. *Phone:* 918-631-2307. *Toll-free phone:* 800-331-3050. *Fax:* 918-631-5003. *E-mail:* admission@utulsa.edu.

See page 2086 for the College Close-Up.

UNIVERSITY OF TULSA

TULSA, OKLAHOMA

The University

The University of Tulsa (TU) is a four-year, private, liberal arts university featuring highly personalized study in the humanities, engineering, natural sciences, business, health professions, and fine and performing arts. TU features three undergraduate colleges: the Henry Kendall College of Arts and Sciences, the College of Business Administration, and the College of Engineering and Natural Sciences.

TU also has a College of Law and master's and doctoral programs in select disciplines. The University is fully accredited by the North Central Association of Colleges and Universities and is an NCAA Division I participant in Conference USA. TU maintains an affiliation with the Presbyterian Church (USA).

A customizable array of majors, minors, concentrations within majors, and certificate programs allows undergraduates to assemble a personalized education, which can include a self-designed major. TU's low 11:1 student-faculty ratio, average class size of 19, and emphasis on individual attention anchor an educational culture where students are rigorously challenged and comprehensively supported.

Long regarded for programs that include accounting; MIS; petroleum, mechanical, and chemical engineering; English; environmental law; and psychology, TU is also emerging as a leader in computer science and information security. TU was the first institution selected by the National Science Foundation for the Federal Cyber Service Initiative (Cyber Corps). The University's strength in computer science extends to its graduate program, which regularly awards Ph.D. degrees in computer security.

Joint bachelors and M.B.A. programs are available, as well as a highly selective six-year joint bachelor's and J.D. (law degree) program.

The University's 34-acre sports and recreation complex features a student fitness facility, competition-grade tennis complex, NCAA soccer and softball fields, multiuse recreational fields, and an NCAA track and field. TU offers ample extracurricular opportunities through 160 campus-based organizations, including intramural sports, special interest clubs, preprofessional organizations, fraternities and sororities, and campus ministry groups. Residence life at TU offers a variety of living arrangements, including traditional residence halls, suite-style halls, premium-style student apartments, and special living communities.

Fall 2007 enrollment was 4,165, with 2,987 undergraduates and 1,178 graduate and law students and a 54:46 ratio of men and women. International and multicultural students made up 28 percent of the student population, with fifty-seven countries represented.

Based on academic reputation and other factors, *U.S. News & World Report* ranks TU among the top 100 national universities of the 1,400 colleges and universities it surveys. *The Princeton Review* ranks TU sixth in the nation for student happiness.

Location

University of Tulsa features a residential campus in midtown Tulsa, Oklahoma. Tulsa's prominent industries include energy, telecommunications and data, finance, medicine, aerospace, transportation, and education—all of which present rich internship opportunities for students and employment opportunities for graduates. *Newsweek* has named Tulsa one of ten "New Frontier" technology cities, and the *New York Times* declared Tulsa "a new economy hotbed." *Southern Living* magazine named Tulsa one of its five favorite Southern cities. Tulsa has more than 550,000 residents and features cultural assets including the Performing Arts Center, ballet, theater, symphony, opera, two nationally renowned museums, and cultural festivals such as Jazzfest, Mayfest, and Oktoberfest. Professional sports in Tulsa include baseball, basketball, golf, hockey, arena football, and horse racing. The extensive River Parks development, 3 miles from the campus, has facilities for outdoor activities, jogging and bicycle trails, and an outdoor floating amphitheater.

Majors and Degrees

The Henry Kendall College of Arts and Sciences grants the Bachelor of Arts, Bachelor of Fine Arts, Bachelor of Music, Bachelor of Music Education, or Bachelor of Science degrees in anthropology, art, art history, arts management, communication, deaf education, economics, education, English, environmental policy, film studies, French, German, history, law and society (an accelerated B.A./J.D. program), music, music education, musical theater, organizational studies, philosophy, political science, psychology, religion, Russian studies, sociology, Spanish, speech/language pathology, and theater. Students can create their own designated area of concentration with the approval of the dean of the college. Teacher certification at the elementary and secondary levels is available through the college.

The College of Business Administration awards the Bachelor of Science in athletic training, business administration (majors in accounting, economics, finance, management, management information systems, and marketing), energy management, exercise and sports science, international business and language (with emphases in French, German, Russian, and Spanish), and nursing. The college offers minors in accounting, business administration, coaching, finance, international business studies, management information systems, and marketing communication. Management majors may choose concentrations in business law, entrepreneurship and family business management, and human resource management. Marketing majors may choose an emphasis in integrated marketing communication. The college is home to several specialized centers, including the Family Owned Business Institute, the Genave King Rogers Center for Business Law, and the Williams Risk Management Center.

The College of Engineering and Natural Sciences offers the Bachelor of Science degree in applied mathematics, biochemistry, biogeosciences, biology, chemical engineering, chemistry, computer information systems, computer science, earth and environmental science, electrical engineering, engineering physics, geology, geosciences, mathematics, mechanical engineering, petroleum engineering, and physics. The college also offers a B.A. in chemistry, earth and environmental science, and geology. The college features state-of-the-art research facilities, including the Center for Information Security and the Williams Communications Fiber Optic Networking Laboratory. From 1995 to 2007, 41 TU engineering students received the prestigious Barry M. Goldwater Scholarship, the nation's premier award for undergraduate students in engineering, math, or science, while 27 students received National Science Fellowships.

Academic Programs

A TU education links a broad, humanities-based core curriculum for all majors and a highly flexible group of majors, minors, concentrations, and certificate programs. With so many program options and a high level of faculty support, TU students can receive an education that is well-rounded, in-depth, and uniquely personalized. Candidates for graduation must complete at least 124 semester hours of course work, with more hours required of students majoring in engineering and business administration.

The University offers a number of special academic programs. The Honors Program engages students in intensive multidisciplinary work and in specialized study culminating in a major research or creative project during the senior year. Honors freshmen may live in the Honors House. The Tulsa Undergraduate Research Challenge program (TURC) combines advanced research, scholarship, and community service. The Federal Cyber Service Initiative (Cyber Corps) prepares students for advanced federal careers in computer security. Other special programs include internships, study abroad, Air Force ROTC, a six-year accelerated law degree, and a five-year M.B.A. program.

Qualified students may receive advanced standing or credit for scores on the tests of the Advanced Placement and College-Level Examination programs. Students who complete the International Baccalaureate diploma with a score of 28 or above receive at least 30 college credits, the equivalent of one year in college.

The University of Tulsa operates on a semester calendar. The fall term begins in late August, the spring term in early January, and the summer session in mid-May.

Off-Campus Programs

TU students can choose from several study-abroad options, including summer, semester, and yearlong programs. TU has direct international exchange partnerships with universities in Australia, Austria, Finland, France, Germany, England, Spain, Switzerland, and New Zealand and is part of the ISEP Exchange Program Network. In addition, TU offers a wide selection of international study options around the world through consortia and study-abroad affiliate programs. All approved study-abroad programs allow students to choose courses in various disciplines, and with their college's approval, they can apply these courses towards their majors or other graduation requirements. Federal financial aid and scholarships are portable with TU's study-abroad programs.

Academic Facilities

The University of Tulsa's libraries (McFarlin Library and the Mabee Legal Information Center) house more than 3.6 million items, including periodical subscriptions to scholarly and popular journals. McFarlin holdings include 850,000 print volumes, 97,000 electronic book titles, and 12,000 journal titles. McFarlin's Special Collections are internationally recognized, particularly for holdings in Native American history and nineteenth- and twentieth-century Irish, English, and American literature. McFarlin is home to the papers of Nobel Laureate V. S. Naipaul. McFarlin is also developing a specialization in World War I literature, correspondence, and artifacts. Special Collections rare book holdings currently number about 125,000 volumes.

Keplinger Hall is the $15-million home to the College of Engineering and Natural Sciences. An array of equipment complements this facility, including a comprehensive multimillion-dollar telecommunications networking laboratory developed with Williams Communications and other industry partners.

The TU Center for Information Security is developing defenses against cyberterrorist attacks and information warfare and supports the University's National Security Agency (NSA)–accredited certificate program in information assurance, a curriculum that integrates information security with computer law and policy issues. TU is designated a Center of Excellence in Information Assurance by the NSA and is one of the original six institutions selected by the National Science Foundation for the Federal Cyber Service Initiative (Cyber Corps).

The Mary K. Chapman Center for Communicative Disorders links the University to the community with its clinical facility and its curricula in education of the deaf and speech/language pathology. The Tulsa Center for the Study of Women's Literature offers concentrated studies in women's literature and in feminist literary critical theory. The National Energy-Environment Law and Policy Institute researches energy, natural resource, and environmental law and policy development. TU's engineering students have the opportunity to participate in research projects through ten consortia funded by the petroleum industry. The Family-Owned Business Institute provides a forum for the development and dissemination of information relevant to the succession and stability of the family business. The TU Innovation Institute combines research and interdisciplinary programs in innovation, product development, and entrepreneurship.

Other facilities include the Genave King Rogers Center for Business Law, which supports the business law specialization within the management major, and the Williams Risk Management Center in the College of Business Administration, an advanced learning environment that combines the latest in trading floor technology and advanced study in risk-management theories and techniques. The performing arts utilize Chapman Theatre, the home of TU's symphony orchestra, concert band, wind ensemble, jazz workshop, modern choir, theater, and opera productions. The Allen Chapman Activity Center, which is the University's student union, features student organization offices, the Great Hall for lectures and entertainment, a food court, and the University bookstore. The Donald W. Reynolds Center serves as the campus arena and convocation center. This $28-million facility is the home for several intercollegiate athletic programs, student concerts, cutting-edge facilities for video editing and strength training, and the state's only accredited academic program in athletic/sports medicine. In 2007, the University opened Collins Hall, which houses administrative, alumni, and admission offices.

Costs

For 2007–08, the typical cost for students living on campus was $29,649, including $21,690 for tuition, $7404 for room and board, and fees of $555. Expenses for books average about $1200 per year.

Financial Aid

In 2007, more than 90 percent of entering full-time freshmen received some form of financial aid (including grants, scholarships, work-study, and loans). Academic, athletic, and performance scholarships are available, as well as federally funded grants, loans, and Federal Work-Study awards. The University of Tulsa participates in the National Merit program and offers full-tuition, room, and board scholarships for selected National Merit Finalists. University Scholarships are also awarded to qualified students. Performance scholarships are available in music, theater, and athletics. Applicants for aid should submit the Free Application for Federal Student Aid (FAFSA) and the TU Financial Aid Application by March 1 for priority consideration.

Faculty

The University has 306 full-time faculty members, with 96 percent having earned the highest degree in their field of study. The faculty is primarily a teaching faculty, although most of its members are also involved in funded research or publishing activities. Many faculty members serve as student advisers and work collaboratively with students in and outside the classroom. The faculty includes a number of distinguished scholars, with 20 endowed chairs, 7 endowed professorships, and 2 visiting chairs.

Student Government

All full-time students are members of the Student Association, which consists of legislative, executive, and judicial branches. Regular elections are held for representatives from each college, who appropriate nearly $500,000 annually for student organizations and special events. The executive cabinet's main function is to schedule speakers, artists, and events on campus that are sponsored by the Student Association.

Admission Requirements

By design, University of Tulsa has a highly personalized admission process. TU seeks students who demonstrate intellectual promise in a challenging curriculum and are committed to the liberal education reflected in the University's mission. TU uses an individualized and holistic approach in evaluating candidates for admission.

Performance in high school college-preparatory subjects and scores on the SAT or ACT are the primary criteria considered in the admission evaluation. Information, including academic and extracurricular achievement, school records, and personal qualities, is carefully considered. The counselor recommendation and information about the applicants' extracurricular activities and job experience are also considered. Campus visits and interviews are highly recommended but not required.

TU looks for students who will appreciate and take advantage of the exceptional educational and extracurricular opportunities TU offers—students who enjoy challenges, who are intellectually curious, and who want to discover more about themselves.

The recommended high school curriculum consists of four years of English and math, three years of science and social science, and a solid foundation in a foreign language and computer science. In addition, students are encouraged to take an active part in their school and community or hone special talents that demonstrate traits such as leadership, initiative, maturity, and creativity.

Application and Information

Students are encouraged to complete an application for admission and scholarships by the priority date of February 1. The admission process is rolling, and applicants are reviewed and notified as their admission files are completed. The reply date for students is May 1. An application, accompanied by a six-semester secondary school transcript, ACT or SAT scores, and a guidance counselor's recommendation are required when applying for admission. Completed applications should be sent to the Office of Admission. For additional information, students should view the online tour (http://www.utulsa.edu/virtualtour) or contact:

John C. Corso
Associate Vice President for Enrollment and Student Services
University of Tulsa
800 South Tucker Drive
Tulsa, Oklahoma 74104-3189

Phone: 918-631-2307 (in Tulsa)
800-331-3050 (toll-free)
Fax: 918-631-5003
E-mail: admission@utulsa.edu
Web site: http://www.utulsa.edu/admission

OREGON

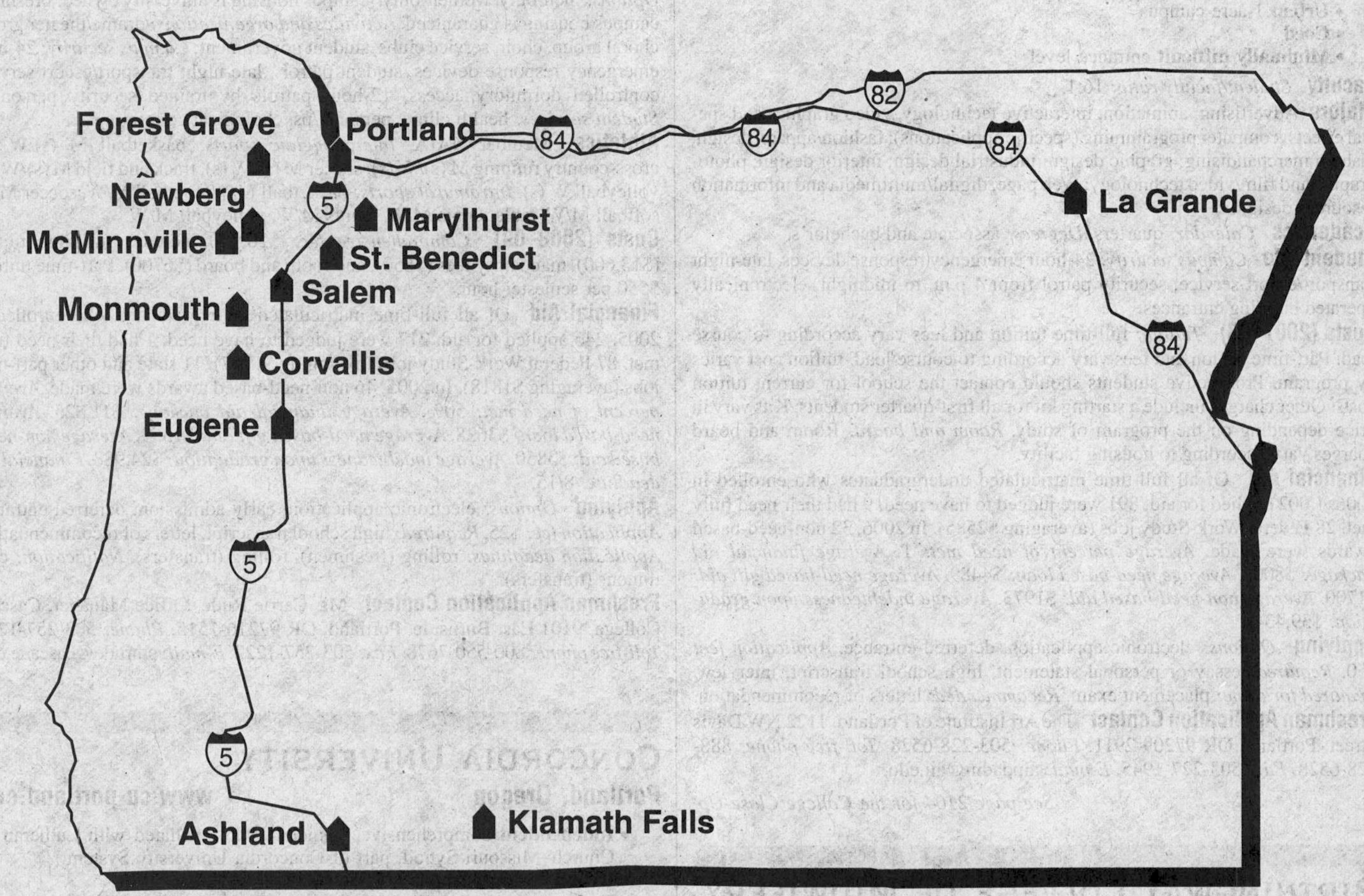
Forest Grove
Portland
Newberg
McMinnville
Marylhurst
St. Benedict
Salem
Monmouth
Corvallis
Eugene
Ashland
Klamath Falls
La Grande
5
84
82

THE ART INSTITUTE OF PORTLAND

Portland, Oregon **www.aipd.artinstitutes.edu/**

- **Proprietary** 4-year, founded 1963, part of Education Management Corporation
- **Urban** 1-acre campus
- **Coed**
- **Minimally difficult** entrance level

Faculty *Student/faculty ratio:* 16:1.

Majors Advertising; animation, interactive technology, video graphics and special effects; computer programming (specific applications); fashion/apparel design; fashion merchandising; graphic design; industrial design; interior design; photographic and film/video technology; Web page, digital/multimedia and information resources design.

Academics *Calendar:* quarters. *Degrees:* associate and bachelor's.

Student Life *Campus security:* 24-hour emergency response devices, late-night transport/escort service, security patrol from 4 p.m. to midnight, electronically operated building entrances.

Costs (2007–08) *Tuition:* full-time tuition and fees vary according to course load. Part-time tuition and fees vary according to course load. tuition cost varies by program. Prospective students should contact the school for current tuition costs. Other charges include a starting kit for all first-quarter students. Kits vary in price depending on the program of study. *Room and board:* Room and board charges vary according to housing facility.

Financial Aid Of all full-time matriculated undergraduates who enrolled in 2006, 1,002 applied for aid, 891 were judged to have need, 9 had their need fully met. 28 Federal Work-Study jobs (averaging $2585). In 2006, 32 non-need-based awards were made. *Average percent of need met:* 1. *Average financial aid package:* $8002. *Average need-based loan:* $4489. *Average need-based gift aid:* $1700. *Average non-need-based aid:* $1973. *Average indebtedness upon graduation:* $39,434.

Applying *Options:* electronic application, deferred entrance. *Application fee:* $50. *Required:* essay or personal statement, high school transcript, interview. *Required for some:* placement exam. *Recommended:* letters of recommendation.

Freshman Application Contact The Art Institute of Portland, 1122 NW Davis Street, Portland, OR 97209-2911. *Phone:* 503-228-6528. *Toll-free phone:* 888-228-6528. *Fax:* 503-227-1945. *E-mail:* aipdadm@aii.edu.

See page 2104 for the College Close-Up.

BIRTHINGWAY COLLEGE OF MIDWIFERY

Portland, Oregon

CASCADE COLLEGE

Portland, Oregon **www.cascade.edu/**

- **Independent** 4-year, founded 1994, affiliated with Church of Christ, administratively affiliated with Oklahoma Christian University
- **Urban** 13-acre campus
- **Endowment** $358,467
- **Coed** 265 undergraduate students, 98% full-time, 58% women, 42% men
- **Noncompetitive** entrance level, 60% of applicants were admitted

Undergraduates 259 full-time, 6 part-time. Students come from 15 states and territories, 8 other countries, 68% are from out of state, 8% African American, 4% Asian American or Pacific Islander, 11% Hispanic American, 1% Native American, 2% international, 16% transferred in, 72% live on campus. *Retention:* 46% of 2006 full-time freshmen returned.

Freshmen *Admission:* 227 applied, 136 admitted, 56 enrolled. *Average high school GPA:* 3.0. *Test scores:* SAT critical reading scores over 500: 50%; SAT math scores over 500: 47%; ACT scores over 18: 67%; SAT critical reading scores over 600: 11%; SAT math scores over 600: 20%; ACT scores over 24: 17%; SAT math scores over 700: 4%; ACT scores over 30: 4%.

Faculty *Total:* 35, 43% full-time, 31% with terminal degrees. *Student/faculty ratio:* 12:1.

Majors Biblical studies; business administration and management; communication and media related; early childhood education; elementary education; English; liberal arts and sciences/liberal studies; marketing/marketing management; psychology.

Academics *Calendar:* semesters. *Degree:* bachelor's. *Special study options:* academic remediation for entering students, accelerated degree program, advanced placement credit, double majors, independent study, internships, off-campus study, services for LD students, study abroad, summer session for credit. *ROTC:* Army (c), Air Force (c).

Computers on Campus 26 computers/terminals are available on campus for general student use. Campuswide network is available.

Student Life *Housing:* on-campus residence required through senior year. *Options:* men-only, women-only. Campus housing is university owned. Freshman campus housing is guaranteed. *Activities and organizations:* drama/theater group, choral group, choir, service clubs, student government. *Campus security:* 24-hour emergency response devices, student patrols, late-night transport/escort service, controlled dormitory access, 12-hour patrols by trained security personnel. *Student services:* health clinic, personal/psychological counseling.

Athletics Member NAIA. *Intercollegiate sports:* basketball M (s)/W (s), cross-country running M (s)/W (s), soccer M (s)/W (s), track and field M (s)/W (s), volleyball W (s). *Intramural sports:* basketball M/W, football M/W, soccer M/W, softball M/W, table tennis M/W, tennis M/W, volleyball M/W.

Costs (2008–09) *Comprehensive fee:* $20,950 includes full-time tuition ($13,600), mandatory fees ($650), and room and board ($6700). Part-time tuition: $550 per semester hour.

Financial Aid Of all full-time matriculated undergraduates who enrolled in 2005, 246 applied for aid, 217 were judged to have need, 1 had their need fully met. 87 Federal Work-Study jobs (averaging $1997). 11 state and other part-time jobs (averaging $1818). In 2005, 46 non-need-based awards were made. *Average percent of need met:* 50%. *Average financial aid package:* $11,825. *Average need-based loan:* $3638. *Average need-based gift aid:* $1559. *Average non-need-based aid:* $3850. *Average indebtedness upon graduation:* $24,988. *Financial aid deadline:* 8/15.

Applying *Options:* electronic application, early admission, deferred entrance. *Application fee:* $25. *Required:* high school transcript, letters of recommendation. *Application deadlines:* rolling (freshmen), rolling (transfers). *Notification:* continuous (transfers).

Freshman Application Contact Ms. Carrie Rude, Office Manager, Cascade College, 9101 East Burnside, Portland, OR 97216-1515. *Phone:* 503-257-1202. *Toll-free phone:* 800-550-7678. *Fax:* 503-257-1222. *E-mail:* cmrude@cascade.edu.

CONCORDIA UNIVERSITY

Portland, Oregon **www.cu-portland.edu/**

- **Independent** comprehensive, founded 1905, affiliated with Lutheran Church–Missouri Synod, part of Concordia University System
- **Urban** 13-acre campus
- **Endowment** $6.4 million
- **Coed** 1,104 undergraduate students, 84% full-time, 66% women, 34% men
- **Moderately difficult** entrance level, 65% of applicants were admitted

Undergraduates 927 full-time, 177 part-time. Students come from 26 states and territories, 12 other countries, 58% are from out of state, 7% African American, 5% Asian American or Pacific Islander, 5% Hispanic American, 1% Native American, 2% international, 13% transferred in, 44% live on campus. *Retention:* 71% of 2006 full-time freshmen returned.

Freshmen *Admission:* 867 applied, 561 admitted, 183 enrolled. *Average high school GPA:* 3.42. *Test scores:* SAT critical reading scores over 500: 52%; SAT math scores over 500: 47%; ACT scores over 18: 88%; SAT critical reading scores over 600: 13%; SAT math scores over 600: 15%; ACT scores over 24: 34%; SAT critical reading scores over 700: 2%; SAT math scores over 700: 1%.

Faculty *Total:* 161, 29% full-time, 34% with terminal degrees. *Student/faculty ratio:* 17:1.

Majors Biological and physical sciences; biology/biological sciences; business administration and management; chemistry; dramatic/theater arts; education; elementary education; English; English/language arts teacher education; environmental studies; health/health care administration; humanities; interdisciplinary studies; kindergarten/preschool education; liberal arts and sciences/liberal studies; mathematics teacher education; natural sciences; nursing (registered nurse training); physical education teaching and coaching; physical sciences; premedical studies; pre-theology/pre-ministerial studies; psychology; religious education; religious studies; science teacher education; secondary education; social sciences; social studies teacher education; social work; sport and fitness administration/management; theology.

Academics *Calendar:* semesters. *Degrees:* certificates, associate, bachelor's, master's, and postbachelor's certificates. *Special study options:* academic remediation for entering students, accelerated degree program, adult/continuing education programs, advanced placement credit, double majors, English as a second language, internships, off-campus study, part-time degree program, student-designed majors, study abroad, summer session for credit. *ROTC:* Air Force (c).

Computers on Campus 100 computers/terminals are available on campus for general student use. Students can access the following: campus intranet, computer help desk, free student e-mail accounts, online (class) grades, online (class) registration, online (class) schedules. Campuswide network is available. 100% of college-owned or -operated housing units are wired for high-speed Internet access. Wireless service is available via entire campus.

Student Life *Housing:* on-campus residence required through sophomore year. *Options:* coed. Campus housing is university owned. Freshman applicants given priority for college housing. *Activities and organizations:* drama/theater group, student-run newspaper, choral group, Drama Club, Business Club, Christian Life Ministry, Service Organization, The Promethean. *Campus security:* 24-hour emergency response devices and patrols, student patrols, late-night transport/escort service, controlled dormitory access. *Student services:* health clinic, personal/psychological counseling.

Athletics Member NAIA. *Intercollegiate sports:* baseball M (s), basketball M (s)/W (s), cross-country running M (s)/W (s), golf M (s)/W (s), soccer M (s)/W (s), softball W (s), track and field M (s)/W (s), volleyball W (s). *Intramural sports:* basketball M/W, volleyball M/W.

Standardized Tests *Required:* SAT or ACT (for admission).

Costs (2008–09) *Comprehensive fee:* $28,500 includes full-time tuition ($21,800), mandatory fees ($300), and room and board ($6400). Part-time tuition: $680 per credit. *College room only:* $3080.

Financial Aid Of all full-time matriculated undergraduates who enrolled in 2006, 680 applied for aid, 603 were judged to have need, 137 had their need fully met. In 2006, 32 non-need-based awards were made. *Average percent of need met:* 85%. *Average financial aid package:* $15,000. *Average need-based loan:* $5000. *Average need-based gift aid:* $9000. *Average non-need-based aid:* $5000. *Average indebtedness upon graduation:* $15,000.

Applying *Options:* electronic application, deferred entrance. *Application fee:* $20. *Required:* essay or personal statement, high school transcript, minimum 2.5 GPA, 1 letter of recommendation. *Required for some:* interview. *Recommended:* interview. *Application deadlines:* rolling (freshmen), rolling (transfers). *Notification:* continuous (freshmen), continuous (transfers).

Freshman Application Contact Ms. Bobi Swan, Dean of Admission, Concordia University, 2811 Northeast Holman, Portland, OR 97211-6099. *Phone:* 503-493-6526. *Toll-free phone:* 800-321-9371. *Fax:* 503-280-8531. *E-mail:* admissions@cu-portland.edu.

CORBAN COLLEGE

Salem, Oregon **www.corban.edu/**

- **Independent religious** 4-year, founded 1935
- **Suburban** 107-acre campus with easy access to Portland
- **Endowment** $1.5 million
- **Coed**
- **Moderately difficult** entrance level

Faculty *Student/faculty ratio:* 13:1.

Academics *Calendar:* semesters. *Degrees:* associate, bachelor's, and master's.

Student Life *Campus security:* 24-hour emergency response devices, student patrols, late-night transport/escort service.

Athletics Member NAIA, NCCAA.

Standardized Tests *Required:* SAT or ACT (for admission).

Costs (2007–08) *Comprehensive fee:* $28,254 includes full-time tuition ($20,420), mandatory fees ($270), and room and board ($7564). Part-time tuition: $850 per credit. Part-time tuition and fees vary according to course load. *Room and board:* Room and board charges vary according to board plan.

Financial Aid Of all full-time matriculated undergraduates who enrolled in 2005, 611 applied for aid, 563 were judged to have need, 78 had their need fully met. 150 Federal Work-Study jobs (averaging $1109). In 2005, 91 non-need-based awards were made. *Average percent of need met:* 62. *Average financial aid package:* $12,148. *Average need-based loan:* $3611. *Average need-based gift aid:* $8797. *Average non-need-based aid:* $7729. *Average indebtedness upon graduation:* $28,021.

Applying *Options:* electronic application, early admission. *Application fee:* $40. *Required:* essay or personal statement, high school transcript, minimum 2.5 GPA, 3 letters of recommendation.

Freshman Application Contact Ms. Heidi Stowman, Director of Admissions, Corban College, 5000 Deer Park Drive, SE, Salem, OR 97301-9392. *Phone:* 503-375-7115. *Toll-free phone:* 800-845-3005. *Fax:* 503-585-4316. *E-mail:* admissions@corban.edu.

DEVRY UNIVERSITY

Portland, Oregon **www.devry.edu/**

- **Proprietary** comprehensive, part of DeVry University
- **Coed** 66 undergraduate students, 59% full-time, 45% women, 55% men
- **Minimally difficult** entrance level

Undergraduates 39 full-time, 27 part-time. 24% are from out of state, 12% African American, 3% Asian American or Pacific Islander, 8% Hispanic American, 12% transferred in. *Retention:* 43% of 2006 full-time freshmen returned.

Freshmen *Admission:* 12 enrolled.

Faculty *Total:* 4. *Student/faculty ratio:* 53:1.

Majors Biomedical technology; business administration, management and operations related; computer systems analysis.

Academics *Calendar:* semesters. *Degrees:* bachelor's and master's. *Special study options:* academic remediation for entering students, accelerated degree program, adult/continuing education programs, advanced placement credit, distance learning, part-time degree program, services for LD students, summer session for credit.

Student Life *Housing:* college housing not available.

Costs (2008–09) *Tuition:* $13,810 full-time, $515 per credit part-time. *Required fees:* $80 full-time.

Applying *Options:* electronic application, early admission, deferred entrance. *Application fee:* $50. *Required:* high school transcript, interview. *Application deadlines:* rolling (freshmen), rolling (transfers). *Notification:* continuous (freshmen), continuous (transfers).

Director of Admissions Admissions Office, DeVry University, 9755 SW Barnes Road, Suite 150, Portland, OR 97225-6651.

EASTERN OREGON UNIVERSITY

La Grande, Oregon **www.eou.edu/**

- **State-supported** comprehensive, founded 1929, part of Oregon University System
- **Rural** 121-acre campus
- **Endowment** $1.7 million
- **Coed**
- **Moderately difficult** entrance level

Faculty *Student/faculty ratio:* 23:1.

Academics *Calendar:* quarters. *Degrees:* bachelor's and master's.

Student Life *Campus security:* 24-hour emergency response devices and patrols, late-night transport/escort service, controlled dormitory access.

Athletics Member NCAA, NAIA. All NCAA Division III.

Standardized Tests *Required:* SAT or ACT (for admission).

Costs (2007–08) *Tuition:* state resident $4653 full-time, $103 per credit hour part-time; nonresident $4653 full-time. Full-time tuition and fees vary according to course load. Part-time tuition and fees vary according to course load. *Required fees:* $1419 full-time. *Room and board:* $8475. Room and board charges vary according to board plan and housing facility.

Financial Aid Of all full-time matriculated undergraduates who enrolled in 2006, 1,558 applied for aid, 1,259 were judged to have need, 427 had their need fully met. 245 Federal Work-Study jobs (averaging $1553). In 2006, 37 non-need-based awards were made. *Average percent of need met:* 59. *Average financial aid package:* $11,762. *Average need-based loan:* $3751. *Average need-based gift aid:* $3698. *Average non-need-based aid:* $1298. *Average indebtedness upon graduation:* $15,447.

Applying *Options:* electronic application, early action, deferred entrance. *Application fee:* $50. *Required:* high school transcript, minimum 3.0 GPA. *Required for some:* essay or personal statement, 2 letters of recommendation.

Freshman Application Contact Mr. Jaime Contraras, Director, Admissions, Eastern Oregon University, One University Boulevard, La Grande, OR 97850. *Phone:* 541-962-3393. *Toll-free phone:* 800-452-8639 (in-state); 800-452-3393 (out-of-state). *Fax:* 541-962-3418. *E-mail:* admissions@eou.edu.

EUGENE BIBLE COLLEGE

Eugene, Oregon **www.ebc.edu/**

- **Independent** 4-year, founded 1925, affiliated with Open Bible Standard Churches
- **Suburban** 40-acre campus
- **Endowment** $925,859

- **Coed** 222 undergraduate students, 68% full-time, 44% women, 56% men
- **Minimally difficult** entrance level, 46% of applicants were admitted

Since 1925, Eugene Bible College has been fulfilling the Great Commission by equipping students for Spirit-empowered leadership and ministry. In addition to the bachelor's degree programs, Eugene Bible College offers students opportunities to participate in community ministry, music, drama, athletics, and other activities that open doors to spiritual growth, fellowship, and life-long friendships.

Undergraduates 152 full-time, 70 part-time. Students come from 15 states and territories, 1 other country, 45% are from out of state, 50% live on campus. *Retention:* 60% of 2006 full-time freshmen returned.

Freshmen *Admission:* 158 applied, 72 admitted, 61 enrolled. *Average high school GPA:* 3.1. *Test scores:* SAT critical reading scores over 500: 70%; SAT math scores over 500: 70%; ACT scores over 18: 75%; SAT critical reading scores over 600: 14%; SAT math scores over 600: 9%; ACT scores over 24: 28%; ACT scores over 30: 2%.

Faculty *Total:* 24, 58% full-time, 29% with terminal degrees. *Student/faculty ratio:* 10:1.

Majors Biblical studies; divinity/ministry; missionary studies and missiology; pastoral studies/counseling; religious education; religious/sacred music; youth ministry.

Academics *Calendar:* quarters. *Degree:* certificates and bachelor's. *Special study options:* academic remediation for entering students, advanced placement credit, cooperative education, distance learning, double majors, independent study, internships, part-time degree program, summer session for credit.

Computers on Campus 18 computers/terminals are available on campus for general student use. Students can access the following: free student e-mail accounts. Campuswide network is available.

Student Life *Housing:* on-campus residence required through junior year. *Options:* men-only, women-only. Campus housing is university owned. Freshman campus housing is guaranteed. *Activities and organizations:* drama/theater group, choral group, Element X. *Campus security:* 24-hour emergency response devices, student patrols, controlled dormitory access. *Student services:* personal/psychological counseling.

Athletics *Intercollegiate sports:* basketball M, soccer M/W, ultimate Frisbee M/W, volleyball M/W. *Intramural sports:* basketball M/W, soccer M/W, ultimate Frisbee M/W, volleyball M/W.

Financial Aid Of all full-time matriculated undergraduates who enrolled in 2006, 140 applied for aid, 140 were judged to have need, 1 had their need fully met. 6 Federal Work-Study jobs (averaging $2123). 23 state and other part-time jobs (averaging $2175). In 2006, 1 non-need-based award was made. *Average percent of need met:* 42%. *Average financial aid package:* $8900. *Average need-based loan:* $3850. *Average need-based gift aid:* $3500. *Average non-need-based aid:* $100. *Average indebtedness upon graduation:* $10,550. *Financial aid deadline:* 9/1.

Applying *Options:* electronic application. *Application fee:* $30. *Required:* essay or personal statement, high school transcript, minimum 2.0 GPA, 2 letters of recommendation. *Application deadlines:* 9/1 (freshmen), 9/1 (transfers). *Notification:* continuous until 9/1 (freshmen), continuous until 9/1 (transfers).

Freshman Application Contact Scott Thomas, Director of Admissions, Eugene Bible College, 2155 Bailey Hill Road, Eugene, OR 97405. *Phone:* 541-485-1780 Ext. 3106. *Toll-free phone:* 800-322-2638. *Fax:* 541-343-5801. *E-mail:* scottthomas@ebc.edu.

GEORGE FOX UNIVERSITY

Newberg, Oregon **www.georgefox.edu/**

- **Independent Friends** university, founded 1891
- **Small-town** 85-acre campus with easy access to Portland
- **Endowment** $22.4 million
- **Coed** 1,934 undergraduate students, 87% full-time, 63% women, 37% men
- **Moderately difficult** entrance level, 83% of applicants were admitted

George Fox University is the only evangelical Christian university in the Pacific Northwest classified by *U.S. News & World Report* as a national university. More than 3,200 students attend classes on the University's campus in Newberg, Oregon, and at teaching centers in Portland, Salem, and Redmond, Oregon, and Boise, Idaho. George Fox offers bachelor's degrees in more than forty majors, degree-completion programs for working adults, five seminary degrees, and twelve master's and doctoral degrees.

Undergraduates 1,673 full-time, 261 part-time. Students come from 27 states and territories, 9 other countries, 28% are from out of state, 1% African American, 5% Asian American or Pacific Islander, 4% Hispanic American, 2% Native American, 2% international, 4% transferred in, 60% live on campus. *Retention:* 80% of 2006 full-time freshmen returned.

Freshmen *Admission:* 1,264 applied, 1,049 admitted, 435 enrolled. *Average high school GPA:* 3.51. *Test scores:* SAT critical reading scores over 500: 70%; SAT math scores over 500: 68%; SAT writing scores over 500: 60%; ACT scores over 18: 86%; SAT critical reading scores over 600: 25%; SAT math scores over 600: 23%; SAT writing scores over 600: 20%; ACT scores over 24: 40%; SAT critical reading scores over 700: 6%; SAT math scores over 700: 2%; SAT writing scores over 700: 2%; ACT scores over 30: 6%.

Faculty *Total:* 348, 48% full-time, 43% with terminal degrees. *Student/faculty ratio:* 11:1.

Majors Acting; art; athletic training; behavioral sciences; biblical studies; biology/biological sciences; broadcast journalism; business administration and management; chemistry; cinematography and film/video production; clinical psychology; cognitive psychology and psycholinguistics; cognitive science; communication/speech communication and rhetoric; computer and information sciences; directing and theatrical production; dramatic/theater arts; economics; electrical, electronics and communications engineering; elementary education; engineering; English; family and consumer sciences/human sciences; fashion merchandising; film/cinema studies; finance; fine/studio arts; foods, nutrition, and wellness; graphic design; health and physical education; health teacher education; history; industrial design; information science/studies; interdisciplinary studies; intermedia/multimedia; international business/trade/commerce; international/global studies; management information systems; marketing/marketing management; mathematics; mechanical engineering; missionary studies and missiology; music; music performance; music teacher education; music theory and composition; nursing (registered nurse training); pastoral studies/counseling; philosophy; physical education teaching and coaching; psychology; public relations/image management; radio and television; religious education; religious studies; social work; sociology; Spanish; sport and fitness administration/management; theater design and technology; youth ministry.

Academics *Calendar:* semesters. *Degrees:* bachelor's, master's, doctoral, first professional, post-master's, and postbachelor's certificates. *Special study options:* academic remediation for entering students, accelerated degree program, adult/continuing education programs, advanced placement credit, double majors, English as a second language, honors programs, independent study, internships, off-campus study, part-time degree program, services for LD students, student-designed majors, study abroad, summer session for credit. *ROTC:* Air Force (c). *Unusual degree programs:* 3-2 engineering.

Computers on Campus 154 computers/terminals and 200 ports are available on campus for general student use. Students can access the following: campus intranet, computer help desk, free student e-mail accounts, online (class) grades, online (class) registration, online (class) schedules. Campuswide network is available. 100% of college-owned or -operated housing units are wired for high-speed Internet access. Wireless service is available via entire campus.

Student Life *Housing:* on-campus residence required through junior year. *Options:* men-only, women-only, disabled students. Campus housing is university owned. Freshman campus housing is guaranteed. *Activities and organizations:* drama/theater group, student-run newspaper, radio station, choral group, Student Government, Intramural Sports, Christian Ministries, Orientation Committee, Outdoor Club and Bruin Ambassadors. *Campus security:* 24-hour emergency response devices and patrols, late-night transport/escort service, controlled dormitory access. *Student services:* health clinic, personal/psychological counseling.

Athletics Member NCAA. All Division III. *Intercollegiate sports:* baseball M, basketball M/W, cross-country running M/W, golf M/W, soccer M/W, softball W, tennis M/W, track and field M/W, volleyball W. *Intramural sports:* badminton M/W, basketball M/W, football M/W, golf M/W, racquetball M/W, rock climbing M/W, soccer M/W, table tennis M/W, tennis M/W, volleyball M/W.

Standardized Tests *Required:* SAT or ACT (for admission).

Costs (2007–08) *Comprehensive fee:* $31,390 includes full-time tuition ($23,470), mandatory fees ($320), and room and board ($7600). Part-time tuition: $730 per hour. Part-time tuition and fees vary according to course load. *College room only:* $4280. Room and board charges vary according to board plan. *Payment plan:* installment. *Waivers:* senior citizens and employees or children of employees.

Financial Aid Of all full-time matriculated undergraduates who enrolled in 2006, 1,555 applied for aid, 1,287 were judged to have need, 255 had their need fully met. 640 Federal Work-Study jobs (averaging $2089). In 2006, 256 non-need-based awards were made. *Average percent of need met:* 63%. *Average financial aid package:* $16,709. *Average need-based loan:* $3941. *Average need-based gift aid:* $12,755. *Average non-need-based aid:* $5273. *Average indebtedness upon graduation:* $17,903.

Applying *Options:* electronic application, early action, deferred entrance. *Application fee:* $40. *Required:* essay or personal statement, high school transcript, 2 letters of recommendation. *Required for some:* interview. *Recommended:* minimum 2.6 GPA, interview. *Application deadlines:* 2/1 (freshmen), 6/1 (transfers), 12/1 (early action). *Notification:* continuous until 10/1 (freshmen), continuous (transfers), 12/15 (early action).

Freshman Application Contact Mr. Ryan Dougherty, Director of Undergraduate Admissions, George Fox University, 414 North Meridian Street, Newberg, OR 97132. *Phone:* 503-554-2240. *Toll-free phone:* 800-765-4369. *Fax:* 503-554-3110. *E-mail:* admissions@georgefox.edu.

See page 2106 for the College Close-Up.

GUTENBERG COLLEGE

Eugene, Oregon **www.gutenberg.edu/**

- **Independent religious** 4-year
- **Urban** campus
- **Coed** 51 undergraduate students, 100% full-time, 45% women, 55% men
- **Moderately difficult** entrance level, 76% of applicants were admitted

Undergraduates 51 full-time. Students come from 15 states and territories, 3 other countries, 53% are from out of state, 2% Hispanic American, 6% international, 75% live on campus. *Retention:* 70% of 2006 full-time freshmen returned.

Freshmen *Admission:* 17 applied, 13 admitted, 5 enrolled. *Test scores:* SAT critical reading scores over 500: 100%; SAT critical reading scores over 600: 57%; SAT critical reading scores over 700: 14%; SAT math scores over 700: 14%.

Faculty *Total:* 10, 80% full-time, 60% with terminal degrees. *Student/faculty ratio:* 6:1.

Majors Liberal arts and sciences/liberal studies.

Academics *Degree:* diplomas and bachelor's.

Computers on Campus 2 computers/terminals are available on campus for general student use.

Student Life *Housing options:* men-only, women-only, cooperative. Campus housing is university owned and leased by the school. Freshman applicants given priority for college housing. *Activities and organizations:* choral group.

Standardized Tests *Required:* SAT (for admission).

Costs (2008–09) *Comprehensive fee:* $16,577 includes full-time tuition ($11,202), mandatory fees ($650), and room and board ($4725).

Applying *Application fee:* $40. *Required:* essay or personal statement, high school transcript, 2 letters of recommendation, interview. *Application deadline:* 3/1 (freshmen). *Notification:* continuous until 9/10 (freshmen).

Freshman Application Contact Mr. Terry Stollar, Director of Admissions and Development, Gutenberg College, 1883 University Street, Eugene, OR 97403. *Phone:* 541-736-9071. *Fax:* 541-683-6997. *E-mail:* tstollar@gutenberg.edu.

ITT TECHNICAL INSTITUTE

Portland, Oregon **www.itt-tech.edu/**

- **Proprietary** primarily 2-year, founded 1971, part of ITT Educational Services, Inc
- **Urban** 4-acre campus
- **Coed**
- **Minimally difficult** entrance level

Academics *Calendar:* quarters. *Degrees:* associate and bachelor's.

Standardized Tests *Required:* Wonderlic aptitude test (for admission).

Financial Aid Of all full-time matriculated undergraduates who enrolled in 2006, 15 Federal Work-Study jobs (averaging $5000).

Applying *Options:* deferred entrance. *Application fee:* $100. *Required:* high school transcript, interview. *Recommended:* letters of recommendation.

Freshman Application Contact Mr. Greg Lester, Director of Recruitment, ITT Technical Institute, 6035 Northeast 78th Court, Portland, OR 97218. *Phone:* 503-255-6500. *Toll-free phone:* 800-234-5488.

LEWIS & CLARK COLLEGE

Portland, Oregon **www.lclark.edu/**

- **Independent** comprehensive, founded 1867
- **Suburban** 137-acre campus
- **Endowment** $224.5 million
- **Coed** 1,964 undergraduate students, 99% full-time, 61% women, 39% men
- **Very difficult** entrance level, 56% of applicants were admitted

Lewis & Clark combines a solid foundation in the liberal arts and sciences with a reputation as a residential college with a global reach. Students come from forty-five states and fifty-three countries. Fifty-five percent participate in overseas and off-campus study programs. Portland provides many internship and community service opportunities. Lewis & Clark also offers a very popular, top-notch College Outdoors program.

Undergraduates 1,952 full-time, 12 part-time. Students come from 45 states and territories, 53 other countries, 79% are from out of state, 2% African American, 6% Asian American or Pacific Islander, 5% Hispanic American, 0.9% Native American, 5% international, 3% transferred in, 67% live on campus. *Retention:* 88% of 2006 full-time freshmen returned.

Freshmen *Admission:* 5,351 applied, 2,998 admitted, 507 enrolled. *Average high school GPA:* 3.69. *Test scores:* SAT critical reading scores over 500: 98%; SAT math scores over 500: 98%; SAT writing scores over 500: 98%; ACT scores over 18: 100%; SAT critical reading scores over 600: 82%; SAT math scores over 600: 73%; SAT writing scores over 600: 73%; ACT scores over 24: 93%; SAT critical reading scores over 700: 27%; SAT math scores over 700: 16%; SAT writing scores over 700: 17%; ACT scores over 30: 33%.

Faculty *Total:* 359, 62% full-time, 69% with terminal degrees. *Student/faculty ratio:* 12:1.

Majors Anthropology; art; Asian studies (East); biochemistry; biology/biological sciences; chemistry; communication/speech communication and rhetoric; computer science; dramatic/theater arts; economics; English; environmental studies; foreign languages and literatures; French; German; Hispanic-American, Puerto Rican, and Mexican-American/Chicano studies; history; international relations and affairs; mathematics; modern languages; music; philosophy; physics; political science and government; pre-engineering; psychology; religious studies; sociology; Spanish.

Academics *Calendar:* semesters. *Degrees:* bachelor's, master's, doctoral, first professional, and post-master's certificates. *Special study options:* accelerated degree program, advanced placement credit, double majors, English as a second language, honors programs, independent study, internships, off-campus study, part-time degree program, services for LD students, student-designed majors, study abroad, summer session for credit. *Unusual degree programs:* 3-2 engineering with Columbia University, Washington University in St. Louis, University of Southern California, Oregon Health Sciences University.

Computers on Campus 158 computers/terminals are available on campus for general student use. Students can access the following: campus intranet, computer help desk, free student e-mail accounts, online (class) grades, online (class) registration, online (class) schedules. Campuswide network is available. Wireless service is available via entire campus.

Student Life *Housing:* on-campus residence required through sophomore year. *Options:* coed, women-only. Campus housing is university owned. Freshman campus housing is guaranteed. *Activities and organizations:* drama/theater group, student-run newspaper, radio and television station, choral group, College Outdoors, Associated Students, Center for Service and Work, musical groups, student radio station. *Campus security:* 24-hour emergency response devices and patrols, student patrols, late-night transport/escort service, controlled dormitory access. *Student services:* health clinic, personal/psychological counseling, women's center.

Athletics Member NCAA, NAIA. All NCAA Division III. *Intercollegiate sports:* baseball M, basketball M/W, crew M/W, cross-country running M/W, football M, golf M/W, lacrosse M (c)/W (c), soccer M (c)/W, softball W, swimming and diving M/W, tennis M/W, track and field M/W, volleyball W. *Intramural sports:* badminton M/W, basketball M/W, cross-country running M/W, fencing M (c)/W (c), football M/W, ice hockey M (c), rock climbing M (c)/W (c), rugby M (c)/W (c), sailing M (c)/W (c), skiing (cross-country) M (c)/W (c), skiing (downhill) M (c)/W (c), softball M/W, swimming and diving M/W, table tennis M/W, tennis M/W, ultimate Frisbee M/W, volleyball M/W, water polo M/W.

Standardized Tests *Required:* SAT, ACT, or academic portfolio (for admission). *Required for some:* SAT or ACT (for admission).

Costs (2007–08) *Comprehensive fee:* $40,290 includes full-time tuition ($31,624), mandatory fees ($216), and room and board ($8450). Part-time tuition: $1592 per credit hour. *College room only:* $4380. Room and board charges vary according to board plan and housing facility. *Payment plan:* installment. *Waivers:* employees or children of employees.

Financial Aid Of all full-time matriculated undergraduates who enrolled in 2007, 1,317 applied for aid, 1,068 were judged to have need, 321 had their need fully met. 674 Federal Work-Study jobs (averaging $2034). In 2007, 259 non-need-based awards were made. *Average percent of need met:* 84%. *Average financial aid package:* $23,801. *Average need-based loan:* $5111. *Average need-based gift aid:* $22,536. *Average non-need-based aid:* $8822. *Average indebtedness upon graduation:* $20,127.

Applying *Options:* electronic application, early action, deferred entrance. *Application fee:* $50. *Required:* essay or personal statement, high school transcript, minimum 2.0 GPA, 2 letters of recommendation. *Required for some:* 4 letters of recommendation, portfolio applicants must submit samples of graded work. *Recommended:* minimum 3.0 GPA, interview. *Application deadlines:* 2/1 (freshmen), 7/1 (transfers), 11/15 (early action). *Notification:* 4/1 (freshmen), continuous (transfers), 1/15 (early action).

Freshman Application Contact Mr. Michael Sexton, Dean of Admissions, Lewis & Clark College, 0615 SW Palatine Hill Road, Portland, OR 97219-7899. *Phone:* 503-768-7040. *Toll-free phone:* 800-444-4111. *Fax:* 503-768-7055. *E-mail:* admissions@lclark.edu.

See page 2108 for the College Close-Up.

LINFIELD COLLEGE

McMinnville, Oregon **www.linfield.edu/**

- **Independent American Baptist Churches in the USA** 4-year, founded 1849
- **Small-town** 193-acre campus with easy access to Portland
- **Endowment** $71.7 million
- **Coed** 1,693 undergraduate students, 97% full-time, 54% women, 46% men
- **Moderately difficult** entrance level, 80% of applicants were admitted

Tracing its roots back to 1858, Linfield College is an independent, four-year institution that is nationally recognized for its strong teaching faculty, outstanding science programs, and extensive study-abroad opportunities. More than 50 percent of graduating students have spent a January term, a semester, or an academic year in another country. Linfield is located in the heart of Oregon's Willamette Valley.

Undergraduates 1,650 full-time, 43 part-time. Students come from 30 states and territories, 21 other countries, 41% are from out of state, 2% African American, 8% Asian American or Pacific Islander, 4% Hispanic American, 0.9% Native American, 2% international, 3% transferred in, 76% live on campus. *Retention:* 81% of 2006 full-time freshmen returned.

Freshmen *Admission:* 2,050 applied, 1,637 admitted, 476 enrolled. *Average high school GPA:* 3.56. *Test scores:* SAT critical reading scores over 500: 72%; SAT math scores over 500: 79%; SAT writing scores over 500: 66%; ACT scores over 18: 96%; SAT critical reading scores over 600: 31%; SAT math scores over 600: 30%; SAT writing scores over 600: 20%; ACT scores over 24: 54%; SAT critical reading scores over 700: 5%; SAT math scores over 700: 6%; SAT writing scores over 700: 3%; ACT scores over 30: 14%.

Faculty *Total:* 186, 59% full-time, 70% with terminal degrees. *Student/faculty ratio:* 12:1.

Majors Accounting; anthropology; area, ethnic, cultural, and gender studies related; art; athletic training; biology/biological sciences; business/commerce; chemistry; communication/speech communication and rhetoric; computer science; creative writing; design and visual communications; dramatic/theater arts; economics; elementary education; English; environmental studies; finance; fine/studio arts; French; German; health and physical education; history; international business/trade/commerce; Japanese; kinesiology and exercise science; mass communication/media; mathematics; music; music performance; music theory and composition; nursing (registered nurse training); philosophy; physical sciences; physics; physics related; political science and government; psychology; religious studies; sociology; Spanish.

Academics *Calendar:* 4-1-4. *Degree:* bachelor's. *Special study options:* adult/continuing education programs, advanced placement credit, distance learning, double majors, English as a second language, external degree program, independent study, internships, off-campus study, part-time degree program, services for LD students, student-designed majors, study abroad, summer session for credit. *ROTC:* Air Force (c). *Unusual degree programs:* 3-2 engineering with Washington State University, Oregon State University, University of Southern California.

Computers on Campus 250 computers/terminals are available on campus for general student use. Students can access the following: computer help desk, free student e-mail accounts, online (class) grades, online (class) registration, online (class) schedules. Campuswide network is available. 95% of college-owned or -operated housing units are wired for high-speed Internet access. Wireless service is available via classrooms, computer centers, computer labs, learning centers, libraries, student centers.

Student Life *Housing:* on-campus residence required through junior year. *Options:* coed, men-only, women-only, disabled students. Campus housing is university owned. Freshman campus housing is guaranteed. *Activities and organizations:* drama/theater group, student-run newspaper, radio station, choral group, Fellowship of Christian Athletes, Linfield Ultimate Players Association, Hawaiian Club, International Club, Outdoor Club, national fraternities, national sororities. *Campus security:* 24-hour emergency response devices and patrols, late-night transport/escort service, controlled dormitory access. *Student services:* health clinic, personal/psychological counseling, women's center.

Athletics Member NCAA. All Division III. *Intercollegiate sports:* baseball M, basketball M/W, cross-country running M/W, football M, golf M/W, lacrosse W, soccer M/W, softball W, swimming and diving M/W, tennis M/W, track and field M/W, volleyball W. *Intramural sports:* basketball M/W, bowling M/W, football M/W, lacrosse M, racquetball M/W, soccer M/W, softball M/W, ultimate Frisbee M/W, volleyball M/W, water polo M/W.

Standardized Tests *Required:* SAT or ACT (for admission).

Costs (2007–08) *Comprehensive fee:* $33,044 includes full-time tuition ($25,390), mandatory fees ($254), and room and board ($7400). Part-time tuition: $790 per semester hour. Part-time tuition and fees vary according to course load. *Required fees:* $77 per term part-time. *College room only:* $3950. Room and board charges vary according to board plan and housing facility. *Payment plan:* installment. *Waivers:* senior citizens and employees or children of employees.

Financial Aid Of all full-time matriculated undergraduates who enrolled in 2006, 1,061 applied for aid, 1,061 were judged to have need, 328 had their need fully met. 708 Federal Work-Study jobs (averaging $2041). 603 state and other part-time jobs (averaging $2060). In 2006, 480 non-need-based awards were made. *Average percent of need met:* 82%. *Average financial aid package:* $20,059. *Average need-based loan:* $4915. *Average need-based gift aid:* $8225. *Average non-need-based aid:* $7951. *Average indebtedness upon graduation:* $25,940.

Applying *Options:* electronic application, early action, deferred entrance. *Application fee:* $40. *Required:* essay or personal statement, high school transcript, 1 letter of recommendation. *Recommended:* interview. *Application deadlines:* 2/15 (freshmen), 4/15 (transfers), 11/15 (early action). *Notification:* 4/1 (freshmen), 5/15 (transfers), 1/15 (early action).

Freshman Application Contact Ms. Lisa Knodle-Bragiel, Director of Admission, Linfield College, 900 SE Baker Street, McMinnville, OR 97128. *Phone:* 503-883-2213. *Toll-free phone:* 800-640-2287. *Fax:* 503-883-2472. *E-mail:* admission@linfield.edu.

See page 2110 for the College Close-Up.

MARYLHURST UNIVERSITY

Marylhurst, Oregon **www.marylhurst.edu/**

- **Independent Roman Catholic** comprehensive, founded 1893
- **Suburban** 73-acre campus with easy access to Portland
- **Endowment** $15.2 million
- **Coed** 837 undergraduate students, 23% full-time, 72% women, 28% men
- **Noncompetitive** entrance level

Undergraduates 194 full-time, 643 part-time. Students come from 13 other countries, 0.6% African American, 0.5% Asian American or Pacific Islander, 1% Hispanic American, 0.1% Native American, 2% international.

Freshmen *Admission:* 23 enrolled.

Faculty *Total:* 179, 21% full-time, 37% with terminal degrees.

Majors Anthropology; art; business administration and management; communication/speech communication and rhetoric; English; environmental science; fine/studio arts; humanities; interior design; mass communication/media; multi-/interdisciplinary studies related; music; music performance; music related; music theory and composition; music therapy; organizational communication; psychology; real estate; religious studies; social sciences; sociology.

Academics *Calendar:* quarters. *Degrees:* bachelor's, master's, post-master's, and postbachelor's certificates. *Special study options:* accelerated degree program, adult/continuing education programs, advanced placement credit, distance learning, double majors, English as a second language, independent study, internships, off-campus study, part-time degree program, services for LD students, student-designed majors, study abroad, summer session for credit.

Computers on Campus 40 computers/terminals are available on campus for general student use. Students can access the following: online (class) grades, online (class) registration, online (class) schedules. Campuswide network is available. Wireless service is available via classrooms, computer labs, libraries, student centers.

Student Life *Housing:* college housing not available. *Activities and organizations:* choral group, Marylhurst's Writer's Club, Marylhurst Gerontology Association, Solutions: Marylhurst Mediation Resource, Marylhurst S.A.F.E. Community: Sexual Acceptance for Everyone, LABY: Labyrinth Alliance Balances You. *Student services:* personal/psychological counseling.

Costs (2007–08) *Tuition:* $15,120 full-time, $336 per credit part-time. Full-time tuition and fees vary according to course load, degree level, and program. Part-time tuition and fees vary according to course load, degree level, and program. *Required fees:* $450 full-time, $10 per credit part-time. *Payment plans:* installment, deferred payment. *Waivers:* employees or children of employees.

Financial Aid Of all full-time matriculated undergraduates who enrolled in 2006, 121 applied for aid, 115 were judged to have need, 1 had their need fully met. 60 Federal Work-Study jobs (averaging $3524). In 2006, 12 non-need-based awards were made. *Average percent of need met:* 45%. *Average financial aid package:* $12,122. *Average need-based loan:* $5080. *Average need-based gift aid:* $8233. *Average non-need-based aid:* $8019. *Average indebtedness upon graduation:* $17,997.

Applying *Options:* electronic application. *Application fee:* $20. *Required:* high school transcript, letters of recommendation, interview. *Recommended:* minimum 2.0 GPA. *Application deadlines:* rolling (freshmen), rolling (transfers). *Notification:* continuous (freshmen), continuous (transfers).

Freshman Application Contact Admissions, Marylhurst University, 17600 Pacific Highway (Highway 43), PO Box 261, Marylhurst, OR 97036. *Phone:* 503-636-8141. *Toll-free phone:* 800-634-9982. *Fax:* 503-635-6585. *E-mail:* admissions@marylhurst.edu.

MOUNT ANGEL SEMINARY

Saint Benedict, Oregon

www.mtangel.edu/seminary/index.html

Director of Admissions Registrar/Admissions Officer, Mount Angel Seminary, Saint Benedict, OR 97373. *Phone:* 503-845-3951 Ext. 14.

MULTNOMAH BIBLE COLLEGE AND BIBLICAL SEMINARY

Portland, Oregon

www.multnomah.edu/

- **Independent interdenominational** comprehensive, founded 1936
- **Urban** 22-acre campus
- **Endowment** $7.6 million
- **Coed** 567 undergraduate students, 92% full-time, 45% women, 55% men
- **Moderately difficult** entrance level, 81% of applicants were admitted

Undergraduates 523 full-time, 44 part-time. Students come from 27 states and territories, 6 other countries, 49% are from out of state, 1% African American, 4% Asian American or Pacific Islander, 2% Hispanic American, 1% Native American, 0.9% international, 18% transferred in, 42% live on campus. *Retention:* 60% of 2006 full-time freshmen returned.

Freshmen *Admission:* 143 applied, 116 admitted, 72 enrolled. *Average high school GPA:* 3.36. *Test scores:* SAT critical reading scores over 500: 68%; SAT math scores over 500: 59%; SAT writing scores over 500: 67%; ACT scores over 18: 91%; SAT critical reading scores over 600: 31%; SAT math scores over 600: 19%; SAT writing scores over 600: 18%; ACT scores over 24: 52%; SAT critical reading scores over 700: 1%; SAT math scores over 700: 2%; ACT scores over 30: 3%.

Faculty *Total:* 53, 45% full-time, 42% with terminal degrees. *Student/faculty ratio:* 16:1.

Majors Ancient/classical Greek; biblical studies; communication/speech communication and rhetoric; Hebrew; history; journalism; missionary studies and missiology; pastoral counseling and specialized ministries related; pastoral studies/counseling; religious education; religious/sacred music; theology; youth ministry.

Academics *Calendar:* early semesters. *Degrees:* bachelor's, master's, first professional, and postbachelor's certificates. *Special study options:* academic remediation for entering students, adult/continuing education programs, advanced placement credit, double majors, internships, part-time degree program, services for LD students, summer session for credit.

Computers on Campus 42 computers/terminals are available on campus for general student use. Students can access the following: campus intranet, computer help desk, free student e-mail accounts, online (class) grades, online (class) registration, online (class) schedules. Campuswide network is available. 80% of college-owned or -operated housing units are wired for high-speed Internet access. Wireless service is available via entire campus.

Student Life *Housing:* on-campus residence required through junior year. *Options:* men-only, women-only. Campus housing is university owned. Freshman campus housing is guaranteed. *Activities and organizations:* drama/theater group, student-run newspaper, choral group. *Campus security:* 24-hour emergency response devices and patrols, late-night transport/escort service, controlled dormitory access. *Student services:* health clinic, personal/psychological counseling.

Athletics Member NCCAA. *Intercollegiate sports:* basketball M/W, volleyball W. *Intramural sports:* basketball M/W, tennis M/W, ultimate Frisbee M/W, volleyball M/W.

Standardized Tests *Required:* SAT or ACT (for admission).

Costs (2007–08) *Comprehensive fee:* $19,080 includes full-time tuition ($13,480) and room and board ($5600). Part-time tuition: $558 per credit. Part-time tuition and fees vary according to course load. *Room and board:* Room and board charges vary according to board plan and housing facility. *Payment plan:* installment. *Waivers:* employees or children of employees.

Financial Aid Of all full-time matriculated undergraduates who enrolled in 2004, 451 applied for aid, 404 were judged to have need, 23 had their need fully met. 85 Federal Work-Study jobs (averaging $2000). In 2004, 66 non-need-based awards were made. *Average percent of need met:* 57%. *Average financial aid package:* $7858. *Average need-based loan:* $3633. *Average need-based gift aid:* $4262. *Average non-need-based aid:* $9903. *Average indebtedness upon graduation:* $19,783.

Applying *Options:* deferred entrance. *Application fee:* $40. *Required:* essay or personal statement, high school transcript, minimum 2.5 GPA, 4 letters of recommendation. *Application deadlines:* 7/15 (freshmen), 7/15 (transfers). *Notification:* continuous (freshmen), continuous (transfers).

Freshman Application Contact Ms. Nancy Gerecz, Admissions Assistant, Multnomah Bible College and Biblical Seminary, 8435 Northeast Glisan Street, Portland, OR 97220-5898. *Phone:* 503-255-0332 Ext. 373. *Toll-free phone:* 800-275-4672. *Fax:* 503-254-1268. *E-mail:* admiss@multnomah.edu.

See page 2112 for the College Close-Up.

NORTHWEST CHRISTIAN COLLEGE

Eugene, Oregon

www.nwcc.edu/

- **Independent Christian** comprehensive, founded 1895
- **Urban** 8-acre campus with easy access to Portland
- **Endowment** $14.3 million
- **Coed** 396 undergraduate students, 77% full-time, 59% women, 41% men
- **Moderately difficult** entrance level, 45% of applicants were admitted

Undergraduates 304 full-time, 92 part-time. Students come from 13 states and territories, 9% are from out of state, 2% African American, 3% Asian American or Pacific Islander, 2% Hispanic American, 2% Native American, 13% transferred in, 28% live on campus. *Retention:* 53% of 2006 full-time freshmen returned.

Freshmen *Admission:* 614 applied, 275 admitted, 53 enrolled. *Average high school GPA:* 3.34. *Test scores:* SAT critical reading scores over 500: 48%; SAT math scores over 500: 46%; SAT writing scores over 500: 44%; ACT scores over 18: 80%; SAT critical reading scores over 600: 19%; SAT math scores over 600: 13%; SAT writing scores over 600: 18%; ACT scores over 24: 20%; SAT critical reading scores over 700: 6%; SAT math scores over 700: 4%; SAT writing scores over 700: 5%; ACT scores over 30: 7%.

Faculty *Total:* 90, 30% full-time, 37% with terminal degrees. *Student/faculty ratio:* 8:1.

Majors Accounting; area, ethnic, cultural, and gender studies related; biblical studies; business administration, management and operations related; communication and journalism related; communication/speech communication and rhetoric; computer and information sciences; computer programming; education (multiple levels); English; general studies; health services administration; history; humanities; human services; liberal arts and sciences and humanities related; management information systems; mathematics; multi-/interdisciplinary studies related; music; music management and merchandising; psychology related; social sciences related; theological and ministerial studies related.

Academics *Calendar:* quarters. *Degrees:* certificates, associate, bachelor's, master's, and postbachelor's certificates. *Special study options:* academic remediation for entering students, accelerated degree program, adult/continuing education programs, advanced placement credit, cooperative education, distance learning, double majors, English as a second language, independent study, internships, off-campus study, part-time degree program, services for LD students, student-designed majors, study abroad, summer session for credit. *ROTC:* Army (c).

Computers on Campus 60 computers/terminals are available on campus for general student use. Students can access the following: campus intranet, computer help desk, free student e-mail accounts, online (class) grades, online (class) schedules. Campuswide network is available. 100% of college-owned or -operated housing units are wired for high-speed Internet access. Wireless service is available via classrooms, computer centers, computer labs, learning centers, libraries.

Student Life *Housing:* on-campus residence required through sophomore year. *Options:* coed, men-only, women-only. Campus housing is university owned and leased by the school. Freshman applicants given priority for college housing. *Activities and organizations:* drama/theater group, student-run newspaper, choral group, Praise Gathering, Spirit Club, Teachers for Tomorrow, Environmental Club, Drama Club. *Campus security:* 24-hour emergency response devices and patrols, late-night transport/escort service, controlled dormitory access, late-night patrols by trained security personnel. *Student services:* health clinic, personal/psychological counseling.

Athletics Member NAIA. *Intercollegiate sports:* basketball M (s)/W (s), soccer M (s)/W (s), softball W (s), volleyball W (s). *Intramural sports:* basketball M/W, volleyball W.

Standardized Tests *Required:* SAT or ACT (for admission). *Required for some:* SAT Subject Tests (for admission).

Costs (2007–08) *Comprehensive fee:* $28,251 includes full-time tuition ($21,481) and room and board ($6770). Full-time tuition and fees vary according to course load and program. Part-time tuition: $716 per credit. Part-time tuition and fees vary according to course load and program. *Room and board:* Room and board charges vary according to board plan and housing facility. *Payment plans:* installment, deferred payment. *Waivers:* employees or children of employees.

Financial Aid Of all full-time matriculated undergraduates who enrolled in 2006, 273 applied for aid, 248 were judged to have need, 52 had their need fully met. In 2006, 21 non-need-based awards were made. *Average percent of need met:* 75%. *Average financial aid package:* $16,807. *Average need-based loan:* $3950. *Average need-based gift aid:* $12,492. *Average non-need-based aid:* $11,252. *Average indebtedness upon graduation:* $14,415.

Applying *Options:* electronic application, deferred entrance. *Required:* essay or personal statement, high school transcript, minimum 2.5 GPA, 2 letters of recommendation. *Recommended:* interview. *Application deadlines:* rolling (freshmen), rolling (transfers). *Notification:* continuous (freshmen), continuous (transfers).

Freshman Application Contact Director of Admissions, Northwest Christian College, 828 East 11th Avenue, Eugene, OR 97401-3745. *Phone:* 541-684-7201. *Toll-free phone:* 877-463-6622. *Fax:* 541-684-7317. *E-mail:* admissions@nwcc.edu.

Oregon College of Art & Craft

Portland, Oregon — **www.ocac.edu/**

- **Independent** 4-year, founded 1907
- **Urban** 11-acre campus
- **Endowment** $4.4 million
- **Coed**
- **Minimally difficult** entrance level

Faculty *Student/faculty ratio:* 9:1.

Academics *Calendar:* semesters. *Degrees:* certificates, bachelor's, and post-bachelor's certificates.

Student Life *Campus security:* 24-hour emergency response devices, late-night transport/escort service.

Standardized Tests *Recommended:* SAT (for admission), ACT (for admission).

Costs (2007–08) *Comprehensive fee:* $26,585 includes full-time tuition ($17,745), mandatory fees ($1340), and room and board ($7500). Part-time tuition: $2325 per course. Part-time tuition and fees vary according to course load. *Required fees:* $50 per course part-time. *College room only:* $3600. Room and board charges vary according to location.

Financial Aid Of all full-time matriculated undergraduates who enrolled in 2005, 75 applied for aid, 75 were judged to have need, 2 had their need fully met. 40 Federal Work-Study jobs (averaging $459). 49 state and other part-time jobs (averaging $622). In 2005, 2 non-need-based awards were made. *Average percent of need met:* 68. *Average financial aid package:* $18,130. *Average need-based loan:* $3980. *Average need-based gift aid:* $6763. *Average non-need-based aid:* $5000. *Average indebtedness upon graduation:* $32,000.

Applying *Options:* deferred entrance. *Application fee:* $35. *Required:* essay or personal statement, high school transcript, minimum 2.5 GPA, 2 letters of recommendation, portfolio. *Required for some:* interview.

Freshman Application Contact Ms. Debrah Spencer, Interim Director of Admissions, Oregon College of Art & Craft, 8245 Southwest Barnes Road, Portland, OR 97225-6349. *Phone:* 503-297-5544 Ext. 129. *Toll-free phone:* 800-390-0632 Ext. 129. *Fax:* 503-297-9651. *E-mail:* admissions@ocac.edu.

Oregon Health & Science University

Portland, Oregon — **www.ohsu.edu/**

- **State-related** upper-level, founded 1974
- **Urban** 116-acre campus
- **Endowment** $365.3 million
- **Coed**
- **Moderately difficult** entrance level

Academics *Calendar:* quarters. *Degrees:* certificates, bachelor's, master's, doctoral, first professional, post-master's, postbachelor's, and first professional certificates.

Student Life *Campus security:* 24-hour emergency response devices and patrols.

Costs (2007–08) *Tuition:* state resident $8676 full-time, $241 per credit part-time; nonresident $15,984 full-time, $444 per credit part-time. Full-time tuition and fees vary according to location. Part-time tuition and fees vary according to location. *Required fees:* $4192 full-time.

Financial Aid Of all full-time matriculated undergraduates who enrolled in 2007, 170 applied for aid, 163 were judged to have need, 8 had their need fully met. 10 Federal Work-Study jobs (averaging $1600). *Average percent of need met:* 60. *Average financial aid package:* $10,706. *Average need-based loan:* $5895. *Average need-based gift aid:* $6780.

Applying *Application fee:* $125.

Application Contact Jennifer Anderson, Registrar and Director of Financial Aid, Oregon Health & Science University, 3181 Southwest Sam Jackson Park Road, Portland, OR 97201-3098. *Phone:* 503-494-0647. *Fax:* 503-494-4350. *E-mail:* andersje@ohsu.edu.

Oregon Institute of Technology

Klamath Falls, Oregon — **www.oit.edu/**

- **State-supported** 4-year, founded 1947, part of Oregon University System
- **Small-town** 173-acre campus
- **Endowment** $12.9 million
- **Coed** 3,134 undergraduate students, 58% full-time, 49% women, 51% men
- **Moderately difficult** entrance level, 88% of applicants were admitted

Undergraduates 1,812 full-time, 1,322 part-time. Students come from 37 states and territories, 13 other countries, 15% are from out of state, 1% African American, 5% Asian American or Pacific Islander, 4% Hispanic American, 2% Native American, 0.9% international, 13% transferred in, 15% live on campus. *Retention:* 67% of 2006 full-time freshmen returned.

Freshmen *Admission:* 651 applied, 575 admitted, 296 enrolled. *Average high school GPA:* 3.42. *Test scores:* SAT critical reading scores over 500: 57%; SAT math scores over 500: 67%; ACT scores over 18: 83%; SAT critical reading scores over 600: 20%; SAT math scores over 600: 31%; ACT scores over 24: 27%; SAT critical reading scores over 700: 3%; SAT math scores over 700: 4%; ACT scores over 30: 4%.

Faculty *Total:* 223, 60% full-time. *Student/faculty ratio:* 14:1.

Majors Accounting; business administration and management; civil engineering; communication/speech communication and rhetoric; computer and information sciences; computer engineering technology; computer programming; counseling psychology; dental hygiene; electrical, electronic and communications engineering technology; environmental studies; industrial radiologic technology; laser and optical technology; liberal arts and sciences/liberal studies; management information systems; mechanical engineering/mechanical technology; pre-medical studies; radiologic technology/science; survey technology.

Academics *Calendar:* quarters. *Degrees:* associate, bachelor's, and master's. *Special study options:* academic remediation for entering students, advanced placement credit, cooperative education, distance learning, double majors, external degree program, internships, off-campus study, part-time degree program, services for LD students, study abroad, summer session for credit. *ROTC:* Army (c).

Computers on Campus 700 computers/terminals are available on campus for general student use. Students can access the following: online (class) grades, online (class) registration. Campuswide network is available.

Student Life *Housing options:* coed. Campus housing is university owned. *Activities and organizations:* student-run newspaper, radio and television station, choral group, Phi Delta Theta, Christian Fellowship, International Club, Society of Women Engineers, Association of Student Mechanical Engineers, national fraternities. *Campus security:* 24-hour emergency response devices and patrols, late-night transport/escort service. *Student services:* health clinic, personal/psychological counseling.

Athletics Member NAIA. *Intercollegiate sports:* baseball M, basketball M (s)/W, cross-country running M (s)/W (s), soccer W, softball W (s), track and field M (s)/W (s), volleyball W (s). *Intramural sports:* basketball M/W, bowling M/W, cheerleading M/W, cross-country running M/W, football M/W, golf M/W, lacrosse M, rugby M/W, soccer W, softball W, track and field M/W, volleyball M/W, water polo M/W.

Standardized Tests *Required:* SAT or ACT (for admission).

Costs (2007–08) *Tuition:* state resident $5811 full-time, $102 per credit part-time; nonresident $16,892 full-time, $102 per credit part-time. Full-time tuition and fees vary according to course level, course load, degree level, location, program, and reciprocity agreements. Part-time tuition and fees vary according to course level, course load, degree level, location, program, and reciprocity agreements. *Required fees:* $1329 full-time. *Room and board:* $7452; room only: $4167. Room and board charges vary according to board plan and housing facility.

Financial Aid Of all full-time matriculated undergraduates who enrolled in 2002, 1,913 applied for aid, 1,796 were judged to have need, 647 had their need fully met. In 2002, 2 non-need-based awards were made. *Average percent of need met:* 17%. *Average financial aid package:* $5791. *Average need-based loan:* $4308. *Average need-based gift aid:* $3951. *Average non-need-based aid:* $9563. *Average indebtedness upon graduation:* $21,620.

Applying *Options:* electronic application, deferred entrance. *Application fee:* $50. *Required:* high school transcript, minimum 3.0 GPA. *Required for some:* letters of recommendation. *Application deadlines:* 10/1 (freshmen), 2/1 (transfers). *Notification:* continuous until 8/1 (freshmen), continuous (transfers).

Director of Admissions Mr. John Duarte, Director of Admissions, Oregon Institute of Technology, 3201 Campus Drive, Klamath Falls, OR 97601. *Phone:* 541-885-1150. *Toll-free phone:* 800-422-2017 (in-state); 800-343-6653 (out-of-state). *E-mail:* oit@oit.edu.

OREGON STATE UNIVERSITY

Corvallis, Oregon **oregonstate.edu/**

- **State-supported** university, founded 1868, part of Oregon University System
- **Small-town** 422-acre campus with easy access to Portland
- **Endowment** $457.1 million
- **Coed** 16,228 undergraduate students, 86% full-time, 47% women, 53% men
- **Moderately difficult** entrance level, 86% of applicants were admitted

Small classes, motivated students, honors-level instruction, and close interaction with some of Oregon State University's finest faculty members create an exciting, challenging University Honors College atmosphere. In honors classes, colloquiums, and other innovative ways, Honors College students explore their majors with an interdisciplinary approach. Students also work with faculty mentors to prepare honors theses. Graduates receive an Honors baccalaureate degree in their major, conferred jointly by the Honors College and their academic college. Honors College graduates enjoy virtually 100 percent placement into graduate and professional programs.

Undergraduates 13,982 full-time, 2,246 part-time. Students come from 50 states and territories, 88 other countries, 11% are from out of state, 2% African American, 9% Asian American or Pacific Islander, 4% Hispanic American, 1% Native American, 2% international, 6% transferred in, 21% live on campus. *Retention:* 81% of 2006 full-time freshmen returned.

Freshmen *Admission:* 8,149 applied, 6,971 admitted, 3,089 enrolled. *Average high school GPA:* 3.47. *Test scores:* SAT critical reading scores over 500: 61%; SAT math scores over 500: 72%; ACT scores over 18: 90%; SAT critical reading scores over 600: 21%; SAT math scores over 600: 29%; ACT scores over 24: 43%; SAT critical reading scores over 700: 3%; SAT math scores over 700: 5%; ACT scores over 30: 7%.

Majors Actuarial science; agricultural/biological engineering and bioengineering; agricultural business and management; agricultural economics; agriculture; agronomy and crop science; American studies; animal sciences; anthropology; applied art; applied mathematics; art; art history, criticism and conservation; athletic training; biochemistry; biological and physical sciences; biology/biological sciences; biophysics; botany/plant biology; business administration and management; cell biology and histology; chemical engineering; chemistry; civil engineering; clinical laboratory science/medical technology; clothing/textiles; comparative literature; computer engineering; computer science; construction engineering; construction management; cultural studies; economics; electrical, electronics and communications engineering; engineering; engineering physics; English; entomology; environmental biology; environmental/environmental health engineering; environmental health; environmental studies; evolutionary biology; family and community services; family and consumer economics related; family and consumer sciences/human sciences; fashion/apparel design; fashion merchandising; finance; fish/game management; fishing and fisheries sciences and management; food science; foods, nutrition, and wellness; forest engineering; forest/forest resources management; forest resources production and management; forestry; French; geography; geological/geophysical engineering; geology/earth science; geophysics and seismology; German; health/health care administration; health science; history; history and philosophy of science and technology; horticultural science; human development and family studies; industrial engineering; information science/studies; interdisciplinary studies; interior design; international business/trade/commerce; international/global studies; international relations and affairs; kindergarten/preschool education; kinesiology and exercise science; liberal arts and sciences/liberal studies; literature; management information systems; marketing/marketing management; mathematics; mechanical engineering; medical microbiology and bacteriology; merchandising, sales, and marketing operations related (general); metallurgical engineering; microbiology; mining and mineral engineering; music; natural resources management and policy; nuclear engineering; occupational safety and health technology; parks, recreation and leisure; parks, recreation and leisure facilities management; philosophy; physical education teaching and coaching; physical sciences; physics; political science and government; pre-pharmacy studies; psychology; public health; radiation protection/health physics technology; range science and management; sociology; soil sciences; Spanish; special products marketing; speech and rhetoric; wildlife and wildlands science and management; wood science and wood products/pulp and paper technology; zoology/animal biology.

Academics *Calendar:* quarters. *Degrees:* certificates, bachelor's, master's, doctoral, first professional, post-master's, postbachelor's, and first professional certificates. *Special study options:* academic remediation for entering students, accelerated degree program, advanced placement credit, cooperative education, distance learning, double majors, English as a second language, external degree program, freshman honors college, honors programs, independent study, internships, off-campus study, part-time degree program, services for LD students, student-designed majors, study abroad, summer session for credit. *ROTC:* Army (b), Navy (b), Air Force (b).

Computers on Campus 1,300 computers/terminals and 150 ports are available on campus for general student use. Students can access the following: campus intranet, computer help desk, free student e-mail accounts, online (class) grades, online (class) registration, online (class) schedules. Campuswide network is available. 95% of college-owned or -operated housing units are wired for high-speed Internet access. Wireless service is available via entire campus.

Student Life *Housing options:* coed, cooperative, disabled students. Campus housing is university owned. Freshman applicants given priority for college housing. *Activities and organizations:* drama/theater group, student-run newspaper, radio and television station, choral group, marching band, Associated Students of OSU, International Students of OSU, Graduate Students Organization, Campus Crusade, MECHA, national fraternities, national sororities. *Campus security:* 24-hour emergency response devices and patrols, student patrols, late-night transport/escort service, controlled dormitory access, crime prevention office. *Student services:* health clinic, personal/psychological counseling, women's center, legal services.

Athletics Member NCAA. All Division I except football (Division I-A). *Intercollegiate sports:* baseball M (s), basketball M (s)/W (s), crew M/W, golf M (s)/W (s), gymnastics W (s), soccer M (s)/W (s), softball W (s), swimming and diving W (s), volleyball W (s), wrestling M (s). *Intramural sports:* archery M/W, badminton M/W, basketball M/W, bowling M/W, crew M/W, cross-country running M/W, equestrian sports M (c)/W (c), fencing M (c)/W (c), football M, golf M/W, lacrosse M (c)/W (c), racquetball M/W, riflery M (c)/W (c), rugby M (c)/W (c), sailing M (c)/W (c), skiing (cross-country) M (c)/W (c), skiing (downhill) M (c)/W (c), soccer M/W, softball M/W, squash M (c), swimming and diving M/W, table tennis M (c)/W (c), tennis M/W, track and field M/W, volleyball M/W, water polo M/W, wrestling M.

Standardized Tests *Required:* SAT or ACT (for admission). *Required for some:* SAT Subject Tests (for admission).

Costs (2007–08) *Tuition:* state resident $4464 full-time, $124 per credit part-time; nonresident $16,740 full-time, $465 per credit part-time. Full-time tuition and fees vary according to course load. Part-time tuition and fees vary according to course load. *Required fees:* $1447 full-time. *Room and board:* $7566. Room and board charges vary according to board plan and housing facility. *Payment plan:* deferred payment. *Waivers:* employees or children of employees.

Financial Aid Of all full-time matriculated undergraduates who enrolled in 2005, 9,085 applied for aid, 6,752 were judged to have need, 1,446 had their need fully met. In 2005, 62 non-need-based awards were made. *Average percent of need met:* 68%. *Average financial aid package:* $9022. *Average need-based loan:* $3108. *Average need-based gift aid:* $2466. *Average non-need-based aid:* $2556. *Average indebtedness upon graduation:* $19,550. *Financial aid deadline:* 5/1.

Applying *Options:* electronic application, early admission, early action, deferred entrance. *Application fee:* $50. *Required:* essay or personal statement, high school transcript, minimum 3.0 GPA. *Application deadlines:* 9/1 (freshmen), 5/1 (transfers), 11/1 (early action). *Notification:* continuous (freshmen), continuous (transfers).

Freshman Application Contact Ms. Michele Sandlin, Director of Admissions, Oregon State University, Corvallis, OR 97331. *Phone:* 541-737-4411. *Toll-free phone:* 800-291-4192. *E-mail:* osuadmit@orst.edu.

See page 2114 for the College Close-Up.

OREGON STATE UNIVERSITY–CASCADES

Bend, Oregon

PACIFIC NORTHWEST COLLEGE OF ART

Portland, Oregon **www.pnca.edu/**

Freshman Application Contact Mr. Chris Sweet Jr., Director of Admissions, Pacific Northwest College of Art, 1241 NW Johnson Street, Portland, OR 97209. *Phone:* 503-821-8972. *Fax:* 503-821-8978. *E-mail:* admissions@pnca.edu.

PACIFIC UNIVERSITY

Forest Grove, Oregon **www.pacificu.edu/**

- **Independent** comprehensive, founded 1849
- **Small-town** 60-acre campus with easy access to Portland
- **Endowment** $44.5 million
- **Coed** 1,452 undergraduate students, 95% full-time, 63% women, 37% men
- **Moderately difficult** entrance level, 83% of applicants were admitted

Undergraduates 1,382 full-time, 70 part-time. Students come from 36 states and territories, 11 other countries, 52% are from out of state, 1% African American, 24% Asian American or Pacific Islander, 4% Hispanic American, 1% Native American, 0.4% international, 6% transferred in, 60% live on campus. *Retention:* 80% of 2006 full-time freshmen returned.

Freshmen *Admission:* 1,258 applied, 1,050 admitted, 372 enrolled. *Average high school GPA:* 3.61. *Test scores:* SAT critical reading scores over 500: 81%; SAT math scores over 500: 74%; ACT scores over 18: 95%; SAT critical reading scores over 600: 28%; SAT math scores over 600: 27%; ACT scores over 24: 53%; SAT critical reading scores over 700: 4%; SAT math scores over 700: 4%; ACT scores over 30: 7%.

Faculty *Total:* 164, 56% full-time, 50% with terminal degrees. *Student/faculty ratio:* 12:1.

Majors Accounting; art; art teacher education; athletic training; biology/biological sciences; broadcast journalism; business administration and management; chemistry; Chinese; computer science; creative writing; dramatic/theater arts; economics; education; elementary education; English; environmental studies; finance; French; German; health science; history; humanities; international relations and affairs; Japanese; journalism; kindergarten/preschool education; kinesiology and exercise science; liberal arts and sciences/liberal studies; literature; marketing/marketing management; mass communication/media; mathematics; modern languages; music; music performance; music teacher education; philosophy; physics; political science and government; pre-dentistry studies; pre-medical studies; pre-veterinary studies; psychology; radio and television; secondary education; social work; sociology; Spanish; telecommunications.

Academics *Calendar:* 4-1-4. *Degrees:* bachelor's, master's, doctoral, and first professional. *Special study options:* advanced placement credit, cooperative education, double majors, English as a second language, independent study, internships, off-campus study, services for LD students, study abroad, summer session for credit. *ROTC:* Army (c), Air Force (c). *Unusual degree programs:* 3-2 engineering with Washington State University, Washington University in St. Louis, Oregon Graduate Institute of Science and Technology, Oregon State University; medical technology, computer science, environmental science with Oregon Graduate Institute of Science and Technology.

Computers on Campus 315 computers/terminals and 5,900 ports are available on campus for general student use. Students can access the following: campus intranet, computer help desk, free student e-mail accounts, online (class) grades, online (class) schedules, Web space, printing, student and academic information, WebCT, computer peripherals. Campuswide network is available. 100% of college-owned or -operated housing units are wired for high-speed Internet access. Wireless service is available via entire campus.

Student Life *Housing:* on-campus residence required through sophomore year. *Options:* coed, women-only, cooperative, disabled students. Campus housing is university owned. Freshman campus housing is guaranteed. *Activities and organizations:* drama/theater group, student-run newspaper, radio station, choral group, Pacific Outback activities, Hawaiian Club, Pacific Christian Fellowship (PCF), Business and Economics Club, Exercise Science Club. *Campus security:* 24-hour emergency response devices and patrols, late-night transport/escort service, controlled dormitory access. *Student services:* health clinic, personal/psychological counseling, women's center.

Athletics Member NCAA, NAIA. All NCAA Division III. *Intercollegiate sports:* baseball M, basketball M/W, cross-country running M/W, golf M/W, lacrosse W, soccer M/W, softball W, swimming and diving M/W, tennis M/W, track and field M/W, volleyball W, wrestling M/W. *Intramural sports:* basketball M/W, cheerleading M/W, crew M/W, football M/W, racquetball W, softball M/W, volleyball M/W.

Standardized Tests *Required:* SAT or ACT (for admission).

Costs (2007–08) *Comprehensive fee:* $33,840 includes full-time tuition ($25,830), mandatory fees ($840), and room and board ($7170). Part-time tuition: $1016 per credit hour. *College room only:* $3720.

Financial Aid Of all full-time matriculated undergraduates who enrolled in 2007, 1,135 applied for aid, 998 were judged to have need, 327 had their need fully met. 789 Federal Work-Study jobs (averaging $1953). 187 state and other part-time jobs (averaging $556). In 2007, 272 non-need-based awards were made. *Average percent of need met:* 78%. *Average financial aid package:* $22,706. *Average need-based loan:* $7885. *Average need-based gift aid:* $11,895. *Average non-need-based aid:* $9561. *Average indebtedness upon graduation:* $24,757.

Applying *Options:* electronic application, deferred entrance. *Application fee:* $40. *Required:* essay or personal statement, high school transcript, minimum 3.0 GPA, 1 letter of recommendation. *Recommended:* interview. *Application deadlines:* 8/15 (freshmen), rolling (transfers). *Notification:* continuous (freshmen), continuous (transfers).

Freshman Application Contact Ms. Karen Dunston, Director of Undergraduate Admission, Pacific University, 2043 College Way, Forest Grove, OR 97116-1797. *Phone:* 503-352-2218. *Toll-free phone:* 877-722-8648. *Fax:* 503-352-2975. *E-mail:* admissions@pacificu.edu.

See page 2116 for the College Close-Up.

PIONEER PACIFIC COLLEGE

Wilsonville, Oregon **www.pioneerpacific.edu/**

- **Proprietary** primarily 2-year, founded 1981
- **Suburban** campus with easy access to Portland
- **Coed**
- **Noncompetitive** entrance level

Faculty *Student/faculty ratio:* 15:1.

Academics *Calendar:* continuous. *Degrees:* diplomas, associate, and bachelor's.

Standardized Tests *Required:* CPAt (for admission).

Costs (2007–08) *Tuition:* $9750 full-time, $228 per credit hour part-time. Full-time tuition and fees vary according to program. *Required fees:* $400 full-time. *Payment plans:* installment, deferred payment.

Applying *Application fee:* $50. *Required:* high school transcript, interview.

Freshman Application Contact Ms. Kristin Lynn, Director of Admissions, Pioneer Pacific College, 27501 Southwest Parkway Avenue, Wilsonville, OR 97070. *Phone:* 866-772-4636. *Toll-free phone:* 866-PPC-INFO. *Fax:* 503-682-1514. *E-mail:* inquiries@pioneerpacific.edu.

PIONEER PACIFIC COLLEGE-EUGENE/SPRINGFIELD BRANCH

Springfield, Oregon

PORTLAND STATE UNIVERSITY

Portland, Oregon **www.pdx.edu/**

- **State-supported** university, founded 1946, part of Oregon University System
- **Urban** 49-acre campus
- **Endowment** $42.7 million

- **Coed** 18,916 undergraduate students, 61% full-time, 54% women, 46% men
- **Moderately difficult** entrance level, 91% of applicants were admitted

Undergraduates 11,504 full-time, 7,412 part-time. Students come from 55 states and territories, 72 other countries, 20% are from out of state, 4% African American, 10% Asian American or Pacific Islander, 5% Hispanic American, 1% Native American, 4% international, 13% transferred in. *Retention:* 68% of 2006 full-time freshmen returned.

Freshmen *Admission:* 3,726 applied, 3,378 admitted, 1,671 enrolled. *Average high school GPA:* 3.25. *Test scores:* SAT critical reading scores over 500: 62%; SAT math scores over 500: 62%; SAT writing scores over 500: 53%; ACT scores over 18: 84%; SAT critical reading scores over 600: 25%; SAT math scores over 600: 21%; SAT writing scores over 600: 15%; ACT scores over 24: 34%; SAT critical reading scores over 700: 4%; SAT math scores over 700: 3%; SAT writing scores over 700: 1%; ACT scores over 30: 5%.

Faculty *Total:* 1,303, 59% full-time, 53% with terminal degrees. *Student/faculty ratio:* 19:1.

Majors Accounting; advertising; African studies; American Indian/Native American studies; anthropology; applied art; architecture; art; art history, criticism and conservation; Asian studies (East); biochemistry; biological and physical sciences; biology/biological sciences; business administration and management; chemistry; child development; Chinese; city/urban, community and regional planning; civil engineering; commercial and advertising art; computer and information sciences; computer engineering; computer science; criminal justice/law enforcement administration; dramatic/theater arts; drawing; economics; electrical, electronics and communications engineering; English; environmental studies; European studies (Central and Eastern); finance; French; geography; geology/earth science; German; health teacher education; history; humanities; human resources management; international relations and affairs; Japanese; Latin American studies; liberal arts and sciences/liberal studies; linguistics; logistics and materials management; marketing/marketing management; mathematics; mechanical engineering; music; Near and Middle Eastern studies; philosophy; physics; political science and government; psychology; Russian; sculpture; social sciences; sociology; Spanish; speech and rhetoric; urban studies/affairs; women's studies.

Academics *Calendar:* quarters. *Degrees:* certificates, bachelor's, master's, doctoral, and postbachelor's certificates. *Special study options:* academic remediation for entering students, accelerated degree program, adult/continuing education programs, advanced placement credit, cooperative education, distance learning, double majors, English as a second language, freshman honors college, honors programs, independent study, internships, off-campus study, part-time degree program, services for LD students, study abroad, summer session for credit. *ROTC:* Army (b), Air Force (c).

Computers on Campus 875 computers/terminals are available on campus for general student use. Students can access the following: online (class) registration. Campuswide network is available. 100% of college-owned or -operated housing units are wired for high-speed Internet access. Wireless service is available via entire campus.

Student Life *Housing:* on-campus residence required for freshman year. *Options:* coed, disabled students. Campus housing is university owned and is provided by a third party. Freshman campus housing is guaranteed. *Activities and organizations:* drama/theater group, student-run newspaper, radio station, choral group, MECHA, Women's Union, Association of African Students, Queers and Allies, Food for Thought, national fraternities, national sororities. *Campus security:* 24-hour emergency response devices and patrols, late-night transport/escort service, controlled dormitory access, self-defense education. *Student services:* health clinic, personal/psychological counseling, women's center, legal services.

Athletics Member NCAA. All Division I except football (Division I-AA). *Intercollegiate sports:* baseball M (s), basketball M (s)/W (s), cross-country running M (s)/W (s), golf M (s)/W (s), soccer W (s), softball W (s), tennis M (s)/W (s), track and field M (s)/W (s), volleyball W (s), wrestling M (s). *Intramural sports:* archery M/W, basketball M/W, bowling M (c)/W (c), crew M (c)/W (c), fencing M (c)/W (c), football M, golf M/W, racquetball M/W, sailing M (c)/W (c), skiing (downhill) M (c)/W (c), soccer M (c)/W, softball M/W, table tennis M (c)/W (c), tennis M (c)/W (c), volleyball M/W, water polo M (c)/W (c).

Standardized Tests *Required:* SAT or ACT (for admission).

Costs (2007–08) *One-time required fee:* $150. *Tuition:* state resident $4314 full-time, $98 per credit part-time; nonresident $16,380 full-time, $364 per credit part-time. Full-time tuition and fees vary according to program and reciprocity agreements. *Required fees:* $1451 full-time, $23 per credit part-time, $59 per term part-time. *Room and board:* $9207; room only: $6489. Room and board charges vary according to board plan and housing facility. *Payment plan:* installment. *Waivers:* minority students, senior citizens, and employees or children of employees.

Financial Aid Of all full-time matriculated undergraduates who enrolled in 2007, 7,586 applied for aid, 6,518 were judged to have need, 843 had their need fully met. 758 Federal Work-Study jobs (averaging $2626). In 2007, 247 non-need-based awards were made. *Average percent of need met:* 57%. *Average financial aid package:* $8149. *Average need-based loan:* $4565. *Average need-based gift aid:* $5025. *Average non-need-based aid:* $3813. *Average indebtedness upon graduation:* $16,445.

Applying *Options:* electronic application, early admission, deferred entrance. *Application fee:* $50. *Required:* high school transcript, minimum 3.0 GPA. *Application deadlines:* rolling (freshmen), rolling (transfers). *Notification:* continuous (freshmen), continuous (transfers).

Freshman Application Contact Portland State University, PO Box 751, Portland, OR 97207-0751. *Phone:* 503-725-3511. *Toll-free phone:* 800-547-8887. *Fax:* 503-725-5525. *E-mail:* admissions@pdx.edu.

REED COLLEGE

Portland, Oregon

www.reed.edu/

- **Independent** comprehensive, founded 1908
- **Urban** 110-acre campus
- **Endowment** $450.5 million
- **Coed** 1,464 undergraduate students, 97% full-time, 55% women, 45% men
- **Most difficult** entrance level, 34% of applicants were admitted

Undergraduates 1,413 full-time, 51 part-time. Students come from 49 states and territories, 43 other countries, 87% are from out of state, 3% African American, 8% Asian American or Pacific Islander, 6% Hispanic American, 1% Native American, 6% international, 3% transferred in, 59% live on campus. *Retention:* 91% of 2006 full-time freshmen returned.

Freshmen *Admission:* 3,365 applied, 1,154 admitted, 346 enrolled. *Average high school GPA:* 3.9. *Test scores:* SAT critical reading scores over 500: 100%; SAT math scores over 500: 99%; SAT writing scores over 500: 100%; ACT scores over 18: 100%; SAT critical reading scores over 600: 98%; SAT math scores over 600: 87%; SAT writing scores over 600: 93%; ACT scores over 24: 100%; SAT critical reading scores over 700: 67%; SAT math scores over 700: 33%; SAT writing scores over 700: 47%; ACT scores over 30: 64%.

Faculty *Total:* 135, 93% full-time, 91% with terminal degrees. *Student/faculty ratio:* 10:1.

Majors American studies; anthropology; art; biochemistry; biology/biological sciences; chemistry; Chinese; classics and languages, literatures and linguistics; dance; dramatic/theater arts; economics; English; fine/studio arts; French; German; history; international relations and affairs; linguistics; literature; mathematics; music; philosophy; physics; political science and government; psychology; religious studies; Russian; sociology; Spanish.

Academics *Calendar:* semesters. *Degrees:* bachelor's and master's. *Special study options:* advanced placement credit, cooperative education, double majors, independent study, internships, off-campus study, part-time degree program, services for LD students, study abroad. *Unusual degree programs:* 3-2 engineering with California Institute of Technology, Rensselaer Polytechnic Institute, Columbia University; forestry with Nicholas School of the Environment of Duke University; computer science with University of Washington; studio art with Pacific Northwest College of Art; applied physics, electronic science with Oregon Graduate Institute.

Computers on Campus 415 computers/terminals are available on campus for general student use. Students can access the following: campus intranet, computer help desk, free student e-mail accounts, online (class) registration, online (class) schedules. Campuswide network is available. 100% of college-owned or -operated housing units are wired for high-speed Internet access. Wireless service is available via entire campus.

Student Life *Housing:* on-campus residence required for freshman year. *Options:* coed, women-only, cooperative, disabled students. Campus housing is university owned and leased by the school. Freshman campus housing is guaranteed. *Activities and organizations:* drama/theater group, student-run newspaper, radio station, choral group, Reed Recycling, Movie Board, Reed Outing Club. *Campus security:* 24-hour emergency response devices and patrols, student patrols, late-night transport/escort service, controlled dormitory access, 24-hour emergency dispatch. *Student services:* health clinic, personal/psychological counseling, women's center.

Athletics *Intercollegiate sports:* basketball M (c), fencing M (c)/W (c), rugby M (c)/W (c), soccer M (c)/W (c), squash M (c)/W (c). *Intramural sports:* basketball M/W, racquetball M/W, rugby M/W, soccer M/W, softball M/W, squash M/W, tennis M/W, ultimate Frisbee M/W.

Standardized Tests *Required:* SAT or ACT (for admission). *Recommended:* SAT Subject Tests (for admission).

Costs (2007–08) *Comprehensive fee:* $45,880 includes full-time tuition ($36,190), mandatory fees ($230), and room and board ($9460). Full-time tuition and fees vary according to course load. Part-time tuition: $6170 per course. Part-time tuition and fees vary according to course load. *College room only:* $4940. Room and board charges vary according to board plan and housing facility. *Payment plan:* installment. *Waivers:* employees or children of employees.

Financial Aid Of all full-time matriculated undergraduates who enrolled in 2007, 810 applied for aid, 702 were judged to have need, 625 had their need fully met. 485 Federal Work-Study jobs (averaging $685). 54 state and other part-time jobs (averaging $687). *Average percent of need met:* 100%. *Average financial aid package:* $32,154. *Average need-based loan:* $4177. *Average need-based gift aid:* $28,108. *Average indebtedness upon graduation:* $17,098. *Financial aid deadline:* 1/15.

Applying *Options:* electronic application, early admission, early decision, deferred entrance. *Application fee:* $50. *Required:* essay or personal statement, high school transcript, 2 letters of recommendation. *Recommended:* interview. *Application deadlines:* 1/15 (freshmen), 3/1 (transfers). *Early decision deadline:* 11/15 (for plan 1), 1/2 (for plan 2). *Notification:* 4/1 (freshmen), 5/15 (transfers), 12/15 (early decision plan 1), 2/1 (early decision plan 2).

Freshman Application Contact Mr. Paul Marthers, Dean of Admission, Reed College, 3203 Southeast Woodstock Boulevard, Portland, OR 97202-8199. *Phone:* 503-777-7511. *Toll-free phone:* 800-547-4750. *Fax:* 503-777-7553. *E-mail:* admission@reed.edu.

See page 2118 for the College Close-Up.

SOUTHERN OREGON UNIVERSITY

Ashland, Oregon **www.sou.edu/**

- **State-supported** comprehensive, founded 1926, part of Oregon University System
- **Small-town** 175-acre campus
- **Endowment** $13.0 million
- **Coed** 4,297 undergraduate students, 75% full-time, 57% women, 43% men
- **Moderately difficult** entrance level, 83% of applicants were admitted

Undergraduates 3,205 full-time, 1,092 part-time. Students come from 45 states and territories, 33 other countries, 22% are from out of state, 2% African American, 4% Asian American or Pacific Islander, 4% Hispanic American, 2% Native American, 2% international, 11% transferred in, 24% live on campus. *Retention:* 66% of 2006 full-time freshmen returned.

Freshmen *Admission:* 1,887 applied, 1,565 admitted, 749 enrolled. *Average high school GPA:* 3.2. *Test scores:* SAT critical reading scores over 500: 55%; SAT math scores over 500: 52%; ACT scores over 18: 88%; SAT critical reading scores over 600: 18%; SAT math scores over 600: 13%; ACT scores over 24: 34%; SAT critical reading scores over 700: 1%; SAT math scores over 700: 1%; ACT scores over 30: 4%.

Faculty *Total:* 289, 67% full-time. *Student/faculty ratio:* 22:1.

Majors Accounting; anthropology; art; biochemistry; biology/biological sciences; business administration and management; business statistics; chemistry; communication/speech communication and rhetoric; computer science; criminology; dramatic/theater arts; economics; English; environmental studies; French; geography; geology/earth science; German; health teacher education; history; hotel/motel administration; interdisciplinary studies; international relations and affairs; liberal arts and sciences/liberal studies; marketing/marketing management; mathematics; mathematics and computer science; music; music management and merchandising; nursing (registered nurse training); physical education teaching and coaching; physics; political science and government; pre-law studies; pre-medical studies; psychology; social sciences; sociology; Spanish.

Academics *Calendar:* quarters. *Degrees:* bachelor's, master's, and postbachelor's certificates. *Special study options:* academic remediation for entering students, accelerated degree program, adult/continuing education programs, advanced placement credit, cooperative education, distance learning, double majors, English as a second language, freshman honors college, honors programs, independent study, internships, off-campus study, part-time degree program, services for LD students, student-designed majors, study abroad, summer session for credit. *Unusual degree programs:* 3-2 engineering with Oregon State University.

Computers on Campus 750 computers/terminals are available on campus for general student use. Students can access the following: online (class) registration. Campuswide network is available.

Student Life *Housing:* on-campus residence required for freshman year. *Options:* coed, disabled students. Campus housing is university owned. Freshman campus housing is guaranteed. *Activities and organizations:* drama/theater group, student-run newspaper, radio and television station, choral group, Native American Student Union, International Student Association, Impact (religious club), Ho'opa'a Hawaii Club, Omicron Delta Kappa. *Campus security:* 24-hour emergency response devices and patrols, student patrols, late-night transport/escort service. *Student services:* health clinic, personal/psychological counseling, women's center, legal services.

Athletics Member NAIA. *Intercollegiate sports:* basketball M (s)/W (s), cross-country running M (s)/W (s), football M (s), skiing (downhill) M/W, soccer W (s), softball W (s), tennis W (s), track and field M (s)/W (s), volleyball W (s), wrestling M (s). *Intramural sports:* basketball M/W, bowling M/W, cheerleading M/W, crew M/W, football M/W, golf M/W, racquetball M/W, rugby M/W, sailing M/W, skiing (cross-country) M/W, soccer M/W, softball M/W, swimming and diving M/W, table tennis M/W, tennis M/W, track and field M/W, ultimate Frisbee M/W, volleyball M/W, water polo M/W.

Standardized Tests *Required:* SAT or ACT (for admission). *Required for some:* SAT Subject Tests (for admission).

Costs (2007–08) *Tuition:* state resident $5409 full-time; nonresident $17,988 full-time. Full-time tuition and fees vary according to course load, location, and reciprocity agreements. Part-time tuition and fees vary according to course load, location, and reciprocity agreements. *Room and board:* $7941. Room and board charges vary according to board plan and housing facility. *Payment plan:* deferred payment. *Waivers:* senior citizens and employees or children of employees.

Financial Aid Of all full-time matriculated undergraduates who enrolled in 2006, 2,313 applied for aid, 1,962 were judged to have need, 273 had their need fully met. 566 Federal Work-Study jobs (averaging $1339). In 2006, 354 non-need-based awards were made. *Average percent of need met:* 65%. *Average financial aid package:* $8196. *Average need-based loan:* $3673. *Average need-based gift aid:* $5781. *Average non-need-based aid:* $9437. *Average indebtedness upon graduation:* $22,851.

Applying *Options:* electronic application, early admission, deferred entrance. *Application fee:* $50. *Required:* high school transcript, 2.75 high school GPA or minimum SAT score of 1010. *Required for some:* essay or personal statement, letters of recommendation. *Application deadlines:* rolling (freshmen), rolling (transfers). *Notification:* continuous (freshmen), continuous (transfers).

Freshman Application Contact Mr. Mark Bottorff, Director of Admissions, Southern Oregon University, 1250 Siskiyou Boulevard, Ashland, OR 97520. *Phone:* 541-552-6411. *Toll-free phone:* 800-482-7672. *Fax:* 541-552-6614. *E-mail:* admissions@sou.edu.

See page 2120 for the College Close-Up.

UNIVERSITY OF OREGON

Eugene, Oregon **www.uoregon.edu/**

- **State-supported** university, founded 1872, part of Oregon University System
- **Urban** 295-acre campus
- **Endowment** $455.6 million
- **Coed** 16,674 undergraduate students, 90% full-time, 52% women, 48% men
- **Moderately difficult** entrance level, 87% of applicants were admitted

Undergraduates 15,077 full-time, 1,597 part-time. Students come from 53 states and territories, 84 other countries, 28% are from out of state, 2% African American, 6% Asian American or Pacific Islander, 4% Hispanic American, 1% Native American, 5% international, 8% transferred in, 21% live on campus. *Retention:* 84% of 2006 full-time freshmen returned.

Freshmen *Admission:* 11,287 applied, 9,813 admitted, 3,587 enrolled. *Average high school GPA:* 3.49. *Test scores:* SAT critical reading scores over 500: 71%; SAT math scores over 500: 75%; SAT critical reading scores over 600: 29%; SAT math scores over 600: 32%; SAT critical reading scores over 700: 5%; SAT math scores over 700: 5%.

Faculty *Total:* 1,167, 70% full-time, 95% with terminal degrees. *Student/faculty ratio:* 18:1.

Majors Accounting; advertising; ancient/classical Greek; ancient studies; anthropology; architecture; area, ethnic, cultural, and gender studies related; art; art history, criticism and conservation; Asian studies; biochemistry; biological and physical sciences; biology/biological sciences; business administration and management; business/commerce; ceramic arts and ceramics; chemistry; Chinese; classics and languages, literatures and linguistics; communication disorders; comparative literature; computer and information sciences; dance; design and visual communications; digital communication and media/multimedia; dramatic/theater arts; economics; education; English; environmental science; environmental studies; fiber, textile and weaving arts; fine/studio arts; French; geography; geology/earth science; German; history; humanities; human services; interior architecture; intermedia/multimedia; international/global studies; Italian; Japanese; jazz/jazz studies; Jewish/Judaic studies; journalism; journalism related;

landscape architecture; Latin; linguistics; marine biology and biological oceanography; mass communication/media; mathematics; mathematics and computer science; medieval and Renaissance studies; metal and jewelry arts; multi-/interdisciplinary studies related; music; music performance; music teacher education; music theory and composition; painting; philosophy; photography; physics; physiology; political science and government; printmaking; psychology; public administration; public policy analysis; public relations/image management; religious studies; Romance languages; Russian studies; sculpture; sociology; Spanish; women's studies.

Academics *Calendar:* quarters. *Degrees:* bachelor's, master's, doctoral, first professional, and postbachelor's certificates. *Special study options:* academic remediation for entering students, accelerated degree program, adult/continuing education programs, advanced placement credit, distance learning, double majors, English as a second language, freshman honors college, honors programs, independent study, internships, off-campus study, part-time degree program, services for LD students, student-designed majors, study abroad, summer session for credit. *ROTC:* Army (b), Air Force (c). *Unusual degree programs:* 3-2 engineering with Oregon State University.

Computers on Campus 1,700 computers/terminals and 500 ports are available on campus for general student use. Students can access the following: campus intranet, computer help desk, free student e-mail accounts, online (class) grades, online (class) registration, online (class) schedules. Campuswide network is available. 100% of college-owned or -operated housing units are wired for high-speed Internet access. Wireless service is available via entire campus.

Student Life *Housing options:* coed, men-only, women-only, disabled students. Campus housing is university owned. Freshman applicants given priority for college housing. *Activities and organizations:* drama/theater group, student-run newspaper, radio station, choral group, marching band, Political and Environmental Action, cultural organizations, Major-Specific Organizations, Community Service Organizations, Club Sports, national fraternities, national sororities. *Campus security:* 24-hour emergency response devices and patrols, student patrols, late-night transport/escort service, controlled dormitory access. *Student services:* health clinic, personal/psychological counseling, women's center, legal services.

Athletics Member NCAA. All Division I except football (Division I-A). *Intercollegiate sports:* badminton M (c)/W (c), baseball M (s), basketball M (s)/W (s), bowling M (c)/W (c), cheerleading W (s), cross-country running M (s)/W (s), equestrian sports M (c)/W (c), golf M (s)/W (s), ice hockey M (c), lacrosse W (s), racquetball M (c)/W (c), rugby M (c)/W (c), soccer W (s), softball W (s), swimming and diving M (c)/W (c), table tennis M (c)/W (c), tennis M (s)/W (s), track and field M (s)/W (s), ultimate Frisbee M (c)/W (c), volleyball M (c)/W (s), water polo M (c)/W (c), wrestling M (s). *Intramural sports:* archery M (c)/W (c), badminton M/W, baseball M (c), basketball M/W, crew M (c)/W (c), cross-country running M/W, equestrian sports M/W, fencing M (c)/W (c), ice hockey M (c), lacrosse M (c)/W (c), racquetball M/W, sailing M (c)/W (c), skiing (downhill) M (c)/W (c), soccer M (c)/W (c), softball W (c), swimming and diving M/W, table tennis M/W, tennis M/W, track and field M/W, ultimate Frisbee M/W, volleyball M/W, wrestling M.

Standardized Tests *Required:* SAT or ACT (for admission).

Costs (2007–08) *One-time required fee:* $250. *Tuition:* state resident $4494 full-time, $111 per credit hour part-time; nonresident $17,250 full-time, $446 per credit hour part-time. Full-time tuition and fees vary according to class time, course load, program, and reciprocity agreements. Part-time tuition and fees vary according to class time, course load, program, and reciprocity agreements. *Required fees:* $1542 full-time. *Room and board:* $7849. Room and board charges vary according to board plan and housing facility. *Payment plan:* installment. *Waivers:* employees or children of employees.

Financial Aid Of all full-time matriculated undergraduates who enrolled in 2007, 8,500 applied for aid, 6,009 were judged to have need, 1,481 had their need fully met. 2,008 Federal Work-Study jobs (averaging $1413). 120 state and other part-time jobs (averaging $1820). In 2007, 770 non-need-based awards were made. *Average percent of need met:* 71%. *Average financial aid package:* $8682. *Average need-based loan:* $5188. *Average need-based gift aid:* $4756. *Average non-need-based aid:* $2112. *Average indebtedness upon graduation:* $18,728.

Applying *Options:* electronic application, early action. *Application fee:* $50. *Required:* high school transcript. *Required for some:* essay or personal statement, 2 letters of recommendation. *Recommended:* minimum 3.25 GPA, 16 units college prep. *Application deadlines:* 1/15 (freshmen), 5/15 (transfers), 11/1 (early action). *Notification:* 4/1 (freshmen), continuous (transfers), 12/15 (early action).

Freshman Application Contact University of Oregon, 1217 University of Oregon, Eugene, OR 97403-1217. *Phone:* 541-346-3201. *Toll-free phone:* 800-232-3825.

See page 2122 for the College Close-Up.

UNIVERSITY OF PHOENIX–OREGON CAMPUS

Tigard, Oregon **www.phoenix.edu/**

- **Proprietary** comprehensive, founded 1976
- **Urban** campus
- **Coed**
- **Noncompetitive** entrance level

Faculty *Student/faculty ratio:* 7:1.

Academics *Calendar:* continuous. *Degrees:* certificates, bachelor's, and master's.

Student Life *Campus security:* late-night transport/escort service.

Costs (2007–08) *Tuition:* $11,100 full-time, $370 per credit part-time. Full-time tuition and fees vary according to course level.

Financial Aid *Average financial aid package:* $4213. *Average need-based gift aid:* $23,181.

Applying *Options:* deferred entrance. *Application fee:* $45. *Required:* 1 letter of recommendation. *Required for some:* high school transcript.

Freshman Application Contact Ms. Beth Barilla, Associate Vice President, Student Admissions and Services, University of Phoenix–Oregon Campus, 4615 East Elwood Street, Mail Stop AA-K101, Phoenix, AZ 85040-1958. *Phone:* 480-317-6000. *Toll-free phone:* 800-776-4867 (in-state); 800-228-7240 (out-of-state). *Fax:* 480-894-1758. *E-mail:* beth.barilla@phoenix.edu.

UNIVERSITY OF PORTLAND

Portland, Oregon **www.up.edu/**

- **Independent Roman Catholic** comprehensive, founded 1901
- **Urban** 125-acre campus
- **Endowment** $96.3 million
- **Coed** 3,027 undergraduate students, 97% full-time, 62% women, 38% men
- **Moderately difficult** entrance level, 59% of applicants were admitted

Undergraduates 2,933 full-time, 94 part-time. Students come from 39 states and territories, 19 other countries, 59% are from out of state, 1% African American, 10% Asian American or Pacific Islander, 4% Hispanic American, 0.8% Native American, 2% international, 3% transferred in, 49% live on campus. *Retention:* 85% of 2006 full-time freshmen returned.

Freshmen *Admission:* 7,139 applied, 4,195 admitted, 805 enrolled. *Average high school GPA:* 3.66. *Test scores:* SAT critical reading scores over 500: 90%; SAT math scores over 500: 91%; SAT critical reading scores over 600: 45%; SAT math scores over 600: 52%; SAT critical reading scores over 700: 10%; SAT math scores over 700: 9%.

Faculty *Total:* 299, 67% full-time, 63% with terminal degrees. *Student/faculty ratio:* 13:1.

Majors Accounting; arts management; biology/biological sciences; business administration and management; chemistry; civil engineering; computer engineering; computer science; criminal justice/safety; dramatic/theater arts; education; electrical, electronics and communications engineering; elementary education; engineering; engineering/industrial management; engineering science; English; environmental studies; finance; history; interdisciplinary studies; international business/trade/commerce; journalism; marketing/marketing management; mass communication/media; mathematics; mechanical engineering; music; music teacher education; nursing (registered nurse training); philosophy; physics; political science and government; pre-dentistry studies; pre-law studies; pre-medical studies; psychology; secondary education; social work; sociology; Spanish; theology.

Academics *Calendar:* semesters. *Degrees:* bachelor's, master's, post-master's, and postbachelor's certificates. *Special study options:* adult/continuing education programs, advanced placement credit, double majors, honors programs, independent study, internships, off-campus study, part-time degree program, services for LD students, study abroad, summer session for credit. *ROTC:* Army (b), Air Force (b).

Computers on Campus 575 computers/terminals and 1,950 ports are available on campus for general student use. Students can access the following: campus intranet, computer help desk, free student e-mail accounts, online (class) grades, online (class) registration, online (class) schedules. Campuswide network is available. 90% of college-owned or -operated housing units are wired for high-speed Internet access. Wireless service is available via classrooms, dorm rooms, learning centers, libraries, student centers.

Student Life *Housing options:* coed, men-only, women-only. Campus housing is university owned. Freshman campus housing is guaranteed. *Activities and* *organizations:* drama/theater group, student-run newspaper, radio station, choral group, English Society, International Club, Hawaiian Club, Rugby Club, Social Science Club. *Campus security:* 24-hour patrols, student patrols, late-night transport/escort service, controlled dormitory access. *Student services:* health clinic, personal/psychological counseling.

Athletics Member NCAA. All Division I. *Intercollegiate sports:* baseball M (s), basketball M (s)/W (s), cross-country running M (s)/W (s), golf M (s)/W (s), rugby M (c), soccer M (s)/W (s), tennis M (s)/W (s), track and field M (s)/W (s), volleyball W (s). *Intramural sports:* basketball M/W, crew M/W, cross-country running M/W, football M/W, rugby M, skiing (cross-country) M/W, skiing (downhill) M/W, soccer M (c)/W, softball M/W, swimming and diving M/W, tennis M/W, track and field M/W, volleyball M/W, water polo M/W, weight lifting M/W.

Standardized Tests *Required:* SAT or ACT (for admission).

Costs (2007–08) *Comprehensive fee:* $37,154 includes full-time tuition ($27,500), mandatory fees ($1354), and room and board ($8300). Full-time tuition and fees vary according to course load. Part-time tuition: $875 per credit hour. Part-time tuition and fees vary according to course load. *College room only:* $4150. Room and board charges vary according to board plan and housing facility. *Payment plans:* installment, deferred payment. *Waivers:* employees or children of employees.

Financial Aid Of all full-time matriculated undergraduates who enrolled in 2006, 1,999 applied for aid, 1,461 were judged to have need, 391 had their need fully met. 848 Federal Work-Study jobs (averaging $1819). 9 state and other part-time jobs (averaging $1660). In 2006, 1,203 non-need-based awards were made. *Average percent of need met:* 94%. *Average financial aid package:* $21,821. *Average need-based loan:* $5511. *Average need-based gift aid:* $14,249. *Average non-need-based aid:* $16,651. *Average indebtedness upon graduation:* $22,253.

Applying *Options:* electronic application, deferred entrance. *Application fee:* $50. *Required:* essay or personal statement, high school transcript, 1 letter of recommendation. *Application deadlines:* 6/1 (freshmen), 6/1 (transfers). *Notification:* continuous (freshmen), continuous (transfers).

Freshman Application Contact Mr. Jason McDonald, Dean of Admissions, University of Portland, 5000 North Willamette Boulevard, Portland, OR 97203. *Phone:* 503-943-7147. *Toll-free phone:* 888-627-5601. *Fax:* 503-943-7315. *E-mail:* admissions@up.edu.

WARNER PACIFIC COLLEGE

Portland, Oregon **www.warnerpacific.edu/**

- **Independent** comprehensive, founded 1937, affiliated with Church of God
- **Urban** 15-acre campus
- **Coed** 736 undergraduate students, 13% full-time, 9% women, 5% men
- **Moderately difficult** entrance level, 48% of applicants were admitted

Undergraduates 98 full-time. Students come from 20 states and territories, 8 other countries, 5% African American, 3% Asian American or Pacific Islander, 5% Hispanic American, 0.3% Native American, 1% international, 32% live on campus. *Retention:* 66% of 2006 full-time freshmen returned.

Freshmen *Admission:* 948 applied, 459 admitted, 98 enrolled. *Average high school GPA:* 3.32.

Faculty *Total:* 57, 74% full-time. *Student/faculty ratio:* 14:1.

Majors American studies; biological and physical sciences; biology/biological sciences; business administration and management; early childhood education; elementary education; English; history; human development and family studies; kinesiology and exercise science; liberal arts and sciences/liberal studies; middle school education; music; music management and merchandising; music teacher education; nursing (registered nurse training); pastoral studies/counseling; physical education teaching and coaching; physical sciences; pre-law studies; premedical studies; pre-veterinary studies; psychology; religious studies; science teacher education; secondary education; social work; theology.

Academics *Calendar:* semesters. *Degrees:* associate, bachelor's, master's, and postbachelor's certificates. *Special study options:* academic remediation for entering students, accelerated degree program, adult/continuing education programs, advanced placement credit, cooperative education, double majors, honors programs, independent study, internships, off-campus study, part-time degree program, services for LD students, student-designed majors, study abroad, summer session for credit. *ROTC:* Army (c), Air Force (c).

Computers on Campus 30 computers/terminals are available on campus for general student use. Campuswide network is available.

Student Life *Housing:* on-campus residence required through sophomore year. *Options:* men-only, women-only. Campus housing is university owned. *Activities and organizations:* drama/theater group, student-run newspaper, choral group, Associated Students of Warner Pacific College, yearbook, College Activities Board, Fellowship of Christian Athletes. *Campus security:* 24-hour emergency response devices and patrols, student patrols, late-night transport/escort service, controlled dormitory access. *Student services:* health clinic, personal/psychological counseling.

Athletics Member NAIA, NCCAA. *Intercollegiate sports:* basketball M (s)/W (s), cross-country running M (s)/W (s), soccer M/W, track and field M/W, volleyball W (s). *Intramural sports:* basketball M/W, football M/W, skiing (cross-country) M/W, skiing (downhill) M/W, soccer M/W, softball M/W, table tennis M/W, volleyball M/W.

Standardized Tests *Required:* SAT or ACT (for admission). *Recommended:* SAT Subject Tests (for admission).

Costs (2007–08) *Comprehensive fee:* $29,745 includes full-time tuition ($21,500), mandatory fees ($2217), and room and board ($6028). Full-time tuition and fees vary according to course load, location, and reciprocity agreements. Part-time tuition and fees vary according to course load, location, and reciprocity agreements. *Room and board:* Room and board charges vary according to board plan and housing facility.

Financial Aid Of all full-time matriculated undergraduates who enrolled in 2007, 326 applied for aid, 308 were judged to have need, 61 had their need fully met. 229 Federal Work-Study jobs (averaging $2016). In 2007, 15 non-need-based awards were made. *Average percent of need met:* 78%. *Average financial aid package:* $17,559. *Average need-based loan:* $4932. *Average need-based gift aid:* $6044. *Average non-need-based aid:* $6137. *Average indebtedness upon graduation:* $21,001.

Applying *Options:* electronic application. *Application fee:* $50. *Required:* essay or personal statement, high school transcript, minimum 2.5 GPA. *Required for some:* 1 letter of recommendation, interview. *Recommended:* minimum 3.0 GPA, interview. *Application deadlines:* rolling (freshmen), rolling (transfers). *Notification:* continuous (freshmen), continuous (transfers).

Freshman Application Contact Mrs. Shannon Mackey, Executive Director of Enrollment Management, Warner Pacific College, 2219 Southeast 68th Avenue, Portland, OR 97215. *Phone:* 503-517-1020. *Toll-free phone:* 800-582-7885 (in-state); 800-804-1510 (out-of-state). *Fax:* 503-517-1352. *E-mail:* admiss@warnerpacific.edu.

See page 2124 for the College Close-Up.

WESTERN OREGON UNIVERSITY

Monmouth, Oregon **www.wou.edu/**

- **State-supported** comprehensive, founded 1856, part of Oregon University System
- **Rural** 157-acre campus with easy access to Portland
- **Endowment** $10.3 million
- **Coed**
- **Moderately difficult** entrance level

Faculty *Student/faculty ratio:* 19:1.

Academics *Calendar:* quarters. *Degrees:* bachelor's, master's, and postbachelor's certificates.

Student Life *Campus security:* 24-hour emergency response devices and patrols, student patrols, late-night transport/escort service, controlled dormitory access.

Athletics Member NCAA. All Division II.

Standardized Tests *Required:* SAT or ACT (for admission).

Costs (2008–09) *Tuition:* state resident $5175 full-time, $115 per credit part-time; nonresident $15,750 full-time, $350 per credit part-time. *Required fees:* $1100 full-time, $91 part-time, $91 part-time. *Room and board:* $7600.

Financial Aid Of all full-time matriculated undergraduates who enrolled in 2007, 2,894 applied for aid, 2,332 were judged to have need, 423 had their need fully met. 250 Federal Work-Study jobs (averaging $912). In 2007, 692 non-need-based awards were made. *Average percent of need met:* 66. *Average financial aid package:* $7605. *Average need-based loan:* $3943. *Average need-based gift aid:* $5077. *Average non-need-based aid:* $8014. *Average indebtedness upon graduation:* $20,498.

Applying *Options:* electronic application, deferred entrance. *Application fee:* $50. *Required:* high school transcript, minimum 2.75 GPA, general college prep program completion.

Freshman Application Contact Mr. Rob Findtner, Assistant Director of Admissions, Western Oregon University, 345 North Monmouth Avenue, Monmouth, OR 97361. *Phone:* 503-838-8211. *Toll-free phone:* 877-877-1593. *Fax:* 503-838-8067. *E-mail:* wolfgram@wou.edu.

WILLAMETTE UNIVERSITY

Salem, Oregon **www.willamette.edu/**

- **Independent United Methodist** comprehensive, founded 1842
- **Urban** 72-acre campus with easy access to Portland
- **Endowment** $284.7 million
- **Coed** 1,932 undergraduate students, 94% full-time, 55% women, 45% men
- **Very difficult** entrance level, 77% of applicants were admitted

Undergraduates 1,813 full-time, 119 part-time. Students come from 43 states and territories, 8 other countries, 62% are from out of state, 1% African American, 5% Asian American or Pacific Islander, 3% Hispanic American, 0.5% Native American, 5% international, 3% transferred in, 69% live on campus. *Retention:* 87% of 2006 full-time freshmen returned.

Freshmen *Admission:* 2,983 applied, 2,301 admitted, 444 enrolled. *Average high school GPA:* 3.68. *Test scores:* SAT critical reading scores over 500: 92%; SAT math scores over 500: 95%; SAT writing scores over 500: 95%; ACT scores over 18: 100%; SAT critical reading scores over 600: 66%; SAT math scores over 600: 56%; SAT writing scores over 600: 56%; ACT scores over 24: 88%; SAT critical reading scores over 700: 23%; SAT math scores over 700: 12%; SAT writing scores over 700: 10%; ACT scores over 30: 24%.

Faculty *Total:* 310, 65% full-time, 45% with terminal degrees. *Student/faculty ratio:* 11:1.

Majors American studies; anthropology; art; art history, criticism and conservation; Asian studies; biology/biological sciences; chemistry; classics and languages, literatures and linguistics; comparative literature; computer science; dramatic/theater arts; economics; English; environmental science; fine/studio arts; French; German; history; humanities; international/global studies; Japanese studies; kinesiology and exercise science; Latin American studies; mathematics; music; music performance; music theory and composition; philosophy; physics; piano and organ; political science and government; psychology; religious studies; science technologies related; sociology; Spanish; speech and rhetoric; violin, viola, guitar and other stringed instruments; voice and opera; women's studies.

Academics *Calendar:* semesters. *Degrees:* bachelor's, master's, first professional, postbachelor's, and first professional certificates. *Special study options:* accelerated degree program, advanced placement credit, cooperative education, double majors, independent study, internships, off-campus study, part-time degree program, services for LD students, student-designed majors, study abroad. *ROTC:* Air Force (c). *Unusual degree programs:* 3-2 engineering with University of Southern California, Washington University in St. Louis, Columbia University; forestry with Duke University.

Computers on Campus 400 computers/terminals are available on campus for general student use. Students can access the following: online (class) registration. Campuswide network is available.

Student Life *Housing:* on-campus residence required through sophomore year. *Options:* coed. Campus housing is university owned. Freshman campus housing is guaranteed. *Activities and organizations:* drama/theater group, student-run newspaper, radio station, choral group, Hawaii Club, Bush Mentor Program, Outdoors Club, Campus Ambassadors, Associated Students, national fraternities, national sororities. *Campus security:* 24-hour emergency response devices and patrols, student patrols, late-night transport/escort service, controlled dormitory access. *Student services:* health clinic, personal/psychological counseling, women's center.

Athletics Member NCAA. All Division III. *Intercollegiate sports:* baseball M, basketball M/W, crew M/W, cross-country running M/W, football M, golf M/W, lacrosse M (c), soccer M/W, softball W, swimming and diving M/W, tennis M/W, track and field M/W, volleyball W. *Intramural sports:* badminton M/W, basketball M/W, bowling M/W, cross-country running M/W, football M/W, golf M/W, racquetball M/W, skiing (cross-country) M (c)/W (c), skiing (downhill) M (c)/W (c), soccer M/W, softball M/W, table tennis M/W, tennis M/W, ultimate Frisbee M/W, volleyball M/W, water polo M/W, weight lifting M/W.

Standardized Tests *Required:* SAT or ACT (for admission).

Costs (2007–08) *Comprehensive fee:* $39,538 includes full-time tuition ($31,760), mandatory fees ($208), and room and board ($7570). Full-time tuition and fees vary according to course load. Part-time tuition: $3972 per course. Part-time tuition and fees vary according to course load. *Room and board:* Room and board charges vary according to board plan and housing facility. *Payment plans:* tuition prepayment, installment. *Waivers:* employees or children of employees.

Financial Aid Of all full-time matriculated undergraduates who enrolled in 2007, 1,285 applied for aid, 1,134 were judged to have need, 220 had their need fully met. 555 Federal Work-Study jobs (averaging $1264). 579 state and other part-time jobs (averaging $1021). In 2007, 563 non-need-based awards were made. *Average percent of need met:* 91%. *Average financial aid package:* $27,209. *Average need-based loan:* $5150. *Average need-based gift aid:* $19,420. *Average non-need-based aid:* $9804. *Average indebtedness upon graduation:* $23,188.

Applying *Options:* electronic application, early action, deferred entrance. *Application fee:* $50. *Required:* essay or personal statement, high school transcript, minimum 2.0 GPA, 1 letter of recommendation. *Required for some:* interview. *Recommended:* interview. *Application deadlines:* 2/1 (freshmen), 2/1 (transfers), 12/1 (early action). *Notification:* 4/1 (freshmen), 4/1 (transfers), 1/15 (early action).

Freshman Application Contact Dr. Robin Brown, Vice President for Enrollment, Willamette University, 900 State Street, Salem, OR 97301-3931. *Toll-free phone:* 877-542-2787. *Fax:* 503-375-5363. *E-mail:* libarts@williamette.edu.

THE ART INSTITUTE OF PORTLAND

PORTLAND, OREGON

The Institute

At The Art Institute of Portland, students and faculty members share ideas and work together to develop skills in the creative arts. Friendships and potential career contacts are made as new designs emerge and become a part of the vibrant creative culture. The Art Institute of Portland is committed to preparing students for entry-level positions in the arts. The school offers bachelor's and associate degree programs.

The Art Institute of Portland provides educational programs created to instruct students in skills useful for everyday performance in the workplace. Education is offered along two main tracks in the fields of design and management. Programs include course work in communications, the humanities, social sciences, natural science, and mathematics. In addition, students receive a wide variety of educational experiences, including workshops, seminars, and internships.

The Art Institute of Portland seeks to provide a diverse, challenging, rewarding educational experience to its students. The Student Affairs Department helps students to enrich their academic experience through student clubs and organizations, school activities, counseling and disability services, and housing services. Student clubs include the American Society of Interior Designers (ASID), Fight Club, Rorschach Writers Guild, and the S.T.A.C. (Student Action Committee).

Students come to The Art Institute of Portland from throughout the United States and abroad. The student population includes recent high school graduates, transfer students, and those who have left a previous employment situation to study and train for a new career. Students are creative, competitive, and open to new ideas. They place great value on an education that prepares them for an exciting entry-level position in the arts.

Assistance is available to help students with resume writing, networking, and keeping abreast of what employers are looking for in job candidates.

The Art Institute of Portland offers housing assistance to all students. School-sponsored housing is available. Resident assistants are trained by the housing staff to help students become acquainted with each other through social and academic activities. Apartment information and roommate referrals are also available for students who choose to live off-campus.

The Art Institute of Portland is accredited by the Northwest Commission on Colleges and Universities (NWCCU) and is exempt from the Oregon Department of Education.

Location

Portland is the largest city in Oregon, located on the Willamette River near its junction with the Columbia River. Since 1888, Portland has been known as the Rose City because of the thousands of flowers that bloom in Washington Park. Natural attractions include the Columbia River Gorge's 3,000-foot-high basaltic cliffs, Multnomah Falls, and Mount Hood—the site of America's longest ski season. Portland also has a wide array of coffee shops, Native American art galleries, bookstores, and brew pubs as well as the Oregon Symphony, Tygres Heart Shakespeare Company, Musical Theater Company, Portland Opera, Baroque Orchestra, Northwest Afrikan American Ballet, Oregon Ballet Theatre, and Mount Hood Festival of Jazz.

Portland is home to many large apparel companies—students in the Apparel Accessory Design and the Apparel Design programs have the advantage of learning from talented professionals in the industry. In addition, The Art Institute of Portland has built valuable relationships with the Oregon Film and Video Office and the Oregon Media Production Association.

Majors and Degrees

Bachelor's degrees are available in advertising, apparel accessory design, apparel design, design management, design studies, design visualization, digital film and video, fashion marketing, game art and design, graphic design, industrial design, interior design, media arts and animation, visual and game programming, visual effects and motion graphics, and Web design and interactive media. Associate of Arts degrees are offered in apparel accessory design, apparel design, graphic design, interior design, and Web design and interactive media.

Academic Programs

The academic year is divided into four quarters, beginning in January, April, July, and October. To earn a bachelor's degree, students must complete 180 academic credits. To earn an associate degree, students must earn 105 academic credits.

Academic Facilities

With more than 80,000 square feet of space, The Art Institute of Portland houses computer labs where students work on Macs and PCs using various software applications related to their programs of study. The Art Institute of Portland Gallery serves as a noncommercial exhibition space that reflects and exemplifies the artwork of professionals, faculty members, students, and graduates. Students learn more about industry-related media gear at the Equipment Cage and create high-quality prints of their projects in the school's Print Service Center. The library's specialized collection is organized around the college curriculum, featuring books, journals and magazines, videos, DVDs, and CD-ROMs.

Costs

Tuition varies by program. Prospective students should contact the school for current tuition costs. Other charges include a starting kit for all first-quarter students. Kits vary in price depending on the program of study.

Financial Aid

Financial aid is available for those who qualify. Students who require financial assistance should first complete and submit a Free Application for Federal Student Aid (FAFSA) and meet with a financial aid officer. The officer determines the student's level of need based on a required federal formula, the cost of education, and other factors. Gift aid is available in the form of Federal Pell Grants, Federal Supplemental Educational Opportunity Grants, and veterans' benefits. Loans include Federal Stafford Loans, Federal PLUS Loans, and alternative loans. Scholarships are available from the school and private sources. Application deadlines and eligibility requirements vary by program.

Faculty

The Art Institute of Portland faculty consists of full-time and part-time instructors, many of whom have degrees and professional experience in their respective fields. The faculty members bring this knowledge and experience to their instruction.

Admission Requirements

Prospective students begin the application process by writing an essay of approximately 150 words to describe ways in which an education at The Art Institute of Portland may help to meet their creative objectives. Portfolios are encouraged but not required. An application for admission and enrollment agreement must be submitted to the school. Applicants who have taken the SAT or ACT should also submit these test scores. Each individual seeking admission is interviewed by an assistant director of admissions in order to explore the applicant's background, interests, and goals. There is a $50 application fee.

Application and Information

To obtain an application or make arrangements for an interview or tour of the school, students should contact:

The Art Institute of Portland
1122 N.W. Davis Street
Portland, Oregon 97209-2911
Phone: 503-228-6528
888-228-6528 (toll-free)
Fax: 503-227-1945
Web site: http://www.artinstitutes.edu/portland

The Art Institute of Atlanta®, GA; The Art Institute of Atlanta®–Decatur, GA; The Art Institute of Austin℠, TX; The Art Institute of California℠–Inland Empire; The Art Institute of California℠–Los Angeles; The Art Institute of California℠–Orange County; The Art Institute of California℠–Sacramento; The Art Institute of California℠–San Diego; The Art Institute of California℠–San Francisco; The Art Institute of California℠–Sunnyvale; The Art Institute of Charleston℠, SC, A branch of The Art Institute of Atlanta, GA; The Art Institute of Charlotte®, NC; The Art Institute of Colorado® (Denver); The Art Institute of Dallas®, TX; The Art Institute of Fort Lauderdale®, FL; The Art Institute of Houston®, TX; The Art Institute of Indianapolis℠, IN*; The Art Institute of Jacksonville℠, FL, A branch of Miami International University of Art & Design; The Art Institute of Las Vegas®, NV; The Art Institute of Michigan℠ (Detroit); The Art Institute of New York City®, NY; The Art Institute of Ohio℠–Cincinnati**; The Art Institute of Philadelphia®, PA; The Art Institute of Phoenix®, AZ; The Art Institute of Pittsburgh®, PA; The Art Institute of Pittsburgh®–Online Division; The Art Institute of Portland®, OR; The Art Institute of Salt Lake City℠, UT; The Art Institute of Seattle®, WA; The Art Institute of Tampa℠, FL, A branch of Miami International University of Art & Design; The Art Institute of Tennessee℠–Nashville, A branch of The Art Institute of Atlanta, GA; The Art Institute of Tucson℠, AZ; The Art Institute of Washington® (Arlington, VA), A branch of The Art Institute of Atlanta, GA; The Art Institute of York–Pennsylvania℠; The Art Institutes International Minnesota℠ (Minneapolis); California Design College℠ (Los Angeles–Wilshire Blvd.); The Illinois Institute of Art®–Chicago; The Illinois Institute of Art®–Schaumburg; Miami International University of Art & Design℠, FL; The New England Institute of Art® (Boston, MA).

*The Art Institute of Indianapolis is licensed by the Indiana Commission on Proprietary Education, 302 W. Washington St., Rm. E201, Indianapolis, IN 46204, AC-0080.

**The Art Institute of Ohio–Cincinnati, 8845 Governors Hill Drive, Suite 100, Cincinnati, OH 45249-3317, OH Reg. #04-01-1698B.

GEORGE FOX UNIVERSITY

NEWBERG, OREGON

The University

George Fox University was founded in 1891 by Quaker pioneers with the purpose of providing students a challenging academic atmosphere within a community of Christian faith. Today, George Fox maintains the same mission and has grown to an enrollment of more than 3,200 students.

Students find George Fox to be a place where spiritual growth and intellectual challenge take place in a friendly, caring environment. This tradition of integration of faith and learning has been recognized by the Templeton Foundation, which named George Fox University to its honor roll of character-building colleges.

The majority of George Fox undergraduate students live in campus residence halls, suites, and apartments. Opportunities for extracurricular involvement are available in music, drama, journalism, student government, radio, clubs, and athletics. George Fox is a member of NCAA Division III and competes in seven men's sports (baseball, basketball, cross-country, golf, soccer, tennis, and track) and eight women's sports (basketball, cross-country, golf, soccer, softball, tennis, track, and volleyball). The University also offers a robust intramural sports program.

Regular chapel services bring the campus community together in worship. Students have the opportunity to put their faith into action on volunteer mission trips and during community outreach activities.

In addition to its undergraduate degrees, George Fox confers graduate degrees in business, counseling, education, organizational leadership, and psychology. George Fox Evangelical Seminary offers five seminary degrees.

Location

George Fox University's residential campus is located in Newberg, a community of 20,000 people. The 85-acre tree-shaded campus is a 30-minute drive from the major metropolitan environment of Portland. The University is situated in the beautiful Pacific Northwest, with scenic Mt. Hood and the rugged Pacific coastline within short driving distances.

Tilikum Retreat Center, which is set on a 90-acre lake and just 10 minutes away, provides students a change of pace from the classroom. Students enjoy hiking, canoeing, and fishing at the camp. Tilikum has an extensive summer day camp program that employs many University students.

George Fox offers adult degree-completion classes and most of its graduate programs at teaching centers in Portland, Salem, and Redmond, Oregon, and in Boise, Idaho.

Majors and Degrees

George Fox confers the Bachelor of Arts and Bachelor of Science degrees. The following undergraduate majors are available: accounting, allied health, applied science, art, athletic training, biblical studies, biology, business administration, chemistry, Christian ministries, cinema and media communications, cognitive science, communication arts, computer and information science, economics, elementary education, engineering, family and consumer sciences, health and human performance, history, interdisciplinary studies, international studies, mathematics, music, music education, nursing, organizational communication, philosophy, political science, psychology, religion, social work, sociology, Spanish, theater, and writing/literature.

The University also offers five professional studies programs for adult students wishing to complete their undergraduate degrees through night and weekend classes.

Academic Programs

The academic year at George Fox University is divided into two semesters of fifteen weeks. In addition to the two semesters, the University sponsors a three-week May Term. For graduation, students are required to earn 126 credit hours, including 54 general education and 42 upper-division credits.

Students may reduce the number of required courses and add flexibility to their undergraduate years with credit earned through Advanced Placement, International Baccalaureate (I.B.), the College-Level Examination Program, and credit by examination. All traditional undergraduates are given a personal computer to use and keep upon graduation.

George Fox demonstrates its commitment to freshmen by providing a Freshman Seminar program to assist students as they integrate themselves into the academic and social life of the University community.

Off-Campus Programs

More than two thirds of George Fox traditional undergraduates study internationally before graduating, ranking the University number 20 out of 1,400 American colleges in study-abroad participation. Each year during May Term, George Fox sponsors three-week study tours led by University faculty members. Transportation costs are subsidized by the University. These international learning experiences are designed for students completing their junior year. Through the Council for Christian Colleges and Universities, students are also given the opportunity to study for a semester in Africa, Australia, China, England, Latin America, the Middle East, Russia, and Washington, D.C.

Membership in the Christian College Consortium enables George Fox University students to attend for a semester one of twelve other colleges located throughout the United States.

Academic Facilities

The Edward F. Stevens Center provides 40,000 square feet of office and classroom space. All student service–oriented offices are now housed under one roof, providing greater efficiency and access for students. The building has been selected as part of the "Ten Shades of Green" by Portland General Electric for its use of recycled materials and minimal environmental impact.

The Murdock Learning Resource Center houses more than 200,000 books and periodicals. Its features include rare-book collections, study carrels, an audiovisual laboratory, and access to 19,000 journal titles in electronic format.

The Edwards/Holman Science Center is home to the University's science programs. The 36,000-square-foot building provides classrooms, offices, and laboratories for biology, chemistry, premedicine, mathematics, computer science, and engineering programs.

The William and Mary Bauman Auditorium seats 1,150 people in a facility that annually hosts the Oregon Symphony and other regional events. Rotating art exhibits appear in the adjoining Lindgren Gallery. All academic buildings and residence halls are equipped with wireless Web access.

Hoover Academic Building was named after former president Herbert Hoover and displays various photos and memorabilia from his life. Hoover was a student at Friends Pacific Academy, the forerunner of George Fox University. The newly remodeled facility houses the nursing program and the undergraduate psychology, religion, and sociology/social work departments.

Costs

Tuition for the 2007–08 year was $23,790. Room, board, and fees were $7600. Books are estimated to cost $700 per year.

Financial Aid

George Fox maintains that every qualified student should be able to attend the university of his or her choice without letting limited finances stand in the way. To this end, federal, state, and institutional need-based funds are available, as are merit awards. About 95 percent of all students receive financial aid.

Faculty

The faculty at George Fox University fosters an atmosphere of discussion and independent thinking in the classroom. Faculty members have found a healthy balance between teaching and research by devoting a majority of their time to educating students. The University employs 167 full-time and 181 part-time faculty members. Seventy percent of full-time faculty members hold doctoral degrees. Faculty members are personally committed Christians who are involved in the lives of their students. The student-faculty ratio is 12:1.

Student Government

The Associated Student Community of George Fox University serves as a unifying force and voice for the campus student community and plays a significant role in organizing cultural, social, and recreational activities.

Admission Requirements

Students admitted to George Fox University must show academic ability, high moral character, and social concern. These qualities are evaluated by consideration of each applicant's academic record, test scores, recommendations, interview reports, and participation in extracurricular activities. The priority application date is February 1. In order to provide a solid foundation for college-level work, it is recommended that the applicant present the equivalent of 16 academic units from an approved high school. The following units are suggested: English, 4; social studies, 3; science, 2; mathematics, 2; foreign language, 2; and health and physical education, 1.

Application and Information

For additional information, students should contact:

Office of Undergraduate Admissions
George Fox University
Newberg, Oregon 97132-2697
Phone: 800-765-4369 Ext. 2240 (toll-free)
E-mail: admissions@georgefox.edu
Web site: http://www.georgefox.edu

LEWIS & CLARK COLLEGE

PORTLAND, OREGON

The College

Founded in 1867 in a small town south of Portland, Lewis & Clark College moved to its present location in Portland's southwest hills in 1942. The 137-acre campus is situated in a wooded residential area 6 miles from the center of the city and overlooks the lush Willamette Valley and Mount Hood in the distance.

The student body is known for its geographic diversity. In fall 2006, of the 1,985 undergraduates, 21 percent were from Oregon, and 79 percent came from forty-five states, plus the District of Columbia, and fifty-three countries. Approximately 70 percent live in housing on campus, most of which is coed (91 percent). Residence halls allow for interaction among students, and the units are governed through student representation and hall councils. There are no fraternities or sororities.

The College offers numerous cocurricular activities, including nine music groups; nine media organizations; eight religious/spiritual life groups; fifteen international, cultural, and diversity groups; and more than forty student organizations. Cultural events such as lectures, symposia, art exhibits, theater productions, concerts, recitals, and dance performances occur on a regular basis. Currently, there are nineteen NCAA Division III varsity athletic teams, eight club teams, and eight to ten intramural sports. Athletic facilities include three basketball courts, a competition-size swimming pool, a weight-training room, a stadium, a baseball/softball complex, and six tennis courts, three of which are covered by an airdome. The renowned College Outdoors Program offers adventures such as backpacking, rafting, skiing, sea kayaking (and more) in Oregon's and Washington's nearby wilderness areas.

Location

Portland has long been known for its livability and its excellent transportation service. Public buses and a free College shuttle run from the Lewis & Clark campus to the center of Portland. The metropolitan area (population 2 million) is bisected by the Willamette River. Mount Hood, offering skiing ten months per year, is 50 miles away, and Oregon's rugged coastline lies 90 miles to the west. The city has 10,447 acres of parks, thirty-three music associations, thirty-five theater and dance companies, more than ninety galleries and museums, and more than 1,000 restaurants. Professional sports teams compete in baseball, hockey, lacrosse, and NBA basketball.

Majors and Degrees

Lewis & Clark offers programs leading to the Bachelor of Arts degree. Academic majors include art, biochemistry and molecular biology, biology, chemistry, communications, computer science and mathematics, East Asian studies, economics, English, environmental studies, foreign languages, French studies, German studies, Hispanic studies, history, international affairs, mathematics, music, philosophy, physics, political science, psychology, religious studies, sociology/anthropology, and theater. Students may also design a major or pursue a double major and numerous minors. Preprofessional programs are available in dentistry, education, law, and medicine.

Dual-degree (3-2 and 4-2) programs in engineering are offered in cooperation with Columbia University, Washington University (St. Louis), the University of Southern California, and the Oregon Graduate Institute. A 4-2 B.A./M.B.A. program is offered in cooperation with the University of Rochester's Simon Graduate School of Business Administration. A 4-1 B.A./M.A.T. program is offered through Lewis & Clark's Graduate School of Education and Counseling.

Academic Programs

The liberal arts curriculum offers sufficient structure to ensure depth and breadth of study, but it also incorporates a high degree of freedom in order to promote creative and critical thinking. In the four-year plan of study, approximately one third of a student's time is devoted to general education, one third to a major program, and one third to elective courses. Students are also encouraged to participate in departmental honors programs, undergraduate research, independent study, and internships.

The academic calendar consists of two 15-week semesters. A normal load is four 4-semester-hour academic courses, plus one or more activity courses. By graduation a student is expected to have earned at least 128 semester hours—equivalent, roughly, to eight different classes a year. The fall semester begins early in September and ends before Christmas, and the spring semester begins in mid-January and ends in early May. There are also a limited number of courses offered during two summer sessions.

The community of scholars at Lewis & Clark College is dedicated to personal and academic excellence. Joining the Lewis & Clark community obligates each member to observe the principles of mutual respect, academic integrity, civil discourse, and responsible decision making.

Off-Campus Programs

Lewis & Clark offers nationally recognized international and off-campus study opportunities that have been in existence for more than forty years. Approximately twenty-five different overseas study programs and two domestic programs are available annually. Usually, 20 to 24 students, plus a faculty leader, participate in each program. Fifty-five percent of the College's graduates have taken advantage of these outstanding programs, often satisfying General Education or major requirements at the same time.

Overseas study may have either a general-culture focus or a specialized academic focus. On general-culture programs, students become immersed in the everyday life of the host country by living with local families, traveling, studying in classes and seminars, and working on independent projects. Programs with a more specific academic focus may include studying German language and literature in Munich; perfecting language skills in France, Ecuador, Russia, Japan, or China; or studying literature in England. Sites for overseas study programs from 2008 through 2011 are Australia, Chile, China, Cuba, Dominican Republic, Ecuador, England, France, Germany, Ghana, Greece, India, Ireland, Italy, Japan, Kenya/Tanzania, New Zealand, Russia, Scotland, Senegal, and Spain. Domestic programs are available in New York and Washington, D.C., for those interested in economics, political science, sociology, theater, or art. Students receive academic credit on all programs, both overseas and domestic.

Academic Facilities

The Aubrey R. Watzek Library (open 24 hours per day when school is in session) houses more than 300,000 volumes and includes electronic access to thousands of periodical titles. Its mission is to provide a solid core of materials designed to support the curriculum and the research needs of the Lewis & Clark community. The library offers individualized reference assistance in the use of both print and electronic resources. The library's Web site provides access to its catalog as well as to a full range of electronic databases and links to useful Internet resources. The library is a member of Summit, a consortium of thirty-three academic libraries that have a unified catalog that enables students to request and receive materials from member libraries within two days.

Music department facilities include Evans Auditorium, a 410-seat recital hall equipped with an orchestra pit and stage elevator; an extensive record, CD, and tape collection; twenty-two practice rooms; forty-three pianos, including several 6- and 7-foot concert grands and a 9-foot Steinway concert grand; two harpsichords; a Baroque organ; an electronic music studio with CD production capability; Zimbabwe marimbas; and an Indonesian gamelan orchestra. The 600-seat chapel houses an 85-rank Casavant organ.

The Fields Center for the Visual Arts is equipped with studio space for painting, drawing, ceramics, sculpture, design, and printmaking as well as a photography lab. The department also has a library of 50,000 slides and several thousand digital images representing artwork from a wide range of media, time periods, world regions, and cultures. The arts center contains gallery and classroom space as well. The humanities and social sciences also enjoy state-of-the-art classroom and lab facilities.

The natural sciences are housed in the Biology/Psychology, BoDine, and Olin Buildings, which are well equipped with modern instrumentation to support the College's emphasis on collaborative student-faculty research. These buildings contain numerous research laboratories and equipment, used by students in classes or research projects, in addition to teaching labs and classrooms. Among the notable facilities are a laboratory for the study of human-computer interactions, a scanning electron microscope, a modern greenhouse, an astronomical observatory with several telescopes, a molecular modeling laboratory equipped with high-speed computers, a laboratory for the study of parallel computing, a laboratory for studying the biomechanics of animal locomotion, and an astrophysics laboratory that is equipped to remotely operate and acquire data from a specialized telescope at Kitts Peak, Arizona. All labs are computerized for acquiring and analyzing data and are networked to allow sharing and acquisition of data remotely. Ecological investigations and studies of the environmental impacts of human activity can be conducted both on the College's heavily wooded campus and at the nearby Tryon Creek State Park.

Computer facilities include several computer laboratories in academic buildings that are for student use. More than 130 Macintosh, IBM, and compatible computers are available for student use, along with peripherals such as color scanners, color printers, digital cameras, and digital video editing. All residence halls have direct Internet access. Parts of the campus also have wireless network capability.

Costs

Tuition and fees for 2007–08 are $31,840. The room and board charge is $8380 for fourteen (flex) meals per week; other meal plans are also available. The estimate for books and personal expenses is $1900.

Financial Aid

In 2006–07, 75 percent of the College's students received some form of financial assistance. Institutional, state, and federal resources, including Federal Pell Grants, Federal Supplemental Educational Opportunity Grants, Federal Perkins Loans, and Federal Work-Study awards, may be part of an aid award. Other options include low-interest Federal Stafford Student Loans and opportunities to work on and off campus. To receive priority consideration for need-based financial aid, students must meet appropriate deadlines for admission and should submit the Free Application for Federal Student Aid (FAFSA) and the CSS/Financial Aid PROFILE application by March 1. Merit-based awards are offered to exceptional students who are selected as Neely Scholars (up to ten full-tuition scholarships), Trustee Scholars (up to fifteen half-tuition scholarships per year), and more than 100 Dean's Scholars ($4000–$10,000 scholarships per year). In addition, more than thirty $5000 Leadership and Service Awards are made annually. Students designated as National Merit finalists with Lewis & Clark officially named as their first choice receive $1000.

Faculty

The 128 full-time members of the faculty are committed to undergraduate teaching and advising and are also active in research, writing, and publishing. Involving students in the research process is of high priority. Ninety-five percent of the full-time faculty members hold a Ph.D. or the highest advanced degree in their discipline. The student-faculty ratio is 13:1. The average class size is 19, with an average size of 25 for first-year-level courses and 14 for upper-division courses.

Student Government

The Associated Students of Lewis & Clark (ASLC) has a decentralized structure that encourages cocurricular participation by students and places a high priority on participation with faculty and staff in the process of enriching the academic environment. ASLC consists of an Executive Council, governing boards, and appointed students who serve on faculty constitutional, standing, and special committees. The 25 members of the Student Academic Affairs Board (SAAB) are appointed on a departmental basis to solicit, evaluate, and support undergraduate and faculty research, instruction, curriculum, and program enhancement. One quarter of the total ASLC budget of more than $330,000 is used by SAAB in support of undergraduate research grants and speakers.

Admission Requirements

Lewis & Clark College seeks first-year and transfer applicants who are committed to academic excellence and personal growth. Admission is competitive. Applications are carefully reviewed and examined for degree of academic preparation, ability to express ideas in essay form, participation in activities, citizenship and community service, and support given by the school through recommendations. Campus visits are encouraged. Interviews are available but not required. Recommended high school preparation includes 4 years of English, 4 years of history or social science, 4 years of mathematics, 3 years of laboratory science, 2 to 3 years of foreign language, and 1 year of fine arts. The SAT or ACT is required, unless the student is applying via the Portfolio Path.

Application and Information

First-year applicants should submit the online Lewis & Clark or the Common Application (online or paper); a personal essay; an official academic transcript, including senior grades from the first marking period; one recommendation from a counselor; and at least one reference from an academic teacher. Lewis & Clark's online application can be found at the College's Web site. The application fee is waived if the applicant uses the College's online option or the online Common Application. Application deadlines are November 1 for Early Action (notification by January 15) and February 1 for Regular Decision (notification by April 1). The optional Portfolio Path admissions program provides an opportunity for applicants who have shown exceptional academic initiative to demonstrate the full extent of their pursuits by presenting a portfolio of their academic work. Under this plan, SAT or ACT scores are optional.

For more information about Lewis & Clark College or to arrange a visit, students should contact:

Office of Admissions
Lewis & Clark College
0615 Southwest Palatine Hill Road
Portland, Oregon 97219-7899
Phone: 503-768-7040
800-444-4111 (toll-free)
Fax: 503-768-7055
E-mail: admissions@lclark.edu
Web site: http://www.lclark.edu

LINFIELD COLLEGE

MCMINNVILLE, OREGON

The College

Linfield College (1858) is an independent, coeducational, residential, comprehensive liberal arts and sciences college dedicated to providing an educational environment conducive to learning and participation. There are 1,750 full-time students on the McMinnville campus. These students come primarily from the thirteen Western states (twenty-six states overall) but also from twenty-one other countries. Members of minority groups make up 11 percent of the student body, and 4 percent of students are international. Most students are between 18 and 22. Linfield is primarily residential, with one residence hall for men, three for women, and twelve that are coeducational, each accommodating between 10 and 100 residents. There are also four fraternity houses. Each hall establishes its own calendar of social, educational, and recreational events throughout the year. Students who reside on campus eat their meals in the College dining hall. Houses and apartments are available for upper-division students. Social clubs, professional organizations, sororities (one local: Sigma Kappa Phi, and three national: Alpha Phi, Phi Sigma Sigma, and Zeta Tau Alpha) and fraternities (one local: Delta Psi Delta, and three national: Kappa Sigma, Pi Kappa Alpha, and Theta Chi), service clubs, and almost forty other organizations play an important role in the daily life of a Linfield student. Linfield's winning athletics tradition fosters participation at all levels of competition. Women compete in intercollegiate basketball, cross-country, golf, lacrosse, soccer, softball, swimming, tennis, track and field, and volleyball. Men compete in intercollegiate baseball, basketball, cross-country, football, golf, soccer, swimming, tennis, and track and field. Water polo, Ultimate Frisbee, and men's lacrosse are club sports. Linfield also has an extensive and active year-round intramural program.

Linfield hosts the Oregon Nobel Laureate Symposium. (There are only five such symposiums worldwide.) At each symposium, several Nobel laureates come to share their backgrounds and expertise within the context of a basic theme.

The Linfield–Good Samaritan School of Nursing, an academic unit of the College at its Portland campus, prepares students for the B.S.N. or a degree in health science. This campus, at the Good Samaritan Hospital and Medical Center, has residence facilities, food service options, and a residence life program. The Portland campus median age is 24.

Location

Located in McMinnville, 40 miles southwest of Portland, Linfield College is a leader in the cultural, educational, and recreational events of the fast-growing community of 30,000. The seat of county government, McMinnville provides Linfield faculty and students with many opportunities to participate in community service activities. Cinemas, a community theater, bowling alleys, coffeehouses, and a wide variety of restaurants welcome Linfield students. Shopping is within walking distance. The central Oregon coast is an hour to the west, and the outdoor activity areas of the Oregon Cascade mountains, including year-round skiing at Mt. Hood, are 2 hours to the east. Salem, the state capital of Oregon, is 25 miles to the southeast, and Eugene is 80 miles south. Rainfall in western Oregon averages 42 inches annually, and the winter temperature averages 41°F.

Majors and Degrees

Linfield offers the Bachelor of Arts degree in art, communication, creative writing, English, European studies–German, French, German, history, Japanese, music, philosophy, political science, religious studies, sociology, Spanish, and theater arts. The Bachelor of Arts or Bachelor of Science degree is offered in accounting, anthropology, applied physics, athletic training, biology, business, chemistry, computing science, economics, elementary education, environmental studies, exercise science, finance, general science, health education, health sciences, international business, mathematics, medical technology, nursing, physical education, physics, and psychology. The College has programs to prepare students for advanced study in dentistry, law, and medicine. The education department offers a strong program of teacher certification at the secondary and elementary levels. A 3-2 engineering program is available in cooperation with Oregon State University, Washington State University, and the University of Southern California.

Academic Programs

The academic year is divided into two 15-week semesters (fall and spring) and an optional four-week winter term in January. The January Term offers regular departmental courses and cultural-epochs study. Academic courses are assigned 1–5 semester credit hours each; 125 credits are required for a B.A. or a B.S. degree. Students divide their time equally among required general education courses, a major area of study, and elective subjects. The Linfield Curriculum courses, selected to provide a solid foundation in the liberal arts, require students to take 6 semester hours in at least two courses in each of the five areas of inquiry. These areas of inquiry are as follows: the Vital Past; Ultimate Questions; Individuals, Systems, and Societies; the Natural World; and Images and Arts. In addition, students are required to take a writing-intensive course, a course addressing global diversity, and a course dealing with American pluralism. Major requirements differ from department to department. Individually designed majors are available with faculty approval. Students majoring in a foreign language spend an academic year in a country in which the language being studied is the native tongue. Language majors have recently studied in such cities as Avignon, Guadalajara, Nantes, Munich, Quebec, and Valencia. The Advanced Placement (AP) Program of the College Board is recognized, and up to 5 semester hours of credit are granted for a score of 4 or 5 on an AP test. AP examinations do not satisfy general education requirements. The College recognizes the International Baccalaureate (IB) Diploma and awards up to 30 semester hours of credit for higher-level courses on a course-by-course basis. Total credit awarded by AP or IB may not exceed 30 semester hours.

The College offers courses in English with the English Language and Culture program. These courses are designed to help international students whose native language is not English to achieve competence in academic and social English skills, so that they may work effectively in their undergraduate classes at Linfield.

Off-Campus Programs

Off-campus educational experiences include the Semester Abroad Program, involving four months of study in San Ramon, Costa Rica; Aix, Angers, or Avignon, France; Vienna, Austria; Yokohama, Japan; Oaxaca, Mexico; Oslo, Norway; Hong Kong, China; Seoul, South Korea; Galway, Ireland; Nottingham, England; Quito and Galapagos, Ecuador; or various locations in Asia, as approved by the Director of International Programs. Sophomores, juniors, and seniors are encouraged to participate, and approximately 20 students are selected for each country each year. The program is designed to serve students who have successfully completed one year of study at Linfield in the appropriate language and who will return to the campus to share their international experiences with the College community. Transportation for the first round trip is included in the cost of tuition, and most of these study programs cost the same as a semester on campus. January Term study-abroad programs for four weeks are also offered. Recent offerings included the Emergence of Modern Ghana (West Africa); Mainland Southeast Asia History (Cambodia, Vietnam, and China); American Expatriate Writers in Europe: The Lost Generation Tour (nine European cities); and Australia: From Colony to Asian Power.

Academic Facilities

Murdock Hall houses the biology and chemistry departments and up-to-date laboratories and equipment. Laboratory and research space is provided for general and advanced chemistry and biology, organic chemistry, biochemistry, microbiology, bacteriology, immunology, ecology, botany, physiology, embryology, and gross and microscopic anatomy. There are approximately 200 IBM and Macintosh computers on campus available for student use. Services on the network that students can use include the two UNIX hosts (available for programming, e-mail, and other communication services), a connection to the Internet, file servers, and both laser and dot-matrix printers. Linfield students benefit from a communications and technology network, including phone service, voice mail, e-mail, and Internet connections in each residence hall room. In addition, there is wireless access in the library and other academic areas of the campus.

The Health and Physical Education/Recreation Complex houses three gymnasiums; weight rooms; fitness laboratories with a hydrostatic weighing tank, a metabolic and pulmonary measuring system, and an electrocardiovascular exercise ECG system; an eight-lane, 25-yard-long indoor pool; handball and racquetball courts; classrooms; offices; and a 28,000-square-foot field house.

Since 2000, there have been many exciting changes at Linfield. The College first opened six apartment buildings as well as the James F. Miller Fine Arts Center. In 2003, Linfield opened Nicholson library and the Marshall Theater and communication arts facility. The library covers 56,000 square feet and combines traditional collections of books and journals with the new and changing digital and electronic technology to provide access to the Web and Web-based designs. There is seating for up to 500 students, as well as thirty-five computer workstations and wireless access to the campus network, the Internet, and the World Wide Web for students who bring their own laptops or check out those available at the library. The studio theater has an audience seating capacity of up to 140, more than double the former facility. It includes space for set construction and design as well as faculty offices. In the fall of 2006, Linfield opened two new residence halls and the Vivian A. Bull Center for Music. Other facilities include art galleries and studios, a 250-watt FM radio station, an experimental psychology laboratory, dance and music studios, a preschool, and a 425-seat auditorium that houses a three-manual, 48-rank Casavant pipe organ.

Costs

For 2007–08, tuition and fees were $25,390 per two-semester year. Board was $3390, and a double room was $3950. There was a $150-per-credit fee for January Term classes.

Financial Aid

Eligibility for most of Linfield's assistance programs is based on need as determined by a federally approved needs analysis processor. The only form required for need-based programs is the Free Application for Federal Student Aid (FAFSA). Linfield participates in the Federal Perkins and Federal Stafford Student Loan programs, Federal Supplemental Educational Opportunity Grants, Federal Work-Study, and other forms of financial assistance on the basis of demonstrated need.

The College awards a number of scholarships to full-time students based on scholastic achievement, independent of financial need. These academic scholarships vary from 20 to 75 percent of tuition. To be considered, students must have a minimum GPA of 3.4. A number of other criteria are used when determining scholarships. Linfield sponsors special scholarships for National Merit finalists. The minimum award is 50 percent of tuition. Awards can range to full tuition, depending on financial need, provided the student has indicated that Linfield is his or her first-choice college. The College also sponsors the annual Academic Competitive Scholarship Program in early spring each year. Participation is limited to high school seniors who meet particular academic requirements. Each academic department offers prizes ranging from $10,000 to $16,000, divided over the student's four years at Linfield, provided the student maintains a grade point average of at least 3.0. Scholarships of varying amounts are awarded to entering students who are particularly talented in music performance. Amounts range from $1500 to $2500 annually. Interested students are required to audition either in person or by cassette tape by February 15. Financial assistance for non-U.S. citizens is limited to partial tuition scholarships and the opportunity to work part-time on campus. Other scholarships are available for students who demonstrate outstanding leadership and community service.

Faculty

There are 114 full-time and 64 part-time faculty members, each of whom is committed to undergraduate teaching and scholarship. Ninety-three percent have doctoral or other terminal degrees within their field. The student-faculty ratio is 12:1, and faculty members serve as academic advisers. There are no teaching assistants.

Student Government

Students have a significant voice in establishing and changing College policies and regulations. The Student Senate, chosen through campus elections, is the focus of student opinion and debate. Students are represented on most College governing councils and committees with faculty members and trustees, and they are encouraged to express and implement their ideas on academic or extracurricular matters.

Admission Requirements

Admission to Linfield College is selective. Admission is granted to students who are likely to grow and succeed in a personal and challenging liberal arts environment. Each applicant is judged on individual merit. A faculty admission committee evaluates candidates in a number of areas that commonly indicate academic potential. These include high school performance, a writing sample, recommendations from teachers and counselors, and precollege standardized test results (ACT or SAT). The committee also considers the depth and quality of an applicant's involvement in community and school activities. It reviews all applications as a group, selecting those students who show the greatest likelihood of benefiting from and contributing to the Linfield community. Linfield is a member of the Common Application Association.

International students whose education has been in a language other than English must submit certified English translations of their academic work. Proficiency in English is required, as demonstrated by an official TOEFL score report, including the Test of Written English (TWE; not available after September 2005, as the TOEFL will then include a test of speaking proficiency).

Application and Information

Early action applicants must apply by November 15, and notification is made by January 15. The priority application deadline for regular admission is February 15, with notification made on or before April 1. Admitted international students must show evidence of financial responsibility and submit a $2000 deposit.

Interviews are not required, but students are encouraged to visit. Appointments should be made in advance and can be requested online at http://www.linfield.edu/stopby. The Office of Admission is open Monday through Friday, 7:30 a.m. to 5:30 p.m., and on Saturdays during the school year from 9 a.m. to 2 p.m. The Linfield Web site provides students with information on student life, academic programs, and athletics. Students may also complete their application for admission online or ask for additional information. Interested students are encouraged to contact:

Director of Admission
Linfield College
McMinnville, Oregon 97128
Phone: 503-883-2213
800-640-2287 (toll-free)
Fax: 503-883-2472
E-mail: admission@linfield.edu
Web site: http://www.linfield.edu

MULTNOMAH BIBLE COLLEGE AND BIBLICAL SEMINARY

PORTLAND, OREGON

The College

Multnomah Bible College and Biblical Seminary has been devoted to teaching the Bible to men and women since the 1930s. The mission of Multnomah Bible College is to produce, through collegiate education, biblically competent, culturally aware, maturing servants of Jesus Christ, whose love for God, His Word, and people shapes their lives into a transforming force in the church and world. Multnomah's education is more than time in the classroom—it's learning through hands-on ministry, late-night talks with friends in the coffee shop, and discovering the heart of God through prayer. At Multnomah, the Bible is central to everything students learn. Whether majoring in journalism or pastoral ministry, students are challenged at the end of the day to think and live biblically. Multnomah offers one of the most comprehensive Bible programs in the nation, requiring each student to complete a comprehensive Bible and theology major. The College is accredited by the Northwest Commission on Colleges and Universities (NWCCU) and the Association of Biblical Higher Education (ABHE) and is recognized by the state of Oregon to award bachelor's degrees.

Effective education teaches the whole person. Community life presents challenges but provides tremendous opportunities to build lifelong friendships and to make service to others a lifelong habit. It allows faculty and staff members to give each student the individual attention befitting one created in God's image. But Multnomah does not leave its populace unprepared for the world's harsh realities. Rather, the College continually seeks ways to train students to have the greatest possible impact on the world today. Students are instructed in and saturated with a biblical, Christian worldview designed to prepare them for any situation encountered. Opportunities to make the world the classroom are offered through cross-cultural experiences and internships in the community. Students can work side-by-side with their instructors as they share the gospel in the community or minister in a home for abused women. The opportunities are endless.

Something is always happening on Multnomah's campus. Opportunities abound for students to get involved in a variety of activities, each designed to cultivate life skills that enhance their college experience. Students can join the student government, intramural sports, the Ambassador Choir, or various chapel worship bands, among other activities.

Multnomah Biblical Seminary was launched to provide a complementary, nonrepetitive seminary option for the Bible college graduate. Programs include the graduate certificate, the Master of Arts in biblical studies or in pastoral studies (emphases in family ministry, intercultural studies, ministry management, spiritual formation, and women's ministry), the Master of Divinity, and the Master of Theology. Multnomah also offers a Master of Arts in Teaching.

Location

The city of Portland offers an endless supply of adventure and excitement. The campus is only 15 minutes from downtown. On weekends, the Saturday Market offers a huge collection of handmade crafts, art, and ethnic food. Waterfront Park hosts the Rose Festival in late May, and many shops and restaurants overlook the Willamette River. The eclectic Hawthorne and northwest Portland districts have unique shopping and restaurants—including thirty-two Starbucks within 5 miles of campus. Portland is home to museums, concert venues, and the Trail Blazer basketball team. Less than 2 hours from Multnomah are Oregon's sandy beaches. An hour east of Portland lie the slopes of Mt. Hood, a favorite for skiers and snowboarders throughout the world. Portland International Airport (PDX) is less than 20 minutes from campus, and Portland has an excellent public transportation system.

Majors and Degrees

In addition to the Bible and theology major, students select a second major or minor in one of fifteen areas of study. Giving the Bible priority in their lives, most Multnomah students carry two majors (one of which is Bible) as they pursue their bachelor's degree. The Bachelor of Arts degree program provides students with more exposure to languages and humanities, while the Bachelor of Science degree program focuses more on social sciences. Areas of study include biblical Hebrew, education, educational ministries, history, intercultural studies, journalism, missionary aviation co-op, music ministry, New Testament Greek, pastoral ministry, speech communication, and youth ministry. Minors are now available in English, psychology, and Teaching English to Speakers of Other Languages (TESOL).

Academic Programs

Multnomah Bible College believes that there is no substitute for a thorough knowledge of the Word of God and that it is basic to all successful Christian service. For that reason, the College has made teaching the Bible its primary objective and enrolls all bachelor's students in the Bible major. As a result of the large proportion of Bible in the curriculum, students are able to obtain a sound and thorough training in the Word of God. A varied program of second majors and minors enables students to specialize in a particular area of interest for more effective Christian service and professional competency. General education provides learning experiences that enhance and complement the academic majors, giving the student an integrated Christian worldview. Students gain an understanding and awareness of broad areas of language, history, philosophy, communication, science, and human development.

Off-Campus Programs

Multnomah offers a South American Studies program through a cooperative program with George Fox University and Bolivian Evangelical University in Santa Cruz, Bolivia's second-largest city. Alternative study-abroad options are available though the Council of Christian Colleges and Universities (CCCU), of which Multnomah Bible College is an affiliate member.

Academic Facilities

The John and Mary Mitchell Library has a rich and developing collection of conventional and electronic resources to support the programs of study at Multnomah Bible College and Biblical Seminary. Multnomah is a member of a consortium of eight libraries with a union database of more than 500,000 library holdings. The library has more than 90,000 volumes and 1,000 full-text journals, a growing collection of videos and DVDs, and many online research tools. The library staff is pleased to assist patrons in locating materials and answer any questions about the library, its resources, and its use.

The upper floor comprises stacks filled with a wide variety of books and a large study area for student and guest use. The lower floor has four classrooms, with seating capacities ranging from 38 to 55. A fifth classroom with auditorium-style seating accommodates 186 people. This classroom also has audiovisual computer capabilities. Two outside classrooms can seat 24 people. The Travis-Lovitt seminary building, the newest addition to campus, houses seven classrooms able to seat from 20 to 60 students. Each classroom is equipped with state-of-the-art audiovisual equipment.

Costs

In 2007–08, tuition and fees were $13,480 per year, and room and board averaged $5600, for a total of approximately $19,080.

Financial Aid

Multnomah provides a variety of aid through many sources, including federal and institutional aid. A variety of scholarships based on academics and experience are awarded. The President's Scholarship, Multnomah's most prestigious award, provides 50 percent of tuition. To qualify, the student must be an entering freshman and have at least a 3.5 GPA and a minimum SAT score of 1800 or ACT score of 27. The student must provide references from 3 people, including a person he or she has worked with in ministry, such as a pastor. The Multnomah Academic Dean's Scholarship is a second-tier scholarship providing 25 percent of tuition costs. Dean's Scholarship applicants must have a high school GPA of at least 3.25 or a minimum college-transfer GPA of 3.0 and an SAT score of at least 1650 or an ACT score of 24 or higher. Multnomah offers a variety of leadership opportunities on-campus that include financial assistance. Each student can apply for leadership opportunities after his or her first year at Multnomah.

Faculty

The faculty members are the foundation upon which programs of academic excellence are built. Though highly educated and respected as scholars, faculty members do not promote "ivory tower" scholarship in their classrooms. Faculty members are skilled communicators who make the ideas and principles they teach relevant to their students' lives. While the faculty members love to teach, they also consistently broaden their knowledge base—indicated by their publishing of books and journal articles and their involvement in various scholarly societies. They serve the church as pastors, church planters, counselors, and conference speakers. The content of their classroom instruction has been tested in the laboratory of experience, allowing them to teach with confidence.

Student Government

STUGO, the student government organization, organizes social events and ministries to help students become mature, Christ-like individuals. STUGO's Multnomah Community Outreach (MCO) provides opportunities for students to serve the surrounding community in after-school programs, workdays, and individual-care services. The Student World Outreach Team (SWOT) facilitates a world missionary vision through Monday chapels and missions-related events throughout the school year. All STUGO activities are designed to enrich the students' lives and contribute to their educational experience.

Admission Requirements

Because the academic load at Multnomah is rigorous, applicants should have a minimum 2.5 GPA. Students must complete the full application packet, which includes a personal statement and four reference forms (from one pastor, one employer or teacher, and two friends). Applicants must also submit official transcripts (from high school or community college), SAT or ACT scores, and the $40 application fee. The admissions committee also examines an applicant's character and his or her demonstrated commitment to Jesus Christ through service, leadership, and other factors.

Application and Information

Applicants should file admission forms well in advance of the enrollment date. Applications must arrive by July 15 for August admission (fall semester) or by November 15 for January admission (spring semester).

Admissions Office
Multnomah Bible College and Biblical Seminary
8435 Northeast Glisan Street
Portland, Oregon 97220
Phone: 503-251-6485
800-275-4672 (toll-free)
E-mail: admiss@multnomah.edu
Web site: http://www.multnomah.edu/

OREGON STATE UNIVERSITY

CORVALLIS, OREGON

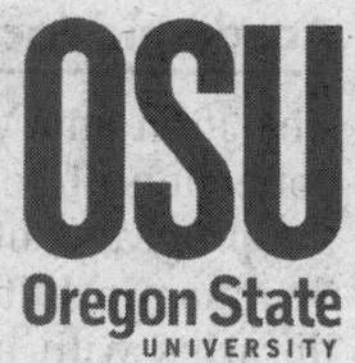

The University

Exceptional students, an outstanding faculty, and a challenging curriculum combine to make Oregon State University (OSU) a nationally and internationally recognized comprehensive university.

OSU has earned the Carnegie Foundation's "Very High Research Activity" designation for commitment to education and research. Widely recognized research programs add to the quality of teaching by bringing new knowledge into the classroom and by encouraging undergraduate students to work with faculty members on research projects in many fields. As a member of the non-tiered Oregon University System, OSU is the premier research university in the state of Oregon. In fact, OSU's economic impact to the state of Oregon exceeds $1.5 billion.

The University's 19,700 students come from all fifty states and more than ninety-three countries around the world to pursue a wide choice of undergraduate programs that prepare them for careers and leadership positions in science, engineering and computer-related fields, natural resources, government, teaching and social service, pharmacy, and other professions. Employers from across the nation recognize the value of an OSU degree, and more of them recruit at Oregon State University each year than at any other university in the state. Oregon State also ranks twenty-fifth nationally in Peace Corps volunteers.

OSU is committed to offering students the resources they need to be successful in their education. In addition to utilizing Blackboard™ as an electronic tool to assist students with class materials, interactive topic conversations, and resources, OSU continues to innovate by systematically adding wireless networks to classrooms, libraries, and common areas on campus. Students also have access to one of the largest open-source software labs in the world, where new shareware is developed, housed, and distributed.

Students also benefit from more than 300 cocurricular activities on campus. These include student government, student media, theater and music, intramural and club sports, and numerous social, academic, cultural, and professional clubs and organizations. In addition, Dixon Recreation Center offers opportunities for swimming and diving, weight training, aerobic exercise, and the largest collegiate rock-climbing center in the Northwest. A campus child-care facility offers educationally oriented day-care programs for children of students and faculty and staff members.

OSU offers a wide range of housing and dining options, including special-program residence halls, cooperative houses, student family housing, and fraternity and sorority housing. Many apartments and houses are available within biking or walking distance of OSU for students who choose to live off campus. There are more than fifteen restaurants on campus.

Graduate degrees are offered through the Colleges of Agricultural Sciences, Business, Engineering, Forestry, Health and Human Sciences, Liberal Arts, and Science. Graduate and professional degrees are also offered through the Colleges of Oceanic and Atmospheric Sciences, Pharmacy, and Veterinary Medicine, and through the School of Education.

Location

The OSU main campus is in Corvallis, which is consistently ranked as one of the safest university communities on the West Coast. Recently, Farmers Insurance named Corvallis the "Most Secure" city in the U.S. for 2007. With about 52,000 residents, Corvallis offers a friendly, university-oriented atmosphere. In fact, students rated OSU as the fifth-friendliest campus in the U.S., according to CampusDirt.com. *Forbes* magazine also rated Corvallis as one of the top 5 smartest cities. Miles of bike lanes and free city bus service make it easy for students to get around town. Within a couple hours of Corvallis are the Oregon Coast; the Cascade Mountains, with skiing, hiking, camping, and snowboarding; and Portland, Oregon's largest city. The OSU Cascades Campus in Bend, Oregon, represents a unique educational partnership involving four distinguished institutions, creating an innovative and collaborative university to serve the needs of central Oregon.

Majors and Degrees

Oregon State is a comprehensive university, with more than 200 academic programs. Undergraduate degrees are offered through the Colleges of Agricultural Sciences, Business, Education, Engineering, Forestry, Health and Human Sciences, Liberal Arts, and Science.

Students in any undergraduate major can strengthen their transcripts by earning an Honors Degree or an International Degree. Almost 600 top students are enrolled in the University Honors College, which offers a small-college atmosphere within the larger University. The University also offers twenty-eight preprofessional programs that prepare students for graduate programs and careers in fields such as health sciences, law, and education.

The OSU Cascades Campus offers a variety of undergraduate and graduate degree opportunities specific to the region. Geology, wildlife biology, botany, business, nursing, education, computer science, engineering, museum studies, outdoor recreation leadership, and tourism are among the many programs available.

Academic Programs

All undergraduate students at Oregon State complete the Baccalaureate Core, which helps develop skills and knowledge in writing, critical thinking, cultural diversity, the arts, science, literature, lifelong fitness, and global awareness, ensuring that as graduates they will be well prepared for life as well as a career.

Many students take advantage of OSU's first-year experience program, called Odyssey, which offers opportunities for new students to interact with faculty members and other students throughout the year, thus easing the transition to college life. The year begins with a five-day "Connect" orientation that features Convocation (the official kickoff to the school year), small-group meetings between faculty members and students, a barbecue, outdoor movies, open houses, and more.

Undergraduate research is an important component of many academic programs, and more than 2,000 OSU undergraduates participate with faculty members and graduate students on research projects each year. One example is the Howard Hughes Medical Institute Summer Research Program, which funds undergraduate researchers to the tune of $1.9 million.

OSU has more majors, minors, and special programs than any other college in Oregon and offers a University Exploratory Studies Program for students who want to try various options before choosing a major field. Oregon State uses the quarter system for its academic year. Most majors require between 180 and 192 credit hours for a bachelor's degree. There are no impacted majors at Oregon State University.

The Academic Success Center helps OSU students deal with problems and develop the skills they need in college and beyond. The Center for Writing and Learning, the Math Learning Center, and departmental resource centers assist students in preparing for assignments in specific areas, while the African American, Hispanic American, Asian American, and Native American education offices, along with the Educational Opportunities Program, help mentor students throughout their college careers. University Counseling and Psychological Services offers learning resource materials and professional assistance to help students deal with problems, both in and out of the classroom. Career Services assists students in locating internships and in finding jobs when they graduate.

Off-Campus Programs

Through the International Degree, study-abroad, and international internship programs, OSU students can study, work, or conduct research almost anywhere in the world. Programs, which range from a term to a full year, are offered in Australia, Canada, China, Denmark, Ecuador, England, France, Germany, Hungary, Italy, Japan, Korea, Mexico, New Zealand, Norway, Russia, Spain, Thailand, Tunisia, and Vietnam.

OSU also participates in the National Student Exchange Program, allowing students to spend up to a year at one of more than 160 colleges and universities in the U.S. and its possessions, while paying in-state tuition and fees.

Academic Facilities

OSU's Valley Library is a state-of-the-art facility that offers modern electronic services, including a wireless computer network, and unique special collections as well as traditional library services to students and the community. The OSU library is the first academic library to be named "Library of the Year" by *Library Journal* (1999). Library holdings include more than 2.5 million books, periodicals, and government documents on paper or microform. A reciprocal agreement makes more than 5 million additional volumes in the Oregon University System available to OSU students and faculty members. OSU's special collections include the papers and memorabilia of Linus Pauling, the only winner of two unshared Nobel Prizes, and the Atomic Energy Collection. The Valley Library is an official depository for U.S. government and state of Oregon publications.

Students at OSU have access to more than 2,200 computers at labs around the campus, including some that are available 24 hours per day. In addition, all rooms in campus residence facilities are wired for high-speed access to the Internet, and wireless networks are located throughout the campus. Special research facilities include OSU's Mark O. Hatfield Marine Science Center, Oregon Nanoscience and Microtechnologies Institute (ONAMI), Center for Gene Research and Biotechnology, Forest Research Laboratory, Radiation Center, and Hinsdale Wave Research Lab.

Costs

In-state undergraduate tuition and fees were approximately $5830 for the 2007–08 academic year, while nonresident charges were about $17,600. The average cost for a residence hall double room and meal plan was approximately $7565. Students who lived in a fraternity or sorority house paid about the same for housing and meals as those students who lived in residence halls.

Financial Aid

OSU offers the full range of scholarships, grants, work-study, and loans from federal, state, and University sources, investing more than $108 million in student aid annually. Some form of financial assistance is received by 80 percent of the students at OSU. To qualify, students must have applied for admission and must submit the Free Application for Federal Student Aid (FAFSA), listing OSU as one of their top six choices (Title IV code: 003210). Some students help meet educational expenses with one of the many part-time jobs available on or near the campus. For financial aid information, interested students should contact the Office of Financial Aid and Scholarships, 218 Kerr Administration Building, Corvallis, Oregon 97331 (phone: 541-737-2241, Web site: http://oregonstate.edu/admin/finaid/).

Through the University Scholars Program, OSU offers a variety of scholarships and additional scholarship search assistance for new students who have strong academic records. University scholarships range from $500 to $6000 annually for up to four years. In addition, most OSU colleges offer scholarships to new students, and the OSU Foundation has a number of University-wide scholarships.

Faculty

Undergraduate education is a priority at OSU, and nationally prominent scholars and scientists regularly teach undergraduate courses at all levels. Students receive individual attention and the chance to know their professors both in and out of the classroom. Faculty members consistently receive awards for teaching and research, and many of them are nationally and internationally renowned. The more than $206 million in external research funds received annually by OSU faculty members exceeds that of all other Oregon public universities combined.

Student Government

The Associated Students of Oregon State University (ASOSU) plays a major role in making policy and regulating activities for students and in governing the University through student participation on more than fifty University-wide committees. In recent years, ASOSU has become more involved with local, state, and national issues that affect the welfare of students.

Admission Requirements

A minimum 3.0 high school GPA (on a 4.0 scale) qualifies students for freshman admission to OSU when all subject requirements are met. Applicants for undergraduate admission are required to complete an "Insight Resume," a written assessment designed to evaluate students' noncognitive attributes. These attributes include self-concept, realistic self-appraisal, handling the system, ability to set long-range goals, leadership, connections with a strong support person, community engagement, and nontraditional learning. High school subject requirements are 4 years of English, 3 years each of mathematics and social studies, and 2 years each of science and of the same foreign language. Students who do not meet the subject requirements may be considered for admission by earning a total score of at least 1410 on three SAT Subject Tests or by successfully completing course work to make up specific deficiencies. The alternatives must by completed by the time of high school graduation.

Transfer admission requires successful completion of at least 36 graded, transferable credits (24 semester credits) from accredited U.S. institutions, with a minimum GPA of 2.25. Grades of C- or better are required in college-level writing and mathematics. Students with less than 36 transferable credits are considered for admission on the basis of their high school records.

Application and Information

Applicants are encouraged to complete OSU's online application, which can be found at the Web site. An *OSU Viewbook*, with information on specific academic programs, housing, financial aid, scholarships, and activities, is sent to students upon request.

Prospective students are encouraged to visit OSU to determine in person whether the University meets their needs. A visit, including a campus tour and an opportunity to talk to faculty members in the student's area of interest, can be arranged by calling the Office of Admissions.

To request more information, students should contact:

Office of Admissions
104 Kerr Administration Building
Oregon State University
Corvallis, Oregon 97331-2106
Phone: 800-291-4192 (toll-free)
Fax: 541-737-2482
E-mail: osuadmit@oregonstate.edu
Web site: http://oregonstate.edu/admissions

PACIFIC UNIVERSITY

FOREST GROVE, OREGON

The University

Pacific University is a private, fully accredited four-year liberal arts university encompassing the undergraduate College of Arts and Sciences and nine graduate programs: seven in the health professions, an M.F.A. in writing, and one in teacher education. Founded in 1849 by Congregational pioneers, Pacific is still a frontier institution, proud of its tradition in liberal arts and sciences and innovative in its programs.

Pacific's 2,400 students come from all over the United States and twenty-eight countries, creating a diverse and dynamic student body. Students are taught by the University's full-time faculty members, each of whom is chosen for his or her distinctive devotion to teaching and an emphasis on individual mentoring.

The College of Arts and Sciences is noted for its exceptionally personalized approach to education that is grounded in a philosophy of service. It is recognized for outstanding programs in the natural sciences, education, business, psychology, world languages, and the humanities. Pacific's select group of graduate health profession programs includes the Pacific Northwest's only College of Optometry, as well as the School of Professional Psychology, School of Occupational Therapy, School of Physical Therapy, Dental Health Sciences, Pharmacy, and School of Physician's Assistant Studies. In addition, the College of Education offers undergraduate and master's-level programs leading to teacher licensure. Graduate programs in the college include the fifth-year M.A.T., M.A.T. Flex, M.Ed., and M.Ed. in visual function and learning (in conjunction with the optometry program).

The lively and vigorous campus springs from the college's residential nature. Freshmen and sophomores under 21 are required to live in one of the University's coed residence facilities. Students living on campus reside in one of four residence halls or Vandervelden Apartments. All on-campus rooms are connected to the campus computer network, which is linked to the Internet. Students who choose to live off campus may live in University-owned housing units or other nearby apartment complexes. Pacific is also the home of an active Greek system, including three fraternities and four sororities.

On campus, the University Center is a hub of activity, housing the dining commons, a new lounge, student government offices, Macintosh and PC lab facilities, the campus radio station, and the newspaper office. The Pacific Undergraduate Community Council (PUCC) provides funding to more than sixty student interest groups, ranging from the Outback program to the Hawaiian Club to the Politics and Law Forum. Pacific Outback provides a multitude of outdoor activities for interested students, such as kayaking, hiking, cross-country and downhill skiing trips, camping, and outings to Portland-area events.

In athletics, Pacific is a member of the NCAA Division III Northwest Conference. Men's intercollegiate sports are baseball, basketball, cross-country, golf, soccer, swimming, tennis, track and field, and wrestling. Women compete in basketball, cross-country, golf, lacrosse, soccer, softball, swimming, tennis, track and field, volleyball, and wrestling. Pacific athletes train and compete in the Pacific Athletic Center, which houses a gymnasium (with three basketball courts), a state-of-the-art fitness center, a versatile field house, three handball/racquetball courts, a dance studio, a wrestling room, and a complete sports medicine training facility.

Pacific and the city of Forest Grove are also partnering to build another outstanding athletic facility for the University and the community. This new facility will feature a 1,100-seat stadium with a nine-lane, 400-meter track and a FieldTurf soccer and lacrosse field; a brand-new Bond baseball field with a permanent grandstand; a new varsity softball field with permanent grandstand seating; and other new park amenities. The Lincoln Park Athletic Complex will be one of the best outdoor facilities of any small college in the Northwest.

In addition to the Forest Grove campus, the University has a satellite campus in Eugene, Oregon, serving the needs of the College of Education and another in Hillsboro, Oregon, serving the needs of the College of Health Professions, and it operates facilities in Portland that support the academic and clinical programs of the College of Optometry and the School of Professional Psychology.

Pacific offers seven graduate programs in the College of Health Professions: professional psychology (M.A. and Psy.D.), Doctor of Physical Therapy (D.P.T.), Master of Occupational Therapy (M.O.T.), dental health science (B.S. and M.S.), Doctor of Pharmacy, Doctor of Optometry, and a physician's assistant studies program (M.S.P.A.). Occupational therapy students spend three years in undergraduate prerequisite work and 2½ years in the master's program. Physical therapy students must have completed a bachelor's degree program with specific course work before applying to the program. The physician's assistant studies master's program is a twenty-eight-month consecutive program. Through the College of Optometry, students receive a degree (O.D.) with four years of graduate work. Optometry students can be admitted into the College of Optometry's four-year doctoral graduate program after completing three years of undergraduate prerequisite work.

Location

Situated in the northwest corner of Oregon between metropolitan Portland and the Pacific Ocean, the University is located in Forest Grove (population 18,000), about 35 minutes from the heart of Portland, a vibrant metropolitan area. The 55-acre, oak-covered campus is surrounded by green countryside and the foothills of the Coast Range Mountains, beyond which is the 300-mile stretch of Oregon coast. Opportunities abound in Oregon for hiking, skiing, camping, fishing, beachcombing, and bicycling. The climate is temperate throughout the year, with winter rainfall tapering off to a pleasant spring and sunny summer.

Majors and Degrees

Major programs leading to the B.A. or B.S. degree are offered through the College of Arts and Sciences in anthropology/sociology, applied science, art, bioinformatics, biology (with an emphasis in ecology and evolution or in molecular and cellular), business administration (with an emphasis in accounting, finance, management, or marketing), chemistry (with an emphasis in biological chemistry or chemical physics), computer science, coordinated studies in humanities, creative writing, economics, education and learning, environmental science (with an emphasis in biology or chemistry), exercise science (with an emphasis in human performance), French studies, German studies, history, international studies, Japanese studies, literature, mathematics, media arts and communications (with an emphasis in film production, film studies, integrated media, journalism, or video production), modern languages (with an emphasis in Chinese, French, German, Japanese, or Spanish), music (with an emphasis in education or performance), philosophy (with an emphasis in bioethics), social work, sociology, Spanish, and theater. A B.M. degree is offered in music. Secondary education certification is available in art, biology, English, French, German, health education (combined endorsement only), integrated science, Japanese, mathematics, music, reading (combined endorsement only), social studies (secondary education students only), and Spanish.

Pacific offers a 3-2 program in engineering, which is designed as a transfer program in which students spend three years at Pacific studying physics, chemistry, mathematics, and computer science (as well as electives in other areas of the liberal arts) and then transfer to an engineering school for their final two years of professional training in engineering. At the end of this period, students receive a B.S. degree in engineering from the engineering school and a B.S. in applied science, physics, chemistry, mathematics, or computer science from Pacific University. Pacific's program currently involves transfer agreements with Washington University in St. Louis, Oregon State University, and Washington State University. However, students can (and do) transfer to other engineering schools of their choice. There is also a 4-1 cooperative program with Oregon Health & Science University (OHSU) that awards a B.S. in environmental science from Pacific and an M.S. degree in environmental science and engineering from OHSU.

Academic Programs

Pacific provides an excellent education in the liberal arts and sciences. The core curriculum in the College of Arts and Sciences emphasizes writing, reasoning, and communication skills, with attention given to cross-cultural education and work in the natural sciences and the fine arts. All freshmen participate in a semester-long first-year seminar program designed to introduce students to college-level writing and research expectations. Pacific has a long tradition of ethical concern that is reflected in its undergraduate courses and its many opportunities for service both on campus and within the broader community. As a small university, Pacific maintains small classes to ensure close contact among students and faculty members.

Special programs in the College of Arts and Sciences include the interdisciplinary Peace and Conflict Studies Program as well as minors in dance, disabilities studies, and feminist studies.

Basic requirements for the B.A. or B.S. degree are 120 semester hours of credit, completion of a major, and completion of the core requirements in the College of Arts and Sciences. The year is divided into two semesters, with a three-week winter term between the two semesters. Students typically take 15 credit hours during each semester and 3 credit hours during the winter term.

Pacific grants credit for both subject and general CLEP examinations. Each department or school at Pacific University determines whether or not a specific examination may substitute for a specific course. Students who score 4 or better on the Advanced Placement examinations of the College Board are given advanced placement and credit toward graduation. Pacific recognizes the International Baccalaureate program as providing college-level work. Six credit hours are awarded for each higher examination passed at a score of 5 or higher.

Off-Campus Programs

Pacific offers study-abroad programs in twelve different countries, as well as an agreement with the Oregon University System (OUS) giving Pacific students additional study-abroad sites. Foreign language and international studies majors are required to spend at least one semester studying abroad and may use financial aid toward their international study. Pacific also emphasizes internships, which are regularly arranged for students in business, communications, political science, psychology, sociology, and other fields. The internships, which may be arranged for periods lasting from fourteen weeks to an entire academic year, offer students the opportunity to become thoroughly acquainted with professional work and often lead to employment upon graduation.

Academic Facilities

The 55-acre Forest Grove campus contains buildings in a picturesque setting with green lawns and tall shade trees. Architecture at Pacific is a pleasant blend of the old and new. Representing the long history of Pacific University, Old College Hall was the first permanent structure; built in 1850, it contains museum galleries and historic exhibits. Modern buildings include the Douglas C. Strain Science Center, Taylor-Meade Performing Arts Center, and professional buildings. Also included are a 90,000-square-foot Pacific Athletic Center and the Tom Reynolds Soccer Field. Historical Marsh Hall, which was originally constructed in 1893 and completely refurbished in 1977, holds classrooms, professors' offices, and administration facilities.

Wireless Internet can be accessed throughout the campus. Built in 2005, the new library houses superior technology, large study areas, and a collection of materials to support the curriculum and student and faculty research in a variety of formats, both traditional and electronic. While the library strives to build a strong core collection, it also participates in SUMMIT, a regional library consortium meeting the considerable research needs of Pacific's students and faculty members by allowing them access to the collections of sixty-two other northwest college and university libraries. Through computer technology, courier services, and interlibrary loans, students and faculty members can efficiently tap the research resources of the region and beyond.

Encompassing the Schools of Dental Health Science, Occupational Therapy, Pharmacy, Physical Therapy, Physician Assistant Studies, and Professional Psychology, Pacific University's College of Health Professions prepares its students through interdisciplinary activities to provide compassionate delivery of exemplary health care for a diverse population in a changing health-care environment. The Pacific University Health Professions Campus opened in fall 2006 and is located on a half-acre site on the Tuality Hospital Hillsboro campus. This location will also be the site of phase two, which will be built in the next five years.

Costs

Tuition and fees for the 2007–08 school year are $26,470. Room and board are approximately $7170 for a double room and include a University meal plan. Books and supplies are estimated at approximately $700. Fees are $582. Pacific has consistently been named one of the best values west of the Mississippi by several national publications, including *U.S. News & World Report.*

Financial Aid

Financial assistance at Pacific is awarded on the basis of demonstrated need, academic merit, and talent. The Free Application for Federal Student Aid (FAFSA) is used in evaluating need. Prospective students are encouraged to apply for financial assistance by submitting the FAFSA to the federal processor as soon after January 1 as possible. Pacific provides financial assistance through grants, scholarships, loans, and part-time employment. Further information is available via e-mail at financialaid@pacificu.edu.

Faculty

Pacific's outstanding faculty members provide the foundation for the University's academic program. A student-faculty ratio of 13:1 allows for personal attention by the professors. Pacific's faculty is made up of 147 dedicated educators, of whom 96 percent hold terminal degrees in their field. As professionals, they uphold the University's standard of academic excellence and work closely with students. Pacific does not use graduate or teaching assistants; all faculty members teach their own courses.

Student Government

Participatory government at Pacific enables students to help shape the campus community in which they live and work. Students are encouraged to voice their opinions and to pursue new ideas that further not only personal growth but also the overall growth and development of the University. Pacific Undergraduate Community Council (PUCC), the official student government body, manages activity funds, reviews and supports student issues, and coordinates student participation within the system.

Admission Requirements

Pacific University is selective in considering new students. Primary consideration is given to a candidate's academic preparation and potential for successful study at the college level, as assessed by evaluating the student's transcripts of college-preparatory work, counselor and teacher recommendations, personal essay, SAT and/or ACT scores, and other student-submitted information. Transfer students must submit high school records and test scores if they have completed less than 30 semester hours, plus official transcripts from any institution previously attended.

Application and Information

Students may apply early and may be notified early through the modified rolling admissions plan. The regular priority deadline for admission is February 15. For additional information, interested students should contact:

Office of Admissions
Pacific University
2043 College Way
Forest Grove, Oregon 97116
Phone: 503-352-2218
800-677-6712 (toll-free)
E-mail: admissions@pacificu.edu
Web site: http://www.pacificu.edu

REED COLLEGE

PORTLAND, OREGON

The College

For its 1,492 students and 125 faculty members, Reed College is foremost an intellectual community. Since its founding in 1911, Reed has attracted students with a high degree of self-discipline and a genuine enthusiasm for academic work and intellectual challenge. Reed attracts a diverse student body; four fifths of Reed's students come from outside the Northwest, with more than 20 percent from the Northeast and 7 percent from outside the United States. A quarter of Reed's incoming students are members of historically underrepresented ethnic groups.

Campus social opportunities are open to all, with no closed clubs or organizations; there are no sororities or fraternities at Reed. Community life is full of activity and variety, with more than seventy student organizations. Although there are club sports at Reed, there are no varsity athletic teams. Fitness and development of lifelong skills take precedence over competition.

Location

Reed's 100-acre wooded campus is located in a quiet, residential section of southeast Portland. The nearby ocean and mountains of the Pacific Northwest provide a balance to the social and cultural offerings of the greater Portland metropolitan area.

Majors and Degrees

Reed awards the Bachelor of Arts degree in a wide variety of fields, based on work in traditional departments or in interdisciplinary combinations. Students may select from the following majors: American studies, anthropology, art, biochemistry and molecular biology, biology, chemistry, chemistry-physics, Chinese, classics, classics-religion, dance-theater, economics, English literature, French literature, German literature, history, history-literature, international and comparative policy studies, linguistics, literature-theater, mathematics, mathematics-economics, mathematics-physics, music, philosophy, physics, political science, psychology, religion, Russian literature, sociology, Spanish literature, and theater.

Students may also design additional interdisciplinary majors. The approval of such special programs, which link two or more disciplines, is reviewed by the student's adviser and the departments concerned.

Reed offers several combined 3-2 programs, which allow the student to earn both a bachelor's degree from Reed and a professional degree from the cooperating institution. Science programs and institutions include engineering (California Institute of Technology, Columbia University, and Rensselaer Polytechnic Institute), computer science (University of Washington), and environmental sciences (Duke University). The College also has a combined program in fine arts (Pacific Northwest College of Art).

Academic Programs

Hallmarks of academic life at Reed include the small-group conference method of teaching and its reliance on active student participation, a de-emphasis of grades, a yearlong interdisciplinary humanities program, and an integrated academic program that balances the breadth of traditional course content and distribution requirements with flexibility in designing an in-depth senior thesis. The development of skills in preparation for a life of learning takes precedence over the mere memorization of facts. In addition to fulfilling the requirements for the major, taking the humanities course, and writing the senior thesis, students must satisfy a distributional requirement, consisting of two core classes from each of the following academic groups: literature, philosophy, and the arts; history, social sciences, and psychology; the natural sciences; and math, foreign language, logic, and linguistics.

Off-Campus Programs

Reed participates in domestic exchange programs with Howard University in Washington, D.C.; Sarah Lawrence College in New York; and Sea Education Association in Massachusetts. In addition, Reed provides study-abroad opportunities for students in Germany (University of Munich, Tübingen University, Freie University), Russia (ACTR Russian Language, Middlebury School in Russia, National Theater Institute of Moscow, Smolny College at St. Petersburg University), Hungary (Budapest Semester in Mathematics), France (Université de Rennes II Haute Bretagne, Université de Paris), Spain (Hamilton College's Madrid Center, Middlebury School in Spain, University of Santiago de Compostela), Greece (College Year in Athens), Italy (Intercollegiate Center for Classical Studies in Rome, Florence Center of Syracuse University, Sarah Lawrence College Foreign Program in Florence), England (Sarah Lawrence College Foreign Programs in London Theater and at Wadham College at Oxford University, University of East Anglia, Sussex University, University of Nottingham), Ireland (Trinity College at the University of Dublin, University College Cork), Israel (Hebrew University), Egypt (American University in Cairo), Morocco (Al Akhawayn University), China (Reed China Program), Costa Rica (Organization for Tropical Studies, University of Costa Rica), South Africa (Organization for Tropical Studies), Ecuador (Ecuador Program), and Argentina (University of Buenos Aires/FLASCO, Universidad de San Andres). Students may also arrange independent study plans in consultation with appropriate faculty members, the director for off-campus studies, and the registrar.

Academic Facilities

Students have access to Reed's substantial library collection (544,616 volumes, 2,700 periodicals, and 340,000 government documents) by searching the online catalog in the library or from any computer on the campus network. Through its participation in PORTALS (Portland Area Library System) and Summit, a union catalog of Oregon and Washington academic libraries, Reed provides online access to other library catalogs and databases. Students may borrow materials directly from academic libraries in the Portland area, and they have access to collections worldwide through interlibrary loan. In addition, the Reed library accommodates a first-rate art gallery, a language lab, and a music listening facility. The Reed library is open 18 hours most days (24 hours a day during examinations).

Computer technology is highly developed at Reed and widely used for instruction, research, and communication by all members of the College community. A state-of-the-art campus network links all residence halls, classrooms, laboratories, offices, and the library to one another and to the global Internet. The Educational Technology Center was completed in 2002; it houses more than 100 computers and a variety of other teaching and technology resources that are used by students and faculty and staff members. The science laboratories at Reed are among the best equipped of any undergraduate college in the United States. These include the A. A. Knowlton Laboratory of Physics, the Arthur F. Scott Laboratory of Chemistry, and the L. E. Griffin Memorial Biology Building, where a recent $10-million renovation includes improved student thesis space, a tiered-seating classroom, and new teaching labs. Reed's research nuclear reactor (the only such reactor in the country that is staffed primarily by undergraduates) and radiochemistry lab are actively used for student research, instruction, and training. For those interested in the arts, the campus houses studio art facilities that recently saw a $2-million expansion, performing arts facilities, twenty instrumental practice rooms, a computer music laboratory, a recording system, and an 800-seat auditorium. Other popular facilities include a radio station and a modern sports center.

Costs

Tuition for 2007–08 was $36,190, and room and board were $9460. The student body fee was $230, bringing the yearly total cost to approximately $45,880. The cost of books and incidental expenses averages $2000.

Financial Aid

About half of the Reed student body receives financial assistance from the College. A full need-based financial aid program makes Reed accessible to students from a wide range of economic backgrounds. The College guarantees to meet the full demonstrated need of all continuing students in good academic standing who file their financial aid applications on time. Reed's own funds are the primary source of grants to students. The College budgeted more than $14 million for this purpose in 2007–08. The average amount awarded to each student receiving financial aid in 2007–08 was $32,154. Reed also administers federal grants and a variety of other awards. Perkins Loans and other federally subsidized loans are available, along with campus employment and work-study programs. The size of a financial aid award is based upon analysis of the student's need. The financial aid program includes grants, loans, and work opportunities.

Faculty

All classes at Reed are taught by professors, about 88 percent of whom hold the highest degree in their field. The average class has 15 students. Reed students point to the opportunity to work closely with faculty members as one of the great benefits of a Reed education. Reed faculty members point to the opportunity to work with students who are serious scholars as one of the great benefits of teaching at Reed. Faculty members commit themselves primarily to teaching, with scholarly and scientific research furthering this primary goal; they view students as partners in learning, often serving as coauthors and coinvestigators on professional papers and research projects. This close association is due, in large part, to a 10:1 student-faculty ratio and the one-on-one relationship between thesis adviser (a professor) and student during the senior year.

Student Government

The Student Senate is the central body in student governance. The Senate consists of the student body president, vice president, and 8 student representatives, all elected by the students. Its two primary functions are to allocate student body funds and to represent student interests and concerns to the faculty, administration, and Board of Trustees. The Senate distributes approximately $40,000 each semester to the many student organizations on campus. As agreed under the community constitution, students participate fully in discussions and decisions on a wide variety of issues. The Student Committee on Academic Policy and Planning participates in debate about the curriculum at Reed; many other committees, from the Library Board to the Reactor Committee, have substantial student input. The Senate and student body president make all student appointments to such committees.

Admission Requirements

Reed welcomes applications from freshman and transfer candidates who are genuinely committed to the pursuit of a liberal arts education and a rigorous academic program. Those applicants are admitted who, in the view of the Committee on Admission, are most likely to become successful members of and contribute significantly to the Reed community. The College is committed to maintaining a student body distinguished by its intellectual passion, yet diversified in its range of backgrounds, interests, and talents.

Admission decisions are based on many integrated factors, but academic accomplishments and talents are given the greatest weight in the selection process. A strong secondary school preparation, including honors and advanced courses where available, improves a student's chances for admission. Such a program usually includes 4 years of English, 3 years of a foreign or classical language, 3 to 4 years of mathematics through precalculus, 3 to 4 years of science, and 3 to 4 years of history or social studies. Given the wide variation in high school programs and quality, however, there are no fixed requirements for secondary school courses. Applicants are expected to have obtained a secondary school diploma prior to enrollment, although exceptions are occasionally made. There are no "cutoff points" for high school or college grades or for examination scores.

Reed recognizes the qualities of character—in particular, motivation, intellectual curiosity, individual responsibility, and social consciousness—as important considerations in the selection process, beyond a demonstrated commitment to academic excellence. Thus, the Committee on Admission looks for students whose accomplishments and interests in various fields of endeavor will contribute to the overall liveliness of the Reed community. Personal interviews, either on or off campus, are not a requirement in the admission process but are strongly recommended whenever possible. Applications for early decision should be submitted by November 15 (Option I) or January 2 (Option II), regular freshman admission by January 15, and transfer candidates by March 1.

Application and Information

The Office of Admission is open Monday through Friday, from 8:30 a.m. until 5 p.m. (Pacific time) all year, except for major holidays. Students may apply online at http://www.reed.edu/apply/apply_reed.html. For further information or to arrange a campus tour, overnight stay, information session, or interview, students should contact:

Office of Admission
Reed College
3203 Southeast Woodstock Boulevard
Portland, Oregon 97202-8199
Phone: 503-777-7511
800-547-4750 (toll-free)
Fax: 503-777-7553
E-mail: admission@reed.edu
Web site: http://www.reed.edu/

Shooting pool in the Pool Hall.

COLLEGE DATA CENTER • OREGON

SOUTHERN OREGON UNIVERSITY

ASHLAND, OREGON

The University

Southern Oregon University (SOU) is a contemporary public liberal arts and sciences university with a growing national reputation for excellence in teaching. It places student learning, inside and outside the classroom, at the heart of all programs and services. SOU is proud of its strengths in the sciences and humanities; its continuing tradition of preparing outstanding teachers, business leaders, and other select professionals; and its designation as Oregon's Center of Excellence in the Fine and Performing Arts. SOU was recently selected by the *New York Times* as one of higher education's "hidden gems," recognizing its commitment to excellence in undergraduate teaching and learning. SOU is also a member of the prestigious Council of Public Liberal Arts Colleges, recognizing the campus as a leader in providing a high-quality liberal arts education.

The University offers undergraduate majors in thirty-five areas of study, minors in fifty-two areas, and eleven graduate programs that include management, applied psychology, and several areas of study in education. SOU also offers certificates in accounting, applied cultural anthropology, applied finance and economics, botany, business information systems, cultural resource management, interactive marketing and e-commerce, management of human resources, and Native American studies. Students may take preprofessional programs for entry into medicine, engineering, agriculture, law, and theology. The University offers nursing through its association with the nationally ranked nursing school at the Oregon Health Sciences University. SOU has an excellent Honors Program as well.

The combination of high-quality academics and a beautiful environment attracts approximately 5,000 students. SOU features small class sizes and a student-faculty ratio of 19:1. Students have special opportunities for research and internships with government agencies, such as the National Fish and Wildlife Forensics Lab on campus; businesses, such as the Bear Creek Corporation in Medford; media, including Jefferson Public Radio; outstanding public schools; and arts organizations, such as the internationally renowned Oregon Shakespeare Festival. Students gain multicultural perspectives in classes, extracurricular activities, and the International Student Exchange and from 150 currently enrolled international students from thirty-three countries. SOU study-abroad programs span more than twenty countries.

SOU offers an impressive variety of extracurricular activities, clubs, and organizations. The University's newspaper, literary publication, honor societies, social issue groups, social clubs, and religious, preprofessional, international, and academic organizations provide students with multiple opportunities for involvement. Extreme sports, including skydiving, bungee jumping, rock climbing, kayaking, and mountain-bike racing, are very popular. More than 65 percent of the student body participates in intramural sports, and many compete in intercollegiate club sports, including skiing (Northern California Intercollegiate Conference), aikido, baseball, climbing, karate, rugby, soccer, swimming, tennis, and wrestling.

The University is a member of NAIA Division II. Women's varsity sports include basketball, cross-country, soccer, softball, tennis, track and field, and volleyball. Men's varsity sports include basketball, cross-country, football, track and field, and wrestling. The campus is a culturally dynamic and stimulating environment. Annual concerts bring world-class musicians and performers to the campus. The theater department has two seasons and performs before capacity crowds. Music groups include the concert and chamber choirs, vocal jazz ensemble, symphonic band, woodwind quintet, gamelan ensemble, saxophone quartets, clarinet ensemble, Rogue Valley symphony, and opera workshop. Five art galleries feature the work of students, faculty members, and locally, nationally, and internationally acclaimed artists. The International Writer Series attracts recognized writers, poets, and novelists from around the world.

Approximately 25 percent of the student body lives in one of fourteen residence halls or in family housing units. Freshmen are required to live on campus. The majority of students living off campus live in the immediate surrounding area. The track; the football field; volleyball, basketball, and tennis courts; climbing walls; a large swimming pool; dance studios; and the student fitness center are all nearby. The Cascade Food Court is open from 7 a.m. to 10 p.m. and offers a variety of healthy and delicious food choices for every range of tastes.

The University's Student ACCESS Center houses student support services, including counseling services, academic advising, career advising, disabled student services, a learning center, a testing center, and tutorial programs—all in one location.

Location

The University's beautiful 175-acre campus is located in the idyllic community of Ashland. SOU was named by *Outside* magazine as one of the "coolest places to work, study, and live," recognizing SOU for its beautiful campus, incredible location, and abundant outdoor activities. Home of the Oregon Shakespeare Festival, the town of 20,000 draws 385,000 visitors each year to enjoy the lively downtown, exquisite Lithia Park, and abundant theater, music events, and other cultural happenings. The Ashland area has five fairs, thirteen festivals, twenty-five art galleries, and twenty-four museums. The town itself has sixty lodging facilities and eighty restaurants. Colorful flags and banners announcing events create a festive environment, and the many boutiques, cafés, coffee shops, movie theaters, and bookstores create an ideal environment for college students. Mt. Ashland and the Siskiyou Mountains serve as the town's backdrop and offer cross-country skiing, downhill skiing, hiking, mountain biking, and snowboarding. The Cascade Mountains, Rogue and Klamath Rivers, Crater Lake National Park, and numerous lakes offer world-class whitewater rafting, camping, hiking, kayaking, rock climbing, and sailing.

Majors and Degrees

The University is organized into five schools: Arts and Letters, Business, Education, Sciences, and Social Science, Health, and Physical Education. Bachelor of Arts (B.A.) and Bachelor of Science (B.S.) degrees are available in the following majors: anthropology, art, arts and letters, biology, business administration† (accounting; hotel, restaurant, and resort management; management; marketing; small-business management), business-chemistry*, business-mathematics*, business-music*, business-physics*, chemistry†, communication† (human communication, journalism, media studies), computer science† (computer information science, computer programming and software, computer science and multimedia, computer security and information assurance), criminal justice†, early childhood development, economics†, education, English and writing†, environmental studies*, geography†, geology, health and physical education† (athletic training, health promotion and fitness management), history†, human services, interdisciplinary studies, international studies*, language and culture† (French, German, Spanish), mathematics†, mathematics–computer science*, music, nursing (with Oregon Health Sciences University), physics†, political science, psychology, science*, social science*, sociology, and theater arts. Bachelor of Fine Arts (B.F.A.) degrees are available in art and theater. (An * indicates interdisciplinary programs; majors with a † offer the accelerated-degree option.)

Preprofessional programs include agriculture, chiropractic medicine, dental hygiene, dentistry, engineering, law, medical technology, medicine, nursing, occupational therapy, optometry, pharmacy, physical therapy, physician's assistant studies, podiatry, resource management and conservation, theology, and veterinary medicine.

Minors include Africa–Middle East history; anthropology; applied multimedia; art history; biology; British literature; business administration; chemistry; communication; computer science; creative writing; criminology; economics; education; English education; European history; film studies; French; general studio art; geography; geology; German; hotel, restaurant, and resort management; human communication; interdisciplinary ethics; international peace studies; journalism; Latin American history; Latin American studies; media studies; mathematics; mathematics education; military science; music; Native American studies; philosophy; photography; physics; political science; psychology; public relations; Shakespeare studies; sociology; Spanish; theater arts; U.S. history; U.S. literature; video production; women's studies; and writing with professional applications.

Academic Programs

Students are required to complete general education requirements in addition to the major requirements. The general education requirements provide students with skills in effective communication, critical judgment, and research and cultivate an awareness of the social, artistic, cultural, and scientific traditions of civilization. The required freshman University Seminar provides a solid foundation in reading, writing, communication, and critical thinking. Class size is limited to 28 students, and the University Seminar professor also serves as their first-year adviser. Students in a four-year bachelor's program must have a minimum of 180 quarter credits to graduate. Students admitted to the Accelerated Baccalaureate Degree Program complete between 135 and 150 quarter credits to graduate.

Off-Campus Programs

Southern Oregon University offers a wide variety of study-abroad and overseas internship opportunities. The University also participates in National Student Exchange, which allows students to attend any of 140 colleges and universities nationwide and pay resident tuition.

Academic Facilities

The Hannon Library completed a significant expansion and renovation project in 2005. The 120,000-square-foot library houses a coffee shop, group study and seminar rooms, classrooms, comfortable study areas, and an art exhibit area. Other recent developments on the SOU campus include the Center for Visual Arts, a 66,000-square-foot complex of modern glass and steel that serves as a showplace for art exhibition and education; a newly acquired biotechnology center featuring state of-the-art molecular biology instrumentation; and the acclaimed Institute for Environmental, Economic and Civic Studies.

SOU provides a strong information technology environment. Students have access to twenty-three computer labs on SOU's campus. The Main Computing Services Center lab is open more than 80 hours a week and houses more than 200 PCs and Macs, as well as printers and scanners. Other discipline-based and multimedia labs offer additional resources. Residence halls have labs, and student rooms are wired for computer access. Altogether, there are more than 600 workstations on the campus accessible to students. E-mail accounts, data storage, and access to the Internet are free of charge. The campus also offers extensive wireless Internet access.

Costs

For full-time undergraduate students taking 12 credits per term, 2006–07 tuition and fees were $5135 for residents and $15,478 for nonresidents. As a member of the Western Undergraduate Exchange, SOU offers most academic programs to residents of Alaska, Arizona, California, Colorado, Hawaii, Idaho, Montana, Nevada, New Mexico, North Dakota, South Dakota, Utah, Washington, and Wyoming for approximately $7703 (150 percent of the cost of in-state tuition and fees). Room and board costs, including a double room and the medium meal plan, were $6951. These prices are estimates at the time of printing and are subject to change.

Financial Aid

Financial aid is available in the form of grants, loans, and/or work-study. Approximately 65 percent of freshmen receive some form of financial aid. Students must file the Free Application for Federal Student Aid (FAFSA) to qualify. To be considered for financial aid at Southern Oregon University, students must have applied to the University for admission and have indicated the institution as one of their first six choices on the FAFSA. Students should mail the FAFSA by February 1 to receive maximum consideration for fall. The University offers merit and diversity scholarships to new freshmen and transfer students. Additional scholarships are available through departments and the Office of Financial Aid. For more information, students should contact the Financial Aid Office at 541-552-6161 or go online to http://www.sou.edu/finaid. For those seeking employment, the Student Employment Office lists the work-study and regular jobs available on and off campus.

Faculty

Ninety-three percent of the faculty members have Ph.D.'s or the highest degree in their field. There are more than 200 full-time faculty members, whose primary emphasis is on teaching and advising undergraduate students. Faculty members frequently include undergraduates in research projects, and many students have coauthored papers and made joint presentations at national conferences. Every student is assigned an adviser when they declare a major; freshmen have their University Seminar professor as their adviser.

Student Government

The Associated Students' governing body implements policies, makes budget recommendations, and participates in the allocation of more than $1.4 million each year to various clubs and organizations. They also work with the Oregon Student Association on issues important in higher education. Elected, appointed, and volunteer positions offer students valuable leadership experience.

Admission Requirements

Applicants for freshman admission must have achieved a minimum 2.75 cumulative high school GPA or a minimum combined math and critical reading score of 1010 on the SAT Reasoning Test or an ACT composite score of at least 21. In addition, applicants must have completed the following high school course requirements (with grades of C- or better, beginning with the high school graduating class of 2005): 4 years of English, 3 years of mathematics (including geometry, algebra I, and algebra II), 3 years of social science, 2 years of science (one of which must have a lab), and 2 years of one foreign language.

Students transferring from an accredited college or university must have earned at least 36 quarter credits of transfer-level credit with a minimum 2.25 GPA and, if a high school graduate of 1997 or later, meet the language requirement. Transfer applicants with less than 36 quarter credits must also meet the freshman admission requirements.

Home-schooled students and graduates of nonstandard or unaccredited high schools are eligible for admission if they meet the following requirements: a minimum combined math and critical reading score of 1010 on the SAT Reasoning Test and a score of at least 470 on the SAT Writing Test or a minimum score of 21 on the ACT. These students must also score an average of 470 or above (940 total) on two SAT Subject Tests (Math Level I or IIC and another test of the student's choice). These students must also satisfy the second-language admission requirement if they graduated from a high school in 1997 or later.

Application and Information

Applicants must submit an application with a $50 nonrefundable application fee and official transcripts from each high school and/or university or college attended. Freshmen must submit official SAT or ACT scores. Students may apply after September 1 for the following academic year. Admission is rolling, but the priority deadline for the fall is June 1. Students may apply using the paper application or online at http://www.sou.edu/admissions.

A campus visit is encouraged. Tours are offered at the Office of Admissions, Monday through Friday at 10 a.m. and 2 p.m. and on select Saturdays at 11 a.m. by appointment. For a tour or more information and summer tour hours, students should contact SOU at:

Office of Admissions
Southern Oregon University
1250 Siskiyou Boulevard
Ashland, Oregon 97520
Phone: 541-552-6411
800-482-7672 (toll-free in Oregon and from area codes 916, 707, and 530)
E-mail: admissions@sou.edu
Web site: http://www.sou.edu

UNIVERSITY OF OREGON

EUGENE, OREGON

UNIVERSITY OF OREGON

The University

The University of Oregon (UO) provides an excellent academic environment that empowers students to go forth into the world and create change in any field, on any scale. For students who want to engage their minds and use their education to move the world, UO is a perfect place to start.

The University has 272 academic programs, many of which are internationally recognized for academic excellence. The College of Education, the architecture program, and the biochemistry, chemistry, economics, English, molecular biology, neuroscience, physics, psychology, and sports marketing departments all rank among the top 10 in the U.S. The UO's School of Journalism and Communication, College of Business, and programs in comparative literature, finance, historic preservation, and mathematics rank in the top 20 in the U.S. The recognition of the University as a best buy in higher education by three national ranking organizations speaks to both the reasonable cost and academic excellence of the University of Oregon.

At the UO, students learn to see the world differently by experiencing culture and language firsthand. UO graduates are uniquely prepared to enter the global job market through 140 study-abroad programs and 100 language-study options on campus. The University has been recognized by the American Council on Education as one of the country's leaders in internationalization—more than 14 percent of the student body studies abroad in more than eighty countries around the world. Students attend classes alongside others from all fifty states, four U.S. territories, and eighty-four other countries. The Global Graduate internship program provides graduates with job placement at international firms and organizations to gain professional experience and global understanding.

Campus buildings date from 1876, when Deady Hall opened, to 2007, with the opening of the new Lokey Integrative Science Complex. The UO campus is also an arboretum, featuring more than 500 species of trees.

The University offers students more than 250 different student organizations, including political, environmental, professional, cultural heritage, performing arts, religious, and service organizations. Intercollegiate athletics, club sports, and intramurals offer students several levels at which to participate in athletics. The UO is a member of the PAC-10 Conference (NCAA Division I) and sponsors ten women's teams, including basketball, lacrosse, soccer, and volleyball, and eight men's teams, including football, golf, and tennis.

UO graduates have gone on to become leaders in environmental law, violence prevention, public service, educational reform, scientific discovery, investigative journalism, performing arts, and many other spheres of influence. The University is among the top universities in the U.S. for Peace Corps volunteers, student voter registration, and the number of graduates who hold high-ranking military offices. The question for prospective students, should they choose to become a part of the UO legacy, is not whether they can change the world, but what world they want to change.

Location

The 295-acre campus is located in the center of Eugene, Oregon, a small city with a metropolitan area population of 256,380, bordered by pristine wilderness areas. The city is small enough to bike across but large enough to offer plenty of cafés and clubs. Eugene is a community known for its commitment to activism, outdoor recreation, arts, and culture. The active arts and music scene brings major acts to Eugene throughout the year. The University is located in a vast outdoor recreation area, with hundreds of miles of bike paths and hiking trails inside the city limits. With the Pacific Ocean an hour to the west and the Cascade Mountains an hour to the east, students have surfing, skiing, snowboarding, river rafting, and rock climbing practically in their own backyard. The Outdoor Program, ranked number 1 in the country, takes advantage of the University's unique location and offers a host of wilderness adventures. Eugene is served by several major airlines and is on the main north-south Amtrak line, which runs between Seattle and San Diego.

Majors and Degrees

The University is organized into the College of Arts and Sciences and six professional schools and colleges (School of Architecture and Allied Arts, Lundquist College of Business, School of Law, College of Education, School of Journalism and Communication, and School of Music). The College of Arts and Sciences serves as a base for a liberal arts education and offers majors in anthropology, Asian studies, biochemistry, biology, chemistry, Chinese, classical civilization, classics, comparative literature, computer and information science, economics, English, environmental science, environmental studies, ethnic studies, French, general science, geography, geological sciences, German, Greek, history, humanities, human physiology, independent study, international studies, Italian, Japanese, Judaic studies, Latin, linguistics, marine biology, mathematics, mathematics and computer science, philosophy, physics, political science, psychology, religious studies, Romance languages, Russian, Russian and East European studies, sociology, Spanish, theater arts, and women's and gender studies. Preparatory programs in the College of Arts and Sciences include business administration, dental hygiene, dentistry, engineering, forensic science, health sciences, law, library science, medical technology, medicine, nursing, occupational therapy, optometry, pharmacy, physical therapy, physician assistant studies, podiatry, social work, teacher education, and veterinary medicine.

The School of Architecture and Allied Arts offers degree programs in architecture, art, art history, ceramics, community arts, digital arts, fibers, historic preservation, interior architecture, landscape architecture, metalsmithing and jewelry, material and product studies, multimedia design, nonprofit administration, painting, photography, planning, printmaking, product design, public policy and management, sculpture, and visual design. The Lundquist College of Business undergraduate program ranks in the top 2 percent of all public universities in the United States, offering majors in accounting, business administration (with concentrations in corporate accounting, entrepreneurship and small business, finance, management, marketing, and sports business), and global management. The School of Journalism and Communication is nationally accredited and offers journalism majors in advertising, communication studies, electronic media, magazine journalism, news–editorial journalism, and public relations. The School of Education offers majors in communication disorders and sciences, educational studies, family and human services, special education, and teacher education*. The School of Music offers degrees in dance, jazz studies, and music (with concentrations in music composition, music education, music education: elementary education, music performance, and music theory). An * denotes preparatory programs.

Academic Programs

In addition to their majors, students must complete general education requirements in the liberal arts and sciences. Students spend about one third of their academic careers on each of three areas of course work: the general requirements, requirements for their major, and their electives or the requirements for completing a minor or a second major. The University is on a quarter system.

First-year programs are an excellent option for new students. First-year Interest Groups (FIGs) bring together a small group of freshmen interested in the same academic area in three related courses. Freshman Seminars are small-group discussion courses taught by some of the University's most outstanding faculty members. Both programs emulate a small-college experience and help first-year students begin their academic career with a solid start.

Off-Campus Programs

The UO offers students overseas opportunities in eighty countries that include Australia, Austria, Belize, Botswana, Cameroon, China, Costa Rica, Cote d'Ivoire, Cuba, the Czech Republic, Denmark, Ecuador, England, Finland, France, Germany, Ghana, Greece, Hungary, India, Israel, Italy, Jamaica, Japan, Jordan, Kenya, Madagascar, Mali, Mexico, Morocco, New Zealand, Norway, Poland, Russia, Scotland, Senegal, South Africa, South Korea, Spain, Sweden, Tanzania, Thailand, Turkey, Uganda, Vietnam, Zimbabwe, and the independent states of the former USSR. Students may study for a maximum of one year at a university overseas, earning UO course credit. The University also participates in the National Student Exchange program, through which students may attend any of 173 colleges or universities in another state and pay that state's resident tuition.

Academic Facilities

The University of Oregon library system consists of the Knight Library, law library, and four branch libraries (science, mathematics, architecture and allied arts, and map and aerial photography). The library system has more than 2 million volumes and subscribes to more than 17,000 journals.

Information Services provides central computing facilities and services, including the VMS cluster for interactive research and several instructional and open-access laboratories that provide connection to network resources. The Yamada Language Center is equipped with state-of-the-art computer-aided audiovisual equipment.

Costs

Resident undergraduate tuition for the 2007–08 academic year was $6174 and nonresident undergraduate tuition was $19,338. On-campus residence halls, including room and board, cost $7848 per academic year for double occupancy.

Financial Aid

Financial aid is available in the form of grants, loans, and/or work-study. To qualify, students must file the Free Application for Federal Student Aid (FAFSA). To be considered for financial aid at the UO, students must have applied for admission to the University and should indicate the UO as one of their first six choices. The UO awards financial aid based on individual need. Scholarships are awarded through the University, academic departments, and private sources. The general University scholarship application is due by January 15. For information on financial aid or scholarships and for applications, students should contact the Office of Student Financial Aid, 1278 University of Oregon, or call 800-760-6955 (toll-free).

For those seeking employment on or off campus, the Office of Student Employment provides several services, both for students who qualify for work-study and for those who do not qualify.

Faculty

At the UO, the student-teacher ratio is 18:1 and the median class size is 22 students. Students have access to teachers who are recognized for their outstanding teaching skills and renowned for their original research. Among them are winners of every major UO teaching award and every major recognition given for research and scholarship, including the Fulbright, Rhodes, Woodrow Wilson, Guggenheim, MacArthur, National Science Foundation, American Council of Learned Societies, and National Endowment for the Humanities awards, as well as membership in the National Academy of Sciences.

Student Government

The Associated Students of the University of Oregon (ASUO) administers a budget of $9.5 million, financing a broad range of academic, political, ethnic, religious, and recreational programs. The ASUO is part of the governing body of the University and also works as a lobbying organization at the state and national levels.

Admission Requirements

To be considered for admission, students must have a minimum high school GPA of 3.0, complete at least fourteen total college-preparatory units, be a graduate of a standard or accredited high school, and submit SAT or ACT scores. For guaranteed admission, applicants must have a minimum high school GPA of 3.25, have at least sixteen total college-preparatory units, and meet the other admission requirements.

Required college-preparatory courses include English, 4 years (English language, literature, speaking and listening, writing); mathematics, 3 years (first-year algebra, 2 additional years of college-preparatory mathematics); science, 2 years; social science, 3 years (1 year of U.S. history, 1 year of global studies such as world history or geography, one elective); and a second language (2 years in one language).

For students who meet the minimum admission standards, UO next looks at such factors as the quality of course work, grade trend, class rank, and senior-year course work. Academic potential and special talents are also considered.

Students with a GPA below 3.0 or who have fewer than 16 total academic units must submit a one-page personal statement with their application.

To be considered as a transfer student, a student must have earned 36 or more quarter hours (24 semester hours) of college transfer credit and have a minimum GPA of 2.25 if an Oregon resident, or 2.5 if a nonresident. Transfer students must have completed one college-level English composition course and one college-level math course (with a prerequisite of intermediate algebra or above) with a grade of C or better. Transfer applicants who do not meet regular admission requirements may be admitted on a special basis and should contact the Office of Admissions for information.

Applicants must submit an application with a $50 nonrefundable application fee, transcripts from each high school and/or college or university attended, and, for freshmen, SAT or ACT scores.

A campus visit is the best way to decide whether the University of Oregon is right for a student. Tours and information sessions are offered twice daily, Monday through Friday, and once on Saturday mornings. Prospective students should visit the University's Web site for more information.

Application and Information

Students may apply any time after September 1 for the following academic year. The freshman application deadline is January 15. The transfer application deadline is May 15. Students planning to enter programs in architecture, fine and applied arts, interior architecture, landscape architecture, or music should inquire directly to the appropriate department or to the Office of Admissions for early deadlines.

For information and an application, students should contact:

Office of Admissions
1217 University of Oregon
Eugene, Oregon 97403-1217
Phone: 541-346-3201
800-BE-A-DUCK (toll-free)
Web site: http://admissions.uoregon.edu

WARNER PACIFIC COLLEGE

PORTLAND, OREGON

The College

Warner Pacific College prepares the next generation of leaders by providing educational experiences in the liberal arts, purposefully taught with a Christian worldview. Its academic programs encourage students to explore life's most significant questions and learn to manage complex answers. The distinctive humanities core curriculum is designed to explore the paradoxes inherent in the human experience through a foundation of faith. Most importantly, Warner Pacific's liberal arts program equips students to lead and serve in a world challenged by a rapidly changing cultural landscape.

Since its founding in 1937, Warner Pacific has developed a diverse liberal arts curriculum. Today, more than twenty-two majors and twenty-seven minors are offered as well as a certificate in family life education, endorsements in six areas of teacher education, four preprofessional programs, an adult degree program, and six master's programs, opening the doors to more than a thousand possible futures.

Students are challenged in the classroom and encouraged to develop leadership skills by participating in on-campus activities and completing internships with organizations throughout the Portland metropolitan area. Applying theory to real life, students are able to maximize their learning experience. In addition, students are empowered to impact their world for Christ by serving in their community and beyond—consequently, Warner Pacific students tutor young children, visit the elderly, work with the homeless, and participate in many other worthwhile projects. Opportunities are also available for study-abroad programs through Warner Pacific's partnership with the Coalition for Christian Colleges and Universities.

The Warner Pacific campus is alive with activity, including residence life events aimed at building community, intramurals, drama, music, multicultural events, and ethics-bowl competition. Warner Pacific is a member of the National Association of Intercollegiate Athletics (NAIA Division II) and the Cascade Collegiate Conference. Women's sports include basketball, cross-country, golf, soccer, track and field, and volleyball. Men compete in basketball, cross-country, golf, soccer, and track and field. In 2004 and 2006, the women's basketball team achieved national ranking, successfully competing in the NAIA Division II national tournament. The men's basketball team has been nationally ranked since 2005, with appearances in the Sweet 16 of the NAIA Division II national tournament for three years in a row.

Total enrollment at Warner Pacific exceeds 832, with students representing eighteen states, nine countries, and twenty-seven denominations. All student residences have been remodeled since 2006; options include traditional men's and women's residence halls, apartments, and houses. Residence rooms offer private phones and individual high-speed Internet connections. Wireless Internet connections are available for students throughout the campus.

Graduate programs are available that lead to a Master of Education, a Master of Arts in biblical and theological studies, and a Master of Religion. A Master of Science in management and organizational leadership, a Master of Accounting, and a Master of Teaching are available through the Adult Degree Program.

Location

Warner Pacific is an urban campus adjacent to 195-acre Mt. Tabor Park, just 10 minutes from downtown Portland, Oregon. Situated in the beautiful Pacific Northwest, the city of Portland was named one of the best places to live in the U.S. by CNN, *Money*, and *Outside* magazines and the greenest city in the U.S. according to SustainLane.com. It is consistently listed in the top 10 for walking, biking, and other fitness activities. In fact, Portland is known as "FitTown, USA" according to *Fit* magazine. With reliable bus and light-rail transportation available, students are able to take advantage of diverse cultural, recreational, employment, and internship opportunities. Snow-capped mountains, rugged coastlines, and the Columbia Gorge are all an hour away, where students enjoy skiing, hiking, kayaking, windsurfing, and exploring nature.

Majors and Degrees

Warner Pacific offers Associate of Arts (A.A.) and Associate of Science (A.S.) degrees as well as Bachelor of Arts (B.A.) and Bachelor of Science (B.S.) degrees. Majors in American studies, English, history, liberal studies, music, music and youth ministries, and religion and Christian ministries lead to the B.A. degree. Majors in accounting, biological science, business administration, developmental psychology, early childhood/elementary education, health and human kinetics, human development, human development and family studies, middle/high school education, music business, music education, physical science, psychology, social science, and social work lead to the B.S. degree.

A.A. degrees are offered in Christian education, general studies, organizational dynamics (through the Adult Degree Program), and youth ministries. A.S. degrees are offered in business administration, health sciences, and social sciences.

The Teacher Education Program is approved by the Oregon Teacher Standards and Practices Commission. The curriculum provides a Christian liberal arts education along with preparation in a teaching specialty. Extended field-based practicums and student-teaching experiences are an integral part of the program. Warner Pacific graduates have established an excellent reputation in the education community and are employed both nationally and internationally.

Academic Programs

In order to provide Christian excellence and an individualized education, students take courses in three categories: core studies, a major area of study, and elective credits. In general, each of these categories requires a third of a student's total program. A minor may be chosen as a part of the elective program. Unique at Warner Pacific is the humanities core curriculum, which is based on an interdisciplinary approach to learning designed to explore the ethical and pragmatic dilemmas of the human experience.

Course work to complete a bachelor's degree is available during the summer. In addition, the Adult Degree Program makes it possible for qualified adult learners to earn a Bachelor of Science in business administration or human development within a nontraditional course design and evening schedule. It is also possible for students at Warner Pacific to personalize their education by designing their own major.

The College operates on a semester calendar. The core studies include a minimum of 42 semester credits divided among specific requirements in communications, humanities, religion, mathematics, laboratory science, social science, fine arts, and physical education/health. The major area of study requires completion of certain courses as specified in the College course catalog. The remainder of the credits may be earned through elective course work and/or a minor concentration, for a total of 124 semester credit hours.

Off-Campus Programs

Through the Oregon Independent Colleges Association, Warner Pacific has cooperative relationships with all of the regionally accredited private colleges and universities in the state. In addition, Warner Pacific accepts the completed Associate of Arts transfer degree from Oregon community colleges and the Associate of Arts direct transfer agreement (DTA) degree from Clark College in Vancouver, Washington, as having fulfilled the core requirements, with the exception of two religion and two upper-division humanities courses.

ROTC programs are available in cooperation with the University of Portland; study opportunities and laboratory access at the Oregon Health Sciences University in Portland are also available. The College participates in a consortium of colleges that maintains the Malheur (eastern Oregon) High Desert Study Center and is a member of the Council for Christian Colleges and Universities, which provides study opportunities in Oxford, England; Cairo, Egypt; Israel (Middle East Studies); Russia; Latin America; China; Sydney, Australia; Uganda; Los Angeles, California (Film Studies); Martha's Vineyard (Contemporary Music Studies); and Washington, D.C. (American Studies).

Academic Facilities

The Otto F. Linn Library provides study areas and housing for a collection of nearly 60,000 books and 450 periodicals. Access to more than 27,000,000 volumes is available through the Orbis Cascade Alliance, a computer network that links the College with major public and private university collections in Oregon and Washington. Two biology, one physics, and two chemistry labs and an electron microscope are available. A large performing arts auditorium features concerts and other performances and the Cellar Theatre delivers teacher- and student-led dramatic productions. There is a student computer lab as well as modem access in every student residence and wireless access in academic buildings.

Costs

Annual costs for the 2008–09 academic year are $16,000 for tuition (12 to 18 credits per semester) and $6328 for room and board.

Financial Aid

Warner Pacific believes that any student who demonstrates the ability and motivation to learn should have access to Christian higher education; therefore, the staff is committed to helping parents and students find the necessary financial resources through federal and state assistance, personal and federally insured loans, private scholarships and programs, institutional assistance, and parental and student contributions. Approximately 97 percent of Warner Pacific students receive some type of aid, whether institutional or otherwise. In order to determine the amount of assistance a student qualifies for, the Financial Aid Office should receive a completed Free Application for Federal Student Aid (FAFSA) by April 15.

The College manages nearly $3 million in institutional assistance each year in the form of competitive academic merit scholarships and fellowships, talent grants in athletics, drama, music, international student awards, assistance designed to enhance ethnic diversity on campus, various types of church-related assistance (including a $1000 grant to members of the Church of God, which is headquartered in Anderson, Indiana), and awards for dependents of alumni. The scholarship priority application deadline is February 1. Students may be eligible to work on campus and are assisted in locating employment off campus.

Faculty

Warner Pacific faculty members are committed to excellence. With a 12:1 student-faculty ratio and small class sizes, students receive the individualized attention that meaningful scholarship requires. Each course is embedded with critical ethical issues relevant to the subject matter. Students are challenged to think critically and reflect deeply to find their place in an increasingly complex world. Students thrive under the leadership of dedicated professors, many of whom serve as mentors, academic advisers, and advisers to student organizations and clubs.

Student Government

Democratic self-government is essential to the development of maturity, judgment, and leadership. Student life at Warner Pacific mirrors this process. Students, administration, and faculty members enter into this process by mutual consent. The Associated Students of Warner Pacific College (ASWPC) is the executive body, composed of duly elected and appointed officers and representatives. The ASWPC, operating under its own grant of powers, creates policy that contributes to the governance of student life and activities and organizes such activities. It develops and coordinates an active social and spiritual life program to meet the needs of all students.

Admission Requirements

Warner Pacific College selects candidates for admissions who value a Christ-centered liberal arts education and provide evidence of academic achievement, aptitude, and the ability to benefit from and contribute to the opportunities at the College. Graduation from an accredited high school (or the test equivalent) is required for admission. A strong college-preparatory program is recommended. A minimum GPA of 2.5 along with a combined SAT score (critical reading and math) of at least 910 or an ACT composite score of at least 19 is required. The GPA of first-time freshmen averages 3.3. The average combined SAT score is 1010, and the average composite ACT score is 22. Official transcripts from each high school, college, or university attended should be sent directly from the institution to the Office of Admissions. An essay and signed community covenant is also required, along with a nonrefundable application fee of $50. A personal interview and references may be required. Students with a GPA of less than 2.5 may be considered for provisional acceptance. Transfer students with more than 20 semester credit hours are required to have a minimum 2.0 cumulative college GPA (4.0 scale).

Application and Information

Warner Pacific has a priority deadline of January 31 and a regular deadline of March 15. Applications are also accepted on a rolling basis throughout the calendar year. The following must be supplied in order for a student to be considered for admission: the application (including a signed community covenant and the nonrefundable $50 fee), a personal essay, an official transcript from high school and each college/university attended, as well as official SAT or ACT scores. Applicants can expect official notification of acceptance status within 24 hours of receipt of ALL required materials. Requests for further information and all forms should be addressed to:

Admissions Office
Warner Pacific College
2219 Southeast 68th Avenue
Portland, Oregon 97215
Phone: 503-517-1020
800-804-1510 (toll-free)
Fax: 503-517-1352
E-mail: admissions@warnerpacific.edu
Web site: http://www.warnerpacific.edu

PENNSYLVANIA

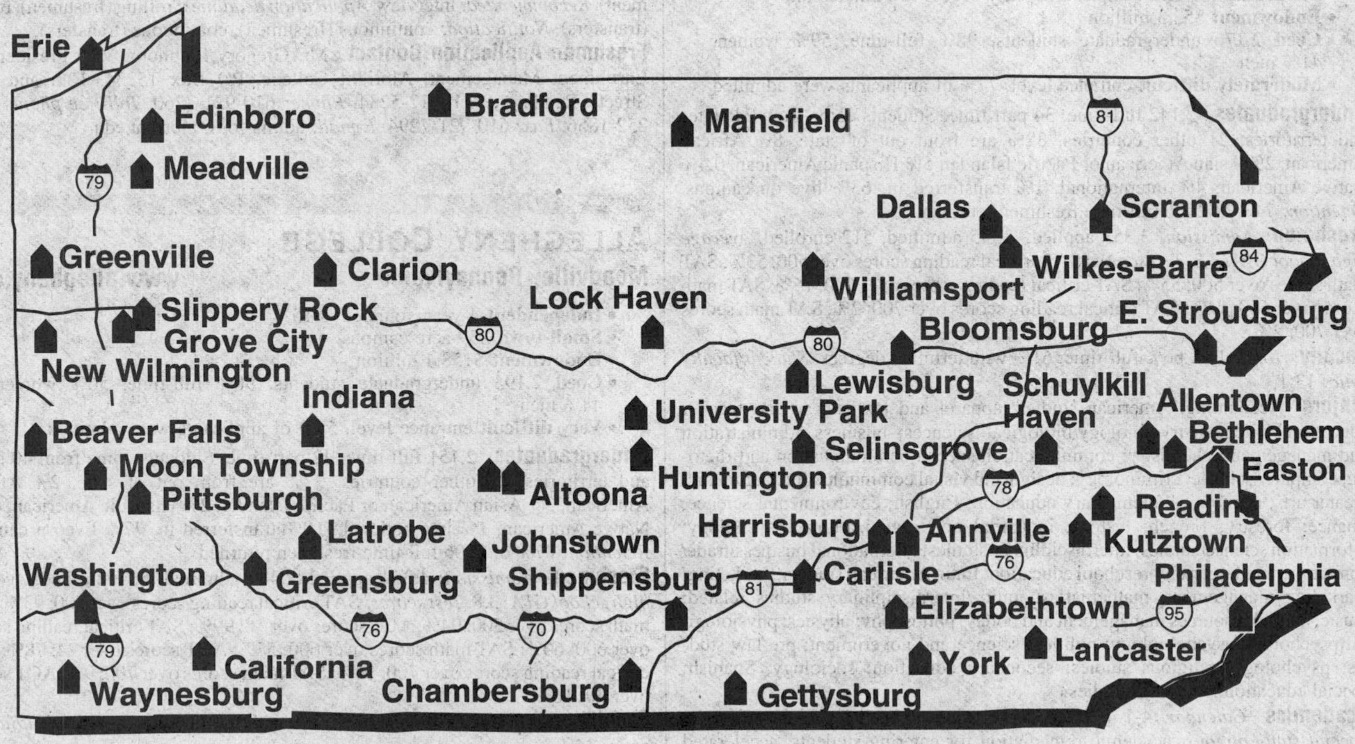

The Philadelphia area includes the towns of Abington, Aston, Bryn Athyn, Bryn Mawr, Chester, Cheyney, Collegeville, Doylestown, Glenside, Gwynedd Valley, Haverford, Immaculata, Langhorne, Media, Melrose Park, Phoenixville, Radnor, Rosemont, St. Davids, Swarthmore, Villanova, West Chester, and Wynnewood.

The Allentown area includes the towns of Center Valley, Fogelsville, and Lincoln University.

The Altoona area includes the towns of Cresson and Loretto.

The Lancaster area includes the town of Millersville.

The Harrisburg area includes the town of Grantham and Middletown.

The Scranton area includes the town of Clarks Summit.

ALBRIGHT COLLEGE

Reading, Pennsylvania **www.albright.edu/**

- **Independent** comprehensive, founded 1856, affiliated with United Methodist Church
- **Suburban** 118-acre campus with easy access to Philadelphia
- **Endowment** $53.3 million
- **Coed** 2,176 undergraduate students, 98% full-time, 59% women, 41% men
- **Moderately difficult** entrance level, 77% of applicants were admitted

Undergraduates 2,142 full-time, 34 part-time. Students come from 24 states and territories, 21 other countries, 32% are from out of state, 8% African American, 2% Asian American or Pacific Islander, 5% Hispanic American, 0.4% Native American, 4% international, 1% transferred in, 63% live on campus. *Retention:* 74% of 2006 full-time freshmen returned.

Freshmen *Admission:* 3,353 applied, 2,595 admitted, 512 enrolled. *Average high school GPA:* 3.3. *Test scores:* SAT critical reading scores over 500: 53%; SAT math scores over 500: 55%; SAT critical reading scores over 600: 15%; SAT math scores over 600: 14%; SAT critical reading scores over 700: 2%; SAT math scores over 700: 2%.

Faculty *Total:* 163, 66% full-time, 61% with terminal degrees. *Student/faculty ratio:* 13:1.

Majors Accounting; American studies; apparel and textiles; art; art teacher education; biochemistry; biology/biological sciences; business administration and management; chemistry; communication/speech communication and rhetoric; computer science; criminology; design and visual communications; dramatic/theater arts; economics; elementary education; English; environmental science; finance; forestry; French; history; industrial and organizational psychology; information science/studies; interdisciplinary studies; international business/trade/commerce; kindergarten/preschool education; Latin American studies; marketing/marketing management; mathematics; multi-/interdisciplinary studies related; music; natural resources management and policy; philosophy; physics; physiological psychology/psychobiology; political science and government; pre-law studies; psychology; religious studies; secondary education; sociology; Spanish; special education; women's studies.

Academics *Calendar:* 4-1-4. *Degrees:* certificates, bachelor's, and master's. *Special study options:* academic remediation for entering students, accelerated degree program, advanced placement credit, English as a second language, honors programs, independent study, internships, off-campus study, part-time degree program, services for LD students, student-designed majors, study abroad, summer session for credit. *Unusual degree programs:* 3-2 forestry with Duke University; natural resource management with University of Michigan.

Computers on Campus 800 computers/terminals and 1,600 ports are available on campus for general student use. Students can access the following: campus intranet, computer help desk, free student e-mail accounts, online (class) grades, online (class) registration, online (class) schedules. Campuswide network is available. 100% of college-owned or -operated housing units are wired for high-speed Internet access. Wireless service is available via entire campus.

Student Life *Housing:* on-campus residence required through sophomore year. *Options:* coed, men-only, women-only. Campus housing is university owned. Freshman campus housing is guaranteed. *Activities and organizations:* drama/theater group, student-run newspaper, radio and television station, choral group, Campus Center Board, Student Government Association, yearbook, newspaper, radio station, national fraternities, national sororities. *Campus security:* 24-hour emergency response devices and patrols, student patrols, late-night transport/escort service, controlled dormitory access. *Student services:* health clinic, personal/psychological counseling, women's center.

Athletics Member NCAA. All Division III. *Intercollegiate sports:* badminton W, baseball M, basketball M/W, cheerleading M/W, cross-country running M/W, field hockey W, football M, golf M, lacrosse M (c)/W (c), rugby M (c)/W (c), soccer M/W, softball W, swimming and diving M/W, tennis M/W, track and field M/W, volleyball W, water polo M (c)/W (c). *Intramural sports:* badminton M/W, basketball M/W, football M, softball M/W, ultimate Frisbee M/W, volleyball M/W.

Standardized Tests *Required:* SAT or ACT (for admission).

Costs (2007–08) *Comprehensive fee:* $37,368 includes full-time tuition ($28,084), mandatory fees ($800), and room and board ($8484). Full-time tuition and fees vary according to program. Part-time tuition: $1435 per course. Part-time tuition and fees vary according to class time. *College room only:* $4830. Room and board charges vary according to board plan and housing facility. *Payment plan:* installment. *Waivers:* children of alumni, adult students, senior citizens, and employees or children of employees.

Financial Aid Of all full-time matriculated undergraduates who enrolled in 2005, 710 applied for aid, 476 were judged to have need, 242 had their need fully met. 548 Federal Work-Study jobs (averaging $1308). 394 state and other part-time jobs (averaging $1391). In 2005, 311 non-need-based awards were made. *Average financial aid package:* $18,291. *Average need-based loan:* $4367. *Average need-based gift aid:* $14,400. *Average non-need-based aid:* $12,601. *Average indebtedness upon graduation:* $30,992.

Applying *Options:* electronic application, early admission, deferred entrance. *Application fee:* $25. *Required:* essay or personal statement, high school transcript, 1 letter of recommendation, secondary school report (guidance department). *Recommended:* interview. *Application deadlines:* rolling (freshmen), rolling (transfers). *Notification:* continuous (freshmen), continuous (transfers).

Freshman Application Contact Mr. Gregory Eichhorn, Vice President for Enrollment Management, Albright College, PO Box 15234, 13th and Bern Streets, Reading, PA 19612-5234. *Phone:* 610-921-7260. *Toll-free phone:* 800-252-1856. *Fax:* 610-921-7294. *E-mail:* admission@albright.edu.

ALLEGHENY COLLEGE

Meadville, Pennsylvania **www.allegheny.edu/**

- **Independent** 4-year, founded 1815
- **Small-town** 259-acre campus
- **Endowment** $158.4 million
- **Coed** 2,193 undergraduate students, 98% full-time, 56% women, 44% men
- **Very difficult** entrance level, 57% of applicants were admitted

Undergraduates 2,151 full-time, 42 part-time. Students come from 40 states and territories, 32 other countries, 37% are from out of state, 2% African American, 3% Asian American or Pacific Islander, 2% Hispanic American, 0.2% Native American, 1% international, 0.9% transferred in, 77% live on campus. *Retention:* 87% of 2006 full-time freshmen returned.

Freshmen *Admission:* 4,354 applied, 2,487 admitted, 584 enrolled. *Average high school GPA:* 3.8. *Test scores:* SAT critical reading scores over 500: 93%; SAT math scores over 500: 94%; ACT scores over 18: 99%; SAT critical reading scores over 600: 60%; SAT math scores over 600: 57%; ACT scores over 24: 78%; SAT critical reading scores over 700: 14%; SAT math scores over 700: 9%; ACT scores over 30: 16%.

Faculty *Total:* 169, 86% full-time, 82% with terminal degrees. *Student/faculty ratio:* 14:1.

Majors Applied economics; art; art history, criticism and conservation; biochemistry; biology/biological sciences; business/managerial economics; chemistry; communication/speech communication and rhetoric; computer science; computer software engineering; creative writing; dramatic/theater arts; economics; education; English; environmental science; environmental studies; fine arts related; fine/studio arts; French; geology/earth science; German; health/medical preparatory programs related; history; international/global studies; international relations and affairs; journalism; mass communication/media; mathematics; multi-/interdisciplinary studies related; music; music performance; neuroscience; philosophy; physics; political science and government; pre-dentistry studies; pre-law studies; pre-medical studies; pre-nursing studies; pre-pharmacy studies; pre-veterinary studies; psychology; religious studies; Spanish; technical and business writing; women's studies.

Academics *Calendar:* semesters. *Degree:* bachelor's. *Special study options:* advanced placement credit, double majors, English as a second language, independent study, internships, off-campus study, services for LD students, student-designed majors, study abroad. *Unusual degree programs:* 3-2 engineering with Columbia University, Case Western Reserve University, Duke University, Washington University, University of Pittsburgh; nursing with Case Western Reserve University; public policy, health care policy, information systems management at Carnegie Mellon University; physician assistant at Chatham.

Computers on Campus 311 computers/terminals and 200 ports are available on campus for general student use. Students can access the following: campus intranet, computer help desk, free student e-mail accounts, online (class) registration, online (class) schedules, online room selection, placement testing, course catalog, class lists, book buy, repair service, transcript review and ordering. Campuswide network is available. 100% of college-owned or -operated housing units are wired for high-speed Internet access. Wireless service is available via computer centers, computer labs, learning centers, libraries, student centers.

Student Life *Housing:* on-campus residence required through junior year. *Options:* coed, men-only, women-only, disabled students. Campus housing is university owned. Freshman campus housing is guaranteed. *Activities and organizations:* drama/theater group, student-run newspaper, radio and television station, choral group, student government, Gators Activity Programming, Orchesis Dance Company, Outing Club, Greek life, national fraternities, national sororities. *Campus security:* 24-hour emergency response devices and patrols, student patrols, late-night transport/escort service, controlled dormitory access, local police patrol. *Student services:* health clinic, personal/psychological counseling.

Athletics Member NCAA. All Division III. *Intercollegiate sports:* baseball M, basketball M/W, cheerleading M (c)/W (c), crew M (c)/W (c), cross-country running M/W, equestrian sports M (c)/W (c), fencing M (c)/W (c), football M, golf M/W, ice hockey M (c), lacrosse M (c)/W, rugby M (c)/W (c), skiing (downhill) M (c)/W (c), soccer M/W, softball W, swimming and diving M/W, table tennis M (c)/W (c), tennis M/W, track and field M/W, ultimate Frisbee M (c)/W (c), volleyball M (c)/W. *Intramural sports:* basketball M/W, bowling M/W, football M/W, golf M/W, racquetball M/W, soccer M/W, softball M/W, tennis M/W, volleyball M/W.

Standardized Tests *Required:* SAT or ACT (for admission).

Costs (2008–09) *Comprehensive fee:* $40,000 includes full-time tuition ($31,680), mandatory fees ($320), and room and board ($8000). Part-time tuition: $1320 per credit hour. *Required fees:* $160 per term part-time. *College room only:* $4200.

Financial Aid Of all full-time matriculated undergraduates who enrolled in 2007, 1,671 applied for aid, 1,465 were judged to have need, 630 had their need fully met. 1,161 Federal Work-Study jobs (averaging $1900). 436 state and other part-time jobs (averaging $2000). In 2007, 619 non-need-based awards were made. *Average percent of need met:* 92%. *Average financial aid package:* $24,183. *Average need-based loan:* $5326. *Average need-based gift aid:* $17,111. *Average non-need-based aid:* $11,044.

Applying *Options:* electronic application, early admission, early decision, deferred entrance. *Application fee:* $35. *Required:* essay or personal statement, high school transcript, 2 letters of recommendation. *Recommended:* interview. *Application deadlines:* 2/15 (freshmen), 7/1 (transfers). *Early decision deadline:* 11/15. *Notification:* 4/1 (freshmen), 8/1 (transfers), 12/15 (early decision).

Freshman Application Contact Ms. Jennifer Winge, Director of Admissions, Allegheny College, 520 North Main Street, Box 5, Meadville, PA 16335. *Phone:* 814-332-4351. *Toll-free phone:* 800-521-5293. *Fax:* 814-337-0431. *E-mail:* admissions@allegheny.edu.

ALVERNIA COLLEGE

Reading, Pennsylvania **www.alvernia.edu/**

- **Independent Roman Catholic** comprehensive, founded 1958
- **Suburban** 85-acre campus with easy access to Philadelphia
- **Endowment** $15.6 million
- **Coed** 2,038 undergraduate students, 78% full-time, 69% women, 31% men
- **Moderately difficult** entrance level, 76% of applicants were admitted

Alvernia is a private college sponsored by the Bernardine Franciscan sisters, a Catholic religious order. Located in Reading, Pennsylvania, Alvernia provides an affordable, high-quality education combining the traditional liberal arts with career and professional opportunities in more than fifty academic programs of study to 2,800 students, including 1,400 traditional undergraduates.

Undergraduates 1,580 full-time, 458 part-time. Students come from 13 states and territories, 14 other countries, 10% are from out of state, 11% African American, 1% Asian American or Pacific Islander, 6% Hispanic American, 0.6% Native American, 0.5% international, 7% transferred in, 42% live on campus. *Retention:* 71% of 2006 full-time freshmen returned.

Freshmen *Admission:* 1,290 applied, 985 admitted, 303 enrolled. *Average high school GPA:* 2.97. *Test scores:* SAT critical reading scores over 500: 33%; SAT math scores over 500: 35%; ACT scores over 18: 66%; SAT critical reading scores over 600: 4%; SAT math scores over 600: 7%; ACT scores over 24: 6%.

Faculty *Total:* 292, 28% full-time, 33% with terminal degrees. *Student/faculty ratio:* 14:1.

Majors Accounting; athletic training; biochemistry; biological and physical sciences; biology/biological sciences; biology teacher education; business administration and management; business/commerce; chemistry; chemistry teacher education; communication/speech communication and rhetoric; computer and information sciences; criminal justice/law enforcement administration; early childhood education; education; elementary education; English; English/language arts teacher education; forensic science and technology; history; human resources management; liberal arts and sciences/liberal studies; marketing/marketing management; mathematics; mathematics teacher education; nursing (registered nurse training); philosophy; political science and government; pre-law studies; premedical studies; psychology; psychology related; religious studies; science teacher education; social sciences; social work; sport and fitness administration/management; substance abuse/addiction counseling.

Academics *Calendar:* semesters. *Degrees:* certificates, associate, bachelor's, master's, post-master's, and postbachelor's certificates. *Special study options:* academic remediation for entering students, accelerated degree program, adult/continuing education programs, advanced placement credit, double majors, honors programs, independent study, internships, off-campus study, part-time degree program, services for LD students, summer session for credit. *ROTC:* Army (c). *Unusual degree programs:* 3-2 occupational therapy.

Computers on Campus 180 computers/terminals are available on campus for general student use. Students can access the following: computer help desk, free student e-mail accounts, online (class) grades, online (class) registration, online (class) schedules. Campuswide network is available. 100% of college-owned or -operated housing units are wired for high-speed Internet access. Wireless service is available via classrooms, computer centers, computer labs, learning centers, libraries, student centers.

Student Life *Housing:* on-campus residence required for freshman year. *Options:* coed, women-only, disabled students. Campus housing is university owned. Freshman campus housing is guaranteed. *Activities and organizations:* drama/theater group, student-run newspaper, choral group, Student Government Association, Student Nurses Association of Alvernia College (SNAAC), Science Association, Sports Management Association, Criminal Justice Association. *Campus security:* 24-hour patrols, late-night transport/escort service, controlled dormitory access. *Student services:* health clinic, personal/psychological counseling.

Athletics Member NCAA. All Division III. *Intercollegiate sports:* baseball M, basketball M/W, cross-country running M/W, field hockey W, golf M, lacrosse M/W, soccer M/W, softball W, tennis M/W, volleyball W. *Intramural sports:* basketball M/W, ice hockey M (c)/W (c), lacrosse M/W, skiing (downhill) M (c)/W (c), volleyball M (c).

Standardized Tests *Required:* SAT or ACT (for admission).

Costs (2007–08) *Comprehensive fee:* $30,144 includes full-time tuition ($21,400), mandatory fees ($214), and room and board ($8530). Full-time tuition and fees vary according to class time and reciprocity agreements. Part-time tuition: $600 per credit. Part-time tuition and fees vary according to class time and course load. *Required fees:* $6 per credit part-time. *Room and board:* Room and board charges vary according to board plan and housing facility. *Payment plan:* installment. *Waivers:* senior citizens and employees or children of employees.

Financial Aid Of all full-time matriculated undergraduates who enrolled in 2007, 1,282 applied for aid, 1,185 were judged to have need, 295 had their need fully met. 233 Federal Work-Study jobs (averaging $2400). 45 state and other part-time jobs (averaging $2400). In 2007, 147 non-need-based awards were made. *Average percent of need met:* 64%. *Average financial aid package:* $15,690. *Average need-based loan:* $6380. *Average need-based gift aid:* $9969. *Average non-need-based aid:* $11,311. *Average indebtedness upon graduation:* $28,364.

Applying *Options:* electronic application, deferred entrance. *Application fee:* $25. *Required:* essay or personal statement, high school transcript. *Required for some:* 2 letters of recommendation, interview. *Recommended:* minimum 2.0 GPA, 1 letter of recommendation. *Application deadlines:* rolling (freshmen), rolling (transfers). *Notification:* continuous (freshmen).

Freshman Application Contact Mr. Jeff Dittman, Vice President for Enrollment Management, Alvernia College, 400 Saint Bernardine Street, Reading, PA 19607. *Phone:* 610-796-8269. *Toll-free phone:* 888-ALVERNIA. *Fax:* 610-796-2873. *E-mail:* admissions@alvernia.edu.

See page 2198 for the College Close-Up.

ARCADIA UNIVERSITY

Glenside, Pennsylvania **www.arcadia.edu/**

- **Independent** comprehensive, founded 1853, affiliated with Presbyterian Church (U.S.A.)
- **Suburban** 71-acre campus with easy access to Philadelphia
- **Endowment** $51.6 million
- **Coed**
- **Moderately difficult** entrance level

Faculty *Student/faculty ratio:* 13:1.

Academics *Calendar:* semesters. *Degrees:* bachelor's, master's, and doctoral.

Student Life *Campus security:* 24-hour emergency response devices and patrols, student patrols, late-night transport/escort service, controlled dormitory access.

Athletics Member NCAA. All Division III.

Standardized Tests *Required:* SAT or ACT (for admission).

Costs (2008–09) *One-time required fee:* $100. *Comprehensive fee:* $39,980 includes full-time tuition ($29,340), mandatory fees ($360), and room and board ($10,280). Part-time tuition: $490 per credit. *College room only:* $7270.

Financial Aid Of all full-time matriculated undergraduates who enrolled in 2007, 1,807 applied for aid, 1,686 were judged to have need, 554 had their need fully met. 872 Federal Work-Study jobs (averaging $1287). 245 state and other part-time jobs (averaging $1196). In 2007, 137 non-need-based awards were made. *Average percent of need met:* 78. *Average financial aid package:* $19,986.

Average need-based loan: $5709. *Average need-based gift aid:* $15,052. *Average non-need-based aid:* $15,237. *Average indebtedness upon graduation:* $33,597.

Applying *Options:* electronic application, deferred entrance. *Application fee:* $30. *Required:* essay or personal statement, high school transcript, 2 letters of recommendation. *Required for some:* portfolio, acting audition. *Recommended:* minimum 3.0 GPA, interview.

Freshman Application Contact Mr. Mark Lapreziosa, Assistant Vice President of Enrollment Management, Arcadia University, 450 South Easton Road, Glenside, PA 19038. *Phone:* 215-572-2910. *Toll-free phone:* 877-ARCADIA. *Fax:* 215-572-4049. *E-mail:* admiss@arcadia.edu.

See page 2200 for the College Close-Up.

THE ART INSTITUTE OF PHILADELPHIA

Philadelphia, Pennsylvania **www.aiph.artinstitutes.edu/**

- **Proprietary** 4-year, founded 1966, part of Education Management Corporation
- **Urban** campus
- **Coed** 3,749 undergraduate students, 69% full-time, 58% women, 42% men
- **Moderately difficult** entrance level, 53% of applicants were admitted

Undergraduates 2,603 full-time, 1,146 part-time. Students come from 30 states and territories, 18 other countries, 49% are from out of state, 16% African American, 4% Asian American or Pacific Islander, 4% Hispanic American, 0.4% Native American, 0.2% international, 27% live on campus. *Retention:* 70% of 2006 full-time freshmen returned.

Freshmen *Admission:* 3,514 applied, 1,845 admitted, 1,070 enrolled. *Average high school GPA:* 2.77. *Test scores:* SAT critical reading scores over 500: 54%; SAT math scores over 500: 54%; SAT critical reading scores over 600: 24%; SAT math scores over 600: 24%; SAT critical reading scores over 700: 1%; SAT math scores over 700: 1%.

Faculty *Total:* 209, 43% full-time. *Student/faculty ratio:* 22:1.

Majors Cinematography and film/video production; culinary arts; film/video and photographic arts related; industrial design; photographic and film/video technology.

Academics *Calendar:* quarters. *Degrees:* associate and bachelor's. *Special study options:* academic remediation for entering students, adult/continuing education programs, advanced placement credit, cooperative education, external degree program, independent study, internships, off-campus study, part-time degree program, services for LD students, summer session for credit.

Computers on Campus 368 computers/terminals are available on campus for general student use. Students can access the following: online (class) registration. Campuswide network is available.

Student Life *Housing options:* coed, disabled students. Campus housing is university owned. Freshman campus housing is guaranteed. *Campus security:* student patrols, controlled dormitory access. *Student services:* personal/psychological counseling.

Athletics *Intramural sports:* basketball M/W, softball M/W, ultimate Frisbee M/W, volleyball M/W.

Costs (2007–08) *Tuition:* $427 per credit part-time. tuition cost varies by program. Prospective students should contact the school for current tuition costs. Other charges include a starting kit for all first-quarter students. Kits vary in price depending on the program of study.

Financial Aid Of all full-time matriculated undergraduates who enrolled in 2006, 230 Federal Work-Study jobs (averaging $3500).

Applying *Options:* electronic application, early admission, early decision, deferred entrance. *Application fee:* $50. *Required:* essay or personal statement, high school transcript, interview. *Recommended:* minimum 2.5 GPA, letters of recommendation. *Application deadlines:* rolling (freshmen), rolling (transfers). *Notification:* continuous (freshmen), continuous (transfers).

Freshman Application Contact Admissions Office, The Art Institute of Philadelphia, 1622 Chestnut Street, Philadelphia, PA 19103. *Toll-free phone:* 800-275-2474. *Fax:* 215-405-6399. *E-mail:* aiphinfo@aii.edu.

See page 2202 for the College Close-Up.

THE ART INSTITUTE OF PITTSBURGH

Pittsburgh, Pennsylvania **www.aip.artinstitutes.edu/**

- **Proprietary** 4-year, founded 1921, part of Education Management Corporation
- **Urban** campus
- **Coed** 10,975 undergraduate students, 29% full-time, 62% women, 38% men
- **Minimally difficult** entrance level, 51% of applicants were admitted

Undergraduates 3,156 full-time, 7,819 part-time. Students come from 51 states and territories, 14 other countries, 68% are from out of state, 2% African American, 0.3% Asian American or Pacific Islander, 0.6% Hispanic American, 0.2% Native American, 0.1% international, 30% live on campus. *Retention:* 64% of 2006 full-time freshmen returned.

Freshmen *Admission:* 6,172 applied, 3,117 admitted, 3,117 enrolled. *Average high school GPA:* 2.84. *Test scores:* SAT critical reading scores over 500: 49%; SAT math scores over 500: 39%; ACT scores over 18: 50%; SAT critical reading scores over 600: 13%; SAT math scores over 600: 8%; SAT critical reading scores over 700: 1%.

Faculty *Total:* 1,014, 23% full-time. *Student/faculty ratio:* 20:1.

Majors Advertising; applied art; architectural drafting and CAD/CADD; CAD/CADD drafting/design technology; food service and dining room management; restaurant, culinary, and catering management.

Academics *Calendar:* quarters. *Degrees:* diplomas, associate, and bachelor's. *Special study options:* academic remediation for entering students, adult/continuing education programs, advanced placement credit, distance learning, English as a second language, external degree program, internships, part-time degree program, services for LD students, study abroad, summer session for credit.

Computers on Campus 580 computers/terminals are available on campus for general student use. Students can access the following: computer help desk, free student e-mail accounts, online (class) grades, online (class) registration, online (class) schedules, open lab schedules. Campuswide network is available. 100% of college-owned or -operated housing units are wired for high-speed Internet access. Wireless service is available via classrooms, computer centers, computer labs, learning centers, libraries, student centers.

Student Life *Housing options:* coed, men-only, women-only. Campus housing is leased by the school. *Activities and organizations:* drama/theater group, student-run newspaper, television station, Graphic Design Club, The Pride Club, Student Council, Hip Hop Dance, Anime Club. *Campus security:* 24-hour emergency response devices and patrols, student patrols, late-night transport/escort service, controlled dormitory access. *Student services:* personal/psychological counseling.

Standardized Tests *Required for some:* ACCUPLACER. *Recommended:* SAT or ACT (for admission).

Costs (2008–09) *Comprehensive fee:* $26,960 includes full-time tuition ($20,405) and room and board ($6555).

Applying *Options:* electronic application, deferred entrance. *Application fee:* $50. *Required:* essay or personal statement, high school transcript, minimum 2.0 GPA. *Required for some:* art portfolio. *Recommended:* interview. *Application deadlines:* rolling (freshmen), rolling (transfers). *Notification:* continuous (freshmen), continuous (transfers).

Freshman Application Contact Mr. Jeffrey A. Bucklew, Director of Admissions, The Art Institute of Pittsburgh, 420 Boulevard of The Allies, Pittsburgh, PA 15219. *Toll-free phone:* 800-275-2470. *Fax:* 412-263-6667. *E-mail:* admissions@aii.edu.

See page 2204 for the College Close-Up.

BAPTIST BIBLE COLLEGE OF PENNSYLVANIA

Clarks Summit, Pennsylvania **www.bbc.edu/**

- **Independent Baptist** comprehensive, founded 1932
- **Suburban** 124-acre campus
- **Endowment** $1.8 million
- **Coed** 675 undergraduate students, 94% full-time, 59% women, 41% men
- **Minimally difficult** entrance level, 76% of applicants were admitted

Undergraduates 635 full-time, 40 part-time. Students come from 30 states and territories, 4 other countries, 63% are from out of state, 0.6% African American, 0.6% Asian American or Pacific Islander, 2% Hispanic American, 0.1% Native American, 2% international, 9% transferred in, 86% live on campus. *Retention:* 69% of 2006 full-time freshmen returned.

Freshmen *Admission:* 452 applied, 344 admitted, 167 enrolled. *Average high school GPA:* 3.26. *Test scores:* SAT critical reading scores over 500: 58%; SAT math scores over 500: 49%; ACT scores over 18: 94%; SAT critical reading scores over 600: 19%; SAT math scores over 600: 13%; ACT scores over 24: 35%; SAT critical reading scores over 700: 2%; ACT scores over 30: 5%.

Faculty *Total:* 51, 69% full-time, 45% with terminal degrees. *Student/faculty ratio:* 16:1.

Majors Administrative assistant and secretarial science; biblical studies; communication/speech communication and rhetoric; divinity/ministry; early childhood education; education; education (multiple levels); elementary education; general studies; mathematics teacher education; missionary studies and missiology; music; music teacher education; pastoral studies/counseling; physical education teaching and coaching; piano and organ; pre-theology/pre-ministerial studies; psychology; religious education; religious/sacred music; science teacher education; secondary education; social studies teacher education; speech/theater education; theological and ministerial studies related; theology and religious vocations related; youth ministry.

Academics *Calendar:* semesters. *Degrees:* certificates, associate, bachelor's, master's, doctoral, and first professional. *Special study options:* academic remediation for entering students, advanced placement credit, internships, part-time degree program, study abroad, summer session for credit. *ROTC:* Army (c).

Computers on Campus 15 computers/terminals are available on campus for general student use. Students can access the following: campus intranet, computer help desk, free student e-mail accounts, online (class) grades, online (class) registration, online (class) schedules. Campuswide network is available. 100% of college-owned or -operated housing units are wired for high-speed Internet access. Wireless service is available via classrooms, computer centers, computer labs, learning centers, libraries, student centers.

Student Life *Housing:* on-campus residence required through senior year. *Options:* men-only, women-only. Campus housing is university owned. Freshman campus housing is guaranteed. *Activities and organizations:* drama/theater group, choral group. *Campus security:* 24-hour patrols, student patrols. *Student services:* health clinic, personal/psychological counseling.

Athletics Member NCAA, NCCAA. All NCAA Division III. *Intercollegiate sports:* baseball M, basketball M/W, cheerleading W, cross-country running M/W, golf M, soccer M/W, softball W, tennis W, track and field M/W, volleyball W. *Intramural sports:* basketball M, golf M, soccer M/W, softball M, volleyball W.

Standardized Tests *Required:* SAT or ACT (for admission).

Costs (2007–08) *Comprehensive fee:* $20,680 includes full-time tuition ($14,040), mandatory fees ($1040), and room and board ($5600). Part-time tuition: $585 per credit. Part-time tuition and fees vary according to course load. *Required fees:* $34 per credit part-time. *College room only:* $2076. Room and board charges vary according to board plan. *Payment plan:* installment. *Waivers:* employees or children of employees.

Financial Aid Of all full-time matriculated undergraduates who enrolled in 2006, 590 applied for aid, 509 were judged to have need, 81 had their need fully met. 12 state and other part-time jobs (averaging $1700). In 2006, 92 non-need-based awards were made. *Average percent of need met:* 60%. *Average financial aid package:* $9225. *Average need-based loan:* $3820. *Average need-based gift aid:* $6667. *Average non-need-based aid:* $7419. *Average indebtedness upon graduation:* $15,000.

Applying *Options:* electronic application, early admission, deferred entrance. *Application fee:* $30. *Required:* essay or personal statement, high school transcript, 3 letters of recommendation, Christian testimony. *Required for some:* interview. *Application deadlines:* 8/15 (freshmen), rolling (transfers).

Freshman Application Contact Ms. Becki Scouten, Admissions Counselor, Baptist Bible College of Pennsylvania, PO Box 800, Clarks Summit, PA 18411-1297. *Phone:* 570-586-2400 Ext. 9389. *Toll-free phone:* 800-451-7664. *Fax:* 570-585-9400. *E-mail:* bscouten@bbc.edu.

BLOOMSBURG UNIVERSITY OF PENNSYLVANIA

Bloomsburg, Pennsylvania www.bloomu.edu/

- **State-supported** comprehensive, founded 1839, part of Pennsylvania State System of Higher Education
- **Small-town** 282-acre campus
- **Endowment** $15.2 million
- **Coed** 7,938 undergraduate students, 93% full-time, 59% women, 41% men
- **Moderately difficult** entrance level, 61% of applicants were admitted

Undergraduates 7,359 full-time, 579 part-time. Students come from 18 states and territories, 27 other countries, 10% are from out of state, 7% African American, 1% Asian American or Pacific Islander, 2% Hispanic American, 0.2% Native American, 0.6% international, 5% transferred in, 46% live on campus. *Retention:* 81% of 2006 full-time freshmen returned.

Freshmen *Admission:* 9,868 applied, 6,009 admitted, 1,685 enrolled. *Average high school GPA:* 3.3. *Test scores:* SAT critical reading scores over 500: 51%; SAT math scores over 500: 62%; SAT writing scores over 500: 43%; SAT critical reading scores over 600: 9%; SAT math scores over 600: 15%; SAT writing scores over 600: 7%; SAT critical reading scores over 700: 1%; SAT math scores over 700: 1%.

Faculty *Total:* 425, 89% full-time, 77% with terminal degrees. *Student/faculty ratio:* 20:1.

Majors Accounting; anthropology; art history, criticism and conservation; audiology and speech-language pathology; biology/biological sciences; business administration and management; business/commerce; business/managerial economics; chemistry; clinical laboratory science/medical technology; communication/speech communication and rhetoric; computer and information sciences; computer and information sciences and support services related; computer science; criminal justice/safety; dramatic/theater arts; early childhood education; economics; economics related; electrical, electronics and communications engineering; elementary education; English; fine/studio arts; French; geography; geology/earth science; German; health and physical education related; health/medical physics; history; mass communication/media; mathematics; medical radiologic technology; music; nursing (registered nurse training); philosophy; physics; political science and government; psychology; sign language interpretation and translation; social sciences; social sciences related; social work; sociology; Spanish; special education; speech and rhetoric.

Academics *Calendar:* semesters. *Degrees:* bachelor's, master's, doctoral, and postbachelor's certificates. *Special study options:* academic remediation for entering students, adult/continuing education programs, advanced placement credit, cooperative education, distance learning, double majors, freshman honors college, honors programs, independent study, internships, off-campus study, part-time degree program, services for LD students, study abroad, summer session for credit. *ROTC:* Army (b), Air Force (c). *Unusual degree programs:* 3-2 engineering with Pennsylvania State University, Wilkes University.

Computers on Campus 800 computers/terminals are available on campus for general student use. Students can access the following: computer help desk, free student e-mail accounts, online (class) grades, online (class) registration, online (class) schedules. Campuswide network is available. Wireless service is available via classrooms, computer centers, computer labs, libraries, student centers.

Student Life *Housing:* on-campus residence required for freshman year. *Options:* coed. Campus housing is university owned. Freshman campus housing is guaranteed. *Activities and organizations:* drama/theater group, student-run newspaper, radio and television station, choral group, marching band, national fraternities, national sororities. *Campus security:* 24-hour emergency response devices and patrols, late-night transport/escort service, controlled dormitory access, monitored surveillance cameras. *Student services:* health clinic, personal/psychological counseling, women's center, legal services.

Athletics Member NCAA. All Division II except wrestling (Division I). *Intercollegiate sports:* baseball M (s), basketball M (s)/W (s), cheerleading M/W, cross-country running M (s)/W (s), equestrian sports M (c)/W (c), field hockey W (s), football M (s), lacrosse W (s), soccer M (s)/W (s), softball W (s), swimming and diving M (s)/W (s), tennis M (s)/W (s), track and field M (s)/W (s), volleyball W, wrestling M (s). *Intramural sports:* archery M (c)/W (c), basketball M/W, fencing M (c)/W (c), field hockey W, football M/W, lacrosse M (c), racquetball M/W, rock climbing M (c)/W (c), rugby M (c)/W (c), skiing (downhill) M (c)/W (c), soccer M/W, softball M/W, tennis M/W, ultimate Frisbee M (c)/W (c), volleyball M/W, water polo M (c)/W (c), weight lifting M (c), wrestling M.

Standardized Tests *Required:* SAT or ACT (for admission).

Costs (2007–08) *Tuition:* state resident $5177 full-time, $216 per credit part-time; nonresident $12,944 full-time, $539 per credit part-time. Full-time tuition and fees vary according to course load. Part-time tuition and fees vary according to course load. *Required fees:* $1446 full-time, $42 per credit part-time, $78 per term part-time. *Room and board:* $6030; room only: $3610. Room and board charges vary according to board plan and housing facility. *Payment plan:* installment. *Waivers:* minority students, senior citizens, and employees or children of employees.

Financial Aid Of all full-time matriculated undergraduates who enrolled in 2007, 6,123 applied for aid, 5,817 were judged to have need, 5,105 had their need fully met. 809 Federal Work-Study jobs (averaging $2678). 839 state and other part-time jobs (averaging $3218). In 2007, 142 non-need-based awards were made. *Average percent of need met:* 70%. *Average financial aid package:* $10,455. *Average need-based loan:* $4053. *Average need-based gift aid:* $4883. *Average non-need-based aid:* $1974. *Average indebtedness upon graduation:* $17,730.

Applying *Options:* electronic application, early admission, early decision, early action, deferred entrance. *Application fee:* $30. *Required:* high school transcript. *Application deadlines:* rolling (freshmen), rolling (transfers), 10/31 (early action). *Early decision deadline:* 11/15. *Notification:* 10/1 (freshmen), continuous (transfers), 12/1 (early decision).

Freshman Application Contact Mr. Christopher Keller, Director of Admissions, Bloomsburg University of Pennsylvania, 104 Student Services Center, Bloomsburg, PA 17815-1905. *Phone:* 570-389-4316. *Fax:* 570-389-4741. *E-mail:* buadmiss@bloomu.edu.

BRYN ATHYN COLLEGE OF THE NEW CHURCH

Bryn Athyn, Pennsylvania www.brynathyn.edu/

- **Independent Swedenborgian** comprehensive, founded 1876, part of The Academy of the New Church
- **Suburban** 130-acre campus with easy access to Philadelphia
- **Endowment** $364.4 million
- **Coed** 120 undergraduate students, 97% full-time, 55% women, 45% men
- **Minimally difficult** entrance level, 97% of applicants were admitted

Undergraduates 116 full-time, 4 part-time. Students come from 13 states and territories, 9 other countries, 19% are from out of state, 2% African American, 3% Asian American or Pacific Islander, 16% international, 2% transferred in, 60% live on campus. *Retention:* 65% of 2006 full-time freshmen returned.

Freshmen *Admission:* 59 applied, 57 admitted, 47 enrolled. *Average high school GPA:* 3.37. *Test scores:* SAT critical reading scores over 500: 70%; SAT math scores over 500: 76%; SAT writing scores over 500: 61%; ACT scores over 18: 80%; SAT critical reading scores over 600: 50%; SAT math scores over 600: 47%; SAT writing scores over 600: 30%; ACT scores over 24: 20%; SAT critical reading scores over 700: 18%; SAT math scores over 700: 6%; SAT writing scores over 700: 6%.

Faculty *Total:* 39, 51% full-time, 49% with terminal degrees. *Student/faculty ratio:* 5:1.

Majors Biology/biological sciences; elementary education; English; history; interdisciplinary studies; liberal arts and sciences/liberal studies; religious studies related.

Academics *Calendar:* trimesters. *Degrees:* associate, bachelor's, master's, first professional, and first professional certificates. *Special study options:* academic remediation for entering students, accelerated degree program, advanced placement credit, cooperative education, English as a second language, independent study, internships, part-time degree program, services for LD students, student-designed majors, study abroad.

Computers on Campus 55 computers/terminals are available on campus for general student use. Students can access the following: computer help desk, free student e-mail accounts. Campuswide network is available. Wireless service is available via entire campus.

Student Life *Housing:* on-campus residence required for freshman year. *Options:* men-only, women-only. Campus housing is university owned. Freshman campus housing is guaranteed. *Activities and organizations:* drama/theater group, student-run newspaper, choral group, C.A.R.E. Community Service, Business Club, International Student Organization, Peer Advisory Council, Outing Club. *Campus security:* 24-hour emergency response devices, controlled dormitory access, 18-hour patrols by trained personnel. *Student services:* health clinic, personal/psychological counseling.

Athletics *Intercollegiate sports:* badminton M (c)/W (c), lacrosse M (c), soccer M, volleyball W. *Intramural sports:* ice hockey M, soccer W (c), volleyball M (c)/W (c).

Standardized Tests *Required:* SAT or ACT (for admission).

Costs (2007–08) *Comprehensive fee:* $15,688 includes full-time tuition ($8264), mandatory fees ($1850), and room and board ($5574). Part-time tuition: $319 per credit. *Required fees:* $70 per credit part-time.

Financial Aid Of all full-time matriculated undergraduates who enrolled in 2003, 64 applied for aid, 57 were judged to have need, 57 had their need fully met. In 2003, 9 non-need-based awards were made. *Average percent of need met:* 100%. *Average financial aid package:* $7248. *Average need-based loan:* $2000. *Average need-based gift aid:* $7248. *Average non-need-based aid:* $1037. *Average indebtedness upon graduation:* $2000.

Applying *Options:* electronic application, deferred entrance. *Application fee:* $30. *Required:* essay or personal statement, high school transcript, minimum 2.2 GPA, 1 letter of recommendation. *Required for some:* interview. *Application deadlines:* 7/1 (freshmen), 7/1 (transfers). *Notification:* continuous (freshmen), continuous (transfers).

Freshman Application Contact Admissions Office, Bryn Athyn College of the New Church, Box 717, Bryn Athyn, PA 19009. *Phone:* 267-502-2511. *Fax:* 267-502-2658. *E-mail:* admissions@brynathyn.edu.

BRYN MAWR COLLEGE

Bryn Mawr, Pennsylvania www.brynmawr.edu/

- **Independent** university, founded 1885
- **Suburban** 135-acre campus with easy access to Philadelphia
- **Endowment** $661.0 million
- **Undergraduate: women only; graduate: coed** 1,287 undergraduate students, 98% full-time, 100% women, 0% men
- **Most difficult** entrance level, 45% of applicants were admitted

Bryn Mawr, a liberal arts college for women located in suburban Philadelphia, is a diverse community of individuals who share an intense intellectual commitment, a self-directed and purposeful vision of their lives, and a desire to make a meaningful contribution to the world. Bryn Mawr benefits from its proximity to Philadelphia, with its rich cultural and social resources, as well as an active academic and social consortium with neighboring Haverford College, nearby Swarthmore College, and the University of Pennsylvania.

Undergraduates 1,267 full-time, 20 part-time. Students come from 49 states and territories, 42 other countries, 82% are from out of state, 6% African American, 12% Asian American or Pacific Islander, 3% Hispanic American, 0.1% Native American, 7% international, 0.5% transferred in, 95% live on campus. *Retention:* 94% of 2006 full-time freshmen returned.

Freshmen *Admission:* 2,106 applied, 958 admitted, 352 enrolled. *Test scores:* SAT critical reading scores over 500: 98%; SAT math scores over 500: 94%; SAT writing scores over 500: 98%; ACT scores over 18: 100%; SAT critical reading scores over 600: 85%; SAT math scores over 600: 69%; SAT writing scores over 600: 82%; ACT scores over 24: 92%; SAT critical reading scores over 700: 42%; SAT math scores over 700: 20%; SAT writing scores over 700: 36%; ACT scores over 30: 38%.

Faculty *Total:* 176, 87% full-time, 93% with terminal degrees. *Student/faculty ratio:* 8:1.

Majors Ancient/classical Greek; anthropology; archeology; art; art history, criticism and conservation; Asian studies (East); astronomy; biology/biological sciences; chemistry; classics and classical languages related; classics and languages, literatures and linguistics; comparative literature; economics; English; French; geology/earth science; German; history; Italian; Latin; mathematics; Middle/Near Eastern and Semitic languages related; music; philosophy; physics; political science and government; psychology; religious studies; Romance languages; Russian; sociology; Spanish; urban studies/affairs.

Academics *Calendar:* semesters. *Degrees:* bachelor's, master's, doctoral, and postbachelor's certificates. *Special study options:* academic remediation for entering students, accelerated degree program, adult/continuing education programs, advanced placement credit, double majors, independent study, internships, off-campus study, services for LD students, student-designed majors, study abroad, summer session for credit. *ROTC:* Air Force (c). *Unusual degree programs:* 3-2 engineering with University of Pennsylvania, California Institute of Technology; city and regional planning with University of Pennsylvania.

Computers on Campus 200 computers/terminals and 1,500 ports are available on campus for general student use. Students can access the following: campus intranet, computer help desk, free student e-mail accounts, online (class) grades, online (class) registration, online (class) schedules. Campuswide network is available. 100% of college-owned or -operated housing units are wired for high-speed Internet access. Wireless service is available via classrooms, computer centers, computer labs, dorm rooms, learning centers, libraries, student centers.

Student Life *Housing:* on-campus residence required for freshman year. *Options:* coed, women-only, cooperative. Campus housing is university owned. Freshman campus housing is guaranteed. *Activities and organizations:* drama/theater group, student-run newspaper, choral group, musical and theater groups, community service, Student Government Association, International Students Association, cultural groups. *Campus security:* 24-hour emergency response devices and patrols, late-night transport/escort service, controlled dormitory access, shuttle bus service, awareness programs, bicycle registration, security Website. *Student services:* health clinic, personal/psychological counseling, women's center.

Athletics Member NCAA. All Division III.

Standardized Tests *Required:* SAT and SAT Subject Tests or ACT (for admission).

Costs (2007–08) *Comprehensive fee:* $45,674 includes full-time tuition ($33,840), mandatory fees ($810), and room and board ($11,024). Part-time tuition: $4190 per course. *College room only:* $6300. *Payment plans:* tuition prepayment, installment.

Financial Aid Of all full-time matriculated undergraduates who enrolled in 2006, 855 applied for aid, 711 were judged to have need, 711 had their need fully met. 610 Federal Work-Study jobs (averaging $1849). 73 state and other part-time jobs (averaging $1872). In 2006, 28 non-need-based awards were made. *Average*

percent of need met: 100%. *Average financial aid package:* $29,169. *Average need-based loan:* $4817. *Average need-based gift aid:* $24,179. *Average non-need-based aid:* $11,302. *Average indebtedness upon graduation:* $18,787. *Financial aid deadline:* 3/1.

Applying *Options:* electronic application, early admission, early decision, deferred entrance. *Application fee:* $50. *Required:* essay or personal statement, high school transcript, 3 letters of recommendation. *Recommended:* interview. *Application deadlines:* 1/15 (freshmen), 3/15 (transfers). *Early decision deadline:* 11/15 (for plan 1), 1/1 (for plan 2). *Notification:* 4/15 (freshmen), 6/1 (transfers), 12/15 (early decision plan 1), 2/1 (early decision plan 2).

Freshman Application Contact Ms. Jody Sanford Sweeney, Director of Admissions, Bryn Mawr College, 101 North Merion Avenue, Bryn Mawr, PA 19010. *Phone:* 610-526-5152. *Toll-free phone:* 800-BMC-1885. *Fax:* 610-526-7471. *E-mail:* admissions@brynmawr.edu.

See page 2206 for the College Close-Up.

BUCKNELL UNIVERSITY

Lewisburg, Pennsylvania www.bucknell.edu/

- **Independent** comprehensive, founded 1846
- **Small-town** 445-acre campus
- **Endowment** $599.4 million
- **Coed** 3,520 undergraduate students, 99% full-time, 51% women, 49% men
- **Most difficult** entrance level, 30% of applicants were admitted

Undergraduates 3,492 full-time, 28 part-time. Students come from 47 states and territories, 41 other countries, 73% are from out of state, 3% African American, 7% Asian American or Pacific Islander, 3% Hispanic American, 0.5% Native American, 3% international, 0.6% transferred in, 87% live on campus. *Retention:* 94% of 2006 full-time freshmen returned.

Freshmen *Admission:* 8,943 applied, 2,673 admitted, 887 enrolled. *Test scores:* SAT critical reading scores over 500: 98%; SAT math scores over 500: 99%; ACT scores over 18: 100%; SAT critical reading scores over 600: 80%; SAT math scores over 600: 89%; ACT scores over 24: 94%; SAT critical reading scores over 700: 23%; SAT math scores over 700: 34%; ACT scores over 30: 39%.

Faculty *Total:* 340, 93% full-time, 93% with terminal degrees. *Student/faculty ratio:* 11:1.

Majors Accounting; animal behavior and ethology; anthropology; area studies; art; art history, criticism and conservation; Asian studies (East); biochemistry; biology/biological sciences; biomedical/medical engineering; biopsychology; business administration and management; cell and molecular biology; chemical engineering; chemistry; civil engineering; classics and languages, literatures and linguistics; computer and information sciences; computer engineering; creative writing; dramatic/theater arts; early childhood education; economics; education; educational statistics and research methods; electrical, electronics and communications engineering; elementary education; English; environmental studies; fine/studio arts; French; geography; geological and earth sciences/geosciences related; geology/earth science; German; history; humanities; interdisciplinary studies; international relations and affairs; kindergarten/preschool education; Latin American studies; mathematics; mechanical engineering; multi-/interdisciplinary studies related; music; music history, literature, and theory; music performance; music teacher education; music theory and composition; philosophy; physics; political science and government; psychology; religious studies; Russian; secondary education; sociology; Spanish; women's studies.

Academics *Calendar:* semesters. *Degrees:* bachelor's and master's. *Special study options:* advanced placement credit, double majors, honors programs, independent study, internships, off-campus study, part-time degree program, services for LD students, student-designed majors, study abroad, summer session for credit. *ROTC:* Army (b).

Computers on Campus 940 computers/terminals are available on campus for general student use. Students can access the following: campus intranet, computer help desk, free student e-mail accounts, online (class) grades, online (class) registration, online (class) schedules. Campuswide network is available. 100% of college-owned or -operated housing units are wired for high-speed Internet access. Wireless service is available via entire campus.

Student Life *Housing:* on-campus residence required through senior year. *Options:* coed, women-only, disabled students. Campus housing is university owned. Freshman campus housing is guaranteed. *Activities and organizations:* drama/theater group, student-run newspaper, radio station, choral group, Alpha Phi Omega, Outing Club, Habitat for Humanity, Activities and Campus Events, Catholic Campus Ministries, national fraternities, national sororities. *Campus security:* 24-hour emergency response devices and patrols, student patrols, late-night transport/escort service, well-lit pathways, self-defense education, safety/security orientation. *Student services:* health clinic, personal/psychological counseling, women's center.

Athletics Member NCAA. All Division I except football (Division I-AA). *Intercollegiate sports:* baseball M, basketball M (s)/W (s), cheerleading M (c)/W (c), crew M (c)/W, cross-country running M/W, equestrian sports M (c)/W (c), field hockey W, golf M/W, ice hockey M (c), lacrosse M/W, rugby M (c)/W (c), skiing (downhill) M (c)/W (c), soccer M/W, softball W, swimming and diving M/W, tennis M/W, track and field M/W, ultimate Frisbee M (c)/W (c), volleyball M (c)/W, water polo M/W, wrestling M. *Intramural sports:* basketball M/W, bowling M/W, cross-country running M/W, golf M/W, racquetball M/W, soccer M/W, softball M/W, squash M/W, table tennis M/W, tennis M/W, ultimate Frisbee M/W, volleyball M/W, weight lifting M.

Standardized Tests *Required:* SAT or ACT (for admission). *Required for some:* SAT Subject Tests (for admission).

Costs (2008–09) *Comprehensive fee:* $48,380 includes full-time tuition ($39,434), mandatory fees ($218), and room and board ($8728). *College room only:* $4912.

Financial Aid Of all full-time matriculated undergraduates who enrolled in 2007, 1,917 applied for aid, 1,625 were judged to have need, 1,625 had their need fully met. 825 Federal Work-Study jobs (averaging $1500). 50 state and other part-time jobs (averaging $1500). In 2007, 79 non-need-based awards were made. *Average percent of need met:* 100%. *Average financial aid package:* $24,200. *Average need-based loan:* $5550. *Average need-based gift aid:* $20,200. *Average non-need-based aid:* $12,681. *Average indebtedness upon graduation:* $17,700. *Financial aid deadline:* 1/1.

Applying *Options:* electronic application, early decision, deferred entrance. *Application fee:* $60. *Required:* essay or personal statement, high school transcript, 1 letter of recommendation. *Application deadlines:* 1/15 (freshmen), 3/15 (transfers). *Early decision deadline:* 11/15 (for plan 1), 1/15 (for plan 2). *Notification:* 4/1 (freshmen), 5/1 (transfers), 12/15 (early decision plan 1), 2/1 (early decision plan 2).

Freshman Application Contact Mr. Kurt M. Thiede, Vice President, Enrollment Management and Dean of Admissions, Bucknell University, Lewisburg, PA 17837. *Phone:* 570-577-1101. *Fax:* 570-577-3538. *E-mail:* admissions@bucknell.edu.

See page 2208 for the College Close-Up.

CABRINI COLLEGE

Radnor, Pennsylvania www.cabrini.edu/

- **Independent Roman Catholic** comprehensive, founded 1957
- **Suburban** 112-acre campus with easy access to Philadelphia
- **Endowment** $28.5 million
- **Coed** 1,878 undergraduate students, 90% full-time, 65% women, 35% men
- **Moderately difficult** entrance level, 75% of applicants were admitted

Undergraduates 1,688 full-time, 190 part-time. Students come from 18 states and territories, 14 other countries, 34% are from out of state, 6% African American, 2% Asian American or Pacific Islander, 3% Hispanic American, 0.4% Native American, 0.9% international, 6% transferred in, 56% live on campus. *Retention:* 66% of 2006 full-time freshmen returned.

Freshmen *Admission:* 4,015 applied, 3,021 admitted, 514 enrolled. *Average high school GPA:* 3.06. *Test scores:* SAT critical reading scores over 500: 40%; SAT math scores over 500: 35%; SAT critical reading scores over 600: 7%; SAT math scores over 600: 4%.

Faculty *Total:* 267, 24% full-time, 35% with terminal degrees. *Student/faculty ratio:* 16:1.

Majors Accounting; American studies; biology/biological sciences; biology teacher education; business administration and management; business, management, and marketing related; chemistry; chemistry teacher education; communication/speech communication and rhetoric; computer and information sciences; computer and information sciences and support services related; criminology; education; elementary education; English; English/language arts teacher education; finance; fine/studio arts; French; graphic design; history; human resources management; information technology; kindergarten/preschool education; kinesiology and exercise science; liberal arts and sciences/liberal studies; marketing/marketing management; mathematics; mathematics teacher education; philosophy; political science and government; psychology; religious studies; social studies teacher education; social work; sociology; Spanish; special education.

Academics *Calendar:* semesters. *Degrees:* certificates, bachelor's, master's, and postbachelor's certificates. *Special study options:* academic remediation for entering students, accelerated degree program, adult/continuing education programs, advanced placement credit, cooperative education, double majors, honors programs, independent study, internships, off-campus study, part-time degree program, services for LD students, student-designed majors, study abroad, summer session for credit. *ROTC:* Army (c), Air Force (c). *Unusual degree programs:* 3-2 physical therapy, occupational therapy with Thomas Jefferson University.

Computers on Campus 460 computers/terminals and 1,050 ports are available on campus for general student use. Students can access the following: campus intranet, computer help desk, free student e-mail accounts, online (class) grades, online (class) registration, online (class) schedules, account balances and other services. Campuswide network is available. 100% of college-owned or -operated housing units are wired for high-speed Internet access. Wireless service is available via entire campus.

Student Life *Housing options:* coed, women-only, disabled students. Campus housing is university owned. Freshman applicants given priority for college housing. *Activities and organizations:* drama/theater group, student-run newspaper, radio station, choral group, Student Government Association, Campus Activities and Programming Board, Ski Club, Psychology Club, Dance Team. *Campus security:* 24-hour emergency response devices and patrols, student patrols, late-night transport/escort service, controlled dormitory access, resident assistants and directors on nightly duty. *Student services:* health clinic, personal/psychological counseling.

Athletics Member NCAA. All Division III. *Intercollegiate sports:* basketball M/W, cross-country running M/W, field hockey W, golf M, lacrosse M/W, soccer M/W, softball W, swimming and diving W, tennis M/W, track and field M/W, volleyball W. *Intramural sports:* badminton M/W, basketball M/W, cheerleading W (c), football M/W, racquetball M/W, rugby M/W, skiing (downhill) M/W, soccer M/W, softball M/W, squash M/W, swimming and diving M/W, tennis M/W, ultimate Frisbee M/W, volleyball M/W.

Standardized Tests *Required:* SAT or ACT (for admission).

Costs (2007–08) *Comprehensive fee:* $38,320 includes full-time tuition ($27,200), mandatory fees ($830), and room and board ($10,290). Part-time tuition: $425 per credit hour. Part-time tuition and fees vary according to course load. *Required fees:* $45 per term part-time. *Room and board:* Room and board charges vary according to board plan and housing facility. *Payment plan:* installment. *Waivers:* children of alumni, senior citizens, and employees or children of employees.

Financial Aid Of all full-time matriculated undergraduates who enrolled in 2006, 1,309 applied for aid, 1,153 were judged to have need, 150 had their need fully met. 176 Federal Work-Study jobs (averaging $1504). In 2006, 421 non-need-based awards were made. *Average percent of need met:* 68%. *Average financial aid package:* $17,029. *Average need-based loan:* $3988. *Average need-based gift aid:* $5883. *Average non-need-based aid:* $8144. *Average indebtedness upon graduation:* $17,515. *Financial aid deadline:* 4/15.

Applying *Options:* electronic application, deferred entrance. *Application fee:* $35. *Required:* high school transcript, minimum 2.0 GPA. *Recommended:* essay or personal statement, minimum 3.0 GPA, 3 letters of recommendation, interview. *Application deadlines:* rolling (freshmen), rolling (transfers).

Freshman Application Contact Mr. Mark Osborn, Vice President for Enrollment Services, Cabrini College, 610 King of Prussia Road, Radnor, PA 19087-3698. *Phone:* 610-902-8552. *Toll-free phone:* 800-848-1003. *Fax:* 610-902-8508. *E-mail:* admit@cabrini.edu.

See page 2210 for the College Close-Up.

CALIFORNIA UNIVERSITY OF PENNSYLVANIA

California, Pennsylvania **www.cup.edu/**

- **State-supported** comprehensive, founded 1852, part of Pennsylvania State System of Higher Education
- **Small-town** 188-acre campus with easy access to Pittsburgh
- **Endowment** $9.0 million
- **Coed**
- **Moderately difficult** entrance level

Cal U offers more than 100 programs. Offerings in science and technology are the University's special mission. Education and human services programs hold a long tradition of excellence. Liberal arts programs offer outstanding opportunities, while providing the general education curriculum. With about 6,000 undergraduate students and a student-faculty ratio of 22:1, education is economical and personal.

Faculty *Student/faculty ratio:* 20:1.

Academics *Calendar:* semesters. *Degrees:* associate, bachelor's, and master's.

Student Life *Campus security:* 24-hour emergency response devices and patrols, student patrols, late-night transport/escort service, residence hall entrances staffed 24/7, fire suppression and smoke detection systems, security staff are trained police officers.

Athletics Member NCAA. All Division II.

Standardized Tests *Required:* SAT or ACT (for admission).

Costs (2007–08) *Tuition:* state resident $5178 full-time, $216 per credit part-time; nonresident $8284 full-time, $345 per credit part-time. Full-time tuition and fees vary according to course load and location. Part-time tuition and fees vary according to course load and location. *Required fees:* $1673 full-time, $282 per credit part-time. *Room and board:* $8540; room only: $5662. Room and board charges vary according to board plan and housing facility.

Financial Aid Of all full-time matriculated undergraduates who enrolled in 2006, 5,023 applied for aid, 4,050 were judged to have need, 242 had their need fully met. In 2006, 718 non-need-based awards were made. *Average percent of need met:* 98. *Average financial aid package:* $9406. *Average need-based loan:* $3995. *Average need-based gift aid:* $4504. *Average non-need-based aid:* $2994. *Average indebtedness upon graduation:* $21,860.

Applying *Options:* electronic application, early admission, deferred entrance. *Application fee:* $25. *Required:* high school transcript, minimum 2.0 GPA. *Required for some:* letters of recommendation, interview. *Recommended:* essay or personal statement, minimum 3.0 GPA.

Freshman Application Contact Mr. William Edmonds, Dean of Enrollment Management and Academic Services, California University of Pennsylvania, 250 University Avenue, California, PA 15419. *Phone:* 724-938-4404. *Fax:* 724-938-4564. *E-mail:* inquiry@cup.edu.

See page 2212 for the College Close-Up.

CARLOW UNIVERSITY

Pittsburgh, Pennsylvania **www.carlow.edu/**

- **Independent Roman Catholic** comprehensive, founded 1929
- **Urban** 14-acre campus
- **Endowment** $7.7 million
- **Coed, primarily women** 1,565 undergraduate students, 74% full-time, 94% women, 6% men
- **Moderately difficult** entrance level, 60% of applicants were admitted

Undergraduates 1,165 full-time, 400 part-time. Students come from 16 states and territories, 6 other countries, 3% are from out of state, 16% African American, 0.7% Asian American or Pacific Islander, 0.9% Hispanic American, 0.7% Native American, 0.4% international, 13% transferred in, 22% live on campus. *Retention:* 70% of 2006 full-time freshmen returned.

Freshmen *Admission:* 1,101 applied, 661 admitted, 226 enrolled. *Average high school GPA:* 3.4. *Test scores:* SAT critical reading scores over 500: 52%; SAT math scores over 500: 40%; ACT scores over 18: 87%; SAT critical reading scores over 600: 10%; SAT math scores over 600: 9%; ACT scores over 24: 28%; SAT critical reading scores over 700: 1%; SAT math scores over 700: 1%; ACT scores over 30: 2%.

Faculty *Total:* 233, 36% full-time. *Student/faculty ratio:* 12:1.

Majors Accounting; art; art history, criticism and conservation; art teacher education; art therapy; auditing; biological and biomedical sciences related; biology/biological sciences; business/commerce; business, management, and marketing related; chemistry; chemistry related; clinical/medical laboratory science and allied professions related; commercial and advertising art; communication and journalism related; communication/speech communication and rhetoric; creative writing; early childhood education; elementary education; English; environmental biology; environmental science; history; information science/studies; intermedia/multimedia; liberal arts and sciences/liberal studies; mass communication/media; mathematics; mathematics related; nursing (registered nurse training); philosophy; photography; political science and government; psychology; public policy analysis; science technologies related; social studies teacher education; social work; sociology; Spanish; special education; technical and business writing; theology.

Academics *Calendar:* semesters. *Degrees:* bachelor's, master's, doctoral, post-master's, and postbachelor's certificates. *Special study options:* academic remediation for entering students, accelerated degree program, adult/continuing education programs, advanced placement credit, cooperative education, distance learning, double majors, honors programs, independent study, internships, off-campus study, part-time degree program, services for LD students, student-designed majors, study abroad, summer session for credit. *ROTC:* Army (c), Navy (c), Air Force (c). *Unusual degree programs:* 3-2 engineering with Carnegie Mellon University; computer animation, computer graphics with Art Institute of Pittsburgh; physical therapy, occupational therapy, athletic training, physician's assistant, environmental science and management with Duquesne University.

Computers on Campus 151 computers/terminals and 72 ports are available on campus for general student use. Students can access the following: campus intranet, computer help desk, free student e-mail accounts, online (class) grades, online (class) registration, online (class) schedules. Campuswide network is

available. 100% of college-owned or -operated housing units are wired for high-speed Internet access. Wireless service is available via entire campus.

Student Life *Housing options:* women-only. Campus housing is university owned. *Activities and organizations:* drama/theater group, student-run newspaper, choral group, Commuter Student Association, Resident Student Association, Student Athletic Association, "Blessed" (gospel choir), Student Government Association. *Campus security:* 24-hour emergency response devices and patrols, late-night transport/escort service, controlled dormitory access. *Student services:* health clinic, personal/psychological counseling, women's center.

Athletics Member NAIA. *Intercollegiate sports:* basketball W (s), crew W (c), soccer W (s), softball W (s), tennis W (s), volleyball W (s).

Standardized Tests *Required:* SAT or ACT (for admission).

Costs (2007–08) *Comprehensive fee:* $27,198 includes full-time tuition ($18,736), mandatory fees ($778), and room and board ($7684). Full-time tuition and fees vary according to course load and program. Part-time tuition: $612 per credit. Part-time tuition and fees vary according to course load and program. *College room only:* $3926. Room and board charges vary according to board plan. *Payment plans:* installment, deferred payment. *Waivers:* adult students and employees or children of employees.

Financial Aid Of all full-time matriculated undergraduates who enrolled in 2003, 431 Federal Work-Study jobs (averaging $776).

Applying *Options:* electronic application, early admission, early action, deferred entrance. *Application fee:* $20. *Required:* high school transcript. *Recommended:* essay or personal statement, minimum 3.0 GPA, letters of recommendation, interview, rank in upper two-fifths of high school class. *Application deadlines:* 7/1 (freshmen), rolling (transfers), 9/30 (early action). *Notification:* continuous (freshmen), continuous (transfers), 10/30 (early action).

Freshman Application Contact Office of Admissions, Carlow University, 3333 Fifth Avenue, Pittsburgh, PA 15213. *Phone:* 412-578-6059. *Toll-free phone:* 800-333-CARLOW. *Fax:* 412-578-6668. *E-mail:* admissions@carlow.edu.

See page 2214 for the College Close-Up.

CARNEGIE MELLON UNIVERSITY

Pittsburgh, Pennsylvania **www.cmu.edu/**

- **Independent** university, founded 1900
- **Urban** 144-acre campus
- **Endowment** $941.5 million
- **Coed** 5,849 undergraduate students, 97% full-time, 39% women, 61% men
- **Most difficult** entrance level, 28% of applicants were admitted

Undergraduates 5,645 full-time, 204 part-time. Students come from 52 states and territories, 49 other countries, 77% are from out of state, 5% African American, 24% Asian American or Pacific Islander, 5% Hispanic American, 0.4% Native American, 14% international, 0.8% transferred in, 64% live on campus. *Retention:* 95% of 2006 full-time freshmen returned.

Freshmen *Admission:* 22,356 applied, 6,259 admitted, 1,416 enrolled. *Average high school GPA:* 3.58. *Test scores:* SAT critical reading scores over 500: 99%; SAT math scores over 500: 100%; SAT writing scores over 500: 100%; ACT scores over 18: 100%; SAT critical reading scores over 600: 84%; SAT math scores over 600: 97%; SAT writing scores over 600: 85%; ACT scores over 24: 97%; SAT critical reading scores over 700: 35%; SAT math scores over 700: 74%; SAT writing scores over 700: 32%; ACT scores over 30: 66%.

Faculty *Total:* 1,012, 82% full-time, 98% with terminal degrees. *Student/faculty ratio:* 11:1.

Majors Anthropology related; applied mathematics; architectural history and criticism; architectural technology; architecture; architecture related; art; astrophysics; behavioral sciences; biological and biomedical sciences related; biology/biological sciences; biomedical/medical engineering; biophysics; biopsychology; business administration and management; business/managerial economics; chemical engineering; chemical physics; chemistry; chemistry related; Chinese; civil engineering; cognitive science; communication and media related; computational mathematics; computer engineering related; computer science; creative writing; dramatic/theater arts; economics; engineering related; English; English as a second/foreign language (teaching); ethics; ethnic, cultural minority, and gender studies related; European history; European studies; foreign languages and literatures; French; German; history related; industrial design; information science/studies; international relations and affairs; Japanese; Latin American studies; liberal arts and sciences/liberal studies; logic; materials science; mathematical statistics and probability; mathematics and statistics related; mechanical engineering; music performance; music theory and composition; natural resources management and policy; operations research; philosophy; physics; physics related; piano and organ; political science and government; psychology; public policy analysis; science, technology and society; social sciences related; Spanish; statistics; systems science and theory; technical and business writing; violin, viola, guitar and other stringed instruments; voice and opera.

Academics *Calendar:* semesters. *Degrees:* bachelor's, master's, doctoral, and post-master's certificates. *Special study options:* advanced placement credit, cooperative education, distance learning, double majors, freshman honors college, independent study, internships, off-campus study, part-time degree program, services for LD students, student-designed majors, study abroad, summer session for credit. *ROTC:* Army (b), Navy (b), Air Force (b). *Unusual degree programs:* 3-2 business administration; engineering; public management and policy.

Computers on Campus 402 computers/terminals are available on campus for general student use. Students can access the following: online (class) registration. Campuswide network is available.

Student Life *Housing:* on-campus residence required for freshman year. *Options:* coed, men-only, women-only, disabled students. Campus housing is university owned and leased by the school. Freshman campus housing is guaranteed. *Activities and organizations:* drama/theater group, student-run newspaper, radio and television station, choral group, marching band, Student Senate, Alpha Phi Omega, Tartan Club, Spirit Club, national fraternities, national sororities. *Campus security:* 24-hour emergency response devices and patrols, late-night transport/escort service, controlled dormitory access. *Student services:* health clinic, personal/psychological counseling, women's center, legal services.

Athletics Member NCAA. All Division III. *Intercollegiate sports:* badminton M (c)/W (c), baseball M (c), basketball M/W, cheerleading M/W, crew M (c)/W (c), cross-country running M/W, fencing M (c)/W (c), football M, golf M, ice hockey M (c)/W (c), lacrosse M (c)/W (c), rugby M (c)/W (c), soccer M/W, softball W (c), squash M (c)/W (c), swimming and diving M/W, tennis M/W, track and field M/W, ultimate Frisbee M (c)/W (c), volleyball M (c)/W, water polo M (c)/W (c). *Intramural sports:* badminton M/W, basketball M/W, bowling M/W, cross-country running M/W, fencing M/W, football M/W, golf M/W, racquetball M/W, soccer M/W, softball M/W, squash M/W, swimming and diving M/W, table tennis M/W, tennis M/W, track and field M/W, ultimate Frisbee M/W, volleyball M/W, water polo M/W.

Standardized Tests *Required:* SAT or ACT (for admission). *Required for some:* SAT and SAT Subject Tests or ACT (for admission).

Costs (2008–09) *Comprehensive fee:* $49,614 includes full-time tuition ($39,150), mandatory fees ($414), and room and board ($10,050). Part-time tuition: $544 per unit. *Required fees:* $207 per term part-time. *College room only:* $5890.

Financial Aid Of all full-time matriculated undergraduates who enrolled in 2005, 3,200 applied for aid, 2,738 were judged to have need, 996 had their need fully met. 2,012 Federal Work-Study jobs (averaging $2355). 19 state and other part-time jobs (averaging $2247). In 2005, 495 non-need-based awards were made. *Average percent of need met:* 81%. *Average financial aid package:* $22,143. *Average need-based loan:* $4853. *Average need-based gift aid:* $16,636. *Average non-need-based aid:* $12,318. *Average indebtedness upon graduation:* $26,500. *Financial aid deadline:* 5/1.

Applying *Options:* electronic application, early admission, early decision, deferred entrance. *Application fee:* $70. *Required:* essay or personal statement, high school transcript, 1 letter of recommendation. *Required for some:* portfolio, audition. *Recommended:* interview. *Application deadlines:* 1/1 (freshmen), 3/1 (transfers). *Early decision deadline:* 11/1 (for plan 1), 12/1 (for plan 2). *Notification:* 4/15 (freshmen), 6/30 (transfers), 12/15 (early decision plan 1), 1/15 (early decision plan 2).

Freshman Application Contact Mr. Michael Steidel, Director of Admissions, Carnegie Mellon University, 5000 Forbes Avenue, Warner Hall, Room 101, Pittsburgh, PA 15213. *Phone:* 412-268-2082. *Fax:* 412-268-7838. *E-mail:* undergraduate-admissions@andrew.cmu.edu.

See page 2216 for the College Close-Up.

CEDAR CREST COLLEGE

Allentown, Pennsylvania **www.cedarcrest.edu/**

- **Independent** comprehensive, founded 1867, affiliated with United Church of Christ
- **Suburban** 84-acre campus with easy access to Philadelphia
- **Endowment** $20.0 million
- **Women only** 1,799 undergraduate students, 54% full-time
- **Moderately difficult** entrance level, 62% of applicants were admitted

The most popular programs include conservation biology, dance, education, forensic science, marketing, nursing, and psychology. A master's in education and a master's in forensic science are currently offered, with a master's in nursing planned for fall 2008. Qualified students may pursue internships with companies and agencies such as the FBI, CNN, and MTV. Students may also

participate in the freshman research and honors program and Division III athletics and cross-register at five area colleges.

Undergraduates 975 full-time, 824 part-time. Students come from 32 states and territories, 20 other countries, 17% are from out of state, 6% African American, 2% Asian American or Pacific Islander, 7% Hispanic American, 0.5% Native American, 0.1% international, 7% transferred in, 80% live on campus. *Retention:* 80% of 2006 full-time freshmen returned.

Freshmen *Admission:* 1,543 applied, 952 admitted, 222 enrolled. *Average high school GPA:* 3.1. *Test scores:* SAT critical reading scores over 500: 76%; SAT math scores over 500: 68%; SAT writing scores over 500: 66%; ACT scores over 18: 87%; SAT critical reading scores over 600: 19%; SAT math scores over 600: 16%; SAT writing scores over 600: 16%; ACT scores over 24: 54%; SAT critical reading scores over 700: 2%; SAT math scores over 700: 1%; SAT writing scores over 700: 2%; ACT scores over 30: 7%.

Faculty *Total:* 175, 53% full-time, 48% with terminal degrees. *Student/faculty ratio:* 11:1.

Majors Accounting; art; biochemistry; biology/biological sciences; business administration and management; chemistry; communication/speech communication and rhetoric; computer and information sciences; criminology; dance; dramatic/theater arts; education; elementary education; English; environmental biology; foods, nutrition, and wellness; forensic science and technology; genetics; Hispanic-American, Puerto Rican, and Mexican-American/Chicano studies; history; liberal arts and sciences/liberal studies; mathematics; music; neuroscience; nuclear medical technology; nursing science; physical sciences related; political science and government; pre-dentistry studies; pre-law studies; pre-medical studies; pre-veterinary studies; psychology; secondary education; social work.

Academics *Calendar:* semesters. *Degrees:* bachelor's, master's, and post-bachelor's certificates. *Special study options:* academic remediation for entering students, accelerated degree program, adult/continuing education programs, advanced placement credit, double majors, honors programs, independent study, internships, off-campus study, part-time degree program, services for LD students, student-designed majors, study abroad, summer session for credit. *ROTC:* Army (c).

Computers on Campus 207 computers/terminals and 587 ports are available on campus for general student use. Students can access the following: campus intranet, computer help desk, free student e-mail accounts, online (class) grades, online (class) registration, online (class) schedules. Campuswide network is available. 100% of college-owned or -operated housing units are wired for high-speed Internet access. Wireless service is available via classrooms, dorm rooms, libraries, student centers.

Student Life *Housing:* on-campus residence required through junior year. *Options:* women-only, disabled students. Campus housing is university owned. Freshman campus housing is guaranteed. *Activities and organizations:* drama/theater group, student-run newspaper, radio and television station, choral group, Alpha Phi Omega, Forensic Science Student Organization, Crestiad Student Newspaper, Student Activities Board, Student Government Association. *Campus security:* 24-hour emergency response devices and patrols, late-night transport/escort service, controlled dormitory access, crime prevention programs. *Student services:* health clinic, personal/psychological counseling.

Athletics Member NCAA. All Division III. *Intercollegiate sports:* basketball W, cross-country running W, equestrian sports W (c), field hockey W, lacrosse W, soccer W, softball W, tennis W, track and field W (c), volleyball W. *Intramural sports:* badminton W, basketball W, soccer W, softball W, tennis W, volleyball W.

Standardized Tests *Required:* SAT or ACT (for admission).

Costs (2007–08) *Comprehensive fee:* $33,964 includes full-time tuition ($25,040), mandatory fees ($300), and room and board ($8624). Part-time tuition: $697 per credit.

Financial Aid Of all full-time matriculated undergraduates who enrolled in 2007, 828 applied for aid, 753 were judged to have need, 151 had their need fully met. 104 Federal Work-Study jobs (averaging $2200). 369 state and other part-time jobs (averaging $2200). In 2007, 91 non-need-based awards were made. *Average percent of need met:* 79%. *Average financial aid package:* $18,747. *Average need-based loan:* $4442. *Average need-based gift aid:* $13,977. *Average non-need-based aid:* $14,325. *Average indebtedness upon graduation:* $25,735.

Applying *Options:* electronic application, early admission, deferred entrance. *Application fee:* $30. *Required:* essay or personal statement, high school transcript. *Required for some:* 2 letters of recommendation. *Recommended:* minimum 2.0 GPA, interview. *Application deadlines:* rolling (freshmen), rolling (transfers).

Director of Admissions Ms. Judith A. Neyhart, Vice President for Enrollment, Cedar Crest College, 100 College Drive, Allentown, PA 18104-6196. *Phone:* 610-740-3780. *Toll-free phone:* 800-360-1222. *E-mail:* cccadmis@cedarcrest.edu.

See page 2218 for the College Close-Up.

CENTRAL PENNSYLVANIA COLLEGE

Summerdale, Pennsylvania **www.centralpenn.edu/**

- **Proprietary** 4-year, founded 1881
- **Small-town** 35-acre campus
- **Coed** 1,103 undergraduate students, 65% full-time, 67% women, 33% men
- **Minimally difficult** entrance level, 41% of applicants were admitted

Undergraduates 722 full-time, 381 part-time. Students come from 16 states and territories, 2 other countries, 13% are from out of state, 20% African American, 1% Asian American or Pacific Islander, 5% Hispanic American, 0.8% Native American, 40% live on campus. *Retention:* 63% of 2006 full-time freshmen returned.

Freshmen *Admission:* 2,517 applied, 1,025 admitted, 135 enrolled.

Faculty *Total:* 115, 26% full-time. *Student/faculty ratio:* 16:1.

Majors Accounting; business administration and management; business/corporate communications; child development; communication/speech communication and rhetoric; computer programming related; consumer merchandising/retailing management; criminal justice/law enforcement administration; criminal justice/police science; design and visual communications; entrepreneurial and small business related; executive assistant/executive secretary; information science/studies; information technology; legal assistant/paralegal; legal professions and studies related; marketing/marketing management; mass communication/media; medical/clinical assistant; physical therapist assistant; securities services administration; tourism and travel services management.

Academics *Calendar:* trimesters. *Degrees:* certificates, associate, and bachelor's. *Special study options:* academic remediation for entering students, adult/continuing education programs, advanced placement credit, distance learning, double majors, honors programs, independent study, internships, part-time degree program, study abroad, summer session for credit.

Computers on Campus 150 computers/terminals are available on campus for general student use. Students can access the following: campus intranet, computer help desk, free student e-mail accounts, online (class) grades, online (class) registration, online (class) schedules. Campuswide network is available. Wireless service is available via classrooms, computer centers, computer labs, dorm rooms, learning centers, libraries, student centers.

Student Life *Housing options:* coed. Campus housing is university owned. *Activities and organizations:* drama/theater group, student-run newspaper, choral group, Campus Christian Fellowship, Student Government Association, Student Ambassadors, Phi Beta Lambda, Travel Club. *Campus security:* 24-hour emergency response devices and patrols. *Student services:* personal/psychological counseling.

Athletics Member NJCAA. *Intercollegiate sports:* basketball M/W, bowling M/W, golf M/W. *Intramural sports:* basketball M/W, football M, tennis M, volleyball M/W.

Costs (2008–09) *Comprehensive fee:* $19,290 includes full-time tuition ($12,600), mandatory fees ($675), and room and board ($6015). *College room only:* $3750.

Financial Aid Of all full-time matriculated undergraduates who enrolled in 2006, 50 Federal Work-Study jobs (averaging $1500). *Financial aid deadline:* 5/1.

Applying *Options:* electronic application. *Required:* essay or personal statement, high school transcript, minimum 2.0 GPA, interview. *Application deadlines:* 9/20 (freshmen), 9/20 (transfers). *Notification:* continuous (freshmen), continuous (transfers).

Freshman Application Contact Ms. Katie Borrelli, Director of Admissions, Central Pennsylvania College, Campus on College Hill and Valley Roads, Summerdale, PA 17093. *Phone:* 717-728-2213. *Toll-free phone:* 800-759-2727 Ext. 2201. *Fax:* 717-732-5254. *E-mail:* admissions@centralpenn.edu.

CHATHAM UNIVERSITY

Pittsburgh, Pennsylvania **www.chatham.edu/**

- **Independent** comprehensive, founded 1869
- **Urban** 32-acre campus
- **Endowment** $62.1 million
- **Undergraduate: women only; graduate: coed** 875 undergraduate students, 68% full-time, 94% women, 6% men
- **Moderately difficult** entrance level, 76% of applicants were admitted

Chatham College for Women at Chatham University emphasizes women's leadership, environmental awareness, and global understanding. One of the nation's oldest women's colleges, Chatham offers a distinctive education

through more than seventy undergraduate, graduate, and certificate programs and its five-year bachelor's/master's degree programs.

Undergraduates 595 full-time, 280 part-time. Students come from 32 states and territories, 21 other countries, 19% are from out of state, 10% African American, 2% Asian American or Pacific Islander, 2% Hispanic American, 0.5% Native American, 6% international, 8% transferred in, 61% live on campus. *Retention:* 69% of 2006 full-time freshmen returned.

Freshmen *Admission:* 600 applied, 453 admitted, 175 enrolled. *Average high school GPA:* 3.33. *Test scores:* SAT critical reading scores over 500: 67%; SAT math scores over 500: 56%; ACT scores over 18: 94%; SAT critical reading scores over 600: 21%; SAT math scores over 600: 13%; ACT scores over 24: 38%; SAT critical reading scores over 700: 4%; ACT scores over 30: 3%.

Faculty *Total:* 259, 33% full-time. *Student/faculty ratio:* 8:1.

Majors Accounting; area, ethnic, cultural, and gender studies related; art history, criticism and conservation; arts management; biochemistry; bioinformatics; biology/biological sciences; broadcast journalism; business administration and management; business/managerial economics; chemistry; communication/speech communication and rhetoric; computer and information sciences; creative writing; dramatic/theater arts; early childhood education; economics; elementary education; English; environmental science; environmental studies; film/video and photographic arts related; fine/studio arts; forensic science and technology; French; history; interior architecture; international business/trade/commerce; international/global studies; international relations and affairs; journalism; kinesiology and exercise science; marketing/marketing management; mathematics; music; nursing (registered nurse training); photography; physics; political science and government; psychology; public policy analysis; social work; Spanish; women's studies.

Academics *Calendar:* 4-4-1. *Degrees:* bachelor's, master's, doctoral, post-master's, and postbachelor's certificates. *Special study options:* accelerated degree program, adult/continuing education programs, advanced placement credit, cooperative education, distance learning, double majors, English as a second language, honors programs, independent study, internships, off-campus study, part-time degree program, services for LD students, student-designed majors, study abroad, summer session for credit. *ROTC:* Army (c), Navy (c), Air Force (c). *Unusual degree programs:* 3-2 business administration; engineering with Carnegie Mellon University, Pennsylvania State University, University of Pittsburgh; biology, counseling psychology, film & digital technology, leadership & organizational transformation, occupational therapy, physician assistant studies, business, teaching, writing & creative writing, architecture-landscape and interior, arts management (Carnegie Mellon Univ), global/public policy.

Computers on Campus 250 computers/terminals are available on campus for general student use. Students can access the following: campus intranet, computer help desk, free student e-mail accounts, online (class) grades, online (class) registration, online (class) schedules. Campuswide network is available. Wireless service is available via classrooms, computer centers, computer labs, learning centers, libraries.

Student Life *Housing:* on-campus residence required through sophomore year. *Options:* women-only. Campus housing is university owned. Freshman campus housing is guaranteed. *Activities and organizations:* drama/theater group, student-run newspaper, choral group, Chatham Student Government, Choir, Chatham Feminist Collective, Students of Community Service, Activities Board. *Campus security:* 24-hour emergency response devices and patrols, late-night transport/escort service, controlled dormitory access, self-defense education, well-lighted pathways and sidewalks. *Student services:* health clinic, personal/psychological counseling.

Athletics Member NCAA. All Division III. *Intercollegiate sports:* basketball W, crew W (c), cross-country running W, ice hockey W, soccer W, softball W, swimming and diving W, tennis W, volleyball W, water polo W. *Intramural sports:* badminton W, basketball W, cross-country running W, football W, golf W, rock climbing W, skiing (downhill) W, softball W, squash W, swimming and diving W, volleyball W, water polo W, weight lifting W.

Costs (2007–08) *Comprehensive fee:* $34,008 includes full-time tuition ($25,216), mandatory fees ($900), and room and board ($7892). Full-time tuition and fees vary according to degree level. Part-time tuition: $612 per credit. Part-time tuition and fees vary according to course load. *College room only:* $4000. Room and board charges vary according to board plan and housing facility. *Payment plan:* installment. *Waivers:* employees or children of employees.

Financial Aid Of all full-time matriculated undergraduates who enrolled in 2007, 491 applied for aid, 461 were judged to have need. In 2007, 128 non-need-based awards were made. *Average percent of need met:* 48%. *Average financial aid package:* $16,201. *Average need-based loan:* $6930. *Average need-based gift aid:* $8678. *Average non-need-based aid:* $11,155.

Applying *Options:* electronic application, early admission, deferred entrance. *Application fee:* $35. *Required:* essay or personal statement, high school transcript, minimum 2.5 GPA, 1 letter of recommendation. *Application deadlines:* rolling (freshmen), rolling (transfers). *Notification:* continuous until 8/1 (freshmen), continuous (transfers).

Freshman Application Contact Ms. Lisa D. Zandier, Director of Admissions, Chatham University, Woodland Road, Pittsburgh, PA 15232. *Phone:* 412-365-1672. *Toll-free phone:* 800-837-1290. *Fax:* 412-365-1609. *E-mail:* lzandier@chatham.edu.

See page 2220 for the College Close-Up.

CHESTNUT HILL COLLEGE

Philadelphia, Pennsylvania **www.chc.edu/**

- **Independent Roman Catholic** comprehensive, founded 1924
- **Suburban** 75-acre campus
- **Endowment** $6.6 million
- **Coed, primarily women** 1,300 undergraduate students, 76% full-time, 67% women, 33% men
- **Moderately difficult** entrance level, 74% of applicants were admitted

Undergraduates 991 full-time, 309 part-time. Students come from 23 states and territories, 3 other countries, 20% are from out of state, 36% African American, 2% Asian American or Pacific Islander, 6% Hispanic American, 0.8% international, 10% transferred in, 67% live on campus. *Retention:* 68% of 2006 full-time freshmen returned.

Freshmen *Admission:* 1,614 applied, 1,193 admitted, 239 enrolled. *Average high school GPA:* 3.04. *Test scores:* SAT critical reading scores over 500: 49%; SAT math scores over 500: 42%; SAT writing scores over 500: 42%; ACT scores over 18: 67%; SAT critical reading scores over 600: 11%; SAT math scores over 600: 10%; SAT writing scores over 600: 8%; ACT scores over 24: 15%; SAT critical reading scores over 700: 3%; SAT math scores over 700: 1%.

Faculty *Total:* 271, 26% full-time, 42% with terminal degrees. *Student/faculty ratio:* 11:1.

Majors Accounting; accounting and business/management; biochemistry; biology/biological sciences; business administration and management; business/corporate communications; chemistry; child care and support services management; communication and journalism related; communications technologies and support services related; computer and information sciences; computer/information technology services administration related; computer science; criminal justice/law enforcement administration; early childhood education; education (multiple levels); elementary education; English; environmental studies; forensic science and technology; French; health/health care administration; history; human resources management; human services; international business/trade/commerce; liberal arts and sciences/liberal studies; marketing/marketing management; mathematics and computer science; molecular biology; multi-/interdisciplinary studies related; music; music teacher education; political science and government; psychology; sociology; Spanish.

Academics *Calendar:* semesters. *Degrees:* certificates, associate, bachelor's, master's, doctoral, post-master's, and postbachelor's certificates (profile includes figures from both traditional and accelerated (part-time) programs). *Special study options:* academic remediation for entering students, adult/continuing education programs, advanced placement credit, cooperative education, double majors, English as a second language, honors programs, independent study, internships, off-campus study, part-time degree program, student-designed majors, study abroad, summer session for credit. *Unusual degree programs:* 3-2 biology, chemistry with the College of Podiatric Medicine of Temple University; biology, chemistry and medical technology with the College of Health Professions of Thomas Jefferson University; education, psychology, computer/applied technology with Chestnut Hill College.

Computers on Campus 45 computers/terminals and 60 ports are available on campus for general student use. Students can access the following: computer help desk, free student e-mail accounts. Campuswide network is available. 90% of college-owned or -operated housing units are wired for high-speed Internet access. Wireless service is available via dorm rooms.

Student Life *Housing options:* men-only, women-only. Campus housing is university owned. Freshman campus housing is guaranteed. *Activities and organizations:* drama/theater group, student-run newspaper, television station, choral group, student government, Hispanics in Action, African American Awareness Society, Campus Ministry Community Service Group, Mosaic of Cultures Club. *Campus security:* 24-hour emergency response devices and patrols, late-night transport/escort service, controlled dormitory access. *Student services:* health clinic, personal/psychological counseling.

Athletics Member NCAA. All Division II. *Intercollegiate sports:* baseball M (s), basketball M (s)/W (s), cross-country running M (s)/W (s), golf M (s)/W (s), lacrosse W (s), soccer M (s)/W (s), softball W (s), tennis M (s)/W (s), volleyball W (s).

Standardized Tests *Required:* SAT or ACT (for admission).

Costs (2008–09) *Comprehensive fee:* $34,550 includes full-time tuition ($26,000) and room and board ($8550). Part-time tuition: $550 per credit.
Financial Aid Of all full-time matriculated undergraduates who enrolled in 2007, 941 applied for aid, 857 were judged to have need, 148 had their need fully met. In 2007, 79 non-need-based awards were made. *Average percent of need met:* 69%. *Average financial aid package:* $16,139. *Average need-based loan:* $5262. *Average need-based gift aid:* $11,872. *Average non-need-based aid:* $13,004. *Average indebtedness upon graduation:* $29,000. *Financial aid deadline:* 3/15.
Applying *Options:* electronic application, early admission, deferred entrance. *Application fee:* $35. *Required:* essay or personal statement, high school transcript, letters of recommendation. *Required for some:* interview. *Recommended:* minimum 2.0 GPA, interview. *Application deadlines:* rolling (freshmen), rolling (transfers). *Notification:* continuous (freshmen), continuous (transfers).
Freshman Application Contact Mr. William Fritz, Director of Admissions, Chestnut Hill College, 9601 Germantown Avenue, Philadelphia, PA 19118-2693. *Phone:* 215-248-7001. *Toll-free phone:* 800-248-0052. *Fax:* 215-248-7082. *E-mail:* chcapply@chc.edu.

See page 2222 for the College Close-Up.

CHEYNEY UNIVERSITY OF PENNSYLVANIA

Cheyney, Pennsylvania — www.cheyney.edu/

- **State-supported** comprehensive, founded 1837, part of Pennsylvania State System of Higher Education
- **Suburban** 275-acre campus with easy access to Philadelphia
- **Endowment** $1.6 million
- **Coed** 1,319 undergraduate students, 95% full-time, 55% women, 45% men
- **Minimally difficult** entrance level, 47% of applicants were admitted

Undergraduates 1,258 full-time, 61 part-time. Students come from 20 states and territories, 5 other countries, 22% are from out of state, 94% African American, 0.1% Asian American or Pacific Islander, 0.6% Hispanic American, 0.4% international, 5% transferred in, 77% live on campus. *Retention:* 56% of 2006 full-time freshmen returned.
Freshmen *Admission:* 3,283 applied, 1,552 admitted, 281 enrolled.
Faculty *Total:* 113, 79% full-time, 64% with terminal degrees. *Student/faculty ratio:* 13:1.
Majors Art; biological and physical sciences; biology/biological sciences; business administration and management; chemistry; clinical laboratory science/medical technology; clothing/textiles; communications technology; computer science; dramatic/theater arts; economics; education; elementary education; English; family and consumer sciences/home economics teacher education; French; geography; hotel/motel administration; industrial technology; kindergarten/preschool education; mass communication/media; mathematics; music; parks, recreation and leisure; political science and government; psychology; secondary education; social sciences; sociology; Spanish; special education.
Academics *Calendar:* 4-1-4. *Degrees:* associate, bachelor's, and master's. *Special study options:* academic remediation for entering students, adult/continuing education programs, cooperative education, distance learning, double majors, honors programs, independent study, internships, off-campus study, part-time degree program, services for LD students, study abroad, summer session for credit. *ROTC:* Army (c).
Computers on Campus 250 computers/terminals and 200 ports are available on campus for general student use. Students can access the following: campus intranet, computer help desk, free student e-mail accounts, online (class) grades, online (class) registration, online (class) schedules, online tutorials, various software packages, online payment/online praxis study guide. Campuswide network is available. 100% of college-owned or -operated housing units are wired for high-speed Internet access.
Student Life *Housing options:* coed, men-only, women-only. Campus housing is university owned. Freshman applicants given priority for college housing. *Activities and organizations:* drama/theater group, student-run newspaper, radio station, choral group, marching band, national fraternities, national sororities. *Campus security:* 24-hour emergency response devices and patrols. *Student services:* health clinic, personal/psychological counseling.
Athletics Member NCAA. All Division II. *Intercollegiate sports:* basketball M (s)/W (s), bowling W (s), cross-country running M (s)/W (s), football M (s), track and field M (s)/W (s), volleyball W (s). *Intramural sports:* basketball M/W, football M.
Standardized Tests *Required:* SAT and SAT Subject Tests or ACT (for admission).
Costs (2007–08) *Tuition:* state resident $5177 full-time, $216 per credit part-time; nonresident $12,944 full-time, $539 per credit part-time. Full-time tuition and fees vary according to reciprocity agreements. Part-time tuition and fees vary according to reciprocity agreements. *Required fees:* $1235 full-time. *Room and board:* $6586; room only: $4500. Room and board charges vary according to board plan. *Payment plan:* deferred payment. *Waivers:* senior citizens and employees or children of employees.
Financial Aid Of all full-time matriculated undergraduates who enrolled in 2003, 1,030 applied for aid, 1,005 were judged to have need, 451 had their need fully met. 215 Federal Work-Study jobs (averaging $1300). 133 state and other part-time jobs (averaging $600). *Average percent of need met:* 87%. *Average financial aid package:* $11,789. *Average need-based loan:* $3700. *Average need-based gift aid:* $1975. *Average non-need-based aid:* $10,000. *Average indebtedness upon graduation:* $21,000.
Applying *Options:* electronic application, early admission. *Application fee:* $20. *Required:* essay or personal statement, high school transcript. *Required for some:* 3 letters of recommendation. *Recommended:* interview. *Application deadlines:* 3/31 (freshmen), rolling (transfers). *Notification:* continuous (freshmen).
Freshman Application Contact Ms. Gemma Stemley, Director of Admissions, Cheyney University of Pennsylvania, 1837 University Circle, Cheyney, PA 19319. *Phone:* 610-399-2275. *Toll-free phone:* 800-CHEYNEY. *Fax:* 610-399-2099. *E-mail:* gstemley@cheyney.edu.

CLARION UNIVERSITY OF PENNSYLVANIA

Clarion, Pennsylvania — www.clarion.edu/

- **State-supported** comprehensive, founded 1867, part of Pennsylvania State System of Higher Education
- **Rural** 100-acre campus
- **Endowment** $17.4 million
- **Coed** 5,873 undergraduate students, 88% full-time, 60% women, 40% men
- **Minimally difficult** entrance level, 69% of applicants were admitted

Clarion University is located in the beautiful town of Clarion, with a historic Main Street and popular outdoor recreational areas nearby. Students from thirty-three states and forty-two countries specialize in more than ninety degree programs. Committed to excellence, Clarion's faculty members are outstanding in their respective disciplines. New apartment-style residences are nearby to enhance the University's living environment.

Undergraduates 5,144 full-time, 729 part-time. Students come from 46 states and territories, 31 other countries, 7% are from out of state, 5% African American, 0.8% Asian American or Pacific Islander, 0.8% Hispanic American, 0.2% Native American, 0.8% international, 6% transferred in, 35% live on campus. *Retention:* 72% of 2006 full-time freshmen returned.
Freshmen *Admission:* 4,297 applied, 2,951 admitted, 1,430 enrolled. *Average high school GPA:* 3.1. *Test scores:* SAT critical reading scores over 500: 38%; SAT math scores over 500: 42%; SAT writing scores over 500: 31%; SAT critical reading scores over 600: 8%; SAT math scores over 600: 9%; SAT writing scores over 600: 7%; SAT critical reading scores over 700: 1%; SAT math scores over 700: 1%.
Faculty *Total:* 311, 76% full-time, 67% with terminal degrees. *Student/faculty ratio:* 19:1.
Majors Accounting; anthropology; art; audiology and speech-language pathology; biological and physical sciences; biology/biological sciences; business administration and management; business/managerial economics; chemistry; clinical laboratory science/medical technology; communication/speech communication and rhetoric; computer and information sciences; dramatic/theater arts; economics; education; elementary education; English; environmental studies; finance; French; geography; geology/earth science; history; humanities; information science/studies; international business/trade/commerce; kindergarten/preschool education; labor and industrial relations; legal administrative assistant/secretary; liberal arts and sciences/liberal studies; library science; management science; marketing/marketing management; mathematics; molecular biology; music management and merchandising; music performance; music teacher education; nursing (registered nurse training); occupational therapist assistant; philosophy; physics; political science and government; psychology; radiologic technology/science; reading teacher education; real estate; science teacher education; social psychology; social sciences; social studies teacher education; sociology; Spanish; special education; speech and rhetoric.
Academics *Calendar:* semesters. *Degrees:* associate, bachelor's, master's, and post-master's certificates. *Special study options:* academic remediation for entering students, accelerated degree program, adult/continuing education programs, advanced placement credit, cooperative education, distance learning, double majors, honors programs, independent study, internships, off-campus study, part-time degree program, services for LD students, study abroad, summer session

for credit. *ROTC:* Army (c). *Unusual degree programs:* 3-2 engineering with University of Pittsburgh, Case Western Reserve University.

Computers on Campus 400 computers/terminals are available on campus for general student use. Students can access the following: online (class) registration. Campuswide network is available.

Student Life *Housing options:* coed, men-only, women-only. Campus housing is university owned. *Activities and organizations:* drama/theater group, student-run newspaper, radio and television station, choral group, marching band, national fraternities, national sororities. *Campus security:* 24-hour emergency response devices and patrols, student patrols, controlled dormitory access. *Student services:* health clinic, personal/psychological counseling, women's center.

Athletics Member NCAA. All Division II except wrestling (Division I). *Intercollegiate sports:* baseball M (s), basketball M (s)/W (s), cross-country running W (s), football M (s), golf M (s), softball W (s), swimming and diving M (s)/W (s), tennis W (s), track and field W (s), volleyball W (s), wrestling M (s). *Intramural sports:* badminton M/W, basketball M/W, bowling M/W, cross-country running W, football M, golf M/W, racquetball M/W, soccer M/W, swimming and diving M/W, tennis M/W, track and field W, volleyball M (c)/W, weight lifting M/W, wrestling M.

Standardized Tests *Required:* SAT or ACT (for admission).

Costs (2007–08) *One-time required fee:* $150. *Tuition:* state resident $5177 full-time, $216 per credit part-time; nonresident $10,354 full-time, $431 per credit part-time. *Required fees:* $1689 full-time, $51 per credit part-time, $80 per term part-time. *Room and board:* $5808; room only: $3990. Room and board charges vary according to board plan. *Payment plan:* installment. *Waivers:* senior citizens and employees or children of employees.

Financial Aid Of all full-time matriculated undergraduates who enrolled in 2006, 4,295 applied for aid, 3,612 were judged to have need, 582 had their need fully met. 325 Federal Work-Study jobs (averaging $1558). 624 state and other part-time jobs (averaging $1661). In 2006, 295 non-need-based awards were made. *Average percent of need met:* 68%. *Average financial aid package:* $7246. *Average need-based loan:* $3460. *Average need-based gift aid:* $5054. *Average non-need-based aid:* $2892. *Average indebtedness upon graduation:* $18,628.

Applying *Options:* deferred entrance. *Application fee:* $30. *Required:* high school transcript. *Required for some:* essay or personal statement, interview. *Recommended:* essay or personal statement, letters of recommendation, interview. *Application deadlines:* rolling (freshmen), rolling (transfers).

Freshman Application Contact Mr. William Bailey, Dean of Enrollment Management, Clarion University of Pennsylvania, 890 Wood Street, Clarion, PA 16214. *Phone:* 814-393-2306. *Toll-free phone:* 800-672-7171. *Fax:* 814-393-2030. *E-mail:* mdunlap@clarion.edu.

See page 2224 for the College Close-Up.

THE CURTIS INSTITUTE OF MUSIC

Philadelphia, Pennsylvania **www.curtis.edu/**

Director of Admissions Mr. Christopher Hodges, Admissions Officer, The Curtis Institute of Music, 1726 Locust Street, Philadelphia, PA 19103-6107. *Phone:* 215-893-5262.

DELAWARE VALLEY COLLEGE

Doylestown, Pennsylvania **www.delval.edu/**

- **Independent** comprehensive, founded 1896
- **Suburban** 600-acre campus with easy access to Philadelphia
- **Endowment** $16.2 million
- **Coed** 1,946 undergraduate students, 85% full-time, 58% women, 42% men
- **Moderately difficult** entrance level, 66% of applicants were admitted

The distinctive Delaware Valley College (DVC) employment program gets results. All students complete twenty-four weeks of hands-on work in jobs related to their academic programs. This on-the-job learning expands resumes, exposes students to real-life work experience in their chosen fields, and allows employers to recognize students' skills and abilities—all before graduation.

Undergraduates 1,661 full-time, 285 part-time. Students come from 23 states and territories, 8 other countries, 38% are from out of state, 3% African American, 1% Asian American or Pacific Islander, 2% Hispanic American, 0.3% Native American, 0.1% international, 3% transferred in, 58% live on campus. *Retention:* 76% of 2006 full-time freshmen returned.

Freshmen *Admission:* 1,932 applied, 1,273 admitted, 476 enrolled. *Average high school GPA:* 3.49. *Test scores:* SAT critical reading scores over 500: 58%; SAT math scores over 500: 56%; SAT writing scores over 500: 48%; ACT scores over 18: 100%; SAT critical reading scores over 600: 13%; SAT math scores over 600: 14%; SAT writing scores over 600: 10%; ACT scores over 24: 41%; SAT critical reading scores over 700: 1%; SAT math scores over 700: 2%; SAT writing scores over 700: 1%; ACT scores over 30: 3%.

Faculty *Total:* 177, 47% full-time, 36% with terminal degrees. *Student/faculty ratio:* 15:1.

Majors Accounting; agribusiness; agronomy and crop science; animal sciences; animal sciences related; applied horticulture/horticultural business services related; biology/biological sciences; business administration and management; business/commerce; chemistry; computer and information sciences; computer and information sciences and support services related; computer programming; criminal justice/law enforcement administration; crop production; culinary arts related; dairy science; English; food science; horticultural science; management information systems; marketing/marketing management; mathematics; ornamental horticulture; secondary education; turf and turfgrass management; wildlife and wildlands science and management; zoology/animal biology.

Academics *Calendar:* semesters. *Degrees:* certificates, associate, bachelor's, and master's. *Special study options:* academic remediation for entering students, adult/continuing education programs, advanced placement credit, cooperative education, distance learning, double majors, honors programs, independent study, internships, part-time degree program, services for LD students, study abroad, summer session for credit.

Computers on Campus 210 computers/terminals are available on campus for general student use. Students can access the following: online (class) registration. Campuswide network is available.

Student Life *Housing options:* coed, women-only. Campus housing is university owned and is provided by a third party. Freshman applicants given priority for college housing. *Activities and organizations:* drama/theater group, student-run newspaper, radio station, choral group, Block and Bridle Club, Community Service Corps, Student Government, Halloween Haunting. *Campus security:* 24-hour patrols, late-night transport/escort service, controlled dormitory access. *Student services:* health clinic, personal/psychological counseling.

Athletics Member NCAA. All Division III. *Intercollegiate sports:* baseball M, basketball M/W, cheerleading W, cross-country running M/W, equestrian sports M/W, field hockey W, football M, golf M, soccer M/W, softball W, track and field M/W, volleyball W, wrestling M. *Intramural sports:* basketball M/W, cross-country running M/W, football M, golf M, lacrosse M, racquetball M/W, soccer M, softball M/W, tennis M/W, volleyball M/W, weight lifting M.

Standardized Tests *Required:* SAT or ACT (for admission).

Costs (2008–09) *Comprehensive fee:* $35,830 includes full-time tuition ($24,728), mandatory fees ($1600), and room and board ($9502). Part-time tuition: $681 per credit. *College room only:* $4308.

Financial Aid Of all full-time matriculated undergraduates who enrolled in 2006, 1,462 applied for aid, 1,257 were judged to have need, 206 had their need fully met. 111 Federal Work-Study jobs (averaging $1621). In 2006, 274 non-need-based awards were made. *Average percent of need met:* 83%. *Average financial aid package:* $17,242. *Average need-based loan:* $4024. *Average need-based gift aid:* $13,027. *Average non-need-based aid:* $8886. *Average indebtedness upon graduation:* $17,482.

Applying *Options:* electronic application, deferred entrance. *Application fee:* $35. *Required:* high school transcript, 1 letter of recommendation. *Required for some:* minimum 3.0 GPA. *Recommended:* minimum 2.75 GPA, interview. *Application deadlines:* 5/1 (freshmen), rolling (transfers). *Notification:* continuous (freshmen), continuous (transfers).

Freshman Application Contact Mr. Stephen Zenko, Director of Admissions, Delaware Valley College, 700 East Butler Avenue, Doylestown, PA 18901-2697. *Phone:* 215-489-2211 Ext. 2211. *Toll-free phone:* 800-2DELVAL. *Fax:* 215-230-2968. *E-mail:* admitme@devalcol.edu.

See page 2226 for the College Close-Up.

DESALES UNIVERSITY

Center Valley, Pennsylvania **www.desales.edu**

- **Independent Roman Catholic** comprehensive, founded 1964
- **Suburban** 400-acre campus with easy access to Philadelphia and New York City
- **Endowment** $47.0 million
- **Coed** 2,207 undergraduate students, 75% full-time, 58% women, 42% men
- **Moderately difficult** entrance level, 77% of applicants were admitted

Undergraduates 1,663 full-time, 544 part-time. Students come from 14 states and territories, 11 other countries, 17% are from out of state, 1% African American, 0.9% Asian American or Pacific Islander, 2% Hispanic American,

0.1% Native American, 3% transferred in, 65% live on campus. *Retention:* 79% of 2006 full-time freshmen returned.

Freshmen *Admission:* 1,797 applied, 1,387 admitted, 391 enrolled. *Average high school GPA:* 3.18. *Test scores:* SAT critical reading scores over 500: 68%; SAT math scores over 500: 72%; ACT scores over 18: 88%; SAT critical reading scores over 600: 24%; SAT math scores over 600: 26%; ACT scores over 24: 12%; SAT critical reading scores over 700: 4%; SAT math scores over 700: 2%.

Faculty *Total:* 181, 57% full-time, 51% with terminal degrees. *Student/faculty ratio:* 13:1.

Majors Accounting; biochemistry; biology/biological sciences; business administration and management; chemistry; cinematography and film/video production; clinical laboratory science/medical technology; computer science; criminal justice/law enforcement administration; criminal justice/safety; dance; dramatic/theater arts; e-commerce; elementary education; English; environmental science; environmental studies; finance; health/medical preparatory programs related; history; human resources management; kinesiology and exercise science; liberal arts and sciences/liberal studies; management information systems; marketing/marketing management; marketing related; mass communication/media; mathematics; nursing (registered nurse training); pharmacy administration/pharmaceutics; philosophy; political science and government; pre-dentistry studies; pre-medical studies; pre-veterinary studies; psychology; Spanish; sport and fitness administration/management; theology.

Academics *Calendar:* semesters. *Degrees:* bachelor's, master's, post-master's, and postbachelor's certificates. *Special study options:* accelerated degree program, adult/continuing education programs, advanced placement credit, distance learning, double majors, honors programs, independent study, internships, off-campus study, part-time degree program, services for LD students, study abroad, summer session for credit. *ROTC:* Army (c).

Computers on Campus 200 computers/terminals are available on campus for general student use. Students can access the following: computer help desk, free student e-mail accounts, online (class) grades, online (class) registration, online (class) schedules. Campuswide network is available. 100% of college-owned or -operated housing units are wired for high-speed Internet access.

Student Life *Housing options:* men-only, women-only. Campus housing is university owned. Freshman campus housing is guaranteed. *Activities and organizations:* drama/theater group, student-run newspaper, radio and television station, choral group, Social Outreach, Best Buddies, Student Nursing Organization, Student Government Association, Outdoor Adventure Club. *Campus security:* 24-hour emergency response devices and patrols, late-night transport/escort service, controlled dormitory access, desk security in residence halls 24 hours per day. *Student services:* health clinic, personal/psychological counseling.

Athletics Member NCAA. All Division III. *Intercollegiate sports:* baseball M, basketball M/W, cheerleading W (c), cross-country running M/W, equestrian sports W (c), field hockey W, golf M, ice hockey M (c), lacrosse M, soccer M/W, softball W, tennis M/W, track and field M/W, volleyball M (c)/W. *Intramural sports:* badminton M/W, basketball M/W, football M/W, golf M, soccer M/W, softball M/W, volleyball M/W, weight lifting M/W.

Standardized Tests *Required:* SAT or ACT (for admission).

Costs (2007–08) *One-time required fee:* $200. *Comprehensive fee:* $32,650 includes full-time tuition ($23,000), mandatory fees ($900), and room and board ($8750). Part-time tuition: $960 per credit. *Room and board:* Room and board charges vary according to board plan and housing facility. *Payment plans:* installment, deferred payment. *Waivers:* senior citizens and employees or children of employees.

Financial Aid Of all full-time matriculated undergraduates who enrolled in 2007, 1,181 applied for aid, 989 were judged to have need, 595 had their need fully met. 324 Federal Work-Study jobs (averaging $631). 234 state and other part-time jobs (averaging $631). In 2007, 387 non-need-based awards were made. *Average percent of need met:* 73%. *Average financial aid package:* $16,684. *Average need-based loan:* $4313. *Average need-based gift aid:* $6249. *Average non-need-based aid:* $6739. *Average indebtedness upon graduation:* $13,977.

Applying *Options:* electronic application, early admission, deferred entrance. *Application fee:* $30. *Required:* high school transcript, 2 letters of recommendation. *Recommended:* essay or personal statement, interview. *Application deadlines:* 8/1 (freshmen), 8/1 (transfers). *Notification:* continuous (freshmen), continuous (transfers).

Freshman Application Contact Mrs. Mary Birkhead, Executive Director of Admissions, DeSales University, 2755 Station Avenue, Center Valley, PA 18034-9568. *Phone:* 610-282-1100. *Toll-free phone:* 877-4DESALES. *Fax:* 610-282-0131. *E-mail:* admiss@desales.edu.

See page 2228 for the College Close-Up.

DeVry University
Chesterbrook, Pennsylvania

DeVry University
Fort Washington, Pennsylvania **www.devry.edu/**

- **Proprietary** comprehensive, founded 2002, part of DeVry University
- **Coed** 813 undergraduate students, 55% full-time, 33% women, 67% men
- **Minimally difficult** entrance level

Undergraduates 449 full-time, 364 part-time. 14% are from out of state, 35% African American, 4% Asian American or Pacific Islander, 6% Hispanic American, 0.5% Native American, 0.7% international, 13% transferred in. *Retention:* 52% of 2006 full-time freshmen returned.

Freshmen *Admission:* 182 enrolled.

Faculty *Total:* 119, 24% full-time. *Student/faculty ratio:* 11:1.

Majors Biomedical technology; business administration and management; business administration, management and operations related; computer engineering technology; computer systems analysis; computer systems networking and telecommunications; electrical, electronic and communications engineering technology; health information/medical records technology.

Academics *Calendar:* semesters. *Degrees:* associate, bachelor's, and master's. *Special study options:* academic remediation for entering students, accelerated degree program, adult/continuing education programs, advanced placement credit, distance learning, part-time degree program, services for LD students, summer session for credit.

Computers on Campus 84 computers/terminals are available on campus for general student use. Students can access the following: online (class) registration. Campuswide network is available.

Student Life *Housing:* college housing not available.

Costs (2008–09) *Tuition:* $14,480 full-time, $540 per credit part-time. *Required fees:* $180 full-time.

Financial Aid Of all full-time matriculated undergraduates who enrolled in 2002, 286 applied for aid, 275 were judged to have need. In 2002, 13 non-need-based awards were made. *Average percent of need met:* 32%. *Average financial aid package:* $6652. *Average need-based loan:* $3657. *Average need-based gift aid:* $4040. *Average non-need-based aid:* $8122.

Applying *Options:* electronic application, early admission, deferred entrance. *Application fee:* $50. *Required:* high school transcript, interview. *Application deadlines:* rolling (freshmen), rolling (transfers). *Notification:* continuous (freshmen), continuous (transfers).

Director of Admissions Admissions Office, DeVry University, 1140 Virginia Drive, Fort Washington, PA 19034-3204.

DeVry University
Pittsburgh, Pennsylvania

Dickinson College
Carlisle, Pennsylvania **www.dickinson.edu/**

- **Independent** 4-year, founded 1773
- **Suburban** 120-acre campus with easy access to Harrisburg
- **Endowment** $287.7 million
- **Coed** 2,381 undergraduate students, 99% full-time, 55% women, 45% men
- **Very difficult** entrance level, 42% of applicants were admitted

Undergraduates 2,355 full-time, 26 part-time. Students come from 41 states and territories, 46 other countries, 75% are from out of state, 4% African American, 5% Asian American or Pacific Islander, 5% Hispanic American, 0.3% Native American, 6% international, 0.6% transferred in, 92% live on campus. *Retention:* 91% of 2006 full-time freshmen returned.

Freshmen *Admission:* 5,844 applied, 2,442 admitted, 621 enrolled. *Test scores:* SAT critical reading scores over 500: 99%; SAT math scores over 500: 98%; SAT critical reading scores over 600: 78%; SAT math scores over 600: 71%; SAT critical reading scores over 700: 24%; SAT math scores over 700: 16%.

Faculty *Total:* 227, 83% full-time, 88% with terminal degrees. *Student/faculty ratio:* 11:1.

Majors American studies; anthropology; archeology; Asian studies (East); biochemistry; biology/biological sciences; chemistry; classics and languages, literatures and linguistics; computer science; dance; dramatic/theater arts; economics; English; environmental science; environmental studies; fine/studio arts; French; geology/earth science; German; history; international business/trade/

commerce; international relations and affairs; Italian; Jewish/Judaic studies; legal studies; mathematics; medieval and Renaissance studies; multi-/interdisciplinary studies related; music; music related; neuroscience; philosophy; physics; political science and government; pre-dentistry studies; pre-medical studies; psychology; public policy analysis; religious studies; Russian; Russian studies; sociology; Spanish; women's studies.

Academics *Calendar:* semesters. *Degree:* bachelor's. *Special study options:* accelerated degree program, adult/continuing education programs, advanced placement credit, double majors, English as a second language, independent study, internships, off-campus study, part-time degree program, services for LD students, student-designed majors, study abroad, summer session for credit. *ROTC:* Army (b). *Unusual degree programs:* 3-2 engineering with Case Western Reserve University, University of Pennsylvania, Rensselaer Polytechnic Institute; pre-law with the Dickinson School of Law of the Pennsylvania State University.

Computers on Campus 600 computers/terminals and 5,000 ports are available on campus for general student use. Students can access the following: campus intranet, computer help desk, free student e-mail accounts, online (class) grades, online (class) registration, online (class) schedules. Campuswide network is available. 100% of college-owned or -operated housing units are wired for high-speed Internet access. Wireless service is available via classrooms, computer centers, computer labs, libraries, student centers.

Student Life *Housing:* on-campus residence required for freshman year. *Options:* coed, disabled students. Campus housing is university owned. Freshman campus housing is guaranteed. *Activities and organizations:* drama/theater group, student-run newspaper, radio station, choral group, Student Senate, College Choir, Alpha Lambda Delta, Multi-Organization Board, Alpha Phi Omega, national fraternities, national sororities. *Campus security:* 24-hour emergency response devices and patrols, student patrols, late-night transport/escort service, controlled dormitory access. *Student services:* health clinic, personal/psychological counseling, women's center.

Athletics Member NCAA. All Division III. *Intercollegiate sports:* baseball M, basketball M/W, cheerleading M (c)/W (c), cross-country running M/W, equestrian sports M (c)/W (c), fencing M (c)/W (c), field hockey W, football M, golf M/W, ice hockey M (c), lacrosse M/W, skiing (downhill) M (c)/W (c), soccer M/W, softball W, squash M (c)/W (c), swimming and diving M/W, tennis M/W, track and field M/W, ultimate Frisbee M (c)/W (c), volleyball M (c)/W, wrestling M (c). *Intramural sports:* badminton M/W, basketball M, bowling M, field hockey W, football M, golf M/W, racquetball M/W, soccer M/W, softball M/W, squash M/W, table tennis M/W, tennis M/W, ultimate Frisbee M/W, volleyball M.

Standardized Tests *Recommended:* SAT or ACT (for admission).

Costs (2008–09) *One-time required fee:* $25. *Comprehensive fee:* $47,834 includes full-time tuition ($37,900), mandatory fees ($334), and room and board ($9600). Part-time tuition: $4740 per course. *Required fees:* $42 per course part-time. *College room only:* $4950.

Financial Aid Of all full-time matriculated undergraduates who enrolled in 2007, 1,226 applied for aid, 1,029 were judged to have need, 772 had their need fully met. 765 Federal Work-Study jobs (averaging $2038). 162 state and other part-time jobs (averaging $3156). In 2007, 214 non-need-based awards were made. *Average percent of need met:* 96%. *Average financial aid package:* $28,455. *Average need-based loan:* $5087. *Average need-based gift aid:* $23,286. *Average non-need-based aid:* $10,902. *Average indebtedness upon graduation:* $22,853. *Financial aid deadline:* 2/1.

Applying *Options:* electronic application, early decision, early action, deferred entrance. *Application fee:* $65. *Required:* essay or personal statement, high school transcript, 2 letters of recommendation. *Recommended:* minimum 3.0 GPA, interview. *Application deadlines:* 2/1 (freshmen), 2/1 (out-of-state freshmen), 4/1 (transfers), 12/1 (early action). *Early decision deadline:* 11/15 (for plan 1), 1/15 (for plan 2). *Notification:* 3/31 (freshmen), 3/31 (out-of-state freshmen), continuous (transfers), 12/15 (early decision plan 1), 2/15 (early decision plan 2), 1/31 (early action).

Freshman Application Contact Catherine Davenport, Acting Dean of Admissions, Dickinson College, PO Box 1773, Carlisle, PA 17013-2896. *Toll-free phone:* 800-644-1773. *Fax:* 717-245-1442. *E-mail:* admit@dickinson.edu.

DREXEL UNIVERSITY

Philadelphia, Pennsylvania **www.drexel.edu/**

- **Independent** university, founded 1891
- **Urban** 42-acre campus
- **Endowment** $638.5 million
- **Coed** 13,194 undergraduate students, 80% full-time, 44% women, 56% men
- **Moderately difficult** entrance level, 72% of applicants were admitted

Undergraduates 10,583 full-time, 2,611 part-time. Students come from 50 states and territories, 93 other countries, 48% are from out of state, 8% African American, 12% Asian American or Pacific Islander, 3% Hispanic American, 0.3% Native American, 7% international, 9% transferred in, 25% live on campus.

Freshmen *Admission:* 16,867 applied, 12,097 admitted, 2,396 enrolled. *Average high school GPA:* 3.5.

Faculty *Student/faculty ratio:* 10:1.

Majors Accounting; architectural engineering; architecture; area studies related; biological and physical sciences; biology/biological sciences; biomedical/medical engineering; business/commerce; business, management, and marketing related; business/managerial economics; chemical engineering; chemistry; cinematography and film/video production; civil engineering; civil engineering related; commercial and advertising art; communication and journalism related; computer engineering; computer science; culinary arts; design and applied arts related; education (specific subject areas) related; electrical, electronics and communications engineering; engineering; English language and literature related; environmental/environmental health engineering; environmental studies; fashion/apparel design; finance; general studies; health/health care administration; history; hospitality administration related; humanities; human resources management; industrial engineering; information science/studies; interior design; international business/trade/commerce; management information systems; marketing/marketing management; materials engineering; mathematics; mechanical engineering; music; nutrition sciences; photography; physics related; playwriting and screenwriting; psychology; social sciences; sociology; taxation; technical and business writing; web page, digital/multimedia and information resources design.

Academics *Calendar:* quarters. *Degrees:* certificates, associate, bachelor's, master's, doctoral, first professional, post-master's, postbachelor's, and first professional certificates. *Special study options:* academic remediation for entering students, accelerated degree program, adult/continuing education programs, advanced placement credit, cooperative education, distance learning, double majors, English as a second language, freshman honors college, honors programs, independent study, internships, part-time degree program, services for LD students, study abroad, summer session for credit. *ROTC:* Army (b), Air Force (c).

Computers on Campus 6,500 computers/terminals are available on campus for general student use. Students can access the following: online (class) registration. Campuswide network is available. Wireless service is available via entire campus.

Student Life *Housing:* on-campus residence required for freshman year. *Options:* coed, disabled students. Freshman campus housing is guaranteed. *Activities and organizations:* drama/theater group, student-run newspaper, radio and television station, choral group, student government, Black Student Union, Society of Hispanic Professional Engineers, Society of Minority Engineers and Scientists, Campus Activities Board, national fraternities, national sororities. *Campus security:* 24-hour emergency response devices and patrols, late-night transport/escort service, controlled dormitory access. *Student services:* health clinic, personal/psychological counseling.

Athletics Member NCAA. All Division I. *Intercollegiate sports:* basketball M (s)/W (s), crew M (s)/W (s), field hockey W (s), golf M (s), lacrosse M (s)/W (s), soccer M (s)/W (s), softball W (s), swimming and diving M (s)/W (s), tennis M (s)/W (s), wrestling M (s). *Intramural sports:* badminton M/W, basketball M/W, fencing M/W, football M, ice hockey M, riflery M/W, sailing M/W, softball M, squash M/W, table tennis M/W, tennis M/W, volleyball M/W, water polo M/W.

Standardized Tests *Required:* SAT or ACT (for admission). *Recommended:* SAT (for admission).

Costs (2008–09) *Comprehensive fee:* $42,575 includes full-time tuition ($28,500), mandatory fees ($1940), and room and board ($12,135). Part-time tuition: $785 per credit hour. *College room only:* $7275.

Financial Aid Of all full-time matriculated undergraduates who enrolled in 2005, 8,758 applied for aid, 6,495 were judged to have need, 702 had their need fully met. In 2005, 1,928 non-need-based awards were made. *Average percent of need met:* 59%. *Average financial aid package:* $15,076. *Average need-based loan:* $4299. *Average need-based gift aid:* $4672. *Average non-need-based aid:* $9206. *Average indebtedness upon graduation:* $25,347. *Financial aid deadline:* 3/15.

Applying *Options:* electronic application, deferred entrance. *Application fee:* $75. *Required:* high school transcript, minimum 2.0 GPA. *Required for some:* essay or personal statement. *Recommended:* 2 letters of recommendation, interview. *Application deadlines:* 3/1 (freshmen), rolling (transfers). *Notification:* continuous (freshmen), continuous (transfers).

Freshman Application Contact Ms. Joan MacDonald, Vice President of Enrollment Management, Drexel University, 3141 Chestnut Street, Philadelphia, PA 19104-2875. *Phone:* 215-895-2400. *Toll-free phone:* 800-2-DREXEL. *Fax:* 215-895-5939. *E-mail:* enroll@drexel.edu.

See page 2230 for the College Close-Up.

DUQUESNE UNIVERSITY

Pittsburgh, Pennsylvania **www.duq.edu/**

- **Independent Roman Catholic** university, founded 1878
- **Urban** 50-acre campus
- **Endowment** $174.7 million
- **Coed** 5,837 undergraduate students, 90% full-time, 58% women, 42% men
- **Moderately difficult** entrance level, 74% of applicants were admitted

Undergraduates 5,250 full-time, 587 part-time. Students come from 49 states and territories, 48 other countries, 18% are from out of state, 3% African American, 2% Asian American or Pacific Islander, 1% Hispanic American, 0.1% Native American, 2% international, 3% transferred in, 57% live on campus. *Retention:* 88% of 2006 full-time freshmen returned.

Freshmen *Admission:* 5,374 applied, 3,993 admitted, 1,361 enrolled. *Average high school GPA:* 3.65. *Test scores:* SAT critical reading scores over 500: 84%; SAT math scores over 500: 81%; SAT writing scores over 500: 80%; ACT scores over 18: 93%; SAT critical reading scores over 600: 26%; SAT math scores over 600: 33%; SAT writing scores over 600: 27%; ACT scores over 24: 53%; SAT critical reading scores over 700: 3%; SAT math scores over 700: 3%; SAT writing scores over 700: 2%; ACT scores over 30: 6%.

Faculty *Total:* 912, 49% full-time. *Student/faculty ratio:* 15:1.

Majors Accounting; accounting related; ancient/classical Greek; art history, criticism and conservation; athletic training; biochemistry; biology/biological sciences; business administration, management and operations related; business/commerce; business/corporate communications; business, management, and marketing related; business/managerial economics; chemistry; chemistry related; classics and languages, literatures and linguistics; communication/speech communication and rhetoric; computer science; computer software and media applications related; dramatic/theater arts; early childhood education; economics; education; education (multiple levels); elementary education; English; English language and literature related; English/language arts teacher education; entrepreneurship; environmental science; finance; fine/studio arts; foreign languages and literatures; French language teacher education; general studies; health/health care administration; history; international business/trade/commerce; international relations and affairs; investments and securities; journalism; Latin; Latin teacher education; liberal arts and sciences and humanities related; logistics and materials management; management information systems; management science; management sciences and quantitative methods related; marketing/marketing management; marketing related; mathematics; mathematics teacher education; music performance; music related; music teacher education; music therapy; non-profit management; nursing (registered nurse training); occupational therapy; operations management; pharmacy, pharmaceutical sciences, and administration related; philosophy; physical therapy; physician assistant; physics; political science and government; pre-medical studies; psychology; public relations, advertising, and applied communication related; public relations/image management; science teacher education; secondary education; securities services administration; social studies teacher education; sociology; Spanish; Spanish language teacher education; special education; speech and rhetoric; speech-language pathology; theology; web/multimedia management and webmaster; web page, digital/multimedia and information resources design.

Academics *Calendar:* semesters. *Degrees:* bachelor's, master's, doctoral, first professional, post-master's, and postbachelor's certificates. *Special study options:* accelerated degree program, adult/continuing education programs, advanced placement credit, distance learning, double majors, English as a second language, external degree program, freshman honors college, honors programs, independent study, internships, off-campus study, part-time degree program, services for LD students, student-designed majors, study abroad, summer session for credit. *ROTC:* Army (b), Navy (c), Air Force (c). *Unusual degree programs:* 3-2 engineering with Case Western Reserve University, University of Pittsburgh.

Computers on Campus 1,000 computers/terminals are available on campus for general student use. Students can access the following: campus intranet, computer help desk, free student e-mail accounts, online (class) grades, online (class) registration, online (class) schedules. Campuswide network is available. 100% of college-owned or -operated housing units are wired for high-speed Internet access. Wireless service is available via classrooms, computer centers, computer labs, learning centers, libraries, student centers.

Student Life *Housing:* on-campus residence required through sophomore year. *Options:* coed, men-only, women-only, disabled students. Campus housing is university owned. Freshman campus housing is guaranteed. *Activities and organizations:* drama/theater group, student-run newspaper, radio and television station, choral group, Duquesne University Volunteers, Red and Blue Crew, Student Government Association, Program Council, Residence Halls Association, national fraternities, national sororities. *Campus security:* 24-hour emergency response devices and patrols, late-night transport/escort service, controlled dormitory access, 24-hour front desk personnel, 24-hour video monitors at residence hall entrances, surveillance cameras throughout the campus. *Student services:* health clinic, personal/psychological counseling.

Athletics Member NCAA. All Division I except football (Division I-AA). *Intercollegiate sports:* baseball M (s), basketball M (s)/W (s), cheerleading M (c)/W (c), crew M (c)/W (s), cross-country running M (s)/W (s), equestrian sports W (c), golf M (s), ice hockey M (c), lacrosse M (c)/W (s), soccer M (s)/W (s), swimming and diving M (s)/W (s), tennis M (s)/W (s), track and field M (s)/W (s), volleyball W (s), wrestling M (s). *Intramural sports:* badminton M/W, basketball M/W, football M/W, skiing (downhill) M/W, soccer M/W, softball M/W, swimming and diving M/W, table tennis M/W, tennis M/W, volleyball M/W, water polo M/W, weight lifting M/W.

Standardized Tests *Required:* SAT or ACT (for admission).

Costs (2007–08) *Comprehensive fee:* $32,496 includes full-time tuition ($22,054), mandatory fees ($1896), and room and board ($8546). Full-time tuition and fees vary according to program. Part-time tuition: $717 per credit. Part-time tuition and fees vary according to program. *Required fees:* $74 per credit part-time. *College room only:* $4662. Room and board charges vary according to board plan and housing facility. *Payment plan:* installment. *Waivers:* senior citizens and employees or children of employees.

Financial Aid Of all full-time matriculated undergraduates who enrolled in 2006, 4,111 applied for aid, 3,514 were judged to have need, 2,084 had their need fully met. 1,539 Federal Work-Study jobs (averaging $2559). In 2006, 1,153 non-need-based awards were made. *Average percent of need met:* 89%. *Average financial aid package:* $15,204. *Average need-based loan:* $4364. *Average need-based gift aid:* $11,403. *Average non-need-based aid:* $7858. *Average indebtedness upon graduation:* $27,080. *Financial aid deadline:* 5/1.

Applying *Options:* electronic application, early admission, early decision, early action, deferred entrance. *Application fee:* $50. *Required:* essay or personal statement, high school transcript, 1 letter of recommendation. *Recommended:* minimum 3.0 GPA, interview. *Application deadlines:* 7/1 (freshmen), 7/1 (transfers), 12/1 (early action). *Early decision deadline:* 11/1. *Notification:* continuous (freshmen), continuous (transfers), 12/15 (early decision), 1/15 (early action).

Freshman Application Contact Mr. Paul-James Cukanna, Associate Vice President for Enrollment Management and Director of Admissions, Duquesne University, 600 Forbes Avenue, Pittsburgh, PA 15282-0201. *Phone:* 412-396-5002. *Toll-free phone:* 800-456-0590. *Fax:* 412-396-5644. *E-mail:* admissions@duq.edu.

EASTERN UNIVERSITY

St. Davids, Pennsylvania **www.eastern.edu/**

- **Independent American Baptist Churches in the USA** comprehensive, founded 1952
- **Small-town** 107-acre campus with easy access to Philadelphia
- **Coed**
- **Moderately difficult** entrance level

Eastern is a coeducational, comprehensive Christian university that integrates faith, reason, and justice for its 3,700 students in undergraduate, graduate, seminary, and accelerated adult programs. Eastern was named to the Templeton Honor Roll of Character-Building Colleges and the Honor Roll of Exemplary First-Year Programs. Eastern has an interdenominational Christian student body and is affiliated with the American Baptist Churches USA. The curriculum is firmly rooted in a Christian worldview. With dramatic growth over the past decade, Eastern has increased its faculty, raised the percentage of faculty members with Ph.D. degrees to 85 percent, built four additional residence halls and two synthetic turf fields, opened a new 30,000-square-foot learning center, and raised the standards of admission. Eastern is located near Philadelphia, Pennsylvania, one of America's educational centers, and is only 2 hours from Washington, D.C., and New York City.

Faculty *Student/faculty ratio:* 13:1.

Academics *Calendar:* semesters. *Degrees:* associate, bachelor's, and master's.

Student Life *Campus security:* 24-hour emergency response devices and patrols, late-night transport/escort service, controlled dormitory access, emergency call boxes.

Athletics Member NCAA. All Division III.

Standardized Tests *Required:* SAT or ACT (for admission).

Costs (2007–08) *One-time required fee:* $45. *Comprehensive fee:* $29,700 includes full-time tuition ($21,350) and room and board ($8350). Full-time tuition and fees vary according to course load, degree level, and program. Part-time tuition: $455 per credit hour. Part-time tuition and fees vary according to degree level and program. *College room only:* $4550. Room and board charges vary according to board plan, housing facility, and location.

Financial Aid Of all full-time matriculated undergraduates who enrolled in 2002, 1,483 applied for aid, 1,253 were judged to have need, 330 had their need fully met. 347 Federal Work-Study jobs (averaging $1050). 811 state and other part-time jobs (averaging $500). In 2002, 228 non-need-based awards were made. *Average percent of need met:* 74. *Average financial aid package:* $11,892. *Average need-based loan:* $3505. *Average need-based gift aid:* $9959. *Average non-need-based aid:* $14,048. *Average indebtedness upon graduation:* $18,057.

Applying *Options:* electronic application, early admission, deferred entrance. *Application fee:* $25. *Required:* essay or personal statement, high school transcript, minimum 2.0 GPA, 1 letter of recommendation. *Recommended:* minimum 3.0 GPA, 2 letters of recommendation, interview.

Freshman Application Contact Mr. Michael Dziedziak, Director of Undergraduate Admissions, Eastern University, 1300 Eagle Road, St. Davids, PA 19087-3696. *Phone:* 610-341-5967. *Toll-free phone:* 800-452-0996. *Fax:* 610-341-1723. *E-mail:* ugadm@eastern.edu.

See page 2232 for the College Close-Up.

EAST STROUDSBURG UNIVERSITY OF PENNSYLVANIA

East Stroudsburg, Pennsylvania **www4.esu.edu/**

- **State-supported** comprehensive, founded 1893, part of Pennsylvania State System of Higher Education
- **Small-town** 213-acre campus
- **Endowment** $13.7 million
- **Coed** 5,959 undergraduate students, 92% full-time, 56% women, 44% men
- **Moderately difficult** entrance level, 66% of applicants were admitted

Undergraduates 5,471 full-time, 488 part-time. Students come from 27 states and territories, 17 other countries, 25% are from out of state, 5% African American, 1% Asian American or Pacific Islander, 5% Hispanic American, 0.3% Native American, 0.3% international, 8% transferred in, 38% live on campus. *Retention:* 82% of 2006 full-time freshmen returned.

Freshmen *Admission:* 5,799 applied, 3,820 admitted, 1,190 enrolled. *Average high school GPA:* 3.26. *Test scores:* SAT critical reading scores over 500: 39%; SAT math scores over 500: 49%; SAT writing scores over 500: 37%; SAT critical reading scores over 600: 4%; SAT math scores over 600: 8%; SAT writing scores over 600: 4%.

Faculty *Total:* 346, 79% full-time, 68% with terminal degrees. *Student/faculty ratio:* 19:1.

Majors Athletic training; audiology and speech-language pathology; biochemistry; biological and physical sciences; biology/biological sciences; biotechnology; business administration and management; chemistry; clinical laboratory science/medical technology; communication/speech communication and rhetoric; communications technology; computer and information sciences; computer and information systems security; dramatic/theater arts; early childhood education; economics; elementary education; English; environmental biology; French; geography; geology/earth science; graphic design; health and physical education related; health services administration; health teacher education; history; hospitality administration; humanities; kinesiology and exercise science; liberal arts and sciences/liberal studies; marine biology and biological oceanography; mathematics; nursing (registered nurse training); parks, recreation and leisure facilities management; philosophy; physical education teaching and coaching; physical sciences; physics; political science and government; psychology; rehabilitation and therapeutic professions related; rehabilitation therapy; secondary education; social sciences; social science teacher education; sociology; Spanish; special education; visual and performing arts.

Academics *Calendar:* semesters. *Degrees:* associate, bachelor's, and master's. *Special study options:* academic remediation for entering students, accelerated degree program, adult/continuing education programs, advanced placement credit, double majors, honors programs, independent study, internships, off-campus study, part-time degree program, services for LD students, student-designed majors, study abroad, summer session for credit. *ROTC:* Army (c), Air Force (c). *Unusual degree programs:* 3-2 engineering with Pennsylvania State University—University Park Campus, University of Pittsburgh.

Computers on Campus 500 computers/terminals are available on campus for general student use. Students can access the following: campus intranet, computer help desk, free student e-mail accounts, online (class) grades, online (class) registration, online (class) schedules, online classes. Campuswide network is available. 100% of college-owned or -operated housing units are wired for high-speed Internet access. Wireless service is available via classrooms, dorm rooms, libraries, student centers.

Student Life *Housing:* on-campus residence required for freshman year. *Options:* coed, men-only. Campus housing is university owned and is provided by a third party. Freshman campus housing is guaranteed. *Activities and organizations:* drama/theater group, student-run newspaper, radio station, choral group, marching band, Student Senate, Stage II, Council for Exceptional Children, United Campus Ministry/ESU Christian Fellowship, University Band/Vocal Performing Choirs, national fraternities, national sororities. *Campus security:* 24-hour emergency response devices and patrols, late-night transport/escort service, controlled dormitory access. *Student services:* health clinic, personal/psychological counseling, women's center.

Athletics Member NCAA. All Division II except wrestling (Division I). *Intercollegiate sports:* baseball M (s), basketball M (s)/W (s), cross-country running M (s)/W (s), field hockey W (s), football M (s), lacrosse W (s), soccer M (s)/W (s), softball W (s), swimming and diving W (s), tennis M (s)/W (s), track and field M (s)/W (s), volleyball M (s)/W (s), wrestling M (s). *Intramural sports:* badminton M/W, basketball M/W, equestrian sports M/W, golf M/W, ice hockey M/W, lacrosse M, racquetball M/W, rugby M/W, soccer M/W, softball W, tennis M/W, track and field M/W, ultimate Frisbee M/W, volleyball M/W, water polo M/W.

Standardized Tests *Required:* SAT or ACT (for admission).

Costs (2007–08) *Tuition:* state resident $5178 full-time, $216 per credit part-time; nonresident $12,944 full-time, $539 per credit part-time. Part-time tuition and fees vary according to course load. *Required fees:* $1631 full-time, $59 per credit part-time. *Room and board:* $5686; room only: $3788. Room and board charges vary according to board plan and housing facility. *Payment plan:* installment. *Waivers:* senior citizens and employees or children of employees.

Financial Aid Of all full-time matriculated undergraduates who enrolled in 2004, 3,902 applied for aid, 2,891 were judged to have need, 2,127 had their need fully met. 346 Federal Work-Study jobs (averaging $1085). 752 state and other part-time jobs (averaging $1285). In 2004, 901 non-need-based awards were made. *Average percent of need met:* 86%. *Average financial aid package:* $5224. *Average need-based loan:* $3780. *Average need-based gift aid:* $3489. *Average non-need-based aid:* $7415. *Average indebtedness upon graduation:* $21,900. *Financial aid deadline:* 3/1.

Applying *Options:* electronic application. *Application fee:* $35. *Required:* high school transcript. *Application deadlines:* 4/1 (freshmen), 5/1 (transfers). *Notification:* continuous until 5/1 (freshmen), continuous (transfers).

Freshman Application Contact Mr. Jeff Jones, East Stroudsburg University of Pennsylvania, 200 Prospect Street, East Stroudsburg, PA 18301. *Phone:* 570-422-3542. *Toll-free phone:* 877-230-5547. *Fax:* 570-422-3933. *E-mail:* undergrads@po-box.esu.edu.

EDINBORO UNIVERSITY OF PENNSYLVANIA

Edinboro, Pennsylvania **www.edinboro.edu/**

- **State-supported** comprehensive, founded 1857, part of Pennsylvania State System of Higher Education
- **Small-town** 585-acre campus
- **Endowment** $3.0 million
- **Coed** 6,412 undergraduate students, 87% full-time, 57% women, 43% men
- **Moderately difficult** entrance level, 82% of applicants were admitted

Undergraduates 5,595 full-time, 817 part-time. Students come from 33 states and territories, 34 other countries, 10% are from out of state, 10% African American, 1% Asian American or Pacific Islander, 1% Hispanic American, 0.3% Native American, 1% international, 7% transferred in, 28% live on campus. *Retention:* 69% of 2006 full-time freshmen returned.

Freshmen *Admission:* 3,612 applied, 2,944 admitted, 1,284 enrolled. *Average high school GPA:* 2.80. *Test scores:* SAT critical reading scores over 500: 36%; SAT math scores over 500: 34%; ACT scores over 18: 57%; SAT critical reading scores over 600: 8%; SAT math scores over 600: 8%; ACT scores over 24: 6%; SAT critical reading scores over 700: 2%; SAT math scores over 700: 2%.

Faculty *Total:* 357, 90% full-time. *Student/faculty ratio:* 17:1.

Majors Adult and continuing education; anthropology; art; biochemistry; biology/biological sciences; broadcast journalism; business administration and management; chemistry; chemistry related; clinical/medical laboratory assistant; clinical/medical laboratory technology; communication disorders; communication/speech communication and rhetoric; computer and information sciences; counselor education/school counseling and guidance; criminal justice/safety; dramatic/theater arts; early childhood education; economics; educational leadership and administration; educational psychology; education (multiple levels); elementary education; English; environmental science; family practice nursing/nurse practitioner; fine/studio arts; geography; geology/earth science; German; health and physical education related; history; industrial technology; information technology; journalism; Latin American studies; liberal arts and sciences/liberal studies;

mathematics; mental and social health services and allied professions related; metal and jewelry arts; music; nursing (registered nurse training); nursing related; operations management; philosophy; physics; political science and government; psychology; reading teacher education; social sciences; social work; sociology; Spanish; special education; sport and fitness administration/management; women's studies.

Academics *Calendar:* semesters. *Degrees:* associate, bachelor's, master's, post-master's, and postbachelor's certificates. *Special study options:* academic remediation for entering students, adult/continuing education programs, advanced placement credit, distance learning, double majors, freshman honors college, honors programs, independent study, internships, off-campus study, part-time degree program, services for LD students, student-designed majors, study abroad, summer session for credit. *ROTC:* Army (b). *Unusual degree programs:* 3-2 engineering with Pennsylvania State University—University Park Campus, University of Pittsburgh, Case Western Reserve University, Pennsylvania State University at Erie, The Behrend College; pre-pharmacy, 2+3 at Lake Erie College of Osteopathic Medicine and School of Pharmacy.

Computers on Campus 934 computers/terminals are available on campus for general student use. Students can access the following: campus intranet, computer help desk, free student e-mail accounts, online (class) grades, online (class) registration, online (class) schedules, software. Campuswide network is available. 100% of college-owned or -operated housing units are wired for high-speed Internet access. Wireless service is available via classrooms, computer centers, computer labs, dorm rooms, learning centers, libraries, student centers.

Student Life *Housing:* on-campus residence required for freshman year. *Options:* coed, men-only, women-only, disabled students. Campus housing is university owned. Freshman campus housing is guaranteed. *Activities and organizations:* drama/theater group, student-run newspaper, radio and television station, choral group, marching band, Student Government Association, AFRICA, Gamma Sigma Sigma, Health and Physical Education Majors Club, national fraternities, national sororities. *Campus security:* 24-hour emergency response devices and patrols, self-defense education. *Student services:* health clinic, personal/psychological counseling, women's center, legal services.

Athletics Member NCAA. All Division II except wrestling (Division I). *Intercollegiate sports:* basketball M (s)/W (s), cross-country running M (s)/W (s), football M (s), ice hockey M (c), soccer W (s), softball W (s), swimming and diving M (s)/W (s), track and field M (s)/W (s), volleyball W (s), wrestling M (s). *Intramural sports:* badminton M (c)/W (c), basketball M (c)/W (c), equestrian sports M (c)/W (c), fencing M (c)/W (c), football M (c)/W (c), golf M (c)/W (c), ice hockey M (c)/W (c), racquetball M (c)/W (c), rock climbing M (c)/W (c), skiing (downhill) M (c)/W (c), soccer M (c)/W (c), softball M (c)/W (c), table tennis M (c)/W (c), tennis M (c)/W (c), track and field M (c)/W (c), ultimate Frisbee M (c)/W (c), volleyball M (c)/W (c), weight lifting M (c)/W (c), wrestling M.

Standardized Tests *Required for some:* SAT or ACT (for admission).

Costs (2008–09) *Tuition:* state resident $5177 full-time, $216 per credit hour part-time; nonresident $7766 full-time, $324 per credit hour part-time. *Required fees:* $1509 full-time, $59 per credit part-time. *Room and board:* $5718; room only: $3600.

Financial Aid Of all full-time matriculated undergraduates who enrolled in 2006, 5,462 applied for aid, 4,759 were judged to have need, 312 had their need fully met. 571 Federal Work-Study jobs (averaging $1281). 801 state and other part-time jobs (averaging $1128). In 2006, 687 non-need-based awards were made. *Average percent of need met:* 81%. *Average financial aid package:* $6402. *Average need-based loan:* $3227. *Average need-based gift aid:* $1825. *Average non-need-based aid:* $1900. *Average indebtedness upon graduation:* $17,034.

Applying *Options:* electronic application, early admission, deferred entrance. *Application fee:* $30. *Required:* high school transcript. *Required for some:* essay or personal statement, letters of recommendation, interview, music auditions. *Recommended:* minimum 2.5 GPA. *Application deadline:* rolling (transfers). *Notification:* 7/1 (freshmen), continuous (transfers).

Freshman Application Contact Mr. J. P. Cooney, Director of Undergraduate Admissions, Edinboro University of Pennsylvania, Biggers House, Edinboro, PA 16444. *Phone:* 814-732-2761. *Toll-free phone:* 888-846-2676 (in-state); 800-626-2203 (out-of-state). *Fax:* 814-732-2420. *E-mail:* eup_admissions@edinboro.edu.

See page 2234 for the College Close-Up.

ELIZABETHTOWN COLLEGE

Elizabethtown, Pennsylvania — www.etown.edu/

- **Independent** comprehensive, founded 1899, affiliated with Church of the Brethren
- **Small-town** 193-acre campus with easy access to Baltimore and Philadelphia
- **Endowment** $52.2 million
- **Coed** 2,322 undergraduate students, 83% full-time, 65% women, 35% men
- **Moderately difficult** entrance level, 58% of applicants were admitted

Elizabethtown College offers liberal arts and professional studies to more than 1,950 students from thirty states and forty countries. Twenty academic departments offer fifty-three academic programs. An engaging faculty encourages students to enjoy experiential learning opportunities, such as research, internships, and off-campus study. Rigorous academics combined with service and leadership opportunities offered through student organizations and athletics prepare graduates for lives of purpose. Interested students are encouraged to visit the campus or the College Web site at http://www.etown.edu.

Undergraduates 1,920 full-time, 402 part-time. Students come from 28 states and territories, 26 other countries, 31% are from out of state, 3% African American, 2% Asian American or Pacific Islander, 2% Hispanic American, 0.2% Native American, 1% international, 0.8% transferred in, 83% live on campus. *Retention:* 86% of 2006 full-time freshmen returned.

Freshmen *Admission:* 3,370 applied, 1,968 admitted, 518 enrolled. *Test scores:* SAT critical reading scores over 500: 81%; SAT math scores over 500: 82%; ACT scores over 18: 100%; SAT critical reading scores over 600: 31%; SAT math scores over 600: 35%; ACT scores over 24: 74%; SAT critical reading scores over 700: 5%; SAT math scores over 700: 5%; ACT scores over 30: 9%.

Faculty *Total:* 210, 62% full-time. *Student/faculty ratio:* 12:1.

Majors Accounting; anthropology; art; biochemistry; biology/biological sciences; biotechnology; business administration and management; chemistry; communication/speech communication and rhetoric; computer engineering; computer science; criminal justice/safety; directing and theatrical production; economics; education; elementary education; engineering; engineering physics; English; environmental studies; French; German; history; industrial engineering; international business/trade/commerce; kindergarten/preschool education; mathematics; modern languages; music; music teacher education; music therapy; occupational therapy; peace studies and conflict resolution; philosophy; physics; political science and government; pre-dentistry studies; pre-law studies; pre-medical studies; pre-veterinary studies; psychology; religious studies; science teacher education; secondary education; social sciences; social work; sociology; Spanish; theater design and technology; theater/theater arts management.

Academics *Calendar:* semesters. *Degrees:* certificates, associate, bachelor's, master's, and postbachelor's certificates. *Special study options:* adult/continuing education programs, advanced placement credit, double majors, English as a second language, external degree program, honors programs, independent study, internships, off-campus study, part-time degree program, services for LD students, study abroad, summer session for credit. *Unusual degree programs:* 3-2 engineering with Pennsylvania State University—University Park Campus; forestry with Duke University; allied health programs with Thomas Jefferson University, Widener University, University of Maryland at Baltimore.

Computers on Campus 200 computers/terminals and 200 ports are available on campus for general student use. Students can access the following: campus intranet, computer help desk, free student e-mail accounts, online (class) grades, online (class) registration, online (class) schedules, file space, personal web page, financial aid, student billing. Campuswide network is available. 100% of college-owned or -operated housing units are wired for high-speed Internet access. Wireless service is available via classrooms, computer labs, learning centers, libraries, student centers.

Student Life *Housing:* on-campus residence required through senior year. *Options:* coed, women-only. Campus housing is university owned. Freshman campus housing is guaranteed. *Activities and organizations:* drama/theater group, student-run newspaper, radio and television station, choral group, Students in Free Enterprise, Emotion Dance Club, Student Senate, Acapella Groups, Religious Groups. *Campus security:* 24-hour emergency response devices and patrols, student patrols, late-night transport/escort service, controlled dormitory access, self-defense workshops, crime prevention program. *Student services:* health clinic, personal/psychological counseling.

Athletics Member NCAA. All Division III. *Intercollegiate sports:* baseball M, basketball M/W, cheerleading M (c)/W (c), cross-country running M/W, field hockey W, golf M, lacrosse M/W, soccer M/W, softball W, swimming and diving M/W, tennis M/W, track and field M/W, volleyball M (c)/W, wrestling M. *Intramural sports:* basketball M/W, racquetball M/W, soccer M/W, softball M/W, tennis M/W, volleyball M/W.

Standardized Tests *Required:* SAT or ACT (for admission).

Costs (2008–09) *Comprehensive fee:* $38,600 includes full-time tuition ($30,650) and room and board ($7950). Part-time tuition: $740 per credit hour. *College room only:* $3950.

Financial Aid Of all full-time matriculated undergraduates who enrolled in 2007, 1,541 applied for aid, 1,342 were judged to have need, 302 had their need fully met. 917 Federal Work-Study jobs (averaging $1337). In 2007, 473 non-need-based awards were made. *Average percent of need met:* 82%. *Average* *financial aid package:* $19,988. *Average need-based loan:* $4440. *Average need-based gift aid:* $15,370. *Average non-need-based aid:* $13,908.

Applying *Options:* electronic application, early admission, deferred entrance. *Application fee:* $30. *Required:* essay or personal statement, high school transcript, minimum 2.0 GPA, 2 letters of recommendation. *Required for some:* interview. *Recommended:* minimum 3.0 GPA, interview. *Application deadlines:* 3/1 (freshmen), 8/1 (transfers). *Notification:* continuous (freshmen), continuous (transfers).

Freshman Application Contact Ms. Debra Murray, Director of Admissions, Elizabethtown College, One Alpha Drive, Elizabethtown, PA 17022. *Phone:* 717-361-1400. *Fax:* 717-361-1365. *E-mail:* admissions@etown.edu.

See page 2236 for the College Close-Up.

FRANKLIN & MARSHALL COLLEGE

Lancaster, Pennsylvania **www.fandm.edu/**

- **Independent** 4-year, founded 1787
- **Suburban** 125-acre campus with easy access to Philadelphia
- **Endowment** $362.9 million
- **Coed** 2,104 undergraduate students, 98% full-time, 49% women, 51% men
- **Very difficult** entrance level, 37% of applicants were admitted

Undergraduates 2,059 full-time, 45 part-time. Students come from 40 states and territories, 47 other countries, 66% are from out of state, 4% African American, 4% Asian American or Pacific Islander, 4% Hispanic American, 0.3% Native American, 8% international, 1% transferred in, 80% live on campus. *Retention:* 91% of 2006 full-time freshmen returned.

Freshmen *Admission:* 5,018 applied, 1,873 admitted, 569 enrolled. *Average high school GPA:* 3.57. *Test scores:* SAT critical reading scores over 500: 100%; SAT math scores over 500: 99%; SAT critical reading scores over 600: 77%; SAT math scores over 600: 86%; SAT critical reading scores over 700: 22%; SAT math scores over 700: 23%.

Faculty *Total:* 238, 77% full-time, 89% with terminal degrees. *Student/faculty ratio:* 10:1.

Majors African studies; American studies; ancient/classical Greek; animal behavior and ethology; anthropology; art history, criticism and conservation; astronomy; astrophysics; biochemistry; biology/biological sciences; business administration and management; chemistry; classics and languages, literatures and linguistics; creative writing; dance; dramatic/theater arts; economics; English; environmental science; environmental studies; fine/studio arts; French; geology/earth science; German; German studies; history; Latin; mathematics; multi-/interdisciplinary studies related; music; neuroscience; philosophy; physics; political science and government; psychology; religious studies; sociology; Spanish.

Academics *Calendar:* semesters. *Degree:* bachelor's. *Special study options:* accelerated degree program, advanced placement credit, double majors, honors programs, independent study, internships, off-campus study, student-designed majors, study abroad, summer session for credit. *Unusual degree programs:* 3-2 engineering with Rensselaer Polytechnic Institute, Washington University in St. Louis, Columbia University, Case Western Reserve University, Penn State University College of Engineering; forestry with Duke University; environmental studies with Duke University.

Computers on Campus 125 computers/terminals are available on campus for general student use. Students can access the following: campus intranet, computer help desk, free student e-mail accounts, online (class) grades, online (class) registration, online (class) schedules, online degree audit, unofficial transcripts, course material. Campuswide network is available. 100% of college-owned or -operated housing units are wired for high-speed Internet access. Wireless service is available via entire campus.

Student Life *Housing:* on-campus residence required through sophomore year. *Options:* coed, men-only, women-only, disabled students. Campus housing is university owned. Freshman campus housing is guaranteed. *Activities and organizations:* drama/theater group, student-run newspaper, radio and television station, choral group, Women's Center, Ware Institute for Community Service, College Reporter, Ben's Underground, F&M Players, national fraternities, national sororities. *Campus security:* 24-hour emergency response devices and patrols, late-night transport/escort service, controlled dormitory access, residence hall security, campus security connected to city police and fire company. *Student services:* health clinic, personal/psychological counseling, women's center.

Athletics Member NCAA. All Division III except wrestling (Division I). *Intercollegiate sports:* baseball M, basketball M/W, crew M (c)/W, cross-country running M/W, equestrian sports W (c), field hockey W, football M, golf M/W, ice hockey M (c), lacrosse M/W, rugby M (c)/W (c), soccer M/W, softball W, squash M/W, swimming and diving M/W, tennis M/W, track and field M/W, ultimate Frisbee M (c), volleyball M (c)/W, wrestling M. *Intramural sports:* archery M/W, badminton M/W, basketball M/W, bowling M/W, football M, soccer M/W, softball M/W, squash M/W, table tennis M/W, tennis M/W, volleyball M/W, wrestling M.

Standardized Tests *Recommended:* SAT or ACT (for admission).

Costs (2007–08) *Comprehensive fee:* $45,654 includes full-time tuition ($36,430), mandatory fees ($50), and room and board ($9174). Full-time tuition and fees vary according to reciprocity agreements. Part-time tuition: $4554 per course. *College room only:* $5880. Room and board charges vary according to board plan, housing facility, and location. *Payment plans:* installment, deferred payment. *Waivers:* employees or children of employees.

Financial Aid Of all full-time matriculated undergraduates who enrolled in 2007, 1,133 applied for aid, 965 were judged to have need, 341 had their need fully met. In 2007, 487 non-need-based awards were made. *Average percent of need met:* 96%. *Average financial aid package:* $28,513. *Average need-based loan:* $5733. *Average need-based gift aid:* $21,392. *Average non-need-based aid:* $13,519. *Average indebtedness upon graduation:* $24,752. *Financial aid deadline:* 3/1.

Applying *Options:* electronic application, early admission, early decision, deferred entrance. *Application fee:* $50. *Required:* essay or personal statement, high school transcript, 2 letters of recommendation. *Recommended:* interview. *Application deadlines:* 2/1 (freshmen), 5/1 (transfers). *Early decision deadline:* 11/15. *Notification:* 4/1 (freshmen), 12/15 (early decision).

Freshman Application Contact Sara Harberson, Vice President for Enrollment Management, Franklin & Marshall College, PO Box 3003, Lancaster, PA 17604-3003. *Phone:* 717-291-3953. *Fax:* 717-291-4389. *E-mail:* admission@fandm.edu.

GANNON UNIVERSITY

Erie, Pennsylvania **www.gannon.edu/**

- **Independent Roman Catholic** comprehensive, founded 1925
- **Urban** 13-acre campus with easy access to Cleveland
- **Endowment** $37.6 million
- **Coed** 2,729 undergraduate students, 84% full-time, 60% women, 40% men
- **Moderately difficult** entrance level, 83% of applicants were admitted

At Gannon, students can custom-tailor their education to meet their specific personal, educational, and spiritual goals. Students explore internships, co-ops, service-learning projects, honors courses, and campus ministry activities while developing a values-centered liberal arts education in one of more than seventy undergraduate majors.

Undergraduates 2,290 full-time, 439 part-time. Students come from 30 states and territories, 8 other countries, 22% are from out of state, 5% African American, 2% Asian American or Pacific Islander, 2% Hispanic American, 0.3% Native American, 0.9% international, 3% transferred in, 48% live on campus. *Retention:* 81% of 2006 full-time freshmen returned.

Freshmen *Admission:* 2,909 applied, 2,423 admitted, 617 enrolled. *Average high school GPA:* 3.42. *Test scores:* SAT critical reading scores over 500: 59%; SAT math scores over 500: 67%; ACT scores over 18: 87%; SAT critical reading scores over 600: 18%; SAT math scores over 600: 23%; ACT scores over 24: 42%; SAT critical reading scores over 700: 2%; SAT math scores over 700: 2%; ACT scores over 30: 6%.

Faculty *Total:* 334, 57% full-time, 49% with terminal degrees. *Student/faculty ratio:* 14:1.

Majors Accounting; accounting technology and bookkeeping; advertising; area studies related; bioinformatics; biology/biological sciences; biology/biotechnology laboratory technician; business administration and management; business/commerce; business teacher education; chemical engineering; chemistry; clinical laboratory science/medical technology; computer and information sciences; computer programming; criminal justice/safety; dietetics; dramatic/theater arts; early childhood education; education (multiple levels); education related; electrical, electronics and communications engineering; elementary education; English literature (British and Commonwealth); environmental/environmental health engineering; environmental science; finance; foreign languages and literatures; foreign language teacher education; funeral service and mortuary science; health/medical preparatory programs related; health professions related; history; industrial engineering; insurance; international business/trade/commerce; journalism; kinesiology and exercise science; legal assistant/paralegal; liberal arts and sciences/liberal studies; management information systems; marketing/marketing management; mathematics; mechanical engineering; medical radiologic technology; merchandising, sales, and marketing operations related (specialized); multi-/interdisciplinary studies related; nursing (registered nurse training); philosophy; physician assistant; political science and government; pre-law studies; premedical studies; psychology; radio and television broadcasting technology; respiratory care therapy; secondary education; social sciences; social studies teacher education; social work; special education; sport and fitness administration/management; theology; visual and performing arts.

Academics *Calendar:* semesters plus 2 summer sessions. *Degrees:* bachelor's, master's, doctoral, post-master's, and postbachelor's certificates (associate). *Special study options:* academic remediation for entering students, accelerated degree program, adult/continuing education programs, cooperative education, distance learning, double majors, English as a second language, external degree program, honors programs, independent study, internships, off-campus study, part-time degree program, services for LD students, study abroad, summer session for credit. *ROTC:* Army (b). *Unusual degree programs:* 3-2 engineering with University of Akron, University of Pittsburgh.

Computers on Campus 300 computers/terminals and 1,225 ports are available on campus for general student use. Students can access the following: campus intranet, computer help desk, free student e-mail accounts, online (class) grades, online (class) registration, online (class) schedules. Campuswide network is available. 100% of college-owned or -operated housing units are wired for high-speed Internet access. Wireless service is available via entire campus.

Student Life *Housing:* on-campus residence required through sophomore year. *Options:* coed, disabled students. Campus housing is university owned and leased by the school. Freshman campus housing is guaranteed. *Activities and organizations:* drama/theater group, student-run newspaper, radio station, choral group, Model United Nations, Vitality Through Exercise, Gannon University Residence Union, national fraternities, national sororities. *Campus security:* 24-hour emergency response devices and patrols, student patrols, late-night transport/escort service, controlled dormitory access, security cameras. *Student services:* health clinic, personal/psychological counseling.

Athletics Member NCAA. All Division II. *Intercollegiate sports:* baseball M (s), basketball M (s)/W (s), cross-country running M (s)/W (s), football M, golf M (s)/W (s), lacrosse W (s), soccer M (s)/W (s), softball W (s), swimming and diving M (s)/W (s), volleyball W (s), water polo M/W, wrestling M (s). *Intramural sports:* badminton M/W, basketball M/W, bowling M/W, cross-country running M/W, football M, golf M/W, racquetball M/W, soccer M/W, softball M/W, swimming and diving M/W, tennis M/W, volleyball M (c)/W, water polo M, weight lifting M, wrestling M.

Standardized Tests *Required:* SAT or ACT (for admission).

Costs (2007–08) *Comprehensive fee:* $29,646 includes full-time tuition ($20,850), mandatory fees ($496), and room and board ($8300). Full-time tuition and fees vary according to class time and program. Part-time tuition: $645 per credit hour. Part-time tuition and fees vary according to class time and program. *Required fees:* $16 per credit hour part-time. *College room only:* $4550. Room and board charges vary according to board plan and housing facility. *Payment plans:* installment, deferred payment. *Waivers:* senior citizens and employees or children of employees.

Financial Aid Of all full-time matriculated undergraduates who enrolled in 2007, 2,140 applied for aid, 1,946 were judged to have need, 701 had their need fully met. 487 Federal Work-Study jobs (averaging $2023). 137 state and other part-time jobs (averaging $1987). In 2007, 296 non-need-based awards were made. *Average percent of need met:* 78%. *Average financial aid package:* $17,005. *Average need-based loan:* $3734. *Average need-based gift aid:* $13,098. *Average non-need-based aid:* $6510. *Average indebtedness upon graduation:* $26,014.

Applying *Options:* electronic application, early admission, deferred entrance. *Application fee:* $25. *Required:* high school transcript, minimum 2.0 GPA. *Required for some:* minimum 3.0 GPA, 3 letters of recommendation, interview. *Recommended:* essay or personal statement, counselor's recommendation. *Application deadlines:* rolling (freshmen), rolling (transfers).

Freshman Application Contact Office of Admissions, Gannon University, University Square, Erie, PA 16541. *Phone:* 814-871-7240. *Toll-free phone:* 800-GANNONU. *Fax:* 814-871-5803. *E-mail:* admissions@gannon.edu.

See page 2238 for the College Close-Up.

GENEVA COLLEGE

Beaver Falls, Pennsylvania **www.geneva.edu/**

- **Independent** comprehensive, founded 1848, affiliated with Reformed Presbyterian Church of North America
- **Small-town** 55-acre campus with easy access to Pittsburgh
- **Endowment** $32.6 million
- **Coed**
- **Moderately difficult** entrance level

Faculty *Student/faculty ratio:* 13:1.

Academics *Calendar:* semesters. *Degrees:* associate, bachelor's, and master's.

Student Life *Campus security:* 24-hour emergency response devices and patrols, late-night transport/escort service, controlled dormitory access.

Athletics Member NAIA, NCCAA.

Standardized Tests *Required:* SAT or ACT (for admission).

Costs (2008–09) *Comprehensive fee:* $27,850 includes full-time tuition ($20,400) and room and board ($7450). Part-time tuition: $680 per credit.

Financial Aid Of all full-time matriculated undergraduates who enrolled in 2007, 1,167 applied for aid, 1,066 were judged to have need, 292 had their need fully met. In 2007, 200 non-need-based awards were made. *Average percent of need met:* 83. *Average financial aid package:* $16,490. *Average need-based loan:* $4191. *Average need-based gift aid:* $12,151. *Average non-need-based aid:* $8920. *Average indebtedness upon graduation:* $25,197.

Applying *Options:* electronic application, early admission, deferred entrance. *Application fee:* $40. *Required:* essay or personal statement, high school transcript, minimum 2.0 GPA. *Required for some:* letters of recommendation, interview. *Recommended:* minimum 3.0 GPA, interview.

Freshman Application Contact Mr. David Layton, Dean for Undergraduate Enrollment, Geneva College, 3200 College Avenue, Beaver Falls, PA 15010-3599. *Phone:* 724-847-6500. *Toll-free phone:* 800-847-8255. *E-mail:* admissions@geneva.edu.

GETTYSBURG COLLEGE

Gettysburg, Pennsylvania **www.gettysburg.edu/**

- **Independent** 4-year, founded 1832, affiliated with Evangelical Lutheran Church in America
- **Small-town** 200-acre campus with easy access to Baltimore and Washington, DC
- **Endowment** $241.5 million
- **Coed** 2,497 undergraduate students, 99% full-time, 53% women, 47% men
- **Most difficult** entrance level, 36% of applicants were admitted

Undergraduates 2,469 full-time, 28 part-time. Students come from 40 states and territories, 35 other countries, 74% are from out of state, 4% African American, 2% Asian American or Pacific Islander, 2% Hispanic American, 2% international, 0.6% transferred in, 94% live on campus. *Retention:* 90% of 2006 full-time freshmen returned.

Freshmen *Admission:* 6,126 applied, 2,180 admitted, 695 enrolled. *Test scores:* SAT critical reading scores over 500: 100%; SAT math scores over 500: 100%; SAT critical reading scores over 600: 82%; SAT math scores over 600: 75%; SAT critical reading scores over 700: 19%; SAT math scores over 700: 10%.

Faculty *Total:* 285, 70% full-time, 61% with terminal degrees. *Student/faculty ratio:* 11:1.

Majors Accounting; African-American/Black studies; American history; American studies; ancient/classical Greek; anthropology; area, ethnic, cultural, and gender studies related; area studies; area studies related; art; art history, criticism and conservation; Asian history; Asian studies (East); Asian studies (South); biochemistry; biological and physical sciences; biology/biological sciences; broadcast journalism; business administration and management; business administration, management and operations related; chemistry; classics and languages, literatures and linguistics; computer science; creative writing; dramatic/theater arts; economics; education; elementary education; engineering related; English; English composition; environmental science; environmental studies; European history; fine/studio arts; French; German; health science; Hispanic-American, Puerto Rican, and Mexican-American/Chicano studies; history; interdisciplinary studies; international business/trade/commerce; international economics; international relations and affairs; Italian; Japanese; Japanese studies; journalism; Latin; Latin American studies; liberal arts and sciences/liberal studies; literature; marine biology and biological oceanography; mathematics; middle school education; modern languages; molecular biology; music; music teacher education; non-profit management; peace studies and conflict resolution; philosophy; physical education teaching and coaching; physics; political science and government; predentistry studies; pre-law studies; pre-medical studies; pre-nursing studies; pre-pharmacy studies; pre-veterinary studies; psychology; religious studies; Romance languages; science teacher education; secondary education; social sciences; social sciences related; sociology; Spanish; visual and performing arts; western civilization; women's studies.

Academics *Calendar:* semesters. *Degree:* bachelor's. *Special study options:* adult/continuing education programs, advanced placement credit, double majors, independent study, internships, off-campus study, student-designed majors, study abroad. *ROTC:* Army (c). *Unusual degree programs:* 3-2 engineering with Rensselaer Polytechnic Institute, Washington University, Columbia University; forestry with Duke University; nursing with Johns Hopkins University.

Computers on Campus Students can access the following: campus intranet, computer help desk, online (class) registration. Campuswide network is available. 100% of college-owned or -operated housing units are wired for high-speed Internet access.

Student Life *Housing:* on-campus residence required through senior year. *Options:* coed, men-only, women-only. Campus housing is university owned. Freshman campus housing is guaranteed. *Activities and organizations:* drama/theater group, student-run newspaper, radio and television station, choral group, marching band, community service, music, athletics, student government, national fraternities, national sororities. *Campus security:* 24-hour emergency response devices and patrols, late-night transport/escort service, controlled dormitory access. *Student services:* health clinic, personal/psychological counseling, women's center.

Athletics Member NCAA. All Division III. *Intercollegiate sports:* baseball M, basketball M/W, cheerleading M/W, cross-country running M/W, field hockey W, football M, golf M/W, lacrosse M/W, soccer M/W, softball W, swimming and diving M/W, tennis M/W, track and field M/W, volleyball W, wrestling M. *Intramural sports:* badminton M/W, basketball M/W, cross-country running M/W, equestrian sports M/W, field hockey W, football M, golf M/W, ice hockey M (c), lacrosse M/W, rugby M (c)/W (c), skiing (cross-country) M/W, skiing (downhill) M/W, soccer M/W, softball M/W, swimming and diving M/W, tennis M/W, track and field M/W, ultimate Frisbee M (c)/W (c), volleyball M/W, wrestling M.

Standardized Tests *Required:* SAT or ACT (for admission). *Recommended:* SAT Subject Tests (for admission).

Costs (2007–08) *Comprehensive fee:* $44,620 includes full-time tuition ($35,640), mandatory fees ($350), and room and board ($8630). *College room only:* $4630. Room and board charges vary according to board plan and housing facility. *Payment plans:* tuition prepayment, installment. *Waivers:* employees or children of employees.

Financial Aid Of all full-time matriculated undergraduates who enrolled in 2007, 1,694 applied for aid, 1,451 were judged to have need, 1,435 had their need fully met. 605 Federal Work-Study jobs (averaging $900). 640 state and other part-time jobs (averaging $933). In 2007, 335 non-need-based awards were made. *Average percent of need met:* 100%. *Average financial aid package:* $27,610. *Average need-based loan:* $4973. *Average need-based gift aid:* $22,731. *Average non-need-based aid:* $9532. *Average indebtedness upon graduation:* $27,440. *Financial aid deadline:* 2/15.

Applying *Options:* electronic application, early admission, early decision, deferred entrance. *Application fee:* $55. *Required:* essay or personal statement, high school transcript, 2 letters of recommendation. *Recommended:* minimum 3.0 GPA, interview, extracurricular activities. *Application deadlines:* 2/1 (freshmen), rolling (transfers). *Early decision deadline:* 11/15 (for plan 1), 1/15 (for plan 2). *Notification:* 4/1 (freshmen), continuous (transfers), 12/15 (early decision plan 1), 2/15 (early decision plan 2).

Freshman Application Contact Ms. Gail Sweezey, Director of Admissions, Gettysburg College, 300 North Washington Street, Gettysburg, PA 17325. *Phone:* 717-337-6100. *Toll-free phone:* 800-431-0803. *Fax:* 717-337-6145. *E-mail:* admiss@gettysburg.edu.

GRATZ COLLEGE

Melrose Park, Pennsylvania — www.gratzcollege.edu/

- **Independent Jewish** comprehensive, founded 1895
- **Suburban** 28-acre campus with easy access to Philadelphia
- **Endowment** $3.1 million
- **Coed**
- **Moderately difficult** entrance level

Academics *Calendar:* semesters. *Degrees:* bachelor's, master's, and post-master's certificates.

Student Life *Campus security:* 24-hour patrols, Locked entrance; people must be buzzed into the building.

Costs (2007–08) *Tuition:* $11,340 full-time, $1600 per course part-time. *Required fees:* $400 full-time.

Financial Aid Of all full-time matriculated undergraduates who enrolled in 2002, 4 applied for aid, 4 were judged to have need. *Average percent of need met:* 86. *Average financial aid package:* $3908. *Average need-based loan:* $3333.

Applying *Options:* electronic application, early admission, deferred entrance. *Application fee:* $50. *Required:* essay or personal statement, high school transcript, letters of recommendation. *Required for some:* interview.

Freshman Application Contact Ms. Ruthann Crosby, Director of Student Life, Gratz College, 7605 Old York Road, Melrose Park, PA 19027. *Phone:* 215-635-7300. *Toll-free phone:* 800-475-4635 Ext. 140. *Fax:* 215-635-7399. *E-mail:* admissions@gratz.edu.

GROVE CITY COLLEGE

Grove City, Pennsylvania — www.gcc.edu/

- **Independent Presbyterian** 4-year, founded 1876
- **Small-town** 150-acre campus with easy access to Pittsburgh
- **Endowment** $120.0 million
- **Coed** 2,504 undergraduate students, 99% full-time, 50% women, 50% men
- **Most difficult** entrance level, 55% of applicants were admitted

Grove City College is the most affordable, top-ranked Christian college. The institution is committed to rigorous academics and Christian values at an amazing value. The school's humanities and social sciences programs emphasize classic books and great thinkers proved across the ages to be of value in the quest for knowledge. Professional studies include excellent mechanical and electrical/computer engineering programs, which are accredited by the Engineering Accreditation Commission of the Accreditation Board for Engineering and Technology, Inc. The Grove City College Information Technology Initiative provides every freshman with a Tablet PC and color printer, which they keep upon graduation and are included in the cost of education.

Undergraduates 2,480 full-time, 24 part-time. Students come from 42 states and territories, 11 other countries, 53% are from out of state, 0.6% African American, 2% Asian American or Pacific Islander, 1% Hispanic American, 0.1% Native American, 0.7% international, 0.8% transferred in, 90% live on campus. *Retention:* 90% of 2006 full-time freshmen returned.

Freshmen *Admission:* 1,916 applied, 1,057 admitted, 655 enrolled. *Average high school GPA:* 3.71. *Test scores:* SAT critical reading scores over 500: 96%; SAT math scores over 500: 96%; ACT scores over 18: 100%; SAT critical reading scores over 600: 70%; SAT math scores over 600: 71%; ACT scores over 24: 88%; SAT critical reading scores over 700: 26%; SAT math scores over 700: 18%; ACT scores over 30: 29%.

Faculty *Total:* 211, 66% full-time, 61% with terminal degrees. *Student/faculty ratio:* 15:1.

Majors Accounting; biochemistry; biology/biological sciences; business administration and management; business/managerial economics; chemistry; computer and information sciences; computer management; divinity/ministry; economics; electrical and electronic engineering technologies related; electrical, electronics and communications engineering; elementary education; English; entrepreneurship; finance; French; history; international business/trade/commerce; kindergarten/preschool education; literature; marketing/marketing management; mass communication/media; mathematics; mechanical engineering; mechanical engineering technologies related; modern languages; molecular biology; music; music management and merchandising; music performance; music teacher education; philosophy; physics; political science and government; pre-dentistry studies; pre-law studies; pre-medical studies; pre-veterinary studies; psychology; religious studies; science teacher education; secondary education; sociology; Spanish.

Academics *Calendar:* semesters. *Degree:* bachelor's. *Special study options:* advanced placement credit, double majors, independent study, internships, student-designed majors, study abroad, summer session for credit. *ROTC:* Army (c).

Computers on Campus 50 computers/terminals are available on campus for general student use. Students can access the following: campus intranet, computer help desk, free student e-mail accounts, online (class) grades, online (class) registration, online (class) schedules. Campuswide network is available. 100% of college-owned or -operated housing units are wired for high-speed Internet access. Wireless service is available via learning centers, student centers.

Student Life *Housing:* on-campus residence required through senior year. *Options:* men-only, women-only. Campus housing is university owned. Freshman campus housing is guaranteed. *Activities and organizations:* drama/theater group, student-run newspaper, radio and television station, choral group, marching band, Salt Company, Warriors for Christ, orientation board, Orchesis, touring choir. *Campus security:* 24-hour emergency response devices and patrols, student patrols, late-night transport/escort service, controlled dormitory access, monitored women's residence hall entrances. *Student services:* health clinic, personal/psychological counseling.

Athletics Member NCAA. All Division III. *Intercollegiate sports:* baseball M, basketball M/W, cheerleading W, cross-country running M/W, football M, golf M/W, soccer M/W, softball W, swimming and diving M/W, tennis M/W, track and field M/W, volleyball W, water polo W. *Intramural sports:* basketball M/W, bowling M/W, football M, golf M/W, racquetball M/W, soccer M, softball M, swimming and diving M/W, table tennis W, tennis M/W, ultimate Frisbee M/W, volleyball M/W, weight lifting M.

Standardized Tests *Required:* SAT or ACT (for admission).

Costs (2007–08) *Comprehensive fee:* $17,634 includes full-time tuition ($11,500) and room and board ($6134). Full-time tuition and fees vary according to course load. Part-time tuition: $365 per credit. *Room and board:* Room and board charges vary according to housing facility. *Payment plan:* installment. *Waivers:* employees or children of employees.

Financial Aid Of all full-time matriculated undergraduates who enrolled in 2007, 1,136 applied for aid, 885 were judged to have need, 103 had their need fully met. 18 state and other part-time jobs (averaging $600). In 2007, 777 non-need-based awards were made. *Average percent of need met:* 58%. *Average financial aid package:* $5845. *Average need-based loan:* $18. *Average need-based gift aid:* $6097. *Average non-need-based aid:* $6520. *Average indebtedness upon graduation:* $24,721. *Financial aid deadline:* 4/15.

Applying *Options:* electronic application, early admission, early decision, deferred entrance. *Application fee:* $50. *Required:* essay or personal statement, high school transcript, 2 letters of recommendation. *Recommended:* interview. *Application deadlines:* 2/1 (freshmen), 8/15 (transfers). *Early decision deadline:* 11/15. *Notification:* 3/15 (freshmen), continuous (transfers), 12/15 (early decision).

Freshman Application Contact Mr. Jeffrey Mincey, Director of Admissions, Grove City College, 100 Campus Drive, Grove City, PA 16127-2104. *Phone:* 724-458-2100. *Fax:* 724-458-3395. *E-mail:* admissions@gcc.edu.

See page 2240 for the College Close-Up.

GWYNEDD-MERCY COLLEGE

Gwynedd Valley, Pennsylvania — www.gmc.edu/

- **Independent Roman Catholic** comprehensive, founded 1948
- **Suburban** 170-acre campus with easy access to Philadelphia
- **Endowment** $11.8 million
- **Coed** 2,017 undergraduate students, 66% full-time, 74% women, 26% men
- **Moderately difficult** entrance level, 57% of applicants were admitted

Gwynedd-Mercy College (GMC) is an independent, coeducational institution. Espousing the ideals of a liberal education, the College continues its commitment to prepare students for professional careers. GMC offers baccalaureate and associate degrees in more than thirty undergraduate majors. In addition, six master's programs in nursing and education are available on a full- or part-time basis.

Undergraduates 1,332 full-time, 685 part-time. Students come from 10 states and territories, 27 other countries, 11% are from out of state, 16% African American, 3% Asian American or Pacific Islander, 1% Hispanic American, 0.3% Native American, 0.7% international, 8% transferred in, 27% live on campus. *Retention:* 75% of 2006 full-time freshmen returned.

Freshmen *Admission:* 1,901 applied, 1,080 admitted, 291 enrolled. *Test scores:* SAT critical reading scores over 500: 43%; SAT math scores over 500: 43%; SAT critical reading scores over 600: 9%; SAT math scores over 600: 9%; SAT critical reading scores over 700: 1%; SAT math scores over 700: 1%.

Faculty *Total:* 305, 27% full-time, 33% with terminal degrees. *Student/faculty ratio:* 11:1.

Majors Accounting; allied health diagnostic, intervention, and treatment professions related; biological and biomedical sciences related; biology/biological sciences; business administration and management; business teacher education; cardiovascular technology; clinical laboratory science/medical technology; computer and information sciences; computer programming; elementary education; English; forensic psychology; gerontology; health information/medical records administration; health information/medical records technology; health science; health services/allied health/health sciences; history; history teacher education; hospital and health care facilities administration; human services; liberal arts and sciences/liberal studies; mathematics; mathematics teacher education; nursing (registered nurse training); psychology; respiratory care therapy; secondary education; social work; sociology; special education.

Academics *Calendar:* semesters. *Degrees:* certificates, associate, bachelor's, master's, post-master's, and postbachelor's certificates. *Special study options:* academic remediation for entering students, accelerated degree program, adult/continuing education programs, advanced placement credit, cooperative education, double majors, English as a second language, freshman honors college, honors programs, independent study, internships, part-time degree program, summer session for credit.

Computers on Campus 218 computers/terminals are available on campus for general student use. Students can access the following: campus intranet, computer help desk, free student e-mail accounts, online (class) grades, online (class) registration, online (class) schedules. Campuswide network is available. 100% of college-owned or -operated housing units are wired for high-speed Internet access. Wireless service is available via classrooms, computer labs, libraries, student centers.

Student Life *Housing options:* coed, disabled students. Campus housing is university owned. Freshman applicants given priority for college housing. *Activities and organizations:* student-run newspaper, choral group, Voices of Gwynedd, Athletic Association, student government, Program Board, Peer Mentors. *Campus security:* 24-hour emergency response devices and patrols, late-night transport/escort service. *Student services:* health clinic, personal/psychological counseling.

Athletics Member NCAA. All Division III. *Intercollegiate sports:* baseball M, basketball M/W, field hockey W, golf M, lacrosse W, soccer M/W, softball W, tennis M/W, track and field M, volleyball W.

Standardized Tests *Required:* SAT or ACT (for admission).

Costs (2008–09) *Comprehensive fee:* $31,780 includes full-time tuition ($22,340), mandatory fees ($450), and room and board ($8990). Part-time tuition: $495 per credit. *Required fees:* $10 per credit part-time.

Financial Aid Of all full-time matriculated undergraduates who enrolled in 2006, 1,170 applied for aid, 988 were judged to have need, 157 had their need fully met. 185 Federal Work-Study jobs (averaging $813). 10 state and other part-time jobs (averaging $1450). In 2006, 246 non-need-based awards were made. *Average percent of need met:* 70%. *Average financial aid package:* $12,676. *Average need-based loan:* $3333. *Average need-based gift aid:* $9909. *Average non-need-based aid:* $11,601. *Average indebtedness upon graduation:* $18,877.

Applying *Options:* electronic application, deferred entrance. *Application fee:* $25. *Required:* high school transcript. *Application deadlines:* rolling (freshmen), rolling (out-of-state freshmen), 8/20 (transfers). *Notification:* continuous (freshmen), continuous (transfers).

Freshman Application Contact Ms. Michelle Diehl, Director of Admissions, Gwynedd-Mercy College, 1325 Sumneytown Pike, Gwynedd Valley, PA 19437-0901. *Phone:* 215-646-7300. *Toll-free phone:* 800-DIAL-GMC. *Fax:* 215-641-5556. *E-mail:* admissions@gmc.edu.

See page 2242 for the College Close-Up.

HARRISBURG UNIVERSITY OF SCIENCE AND TECHNOLOGY

Harrisburg, Pennsylvania — www.harrisburgu.net/

- **Independent** comprehensive, founded 2005
- **Urban** campus
- **Coed** 141 undergraduate students, 46% full-time, 52% women, 48% men
- **Minimally difficult** entrance level, 86% of applicants were admitted

Undergraduates 65 full-time, 76 part-time. Students come from 5 states and territories, 5% are from out of state, 42% African American, 4% Asian American or Pacific Islander, 14% Hispanic American, 2% international, 6% transferred in. *Retention:* 40% of 2006 full-time freshmen returned.

Freshmen *Admission:* 203 applied, 175 admitted, 87 enrolled. *Average high school GPA:* 2.79.

Faculty *Total:* 26, 35% full-time, 42% with terminal degrees. *Student/faculty ratio:* 5:1.

Majors Biology/biological sciences; computer and information sciences; e-commerce; geography; interdisciplinary studies.

Academics *Calendar:* semesters. *Degrees:* certificates, bachelor's, and master's. *Special study options:* academic remediation for entering students, adult/continuing education programs, advanced placement credit, double majors, independent study, internships, part-time degree program, services for LD students, student-designed majors, summer session for credit.

Computers on Campus 10 computers/terminals and 80 ports are available on campus for general student use. Students can access the following: campus intranet, computer help desk, free student e-mail accounts. Campuswide network is available. Wireless service is available via entire campus.

Student Life *Housing:* college housing not available. *Campus security:* trained security personnel during all university operating hours.

Standardized Tests *Recommended:* SAT or ACT (for admission).

Costs (2008–09) *Tuition:* $14,750 full-time, $500 per credit part-time.

Financial Aid Of all full-time matriculated undergraduates who enrolled in 2006, 5 Federal Work-Study jobs (averaging $1000).

Applying *Options:* electronic application. *Required:* high school transcript. *Recommended:* essay or personal statement, interview. *Application deadline:* rolling (out-of-state freshmen).

Freshman Application Contact Office of Admissions, Harrisburg University of Science and Technology, 304 Market Street, Harrisburg, PA 17101. *Phone:* 717-901-5160. *Toll-free phone:* 866-HBG-UNIV. *Fax:* 717-901-3160. *E-mail:* admissions@harrisburgu.net.

See page 2244 for the College Close-Up.

HAVERFORD COLLEGE

Haverford, Pennsylvania **www.haverford.edu/**

- **Independent** 4-year, founded 1833
- **Suburban** 200-acre campus with easy access to Philadelphia
- **Endowment** $539.6 million
- **Coed** 1,169 undergraduate students, 100% full-time, 54% women, 46% men
- **Most difficult** entrance level, 25% of applicants were admitted

Undergraduates 1,169 full-time. Students come from 48 states and territories, 44 other countries, 87% are from out of state, 8% African American, 11% Asian American or Pacific Islander, 8% Hispanic American, 0.7% Native American, 4% international, 0.2% transferred in, 99% live on campus. *Retention:* 96% of 2006 full-time freshmen returned.

Freshmen *Admission:* 3,492 applied, 877 admitted, 315 enrolled. *Test scores:* SAT critical reading scores over 500: 100%; SAT math scores over 500: 100%; SAT writing scores over 500: 100%; SAT critical reading scores over 600: 92%; SAT math scores over 600: 88%; SAT writing scores over 600: 91%; SAT critical reading scores over 700: 55%; SAT math scores over 700: 49%; SAT writing scores over 700: 52%.

Faculty *Total:* 129, 88% full-time, 91% with terminal degrees. *Student/faculty ratio:* 8:1.

Majors African studies; anthropology; archeology; art; art history, criticism and conservation; Asian studies (East); astronomy; biochemistry; biology/biological sciences; biophysics; chemistry; classics and languages, literatures and linguistics; comparative literature; computer science; econometrics and quantitative economics; economics; education; English; French; geology/earth science; German; history; Italian; Latin; Latin American studies; mathematics; modern Greek; music; neuroscience; peace studies and conflict resolution; philosophy; physics; political science and government; pre-law studies; pre-medical studies; preveterinary studies; psychology; religious studies; Romance languages; Russian; sociology; Spanish; urban studies/affairs; women's studies.

Academics *Calendar:* semesters. *Degree:* bachelor's. *Special study options:* advanced placement credit, double majors, independent study, internships, off-campus study, services for LD students, student-designed majors, study abroad. *Unusual degree programs:* 3-2 engineering with California Institute of Technology.

Computers on Campus 300 computers/terminals and 1,600 ports are available on campus for general student use. Students can access the following: campus intranet, computer help desk, free student e-mail accounts, online (class) grades, online (class) registration, online (class) schedules. Campuswide network is available. 100% of college-owned or -operated housing units are wired for high-speed Internet access. Wireless service is available via classrooms, computer centers, computer labs, dorm rooms, learning centers, libraries, student centers.

Student Life *Housing:* on-campus residence required for freshman year. *Options:* coed, disabled students. Campus housing is university owned. Freshman campus housing is guaranteed. *Activities and organizations:* drama/theater group, student-run newspaper, radio station, choral group, Volunteer Programs, Student Government, Choral Groups, Multicultural Groups, Orientation Team/Residential Life Leaders. *Campus security:* 24-hour emergency response devices and patrols, late-night transport/escort service, controlled dormitory access. *Student services:* health clinic, personal/psychological counseling, women's center.

Athletics Member NCAA. All Division III. *Intercollegiate sports:* badminton W (c), baseball M, basketball M/W, crew M (c)/W (c), cross-country running M/W, fencing M/W, field hockey W, golf M (c)/W (c), lacrosse M/W, rugby M (c), soccer M/W, softball W, squash M/W, tennis M/W, track and field M/W, ultimate Frisbee M (c)/W (c), volleyball M (c)/W, wrestling M (c). *Intramural sports:* basketball M/W, ice hockey M (c)/W (c), sailing M (c)/W (c), soccer M/W, softball M/W, tennis M/W, volleyball W.

Standardized Tests *Required:* SAT Reasoning Test or ACT and two SAT Subject Tests (for admission).

Costs (2007–08) *One-time required fee:* $180. *Comprehensive fee:* $46,260 includes full-time tuition ($35,058), mandatory fees ($322), and room and board ($10,880). *College room only:* $6150. *Payment plan:* installment. *Waivers:* employees or children of employees.

Financial Aid Of all full-time matriculated undergraduates who enrolled in 2007, 581 applied for aid, 528 were judged to have need, 528 had their need fully met. *Average percent of need met:* 100%. *Average financial aid package:* $29,072. *Average need-based loan:* $4291. *Average need-based gift aid:* $27,643. *Average indebtedness upon graduation:* $17,125. *Financial aid deadline:* 2/1.

Applying *Options:* electronic application, early admission, early decision, deferred entrance. *Application fee:* $60. *Required:* essay or personal statement, 2 letters of recommendation. *Recommended:* interview. *Application deadlines:* 1/15 (freshmen), 3/31 (transfers). *Early decision deadline:* 11/15. *Notification:* 4/15 (freshmen), 6/1 (transfers), 12/15 (early decision).

Freshman Application Contact Mr. Jess Lord, Dean of Admissions and Financial Aid, Haverford College, 370 Lancaster Avenue, Haverford, PA 19041-1392. *Phone:* 610-896-1350. *Fax:* 610-896-1338. *E-mail:* admitme@haverford.edu.

See page 2246 for the College Close-Up.

HOLY FAMILY UNIVERSITY

Philadelphia, Pennsylvania **www.holyfamily.edu/**

- **Independent Roman Catholic** comprehensive, founded 1954
- **Suburban** 47-acre campus
- **Endowment** $8.6 million
- **Coed** 2,320 undergraduate students, 62% full-time, 75% women, 25% men
- **Moderately difficult** entrance level, 63% of applicants were admitted

Undergraduates 1,448 full-time, 872 part-time. Students come from 9 states and territories, 5 other countries, 11% are from out of state, 7% African American, 5% Asian American or Pacific Islander, 3% Hispanic American, 0.3% Native American, 0.5% international, 9% transferred in, 13% live on campus. *Retention:* 85% of 2006 full-time freshmen returned.

Freshmen *Admission:* 1,097 applied, 694 admitted, 297 enrolled. *Average high school GPA:* 3.02. *Test scores:* SAT critical reading scores over 500: 35%; SAT math scores over 500: 39%; SAT critical reading scores over 600: 8%; SAT math scores over 600: 4%.

Faculty *Total:* 373, 27% full-time, 41% with terminal degrees. *Student/faculty ratio:* 15:1.

Majors Accounting; art; biochemistry; biology/biological sciences; business administration and management; chemistry; clinical/medical laboratory technology; communication/speech communication and rhetoric; computer and information sciences; computer management; criminal justice/law enforcement administration; economics; education; elementary education; English; fire science; French; history; humanities; industrial and organizational psychology; international business/trade/commerce; kindergarten/preschool education; liberal arts and sciences/liberal studies; literature; marketing/marketing management; mathematics; nursing science; physiological psychology/psychobiology; pre-dentistry studies; pre-law studies; pre-medical studies; pre-pharmacy studies; pre-veterinary studies; psychology; radiologic technology/science; religious education; religious studies; secondary education; social sciences; social studies teacher education; social work; sociology; Spanish; special education; sport and fitness administration/management.

Academics *Calendar:* semesters. *Degrees:* certificates, associate, bachelor's, master's, and postbachelor's certificates. *Special study options:* academic remediation for entering students, accelerated degree program, adult/continuing education programs, advanced placement credit, cooperative education, double majors, freshman honors college, honors programs, independent study, internships, part-time degree program, services for LD students, study abroad, summer session for credit.

Computers on Campus 350 computers/terminals and 250 ports are available on campus for general student use. Students can access the following: campus intranet, computer help desk, free student e-mail accounts, online (class) grades, online (class) registration, online (class) schedules. Campuswide network is available. 100% of college-owned or -operated housing units are wired for high-speed Internet access. Wireless service is available via entire campus.

Student Life *Housing options:* coed, cooperative, disabled students. Campus housing is university owned. Freshman applicants given priority for college housing. *Activities and organizations:* drama/theater group, student-run newspaper, radio and television station, choral group, Students at Your Service (S.A.Y.S.), Rainbow Connections, Campus Ministry Team, Folio, Tri-lite. *Campus security:* 24-hour emergency response devices and patrols, student patrols, late-night transport/escort service. *Student services:* health clinic, personal/psychological counseling.

Athletics Member NCAA. All Division II. *Intercollegiate sports:* basketball M (s)/W (s), cheerleading W, cross-country running M (s)/W (s), golf M (s), lacrosse W (s), soccer M (s)/W (s), softball W (s), tennis W (s), track and field M (s)/W (s), volleyball W (s). *Intramural sports:* basketball M/W, football M, racquetball M/W, table tennis M/W, ultimate Frisbee M/W, volleyball M/W.

Standardized Tests *Required:* SAT or ACT (for admission).

Costs (2008–09) *Comprehensive fee:* $30,990 includes full-time tuition ($20,990), mandatory fees ($600), and room and board ($9400). Part-time tuition: $460 per credit hour. *Required fees:* $60 per term part-time. *College room only:* $5600.

Financial Aid Of all full-time matriculated undergraduates who enrolled in 2007, 1,310 applied for aid, 1,310 were judged to have need, 1,181 had their need fully met. 423 Federal Work-Study jobs (averaging $1422). In 2007, 349 non-need-based awards were made. *Average percent of need met:* 85%. *Average financial aid package:* $8627. *Average need-based loan:* $4264. *Average need-based gift aid:* $8048. *Average non-need-based aid:* $1375. *Average indebtedness upon graduation:* $17,125.

Applying *Options:* electronic application, deferred entrance. *Application fee:* $25. *Required:* essay or personal statement, high school transcript, 1 letter of recommendation. *Recommended:* interview. *Application deadlines:* rolling (freshmen), rolling (transfers).

Freshman Application Contact Ms. Lauren McDermott-Campbell, Director of Admissions, Holy Family University, Grant and Frankford Avenues, Philadelphia, PA 19114-2094. *Phone:* 215-637-3050. *Toll-free phone:* 800-637-1191. *Fax:* 215-281-1022. *E-mail:* admissions@holyfamily.edu.

HUSSIAN SCHOOL OF ART

Philadelphia, Pennsylvania **www.hussianart.edu/**

- **Proprietary** 4-year, founded 1946
- **Urban** 1-acre campus
- **Coed** 142 undergraduate students, 100% full-time, 30% women, 70% men
- **Minimally difficult** entrance level, 95% of applicants were admitted

Undergraduates 142 full-time. Students come from 4 states and territories, 20% are from out of state, 13% African American, 6% Hispanic American. *Retention:* 75% of 2006 full-time freshmen returned.

Freshmen *Admission:* 108 applied, 103 admitted, 48 enrolled. *Average high school GPA:* 2.7.

Faculty *Total:* 24, 13% full-time, 13% with terminal degrees. *Student/faculty ratio:* 18:1.

Majors Advertising; commercial and advertising art.

Academics *Calendar:* semesters. *Degree:* associate. *Special study options:* independent study, internships.

Computers on Campus 58 computers/terminals are available on campus for general student use. Campuswide network is available.

Student Life *Housing:* college housing not available. *Campus security:* security guard during open hours.

Costs (2008–09) *Tuition:* $11,000 full-time. *Required fees:* $825 full-time.

Applying *Options:* deferred entrance. *Application fee:* $25. *Required:* high school transcript, interview, art portfolio. *Application deadlines:* rolling (freshmen), rolling (transfers). *Notification:* continuous (freshmen), continuous (transfers).

Freshman Application Contact Ms. Lynne Wartman, Director of Admissions, Hussian School of Art, 1118 Market Street, Philadelphia, PA 19107. *Phone:* 215-981-0900. *Fax:* 215-864-9115. *E-mail:* info@hussianart.edu.

IMMACULATA UNIVERSITY

Immaculata, Pennsylvania **www.immaculata.edu/**

- **Independent Roman Catholic** comprehensive, founded 1920
- **Suburban** 400-acre campus with easy access to Philadelphia
- **Endowment** $13.9 million
- **Coed, primarily women** 2,918 undergraduate students, 36% full-time, 77% women, 23% men
- **Moderately difficult** entrance level, 80% of applicants were admitted

Immaculata University is a Catholic, coeducational, comprehensive liberal arts university dedicated to educating students of all faiths. Founded in 1920, Immaculata now enrolls more than 4,000 students. Immaculata is composed of three areas: the College of Undergraduate Studies, the College of Lifelong Learning, and the College of Graduate Studies. Approximately 900 men and women attend the College of Undergraduate Studies; 90 percent live in campus housing. A fixed tuition rate is offered to all full-time students entering the College of Undergraduate Studies. The University is located 20 miles west of Philadelphia.

Undergraduates 1,048 full-time, 1,870 part-time. Students come from 19 states and territories, 12 other countries, 31% are from out of state, 10% African American, 2% Asian American or Pacific Islander, 2% Hispanic American, 0.1% Native American, 0.8% international, 1% transferred in, 71% live on campus. *Retention:* 70% of 2006 full-time freshmen returned.

Freshmen *Admission:* 1,335 applied, 1,071 admitted, 365 enrolled. *Average high school GPA:* 3.1. *Test scores:* SAT critical reading scores over 500: 48%; SAT math scores over 500: 37%; SAT critical reading scores over 600: 10%; SAT math scores over 600: 6%; SAT critical reading scores over 700: 1%.

Faculty *Total:* 421, 24% full-time, 38% with terminal degrees. *Student/faculty ratio:* 10:1.

Majors Accounting; biochemistry; biology/biological sciences; biopsychology; business administration and management; chemistry; communication/speech communication and rhetoric; computer science; computer teacher education; criminology; dietetics; economics; elementary education; English; environmental studies; family and consumer sciences/home economics teacher education; fashion merchandising; finance; foods, nutrition, and wellness; French; health/health care administration; health services/allied health/health sciences; history; human resources management; information science/studies; intercultural/multicultural and diversity studies; international business/trade/commerce; international relations and affairs; kinesiology and exercise science; mathematics; mathematics and computer science; modern languages; music; music performance; music teacher education; music therapy; nursing science; pre-dentistry studies; pre-law studies; pre-veterinary studies; psychology; public policy analysis; religious/sacred music; social work; sociology; Spanish; theology.

Academics *Calendar:* semesters. *Degrees:* associate, bachelor's, master's, and doctoral. *Special study options:* academic remediation for entering students, accelerated degree program, adult/continuing education programs, advanced placement credit, double majors, English as a second language, external degree program, honors programs, independent study, internships, off-campus study, part-time degree program, services for LD students, study abroad, summer session for credit.

Computers on Campus 254 computers/terminals are available on campus for general student use. Campuswide network is available.

Student Life *Housing options:* coed, men-only, women-only, disabled students. Campus housing is university owned. Freshman campus housing is guaranteed. *Activities and organizations:* drama/theater group, student-run newspaper, choral group, Campus Ministry, Student Association, chorale, Honor Society, Cue and Curtain. *Campus security:* 24-hour emergency response devices and patrols, late-night transport/escort service, controlled dormitory access. *Student services:* health clinic, personal/psychological counseling.

Athletics Member NCAA. All Division III. *Intercollegiate sports:* basketball W, cross-country running W, field hockey W, lacrosse W, soccer W, softball W, tennis W, volleyball W. *Intramural sports:* archery W, badminton W, cheerleading W (c), equestrian sports W (c), fencing W, swimming and diving W.

Standardized Tests *Required:* SAT or ACT (for admission).

Costs (2007–08) *Comprehensive fee:* $32,450 includes full-time tuition ($22,650) and room and board ($9800). Full-time tuition and fees vary according to student level. Part-time tuition: $380 per credit hour. No tuition increase for student's term of enrollment. *College room only:* $5260. Room and board charges vary according to housing facility. *Payment plan:* installment. *Waivers:* employees or children of employees.

Financial Aid Of all full-time matriculated undergraduates who enrolled in 2007, 810 applied for aid, 697 were judged to have need, 201 had their need fully met. *Average percent of need met:* 24%. *Average financial aid package:* $15,657. *Average need-based loan:* $4132. *Average need-based gift aid:* $5516. *Average non-need-based aid:* $6508.

Applying *Options:* electronic application, early admission, deferred entrance. *Application fee:* $35. *Required:* high school transcript, minimum 2.0 GPA. *Required for some:* essay or personal statement. *Recommended:* minimum 3.0 GPA, interview. *Application deadlines:* rolling (freshmen), rolling (transfers). *Notification:* continuous (freshmen), continuous (transfers).

Freshman Application Contact Ms. Rebecca Bowlby, Director of Admissions, Immaculata University, PO Box 642, Immaculata, PA 19345-0642. *Phone:* 610-647-4400 Ext. 3046. *Toll-free phone:* 877-428-6328. *Fax:* 610-640-0836. *E-mail:* admiss@immaculata.edu.

See page 2248 for the College Close-Up.

INDIANA UNIVERSITY OF PENNSYLVANIA

Indiana, Pennsylvania **www.iup.edu/**

- **State-supported** university, founded 1875, part of Pennsylvania State System of Higher Education
- **Small-town** 350-acre campus with easy access to Pittsburgh
- **Coed** 11,724 undergraduate students, 92% full-time, 55% women, 45% men
- **Moderately difficult** entrance level, 65% of applicants were admitted

Undergraduates 10,741 full-time, 983 part-time. Students come from 30 states and territories, 56 other countries, 6% are from out of state, 11% African

American, 0.9% Asian American or Pacific Islander, 2% Hispanic American, 0.3% Native American, 2% international, 5% transferred in, 31% live on campus. *Retention:* 73% of 2006 full-time freshmen returned.

Freshmen *Admission:* 9,322 applied, 6,013 admitted, 2,560 enrolled. *Test scores:* SAT critical reading scores over 500: 41%; SAT math scores over 500: 42%; SAT writing scores over 500: 37%; SAT critical reading scores over 600: 9%; SAT math scores over 600: 9%; SAT writing scores over 600: 7%; SAT critical reading scores over 700: 1%; SAT math scores over 700: 1%; SAT writing scores over 700: 1%.

Faculty *Total:* 720, 90% full-time. *Student/faculty ratio:* 16:1.

Majors Accounting; anthropology; applied mathematics; art; art teacher education; audiology and speech-language pathology; biochemistry; biological and physical sciences; biology/biological sciences; business administration and management; chemistry; city/urban, community and regional planning; clinical laboratory science/medical technology; communication/speech communication and rhetoric; computer and information sciences; consumer economics; criminology; dietetics; dramatic/theater arts; early childhood education; economics; educational psychology; electrical and electronic engineering technologies related; elementary education; English; environmental health; family and consumer sciences/home economics teacher education; fashion merchandising; finance; fine/studio arts; foods, nutrition, and wellness; foreign languages related; French; general studies; geography; geology/earth science; German; health and physical education; history; hospitality administration; human development and family studies; human resources management; interior design; intermedia/multimedia; international business/trade/commerce; international relations and affairs; journalism; kindergarten/preschool education; management information systems; marketing/marketing management; mathematics; mathematics and statistics related; music; music performance; nuclear medical technology; nursing (registered nurse training); occupational safety and health technology; office management; optical sciences; philosophy; physical education teaching and coaching; physical sciences; physics; physics related; political science and government; psychology; rehabilitation and therapeutic professions related; religious studies; respiratory care therapy; science teacher education; secondary education; social science teacher education; sociology; Spanish; special education; special education (hearing impaired); trade and industrial teacher education.

Academics *Calendar:* semesters. *Degrees:* certificates, associate, bachelor's, master's, doctoral, post-master's, and postbachelor's certificates. *Special study options:* academic remediation for entering students, accelerated degree program, adult/continuing education programs, advanced placement credit, cooperative education, distance learning, double majors, English as a second language, freshman honors college, honors programs, independent study, internships, off-campus study, part-time degree program, services for LD students, study abroad, summer session for credit. *ROTC:* Army (b). *Unusual degree programs:* 3-2 engineering with Drexel University, University of Pittsburgh; forestry with Duke University.

Computers on Campus 3,500 computers/terminals are available on campus for general student use. Students can access the following: online (class) registration. Campuswide network is available. Wireless service is available via entire campus.

Student Life *Housing:* on-campus residence required for freshman year. *Options:* coed, women-only, disabled students. Campus housing is university owned and is provided by a third party. Freshman campus housing is guaranteed. *Activities and organizations:* drama/theater group, student-run newspaper, radio and television station, choral group, marching band, Student Government Association, Panhellenic Association, Interfraternity Council, NAACP, Alpha Phi Omega Services Fraternity, national fraternities, national sororities. *Campus security:* 24-hour emergency response devices and patrols, late-night transport/escort service, controlled dormitory access. *Student services:* health clinic, personal/psychological counseling, women's center, legal services.

Athletics Member NCAA. All Division II. *Intercollegiate sports:* baseball M (s), basketball M (s)/W (s), cross-country running M (s)/W (s), field hockey W (s), football M (s), golf M (s), lacrosse W (s), soccer W (s), softball W (s), swimming and diving M/W (s), tennis W (s), track and field M (s)/W (s), volleyball W (s). *Intramural sports:* archery M/W, badminton M/W, basketball M/W, bowling M/W, cheerleading M (c)/W (c), equestrian sports M (c)/W (c), fencing M (c), football M/W, golf M/W, ice hockey M (c)/W (c), lacrosse M (c), racquetball M/W, riflery M (c)/W (c), rugby M (c)/W (c), sailing M (c)/W (c), skiing (downhill) M (c)/W (c), soccer M (c)/W (c), softball M/W, table tennis M/W, tennis M/W, ultimate Frisbee M (c)/W (c), volleyball M (c)/W, water polo M (c)/W (c), weight lifting M/W.

Standardized Tests *Required:* SAT or ACT (for admission).

Costs (2007–08) *Tuition:* state resident $5178 full-time, $216 per credit part-time; nonresident $12,944 full-time, $539 per credit part-time. Full-time tuition and fees vary according to course load, location, and reciprocity agreements. Part-time tuition and fees vary according to course load, location, and reciprocity agreements. *Required fees:* $1517 full-time, $22 per credit part-time, $206 per term part-time. *Room and board:* $5436; room only: $3340. Room and board charges vary according to board plan, housing facility, and location. *Payment plans:* installment, deferred payment. *Waivers:* minority students and employees or children of employees.

Financial Aid Of all full-time matriculated undergraduates who enrolled in 2006, 9,113 applied for aid, 7,064 were judged to have need, 884 had their need fully met. 1,437 Federal Work-Study jobs (averaging $1383). 1,807 state and other part-time jobs (averaging $2209). In 2006, 332 non-need-based awards were made. *Average percent of need met:* 75%. *Average financial aid package:* $8185. *Average need-based loan:* $3640. *Average need-based gift aid:* $4745. *Average non-need-based aid:* $2430. *Average indebtedness upon graduation:* $22,431. *Financial aid deadline:* 4/15.

Applying *Options:* electronic application, early admission, deferred entrance. *Application fee:* $35. *Required:* high school transcript. *Recommended:* essay or personal statement, letters of recommendation. *Application deadlines:* rolling (freshmen), rolling (transfers). *Notification:* 9/15 (freshmen), continuous (transfers).

Freshman Application Contact Office of Admissions, Indiana University of Pennsylvania, 1011 South Drive, Sutton Hall 214, Indiana, PA 15705. *Phone:* 724-357-2230. *Toll-free phone:* 800-442-6830. *Fax:* 724-357-6281. *E-mail:* admissions-inquiry@iup.edu.

See page 2250 for the College Close-Up.

JUNIATA COLLEGE

Huntingdon, Pennsylvania **www.juniata.edu/**

- **Independent** 4-year, founded 1876, affiliated with Church of the Brethren
- **Small-town** 110-acre campus
- **Endowment** $71.1 million
- **Coed** 1,506 undergraduate students, 95% full-time, 54% women, 46% men
- **Moderately difficult** entrance level, 67% of applicants were admitted

Juniata has a flexible curriculum in which students can combine their intellectual interests and passions into a self-designed academic program. Two academic advisers provide advice and support to ensure preparedness for graduate work, professional school, research, and the job market. Hands-on learning through internships, study abroad, research, and even business start-ups give students real-world experiences while still in college. Juniata is a diverse, friendly, and open community where students feel at home.

Undergraduates 1,431 full-time, 75 part-time. Students come from 36 states and territories, 34 other countries, 32% are from out of state, 1% African American, 1% Asian American or Pacific Islander, 1% Hispanic American, 0.1% Native American, 5% international, 2% transferred in, 82% live on campus. *Retention:* 84% of 2006 full-time freshmen returned.

Freshmen *Admission:* 1,958 applied, 1,318 admitted, 377 enrolled. *Average high school GPA:* 3.78. *Test scores:* SAT critical reading scores over 500: 88%; SAT math scores over 500: 91%; SAT critical reading scores over 600: 38%; SAT math scores over 600: 42%; SAT critical reading scores over 700: 8%; SAT math scores over 700: 4%.

Faculty *Total:* 133, 73% full-time, 74% with terminal degrees. *Student/faculty ratio:* 13:1.

Majors Accounting; anthropology; art history, criticism and conservation; biochemistry; biology/biological sciences; biology teacher education; botany/plant biology; business administration and management; business/commerce; cell biology and histology; chemistry; chemistry teacher education; communication and journalism related; communication/speech communication and rhetoric; computer and information sciences; criminal justice/safety; criminology; early childhood education; ecology; economics; education; education (multiple levels); elementary education; engineering; engineering physics; English; English/language arts teacher education; environmental science; environmental studies; finance; fine/studio arts; foreign languages and literatures; foreign language teacher education; French; French language teacher education; geology/earth science; German; German language teacher education; health communication; health/medical preparatory programs related; history; humanities; human resources management; information resources management; information technology; international business/trade/commerce; international relations and affairs; kindergarten/preschool education; liberal arts and sciences/liberal studies; marine biology and biological oceanography; marketing/marketing management; mathematics; mathematics teacher education; microbiology; molecular biology; museum studies; natural sciences; peace studies and conflict resolution; philosophy; philosophy and religious studies related; physical sciences; physics; physics teacher education; political science and government; pre-dentistry studies; pre-law studies; pre-medical studies; pre-nursing studies; pre-pharmacy studies; pre-theology/pre-ministerial studies; pre-veterinary studies; psychology; public administration; religious studies; Russian; science teacher education; secondary education; social sciences; social studies teacher education; social work; sociology; Spanish; Spanish language teacher education; special education (early childhood); special education related; theater/theater arts management; zoology/animal biology.

Academics *Calendar:* semesters. *Degree:* bachelor's. *Special study options:* accelerated degree program, adult/continuing education programs, advanced placement credit, double majors, English as a second language, freshman honors college, honors programs, independent study, internships, off-campus study, part-time degree program, services for LD students, student-designed majors, study abroad, summer session for credit. *Unusual degree programs:* 3-2 engineering with Pennsylvania State University—University Park Campus, Columbia University, Washington University in St. Louis, Clarkson University; nursing with Johns Hopkins University, Case Western Reserve University, Jefferson College of Health Professions; biotechnology; cytotechnology; radiological science; medical technology; occupational therapy, physical therapy with Jefferson College of Health Professions; Widener University; Drexel University; Peace and Conflict Studies.

Computers on Campus 360 computers/terminals are available on campus for general student use. Students can access the following: campus intranet, computer help desk, free student e-mail accounts, online (class) grades, online (class) registration, online (class) schedules. Campuswide network is available. 100% of college-owned or -operated housing units are wired for high-speed Internet access. Wireless service is available via entire campus.

Student Life *Housing:* on-campus residence required through senior year. *Options:* coed, women-only. Campus housing is university owned. Freshman campus housing is guaranteed. *Activities and organizations:* drama/theater group, student-run newspaper, radio station, choral group, Student Government, Activities Board, HOSA, International Club, Habitat for Humanity. *Campus security:* 24-hour emergency response devices and patrols, student patrols, late-night transport/escort service, fire safety training, adopt-an-officer program, security website, weather/terror alerts, travel forecast, crime statistics. *Student services:* health clinic, personal/psychological counseling, women's center.

Athletics Member NCAA. All Division III. *Intercollegiate sports:* baseball M, basketball M/W, cross-country running M/W, equestrian sports M (c)/W (c), field hockey W, football M, golf M (c)/W (c), ice hockey M (c), lacrosse M (c), rugby M (c)/W (c), soccer M/W, softball W, swimming and diving W, tennis M/W, track and field M/W, ultimate Frisbee M (c)/W (c), volleyball M/W. *Intramural sports:* basketball M/W, bowling M/W, field hockey M (c)/W (c), gymnastics M (c)/W (c), lacrosse W (c), skiing (cross-country) M/W, skiing (downhill) M (c)/W (c), soccer M/W, volleyball M/W, water polo M (c)/W (c).

Standardized Tests *Recommended:* SAT or ACT (for admission).

Costs (2007–08) *Comprehensive fee:* $38,700 includes full-time tuition ($29,610), mandatory fees ($670), and room and board ($8420). Part-time tuition: $1175 per credit hour. *College room only:* $4420. *Payment plan:* installment. *Waivers:* adult students and employees or children of employees.

Financial Aid Of all full-time matriculated undergraduates who enrolled in 2007, 1,129 applied for aid, 999 were judged to have need, 320 had their need fully met. 363 Federal Work-Study jobs (averaging $540). 432 state and other part-time jobs (averaging $668). In 2007, 402 non-need-based awards were made. *Average percent of need met:* 84%. *Average financial aid package:* $22,439. *Average need-based loan:* $5174. *Average need-based gift aid:* $17,035. *Average non-need-based aid:* $16,475. *Average indebtedness upon graduation:* $21,426. *Financial aid deadline:* 3/1.

Applying *Options:* electronic application, early admission, early decision, early action, deferred entrance. *Application fee:* $30. *Required:* essay or personal statement, high school transcript, minimum 3.0 GPA, 1 letter of recommendation. *Recommended:* interview. *Application deadlines:* 3/1 (freshmen), 6/15 (transfers). *Early decision deadline:* 11/1. *Notification:* continuous (freshmen), continuous (transfers), 12/30 (early decision).

Freshman Application Contact Terry Bollman-Dalansky, Director of Admissions, Juniata College, 1700 Moore Street, Huntingdon, PA 16652. *Phone:* 814-641-3424. *Toll-free phone:* 877-JUNIATA. *Fax:* 814-641-3100. *E-mail:* admissions@juniata.edu.

See page 2252 for the College Close-Up.

KAPLAN CAREER INSTITUTE–HARRISBURG

Harrisburg, Pennsylvania **www.kci-Harrisburg.com/**

Director of Admissions Mr. Charles Zimmerman, Admissions Director, Kaplan Career Institute–Harrisburg, 5650 Derry Street, Harrisburg, PA 17111. *Phone:* 717-564-4112. *Toll-free phone:* 800-431-1995.

KEYSTONE COLLEGE

La Plume, Pennsylvania **www.keystone.edu/**

- **Independent** 4-year, founded 1868
- **Rural** 270-acre campus
- **Endowment** $8.8 million
- **Coed** 1,796 undergraduate students, 74% full-time, 62% women, 38% men
- **Minimally difficult** entrance level, 95% of applicants were admitted

Undergraduates 1,334 full-time, 462 part-time. Students come from 12 states and territories, 7 other countries, 10% are from out of state, 2% African American, 0.5% Asian American or Pacific Islander, 1% Hispanic American, 0.1% Native American, 0.6% international, 6% transferred in, 22% live on campus. *Retention:* 70% of 2006 full-time freshmen returned.

Freshmen *Admission:* 932 applied, 884 admitted, 369 enrolled. *Average high school GPA:* 2.69. *Test scores:* SAT critical reading scores over 500: 25%; SAT math scores over 500: 23%; SAT writing scores over 500: 21%; ACT scores over 18: 42%; SAT critical reading scores over 600: 3%; SAT math scores over 600: 3%; SAT writing scores over 600: 2%; ACT scores over 24: 5%; SAT critical reading scores over 700: 1%.

Faculty *Total:* 248, 24% full-time, 15% with terminal degrees. *Student/faculty ratio:* 12:1.

Majors Accounting; accounting and business/management; accounting related; art; art teacher education; biological and physical sciences; biology/biological sciences; business administration and management; business/commerce; communication and journalism related; communication and media related; communication/speech communication and rhetoric; computer/information technology services administration related; computer programming; criminal justice/law enforcement administration; criminal justice/safety; culinary arts; culinary arts related; data processing and data processing technology; diagnostic medical sonography and ultrasound technology; drawing; early childhood education; education (K-12); elementary education; environmental biology; environmental science; environmental studies; family and community services; fine/studio arts; food preparation; forensic science and technology; forestry; forestry technology; graphic design; hotel/motel administration; human resources management; illustration; information technology; journalism; kindergarten/preschool education; landscape architecture; liberal arts and sciences/liberal studies; mathematics teacher education; medical radiologic technology; natural resources management; occupational therapy; painting; parks, recreation and leisure facilities management; photography; physical therapy; pre-nursing studies; printmaking; public relations, advertising, and applied communication related; radio and television; radiologic technology/science; radio, television, and digital communication related; restaurant, culinary, and catering management; restaurant/food services management; sculpture; social studies teacher education; sport and fitness administration/management; therapeutic recreation; water, wetlands, and marine resources management; wildlife and wildlands science and management; wildlife biology.

Academics *Calendar:* semesters. *Degrees:* certificates, associate, bachelor's, and postbachelor's certificates. *Special study options:* academic remediation for entering students, adult/continuing education programs, advanced placement credit, cooperative education, distance learning, external degree program, honors programs, independent study, internships, part-time degree program, services for LD students, student-designed majors, study abroad, summer session for credit. *ROTC:* Army (c), Air Force (c).

Computers on Campus 120 computers/terminals are available on campus for general student use. Students can access the following: campus intranet, computer help desk, free student e-mail accounts, online (class) grades, online (class) registration, online (class) schedules. Campuswide network is available. 100% of college-owned or -operated housing units are wired for high-speed Internet access. Wireless service is available via entire campus.

Student Life *Housing:* on-campus residence required for freshman year. *Options:* coed, women-only, disabled students. Campus housing is university owned. Freshman campus housing is guaranteed. *Activities and organizations:* drama/theater group, student-run newspaper, radio station, choral group, Campus Activity Board, Student Senate, Art Society, Inter-Hall Council, Commuter Council. *Campus security:* 24-hour emergency response devices and patrols, student patrols, late-night transport/escort service, controlled dormitory access. *Student services:* health clinic, personal/psychological counseling, women's center.

Athletics Member NCAA. All Division III. *Intercollegiate sports:* baseball M, basketball M/W, cross-country running M/W, field hockey W, golf M, soccer M/W, softball W, tennis M/W, track and field M/W. *Intramural sports:* basketball M/W, cheerleading M (c)/W (c), football M/W, lacrosse M/W, skiing (downhill) M (c)/W (c), soccer M/W, softball M/W, table tennis M/W, tennis M/W, volleyball M/W, weight lifting M/W, wrestling M (c)/W (c).

Standardized Tests *Required:* SAT or ACT (for admission).

Costs (2008–09) *Comprehensive fee:* $26,385 includes full-time tuition ($16,630), mandatory fees ($1175), and room and board ($8580). Part-time tuition: $375 per credit. *Required fees:* $200 per term part-time. *College room only:* $4400.

Financial Aid Of all full-time matriculated undergraduates who enrolled in 2006, 125 Federal Work-Study jobs (averaging $1000). 100 state and other part-time jobs (averaging $1000).

Applying *Options:* electronic application, early admission, deferred entrance. *Application fee:* $30. *Required:* essay or personal statement, high school transcript, 1 letter of recommendation. *Required for some:* interview, art portfolio. *Recommended:* interview. *Application deadlines:* 7/1 (freshmen), 8/1 (transfers).

Freshman Application Contact Ms. Sarah Keating, Assistant Vice President for Enrollment, Keystone College, One College Green, La Plume, PA 18440-1099. *Phone:* 570-945-8112. *Toll-free phone:* 877-4COLLEGE Ext. 1. *Fax:* 570-945-7916. *E-mail:* admissions@keystone.edu.

See page 2254 for the College Close-Up.

KING'S COLLEGE

Wilkes-Barre, Pennsylvania **www.kings.edu/**

- **Independent Roman Catholic** comprehensive, founded 1946
- **Urban** 48-acre campus
- **Endowment** $60.7 million
- **Coed** 2,273 undergraduate students, 85% full-time, 49% women, 51% men
- **Moderately difficult** entrance level, 78% of applicants were admitted

King's College is a Catholic liberal arts college that was founded more than sixty years ago by the Holy Cross Fathers and Brothers of the University of Notre Dame. There are thirty-five undergraduate majors in the arts and sciences and in the William G. McGowan School of Business. Graduate degrees are offered in education and health-care administration, and a five-year physician assistant studies program is available. There is an innovative program of career development across the curriculum. Within six months of graduation, 95 percent of King's graduates are employed or attend graduate school. More than 95 percent of King's students receive financial aid.

Undergraduates 1,942 full-time, 331 part-time. Students come from 18 states and territories, 6 other countries, 25% are from out of state, 2% African American, 0.8% Asian American or Pacific Islander, 3% Hispanic American, 0.1% Native American, 0.3% international, 4% transferred in, 48% live on campus. *Retention:* 82% of 2006 full-time freshmen returned.

Freshmen *Admission:* 2,107 applied, 1,651 admitted, 557 enrolled. *Average high school GPA:* 3.24. *Test scores:* SAT critical reading scores over 500: 57%; SAT math scores over 500: 60%; SAT writing scores over 500: 49%; SAT critical reading scores over 600: 15%; SAT math scores over 600: 16%; SAT writing scores over 600: 12%; SAT critical reading scores over 700: 2%; SAT math scores over 700: 2%; SAT writing scores over 700: 1%.

Faculty *Total:* 208, 60% full-time, 58% with terminal degrees. *Student/faculty ratio:* 13:1.

Majors Accounting; athletic training; biological and physical sciences; biology/biological sciences; business administration and management; chemistry; clinical laboratory science/medical technology; communication and media related; computer and information sciences; computer science; criminal justice/safety; dramatic/theater arts; early childhood education; economics; elementary education; English; environmental science; environmental studies; finance; French; health professions related; history; human resources management; international business/trade/commerce; marketing/marketing management; mathematics; neuroscience; philosophy; political science and government; pre-dentistry studies; pre-law studies; pre-medical studies; pre-pharmacy studies; pre-veterinary studies; psychology; secondary education; sociology; Spanish; special education; theology.

Academics *Calendar:* semesters. *Degrees:* certificates, associate, bachelor's, master's, and postbachelor's certificates. *Special study options:* accelerated degree program, adult/continuing education programs, advanced placement credit, distance learning, double majors, English as a second language, honors programs, independent study, internships, off-campus study, part-time degree program, services for LD students, student-designed majors, study abroad, summer session for credit. *ROTC:* Army (b).

Computers on Campus 350 computers/terminals are available on campus for general student use. Students can access the following: computer help desk, free student e-mail accounts. Campuswide network is available. 100% of college-owned or -operated housing units are wired for high-speed Internet access. Wireless service is available via computer labs, libraries, student centers.

Student Life *Housing:* on-campus residence required through sophomore year. *Options:* coed, men-only, women-only, cooperative, disabled students. Campus housing is university owned. Freshman campus housing is guaranteed. *Activities and organizations:* drama/theater group, student-run newspaper, radio station, choral group, Association of Campus Events, Student Government Association, Accounting Association, International/Multicultural Club, Biology Club. *Campus security:* 24-hour emergency response devices and patrols, student patrols, late-night transport/escort service, bicycle patrols. *Student services:* health clinic, personal/psychological counseling, women's center.

Athletics Member NCAA. All Division III. *Intercollegiate sports:* baseball M, basketball M/W, cheerleading M/W, cross-country running M/W, field hockey W, football M, golf M, lacrosse M/W, soccer M/W, softball W, swimming and diving M/W, tennis M/W, volleyball W, wrestling M. *Intramural sports:* basketball M/W, ice hockey M (c), soccer M/W, track and field M (c)/W (c).

Standardized Tests *Recommended:* SAT or ACT (for admission).

Costs (2007–08) *Comprehensive fee:* $32,380 includes full-time tuition ($23,450) and room and board ($8930). Part-time tuition: $460 per credit hour. *College room only:* $4180. Room and board charges vary according to board plan. *Payment plans:* installment, deferred payment. *Waivers:* senior citizens and employees or children of employees.

Financial Aid Of all full-time matriculated undergraduates who enrolled in 2007, 1,742 applied for aid, 1,545 were judged to have need, 1,189 had their need fully met. 300 Federal Work-Study jobs (averaging $1029). 245 state and other part-time jobs (averaging $1073). In 2007, 363 non-need-based awards were made. *Average percent of need met:* 75%. *Average financial aid package:* $15,356. *Average need-based loan:* $4733. *Average need-based gift aid:* $12,325. *Average non-need-based aid:* $9247. *Average indebtedness upon graduation:* $28,139.

Applying *Options:* electronic application, early admission, deferred entrance. *Application fee:* $30. *Required:* essay or personal statement, high school transcript. *Recommended:* 2 letters of recommendation, interview. *Application deadlines:* rolling (freshmen), rolling (transfers). *Notification:* continuous (freshmen), continuous (transfers).

Freshman Application Contact Ms. Michelle Lawrence-Schmude, Director of Admissions, King's College, 133 North River Street, Wilkes-Barre, PA 18711-0801. *Phone:* 570-208-5858. *Toll-free phone:* 888-KINGSPA. *Fax:* 570-208-5971. *E-mail:* admissions@kings.edu.

See page 2256 for the College Close-Up.

KUTZTOWN UNIVERSITY OF PENNSYLVANIA

Kutztown, Pennsylvania **www.kutztown.edu/**

- **State-supported** comprehensive, founded 1866, part of Pennsylvania State System of Higher Education
- **Rural** 326-acre campus with easy access to Philadelphia
- **Endowment** $13.8 million
- **Coed** 9,311 undergraduate students, 90% full-time, 59% women, 41% men
- **Moderately difficult** entrance level, 65% of applicants were admitted

Kutztown University opened the new Student Recreation Center in fall 2006, which features an indoor track, racquetball courts, a rock-climbing wall, and more than 100 pieces of cardio and fitness equipment. Opened in January 2007, the Academic Forum is wired with state-of-the-art technology in seven lecture-style classrooms and houses a new full-service food court. A new 865-bed residence hall and renovations of the Sharadin Arts Building are scheduled to be completed in fall 2008.

Undergraduates 8,387 full-time, 924 part-time. Students come from 20 states and territories, 59 other countries, 10% are from out of state, 7% African American, 1% Asian American or Pacific Islander, 4% Hispanic American, 0.3% Native American, 0.7% international, 8% transferred in, 46% live on campus. *Retention:* 78% of 2006 full-time freshmen returned.

Freshmen *Admission:* 9,064 applied, 5,901 admitted, 1,902 enrolled. *Average high school GPA:* 3.04. *Test scores:* SAT critical reading scores over 500: 43%; SAT math scores over 500: 45%; SAT writing scores over 500: 38%; ACT scores over 18: 74%; SAT critical reading scores over 600: 8%; SAT math scores over 600: 8%; SAT writing scores over 600: 6%; ACT scores over 24: 7%; SAT critical reading scores over 700: 1%; ACT scores over 30: 1%.

Faculty *Total:* 513, 89% full-time, 50% with terminal degrees. *Student/faculty ratio:* 19:1.

Majors Accounting; anthropology; art teacher education; biochemistry; biology/biological sciences; biology teacher education; business administration and management; chemistry; chemistry teacher education; clinical laboratory science/medical technology; commercial and advertising art; computer science; crafts, folk art and artisanry; criminal justice/safety; digital communication and media/multimedia; dramatic/theater arts; elementary education; English; English/

language arts teacher education; environmental science; finance; fine/studio arts; French; French language teacher education; general studies; geography; geology/earth science; German language teacher education; German studies; history; human resources management; information technology; international business/trade/commerce; kindergarten/preschool education; library science; marketing/marketing management; mathematics; mathematics teacher education; music; music teacher education; nursing (registered nurse training); oceanography (chemical and physical); parks, recreation and leisure; philosophy; physics; physics teacher education; political science and government; pre-engineering; psychology; public administration; science teacher education; secondary education; social sciences; social science teacher education; social work; sociology; Spanish; Spanish language teacher education; special education; special education (speech or language impaired); special education (vision impaired); speech and rhetoric; technical and business writing; telecommunications; visual and performing arts; visual and performing arts related.

Academics *Calendar:* semesters. *Degrees:* bachelor's, master's, and post-bachelor's certificates. *Special study options:* academic remediation for entering students, accelerated degree program, adult/continuing education programs, advanced placement credit, distance learning, double majors, honors programs, independent study, internships, off-campus study, part-time degree program, services for LD students, student-designed majors, study abroad, summer session for credit. *ROTC:* Army (c). *Unusual degree programs:* 3-2 engineering with Pennsylvania State University—University Park Campus.

Computers on Campus 950 computers/terminals and 100 ports are available on campus for general student use. Students can access the following: computer help desk, free student e-mail accounts, online (class) grades, online (class) registration, online (class) schedules. Campuswide network is available. 100% of college-owned or -operated housing units are wired for high-speed Internet access. Wireless service is available via classrooms, learning centers, libraries, student centers.

Student Life *Housing options:* coed, women-only, cooperative. Campus housing is university owned and leased by the school. Freshman campus housing is guaranteed. *Activities and organizations:* drama/theater group, student-run newspaper, radio and television station, choral group, marching band, Student Government Board, Student Pennsylvania State Education Association, National Art Education Association, Residence Hall Association, Association of Campus Events, national fraternities, national sororities. *Campus security:* 24-hour emergency response devices and patrols, student patrols, late-night transport/escort service, secondary door electronic alarm system in residence halls, 24-hour student desk personnel at main entrance of residence halls. *Student services:* health clinic, personal/psychological counseling, women's center.

Athletics Member NCAA. All Division II. *Intercollegiate sports:* baseball M (s), basketball M (s)/W (s), bowling M, cheerleading W (s), cross-country running M (s)/W (s), equestrian sports W (c), field hockey W (s), football M (s), golf W (s), ice hockey M (c), lacrosse M (c)/W, rugby M (c)/W (c), soccer M (s)/W (s), softball W (s), swimming and diving M (s)/W (s), tennis M (s)/W (s), track and field M (s)/W (s), volleyball M (c)/W (s), wrestling M (s). *Intramural sports:* badminton M/W, basketball M/W, cross-country running M/W, football M/W, golf M/W, lacrosse M/W, racquetball M/W, skiing (cross-country) W, skiing (downhill) M/W, soccer M/W, softball M/W, swimming and diving M/W, table tennis M/W, tennis M/W, volleyball M/W, water polo M/W, weight lifting M/W.

Standardized Tests *Required:* SAT or ACT (for admission). *Required for some:* SAT Subject Tests (for admission).

Costs (2007–08) *Tuition:* state resident $5177 full-time, $216 per credit part-time; nonresident $12,944 full-time, $539 per credit part-time. *Required fees:* $1696 full-time, $90 per credit part-time, $40 per term part-time. *Room and board:* $6960; room only: $4288. Room and board charges vary according to board plan and housing facility. *Payment plans:* installment, deferred payment. *Waivers:* senior citizens and employees or children of employees.

Financial Aid Of all full-time matriculated undergraduates who enrolled in 2006, 6,881 applied for aid, 4,900 were judged to have need, 2,539 had their need fully met. 425 Federal Work-Study jobs (averaging $1017). In 2006, 258 non-need-based awards were made. *Average percent of need met:* 59%. *Average financial aid package:* $6653. *Average need-based loan:* $3558. *Average need-based gift aid:* $4533. *Average non-need-based aid:* $1955. *Average indebtedness upon graduation:* $15,559.

Applying *Options:* electronic application, early admission, deferred entrance. *Application fee:* $35. *Required:* high school transcript, minimum 2.0 GPA. *Required for some:* audition required for music program; portfolio and/or art test required for art education, communication design, crafts, and fine arts programs. *Application deadlines:* rolling (freshmen), rolling (transfers). *Notification:* continuous (freshmen), continuous (transfers).

Freshman Application Contact Dr. William Stahler, Director of Admissions, Kutztown University of Pennsylvania, 15200 Kutztown Road, Kutztown, PA 19530-0730. *Phone:* 610-683-4060. *Toll-free phone:* 877-628-1915. *Fax:* 610-683-1375. *E-mail:* admission@kutztown.edu.

See page 2258 for the College Close-Up.

LAFAYETTE COLLEGE

Easton, Pennsylvania **www.lafayette.edu/**

- **Independent** 4-year, founded 1826, affiliated with Presbyterian Church (U.S.A.)
- **Suburban** 340-acre campus with easy access to New York City and Philadelphia
- **Endowment** $780.2 million
- **Coed** 2,403 undergraduate students, 98% full-time, 48% women, 52% men
- **Most difficult** entrance level, 35% of applicants were admitted

Undergraduates 2,349 full-time, 54 part-time. Students come from 38 states and territories, 41 other countries, 70% are from out of state, 5% African American, 3% Asian American or Pacific Islander, 5% Hispanic American, 0.1% Native American, 6% international, 0.5% transferred in, 98% live on campus. *Retention:* 95% of 2006 full-time freshmen returned.

Freshmen *Admission:* 6,364 applied, 2,224 admitted, 592 enrolled. *Average high school GPA:* 3.44. *Test scores:* SAT critical reading scores over 500: 97%; SAT math scores over 500: 99%; ACT scores over 18: 100%; SAT critical reading scores over 600: 66%; SAT math scores over 600: 80%; ACT scores over 24: 88%; SAT critical reading scores over 700: 12%; SAT math scores over 700: 24%; ACT scores over 30: 20%.

Faculty *Total:* 234, 85% full-time, 92% with terminal degrees. *Student/faculty ratio:* 11:1.

Majors American studies; anthropology; art; art history, criticism and conservation; biochemistry; biology/biological sciences; business/managerial economics; chemical engineering; chemistry; civil engineering; computer science; economics; electrical, electronics and communications engineering; engineering; English; environmental/environmental health engineering; fine/studio arts; French; geology/earth science; German; history; international relations and affairs; mathematics; mechanical engineering; music; music history, literature, and theory; philosophy; physics; political science and government; psychology; religious studies; Russian studies; sociology; Spanish.

Academics *Calendar:* semesters plus interim January program. *Degree:* bachelor's. *Special study options:* academic remediation for entering students, accelerated degree program, adult/continuing education programs, advanced placement credit, honors programs, internships, off-campus study, part-time degree program, services for LD students, student-designed majors, study abroad, summer session for credit. *ROTC:* Army (c).

Computers on Campus 600 computers/terminals and 600 ports are available on campus for general student use. Students can access the following: computer help desk, free student e-mail accounts, online (class) grades, online (class) registration, online (class) schedules. Campuswide network is available. 100% of college-owned or -operated housing units are wired for high-speed Internet access.

Student Life *Housing:* on-campus residence required through senior year. *Options:* coed. Campus housing is university owned. Freshman campus housing is guaranteed. *Activities and organizations:* drama/theater group, student-run newspaper, radio station, choral group, Association of Biscer Collegians, International Student Association, Activities Forum, national fraternities, national sororities. *Campus security:* 24-hour emergency response devices and patrols, student patrols, late-night transport/escort service, controlled dormitory access. *Student services:* health clinic, personal/psychological counseling, women's center.

Athletics Member NCAA. All Division I except football (Division I-AA). *Intercollegiate sports:* baseball M, basketball M/W, crew M (c)/W (c), cross-country running M/W, equestrian sports M (c)/W (c), fencing M/W, field hockey W, golf M, ice hockey M (c), lacrosse M/W, rugby M (c)/W (c), skiing (downhill) M (c)/W (c), soccer M/W, softball W, squash M (c), swimming and diving M/W, tennis M/W, track and field M/W, volleyball W, weight lifting M (c)/W (c), wrestling M (c). *Intramural sports:* badminton M/W, baseball M, basketball M/W, bowling M/W, cross-country running M/W, fencing M/W, field hockey W, football M, golf M/W, lacrosse M/W, racquetball M/W, sailing M (c)/W (c), skiing (cross-country) M (c)/W (c), soccer M/W, softball M/W, squash M/W, swimming and diving M/W, table tennis M/W, tennis M/W, track and field M/W, volleyball M/W, weight lifting M/W, wrestling M.

Standardized Tests *Required:* SAT or ACT (for admission). *Recommended:* SAT Subject Tests (for admission).

Costs (2008–09) *Comprehensive fee:* $47,400 includes full-time tuition ($36,000), mandatory fees ($200), and room and board ($11,200). *College room only:* $6800.

Financial Aid Of all full-time matriculated undergraduates who enrolled in 2003, 1,374 applied for aid, 1,251 were judged to have need, 1,225 had their need fully met. In 2003, 158 non-need-based awards were made. *Average percent of need met:* 99%. *Average financial aid package:* $22,888. *Average need-based loan:* $4313. *Average need-based gift aid:* $20,754. *Average non-need-based aid:* $12,964. *Average indebtedness upon graduation:* $17,995. *Financial aid deadline:* 3/15.

Applying *Options:* electronic application, early admission, early decision, deferred entrance. *Application fee:* $60. *Required:* essay or personal statement, high school transcript, 1 letter of recommendation. *Recommended:* interview. *Application deadlines:* 1/1 (freshmen), 6/1 (transfers). *Early decision deadline:* 12/1. *Notification:* continuous until 4/1 (freshmen), continuous (transfers), 3/15 (early decision).

Freshman Application Contact Ms. Carol Rowlands, Director of Admissions, Lafayette College, Easton, PA 18042-1798. *Phone:* 610-330-5100. *Fax:* 610-330-5355. *E-mail:* admissions@lafayette.edu.

See page 2260 for the College Close-Up.

LANCASTER BIBLE COLLEGE

Lancaster, Pennsylvania **www.lbc.edu/**

- **Independent nondenominational** comprehensive, founded 1933
- **Suburban** 100-acre campus with easy access to Philadelphia
- **Endowment** $5.6 million
- **Coed**
- **Minimally difficult** entrance level

Faculty *Student/faculty ratio:* 15:1.

Academics *Calendar:* semesters. *Degrees:* certificates, associate, bachelor's, master's, and postbachelor's certificates.

Student Life *Campus security:* student patrols, late-night transport/escort service, controlled dormitory access.

Athletics Member NCCAA.

Standardized Tests *Required:* SAT or ACT (for admission).

Costs (2007–08) *Comprehensive fee:* $20,690 includes full-time tuition ($13,920), mandatory fees ($600), and room and board ($6170). Part-time tuition: $460 per credit. *Required fees:* $25 per credit part-time. *College room only:* $2720. Room and board charges vary according to board plan.

Financial Aid Of all full-time matriculated undergraduates who enrolled in 2007, 517 applied for aid, 462 were judged to have need, 53 had their need fully met. 82 Federal Work-Study jobs (averaging $2000). In 2007, 95 non-need-based awards were made. *Average percent of need met:* 65. *Average financial aid package:* $10,395. *Average need-based loan:* $4151. *Average need-based gift aid:* $7564. *Average non-need-based aid:* $4900. *Average indebtedness upon graduation:* $20,604.

Applying *Options:* early admission, deferred entrance. *Application fee:* $25. *Required:* essay or personal statement, high school transcript, minimum 2.0 GPA, 3 letters of recommendation. *Required for some:* interview.

Freshman Application Contact Mrs. Joanne M. Roper, Associate Vice President for Admissions, Lancaster Bible College, 901 Eden Road, Lancaster, PA 17601-5036. *Phone:* 717-560-8271. *Toll-free phone:* 866-LBC4YOU. *Fax:* 717-560-8213. *E-mail:* admissions@lbc.edu.

LA ROCHE COLLEGE

Pittsburgh, Pennsylvania **www.laroche.edu/**

- **Independent** comprehensive, founded 1963, affiliated with Roman Catholic Church
- **Suburban** 80-acre campus
- **Endowment** $3.2 million
- **Coed** 1,359 undergraduate students, 84% full-time, 67% women, 33% men
- **Minimally difficult** entrance level, 73% of applicants were admitted

Undergraduates 1,139 full-time, 220 part-time. Students come from 17 states and territories, 45 other countries, 5% are from out of state, 5% African American, 0.7% Asian American or Pacific Islander, 1% Hispanic American, 0.5% Native American, 12% international, 10% transferred in, 36% live on campus. *Retention:* 66% of 2006 full-time freshmen returned.

Freshmen *Admission:* 944 applied, 685 admitted, 295 enrolled. *Average high school GPA:* 3.10. *Test scores:* SAT critical reading scores over 500: 31%; SAT math scores over 500: 30%; ACT scores over 18: 47%; SAT critical reading scores over 600: 4%; SAT math scores over 600: 7%; ACT scores over 24: 4%; SAT math scores over 700: 1%.

Faculty *Total:* 192, 33% full-time, 39% with terminal degrees. *Student/faculty ratio:* 12:1.

Majors Accounting; architecture related; biology/biological sciences; business administration, management and operations related; chemistry; commercial and advertising art; communication and media related; computer and information sciences; computer science; corrections and criminal justice related; criminal justice/safety; dance; elementary education; English; English composition; English/language arts teacher education; film/video and photographic arts related; finance; general studies; history; human services; information technology; interior architecture; international business/trade/commerce; international relations and affairs; liberal arts and sciences/liberal studies; management science; marketing/marketing management; mathematics; medical radiologic technology; nursing (registered nurse training); psychology; religious education; religious studies; respiratory care therapy; sociology; Spanish.

Academics *Calendar:* semesters plus summer term. *Degrees:* certificates, associate, bachelor's, and master's. *Special study options:* academic remediation for entering students, accelerated degree program, adult/continuing education programs, advanced placement credit, distance learning, double majors, English as a second language, independent study, internships, part-time degree program, services for LD students, student-designed majors, study abroad, summer session for credit. *ROTC:* Army (c), Air Force (c). *Unusual degree programs:* 3-2 engineering with University of Pittsburgh; physical therapy, physician's assistant, speech language pathologist, athletic trainer, occupational therapy with Duquesne University.

Computers on Campus 186 computers/terminals are available on campus for general student use. Students can access the following: campus intranet, computer help desk, free student e-mail accounts, online (class) grades, online (class) registration, online (class) schedules. Campuswide network is available. 100% of college-owned or -operated housing units are wired for high-speed Internet access. Wireless service is available via classrooms, computer labs, learning centers, libraries, student centers.

Student Life *Housing options:* coed. Campus housing is university owned. Freshman campus housing is guaranteed. *Activities and organizations:* drama/theater group, student-run newspaper, radio station, choral group, American Society of Interior Design, student government, Visions (environmental club), Helping Hands, Project Achievement. *Campus security:* 24-hour emergency response devices and patrols, student patrols, late-night transport/escort service, controlled dormitory access. *Student services:* health clinic, personal/psychological counseling.

Athletics Member NCAA. All Division III. *Intercollegiate sports:* baseball M, basketball M/W, cross-country running M/W, soccer M/W, softball W, volleyball W. *Intramural sports:* basketball M/W, weight lifting M/W.

Standardized Tests *Required:* SAT or ACT (for admission).

Costs (2007–08) *Comprehensive fee:* $27,412 includes full-time tuition ($18,600), mandatory fees ($870), and room and board ($7942). Full-time tuition and fees vary according to program. Part-time tuition: $557 per credit. Part-time tuition and fees vary according to program. *Required fees:* $23 per credit part-time. *College room only:* $4974. Room and board charges vary according to board plan. *Payment plan:* installment. *Waivers:* senior citizens and employees or children of employees.

Financial Aid Of all full-time matriculated undergraduates who enrolled in 2007, 1,116 applied for aid, 1,116 were judged to have need. 185 Federal Work-Study jobs (averaging $2000). In 2007, 23 non-need-based awards were made. *Average percent of need met:* 88%. *Average financial aid package:* $7969. *Average need-based loan:* $4400. *Average need-based gift aid:* $2235. *Average non-need-based aid:* $5131. *Average indebtedness upon graduation:* $18,750. *Financial aid deadline:* 5/1.

Applying *Options:* electronic application, early admission, deferred entrance. *Application fee:* $50. *Required:* high school transcript, minimum 2.0 GPA, letters of recommendation. *Recommended:* essay or personal statement, minimum 3.0 GPA, interview. *Application deadlines:* rolling (freshmen), rolling (transfers). *Notification:* 9/15 (freshmen).

Freshman Application Contact Mr. Thomas Hassett, Director of Admissions, La Roche College, 9000 Babcock Boulevard, Pittsburgh, PA 15237. *Phone:* 412-536-1275. *Toll-free phone:* 800-838-4LRC. *Fax:* 412-536-1048. *E-mail:* admissions@laroche.edu.

See page 2262 for the College Close-Up.

LA SALLE UNIVERSITY

Philadelphia, Pennsylvania **www.lasalle.edu/**

- **Independent Roman Catholic** comprehensive, founded 1863
- **Urban** 100-acre campus
- **Endowment** $70.1 million

- **Coed** 4,189 undergraduate students, 76% full-time, 62% women, 38% men
- **Moderately difficult** entrance level, 68% of applicants were admitted

Undergraduates 3,194 full-time, 995 part-time. Students come from 36 states and territories, 11 other countries, 44% are from out of state, 16% African American, 4% Asian American or Pacific Islander, 8% Hispanic American, 0.1% Native American, 0.6% international, 3% transferred in, 61% live on campus. *Retention:* 83% of 2006 full-time freshmen returned.

Freshmen *Admission:* 5,268 applied, 3,558 admitted, 825 enrolled. *Test scores:* SAT critical reading scores over 500: 67%; SAT math scores over 500: 65%; SAT critical reading scores over 600: 20%; SAT math scores over 600: 18%; SAT critical reading scores over 700: 2%; SAT math scores over 700: 1%.

Faculty *Total:* 373, 61% full-time. *Student/faculty ratio:* 13:1.

Majors Accounting; Air Force R.O.T.C./air science; applied mathematics; Army R.O.T.C./military science; art history, criticism and conservation; audiology and speech-language pathology; biochemistry; biology/biological sciences; broadcast journalism; business administration and management; business/managerial economics; business teacher education; chemistry; classics and languages, literatures and linguistics; computer and information sciences; computer programming; computer science; criminal justice/safety; economics; education; elementary education; English; environmental studies; film/cinema studies; finance; French; general studies; geology/earth science; German; history; human resources management; information science/studies; Italian; journalism; management information systems; marketing/marketing management; mass communication/media; mathematics; modern languages; nursing (registered nurse training); nutrition sciences; philosophy; political science and government; pre-dentistry studies; pre-medical studies; pre-veterinary studies; psychology; public administration; public relations/image management; radio and television; religious education; religious studies; Russian; Russian studies; science teacher education; secondary education; social sciences; social work; sociology; Spanish; special education.

Academics *Calendar:* semesters. *Degrees:* associate, bachelor's, master's, doctoral, post-master's, and postbachelor's certificates. *Special study options:* accelerated degree program, adult/continuing education programs, advanced placement credit, cooperative education, double majors, freshman honors college, honors programs, independent study, internships, off-campus study, part-time degree program, services for LD students, student-designed majors, study abroad, summer session for credit. *ROTC:* Army (c), Air Force (c). *Unusual degree programs:* 3-2 occupational therapy with Thomas Jefferson University, speech pathology.

Computers on Campus 1,100 computers/terminals are available on campus for general student use. Students can access the following: campus intranet, computer help desk, free student e-mail accounts, online (class) grades, online (class) registration, online (class) schedules, Blackboard Course Management System. Campuswide network is available. 100% of college-owned or -operated housing units are wired for high-speed Internet access. Wireless service is available via classrooms, computer centers, computer labs, dorm rooms, learning centers, libraries, student centers.

Student Life *Housing options:* coed, men-only, women-only, disabled students. Campus housing is university owned and leased by the school. Freshman campus housing is guaranteed. *Activities and organizations:* drama/theater group, student-run newspaper, radio and television station, choral group, Student Government Association, Community service organization, La Salle Entertainment Organization, The Explorer (yearbook), The Masque (theater group), national fraternities, national sororities. *Campus security:* 24-hour emergency response devices and patrols, student patrols, late-night transport/escort service, controlled dormitory access. *Student services:* health clinic, personal/psychological counseling, women's center.

Athletics Member NCAA. All Division I. *Intercollegiate sports:* baseball M (s), basketball M (s)/W (s), crew M (s)/W (s), cross-country running M (s)/W (s), field hockey W (s), golf M (s)/W (s), lacrosse W (s), soccer M (s)/W (s), softball W (s), swimming and diving M (s)/W (s), tennis M (s)/W (s), track and field M (s)/W (s), volleyball W (s). *Intramural sports:* baseball M, basketball M/W, crew M/W, field hockey W, football M/W, golf M/W, ice hockey M (c), lacrosse M (c), rugby M (c)/W (c), soccer M/W, softball W, swimming and diving M/W, tennis M/W, track and field M/W, volleyball M/W.

Standardized Tests *Required:* SAT or ACT (for admission).

Costs (2007–08) *One-time required fee:* $150. *Comprehensive fee:* $39,700 includes full-time tuition ($29,200), mandatory fees ($200), and room and board ($10,300). Full-time tuition and fees vary according to class time, course load, and program. Part-time tuition: $410 per credit. Part-time tuition and fees vary according to class time and course load. *College room only:* $5120. Room and board charges vary according to board plan, housing facility, and location. *Payment plans:* installment, deferred payment. *Waivers:* employees or children of employees.

Financial Aid Of all full-time matriculated undergraduates who enrolled in 2006, 2,841 applied for aid, 2,555 were judged to have need, 577 had their need fully met. In 2006, 601 non-need-based awards were made. *Average percent of need met:* 82%. *Average financial aid package:* $17,373. *Average need-based loan:* $4663. *Average need-based gift aid:* $13,462. *Average non-need-based aid:* $9373. *Average indebtedness upon graduation:* $24,345.

Applying *Options:* electronic application, early admission, early decision, early action, deferred entrance. *Application fee:* $35. *Required:* essay or personal statement, high school transcript, 1 letter of recommendation. *Recommended:* interview. *Application deadlines:* 8/15 (transfers), 11/15 (early action). *Notification:* continuous (freshmen), continuous (transfers), 12/15 (early action).

Freshman Application Contact Mr. Robert G. Voss, Dean of Admission and Financial Aid, La Salle University, 1900 West Olney Avenue, Philadelphia, PA 19141-1199. *Phone:* 215-951-1500. *Toll-free phone:* 800-328-1910. *Fax:* 215-951-1656. *E-mail:* admiss@lasalle.edu.

LEBANON VALLEY COLLEGE

Annville, Pennsylvania **www.lvc.edu/**

- **Independent United Methodist** comprehensive, founded 1866
- **Small-town** 340-acre campus
- **Endowment** $50.8 million
- **Coed** 1,793 undergraduate students, 91% full-time, 55% women, 45% men
- **Moderately difficult** entrance level, 71% of applicants were admitted

Undergraduates 1,636 full-time, 157 part-time. Students come from 22 states and territories, 5 other countries, 21% are from out of state, 1% African American, 2% Asian American or Pacific Islander, 2% Hispanic American, 0.3% Native American, 0.6% international, 3% transferred in, 74% live on campus. *Retention:* 83% of 2006 full-time freshmen returned.

Freshmen *Admission:* 2,131 applied, 1,514 admitted, 451 enrolled.

Faculty *Total:* 191, 52% full-time, 59% with terminal degrees. *Student/faculty ratio:* 13:1.

Majors Accounting; actuarial science; American studies; art history, criticism and conservation; biochemistry; biochemistry/biophysics and molecular biology; biology/biological sciences; business administration and management; chemistry; clinical/medical laboratory science and allied professions related; computer science; criminology; digital communication and media/multimedia; economics; elementary education; English; fine/studio arts; French; general studies; German; health/health care administration; health services/allied health/health sciences; history; liberal arts and sciences/liberal studies; mathematics; multi-/interdisciplinary studies related; music management and merchandising; music performance; music teacher education; philosophy; physics; physiological psychology/psychobiology; political science and government; psychology; recording arts technology; religious studies; sociology; Spanish.

Academics *Calendar:* semesters. *Degrees:* certificates, associate, bachelor's, master's, doctoral, and postbachelor's certificates. *Special study options:* academic remediation for entering students, adult/continuing education programs, advanced placement credit, double majors, independent study, internships, off-campus study, part-time degree program, services for LD students, student-designed majors, study abroad, summer session for credit. *Unusual degree programs:* 3-2 engineering with Case Western Reserve University, The Pennsylvania State University; forestry with Duke University.

Computers on Campus 195 computers/terminals are available on campus for general student use. Students can access the following: campus intranet, computer help desk, free student e-mail accounts, online (class) grades, online (class) registration, online (class) schedules. Campuswide network is available. 100% of college-owned or -operated housing units are wired for high-speed Internet access. Wireless service is available via classrooms, computer centers, computer labs, learning centers, libraries, student centers.

Student Life *Housing:* on-campus residence required through senior year. *Options:* coed, women-only, disabled students. Campus housing is university owned. Freshman campus housing is guaranteed. *Activities and organizations:* drama/theater group, student-run newspaper, radio station, choral group, marching band, LVC PSEA, Council of Christian Organization, Tae Kwon Do Club, Phi Beta Lambda, Wig and Buckle (theatrical group), national fraternities, national sororities. *Campus security:* 24-hour emergency response devices and patrols, late-night transport/escort service, controlled dormitory access, dormitory entrances locked at midnight. *Student services:* health clinic, personal/psychological counseling.

Athletics Member NCAA. All Division III. *Intercollegiate sports:* baseball M, basketball M/W, cross-country running M/W, field hockey W, football M, golf M, ice hockey M, soccer M/W, softball W, swimming and diving M/W, tennis M/W, track and field M/W, volleyball W. *Intramural sports:* basketball M/W, football M/W, racquetball M/W, rugby W (c), softball M/W, volleyball M (c).

Costs (2007–08) *Comprehensive fee:* $35,230 includes full-time tuition ($27,125), mandatory fees ($675), and room and board ($7430). Part-time tuition:

$475 per credit. Part-time tuition and fees vary according to class time and degree level. *College room only:* $3630. Room and board charges vary according to board plan and housing facility. *Payment plans:* tuition prepayment, installment. *Waivers:* senior citizens and employees or children of employees.

Financial Aid Of all full-time matriculated undergraduates who enrolled in 2006, 1,439 applied for aid, 1,252 were judged to have need, 417 had their need fully met. 804 Federal Work-Study jobs (averaging $1196). In 2006, 315 non-need-based awards were made. *Average percent of need met:* 87%. *Average financial aid package:* $19,056. *Average need-based loan:* $4098. *Average need-based gift aid:* $16,038. *Average non-need-based aid:* $10,607. *Average indebtedness upon graduation:* $28,051.

Applying *Options:* electronic application. *Application fee:* $30. *Required:* high school transcript. *Required for some:* essay or personal statement, audition for music majors. *Recommended:* 2 letters of recommendation, interview. *Application deadlines:* rolling (freshmen), rolling (transfers). *Notification:* continuous (freshmen), continuous (transfers).

Freshman Application Contact Ms. Susan Sarisky, Director of Admission, Lebanon Valley College, 101 North College Avenue, Annville, PA 17003-1400. *Toll-free phone:* 866-LVC-4ADM. *Fax:* 717-867-6026. *E-mail:* admission@lvc.edu.

See page 2264 for the College Close-Up.

LEHIGH UNIVERSITY

Bethlehem, Pennsylvania www.lehigh.edu/

- **Independent** university, founded 1865
- **Suburban** 1600-acre campus with easy access to Philadelphia
- **Endowment** $1.1 billion
- **Coed** 4,756 undergraduate students, 98% full-time, 41% women, 59% men
- **Most difficult** entrance level, 32% of applicants were admitted

Undergraduates 4,662 full-time, 94 part-time. Students come from 49 states and territories, 44 other countries, 76% are from out of state, 3% African American, 6% Asian American or Pacific Islander, 4% Hispanic American, 0.1% Native American, 2% international, 1% transferred in, 71% live on campus. *Retention:* 93% of 2006 full-time freshmen returned.

Freshmen *Admission:* 12,155 applied, 3,882 admitted, 1,166 enrolled. *Test scores:* SAT critical reading scores over 500: 96%; SAT math scores over 500: 99%; SAT critical reading scores over 600: 76%; SAT math scores over 600: 87%; SAT critical reading scores over 700: 18%; SAT math scores over 700: 34%.

Faculty *Total:* 629, 70% full-time, 69% with terminal degrees. *Student/faculty ratio:* 9:1.

Majors Accounting; African-American/Black studies; American studies; anthropology; architecture; art; art history, criticism and conservation; Asian studies; astronomy; astrophysics; biochemistry; biological and biomedical sciences related; biological and physical sciences; biology/biological sciences; biomedical/medical engineering; biopsychology; business administration and management; business/commerce; business/managerial economics; chemical engineering; chemistry; chemistry related; civil engineering; classics and languages, literatures and linguistics; communication and journalism related; computer and information sciences and support services related; computer engineering; computer science; design and applied arts related; design and visual communications; dramatic/theater arts; dramatic/theater arts and stagecraft related; ecology; education; electrical, electronics and communications engineering; engineering mechanics; engineering physics; engineering related; English; environmental/environmental health engineering; environmental science; environmental studies; finance; French; geological and earth sciences/geosciences related; German; history; industrial engineering; information science/studies; international relations and affairs; journalism; logistics and materials management; management information systems; marketing/marketing management; materials engineering; mathematics; mechanical engineering; molecular biology; music; music theory and composition; neuroscience; philosophy; physical and theoretical chemistry; physics; political science and government; pre-dentistry studies; pre-medical studies; psychology; religious studies; Russian studies; science technologies related; social sciences; social sciences related; sociology; Spanish; statistics; structural engineering; urban studies/affairs; women's studies.

Academics *Calendar:* semesters. *Degrees:* bachelor's, master's, doctoral, post-master's, and postbachelor's certificates. *Special study options:* accelerated degree program, adult/continuing education programs, advanced placement credit, cooperative education, distance learning, double majors, English as a second language, external degree program, honors programs, independent study, internships, off-campus study, services for LD students, study abroad, summer session for credit. *ROTC:* Army (b). *Unusual degree programs:* 3-2 education.

Computers on Campus 629 computers/terminals are available on campus for general student use. Students can access the following: campus intranet, computer help desk, free student e-mail accounts, online (class) grades, online (class) registration, online (class) schedules. Campuswide network is available. 100% of college-owned or -operated housing units are wired for high-speed Internet access. Wireless service is available via classrooms, computer centers, computer labs, learning centers, libraries, student centers.

Student Life *Housing:* on-campus residence required for freshman year. *Options:* coed, disabled students. Campus housing is university owned. Freshman campus housing is guaranteed. *Activities and organizations:* drama/theater group, student-run newspaper, radio station, choral group, marching band, Student Senate, University Productions, Graduate Student Council, Residence Hall Association, Global Union, national fraternities, national sororities. *Campus security:* 24-hour emergency response devices and patrols, student patrols, late-night transport/escort service, controlled dormitory access. *Student services:* health clinic, personal/psychological counseling, women's center.

Athletics Member NCAA. All Division I except football (Division I-AA). *Intercollegiate sports:* baseball M (s), basketball M (s)/W (s), bowling M (c)/W (c), cheerleading M (c)/W (c), crew M (c)/W (s), cross-country running M (s)/W (s), equestrian sports M (c)/W (c), field hockey W (s), football M (s)/W (c), golf M (s)/W, ice hockey M (c), lacrosse M (s)/W (s), rugby M (c), skiing (downhill) M (c)/W (c), soccer M (s)/W (s), softball W (s), squash M (c), swimming and diving M (s)/W (s), tennis M (s)/W (s), track and field M (s)/W (s), volleyball M (c)/W (s), wrestling M (s). *Intramural sports:* basketball M/W, fencing M (c)/W (c), football M/W, gymnastics M (c)/W (c), ice hockey M (c), lacrosse M (c)/W (c), racquetball M/W, rock climbing M/W, rugby W (c), sailing M (c)/W (c), skiing (cross-country) M (c)/W (c), soccer M (c)/W (c), softball M/W, tennis M (c)/W (c), ultimate Frisbee M (c)/W (c), volleyball M/W, water polo M (c)/W (c).

Standardized Tests *Required:* SAT or ACT (for admission).

Costs (2008–09) *Comprehensive fee:* $47,320 includes full-time tuition ($37,250), mandatory fees ($300), and room and board ($9770). Part-time tuition: $1555 per credit. *College room only:* $5660.

Financial Aid Of all full-time matriculated undergraduates who enrolled in 2007, 2,699 applied for aid, 2,067 were judged to have need, 1,507 had their need fully met. 1,175 Federal Work-Study jobs (averaging $1579). 158 state and other part-time jobs (averaging $4841). In 2007, 345 non-need-based awards were made. *Average percent of need met:* 97%. *Average financial aid package:* $29,498. *Average need-based loan:* $4628. *Average need-based gift aid:* $23,960. *Average non-need-based aid:* $10,456. *Average indebtedness upon graduation:* $26,768. *Financial aid deadline:* 2/1.

Applying *Options:* electronic application, early admission, early decision, deferred entrance. *Application fee:* $65. *Required:* essay or personal statement, high school transcript, 1 letter of recommendation, graded writing sample. *Recommended:* interview. *Application deadlines:* 1/1 (freshmen), 4/1 (transfers). *Early decision deadline:* 11/15 (for plan 1), 1/15 (for plan 2). *Notification:* 4/1 (freshmen), 5/1 (transfers), 12/15 (early decision plan 1), 2/15 (early decision plan 2).

Freshman Application Contact J. Bruce Gardiner, Director of Admissions, Lehigh University, 27 Memorial Drive West, Bethlehem, PA 18015. *Phone:* 610-758-3100. *Fax:* 610-758-4361. *E-mail:* admissions@lehigh.edu.

LINCOLN UNIVERSITY

Lincoln University, Pennsylvania www.lincoln.edu/

- **State-related** comprehensive, founded 1854
- **Rural** 422-acre campus with easy access to Philadelphia
- **Endowment** $24.6 million
- **Coed** 1,904 undergraduate students, 98% full-time, 60% women, 40% men
- **Moderately difficult** entrance level, 38% of applicants were admitted

Undergraduates 1,863 full-time, 41 part-time. Students come from 27 states and territories, 23 other countries, 57% are from out of state, 96% African American, 0.6% Hispanic American, 3% international, 2% transferred in, 98% live on campus. *Retention:* 66% of 2006 full-time freshmen returned.

Freshmen *Admission:* 5,488 applied, 2,068 admitted, 633 enrolled. *Average high school GPA:* 2.79. *Test scores:* SAT critical reading scores over 500: 12%; SAT math scores over 500: 12%; ACT scores over 18: 33%; SAT critical reading scores over 600: 1%; SAT math scores over 600: 1%.

Faculty *Total:* 194, 51% full-time, 50% with terminal degrees. *Student/faculty ratio:* 18:1.

Majors Accounting; actuarial science; anthropology; art teacher education; biology/biological sciences; business administration and management; chemistry; Chinese; communication/speech communication and rhetoric; computer and information sciences; criminal justice/safety; economics; education; elementary education; English; English/language arts teacher education; environmental science; finance; foreign language teacher education; French; health and physical education; health and physical education related; history; human services; industrial and organizational psychology; international relations and affairs; Japanese; journalism; kindergarten/preschool education; mathematics; mathematics teacher education; music; music teacher education; philosophy; physical sciences; physics; physiological psychology/psychobiology; political science and government; psychology; public administration; religious studies; secondary education; sociology; Spanish; special education; therapeutic recreation.

Academics *Calendar:* semesters. *Degrees:* bachelor's and master's. *Special study options:* academic remediation for entering students, accelerated degree program, adult/continuing education programs, advanced placement credit, cooperative education, double majors, honors programs, independent study, internships, off-campus study, part-time degree program, student-designed majors, study abroad, summer session for credit. *ROTC:* Army (c), Air Force (c). *Unusual degree programs:* 3-2 engineering with Drexel University, Pennsylvania State University—University Park Campus, Lafayette College, New Jersey Institute of Technology, University of Delaware, Howard University, Rensselaer Polytechnic Institute.

Computers on Campus 167 computers/terminals are available on campus for general student use. Campuswide network is available.

Student Life *Housing options:* coed, men-only, women-only. Campus housing is university owned. Freshman applicants given priority for college housing. *Activities and organizations:* drama/theater group, student-run newspaper, radio and television station, choral group, The Gospel Ensemble, Ziana Fashion Club, We R One, Council of Independent Organizations, national fraternities, national sororities. *Campus security:* 24-hour emergency response devices and patrols, late-night transport/escort service. *Student services:* health clinic, personal/psychological counseling, women's center.

Athletics Member NCAA. All Division III. *Intercollegiate sports:* baseball M, basketball M/W, bowling M/W, cross-country running M/W, soccer M/W, tennis M/W, track and field M/W, volleyball W. *Intramural sports:* baseball M, basketball M/W, bowling M/W, cheerleading W, cross-country running M/W, football M, softball M/W, swimming and diving M/W, tennis M/W, track and field M/W, volleyball M/W.

Standardized Tests *Required:* SAT or ACT (for admission).

Costs (2007–08) *Tuition:* state resident $5472 full-time, $228 per credit hour part-time; nonresident $9312 full-time, $388 per credit hour part-time. Part-time tuition and fees vary according to course load. *Required fees:* $2422 full-time, $80 per credit hour part-time. *Room and board:* $7392; room only: $3956. Room and board charges vary according to board plan. *Payment plans:* installment, deferred payment. *Waivers:* employees or children of employees.

Financial Aid Of all full-time matriculated undergraduates who enrolled in 2007, 1,763 applied for aid, 1,643 were judged to have need, 314 had their need fully met. 257 Federal Work-Study jobs (averaging $798). In 2007, 77 non-need-based awards were made. *Average percent of need met:* 48%. *Average financial aid package:* $10,369. *Average need-based loan:* $4376. *Average need-based gift aid:* $5434. *Average non-need-based aid:* $7689. *Average indebtedness upon graduation:* $28,582. *Financial aid deadline:* 5/1.

Applying *Options:* electronic application, early admission, deferred entrance. *Application fee:* $20. *Required:* essay or personal statement, high school transcript, minimum 2.0 GPA, 2 letters of recommendation. *Recommended:* interview. *Application deadlines:* rolling (freshmen), rolling (transfers). *Notification:* 2/15 (freshmen), continuous (transfers).

Freshman Application Contact Mr. Michael Taylor, Director of Admissions, Lincoln University, PO Box 179, MSC 147, Lincoln University, PA 19352-0999. *Phone:* 484-365-7206. *Toll-free phone:* 800-790-0191. *Fax:* 484-365-8109. *E-mail:* admiss@lincoln.edu.

See page 2266 for the College Close-Up.

LOCK HAVEN UNIVERSITY OF PENNSYLVANIA

Lock Haven, Pennsylvania **www.lhup.edu/**

- **State-supported** comprehensive, founded 1870, part of Pennsylvania State System of Higher Education
- **Rural** 165-acre campus
- **Coed** 4,982 undergraduate students, 92% full-time, 56% women, 44% men
- **Moderately difficult** entrance level, 74% of applicants were admitted

Undergraduates 4,568 full-time, 414 part-time. 10% are from out of state, 7% African American, 0.8% Asian American or Pacific Islander, 2% Hispanic American, 0.2% Native American, 1% international, 4% transferred in, 38% live on campus. *Retention:* 70% of 2006 full-time freshmen returned.

Freshmen *Admission:* 4,480 applied, 3,331 admitted, 1,233 enrolled. *Average high school GPA:* 3.12. *Test scores:* SAT critical reading scores over 500: 33%; SAT math scores over 500: 40%; SAT writing scores over 500: 29%; ACT scores over 18: 62%; SAT critical reading scores over 600: 4%; SAT math scores over 600: 7%; SAT writing scores over 600: 4%; ACT scores over 24: 13%; SAT writing scores over 700: 1%; ACT scores over 30: 1%.

Faculty *Total:* 255, 93% full-time, 66% with terminal degrees. *Student/faculty ratio:* 20:1.

Majors Accounting; anthropology; art; athletic training; biological and physical sciences; biology/biological sciences; business administration and management; business/managerial economics; chemistry; computer and information sciences; computer science; criminal justice/law enforcement administration; curriculum and instruction; dramatic/theater arts; economics; education; elementary education; engineering; English; French; geography; geology/earth science; German; health professions related; health science; history; humanities; international relations and affairs; journalism; kindergarten/preschool education; Latin American studies; legal assistant/paralegal; liberal arts and sciences/liberal studies; management information systems; mathematics; music; natural sciences; nursing (registered nurse training); parks, recreation and leisure; philosophy; physical education teaching and coaching; physical sciences; physics; political science and government; pre-dentistry studies; pre-medical studies; pre-veterinary studies; psychology; secondary education; social sciences; social work; sociology; Spanish; special education; special education related; speech and rhetoric.

Academics *Calendar:* semesters. *Degrees:* associate, bachelor's, and master's. *Special study options:* academic remediation for entering students, adult/continuing education programs, advanced placement credit, cooperative education, distance learning, double majors, English as a second language, honors programs, independent study, internships, off-campus study, part-time degree program, services for LD students, student-designed majors, study abroad, summer session for credit. *ROTC:* Army (b). *Unusual degree programs:* 3-2 engineering with Pennsylvania State University—University Park Campus; nursing with Clarion University of Pennsylvania.

Computers on Campus 290 computers/terminals are available on campus for general student use. Students can access the following: online (class) registration. Campuswide network is available.

Student Life *Housing:* on-campus residence required for freshman year. *Options:* coed. Campus housing is university owned and is provided by a third party. Freshman applicants given priority for college housing. *Activities and organizations:* drama/theater group, student-run newspaper, radio and television station, choral group, marching band, student government, Residence Hall Association, national fraternities, national sororities. *Campus security:* 24-hour emergency response devices and patrols. *Student services:* health clinic, personal/psychological counseling.

Athletics Member NCAA. All Division II except field hockey (Division I), wrestling (Division I). *Intercollegiate sports:* baseball M (s), basketball M (s)/W (s), cross-country running M (s)/W (s), field hockey W (s), football M (s), lacrosse W (s), soccer M (s)/W (s), softball W (s), swimming and diving W (s), track and field M (s)/W (s), volleyball W (s), wrestling M (s). *Intramural sports:* badminton M/W, basketball M/W, cross-country running M/W, fencing M/W, field hockey W, football M, golf M/W, ice hockey M, lacrosse M/W, racquetball M/W, rugby M/W, skiing (cross-country) M/W, skiing (downhill) M/W, soccer M/W, softball M/W, swimming and diving M/W, tennis M/W, track and field M/W, ultimate Frisbee M/W, volleyball M/W, water polo M, weight lifting M/W, wrestling M.

Standardized Tests *Required:* SAT or ACT (for admission).

Costs (2007–08) *One-time required fee:* $25. *Tuition:* state resident $5177 full-time, $216 per credit part-time; nonresident $10,944 full-time, $456 per credit part-time. Full-time tuition and fees vary according to course load and location. Part-time tuition and fees vary according to course load and location. *Required fees:* $1501 full-time, $54 per credit part-time, $58 per term part-time. *Room and board:* $5900; room only: $3360. Room and board charges vary according to board plan and housing facility. *Payment plans:* installment, deferred payment. *Waivers:* minority students, senior citizens, and employees or children of employees.

Financial Aid Of all full-time matriculated undergraduates who enrolled in 2007, 4,283 applied for aid, 3,340 were judged to have need, 1,836 had their need fully met. 253 Federal Work-Study jobs (averaging $1174). 951 state and other part-time jobs (averaging $711). In 2007, 239 non-need-based awards were made. *Average percent of need met:* 77%. *Average financial aid package:* $7940. *Average need-based loan:* $4500. *Average need-based gift aid:* $5955. *Average non-need-based aid:* $932. *Average indebtedness upon graduation:* $22,407. *Financial aid deadline:* 3/15.

Applying *Options:* electronic application, deferred entrance. *Application fee:* $25. *Required:* high school transcript. *Required for some:* essay or personal statement, letters of recommendation. *Recommended:* interview. *Application deadlines:* rolling (freshmen), rolling (transfers). *Notification:* continuous (freshmen), continuous (transfers).

Freshman Application Contact Mr. Steven Lee, Director of Admissions, Lock Haven University of Pennsylvania, Office of Admission, Akeley Hall, Lock

Haven, PA 17745. *Phone:* 570-484-2027. *Toll-free phone:* 800-332-8900 (in-state); 800-233-8978 (out-of-state). *Fax:* 570-484-2201. *E-mail:* admissions@lhup.edu.

LYCOMING COLLEGE

Williamsport, Pennsylvania **www.lycoming.edu/**

- **Independent United Methodist** 4-year, founded 1812
- **Small-town** 35-acre campus
- **Endowment** $135.1 million
- **Coed** 1,431 undergraduate students, 98% full-time, 55% women, 45% men
- **Moderately difficult** entrance level, 78% of applicants were admitted

Undergraduates 1,399 full-time, 32 part-time. Students come from 29 states and territories, 13 other countries, 31% are from out of state, 3% African American, 1% Asian American or Pacific Islander, 2% Hispanic American, 0.5% Native American, 0.9% international, 2% transferred in, 92% live on campus. *Retention:* 80% of 2006 full-time freshmen returned.

Freshmen *Admission:* 1,585 applied, 1,236 admitted, 399 enrolled. *Test scores:* SAT critical reading scores over 500: 62%; SAT math scores over 500: 62%; SAT writing scores over 500: 56%; ACT scores over 18: 93%; SAT critical reading scores over 600: 17%; SAT math scores over 600: 18%; SAT writing scores over 600: 17%; ACT scores over 24: 41%; SAT critical reading scores over 700: 1%; SAT math scores over 700: 2%; SAT writing scores over 700: 1%; ACT scores over 30: 1%.

Faculty *Total:* 123, 68% full-time, 67% with terminal degrees. *Student/faculty ratio:* 14:1.

Majors Accounting; actuarial science; American studies; anthropology; applied mathematics related; archeology; area studies related; art; art history, criticism and conservation; astronomy; biology/biological sciences; business administration and management; chemistry; classical, ancient Mediterranean and Near Eastern studies and archaeology; commercial and advertising art; communication/speech communication and rhetoric; computer and information sciences; creative writing; dramatic/theater arts; economics; English; finance; fine/studio arts; foreign languages and literatures; French; German; history; international business/trade/commerce; international relations and affairs; literature; marketing/marketing management; mathematics; multi-/interdisciplinary studies related; music; philosophy; physics; political science and government; pre-dentistry studies; pre-law studies; pre-medical studies; pre-veterinary studies; psychology; religious studies; social sciences; sociology.

Academics *Calendar:* semesters. *Degree:* bachelor's. *Special study options:* accelerated degree program, advanced placement credit, double majors, honors programs, independent study, internships, off-campus study, part-time degree program, services for LD students, student-designed majors, study abroad, summer session for credit. *ROTC:* Army (c). *Unusual degree programs:* 3-2 forestry with Duke University; environmental management with Duke University.

Computers on Campus 140 computers/terminals are available on campus for general student use. Students can access the following: campus intranet, computer help desk, free student e-mail accounts, online (class) grades, online (class) registration, online (class) schedules. Campuswide network is available. 100% of college-owned or -operated housing units are wired for high-speed Internet access. Wireless service is available via entire campus.

Student Life *Housing:* on-campus residence required through senior year. *Options:* coed, women-only. Campus housing is university owned. Freshman campus housing is guaranteed. *Activities and organizations:* drama/theater group, student-run newspaper, radio station, choral group, Campus Activities Board, Lycoming Dance Club, Habitat for Humanity, Circle K, United Campus Ministry, national fraternities, national sororities. *Campus security:* 24-hour emergency response devices and patrols, student patrols, late-night transport/escort service, controlled dormitory access. *Student services:* health clinic, personal/psychological counseling.

Athletics Member NCAA. All Division III. *Intercollegiate sports:* basketball M/W, cheerleading M (c)/W (c), crew M (c)/W (c), cross-country running M/W, equestrian sports M (c)/W (c), fencing M (c)/W (c), football M, golf M, lacrosse M/W, soccer M/W, softball W, swimming and diving M/W, tennis M/W, ultimate Frisbee M (c)/W (c), volleyball W, water polo M (c)/W (c), wrestling M. *Intramural sports:* basketball M/W, football M/W, soccer M/W, softball M/W, table tennis M/W, volleyball M/W.

Standardized Tests *Required:* SAT or ACT (for admission).

Costs (2007–08) *Comprehensive fee:* $34,367 includes full-time tuition ($26,624), mandatory fees ($505), and room and board ($7238). Full-time tuition and fees vary according to course load. Part-time tuition: $832 per credit hour. Part-time tuition and fees vary according to course load. *College room only:* $3692. Room and board charges vary according to housing facility. *Payment plan:* installment. *Waivers:* employees or children of employees.

Financial Aid Of all full-time matriculated undergraduates who enrolled in 2007, 1,253 applied for aid, 1,142 were judged to have need, 239 had their need fully met. 489 Federal Work-Study jobs (averaging $1201). In 2007, 208 non-need-based awards were made. *Average percent of need met:* 79%. *Average financial aid package:* $20,288. *Average need-based loan:* $4929. *Average need-based gift aid:* $15,556. *Average non-need-based aid:* $9438. *Average indebtedness upon graduation:* $26,538.

Applying *Options:* electronic application, deferred entrance. *Application fee:* $35. *Required:* essay or personal statement, high school transcript, 2 letters of recommendation. *Recommended:* minimum 2.3 GPA, interview. *Application deadlines:* 5/1 (freshmen), rolling (transfers). *Notification:* continuous (freshmen), continuous (transfers).

Freshman Application Contact Mr. James Spencer, Vice President of Admissions and Financial Aid, Lycoming College, 700 College Place, Box 164, Williamsport, PA 17701. *Phone:* 570-321-4026. *Toll-free phone:* 800-345-3920 Ext. 4026. *Fax:* 570-321-4317. *E-mail:* admissions@lycoming.edu.

MANSFIELD UNIVERSITY OF PENNSYLVANIA

Mansfield, Pennsylvania **www.mansfield.edu/**

- **State-supported** comprehensive, founded 1857, part of Pennsylvania State System of Higher Education
- **Small-town** 205-acre campus
- **Endowment** $8.8 million
- **Coed** 2,921 undergraduate students, 91% full-time, 62% women, 38% men
- **Moderately difficult** entrance level, 70% of applicants were admitted

Undergraduates 2,672 full-time, 249 part-time. Students come from 5 states and territories, 17 other countries, 21% are from out of state, 5% African American, 0.6% Asian American or Pacific Islander, 2% Hispanic American, 0.7% Native American, 1% international, 8% transferred in, 43% live on campus. *Retention:* 66% of 2006 full-time freshmen returned.

Freshmen *Admission:* 3,367 applied, 2,349 admitted, 670 enrolled. *Test scores:* SAT critical reading scores over 500: 47%; SAT math scores over 500: 47%; SAT writing scores over 500: 38%; SAT critical reading scores over 600: 10%; SAT math scores over 600: 11%; SAT writing scores over 600: 8%; SAT critical reading scores over 700: 1%; SAT math scores over 700: 1%; SAT writing scores over 700: 1%.

Faculty *Total:* 210, 72% full-time, 64% with terminal degrees. *Student/faculty ratio:* 16:1.

Majors Accounting; anthropology; applied art; art; art teacher education; biochemistry; biological and physical sciences; biology/biological sciences; biology teacher education; business administration and management; cell biology and histology; chemistry; chemistry teacher education; city/urban, community and regional planning; clinical laboratory science/medical technology; clinical psychology; computer and information sciences; computer science; criminal justice/law enforcement administration; dietetics; economics; education; elementary education; English; English/language arts teacher education; environmental studies; fishing and fisheries sciences and management; French; French language teacher education; geography; geology/earth science; German; German language teacher education; history; human resources management; information science/studies; international business/trade/commerce; international relations and affairs; journalism; kindergarten/preschool education; liberal arts and sciences/liberal studies; marketing/marketing management; mass communication/media; mathematics; mathematics teacher education; music; music management and merchandising; music performance; music teacher education; nursing (registered nurse training); philosophy; physics; physics teacher education; political science and government; pre-law studies; psychology; public relations/image management; radiologic technology/science; respiratory care therapy; science teacher education; secondary education; social sciences; social science teacher education; social studies teacher education; social work; sociology; Spanish; Spanish language teacher education; special education; tourism and travel services management.

Academics *Calendar:* semesters. *Degrees:* certificates, diplomas, associate, bachelor's, and master's. *Special study options:* academic remediation for entering students, accelerated degree program, adult/continuing education programs, advanced placement credit, distance learning, double majors, freshman honors college, honors programs, independent study, internships, off-campus study, part-time degree program, services for LD students, student-designed majors, study abroad, summer session for credit. *Unusual degree programs:* 3-2 engineering.

Computers on Campus 661 computers/terminals and 4,600 ports are available on campus for general student use. Students can access the following: campus intranet, computer help desk, free student e-mail accounts, online (class) grades, online (class) registration, online (class) schedules. Campuswide network is available. 100% of college-owned or -operated housing units are wired for high-speed Internet access. Wireless service is available via classrooms, computer centers, computer labs, dorm rooms, learning centers, libraries, student centers.

Student Life *Housing:* on-campus residence required through sophomore year. *Options:* coed. Campus housing is university owned. Freshman campus housing is guaranteed. *Activities and organizations:* drama/theater group, student-run newspaper, radio and television station, choral group, marching band, Mansfield International Student Organization, P.R. Society, PSEA, Ski Club, Activities Council, national fraternities, national sororities. *Campus security:* 24-hour emergency response devices and patrols, student patrols, late-night transport/ escort service, controlled dormitory access. *Student services:* health clinic, personal/psychological counseling, women's center.

Athletics Member NCAA. All Division II. *Intercollegiate sports:* baseball M (s), basketball M (s)/W (s), cross-country running M (s)/W (s), field hockey W (s), soccer W (s), softball W (s), swimming and diving W, track and field M (s)/W (s). *Intramural sports:* badminton M/W, basketball M/W, bowling M/W, cheerleading W, cross-country running M/W, equestrian sports M/W, football M/W, golf M/W, racquetball M/W, skiing (cross-country) M/W, skiing (downhill) M/W, soccer M/W, softball M/W, swimming and diving M/W, tennis M/W, track and field M/W, volleyball M/W, water polo M/W, weight lifting M/W.

Standardized Tests *Required:* SAT or ACT (for admission).

Costs (2007–08) *Tuition:* state resident $5177 full-time, $216 per credit hour part-time; nonresident $12,944 full-time, $539 per credit hour part-time. Part-time tuition and fees vary according to course load. *Required fees:* $1827 full-time, $21 per credit hour part-time, $348 per term part-time. *Room and board:* $6236; room only: $2326. Room and board charges vary according to board plan. *Payment plans:* installment, deferred payment. *Waivers:* senior citizens and employees or children of employees.

Financial Aid Of all full-time matriculated undergraduates who enrolled in 2005, 75 had their need fully met. In 2005, 155 non-need-based awards were made. *Average percent of need met:* 48%. *Average financial aid package:* $5120. *Average need-based loan:* $3709. *Average need-based gift aid:* $4025. *Average non-need-based aid:* $2075. *Average indebtedness upon graduation:* $19,262.

Applying *Options:* electronic application, early admission, deferred entrance. *Application fee:* $25. *Required:* high school transcript. *Required for some:* interview. *Recommended:* essay or personal statement, minimum 2.5 GPA, letters of recommendation. *Application deadlines:* rolling (freshmen), rolling (transfers). *Notification:* continuous (freshmen), continuous (transfers).

Freshman Application Contact Mr. Brian Barden, Director of Admissions, Mansfield University of Pennsylvania, Alumni Hall, Mansfield, PA 16933. *Phone:* 570-662-4813. *Toll-free phone:* 800-577-6826. *E-mail:* admissions@mnsfld.edu.

MARYWOOD UNIVERSITY

Scranton, Pennsylvania **www.marywood.edu/**

- **Independent Roman Catholic** comprehensive, founded 1915
- **Suburban** 115-acre campus
- **Endowment** $34.2 million
- **Coed** 2,002 undergraduate students, 92% full-time, 71% women, 29% men
- **Moderately difficult** entrance level

Building on its tradition of preparing students from around the world to be successful in professional life and to contribute to the welfare of others, Marywood University offers more than sixty undergraduate programs and more than thirty graduate programs. Using its attractive 115-acre campus in northeastern Pennsylvania creatively, Marywood continues to expand its facilities, including a new health and recreation facility that addresses the physical education needs and expectations of the growing student population. Marywood is also committed to making college affordable through a remarkable scholarship/grant program.

Undergraduates 1,838 full-time, 164 part-time. Students come from 20 states and territories, 21 other countries, 24% are from out of state, 1% African American, 2% Asian American or Pacific Islander, 3% Hispanic American, 0.4% Native American, 1% international, 6% transferred in. *Retention:* 80% of 2006 full-time freshmen returned.

Freshmen *Admission:* 416 enrolled. *Average high school GPA:* 3.07. *Test scores:* SAT critical reading scores over 500: 60%; SAT math scores over 500: 61%; SAT writing scores over 500: 57%; ACT scores over 18: 93%; SAT critical reading scores over 600: 16%; SAT math scores over 600: 14%; SAT writing scores over 600: 13%; ACT scores over 24: 20%; SAT critical reading scores over 700: 2%; SAT math scores over 700: 1%; SAT writing scores over 700: 1%.

Faculty *Total:* 307, 43% full-time, 35% with terminal degrees. *Student/faculty ratio:* 13:1.

Majors Accounting; arts management; art teacher education; art therapy; athletic training; audiology and speech-language pathology; aviation/airway management; biology/biological sciences; biology teacher education; biotechnology; business administration and management; ceramic arts and ceramics; clinical laboratory science/medical technology; computer/information technology services administration related; criminal justice/safety; dietetics; digital communication and media/multimedia; dramatic/theater arts; early childhood education; education (specific subject areas) related; elementary education; English; English/ language arts teacher education; environmental science; family and consumer sciences/home economics teacher education; financial planning and services; French; French language teacher education; graphic design; health and physical education; health/health care administration; health services/allied health/health sciences; history; hospitality administration; illustration; industrial and organizational psychology; interior design; international business/trade/commerce; marketing/ marketing management; mathematics; mathematics teacher education; multi-/ interdisciplinary studies related; music performance; music teacher education; music therapy; nursing (registered nurse training); painting; photography; psychology; public relations, advertising, and applied communication related; religious studies; science teacher education; sculpture; social sciences; social sciences related; social science teacher education; social work; Spanish; Spanish language teacher education; special education; special education (emotionally disturbed); visual and performing arts related.

Academics *Calendar:* semesters. *Degrees:* bachelor's, master's, doctoral, post-master's, and postbachelor's certificates. *Special study options:* academic remediation for entering students, accelerated degree program, adult/continuing education programs, advanced placement credit, distance learning, double majors, English as a second language, external degree program, honors programs, independent study, internships, off-campus study, part-time degree program, services for LD students, student-designed majors, study abroad, summer session for credit. *ROTC:* Army (c), Air Force (c). *Unusual degree programs:* 3-2 physician assistant, communication sciences disorders, criminal justice.

Computers on Campus 367 computers/terminals are available on campus for general student use. Students can access the following: computer help desk, free student e-mail accounts, online (class) registration, online (class) schedules. Campuswide network is available. 100% of college-owned or -operated housing units are wired for high-speed Internet access. Wireless service is available via classrooms, computer centers, computer labs, learning centers, libraries, student centers.

Student Life *Housing:* on-campus residence required through sophomore year. *Options:* coed, men-only, women-only, disabled students. Campus housing is university owned. Freshman campus housing is guaranteed. *Activities and organizations:* drama/theater group, student-run newspaper, radio and television station, choral group, marching band, Outdoor Adventure Club, Volunteers in Action, International Club, Peer Mediators, Speech and Hearing Club. *Campus security:* 24-hour emergency response devices and patrols, late-night transport/ escort service, controlled dormitory access, apartments with deadbolts, self-defense education, lighted pathways, seminars on safety. *Student services:* health clinic, personal/psychological counseling.

Athletics Member NCAA. All Division III. *Intercollegiate sports:* baseball M, basketball M/W, cheerleading M (c)/W (c), cross-country running M/W, field hockey W, golf M (c)/W (c), lacrosse M/W, soccer M/W, softball W, swimming and diving M (c)/W (c), tennis M/W, volleyball M (c)/W (c). *Intramural sports:* badminton M/W, baseball M, basketball M/W, field hockey W, football M, racquetball M/W, skiing (downhill) M (c)/W (c), soccer M (c)/W (c), softball M/W, table tennis M/W, tennis M/W, ultimate Frisbee M/W, volleyball M/W, water polo M/W.

Standardized Tests *Required:* SAT or ACT (for admission).

Costs (2007–08) *Comprehensive fee:* $34,500 includes full-time tuition ($23,040), mandatory fees ($1050), and room and board ($10,410). Part-time tuition: $550 per credit. *Required fees:* $200 per term part-time. *College room only:* $5980. Room and board charges vary according to board plan and housing facility. *Payment plans:* installment, deferred payment. *Waivers:* senior citizens and employees or children of employees.

Financial Aid Of all full-time matriculated undergraduates who enrolled in 2006, 1,543 applied for aid, 1,422 were judged to have need, 223 had their need fully met. 643 Federal Work-Study jobs (averaging $1724). In 2006, 276 non-need-based awards were made. *Average percent of need met:* 73%. *Average financial aid package:* $16,952. *Average need-based loan:* $4332. *Average need-based gift aid:* $12,214. *Average non-need-based aid:* $8818. *Average indebtedness upon graduation:* $34,364.

Applying *Options:* electronic application, early admission, deferred entrance. *Application fee:* $35. *Required:* high school transcript, 1 letter of recommendation. *Required for some:* essay or personal statement, interview. *Recommended:* essay or personal statement, interview. *Application deadlines:* rolling (freshmen), rolling (transfers). *Notification:* continuous (freshmen), continuous (transfers).

Freshman Application Contact Mr. Robert W. Reese, Director of University Admissions, Marywood University, 2300 Adams Avenue, Scranton, PA 18509-1598. *Phone:* 570-348-6234. *Toll-free phone:* 800-346-5014. *Fax:* 570-961-4763. *E-mail:* yourfuture@marywood.edu.

See page 2268 for the College Close-Up.

MERCYHURST COLLEGE

Erie, Pennsylvania **www.mercyhurst.edu/**

- **Independent Roman Catholic** comprehensive, founded 1926
- **Suburban** 88-acre campus with easy access to Buffalo
- **Endowment** $26.9 million
- **Coed** 3,970 undergraduate students, 89% full-time, 58% women, 42% men
- **Moderately difficult** entrance level, 66% of applicants were admitted

Undergraduates 3,518 full-time, 452 part-time. Students come from 43 states and territories, 26 other countries, 38% are from out of state, 5% African American, 0.7% Asian American or Pacific Islander, 2% Hispanic American, 0.4% Native American, 5% international, 2% transferred in, 73% live on campus. *Retention:* 80% of 2006 full-time freshmen returned.

Freshmen *Admission:* 3,583 applied, 2,354 admitted, 671 enrolled. *Average high school GPA:* 3.4. *Test scores:* SAT critical reading scores over 500: 64%; SAT math scores over 500: 67%; ACT scores over 18: 93%; SAT critical reading scores over 600: 19%; SAT math scores over 600: 19%; ACT scores over 24: 41%; SAT critical reading scores over 700: 2%; SAT math scores over 700: 1%; ACT scores over 30: 3%.

Faculty *Total:* 302, 56% full-time, 29% with terminal degrees. *Student/faculty ratio:* 17:1.

Majors Accounting; anthropology; archeology; art; arts management; art teacher education; art therapy; athletic training; biochemistry; biology/biological sciences; biology teacher education; business, management, and marketing related; business teacher education; chemistry; chemistry teacher education; clinical laboratory science/medical technology; communication/speech communication and rhetoric; computer and information sciences; computer science; corrections; corrections and criminal justice related; creative writing; criminal justice/safety; dance; dietetics; education; elementary education; English; English/language arts teacher education; family and consumer sciences/home economics teacher education; family and consumer sciences/human sciences; fashion merchandising; fiber, textile and weaving arts; finance; fine/studio arts; foreign languages and literatures; foreign language teacher education; forensic science and technology; geology/earth science; health information/medical records technology; health/medical preparatory programs related; history; history related; hospitality administration; human development and family studies; human ecology; humanities; human resources management; information science/studies; interior design; journalism; marketing/marketing management; mass communication/media; mathematics; mathematics teacher education; medical administrative assistant and medical secretary; medical transcription; multi-/interdisciplinary studies related; music; music performance; music teacher education; office management; paleontology; petroleum technology; philosophy; physical therapist assistant; physical therapy; physics; political science and government; pre-dentistry studies; pre-law studies; pre-medical studies; pre-veterinary studies; psychology; public relations/image management; purchasing, procurement/acquisitions and contracts management; radio and television; religious studies; science teacher education; sculpture; secondary education; social sciences; social science teacher education; social work; sociology; special education; sport and fitness administration/management; statistics; voice and opera; wind/percussion instruments.

Academics *Calendar:* 4-3-3. *Degrees:* certificates, associate, bachelor's, master's, and postbachelor's certificates. *Special study options:* academic remediation for entering students, accelerated degree program, adult/continuing education programs, advanced placement credit, cooperative education, double majors, honors programs, independent study, internships, off-campus study, part-time degree program, services for LD students, student-designed majors, study abroad, summer session for credit. *ROTC:* Army (c), Air Force (c). *Unusual degree programs:* law with Duquesne University.

Computers on Campus 350 computers/terminals and 150 ports are available on campus for general student use. Students can access the following: campus intranet, computer help desk, free student e-mail accounts, online (class) grades, online (class) registration, online (class) schedules. Campuswide network is available. 100% of college-owned or -operated housing units are wired for high-speed Internet access. Wireless service is available via entire campus.

Student Life *Housing:* on-campus residence required through sophomore year. *Options:* men-only, women-only. Campus housing is university owned and leased by the school. Freshman campus housing is guaranteed. *Activities and organizations:* drama/theater group, student-run newspaper, radio and television station, choral group; student government, chorus, Admission Ambassadors, Amnesty International, The Merciad. *Campus security:* 24-hour emergency response devices and patrols, campus-wide camera system. *Student services:* health clinic, personal/psychological counseling.

Athletics Member NCAA, NCCAA. All NCAA Division II. *Intercollegiate sports:* baseball M (s), basketball M (s)/W (s), crew M (s)/W (s), cross-country running M (s)/W (s), field hockey W (s), football M (s), golf M (s)/W (s), ice hockey M (s)/W (s), lacrosse M (s)/W (s), soccer M (s)/W (s), softball W (s), tennis M (s)/W (s), volleyball M (s)/W (s), water polo M (s)/W (s), wrestling M (s). *Intramural sports:* basketball M/W, football M, skiing (cross-country) M/W, skiing (downhill) M/W, volleyball M/W.

Standardized Tests *Required:* SAT or ACT (for admission).

Costs (2007–08) *Comprehensive fee:* $28,633 includes full-time tuition ($19,561), mandatory fees ($1614), and room and board ($7458). Part-time tuition and fees vary according to course load and location. *College room only:* $3750. Room and board charges vary according to board plan and housing facility. *Payment plan:* installment. *Waivers:* adult students and employees or children of employees.

Financial Aid Of all full-time matriculated undergraduates who enrolled in 2005, 3,079 applied for aid, 2,581 were judged to have need, 2,084 had their need fully met. 248 Federal Work-Study jobs (averaging $1400). 1,404 state and other part-time jobs (averaging $1202). *Average percent of need met:* 89%. *Average financial aid package:* $10,261. *Average need-based loan:* $3224. *Average need-based gift aid:* $5433. *Average indebtedness upon graduation:* $21,000. *Financial aid deadline:* 5/1.

Applying *Options:* electronic application, deferred entrance. *Application fee:* $30. *Required:* high school transcript. *Required for some:* letters of recommendation. *Recommended:* essay or personal statement, interview. *Application deadlines:* rolling (freshmen), rolling (transfers). *Notification:* continuous until 8/1 (freshmen), continuous until 8/30 (transfers).

Freshman Application Contact Emily Crawford, Director of Undergraduate Admissions, Mercyhurst College, 501 East 38th Street, Erie, PA 16546-0001. *Phone:* 814-824-3317. *Toll-free phone:* 800-825-1926 Ext. 2202. *Fax:* 814-824-2071. *E-mail:* ecrawford@mercyhurst.edu.

See page 2270 for the College Close-Up.

MESSIAH COLLEGE

Grantham, Pennsylvania **www.messiah.edu/**

- **Independent interdenominational** 4-year, founded 1909
- **Small-town** 485-acre campus
- **Endowment** $128.1 million
- **Coed** 2,837 undergraduate students, 98% full-time, 63% women, 37% men
- **Moderately difficult** entrance level, 79% of applicants were admitted

Undergraduates 2,778 full-time, 59 part-time. Students come from 37 states and territories, 23 other countries, 46% are from out of state, 2% African American, 2% Asian American or Pacific Islander, 1% Hispanic American, 0.1% Native American, 2% international, 3% transferred in, 85% live on campus. *Retention:* 86% of 2006 full-time freshmen returned.

Freshmen *Admission:* 2,496 applied, 1,961 admitted, 696 enrolled. *Average high school GPA:* 3.71. *Test scores:* SAT critical reading scores over 500: 83%; SAT math scores over 500: 82%; SAT writing scores over 500: 81%; ACT scores over 18: 96%; SAT critical reading scores over 600: 38%; SAT math scores over 600: 37%; SAT writing scores over 600: 35%; ACT scores over 24: 57%; SAT critical reading scores over 700: 8%; SAT math scores over 700: 6%; SAT writing scores over 700: 6%; ACT scores over 30: 13%.

Faculty *Total:* 288, 60% full-time. *Student/faculty ratio:* 13:1.

Majors Accounting; art history, criticism and conservation; art teacher education; athletic training; biblical studies; biochemistry; biology/biological sciences; biology teacher education; biopsychology; business administration and management; business, management, and marketing related; business/managerial economics; chemistry; chemistry teacher education; civil engineering; clinical nutrition; communication/speech communication and rhetoric; computer science; criminal justice/safety; dramatic/theater arts; early childhood education; e-commerce; economics; elementary education; engineering; English; English/language arts teacher education; entrepreneurship; environmental science; environmental studies; family and community services; fine/studio arts; French; French language teacher education; German; German language teacher education; history; humanities; human resources management; information science/studies; international business/trade/commerce; journalism; kinesiology and exercise science; marketing/marketing management; mathematics; mathematics teacher education; multi-/interdisciplinary studies related; music; music teacher education; nursing (registered nurse training); parks, recreation and leisure; philosophy; physical education teaching and coaching; physics; political science and government; psychology; radio and television; religious education; religious studies; social studies teacher education; social work; sociology; Spanish; Spanish language teacher education; sport and fitness administration/management.

Academics *Calendar:* semesters. *Degree:* bachelor's. *Special study options:* academic remediation for entering students, accelerated degree program, adult/continuing education programs, advanced placement credit, double majors, English as a second language, honors programs, independent study, internships, off-campus study, part-time degree program, services for LD students, student-designed majors, study abroad, summer session for credit.

Computers on Campus 571 computers/terminals are available on campus for general student use. Students can access the following: campus intranet, computer help desk, free student e-mail accounts, online (class) grades, online (class) registration, online (class) schedules, access to software. Campuswide network is available. 100% of college-owned or -operated housing units are wired for high-speed Internet access. Wireless service is available via entire campus.

Student Life *Housing:* on-campus residence required through senior year. *Options:* coed, men-only, women-only, disabled students. Campus housing is university owned. Freshman campus housing is guaranteed. *Activities and organizations:* drama/theater group, student-run newspaper, radio station, choral group, outreach teams, student government, music ensembles, Small Group Program, Outdoors Club. *Campus security:* 24-hour emergency response devices and patrols, student patrols, late-night transport/escort service, controlled dormitory access, bicycle patrols, security lighting, self-defense classes, prevention/awareness programs. *Student services:* health clinic, personal/psychological counseling.

Athletics Member NCAA. All Division III. *Intercollegiate sports:* baseball M, basketball M/W, cross-country running M/W, field hockey W, golf M, lacrosse M/W, soccer M/W, softball W, tennis M/W, track and field M/W, volleyball W, wrestling M. *Intramural sports:* basketball M/W, football M/W, ice hockey M (c), racquetball M/W, soccer M/W, softball M/W, ultimate Frisbee M/W, volleyball M/W.

Standardized Tests *Required for some:* SAT or ACT (for admission).

Costs (2007–08) *Comprehensive fee:* $31,760 includes full-time tuition ($23,710), mandatory fees ($710), and room and board ($7340). Part-time tuition: $990 per credit. *Required fees:* $30 per credit part-time. *College room only:* $3840. Room and board charges vary according to board plan, housing facility, and location. *Payment plan:* installment. *Waivers:* minority students, children of alumni, adult students, senior citizens, and employees or children of employees.

Financial Aid Of all full-time matriculated undergraduates who enrolled in 2007, 2,178 applied for aid, 1,904 were judged to have need, 311 had their need fully met. 754 Federal Work-Study jobs (averaging $1866). 919 state and other part-time jobs (averaging $2052). In 2007, 742 non-need-based awards were made. *Average percent of need met:* 70%. *Average financial aid package:* $15,442. *Average need-based loan:* $4747. *Average need-based gift aid:* $10,855. *Average non-need-based aid:* $8077. *Average indebtedness upon graduation:* $33,283.

Applying *Options:* electronic application, deferred entrance. *Application fee:* $30. *Required:* essay or personal statement, high school transcript, 2 letters of recommendation. *Recommended:* interview. *Application deadline:* rolling (freshmen). *Notification:* continuous (freshmen), continuous (transfers).

Freshman Application Contact Mr. John Chopka, Dean for Enrollment Management, Messiah College, PO Box 3005, One College Avenue, Grantham, PA 17027. *Phone:* 717-691-6000. *Toll-free phone:* 800-233-4220. *Fax:* 717-796-5374. *E-mail:* admiss@messiah.edu.

See page 2272 for the College Close-Up.

MILLERSVILLE UNIVERSITY OF PENNSYLVANIA

Millersville, Pennsylvania **www.millersville.edu/**

- **State-supported** comprehensive, founded 1855, part of Pennsylvania State System of Higher Education
- **Small-town** 220-acre campus
- **Endowment** $2.4 million
- **Coed** 7,259 undergraduate students, 91% full-time, 56% women, 44% men
- **Moderately difficult** entrance level, 57% of applicants were admitted

Undergraduates 6,592 full-time, 667 part-time. Students come from 17 states and territories, 53 other countries, 4% are from out of state, 7% African American, 2% Asian American or Pacific Islander, 4% Hispanic American, 0.2% Native American, 0.4% international, 7% transferred in, 32% live on campus. *Retention:* 83% of 2006 full-time freshmen returned.

Freshmen *Admission:* 6,723 applied, 3,820 admitted, 1,345 enrolled. *Test scores:* SAT critical reading scores over 500: 61%; SAT math scores over 500: 66%; SAT writing scores over 500: 56%; SAT critical reading scores over 600: 15%; SAT math scores over 600: 19%; SAT writing scores over 600: 12%; SAT critical reading scores over 700: 2%; SAT math scores over 700: 2%; SAT writing scores over 700: 1%.

Faculty *Total:* 462, 72% full-time, 76% with terminal degrees. *Student/faculty ratio:* 19:1.

Majors Anthropology; area studies; art; art teacher education; atmospheric sciences and meteorology; biology/biological sciences; business administration and management; chemical technology; chemistry; communication/speech communication and rhetoric; computer and information sciences; early childhood education; earth sciences; economics; elementary education; English; English/language arts teacher education; foreign language teacher education; French; geography; geology/earth science; German; history; industrial production technologies related; mathematics; mathematics teacher education; music; music teacher education; nursing (registered nurse training); nursing science; occupational safety and health technology; oceanography (chemical and physical); philosophy; physics; political science and government; psychology; reading teacher education; science teacher education; secondary education; social sciences related; social studies teacher education; social work; sociology; Spanish; special education; technology/industrial arts teacher education.

Academics *Calendar:* 4-1-4. *Degrees:* associate, bachelor's, master's, post-master's, and postbachelor's certificates. *Special study options:* academic remediation for entering students, accelerated degree program, adult/continuing education programs, advanced placement credit, cooperative education, distance learning, double majors, honors programs, independent study, internships, off-campus study, part-time degree program, services for LD students, study abroad, summer session for credit. *ROTC:* Army (b). *Unusual degree programs:* 3-2 engineering with Pennsylvania State University—University Park Campus, and University of Pennsylvania.

Computers on Campus 580 computers/terminals are available on campus for general student use. Students can access the following: computer help desk, free student e-mail accounts, online (class) registration. Campuswide network is available. 100% of college-owned or -operated housing units are wired for high-speed Internet access.

Student Life *Housing:* on-campus residence required through sophomore year. *Options:* coed. Campus housing is university owned. Freshman campus housing is guaranteed. *Activities and organizations:* drama/theater group, student-run newspaper, radio and television station, choral group, marching band, University Christian Fellowship, John Newman Association, Marching Band, Phi Eta Sigma, WIQX—Radio Station, national fraternities, national sororities. *Campus security:* 24-hour emergency response devices and patrols, student patrols, late-night transport/escort service, controlled dormitory access, crime awareness programs, self-defense education, shuttle buses. *Student services:* health clinic, personal/psychological counseling, women's center.

Athletics Member NCAA. All Division II except wrestling (Division I). *Intercollegiate sports:* baseball M (s), basketball M (s)/W (s), cheerleading W, cross-country running M (s)/W (s), field hockey W (s), football M (s), golf M (s), lacrosse W (s), soccer M (s)/W (s), softball W (s), swimming and diving W (s), tennis M (s)/W (s), track and field M (s)/W (s), volleyball W (s), wrestling M (s). *Intramural sports:* badminton M/W, basketball M/W, bowling M (c)/W (c), fencing M (c)/W (c), golf M/W, ice hockey M (c), lacrosse M (c), racquetball M/W, rock climbing M (c)/W (c), rugby M/W, soccer M/W, softball M/W, tennis M/W, ultimate Frisbee M/W, volleyball M (c)/W, water polo M (c)/W (c).

Standardized Tests *Required:* SAT or ACT (for admission).

Costs (2007–08) *Tuition:* area resident $5177 full-time; state resident $216 per credit part-time; nonresident $12,944 full-time, $539 per credit part-time. Full-time tuition and fees vary according to degree level. Part-time tuition and fees vary according to course load and degree level. *Required fees:* $1447 full-time, $53 per credit part-time, $43 per term part-time. *Room and board:* $6876; room only: $4166. Room and board charges vary according to board plan and housing facility. *Payment plan:* installment. *Waivers:* senior citizens and employees or children of employees.

Financial Aid Of all full-time matriculated undergraduates who enrolled in 2006, 4,910 applied for aid, 3,510 were judged to have need, 636 had their need fully met. 188 Federal Work-Study jobs (averaging $1307). 1,780 state and other part-time jobs (averaging $1302). In 2006, 177 non-need-based awards were made. *Average percent of need met:* 76%. *Average financial aid package:* $7081. *Average need-based loan:* $3712. *Average need-based gift aid:* $4417. *Average non-need-based aid:* $2467. *Average indebtedness upon graduation:* $19,555. *Financial aid deadline:* 3/15.

Applying *Options:* electronic application, early admission, deferred entrance. *Application fee:* $50. *Required:* high school transcript, minimum 2.0 GPA. *Required for some:* essay or personal statement, letters of recommendation, interview. *Recommended:* essay or personal statement, letters of recommendation.

Application deadlines: rolling (freshmen), rolling (transfers). *Notification:* continuous (freshmen), continuous (transfers).

Freshman Application Contact Mr. Douglas Zander, Director of Admissions, Millersville University of Pennsylvania, PO Box 1002, Millersville, PA 17551-0302. *Phone:* 717-872-3371. *Toll-free phone:* 800-MU-ADMIT. *Fax:* 717-871-2147. *E-mail:* admissions@millersville.edu.

See page 2274 for the College Close-Up.

MISERICORDIA UNIVERSITY

Dallas, Pennsylvania **www.misericordia.edu/**

- **Independent Roman Catholic** comprehensive, founded 1924
- **Small-town** 100-acre campus
- **Endowment** $15.8 million
- **Coed, primarily women** 2,075 undergraduate students, 71% full-time, 73% women, 27% men
- **Moderately difficult** entrance level, 74% of applicants were admitted

Misericordia University (MU) scores among the best schools nationally in important areas of the National Survey of Student Engagement (NSSE), one of the best measures of undergraduate success. MU students report a unique blend of personal attention, preparation for a career, and service leadership. Misericordia offers a guaranteed career placement program that ensures a paid internship to graduates who are not employed or enrolled in graduate or professional school within six months of graduation.

Undergraduates 1,476 full-time, 599 part-time. Students come from 21 states and territories, 2 other countries, 17% are from out of state, 1% African American, 0.6% Asian American or Pacific Islander, 1% Hispanic American, 0.5% Native American, 0.1% international, 6% transferred in, 38% live on campus. *Retention:* 81% of 2006 full-time freshmen returned.

Freshmen *Admission:* 1,289 applied, 949 admitted, 372 enrolled. *Average high school GPA:* 3.21. *Test scores:* SAT critical reading scores over 500: 57%; SAT math scores over 500: 55%; ACT scores over 18: 90%; SAT critical reading scores over 600: 8%; SAT math scores over 600: 12%; ACT scores over 24: 33%; SAT critical reading scores over 700: 1%; SAT math scores over 700: 1%.

Faculty *Total:* 253, 37% full-time, 36% with terminal degrees. *Student/faculty ratio:* 12:1.

Majors Accounting; biochemistry; biology/biological sciences; biology teacher education; business administration and management; chemistry; clinical laboratory science/medical technology; communication/speech communication and rhetoric; computer science; elementary education; English; English/language arts teacher education; health/health care administration; health science; history; information science/studies; interdisciplinary studies; liberal arts and sciences/liberal studies; management information systems; marketing/marketing management; mathematics; mathematics teacher education; medical informatics; medical radiologic technology; nursing (registered nurse training); philosophy; psychology; social studies teacher education; social work; special education; sport and fitness administration/management.

Academics *Calendar:* semesters. *Degrees:* bachelor's, master's, doctoral, post-master's, and postbachelor's certificates. *Special study options:* academic remediation for entering students, accelerated degree program, adult/continuing education programs, advanced placement credit, cooperative education, distance learning, double majors, English as a second language, external degree program, honors programs, independent study, internships, off-campus study, part-time degree program, services for LD students, student-designed majors, study abroad, summer session for credit. *ROTC:* Army (c), Air Force (c). *Unusual degree programs:* 3-2 occupational therapy, physical therapy, speech-language pathology.

Computers on Campus 100 computers/terminals and 1,000 ports are available on campus for general student use. Students can access the following: campus intranet, computer help desk, free student e-mail accounts, online (class) grades, online (class) registration, online (class) schedules, Student Leadership Transcript. Campuswide network is available. 100% of college-owned or -operated housing units are wired for high-speed Internet access. Wireless service is available via computer labs, learning centers, libraries, student centers.

Student Life *Housing options:* coed. Campus housing is university owned. Freshman applicants given priority for college housing. *Activities and organizations:* drama/theater group, student-run newspaper, radio station, choral group, Circle K, SOAR—Student Outdoor Adventure and Recreation, BACCHUS, Peer Advocates, Commuter Council. *Campus security:* 24-hour emergency response devices and patrols, late-night transport/escort service. *Student services:* health clinic, personal/psychological counseling, women's center.

Athletics Member NCAA. All Division III. *Intercollegiate sports:* baseball M, basketball M/W, cheerleading W, cross-country running M/W, field hockey W, golf M, lacrosse M/W, soccer M/W, softball W, swimming and diving M/W, tennis W, track and field M/W, volleyball W. *Intramural sports:* basketball M/W, cross-country running M/W, football M/W, racquetball M/W, soccer M/W, softball M/W, tennis M/W, ultimate Frisbee M/W, volleyball M/W.

Standardized Tests *Required:* SAT or ACT (for admission).

Costs (2007–08) *Comprehensive fee:* $31,050 includes full-time tuition ($20,830), mandatory fees ($1120), and room and board ($9100). Part-time tuition: $425 per credit. Part-time tuition and fees vary according to location. *College room only:* $5250. Room and board charges vary according to board plan and housing facility. *Payment plans:* installment, deferred payment. *Waivers:* employees or children of employees.

Financial Aid Of all full-time matriculated undergraduates who enrolled in 2007, 1,381 applied for aid, 1,237 were judged to have need, 219 had their need fully met. 130 Federal Work-Study jobs (averaging $1400). In 2007, 132 non-need-based awards were made. *Average percent of need met:* 73%. *Average financial aid package:* $15,030. *Average need-based loan:* $5485. *Average need-based gift aid:* $10,317. *Average non-need-based aid:* $5661. *Average indebtedness upon graduation:* $20,006.

Applying *Options:* electronic application, early admission, deferred entrance. *Application fee:* $25. *Required:* high school transcript. *Required for some:* essay or personal statement, minimum 2.0 GPA, 2 letters of recommendation. *Recommended:* interview. *Application deadlines:* rolling (freshmen), rolling (transfers). *Notification:* continuous (freshmen), continuous (transfers).

Freshman Application Contact Mr. Glenn Bozinski, Director of Admissions, Misericordia University, 301 Lake Street, Dallas, PA 18612-1098. *Phone:* 570-675-6264. *Toll-free phone:* 866-262-6363. *Fax:* 570-674-6232. *E-mail:* admiss@misericordia.edu.

See page 2276 for the College Close-Up.

MOORE COLLEGE OF ART & DESIGN

Philadelphia, Pennsylvania **www.moore.edu/**

- **Independent** 4-year, founded 1848
- **Urban** 3-acre campus
- **Endowment** $10.0 million
- **Women only**
- **Moderately difficult** entrance level

Moore College of Art & Design sets the standard of excellence in educating women for careers in the arts and design. Located in the Museum District of Center City, Philadelphia, Moore's fully accredited B.F.A. program offers degrees in ten fine arts and design disciplines taught by an award-winning faculty of practicing artists, designers, and scholars.

Faculty *Student/faculty ratio:* 8:1.

Academics *Calendar:* semesters. *Degrees:* certificates, bachelor's, and post-bachelor's certificates.

Student Life *Campus security:* 24-hour patrols, late-night transport/escort service.

Standardized Tests *Required for some:* SAT or ACT (for admission).

Costs (2008–09) *Comprehensive fee:* $38,350 includes full-time tuition ($26,800), mandatory fees ($1048), and room and board ($10,502). Part-time tuition: $1118 per credit. *Required fees:* $488 per credit part-time. *College room only:* $6322.

Financial Aid Of all full-time matriculated undergraduates who enrolled in 2006, 383 applied for aid, 357 were judged to have need, 9 had their need fully met. 87 Federal Work-Study jobs (averaging $1500). In 2006, 93 non-need-based awards were made. *Average percent of need met:* 45. *Average financial aid package:* $14,823. *Average need-based loan:* $4355. *Average need-based gift aid:* $10,180. *Average non-need-based aid:* $9729. *Average indebtedness upon graduation:* $36,778.

Applying *Options:* electronic application, early admission, early decision, deferred entrance. *Application fee:* $40. *Required:* essay or personal statement, high school transcript, minimum 2.5 GPA, 1 letter of recommendation, portfolio. *Required for some:* minimum 3.0 GPA. *Recommended:* interview.

Freshman Application Contact Ms. Heesung Lee, Director of Admissions, Moore College of Art & Design, 20th and The Parkway, Philadelphia, PA 19103-1179. *Phone:* 215-965-4014. *Toll-free phone:* 800-523-2025. *Fax:* 215-965-8544. *E-mail:* enroll@moore.edu.

See page 2278 for the College Close-Up.

MORAVIAN COLLEGE

Bethlehem, Pennsylvania **www.moravian.edu/**

- **Independent** comprehensive, founded 1742, affiliated with Moravian Church
- **Suburban** 60-acre campus with easy access to Philadelphia
- **Endowment** $93.9 million
- **Coed** 1,784 undergraduate students, 89% full-time, 58% women, 42% men
- **Moderately difficult** entrance level, 64% of applicants were admitted

Undergraduates 1,588 full-time, 196 part-time. Students come from 20 states and territories, 15 other countries, 43% are from out of state, 2% African American, 2% Asian American or Pacific Islander, 3% Hispanic American, 0.2% Native American, 1% international, 4% transferred in, 71% live on campus. *Retention:* 86% of 2006 full-time freshmen returned.

Freshmen *Admission:* 2,189 applied, 1,401 admitted, 401 enrolled. *Test scores:* SAT critical reading scores over 500: 78%; SAT math scores over 500: 80%; SAT writing scores over 500: 71%; SAT critical reading scores over 600: 26%; SAT math scores over 600: 31%; SAT writing scores over 600: 24%; SAT critical reading scores over 700: 3%; SAT math scores over 700: 5%; SAT writing scores over 700: 4%.

Faculty *Total:* 201, 59% full-time, 69% with terminal degrees. *Student/faculty ratio:* 11:1.

Majors Accounting; art; art history, criticism and conservation; art teacher education; biochemistry; biology/biological sciences; biology teacher education; business administration and management; chemistry; chemistry teacher education; classics and languages, literatures and linguistics; clinical laboratory science/medical technology; clinical psychology; computer science; creative writing; criminal justice/law enforcement administration; dramatic/theater arts; economics; education; elementary education; English; English language and literature related; environmental studies; experimental psychology; fine/studio arts; foreign language teacher education; French; French language teacher education; geology/earth science; German; German language teacher education; German studies; graphic design; history; history teacher education; industrial and organizational psychology; international business/trade/commerce; mathematics; mathematics teacher education; music; music performance; music teacher education; music theory and composition; natural resources management; nursing (registered nurse training); philosophy; physics; physics teacher education; political science and government; psychology; religious/sacred music; religious studies; science teacher education; secondary education; social psychology; social sciences; social studies teacher education; sociology; Spanish; Spanish language teacher education; theater literature, history and criticism.

Academics *Calendar:* semesters. *Degrees:* bachelor's, master's, first professional, and postbachelor's certificates. *Special study options:* adult/continuing education programs, advanced placement credit, double majors, honors programs, independent study, internships, off-campus study, part-time degree program, services for LD students, student-designed majors, study abroad, summer session for credit. *ROTC:* Army (c). *Unusual degree programs:* 3-2 engineering with Washington University in St. Louis; forestry with Duke University; occupational therapy with Thomas Jefferson University, Dental School, Temple University.

Computers on Campus 263 computers/terminals and 150 ports are available on campus for general student use. Students can access the following: campus intranet, computer help desk, free student e-mail accounts, online (class) grades, online (class) schedules. Campuswide network is available. 100% of college-owned or -operated housing units are wired for high-speed Internet access. Wireless service is available via classrooms, computer centers, computer labs, learning centers, libraries, student centers.

Student Life *Housing:* on-campus residence required through junior year. *Options:* coed, men-only, women-only. Campus housing is university owned. Freshman campus housing is guaranteed. *Activities and organizations:* drama/theater group, student-run newspaper, radio station, choral group, marching band, Student Alumni Association, United Student Government, Moravian College Choir, Twenty-six Points (student ambassador group), International Club, national fraternities, national sororities. *Campus security:* 24-hour emergency response devices and patrols, late-night transport/escort service, controlled dormitory access. *Student services:* health clinic, personal/psychological counseling.

Athletics Member NCAA. All Division III. *Intercollegiate sports:* baseball M, basketball M/W, cheerleading W (c), cross-country running M/W, equestrian sports W (c), field hockey W, football M, golf M/W (c), ice hockey M (c)/W (c), lacrosse M/W, soccer M/W, softball W, tennis M/W, track and field M/W, volleyball W. *Intramural sports:* badminton M/W, basketball M/W, football M/W, racquetball M/W, skiing (downhill) M (c)/W (c), soccer M/W, softball M/W, table tennis M/W, tennis M/W, volleyball M/W, wrestling M.

Standardized Tests *Required:* SAT or ACT (for admission).

Costs (2007–08) *Comprehensive fee:* $36,381 includes full-time tuition ($27,873), mandatory fees ($515), and room and board ($7993). Part-time tuition: $774 per credit hour. Part-time tuition and fees vary according to class time. *College room only:* $4491. Room and board charges vary according to board plan and housing facility. *Payment plan:* installment. *Waivers:* employees or children of employees.

Financial Aid Of all full-time matriculated undergraduates who enrolled in 2006, 1,256 applied for aid, 1,112 were judged to have need, 216 had their need fully met. 905 Federal Work-Study jobs (averaging $1464). 269 state and other part-time jobs (averaging $1092). In 2006, 306 non-need-based awards were made. *Average percent of need met:* 75%. *Average financial aid package:* $18,154. *Average need-based loan:* $4288. *Average need-based gift aid:* $13,070. *Average non-need-based aid:* $13,068.

Applying *Options:* electronic application, early admission, early decision, deferred entrance. *Application fee:* $40. *Required:* essay or personal statement, high school transcript, 3 letters of recommendation. *Recommended:* interview. *Application deadlines:* 3/1 (freshmen), 3/1 (transfers). *Early decision deadline:* 2/1. *Notification:* 3/15 (freshmen), continuous (transfers), 12/15 (early decision).

Freshman Application Contact Mr. James Mackin, Director of Admission, Moravian College, 1200 Main Street, Bethlehem, PA 18018. *Phone:* 610-861-1320. *Toll-free phone:* 800-441-3191. *Fax:* 610-625-7930. *E-mail:* admissions@moravian.edu.

See page 2280 for the College Close-Up.

MOUNT ALOYSIUS COLLEGE

Cresson, Pennsylvania **www.mtaloy.edu/**

- **Independent Roman Catholic** comprehensive, founded 1939
- **Small-town** 165-acre campus
- **Endowment** $16.2 million
- **Coed** 1,544 undergraduate students, 74% full-time, 72% women, 28% men
- **Minimally difficult** entrance level, 87% of applicants were admitted

Mount Aloysius College is a small, private Catholic college specializing in both undergraduate and graduate education. Offering more than fifty academic programs of study, Mount Aloysius College provides solid career-directed study within the liberal arts tradition. With more than 150 years of academic excellence, Mount Aloysius College is committed to providing small classroom size, plenty of individual attention, and high job placement rates.

Undergraduates 1,150 full-time, 394 part-time. Students come from 21 states and territories, 12 other countries, 4% are from out of state, 2% African American, 0.3% Asian American or Pacific Islander, 0.7% Hispanic American, 0.1% Native American, 0.7% international, 9% transferred in, 24% live on campus. *Retention:* 66% of 2006 full-time freshmen returned.

Freshmen *Admission:* 951 applied, 830 admitted, 307 enrolled. *Average high school GPA:* 3.1. *Test scores:* SAT critical reading scores over 500: 30%; SAT math scores over 500: 31%; SAT writing scores over 500: 25%; ACT scores over 18: 56%; SAT critical reading scores over 600: 5%; SAT math scores over 600: 7%; SAT writing scores over 600: 4%; ACT scores over 24: 4%; SAT critical reading scores over 700: 1%.

Faculty *Total:* 170, 34% full-time. *Student/faculty ratio:* 14:1.

Majors Accounting; accounting and business/management; behavioral sciences; business administration and management; child care and support services management; computer science; criminal justice/safety; criminology; English; general studies; health services/allied health/health sciences; history; humanities; information science/studies; kindergarten/preschool education; legal assistant/paralegal; liberal arts and sciences/liberal studies; medical/clinical assistant; medical office assistant; nursing (registered nurse training); nursing science; occupational therapist assistant; occupational therapy; pharmacy technician; physical therapist assistant; physical therapy; political science and government; pre-law studies; professional studies; psychology; radiologic technology/science; sign language interpretation and translation; social sciences; surgical technology.

Academics *Calendar:* semesters. *Degrees:* certificates, associate, bachelor's, and master's. *Special study options:* academic remediation for entering students, accelerated degree program, adult/continuing education programs, advanced placement credit, distance learning, double majors, honors programs, independent study, internships, part-time degree program, student-designed majors, study abroad, summer session for credit.

Computers on Campus 149 computers/terminals are available on campus for general student use. Campuswide network is available.

Student Life *Housing:* on-campus residence required for freshman year. *Options:* Campus housing is university owned. Freshman campus housing is guaranteed. *Activities and organizations:* drama/theater group, student-run newspaper, choral group, Phi Theta Kappa, Student Nursing Association, Student Government, Delta Epsilon Sigma, Residence Hall Association. *Campus security:* 24-hour emergency response devices and patrols, student patrols, late-night transport/escort service, controlled dormitory access. *Student services:* health clinic, personal/psychological counseling, women's center.

Athletics Member NCAA. *Intercollegiate sports:* baseball M, basketball M/W, cross-country running M/W, golf M/W, soccer M/W, softball W, volleyball W. *Intramural sports:* baseball M, basketball M/W, cheerleading M (c)/W (c), football M/W, skiing (cross-country) M/W, skiing (downhill) M/W, soccer M/W, softball M/W, table tennis M/W, tennis M/W, ultimate Frisbee M/W, volleyball M/W, weight lifting M/W.

Standardized Tests *Required:* SAT or ACT (for admission).

Costs (2008–09) *Comprehensive fee:* $23,530 includes full-time tuition ($15,930), mandatory fees ($650), and room and board ($6950). Part-time tuition: $450 per credit. *Required fees:* $175 per term part-time. *College room only:* $3520.

Financial Aid Of all full-time matriculated undergraduates who enrolled in 2006, 1,250 applied for aid, 1,214 were judged to have need. 169 Federal Work-Study jobs (averaging $1640). In 2006, 36 non-need-based awards were made. *Average percent of need met:* 25%. *Average financial aid package:* $10,545. *Average need-based loan:* $3205. *Average need-based gift aid:* $1749. *Average non-need-based aid:* $1850. *Average indebtedness upon graduation:* $23,672.

Applying *Options:* electronic application, early admission, deferred entrance. *Application fee:* $30. *Required:* high school transcript, minimum 2.5 GPA. *Required for some:* essay or personal statement, 3 letters of recommendation, interview. *Recommended:* interview. *Application deadlines:* rolling (freshmen), rolling (transfers). *Notification:* continuous (freshmen), continuous (transfers).

Freshman Application Contact Mr. Francis C. Crouse Jr., Vice President for Enrollment, Mount Aloysius College, 7373 Admiral Peary Highway, Cresson, PA 16630. *Phone:* 814-886-6383. *Toll-free phone:* 888-823-2220. *Fax:* 814-886-6441. *E-mail:* admissions@mtaloy.edu.

See page 2282 for the College Close-Up.

MUHLENBERG COLLEGE

Allentown, Pennsylvania **www.muhlenberg.edu/**

- **Independent** 4-year, founded 1848, affiliated with Lutheran Church
- **Suburban** 75-acre campus with easy access to Philadelphia
- **Endowment** $135.4 million
- **Coed** 2,457 undergraduate students, 93% full-time, 59% women, 41% men
- **Very difficult** entrance level, 37% of applicants were admitted

"Friendly" and "challenging" are the words that students use most often to describe Muhlenberg. The educational experience is active and hands-on, with small classes, a caring environment, and easy access to faculty members. Internships, field study, study abroad, and a Washington semester supplement traditional classroom experiences. Students are taught to analyze critically, think creatively, and express themselves effectively in person and in writing—the most prized outcomes of a Muhlenberg education.

Undergraduates 2,275 full-time, 182 part-time. Students come from 24 states and territories, 5 other countries, 70% are from out of state, 2% African American, 2% Asian American or Pacific Islander, 4% Hispanic American, 0.2% Native American, 0.2% international, 0.5% transferred in, 92% live on campus. *Retention:* 92% of 2006 full-time freshmen returned.

Freshmen *Admission:* 4,703 applied, 1,750 admitted, 551 enrolled. *Average high school GPA:* 3.41. *Test scores:* SAT critical reading scores over 500: 94%; SAT math scores over 500: 95%; ACT scores over 18: 100%; SAT critical reading scores over 600: 55%; SAT math scores over 600: 61%; ACT scores over 24: 79%; SAT critical reading scores over 700: 10%; SAT math scores over 700: 12%; ACT scores over 30: 16%.

Faculty *Total:* 275, 59% full-time, 57% with terminal degrees. *Student/faculty ratio:* 12:1.

Majors Accounting; American studies; anthropology; art; biochemistry; biology/biological sciences; business administration and management; chemistry; dance; dramatic/theater arts; economics; economics related; English; environmental science; French; German; history; international relations and affairs; mathematics; music; natural sciences; neuroscience; philosophy; physical sciences; physics; political science and government; political science and government related; psychology; religious studies; Russian studies; social sciences; sociology; Spanish.

Academics *Calendar:* semesters. *Degrees:* certificates, associate, and bachelor's. *Special study options:* accelerated degree program, adult/continuing education programs, advanced placement credit, double majors, honors programs, independent study, internships, off-campus study, part-time degree program, services for LD students, student-designed majors, study abroad, summer session for credit. *ROTC:* Army (c). *Unusual degree programs:* 3-2 engineering with Columbia University, Washington University in St. Louis; forestry with Duke University.

Computers on Campus 486 computers/terminals and 100 ports are available on campus for general student use. Students can access the following: campus intranet, computer help desk, free student e-mail accounts, online (class) grades, online (class) registration, online (class) schedules. Campuswide network is available. 100% of college-owned or -operated housing units are wired for high-speed Internet access. Wireless service is available via classrooms, dorm rooms, libraries, student centers.

Student Life *Housing:* on-campus residence required for freshman year. *Options:* coed, women-only, disabled students. Campus housing is university owned and leased by the school. Freshman campus housing is guaranteed. *Activities and organizations:* drama/theater group, student-run newspaper, radio and television station, choral group, Theater Association, Environmental Action Team, Jefferson School Partnership, Select Choir, Habitat for Humanity, national fraternities, national sororities. *Campus security:* 24-hour emergency response devices and patrols, late-night transport/escort service, controlled dormitory access. *Student services:* health clinic, personal/psychological counseling.

Athletics Member NCAA. All Division III. *Intercollegiate sports:* baseball M, basketball M/W, cheerleading M/W, cross-country running M/W, field hockey W, football M, golf M/W, lacrosse M/W, soccer M/W, softball W, tennis M/W, track and field M/W, volleyball W, wrestling M. *Intramural sports:* basketball M/W, cross-country running M/W, football M/W, ice hockey M, racquetball M/W, rugby M/W, soccer M/W, softball M, swimming and diving M/W, tennis M/W, ultimate Frisbee M, volleyball M/W.

Standardized Tests *Required for some:* SAT or ACT (for admission).

Costs (2007–08) *Comprehensive fee:* $40,880 includes full-time tuition ($32,850), mandatory fees ($240), and room and board ($7790). Part-time tuition: $3865 per course. Part-time tuition and fees vary according to program. *Required fees:* $265 per year part-time. *College room only:* $4480. Room and board charges vary according to board plan, housing facility, and location. *Payment plan:* installment. *Waivers:* employees or children of employees.

Financial Aid Of all full-time matriculated undergraduates who enrolled in 2003, 1,206 applied for aid, 973 were judged to have need, 895 had their need fully met. In 2003, 372 non-need-based awards were made. *Average percent of need met:* 95%. *Average financial aid package:* $16,847. *Average need-based loan:* $3894. *Average need-based gift aid:* $13,931. *Average non-need-based aid:* $9718. *Average indebtedness upon graduation:* $16,642. *Financial aid deadline:* 2/15.

Applying *Options:* electronic application, early admission, early decision, deferred entrance. *Application fee:* $50. *Required:* essay or personal statement, high school transcript, 2 letters of recommendation. *Required for some:* interview, graded paper. *Recommended:* interview. *Application deadlines:* 2/15 (freshmen), 6/15 (transfers). *Early decision deadline:* 2/1. *Notification:* 3/15 (freshmen), continuous until 7/1 (transfers).

Freshman Application Contact Mr. Christopher Hooker-Haring, Director of Undergraduate Admissions, Muhlenberg College, 2400 Chew Street, Allentown, PA 18104-5586. *Phone:* 484-664-3245. *Fax:* 484-664-3234. *E-mail:* adm@muhlenberg.edu.

See page 2284 for the College Close-Up.

NEUMANN COLLEGE

Aston, Pennsylvania **www.neumann.edu/**

- **Independent Roman Catholic** comprehensive, founded 1965
- **Suburban** 50-acre campus with easy access to Philadelphia
- **Endowment** $17.2 million
- **Coed** 2,499 undergraduate students, 79% full-time, 65% women, 35% men
- **Moderately difficult** entrance level, 95% of applicants were admitted

Undergraduates 1,968 full-time, 531 part-time. Students come from 18 states and territories, 8 other countries, 30% are from out of state, 13% African American, 1% Asian American or Pacific Islander, 2% Hispanic American, 0.2% Native American, 2% international, 3% transferred in, 40% live on campus. *Retention:* 74% of 2006 full-time freshmen returned.

Freshmen *Admission:* 2,490 applied, 2,359 admitted, 540 enrolled. *Average high school GPA:* 3.25. *Test scores:* SAT critical reading scores over 500: 22%; SAT math scores over 500: 23%; SAT critical reading scores over 600: 3%; SAT math scores over 600: 2%; SAT critical reading scores over 700: 1%.

Faculty *Total:* 289, 31% full-time, 38% with terminal degrees. *Student/faculty ratio:* 14:1.

Majors Accounting; athletic training/sports medicine; biology/biological sciences; business administration and management; communication/speech communication and rhetoric; computer and information sciences; criminal justice/safety; elementary education; English; environmental studies; international business/trade/commerce; kindergarten/preschool education; liberal arts and sciences/liberal studies; marketing/marketing management; nursing (registered nurse training); political science and government; psychology; radio, television, and digital communication related; sport and fitness administration/management.

Academics *Calendar:* semesters. *Degrees:* certificates, associate, bachelor's, and master's. *Special study options:* academic remediation for entering students, accelerated degree program, adult/continuing education programs, advanced placement credit, cooperative education, distance learning, double majors, freshman honors college, honors programs, independent study, internships, off-campus study, part-time degree program, services for LD students, student-designed majors, study abroad, summer session for credit. *ROTC:* Army (c).

Computers on Campus 400 computers/terminals are available on campus for general student use. Students can access the following: campus intranet, computer help desk, free student e-mail accounts, online (class) grades, online (class) registration, online (class) schedules. Campuswide network is available. 100% of college-owned or -operated housing units are wired for high-speed Internet access. Wireless service is available via computer centers, libraries.

Student Life *Housing options:* coed. Campus housing is university owned and leased by the school. Freshman applicants given priority for college housing. *Activities and organizations:* drama/theater group, student-run newspaper, radio station, choral group, Professional Education Society, Student Nurses Association, theater ensemble, Environmental Club, community chorus. *Campus security:* 24-hour emergency response devices and patrols, late-night transport/escort service, controlled dormitory access. *Student services:* health clinic, personal/psychological counseling.

Athletics Member NCAA. All Division III. *Intercollegiate sports:* baseball M, basketball M/W, field hockey W, golf M, ice hockey M/W, lacrosse M/W, soccer M/W, softball W, tennis M/W, volleyball W. *Intramural sports:* basketball M/W, lacrosse M, softball W, tennis M/W, volleyball M/W.

Standardized Tests *Required:* SAT or ACT (for admission).

Costs (2007–08) *Comprehensive fee:* $28,324 includes full-time tuition ($18,846), mandatory fees ($640), and room and board ($8838). Part-time tuition: $431 per credit. *College room only:* $5248. Room and board charges vary according to board plan. *Payment plan:* installment. *Waivers:* employees or children of employees.

Financial Aid Of all full-time matriculated undergraduates who enrolled in 2006, 1,600 applied for aid, 1,600 were judged to have need, 960 had their need fully met. 120 Federal Work-Study jobs (averaging $1200). *Average percent of need met:* 65%. *Average financial aid package:* $17,000. *Average need-based loan:* $1200. *Average need-based gift aid:* $17,000. *Average indebtedness upon graduation:* $20,000.

Applying *Options:* early admission, deferred entrance. *Application fee:* $35. *Required:* high school transcript, minimum 2.0 GPA. *Recommended:* interview. *Application deadlines:* 4/1 (freshmen), rolling (transfers). *Notification:* continuous (freshmen), continuous (transfers).

Freshman Application Contact Mr. Dennis J. Murphy, Vice President for Enrollment Management, Neumann College, One Neumann Drive, Aston, PA 19014-1298. *Phone:* 610-361-2448. *Toll-free phone:* 800-963-8626. *Fax:* 610-558-5652. *E-mail:* neumann@neumann.edu.

See page 2286 for the College Close-Up.

Peirce College

Philadelphia, Pennsylvania www.peirce.edu/

- **Independent** 4-year, founded 1865
- **Urban** 1-acre campus
- **Endowment** $13.6 million
- **Coed** 2,181 undergraduate students, 41% full-time, 73% women, 27% men
- **Noncompetitive** entrance level

Undergraduates 887 full-time, 1,294 part-time. Students come from 37 states and territories, 28 other countries, 18% are from out of state, 55% African American, 1% Asian American or Pacific Islander, 6% Hispanic American, 0.3% Native American, 2% international, 12% transferred in. *Retention:* 60% of 2006 full-time freshmen returned.

Freshmen *Admission:* 95 enrolled.

Faculty *Total:* 167, 18% full-time, 26% with terminal degrees. *Student/faculty ratio:* 17:1.

Majors Accounting technology and bookkeeping; business administration and management; computer and information systems security; computer programming (vendor/product certification); data processing and data processing technology; entrepreneurship; human resources management; information science/studies; legal assistant/paralegal; management information systems; marketing/marketing management; pre-law studies; system administration.

Academics *Calendar:* continuous. *Degrees:* certificates, associate, bachelor's, and postbachelor's certificates. *Special study options:* accelerated degree program, advanced placement credit, cooperative education, distance learning, independent study, internships, part-time degree program, services for LD students, summer session for credit.

Computers on Campus 228 computers/terminals are available on campus for general student use. Students can access the following: computer help desk, online (class) grades, online (class) registration, online (class) schedules. Campuswide network is available. Wireless service is available via classrooms, computer labs, libraries.

Student Life *Housing:* college housing not available. *Campus security:* 24-hour emergency response devices and patrols, late-night transport/escort service, 24-hour security cameras.

Costs (2007–08) *Tuition:* $12,750 full-time, $425 per credit hour part-time. Full-time tuition and fees vary according to course load. Part-time tuition and fees vary according to course load. *Required fees:* $1000 full-time, $100 per course part-time. *Payment plan:* installment. *Waivers:* children of alumni and employees or children of employees.

Financial Aid Of all full-time matriculated undergraduates who enrolled in 2005, 560 applied for aid, 560 were judged to have need, 530 had their need fully met. 35 Federal Work-Study jobs (averaging $2175). In 2005, 52 non-need-based awards were made. *Average percent of need met:* 68%. *Average financial aid package:* $4206. *Average need-based loan:* $3000. *Average need-based gift aid:* $2193. *Average non-need-based aid:* $2311. *Average indebtedness upon graduation:* $15,662.

Applying *Options:* electronic application. *Application fee:* $50. *Required:* high school transcript. *Application deadlines:* rolling (freshmen), rolling (transfers). *Notification:* continuous (freshmen), continuous (transfers).

Freshman Application Contact Mr. Steve W. Bird, Supervisor, Admissions, Peirce College, 1420 Pine Street, Philadelphia, PA 19102. *Phone:* 215-670-9375. *Toll-free phone:* 888-467-3472. *Fax:* 215-670-9366. *E-mail:* info@peirce.edu.

Penn State Abington

Abington, Pennsylvania www.abington.psu.edu/

- **State-related** 4-year, founded 1950, part of Pennsylvania State University
- **Small-town** 45-acre campus with easy access to Philadelphia
- **Endowment** $1.7 billion
- **Coed** 3,351 undergraduate students, 79% full-time, 50% women, 50% men
- **Very difficult** entrance level, 80% of applicants were admitted

Undergraduates 2,634 full-time, 717 part-time. Students come from 16 states and territories, 10 other countries, 5% are from out of state, 13% African American, 15% Asian American or Pacific Islander, 6% Hispanic American, 0.2% Native American, 0.6% international, 3% transferred in. *Retention:* 73% of 2006 full-time freshmen returned.

Freshmen *Admission:* 3,604 applied, 2,870 admitted, 870 enrolled. *Average high school GPA:* 3.00. *Test scores:* SAT critical reading scores over 500: 34%; SAT math scores over 500: 42%; SAT critical reading scores over 600: 7%; SAT math scores over 600: 12%; SAT math scores over 700: 1%.

Faculty *Total:* 210, 50% full-time, 45% with terminal degrees. *Student/faculty ratio:* 21:1.

Majors Accounting; acting; actuarial science; adult and continuing education administration; advertising; aerospace, aeronautical and astronautical engineering; African-American/Black studies; agribusiness; agricultural and extension education; agricultural/biological engineering and bioengineering; agricultural business and management related; agricultural mechanization; agriculture; agronomy and crop science; American studies; animal sciences; animal sciences related; anthropology; applied economics; archeology; architectural engineering; art; art history, criticism and conservation; art teacher education; Asian studies (East); astronomy; atmospheric sciences and meteorology; biochemistry; biological and biomedical sciences related; biological and physical sciences; biology/biological sciences; biology/biotechnology laboratory technician; biomedical/medical engineering; business/commerce; business/corporate communications; business/managerial economics; chemical engineering; chemistry; civil engineering; classics and languages, literatures and linguistics; communication and journalism related; communication disorders; communication/speech communication and rhetoric; comparative literature; computer and information sciences; computer engineering; criminal justice/law enforcement administration; criminal justice/safety; economics; electrical, electronic and communications engineering technology; electrical, electronics and communications engineering; elementary education; engineering science; English; environmental/environmental health engineering; film/cinema studies; finance; food science; foreign language teacher education; forestry technology; forest sciences and biology; French; geography; geological and earth sciences/geosciences related; geology/earth science; German; graphic design; health/health care administration; history; horticultural science; hospitality administration related; human development and family studies; human nutrition; industrial engineering; information science/studies; international relations and affairs; Italian; Japanese; Jewish/Judaic studies; journalism; kinesiology and exercise science; labor and industrial relations; landscaping and groundskeeping; Latin American studies; liberal arts and sciences/liberal studies; management information systems; marketing/marketing management; materials science; mathematics; mechanical engineering; medical microbiology and bacteriology; medieval and Renaissance studies; mining and mineral engineering; natural resources and conservation related; natural resources/conservation; nuclear engineering; nursing (registered nurse training); organizational behavior; parks, recreation and leisure facilities management; petroleum engineering; philosophy; physics; political science and government; pre-medical studies; psychology; rehabilitation and therapeutic professions related; religious studies; Russian; secondary education; social psychology; sociology; soil science and agronomy; Spanish; special education; statistics; theater design and technology; turf and turfgrass management; visual and performing arts; women's studies.

Academics *Calendar:* semesters. *Degrees:* associate and bachelor's. *Special study options:* academic remediation for entering students, accelerated degree program, adult/continuing education programs, advanced placement credit, cooperative education, distance learning, double majors, English as a second language, external degree program, freshman honors college, honors programs, independent study, internships, off-campus study, part-time degree program, services for LD students, student-designed majors, study abroad, summer session for credit. *ROTC:* Army (c), Air Force (c). *Unusual degree programs:* 3-2 biotechnology, cytotechnology, medical technology, occupational therapy with Thomas Jefferson University, Jefferson College of Health Professions; clinical health psychology with Philadelphia College of Osteopathic Medicine.

Computers on Campus 150 computers/terminals are available on campus for general student use. Students can access the following: campus intranet, computer help desk, free student e-mail accounts, online (class) grades, online (class) registration, online (class) schedules. Campuswide network is available.

Student Life *Housing:* college housing not available. *Activities and organizations:* drama/theater group, student-run newspaper. *Campus security:* 24-hour emergency response devices and patrols. *Student services:* health clinic, personal/psychological counseling.

Athletics *Intercollegiate sports:* baseball M, basketball M/W, golf M, soccer M/W, softball W, tennis M/W, volleyball W. *Intramural sports:* basketball M/W, cross-country running M/W, football M, soccer M/W, softball M, tennis M/W, volleyball M/W.

Standardized Tests *Required:* SAT or ACT (for admission).

Costs (2007–08) *Tuition:* state resident $10,454 full-time, $423 per credit hour part-time; nonresident $15,954 full-time, $665 per credit hour part-time. Full-time tuition and fees vary according to course level, location, program, and student level. Part-time tuition and fees vary according to course level, course load, location, program, and student level. *Required fees:* $552 full-time, $205 per term part-time. *Room and board:* $3360. *Payment plans:* installment, deferred payment. *Waivers:* senior citizens and employees or children of employees.

Financial Aid Of all full-time matriculated undergraduates who enrolled in 2006, 1,849 applied for aid, 1,465 were judged to have need, 91 had their need fully met. 91 Federal Work-Study jobs (averaging $1222). In 2006, 70 non-need-based awards were made. *Average percent of need met:* 67%. *Average financial aid package:* $8499. *Average need-based loan:* $3448. *Average need-based gift aid:* $6032. *Average non-need-based aid:* $1944. *Average indebtedness upon graduation:* $26,300.

Applying *Options:* electronic application, early admission, deferred entrance. *Application fee:* $50. *Required:* high school transcript. *Required for some:* letters of recommendation, interview. *Recommended:* essay or personal statement. *Application deadlines:* rolling (freshmen), rolling (transfers). *Notification:* continuous until 11/1 (freshmen), continuous (transfers).

Freshman Application Contact Anne L. Rohrbach, Executive Director for Undergraduate Admissions, Penn State Abington, 106 Sutherland, 1600 Woodland Road, Abington, PA 19001-3990. *Phone:* 814-865-4700. *Fax:* 814-863-7590. *E-mail:* admissions@psu.edu.

PENN STATE ALTOONA

Altoona, Pennsylvania **www.aa.psu.edu/**

- **State-related** 4-year, founded 1939, part of Pennsylvania State University
- **Suburban** 150-acre campus
- **Endowment** $1.7 billion
- **Coed** 4,031 undergraduate students, 93% full-time, 49% women, 51% men
- **Very difficult** entrance level, 70% of applicants were admitted

Undergraduates 3,750 full-time, 281 part-time. Students come from 30 states and territories, 13 other countries, 15% are from out of state, 6% African American, 2% Asian American or Pacific Islander, 2% Hispanic American, 0.1% Native American, 0.6% international, 2% transferred in, 22% live on campus. *Retention:* 84% of 2006 full-time freshmen returned.

Freshmen *Admission:* 5,930 applied, 4,122 admitted, 1,494 enrolled. *Average high school GPA:* 3.06. *Test scores:* SAT critical reading scores over 500: 49%; SAT math scores over 500: 60%; SAT critical reading scores over 600: 10%; SAT math scores over 600: 15%; SAT critical reading scores over 700: 1%; SAT math scores over 700: 1%.

Faculty *Total:* 300, 50% full-time, 48% with terminal degrees. *Student/faculty ratio:* 19:1.

Majors Accounting; acting; actuarial science; adult and continuing education administration; advertising; aerospace, aeronautical and astronautical engineering; African-American/Black studies; agribusiness; agricultural and extension education; agricultural/biological engineering and bioengineering; agricultural business and management related; agricultural mechanization; agriculture; agronomy and crop science; American studies; animal sciences; animal sciences related; anthropology; applied economics; archeology; architectural engineering; art; art history, criticism and conservation; art teacher education; Asian studies (East); astronomy; atmospheric sciences and meteorology; biochemistry; biological and biomedical sciences related; biological and physical sciences; biology/biological sciences; biology/biotechnology laboratory technician; biomedical/medical engineering; biomedical technology; business administration and management; business/commerce; business/managerial economics; chemical engineering; chemistry; civil engineering; classics and languages, literatures and linguistics; communication disorders; communication/speech communication and rhetoric; comparative literature; computer and information sciences; computer engineering; criminal justice/law enforcement administration; criminal justice/safety; economics; electrical, electronic and communications engineering technology; electrical, electronics and communications engineering; elementary education; engineering science; English; environmental/environmental health engineering; environmental studies; film/cinema studies; finance; food science; foreign language teacher education; forestry technology; forest sciences and biology; French; geography; geological and earth sciences/geosciences related; geology/earth science; German; graphic design; health/health care administration; history; horticultural science; hospitality administration related; human development and family studies; human nutrition; industrial engineering; information science/studies; international relations and affairs; Italian; Japanese; Jewish/Judaic studies; journalism; kinesiology and exercise science; labor and industrial relations; landscaping and groundskeeping; Latin American studies; liberal arts and sciences/liberal studies; management information systems; marketing/marketing management; materials science; mathematics; mechanical engineering; mechanical engineering/mechanical technology; medical microbiology and bacteriology; medieval and Renaissance studies; metallurgical technology; mining and mineral engineering; natural resources and conservation related; natural resources/conservation; nuclear engineering; nursing (registered nurse training); organizational behavior; parks, recreation and leisure facilities management; petroleum engineering; philosophy; physics; political science and government; pre-medical studies; psychology; rehabilitation and therapeutic professions related; religious studies; Russian; secondary education; sociology; soil science and agronomy; Spanish; special education; statistics; telecommunications technology; theater design and technology; turf and turfgrass management; visual and performing arts; women's studies.

Academics *Calendar:* semesters. *Degrees:* associate and bachelor's. *Special study options:* academic remediation for entering students, adult/continuing education programs, advanced placement credit, cooperative education, distance learning, double majors, English as a second language, external degree program, freshman honors college, honors programs, independent study, internships, off-campus study, part-time degree program, services for LD students, student-designed majors, study abroad, summer session for credit. *ROTC:* Army (b), Air Force (b).

Computers on Campus 450 computers/terminals are available on campus for general student use. Students can access the following: campus intranet, computer help desk, free student e-mail accounts, online (class) grades, online (class) registration, online (class) schedules. Campuswide network is available.

Student Life *Housing options:* coed, disabled students. Campus housing is university owned. *Activities and organizations:* drama/theater group, student-run newspaper, choral group, national fraternities, national sororities. *Campus security:* 24-hour emergency response devices and patrols, late-night transport/escort service. *Student services:* health clinic, personal/psychological counseling.

Athletics Member NCAA. All Division III. *Intercollegiate sports:* baseball M, basketball M/W, cross-country running M/W, golf M/W, soccer M/W, softball W, swimming and diving M/W, tennis M/W. *Intramural sports:* badminton M/W, baseball M/W, basketball M/W, football M/W, golf M/W, racquetball M/W, soccer M/W, softball M/W, table tennis M/W, tennis M/W, track and field M/W, volleyball M/W, weight lifting M/W.

Standardized Tests *Required:* SAT or ACT (for admission).

Costs (2007–08) *Tuition:* state resident $10,912 full-time, $455 per credit hour part-time; nonresident $16,694 full-time, $696 per credit hour part-time. Full-time tuition and fees vary according to course level, location, program, and student level. Part-time tuition and fees vary according to course level, course load, location, program, and student level. *Required fees:* $552 full-time, $205 per term part-time. *Room and board:* $7180; room only: $3820. Room and board charges vary according to board plan, housing facility, and location. *Payment plans:* installment, deferred payment. *Waivers:* senior citizens and employees or children of employees.

Financial Aid Of all full-time matriculated undergraduates who enrolled in 2006, 2,861 applied for aid, 2,358 were judged to have need, 208 had their need fully met. 265 Federal Work-Study jobs (averaging $1692). 1 state and other part-time job (averaging $1107). In 2006, 83 non-need-based awards were made. *Average percent of need met:* 67%. *Average financial aid package:* $8526. *Average need-based loan:* $3594. *Average need-based gift aid:* $5204. *Average non-need-based aid:* $1332. *Average indebtedness upon graduation:* $26,300.

Applying *Options:* electronic application, early admission, deferred entrance. *Application fee:* $50. *Required:* high school transcript. *Required for some:* letters of recommendation, interview. *Recommended:* essay or personal statement. *Application deadlines:* rolling (freshmen), rolling (transfers). *Notification:* continuous until 11/1 (freshmen), continuous (transfers).

Freshman Application Contact Anne L. Rohrbach, Executive Director for Undergraduate Admissions, Penn State Altoona, E108 E. Raymond Smith Building, Altoona, PA 16601-3760. *Phone:* 814-865-4700. *Toll-free phone:* 800-848-9843. *Fax:* 814-863-7590. *E-mail:* admissions@psu.edu.

PENN STATE BEAVER

Monaca, Pennsylvania **www.br.psu.edu/**

- **State-related** primarily 2-year, founded 1964, part of Pennsylvania State University
- **Small-town** 91-acre campus with easy access to Pittsburgh
- **Endowment** $1.2 billion
- **Coed**
- **Moderately difficult** entrance level

Faculty *Student/faculty ratio:* 16:1.

Academics *Calendar:* semesters. *Degrees:* associate and bachelor's.

Student Life *Campus security:* 24-hour patrols, controlled dormitory access.

Athletics Member NJCAA.

Standardized Tests *Required:* SAT or ACT (for admission).

Costs (2007–08) *Tuition:* state resident $10,454 full-time, $423 per credit hour part-time; nonresident $15,954 full-time, $665 per credit hour part-time. Full-time tuition and fees vary according to course level, location, program, and student level. Part-time tuition and fees vary according to course level, course load, location, program, and student level. *Required fees:* $424 full-time, $72 per term part-time. *Room and board:* $7180; room only: $3820. Room and board charges vary according to board plan, housing facility, and location. *Payment plans:* installment, deferred payment.

Financial Aid Of all full-time matriculated undergraduates who enrolled in 2006, 34 Federal Work-Study jobs (averaging $1471).

Applying *Options:* electronic application, early admission, deferred entrance. *Application fee:* $50. *Required:* high school transcript. *Required for some:* letters of recommendation, interview. *Recommended:* essay or personal statement.

Director of Admissions Mr. Randall C. Deike, Assistant Vice President for Enrollment Management, Penn State Beaver, 100 University Drive, Suite 113, Monaca, PA 15061-2799. *Phone:* 814-865-5471. *E-mail:* admissions@psu.edu.

PENN STATE BERKS

Reading, Pennsylvania **www.bk.psu.edu/**

- **State-related** 4-year, founded 1924, part of Pennsylvania State University
- **Suburban** 258-acre campus with easy access to Philadelphia
- **Endowment** $1.7 billion
- **Coed** 2,759 undergraduate students, 89% full-time, 43% women, 57% men
- **Very difficult** entrance level, 75% of applicants were admitted

Undergraduates 2,446 full-time, 313 part-time. Students come from 18 states and territories, 8 other countries, 8% are from out of state, 8% African American, 4% Asian American or Pacific Islander, 4% Hispanic American, 0.6% international, 4% transferred in, 29% live on campus. *Retention:* 80% of 2006 full-time freshmen returned.

Freshmen *Admission:* 3,354 applied, 2,532 admitted, 929 enrolled. *Average high school GPA:* 2.85. *Test scores:* SAT critical reading scores over 500: 41%; SAT math scores over 500: 51%; SAT critical reading scores over 600: 9%; SAT math scores over 600: 14%; SAT math scores over 700: 1%.

Faculty *Total:* 190, 57% full-time, 45% with terminal degrees. *Student/faculty ratio:* 19:1.

Majors Accounting; acting; actuarial science; adult and continuing education administration; advertising; aerospace, aeronautical and astronautical engineering; African-American/Black studies; agribusiness; agricultural and extension education; agricultural/biological engineering and bioengineering; agricultural business and management related; agricultural mechanization; agriculture; agronomy and crop science; American studies; animal sciences; animal sciences related; anthropology; applied economics; archeology; architectural engineering; art; art history, criticism and conservation; art teacher education; Asian studies (East); astronomy; atmospheric sciences and meteorology; biochemistry; biological and biomedical sciences related; biological and physical sciences; biology/biological sciences; biology/biotechnology laboratory technician; biomedical/medical engineering; biomedical technology; business administration and management; business/commerce; business/managerial economics; chemical engineering; chemistry; civil engineering; classics and languages, literatures and linguistics; communication and journalism related; communication disorders; communication/speech communication and rhetoric; comparative literature; computer and information sciences; computer engineering; criminal justice/law enforcement administration; criminal justice/safety; economics; electrical, electronic and communications engineering technology; electrical, electronics and communications engineering; elementary education; engineering science; English; environmental/environmental health engineering; film/cinema studies; finance; food science; foreign languages and literatures; foreign language teacher education; forestry technology; forest sciences and biology; French; geography; geological and earth sciences/geosciences related; geology/earth science; German; graphic design; health/health care administration; history; horticultural science; hospitality administration related; human development and family studies; human nutrition; industrial engineering; information science/studies; international relations and affairs; Italian; Japanese; Jewish/Judaic studies; journalism; kinesiology and exercise science; labor and industrial relations; landscaping and groundskeeping; Latin American studies; liberal arts and sciences/liberal studies; management information systems; marketing/marketing management; materials science; mathematics; mechanical engineering; mechanical engineering/mechanical technology; medical microbiology and bacteriology; medieval and Renaissance studies; metallurgical technology; mining and mineral engineering; natural resources and conservation related; natural resources/conservation; nuclear engineering; nursing (registered nurse training); occupational therapist assistant; organizational behavior; parks, recreation and leisure facilities management; petroleum engineering; philosophy; physics; political science and government; pre-medical studies; psychology; rehabilitation and therapeutic professions related; religious studies; Russian; secondary education; sociology; soil science and agronomy; Spanish; special education; statistics; technical and business writing; telecommunications technology; theater design and technology; turf and turfgrass management; visual and performing arts; women's studies.

Academics *Calendar:* semesters. *Degrees:* certificates, associate, and bachelor's. *Special study options:* academic remediation for entering students, accelerated degree program, adult/continuing education programs, advanced placement credit, cooperative education, distance learning, external degree program, freshman honors college, honors programs, independent study, internships, off-campus study, part-time degree program, services for LD students, study abroad, summer session for credit. *ROTC:* Army (c).

Computers on Campus 300 computers/terminals are available on campus for general student use. Students can access the following: campus intranet, computer help desk, free student e-mail accounts, online (class) grades, online (class) registration, online (class) schedules. Campuswide network is available.

Student Life *Housing options:* coed, disabled students. Campus housing is university owned. *Activities and organizations:* drama/theater group, student-run newspaper, radio station, choral group. *Campus security:* 24-hour emergency response devices and patrols, late-night transport/escort service, controlled dormitory access. *Student services:* health clinic, personal/psychological counseling.

Athletics Member NJCAA. *Intercollegiate sports:* baseball M, basketball M/W, cheerleading M/W, cross-country running M/W, golf M, soccer M/W, softball W, tennis M/W, volleyball W. *Intramural sports:* badminton M/W, basketball M/W, football M/W, golf M/W, table tennis M/W, volleyball M/W.

Standardized Tests *Required:* SAT or ACT (for admission).

Costs (2007–08) *Tuition:* state resident $10,912 full-time, $455 per credit hour part-time; nonresident $16,694 full-time, $696 per credit hour part-time. Full-time tuition and fees vary according to course level, location, program, and student level. Part-time tuition and fees vary according to course level, course load, location, program, and student level. *Required fees:* $552 full-time, $205 per term part-time. *Room and board:* $7850; room only: $4490. Room and board charges vary according to board plan, housing facility, and location. *Payment plans:* installment, deferred payment. *Waivers:* senior citizens and employees or children of employees.

Financial Aid Of all full-time matriculated undergraduates who enrolled in 2006, 1,747 applied for aid, 1,294 were judged to have need, 77 had their need fully met. 76 Federal Work-Study jobs (averaging $1110). In 2006, 42 non-need-based awards were made. *Average percent of need met:* 63%. *Average financial aid package:* $7530. *Average need-based loan:* $3378. *Average need-based gift aid:* $5470. *Average non-need-based aid:* $1984. *Average indebtedness upon graduation:* $26,300.

Applying *Options:* electronic application, early admission, deferred entrance. *Application fee:* $50. *Required:* high school transcript. *Required for some:* letters of recommendation, interview. *Recommended:* essay or personal statement. *Application deadlines:* rolling (freshmen), rolling (transfers). *Notification:* continuous until 11/1 (freshmen), continuous (transfers).

Freshman Application Contact Anne L. Rohrbach, Executive Director for Undergraduate Admissions, Penn State Berks, Tulpehocken Road, PO Box 7009, Reading, PA 19610-6009. *Phone:* 814-865-4700. *Fax:* 814-863-7590. *E-mail:* admissions@psu.edu.

PENN STATE DELAWARE COUNTY

Media, Pennsylvania **www.de.psu.edu/**

- **State-related** primarily 2-year, founded 1966, part of Pennsylvania State University
- **Small-town** 87-acre campus with easy access to Philadelphia
- **Endowment** $1.2 billion
- **Coed**
- **Moderately difficult** entrance level

Faculty *Student/faculty ratio:* 18:1.

Academics *Calendar:* semesters. *Degrees:* associate and bachelor's.

Student Life *Campus security:* late-night transport/escort service, part-time trained security personnel.

Athletics Member NJCAA.

Standardized Tests *Required:* SAT or ACT (for admission).

Costs (2007–08) *Tuition:* state resident $10,454 full-time, $423 per credit hour part-time; nonresident $15,954 full-time, $665 per credit hour part-time. Full-time tuition and fees vary according to course level, location, program, and student level. Part-time tuition and fees vary according to course level, course load, location, program, and student level. *Required fees:* $424 full-time, $72 per term part-time. *Payment plans:* installment, deferred payment.

Financial Aid Of all full-time matriculated undergraduates who enrolled in 2006, 45 Federal Work-Study jobs (averaging $1137).

Applying *Options:* electronic application, early admission, deferred entrance. *Application fee:* $50. *Required:* high school transcript. *Required for some:* letters of recommendation, interview. *Recommended:* essay or personal statement.

Director of Admissions Mr. Randall C. Deike, Assistant Vice President for Enrollment Management, Penn State Delaware County, 25 Yearsley Mill Road, Media, PA 19063-5596. *Phone:* 814-865-5471. *E-mail:* admissions@psu.edu.

PENN STATE DUBOIS

DuBois, Pennsylvania **www.ds.psu.edu/**

- **State-related** primarily 2-year, founded 1935, part of Pennsylvania State University
- **Small-town** 20-acre campus
- **Endowment** $1.2 billion
- **Coed**
- **Moderately difficult** entrance level

Faculty *Student/faculty ratio:* 12:1.

Academics *Calendar:* semesters. *Degrees:* associate and bachelor's.

Athletics Member NJCAA.

Standardized Tests *Required:* SAT or ACT (for admission).

Costs (2007–08) *Tuition:* state resident $10,454 full-time, $423 per credit hour part-time; nonresident $15,954 full-time, $665 per credit hour part-time. Full-time tuition and fees vary according to course level, location, program, and student level. Part-time tuition and fees vary according to course level, course load, location, program, and student level. *Required fees:* $424 full-time, $72 per term part-time. *Payment plans:* installment, deferred payment.

Financial Aid Of all full-time matriculated undergraduates who enrolled in 2006, 67 Federal Work-Study jobs (averaging $1509). 2 state and other part-time jobs (averaging $1675).

Applying *Options:* electronic application, early admission, deferred entrance. *Application fee:* $50. *Required:* high school transcript. *Required for some:* letters of recommendation, interview. *Recommended:* essay or personal statement.

Director of Admissions Mr. Randall C. Deike, Assistant Vice President for Enrollment Management, Penn State DuBois, 101 Hiller Building, College Place, DuBois, PA 15801-3199. *Phone:* 814-865-5471. *Toll-free phone:* 800-346-7627. *E-mail:* admissions@psu.edu.

PENN STATE ERIE, THE BEHREND COLLEGE

Erie, Pennsylvania **www.pserie.psu.edu/**

- **State-related** comprehensive, founded 1948, part of Pennsylvania State University
- **Suburban** 725-acre campus
- **Endowment** $1.7 billion
- **Coed** 4,031 undergraduate students, 93% full-time, 35% women, 65% men
- **Very difficult** entrance level, 79% of applicants were admitted

Students benefit from small classes and participation in undergraduate research as they earn an internationally recognized Penn State degree. Modern facilities include a high-technology business park, a recreation center, and residence halls. A new $30-million academic center for business and engineering just opened. Twenty-one NCAA Division III teams are offered.

Undergraduates 3,745 full-time, 286 part-time. Students come from 35 states and territories, 20 other countries, 8% are from out of state, 3% African American, 2% Asian American or Pacific Islander, 2% Hispanic American, 0.1% Native American, 1% international, 3% transferred in, 41% live on campus. *Retention:* 83% of 2006 full-time freshmen returned.

Freshmen *Admission:* 3,689 applied, 2,908 admitted, 1,162 enrolled. *Average high school GPA:* 3.18. *Test scores:* SAT critical reading scores over 500: 56%; SAT math scores over 500: 70%; SAT critical reading scores over 600: 15%; SAT math scores over 600: 24%; SAT critical reading scores over 700: 1%; SAT math scores over 700: 2%.

Faculty *Total:* 280, 74% full-time, 48% with terminal degrees. *Student/faculty ratio:* 17:1.

Majors Accounting; acting; actuarial science; adult and continuing education administration; advertising; aerospace, aeronautical and astronautical engineering; African-American/Black studies; agribusiness; agricultural and extension education; agricultural/biological engineering and bioengineering; agricultural business and management related; agricultural mechanization; agriculture; agronomy and crop science; American studies; animal sciences; animal sciences related; anthropology; applied economics; archeology; architectural engineering; art; art history, criticism and conservation; art teacher education; Asian studies (East); astronomy; atmospheric sciences and meteorology; biochemistry; biological and biomedical sciences related; biological and physical sciences; biology/biological sciences; biology/biotechnology laboratory technician; biomedical/medical engineering; biomedical technology; business administration and management; business/commerce; business/managerial economics; chemical engineering; chemistry; civil engineering; classics and languages, literatures and linguistics; communication and journalism related; communication and media related; communication disorders; communication/speech communication and rhetoric; comparative literature; computer and information sciences; computer engineering; computer science; computer software engineering; criminal justice/law enforcement administration; criminal justice/safety; economics; electrical, electronic and communications engineering technology; electrical, electronics and communications engineering; elementary education; engineering science; English; environmental/environmental health engineering; film/cinema studies;

finance; food science; foreign language teacher education; forestry technology; forest sciences and biology; French; geography; geological and earth sciences/ geosciences related; geology/earth science; German; graphic design; health/ health care administration; history; horticultural science; hospitality administration related; human development and family studies; human nutrition; industrial engineering; information science/studies; international business/trade/commerce; international relations and affairs; Italian; Japanese; Jewish/Judaic studies; journalism; kinesiology and exercise science; labor and industrial relations; landscaping and groundskeeping; Latin American studies; liberal arts and sciences/liberal studies; management information systems; manufacturing technology; marketing/ marketing management; materials science; mathematics; mechanical engineering; mechanical engineering/mechanical technology; medical microbiology and bacteriology; medieval and Renaissance studies; metallurgical technology; mining and mineral engineering; multi-/interdisciplinary studies related; natural resources and conservation related; natural resources/conservation; nuclear engineering; nursing (registered nurse training); organizational behavior; parks, recreation and leisure facilities management; petroleum engineering; philosophy; physical sciences; physics; plastics engineering technology; political science and government; polymer/plastics engineering; pre-medical studies; psychology; rehabilitation and therapeutic professions related; religious studies; Russian; secondary education; sociology; soil science and agronomy; Spanish; special education; statistics; telecommunications technology; theater design and technology; turf and turfgrass management; visual and performing arts; women's studies.

Academics *Calendar:* semesters. *Degrees:* certificates, associate, bachelor's, and master's. *Special study options:* academic remediation for entering students, accelerated degree program, adult/continuing education programs, advanced placement credit, cooperative education, distance learning, double majors, external degree program, freshman honors college, honors programs, independent study, internships, off-campus study, part-time degree program, services for LD students, study abroad, summer session for credit. *ROTC:* Army (c).

Computers on Campus 700 computers/terminals are available on campus for general student use. Students can access the following: campus intranet, computer help desk, free student e-mail accounts, online (class) grades, online (class) registration, online (class) schedules. Campuswide network is available.

Student Life *Housing options:* coed, men-only, women-only, disabled students. Campus housing is university owned. *Activities and organizations:* drama/theater group, student-run newspaper, radio station, choral group, national fraternities, national sororities. *Campus security:* 24-hour emergency response devices and patrols, student patrols, late-night transport/escort service, controlled dormitory access. *Student services:* health clinic, personal/psychological counseling.

Athletics Member NCAA. All Division III. *Intercollegiate sports:* baseball M, basketball M/W, cheerleading M/W, cross-country running M/W, golf M/W, ice hockey M (c), lacrosse M (c), skiing (downhill) M (c)/W (c), soccer M/W, softball W, swimming and diving M/W, tennis M/W, track and field M/W, volleyball M (c)/W, water polo M/W. *Intramural sports:* badminton M/W, basketball M/W, bowling M/W, cross-country running M/W, football M/W, golf M/W, skiing (downhill) M/W, soccer M/W, softball M/W, swimming and diving M/W, table tennis M/W, tennis M/W, volleyball M/W.

Standardized Tests *Required:* SAT or ACT (for admission).

Costs (2007–08) *Tuition:* state resident $10,912 full-time, $455 per credit hour part-time; nonresident $16,694 full-time, $696 per credit hour part-time. Full-time tuition and fees vary according to course level, location, program, and student level. Part-time tuition and fees vary according to course level, course load, location, program, and student level. *Required fees:* $552 full-time, $205 per term part-time. *Room and board:* $7180; room only: $3820. Room and board charges vary according to board plan, housing facility, and location. *Payment plans:* installment, deferred payment. *Waivers:* senior citizens and employees or children of employees.

Financial Aid Of all full-time matriculated undergraduates who enrolled in 2006, 2,816 applied for aid, 2,302 were judged to have need, 210 had their need fully met. 214 Federal Work-Study jobs (averaging $1517). In 2006, 114 non-need-based awards were made. *Average percent of need met:* 70%. *Average financial aid package:* $8793. *Average need-based loan:* $3995. *Average need-based gift aid:* $5181. *Average non-need-based aid:* $2394. *Average indebtedness upon graduation:* $26,300.

Applying *Options:* electronic application, early admission, deferred entrance. *Application fee:* $50. *Required:* high school transcript. *Required for some:* letters of recommendation, interview. *Recommended:* essay or personal statement. *Application deadlines:* rolling (freshmen), rolling (transfers). *Notification:* continuous until 11/1 (freshmen), continuous (transfers).

Freshman Application Contact Anne L. Rohrbach, Executive Director for Undergraduate Admissions, Penn State Erie, The Behrend College, 5091 Station Road, Erie, PA 16563-0105. *Phone:* 814-865-4700. *Toll-free phone:* 866-374-3378. *Fax:* 814-863-7590. *E-mail:* admissions@psu.edu.

See page 2288 for the College Close-Up.

PENN STATE FAYETTE, THE EBERLY CAMPUS

Uniontown, Pennsylvania **www.fe.psu.edu/**

- **State-related** primarily 2-year, founded 1934, part of Pennsylvania State University
- **Small-town** 92-acre campus
- **Endowment** $1.2 billion
- **Coed**
- **Moderately difficult** entrance level

Faculty *Student/faculty ratio:* 14:1.

Academics *Calendar:* semesters. *Degrees:* associate and bachelor's.

Student Life *Campus security:* student patrols, 8-hour patrols by trained security personnel.

Athletics Member NJCAA.

Standardized Tests *Required:* SAT or ACT (for admission).

Costs (2007–08) *Tuition:* state resident $10,454 full-time, $423 per credit hour part-time; nonresident $15,954 full-time, $665 per credit hour part-time. Full-time tuition and fees vary according to course level, location, program, and student level. Part-time tuition and fees vary according to course level, course load, location, program, and student level. *Required fees:* $424 full-time, $72 per term part-time. *Payment plans:* installment, deferred payment.

Financial Aid Of all full-time matriculated undergraduates who enrolled in 2006, 66 Federal Work-Study jobs (averaging $1636).

Applying *Options:* electronic application, early admission, deferred entrance. *Application fee:* $50. *Required:* high school transcript. *Required for some:* letters of recommendation, interview. *Recommended:* essay or personal statement.

Director of Admissions Mr. Randall C. Deike, Assistant Vice President for Enrollment Management, Penn State Fayette, The Eberly Campus, PO Box 519, Route 119 North, 108 Williams Building, Uniontown, PA 15401-0519. *Phone:* 814-865-5471. *Toll-free phone:* 877-568-4130. *E-mail:* admissions@psu.edu.

PENN STATE HARRISBURG

Middletown, Pennsylvania **www.hbg.psu.edu/**

- **State-related** comprehensive, founded 1966, part of Pennsylvania State University
- **Small-town** 218-acre campus
- **Endowment** $1.7 billion
- **Coed** 2,435 undergraduate students, 80% full-time, 46% women, 54% men
- **Very difficult** entrance level, 70% of applicants were admitted

Penn State Harrisburg is an undergraduate college and graduate school of Penn State University, one of the largest and most widely recognized institutions in the nation. At the undergraduate level, the College offers two associate and thirty baccalaureate degrees, as well as the first two years of study leading to more than 160 undergraduate majors available throughout the Penn State system. The College features all the resources of a major research university in a smaller setting in the capital region of the state. For more information, students can visit the Web site at http://www.hbg.psu.edu and can apply online.

Undergraduates 1,955 full-time, 480 part-time. Students come from 26 states and territories, 17 other countries, 12% are from out of state, 9% African American, 7% Asian American or Pacific Islander, 4% Hispanic American, 0.2% Native American, 2% international, 10% transferred in, 13% live on campus. *Retention:* 82% of 2006 full-time freshmen returned.

Freshmen *Admission:* 2,689 applied, 1,882 admitted, 422 enrolled. *Average high school GPA:* 3.10. *Test scores:* SAT critical reading scores over 500: 58%; SAT math scores over 500: 63%; SAT critical reading scores over 600: 15%; SAT math scores over 600: 20%; SAT critical reading scores over 700: 1%; SAT math scores over 700: 2%.

Faculty *Total:* 296, 66% full-time, 69% with terminal degrees. *Student/faculty ratio:* 12:1.

Majors American studies; applied mathematics; business administration and management; business/commerce; communication/speech communication and rhetoric; computer and information sciences; criminal justice/safety; electrical, electronics and communications engineering; elementary education; English; environmental/environmental health engineering; finance; health/health care administration; humanities; information science/studies; international business/trade/ commerce; liberal arts and sciences/liberal studies; management information systems; marketing/marketing management; mechanical engineering; nursing (registered nurse training); organizational behavior; psychology; public policy analysis; social studies teacher education; sociology; structural engineering.

Academics *Calendar:* semesters. *Degrees:* certificates, associate, bachelor's, master's, doctoral, and postbachelor's certificates. *Special study options:* academic remediation for entering students, accelerated degree program, adult/continuing education programs, advanced placement credit, cooperative education, distance learning, double majors, freshman honors college, honors programs, independent study, internships, off-campus study, part-time degree program, services for LD students, student-designed majors, study abroad, summer session for credit. *ROTC:* Army (c).

Computers on Campus 500 computers/terminals are available on campus for general student use. Students can access the following: campus intranet, computer help desk, free student e-mail accounts, online (class) grades, online (class) registration, online (class) schedules. Campuswide network is available.

Student Life *Housing options:* men-only, women-only, disabled students. Campus housing is university owned. *Activities and organizations:* drama/theater group, student-run newspaper, radio station, choral group. *Campus security:* 24-hour emergency response devices and patrols, student patrols, late-night transport/escort service, controlled dormitory access. *Student services:* health clinic, personal/psychological counseling.

Athletics *Intercollegiate sports:* baseball M, basketball M/W, cross-country running M/W, golf M/W, soccer M/W, softball W, tennis M/W, volleyball W. *Intramural sports:* badminton M/W, basketball M/W, racquetball M/W, tennis M/W.

Standardized Tests *Required:* SAT or ACT (for admission).

Costs (2007–08) *Tuition:* state resident $10,912 full-time, $455 per credit hour part-time; nonresident $16,694 full-time, $696 per credit hour part-time. Full-time tuition and fees vary according to course level, location, program, and student level. Part-time tuition and fees vary according to course level, course load, location, program, and student level. *Required fees:* $542 full-time, $205 per term part-time. *Room and board:* $8610; room only: $5500. Room and board charges vary according to board plan, housing facility, and location. *Payment plans:* installment, deferred payment. *Waivers:* senior citizens and employees or children of employees.

Financial Aid Of all full-time matriculated undergraduates who enrolled in 2006, 1,395 applied for aid, 1,134 were judged to have need, 124 had their need fully met. 51 Federal Work-Study jobs (averaging $1313). In 2006, 22 non-need-based awards were made. *Average percent of need met:* 66%. *Average financial aid package:* $9301. *Average need-based loan:* $4375. *Average need-based gift aid:* $5314. *Average non-need-based aid:* $2285. *Average indebtedness upon graduation:* $26,300.

Applying *Options:* electronic application, early admission, deferred entrance. *Application fee:* $50. *Required:* high school transcript. *Required for some:* letters of recommendation, interview. *Recommended:* essay or personal statement. *Application deadlines:* rolling (freshmen), rolling (transfers). *Notification:* continuous until 11/1 (freshmen), continuous (transfers).

Freshman Application Contact Anne L. Rohrbach, Executive Director for Undergraduate Admissions, Penn State Harrisburg, Swatapa Building, 777 West Harrisburg Pike, Middletown, PA 17057-4898. *Phone:* 814-865-4700. *Toll-free phone:* 800-222-2056. *Fax:* 814-863-7590. *E-mail:* admissions@psu.edu.

PENN STATE HAZLETON

Hazleton, Pennsylvania **www.hn.psu.edu/**

- **State-related** primarily 2-year, founded 1934, part of Pennsylvania State University
- **Small-town** 98-acre campus
- **Endowment** $1.2 billion
- **Coed**
- **Moderately difficult** entrance level

Faculty *Student/faculty ratio:* 18:1.

Academics *Calendar:* semesters. *Degrees:* associate and bachelor's.

Student Life *Campus security:* 24-hour patrols, late-night transport/escort service, controlled dormitory access.

Athletics Member NJCAA.

Standardized Tests *Required:* SAT or ACT (for admission).

Costs (2007–08) *Tuition:* state resident $10,454 full-time, $423 per credit hour part-time; nonresident $15,954 full-time, $665 per credit hour part-time. Full-time tuition and fees vary according to course level, location, program, and student level. Part-time tuition and fees vary according to course level, course load, location, program, and student level. *Required fees:* $424 full-time, $72 per term part-time. *Room and board:* $7180; room only: $3820. Room and board charges vary according to board plan, housing facility, and location. *Payment plans:* installment, deferred payment.

Financial Aid Of all full-time matriculated undergraduates who enrolled in 2006, 61 Federal Work-Study jobs (averaging $1710). 12 state and other part-time jobs (averaging $5850).

Applying *Options:* electronic application, early admission, deferred entrance. *Application fee:* $50. *Required:* high school transcript. *Required for some:* letters of recommendation, interview. *Recommended:* essay or personal statement.

Director of Admissions Mr. Randall C. Deike, Assistant Vice President for Enrollment Management, Penn State Hazleton, 110 Administration Building, 76 University Drive, Hazleton, PA 18202-1291. *Phone:* 814-865-5471. *Toll-free phone:* 800-279-8495. *E-mail:* admissions@psu.edu.

PENN STATE LEHIGH VALLEY

Fogelsville, Pennsylvania **www.lv.psu.edu/**

- **State-related** primarily 2-year, founded 1912, part of Pennsylvania State University
- **Small-town** 42-acre campus
- **Coed**
- **Moderately difficult** entrance level

Faculty *Student/faculty ratio:* 15:1.

Academics *Calendar:* semesters. *Degrees:* associate and bachelor's.

Athletics Member NJCAA.

Standardized Tests *Required:* SAT or ACT (for admission).

Costs (2007–08) *Tuition:* state resident $10,454 full-time, $423 per credit hour part-time; nonresident $15,954 full-time, $665 per credit hour part-time. Full-time tuition and fees vary according to course level, location, program, and student level. Part-time tuition and fees vary according to course level, course load, location, program, and student level. *Required fees:* $424 full-time, $72 per term part-time. *Payment plans:* installment, deferred payment.

Financial Aid Of all full-time matriculated undergraduates who enrolled in 2003, 391 applied for aid, 301 were judged to have need, 21 had their need fully met. 23 Federal Work-Study jobs (averaging $6445). In 2003, 29 non-need-based awards were made. *Average percent of need met:* 67. *Average financial aid package:* $9068. *Average need-based loan:* $3196. *Average need-based gift aid:* $4017. *Average non-need-based aid:* $1379. *Average indebtedness upon graduation:* $18,600.

Applying *Options:* electronic application, early admission, deferred entrance. *Application fee:* $50. *Required:* high school transcript.

Director of Admissions Mr. Randall C. Deike, Assistant Vice President for Enrollment Management, Penn State Lehigh Valley, 8380 Mohr Lane, Academic Building, Fogelsville, PA 18051-9999. *Phone:* 814-865-5471.

PENN STATE MCKEESPORT

McKeesport, Pennsylvania **www.mk.psu.edu/**

- **State-related** primarily 2-year, founded 1947, part of Pennsylvania State University
- **Small-town** 40-acre campus with easy access to Pittsburgh
- **Endowment** $1.2 billion
- **Coed**
- **Moderately difficult** entrance level

Faculty *Student/faculty ratio:* 14:1.

Academics *Calendar:* semesters. *Degrees:* associate and bachelor's.

Student Life *Campus security:* 24-hour patrols, controlled dormitory access.

Athletics Member NJCAA.

Standardized Tests *Required:* SAT or ACT (for admission).

Costs (2007–08) *Tuition:* state resident $10,454 full-time, $423 per credit hour part-time; nonresident $15,954 full-time, $665 per credit hour part-time. Full-time tuition and fees vary according to course level, location, program, and student level. Part-time tuition and fees vary according to course level, course load, location, program, and student level. *Required fees:* $424 full-time, $72 per term part-time. *Room and board:* $7180; room only: $3820. Room and board charges vary according to board plan, housing facility, and location. *Payment plans:* installment, deferred payment.

Financial Aid Of all full-time matriculated undergraduates who enrolled in 2006, 43 Federal Work-Study jobs (averaging $1511).

Applying *Options:* electronic application, early admission, deferred entrance. *Application fee:* $50. *Required:* high school transcript. *Required for some:* letters of recommendation, interview. *Recommended:* essay or personal statement.

Director of Admissions Mr. Randall C. Deike, Assistant Vice President for Enrollment Management, Penn State McKeesport, 101 Frable Building, 4000 University Drive, McKeesport, PA 15132-7698. *Phone:* 814-865-5471. *E-mail:* admissions@psu.edu.

PENN STATE MONT ALTO

Mont Alto, Pennsylvania www.ma.psu.edu/

- **State-related** primarily 2-year, founded 1929, part of Pennsylvania State University
- **Small-town** 64-acre campus
- **Endowment** $1.2 billion
- **Coed**
- **Moderately difficult** entrance level

Faculty *Student/faculty ratio:* 13:1.

Academics *Calendar:* semesters. *Degrees:* associate and bachelor's.

Student Life *Campus security:* 24-hour patrols, controlled dormitory access.

Athletics Member NJCAA.

Standardized Tests *Required:* SAT or ACT (for admission).

Costs (2007–08) *Tuition:* state resident $10,454 full-time, $423 per credit hour part-time; nonresident $15,954 full-time, $665 per credit hour part-time. Full-time tuition and fees vary according to course level, location, program, and student level. Part-time tuition and fees vary according to course level, course load, location, program, and student level. *Required fees:* $424 full-time, $72 per term part-time. *Room and board:* $7180; room only: $3820. Room and board charges vary according to board plan, housing facility, and location. *Payment plans:* installment, deferred payment.

Financial Aid Of all full-time matriculated undergraduates who enrolled in 2006, 41 Federal Work-Study jobs (averaging $1393).

Applying *Options:* electronic application, early admission, deferred entrance. *Application fee:* $50. *Required:* high school transcript. *Required for some:* letters of recommendation, interview. *Recommended:* essay or personal statement.

Director of Admissions Mr. Randall C. Deike, Assistant Vice President for Enrollment Management, Penn State Mont Alto, 1 Campus Drive, Mont Alto, PA 17237-9703. *Phone:* 814-865-5471. *Toll-free phone:* 800-392-6173. *E-mail:* admissions@psu.edu.

PENN STATE NEW KENSINGTON

New Kensington, Pennsylvania www.nk.psu.edu/

- **State-related** primarily 2-year, founded 1958, part of Pennsylvania State University
- **Small-town** 71-acre campus with easy access to Pittsburgh
- **Endowment** $1.2 billion
- **Coed**
- **Moderately difficult** entrance level

Faculty *Student/faculty ratio:* 13:1.

Academics *Calendar:* semesters. *Degrees:* associate and bachelor's.

Student Life *Campus security:* part-time trained security personnel.

Athletics Member NJCAA.

Standardized Tests *Required:* SAT or ACT (for admission).

Costs (2007–08) *Tuition:* state resident $10,454 full-time, $423 per credit hour part-time; nonresident $15,954 full-time, $665 per credit hour part-time. Full-time tuition and fees vary according to course level, location, program, and student level. Part-time tuition and fees vary according to course level, course load, location, program, and student level. *Required fees:* $424 full-time, $72 per term part-time. *Payment plans:* installment, deferred payment.

Financial Aid Of all full-time matriculated undergraduates who enrolled in 2006, 29 Federal Work-Study jobs (averaging $1521).

Applying *Options:* electronic application, early admission, deferred entrance. *Application fee:* $50. *Required:* high school transcript. *Required for some:* letters of recommendation, interview. *Recommended:* essay or personal statement.

Director of Admissions Mr. Randall C. Deike, Assistant Vice President for Enrollment Management, Penn State New Kensington, 3550 7th Street Road, Route 780, New Kensington, PA 15068-1765. *Phone:* 814-865-5471. *Toll-free phone:* 888-968-7297. *E-mail:* admissions@psu.edu.

PENN STATE SCHUYLKILL

Schuylkill Haven, Pennsylvania www.sl.psu.edu/

- **State-related** primarily 2-year, founded 1934, part of Pennsylvania State University
- **Small-town** 42-acre campus
- **Coed**
- **Moderately difficult** entrance level

Faculty *Student/faculty ratio:* 17:1.

Academics *Calendar:* semesters. *Degrees:* associate and bachelor's (bachelor's degree programs completed at the Harrisburg campus).

Student Life *Campus security:* 24-hour patrols, controlled dormitory access.

Athletics Member NJCAA.

Standardized Tests *Required:* SAT or ACT (for admission).

Costs (2007–08) *Tuition:* state resident $10,454 full-time, $423 per credit hour part-time; nonresident $15,954 full-time, $665 per credit hour part-time. Full-time tuition and fees vary according to course level, location, program, and student level. Part-time tuition and fees vary according to course level, course load, location, program, and student level. *Required fees:* $424 full-time, $72 per term part-time. *Room and board:* $7740; room only: $3816. Room and board charges vary according to board plan, housing facility, and location. *Payment plans:* installment, deferred payment.

Financial Aid Of all full-time matriculated undergraduates who enrolled in 2003, 665 applied for aid, 563 were judged to have need, 39 had their need fully met. 57 Federal Work-Study jobs (averaging $1657). 7 state and other part-time jobs (averaging $4134). In 2003, 29 non-need-based awards were made. *Average percent of need met:* 68. *Average financial aid package:* $11,204. *Average need-based loan:* $3285. *Average need-based gift aid:* $4384. *Average non-need-based aid:* $2087. *Average indebtedness upon graduation:* $18,600.

Applying *Options:* electronic application, early admission, deferred entrance. *Application fee:* $50. *Required:* high school transcript.

Director of Admissions Mr. Randall C. Deike, Assistant Vice President for Enrollment Management, Penn State Schuylkill, 200 University Drive, A102 Administration Building, Schuylkill Haven, PA 17972-2208. *Phone:* 814-865-5471. *E-mail:* admissions@psu.edu.

PENN STATE SHENANGO

Sharon, Pennsylvania www.shenango.psu.edu/

- **State-related** primarily 2-year, founded 1965, part of Pennsylvania State University
- **Small-town** 14-acre campus
- **Endowment** $1.2 billion
- **Coed**
- **Moderately difficult** entrance level

Faculty *Student/faculty ratio:* 14:1.

Academics *Calendar:* semesters. *Degrees:* associate and bachelor's.

Student Life *Campus security:* part-time trained security personnel.

Standardized Tests *Required:* SAT or ACT (for admission).

Costs (2007–08) *Tuition:* state resident $10,454 full-time, $423 per credit hour part-time; nonresident $15,954 full-time, $665 per credit hour part-time. Full-time tuition and fees vary according to course level, location, program, and student level. Part-time tuition and fees vary according to course level, course load, location, program, and student level. *Required fees:* $424 full-time, $72 per term part-time. *Payment plans:* installment, deferred payment.

Financial Aid Of all full-time matriculated undergraduates who enrolled in 2006, 40 Federal Work-Study jobs (averaging $1807).

Applying *Options:* electronic application, early admission, deferred entrance. *Application fee:* $50. *Required:* high school transcript. *Required for some:* letters of recommendation, interview. *Recommended:* essay or personal statement.

Director of Admissions Mr. Randall C. Deike, Assistant Vice President for Enrollment Management, Penn State Shenango, 147 Shenango Avenue, Sharon, PA 16146-1597. *Phone:* 814-865-5471. *E-mail:* admissions@psu.edu.

PENN STATE UNIVERSITY PARK

State College, Pennsylvania www.psu.edu/

- **State-related** university, founded 1855, part of Pennsylvania State University
- **Small-town** 15,984-acre campus
- **Endowment** $1.7 billion

- **Coed** 36,815 undergraduate students, 96% full-time, 45% women, 55% men
- **Very difficult** entrance level, 51% of applicants were admitted

Undergraduates 35,447 full-time, 1,368 part-time. Students come from 52 states and territories, 80 other countries, 24% are from out of state, 4% African American, 5% Asian American or Pacific Islander, 4% Hispanic American, 0.1% Native American, 2% international, 1% transferred in, 36% live on campus. *Retention:* 94% of 2006 full-time freshmen returned.

Freshmen *Admission:* 39,551 applied, 20,156 admitted, 6,495 enrolled. *Average high school GPA:* 3.58. *Test scores:* SAT critical reading scores over 500: 86%; SAT math scores over 500: 92%; SAT critical reading scores over 600: 43%; SAT math scores over 600: 60%; SAT critical reading scores over 700: 7%; SAT math scores over 700: 14%.

Faculty *Total:* 2,651, 88% full-time, 72% with terminal degrees. *Student/faculty ratio:* 17:1.

Majors Accounting; acting; actuarial science; adult and continuing education administration; advertising; aerospace, aeronautical and astronautical engineering; African-American/Black studies; agribusiness; agricultural and extension education; agricultural/biological engineering and bioengineering; agricultural business and management related; agricultural mechanization; agriculture; agronomy and crop science; animal sciences; animal sciences related; anthropology; applied economics; archeology; architectural engineering; architecture; art; art history, criticism and conservation; art teacher education; Asian studies (East); astronomy; atmospheric sciences and meteorology; biochemistry; biological and biomedical sciences related; biological and physical sciences; biology/biological sciences; biology/biotechnology laboratory technician; biomedical/medical engineering; business/commerce; business/managerial economics; chemical engineering; chemistry; civil engineering; classics and languages, literatures and linguistics; communication and journalism related; communication disorders; communication/speech communication and rhetoric; comparative literature; computer and information sciences; computer engineering; criminal justice/law enforcement administration; dietitian assistant; economics; electrical, electronics and communications engineering; elementary education; engineering science; English; environmental/environmental health engineering; film/cinema studies; finance; food science; foreign language teacher education; forestry technology; forest sciences and biology; French; geography; geological and earth sciences/geosciences related; geology/earth science; German; graphic design; health/health care administration; history; horticultural science; hospitality administration related; human development and family studies; human nutrition; industrial engineering; information science/studies; international business/trade/commerce; international relations and affairs; Italian; Japanese; Jewish/Judaic studies; journalism; kinesiology and exercise science; labor and industrial relations; landscape architecture; landscaping and groundskeeping; Latin American studies; liberal arts and sciences/liberal studies; management information systems; management sciences and quantitative methods related; marketing/marketing management; materials science; mathematics; mechanical engineering; medical microbiology and bacteriology; medieval and Renaissance studies; mining and mineral engineering; music; music performance; music teacher education; natural resources and conservation related; natural resources/conservation; nuclear engineering; nursing (registered nurse training); organizational behavior; parks, recreation and leisure facilities management; petroleum engineering; philosophy; physics; political science and government; pre-medical studies; psychology; rehabilitation and therapeutic professions related; religious studies; Russian; secondary education; sociology; soil science and agronomy; Spanish; special education; statistics; theater design and technology; toxicology; turf and turfgrass management; visual and performing arts; women's studies.

Academics *Calendar:* semesters. *Degrees:* certificates, associate, bachelor's, master's, doctoral, first professional, and postbachelor's certificates. *Special study options:* academic remediation for entering students, accelerated degree program, adult/continuing education programs, advanced placement credit, cooperative education, distance learning, double majors, English as a second language, external degree program, freshman honors college, honors programs, independent study, internships, off-campus study, part-time degree program, services for LD students, student-designed majors, study abroad, summer session for credit. *ROTC:* Army (b), Navy (b), Air Force (b). *Unusual degree programs:* 3-2 engineering.

Computers on Campus 3,800 computers/terminals and 1,000 ports are available on campus for general student use. Students can access the following: campus intranet, computer help desk, free student e-mail accounts, online (class) grades, online (class) registration, online (class) schedules. Campuswide network is available.

Student Life *Housing:* on-campus residence required for freshman year. *Options:* coed, men-only, women-only, disabled students. Campus housing is university owned. *Activities and organizations:* drama/theater group, student-run newspaper, radio and television station, choral group, marching band, national fraternities, national sororities. *Campus security:* 24-hour emergency response devices and patrols, student patrols, late-night transport/escort service, controlled dormitory access. *Student services:* health clinic, personal/psychological counseling, women's center.

Athletics Member NCAA. All Division I except football (Division I-A). *Intercollegiate sports:* archery M (c)/W (c), badminton M (c)/W (c), baseball M (s), basketball M (s)/W (s), bowling M (c), cheerleading M/W, cross-country running M (s)/W (s), equestrian sports M (c)/W (c), fencing M (s)/W (s), field hockey W (s), golf M (s)/W (s), gymnastics M (s)/W (s), ice hockey M (c)/W (c), lacrosse M (s)/W (s), rugby M (c)/W (c), skiing (downhill) M (c)/W (c), soccer M (s)/W (s), softball W, swimming and diving M (s)/W (s), table tennis M (c), tennis M (s)/W (s), track and field M (s)/W (s), volleyball M (s)/W (s), water polo M (c)/W (c), weight lifting M (c)/W (c), wrestling M (s). *Intramural sports:* badminton M/W, basketball M/W, bowling M/W, crew M (c)/W (c), cross-country running M/W, fencing M (c)/W (c), field hockey W, football M, golf M/W, gymnastics M (c)/W (c), lacrosse M (c)/W (c), racquetball M/W, riflery M (c)/W (c), sailing M (c)/W (c), soccer M/W, softball M/W, squash M/W, tennis M/W, track and field M/W, ultimate Frisbee M (c)/W (c), volleyball M/W, wrestling M.

Standardized Tests *Required:* SAT or ACT (for admission).

Costs (2007–08) *Tuition:* state resident $12,284 full-time, $512 per credit hour part-time; nonresident $23,152 full-time, $965 per credit hour part-time. Full-time tuition and fees vary according to course level, location, program, and student level. Part-time tuition and fees vary according to course level, course load, location, program, and student level. *Required fees:* $560 full-time, $208 per term part-time. *Room and board:* $7180; room only: $3820. Room and board charges vary according to board plan, housing facility, and location. *Payment plans:* installment, deferred payment. *Waivers:* senior citizens and employees or children of employees.

Financial Aid Of all full-time matriculated undergraduates who enrolled in 2006, 23,699 applied for aid, 17,549 were judged to have need, 1,980 had their need fully met. 1,183 Federal Work-Study jobs (averaging $1529). 6 state and other part-time jobs (averaging $749). In 2006, 2,478 non-need-based awards were made. *Average percent of need met:* 67%. *Average financial aid package:* $9035. *Average need-based loan:* $4204. *Average need-based gift aid:* $5475. *Average non-need-based aid:* $3124. *Average indebtedness upon graduation:* $26,300.

Applying *Options:* electronic application, early admission, deferred entrance. *Application fee:* $50. *Required:* high school transcript. *Required for some:* letters of recommendation, interview. *Recommended:* essay or personal statement. *Application deadlines:* rolling (freshmen), rolling (transfers). *Notification:* continuous (freshmen), continuous (transfers).

Freshman Application Contact Anne L. Rohrbach, Director for Undergraduate Admissions, Penn State University Park, 201 Shields Building, Box 3000, University Park, PA 16804-3000. *Phone:* 814-865-4700. *Fax:* 814-863-7590. *E-mail:* admissions@psu.edu.

PENN STATE WILKES-BARRE

Lehman, Pennsylvania — www.wb.psu.edu/

- **State-related** primarily 2-year, founded 1916, part of Pennsylvania State University
- **Rural** 156-acre campus
- **Endowment** $1.2 billion
- **Coed**
- **Moderately difficult** entrance level

Faculty *Student/faculty ratio:* 15:1.

Academics *Calendar:* semesters. *Degrees:* associate, bachelor's, and postbachelor's certificates.

Student Life *Campus security:* part-time trained security personnel.

Athletics Member NJCAA.

Standardized Tests *Required:* SAT or ACT (for admission).

Costs (2007–08) *Tuition:* state resident $10,454 full-time, $423 per credit hour part-time; nonresident $15,954 full-time, $665 per credit hour part-time. Full-time tuition and fees vary according to course level, location, program, and student level. Part-time tuition and fees vary according to course level, course load, location, program, and student level. *Required fees:* $424 full-time, $72 per term part-time. *Payment plans:* installment, deferred payment.

Financial Aid Of all full-time matriculated undergraduates who enrolled in 2006, 21 Federal Work-Study jobs (averaging $1149).

Applying *Options:* electronic application, early admission, deferred entrance. *Application fee:* $50. *Required:* high school transcript. *Required for some:* letters of recommendation, interview. *Recommended:* essay or personal statement.

Director of Admissions Mr. Randall C. Deike, Assistant Vice President for Enrollment Management, Penn State Wilkes-Barre, PO Box PSU, Old Route 115,

Lehman, PA 18627-9999. *Phone:* 814-865-5471. *Toll-free phone:* 800-966-6613. *E-mail:* admissions@psu.edu.

PENN STATE WORTHINGTON SCRANTON

Dunmore, Pennsylvania **www.sn.psu.edu/**

- **State-related** primarily 2-year, founded 1923, part of Pennsylvania State University
- **Small-town** 43-acre campus
- **Endowment** $1.2 billion
- **Coed**
- **Moderately difficult** entrance level

Faculty *Student/faculty ratio:* 16:1.

Academics *Calendar:* semesters. *Degrees:* associate and bachelor's.

Student Life *Campus security:* part-time trained security personnel.

Athletics Member NJCAA.

Standardized Tests *Required:* SAT or ACT (for admission).

Costs (2007–08) *Tuition:* state resident $10,454 full-time, $423 per credit hour part-time; nonresident $15,954 full-time, $665 per credit hour part-time. Full-time tuition and fees vary according to course level, location, program, and student level. Part-time tuition and fees vary according to course level, course load, location, program, and student level. *Required fees:* $424 full-time, $72 per term part-time. *Payment plans:* installment, deferred payment.

Financial Aid Of all full-time matriculated undergraduates who enrolled in 2006, 24 Federal Work-Study jobs (averaging $1298).

Applying *Options:* electronic application, early admission, deferred entrance. *Application fee:* $50. *Required:* high school transcript. *Required for some:* letters of recommendation, interview. *Recommended:* essay or personal statement.

Director of Admissions Mr. Randall C. Deike, Assistant Vice President for Enrollment Management, Penn State Worthington Scranton, 120 Ridge View Drive, Dunmore, PA 18512-1699. *Phone:* 814-865-5471. *E-mail:* admissions@psu.edu.

PENN STATE YORK

York, Pennsylvania **www.yk.psu.edu/**

- **State-related** primarily 2-year, founded 1926, part of Pennsylvania State University
- **Suburban** 53-acre campus
- **Endowment** $1.2 billion
- **Coed**
- **Moderately difficult** entrance level

Faculty *Student/faculty ratio:* 14:1.

Academics *Calendar:* semesters. *Degrees:* associate and bachelor's (also offers up to 2 years of most bachelor's degree programs offered at University Park campus).

Student Life *Campus security:* part-time trained security personnel.

Athletics Member NJCAA.

Standardized Tests *Required:* SAT or ACT (for admission).

Costs (2007–08) *Tuition:* state resident $10,454 full-time, $423 per credit hour part-time; nonresident $15,954 full-time, $665 per credit hour part-time. Full-time tuition and fees vary according to course level, location, program, and student level. Part-time tuition and fees vary according to course level, course load, location, program, and student level. *Required fees:* $424 full-time, $72 per term part-time. *Payment plans:* installment, deferred payment.

Financial Aid Of all full-time matriculated undergraduates who enrolled in 2006, 31 Federal Work-Study jobs (averaging $1152).

Applying *Options:* electronic application, early admission, deferred entrance. *Application fee:* $50. *Required:* high school transcript. *Required for some:* letters of recommendation, interview. *Recommended:* essay or personal statement.

Director of Admissions Mr. Randall C. Deike, Assistant Vice President for Enrollment Management, Penn State York, 1031 Edgecomb Avenue, York, PA 17403-3398. *Phone:* 814-865-5471. *Toll-free phone:* 800-778-6227. *E-mail:* admissions@psu.edu.

PENNSYLVANIA COLLEGE OF ART & DESIGN

Lancaster, Pennsylvania **www.pcad.edu/**

- **Independent** 4-year, founded 1982
- **Urban** campus with easy access to Philadelphia and Wilmington
- **Endowment** $584,038
- **Coed** 253 undergraduate students, 93% full-time, 60% women, 40% men
- **Moderately difficult** entrance level, 56% of applicants were admitted

Undergraduates 236 full-time, 17 part-time. Students come from 8 states and territories, 18% are from out of state, 4% African American, 3% Asian American or Pacific Islander, 3% Hispanic American, 1% Native American, 8% transferred in. *Retention:* 85% of 2006 full-time freshmen returned.

Freshmen *Admission:* 203 applied, 114 admitted, 61 enrolled. *Average high school GPA:* 3.02.

Faculty *Total:* 46, 26% full-time, 57% with terminal degrees. *Student/faculty ratio:* 9:1.

Majors Fine/studio arts; graphic design; illustration; photography.

Academics *Calendar:* semesters. *Degree:* certificates and bachelor's. *Special study options:* advanced placement credit, internships, part-time degree program.

Computers on Campus 42 computers/terminals are available on campus for general student use. Wireless service is available via entire campus.

Student Life *Housing:* college housing not available. *Activities and organizations:* Student Council, Anime Club. *Campus security:* late-night transport/escort service, trained evening/weekend security personnel.

Costs (2007–08) *Tuition:* $14,425 full-time, $601 per credit part-time. Part-time tuition and fees vary according to course load. *Required fees:* $780 full-time, $175 per term part-time. *Payment plan:* installment. *Waivers:* employees or children of employees.

Applying *Options:* deferred entrance. *Application fee:* $40. *Required:* essay or personal statement, high school transcript, interview, portfolio. *Required for some:* 2 letters of recommendation. *Recommended:* minimum 2.0 GPA. *Application deadlines:* rolling (freshmen), rolling (transfers). *Notification:* continuous (transfers).

Freshman Application Contact Director of Admissions and Marketing, Pennsylvania College of Art & Design, 204 North Prince Street, PO Box 59, Lancaster, PA 17608. *Phone:* 717-396-7833. *Fax:* 717-396-1339. *E-mail:* admissions@pcad.edu.

PENNSYLVANIA COLLEGE OF TECHNOLOGY

Williamsport, Pennsylvania **www.pct.edu/**

- **State-related** 4-year, founded 1965, administratively affiliated with Pennsylvania State University
- **Small-town** 981-acre campus
- **Endowment** $606,992
- **Coed** 6,682 undergraduate students, 85% full-time, 34% women, 66% men
- **Noncompetitive** entrance level, 95% of applicants were admitted

Pennsylvania College of Technology, Pennsylvania's premier technical college, is a special mission affiliate of Penn State and is committed to applied technology education. More than 6,500 students are enrolled in Penn College's bachelor's and associate degree and certificate program majors, which combine hands-on experience with theory and management. "Degrees that work" represents more than 100 career fields.

Undergraduates 5,689 full-time, 993 part-time. Students come from 33 states and territories, 15 other countries, 9% are from out of state, 3% African American, 1% Asian American or Pacific Islander, 1% Hispanic American, 0.6% Native American, 0.4% international, 9% transferred in, 24% live on campus. *Retention:* 69% of 2006 full-time freshmen returned.

Freshmen *Admission:* 3,066 applied, 2,911 admitted, 1,631 enrolled.

Faculty *Total:* 493, 59% full-time, 13% with terminal degrees. *Student/faculty ratio:* 19:1.

Majors Accounting technology and bookkeeping; administrative assistant and secretarial science; adult health nursing; aeronautical/aerospace engineering technology; aircraft powerplant technology; allied health diagnostic, intervention, and treatment professions related; applied art; applied horticulture; applied horticulture/horticultural business services related; architectural engineering technology; autobody/collision and repair technology; baking and pastry arts; banking and financial support services; biology/biological sciences; biomedical technology; broadcast journalism; business administration and management; business administration, management and operations related; business automation/technology/data entry; cabinetmaking and millwork; cardiovascular technology; carpentry; child care and support services management; child care provision; computer and information sciences; computer and information sciences and support services related; computer and information systems security; computer engineering technologies related; computer/information technology services administration related; computer programming (specific applications); computer systems analysis; computer technology/computer systems technology; construction management; dental services and allied professions related; diesel mechanics technology; dietitian assistant; drafting and design technology; drafting/design engineering technologies related; early childhood education; education (specific subject areas) related; electrical and power transmission installation related; electrician; emergency medical technology (EMT paramedic); engineering science; engineering technologies related; entrepreneurial and small business related; environmental control technologies related; fine/studio arts; forestry technology; general studies; graphic design; health and medical administrative services related; health and physical education related; health information/medical records administration; health information/medical records technology; health professions related; health services/allied health/health sciences; heavy equipment maintenance technology; heavy/industrial equipment maintenance technologies related; hospitality administration; human resources management; industrial electronics technology; industrial mechanics and maintenance technology; information technology; institutional food workers; instrumentation technology; kinesiology and exercise science; landscaping and groundskeeping; laser and optical technology; legal assistant/paralegal; legal professions and studies related; legal studies; liberal arts and sciences and humanities related; liberal arts and sciences/liberal studies; machine shop technology; management information systems; management science; marketing/marketing management; masonry; mass communication/media; mechanical engineering/mechanical technology; mechanic and repair technologies related; medical administrative assistant and medical secretary; medical/clinical assistant; medical radiologic technology; mental and social health services and allied professions related; multi-/interdisciplinary studies related; nursing (licensed practical/vocational nurse training); occupational therapist assistant; office occupations and clerical services; ornamental horticulture; physical sciences; plant nursery management; platemaking/imaging; plumbing technology; quality control technology; radiologic technology/science; robotics technology; solar energy technology; surgical technology; survey technology; technical and business writing; tool and die technology; tourism and travel services management; turf and turfgrass management; vehicle and vehicle parts and accessories marketing; vehicle maintenance and repair technologies related; web page, digital/multimedia and information resources design.

Academics *Calendar:* semesters. *Degrees:* certificates, associate, and bachelor's. *Special study options:* academic remediation for entering students, advanced placement credit, cooperative education, distance learning, double majors, English as a second language, independent study, internships, off-campus study, part-time degree program, services for LD students, student-designed majors, summer session for credit. *ROTC:* Army (c).

Computers on Campus 1,500 computers/terminals are available on campus for general student use. Students can access the following: campus intranet, computer help desk, free student e-mail accounts, online (class) grades, online (class) registration, online (class) schedules. Campuswide network is available. 100% of college-owned or -operated housing units are wired for high-speed Internet access. Wireless service is available via entire campus.

Student Life *Housing options:* coed, disabled students. Campus housing is university owned. *Activities and organizations:* student-run radio station, Student Government Association, Residence Hall Association (RHA), Wildcats Event Board (WEB), Penn College Construction Association, Campus Crusade for Christ, national fraternities. *Campus security:* 24-hour emergency response devices and patrols, late-night transport/escort service, controlled dormitory access. *Student services:* health clinic, personal/psychological counseling.

Athletics *Intercollegiate sports:* archery M/W, baseball M, basketball M/W, bowling M/W, cross-country running M/W, golf M/W, soccer M/W, softball W, tennis M/W, volleyball M/W. *Intramural sports:* archery M/W, badminton M/W, basketball M/W, bowling M/W, football M/W, golf M/W, lacrosse M/W, racquetball M/W, soccer M/W, softball M/W, table tennis M/W, tennis M/W, ultimate Frisbee M/W, volleyball M/W, weight lifting M/W, wrestling M.

Standardized Tests *Required for some:* SAT (for admission).

Costs (2007–08) *Tuition:* state resident $9570 full-time, $375 per credit hour part-time; nonresident $12,450 full-time, $471 per credit hour part-time. Full-time tuition and fees vary according to course load and program. Part-time tuition and fees vary according to course load and program. *Required fees:* $1680 full-time. *Room and board:* $7700; room only: $4870. Room and board charges vary according to board plan, housing facility, and location. *Payment plan:* deferred payment. *Waivers:* employees or children of employees.

Financial Aid Of all full-time matriculated undergraduates who enrolled in 2006, 242 Federal Work-Study jobs (averaging $1502). 331 state and other part-time jobs (averaging $1398). *Average percent of need met:* 77%. *Average financial aid package:* $11,302. *Average need-based gift aid:* $2638.

Applying *Options:* electronic application, early admission, deferred entrance. *Application fee:* $50. *Required:* high school transcript. *Application deadlines:* 7/1 (freshmen), rolling (transfers).

Freshman Application Contact Mr. Chester Schuman, Director of Admissions, Pennsylvania College of Technology, One College Avenue, DIF #119, Williamsport, PA 17701. *Phone:* 570-327-4761. *Toll-free phone:* 800-367-9222. *Fax:* 570-321-5551. *E-mail:* cschuman@pct.edu.

See page 2290 for the College Close-Up.

PHILADELPHIA BIBLICAL UNIVERSITY

Langhorne, Pennsylvania **www.pbu.edu/**

- **Independent nondenominational** comprehensive, founded 1913
- **Suburban** 105-acre campus with easy access to Philadelphia
- **Endowment** $9.2 million
- **Coed** 1,069 undergraduate students, 93% full-time, 54% women, 46% men
- **Moderately difficult** entrance level, 98% of applicants were admitted

Undergraduates 993 full-time, 76 part-time. Students come from 40 states and territories, 17 other countries, 52% are from out of state, 12% African American, 3% Asian American or Pacific Islander, 2% Hispanic American, 0.2% Native American, 2% international, 15% transferred in, 61% live on campus. *Retention:* 82% of 2006 full-time freshmen returned.

Freshmen *Admission:* 366 applied, 357 admitted, 202 enrolled. *Average high school GPA:* 3.32. *Test scores:* SAT critical reading scores over 500: 63%; SAT math scores over 500: 52%; ACT scores over 18: 88%; SAT critical reading scores over 600: 20%; SAT math scores over 600: 12%; ACT scores over 24: 38%; SAT critical reading scores over 700: 4%; SAT math scores over 700: 2%.

Faculty *Total:* 131, 40% full-time, 36% with terminal degrees. *Student/faculty ratio:* 14:1.

Majors Biblical studies; business administration and management; elementary education; English/language arts teacher education; kindergarten/preschool education; mathematics teacher education; music; physical education teaching and coaching; religious studies; social studies teacher education; social work.

Academics *Calendar:* semesters. *Degrees:* certificates, bachelor's, master's, and first professional. *Special study options:* academic remediation for entering students, accelerated degree program, adult/continuing education programs, advanced placement credit, double majors, honors programs, independent study, internships, off-campus study, part-time degree program, services for LD students, study abroad, summer session for credit. *ROTC:* Air Force (c).

Computers on Campus 90 computers/terminals and 1,095 ports are available on campus for general student use. Students can access the following: campus intranet, computer help desk, free student e-mail accounts, online (class) grades, online (class) registration, online (class) schedules. Campuswide network is available. 62% of college-owned or -operated housing units are wired for high-speed Internet access. Wireless service is available via classrooms, computer labs, dorm rooms, learning centers, libraries.

Student Life *Housing:* on-campus residence required through senior year. *Options:* men-only, women-only, disabled students. Campus housing is university owned and leased by the school. Freshman campus housing is guaranteed. *Activities and organizations:* drama/theater group, student-run newspaper, choral group, Student Theological Society, Student Missionary Fellowship, Cultural Awareness Association, University Social Committee, Student Senate. *Campus security:* 24-hour emergency response devices and patrols, student patrols, late-night transport/escort service, controlled dormitory access. *Student services:* health clinic, personal/psychological counseling.

Athletics Member NCAA, NCCAA. All NCAA Division III. *Intercollegiate sports:* baseball M, basketball M/W, field hockey W, golf M, soccer M/W, softball W, tennis M/W, volleyball M/W. *Intramural sports:* basketball M/W, soccer M/W, table tennis M/W, tennis M/W, volleyball M/W.

Standardized Tests *Required:* SAT or ACT (for admission).

Costs (2008–09) *Comprehensive fee:* $24,935 includes full-time tuition ($17,450), mandatory fees ($335), and room and board ($7150). Part-time tuition: $526 per credit. *College room only:* $3750.

Financial Aid Of all full-time matriculated undergraduates who enrolled in 2007, 715 applied for aid, 644 were judged to have need, 177 had their need fully met. 81 Federal Work-Study jobs (averaging $1106). In 2007, 175 non-need-based awards were made. *Average percent of need met:* 78%. *Average financial aid package:* $13,833. *Average need-based loan:* $4844. *Average need-based gift aid:* $9857. *Average non-need-based aid:* $8789.

Applying *Options:* electronic application, early admission, deferred entrance. *Application fee:* $25. *Required:* essay or personal statement, high school transcript, minimum 2.0 GPA. *Required for some:* interview. *Recommended:* interview. *Application deadlines:* rolling (freshmen), rolling (transfers). *Notification:* continuous (freshmen), continuous (transfers).

Freshman Application Contact Ms. Lisa Yoder, Director of Undergraduate Admissions, Philadelphia Biblical University, 200 Manor Avenue, Langhorne, PA 19047. *Phone:* 215-702-4550. *Toll-free phone:* 800-366-0049. *Fax:* 215-702-4248. *E-mail:* admissions@pbu.edu.

See page 2292 for the College Close-Up.

PHILADELPHIA UNIVERSITY

Philadelphia, Pennsylvania **www.philau.edu/**

- **Independent** comprehensive, founded 1884
- **Suburban** 100-acre campus
- **Endowment** $23.2 million
- **Coed** 2,810 undergraduate students, 91% full-time, 69% women, 31% men
- **Moderately difficult** entrance level, 64% of applicants were admitted

Undergraduates 2,570 full-time, 240 part-time. Students come from 42 states and territories, 26 other countries, 48% are from out of state, 10% African American, 4% Asian American or Pacific Islander, 3% Hispanic American, 0.2% Native American, 2% international, 3% transferred in, 47% live on campus. *Retention:* 73% of 2006 full-time freshmen returned.

Freshmen *Admission:* 4,015 applied, 2,574 admitted, 743 enrolled. *Average high school GPA:* 3.46. *Test scores:* SAT critical reading scores over 500: 68%; SAT math scores over 500: 74%; SAT writing scores over 500: 65%; SAT critical reading scores over 600: 17%; SAT math scores over 600: 25%; SAT writing scores over 600: 14%; SAT critical reading scores over 700: 1%; SAT math scores over 700: 1%; SAT writing scores over 700: 1%.

Faculty *Total:* 446, 25% full-time. *Student/faculty ratio:* 13:1.

Majors Accounting; apparel and accessories marketing; architecture; biochemistry; biology/biological sciences; biopsychology; business administration and management; chemistry; clothing/textiles; commercial and advertising art; computer and information sciences; computer science; conservation biology; e-commerce; environmental biology; fashion/apparel design; fashion merchandising; fiber, textile and weaving arts; finance; graphic design; industrial design; information science/studies; interior architecture; interior design; international business/trade/commerce; landscape architecture; management information systems; marketing/marketing management; physician assistant; pre-medical studies; psychology; textile sciences and engineering.

Academics *Calendar:* semesters. *Degrees:* certificates, associate, bachelor's, master's, doctoral, post-master's, and postbachelor's certificates. *Special study options:* academic remediation for entering students, accelerated degree program, adult/continuing education programs, advanced placement credit, cooperative education, English as a second language, freshman honors college, honors programs, independent study, internships, off-campus study, part-time degree program, services for LD students, study abroad, summer session for credit.

Computers on Campus 400 computers/terminals are available on campus for general student use. Students can access the following: online (class) registration. Campuswide network is available.

Student Life *Housing options:* coed, women-only, disabled students. Campus housing is university owned and leased by the school. Freshman campus housing is guaranteed. *Activities and organizations:* drama/theater group, student-run newspaper, choral group, Gemini Theatre, Black Student Union, Cornerstone, Phila'cappella, Global Friends, national fraternities, national sororities. *Campus security:* 24-hour emergency response devices and patrols, late-night transport/escort service, controlled dormitory access. *Student services:* health clinic, personal/psychological counseling.

Athletics Member NCAA. All Division II except soccer (Division I). *Intercollegiate sports:* baseball M (s), basketball M (s)/W (s), field hockey W (s), golf M (s), lacrosse W (s), soccer M (s)/W (s), softball W (s), tennis M (s)/W (s), volleyball W (s). *Intramural sports:* basketball M/W, cross-country running M/W, football M, skiing (downhill) M (c)/W (c), soccer M/W, softball M/W, swimming and diving M/W, table tennis M/W, tennis M/W, volleyball M/W, weight lifting M/W.

Standardized Tests *Required:* SAT or ACT (for admission).

Costs (2007–08) *Comprehensive fee:* $33,814 includes full-time tuition ($25,386), mandatory fees ($70), and room and board ($8358). Full-time tuition and fees vary according to program. Part-time tuition: $450 per credit hour. Part-time tuition and fees vary according to class time and program. *College room only:* $4258. Room and board charges vary according to board plan and housing facility. *Payment plans:* installment, deferred payment. *Waivers:* employees or children of employees.

Financial Aid Of all full-time matriculated undergraduates who enrolled in 2006, 1,985 applied for aid, 1,692 were judged to have need, 158 had their need fully met. 992 Federal Work-Study jobs (averaging $2000). In 2006, 665 non-need-based awards were made. *Average percent of need met:* 72%. *Average financial aid package:* $16,592. *Average need-based loan:* $4228. *Average need-based gift aid:* $10,870. *Average non-need-based aid:* $4164. *Average indebtedness upon graduation:* $27,991. *Financial aid deadline:* 4/15.

Applying *Options:* electronic application, deferred entrance. *Application fee:* $35. *Required:* high school transcript. *Recommended:* essay or personal statement, 2 letters of recommendation, interview. *Application deadlines:* rolling (freshmen), rolling (transfers). *Notification:* continuous (freshmen).

Freshman Application Contact Ms. Christine Greb, Director of Admissions, Philadelphia University, School House Lane and Henry Avenue, Philadelphia, PA 19144-5497. *Phone:* 215-951-2800. *Fax:* 215-951-2907. *E-mail:* admissions@philau.edu.

See page 2294 for the College Close-Up.

POINT PARK UNIVERSITY

Pittsburgh, Pennsylvania **www.pointpark.edu/**

- **Independent** comprehensive, founded 1960
- **Urban** campus
- **Endowment** $20.7 million
- **Coed** 3,109 undergraduate students, 79% full-time, 60% women, 40% men
- **Moderately difficult** entrance level, 75% of applicants were admitted

Point Park University offers students the opportunity to attend small, personalized classes in the heart of downtown Pittsburgh, ranked as America's most livable city. Long recognized for providing a liberal arts education with career preparation, Point Park's location means students have convenient access to internships providing valuable professional-level experience that complements classroom learning.

Undergraduates 2,446 full-time, 663 part-time. Students come from 48 states and territories, 18 other countries, 17% are from out of state, 19% African American, 1% Asian American or Pacific Islander, 2% Hispanic American, 0.4% Native American, 1% international, 17% transferred in, 24% live on campus. *Retention:* 73% of 2006 full-time freshmen returned.

Freshmen *Admission:* 2,681 applied, 2,021 admitted, 460 enrolled. *Average high school GPA:* 3.16. *Test scores:* SAT critical reading scores over 500: 60%; SAT math scores over 500: 47%; SAT writing scores over 500: 53%; ACT scores over 18: 86%; SAT critical reading scores over 600: 19%; SAT math scores over 600: 10%; SAT writing scores over 600: 16%; ACT scores over 24: 34%; SAT critical reading scores over 700: 3%; SAT math scores over 700: 1%; SAT writing scores over 700: 2%; ACT scores over 30: 3%.

Faculty *Total:* 321, 34% full-time. *Student/faculty ratio:* 17:1.

Majors Accounting; acting; advertising; area, ethnic, cultural, and gender studies related; arts management; behavioral sciences; biology/biological sciences; biology/biotechnology laboratory technician; biology teacher education; biotechnology; broadcast journalism; business administration and management; business administration, management and operations related; business/corporate communications; business, management, and marketing related; cinematography and film/video production; civil engineering technology; communication and journalism related; communication and media related; computer/information technology services administration related; criminal justice/law enforcement administration; criminal justice/safety; dance; design and applied arts related; drama and dance teacher education; dramatic/theater arts; early childhood education; education; education related; education (specific subject areas) related; electrical and electronic engineering technologies related; electrical, electronic and communications engineering technology; elementary education; English; English/language arts teacher education; environmental science; funeral service and mortuary science; general studies; health/health care administration; history; human resources management; information technology; journalism; legal studies; mass communication/media; mathematics teacher education; mechanical engineering/mechanical technology; photography; photojournalism; political science and government; psychology; public administration; radio and television; secondary education; security and protective services related; social sciences; social science teacher education.

Academics *Calendar:* semesters. *Degrees:* certificates, associate, bachelor's, master's, post-master's, and postbachelor's certificates. *Special study options:* academic remediation for entering students, accelerated degree program, adult/continuing education programs, advanced placement credit, distance learning, double majors, honors programs, independent study, internships, off-campus study, part-time degree program, services for LD students, student-designed majors, study abroad, summer session for credit. *ROTC:* Army (c), Air Force (c).

Computers on Campus 170 computers/terminals and 112 ports are available on campus for general student use. Students can access the following: campus intranet, computer help desk, free student e-mail accounts, online (class) grades, online (class) schedules. Campuswide network is available. 100% of college-owned or -operated housing units are wired for high-speed Internet access. Wireless service is available via libraries, student centers.

Student Life *Housing options:* coed. Campus housing is university owned. Freshman campus housing is guaranteed. *Activities and organizations:* drama/theater group, student-run newspaper, radio and television station, choral group, Black Student Union, student radio station, Dance Club, Alpha Phi Omega, College Students in Broadcasting. *Campus security:* 24-hour emergency response devices and patrols, late-night transport/escort service, 24-hour security desk, video security. *Student services:* health clinic, personal/psychological counseling.

Athletics Member NAIA. *Intercollegiate sports:* baseball M (s), basketball M (s)/W (s), cross-country running M (s)/W (s), soccer M (s), softball W (s), volleyball W (s). *Intramural sports:* basketball M, football M, golf M, tennis M/W, volleyball M/W, weight lifting M/W.

Standardized Tests *Required:* SAT or ACT (for admission).

Costs (2007–08) *Comprehensive fee:* $27,430 includes full-time tuition ($18,460), mandatory fees ($530), and room and board ($8440). Full-time tuition and fees vary according to program. Part-time tuition: $510 per credit. Part-time tuition and fees vary according to program. *Required fees:* $15 per credit part-time. *College room only:* $3980. Room and board charges vary according to board plan and housing facility. *Payment plans:* installment, deferred payment. *Waivers:* children of alumni and employees or children of employees.

Financial Aid Of all full-time matriculated undergraduates who enrolled in 2006, 2,129 applied for aid, 1,876 were judged to have need, 454 had their need fully met. 213 Federal Work-Study jobs (averaging $2205). 264 state and other part-time jobs (averaging $1965). In 2006, 484 non-need-based awards were made. *Average percent of need met:* 69%. *Average financial aid package:* $14,691. *Average need-based loan:* $5748. *Average need-based gift aid:* $8417. *Average non-need-based aid:* $10,176. *Average indebtedness upon graduation:* $29,989. *Financial aid deadline:* 5/1.

Applying *Options:* electronic application, early admission, deferred entrance. *Application fee:* $40. *Required:* high school transcript. *Required for some:* 2 letters of recommendation, interview, audition. *Recommended:* essay or personal statement, minimum 2.0 GPA. *Application deadlines:* rolling (freshmen), rolling (transfers).

Freshman Application Contact Ms. Joell Minford, Director, Full-Time Admissions, Point Park University, 201 Wood Street, Pittsburgh, PA 15222. *Phone:* 412-392-3430. *Toll-free phone:* 800-321-0129. *Fax:* 412-392-3902. *E-mail:* enroll@pointpark.edu.

See page 2296 for the College Close-Up.

THE RESTAURANT SCHOOL AT WALNUT HILL COLLEGE

Philadelphia, Pennsylvania **www.walnuthillcollege.edu/**

Freshman Application Contact Mr. Karl D. Becker, Director of Admissions, The Restaurant School at Walnut Hill College, 4207 Walnut Street, Philadelphia, PA 19104. *Phone:* 267-295-2373. *Toll-free phone:* 877-925-6884 Ext. 3011. *Fax:* 215-222-4219. *E-mail:* kbecker@walnuthillcollege.edu.

See page 2298 for the College Close-Up.

ROBERT MORRIS UNIVERSITY

Moon Township, Pennsylvania **www.rmu.edu/**

- **Independent** university, founded 1921
- **Suburban** 230-acre campus with easy access to Pittsburgh
- **Endowment** $19.8 million
- **Coed** 3,984 undergraduate students, 80% full-time, 47% women, 53% men
- **Moderately difficult** entrance level, 76% of applicants were admitted

Undergraduates 3,207 full-time, 777 part-time. Students come from 39 states and territories, 16 other countries, 13% are from out of state, 8% African American, 1% Asian American or Pacific Islander, 1% Hispanic American, 0.1% Native American, 2% international, 11% transferred in, 30% live on campus. *Retention:* 73% of 2006 full-time freshmen returned.

Freshmen *Admission:* 2,938 applied, 2,223 admitted, 666 enrolled. *Average high school GPA:* 3.23. *Test scores:* SAT critical reading scores over 500: 45%; SAT math scores over 500: 58%; ACT scores over 18: 84%; SAT critical reading scores over 600: 8%; SAT math scores over 600: 18%; ACT scores over 24: 27%; SAT critical reading scores over 700: 1%; SAT math scores over 700: 3%; ACT scores over 30: 2%.

Faculty *Total:* 354, 49% full-time, 56% with terminal degrees. *Student/faculty ratio:* 16:1.

Majors Accounting; actuarial science; applied mathematics; business administration and management; business teacher education; computer/information technology services administration related; computer software engineering; design and visual communications; economics; elementary education; engineering; English; environmental science; finance; health and medical administrative services related; health services administration; hospitality administration; information science/studies; management information systems; manufacturing engineering; marketing/marketing management; mass communication/media; multi-/interdisciplinary studies related; nuclear medical technology; nursing (registered nurse training); organizational behavior; psychology; social sciences; sport and fitness administration/management.

Academics *Calendar:* semesters. *Degrees:* certificates, bachelor's, master's, doctoral, and postbachelor's certificates. *Special study options:* academic remediation for entering students, accelerated degree program, adult/continuing education programs, advanced placement credit, cooperative education, distance learning, double majors, honors programs, independent study, internships, off-campus study, part-time degree program, services for LD students, study abroad, summer session for credit. *ROTC:* Army (b), Air Force (c).

Computers on Campus 300 computers/terminals are available on campus for general student use. Students can access the following: campus intranet, computer help desk, free student e-mail accounts, online (class) grades, online (class) registration, online (class) schedules, online payment. Campuswide network is available. 100% of college-owned or -operated housing units are wired for high-speed Internet access. Wireless service is available via classrooms, computer centers, computer labs, learning centers.

Student Life *Housing options:* coed, men-only, women-only, disabled students. Campus housing is university owned. Freshman applicants given priority for college housing. *Activities and organizations:* drama/theater group, student-run newspaper, television station, choral group, marching band, Student Government Association, Residence Hall Association, R-MOVE, National Society of Collegiate Scholars, Black Student Union, national fraternities, national sororities. *Campus security:* 24-hour emergency response devices and patrols, late-night transport/escort service, controlled dormitory access. *Student services:* health clinic, personal/psychological counseling.

Athletics Member NCAA. All Division I except football (Division I-AA). *Intercollegiate sports:* baseball M (c), basketball M (s)/W (s), cheerleading M (c)/W (c), crew W (s), field hockey W (s), golf M (s)/W (s), ice hockey M (s)/W (s), lacrosse M (s)/W (s), soccer M (s)/W (s), softball W (s), tennis M (s)/W (s), track and field M (s)/W (s), volleyball W (s). *Intramural sports:* basketball M/W, bowling M (c)/W (c), football M, ice hockey M (c), rock climbing M (c), softball M/W, volleyball M (c)/W.

Standardized Tests *Required:* SAT or ACT (for admission).

Costs (2007–08) *Comprehensive fee:* $26,420 includes full-time tuition ($17,600), mandatory fees ($300), and room and board ($8520). Full-time tuition and fees vary according to program. Part-time tuition: $590 per credit. Part-time tuition and fees vary according to course load and program. *Required fees:* $10 per credit part-time. *College room only:* $4940. Room and board charges vary according to board plan and housing facility. *Payment plans:* installment, deferred payment. *Waivers:* employees or children of employees.

Financial Aid Of all full-time matriculated undergraduates who enrolled in 2006, 2,628 applied for aid, 2,341 were judged to have need, 758 had their need fully met. In 2006, 581 non-need-based awards were made. *Average percent of need met:* 73%. *Average financial aid package:* $16,027. *Average need-based loan:* $7225. *Average need-based gift aid:* $8312. *Average non-need-based aid:* $10,907. *Average indebtedness upon graduation:* $25,960.

Applying *Options:* electronic application, deferred entrance. *Application fee:* $30. *Required:* high school transcript, minimum 2.5 GPA. *Required for some:* interview. *Recommended:* minimum 3.0 GPA, letters of recommendation, interview. *Application deadlines:* 7/1 (freshmen), 7/1 (transfers). *Notification:* continuous (freshmen), continuous (transfers).

Freshman Application Contact Enrollment Services Department, Robert Morris University, 6001 University Boulevard, Moon Township, PA 15108-1189. *Phone:* 412-397-5200. *Toll-free phone:* 800-762-0097. *Fax:* 412-397-2425. *E-mail:* admissions@rmu.edu.

See page 2300 for the College Close-Up.

ROSEMONT COLLEGE

Rosemont, Pennsylvania www.rosemont.edu/

- **Independent Roman Catholic** comprehensive, founded 1921
- **Suburban** 56-acre campus with easy access to Philadelphia
- **Endowment** $9.3 million
- **Undergraduate: women only; graduate: coed** 551 undergraduate students, 72% full-time, 95% women, 5% men
- **Moderately difficult** entrance level, 60% of applicants were admitted

Rosemont College was founded in 1921 as a women's college in the Catholic tradition. The College's reputation for academic excellence in an intimate setting is its hallmark.

Undergraduates 395 full-time, 156 part-time. Students come from 14 states and territories, 11 other countries, 30% are from out of state, 36% African American, 6% Asian American or Pacific Islander, 8% Hispanic American, 1% international, 5% transferred in, 70% live on campus. *Retention:* 76% of 2006 full-time freshmen returned.

Freshmen *Admission:* 367 applied, 221 admitted, 68 enrolled. *Average high school GPA:* 3.6. *Test scores:* SAT critical reading scores over 500: 41%; SAT math scores over 500: 26%; SAT writing scores over 500: 28%; ACT scores over 18: 100%; SAT critical reading scores over 600: 8%; SAT writing scores over 600: 4%.

Faculty *Total:* 165, 16% full-time, 22% with terminal degrees. *Student/faculty ratio:* 8:1.

Majors Accounting; art history, criticism and conservation; biochemistry; biology/biological sciences; business administration and management; chemistry; communication/speech communication and rhetoric; criminal justice/safety; economics; English; fine/studio arts; French; German; history; humanities; Italian; mathematics; philosophy; political science and government; psychology; religious studies; social sciences; sociology; Spanish; women's studies.

Academics *Calendar:* semesters. *Degrees:* certificates, bachelor's, master's, and postbachelor's certificates. *Special study options:* accelerated degree program, adult/continuing education programs, advanced placement credit, double majors, English as a second language, honors programs, independent study, internships, off-campus study, part-time degree program, services for LD students, student-designed majors, study abroad, summer session for credit. *ROTC:* Army (c). *Unusual degree programs:* 3-2 engineering with Villanova University; nursing with Villanova University, Drexel University; counseling psychology, dentistry, art therapy, physical therapy, master of arts-creative arts in therapy with Drexel University; B.S. Nursing, in cooperation with Drexel University.

Computers on Campus 100 computers/terminals and 250 ports are available on campus for general student use. Students can access the following: campus intranet, computer help desk, free student e-mail accounts, online (class) grades, online (class) registration, online (class) schedules. Campuswide network is available. 100% of college-owned or -operated housing units are wired for high-speed Internet access. Wireless service is available via classrooms, computer centers, dorm rooms, learning centers, libraries, student centers.

Student Life *Housing:* on-campus residence required through junior year. *Options:* women-only. Campus housing is university owned. Freshman campus housing is guaranteed. *Activities and organizations:* drama/theater group, student-run newspaper, choral group, student government, Triad, Jest and Gesture, Best Buddies, Political Science Club. *Campus security:* 24-hour emergency response devices and patrols, late-night transport/escort service, controlled dormitory access. *Student services:* health clinic, personal/psychological counseling, women's center, legal services.

Athletics Member NCAA. All Division III. *Intercollegiate sports:* basketball W, field hockey W, softball W, tennis W, volleyball W.

Standardized Tests *Required:* SAT or ACT (for admission).

Costs (2007–08) *Comprehensive fee:* $32,035 includes full-time tuition ($21,630), mandatory fees ($1205), and room and board ($9200). Part-time tuition: $830 per credit. *Required fees:* $310 per term part-time. *Room and board:* Room and board charges vary according to housing facility. *Payment plan:* installment. *Waivers:* senior citizens and employees or children of employees.

Financial Aid Of all full-time matriculated undergraduates who enrolled in 2007, 319 applied for aid, 290 were judged to have need, 52 had their need fully met. 97 Federal Work-Study jobs (averaging $1175). In 2007, 65 non-need-based awards were made. *Average percent of need met:* 71%. *Average financial aid package:* $18,345. *Average need-based loan:* $3780. *Average need-based gift aid:* $15,046. *Average non-need-based aid:* $11,592. *Average indebtedness upon graduation:* $21,515.

Applying *Options:* electronic application, early admission, deferred entrance. *Application fee:* $35. *Required:* essay or personal statement, high school transcript, 2 letters of recommendation. *Recommended:* minimum 3.0 GPA, interview. *Application deadlines:* rolling (freshmen), rolling (transfers). *Notification:* continuous until 8/1 (freshmen), continuous until 8/1 (transfers).

Freshman Application Contact Ms. Rennie Andrews, Dean, Undergraduate Women's College Admissions, Rosemont College, 1400 Montgomery Avenue, Main Building, Rosemont, PA 19010. *Phone:* 610-527-0200. *Toll-free phone:* 800-331-0708. *Fax:* 610-520-4399. *E-mail:* admissions@rosemont.edu.

See page 2302 for the College Close-Up.

ST. CHARLES BORROMEO SEMINARY, OVERBROOK

Wynnewood, Pennsylvania www.scs.edu/

- **Independent Roman Catholic** comprehensive, founded 1832
- **Suburban** 77-acre campus with easy access to Philadelphia
- **Endowment** $19.5 million
- **Undergraduate: men only; graduate: coed** 113 undergraduate students, 68% full-time, 22% women, 78% men
- **Moderately difficult** entrance level, 100% of applicants were admitted

Undergraduates 77 full-time, 36 part-time. Students come from 13 states and territories, 3 other countries, 42% are from out of state, 1% African American, 4% Hispanic American, 3% international, 12% transferred in, 97% live on campus. *Retention:* 100% of 2006 full-time freshmen returned.

Freshmen *Admission:* 7 applied, 7 admitted, 7 enrolled.

Faculty *Total:* 28, 64% full-time, 54% with terminal degrees. *Student/faculty ratio:* 7:1.

Majors Philosophy.

Academics *Calendar:* semesters. *Degrees:* certificates, bachelor's, master's, and first professional (also offers coed part-time programs). *Special study options:* academic remediation for entering students, accelerated degree program, adult/continuing education programs, advanced placement credit, English as a second language, independent study, summer session for credit.

Computers on Campus 60 computers/terminals are available on campus for general student use. Students can access the following: campus intranet, free student e-mail accounts, online (class) registration. Campuswide network is available.

Student Life *Housing:* on-campus residence required through senior year. *Options:* men-only. Campus housing is university owned. Freshman campus housing is guaranteed. *Activities and organizations:* drama/theater group, student-run newspaper, choral group, Seminarians for Life, student council. *Campus security:* 24-hour emergency response devices and patrols. *Student services:* health clinic, personal/psychological counseling.

Athletics *Intramural sports:* basketball M, football M, soccer M, volleyball M.

Costs (2007–08) *Comprehensive fee:* $20,590 includes full-time tuition ($12,321) and room and board ($8269). Part-time tuition: $220 per credit. *Payment plan:* installment. *Waivers:* employees or children of employees.

Applying *Options:* deferred entrance. *Required:* essay or personal statement, high school transcript, minimum 2.0 GPA, 3 letters of recommendation, interview, sponsorship by diocese or religious community. *Application deadlines:* 7/15 (freshmen), 7/15 (transfers). *Notification:* continuous (freshmen).

Freshman Application Contact Rev. David E. Diamond, Vice Rector, St. Charles Borromeo Seminary, Overbrook, 100 East Wynnewood Road, Wynnewood, PA 19096. *Phone:* 610-785-6271. *Fax:* 610-617-9267. *E-mail:* cao@adphila.org.

SAINT FRANCIS UNIVERSITY

Loretto, Pennsylvania www.francis.edu/

- **Independent Roman Catholic** comprehensive, founded 1847
- **Rural** 600-acre campus
- **Endowment** $25.3 million
- **Coed** 1,594 undergraduate students, 89% full-time, 64% women, 36% men
- **Moderately difficult** entrance level, 85% of applicants were admitted

Saint Francis University has continued its service of caring for the Earth by becoming the only Pennsylvania university to develop its own wind-energy facility. The project offers energy conservation and innovative education, including a new academic program offering in interdisciplinary environmental science. Students team with faculty members to work on unique undergraduate research projects that focus on environmental protection and rural economic development.

Undergraduates 1,425 full-time, 169 part-time. Students come from 31 states and territories, 5 other countries, 21% are from out of state, 5% African American, 1% Asian American or Pacific Islander, 1% Hispanic American, 0.3% Native American, 0.1% international, 2% transferred in, 80% live on campus. *Retention:* 82% of 2006 full-time freshmen returned.

Freshmen *Admission:* 1,342 applied, 1,146 admitted, 418 enrolled. *Average high school GPA:* 3.45. *Test scores:* SAT critical reading scores over 500: 55%; SAT math scores over 500: 65%; ACT scores over 18: 93%; SAT critical reading scores over 600: 14%; SAT math scores over 600: 16%; ACT scores over 24: 36%; SAT critical reading scores over 700: 1%; SAT math scores over 700: 3%; ACT scores over 30: 5%.

Faculty *Total:* 178, 56% full-time, 51% with terminal degrees. *Student/faculty ratio:* 16:1.

Majors Accounting; accounting and finance; American studies; anthropology; biology/biological sciences; biology teacher education; business administration and management; chemistry; chemistry teacher education; clinical laboratory science/medical technology; computer programming; computer science; criminal justice/law enforcement administration; criminology; economics; education; elementary education; engineering; English; English/language arts teacher education; environmental science; environmental studies; exercise physiology; finance; fine arts related; foreign language teacher education; forensic science and technology; French; French language teacher education; history; history teacher education; human resources management; international business/trade/commerce; international relations and affairs; journalism; labor and industrial relations; literature; management information systems; marine biology and biological oceanography; marketing/marketing management; mass communication/media; mathematics; mathematics and computer science; mathematics teacher education; modern languages; nursing (registered nurse training); occupational therapy; pastoral studies/counseling; philosophy; physical therapy; physician assistant; political science and government; pre-dentistry studies; pre-law studies; premedical studies; pre-veterinary studies; psychology; public administration; public relations/image management; real estate; religious studies; science teacher education; secondary education; social studies teacher education; social work; sociology; Spanish; special education.

Academics *Calendar:* semesters. *Degrees:* certificates, associate, bachelor's, and master's. *Special study options:* academic remediation for entering students, accelerated degree program, adult/continuing education programs, advanced placement credit, distance learning, double majors, external degree program, freshman honors college, honors programs, internships, off-campus study, part-time degree program, student-designed majors, study abroad, summer session for credit. *ROTC:* Army (c). *Unusual degree programs:* 3-2 engineering with Pennsylvania State University—University Park Campus, University of Pittsburgh, Clarkson University; forestry with Duke University; occupational therapy, physical therapy, physician assistant, all at Saint Francis University.

Computers on Campus 60 computers/terminals are available on campus for general student use. Students can access the following: campus intranet, computer help desk, free student e-mail accounts, online (class) grades, billing and schedules. Campuswide network is available. 90% of college-owned or -operated housing units are wired for high-speed Internet access. Wireless service is available via entire campus.

Student Life *Housing:* on-campus residence required through senior year. *Options:* men-only, women-only. Campus housing is university owned. Freshman campus housing is guaranteed. *Activities and organizations:* drama/theater group, student-run newspaper, radio and television station, choral group, Student Activities Organization, New Theatre, Student Government Association, Best Buddies, Newspaper, national fraternities, national sororities. *Campus security:* 24-hour emergency response devices and patrols, late-night transport/escort service, controlled dormitory access. *Student services:* health clinic, personal/psychological counseling.

Athletics Member NCAA. All Division I. *Intercollegiate sports:* basketball M (s)/W (s), cross-country running M (s)/W (s), field hockey W (s), football M, golf M (s)/W (s), lacrosse W (s), soccer M (s)/W (s), softball W (s), swimming and diving M (s)/W (s), tennis M (s)/W (s), track and field M (s)/W (s), volleyball M (s)/W (s). *Intramural sports:* basketball M/W, bowling M/W, cheerleading M/W, cross-country running M/W, football M, golf M/W, lacrosse W, racquetball M/W, skiing (cross-country) M/W, skiing (downhill) M/W, soccer M/W, softball W, swimming and diving M/W, table tennis M/W, tennis M/W, track and field M/W, ultimate Frisbee M/W, volleyball M/W.

Standardized Tests *Required:* SAT or ACT (for admission).

Costs (2007–08) *Comprehensive fee:* $31,478 includes full-time tuition ($22,444), mandatory fees ($1050), and room and board ($7984). Full-time tuition and fees vary according to course load and program. Part-time tuition: $701 per credit. Part-time tuition and fees vary according to class time. *Required fees:* $333 per credit part-time, $30 per term part-time. *College room only:* $4032. Room and board charges vary according to board plan and housing facility. *Payment plan:* installment. *Waivers:* employees or children of employees.

Financial Aid Of all full-time matriculated undergraduates who enrolled in 2006, 1,270 applied for aid, 1,142 were judged to have need, 387 had their need fully met. 693 Federal Work-Study jobs (averaging $906). In 2006, 182 non-need-based awards were made. *Average percent of need met:* 76%. *Average financial aid package:* $17,459. *Average need-based loan:* $4458. *Average need-based gift aid:* $13,786. *Average non-need-based aid:* $13,211. *Average indebtedness upon graduation:* $15,600.

Applying *Options:* electronic application, deferred entrance. *Application fee:* $30. *Required:* essay or personal statement, high school transcript, 1 letter of recommendation. *Required for some:* 3 letters of recommendation, interview. *Recommended:* interview. *Application deadlines:* rolling (freshmen), rolling (transfers). *Notification:* continuous (transfers).

Freshman Application Contact Robert Beener, Associate Dean for Enrollment Management, Saint Francis University, PO Box 600, 117 Evergreen Drive, Loretto, PA 15940-0600. *Phone:* 814-472-3100. *Toll-free phone:* 800-342-5732. *E-mail:* rbeener@francis.edu.

See page 2304 for the College Close-Up.

SAINT JOSEPH'S UNIVERSITY

Philadelphia, Pennsylvania **www.sju.edu/**

- **Independent Roman Catholic (Jesuit)** comprehensive, founded 1851
- **Suburban** 65-acre campus
- **Endowment** $141.8 million
- **Coed** 4,998 undergraduate students, 83% full-time, 52% women, 48% men
- **Moderately difficult** entrance level, 62% of applicants were admitted

Founded by the Society of Jesus in 1851, Saint Joseph's University advances the professional and personal ambitions of men and women by providing a demanding and supportive experience. One of only 142 schools with a Phi Beta Kappa chapter and AACSB International accreditation, Saint Joseph's is home to 4,211 full-time undergraduates and 2,600 graduate, part-time, and doctoral students.

Undergraduates 4,161 full-time, 837 part-time. Students come from 37 states and territories, 35 other countries, 49% are from out of state, 8% African American, 3% Asian American or Pacific Islander, 3% Hispanic American, 0.2% Native American, 2% international, 2% transferred in, 59% live on campus. *Retention:* 88% of 2006 full-time freshmen returned.

Freshmen *Admission:* 8,779 applied, 5,407 admitted, 1,090 enrolled. *Average high school GPA:* 3.32. *Test scores:* SAT critical reading scores over 500: 89%; SAT math scores over 500: 90%; ACT scores over 18: 99%; SAT critical reading scores over 600: 39%; SAT math scores over 600: 43%; ACT scores over 24: 71%; SAT critical reading scores over 700: 5%; SAT math scores over 700: 5%; ACT scores over 30: 4%.

Faculty *Total:* 614, 45% full-time. *Student/faculty ratio:* 12:1.

Majors Accounting; actuarial science; biochemistry; biology/biological sciences; business administration and management; chemistry; communication/speech communication and rhetoric; computer and information sciences; criminology; economics; elementary education; English; English/language arts teacher education; environmental studies; European studies; finance; foreign language teacher education; French; French studies; German; health services/allied health/health sciences; history; hospital and health care facilities administration; humanities; information science/studies; international business/trade/commerce; international marketing; international relations and affairs; Italian; Latin; legal studies; liberal arts and sciences/liberal studies; management information systems; marketing/marketing management; mathematics; mathematics teacher education; philosophy; physics; political science and government; psychology; public administration; purchasing, procurement/acquisitions and contracts management; religious studies; science teacher education; secondary education; social sciences; social studies teacher education; sociology; Spanish; special education; special products marketing; visual and performing arts.

Academics *Calendar:* semesters. *Degrees:* certificates, associate, bachelor's, master's, doctoral, post-master's, and postbachelor's certificates. *Special study options:* academic remediation for entering students, accelerated degree program, adult/continuing education programs, advanced placement credit, cooperative education, distance learning, double majors, English as a second language, honors programs, independent study, internships, off-campus study, part-time degree program, services for LD students, student-designed majors, study abroad, summer session for credit. *ROTC:* Army (c), Navy (c), Air Force (b).

Computers on Campus 670 computers/terminals are available on campus for general student use. Students can access the following: campus intranet, computer help desk, free student e-mail accounts, online (class) grades, online (class) registration, online (class) schedules. Campuswide network is available. 100% of college-owned or -operated housing units are wired for high-speed Internet access. Wireless service is available via entire campus.

Student Life *Housing:* on-campus residence required through sophomore year. *Options:* coed, men-only, women-only, disabled students. Campus housing is university owned, leased by the school and is provided by a third party. Freshman campus housing is guaranteed. *Activities and organizations:* drama/theater group, student-run newspaper, radio station, choral group, University Student Senate, Student Union Board, Cap and Bells Dramatic Arts Society, Hand-in-Hand, Up 'til Dawn, national fraternities, national sororities. *Campus security:* 24-hour emergency response devices and patrols, late-night transport/escort service, controlled dormitory access, 24-hour shuttle/escort service, bicycle patrols. *Student services:* health clinic, personal/psychological counseling.

Athletics Member NCAA. All Division I. *Intercollegiate sports:* baseball M (s), basketball M (s)/W (s), crew M (s) (c)/W (s) (c), cross-country running M (s)/W (s), field hockey W (s), golf M (s), lacrosse M (s)/W (s), soccer M (s)/W (s), softball W (s), tennis M (s)/W (s), track and field M (s)/W (s). *Intramural sports:* basketball M/W, field hockey W (c), football M/W, golf M/W (c), ice hockey M (c), racquetball M/W, rugby M (c)/W (c), tennis M/W, ultimate Frisbee M (c)/W (c), volleyball M (c)/W (c).

Standardized Tests *Required:* SAT or ACT (for admission).

Costs (2007–08) *One-time required fee:* $210. *Comprehensive fee:* $41,535 includes full-time tuition ($30,850), mandatory fees ($135), and room and board ($10,550). Full-time tuition and fees vary according to student level. Part-time tuition: $1012 per credit. *College room only:* $6750. Room and board charges vary according to board plan and housing facility. *Payment plans:* installment, deferred payment. *Waivers:* employees or children of employees.

Financial Aid Of all full-time matriculated undergraduates who enrolled in 2007, 2,311 applied for aid, 1,832 were judged to have need, 388 had their need fully met. In 2007, 1,806 non-need-based awards were made. *Average percent of need met:* 86%. *Average financial aid package:* $17,132. *Average need-based loan:* $4080. *Average need-based gift aid:* $12,899. *Average non-need-based aid:* $9538.

Applying *Options:* electronic application, early action, deferred entrance. *Application fee:* $60. *Required:* essay or personal statement, high school transcript, 1 letter of recommendation. *Recommended:* minimum 3.0 GPA. *Application deadlines:* 2/1 (freshmen), 3/1 (transfers), 11/15 (early action). *Notification:* 3/1 (freshmen), continuous until 5/1 (transfers), 1/15 (early action).

Freshman Application Contact Saint Joseph's University, 5600 City Avenue, Philadelphia, PA 19131-1395. *Phone:* 610-660-1300. *Toll-free phone:* 888-BEAHAWK. *Fax:* 610-660-1314. *E-mail:* admit@sju.edu.

See page 2306 for the College Close-Up.

SAINT VINCENT COLLEGE

Latrobe, Pennsylvania www.stvincent.edu/

- **Independent Roman Catholic** comprehensive, founded 1846
- **Suburban** 200-acre campus with easy access to Pittsburgh
- **Endowment** $60.2 million
- **Coed** 1,705 undergraduate students, 94% full-time, 50% women, 50% men
- **Moderately difficult** entrance level, 62% of applicants were admitted

Undergraduates 1,601 full-time, 104 part-time. Students come from 24 states and territories, 15 other countries, 12% are from out of state, 3% African American, 1% Asian American or Pacific Islander, 2% Hispanic American, 0.2% Native American, 1% international, 4% transferred in, 74% live on campus. *Retention:* 84% of 2006 full-time freshmen returned.

Freshmen *Admission:* 1,855 applied, 1,146 admitted, 423 enrolled. *Average high school GPA:* 3.55. *Test scores:* SAT critical reading scores over 500: 67%; SAT math scores over 500: 72%; SAT writing scores over 500: 61%; ACT scores over 18: 93%; SAT critical reading scores over 600: 23%; SAT math scores over 600: 26%; SAT writing scores over 600: 18%; ACT scores over 24: 43%; SAT critical reading scores over 700: 4%; SAT math scores over 700: 3%; SAT writing scores over 700: 2%; ACT scores over 30: 6%.

Faculty *Total:* 203, 45% full-time, 53% with terminal degrees. *Student/faculty ratio:* 13:1.

Majors Accounting; anthropology; art history, criticism and conservation; art teacher education; biochemistry; bioinformatics; biology/biological sciences; business administration and management; business, management, and marketing related; business teacher education; chemistry; communication/speech communication and rhetoric; computer and information sciences; dramatic/theater arts; economics; engineering; English; environmental science; environmental studies; finance; fine/studio arts; French; history; international business/trade/commerce; liberal arts and sciences/liberal studies; marketing/marketing management; mathematics; music; music performance; music teacher education; occupational therapy; pharmacy; philosophy; physical therapy; physician assistant; physics; physics teacher education; political science and government; psychology; public policy analysis; religious education; sociology; Spanish; theology.

Academics *Calendar:* semesters. *Degrees:* certificates, bachelor's, master's, and postbachelor's certificates. *Special study options:* accelerated degree program, adult/continuing education programs, advanced placement credit, cooperative education, honors programs, independent study, internships, off-campus study, part-time degree program, study abroad, summer session for credit. *ROTC:* Air Force (c). *Unusual degree programs:* 3-2 engineering with University of Pittsburgh, Pennsylvania State University, Boston University, The Catholic University of America; physician assistant, physical therapy, occupational therapy with Duquesne University.

Computers on Campus Students can access the following: campus intranet, computer help desk, free student e-mail accounts, online (class) grades, online (class) registration, online (class) schedules. Campuswide network is available. 100% of college-owned or -operated housing units are wired for high-speed Internet access. Wireless service is available via classrooms, computer labs, libraries, student centers.

Student Life *Housing:* on-campus residence required for freshman year. *Options:* coed. Campus housing is university owned. Freshman applicants given priority for college housing. *Activities and organizations:* drama/theater group, student-run newspaper, radio and television station, choral group, The Company (student theatre group), Activities Programming Board, Best Buddies, Women in Business, Ultimate Frisbee. *Campus security:* 24-hour emergency response devices and patrols, late-night transport/escort service, controlled dormitory access, limited access to residence halls on weekends. *Student services:* health clinic, personal/psychological counseling.

Athletics Member NCAA. All Division III. *Intercollegiate sports:* baseball M, basketball M/W, cross-country running M/W, equestrian sports M (c)/W (c), fencing M (c)/W (c), field hockey W, golf M/W, ice hockey M (c), lacrosse M/W, soccer M/W, softball W, swimming and diving M/W, tennis M/W, volleyball W. *Intramural sports:* basketball M/W, football M/W, softball M/W, ultimate Frisbee M/W, volleyball M/W.

Standardized Tests *Required:* SAT or ACT (for admission).

Costs (2007–08) *Comprehensive fee:* $31,686 includes full-time tuition ($23,456), mandatory fees ($650), and room and board ($7580). Part-time tuition: $734 per credit. *Required fees:* $45 per term part-time. *College room only:* $3880. Room and board charges vary according to board plan and student level. *Payment plan:* installment. *Waivers:* senior citizens and employees or children of employees.

Financial Aid Of all full-time matriculated undergraduates who enrolled in 2006, 1,314 applied for aid, 1,158 were judged to have need, 261 had their need fully met. 181 Federal Work-Study jobs (averaging $1000). 578 state and other part-time jobs (averaging $975). In 2006, 283 non-need-based awards were made. *Average percent of need met:* 82%. *Average financial aid package:* $18,515. *Average need-based loan:* $3291. *Average need-based gift aid:* $13,671. *Average non-need-based aid:* $8270. *Financial aid deadline:* 5/1.

Applying *Options:* early admission, deferred entrance. *Application fee:* $25. *Required:* essay or personal statement, high school transcript, minimum 2.5 GPA. *Required for some:* interview. *Recommended:* minimum 3.2 GPA, 3 letters of recommendation, interview. *Application deadlines:* 5/1 (freshmen), 7/1 (transfers). *Notification:* continuous (freshmen), continuous (transfers).

Freshman Application Contact Mr. David A. Collins, Assistant Vice President of Admission and Financial Aid, Saint Vincent College, 300 Fraser Purchase Road, Latrobe, PA 15650. *Phone:* 724-532-5089. *Toll-free phone:* 800-782-5549. *Fax:* 724-532-5069. *E-mail:* admission@stvincent.edu.

See page 2308 for the College Close-Up.

SETON HILL UNIVERSITY

Greensburg, Pennsylvania www.setonhill.edu/

- **Independent Roman Catholic** comprehensive, founded 1883
- **Small-town** 200-acre campus with easy access to Pittsburgh
- **Endowment** $14.7 million
- **Coed** 1,615 undergraduate students, 80% full-time, 63% women, 37% men
- **Moderately difficult** entrance level, 63% of applicants were admitted

Undergraduates 1,288 full-time, 327 part-time. Students come from 36 states and territories, 20 other countries, 22% are from out of state, 8% African American, 0.5% Asian American or Pacific Islander, 2% Hispanic American, 0.4% Native American, 2% international, 4% transferred in, 61% live on campus. *Retention:* 73% of 2006 full-time freshmen returned.

Freshmen *Admission:* 1,701 applied, 1,079 admitted, 329 enrolled. *Average high school GPA:* 3.33. *Test scores:* SAT critical reading scores over 500: 49%;

SAT math scores over 500: 55%; ACT scores over 18: 73%; SAT critical reading scores over 600: 14%; SAT math scores over 600: 17%; ACT scores over 24: 15%; SAT critical reading scores over 700: 2%; SAT math scores over 700: 1%; ACT scores over 30: 1%.

Faculty *Total:* 205, 34% full-time, 56% with terminal degrees. *Student/faculty ratio:* 14:1.

Majors Accounting; acting; actuarial science; art history, criticism and conservation; arts management; art therapy; biochemistry; biology/biological sciences; biology teacher education; business administration and management; business/managerial economics; ceramic arts and ceramics; chemistry; chemistry teacher education; child care and support services management; child development; clinical laboratory science/medical technology; commercial and advertising art; communication/speech communication and rhetoric; community health services counseling; community psychology; computer science; creative writing; criminal justice/law enforcement administration; dietetics; dramatic/theater arts; dramatic/theater arts and stagecraft related; drawing; early childhood education; economics; educational/instructional media design; elementary education; engineering; English; English/language arts teacher education; entrepreneurship; family and consumer sciences/home economics teacher education; family and consumer sciences/human sciences; finance; fine/studio arts; foreign language teacher education; forensic science and technology; French language teacher education; general studies; history; hospitality administration; human resources management; human services; international business/trade/commerce; international relations and affairs; journalism; kindergarten/preschool education; management information systems; marketing/marketing management; marriage and family therapy/counseling; mathematics; mathematics related; mathematics teacher education; metal and jewelry arts; music; music performance; music teacher education; music theory and composition; nursing (registered nurse training); painting; physician assistant; physics; piano and organ; political science and government; pre-dentistry studies; pre-law studies; pre-medical studies; pre-veterinary studies; printmaking; psychology; religious/sacred music; religious studies; sales, distribution and marketing; sculpture; social studies teacher education; social work; sociology; Spanish; Spanish language teacher education; special education; theater design and technology; theater/theater arts management; violin, viola, guitar and other stringed instruments; voice and opera; wind/percussion instruments.

Academics *Calendar:* semesters. *Degrees:* certificates, bachelor's, master's, post-master's, and postbachelor's certificates. *Special study options:* academic remediation for entering students, accelerated degree program, adult/continuing education programs, advanced placement credit, distance learning, double majors, English as a second language, honors programs, independent study, internships, off-campus study, part-time degree program, student-designed majors, study abroad, summer session for credit. *ROTC:* Army (c), Air Force (c). *Unusual degree programs:* 3-2 engineering with University of Pittsburgh, Pennsylvania State University—University Park Campus, Georgia Institute of Technology; nursing with Catholic University of America; physician assistant-Seton Hill University.

Computers on Campus 300 computers/terminals are available on campus for general student use. Students can access the following: campus intranet, computer help desk, free student e-mail accounts, online (class) grades, online (class) registration, online (class) schedules. Campuswide network is available. 100% of college-owned or -operated housing units are wired for high-speed Internet access. Wireless service is available via classrooms, computer centers, computer labs, dorm rooms, learning centers, libraries, student centers.

Student Life *Housing options:* coed, men-only, women-only. Campus housing is university owned. Freshman campus housing is guaranteed. *Activities and organizations:* drama/theater group, student-run newspaper, choral group, marching band, Intercultural Student Organization, Biology/Environmental Club, Association of Black Collegians, Chemistry Club, Pennsylvania Student Education Association. *Campus security:* 24-hour emergency response devices and patrols, late-night transport/escort service, controlled dormitory access, student personnel at entrances during evening hours, 15-hour overnight patrols by trained police officers. *Student services:* health clinic, personal/psychological counseling.

Athletics Member NCAA except baseball (Division II), men's and women's basketball (Division II), men's and women's cross-country running (Division II), men's and women's equestrian sports (Division II), field hockey (Division II), men's and women's soccer (Division II), softball (Division II), men's and women's tennis (Division II), men's and women's track and field (Division II), volleyball (Division II), wrestling (Division II) *Intercollegiate sports:* baseball M (s), basketball M (s)/W (s), cross-country running M (s)/W (s), equestrian sports M (s)/W (s), field hockey W (s), football M (s), golf M (s)/W (s), lacrosse M (s)/W (s), soccer M (s)/W (s), softball W (s), tennis M (s)/W (s), track and field M (s)/W (s), volleyball W (s), wrestling M. *Intramural sports:* basketball W, skiing (cross-country) M (c)/W (c), skiing (downhill) M (c)/W (c).

Standardized Tests *Recommended:* SAT or ACT (for admission).

Costs (2007–08) *Comprehensive fee:* $32,746 includes full-time tuition ($24,806), mandatory fees ($200), and room and board ($7740). Part-time tuition: $660 per credit. Part-time tuition and fees vary according to course load. *Required fees:* $100 per term part-time. *Room and board:* Room and board charges vary according to board plan and housing facility. *Payment plans:* installment, deferred payment. *Waivers:* employees or children of employees.

Financial Aid Of all full-time matriculated undergraduates who enrolled in 2007, 1,139 applied for aid, 1,080 were judged to have need, 227 had their need fully met. 346 Federal Work-Study jobs (averaging $1236). 211 state and other part-time jobs (averaging $1500). In 2007, 92 non-need-based awards were made. *Average percent of need met:* 76%. *Average financial aid package:* $20,622. *Average need-based loan:* $5245. *Average need-based gift aid:* $15,597. *Average non-need-based aid:* $14,640. *Average indebtedness upon graduation:* $26,872.

Applying *Options:* electronic application, early admission, deferred entrance. *Application fee:* $35. *Required:* essay or personal statement, high school transcript, minimum 2.0 GPA, letters of recommendation, portfolio for art program, audition for music and theater programs, separate application process for physician assistant program. *Recommended:* interview. *Application deadlines:* 8/15 (freshmen), rolling (transfers). *Notification:* continuous (freshmen), continuous (transfers).

Freshman Application Contact Ms. Sherri Bett, Director of Admissions, Seton Hill University, Seton Hill Drive, Greensburg, PA 15601. *Phone:* 724-838-4255. *Toll-free phone:* 800-826-6234. *Fax:* 724-830-1294. *E-mail:* admit@setonhill.edu.

See page 2310 for the College Close-Up.

SHIPPENSBURG UNIVERSITY OF PENNSYLVANIA

Shippensburg, Pennsylvania **www.ship.edu/**

- **State-supported** comprehensive, founded 1871, part of Pennsylvania State System of Higher Education
- **Rural** 200-acre campus
- **Endowment** $28.2 million
- **Coed** 6,621 undergraduate students, 95% full-time, 53% women, 47% men
- **Moderately difficult** entrance level, 75% of applicants were admitted

Recognized for its academic excellence, Shippensburg University has a national reputation for providing students with opportunities for student-faculty research, volunteer community service projects, and internships. Talented and dedicated faculty members offer a personalized education, and recent renovations of several academic buildings further complement the high quality of academics.

Undergraduates 6,307 full-time, 314 part-time. Students come from 21 states and territories, 14 other countries, 5% are from out of state, 6% African American, 1% Asian American or Pacific Islander, 2% Hispanic American, 0.3% Native American, 0.2% international, 6% transferred in, 40% live on campus. *Retention:* 74% of 2006 full-time freshmen returned.

Freshmen *Admission:* 6,164 applied, 4,648 admitted, 1,726 enrolled. *Average high school GPA:* 3.2. *Test scores:* SAT critical reading scores over 500: 49%; SAT math scores over 500: 51%; ACT scores over 18: 76%; SAT critical reading scores over 600: 10%; SAT math scores over 600: 14%; ACT scores over 24: 15%; SAT critical reading scores over 700: 1%; SAT math scores over 700: 1%.

Faculty *Total:* 382, 86% full-time, 81% with terminal degrees. *Student/faculty ratio:* 19:1.

Majors Accounting; art; biology/biological sciences; business administration and management; business/commerce; chemistry; computer and information sciences; computer systems analysis; criminal justice/safety; economics; elementary education; English; environmental studies; finance; French; geography; geology/earth science; health/health care administration; history; journalism; kinesiology and exercise science; management science; marketing/marketing management; mathematics; multi-/interdisciplinary studies related; physics; political science and government; psychology; public administration; social work; sociology; Spanish; speech and rhetoric.

Academics *Calendar:* semesters. *Degrees:* certificates, bachelor's, master's, post-master's, and postbachelor's certificates. *Special study options:* academic remediation for entering students, accelerated degree program, advanced placement credit, cooperative education, distance learning, double majors, honors programs, independent study, internships, off-campus study, part-time degree program, services for LD students, study abroad, summer session for credit. *ROTC:* Army (b). *Unusual degree programs:* 3-2 engineering with Pennsylvania State University—University Park and Harrisburg Campus, University of Maryland College Park.

Computers on Campus 800 computers/terminals are available on campus for general student use. Students can access the following: campus intranet, free student e-mail accounts, online (class) grades, online (class) registration, online (class) schedules, personal Web pages. Campuswide network is available. 100% of college-owned or -operated housing units are wired for high-speed Internet access. Wireless service is available via classrooms, computer centers, computer labs, learning centers, libraries, student centers.

Student Life *Housing:* on-campus residence required for freshman year. *Options:* coed, women-only. Campus housing is university owned and leased by the school. Freshman campus housing is guaranteed. *Activities and organizations:* drama/theater group, student-run newspaper, radio and television station, choral group, marching band, Band, Christian Fellowship, Residence Hall Association, United Campus Ministry, African-American Organization, national fraternities, national sororities. *Campus security:* 24-hour emergency response devices and patrols, student patrols, late-night transport/escort service, controlled dormitory access, surveillance cameras in certain parking lots and buildings, foot, vehicular and bicycle patrols by security officers. *Student services:* health clinic, personal/psychological counseling, women's center.

Athletics Member NCAA. All Division II. *Intercollegiate sports:* baseball M (s), basketball M (s)/W (s), cross-country running M (s)/W (s), field hockey W (s), football M (s), lacrosse W (s), soccer M (s)/W (s), softball W (s), swimming and diving M (s)/W (s), tennis W (s), track and field M (s)/W (s), volleyball W (s), wrestling M (s). *Intramural sports:* basketball M/W, bowling M (c)/W (c), ice hockey M (c), lacrosse M (c), racquetball M/W, rugby M (c)/W (c), soccer M/W, softball M/W, swimming and diving W, tennis M/W, ultimate Frisbee M/W, volleyball W, water polo M (c)/W (c).

Standardized Tests *Required:* SAT or ACT (for admission).

Costs (2007–08) *Tuition:* state resident $5178 full-time, $216 per credit hour part-time; nonresident $12,944 full-time, $539 per credit hour part-time. *Required fees:* $1671 full-time, $165 per course part-time, $43 per term part-time. *Room and board:* $6272; room only: $3540. Room and board charges vary according to board plan and housing facility. *Payment plan:* installment. *Waivers:* senior citizens and employees or children of employees.

Financial Aid Of all full-time matriculated undergraduates who enrolled in 2007, 4,307 applied for aid, 2,864 were judged to have need, 654 had their need fully met. 137 Federal Work-Study jobs (averaging $1821). 264 state and other part-time jobs (averaging $2028). In 2007, 582 non-need-based awards were made. *Average percent of need met:* 73%. *Average financial aid package:* $7211. *Average need-based loan:* $3796. *Average need-based gift aid:* $4765. *Average non-need-based aid:* $3356. *Average indebtedness upon graduation:* $20,256.

Applying *Options:* electronic application, early admission, early action, deferred entrance. *Application fee:* $30. *Required:* high school transcript. *Required for some:* interview. *Recommended:* essay or personal statement, letters of recommendation, class rank. *Application deadlines:* rolling (freshmen), rolling (transfers). *Notification:* continuous (freshmen), continuous (transfers).

Freshman Application Contact Dr. Thomas Speakman, Dean of Enrollment Services, Shippensburg University of Pennsylvania, 1871 Old Main Drive, Shippensburg, PA 17257-2299. *Phone:* 717-477-1231. *Toll-free phone:* 800-822-8028. *Fax:* 717-477-4016. *E-mail:* admiss@ship.edu.

See page 2312 for the College Close-Up.

SLIPPERY ROCK UNIVERSITY OF PENNSYLVANIA

Slippery Rock, Pennsylvania — www.sru.edu/

- **State-supported** comprehensive, founded 1889, part of Pennsylvania State System of Higher Education
- **Rural** 600-acre campus with easy access to Pittsburgh
- **Endowment** $17.9 million
- **Coed** 7,585 undergraduate students, 93% full-time, 56% women, 44% men
- **Moderately difficult** entrance level, 70% of applicants were admitted

Slippery Rock University of Pennsylvania (SRU) offers a "Rock Solid Education." Some of the areas of distinction include communication and information technology; environmental sciences and studies; health, wellness, and recreation; teacher education; and fine and performing arts. Students become leaders, think globally, and live and learn on this midsized premier residential campus. Located in a college town, SRU is an affordable choice and is located just an hour north of the city of Pittsburgh. The campus and its surrounding area are beautiful, offering a mix of modern and stately architecture, blending tradition and technology.

Undergraduates 7,033 full-time, 552 part-time. Students come from 32 states and territories, 38 other countries, 7% are from out of state, 5% African American, 0.6% Asian American or Pacific Islander, 1% Hispanic American, 0.2% Native American, 1% international, 8% transferred in, 33% live on campus. *Retention:* 78% of 2006 full-time freshmen returned.

Freshmen *Admission:* 4,736 applied, 3,324 admitted, 1,508 enrolled. *Average high school GPA:* 3.26. *Test scores:* SAT critical reading scores over 500: 46%; SAT math scores over 500: 56%; ACT scores over 18: 89%; SAT critical reading scores over 600: 7%; SAT math scores over 600: 11%; ACT scores over 24: 17%; SAT critical reading scores over 700: 1%; ACT scores over 30: 1%.

Faculty *Total:* 366, 90% full-time, 80% with terminal degrees. *Student/faculty ratio:* 20:1.

Majors Adapted physical education; anthropology; art; athletic training; biology/biological sciences; business administration and management; chemistry; clinical/medical laboratory technology; clinical/medical social work; communication/speech communication and rhetoric; computer and information sciences; counselor education/school counseling and guidance; cytotechnology; dance; dramatic/theater arts; economics; elementary education; English; environmental science; environmental studies; French; geography; geology/earth science; health and physical education; history; information technology; kinesiology and exercise science; mathematics; medical informatics; modern languages; music; music performance; music therapy; natural resources/conservation; nursing (registered nurse training); occupational safety and health technology; parks, recreation and leisure facilities management; philosophy; physical education teaching and coaching; physics; political science and government; psychology; public health; public relations, advertising, and applied communication related; science, technology and society; secondary education; social work; sociology; Spanish; special education; sport and fitness administration/management.

Academics *Calendar:* semesters. *Degrees:* bachelor's, master's, doctoral, and postbachelor's certificates. *Special study options:* academic remediation for entering students, adult/continuing education programs, advanced placement credit, distance learning, double majors, honors programs, independent study, internships, off-campus study, part-time degree program, services for LD students, study abroad, summer session for credit. *ROTC:* Army (b). *Unusual degree programs:* 3-2 engineering with Pennsylvania State University, University Park Campus.

Computers on Campus 1,253 computers/terminals are available on campus for general student use. Students can access the following: computer help desk, free student e-mail accounts, online (class) grades, online (class) registration, online (class) schedules. Campuswide network is available. 100% of college-owned or -operated housing units are wired for high-speed Internet access.

Student Life *Housing:* on-campus residence required for freshman year. *Options:* coed, women-only, disabled students. Campus housing is university owned. Freshman campus housing is guaranteed. *Activities and organizations:* drama/theater group, student-run newspaper, radio and television station, choral group, marching band, Association of Residence Hall Students, University Program Board, Student Union for Minority Affairs, Student Government Association, national fraternities, national sororities. *Campus security:* 24-hour emergency response devices and patrols, late-night transport/escort service, controlled dormitory access. *Student services:* health clinic, personal/psychological counseling, women's center, legal services.

Athletics Member NCAA. All Division II. *Intercollegiate sports:* baseball M (s), basketball M (s)/W (s), cheerleading M/W, cross-country running M (s)/W (s), field hockey W (s), football M (s), soccer M (s)/W (s), softball W (s), tennis W (s), track and field M (s)/W (s), volleyball W (s), water polo W. *Intramural sports:* basketball M/W, cross-country running M/W, equestrian sports W (c), football M/W, golf M/W, ice hockey M (c)/W (c), lacrosse M (c)/W (c), racquetball M (c)/W (c), rugby M (c)/W (c), soccer M/W, softball M/W, swimming and diving W, tennis M/W, track and field M/W, ultimate Frisbee M/W, volleyball M (c)/W, water polo W, weight lifting M/W, wrestling M/W.

Standardized Tests *Required:* SAT or ACT (for admission).

Costs (2007–08) *Tuition:* state resident $5178 full-time, $216 per credit hour part-time; nonresident $7767 full-time, $539 per credit hour part-time. Full-time tuition and fees vary according to course load and degree level. Part-time tuition and fees vary according to course load and degree level. *Required fees:* $1493 full-time, $67 per credit hour part-time, $43 per term part-time. *Room and board:* $7862; room only: $5618. Room and board charges vary according to board plan, housing facility, and location. *Payment plan:* installment. *Waivers:* minority students, senior citizens, and employees or children of employees.

Financial Aid Of all full-time matriculated undergraduates who enrolled in 2007, 6,296 applied for aid, 4,709 were judged to have need, 2,102 had their need fully met. In 2007, 1,262 non-need-based awards were made. *Average percent of need met:* 71%. *Average financial aid package:* $8094. *Average need-based loan:* $3813. *Average need-based gift aid:* $3346. *Average non-need-based aid:* $5993. *Average indebtedness upon graduation:* $21,680.

Applying *Options:* electronic application, deferred entrance. *Application fee:* $30. *Required:* high school transcript, minimum 2.0 GPA. *Notification:* 9/1 (freshmen), continuous (transfers).

Freshman Application Contact Slippery Rock University of Pennsylvania, 1 Morrow Way, 146 North Hall, Slippery Rock, PA 16057. *Phone:* 724-738-2015. *Toll-free phone:* 800-SRU-9111. *Fax:* 724-738-2913. *E-mail:* asktherock@sru.edu.

SUSQUEHANNA UNIVERSITY

Selinsgrove, Pennsylvania **www.susqu.edu/**

- **Independent** 4-year, founded 1858, affiliated with Evangelical Lutheran Church in America
- **Suburban** 220-acre campus with easy access to Harrisburg
- **Endowment** $127.9 million
- **Coed** 2,039 undergraduate students, 97% full-time, 54% women, 46% men
- **Moderately difficult** entrance level, 86% of applicants were admitted

Undergraduates 1,985 full-time, 54 part-time. Students come from 31 states and territories, 10 other countries, 43% are from out of state, 3% African American, 2% Asian American or Pacific Islander, 2% Hispanic American, 0.1% Native American, 1% international, 1% transferred in, 77% live on campus. *Retention:* 84% of 2006 full-time freshmen returned.

Freshmen *Admission:* 2,373 applied, 2,042 admitted, 593 enrolled. *Test scores:* SAT critical reading scores over 500: 83%; SAT math scores over 500: 87%; SAT critical reading scores over 600: 35%; SAT math scores over 600: 35%; SAT critical reading scores over 700: 4%; SAT math scores over 700: 4%.

Faculty *Total:* 189, 64% full-time, 68% with terminal degrees. *Student/faculty ratio:* 14:1.

Majors Accounting; art; art history, criticism and conservation; biochemistry; biology/biological sciences; broadcast journalism; business administration and management; business/managerial economics; chemistry; communication/speech communication and rhetoric; computer science; creative writing; dramatic/theater arts; ecology; economics; elementary education; English; entrepreneurship; finance; French; geology/earth science; German; graphic design; history; human resources management; information science/studies; international relations and affairs; journalism; kindergarten/preschool education; marketing/marketing management; mass communication/media; mathematics; music; music teacher education; philosophy; physics; piano and organ; political science and government; pre-dentistry studies; pre-law studies; pre-medical studies; pre-veterinary studies; psychology; public relations/image management; radio and television; religious/sacred music; religious studies; secondary education; sociology; Spanish; speech and rhetoric; violin, viola, guitar and other stringed instruments; voice and opera; wind/percussion instruments.

Academics *Calendar:* semesters. *Degrees:* bachelor's (also offers evening associate degree program limited to local adult students). *Special study options:* accelerated degree program, adult/continuing education programs, advanced placement credit, distance learning, double majors, honors programs, independent study, internships, off-campus study, part-time degree program, student-designed majors, study abroad, summer session for credit. *ROTC:* Army (c). *Unusual degree programs:* 3-2 forestry with Duke University; environmental management with Duke University, allied health programs with Thomas Jefferson University, dentistry with Temple University.

Computers on Campus 440 computers/terminals are available on campus for general student use. Students can access the following: computer help desk, free student e-mail accounts, online (class) grades, online (class) registration, online (class) schedules, class listings and assignments, online voting booth. Campuswide network is available. 100% of college-owned or -operated housing units are wired for high-speed Internet access. Wireless service is available via entire campus.

Student Life *Housing:* on-campus residence required through junior year. *Options:* coed. Campus housing is university owned. Freshman campus housing is guaranteed. *Activities and organizations:* drama/theater group, student-run newspaper, radio station, choral group, Student Government Association, community service organizations, music performance groups, theater performance groups, intramurals and outdoor recreation, national fraternities, national sororities. *Campus security:* 24-hour patrols, late-night transport/escort service, controlled dormitory access. *Student services:* health clinic, personal/psychological counseling, women's center.

Athletics Member NCAA. All Division III. *Intercollegiate sports:* baseball M, basketball M/W, cheerleading M (c)/W (c), crew M (c)/W (c), cross-country running M/W, equestrian sports M (c)/W (c), field hockey W, football M, golf M/W, lacrosse M/W, rugby M (c)/W (c), soccer M/W, softball W, swimming and diving M/W, tennis M/W, track and field M/W, volleyball M (c)/W. *Intramural sports:* basketball M/W, bowling M/W, football M/W, racquetball M/W, soccer M/W, softball M/W, table tennis M/W, tennis M/W, ultimate Frisbee M/W, volleyball M/W.

Standardized Tests *Recommended:* SAT or ACT (for admission).

Costs (2008–09) *Comprehensive fee:* $39,480 includes full-time tuition ($30,700), mandatory fees ($380), and room and board ($8400). *College room only:* $4400.

Financial Aid Of all full-time matriculated undergraduates who enrolled in 2004, 1,429 applied for aid, 1,230 were judged to have need, 294 had their need fully met. 905 Federal Work-Study jobs (averaging $1574). 64 state and other part-time jobs (averaging $3816). In 2004, 550 non-need-based awards were made. *Average percent of need met:* 83%. *Average financial aid package:* $17,743. *Average need-based loan:* $3737. *Average need-based gift aid:* $13,961. *Average non-need-based aid:* $11,878. *Average indebtedness upon graduation:* $18,119.

Applying *Options:* electronic application, early admission, early decision, deferred entrance. *Application fee:* $35. *Required:* essay or personal statement, high school transcript, minimum 2.5 GPA, 1 letter of recommendation. *Required for some:* writing portfolio, auditions for music programs. *Recommended:* minimum 3.0 GPA, interview. *Application deadlines:* 3/1 (freshmen), 7/1 (transfers). *Early decision deadline:* 11/15 (for plan 1), 1/1 (for plan 2). *Notification:* 1/15 (freshmen), 8/1 (transfers), 12/1 (early decision plan 1), 1/15 (early decision plan 2).

Freshman Application Contact Mr. Chris Markle, Director of Admissions, Susquehanna University, 514 University Avenue, Selinsgrove, PA 17870-1040. *Phone:* 570-372-4260. *Toll-free phone:* 800-326-9672. *Fax:* 570-372-2722. *E-mail:* suadmiss@susqu.edu.

See page 2314 for the College Close-Up.

SWARTHMORE COLLEGE

Swarthmore, Pennsylvania **www.swarthmore.edu/**

- **Independent** 4-year, founded 1864
- **Suburban** 357-acre campus with easy access to Philadelphia
- **Endowment** $1.4 billion
- **Coed** 1,491 undergraduate students, 100% full-time, 52% women, 48% men
- **Most difficult** entrance level, 18% of applicants were admitted

Consistently ranked among the top three small liberal arts colleges, Swarthmore is a coeducational institution located 11 miles southwest of Philadelphia. It has a student-faculty ratio of 8:1, an engineering department, and need-blind admission. More than 33 percent of the students identify themselves as members of minority groups, and 8 percent are international students.

Undergraduates 1,485 full-time, 6 part-time. Students come from 48 states and territories, 35 other countries, 87% are from out of state, 8% African American, 17% Asian American or Pacific Islander, 10% Hispanic American, 0.9% Native American, 7% international, 0.9% transferred in, 95% live on campus. *Retention:* 97% of 2006 full-time freshmen returned.

Freshmen *Admission:* 5,242 applied, 930 admitted, 365 enrolled. *Test scores:* SAT critical reading scores over 500: 100%; SAT math scores over 500: 99%; SAT writing scores over 500: 100%; ACT scores over 18: 100%; SAT critical reading scores over 600: 94%; SAT math scores over 600: 94%; SAT writing scores over 600: 91%; ACT scores over 24: 97%; SAT critical reading scores over 700: 71%; SAT math scores over 700: 64%; SAT writing scores over 700: 64%; ACT scores over 30: 62%.

Faculty *Total:* 203, 83% full-time, 95% with terminal degrees. *Student/faculty ratio:* 8:1.

Majors Ancient/classical Greek; ancient studies; anthropology; art history, criticism and conservation; Asian studies; astronomy; astrophysics; biochemistry; biology/biological sciences; chemical physics; chemistry; Chinese; classics and languages, literatures and linguistics; comparative literature; computer and information sciences; dance; dramatic/theater arts; economics; education related; engineering; English; film/video and photographic arts related; fine/studio arts; French; German; German studies; history; Latin; linguistics; mathematics; medieval and Renaissance studies; music; philosophy; physics; physiological psychology/psychobiology; political science and government; psychology; religious studies; Russian; social sciences related; sociology; Spanish.

Academics *Calendar:* semesters. *Degree:* bachelor's. *Special study options:* advanced placement credit, double majors, honors programs, independent study, internships, off-campus study, services for LD students, student-designed majors, study abroad. *ROTC:* Army (c), Air Force (c).

Computers on Campus 206 computers/terminals and 3,300 ports are available on campus for general student use. Students can access the following: campus intranet, computer help desk, free student e-mail accounts, online (class) grades, online (class) registration, online (class) schedules. Campuswide network is available. 100% of college-owned or -operated housing units are wired for high-speed Internet access. Wireless service is available via entire campus.

Student Life *Housing:* on-campus residence required for freshman year. *Options:* coed, men-only, women-only. Campus housing is university owned. Freshman campus housing is guaranteed. *Activities and organizations:* drama/theater group, student-run newspaper, radio station, choral group, community service and activist groups, club sports and intramurals, music/acapella groups, social/cultural clubs, political and debate clubs, national fraternities. *Campus security:* 24-hour emergency response devices and patrols, student patrols, late-night transport/escort service. *Student services:* health clinic, personal/psychological counseling, women's center.

Athletics Member NCAA. All Division III. *Intercollegiate sports:* badminton M (c)/W, baseball M, basketball M/W, cross-country running M/W, fencing M (c)/W (c), field hockey W, golf M, ice hockey M (c)/W (c), lacrosse M/W, rugby M (c)/W (c), soccer M/W, softball W, squash M (c)/W (c), swimming and diving M/W, tennis M/W, track and field M/W, ultimate Frisbee M (c)/W (c), volleyball M (c)/W. *Intramural sports:* basketball M/W, football M/W, soccer M/W, softball M/W, table tennis M/W, tennis M/W, volleyball M/W.

Standardized Tests *Required:* SAT and SAT Subject Tests or ACT (for admission).

Costs (2007–08) *Tuition:* $34,564 full-time. *Required fees:* $320 full-time. *Room only:* $5544.

Financial Aid Of all full-time matriculated undergraduates who enrolled in 2006, 793 applied for aid, 719 were judged to have need, 719 had their need fully met. 632 Federal Work-Study jobs (averaging $1574). In 2006, 11 non-need-based awards were made. *Average percent of need met:* 100%. *Average financial aid package:* $30,369. *Average need-based loan:* $3121. *Average need-based gift aid:* $26,411. *Average non-need-based aid:* $32,912. *Average indebtedness upon graduation:* $13,404. *Financial aid deadline:* 2/15.

Applying *Options:* electronic application, early admission, early decision, deferred entrance. *Application fee:* $60. *Required:* essay or personal statement, high school transcript, 3 letters of recommendation. *Recommended:* interview. *Application deadlines:* 1/2 (freshmen), 4/1 (transfers). *Early decision deadline:* 11/15 (for plan 1), 1/2 (for plan 2). *Notification:* 4/1 (freshmen), 5/15 (transfers), 12/15 (early decision plan 1), 2/15 (early decision plan 2).

Freshman Application Contact Mr. Jim Bock, Dean of Admissions and Financial Aid, Swarthmore College, Swarthmore, PA 19081. *Phone:* 610-328-8300. *Toll-free phone:* 800-667-3110. *Fax:* 610-328-8580. *E-mail:* admissions@swarthmore.edu.

TALMUDICAL YESHIVA OF PHILADELPHIA

Philadelphia, Pennsylvania

Freshman Application Contact Rabbi Shmuel Kamenetsky, Co-Dean, Talmudical Yeshiva of Philadelphia, 6063 Drexel Road, Philadelphia, PA 19131-1296. *Phone:* 215-473-1212.

TEMPLE UNIVERSITY

Philadelphia, Pennsylvania www.temple.edu/

- **State-related** university, founded 1884
- **Urban** 110-acre campus
- **Endowment** $236.7 million
- **Coed** 25,505 undergraduate students, 87% full-time, 55% women, 45% men
- 63% of applicants were admitted

Temple University is a major teaching and research university that is 1½ miles from dynamic Center City Philadelphia. With 125 undergraduate majors, 110 master's programs, and fifty doctoral degrees, Temple has what students need for success. In addition, life on campus is booming: more than 10,000 students live on and around Temple's main campus.

Undergraduates 22,306 full-time, 3,199 part-time. Students come from 49 states and territories, 94 other countries, 22% are from out of state, 17% African American, 10% Asian American or Pacific Islander, 3% Hispanic American, 0.3% Native American, 3% international, 10% transferred in, 20% live on campus. *Retention:* 85% of 2006 full-time freshmen returned.

Freshmen *Admission:* 16,659 applied, 10,559 admitted, 4,089 enrolled. *Average high school GPA:* 3.35. *Test scores:* SAT critical reading scores over 500: 71%; SAT math scores over 500: 75%; SAT writing scores over 500: 69%; ACT scores over 18: 91%; SAT critical reading scores over 600: 23%; SAT math scores over 600: 25%; SAT writing scores over 600: 20%; ACT scores over 24: 37%; SAT critical reading scores over 700: 3%; SAT math scores over 700: 3%; SAT writing scores over 700: 2%; ACT scores over 30: 4%.

Faculty *Total:* 2,753, 47% full-time, 33% with terminal degrees. *Student/faculty ratio:* 17:1.

Majors Accounting; acting; actuarial science; advertising; African-American/Black studies; American studies; anthropology; applied horticulture; architecture; art; art history, criticism and conservation; art teacher education; Asian studies; audiology and speech-language pathology; biochemistry; biology/biological sciences; biophysics; business administration and management; business/commerce; business teacher education; ceramic arts and ceramics; chemistry; city/urban, community and regional planning; civil engineering; civil engineering technology; classics and languages, literatures and linguistics; computer and information sciences; criminal justice/safety; dance; dramatic/theater arts; economics; electrical, electronics and communications engineering; elementary education; engineering technology; English; English/language arts teacher education; entrepreneurship; environmental engineering technology; environmental studies; fiber, textile and weaving arts; film/cinema studies; finance; foreign language teacher education; French; general studies; geography; geology/earth science; German; graphic design; health information/medical records administration; Hebrew; history; horticultural science; hospitality administration; information technology; insurance; international business/trade/commerce; Italian; jazz/jazz studies; Jewish/Judaic studies; journalism; labor and industrial relations; landscape architecture; Latin American studies; liberal arts and sciences/liberal studies; linguistics; management information systems; marketing/marketing management; mathematics; mathematics teacher education; mechanical engineering; metal and jewelry arts; music; music history, literature, and theory; music pedagogy; music performance; music teacher education; music theory and composition; music therapy; nursing (registered nurse training); organizational communication; painting; parks, recreation and leisure; philosophy; photography; physical education teaching and coaching; physics; political science and government; printmaking; psychology; public health education and promotion; public relations/image management; real estate; religious studies; Russian; science teacher education; sculpture; social studies teacher education; social work; sociology; Spanish; speech and rhetoric; therapeutic recreation; trade and industrial teacher education; voice and opera; wind/percussion instruments; women's studies.

Academics *Calendar:* semesters. *Degrees:* certificates, diplomas, associate, bachelor's, master's, doctoral, first professional, post-master's, postbachelor's, and first professional certificates. *Special study options:* academic remediation for entering students, adult/continuing education programs, advanced placement credit, cooperative education, distance learning, double majors, English as a second language, honors programs, independent study, internships, off-campus study, part-time degree program, services for LD students, student-designed majors, study abroad, summer session for credit. *ROTC:* Army (b), Navy (c), Air Force (c). *Unusual degree programs:* 3-2 physical therapy, pharmacy.

Computers on Campus 3,565 computers/terminals are available on campus for general student use. Students can access the following: computer help desk, free student e-mail accounts, online (class) grades, online (class) registration, online (class) schedules, student accounts, library, Web hosting. Campuswide network is available. Wireless service is available via entire campus.

Student Life *Housing options:* coed. Campus housing is university owned, leased by the school and is provided by a third party. Freshman campus housing is guaranteed. *Activities and organizations:* drama/theater group, student-run newspaper, radio station, choral group, marching band, Black Student Union, American Medical Student Association, Campus Crusade for Christ, Indian Students Association, Student Organization for Caribbean Awareness, national fraternities, national sororities. *Campus security:* 24-hour emergency response devices and patrols, late-night transport/escort service, controlled dormitory access. *Student services:* health clinic, personal/psychological counseling, legal services.

Athletics Member NCAA. All Division I except football (Division I-A). *Intercollegiate sports:* baseball M (s); basketball M (s)/W (s), cheerleading M (s)/W (s), crew M (s)/W (s), cross-country running M/W, fencing W (s), field hockey W (s), golf M (s), gymnastics M (s)/W (s), lacrosse W (s), soccer M (s)/W (s), softball W (s), tennis M (s)/W (s), track and field M (s)/W (s), volleyball W (s). *Intramural sports:* badminton M (c)/W (c), basketball M/W, equestrian sports M (c)/W (c), football M/W, lacrosse M (c)/W (c), racquetball M/W, rugby M (c)/W (c), soccer M, softball M, swimming and diving M (c)/W (c), table tennis M/W, tennis M/W, volleyball M/W, water polo M/W.

Standardized Tests *Required:* SAT or ACT (for admission).

Costs (2007–08) *Tuition:* state resident $10,252 full-time, $397 per credit part-time; nonresident $18,770 full-time, $668 per credit part-time. Full-time tuition and fees vary according to course load, program, and reciprocity agreements. Part-time tuition and fees vary according to course load, program, and reciprocity agreements. *Required fees:* $550 full-time, $140 per term part-time. *Room and board:* $8518; room only: $5604. Room and board charges vary according to board plan and housing facility. *Payment plan:* installment. *Waivers:* employees or children of employees.

Financial Aid Of all full-time matriculated undergraduates who enrolled in 2005, 18,741 applied for aid, 14,277 were judged to have need, 4,956 had their need fully met. In 2005, 4,437 non-need-based awards were made. *Average percent of need met:* 89%. *Average financial aid package:* $13,308. *Average need-based loan:* $3500. *Average need-based gift aid:* $4746. *Average non-need-based aid:* $4603. *Average indebtedness upon graduation:* $27,355.

Applying *Options:* electronic application, early admission, deferred entrance. *Application fee:* $50. *Required:* essay or personal statement, high school transcript. *Required for some:* interview, portfolio, audition. *Application deadlines:* 4/1 (freshmen), 6/15 (transfers). *Notification:* continuous (freshmen), continuous (transfers).

Freshman Application Contact Dr. Timm Rinehart, Associate Vice President Enrollment Management, Temple University, 1801 North Broad Street, Philadelphia, PA 19122-6096. *Phone:* 215-204-8556. *Toll-free phone:* 888-340-2222. *Fax:* 215-204-5694. *E-mail:* tuadm@temple.edu.

See page 2316 for the College Close-Up.

THIEL COLLEGE

Greenville, Pennsylvania **www.thiel.edu/**

- **Independent** 4-year, founded 1866, affiliated with Evangelical Lutheran Church in America
- **Rural** 135-acre campus with easy access to Cleveland and Pittsburgh
- **Endowment** $27.3 million
- **Coed** 1,219 undergraduate students, 94% full-time, 46% women, 54% men
- **Moderately difficult** entrance level, 75% of applicants were admitted

Undergraduates 1,144 full-time, 75 part-time. Students come from 21 states and territories, 10 other countries, 28% are from out of state, 6% African American, 0.8% Asian American or Pacific Islander, 0.9% Hispanic American, 0.3% Native American, 4% international, 4% transferred in, 82% live on campus. *Retention:* 57% of 2006 full-time freshmen returned.

Freshmen *Admission:* 1,328 applied, 999 admitted, 371 enrolled. *Average high school GPA:* 2.9. *Test scores:* SAT critical reading scores over 500: 35%; SAT math scores over 500: 36%; ACT scores over 18: 74%; SAT critical reading scores over 600: 7%; SAT math scores over 600: 11%; ACT scores over 24: 18%; ACT scores over 30: 2%.

Faculty *Total:* 117, 58% full-time, 46% with terminal degrees. *Student/faculty ratio:* 16:1.

Majors Accounting; actuarial science; art; audiology and speech-language pathology; biology/biological sciences; business administration and management; chemical engineering; chemistry; clinical laboratory science/medical technology; communication/speech communication and rhetoric; computer science; criminal justice/safety; cytotechnology; e-commerce; elementary education; engineering physics; English; environmental studies; funeral service and mortuary science; history; information science/studies; international business/trade/commerce; liberal arts and sciences/liberal studies; management information systems; mass communication/media; mathematics; philosophy; physics; political science and government; pre-dentistry studies; pre-law studies; pre-medical studies; pre-veterinary studies; psychology; religious education; religious studies; secondary education; sociology; web page, digital/multimedia and information resources design.

Academics *Calendar:* semesters. *Degrees:* associate and bachelor's. *Special study options:* academic remediation for entering students, adult/continuing education programs, advanced placement credit, cooperative education, distance learning, double majors, English as a second language, freshman honors college, honors programs, internships, off-campus study, part-time degree program, services for LD students, study abroad, summer session for credit. *Unusual degree programs:* 3-2 engineering with Case Western Reserve University, Point Park College, University of Pittsburgh; forestry with Duke University.

Computers on Campus 220 computers/terminals are available on campus for general student use. Students can access the following: campus intranet, computer help desk, free student e-mail accounts, online (class) grades, online (class) registration, online (class) schedules. Campuswide network is available. 100% of college-owned or -operated housing units are wired for high-speed Internet access. Wireless service is available via entire campus.

Student Life *Housing:* on-campus residence required through senior year. *Options:* coed, men-only, women-only. Campus housing is university owned and leased by the school. Freshman campus housing is guaranteed. *Activities and organizations:* drama/theater group, student-run newspaper, radio and television station, choral group, Thiel Players Theatre Group, student government, Thiel Choir, sororities and fraternities, Thiel Christian Fellowship, national fraternities, national sororities. *Campus security:* 24-hour emergency response devices and patrols, late-night transport/escort service, controlled dormitory access. *Student services:* health clinic, personal/psychological counseling, women's center.

Athletics Member NCAA. All Division III. *Intercollegiate sports:* baseball M, basketball M/W, cheerleading M/W, cross-country running M/W, football M, golf M/W, soccer M/W, softball W, track and field M/W, volleyball W, wrestling M. *Intramural sports:* badminton M/W, basketball M/W, football M, soccer M, softball M/W, volleyball M/W.

Standardized Tests *Required:* SAT or ACT (for admission).

Costs (2007–08) *Comprehensive fee:* $28,054 includes full-time tuition ($18,654), mandatory fees ($1560), and room and board ($7840). Full-time tuition and fees vary according to course load. Part-time tuition: $600 per credit hour. Part-time tuition and fees vary according to course load. *Required fees:* $45 per credit hour part-time, $60 per term part-time. *College room only:* $4000. Room and board charges vary according to board plan and housing facility. *Payment plan:* installment. *Waivers:* senior citizens and employees or children of employees.

Financial Aid Of all full-time matriculated undergraduates who enrolled in 2006, 1,136 applied for aid, 1,068 were judged to have need, 359 had their need fully met. 154 Federal Work-Study jobs (averaging $1013). 416 state and other part-time jobs (averaging $1014). In 2006, 45 non-need-based awards were made. *Average percent of need met:* 71%. *Average financial aid package:* $11,403. *Average need-based loan:* $3358. *Average need-based gift aid:* $10,713. *Average non-need-based aid:* $7292. *Average indebtedness upon graduation:* $21,427.

Applying *Options:* electronic application, deferred entrance. *Application fee:* $35. *Required:* essay or personal statement, high school transcript, minimum 2.0 GPA, 1 letter of recommendation. *Required for some:* interview. *Recommended:* interview. *Application deadlines:* 6/30 (freshmen), rolling (transfers). *Notification:* continuous (freshmen), continuous (transfers).

Freshman Application Contact Sonya Lapikas, Chief Admissions Officer, Thiel College, 75 College Avenue, Greenville, PA 16125. *Phone:* 724-589-2172. *Toll-free phone:* 800-248-4435. *Fax:* 724-589-2013. *E-mail:* admissions@thiel.edu.

THOMAS JEFFERSON UNIVERSITY

Philadelphia, Pennsylvania **www.jefferson.edu/**

- **Independent** university, founded 1824
- **Urban** 13-acre campus
- **Endowment** $18.2 million
- **Coed**
- **Moderately difficult** entrance level

Faculty *Student/faculty ratio:* 10:1.

Academics *Calendar:* semesters. *Degrees:* bachelor's, master's, doctoral, and postbachelor's certificates.

Student Life *Campus security:* 24-hour emergency response devices and patrols, late-night transport/escort service, controlled dormitory access.

Standardized Tests *Required for some:* NET. *Recommended:* SAT or ACT (for admission).

Financial Aid Of all full-time matriculated undergraduates who enrolled in 2006, 150 Federal Work-Study jobs (averaging $2500). In 2006, 9 non-need-based awards were made. *Average need-based loan:* $10,993. *Average non-need-based aid:* $5000. *Average indebtedness upon graduation:* $32,000.

Applying *Options:* deferred entrance. *Application fee:* $50. *Required:* essay or personal statement, minimum 3.0 GPA, 2 letters of recommendation, interview. *Required for some:* high school transcript.

Freshman Application Contact Ms. Karen Jacobs, Director of Admissions, Thomas Jefferson University, Edison Building, Suite 1610, 130 South Ninth Street, Philadelphia, PA 19107. *Phone:* 215-503-8890. *Toll-free phone:* 877-533-3247. *Fax:* 215-503-7241. *E-mail:* chpadmissions@mail.tju.edu.

See page 2318 for the College Close-Up.

UNIVERSITY OF PENNSYLVANIA

Philadelphia, Pennsylvania **www.upenn.edu/**

- **Independent** university, founded 1740
- **Urban** 269-acre campus
- **Endowment** $5.3 billion
- **Coed** 9,687 undergraduate students, 97% full-time, 49% women, 51% men
- **Most difficult** entrance level, 16% of applicants were admitted

Undergraduates 9,403 full-time, 284 part-time. Students come from 54 states and territories, 111 other countries, 81% are from out of state, 8% African American, 17% Asian American or Pacific Islander, 6% Hispanic American, 0.4% Native American, 10% international, 2% transferred in, 64% live on campus. *Retention:* 98% of 2006 full-time freshmen returned.

Freshmen *Admission:* 22,645 applied, 3,628 admitted, 2,385 enrolled. *Average high school GPA:* 3.83. *Test scores:* SAT critical reading scores over 500: 100%; SAT math scores over 500: 100%; SAT writing scores over 500: 100%; ACT scores over 18: 100%; SAT critical reading scores over 600: 93%; SAT math scores over 600: 95%; SAT writing scores over 600: 93%; ACT scores over 24: 97%; SAT critical reading scores over 700: 53%; SAT math scores over 700: 65%; SAT writing scores over 700: 57%; ACT scores over 30: 70%.

Faculty *Total:* 2,088, 67% full-time, 100% with terminal degrees. *Student/faculty ratio:* 6:1.

Majors Accounting; actuarial science; African-American/Black studies; African studies; American studies; anthropology; architecture; art history, criticism and conservation; Asian studies (East); Asian studies (South); biochemistry; bioinformatics; biology/biological sciences; biomedical/medical engineering; biomedical sciences; biophysics; business administration and management; business administration, management and operations related; chemical engineering; chemistry; classics and languages, literatures and linguistics; cognitive science; communication/speech communication and rhetoric; community health services counseling; comparative literature; computer engineering; computer graphics; computer systems networking and telecommunications; dramatic/theater arts; East Asian languages; e-commerce; economics; electrical, electronics and communications engineering; elementary education; engineering related; English; English language and literature related; environmental design/architecture; environmental/environmental health engineering; environmental studies; film/cinema studies; finance; fine/studio arts; French; geology/earth science; German; health/health care administration; health professions related; history; history and philosophy of science and technology; humanities; human resources management; insurance; international business/trade/commerce; international/global studies; international relations and affairs; Italian; Jewish/Judaic studies; Latin American studies; legal professions and studies related; liberal arts and sciences/liberal studies; linguistics; logic; management information systems; management sciences and quantitative methods related; marketing/marketing management; materials engineering; materials science; mathematics; mechanical engineering; music; natural sciences; neuroscience; nursing (registered nurse training); nursing related; operations management; philosophy; philosophy related; physics; political science and government; psychology; public policy analysis; real estate; religious studies; Romance languages related; Russian; sales, distribution and marketing; Semitic languages; social sciences; sociology; Spanish; statistics; systems engineering; transportation management; urban studies/affairs; visual and performing arts; women's studies.

Academics *Calendar:* semesters plus 2 5-week summer sessions. *Degrees:* associate, bachelor's, master's, doctoral, first professional, post-master's, postbachelor's, and first professional certificates (also offers evening program with significant enrollment not reflected in profile). *Special study options:* academic remediation for entering students, accelerated degree program, adult/continuing education programs, advanced placement credit, distance learning, double majors, English as a second language, honors programs, independent study, internships, off-campus study, part-time degree program, services for LD students, student-designed majors, study abroad, summer session for credit. *ROTC:* Army (c), Navy (b), Air Force (c).

Computers on Campus 1,295 computers/terminals and 1,472 ports are available on campus for general student use. Students can access the following: campus intranet, computer help desk, free student e-mail accounts, online (class) grades, online (class) registration, online (class) schedules, billing information, financial aid application, status, academic records, student services. Campuswide network is available. 100% of college-owned or -operated housing units are wired for high-speed Internet access. Wireless service is available via classrooms, computer centers, computer labs, dorm rooms, learning centers, libraries, student centers.

Student Life *Housing options:* coed, disabled students. Campus housing is university owned. Freshman campus housing is guaranteed. *Activities and organizations:* drama/theater group, student-run newspaper, radio and television station, choral group, marching band, Kite and Key Society, Social Planning and Events Committee, Hillel at Penn, Sports Club Council, national fraternities, national sororities. *Campus security:* 24-hour emergency response devices and patrols, late-night transport/escort service, controlled dormitory access. *Student services:* health clinic, personal/psychological counseling, women's center.

Athletics Member NCAA. All Division I except football (Division I-AA). *Intercollegiate sports:* baseball M, basketball M/W, crew M/W, cross-country running M/W, fencing M/W, field hockey W, golf M/W, gymnastics W, lacrosse M/W, soccer M/W, softball W, squash M/W, swimming and diving M/W, tennis M/W, track and field M/W, volleyball W, wrestling M. *Intramural sports:* badminton M/W, baseball M (c), basketball M/W, cheerleading M/W, equestrian sports M (c)/W (c), field hockey W (c), football M/W, golf M/W, gymnastics M (c), ice hockey M (c)/W (c), lacrosse M/W, rock climbing M/W, rugby M (c)/W (c), sailing M (c)/W (c), skiing (downhill) M (c)/W (c), soccer M/W, softball M/W, squash M/W, swimming and diving M/W, table tennis M/W, tennis M/W, track and field M/W, ultimate Frisbee M (c)/W (c), volleyball M/W, water polo M (c)/W (c).

Standardized Tests *Required:* SAT and SAT Subject Tests or ACT (for admission).

Costs (2007–08) *Comprehensive fee:* $46,124 includes full-time tuition ($32,160), mandatory fees ($3756), and room and board ($10,208). Part-time tuition: $4107 per course. Part-time tuition and fees vary according to course load. the College, Engineering, Nursing and Wharton part-time undergrad tuition is $3708 per course unit ($389 fees). The College of General Studies which has the largest part-time undergraduate population is $1384 ($194 fees). *Required fees:* $440 per course part-time. *College room only:* $6324. Room and board charges vary according to board plan and housing facility. *Payment plan:* installment. *Waivers:* employees or children of employees.

Financial Aid Of all full-time matriculated undergraduates who enrolled in 2005, 4,632 applied for aid, 4,183 were judged to have need, 4,183 had their need fully met. *Average percent of need met:* 100%. *Average financial aid package:* $28,633. *Average need-based loan:* $3713. *Average need-based gift aid:* $23,580. *Average indebtedness upon graduation:* $20,927.

Applying *Options:* electronic application, early admission, early decision, deferred entrance. *Application fee:* $75. *Required:* essay or personal statement, high school transcript, 2 letters of recommendation. *Application deadlines:* 1/1 (freshmen), 3/15 (transfers). *Early decision deadline:* 11/1. *Notification:* 4/1 (freshmen), continuous (transfers), 12/15 (early decision).

Freshman Application Contact Eric J. Kaplan, Interim Dean of Admissions, University of Pennsylvania, 1 College Hall, Levy Park, Philadelphia, PA 19104. *Phone:* 215-898-7507. *E-mail:* info@admissions.ugao.upenn.edu.

UNIVERSITY OF PHOENIX–PHILADELPHIA CAMPUS

Wayne, Pennsylvania **www.phoenix.edu/**

- **Proprietary** comprehensive, founded 1999
- **Urban** campus
- **Coed**
- **Noncompetitive** entrance level

Faculty *Student/faculty ratio:* 9:1.

Academics *Calendar:* continuous. *Degrees:* bachelor's and master's.

Student Life *Campus security:* late-night transport/escort service.

Costs (2007–08) *Tuition:* $12,900 full-time, $430 per credit part-time. Full-time tuition and fees vary according to course level.

Financial Aid *Average financial aid package:* $3973. *Average need-based gift aid:* $2014.

Applying *Options:* deferred entrance. *Application fee:* $45. *Required:* 1 letter of recommendation. *Required for some:* high school transcript.

Freshman Application Contact Ms. Beth Barilla, Associate Vice President, Student Admissions and Services, University of Phoenix–Philadelphia Campus, 4615 East Elwood Street, Mail Stop AA-K101, Phoenix, AZ 85040-1958. *Phone:* 480-317-6000. *Toll-free phone:* 800-776-4867 (in-state); 800-228-7240 (out-of-state). *Fax:* 480-894-1758. *E-mail:* beth.barilla@phoenix.edu.

UNIVERSITY OF PHOENIX–PITTSBURGH CAMPUS

Pittsburgh, Pennsylvania **www.phoenix.edu/**

- **Proprietary** comprehensive, founded 2001
- **Urban** campus
- **Coed**
- **Noncompetitive** entrance level

Faculty *Student/faculty ratio:* 4:1.

Academics *Calendar:* continuous. *Degrees:* bachelor's and master's.

Student Life *Campus security:* late-night transport/escort service.

Costs (2007–08) *Tuition:* $12,900 full-time, $430 per credit part-time. Full-time tuition and fees vary according to course level.

Financial Aid *Average financial aid package:* $3829. *Average need-based gift aid:* $1920.

Applying *Options:* deferred entrance. *Application fee:* $45. *Required:* 1 letter of recommendation. *Required for some:* high school transcript.

Freshman Application Contact Ms. Beth Barilla, Associate Vice President, Student Admissions and Services, University of Phoenix–Pittsburgh Campus, 4615 East Elwood Street, Mail Stop AA-K101, Phoenix, AZ 85040-1958. *Phone:* 480-317-6000. *Toll-free phone:* 800-776-4867 (in-state); 800-228-7240 (out-of-state). *Fax:* 480-894-1758. *E-mail:* beth.barilla@phoenix.edu.

UNIVERSITY OF PITTSBURGH

Pittsburgh, Pennsylvania **www.pitt.edu/**

- **State-related** university, founded 1787, part of Commonwealth System of Higher Education
- **Urban** 132-acre campus
- **Endowment** $2.3 billion
- **Coed** 17,208 undergraduate students, 91% full-time, 51% women, 49% men
- **Moderately difficult** entrance level, 56% of applicants were admitted

Undergraduates 15,662 full-time, 1,546 part-time. Students come from 50 states and territories, 40 other countries, 17% are from out of state, 8% African American, 5% Asian American or Pacific Islander, 1% Hispanic American, 0.2% Native American, 0.8% international, 5% transferred in, 45% live on campus. *Retention:* 90% of 2006 full-time freshmen returned.

Freshmen *Admission:* 19,056 applied, 10,591 admitted, 3,432 enrolled. *Test scores:* SAT critical reading scores over 500: 97%; SAT math scores over 500: 97%; ACT scores over 18: 99%; SAT critical reading scores over 600: 60%; SAT math scores over 600: 69%; ACT scores over 24: 83%; SAT critical reading scores over 700: 18%; SAT math scores over 700: 18%; ACT scores over 30: 26%.

Faculty *Total:* 2,157, 73% full-time. *Student/faculty ratio:* 16:1.

Majors Accounting; African-American/Black studies; anthropology; applied mathematics; art history, criticism and conservation; audiology and speech-language pathology; biological and physical sciences; biology/biological sciences; biomedical/medical engineering; business/commerce; chemical engineering; chemistry; Chinese; civil engineering; classics and languages, literatures and linguistics; computer and information sciences and support services related; computer engineering; computer science; corrections; creative writing; dental hygiene; dietetics; dramatic/theater arts; ecology; economics; educational psychology; electrical, electronics and communications engineering; engineering; engineering physics; English; English literature (British and Commonwealth); ethnic, cultural minority, and gender studies related; film/cinema studies; finance; fine/studio arts; French; geological and earth sciences/geosciences related; geology/earth science; German; health information/medical records administration; health professions related; history; history and philosophy of science and technology; humanities; industrial engineering; information science/studies; interdisciplinary studies; Italian; Japanese; legal studies; liberal arts and sciences/liberal studies; linguistics; marketing/marketing management; materials engineering; mathematics; mathematics and statistics related; mathematics related; mechanical engineering; metallurgical engineering; microbiology; molecular biology; multi-/interdisciplinary studies related; music; neuroscience; nursing (registered nurse training); occupational therapy; pharmacy; philosophy; physical education teaching and coaching; physical sciences; physics; political science and government; psychology; public administration; rehabilitation and therapeutic professions related; religious studies; Russian; Slavic languages; social sciences; social work; sociology; Spanish; speech and rhetoric; statistics; urban studies/affairs.

Academics *Calendar:* semesters plus summer term. *Degrees:* certificates, bachelor's, master's, doctoral, first professional, post-master's, and postbachelor's certificates. *Special study options:* academic remediation for entering students, accelerated degree program, adult/continuing education programs, advanced placement credit, cooperative education, distance learning, double majors, English as a second language, external degree program, freshman honors college, honors programs, independent study, internships, off-campus study, part-time degree program, services for LD students, student-designed majors, study abroad, summer session for credit. *ROTC:* Army (b), Navy (c), Air Force (b). *Unusual degree programs:* 3-2 engineering; statistics.

Computers on Campus 1,150 computers/terminals and 1,150 ports are available on campus for general student use. Students can access the following: campus intranet, computer help desk, free student e-mail accounts, online (class) grades, online (class) schedules, online class listings, online tuition payment. Campus-wide network is available. 100% of college-owned or -operated housing units are wired for high-speed Internet access. Wireless service is available via entire campus.

Student Life *Housing options:* coed, women-only. Campus housing is university owned. Freshman campus housing is guaranteed. *Activities and organizations:* drama/theater group, student-run newspaper, radio and television station, choral group, marching band, Pitt Program Council, Quo Vadis, Black Action Society, Pitt Crew (rowing club), Blue and Gold Society, national fraternities, national sororities. *Campus security:* 24-hour emergency response devices and patrols, late-night transport/escort service, controlled dormitory access, on-call van transportation. *Student services:* health clinic, personal/psychological counseling, women's center.

Athletics Member NCAA. All Division I except football (Division I-A). *Intercollegiate sports:* baseball M (s), basketball M (s)/W (s), cross-country running M (s)/W (s), gymnastics W (s), soccer M (s)/W (s), softball W (s), swimming and diving M (s)/W (s), tennis W (s), track and field M (s)/W (s), volleyball W (s), wrestling M (s). *Intramural sports:* badminton M/W, baseball M (c)/W (c), basketball M/W, crew M (c)/W (c), equestrian sports M (c)/W (c), football M, ice hockey M (c)/W (c), lacrosse M (c)/W (c), racquetball M/W, soccer M/W, softball W (c), squash M/W, swimming and diving M/W, ultimate Frisbee M/W, volleyball M/W, water polo W (c), wrestling M.

Standardized Tests *Required:* SAT or ACT (for admission).

Costs (2007–08) *Tuition:* state resident $12,106 full-time, $504 per credit part-time; nonresident $21,616 full-time, $900 per credit part-time. Full-time tuition and fees vary according to degree level and program. Part-time tuition and fees vary according to degree level and program. *Required fees:* $770 full-time, $189 per term part-time. *Room and board:* $8300; room only: $4950. Room and board charges vary according to board plan and housing facility. *Payment plans:* installment, deferred payment. *Waivers:* employees or children of employees.

Financial Aid Of all full-time matriculated undergraduates who enrolled in 2006, 11,048 applied for aid, 8,767 were judged to have need, 3,194 had their need fully met. In 2006, 1,020 non-need-based awards were made. *Average percent of need met:* 79%. *Average financial aid package:* $9087. *Average need-based loan:* $4673. *Average need-based gift aid:* $7273. *Average non-need-based aid:* $11,038. *Financial aid deadline:* 6/1.

Applying *Options:* electronic application, early admission. *Application fee:* $45. *Required:* high school transcript. *Recommended:* essay or personal statement, letters of recommendation, interview. *Application deadlines:* rolling (freshmen), rolling (transfers). *Notification:* continuous (freshmen), continuous (transfers).

Freshman Application Contact Dr. Betsy A. Porter, Director of Office of Admissions and Financial Aid, University of Pittsburgh, 4227 Fifth Avenue, First Floor, Alumni Hall, Pittsburgh, PA 15260. *Phone:* 412-624-7488. *Fax:* 412-648-8815. *E-mail:* oafa@pitt.edu.

UNIVERSITY OF PITTSBURGH AT BRADFORD

Bradford, Pennsylvania **www.upb.pitt.edu/**

- **State-related** 4-year, founded 1963, part of University of Pittsburgh System
- **Small-town** 317-acre campus with easy access to Buffalo
- **Endowment** $16.2 million
- **Coed** 1,407 undergraduate students, 85% full-time, 58% women, 42% men
- **Minimally difficult** entrance level, 84% of applicants were admitted

Undergraduates 1,193 full-time, 214 part-time. Students come from 28 states and territories, 9 other countries, 15% are from out of state, 4% African American, 2% Asian American or Pacific Islander, 0.9% Hispanic American, 0.3% Native American, 0.2% international, 7% transferred in, 52% live on campus. *Retention:* 71% of 2006 full-time freshmen returned.

Freshmen *Admission:* 737 applied, 620 admitted, 322 enrolled. *Average high school GPA:* 3.10. *Test scores:* SAT critical reading scores over 500: 45%; SAT math scores over 500: 50%; SAT writing scores over 500: 39%; ACT scores over 18: 71%; SAT critical reading scores over 600: 7%; SAT math scores over 600: 12%; SAT writing scores over 600: 5%; ACT scores over 24: 12%; ACT scores over 30: 2%.

Faculty *Total:* 135, 51% full-time, 40% with terminal degrees. *Student/faculty ratio:* 14:1.

Majors Accounting; applied mathematics; athletic training; athletic training/sports medicine; biology/biological sciences; business administration and management; chemistry; computer science; creative writing; criminal justice/law enforcement administration; economics; elementary education; engineering science; English; entrepreneurship; environmental studies; history; humanities; information science/studies; liberal arts and sciences/liberal studies; nursing (registered nurse training); petroleum technology; physical education teaching and coaching; physical sciences; political science and government; psychology; public relations/image management; radio and television; radiologic technology/science; secondary education; social sciences; sociology; sport and fitness administration/management.

Academics *Calendar:* semesters. *Degrees:* associate and bachelor's. *Special study options:* academic remediation for entering students, accelerated degree program, adult/continuing education programs, advanced placement credit, distance learning, double majors, independent study, internships, off-campus study, part-time degree program, services for LD students, study abroad, summer session for credit. *ROTC:* Army (c).

Computers on Campus 186 computers/terminals and 974 ports are available on campus for general student use. Students can access the following: computer help desk, free student e-mail accounts, online (class) grades, Online bills.

Campuswide network is available. 100% of college-owned or -operated housing units are wired for high-speed Internet access.

Student Life *Housing:* on-campus residence required for freshman year. *Options:* coed, disabled students. Campus housing is university owned. Freshman campus housing is guaranteed. *Activities and organizations:* drama/theater group, student-run newspaper, radio station, choral group, Student Government Association, Student Activities Board, The Source (student newspaper), Alpha Phi Omega (national service fraternity), WDRQ (student radio station). *Campus security:* 24-hour emergency response devices and patrols, late-night transport/escort service, controlled dormitory access. *Student services:* health clinic, personal/psychological counseling.

Athletics Member NCAA. All Division III. *Intercollegiate sports:* baseball M, basketball M/W, cross-country running M/W, golf M/W, soccer M/W, softball W, swimming and diving M/W, tennis M/W, volleyball W. *Intramural sports:* basketball M/W, bowling M/W, cheerleading W (c), equestrian sports M/W, football M/W, golf M/W, rock climbing M/W, rugby M (c)/W (c), skiing (cross-country) M/W, soccer M/W, softball M/W, swimming and diving M/W, table tennis M/W, tennis M/W, ultimate Frisbee M/W, volleyball M/W, water polo M/W.

Standardized Tests *Required:* SAT or ACT (for admission).

Costs (2007–08) *Tuition:* state resident $10,590 full-time, $441 per credit part-time; nonresident $20,170 full-time, $840 per credit part-time. Full-time tuition and fees vary according to course load and program. Part-time tuition and fees vary according to course load and program. *Required fees:* $710 full-time, $105 per term part-time. *Room and board:* $6850. Room and board charges vary according to board plan and housing facility. *Payment plan:* installment. *Waivers:* employees or children of employees.

Financial Aid Of all full-time matriculated undergraduates who enrolled in 2007, 1,120 applied for aid, 1,036 were judged to have need, 227 had their need fully met. 154 Federal Work-Study jobs (averaging $1725). 10 state and other part-time jobs (averaging $1540). In 2007, 130 non-need-based awards were made. *Average percent of need met:* 79%. *Average financial aid package:* $11,214. *Average need-based loan:* $3925. *Average need-based gift aid:* $4947. *Average non-need-based aid:* $5209. *Average indebtedness upon graduation:* $24,910.

Applying *Options:* electronic application, deferred entrance. *Application fee:* $45. *Required:* high school transcript, minimum 2.0 GPA. *Required for some:* minimum 3.0 GPA. *Recommended:* essay or personal statement, letters of recommendation, interview. *Application deadlines:* rolling (freshmen), rolling (out-of-state freshmen), rolling (transfers). *Notification:* continuous (freshmen), continuous (out-of-state freshmen), continuous (transfers).

Freshman Application Contact Ms. Vicky Pingie, Associate Director of Admissions, University of Pittsburgh at Bradford, 300 Campus Drive, Bradford, PA 16701. *Phone:* 814-362-7552. *Toll-free phone:* 800-872-1787. *Fax:* 814-362-5150. *E-mail:* monti@upb.pitt.edu.

See page 2320 for the College Close-Up.

UNIVERSITY OF PITTSBURGH AT GREENSBURG

Greensburg, Pennsylvania **www.upg.pitt.edu/**

- **State-related** 4-year, founded 1963, part of University of Pittsburgh System
- **Small-town** 219-acre campus with easy access to Pittsburgh
- **Endowment** $2.2 million
- **Coed**
- **Moderately difficult** entrance level

Faculty *Student/faculty ratio:* 18:1.

Academics *Calendar:* semesters. *Degree:* certificates and bachelor's.

Student Life *Campus security:* 24-hour emergency response devices and patrols, late-night transport/escort service, controlled dormitory access.

Athletics Member NCAA. All Division III.

Standardized Tests *Required:* SAT or ACT (for admission).

Costs (2007–08) *Tuition:* state resident $10,590 full-time, $441 per credit hour part-time; nonresident $20,170 full-time, $840 per credit hour part-time. *Required fees:* $730 full-time, $126 per term part-time. *Room and board:* $7000.

Financial Aid Of all full-time matriculated undergraduates who enrolled in 2007, 1,240 applied for aid, 1,010 were judged to have need, 158 had their need fully met. In 2007, 52 non-need-based awards were made. *Average percent of need met:* 63. *Average financial aid package:* $9572. *Average need-based loan:* $4624. *Average need-based gift aid:* $5212. *Average non-need-based aid:* $3284. *Average indebtedness upon graduation:* $24,080.

Applying *Options:* electronic application, early admission, deferred entrance. *Application fee:* $45. *Required:* high school transcript, minimum 2.5 GPA. *Required for some:* letters of recommendation. *Recommended:* essay or personal statement, interview.

Freshman Application Contact University of Pittsburgh at Greensburg, 1150 Mount Pleasant Road, Greensburg, PA 15601-5860. *Phone:* 724-836-9880.

UNIVERSITY OF PITTSBURGH AT JOHNSTOWN

Johnstown, Pennsylvania **www.upj.pitt.edu/**

- **State-related** 4-year, founded 1927, part of University of Pittsburgh System
- **Suburban** 650-acre campus with easy access to Pittsburgh
- **Coed** 3,121 undergraduate students, 94% full-time, 47% women, 53% men
- **Moderately difficult** entrance level, 88% of applicants were admitted

Undergraduates 2,937 full-time, 184 part-time. Students come from 1 other country, 1% are from out of state, 2% African American, 1% Asian American or Pacific Islander, 0.7% Hispanic American, 4% transferred in, 61% live on campus. *Retention:* 73% of 2006 full-time freshmen returned.

Freshmen *Admission:* 1,749 applied, 1,542 admitted, 840 enrolled. *Average high school GPA:* 3.33. *Test scores:* SAT critical reading scores over 500: 51%; SAT math scores over 500: 61%; SAT writing scores over 500: 38%; ACT scores over 18: 79%; SAT critical reading scores over 600: 8%; SAT math scores over 600: 16%; SAT writing scores over 600: 6%; ACT scores over 24: 17%; SAT critical reading scores over 700: 1%; SAT math scores over 700: 1%; SAT writing scores over 700: 1%.

Faculty *Total:* 194, 74% full-time, 60% with terminal degrees. *Student/faculty ratio:* 19:1.

Majors Accounting; American studies; biology/biological sciences; biology teacher education; biopsychology; business administration and management; business/managerial economics; chemistry; chemistry teacher education; civil engineering technology; computer science; creative writing; dramatic/theater arts; ecology; economics; education; electrical, electronic and communications engineering technology; elementary education; emergency medical technology (EMT paramedic); engineering technology; English; English/language arts teacher education; environmental biology; environmental studies; finance; geography; geology/earth science; history; history teacher education; humanities; journalism; literature; mass communication/media; mathematics; mathematics teacher education; mechanical engineering/mechanical technology; natural sciences; political science and government; pre-dentistry studies; pre-law studies; pre-medical studies; pre-veterinary studies; psychology; respiratory care therapy; science teacher education; secondary education; social sciences; social studies teacher education; sociology; surgical technology.

Academics *Calendar:* semesters. *Degrees:* associate and bachelor's. *Special study options:* accelerated degree program, adult/continuing education programs, advanced placement credit, cooperative education, distance learning, double majors, independent study, internships, off-campus study, part-time degree program, services for LD students, student-designed majors, study abroad, summer session for credit.

Computers on Campus 222 computers/terminals and 100 ports are available on campus for general student use. Campuswide network is available. 100% of college-owned or -operated housing units are wired for high-speed Internet access. Wireless service is available via entire campus.

Student Life *Housing options:* coed. Campus housing is university owned. Freshman campus housing is guaranteed. *Activities and organizations:* drama/theater group, student-run newspaper, radio and television station, choral group, Dance Ensemble, Student Senate, Programming Board, academic clubs, national fraternities, national sororities. *Campus security:* 24-hour emergency response devices and patrols, late-night transport/escort service, controlled dormitory access. *Student services:* health clinic, personal/psychological counseling.

Athletics Member NCAA. All Division II. *Intercollegiate sports:* baseball M, basketball M (s)/W (s), cheerleading W, cross-country running W, soccer M/W, track and field W, volleyball W, wrestling M (s). *Intramural sports:* archery M (c)/W (c), basketball M/W, football M/W, ice hockey M (c), lacrosse M (c), rock climbing M (c)/W (c), sailing M (c)/W (c), skiing (downhill) M (c)/W (c), softball M/W, ultimate Frisbee M (c)/W (c), volleyball M/W.

Standardized Tests *Required:* SAT or ACT (for admission). *Required for some:* SAT or ACT (for placement).

Costs (2007–08) *Tuition:* state resident $10,590 full-time, $441 per credit part-time; nonresident $20,170 full-time, $840 per credit part-time. Full-time tuition and fees vary according to program. Part-time tuition and fees vary according to program. *Required fees:* $742 full-time, $87 per term part-time.

Room and board: $6400; room only: $3930. Room and board charges vary according to board plan and housing facility. *Payment plan:* installment. *Waivers:* employees or children of employees.

Financial Aid Of all full-time matriculated undergraduates who enrolled in 2007, 2,558 applied for aid, 2,287 were judged to have need, 54 had their need fully met. 242 Federal Work-Study jobs (averaging $1715). 158 state and other part-time jobs (averaging $2874). In 2007, 59 non-need-based awards were made. *Average percent of need met:* 54%. *Average financial aid package:* $8464. *Average need-based loan:* $4438. *Average need-based gift aid:* $5005. *Average non-need-based aid:* $5783. *Average indebtedness upon graduation:* $23,412.

Applying *Options:* electronic application, early admission, deferred entrance. *Application fee:* $45. *Required:* high school transcript, minimum 2.0 GPA. *Required for some:* interview. *Recommended:* essay or personal statement, 3 letters of recommendation. *Application deadlines:* rolling (freshmen), rolling (out-of-state freshmen), rolling (transfers). *Notification:* continuous (freshmen), continuous (out-of-state freshmen), continuous (transfers).

Freshman Application Contact Office of Admissions, University of Pittsburgh at Johnstown, 157 Blackington Hall, 450 Schoolhouse Road, Johnstown, PA 15904-2990. *Phone:* 814-269-7050. *Toll-free phone:* 800-765-4875. *E-mail:* upjadmit@pitt.edu.

See page 2322 for the College Close-Up.

The University of Scranton

Scranton, Pennsylvania **www.scranton.edu/**

- **Independent Roman Catholic (Jesuit)** comprehensive, founded 1888
- **Urban** 50-acre campus
- **Endowment** $120.1 million
- **Coed** 4,081 undergraduate students, 94% full-time, 57% women, 43% men
- **Moderately difficult** entrance level, 66% of applicants were admitted

Undergraduates 3,848 full-time, 233 part-time. Students come from 25 states and territories, 18 other countries, 52% are from out of state, 1% African American, 2% Asian American or Pacific Islander, 5% Hispanic American, 0.2% Native American, 0.4% international, 2% transferred in, 53% live on campus. *Retention:* 90% of 2006 full-time freshmen returned.

Freshmen *Admission:* 7,609 applied, 5,033 admitted, 1,027 enrolled. *Average high school GPA:* 3.36. *Test scores:* SAT critical reading scores over 500: 82%; SAT math scores over 500: 85%; SAT critical reading scores over 600: 25%; SAT math scores over 600: 33%; SAT critical reading scores over 700: 4%; SAT math scores over 700: 4%.

Faculty *Total:* 512, 50% full-time, 51% with terminal degrees. *Student/faculty ratio:* 11:1.

Majors Accounting; ancient/classical Greek; biology/biological sciences; biomathematics and bioinformatics related; biophysics; business administration and management; business administration, management and operations related; chemistry; chemistry related; clinical laboratory science/medical technology; communication/speech communication and rhetoric; communications technologies and support services related; computer and information sciences and support services related; computer engineering; computer science; criminal justice/safety; dramatic/theater arts; early childhood education; economics; electrical, electronics and communications engineering; elementary education; English; entrepreneurship; finance; foreign languages and literatures; French; German; gerontology; health/health care administration; history; human resources management; human services; information science/studies; international business/trade/commerce; international relations and affairs; Italian; kindergarten/preschool education; kinesiology and exercise science; Latin; management science; marketing/marketing management; mathematics; mathematics and statistics related; neuroscience; nursing (registered nurse training); operations management; philosophy; physics; political science and government; psychology; religious studies; secondary education; sociology; Spanish; special education.

Academics *Calendar:* 4-1-4. *Degrees:* certificates, associate, bachelor's, master's, doctoral, post-master's, and postbachelor's certificates. *Special study options:* academic remediation for entering students, accelerated degree program, adult/continuing education programs, advanced placement credit, distance learning, double majors, external degree program, honors programs, independent study, internships, off-campus study, part-time degree program, services for LD students, student-designed majors, study abroad, summer session for credit. *ROTC:* Army (b), Air Force (c). *Unusual degree programs:* 3-2 engineering with University of Detroit Mercy, Widener University.

Computers on Campus 927 computers/terminals are available on campus for general student use. Students can access the following: computer help desk, free student e-mail accounts, online (class) grades, online (class) registration, online (class) schedules. Campuswide network is available. 100% of college-owned or -operated housing units are wired for high-speed Internet access. Wireless service is available via classrooms, computer centers, computer labs, dorm rooms, learning centers, libraries, student centers.

Student Life *Housing:* on-campus residence required through sophomore year. *Options:* coed, men-only, women-only, disabled students. Campus housing is university owned. Freshman campus housing is guaranteed. *Activities and organizations:* drama/theater group, student-run newspaper, radio and television station, choral group, Service-Oriented Students Club, United Colors, retreat program, Biology/Pre-Medicine Club, Pre-Law Society. *Campus security:* 24-hour emergency response devices and patrols, student patrols, late-night transport/escort service, controlled dormitory access. *Student services:* health clinic, personal/psychological counseling, women's center.

Athletics Member NCAA. All Division III. *Intercollegiate sports:* baseball M, basketball M/W, bowling M (c)/W (c), crew M (c)/W (c), cross-country running M/W, equestrian sports M (c)/W (c), field hockey W, golf M, ice hockey M, lacrosse M/W (c), rugby M (c)/W (c), skiing (downhill) M (c)/W (c), soccer M/W, softball W, swimming and diving M/W, tennis M/W, track and field M (c)/W (c), volleyball M (c)/W, wrestling M. *Intramural sports:* badminton M/W, baseball M, basketball M/W, bowling M/W, cross-country running M/W, football M, golf M/W, racquetball M/W, soccer M/W, softball M/W, swimming and diving M/W, table tennis M/W, tennis M/W, ultimate Frisbee M/W, volleyball M/W, water polo M/W, weight lifting M/W, wrestling M.

Standardized Tests *Required:* SAT or ACT (for admission).

Costs (2007–08) *Comprehensive fee:* $39,368 includes full-time tuition ($28,458), mandatory fees ($300), and room and board ($10,610). Full-time tuition and fees vary according to student level. Part-time tuition: $758 per credit. *College room only:* $6256. Room and board charges vary according to board plan and housing facility. *Payment plan:* installment. *Waivers:* senior citizens and employees or children of employees.

Financial Aid Of all full-time matriculated undergraduates who enrolled in 2004, 2,961 applied for aid, 2,577 were judged to have need, 336 had their need fully met. 1,005 Federal Work-Study jobs (averaging $1800). 255 state and other part-time jobs (averaging $1500). In 2004, 211 non-need-based awards were made. *Average percent of need met:* 72%. *Average financial aid package:* $15,558. *Average need-based loan:* $4375. *Average need-based gift aid:* $11,250. *Average non-need-based aid:* $7813. *Average indebtedness upon graduation:* $15,800.

Applying *Options:* electronic application, early admission, early action, deferred entrance. *Application fee:* $40. *Required:* essay or personal statement, high school transcript, letters of recommendation. *Required for some:* interview. *Application deadlines:* 3/1 (freshmen), rolling (transfers), 11/15 (early action). *Notification:* continuous until 5/1 (freshmen), continuous (transfers), 12/15 (early action).

Freshman Application Contact Mr. Joseph Roback, Associate Vice President, Undergraduate Admissions and Enrollment, The University of Scranton, Scranton, PA 18510-4622. *Phone:* 570-941-7540. *Toll-free phone:* 888-SCRANTON. *Fax:* 570-941-4370. *E-mail:* admissions@scranton.edu.

See page 2324 for the College Close-Up.

The University of the Arts

Philadelphia, Pennsylvania **www.uarts.edu/**

- **Independent** comprehensive, founded 1870
- **Urban** 18-acre campus
- **Endowment** $21.5 million
- **Coed**
- **Moderately difficult** entrance level

The only university devoted exclusively to educating creative individuals in art and design, the performing arts, and media and communication, the University of the Arts (UArts) is located in the heart of Philadelphia's vibrant arts community. More than 2,300 students are enrolled in the University's undergraduate and graduate programs. For more than 135 years, UArts has defined creativity.

Faculty *Student/faculty ratio:* 10:1.

Academics *Calendar:* semesters. *Degrees:* certificates, diplomas, bachelor's, master's, and postbachelor's certificates.

Student Life *Campus security:* 24-hour emergency response devices and patrols, late-night transport/escort service, crime prevention workshops and seminars.

Standardized Tests *Required:* SAT or ACT (for admission).

Costs (2008–09) *Tuition:* $29,500 full-time, $1440 per credit part-time. *Required fees:* $1100 full-time. *Room only:* $7047.

Financial Aid In 2002, 561 non-need-based awards were made. *Average percent of need met:* 65. *Average financial aid package:* $16,500. *Average indebtedness upon graduation:* $17,000.

Applying *Options:* electronic application, early admission, deferred entrance. *Application fee:* $60. *Required:* essay or personal statement, high school transcript, minimum 2.0 GPA, 1 letter of recommendation, portfolio or audition. *Required for some:* interview. *Recommended:* interview.

Freshman Application Contact Ms. Susan Gandy, Director of Admission, The University of the Arts, 320 South Broad Street, Philadelphia, PA 19102-4944. *Phone:* 215-717-6030. *Toll-free phone:* 800-616-ARTS. *Fax:* 215-717-6045. *E-mail:* admissions@uarts.edu.

See page 2326 for the College Close-Up.

UNIVERSITY OF THE SCIENCES IN PHILADELPHIA

Philadelphia, Pennsylvania **www.usip.edu/**

- **Independent** university, founded 1821
- **Urban** 35-acre campus
- **Endowment** $149.5 million
- **Coed** 2,128 undergraduate students, 98% full-time, 59% women, 41% men
- **Moderately difficult** entrance level, 58% of applicants were admitted

The University of the Sciences in Philadelphia (USP), located in the University City section of historic Philadelphia, is a private university of more than 2,500 students. USP offers twenty-one majors in three colleges: Philadelphia College of Pharmacy, College of Health Sciences, and Misher College of Arts and Sciences. All students are admitted directly into their major of choice for the entire program length and are not required to reapply for admission at a later date. Prospective students should contact the Admission Office at 888-996-8747 (toll-free).

Undergraduates 2,089 full-time, 39 part-time. Students come from 32 states and territories, 16 other countries, 48% are from out of state, 5% African American, 34% Asian American or Pacific Islander, 2% Hispanic American, 0.4% Native American, 1% international, 3% transferred in, 35% live on campus. *Retention:* 91% of 2006 full-time freshmen returned.

Freshmen *Admission:* 3,963 applied, 2,307 admitted, 557 enrolled. *Average high school GPA:* 3.62. *Test scores:* SAT critical reading scores over 500: 87%; SAT math scores over 500: 97%; ACT scores over 18: 100%; SAT critical reading scores over 600: 31%; SAT math scores over 600: 54%; ACT scores over 24: 71%; SAT critical reading scores over 700: 3%; SAT math scores over 700: 11%; ACT scores over 30: 3%.

Faculty *Total:* 255, 60% full-time. *Student/faculty ratio:* 13:1.

Majors Biochemistry; bioinformatics; biology/biological sciences; chemistry; clinical laboratory science/medical technology; computer science; environmental science; health/medical psychology; health services/allied health/health sciences; marketing/marketing management; medical pharmacology and pharmaceutical sciences; medicinal and pharmaceutical chemistry; microbiology; pharmacology and toxicology; pharmacy, pharmaceutical sciences, and administration related; psychology.

Academics *Calendar:* semesters. *Degrees:* bachelor's, master's, doctoral, first professional, and postbachelor's certificates. *Special study options:* academic remediation for entering students, adult/continuing education programs, advanced placement credit, cooperative education, distance learning, double majors, English as a second language, honors programs, internships, off-campus study, part-time degree program, services for LD students, summer session for credit. *ROTC:* Army (c), Air Force (c). *Unusual degree programs:* 3-2 occupational therapy, pharmacy, physical therapy.

Computers on Campus 130 computers/terminals are available on campus for general student use. Campuswide network is available.

Student Life *Housing:* on-campus residence required through sophomore year. *Options:* coed. Campus housing is university owned and leased by the school. Freshman campus housing is guaranteed. *Activities and organizations:* drama/theater group, student-run newspaper, choral group, student government, Bharat, Academy of Students of Pharmacy, Student Physical Therapy Association, Asian Student Association, national fraternities, national sororities. *Campus security:* 24-hour emergency response devices and patrols, late-night transport/escort service, controlled dormitory access. *Student services:* health clinic, personal/psychological counseling.

Athletics Member NCAA, NAIA. All NCAA Division II. *Intercollegiate sports:* baseball M (s), basketball M (s)/W (s), cross-country running M/W, golf M/W, riflery M/W, softball W (s), tennis M/W, volleyball W (s). *Intramural sports:* archery M/W, basketball M/W, bowling M/W, riflery M/W, softball M/W, table tennis M/W, volleyball M/W.

Standardized Tests *Required:* SAT or ACT (for admission). *Recommended:* SAT (for admission).

Costs (2007–08) *Comprehensive fee:* $37,454 includes full-time tuition ($25,618), mandatory fees ($1312), and room and board ($10,524). Full-time tuition and fees vary according to degree level and program. Part-time tuition: $1067 per credit. Part-time tuition and fees vary according to course load and degree level. *Required fees:* $41 per credit part-time. *College room only:* $6430. Room and board charges vary according to board plan. *Payment plans:* tuition prepayment, installment. *Waivers:* employees or children of employees.

Financial Aid Of all full-time matriculated undergraduates who enrolled in 2006, 1,523 applied for aid, 1,367 were judged to have need, 641 had their need fully met. 975 Federal Work-Study jobs (averaging $682). In 2006, 716 non-need-based awards were made. *Average percent of need met:* 52%. *Average financial aid package:* $11,801. *Average need-based loan:* $4561. *Average need-based gift aid:* $8744. *Average non-need-based aid:* $6432. *Average indebtedness upon graduation:* $36,145. *Financial aid deadline:* 3/15.

Applying *Options:* electronic application, deferred entrance. *Application fee:* $45. *Required:* high school transcript. *Recommended:* minimum 3.0 GPA. *Application deadline:* rolling (freshmen). *Notification:* continuous (freshmen), continuous (transfers).

Freshman Application Contact Mr. Louis Hegyes, Director of Admission, University of the Sciences in Philadelphia, 600 South 43rd Street, Philadelphia, PA 19104-4495. *Phone:* 215-596-8810. *Toll-free phone:* 888-996-8747. *Fax:* 215-596-8821. *E-mail:* admit@usip.edu.

See page 2328 for the College Close-Up.

URSINUS COLLEGE

Collegeville, Pennsylvania **www.ursinus.edu/**

- **Independent** 4-year, founded 1869
- **Suburban** 168-acre campus with easy access to Philadelphia
- **Endowment** $150.0 million
- **Coed** 1,583 undergraduate students, 99% full-time, 52% women, 48% men
- **Very difficult** entrance level, 53% of applicants were admitted

Ursinus, a highly selective, coeducational liberal arts college founded in 1869, offers an innovative curriculum emphasizing student achievement and independent, faculty-mentored research. A distinctive aspect of the program is the Common Intellectual Experience, or CIE, in which all freshmen explore questions of human existence through readings and small-group discussion.

Undergraduates 1,560 full-time, 23 part-time. Students come from 28 states and territories, 14 other countries, 38% are from out of state, 6% African American, 5% Asian American or Pacific Islander, 3% Hispanic American, 0.2% Native American, 1% international, 0.8% transferred in, 95% live on campus. *Retention:* 88% of 2006 full-time freshmen returned.

Freshmen *Admission:* 5,141 applied, 2,711 admitted, 468 enrolled. *Test scores:* SAT critical reading scores over 500: 96%; SAT math scores over 500: 95%; SAT writing scores over 500: 90%; ACT scores over 18: 96%; SAT critical reading scores over 600: 65%; SAT math scores over 600: 57%; SAT writing scores over 600: 52%; ACT scores over 24: 57%; SAT critical reading scores over 700: 18%; SAT math scores over 700: 12%; SAT writing scores over 700: 11%; ACT scores over 30: 13%.

Faculty *Total:* 159, 75% full-time, 80% with terminal degrees. *Student/faculty ratio:* 12:1.

Majors American studies; anthropology; art; Asian studies (East); biological and physical sciences; biology/biological sciences; business administration and management; chemistry; civil engineering; classics; classics and languages, literatures and linguistics; computer science; economics; electrical, electronics and communications engineering; English; environmental studies; fine arts related; French; German; health and physical education; history; international relations and affairs; mass communication/media; mathematics; mechanical engineering; metallurgical engineering; multi-/interdisciplinary studies related; neuroscience; philosophy; physics; political science and government; psychology; social sciences related; sociology; Spanish.

Academics *Calendar:* semesters. *Degree:* bachelor's. *Special study options:* adult/continuing education programs, advanced placement credit, double majors, English as a second language, honors programs, independent study, internships, off-campus study, part-time degree program, student-designed majors, study abroad. *Unusual degree programs:* 3-2 engineering with Columbia University, Washington University of St. Louis.

Computers on Campus 1,655 computers/terminals and 1,100 ports are available on campus for general student use. Students can access the following: campus intranet, computer help desk, free student e-mail accounts, online (class) grades, online (class) registration, online (class) schedules. Campuswide network is available. 100% of college-owned or -operated housing units are wired for high-speed Internet access. Wireless service is available via classrooms, computer centers, computer labs, dorm rooms, libraries, student centers.

Student Life *Housing options:* coed, men-only, women-only. Campus housing is university owned. Freshman campus housing is guaranteed. *Activities and organizations:* drama/theater group, student-run newspaper, radio and television station, choral group, Environmental Action Committee, Habitat for Humanity, Campus Activities Board, Relay for Life, Multicultural Student Union, national fraternities, national sororities. *Campus security:* 24-hour emergency response devices and patrols, late-night transport/escort service, student EMT Corps for first aid/emergency first response. *Student services:* health clinic, personal/psychological counseling.

Athletics Member NCAA. All Division III. *Intercollegiate sports:* baseball M, basketball M/W, cross-country running M/W, field hockey W, football M, golf M/W, gymnastics W, lacrosse M/W, rugby M (c)/W (c), soccer M/W, softball W, swimming and diving M/W, tennis M/W, track and field M/W, volleyball W, wrestling M. *Intramural sports:* basketball M/W, cheerleading W, cross-country running W, fencing M/W, field hockey W, football M/W, lacrosse M, racquetball M/W, rugby M/W, sailing M/W, skiing (cross-country) M/W, skiing (downhill) M/W, softball M/W, squash M/W, swimming and diving M/W, tennis M/W, ultimate Frisbee M/W, volleyball M/W, water polo M/W, weight lifting M/W.

Standardized Tests *Required for some:* SAT or ACT (for admission).

Costs (2007–08) *Comprehensive fee:* $43,160 includes full-time tuition ($35,000), mandatory fees ($160), and room and board ($8000). Full-time tuition and fees vary according to course load. Part-time tuition: $1094 per credit hour. Part-time tuition and fees vary according to course load. *Required fees:* $160 per year part-time. *College room only:* $4000. *Payment plan:* installment. *Waivers:* senior citizens and employees or children of employees.

Financial Aid Of all full-time matriculated undergraduates who enrolled in 2007, 1,277 applied for aid, 1,089 were judged to have need, 241 had their need fully met. 637 Federal Work-Study jobs (averaging $1540). In 2007, 359 non-need-based awards were made. *Average percent of need met:* 84%. *Average financial aid package:* $23,300. *Average need-based loan:* $4936. *Average need-based gift aid:* $17,173. *Average non-need-based aid:* $11,909. *Average indebtedness upon graduation:* $18,509. *Financial aid deadline:* 2/15.

Applying *Options:* electronic application, early admission, early decision, early action, deferred entrance. *Application fee:* $50. *Required:* essay or personal statement, high school transcript, 2 letters of recommendation, graded paper. *Recommended:* interview. *Application deadlines:* 2/15 (freshmen), 8/15 (transfers), 12/15 (early action). *Early decision deadline:* 1/15. *Notification:* 4/1 (freshmen), 2/1 (early decision), 1/15 (early action).

Freshman Application Contact Mr. Robert McCullough, Dean of Admissions, Ursinus College, Box 1000, Main Street, Collegeville, PA 19426. *Phone:* 610-409-3200. *Fax:* 610-409-3662. *E-mail:* admissions@ursinus.edu.

See page 2330 for the College Close-Up.

VALLEY FORGE CHRISTIAN COLLEGE

Phoenixville, Pennsylvania — www.vfcc.edu/

- **Independent Assemblies of God** 4-year, founded 1938
- **Small-town** 77-acre campus with easy access to Philadelphia
- **Endowment** $806,118
- **Coed**
- **Minimally difficult** entrance level

Faculty *Student/faculty ratio:* 19:1.

Academics *Calendar:* semesters. *Degrees:* certificates, associate, and bachelor's.

Student Life *Campus security:* 24-hour emergency response devices and patrols, student patrols, late-night transport/escort service, controlled dormitory access, 16-hour patrols by trained security personnel.

Athletics Member NCCAA.

Standardized Tests *Required:* SAT or ACT (for admission).

Costs (2007–08) *Comprehensive fee:* $19,342 includes full-time tuition ($11,650), mandatory fees ($950), and room and board ($6742). Part-time tuition: $449 per credit. *College room only:* $3282.

Financial Aid Of all full-time matriculated undergraduates who enrolled in 2007, 756 applied for aid, 688 were judged to have need, 85 had their need fully met. 56 Federal Work-Study jobs (averaging $1243). In 2007, 190 non-need-based awards were made. *Average percent of need met:* 54. *Average financial aid package:* $8956. *Average need-based loan:* $4071. *Average need-based gift aid:* $5474. *Average non-need-based aid:* $5708. *Average indebtedness upon graduation:* $33,120.

Applying *Options:* electronic application, early admission, deferred entrance. *Application fee:* $25. *Required:* essay or personal statement, high school transcript, 1 letter of recommendation. *Required for some:* interview.

Freshman Application Contact Rev. William Chenco, Director of Admissions, Valley Forge Christian College, 1401 Charlestown Road, Phoenixville, PA 19460. *Phone:* 610-935-0450 Ext. 1430. *Toll-free phone:* 800-432-8322. *Fax:* 610-935-9353. *E-mail:* admissions@vfcc.edu.

VILLANOVA UNIVERSITY

Villanova, Pennsylvania — www.villanova.edu/

- **Independent Roman Catholic** comprehensive, founded 1842
- **Suburban** 254-acre campus with easy access to Philadelphia
- **Endowment** $335.4 million
- **Coed** 7,350 undergraduate students, 91% full-time, 51% women, 49% men
- **Very difficult** entrance level, 42% of applicants were admitted

Undergraduates 6,673 full-time, 677 part-time. Students come from 46 states and territories, 41 other countries, 71% are from out of state, 4% African American, 6% Asian American or Pacific Islander, 6% Hispanic American, 0.2% Native American, 2% international, 2% transferred in, 72% live on campus. *Retention:* 94% of 2006 full-time freshmen returned.

Freshmen *Admission:* 13,760 applied, 5,718 admitted, 1,604 enrolled. *Average high school GPA:* 3.76. *Test scores:* SAT critical reading scores over 500: 97%; SAT math scores over 500: 97%; ACT scores over 18: 100%; SAT critical reading scores over 600: 69%; SAT math scores over 600: 79%; ACT scores over 24: 92%; SAT critical reading scores over 700: 15%; SAT math scores over 700: 27%; ACT scores over 30: 48%.

Faculty *Total:* 932, 61% full-time, 69% with terminal degrees. *Student/faculty ratio:* 14:1.

Majors Accounting; art history, criticism and conservation; astronomy; astrophysics; biology/biological sciences; business administration and management; business/managerial economics; chemical engineering; chemistry; civil engineering; classics and languages, literatures and linguistics; computer engineering; computer science; criminal justice/law enforcement administration; economics; education; electrical, electronics and communications engineering; elementary education; English; finance; French; geography; German; history; human services; information science/studies; international business/trade/commerce; Italian; liberal arts and sciences/liberal studies; management information systems; marketing/marketing management; mass communication/media; mathematics; mechanical engineering; nursing (registered nurse training); philosophy; physics; political science and government; psychology; religious studies; secondary education; sociology; Spanish.

Academics *Calendar:* semesters. *Degrees:* certificates, associate, bachelor's, master's, doctoral, and first professional. *Special study options:* accelerated degree program, adult/continuing education programs, advanced placement credit, cooperative education, distance learning, double majors, English as a second language, honors programs, independent study, internships, off-campus study, part-time degree program, services for LD students, study abroad, summer session for credit. *ROTC:* Army (c), Navy (b), Air Force (c). *Unusual degree programs:* 3-2 engineering; political science, biology, computer science, mathematics, physics.

Computers on Campus 6,466 computers/terminals and 18,000 ports are available on campus for general student use. Students can access the following: campus intranet, computer help desk, free student e-mail accounts, online (class) grades, online (class) registration, online (class) schedules, learning management system, Web-based laundry reservation, electronic library reserves, electronic portfolios, data vaulting, calendar system, basketball ticket lottery, printing. Campuswide network is available. 100% of college-owned or -operated housing units are wired for high-speed Internet access. Wireless service is available via classrooms, computer centers, computer labs, dorm rooms, learning centers, libraries, student centers.

Student Life *Housing options:* coed, men-only, women-only, disabled students. Campus housing is university owned. Freshman campus housing is guaranteed. *Activities and organizations:* drama/theater group, student-run newspaper, radio and television station, choral group, marching band, Blue Key Society, orientation counselor program, Special Olympics, campus activities team, national fraternities, national sororities. *Campus security:* 24-hour emergency response devices and patrols, student patrols, late-night transport/escort service, controlled dormitory access. *Student services:* health clinic, personal/psychological counseling, legal services.

Athletics Member NCAA. All Division I except football (Division I-AA). *Intercollegiate sports:* baseball M (s), basketball M (s)/W (s), cheerleading M/W, crew M (c)/W (s), cross-country running M (s)/W (s), field hockey W (s), golf M, ice hockey M (c), lacrosse M/W, rugby M (c), sailing M (c)/W (c), skiing (downhill) M (c)/W (c), soccer M (s)/W (s), softball W (s), swimming and diving M/W (s), tennis M/W, track and field M (s)/W (s), volleyball M (c)/W (s), water polo M (c)/W, weight lifting M (c)/W (c). *Intramural sports:* baseball M (c), basketball M/W, equestrian sports W (c), field hockey W (c), football M/W, golf M (c), lacrosse M (c)/W (c), soccer M/W, softball M/W, swimming and diving M (c)/W (c), tennis M/W, track and field M/W, ultimate Frisbee M/W, volleyball M/W.

Standardized Tests *Required:* SAT or ACT (for admission).

Costs (2007–08) *Comprehensive fee:* $44,710 includes full-time tuition ($34,320), mandatory fees ($580), and room and board ($9810). Full-time tuition and fees vary according to class time, course level, program, and student level. Part-time tuition: $1430 per credit hour. Part-time tuition and fees vary according to class time, course level, and program. *Required fees:* $30 per term part-time. *College room only:* $5200. Room and board charges vary according to board plan and housing facility. *Payment plan:* installment. *Waivers:* senior citizens and employees or children of employees.

Financial Aid Of all full-time matriculated undergraduates who enrolled in 2007, 3,733 applied for aid, 3,013 were judged to have need, 537 had their need fully met. 1,600 Federal Work-Study jobs (averaging $2367). 35 state and other part-time jobs (averaging $2590). In 2007, 389 non-need-based awards were made. *Average percent of need met:* 79%. *Average financial aid package:* $23,433. *Average need-based loan:* $5270. *Average need-based gift aid:* $18,881. *Average non-need-based aid:* $10,698. *Average indebtedness upon graduation:* $28,107.

Applying *Options:* electronic application, early admission, early action, deferred entrance. *Application fee:* $75. *Required:* essay or personal statement, high school transcript, letters of recommendation, activities resume. *Application deadlines:* 1/7 (freshmen), 6/1 (transfers), 11/1 (early action). *Notification:* 4/1 (freshmen), continuous (transfers), 12/20 (early action).

Freshman Application Contact Mr. Michael Gaynor, Director of University Admission, Villanova University, 800 Lancaster Avenue, Villanova, PA 19085-1672. *Phone:* 610-519-4000. *Fax:* 610-519-6450. *E-mail:* gotovu@villanova.edu.

See page 2332 for the College Close-Up.

WASHINGTON & JEFFERSON COLLEGE

Washington, Pennsylvania **www.washjeff.edu/**

- **Independent** 4-year, founded 1781
- **Small-town** 51-acre campus with easy access to Pittsburgh
- **Endowment** $104.5 million
- **Coed** 1,531 undergraduate students, 99% full-time, 47% women, 53% men
- **Very difficult** entrance level, 34% of applicants were admitted

Now in its third century, Washington & Jefferson College (W&J) continues to be one of America's premier liberal arts colleges. High-quality academic programs and a student-centered approach characterize a W&J education. Programs in prehealth and prelaw are nationally recognized, with medical and law school acceptance rates among the highest in the country.

Undergraduates 1,517 full-time, 14 part-time. Students come from 34 states and territories, 6 other countries, 24% are from out of state, 2% African American, 1% Asian American or Pacific Islander, 1% Hispanic American, 0.1% Native American, 0.8% international, 0.7% transferred in, 94% live on campus. *Retention:* 84% of 2006 full-time freshmen returned.

Freshmen *Admission:* 7,377 applied, 2,529 admitted, 407 enrolled. *Average high school GPA:* 3.46. *Test scores:* SAT critical reading scores over 500: 89%; SAT math scores over 500: 85%; ACT scores over 18: 99%; SAT critical reading scores over 600: 42%; SAT math scores over 600: 37%; ACT scores over 24: 66%; SAT critical reading scores over 700: 5%; SAT math scores over 700: 4%; ACT scores over 30: 10%.

Faculty *Total:* 154, 71% full-time, 77% with terminal degrees. *Student/faculty ratio:* 12:1.

Majors Accounting; art; art teacher education; biochemistry; biology/biological sciences; biophysics; business/commerce; cell biology and anatomical sciences related; chemistry; chemistry related; economics; education; English; environmental studies; French; German; history; information technology; international business/trade/commerce; international/global studies; mathematics; multi-/interdisciplinary studies related; music; philosophy; physics; political science and government; psychology; sociology; Spanish; theater literature, history and criticism.

Academics *Calendar:* 4-1-4. *Degrees:* associate and bachelor's. *Special study options:* academic remediation for entering students, accelerated degree program, advanced placement credit, double majors, honors programs, independent study, internships, off-campus study, part-time degree program, services for LD students, student-designed majors, study abroad, summer session for credit. *ROTC:* Army (c), Air Force (c). *Unusual degree programs:* 3-2 engineering with Columbia University in New York; Case Western Reserve University, Washington University in St. Louis; podiatry with Pennsylvania and Ohio colleges; optometry with Pennsylvania College of Optometry; integrated pre-health enrichment program, physical therapy program, pre-occupational therapy program, physician assistant program; law with Duquesne University and University of Pittsburgh.

Computers on Campus 450 computers/terminals and 2,000 ports are available on campus for general student use. Students can access the following: campus intranet, computer help desk, free student e-mail accounts, online (class) grades, online (class) registration, online (class) schedules. Campuswide network is available. 100% of college-owned or -operated housing units are wired for high-speed Internet access. Wireless service is available via entire campus.

Student Life *Housing:* on-campus residence required through senior year. *Options:* coed, men-only, women-only, disabled students. Campus housing is university owned and leased by the school. Freshman campus housing is guaranteed. *Activities and organizations:* drama/theater group, student-run newspaper, radio station, choral group, Student Government Association, Student Activities Board, The Newman Club, Asian Student Association, Accounting Society, national fraternities, national sororities. *Campus security:* 24-hour emergency response devices and patrols, late-night transport/escort service, controlled dormitory access. *Student services:* health clinic, personal/psychological counseling.

Athletics Member NCAA. All Division III. *Intercollegiate sports:* baseball M, basketball M/W, cheerleading M/W, cross-country running M/W, field hockey W, football M, golf M/W, ice hockey M (c), lacrosse M/W, soccer M/W, softball W, swimming and diving M/W, tennis M/W, track and field M/W, volleyball W, water polo M/W, wrestling M. *Intramural sports:* basketball M/W, bowling M/W, cross-country running M/W, equestrian sports M (c)/W (c), fencing M (c)/W (c), football M/W, racquetball M/W, rugby M (c)/W (c), skiing (downhill) M (c)/W (c), soccer M/W, softball M/W, table tennis M/W, tennis M/W, ultimate Frisbee M/W, volleyball M/W.

Standardized Tests *Required:* SAT or ACT (for admission).

Costs (2007–08) *Comprehensive fee:* $37,562 includes full-time tuition ($29,132), mandatory fees ($400), and room and board ($8030). Part-time tuition: $730 per credit hour. Part-time tuition and fees vary according to course load. *College room only:* $4734. Room and board charges vary according to board plan and housing facility. *Payment plans:* installment, deferred payment. *Waivers:* employees or children of employees.

Financial Aid Of all full-time matriculated undergraduates who enrolled in 2007, 1,263 applied for aid, 1,105 were judged to have need, 217 had their need fully met. 600 Federal Work-Study jobs (averaging $1695). 270 state and other part-time jobs (averaging $900). In 2007, 344 non-need-based awards were made. *Average percent of need met:* 81%. *Average financial aid package:* $21,882. *Average need-based loan:* $4503. *Average need-based gift aid:* $9020. *Average non-need-based aid:* $9971. *Average indebtedness upon graduation:* $20,000.

Applying *Options:* electronic application, early admission, early decision, early action, deferred entrance. *Application fee:* $25. *Required:* essay or personal statement, high school transcript, 1 letter of recommendation. *Required for some:* interview. *Recommended:* interview. *Application deadlines:* 3/1 (freshmen), rolling (transfers), 1/1 (early action). *Early decision deadline:* 12/1. *Notification:* 3/15 (freshmen), 12/15 (early decision), 1/15 (early action).

Freshman Application Contact Mr. Alton E. Newell, Vice President for Enrollment Management, Washington & Jefferson College, 60 South Lincoln Street, Washington, PA 15301. *Phone:* 724-223-6025. *Toll-free phone:* 888-WANDJAY. *Fax:* 724-223-6534. *E-mail:* admission@washjeff.edu.

WAYNESBURG UNIVERSITY

Waynesburg, Pennsylvania **www.waynesburg.edu/**

- **Independent** comprehensive, founded 1849, affiliated with Presbyterian Church (U.S.A.)
- **Small-town** 30-acre campus with easy access to Pittsburgh
- **Endowment** $30.8 million
- **Coed** 1,616 undergraduate students, 82% full-time, 62% women, 38% men
- **Moderately difficult** entrance level, 74% of applicants were admitted

Undergraduates 1,332 full-time, 284 part-time. Students come from 17 states and territories, 4 other countries, 3% African American, 0.2% Asian American or Pacific Islander, 0.6% Hispanic American, 0.1% Native American, 3% transferred in, 59% live on campus. *Retention:* 76% of 2006 full-time freshmen returned.

Freshmen *Admission:* 1,518 applied, 1,124 admitted, 380 enrolled. *Average high school GPA:* 3.36.

Faculty *Total:* 135, 46% full-time, 41% with terminal degrees. *Student/faculty ratio:* 13:1.

Majors Accounting; advertising; art; arts management; athletic training; biology/biological sciences; biology teacher education; business administration and management; chemistry; chemistry teacher education; commercial and advertising art; communication/speech communication and rhetoric; computer and information sciences; computer science; creative writing; criminal justice/law enforcement administration; elementary education; engineering related; English; English/language arts teacher education; environmental studies; finance; forensic science and technology; graphic design; health/health care administration; history; international business/trade/commerce; journalism; kinesiology and exercise science; liberal arts and sciences/liberal studies; marine biology and biological oceanography; marketing/marketing management; mathematics; mathematics teacher education; nursing (registered nurse training); pre-dentistry studies; pre-engineering; pre-law studies; pre-medical studies; pre-theology/pre-ministerial studies; pre-veterinary studies; psychology; public administration; radio and television; science teacher education; secondary education; social sciences; social studies teacher education; sociology; special education.

Academics *Calendar:* semesters. *Degrees:* associate, bachelor's, and master's. *Special study options:* academic remediation for entering students, accelerated degree program, adult/continuing education programs, advanced placement credit, distance learning, double majors, honors programs, independent study, internships, part-time degree program, study abroad. *ROTC:* Army (c). *Unusual degree programs:* 3-2 engineering with Case Western Reserve University, Washington University in St. Louis, Pennsylvania State University—University Park Campus.

Computers on Campus 150 computers/terminals are available on campus for general student use. Students can access the following: online (class) registration. Campuswide network is available.

Student Life *Housing:* on-campus residence required through junior year. *Options:* men-only, women-only. Campus housing is university owned. Freshman campus housing is guaranteed. *Activities and organizations:* drama/theater group, student-run newspaper, radio and television station, choral group, marching band, Student Senate, Student Activities Board (SAB), Student Nurses Association, Christian Fellowship. *Campus security:* 24-hour emergency response devices and patrols, late-night transport/escort service, controlled dormitory access. *Student services:* health clinic, personal/psychological counseling.

Athletics Member NCAA. All Division III. *Intercollegiate sports:* baseball M, basketball M/W, cross-country running M/W, football M, golf M/W, soccer M/W, softball W, tennis M/W, track and field M/W, volleyball W, wrestling M. *Intramural sports:* basketball M/W, bowling M/W, racquetball M/W, softball M/W, table tennis M/W, volleyball M/W.

Standardized Tests *Required:* SAT or ACT (for admission).

Costs (2008–09) *Comprehensive fee:* $24,130 includes full-time tuition ($16,730), mandatory fees ($350), and room and board ($7050). Part-time tuition: $700 per credit. *College room only:* $3600.

Financial Aid Of all full-time matriculated undergraduates who enrolled in 2007, 1,483 applied for aid, 1,281 were judged to have need, 417 had their need fully met. 275 Federal Work-Study jobs (averaging $1300). In 2007, 244 non-need-based awards were made. *Average percent of need met:* 83%. *Average financial aid package:* $12,836. *Average need-based loan:* $4019. *Average need-based gift aid:* $9895. *Average non-need-based aid:* $10,969. *Average indebtedness upon graduation:* $19,000.

Applying *Options:* early admission. *Application fee:* $20. *Required:* high school transcript, minimum 2.75 GPA. *Required for some:* essay or personal statement, letters of recommendation. *Recommended:* minimum 3.0 GPA, interview. *Application deadlines:* rolling (freshmen), rolling (transfers). *Notification:* continuous (freshmen), continuous (transfers).

Freshman Application Contact Ms. Robin L. King, Dean of Admissions, Waynesburg University, 51 West College Street, Waynesburg, PA 15370. *Phone:* 724-852-3333. *Toll-free phone:* 800-225-7393. *Fax:* 724-627-8124. *E-mail:* admissions@waynesburg.edu.

WEST CHESTER UNIVERSITY OF PENNSYLVANIA

West Chester, Pennsylvania www.wcupa.edu/

- **State-supported** comprehensive, founded 1871, part of Pennsylvania State System of Higher Education
- **Suburban** 547-acre campus with easy access to Philadelphia
- **Endowment** $14.9 million
- **Coed** 11,109 undergraduate students, 90% full-time, 61% women, 39% men
- **Moderately difficult** entrance level, 48% of applicants were admitted

Undergraduates 9,975 full-time, 1,134 part-time. Students come from 30 states and territories, 57 other countries, 12% are from out of state, 9% African American, 2% Asian American or Pacific Islander, 3% Hispanic American, 0.3% Native American, 0.3% international, 9% transferred in, 41% live on campus. *Retention:* 86% of 2006 full-time freshmen returned.

Freshmen *Admission:* 12,237 applied, 5,834 admitted, 1,964 enrolled. *Average high school GPA:* 3.35. *Test scores:* SAT critical reading scores over 500: 69%; SAT math scores over 500: 72%; SAT writing scores over 500: 65%; SAT critical reading scores over 600: 15%; SAT math scores over 600: 19%; SAT writing scores over 600: 14%; SAT critical reading scores over 700: 1%; SAT math scores over 700: 1%; SAT writing scores over 700: 1%.

Faculty *Total:* 829, 69% full-time. *Student/faculty ratio:* 17:1.

Majors Accounting; American studies; analytical chemistry; anthropology; art; athletic training; audiology and speech-language pathology; biochemistry; biology/biological sciences; business administration and management; business/commerce; business/managerial economics; chemistry; clinical nutrition; communication/speech communication and rhetoric; computer and information sciences; counselor education/school counseling and guidance; criminal justice/safety; dietetics; dramatic/theater arts; early childhood education; elementary education; English; finance; fine/studio arts; French; geography; geology/earth science; German; health and physical education; health/health care administration; health teacher education; history; international relations and affairs; Latin; liberal arts and sciences/liberal studies; mathematics; mathematics teacher education; medical pharmacology and pharmaceutical sciences; music; music performance; music teacher education; music theory and composition; nursing (registered nurse training); philosophy; physical education teaching and coaching; physics; piano and organ; political science and government; pre-medical studies; psychology; public health; reading teacher education; Russian; sales, distribution and marketing; secondary education; social studies teacher education; social work; sociology; Spanish; special education; special education (speech or language impaired); speech and rhetoric; voice and opera; women's studies.

Academics *Calendar:* semesters. *Degrees:* bachelor's, master's, and post-bachelor's certificates. *Special study options:* academic remediation for entering students, accelerated degree program, adult/continuing education programs, advanced placement credit, distance learning, double majors, English as a second language, honors programs, independent study, internships, off-campus study, part-time degree program, services for LD students, student-designed majors, study abroad, summer session for credit. *ROTC:* Army (c), Air Force (c). *Unusual degree programs:* engineering with Pennsylvania State University.

Computers on Campus 1,100 computers/terminals are available on campus for general student use. Students can access the following: campus intranet, computer help desk, free student e-mail accounts, online (class) grades, online (class) registration, online (class) schedules. Campuswide network is available. 100% of college-owned or -operated housing units are wired for high-speed Internet access. Wireless service is available via classrooms, computer centers, computer labs, learning centers, libraries, student centers.

Student Life *Housing options:* coed, men-only, women-only, disabled students. Campus housing is university owned and is provided by a third party. Freshman applicants given priority for college housing. *Activities and organizations:* drama/theater group, student-run newspaper, radio and television station, choral group, marching band, Off Campus and Commuter Association, Residence Hall Association, Student Government Association, Sports Club Council, national fraternities, national sororities. *Campus security:* 24-hour emergency response devices and patrols, late-night transport/escort service, controlled dormitory access. *Student services:* health clinic, personal/psychological counseling, women's center, legal services.

Athletics Member NCAA. All Division II except field hockey (Division I). *Intercollegiate sports:* baseball M (s), basketball M (s)/W (s), cheerleading W (c), cross-country running M (s)/W (s), equestrian sports M (c)/W (c), fencing M (c)/W (c), field hockey W (s), football M (s), golf M (s)/W (s), gymnastics W (s), ice hockey M (c)/W (c), lacrosse M (c)/W (s), rugby M (c)/W (s), skiing (downhill) M (c)/W (c), soccer M (s)/W (s), softball W (s), swimming and diving M (s)/W (s), tennis M (s)/W (s), track and field M (s)/W (s), volleyball M (c)/W (s), water polo M (c)/W (c). *Intramural sports:* basketball M/W, field hockey M/W, football M/W, soccer M/W, softball M/W, tennis M/W, volleyball M/W.

Standardized Tests *Required:* SAT or ACT (for admission).

Costs (2007–08) *One-time required fee:* $1499. *Tuition:* state resident $5177 full-time, $216 per credit part-time; nonresident $12,944 full-time, $539 per credit part-time. Full-time tuition and fees vary according to course load and student level. Part-time tuition and fees vary according to course load and student level. *Required fees:* $1499 full-time, $49 per credit part-time. *Room and board:* $6590; room only: $4388. Room and board charges vary according to board plan and housing facility. *Payment plan:* installment. *Waivers:* senior citizens and employees or children of employees.

Financial Aid *Average indebtedness upon graduation:* $17,500.

Applying *Options:* electronic application, early admission, deferred entrance. *Application fee:* $35. *Required:* essay or personal statement, high school transcript. *Required for some:* letters of recommendation, interview. *Recommended:* minimum 3.0 GPA. *Application deadlines:* rolling (freshmen), rolling (transfers). *Notification:* continuous (freshmen), continuous (transfers).

Freshman Application Contact Ms. Marsha Haug, Vice President of Enrollment Services and Admissions, West Chester University of Pennsylvania,

Messikomer Hall, Rosedale Avenue, West Chester, PA 19383. *Phone:* 610-436-3414. *Toll-free phone:* 877-315-2165. *Fax:* 610-436-2907. *E-mail:* ugadmiss@wcupa.edu.

See page 2334 for the College Close-Up.

WESTMINSTER COLLEGE

New Wilmington, Pennsylvania **www.westminster.edu/**

Westminster College, an independent, coeducational liberal arts college affiliated with the Presbyterian Church (USA), was founded in 1852. Westminster's liberal arts foundation thrives in a caring environment supported by an integrative curriculum featuring state-of-the-art technology and opportunities for involvement to prepare students for a diverse world while they choose from more than forty different majors.

Freshman Application Contact Bradley Tokar, Director of Admissions, Westminster College, 319 South Market Street, New Wilmington, PA 16172-0001. *Phone:* 724-946-7100. *Toll-free phone:* 800-942-8033. *Fax:* 724-946-7171. *E-mail:* tokarbp@westminster.edu.

See page 2336 for the College Close-Up.

WIDENER UNIVERSITY

Chester, Pennsylvania **www.widener.edu/**

- **Independent** comprehensive, founded 1821
- **Suburban** 110-acre campus with easy access to Philadelphia
- **Endowment** $86.1 million
- **Coed** 3,424 undergraduate students, 77% full-time, 58% women, 42% men
- **Moderately difficult** entrance level, 66% of applicants were admitted

Located just 12 miles from the historic and culturally rich city of Philadelphia, Widener University provides a unique combination of liberal arts and professional education. Having benefited from service-learning and civic engagement, Widener graduates leave the University well-prepared for a successful life of responsible citizenship in a global society.

Undergraduates 2,651 full-time, 773 part-time. Students come from 22 states and territories, 17 other countries, 38% are from out of state, 13% African American, 3% Asian American or Pacific Islander, 3% Hispanic American, 0.3% Native American, 2% international, 3% transferred in, 50% live on campus. *Retention:* 76% of 2006 full-time freshmen returned.

Freshmen *Admission:* 4,394 applied, 2,913 admitted, 800 enrolled. *Average high school GPA:* 3.30. *Test scores:* SAT critical reading scores over 500: 45%; SAT math scores over 500: 56%; SAT critical reading scores over 600: 8%; SAT math scores over 600: 15%; SAT critical reading scores over 700: 1%; SAT math scores over 700: 2%.

Faculty *Total:* 657, 47% full-time, 70% with terminal degrees. *Student/faculty ratio:* 12:1.

Majors Accounting; advertising; allied health and medical assisting services related; anthropology; behavioral sciences; biochemistry; biology/biological sciences; biology teacher education; business administration and management; business administration, management and operations related; business/managerial economics; chemical engineering; chemistry; chemistry teacher education; civil engineering; computer and information sciences; computer science; criminal justice/law enforcement administration; early childhood education; economics; educational/instructional media design; electrical, electronics and communications engineering; elementary education; engineering; engineering/industrial management; English; English/language arts teacher education; environmental studies; financial planning and services; fine arts related; foreign languages and literatures; French; French language teacher education; general studies; health services/allied health/health sciences; history; history teacher education; hospitality administration related; hotel/motel administration; humanities; human resources management and services related; industrial radiologic technology; information science/studies; international business/trade/commerce; international relations and affairs; kindergarten/preschool education; legal assistant/paralegal; management information systems and services related; marketing/marketing management; mass communication/media; mathematics; mathematics teacher education; mechanical engineering; modern languages; nursing (registered nurse training); operations management; physics; political science and government; pre-dentistry studies; pre-medical studies; pre-veterinary studies; psychology; psychology teacher education; radiologic technology/science; science teacher education; social sciences; social studies teacher education; social work; sociology; Spanish; Spanish language teacher education; special education; sport and fitness administration/management.

Academics *Calendar:* semesters. *Degrees:* associate, bachelor's, master's, doctoral, and first professional. *Special study options:* academic remediation for entering students, accelerated degree program, adult/continuing education programs, advanced placement credit, cooperative education, distance learning, double majors, English as a second language, honors programs, independent study, internships, off-campus study, part-time degree program, services for LD students, student-designed majors, study abroad, summer session for credit. *ROTC:* Army (b), Navy (c), Air Force (c). *Unusual degree programs:* 3-2 business administration; engineering; social work; physical therapy, education.

Computers on Campus 345 computers/terminals are available on campus for general student use. Students can access the following: campus intranet, computer help desk, free student e-mail accounts, online (class) grades, online (class) registration, online (class) schedules, all library resources and special journals and services. Campuswide network is available. 100% of college-owned or -operated housing units are wired for high-speed Internet access. Wireless service is available via classrooms, computer centers, computer labs, dorm rooms, learning centers, libraries, student centers.

Student Life *Housing:* on-campus residence required through sophomore year. *Options:* coed, men-only, women-only, cooperative, disabled students. Campus housing is university owned. Freshman campus housing is guaranteed. *Activities and organizations:* drama/theater group, student-run newspaper, radio and television station, choral group, WDNR Radio, Black Student Union, volunteer services, Rugby Club, Theatre Widener, national fraternities, national sororities. *Campus security:* 24-hour emergency response devices and patrols, late-night transport/escort service, controlled dormitory access, "blue light" emergency phones located throughout campus. *Student services:* health clinic, personal/psychological counseling.

Athletics Member NCAA. All Division III. *Intercollegiate sports:* baseball M, basketball M/W, cheerleading W, cross-country running M/W, field hockey W, football M, golf M, lacrosse M/W, soccer M/W, softball W, swimming and diving M/W, tennis M/W, track and field M/W, volleyball W. *Intramural sports:* crew M, ice hockey M (c), rock climbing M (c)/W (c), skiing (downhill) M (c)/W (c), soccer M, volleyball M (c), water polo M (c)/W (c).

Standardized Tests *Required:* SAT or ACT (for admission).

Costs (2007–08) *Comprehensive fee:* $38,870 includes full-time tuition ($28,180), mandatory fees ($450), and room and board ($10,240). Full-time tuition and fees vary according to class time, course load, and program. Part-time tuition: $940 per credit. *College room only:* $5200. Room and board charges vary according to board plan and housing facility. *Payment plan:* installment. *Waivers:* senior citizens and employees or children of employees.

Financial Aid Of all full-time matriculated undergraduates who enrolled in 2007, 2,257 applied for aid, 2,063 were judged to have need, 642 had their need fully met. 1,437 Federal Work-Study jobs (averaging $1864). 350 state and other part-time jobs (averaging $1200). In 2007, 401 non-need-based awards were made. *Average percent of need met:* 78%. *Average financial aid package:* $21,555. *Average need-based loan:* $5127. *Average need-based gift aid:* $8662. *Average non-need-based aid:* $9391. *Average indebtedness upon graduation:* $32,215.

Applying *Options:* electronic application, deferred entrance. *Application fee:* $35. *Required:* essay or personal statement, high school transcript. *Required for some:* minimum 2.85 GPA. *Recommended:* interview. *Application deadlines:* rolling (freshmen), rolling (transfers). *Notification:* continuous (freshmen), continuous (transfers).

Freshman Application Contact Office of Admissions, Widener University, One University Place, Chester, PA 19013. *Phone:* 610-499-4126. *Toll-free phone:* 888-WIDENER. *Fax:* 610-499-4676. *E-mail:* admissions.office@widener.edu.

See page 2338 for the College Close-Up.

WILKES UNIVERSITY

Wilkes-Barre, Pennsylvania **www.wilkes.edu/**

- **Independent** comprehensive, founded 1933
- **Urban** 25-acre campus
- **Endowment** $42.7 million
- **Coed** 2,336 undergraduate students, 90% full-time, 50% women, 50% men
- **Moderately difficult** entrance level, 79% of applicants were admitted

A comprehensive private university of intimate size, Wilkes University offers high-quality academic programs in business, education, engineering, nursing, liberal arts, and the sciences; preprofessional programs in dentistry, law, medicine, occupational therapy, optometry, osteopathic medicine, physical therapy, podiatry, and veterinary science; and a six-year Doctor of Pharmacy degree. Students have easy access to faculty members and research oppor-

tunities, and 99 percent gain employment or attend graduate/professional school within six months of graduation.

Undergraduates 2,110 full-time, 226 part-time. Students come from 28 states and territories, 10 other countries, 22% are from out of state, 3% African American, 2% Asian American or Pacific Islander, 2% Hispanic American, 0.3% Native American, 2% international, 5% transferred in, 42% live on campus. *Retention:* 79% of 2006 full-time freshmen returned.

Freshmen *Admission:* 2,668 applied, 2,102 admitted, 623 enrolled. *Test scores:* SAT critical reading scores over 500: 58%; SAT math scores over 500: 64%; SAT writing scores over 500: 52%; SAT critical reading scores over 600: 15%; SAT math scores over 600: 26%; SAT writing scores over 600: 12%; SAT critical reading scores over 700: 2%; SAT math scores over 700: 2%; SAT writing scores over 700: 1%.

Faculty *Total:* 413, 33% full-time. *Student/faculty ratio:* 15:1.

Majors Accounting; biochemistry; biology/biological sciences; business administration and management; chemistry; clinical laboratory science/medical technology; communication/speech communication and rhetoric; computer and information sciences; criminal justice/safety; digital communication and media/multimedia; dramatic/theater arts; education; electrical, electronics and communications engineering; elementary education; engineering; engineering/industrial management; English; entrepreneurship; environmental/environmental health engineering; French; geology/earth science; history; information science/studies; international relations and affairs; liberal arts and sciences/liberal studies; mathematics; mechanical engineering; multi-/interdisciplinary studies related; nursing (registered nurse training); pharmacy; pharmacy, pharmaceutical sciences, and administration related; philosophy; political science and government; psychology; sociology; Spanish.

Academics *Calendar:* semesters. *Degrees:* bachelor's, master's, and first professional. *Special study options:* academic remediation for entering students, accelerated degree program, adult/continuing education programs, advanced placement credit, cooperative education, distance learning, double majors, English as a second language, external degree program, honors programs, independent study, internships, off-campus study, part-time degree program, services for LD students, student-designed majors, study abroad, summer session for credit. *ROTC:* Army (c), Air Force (b).

Computers on Campus 530 computers/terminals are available on campus for general student use. Students can access the following: campus intranet, computer help desk, free student e-mail accounts, online (class) grades, online (class) registration, online (class) schedules. Campuswide network is available. Wireless service is available via libraries, student centers.

Student Life *Housing:* on-campus residence required through sophomore year. *Options:* coed, men-only, women-only. Campus housing is university owned. *Activities and organizations:* drama/theater group, student-run newspaper, radio and television station, choral group. *Campus security:* 24-hour emergency response devices and patrols, late-night transport/escort service, controlled dormitory access. *Student services:* health clinic, personal/psychological counseling.

Athletics Member NCAA. All Division III. *Intercollegiate sports:* baseball M, basketball M/W, field hockey W, football M, golf M, lacrosse W, soccer M/W, softball W, tennis M/W, volleyball W, wrestling M. *Intramural sports:* basketball M/W, football M, racquetball M/W, volleyball M/W, weight lifting M/W.

Standardized Tests *Required:* SAT or ACT (for admission).

Costs (2007–08) *Comprehensive fee:* $34,390 includes full-time tuition ($22,820), mandatory fees ($1260), and room and board ($10,310). Part-time tuition: $630 per credit. *Required fees:* $55 per credit part-time. *College room only:* $6210. Room and board charges vary according to board plan and housing facility. *Payment plans:* installment, deferred payment. *Waivers:* employees or children of employees.

Financial Aid Of all full-time matriculated undergraduates who enrolled in 2007, 2,025 applied for aid, 1,821 were judged to have need, 126 had their need fully met. In 2007, 170 non-need-based awards were made. *Average percent of need met:* 79%. *Average financial aid package:* $18,718. *Average need-based loan:* $3480. *Average need-based gift aid:* $13,330. *Average non-need-based aid:* $8725. *Average indebtedness upon graduation:* $29,478.

Applying *Options:* electronic application, early admission, deferred entrance. *Application fee:* $45. *Required:* high school transcript. *Required for some:* letters of recommendation. *Recommended:* interview. *Application deadlines:* rolling (freshmen), rolling (transfers). *Notification:* continuous until 8/30 (freshmen), continuous until 8/30 (transfers).

Freshman Application Contact Mr. Michael Frantz, Vice President of Enrollment Services, Wilkes University, 84 West South Street, Wilkes-Barre, PA 18766. *Phone:* 570-408-4400. *Toll-free phone:* 800-945-5378 Ext. 4400. *Fax:* 570-408-4904. *E-mail:* admissions@wilkes.edu.

See page 2340 for the College Close-Up.

WILSON COLLEGE

Chambersburg, Pennsylvania **www.wilson.edu/**

- **Independent** 4-year, founded 1869, affiliated with Presbyterian Church (U.S.A.)
- **Small-town** 300-acre campus
- **Endowment** $66.0 million
- **Women only** 714 undergraduate students, 51% full-time
- **Moderately difficult** entrance level, 48% of applicants were admitted

Undergraduates 365 full-time, 349 part-time. Students come from 16 states and territories, 22 other countries, 23% are from out of state, 4% African American, 0.1% Asian American or Pacific Islander, 2% Hispanic American, 0.1% Native American, 5% international, 4% transferred in, 54% live on campus. *Retention:* 61% of 2006 full-time freshmen returned.

Freshmen *Admission:* 479 applied, 229 admitted, 83 enrolled. *Average high school GPA:* 3.3. *Test scores:* SAT critical reading scores over 500: 46%; SAT math scores over 500: 45%; SAT writing scores over 500: 41%; ACT scores over 18: 88%; SAT critical reading scores over 600: 13%; SAT math scores over 600: 7%; SAT writing scores over 600: 11%; ACT scores over 24: 12%; SAT critical reading scores over 700: 1%; SAT math scores over 700: 1%; SAT writing scores over 700: 3%.

Faculty *Total:* 87, 46% full-time, 46% with terminal degrees. *Student/faculty ratio:* 9:1.

Majors Accounting; art; behavioral sciences; biology/biological sciences; business administration and management; chemistry; elementary education; English; environmental studies; equestrian studies; French; international relations and affairs; kinesiology and exercise science; liberal arts and sciences/liberal studies; management information systems; mass communication/media; mathematics; philosophy and religious studies related; physiological psychology/psychobiology; rehabilitation and therapeutic professions related; social sciences; Spanish; veterinary/animal health technology.

Academics *Calendar:* 4-1-4. *Degrees:* associate and bachelor's. *Special study options:* academic remediation for entering students, adult/continuing education programs, advanced placement credit, cooperative education, double majors, English as a second language, external degree program, honors programs, independent study, internships, off-campus study, part-time degree program, services for LD students, student-designed majors, study abroad, summer session for credit. *ROTC:* Army (c).

Computers on Campus 112 computers/terminals are available on campus for general student use. Students can access the following: campus intranet, computer help desk, free student e-mail accounts, online (class) grades, online (class) registration, online (class) schedules. Campuswide network is available. 100% of college-owned or -operated housing units are wired for high-speed Internet access. Wireless service is available via classrooms, learning centers, libraries, student centers.

Student Life *Housing:* on-campus residence required through junior year. *Options:* women-only. Campus housing is university owned. Freshman campus housing is guaranteed. *Activities and organizations:* drama/theater group, student-run newspaper, radio station, choral group, Muhibbah Club, Orchesis Club, student newspaper, student government, Black Student Union. *Campus security:* 24-hour emergency response devices and patrols, late-night transport/escort service, controlled dormitory access. *Student services:* health clinic, personal/psychological counseling, women's center.

Athletics Member NCAA. All Division III. *Intercollegiate sports:* basketball W, field hockey W, gymnastics W, soccer W, softball W. *Intramural sports:* archery W, equestrian sports W, lacrosse W, tennis W.

Costs (2008–09) *Comprehensive fee:* $34,530 includes full-time tuition ($25,350), mandatory fees ($550), and room and board ($8630). Part-time tuition: $2540 per course. *Required fees:* $40 per course part-time, $40 per course part-time. *College room only:* $4470.

Financial Aid Of all full-time matriculated undergraduates who enrolled in 2007, 297 applied for aid, 260 were judged to have need, 32 had their need fully met. 60 Federal Work-Study jobs (averaging $1500). 101 state and other part-time jobs (averaging $1500). In 2007, 101 non-need-based awards were made. *Average percent of need met:* 76%. *Average financial aid package:* $18,021. *Average need-based loan:* $5223. *Average need-based gift aid:* $13,809. *Average non-need-based aid:* $15,316. *Average indebtedness upon graduation:* $24,443.

Applying *Options:* electronic application, early admission, deferred entrance. *Application fee:* $35. *Required:* essay or personal statement, high school transcript, letters of recommendation. *Recommended:* minimum 2.7 GPA, interview. *Application deadlines:* rolling (freshmen), rolling (transfers). *Notification:* continuous (freshmen), continuous (transfers).

Freshman Application Contact Deborah Arthur, Admissions Administrator, Wilson College, 1015 Philadelphia Avenue, Chambersburg, PA 17201. *Phone:* 717-262-2002. *Toll-free phone:* 800-421-8402. *Fax:* 717-262-2546. *E-mail:* admissions@wilson.edu.

YESHIVA BETH MOSHE

Scranton, Pennsylvania

Director of Admissions Rabbi I. Bressler, Dean, Yeshiva Beth Moshe, 930 Hickory Street, PO Box 1141, Scranton, PA 18505-2124. *Phone:* 717-346-1747.

YORK COLLEGE OF PENNSYLVANIA

York, Pennsylvania www.ycp.edu/

- **Independent** comprehensive, founded 1787
- **Suburban** 118-acre campus with easy access to Baltimore
- **Endowment** $69.3 million
- **Coed** 5,444 undergraduate students, 85% full-time, 56% women, 44% men
- **Moderately difficult** entrance level, 64% of applicants were admitted

Undergraduates 4,639 full-time, 805 part-time. Students come from 36 states and territories, 43% are from out of state, 2% African American, 1% Asian American or Pacific Islander, 2% Hispanic American, 0.2% Native American, 0.5% international, 5% transferred in, 45% live on campus. *Retention:* 77% of 2006 full-time freshmen returned.

Freshmen *Admission:* 7,009 applied, 4,462 admitted, 1,262 enrolled. *Average high school GPA:* 3.50. *Test scores:* SAT critical reading scores over 500: 69%; SAT math scores over 500: 80%; SAT writing scores over 500: 66%; SAT critical reading scores over 600: 18%; SAT math scores over 600: 25%; SAT writing scores over 600: 15%; SAT critical reading scores over 700: 2%; SAT math scores over 700: 2%; SAT writing scores over 700: 1%.

Faculty *Total:* 419, 37% full-time, 42% with terminal degrees. *Student/faculty ratio:* 15:1.

Majors Accounting; biology/biological sciences; biology teacher education; business administration and management; business/commerce; business, management, and marketing related; chemistry; clinical laboratory science/medical technology; communication/speech communication and rhetoric; computer and information sciences; computer and information sciences and support services related; computer engineering; computer science; corrections; criminalistics and criminal science; digital communication and media/multimedia; dramatic/theater arts; education related; electrical, electronics and communications engineering; elementary education; engineering/industrial management; English; English/language arts teacher education; entrepreneurship; finance; fine arts related; fine/studio arts; forensic science and technology; general studies; graphic design; history; history teacher education; humanities; management information systems and services related; marketing/marketing management; mass communication/media; mathematics; mathematics teacher education; mechanical engineering; medical insurance coding; multi-/interdisciplinary studies related; music; music teacher education; nuclear medical technology; nursing (registered nurse training); parks, recreation and leisure; philosophy; physics; political science and government; psychology; public relations/image management; recording arts technology; respiratory care therapy; science teacher education; secondary education; social sciences; social studies teacher education; sociology; Spanish; special education; speech and rhetoric; sport and fitness administration/management; technical and business writing.

Academics *Calendar:* semesters. *Degrees:* associate, bachelor's, and master's. *Special study options:* academic remediation for entering students, accelerated degree program, adult/continuing education programs, advanced placement credit, cooperative education, distance learning, double majors, honors programs, independent study, internships, part-time degree program, student-designed majors, study abroad, summer session for credit. *ROTC:* Army (c).

Computers on Campus 400 computers/terminals are available on campus for general student use. Students can access the following: campus intranet, computer help desk, free student e-mail accounts, online (class) grades, online (class) registration, online (class) schedules. Campuswide network is available. 100% of college-owned or -operated housing units are wired for high-speed Internet access. Wireless service is available via classrooms, computer centers, computer labs, dorm rooms, learning centers, libraries, student centers.

Student Life *Housing:* on-campus residence required through junior year. *Options:* coed, men-only, women-only. Campus housing is university owned. Freshman campus housing is guaranteed. *Activities and organizations:* drama/theater group, student-run newspaper, radio station, choral group, Student Senate, Theater Company, Ski and Outdoor Club, Marketing Club, Student Education Association, national fraternities, national sororities. *Campus security:* 24-hour emergency response devices and patrols, late-night transport/escort service. *Student services:* health clinic, personal/psychological counseling.

Athletics Member NCAA. All Division III. *Intercollegiate sports:* baseball M, basketball M/W, cheerleading W, cross-country running M/W, field hockey W, golf M, ice hockey M (c), lacrosse M/W, soccer M/W, softball W, swimming and diving M/W, tennis M/W, track and field M/W, volleyball M (c)/W, wrestling M. *Intramural sports:* badminton M/W, basketball M/W, football M/W, lacrosse M (c)/W (c), rugby M (c)/W (c), skiing (downhill) M (c)/W (c), soccer M/W, softball M/W, swimming and diving M/W, table tennis M, tennis M/W, track and field M/W, volleyball M/W, water polo M/W, weight lifting M (c)/W (c), wrestling M.

Standardized Tests *Required:* SAT or ACT (for admission).

Costs (2007–08) *Comprehensive fee:* $20,160 includes full-time tuition ($11,500), mandatory fees ($1250), and room and board ($7410). Part-time tuition: $360 per credit hour. *Required fees:* $278 per term part-time. *College room only:* $4160. Room and board charges vary according to housing facility. *Payment plans:* tuition prepayment, installment. *Waivers:* employees or children of employees.

Financial Aid Of all full-time matriculated undergraduates who enrolled in 2006, 3,517 applied for aid, 2,360 were judged to have need, 720 had their need fully met. 267 Federal Work-Study jobs (averaging $1458). 37 state and other part-time jobs (averaging $1277). In 2006, 472 non-need-based awards were made. *Average percent of need met:* 73%. *Average financial aid package:* $8670. *Average need-based loan:* $5147. *Average need-based gift aid:* $4342. *Average non-need-based aid:* $3055. *Average indebtedness upon graduation:* $20,639.

Applying *Options:* electronic application, early admission, deferred entrance. *Application fee:* $30. *Required:* essay or personal statement, high school transcript, minimum 2.0 GPA. *Required for some:* interview. *Recommended:* 1 letter of recommendation. *Application deadlines:* 8/1 (freshmen), rolling (transfers). *Notification:* continuous (freshmen), continuous (transfers).

Freshman Application Contact Mrs. Nancy L. Spataro, Director of Admissions, York College of Pennsylvania, York, PA 17405-7199. *Phone:* 717-849-1600. *Toll-free phone:* 800-455-8018. *Fax:* 717-849-1607. *E-mail:* admissions@ycp.edu.

ALVERNIA COLLEGE

READING, PENNSYLVANIA

The College

Alvernia College, a regional Franciscan private college with a total enrollment of more than 2,800 men and women, is a rigorous, caring, and inclusive learning community committed to academic excellence rooted in the Catholic and liberal arts traditions. With a student-faculty ratio of 13:1, Alvernia offers a personalized environment where the faculty members know and care about each student. Located on a beautiful 55-acre campus on the outskirts of Reading, Alvernia offers a setting conducive to learning and is conveniently accessible. It is chartered by the commonwealth of Pennsylvania, fully accredited by the Middle States Association of Colleges and Schools, and sponsored by the Bernardine Franciscan Sisters.

Alvernia participates in a full range of intercollegiate sports, including baseball, basketball, cross-country, field hockey, golf, ice hockey, lacrosse, soccer, softball, tennis, and volleyball. The College is a member of the NCAA Division III, the ECAC, and the Pennsylvania Athletic Conference. Alvernia will become a member of the Middle Atlantic States Athletic Conference (MAC), a highly competitive Division III intercollegiate conference, beginning in the 2008–09 season.

Alvernia offers more than thirty-five student organizations, including the Black Student Union, College Thespians, Honors Council, International Club, Phi Beta Lambda, Science Association, Sigma Tau Delta, and Student Government Association. Formal and informal dances, formal and buffet dinners, informal club socials, picnics, parties, coffeehouses, and student entertainment all provide occasions for social development and friendly relationships. Resident students have several attractive housing options, including traditional and suite-style residence halls and town houses. New residence halls opened in 2001, 2003, and 2005. A student center is the hub of campus life, with the dining hall, the new student-run Crusader Café, wireless Internet access, 24/7 availability for late-night study breaks or between classes, and a lounge with a big-screen television and game room.

In addition to its undergraduate programs, Alvernia offers a Master of Social Work through Marywood University. A Doctor of Philosophy in Leadership is also available.

Location

Many first-time visitors are surprised to find Alvernia's peaceful, tree-lined grounds and modern campus buildings in Reading, Pennsylvania, a city of 81,000 once known for its national importance to the mining and railroad industries. Downtown Reading, about 3 miles from the campus, offers a mix of cultural and entertainment destinations. Located in the scenic Blue Mountain area of eastern Pennsylvania, Alvernia's campus overlooks Angelica Lake, noted for its rustic beauty. Beyond Reading lies Pennsylvania's famous Amish country. The College also has easy access to the metropolitan areas of New York, Philadelphia, Baltimore, and Washington, D.C., where students can take advantage of the cultural, historical, and educational attractions these cities have to offer.

Majors and Degrees

Alvernia College offers the Bachelor of Arts, Bachelor of Science, Bachelor of Science in Nursing, and Associate in Science degrees. Bachelor of Arts or Bachelor of Science candidates can major in the following areas: accounting, addiction studies, athletic training, biochemistry, biology, biology/medical technology, chemistry, chemistry/medical technology, communication, computer information systems, criminal justice administration, education (early childhood, elementary, special, and secondary, with major areas in biology, business computers and information technology, chemistry, English, mathematics, and social studies), English, forensic science, general science, history, human resource management, liberal studies, management, marketing, mathematics, nursing, occupational therapy, philosophy, political science, psychology, social work, sport management, and theology. Students can take double majors in areas that are closely related.

Alvernia College also offers five-year programs leading to the Master of Education, the Master of Business Administration, the Master of Arts in liberal studies, and the Master of Occupational Therapy.

Academic Programs

The academic program is designed to help students to think logically and critically, to comprehend accurately, and to communicate effectively. The College concentrates on the personal development of its students by fostering academic integrity, social responsibility, and moral values. The educational program is based on a commitment to develop the whole person into a responsible individual. Therefore, students not only are required to demonstrate proficiency in those skills demanded by their chosen professional concentration but also are expected to take advantage of the opportunity to grow intellectually and spiritually and to be responsible to themselves and to society.

The Honors Program invites qualified students into an enhanced academic experience. Opportunities include a First Year Honors seminar; service opportunities; intellectual and social support; summer internships in Washington, D.C.; and a variety of imaginative courses. Honor students must complete at least three Honors courses plus a senior thesis.

To earn a bachelor's degree, students must complete a minimum of 123 credits, with 54 credits in the liberal arts. Additional requirements vary according to the major program.

Academic Facilities

Alvernia's library facility holds more than 100,000 volumes, including reference works, books for general circulation, and bound periodicals. The library currently subscribes to 850 periodicals covering all areas of study taught at the College, and more than 1,440 volumes of back issues are in the microfilm collection. The library also houses the Audio-Visual Center, which has 23,000 pieces of audiovisual material, including more than 4,750 music records and scores. A new science wing opened in fall 2006 and houses several modern laboratories for science majors and research facilities for psychology majors. Nursing students have practice clinics featuring current medical equipment and life-sized computer-driven patient simulators.

Costs

For 2007–08, the basic tuition fee was $21,400; room and board were $8530.

Financial Aid

More than 85 percent of the students attending Alvernia receive some type of financial aid. The types of aid most commonly received are Pennsylvania Higher Education Assistance Agency grants for Pennsylvania residents, Federal Pell Grants, and numerous scholarships from private sources, as well as grants and scholarships from the College itself. This aid is awarded on the basis of academic performance and financial need. The deadline for application for Alvernia College aid is April 1. In addition, Alvernia participates in the federally funded Federal Work-Study Program. Student loans are also available.

Faculty

The faculty consists of 83 full-time and 190 part-time members, each dedicated to teaching and serving the needs of every student. The faculty is as diversified as the many fields of interest that its members represent. Alvernia faculty members publish widely in professional journals and other media; they present papers and moderate conferences in the region and as far away as India, Italy, Mexico, and South Africa; and they serve on boards and committees of professional associations and corporate and community boards. The use of such faculty members is intended to enhance the theoretical portions of professional training with practical professional knowledge.

Student Government

The Student Government Association (SGA) provides an opportunity for individual leadership and development while also determining, in cooperation with the administration and faculty, suitable standards for College and community life. SGA leaders, elected annually by the student body, are responsible for maintaining the student voice when issues on campus arise. Other duties include activities such as social events, a speakers series, and club activities. The SGA also acts as an intermediary between the administration, the faculty, and the student body and maintains order on campus by proposing rules and regulations for the welfare of the College community. It is composed of a president, vice president, secretary, treasurer, and chief justice elected by the student body and is augmented by 2 representatives from each class.

Admission Requirements

Admission requirements normally include a high school diploma with 16 Carnegie units in the following subjects: English, 4 units; mathematics, 2 units; science, 2 units; social studies, 2 units; and modern languages, 2 units. The remaining units may be made up of academic electives. The College is willing to consider good students whose preparation does not include all of these subjects. Nursing students must fulfill the admission requirements established by the Pennsylvania State Board of Nurse Examiners. The State High School Equivalency Diploma is generally recognized as fulfilling the minimum entrance requirements. Applicants to the freshman class are required to take the SAT; the ACT is also acceptable. Outstanding candidates are considered for entrance to Alvernia at the end of their junior year of high school on the basis of requests made by the candidate and the high school. With the approval of their school officials, students may also be admitted to certain courses during their senior year in high school, simultaneously earning credit toward the high school diploma and a college degree.

Application and Information

Applicants should submit an application for admission and enclose the nonrefundable $25 processing fee. The application form may be obtained from the Office of Admissions or from the College's Web site. Applicants should have an official copy of their high school record sent to the Office of Admissions, along with the official results of the SAT or ACT.

A personal interview, while not required, is often desirable for the prospective student. All interested students and their families are invited to visit Alvernia for a tour of the campus and a personal interview with a member of the Admissions Office staff. It is advisable to make an appointment by mail or phone at least one week in advance. The College reserves the right to request an interview if certain aspects of an application need clarification.

Because Alvernia has a rolling admission policy, an applicant is notified of acceptance by the Director of Admissions shortly after the necessary credentials are on file and have been reviewed, generally within one month of the time an application has been completed. To reserve a place in the freshman class, all students must make a $300 deposit by May 1. This deposit is credited to the student's account for the first semester but is not refunded if the student fails to attend. Transfer students should have a grade point average of 2.0 or higher on a 4.0 scale and should be aware that only grades of C or better are eligible for credit transfer. Alvernia accepts a maximum of 75 transfer credits; at least 45 credits that are required for graduation must be earned at Alvernia and must satisfy all graduation requirements. A detailed analysis of credits to be transferred is done only after students have been accepted by the College. For more information or to schedule a visit, students should contact:

Director of Admissions
Alvernia College
Reading, Pennsylvania 19607
Phone: 888-ALVERNIA (258-3764, toll-free)
Fax: 610-790-2873
E-mail: admissions@alvernia.edu
Web site: http://www.alvernia.edu

Friends outside historic Francis Hall on Alvernia's peaceful, tree-lined campus.

COLLEGE DATA CENTER • PENNSYLVANIA

ARCADIA UNIVERSITY

GLENSIDE, PENNSYLVANIA

The University

Founded in 1853, Arcadia University has the characteristics of a university yet retains a small-college atmosphere. Its diverse student population represents a cross section of cultural and socioeconomic backgrounds. Enrollment includes 1,900 undergraduates and 1,800 graduate students. At present, Arcadia students come from forty-six states and nineteen other countries, and 80 percent of the full-time undergraduate population reside on campus. Adult students attend classes through Continuing Education, take noncredit courses through the Community Scholars Program, or pursue bachelor's degrees during the day or evening.

Campus life, including more than forty-five clubs and organizations, athletics, and cultural and social events, is rich and varied. Community service is an integral part of the Arcadia University experience. Students volunteer on neighborhood improvement projects, work at literacy or gerontology centers, and assist disadvantaged or disabled children. NCAA Division III intercollegiate competition is offered in basketball, field hockey, lacrosse, soccer, softball, swimming, tennis, and volleyball for women and baseball, basketball, golf, soccer, swimming, and tennis for men. Cheerleading and equestrian are offered as club sports, while intramural sports offer many other athletic opportunities.

Arcadia offers master's programs in the fields of business administration, counseling psychology, education, English, environmental education, forensic science, genetic counseling, health education, humanities, international peace and conflict resolution, physician assistant studies, and public health. Doctor of Physical Therapy (D.P.T.) and Doctor of Education (Ed.D.) in special education degrees are also offered.

Location

Set on a former private estate in Glenside, a suburb of Philadelphia, Arcadia University offers a beautiful campus in a peaceful residential neighborhood. The focal point of the campus is the unique Grey Towers Castle, a National Historic Landmark. The University is only 25 minutes from Center City Philadelphia, allowing Arcadia students ready access to the dozens of museums, galleries, performing arts centers, night spots, and historic, government, and commercial sites in this vital metropolitan area. New York City and Washington, D.C., are just a few hours away by car or train, as are recreation areas such as the New Jersey shore and the Pocono Mountains.

Majors and Degrees

Arcadia offers Bachelor of Arts degrees in art, art history, biology (allied health, biomedical, conservation, forensics, molecular), business administration (economics, finance, human resources administration, management, marketing), chemistry, communications (corporate, print, video), computer science, computing technology, criminal justice (crime and deviance, individualized, punishment and social control), digital media, education (early childhood, elementary, secondary), English (creative writing, professional writing), fashion studies, global legal studies, health administration, history, interdisciplinary science, international business and culture, international studies, management information systems, mathematics (actuarial science), media industries, philosophy, political science (international politics, prelaw and political theory, U.S. politics and policy), psychobiology, psychology, scientific illustration, sociology, sound and music, Spanish, Spanish cultural studies, sport psychology, and theater arts and English. Bachelor of Science degrees are offered in accounting, business administration, chemistry, chemistry and business, computer science, finance, health administration, human resources administration, management, management information systems, marketing, and mathematics. Bachelor of Fine Arts degrees are awarded to students majoring in acting or studio arts with concentrations in ceramics, graphic design, interior design, metals and jewelry, painting, photography, and printmaking. Preparation for certification in art education is offered in conjunction with the B.F.A. program, as is preparation for graduate study in art therapy. A five-year program combines the Bachelor of Arts in education with a Master of Education in special education.

Arcadia's physician assistant studies 4+2 program provides a four-year undergraduate degree in a related field, followed by two years of study in the Master of Medical Science: Physician Assistant Program at Arcadia. Arcadia undergraduates are assured admission to the program. The University also offers a combined undergraduate and graduate (4+2.5) program leading to the Doctor of Physical Therapy. Arcadia University undergraduates who meet established criteria are assured admission to the D.P.T. program. The International Peace and Conflict Resolution Program provides a four-year undergraduate degree followed by two years of study in the Master of Arts in international peace and conflict resolution. The forensic science program provides a four-year undergraduate program in a related field followed by two years in the Master of Science in Forensic Science (M.S.F.S.) program.

A dual-degree (3-2) program in engineering is offered in conjunction with Columbia University. An accelerated (3+4) program with Pennsylvania College of Optometry leads to the Bachelor of Arts and Doctor of Optometry degrees. A 3+2 program in environmental science leads to a B.A. in psychology and a Master of Arts in Education in environmental education. Preprofessional preparation is offered for dentistry, law, medicine, optometry, and veterinary medicine, as well as in other areas.

Academic Programs

Arcadia's academic program provides students with a solid background of liberal arts and sciences integrated with courses in their chosen fields. Students explore a variety of interests and can engage in research, internships, or cooperative education placements. Such experiences enable students to gain relevant work experience while putting their academic training to use. The Cooperative Education Program, for instance, provides students with the opportunity to combine on-campus study with off-campus employment in a program that helps them earn both credit and income.

Highly qualified students may enhance their education through the Honors Program, which includes specially designed cross-curricular courses and overseas experience, as well as cultural and social activities. Admission to the Honors Program may occur at the time of acceptance to the University or after the student has been enrolled at the University for one or more semesters.

Credit toward graduation is granted for scores of 3 or better on Advanced Placement examinations. Exemption from or credit for courses may also be earned through the College-Level Examination Program (CLEP) and locally administered examinations at the discretion of the department concerned.

Arcadia's academic year is divided into two semesters. Three summer sessions are offered, beginning in May and continuing through early August. Most full-time students carry four academic courses in each regular semester; 128 semester hours are required for graduation.

Off-Campus Programs

Arcadia's Center for Education Abroad (CEA), top-ranked in the nation by *U.S. News & World Report*, is one of the largest campus-based international study programs in the United States. With more than 100 programs around the world, the Center for Education Abroad supports and implements the University's commitment to international education. Students have the opportunity to study overseas for a summer, semester, or full year for approximately the same cost as remaining on the Glenside campus.

Arcadia offers two distinct opportunities for students to study abroad during their first year of college. The University's London/Scotland/Spain Preview program enables first-year students in good academic standing to spend their spring break in London, Scotland, or Spain for just $245, which includes round-trip airfare, accommodations, and programming. The unique First Year Study Abroad Experience (FY-SAE) gives select incoming students the chance to spend their first or second semester in London, Scotland, or Ireland. Arcadia's First Year Study Abroad Experience and Preview programs have been recognized as among the most innovative international programs in the country by the American Council on Education, *U.S. News & World Report,* and *The Princeton Review.*

In 2007, Arcadia introduced Majors Abroad Programs. Seven new majors are approved, with more planned. Students in these majors spend a year (two semesters) abroad, taking general courses as well as major-related courses at an overseas institution. These new majors are digital media, fashion studies, global legal studies, media industries, sound and music, Spanish cultural studies, and sport psychology.

Off-campus study in the Philadelphia area includes internships and fieldwork in most majors. The University also offers the Washington Semester Program at American University.

Academic Facilities

A prime academic resource on Arcadia's campus is the Landman Library, which offers students and faculty members increased technology and access to resources both on campus and around the globe. The 85-acre campus includes historical buildings as well as extensive modern facilities, like the state-of-the-art Health Sciences Center and Brubaker Hall, which houses the Business Department and the Physician Assistant Program.

Wireless Internet access is available everywhere on campus. The campus network extends to each room in the residence halls. Computer facilities include an Alpha mainframe with Ethernet connections to more than thirty on-site and dial-up workstations. There are also four computer labs and a Mac lab.

Costs

The charge for tuition in 2007–08 was $27,440. Student fees are $360 per year. Room and board charges are $9980 per year. Books and supplies for most students are between $300 and $500 per semester.

Financial Aid

Every effort is made to see that students requiring financial assistance are able to attend Arcadia. Aid is awarded on the basis of need, as determined by the Free Application for Federal Student Aid (FAFSA) and the Arcadia University Financial Aid Application, and is available in the form of grants, loans, and part-time campus employment or some combination of the three. On average, 98 percent of full-time undergraduates receive financial aid, and 95 percent receive grants and scholarships. Scholarships are presented annually to entering first-year and transfer students who have achieved academic distinction or have been recognized for outstanding extracurricular accomplishments. Distinguished Scholarships, ranging from $50,000 to $60,000 over four years, and the Arcadia University Achievement Awards, ranging from $4000 to $48,000 over four years, recognize academic excellence, leadership, and extracurricular accomplishments. A limited number of full-tuition scholarships are available to the top entering first-year undergraduates in the applicant pool. To receive full consideration for financial aid, students should complete their applications and submit the FAFSA and the Arcadia University Financial Aid Application by March 1.

A new, unique online financial aid calculator for students considering full-time undergraduate enrollment is now available at http://www.arcadia.edu/calculator. This online calculator gives them the chance to estimate their eligibility for federal, state, and Arcadia University financial aid (including merit scholarships)—truly allowing them to get an idea of their actual costs, in real time.

Faculty

Arcadia University has a faculty with a primary commitment to teaching. The average class size is 16 students, and the ratio of students to faculty members is 13:1, allowing professors the opportunity to know and care about their students. This fosters an environment in which students and faculty members collaborate on research and writing and engage in informal discussions, field trips, and other special activities outside the classroom. Eighty-nine percent of Arcadia faculty members hold doctorates or terminal degrees in their field, and all courses are taught by faculty members.

Student Government

Student life is largely self-regulated by the Student Government Organization (SGO) through the Student Senate. Most students feel that the SGO has proved effective in working with the faculty and administration on matters of student concern, as well as in developing the social climate of the University. Students serve on most major faculty committees, and student leaders attend Board of Trustees meetings.

Admission Requirements

Students are carefully selected on the basis of educational preparation, intellectual promise, and potential. Each candidate's credentials are reviewed individually by members of the Enrollment Management staff. Particular emphasis is placed on the candidate's academic record, including the type of program followed and the grades and class rank earned. Standardized test scores, counselor and teacher recommendations, participation in school and community activities, and other supporting credentials are also considered.

Freshman applicants must submit an official high school transcript, standardized test scores (SAT or ACT), and counselor and teacher recommendations. Applicants should pursue a college-preparatory program, usually consisting of 16 academic units. Early admission, early decision, deferred admission, and advanced placement are available. Students are encouraged to visit the campus for an admissions interview and a student-guided tour.

Transfer applicants may apply for the fall term or at midyear and must submit official college transcripts. In some cases, transfer applicants are required to submit high school transcripts and SAT or ACT scores.

Application and Information

Students are encouraged to submit their applications as early as possible in the senior year. Admission decisions are made on a rolling basis, and applicants are usually notified within four to six weeks of the date of submission of the completed application. For freshman applicants, the priority admission application deadline for Distinguished Scholarship consideration is January 15. The priority admission application deadline for Achievement Award consideration is March 1. The admission application deadline is also March 1. The transfer student deadline for portfolio review, Honors Program and Distinguished Scholarship consideration, and priority admission is June 15 for fall-term admission.

Requests for further information should be directed to:

Office of Enrollment Management
Arcadia University
450 South Easton Road
Glenside, Pennsylvania 19038-3295
Phone: 215-572-2910
877-ARCADIA (877-272-2342, toll-free)
E-mail: admiss@arcadia.edu
Web site: http://www.arcadia.edu/pet.asp

Grey Towers Castle, Arcadia University.

COLLEGE DATA CENTER • PENNSYLVANIA

THE ART INSTITUTE OF PHILADELPHIA

PHILADELPHIA, PENNSYLVANIA

The Art Institute of Philadelphia®

The Institute

The Art Institute of Philadelphia trains students with the skills needed to be prepared for an entry-level job in the creative arts. Employers consistently return to hire qualified graduates—a testament to the school's educational philosophies and how well it prepares students for the increasingly competitive career market.

Students come to The Art Institute of Philadelphia from across the country and abroad. The student body includes a diverse population—from men and women who enrolled directly after completing high school to those who transferred in from colleges and universities to those who have left employment to prepare for new careers.

Students at The Art Institute of Philadelphia have the opportunity to join such professional organizations as the American Society of Interior Designers (ASID), the CLIQUE Photography Club, and the Future Fashion Association.

Whether in the student lounge, the gallery, The Art Institute of Philadelphia Supply Store, or the extensive resource center, the daily gathering of students and faculty and staff members makes it easy to feel the energy, caring, and commitment that underlie an education at The Art Institute of Philadelphia. Classes are structured to be as close to a professional work environment as possible. Students practice their skills in labs and studios featuring industry-relevant technologies.

Assistance is available to help students with resume writing, networking, and keeping abreast of what employers are looking for in job candidates. The school offers a skills-enhancement program designed to help students prepare for college-level English and math courses, and confidential counseling is available when academic or personal problems create roadblocks to success.

The Student Services Department helps enrolled students to locate appropriate housing. Options include school-sponsored, apartment-style housing and independent apartment living.

The Art Institute of Philadelphia is accredited by the Accrediting Council for Independent Colleges and Schools (ACICS; 750 First Street NE, Suite 980, Washington, D.C. 20002, phone: 202-336-6780) to award bachelor's degrees, associate degrees, and diplomas. ACICS is listed as a nationally recognized accrediting agency by the U.S. Department of Education. Its accreditation of degree granting institutions is recognized by the Council for Higher Education Accreditation. The Associate of Science in Culinary Arts degree program is accredited by the American Culinary Federation (ACF).

Location

Philadelphia is the birthplace of American Democracy. The City of Brotherly Love surrounds the largest municipal landscaped park in the world, with tree-lined streets and an elegant blend of contemporary and historic architecture. Philadelphia has a renowned symphony orchestra, theater, film, jazz, and opera. With thirty-two major museums—including the expansive collections at the Museum of Art—the city is also home to fine shopping at locations such as the European-style Bourse, with its fifty international boutiques and restaurants, and to sports teams, such as baseball's Phillies, the NFL's Eagles, the NBA's 76ers, and the NHL's Flyers.

Majors and Degrees

The Art Institute of Philadelphia offers bachelor's degree programs (thirty-six months) in culinary management, digital filmmaking and video production, fashion design, fashion marketing, graphic design, industrial design technology, interior design, media arts and animation, photography, visual effects and motion graphics, and Web design and interactive media. Associate degree programs (twenty-one to twenty-four months, depending on the program) are offered in culinary arts, digital filmmaking and video production, fashion design, fashion marketing, graphic design, interior design, photography, visual merchandising, and Web design and interactive media. Diploma programs in baking and pastry, culinary arts, and digital print production are also available.

Academic Programs

School quarters are eleven weeks long, and academic programs are between six and twelve quarters in length. Programs are offered on a year-round basis, allowing for strong continuity and the ability to work uninterrupted toward a degree.

The Art Institute of Philadelphia arranges student trips to local cultural and commercial sites. These visits are an integral part of each student's learning experience. In addition to local student trips to support the curriculum, out-of-town seminars and visits are planned within individual programs.

Academic Facilities

The Art Institute of Philadelphia occupies nearly 86,000 square feet of space on Chestnut Street. Designated a historical site by the Philadelphia Historical Commission, the Art Deco building became home to The Art Institute of Philadelphia in 1982. In addition to classrooms, studios, laboratories, offices, a learning resource center, and the exhibition gallery, the school maintains an impressive gallery and an art supply store for the convenience of students. A recently acquired space at 1610 Chestnut Street adds approximately 40,000 square feet for offices, classrooms, and computer labs for all bachelor's and associate degree programs.

The general education, fashion, interior design, and culinary arts programs are housed at 2300 Market Street. Three large kitchens are contained within the building, along with a bake shop, a skills kitchen, and an à la carte kitchen.

Computer lab facilities at the school include the PAD System (computerized patternmaking) as well as Intergraph Visual Workstations, PCs and Macs, Avid video labs, and a television station.

Costs

Tuition cost varies by program. Prospective students should contact the school for current tuition costs. Other charges include a starting kit for all first-quarter students. Kits vary in price depending on the program of study.

Financial Aid

Financial aid is available for those who qualify. Students who require financial assistance should first complete and submit a Free Application for Federal Student Aid (FAFSA) and meet with a financial aid officer. The officer determines the student's level of need based on a required federal formula, the cost of education, and other factors. Gift aid is available in the form of Federal Pell Grants, Federal Supplemental Educational Opportunity Grants, and veterans' benefits. Loans include Federal Stafford Loans, Federal PLUS Loans, and alternative loans. Scholarships are available from the school and private sources. Application deadlines and eligibility requirements vary by program.

Faculty

The school employs full-time and part-time faculty members. The Art Institute of Philadelphia faculty members, many of whom have professional experience in their industry, have credentials and reputations within their respective fields. Faculty members, the academic department director, and the dean of education provide academic counseling, evaluating student projects for the purpose of helping students to prepare a professional portfolio.

Admission Requirements

High school graduation or a General Educational Development (GED) certificate is a prerequisite for admission. All applicants are evaluated on the basis of previous education and their background/interest in the program of interest. Portfolios are welcomed but not required.

The Art Institute of Philadelphia operates on a rolling admissions basis. High school and/or college transcripts must be submitted to The Art Institute of Philadelphia at least one month prior to starting classes. There is a $50 application fee.

Application and Information

To obtain an application, make arrangements for an interview, or tour the school, students should contact:

The Art Institute of Philadelphia
1622 Chestnut Street
Philadelphia, Pennsylvania 19103-5119
Phone: 215-567-7080
800-275-2474 (toll-free)
Fax: 215-405-6399
Web site: http://www.artinstitutes.edu/philadelphia

The Art Institute of Atlanta®, GA; The Art Institute of Atlanta®–Decatur, GA; The Art Institute of Austin℠, TX; The Art Institute of California℠–Inland Empire; The Art Institute of California℠–Los Angeles; The Art Institute of California℠–Orange County; The Art Institute of California℠–Sacramento; The Art Institute of California℠–San Diego; The Art Institute of California℠–San Francisco; The Art Institute of California℠–Sunnyvale; The Art Institute of Charleston℠, SC, A branch of The Art Institute of Atlanta, GA; The Art Institute of Charlotte®, NC; The Art Institute of Colorado® (Denver); The Art Institute of Dallas®, TX; The Art Institute of Fort Lauderdale®, FL; The Art Institute of Houston®, TX; The Art Institute of Indianapolis℠, IN*; The Art Institute of Jacksonville℠, FL, A branch of Miami International University of Art & Design; The Art Institute of Las Vegas®, NV; The Art Institute of Michigan℠ (Detroit); The Art Institute of New York City®, NY; The Art Institute of Ohio℠–Cincinnati**; The Art Institute of Philadelphia®, PA; The Art Institute of Phoenix®, AZ; The Art Institute of Pittsburgh®, PA; The Art Institute of Pittsburgh®–Online Division; The Art Institute of Portland®, OR; The Art Institute of Salt Lake City℠, UT; The Art Institute of Seattle®, WA; The Art Institute of Tampa℠, FL, A branch of Miami International University of Art & Design; The Art Institute of Tennessee℠–Nashville, A branch of The Art Institute of Atlanta, GA; The Art Institute of Tucson℠, AZ; The Art Institute of Washington® (Arlington, VA), A branch of The Art Institute of Atlanta, GA; The Art Institute of York–Pennsylvania℠; The Art Institutes International Minnesota℠ (Minneapolis); California Design College℠ (Los Angeles–Wilshire Blvd.); The Illinois Institute of Art®–Chicago; The Illinois Institute of Art®–Schaumburg; Miami International University of Art & Design℠, FL; The New England Institute of Art® (Boston, MA).

*The Art Institute of Indianapolis is licensed by the Indiana Commission on Proprietary Education, 302 West Washington Street, Room E201, Indianapolis, IN 46204, AC-0080.

**The Art Institute of Ohio–Cincinnati, 8845 Governors Hill Drive, Suite 100, Cincinnati, OH 45249-3317, Reg. #04-01-1698B.

THE ART INSTITUTE OF PITTSBURGH

PITTSBURGH, PENNSYLVANIA

The Institute

At The Art Institute of Pittsburgh, students are given the opportunity to learn new ways to apply creative talent, energy, and skills to a world of commercial and culinary arts, design, and technology. With fourteen bachelor's and associate degrees and diploma programs, the school prepares students for entry-level positions in the creative arts.

The school is located within a renovated historic landmark building with ten floors of fully networked, industry-standard computer labs and specialty facilities. Four kitchens, editing suites, digital photography labs, a television production studio, and an industrial design machine shop allow students to gain expertise in their fields of study.

The student population includes recent high school graduates, transfer students, and those who have left a previous employment situation to study and train for a new career. Students are creative, competitive, and open to new ideas. They place great value on an education that prepares them for an exciting entry-level position in the arts. The Art Institute of Pittsburgh Student Affairs Department arranges school activities and events. The department also employs a student activities coordinator who plans various events, theme parties, and clubs. Events are communicated via weekly and quarterly newsletters as well as through a television network. A cross-program Student Council represents the needs and issues of the entire student body. The school also supports approximately twenty clubs and intramural sports teams and oversees the activities and concerns of school-sponsored housing residents. The Student Life Department offers counseling services.

Students at The Art Institute of Pittsburgh may find reasonably priced housing within a 5- to 10-minute walk of the school through the school's Housing Department. Amenities include cable/Internet service, laundry facilities, and easy access to public transportation.

The Art Institute of Pittsburgh is accredited by the Accrediting Council for Independent Colleges and Schools (ACICS) to award bachelor's degrees, associate degrees, and diplomas. ACICS is listed as a nationally recognized accrediting agency by the U.S. Department of Education. Its accreditation of degree-granting institutions is recognized by the Council for Higher Education Accreditation. ACICS can be contacted at 750 First Street NE, Suite 980, Washington, D.C. 20002; telephone: 202-336-6780. The Bachelor of Science in interior design degree program is accredited by the Council for Interior Design Accreditation. The Associate of Science in culinary arts degree is accredited by the American Culinary Federation Foundation Accrediting Commission.

Location

The Art Institute of Pittsburgh is nestled in the heart of downtown Pittsburgh's Golden Triangle. Pittsburgh is a thriving metropolis, sprawling over 55 square miles. It is situated halfway between New York City and Chicago and is within a 2-hour flight or a one-day drive of more than 70 percent of the U.S. population.

Pittsburgh is the international headquarters of many technology-driven businesses. Culture abounds, with free summer concerts in the downtown's Market Square, new theaters, thriving nightlife districts, quaint coffee shops, and retail merchants on every corner. The Pittsburgh Steelers' stadium and the Pirates' waterfront PNC Park adorn the city's North Shore. Pittsburgh is serviced by Greater Pittsburgh International Airport, one of the largest and most retail-developed airports in the country.

Majors and Degrees

The Art Institute of Pittsburgh offers bachelor's degree programs (thirty-six months) in advertising, culinary management, digital media production, entertainment design, fashion and retail management, game art and design, graphic design, hotel and restaurant management, industrial design, interior design, media arts and animation, photography, visual effects and motion graphics, and Web design and interactive media.

Associate of Science degree programs (twenty-one months) are offered in culinary arts, graphic design, industrial design technology, photography, video production, and Web design and interactive media.

Diploma programs (twelve months) are offered in the art of cooking, digital design, residential planning, and Web design.

Academic Facilities

The Art Institute of Pittsburgh is located in a fully networked, 170,000-square-foot historic landmark building. The facility has interchangeable classroom, computer, and cell animation labs with extended access to Macintosh and PC computers and design and animation software. Photography students use a digital darkroom as well as traditional wet labs and printing stations. Interior design students have access to a fabric and textile research facility and computer-aided drawing software. The building is equipped with a television studio, digital editing suites, and Foley audio studio to support the video production curriculum. A full industrial design shop is available. The Art Institute of Pittsburgh also contains a program-oriented library.

Costs

Tuition cost varies by program. Prospective students should contact the school for current tuition costs. Other charges include a starting kit for all first-quarter students. Kits vary in price depending on the program of study.

Financial Aid

Financial aid is available for those who qualify. Students who require financial assistance should first complete and submit a Free Application for Federal Student Aid (FAFSA) and meet with a financial aid officer. The officer determines the student's level of need based on a required federal formula, the cost of education, and other factors. Gift aid is available in the form of Federal Pell Grants, Federal Supplemental Educational Opportunity Grants, and veterans' benefits. Loans include Federal Stafford Loans, Federal PLUS Loans, and alternative loans. Scholarships are available from the school and private sources. Application deadlines and eligibility requirements vary by program.

Faculty

The Art Institute of Pittsburgh faculty and staff members are professionals, many of whom are drawn from the ranks of industry. The school's faculty consists of full-time and part-time instructors who teach students how to cultivate conceptual, creative, and problem-solving skills.

In addition, assistance is available to help students with resume writing, networking, and keeping abreast of what employers are looking for in job candidates.

Admission Requirements

A prospective student must be a high school graduate with a high school QPA of 2.0 or higher (2.5 or higher QPA required for admission into game art and design), hold a General Educational Development (GED) certificate, or have a bachelor's degree or higher as a prerequisite for admission. Students who have completed high school or its equivalent but cannot provide the necessary documentation may provide alternate documentation to satisfy this requirement. The president of The Art Institute of Pittsburgh must approve all exceptions. A student who holds a bachelor's degree or higher may submit proof of the degree to satisfy the high school graduation or General Educational Development (GED) requirement. There is a portfolio requirement for media arts and animation and game art and design program candidates.

All applicants are evaluated on the basis of their previous education, background, and stated or demonstrated interest in their program of choice. Applicants who have taken the SAT or ACT are encouraged to submit scores to the Admissions Office for evaluation.

Applications are accepted on a rolling basis. An application for admission must be completed and signed by the applicant and be submitted along with an essay stating how The Art Institute of Pittsburgh can help the student to attain his or her creative goals. There is a $50 application fee.

Application and Information

To obtain an application, make arrangements for an interview, or tour the school, students should contact:

The Art Institute of Pittsburgh
420 Boulevard of the Allies
Pittsburgh, Pennsylvania 15219-1301
Phone: 412-263-6600
800-275-2470 (toll-free)
Fax: 412-263-6667
Web site: http://www.artinstitutes.edu/pittsburgh

The Art Institute of Atlanta®, GA; The Art Institute of Atlanta®–Decatur, GA; The Art Institute of Austin℠, TX; The Art Institute of California℠–Inland Empire; The Art Institute of California℠–Los Angeles; The Art Institute of California℠–Orange County; The Art Institute of California℠–Sacramento; The Art Institute of California℠–San Diego; The Art Institute of California℠–San Francisco; The Art Institute of California℠–Sunnyvale; The Art Institute of Charleston℠, SC, A branch of The Art Institute of Atlanta, GA; The Art Institute of Charlotte®, NC; The Art Institute of Colorado® (Denver); The Art Institute of Dallas®, TX; The Art Institute of Fort Lauderdale®, FL; The Art Institute of Houston®, TX; The Art Institute of Indianapolis℠, IN*; The Art Institute of Jacksonville℠, FL, A branch of Miami International University of Art & Design; The Art Institute of Las Vegas®, NV; The Art Institute of Michigan℠ (Detroit); The Art Institute of New York City®, NY; The Art Institute of Ohio℠–Cincinnati**; The Art Institute of Philadelphia®, PA; The Art Institute of Phoenix®, AZ; The Art Institute of Pittsburgh®, PA; The Art Institute of Pittsburgh®–Online Division; The Art Institute of Portland®, OR; The Art Institute of Salt Lake City℠, UT; The Art Institute of Seattle®, WA; The Art Institute of Tampa℠, FL, A branch of Miami International University of Art & Design; The Art Institute of Tennessee℠–Nashville, A branch of The Art Institute of Atlanta, GA; The Art Institute of Tucson℠, AZ; The Art Institute of Washington® (Arlington, VA), A branch of The Art Institute of Atlanta, GA; The Art Institute of York–Pennsylvania℠; The Art Institutes International Minnesota℠ (Minneapolis); California Design College℠ (Los Angeles–Wilshire Blvd.); The Illinois Institute of Art®–Chicago; The Illinois Institute of Art®–Schaumburg; Miami International University of Art & Design℠, FL; The New England Institute of Art® (Boston, MA).

*The Art Institute of Indianapolis is licensed by the Indiana Commission on Proprietary Education, 302 W. Washington St., Rm. E201, Indianapolis, IN 46204, AC-0080.

**The Art Institute of Ohio–Cincinnati, 8845 Governors Hill Drive, Suite 100, Cincinnati, OH 45249-3317, OH Reg. #04-01-1698B.

BRYN MAWR COLLEGE
BRYN MAWR, PENNSYLVANIA

The College

Bryn Mawr women are leaders in the classroom, in the studio, in the laboratory, and on the field. They are women who share an intense intellectual commitment, a purposeful vision for their lives, and a common desire to make a meaningful contribution to the world.

Bryn Mawr women empower each other to engage with the world beyond the campus, too, by testing the boundaries of knowledge in a number of ways. Through advanced research projects, summer internships, and collaborative research with faculty members, students are involved in the local, national, and global communities. Bryn Mawr's Centers for 21st Century Inquiry, the Katherine Houghton Hepburn Center for Women in Public Life, and the Praxis Program, which integrates fieldwork with theoretical study, provide students with extensive opportunities for internships in Philadelphia, where they may apply knowledge far beyond the classroom. Many students pursue independent and interdepartmental majors with faculty permission. Joint academic programs also exist with Haverford, Swarthmore, and the University of Pennsylvania.

Bryn Mawr alumnae are physicians, economists, entrepreneurs, scholars, filmmakers, journalists, jurists, writers, and scientists whose achievements are marked by originality of thought and direction. Bryn Mawr's prestigious alumnae include the first woman to be president of Harvard University, one of the first women to receive the Nobel Peace Prize, the first woman neurosurgeon, and the first and only woman to receive four Academy Awards. Bryn Mawr women have also been recipients of the MacArthur ("genius grant") Fellowships and Pulitzer Prizes and are continually awarded Fulbright and Watson Fellowships. A recent alumna won an international competition to design the future September 11 Memorial at the Pentagon.

Bryn Mawr prides itself on diversity; students who are members of minority groups and international students make up more than a third of the undergraduate enrollment. Bryn Mawr's student body is composed of women from forty-nine states and forty other countries. Above all else, Bryn Mawr women share a tremendous respect for individual differences, not merely a passive tolerance of other lifestyles and points of view. The result is a community that resounds with the energy, healthy friction, and range of perspectives that can only come from true cultural and ideological diversity. These women share a commitment to a community that is based on inclusion and support, reinforced by Bryn Mawr's Honor Code, a set of principles stressing personal integrity and mutual respect. In the words of one graduating senior, "This is a place where being yourself makes you feel part of something larger than yourself. A strong sense of self is what we all have in common."

Bryn Mawr is home to varsity athletic teams in badminton, basketball, crew, cross-country, field hockey, lacrosse, soccer, swimming, tennis, track and field, and volleyball. Students participate in more than 100 active student organizations at Bryn Mawr. The tricollege community of Haverford, Swarthmore, and Bryn Mawr Colleges also sponsors many students groups and activities.

Cambrian Row, a group of homes built in the late 1900s, has recently been renovated and restored to support student life on campus. The houses include the Multicultural Center, the Office of Civic Engagement, and offices to house religious advisers and the Student Government Association. Dalton Hall was restored and reopened in 2007 and offers state-of-the-art classrooms, meeting spaces, and laboratory spaces for all of the social sciences. Renovation and improvement of the Goodhart Theatre is scheduled to begin in spring 2008. Its interior spaces will be upgraded to accommodate students' growing interest in performing arts.

Location

Bryn Mawr College is located on a 135-acre suburban campus, 11 miles west of Philadelphia. Bryn Mawr's campus is graceful and serene and has a deep engagement with the wider world. Bryn Mawr women enjoy a rich academic and social life on their own campus and at neighboring tricollege partners Haverford and Swarthmore Colleges as well as the University of Pennsylvania. This network allows Bryn Mawr students to experience the benefits of attending a small liberal arts college while also having access to nearly 5,000 courses. Bryn Mawr's relationship with Haverford College is particularly close. A 20-minute walk or a 5-minute ride on the bicollege "Blue Bus" brings students from one campus to the other. There are nearly 3,000 course exchanges between the institutions each year, selected from a jointly published course list. Students are encouraged to participate in many bicollege extracurricular activities, including the orchestra, the chorus, the drama program, and one of the major newspapers.

Almost all students live on campus in one of sixteen main residence halls. These buildings, which include a multicultural residence for students interested in foreign languages and culture, range from university Gothic to postmodern in style. Two of the buildings are listed on the National Register of Historic Places, and one is also a National Historic Landmark.

Majors and Degrees

Bryn Mawr College grants the Bachelor of Arts (A.B.) degree with majors, minors, and concentrations in more than forty areas: Africana studies, anthropology, astronomy, biology, chemistry, classical and Near Eastern archaeology, classical languages, classical studies, comparative literature, computational methods, computer science, creative writing, dance, East Asian studies, economics, education, English, environmental studies, film studies, fine arts, French and French studies, gender and sexuality, geology, German and German studies, Greek, growth and structure of cities, Hebrew and Judaic studies, Hispanic and Hispanic-American studies, history, history of art, international studies, Italian, Latin, linguistics, mathematics, music, neural and behavioral sciences, peace and conflict studies, philosophy, physics, political science, psychology, religion, Romance languages, Russian, sociology, Spanish, and theater and theater studies.

Through an unusually broad cooperative arrangement with Haverford College, Bryn Mawr students may major in any of Haverford's coordinate departments or in astronomy, classics, music, or religion while earning a Bachelor of Arts degree from Bryn Mawr. A new major in linguistics offered through Swarthmore College is also available. Finally, Haverford, Swarthmore, and Bryn Mawr have joined together to form the Middle East Studies Initiative.

Academic Programs

Having the freedom to shape one's education is a central part of the Bryn Mawr experience—and excellent preparation for creating a purposeful life after graduation. The College's divisional requirements are designed to encourage students to explore extensively while allowing a good deal of flexibility in shaping their course work. A total of 32 units of work is required for graduation, including one course to meet the quantitative skills requirement, work to demonstrate proficiency in a foreign language, 2 units in the humanities, 2 units in natural or physical sciences, 2 units in the social sciences, a major subject sequence, and elective units. Each student chooses and plans her major in consultation with her Dean and faculty adviser. Some students take advantage of this freedom to design an independent major, while others fashion their own intellectual perspectives by enrolling in courses that span academic fields (such as The Growth and Structure of Cities) or assisting with a faculty member's research project.

Off-Campus Programs

Bryn Mawr is only 20 minutes by car or train from the vast cultural and professional resources of Philadelphia, the nation's fifth-largest city. Philadelphia is an incredible resource for Bryn Mawr—a truly accessible city rich with cultural and professional resources, including the Philadelphia Museum of Art, the Philadelphia Orchestra, the Pennsylvania Ballet, numerous theaters, professional and collegiate athletics, and some of the nation's most important historic sites, as well as internship opportunities in Center City law firms, art galleries, government agencies, hospitals, TV studios, banks, and schools. When Philadelphia seems too small, 1 in 3 Bryn Mawr students participate in one of more than seventy study-abroad programs from Stockholm to South Africa.

Academic Facilities

Bryn Mawr students have unlimited access to libraries and laboratories equal to those of many graduate programs, allowing students to pursue independent research at a level unimaginable at most undergraduate institutions. These resources include more than 1 million volumes in a network of open-stack libraries at Bryn Mawr as well as access to the libraries of both Haverford and Swarthmore Colleges via the Tripod Library System. In addition, the College recently renovated and enhanced a 1913 Colonial Revival home on campus into a new Psychology Center. The facility houses offices, labs, classrooms, student offices and lounges, and state-of-the-art computer facilities. Four former faculty residences have also been renovated to house the student activities village, Cambrian Row. The Rhys Carpenter Library for Art, Archaeology, and Cities opened in 1997 and houses seminar rooms, research facilities, and a state-of-the-art Visual Resources Center. Special departmental research collections include American and European anthropological and archaeological artifacts; recordings of the music of native peoples from all parts of the world; an extensive and important geologic collection of minerals and maps; a collection of Greek and Roman minor arts, especially vases and coins; medieval manuscripts and late medieval printed books (the third-largest collection of incunabula in the nation); and distinguished library holdings of American, Asian, and African books. Other resources include a language laboratory; high-speed Internet connections in its residence halls, computing labs, and networked classrooms; and wireless access in its libraries, campus center, and public labs across the campus.

Costs

In 2007–08, Bryn Mawr tuition, room and board, and fees totaled $45,674.

Financial Aid

To apply for financial aid, students must submit the Free Application for Federal Student Aid (FAFSA) and the Financial Aid PROFILE from the College Scholarship Service, both available on Bryn Mawr's Web site. In addition, the College requires a copy of the family's most recent tax return and W-2 forms. Applicants who are not citizens of the U.S. must instead file the Foreign Student Financial Aid Application. Prospective freshmen are notified of the admission and financial aid decisions at the same time.

Faculty

The Bryn Mawr faculty has 153 full-time members, of whom 51 percent are women and 17 percent are professors of color. The College's student-faculty ratio is 8:1. Few colleges or universities can genuinely claim the intellectual curiosity, intensity, and passion found at Bryn Mawr. Classes are small (many have fewer than 15 students), and faculty members come to know their students as individuals. That means more than just being on a first-name basis. In fact, Bryn Mawr faculty members, world-renowned leaders in their fields, regard their students as junior colleagues, fully capable of working at a high level, developing their own ideas, and making important contributions. It is in this way that, perhaps more than at any other school, Bryn Mawr feels like a graduate school on an undergraduate level.

Student Government

Bryn Mawr's culture of innovative leadership dates back to 1892. That year, the Self-Government Association, the oldest undergraduate governing body in the country, was founded, giving Bryn Mawr students the responsibility of running many campus organizations and activities and participating in discussion and resolution of important issues, such as curriculum and faculty appointments.

Admission Requirements

Bryn Mawr's freshman class of about 350 is selected from applicants from all parts of the United States and the world. The Admissions Committee, composed of admissions officers, professors, and current students, looks for an excellent school and test record and asks the applicant's counselor and teachers for an estimate of her character and readiness for college. Such qualities as integrity, vitality, a sense of humor, independence, and sensitivity to others are important, as are any special talents or interests. Early decision, early admission, deferred entrance, and advanced placement options are available to qualified students.

Basic high school academic requirements include 4 years of English, 3 years of mathematics, at least 1 year each of a laboratory science and history, and a solid foundation in at least one foreign language. However, most applicants are well prepared for the academic rigor of Bryn Mawr and have taken at least three lab science courses as well as mathematics courses that include trigonometry. The SAT and SAT Subject Tests in two other areas must be taken by November of the senior year for early decision applicants and January for regular decision applicants. The ACT may be substituted. The writing option is highly recommended. An interview, either at the College or with a local alumnae representative, is also strongly recommended. Application forms should be submitted by November 15 for fall early decision applicants, by January 1 for winter early decision applicants, and by January 15 for regular decision applicants.

Transfer students must complete a minimum of two years of work at Bryn Mawr to qualify for the A.B. degree.

Application and Information

The Admissions Office is open from 9 a.m. to 5 p.m. on weekdays and, during the fall, from 9 a.m. to 1 p.m. on Saturdays. For further information, an application form, or the name of a local alumnae representative, prospective students should contact:

Jennifer J. Rickard
Dean of Admissions and Financial Aid
Bryn Mawr College
101 North Merion Avenue
Bryn Mawr, Pennsylvania 19010-2899
Phone: 610-526-5152
Fax: 610-526-7471
E-mail: admissions@brynmawr.edu
Web site: http://www.brynmawr.edu
http://www.brynmawr.edu/admissions/applicationoptions.shtml (to apply online)

BUCKNELL UNIVERSITY

LEWISBURG, PENNSYLVANIA

The University

Founded in 1846 as a "literary institution" in the "wilds of Pennsylvania," Bucknell University has long embraced academic vigor. From its beginnings, Bucknell set a high standard for the teaching of the classics, the arts, and music. Today, the University is ranked among the top liberal arts institutions in the nation, offering a broad curriculum that includes professional programs in accounting, management, education, engineering, and music and preprofessional programs in law and medicine.

Bucknell distinguishes itself by combining the best characteristics of the traditional liberal arts college—selectivity, personalized education, residential living, and a commitment to the teacher-scholar model—with the advantages of a larger university—research opportunities and facilities, diverse curricula, and extensive cocurricular resources. Bucknell's 3,400 undergraduates have many more options, especially for research (250 labs campuswide), than those found in a traditional liberal arts college. Bucknell also offers an array of experiential learning opportunities, from the Student Managed Investment Fund, a yearlong class in which students take charge of real-money investments, to the Bucknell Brigade, a biannual service trip to Nicaragua, where in the past eight years, Bucknellians have helped to rebuild a community that was devastated by Hurricane Mitch.

The University believes in the totality of the learning experience, that personal growth and development occur not only in the classroom but also outside of it. The University strongly supports and encourages service—students contribute time, supplies, and money for projects ranging from rebuilding efforts in the area affected by Hurricane Katrina to volunteering with the local fire and rescue company. Students can choose from more than 150 clubs and organizations or start their own. A large number of students participate in intercollegiate Division I and intramural athletics; work on one of the numerous publications, host a show at the radio station; participate in student government; help with community volunteer projects; perform with one of the many music, drama, and dance groups; or join one of the thirteen fraternities or six sororities.

Location

With its green spaces, red brick buildings, and striking vistas, Bucknell's campus is a quintessential college environment in the heart of scenic central Pennsylvania. The University is located within 3 to 4 hours of most of the major Eastern cities, including New York City; Washington, D.C.; Baltimore; Philadelphia; and Pittsburgh.

Majors and Degrees

Bucknell provides students with a choice of more than fifty majors in a variety of liberal arts and professional fields. The University offers the Bachelor of Arts degree in animal behavior, anthropology, art, art history, biology, chemistry, classics (Greek and Latin), comparative humanities, computer science, East Asian studies (China or Japan), economics, education, English, environmental studies, French, geography, geology/ environmental geology, German, history, international relations, Latin American studies, mathematics, music (music composition, music education, music history, and performance), philosophy, physics, political science, psychology, religion, Russian, sociology (general, human services, and legal studies), Spanish, theater, and women's and gender studies; the Bachelor of Music degree; the Bachelor of Science degree in animal behavior, biology, cell biology and biochemistry, chemistry, computer engineering, computer science, engineering (biomedical, chemical, civil and environmental, computer science, electrical, and mechanical), environmental geology, environmental studies, mathematics, mathematics-economics, neuroscience, and physics; the Bachelor of Science in Business Administration degree in accounting and management; and Bachelor of Science in Education degrees in early childhood development, elementary education, and secondary education. In consultation with an academic adviser, students also may design their own major based around their individualized educational goals. Select engineering students also have the option of completing one of two five-year interdisciplinary programs; these programs lead to a B.S. in an engineering field and either a B.A. in another discipline or a specially designed Bachelor of Management for Engineers degree.

Academic Programs

Although requirements for each degree vary, all students are required to successfully complete three writing courses. Special programs are offered to encourage each student's personal and intellectual development. Examples are the first-year foundation seminars, an introductory engineering course open to students in the College of Arts and Sciences, and Bucknell's Residential College program. The Residential Colleges are six themed-based options for first-year students that combine classroom and out-of-class activities into a living and learning experience. The themes are the arts, environmental issues, global affairs, humanities, social justice, and society and technology.

Bucknell prepares students for the challenges of the twenty-first century–and the proof is in the numbers. Ninety-six percent of graduates are employed or pursue advanced degrees within six months of graduation. Whether students plan to begin their careers immediately after graduating or go on to professional or graduate schools, professors strive to help them to use their skills and abilities to succeed and contribute as global citizens in an increasingly complex society.

Off-Campus Programs

Nearly 45 percent of each graduating class has spent a summer, a semester, or more studying through approved programs in Europe, Asia, the Middle East, Africa, Australia, New Zealand, and Central or South America. Bucknell's off-campus study offers one of the largest overseas learning programs available at any university of Bucknell's size. Bucknell sponsors four of its own programs in England, France, Spain, and Barbados and is affiliated with 130 other programs worldwide. About 10 percent of those studying off campus attend internship programs in Philadelphia or Washington, D.C. Institutional financial aid is available for off-campus study.

Academic Facilities

Bucknell provides unusually fine facilities to students, including recently completed buildings for music, engineering, and psychology/geology; an athletics and recreation center with a modern fitness center, pool, and 4,000-seat arena; an outstanding library; a performing arts center with a 1,200-seat concert hall; and computer labs throughout the campus. Most of campus is wireless-accessible, including many green spaces. Many classrooms are equipped with projectors and computers, some with computers for each student. All student residences are connected to the residential network, featuring a high-speed data connection for each student.

Costs

The cost of tuition and fees for 2007–08 is $46,186, including $37,934 for tuition, $8052 for room and board, and $200 for student fees.

Financial Aid

More than $50 million in total financial aid was awarded to students in 2006, with an average award of $23,500, which includes scholarships, loans, and part-time jobs. More than 65 percent of all students received some sort of aid, including government grants and loans. Financial aid applicants must file the Financial Aid PROFILE with the College Scholarship Service before January 1.

Faculty

Bucknell has 301 full-time and 20 part-time members on the teaching faculty; 97 percent of full-time faculty members hold doctorates or appropriate terminal degrees. The student-faculty ratio is 11:1. The most celebrated professors teach first-year students as well as advanced students.

Bucknell's professors uphold the teacher-scholar ideal, through which they are committed to providing an excellent undergraduate education while at the same time actively pursuing their scholarly work. Many students collaborate with faculty members in research, and projects regularly lead to joint publications or presentations at professional meetings.

Student Government

The Bucknell Student Government serves as the official voice of Bucknell's students. It dispenses funds for most student clubs and organizations, and its representatives serve on standing committees of the Board of Trustees and other University governance groups.

Admission Requirements

Admission decisions focus on the quality of preparation as demonstrated by achievement in rigorous high school courses, SAT or ACT scores, special talent, significant contribution to school or community, and evidence of strong character and integrity. The University seeks qualified students from throughout the United States and abroad.

Application and Information

Applications should be filed before January 1 of the senior year in high school for notification by March 25. SAT or ACT results must be submitted before March 1. Early decision candidates may apply for Early Decision–Round One consideration by November 15 or Early Decision–Round Two consideration by January 1. Applications for transfer students should be submitted by April 1 for studies beginning in the following fall and by December 1 for the spring semester.

Kurt M. Thiede
Vice President for Enrollment Management and Dean of Admissions
Bucknell University
Lewisburg, Pennsylvania 17837
Phone: 570-577-1101
Fax: 570-577-3538
E-mail: admissions@bucknell.edu
Web site: http://www.bucknell.edu

Bucknell students often say that they fell in love with the campus when they saw it for the first time. The Academic Quad, shown here, is one of their favorite spots.

CABRINI COLLEGE

RADNOR, PENNSYLVANIA

The College

Cabrini College, a Catholic institution for men and women, is concerned with the full intellectual, personal, and social development of each student. The College's programs are organized to help students welcome the changes in their lives with vigor, initiative, and confidence. While academic excellence is the priority at Cabrini, students are encouraged to participate in activities that will help them develop socially, culturally, and spiritually. Although founded as a private Catholic college, the institution is proud of its diverse student body and accepts students of all denominations. Cabrini enrolls 2,361 men and women. The student community is a friendly one, characterized by close and long-standing ties to the faculty. Cabrini College is sponsored by the Missionary Sisters of the Sacred Heart of Jesus and is named for that institution's founder, St. Frances Xavier Cabrini, the first U.S. citizen to be canonized. Mother Cabrini's commitment to service to others and education of the heart are key parts of the College's programs.

More than 66 percent of Cabrini's full-time students live on campus in a variety of housing accommodations, including traditional residence halls for men and women, residential houses, and a 120-bed, apartment-style complex. The College provides a full range of services to students, including placement, career, and personal counseling; a tutoring program; and health services. Students can participate in seventeen intercollegiate sports for men and women as well as an intramural sports program. Other popular extracurricular activities are the theater program, the College chorus, the ethnic student alliance, departmental clubs, and campus ministry. Students are encouraged to join the College's award-winning newspaper, the literary journal, and the yearbook. The campus radio station, WYBF-FM, and television studio are available to all students.

Cabrini also provides a Master of Education degree, certification, a Master of Science degree in organization leadership, and a new Master of Science degree in instructional systems and technology.

Location

Cabrini offers students the best of both worlds—a wooded, spacious 112-acre suburban campus minutes from the King of Prussia shopping mall and a half hour from Philadelphia. The College is close enough for students to take advantage of the many cultural, social, and educational opportunities of the city. Students may visit Philadelphia's art museums or historic sites or travel to the Wachovia Center to see national sporting events or performances by professional musicians. Cabrini also is close to many other Philadelphia-area colleges, which sponsor activities of interest to students.

Majors and Degrees

Cabrini offers the Bachelor of Arts degree, with major programs in American studies, communication, English, French (through an affiliate agreement with Eastern University), graphic design, history, liberal arts, organizational management accelerated degree program for adult students, philosophy, political science, psychology, religious studies, sociology, and Spanish. The Bachelor of Science degree is offered, with major programs in accounting, biology, business administration, chemistry, computer information science, exercise science and health promotion, finance, human resource management, marketing, and mathematics. An individualized major, which is designed by the student using existing courses, can lead to a B.A. degree. The Bachelor of Social Work degree, which is accredited by the Council on Social Work Education, is awarded to graduates completing the social work major. The Bachelor of Science in Education degree is available, with majors in early childhood, educational studies, elementary, and special education; these programs also lead to teacher certification in each of the three fields (except for the educational studies major). Education majors are certified to teach in Pennsylvania and reciprocating states. Teacher certification for secondary education is offered in biology, chemistry, communications, English, mathematics, and social studies (concentration in history or sociology). Preprofessional programs in dentistry, nursing, occupational therapy, pharmacy, and physical therapy are designed by faculty advisers to meet the needs of individual students. Academic concentrations include advertising, economics, environmental science, international business, journalism and writing, nonprofit management, professional communication, public administration, social justice, theater, and video/audio/recording arts/photography/new communication technology.

Academic Programs

Cabrini College's academic program gives students a well-rounded educational experience—one that includes a strong liberal arts and science base as well as professional development in a specific career field. All students take core curriculum competency and distribution requirement courses to supplement the in-depth knowledge acquired within each major. The core distribution requirements include courses in the following areas: contemporary issues, cultural diversity, heritage, aesthetic appreciation, natural science, the individual and society, religious studies, and values and commitments. In addition, students take two seminar classes, Self-Understanding and the Common Good, in their freshman and junior years, respectively. The Common Good seminar includes a service-learning component. Cabrini's core curriculum has been developed by its faculty to help students understand themselves, their society, and the world around them.

Within each major, Cabrini's curriculum is designed to help students develop professional skills in their chosen career field. Classroom instruction in all majors is supplemented by various forms of experiential learning. Many programs have required internships, through which upperclass students can earn academic credit for working in a job related to their major program.

Cooperative Education is another form of experiential learning for all students to gain on-the-job experience in a field they may wish to pursue, and most co-ops are paid positions.

All education majors participate in fieldwork beginning in the sophomore year. Social work majors spend 600 hours in direct practice before graduation. Cabrini students can choose a double major, and a free elective system encourages students to broaden their academic backgrounds.

Students may pursue their studies on a full-time or part-time basis during the school year. The College enables students to take courses in the evening, on Saturday, or during the summer and offers an accelerated degree program in organizational management. The College also is beginning to offer more courses online.

Off-Campus Programs

Cabrini participates with area colleges in a number of cooperative programs that enrich educational opportunities. Through an exchange program with nearby Eastern University, Rosemont College, Valley Forge Military College, and all institutions in the Southeastern Pennsylvania Consortium of Higher Education (SEPCHE), full-time students may elect courses offered on the other campuses; no additional tuition fees are charged, and credit is automatically transferred. Cabrini also maintains affiliations with the Pennsylvania College of Podiatric Medicine for an accelerated medical program and KAJEM Recording Arts Studio for communication.

Academic Facilities

Cabrini's 210,000-volume library, which includes subscription to 240 periodicals, serves as a comprehensive resource for students. The library continues to expand its collection of electronic resources and now provides access to more than 21,000 electronic periodicals in a wide range of disciplines. Cabrini is a member of the Tri-State College Library Cooperative and the Online Computer Library Center (OCLC), so additional resources at other libraries in the area are just a keystroke away. The College's computer laboratory, which is open to all students, and five state-of-the-art-computer classroom facilities are equipped with IBM or Macintosh computers. Research facilities include the biology, chemistry, and psychology laboratories. A modern, fully equipped communication center houses the College's television studio, FM radio station, newsroom (with facilities for desktop publishing), and graphic design laboratory.

A great resource for education majors is the Children's School. Education majors have the opportunity to observe, do fieldwork, and student teach at the school. The College's educational resource center provides students with access to teaching materials, ranging from videos and transparencies to children's literature.

The new Center for Science, Education, and Technology provides the ideal setting for learning and discovery. The three-story facility underscores Cabrini's commitment to the sciences by providing state-of-the-art equipment, study space and training, and research and experimentation opportunities. The facility is designed to provide labs and classrooms for science majors and nonmajors, with smart technology in every lab, enhancing the learning experience. The building also includes a high-tech sixty-seat lecture hall, which features stadium seating for classes, seminars, workshops, and outreach programs.

In the Information Science and Technology Department, there are an undergraduate lab, two graduate labs, and three computer-based classrooms.

The science education classroom is designed specifically for education majors and secondary education certification; this classroom helps students learn innovative ways to teach science to children in grades K–12. Labs for anatomy and physiology, microbiology, life sciences, and biotechnology complement research labs and a resource center for faculty members and students. Equipment includes fluorescent, phase, and inverted microscopes; a flow cytometer; and recombinant DNA and cell facilities. The center's top floor houses the general chemistry, organic chemistry, and analytical chemistry labs; specialized instrumentation rooms; and a chemistry resource center as well as research labs for faculty members and students.

In addition, the College has included research labs for outside scientists with the intent of working with biotech companies in the area, providing opportunities for real-life experiences for students. Majors include biology, biology/premedicine, biotechnology, chemistry, and clinical laboratory science/medical technology. Pre–allied health programs include those in nursing, occupational therapy, pharmacy, and physical therapy. Various science and technology-focused minors and concentrations are also available for students to explore science within the context of their chosen area of study.

Costs

Tuition for full-time students in 2007–08 is $27,200; average room and board cost $10,290 for the year. A general fee of $830 covers student registration, health services, activities, library use, testing, and publications. Textbooks and supplies are approximately $960 per year, and fees of $30 and $85 are charged for laboratory and other miscellaneous courses. Students with cars secure an $85 parking permit annually.

Financial Aid

Last year, 96 percent of Cabrini's undergraduates shared more than $23 million in financial aid in the form of scholarship, grant, loan, and work-study funds. The College itself offered more than $10 million through a variety of institutional scholarship programs. In addition, eligible students can receive funds through federal programs such as Pell Grants, Supplemental Educational Opportunity Grants, and the Federal Work-Study Program, which is a student employment program. Pennsylvania students may also be eligible for a Pennsylvania State Grant. Sometimes out-of-state students may be able to receive grants from their own states. In addition to the Federal Work-Study Program, the College offers its own Work-Grant Program to help students with tuition costs. Applicants for all federal financial aid, plus any aid that is based on financial need, must submit the Free Application for Federal Student Aid (FAFSA) as soon as the form becomes available on January 1. The FAFSA is available by going online to http://www.fafsa.ed.gov. All financial aid is offered for a one-year period but is renewable.

Faculty

Cabrini's average class size is 19 students, and the College's faculty members are committed to developing and challenging the individual skills of each student. Faculty members are known for their dedication to teaching and getting to know their students personally. Each full-time student has a faculty adviser who assists in arranging a program that is designed to meet the student's objectives.

Student Government

The Student Government Association (SGA) of Cabrini College facilitates all communication pertaining to students within the College community. The association exists to make known the views of the student body and to look after its interests with respect to the faculty members, administration, and educational policies of the College.

Admission Requirements

The Admissions Committee considers applicants on the basis of their high school record, SAT or ACT scores, class rank, and other indicators of potential to succeed in college-level studies, such as recommendations. Applications for admission are reviewed without regard to sex, race, creed, color, national origin, age, or handicap. Applicants should be graduates of an accredited high school (or present equivalent credentials) and have a minimum of 15 units of credit: 4 in English, 2 in a foreign language, 3 in college-preparatory mathematics, 3 in science, and 3 in social studies. Cabrini also conducts an early admission program through which students with superior ability and a sound academic background may begin college studies at the end of the junior year in high school. Applicants may apply for advanced standing at Cabrini through the Advanced Placement (AP) Program and the College-Level Examination Program (CLEP) of the College Board. The College's Graduate and Continuing Studies Office administers CLEP and DANTES tests.

Cabrini welcomes transfer students from other accredited institutions. Applicants should have a minimum GPA of 2.0 to be considered for transfer. Students transferring from Bucks County Community College, Community College of Philadelphia, Manor College, Delaware County Community College, Montgomery County Community College, Harcum College, Harrisburg Area Community College, Peirce College, Reading Community College, or Valley Forge Military College with an A.A. or A.S. degree and a minimum 2.5 GPA receive credit for all previous course work. Two-year-college students are encouraged to follow a course of liberal and general studies during their first two years at another institution if they expect to continue their studies at a four-year college such as Cabrini.

A campus visit, while not required, is recommended for prospective students. The Admissions Office offers individual interviews and group information sessions on weekdays and select Saturdays. Students conduct campus tours, which may include class visits and informal meetings with faculty members and administrators. Those planning to visit the campus should contact a member of the Admissions Office staff for information. In addition, representatives of the College visit high schools in various cities.

Application and Information

Applicants for freshman admission are requested to have SAT or ACT scores and official high school transcripts sent to the Admissions Office along with the application for admission. Transfer students must submit an application and high school and college transcripts. A nonrefundable application fee of $35 must accompany the application. The Admissions Office maintains a rolling admission policy until the class is filled and takes action on an application when all the necessary credentials are on file. For more information, students may contact:

Admissions Office
Cabrini College
610 King of Prussia Road
Radnor, Pennsylvania 19087-3698
Phone: 610-902-8552
800-848-1003 (toll-free)
E-mail: admit@cabrini.edu
Web site: http://www.cabrini.edu

CALIFORNIA UNIVERSITY OF PENNSYLVANIA

CALIFORNIA, PENNSYLVANIA

The University

California University of Pennsylvania, a member of Pennsylvania's State System of Higher Education, traces its origin to the establishment of an academy in the town of California, Pennsylvania, in 1852. It has as its mission Building Character and Building Careers. California University began as a teacher-preparation school and has evolved into a multipurpose university that grants both undergraduate and graduate degrees.

In 2007, California was included in the *Princeton Review*'s "Best Northeastern Colleges." California University was also included in the *Templeton Guide to Character Building Colleges* and the *Making a Difference College and Graduate Guide,* the distinctive guide for students who want to use their education to make a better world. The University adopted Integrity, Civility, and Responsibility as its core values in 1998 and encourages all members of the community to aspire to these high ideals in order to make the University community, and the world, a better place.

The campus and recreational facilities, consisting of 188 acres with thirty-four primary buildings, are nestled on a bend of the Monongahela River. The Natali Student Center, which is located in the center of the campus, houses the student information center, dining facilities, movie theater, convenience store, food court, bookstore, ATM machine, and a variety of student organizations, including the Commuter Center and the University radio (WCAL) and television (CUTV) stations. The recreational complex, Roadman Park, is located just 1½ miles from the campus. Tennis courts; running tracks; picnic areas; baseball, softball, rugby, and soccer fields; and the football stadium are located there.

The current enrollment is about 6,000 undergraduate and 1,250 graduate students. About 3,700 undergraduate students commute, 1,500 live on campus in five recently completed air-conditioned residence halls, 750 live off campus in a new garden-style apartment complex that is affiliated with the University, and the rest live in off-campus fraternity or sorority houses, rental units, or private homes.

At the University, students have the opportunity to select the living arrangement that best fits their personal needs and preferences. Lower-campus residence halls provide the perfect environment for being in the center of all academic and recreational activities. On-campus living also provides an environment that offers structure, with tremendous convenience to classrooms, dining, Natali Student Center, and Manderino Library. A variety of room configurations allows students to choose from 1, 2, or 3 roommates or suitemates.

Great for more independent living, the apartments at Jefferson@ California are located less than 1½ miles from the campus, adjacent to Roadman Park. There are a variety of configurations, most of which have private baths. Jefferson also provides a clubhouse with a fully equipped fitness center, a recreation room with various games, a computer lab, and a media room. Other amenities include an outdoor swimming pool and sand volleyball and basketball courts. A shuttle service connects Jefferson to the main campus.

The University offers students the convenience of an on-campus Health Center, which is staffed by registered nurses and a nurse practitioner. A medical director/physician has regularly scheduled office hours.

The counseling center, which is staffed by professionals, is available to all students and provides psychological services. The University also offers drug and alcohol education programs that include consultation, intervention, counseling, education, awareness programs, and substance-free activities.

Location

The campus is located in the borough of California, Pennsylvania, a community of 6,000 people. It is approximately 35 miles south of Pittsburgh in the foothills of the Allegheny Mountains, near Pennsylvania's Laurel Highlands recreational area. Professional baseball, football, and hockey, as well as a variety of cultural activities, are available in Pittsburgh. The area in which the University is located has a number of significant historical sites related to the pre–Revolutionary War era. The University also offers students the option of off-campus sites located in Canonsburg at the Southpointe Technology Park and at the Regional Enterprise Tower in Pittsburgh.

Majors and Degrees

California University of Pennsylvania offers the following baccalaureate degrees: Bachelor of Arts, Bachelor of Fine Arts, Bachelor of Science, Bachelor of Science in Athletic Training, Bachelor of Science in Education, Bachelor of Science in Nursing, Bachelor of Science in Sports Management. Associate of Arts, Associate of Science, and Associate of Applied Science degrees are also offered.

The liberal arts majors include art, communication studies (language and literacy, public relations, radio/television, and speech concentrations available), criminal justice, English (creative writing, journalism, and literature concentrations available), French, graphic design, history, international studies (business and economics, geography, modern languages, and political science concentrations available),philosophy, political science (campaign management, prelaw, and public policy concentrations available), psychology (industrial-organizational psychology concentration available), sociology (applied sociology concentration available), Spanish, and theater.

The Bachelor of Science in Education includes majors in athletic training, communication disorders, early childhood education, elementary education, secondary education (art, biology, chemistry, communication, comprehensive social sciences, earth and space science, English, French, mathematics, physics, and Spanish), special education, and technology education. Dual majors are available in many education programs. The College of Education and Human Services also offers bachelor's degrees in gerontology, social work, and sport management, with concentrations in professional golf management and wellness and fitness.

The Eberly College of Science and Technology offers majors in the areas of administration and management, biology, business administration (accounting, business administration, business economics, computer-based systems management, finance, human resources management, management, and marketing), computer information systems, computer science, earth science, electrical engineering technology, environmental earth science, environmental studies (ecology, environmental science, and fisheries and wildlife concentrations) geography (geographic information systems and travel and tourism concentrations), geology, graphic communication technology, natural sciences (biology, chemistry, earth science, geology, mathematics, natural sciences interdisciplinary, and physics), parks and recreation management, and prehealth professions (pre-chiropractic medicine, predentistry, premedicine, pre-mortuary science, preoptometry, pre-osteopathic medicine, prepharmacy, pre-podiatric medicine, and preveterinary medicine). A cooperative nursing program is offered with the Community College of Allegheny County. The University offers an upper-division Bachelor of Science in Nursing degree program for students who have completed an RN program.

Academic Programs

Each bachelor's degree requires a minimum of 120 semester hours of credit. A general education requirement of 51 credits is distributed among the following areas: building a sense of community (1 credit), communication skills (9 credits), critical-thinking skills (3 credits), fine arts (3 credits), health and wellness (3 credits), humanities (3 credits), mathematics (3 credits), multicultural awareness (3 credits), natural sciences (8 credits), social sciences (6 credits), technological literacy (6 credits), and values (3 credits). An honors program provides an opportunity for an enhanced educational experience to students who meet the criteria. Honors students have the option of living in the new Honors Residence Hall, which offers numerous outstanding amenities, including a private library. Wireless Internet connections are available throughout campus. Applications of all incoming first-year and transfer students are reviewed, and those with the highest indicators of past and future academic success are invited to participate in the honors program.

Academic Facilities

The University has traditional library holdings of more than 360,000 volumes, more than 1 million microform units, nearly 1,500 periodical titles, and U.S. government documents. It is a member of the Keystone Library Network, which provides access to library holdings, databases, and electronic resources among fourteen State System of Higher Education libraries. This virtual library electronically links users to a variety of information sources and delivers both text and multimedia sources immediately and seamlessly from any location. The 80,400-square-foot Eberly Science and Technology Center features state-of-the-art science and computer laboratories and is one of the premier teaching facilities on campus. Every residence hall room is wired with fiber optics so that students can bring computers, plug them in, and have immediate access to the Internet and all of its resources. For students who do not have computers of their own, there is a computer lab on every floor of the residence halls. Numerous specialized computer facilities are available across the campus, including ones devoted to meteorology, math and computer science, word processing, accounting, CAD-CAM, robotics, teacher education, art, and chemistry.

Costs

The 2007–08 tuition for a resident of Pennsylvania attending full-time (12 to 18 credits) was $2589 per semester. For a full-time nonresident, tuition was $4142 per semester. Room costs for 2007–08 ranged from $2494 to $3638. Board prices ranged from $1188 to $1439. Based on a full-time schedule, fees for 2007–08 included a $62.50 technology fee, an $85 service fee, a $210 Student Association fee, an $81 student union building fee, an $84 student center operations and maintenance fee, and a $251.90 academic support fee. The cost of books, materials, and supplies varies with each program.

Financial Aid

California University of Pennsylvania has available a number of types of financial aid, including student employment, grant and scholarship aid through the Pennsylvania Higher Education Assistance Agency, federal grants, and student loans. A number of non-need-based academic scholarships are available for talented students. All students must complete the Pennsylvania State Grant and federal financial aid application for need-based aid. The Director of Financial Aid at the University administers all student aid. Overall, 98 percent of student need is met for students who are awarded need-based aid.

Faculty

Classes are taught by 238 full-time faculty members; no classes are taught by graduate assistants. Terminal degrees are held by more than 84 percent of the full-time faculty members. Faculty advisers are assigned based on the student's major, department, or school.

Student Government

Student government at California University of Pennsylvania regulates cocurricular activities. It furthers the quality of student life by encouraging and funding diverse student activities, providing experiences in the principles and practices of democratic government, supplying a forum for general student interest, and improving and promoting the cultural standards of the University. Students sit on many important University committees, including the University Forum, and have a voice in most policy decisions.

Admission Requirements

California University of Pennsylvania welcomes applications from all qualified persons. Admission standards have been established by California University of Pennsylvania for the purpose of ascertaining which prospective students are most likely to succeed at the University. An applicant for admission should have graduated from an accredited four-year high school or should possess an equivalency diploma issued by a state department of education. All applicants should submit to the University evidence of their ability to do college-level work, as indicated by such tests as the College Board's SAT. All applicants are required to have a Social Security number.

Application and Information

Prospective students should obtain, complete, and return an application form, along with the Secondary School Record (which is completed by the high school guidance counselor). A nonrefundable application fee of $25 must accompany the application. Students can apply and pay online at the University's Web site. A student who wants to transfer to California University of Pennsylvania should complete the application form (hard copy or online) and forward it to the Admissions Office with a nonrefundable check or money order for $25 or pay online. Official transcripts from all colleges and universities attended must be sent to the Admissions Office.

For additional information regarding admission, students should contact:

Mr. Bill Edmonds
Director of Admissions
California University of Pennsylvania
250 University Avenue
California, Pennsylvania 15419
Phone: 724-938-4404
888-412-0479 (toll-free)
E-mail: inquiry@cup.edu
Web site: http://www.cup.edu

Students on the campus of California University of Pennsylvania.

CARLOW UNIVERSITY

PITTSBURGH, PENNSYLVANIA

The University

Carlow University was founded in 1929 in response to a local need for a Catholic women's college. The mission of the University is to involve people, primarily women, in a process of self-directed lifelong learning that frees them to think clearly and creatively, to discover and to challenge or affirm cultural and aesthetic values, to respond reverently to God and others, and to render competent and compassionate service in personal and professional life. Although Carlow makes explicit its strong continuing commitment to the education of women, it welcomes men. The University's mission has been confirmed over the years by the growing number of students who come seeking a solid liberal arts education as well as strong career preparation. In addition to its undergraduate programs, the University offers an M.B.A., an M.F.A., and other graduate degrees.

Current enrollment exceeds 2,300 students. Carlow's students have various backgrounds and come mainly from the Middle Atlantic states; the majority are from western Pennsylvania.

Placement and career counseling, free professional and peer tutorial services, the Center for Academic Achievement, the Disabilities Service Office, student health, personal counseling programs, and campus ministry are support services available to students.

Cocurricular organizations include the Student Government Association, the Commuter Student Association, the International Student Association, the *Purple Menace* newspaper, and United Black Students, among many others.

The University has a large group of students involved in community service and volunteerism. Spring break service projects have taken students to Jamaica, the Virgin Islands, Arizona, Arkansas, Ireland, and many other locations. Academic- or career-oriented organizations include Alpha Phi Omega (national service/honor society), American Chemical Society, Beta Beta Beta (biology club), Business Leaders of Carlow, the Council for Exceptional Children, Kappa Delta Epsilon (for education majors), Social Work Organization, Student Nurses Association of Pennsylvania, Phi Chi Theta (business fraternity), and the Psychology Club. Special-interest groups include Blessed, the Gospel choir; the Environmental Clean-up Organization; Pep Band; Spirit; Student Athlete Association; Theater Group; and Women in Communication (WIC).

The athletic program includes women's intercollegiate basketball, soccer, softball, tennis, and volleyball as well as a selection of physical education courses, including aerobics, fitness and weight control, martial arts/self-defense, modern dance, water aerobics, weight training, and yoga. Wellness and fitness services include individual health assessment, fitness programming, and nutrition counseling.

Popular campus events include entertainment, film series, carnivals, Homecoming, Mercy Founders Week, a St. Patrick's Day celebration and parade, the International Festival, Black History Month events, Women's History Month events, and theater productions.

The University's central location gives students opportunities for internships in various businesses and agencies. Students in health-related fields complete their clinical experiences in the many fine teaching hospitals and private health-care facilities in the city of Pittsburgh. City buses stop in front of the campus, and campus parking is available for commuting students.

Location

Carlow University is located on a 15-acre campus in the heart of Oakland, one of the nation's biggest college towns and the educational, cultural, and medical center of Pittsburgh. Nine other colleges and universities at which students can cross-register are within walking distance or just minutes away by bus. Schenley Park, Carnegie Library and Museums, Phipps Conservatory, Carnegie Music and Lecture Halls, and the Oakland shopping district are all a short walk from the campus. Downtown Pittsburgh is only a 10-minute bus ride away. Greater Pittsburgh International Airport is a 30-minute drive from the Carlow campus.

Majors and Degrees

Carlow University grants the undergraduate degrees of Bachelor of Arts, Bachelor of Science, Bachelor of Science in Nursing, and Bachelor of Social Work. Programs include accounting, art, art/art education, art/art history, art/ceramics, art/graphic design, art/interactive media design, art/painting and drawing, art/photography, art with a certificate in art therapy preparation, biology (with concentrations in forensic medical and legal investigations/autopsy specialization, human biology, molecular cell and biotechnology, and organismal/ecological biology), business management, business management/communication, chemistry, communication studies, creative writing, early childhood education, elementary education, English, forensic accounting, health science (available to students who have previously earned an associate degree), history, human resource management and technology, information systems management, liberal studies, marketing, mathematics, nursing, philosophy, political science, professional writing, professional writing/business, psychology, public policy and leadership, scientific/medical marketing, social work, sociology, sociology/criminal justice, Spanish, special education, and theology. An independent major, designed by the student, may also be arranged.

Certification programs are offered in forensic accounting, perfusion technology (biology majors only) and secondary education (biology, chemistry, English, general science, mathematics, and social studies).

Preprofessional programs include athletic training, dentistry, law, medicine, occupational therapy, optometry, osteopathy, pharmacy, physical therapy, physician assistant studies, podiatry, and veterinary medicine.

The University offers 3-2 programs in engineering in three areas: biology/environmental engineering, chemistry/chemical engineering, and mathematics/engineering. In addition, there are a 3-2 program in environmental science and a 3-3 B.A./J.D. law program.

Academic Programs

Carlow's primary concern is the development of the student as a lifelong learner. To this end, members of the Carlow community—students, faculty, and staff—recognize the integrity and value of each person in the daily life and work of the University. The academic programs are broad and flexible, including opportunities for double majors, single majors with certification in education, minors, certificate programs, and changes of major. Transfer students are warmly welcomed.

The University operates on the two-semester system, August to December and January to May. Summer sessions, a variable number of weeks in length, are offered every year. Most courses carry 3 credits (laboratory courses, among others, carry 4 credits). Students normally take five courses each semester. Each student must demonstrate basic competence in English composition, speech and interpersonal communication, reading comprehension, and mathematics. Required of all students is one course each in a lab science, history, literature, mathematics, social/

behavioral science (such as psychology or sociology), theology, fine arts, philosophy, women's studies, and political science or economics, as well as one global perspective course. Students are also required to take an interdisciplinary course, which is selected from a variety of subject areas. Students in nursing, education, social work, psychology, management, and perfusion technology are required to do fieldwork as part of their program. Field placements and internships are guaranteed and encouraged in all areas of study. An honors program is open to eligible students. After the first semester of the first year, one course per semester (outside of the major) may be taken on a pass-fail basis. Some courses may be challenged, for credit or exemption, by passing an examination. CLEP general exam credits may be used for this purpose as well.

The University gives women and men the opportunity to return to the classroom at various stages of their lives. Adult learners may enroll in full-time and part-time degree programs, noncredit enrichment courses, seminars, and workshops. Scheduling options include day, evening, accelerated, weekend, and online courses.

Academic Facilities

Grace Library, a five-level multipurpose learning center in the heart of the campus, currently contains more than 100,000 books, subscribes to over 350 print journals, and offers access to more than 4,500 online journals. The library houses the offices of the President and Provost. The Center for Academic Achievement, the mail room, the bookstore, Academic Affairs, the Center for Career Enrichment, Printing Services, the International Poetry Forum, University Archives, and computer laboratories are also located here. Kresge Theatre, a 300-seat auditorium, is located on the fifth level as well.

Curran Hall houses the School of Nursing and includes a state-of-the-art nursing skills lab and conference and seminar rooms. Frances Warde Hall is a residence hall that also houses the School of Education, art labs, student affairs offices, and the campus café. Antonian Hall houses the 1,000-seat Sister Rosemary Heyl Theatre, the School for Social Change, the fine arts department, and classrooms as well as administrative offices for admissions, financial aid, advising, the registrar, and student accounts.

The cafeteria and the Campus School of Carlow University (kindergarten through grade 8) are located in Tiernan Hall. St. Joseph Hall contains the gymnasium, fitness center, and swimming pool, and Aquinas Hall houses classrooms, the humanities division, the International Student Center, and faculty and staff offices.

Carlow's A. J. Palumbo Hall of Science and Technology houses state-of-the-art teaching/research laboratories in physics, organic and advanced chemistry, genetics, cell biology, and gross anatomy; a herbarium to store dry plant specimens; a greenhouse; an amphitheater for scientific presentations; and the Bayer Children's Science Learning Laboratory.

Carlow University's campus computer network features Internet accounts and e-mail, network and Internet access from any location on campus. There is one network port per pillow in the residence halls.

Costs

Tuition and fees for 2007–08 were $18,736 for full-time students. Room and board charges for the year were $7684 for double occupancy.

Financial Aid

Financial aid in the form of grants, scholarships, loans, and student employment is available to eligible applicants. More than 90 percent of all full-time students receive some type of financial assistance. Academic and/or leadership scholarships ranging from $1000 to full tuition are available for qualified students. The University expects that most aid recipients assume a portion of their expenses through loans and/or part-time employment. Job opportunities are available on campus in a wide variety of positions, and students are placed, whenever possible, in positions that coincide with their skills and interests. Basketball, soccer, softball, tennis, and volleyball scholarships are also available.

Faculty

Carlow's student-faculty ratio is 12:1, and faculty members are readily available to help plan individualized programs of study, to provide assistance relating to field placements and internships, and to assist in career preparation. The student's major adviser is normally a faculty member in the department.

Student Government

All registered students are members of the Student Government Association (SGA). Through the SGA, students act as equal participants with the administration, faculty, and staff in general governance. The SGA promotes the general welfare of the students and is the advocate to ensure that the academic, social, and spiritual needs of students are met. SGA is empowered to charter all student organizations.

Admission Requirements

Applicants are evaluated on the basis of their secondary school record, class rank, and scores on the SAT or ACT. The Committee on Admissions recognizes that school curricula vary greatly and always gives careful consideration to the application of an able student whose course work or grading scale is more challenging or whose preparation differs from the traditional program. A personal interview is strongly recommended but not required. Overnight visits, a day of classes, campus tours, and meals are available and are strongly encouraged. Throughout the year, the University sponsors programs that give candidates the opportunity to tour the campus and meet faculty and staff members and Carlow students.

Application and Information

Although Carlow subscribes to the rolling admission plan, high school students are encouraged to submit an application early in the first semester of the senior year. Students interested in early notification should apply by September 30. The University's priority admission and scholarship deadline is February 15.

Students may apply online or request an application form by contacting:

Office of Admissions
Carlow University
3333 Fifth Avenue
Pittsburgh, Pennsylvania 15213
Phone: 412-578-6059
800-333-CARLOW (toll-free)
E-mail: admissions@carlow.edu
Web site: http://www.carlow.edu

CARNEGIE MELLON UNIVERSITY

CarnegieMellon

PITTSBURGH, PENNSYLVANIA

The University

Since its beginning more than 100 years ago, Carnegie Mellon has evolved into an institution consistently ranked in the top twenty-five for its unique approach to education and research. Students become experts in fields ranging from business, the fine arts, and computer science to humanities, the sciences, and engineering—far more than steel magnate and philanthropist Andrew Carnegie first envisioned when he founded Carnegie Mellon as a technical school in 1900.

Carnegie Mellon is world renowned for its left-brain and right-brain thinking that unite within the University's collaborative culture and are the foundation of learning at Carnegie Mellon. Students acquire a depth and breadth of knowledge while sharpening problem-solving, critical-thinking, creative, and quantitative skills. The University's unique approach to education develops sound critical judgment, resourcefulness, and professional ethics through interdisciplinary and hands-on experiences. Graduates go on to become the innovative leaders and problem solvers of tomorrow.

Students in this private coeducational university come from all fifty states and more than forty countries. Each year, Carnegie Mellon enrolls a diverse freshman class of approximately 1,400 students. The total undergraduate population is 5,200. Students come from a variety of different social and cultural backgrounds and also represent a wide range of academic and artistic interests. Approximately 11 percent of the student body identifies with an ethnic minority population such as African American, Hispanic/Latin American, or Native American.

Carnegie Mellon spans the best of both worlds; its traditional 110-acre campus is located minutes from downtown Pittsburgh, yet it is surrounded by residential neighborhoods. Student activities include more than 150 clubs and organizations, varsity and intramural sports, fraternities and sororities, and student government. Off campus, students can take advantage of three culturally active neighborhoods (all within walking distance), the largest public park in Pittsburgh, urban and suburban shopping, excellent sightseeing, professional sports, museums, art galleries, and amusement parks.

Approximately 80 percent of students live in University housing, which is guaranteed for all four years, provided students remain in the housing system, and ranges from traditional residence halls, special-interest housing, and apartment buildings to fraternity and sorority housing. Freshmen are required to live in University housing.

Carnegie Mellon students come away from their undergraduate experience poised to be trendsetters, whether in the business world, the art community, or graduate school. Students not only gain the knowledge necessary to succeed professionally, they also learn how to maximize their creativity, intellectual playfulness, and analytical skills in order to survive in an ever-changing global environment. The University strives to produce graduates who are adaptable, resourceful, and independent—graduates who communicate effectively, strive to be leaders, and understand their professional and social responsibilities.

High school juniors can participate in Carnegie Mellon's six-week summer Pre-College programs, in which students have the opportunity to take college course work, meet people from all over the country, live like true college students, and explore the city of Pittsburgh. Students can take two regular Carnegie Mellon courses for full credit in disciplines such as engineering, humanities, computer science, or the sciences; immerse themselves in the fine arts studio or conservatory-based courses to determine their level of interest for study at the college level in architecture, art, design, drama, or music; or attend the National High School Game Academy, in which students learn interactive digital game development through hands-on experience.

In addition to bachelor's degrees, Carnegie Mellon offers master's and doctoral degrees.

Location

Carnegie Mellon is located 5 miles from the downtown area in the Oakland neighborhood of Pittsburgh. Home to several of the city's colleges, universities, museums, and hospitals, Oakland offers many activities and resources to area students. Although Carnegie Mellon has the collegiate feel of a suburban campus, the surrounding Pittsburgh community provides all of the cultural and social advantages of a big city. The University is approximately 1 hour from some of the best skiing in the East and is only a short plane ride from many major metropolitan areas, including Boston, New York City, Chicago, Philadelphia, and Washington, D.C.

Majors and Degrees

Undergraduate majors at Carnegie Mellon include business administration, computer science, engineering (biomedical engineering*, chemical engineering, civil and environmental engineering, electrical and computer engineering, engineering and public policy*, materials science, and mechanical engineering), fine and performing arts (architecture, art, design, drama, and music), information systems, liberal arts and professional studies (economics, English, history, information systems, modern languages, philosophy, political science, psychology, social and decision sciences, and statistics), and the sciences (biological sciences, chemistry, mathematical sciences, and physics). The Bachelor of Humanities and Arts (B.H.A.) and Bachelor of Science and Arts (B.S.A.) degree programs also are available, as are many interdepartmental majors. (* indicates double majors only.)

Academic Programs

There is no core curriculum at Carnegie Mellon. The only required classes are Computing@CarnegieMellon (C@CM) and a first-year writing course. Each college has its own requirements for graduation.

Students at Carnegie Mellon have the freedom to design courses of study that cross over majors and disciplines. In fact, some students have double majors, minors, or concentrations in areas other than their principal major. It is not unusual to find an engineering student with a double major in music or an English major with a minor in business administration.

The Bachelor of Humanities and Arts and Bachelor of Science and Arts degree programs are unique, non-performance-based programs at Carnegie Mellon that allow students to pursue interdisciplinary programs in the fine arts and either the humanities and social sciences or the pure sciences. Other special programs include Army, Navy, and Air Force ROTC; self-defined majors and interdepartmental major options in the College of Humanities and Social Sciences; prelaw and premedicine advising programs; and five-year combined bachelor's/master's degree programs.

Carnegie Mellon has nearly unlimited opportunities for students to participate in undergraduate research, sometimes as early as the second semester of the freshman year. Many departments offer research training courses and research programs during the academic year and summer. Students can work on research in groups, individually with a professor, or independently through Carnegie Mellon's Small Undergraduate Research Grant (SURG) program.

Off-Campus Programs

Carnegie Mellon students can take one course per semester at any of the following colleges and universities in Pittsburgh for full credit: the University of Pittsburgh, Carlow College, Chatham College, Duquesne University, La Roche College, Point Park University, Robert Morris University, Pittsburgh Theological Seminary, and the Community College of Allegheny County.

Carnegie Mellon has numerous study-abroad programs, including university exchange programs in Chile, Singapore, Mexico, Japan, and Switzerland. More than 300 students take advantage of study abroad each year. Students may also take advantage of study-abroad opportunities through their department or another university.

Academic Facilities

Carnegie Mellon has a 110-acre main campus with a few outlying research buildings. The campus contains more than fifty academic and administrative buildings and three libraries. The Hunt, Engineering and Science, and Mellon Institute Libraries contain more than 1 million volumes and thousands of periodicals. An international online resource sharing system and reciprocal borrowing between Carnegie Mellon and other local universities provide students with almost unlimited library resources.

A wireless network spans all academic, administrative, and residence hall buildings as well as key outdoor areas across campus. Public computing labs, known as "clusters," offer approximately 400 Macintosh, Windows, and Linus computers equipped with hundreds of software packages that range from basic productivity to high-end engineering and multimedia.

For students with their own computers, all of the residence hall rooms are wired to the Andrew network—Carnegie Mellon's high-speed computer network that links the campus and provides access to the outside world. Carnegie Mellon was the first university campus to offer wireless networking.

In addition to academic facilities, Carnegie Mellon features the University Center—a centralized building with eateries and recreational facilities, the historic Kresge Theater for Performing Arts, studio and black-box theaters, art galleries, abundant studio and rehearsal space, a gymnasium, and numerous research laboratories.

Costs

Carnegie Mellon's costs for the 2007–08 academic year include tuition and fees in the amount of $37,544 and room and board totaling $9660. The cost of books, supplies, and personal expenses are estimated at $2301. The total cost is approximately $49,498. International students must also pay an additional $1816 for required health insurance.

Financial Aid

Carnegie Mellon is a need-blind institution, meaning that students' personal financial information is not considered in the admission process. Approximately 52 percent of the freshman class receive financial aid (U.S. citizens and eligible noncitizens).

Carnegie Mellon uses Federal Methodology to determine financial aid eligibility. The forms required to apply for financial assistance are the Free Application for Federal Student Aid (FAFSA), the Carnegie Mellon Financial Aid Form, parental W-2s, and both parental and student tax returns. Financial aid packages usually include a combination of loans, grants, and work-study allowances.

Three merit-based scholarships are offered, with awards ranging up to the cost of tuition. A need- and merit-based scholarship is also offered. Every student is eligible for merit-based scholarship consideration with no separate application process. Students are also encouraged to apply for outside scholarships as a source of aid.

Faculty

Carnegie Mellon has more than 1,200 teaching and research faculty members and a student-faculty ratio of 10:1. The average class size is 25 to 35 students. Faculty members are practicing professionals at the forefront of their respective fields. More often than not, faculty members teach both undergraduate and graduate courses. Carnegie Mellon's classes are taught by faculty members, not teaching assistants. Professors, instructors, and lecturers are in the classroom, lab, studio, or workplace creating new knowledge on a daily basis and passing that knowledge on to their students. Undergraduates have the opportunity to work on groundbreaking research projects with award-winning faculty members, many times one-on-one, through assistantships, internships, work-study positions, and extracurricular organizations.

Student Government

Carnegie Mellon's Student Senate is composed of representatives from each college at Carnegie Mellon and exists to promote the welfare of the campus community, distribute budget funds to student groups, provide a liaison between students and the administration, and inform the student body of proposals and changes.

Admission Requirements

Carnegie Mellon looks for strong students, both academically and socially, who have a wide range of interests and activities. There are no minimum grade requirements or standardized test scores, although most of Carnegie Mellon's students tend to have strong test scores and are at the top of their classes. The University uses standardized test scores, including the SAT (or ACT with Writing Test) and SAT Subject Tests; high school performance; evidence of leadership; honors and awards earned; and extracurricular activities to make admission decisions. Recommendations from a guidance counselor and a teacher are required along with a personal statement and essay. Interviews with admission counselors are recommended but not required.

Carnegie Mellon strives to build a class of students that is racially, socially, economically, and geographically diverse. The University is committed to recruiting students from traditionally underrepresented backgrounds, including African Americans, Hispanic/Latin Americans, and Native Americans. Transfer students are also welcome.

Application and Information

Carnegie Mellon has three types of decision plans: early admission, early decision, and regular decision.

Early admission is offered for high school juniors who wish to skip their senior year to go directly to college. In addition to academic strength, early admission candidates must display maturity and have strong teacher and guidance counselor recommendations. The application deadline for early admission is January 1 (December 1 for fine arts), and candidates are notified of a decision between March 15 and April 15.

Early decision is offered for students who declare Carnegie Mellon as their first choice. Early decision is a binding agreement; if admitted, students are expected to enroll. The University offers two early decision plans. The deadline for Early Decision I is November 1 (there is no Early Decision I for drama, composition, voice, flute, or B.H.A./B.S.A.), and candidates are notified of a decision by December 15. The deadline for Early Decision II is December 1, (there is no Early Decision II for architecture, art, design, drama, music, or B.H.A./B.S.A.), and candidates are notified by January 15.

Regular decision is the most popular plan. Applications are due by January 1 (December 1 for fine arts), and notification occurs between March 15 and April 15.

Students interested in learning more about Carnegie Mellon can arrange to visit the campus. Throughout most of the year, the University offers group information sessions, campus tours, and personal interviews, which are recommended, but not required, for admission.

Group information sessions and hometown or alumni interviews are available for students who cannot come to Pittsburgh. University representatives travel across the United States during the fall of every year. Students should visit http://www.cmu.edu/admission to see the current travel schedule.

For more information, students should contact:

Carnegie Mellon Office of Admission
5000 Forbes Avenue
Pittsburgh, Pennsylvania 15213-3890
Phone: 412-268-2082
Fax: 412-268-7838
E-mail: undergraduate-admissions@andrew.cmu.edu
Web site: http://www.cmu.edu/admission/

Carnegie Mellon University, located in Pittsburgh, Pennsylvania, is one of America's leading universities.

CEDAR CREST COLLEGE

ALLENTOWN, PENNSYLVANIA

The College

Since its founding in 1867 as an independent liberal arts college for women, Cedar Crest has educated women for leadership in a changing world. Approximately 1,900 students come to the College annually from thirty-two states and twenty other countries. The 11:1 student-faculty ratio provides for small classes, individual advising, and independent work in an environment that emphasizes interdisciplinary, values-oriented education. The Honor Philosophy is a most compelling statement of each student's rights and responsibilities for her own academic and cocurricular performance.

Cedar Crest's science programs, including conservation biology, forensic science, genetic engineering, neuroscience, nuclear medicine, nursing, and nutrition, generate the largest student enrollment. Business and marketing, psychology, and education generate the next largest enrollments. The genetic engineering major was the first such program at a women's college and the second at an undergraduate institution.

Cedar Crest has a national Gold Award program for health and wellness that includes personal sports training, nutrition counseling, and a full schedule of dance classes plus yoga and aerobics. The Rodale Aquatic Center for Civic Health, a state-of-the-art two-pool complex, offers health and fitness opportunities for the entire campus community. The campus also includes tennis courts and regulation fields for field hockey, lacrosse, soccer, and softball.

Student Affairs sponsors workshops and retreats on leadership and service throughout the year. More than forty-five campus organizations offer opportunities in the performing arts, preprofessional areas, environmental awareness, cultural diversity, and much more. An active community service program is made up of student and faculty volunteers with many groups, from Habitat for Humanity to the Girls Club. Healthy lifestyle, community building, and innovative quality-of-life programs are held regularly in the four residence halls.

The Office of Career Planning offers placement opportunities, internships at nearly 350 companies worldwide, and four-year guidance in preparing resumes and interviewing for employment and graduate schools.

The Cedar Crest Falcons compete in eight NCAA Division III intercollegiate sports: basketball, cross-country, field hockey, lacrosse, soccer, softball, tennis, and volleyball. Intramural activities include badminton, basketball, soccer, softball, and tennis. The Equestrian Club competes in collegiate horse shows.

Cedar Crest's academic programs are fully accredited by the Middle States Association of Colleges and Schools and, where appropriate, by the American Academy of Forensic Science, American Medical Association, American Dietetic Association, American Bar Association, National League for Nursing Accrediting Commission, and National Council on Social Work Education and by the Departments of Education of New York, New Jersey, and Pennsylvania.

In addition to its undergraduate offerings, Cedar Crest offers a master's degree in forensic science. A master's degree in nursing is planned for fall 2008.

Location

Cedar Crest's 84-acre campus, a nationally registered arboretum, is situated in a well-established residential section of Allentown, a midsized city (105,000) in the Lehigh Valley of eastern Pennsylvania. In Allentown, students enjoy the Allentown Art Museum, three professional orchestras, numerous community theater companies, and public parks with jogging paths, riding trails, picnic areas, and other recreational facilities. Sites for skiing, white-water rafting, and hiking are nearby. By car or bus, Cedar Crest is less than 2 hours from New York City; 1 hour from Philadelphia; just under 3 hours from Washington, D.C.; and 2 hours from the Jersey Shore. The Pocono Mountains are less than an hour away. The Lehigh Valley International Airport, only 10 minutes away, is served by major airlines with connecting flights to most major cities in the United States.

Majors and Degrees

Cedar Crest offers programs in accounting, applied sociology, art, biochemistry, biology, business administration, chemistry, communications, computer information systems, conservation biology, criminal justice, dance, education (elementary and secondary), English, fine arts, forensic science, gender studies, genetic engineering, Hispanic and Latino studies, history, marketing, mathematics, music, neuroscience, nuclear medicine, nursing, nutrition, philosophy, political science, psychology, religion, social work, theater, and writing. With committee approval, a student may pursue a self-designed major.

Preprofessional programs include dentistry, law, medicine, and veterinary medicine.

Certificate programs are offered in gerontology, human resource management, and nuclear medicine.

A five-year B.S./master's program in education is also available.

Academic Programs

Self-designed majors, double majors, minors, independent-study programs, and individual and group research projects support serious concentration at the undergraduate level. Working with her adviser, each student designs a program of study that meets the major requirements as well as her personal interests and professional goals. The College's curriculum is structured to provide course work in the areas that define a liberal arts education. The Ethical Life Course integrates applied ethics and service-learning opportunities. Science majors begin conducting advanced research at the freshman level, opening opportunities that often lead to internships at major research institutions.

Highly motivated students with records of academic excellence may participate in the four-year Honors Program. The program incorporates seminars not offered in the regular course schedule with off-campus activities and advanced creative and research projects.

Each major has a Capstone experience that reflects on previous learning and experience and explores issues emerging in the present and expected in the future. The academic program emphasizes independent and faculty-supported student research.

Off-Campus Programs

Internship opportunities enable Cedar Crest students to explore career options and gain practical experience at major corporations, national nonprofit organizations, and health-care facilities. Students have completed internships as a CNN foreign correspondent with the United Nations, as an FBI honors intern working on a database for DNA fingerprinting, and as research assistants at Cold Spring Harbor Laboratory and nationally recognized cancer research laboratories. Students may also participate in the Washington Semester at American University or study-abroad programs for a summer, a semester, or an entire year or do fieldwork through the School for Field Studies or at nearby Hawk Mountain Wildlife Sanctuary.

At no added cost, Cedar Crest upperclass students may cross-register at Lehigh and DeSales Universities and Lafayette, Moravian, and Muhlenberg Colleges, all nearby schools.

Academic Facilities

Cressman Library collections include books, periodicals, and electronic and audiovisual resources. Access to the collections is through an online catalog that also provides access to the Library of Congress, OCLC, remote data and indexing sources, and 1.75 million volumes available with daily delivery through the local academic consortium. Campuswide Internet/World Wide Web connections provide access to full-text reference tools and journals.

Other buildings on the campus house theaters, art galleries, sculpture gardens, student exhibit space, computer labs, hospital simulation labs, multimedia classrooms, a multimedia development lab, music practice rooms, a video production studio, dance and art studios and workshops, a ceramics studio, a papermaking studio, a state-of-the art nutrition laboratory, spectrophotometry equipment, up-to-date genetic engineering laboratories, a greenhouse, dining services, a bookstore, a post office, a gymnasium, a fitness center, an aquatics center, and a computational biology center.

Costs

For 2007–08, the comprehensive resident fee was $33,664, including $25,040 for tuition and $8624 for room and board.

Financial Aid

Cedar Crest offers a generous program of financial aid based on academic achievement and financial need, including scholarships, grants, loans, and employment. Federal funds available are Federal Pell Grants, Federal Supplemental Educational Opportunity Grants, Federal Perkins Loans, Federal Work-Study Program awards, and Nursing Student Loans. The size of an award varies with need. More than 90 percent of the students at Cedar Crest receive aid. Students applying for financial aid should file the Free Application for Federal Student Aid (FAFSA). Outstanding international students may also qualify for financial aid.

Applicants who rank in the top 25 percent of their class and score 1100 or higher on the critical reading and math sections of the SAT (24 on the ACT) can qualify for a scholarship of up to one-half tuition per year. Sibling grants are awarded to students when 2 siblings are attending Cedar Crest full-time, concurrently.

Recipients of Girl Scout Gold awards, graduates of Governor's School of Excellence programs, and HOBY alumnae are also eligible for scholarship recognition.

Students can receive an early estimate of aid eligibility by completing a Cedar Crest financial aid application/planner.

Faculty

Of the 89 full-time faculty members, 75 percent have doctorates or other terminal degrees in their field, and 58 percent are women. Excellence in teaching is the first priority of the Cedar Crest faculty. At Cedar Crest, research grows out of teaching and becomes part of the learning process. In the last six years, Cedar Crest faculty members have published books and many articles; won Fulbright fellowships, fellowships from the National Education Association and the National Endowment for the Arts, and grants from the National Science Foundation, Allen Foundation, Pennsylvania Department of Education, and United Church of Christ; served as officers in national professional organizations; and presented research at conferences worldwide.

Student Government

Student Government is a strong and vigorous organization at Cedar Crest. Regular meetings are held to discuss policy, plan student activities, and initiate legislation. Students serve as voting members of College and faculty committees and on the Board of Trustees.

Admission Requirements

Cedar Crest seeks students who have shown academic achievement and promise and those with varied interests, talents, and backgrounds. An academic program providing a good foundation usually includes 4 years of English, 3 of mathematics, 3 of social science, 2 of a laboratory science, 2 of a foreign language, and 3 or 4 academic electives. The College considers good students whose preparation does not include all of these subjects. Through the Advanced Placement Program, qualified applicants may apply for advanced study credits at Cedar Crest.

Application and Information

Students need to submit the application form, an official transcript of the secondary school record, examination results from the SAT or ACT, recommendations, and a personal essay.

Cedar Crest has a rolling admission policy; applications are reviewed on a continuing basis. Students are encouraged to apply early in their senior year of high school. Admission is awarded for the fall or spring semester.

Transfer students applying to Cedar Crest must fulfill all of the requirements stated above. They must also submit official transcripts and a catalog from each college previously attended.

International students must complete the international student application form; students educated in non-English-speaking countries must also submit TOEFL examination scores.

An application, financial aid forms, and additional information may be obtained online or by contacting:

Vice President for Enrollment
Cedar Crest College
100 College Drive
Allentown, Pennsylvania 18104-6196
Phone: 800-360-1222 (toll-free)
Fax: 610-606-4647
E-mail: cccadmis@cedarcrest.edu
Web site: http://www.cedarcrest.edu

CHATHAM UNIVERSITY

PITTSBURGH, PENNSYLVANIA

chatham UNIVERSITY

The University

Founded in 1869, Chatham University is a coed university with a women's college as its historic heart. Chatham University provides students with a solid education built upon strong academics, public leadership, and global understanding. Chatham's 35-acre arboretum campus is located on historic Woodland Road in Pittsburgh's Shadyside neighborhood, where students have easy access to Pittsburgh's dynamic career, cultural, and entertainment opportunities and can share in the educational and social offerings of the other nine area colleges and universities.

The University houses three distinctive colleges. Chatham College for Women houses academic and cocurricular programs for undergraduate women and embodies the traditions and rituals of one of the nation's oldest colleges for women. The College for Graduate Studies offers women and men both master's and doctoral programs. Programs within the College for Graduate Studies include concentrations in art and architecture, business, counseling psychology, health sciences and nursing, teaching, and writing. The College for Continuing and Professional Studies provides online and hybrid undergraduate and graduate degree programs for women and men, certificate programs, and community programming.

The student body of almost 1,800 represents twenty-eight states and eighteen other countries. Members of minority groups and international students compose 20 percent of the student body. Resident and commuting students participate actively in the numerous professional, academic, social, and special-interest organizations at the University. Each year, Chatham students complete thousands of hours of community service with organizations throughout the region. Health services and personal and career counseling services are available on campus. There are several student publications, and Chatham sponsors frequent programs and speakers in the arts, environment, sciences, and public leadership arena.

Chatham College for Women offers NCAA Division III intercollegiate competition in basketball, ice hockey, soccer, softball, swimming, tennis, and volleyball as well as intramural and recreational competition in other sports. Chatham has a new athletic facility with an eight-lane competition pool, a gymnasium, squash courts, cardio rooms, a climbing wall, a running track, and exercise and dance studios.

All incoming first-year undergraduate students receive Hewlett-Packard (HP) tablet PCs that can access the University's wireless network and are incorporated into the curriculum for in-class note-taking, research, and online learning. Students are assessed a technology fee each year to lease the computers, which they own upon graduation.

All residence halls have computer labs and high-speed network printers as well as network ports in each room. Central computer equipment supports e-mail, computer-mediated courseware, personal Web pages, and file and print servers. Public computer labs throughout the University supply high-end personal computer workstations, Macintosh G-5s, laser printers, scanners, and CD-ROM burners. Chatham participates in campuswide software license agreements that permit students to install select productivity software on their personal machines at no additional cost.

Location

Chatham's suburban campus is located minutes from downtown Pittsburgh. Steeped in history, the campus features towering trees, wandering paths, and century-old mansions that serve as networked residence halls.

Pittsburgh is one of the safest and most dynamic cities in the country and is headquarters to major businesses and industries in finance, health care, and technology. Students find eclectic neighborhoods that reflect Pittsburgh's historic qualities yet appeal to a wide audience. The city offers numerous arts and entertainment options in the Pittsburgh Symphony and world-renowned opera, ballet, and theater companies. Nearby parks and ski areas and the city's three rivers provide ample opportunities for such activities as hiking, biking, kayaking, skiing, whitewater rafting, and more. For sports enthusiasts, Pittsburgh offers the Penguins, Pirates, and Steelers professional ice hockey, baseball, and football teams. Excellent bus, rail, and air connections are available to and from most major cities. For more information, students should visit http://www.pittsburghregion.org.

Majors and Degrees

Chatham University offers the following majors leading to a Bachelor of Arts or Bachelor of Science degree: accounting, art (electronic media, photography, studio arts), art history, arts management, biochemistry, biology, business economics, chemistry, cultural studies, economics, education, English, environmental studies, exercise science, film and digital video-making, forensics, French, global policy studies, history, interior architecture, international business, management, marketing, mathematics, music, physics, political science, professional communication (broadcast journalism, print journalism, professional writing, public relations), psychology, public policy studies, social work, Spanish, theater, and women's studies. Students may choose a traditional major, an interdisciplinary major, a double major, or a self-designed major.

Preprofessional programs are offered in education with law, medicine and health professions, physical therapy, teaching certification, and veterinary medicine. A joint-degree engineering program is offered with Carnegie Mellon University. Teacher certification is available through the education program in early childhood, elementary, environmental, school counseling, secondary education, and special education.

The Five-Year Master's Program enables every undergraduate student to apply to one of the University's graduate programs during their junior year, enabling them to earn both a bachelor's and master's degree in as little as five years. The following degree programs are included: Master of Arts in Landscape Studies, Master of Arts in Teaching, Master of Business Administration, Master of Fine Arts in film and digital technology, Master of Fine Arts in writing, Master of Occupational Therapy, Master of Physician Assistant Studies, and Master of Science in Counseling Psychology.

Chatham also offers a five-year master's program with the prestigious H. John Heinz III School of Public Policy at Carnegie Mellon University. Students may apply during their junior year to one of the following Heinz School programs: Master of Arts Management, Master of Information Systems Management, Master of Science in Healthcare Policy and Management, and Master of Science in Public Policy and Management. Accepted students take courses at both Chatham and the Heinz School during their senior year and earn a bachelor's degree from Chatham and a master's degree from Carnegie Mellon.

Academic Programs

Chatham's general education curriculum includes six required interdisciplinary courses, plus analytical reasoning, an international or intercultural experience, and wellness courses. Graduation requirements include the general education courses, a major, and the senior tutorial—an original research/capstone project. Students are mentored one-on-one by a faculty member throughout the tutorial process. The project provides an excellent bridge to graduate and professional schools and strong preparation for law and medical schools.

The University's 4-4-1 academic calendar consists of fall and spring terms plus a three-week "Maymester," which features study abroad, concentrated study, experimental projects, travel and field experiences, internships, interdisciplinary study, and student exchanges with other institutions.

The First-Year Student Sequence introduces students to the College community and its culture and provides opportunities to learn about the resources of the urban environment and study issues of concern to women. These courses provide students with the analytical and communication skills essential for successful academic performance.

Chatham's Programs for Academic Advising, Career Development, and Educational Enrichment (PACE) offers students a comprehensive approach to academic and career planning as well as an academic-support network designed to maximize each student's academic success. Career services include counseling for undecided students, student internships, placement, workshops, recruitment, and mentor programs.

The Rachel Carson Institute honors Chatham's 1929 alumna and her commitment to the environment. Its focus is on global environmental issues, with a concentration on the impact of environmental degradation on women's health and societal roles and the promotion of women's leadership in the environmental movement.

The Pennsylvania Center for Women, Politics, and Public Policy introduces students to the world of politics, public policy, and civic engagement. It provides opportunities for one-on-one mentoring with local politicians, judges, and state-level policy makers. Students may also participate in seminars and internships in Washington, D.C.

The Center for Women's Entrepreneurship provides support for women entrepreneurs in the Pittsburgh region. Designed to assist current and future women business owners, the center provides innovative services and programs.

Off-Campus Programs

Chatham students may at no additional cost register for classes at any of Pittsburgh's eight other colleges and universities, including Carnegie Mellon and the University of Pittsburgh, both of which are within walking distance of the campus. Chatham Abroad involves a three-week travel experience with faculty members during Maymester of sophomore year; past Chatham Abroad trips featured Belize, Egypt, England, France, the Galapagos Islands, Ireland, Italy, Morocco, Russia, and Spain for an additional fee.

Chatham students may participate in up to six internships related to their major and career goals before they graduate. Recent examples include World Bank, Pittsburgh Council of International Visitors, PPG Industries, Senator H. J. Heinz III History Center (affiliated with the Smithsonian Institution), Pittsburgh Children's Hospital, Carnegie Museum, the Pennsylvania Senate, Coro Center for Civic Leadership, WQED, Pittsburgh Zoo and Aquarium, YMCA Legal Resources for Women, Women's Law Project, UPMC Rehabilitation Hospital, and numerous sites in Pittsburgh's corporate, nonprofit, government, health-care, and communications communities.

Academic Facilities

The Jennie King Mellon (JKM) Library has approximately 90,000 volumes, more than 300 current print journals, over 10,000 electronic journals, and nearly forty online databases. It offers individual study areas, special seminar rooms, and a 24/7 study room. Through consortium memberships, the library provides access to print materials from hundreds of academic libraries nationwide.

The Science Laboratory Complex houses state-of-the-art science laboratories and individual laboratory units. Psychology and language laboratories and audiovisual facilities are also available. The new Broadcast Studio contains sophisticated audio- and video-editing technology, including Macintosh G-5 computers, as well as a multifunctional studio. Chatham's new Art and Design Center features fine and applied art studios, a computer lab, and classroom space as well as gallery and student exhibition space.

Costs

For 2007–08, full-time tuition is $25,215 per year, and room and board are approximately $7890. A one-time deposit of $100 for tuition and $100 for on-campus housing is paid by newly admitted students and is applied to first-semester charges. Regularly enrolled full-time students pay no additional costs for Maymester courses, except for special supplies or travel. Music lessons and art supplies are additional costs. Students must have health and accident insurance. A technology fee is assessed for the HP laptop PC program.

Financial Aid

Financial aid is awarded on the basis of an individual's financial need, as determined through the Free Application for Federal Student Aid. The awards combine grants, loans, and employment. The priority financial aid deadline is May 1.

Sources of financial aid include Chatham University grants and loans, state grants, Federal Pell Grants, Federal Supplemental Educational Opportunity Grants, federally funded student loans, and jobs provided under the Federal Work-Study Program. Chatham Merit scholarships for entering students are awarded without regard to need on the basis of high academic achievement and an on-campus interview. Scholarships begin at approximately $4000 and are awarded based on the student's match with Chatham's mission, as well as the academic merits on her application for admission. Minna Kaufmann Ruud Scholarships are available for students with exceptional ability in vocal music, based on an on-campus audition. Approximately 90 percent of undergraduate students receive aid administered by the University.

Faculty

The undergraduate student-teacher ratio of 18:1 ensures individual consideration and interaction between students and faculty members. Each student is assigned a faculty member who serves as her adviser through the completion of her degree program, including the Senior Tutorial capstone project. Ninety-four percent of all undergraduate faculty members hold terminal degrees.

Admission Requirements

Evaluation is made on the basis of the prospective student's academic record, recommendations, essay, involvement in activities, and other submitted material. Chatham seeks to enroll students representing a variety of cultural, geographical, racial, religious, and socioeconomic backgrounds, with diverse talents in academic and creative areas.

The admissions requirements now include a Standardized Test-Optional Policy. Applicants may choose to submit a graded writing sample and resume or a list of curricular and cocurricular activities as well as a portfolio or special project/activity, in lieu of SAT or ACT scores. These materials are reviewed by Chatham faculty members and may be applied toward the scholarship-review process.

It is strongly recommended that candidates arrange to visit the University for a personal appointment, a student-guided campus tour, observation of one or more classes, and conversations with faculty and staff members and students. Early entrance is available for well-qualified and mature students who wish to begin at the end of their junior year in high school; early-entrance candidates must have an on-campus interview. Chatham welcomes the opportunity to discuss future educational plans with transfer candidates in good academic standing, including junior college and community college graduates. Chatham grants college course credit for grades of 4 or 5 on the Advanced Placement (AP) examinations. Certain prerequisites in course offerings may be fulfilled by attaining scores of 3, 4, or 5.

Application and Information

Candidates for admission must file an application with the Admissions Office, together with a $35 nonrefundable processing fee. A free online application is available on the University's Web site. Applications are accepted on a rolling basis.

Vice President of Admissions and Financial Aid
Office of Admissions
Chatham University
Woodland Road
Pittsburgh, Pennsylvania 15232
Phone: 412-365-1290
800-837-1290 (toll-free)
Fax: 412-365-1609
E-mail: admissions@chatham.edu
Web site: http://www.chatham.edu

View of the Chatham University campus.

CHESTNUT HILL COLLEGE

PHILADELPHIA, PENNSYLVANIA

The College

Chestnut Hill College is a four-year, coeducational, Catholic liberal arts college. Founded in 1924 by the Sisters of St. Joseph, it is situated on a 75-acre campus overlooking the Wissahickon Creek. Enrolling more than 1,500 students, Chestnut Hill College is a diverse community of learners. Working adults are enrolled in the accelerated evening and weekend undergraduate program (School of Continuing and Professional Studies). In addition to its undergraduate degrees, Chestnut Hill awards the M.Ed., M.A., and M.S. (School of Graduate Studies) in six fields, including administration of human services, applied technology, counseling psychology and human services, education, holistic spirituality, and holistic spirituality and health care. The College also awards a doctoral degree in clinical psychology (Psy.D.).

When it comes to student activities, students enthusiastically engage in the many clubs and organizations available and participate in everything from aerobics and horseback riding to golf and archery. The College is an NCAA Division II provisional member and competes in baseball (men), basketball (men and women), cross-country (men and women), golf (men and women), lacrosse (women), soccer (men and women), softball (women), tennis (men and women), and volleyball (women). A swimming pool, a gymnasium, a fitness room, and outdoor basketball and tennis courts provide excellent athletic facilities for Chestnut Hill's students.

Location

Chestnut Hill College is situated in a beautiful historical area at the northwestern edge of Philadelphia. The College is bounded by the wooded hills of Fairmount Park, yet it is only a 30-minute ride by train or car to downtown Philadelphia where students can enjoy a wide variety of dining, cultural, and sporting events. Among the many attractions are the museums that grace Philadelphia, from its landmark Art Museum to the Rodin Museum, the Living History Museum, the Franklin Institute, and numerous others. The city's history is reflected throughout but is most prominent in the areas surrounding Independence Hall, Society Hill, and Penn's Landing. In addition, more than seventy colleges, universities, and medical schools in the area offer opportunities for socialization and an extensive range of activities.

One mile beyond Chestnut Hill College on Germantown Avenue is the well-known area of Philadelphia also called Chestnut Hill. Reminiscent of a colonial village, this section of Philadelphia provides convenient opportunities for shopping, cultural experiences, and transportation to downtown Philadelphia. Chestnut Hill is a school in a suburban setting with all the advantages of a cosmopolitan experience—located where the northwest corner of the city meets the suburbs.

Majors and Degrees

The Bachelor of Arts and Bachelor of Science degrees are offered with majors in accounting; biochemistry; biology; business administration; chemistry; communications and technology; computer and information science; computer and information technology; criminal justice; early childhood education (with an option of Montessori certification); early childhood and elementary education; elementary education; English literature; English literature and communications; environmental science; forensic sciences; French; history; human services; international business, language, and culture; marketing; mathematics; mathematical and computer science; molecular biology; music; music education; political science; psychology; secondary education certification in various disciplines; sociology (with a professional option in criminal justice); and Spanish.

Dual degrees (B.S./M.S.) are offered in education, human services, psychology, and technology.

Academic Programs

The academic year consists of two 15-week semesters. There are also two 6-week summer sessions.

As a liberal arts college, Chestnut Hill offers courses of study that provide the student with a broad background in the fine arts and humanities, a knowledge of science, and a keen awareness of the social problems of the day, as well as intensive, in-depth study in a major field.

Chestnut Hill College confers a B.S. or B.A. degree to students who earn 120 semester hours of credit and satisfy specific requirements set by the faculty. Core seminars are interdisciplinary and provide opportunities for experiential learning. In addition, students must take 6 semester hours of religious studies, 6 hours beyond the elementary level in a classical or modern foreign language, and 3 hours in a writing course (unless exempted by the English department). Focused on six perspectives (historical, literary, artistic, scientific, behavior, and problem solving and analysis), the Ways of Knowing component of the core curriculum is designed to introduce students to different learning methodologies and strategies.

A student with the ability and proper motivation may be permitted to major in two departments. The student must consult with the chair of each department to determine the feasibility of the proposal and then submit it to the dean of the college for approval. It is understood that the student will satisfy the requirements of both departments.

Each year, selected first-year students and sophomores are invited into an interdepartmental honors program that challenges intellectual initiative and provides the opportunity for independent study and seminar discussion. The completion of the four honors courses and an honors paper satisfies all distributional requirements. Students may apply for admission at the beginning of their first year or sophomore year.

Sophomores of high scholastic standing are invited by their major departments to engage in a program of independent study during their junior and senior years. This opportunity for independent study and original research culminates in an honors thesis, which is a prerequisite for the conferring of honors at graduation.

Off-Campus Programs

Students have the advantages of two campuses and two curricula through an agreement with La Salle University, which allows students from either school to register for courses at the other institution for full credit without paying extra tuition. Public transportation is available between the two schools.

At Chestnut Hill College, a student may take advantage of the monthlong interim between semesters by coordinating travel and study. Students, with the assistance of one or more of their professors, can use their imagination and interests to develop an off-campus program. Should the program be more lengthy than the interim allows, students may schedule their travel and study for the summer. Past intersession programs have included studies of French culture in Paris, women in English literature in London, and marine biology in Florida.

Chestnut Hill College participates in a consortium arrangement with seven colleges throughout the nation, founded by the Sisters of St. Joseph. As participants, students can study at any other member institution for a semester or a year, while maintaining status as full-time Chestnut Hill students.

An average of B or above and approval of the academic dean allow an upperclass student to pursue organized study in another country. The major department must approve the course of study. In recent years, Chestnut Hill College students have enrolled in institutions in London, Madrid, Rome, Salzburg, Vienna, and other European centers. Chestnut Hill College maintains agreements with Regent's College London, the Sorbonne and the American Business School in Paris, the Centre d'Etudes Franco-Americain de Management in Lyons, and Seisen University in Japan for study abroad.

The growing interest of students in acquiring on-the-job experience while still in college has prompted the development of many departmental internship programs, which provide students with the opportunity to gain professional experience in their major while earning academic credit. Chestnut Hill has also established an office of experiential education, through which Chestnut Hill College students are assisted in finding jobs that correspond to their career interests and academic pursuits. Co-op students work and attend classes in alternate periods, earning academic credit for their practical experience.

Academic Facilities

Chestnut Hill College's Logue Library houses a collection of approximately 139,585 volumes and 544 current periodicals, a rare book room that contains first editions and special editions, the Gruber Theater, the fine Curriculum Library for elementary education, and an Irish literature collection. Well-equipped science laboratories, a math center, a multimedia technology center, a writing enrichment center, individual practice rooms for music students, a spacious art studio, a planetarium, and an observatory are among the many other outstanding facilities on campus. Martino Hall, which opened in 2000 and was designed to maintain the architectural history of the College, provides room for a performance center, gymnasium, or convocation center. The second and third floors house cutting-edge "smart" classrooms. New Hall opened its doors in fall 2006 offering resident students suite-style living accommodations.

Costs

General expenses for 2007–08 are tuition $24,900 and room and board between $8000 and $9000.

Financial Aid

Financial aid is available in the form of academic scholarships, loans, work-study programs, federal grants, and Chestnut Hill College grants. Most of these are based on financial need and are awarded in financial aid packages that combine various forms of aid and are tailored to each student's need. More than 75 percent of Chestnut Hill College students receive financial aid to meet College costs. All applicants for aid should file a copy of the Free Application for Federal Student Aid (FAFSA). Merit-based scholarships and awards are granted for academic achievement.

Faculty

Evidence of Chestnut Hill's vitality can be seen in its faculty. While their primary interest is teaching, faculty members are also engaged in research, publication, travel, and other professional activities. More than 82 percent of the faculty members hold terminal degrees. The men and women who make up this group are deeply interested in both their subject and their students. Their qualifications include international degrees from Bangalore University (India), the University of London, and the University of Paris, and domestic degrees from Boston College, Bryn Mawr College, Catholic University of America, Columbia University, Creighton University, Duke University, Fordham University, Harvard University, Middlebury College, the New School for Social Research, New York University, Purdue University, Saint Louis University, Temple University, and the Universities of Arizona, Delaware, Massachusetts, Minnesota, Montana, New Mexico, North Carolina, Notre Dame, and Pennsylvania. Chestnut Hill College's faculty-student ratio is 1:12.

Student Government

A student at Chestnut Hill College has the opportunity to think independently and approach decisions creatively. Students, in conjunction with members of the faculty and administration, make judgments concerning all collegiate affairs. Several organizations provide structure for the decision-making process. Students join members of the faculty and administration on the Curriculum Committee and the College Council. The Academic, Social-Cultural, and Student Affairs Committees of the Student Organization identify, represent, and meet campus needs.

Admission Requirements

Chestnut Hill College welcomes students whose aptitudes and academic records show a desire to accept a challenge. Applications are judged by the Admissions Committee on the basis of intellectual ability, academic achievement (class rank and performance in high school, including completion of 16 academic units), and SAT or ACT results. Chestnut Hill has early decision, early admission, and advanced placement programs.

Students should submit a completed application, application fee, SAT or ACT scores, and a high school transcript. Letters of recommendation, a personal statement, and other supporting documentation are strongly encouraged. An interview is recommended and may be required. A student wishing to transfer to Chestnut Hill College is asked to submit a transcript from all colleges previously attended.

Application and Information

Applications are processed on a rolling admission system. To arrange an interview or to obtain more detailed information about the academic program, students should contact:

Office of Admissions
School of Undergraduate Studies
Chestnut Hill College
9601 Germantown Avenue
Philadelphia, Pennsylvania 19118
Phone: 215-248-7001
800-248-0052 (toll-free)
E-mail: chcapply@chc.edu
Web site: http://www.chc.edu

CLARION UNIVERSITY OF PENNSYLVANIA

CLARION, PENNSYLVANIA

The University

Clarion University of Pennsylvania is fully accredited by the Middle States Association of Colleges and Schools. It was founded in 1867 and is one of fourteen state-owned institutions of higher education in Pennsylvania. Its programs in education are accredited by the National Council for Accreditation of Teacher Education and the National Academy of Early Childhood Programs, and its chemistry program is approved by the American Chemical Society. The University is a member of the Association to Advance Collegiate Schools of Business, the American Association of Colleges for Teacher Education, and the American Association of State Colleges and Universities and is an Educational Associate of the Institute of International Education. The Bachelor of Science in Nursing and the Associate of Science in Nursing degree programs have the accreditation of the National League for Nursing. Clarion's program in library science is accredited by the prestigious American Library Association, and its program in speech pathology and audiology is accredited by the Education Standards Board of the American Speech-Language-Hearing Association. The legal business studies program at the Venango campus is approved by the American Bar Association. The Graduate School offers twelve advanced degree programs. Master's degrees are offered in biology (M.S.), business administration (M.B.A.), English (M.A.), library science (M.S.L.S.), nursing (M.S.N.), special education (M.S.), and speech pathology and audiology (M.S.). The Master in Education (M.Ed.) degree is awarded in elementary education, mathematics, reading education, and science education.

The University's total enrollment is approximately 6,500 women and men, including students on the main campus at Clarion, on the Venango campus in Oil City, and on the site at West Penn Hospital in Pittsburgh. Five residence hall facilities are available for students living on the main campus. As of fall 2004, the Clarion and Venango campuses have brand new apartment-style living available. The Reinhard Villages, located off campus at Clarion, offers fully furnished two- and four-bedroom units, with private bedrooms and individual leases. The all-inclusive utility package, full-size washers and dryers, and fully equipped modern kitchens provide students with comfortable, convenient, carefree living. The student apartments at the Venango Campus include two- and three-story buildings with two apartments on each floor. Each apartment houses four students. Students have a private bedroom, semiprivate bathroom, a full-size washer and dryer, and a fully equipped modern kitchen.

Clarion University's lifestyle of learning is attractive to many people. The educational experience includes not only academics but also social and cultural growth. Personal interaction allows students to become familiar with diverse backgrounds and helps develop understanding and cooperation in community living. The activities on campus include the Autumn Leaf Festival and Homecoming Weekend, coffeehouses, campus movies, rock concerts, intercollegiate and intramural athletics, music and drama performances by Clarion University students and staff members, clubs, Greek organizations, art exhibits, and special performances by noted orchestras, drama groups, and speakers. More than 130 clubs and organizations serve a wide range of student interests. The University recreation center offers many opportunities for students, including a four-lane indoor track, three multisport courts, a climbing wall, and a weight room.

Starting in the spring of 2007, Clarion is constructing a new Science Center that will be a Leadership in Energy and Environmental Design (LEED)-certified building that is environmentally friendly and one of only a few LEED-certified buildings in the state of Pennsylvania. Stressing an emphasis on student research, the new building expects to have forty laboratories, seven classrooms, and two seminar rooms.

Location

Located high on the Allegheny plateau, Clarion University and the Clarion community have much to offer those who seek a place to study undisturbed by the hectic pace of urban life. Regarded as the "Autumn Leaf Capital of the World," the spectacular fall foliage makes the annual Autumn Leaf Festival a major attraction, drawing 150,000 visitors or more each year. The scenic Clarion River and its tributaries offer ideal settings for summer boating, fishing, and other water sports. Excellent opportunities for skiing, hiking, camping, and canoeing also exist. The beautiful university town of Clarion has 7,000 residents, with a historic Main Street, specialty shops, and two national wild and scenic rivers. Clarion is just off Interstate 80 nestled in the rolling wooded mountains and countryside near popular outdoor recreational areas, within an easy 2-hour drive of urban centers in Erie and Pittsburgh and an hour from Youngstown, Ohio.

Majors and Degrees

Clarion University offers more than ninety degree programs, including the Bachelor of Arts (B.A.), the Bachelor of Science (B.S.), the Bachelor of Science in Business Administration (B.S.B.A.), the Bachelor of Fine Arts (B.F.A.), the Bachelor of Science in Nursing (B.S.N.), and the Bachelor of Science in Education (B.S.Ed.).

Undergraduate majors in the College of Arts and Sciences include anthropology, art, biology, chemistry, computer science, economics, English, environmental biology, environmental geosciences, French, geology, history, industrial mathematics, information systems, liberal studies, mass media arts and journalism, mathematics, medical technology, molecular biology/biotechnology, philosophy, physics, political science, psychology, sociology, sociology-psychology, Spanish, speech communication, and theater. A Bachelor of Science degree in athletic training is now offered in conjunction with California University of Pennsylvania.

Undergraduate majors in the College of Business Administration include accounting, business economics, finance, industrial relations, international business, management, marketing, and real estate.

Undergraduate majors in the College of Education and Human Services include early childhood education, elementary education, music education, rehabilitative science, secondary education (with certification available in nine areas), special education, and speech pathology and audiology. Numerous minors, concentrations, and dual certificate programs are available to enhance the student's academic major.

The School of Nursing at the Venango campus in Oil City offers both the Associate and the Bachelor of Science in Nursing degrees. Clarion now offers a Bachelor of Science degree in radiological sciences at the Venango or Clarion campus. The School of Nursing at the Pittsburgh site (West Penn Hospital) offers a diploma and a nondegree program in general studies. In addition, the Venango campus offers the Associate of Science (A.S.) degree in business administration (with concentrations in accounting, computer processing, general business management, and office management), criminal justice, early childhood, industrial technology, legal business studies (legal assistant studies), and rehabilitative services. The Associate of Arts (A.A.) degree may also be earned at the Venango campus.

The Venango campus now offers an Associate of Science in criminal justice as well as an Associate of Applied Science in industrial technology designed to prepare students in technical, industrial, and other related fields.

Academic Programs

A philosophy of liberal education at Clarion allows students to become intellectually well rounded while specializing in their field. The flexibility of the academic program also enables students to have dual majors. In most cases, students must complete 120 credits to earn a bachelor's degree and 60 credits to earn an associate degree, but requirements vary according to the specific program.

An honors program for high-achieving students is offered. In addition to this program, scholastic excellence may also be recognized through awards and admission to honorary societies.

The school year is on a semester basis. Entering students may apply for college credit through Advanced Placement programs, by examination, or by taking college courses at an accredited college or university.

Clarion University also offers a Leaders' Early Admission Program (L.E.A.P.) for qualified high school students in tenth, eleventh, and twelfth grade. L.E.A.P. is designed to admit selected students on a part-time or full-time basis for summer, fall, and/or spring. To find out more about L.E.A.P. and the admission criteria, students should go online to http://www.clarion.edu/admiss and click on the L.E.A.P. link.

Off-Campus Programs

Study-abroad, cooperative education, and internship programs with credit are available for students who want to broaden their educational experience. International studies have given students the opportunity to visit Costa Rica, France, Malta, Spain, and many other countries. Internships have included MTV, CNN, Big Four accounting firms, and Disney World.

Academic Facilities

A farsighted building program has transformed Clarion into one of the most up-to-date campuses in Pennsylvania. However, many of the historic buildings remain, preserving the historical beauty. Campus facilities include a communications center with a color TV studio, a newly renovated digital FM radio station, and a large computer center; a fine arts center, housing a theater, an auditorium, music practice rooms and art studios; the business administration building, housing case-study classrooms, a computer center, and an auditorium; two libraries, containing more than 1 million resources; and a physical education complex with swimming and diving pools, a gymnasium-auditorium, racquetball courts, and weight-training and fitness rooms.

Costs

Total expenses for full-time students in the 2006–07 academic year were $12,342 for Pennsylvania residents and $17,446 for out-of-state students. These costs included tuition, fees, on-campus housing, and meals. Books, transportation, entertainment, and personal expenses cost an estimated $1500 for one academic year.

Financial Aid

Clarion University participates in three campus-based federal aid programs: the Federal Perkins Loan, Federal Work-Study, and Federal Supplemental Educational Opportunity Grant (SEOG) programs. The institution also participates in the Federal Pell Grant and Federal Stafford Student Loan programs. Students who are residents of Pennsylvania are potentially eligible for grants and loans through the Pennsylvania Higher Education Assistance Agency (PHEAA) program. In addition, numerous academic scholarships are available to qualified students.

All aid applicants must file the Free Application for Federal Student Aid (FAFSA). This form is available in all high school guidance offices and the Clarion University Financial Aid Office. It is from this form that a student's financial need is determined. For further information, applicants should contact the University's financial aid director at 814-393-2315.

Faculty

Over the years, the Clarion faculty has included a number of Fulbright lecture appointees. An educational and cultural profile of the faculty indicates a diversity of backgrounds, with members who have graduated from colleges and universities throughout the United States and from such international institutions as the Universities of Heidelberg, Baghdad, Leningrad, Paris, and Bombay. The low student-faculty ratio makes it possible to maintain a learning environment in which there is close interaction between students and faculty members. Members of the counseling staff are always available for academic and personal counseling, and all students may take advantage of the career-counseling program. Clarion University counselors are accredited through the International Association of Counseling Services.

Student Government

The Student Senate at Clarion is a vital and active campus organization. Its members allocate all athletic and activity funds, initiate academic and campus policy, and serve on search committees for faculty and administrative positions.

Admission Requirements

Applicants must show evidence of graduation from an approved secondary school or an equivalent preparation. Standardized test results from the SAT or ACT must be submitted with the application. Students may fill out the paper application or apply online at http://www.clarion.edu/admiss. Clarion University does not discriminate on the basis of race, creed, color, sex, or national origin and is an Equal Opportunity/Affirmative Action employer.

Application and Information

Clarion University offers rolling admission. Applications are reviewed within two weeks, and an Admissions Counselor calls to personally answer any questions and notify the applicant of his or her acceptance status. The admissions staff offers different types of acceptances, working with applicants to match their academic needs. The goal is to provide students with the greatest opportunities, helping them invest in their success at Clarion University.

As of March 2005, the College Board began administering a new SAT, but Clarion will continue to accept the old SAT scores. For the new SAT, students should be aware that the Office of Admissions is only looking at the Critical Reading and Math scores to make the combined total score for the admissions decision.

Campus visits are welcome, and appointments should be arranged between 9 and 4, Monday through Friday, and on some Saturdays. Campus visitation days, which parents and prospective students are encouraged to attend, are conducted throughout the year.

Application forms and additional information may be obtained by contacting:

Office of Admissions
Clarion University of Pennsylvania
840 Wood Street
Clarion, Pennsylvania 16214
Phone: 814-393-2306
800-672-7171 (toll-free, selection #1)
E-mail: admissions@clarion.edu
Web site: http://www.clarion.edu/admiss/

DELAWARE VALLEY COLLEGE

DOYLESTOWN, PENNSYLVANIA

The College

Founded in 1896, Delaware Valley College (DVC) is a private, coeducational four-year college enrolling approximately 1,650 full-time students. Over the years, the College has concentrated on producing graduates who can fill employers' needs. Today, DVC's curriculum has expanded to include a broad range of programs in agriculture, business, science, education, and liberal arts.

Students attend Delaware Valley College, first and foremost, to prepare themselves for a professional career. The placement record of Delaware Valley College graduates is outstanding, proving that the time-honored educational philosophy of "scholarship with applied experience" works. An extremely high proportion of graduates find employment in their major field of study or enter graduate school within six months of graduation.

In addition to its academic programs, the College offers a wide range of extracurricular activities and events. More than fifty special-interest organizations exist, many of which are linked with a specific major. Student publications include the weekly *RamPages* (newspaper), the *Cornucopia* (yearbook), and the *Gleaner* (literary magazine). The College band and chorale give students the chance to demonstrate their musical talents. There are active minority and international clubs on campus. The DVC Volunteer Corps lines up opportunities for student service to the community in a variety of settings that are relevant to the student's academic major. A-Day, the student-run campuswide fair, annually attracts 50,000 visitors who enjoy the festival, the entertainment, and the academically oriented projects. Such projects as livestock judging, plant sales, chemistry magic shows, computer-aided design demonstrations, a model rain-forest habitat, and equestrian events all demonstrate the expertise of DVC students.

Seventy percent of students live on campus in ten residence halls. A full range of intercollegiate and intramural athletics programs (NCAA Division III, ECAC, and MAC) for both women and men is offered. All elements of the College's educational and recreational programs are in place to develop students as open-minded professionals who are capable of expanding their horizons in a future of unlimited possibilities.

On the graduate level, Delaware Valley College offers a Master in Business Administration degree program, a Master of Business Administration in Food and Agribusiness, as well as a Master of Educational Leadership.

Location

The College is located in historic Bucks County, Pennsylvania, approximately 30 miles north of Philadelphia and 70 miles southwest of New York City. Bucks County is one of the fastest-growing areas in the United States, yet it maintains its rich historical and agricultural heritage. The central Bucks County area is also rich in libraries, museums, and additional cultural resources, further enhancing the educational opportunities of Delaware Valley College students. The Pennsylvania and New Jersey Turnpikes provide quick access to the College. A commuter railway system links the College with Philadelphia, providing daily scheduled arrivals and departures. The College enjoys a mutually beneficial relationship with its surrounding community. Many students find convenient employment opportunities with local businesses, and the community benefits from the many events and activities that are held on campus.

Majors and Degrees

Delaware Valley College awards Bachelor of Science degrees in agribusiness, agronomy and environmental science, animal science, biochemistry, biology, business administration, chemistry, criminal justice, dairy science, environmental design, food science and management, horticulture, information technology and management, ornamental horticulture, psychology, and secondary education. A Bachelor of Arts degree is awarded in English. Within the degree programs, students are given the opportunity to focus their attention on a number of options, minors, and specializations, such as accounting, biotechnology, business management, ecological landscape design, ecology, equine science and management, equine studies, floriculture, food service systems management, food technology, landscape contracting and management, marketing, microbiology, plant science, small-animal science, sports management, turfgrass management, media and communication, and zoo science.

DVC also offers preprofessional preparation in dentistry, law, medicine, optometry, and veterinary medicine.

Academic Programs

All courses are taught from a liberal arts perspective, which broadens the students' appreciation of their cultural heritage. The College is committed to producing graduates who are not only technically competent but also skilled in the use of language, mathematics, and computers. The entire academic program is designed to contribute to the total educational growth of the student and provides him or her with the opportunity to participate in special methods and techniques courses that coordinate theory with practice. The College stresses a practical, hands-on approach to learning. The curriculum includes a required 24-week Employment Program, through which students gain practical work experience in their field while still in college. The Employment Program provides valuable entries on student resumes as it builds meaningful skills.

The academic calendar consists of two 15-week semesters, a January term, and two 6-week summer sessions.

Academic Facilities

Many of the courses taught at Delaware Valley College are laboratory or field oriented. Facilities include many lecture rooms, laboratories containing the most up-to-date equipment, and approximately 550 acres of cultivated and forested lands, which offer a variety of field laboratory situations. In addition, the recently acquired 174-acre Roth Farm is being developed and maintained with the help of students and various DVC departments as a "working history farm" to demonstrate agricultural and food production practices from the 1890–1910 era.

Delaware Valley College students benefit from the low student-laboratory ratio. This enables ready access to equipment, which is imperative to learning. Specifically, the College utilizes biology, chemistry, physics, plant science, and animal science laboratories. Facilities include a tissue culture laboratory, a food processing plant, a greenhouse-laboratory complex, a dairy, a small-animal science center, equine breeding barns, and an indoor equestrian center. The campus is itself a recognized arboretum that is managed by students and faculty members. These facilities are all supported by the Krauskopf Memorial Library, which houses some 80,000 publications.

Costs

For 2007–08, tuition and fees were $24,710, room was $4064, and board was $4900 for a twenty-one-meal plan.

Financial Aid

The College is committed to providing financial assistance so that every student is able to meet the costs of obtaining a college education. DVC offers to students of academic promise faculty scholarships and faculty grants. It participates with the federal government in the Federal Pell Grant Program, the Federal Supplemental Educational Opportunity Grant Program, the Federal Perkins Loan Program, and the Federal Work-Study Program. More than 90 percent of the College's total student body receives some type of financial aid; the average award package totaled $19,100 for 2006–07.

Faculty

All courses at Delaware Valley College are taught by faculty members who combine professional expertise with deep theoretical knowledge and are devoted to the teaching profession. Courses are never taught by graduate students. The faculty numbers approximately 200 full- and part-time instructors, who are friendly and accessible and always ready to help individual students make the most of the educational opportunities offered by the College. The teacher-student ratio is 1:18.

Student Government

Students are encouraged to make the most of extracurricular activities to ensure that their education includes as many different experiences as possible. The student government acts to coordinate the activities of all organizations on campus and sponsors a variety of mixers, movies, concerts, and speakers.

Admission Requirements

In reviewing applications for admission, the College takes into consideration the quality of a student's high school work, scores on the SAT or ACT, class rank, the guidance counselor's recommendation, and the level of a student's motivation, as determined by extracurricular activities. A personal interview is recommended.

Application and Information

For more information about Delaware Valley College and its academic, athletic, and financial aid programs, students should contact:

Office of Admissions
Delaware Valley College
700 East Butler Avenue
Doylestown, Pennsylvania 18901-2697
Phone: 215-489-2211
800-2DELVAL (toll-free)
Fax: 215-230-2968
E-mail: admitme@delval.edu
Web site: http://www.delval.edu

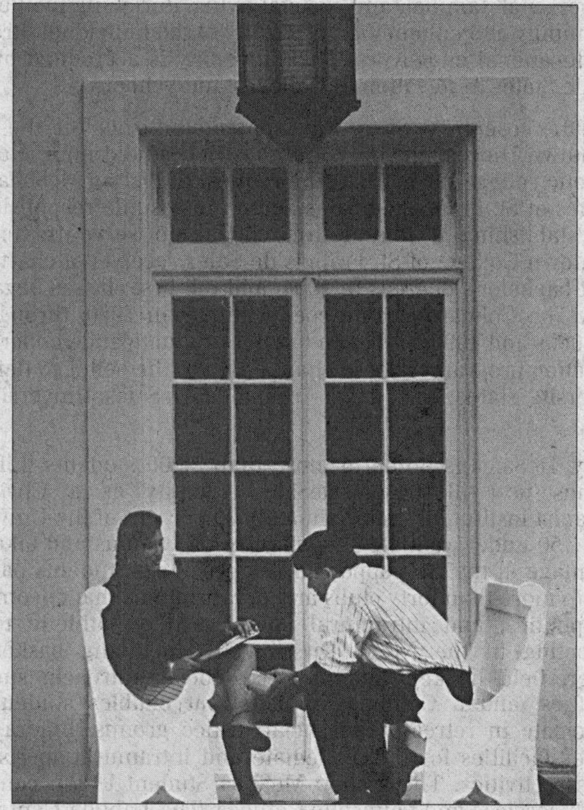

Students relaxing in front of Lasker Hall.

COLLEGE DATA CENTER • PENNSYLVANIA

DESALES UNIVERSITY
CENTER VALLEY, PENNSYLVANIA

The University

DeSales University is a private, four-year Catholic university for men and women that is administered by the Oblates of St. Francis de Sales. Its mission is to provide high-quality higher education according to the philosophy of Christian humanism. The University imparts knowledge about, and develops talents for, personal, familial, and societal living, enriching the human community and enhancing the dignity of the individual through its educational endeavors. The University is accredited by the Middle States Association of Colleges and Schools.

In 1961, Joseph McShea was appointed Bishop of the new Allentown Diocese. At the time, the Diocese did not include a Catholic college for men. At the request of Bishop McShea, the Oblates of St. Francis de Sales agreed to assume responsibility for establishing a liberal arts college to serve this need. Allentown College of St. Francis de Sales received a charter to grant bachelor's degrees in 1964, and the first classes began in 1965. The College became coeducational in 1970; throughout the 1980s and 1990s, it began to offer graduate and cooperative education programs. These changes led to the college attaining university status, and it was renamed DeSales University in 2001.

Today, DeSales is home to more than 2,200 students. Life on campus best illustrates DeSales' identity as a Christian humanist institution. Approximately 70 percent of the University's 1,450 undergraduate students live on campus and take full advantage of the rich opportunities provided. Students participate in more than forty clubs and organizations that encompass art, politics, and intramural sports; sixteen athletic teams competing in the NCAA Division III, including basketball, soccer, field hockey, and lacrosse; social outreach; student activities; and a Campus Ministry that enables students to participate in retreats and social justice groups. Billera Hall houses facilities for intercollegiate and intramural sports and fitness activities. The Bishop McShea Student Union contains health services and counseling offices. The Labuda Center for the Performing Arts houses the largest department in the University and is proud of its thirty-five-year history of success. The newly expanded University Center includes the University bookstore and expanded meeting space in addition to the food court, student dining facility, and student lounge. Eight residence halls offer a range of living options, including living-learning communities, which allows students with common interests to live together.

Location

The Lehigh Valley contains three cities, including Allentown, the third-largest city in Pennsylvania; Bethlehem; and Easton. The region offers a wide range of year-round recreational activities, from skiing and skating in the winter to golf and swimming in the summer, and theater, dance, fine dining, shopping, and music year-round. Historic walking tours might include a wine tasting at one of nine wineries or a trek over the famous seven covered bridges.

The Lehigh Valley has a wide variety of museums, art galleries, and concert venues for every taste and age group, while farmers' markets are a common sight throughout the region. Amusement parks like Dorney Park and Wildwater Kingdom and the Crayola Factory are nearby, as are Kutztown Festival and other annual celebrations. For those wanting to travel beyond the region, the Lehigh Valley is less than 2 hours from New York City and 1 hour from Philadelphia.

Majors and Degrees

The University offers undergraduate degrees in more than thirty programs: accounting, biochemistry, biology, chemistry, communications, computer science, criminal justice, dance, digital art, elementary education, English, finance, history, law and society, liberal studies, management, management of information technology, marketing, marriage and family studies, mathematics, nursing, pharmaceutical marketing, philosophy, physician assistant studies, political science, premedicine, psychology, Spanish, special education, sport and exercise science, sport management, television and film, theater, and theology.

Academic Programs

Students must complete a total of forty courses with a minimum GPA of 2.0 to earn a bachelor's degree. Each degree program has three components. The General Education Core requires completion of sixteen courses, including two courses in English; three physical education courses; two courses in a foreign language or world cultures; two courses in history or political science; one course in art or music; one course in literature; five courses in modes of thinking, concentrating on literature, mathematics, natural science, philosophy, and social science; and three courses in theology. The major provides a thorough and systematic study of one subject area. The major requires completion of sixteen courses. As an alternative, a student may choose to enroll in a special degree program, which may extend the number of required courses. Electives comprise the remaining eight course requirements. Electives provide opportunities for learning in areas of special interest outside the student's major. Some students may want to consider a dual major, in which case the student must complete the requirements of both fields of study. Students who wish to complete a minor must take six courses within that field of study.

Off-Campus Programs

DeSales encourages qualified students to study abroad during the summer and/or the academic year. Through an affiliation with the Lehigh Valley Association of Independent Colleges, the University offers qualified students in a number of disciplines the opportunity to spend a summer or semester in Germany, Italy, Mexico, Spain, or other countries. During the fall semester of their junior year, full-time students majoring in theology, philosophy, marriage and family studies, and history are encouraged to study abroad in DeSales University's program at the American University of Rome. Shorter, more intensive trips are offered to all students through a variety of clubs, organizations, and academic programs. Recent trips have taken DeSales students to South Africa, India, Peru, Romania, and other countries.

Academic Facilities

The campus contains nineteen buildings. A state-of-the-art 37,000-square-foot Science Center houses classrooms and laboratories for the natural sciences. Trexler Library contains more than 550,000 items, including 132,000 volumes and 40,000 electronic books, more than 12,000 electronic journals and newspapers, and 400,000 microfiche items. The periodical collection includes 550 paper and microform subscriptions. Collections of the other five independent colleges of the Lehigh Valley, totaling more than 1 million volumes, are available through an interlibrary loan system.

The University maintains ten computing laboratories or classrooms. The Academic Computing Center contains approximately sixty PCs in its main area, while ACC Computing Classroom houses twenty-three systems. Dooling Hall has three dedicated computing classrooms, each containing approximately twenty-five workstations. Trexler Technology Center contains forty-nine PC systems for both public use and classroom support. Each computing area is supported by at least one high-volume laser printer. All systems have Internet access and contain a suite of both application and network software.

Costs

In 2007–08, full-time tuition is $23,000 per academic year. Other annual fees include a Student Center fee of $550 and a technology fee of $250. For students living on campus, room and board cost $8750 per year.

Financial Aid

Nearly 90 percent of incoming students receive some form of financial aid. Students must complete the Free Application for Federal Student Aid and mail it to the processing center indicated on the form with DeSales University's Title IV code number, which is 003986, after January 1 of the student's senior year. The Office of Financial Aid processes requests for assistance on both a date priority and a financial need basis. The types and amounts of assistance a student will receive are specified in an award letter. The package also provides students and parents with a payment options letter, which outlines the three ways a student can finance the remaining cost of education. Parents may apply for a Federal Parent Loan for Undergraduate Students, students may apply for an alternative loan, or they may take advantage of a monthly billing plan.

All applicants are automatically considered for merit scholarships, which are awarded to incoming first-year students based upon academic achievement. Priority consideration is given to students who apply by December 1 of their senior year. Scholarships include Presidential Scholarships, which can award up to full tuition to students who earn a combined SAT score (math and critical reasoning sections) of at least 1300 (29 ACT) and rank in the top 5 percent of their high school class; Trustee Scholarships of $6000 for students who achieve a combined SAT score (math and critical reasoning sections) of at least 1200 (27 ACT) and rank in the top 15 percent of their high school class; and DeSales Scholarships of $4000 for students who achieve a combined SAT score (math and critical reasoning sections) of at least 1100 (24 ACT) and rank in the top 25 percent of their high school class. Department Scholarships are awarded to students who attend scholarship day and demonstrate excellence in their field of study.

Faculty

There are 97 full-time faculty members teaching at the University. Eighty-five percent of the professors have a doctorate or the highest degree in their specialty. The average class size is 18 students, and the student-faculty ratio is 15:1. Students are assigned a faculty member from their chosen field of study to serve as an academic adviser; undeclared students are assigned to a faculty member who assists them in planning courses, deciding upon a major, and moving toward declaring a major.

Student Government

The Student Government Association is the liaison between the students and the administration. The Executive Board and each of the four undergraduate classes elect a president, vice president, secretary, and treasurer, for a total of 20 officers.

Admission Requirements

Admission is based on past academic achievement, particularly within a college-preparatory course of study, as well as the student's potential for future growth. Preferably, this includes four years of English; three to four years of college-preparatory mathematics; two years of modern, foreign, or classical language; and at least two laboratory science courses. Quality of academic performance is the single most important factor in the decision-making process.

Application and Information

DeSales University uses a rolling admissions process; the school notifies applicants of their admission status within four weeks of receiving all application materials. To apply, students must submit a completed application, official high school or home school transcripts, official SAT or ACT scores, two letters of recommendation, and the $30 application fee. An on-campus interview is recommended but not required. For maximum consideration for scholarships, students are encouraged to apply by December 1.

Prospective students may direct their applications or requests for additional information to:

Admissions Office
DeSales University
2755 Station Avenue
Center Valley, Pennsylvania 18034-9568
Phone: 610-282-1100
E-mail: admiss@desales.edu
Web site: http://www.desales.edu

DREXEL UNIVERSITY

PHILADELPHIA, PENNSYLVANIA

The University

Drexel, a private, nonsectarian, coeducational university, has maintained a reputation for academic excellence since its founding in 1891. Its technologically focused academic programs prepare undergraduates for graduate school and a variety of careers. Full-time professional experience through Drexel's cooperative education program is a vital part of a Drexel education. Students gain professional experience in jobs related to their career interests by alternating classroom study with periods of professional experience.

Drexel University grants bachelor's, master's, and doctoral degrees. Last year's undergraduate enrollment numbered 12,906 full-time students representing forty states and fifty-three countries.

In 2006, Drexel admitted 181 students to the new College of Law. The College of Law is the first law school to be founded by a major research university in thirty years. Traditionally, Drexel University has great strength in the areas of engineering, science, business, and health care. The J.D. program has been designed around these innovative fields to prepare law students for the challenges of twenty-first-century practice.

Eight residential halls house more than 2,600 students on campus. In conjunction with Drexel's fourteen fraternities and ten sororities, the Campus Activities Board sponsors events such as dances, lectures, excursions, and films. Students take part in a variety of extracurricular activities, including musical groups, a recording studio, Mad Dragon Records, a dance ensemble, theatrical productions, a student-run newspaper, a radio station, and a cable TV station. Drexel offers sixteen NCAA Division I varsity athletic programs, competes in the Colonial Athletic Association Conference, and produces some of the nation's top student athletes in both the academic and athletic arenas. The University sponsors intramural and club sports.

Location

Drexel sits at the heart of the nation's fifth-largest metropolitan area. Philadelphia offers history, culture, nightlife, major-league sports, and great food. The region is also a huge college town, with the highest concentration of universities and colleges in the country. Drexel's immediate neighbor is the University of Pennsylvania, and the neighborhood they share is called "University City." With thousands of student residents, University City is a great place for students to spend their college years. The whole region is accessible. Public transportation runs right through the campus. A short walk takes students to Amtrak's 30th Street Station to catch a commuter train to the suburbs; New York City; Washington, D.C.; or beyond.

Majors and Degrees

From computer engineering to media arts and design and from health sciences to business administration, whatever their major, students at Drexel are at the forefront of their field. Offering seventy-three undergraduate programs, Drexel University comprises thirteen colleges and schools, including the Pennoni Honors College. Drexel's academic majors and concentrations include accounting, anthropology, applied engineering technology, appropriate technology, architectural engineering, architecture, behavioral health counseling, biological sciences, biomedical engineering, business, business administration, cardiovascular perfusion technology, chemical engineering, chemistry, civil engineering, commerce and engineering, communication, computer engineering, computer science, construction management, criminal justice, culinary arts, design and merchandising, digital media, economics, education, electrical engineering, engineering for still-deciding students®, English, entertainment and arts management, entrepreneurship, environmental engineering, environmental science, fashion design, film and video, finance, general business for still-deciding students®, general humanities and social sciences for still-deciding students®, graphic design, health services administration, history and politics, hospitality management, information systems, information technology, interior design, international area studies, international business, management information systems, marketing, materials engineering, mathematics, mechanical engineering, music industry, nursing, nutrition and food science, operations management, pathway to health professions, photography, physics, psychology, radiologic technology, science for still-deciding students®, screenwriting and playwriting, sociology, software engineering, sport management, and urban environmental studies.

Qualified Drexel applicants can also choose from fifteen accelerated degree programs, including B.A./B.S./J.D. in law; B.S./D.P.T. in physical therapy; B.S./M.B.A. in business, design and merchandising, and music industry; B.S./M.D. in medicine; B.S./M.H.S. for physician assistant studies; B.S./M.S. programs in biomedical engineering, engineering, higher education, information systems, psychology, and science of instruction; B.S.N./M.S.N. in nursing; or B.S./Ph.D. in engineering.

Academic Programs

Students with high ability can apply to the Pennoni Honors College, which is open to students in every major. Honors sections of general and required courses and honors colloquia and seminars are available. Special living communities designed for the exceptional student and independent projects characterize the program.

At Drexel, students have opportunities to conduct research. Students Tackling Advanced Research (STAR) allows students to participate in research projects in their field as early as the freshman year. Students who take part in these research opportunities may be eligible for stipends or academic credit for their work.

Off-Campus Programs

Drexel has an active study-abroad program that allows students to spend a term or several terms studying abroad, earning credits toward their degree and gaining valuable international experience. Since this is a Drexel-sponsored program, students pay their regular Drexel tuition and receive their regular Drexel financial aid while they are abroad.

Classroom study is essential, challenging, and inspiring. But experience makes all of the difference. Drexel Co-op allows students to alternate periods of full-time work experience with periods of classroom study. With Drexel Co-op, students have the opportunity to explore how they will use their degree in a professional setting. Fortune 500 companies, major pharmaceutical companies, and top design firms are among the workplaces where students can gain up to eighteen months of experience before graduation. More than 2,800 employers from forty-one states and fifteen other countries participate in this program.

Academic Facilities

Drexel comprises three campuses: University City Main, Hahnemann Center City, and the Queen Lane Medical Campus. Buildings contain dozens of state-of-the-art laboratories for classes and research. Drexel University's library system comprises a main library (W. W. Hagerty Library) on the University City Main Campus site as well as three health sciences libraries to serve the needs of students and faculty and staff members. The W. W. Hagerty Library, the University's central library, houses 1.4 million volumes and maintains subscriptions to nearly 12,000 electronic journals. The library provides access via its Web site to these journals and 200 databases from library computers or remotely through the Internet. The library circulates laptops for use with its wireless network. The additional libraries on the health sciences campuses provide study space, 75,000 books, and network access to the same set of online journals and databases.

As early as 1983, Drexel required incoming freshmen to have personal access to a microcomputer. By 2000, the University had created one of the nation's first fully wireless campuses, including all health sciences campuses. The University has most recently launched a new high-performance parallel computing facility available for faculty and student research. The parallel machine, an IBM RS/6000 S-80 Enterprise Server, offers high-speed performance and scalability. This server provides a shared memory computing environment with low latency, high bandwidth communication between processors.

The Edmund D. Bossone Research Enterprise Center, a $37-million, 155,000-square-foot, multistory facility, strengthens the research capabilities of faculty members and students in the engineering and biomedical engineering fields. Recently opened is the new College of Law building, a four-story facility in the heart of Drexel's campus.

Costs

Depending on the course of study, a student at Drexel may enroll in a four- or five-year degree program. Typically, students enroll in a five-year program, spending eighteen months of that time on co-op gaining valuable work experience; the income earned during co-op can help make the cost of education more affordable for Drexel students. The full-time undergraduate tuition for the 2006–07 academic year was $26,000 for a student in the five-year program and $32,000 for a student in the four-year program. On-campus housing cost $6555, and the campus meal plan was $4455 per year. Fees are approximately $1670 per year, depending on the degree program.

Financial Aid

Approximately 90 percent of all freshmen receive financial aid. The aid package may contain academic, athletic, or performing arts scholarships; grants; loans; or part-time employment. Federal programs are also included. All students applying for aid must submit the Free Application for Federal Student Aid (FAFSA) by March 1. Notification to incoming freshmen and transfer students begins mid-March. Drexel offers a unique achievement-based award, the A. J. Drexel Scholarship, to all qualified incoming freshmen and transfer students. With an annual award value of up to $26,000, the A. J. Drexel Scholarship is renewable on a yearly basis, provided the student maintains at least a 3.0 GPA and full-time status. Criteria include a strong academic record and involvement in extracurricular and community service activities.

Faculty

Approximately 94 percent of Drexel's full-time faculty members hold a Ph.D. or the highest degree in their field. Many of the engineering faculty members are registered professional engineers. As a matter of policy, faculty members engaged in research and graduate teaching are also required to teach at the undergraduate level. Thus, the undergraduate student benefits from the research activities of the faculty. Specially selected faculty members serve as advisers for freshmen. The student-faculty ratio is 10:1.

Admission Requirements

All colleges within the University require completion of a college-preparatory program in high school that includes at least 3 years of mathematics and 1 year of laboratory science. Students applying to major in engineering, the sciences, and business and engineering are required to take 4 years of mathematics (through trigonometry) and 2 years of laboratory science. Engineering requires four years of mathematics (through trigonometry and precalculus), chemistry, and physics. The quality of academic performance is more important than merely meeting minimum requirements. The strength of preparation is judged primarily by rank in class or relative grade point average, by the degree of improvement in the quality of the academic record, and by the comments and recommendations from principals, guidance counselors, or teachers. Freshman applicants are required to take the SAT or the ACT. Transfer applicants must have a minimum 2.5 cumulative average (2.75 for engineering, information systems, information technology, and nursing) for consideration and generally are expected to complete at least 24 credits at a regionally accredited four-year college or two-year community college in a program of study comparable to the one being sought at Drexel.

Application and Information

Applications to Drexel are available online (http://www.drexel.edu/apply) or from the address listed. Each application must be accompanied by a nonrefundable application fee of $75; however, the fee is waived for online applications or if submitted during a campus visit. Applications for regular full-time undergraduate status are accepted throughout the senior year until March 1. Applications for Drexel's premier scholarship program—the A. J. Drexel scholarship—are due on January 15. Applications for accelerated degree options are due on December 1. Drexel subscribes to the College Board's Candidates Reply Date of May 1. Transfer students should apply at least three months before the beginning of the term in which they wish to enroll.

An essay or personal statement is required, with its subject dependent on the major and program. Interviews are optional.

Undergraduate Admissions
Drexel University
3141 Chestnut Street
Philadelphia, Pennsylvania 19104-2876
Phone: 215-895-2400
800-2-DREXEL (toll-free)
Web site: http://www.drexel.edu/em

Ms. Joan McDonald
Vice President of Enrollment Management
Drexel University
Phone: 800-2-DREXEL (toll-free)
Fax: 215-895-5939
E-mail: enroll@drexel.edu

EASTERN UNIVERSITY

ST. DAVIDS, PENNSYLVANIA

The University

Eastern University is a Christian university committed to the integration of faith, reason, and justice. In all of its undergraduate, graduate, professional, and international programs, the University's mission is to produce Christians who are capable of confronting injustice and indifference. Viewing education through the lens of a Christian worldview, Eastern challenges students to look outside themselves and strive to change the world that is into the world that ought to be.

Eastern University values its affiliation with the American Baptist Churches USA and also welcomes an interdenominational student body, faculty, and campus community. As a result, everyone at the University can actively pursue the full dynamic of abundant Christian life with freedom and confidence.

The academic curriculum at Eastern University emphasizes the liberal arts and sciences while helping a student pursue a major field of study. Classroom experience is intellectually rigorous and practical experience is gained through a variety of internships and practicums.

More than 1,700 full-time undergraduates are enrolled at Eastern in the College of the Arts and Sciences. The total enrollment at the University, including adult education, seminary, and graduate programs, is approximately 3,700 students. These programs take place in the Campolo College for Graduate and Professional Studies, Esperanza College, and Palmer Theological Seminary.

On-campus housing at the St. Davids campus accommodates more than 1,300 students in eight residence halls. Rooms are structured as singles, doubles, quads, suites, and apartments. The entire St. Davids campus is wireless, including dorms and living areas.

Athletics at Eastern University are NCAA Division III and the teams compete in the MAC Conference. Intercollegiate teams for men are fielded in baseball, basketball, cross-country, Frisbee (club), golf, lacrosse, soccer, swimming (club), tennis, and volleyball (club). The intercollegiate program for women offers basketball, cheerleading (club), cross-country, field hockey, Frisbee (club), lacrosse, soccer, softball, swimming (club), tennis, and volleyball. An intramural program also offers numerous opportunities for students to actively participate in sports.

Eastern provides students with a well-developed Student Ministry Program that challenges students and helps them grow in their faith. Student ministries include weekly chapel, "Sunday Night Live" worship led by students, grow groups, and student chaplains. Among the outreach opportunities available are Evangelicals for Social Action, Fellowship of Christian Athletes (FCA), Youth Against Complacency and Homelessness Today (YACHT), and Habitat for Humanity. Although it is an independent mission organization, the Evangelical Association for the Promotion of Education (EAPE) works closely with the Student Ministry Program and welcomes Eastern student volunteers to staff its programs in inner-city Philadelphia and Camden.

Location

Eastern University is located 25 minutes west of Philadelphia, Pennsylvania, and within 2½ hours of New York City; Washington, D.C.; and Baltimore, Maryland. Sitting in the historic Philadelphia Main Line in the town of Wayne, Eastern's convenient suburban setting provides easy access to Philadelphia via SEPTA trains that run every half hour from the St. Davids station.

Eastern University has one of the most picturesque campuses in America, with its three lakes, wooded walking trails, historic buildings, and working waterwheel. Besides major metropolitan centers, the campus is also within an hour of Lancaster, Pennsylvania, the Jersey Shore, and the Pocono Mountains and within 20 minutes of Valley Forge National Park.

Majors and Degrees

Undergraduate degrees include the Bachelor of Arts, Bachelor of Science, Bachelor of Science in Nursing, and Bachelor of Social Work degrees. Majors are offered in accounting and finance, astronomy, athletic training, biblical studies (biblical languages/without biblical languages), biochemistry, biokinetics (exercise science, sports medicine, pre–occupational/pre-physical therapy), biological studies, biology, chemistry, chemistry business, communication studies (communication in society, dance, public relations/advertising, theater), dance, economic development, economics, elementary education (early childhood, special education), English (journalism, literature, writing), environmental studies, French, history, , international area studies and business, management, marketing, mathematics, missions and anthropology, music (church music, composition/electronic music, cross-cultural music, performance, teaching), political science, psychology, secondary education (five-year M.Ed. option), social work, sociology, Spanish, theological studies, urban studies, and youth ministry.

Minors are offered in accounting, American history, anthropology, astronomy, biblical studies, biology, chemistry, communication studies, dance, economics, English (journalism, literature, writing), environmental studies, European history, finance, fine arts, French, French civilization, gender studies, information technology, Latin American studies, leadership, legal studies, management, marketing, mathematics, missions, music, philosophy, political science, psychology, social welfare, sociology, Spanish, sports and coaching, teaching English as a second language, theological studies, and urban studies. Preprofessional programs are offered in dentistry, law, and medicine.

Academic Programs

In the core curriculum, students take courses designed to fulfill the basic mission of Eastern: to provide a biblical foundation for all learning and action, to ensure the acquisition of basic skills, and to broaden the student's view of the world. The central themes of the Christian faith are integrated into the course content of the core curriculum, which includes courses such as Justice and Diversity in a Pluralistic Society and Science, Technology and Values.

The Templeton Honors College, "a college within the University," offers a rigorous, classically oriented curriculum designed to challenge academically gifted students and prepare them for leadership and service in all areas of culture and society. The honors college includes special events and a required study-abroad, study-away semester. Enrollment in the honors college is highly competitive and limited to 24–30 new students each academic year. Students qualify to apply to the Templeton Honors College by achieving a combined score of 1350 or higher on the SAT or 30 or higher on the ACT or by ranking in the top 9 percent of their high school class.

Off-Campus Programs

Eastern students are encouraged to study abroad or participate in special programs recognized by the University. Academic study abroad is required of language majors. Nonlanguage majors may select from many options, including (but not limited to) Austria, Canada, England, Israel, Kenya, Peru, South Africa, and Uganda. At the AuSable Institute in Michigan, students may apply for certificate programs leading to the designation of naturalist, land resources analyst, water resources analyst, or environmental analyst.

The American Studies Program, sponsored by the Coalition of Christian Colleges and Universities, provides an opportunity for students to study or serve as interns in Washington, D.C., with the nation's leaders. In the Latin American Studies Program, students live with native families; study Spanish and the local culture, history, politics, economics, and religious life; participate in service projects; and travel in Central America. The coalition also operates a film-study center in California and offers Russian and Middle East studies programs.

The Oregon Extension offers a semester of community living and liberal arts studies in the Cascade Mountains of southern Oregon. The Honors Research Program at the Argonne National Laboratory in Chicago provides junior and senior biology, chemistry, and math majors an opportunity for advanced research at a nationally recognized laboratory. Through the Goshen Study Service Trimester, students and faculty members study the history and culture of Caribbean nations and engage in a service project. Exchange programs with selected American Baptist colleges allow upperclass students to spend a semester or a year at another college. May Term opportunities include special courses, semesters, and study tours. Eastern Baptist Theological Seminary offers students the chance to take selected course work.

Academic Facilities

Of Eastern's twenty-six buildings, the primary academic facility is the McInnis Learning Center. In addition to classrooms and offices for faculty members and administrators, the main floor includes a 300-seat auditorium and several music practice rooms. Other features are the biology center; a highly regarded curriculum laboratory for those preparing to be teachers; a technology classroom for distance learning; the Julia Fowler Planetarium, containing a digital projector "Scidome" powered by Starry Night; a media services center; a computer-assisted language laboratory; fully equipped "smart" classrooms; and three student computer centers. The state-of-the-art Bradstreet Observatory is located on the roof of the McInnis Learning Center.

Heritage House offers an acoustically designed Great Room for music performances as well as smart classrooms with the latest computer technology.

The recently constructed Harold Howard Center is a 25,000-square-foot addition to the Warner Library. In addition to more space for the library, the addition features wireless technology, smart classrooms, and more study and office space. Eastern students have direct access to libraries throughout the region and around the world via the computer and more than 50 electronic databases.

Facilities for chemistry, physics, and computer science are located in Andrews Hall. In addition to offices and classroom space, Andrews houses six teaching laboratories, a computer center, and scientific equipment generally found only at larger colleges and universities. Instrumentation includes 300 MHz FT-NMR, FT-IR, GC-MS, AAS, Diode-array UV-Vis, HPLC, PCR, 96-well microplate reader, and molecular modeling.

Costs

For the academic year 2007–08, tuition was $21,350 and room and board are $8350. Total costs for the year were approximately $29,700.

Financial Aid

Eastern is committed to providing education to qualified students regardless of their means. The financial aid program offers scholarships, grants, loans, and employment. The University utilizes the Pennsylvania Higher Education Assistance Agency (PHEAA) for needs analysis forms processing. The student is required to complete the Free Application for Federal Student Aid (FAFSA) to determine financial aid eligibility.

Overall, the University views financial assistance to students as a cooperative investment. If parents contribute to the maximum of their ability and the student contributes a fair share through earnings and personal savings, the University attempts to complete the partnership.

Non-need academic scholarships ranging from $500 to full tuition are available. These scholarships are awarded on the basis of SAT or ACT scores and high school class rank information. Music, leadership, Templeton Honors College, FCA, Young Life, and church matching grants are other University-based grant programs.

Faculty

Eastern University employs more than 125 full- and part-time faculty members. More than 85 percent have earned doctorates. With an emphasis on teaching and a commitment to research, faculty members have authored more than 300 scholarly publications. Some faculty members teach both graduate and undergraduate courses, and almost all serve as academic advisers. Classes are kept small, with a student-faculty ratio of 15:1.

Admission Requirements

The University seeks applicants who present acceptable academic records. The average applicant has a GPA of 3.4 and a score of 1100 out of 1600 on the SAT. A campus visit and interview are recommended. Transfer applicants are welcome.

Application and Information

Applications are generally accepted until the beginning of each term. Admission decisions are made on a rolling basis. For more information, students should visit Eastern's Web site at http://www.eastern.edu. Students should contact:

David Urban, M.B.A.
Vice President for Enrollment
Eastern University
1300 Eagle Road
St. Davids, Pennsylvania 19087-3696
Phone: 800-452-0996 (toll-free)
E-mail: ugadm@eastern.edu
Web site: http://www.eastern.edu

EDINBORO UNIVERSITY OF PENNSYLVANIA

EDINBORO, PENNSYLVANIA

The University

Edinboro University, a part of the Pennsylvania State System of Higher Education, is located in the borough of Edinboro, Erie County, Pennsylvania. It is the oldest teacher-training institution in Pennsylvania west of the Allegheny Mountains and the second-oldest in the state. Edinboro Academy was chartered in 1856. After the passage of the State Normal Act in 1857, the school opened as Edinboro Normal School for the preparation of teachers. Under its original charter, the school was privately administered until 1861, when the commonwealth chartered it as a state normal school. The school was purchased by the commonwealth of Pennsylvania in 1914. The state recognized Edinboro State Teachers College as a four-year college in 1926 and granted it the right to offer a Bachelor of Science in Education degree in the areas of elementary, secondary, and art education. The name of the institution was changed to Edinboro State College in 1960. In 1983, university status was given to each of the state colleges, and a comprehensive commonwealth university system was established.

Edinboro's graduate school offers the Master of Arts, Master of Fine Arts, Master of Education, Master of Science, Master of Science in Nursing, Master of Social Work, and post-master's certifications.

The University is accredited by the Commission on Higher Education of the Middle States Association of Colleges and Schools (3624 Market Street, Philadelphia, Pennsylvania 19104; phone: 215-662-5606). The commission is an institutional accrediting agency that is recognized by the U.S. Secretary of Education and the Commission on Recognition of Postsecondary Accreditation. Other University accreditations and program approvals include the American Dietetic Association, the Council on Rehabilitation Education, the Council for Accreditation of Counseling and Related Educational Programs, the American Speech-Language-Hearing Association, the Council on Social Work Education, the National Association of Collegiate Business Schools and Programs, the Commission on Collegiate Nursing Education, the National League for Nursing Accrediting Commission, and the National Council for Accreditation of Teacher Education.

Of the 7,579 students at Edinboro, 6,443 are undergraduates. The University maintains on-campus residence. Each residence hall is wired for digital satellite cable television services, two high-speed data connections, and a telephone connection. Edinboro University has undertaken a $115-million housing project on campus that when finished in 2009 will provide suite- and semisuite-style housing units as well as new dining facilities for students.

There are more than forty-three buildings situated on the spacious 585-acre campus, which includes open fields, a 5-acre lake, and many acres of woods.

Edinboro University in Erie–The Porreco Center and Edinboro University in Meadville offer classes and University services at convenient off-campus locations.

Location

Located adjacent to the business district of Edinboro, Pennsylvania, the University is accessible by automobile from all sections of the state and is near the intersection of Interstates 90 and 79. Passenger service of all kinds operates on frequent schedules, connecting Edinboro with nearby cities and towns, including Erie, Pennsylvania's fourth-largest city. The Erie Airport is approximately 15 miles to the north. Within walking distance of the campus, the community of Edinboro has eight churches of various denominations.

Majors and Degrees

The University awards the Associate of Arts, Associate of Engineering Technology, Associate of Science, Bachelor of Arts, Bachelor of Fine Arts, Bachelor of Science, Bachelor of Science in Education, and Bachelor of Science in Nursing. These degrees permit majors in the following areas: anthropology, applied media arts (with concentrations in animation, cinema, graphic design, and photography), fine arts/crafts (with concentrations in ceramics, drawing, jewelry/metalry, painting, printmaking, sculpture, weaving/fibers, and wood/furniture design), art education, art history, biology, biology/premedical, broadcast journalism, business administration/accounting, business administration/administration, business administration/financial services, business administration/forensic accounting, business administration/marketing, business administration/management information systems, chemistry, chemistry/forensic sciences, chemistry/industrial biochemistry, communication studies (with concentrations in broadcasting, organizational communication, and public relations/advertising), computer science, criminal justice, drama, earth sciences, economics, elementary education, elementary/early childhood education, elementary/special education, English/literature, English/writing, environmental science/biology, environmental studies/geography, environmental science/geology, foreign language, general business administration, general studies, geography, geology, German, health and physical education (with concentrations in health promotion, recreation administration, sport administration, and teacher education), history, humanities, human services/developmental disabilities, human services/social services, innovative nursing, Latin American studies, liberal studies, manufacturing engineering technology, mathematics, medical technology, music, music education, natural science and math, natural science and math/wildlife, nuclear medicine technology, nursing, nursing/RN, nutrition, philosophy, physics 3-2 engineering, physics/liberal arts, physics/theoretical, political science, preschool education, print journalism, psychology, secondary education (biology, chemistry, earth and space science, English, general science, German, mathematics, physics, social studies, and Spanish), social science, social work, sociology, Spanish, special education, special education/elementary education, specialized studies, speech and hearing sciences, and women's studies. Preprofessional programs are offered in dentistry, law, medicine, pharmacy, and veterinary science. Minors also exist in fifty-seven specializations.

Academic Programs

Associate degrees require a minimum of 60 semester hours of credit, including a general education component.

Baccalaureate degrees require a minimum of 120 semester hours of credit. A general education requirement of 60 semester hours is distributed among the arts, humanities, and science and technology to ensure a basic liberal arts foundation. The remaining 60 semester hours are devoted to specialization and may include major and professional courses, a minor, and other concomitant courses.

Advanced Placement credit and honors courses are available.

The Office of Extended Learning offers a variety of workshops and special-interest courses. The Office of Adult Student Information Services enables nontraditional students to enroll for academic programs at convenient times and locations on a full- or part-time basis.

An Army Reserve Officers' Training Corps (ROTC) program is available.

The Office for Students with Disabilities provides services that are essential for physically disabled, hearing-impaired, visually impaired, and learning-disabled individuals. Edinboro University has one of the finest programs in the nation for students with disabilities.

Academic Facilities

The seven-story Baron-Forness Library is the focal point of the University campus. The library houses more than 500,000 bound volumes and more than 1.4 million microform units. Technology and Communications supports and manages thirty-seven computer labs.

Costs

For 2007–08, the tuition fee for a resident of Pennsylvania was $5177 per year; for nonresident students, the cost per year was $7766. Room rent per year was $3800 and meals were $2176. Additional annual fees include a student activity fee of $327, a University Center fee of $430, a health fee of $140, an instructional service fee of $518, and an instructional technology fee of $175. The cost of books and supplies varies with the academic major. Costs are subject to change.

Financial Aid

With more than $58 million in financial aid for eligible students, Edinboro offers student employment, loans, grants, and scholarships. In most cases, Pennsylvania State Grant and Free Application for Federal Student Aid forms are used to determine eligibility for these programs. Federal aid administered by the University is available for both the regular academic year and the summer sessions. The application deadline for upperclass students for these programs is normally May 1 for the following academic year. Freshmen may apply for aid upon acceptance by the University. Financial aid is also available through the University's ROTC program. For additional information, students should contact the Assistant Vice President for Student Financial Support and Services at 888-611-2680 (toll-free) or access the information online at http://piper.edinboro.edu/cwis/studaff/emr/finaid/.

Faculty

Edinboro's student-faculty ratio of 18:1 makes it possible to maintain close interaction between students and the highly qualified faculty members. A large percentage of the faculty has completed terminal degrees in their area of specialization.

Student Government

The Student Government Association is a vital and active organization on the campus and serves as the official student voice in all University matters. Student Government Association representatives serve on nearly all University committees and participate in the University governance system. This organization sponsors special events, activities, and student clubs to satisfy a variety of student interests. The Student Government Association participates in the annual budget recommendations regarding the budgeting of the student activity fund.

Admission Requirements

Edinboro University grants admission on the basis of general scholarship, character, interest, and motivation as they may be determined by graduation from an approved high school, home school, or institution of equivalent grade or equivalent preparation, as determined by the Credentials Division of the Department of Education; official scholastic records; aptitude tests; recommendations; and interviews. To fully prepare for a University program of study and increase the probability for academic success, students should pursue a college-preparatory curriculum at the secondary level and provide evidence of scholastic aptitude, as measured by scores on the SAT or ACT. Submission of aptitude scores can be waived for nontraditional adult learners. An audition is required for all applicants to any music curriculum; music students are invited to participate in the audition some time after the application for admission is received by the Office of Undergraduate Admissions.

Application and Information

Students may apply for admission as early as July 1, after finishing the junior year of high school; the application can be found online at the University's Web site. Requests for application papers, viewbooks, financial aid forms, and further information should be addressed to:

Admissions Office
Edinboro University of Pennsylvania
Edinboro, Pennsylvania 16444
Phone: 814-732-2761
888-8GO-BORO (toll-free)
Fax: 814-732-2420
Web site: http://www.edinboro.edu

A view of the campus at Edinboro University of Pennsylvania.

ELIZABETHTOWN COLLEGE

ELIZABETHTOWN, PENNSYLVANIA

The College

Founded in 1899, Elizabethtown College is committed to an academic program of liberal arts and professional training built upon a core curriculum that focuses on teaching students to think, analyze, and communicate. The more than 1,950 students at Elizabethtown come from thirty states and forty countries, providing a diversity of backgrounds that enhances the College as a whole.

Elizabethtown is a residential college, where 85 percent of students live on the 195-acre campus in eight residence halls and senior town houses. Student-run residence hall councils plan programs and provide service and leadership opportunities. A wide variety of campus cultural events and other activities keep 80 percent of the students on campus throughout the weekends. The College maintains an active intramural sports program and fields ten NCAA Division III teams for men (baseball, basketball, cross-country, golf, lacrosse, soccer, swimming, tennis, track and field, and wrestling) and ten for women (basketball, cross-country, field hockey, lacrosse, soccer, softball, swimming, tennis, track and field, and volleyball), several of which contend for national titles each year.

The College offers effective academic, personal, and career counseling services through the Center for Student Success, which encourages students to make use of its office as early as their first year. Ninety-five percent of students who graduate from Elizabethtown are employed or enrolled in graduate school within eight months after graduation.

In addition to its undergraduate degree programs, Elizabethtown also offers a Master of Science degree in occupational therapy.

Location

Elizabethtown is a community of 20,000 people located in southeastern Pennsylvania, within 20 minutes of Harrisburg (the state capital), Hershey, and Lancaster. Philadelphia and Baltimore are within 1½ hours of Elizabethtown; New York and Washington are within 4 hours. Elizabethtown is easily accessible by Amtrak train service from New York, Philadelphia, and Pittsburgh, and the Harrisburg International Airport is 15 minutes away.

Majors and Degrees

Bachelor of Arts degrees are awarded in art, communications, criminal justice, economics, engineering, English, French, German, history, international business, Japanese, music, philosophy, political philosophy and legal studies, political science, psychology, religious studies, secondary education, social work, sociology-anthropology, Spanish, and theater.

Bachelor of Science degrees are offered in accounting, actuarial science, biochemistry, biology, biotechnology, business administration, chemistry, citizenship education, computer engineering, computer science, elementary education, engineering, environmental science, forensic science, forestry and environmental management, general science education, health and occupation, industrial engineering, information systems, mathematics, physics, secondary education, social sciences, and social studies.

Bachelor of Music degrees are offered in music education and music therapy. More than eighty minors and concentrations as well as eight certification programs in secondary education are available.

The College offers joint 3-2 programs with Duke University, leading to a Master of Forestry or Master of Environmental Management. A 3-2 program in engineering with Pennsylvania State University is also offered, leading to a Bachelor of Arts in physics from Elizabethtown and a Bachelor of Science in engineering from Penn State.

Elizabethtown offers cooperative programs in biology and allied health with Thomas Jefferson University, University of Maryland at Baltimore, and Widener University. These programs lead to a Bachelor of Science degree from Elizabethtown and a master's or doctoral degree from the cooperating university. The College also has a cooperative program in invasive cardiovascular technology with Lancaster General Hospital.

Preprofessional majors are offered in dentistry, law, medicine and osteopathy, the ministry, and veterinary medicine.

The Primary Care Pre-Admissions Program through the Pennsylvania State University College of Medicine at the Milton S. Hershey Medical Center provides options for Elizabethtown students (who are Pennsylvania residents) pursuing careers in internal medicine, family practice, and pediatrics.

Academic Programs

Through Elizabethtown's core program of traditional and innovative liberal arts, students develop skills for critical analysis, effective communication, and habits of mind that ensure adaptability in the ever-changing global job market. Independent and directed studies and extensive internship and externship possibilities are available.

The Elizabethtown College Honors Program offers top academic students a highly selective program of study with the opportunity for a stipend to fund professional development, research, or travel-related study.

The College operates on a semester calendar. First-year students arrive in the last week of August, and examinations are given prior to the winter break. The spring semester begins in the middle of January and runs through early May. Intensive summer-session courses are available for students who wish to accelerate their academic program. Students may earn credit toward graduation through Advanced Placement examinations, College-Level Examination Program tests, or tests administered by the individual departments.

Off-Campus Programs

Through Brethren Colleges Abroad (BCA), students may spend all or part of a year studying in Australia, Belgium, China, Ecuador, England, France, Germany, Greece, Ireland, Italy, Japan, Mexico, New Zealand, or Spain. Elizabethtown also has agreements of affiliation with the Queens University International Study Centre at Herstmonceux Castle in England and with Nihon University in Japan.

A number of short-term opportunities are available as well, including two- to three-week study tours at England's Oxford University and in Beijing, China; Costa Rica; Ecuador; and

Prague. In addition, students majoring in programs including occupational therapy, music therapy, and social work are required to complete extensive fieldwork in on- and off-campus facilities.

Academic Facilities

Academic buildings include the High Library; Zug Memorial Hall, home of Hess Gallery and the Department of Fine and Performing Arts; Wenger Center for the Humanities; Steinman Center for the Communications and Art; Nicarry Hall; and the James B. Hoover Center for Business. The Masters Center for Science, Mathematics and Engineering, which includes the new Lyet Wing for Biological Sciences as well as renovations to Musser and Esbenshade Halls, opened in fall 2007. In addition, the student center, Brossman Commons, is the location for the Tempest Theatre and a dance studio.

Costs

For 2007–08, tuition was $29,000 and room and board were $7600, for a total comprehensive fee of $36,600. Students should also plan on an additional cost of about $1650 for books, transportation, and personal expenses, for a total cost of $38,250. Financial aid is based on this figure.

Financial Aid

Financial aid packages are typically a combination of scholarships, grants, loans, and student employment; 90 percent of the students receive some form of aid. To apply for financial aid, students must file the Free Application for Federal Student Aid (FAFSA) and the Elizabethtown College Verification Form. Estimated data should not be filed. Signed copies of the parent's (and student's, if applicable) most recent federal income tax form, including all schedules, must also be submitted to the financial aid office.

More than one third of Elizabethtown's first-year students with the strongest academic credentials receive merit-based scholarships, which are awarded on a competitive basis and without regard to need.

Elizabethtown's deadline for financial consideration is March 15.

Faculty

Elizabethtown has a teaching faculty of nearly 130 full-time professors. The student-faculty ratio is 11:1. More than 90 percent of the full-time faculty members hold a Ph.D. or the highest earned degree in their field. In addition to being assigned a faculty adviser through the First-Year Seminar program, when students declare a major, they are assigned a new faculty adviser within that department.

Student Government

Students play an active role in campus governance through the Student Senate, the Campus Residence Association, and other organizations. Members of the Student Senate are elected from each class to advocate for students, coordinate special events, and allocate funds for student activities and more than eighty student-run clubs and organizations. Students Working to Entertain E-town (SWEET) allocates funding for weekend programs, campus social activities, and entertainment for the College community.

Admission Requirements

Decisions about admission to Elizabethtown are made without regard to sex, sexual orientation, race, religion, physical handicap, or place of residence. Fewer than 60 percent of all applicants are accepted. Students should have followed an academic curriculum, with the completion of at least 18 college-preparatory units recommended. The middle 50 percent of enrolled students scored between 1030 and 1230 on the critical reading and mathematics sections of the SAT, and 33 percent were in the top 10 percent of their high school class.

The College seeks diversity, and students who display leadership abilities or special talents are considered highly desirable. Campus interviews are highly recommended but not required for most students, although the College reserves the right to require interviews in special cases. Students applying to the Honors Program are required to interview, as are occupational therapy students. Auditions are required for music students.

Early admission is available for highly qualified high school juniors.

Application and Information

The College operates on a rolling admission basis—applications are processed as they are received—and the application deadline is March 1. Students can apply using the Common Application or online at the College's Web site. Applicants must submit a high school transcript, first-quarter grades, SAT or ACT scores, two letters of recommendation, and a personal statement, essay, or graded paper. Early application is strongly recommended. Accepted students should notify the College of their decision to attend by May 1; matriculation after that date is on a space-available basis. Students who are interested in the Elizabethtown College Honors Program must submit a completed application by January 15.

For more information, students should contact:

Debra Murray
Director of Admissions
Elizabethtown College
One Alpha Drive
Elizabethtown, Pennsylvania 17022-2298
Phone: 717-361-1400
Fax: 717-361-1365
E-mail: admissions@etown.edu
Web site: http://www.etown.edu

Elizabethtown offers more than 1,950 students liberal arts and professional programs through fifty-three majors and eighty minors and concentrations.

GANNON UNIVERSITY

ERIE, PENNSYLVANIA

The University

Gannon University, which is consistently named one of America's Best Colleges by *U.S. News & World Report,* is dedicated to excellence in holistic education. The oldest part of the University is Villa Maria College, which was founded in 1925 by the Sisters of St. Joseph. In 1933, Archbishop John Mark Gannon established Cathedral College, a two-year institution, which by 1941 had evolved into a four-year college, the Gannon School of Arts and Sciences. The name Gannon College was adopted in 1944, and Gannon achieved university status in 1979. Villa Maria College subsequently merged with Gannon University in 1989.

Gannon's campus is located in the heart of downtown Erie, giving students the benefit of internships with businesses, law and law-enforcement agencies, health-care facilities, industries, and social service organizations. It is also within walking distance of stores, shops, restaurants, and theaters. The campus consists of more than thirty buildings located within six city blocks. Among these buildings is the Carneval Athletic Pavilion, which has a pool; three gyms; a running track; a weight room; courts for racquetball, handball, volleyball and basketball; and other facilities. Also on campus are two residence halls, nine apartment buildings, classroom and faculty office buildings, an administration building, and a multipurpose chapel building. The Waldron Campus Center is a focal point that gives students the opportunity to meet and socialize between classes with faculty members and other students.

Gannon offers students a broad intramural sports program that runs throughout the entire year. In Division II intercollegiate athletics, Gannon offers men's baseball, basketball, cross-country, football, golf, soccer, water polo, and wrestling and women's basketball, cross-country, golf, lacrosse, soccer, softball, volleyball, and water polo. There is also an intercollegiate coed swimming and diving team. Gannon's athletes utilize the Gannon University Field, a multipurpose athletic facility that is conveniently located on campus.

There are approximately 4,100 students at Gannon, more than 2,700 of whom are undergraduates. The ratio of commuters to resident students is approximately 1:4. The University has a Career Development and Employment Services Office to aid students in locating internships and part-time work during school and full-time work after graduation.

Location

Erie is Pennsylvania's fourth-largest city and is located in the northwestern corner of the state on the shore of Lake Erie. Erie is approximately 120 miles north of Pittsburgh, Pennsylvania; 90 miles east of Cleveland, Ohio; and 90 miles southwest of Buffalo, New York. The campus is within 5 miles of Interstates 79 and 90 and 5 miles from Erie International Airport. Erie is also serviced by rail and bus transportation.

Majors and Degrees

The College of Humanities, Business and Education awards the Bachelor of Arts and Bachelor of Science degrees.

In the School of Humanities, the areas of study from which students may select a major are communication arts, criminal justice, English (with concentrations in applied communications, literature, and writing), foreign language and international studies, foreign language and literature, foreign language teaching (Spanish only), history, journalism communications, legal studies, liberal arts, mortuary science, philosophy, political science, prelaw, a 3+3 prelaw program that includes early admission to Duquesne University, psychology, social work, theater, theater and communication arts, and theology.

In the School of Business, students may choose to major in accounting, advertising communications, business administration, finance, international business, management, marketing, risk management, and sports management and marketing.

In the School of Education, the areas of study from which students may select a major are early childhood education, elementary education, secondary education (in biology, English, foreign language (Spanish only), mathematics, and social studies), and special education.

The College of Sciences, Engineering and Health Sciences awards the Bachelor of Science degree.

In the School of Sciences and Engineering, students may choose to major in bioinformatics, biology, chemistry, chemical engineering, computer science, electrical engineering, electrical engineering (five-year co-op program), environmental engineering, environmental science, management information systems, mathematics, mechanical engineering, mechanical engineering (five-year co-op program), science, scientific and technical sales, and software engineering. A minor is offered in environmental and occupational science and health. Preprofessional programs of study are offered in chiropractic, dentistry, medicine, optometry, osteopathy, pharmacy, physical therapy, podiatry, and veterinary medicine; seven-year accelerated programs are offered in optometry and podiatry. Additional accelerated programs include accelerated pharmacy options through Duquesne University (2+4), the University of Charleston (2+4 and 3+4), and the Lake Erie College of Osteopathic Medicine (LECOM) (2+3) and a conditionally guaranteed medical school 4+4 program with LECOM and the Philadelphia College of Osteopathic Medicine (PCOM). There are also accelerated options in allopathic medicine and veterinary medicine through Ross University in the Caribbean. Students who are interested in earning their Doctor of Physical Therapy degree can complete an accelerated (3+3) program at Gannon.

In the School of Health Sciences and the Villa Maria School of Nursing, the areas of study from which students may select a major are medical technology, nursing, occupational therapy, physician assistant studies, radiologic sciences, respiratory care, and sport and exercise science. A minor is also offered in athletic coaching.

The associate degree program offers Associate of Science and Associate of Arts degrees. Areas of study in which students may major are accounting, business administration, criminal justice, early childhood education, legal studies, radiologic sciences, and respiratory care.

Academic Programs

Each undergraduate program has its own sequence of requirements. Students in all programs must complete credits in liberal studies. A faculty adviser is assigned to each student to assist with academic planning. A department chairperson and faculty adviser also assist each student in selecting courses that fulfill requirements and best meet the student's desired career objectives. The basic graduation requirements for bachelor's degree candidates are 128 credit hours, including completion of requirements for their major and the liberal studies program. To earn an associate degree, students must usually complete 60 to 68 credit hours, depending on the program. Students may receive credit through the Advanced Placement Program.

Gannon offers a program for students with learning disabilities (PSLD) and an Army ROTC program that is open to interested students.

Gannon's academic calendar consists of two full semesters, running from August to December and from January to May. There are also optional summer classes.

Academic Facilities

The Nash Library currently has more than 250,000 bound volumes. The library subscribes to more than 1,000 periodicals and has book and periodical materials on various forms of microfilms and microcards. The wireless library contains a personal computer lab; a lecture room; a curriculum library; the Founder's Room for fine and rare books; the Cyber Café, containing personal computers, laptop ports, and cappuccino and juice machines; lounges; study rooms; typing rooms; an information-retrieval system; a TV studio; the latest audiovisual and tape equipment; and a multimedia studio classroom. In addition, students may use the facilities and resources of the Erie County Law Library and the Erie County Library. For specialized research projects, an efficient interlibrary loan service is available.

The A. J. Palumbo Academic Center houses the Schools of Health Sciences, Education, and Humanities. It offers some of the finest laboratories, technology, and classrooms available today. From education to nursing and foreign language programs, the faculty members and facilities in Palumbo provide high-quality education. The University's Honors Program also has a home in the Palumbo Center.

The Zurn Science Center has laboratories for research in biology, anatomy, physics, chemistry, and engineering. The building also houses three computer laboratories, including the Computer Integrated Enterprise Center and an IBM PC lab. There are numerous classrooms and two auditoriums in the building. Among other University facilities are additional classroom buildings, a radio station, and a theater. All academic buildings are wireless.

Costs

For 2007–08, full-time tuition was $10,425 per semester ($11,055 for engineering and health sciences), or $20,850 per academic year ($22,110 for engineering and health sciences). Tuition for part-time students was $645 to $675 per credit hour. Room and board were approximately $4105 per semester. The total cost for the academic year at Gannon was between $21,745 and $23,005 for commuting students and $29,955 and $31,761 for resident students, depending on the program of study.

Financial Aid

In order to bring a Gannon education to qualified students who could not otherwise afford it, the University offers an integrated financial aid program of scholarships, grants, loans, and employment. Gannon's financial aid program is open to all full-time students attending classes during the period from August to May. It is highly recommended that all students seeking financial aid should file the admissions and financial aid applications no later than March 15.

Faculty

Gannon's faculty consists of 312 lay and religious men and women, and 58 percent of the full-time faculty members have doctoral degrees. The student-faculty ratio is about 14:1, and there are approximately 25 students in each class. Most faculty members assist in the faculty adviser program, giving each student individual attention and counseling on academic and personal matters.

Student Government

The Student Government Association (SGA) is composed of students elected by members of their class. Through the SGA, students can play a responsible role in the planning and working of the University. SGA has voting representatives on all of the standing committees of the University. Members of the SGA not only research existing policies and problems, they also look for new ways to improve the academic life of students. The SGA also plans social events for the student body.

Admission Requirements

Gannon University actively recruits students of all races, creeds, and ages from all geographic regions. Transfer and international students are encouraged to seek admission. Applicants are required to submit scores (including senior-year scores) on either the SAT or ACT; an up-to-date transcript of the high school record, showing rank in class (plus a college transcript for transfer applicants); a completed application form; and a nonrefundable $25 fee. Admission decisions are based upon numerous factors, central of which is the strength of the high school record, as demonstrated through grades and relative class standing and SAT and/or ACT scores and other test scores that may be available. Recommendations and personal statements also affect admission decisions. Transfer and international students should check with the admissions office for special application procedures.

Application and Information

Students applying for admission in the fall semester should start the application process at the beginning of their senior year in high school. Gannon operates on a rolling admissions basis, which means that there is no deadline for filing applications, with the exceptions of the LECOM and PCOM 4+4 Medical Programs and the accelerated pharmacy options, which have a deadline of January 15 for the fall semester. Due to the competitiveness of the program, students who are interested in the physician's assistant studies program are highly encouraged to file their applications in September. Early applications are recommended, as are enrollment deposits.

For further information, students should contact:

Office of Admissions
Gannon University
109 University Square
Erie, Pennsylvania 16541
Phone: 814-871-7240
800-GANNON-U (426-6668, toll-free)
Fax: 814-871-5803
E-mail: admissions@gannon.edu
Web site: http://www.gannon.edu

Gannon University's faculty advisers are always available to help students chart their personal, educational, and professional accomplishments and potential.

GROVE CITY COLLEGE

GROVE CITY, PENNSYLVANIA

The College

The beautifully landscaped campus of Grove City College (GCC) stretches more than 150 acres and includes twenty-seven neo-Gothic buildings valued at more than $100 million. The campus is considered one of the loveliest in the nation. While the College has changed to meet the needs of the society it serves, its basic philosophy has remained unchanged since its founding in 1876. It is a Christian liberal arts and sciences institution of ideal size and dedicated to the principle of providing the highest-quality education at the lowest possible cost. Wishing to remain truly independent and to retain its distinctive qualities as a private school governed by private citizens (trustees), it is one of the very few colleges in the country that does not accept any state or federal monies. Affiliated with the Presbyterian Church (U.S.A.) but not narrowly denominational, the College believes that to be well educated a student should be exposed to the central ideas of the Judeo-Christian tradition. A 20-minute chapel program offered Tuesday and Thursday mornings, along with a Sunday evening worship service, challenges students in their faith. Sixteen chapel services per semester are required out of fifty opportunities. Religious organizations and activities exist to provide fellowship and spiritual growth.

Grove City students generally come from middle-income families. The greatest number comes from Pennsylvania, Ohio, New Jersey, Virginia, and New York, although forty-one states and twelve other countries were represented in 2006–07. Eighty-eight percent of the women and 71 percent of the men in the most recent freshman class ranked in the top fifth of their high school class. Their average SAT combined score was 1279; the average ACT composite score was 28.

Ninety-three percent of the 2,500 students live in separate men's and women's residence halls. All others are regular commuters or married students. A full program of cultural, professional, athletic, and social activities is offered. An arena, Crawford Auditorium, and the J. Howard Pew Fine Arts Center are used for athletics, concerts, movies, plays, and lectures. The Physical Learning Center is one of the finest among the nation's small colleges and includes an eight-lane bowling alley, two swimming pools, handball/racquetball courts, playing surfaces, fitness rooms with free weights, aerobic equipment and Cybex machines, an indoor three-lane running track, and the basketball arena. A Student Union, which includes an eatery, mailroom, bookstore, and commuters' lounge, and Ketler Recreation Lounge are also available. There are more than 100 organizations and special interest groups, including local fraternities and sororities. No alcohol or drugs are permitted on campus. The athletic activities include an extensive intramural, club, and varsity sports program that provides nineteen intercollegiate teams that compete at the NCAA Division III level for men and women.

The College's well-established placement services are used constantly by students who are interested in business and industrial employment and by those seeking educational positions in the teaching field. A complete file of personal data, scholastic records, and recommendations is prepared for each registrant. These files are available to the scores of prospective employers who visit the campus annually to interview the graduating seniors. One of Grove City's strengths is placing students in business, industrial, and teaching positions, as well as in professional institutions such as medical schools.

Location

Grove City, a town of 8,000 people, is 60 miles north of Pittsburgh. Convenient to I-79 and I-80, Grove City is only a day's drive from Chicago, New York City, Toronto, and Washington, D.C. The municipal airport has a 3,500-foot runway, and there is bus service to Pittsburgh.

Majors and Degrees

Grove City College offers undergraduate degrees in liberal arts, sciences, engineering, and music. The Bachelor of Arts is offered with majors in Christian thought, communication, economics, English, English/communication, history, modern language (French, Spanish, and international business), philosophy, political science, psychology, secondary education, and sociology. Preprofessional students in Christian education, law, or theology usually earn the B.A. degree. Interdisciplinary major programs are also available for qualified students.

The Bachelor of Science is granted with majors in accounting, applied physics, applied physics/computer, biochemistry, biology, business management, chemistry, computer information systems, computer science, early childhood education, elementary education, entrepreneurship, financial management, industrial management, international business, marketing management, mathematics, and molecular biology. Preprofessional students often select one of these majors for dentistry, medicine, or other health fields.

The Bachelor of Science in Electrical and Computer Engineering degree is also offered. The Bachelor of Science in Mechanical Engineering major provides for mechanical systems design and/or thermal systems design. The electrical and computer and mechanical engineering programs are accredited by the Accreditation Board for Engineering and Technology, Inc. (ABET).

The Bachelor of Music degree is awarded to those who major in music. Programs may also include concentrations in business, education, performing arts, or religion.

Academic Programs

Grove City College's goal is to assist young men and women in developing as complete individuals—academically, spiritually, and physically. The general education requirements provide all students with a high level of cultural literacy and communication skills. They include 38–50 semester hours of courses with emphases in the humanities, social sciences, and natural sciences and in quantitative and logical reasoning, as well as a language requirement for nonengineering and science majors. Degree candidates must also complete the requirements in their field of concentration, physical education, electives, and convocation. To graduate, a student must have completed 128 semester hours (132 hours for electrical engineering) plus 4 convocation credits. Seventy-five percent of those entering as freshmen stay and receive a diploma in four years.

A distinctive liberal arts–engineering program includes engineering courses plus courses in the humanities to provide students with a well-grounded preparation for entering the engineering field, as well as the civic and cultural life of society. The economics program exposes students to all economic philosophies, yet strongly advocates economic freedoms and free markets.

Grove City follows the early semester calendar plan. Academic credit may be granted to incoming freshmen on the basis of scores on appropriate Advanced Placement tests, International Baccalaureate tests, or College-Level Examination Program tests. Honors courses, independent study, seminars, and the opportunity for juniors to study abroad for credit are also offered.

Academic Facilities

The Hall of Arts and Letters opened in 2003. This state-of-the-art teaching facility features a 200-seat lecture hall, forty classrooms (including multimedia-equipped rooms and tiered "case study" rooms), eighty faculty offices, the Early Education Center, the Curriculum Library, and language, computer, and video production labs.

The College library houses 158,000 books and 270,000 microfilm/microfiche units. Modern, well-equipped laboratories for biology, chemistry, engineering, and physics are available, as are facilities for language and piano studies.

The Technological Learning Center, which consists of forty microcomputers and three big-screen projection systems, has received national recognition. All freshmen receive their own tablet PC.

The J. Howard Pew Fine Arts Center has art, photography, and music studios; a rehearsal hall; a little theater; a museum; an art gallery; music practice rooms; and an auditorium and stage large enough to accommodate the most elaborate drama productions and concerts. An addition completed in 2002 contains additional classrooms, practice rooms, and a 188-seat recital hall.

Costs

As a relatively small, financially sound college, Grove City is able to charge an unusually low tuition in comparison to other independent institutions of similar quality. The 2007–08 annual tuition charge was $11,500 for all degrees. The cost of a tablet PC for all freshmen is included in the tuition fees. There is no comprehensive fee. Part-time tuition is $365 per credit. Room and board are $6134. Expenses for books, laundry, transportation, and personal needs vary considerably with the lifestyle of the individual.

Financial Aid

Because the College's tuition charges are low, every student, in effect, receives significant financial assistance. Sixty-two percent of the freshmen receive additional aid from GCC. Students applying for financial assistance must complete Grove City College's financial aid form. Job opportunities are available both on and off campus.

Faculty

The focus of the Grove City faculty members is on teaching students, although many members are involved with research and writing. Eighty percent of the faculty members hold doctorates. Most of the administrative staff members also teach part-time in various departments. The student-faculty ratio is approximately 17:1. Faculty members emphasize teaching and attention to the students' individual needs; they also participate extensively in the College's extracurricular programs.

Student Government

The Student Government Association provides an opportunity for direct student interaction with the faculty members and administration in matters relating to campus activities. Students serve on regular College committees (library, publications, religious activities, and student activities) and also on the Men's and Women's Governing Board and the Discipline Committee.

Admission Requirements

The College seeks academically qualified students without regard to race, color, sex, religion, or national or ethnic origin. An applicant for admission should be a high school graduate with the following recommended units: English, 4; foreign language, 3; mathematics, 3; history, 2; and science, 2. Engineering, science, and mathematics majors should have 4 units each in both mathematics and science. Auditions are required for music majors. An interview is highly recommended, especially for those who live within a day's drive (400 miles).

Transfer students may receive advanced standing if they have been in good standing at their previous institutions and have maintained a minimum grade point average of 2.0 (on a 4.0 scale).

Application and Information

A regular admission applicant should take the SAT or ACT by October or November of the senior year in high school. The application should include scores on the SAT (preferred) or the ACT, a high school transcript, references, a recommendation from the student's principal or counselor, and a nonrefundable application fee of $50. An application may be submitted after the eleventh grade. An early decision applicant should take the entrance test in the eleventh grade, visit the College for an interview, and submit the application by November 15; notification of the admission decision is mailed on December 15. Approved early decision applicants must accept by January 15 and submit a nonrefundable deposit of $200.

Applicants seeking regular decision must submit the completed application and supporting documents by February 1 of their senior year. Notification of the admission decision is mailed on March 15. Students who are offered admission should reply as soon as possible, but no later than May 1, and include a nonrefundable deposit of $200. Applications received after February 1 are considered as space permits. The College receives three applications for every freshman vacancy.

Additional information may be obtained from:

Jeffrey C. Mincey
Director of Admissions
Grove City College
100 Campus Drive
Grove City, Pennsylvania 16127-2104
Phone: 724-458-2100
Fax: 724-458-3395
E-mail: admissions@gcc.edu
Web site: http://www.gcc.edu

A view of the campus at Grove City College.

COLLEGE DATA CENTER • PENNSYLVANIA

GWYNEDD-MERCY COLLEGE

GWYNEDD VALLEY, PENNSYLVANIA

The College

The dedication of the Sisters of Mercy to higher education led to the founding of Gwynedd-Mercy College in suburban Philadelphia in 1948. Gwynedd-Mercy is a four-year coeducational college with majors in both the liberal arts and professional fields of study. Gwynedd-Mercy was the first Catholic college in the United States to establish a sequential associate degree to bachelor's degree program in nursing, and it has recently established the first such progressive program in health information technology.

Gwynedd-Mercy College is recognized in *U.S. News & World Report's Best Colleges* issue as a top Northern University at the master's level. Students at Gwynedd-Mercy establish strong cooperative relationships, encouraging and mentoring one another at all levels. A high degree of interaction and cooperation is also evident between faculty members and students. This may help to explain the high retention rate.

Gwynedd-Mercy offers participation in twenty NCAA Division III athletic teams. Two sports have conference Coaches of the Year. Gwynedd-Mercy's recognized excellence in the health fields provides a basis for its commitment to physical as well as spiritual wellness.

A special effort is made to encourage the participation of all students in activities and student government. Opportunities are available through the drama club, campus ministry, a nationally renowned choir, the yearbook staff, and social committees. The first Catholic college chapter of Habitat for Humanity, which has been endorsed by former President Jimmy Carter, gives students the chance to help in the actual construction of homes for the less fortunate. Students can write for the College newspaper, the *Gwynmercian*, which has received a first-place rating with special merit from the American Scholastic Press Association. Through the on-campus chapter of Mercy Corps, students can help the poor with fund-raising efforts and adopt-a-family programs at the Thanksgiving and Christmas holidays. Some students decide to give a year of service after graduation to Mercy Corps' nationwide outreach program.

A student lounge dedicated as an International Center for Understanding and Culture (ICUC) was opened in 1986. It gives American students the opportunity to meet, socialize with, and get to know young people from other countries. This diversified international student group includes 63 students representing thirty countries. The ICUC quickly became a popular campus meeting place for students to confide their hopes and dreams.

On the graduate level, Gwynedd-Mercy offers a master's degree program in education (educational administration, reading, school counseling, special education, and a Master Teacher program) and nursing (geriatrics, oncology, and pediatrics).

Location

Gwynedd-Mercy's idyllic 160-acre campus is located in Gwynedd Valley, Pennsylvania, a suburb 20 miles from Center City Philadelphia. Old City, South Street, and sports arenas are a 25- to 30-minute car ride from the campus. The College is situated just minutes from several major highways, including the Pennsylvania Turnpike. The immediate area is rich in the history of Colonial America, and two of the oldest homes in Pennsylvania are located on the Gwynedd campus.

Majors and Degrees

Gwynedd-Mercy offers baccalaureate degrees in accounting, behavioral/social gerontology, biology, business administration, business education, computer information sciences, criminal justice, elementary education, English, history, human services, mathematics, nursing, psychology, sociology, and special education. Seven certification options are available through the School of Education.

Associate in Science degrees are awarded in the allied health fields of cardiovascular technology, health information technology, and respiratory care. Associate degrees are also granted in accounting, business administration, computer programming, liberal studies, natural science, and nursing.

Academic Programs

The school year is divided into two semesters, and most baccalaureate degree programs require the completion of a minimum of 125 credit hours. Gwynedd-Mercy maintains a strong liberal arts component in all of its degree programs. Whether the student chooses to major in one of the liberal arts or to pursue a professionally oriented degree, courses are required in language, literature and the fine arts, humanities, and behavioral, social, and natural sciences.

Individualized internships and work-experience programs are available and recommended in all majors to give students first-hand experience in their chosen major. Nearby Fortune 500 companies offer a wide variety of experience to students in business and accounting. TAP, the Teacher Assistant Program, places every education major in the classroom one day a week beginning in the freshman year. All allied health and nursing programs require clinical experience. The 2+2 programs—those with an associate degree to bachelor's degree progression—offer allied health and nursing students the opportunity to gain employment in their field while continuing toward the baccalaureate degree. The School of Business and Computer and Information Sciences maintains a successful work-experience semester. Through this paid internship, students earn credit while gaining valuable experience in challenging positions.

The tutoring program, which was begun for science and health majors, has expanded so that free tutoring is now available in other academic areas for students who need it. This program complements the close student-faculty relationship that is part of the Gwynedd-Mercy milieu.

Off-Campus Programs

The excellent on-campus laboratory facilities are extended by affiliations with more than 200 hospitals and health-care agencies in Pennsylvania, New Jersey, and Delaware, where students may complete their clinical experience. Merck provides a one-semester industrial laboratory experience for qualified biology majors. Gwynedd maintains a close relationship with nearby companies, such as Unisys, McNeil, and Sun Company, for work-experience programs.

Academic Facilities

Gwynedd-Mercy has expanded its physical facilities as its student enrollment has increased. The Sister Isabelle Keiss Center for Health and Science opened in fall 1999 and houses the Schools of Nursing and Allied Health Professions and the Division of Natural Sciences. The 50,000-square-foot state-of-the-art facility offers laboratories for areas such as nursing skills, respiratory care, cardiovascular technology, radiation therapy, health information technology, organic chemistry, and microbiology. The College's Griffin Complex houses the College's Student Union—which is equipped with a game room, full gymnasium and track, racquetball court, and weight room. Three newly built residence halls have been added to the existing Loyola Hall. The College now offers three residence facilities that house 40 percent of the school population. The Lincoln Library, which is a large adjunct collection of books on Lincoln and the Civil War, is housed in Assumption Hall. Theaters include the Julia Ball Auditorium, a small in-the-round theater, and a TV production studio. One computer laboratory is reserved for computer majors. A separate facility is maintained for use by the general student body. Both are staffed and open at hours that are convenient to student use. The Valie Genuardi Hobbit House, a private school for preschoolers where students in the School of Education are trained, is situated on campus.

Costs

The 2007–08 academic-year tuition (two semesters) for full-time students (12 to 18 credits per semester) was $20,500. Allied health and nursing students paid $22,000. Room and board are, on average, $8200. Professional liability fees for students enrolled in clinical components and lab fees are extra.

Financial Aid

Gwynedd-Mercy's financial aid program is designed to provide financial assistance to academically qualified students whose resources are inadequate to meet the costs of attending the College. The student Financial Aid Committee endeavors to assist as many students as possible, using Gwynedd-Mercy funds as well as federal, state, and other available funds. Aid is awarded on the basis of demonstrated financial need, academic proficiency, and responsible campus citizenship.

A financial aid packet is sent, with instructions, to those who request it on their application form. High school students should request the Free Application for Federal Student Aid (FAFSA) from their guidance office. In 2006–07, 91 percent of Gwynedd-Mercy full-time students received some form of financial aid. March 15 is the deadline for freshmen entering in the fall semester. The deadline for Academic Scholarships is February 15.

Faculty

The student-faculty ratio is 13:1, allowing for personal contact, advising, and after-class instruction. This is a widely acknowledged strength of the Gwynedd-Mercy experience. For nursing students in the clinical setting, there are never more than 8 students to 1 clinical adviser; in the allied health programs, there often is one-to-one instruction. The quality of teaching is enhanced by the diversified interests of the faculty. The 181 faculty members teach both day and evening classes, allowing students the greatest flexibility in scheduling. Free tutoring is available in all disciplines.

Student Government

All students are encouraged to take part in the responsibilities of student government. This student participation and shared responsibility for the welfare of the College are promoted through a framework of committees. The student government president and 3 other students are members of the College Council, which is responsible for the continuing self-evaluation of the College and for policy formation. In addition, students share membership in the Educational Planning Committee, Faculty/Student Committee, Financial Aid Committee, and Library Committee.

Admission Requirements

Admission to Gwynedd-Mercy is based on a student's high school record, rank in class, SAT or ACT scores, counselor's recommendation, and choice of major. Entrance requirements vary with the program. For the fall 2008 entering class, the College bases admission decisions on the critical reading and mathematics scores on the SAT. The rolling admission policy allows the student to be informed of the admission decision within two to three weeks after the file is complete.

Gwynedd-Mercy awards College credit for satisfactory completion of Advanced Placement courses. The exam score must be 3 or above.

A minimum 2.0 grade point average (on a 4.0 scale) is generally required to transfer from another college. Gwynedd-Mercy does, however, retain the right to require a higher GPA for admission to some programs.

Gwynedd-Mercy selects all students on the basis of academic achievement and does not discriminate on the basis of race, religion, gender, handicap, or sexual orientation.

Application and Information

All prospective applicants are urged to visit the campus to meet and talk with an admission counselor, a dean, or a program director. To apply for admission, applicants should complete the application form and submit it to the admissions office along with the required nonrefundable $25 application fee. First-time freshmen must also submit an official high school transcript or equivalency certificate; a written recommendation from a principal, teacher, guidance counselor, or employer; and results of the SAT or ACT (for recent high school graduates). All applicants should verify that they meet the specific requirements and have the necessary high school prerequisites for admission.

Students who wish to transfer to Gwynedd should complete the application form and submit it to the admissions office along with the required nonrefundable $25 application fee, high school and college transcripts, and a letter of recommendation.

For additional information or to schedule campus tours and visits, students are encouraged to contact:

Office of Admissions
Gwynedd-Mercy College
1325 Sumneytown Pike
P.O. Box 901
Gwynedd Valley, Pennsylvania 19437-0901
Phone: 800-DIAL-GMC (toll-free)
E-mail: admissions@gmc.edu
Web site: http://www.gmc.edu

Aerial view of Gwynedd-Mercy College.

HARRISBURG UNIVERSITY OF SCIENCE AND TECHNOLOGY

HARRISBURG, PENNSYLVANIA

The University

The Harrisburg University of Science and Technology (HU) is an independent educational institution offering applied academic programs designed to educate career-minded individuals in the science, technology, engineering, and math disciplines. A private, nonprofit university, HU offers Bachelor of Science (B.S.) degrees in high-demand fields such as biotechnology, computer and information sciences, e-business and management, environmental chemistry, forensics, geography and geospatial imaging, integrative sciences, new media design, and software development.

More and more companies throughout the nation are looking for employees who can offer a combination of professional expertise, interpersonal skills, and a solid understanding of technology. However, there is a shortage of college-educated students with these traits. The University created its academic programs to prepare graduates to fill this need. Harrisburg University offers an applied science and technology education dedicated to careers that recognizes students' unique qualities. With its mentoring and internship programs, HU students may start their careers before graduation.

With a low student-faculty ratio (7:1), small class sizes, and corporate connections, students are assured of personal attention to their education and a helping hand if they need it. That help includes generous financial aid and academic advising.

Regional organizations, such as Gannett Fleming, the Technology Council of Central Pennsylvania, GeoDecisions, and Commerce Bank, have helped write and develop the academic programs, and many individuals with these companies teach courses as well. Additional organizations provide lab space and research opportunities. Still others—Hershey Foods, PPL, Penn National Insurance, and Wachovia Foundation, to name a few—provide scholarship and internship support.

The Harrisburg University of Science and Technology was incorporated in the Commonwealth of Pennsylvania on December 12, 2001, making it the first science and technology–focused, nonprofit, comprehensive university to be established in Pennsylvania in more than 100 years. Established to address the Capital Region's need for increased educational opportunities in science, technology, engineering, and math (STEM) careers, Harrisburg University represents a major step to attract, educate, and retain Pennsylvania's diverse twenty-first-century, knowledge-based workforce.

Students can maintain their own apartments, commute from home, or live at the Harrisburg International House (http://www.ihousehbg.org), a fully furnished, independent student-living complex that is one city block from the campus. With accommodations that are more like apartments than traditional residence hall rooms, the International House provides a safe and friendly environment. About 25 percent of the University's students live in these apartments, which are ideal for those who enjoy the independence of college living but seek a more sophisticated and supportive residential environment.

Along with its bachelor's degree programs, the University also offers the only Master of Science degree in IT project management and the only Master of Science degree in learning technologies in central Pennsylvania.

HU graduates possess an increasingly rare combination of STEM skills—capabilities in science, technology, engineering, and mathematics—coupled with core competencies from the humanities in writing, teamwork, cultural understanding, and other areas. Students leave Harrisburg University with experiences that make them more prepared and competitive in their careers and their lives.

Location

Located in downtown Harrisburg, the University is close to Interstates 83 and 81 and the Pennsylvania Turnpike, making it an easy drive from any of Pennsylvania's major cities. It is only a 2-hour drive from Philadelphia, Baltimore, or Washington, D.C. The University is easily accessible by Amtrak, Greyhound bus, or air.

The dynamic downtown Harrisburg location connects students to a diverse and exciting community that *Money* magazine rates as one of the nation's top "Up and Coming Cities," and the area is ranked twelfth among *Kiplinger's Personal Finance* magazine's "Best Places to Live."

The area is rich in cultural resources, museums, shopping malls, dance clubs, and restaurants. The scenic nature areas along the nearby Susquehanna River offer a relaxing escape from classes and are the site for local concerts, art festivals, and shows. Students can also tour Harrisburg's many historic museums, work out at the local fitness clubs, visit the theaters, or take in a minor-league baseball game. The location puts students close to hockey arenas, ski resorts, and amusement parks such as Hersheypark.

Majors and Degrees

Harrisburg University offers programs that lead to Bachelor of Science degrees. Majors include computer and information sciences, e-business and management, environmental chemistry, forensics, geography and geospatial imaging, integrative sciences, molecular and microbial biotechnology, new media design, and software development. The University also offers nondegree, postbaccalaureate certificate programs and professional development courses.

Academic Programs

The academic program followed by Harrisburg University was chosen to provide a science and technology education melded with the liberal arts. The University operates on a trimester system. A minimum of 120 semester hours is required for a baccalaureate degree. Students have a 45-hour general education requirement, including a sequence of courses that integrates science and engineering principles with humanities topics such as The Civic Mind, The Learned Mind, The Entrepreneurial Mind, and The Political Mind—which looks at history and economics through a science lens. Courses are designed to be team taught, and professors are encouraged to run classes in a seminar style. Public speaking is emphasized and group projects are mandatory. The idea is to simulate what it is like to work with colleagues in a business setting. Students are required to complete three internship or out-of-classroom projects to graduate.

Off-Campus Programs

Students leave Harrisburg University with experiences that make them more prepared and competitive in their careers and in life. During a student's first year, the University begins pairing each student with a business mentor. Together, the student and mentor network at professional events and mixers, and they visit businesses and organizations related to the field of study. Throughout the student's education at HU, the mentor guides the student, simultaneously building the student's confidence and contacts. The HU staff works closely to match students with regional businesses, so students can connect classwork to related work experiences.

Harrisburg University utilizes a top executive search and staffing firm to facilitate internships. Professionals with Arcus, LLC, interview students, help with resume preparation and interviewing skills, and even market students to prospective employers. This gives students access to exceptional internship opportunities that lead to long-term employment after graduation. Although the academic professors challenge students to strive toward greater knowledge in their chosen fields, the University connects students with corporate faculty members who come to the campus with extensive professional expertise in the University's competitive fields of study. They may be CEOs, project leaders, research scientists, or clinicians. Their experience and wisdom enable students to see how their education applies to the career world as they guide students toward a successful transition to the workplace.

Many social and professional opportunities arise from the University's partnerships with various civic groups in the area, including the Harrisburg Young Professionals (HYP). Each student receives a membership in HYP, which comprises a group of young, active, civic-minded professionals who create events and programs that make Harrisburg a great place to live, work, play, and shop. HYP is an influential group in Harrisburg, and they coordinate community projects as well as many different kinds of social activities.

Academic Facilities

Harrisburg University connects directly with Strawberry Square, a distinctive retail complex located in a 1-million-square-foot office facility in the heart of Pennsylvania's capital city. A unique mix of atrium shops, clothing stores, eateries, and even a fitness center, Strawberry Square is an energetic hub for students and the city's affluent professionals, and HU's connection to it makes the University truly a one-of-a-kind campus.

The University's new sixteen-story, $73-million Academic Center is set to open in winter 2008. The ultramodern, 371,000-square-foot facility is designed to provide state-of-the-art classroom space for 1,600 students. Housing a library, a 125-seat auditorium, a one-stop-shop student services center, numerous laboratories, businesses, the National Center for Science and Civic Engagement, the Center for Advanced Entertainment and Learning Technologies, and hundreds of parking spaces, the Academic Center provides a home for the growing University over the next decade.

Faculty

The average class size is 13, and the student-faculty ratio is 7:1. Of the University's full-time professors, 100 percent hold the terminal degree in their field.

Costs

For 2007, the tuition was $14,000. The cost for housing at the Harrisburg International House is approximately $2450 per semester. There is no application fee.

Financial Aid

Financial aid is available for undergraduate students. Ninety-six percent of HU students receive financial aid. The University reviews all admissions applications for generous University scholarships as well as for need-based financial and state aid, such as grants, loans, and employment opportunities. Harrisburg University is approved for training veterans under the provisions of the various public laws commonly called the G.I. Bill.

Admission Requirements

The University seeks students from a variety of backgrounds who can contribute to a vibrant and diverse University community. Students can demonstrate their academic potential through their high school record, scores on standardized tests, and written recommendations from teachers or adult mentors. The SAT reporting code for HU is 4511, and the ACT code is 3637. Students may have the requirement for test scores waived upon review by the Director of Admissions. All undergraduate candidates must provide a high school transcript. Students who have been out of high school for four or more years and students who have completed at least 24 undergraduate credits are automatically waived from the standardized test requirement.

No single particular factor can measure a student's potential; therefore, the University gives equal consideration to all aspects of a student's admissions application. HU has a rolling admission policy and notifies qualified applicants after immediate review of completed application packages. There is no application deadline at this time, and students are accepted provided ample time is allowed to develop the student's schedule prior to the start of the semester. Full consideration is given to candidates who submit applications prior to June 15 for fall enrollment and by November 1 for spring enrollment.

Application and Information

For application forms, a catalog, or further information, students should contact:

Office of Admission
Harrisburg University of Science and Technology
304 Market Street
Harrisburg, Pennsylvania 17101
Phone: 717-901-5101
866-424-8648 (toll-free)
Fax: 717-901-3110
E-mail: Connect@HarrisburgU.net
Web site: http://www.harrisburgu.net/

Harrisburg University is the right place for young adults who are drawn to science, math, and technology.

COLLEGE DATA CENTER • PENNSYLVANIA

HAVERFORD COLLEGE
HAVERFORD, PENNSYLVANIA

The College

Founded in 1833 as the first college established by members of the Society of Friends (Quakers), Haverford College has chosen to remain small, undergraduate, and residential in order to offer students remarkable classroom and research opportunities while maintaining a strong sense of community. Haverford's Honor Code, created and implemented by students, is an important part of the College's identity. The Code allows students to directly confront academic and social issues in a spirit of cooperation and mutual respect.

Haverford's 1,169 students represent forty-six states, Puerto Rico, the District of Columbia, and forty-four countries. Thirty-one percent of the students are students of color, while an additional 6 percent are international students.

Haverford is a residential campus with 99 percent of the students and 50 percent of the faculty living on campus. Housing on Haverford's campus is single-sex or coed, and residence halls vary in accommodations from 4-person apartments to suites and singles. Other choices of residence facilities include the Ira De A. Reid House (Black Cultural Center), La Casa Hispanica, and an environmental house.

Haverford's athletic teams participate in Division III of the NCAA. Intercollegiate sports include baseball, basketball, cricket, cross-country, fencing, field hockey, lacrosse, soccer, softball, squash, tennis, track and field, and volleyball. Haverford also sponsors several junior varsity, club, and intramural sports teams. Athletic facilities include the Alumni Field House, the Ryan Gymnasium, and the new Douglas B. Gardner Integrated Athletic Center.

Location

The College is located 10 miles (16 kilometers) west of Center City Philadelphia on a wooded campus of 216 acres. Haverford's proximity to the fifth-largest city in the United States allows its students to take advantage of the many social, cultural, and educational resources that this historic area offers. Extensive public transportation allows students easy access to the city and environs.

Majors and Degrees

Majors leading to a B.A. or B.S. degree are offered in thirty departments: anthropology, archaeology, astronomy, biology, chemistry, classics, comparative literature, computer science, East Asian studies (including Chinese and Japanese), economics, English, fine arts, French, geology, German, growth and structure of cities, history, history of art, Italian, mathematics, music, philosophy, physics, political science, psychology, religion, Romance languages, Russian, sociology, and Spanish. Students may minor, arrange an interdepartmental or double major, or design an individual major. Approximately 30 percent of the students major in the sciences or mathematics, 40 percent in the social sciences, and 30 percent in the humanities. Ten percent have double, interdepartmental, or special majors. A 3-2 engineering program with Caltech is available to students who qualify.

Other programs that students may incorporate into their curricula include Africana studies, biochemistry and biophysics, creative writing, dance, education, environmental studies, gender and sexuality studies, Hebrew and Judaic studies, Hispanic and Hispanic American studies, international economic relations, Latin American and Iberian studies, linguistics, mathematical economics, neural and behavioral science, peace and conflict studies, prebusiness, prelaw, premedicine, and theater.

Academic Programs

The academic experience at Haverford is centered around a deep commitment to the core values of a liberal arts education and its emphasis on the dual pursuit of a breadth of study and in-depth work. While the College mandates that all students take classes across the academic spectrum, there is no core curriculum of specific required courses. Instead, Haverford's system of distribution requirements ensures that students will take at least three classes in each of the divisions of the College (humanities, natural sciences, and social sciences) while allowing them the flexibility to choose courses they find truly interesting. In addition, students must fulfill requirements in foreign language, social justice, writing, and quantitative course work. Majors are selected at the end of the sophomore year.

Haverford's small size and exclusive focus on undergraduate education allow students to count on discussion-based classes and research opportunities that students at most colleges would not be able to experience until graduate school. It is common for Haverford students to pursue independent study and approximately half will study abroad, typically during the junior year.

Haverford's three academic centers—the John B. Hurford Humanities Center, the Marian E. Koshland Integrated Natural Sciences Center, and the Center for Peace and Global Citizenship—provide opportunities for integrated learning, bringing students and faculty in related fields together and promoting conversation and collaboration across disciplines. The centers also help to bring an outward view to students' education by sponsoring speaker series, artists in residence, and colloquia on campus.

One of Haverford's distinctive features is its extensive academic and social cooperation with Bryn Mawr College. Students may take courses or major at either school, live on either campus, and eat on either campus. There are more than 3,500 cross-registrations annually. Both colleges jointly operate a weekly newspaper, a drama club, a radio station, an orchestra, social action groups, and intramural sports. A free bus service between the two campuses, which are a mile apart, facilitates cooperative arrangements. Haverford and Bryn Mawr also share library resources with nearby Swarthmore College. All three college libraries are linked electronically, and students have instant access to library resources through the campus computer network. Combined holdings are in excess of 1.5 million volumes.

Off-Campus Programs

Haverford students may take advantage of course offerings at Swarthmore College and the University of Pennsylvania in addition to courses at Bryn Mawr. Students may also enhance their college experiences by arranging study abroad at one of seventy-six programs overseas or study away at Claremont McKenna, Fisk, Spelman, or Pitzer colleges.

Academic Facilities

Major facilities include the James P. Magill Library (580,000 volumes); computer centers; the Koshland Integrated Natural Sciences Center for the physical sciences, biology, and psychology; the Strawbridge Observatory for astronomy; the Music Center; Gest Center for Cross-Cultural Study of Religion; the Fine Arts Center; Marshall Auditorium; and the Language Learning Center. Academic buildings and dormitories are linked by a campuswide computer network.

Costs

The total approximate costs for 2007–08 were $46,450 for new students and $46,270 for returning students. This consisted of $35,058 for tuition, $10,880 for room and board, and a student association fee of $332. New students have a one-time orientation fee of $180.

Financial Aid

Fifty-four percent of Haverford's students receive financial aid, which is awarded solely based on need. Candidates for Haverford College–funded aid must file the online College Board PROFILE application and the online Free Application for Federal Student Aid (FAFSA), along with other forms. Complete information on forms and deadlines to apply for financial aid at Haverford, including links to the PROFILE and FAFSA, are available at http://www.haverford.edu/financialaid. Early decision applicants must file for financial aid by November 15 and regular decision applicants by January 31. Further details are available on the Web site. Haverford's PROFILE code is 2289, and the FAFSA code is 003274.

Faculty

The student-faculty ratio is 8:1. The faculty devotes its full teaching time to undergraduates. There are no graduate assistants. The regular faculty is supplemented by 90 to 100 scholars, artists, and public figures who visit the College annually under the auspices of seven specially endowed funds.

Student Government

The Students' Association has responsibility for nearly all aspects of student life. The Haverford Honor Code, established and administered by students, has been in existence since 1897. The Honor Code makes possible a climate of trust, concern, and respect, which produces a campus atmosphere conducive to learning and personal growth. The code provides for students' academic and social freedom within the confines of agreed-upon community standards. Exams are not proctored, and the students schedule their own final exams. The code is administered by an elected Honor Council of 16 students—4 from each class at the College. Each year, the students meet to discuss resolutions and changes in the Honor Code and to approve its adoption. The students also elect several members of the student body to serve on faculty committees and as nonvoting representatives to the Board of Managers (trustees).

Admission Requirements

Admission to Haverford is highly competitive. Admitted students have strong academic records and represent a diversity of backgrounds and interests. The primary criteria for admission are academic and personal qualities as shown by the school record, standardized test scores, extracurricular achievement, and personal recommendations. A combination of qualities that indicate academic and personal promise and potential for growth at Haverford is more significant than any single factor. Of the most recent first-year class, 89 percent rank in the top 10 percent of their high school class, and their SAT scores range from 500 to 800. The mean SAT ranges are 650–750 critical reasoning, 640–740 math, and 650–740 writing. All candidates are required to take the new SAT and two SAT Subject Tests. The ACT with the writing component may be substituted for the SAT. A visit to campus to meet students, observe classes, and have an interview is recommended. Students who live within 150 miles of the campus are strongly recommended to arrange an on-campus interview. A first-choice early decision plan and a deferred matriculation plan are offered.

Admission of transfer students to Haverford is also highly competitive. A limited number of transfer students are accepted each year. Candidates must have completed one full year of college, with a minimum grade point average of 3.0 (B). Campus visits are strongly recommended for those wishing to transfer. A transfer student must spend a minimum of two years at Haverford in order to receive a degree.

Application and Information

The application deadlines for admission are November 15 for early decision candidates, January 15 for regular decision candidates, and March 31 for transfer candidates. Haverford uses the Common Application, which is available in school guidance offices and online. The admission office is open from 9 a.m. to 5 p.m. on weekdays (8:30 a.m. to 4:30 p.m. from June through August) and, during the fall, from 10 a.m. to 1 p.m. on Saturday. For more information or to arrange an interview or tour appointment, students should contact:

Office of Admission and Financial Aid
Haverford College
370 Lancaster Avenue
Haverford, Pennsylvania 19041-1392
Phone: 610-896-1350
610-896-1436 (TTY/TDD)
Fax: 610-896-1338
E-mail: admission@haverford.edu (Admission)
finaid@haverford.edu (Financial Aid)
Web site: http://www.haverford.edu

IMMACULATA UNIVERSITY

IMMACULATA, PENNSYLVANIA

The University

Immaculata University (IU), a comprehensive Catholic liberal arts university for students of all faiths, offers a high-quality education that is firmly grounded in values and tradition. Immaculata graduates are known for their skills and knowledge and also for their desire to serve. The University was founded in 1920 and has since grown to enroll almost 4,000 students in bachelor's, master's, and doctoral degree programs and accelerated degree-completion programs.

Approximately 900 traditional-age men and women attend the College of Undergraduate Studies, with 90 percent of them living in University-sponsored housing. The College of Lifelong Learning includes undergraduate programs that are open to adult men and women. Students represent sixteen states and thirteen countries, giving the campus both ethnic and geographic diversity. Resident students live in four residence halls containing double rooms. Both resident and nonresident students participate in more than fifty student clubs and organizations that represent interests in athletics, student government, academic disciplines, community action, music, dance, theater, and student publications.

Intercollegiate sports include women's basketball, cross-country, field hockey, golf, lacrosse, soccer, softball, tennis, and volleyball and men's basketball, cross-country, golf, lacrosse, soccer, and tennis. Immaculata competes in Division III athletics as part of the Pennsylvania Athletic Conference. A new turf field, stadium, gymnasia, fitness room, and pool are available for student use and provide numerous opportunities for physical activities and wellness programs. The Student Association of Immaculata University provides the unity, enthusiasm, and leadership that are integral parts of the traditional undergraduate experience.

Immaculata University celebrates unique traditions as a part of the overall collegiate experience, such as Freshman Investiture, the academic capping of the newest members of the University community. Carol Night, one of Immaculata's best-loved traditions, involves students, faculty members, alumni, and families singing around the Christmas tree in the rotunda of Villa Maria Hall.

The main building, Villa Maria Hall, is of neo-Renaissance architecture in gray stone with a red tile roof. The other thirteen major campus buildings are also of gray stone with red tile roofs, unifying the aesthetic appearance of the campus.

Graduate degrees offered in the College of Graduate Studies include the Master of Arts in counseling psychology, cultural and linguistic diversity, educational leadership and administration, music therapy, nursing, nutrition education, and organization leadership. Doctoral degrees are offered in educational administration, clinical psychology, and school psychology. ACCEL, the accelerated degree-completion program, offers bachelor's degrees in financial management, human performance management, and information technology.

Location

Immaculata's 375-acre campus is located in historic Chester County, 20 miles west of Philadelphia and 10 miles south of Valley Forge. The area is primarily suburban, with numerous colleges and universities offering a wide range of cultural and social activities. Many places of interest in Philadelphia and Lancaster are easily reached by car, train, or bus. The campus is 15 minutes from the King of Prussia Mall, the second largest mall in the U.S. Southern New Jersey shore resorts and New York City are within 1½ hours by car, with Pocono Mountain ski resorts and Washington, D.C., only 2½ hours away by car or train. The University provides numerous opportunities for internships in the business, educational, and scientific communities throughout the area.

Majors and Degrees

The College of Undergraduate Studies at Immaculata offers the Bachelor of Arts, Bachelor of Music, Bachelor of Science, Associate of Arts, and Associate of Science degrees as well as certification in education for preschool through grade 12. Undergraduate major fields of study include accounting, allied health, biology, biology/psychology, business administration, chemistry, communication, criminology/sociology, education, English, exercise science, family and consumer sciences, fashion marketing, finance, French, general science, health-care management, history, information technology, international business/foreign language, marketing management, mathematics, mathematics/computer science, music, music education, music therapy, nutrition/dietetics, political science/international relations, prelaw, premedicine, pre–physical therapy, pre–veterinary medicine, psychology, sociology, sociology/social work, Spanish, Spanish/psychology, Spanish/social work, and theology. Allied health concentrations include: clinical laboratory science, diagnostic medical sonography, invasive cardiovascular technology, nuclear medicine technology, and surgical technology. IU also offers partnership programs with Thomas Jefferson University (TJU) in physical therapy, occupational therapy, bioscience technologies, radiologic sciences, and the Doctor of Pharmacy (Pharm.D.) degree. These programs allow students to seamlessly matriculate into TJU after three years of study at IU.

Academic Programs

Two factors are emphasized in the educational program at Immaculata: a comprehensive liberal arts background and a major field of concentration that prepares students to begin a career or to attend graduate school. The honors program, an option for gifted students, offers an array of courses designed to give those who participate a special involvement in the learning process.

The Mary Bruder Center houses the offices for personal, career, and graduate study counseling and for educational and career testing. Workshops and seminars in resume writing, interviewing, career options, internship opportunities, and graduate fellowships are offered at regular intervals.

Off-Campus Programs

Both summer-abroad and junior-year-abroad programs combine travel with academic study to heighten the experience of students who seek these opportunities.

Every undergraduate major department offers numerous internship opportunities for students in agencies, businesses, institutions, or corporations related to their study. Some majors, such as dietetics, nutrition, fashion marketing, and music therapy, require a multiweek internship for the degree to be granted.

Academic Facilities

The Gabriele Library houses 130,000 volumes and offers 714 periodical subscriptions. In addition to the computer center, students have access to networked computers in the library, an interactive language lab with a video screen, and a multifaceted science lab with computer-simulated experiments; they also have Internet/Intranet access from their residence halls. Well-equipped laboratories, art studios, media centers, and a 1,150-seat theater give students a variety of settings in which to pursue their interests.

State-of-the-art computer labs include the Campus Learning and Language Laboratory, the Sister Maria Socorro Studio Laboratory for Mathematics and Science, a new Biology Laboratory, and the Loyola Executive Technology Center. Classrooms and the library utilize wireless technology in the smart classrooms.

Costs

For 2006–07, tuition and fees were $22,560 and room and board were $9000. An additional $1000 is estimated to cover books and personal spending. A fixed tuition rate guarantees the same tuition cost for a maximum of four years for all full-time students entering the College of Undergraduate Studies.

Financial Aid

Financial aid is available in the form of scholarships, grants, loans, and part-time campus employment through the resources of Immaculata, federal and state governments, and private endowments. Scholarships are awarded for academic excellence. Approximately 90 percent of the students receive some form of aid, and all students who demonstrate need are offered financial aid packages. The University requires that students submit the Free Application for Federal Student Aid (FAFSA) to be considered for financial aid. The University sends financial aid packages to accepted students as their files are completed by the middle of March. The FAFSA reporting code is 003276.

Faculty

The faculty has more than 80 full-time and 200 part-time members, more than half of whom hold doctorates. Several members of the Immaculata faculty conduct research and present papers in various disciplines, both nationally and internationally. High-quality teaching is of the greatest importance to Immaculata's academic program. Full-time faculty members serve as academic counselors and activity moderators. The student-faculty ratio is 11:1.

Student Government

The Student Association of Immaculata University (SAIU) governs most aspects of student life for both resident and commuter students. The resident assistant program moderates residence life by holding open meetings to discuss safety issues and to set residence hall regulations. Students serve on the various University policymaking committees and handle all student activity funds.

Admission Requirements

In order to be considered for admission to the College of Undergraduate Studies, students must submit an official secondary school transcript indicating course selection for the senior year and SAT or ACT scores. The reporting code for the SAT is 2320, and the reporting code for the ACT is 3596. An essay and recommendations can enhance a candidate's application. The Admission Committee requires 14 or more course units, as follows: 4 units of English, 2 units of social science, 2 units of mathematics, 2 units of science (1 lab), and 2 consecutive years of the same foreign language. Most candidates exceed this curriculum. The mid-range GPA for the past two years was 3.2.

All admission credentials should be sent to the College of Undergraduate Studies. Students can apply online at the University's Web site. The application fee is waived for students who apply prior to December 15 or who visit the campus and complete an application during their visit.

Application and Information

Applications are accepted from prospective freshman and transfer students on a rolling admissions basis, and decisions are made three to four weeks after an applicant's file is complete.

For further information, students should contact:

The College of Undergraduate Studies
Immaculata University
P.O. Box 642
Immaculata, Pennsylvania 19345-0642
Phone: 610-647-4400 Ext. 3015
877-428-6329 (toll-free)
Fax: 610-640-0836
E-mail: admis@immaculata.edu
Web site: http://www.immaculata.edu

Students at Immaculata University.

COLLEGE DATA CENTER • PENNSYLVANIA

INDIANA UNIVERSITY OF PENNSYLVANIA

INDIANA, PENNSYLVANIA

The University

Founded in 1875, Indiana University of Pennsylvania (IUP) draws its enrollment of 14,018 students from nearly every state and from scores of other countries. With three campuses located in the foothills of the Allegheny Mountains, IUP is the largest of the fourteen universities in the State System of Higher Education and the only one that grants doctoral degrees.

Recognized as a "public ivy," the University sustains a tradition of high academic quality at an affordable cost. In forty-five academic departments located within six colleges and two schools, IUP offers approximately 100 major fields of study. Graduate programs in many professional and applied areas are available, as are eight doctoral programs. IUP has one of the largest internship programs in Pennsylvania, providing students with professional experience to supplement their classroom learning.

The following publications have recognized IUP for its high academic standards and competitive costs: *Consumers Digest* Top 50 Best Values for Public Colleges and Universities, *Kiplinger's Personal Finance* magazine's annual *100 Best Values in Public Colleges, Two Hundred Most Selective Colleges: The Definitive Guide to America's First-Choice Schools,* Princeton Review's *The Best 366 Colleges,* Princeton Review's *Best 237 Business Schools,* and *U.S. News & World Report.*

Location

Located 50 miles northeast of Pittsburgh in the borough of Indiana, the seat of Indiana County, the main campus of IUP is just three blocks from the town's business district. The University is easily accessible by automobile from all sections of the state. The campus's residential facilities are being transformed from traditional double rooms with communal bathrooms to multiroom suites and bathrooms shared by no more than 2 students. The community of Indiana has more than thirty churches that represent all major faiths. All churches are within walking distance of the campus.

Majors and Degrees

IUP awards B.A., B.S., B.F.A., B.S.Ed., and B.S.N. degrees in approximately 100 majors in the areas of the arts and sciences, business, consumer services, elementary and secondary education, fine arts, food and nutrition, health and physical education, home economics, medical technology, nursing, respiratory therapy, and safety sciences. IUP also offers the Associate of Arts degree in business. Dual majors are available to students who wish to augment their academic background.

Academic Programs

IUP provides for the nourishment of the whole person through its Liberal Studies Program. In addition to fulfilling the minimum 48-semester-hour Liberal Studies Program requirement, each student must complete the necessary major and minor requirements to reach the minimum total of 120 credits necessary for graduation.

Courses taken by students under the Advanced Placement program of the College Board prior to admission may be recognized by the awarding of college credit or by the exemption of required subjects from the student's curriculum. For students who have acquired learning in nontraditional or other ways or who have advanced in a given field, an opportunity to gain exemption from a course is offered through examinations given at the discretion of each department.

The University offers an Army Reserve Officers' Training Corps (ROTC) program.

IUP operates on two 14-week semesters—September through December and January through May—plus two 5-week summer sessions. The University also offers a Pre-Summer Session.

Off-Campus Programs

The University participates in joint programs with other colleges and universities. Included in these cooperative programs are one in family medicine with Jefferson Medical College of Thomas Jefferson University, one in forestry with Duke University, two in engineering with Drexel University and the University of Pittsburgh, one in graphic arts with the Art Institute of Pittsburgh, one in jewelry with the Bowman Technical School, one in optometry with Pennsylvania College of Optometry, and one in podiatry with Philadelphia School of Podiatry.

The Office of International Affairs has arrangements for students to study in numerous countries. Each year, approximately 200 students study abroad. Other opportunities for off-campus study include the marine science consortium, the graphic arts exchange program, internships, and studies in the health services, which are offered through the University's affiliations with hospitals and other universities.

Academic Facilities

Information Technology Services provides computational support for undergraduate and graduate courses, faculty and student research, and the administrative requirements of the University. Terminals may be found in various locations on campus.

The University's campuswide cable system and fiber-optic backbone are fully connected to all academic buildings and each residence hall room, allowing immediate connection to the University's mainframe computer and access to the University's television station and educational programming.

The Stapleton-Stabley Library complex provides study space for about 1,200 students. The monograph holdings total more than 852,000 volumes. The general holdings are enhanced by the reference collection, which has more than 16,000 current serial titles and 15,000 electronic serials publications, 2.3 million items of microform materials, and an extensive media collection. IUP is a designated select depository for federal and state publications and is currently housing more than 37,000 volumes of governmental publications. The Special Collections and Archives collections highlight the labor history and industrial heritage of western Pennsylvania. Media Resources provides children's and curricular material to support the teacher preparation programs. The Cogswell Music Library houses approximately 11,000 books, 22,000 scores, 10,000 recordings, and 3,000 CDs.

There are a public computer lab in Stapleton and more than 118 public computers throughout the library. An increasing percentage of resources are available in full text electronically. The Instructional Design Center actively supports the growing distance education courses.

Costs

The basic costs that in-state students incurred per year in 2007–08 included $6695 for tuition and fees, $5436 for room and board, and approximately $1000 for books and supplies. Additional costs included $2633 for personal expenses. Tuition and fees for out-of-state students were $14,550 per year. All costs are subject to change.

Financial Aid

More than 81 percent of IUP students received some type of financial assistance during the 2006–07 academic year. The types of financial aid offered by IUP include student employment, loans, grants, and scholarships. In most cases, the Free Application for Federal Student Aid (FAFSA) serves as the application used to determine eligibility for these programs. Federal student assistance is available during the fall, spring, and summer terms. The application deadline for all students for the FAFSA is April 15, with award notifications to accepted freshmen beginning on March 15. Financial assistance is also available through IUP's Army ROTC program.

Faculty

There are 644 full-time and 75 part-time teaching faculty members. The student-faculty ratio is 16:1. While primarily serving as instructors, faculty members also aid students in course selections and career planning and advise student organizations and clubs.

Student Government

IUP students actively participate in the governance of the University through the Student Government Association, the elected members of which represent students in the University Senate.

Admission Requirements

Any graduate of an accredited four-year high school or holder of a high school equivalency diploma is qualified to apply for admission to IUP. Applicants are reviewed by the Admissions Committee on the basis of high school records, recommendations, and scores earned on the SAT or the ACT. Applicants are expected to name their major field upon application, but a change in major can be made prior to or during the freshman year.

Application and Information

Applications are accepted for consideration for the fall and spring semesters after August 1 of the preceding year. Applications are reviewed on a rolling basis beginning on September 15 until vacancies are filled.

To request an application or further information, students should contact:

Office of Admissions
117 Sutton Hall
Indiana University of Pennsylvania
1011 South Drive
Indiana, Pennsylvania 15705
Phone: 724-357-2230
800-442-6830 (toll-free)
Fax: 724-357-6281
E-mail: admissions-inquiry@iup.edu
Web site: http://www.iup.edu/admissions

JUNIATA COLLEGE
HUNTINGDON, PENNSYLVANIA

The College

Juniata College is an independent, coeducational college of liberal arts and sciences, founded in 1876 by members of the Church of the Brethren to prepare individuals "for the useful occupations of life." Juniata College holds a place of national prominence in higher education. Recent studies rank the College highly in the percentage of graduates that eventually earn doctoral degrees; one, in fact, ranked Juniata in the top 10 percent in the nation among all four-year private undergraduate institutions. Juniata's national reputation is strongest in several fields, including biology, chemistry, environmental science and education, health sciences, peace and conflict studies, and prelaw. The College is known for the personal attention it gives students. Each student is assigned 2 faculty advisers, and the average student-faculty ratio is 13:1.

Juniata is a very strong community where student involvement is paramount. There are no fraternities or sororities so the entire campus gets involved. School spirit and campus activities are the heart and soul of the institution. The 100 clubs and service organizations not only impact the Juniata community but also the larger community of Huntingdon and the surrounding area.

Location

Juniata is located in Huntingdon, which lies in the scenic Allegheny Mountains of central Pennsylvania. Huntingdon is a charming community of 10,000 residents. It is 30 minutes from the cities of Altoona (pop. 65,000) and State College (pop. 55,000), Pennsylvania. The 110 acres on College Hill overlook the historic architecture of a classic river town. Juniata's campus also consists of a 365-acre field station and a 315-acre nature preserve. The surrounding area is suited for many outdoor activities, including swimming, fishing, hunting, rock climbing, and hiking. Raystown Lake, the largest recreational lake wholly in Pennsylvania, is only 15 minutes from Juniata. Several major cities lie within a short drive of the campus—3 hours to Pittsburgh, Baltimore, and Washington, D.C.; 4 hours to Philadelphia; and 5 hours to New York City. The nearest commercial airport is in State College, the location of Penn State University. In addition, Huntingdon is on the main U.S. east-west railway line, with travel by train to East and West Coast cities available.

Majors and Degrees

Juniata awards B.A. and B.S. degrees in the arts, humanities, natural sciences, and social sciences. Rather than complete a traditional major, each Juniata student designs a Program of Emphasis (POE) that is tailored to the student's own goals and often crosses departmental lines. Working closely with 2 academic advisers, students select courses for either a designated or an individualized POE.

Current areas of study include accounting; anthropology; art (art history; museum studies, with an art history focus; and studio fine arts); arts management; biological sciences (biochemistry, biology, botany, ecology, microbiology, molecular and cell physiology, and zoology); business (business and IT, finance, human resource management, international business, management, and marketing); chemistry; communication; communication and conflict resolution; computer science; criminal justice; digital media; early childhood education; early childhood and special education; earth and space science; economics; elementary education; elementary and special education; English; entrepreneurial studies; environmental science; environmental studies; exploratory studies; geology; health communication; history; interdisciplinary studies (humanities, liberal arts, natural sciences, and social sciences); information technology; international politics; international studies; languages (French, German, Russian, and Spanish); marine science; mathematics; peace and conflict studies; philosophy, politics, and economics; philosophy and religious studies; physics (engineering physics, physics, and pre-engineering); politics; prehealth (art therapy, biotechnology, cardiovascular technology, cytotechnology, diagnostic imaging/radiography, genetic counseling, health administration, medical technology, nursing, occupational therapy, physical therapy, and physician's assistant studies); pre–health professions (chiropractic medicines, dentistry, medicine, optometry, pharmacy, podiatry, public health, and veterinary science); prelaw; preministry; psychology; public administration; religion; secondary education (biology, chemistry, communication, earth and space science, English, French, general science, German, mathematics, physics, social studies, and Spanish); social work; sociology; and theater (performing arts management and theater performance).

Academic Programs

Designed to foster individual responsibility, Juniata's flexible and academically rigorous program allows both acquisition of a broad range of knowledge and in-depth examination of a particular field. Almost 50 percent of the students attending Juniata develop their own program through a flexible program of emphasis (POE).

Students must satisfactorily complete 120 semester credit hours. Writing, computer and bibliographic skills, and the transition to college are addressed in the freshman year. Graduation requirements also include a two-course cultural analysis sequence, advanced communication/writing skills, quantitative studies, social sciences, humanities, international, fine arts, and natural sciences and an optional service learning component. In addition, all students complete a 45–60 credit POE, and many choose to complete an integrative senior project to graduate with distinction.

Many students include independent study and independent research in their POEs. Although not required, 87 percent of students participate in internships. The Juniata College Center for International Education provides excellent study-abroad opportunities that are taken advantage of by approximately 40 percent of the junior class. Experiences include summer, semester, and year-long opportunities.

Academic Facilities

Juniata's academic programs are complemented by up-to-date technology, labs, and bibliographic resources. In addition to the College's academic computer center, the campus has high-tech classroom/laboratory and computer labs devoted specifically to business, education, psychology, and world languages. The College supports the Juniata Center for Entrepreneurial Leadership (JCEL), a unique opportunity for students of all academic areas to pursue developing their own business. JCEL provides students with hands-on experience in every aspect of entrepreneurial endeavors. A human interaction lab offers students the opportunity to study communication and group interaction. In addition, the College has a distance learning and teleconferencing facility, multimedia classrooms, and a teaching and learning technology center (Solutions Center) for both student and faculty member use. The Solutions Center was designed to give faculty members and students the resources for utilizing advanced technology in their course work and presentations. The William J. von Liebig Center for Science is a $20-million facility that provides state-of-the-art facilities for teaching and learning in chemistry and biology. The Brumbaugh Academic Center houses the business, communications, computer science, environmental sciences, information technology, mathematics, and physical sciences departments.

For research projects, students in the natural sciences use laboratories equipped with sophisticated instrumentation typically reserved for graduate students. Juniata's Raystown Field Station serves as an ecology, zoology, and environmental science laboratory. The field station recently expanded facilities to allow students to live and learn at an on-site field laboratory. Juniata's Beeghly Library provides the College with an online public-access catalog that is accessible campuswide and an extensive CD-ROM network.

Costs

For 2008–09, the general fee is approximately $38,720, with tuition costs of $30,300, and room, board, and fee costs of $8420. Several special and occasional fees of $30–$300 for laboratory or studio use are also required.

Financial Aid

The Juniata College Office of Student Financial Planning is committed to building relationships with families striving to meet the long-term investment needs associated with quality education. Juniata succeeds by maximizing available assistance opportunities from Juniata programs as well as state and federal government programs in the form of grants, loans, and work-study initiatives. The College's commitment includes scholarship and loan programs. Juniata's Academic Scholarship Program offers aggressive scholarship programs designed to recognize and reward academic achievement. Students who exhibit promise of future success may be eligible for academic awards ranging from $8000 to full tuition, room, and board. Students who wish to be considered for Nomination Scholarships should have their admission applications postmarked no later than January 4 of their senior year.

Juniata representatives work with each family, matching their individual circumstances to all applicable aid programs. For need-based aid, individual plans are developed using the Free Application for Federal Student Aid (FAFSA) as the basis for determining need. The results of the FAFSA needs analysis should reach Juniata by March 1.

Faculty

Juniata has 99 full-time and 31 part-time faculty members, of whom 91 percent hold a doctoral or terminal degree in their field. The student-faculty ratio is 13:1. Although faculty members engage in numerous scholarly pursuits and maintain professional ties to their academic fields, they consider teaching and advising their primary functions.

Student Government

Juniata seeks to provide an environment within which students can mature intellectually, socially, and personally in a manner consistent with academic programs. In campus life as well as in the classroom, many opportunities for growth and self-exploration exist. Students have a voice—and in most cases a vote—in all essential areas of campus governance.

Admission Requirements

Juniata seeks students who show strong academic promise, motivation, and maturity. The College seeks a wide geographic representation and a variety of cultural, social, and economic backgrounds. Selection is made without regard to race, sex, religion, creed, color, handicap, or the ability to afford a private college education. Careful consideration is given to the academic record, test results, and personal qualities of applicants. Applicants should have completed a minimum of sixteen college-preparatory courses in mathematics, social studies, world language, and laboratory science. International student candidates may be required to submit TOEFL scores. Interviews and campus visits are strongly recommended.

Transfer students who have completed A.A. or A.S. requirements in an approved collegiate transfer program at an accredited community or junior college may enter Juniata with junior-class standing and receive transfer credit for two years of course work. Students who transfer without a degree receive credit on a course-by-course basis. Students whose college has a formal transfer agreement with Juniata College should consult with their transfer coordinator to review requirements for that agreement. It is strongly recommended that transfer students have an interview.

Application and Information

Students may apply to Juniata after completion of their junior year in secondary school. A nonrefundable $30 fee must accompany the application. A complete secondary school transcript that indicates courses and grades (with a list of senior courses, if required) must be sent from the applicant's guidance office along with SAT or ACT scores or SAT Alternative Program, an essay, and a letter of recommendation. An on-campus interview is highly recommended but not required. Transfer students must complete the normal application requirements and submit an official transcript from each college previously attended.

Candidates for freshman admission can choose from three application deadlines: Early Decision, Early Action, and Regular Decision.

Early Decision is designed for students who believe that Juniata College is their first choice. The early decision application deadline is December 1 of the student's senior year in secondary school, with notification no later than December 31. The student is asked to complete Juniata's institutional aid form in order to receive an early financial planning award. Students are required to submit a nonrefundable $300 matriculation deposit by February 24.

Early Action allows students to apply and get a response earlier than Regular Decision while still adhering to the May 1 deposit deadline. The Early Action application deadline is January 1 of the student's senior year, with notification of a decision by January 31. Financial aid award packages are determined after the Free Application for Federal Student Aid (FAFSA) has been completed. (Juniata's FAFSA Code is 003279.) Students should fill out the FAFSA form as soon as possible after January 1 of their senior year in order to have it completed by the March 1 deadline.

The Regular Decision application deadline is March 15 of the student's senior year. First notification for Regular Decision begins February 28. As with Early Action applicants, financial award packages are determined after the FAFSA has been completed. Students should fill out the FAFSA form as soon as possible after January 1 of their senior year in order to have it completed by the March 1 deadline

Juniata accepts applications for transfer admission for either the spring or fall semesters. The application due date for fall applicants is June 1; the due date for spring applicants is December 1. It is to the student's benefit to submit all application materials before the due date. Juniata's transfer admission policy is rolling. In most cases, transfer students receive an admission decision within one month of receipt of all credentials. Necessary credentials include an essay, a statement of interest, a secondary school transcript, SAT or ACT scores, and college transcripts.

Application forms and additional information may be obtained from:

Enrollment Center
Juniata College
1700 Moore Street
Huntingdon, Pennsylvania 16652
Phone: 814-641-3420
877-JUNIATA (877-586-4282, toll-free)
Fax: 814-641-3100
E-mail: admissions@juniata.edu
Web site: http://www.juniata.edu/

On the campus of Juniata College.

COLLEGE DATA CENTER • PENNSYLVANIA

KEYSTONE COLLEGE

LA PLUME, PENNSYLVANIA

The College

Keystone College was founded in 1868 as Keystone Academy in La Plume, Pennsylvania. Initially opened as the only high school between Binghamton, New York, and Scranton, Pennsylvania, Keystone flourished as a secondary school for more than sixty-five years. Rechartered as Scranton-Keystone Junior College in 1934 and then Keystone Junior College in 1944, the College served as one of the premier two-year institutions in the Northeast until 1995. In this year the school was again renamed, as Keystone College, and began its tenure as an "ideal" four-year degree-granting college. Keystone College has a current enrollment of 1,700, including students from fourteen states and seven countries. Students can choose from over forty programs of study.

Location

Located at the foot of the Endless Mountains in northeastern Pennsylvania, the 270-acre campus is both scenic and historic, with buildings dating back to 1870. Located 13 miles from Scranton, Pennsylvania, the campus offers easy access to major East Coast cities, including New York, Philadelphia, and Baltimore.

Majors and Degrees

The Bachelor of Arts degree is offered in communications and visual arts. The Bachelor of Science degree is offered in accounting; biology, with tracks in the medical professions; business; criminal justice, with a track in prelaw; early childhood education; elementary education; environmental biology; environmental resource management; forensic biology; information technology; organizational leadership; social sciences; sport and recreation management; teaching: art education; teaching: child and society; teaching: math education; and teaching: social studies education.

Postbaccalaureate certification is available in elementary education, early childhood education, teaching: art education (K–12), teaching: math education, and teaching: social studies education.

Associate of Applied Science degrees are offered in accounting, culinary arts, hotel and restaurant management, and information technology. The Associate in Fine Arts is offered in art. The Associate in Arts is offered in communications, forest/resource management, landscape architecture, liberal studies, liberal studies–education emphasis, and wildlife biology. The Associate in Science is offered in biology; business; criminal justice; early childhood education; health sciences with emphasis in medical technology, nursing/cytotechnology, occupational therapy/respiratory care, and radiotherapy/medical imaging/cardiac perfusion; and sport and recreation management. In addition, there are one-year programs in Cisco, forestry technology, Microsoft Certified Systems Administrator, Microsoft Certified Systems Engineer, and pre–major studies (undeclared major).

Academic Programs

The College runs on a two-semester schedule (fall and spring) and has night and weekend classes available. The number of credit hours required to earn a degree is dependent on the field of study chosen, and students must have attained a minimum cumulative GPA of 2.0. Every student must complete a set of general core curriculum requirements as well as the courses specific to his or her major course of study. Depending on their course of study, students may be required to complete an internship or co-op before graduation.

Students have the opportunity to participate in both the Army and Navy ROTC programs in conjunction with other local participating institutions. There are opportunities for double majors as well as minors in various fields of study.

Academic Facilities

The Harry K. Miller Library is available on campus to all students. This facility offers standard print and online research opportunities. The Hibbard Campus Center is the setting for the student cafeteria, a full-service restaurant, The Chef's Table (a student-run restaurant), as well as a U.S. post office, a print shop, a student-run radio station (WKCV), and reception halls. The campus also boasts an art gallery, a celestial observatory, early childhood center, career development center, theater, and the Poinsard Greenhouse. Keystone College also serves as the home for the Urban Forestry Center, Willary Water Discovery Center, and the Countryside Conservancy.

There are more than 120 computers available on campus for general student use, and both the Internet and campus network can be accessed from all residence halls and most buildings on campus.

Costs

Tuition and fees for Keystone College for the 2006–07 academic year are $17,144, while room and board costs are $8,400. Books and general supplies average $500 per semester and vary according to major.

Financial Aid

The Financial Aid Office provides adequate funds and resources to meet the financial needs of students from all income categories. In fact, 88 percent of incoming freshmen receive financial aid. Scholarships are awarded based on merit, academic performance, and extracurricular involvement. Keystone College also participates in the following federally sponsored programs: Federal Perkins Loan, Federal Pell Grant, Federal Supplemental Educational Opportunity Grant (FSEOG), Federal PLUS Loan, and Federal Stafford Student Loan. The College also offers college employment programs to students and alternative loans as well as state grants and Keystone grants. In order to be considered for financial aid, students must complete the Free Application for Federal Student Aid (FAFSA). Keystone's financial aid code is 003280.

Faculty

The student-faculty ratio is 13:1, and the average class size is 22 students. Counseling is available for academic, personal, and vocational issues. Keystone College is supported by strong interpersonal relationships among its students and faculty and staff members. All faculty members post regular office hours and are generally available outside of these hours.

Student Government

Student Senate is the central governing body of all student government organizations on the campus. It serves as the liaison between the student body and the College administration. Members of Student Senate are chosen by their peers and are responsible for improving and maintaining student life both on and off campus. Students may choose from more than twenty-five different clubs and organizations, including those with academic, service-oriented, and social interests.

Admission Requirements

Keystone accepts qualified students regardless of race, religion, handicap, or national origin, and admissions are on a rolling basis. Admission is based on prior academic performance and the ability of the applicant to profit from and contribute to the academic, interpersonal, and extracurricular life of the College. Keystone considers applicants who meet the following criteria: graduation from an approved secondary school or the equivalent (with official transcripts), satisfactory scores on the SAT or ACT, one letter of recommendation, essay, and evidence of potential for successful college achievement. All students are strongly encouraged to visit the campus for a personal interview with the admissions staff and a member of the faculty from the student's area of interest. Students applying to the art and teaching–art education programs are required to participate in a portfolio interview.

Transfer students in good academic and financial standing at their current institution are also encouraged to apply to Keystone. Transfer students should contact the Office of Admissions and may be required to submit either high school transcripts or transcripts from each college attended or both.

Admissions decisions are made within two weeks from the day all required materials are received in the Office of Admissions.

Application and Information

Students wishing to be considered for admission must submit an application and a $25 processing fee, along with official high school transcripts, college transcripts (if applicable), a letter of recommendation from someone other than a friend or relative, essay, and scores from either the SAT or ACT (submitted directly to the Office of Admissions; Keystone's CEEB code numbers are 2351 for the SAT, 2602 for the ACT).

Applications and any additional information about Keystone College may be obtained by contacting:

Office of Admissions
Keystone College
One College Green
La Plume, Pennsylvania 18440
Phone: 570-945-8111
800-824-2764 Option 1 (toll-free)
E-mail: admissions@keystone.edu
Web site: http://www.keystone.edu

Students on the campus of Keystone College.

KING'S COLLEGE
WILKES-BARRE, PENNSYLVANIA

The College

King's College is an independent, coed, four-year, Catholic college with 2,400 students. Founded by the Holy Cross Fathers and Brothers of the University of Notre Dame in 1946, King's prepares students for a purposeful life with an education that integrates the human values inherent in a broadly based liberal arts curriculum. The College encourages the religious, moral, personal, and social development of its students.

In addition to the undergraduate degrees, King's College offers a Master of Science (M.S.) degree, a Master of Education (M.Ed.) degree (with a concentration in reading), and a five-year physician assistant studies program leading to a master's degree.

Academic advising begins before students enroll and continues with an innovative program of career development across the curriculum. King's Academic Skills Center includes a nationally certified tutoring program and a faculty-staffed writing center. More than 80 percent of King's first-year students return for their sophomore year. Over 70 percent of students who attend King's graduate from the College, which is well above the national average, and 99 percent are employed or attend graduate school within six months of graduation.

Campus features include the Charles E. and Mary Parente Life Sciences Center, the Mulligan Physical Sciences Center, the William G. McGowan School of Business, and Robert L. Betzler Fields, a 33.5-acre athletic complex that includes a field house and fields for baseball, softball, men's and women's soccer, football, and field hockey. The 15-acre campus also includes Monarch Court; the Sheehy-Farmer Campus Center, which includes an art gallery, an outdoor waterfall, a student restaurant, and marketplace dining; the J. Carroll McCormick Campus Ministry Center; and the William S. Scandlon Physical Education Center, which includes a 3,200-seat basketball arena, wrestling facilities, racquetball and handball courts, an Olympic-size swimming pool, a rifle range, and a state-of-the-art sports medicine facility. The College also has a 5,000-square-foot weight room, with more than 13,000 pounds of free weights, that is approved by the American Weightlifting Federation, and a strength and fitness center. The Student Health Center is located in Hafey-Marian Hall, a modern six-story building housing classrooms and faculty offices, and a consulting physician is on call at all times. The six-story administration and science buildings form a unit that houses the College's theater, a cafeteria, administrative offices, science laboratories, and classrooms. Residence halls have cable television, Internet access, 24-hour computer labs, and individual phone service in the rooms.

More than forty student organizations provide King's students with the opportunity to explore interests outside the classroom. Student athletics include intercollegiate competition in men's baseball, basketball, football, golf, lacrosse, soccer, swimming, tennis, and wrestling; women's basketball, field hockey, lacrosse, soccer, softball, swimming, tennis, and volleyball; and coed cross-country. Club sports include cheerleading and ice hockey. Intramural sports include basketball, bowling, field hockey, flag football, racquetball, softball, street hockey, and volleyball. Other cocurricular activities include academic clubs in almost every department, the King's Players (theater), the nationally ranked debate team, Cantores Christi Regis, Campus Ministry, the Experiencing the Arts Series, *The Crown* (student newspaper), the *Regis* (yearbook), and *SCOP* (literary magazine).

Location

The King's campus is located in a residential area near downtown Wilkes-Barre, Pennsylvania, a city of approximately 50,000 on the banks of the Susquehanna River. A growing city, Wilkes-Barre has developed both economically and culturally, yet it has avoided many typical urban problems. The crime rate in the city is one of the lowest in the nation. Local events include the Cherry Blossom Festival, a national ice carving competition, and the Fine Arts Fiesta. Shopping malls, multiplex theaters, parks, art galleries, and restaurants are nearby. Two blocks from King's is the F. M. Kirby Center, which has hosted national performances, music groups, traveling theater, and more. National recording acts regularly perform in nearby venues.

King's is a short drive from several ski resorts, state parks, and major lakes, as well as the stadium of the New York Yankees' AAA baseball team, the Pocono International Raceway, and the Wachovia Arena, which is home to the Pittsburgh Penguins' minor-league ice hockey team and features regular concerts and is the site of the King's commencement. New York City and Philadelphia are within a 2½-hour drive; Harrisburg, Pennsylvania, and Morristown, New Jersey, are within 2 hours; and New England and Washington, D.C., are within 4 hours.

Majors and Degrees

King's awards Bachelor of Arts, Bachelor of Science, Associate in Arts, and Associate in Science degrees. The College's thirty-five major programs are offered in the arts and sciences and the William G. McGowan School of Business, which is accredited by AACSB International–The Association to Advance Collegiate Schools of Business.

Arts and sciences include the humanities and social sciences division (computers and information systems, criminal justice, economics, English-literature, English–professional writing, French, history, mass communication, philosophy, political science, psychology, sociology, Spanish, theater, and theology); the education division (early childhood, elementary, secondary certification, and special education), which is a candidate for NCATE accreditation; the science division (biology, chemistry, computer science, environmental science, environmental studies, general science, mathematics, and neuroscience); and the allied health division (clinical lab science, physician assistant studies, and athletics training education/sports medicine accredited by CAAHEP). Available majors in the William G. McGowan School of Business are accounting, business administration, finance, human resource management, international business, and marketing. King's offers preprofessional programs in chiropractic, dentistry, law, medicine, optometry, pharmacy, and veterinary science.

Academic Programs

The general education program at King's is recognized nationwide by its peers. King's is included in *Barron's Best Buys in College Education* and fourteen consecutive issues of *U.S. News & World Report*'s *Best Colleges Guide.* The College was also recognized by the John Templeton Foundation Honor Roll for Character-Building Colleges and is one of sixteen institutions nationwide named to the Greater Expectations initiative. The core curriculum is recognized as a model curriculum. It incorporates traditional and new concepts in liberal arts education, develops competence in such areas as communications and problem solving, and measures students' progress throughout the program.

The honors program offers highly motivated students the challenge of learning in discussion-centered courses that explore distinctive subject matter with exciting and innovative approaches. Sixteen honor societies encourage students to excel in their chosen fields and recognize students for their academic distinction; members are honored each year at the All-College Honors Convocation. Science students receive hands-on lab training much earlier than students at other institutions and work together with faculty members on real-world research projects.

Off-Campus Programs

Experiential learning (via internships) is available in conjunction with almost every major. Placement possibilities include CNN, the New York Stock Exchange, PricewaterhouseCoopers, the Pennsylvania Department of Education, the Pennsylvania State House of Representatives, the U.S. House of Representatives, U.S. Senators' offices, the U.S. Department of Energy, Walt Disney World, and Xerox Corporation. Every year students are placed with local, regional, and national companies around the globe.

The International Internship Program and Study-Abroad Program are also options for King's students who work in a variety of professions. Many of King's students have studied on campuses throughout Europe, Thailand, China, and Australia.

Academic Facilities

King's facilities include the 51,000-square-foot, three-story D. Leonard Corgan Library, which contains several study rooms, a 100-seat auditorium, and a 160,000-volume collection accessed by a computerized catalog. The library uses its affiliation with the Online Computer Library Center to provide students and faculty members with access to college and research libraries throughout the United States. The library provides full-text databases from every computer on campus. Students and faculty members have direct access to more than 1 million volumes through the local library cooperative (NEPBC).

King's features computer labs with more than 440 PCs; 24-hour labs in residence halls; e-mail accounts for all students; computerized library databases; multimedia classrooms with a variety of instructional aids; course discussions on electronic bulletin boards and chats via e-mail outside of the traditional classroom; a technology component of the core curriculum that requires all students to learn to access, process, and develop their own computer and information presentation skills; distance learning facilities for teleconferencing; satellite down-link capabilities in the 220-seat Burke Auditorium of the William G. McGowan School of Business; and cross-registration with area colleges that enables students to take courses complementary to their majors.

The $6.4-million Charles E. and Mary Parente Life Sciences Center, which contains a molecular biology laboratory and a genomics center, includes computer facilities, instrumentation rooms, a rooftop greenhouse, and environmental chambers. The $6-million Mulligan Physical Sciences Center includes modern research laboratories, computer facilities, and state-of-the-art instrumentation used for molecular identification.

Costs

For the 2007–08 academic year, tuition for full-time students was $23,720. Room and board totaled $8950.

Financial Aid

King's assists all qualified students through its financial aid programs. Currently, more than 95 percent of King's students currently receive financial aid in the form of scholarships, grants, work-study, or loans. Aid is awarded on the basis of demonstrated financial need, the difference between the total cost of education and the expected family contribution. Usually, a combination of financial aid sources and types are used in a student's financial aid package. Of all financial aid awarded to its students, grants and scholarships funded by King's comprise approximately 40 percent of the total aid awarded.

In addition to financial aid programs, installment payment plans are available, offering students and/or their families the ability to make monthly payments throughout the academic year. Students who wish to be considered for financial aid must fill out the Free Application for Federal Student Aid (FAFSA) and the King's College Financial Aid Application. The preferred filing deadline for new freshmen is February 15. Forms are mailed to students accepted for admission but can be completed prior to acceptance.

Faculty

King's College has 125 full-time and 83 part-time faculty members. Eighty-one percent of the full-time faculty members have a Ph.D. or an equivalent terminal degree. Graduate assistants do not teach courses. The student-faculty ratio is 13:1.

Student Government

The student government coordinates and participates in numerous activities for both the student body and the surrounding community. It regularly holds open forums for students and senior administrators at the College, coordinates informal socials for the students with the College president, and makes presentations at each meeting of the Board of Directors. In addition, the student government sponsors events that foster awareness for social and justice issues and a celebration of cultural diversity. Community projects, which incorporate a strong service component, include CitySERVE, National Collegiate Alcohol Awareness Week, and fund-raisers for the United Way. The Association for Campus Events, a student-operated organization, also sponsors comedians, movies, and performers throughout the year.

Admission Requirements

King's encourages applications from qualified high school students and those who wish to transfer from another institution. To be considered for admission, students must be prepared to pursue successfully a program of study at the College, as evidenced by the quality of previous academic and extracurricular performance, the recommendation of school officials and character references, and the student's display of personal promise, maturity, and motivation. King's admits students of any race, sex, color, creed, or national or ethnic origin.

Admission decisions are made for both high school students and transfer students with the understanding that all current courses and examinations will be completed satisfactorily. Candidates should complete four years of mathematics (through trigonometry or precalculus). One year of high school chemistry and biology and physics is also strongly recommended.

The Office of Admission offers two methods for candidates to apply for admission: the SAT/ACT Traditional Choice and the Standardized Test Option/Essay Choice. Applicants are required to state their preference prior to the application review, and the decision is nonreversible. Students who select the SAT/ACT Traditional Choice must submit a completed application, official high school transcripts, SAT or ACT scores, guidance counselor recommendation, an essay, and the $30 application fee. Students who choose the Standardized Test Option/Essay Choice must submit a completed application, official high school transcripts, an official graded writing sample from either their junior or senior year—submitted and notarized by the high school guidance office, guidance counselor recommendation, an essay, and the $30 application fee.

Application and Information

Applicants should forward a completed application and the $30 fee to the Office of Admission or apply online at http://www.kings.edu. Secondary and postsecondary (if applicable) transcripts must be sent. Admission decisions are not made until all credentials are received. King's subscribes to a rolling admission policy. Decisions are announced within two weeks from the date of application. Upon notification of acceptance, a $200 nonrefundable deposit is requested to reserve a place in the class. The deposit deadline is May 1 but may be extended upon request. To schedule an interview, obtain an application form, or for more information, students should contact:

Office of Admission
King's College
133 North River Street
Wilkes-Barre, Pennsylvania 18711
Phone: 570-208-5858
888-KINGS-PA (toll-free)
E-mail: admissions@kings.edu
Web site: http://www.kings.edu

KUTZTOWN UNIVERSITY OF PENNSYLVANIA

KUTZTOWN, PENNSYLVANIA

The University

In an independent survey, 93 percent of students and recent alumni rated their education at Kutztown University (KU) as excellent or good in regard to their overall college experience, the quality of instruction they received, and the quality of the faculty. KU offers excellent academic programs through its undergraduate Colleges of Liberal Arts and Sciences, Visual and Performing Arts, Business, and Education and through its graduate studies program. A wide range of student support services complements the high-quality classroom instruction.

Students have the advantage of a well-rounded program of athletic, cultural, and social events at KU. There are clubs, organizations, and activities to satisfy nearly every taste. Currently, more than 10,000 full- and part-time students are enrolled at the University. About half of the full-time undergraduates live in residence halls; the rest live at home in nearby communities.

Kutztown University's attractive 330-acre campus includes a mix of old and new buildings, including stately Old Main, the historic building known to generations of Kutztown's students; University Place, a modern residence hall in a courtyard setting; and the McFarland Student Union. The new Student Recreation Center opened in fall 2006, and the state-of-the-art Academic Forum opened in January 2007. In fall 2008, renovations of the Sharadin Arts Building are planned to be completed and a new 865-bed suite-style residence hall is slated for opening.

In addition to its undergraduate program, the University's graduate program awards master's degrees in a number of fields. The Master of Science is awarded in computer and information science and electronic media. The Master of Arts is awarded in counseling psychology and English. The Master of Education is awarded in art education, elementary education, elementary school counseling (certification and licensure), instructional technology, reading specialist, secondary education (with specializations), secondary school counseling (certification and licensure), and student affairs in higher education (administration and college counseling licensure). The Master of Library Science, Master of Business Administration, Master of Public Administration, and Master of Social Work are also awarded.

Location

The University is located in a beautiful, rural Pennsylvania Dutch community, midway between the cities of Allentown and Reading. Both cities are a short drive from the campus and have major shopping and recreational facilities. Kutztown borough, an easy walk from the campus, has ample stores and shops to meet the needs of students. Philadelphia is about 1½ hours away and New York City, about 2½ hours.

Majors and Degrees

Undergraduate degrees are offered in a wide variety of fields. The Bachelor of Arts is awarded in anthropology, English, French, geography, history, music, philosophy, political science, sociology, Spanish, speech communication, and theater. The Bachelor of Fine Arts is awarded in communication design, crafts, and studio art. The Bachelor of Science is awarded in art education, biology, biochemistry, chemistry, computer and information science, criminal justice, electronic media, environmental science, geology, leisure and sport studies, library science, marine science, mathematics, medical technology, music education, physics, pre-engineering (with Penn State), psychology, and public administration. The Bachelor of Science in Business Administration is awarded in accounting, finance, general business, international business, management, and marketing. The Bachelor of Science in Education is awarded in elementary education, with concentrations in coaching education, early childhood development, English, French, German, instructional technology, mathematics, psychology, reading, science, social studies, Spanish, and urban education; in secondary education, with specializations in biological science, chemistry, citizenship, communications, earth and space science, English, French, German, general science, mathematics, physics, physics and mathematics, social sciences, social studies, and Spanish; in special education, with concentrations in mentally/physically handicapped and visually impaired; and in library science. The Bachelor of Social Work also is awarded, and there is a B.S.N. completion program for registered nurses. The four most popular majors are criminal justice, communication design, psychology, and elementary education. The most popular minors are psychology and public relations.

Academic Programs

The University observes a two-semester calendar, and first-semester examinations are completed by mid-December. A minimum of 120 semester hours and a cumulative quality point average (QPA) of at least 2.0 are required for graduation. In the College of Liberal Arts and Sciences and College of Business, a quality point average of at least 2.0 in the major is also required.

Students seeking admission to teacher education must complete a three-stage process. (1) Applicants must have a projected grade point average (PGPA) of at least 2.2. Students with less than a 2.2 PGPA may be granted admission to their second-choice major and can reapply to the education program once they earn a minimum QPA of 3.0. (2) Once admitted to the major and by the fourth semester (or after completing 64 semester hours), applicants must present evidence of 30 hours of classroom observation. They must also achieve at least a 3.0 overall average, pass a speech screening test, and complete basic speech, mathematics, English composition, EDU 100, student teaching, and professional education courses, as determined by each major, with a minimum grade of C. (3) Prior to student teaching, applicants must complete a professional semester or early field experience, have achieved at least a 3.0 GPA as well as a 3.0 QPA in all courses in the major required for student teaching, and be recommended by the department screening committee. Students are required to pass the National Teachers Examination (three core batteries and a specialty area) at the end of their academic program before the Pennsylvania Department of Education will issue an Instructional I (Probationary) Certificate.

The distinctive University Honors Program is available to qualified students in all areas of study. Freshmen who have been identified as potential honors students based on their high school records and SAT scores, transfer students from other honors programs, and incumbent students who have at least a 3.25 GPA are invited to enroll in the program. The 21 semester hours in honors work, which include a senior thesis project, count toward the 120 hours required for graduation. Honors students select specially designed courses, independent study, and internships. The honors program awards several merit-based scholarships, and students who complete the program receive an honors diploma upon graduation.

Kutztown University and the Colleges of Engineering and Earth and Mineral Studies of Penn State University cooperate in a 3-2 program in liberal arts and engineering. Three years or the equivalent are spent at Kutztown University, where the student takes liberal arts courses along with pre-engineering courses. Upon satisfactory completion of this program and recommendation by the faculty, the student enters Penn State and fulfills the specified course requirements. Successful completion of these programs leads to appropriate baccalaureate degrees from both institutions.

Kutztown University provides an opportunity for higher education for students who, because of economic need, cultural disadvantage, or inadequate preparation, have previously been unable to attend college. Students admitted to the University under the Developmental Summer Program attend a preparatory program designed to introduce them to university study and to provide supportive services in counseling and tutoring as well as special instruction in study skills, reading, and writing.

Off-Campus Programs

Students majoring in education spend one semester of their senior year student teaching in area schools under the guidance of an experienced teacher. Additional teaching field experiences are available in the junior year during the "professional semester." Internships in other programs provide students with one semester of practical experience in their specialty. For example, political science students may work in local, state, or federal government agencies; psychology students in area psychiatric hospitals, clinics, and rehabilitation centers; social welfare and criminal justice students in various social agencies; electronic media students in commercial or public broadcasting, cable television, and industrial, medical, or institutional television; and medical technology students in area hospitals.

The University has exchange and study-abroad programs with colleges and universities in fourteen countries. In addition, through the International Student Exchange Program, KU students may study for a year in any of sixty institutions in twenty-seven countries. Kutztown is now in its eighth year of a cooperative program with the Diplomatic Academy of the Russian Foreign Ministry, Moscow, in which prominent Russian scholars and foreign affairs experts visit KU to meet with classes and give public lectures. KU also has cooperative programs with institutions in England, Germany, the Netherlands, Hungary, Italy, Spain, and China.

Through consortium arrangements with colleges and universities in three states, Kutztown participates in the operation of a marine science research center at Wallops Island, Virginia, which has laboratories, research equipment, and coastal research ships. Through this facility, students in marine science classes are able to gain firsthand knowledge of the ocean environment. The University's participation in the Pennsylvania Consortium for International Education provides opportunities for study abroad during the summer.

Academic Facilities

The Rohrbach Library is a modern facility that provides many attractive and functional areas that greatly enhance the learning environment for all students. Its technologies are state-of-the-art, and it is the first completely wireless building on the campus. In addition to the 500 computer connection points that were installed when the building was expanded in 1998, students may bring their own laptops to access the Web or use one of the 100 that are available for circulation. The library has both Macintosh and PC public-access computers throughout the building. The library has more than 500,000 books and bound periodicals, subscriptions to 1,308 current periodicals and newspapers, access to 14,344 electronic full-text journals, and more than 1 million microform units. Electronic access to these library materials is provided through the online catalog, Quincy, and the library's Web page, which provides students with easy access to all of its resources and links them to electronic resources available throughout the world. The map collection is one of the finest in Pennsylvania, with 40,379 sheets, and includes Braille maps, city plans, and geographic and raised-relief maps.

The Audiovisual Center maintains a comprehensive collection of more than 15,000 items, including microcomputer software, films, filmstrips, videocassettes, records, audiocassettes, digital cameras, projectors, and laptops, that circulate to students. The Curriculum Materials Center provides preservice and in-service teachers with current teaching and learning resources and includes one of the most coveted collections of children's literature in the country. Supplementing this collection is the Dornish Collection, which features first-edition signed books from top writers in the children's literature field. Kutztown's resources are supplemented by a traditional interlibrary loan service, a rapid document delivery service, and a direct borrowing system (PALCI) that links students with the collections of more than forty academic libraries in the state of Pennsylvania.

Other resources include a modern science complex, an astronomical observatory and planetarium, a seismic observatory, the Sharadin Art Gallery, a television studio, a modern language laboratory, and a speech clinic.

All residence hall rooms are wired for Internet usage, and multistation computer labs are available in buildings across the campus.

Costs

In 2007–08, tuition was $5177 for Pennsylvania residents and $12,944 for out-of-state residents. The average cost of room and board for an incoming freshman was $6500. Fees were $1695 for Pennsylvania residents and $1784.70 for out-of-state residents. (Books, travel expenses, and other supplies are additional.)

Financial Aid

KU believes that no student who is eligible to enroll at the University should be denied the opportunity for an education solely because of lack of funds. Financial assistance is available through grants, private and institutional scholarships, military officer training programs, on-campus part-time employment, and loans. A booklet describing financial aid opportunities may be obtained by writing to the Director of Financial Aid. Any student wishing to investigate financial aid opportunities should do so when applying for admission, as most programs have application deadlines. The only form needed to apply for financial aid is the FAFSA. KU has a priority filing date of February 15. Pennsylvania residents should file the FAFSA no later than May 1 to qualify for Pennsylvania state grants.

Faculty

Although many professors at KU are involved in important research and are leaders in their fields, their primary interest is in the classroom. The University has more than 320 full-time instructors and a favorable 19:1 student-faculty ratio. The average class size is 29. Upon enrollment in the University, each student is assigned a faculty adviser to help plan their academic career. Many faculty members are active in campus groups as members or advisers, creating a close and friendly working relationship with students.

Student Government

All students are members of the Student Government Association and elect representatives who form the Student Government Board (SGB). Students at Kutztown are regarded as mature individuals who can be, in great measure, responsible for the control of their own environment. For that reason, the SGB exercises considerable discretion in coordinating and funding student organizations. Most University committees, including the Council of Trustees, have student members with full voting rights.

Admission Requirements

The main criteria for admission are achievement as indicated on scholastic records and standardized and aptitude tests. Candidates must have graduated from an approved secondary school or demonstrate equivalent preparation. Scores on either the SAT or the ACT are required and are regarded as evidence of ability to do university-level work. It is the responsibility of the applicant to request that his or her scores be forwarded to the Admissions Office. Either test should be taken no later than the fall of the senior year; sitting for these exams during the junior year is encouraged. For admission to a special curriculum, the candidate may be required to take an appropriate aptitude test or to supply additional evidence of ability to succeed in the given field. Specific requirements and instructions are included in the admission application materials.

Application and Information

The completed application and all other required materials must be mailed to the Director of Admissions. No action is taken by the Admission Committee until all necessary steps have been completed. For additional information and application forms, students should contact:

Dr. William Stahler
Director of Admissions
Kutztown University of Pennsylvania
Kutztown, Pennsylvania 19530
Phone: 610-683-4060
E-mail: admission@kutztown.edu
Web site: http://www.kutztown.edu/admissions

LAFAYETTE COLLEGE

EASTON, PENNSYLVANIA

The College

Lafayette is classified as one of the nation's most academically competitive colleges and is committed to providing the best undergraduate education in the liberal arts, sciences, and engineering for men and women who can benefit most from the Lafayette experience. The current undergraduate enrollment is 2,300. Students from thirty-nine states and forty-one other countries currently attend Lafayette. They represent a wide range of interests, special talents, and aspirations. The College draws strength from the diversity of its students.

Primarily residential in nature, Lafayette guarantees on-campus housing to all students who choose to take advantage of the varied living options available to them. More than 96 percent of the students live on the 110-acre main campus in single-sex or coeducational residence halls, social residence halls, fraternities, or sororities, and another 2 percent live close to the campus. An array of student organizations, cultural events, social opportunities, and varsity and intramural sports programs are available to all students.

Recent trends indicate that approximately two thirds of Lafayette graduates go on to obtain a graduate or professional degree. About 20 percent pursue full-time graduate or professional study immediately. A large and growing number obtain practical experience through employment and then undertake full-time study for an advanced degree, often with an employer's financial support. Others continue academic pursuits on a part-time basis.

Location

Lafayette is located in a picturesque setting atop a hill overlooking the Delaware and Lehigh Rivers and Easton, a progressive city of 30,000. Allentown and Bethlehem are located near Easton, and, together with the city and adjacent areas, they make up the Lehigh Valley, the third-largest metropolitan area in Pennsylvania. Various business establishments that serve the needs of students are available near the campus and in downtown Easton. Beyond Easton to the west and north are rolling farmland, beautiful countryside, and the Pocono Mountains. New York City is 70 miles east of the campus and Philadelphia is 60 miles south.

Majors and Degrees

Lafayette awards the Bachelor of Science (B.S.) degree in the following fields: behavioral neuroscience, biochemistry, biology, chemical engineering, chemistry, civil engineering, computer science, electrical and computer engineering, geology, mathematics, mechanical engineering, physics, and psychology. The Bachelor of Arts (A.B.) degree is awarded in the following majors: American studies, anthropology and sociology, art, biochemistry, biology, chemistry, computer science, economics and business, engineering, English, French, geology, German, government and law, history, international affairs, mathematics, mathematics/economics, music, philosophy, physics, policy studies, psychology, religion, Russian and East European studies, and Spanish.

In addition, Lafayette students may enroll in a five-year program leading to either a B.S. and an A.B. or two B.S. degrees.

Academic Programs

Students work together one-on-one with faculty advisers to ensure the planning of a program that is both educationally sound and responsive to the student's individual interests and needs. Each academic department specifies core curriculum requirements for its majors. All A.B. candidates must satisfy a course-distribution requirement, which can be met through advanced placement, transfer credit, or a broad selection of college course work.

In combining arts, sciences, and engineering in one undergraduate institution and in having one faculty with a unified educational approach, Lafayette has a distinctive capability to exercise a broadening influence on all students. Approximately one half of Lafayette's students major in the humanities and social sciences, while the other half specialize in the natural sciences and engineering. Flexible curricular arrangements enable students to defer their final decision on a major until the end of the sophomore year.

In addition to the formal majors offered at the College, interdisciplinary minor programs are offered in ten areas: Black studies, classical civilization, East Asian studies, environmental science, ethical studies, health care and society, Jewish studies, Latin American and Caribbean studies, technology studies, and women's studies. A number of internships can also be arranged through the various academic departments.

Students planning to continue their study in a professional school are assisted by faculty preprofessional advisers in designing a program of study that provides an appropriate foundation for advanced work.

Army ROTC programs are offered for both men and women.

The College observes a two-semester academic calendar. An optional January interim session is offered. Classes are available on campus as well as off campus, including study overseas.

Off-Campus Programs

Students are encouraged to spend a semester or a year in a study-abroad program sponsored by the College or another institution. The College has recently established affiliations with four universities overseas. Groups of students led by Lafayette professors attend Vesalius College at the University of Brussels, l'Université de Bourgogne in Dijon, Middlesex University in London, the University College in London, and the Sweet Briar junior-year-abroad program in Paris.

Students also travel widely during the Lafayette interim session. Two faculty members have accompanied each group of students in their pursuit of knowledge in China, England, Germany, France, Israel, and Russia as well as in Eastern Europe and sub-Saharan Africa.

Lafayette is a member of the American Collegiate Consortium, an association of some sixty American colleges and universities that operates a prestigious study-abroad program at the Universities of Voronezh and Yaroslavl in Russia. Students may take a full semester of courses in the fields of their choice alongside Russian students.

Academic Facilities

The recently expanded $22-million Skillman Library contains more than 525,000 hardbound volumes as well as numerous pamphlets, periodicals, electronic databases, CD-ROMs, electronic journals, microfilms, audiovisual materials, and special collections. The library operates on an open-stack policy. Cooperative arrangements with other Lehigh Valley colleges make more than 1 million books available to Lafayette students.

Ten additional classroom, laboratory, and departmental buildings house specialized libraries, modern scientific and engineering equipment, studio rooms, galleries, classrooms, seminar rooms, and faculty offices.

The College's rapidly growing Academic Computing Services facilities include a campuswide network with connections in every residence hall, office, and classroom, and to more than 600 public microcomputers available for student use (many of them for 24 hours a day). At no charge, students can have access to e-mail and the Internet and to general and course software from the computing sites or from their rooms.

Costs

The comprehensive fee for 2007–08 was $33,634. Additional costs included a room fee of $6155, a board fee of $4222, and an estimated $1625 for books, travel, and miscellaneous expenses.

Financial Aid

Substantial amounts of financial aid are available for students with demonstrated need. Approximately 60 percent of the student body receives financial aid—more than 40 percent of Lafayette's students receive financial aid directly from the College in the form of grants, loans, and work opportunities and almost 20 percent are assisted by government grants or other awards not funded by the College. Detailed information regarding financial assistance is available from the Office of Student Financial Aid, Lafayette College, Easton, Pennsylvania 18042-1777 (phone: 610-330-5055). Each year, through the Marquis Scholars Program, Lafayette offers merit scholarships to 60 entering first-year students who have demonstrated academic excellence. Each recipient is awarded a minimum of $16,000 each year with a scholarship up to full need each year if need exceeds $16,000. In addition, 32 entering freshmen receive $8000 Trustee Scholarships.

Faculty

Of the College's 199 full-time faculty members, all hold a doctoral degree or the terminal degree in their fields. Many have earned wide recognition for their research and scholarship or have won awards for superior teaching. Some hold faculty chairs endowed to attract or retain professors of exceptional ability. Students benefit from a student-faculty ratio of about 11:1 and from the fact that all faculty members—full professors and heads of departments as well as junior faculty members—teach classes and advise students on an individual basis.

Student Government

Traditionally, students have contributed to major policy decisions at Lafayette. Student Government is responsible for formulating student activity policy, distributing funds to student organizations, and maintaining liaison with the Board of Trustees, the faculty, and the administration. Voting student members sit on four trustee committees and on almost all faculty committees, and student representatives participate in faculty meetings.

Admission Requirements

Lafayette admits students without regard to sex, race, religion, or physical handicap. All Lafayette students pursued a strong college-preparatory program of studies, and approximately one half graduated in the top tenth of their secondary school class. Many held leadership positions in school or community organizations or on sports teams. They are encouraged—and expected—to assume major responsibility for all aspects of their lives at the College and to continue to develop those attributes and talents on which their admission was based.

Students applying for admission to Lafayette College should submit the results of the SAT or the ACT (with writing). SAT Subject Test results are recommended but not required. A student may submit as few or as many Subject Test results as desired, and these tests may be taken in any subject. Some academic departments use scores from these tests for placement purposes. Students are strongly encouraged to visit the Lafayette campus for an admission interview and a student-guided tour.

Application and Information

Applications for admission should be filed by January 1. Candidates are notified of the admission decision around April 1. If a student requests consideration of their application under the Early Decision Plan, a decision is normally made within thirty days of receipt of completed application forms. February 15 is the deadline to request early decision. Applicants accepted under early decision are obligated to enroll at Lafayette unless their financial needs are not met.

Office of Admissions
Lafayette College
Easton, Pennsylvania 18042-1770
Phone: 610-330-5100
Web site: http://www.lafayette.edu

A view of Lafayette College's campus.

LA ROCHE COLLEGE

PITTSBURGH, PENNSYLVANIA

The College

La Roche College invites students to experience learning that brings their world together. International in dimension, La Roche College is a growing global community of learners offering an education that enables students to reach their potential in an atmosphere of support and encouragement. Students at the College number approximately 1,500 and come from across the nation and around the globe. In 2005, 2006, and 2007, the Princeton Review rated La Roche College as one of the nation's "Best Northeastern Colleges," a designation reserved for superior colleges and universities in eleven states and the District of Columbia.

Founded in 1963 by the Sisters of Divine Providence, La Roche is a Catholic, coeducational, international four-year institution and is fully accredited by the Middle States Association of Colleges and Schools. It is chartered by the Commonwealth of Pennsylvania, and its programs have been approved by the Pennsylvania Department of Education. The College holds memberships in the Council for Independent Colleges, the National Association for Independent Colleges and Universities, the American Council on Education, the Pittsburgh Council on Higher Education, and the National Collegiate Athletic Association (NCAA). The College's business program is accredited by the Association of Collegiate Business Schools and Programs (ACBSP). La Roche's nursing program is accredited by the National League for Nursing Accrediting Commission (NLNAC), the American Association of Nurse Anesthetists (AANA), and the Joint Review Committee on Education in Radiologic Technology (JCERT). Its interior design and graphic design majors are accredited by the National Association of Schools of Art and Design (NASAD), and its interior design major is also accredited by the Council for Interior Design Accreditation (CIDA). The Center for Teacher Education is fully accredited by the Pennsylvania Department of Education in elementary education, nursing education, secondary English, Spanish (K–12), and special education.

Campus clubs and organizations give students an opportunity to participate in a variety of activities, including athletics, social clubs, academic societies, and student chapters of professional associations. In addition to intramural sports, La Roche participates in ten NCAA Division III (Allegheny Mountain Collegiate Conference) intercollegiate sports: men's varsity baseball and golf, women's softball and volleyball, and men's and women's basketball, cross-country, and soccer.

Students are encouraged to live on campus in one of four residence halls, where apartment-style suites promote group interaction and a sense of community. With the guidance of a residence life director, students plan a variety of programs, including guest speakers, recreational events, and social activities. All residence hall rooms are wired for Internet access. All residence halls provide students with microwave and refrigerator units and free laundry facilities.

A number of certificate programs and several master's degree programs are currently available, and several are under review by the College's Academic Senate.

Location

La Roche College's attractive 80-acre wooded campus is located in the North Hills of Pittsburgh, just 10 minutes from the center of the city. The College was recently named one of the safest four-year private college campuses in the United States by the APBnews.com/GAP Index study. Pittsburgh is the second-largest city in Pennsylvania and the headquarters of several of the largest corporations in the United States, including U.S. Steel, Bank of New York/Mellon Bank, and the H. J. Heinz Company. A lively, dynamic city, Pittsburgh has outstanding facilities and attractions, including the Pittsburgh Symphony, the Civic Light Opera, Carnegie Music Hall and Museum, and Heinz Hall for the Performing Arts. Pittsburgh has a host of professional sports teams—the Pittsburgh Pirates make their home at PNC Park, the Pittsburgh Steelers play at Heinz Field, and the Pittsburgh Penguins call Mellon Arena their home ice. In addition to the recreational benefits, proximity to a large metropolitan area offers students a number of internship and career opportunities.

Majors and Degrees

Students at La Roche College may choose from fifty majors as they earn their Bachelor of Arts, Bachelor of Science, or Bachelor of Science in Nursing degrees in the College's two schools: the School of Arts and Sciences and the School of the Professions. In the School of Arts and Sciences, the following majors are offered: athletic training (2-2 program); biology (liberal arts); biology (sciences); biology/forensic science; chemistry; chemistry/chemical engineering (3-2 program); chemistry/forensic science; chemistry/material sciences engineering (3-2 program); communication, media, and technology; comprehensive chemistry; computer science; computer science/industrial engineering (3-2 program); criminal justice; English education; English studies: language and literature; English studies: professional writing; environmental chemistry/environmental management (3-2 program); film, video, and media; history; human services; international studies; liberal studies; mathematics (liberal arts); mathematics (sciences); mathematics/industrial engineering (3-2 program); national security studies; occupational therapy (2-3 program); performing arts/dance; performing arts/pedagogy; physical therapy (3-3 program); physician assistant studies (2-3 program); psychology; radiography (degree completion); radiologic technology (associate degree); religious education/catechetics; religious studies; respiratory therapy (degree completion); sociology; speech and language pathology (1.5-3.5 program); and undeclared.

In the School of the Professions, students can choose from these majors: accounting, computer information systems, elementary education, facility management, finance, graphic and communication design, information technology, interior design, international management, leadership and administrative development (degree completion), management, marketing, nursing (associate degree), nursing–traditional program (RN-B.S.N.), professional studies (degree completion), and real estate.

Academic Programs

La Roche College offers students a blend of liberal arts studies and professional preparation, a combination that allows students to develop broad perspectives and understanding while acquiring professional skills. Students can gain practical field experience through an internship in one of Pittsburgh's many businesses or corporations. Study-abroad programs are also available.

In La Roche's highly individualized program, students work closely with faculty members, who help identify and foster each student's talents and assist students in applying knowledge acquired at La Roche to the world of work. The student-faculty ratio at La Roche is 12:1. Faculty advisers at La Roche mentor and guide students during their time at the College.

Degree requirements in most majors total a minimum of 120 credits. Students must demonstrate competence in English, mathematics, and practical computer application and must complete a core curriculum.

Academic Facilities

La Roche College is positioned to prepare students for the information age and a twenty-first-century global economy. The College employs "smart" classroom technology in many of its classrooms, which are wired for Internet access, telecommunications, data transmission, and cable TV. Students can bring their laptop computers to class and tap into the system. The "smart" classroom technology acts as a perfect complement to a dynamic and engaging faculty.

La Roche has three instructional computer labs and one general-purpose lab that each house IBM and IBM-compatible personal computers for student use. For graphic design students, two computer labs provide students access to Macintosh systems that use QuarkXpress, Illustrator, and Photoshop, among others. Each student also has access to the Internet at any of La Roche's state-of-the-art computer labs and in their residence halls.

The John J. Wright Library and Learning Center offers tutoring and academic support programs and a Writers' Center. The library is an official repository for government documents and participates in an interlibrary loan system that circulates materials through the ten higher education institutions in Pittsburgh.

Costs

Full-time tuition for the 2007–08 academic year was approximately $18,600. Room and board costs were approximately $7940.

Financial Aid

A La Roche College education is an investment that can produce a lifetime of dividends, yet the cost continues to be well below the national average for private colleges. La Roche College is committed to helping its students find ways to bridge the gap between what they can afford and what their education will cost. Aid is available through various scholarships, grants, loans, work-study awards, and special benefits made available by the federal and state governments, La Roche College, and private organizations. In addition, the College awards full- and partial-tuition scholarships to students who qualify on the basis of academic achievements. Financial aid counselors are available to answer questions and assist students. La Roche also offers several payment plans. Information on these options may be obtained from the College's admissions office.

All students who intend to apply for financial aid must submit the Free Application for Federal Student Aid (FAFSA). Students who live outside of Pennsylvania should also submit their own state grant form, if applicable. All students are encouraged to submit the proper forms as soon after January 1 as possible so that they are processed prior to La Roche College's May 1 deadline.

Faculty

At La Roche, faculty members are an acclaimed group of scholars. Eighty-five percent of the College's full-time faculty members have earned terminal degrees in their fields. They work closely with students, challenging them and encouraging them. With a 12:1 student-faculty ratio, it's common for students and faculty members to get to know each other well during their time together. La Roche's faculty members are experts in their fields. Many have earned distinguished honors, such as the graphic design professor who was awarded a Fulbright Scholar Grant and the former FBI agent with more than two decades of investigative experience.

La Roche's faculty is engaged in research and is equally committed to teaching. These highly trained and experienced people spend time in classrooms, laboratories, and studios, imparting wisdom and encouraging students to reach beyond the classroom to achieve their goals and educational pursuits.

Student Government

The Student Government Association (SGA) is a central and vital organization at the College. It is a legislative body that is responsible for all areas of student life. All enrolled students are represented by the SGA, and all full-time students are eligible for election. Students are also represented on various administrative committees within the College, including the College Cabinet and the Academic Senate.

Admission Requirements

La Roche is selective in its admission process. The College seeks students who demonstrate a strong desire to fulfill their academic potential and have a clear commitment to personal growth and achievement. Because the College values a commitment to community and lifelong learning, the admission staff also considers a student's extracurricular and volunteer activities in such areas as school, church, and community. The admission committee reviews each applicant individually, assessing personal and academic strengths in light of a student's background and opportunities. Committee members carefully examine high school records (course work, grade point average, and class rank), letters of recommendation, and SAT or ACT scores. La Roche's code numbers are 2379 for the SAT and 3607 for the ACT.

Application and Information

Candidates for admission should submit a completed application, a copy of their high school transcript, and a school report completed by a guidance counselor. Each application requires a $50 nonrefundable fee. Applications may also be completed online. SAT and ACT scores should be sent directly to the College. La Roche adheres to a rolling admission system by which students receive decisions once their application credentials are complete. To ensure appropriate financial aid and housing opportunities, students are encouraged to apply no later than March 31 for the fall semester and December 31 for the spring semester. For additional information regarding La Roche admission, prospective students should contact:

Office of Admissions
La Roche College
9000 Babcock Boulevard
Pittsburgh, Pennsylvania 15237
Phone: 412-536-1272
800-838-4LRC (toll-free)
Fax: 412-847-1820
E-mail: admissions@laroche.edu
Web site: http://www.laroche.edu

Students on the campus of La Roche College.

LEBANON VALLEY COLLEGE

ANNVILLE, PENNSYLVANIA

The College

With 141 years of tradition, an outstanding student body and faculty, and exceptional facilities, this private liberal arts college stands out among other schools. Founded in 1866, Lebanon Valley College (LVC) is steeped in a tradition of providing students with an educational foundation that transcends time and embraces new technology. The College has instilled in its graduates the desire and ability to think, ask questions, solve problems, and communicate effectively. These qualities, combined with a love for education and learning, prepare students to be competitive in a world that is constantly changing. A supportive community provides the final ingredient students need to achieve success in the job market and professional or graduate school.

The Lebanon Valley College family of 1,660 students is growing. The new freshmen and transfer students have become part of a student body that represents twenty-one states and five countries. Technology connects them to the world and prepares them for the future. Beautiful spaces foster quiet reflection, where students work and play together, building friendships that last a lifetime.

Students' efforts and accomplishments are being recognized. Few other small colleges have received more Fulbright awards than Lebanon Valley College—fourteen awards in the past thirty-seven years—with mathematics majors receiving five during that period. For the thirteenth consecutive year, *U.S. News & World Report* rated Lebanon Valley College among the top-tier schools in the Northern Universities–Master's: Top Schools category. LVC also ranked eighth on its list of Great Schools at Great Prices.

Lebanon Valley's tree-lined campus feels like a college of yesteryear—with twenty-first-century accoutrements. Students enjoy state-of-the-art facilities whether they are studying in the atrium of the Bishop Library, using a workstation in the molecular modeling lab, or performing student-faculty research in the science center that is scheduled for an $18-million transformation. The College's forty-five buildings provide for every facet of college life with thirty-two residence halls, including four apartment-style halls; classroom buildings, including a revitalized academic center with all of the latest technology for teaching and learning; two student centers; a recreational sports center; a new varsity gymnasium; a library; a music center; an art gallery and recital hall; an art studio; and a chapel. One of the keys to providing students with a rich, well-rounded experience is to offer a wealth of opportunities for learning and growth beyond the classroom. There are award-winning athletic fields; gardens and plazas; soccer, baseball, field hockey, and softball parks; and a physical therapy facility. The baseball and soccer fields were each named National Collegiate Athletic Association (NCAA) field of the year in their respective categories, and the softball park is a two-time regional field of the year.

The staff of the Career Services Office helps students to research careers and establish contacts with potential employers. Seminars are offered on resume writing and interviewing skills. The Career Connections alumni database provides students personal access to individuals who are working in their prospective fields.

The College's mission is to continue to carry out the art of teaching and learning with the same dedication and love that has come to be identified with the educators of the Valley.

Lebanon Valley offers master's degree programs in business, music education, and science education; a doctoral program in physical therapy; and preprofessional programs in dentistry, law, medicine, ministry, pharmacy, and veterinary medicine.

Location

Annville, founded in 1799, is a small town of approximately 5,000. Located near Pennsylvania Dutch country, the town is just 10 minutes east of Hershey and within a 2- to 3-hour drive of Philadelphia, Baltimore, New York, and Washington, D.C. Nestled in a valley, the College sits on 345 beautiful acres. A wide variety of cultural events and activities are offered on campus and within the community.

Majors and Degrees

The College confers five baccalaureate degrees. The Bachelor of Arts is available in the following major programs: American studies, art and art history, criminal justice, economics, English, French, German, historical communications, history, music, philosophy, political science, psychology, religion, sociology, Spanish, and certain individualized majors. The Bachelor of Science is available in the following major programs: accounting, actuarial science, biochemistry and molecular biology, biology, business administration, chemistry, computer science, cooperative engineering, cooperative forestry, digital communications, elementary education, health-care management, mathematics, music business, music education, physics, psychobiology, and certain individualized majors. The Bachelor of Science in chemistry, the Bachelor of Science in medical technology, and the Bachelor of Music (with an emphasis in music recording technology) are also available.

Academic Programs

Lebanon Valley has long been known for the strength of its academic programs and the achievement of its faculty members and alumni. The science program is particularly strong, with exceptionally well-equipped laboratories. In the latest numbers released by the National Science Foundation, the College ranked among the top 15 percent in the nation for Ph.D.'s produced at "Private, Predominantly Undergraduate Institutions" for biology, biochemistry, and chemistry in the past ten years. Lebanon Valley's mission arises directly from its historical traditions and a relationship with the United Methodist Church. The College's aim is to enable its students to become people of broad vision capable of making informed decisions and prepared for a life of service to others. To that end, the College provides an education that helps students to acquire the knowledge, skills, attitudes, and values necessary to live and work in a changing, diverse, and fragile world. The general education core provides students with the breadth of knowledge and experience across the curriculum, in addition to their major course work. Each student's academic program is fully complemented by a wide range of extracurricular activities, including guest lectures; concerts; Division III athletics; trips to New York and Washington, D.C.; and a variety of cultural activities.

Off-Campus Programs

Domestic students are encouraged to take advantage of the numerous study-abroad opportunities in Argentina, Australia, England, France, Germany, Greece, Italy, the Netherlands, New Zealand, Spain, and Sweden. Scholarship money and financial aid can be transferred to the programs, making the cost of study abroad the same as the cost of attendance at Lebanon Valley. Students can focus on becoming fluent in a language or join their classmates and a faculty adviser in a classroom experience. Internships both abroad and in the U.S. are a very popular method for students to research possible professions, establish early contacts, and gain valuable experience within their professional field.

Academic Facilities

Lebanon Valley has beautiful facilities and provides a safe environment in which students can live and learn. The Bishop Library houses more than 215,000 cataloged items, including books, journals, microfilm, and media collections. Most importantly, the library, residence halls, classrooms, and administrative offices are linked to the campus network, providing state-of-the-art technology and Internet access. There are smart classrooms and wireless capabilities throughout the campus, including in the College's newest academic center, Lynch Memorial Hall. Well-equipped laboratories provide students with hands-on experience and numerous opportunities for research.

Costs

Annual tuition and fees for the 2007–08 school year are $27,125. Room and board charges are $7430, and fees are $675.

Financial Aid

Lebanon Valley is committed to helping families finance a college education and has received national recognition for its outstanding merit-based scholarship program. High school achievement is rewarded at Lebanon Valley. Students who graduate in the top 30 percent of their high school class automatically receive one of the College's academic scholarships for up to half of the cost of tuition. Additional need-based financial aid is available, and 98 percent of students receive some form of financial aid. The College committed more than $17.8 million last year to institutional aid. The Free Application for Federal Student Aid (FAFSA) and the LVC Undergraduate Financial Aid Application must be completed to determine eligibility. The priority deadline for filing for financial aid is March 1.

Faculty

Lebanon Valley College's faculty members are dedicated to teaching. The close-knit community and an opportunity to be actively involved in the students' educational growth have drawn talented, multifaceted faculty members from all over the world. Many professors choose to live in the area and take an active role in supporting students' growth and development both in and out of the classroom. Faculty members are very involved in professional organizations and play an active role in helping students find internships and get started with research. Of the 100 professors at Lebanon Valley, 85 percent have earned a Ph.D. or equivalent terminal degree. The College is committed to maintaining a low student-teacher ratio of 14:1 (FTE). The average class size is 20.

Student Government

Lebanon Valley students participate in the College's governing system through Student Government and the Student Programming Board. Student Government includes 26 students who are elected from the student body each year for a one-year term beginning in September. Among the government's major responsibilities is fostering understanding, communication, and cooperation among the students, faculty members, and administration. It serves as the channel for all students' recommendations for establishing or changing policy and routes these recommendations to the appropriate administrative offices or faculty committees. The Student Programming Board organizes trips and schedules comedians and other entertainment on campus.

Admission Requirements

The admission process is selective, and the student's academic record is the most important factor. Lebanon Valley seeks students from diverse backgrounds and those who display leadership abilities, a commitment to community service, and special talents. All applicants should have completed 16 credit units and graduated from an accredited secondary school or present an equivalency certificate (GED). Of the 16 units, 4 should be in English, 2 in foreign language, 2 in mathematics, 1 in science, and 1 in social studies. Additional course work in math and science is strongly recommended. More than 70 percent of the freshman class rank in the top 30 percent of their high school class. Submission of SAT or ACT scores is optional. Advanced standing is offered through CLEP and AP examinations.

Application and Information

To apply, students should submit a completed application, a $30 application fee, and official copies of their high school transcript. Lebanon Valley has a rolling admission process. However, students are encouraged to apply during the fall of their senior year. The Admission Advisory Group gives careful consideration to scholastic credentials such as course selection and classroom performance as well as to the nonacademic qualities of each applicant. Personal visits to the campus are also encouraged.

For more information, applicants should contact:

Susan Sarisky
Director of Admission
Lebanon Valley College
101 North College Avenue
Annville, Pennsylvania 17003-1400
Phone: 866-LVC-4ADM (866-582-4236, toll-free)
Fax: 717-867-6026
E-mail: admission@lvc.edu
Web site: http://www.lvc.edu

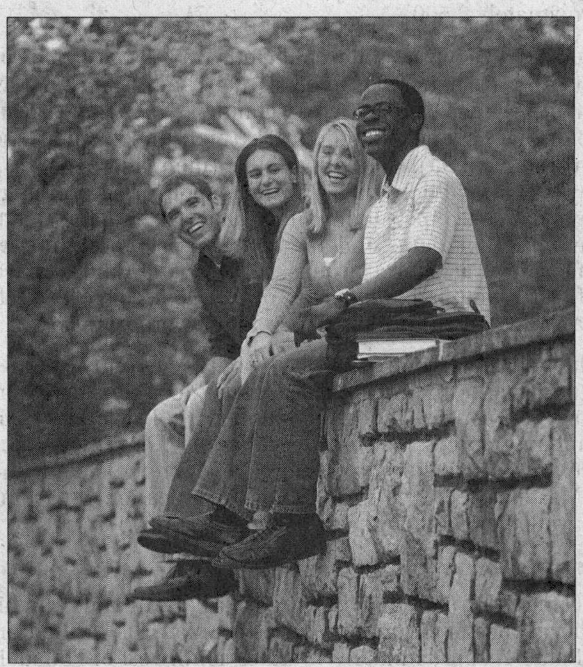

LVC students enjoy a spring afternoon on the College's Academic Quad.

LINCOLN UNIVERSITY

LINCOLN UNIVERSITY, PENNSYLVANIA

The University

Lincoln University is a nonsectarian, coeducational, state-related four-year liberal arts institution. Founded in 1854, it is the oldest college in the United States to have as its original purpose the higher education of youth of African descent. Today, it provides a superior education to people of all races.

On Lincoln's well-maintained campus, modern architectural styles blend with designs from an older era. There are fourteen residence halls (seven for women, six for men, and one that is coed); a student union building with a bookstore, a mailroom, several student offices and activity rooms, and a state-of-the-art radio station and television station; a University chapel; Manuel Rivero Hall, which houses an Olympic-size swimming pool, a 2,400-seat gymnasium, a bowling alley, a dance studio, a large game room, and two weight rooms; John Miller Dickey Hall, a $5.4-million computer center and humanities complex; and the $17-million state-of-the-art Thurgood Marshall Living and Learning Center. A new, state-of-the-art science center is currently under construction and is scheduled to open in the near future. Students may also use one of the fifteen well-equipped computer labs, which have a 6:1 student-computer ratio. The current total student enrollment is approximately 2,500.

Lincoln's Division II intercollegiate varsity sports program consists of baseball, basketball (men and women), bowling (women), cheerleading, cross-country (men and women), football, indoor and outdoor track (men and women), soccer (men and women), softball, tennis (men and women), and volleyball. In addition, the University sponsors a drama group, student dance troupe, student newspaper, drill team, step team, student fashion club, and an active music program, which includes several choral groups, a jazz band, and a marching band. The campus is the scene of frequent concerts, lectures, and a variety of cultural and recreational programs.

At the graduate level, the University currently offers four master's degree programs: Master of Education, with concentrations in early childhood, elementary, and secondary; Master of Human Services; Master of Science in Administration, with concentrations in human resource management and finance; and Master of Science in Reading. Certification programs are also available in reading and teacher certification.

Location

The campus is surrounded by the rolling farmlands and hills of southern Chester County in Pennsylvania. It is located on Old U.S. Route 1, approximately 45 miles southwest of Philadelphia; 25 miles west of Wilmington, Delaware; and 55 miles north of Baltimore, Maryland. These three major cities provide excellent cultural and recreational resources. Oxford, Pennsylvania, the town nearest to Lincoln University, is located 4 miles south of the campus. There are shopping centers, banks, churches, and restaurants located in and around the University area. Lincoln's master's degree programs are held at the Lincoln University Graduate Center, 3020 Market Street, in Philadelphia, Pennsylvania.

Majors and Degrees

Lincoln University offers four-year programs leading to an undergraduate Bachelor of Arts or Bachelor of Science degree. Majors available to students are as follows: accounting, anthropology, biology, biopsychosocial health psychology, chemistry, clinical/counseling psychology, computer science, criminal justice, early childhood education, elementary education, engineering (dual degree), English education, English–liberal arts, environmental issues, finance, French, general science, health and physical education (K–12), health science (several areas), history, human services, information technology, management, mass communications (several areas), mathematics, music (B.A., performance), music education (B.S.), organizational psychology, philosophy, physics, political science, religion, secondary education (several areas), sociology, Spanish, and studio arts. Preprofessional programs in dentistry, engineering, law, medicine, and veterinary science are also offered.

Lincoln offers a 3-3 (dual degree) program in engineering in cooperation with Drexel University and Temple University and a 3-2 (dual degree) program in engineering in cooperation with Pennsylvania State University, Lafayette College, New Jersey Institute of Technology, the University of Delaware, Howard University, and Rensselaer Polytechnic Institute. These programs lead to a B.A. from Lincoln University and a B.S. degree from one of the engineering schools.

Academic Programs

The University operates on a semester calendar system. It is accredited by the College and University Council of the State of Pennsylvania and by the Middle States Association of Colleges and Schools, and its health-related programs are accredited by the American Medical Association.

Lincoln requires the study in depth of a single field of concentration. New students are assigned faculty advisers by the Academic Advising Center when they enroll, based upon their career intent (and other information) as expressed in their application for admission. The normal load for a full-time student each semester is 15 credit hours plus physical education. The minimum load necessary to be registered as a full-time student is 12 credit hours. Students are not permitted to carry more than 5½ courses, or 18 credit hours, without the consent of their adviser and the approval of the Registrar. Upon satisfactory completion of a minimum of 124 credit hours, the student is recommended by the faculty to the Board of Trustees for the degree of Bachelor of Arts or Bachelor of Science.

The Act–101 Achievement Program, funded by the Commonwealth of Pennsylvania Legislative Act 101, is one of Lincoln University's supportive services programs providing counseling and tutorial support in mathematics, reading, writing, and content courses for qualified Pennsylvania students only.

Another of the University's many exceptional programs, Lincoln's Excellent Academic Program in Science (LEAPS), is designed to meet the challenges of those students who are interested in pursuing a rigorous background in either the physical or natural sciences.

Off-Campus Programs

Through a study-abroad program, students are offered the opportunity to visit a number of other countries, including the People's Republic of China, the Commonwealth of Independent States, Taiwan, and several African and European countries.

Academic Facilities

The 422-acre campus contains a library with 178,750 volumes, 580 current periodicals, and 45,104 microforms. Lincoln's state-of-the-art facilities also include Harold Grim Hall, a life sciences building; Ware Center, dedicated to the fine arts; Wright Hall, dedicated to the physical sciences; John Miller Dickey Hall; University Hall, for English and mass communications majors; and a learning resource center.

Costs

Tuition and fees for 2007–08 were $8224 for Pennsylvania residents and $12,654 for out-of-state students. Total costs, including room and board, were $15,816 for Pennsylvania residents and $20,246 for out-of-state students. Tuition and fees are subject to change without notice.

Financial Aid

Financial aid awards are based on need. An applicant for aid is required to file the Free Application for Federal Student Aid (FAFSA). The application may be mailed but should be completed online for a much faster response. Lincoln University's federal code number is 003290. The priority filling deadline for the financial aid application is April 1.

More than 90 percent of the students at Lincoln receive some type of financial assistance. Aid is awarded in the form of packages, which may include scholarships, federal grants, state grants, Federal Perkins Loans, Federal Stafford Student Loans, Federal Work-Study Program awards, and institutional aid.

Scholarships are offered to prospective students with outstanding academic potential. The minimum requirements are a combined SAT score of 900 or above (from the critical reading and math sections only), at least a 3.0 or B average, and significant school and community involvement. Students should write to the Office of Admissions for further information.

Faculty

The student-faculty ratio is 16:1. There are 97 full-time and 34 part-time faculty members. Seventy-five percent have doctoral degrees.

Student Government

The members of the Student Government Association (SGA) are elected by the student body as representatives of and for all the students. It is the responsibility of the Student Government Association to make use of all channels of communication between the student body, its elected officials, the administration, and the faculty for the purpose of alleviating campus problems and for the implementation of programs, regulations, and long- and short-range planning.

Admission Requirements

Lincoln University welcomes admission applications from prospective freshmen any time after they have completed their junior year in high school. The University employs the rolling admissions system in which there is no firm deadline for applications. However, students are strongly encouraged to apply by April 15 if admission is desired in August and by December 15 if admission is desired in January. Lincoln also accepts the General Educational Development credential. Required documents for admissions consideration are a completed application for admission, an official high school transcript, SAT/ACT test results, two letters of recommendation, an application essay, and a $20 application fee.

Application and Information

To receive an application and other relevant information about the admissions process, students should contact:

Office of Admissions
MSC 147
Lincoln University
P.O. Box 179
Lincoln University, Pennsylvania 19352-0999
Phone: 484-365-8000
800-790-0191 (toll-free)
E-mail: admiss@lu.lincoln.edu
Web site: http://www.lincoln.edu

Thurgood Marshall Living and Learning Center on the campus of Lincoln University.

COLLEGE DATA CENTER • PENNSYLVANIA

MARYWOOD UNIVERSITY

SCRANTON, PENNSYLVANIA

The University

Marywood University is coeducational, comprehensive, residential, and Catholic. Founded in 1915 by the Sisters, Servants of the Immaculate Heart of Mary, the University serves men and women from a variety of backgrounds and religions. The University enrolls more than 3,300 students in an array of undergraduate and graduate programs. Motivated by a pioneering, progressive spirit, Marywood provides a framework for educational excellence that enables students to develop fully as persons and to master professional and leadership skills that are necessary for meeting human needs.

Students at Marywood have the opportunity to build on their academic interests and proactively shape their educational experience. Students' energy and intellectual curiosity guides their work, growth, and success. Marywood believes in the power of the individual and in the premise that education is the most empowering tool.

Marywood is fully accredited by the Commission on Higher Education of the Middle States Association of Colleges and Schools. Accreditations/approvals have been granted by Accreditation Review Commission on Education for the Physician Assistant, American Psychological Association, American Art Therapy Association, American Music Therapy Association, Commission on Accreditation for Dietetics Education, American Dietetic Association, Council on Academic Accreditation, American Speech-Language-Hearing Association, Association of Collegiate Business Schools and Programs, Commission on Accreditation of Athletic Training Education, Council for Accreditation of Counseling and Related Educational Programs, Council on Social Work Education, National Association of Schools of Art and Design, National Association of Schools of Music, National Council for Accreditation of Teacher Education, and National League for Nursing Accrediting Commission.

The athletic program for women and men at Marywood provides students with opportunities to play on competitive intercollegiate, club, and intramural teams. Students compete on an intercollegiate basis in baseball, basketball, cross-country, field hockey, lacrosse, soccer, softball, tennis, and volleyball. Marywood is a member of the NCAA Division III and the Pennsylvania Athletic Conference (PAC). Marywood's teams have been successful, winning titles in basketball, field hockey, softball, tennis, and volleyball. In addition, Marywood teams and individuals have participated in tournaments at the national level.

Location

Situated on a hilltop, Marywood's scenic 115-acre campus is part of an attractive residential area of the city of Scranton, in northeastern Pennsylvania. With a population of 78,000, Scranton is the fifth-largest city in Pennsylvania and is the county seat of Lackawanna County (the county population is approximately 213,000). Marywood is relatively close to many major cities of the Northeast; traveling by car, it is 1 hour to Binghamton; 2½ hours to New York and Philadelphia; 4 hours to Washington, D.C.; and 5½ hours to Boston. Several airlines serve the Wilkes-Barre/Scranton International Airport, which is 20 minutes from the campus. The Pocono Mountains, offering spectacular scenery and an abundance of outdoor recreational opportunities, including downhill skiing, are a short distance from the campus.

Majors and Degrees

Marywood University offers a variety of majors and minors at the undergraduate level. Individually designed majors, developed with faculty guidance, and double and interdisciplinary majors are also available. Several five-year bachelor's/master's degree programs are offered.

At the undergraduate level, Marywood University awards the Bachelor of Arts (B.A.), Bachelor of Business Administration (B.B.A.), Bachelor of Fine Arts (B.F.A.), Bachelor of Music (B.M.), Bachelor of Science (B.S.), Bachelor of Science in Nursing (B.S.N.), and Bachelor of Social Work (B.S.W.).

Marywood offers majors and minors in the following areas of study: accounting, ad hoc (self-designed), advertising and public relations, art (studio: ceramics, painting, sculpture; design: graphic design, illustration, architecture/interior design, photography), art education, art therapy, arts administration (art, music, theater), aviation management, biology, biotechnology, church music, communication sciences and disorders (audiology, deaf studies, speech-language pathology), comprehensive social sciences (general, history, sociology), computer information and telecommunications systems, computer science (minor), criminal justice, dance/movement (minor), digital media and broadcast production (broadcast, corporate), early childhood special education, education (elementary, secondary), English, environmental science, family and consumer sciences education, financial planning, French, general science education, health and physical education (athletic training, education, physical activity), health services administration, history/political science, hospitality management, industrial/organizational psychology, international business, journalism (minor), management, marketing, mathematics, medical technology/clinical laboratory science, multimedia (minor), music, music education, music therapy, nursing (preservice, post-RN), nutrition and dietetics (coordinated program, didactic program), performance, performing arts, philosophy (minor), physician assistant studies, psychology, psychology/clinical practice, public administration, religious studies, retail business management, science, social sciences secondary education, social work, Spanish, special education of the mentally/physically disabled, special education/elementary education (dual certification), theater, and women's studies (minor).

Preprofessional programs are offered in chiropractic, communication sciences and disorders, dentistry, law, medicine, physician assistant studies, and veterinary medicine. A joint seven-year bachelor's/doctoral program in chiropractic involves three years of study on the Marywood campus and additional work at New York Chiropractic College, which is located in Seneca Falls, New York.

Academic Programs

Undergraduate degrees are offered in more than sixty academic programs, including the arts, sciences, music, fine arts, social work, and nursing. All students are required to complete a core curriculum in the liberal arts in addition to the courses in their major. Opportunities for undergraduates abound through double majors, honors and independent-study programs, practicums, internships, and study abroad. Army and Air Force ROTC programs are available.

Off-Campus Programs

Study-abroad opportunities are available in such countries as Australia, Canada, England, France, Mexico, and Spain. A visiting student program allows Marywood retail business management students to study at the Fashion Institute of Technology in New York City. Through Studio Art Centers International (SACI), art students may study in Florence, Italy. Students can also earn credits toward a degree through the distance learning program.

Academic Facilities

Marywood continues to expand its facilities with the newly built $13.8-million Mellow Center for Athletics and Wellness, which is designed to provide the newest recreational opportunities for students and clinical space for Marywood's burgeoning health research programs.

Marywood's Learning Resources Center (LRC) houses library services, media services, and academic computing services. The library collection includes more than 216,000 volumes, nearly 1,000 current journal subscriptions, and more than 43,000 media items. The LRC provides CD-ROM and full-text databases. It also participates in the interlibrary loan network with 8,650 libraries. The research collection includes many index and abstract services.

Costs

Tuition for full-time students (12–18 credits per semester) for the 2007–08 academic year was a flat fee of $23,040. There was also a general fee of $850 for full-time students. Costs for room and board for a full academic year were approximately $10,400, depending on which meal plan is selected and the desired room occupancy. Costs of books and supplies were estimated at $900.

Financial Aid

Marywood offers a comprehensive program of financial aid to assist students in meeting educational costs. Eligibility for federal and state programs is based on demonstrated financial need, as determined by a federal eligibility formula that analyzes family income and assets. In addition, approximately $18 million in institutional aid is awarded annually to Marywood students. Applicants to Marywood are considered for all financial assistance programs for which they qualify. Candidates are required to submit the Free Application for Federal Student Aid (FAFSA) and the Marywood application form, preferably by February 15.

Faculty

Among faculty members at Marywood, 153 are full-time, and 88 percent of these hold the Ph.D. or the highest degree in their field. The student-faculty ratio is 12:1. Faculty members are evaluated on their teaching and on their scholarly and artistic activities.

Student Government

All matriculated students in the undergraduate school are members of the Student Government Association (SGA). The SGA operates with a number of committees, including the Student Council, the Resident Committee, and the Commuter Committee. The association plays a key role in establishing a positive campus environment.

Admission Requirements

Candidates for admission should demonstrate reasonable progress toward graduation in an accredited secondary school, have graduated from a secondary school, or offer evidence of an equivalent secondary education. Each candidate should show satisfactory academic preparation in 16 units of subject matter, including 4 units of English, 3 units of social studies, 2 units of mathematics, 1 unit of science with laboratory, and 6 additional units. Either SAT or ACT scores are required for those who wish to enter as freshmen.

In addition to fulfilling general admission requirements, candidates for admission to a degree program in art, education, music, nursing, and pre–physician assistant studies must meet special standards established by the department. Prior to enrollment, music, theater, and art candidates are required to audition or to present an art portfolio.

For certain programs, candidates without the recommended distribution of units may be eligible for admission if their course work as a whole and the results of their tests offer evidence of a strong foundation for college work. Candidates who are deficient in required course work may complete the appropriate work during the summer or the first year in college.

A student who demonstrates satisfactory academic performance at another college may apply for admission as a transfer student. Academic courses presented for transfer should be equivalents of courses required by the programs of study at Marywood. Students should have earned a grade of C or higher in their course work; C– will not transfer. A student should expect to earn a minimum of 60 credits at Marywood University; ordinarily, at least one half of the credits required for a major must also be earned at Marywood.

International candidates are required to meet the academic standards for admission, demonstrate proficiency in the use of the English language, and submit documentation of having sufficient funds to cover educational and living expenses for the duration of study. To certify proficiency in the use of English, international applicants whose primary language is not English must submit scores from the Test of English as a Foreign Language (TOEFL).

Application and Information

Applications for admission are considered on a rolling basis; however, candidates are strongly encouraged to submit applications by March 1. Applications received after March 1 are considered on the basis of available space in particular programs. To be considered for admission, freshman applicants must submit to the Office of Admissions a completed application (paper or online), a nonrefundable $35 application fee, an official high school transcript with an indication of class rank, an official report of scores from the SAT or ACT, and at least one letter of recommendation. Students can apply online at http://www.mymarywood.com/apply_now.asp.

Transfer students must submit a completed application, a nonrefundable $35 application fee, an official high school transcript, official academic transcript(s) reflecting all college course work for which the candidate has enrolled, and at least one letter of recommendation.

All submitted credentials become the property of Marywood and are not returnable to the applicant. Admission standards and policies are free of discrimination on grounds of race, color, national origin, sex, age, or disability.

For further information, interested students should contact:

Robert Reese, Director
University Admissions
Marywood University
2300 Adams Avenue
Scranton, Pennsylvania 18509
Phone: 570-348-6234
TO-MARYWOOD (866-279-9663, toll-free)
Fax: 570-961-4763
E-mail: yourfuture@marywood.edu
Web site: http://www.mymarywood.com

The Liberal Arts Center on Marywood's campus.

MERCYHURST COLLEGE

ERIE, PENNSYLVANIA

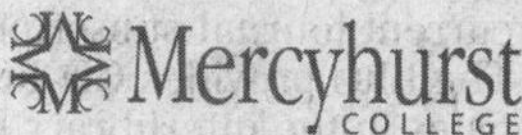

The College

Excellence in education, a strong sense of tradition and a beautiful campus are just a few reasons why students from across the country and around the world come to Mercyhurst College. Located in Erie, Pennsylvania, and founded by the Sisters of Mercy in 1926, Mercyhurst College is a fully accredited, four-year Catholic liberal arts institution. The 70-acre Erie campus offers fifty undergraduate majors with sixty-seven concentrations, as well as unique adult programs and six graduate programs. In addition, Mercyhurst maintains its one- and two-year programs at three additional locations, including a residential campus in scenic North East, Pennsylvania, just 20 minutes from Erie; Mercyhurst West, in neighboring Girard, Pennsylvania; and Mercyhurst Corry in Corry, Pennsylvania.

Nearly 4,000 students, from across the United States and thirty-seven countries, attend classes at one of the four locations, with about 3,000 at the Erie campus.

The College supports a wide range of traditional four-year programs, from dance and art to geology and international business. Mercyhurst also is home to several nationally renowned undergraduate and graduate programs, including archaeology/anthropology, applied forensic science, and intelligence studies, and offers unique programs such as art therapy, fashion merchandising, and ecosystem management. Graduate programs in applied intelligence, organizational leadership, administration of justice, anthropology, special education, and secondary math and science education offer outstanding opportunities for those seeking advanced degrees. Mercyhurst also offers teaching certifications, advanced certificates, and graduate certificates.

Mercyhurst College has consistently been ranked highly by *U.S. News & World Report* and *Princeton Review.* Alumni of Mercyhurst are found in every major profession and in every state in the nation as well as several countries around the world. A Mercyhurst education combines a rich sense of tradition with a progressive liberal arts approach to career preparation. Once enrolled, students work closely with academic advisers and academic support and career services personnel to ensure they reach their individual aspirations and objectives.

Mercyhurst's sense of tradition and excellence is also reflected in its beautiful Tudor-Gothic college setting. More than fifty-seven buildings surround stately Old Main, the College's epicenter since 1926. Facilities abound for academics, the arts, athletics, student services, student recreation, and student housing.

The College's athletic facilities include the Mercyhurst Athletic Center, the Student Recreation Center, the Mercyhurst Ice Center, Tullio Field, and several additional playing fields. The Athletic Center houses a gymnasium complex, rowing tanks, and a fully equipped athletic training facility. The Ice Center includes a rink, four locker rooms, and seating for 1,500 people. The Recreation Center is the home of most Mercyhurst intramural programs and contains a large physical fitness area and two all-purpose floors for basketball, volleyball, and other indoor uses.

Mercyhurst fields twenty-five NCAA athletic teams, including Division I men's and women's ice hockey. Division II sports include men's and women's basketball, cross-country, golf, lacrosse, rowing, soccer, tennis, volleyball, and water polo. Other Division II sports fielded are baseball, field hockey, football, softball, and wrestling. In 2007, the women's hockey team advanced to the NCAA Division I quarterfinals, and enjoyed an 11-week reign as #1 in the nation.

At Mercyhurst, learning extends beyond the classroom. With more than 100 clubs and organizations, service learning opportunities, study-abroad programs, and on-campus housing, Mercyhurst graduates leave with more than just a diploma—they leave with the skills to succeed in employment, graduate and professional schools, community service, and most importantly—life.

Location

The Mercyhurst campus is situated on a beautiful site overlooking Lake Erie. One block from the Erie city limits, the College enjoys the advantages of a suburban pastoral setting only minutes from downtown's bustling shopping and entertainment district. These areas are accessible to Mercyhurst students up to five days a week through the use of the Mercyhurst Shuttle Bus.

Erie is a short drive from Cleveland, Pittsburgh, and Buffalo, and the campus is located just 10 miles from the Erie International Airport.

Majors and Degrees

Mercyhurst College awards the Bachelor of Arts degree in accounting; anthropology/archaeology (archaeology); art (graphic design, studio); art education; art therapy; biochemistry; biology (ecosystem conservation, predental, premedical, preosteopathy, prepharmacy, and pre–veterinary medicine); business (advertising, business/chemistry, business/computer information technology, finance, management, marketing, and sport business management); biology education, chemistry (environmental science); chemistry education, communication (journalism, production, and public relations); computer systems (computer information systems, management information systems, and Web information systems); criminal justice (corrections, juvenile justice, law enforcement, and prelaw); dance (applied theory choreography track, applied theory pedagogy track, and performance); early childhood education, earth/space science education, elementary education, elementary education/early childhood education, elementary education/special education, English (creative writing, secondary education, prelaw, and writing); general science education, geology (environmental geology/hydrogeology and geoarchaeology); history (public history and social studies education); hotel, restaurant, and institutional management (facilities and property management, food and beverage management, hotel management, professional clubhouse and golf management, and professional convention management); intelligence studies, international business, mathematics (secondary education); music, philosophy, political science (environmental studies and politics, international relations, and prelaw); psychology (neuroscience); religious education and lay ministry, religious studies, sociology (criminology); social work, special education, world languages and cultures, and world language education (French and Spanish).

The Bachelor of Science is conferred in anthropology/archaeology (archaeology and bioarchaeology), applied forensic science (criminalistics, forensic anthropology, forensic chemistry and toxicology, and forensic wildlife investigation), biochemistry, biology (medical technology), chemistry, earth/space science education, family and consumer sciences (fashion merchandising, interior design, and marriage and family studies), general science education, geology, and sports medicine (athletic training, health/fitness promotion, premedical, and pre–physical therapy).

The Bachelor of Music is awarded in applied music and music education.

Academic Programs

Core requirements, which include a select, limited number of courses from the liberal arts disciplines, furnish students with a broad base of skills and knowledge. In addition to completing the core program, students must complete a major. Graduation requirements for the Bachelor of Arts, Bachelor of Science, and Bachelor of Music degrees range from 120 to 140 credits, depending upon the chosen major.

Mercyhurst College offers and honors program, cooperative education, contract majors, independent/tutorial study, and off-campus study, including study abroad. Students may earn credit or advanced placement through challenge examinations, life experience, Advanced Placement tests (scores of 4 or 5 are accepted), and CLEP tests.

The College operates on a three-term calendar (fall, winter and spring), with an academic year that generally runs from the last week in August through the third week of May.

Off-Campus Programs

Mercyhurst College has an increasingly active study-abroad program that is open to all students, irrespective of the (academic) program. Up to half of a student's financial aid is available to transfer to the destination school. Mercyhurst students have studied all over the globe, including Australia, Europe, Central America, and Russia. Students may also choose to pursue internships abroad.

For further information, prospective students should contact Eric Evans, Director, International Admissions and Services, at the main phone number, Ext. 2478, or by e-mail at eevans@mercyhurst.edu.

Academic Facilities

Some of the nation's best science facilities are housed in Mercyhurst's Zurn Hall. The College has one of the finest archaeology/anthropology programs in the country and is the home of the Mercyhurst Archaeological Institute (MAI). Its state-of-the-art facilities include an artifact processing and curation laboratory, a lithics laboratory, a faunal analysis laboratory, and the R. L. Andrews Center for Perishables Analysis—the only laboratory in North America fully dedicated to the analysis of basketry, textiles, cordage, netting, sandals, and related perishable material. A customized DNA lab, the Donald and Judith Alstadt Laboratory for Molecular and Cellular Research, dedicated February 1, 2005, features a lab, a prep room, and DNA clean room.

In the DNA lab, students learn to use a geospatial information system (GIS) to plot sites for archaeological digs, a task formerly accomplished using ropes and stakes. Mercyhurst also has a museum-quality collection of prehistoric casts and fossils, including a cast of a *T. rex* skull, a set of 7-foot shark jaws, casts of several other skulls of large reptiles from the Jurassic period, a 2-ton section of petrified wood from Indonesia, a fossilized elephant specimen from Java, a dinosaur egg nest, and a stalactite from China. The collection was donated by Michael and Barbara Sincak, who have spent nearly twenty years traveling the globe to acquire specimens for their business and personal collections.

The Mary D'Angelo Performing Arts Center is a gorgeous facility built in 1996. The center seats 825 and has a performance stage of 3,400 square feet. As such, it is the only facility in the Erie-Cleveland-Pittsburgh-Buffalo area capable of handling the technical requirements of the most elaborate productions, including ballet and opera. Especially renowned for its acoustics, it was designed as a showcase for the performing arts. It is conducive not only to the cultural aspirations of the College and the Erie community, but also as a venue for students and faculty members to perform in a magnificent professional setting.

In 2003, the College unveiled a newly built bookstore and coffee bar. Textbooks, trade books, periodicals, and a sizeable inventory of sundries, school needs, and clothing occupy a good part of the space, but the Starbucks coffee bar and the wireless environment make this cybercafé a popular place to relax.

The Audrey Hirt Academic Center, which opened in 2002, contains an atrium, technology-rich classroom and lecture halls, faculty offices, the Walker Recital Hall, special facilities for the graphic arts and communications, the comfortable Honors Lounge, and studios and working areas for the College's newspaper, yearbook, and radio and television organizations.

Costs

Tuition for 31 credits in the 2007–08 academic year totaled $21,049 ($679 per credit). In addition to tuition, various fees totaled $1686. Room and board totaled $7800. The total for room, board, tuition, and fees was roughly $30,535. Students should budget an additional $2000 for books, supplies, and personal expenses.

Financial Aid

Mercyhurst is dedicated to assisting students with the cost of their education. Financial aid awards are both need- and merit-based (http://merit.mercyhurst.edu). In addition to federal and state programs, Mercyhurst awards nearly $25 million in institutional scholarships, grants, and loans annually. More than 97 percent of Mercyhurst's students receive financial aid in the form of grants, scholarships, part-time on-campus employment, and/or long-term loans to be repaid after leaving the College. The typical student's financial aid award consists of aid from one or more of these sources.

Financing a college education is a challenging task and an important part of making a good enrollment decision. Mercyhurst's experienced admission and financial aid counselors look forward to assisting families in making Mercyhurst College affordable. Any questions that arise during the process should be directed to an admissions counselor at the telephone numbers listed below, Ext. 2202.

Faculty

There are 131 full-time and 75 part-time faculty members who staff undergraduate programs at Mercyhurst. More than 60 percent of the faculty members hold a Ph.D. or the terminal degree in their fields of study. The primary faculty function is teaching, but faculty members are also active in research, publishing, and service to their community. The faculty-student ratio is 1:17.

Student Government

A student government organization is designed to help meet the academic, cultural, and social needs of the student body and is financed by an activity fee. Student government comprises an executive committee, a study activities committee, representatives from each major and club on campus, and 7 College senators.

Admission Requirements

In selecting a student for admission, Mercyhurst College looks for evidence of academic ability and readiness as demonstrated by high school course work, grades earned, performance on standardized tests, and personal characteristics that relate to a student's ability to succeed.

The College's entrance policy is free of discrimination on the grounds of race, creed, color, sex, or national origin. In fact, the student body reflects this diversity; students come from thirty-seven countries, and five continents.

Application and Information

The College operates on a rolling admission cycle. Beginning in November, notification is given as soon as possible after all credentials reach the Admissions Office.

Students applying to Mercyhurst may apply online at the College's Web site for free or complete traditional paper applications and send them to the Admissions Office with a $30 processing fee. Applicants must submit an official copy of all high school transcripts, official copies of SAT and/or ACT scores, and two letters of recommendation. Applicants should also complete any required audition or portfolio review required by individual majors.

While interviews are not required, students in their junior or senior year of high school are strongly encouraged to schedule a campus visit and an interview. Campus tours are available by appointment Monday through Friday at 9, 10, 11, 1, and 2. Saturday tours are scheduled at 9, 10, 11, and noon.

For additional information about Mercyhurst College, students should contact:

Mercyhurst College Admissions
501 East 38th Street
Erie, Pennsylvania 16546-0001
Phone: 814-824-2202
800-825-1926 (toll-free)
E-mail: admissions@mercyhurst.edu
Internet: http://admissions.mercyhurst.edu

MESSIAH COLLEGE

GRANTHAM, PENNSYLVANIA

The College

Messiah College is a place where students' minds are strengthened in unison with their character, where there is no separation between intellectual and spiritual life, and where students can make the connection between what they think and what they believe. At Messiah College, students are encouraged to engage both their heads and their hearts to pursue a higher education and discover their calling.

A Christian college of the liberal and applied arts and sciences, Messiah College takes its mission seriously: to educate men and women toward maturity of intellect, character, and Christian faith to prepare them for lives of service and reconciliation in church and society. More than 2,850 students from forty states, twenty-five countries, and several denominations choose to take on the rigors of academic pursuit while strengthening their faith and putting it into meaningful action.

Alumni and faculty members include a Rhodes Scholar, a Marshall Scholar, a Truman Scholar, and several Fulbright Fellowship and award recipients. In addition, Messiah has been listed for more than ten consecutive years on the Templeton Foundation's "Honor Roll of Character-Building Colleges."

At Messiah College, more than 86 percent of students live on campus, creating a vibrant community life and lasting friendships. More than sixty extracurricular activities, from national honor societies to special interest clubs to service and outreach teams, allow students the opportunity to enhance their classroom experiences and hone their leadership and team skills. In fact, in a recent year, students volunteered more than 60,000 hours in service and mission projects. Student government, the yearbook, the student-run weekly newspaper, the College radio station, theatrical productions, traveling musical groups, Habitat for Humanity, and residence hall activities are among the many opportunities offered by Messiah College for students to get involved.

Messiah encourages fitness for the body, mind, and spirit, offering active club and recreational sports programs as well as fielding twenty intercollegiate sports teams: ten for men and ten for women. Several of the NCAA Division III teams attain national rankings each year. In 2006, 2005, 2004, 2002, and 2000, the men's soccer team won the national championship. In 2005, the women's soccer team won the national championship. In 2005, the women's field hockey team was a national finalist. *USA Today* not only recognized the College for the success of its teams on the field, but also ranked Messiah fifth in the country for its high graduation rate of student athletes in Division III. Top-notch athletics facilities include a competition-size indoor pool, a diving pool, two gymnasiums, an artificial-turf field hockey field, a weight-training center, exercise machines, a human-performance laboratory, competition tennis courts, a demonstration tennis court, and an indoor track as well as an expansive soccer stadium, manicured baseball and softball diamonds, a high ropes course, a fitness trail, and an outdoor track and field stadium.

Location

Located just 12 miles southwest of the state capital, Harrisburg, Messiah College's beautiful, 485-acre campus provides an ideal setting for outdoor recreation with easy access to urban centers such as Baltimore, Philadelphia, and Washington, D.C. Students enjoy picnics and canoeing on the Yellow Breeches Creek that passes through campus. The thriving suburban environment of central Pennsylvania affords students the opportunity to participate in the cultural, internship, and service options provided by the state capital and other major East Coast urban hubs.

Majors and Degrees

Messiah College awards both Bachelor of Arts and Bachelor of Science degrees in more than sixty majors: accounting, adventure education, art education, art history, athletic training, biblical and religious studies, biochemistry and molecular biology, biology, biopsychology, broadcasting, business administration, business information systems, chemistry, Christian ministries, communication, computer science, criminal justice, early childhood education (N–3), economics, elementary education (K–6), e-marketing, engineering, English, entrepreneurship, environmental science, environmental studies, family and consumer sciences education, French, German, health and exercise science, health and physical education (K–12), history, human development and family science, human resource management, humanities, international business, journalism, marketing, mathematics, music, nursing, nutrition and dietetics, nutrition science, philosophy, physics, politics, psychology, religion, social work, sociology, Spanish, Spanish business, sport management, studio art, and theater. Individualized majors are also available.

Students may also pursue teaching certification in art, biology and environmental education, chemistry, early childhood education, elementary education, elementary and special education, English, environmental education, French, German, health and physical education, mathematics, music education, social studies, and Spanish.

Preprofessional programs of study include allied health, dental, law, medical, physical therapy, and veterinary science.

In addition, students may choose from more than fifty different minors that include coaching, African American religion and culture, peace and conflict, and urban studies.

Academic Programs

Messiah's unique approach to academics combines a solid liberal arts foundation with study in one or more academic major. In addition to courses required in their major, students complete required general courses in writing, the sciences, the arts, language and culture, Christian faith, and physical education as well as electives to broaden their understanding and skills.

The College's academic year consists of two semesters, fall and spring, with a month long January term offering concentrated study in a single course or numerous cross-cultural trips to expand horizons. The College Honors Program, independent study, service learning, and internships enrich students' academic studies.

U.S. News & World Report has repeatedly ranked Messiah College among the top ten best colleges in the Northern Comprehensive Colleges–Bachelor's category. But more important, Messiah's approach allows students to seek top-quality higher education to equip them for a higher calling. Ninety-nine percent of Messiah graduates are employed full-time, attending graduate school, or in voluntary service within six months of graduation.

Off-Campus Programs

Through the College's EpiCenter (experiential learning center), Messiah students have many opportunities for off-campus study. In fact, the *Open Doors Report* ranked Messiah ninth among the nation's undergraduate institutions in sending students to study abroad.

In addition to a satellite campus in conjunction with Temple University in Philadelphia, students may also study in the following semester-long programs: American Studies Program (Washington, D.C.), AuSable Institute of Environmental Studies (Michigan), Australia Studies Centre (Sydney, Australia), Central American Study and Service, China Studies Program, Creation Care Study Program, Jerusalem University College, Latin American Studies Program (Costa Rica), Los Angeles Film Studies Center, Oxford Semester

(England), Russian Studies Program, Middle East Studies Program, Oregon Extension, and International Business Institute (Europe and Russia).

Messiah students may also participate in the Brethren Colleges Abroad program in locations such as China, Ecuador, England, France, Germany, Greece, Japan, and Spain. Annual cross-cultural study tours to locales including the Bahamas, Greece, Guatemala, and Israel provide additional educational opportunities during January or summer terms.

Academic Facilities

Messiah College is committed to providing modern academic facilities with state-of-the-art technology and equipment for students in all fields of study. In addition to a library with more than 300,000-volumes and access to information, literature, and publications from around the globe, academic buildings include a new science center; a renovated and expanded nursing hall; a hall of engineering, mathematics, and business; a fine arts center; and a sports center, all constructed or renovated within the last twenty years. Two new facilities opened in fall 2003: a 95,000-square-foot academic building and a 35,000-square-foot student union. More than 500 computers in various academic and residence hall labs are connected to a campuswide network, along with fully wired residence hall rooms, enabling students to have access to research and important communication.

Costs

Tuition and fees for 2007–08 total $23,710, and room and board average $7340. Additional fees total $710.

Financial Aid

Keeping a Messiah education affordable for all students who desire it continues to be a high priority for the College. Tuition, room, and board costs remain competitive, with costs at about the average of comparable four-year, private colleges in Pennsylvania. Financial aid counselors help students and families find available resources and create aid packages designed to meet needs. In addition to federal and state grants and loans and on-campus employment programs, Messiah students benefit from about $20 million in institutional merit scholarships and need-based aid. About 97 percent of Messiah students receive financial aid, with the average annual award per recipient (from all sources of aid) being nearly $17,000. Students should apply for institutional aid by the March 1 deadline for the following fall semester.

The College also offers both a semester and a monthly payment plan, allowing students and their families to choose the payment option most suitable to their needs.

Faculty

Professors, not teaching assistants, teach all classes at Messiah College. Representing nearly 150 graduate schools in five countries as well as a variety of denominational affiliations, more than 70 percent of the professors have earned the terminal degree in their field. While Messiah's faculty members are serious scholars who pursue original research, present findings, and publish widely, they are first and foremost committed to teaching. Chosen for their scholarship, Christian commitment, and teaching ability, Messiah's 173 full-time and more than 111 part-time faculty members lead by example, encouraging students to dig deeper, seek truth, pursue academic excellence, and grow in all areas of their lives. A low student-faculty ratio of 14:1 enables professors and students to forge close relationships while learning from each other.

Student Government

The self-governing Messiah College Student Government Association (SGA) is the vital force behind many campus activities. SGA also provides student services such as outreach opportunities, social events, and book sales. Encouraging trial by peers rather than the College administration, the student judicial council hears cases of rule violations on a regular basis. Messiah also values student input for critical College decisions, inviting student representatives to sit on almost every standing and ad hoc committee on the campus.

Admission Requirements

Messiah College seeks student applicants who are serious about their intellectual, spiritual, and personal development—those who strive to excel in many areas of their life and who will make a contribution to the campus community. Transfer, international, and ethnic minority students are highly encouraged to apply.

Selective in its admissions policy, the College examines academic achievement, extracurricular involvement, leadership skills, and Christian service. Nearly thirty percent of last year's freshman class ranked in the top 10 percent of their high school class. Forty were valedictorians or salutatorians, 8 were National Merit Scholars, and 21 percent had SAT scores of more than 1300, and 30 percent had ACT scores of more than 28.

Applicants should have taken at least 4 years of English, 3 years of mathematics, 2 years each of science and social studies, and 6 electives, preferably 2 in a foreign language. A large majority of students accepted at Messiah College exceed these minimum requirements. Students should take the SAT or the ACT by January of their senior year in high school. The Write Choice option, where a required interview replaces the standardized test score, is available to students who rank in the upper 20 percent of their high school class. One Christian Life recommendation is required. Students are invited to attend on-campus information sessions and tours.

Application and Information

Messiah College makes admissions decisions on a rolling basis beginning July 1 prior to the student's senior year. The Admissions Office is open from 8 to 5 on weekdays. For more information, to arrange a campus tour and an interview, or to request a catalog and application, students should contact:

Admissions Office
Messiah College
Box 3005
One College Avenue
Grantham, Pennsylvania 17027
Phone: 717-691-6000
800-233-4220 (toll-free)
Fax: 717-796-5374
E-mail: admiss@messiah.edu
Web site: http://www.messiah.edu

Messiah's faculty members mentor and prepare students to excel in their professions. In 2006, Messiah's accounting program ranked seventh in the nation for the percentage of students who passed the CPA exam on their first attempt. That same year, 100 percent of nursing graduates passed the National Council Licensure Examination for registered nurses on their first attempt.

MILLERSVILLE UNIVERSITY OF PENNSYLVANIA

MILLERSVILLE, PENNSYLVANIA

Millersville University
SEIZE THE OPPORTUNITY

The University

Millersville University is a multifaceted public institution with a wide range of programs and a primary commitment to high-quality undergraduate instruction. Millersville's student body of approximately 8,000, including 7,000 undergraduates, is large enough for the University to offer a wide variety of programs. The University is small enough, however, to provide friendly service and individual attention. Students report that the relaxed, friendly campus atmosphere is one of the things they like best. The Millersville campus features a beautiful green and flowered landscape, a lake with resident swans, and clean, well-maintained facilities.

Millersville University was established more than 150 years ago, in 1855, as a normal school, the first one in Pennsylvania. It remained a teachers' college until 1962, when it was authorized to offer liberal arts degrees. It has been Millersville University of Pennsylvania since 1983.

The two reasons students most frequently cite for choosing Millersville are its excellent academic reputation and affordable tuition. The most popular majors are elementary education, business administration, biology, psychology, and speech communication/theater. Millersville's undergraduates are diverse; 1 in 8 students attends part-time, 12 percent are members of a racial/ethnic minority group, and 12 percent are more than 25 years old. Thirty-five percent of Millersville undergraduates are from Lancaster County, 60 percent from elsewhere in Pennsylvania, 4 percent from out of state, and 1 percent from other countries.

The University offers a wide range of intercollegiate varsity, intramural, and club sports; special interest clubs; fraternities and sororities; musical organizations; and publications. A broad program of cultural events is offered, with alcohol-free nightclubs particularly popular.

Thirty-five percent of undergraduates live in campus residence halls, with the rest commuting from home or living nearby. Coed dormitories are provided. University-affiliated apartments are adjacent to campus. Freshmen and sophomores not commuting from home are required to live on campus. The possession, use, or sale of alcoholic beverages and illegal drugs is prohibited on the University campus. Smoking is prohibited in all academic and residential buildings on campus. Freshmen and sophomores living on campus are not permitted to have motor vehicles.

Special services provided for students include free tutoring, academic advisement, career planning and placement, personal counseling, health services, wellness activities, fee-for-service child care, and special facilities for commuters.

Location

Millersville, in the heart of Pennsylvania Dutch country, is 3 miles from Lancaster city, a growing metropolitan area. Lancaster County is an exceptionally friendly and beautiful area with a large number of stores, restaurants, theaters, parks, and tourist attractions. The campus is served by the area bus system, and Lancaster has train and air service.

Lancaster County is one of the fastest-growing counties in Pennsylvania and has one of the lowest unemployment rates in the state. The local economy is unusually sound and diverse. Sixty percent of Millersville graduates settle within the county.

Majors and Degrees

Millersville offers the Bachelor of Arts degree in anthropology, art, biology, chemistry, earth sciences, economics, English, French, geography, German, government and political affairs, history, international studies, mathematics, music, philosophy, physics, psychology, social work, sociology, and Spanish.

The Bachelor of Science degree is offered in biology, business administration, chemistry, communications and theater, computer science, earth sciences, geology, industrial technology, mathematics, meteorology, occupational safety and environmental health, oceanography, and physics.

The Bachelor of Science in Education degree with teaching certification is offered in art education, biology, chemistry, earth sciences, elementary education, English, French, German, mathematics, music education, physics, social studies, Spanish, special education, and technology education.

The University also offers the Bachelor of Fine Arts degree in art, the Bachelor of Science in Nursing degree for RNs only, the Associate of Science degree in chemistry and in computer science, and the Associate of Technology degree in industrial technology.

Most majors offer several options that permit specialization, including accounting, finance, international business, management, and marketing in business. Students should refer to the Web site for a complete listing. More than thirty minors are offered along with 3-2 engineering programs for chemistry and physics majors. Special advisement is available for students interested in premedicine and prelaw.

Academic Programs

Millersville University places a strong emphasis on the liberal arts. Nearly half of the courses required for all its undergraduate degrees, including those with technical or professional majors, are in the liberal arts. This prepares students for a lifetime of learning and gives them a background in writing, speaking, analysis, and critical thinking across a broad range of subjects.

Millersville's baccalaureate degree programs have four common curricular elements: proficiency requirements in English composition and speech; the general education program, which constitutes about half the curriculum; the major field of study; and elective courses, if needed, to meet the minimum of 120 credits required for graduation. Within this framework, students have many choices in developing programs of study.

The general education program has requirements in writing, speaking, humanities, natural sciences and mathematics, social sciences, and interdisciplinary and/or multicultural study. There is also a health and physical education requirement.

Millersville offers a University Honors College, departmental honors programs, independent study, a pass/fail option, remedial courses, and special advisement to students who are undecided about a major.

The University operates on a 4-1-4 academic calendar with summer sessions.

Off-Campus Programs

An exchange agreement with Franklin and Marshall College allows Millersville students to take Franklin and Marshall courses not offered at Millersville. Cooperative education internships are available to students in most majors, and some majors offer or require specialized internships. Millersville has study-abroad pro-

COLLEGE DATA CENTER • PENNSYLVANIA

grams in Chile, England, France, Germany, Ireland, Japan, Peru, Scotland, South Africa, and Spain. Qualified students who wish to study abroad elsewhere may do so through the University's cooperative arrangements with other colleges and universities.

Academic Facilities

Ganser Library houses more than 495,000 books and more than 558,000 other items and subscribes to more than 4,000 periodicals. Materials from other libraries are available through interlibrary loan. The library also houses computerized database-searching facilities, a curriculum center, a listening room, and archives.

Millersville's computing facilities include IBM and VAX mainframes and SUN Workstations. There are 450 terminals and microcomputers available, including IBM and Macintosh models. Users with their own microcomputers can access University mainframes through telephone lines. On-campus access to the Internet is available for all faculty members and students. Wireless access is available in the library, the Student Center, and the cybercafé in Roddy Science Center.

Other University facilities include an extensive scientific instrumentation inventory, industry and technology laboratories, a variety of art studios and galleries, a large auditorium and a small theater, two gymnasiums and swimming pools, radio and television production facilities, soundproof music practice modules, and a language laboratory. The University's day-care center and prekindergarten provide field experiences in early childhood education.

Costs

Annual tuition and fees in 2007–08 were $6624 for Pennsylvania residents and $14,480 for out-of-state students. Annual room and board charges for 2007–08 were $6876. Students paid approximately $900 for books and incidentals.

Financial Aid

Approximately 72 percent of Millersville undergraduates receive financial aid through grants, scholarships, employment, and loans. Scholarships are available on the basis of academic performance. Federal Pell and Federal Supplemental Educational Opportunity grants and Pennsylvania Higher Education Assistance Agency (PHEAA) grants are awarded on the basis of need. Students may also qualify for Federal Perkins Loans and Federal Stafford Student Loans. On-campus and off-campus job opportunities are plentiful.

Students applying for a federal or state grant, Federal Work-Study, or a Federal Perkins Loan must complete the Free Application for Federal Student Aid. The forms are available from high school guidance offices, from the Financial Aid Office, or online at http://www.fafsa.ed.gov. Deadlines are given in the forms' instructions.

Faculty

Millersville University faculty members are dedicated to teaching and to offering individual attention. They take a personal interest in their students' lives and careers and are solely responsible for providing academic advisement. The University keeps a relatively low student-faculty ratio of 18:1 and an average class size of 26. No classes are taught by graduate assistants. Ninety-six percent of the 325 full-time faculty members hold a doctorate or the terminal degree in their field.

Student Government

Millersville University students participate in University governance through the Student Senate, faculty-student committees, and representation on the Faculty Senate, the Council of Trustees, and the Millersville Borough Council. The Student Senate works with faculty members and the administration on major University policies.

Admission Requirements

Millersville University admits approximately half its applicants. More than 80 percent of its full-time freshmen rank in the top 40 percent of their high school class. Academic records are the most important factor in admission decisions. Applicants must have successfully completed at least 4 years of high school English, 3 years of social studies, 3 years of mathematics (including a minimum of algebra I and II and geometry), and 3 years of science (2 units must be labs). In addition, 2 years of foreign language and 1 additional year each of math and science are strongly recommended.

Because an important part of the college experience is meeting people with backgrounds and interests different from one's own, Millersville University is committed to recruiting a diversified student body. SAT or ACT scores are required. Interviews, recommendations, and essays are not required. Out-of-state, international, and transfer applicants are welcome. Exceptional high school students may apply for early admission at the end of their junior year. Admitted applicants may request to defer their admission for one semester. Advanced standing is offered through CLEP and AP examinations.

Application and Information

To apply, students should submit a completed application form along with a $50 processing fee and official copies of the high school record and SAT or ACT scores. The University has a rolling admission policy, and students are encouraged to apply early (by mid-November) in their senior year for fall admission. Applicants are usually notified of a decision within a month after a completed application is received.

For application forms and additional information, students should contact:

Office of Admissions
Millersville University of Pennsylvania
P.O. Box 1002
Millersville, Pennsylvania 17551-0302
Phone: 717-872-3371
800-MU-ADMIT (toll-free)
E-mail: admissions@millersville.edu
Web site: http://www.millersville.edu

Millersville University's campus includes shaded areas that invite students to study or relax with friends.

MISERICORDIA UNIVERSITY
DALLAS, PENNSYLVANIA

The University

Misericordia University is a high-quality liberal arts and professional studies institution rooted in a foundation of service to others and committed to providing academic challenge and the personal attention to help students meet that challenge. Founded by the Sisters of Mercy, Misericordia offers undergraduate and graduate programs to resident and commuter students. Current enrollment is about 2,358 men and women.

Misericordia provides an academic atmosphere designed to stimulate critical thinking, independent judgment, and creativity as well as encourage the development of curiosity, good study habits, and personal values. The University also cultivates a spirit of community service and a lifelong love of learning in its students through extracurricular activities and challenging academic programs. In the National Survey of Student Engagement, Misericordia students say they are more involved in learning and have better relationships with faculty members and peers than students at other institutions.

The University is fully accredited by the Middle States Association of Colleges and Schools. Its programs in nursing, social work, medical imaging, occupational therapy, and physical therapy are accredited by the National League for Nursing Accrediting Commission, the Council on Social Work Education, the Joint Review Committee on Education in Radiologic Technology, the American Occupational Therapy Association, and the American Physical Therapy Association, respectively.

Misericordia operates three residential facilities and eighteen townhouse units with a total capacity for 760 students. A new residence hall is under construction. Two nearby homes are reserved for upper-level students. Residents have a number of options, including single rooms and wellness housing, and students living in campus housing hold average GPAs of more than 3.2. Each residence hall offers study rooms, laundry facilities, and recreational lounges. The new dining hall is located in the Banks Student Life Center, which also houses the Cougar's Den coffeehouse and snack bar.

There are numerous opportunities for students to become involved in campus activities. Besides Student Government, there are twenty-four chartered student clubs and organizations. Cultural events, Campus Ministry, intramural and intercollegiate athletic programs for men and women, performing arts shows, and many other social activities complement and reinforce the academic experience. In keeping with the University's tradition of mercy, justice, service, and hospitality, students also have opportunities to develop leadership potential through a variety of volunteer service projects that benefit the surrounding communities. The University's Service Leadership Center engages students in the development of lifelong civic responsibility through academic course work.

Campus Ministry provides opportunities to participate in campus and community programs. These programs are designed to promote social awareness in students. On spring break, students have elected to serve the poor in rural Appalachia, the storm-ravaged Gulf Coast, and the South Bronx. A six-week summer Cross-Cultural Ministry Experience in Guyana, South America, awaits selected participants.

Personalized attention is the key to the support available in the Learning Resource Center. A psychologist, counselors, therapists, and peer counselors form a dedicated team of professionals who conduct workshops for students each semester on a variety of topics, including test anxiety, stress management, time management, and goal setting. All services are free of charge to students, and contacts are strictly confidential.

First-year students may join the Guaranteed Placement Program through the Insalaco Center for Career Development. The program includes academic standards; cocurricular activities, such as leadership and service projects; internships; resume development; and interviewing skills. If a student fulfills the requirements of the program and is not employed in his or her field or enrolled in graduate or professional school within six months of graduation, a paid internship is assured. The center also co-presents the Choice Program, offering special guidance for students who have not chosen a major. Opportunities for career exploration, cooperative education, and internships are available for students to develop the knowledge and skills they need to enter the working world.

Student Health Services occupies a state-of-the-art facility. Health-care staff members provide first aid, assessment and treatment of common illnesses, and referrals for more serious health conditions. Health center activities are directed by a registered nurse with a master's degree in nursing administration under the guidance of a physician. A nurse practitioner is also available. A self-care room offers reference materials and up-to-date information on personal health concerns. All services are confidential.

A rapidly evolving world and development of new technologies have increased the number of adults who seek higher education. Misericordia offers special undergraduate and graduate programs for adults, including the Expressway Program, an accelerated bachelor's degree program; Women with Children, which provides housing and support services for single women with children; and evening and weekend formats for people with families and full-time jobs.

At Misericordia University, students can earn a master's degree by attending classes in the evening and/or on weekends. The small-class format enhances critical thinking and decision-making skills and draws out a variety of viewpoints that help broaden the perspectives of the student. Master's degrees are available in education, nursing, occupational therapy, physical therapy, speech-language pathology, business administration, and organizational management. A doctoral program in physical therapy is available to students entering in a full-time format. A doctorate in occupational therapy is planned for 2008.

Location

Located on a 123-acre campus in northeastern Pennsylvania, Misericordia University is the oldest institution of higher education in Luzerne County. Expansive lawns and thick stands of trees dominate the campus. It is 9 miles from the city of Wilkes-Barre. The area provides shopping centers, malls, cinemas, skiing, professional sporting events, and a variety of cultural activities. Pennsylvania's largest natural lake and two state parks are nearby, as are Pocono ski resorts. Metropolitan New York and Philadelphia are each within a 3-hour drive. Public and college-sponsored transportation is available to and from the campus.

Majors and Degrees

Misericordia University awards the Bachelor of Arts (B.A.) degree in English, history, and liberal studies. The Bachelor of Science (B.S.) degree is awarded in accounting, biochemistry, biology, business administration, chemistry, clinical laboratory science, communications, computer science, elementary education, health-care management, information technology, interdisciplinary studies, management, marketing, mathematics, math/computer science, medical imaging, philosophy, professional studies, psychology, secondary education, special education, and sport management. A Bachelor of Science in Nursing (B.S.N.) is awarded to nursing majors, and a Bachelor of Science in Social Work (B.S.W.) is awarded to social work majors. Specializations in accounting, early childhood education, pre-law, special education, and preprofessional occupations are also available. Certification programs include addictions counseling, child welfare services, gerontology, health-care informatics, and secondary education and may be taken in support of several degrees offered by Misericordia or as stand-alone programs.

The University offers five-year entry-level graduate majors in occupational therapy and speech-language pathology. Students graduate with a master's degree in speech-language pathology or occupational therapy and a bachelor's degree in health sciences. The physical therapy program is a 6½-year doctoral program. Students graduate with a bachelor's degree in one of several areas and a Doctor of Physical Therapy (D.P.T.) degree.

Academic Programs

Candidates for the B.A., B.S., B.S.N., or B.S.W. must fulfill a 48-credit liberal arts core curriculum in addition to the requirements of their chosen major to graduate. They must earn at least 36 credit hours in a chosen field. For regularly enrolled students, the average requirement for a baccalaureate degree is a total of 126 credits. Other options open to students include minors, specializations, certifications, and electives.

Courses are offered on a semester basis, beginning in August and January and ending in December and May. Summer, weekend, and accelerated courses are also available.

Academic Facilities

The chemistry, physics, and biology departments all have modern, fully equipped research laboratories available to students in these fields of concentration. State-of-the-art equipment includes high-performance liquid chromatography (HPLC), a rotary evaporator, an infrared spectrophotometer, and gas chromatography. The University also houses an energized radiation laboratory for the medical imaging program. The Anderson Sports and Health Center provides classrooms and laboratories for the occupational therapy, physical therapy, and nursing programs.

In addition to the four main computer labs, the Banks Student Life Center and Bevevino Library have more than 200 network access ports for Internet access as well as a wireless network. The University operates e-MU, a secure online portal where students can access e-mail, course schedules, group and chat functions, and student account and registration information from a single sign-on. The Munson Center for Communications features the area's only all-digital television control room and editing bays

Mercy Hall, the University's original administrative building, underwent extensive renovations in 2002 with new multipurpose classrooms and facilities for the speech-language pathology program. In addition, many key student service departments, including the registrar, student accounts, and financial aid are now centralized in one area in Mercy Hall.

McGowan Hall, a new 120-bed residence hall, is currently under construction. Insalaco Hall is also under construction. A new state-of-the-art classroom and conference building, Insalaco Hall is expected to be complete in fall 2008.

The three-story Bevevino Library covers 37,500 square feet and houses stacks for 90,000 volumes. Materials include information and communication technology and a reference section that offers books, serials, and a variety of periodicals as well as reference search tools, CD-ROMs, and multiple online databases and microfilm. The Bevevino Library is a member of the Northeastern Pennsylvania Library Network, which provides users access to the 1.5-million-volume collections of participating libraries via its new virtual online catalog.

Costs

Tuition for 2007–08 is $20,830 per year. The general fee, including the technology fee, is $1120. Housing options include traditional rooms, suites, town houses, and wellness housing. The average room cost is $5200. All resident students must participate in a meal plan. Residents may choose from a ten-, fourteen-, or nineteen-meal plan. In addition, town-house residents are eligible to choose a five-meal plan. The average board cost was $3680.

Financial Aid

All students applyihg for financial aid must complete the Free Application for Federal Student Aid (FAFSA) by May 1. The application is used for Federal Pell Grants, Federal Supplemental Educational Opportunity Grants (FSEOG), subsidized and unsubsidized Federal Stafford Student Loans, Federal Perkins Loans, nursing loans, and Federal Work-Study Program awards. This application is also the basis upon which state and institutional aid is awarded. The University also offers a no-interest monthly payment plan. In addition, many scholarships are available for qualified students, including $4 million in honors scholarships based on academic abilities and $2.2 million in McAuley Awards for students who have experience in leadership roles and volunteer service.

Faculty

There are 97 full-time faculty members. A student-faculty ratio of 11:1 results in students receiving a great deal of individual attention from a highly qualified faculty. Eighty-four percent of the faculty members hold doctorates. Besides student academic advising, the faculty members also serve as advisers to clubs.

Student Government

An active student government organization serves as a liaison between the students and the faculty and staff members. The administration enables students to become involved by serving as student representatives on various University committees.

Admission Requirements

Misericordia University admits applicants based on their secondary school record, high school recommendation, extracurricular activities, and personal promise. The University requires SAT or ACT scores. Although a personal interview is highly recommended, it is not necessary for all majors. Misericordia offers both early decision and early admissions programs.

Transfer students with a cumulative average of at least 2.0 (on a 4.0 scale) may be considered for admission and may receive advanced standing. Some majors require a 2.5 or higher cumulative average. Transfer students must submit official high school transcripts. A transcript of work completed at other colleges and universities and proof of honorable dismissal are also required.

Application and Information

Applicants must submit an official application form (available upon request), transcripts, and SAT or ACT scores. Applicants may also apply for admission online at the University's Web address. There is a nonrefundable application fee of $25, which is waived for students who visit the campus.

The University considers applications on a rolling basis. Usually, candidates are notified of the admission decision within three weeks of receipt of all required materials.

Office of Admissions
Misericordia University
301 Lake Street
Dallas, Pennsylvania 18612-1090
Phone: 570-674-6461
866-262-6363 (toll free)
Fax: 570-675-2441
E-mail: admiss@misericordia.edu
Internet: http://admissions.misericordia.edu

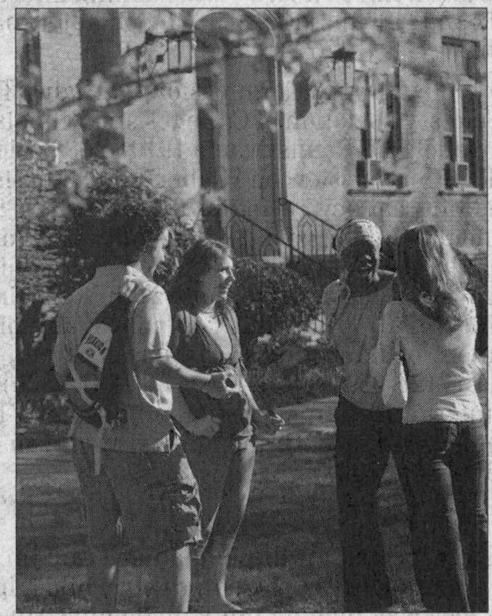

Students at Misericordia University pursue their studies with an emphasis on academic excellence, service leadership, and professional preparation.

MOORE COLLEGE OF ART & DESIGN

PHILADELPHIA, PENNSYLVANIA

The College

Moore College of Art & Design sets the standard of excellence in educating women for careers in art and design. It is the only women's college for the visual arts in the nation, and students enjoy Moore's accessible, supportive, small-college community and are taught by a dedicated faculty of award-winning artists, designers, and scholars.

Moore offers ten Bachelor of Fine Arts (B.F.A.) degree majors, emphasizing career and leadership skills throughout the academic programs. Each major provides strong career preparation for its field and offers internships coordinated with the Locks Career Center for Women in the Arts. The Locks Center also provides extensive career resources for students and alumnae, such as one-on-one career counseling, mentoring, job bulletins, and workshops on topics ranging from networking to resume writing.

On-campus leadership organizations provide the opportunity to learn about and utilize leadership skills and to develop self-confidence. Leadership fellowships provide financial support for students to work either with an individual leader in the arts community or within an innovative organization. Other experiences are available through community service or study abroad.

Approximately 70 percent of first-year students live in College housing, which includes Main Residence and Sartain Hall. Some students choose to rent apartments near the campus or in one of Philadelphia's many residential neighborhoods.

Moore alumnae are accomplished artists and designers who use their creativity, skills, and talent to excel in a wide variety of industries. Among Moore's notable graduates are fashion designer and business icon, Adrienne Vittadini; renowned twentieth-century portraitist, Alice Neel; award-winning interior designer, Karon Daroff; and Pulitzer Prize-winning photojournalist, Sharon J. Wohlmuth.

Moore is accredited by the Commission on Higher Education of the Middle States Association of Colleges and Schools (3624 Market Street, Philadelphia, Pennsylvania 19104-2680, telephone: 215-662-5606). The Commission on Higher Education is an institutional accrediting agency recognized by the U.S. Secretary of Education and the Commission on Recognition of Postsecondary Accreditation; by the National Association of Schools of Art and Design (11250 Roger Bacon Drive, Suite 21, Reston, Virginia 20190, telephone: 703-437-0700); by the Commonwealth of Pennsylvania, Department of Education (333 Market Street, Harrisburg, Pennsylvania 17126-0333, telephone: 717-787-5820); and by the Council for Interior Design Accreditation (formerly FIDER) (146 Monroe Center NW, #1318, Grand Rapids, Michigan 49503-2822, telephone: 616-458-0400).

Location

Moore is ideally located on the Benjamin Franklin Parkway in the scenic Museum District of Center City, Philadelphia. Neighbors on The Parkway include the Philadelphia Museum of Art, the Rodin Museum, the Academy of Natural Sciences, the Franklin Institute, and the Free Library of Philadelphia. The Parkway is also the future site of the new Barnes Foundation which has one of the largest collections of impressionist and post-impressionist art in the world.

Philadelphia is also the home of Independence National Historical Park and to dozens of art galleries, diverse neighborhoods, and shops and restaurants of every variety. This artistic and cultural vitality provides Moore students with a multitude of resources and recreation in a stimulating urban setting. Nearly eighty nearby colleges and universities form one of the largest higher-education communities in the nation, second only to New York City.

Philadelphia is 100 miles south of New York City and 133 miles north of Washington, D.C., a short journey by car, bus, or train. Faculty members regularly organize classroom trips to take advantage of these cities' additional galleries, museums, and designer showrooms.

Majors and Degrees

Moore College of Art & Design offers a four-year program leading to a Bachelor of Fine Arts degree, with concentrations in art education, art history, curatorial studies, fashion design, fine arts (with 2-D and/or 3-D emphasis), graphic design, illustration, interior design, photography and digital arts, and textile design. Students can minor in any major offered except art education.

In most majors, students are required to participate in an internship to acquire practical experience in their chosen field. In addition to Bachelor of Fine Arts degree programs, Moore also offers postbaccalaureate certificates in art education and interior design.

Academic Programs

The College operates on a two-semester academic year. In B.F.A. programs, approximately two thirds of the required credits are in studio courses. One third of the credits are in academic courses.

A student's first year includes a broadly based core of studies in art history, two- and three-dimensional basic design, color, drawing, computer applications, figure drawing, and the humanities. Introductory courses to the fine and design arts are also offered.

Tutorial support is available for all students. At the end of the first year, the student chooses a design or fine arts concentration.

While instruction in the core studies is highly directive, advanced studio courses require more initiative and self-discipline, because the College provides each student with an increasingly personal program of study and assistance. Seniors in both the fine arts and design arts acquire practical experience in their fields through internships, apprenticeships, and the College's cooperative education program.

The College participates in the Association of Independent Colleges of Art and Design (AICAD) Student Mobility Exchange Program. A student who meets eligibility requirements may apply for one semester's study at an AICAD member school's program.

In addition to Bachelor of Fine Arts programs, Moore also offers leading continuing education (CE) programs. Moore's adult CE courses for men and women, offered mainly in the evening and on weekends, include certificate programs in digital media and decorative arts for interiors. The 84-year-old Young Artists Workshop (YAW) provides art education opportunities for girls and boys in grades 1–12. The Summer Art and Design Institute is a four-week summer residency program that offers high school-age women a program that earns 3 college credits. For CE information, students should call 215-965-4029 or contact CE via e-mail at ce@moore.edu.

Academic Facilities

The main campus is a complex of interconnected buildings that includes Wilson Hall, Sarah Peter Hall, and the Stahl Residence Hall. Sartain Residence Hall is located two blocks from the main campus.

Main campus includes expansive studios and classrooms, technology centers, MAC and PC computer labs, a professional woodshop, ferrous and nonferrous metal workshops, ceramic studios with indoor and outdoor kilns, abundant student exhibition space, two contemporary art galleries, several outdoor courtyards and student lounges, a sculpture park, The Art Shop, a dining café, and two auditoriums.

The Connolly Library's extensive holdings include 40,000 volumes reflecting subjects in the curriculum, artists' books, rare design folios, a slide collection of more than 123,000 images, reference materials, exhibition catalogs and annuals, and subscriptions to 185 local, national, and international periodicals.

The Galleries at Moore are internationally known and present a wide range of exhibitions and educational programs of both established and emerging artists. The Paley Gallery exhibits challenging and innovative work by national and international artists, while the Levy Gallery showcases artists from the Philadelphia area. The galleries also provide a professional exhibition space for shows by Moore students, faculty members, and alumnae.

In addition, Moore has two galleries showing student, alumnae, and faculty work at Philadelphia's landmark Kimmel Center for the Performing Arts as well as galleries in the Lincoln Financial Field sports complex.

Costs

Tuition and fees for 2007–08 were $26,156. Room and board for students living in College residence halls were $9906. Books, supplies, and personal expenses (excluding transportation) are estimated to be approximately $3500 per year for most students.

Financial Aid

Moore offers financial aid based on financial need as established by information provided on the Free Application for Federal Student Aid (FAFSA).

The principal forms of financial aid are Federal Pell Grants, Federal Supplemental Educational Opportunity Grants, Federal Perkins Loans, and Moore College of Art & Design scholarships and grants. Assistance is also available through the Federal Work-Study program. For full consideration, students are encouraged to apply for financial aid by March 1.

Moore College annually grants $3.5 million in scholarship aid to students who demonstrate excellence both academically and artistically. Awards are granted on the basis of the portfolio review and academic merit.

Faculty

Moore College of Art & Design has 142 faculty members, 36 in academic and 106 in studio areas. All studio classes are taught by practicing professionals. The student-faculty ratio is approximately 8:1.

Student Government

On-campus leadership organizations provide the chance to learn about and utilize leadership skills and to develop self-confidence participating in groups such as Student Government, Student Mentors, Residence Life Staff, and the Student Judiciary Committee. Students are trained in areas such as teambuilding, presentation skills, ethics, diversity, time management, and creating community on campus.

Admission Requirements

The admission decision is based on an evaluation of the following required materials: transcripts from high schools and any colleges attended, SAT or ACT scores, and a portfolio of between twelve and twenty pieces of original artwork that must include some observational drawings. (International students should submit TOEFL scores instead of SAT or ACT scores.) First-year students may enter in the fall and spring semesters.

Transfer students are encouraged to apply for advanced class standing at Moore. Class standing is determined on the basis of acceptable transfer credits and an evaluation of the applicant's portfolio. All transfers who are applying for advanced standing must submit their portfolio in slide or digital form, accompanied by a detailed description letter. Upper-level transfer students may enter in the fall or spring semester.

Application and Information

Although Moore has a rolling admissions policy and therefore no application deadline, students seeking admission in the fall semester are encouraged to submit applications to the Admissions Office by March 1. For application forms, catalogs, and additional information, students should contact:

Director of Admissions
Moore College of Art & Design
20th Street and The Parkway
Philadelphia, Pennsylvania 19103-1179
Phone: 215-965-4014
800-523-2025 (toll-free)
Fax: 215-568-3547
E-mail: enroll@moore.edu
Web site: http://www.moore.edu

Moore College of Art & Design sets the standard for educating women for careers in art and design as the first and only visual arts college for women in the United States.

MORAVIAN COLLEGE

BETHLEHEM, PENNSYLVANIA

The College

Moravian College is the nation's sixth-oldest college, tracing its origins to a women's program begun in 1742. Settlers from Eastern Europe, known as Moravians, founded both the College and the community of Bethlehem and brought to America a rich cultural heritage of architecture, music, scholarship, and craftsmanship. The strength of Moravian's music program and the community's famed Bach Choir are aspects of the continuing influence of this heritage.

Moravian College is a selective, coeducational institution offering more than fifty programs with foundations in the liberal arts and sciences. Among its strengths and distinctions are an outstanding faculty with a personal and professional commitment to teaching, a demanding academic program recognized for its excellence and high standards, and close working relationships among students and faculty and staff members. Moravian has won national recognition for the depth and effectiveness of its career-counseling and placement programs. Opportunities for field studies and internships enhance career preparation in much the same way that independent study and honors programs enhance all aspects of the academic program.

The majority of the 1,515 students enrolled come from the mid-Atlantic region, but more than twenty states and fifteen countries are represented in the student body. Moravian's students are involved in a wide range of activities and athletics. Men compete in intercollegiate baseball, basketball, cross-country, football, golf, lacrosse, soccer, tennis, and track and field; women compete in basketball, cross-country, field hockey, lacrosse, soccer, softball, tennis, track and field, and volleyball. Intramural sports include basketball, floor hockey, indoor soccer, racquetball, softball, table tennis, touch football, and volleyball. Club sports include equitation, ice hockey, and skiing.

Activities range from participation in an outing club to modern dancing. There are departmental clubs, honor societies, fraternities, sororities, and service organizations. Communications opportunities include a student newspaper, a yearbook, WRMC (radio station), a literary magazine, and work in the Media Center. Performance groups include the Moravian College Theatre Company, a wind ensemble, an orchestra, and the Moravian College Choir, which in recent years has toured Europe, including England, Germany, and Scandinavia; Israel; and the Caribbean and performed at the Kennedy Center in Washington, D.C. Nationally known lecturers, scholars, authors, and artists are brought to the campus, and, through the College-Community Concert series, many major European and American touring orchestras have appeared on campus. Many students participate in volunteer activities related to political, social welfare, health, and teaching fields.

Approximately 71 percent of Moravian's students reside on campus in housing that ranges from the traditional dormitory to apartment and town-house accommodations.

An M.B.A. degree is offered by the Department of Economics and Business through the Division of Continuing and Graduate Studies. As a corporate institution, Moravian College also includes a theological seminary, offering programs leading to the Master of Divinity (M.Div.) degree and Master of Arts (M.A.) degrees in theological studies and pastoral counseling; a cooperative program leading to the M.A. in Christian education is also offered. While campus facilities are shared with the undergraduate program, the faculty, administration, and fee schedules are separate.

Location

Moravian College is located in Bethlehem, Pennsylvania, a city of 75,000 people. Bethlehem's location in the Lehigh Valley area (Allentown-Bethlehem-Easton) and its proximity to New York City and Philadelphia allow it to combine the advantages of these cities with the accessibility and friendliness of a smaller community. Moravian shares its Lehigh Valley location with the world headquarters of Air Products, Mack Truck, Rodale, Agere Systems, and other businesses and industries as well as with five other private colleges: Lafayette, Muhlenberg, and Cedar Crest Colleges and DeSales and Lehigh Universities. Bethlehem, with its distinctive history, is carefully preserving its past while engaging in twenty-first-century expansion.

Majors and Degrees

Moravian College offers the Bachelor of Arts, Bachelor of Science, and Bachelor of Music degrees with programs of study in fifty areas. The following programs of study are offered: accounting, art education, art history and criticism, biochemistry, biology, business management, chemistry, classics, computer science, drama and theater, economics, elementary education, English language and literature, environmental policy and economics, environmental science, financial economics, French, German, German studies, graphic and interactive design, history, international management, law and society, mathematics, music, music composition, music education, music performance, neuroscience, nursing, philosophy, physics, political science, psychology, religion, sacred music, secondary education, sociology, Spanish, studio art, and writing. (Engineering, geology, medical technology, natural resource management, occupational therapy, and physical therapy are offered in cooperation with other institutions.)

The College offers preprofessional programs in dentistry, law, medicine, ministry, and veterinary medicine. Students can also structure interdepartmental majors, individually designed majors, double majors, and minors in all areas.

Academic Programs

The academic year consists of fall and spring terms of fifteen weeks each. The typical course load per term is 4 course units, equivalent to 4 semester-credit hours per unit.

To earn a baccalaureate degree, students are required to complete 32 course units (128 semester-credit hours). By following Moravian's general education curriculum, Learning in Common, students are given a coherent introduction to the liberal arts and sciences. Special programs available include independent study, field study, study-abroad and exchange programs, a special honors program in the senior year, Rokke Scholars, and the Student Opportunities for Academic Research (SOAR) program.

The Learning in Common (LINC) curriculum includes a multidisciplinary approach designed to sharpen such critical skills as writing, computer competence, knowledge of economic and social systems, science experimentation, moral and ethical issues, international and historical perspectives, and quantitative reasoning.

Off-Campus Programs

Moravian students may participate in the Washington Semester, study at Oxford University, and experience a variety of other study-abroad opportunities for a summer, a term, or a full academic year. In addition, students may cross-register for courses offered by Lehigh and DeSales Universities and Lafayette, Muhlenberg, and Cedar Crest Colleges through the Lehigh Valley Association of Independent Colleges. Two- and four-year U.S. Army ROTC programs are available through cross-registration with Lehigh University. All programs carry academic credit. Students may also participate in courses and programs offered through the Lehigh Valley Center for Jewish Studies.

Academic Facilities

The Priscilla Payne Hurd Academic Complex, a $19-million technology-enhanced teaching facility, opened in 2003 for the Departments of Education, Psychology, Sociology, Mathematics, and Computer Science. The facility is used for classroom teaching, conferences, laboratories, research, lectures, and special events.

Reeves Library houses more than 263,000 volumes and operates on an open-stack policy, with reading areas throughout the building. Cooperation with other Lehigh Valley colleges makes more than 2 million volumes readily accessible to Moravian College students. An automated online catalog with remote access is available, as are other online reference services. The library is open until midnight.

Collier Hall of Science, which has been recognized for its architectural design and function, provides lecture halls, teaching laboratories, specialized collections and reading rooms, a greenhouse, and individual research laboratories for faculty members and advanced students in physics, earth science, chemistry, biology, and computer science.

All members of the College community are provided a full range of computer network privileges, including e-mail, Internet access, and networked data storage. All residence hall rooms provide data network connections. Approximately 175 Windows, Macintosh, and UNIX computers are available for student use in labs and classrooms. Standard office software, Web browsers, statistical packages, graphic design software, and miscellaneous courseware are available on these machines. Free laser printing is provided to all students as well. Seventeen of Moravian's classrooms have full multimedia capabilities. Course management software by Blackboard offers professors a full suite of teaching and communication tools for their classes.

The Center for Music and Art is located on the College's historic Priscilla Payne Hurd campus, in an area that reflects the grace of Colonial and Victorian architecture. The center has been extensively renovated for practice and performance needs and includes a changing-exhibition art gallery.

Costs

The cost of tuition and fees, including a student activity fee, is $30,062 for 2008–09. Room and board are $8312. Books, travel, and miscellaneous expenses are estimated at $2725 for resident students, $4630 for students commuting from home, and $5875 for off-campus residents. Expenses for international students are the same as those for resident students. A one-time freshman orientation fee of $125 is also charged.

Financial Aid

Moravian College, together with state and federal programs, offers financial aid to qualified students through scholarships, loans, grants, and employment. The purpose of these programs is to provide financial assistance to supplement that given by the student's family. Applications for financial aid, filed with the College and with state and federal agencies, allow students to be considered for each program for which they are eligible. All financial aid awards generally involve both grants and student self-help in the form of loans and student employment. Endowed scholarships are also available in several areas of study. Academic achievement, future promise, and leadership potential play a role in the type of award made. The College also offers limited funding to qualified international students each year.

The College awards approximately $24 million annually in financial aid (grants, campus jobs, and loans) to an average of 90 percent of the student body. Incoming freshmen and upperclassmen applying for need-based financial aid are required to file the College Scholarship Service Financial Aid PROFILE with signed copies of federal income taxes for both parents and student, and the Free Application for Federal Student Aid (FAFSA).

The College offers merit scholarship programs, awarded to students without regard to financial need, based on superior academic performance. Scholarships range from $1000 to full tuition.

Faculty

Of Moravian's 120 full-time faculty members, 92 percent hold earned doctoral or other terminal degrees. The student-faculty ratio is 11:1. Many Moravian faculty members have distinguished themselves in research, publication, and public service, but the primary focus of their endeavors is on effective teaching and advising of students.

Student Government

The United Student Government represents students' interests, allocates activity funds to student organizations, and appoints students to student-faculty committees. Self-governance is developed through the appointment of an undergraduate resident staff and a student-dominated College Discipline Committee. Two students are elected annually as voting members of the Board of Trustees. The Haupert Union Program Board, composed entirely of students, provides a major part of the College's social program and, through its various committees, is a vehicle for the development of leadership.

Admission Requirements

Moravian welcomes students from diverse backgrounds and geographic locations. The Admissions Committee carefully evaluates the preparation and potential of each applicant, placing emphasis on academic achievement in secondary school. Other factors considered include a student's test scores, recommendations, extracurricular activities, and demonstrated interest in the College. Graduation from an accredited secondary school or a high school equivalency certificate is required. Of the students entering Moravian in 2007, nearly a third ranked in the top 10 percent of their secondary school class, with 46 percent in the top fifth. Of the 2,189 applicants, 1,401 were accepted. Of those who were accepted, 401 enrolled.

Transfer and international students are welcome and are encouraged to apply. International applicants must demonstrate English proficiency and the ability to assume expenses and must provide transcripts (originals and certified translations) documenting secondary and postsecondary school study. Each transfer student's credentials are considered individually to determine the number of credits to be accepted. Transfer applicants must present a minimum 3.0 grade point average (4.0 scale).

Students are strongly encouraged to visit the campus. Interviews, tours of the College, and visits with faculty members may be arranged by contacting the Admission Office prior to the visit.

Application and Information

Each prospective student should submit a completed application and a nonrefundable $40 application fee as early as possible in the senior year, preferably by February 1. The deadline is March 1. An official high school transcript, an essay, letters of recommendation, and reports from either the SAT or ACT are required. The TOEFL is required of all applicants for whom English is not the native language. Applicants are notified of the Admissions Committee decision on March 15. Early decision applicants must apply by February 1. The committee notifies these applicants of its decision between December 15 and February 15.

For an application form or additional information, students should contact:

James P. Mackin
Director of Admission
Moravian College
Bethlehem, Pennsylvania 18018
Phone: 610-861-1320
800-441-3191 (toll-free)
Fax: 610-625-7930
E-mail: admissions@moravian.edu
Web site: http://www.moravian.edu

MOUNT ALOYSIUS COLLEGE

CRESSON, PENNSYLVANIA

The College

Mount Aloysius College is a small, private, comprehensive, Catholic liberal arts college sponsored by the Sisters of Mercy. Established in 1853, the College today specializes in both undergraduate and graduate education. Since the founding of the College, more than 12,000 students have become proud Mount Aloysius College graduates. The College is committed to providing a small classroom size and a highly structured environment. Mount Aloysius College students come from the commonwealth of Pennsylvania, but many other states are represented on campus, including Connecticut, Delaware, Maine, Maryland, Missouri, New Jersey, New York, Vermont, Virginia, and West Virginia. Approximately 65 percent of the College's students are women. There are approximately 1,200 full-time and 400 part-time students enrolled.

Mount Aloysius College is one of eighteen Mercy Colleges nationwide. As part of the Mercy College curriculum, students are encouraged to evaluate ethical issues and form a sound character consistent with traditional, Judeo-Christian values. Social growth is seen as a vital element of a complete liberal arts education, encompassing the important ability to relate closely to people.

The College recognizes that student activities play a distinctive role in the total campus educational program. There are approximately 100 organized clubs, groups, honor societies, and intramural sports programs, including a newspaper, residence hall associations, student government, cheerleading, dance team, scholarship-funded theater and choir programs, and a student activities planning board. Student activities include many social events, intramural sports programs, NCAA Division III athletic events, comedians, cultural and educational events, campus forums, and lectures by guest speakers.

Mount Aloysius College is a member of NCAA Division III. The following athletic programs are available to both women and men: basketball, cross-country, golf, and soccer. Men's baseball and women's softball and volleyball are also offered. Both intercollegiate and intramural athletes benefit from the Ray S. and Louise S. Walker Athletic Field Complex, which includes a softball field and one of the finest soccer fields in the area. The most recent addition is the Calandra-Smith baseball field.

Many buildings make up the 165-acre campus. The main building is a picturesque structure dating to 1897; it houses the admissions, financial aid, security, health, and academic offices, along with the Office of the President, classrooms, telenursing research facilities, and the Wolf-Kuhn art gallery. Cosgrave Center is the main hub on campus, serving as the Student Union. The building contains the dining hall, snack bar, bookstore, child-care center (part of the elementary education/early childhood program at the College), lounges, recreational rooms, student affairs offices, and meeting rooms. The College's Health and Physical Fitness Center is adjacent to Cosgrave Center. Its main athletic arena has a seating capacity of approximately 2,000 and serves as the home to all Mounties fans. The facility provides space for three basketball courts, three volleyball courts, a tennis court, a weight and exercise room equipped with a sauna, two locker rooms, office areas, changing rooms for sports officials, public restrooms, a lobby, and a vestibule. Ihmsen Halls are key housing facilities for residential students. Misciagna Residence is a state-of-the-art residence hall, providing twenty-five suites and private bathrooms. Slated for completion by fall 2009, Mount Aloysius is currently constructing a new residence hall that will feature both double and single rooms. This new hall will also house a large multipurpose room as well as study lounges on each of its three floors. Alumni Hall is a historic, multipurpose room that is used for College drama, musicals, and many performing arts events. The College operates twelve months per year and opens its facilities to the outside community as well.

The campus offers 100 percent wireless Internet access for laptops and PDAs. Wireless access points are installed in all buildings throughout the campus. In addition, several smart classrooms are located around campus.

Mount Aloysius is a comprehensive college that is fully accredited by the Middle States Association of Colleges and Schools and approved by the Pennsylvania Department of Education. All nursing programs and health studies programs are fully accredited by their professional accrediting bodies, including the National League for Nursing Accrediting Commission, the Commission on Accreditation in Physical Therapy Education, the American Association of Medical Assistants, and the Joint Commission on Accreditation for Programs of Surgical Technology.

In addition to its undergraduate programs, Mount Aloysius offers master's degrees in criminal justice management in correctional administration, health and human services administration, and psychology.

Location

Mount Aloysius College is located in the scenic southern Allegheny Mountains of west-central Pennsylvania, in the small town of Cresson, which is adjacent to U.S. Route 22. The College's setting is rural, with two midsized cities, Altoona and Johnstown, within a very short distance. The area has warm, beautiful summers; brisk, breathtaking autumns; invigorating, snowy winters; and cool, blooming springs. Facilities in the area are available for outdoor activities, including biking, golfing, swimming, horseback riding, waterskiing and water activities, hiking, spelunking, picnicking, and amusement and water parks.

Majors and Degrees

Mount Aloysius College awards bachelor's and associate degrees in the arts, sciences, and health studies fields in both career-oriented and traditional liberal arts programs. Baccalaureate degrees are available in accounting, behavioral and social science, biology and general science, business administration, computer science, criminology, elementary/early childhood education and secondary education (with certifications), English, general science, history/political science, humanities, information technology, math/science, medical imaging, nursing (RN-B.S.N. program), nursing (2-2), occupational therapy (3-2), physical therapy (4-2), physician assistant studies (3-2), prelaw, psychology, sign language/interpreter education, and undecided/exploratory. Associate degrees are offered in applied technology, business administration, criminology, early childhood studies, general studies, legal studies, liberal arts, medical assistant studies, nursing, nursing (LPN to RN), physical therapist assistant studies, prenursing, radiography/medical imaging, sign language/deaf studies, and surgical technology.

Academic Programs

Whether preparing students for careers upon graduation or for graduate school, Mount Aloysius recognizes the importance of a broad and liberal education. Thus, in addition to receiving solid preparation for a chosen career, every student at the College receives a foundation in the arts, sciences, and humanities through an outstanding core curriculum. Strong emphasis is placed on the specialized courses within each program of study, and many academic programs combine classroom experience with internships and related training at area clinical sites, agencies, and institutions. In addition to its regular academic programs, Mount Aloysius offers independent and directed study with a commitment to service, which is a key ingredient in a Mercy education. The College has an excellent honors program and academic services area. The academic calendar has two traditional semesters and two or three optional summer sessions.

Off-Campus Programs

An important feature of many academic programs is off-campus training. The majority of the College's programs of study require credit-yielding practicums, through which students work and receive training at local and regional hospitals, public and private schools, or health or human service agencies. Students in all health programs participate in required on-the-job training during their time at the College.

Academic Facilities

In 1995, Mount Aloysius College opened both a new library and a new era, signifying greater access to information for the College community. This state-of-the-art facility is the campus hub for technology and studying. With a Buhl Electronic Classroom and more than 80,000 print and nonprint titles, the library is an impressive, 31,000-square-foot facility with ample seating space, four group-study rooms, a reading lounge, a law library and classroom, an unparalleled 17,000-volume ecumenical collection that was donated by Pastor Gerald Myers, and additional room for future expansion. This facility is completely automated, with an online catalog and access to remote libraries and the World Wide Web at more than thirty public workstations. Also located in the library is the Information Technology Center, home to fifteen multimedia computer workstations and some of the latest offerings in educational software.

Pierce Hall serves as the science center on campus and is a state-of-the-art, 31,000-square-foot facility that was completed in 1997 and houses all science laboratories, health science centers, and offices of faculty members in the health studies programs. Academic Hall is an impressive facility that is home to the College Honors Program. It also has classrooms, labs, seminar rooms, faculty offices, and electronic rooms. The College is proud of its bridge to the past and its progress in providing twenty-first-century buildings.

Costs

Annual tuition and fees for the 2007–08 academic year for full-time students were $15,390, and room and board were $6700.

Financial Aid

Mount Aloysius recognizes the expense involved in acquiring a liberal arts education and encourages all students to apply for all available aid. Through the Office of Financial Aid, the College assists students in applying for state and federal grants, loans, work-study awards, and College merit scholarships and grants. The College awards academic monies based on GPA and SAT or ACT scores; these awards are renewable over a four-year period and range from $1000 to $8000 per year. Mount Aloysius College participates in all federal and state programs; 90 percent of the College's students receive some form of financial aid. *U.S. News & World Report* has ranked Mount Aloysius College as one of the best-priced private liberal arts colleges in the U.S.

Faculty

The Mount Aloysius faculty consists of approximately 60 full-time members, whose primary responsibility is teaching and advising students. Most full-time faculty members hold advanced or terminal degrees and are expected to maintain close instructional ties with students. Many professors hold national professional certificates in such disciplines as criminology, education, law, and nursing. The Mount Aloysius student-faculty ratio of 14:1 allows close contact between students and faculty members, providing personal attention in a highly structured environment—a key ingredient in the College's academic philosophy.

Student Government

The Student Representative Government (SRG) represents students on all issues that concern the College. The SRG appoints student representatives to all student-oriented College committees. The College encourages active student participation in the general governance structure and in other matters concerning the development and implementation of policies on residential student life.

Admission Requirements

The College admits a freshman class of approximately 350 students, which amounts to a total class of 500 with transfer students. Admission is selective and is based on academic promise, as indicated by a student's secondary school performance and activities, standardized test scores, and special experience and talents. Applicants are required to have, or expect to earn, a diploma from an approved secondary school or a GED diploma. Submission of official transcripts and SAT or ACT scores is required. In addition to the general admission requirements, specific admission requirements exist for the health programs; students should visit the College's Web site (http://www.mtaloy.edu) for further information. Prospective students are highly encouraged to visit the scenic 165-acre campus. The College is open Monday to Friday from 8:30 to 4 and on select Saturdays.

Application and Information

To apply for admission to Mount Aloysius College, candidates are encouraged to submit their application and $30 application fee to the Office of Undergraduate and Graduate Admissions. In addition, students may apply online. For further information, students should contact:

Office of Undergraduate and Graduate Admissions
Mount Aloysius College
7373 Admiral Peary Highway
Cresson, Pennsylvania 16630
Phone: 814-886-6383
888-823-2220 (toll-free)
Fax: 814-886-6441
E-mail: admissions@mtaloy.edu
Web site: http://www.mtaloy.edu

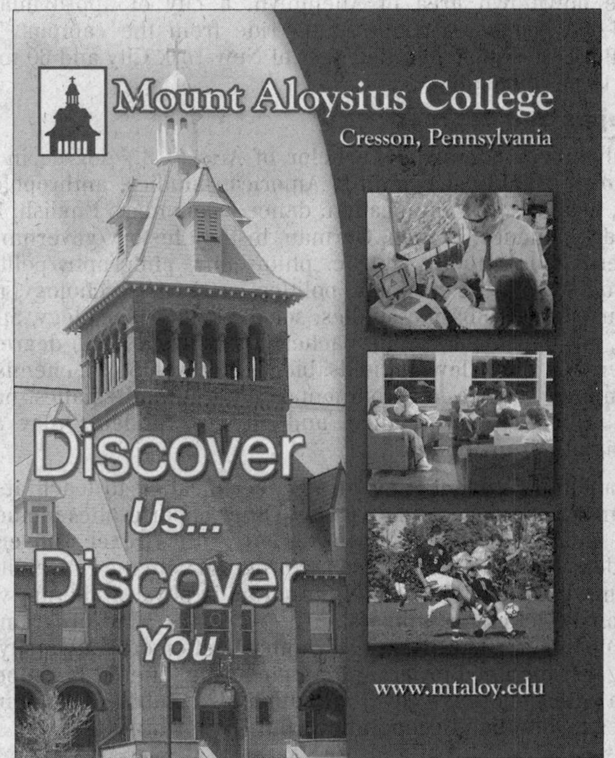

Student activities abound on the Mount Aloysius College campus.

MUHLENBERG COLLEGE

ALLENTOWN, PENNSYLVANIA

The College

Founded in 1848, Muhlenberg College aims to develop independent critical thinkers who are intellectually agile, characterized by a zeal for reasoned and civil debate, knowledgeable about the achievements and traditions of diverse civilizations and cultures, able to express ideas with clarity and grace, committed to lifelong learning, equipped with ethical values, and prepared for lives of leadership and service.

Muhlenberg students achieve the College's goals by assuming strong individual responsibility for intense involvement in vigorous academic work and for personal involvement within the College community. The more than 100 student organizations provide outlets for the diversified cultural, athletic, religious, social, leadership, and service interests of the students. The campus is primarily residential; more than 90 percent of the 2,150 students live on campus. A close sense of community develops naturally, one in which their diversified academic and personal interests enable students to contribute positively to the intellectual and personal growth of their peers.

Students are aided by an active Career Planning and Placement Service in relating academic and personal knowledge and skills to appropriate career goals and in obtaining positions upon graduation. About one third of a typical graduating class proceeds immediately to graduate or professional school.

Location

Muhlenberg College is located in suburban west Allentown, an area made up primarily of attractive family homes and parks. The downtown area of Allentown, a city of approximately 104,000 people, is a 10-minute ride from the campus. The College is located 90 miles west of New York City and 60 miles north of Philadelphia.

Majors and Degrees

Muhlenberg offers the Bachelor of Arts (A.B.) degree in the following fields: accounting, American studies, anthropology, art, business, communication, dance, economics, English, film studies, finance, French, German, history, history/government, international studies, music, philosophy, philosophy/political thought, political economy, political science, psychology, religious studies, Russian studies, social science, sociology, Spanish, and theater arts. The Bachelor of Science (B.S.) degree is offered in the following fields: biochemistry, biology, chemistry, computer science, environmental science, mathematics, natural sciences, neuroscience, and physics. Students may also design their own major.

In addition, students may receive certification to teach at the elementary and secondary levels. Other opportunities include a 4-4 guaranteed-admission program with Drexel University College of Medicine; a 3-4 dental program with the University of Pennsylvania; a 3-3 B.S./Ph.D. program in physical therapy with Thomas Jefferson University; a 3-2½ B.S./M.S. program in occupational therapy with Thomas Jefferson University; a 3-2/4-2 combined program in engineering, offered in cooperation with Columbia University; and a 3-2 combined program in forestry, offered in cooperation with Duke University.

Academic Programs

The A.B. and B.S. programs emphasize breadth of study in the liberal arts as well as in-depth study of a particular academic major. All students must fulfill requirements in foreign culture, the humanities, social sciences, and natural sciences. Strong achievement on Advanced Placement examinations may enable a student to receive advanced placement, possibly with credit. Scores of 4 or 5 earn automatic credit. Scores of 3 are evaluated by the appropriate department.

Students work closely with academic advisers to formulate programs well suited to their individual interests, abilities, needs, and goals. Generally, students are expected to declare their major at the end of the freshman year; however, many students later change their academic major with no difficulty. A double major is possible, and several fields are available as minor programs. These minor fields are accounting, African American studies, anthropology, business, chemistry, computer science, economics, English, French, German, history, Jewish studies, mathematics, music, philosophy, physics, political science, public health, religion, sociology, Spanish, and women's studies. In addition, independent study and research are available. The College also enriches the freshman-year experience through more than thirty special-focus Freshman Seminars.

Off-Campus Programs

Study abroad is available through Muhlenberg's Semester-in-London Program, Netherlands Semester, or more than sixty affiliate agreements with international universities all over the world. In addition, the Lehigh Valley Association of Independent Colleges sponsors summer study-abroad options in England, France, Germany, Israel, and Spain. Credit for study-abroad programs sponsored by other institutions or by private agencies may also be transferred to Muhlenberg by special arrangement.

Students may participate in a variety of internships in local businesses, health-care facilities, schools, public agencies, theaters, broadcasting stations, and magazines. Government internships in Harrisburg, Pennsylvania, and Washington, D.C., and an Ethics and Public Affairs semester in Washington, D.C., are also available.

Students may enroll in courses offered at any of the five other member institutions of the Lehigh Valley Association of Independent Colleges: Lafayette College, Lehigh University, Cedar Crest College, DeSales University, and Moravian College.

Academic Facilities

Muhlenberg's library collection contains more than 200,000 volumes as well as numerous government documents, periodicals, and microforms. The $12-million Harry C. Trexler Library, a state-of-the-art library facility, opened in 1988. Students may also use library materials owned by the other institutions participating in the Lehigh Valley Association of Independent Colleges.

The Baker Center for the Arts was designed for Muhlenberg by the well-known architect Philip Johnson. It houses a modern theater complex, a recital hall, classrooms, art studios, and a fine arts gallery. The Trexler Performing Arts Pavilion opened in 2000 and provides dance performance and studio space, a new theater, a Black Box, and additional arts spaces.

Life science facilities include numerous laboratories, classrooms, two electron microscopes, a DNA sequencer, an isolation room used for growing and studying viruses, and a museum of natural history. Facilities supporting students in the physical sciences include equipment for optics, electronics, and atomic, nuclear, and solid-state physics. A new 40,000-square-foot addition to the science facilities opened in fall 2006. The College uses a UNIX/Windows computer system with Novell software.

Costs

The comprehensive tuition fee for 2007–08 was $33,090. The room and board fee was $7790. The total cost for a resident student was $40,880.

Financial Aid

Muhlenberg College endeavors to make its educational opportunities available to all qualified students regardless of their financial circumstances. While most financial aid at Muhlenberg is based on financial need as demonstrated by the College Scholarship Service Financial Aid PROFILE, there is also significant merit aid available. Typically, about 65 percent of Muhlenberg's students qualify for and receive financial aid.

Faculty

The Muhlenberg faculty consists of 155 full-time and 109 part-time members. Ninety percent of full-time faculty members hold doctoral or terminal degrees. While many faculty members are distinguished for their scholarly research, teaching is the main emphasis of their work. Professors at all levels work closely with students both inside and outside of the classroom. Most department heads teach introductory courses.

Student Government

Muhlenberg students are expected to demonstrate a high level of responsibility with regard to their own governance and to participate extensively in internal decision-making and communication processes throughout the campus. These responsibilities are coordinated by the Student Council, which transacts all business pertaining to the student body. This organization is in charge of a student activities budget of more than $350,000. In addition, 2 students serve as representatives to the Board of Trustees, and students hold full voting privileges on many faculty committees.

Admission Requirements

The College selects students who give evidence of ability and scholastic achievement, seriousness of purpose, and the capacity to make constructive contributions to the College community. Approximately 65 percent of a typical freshman class ranked in the top fifth of their secondary school class. SAT scores for entering freshmen average approximately 605 verbal, 615 math, and 610 writing.

Submission of SAT or ACT scores is optional. An on-campus interview is strongly recommended for all applicants and required for students who choose not to submit standardized test scores.

Application and Information

Students who wish to be considered for admission should submit a completed application form as early as possible during their senior year of secondary school and no later than February 15. Candidates receive notice of admission decisions in late March. Early decision plans and transfer admission are possible.

For further information, interested students should contact:

Christopher Hooker-Haring
Dean of Admission and Financial Aid
Muhlenberg College
Allentown, Pennsylvania 18104-5586
Phone: 484-664-3200
E-mail: admissions@muhlenberg.edu
Web site: http://www.muhlenberg.edu

The Bell Tower of the Haas College Center stands as the focal point of the Muhlenberg College campus.

NEUMANN COLLEGE

ASTON, PENNSYLVANIA

The College

Neumann College, a Catholic coeducational institution in the Franciscan tradition, recognizes the value of developing intellectual excellence, professional competence, and strong community life. As a college that balances the liberal arts with the professions, Neumann was founded to meet and expand the educational and professional horizons of men and women through instruction that is based on values, ethical behavior, and service to others. With the addition of the Living and Learning Center (multimedia-capable residences), Neumann College serves a diverse geographic and demographic population.

Founded and sponsored by the Sisters of St. Francis of Philadelphia, the College is committed to a varied student body and welcomes students of all denominations. Current enrollment is 3,084.

The Life Center houses the Meagher Theatre, the Bruder Athletic Center, and the Crossroads Cafe dining facility. Intercollegiate sports include women's basketball, field hockey, ice hockey, lacrosse, soccer, softball, tennis, and volleyball and men's baseball, basketball, golf, ice hockey, lacrosse, soccer, and tennis. Neumann College competes as a member of the National Collegiate Athletic Association (NCAA) Division III, the Pennsylvania Athletic Conference (PAC), and the Eastern Collegiate Athletic Conference (ECAC). Intramural sports are available to all members of the campus community.

The Living and Learning Center is designed to provide a state-of-the-art residential experience, with a focus on education within a real-world living environment. Technologically smart, the center connects students to both faculty members and friends via the Internet, which is available in every suite and apartment. The system provides full access to campus resources and activities, as well as activities and resources worldwide. The center also houses a separate computer lab, a fitness center, a reflection room, various study rooms with warming kitchens for group study or meetings, and a laundry.

The College provides a full range of services to students, including career placement, which averages above 95 percent within six months of graduation; career and personal counseling; a tutoring program; and health services.

Neumann students are involved in a wide variety of campus and community activities. Major and special interest clubs are available for student participation. Clubs bring together students who share common interests and help foster new friendships.

At Neumann, the spiritual dimension of one's life is recognized as integral to total human development. The Ministry Team provides a pastoral presence on campus and promotes a sense of community. The entire College community is invited to serve the needs of the poor and neglected in society through various outreach programs, with special attention to the need for peace and justice in the world today.

Neumann is well positioned to respond to the academic and extracurricular needs of students who are of traditional or nontraditional age, commuters or residents, and full-time or part-time.

In addition to undergraduate programs, Neumann confers master's degrees in education, nursing, pastoral counseling, sport management, and strategic leadership as well as doctoral degrees in education (Ed.D.) and physical therapy (D.P.T.).

Location

Neumann, with a beautiful 63-acre suburban campus in Aston, Delaware County, Pennsylvania, is a short distance from Philadelphia; Wilmington, Delaware; southern New Jersey; and Maryland. It is easily accessible from major arteries such as I-95, Route 476, Route 1, and the Pennsylvania Turnpike.

Majors and Degrees

Neumann offers strong academic majors leading to a Bachelor of Arts degree or a Bachelor of Science degree in accounting, arts production and performance, athletic training, biology, business administration, communication and media arts, computer and information management, criminal justice, education, English, environmental studies, international business, liberal arts, marketing, nursing, political science, psychology, and sport management. The education programs lead to teacher certification in Pennsylvania and reciprocating states, with secondary certification in biology/general science, English, social studies, and special education. Preprofessional programs in law and medicine are also available. An accelerated evening program for adults using a 6-credit seminar format leads to an Associate of Arts, Bachelor of Arts, or Bachelor of Science degree in liberal studies.

Academic Programs

The academic program at Neumann College is composed of a core curriculum (required of all students), a major area of study (chosen by each student), and a wide range of elective offerings. Students may also choose a minor area of study. The College's broad base of liberal arts offerings prepares students for the intellectual and social challenges they will face in the employment marketplace and throughout their lives. The core is intended to provide basic knowledge of the liberal arts and sciences; develop verbal, written, and symbolic communication skills; and stimulate interest in a broad range of topics for the purpose of enhancing the individual's contributions to society, thereby enabling the individual to realize full human potential.

Classroom instruction is supplemented by cooperative education and internships, through which students can earn credit and gain experience by working in a job related to their career interest. Fieldwork and student teaching are required of all education majors. Clinical practice for the nursing major occurs in a variety of health-care facilities in the tristate area.

The honors program is an opportunity for academically talented students to explore imaginative and innovative perspectives on learning. It is also an opportunity to stimulate and motivate students to expand their knowledge and interest and to strive for greater excellence. Moreover, it is a reward for prior perseverance and dedication as well as an obligation to use skills and abilities in service to others. Admission to the honors program is by invitation.

Neumann College has transfer articulation agreements with numerous colleges throughout the area.

Academic Facilities

The Child Development Center is a state-of-the-art, octagonal-shaped building, specifically designed to house an educational program for preschoolers. As a state-licensed day-care facility, it enrolls children of Neumann students, the faculty, and the community. The Child Development Center is part of the Division of Education and Human Services. Students enrolled in education courses use the center for observation, practical experience, and student teaching.

The Academic Computer Center is located on the ground floor of the College. The computers are viewed as tools to support all fields of study and all students and faculty members. Neumann College has installed a wireless Local Area Network (LAN) that connects various computers and provides shared services such as printing, e-mail, and support for the instructional use of computers by providing for the sharing of files. Computers are available to all students, as is software related to various academic disciplines. Access to the Web and the Internet is available.

The Academic Resource Center is a service that enables students to meet Neumann's academic standards and successfully attain their personal educational goals.

The College library contains a balanced collection of more than 70,000 volumes, 95,000 microfilm units, 2,000 videos, and 400 periodical subscriptions. Private study rooms and conference rooms are available for both student and faculty use. In addition to traditional media services support, a full-color video studio and a graphics production area are available. Serving as a comprehensive resource for students, other holdings include Neumann's online catalog system, Francis, which is accessible via the Web. The library is a member of the Tri-State College Library Cooperative, the Consortium for Health Information and Library Services, SEPCHE, and the Online Computer Library Center, which provide additional convenient resources for students. The library subscribes to various online research services.

Costs

Tuition for full-time students (12 to 18 credits per semester) in 2007–08 was $18,846. Room and board were $8838 (full meal plan).

Financial Aid

Typically, about 95 percent of Neumann undergraduate students receive some form of financial aid (scholarships, grants, and student loans).

Neumann offers a variety of renewable scholarships each year to entering full-time freshmen. Interested applicants should contact the Office of Admissions and Financial Aid as soon as possible to determine eligibility.

In addition to Neumann scholarships, funds are available through the Federal Pell Grant, Federal Supplemental Educational Opportunity Grant, and Federal Work-Study Programs. Many states provide grant money to attend Neumann (non-Pennsylvania residents should check with their state's higher education agency for details). Veterans Administration benefits can be received by qualified veterans or their dependents. Federal Stafford Student Loans and Federal PLUS Program loans are available and can be applied for through Neumann's preferred lender or any participating bank. Neumann also offers institutional need-based grants. All students requesting financial aid must complete the Free Application for Federal Student Aid (FAFSA) each year to determine eligibility. In order to expedite processing, the FAFSA should be submitted by March 15 for the following school year. Financial aid funds are renewable annually based on need, as determined by the FAFSA results.

Faculty

Neumann students describe faculty members as sincere, hard working, determined, and energetic. Faculty members view themselves, first and foremost, as teachers and are proud partners in their students' journeys toward professional careers. Each student has a faculty adviser, who assists in arranging a program designed to meet the student's educational goals. Many faculty members serve as moderators of student clubs. The student-faculty ratio is 14:1.

Student Government

The Student Government Association (SGA) is the representative body for all students. Its function is to implement the aims and purposes of the College, foster cooperation in student relationships, assist the College in being responsive to the needs of the student body, and encourage personal responsibility for an intelligent system of student self-government. Through the Student Activities Board, social functions are planned throughout the year. Students serve on various College committees, including the Student Affairs Committee of the Board, Academic Advising Committee, Honors Program Committee, Registration/Orientation Task Force, and Student Judicial Board. For full-time students, a Student Government Association fee of $60 per semester is required.

Admission Requirements

Neumann has a rolling admission policy and accepts applications throughout the year. Applicants are considered on the basis of high school record, SAT or ACT scores, recommendations, class rank, and other indicators of potential to succeed in college-level studies. Applications for admission are reviewed without regard to sex, race, creed, color, national origin, age, sexual orientation, pregnancy, military status, religion, or disability. Applicants should be graduates of an accredited high school (or present equivalent credentials) and have a recommended curriculum of 16 units of high school course work, distributed as follows: 4 in English, 2 to 3 in science, 2 in mathematics, 2 in social studies, 2 in foreign language, and 4 in electives. Students intending to pursue a major in biology or clinical laboratory science must have at least 1 year of high school biology and chemistry, and high school physics is also highly recommended.

Neumann participates in the Advanced Placement (AP) Program and the College-Level Examination Program (CLEP). Students with superior ability and a sound academic background may begin College studies at the end of the junior year in high school.

An interview and tour of the campus are highly recommended for all prospective students and parents. Visits can be arranged by contacting the Office of Admissions.

Application and Information

Applicants for freshman admission are requested to have SAT or ACT scores and high school transcripts sent to the Office of Admissions. A nonrefundable $35 application fee should accompany the completed application. A free application is available online at http://www.neumann.edu.

Neumann College welcomes applications from students who have attended or are currently attending either two-year or four-year regionally accredited institutions of higher learning.

For further information, students should contact:

Office of Admissions
Neumann College
One Neumann Drive
Aston, Pennsylvania 19014-1298
Phone: 610-558-5616
800-9NEUMANN (toll-free)
E-mail: neumann@neumann.edu

PENN STATE ERIE, THE BEHREND COLLEGE

ERIE, PENNSYLVANIA

The College

Penn State Erie, The Behrend College, is committed to providing the best possible education in the disciplines of business, engineering, engineering technology, the humanities, science, and the social sciences. Students benefit from the resources and opportunities provided by a major research institution while they enjoy the advantages of learning in a small university setting. The College offers thirty-two 4-year baccalaureate degree programs, six 2-year associate degree programs, and two graduate degree programs—Master of Business Administration (M.B.A.) and a Master of Project Management (M.P.M.).

Among all public colleges and universities in Pennsylvania, Penn State Behrend ranks in the top three in the student-to-faculty ratio, freshman retention rate, and SAT scores.

More than $100 million in new facilities are transforming the Penn State Behrend experience, including three new residence halls, an athletics center, a chapel, an observatory, a child-care center, a baseball and softball complex, intramural fields, a research center, and a high-technology park.

Established in 1948 when Mary Behrend donated her Glenhill Farm estate in memory of her husband, Ernst, the campus is magnificent, with 725 acres overlooking Lake Erie and Presque Isle State Park, which has miles of sandy beaches and some of the most beautiful sunsets in the world. Penn State Behrend's campus has extensive woodlands, deep gorges, and beautiful streams. It also features cross-country skiing and fitness trails.

More than 4,000 students attend classes in modern academic buildings and labs, and 1,650 students live on campus in traditional student housing, four-bedroom suites, and two-bedroom apartments.

Penn State Behrend participates in twenty-one varsity sports, and it is an NCAA Division III member and a member of the Allegheny Mountain Collegiate Conference. Varsity sports include ten teams for men (baseball, basketball, cross-country, golf, indoor track, soccer, swimming, tennis, track and field, and water polo) and eleven for women (basketball, cross-country, golf, indoor track, soccer, softball, swimming, tennis, track and field, volleyball, and water polo). More than 65 percent of students participate in a comprehensive intramural program. The Junker Athletics Center features a swimming pool, gymnasium, and exercise equipment.

A multifaith chapel and carillon is designed to inspire quiet reflection and offer enrichment opportunities provided by campus ministries.

Knowledge Park at Penn State Behrend is a 200-acre research and development park housing knowledge-based companies that benefit from the site's technological infrastructure and the University's strengths in applied research and technology transfer. A number of students work as interns for companies in the park.

Location

Penn State Behrend students benefit from the college's convenient location near I-90 (and close to I-79 and I-86) in a suburb of Erie, Pennsylvania. The population of the area is more than 280,000.

Public transportation departs from campus every half hour to other points throughout the Erie area, including dozens of movie theaters, ethnic restaurants, a philharmonic orchestra, museums, theaters, and a zoo. A convention center in downtown Erie features Broadway plays and top-name performers in rock, classical, and country music. Erie is located within 2 hours of Buffalo, Cleveland, and Pittsburgh and is a comfortable 4-hour drive from Toronto.

Majors and Degrees

Penn State Behrend confers the Bachelor of Arts degree in communication, economics, English, general arts and sciences, history, political science, psychology, and science. The Bachelor of Fine Arts degree is offered in creative writing. The Bachelor of Science degree is offered in accounting; biology; business economics; business, liberal arts, and science; chemistry; computer engineering; computer science; electrical engineering; electrical engineering technology; finance; international business; management; management information systems; marketing; mathematics; mathematics education; mechanical engineering; mechanical engineering technology; physics; plastics engineering technology; psychology; science; and software engineering.

The Associate in Arts degree is awarded in one major—letters, arts, and sciences. The Associate in Science degree is offered in business, and the Associate in Engineering degree is offered in electrical engineering technology, mechanical engineering technology, and plastics engineering technology. The College also offers an associate degree in nursing.

Academic Programs

Each baccalaureate program has two components: at least 46 credits in general education and at least 78 credits in specific requirements for the major. Students must complete a minimum of 124 semester hours to earn a bachelor's degree; the exact number depends on the program. Associate degrees require a minimum of 60 semester hours. All Penn State Behrend majors require an overall grade point average of at least 2.0 and a grade of C or better in all upper-level courses in the major. An honors program and the Schreyer Scholars Program are available to students who show exceptional promise. Several majors serve as excellent preparation for law or medical school. Special prelaw and premed advisers assist students in planning their programs. The Division of Undergraduate Studies enables those who have not yet decided on an academic major to explore several areas of study before selecting a specific program.

The Bachelor of Fine Arts degree in creative writing is one of few such programs in the country. It is an intensive course of study in the art of writing. Students have the opportunity to serve on the editorial staff of the national literary journal, *Lake Effect*.

The Plastics Engineering Technology program and its facilities are among the nation's best. The program is one of only four in the country to earn accreditation. The School of Engineering and Engineering Technology also has nationally accredited programs in electrical engineering technology, mechanical engineering technology, and electrical, mechanical, and computer engineering.

The College's chemistry program has earned approval from the American Chemical Society, making Penn State Behrend one of only 619 colleges and universities in the United States to achieve such approval.

The Sam and Irene Black School of Business is the first and only school of business in the Erie region to receive accreditation from AACSB International, the premier accrediting agency for programs in management and accounting. The school was named for Sam and Irene Black following a $20-million endowment bequest.

The fall and spring semesters are each fifteen weeks in length. Registration and advising take place before the first week of classes, and the final examinations are given after the last week. There are also three summer sessions. The Division of Undergraduate Studies provides a summer preregistration and counseling service for all entering freshmen and their parents.

Many students present their undergraduate research at regional and national conferences, and others publish in refereed journals. This provides Penn State Behrend students with an advantage when looking for a job or applying to professional or graduate school. The

Career Development Center works closely with employers, and each fall it hosts recruiters on campus at its successful engineering and business career fairs.

Academic Facilities

Penn State Behrend features a mix of contemporary and traditional buildings in a parklike setting. Facilities include a science complex, library, academic buildings, observatory, and science labs. A Research and Economic Development Center just opened and houses the Black School of Business and the School of Engineering and Engineering Technology.

In addition to using Penn State Behrend's library collection, students can draw on the resources of the entire Penn State University Libraries collection through the computerized Library Information Access System. The collection comprises 4.3 million cataloged items, 38,500 serial titles, and 2.5 million government documents. Computers connect students to major databases throughout the world.

The General Electric Foundation Computer Center provides a sophisticated, high-speed electronic link from Penn State's mainframe computer—one of the most up-to-date in the country—to supercomputing. Students benefit from T-3 Internet access, technology classrooms, and e-Lion, the University's online student advising system. In addition, the College has more than thirty microcomputer labs with IBM-compatible personal computers running both Windows and LINUX operating systems, Silicon Graphics workstations, and computer-aided design systems. Wireless computing is available in many locations on campus.

Costs

Educational costs at Penn State Behrend vary depending on whether the student is a resident of Pennsylvania, whether enrollment is in the upper or lower division, and whether he or she lives off campus or in a residence hall. The 2007–08 tuition at Penn State Behrend for Pennsylvania residents (lower division) was $10,912 for the academic year. For out-of-state students, the tuition was $16,694 for the academic year. On-campus rooms are a fixed cost, but board and all other costs are variable and fluctuate according to each student's spending habits. These variable costs are approximately $6000 for room and board, $800 for books and supplies, and $1200 to $2400 for personal expenses, including clothing, laundry, travel, and miscellaneous items. Other costs are a nonrefundable $50 application fee, a nonrefundable $200 enrollment fee and general fee, and a $100 housing fee for students living in on-campus residences.

Financial Aid

Students benefit from more than $1 million in annual Penn State Behrend scholarships, and more than 75 percent of students receive some form of financial aid. Awards are based on an analysis of the student's financial need. Students should file the Free Application for Federal Student Aid (FAFSA) by February 15 of their senior year of high school. Penn State's school code is 003329. Students are encouraged to seek grant assistance from their home state. Financial aid applications are available from high school counselors and financial aid offices at colleges and other institutions. These forms and the application for admission are the only forms that incoming freshmen need to complete to be considered for federal, state, and University aid. Aid includes Federal Pell Grants, Pennsylvania Higher Education Assistance Agency Grants, Federal Work-Study Program awards, Federal Perkins Loans, Federal Supplemental Educational Opportunity Grants, Federal Stafford Student Loans, and Penn State awards and scholarships.

Faculty

A first-rate faculty is at the heart of the Penn State Behrend experience. Of the 275 faculty members who teach both graduate and undergraduate students, almost all have earned the terminal degree in their major field. There are no graduate teaching assistants, and the use of part-time professors is limited. The faculty members are distinguished scholars and superb teachers. They are extensively involved in research and publishing, and they are caring people with a record of excellence in advising students. Professors and students get to know each other, and such close relationships have many educational and career advantages.

Student Government

The Student Government Association is the official representative of the student body at Penn State Behrend. In addition to representing students to the administration and faculty, the Student Government Association charters all student organizations and allocates funds to support and promote student activities. The association also appoints student representatives to serve on key administrative and faculty committees and the appropriate adjudicatory boards.

Admission Requirements

As part of Penn State University, and in compliance with federal and state laws, Penn State Behrend is committed to the policy that all persons shall have equal access to admission without regard to race, religion, sex, national origin, ancestry, color, sexual orientation, handicap, age, or status as a disabled or Vietnam veteran. Each applicant is evaluated on the basis of his or her high school record and the results of the SAT or scores from the ACT. The high school grade point average, when combined with the SAT score, produces an evaluation index, and students are admitted on the basis of that index.

Application and Information

Students interested in freshman admission to Penn State Behrend may obtain a Web application at http://www.admissions.psu.edu. Students who do not wish to file a Web application can obtain an admission application form from any Penn State campus or by writing to Penn State Behrend. Application forms are available in late summer. The recommended deadline for submitting an application is November 30. Applicants admitted to Penn State Behrend are notified approximately four to six weeks after the application and credentials are received. The student must make certain that the Educational Testing Service forwards the SAT scores to the Undergraduate Admissions Office, Pennsylvania State University, University Park, Pennsylvania 16802.

This description is available in alternative media upon request. For application forms, more information, or a campus visit, interested students should contact:

Office of Admissions
Penn State Erie, The Behrend College
5091 Station Road
Erie, Pennsylvania 16563-0105
Phone: 814-898-6100
866-374-3378 (toll-free)
E-mail: behrend.admissions@psu.edu
Web site: http://www.behrend.psu.edu

The library at Penn State Behrend features access to all of the holdings in the Penn State system.

PENNSYLVANIA COLLEGE OF TECHNOLOGY

An Affiliate of The Pennsylvania State University

WILLIAMSPORT, PENNSYLVANIA

Pennsylvania College of Technology
PENNSTATE

The College

Pennsylvania College of Technology (Penn College) is a special-mission affiliate of Penn State committed to applied technology education. The College has a national reputation for "degrees that work" in the high quality and diversity of its traditional and advanced technology majors. Partnerships with industry leaders, including Honda, Ford, Mack Trucks, and Caterpillar, provide students unique opportunities to build relationships that can advance their careers.

Excellent graduate placement rates exceed 95 percent annually (100 percent in some majors). Among the keys to graduate success are Penn College's emphasis on small classes, personal attention, and hands-on experience using the latest technology. State-of-the-art classrooms and laboratories reflect the expectations of the modern workforce. A number of campus buildings, including a conference center, a Victorian guest house, an athletics field house, and a rustic retreat used for professional gatherings, have been designed, constructed, and maintained by students.

More than 6,500 students attend Penn College. More than 3,000 additional men and women take part in noncredit classes, including customized business and industry courses offered through Workforce Development and Continuing Education.

The Penn College Wildcats compete in the Penn States University Athletic Conference. Varsity sports include archery, baseball, basketball, bowling, cross-country, dance team, golf, soccer, softball, team tennis, and volleyball. Penn College's men's compound-bow archery team is a former two-time national champion in the National Archery Association (NAA).

Location

Penn College is located in north-central Pennsylvania. The main campus is in Williamsport, a city known around the world as the home of the Little League Baseball World Series. Penn College offers credit classes at three other locations: the Advanced Automotive Technology Center in the Wahoo Drive Industrial Park in Williamsport, the Aviation Center at the Williamsport Regional Airport in Montoursville, and the Earth Science Center, 10 miles south of Williamsport near Allenwood. Noncredit classes are offered from locations in Williamsport and Wellsboro.

Majors and Degrees

Bachelor of Science (B.S.) degrees focus on applied technology in traditional and emerging career fields. Majors include accounting; applied health studies; applied human services; automotive technology management; aviation maintenance technology; building automation technology; business administration (concentrations in banking and finance, human resource management, management, management information systems, marketing, and small business and entrepreneurship); civil engineering technology; computer-aided product design; construction management; culinary arts and systems; dental hygiene (concentrations in health policy and administration and special-population care); electronics and computer engineering technology; graphic communications management; graphic design; heating, ventilation, and air conditioning (HVAC) technology; information technology (concentrations in IT security specialist studies, network specialist studies, and Web and applications development); legal assistant/paralegal studies; manufacturing engineering technology; nursing; physician assistant studies; plastics and polymer engineering technology; residential construction technology and management; technology management; and welding and fabrication engineering technology.

Associate degrees (A.A.S., A.A.A., or A.A.) are offered in accounting; advertising art; architectural technology; automated manufacturing technology; automotive service sales and marketing; automotive technology (including Ford ASSET and Honda PACT industry-sponsored majors); aviation technology; baking and pastry arts; building construction technology; building construction technology/masonry; business management; civil engineering technology; collision repair technology; computer-aided drafting technology; culinary arts technology; dental hygiene; diesel technology (including a Mack industry-sponsored major); early childhood education; electric power generation technology; electrical technology; electromechanical maintenance technology; electronics and computer engineering technology (emphases in Cisco systems, communications and fiber optics, nanofabrication technology, and robotics and automation); emergency medical services; forest technology; general studies; graphic communications technology; health arts; health arts/practical nursing; health information technology; heating, ventilation, and air conditioning (HVAC) technology; heavy construction equipment technology (emphases in Caterpillar industry-sponsored, operator, and technician); hospitality management; human services; individual studies; information technology (emphases in Cisco technology, network technology, technical support technology, and Web and applications technology); legal assistant/paralegal studies; mass media communication; nursing; occupational therapy assistant studies; office information technology (medical office information and specialized office information emphases); ornamental horticulture (emphases in horticulture retail management, landscape technology, and plant productions); physical fitness specialist studies; plastics and polymer technology; radiography; studio arts; surgical technology; surveying technology; toolmaking technology; transmission and distribution technology; and welding technology.

Certificate majors are offered in automotive service technician studies, aviation maintenance technician studies, collision repair technician studies, construction carpentry, diesel technician studies, electrical occupations, health information coding specialist studies, machinist general, nurse/health-care paralegal studies; paramedic technician studies, plumbing, practical nursing, and welding.

Academic Programs

Penn College offers unique bachelor's degrees that are designed to prepare students for employment or serve as the basis for additional educational opportunities. The bachelor's degree offerings either parallel or build upon two-year majors or stand as their own unique majors. Five B.S. degrees are offered via distance learning: applied health studies, automotive technology management, dental hygiene, nursing (requires periodic visits to campus), and technology management.

While associate degrees primarily emphasize practical applications, the bachelor's degree curricula complete a larger educational base by adding advanced practical applications, broader liberal arts study, systematic problem solving, writing-enriched courses, cultural diversity, senior-year capstone projects, and interdisciplinary courses that develop appreciation for the relationships between science, technology, and society.

Off-Campus Programs

Penn College students earn academic credit for real work experience if they choose to participate in an internship. Many majors require internships. Penn College students have worked throughout Pennsylvania and the United States and around the world.

Academic Facilities

The hands-on experience offered at Penn College creates a need for a variety of special academic facilities. Campus computers are very accessible. Wireless zones and networked on-campus residences make study across campus very convenient. Besides extensive, accessible computer labs, the main campus has an automated manufacturing center, a plastics manufacturing center, a printing and publishing facility, a dental hygiene clinic, automotive and collision repair centers, a machine shop, a welding shop, a building technologies center, an architectural studio, computer-aided drafting labs, a broadcast studio, a video production studio, modern science laboratories, a fine-dining restaurant and campus guest house, an aviation and avionics instructional facility located at the regional airport, greenhouses, a working sawmill, a diesel center, and a heavy-equipment training site.

Off-campus sites include the Aviation Center, one of the nation's finest aviation instructional facilities, located at the regional airport; the Earth Science Center, located on 180 acres of wooded land and featuring greenhouses, a working sawmill, a diesel center, and a heavy-equipment training site; and an Advanced Automotive Technology Center, with motorsports and other advanced laboratories.

The Madigan Library on the main campus is open every day during the academic semesters and offers an impressive selection of print and electronic resources. Services available include a professional reference staff, a well-developed instructional program, reciprocal borrowing with regional libraries, interlibrary loans, and paper and electronic reserves. The library also houses fourteen study areas, two computer laboratories, a 100-seat open computer lab complex, the Student Help Desk, a café, and the art gallery.

Costs

Tuition and related fees are based on a per-credit-hour charge. Pennsylvania residents attending Penn College in 2007–08 paid approximately $19,720 per year, and out-of-state residents paid approximately $22,600 per year. These estimated costs are based on tuition and fees for an average 15 credits per semester plus estimated expenses for housing, meals, books, and supplies. Rates vary according to specific choices for classes, housing, meal plans, and other costs.

All on-campus housing is apartment-style (kitchen, living room, bedrooms, and bathroom). On-campus housing is alcohol free, drug free, noise controlled, and secure. Students are offered a variety of meal plans, which are accepted in the College's dining facilities, including the main dining hall, an all-you-can-eat buffet, a gourmet restaurant, a convenience store, snack bars, and a café.

Financial Aid

Approximately 4 out of 5 Penn College students receive some form of financial assistance. Types of aid available include Federal Pell Grants, Pennsylvania Higher Education Assistance Agency Grants, Federal Supplemental Educational Opportunity Grants, Federal Work-Study Program awards, Federal Stafford Student Loans, Federal PLUS Loans, veterans' benefits, and Bureau of Vocational Rehabilitation benefits. A deferred-payment plan allows students to spread their tuition over two payments each semester. Penn College offers a variety of academic, need-based, and technical scholarships to qualified students. Detailed information on scholarships can be obtained from the Financial Aid Office or on the Web at http://www.pct.edu/finaid.

Faculty

Penn College's faculty members (304 full-time and 207 part-time) provide the kind of individual attention students need to be successful in the classroom and in the workplace. Faculty members are both educated and experienced in their field. Penn College recognizes excellence among the faculty members through distinguished faculty award programs. Small class sizes (fewer than 20 students in most classes) provide individual attention and promote student success. In addition, advisory committees of business and industry leaders and faculty and staff members work together to ensure that programs of study meet current workplace needs.

Student Government

Student Government Association (SGA) and Wildcat Events Board (WEB) represent the student body in matters related to College policy and social activities. All enrolled students are members of SGA and WEB. Active participation offers the opportunity to develop leadership skills while contributing to the well-being of the College and the student body. In addition, more than fifty student organizations, including the Residence Hall Association, which represents all on-campus student residents, offer opportunities for organized campus activity and leadership experiences.

Admission Requirements

The application deadline for fall is July 1. Students may submit applications and the $50 application fee online at http://www.pct.edu or they may contact the Admissions Office for an application form. Applicants for bachelor's degree majors must submit SAT/ACT scores in addition to high school transcripts to be considered for admission. Applicants must satisfactorily complete placement testing and satisfy other major-specific admission criteria in order to be offered acceptance into a major program of study.

Penn College offers educational opportunities to anyone who has the interest, desire, and ability to pursue advanced study. Due to the wide variety of majors, admission criteria vary according to the major. At a minimum, applicants must have a high school diploma or its equivalent. Some majors are restricted to people who meet certain academic skills and prerequisites, who have attained high levels of academic achievement, and who have achieved acceptable scores on the SAT or ACT. Questions regarding the admission standards for specific majors should be directed to the Admissions Office.

To ensure that applicants have the entry-level skills needed for success in Penn College majors, all students are required to take placement examinations, which are used to assess skills in math, English, and reading. The College provides opportunities for students to develop the basic skills necessary for enrollment in associate degree and certificate programs when the placement tests indicate that such help is needed. International students whose native language is not English are required to take the TOEFL, submit an affidavit of support, and comply with test regulations of the Immigration and Naturalization Service, along with meeting all other admission requirements.

Penn College offers opportunities for students to transfer course credit earned at other institutions, college credit earned before high school graduation, service credit, DANTES credit, and credit earned through the College-Level Examination Program (CLEP). The College offers equal opportunity for admission without regard to age, race, color, creed, sex, national origin, handicap, veteran status, or political affiliation.

Application and Information

College catalogs, viewbooks, financial aid information, and other informative brochures as well as applications for admission are available from the Admissions Office. The College invites prospective students and their families to contact the Admissions Office to arrange a personal interview or campus tour. Annual fall and spring open house events offer the best opportunity to see the entire campus in action. Interested students should visit the College's Web site or contact the Admissions Office for dates or to schedule a tour at any time.

All inquiries should be addressed to:

Admissions Office
Pennsylvania College of Technology
One College Avenue
Williamsport, Pennsylvania 17701-5799
Phone: 570-327-4761
800-367-9222 (toll-free)
E-mail: PCTinfo@pct.edu
Web site: http://www.pct.edu/peter4

Banners representing each of the eight academic schools at Penn College adorn lampposts on the road leading from the main entrance to the heart of the campus.

COLLEGE DATA CENTER • PENNSYLVANIA

PHILADELPHIA BIBLICAL UNIVERSITY

LANGHORNE, PENNSYLVANIA

The University

Philadelphia Biblical University (PBU) is the result of the merger of two Bible schools: the Bible Institute of Pennsylvania and Philadelphia School of the Bible. In 1951, the schools became the Philadelphia Bible Institute, which offered a three-year Bible diploma. In 1958, Pennsylvania granted the institute approval to offer the Bachelor of Science in Bible degree. The institute then changed its name to Philadelphia College of Bible. In 2000, Pennsylvania granted the college approval to become a university, and the college became Philadelphia Biblical University.

PBU is regionally accredited by the Middle States Association of Colleges and Schools and is professionally accredited by the Association for Biblical Higher Education. PBU is an institutional member of the National Association of Schools of Music. The Bachelor of Social Work program is accredited by the Council on Social Work Education, the teacher education programs are accredited by the Association of Christian Schools International, and the business program is accredited by the International Assembly for Collegiate Business Education. PBU was approved in 1958 by the State Council on Education, Commonwealth of Pennsylvania, to confer the Bachelor of Science in Bible degree and by the Department of Education to confer the remaining bachelor's and master's degrees listed below and to offer both public and private school teacher certification programs. The University is listed in publications of the United States Office of Education, the Office of Chief of Chaplains, and the Justice Department and is approved for veterans' education. PBU maintains appropriate relationships with the Association of Independent Colleges and Universities of Pennsylvania, Council for the Advancement and Support of Education, National Association of Independent Colleges and Universities, Commission for Independent Colleges and Universities, and the Council for Christian Colleges and Universities.

In addition to its undergraduate degrees, PBU offers the following graduate degrees: Master of Divinity, Master of Science in Bible, Master of Science in Christian Counseling, Master of Science in Education, Master of Science in Educational Leadership and Administration, and Master of Science in Organizational Leadership.

PBU has an intercollegiate athletic program for both men and women. PBU participates in the National Collegiate Athletic Association (NCAA) Division III, the National Christian College Athletic Association (NCCAA) Division II, and the North Eastern Athletic Conference (NEAC). Sports include men's baseball, men's and women's basketball, men's and women's cross-country, women's field hockey, men's golf, men's and women's soccer, women's softball, men's and women's tennis, and men's and women's volleyball. Intramural sports include a variety of individual and team sports for men and women as well as several coeducational sports. Recreational facilities include a fitness center, gymnasium, field space, and four tennis courts.

The University's residential facilities can be described in three distinct groupings. Centrally located on the campus are five dormitories, each designed to accommodate 40 students. Students live in two-bedroom suites that share a bathroom. These dormitories are occupied primarily by entering students. PBU's largest dormitory, Heritage Hall, features eight residential wings that have double and single rooms, most of which have private baths. The University's sixty-six-unit apartment complex is located approximately ¼ mile from the main campus. Most of the apartments are two-bedroom units. Several buildings are used as single-student residences, and the remaining apartments are available for rent by older or married students.

The Dining Commons seats more than 500 people and provides a comfortable, casual atmosphere in which to enjoy a wide selection of food.

Location

PBU's main campus is a 120-acre facility located in Bucks County. It is 30 minutes from Center City Philadelphia; 15 minutes from Trenton, New Jersey; and 2 hours from New York City. The Langhorne train station is within walking distance, and Philadelphia International Airport is a 45-minute drive.

Majors and Degrees

The School of Biblical Studies offers biblical studies and Bible ministries programs leading to a Bachelor of Science in Bible degree.

The School of Church and Community Ministries offers a Bachelor of Social Work* degree program and a Bachelor of Science in Bible degree, with programs in camping ministries, children's ministries, church ministries interdisciplinary, discipleship counseling, missions ministry, pastoral ministries, preseminary, social service interdisciplinary, and youth ministries.

The School of Music and Performing Arts offers a Bachelor of Science in Bible degree with a church music minor, as well as a Bachelor of Music degree with programs in church music,* church music/worship leader,* composition,* music education,* and performance.*

The School of Education offers programs leading to a Bachelor of Science in Bible degree in Bible education, early childhood education–preschool/kindergarten, and secondary education–Bible and history. An additional degree, the Bachelor of Science in Education, can be earned in elementary education;* elementary education–early childhood;* health and physical education;* music education;* secondary education–English;* secondary education–math;* secondary education–social sciences;* and secondary education–social studies.*

The School of Business and Leadership offers a Bachelor of Science in Business Administration* degree program.

A Bachelor of Science in Bible degree program in networking technology is offered in cooperation with Bucks County Community College (BCCC).

An asterisk (*) designates dual-degree programs.

Academic Programs

Students choose PBU for its emphasis on biblical and practical education. Each student receives a core curriculum of Bible classes in addition to those in their areas of professional study. PBU students are expected to apply the knowledge gained in the classroom to their spiritual lives and to practice godly character. The undergraduate degree programs are structured to provide every student with a thorough grounding in Bible, doctrine, and church history. Up to 6 additional elective credits may be stipulated for graduation. The curriculum also provides the student with a foundation in arts and sciences through knowledge of the history, language, behavior, expression, and thought of both past and present cultures. To complete the undergraduate curriculum, the student specializes in an elected professional area. These professional programs are designed to equip the student with a foundational knowledge of the history, philosophy, content, literature, and skills in each respective field.

The Honors Program seeks to develop Christian scholars who integrate their biblical studies with their arts and sciences and professional education. The capstone of the Honors Program is the honors thesis. Students choose a research topic designed to bring together all of their education. Working closely with an adviser, the students learn and apply the fundamentals of researching and writing a thesis. The University faculty is involved in mentoring the honors students. The development of student-faculty relationships provides an important scaffolding for the student's intellectual development. Faculty members advise students in honors course work, colloquium topics, and the honors project. The director plans colloquia and honors activities for interested students.

The Friends of Israel Institute of Jewish Studies (IJS) is a PBU program where students study the Scriptures from a Jewish perspective and take courses in Jewish history, culture, and the geography of the land of Israel, both ancient and modern. Students engage in practical outreach courses taught by experienced Friends of Israel staff members and have opportunities to be involved in ministries to Jewish people.

PBU students are eligible to participate in the Air Force Reserve Officer Training Corps (AFROTC) through a collaborative agreement with Saint Joseph's University. The AFROTC program enables a college student to earn a commission as an Air Force officer while concurrently satisfying requirements for the baccalaureate degree.

Off-Campus Programs

The Wisconsin Wilderness Campus (WWC) of PBU offers an accredited alternative to a traditional college year. The curriculum is primarily biblical with some arts and sciences and professional studies. The enrollment is limited in order to provide increased opportunities for personal guidance and discipleship, formal and informal interaction with professors, the development of interpersonal skills, and involvement in outdoor recreational/educational experiences.

Academic Facilities

The Masland Learning Resource Center offers 167,093 volumes in the main collection, along with reference works, periodicals, sound recordings, microforms, and other media. Two computer labs are available for use by students and staff members. A teacher education curriculum lab is available for study and instruction, and two conference rooms are available for group study.

Costs

For 2007–08, tuition was $8197.50 per semester for full-time students (12–18 credits). Room and board costs vary among residence halls from $3250 to $3500 per semester. Other fees vary by program.

Financial Aid

Admitted students who complete the FAFSA are considered for PBU Grants. These grants are awarded in various amounts (up to 50 percent of tuition) based on demonstrated need after considering all other sources of aid available. PBU Grants are renewable each year for full-time students whose annual FAFSA results document continuing financial need.

Students should contact the University Admissions Office for academic scholarship details. PBU offers academic scholarships with awards ranging from $1000 to $8500 per year. Transfer students are also considered for these scholarships. Students awarded scholarships for 2008–09 must enroll full-time for the fall 2008 semester. Students who are dependents of a full-time Christian worker (pastor or church staff, missionary, Christian school, or para–church organization employee) may also qualify for the PBU Christian Worker Scholarship. This scholarship is a supplement to other types of aid, with awards ranging up to $3000 or 50 percent of unmet need after all other aid is considered. Admitted students are eligible to be considered if the parent in the full-time Christian vocation is the primary wage earner of the family.

On-campus employment is available in many areas, including maintenance, security, food service, housekeeping, and clerical services.

Faculty

Of the 156 faculty members, 62 are engaged in full-time teaching and service to the student body. The majority possess doctoral degrees. The faculty-student ratio is 1:15.

Student Government

Students at PBU have an opportunity to influence the decisions that are made on campus and provide leadership for their fellow classmates through involvement in student government. The umbrella for government leadership is the Student Senate Cabinet. This group serves as the student representative body and liaison between students and the administration and faculty. The cabinet promotes school functions, helps to acclimate new students, and plans student gatherings. Involvement in student government can also be accessed through serving one's class. Each class has a cabinet that works to improve the students' experience and serves as a mediator between the Student Senate and the class. One role of the class leadership team is to organize activities, plan class chapels, and voice the concerns of those with whom they come in contact.

Admission Requirements

Three factors are considered in relation to the applicant's high school grades: overall grade point average, class rank and school size, and grade pattern from freshman to senior year. It is normally expected that the applicant should rank in the upper half of the high school class and have at least a 2.0 grade point average. To determine whether the applicant can benefit from the programs and environment of the University, three areas are reviewed: conversion, lifestyle, and beliefs. It is expected that students at the University have confessed faith in Jesus Christ as personal Savior. It is also expected that the applicant understands the theological perspective of the University, and the applicant's lifestyle should reflect Christian principles. A personal interview with an admissions counselor is recommended if an applicant is visiting the campus. On occasion, an interview is required in order to clarify personal or academic issues pertaining to the application.

Applicants must submit an application form, which is also available online, with an autobiography and a $25 application fee, along with official high school transcripts, official SAT or ACT scores, and a pastor's reference. Transfer students should enclose official transcripts for work completed at other colleges. International students should also submit TOEFL scores, an International Financial Aid Form, and proof of financial support.

Application and Information

For more information, prospective students should contact:

Academic Communications Department
Philadelphia Biblical University
200 Manor Avenue
Langhorne, Pennsylvania 19047-2990
Phone: 800-366-0049 (toll-free)
Fax: 215-702-4248
E-mail: inquiries@pbu.edu
Web site: http://www.pbu.edu

PHILADELPHIA UNIVERSITY

PHILADELPHIA, PENNSYLVANIA

The University

Founded in 1884, Philadelphia University is a private institution of higher learning for students with high motivation and academic ability. Philadelphia University is professionally oriented and offers undergraduate and graduate degree programs in the areas of architecture, business, design, engineering, fashion, general sciences, health sciences, and textile engineering technology. The University's enrollment of approximately 2,500 undergraduates represents a diverse and talented group of students from thirty-eight states and thirty countries. With an average class size of 18 and a 14:1 student-faculty ratio, students receive the personal attention so important to social and professional growth.

Through a unique blend of liberal and specialized education with an interdisciplinary focus, the University prepares students for today's complex, global workplace. Recognized as a premier professional university, Philadelphia University has established a phenomenal record of career success for its graduates. The University is committed to a technologically advanced approach to career planning, and students have full access to the Career Services Center's CareerLink, an Internet-based resume and job-listing management system that electronically stores resumes, job listings, and employer information. Nearly 2,000 job titles were posted in 2007. Students have access to job-search resources, including ReferenceUSA, a database of 1.5 million companies nationwide. Prospective employers gain access to students through the various career fairs and industry spotlights hosted by the center annually. The University's innovative academic programs that meet emerging needs in the marketplace, extensive networking with prospective employers (connecting students with 150 employers on campus and 1,200 employers electronically last year), and extensive career and professional development opportunities for students all add up to a nearly 90 percent placement rate within just a few months of graduation.

Philadelphia University believes the college experience of every student should extend well beyond the classroom. The Student Life Programs at Philadelphia University build bridges between the classroom and out-of-class experiences to create a dynamic learning community for students. Fifteen varsity teams compose the intercollegiate athletics program. Men participate in baseball, basketball, cross-country, golf, rowing, soccer, and tennis. Women's teams include basketball, cross-country, field hockey, lacrosse, rowing, soccer, softball, tennis, and volleyball. An extensive intramural sports program is available to all students. Students are actively engaged in campus life, whether through one of the nationally ranked athletic teams, events sponsored by Student Government, a wide array of community service opportunities, an extensive intramural program, or participation in the more than thirty student clubs and organizations.

More than 1,200 students live on campus in residence halls, apartments, and townhouses. Professional and paraprofessional staff members live within each residential area to assist students with daily concerns and program activities to enhance residential living.

The University holds accreditation from the Middle States Association of Colleges and Schools, the National Architectural Accrediting Board (NAAB), Council for Interior Design Accreditation (CIDA), the American Chemical Society (ACS), Accreditation Review Commission on Education for the Physician Assistant (ARC-PA), National Association of Schools of Art and Design (NASAD), and the Engineering Accreditation Commission of the Accreditation Board for Engineering and Technology (ABET), Inc., as well as certification from the International College Reading and Learning Center Association.

Location

The University's sprawling, 100-acre campus is adjacent to Fairmount Park, the largest urban park system in the country. Students enjoy the best of both worlds—a beautiful campus with tree-lined walkways, spacious lawns, and classical architecture, and easy access to Philadelphia (just minutes away) for entertainment, cultural events, great night spots, and more than 300 years of American history.

Philadelphia also serves as a "living lab" where students frequently interact with area professionals for class projects, internships, and off-campus jobs.

Majors and Degrees

Philadelphia University offers the Bachelor of Science in more than thirty areas, including accounting, architectural engineering, architectural studies, architecture, biochemistry, biology, biopsychology, chemistry, digital animation, digital design, engineering (with minor tracks in architectural, environmental, industrial, mechanical, and textile), environmental and conservation biology, environmental sustainability, fashion design, fashion industry management, fashion merchandising, finance, financial information systems, graphic design communication, health sciences, industrial and systems engineering, industrial design, interior design, international business, landscape architecture, law and society, management, management information systems, marketing, mechanical engineering, physician assistant studies, premedical studies, professional communication, psychology, science and business, textile design, and textile engineering technology.

The University also offers several five-year B.S./M.B.A. joint-degree programs and a five-year B.S./M.S. physician assistant studies program. The five-year architecture program leads to a Bachelor of Architecture (B.Arch.), and the five-year landscape architecture program leads to the Bachelor of Landscape Architecture (B.L.A.). For students wishing to keep their choices open, an undeclared option offers an introduction to college courses in preparation for entering a specific major in the sophomore year.

Academic Programs

Philadelphia University's commitment to quality professional education is realized in curricula that combine a solid foundation in liberal studies with career preparation. These curricula are designed to enhance students' ability and desire to learn; to ensure them an understanding of the ideas, traditions, and values of their own and other cultures; and to prepare them to apply the concepts and techniques of both general and specialized learning to their lives as citizens with productive careers. Degree requirements include successful completion of 121 to 138 credits (depending upon the major chosen), successful completion of both major and general education programs, and the satisfactory completion of at least 60 credits in residence at the University. All students have the option to participate in the University's Internship Program, through which they earn both academic credit and a salary.

As a rule, the University grants credit to students who obtain satisfactory grades in subject examinations developed by the Advanced Placement Program, the College-Level Examination

Program, and the Proficiency Examination Program. Students may, by invitation, participate in the honors program, which offers a number of courses expressly for honors students.

The University's academic calendar consists of two semesters and two summer sessions.

Off-Campus Programs

Internships are available, and the University's Internship Office has affiliations with a wide variety of organizations, such as L. L. Bean, Isdaner & Company, the Hillier Group, Citizens Bank, Burlington Industries, J. Crew, and Federated Department Stores.

Study abroad at Philadelphia University prepares students for successful participation and competition in an increasingly interdependent world and to perform with distinction in the international and multicultural contexts that are increasingly shaping professional life. Students at Philadelphia University may study abroad and receive credit for courses that apply directly to their challenging, professions-oriented curricula. Opportunities are available for fall, spring, and summer semesters. The University has its own programs in Rome and Milan, Italy, and affiliations with more than twenty-five programs all over the world and in most majors.

Academic Facilities

In fall 2006, the University opened the Kanbar Campus Center, a 72,000-square-foot building with an open design, featuring walls of windows to optimize the spectacular natural setting. In addition, the University opened a new recreation center.

The Tuttleman Center at Philadelphia University, a 31,500-square-foot academic building, provides students and faculty members with access to the most sophisticated technologies for teaching and learning.

Many major labs and studios enable students to gain practical experience in engineering, design, textiles, apparel manufacturing, foreign languages, the sciences, computer technologies, and physician assistant studies. The University's Paul J. Gutman Library is a state-of-the-art information center. Through the contemporary information system, students can search the library's collections, as well as major indexes and full-text journals, from on or off campus. An international computer network links Philadelphia University to the resources of more than 14,000 libraries worldwide. With more than 400 study spaces and nine group study rooms, the library provides an ideal environment for reading and research. The Architecture and Design Center houses studio space, a photo lab, and computer-aided design labs. The Design Center at Philadelphia University houses an extensive collection of textile artifacts and hosts changing exhibits in its galleries.

General-purpose and departmental computing labs are updated using a multiyear migration strategy as changes in technology dictate. The labs are currently equipped with Pentium PCs and Macintoshes running at speeds from 1.0 to 1.8 MHz. The University operates a switched, 100-megabit network with building-to-building gigabit (1000-megabit) connections in high-traffic areas. The network provides students with access to the Internet, e-mail service, network storage (300 MB per student), digital library resources, online databases, and the Blackboard course management system.

Costs

The University's 2007–08 cost for regular tuition was $25,386. Room was $4258 and board was $4312.

Financial Aid

In 2007–08, Philadelphia University's total financial aid program amounted to more than $60 million; about $20.2 million came from the University itself and the remainder came from federal, state, and private sources. While 96 percent of the University's full-time day students receive direct institutional scholarship assistance, 97 percent receive some form of aid each year (e.g., other scholarships, loans, and job opportunities). Candidates for aid should complete the Free Application for Federal Student Aid by April 15. The University offers a wide range of institutional scholarships and grants to incoming students each year. Award amounts vary according to the quality of each student's academic record. The University's scholarship program is available to all prospective students (freshmen and transfer students). Scholarships are awarded regardless of financial need. Students and parents are strongly encouraged to call the admissions or financial aid offices for further information.

Faculty

Primarily a teaching institution, the University encourages close connections between the faculty and students. Classes intentionally are kept small, and faculty members make a practice of being available to students outside the classroom. Often, students can partner with faculty members to pursue joint research interests and gain career experience. The University's faculty is composed of a diverse group of professionals who not only hold strong academic credentials but also frequently possess impressive work experience. They are often sought out as consultants in their fields.

Student Government

The Student Government Association (SGA) is an independent, self-governing student group. In addition to the basic responsibility of protecting students' rights, SGA recommends students to University-wide committees, addresses student grievances, and sponsors campuswide events. The Campus Activities Board is the major programming organization on campus. Its primary responsibility is to provide a wide variety of cultural, scholastic, social, educational, and recreational programs.

Admission Requirements

The University evaluates applicants on the basis of their high school record (including GPA and quality of courses taken), scores on either the SAT or the ACT, and extracurricular activities. Normally, 15 units of secondary school preparation are required for admission. Three units of mathematics (including algebra II and geometry) are required for admission. Students who wish to enter a science curriculum are strongly encouraged to take 4 units of mathematics and 4 units of science. The University actively recruits qualified transfer students, who represent approximately one fifth of the incoming class each fall. The University also has a large international student population. These students must score at least 170 (computer-based) on the TOEFL in order to be considered for admission.

Application and Information

The University maintains a rolling admission plan. Applications are reviewed and decisions are made soon after an application, academic credentials, and standardized test scores are received. Students are encouraged to submit applications early in the senior year; applications received after March 1 are considered on a space-available basis. All applicants are encouraged to come to the campus for an interview with a member of the professional admission staff.

Christine E. Greb
Dean of Admissions
Philadelphia University
School House Lane and Henry Avenue
Philadelphia, Pennsylvania 19144
Phone: 215-951-2800
800-951-7287 (toll-free)
Fax: 215-951-2907
E-mail: admissions@PhilaU.edu
Web site: http://www.PhilaU.edu

POINT PARK UNIVERSITY

PITTSBURGH, PENNSYLVANIA

The University

Point Park University, founded in 1960, has undergone vigorous growth in the last decade. It is accredited by the Middle States Association of Colleges and Schools. Enrollment has grown to 3,600, and the number of majors available totals more than fifty, including a Master of Arts in educational administration, Master of Arts degree programs in journalism and mass communications, a Master of Arts in curriculum and instruction, a Master of Science in criminal justice, a Master of Science in engineering management, an accelerated M.B.A., and an M.F.A. in theater arts.

Characterized by a willingness to innovate, the University, since its inception, has actively established internship possibilities with the many resources for career preparation in Pittsburgh. Internship opportunities can be found in the performing arts, local broadcasting stations, area hospitals, and the government and with such corporate giants as USX and PPG Industries. The University's numerous activities are designed to meet the needs of a diversified student body, representing forty-two states and thirty-nine countries. Fraternities, sororities, clubs associated with specific majors, the Point Park University Singers, and the United Student Government are a few of the organizations that students may join. Intramural sports include basketball, billiards, flag football, soccer, table tennis, tennis, volleyball, and weight lifting. The men's intercollegiate basketball and baseball teams are perennially included in the National Association of Intercollegiate Athletics (NAIA) national rankings and district and national playoffs. Point Park also has men's intercollegiate cross-country and soccer teams (NAIA). The women's basketball, cross-country, soccer, softball, and volleyball teams add another strong tradition to the Point Park Pioneer sports program. The University's teams compete in the NAIA's American Mideast Conference (AMC).

Location

Metropolitan Pittsburgh has a population of more than 2 million. In the Golden Triangle, gleaming office towers loom high above landscaped plazas, fountains, and a 36-acre park fronting on Pittsburgh's three rivers. More than 100 major corporations have their headquarters in the city, making it the fifth-largest corporate center in the nation. Through its prominence as a corporate hub, a home for high-tech industries, and a major production center for steel, the city provides a vast array of career opportunities, as well as a distinctive population mix. Pittsburgh continues to be named one of the most livable cities in the United States in *Places Rated Almanac.*

Through the philanthropic efforts of such financial entrepreneurs as Carnegie and Frick, Pittsburgh has enjoyed a long tradition as a cultural center. The city has an excellent opera and ballet companies and the Pittsburgh Opera is world renowned. Theaters, ethnic festivals, and club attractions fill out the entertainment spectrum. In addition, the nation's first educational television station, WQED, provides a wealth of stimulating offerings. PNC Park, Heinz Field, and Mellon Arena are homes of Pittsburgh's professional sports teams and also host concerts and other special events; all are within walking distance of the University. Also within walking distance of the campus is the downtown YMCA, where a nominal fee entitles students to the use of extensive and varied facilities the year round. A short bus ride away is the Oakland section of Pittsburgh, the location of several renowned museums.

Majors and Degrees

The Bachelor of Arts degree is offered in advertising/public relations; applied arts; applied history; behavioral sciences; broadcasting; cinema and digital arts; dance; dance pedagogy; early childhood education; elementary education; English; film and video production; general studies; journalism; legal studies; mass communication; photojournalism; political science; psychology; secondary education; sport, arts, and entertainment management; and theater arts.

The Bachelor of Fine Arts degree is conferred in dance, film and video production and photography (in conjunction with Pittsburgh Filmmakers), and theater arts.

The Bachelor of Science degree is conferred in accounting, biological sciences, biotechnology, business management, civil engineering technology, criminal justice, electrical engineering technology, environmental health science and protection, general studies, health services, human resources management, information technology, management services, mathematics/secondary education, mechanical engineering technology, public administration, specialized professional studies–funeral service, and sport, arts, and entertainment management.

Preparation for teachers in secondary education is a cooperative effort of the Department of Education and the department of the student's major subject. Programs in predental, prelaw, and premedical studies are arranged within suitable majors.

Academic Programs

Point Park is an innovative institution. Its philosophy is one of meeting and adapting to individual requirements within the framework of a sound humanistic education. This commitment is reflected in programs that, while providing for the expansion of mind and spirit that the liberal arts alone can give, places strong emphasis on developing career skills. Thus, all degree programs, with the exception of the B.F.A. programs, include a core curriculum requirement of 42 credit hours. The core curriculum includes choices in the humanities as well as in the social, behavioral, and natural sciences. Aside from completing the prerequisites for major offerings, students may elect to fulfill their core requirements on a schedule of their own choosing. At the same time, the student's introduction to specific career preparation can begin in the first semester. Indeed, this is typical for students majoring in computer science, dance, engineering technology, film production, journalism and communications, and theater arts. In order to encourage student experimentation, the University permits eight courses from the core curriculum to be taken under a pass/fail option.

With the approval of their guidance offices, high school students may take courses at Point Park for full college credit. The University grants advanced standing on the basis of the College Board's Advanced Placement tests, the CLEP examinations, and educational experiences in the armed forces. In addition, the University has long-standing experience in meeting the needs of transfer students.

The academic calendar consists of two semesters and a summer schedule offering two 6-week sessions and one 12-week session. This year-round utilization of facilities, combined with the University's extensive evening and Saturday programs, provides students with maximum flexibility in planning their schedules.

Off-Campus Programs

Point Park's membership in the Pittsburgh Council on Higher Education gives students the chance to cross-register at any of nine area institutions, including Duquesne University, the University of Pittsburgh, and Carnegie Mellon University.

Point Park University gives students the opportunity to earn a number of credits at various off-campus sites.

Academic Facilities

The University Center of Point Park University opened in downtown Pittsburgh in May 1997. The University Center houses Point Park University's television studio and cinema and digital arts labs. The Point Park University Library supports the University's curriculum through its print, multimedia, and electronic collections. Students have access to the library's online resources from on and off campus. The library has computers for students' use on the first floor and in the library's instruction lab. A science and journalism laboratory complex, an on-campus radio station, a student-run newspaper and magazine, an on-campus laboratory school, on-campus dance studios, numerous computer terminal rooms, a CADD lab, a new biotechnology lab, and other facilities and programs contribute to the University's philosophy of carefully balancing theory with practical experience. The University's location in the heart of Pittsburgh's business district opens numerous opportunities for practical learning. Point Park owns and operates the Pittsburgh Playhouse of Point Park University, which presents more than twenty dance and theater productions per year.

Costs

For 2007–08, tuition and fees for full-time study totaled $9495 per semester. The charge for part-time study was $510 per credit hour. Room and board were $4220 per term for double occupancy. The majority of rooms are for double occupancy with private bath, Ethernet and cable access, and phone.

Financial Aid

Point Park makes a sincere effort to ensure that each student who desires to attend is able to do so. Accordingly, the University administers a generous program of financial aid, including Federal Work-Study awards and Point Park, Federal Pell, and Federal Supplemental Educational Opportunity grants. The University administers loans under the Federal Perkins Loan Program and the Federal Stafford Student Loan Program. Academic, talent, and athletic scholarships are also available for all students, including transfer students.

Applicants for financial aid must demonstrate financial need and show evidence of academic promise or achievement. To apply, students must submit a completed University application form. All students must submit applications for federal, state, and Point Park financial aid through the Pennsylvania Higher Education Assistance Agency (PHEAA).

Faculty

Full- and part-time faculty members provide undergraduate instruction at an average faculty-student ratio of 1:15. Forty-four percent of full-time faculty members in the academic disciplines hold doctoral degrees. Faculty members in the performing arts and practical disciplines are involved in their professions outside of the University as well as in the classroom. The top priority among this faculty group is the instruction of undergraduate students rather than specialized research and publication. Students are advised throughout their college career by a designated faculty member in their major area.

Student Government

The United Student Government actively participates in the affairs of the University. The Student Affairs Committee acts in conjunction with the Dean of Students to coordinate social programs on the campus as well as to provide input for University policy.

Admission Requirements

Point Park University is very much concerned with the needs and interests of its students. This concern is extended not only to matriculated students but also to prospective students. For this reason, the admissions staff pursues a policy that is individualized, personal, and humanistic. Each student is viewed in terms of his or her own personal and academic potential. Recommendations from guidance counselors and teachers and an interview, while not required, are considered, along with motivational factors and relative maturity, in conjunction with the traditional objective criteria, such as class rank, high school record, and standardized test scores. All candidates are required to take either the SAT or the ACT.

Application and Information

Applications for the fall semester are taken on a rolling basis; however, students are urged to apply early in their senior year of secondary school. Early application is particularly important for students desiring residence hall accommodations and financial aid. Applications from freshman and transfer candidates are also considered for the spring semester and should be filed by December 15. The University requires each freshman applicant to submit an application, a nonrefundable $40 fee, SAT or ACT scores, and an official high school transcript. Transfer applicants must also submit official transcripts from all colleges and postsecondary schools attended.

Application forms and additional information may be obtained by writing to:

Office of Admission
Point Park University
201 Wood Street
Pittsburgh, Pennsylvania 15222-1984
Phone: 412-392-3430
800-321-0129 (toll-free)
Fax: 412-392-3902
E-mail: enroll@pointpark.edu
Web site: http://www.pointpark.edu

Point Park students enjoy the many social and sporting activities that Pittsburgh has to offer.

COLLEGE DATA CENTER • PENNSYLVANIA

THE RESTAURANT SCHOOL AT WALNUT HILL COLLEGE

PHILADELPHIA, PENNSYLVANIA

The School

The Restaurant School at Walnut Hill College was established in 1974 and is dedicated to inspiring the future of the restaurant and hotel industry through training that is dynamic, timely, and insightful, with a commitment of service to its students. The Restaurant School at Walnut Hill College combines both intensive classroom training and practical experience: students use their knowledge while they learn.

A student's education is cultivated by the College's philosophy that hands-on training is an essential part of education. This approach has multiple benefits—it enhances learning abilities, creates marketable skills and experience for a resume, brings education to life, and, most importantly, puts the student at the center of it all.

The Restaurant School at Walnut Hill College is accredited by the Accrediting Commission of Career Schools and Colleges of Technology, certified for veteran's training by the Veterans Administration, approved by the United States Department of Justice to grant student visas, and recognized as a Professional Management Development Partner of the Educational Foundation of the National Restaurant Association.

There is a diverse population at the Restaurant School at Walnut Hill College, with students coming from throughout the United States and abroad and ranging in age from the high school graduate to the adult who wants to change careers.

Whether it is a celebrity chef's cooking demonstration, dinner and a tour at a notable restaurant or hotel, or a winery tour and tasting, students at the Restaurant School are exposed to the very best Philadelphia has to offer. There are activities and weekly special events that are sponsored by student clubs. The Student Culinary Team has been the winner of several major competitions in recent years—both nationally and internationally. Activities are both educational and fun, combining opportunities to learn and to establish camaraderie and professional development. Events are listed in the student newsletter and monthly calendar.

Location

Philadelphia is a great place to live and learn. As the fourth-largest city in the United States, Philadelphia has much to offer and is a city of firsts—the first public library, the first college, and the first zoo—all in a first-class city.

The Restaurant School at Walnut Hill College is located in the University City section of Philadelphia, neighboring both the University of Pennsylvania and Drexel University. Located just across the Schuylkill River from Center City, University City has a wonderful college-town ambiance. Restaurants, museums, shops, and theaters abound, with local merchants offering discounts to students. The Amtrak train station is within walking distance of the campus, and the airport is 20 minutes away by car.

Center City is located just minutes from campus. Here, students find a bustling shopping and business district, complete with an award-winning restaurant row, luxury hotels, and exclusive boutiques.

Diversity abounds in this city of neighborhoods, including Chinatown, complete with exotic restaurants and shops; South Philadelphia, with its famed Italian market; and the ever-eclectic South Street, with blocks of restaurants, galleries, shops, and entertainment—not to mention the Historic District, which was the birthplace of the nation, and a waterfront that features an exciting nightlife.

Philadelphia is rich in culture and heritage. Students find world-class art and science museums, theaters that feature major Broadway shows and renowned regional production, and music, which includes everything from jazz to pop to the internationally acclaimed Philadelphia Orchestra.

Majors and Degrees

The College offers associate and bachelor's degrees in four program majors: hotel management (101 A.S. and 202 B.S. credits), restaurant management (101 A.S. and 202 B.S. credits), culinary arts (103 A.S. and 201 B.S. credits), and pastry arts (106 A.S. and 199 B.S. credits). Each major provides students with a broad-based knowledge of the overall workings of a fine restaurant or hotel. Beyond that, the programs prepare students with the day-to-day skills and specific knowledge required as they develop careers as restaurant managers, chefs, pastry chefs, hotel managers, or restaurateurs. In partnership with the Educational Foundation of the National Restaurant Association, the College's curriculum includes up to twelve nationally recognized food-service and hospitality-management courses. Upon successful completion of the courses and the certification exam, students receive national certification.

Academic Programs

All students must successfully complete twelve 10-week terms to be awarded a Bachelor of Science degree or six 10-week terms to be awarded an Associate of Science degree in their field of study. Each academic year consists of three terms. A student must fulfill the required term hours in a major as well as the basic requirements of the core curriculum. All students are required to participate in special service programs prior to graduating.

Off-Campus Programs

The Restaurant School at Walnut Hill College was one of the first schools in the country to offer a travel experience as part of a curriculum. Culinary and pastry students participate in an eight-day tour of France, and hotel and restaurant management students participate in an eight-day Orlando resort and cruise tour. This travel experience enhances both training and resumes.

A capstone program to England is in place for all baccalaureate students. Students may contact the College for detailed information.

Academic Facilities

Recently completing a yearlong renovation, the Restaurant School at Walnut Hill College is poised to offer one of the most dynamic hands-on learning opportunities in the country. The dining experience, situated in the breathtakingly restored 1855 Allison Mansion, turns into a dining event, with the addition of three theme restaurants, including the Italian Trattoria, which is a casual Italian restaurant that features classic pasta presentations set amidst an Italian terrace. Guests are invited to sit inside the restaurant, where they can enjoy homemade pasta or dine outside among the twinkling lights in the European courtyard.

American cuisine is presented in an innovative new style of the American Heartland. Depicting a country farm with a painted blue sky and cornfields, this restaurant allows students to explore some of America's best cooking while guests enjoy the comfort of a country dining or veranda setting.

Most notable is the elegant Great Chefs of Philadelphia restaurant. Amidst glittering crystal chandeliers and a rich tapestry motif, guests enjoy wonderful cuisine and service designed by some of Philadelphia and America's top chefs.

Also in the mansion is the Student Resource Center, featuring state-of-the-art computer lab stations as well as the Alumni Library, which encompasses thousands of books, magazines, and videotapes on cooking, management, and wine. The building also houses a student conference room and a wine lab.

The Pastry Shop and Café is filled each morning with buttery croissants, crisp French baguettes, and glistening pastries that are prepared by the pastry arts students. Also available is a selection of pastas, salads, soups, and entrees for an informal café lunch, prepared by the culinary arts students.

The education and the Center for Hospitality Studies buildings are the focal points of the student's training. They house six modern classroom kitchens, four lecture halls, and the College's purchasing center and school store.

Hunter Hall is a turn-of-the-century masterpiece that features magnificent carved mahogany, marble, and fireplaces. The College's Offices of Admissions, Financial Aid, and Independent Student Housing are located in this building.

Costs

Tuition for students who start September 2008 is $34,500 ($17,250 per academic year) for the two-year Associate of Science degree program or $69,000 ($17,250 per academic year) for the four-year Bachelor of Science degree program. Equipment, activity fees, culinary whites, and management dining room attire cost approximately $1200. Students may contact the College for information on on-campus housing.

Financial Aid

Financial aid programs are available for those who qualify. It is recommended that students apply early. The College participates in the Federal Pell Grant, the Pennsylvania PHEAA State Grant, the subsidized Federal Stafford Student Loan, and parents' Federal PLUS Loan, in addition to other alternative loans. The financial aid officers assist students and their families with the creation of a personal plan that outlines expenses and identifies financial resources available to incoming students. For more specific information, students may contact the College.

Faculty

Learning comes to life under the guiding hands and encouragement of the highly trained, technically skilled faculty. The faculty members are seasoned professionals, having logged many years of experience in restaurants and food service. Through their instruction, students gain professional insight that gives them a competitive edge on entering the hospitality field. The chefs and instructors are committed to helping students achieve success. As professionals, they continuously keep pace with current trends in the hospitality industry and convey their professional dedication and work ethic to their students.

Admission Requirements

Typically, the admissions procedure begins with a visit to the College. At that time, prospective students and their families tour the campus, watch hands-on classes in action, and get a feel for campus life. Application for admission to the College is available to any individual with a high school diploma or its equivalent and an interest in developing a career or ownership options in the fine restaurant, food service, or hospitality field. Applicants are evaluated on their educational background and demonstrated or stated interest in their chosen field. Two references are required, as are high school transcripts and an essay.

Students may contact the College for information on the early decision program for high school juniors and seniors.

Application and Information

The Restaurant School at Walnut Hill College practices rolling admission; qualified applicants are accepted at any time. Applications for admission are submitted with a $50 application fee and a $150 registration fee. Prospective students should contact:

Office of Admissions
The Restaurant School at Walnut Hill College
4207 Walnut Street
Philadelphia, Pennsylvania 19104
Phone: 215-222-4200 Ext. 3011
877-925-6884 Ext. 3011 (toll-free)
Fax: 215-222-4219
E-mail: info@walnuthillcollege.edu
Web site: http://www.walnuthillcollege.edu

The Restaurant School at Walnut Hill College.

ROBERT MORRIS UNIVERSITY

PITTSBURGH AND MOON TOWNSHIP, PENNSYLVANIA

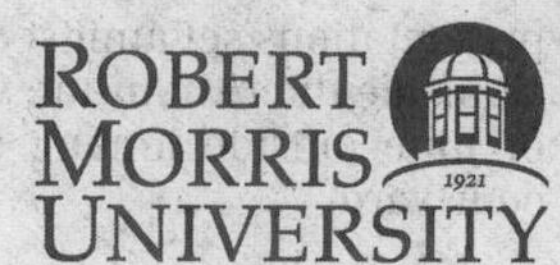

The University

Robert Morris University (RMU), founded in 1921, is one of the leading universities in the Pittsburgh region and among the largest private institutions of higher learning in Pennsylvania. RMU built its reputation by offering strong academic programs in traditional business fields such as accounting, finance, marketing, and management. To prepare students for success in a changing and competitive workforce, the University has created programs in communications, information systems, engineering, mathematics, science, education, social sciences, and nursing during the past decade. The University also offers students the opportunity to gain a global perspective by studying abroad.

Because Robert Morris University is a teaching-centered institution, classes are small and are taught by faculty members, not teaching assistants. The student-faculty ratio is 16:1, and the University has an average class size of 24. More than 5,000 full- and part-time undergraduate and graduate students from thirty-seven states and fourteen countries are enrolled at Robert Morris University.

The 78,000-square-foot Nicholson Center, which opened in 1999, is located at the heart of the campus and provides a gathering place for students, alumni, and faculty and staff members. The center is the hub for student activities and programs, and it houses a food court, a café, a bookstore, and administrative offices.

Nearly ninety activities and organizations help students to develop leadership skills, network professionally, and meet new friends. Student activities include varsity, club, and intramural sports; fraternities and sororities; student government; and community service projects. RMU offers twenty-three NCAA Division I men's and women's varsity sports, including the only Division I men's and women's ice hockey programs in Pittsburgh. In 2003, the University purchased the Island Sports Center, a 32-acre sports and recreation complex with two ice rinks, two multipurpose rinks, an indoor golf driving range, a miniature golf course, batting cages, a fitness center, a pro shop, and a bistro.

The Student Life Office organizes dances, parties, movie screenings, comedy acts, health and wellness fairs, educational programs, and day trips. Business organizations, professional clubs, and honor societies provide students with career preparation opportunities. RMU students also get involved in the community, organizing Habitat for Humanity projects, coordinating blood drives, collecting food donations, and organizing holiday parties for needy youngsters.

Robert Morris University offers nineteen graduate degree programs, including the Master of Science (M.S.) in business education, communications and information systems, competitive intelligence systems, engineering management, human resource management, information security and assurance, information systems management, information technology project management, instructional leadership, Internet information systems, nonprofit management, nursing, organizational studies, and taxation; the Master of Business Administration (M.B.A.); the Doctor of Nursing Practice (D.N.P.); the Doctor of Science (D.Sc.) in information systems and communications; and the Doctor of Philosophy (Ph.D.) in engineering and in instructional management and leadership.

Location

The 230-acre main campus is located in Moon Township, Pennsylvania, just 15 minutes from Pittsburgh International Airport and 17 miles from downtown Pittsburgh. The RMU Island Sports Center, a 32-acre sports and recreation complex, is located 15 minutes from campus on Neville Island, while the University's Center for Adult and Continuing Education is located in downtown Pittsburgh.

Majors and Degrees

Robert Morris University offers thirty undergraduate degree programs, many of which offer multiple specializations. Bachelor's degree programs include the Bachelor of Arts (B.A.) in applied mathematics, communications, English, environmental science, media arts, and social science; the Bachelor of Fine Arts (B.F.A.) in media arts; the Bachelor of Science (B.S.) in actuarial science, applied mathematics, applied psychology, business education, competitive intelligence systems, computer information systems, elementary education, engineering (industrial, mechanical, and software), environmental science, health services administration, information sciences, manufacturing engineering, nursing, organizational studies, professional communications and information systems, and social science; and the Bachelor of Science in Business Administration (B.S.B.A.) in accounting, economics, finance, hospitality and tourism management, management, marketing, and sport management. In addition, RMU offers preparation for secondary teacher certification in biology, business, communication, English, mathematics, and social studies education.

Academic Programs

Robert Morris is on a two-semester schedule with various summer sessions. A total of 126 credits are required for the bachelor's degree. Internship or co-op credits of 3 to 12 hours may be used toward degree requirements. The University participates in a cross-registration program with nine local colleges through the Pittsburgh Council on Higher Education consortium.

Academic Facilities

Learning resources include a traditional library with more than 137,000 bound volumes, more than 80 reference databases, and nearly 600 periodical subscriptions.

The Academic Media Center, with full production facilities, provides students with opportunities to collaborate on projects in all areas of media, including television/video production, audio production, and photography.

State-of-the-art laboratory facilities were recently opened to support the engineering, mathematics, science, and nursing programs. Graphic and Web design students benefit from a cutting-edge design studio.

Costs

Annual tuition for the 2007–08 year was a $17,600 flat rate based on a 24- to 36-credit, two-semester schedule. Room and board fees were $8520 based on double occupancy and a full meal plan.

Financial Aid

More than 90 percent of RMU undergraduates receive some sort of financial aid, including scholarships, grants, loans, and work-study programs. Both need-based and achievement-based awards are available. All applicants must complete the admissions application, the Free Application for Federal Student Aid, and the grant forms from their own state.

Faculty

The University has nearly 400 full- and part-time faculty members, 82 percent of whom hold terminal degrees. The student-faculty ratio is 16:1 and the average class size is 24. Students may take advantage of the expertise offered by the faculty in academic advisement and counseling, as well as counseling from the staff at the Center for Student Success.

Student Government

The Student Government Association represents all student organizations, including fraternities and sororities. Members participate in the planning of all social and cultural events on campus.

Admission Requirements

First-time freshmen must submit an application for admission with a $30 application fee (waived for online applicants), official high school transcripts or GED credential, and official SAT or ACT scores. Preference is given to applicants with a minimum 3.0 high school GPA and a combined SAT score of 1000 or a composite ACT score of 22.

Transfer students who have earned credits from another regionally accredited institution must submit transcripts from all postsecondary institutions attended and must have a minimum 2.0 GPA. Students with less than 30 college credits must also submit high school transcripts or GED credential.

Interviews are not required for admission except for students interested in the engineering, elementary education, and nursing programs. Students are encouraged to arrange for a campus visit with an enrollment manager.

Robert Morris University is committed to a policy of nondiscrimination on the basis of race, sex, color, religion, national origin, or handicap.

Application and Information

Students are encouraged to submit applications in the fall of their senior year of high school. Official transcripts and counselor recommendations should accompany the application; there is a $30 application processing fee that is waived for online applicants.

Robert Morris uses a rolling admission system; students are considered for acceptance as soon as all application materials have been received and evaluated.

For additional information and application materials, students should contact:

Kellie Laurenzi
Dean of Admissions
Robert Morris University
6001 University Boulevard
Moon Township, Pennsylvania 15108
Phone: 800-762-0097 (toll-free)
Web site: http://www.rmu.edu

Robert Morris University's Nicholson Center.

COLLEGE DATA CENTER • PENNSYLVANIA

ROSEMONT COLLEGE

ROSEMONT, PENNSYLVANIA

The College

Founded in 1921, Rosemont College is an independent liberal arts institution in the Catholic tradition. Rosemont's reputation for academic excellence in an intimate setting is its hallmark. Rosemont College's community of students and faculty members are dedicated to developing the intellect and abilities of every student.

Rosemont College welcomes persons of all beliefs. It is committed to excellence and joy in teaching and learning. Rosemont seeks to develop open and critical minds and reasoned moral positions in all members of the community and to assist them in becoming persons capable of independent and reflective thought and action. It seeks also to prepare women and men for the world of work so that they can make a significant contribution.

Rosemont is consistently highly ranked by *U.S. News & World Report*. It has been named to the John Templeton Foundation Honor Roll for Character-Building Colleges, a designation that recognizes colleges and universities that emphasize character building as an integral part of the college experience.

Rosemont is one college with three schools: the Undergraduate Women's College, the School of Graduate Studies, and the School of Continuing Studies. The nationally acclaimed, traditional Undergraduate Women's College confers the Bachelor of Arts, the Bachelor of Fine Arts, and the Bachelor of Science degrees in twenty-three majors. Rosemont has approximately 7,000 living alumnae, many of whom have been in the vanguard of expanding career and professional opportunities for women. They can be found in high-ranking positions in science and medicine, law, business, education, the social sciences, publishing, and the arts.

Building on its historic commitment to the undergraduate education of women, Rosemont has expanded to include a School of Continuing Studies and a School of Graduate Studies, which are open to both women and men. The School of Continuing Studies offers seven undergraduate business degrees and two graduate business degrees, all in an accelerated format. Rosemont's School of Graduate Studies offers the Master of Arts degree in curriculum and instruction, counseling psychology, English, and English and publishing. A Master of Fine Arts degree is offered in creative writing.

In the spirit of Cornelia Connelly, founder of the Society of the Holy Child Jesus, Rosemont is committed to preparing individuals to meet the challenges of the times and to act responsibly and effectively in an ever-changing world. Rosemont College looks forward to meeting the demands of the new century—and beyond.

Rosemont participates in NCAA Division III varsity teams of basketball, field hockey, lacrosse, softball, tennis, and volleyball.

Location

Rosemont's 56-acre campus is located in the town of Rosemont, a historic suburban community with many shops, movie theaters, restaurants, and bookstores. The city of Philadelphia is 11 miles east of Rosemont and just a 20-minute train ride from the campus. Rosemont's proximity to Philadelphia provides students with a vast array of cultural and social opportunities, such as the Philadelphia Museum of Art, the Philadelphia Orchestra, the Pennsylvania Ballet, and various professional sports events, including Phillies, Flyers, and Eagles games. Within the Philadelphia area there are approximately eighty other colleges and universities. Rosemont is ideally located for recreational activities; it is only a short distance from both the Pocono Mountains and the New Jersey shore.

Majors and Degrees

Rosemont College awards the Bachelor of Arts, the Bachelor of Fine Arts, and the Bachelor of Science degrees. Majors are offered in the following fields: accounting, biochemistry, biology, business, chemistry, communication, economics, education, English, French, German, history, history of art, international business, mathematics, philosophy, political science, psychology, religious studies, sociology, Spanish, studio art, and women's studies. Interdisciplinary majors are offered in humanities, Italian studies, and social science. Prelaw and premedical programs and teacher certification for art, early childhood, elementary, secondary, and special education areas are available. Minors are available in most majors in addition to theater. Students may also choose to pursue a double major or create their own cross-disciplinary individualized major. Other special programs include art therapy, medical, nursing, and physician assistant degree programs with Drexel University; a dual-degree program in chemical engineering and a transfer nursing program with nearby Villanova University; and a transfer dental program with Temple University.

In addition, Rosemont offers a combined B.A./M.A. in English and publishing and a combined B.A./M.A. in counseling psychology.

Academic Programs

To earn a Rosemont undergraduate degree, each candidate must complete 128 credits. In addition to the requirements of a major concentration, all students must complete general requirements. An internship, service-learning, or study-abroad experience is required prior to graduation. During their senior year, all students must successfully complete a comprehensive exam exhibiting competency in their declared major.

Rosemont College offers two joint-admissions medical programs with the Drexel University College of Medicine. These programs are highly selective, and a December 1 deadline applies.

For students interested in a French and business major, Rosemont offers specialized courses in business French to prepare students for the examination of the Chambre de Commerce et d'Industrie de Paris. The Certificat Pratique de Français Commercial et Économique is awarded to students who successfully complete this exam.

Rosemont offers programs granting certification in the following teaching areas: art education, early childhood education/elementary education, elementary education, secondary education, and special education with a concentration in hearing impaired.

Off-Campus Programs

Through academic exchange programs that expand course offerings, students may take courses at neighboring Villanova University, Eastern University, Arcadia University, Cabrini College, Chestnut Hill College, Gwynedd-Mercy College, Holy Family College, Immaculata University, and Neumann College. The Art Institutes International Exchange Program, which allows studio art candidates to apply for admission into the commercial art program offered at any one of the eight Art Institute International Schools located in Atlanta, Dallas, Denver, Fort Lauderdale, Houston, Philadelphia, Pittsburgh, and Seattle, is also available.

Rosemont students may participate in any of a variety of study-abroad programs. These programs give students the opportunity to combine travel with academic and cultural study. Students receive full credit at Rosemont for course work successfully completed on an approved program. Rosemont, in cooperation with Villanova University, sponsors its own summer study-abroad program to Siena, Italy. This program focuses on course work in studio art, Italian Renaissance art history, and Italian language and literature.

There are many opportunities for full-semester internships in various fields of study. Each candidate must be academically qualified and meet the approval of the appropriate faculty member. Fieldwork and practicums, as well as summer internships, are also available.

Academic Facilities

The Student Academic Support Center, located in the Brown Science Building, is the comprehensive source for academic assistance. The center offers a wide range of advising, experiential learning, and learning support services to enhance students' educational experiences at the College. All services are offered to all students at no cost.

The Gertrude Kistler Memorial Library creates a setting that is conducive to study and research. The library was the first academic building erected on the campus and was renovated in 1998. It houses more than 159,000 volumes, approximately 563 current periodicals, and numerous electronic indexes and databases as well as access to the Internet. The library also houses a 10,000 volume collection of children's literature. The online catalog, the Rosemont Electronic Learning and Library System (TRELLIS), is the basic index to the library's collections. TRELLIS includes a number of computerized periodical indexes and encyclopedias and provides access to the Internet's World Wide Web.

The renovated science building is composed of the Dorothy McKenna Brown Science Building and the McShain Performing Arts Center. The Brown Science Building provides laboratory facilities and lecture rooms for the natural sciences. State-of-the-art equipment includes a phase microscope with video camera and color TV monitor, physiographs, spectrophotometers, and an environment chamber. The building also houses two electronic classrooms equipped with the latest in Windows PC and Macintosh technology. Students have access to laser and full-color printers, scanners, zip drives, and CD burners as well as numerous software resources for word processing, desktop publishing, indexing, and graphic arts. A mobile cart containing eleven wireless laptop computers is also housed in the Brown Science Building and is available for use throughout the building. The McShain Performing Arts Center is a 400-seat auditorium used for special forums, theatrical performances, and ceremonies.

The Global Curriculum Classroom located in Good Counsel Hall, houses a sympodium, an interactive smart-computer/touchsceen; integrated projector DVD/VCR; and sound system. A mobile cart equipped with twenty-four wireless laptop computers is also located in the Global Curriculum Classroom.

Costs

For 2007–08, costs for full-time students included tuition, $21,630; room and board, $9200; and fees, approximately $1185.

Financial Aid

Many Rosemont students receive some form of financial aid. Financial aid includes scholarships, grants, loans, and work-study awards. Most financial packages are a combination of various forms of aid. To apply for aid, students should submit the Free Application for Federal Student Aid (FAFSA) by February 15.

Faculty

The faculty is one of Rosemont's most important assets. The faculty members are dedicated individuals who believe the student must be engaged to learn; therefore, all classes at Rosemont are small, which lends to the discussion or seminar format. Approximately 90 percent of the faculty members hold either the Ph.D. or the highest degree in their field.

Student Government

The student government at Rosemont coordinates the ongoing governing processes to be responsive to the needs and opinions of students, to stimulate change as needed, to provide a range of programs and activities, and to represent students to Rosemont College as a whole.

Admission Requirements

Rosemont College seeks to enroll women interested in the liberal arts and who have the capacity and the desire to pursue a rigorous academic program. Students are considered without regard to race, religion, disability, or ethnic or national origin. A candidate for admission must present a satisfactory record of scholastic ability and personal integrity from an accredited high school as well as acceptable scores on the SAT. Applicants' records are reviewed by the Admissions Committee. The student must have an official copy of her high school transcript sent to Rosemont's Office of Admissions. An applicant's secondary school preparation should include sixteen college-preparatory courses. For admission to the traditional college program, all applicants are advised to include in their high school program a minimum of 4 units of English, 2 units of foreign language, 2 units of social studies, 2 units of college-preparatory math, and 2 units of laboratory science, one of which must be a lab science. Prospective business majors must present additional units of college-preparatory math. Applicants are expected to carry a full academic program during their senior year of high school.

Two recommendations are required in support of the student's application. The applicant should ask her guidance counselor or other adult who knows the student well (coach, mentor, etc.) and a teacher who has taught the student an academic subject to submit recommendations on her behalf and forward them to Rosemont's Office of Admissions. All applicants are required to submit results of the SAT. The applicant may obtain the registration form for the test from her school or by writing to the College Board, Box 592, Princeton, New Jersey 08540. The code for Rosemont College is 2763. Puerto Rican students may submit scores from the Prueba de Aptitud Académica (PAA) in place of the SAT. Students may also submit ACT scores. The code for Rosemont College is 3676. More information can be obtained by writing to ACT Registration–81, Box 414, Iowa City, Iowa 53343-0414. A personal interview with a member of the admissions staff is strongly recommended as an important part of the application process. Students who are seriously considering Rosemont should visit the campus to enhance their understanding of the academic and social atmosphere. Prospective students are also encouraged to make arrangements to visit classes, meet Rosemont students, and whenever possible, stay overnight. Arrangements can be made by calling the Office of Admissions.

Application and Information

Applications are accepted on a rolling basis. Those interested in scholarships should apply no later than February 15. To arrange for an interview and a tour, or to receive additional information, students should contact:

R. Lizzie Wahab
VP, Enrollment Management
Rosemont College
1400 Montgomery Avenue
Rosemont, Pennsylvania 19010-1699
Phone: 610-526-2966
888-2ROSEMONT (toll-free)
E-mail: admissions@rosemont.edu
Web site: http://www.rosemont.edu

Rosemont College—linking strong traditions with the future.

SAINT FRANCIS UNIVERSITY

LORETTO, PENNSYLVANIA

The University

Saint Francis University is a small, coeducational, liberal arts university. The University was founded in 1847 and conducted under the tradition of the Franciscan Friars of the Third Order Regular. The University is concerned with the development of each student for the world of today. For more than 150 years, the University's philosophy of education and student life has continued to emphasize two values: instruction of high quality and respect for the student as an individual. The University believes that a liberal arts education, encompassing a major field of study, is the soundest kind of preparation a student can have for a productive life. The University is accredited by the Middle States Association of Colleges and Schools. The social work program is accredited by the Council on Social Work Education, and the programs in teacher education have been approved by the Pennsylvania State Department of Education. The physician assistant science program is accredited by the Accreditation Review Commission on Education for Physician Assistants. The nursing program has full approval by the Pennsylvania State Board of Nurse Examiners and is fully accredited by the National League for Nursing Accrediting Commission (NLNAC). The physical therapy program is fully accredited by the Commission on Accreditation in Physical Therapy Education.

Students at Saint Francis University can find a number of outlets for their talents, interests, and abilities. Departmental clubs; volunteer organizations; social, business, and service fraternities; social sororities; and a service sorority are part of campus life. Athletics have played a major role in the University's history, and the athletics program offers twenty-one NCAA Division I sports for men and women as well as intramural sports. The Student Activities Organization sponsors an impressive program of lectures, films, and concerts. The Southern Alleghenies Museum of Art, separately chartered, is located on the campus as well.

The full-time undergraduate enrollment is 509 men and 805 women; the University as a whole enrolls 2,200 students. Saint Francis University offers Associate of Science degrees in business administration, and religious education. On the graduate level, Saint Francis grants a Master of Arts degree in human resource management and industrial relations. The University also offers the Master of Business Administration, Master of Education, Master of Medical Science, Master of Science in physician assistant sciences, and Master of Science in Occupational Therapy degrees. A doctoral degree in physical therapy is also available.

Location

Saint Francis University is situated on 600 acres in the heart of the Allegheny Mountains. The campus is located in the borough of Loretto, which has a population of approximately 1,400. The campus is 6 miles from the county seat of Ebensburg, which has a population of 4,000. The cities of Johnstown and Altoona are within 25 miles of Loretto and have populations of 35,000 and 55,000, respectively. The University is a 90-minute drive east of Pittsburgh.

Majors and Degrees

Saint Francis University grants the Bachelor of Arts degree and offers majors in American studies, biology, computer science, engineering (3-2 program), English, English/communications, history, mathematics, philosophy, political science, psychology, public administration/government service, religious studies, and sociology. The Bachelor of Science degree is also granted, with majors in accounting, biology, chemistry, computer science, economics and finance, elementary education/special education, environmental management (3-2 program), environmental studies (interdisciplinary), exercise physiology, management information systems, marketing, mathematics, medical technology, nursing, occupational therapy (five-year master's), pharmacy (3+2 or 3+3), physical therapy (six-year doctoral degree), physician assistant science (five-year master's), podiatric science, psychology, public administration/government service, social work, and sociology.

Areas of preprofessional study include dentistry, engineering (3-2 program), law, medicine, optometry, podiatry, and veterinary medicine. Areas of concentration within majors include anthropology, biochemistry, bioinformatics, communications, computer science, criminal justice, environmental politics, environmental science, forensics, international studies, management information systems, marine and environmental education specialties, marine biology, molecular biology, political communications, public management, public relations, and systems/languages. The University also grants secondary education certification in the areas of biology, chemistry, English, general science, mathematics, and social studies. A 3-2 cooperative program with Duke University in forestry and environmental management, a 3+4 accelerated program in primary care, a 2+3 accelerated program and a 3+3 program in pharmacy with Lake Erie College of Osteopathic Medicine, and a 3+4 accelerated program leading to the baccalaureate and Doctor of Dental Medicine degrees with Temple University are also offered.

It is possible for students to major in one area and minor in another or to have a double major. A self-designed major program is available as well. The University offers an honors program to challenge intellectually ambitious students from all disciplines. While pursuing their major field of study, students enroll in the full four-year curriculum, which allows in-depth, creative study in a variety of subject areas.

A continuing education program provides credit and noncredit courses on campus as well as in the communities surrounding Loretto. The Office of Continuing Education offers Associate of Science degrees in business administration and religious education and Bachelor of Science degrees in accounting and management.

Academic Programs

The program of study leading to a bachelor's degree is usually completed in eight semesters. To qualify for graduation, a student must follow a program of study, approved by the Vice President for Academic Affairs, that totals at least 128 credits distributed among liberal arts courses, major requirements, collateral requirements, and general electives. All students, regardless of major, are required to complete the University's general education program of 58 credits.

The academic calendar is divided into two semesters and three summer sessions.

Electronic capabilities at Saint Francis University enable students to access library holdings and communicate with professors, fellow students, and the world through the use of personal computers via e-mail and the Internet. Every classroom and residence hall room is wired for Internet access or can be accessed through the wireless network. The University has several classrooms equipped with state-of-the-art equipment that allows videoconferencing. All incoming freshmen receive a laptop computer as part of their tuition.

Off-Campus Programs

Students at Saint Francis University may, with permission of the University's administration, spend their junior year of study abroad or may earn credit for participation in summer programs conducted in Canada, France, Germany, Spain, and other countries by accredited American colleges and universities.

Students are encouraged to take advantage of the University's study abroad facility in Ambialet, France.

A number of departments offer students the opportunity for off-campus study. For some majors, such as nursing, occupational therapy, physical therapy, physician assistant science, education, medical technology, and social work, off-campus study is required;

in all other majors, an internship is available as an elective. Such an internship can be a meaningful experience and can significantly enhance a student's career preparation.

Academic Facilities

The six-story Pasquerilla Library contains more than 176,000 volumes, 582 periodicals, and a substantial microfilm collection. Other features of the library are typing areas, seminar rooms, reading rooms, microfilm reading rooms, several multimedia classrooms, technologically equipped study rooms, and a collection of study items and educational materials for elementary and secondary education majors. Special features of the library include a PC laboratory with printers, an automated card catalog, periodical search systems, and a satellite hookup.

Scotus and Padua halls contain modern classroom facilities, language laboratories, two computer laboratories, a recording studio for radio and television, and lecture facilities (halls and an amphitheater). Sullivan Science Hall contains twelve well-equipped biology, chemistry, and physics laboratories; fully equipped electronic classrooms; a greenhouse for botanical research; an examining room for use in the physician assistant science program; and other facilities.

Costs

For 2007–08, tuition is $22,444, room and board are $7984, and technology program is $1050, for a total of $31,478.

Financial Aid

Approximately 90 percent of the Saint Francis University student body receive financial aid. In addition to participating in federal and state need-based student aid programs, Saint Francis University offers its own substantial grant program and a generous scholarship program that is based on SAT or ACT scores, high school average, and class rank. Academic awards range from $1000 to $14,500.

Faculty

Faculty members are chosen for their knowledge of subject matter, as well as for their ability to communicate. Of the teaching faculty at Saint Francis University, 79 percent hold a doctorate or the highest degree attainable in their specific field of expertise. No graduate students teach classes at Saint Francis University.

Student Government

The Student Government Association's Steering Committee involves students who are interested in self-government. Students also serve on a number of committees in the Faculty Senate. The Student Government offices are located in the John F. Kennedy Student Center, which also houses a 600-seat auditorium, a campus bookstore and post office, a study lounge, and a café.

Admission Requirements

The admission committee considers applicants and renders decisions on the basis of the secondary school record, the recommendation of the secondary school principal or counselor, and the results of the SAT or ACT. Applicants should have a minimum of 16 academic units and are strongly encouraged to visit the University campus for an admission interview and tour. Interviews and campus tours are available Monday through Friday throughout the year and select Saturday mornings while classes are in session.

Transfer students must submit a formal transfer application and a college clearance form in addition to official transcripts from each high school and college previously attended. Transfer students receive an advanced standing evaluation after an offer of admission has been made.

Saint Francis University, an equal opportunity/affirmative action employer, complies with applicable federal and state laws regarding nondiscrimination and affirmative action, including Title IX of the Educational Amendments of 1972, Titles VI and VII of the Civil Rights Act of 1964, and Section 504 of the Rehabilitation Act of 1973. Saint Francis University is committed to a policy of nondiscrimination and equal opportunity in employment, education programs and activities, and admissions that includes all persons regardless of race, gender, color, religion, national origin or ancestry, age, marital status, disability, or Vietnam-era veteran status. Inquiries or complaints may be addressed to the University's Director of Human Resources/Affirmative Action/Title IX Coordinator, Saint Francis University, Loretto, Pennsylvania 15940; telephone: 814-472-3264. For other University information, students should call 814-472-3000.

Application and Information

The University operates under a rolling admission policy. The application deadline for the physical therapy, occupational therapy, and physician assistant programs is January 15. For more information about Saint Francis University, students should contact:

Dean for Enrollment Management
Saint Francis University
P.O. Box 600
Loretto, Pennsylvania 15940
Phone: 814-472-3100
866-342-5738 (toll-free)
E-mail: admissions@francis.edu
Web site: http://www.francis.edu

Christian Hall.

SAINT JOSEPH'S UNIVERSITY

PHILADELPHIA, PENNSYLVANIA

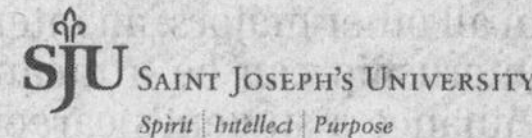

The University

Saint Joseph's University is a nationally recognized, Catholic, Jesuit university. For more than 150 years, Saint Joseph's has advanced the professional and personal ambitions of men and women by providing a rigorous Jesuit education—one that demands high achievement, expands knowledge, deepens understanding, stresses effective reasoning and communication, develops moral and spiritual character, and imparts enduring pride. One of only 142 schools with a Phi Beta Kappa chapter and business school accreditation by AACSB International–The Association to Advance Collegiate Schools of Business, Saint Joseph's is the home of 4,200 full-time undergraduates and 2,600 graduate, part-time, and doctoral students.

As a Jesuit university, Saint Joseph's believes each student realizes his or her fullest potential through challenging classroom study, hands-on learning opportunities, and a commitment to excellence in all endeavors. The University also reinforces the individual's lifelong engagement with the wider world. Graduates of Saint Joseph's attain success in their careers with the help of an extensive network of alumni who have become leading figures in business, law, medicine, education, the arts, technology, government, and public service.

A Saint Joseph's education encompasses all aspects of personal growth and development, reflecting the Ignatian credo of *cura personalis*. Guided by a faculty that is committed to both teaching and scholarship, students develop intellectually through an intense Jesuit liberal arts curriculum and advanced study in a chosen discipline. Students mature socially by participating in Saint Joseph's campus life, noted for its rich variety of activities, infectious enthusiasm, and mutual respect. Students grow ethically and spiritually by living their own values in the larger society beyond the campus.

Steeped in the Jesuit, Catholic tradition, Saint Joseph's provides a rigorous, intensive education that both disciplines and expands the mind. Students develop a lifelong desire to learn and grow while also acquiring the skills and knowledge necessary for success in their professional lives. At the core of this education is a general education requirement, which exposes students to primary fields of inquiry and the cultural values that shape their world. A Jesuit emphasis on engaged teaching and mentoring permeates the university. Faculty members at Saint Joseph's, many of whom are leading scholars in their disciplines, expect students to perform at the highest level and set demanding standards in the classroom.

Saint Joseph's is at the forefront of utilizing innovative technologies to enhance and promote learning. These technologies are widely integrated into the educational process both in class and beyond, where they are also used for individual and collaborative research projects. By mastering these tools and achieving technological fluency, Saint Joseph's students gain a valuable edge in their careers.

Saint Joseph's students engage enthusiastically in all facets of campus life—academic, social, athletic, ethical, and spiritual. Their active participation creates a vibrant, dynamic campus community. In all their activities, students emphasize personal integrity as well as a respect and concern for others. This produces a mutually supportive, humane, and tolerant environment for individual success and service to others.

Location

Located on the edge of metropolitan Philadelphia, Saint Joseph's provides ready access to the vast career opportunities and cultural resources of America's sixth-largest city, while affording students a cohesive and intimate campus experience.

Because of its location, Saint Joseph's has close ties to the people, professional opportunities, and cultural life of Philadelphia. Students enjoy direct access to internships, cooperative programs, and positions in virtually all careers, most of which have a major presence in the Philadelphia area. Saint Joseph's location also offers ample outlets for community involvement and service, and students can easily partake of Philadelphia's professional sports, entertainment, and cultural events.

Majors and Degrees

Saint Joseph's offers full-time baccalaureate degree programs in forty major fields of study and numerous specialty programs, which are administered by two separate colleges.

The College of Arts and Sciences awards the Bachelor of Arts degree in art education, classics, economics, English, fine and performing arts, French, French studies, German, history, international relations, Italian, Latin, philosophy, political science, Spanish, and theology and the Bachelor of Science degree in actuarial science, biology, chemical biology, chemistry, computer science, criminal justice, education, environmental science, interdisciplinary health services, labor studies, mathematics, physics, psychology, public administration, and sociology.

The Erivan K. Haub School of Business awards the Bachelor of Science degree in accounting, decision and system sciences, finance, food marketing, information systems, international business, international marketing, management, marketing, pharmaceutical marketing, and public administration. A co-op program is available for all business majors.

Five-year B.S./M.S. programs are offered in education, international marketing, psychology, and writing studies. The University also offers special academic programs in aerospace studies (Air Force ROTC); allied health (bioscience technologies, nursing, occupational therapy, physical therapy (D.P.T.), and radiologic sciences); American, European, gender, Latin American, medieval, Renaissance, and Russian and East Central European studies; writing studies; and teacher certification at the elementary and secondary levels. Preprofessional study is available in most major fields.

Academic Programs

At Saint Joseph's University, the aim of providing the student with the qualities of a liberally educated individual is pursued through a threefold plan encompassing 120 academic credits. The major concentration (30–45 credits) is intended to provide students with depth in a given field in order to prepare them for effective work in that field or for graduate study. The general education requirement (60 credits) is intended to ensure that students have mastered basic skills necessary for further work, have been exposed to the main divisions of learning, and have been introduced to several new fields of study. Languages and literature, mathematics, natural sciences, history, social sciences, philosophy, and theology are among the areas of study included in the general education requirement. Free electives (15–30 credits) are intended to provide flexibility by encouraging students to pursue studies in areas they have found interesting, to test their interest in an unexplored area, or to deepen their knowledge in the major field.

A competitive honors program is available for qualified students, as are independent and interdisciplinary study options. Claver House provides a place for honors students to have meetings, study, and conduct research.

Off-Campus Programs

Saint Joseph's offers to an increasing number of students the opportunity to study abroad and directly sponsors programs each year in Europe, Africa, Asia, Australia, Latin America, and the UK. International study tours have been made to Africa, Australia, Brazil, Canada, Greece, Ireland, Italy, Japan, Scotland, and Spain.

Students may take advantage of an arrangement with the Washington Center for Internships and Academic Seminars, which allows for a one-semester internship in the nation's capital.

Fieldwork experiences are required in several majors, and the University's location provides for internship opportunities to support virtually all other disciplines. The Career Services Center has a full-time internship coordinator and provides opportunities for on-campus interviews. The Alumni Mentor Alliance matches students with alumni in their fields of interest to gain real-world perspectives.

Academic Facilities

The facilities at Saint Joseph's are a blend of the old and the new. Barbelin/Lonergan Hall is a fine example of collegiate Gothic architecture. Its spired carillon tower rises above the campus and is easily the most recognizable landmark at Saint Joseph's. Mandeville Hall, a modern international academic center, opened in fall 1998. Home of the Haub School of Business, Mandeville offers distance learning technology and unique learning environments. The Francis A. Drexel Library and the Campbell Collection in Food Marketing house a collection of approximately 352,500 volumes, 1,450 print journals, 7,500 full-text electronic journals, 2,700 online books, and 848,000 microforms.

Costs

For the 2007–08 academic year, tuition was $30,850. Room fees ranged from $6430 to $8400 per year, and board fees cost $3690 per year.

Financial Aid

The majority of Saint Joseph's students receive merit and/or federal financial assistance. In the 2006–07 academic year, approximately 85 percent of the University's student body received assistance in the form of academic and athletic scholarships, grants, loans, and work-study funds, either singly or in combination.

Students are automatically considered for merit scholarships upon application to the University. Students who wish to be considered for federal financial assistance should submit the Free Application for Federal Student Aid (FAFSA). Residents from states other than Pennsylvania should file the FAFSA and the proper state grant application from the Education Assistance Agency of their resident state.

Faculty

Saint Joseph's possesses an esteemed research faculty that is committed to undergraduate teaching. A student-faculty ratio of 15:1 and an average class size of 25 offer excellent opportunities for student–faculty member exchange, both inside and outside the classroom. Approximately 98 percent of the full-time faculty members hold a doctorate or terminal degree in their field.

Student Government

The Office of Student Leadership and Activities is dedicated to enhancing the educational development of students by providing opportunities for involvement in cocurricular programs and services. These include leadership programs, student clubs and organizations, Greek life, event programming and planning, and the University Student Senate. Through innovative programming that complements academic and personal development, the University nurtures the mind, body, and spirit of each individual student while enhancing the Jesuit mission of the University.

The University Student Senate, the governing board for the student body, is dedicated to addressing student issues through advocacy and policy recommendations. The Senate consists of an executive board that includes the president, executive vice president, speaker of the Senate, vice president for financial affairs, vice president for student life, four elected representatives from each class, and five appointed at-large members. The Senate has four standing committees: Academic Affairs, Student Budget Allocations, Campus Life, and Administrative Services. Elections for the Senate take place in December. Freshman representatives are elected in September.

The Student Union Board, known as SUB, is a student-run organization that encourages the development of student leadership, responsibility, and social competency by planning and participating in campus programs. These activities are designed to enhance the educational, recreational, cultural, and social aspects of the collegiate experience. All registered undergraduate students are welcome to take part in the activities and to be a part of the standing committees that are responsible for the programming.

Admission Requirements

Candidates for admission to the freshman class must submit evidence of academic achievement in a college-preparatory program, which should emphasize study in English, mathematics, foreign languages (classical or modern), science, history, and social studies. Successful candidates have traditionally completed a secondary school background that included the following: English, 4 units; foreign languages, 2 units; history and social studies, 3 units; mathematics, 3 units (4 units for students interested in the natural sciences or math); and science, 2 units. Applicants are required to submit scores on the SAT or the ACT.

Application and Information

A completed application form may be submitted with the $60 application fee at any time after the student's junior year. Students are accepted to the University and merit scholarships are awarded within the context of a deadline admissions policy with an early action date of November 15 and a regular decision deadline of February 1. Students should visit the admissions Web site at http://www.sju.edu/admissions for current admission information.

Office of Undergraduate Admissions
Saint Joseph's University
5600 City Avenue
Philadelphia, Pennsylvania 19131-1395
Phone: 610-660-1300
888-BE-A-HAWK (232-4295) (toll-free)
Fax: 610-660-1314
E-mail: admit@sju.edu
Web site: http://www.sju.edu/admissions/

Mandeville Hall, Saint Joseph's international academic center and home of the Haub School of Business.

SAINT VINCENT COLLEGE

LATROBE, PENNSYLVANIA

The College

Founded in 1846, Saint Vincent College is the first Benedictine college in the United States. It is an educational community rooted in the tradition of the Catholic faith, the heritage of Benedictine monasticism, and the love of values inherent in the liberal approach to life and learning. There are 1,652 full-time students and 175 part-time students, of whom 82.5 percent reside on campus in five residence halls. The College has students from more than twenty-six states and nineteen other countries. In addition to more than fifty programs in the liberal arts and sciences, the College offers graduate programs in education curriculum and instruction, environmental education, library media management, special education, and school administration and supervision. Student services include advising, athletics, career placement and planning, computer assistance, and a counseling center. Saint Vincent College is accredited by the Department of Education of the commonwealth of Pennsylvania, the Middle States Association of Colleges and Schools, and the Association of Collegiate Business Schools and Programs.

Location

Saint Vincent College is located on 200 acres in the Laurel Highlands of southwestern Pennsylvania. Noted for its beautiful countryside, the region offers abundant opportunities for outdoor recreation and adventure. Excellent sites for hiking, mountain biking, skiing, camping, and white-water rafting are less than half an hour from the campus in ten state forests. Pittsburgh, a regional center of culture and the arts, is only 35 miles to the west. The city offers music, museums, theater, shopping, nightlife, and sports.

Majors and Degrees

The College is organized into four schools: the Alex G. McKenna School of Business, Economics, and Government; the Herbert W. Boyer School of Natural Sciences, Mathematics, and Computing; the School of Humanities and Fine Arts; and the School of Communication, Education, and Social Sciences. The McKenna School includes majors in the areas of business administration, economics, political science, and public policy. The School of Natural Sciences, Mathematics, and Computing encompasses the Departments of Biology, Chemistry, Computing and Information Science, Environmental Science, Mathematics, and Physics. The School of Humanities and Fine Arts includes the Departments of English, Fine Arts (art and music), History, Liberal Arts, Modern and Classical Languages, Philosophy, and Religious Studies. The School of Communication, Education, and Social Sciences combines the Departments of Communication, Education, Psychology, and Sociology/Anthropology. Education certification is offered in art, biology, business, chemistry, citizenship, computer and information science, early childhood education, elementary education, English, environmental education, French, mathematics, physics, social science, social studies, and Spanish. Bachelor's degrees are offered in more than twenty fields.

The College offers a law school 3+3 program in cooperation with Duquesne University. Students complete the requirements of their majors at Saint Vincent College in English, history, political science, public policy analysis, or sociology. In addition, in conjunction with university schools of engineering, the College offers a five-year cooperative liberal arts and engineering program.

Saint Vincent offers prehealth training in accelerated osteopathic medicine, accelerated podiatric medicine, occupational therapy, pharmacy, physician assistant studies, and physical therapy in cooperation with various professional schools. Certificate programs are offered, including accounting, addiction specialist training, business management, communication, and computing and information science.

Students may select minor areas of study in accounting, anthropology, art history, arts administration, biochemistry, biology, chemistry, communication, computing and information science, economics, education, English, environmental affairs, environmental chemistry, environmental science, finance, fine arts, French, general administration of justice, German, graphic arts, history, international business, international studies, Italian, liberal arts, management, marketing, mathematics, music, music history, philosophy, physics, political science, public administration, psychology, sociology, Spanish, studio arts, and theology.

Academic Programs

An academic year consists of two semesters, with the opportunity to earn credits in the summer. Saint Vincent College requires each student to complete a minimum of 124 credits, satisfy the requirements for the major(s) as specified by the department(s) or school(s), achieve an overall grade point average of at least 2.0 as well as a grade point average of at least 2.0 in the major and satisfy the capstone requirement as specified by the major department(s) or school(s). Each student must complete a core curriculum. The core curriculum provides all students with a broadly based education that provides a general body of knowledge in the humanities, social sciences, natural sciences, and mathematics; an interdisciplinary view of that knowledge base; and the skills to increase that general body of knowledge throughout their lives. Special programs include national and international academic honor societies, a cooperative education and internship program, an interdisciplinary writing program, and an honors program.

Off-Campus Programs

Saint Vincent has a sister college relationship with Fu Jen Catholic University in Taiwan. The College is also a cooperating institution with Central College of Iowa, through which programs are offered in Austria, England, France, Germany, Holland, Mexico, Spain, and Wales. Students may enroll for summer study at Cuauhnahuac Institute of Language and Culture in Cuernavaca, Mexico. Each May and June, after the spring semester, Saint Vincent College students have the opportunity to participate in a three-week East Asian study tour of Taiwan and Japan. Students may also enroll in well-designed academic programs sponsored by recognized universities and institutes.

Academic Facilities

Saint Vincent College has coupled extensive renovation and new construction with the introduction of state-of-the-art technology in virtually every area of College life. The result is a modern, student-friendly campus that features accessible computer laboratories and workstations, fiber-optic cabling among buildings, and specialized laboratories for the study of astronomy, ecology, genetics, geology, human anatomy, life sciences, microbiology, optics, organic chemistry, physiology, and other subjects.

Traditionally, Benedictine institutions have granted a place of honor to the library. A central reference room provides access to more than 3,500 resource titles, such as encyclopedias, abstracts, dictionaries, indexes, handbooks, atlases, concordances, and gazetteers. The periodical area displays some 790 current periodical subscriptions, and the adjoining stacks contain more than 269,000 volumes.

Prep Hall houses the Instructional Technology Resource Center, with smart classrooms, a multimedia laboratory, a media suite, and a seminar room for videoconferencing. In addition, the College features a science center with a planetarium, an amphitheater, and a life sciences research laboratory building. The Robert S. Carey Student Center, covering more than 2 acres of ground, contains the Frank and Elizabeth Resnik Swimming Pool, a gymnasium, a performing arts center, a wellness center, a bookstore, a fitness center, locker rooms and training rooms, a snack bar, a student lounge, a chapel, a billiards room, an art gallery, art studios, and music practice rooms.

Costs

Tuition and fees at Saint Vincent are $11,728 per semester, and room and board costs average $3950 per semester, depending on accommodations and meal plan. Books and supplies cost $800–$1200 per year. Costs are subject to change.

Financial Aid

The financial aid program at Saint Vincent College offers a comprehensive program of financial aid in the form of scholarships, grants, loans, part-time employment, and deferred-payment schedules and coordinates programs from the federal and state financial aid program. In 2006–07, more than 90 percent of the students who applied for financial aid were offered assistance. The College annually awards qualified freshmen academic scholarships for excellence in academic achievement and grants in recognition of leadership abilities. In addition, the College offers international student grants, Benedictine grants, and scholarships based on competitive examinations. Other financial aid opportunities include Federal Stafford Student Loans and Federal PLUS loans. Residents of Pennsylvania may be eligible for the Pennsylvania Higher Education Assistance Agency Grant Program. In order to be considered for financial aid, students must complete the Free Application for Federal Student Aid (FAFSA).

Faculty

The faculty numbers 153 members, of whom 90 are ranked. Eighty-one percent of the faculty members hold terminal degrees. Members of the faculty have earned doctorates or terminal degrees at such schools as Catholic University of America, Catholic University of Louvain (Belgium), Cornell, Duke, Ecole Biblique, Fordham, Northwestern, Notre Dame, NYU, Stanford, and the Universities of California, Chicago, Pennsylvania, and Yale. Faculty members are engaged as principal investigators in research and other projects funded through government agencies such as the National Science Foundation and the U.S. Department of Education and private foundations. The student-faculty ratio is 15:1. Faculty members have chosen to teach at Saint Vincent in part because they value the quality of student-teacher interaction, specifically the emphasis on high standards, personalized learning, fieldwork, hands-on experience, and the high level of classroom participation.

Student Government

The Student Government Association (SGA) builds community at the College by providing opportunities for the students, faculty members, and administrators to share in their common interests. All class officers, senators, and representatives can vote in the unicameral senate that composes the student government. Each senator (every voting member of the SGA) has one vote and can vote for or against or abstain from voting on all issues brought before the senate. Students choose from more than fifty academic clubs and student organizations.

Admission Requirements

Saint Vincent College has a rolling admission policy. Adequate preparation for college is an important determinant for a successful college education. Fifteen secondary school academic units are required for admission to Saint Vincent College. These 15 units must include 4 units of English, 3 or more units of college-preparatory mathematics, 1 unit of laboratory science, and 3 units of social science; 2 units of a foreign language are preferred among 5 elective units. Engineering students must have 1 unit in plane algebra, 1 unit in intermediate algebra, 1 unit in physics, and ½ unit in trigonometry in addition to those listed above. Art education majors must submit a portfolio for review. Music and music performance students must audition for acceptance, and studio arts students must submit a portfolio for acceptance to the Fine Arts Department.

Transfer students are invited to apply to Saint Vincent College. The applicant's academic achievement and personal history at the postsecondary schools previously attended are of primary importance in the decision for admission. The secondary school record is requested as background information for academic counseling.

Application and Information

To be considered for admission, a freshman applicant must submit a completed application form with the nonrefundable $25 application fee, an official transcript sent directly to Saint Vincent College from the guidance office at the secondary school of graduation, and an official copy of the test results from the SAT or ACT.

To be considered for admission, a transfer applicant must submit a completed application form with the nonrefundable $25 application fee, an official transcript sent directly to Saint Vincent College from the postsecondary school(s) previously attended, and a secondary school transcript sent directly to Saint Vincent College from the secondary school of graduation.

An application and additional information may be obtained by contacting:

Office of Admission and Financial Aid
Saint Vincent College
300 Fraser Purchase Road
Latrobe, Pennsylvania 15650-2690
Phone: 800-782-5549 (toll-free)
E-mail: admission@stvincent.edu
Web site: http://www.stvincent.edu

The Robert S. Carey Student Center is located on the campus of Saint Vincent College in Latrobe, Pennsylvania.

SETON HILL UNIVERSITY

GREENSBURG, PENNSYLVANIA

The University

Seton Hill was founded by the Sisters of Charity in 1883 and chartered as a college by the commonwealth of Pennsylvania in 1918. In 2002, it became Seton Hill University.

Seton Hill, a liberal arts and sciences, coeducational institution, is situated in the Laurel Highlands, an area of southwestern Pennsylvania known for its beautiful scenery and wealth of outdoor activities such as skiing, cycling, hiking, and white-water rafting. Recreational opportunities include on-campus lectures, theater productions, a fitness center, and aerobics classes, as well as University-sponsored trips to Pittsburgh for cultural and sports events. A new performing arts venue is in the works, and recently constructed are two new residence halls and a new recreation facility that includes new athletic fields.

Seton Hill has varsity teams for women in basketball, cross-country, equestrian competition, field hockey, golf, lacrosse, soccer, softball, tennis, track and field, and volleyball and for men in baseball, basketball, cross-country, equestrian competition, football, golf, lacrosse, soccer, and tennis, track and field, and wrestling, as well as a variety of intramural teams.

At the graduate level, Seton Hill grants the Master of Arts degree in art therapy, elementary education, marriage and family therapy, special education, and writing popular fiction; a Master of Business Administration; a Master of Education in instructional design; and a Master of Science in physician assistant studies.

Location

Seton Hill University's beautiful 200-acre campus is located in Greensburg, Pennsylvania. As a private university, Seton Hill is able to maintain a safe, secure environment that allows students to concentrate on academics.

Seton Hill is easily accessible by car, train, or plane. Just 35 miles east of Pittsburgh, Greensburg enjoys all the advantages of a large city while maintaining a small-town atmosphere. The seat of Westmoreland County, Greensburg is home to the Westmoreland Museum of Art, the Westmoreland Symphony Orchestra, a large mall, several shopping centers, and a hospital.

Majors and Degrees

The University grants the Bachelor of Arts, Bachelor of Fine Arts, Bachelor of Science, Bachelor of Music, and Bachelor of Social Work degrees.

Students choose from the following programs: accounting; art, including art and technology, art education, art history, art therapy, graphic design, studio art, and visual arts management; biology; chemistry, including biochemistry; communication; business, including entrepreneurial studies, human resources, information management, international organization, and marketing; computer science; criminal justice; dietetics; education, including early childhood, elementary, secondary, and special education; English, including creative writing, journalism/new media, and literature; family and consumer sciences (including child care) and forensic science; history; hospitality and tourism; international studies; mathematics, including actuary science and a 3+2 engineering program; medical technology; music, including music education, music therapy, performance, and sacred music; a 2+2 nursing program; political science; psychology; religious studies/theology; social work; sociology; Spanish; and theater, including music theater, technical theater, theater arts, theater business, theater education, and theater performance.

The University offers preprofessional preparation for dentistry, law, medicine, occupational therapy, optometry, physical therapy, podiatry, and veterinary medicine.

Academic Programs

Seton Hill offers five academic divisions, with the opportunity to self-design a major, all enhanced by the University's award-winning liberal arts core curriculum. Special programs are available for students who are undecided about their major.

The Seton Hill University Honors Program is available for students who have distinguished themselves academically in high school. It includes scholarship money as well as housing for qualified candidates.

Prior to graduation, all undergraduate students complete a portfolio, a four-year compilation of their academic, professional, and personal achievements at Seton Hill. Portfolios allow students to showcase their learning and assist them in documenting their accomplishments as they transition from students to practicing professionals.

Students hoping to one day own a business may be interested in Seton Hill University's E-Magnify, a center for entrepreneurs. The center is the first organization of its kind in the United States to offer courses in business ownership and entrepreneurial activities to students in any major.

Off-Campus Programs

Seton Hill University recognizes that important learning experiences occur in nonacademic settings. For this reason, the University offers a variety of internships, fieldwork experiences, and cooperative education opportunities. The Office of Career Development and University faculty members assist students in finding an off-campus placement where practical experience related to the major and valuable job contacts for the future may be gained.

In addition, students may opt to spend a semester or year studying abroad. Seton Hill also offers many travel-abroad opportunities during J-term and M-term semesters.

Academic Facilities

At the center of the Seton Hill campus is Reeves Hall, housing a theater, art gallery, and spacious library that serves as the University's information center. Access to the library holdings is available via the library's online catalog which is also accessible through the Internet. Many online and CD-ROM research subscriptions are also available to students. In addition, students have access to six Pentium labs, a Power Mac lab, a multimedia lab, a Silicon Graphics lab, and clusters of computers in all residence halls. All students receive an Internet account for e-mail, navigating the Web, and conducting research.

In order to provide the maximum benefits possible, Seton Hill's nineteen academic and residence facilities have been specially designed with students' convenience in mind.

Costs

For full-time students, approximate costs for the 2007–08 academic year included tuition of $24,806, room and board fees of $7740, and books and personal expenses amounting to $1000 to $2000.

Financial Aid

Seton Hill's Financial Aid Office works with each student to develop an aid package from the wide variety of scholarships, grants, loans, and work-study programs available.

Seton Hill offers Presidential Scholarships valued between 15 percent and 50 percent of tuition. These are automatically awarded to students who rank in the top 10 percent, 20 percent, or 30 percent of their high school class and meet the admission criteria. In addition, valedictorian, leadership, community service, art, music, theater, biology, chemistry, math, and athletic scholarships are awarded based on merit. Honors scholarships are also available to qualified candidates, and there is also a scholarship for students graduating from a Catholic high school.

Faculty

With a student-faculty ratio of 16:1, Seton Hill faculty members can explore the needs of each student and offer individual attention. The low student-faculty ratio allows each student to become personally acquainted with the instructor. In addition, Seton Hill faculty members understand the importance of being accessible to their students.

The Seton Hill faculty consists of 70 full-time professors, 81 percent of whom have doctoral or terminal degrees.

Student Government

Through the Seton Hill Government Association, students participate in the government of the University and enjoy voting representation on a number of faculty committees. Each residence hall floor is represented by a senator who acts as a liaison between the student senate and the student body. Participation in student government is a valuable experience that develops leadership skills and a working understanding of government.

In addition, the student government helps to sponsor numerous on-campus political, cultural, and social events. Off-campus activities include trips to Pittsburgh, New York City, and Washington, D.C.

Admission Requirements

Acceptance to the University is based on the successful completion of a college-preparatory curriculum in high school. Applicants should have completed at least 15 secondary school academic units. These units should include 4 units of English, 2 units of college-preparatory mathematics, 2 units of social science, 2 units of the same foreign language, 1 unit of laboratory science, and 4 academic electives.

Students who wish to transfer credits to Seton Hill from another college or university must present their transcripts for evaluation on a course-by-course basis. A transfer student will receive a credit evaluation upon admission to the University.

Application and Information

Seton Hill University has a rolling admissions policy. Decisions of the Admissions Committee are rendered shortly after all application materials have been submitted.

The first-time freshman applicant should submit a completed application form, a $35 nonrefundable application fee, an official secondary school transcript that includes the applicant's rank and cumulative grade point average, official score reports from either the SAT or ACT, an essay, and a recommendation form or letter from a guidance counselor or teacher.

Prospective students who do not have SAT or ACT scores may submit two graded written assignments from their junior or senior year for consideration.

For more information, students should contact:

Sherri Bett
Director of Admissions
One Seton Hill Drive
Box 991
Seton Hill University
Greensburg, Pennsylvania 15601

Phone: 800-826-6234 (toll-free)
Fax: 724-830-1294
E-mail: admit@setonhill.edu
Web site: http://www.setonhill.edu

The Administration Building is a picturesque focal point on the Seton Hill campus.

SHIPPENSBURG UNIVERSITY OF PENNSYLVANIA

SHIPPENSBURG, PENNSYLVANIA

The University

Shippensburg University, founded in 1871, is a comprehensive public institution in south-central Pennsylvania enrolling more than 6,600 undergraduate students and approximately 1,000 graduate students. Of the undergraduates, 52 percent are women and 48 percent are men. The University is divided into the College of Arts and Sciences, the College of Education and Human Services, the John L. Grove College of Business, and the School of Graduate Studies. There is also a School of Academic Programs and Services, which includes the Office of Undeclared Students.

Shippensburg University is a member of the Pennsylvania State System of Higher Education and is accredited by the Middle States Association of Colleges and Schools. Other accreditation is by AACSB International–The Association to Advance Collegiate Schools of Business; ABET, Inc. (computer science); the American Chemical Society; the Council on Social Work Education; the Council for the Accreditation of Counseling and Related Educational Programs; the International Association of Counseling Services; the Council for Exceptional Children; the National Council for the Accreditation of Coaching Education; and the National Council for the Accreditation of Teachers. Shippensburg University is a member of the Council of Graduate Schools.

Graduate degrees conferred are the Master of Art, Master of Business Administration, Master of Education, Master of Science, Master of Social Work, and Master of Public Administration. Programs are as follows: Master of Art in applied history; Master of Science in administration of justice, biology, communication studies, computer science, counseling (college, community, mental health, student personnel), geoenvironmental studies, organizational development and leadership (business, communication, education, environmental management, higher education, individual and organizational development, public organizations), and psychology; Master of Science in business administration; Master of Public Administration in public administration; Master of Social Work in social work; and Master of Education in counseling (elementary and secondary), curriculum and instruction (biology, early childhood education, elementary education, English, geography/earth science, history, mathematics, middle-level education), educational leadership and policy, reading, and special education (comprehensive, mental retardation, learning disabilities, behavior disorders). The School of Graduate Studies also offers post-master's degree curricula leading to various types of education certification, including supervisory certification, and is one of twenty-three national sites for a post-graduate academic training program in Reading Recovery.

More than 200 student clubs, organizations, and activity groups, resulting in nearly 600 leadership opportunities, are available. Organizations include academic clubs, community service groups, special interest organizations, media organizations, musical groups, performing arts troupes, and national or local fraternities and sororities.

Student activities are complemented by programs that bring nationally and internationally known figures to campus. Pulitzer Prize–winning author David McCullough, Nobel Peace Prize recipient Archbishop Desmond Tutu, Rev. Jesse Jackson, actor Danny Glover, actor Sidney Poitier, author and poet Maya Angelou, Vice President Dick Cheney, jazz musician Wynton Marsalis, and astronaut Buzz Aldrin have all appeared on campus.

Each of the eight residence halls is equipped with lounges, exercise rooms, music practice rooms, study rooms, and computer connections to the online library catalog system. Each residence hall room has one cable television and two direct computer network connections. Most residence hall rooms are double occupancy; some single rooms are available. Seavers Complex houses six students in each unit. Student safety is emphasized through controlled access to the residence halls, trained supervisory personnel, and a keycard entry system. There is also an apartment-style student housing facility with one, two, or four bedrooms, living room, bathroom, and full kitchen.

The University offers a variety of athletic facilities for both intercollegiate and intramural sports. These include a 2,768-seat field house, an 8,000-seat stadium, a gymnasium, outdoor tennis courts, indoor and outdoor tracks, an indoor swimming pool, squash and handball courts, a physical fitness center, a rehabilitation center, and sand volleyball courts. The University is a member of the Pennsylvania State Athletic Conference and NCAA Division II. Men's intercollegiate sports include baseball, basketball, cross-country, football, soccer, swimming, track and field, and wrestling. Women's intercollegiate sports include basketball, cross-country, field hockey, lacrosse, soccer, softball, swimming, tennis, track and field, and volleyball. There are thirteen intramural sports, which include street hockey, and seventeen club sports, which include men's and women's rugby.

Etter Health Center provides 24-hour access to medical services. The eight-bed infirmary is staffed by a team of physicians and nurses. Chambersburg Hospital is only 20 minutes from campus.

Students have access to comprehensive counseling services on request in academic, career, psychological, social, personal growth, and religious areas. The Career Development Center offers career counseling, workshops in resume preparation, job interview techniques, and job search assistance.

Location

Shippensburg University is on 200 acres overlooking its namesake community, a borough of approximately 6,700 people in the Cumberland Valley. The University is about 40 minutes southwest of Harrisburg, 2 hours from both Baltimore and Washington, D.C., and 2½ hours from Philadelphia. The campus is within easy walking distance of the center of town.

Majors and Degrees

Undergraduate degrees conferred are the Bachelor of Arts (B.A.), Bachelor of Science (B.S.), Bachelor of Science in Business Administration (B.S.B.A.), Bachelor of Science in Education (B.S.Ed.), and Bachelor of Social Work (B.S.W.). The College of Arts and Sciences awards the B.A. degree in art (computer graphics); communication/journalism (electronic media, print media, public relations); English (writing); French; history (public history); human communication studies; interdisciplinary arts; political science; psychology; secondary certification (art, English, French, and Spanish); sociology; and Spanish. The B.S. degree is awarded in applied physics (nanofabrication); biology (biotechnology, ecology and environment, medical technology); chemistry (biochemistry, medical technology); computer science (computer graphics, embedded programming, related discipline, software engineering, systems programming); economics (business, mathematics, political science, social studies); geoenvironmental studies; geography (geographic information systems, land use, regional development and tourism); health-care administration; mathematics (applied, computer science, statistics); physics (nanofabrication); public administration; and secondary education (biology, biology/environmental education, chemistry, mathematics). The B.S.Ed. degree is awarded in earth science, physics, social studies/economics, social studies/geography, social studies/history, and social studies/political science.

The John L. Grove College of Business awards the B.S.B.A. degree in accounting, business administration (general), finance (personal financial planning), supply chain management (logistics), information technology for business education, management (entrepreneurship and corporate entrepreneurship, general, human resource, international), management information systems, and marketing.

The College of Education and Human Services awards the B.S. degree in criminal justice and exercise science; the B.S.W. degree in social work; and the B.S.Ed. degree in elementary education (biology, chemistry, environmental education, mathematics, multicultural education, sociology, TESOL).

Preprofessional preparation is available for admission to schools of chiropractic, dentistry, engineering, forensic science, law, medicine, optometry, pharmacy, physical therapy, podiatry, and veterinary medicine.

Shippensburg University offers 2+2, 3+3, and 4+3 transfer programs in the allied health fields of biotechnology, cytogenetic technology, cytotechnology, diagnostic imaging-multicompetency, nursing, occupational therapy, P.A.C.E. Program, and physical therapy.

Academic Programs

The University is on the semester system with a fall semester beginning in late August and a spring semester beginning in mid-January. Three terms, one of three weeks and two of five weeks, comprise the summer program.

The general education program, which comprises one half of the credits required for graduation, is the core of the undergraduate curriculum. It includes courses to develop competence in writing, speaking, mathematics, and reading. The program ensures exposure to history; language and numbers; literary, artistic, and cultural traditions; laboratory science; biological and physical sciences; political, economic, and geographic sciences; and social and behavioral sciences. Ample elective opportunities are available.

The University requires students to take one approved diversity course for a total of 3 credit hours.

Academic options include an honors program, independent study and research, internships, field experience (mandatory in such areas as teacher education, social work, and medical technology), the Marine Science Consortium Program at Wallops Island, a 3+2 engineering program with several major schools of engineering, and Army ROTC.

Academic Facilities

Ezra Lehman Memorial Library has a computerized library system that includes access to full-text journal articles and electronic indexes to journal literature. The library also provides access to the Internet and many CD-ROM databases. The library's collection of more than 2 million items includes books, journals, government documents, maps, and audiovisual material. The library participates in several consortia that have reciprocal borrowing privileges for students.

Student instruction is supported by multiple computer systems for student e-mail and computer network connections to the Internet. Several hundred terminals or personal computers for student use are available in residence halls, the library, academic buildings, microcomputer labs, and the Computing Technologies Center. Students with their own computers also have access to the systems. All students can use the systems 24 hours a day and have unlimited computer time at no additional expense. Several buildings have wireless network capabilities and satellite capability for distance education. The University also has its own campuswide information system available on and off campus.

Costs

For Pennsylvania residents, the cost per semester in 2007–08 included tuition of $2589; room and board, $2992; educational services fee, $258; technology fee, $87.50; student activities fee, $135; student union fee, $108; health services fee, $90; and recreation center fee, $157. Nonresidents paid tuition of $6472 per semester and a technology fee of $132; the remaining fees were the same.

Financial Aid

The University's extensive financial aid program helps students who deserve a college education but who cannot afford to pay the full cost themselves. Shippensburg offers a wide range of aid in the form of grants, scholarships, loans, and campus employment. Most aid is awarded as a package consisting of all types for which the applicant is qualified. Nearly 80 percent of undergraduates receive some form of financial assistance.

Faculty

The University has 370 full- and part-time faculty members. The undergraduate student-faculty ratio is 20:1. Nearly 90 percent of the full-time instructional faculty members hold a doctorate or other terminal degree in their field. Each student has a faculty adviser.

Student Government

Shippensburg's strong student organization, built around a Student Senate, standing committees, and an Activities Program Board, provides a highly diversified program of student activities. Students sit on many policymaking administration-faculty committees and administer their own budget for the Student Services, Inc.

Admission Requirements

Shippensburg University, in compliance with federal and state laws and University policy, provides equal educational, employment, and economic opportunities for all people without regard to race, color, sex, age, creed, national origin, religion, veteran status, or disability. A student's potential for success is judged by the high school average, rank in class, aptitude test scores (SAT or ACT), and recommendations. The high school record is generally considered the most important factor. A college-preparatory program, consisting of 4 units of English, at least 3 units of math, 3 units in the sciences, 2 units of social studies, and 2 units in the same foreign language, is strongly recommended. A campus interview and visit are encouraged. Transfer students in good standing are welcome.

Application and Information

To be considered for admission, a student should submit the application form with a $30 application fee. The high school transcript, recommendations, and aptitude test results should be sent by the high school. Transfer students must submit college transcripts. The Admissions Office operates on a rolling basis.

For application materials and additional information, students should contact:

Dean of Enrollment Services
Shippensburg University of Pennsylvania
1871 Old Main Drive
Shippensburg, Pennsylvania 17257
Phone: 717-477-1231
800-822-8028 (toll-free)
Fax: 717-477-4016
E-mail: admiss@ship.edu
Web site: http://www.ship.edu

The 200-acre Shippensburg University campus is located 40 miles southwest of Harrisburg, Pennsylvania.

SUSQUEHANNA UNIVERSITY

SELINSGROVE, PENNSYLVANIA

The University

Susquehanna is a national liberal arts college enrolling approximately 1,900 undergraduates in its three schools: the School of Arts, Humanities, and Communications; the Sigmund Weis School of Business; and the School of Natural and Social Sciences. The University offers the best qualities of a residential college and a challenging university. Distinctive liberal arts programs such as biology and writing are enhanced by equally strong professional programs in areas like music and business. A Susquehanna education builds the broad base of knowledge to help students become educated citizens of the world while offering the in-depth preparation needed to succeed in graduate or professional school or in a career after graduation. Susquehanna is affiliated with the Evangelical Lutheran Church in America, and since its founding in 1858, the University has welcomed students and faculty and staff members from all racial, ethnic, and religious backgrounds.

As a residential university, Susquehanna believes that extracurricular activities should be an integral part of each student's experience. There are twenty-three varsity sports teams as well as an extensive intramural program, numerous academic clubs, one of the most powerful student-run radio stations in Pennsylvania, a host of musical activities, and many other organizations, ranging from the French Club to the Students in Free Enterprise. Approximately 80 percent of the students live on campus in seven residence halls, six apartment-style units, several academic and volunteer student project suites and houses, a scholars' house, five fraternity houses, and five sorority houses.

Location

Selinsgrove, Pennsylvania, is a town of about 6,000 inhabitants. It is approximately 90 minutes west of the Pocono Mountain resort areas; about an hour from State College and Harrisburg; about a 3-hour drive from Philadelphia, New York City, and Washington, D.C.; and about a 4-hour drive from Pittsburgh. Located on U.S. Routes 11 and 15 and near I-80, the area is readily accessible, and public transportation is available. Cultural, dining, recreational, and shopping opportunities abound. Susquehanna has close ties with the community, where a number of students participate in internships and many take part in the University's extensive, award-winning volunteer program. Susquehanna is one of three universities in the area.

Majors and Degrees

Susquehanna University offers the Bachelor of Science degree with majors in biochemistry, biology, chemistry, computer science, earth and environmental sciences, ecology, physics, and psychology.

The University offers the Bachelor of Arts degree with majors in art, art history, chemistry, communications, computer science, earth and environmental sciences, economics, English, French, German, graphic design, history, information systems, international studies, liberal studies (education), mathematics, music, philosophy, physics, political science, psychology, religion, sociology, Spanish, theater, and writing.

The Bachelor of Science in Business is offered in accounting, business administration (with emphases in entrepreneurship, finance, global or human resource management, information systems, or marketing), and economics.

The Bachelor of Music degree is offered in music education and performance.

Students may pursue interdisciplinary and self-designed majors and develop major-minor combinations. The fifty minors range from Asian studies to health-care studies to journalism to music technology.

Two dual-degree programs are available: a joint-degree program with Temple University's School of Dentistry and a 3-2 program in forestry or environmental management with Duke University. Also, a number of 2+2 and 2+3 programs in allied health are offered with Thomas Jefferson University.

Academic Programs

Susquehanna's core curriculum, which provides the breadth of knowledge needed for graduate school or a career, includes traditional and contemporary components. The traditional courses offer exposure to the humanities, social sciences, and natural sciences. Contemporary courses help students understand relationships among individuals, organizations, and the natural world. Susquehanna's core curriculum also has an extensive personal development sequence, which includes the nation's first required course on career planning.

Susquehanna offers a competitive four-year interdisciplinary Honors Program affiliated with the National Collegiate Honors Council. Preprofessional studies may be pursued in law, medicine and allied health fields, and the ministry. Teaching certification is offered at the elementary and secondary levels in all of the usual subjects. Teachers are certified for grades K–12 in music and modern foreign languages (French, German, and Spanish). Army ROTC is available under a cross-enrollment program with Bucknell University.

Off-Campus Programs

Susquehanna students may participate in a variety of off-campus programs, including the Washington Center in the nation's capital, the Washington Semester of American University, the United Nations Semester of Drew University, and the Philadelphia Center Program. Each semester, the University approves numerous off-campus departmental internships, some of which are in other countries. Students are encouraged to study abroad, and Susquehanna is a participating member of the Institute of European Studies. The University is a coordinating institution with Senshu University in Japan and offers a semester in London for juniors majoring in business. Susquehanna-designed Focus programs complement special groups of courses with travel to the country being studied. Recent trips have included southern Africa, Australia, and Martinique. All of these programs carry academic credit.

Academic Facilities

Susquehanna is an undergraduate university. All facilities and equipment are for the exclusive use of undergraduate students. The Blough-Weis Library houses Susquehanna's media center and the Film Institute. The library collection exceeds 290,000 volumes and other items, including microforms and records. More than 15,000 periodicals and newspapers are received, and more than 500 individual study spaces are maintained. Music listening and video viewing areas are also available. Fisher Science Hall provides facilities for all the sciences, including experimental psychology. General classrooms are in Steele and Bogar Halls. The Cunningham Center for Music and Art, completed in 2002, includes music and art studios and a performance hall. Seibert Hall houses the University Computer Center. Apfelbaum Hall provides the business and communications programs with multimedia computer labs, video studios, offices, and conference, presentation, and seminar rooms. The Charles B. Degenstein Campus Center houses the Lore Degenstein Gallery and a state-of-the-art 450-seat teaching theater. The James W. Garrett Sports Complex, completed in 2001, includes a 51,000-square-foot field house, a fitness center, racquetball courts, and a football and track stadium.

Costs

Tuition and fees for 2007–08 were $29,000. Room and board costs were $8000. A student's personal expenses, including books, travel, and other costs, are estimated at $1600 to $1900 per year.

Financial Aid

Susquehanna University offers renewable academic and music scholarships, which are awarded on a competitive basis without regard to financial need. In addition, need-based financial aid is awarded to permit attendance by full-time students whose personal and family resources are not sufficient to meet the costs. The amount of financial aid is based on need, not on family income alone. The level of need is determined annually by information provided on the PROFILE and the Free Application for Federal Student Aid (FAFSA). More than half of all students receive financial assistance that ranges from $1000 to full need. Aid is provided in packages that may include grants, scholarships, loans, and jobs. The various state and federal assistance programs are also taken into consideration when aid packages are created. International applicants may be considered for merit-based scholarships but are not eligible for financial aid based on need.

Faculty

Susquehanna's teaching faculty members help students develop their views of themselves and of the world and play an important part in preparing them for life after college. The faculty-student ratio is about 1:14, and 93 percent of the full-time faculty members hold an earned doctorate. Most faculty members serve as student advisers, and full-time counseling services are also available. There are no graduate assistants at Susquehanna.

Student Government

The Student Government Association provides a representative student organization to assure students a voice in University governance. The Student Senate, the legislative branch, provides a forum for student opinion, deals with issues of concern to the entire student body, and seeks solutions to campus problems. The senate is responsible for the allocation of funds collected through the student activity fee and is the body that designates student representatives for University committees and the Board of Trustees, of which one student is a voting member.

Admission Requirements

Susquehanna admits students without regard to race, color, religion, national or ethnic origin, age, sex, sexual orientation, or handicap. Students who gain admission are those whom the Admissions Committee deems able to profit from and contribute to the Susquehanna experience. Graduation from an accredited secondary school or a high school equivalency certificate is required. Experience has shown that the best preparation includes at least 4 years of English, 4 years of mathematics, 3 years of social science, 2 or 3 years of one foreign language, 2 or 3 years of laboratory science, and 3 or more units of electives.

In evaluating a candidate, the committee considers academic performance, major interests, test scores, recommendations, extracurricular activities, and demonstrated interest in the University. In addition to the application and secondary school records, the candidate must submit scores from either the SAT or the ACT, unless he or she chooses the Write Option and submits two graded writing samples instead of standardized test scores. Students for whom English is not their native language must submit official score reports of the TOEFL.

Applications for early decision are encouraged, and deferred admission is available. Interviews and campus tours are strongly suggested for all students interested in Susquehanna. Applicants to the Bachelor of Music program and to the Bachelor of Arts program in music must audition. Applicants to the Bachelor of Arts in writing program must also submit a portfolio. Graphic design applicants are also required to submit portfolios. Transfer candidates can be considered for either semester, and the University recognizes the Advanced Placement and CLEP programs of the College Board and the International Baccalaureate program.

Application and Information

Application materials and introductory and departmental information may be obtained by contacting the Office of Admissions. All interview appointments should be made two weeks in advance to allow time for faculty contact and the scheduling of student-conducted tours. The priority application deadline is March 1 (for Early Decision I, November 15; for Early Decision II, January 1). The University adheres to the Candidates Reply Date of May 1 and is a Common Application participant.

Office of Admissions
Susquehanna University
514 University Avenue
Selinsgrove, Pennsylvania 17870-1164
Phone: 570-372-4260
800-326-9672 (toll-free)
Fax: 570-372-2722
E-mail: suadmiss@susqu.edu
Web site: http://www.susqu.edu

Historic Seibert Hall at Susquehanna University.

TEMPLE UNIVERSITY

PHILADELPHIA, PENNSYLVANIA

The University

Students who visit Temple University's Main Campus find they are quite impressed. Cutting-edge facilities and great faculty members create a dynamic academic environment that draws students from around the world. But what can transform a student's life at Temple happens outside the classroom as well. Temple is located in Philadelphia, a dynamic, world-class city with a diverse ethnic mix, a robust economy, and a thriving music and art scene. It is the perfect place to live and study.

Students who prefer not to attend college in the city should take a look at the Ambler campus, Temple's 187-acre suburban home. Just about all undergraduate programs can be started there, and eighteen can be fully completed there. Ambler's $17-million Learning Center includes smart classrooms; fully integrated technology, including wireless access throughout the building; five computer lab/classrooms; a math, science, and writing center; a video editing lab; a café; and a 300-seat auditorium.

Temple's other local campus is the Health Sciences Center, where the College of Health Professions, Temple University Hospital, Temple University School of Medicine, and Temple Dental School are located.

Temple is in the city, but it has a large residential student population—about 10,000 students living on and around Main Campus. The calendar is crammed with theater, dance, and music performances. The Liacouras Center, Temple's 10,200-seat entertainment complex, hosts the University's NCAA Division I basketball games (free tickets for students!) as well as concerts. Great performers like Kanye West, Green Day, Maroon 5, John Mayer, Counting Crows, Rusted Root, Alicia Keys, and Bob Dylan have performed at the Liacouras Center. Temple has every type of student doing every type of activity. Beyond sports, students can join one of 100 or so clubs and organizations and take full advantage of the rich resources and recreation activities offered by Philadelphia and the surrounding area.

Location

Philadelphia has a lot more than juicy sandwiches and cream cheese. With more than 100 museums, 700 Zagat-rated restaurants, and the largest landscaped park in the country—Fairmount Park at 4,180 acres—Philly has a lot to offer. It is a walkable, manageable city that is just 1.5 miles from Temple's Main Campus. Just four stops on a quick subway ride and students are in Center City—or what most would call downtown. Shop, eat, play, or just chill. In addition, students can find a variety of internships in all fields in the Philadelphia area, and Temple has more than 100,000 alumni in the region who love to hire Temple students.

Majors and Degrees

The Tyler School of Art offers the Bachelor of Fine Arts with concentrations in ceramics/glass, fibers, graphic and interactive design, metals/jewelry/CAD-CAM, painting, photography, printmaking, and sculpture; the Bachelor of Arts in art history and art; and the Bachelor of Science in art education. Tyler's Architecture Program confers the Bachelor of Architecture and the Bachelor of Science in architecture.

The Fox School of Business and Management offers the Bachelor of Business Administration in accounting, actuarial science, business management, economics, entrepreneurship, finance, human resource management, international business administration, law and business, management information systems, marketing, real estate, and risk management and insurance.

The School of Communications and Theater offers the Bachelor of Arts in advertising; American culture and media arts; broadcasting, telecommunications, and mass media; communication; film and media arts; journalism; strategic and organizational communications; and theater.

The College of Education offers the Bachelor of Science in applied communications, career and technical education, elementary education, secondary education, and kinesiology.

The College of Engineering offers the Bachelor of Science in Engineering in civil engineering, electrical engineering, and mechanical engineering. The Bachelor of Science is offered in civil/construction engineering technology, environmental engineering technology, and general engineering technology.

The College of Health Professions offers the Bachelor of Science in communication sciences; health information management; linguistics; nursing; public health; speech, language, and hearing; and therapeutic recreation.

The College of Liberal Arts offers the Bachelor of Arts in African American studies, American studies, anthropology, Asian studies, classics, criminal justice, economics, English, French, geography and urban studies, German, Hebrew, history, Italian, linguistics, philosophy, political science, Portuguese, psychology, religion, Russian, sociology, Spanish, and women's studies.

The Boyer College of Music and Dance offers the Bachelor of Music in composition, dance, jazz studies, music education, music history, music therapy, performance (specific instrument or voice), and theory; the Bachelor of Fine Arts is offered in dance.

The College of Science and Technology offers the Bachelor of Science in biochemistry, biology, biophysics, chemistry, computer and information sciences, environmental studies, geology, mathematical economics, mathematics, physics, and prepharmacy.

The School of Social Administration offers the Bachelor of Social Work degree.

The School of Tourism and Hospitality Management offers the Bachelor of Science in sport and recreation management and in tourism and hospitality management.

In addition, Ambler College offers Bachelor of Science degree programs in horticulture and landscape architecture and in community and regional planning.

Academic Programs

Temple provides an excellent and affordable education, which not only prepares the student for the specific demands of a career, but also enhances an understanding of the world and the ability to continue learning throughout life.

All students are required to complete the core curriculum, a cross-section of liberal arts courses that form the intellectual foundation of a Temple education. Many first-year students take advantage of Learning Communities—groups of 20 to 30 participants who pursue common studies under the direction of a faculty team. They spend a semester together, taking a few common courses, participating in faculty-led discussion groups, studying together, and taking field trips related to their studies.

University Studies is a home for the many students who have not declared a major and for students interested in graduate or professional programs in health fields. Academically qualified students may seek extra intellectual challenge through the honors program, taking about a quarter of their course work in the program's smaller, more demanding classes.

After graduation, students are well-prepared for the job world. Temple's Career Development Services arranges cooperative education assignments, schedules on-campus interviews with employers and graduate schools, offers employment skills workshops, provides career and graduate school advisement, and maintains a network of thousands of successful Temple alumni.

Academic Facilities

With more than fifty computer labs and a 90 percent wireless campus, information is more accessible than ever. An exciting new addition to the Main Campus is the Teaching, Education, Collaboration and Help (TECH) Center. With up to 700 computers (600 fixed workstations and up to 100 laptop loaners), the TECH Center is one of the largest of its kind in the nation; thirteen breakout rooms where students can work on group projects and practice presentations; six specialized labs within the primary center, including video editing, graphic design/CAD, music composition, language/interactive audio, "quiet" zone, and software development facility; a 24-hour computer help desk for students and faculty and staff members; a 4,260-square-foot Temple Welcome Center (run by the Admissions Office) to host visits to the University by prospective students and their families; and a Starbucks café.

Costs

Tuition and fees for the 2007–08 academic year were $10,802 for Pennsylvania residents and $19,320 for out-of-state residents. Room and board for the academic year were about $8000.

Financial Aid

Scholarships, grants, loans, and work-study programs are available; 2 out of every 3 Temple students receive financial aid. Four-year academic merit scholarships for talented entering freshmen begin at $1000. Students need only apply for admission to be eligible for these scholarships. Applicants for need-based aid must file the Free Application for Federal Student Aid (FAFSA). Transfer students must file a financial aid transcript, even if they have received no aid from their previous school.

Faculty

At Temple, faculty members are valued not only for their ability to pursue knowledge, but also to share that knowledge with students. Full-time faculty members teach many introductory courses, and often act as academic advisers; from their first semester students can expect to have contact with the people at the forefront of their fields, winners of prestigious teaching and research awards such as the Lindback, the Golden Apple, the Sowell, the Fulbright, the Guggenheim, the Carnegie, and the National Endowment.

In 2005, Temple officially welcomed the largest group of new tenured and tenure-track faculty members in recent history. Faculty members were hired away from leading universities and research centers, including Princeton University, Brown University, the University of Wisconsin–Madison, the University of Maryland, Wellesley College, and the Cleveland Clinic. Nearly every college at Temple has been joined by at least one new presidential faculty recruit.

In addition to being superlative teachers and researchers, Temple faculty members are also known for their practical experience. For example, a marketing class may be led by a successful entrepreneur, or music lessons given by a member of the Philadelphia Orchestra. Marine biologists, newspaper editors, published authors, practicing architects, and health-care professionals all bring their expertise to the classroom to enhance students' education.

Admission Requirements

For freshman admissions, high school grades (quality of courses, grade trends), standardized test scores, and other factors (the required essay, recommendations, extracurricular activities, work or leadership experience, and other personal circumstances) are considered. Temple uses a sliding scale rather than absolute cut-offs for GPA and test scores. SAT Subject Tests and personal interviews are not required. The deadline for freshman admission is March 1; however, students should apply in the fall of their senior year. Official copies of high school transcripts and standardized test scores must be sent directly to the admissions office. Counselor forms are not required. The deadline for spring admission is November 1.

Temple has rolling admissions. Freshman decisions begin in late fall, and letters are sent four to six weeks after that point. Temple's admissions process is holistic; every aspect of the student's academic history is considered. Typically, students with a B average or better in a strong, college-prep curriculum in grades 9–12 and in the top 40 percent of their graduating classes are accepted. The SAT is required, but the writing portion is not considered—just the critical reading and math sections. Students should have a combined score from these two sections of between 1050 and 1150.

Freshman students who apply are automatically considered for merit-based scholarships and honors. Recommendations are not required but are accepted and considered. There is no recommendation form. The best way to apply is online. The online application fee is $25; the paper application fee is $50.

Temple University welcomes transfer applicants from both two-year and four-year colleges and universities around the country and the world. Transfer students comprise more than half of each entering class and are a vital part of the vibrant campus community. Applicants are considered transfer students if they will have attempted 15 or more college-level credits by the time they apply. If this is not the case, they should apply as freshman students. In making admissions decisions, careful consideration is given to the quality of a student's program and the number of credits earned and the grade point average achieved. A cumulative GPA of at least 2.3 (on a 4.0 scale) is required for consideration but is not a guarantee of admission. A 2.5 cumulative GPA is preferred for most programs of study. The following programs have higher minimum grade point average requirements: architecture, nursing, pharmacy, and film and media arts. For most programs, transfer students must complete the application process by June 1 for the fall semester or by November 1 for the spring semester. The fall semester transfer application deadline for music is March 1. The fall priority deadline for nursing and health information management is February 1. Transfer applicants must request that all high schools and colleges that they previously attended send official transcripts to the Undergraduate Admissions Office at Temple University by these deadlines. SAT or ACT scores are not required if an applicant has earned at least 15 college-level credits.

Application and Information

A completed file should contain an application form accompanied by a nonrefundable application fee, a secondary school transcript (sent by the student's school), and SAT or ACT scores. The University has a rolling admission policy; applicants are notified of the admission decision as soon as possible after all credentials have been received and reviewed.

For additional information, students may contact:

Office of Undergraduate Admissions
Temple University (041-09)
Philadelphia, Pennsylvania 19122-1803
Phone: 215-204-7200
888-340-2222 (toll-free)
E-mail: tuadm@temple.edu
Web site: http://www.temple.edu/undergrad

THOMAS JEFFERSON UNIVERSITY
Jefferson College of Health Professions
PHILADELPHIA, PENNSYLVANIA

Jefferson College of Health Professions

The University and The College

Jefferson College of Health Professions (JCHP) is an integral part of one of the nation's first academic health centers, Thomas Jefferson University, which also includes Jefferson Medical College and Jefferson College of Graduate Studies. JCHP has three schools: the School of Health Professions (consisting of the Departments of Bioscience Technologies, General Studies, Couple and Family Therapy, Occupational Therapy, Physical Therapy, and Radiologic Sciences), the School of Nursing, and the School of Pharmacy (scheduled to start in fall 2008).

JCHP is part of a campuswide commitment to excellence in educating health-care professionals and discovering knowledge to define the future of clinical care. Scholarship and applied, collaborative, and interdisciplinary research are integral to generating this new health-care knowledge.

JCHP is an upper-division college, meaning that students generally transfer into a program in their junior year. High school students can reserve a seat in a future class by applying to JCHP through the PACE (Plan a College Education) program and attending an affiliated school for two years. Those interested in physical therapy, occupational therapy, radiologic sciences, or bioscience technologies can take advantage of special agreements with Elizabethtown College, Immaculata University, Muhlenberg College, Penn State Abington, Saint Joseph's University, University of Delaware, and Villanova University. An associate degree program in nursing is also available for high school graduates.

The University shares its campus with Thomas Jefferson University Hospital, one of the nation's premier health-care facilities. It is also the primary academic affiliate of the Jefferson Health System, a regional, integrated health-care delivery system.

Most JCHP students come from the Middle Atlantic states. In 2005–06, there were 979 undergraduate students and 428 graduate students. More than 22 percent are members of minority groups.

In addition to its undergraduate degree programs, JCHP offers numerous graduate degree programs, many of which students can enter in their third year of undergraduate school. The School of Health Professions offers master's degrees in bioscience technologies (3+2 entry-level master's, accelerated professional master's, and advanced master's degrees), couple and family therapy, occupational therapy (entry-level master's, advanced master's, and doctorate in occupational therapy), and radiologic sciences (executive-style master's degree and a certificate in PET/CT) and a Doctor of Physical Therapy (D.P.T.) degree. The School of Nursing offers master's degrees in nursing, post-master's certificates in several areas of nursing, and a Doctor of Nursing Practice (D.N.P.). The School of Pharmacy offers the Doctor of Pharmacy degree in 2008. The Master's in Family Therapy (M.F.T.) program is a collaboration between Jefferson and the Council for Relationships, a pioneering institution in the field of couple and family therapy treatment and training.

Location

Jefferson is in Center City, Philadelphia, stretching from 8th to 11th streets and from Chestnut to Locust streets. In this prime location, a short walk can take students almost anywhere they need to go. Students can walk four blocks to Independence Hall and the Liberty Bell, three blocks to Chinatown, seven blocks to South Street's funky shops and restaurants, and eight blocks to Rittenhouse Square's popular park and shopping area. In addition, students can easily catch a bus (several lines run through campus) or subway (only two blocks away) to get across town. Getting out of town is a breeze—the Market East regional rail station is two blocks away, Amtrak's 30th Street Station is less than a mile away, and the Philadelphia International Airport is a 30-minute train ride.

Living on campus means that classes, the hospital, and the library are within easy walking distance. From studios to luxury three-bedroom apartments, Jefferson Housing offers something to match almost any budget. The on-campus community includes students from JCHP, Jefferson Medical College, and Jefferson College of Graduate Studies as well as postdoctoral fellows and medical residents.

Majors and Degrees

JCHP has three schools: the Jefferson School of Health Professions, the Jefferson School of Nursing, and the Jefferson School of Pharmacy, scheduled to open in 2008. The School of Health Professions offers baccalaureate degrees in bioscience technologies (biotechnology, cytotechnology, medical technology) and radiologic sciences. The School of Nursing offers associate and baccalaureate degrees in nursing.

Academic Programs

The Department of Bioscience Technologies offers B.S., and B.S./M.S. undergraduate degrees in three programs: biotechnology/molecular sciences, cytotechnology/cell sciences, and medical technology/clinical laboratory sciences. The biotechnology/molecular sciences program educates students for health-care-related laboratory careers in the development of products using biologic and engineering principles. Through a combination of classroom and laboratory experiences, students are prepared to work with DNA, molecular modeling, and related areas.

In the cytotechnology/cell sciences program, students learn the specific microscopy skills necessary to study slides for evidence of normality or disease. Electron microscopy, cytogenetics, and the preparation and study of tissues prepare the student for further study, research, or teaching.

The medical technology/clinical laboratory sciences curriculum provides a thorough background in the physical and biological sciences, culminating in the application of research, theory, and principles to the performance of clinical laboratory procedures. The curriculum provides a firm foundation for teaching, supervisory functions, or graduate study. JCHP offers one- or two-year baccalaureate degree programs. Postbaccalaureate specialty-track certificate programs are available in molecular biology, immunohematology, clinical chemistry, microbiology, and hematology.

The radiologic sciences program prepares students for the expanding and multifaceted role of diagnostic imager. Recent trends in the delivery of health care indicate that the radiologic sciences curriculum must provide students with opportunities to develop skills in more than one modality. JCHP multicompetency students earn a B.S. in radiologic sciences while studying their choice of two modalities from a total of ten: cardiac sonography, computed tomography, general sonography, invasive cardiovascular technology, magnetic resonance imaging, medical dosimetry, nuclear medicine, radiography, radiation therapy, and vascular sonography. Students may also choose education, health management, or health information systems in place of one modality. A one-year Advanced Placement baccalaureate program is available for students with a bachelor's degree in another field.

The occupational therapy program provides students with an understanding of treatment that helps people achieve independence in their lives. Emphasis is placed on a bio-psycho-social approach to health care that concentrates on an individual's ability to perform daily-living activities, including self-care, work, and leisure. Course work is supplemented by six to nine months of supervised fieldwork. The program gives students the foundation necessary to successfully complete the national certification examination after graduation and develop skills in the areas of clinical practice, teaching, administration, or research. Degree programs include the combined B.S./M.S. in occupational therapy.

The physical therapy program's curriculum integrates lecture and laboratory classwork with carefully supervised clinical practice. It also provides a firm foundation in administration, research, consultation, planning, and education.

Jefferson's Department of General Studies offers general courses in arts, humanities, and sciences as well as certificate programs in medical coding, medical practice management, human resources management, professional communication, and health-care information systems; associate degrees in EMS, business, information systems, and medical practice management; and bachelor's degrees in health services management, health professions management, and health services management information systems.

The Jefferson School of Nursing prepares men and women to become effective professional nurses with the background necessary to be responsible, self-directed practitioners of nursing. Jefferson provides a continuum of nursing education, offering degrees at the associate (A.S.N.), bachelor's (B.S.N.), master's (M.S.N.), and Doctor of Nursing Practice (D.N.P) levels, as well as post-master's certificates. There are no prerequisites to enter the A.S.N. to B.S.N. program, which prepares students for bedside nursing. The B.S.N. offers a background in nursing theory in addition to hands-on practice. Both programs provide students with the knowledge and clinical skills necessary to plan, implement, and evaluate nursing care for individuals, families, and communities. Part-time and full-time programs are available.

Starting in 2008, the Jefferson School of Pharmacy offers the doctorate in pharmacy (Pharm.D.). After completing two years of prerequisite undergraduate work, students will come to JCHP to complete the degree in four years.

Academic Facilities

Administrative and academic offices, classrooms, laboratories, and a Learning Resource Center, including a computer laboratory, are located in Jefferson's Edison Building. Jefferson Alumni Hall, a basic medical science/student commons building, houses Jefferson College of Graduate Studies, basic science departments, classrooms, and research laboratories. The University library and administrative offices are located in the Scott Building. Clinical experience is acquired at Thomas Jefferson University Hospital or at more than 1,800 clinical affiliate sites.

Professional counseling services are available for all students who need assistance in resolving academic, vocational, and personal concerns.

Costs

Tuition for 2007–08 is $23,685 for full-time baccalaureate degree students. Fees for associate and advanced placement programs vary. On-campus housing costs range from $328 to $1690 per month for one-, two-, and three-bedroom accommodations.

Financial Aid

About 79 percent of current Jefferson students receive financial assistance. Aid includes Federal Pell Grants, Federal Perkins Loans, Federal Work-Study Program awards, Air Force ROTC scholarships, Nursing Scholarships, Nursing Loans, state grants or scholarships, and state-guaranteed loans. To apply for aid, students must submit the Free Application for Federal Student Aid (FAFSA) as well as a Thomas Jefferson University application. Completed applications must be received by the Financial Aid Office no later than May 1.

Faculty

Jefferson College of Health Professions has 90 full-time and 232 part-time faculty members. Most of the part-time faculty members serve in clinical teaching positions.

Student Government

Students are free to express their views on issues of institutional policy and on matters of student interest. Active membership on faculty and administrative committees enables students to participate in the formulation and application of University and College policy.

Admission Requirements

Admission for high school students is available three ways: through PACE (Plan A College Education), a program in which talented and ambitious high school seniors can reserve a seat in a future class; through the associate degree program in nursing; or through special physical therapy, occupational therapy, radiologic sciences, and bioscience technologies agreements with Elizabethtown College, Immaculata University, Muhlenberg College, Penn State Abington, Saint Joseph's University, University of Delaware, and Villanova University. Approximately two years of college-level course work are required for transfer admission. For a list of specific prerequisite courses and application deadlines for each program, prospective students should contact the Office of Admissions.

Interviews are required for all academically eligible applicants. An evaluation of foreign transcripts by the World Education Service (WES) is required. All international students and U.S. permanent residents must demonstrate English language proficiency as outlined by the Office of Admissions. The nonrefundable application fee is $50 (reduced to $25 for online applications).

Jefferson College of Health Professions offers an equal opportunity for admission to all candidates who meet the admission requirements, without regard to race, color, national or ethnic origin, marital status, religion, sex, sexual orientation, gender identity, age, disability, or veteran's status.

Application and Information

Jefferson College of Health Professions uses the self-managed application process. The application, fee, recommendation letters, transcripts, and other documents must be returned to the Office of Admission in a single envelope and at the same time. Admission and financial aid application forms and further information can be obtained by contacting:

JCHP Office of Admissions
Jefferson College of Health Professions
Thomas Jefferson University
Edison Building, Suite 100
130 South 9th Street
Philadelphia, Pennsylvania 19107-5233
Phone: 215-503-8890
877-JEFF-CHP (toll-free)
Web site: http://www.jefferson.edu/jchp

Thomas Jefferson University is located within walking distance of many places of cultural interest.

UNIVERSITY OF PITTSBURGH AT BRADFORD

BRADFORD, PENNSYLVANIA

The University

The University of Pittsburgh at Bradford (Pitt-Bradford) can take students beyond—beyond the classroom by offering internships and research opportunities; beyond the degree by providing a robust Career Services Office and an informal alumni network; beyond 9 to 5 by offering an active student life, a friendly residence-life environment, excellent athletic and cultural facilities, and a wide range of recreational opportunities; beyond place by exposing students to the world and offering many study-abroad opportunities; and beyond students' expectations by giving them a college experience that can transform them.

At Pitt-Bradford, students live and learn on a safe, intimate campus, where they receive individual and personalized attention from committed professors who work at their side. In addition, students earn a degree from the University of Pittsburgh, which commands respect around the world.

Students can work out in a state-of-the-art fitness center or swim in the six-lane swimming pool in the Sport and Fitness Center. The building also houses facilities for intercollegiate and intramural athletic events.

The Frame-Westerberg Commons offers students a place to eat, gather, and participate in campus life. The building houses the dining hall, where students can help themselves to a wide assortment of meals; a bookstore, which features an after-hours convenience store; offices for many student clubs and organizations; and areas to read or relax.

There are more than forty clubs and organizations, varying from the campus radio station and newspaper to academic clubs, honor societies, and fraternities and sororities. Pitt-Bradford competes in Division III of the NCAA and fields six men's teams in baseball, basketball, cross-country, golf, soccer, and swimming and seven women's teams in basketball, cross-country, golf, soccer, softball, swimming, and volleyball. Men's and women's tennis teams will begin competing at the Division III level in fall 2008.

Location

Pitt-Bradford is nestled on 317 acres in the foothills of the Allegheny Mountains, only steps from the Allegheny National Forest. Pitt-Bradford also is a short drive from larger cities such as Buffalo, New York (80 miles north); Pittsburgh (160 miles southeast); and Erie, Pennsylvania (90 miles west). Pitt-Bradford can also be reach easily by car and plane.

At Pitt-Bradford, students have many opportunities to participate in cocurricular opportunities in the region, including cross-country and downhill skiing, snowboarding, snowshoeing, ice skating, biking, fishing, hiking, and hunting.

Majors and Degrees

Students may pursue four-year degrees in accounting, applied mathematics, athletic training, biology, biology education 7–12, broadcast communications, business education K–12, business management, chemistry, chemistry education 7–12, criminal justice, economics, elementary education, English, English education 7–12, entrepreneurship, environmental studies, environmental studies education 7–12, health and physical education, history/political science, hospitality management, human relations, interdisciplinary arts, mathematics education 7–12, nursing, physical sciences, psychology, public relations, radiological science, social sciences, social studies education 7–12, sociology, sport and recreation management, sports medicine, and writing.

Pitt-Bradford also offers associate degrees in engineering science, information systems, liberal studies, nursing (RN), and petroleum technology.

Students may also study engineering for up to two years at Pitt-Bradford and then complete a program at the Oakland campus in bioengineering, chemical and petroleum engineering, civil and environmental engineering, electrical and computer engineering, industrial engineering, materials science and engineering, or mechanical engineering.

Pitt-Bradford also provides programs offered in conjunction with the University of Pittsburgh School of Dental Medicine and the Pennsylvania College of Optometry. Students begin their studies at Pitt-Bradford and, after three years, transfer to the appropriate graduate school to complete four more years of study.

Pitt-Bradford also offers the first two years of study leading to the doctorate in pharmacy. Students must complete the program at the Oakland campus, where admission is competitive. The Pittsburgh School of Pharmacy pre-admits some qualified high school seniors, pending completion of the first two years of the preprofessional program at Pitt-Bradford.

Academic Programs

The academic programs stress critical-thinking and communication skills and encourage hands-on learning through field experience, internships, and faculty-student collaboration on research. A Pitt-Bradford bachelor's degree requires 120–128 credit hours (requirements differ slightly among programs). Students need to complete between 60 and 70 credit hours to earn an associate degree.

The accounting major prepares students for the workplace, which has a growing need for accountants. The major also prepares students to earn a master's degree in either professional accountancy or business administration.

The biology program prepares students for careers in health-related professions, education, and research; technical positions in governmental agencies; and careers with food, pharmaceutical, chemical, and biotechnology companies. Most students interested in medicine, dentistry, optometry, pharmacy, osteopathy, physical therapy, occupational therapy, podiatry, chiropractic medicine, veterinary medicine, preclinical dietetics and nutrition, and a variety of careers in health and rehabilitation sciences are biology majors.

Students who choose to major in broadcast communications, English, public relations, or writing are able to work on the award-winning student newspaper, *The Source;* broadcast over the college radio station, WDRQ; and publish original works in the award-winning student literary magazine, *Baily's Beads.* Students also have access to an all-digital television studio and two digital radio facilities.

The business management program places a strong emphasis on teaching practical applications; courses often focus on cases taken from real business situations. Students may concentrate in accounting, finance, international business, or management information systems.

In the criminal justice program, students are able to intern with local and regional police departments, county court and probation offices, and a federal prison. New, state-of-the-art crime-scene investigatory tools enable students to "work a crime scene" using many of the same tools as professional law enforcement agents. During the 2007–08 academic year, the University plans to add a Crime Science Investigation (CSI) House to enable students to process simulated crime scenes and collect "evidence" just like the pros.

An education major prepares a student for a career as a teacher in a world of rapid political, economic, scientific, and cultural change. The Education Department seeks to graduate students who have general knowledge and specific content knowledge, as well as sound theory and practice.

Students who graduate from the hospitality management program are prepared to work in a large hotel or resort, in a convention bureau or center, in the areas of event or banquet management, or on a cruise ship. As part of the program, students complete 800 hours of field work at such places as the ski resort in nearby Ellicottville, New York, and Glendorn, a luxurious mountain resort in Bradford.

The nursing program at Pitt-Bradford offers an Associate of Science degree that can be completed in two years and a Bachelor of Science in Nursing degree that requires two additional years. Students may commence this program upon completion of the associate degree. The University also offers a School Nurse Certification program for registered nurses who wish to work in the school system.

In psychology, students gain knowledge in the scientific and theoretical aspects of psychology as well as the application of this knowledge. The major prepares students for graduate work in psychology and related disciplines and for employment in social service agencies, mental health centers, industries, and not-for-profit and governmental agencies.

Students may relocate to another University of Pittsburgh campus to complete academic programs not offered at Pitt-Bradford, but they may earn no more than 70 credits before transferring. All students in the arts and sciences may relocate, provided they are in good standing. Engineering students may relocate if they maintain a grade point average of at least 2.5.

Academic Facilities

In addition to the T. Edward and Tullah Hanley Library on campus, Pitt-Bradford students have online access to the entire University of Pittsburgh library system.

Blaisdell Hall, the fine arts and communication arts building, houses the communication arts, theater, and music programs and features state-of-the-art equipment. Students can find a computer-graphics lab, two art studios, a music/theater rehearsal hall, and a radio and television studio. The building also houses a multipurpose theater and serves as the cultural center for the region by housing plays, concerts, lectures, and other arts-related events.

Costs

For 2007–08, tuition for full-time students was $5295 per fifteen-week term for Pennsylvania residents and $10,085 for out-of-state students. Nursing tuition was $6781 per term for Pennsylvania residents and $12,861 for out-of-state students. Room and board expenses were $3425 per term. Other costs include an activity fee of $85 per term, a health fee of $50 per term, and a computer fee of $150 per term. Books and supplies cost approximately $500 per term.

Financial Aid

Pitt-Bradford believes that the cost of a college education should not be a deterrent to any student regardless of family financial circumstances. A variety of grants, scholarships, loans, and work-study opportunities are administered through the Financial Aid Office. All aid applicants must submit the Free Application for Federal Student Aid (FAFSA) by March 1 to receive priority consideration. Pennsylvania residents who complete the FAFSA by March 1 are also eligible for Pennsylvania Higher Education Assistance Agency (PHEAA) grants. Students who live outside of Pennsylvania should contact their state agency to learn more about the prerequisites for grants.

The University awards merit-based scholarships upon entry to those who demonstrate exceptional academic achievement. The University ROTC program is another possible source of financial aid. The University encourages veterans to contact the VA about educational benefits.

To learn more about financial assistance, students should contact the Financial Aid Office or visit the financial aid Web site at http://www.upb.pitt.edu/financialaid.aspx.

Faculty

Pitt-Bradford's 71 full-time faculty members hold doctorates and master's degrees from some of the most prestigious universities in the nation, including Cornell, Harvard, Stanford, and the University of Pittsburgh. Teaching is the primary activity of the faculty, and personal attention is emphasized in the classroom. Faculty members welcome the chance to meet with their students and know them by name. The student-faculty ratio is 14:1.

Student Government

Because Pitt-Bradford is a personalized campus, opportunities for leadership abound. Many students become campus leaders as early as their sophomore year. Regardless of students' background or interests, most find many places to become involved at Pitt-Bradford.

The Student Activities Council schedules comedy performances, lectures, art exhibits, movies, and trips to such places as Toronto, Canada; Niagara Falls, New York; Cooperstown, New York; and New York City.

Admission Requirements

In reviewing applications, the Admissions Committee considers three primary factors in evaluating an applicant's ability to succeed in college work: the high school record, the results of standardized tests (SAT or ACT), and the high school's recommendations. In addition, personal qualifications, extracurricular activities, and potential to contribute to the college community may be taken into consideration.

Application and Information

Pitt-Bradford has a rolling admissions program, and students may apply at any time. All candidates are notified as soon as action is taken on their application.

Candidates for admission should complete and return the application with a nonrefundable $45 fee. Students must also submit an official copy of their high school record and scores from either the SAT or ACT. In addition to fulfilling the above requirements, transfer applicants must submit all official college transcripts and must have a minimum cumulative grade point average of 2.0.

The Office of Admissions welcomes campus visits by students and their families; such visits help students arrive at a final decision about Pitt-Bradford. Interviews and tours are scheduled Monday through Friday, 9 a.m. to 3 p.m., and on selected Saturdays. Arrangements for these visits can be made by contacting the Office of Admissions or by going online to http://www.upb.pitt.edu/visit.aspx.

For application forms, catalogs, and further information, students should contact:

Office of Admissions
University of Pittsburgh at Bradford
300 Campus Drive
Bradford, Pennsylvania 16701-2898
Phone: 814-362-7555
800-872-1787 (toll-free)
Web site: http://www.upb.pitt.edu

The University of Pittsburgh at Bradford.

UNIVERSITY OF PITTSBURGH AT JOHNSTOWN

University of Pittsburgh at Johnstown

JOHNSTOWN, PENNSYLVANIA

The University

Founded in 1927 as one of the first regional campuses of a major university in the United States, the University of Pittsburgh at Johnstown (Pitt-Johnstown) is a four-year, degree-granting, fully accredited, coeducational, residential undergraduate college of the University of Pittsburgh. With 2,900 well-qualified full-time students and a suburban campus of striking beauty, Pitt-Johnstown combines the strong academic reputation and outstanding resources of a major research university with the personal appeal of a smaller college.

There are thirty-one campus buildings, including a library, student union, sports center, performing arts center, and chapel, in addition to a 40-acre nature preserve and outdoor recreation areas. The college has six different styles of housing, including residence halls, small-group lodges, apartments, and a new state-of-the-art living/learning center. An aquatic center includes a weight room and exercise rooms.

In addition to the undergraduate degrees listed in the Majors and Degrees section, the University also offers postbaccalaureate nondegree teaching certificates.

Location

Located in a suburb of Johnstown, a city of 25,000 only 70 miles east of Pittsburgh, the spacious 650-acre campus is the third largest in Pennsylvania and is recognized as one of the most attractive in the Eastern states. The University's facilities blend easily with the rustic wooded setting, creating a campus of distinctive natural beauty. Shops, entertainment, and cultural activities are conveniently available, and the city is in the heart of Pennsylvania ski country.

Majors and Degrees

Pitt-Johnstown offers the Bachelor of Arts (B.A.) degree in American studies, business (accounting, economics, finance, marketing, and management), communication, creative writing, economics, English literature, environmental studies, geography, history, humanities, journalism, professional writing, secondary education (citizenship education with several social science strands, communication, and English), social sciences, sociology, and theater arts. The Bachelor of Science (B.S.) degree is awarded in biology, chemistry, civil engineering technology, computer science, ecology, electrical engineering technology, elementary education, geology, mathematics, mechanical engineering technology, natural sciences, psychology, and secondary education (biology, chemistry, earth and space science, general science, mathematics, and physics).

An Associate of Science (A.S.) degree is available in emergency medical services, respiratory care, and surgical technology.

Dual teaching certification and dual education degree programs are offered. A cooperative program with a local hospital allows students to combine a B.S. in biology with a certificate in medical technology. A certificate in international studies can be earned in conjunction with any major.

With the assistance of academic advisers, Pitt-Johnstown students can construct interdisciplinary majors, double majors, and self-designed majors. They can also develop their specific fields of study with preprofessional preparation for advanced study in such areas as dental medicine, law, medicine, optometry, physical therapy, and veterinary medicine.

Academic Programs

Pitt-Johnstown seeks to provide contemporary, innovative academic programs that combine the practical concerns of career orientation with the spirit of inquiry and the traditional goals of higher education. Practical experience of all types is encouraged, including campus activities, community service, media work, and research projects. A seminar series introduces freshmen to rigorous intellectual work through small-group elective seminars. Students who show extra potential receive special advising, registration privileges, and scholarships through the President's Scholars Program. Students may complete preliminary requirements for upper-division programs that require relocation to the Pittsburgh campus, including requirements for programs in pharmacy and other health-related areas. In some programs, guaranteed admission is offered to qualified students.

Off-Campus Programs

The study-abroad program, in conjunction with the University Center for International Studies (UCIS), is a program that promotes the integration and synthesis of international knowledge. A wide range of internship projects on campus and at nearby sites is also offered.

Academic Facilities

In addition to the more than 145,500 volumes housed in the Pitt-Johnstown library, students have online request and retrieval access to the extensive collections contained in the University Libraries system, including more than 550 electronic journals and 147,000 electronic books. The college maintains computer classrooms and laboratories equipped with more than 150 computers, including Windows-based PC's, Macintosh computers, and powerful UNIX-based workstations. All classrooms are wired for Internet access, and all computers at Pitt-Johnstown are connected to the Internet, allowing students access to information from around the world and to a large suite of software shared with the University's other campuses. In addition to microcomputer facilities, which include both UNIX and VMS time-sharing systems, Pitt-Johnstown supports off-campus access to the network. To ensure compatibility with the latest technology, computers are replaced on a four-year cycle.

Costs

For full-time students in arts and sciences and education programs, 2007–08 tuition was $5295 per fifteen-week term for Pennsylvania residents and $10,085 for nonresidents. For full-time students in engineering programs, tuition was $5679 per fifteen-week term for Pennsylvania residents and $10,035 for nonresidents. Room and board expenses were approximately $3200 per term, depending on housing style and meal plan. Other costs included activities and facilities fees of $181 per term and a computing service fee of $150 per term. A $10 fee was charged for each physical education course. Books and supplies were estimated at $450 each term. All costs are subject to change.

Financial Aid

Nearly 80 percent of all Pitt-Johnstown students receive some form of financial assistance. In addition to the Pennsylvania Higher Education Assistance Agency (PHEAA) state grant, the Federal Pell Grant, and the Federal Stafford Student Loan, a variety of loans, grants, scholarships, and student-employment positions are awarded through the University. Applicants for all types of financial aid must submit the Free Application for Federal Student Aid (FAFSA) by April 1 prior to the academic year for which assistance is requested.

Faculty

Holding degrees from more than 100 distinguished American and international universities, the 137 full-time members of the Johnstown faculty represent a broad diversity in background and experience. Personally committed to undergraduate teaching, each faculty member is actively involved in a full range of intellectual activities as well as student advising, curriculum development, and the extracurricular and cultural life of the University community. Classes at Pitt-Johnstown are small, and opportunities for faculty-student interaction outside of the classroom are plentiful. Personalized instruction is emphasized. Full-time faculty members teach almost all courses. The student-faculty ratio is 19:1, and the typical class size is 25–30.

Student Government

The Student Senate plays a significant role in building cooperation among all members of the University community. It deals with matters affecting the entire student body and formally represents students in relations with the administration, faculty, and other nonstudent groups. The Programming Board, an administrative branch of the senate, schedules diversified entertainment.

Admission Requirements

All applicants for full-time study must have completed, or be in the process of completing, at least 15 units of work in an accredited secondary school. In addition, candidates must take either the SAT or the ACT. Writing sections of the entrance exams are considered for placement in freshman composition courses. Admission decisions are made after careful study of each applicant's high school record, performance on college entrance examinations, high school recommendations, and personal qualifications. Interviews are not required; however, applicants are encouraged to arrange a visit to the campus by phoning or writing the Office of Admissions.

Application requirements for transfer students include high school and college transcripts. Transfer students should have a minimum quality point average of 2.0.

High school graduates and transfer students must file an application, with a $45 fee, on forms provided by the school.

Application and Information

The candidate is notified as soon as action is taken on the application.

For more information about University of Pittsburgh at Johnstown, students should contact:

Office of Admissions
157 Blackington Hall
University of Pittsburgh at Johnstown
Johnstown, Pennsylvania 15904
Phone: 814-269-7050
800-765-4875 (toll-free)
Web site: http://www.upj.pitt.edu

THE UNIVERSITY OF SCRANTON
SCRANTON, PENNSYLVANIA

The University

At The University of Scranton, all of the programs and services provided are developed with the student in mind. The faculty and staff members and advisers are committed to offering students the best possible educational experience and opportunities both inside and outside the classroom. This balanced focus helps give students all of the tools and training necessary for a successful career and a lifetime of learning. It has also gained the University national recognition. For fourteen consecutive years, *U.S. News & World Report* has ranked Scranton among the ten finest master's universities in the North. For the fourth consecutive year, *U.S. News & World Report* has included Scranton among the fifteen colleges listed as "Great Schools at a Great Price" and named Scranton among the five schools in the North with the "Highest Graduation Rates." For the past six years, The Princeton Review has included Scranton among its "366 Best Colleges." For the second consecutive year, Scranton's Kania School of Management has been included among the elite colleges listed in The Princeton Review's "Best 282 Business Schools." Other national recognition includes Kaplan/Newsweek's 2008 "372 Most Interesting Schools and *Barron's Best Buys in College Education.* Only nineteen schools in Pennsylvania were listed. In addition, Scranton is one of only 100 schools in the nation on Templeton's Honor Roll of Character-Building Colleges.

The University proudly shares in the 450-year-old tradition of Jesuit education, which is renowned for unparalleled quality and prepares young men and women to make a difference in their fields and in the world. Scranton educates the whole person intellectually, socially, physically, and spiritually.

The University historically has achieved both a high graduation rate and a high retention rate. The University's five-year graduation rate averages 79 percent; the national average for selective bachelor's/master's institutions is 64 percent. The University's retention rate, the percentage of students continuing their education after the first year of college, is 90.4 percent. Employment outcomes for Scranton graduates are equally strong. Ninety-eight percent of the Class of 2006 was employed, pursuing graduate or professional studies, or volunteering within six months of graduation.

From 2003 to 2006, more than 200 Scranton graduates have received acceptance into over sixty-five schools, including some of the nation's most prestigious. These include the University of California at Berkeley, Boston College, Cornell University, Duke University, Fordham University, Georgetown University, New York University, the University of Notre Dame, and the University of Pennsylvania. Of the 319 senior applicants to medical schools over the last eight years, an average of 81 percent were accepted. Well over half of successful applicants in the past eight years have received more than one acceptance. Several students received scholarship support through M.D./Ph.D. programs, the National Health Service Corps, or armed services scholarships.

There is yet another success story at Scranton—the Fulbright story. Since 1972, 117 Scranton graduates have earned Fulbrights or other prestigious international fellowships. In the last five years alone, Scranton students earned four Truman Scholarships and six Goldwater Scholarships, and 5 students were named to *USA Today*'s All-USA College Academic Team. These numbers are unparalleled among universities of similar size.

University of Scranton students can choose from more than seventy-five social, academic, religious, volunteer, and honorary organizations and activities. Through the Community Outreach Office, students can participate in a wide range of community service activities. Scranton students perform well over 165,000 hours of service each year.

The University of Scranton is a campus with culture. Students can perform with the University Players or the University Band, Jazz Band, Singers, and String Ensemble. There are exhibitions and lectures at the Hope Horn Gallery. Students can become involved in *The Aquinas* (Scranton's weekly student newspaper), *Windhover* (the yearbook), *Esprit* (the literary magazine), *Retrospect* (the student history journal), WUSR-FM (University broadcast radio station), or *Royal Network News* (the student-operated news telecast).

The University of Scranton has enjoyed a rich tradition of athletic and academic excellence throughout its history, qualifying for NCAA Division III championships in ten different sports, including two national titles in men's basketball (1976, 1983) and one in women's basketball (1985). The focus of the University's nineteen-sport athletics program, however, has always been the overall development of the student-athlete. More importantly, 21 student-athletes have been named academic all-American and 13 have received prestigious NCAA postgraduate scholarships. After a long tenure as a member of the Middle Atlantic States Collegiate Athletic Corporation, Scranton is now a member of the newly formed Landmark Conference, whose members are similar in size and educational philosophy, with a belief that athletics are an important component of the undergraduate experience.

Location

The University's 54-acre hillside campus is nestled in the heart of Scranton, a community of 70,000 within a greater metropolitan area of 750,000 people. Its location in Pennsylvania's Pocono Northeast places it in one of the East Coast's premier vacation spots and a growing center for major corporations looking for locations outside of—but still comfortably close to—major metropolitan areas. The University is just 2 hours from New York City, Philadelphia, Syracuse, and Danbury. The campus is easily accessible by a network of interstate highways and a local airport.

Nearby shopping and historical and cultural attractions include the Scranton Cultural Center, Steamtown Mall, Steamtown National Historic Site, and the Lackawanna Coal Mine Tour. Just a 10-minute drive away is PNC Field, home to the New York Yankees Triple A baseball team; a winter ski area, Sno Mountain; and a concert amphitheater. Other local attractions include professional ice hockey, the Pocono Motor Speedway, several state parks, and three museums.

Majors and Degrees

The University of Scranton offers sixty bachelor's degree programs through three colleges and schools. There are forty-four undergraduate minors and thirty-one undergraduate concentrations or tracks.

In addition to the baccalaureate programs, incoming freshmen may apply directly to the five-year Master of Science program in occupational therapy and for a guaranteed seat in the three-year Doctor of Physical Therapy program. The University offers twenty-two master's degree programs.

Bachelor of Arts degrees are available in classical languages, communication, English, French, German, history, interdisciplinary studies, international language/business, philosophy, Spanish, theater, and theology and religious studies.

Bachelor of Science degrees are offered in accounting; accounting information systems; biochemistry; biochemistry, cell and molecular biology; biology; biomathematics; biophysics; business administration; chemistry; chemistry-business; chemistry-computers; community health education; computer engineering; computer information systems; computer science; counseling and human services; criminal justice; early childhood-special education; economics; electrical engineering; electronic commerce; electronics-business; elementary-early childhood education; elementary-special education, environmental science; exercise science; finance; forensic chemistry; gerontology; health administration; human resources studies; international business; international studies; management; marketing; mathematics; media and information technology; medical technology; neuroscience; nursing; operations management; physics; political science; psychology; secondary education; and sociology.

Academic Programs

In addition to the traditional academic areas, students can enhance their study through minors, concentrations, double majors, bachelor's/master's degree combinations, premedical and prelaw programs, ROTC, study abroad, internships, clinicals, and research. Highly motivated students can also take advantage of special programs of excellence. The Honors Program provides an interdisciplinary approach as well as a greater depth and breadth in a subject area through special courses, seminars, and independent work. The Special Jesuit Liberal Arts Program (SJLA), available to incoming freshmen by invitation, fulfills general education requirements in a distinctive way with a focus on critical thinking and key liberal arts subjects. The Business Leadership Program helps students hone the talents and skills needed in leadership settings, with special emphasis on the corporate world.

The Faculty/Student Research Program provides opportunities to be involved in faculty research in fields as diverse as the natural sciences, humanities, social sciences, and business. In 2006–07, 95 students and 37 faculty members participated in the Faculty/Student Research Program, in many cases with results presented at national conferences or published in distinguished journals.

Academic Facilities

The University is in the midst of more than $60 million in campus improvements. Scranton has built twenty-five new buildings and renovated thirty-eight others since 1984. Currently under construction is the new DeNaples Center, a $35-million, 118,000 square-foot campus center that is scheduled to open in January 2008. Construction is also underway on Condron Hall, a 386-bed suite-style dormitory scheduled to open for the fall 2008 semester.

The University of Scranton is one of the nation's most technologically savvy campuses. It is served by a robust network consisting of a gigabit fiber backbone, switched Ethernet ports, a 50mb Internet connection, and a new 20mb connection to Internet2. Wireless Internet (Wi-Fi) services are available to nearly 100 percent of outdoor campus space and residence halls and in 35 percent of the academic and administrative buildings on campus. Scranton has 915 PC's publicly available. All of the classrooms are Internet accessible. There are fifty fully mediated classrooms, twenty-seven instructional labs, and two cyber cafes.

The Harry and Jeanette Weinberg Memorial Library, which houses more than 484,300 volumes and 15,078 nonprint items, is the leading academic library in Northeastern Pennsylvania. Through the My.Scranton portal, the library is fully integrated into the University's campuswide voice, video, and data network. It offers such electronic resources as an online catalog, over 135 Internet index/databases, over 15,630 full-text journals, 13,900 full-text books online, 24/7 chat reference assistance, online request forms, and document delivery. There are 120 workstations and seventeen laptops available for loan in the library. The entire building has wireless connection to the Internet.

Costs

Annual tuition for the 2007–08 academic year was $28,458. Room and board charges were approximately $10,610. Expenses for books, travel, and personal supplies are estimated at about $2000 for the year.

Financial Aid

A comprehensive financial aid and scholarship program assists approximately 60 percent of the full-time undergraduate body in the form of scholarships, grants, loans, and work-study opportunities. An aid package may consist of any or all of these sources. The average freshman financial aid package for 2007–08, exclusive of parent loans, was $17,509. Both full- and partial-tuition academic scholarships are available and are awarded on the basis of strong academic achievement. To be considered for academic scholarships, students need only apply for admission; scholarships are need-blind and do not require any separate applications or interviews. The University also offers two awards for underrepresented groups of students: the Claver Award for students demonstrating financial need and the Arrupe scholarship for high-achieving students. Freshman and transfer applicants who wish to be considered must complete the Free Application for Federal Student Aid (FAFSA). The preferred filing deadline is February 15.

Faculty

Scranton's professors are known for their excellence in teaching and for the personal attention they give to students. Approximately 86 percent of the University's 263 full-time faculty members hold doctoral or other terminal degrees in their field. With a student-faculty ratio of 11:1 and an average class size of 23, students have ample opportunity to ask questions, participate in research, and meet with faculty members.

Student Government

Student government gives students a chance to put their ideas into action, from sponsoring speakers' visits and other campus events to working side-by-side with administrators. Students are elected by the student body and serve on the Student Senate and University Council and sit on important committees where they represent the entire student body. Student government plans student activities and entertainment by working with class officers, club presidents, and the director of student activities and represents student opinion on various campus and community issues.

Admission Requirements

The University welcomes men and women of all races, national origins, and religious beliefs. In reaching the admission decision, the Admissions Committee considers a number of factors: demonstrated evidence of a student's academic ability, intellectual curiosity, strength of character, and motivation, as evidenced by the student's high school classes, cumulative GPA, class rank, extracurricular activities, essay, letter of recommendation, and SAT and/or ACT scores. The Admissions Committee encourages a comprehensive college preparatory program in high school. For more detailed information, students should refer to The University of Scranton's *2007-08 Undergraduate Catalog.* Students are strongly encouraged to visit the campus for a tour and group presentation or a personal appointment.

The University of Scranton welcomes transfer students from accredited two- and four-year colleges and universities. As a guideline for admission, transfer applicants should have a minimum grade point average of 3.0 (on a 4.0 scale) for consideration. No transfer credit is given for grades below 2.0.

Application and Information

Students seeking freshman admission must complete the application form and a personal statement and have an official copy of their high school transcript and a letter of recommendation sent to the Admissions Office. Scores from the SAT or ACT are also required. Early action, advanced standing (through AP, CLEP, and college transfer credit), and deferred entrance are available. The Test of English as a Foreign Language (TOEFL) is a prerequisite for international students. International students seeking scholarships need to submit SAT scores in order to be considered.

Students may also apply online, with no application fee, at http://www.scranton.edu/apply. Transfer students should follow the same procedures as freshman applicants and submit an official transcript from all colleges previously attended.

There is an early action program with a November 15 deadline; students who apply by this date receive early notification by December 15. For students who choose not to apply for early action, the University operates on a rolling admissions basis, with an application deadline of March 1. The preferred deadline for transfer students is August 1 for the fall semester and December 15 for the spring semester. The deadline for submission of class confirmation fees is May 1.

For further information, students should contact:

Office of Admissions
The University of Scranton
800 Linden Street
Scranton, Pennsylvania 18510-4699
Phone: 570-941-7540
888-SCRANTON (toll-free)
Fax: 570-941-5928
E-mail: admissions@scranton.edu
Web site: http://www.scranton.edu

THE UNIVERSITY OF THE ARTS

College of Art and Design, College of Performing Arts, College of Media and Communication

PHILADELPHIA, PENNSYLVANIA

The University

The only university in the nation devoted exclusively to educating creative individuals in art and design, the performing arts, and media and communication, The University of the Arts (UArts) is located in the heart of Philadelphia's vibrant professional arts community. More than 2,300 students from forty states and thirty countries are enrolled in the undergraduate and graduate programs. For more than 135 years, UArts has defined creativity. Composed of the College of Art and Design, the College of Performing Arts, and the College of Media and Communication, the University offers intensive concentration within a major field as well as creative challenges in multidisciplinary exploration. Founded in 1876, the College of Art and Design is one of the country's leading art colleges, with nationally renowned design, fine arts, and crafts departments. Since its founding in 1870 as the Philadelphia Musical Academy, the College of Performing Arts has expanded to include a School of Dance, with programs in ballet, modern, jazz, and tap, as well as a School of Theater Arts, with acting, applied theater arts, theater design and technology, and musical theater. In 1996, the University inaugurated the College of Media and Communication to prepare students for careers in emerging fields, such as multimedia design, electronic communication, information architecture, computer-generated design, electronic arts and performance, and writing for film/TV.

The University sponsors a variety of activities and regular gallery and museum trips to New York City and Washington, D.C. One fourth of the students live in University housing, which provides coed apartment-style accommodations with complete kitchen and bath facilities and laundry rooms on the premises. Resident advisers live on each floor, and there is 24-hour security. Out-of-town freshmen are guaranteed housing if their contracts are received by June 1. The University also assists students in finding off-campus residences.

The graduate programs of the University of the Arts offer an impressive combination of strengths: exceptionally accomplished faculty members, a remarkably individualized and interactive learning environment, access to outstanding facilities and resources, specialized studios, and programs of study that are both highly focused and highly flexible. UArts offers graduate degrees in art education, book arts/printmaking, ceramics, industrial design, jazz studies, museum communication, museum education, museum exhibition, music education, painting and sculpture, planning and design, and teaching visual arts. A postbaccalaureate certificate in crafts is also offered.

Location

The UArts campus spans the Avenue of the Arts from South Street to Walnut Street and is part of the business and cultural hub of Center City Philadelphia. Next door to the University's historic Hamilton Hall is the city's magnificent Kimmel Regional Performing Art Center; in adjacent blocks are the famous Academy of Music, Wilma Theater, and the University's Merriam Theater, which books touring Broadway shows for the general public and hosts UArts student performances. The area also has world-class museums (Philadelphia Museum of Art and Barnes Museum), galleries, music and dance facilities, superb restaurants, and retail stores. Of historic importance, but also modern and sophisticated, the city is at the same time a series of small, close-knit neighborhoods with verdant squares. Fairmount Park provides facilities for sports activities and picnicking. UArts has the reputation of being the safest campus in the city.

Majors and Degrees

The College of Art and Design confers the B.F.A. degree in animation, crafts, film/animation, film/digital video, graphic design, illustration, multidisciplinary fine arts, painting/drawing, photography, printmaking, and sculpture and the B.S. in industrial design. It also offers a certificate program in art education and a concentration in art therapy. The School of Music confers the B.M. in composition, instrumental performance (with a jazz/contemporary focus), and vocal performance. A four-year diploma in music is also available. The School of Dance offers the B.F.A. in ballet, dance education, jazz dance, and modern dance. The School of Theater Arts offers the B.F.A. in acting, musical theater, theater design and technology, and theater management and production. A two-year certificate is available in dance and music. The College of Media and Communication also confers the B.F.A. in multimedia and in writing for film and television and the B.S. in communication.

Academic Programs

Students are attracted to UArts because of its dynamic, creative atmosphere. Whether majoring in dance, sculpture, graphic design, or multimedia, they enjoy interacting with their talented peers in other disciplines. The Freshman Project, the culmination of the required first-year writing course in liberal arts, provides the first opportunity for freshmen to work with students in other majors on a cross-disciplinary creative project. Students are further encouraged, to the extent that their busy schedules allow, to take elective courses outside their chosen major. All students take a total of 42 credits in liberal arts, which gives them vital exposure to humanities, social science, and science and provides them with the historical and theoretical framework of their major field.

The freshman year in the College of Art and Design is devoted to the Foundation Program; its focus is exploratory, allowing students to investigate various disciplines before deciding on a specific major. Students are assigned to small sections, each with a team of 3 instructors. In the fall, students take two-dimensional design, three-dimensional design, and drawing; in the spring, they may substitute a Time and Motion course for one of these. General program requirements vary from department to department. At the end of the freshman year, students select a major in animation, crafts, film/animation, film/digital video, graphic design, illustration, painting/drawing, photography, printmaking/book arts, or sculpture, and they may add a concentration in art education or art therapy. A wide variety of internship experiences is available to qualified students. A minimum of 123 credits is required for graduation, including 18 credits in the Foundation Program, 42 credits in the major, 42 credits in liberal arts, 15 credits in electives (9 credits of which must be taken in a department other than the major), and 6 credits in other areas outside the major. Students may request credit by exam in liberal arts subjects and by portfolio exam in studio art subjects.

In the College of Performing Arts, the School of Music program stresses individualized training, with a performance emphasis. Students undergo intensive training in theory and musicianship. Private lessons are supplemented by master classes and ensemble work. In the School of Dance, two years of ballet, modern, and jazz dance are required before students choose a major in the junior year. Electives include improvisation, repertory, partnering, Spanish dance, ethnic dance, character, and mime. In the School of Theater Arts students can choose one of three majors. Acting majors focus on developing a strong rehearsal and performance process through a wide range of acting, speech, and movement techniques. Musical theater majors train in a similar foundation technique while strengthening their skills in music and dance. Theater management and production majors study a range of disciplines, such as stage management, directing, playwriting, dramaturgy, production and arts administration, and mask and stage combat, preparing for careers or graduate study in these or related fields. The design and technology major explores the full spectrum of theatrical design and technical production. In the College of Performing Arts, a minimum of 126 to 130 credits is required for graduation, 42 of which must be in liberal arts. Participation in the 17-credit MATPREP Program enables students to complete bachelor's and master's degrees in teaching music in five years. The University has close working relationships, including internships, with professional theater, dance, and music groups in Philadelphia and elsewhere. Students are also encouraged to seek professional roles.

The College of Media and Communication was inaugurated in 1996 in recognition of new artistic opportunities that have arisen from advances in digital technology. In the College's B.F.A. program, Writing for Film and Television, students learn to create feature length screenplays, episodic television series, and movies for television. In addition, students take courses in film history, history of television, video production, and cinema arts. In the B.F.A. program in multimedia students receive a broad education that focuses on the integration of image, sound, text, and interactivity into works that tell stories. The program is designed to prepare students to work in fields in which close interaction among arts disciplines, digital fluency, collaboration, and effective communication are key components. The B.S. in communication is for students who wish to work in media related industries—television, documentary, Web-based, advertising, and writing. It is designed to be flexible, allowing students to create their own areas of emphasis, working both collaboratively and individually in the studio and on location. Students choose skills drawn from areas ranging from sound and video editing to photography, writing for film, producing streaming media, and visual and Web design. They take two application areas drawn from documentary video, narrative video, screenwriting, strategic advertising, digital journalism, Web design, and game design. By their senior year, they produce portfolio quality work and learn to collaborate as well as to combine different application areas. Internships in professional settings provide students with real-life experience in the field. In short, the program provides the skills, the applications, the theory, and the experience required to succeed in media and communication.

Students who want to learn more about the world of media and communication before choosing a major can enroll in the CMAC Discovery Year. This is a 30-credit program offered to entering freshmen. It was created for students who have not yet decided on a major focus but are certain that their interests lie within the fields of media and communication. The program provides students an overview of media and communication and gives them an opportunity to take courses in the college's three majors—communication, multimedia, and writing for film and television—before they finally decide on a major. Students also take foundation courses in liberal arts to satisfy their general education requirements.

Academic Facilities

The University facilities are composed of numerous buildings, with studios, classrooms, galleries, theaters, lounges, cafes, dormitories, and administrative offices. The Terra Building provides seventeen floors of studios, computer labs, classrooms, performing spaces, and TV and video production and recording studios. All design departments provide individual workstations for seniors and exhibition spaces that feature student and faculty work throughout the year. The University also maintains several public galleries, where students may exhibit their work along with curator-managed exhibitions of the work of distinguished guest artists. These include the Rosenwald-Wolf Gallery, the Arronson and Great Hall Galleries, and the Mednick Gallery. Student performances are held in the University's formal theaters, such as the 200-seat Dance Theater, the historic 1,800-seat Merriam Theater, the black box theater, the music recital hall, the Arts Bank, and a 239-seat state-of-the-art theater and rehearsal hall, and in the many informal spaces on campus.

As part of a multimillion-dollar telecommunications project, the campus has installed a multifunctional telephone system and a campus-wide data network, which provides Internet access for every computer attached to the network. Academic computing resources include more than twenty labs on Macintosh and PC platforms that are used for special applications, such as animation, digital imaging, 3-D modeling, multimedia, music, CAD, Web page design, and more, as well as some for word processing and general purposes. Several "smart" classrooms enable faculty members to use computer applications and Internet access in their presentations; smart studios allow students to function as they would in the professional world, with a computer in the studio or office.

Students work in a large number and variety of specialized facilities—both high and low technology—throughout the campus that support the learning of their craft. Among these are the Typography Lab, the Borowsky Center for Publication Arts, digital video editing suites, photo/film/animation labs and darkrooms, a scanner lab, an SGI lab, a bronze foundry and plaster workshop, and crafts studios and workshops for ceramics, metals, wood, glassblowing, papermaking, and fibers. The performing arts facilities include a recording studio; music technology (MIDI) studios; editing suites; chamber music studios and practice rooms; computer labs; dance and movement studios, with barres, mirrors, and resilient floors; and acting studios.

Library facilities include Albert M. Greenfield Library, which contains an extensive collection of books, journals, photographs, and videotapes devoted to the arts; a Picture Resource File; Special Collections, with special strengths in book arts and textiles; a slide library with a collection of more than 140,000 slides of art works and historical images; and a music library with manuscripts, journals, scores, and listening and viewing facilities. Holdings include books and periodicals, music scores, mounted pictures, slides, music recorded in LP and CD formats, videocassettes, videodiscs, and multimedia formats.

Costs

Tuition for the 2008–09 academic year is $29,500 plus a general student fee of $950. Accommodations in 3- or 4-person apartment-style dormitory units average $6600.

Financial Aid

Last year, UArts provided more than $7 million in scholarships and grants to new students, alone. Roughly one third went to those demonstrating financial need; the balance was awarded in talent- or merit-based scholarships. Overall, UArts students receive $30 million in scholarships, grants, loans, and part-time employment each year. Typically, 80 percent of the students enrolled on a full-time basis are eligible for some type of need-based aid. All students should apply. Financial need is defined as the difference between the cost of education and the family's federally calculated contribution to those costs, called the Expected Family Contribution (ECF). Where need exists, UArts assists in meeting costs within its available resources.

The University funds Presidential Scholarships, based on artistic potential and academic achievement. Financial aid is also available on the basis of the applicant's demonstrated financial need. Applicants must submit the Free Application for Federal Student Aid (FAFSA). March 1 is the suggested filing date. The University administers the following federal, campus-based student assistance programs: Federal Perkins Loans, Federal Work-Study, and Federal Supplemental Educational Opportunity Grants. Applicants who wish to be considered for scholarships should complete applications for admission and financial aid prior to March 31. Families from many different income levels can qualify for some type of financial assistance. In addition, the University's location in a large, active city provides students with diverse opportunities for part-time employment.

Faculty

Faculty members are practicing professionals who are deeply committed to the development of their students. As active participants in the arts, they have successfully achieved recognition in their specific fields of study. It is this real-world experience that gives them the knowledge and understanding so vital in the training of young, emerging artists, not just professionally but also in terms of personal growth. The faculty consists of 381 full- and part-time members; the majority hold advanced degrees. The faculty-student ratio is about 1:9.

Student Government

Student Council serves as the voice of the students from all three colleges within the University. It also supports a variety of arts-oriented student organizations, including a dance/step troupe, a Web radio station, and a student-run gallery, among many others.

Admission Requirements

In addition to submitting a portfolio or auditioning, applicants should submit their high school transcript, SAT or ACT scores, one letter of recommendation, and a personal statement of purpose.

The placement of transfer students is made after an evaluation of their portfolio or audition and a determination of their approved credits. Transfer students may be given advanced standing.

International applicants are required to submit scores on the Test of English as a Foreign Language (TOEFL); a minimum score of 550 on the paper-based TOEFL or 213 on the computer-based TOEFL is required. Early entrance and deferred entrance are possible.

Application and Information

The University of the Arts follows a system of rolling admission. All students are notified within two weeks of the receipt of all required materials. Students are encouraged to submit applications by March 15 for fall admission and December 1 for spring admission. For additional information, students should contact:

Office of Admission
University of the Arts
320 South Broad Street
Philadelphia, Pennsylvania 19102
Phone: 215-717-6030
800-616-ARTS (toll-free)
Fax: 215-717-6045
Web site: http://www.uarts.edu

UNIVERSITY OF THE SCIENCES IN PHILADELPHIA

USP

PHILADELPHIA, PENNSYLVANIA

The University

The University of the Sciences in Philadelphia (USP) was founded in 1821 as the Philadelphia College of Pharmacy, America's first college of pharmacy. The University of the Sciences in Philadelphia is located on a 25-acre campus in the academic section of historic Philadelphia known as University City. Besides USP, the University of Pennsylvania and Drexel University also call University City home. USP currently enrolls more than 2,500 undergraduate students in twenty-one majors and 300 students in thirteen graduate programs. The campus consists of nineteen buildings, including the recently completed Science and Technology Center. The University offers a wide variety of cocurricular activities that include intercollegiate and intramural athletics; literary publications; social, professional, religious, and honors organizations; and musical and drama groups. USP competes athletically at the NCAA Division II level and is a member of the Central Atlantic Collegiate Conference.

Location

USP's location in the University City section of Philadelphia offers considerable advantage and appeal. It not only offers a wide variety of educational opportunities, it also is a culturally, architecturally, and socially diverse community that caters to the local college student population. The University of the Sciences in Philadelphia is also actively involved with a number of local community organizations that are designed to foster improvement, development, and unity in the University City community. The Philadelphia metropolitan area is the home of more than forty other colleges and universities. USP students realize that Philadelphia and its immediate region provide abundant off-campus clinical and scientific opportunities, which are required in a number of programs. Within a short 20-minute trolley ride to the Center City area are the vast cultural, historical, and shopping attractions of the fifth-largest city in the United States.

Majors and Degrees

The University of the Sciences in Philadelphia includes three undergraduate colleges: the Philadelphia College of Pharmacy, which offers programs in pharmacy, pharmaceutical marketing and management, pharmaceutical sciences, and pharmacology and toxicology; the College of Health Sciences, which offers programs in fitness and health management, health science, medical technology, occupational therapy, physical therapy, and physician assistant studies; and the Misher College of Arts and Sciences, which offers majors in biochemistry, bioinformatics, biology, computer science, chemistry, environmental science, humanities and science, microbiology, pharmaceutical chemistry, and psychology. Students with strong academic interests in multiple areas may pursue double degrees, including two B.S. degrees or one B.S. degree and one entry-level professional degree.

Academic Programs

Four majors are offered in the Philadelphia College of Pharmacy: a six-year Doctor of Pharmacy (Pharm.D.) program and four-year B.S. degree programs in pharmacy and toxicology, pharmaceutical sciences, and pharmaceutical marketing and management. In the Doctor of Pharmacy program, students are guaranteed a seat in the professional phase (years 3–6) as long as the preprofessional phase (years 1–2) is successfully completed and an acceptable academic record is maintained. The pharmacy program at USP is recognized worldwide and prepares students for the increasingly clinical nature of pharmacy practice.

Pharmacology and toxicology, pharmaceutical sciences, and pharmaceutical marketing and management are unique B.S. degree programs that provide excellent career opportunities and address specific manpower needs within the pharmaceutical industry. Many graduates pursue postgraduate study as well as enter careers in research, manufacturing, and business.

Six programs of study are available in the College of Health Sciences: fitness and health management, health science, medical technology, occupational therapy, physical therapy, and physician assistant studies. Both physical therapy and occupational therapy programs are direct-entry, integrated undergraduate/professional degree programs that lead to the Doctor of Physical Therapy (D.P.T.) and Master of Occupational Therapy (M.O.T.), respectively. The physical therapy program was one of America's first programs to receive approval to offer the six-year, direct-entry D.P.T. In both the physical therapy and occupational therapy programs, students are admitted as first-year students and are guaranteed a professional-phase seat, provided an acceptable academic record is maintained. In the newest major in the College of Health Sciences, the B.S. degree in fitness and health management, students learn about healthy lifestyles and living as well as how sports and leisure activities improve community well-being.

The physician assistant studies program at the University of the Sciences in Philadelphia is a five-year program that leads to the Bachelor of Science and Master of Science degrees in health science and is in partnership with the Philadelphia College of Osteopathic Medicine (PCOM). Students enrolled in the physician assistant studies program complete their preprofessional component (years 1–3) in the natural sciences, social sciences, and humanities at USP. The professional component of the program (years 4–5) is completed at PCOM. A four-year B.S. degree in health science for students who want to focus on general health care and community service is also available.

Medical technology students at the University of the Sciences in Philadelphia receive an excellent three-year academic foundation in preparation for their fourth year, which is spent in a clinical setting at an approved hospital school of medical technology.

Ten different four-year Bachelor of Science degree programs are offered in the Misher College of Arts and Sciences. They include biochemistry, bioinformatics, biology, computer science, chemistry, environmental science, humanities and science, microbiology, and pharmaceutical chemistry. Psychology students may elect to remain at USP for an additional year and qualify for the M.S. in health psychology program. The College of Arts and Sciences combines the expertise of an outstanding group of scientists, researchers, and educators with academic facilities that are not often found at an institution the size of USP. This combination creates an academic atmosphere of especially high quality. The newest major in the Misher College of Arts and Sciences is the B.S. in humanities and science. This major provides a unique combination of scientific and humanistic study, which is particularly attractive to students who want to pursue medical, dental, or veterinary studies.

The University of the Sciences in Philadelphia's strong tradition of excellence prepares graduates to enter postbaccalaureate degrees in medicine, dentistry, veterinary medicine, and other health professions. Traditionally, premed students choose to major in chemistry, biochemistry, biology, microbiology, pharmacology and toxicology, or psychology. The curricula in these and most of the other programs include the basic courses required for admission to medical school. Beginning with the first year, premed students receive individualized counseling by the Pre-Professional Advisor and their faculty adviser in selecting courses to meet their career goals. Premed students may also elect to take advantage of USP's agreement with Philadelphia College of Osteopathic Medicine, which reserves five seats each year for USP students.

An innovative Science Teacher Certification program is available for those students who are majoring in biology or chemistry and wish to pursue teaching careers. The areas of certification include biology, chemistry, environmental science, and general science.

Students may enroll at the University of the Sciences in the one-year undeclared program and select from pre-medical, predental, pre-veterinarian, or science and technology options. Through a special orientation program, undeclared students are introduced to the various academic disciplines and career opportunities available to them. Undeclared students formally declare a major during the spring semester of the first year.

Academic Facilities

Classes and laboratory course work are conducted in ten academic buildings on the University of the Sciences in Philadelphia's campus, while the remaining buildings serve as residence halls or support-service facilities. USP houses more than 100 scientific laboratories and many computer terminals for student use. The Joseph W. England Library contains more than 84,000 volumes and 8,400 periodicals in addition to numerous electronic information programs.

Costs

Tuition for the 2007–08 academic year was $25,600; room and board were $10,500. Costs are subject to change.

Financial Aid

Currently, 98 percent of the undergraduates at USP receive financial assistance, amounting in the aggregate to more than $8 million. Types and sources of aid include Federal Perkins Loans; Health Professions Loans; Federal Work-Study Program; USP Merit Scholarships, Athletic Scholarships, Grants, student employment, and institutional loan funds; deferred tuition payment plans; student loans; and scholarships received from states, municipalities, and service clubs or other organizations. All applicants who seek financial assistance must complete the Free Application for Federal Student Aid (FAFSA). USP's merit scholarship and grant program provides awards for both first-year and transfer candidates.

Faculty

There are 160 full-time faculty members. Of these, more than 100 have doctoral degrees. All full-time faculty members teach undergraduates, and many also teach graduate students and conduct research. Graduate assistants do not teach but serve as laboratory aides.

Student Government

Student government is composed of representatives from all undergraduate classes and class officers. It takes an active part in governance through participation in faculty and administrative committees and sponsors a number of campus activities and functions.

Admission Requirements

The University of the Sciences in Philadelphia seeks students whose aptitudes and achievements are in the areas of science, mathematics, and humanities. Sixteen total high school credits are required and must include English (4 credits), mathematics (3 credits, including algebra I and II and plane geometry), and science (3 credits of laboratory science, including at least two of the following: biology, chemistry, and physics). Physical science, IPS, general science, or similar courses do not fulfill the laboratory science requirement. Class rank, if provided by the applicant's high school, and grade point average are also considered in the admission decision process. Candidates are required to submit the results of their SAT and/or ACT examinations. Supplemental testing or an interview may be requested to clarify a specific aspect of a candidate's record. For students whose first language is not English, the Test of English as a Foreign Language (TOEFL) is suggested. Applications for transfer are welcome, although the number of seats available each year is less than that for first-year students, since all students admitted to USP are admitted for the entire program length. Advanced standing may be achieved through the College Board's Advanced Placement Program, the International Baccalaureate Program, or earned college credit.

The University of the Sciences in Philadelphia does not discriminate in the administration of its educational policies, admission policies, scholarship and loan programs, or athletic and other University-administered programs on the basis of sex, age, handicap, race, creed, color, or national origin. All students are entitled to all of the rights, privileges, programs, and activities generally accorded or made available to students at the University. This institutional policy complies with the requirements of Title IX of the Education Amendments of 1972 (45 CRF 86), Section 504 of the Rehabilitation Act of 1973, and other applicable statutes and regulations.

Application and Information

An Admission Application Booklet may be obtained by calling the Admission Office. Applicants may submit an online application at http://www.usip.edu/applying. Each application must be accompanied by a nonrefundable $45 application fee. First-year applications for admission are considered until the entering class roster has been completed. USP follows a rolling admission policy, and applicants are notified of the admission decision after the University has received all required data. Students accepted into any of the programs have until May 1 to submit a nonrefundable deposit of $150 to hold a place in the class. Applicants accepted after May 1 have two weeks to submit a tuition deposit.

Applicants for transfer to the professional programs should submit completed applications no later than the following dates: physical therapy (January 1), pharmacy (January 15), occupational therapy (March 1), and physician assistant studies (March 15). Applications for transfer may be submitted after the priority filings deadlines. However, they are considered only after those received by the priority filing deadlines are reviewed. All transfer applications are reviewed on a rolling basis except for physical therapy and pharmacy, which are reviewed during the spring semester.

Director of Admission
University of the Sciences in Philadelphia
600 South 43rd Street
Philadelphia, Pennsylvania 19104-4495
Phone: 215-596-8810
888-996-8747 (toll-free)
Fax: 215-596-8821
E-mail: admit@usp.edu
Web site: http://www.usp.edu

URSINUS COLLEGE

COLLEGEVILLE, PENNSYLVANIA

The College

The Ursinus experience has been termed "nothing short of astonishing" by the most recent team of accreditors to review the College's programs. With its highly dedicated faculty and top-flight, innovative yet classic academic curriculum, Ursinus ensures that its students complete their four years well prepared to take on the toughest professional and graduate school programs or to embark upon meaningful and challenging careers. The two most outstanding features of the Ursinus curriculum are the Common Intellectual Experience, a wide-ranging seminar course in which first-year students examine basic questions of life, philosophy, history, art, and culture through the ages, and the Independent Learning Experience, which is fulfilled through independent research, a summer fellowship, study abroad, or student teaching. It is little wonder Ursinus has been selected by the National Survey of Student Engagement as a national model of transformative education. In addition, Ursinus participates in Project Pericles for civic engagement, is on the prestigious Watson Foundation list for fellowships abroad, and is a member of the Annapolis Group of distinctive liberal arts colleges and the Centennial Conference, which is known for students who excel as both scholars and athletes. It is, in the words of a former *New York Times* editor, a college that changes lives. The Ursinus program does not stop at the classroom door but touches every area of its students' lives, as 95 percent of students live on campus. Residence halls are well resourced with network connections and group study areas, and the College's free laptop program ensures that all students have access to the best technological tools to do high-quality work.

As one of 240 colleges granted a chapter of the national academic honor society Phi Beta Kappa, Ursinus College joins together some of the very best students and professors in the nation in a wooded suburban setting that features outstanding facilities. Three out of four Ursinus graduates eventually go on to graduate study. Ursinus alumni are well represented as doctors, attorneys, college professors, high school teachers, artists, scientific researchers, writers, and corporate leaders. The College ranks seventeenth in the nation in the percentage of its graduates who have attended medical school. Historically, 90 percent of those who apply to medical, dental, and veterinary schools gain acceptance. College graduates also have a law school admissions record better than 90 percent. Among Ursinus' 15,000 living alumni are 1972 Nobel laureate Gerald Edelman; NASA Magellan Mission Director James F. Scott III; Ismar Schorsch, Chancellor of the Jewish Theological Seminary of New York; two ambassadors—ambassador and architect of the Camp David Peace Accord Hermann F. Eilts and former U.S. Ambassador to Sierra Leone Joseph H. Melrose Jr., now a member of the Ursinus faculty; Geoff Bloom, president and CEO of Wolverine Worldwide, the maker of Hush Puppies; and pediatric AIDS researcher Loretta P. Finnegan.

Since its founding in 1869, Ursinus has combined a residential experience with an uncompromising drive toward academic quality. Ursinus students are intelligent, motivated, and academically curious. The student body at Ursinus numbers approximately 1,600, with equal numbers of men and women. Ursinus receives over 6,000 applications each year and enrolls 475 students each fall. Forty-one percent of those enrolled in fall 2007 were ranked in the top 10 percent in their high school classes. The class was composed of several captains of varsity sports teams, editors of publications, officers of clubs, and members of distinguished honor societies. Thirteen percent of the entering class is composed of members of minority groups, and 1 percent of the class is composed of international students. The student body comes from across the United States, with a small percentage from other countries.

The Ursinus College graduating class of 2007 achieved exceptional results. Forty students published research papers, 130 gave presentations of their research and internship results via conferences, and 25 received grants and fellowships to graduate schools. Graduates of the class of 2007 attend some of the best medical, law, veterinary, and other graduate schools in the country.

Ursinus provides a variety of activities for students. The nationally recognized Berman Museum of Art is open to the public and is known for its diverse collection and innovative educational programming as well as a wildly popular Annual Student Exhibition and a celebrated Outdoor Sculpture Garden on campus. Students curate exhibitions as well as learn museum programming. The Kaleidoscope, a new $25-million, 55,000-square-foot performing arts center, provides music and dance rooms and two theaters for students majoring in dance and theater and for those interested in taking performing arts courses outside their fields of study. Each year there are four student theater productions in addition to choir, band, and dance concerts. The Floy Lewis Bakes Recreation Center features a four-lane indoor track, indoor tennis courts, and a fully equipped recreation and weight room. Wismer Student Center houses the student cafeteria, a food court, the Ursinus Bookstore operated by Barnes and Noble, a game room, a television lounge, dance and movie facilities, and the Student Activities, Student Government Association (SGA), and Campus Activities Board (CAB) offices. The Residential Village, comprising twenty-five renovated Victorian homes, complements the campus culture. Ursinus students may live in these houses or in one of the residence halls. Six of the homes are special interest houses: Wicks House, Musser International House, Service Learning House, Wellness House, the Java Trench (coffeehouse), and Biology House. Ursinus students, 95 percent of whom live on campus, enjoy their involvement in College activities. Willing to assume leadership roles, all students participate in at least one of the eighty-five special interest clubs and organizations, honorary academic societies, theater and musical programs, service opportunities, and preprofessional advisory groups. Publications include the weekly *Grizzly* newspaper and the *Lantern* literary magazine. The Literary Society meets weekly. The College offers fraternities and sororities and an extensive athletic program, including twenty-six Division III intercollegiate varsity sports, club sports, and intramural activities.

Location

Ursinus is located in the town of Collegeville, 25 miles northwest of Philadelphia along the Route 422 corridor. Its location offers both the charm of a suburban small-town community and the convenience of restaurants, theaters, shops, and cultural and sports events in Philadelphia and nearby. Interests of all kinds can be explored within a 50-mile radius of the College. The College is convenient to skiing, hiking, the retail hub of King of Prussia, and the historic Valley Forge National Park as well as all the history and culture Philadelphia has to offer. The presence of two major pharmaceutical companies in the immediate area provides research and internship opportunities for students.

Majors and Degrees

Ursinus offers undergraduate degrees in arts and sciences. The Bachelor of Arts (B.A.) is awarded to students with majors in American studies, anthropology/sociology, art, business and economics, classical studies, dance, East Asian studies, English, environmental studies, French, German, history, international relations, media and communication studies, philosophy and religion, politics, Spanish, and theater. The Bachelor of Science (B.S.) is awarded to students with majors in biochemistry, biology, chemistry, computer science, exercise and sport science, mathematics, neuroscience, physics, and psychology. In addition, interdisciplinary majors may be arranged. The College offers a cooperative 3-2 engineering program with Columbia University in New York City and Washington University in St. Louis. Secondary teaching certification is offered in many areas.

A new Certificate in International Studies allows students to add a global perspective to a variety of majors and interests. Ursinus has recently entered into an agreement with the University of Rochester's Simon School of Business, enabling talented graduates to enter the M.B.A. program directly after graduation from Ursinus.

Academic Programs

Ursinus is committed to undergraduate liberal education and requires students to select from among choices in a core curriculum, with a minimum of 128 credits for the bachelor's degree. While completing departmental requirements in one of the major fields, students may add one or more minors. All students are required to complete an internship, an independent research project, a study-abroad program, or a student teaching experience. The College operates on a semester calendar. The fall term begins in late August and the spring term ends in mid-May. The College offers funded summer research opportunities in all disciplines with its aggressive undergraduate research scholars program called Summer Fellows.

Off-Campus Programs

Ursinus believes that students in all fields can be transformed by contact with other cultures, so it has created both national and international academic, research, and volunteered internship programs that turn the College into a global gateway. Ursinus sponsors international study programs to Costa Rica, England, France, Germany, Ireland, Japan, Mexico, New Zealand, Scotland, and Senegal. Ursinus also works with the Council on International Education Exchange to provide international experiences to various sites, including Argentina, Australia, Belgium, the Czech Republic, Ghana, Hungary, Indonesia, the Netherlands, Poland, Russia, and Tunisia.

Academic Facilities

Myrin Library's open-stack structure houses 400,000 volumes, 200,000 microforms, 3,500 audiovisual materials, and 3,500 e-books and offers on-site and remote access to some 2,900 print, microform, and electronic periodical titles. Students also have access to more than 3.7 million volumes through the Tri-State College Library Cooperative and countless online reference materials. Pfahler Hall of Science recently underwent a $15-million renovation and addition. Within Pfahler Hall, the Musser Lecture Hall features the latest in videoconferencing and audiovisual technology, the observatory features excellent high-resolution telescopes, and the laboratories are designed for faculty and student collaborative research. The new environmental studies major is housed in Pfahler Hall. The F. W. Olin Academic Building is the home of all departments in the humanities and contains a 320-seat lecture hall, classrooms, seminar rooms, two microcomputer centers, the Writing Center, and faculty offices and research space. Bomberger Hall, which underwent a complete renovation and expansion in 2007, provides classrooms for business and economics, political science and international relations, anthropology and sociology, and education and houses the music department. Thomas Hall houses the psychology and biology departments and provides recently renovated facilities for independent student laboratory research as well as regular course work. Major pieces of scientific instrumentation include infrared spectrometers, a flow cytometer, liquid chromatographs, and a scanning electron microscope. Ritter Center houses a television studio, a new media laboratory, and various other technical facilities for media and communication. Helfferich Hall offers a swimming pool, a studio, and a fully mirrored weight room with hydra equipment. The Floy Lewis Bakes Field House features a four-lane indoor track, indoor tennis courts, and a fully equipped recreation and weight room. Outdoor sports facilities include eight tennis courts, an all-weather track and steeplechase pit, and nine oversized athletics fields for intramural and intercollegiate sports.

Costs

The comprehensive cost for the 2007–08 academic year for entering first-year students was $43,150. Tuition, which includes a laptop computer, was $35,000, and room and board were $8000.

Financial Aid

Approximately 85 percent of Ursinus students receive financial aid in the form of scholarships, grants, loans, campus employment, and state or federal aid. Eligibility for need-based financial aid is determined by the Ursinus Office of Financial Services using the Free Application for Federal Student Aid (FAFSA) and the CSS PROFILE, which is only needed for early decision applicants. Approximately half of the College's students work part-time on campus each year. Merit- and talent-based scholarships, which are awarded regardless of need, include a number of awards of up to $18,000, with a select number of larger scholarships available to especially exceptional candidates. The FAFSA should reach the Office of Financial Services by February 15, which is the College's preferred filing date. No student is denied admission because of financial need.

Faculty

The focus of the College's 165 full- and part-time professors and instructors is on teaching students. All faculty members are also involved in research and writing. Ninety-three percent of the full-time faculty members have earned doctorates or the highest degree in their fields, and all members are encouraged to explore their fields of study. The student-faculty ratio is 12:1. Most faculty members serve as academic advisers, and many serve as advisers to academically oriented clubs and interest groups.

Student Government

Through the Ursinus Student Government Association (USGA), students have responsibility in all essential areas of campus governance. Through the USGA committees, students may participate in the development of the academic, residential, and extracurricular life of the College. Great emphasis is placed on fostering responsibility in campus life.

Admission Requirements

Ursinus students are intelligent, motivated, and academically curious. All admitted freshmen have successfully completed advanced college-prep high school programs and are active outside the classroom. Forty-one percent achieved a rank in the top 10 percent of their high school classes. For fall 2007, the middle 50 percent of the SAT math scores ranged from 550 to 660 and critical reading scores ranged from 550 to 660. SAT or ACT results are required. Students who rank in the top 10 percent of their high school class, or those who have achieved a minimum 3.5 GPA on a 4.0 scale at a high school that does not rank its students, have the option to waive their standardized test scores. Most Ursinus students have taken one or more AP courses, and Ursinus recognizes the AP and I.B. programs for college credit. All applicants are encouraged to arrange for a visit and personal interview on campus. Merit scholarship applicants are strongly recommended to have an on-campus interview.

Application and Information

In addition to its own application, Ursinus College accepts the Common Application and the Universal College Application. Candidates are asked to send a completed application accompanied by the nonrefundable $50 application fee no later than February 15. The fee is waived for online applications. Candidates who wish to be considered for early decision must submit an application and complete their credentials prior to January 15. Those wishing to participate in the Early Action program must apply by December 1. Academic program brochures and application forms may be obtained by contacting:

Office of Admissions
Ursinus College
P.O. Box 1000
Collegeville, Pennsylvania 19426
Phone: 610-409-3200
Fax: 610-409-3662
E-mail: admissions@ursinus.edu
Web site: http://www.ursinus.edu

VILLANOVA UNIVERSITY
VILLANOVA, PENNSYLVANIA

The University

Since 1842, Villanova University has been under the direction of the Order of St. Augustine, better known as the Augustinians, one of the oldest religious teaching orders of the Roman Catholic Church. The University's 254-acre campus is located 12 miles west of downtown Philadelphia in an attractive residential area. There are approximately 10,000 men and women currently enrolled; 6,000 are undergraduates.

Campus life encompasses a wide range of activities and groups. The Campus Activities Team provides a full schedule of films, concerts, and social events throughout the year. Special interest organizations are available in many areas; these include publications, music, theater, professional societies, fraternities and sororities, cultural and political groups, and volunteer organizations.

Location

Philadelphia, America's fifth-largest city, offers unparalleled opportunities to supplement campus life with cultural, recreational, and social service activities. The city offers professional sports in the form of basketball's 76ers, football's Eagles, hockey's Flyers, and baseball's Phillies. Philadelphia is the home of the world-renowned Philadelphia Orchestra and also the location of a wealth of museums, theaters, galleries, and historic attractions.

Majors and Degrees

Villanova University grants the Bachelor of Arts degree in the following majors: art history, classical studies, communication, criminal justice, economics, education (secondary), English, environmental studies, French and Francophone studies, geography, German, Hispanic studies, history, honors, human services, humanities, Italian, philosophy, political science, psychology, sociology, and theology and religious studies. Instruction in Arabic, Chinese, Italian, Japanese, and Russian is also available.

The Bachelor of Science is awarded in the following majors: astronomy and astrophysics, biochemistry, biology, chemistry, comprehensive science, computer science, environmental science, honors, mathematics, and physics. Also offered are the following professional degrees: B.S./D.M.D. (seven-year Doctor of Medical Dentistry program in conjunction with the University of Pennsylvania's School of Dental Medicine), B.S./D.P.T. (seven-year Doctor of Physical Therapy program with the Jefferson College of Health Professions of Thomas Jefferson University), B.S./M.D. (seven-year Doctor of Medicine program in conjunction with Drexel University School of Medicine), and B.S./O.D. (seven-year Doctor of Optometry program in conjunction with the Pennsylvania College of Optometry). Allied health programs are offered in occupational therapy, bioscience technologies, and radiologic technologies (six-year Master of Science programs in conjunction with the Jefferson College of Health Professions of Thomas Jefferson University).

The College of Liberal Arts and Sciences offers interdisciplinary concentrations in Africana studies, Arab and Islamic studies, Augustine in dialogue with faith and culture, cognitive science, East Asian studies, elementary education (in cooperation with Rosemont College), environmental studies, ethics, honors (liberal arts), Irish studies, Latin American studies, peace and justice, Russian area studies, women's studies, and writing and rhetoric.

The Villanova School of Business grants the Bachelor of Science degree in accountancy, business administration, business honors, and economics. The degree program in business administration has majors in finance, international business (co-major), management, management information systems, and marketing.

The College of Engineering offers degrees in chemical, civil, computer, electrical, and mechanical engineering. The College of Engineering offers a concentration in business and a dual degree with the College of Liberal Arts.

The College of Nursing grants a Bachelor of Science in Nursing degree.

The Honors Program sequence in liberal studies is available to students in all four colleges.

Academic Programs

The principal aim of the College of Liberal Arts and Sciences is to assist persons in educating themselves. To achieve this, the College offers a traditional liberal arts and sciences curriculum with a great deal of flexibility built into it, including a Villanova Seminar Program with class sizes of 10 to 15 students. Both general and specialized courses are provided. Stress is laid on critical thinking and effective communication. Accordingly, hundreds of theoretical and practical courses are offered in the arts, the humanities, and the physical and social sciences. Required components of the curriculum include ethics, fine arts, and courses designed to develop students' writing abilities. The College of Liberal Arts and Sciences is the home of a chapter of the prestigious national honor society, Phi Beta Kappa. This distinction is only given to 262 colleges and universities—only eighteen of which are Catholic institutions.

Emphasizing the analytical approach to business, the curriculum in the Villanova School of Business combines broad educational foundation courses with in-depth study of major functional fields of business and business processes, such as accounting information systems, financial flows and markets, management, and the impact of economic variables upon business and social issues. Foundation courses aim at developing proficiency in oral and written communications, the ability to apply the tools of quantitative analysis to the solution of business problems, and awareness of and sensitivity to moral values and law, the need for social responsibility, and the exercise of conscience. Both undergraduate and graduate programs in the Villanova School of Business are accredited by AACSB International—The Association to Advance Collegiate Schools of Business. This accreditation represents the standard of achievement in business schools worldwide. In 2007, the Villanova School of Business was recognized by *Business Week* as number 12 in the top 20 undergraduate business programs in the United States.

In the first two years of the College of Engineering curriculum, work concentrates on such basic areas as chemistry, engineering science, mathematics, and physics, while in the last two years, engineering analysis and design are stressed. Courses in the humanities are included in each engineering curriculum to make the young engineer more fully aware of social responsibilities and better able to consider nontechnical factors in the engineering decision-making process. Students learn the theoretical foundations of the engineering field through lectures and discussions, which are integrated with extensive hands-on laboratory and computer experience. Individual and group design projects utilize state-of-the-art equipment and instrumentation. *U.S. News & World Report* continually ranks the College of Engineering among the ten best engineering schools in the country (master's level).

The College of Nursing curriculum consists of academic and professional study, including laboratory and health-agency experience under the guidance of qualified faculty members. Clinical facilities are selected on the basis of the educational objectives of the curriculum. The program provides clinical experiences beginning in the sophomore year in a variety of settings, including medical centers, community hospitals, and community health agencies. The curriculum builds upon a strong foundation of liberal arts and physical and behavioral sciences. The College of Nursing has been distinguished by the National League of Nursing as a Center of Excellence for Nursing Education.

Naval and Marine ROTC programs are available for men and women on campus, Air Force ROTC through St. Joseph's University, and Army ROTC through Widener University on campus.

Off-Campus Programs

The Office of International Studies assists undergraduates in studying overseas in Africa, Asia, Europe, Latin America, and the Middle East for a summer, semester, or full academic year. All overseas programs must be affiliated with an overseas four-year college or university, have overseas faculty members, and provide bicultural experiences such as homestays. Students usually study overseas in their sophomore or junior year. Villanova's summer programs support language studies and area studies at such sites as Athens-Corinth (Greece), Bethlehem (Palestine), Cádiz (Spain), Dijon (France), Edinburgh (U.K.), Galway (Ireland), London (U.K.), Mafraq (Jordan), Megiddo (Israel), Nizhni Novgorod (Russia), Rome (Italy), Shanghai (China), Siena (Italy), Tübingen (Germany), Urbino (Italy), and Valparaíso (Chile). Villanova also has special relations with Bethlehem University and Birzeit University (Palestine), University of Cádiz (Spain), University College of Galway (Ireland), University of Glasgow (Scotland), University of Urbino (Italy), and Victoria University of Manchester (England). Nursing majors may complete a year at King's College, London. College of Commerce and Finance students can spend a year at European School of Business (Germany), University of Lille–Nice ESPEME (France), or University of Maastricht (Netherlands). College of Liberal Arts and Sciences students may spend a year studying at National University of Ireland-Galway (Ireland); Queens University, Belfast (U.K.); Sophia University (Japan); Universidad Popular Autonóma del Estado de Puebla (Mexico); Universita degli Studi Urbino (Italy); University Colleges Cork and Dublin (Ireland); Trinity College, Dublin (Ireland); and Westfield College, London (U.K.). Of the class of 2006, 33 percent participated in a study-abroad experience.

Academic Facilities

The Falvey Memorial Library provides resources and facilities for study and research by undergraduate students, graduate students, faculty members, and visiting scholars. The library's total seating capacity is 1,200. Its holdings include more than 800,000 volumes, 5,400 serial subscriptions, and more than a million microform items.

Costs

Tuition costs, including fees, averaged $34,320 for the 2007–08 academic year. Room and board costs for the full academic year averaged $9810. Expenses for books, travel, and personal supplies are estimated at $1000 for the year.

Financial Aid

Financial assistance is granted on the basis of need. The aid applicant must file the Free Application for Federal Student Aid (FAFSA) no later than February 7, with the request that the results be sent to the Villanova University Office of Financial Assistance. The family's income tax return for the previous year and Villanova's institutional financial aid application should be sent to Villanova's Office of Financial Assistance by February 7. Academic and athletic merit scholarships are also available.

Faculty

Villanova has 511 full-time and 309 part-time faculty members; 90 percent hold doctorates or the equivalent. The student-faculty ratio is 12:1.

Student Government

The Student Government of Villanova is a representative body of all students. Its purpose is to provide a channel of communication between students and the University, to promote student legislation, and to assist in concerns involving students and the Villanova community. The Student Government performs the double role of providing student representation in the formulation of University policies and of expanding student services. Student senators provide input on matters of policy as voting members of the University Senate and its committees.

Admission Requirements

The basic criteria for admission are the applicant's high school record and class standing, scores on the SAT and/or ACT (including the writing section), Villanova essay, and secondary-school counselor recommendation. In addition to the above items, a student must submit the Villanova Preliminary Application for Undergraduate Admission with the application fee and a completed Common Application by the appropriate deadline.

Application and Information

The regular decision deadline for receipt of the application by the Office of University Admission is January 7. The deadline for Early Action, Presidential Scholarship consideration, and Health Affiliation programs is November 1. Prospective students are encouraged to apply online at the University's Web site.

Office of University Admission
Villanova University
800 Lancaster Avenue
Villanova, Pennsylvania 19085-1672
Phone: 610-519-4000
Fax: 610-519-6450
E-mail: gotovu@villanova.edu
Web site: http://www.admission.villanova.edu

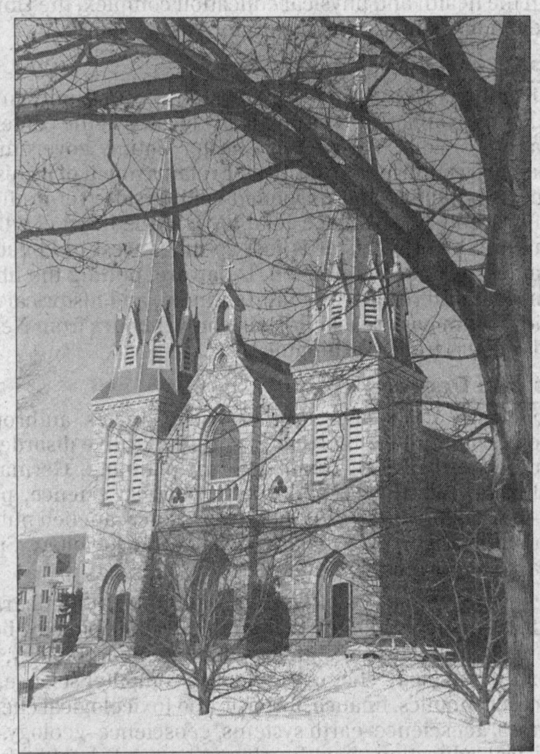

St. Thomas of Villanova Church.

WEST CHESTER UNIVERSITY OF PENNSYLVANIA

WEST CHESTER, PENNSYLVANIA

The University

West Chester University of Pennsylvania (WCU) is the second largest of the fourteen institutions in the Pennsylvania State System of Higher Education and the fourth-largest university in the Philadelphia metropolitan area. Officially founded in 1871, the University traces its heritage to the West Chester Academy, which existed from 1812 to 1869. The University's 402-acre campus has well-maintained facilities, including nine residence halls and two garden-style apartment complexes, plus a new performing arts center. In keeping with West Chester's rich heritage, the University's Quadrangle buildings, part of the original campus, are on the National Register of Historic Places.

While the University attracts the majority of its students from Pennsylvania, New Jersey, and Delaware, it also enrolls many students from other areas across the United States and from more than fifty countries. The undergraduate enrollment includes approximately 11,113 women and men full-time and 1,158 part-time.

Each year, the University community schedules an impressive series of events, including programs with well-known musicians, authors, political figures, and others. More than 210 campus groups in music, theater, athletics, and other activities, as well as clubs, fraternities, sororities, service organizations, and honor societies, provide students with the opportunity to participate in a full range of programs. The University offers twenty-three intercollegiate sports and eleven club sports for men and women. In addition to the facilities in the health and physical education complex, the University has a field house and a gymnasium for varsity sports.

Location

The University is located in West Chester, a community in southeastern Pennsylvania that is strategically located at the center of the mid-Atlantic corridor. The seat of Chester County government for more than two centuries, West Chester retains much of its historical charm in its buildings and unspoiled countryside, yet it offers the twenty-first-century advantages of a town in the heart of a thriving suburban area. West Chester is just 25 miles west of Philadelphia and 17 miles north of Wilmington, Delaware, putting the libraries, museums, cultural resources, entertainment, and historical sites of both cities within easy reach. It is also only 2 hours from New York City and 3 hours from Washington, D.C.

Majors and Degrees

The Bachelor of Arts is offered in American studies, anthropology, art, biology, communication studies, communicative disorders, English, French, geography–urban/regional planning, German, history, Latin, liberal studies, philosophy, political science, political science–international relations, political science–applied public administration, psychology, Russian, social work, sociology, Spanish, theater arts, and women's studies.

The Bachelor of Science is offered in accounting, athletic training, biochemistry, biology, biology–cell and molecular biology, biology-ecology, biology–medical technology, biology-microbiology, chemistry, chemistry–biology, chemistry–clinical, computer science, criminal justice, economics, finance, forensic and toxicological chemistry, geosciences, geoscience–earth systems, geoscience–geology, health and physical education, health science–general, health science–respiratory care, liberal studies–arts and sciences, liberal studies–science and mathematics, liberal studies–professional studies, management, marketing, nutrition and dietetics, pharmaceutical product development, physics, physics–engineering, public health–environmental, and public health–health promotion.

The Bachelor of Science in Nursing, the Bachelor of Fine Arts (studio arts), the Bachelor of Music (composition, music education, performance, theory and studies in an outside field) and the Bachelor of Social Work degrees are also offered.

The Bachelor of Science in Education degree is offered in biology, chemistry, communication, early childhood education, earth-space science–astronomy, earth-space science–geology, elementary education, English, mathematics, physics, and special education.

Paraprofessional studies are available in medicine. In cooperation with the Pennsylvania State University, West Chester University offers a 3-2 dual-degree program combining liberal arts, physics, and engineering. Also available are early admission assurance programs with Drexel School of Medicine, Pennsylvania State University College of Medicine, Philadelphia College of Osteopathic Medicine, Temple University School of Dental Medicine, and Arcadia University Physician Assistant Program. As a member of the State System of Higher Education (PASSHE), special admission opportunities for scholarships to the Widener School of Law–Harrisburg Campus are also available.

Certification programs are available in French, general science, health and physical education, Latin, Russian, social studies, and Spanish education teacher certification.

Interdisciplinary areas of study with transcript recognition include computer security certificate, ethnic studies, Honors College, Latin American studies, and Russian studies. Minors are available in most majors and in several interdisciplinary areas. The University also offers ROTC programs with cross-enrollment agreement with Widener University for Army ROTC and with St. Joseph's University for Air Force ROTC.

Academic Programs

West Chester University is a comprehensive, multipurpose institution now in its second century. The University comprises the College of Arts and Sciences, the College of Business and Public Affairs, the College of Education, the College of Health Sciences, and the College of Visual and Performing Arts. It operates on a two-semester basis; summer sessions are available.

An honors program is available to qualified students for both upper and lower division study; internships and field experiences, self-designed majors, and independent study are also offered. A variety of credit-by-examination programs are available.

Off-Campus Programs

Through the Study Abroad Program, students may spend one or more semesters in countries such as England, Italy, France, Australia, Spain, and Ireland. West Chester also sponsors a number of annual courses that include study abroad during spring, summer, and winter breaks.

West Chester University participates in the National Student Exchange Program, in which students spend up to a year at any one of more than 170 member schools across the United States, broadening their cultural and academic horizons. Automatic transfer of credit is arranged.

Academic Facilities

There are two libraries on the campus: the Francis Harvey Green Library and the Presser Music Library. Library collections include more than 890,000 print and electronic volumes, 9,200 print and electronic periodicals, 880,000 microforms, 48,000 sound recordings, and 7,900 films, videos, and DVDs. Services include interlibrary loan, electronic and print reserves, more than ninety public computer workstations, twenty laptops, a coffee café, and Internet access to more than 100 databases.

The University's extensive state-of-the-art computer facilities include more than 700 IBM and Apple workstations that are available to students and Internet access from residence halls and computer labs. The University has Braille printers, translators, and speech synthesizers for its visually impaired students. Students can use the computing facilities 16 hours a day.

The Boucher Science Center offers modern multimedia lecture halls, extensive laboratories, and study areas where students can work together. Boucher Science Center is connected to the Schmucker Science Center, which houses a fully equipped observatory and planetarium. The center's extensive laboratories have such instrumentation as automated spectrophotometers, electron analytical equipment, atomic absorption spectrometers, and a variety of chromatographs, including gas chromatograph–mass spectrometers.

The campus includes a 100-acre natural area for environmental studies; speech and hearing and reading clinics; two theaters; music facilities with practice, rehearsal, and listening rooms; a large, modern health and physical education complex that houses a gymnasium and a natatorium with two pool areas and a diving well; dance studios; research laboratories; physical therapy rooms; saunas; and a health resource center.

West Chester University is committed to providing barrier-free facilities for persons with impaired mobility.

Costs

West Chester University provides a high-quality education at an affordable cost. Full-time undergraduate students who are legal residents of Pennsylvania paid $5177 per year for tuition for 12 to 18 semester hours in 2006–07. For more than 18 semester hours or fewer than 12, the cost was $216 per semester hour. Out-of-state students were charged $12,994 per year for 12 to 18 semester hours and $539 per semester hour for more than 18 or fewer than 12. Room and board were $6590 per year for on-campus residents. Student fees were $1499 per year, plus a technology fee of $125 for in-state students and $188 for out-of-state students. Tuition is determined by the state.

Financial Aid

The financial aid available to students includes work-study programs, grants, loans, special awards, and scholarships. A limited number of merit scholarships are awarded based on the student's academic standing and accomplishments in high school. Students who qualify are invited to apply. About 73 percent of all full-time undergraduate students receive some form of aid.

Faculty

West Chester University has a faculty of nearly 800 members. The majority hold doctoral degrees, and many are engaged in research and serve as consultants in their field of expertise. The student-faculty ratio is 18:1.

Student Government

The Student Governmental Association represents all students on the West Chester campus. In addition, the Residence Hall Association represents resident students, and the Off Campus Student Association represents commuting students.

Admission Requirements

Applicants to West Chester University are evaluated on the basis of scholarship, character, and potential for achievement. The requirements for freshman admission consideration include graduation from an approved secondary school or a General Educational Development (GED) certificate from an approved agency; satisfactory scores on either the SAT, ACT, or TOEFL (for international applicants); and completion of a personal statement. Transfer applicants must have a minimum cumulative grade point average of 2.0 for admissions consideration. Certain academic programs may require an interview or specific course prerequisites. The University does have several other admissions options such as early admission and special admissions programs, including ACT 101. Based on the scores received on Advanced Placement (AP) tests and subject examinations administered through the College-Level Examination Program (CLEP), students may receive advanced placement or credit.

Application and Information

Students are admitted for the fall or spring semester. Freshman applicants for the fall semester are urged to begin the application procedure at the start of their senior year in high school. Transfers should begin the process beginning in January for the fall semester. Applicants for the spring semester should apply by November 1. International students must apply by March 1 for the fall semester and September 1 for the spring semester. The University operates on a modified rolling admission policy; applicants with the strongest qualifications are given priority, and their applications are processed expeditiously. Students are encouraged to visit WCU's campus. To arrange a visit or to attend an information session, students may call the Office of Admissions. For updated information or directions, students should visit the University's Web site.

For additional information and required forms, students may contact:

Office of Admissions
Emil J. Messikomer Hall
West Chester University of Pennsylvania
100 West Rosedale Avenue
West Chester, Pennsylvania 19383
Phone: 610-436-3411
877-315-2165 (toll-free)
E-mail: ugadmiss@wcupa.edu
Web site: http://www.wcupa.edu

A view of the west side of the Quadrangle at West Chester University.

WESTMINSTER COLLEGE

NEW WILMINGTON, PENNSYLVANIA

The College

Westminster College, an independent, coeducational liberal arts college related to the Presbyterian Church (U.S.A.), was founded in 1852. Westminster's liberal arts foundation thrives in a caring environment supported by an integrative curriculum featuring state-of-the-art technology and opportunities for involvement to prepare students for a diverse world. Westminster College is annually recognized among the nation's best liberal arts colleges by *U.S. News & World Report* and as one of the nation's best college buys by *Money*. Nearly 1,400 students benefit from individualized attention from dedicated faculty members while choosing from more than forty majors and nearly 100 campus organizations on the New Wilmington, Pennsylvania, campus. The College provides many programs to augment the academic and social life of the academic community, including lectures, dramatic productions, art exhibitions, concerts, symposia, dances, films, and other activities. Students may choose to participate in a wide variety of groups and activities, such as dramatics, publications, volunteer and social service teams, athletics, religious groups, musical groups, radio and television stations, fraternities and sororities, honoraries, and special interest groups.

A natatorium and physical education and fitness center are included among Westminster's major buildings, and athletics are carefully integrated into the overall educational program. A full range of intercollegiate and intramural sports for men and women gives each student the opportunity to participate at the level of his or her interest and ability. Westminster students compete in twenty varsity sports as Division III members of the NCAA. Westminster has been called the most successful football program at any level, based on its six national championships and eleven undefeated seasons, and the men's basketball team has had more wins than any other program in NAIA history. Nearly 99 percent of student athletes who letter in a varsity sport graduate.

Location

Westminster is located in New Wilmington, a small residential town in western Pennsylvania. The campus is surrounded by wooded hills, Amish farmlands, scenic country roads, and streams. The town is not far from several large cities. It is 60 miles north of Pittsburgh, 80 miles south of Erie, and 85 miles southeast of Cleveland. New Castle is 9 miles to the south, and Youngstown, Ohio, is 17 miles to the west. The College is within a few miles of I-79, I-80, and the Ohio and Pennsylvania turnpikes. Nearby cities provide transportation to all points by bus, and transportation is available from the Pittsburgh and Youngstown airports.

Majors and Degrees

Westminster College grants three undergraduate degrees: the Bachelor of Arts, the Bachelor of Science, and the Bachelor of Music. The choice of major field can be made from the following: accounting, biochemistry, biology, broadcast communications, business administration (finance, health administration, human resource management, and marketing), chemistry (forensic science), Christian education, communication studies, computer information systems, computer science, economics, elementary education (special education), English, fine art, French, history, Latin, mathematics, media art, molecular biology, music, music education, music performance, philosophy, physics, political science, psychology, public relations, religion, sacred music, sociology (criminal justice), Spanish, and theater. Interdisciplinary majors are available in environmental science, financial economics, intercultural studies, international business, international politics, neuroscience, and quantitative economics. Preprofessional programs are offered in dentistry, environmental science, health management systems, law, medicine, the ministry, occupational therapy, physical therapy, physician's assistant, and veterinary medicine. A 3-2 engineering program is offered in cooperation with Case Western Reserve University and Washington University in St. Louis.

Secondary education certification with a major in an academic discipline is offered.

Academic Programs

The liberal arts degree offered by Westminster College reflects the diversity and depth of the classical education and the practicality of its application. Good writing and speaking skills are emphasized, and science and philosophy become a part of life at Westminster.

Course requirements for graduation vary according to the major fields, but all-College requirements include courses in writing, oral communication, religion, computer science, foreign language, and physical education as well as courses from categories covering the humanities, fine arts, social sciences, natural sciences, and literature. Double majors, minors, and individual interdisciplinary programs are possible.

Westminster operates on a two-term academic year. The fall term runs from September through December, and the spring term runs from January through May.

Every four years since 1936, in conjunction with the Presidential election year, Westminster has held a Mock National Political Convention (for the party out of office) in which more than three fourths of the students have participated, naming their own "candidate."

Off-Campus Programs

Westminster engages in several cooperative programs with other colleges and institutions to provide students with opportunities for in-depth study off campus. Among these is a program at Berea College in Kentucky, in which students study the culture of southern Appalachia. Westminster also offers a Washington Semester in the nation's capital and a Sea Semester in conjunction with Boston University. In addition, it is possible to spend a semester or year studying in France, Germany, Spain, and other countries.

Academic Facilities

McGill Library and the J. S. Mack Science Library contain more than 220,000 volumes and receive about 970 periodicals per year. These library collections are supplemented through the College's membership in the Library Consortium and two computerized networks (one regional and the other national), which provide the best services possible through interlibrary loans and other library activities.

Westminster's campus extends more than 300 rolling acres and has more than twenty major buildings. The facilities include classrooms, a 300-seat theater, a 1,750-seat auditorium, radio and TV stations, and an outdoor environmental-science field laboratory. The Hoyt Science Resource Center contains modern science areas, including electron microscopes and an X-ray diffractor, expanded computer science facilities, and a planetarium.

Costs

Westminster College is one of the most affordable national liberal arts colleges in Pennsylvania and is annually listed as one of America's best college buys. For the academic year 2007–08, tuition and fees were $25,530, and room and board were $7660, bringing the total cost for the year to $33,190.

Financial Aid

About 98 percent of Westminster's students receive some sort of financial aid. Scholarships, Federal Stafford Student Loans, grants, and campus employment are offered to students who have financial need. The student's eligibility for financial aid is determined by the Free Application for Federal Student Aid (FAFSA) form. Also, non-need scholarships of up to more than 50 percent of tuition are awarded to students of high academic ability; these are renewable each year if the student maintains good academic standing. Activity grants in music and theater are also available. Information is available through the Dean of Admissions or Director of Financial Aid.

Faculty

There are 99 full-time faculty members at Westminster College, 91 percent of whom hold earned doctorates or the highest terminal degree in their field. The student-faculty ratio is 12:1. The faculty members are characterized by their interest in and concern for their students.

Student Government

All students, by virtue of their undergraduate registration and payment of fees, are members of the Student Government Association. The Student Senate, the central representative and legislative organization of the Student Government Association, recognizes student organizations, allocates money appropriated by the Board of Trustees, and carries out other responsibilities. In cooperation with the staff of the Dean of Student Affairs, the student senators, through the Campus Programming Committee, plan an extensive student activities program.

Admission Requirements

Students admitted to the College should have received a high school diploma and should have completed a college-preparatory program of study in secondary school, consisting of a minimum of 16 units (including at least 4 units of English, 2 units of a foreign language, 3 units of mathematics, and 2 units each of lab science and social studies). Each new applicant is required to take the SAT or the ACT, preferably during the junior year of high school or early in the senior year.

Application and Information

A completed application with the $35 application fee may be submitted anytime after the student's junior year in secondary school. The student should also see that the required SAT or ACT scores and a high school transcript are sent to the College. The transcript should include grades from the ninth grade through the eleventh grade.

For application forms and further information, students should contact:

Dean of Admissions
Westminster College
New Wilmington, Pennsylvania 16172
Phone: 800-942-8033 (toll-free)
E-mail: admis@westminster.edu
Web site: http://www.westminster.edu

A student takes a break from studying and gets her feet wet at Westminster College.

WIDENER UNIVERSITY

CHESTER, PENNSYLVANIA

Widener University

The University

Widener University is a leading metropolitan university that connects curricula to social issues through civic engagement. It comprises eight school and colleges that offer liberal arts and sciences, professional, and preprofessional curricula leading to associate, baccalaureate, master's, and doctoral degrees. The University's campuses are located in Chester, Exton, and Harrisburg, Pennsylvania, and Wilmington, Delaware, and serve some 6,500 students.

Widener provides a unique combination of liberal arts and professional education in a challenging, scholarly, and culturally diverse learning environment. More than 100 programs of study leading to associate, baccalaureate, master's, and doctoral degrees are available. Currently, there are 6,571 students, including 1,714 graduate students, 2,775 full-time undergraduate students, and 635 evening and weekend undergraduate students. Widener University's School of Law is housed at the Wilmington, Delaware, and Harrisburg, Pennsylvania, campuses, where 1,447 students are enrolled.

In the fall of 2004, Widener opened the Exton Campus, which houses adult undergraduate education and the Osher Lifelong Learning Institute, a learning cooperative for area retirees. The institute is the first facility of its kind in the Philadelphia metropolitan region.

Widener offers diverse, high-quality extracurricular activities. More than eighty student organizations are recognized at Widener, including student government, musical groups, honor societies, fraternities, sororities, academic and professional associations, publications, social and recreational clubs, and an FM radio station, recording studio, and TV production studio. Widener offers ten varsity sports for women and ten for men, as well as several intramural sports. Widener's student-athletes compete at the NCAA Division III intercollegiate level. Traditional residence halls, apartments, and theme houses are available. Housing is guaranteed for all four years of undergraduate study.

Location

Located in Delaware County, Pennsylvania, Widener's Main Campus is easily accessible from I-95, I-476, and Philadelphia International Airport and is an easy commute from southern New Jersey and Delaware. The University is only 15 minutes from historic Philadelphia; approximately 2 hours from either New York City or Washington, D.C.; and about 1 hour from Baltimore or the New Jersey beaches.

Majors and Degrees

Widener offers Bachelor of Arts and Bachelor of Science degrees in the following fields: accounting, anthropology, biochemistry, biology, chemical engineering, chemistry, civil engineering, communication studies, computer information systems, computer science, creative writing, criminal justice, early childhood education, economics, electrical engineering, elementary education, English, environmental science, fine arts, French, government and politics, history, hospitality management, international business, international relations, management, mathematics, mechanical engineering, nursing, physics, psychology, science administration, science education, social work, sociology, Spanish, special education, and women's studies.

Dual majors may also be taken in many areas, and a multidisciplinary (open) major may be created by any degree-seeking candidate in consultation with a faculty adviser. Freshmen who are undecided about a major may elect the Exploratory Studies program during the first year. In addition, options exist in the School of Business Administration and the Center for Education for accelerated programs leading to combined undergraduate and M.B.A., Master of Science, or Master of Education degrees.

The Center for Education offers two options for students seeking certification in elementary and/or early childhood education: the bachelor's degree in elementary and/or early childhood education or the bachelor's degree in an academic major with certification. Students can also choose the bachelor's degree in special education. Multiple secondary certifications include bilingual education, biology, chemistry, earth and space science, English, French, general science, math, physics, social studies, Spanish, and special education.

Academic Programs

The distribution of required courses and the quantitative requirements are set by the College of Arts and Sciences, the School of Engineering, the School of Human Service Professions, the School of Business Administration, the School of Hospitality Management, and the School of Nursing. All students are required to complete a minimum of 12 semester hours in each of the three areas of humanities, social science, and science/mathematics. (A semester hour consists of 1 hour per week in the classroom each semester or 2 to 3 hours per week in laboratory or fieldwork each semester.) An overall academic average of at least 2.0 is required for graduation. In addition to satisfying all other degree requirements, a candidate must complete in residence at Widener the final 45 semester hours required for that degree.

High school students who participate in the Advanced Placement (AP) Program of the College Board and earn scores of 3 or better may receive degree credit for the subjects concerned upon submission of the examination results.

Widener operates on a two-semester calendar. The first semester begins in early September and ends before Christmas; the second semester runs from mid-January to mid-May. The summer sessions include one presession of three weeks and two regular sessions of five weeks each, providing fully accredited courses in economics and management, engineering, the humanities, the physical sciences, and the social sciences.

Off-Campus Programs

Four-year cooperative education programs are offered to computer science majors and students in the Schools of Engineering and Business Administration. These programs are designed to augment the curricula with two periods of full-time, off-campus work experience (totaling twelve months of employment) while enabling the student to earn a bachelor's degree within the normal four-year period. Field experience is also offered in education, psychology, and social work. Experiential education opportunities are available in all areas of study.

Academic Facilities

The academic buildings on Widener's Main Campus provide an eclectic mix of tradition and cutting-edge technology. A 50,000-square-foot addition to Kirkbride Hall, the University's science and engineering building, opened in December 2004. The addition provides new classrooms, state-of-the-art teaching and research laboratories for biology and engineering, and a rooftop astronomical observatory. The Leslie C. Quick Jr. Center, which opened in 2002, is home to the School of Business Administration and houses offices, multimedia classrooms, an information systems lab, and a simulated Wall Street trading room. Beautiful Old Main, built in 1867 and featured on the National Register of Historic Places, houses the School of Nursing as well as a variety of administrative offices. Other academic buildings include the Robert J. Bruce Graduate Center, home to the School of Human Service Professions; Academic Center North, which houses the School of Hospitality Management; and Kapelski Learning Center, a modern classroom facility. At the center of the campus is the Wolfgram Memorial Library, which currently houses more than 200,000 volumes and 170,000 microforms. Through interlibrary loan, students also have access to resources of the School of Law Library, which holds an additional 570,000 volumes.

University Center is the hub of campus activity, with student and faculty dining rooms, a convenience store, coffee shop, TV lounge, post office, bookstore, bank branch, and Student Life Center. Alumni Auditorium—built with funds donated by the Alumni Association—houses the Burt Mustin Memorial Theatre, a 400-seat auditorium for dramatics, lectures, movies, and mass meetings. The University also has a modern, all-weather sports facility, the Schwartz Athletic Center, which features an indoor track and a 3,000-seat athletic stadium.

Costs

Tuition for the 2007–08 academic year for most students was $28,180. The cost of room and board averaged about $10,240, depending on the accommodations selected. Families may spread the payment of tuition over several months each semester or year.

Financial Aid

The goal of Widener's financial aid program is to make sure that every qualified student who wants to attend Widener has the financial resources to do so. Widener University offers both need-based and merit-based financial aid. Currently, 90 percent of the student body receives some form of financial assistance. Financial aid consists of scholarships, grants, loans, and employment, which may be offered to students singly or in various combinations. Special merit scholarships are available to incoming students of exceptional academic ability or achievement. Scholarships are also awarded to students with talent in music or student leadership. Awards range from $2000 per year to full tuition.

Students who submit an application for financial aid are considered for all aid and scholarship programs for which they are eligible. Financial aid applicants are notified of their aid in the spring prior to their enrollment at the University. Students are required to file the Free Application for Federal Student Aid (FAFSA) and the Widener University Undergraduate Financial Aid Application. The priority deadline for new students is February 15.

Faculty

The University's full-time faculty of 309 members is drawn from leading national and international graduate schools. Doctoral and terminal degrees are held by 90 percent of the faculty members. The student-faculty ratio is 12:1, and the average class size is 16.

Student Government

The Student Government Association (SGA) coordinates student activities and exercises legislative, executive, and judicial authority. Participation benefits the students' total collegiate experience, and students are encouraged to become active in the SGA.

Admission Requirements

Admission to Widener is competitive and is based primarily upon the quality of the high school and previous educational record. Recommendations, extracurricular involvement, the personal essay, and the pattern of test scores are also weighed in the decision.

Application and Information

The University offers a nonbinding early action program and has a priority application deadline of February 15 for fall admission. Transfer applicants are encouraged to apply and are also admitted on a rolling basis.

For more information or an appointment, students should contact:

Office of Admissions
Widener University
One University Place
Chester, Pennsylvania 19013-5792
Phone: 610-499-4126
E-mail: admissions.office@widener.edu
Web site: http://www.widener.edu

WILKES UNIVERSITY

WILKES-BARRE, PENNSYLVANIA

The University

Located at the foothills of the Pocono Mountains, along the shore of the Susquehanna River and within walking distance of downtown Wilkes-Barre, Pennsylvania, Wilkes University is a private, comprehensive institution with 2,400 undergraduate students. The University is structured into the College of Arts, Humanities, and Social Sciences; the College of Science and Engineering; the Nesbitt College of Pharmacy and Nursing; the Sidhu School of Business and Leadership; and University College (for undecided students). Wilkes offers a broad range of bachelor's and master's degree programs in the humanities, social and natural sciences, engineering, business administration, nursing, and education as well as the Doctor of Pharmacy degree.

The Wilkes campus features a parklike quadrangle surrounded by modern classroom buildings and historic nineteenth-century mansions that have been restored as student residences and academic buildings. Campus facilities include a sports and conference center, an outdoor athletic complex and field house, a state-of-the-art science classroom building, a modern academic classroom/office building, a performing arts center, an indoor recreation center, and a student center with a food court, café, entertainment rooms, post office, and ballroom.

Hands-on learning, small classes, and strong student-professor relationships are the hallmarks of the Wilkes experience. Programs are designed to prepare students with a well-rounded liberal arts foundation that cultivates independent thinking and gives students the credentials necessary for entrance into graduate and professional schools and professional life. Academic advising integrated with career planning is stressed, and hands-on experiences are provided in laboratory, internship, and cooperative education settings. Free tutorial services are available to all students as well.

The University is accredited by the Middle States Association of Colleges and Schools and has specialized accreditation in the sciences, engineering, nursing, education, and business. The Nesbitt College of Pharmacy and Nursing was granted full accreditation by the American Council on Pharmaceutical Education. More than 99 percent of students are employed or attending graduate/professional school within six months of receiving their degrees.

First-year students enrolling prior to May 1 are guaranteed housing. Campus housing is available for all four years. Architecturally, residence halls vary from modern, multifloor buildings to mansions listed on the National Register of Historic Places. Medical and dental care, department stores, specialty shops, a multiscreen theater, restaurants, a bowling alley, a bus station, and other services are available within three blocks of the campus. A large number of nearby houses of religious worship welcome students' participation.

At Wilkes University, student activities complement academic life. Intercollegiate athletics encompass fifteen Division III sports, and an active and varied intramural program is offered. More than seventy clubs and organizations recognize student achievement and provide opportunities for leadership development, professional growth, and community service. The student-run Programming Board schedules movies and performances by comedians, musicians, and other entertainers, while other organizations sponsor dinner dances, block parties, and special events. The professionally run Student Development Office organizes various activities based on leadership, adventure, or cultural themes, as well as coordinates a unique e-mentor program designed to assist freshmen with the transition to college life. Wilkes students are active community volunteers, participating in numerous local and national service projects each year.

Master's degrees are awarded in business administration, creative writing, education, electrical engineering, engineering operations and strategy, and nursing. The University offers a six-year program leading to the Doctor of Pharmacy degree. Wilkes is the first school in Pennsylvania to offer a dual Doctor of Pharmacy and Master of Business Administration degree. The University also offers doctoral degrees in educational leadership and nursing.

Location

The Luzerne County seat, Wilkes-Barre is a medium-sized city of 50,000 in the midst of a metropolitan area of 400,000. A wide range of recreational facilities are minutes away, including the Lackawanna County Multi-Purpose Stadium (home of the Wilkes-Barre/Scranton Yankees Triple A baseball team); the Wachovia Arena, which serves as home for the Wilkes-Barre/Scranton Penguins hockey team and Pioneers arena football team; the Pocono Mountain ski resorts; numerous golf courses; state parks; outdoor tennis courts; and Pocono Downs harness racing, with the Mohegan Sun casino.

The University is located in the historical district, between the entertainment and residential sections of the city. The entertainment district begins at the F. M. Kirby Center of Performing Arts, featuring symphony, ballet, theatrical, and musical performances, and encompasses the Wilkes University/King's College Barnes and Noble bookstore and café. Other area cultural offerings include art galleries, ethnic and community festivals, and numerous libraries and museums. The city is also approximately 2 hours from the cultural resources of both New York City and Philadelphia.

Wilkes-Barre is in proximity to the intersection of Interstates 80, 81, and 476 and within 3 to 6 hours of other major cities, such as Washington, D.C.; Baltimore; and Boston. The Wilkes-Barre/Scranton International Airport enables travelers to arrive at most domestic destinations via one-stop or nonstop flights.

Majors and Degrees

Wilkes University offers Bachelor of Arts, Bachelor of Business Administration, Bachelor of Science, and Bachelor of Fine Arts degrees. Majors include accounting; applied and engineering sciences; biochemistry; biology; business administration (concentrations in economics, finance, international business, and marketing); chemistry; clinical laboratory sciences; communications (concentrations in journalism, organizational communications, public relations, rhetoric and public communications, and telecommunications); computer information systems; computer science; criminology; earth and environmental sciences; electrical engineering; elementary, secondary, and special education (all with certification); engineering management; English (concentrations in literature and writing); entrepreneurship; environmental engineering; history; integrative media; international studies; mathematics; mechanical engineering; musical theater; nursing; philosophy; political science; psychology; sociology; and theater arts.

The premedical and prelaw preparation programs are particularly strong. In addition to the University's prepharmacy program, other preprofessional programs are available in dentistry, optometry, podiatry, and veterinary science. The University offers affiliated programs in medicine with the Philadelphia College of Osteopathic Medicine; in optometry with the Pennsylvania College of Optometry and the State University of New York (SUNY) College of Optometry; in podiatry with Temple University School of Podiatric Medicine; in occupational therapy with Temple University; in physical therapy with Drexel University, Temple University, and Widener University; in medical technology/clinical laboratory sciences with Robert Packer Hospital; and in psychology with Widener University.

Academic Programs

Through a rigorous curriculum that emphasizes hands-on experience and training, Wilkes helps students to prepare in all majors to adapt to a technologically and socially evolving world. To graduate, students are required to complete a core curriculum and must complete from 120 to 136 credits, depending upon their major field. Graduates demonstrate mastery of the fundamental intellectual skills as well as the essential concepts and techniques of their field. Wilkes also teaches students responsibility and independence by expecting and encouraging active participation in the classroom and laboratory.

The University operates on a dual-semester calendar, with optional summer sessions and a January intersession. Advanced Placement test credits are accepted.

Off-Campus Programs

An extensive cooperative education program is available to all students, with credit applicable in most major fields. Many government offices and private businesses in northeastern Pennsylvania, as well as in New York City, Philadelphia, Harrisburg, and Washington, D.C., employ Wilkes students. The study-abroad adviser works with interested students, placing them in the situation best suited to their academic pursuits. Most recently, students have attended programs in Austria, the Dominican Republic, England, France, Germany, Italy, and Spain.

Academic Facilities

The Eugene S. Farley Library has more than 220,000 volumes of books and bound journals, 857 current print journal and newspaper subscriptions, hundreds of database searches, and 800,000 microforms. Complete laboratory facilities are available for biology, chemistry, earth and environmental sciences, engineering, integrative media, nursing, pharmacy, and psychology. Student-produced programming is broadcast from WCLH-FM, the University's 2,000-watt radio station, and transmitted from a professional-quality television studio via a local cable provider. Technology-enhanced classrooms contain the new Intel-based Apple computers for student use. The Sordoni Art Gallery is professionally equipped and staffed and produces exhibits each year by regionally, nationally, and internationally known artists. The Dorothy Dickson Darte Center for the Performing Arts contains a fully equipped 500-seat theater for the presentation of plays, concerts, ballet, and other performances and lectures. Adjoining the center are studios, practice and rehearsal rooms, and faculty offices for the Department of Visual and Performing Arts. Breiseth Hall accommodates extensive computer facilities, psychology research laboratories, an integrative media lab, and modern classrooms with the latest audiovisual equipment. The University also operates a state-of-the-art distance learning facility that allows global conferencing and study using Internet and videoconferencing technology.

Costs

For the 2007–08 academic year, tuition and fees were $23,970 per year, and room and board were $10,127. Books cost approximately $700 per year.

Financial Aid

Financial aid is available to those students who demonstrate quality academic ability and/or financial need, as verified by the Free Application for Federal Student Aid (FAFSA). Merit-based and need-based aid is available from Wilkes University for qualified students. Scholarships ranging from $5000 to $13,000 per year are available to students solely on the basis of academic ability. Approximately 96 percent of the student body receive some type of financial assistance, including scholarships, grants, loans, and work-study awards.

Faculty

Wilkes University has a nationally recruited full-time faculty of 133 members, approximately 91 percent of whom have earned Ph.D.'s or terminal degrees in their chosen field. Faculty evaluation criteria emphasize teaching excellence and effective advising, while recognizing continued scholarly activities. The student-faculty ratio is 13:1.

Student Government

An active student government provides a structure for student participation in University governance and student discipline. The Inter-Residence Council and Commuter Council coordinate extracurricular activities for on-campus and commuter students.

Admission Requirements

Admission to Wilkes University is traditional. SAT or ACT scores are required. In cases where a student has taken the examination more than once, scores from the highest testing in each category are used in the evaluation process. Applicants for the freshman class should either have completed or be in the process of completing a college-preparatory course of study, including 3 to 4 years of mathematics, social studies, science, and English. Additional courses should be elected in academic subjects according to individual interests. Acceptable electives include foreign language and computing, among others. Students who have not followed this pattern may still qualify for admission if there is other strong evidence of preparation for college work. Letters of recommendation are not required but may be submitted. Students intending to pursue a major in pharmacy or pharmaceutical science or a major in the College of Science and Engineering should have completed algebra I and II, geometry, and trigonometry prior to enrollment. Students intending to major in nursing should have completed courses in biology and chemistry. An audition is required for all prospective musical theater and theater arts students. Transfer students must submit a transcript from every college previously attended. All students are admitted to the University and not to specific departments, with the exception of the professional Nesbitt College of Pharmacy and Nursing and the Department of Visual and Performing Arts. Students individually receive academic advisement at the time of registration and throughout their enrollment.

Wilkes University is an Equal Opportunity/Affirmative Action institution. No applicant shall be denied admission to the University because of race, color, gender, religion, national or ethnic origin, sexual orientation, or handicap.

Application and Information

Applications for admission should be completed early in the senior year of secondary school and sent to the Admissions Office. Applications are reviewed after all of the student's credentials have been received. The review of applications generally begins on September 15, and notification of the University's decision reaches the student two to four weeks after the application file is complete. The priority deadline for all applications is March 1; applications for the Guaranteed Seat Pharmacy Program must be received by February 1. Other health science programs may have additional deadlines; students should contact the Admissions Office for more information.

Admissions Office
Wilkes University
84 West South Street
Wilkes-Barre, Pennsylvania 18766
Phone: 570-408-4400
800-945-5378 Ext. 4400 (toll-free)
Web site: http://www.wilkes.edu

PUERTO RICO

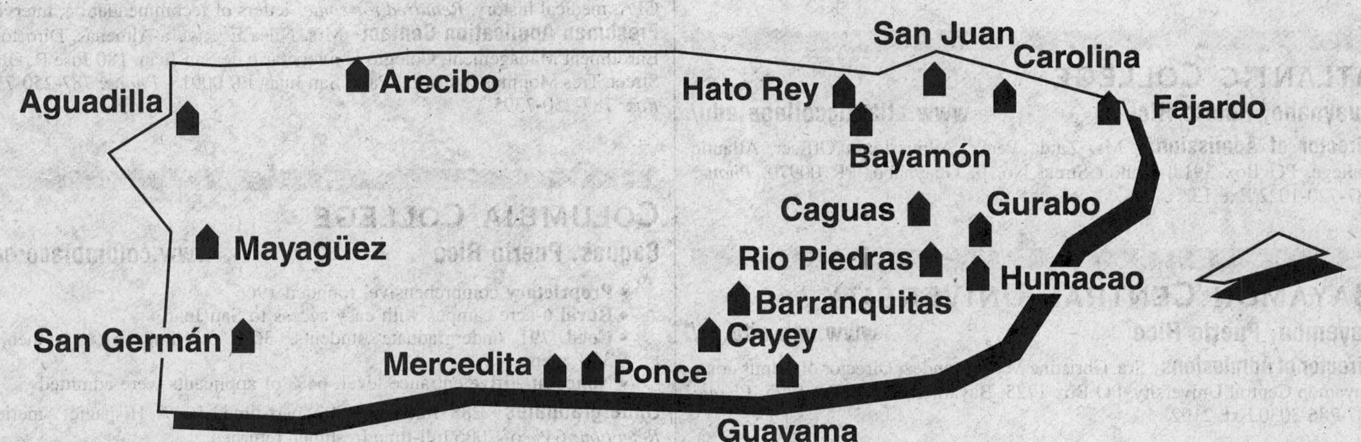
San Juan
Carolina
Aguadilla
Arecibo
Hato Rey
Fajardo
Bayamón
Caguas
Gurabo
Mayagüez
Rio Piedras
Humacao
Barranquitas
San Germán
Cayey
Mercedita
Ponce
Guayama

AMERICAN UNIVERSITY OF PUERTO RICO

Bayamón, Puerto Rico **www.aupr.edu/**

Freshman Application Contact Ms. Margarita Cruz, Director of Admissions, American University of Puerto Rico, PO Box 2037, Bayamón, PR 00960-2037. *Phone:* 787-740-6410. *Fax:* 787-785-7377.

ATLANTIC COLLEGE

Guaynabo, Puerto Rico **www.atlanticcollege.edu/**

Director of Admissions Ms. Zaida Perez, Admission's Officer, Atlantic College, PO Box 3918, Colton Street No. 9, Guaynabo, PR 00970. *Phone:* 787-720-1022 Ext. 13.

BAYAMÓN CENTRAL UNIVERSITY

Bayamón, Puerto Rico **www.ucb.edu.pr/**

Director of Admissions Sra. Christine M. Hernandez, Director of Admissions, Bayamón Central University, PO Box 1725, Bayamón, PR 00960-1725. *Phone:* 787-786-3030 Ext. 2102.

CARIBBEAN UNIVERSITY

Bayamón, Puerto Rico **www.caribbean.edu/**

Director of Admissions Mr. Hector Gracia, Director of Admissions, Caribbean University, Box 493, Bayamón, PR 00960-0493. *Phone:* 787-780-0070 Ext. 226.

CARLOS ALBIZU UNIVERSITY

San Juan, Puerto Rico **www.albizu.edu/**

Director of Admissions Mr. Carlos Rodriguez, Admissions Department, Carlos Albizu University, 151 Tanca Street, San Juan, PR 00901. *Phone:* 787-725-6500 Ext. 1521. *Fax:* 787-721-7187. *E-mail:* crodriguez@albizu.edu.

COLEGIO BIBLICO PENTECOSTAL

St. Just, Puerto Rico **www.cbp.edu/**

Director of Admissions Ms. Carolyn Figueroa, Registrar, Colegio Biblico Pentecostal, PO Box 901, St. Just, PR 00978-0901. *Phone:* 787-761-0640 Ext. 231. *Fax:* 787-748-9220. *E-mail:* registraduriachp@yahoo.com.

COLEGIO PENTECOSTAL MIZPA

Río Piedras, Puerto Rico

Director of Admissions Admissions Department, Colegio Pentecostal Mizpa, Bo Caimito Road 199, Apartado 20966, Río Piedras, PR 00928-0966.

COLEGIO UNIVERSITARIO DE SAN JUAN

San Juan, Puerto Rico **www.cunisanjuan.edu/**

- **City-supported** primarily 2-year, founded 1971
- **Urban** 5-acre campus
- **Endowment** $14.0 million
- **Coed**
- **Noncompetitive** entrance level

Faculty *Student/faculty ratio:* 13:1.
Academics *Calendar:* semesters. *Degrees:* certificates, diplomas, associate, and bachelor's.
Student Life *Campus security:* 24-hour patrols.
Standardized Tests *Required for some:* SAT (for admission), CEEB.
Costs (2007–08) *Tuition:* nonresident $2950 full-time. Full-time tuition and fees vary according to course load. Part-time tuition and fees vary according to course load. *Required fees:* $330 full-time. *Room and board:* $4850; room only: $1500.
Financial Aid Of all full-time matriculated undergraduates who enrolled in 2006, 127 Federal Work-Study jobs (averaging $618). 12 state and other part-time jobs (averaging $2991).
Applying *Application fee:* $15. *Required:* high school transcript, minimum 2.0 GPA, medical history. *Required for some:* letters of recommendation, interview.
Freshman Application Contact Mrs. Nilsa E. Rivera-Almenas, Director of Enrollment Management, Colegio Universitario de San Juan, 180 Jose R. Oliver Street, Tres Monjitas Industrial Park, San Juan, PR 00918. *Phone:* 787-250-7111. *Fax:* 787-250-7395.

COLUMBIA COLLEGE

Caguas, Puerto Rico **www.columbiaco.edu/**

- **Proprietary** comprehensive, founded 1966
- **Rural** 6-acre campus with easy access to San Juan
- **Coed** 791 undergraduate students, 36% full-time, 67% women, 33% men
- **Noncompetitive** entrance level, 64% of applicants were admitted

Undergraduates 288 full-time, 503 part-time. 100% Hispanic American. *Retention:* 64% of 2006 full-time freshmen returned.
Freshmen *Admission:* 479 applied, 307 admitted, 101 enrolled. *Average high school GPA:* 2.0.
Faculty *Total:* 91, 15% full-time, 4% with terminal degrees. *Student/faculty ratio:* 14:1.
Majors Administrative assistant and secretarial science; business administration and management; business/commerce; electrical, electronic and communications engineering technology; management information systems; nursing (registered nurse training); nursing science.
Academics *Calendar:* semesters. *Degrees:* certificates, associate, bachelor's, and master's. *Special study options:* accelerated degree program, adult/continuing education programs, external degree program, independent study, part-time degree program.
Computers on Campus 55 computers/terminals are available on campus for general student use.
Student Life *Housing:* college housing not available. *Campus security:* 24-hour patrols. *Student services:* personal/psychological counseling.
Costs (2007–08) *Tuition:* $5775 full-time, $145 per unit part-time. *Required fees:* $655 full-time, $655 per term part-time.
Applying *Application fee:* $50. *Required:* high school transcript. *Required for some:* essay or personal statement, minimum 2.0 GPA, 3 letters of recommendation, interview. *Application deadline:* rolling (freshmen). *Notification:* continuous (freshmen).
Freshman Application Contact Mrs. Xiomara Sanchez, Admission Coordinator, Columbia College, PO Box 8517, Caguas, PR 00726. *Phone:* 787-743-4041 Ext. 239. *Toll-free phone:* 800-981-4877 Ext. 239. *Fax:* 787-744-7031. *E-mail:* xsanchez@columbianco.edu.

COLUMBIA COLLEGE

Yauco, Puerto Rico **www.columbiaco.edu/**

- **Proprietary** primarily 2-year, founded 1976
- **Coed** 440 undergraduate students, 100% full-time, 30% women, 70% men
- 80% of applicants were admitted

Undergraduates 440 full-time. 100% Hispanic American.
Freshmen *Admission:* 676 applied, 539 admitted. *Average high school GPA:* 2.0.
Faculty *Total:* 41, 27% full-time, 7% with terminal degrees. *Student/faculty ratio:* 11:1.
Majors Administrative assistant and secretarial science; business administration and management; business/commerce; electrical, electronic and communications engineering technology; management information systems; nursing (registered nurse training); nursing science.
Academics *Calendar:* semesters. *Degrees:* certificates, associate, and bachelor's.

Computers on Campus 44 computers/terminals are available on campus for general student use.
Student Life *Housing:* college housing not available. *Activities and organizations:* Nursing Group, Librarian Group. *Student services:* personal/psychological counseling.
Costs (2007–08) *Tuition:* $5540 full-time, $140 per unit part-time. *Required fees:* $440 full-time, $655 per term part-time.
Applying *Application fee:* $50. *Application deadline:* rolling (freshmen). *Notification:* continuous (freshmen).
Freshman Application Contact Ms. Rosario Padilla, Admissions, Columbia College, Box 3062, Yauco, PR 00698. *Phone:* 787-856-0845 Ext. 11. *Fax:* 787-267-2335. *E-mail:* rpadilla@columbiaco.edu.

CONSERVATORIO DE MUSICA

San Juan, Puerto Rico **www.cmpr.edu/**

Director of Admissions Eutimia Santiago, Admissions Department, Conservatorio de Musica, Calle Rafael Lamar #350, Esquina F. D. Roosevelt, San Juan, PR 00918-2199. *Phone:* 787-751-0160 Ext. 275. *Fax:* 787-754-6284. *E-mail:* esantiago@cmpr.gobierno.pr.

CONSERVATORY OF MUSIC OF PUERTO RICO

San Juan, Puerto Rico **www.cmpr.edu/**

Freshman Application Contact Ms. Sandra Rodriquez, Marketing and Recruitment Officer, Conservatory of Music of Puerto Rico, 350 Calle Rafael Lamar, San Juian, PR 00718. *Phone:* 787-751-6180 Ext. 285.

ELECTRONIC DATA PROCESSING COLLEGE OF PUERTO RICO

Hato Rey, Puerto Rico **www.edpcollege.edu/**

- **Proprietary** comprehensive, founded 1968
- **Urban** 1-acre campus
- **Coed** 828 undergraduate students, 77% full-time, 53% women, 47% men
- **Minimally difficult** entrance level, 100% of applicants were admitted

Undergraduates 639 full-time, 189 part-time. Students come from 1 other state, 100% Hispanic American, 21% transferred in. *Retention:* 92% of 2006 full-time freshmen returned.
Freshmen *Admission:* 204 applied, 204 admitted, 204 enrolled. *Average high school GPA:* 2.00.
Faculty *Total:* 75, 17% full-time, 11% with terminal degrees. *Student/faculty ratio:* 19:1.
Majors Administrative assistant and secretarial science; business administration and management; computer programming; computer systems networking and telecommunications; digital communication and media/multimedia; electrical, electronic and communications engineering technology.
Academics *Calendar:* semesters. *Degrees:* associate, bachelor's, and master's. *Special study options:* academic remediation for entering students, accelerated degree program, adult/continuing education programs, distance learning, English as a second language, independent study, internships, part-time degree program, services for LD students, summer session for credit. *ROTC:* Army (c), Air Force (c).
Computers on Campus 24 computers/terminals are available on campus for general student use. Campuswide network is available. Wireless service is available via entire campus.
Student Life *Housing:* college housing not available. *Activities and organizations:* Student Council, Graduate Student Association. *Campus security:* security and emergency telephones in working hours. *Student services:* personal/psychological counseling.
Standardized Tests *Required:* CEEB Placement Test (for admission).
Costs (2008–09) *Tuition:* $4380 full-time, $146 per credit part-time. *Required fees:* $520 full-time, $260 per term part-time.
Applying *Options:* deferred entrance. *Application fee:* $15. *Required:* high school transcript, minimum 2.0 GPA, placement test or College Board exam, vaccination certificate, copy of social security number. *Required for some:* letters of recommendation, interview, placement test or College Board exam, vaccination certificate, copy of social security number. *Application deadlines:* rolling (freshmen), rolling (transfers).
Freshman Application Contact Ms. Leila M. Andino, Electronic Data Processing College of Puerto Rico, 555 Munoz Rivera Avenue, San Juan, PR 00919-2303. *Phone:* 787-765-3560. *Fax:* 787-777-0024. *E-mail:* landino@edpcollege.edu.

ELECTRONIC DATA PROCESSING COLLEGE OF PUERTO RICO–SAN SEBASTIAN

San Sebastian, Puerto Rico **www.edpcollege.edu/**

Director of Admissions Admissions Department, Electronic Data Processing College of Puerto Rico–San Sebastian, Avenue Betances #49, San Sebastian, PR 00685. *Phone:* 787-896-2252 Ext. 238. *Fax:* 787-896-0066.

ESCUELA DE ARTES PLASTICAS DE PUERTO RICO

San Juan, Puerto Rico **www.eap.edu/**

- **Commonwealth-supported** 4-year, founded 1966
- **Urban** campus
- **Endowment** $323,000
- **Coed**
- **Moderately difficult** entrance level

Faculty *Student/faculty ratio:* 11:1.
Academics *Calendar:* semesters. *Degree:* bachelor's.
Student Life *Campus security:* 24-hour emergency response devices and patrols, security cameras, private police.
Standardized Tests *Required:* SAT (for admission).
Costs (2007–08) *Tuition:* area resident $2250 full-time, $75 per credit part-time. Full-time tuition and fees vary according to course load. Part-time tuition and fees vary according to course load. *Required fees:* $212 full-time, $212 per year part-time. *Room and board:* Room and board charges vary according to housing facility.
Financial Aid Of all full-time matriculated undergraduates who enrolled in 2000, 256 applied for aid, 256 were judged to have need. 10 Federal Work-Study jobs (averaging $1800). *Average percent of need met:* 82.
Applying *Application fee:* $20. *Required:* essay or personal statement, high school transcript, minimum 2.0 GPA, interview, portfolio. *Recommended:* letters of recommendation.
Freshman Application Contact Mrs. Nadja Crespo; Mrs. Yvette Munoz, Admission Assistant, Escuela de Artes Plasticas de Puerto Rico, PO Box 9021112, San Juan, PR 00902-1112. *Phone:* 787-729-0007. *Fax:* 787-725-8111. *E-mail:* nadjac_eap@yahoo.com.

INTER AMERICAN UNIVERSITY OF PUERTO RICO, AGUADILLA CAMPUS

Aguadilla, Puerto Rico **www.aguadilla.inter.edu/**

- **Independent** comprehensive, founded 1957, part of Inter American University of Puerto Rico
- **Small-town** 50-acre campus
- **Endowment** $981,667
- **Coed** 3,953 undergraduate students, 85% full-time, 56% women, 44% men
- **Moderately difficult** entrance level

Undergraduates 3,357 full-time, 596 part-time. Students come from 1 other state, 100% Hispanic American.
Freshmen *Admission:* 791 enrolled. *Average high school GPA:* 2.42.
Faculty *Total:* 244, 31% full-time, 18% with terminal degrees.
Majors Biology/biological sciences; biology teacher education; biotechnology research; computer hardware technology; criminal justice/safety; early childhood education; electrical, electronic and communications engineering technology; elementary education; English as a second/foreign language (teaching); hotel/motel administration; kindergarten/preschool education; management informa-

tion systems; marketing/marketing management; microbiology; parks, recreation and leisure facilities management; pharmacy technician; social psychology; Spanish language teacher education.

Academics *Calendar:* semesters. *Degrees:* certificates, associate, bachelor's, and master's. *Special study options:* academic remediation for entering students, adult/continuing education programs, advanced placement credit, cooperative education, distance learning, double majors, external degree program, honors programs, independent study, internships, part-time degree program, services for LD students, summer session for credit. *ROTC:* Army (b), Air Force (b).

Computers on Campus 531 computers/terminals are available on campus for general student use. Students can access the following: online (class) registration, online (class) schedules. Campuswide network is available. Wireless service is available via entire campus.

Student Life *Housing:* college housing not available. *Activities and organizations:* drama/theater group, choral group, Criminal Justice Association, Secretarial Sciences Association, Future Teachers Association, Psychosocial Human Services Association, IPDAS (Drugs, Alcohol and Aids Prevention Institute). *Campus security:* 24-hour emergency response devices and patrols. *Student services:* health clinic, personal/psychological counseling, women's center.

Athletics *Intercollegiate sports:* baseball M (s), basketball M (s)/W (s), cheerleading M/W, cross-country running M (s)/W (s), soccer M (s), softball M (s)/W (s), table tennis M (s)/W (s), tennis M (s)/W (s), track and field M (s)/W (s), volleyball M (s)/W (s), weight lifting M (s)/W (s). *Intramural sports:* basketball M/W, cross-country running M/W, softball M/W, table tennis M/W, tennis M/W, track and field M/W, volleyball M/W, weight lifting M/W.

Standardized Tests *Required:* PAA (for admission). *Required for some:* SAT (for admission).

Costs (2007–08) *Tuition:* $3528 full-time, $147 per credit hour part-time. Full-time tuition and fees vary according to course load. Part-time tuition and fees vary according to course load. *Required fees:* $464 full-time, $232 per term part-time. *Payment plan:* deferred payment. *Waivers:* employees or children of employees.

Applying *Options:* electronic application, early admission. *Required:* high school transcript, minimum 2.0 GPA. *Application deadlines:* rolling (freshmen), rolling (transfers).

Freshman Application Contact Ms. Doris Perez, Admissions Director, Inter American University of Puerto Rico, Aguadilla Campus, PO Box 20,000, Road 459 Intersection 463, Aguadilla, PR 00605. *Phone:* 787-891-0925 Ext. 2101. *Fax:* 787-882-3020.

INTER AMERICAN UNIVERSITY OF PUERTO RICO, ARECIBO CAMPUS

Arecibo, Puerto Rico **www.arecibo.inter.edu/**

Freshman Application Contact Ms. Provi Montalvo, Admission Director, Inter American University of Puerto Rico, Arecibo Campus, PO Box 4050, Arecibo, PR 00614-4050. *Phone:* 787-878-5475. *Fax:* 787-880-1624. *E-mail:* pmontalvo@arecibo.inter.edu.

INTER AMERICAN UNIVERSITY OF PUERTO RICO, BARRANQUITAS CAMPUS

Barranquitas, Puerto Rico **www.br.inter.edu/**

- **Independent** comprehensive, founded 1957, part of Inter American University of Puerto Rico
- **Small-town** campus with easy access to San Juan
- **Endowment** $3.0 million
- **Coed**
- **Moderately difficult** entrance level

Faculty *Student/faculty ratio:* 18:1.

Academics *Calendar:* semesters. *Degrees:* associate, bachelor's, and post-bachelor's certificates.

Student Life *Campus security:* 24-hour patrols.

Standardized Tests *Required:* CEEB (for admission). *Required for some:* SAT or ACT (for admission).

Costs (2007–08) *Tuition:* $3920 full-time, $140 per credit part-time. *Required fees:* $850 full-time, $150 per term part-time.

Financial Aid Of all full-time matriculated undergraduates who enrolled in 2000, 1,350 applied for aid, 1,350 were judged to have need. 466 Federal Work-Study jobs.

Applying *Options:* deferred entrance. *Required:* high school transcript, interview.

Freshman Application Contact Mrs. Aramilda Cartagena, Dean of Students, Inter American University of Puerto Rico, Barranquitas Campus, Box 517, Barranquitas, PR 00794. *Phone:* 787-857-3600 Ext. 2009. *Fax:* 787-857-2125. *E-mail:* acartagena@br.inter.edu.

INTER AMERICAN UNIVERSITY OF PUERTO RICO, BAYAMÓN CAMPUS

Bayamón, Puerto Rico **bc.inter.edu/**

- **Independent** comprehensive, founded 1912, part of Inter American University of Puerto Rico
- **Urban** 51-acre campus with easy access to San Juan
- **Endowment** $4.4 million
- **Coed** 5,021 undergraduate students, 83% full-time, 43% women, 57% men
- 39% of applicants were admitted

Undergraduates 4,190 full-time, 831 part-time. Students come from 1 other state, 4 other countries, 100% Hispanic American, 2% transferred in.

Freshmen *Admission:* 4,081 applied, 1,609 admitted, 1,115 enrolled. *Average high school GPA:* 3.0.

Faculty *Total:* 314, 32% full-time, 15% with terminal degrees. *Student/faculty ratio:* 23:1.

Majors Accounting; administrative assistant and secretarial science; aeronautics/aviation/aerospace science and technology; aerospace, aeronautical and astronautical engineering; airline pilot and flight crew; air traffic control; applied mathematics; aviation/airway management; biochemistry; biological and biomedical sciences related; biology/biological sciences; business administration and management; business automation/technology/data entry; business, management, and marketing related; business/managerial economics; chemical technology; chemistry; communication/speech communication and rhetoric; communications technology; computer and information sciences and support services related; computer installation and repair technology; computer programming; computer science; computer systems analysis; electrical, electronic and communications engineering technology; electrical, electronics and communications engineering; engineering; entrepreneurship; environmental biology; environmental control technologies related; executive assistant/executive secretary; finance; forensic science and technology; human resources management; industrial engineering; management information systems; management science; marketing/marketing management; marketing research; mass communication/media; mathematics; mechanical engineering; medical microbiology and bacteriology; pre-medical studies; telecommunications.

Academics *Calendar:* semesters. *Degrees:* certificates, associate, bachelor's, and master's. *Special study options:* academic remediation for entering students, accelerated degree program, adult/continuing education programs, advanced placement credit, cooperative education, distance learning, double majors, English as a second language, external degree program, honors programs, independent study, internships, part-time degree program, services for LD students, summer session for credit. *ROTC:* Army (c).

Computers on Campus 85 computers/terminals are available on campus for general student use. Students can access the following: computer help desk, free student e-mail accounts, online (class) registration. Campuswide network is available.

Student Life *Housing:* college housing not available. *Activities and organizations:* student-run newspaper, choral group, Associacion de Estudiantes de Administracion de Empresas, Estudiantes Unidos por la Ciencia, Associacion Estudiantes de Aviacion, Consejo de Estudiante, Asociacion Estudiantes de Ingenieria. *Campus security:* 24-hour patrols. *Student services:* health clinic, personal/psychological counseling.

Athletics *Intercollegiate sports:* baseball M (s), basketball M (s)/W (s), cross-country running M (s)/W (s), softball M (s)/W (s), swimming and diving M (s)/W (s), table tennis M (s)/W (s), track and field M (s)/W (s), volleyball M (s)/W (s), weight lifting M (s). *Intramural sports:* basketball M/W, cross-country running M/W, softball M/W, swimming and diving M/W, table tennis M/W, tennis M/W, track and field M/W, volleyball M/W, weight lifting M.

Standardized Tests *Required:* CEEB (for admission). *Required for some:* SAT (for admission).

Costs (2008–09) *Tuition:* $4110 full-time, $147 per credit part-time.

Applying *Options:* electronic application. *Required:* high school transcript, minimum 2.0 GPA, 2.5 GPA for engineering programs. *Application deadline:* 7/30 (freshmen). *Notification:* continuous (freshmen), continuous (transfers).

Freshman Application Contact Mr. Carlos Alicea, Director of Admissions, Inter American University of Puerto Rico, Bayamón Campus, 500 Road 830,

Bayamon, PR 00957. *Phone:* 787-279-1912 Ext. 2017. *Fax:* 787-279-2205. *E-mail:* calicea@bc.inter.edu.

INTER AMERICAN UNIVERSITY OF PUERTO RICO, FAJARDO CAMPUS

Fajardo, Puerto Rico **fajardo.inter.edu/**

- **Independent** comprehensive, founded 1965, part of Inter American University of Puerto Rico
- **Small-town** 11-acre campus with easy access to San Juan
- **Coed** 2,234 undergraduate students
- **Moderately difficult** entrance level, 45% of applicants were admitted

Undergraduates 100% Hispanic American.

Freshmen *Admission:* 973 applied, 439 admitted. *Average high school GPA:* 2.0.

Faculty *Total:* 163, 25% full-time. *Student/faculty ratio:* 15:1.

Majors Accounting; administrative assistant and secretarial science; art teacher education; aviation/airway management; avionics maintenance technology; biology/biological sciences; business administration and management; business teacher education; clinical laboratory science/medical technology; computer science; criminal justice/law enforcement administration; criminal justice/police science; economics; education; electrical, electronics and communications engineering; elementary education; English as a second/foreign language (teaching); history; hotel/motel administration; marketing/marketing management; music; nursing (registered nurse training); physical education teaching and coaching; social work; sociology; special education; tourism and travel services management.

Academics *Calendar:* semesters. *Degrees:* associate, bachelor's, and master's. *Special study options:* academic remediation for entering students, adult/continuing education programs, advanced placement credit, distance learning, English as a second language, freshman honors college, honors programs, independent study, internships, off-campus study, part-time degree program, services for LD students, summer session for credit.

Computers on Campus 90 computers/terminals are available on campus for general student use.

Student Life *Housing:* college housing not available. *Activities and organizations:* Future Teachers Association, Criminal Justice Student Association, Honor Program Association, Practical Teaching Association. *Campus security:* 24-hour patrols. *Student services:* personal/psychological counseling.

Standardized Tests *Required:* College Board (for admission).

Costs (2007–08) *Tuition:* $4200 full-time, $147 per credit part-time. *Required fees:* $424 full-time. *Payment plan:* installment. *Waivers:* employees or children of employees.

Applying *Options:* early admission, deferred entrance. *Required:* high school transcript. *Required for some:* interview. *Application deadlines:* rolling (freshmen), rolling (transfers). *Notification:* 5/1 (freshmen).

Freshman Application Contact Ms. Jackeline Melèndez, Secretary III, Inter American University of Puerto Rico, Fajardo Campus, Call Box 70003, Fajaido, PR 00738-7003. *Phone:* 787-863-2390 Ext. 2210. *E-mail:* jackmel@inter.edu.

INTER AMERICAN UNIVERSITY OF PUERTO RICO, GUAYAMA CAMPUS

Guayama, Puerto Rico **www.guayama.inter.edu/**

Director of Admissions Mrs. Laura E. Ferrer, Director of Admissions, Inter American University of Puerto Rico, Guayama Campus, Interamerican University of Puerto Rico, Guayoma Campus, Call Box 10004 Attention: Laura Ferrer, Guayama, PR 00785. *Phone:* 787-864-2222 Ext. 220. *Toll-free phone:* 787-864-2222 Ext. 2243.

INTER AMERICAN UNIVERSITY OF PUERTO RICO, METROPOLITAN CAMPUS

San Juan, Puerto Rico **metro.inter.edu/**

Freshman Application Contact Ms. Ida G. Betancourt, Official Admission, Inter American University of Puerto Rico, Metropolitan Campus, Metropolitan Campus—Admission Office, PO Box 191293, San Juan, PR 00919-1293. *Phone:* 787-250-1912 Ext. 2188. *Fax:* 787-250-1025. *E-mail:* jbetancourt@metro.inter.edu.

INTER AMERICAN UNIVERSITY OF PUERTO RICO, PONCE CAMPUS

Mercedita, Puerto Rico **www.ponce.inter.edu/**

Freshman Application Contact Mr. Franco Diaz, Admissions Officer, Inter American University of Puerto Rico, Ponce Campus, Ponce Campus, 104 Turpo Industrial Park Road #1, Mercedita, PR 00715-1602. *Phone:* 787-284-1912 Ext. 2025. *Fax:* 787-841-0103. *E-mail:* fidiaz@ponce.inter.edu.

INTER AMERICAN UNIVERSITY OF PUERTO RICO, SAN GERMÁN CAMPUS

San Germán, Puerto Rico **www.sg.inter.edu/**

- **Independent** university, founded 1912, part of Inter American University of Puerto Rico
- **Small-town** 260-acre campus
- **Endowment** $793,677
- **Coed** 4,645 undergraduate students, 85% full-time, 52% women, 48% men
- **Moderately difficult** entrance level, 99% of applicants were admitted

Undergraduates 3,938 full-time, 707 part-time. Students come from 2 states and territories, 5 other countries, 1% are from out of state, 100% Hispanic American, 2% transferred in, 10% live on campus. *Retention:* 74% of 2006 full-time freshmen returned.

Freshmen *Admission:* 1,107 applied, 1,097 admitted, 917 enrolled. *Average high school GPA:* 2.84.

Faculty *Total:* 326, 40% full-time, 25% with terminal degrees. *Student/faculty ratio:* 17:1.

Majors Accounting; administrative assistant and secretarial science; advertising; applied art; applied mathematics; architecture; art; art history, criticism and conservation; art teacher education; behavioral sciences; biology/biological sciences; biology teacher education; biomedical sciences; business administration and management; business/managerial economics; ceramic arts and ceramics; chemistry; chemistry teacher education; clinical laboratory science/medical technology; computer programming; computer science; drawing; early childhood education; economics; education; electrical, electronic and communications engineering technology; elementary education; engineering; English; English as a second/foreign language (teaching); environmental studies; finance; health information/medical records administration; health science; human resources management; information science/studies; kindergarten/preschool education; linguistics; literature; marketing/marketing management; marketing related; mathematics; mathematics teacher education; medical microbiology and bacteriology; medical radiologic technology; music; music teacher education; natural sciences; nursing (registered nurse training); photography; physical education teaching and coaching; piano and organ; political science and government; psychology; public administration; science teacher education; sculpture; secondary education; selling skills and sales; social sciences; social studies teacher education; sociology; Spanish; violin, viola, guitar and other stringed instruments; voice and opera; wind/percussion instruments.

Academics *Calendar:* semesters. *Degrees:* certificates, associate, bachelor's, master's, doctoral, and postbachelor's certificates. *Special study options:* academic remediation for entering students, accelerated degree program, adult/continuing education programs, advanced placement credit, cooperative education, distance learning, double majors, English as a second language, external degree program, honors programs, independent study, internships, off-campus study, part-time degree program, services for LD students, summer session for credit. *ROTC:* Army (c), Navy (c), Air Force (c).

Computers on Campus 1,800 computers/terminals are available on campus for general student use. Students can access the following: free student e-mail accounts, online (class) grades, online (class) registration, online (class) schedules. Campuswide network is available. Wireless service is available via computer centers, computer labs, dorm rooms, libraries, student centers.

Student Life *Housing options:* men-only, women-only. Campus housing is university owned. *Activities and organizations:* drama/theater group, student-run newspaper, choral group, Future Teachers Association, PolyNature, Association for Computer Machinery, International Association of Administrative Professionals, Biology Honor Society, national fraternities, national sororities. *Campus security:* 24-hour emergency response devices and patrols. *Student services:* personal/psychological counseling.

Athletics *Intercollegiate sports:* baseball M (s), basketball M (s)/W (s), cross-country running M (s)/W (s), soccer M (s), softball M/W, swimming and diving M/W, table tennis M (s)/W (s), tennis M (s)/W (s), track and field M (s)/W (s), volleyball M (s)/W (s), weight lifting M (s). *Intramural sports:* badminton M/W, basketball M/W, cross-country running M/W, softball M/W, table tennis M/W, tennis M/W, track and field M/W, volleyball M/W.

Standardized Tests *Required:* CEEB (for admission).

Costs (2007–08) *Comprehensive fee:* $7326 includes full-time tuition ($4410), mandatory fees ($516), and room and board ($2400). Part-time tuition: $147 per credit. *Required fees:* $258 per term part-time. *College room only:* $900. Room and board charges vary according to board plan and student level. *Payment plan:* installment. *Waivers:* employees or children of employees.

Financial Aid Of all full-time matriculated undergraduates who enrolled in 2003, 3,011 applied for aid, 2,887 were judged to have need, 24 had their need fully met. *Average percent of need met:* 33%. *Average financial aid package:* $1556. *Average need-based loan:* $1756. *Average need-based gift aid:* $567.

Applying *Options:* early admission. *Required:* high school transcript, medical history. *Required for some:* 1 letter of recommendation, interview. *Recommended:* essay or personal statement, minimum 2.5 GPA. *Application deadlines:* 5/15 (freshmen), 5/15 (transfers). *Notification:* continuous (freshmen), continuous (transfers).

Freshman Application Contact Mrs. Mildred Camacho, Director of Admissions, Inter American University of Puerto Rico, San Germán Campus, PO Box 5100, San Germán, PR 00683-5008. *Phone:* 787-264-1912 Ext. 7283. *Fax:* 787-892-7020. *E-mail:* milcama@sg.inter.edu.

NATIONAL COLLEGE

Bayamón, Puerto Rico **www.nationalcollegepr.edu/**

Freshman Application Contact Sra. Mercedes Pagán, National College, National College Plaza Building, PO Box 2036, Bayamon, PR 00960. *Phone:* 787-780-5134. *Toll-free phone:* 800-780-5134. *E-mail:* rnieves@nationalcollegepr.edu.

POLYTECHNIC UNIVERSITY OF PUERTO RICO

Hato Rey, Puerto Rico **www.pupr.edu/**

- **Independent** comprehensive, founded 1966
- **Urban** 10-acre campus with easy access to San Juan
- **Endowment** $11.5 million
- **Coed** 5,195 undergraduate students, 53% full-time, 23% women, 77% men
- **Minimally difficult** entrance level, 97% of applicants were admitted

Undergraduates 2,735 full-time, 2,460 part-time. Students come from 2 states and territories, 100% Hispanic American. *Retention:* 74% of 2006 full-time freshmen returned.

Freshmen *Admission:* 973 applied, 948 admitted, 723 enrolled. *Average high school GPA:* 3.0.

Faculty *Total:* 294, 54% full-time, 29% with terminal degrees. *Student/faculty ratio:* 17:1.

Majors Architecture; business administration and management; chemical engineering; civil engineering; computer engineering; electrical, electronics and communications engineering; environmental/environmental health engineering; finance; industrial engineering; marketing/marketing management; mechanical engineering; survey technology.

Academics *Calendar:* trimesters. *Degrees:* bachelor's and master's. *Special study options:* academic remediation for entering students, English as a second language, independent study, part-time degree program, student-designed majors, summer session for credit. *ROTC:* Army (c).

Computers on Campus 375 computers/terminals are available on campus for general student use. Students can access the following: free student e-mail accounts. Campuswide network is available. Wireless service is available via entire campus.

Student Life *Housing:* college housing not available. *Activities and organizations:* drama/theater group, choral group, Society of Women Engineers, American Civil Engineering—Student Chapter, Society of Hispanic Professional Engineers, Society of Automotive Engineers, Capitulo Estuadiantil Ingenieros Electricos. *Campus security:* 24-hour patrols. *Student services:* health clinic, personal/psychological counseling.

Athletics *Intercollegiate sports:* basketball M/W, cross-country running M/W, soccer M, softball M/W, table tennis M/W, tennis M/W, track and field M/W, volleyball M/W. *Intramural sports:* basketball M, cross-country running M/W, soccer M/W, table tennis M/W, tennis M/W, volleyball M/W.

Standardized Tests *Required for some:* SAT (for admission).

Costs (2007–08) *Comprehensive fee:* $16,653 includes full-time tuition ($5508), mandatory fees ($495), and room and board ($10,650). Full-time tuition and fees vary according to program. Part-time tuition: $155 per credit. Part-time tuition and fees vary according to program. *Required fees:* $195 per term part-time. *Payment plan:* deferred payment. *Waivers:* employees or children of employees.

Financial Aid Of all full-time matriculated undergraduates who enrolled in 2003, 2,206 applied for aid, 2,194 were judged to have need. *Average percent of need met:* 19%. *Average financial aid package:* $4363. *Average need-based loan:* $2334. *Average need-based gift aid:* $4340. *Financial aid deadline:* 5/15.

Applying *Options:* early admission, deferred entrance. *Application fee:* $30. *Required:* high school transcript. *Application deadline:* 8/15 (freshmen).

Freshman Application Contact Ms. Teresa Cardona, Director of Admissions, Polytechnic University of Puerto Rico, PO Box 192017, San Juan, PR 00919-2017. *Phone:* 787-754-8000 Ext. 240. *Fax:* 787-764-8712. *E-mail:* tcardona@pupr.edu.

PONTIFICAL CATHOLIC UNIVERSITY OF PUERTO RICO

Ponce, Puerto Rico **www.pucpr.edu/**

- **Independent Roman Catholic** university, founded 1948
- **Urban** 120-acre campus with easy access to San Juan
- **Endowment** $16.2 million
- **Coed**
- **Moderately difficult** entrance level

Faculty *Student/faculty ratio:* 26:1.

Academics *Calendar:* semesters. *Degrees:* associate, bachelor's, master's, doctoral, and first professional (branch locations in Arecibo, Guayana, Mayagüez).

Student Life *Campus security:* 24-hour emergency response devices and patrols.

Athletics Member NAIA.

Standardized Tests *Required:* SAT (for admission).

Costs (2007–08) *Comprehensive fee:* $8008 includes full-time tuition ($4500), mandatory fees ($518), and room and board ($2990). Full-time tuition and fees vary according to course load. Part-time tuition: $150 per credit. Part-time tuition and fees vary according to course load. *College room only:* $1290.

Financial Aid Of all full-time matriculated undergraduates who enrolled in 2005, 6,014 applied for aid, 5,912 were judged to have need, 102 had their need fully met. 1,100 Federal Work-Study jobs (averaging $750). *Average percent of need met:* 71. *Average financial aid package:* $6930. *Average need-based loan:* $1500. *Average need-based gift aid:* $4500. *Average indebtedness upon graduation:* $3500.

Applying *Options:* early admission, deferred entrance. *Application fee:* $15. *Required:* high school transcript, minimum 2.5 GPA. *Required for some:* essay or personal statement, minimum 3.0 GPA, 1 letter of recommendation, interview.

Freshman Application Contact Sra. Ana O. Bonilla, Director of Admissions, Pontifical Catholic University of Puerto Rico, 2250 Avenida Las Americas, Ponce, PR 00717-0777. *Phone:* 787-841-2000 Ext. 1004. *Toll-free phone:* 800-981-5040. *Fax:* 787-840-4295. *E-mail:* admissions@email.pucpr.edu.

UNIVERSIDAD ADVENTISTA DE LAS ANTILLAS

Mayagüez, Puerto Rico **www.uaa.edu/**

- **Independent Seventh-day Adventist** comprehensive, founded 1957
- **Rural** 284-acre campus
- **Endowment** $10,000
- **Coed**
- **Minimally difficult** entrance level

Faculty *Student/faculty ratio:* 14:1.

Academics *Calendar:* semesters. *Degrees:* associate, bachelor's, and master's.

Student Life *Campus security:* 24-hour emergency response devices and patrols, student patrols, controlled dormitory access.

Standardized Tests *Recommended:* SAT or ACT (for admission), PAA.

Costs (2007–08) *Comprehensive fee:* $8710 includes full-time tuition ($4200), mandatory fees ($1210), and room and board ($3300). Part-time tuition: $140 per credit. No tuition increase for student's term of enrollment. *College room only:* $900. Room and board charges vary according to board plan. *Payment plans:* tuition prepayment, installment.

Financial Aid Of all full-time matriculated undergraduates who enrolled in 2002, 723 applied for aid, 723 were judged to have need. *Average percent of need* *met:* 70. *Average need-based loan:* $2500. *Average need-based gift aid:* $6624. *Average indebtedness upon graduation:* $3500.

Applying *Options:* early admission. *Application fee:* $20. *Required:* high school transcript, minimum 2.0 GPA, letters of recommendation. *Required for some:* interview.

Freshman Application Contact Ms. Evelyn del Valle, Director of Admissions, Universidad Adventista de las Antillas, Oficina de Admisiones, PO Box 118, Mayaguez, PR 00681-0118. *Phone:* 787-834-9595 Ext. 2331. *Fax:* 787-834-9597. *E-mail:* admissions@uaa.edu.

Universidad del Este

Carolina, Puerto Rico **www.suagm.edu/une/**

Freshman Application Contact Carmen Rodríguez, Associate Director, Universidad del Este, PO Box 2010, Carolina, PR 00984-2010. *Phone:* 787-257-7373 Ext. 3300.

Universidad del Turabo

Gurabo, Puerto Rico **www.suagm.edu/ut/**

Director of Admissions Sr. Jesús Torres, Director of Admissions, Universidad del Turabo, PO Box 3030, Gurabo, PR 00778-3030. *Phone:* 787-743-7979 Ext. 4351. *E-mail:* ac_msantana@suagm.edu.

Universidad Metropolitana

San Juan, Puerto Rico **www.suagm.edu/umet/**

Director of Admissions Mr. Julio Rodriguez Soiza, Director of Admissions, Universidad Metropolitana, Apartado 21150, San Juan, PR 00928-1150. *Phone:* 787-766-1717 Ext. 540. *Toll-free phone:* 800-747-8362. *E-mail:* um_frivera@suagm1.suagm.edu.

University of Phoenix–Puerto Rico Campus

Guaynabo, Puerto Rico **www.phoenix.edu/**

- **Proprietary** comprehensive, founded 1995
- **Urban** campus
- **Coed**
- **Noncompetitive** entrance level

Faculty *Student/faculty ratio:* 14:1.

Academics *Calendar:* continuous. *Degrees:* bachelor's and master's (courses conducted at 121 campuses and learning centers in 25 states).

Student Life *Campus security:* late-night transport/escort service.

Costs (2007–08) *Tuition:* $6240 full-time, $208 per credit part-time. Full-time tuition and fees vary according to course level.

Financial Aid *Average financial aid package:* $5862. *Average need-based gift aid:* $2624.

Applying *Options:* deferred entrance. *Application fee:* $45. *Required:* 1 letter of recommendation. *Required for some:* high school transcript.

Freshman Application Contact Ms. Beth Barilla, Associate Vice President, Student Admissions and Services, University of Phoenix–Puerto Rico Campus, 4615 East Elwood Street, Mail Stop AA-K101, Phoenix, AZ 85040-1958. *Phone:* 480-317-6000. *Toll-free phone:* 800-776-4867 (in-state); 800-228-7240 (out-of-state). *Fax:* 480-894-1758. *E-mail:* beth.barilla@phoenix.edu.

University of Puerto Rico, Aguadilla University College

Aguadilla, Puerto Rico **www.uprag.edu/**

Director of Admissions Ms. Melba Serrano Lugo, Admissions Officer, University of Puerto Rico, Aguadilla University College, Admission Office, PO Box 250160, Aguadilla, PR 00604-0160. *Phone:* 787-890-2681 Ext. 280.

University of Puerto Rico at Arecibo

Arecibo, Puerto Rico **www.upra.edu/**

Freshman Application Contact Mrs. Delma Barrios, Director of Admissions, University of Puerto Rico at Arecibo, PO Box 4010, Arecibo, PR 00613. *Phone:* 787-878-2830 Ext. 3023.

University of Puerto Rico at Bayamón

Bayamón, Puerto Rico **www.uprb.edu/**

Freshman Application Contact Ms. Vivian Rivera, Officer of Admission, University of Puerto Rico at Bayamón, 170 Carretera 174 Parque Industrial Minillas, Bayamón, PR 00959. *Phone:* 787-786-2885 Ext. 2425. *E-mail:* e_velez@cutb.upr.clu.edu.

University of Puerto Rico at Carolina

Carolina, Puerto Rico **uprc.edu/**

- **Commonwealth-supported** primarily 2-year, founded 1974, part of University of Puerto Rico System
- **Urban** 60-acre campus with easy access to San Juan
- **Coed**
- **Moderately difficult** entrance level

Academics *Calendar:* quarters. *Degrees:* associate and bachelor's.

Standardized Tests *Required:* SAT (for admission), ACT (for admission), SAT Subject Tests (for admission).

Costs (2007–08) *Tuition:* commonwealth resident $2295 full-time, $40 per credit part-time; nonresident $3596 full-time, $100 per credit part-time. Full-time tuition and fees vary according to class time. Part-time tuition and fees vary according to class time. *Required fees:* $216 full-time, $74 per term part-time. *Room and board:* $7580; room only: $2300. Room and board charges vary according to board plan, housing facility, and location.

Applying *Application fee:* $20. *Required:* high school transcript.

Director of Admissions Ms. Celia Mendez, Admissions Officer, University of Puerto Rico at Carolina, PO Box 4800, Carolina, PR 00984-4800. *Phone:* 787-757-1485.

University of Puerto Rico at Humacao

Humacao, Puerto Rico **www.uprh.edu/**

- **Commonwealth-supported** 4-year, founded 1962, part of University of Puerto Rico System
- **Suburban** 62-acre campus with easy access to San Juan
- **Coed** 4,542 undergraduate students, 86% full-time, 70% women, 30% men
- **Moderately difficult** entrance level, 45% of applicants were admitted

Undergraduates 3,917 full-time, 625 part-time. 0.1% Asian American or Pacific Islander, 99% Hispanic American, 0.5% international, 0.4% transferred in. *Retention:* 89% of 2006 full-time freshmen returned.

Freshmen *Admission:* 2,705 applied, 1,204 admitted, 1,105 enrolled. *Average high school GPA:* 3.52. *Test scores:* SAT critical reading scores over 500: 68%; SAT math scores over 500: 67%; SAT critical reading scores over 600: 18%; SAT math scores over 600: 23%; SAT critical reading scores over 700: 1%; SAT math scores over 700: 3%.

Faculty *Total:* 296, 90% full-time, 39% with terminal degrees. *Student/faculty ratio:* 15:1.

Majors Biology/biological sciences; business/commerce; chemical technology; chemistry; communications technology; electrical, electronic and communications engineering technology; elementary education; engineering; English as a second/foreign language (teaching); human resources management; marine biology and biological oceanography; mathematics and computer science; medical microbiology and bacteriology; physical therapist assistant; physics; social work; wildlife and wildlands science and management.

Academics *Calendar:* semesters. *Degrees:* associate and bachelor's. *Special study options:* academic remediation for entering students, advanced placement credit, English as a second language, honors programs, internships, part-time degree program, services for LD students, summer session for credit. *ROTC:* Army (c).

Computers on Campus Students can access the following: free student e-mail accounts, online (class) grades, online (class) registration, online (class) schedules. Campuswide network is available. Wireless service is available via computer centers, libraries.

Student Life *Housing:* college housing not available. *Activities and organizations:* drama/theater group, student-run radio station, choral group, marching band, Recreational Organization, Accounting Students Association, Management Students Association, Microbiology Students Association, Human Resources Students Association, national sororities. *Campus security:* 24-hour patrols, 24-hour gate security. *Student services:* personal/psychological counseling, women's center.

Athletics *Intercollegiate sports:* baseball M (s), basketball M (s)/W (s), cheerleading M/W, cross-country running M (s)/W (s), softball W (s), swimming and diving M (s)/W (s), tennis W (s), track and field M (s)/W (s), volleyball M (s)/W (s), weight lifting M (s)/W (s), wrestling M (s). *Intramural sports:* basketball M/W, softball W, volleyball M/W, weight lifting M/W.

Standardized Tests *Required:* CEEB (for admission). *Required for some:* SAT or ACT (for admission).

Costs (2007–08) *Tuition:* commonwealth resident $1530 full-time, $45 per credit part-time; nonresident $3192 full-time. Full-time tuition and fees vary according to class time, course load, and student level. Part-time tuition and fees vary according to class time, course load, and student level. No tuition increase for student's term of enrollment. non-residents who are US citizens pay an amount equal to the rate for non-residents at a state university in their home state. *Required fees:* $347 full-time. *Room and board:* Room and board charges vary according to housing facility. *Payment plan:* deferred payment. *Waivers:* senior citizens and employees or children of employees.

Financial Aid Of all full-time matriculated undergraduates who enrolled in 2001, 3,515 applied for aid, 2,883 were judged to have need, 7 had their need fully met. 278 Federal Work-Study jobs (averaging $1318). *Average percent of need met:* 50%. *Average financial aid package:* $3929. *Average need-based loan:* $3295. *Average need-based gift aid:* $3664. *Average indebtedness upon graduation:* $2749. *Financial aid deadline:* 6/30.

Applying *Options:* deferred entrance. *Application fee:* $20. *Required:* high school transcript. *Required for some:* interview. *Application deadlines:* 12/15 (freshmen), 2/15 (transfers). *Notification:* continuous until 4/15 (freshmen), continuous until 7/30 (transfers).

Freshman Application Contact Mrs. Milagros Alvarez, Director of Admissions, University of Puerto Rico at Humacao, CUH Station 100 Road 908, Humacao, PR 00791-4300. *Phone:* 787-850-9301. *Fax:* 787-850-9428. *E-mail:* m_alvarez@uprh.edu.

University of Puerto Rico at Ponce

Ponce, Puerto Rico upr-ponce.upr.edu/

Freshman Application Contact Mr. William Rodriguez Mercado, Admissions Officer, University of Puerto Rico at Ponce, PO Box 7186, Ponce, PR 00732-7186. *Phone:* 787-844-8181. *Fax:* 787-842-3875.

University of Puerto Rico at Utuado

Utuado, Puerto Rico upr-utuado.upr.clu.edu/

- **Commonwealth-supported** 4-year, founded 1979, part of University of Puerto Rico System
- **Small-town** 180-acre campus with easy access to San Juan
- **Coed** 1,604 undergraduate students, 90% full-time, 60% women, 40% men
- **Moderately difficult** entrance level, 51% of applicants were admitted

Undergraduates 1,437 full-time, 167 part-time. 100% Hispanic American, 0.1% transferred in. *Retention:* 67% of 2006 full-time freshmen returned.

Freshmen *Admission:* 2,018 applied, 1,025 admitted, 599 enrolled. *Average high school GPA:* 2.5.

Faculty *Total:* 115, 77% full-time, 26% with terminal degrees. *Student/faculty ratio:* 17:1.

Majors Accounting; agricultural production; animal sciences; biological and biomedical sciences related; biology/biological sciences; business administration and management; chemistry; computational mathematics; education; education related; elementary education; English/language arts teacher education; environmental control technologies related; fine/studio arts; food science; forensic psychology; French; history; history teacher education; horticultural science; humanities; industrial production technologies related; mathematics teacher education; natural sciences; nursing (registered nurse training); office management; physical education teaching and coaching; physics related; plant protection and integrated pest management; political science and government; psychology related; quality control technology; radio and television broadcasting technology; science teacher education; social sciences; social sciences related; social work; sociology; Spanish; Spanish language teacher education; visual and performing arts related.

Academics *Calendar:* semesters. *Degrees:* associate and bachelor's. *Special study options:* academic remediation for entering students, cooperative education, honors programs, services for LD students, summer session for credit.

Computers on Campus 40 computers/terminals are available on campus for general student use. Campuswide network is available. Wireless service is available via classrooms, computer centers, computer labs, learning centers, libraries, student centers.

Student Life *Housing:* college housing not available. *Activities and organizations:* drama/theater group, choral group, national fraternities, national sororities. *Campus security:* 24-hour emergency response devices and patrols. *Student services:* health clinic, personal/psychological counseling.

Athletics *Intercollegiate sports:* basketball M (s)/W (s), cross-country running M (s)/W (s), softball M (s)/W (s), table tennis M (s)/W (s), track and field M (s)/W (s), volleyball M (s)/W (s), weight lifting M (s)/W (s). *Intramural sports:* softball M/W.

Standardized Tests *Required:* SAT Subject Tests (for admission), CEEB required (for admission).

Costs (2008–09) *Tuition:* $50 per credit part-time. *Required fees:* $50 per credit part-time.

Financial Aid Of all full-time matriculated undergraduates who enrolled in 2006, 143 Federal Work-Study jobs. *Financial aid deadline:* 6/15.

Applying *Options:* electronic application, early admission, deferred entrance. *Application fee:* $20. *Application deadlines:* rolling (freshmen), rolling (transfers).

Freshman Application Contact Mrs. Maria Robles Serrano, Admissions Officer, University of Puerto Rico at Utuado, PO Box 2500, Utuado, PR 00641-2500. *Phone:* 787-894-2828 Ext. 2240.

University of Puerto Rico, Cayey University College

Cayey, Puerto Rico www.cayey.upr.edu/

- **Commonwealth-supported** 4-year, founded 1967, part of University of Puerto Rico System
- **Urban** 177-acre campus with easy access to San Juan
- **Coed** 3,659 undergraduate students, 88% full-time, 71% women, 29% men
- **Moderately difficult** entrance level, 34% of applicants were admitted

Undergraduates 3,202 full-time, 457 part-time. Students come from 1 other state, 100% Hispanic American, 2% transferred in. *Retention:* 88% of 2006 full-time freshmen returned.

Freshmen *Admission:* 2,544 applied, 863 admitted, 800 enrolled. *Average high school GPA:* 3.67.

Faculty *Total:* 174, 80% full-time, 48% with terminal degrees. *Student/faculty ratio:* 21:1.

Majors Accounting; administrative assistant and secretarial science; biology/biological sciences; business/commerce; chemistry; economics; English; English/language arts teacher education; history; history teacher education; humanities; mathematics; mathematics teacher education; natural sciences; office occupations and clerical services; physical education teaching and coaching; psychology; psychology related; science teacher education; social science teacher education; social studies teacher education; sociology; Spanish; Spanish language teacher education; special education.

Academics *Calendar:* semesters. *Degrees:* associate and bachelor's. *Special study options:* academic remediation for entering students, accelerated degree program, advanced placement credit, honors programs, off-campus study, part-time degree program, study abroad, summer session for credit. *ROTC:* Army (b).

Computers on Campus 1,000 computers/terminals are available on campus for general student use. Students can access the following: campus intranet,

computer help desk, free student e-mail accounts, online (class) grades, online (class) registration, online (class) schedules. Campuswide network is available. Wireless service is available via entire campus.

Student Life *Housing:* college housing not available. *Activities and organizations:* drama/theater group, choral group, marching band, Asociacion de Estudiantes de Psicologia Psy-Chi, Sociedad Honoraria de Biologia—Tri Beta, Asociacion Cristiana Universitaria—CONFRA, Asociacion de Estudiantes del Programa de Estudios de Honor, GAIA, national fraternities, national sororities. *Campus security:* 24-hour emergency response devices and patrols, late-night transport/escort service. *Student services:* health clinic, personal/psychological counseling, women's center.

Athletics Member NCAA. *Intercollegiate sports:* basketball M (s)/W (s), cross-country running M (s)/W (s), soccer M (s), softball M (s)/W (s), swimming and diving M (s)/W, table tennis M (s), tennis M (s)/W (s), track and field M (s)/W (s), volleyball M (s)/W (s), weight lifting M (s)/W (s), wrestling M (s). *Intramural sports:* basketball M/W, cross-country running M/W, soccer M/W, softball M/W, swimming and diving M/W, tennis M/W, track and field M/W, volleyball M/W, weight lifting M/W, wrestling M.

Standardized Tests *Required:* CEEB (for admission). *Required for some:* SAT (for admission).

Costs (2008–09) *Tuition:* commonwealth resident $1360 full-time; nonresident $3596 full-time. *Required fees:* $144 full-time.

Financial Aid Of all full-time matriculated undergraduates who enrolled in 2000, 2,866 applied for aid, 2,819 were judged to have need. 281 Federal Work-Study jobs. *Average financial aid package:* $4200. *Average need-based loan:* $3000. *Average need-based gift aid:* $3300.

Applying *Options:* early admission, early decision. *Application fee:* $20. *Required:* high school transcript. *Application deadlines:* 12/15 (freshmen), 2/15 (transfers). *Notification:* continuous until 5/5 (freshmen).

Director of Admissions Mr. Wilfredo Lopez, Admissions Director, University of Puerto Rico, Cayey University College, Avenue Antonio R. Barcelo, Cayey, PR 00736. *Phone:* 787-738-2161 Ext. 2233. *Fax:* 878-738-5633. *E-mail:* wilopez@cayey.upr.edu.

UNIVERSITY OF PUERTO RICO, MAYAGÜEZ CAMPUS

Mayagüez, Puerto Rico **www.uprm.edu**

- **Commonwealth-supported** university, founded 1911, part of University of Puerto Rico System
- **Urban** 315-acre campus
- **Coed**
- **Moderately difficult** entrance level

Faculty *Student/faculty ratio:* 17:1.

Academics *Calendar:* semesters. *Degrees:* bachelor's, master's, and doctoral.

Student Life *Campus security:* 24-hour emergency response devices and patrols.

Standardized Tests *Required:* SAT Subject Tests (for admission), PEAU (for admission).

Costs (2007–08) *Tuition:* commonwealth resident $1702 full-time, $40 per credit part-time; nonresident $3192 full-time, $133 per credit part-time. Full-time tuition and fees vary according to course load. Part-time tuition and fees vary according to course load. No tuition increase for student's term of enrollment. *Required fees:* $149 full-time, $149 per term part-time.

Financial Aid Of all full-time matriculated undergraduates who enrolled in 2004, 7,756 applied for aid, 6,629 were judged to have need. 420 Federal Work-Study jobs (averaging $1560). 425 state and other part-time jobs. *Average percent of need met:* 38. *Average financial aid package:* $4293. *Average need-based loan:* $3875. *Average need-based gift aid:* $4293. *Average indebtedness upon graduation:* $6400.

Applying *Options:* early action. *Application fee:* $15. *Required:* high school transcript, CEEB Test.

Freshman Application Contact Ms. Sheila Marty-Rodriquez, Director, Admissions Office, University of Puerto Rico, Mayagüez Campus, PO Box 9021, Mayaguez, PR 00681-9021. *Phone:* 787-265-5465. *Fax:* 787-265-5465. *E-mail:* smarty@uprm.edu.

UNIVERSITY OF PUERTO RICO, MEDICAL SCIENCES CAMPUS

San Juan, Puerto Rico **www.rcm.upr.edu/**

Application Contact Mrs. Rosa Vèlez, Acting Director of Admission Office, University of Puerto Rico, Medical Sciences Campus, PO Box 365067, San Juan, PR 00936-5067. *Phone:* 787-758-2525 Ext. 5211.

UNIVERSITY OF PUERTO RICO, RÍO PIEDRAS

San Juan, Puerto Rico **www.uprrp.edu/**

- **Commonwealth-supported** university, founded 1903, part of University of Puerto Rico System
- **Urban** 281-acre campus
- **Coed**
- **Very difficult** entrance level

Faculty *Student/faculty ratio:* 15:1.

Academics *Calendar:* semesters. *Degrees:* bachelor's, master's, doctoral, first professional, post-master's, postbachelor's, and first professional certificates.

Student Life *Campus security:* 24-hour emergency response devices, late-night transport/escort service.

Athletics Member NCAA, NAIA. All NCAA Division II.

Standardized Tests *Required:* SAT (for admission).

Costs (2007–08) *Tuition:* commonwealth resident $960 full-time, $40 per credit part-time; nonresident $3192 full-time, $133 per credit part-time. *Required fees:* $144 full-time, $72 per term part-time. *Room and board:* $4940.

Financial Aid Of all full-time matriculated undergraduates who enrolled in 2006, 637 Federal Work-Study jobs. *Average financial aid package:* $4680. *Average need-based loan:* $3916. *Financial aid deadline:* 4/25.

Applying *Options:* electronic application. *Application fee:* $15. *Required:* high school transcript. *Required for some:* letters of recommendation, interview.

Director of Admissions Mrs. Cruz B. Valentin, Director of Admissions, University of Puerto Rico, Río Piedras, PO Box 21907, San Juan, PR 00931-1907. *Phone:* 787-764-0000 Ext. 5666.

UNIVERSITY OF THE SACRED HEART

San Juan, Puerto Rico **www.sagrado.edu/**

- **Independent Roman Catholic** comprehensive, founded 1935
- **Urban** 33-acre campus
- **Endowment** $18.5 million
- **Coed** 4,463 undergraduate students, 81% full-time, 64% women, 36% men
- **Moderately difficult** entrance level, 34% of applicants were admitted

Undergraduates 3,610 full-time, 853 part-time. 2% are from out of state, 100% Hispanic American, 7% transferred in. *Retention:* 75% of 2006 full-time freshmen returned.

Freshmen *Admission:* 5,924 applied, 2,038 admitted, 798 enrolled. *Average high school GPA:* 2.99.

Faculty *Total:* 364, 33% full-time, 29% with terminal degrees. *Student/faculty ratio:* 19:1.

Majors Accounting; administrative assistant and secretarial science; advertising; bilingual and multilingual education; biology/biological sciences; business administration and management; chemistry; clinical laboratory science/medical technology; communication/speech communication and rhetoric; computer science; criminal justice/safety; dramatic/theater arts; education; elementary education; foreign languages related; humanities; information science/studies; interdisciplinary studies; journalism; kinesiology and exercise science; literature; marketing/marketing management; mass communication/media; office management; psychology; secondary education; social sciences; social work; telecommunications; telecommunications technology; tourism and travel services management; tourism and travel services marketing; visual and performing arts.

Academics *Calendar:* semesters. *Degrees:* certificates, associate, bachelor's, master's, and postbachelor's certificates. *Special study options:* academic remediation for entering students, accelerated degree program, adult/continuing education programs, advanced placement credit, cooperative education, honors programs, internships, part-time degree program, services for LD students, study abroad, summer session for credit.

Computers on Campus 500 computers/terminals are available on campus for general student use. Students can access the following: campus intranet, online (class) registration, online (class) schedules. Campuswide network is available.

Student Life *Housing options:* men-only, women-only. Campus housing is university owned. *Activities and organizations:* drama/theater group, student-run newspaper, television station, choral group, La Red (personal development center), Student Council, Judo Club, Athletic Association. *Campus security:* 24-hour patrols. *Student services:* health clinic, personal/psychological counseling.

Athletics *Intercollegiate sports:* basketball M (s)/W (s), swimming and diving M (s)/W (s), tennis M (s)/W (s), track and field M (s)/W (s), ultimate Frisbee M (s)/W (s), volleyball M (s)/W (s), weight lifting M (s)/W (s). *Intramural sports:* basketball M/W, softball M/W, table tennis M/W, tennis M/W, ultimate Frisbee M/W, volleyball M/W, weight lifting M/W.

Standardized Tests *Required:* PAA, CEEB (for admission).

Costs (2008–09) *Tuition:* $3960 full-time, $165 per credit part-time. *Required fees:* $870 full-time, $435 per semester part-time. *Room only:* $2400.

Applying *Options:* early admission. *Application fee:* $15. *Required:* high school transcript, minimum 2.5 GPA, 1 letter of recommendation. *Application deadlines:* 6/30 (freshmen), 6/30 (transfers).

Director of Admissions Mr. Luis Heviquez, Director of Admissions, University of the Sacred Heart, PO Box 12383, San Juan, PR 00914-0383. *Phone:* 787-728-1515 Ext. 3237.

RHODE ISLAND

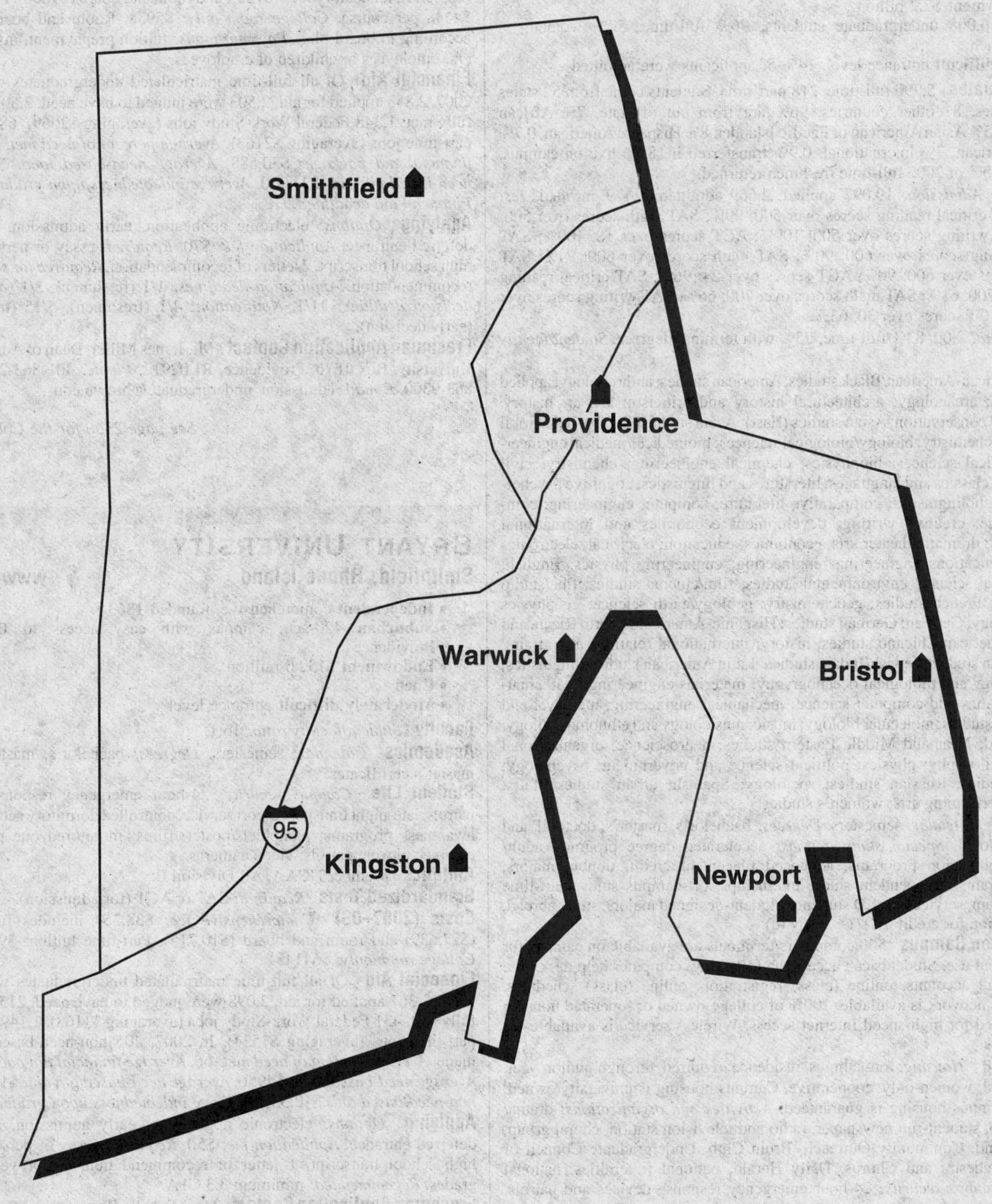

BROWN UNIVERSITY

Providence, Rhode Island www.brown.edu/

- **Independent** university, founded 1764
- **Urban** 140-acre campus with easy access to Boston
- **Endowment** $2.2 billion
- **Coed** 6,008 undergraduate students, 96% full-time, 52% women, 48% men
- **Most difficult** entrance level, 14% of applicants were admitted

Undergraduates 5,790 full-time, 218 part-time. Students come from 52 states and territories, 81 other countries, 96% are from out of state, 7% African American, 15% Asian American or Pacific Islander, 8% Hispanic American, 0.7% Native American, 7% international, 0.9% transferred in, 85% live on campus. *Retention:* 98% of 2006 full-time freshmen returned.

Freshmen *Admission:* 19,097 applied, 2,669 admitted, 1,479 enrolled. *Test scores:* SAT critical reading scores over 500: 99%; SAT math scores over 500: 100%; SAT writing scores over 500: 100%; ACT scores over 18: 100%; SAT critical reading scores over 600: 90%; SAT math scores over 600: 94%; SAT writing scores over 600: 90%; ACT scores over 24: 96%; SAT critical reading scores over 700: 61%; SAT math scores over 700: 66%; SAT writing scores over 700: 62%; ACT scores over 30: 63%.

Faculty *Total:* 800, 83% full-time, 95% with terminal degrees. *Student/faculty ratio:* 9:1.

Majors African-American/Black studies; American studies; anthropology; applied mathematics; archeology; architectural history and criticism; art; art history, criticism and conservation; Asian studies (East); Asian studies (South); behavioral sciences; biochemistry; biology/biological sciences; biomedical/medical engineering; biomedical sciences; biophysics; chemical engineering; chemistry; civil engineering; classics and languages, literatures and linguistics; cognitive psychology and psycholinguistics; comparative literature; computer engineering; computer science; creative writing; development economics and international development; dramatic/theater arts; economics; education; electrical, electronics and communications engineering; engineering; engineering physics; English; environmental science; environmental studies; film/cinema studies; fine/studio arts; French; French studies; geochemistry; geology/earth science; geophysics and seismology; German; German studies; Hispanic-American, Puerto Rican, and Mexican-American/Chicano studies; history; international relations and affairs; Italian; Italian studies; Jewish/Judaic studies; Latin American studies; linguistics; marine biology and biological oceanography; materials engineering; mathematics; mathematics and computer science; mechanical engineering; medieval and Renaissance studies; molecular biology; music; musicology and ethnomusicology; music related; Near and Middle Eastern studies; neuroscience; organizational behavior; philosophy; physics; political science and government; psychology; religious studies; Russian studies; sociology; Spanish; urban studies/affairs; visual and performing arts; women's studies.

Academics *Calendar:* semesters. *Degrees:* bachelor's, master's, doctoral, and first professional. *Special study options:* accelerated degree program, adult/continuing education programs, advanced placement credit, double majors, honors programs, independent study, internships, off-campus study, part-time degree program, services for LD students, student-designed majors, study abroad, summer session for credit. *ROTC:* Army (c).

Computers on Campus 500 computers/terminals are available on campus for general student use. Students can access the following: computer help desk, free student e-mail accounts, online (class) registration, online (class) schedules. Campuswide network is available. 100% of college-owned or -operated housing units are wired for high-speed Internet access. Wireless service is available via entire campus.

Student Life *Housing:* on-campus residence required through junior year. *Options:* coed, women-only, cooperative. Campus housing is university owned. Freshman campus housing is guaranteed. *Activities and organizations:* drama/theater group, student-run newspaper, radio and television station, choral group, marching band, Community Outreach, Bruin Club, Undergraduate Council of Students, Orchestra and Chorus, Daily Herald, national fraternities, national sororities. *Campus security:* 24-hour emergency response devices and patrols, late-night transport/escort service, controlled dormitory access. *Student services:* health clinic, personal/psychological counseling, women's center.

Athletics Member NCAA. All Division I except football (Division I-AA). *Intercollegiate sports:* baseball M, basketball M/W, crew M/W, cross-country running M/W, equestrian sports W, fencing M/W, field hockey W, golf M/W, gymnastics W, ice hockey M/W, lacrosse M/W, rugby M (c)/W (c), sailing M (c)/W (c), skiing (downhill) M (c)/W, soccer M/W, softball W, squash M/W, swimming and diving M/W, tennis M/W, track and field M/W, volleyball M (c)/W, water polo M/W, wrestling M. *Intramural sports:* badminton M (c)/W (c), basketball M/W, cheerleading M/W, fencing M/W, field hockey W, football M, ice hockey M/W, lacrosse M/W, racquetball M (c)/W (c), rugby M/W, skiing (downhill) M/W, soccer M/W, softball M/W, squash M/W, swimming and diving M/W, table tennis M (c)/W (c), tennis M/W, ultimate Frisbee M (c)/W (c), volleyball M/W, water polo M/W.

Standardized Tests *Required:* SAT and SAT Subject Tests or ACT (for admission).

Costs (2007–08) *Comprehensive fee:* $45,948 includes full-time tuition ($35,584), mandatory fees ($758), and room and board ($9606). Part-time tuition: $4448 per course. *College room only:* $5958. Room and board charges vary according to board plan. *Payment plans:* tuition prepayment, installment. *Waivers:* employees or children of employees.

Financial Aid Of all full-time matriculated undergraduates who enrolled in 2007, 2,843 applied for aid, 2,503 were judged to have need, 2,503 had their need fully met. 1,348 Federal Work-Study jobs (averaging $2069). 68 state and other part-time jobs (averaging $2163). *Average percent of need met:* 100%. *Average financial aid package:* $30,588. *Average need-based loan:* $5254. *Average need-based gift aid:* $24,730. *Average indebtedness upon graduation:* $18,610. *Financial aid deadline:* 2/1.

Applying *Options:* electronic application, early admission, early decision, deferred entrance. *Application fee:* $70. *Required:* essay or personal statement, high school transcript, 2 letters of recommendation. *Required for some:* 3 letters of recommendation. *Application deadlines:* 1/1 (freshmen), 3/1 (transfers). *Early decision deadline:* 11/1. *Notification:* 4/1 (freshmen), 5/15 (transfers), 12/15 (early decision).

Freshman Application Contact Mr. James Miller, Dean of Admission, Brown University, Box 1876, Providence, RI 02912. *Phone:* 401-863-2378. *Fax:* 401-863-9300. *E-mail:* admission_undergraduate@brown.edu.

See page 2360 for the College Close-Up.

BRYANT UNIVERSITY

Smithfield, Rhode Island www.bryant.edu/

- **Independent** comprehensive, founded 1863
- **Suburban** 420-acre campus with easy access to Boston and Providence
- **Endowment** $152.0 million
- **Coed**
- **Moderately difficult** entrance level

Faculty *Student/faculty ratio:* 16:1.

Academics *Calendar:* semesters. *Degrees:* bachelor's, master's, and post-master's certificates.

Student Life *Campus security:* 24-hour emergency response devices and patrols, late-night transport/escort service, controlled dormitory access, prevention/awareness programs; pamphlets/posters/films; monitored one point access to campus; bicycle patrols; video cameras.

Athletics Member NCAA. All Division II.

Standardized Tests *Required:* SAT or ACT (for admission).

Costs (2007–08) *Comprehensive fee:* $38,354 includes full-time tuition ($27,639) and room and board ($10,715). Part-time tuition: $987 per course. *College room only:* $6414.

Financial Aid Of all full-time matriculated undergraduates who enrolled in 2007, 2,367 applied for aid, 2,098 were judged to have need, 215 had their need fully met. 431 Federal Work-Study jobs (averaging $1168). 1,149 state and other part-time jobs (averaging $1534). In 2007, 405 non-need-based awards were made. *Average percent of need met:* 66. *Average financial aid package:* $17,226. *Average need-based loan:* $4956. *Average need-based gift aid:* $10,077. *Average non-need-based aid:* $12,535. *Average indebtedness upon graduation:* $33,461.

Applying *Options:* electronic application, early admission, early decision, deferred entrance. *Application fee:* $50. *Required:* essay or personal statement, high school transcript, 1 letter of recommendation, senior year first-quarter grades. *Recommended:* minimum 3.3 GPA.

Freshman Application Contact Ms. Michelle Beauregard, Director of Admission, Bryant University, 1150 Douglas Pike, Smithfield, RI 02917. *Phone:* 401-232-6100. *Toll-free phone:* 800-622-7001. *Fax:* 401-232-6741. *E-mail:* admission@bryant.edu.

See page 2362 for the College Close-Up.

JOHNSON & WALES UNIVERSITY

Providence, Rhode Island **www.jwu.edu/**

- **Independent** comprehensive, founded 1914
- **Urban** 47-acre campus with easy access to Boston
- **Endowment** $236.3 million
- **Coed**
- **Minimally difficult** entrance level

Faculty *Student/faculty ratio:* 27:1.

Academics *Calendar:* quarters. *Degrees:* certificates, diplomas, associate, bachelor's, master's, doctoral, and post-master's certificates (branch locations in Charleston, SC; Denver, CO; North Miami, FL; Norfolk, VA; Gothenberg, Sweden).

Student Life *Campus security:* 24-hour emergency response devices and patrols, student patrols, late-night transport/escort service.

Athletics Member NCAA. All Division III.

Standardized Tests *Required for some:* SAT or ACT (for admission). *Recommended:* SAT or ACT (for admission).

Costs (2008–09) *Comprehensive fee:* $31,477 includes full-time tuition ($21,297), mandatory fees ($1288), and room and board ($8892). Part-time tuition: $394 per quarter hour.

Financial Aid Of all full-time matriculated undergraduates who enrolled in 2005, 6,924 applied for aid, 6,077 were judged to have need, 291 had their need fully met. In 2005, 1105 non-need-based awards were made. *Average percent of need met:* 64. *Average financial aid package:* $12,009. *Average need-based loan:* $5788. *Average need-based gift aid:* $4900. *Average non-need-based aid:* $4455. *Average indebtedness upon graduation:* $17,704.

Applying *Options:* electronic application, early admission, deferred entrance. *Required:* high school transcript. *Required for some:* essay or personal statement, minimum 2.75 GPA, letters of recommendation, interview. *Recommended:* minimum 2.0 GPA.

Freshman Application Contact Ms. Maureen Dumas, Dean of Admissions, Johnson & Wales University, 8 Abbott Park Place, Providence, RI 02903-3703. *Phone:* 401-598-2310. *Toll-free phone:* 800-598-1000 (in-state); 800-342-5598 (out-of-state). *Fax:* 401-598-2948. *E-mail:* admissions.pvd@jwu.edu.

See page 2364 for the College Close-Up.

NEW ENGLAND INSTITUTE OF TECHNOLOGY

Warwick, Rhode Island **www.neit.edu/**

- **Independent** primarily 2-year, founded 1940
- **Suburban** 10-acre campus with easy access to Boston
- **Coed**
- **Noncompetitive** entrance level

Academics *Calendar:* quarters. *Degrees:* associate and bachelor's.

Student Life *Campus security:* security personnel during open hours.

Costs (2007–08) *Tuition:* $15,300 full-time, $385 per credit part-time. *Required fees:* $1415 full-time.

Financial Aid Of all full-time matriculated undergraduates who enrolled in 2006, 250 Federal Work-Study jobs (averaging $2290).

Applying *Options:* early admission, deferred entrance. *Application fee:* $25. *Required:* high school transcript, interview.

Freshman Application Contact Mr. Michael Kwiatkowski, Director of Admissions, New England Institute of Technology, 2500 Post Road, Warwick, RI 02886-2266. *Phone:* 401-739-5000. *E-mail:* neit@ids.net.

PROVIDENCE COLLEGE

Providence, Rhode Island **www.providence.edu/**

- **Independent Roman Catholic** comprehensive, founded 1917
- **Suburban** 105-acre campus with easy access to Boston
- **Endowment** $156.7 million
- **Coed** 3,966 undergraduate students, 100% full-time, 56% women, 44% men
- **Very difficult** entrance level, 41% of applicants were admitted

Providence College (PC) is the only liberal arts college in the U.S. that was founded and administered by the Dominican Friars, a Catholic teaching order whose heritage spans nearly 800 years. The College not only is concerned with the rigors of intellectual life but also recognizes the importance of students' experiences outside the classroom, including service to others. Scholarship, service, and the exuberant PC spirit—these are the qualities that shape the character of Providence College.

Undergraduates 3,951 full-time, 15 part-time. Students come from 16 states and territories, 37 other countries, 87% are from out of state, 2% African American, 2% Asian American or Pacific Islander, 2% Hispanic American, 0.1% Native American, 0.9% international, 1% transferred in, 78% live on campus. *Retention:* 92% of 2006 full-time freshmen returned.

Freshmen *Admission:* 9,802 applied, 4,064 admitted, 988 enrolled. *Average high school GPA:* 3.47. *Test scores:* SAT critical reading scores over 500: 87%; SAT math scores over 500: 89%; SAT writing scores over 500: 90%; ACT scores over 18: 98%; SAT critical reading scores over 600: 43%; SAT math scores over 600: 51%; SAT writing scores over 600: 49%; ACT scores over 24: 71%; SAT critical reading scores over 700: 7%; SAT math scores over 700: 6%; SAT writing scores over 700: 9%; ACT scores over 30: 14%.

Faculty *Total:* 387, 75% full-time, 78% with terminal degrees. *Student/faculty ratio:* 12:1.

Majors Accounting; American studies; art history, criticism and conservation; banking and financial support services; biochemistry; biology/biological sciences; business administration and management; ceramic arts and ceramics; chemistry; community organization and advocacy; computer science; divinity/ministry; drawing; economics; engineering physics; English; finance; fine/studio arts; fire science; French; general studies; health/health care administration; history; humanities; international/global studies; Italian; liberal arts and sciences/liberal studies; marketing/marketing management; mathematics; multi-/interdisciplinary studies related; music; music teacher education; painting; philosophy; political science and government; psychology; secondary education; social sciences; social work; sociology; Spanish; special education; systems engineering; theology; visual and performing arts; visual and performing arts related.

Academics *Calendar:* semesters. *Degrees:* certificates, associate, bachelor's, and master's. *Special study options:* adult/continuing education programs, advanced placement credit, cooperative education, double majors, honors programs, independent study, internships, part-time degree program, services for LD students, student-designed majors, study abroad, summer session for credit. *ROTC:* Army (b). *Unusual degree programs:* 3-2 engineering with Columbia University, Washington University in St. Louis.

Computers on Campus 278 computers/terminals and 5,000 ports are available on campus for general student use. Students can access the following: campus intranet, computer help desk, free student e-mail accounts, online (class) grades, online (class) registration, online (class) schedules. Campuswide network is available. 100% of college-owned or -operated housing units are wired for high-speed Internet access. Wireless service is available via classrooms, computer centers, computer labs, learning centers, libraries, student centers.

Student Life *Housing options:* coed, men-only, women-only, disabled students. Campus housing is university owned. Freshman campus housing is guaranteed. *Activities and organizations:* drama/theater group, student-run newspaper, radio and television station, choral group, Board of Programmers, Student Congress, student newspaper, Big Brothers/Big Sisters, Pastoral Council. *Campus security:* 24-hour emergency response devices and patrols, student patrols, late-night transport/escort service, controlled dormitory access. *Student services:* health clinic, personal/psychological counseling.

Athletics Member NCAA. All Division I. *Intercollegiate sports:* basketball M (s)/W (s), crew M (c)/W (c), cross-country running M (s)/W (s), field hockey W (s), golf M (c)/W (c), ice hockey M (s)/W (s), lacrosse M (s), racquetball M (c)/W (c), rugby M (c)/W (c), sailing M (c)/W (c), skiing (cross-country) M (c)/W (c), skiing (downhill) M (c)/W (c), soccer M (s)/W (s), softball W (s), swimming and diving M (s)/W (s), tennis W (s), track and field M (s)/W (s), volleyball M (c)/W (s). *Intramural sports:* basketball M/W, field hockey M/W, football M/W, ice hockey M/W, lacrosse M/W, racquetball M/W, soccer M/W, softball M/W, tennis M/W, ultimate Frisbee M/W, volleyball M/W.

Standardized Tests *Required for some:* SAT or ACT (for admission).

Costs (2007–08) *Comprehensive fee:* $39,834 includes full-time tuition ($28,920), mandatory fees ($579), and room and board ($10,335). Part-time tuition: $964 per credit. *College room only:* $5785. Room and board charges vary according to board plan and housing facility. *Payment plan:* installment. *Waivers:* senior citizens and employees or children of employees.

Financial Aid Of all full-time matriculated undergraduates who enrolled in 2007, 2,543 applied for aid, 2,166 were judged to have need, 674 had their need fully met. 700 Federal Work-Study jobs (averaging $1800). 700 state and other part-time jobs (averaging $1800). In 2007, 258 non-need-based awards were made. *Average percent of need met:* 83%. *Average financial aid package:* $19,185. *Average need-based loan:* $5285. *Average need-based gift aid:* $12,380.

Average non-need-based aid: $17,583. *Average indebtedness upon graduation:* $35,216. *Financial aid deadline:* 2/1.

Applying *Options:* electronic application, early admission, early action, deferred entrance. *Application fee:* $55. *Required:* essay or personal statement, high school transcript, 2 letters of recommendation. *Application deadlines:* 1/15 (freshmen), 4/1 (transfers), 11/1 (early action). *Notification:* 4/1 (freshmen), 5/30 (transfers), 1/1 (early action).

Freshman Application Contact Providence College, River Avenue and Eaton Street, Providence, RI 02918. *Phone:* 401-865-2535. *Toll-free phone:* 800-721-6444.

See page 2366 for the College Close-Up.

RHODE ISLAND COLLEGE

Providence, Rhode Island www.ric.edu/

- **State-supported** comprehensive, founded 1854
- **Suburban** 180-acre campus with easy access to Boston
- **Endowment** $21.7 million
- **Coed** 7,650 undergraduate students, 71% full-time, 68% women, 32% men
- **Moderately difficult** entrance level, 72% of applicants were admitted

Undergraduates 5,431 full-time, 2,219 part-time. Students come from 29 states and territories, 5 other countries, 13% are from out of state, 6% African American, 2% Asian American or Pacific Islander, 6% Hispanic American, 0.3% Native American, 0.5% international, 9% transferred in, 17% live on campus. *Retention:* 75% of 2006 full-time freshmen returned.

Freshmen *Admission:* 3,636 applied, 2,624 admitted, 1,127 enrolled. *Test scores:* SAT critical reading scores over 500: 40%; SAT math scores over 500: 39%; SAT writing scores over 500: 39%; ACT scores over 18: 80%; SAT critical reading scores over 600: 7%; SAT math scores over 600: 7%; SAT writing scores over 600: 7%; ACT scores over 24: 2%; SAT math scores over 700: 1%; ACT scores over 30: 2%.

Faculty *Total:* 683, 46% full-time. *Student/faculty ratio:* 16:1.

Majors Accounting; African-American/Black studies; anthropology; art history, criticism and conservation; art teacher education; biology/biological sciences; biology teacher education; business administration and management; chemistry; chemistry teacher education; clinical laboratory science/medical technology; communication/speech communication and rhetoric; computer and information sciences; criminal justice/safety; dance; dramatic/theater arts; early childhood education; economics; education (multiple levels); education related; education (specific levels and methods) related; elementary education; English; English/language arts teacher education; film/cinema studies; finance; fine/studio arts; foreign languages and literatures; French; French language teacher education; geography; health teacher education; history; history teacher education; kindergarten/preschool education; labor and industrial relations; liberal arts and sciences and humanities related; liberal arts and sciences/liberal studies; management information systems; marketing/marketing management; mathematics; mathematics teacher education; music; music performance; music teacher education; nursing (registered nurse training); philosophy; physical education teaching and coaching; physics; physics teacher education; political science and government; psychology; psychology related; public administration; science teacher education; secondary education; social science teacher education; social work; sociology; Spanish; Spanish language teacher education; special education; technical teacher education; technology/industrial arts teacher education; women's studies.

Academics *Calendar:* semesters. *Degrees:* certificates, bachelor's, master's, doctoral, and post-master's certificates. *Special study options:* academic remediation for entering students, adult/continuing education programs, advanced placement credit, double majors, freshman honors college, honors programs, independent study, internships, off-campus study, part-time degree program, services for LD students, student-designed majors, study abroad, summer session for credit. *ROTC:* Army (c).

Computers on Campus 350 computers/terminals are available on campus for general student use. Students can access the following: campus intranet, computer help desk, free student e-mail accounts, online (class) grades, online (class) registration, online (class) schedules. Campuswide network is available. 100% of college-owned or -operated housing units are wired for high-speed Internet access. Wireless service is available via classrooms, computer centers, computer labs, dorm rooms, learning centers, libraries, student centers.

Student Life *Housing options:* coed, women-only, disabled students. Campus housing is university owned. *Activities and organizations:* drama/theater group, student-run newspaper, radio station, choral group, Student government, Newspaper, Campus radio station (WXIN), RSA (Resident Student Association), Harambe. *Campus security:* 24-hour emergency response devices and patrols, late-night transport/escort service, controlled dormitory access. *Student services:* health clinic, personal/psychological counseling, women's center.

Athletics Member NCAA. All Division III. *Intercollegiate sports:* baseball M, basketball M/W, cross-country running M/W, golf M, gymnastics W, lacrosse W, soccer M/W, softball W, tennis M/W, track and field M/W, volleyball W, wrestling M. *Intramural sports:* basketball M/W, bowling M/W, football M, gymnastics M/W, softball M/W, tennis M/W, volleyball M/W.

Standardized Tests *Required:* SAT or ACT (for admission).

Costs (2008–09) *One-time required fee:* $25. *Tuition:* state resident $4700 full-time, $202 per credit part-time; nonresident $13,600 full-time, $570 per credit part-time. *Required fees:* $852 full-time, $21 per credit part-time, $68 per term part-time. *Room and board:* $8250; room only: $4600.

Financial Aid Of all full-time matriculated undergraduates who enrolled in 2007, 3,648 applied for aid, 2,635 were judged to have need, 789 had their need fully met. In 2007, 113 non-need-based awards were made. *Average percent of need met:* 37%. *Average financial aid package:* $7478. *Average need-based loan:* $3447. *Average need-based gift aid:* $4930. *Average non-need-based aid:* $2092. *Average indebtedness upon graduation:* $15,518.

Applying *Options:* electronic application, early admission. *Application fee:* $50. *Required:* essay or personal statement, high school transcript, letters of recommendation. *Required for some:* interview. *Application deadlines:* 5/1 (freshmen), 6/1 (transfers). *Notification:* continuous (freshmen), continuous (transfers).

Freshman Application Contact Dr. Holly Shadoian, Director of Admissions, Rhode Island College, 600 Mount Pleasant Avenue, Providence, RI 02908-1924. *Phone:* 401-456-8234. *Toll-free phone:* 800-669-5760. *Fax:* 401-456-8817. *E-mail:* admissions@ric.edu.

RHODE ISLAND SCHOOL OF DESIGN

Providence, Rhode Island www.risd.edu/

- **Independent** comprehensive, founded 1877
- **Urban** 13-acre campus with easy access to Boston
- **Endowment** $293.3 million
- **Coed**
- **Very difficult** entrance level

Faculty *Student/faculty ratio:* 9:1.

Academics *Calendar:* 4-1-4. *Degrees:* bachelor's, master's, and first professional.

Student Life *Campus security:* 24-hour emergency response devices and patrols, late-night transport/escort service, controlled dormitory access.

Standardized Tests *Required:* SAT or ACT (for admission).

Costs (2007–08) *Comprehensive fee:* $42,978 includes full-time tuition ($32,858), mandatory fees ($260), and room and board ($9860). *College room only:* $5630.

Financial Aid Of all full-time matriculated undergraduates who enrolled in 2004, 1,120 applied for aid, 915 were judged to have need, 85 had their need fully met. 511 Federal Work-Study jobs (averaging $1408). 350 state and other part-time jobs (averaging $1400). In 2004, 34 non-need-based awards were made. *Average percent of need met:* 69. *Average financial aid package:* $17,000. *Average need-based loan:* $5900. *Average need-based gift aid:* $11,100. *Average non-need-based aid:* $4700. *Average indebtedness upon graduation:* $22,500.

Applying *Options:* electronic application, early admission, early action, deferred entrance. *Application fee:* $50. *Required:* essay or personal statement, high school transcript, portfolio, drawing assignments. *Recommended:* 3 letters of recommendation.

Freshman Application Contact Mr. Edward Newhall, Director of Admissions, Rhode Island School of Design, 2 College Street, Providence, RI 02905-2791. *Phone:* 401-454-6307. *Toll-free phone:* 800-364-7473. *Fax:* 401-454-6309. *E-mail:* admissions@risd.edu.

ROGER WILLIAMS UNIVERSITY

Bristol, Rhode Island www.rwu.edu/

- **Independent** comprehensive, founded 1956
- **Small-town** 140-acre campus with easy access to Boston
- **Endowment** $100.0 million
- **Coed** 4,353 undergraduate students, 88% full-time, 49% women, 51% men
- **Moderately difficult** entrance level, 68% of applicants were admitted

Roger Williams University (RWU) is a leading liberal arts university located in historic Bristol, Rhode Island. The modern, secure campus is situated on 140 breathtaking waterfront acres. The University is accredited by the New England Association of Schools and Colleges. Current undergraduate enrollment is

approximately 3,775. Students benefit from small class sizes, ensuring students access to attentive, mentoring faculty members. The Roger Williams University School of Law enrolls almost 600 students, and 230 students are currently part of the Graduate Studies division.

Undergraduates 3,827 full-time, 526 part-time. Students come from 41 states and territories, 41 other countries, 82% are from out of state, 1% African American, 1% Asian American or Pacific Islander, 2% Hispanic American, 0.3% Native American, 2% international, 2% transferred in, 79% live on campus. *Retention:* 77% of 2006 full-time freshmen returned.

Freshmen *Admission:* 7,335 applied, 4,984 admitted, 1,045 enrolled. *Average high school GPA:* 3.16. *Test scores:* SAT critical reading scores over 500: 73%; SAT math scores over 500: 82%; SAT writing scores over 500: 72%; ACT scores over 18: 96%; SAT critical reading scores over 600: 16%; SAT math scores over 600: 27%; SAT writing scores over 600: 18%; ACT scores over 24: 46%; SAT critical reading scores over 700: 1%; SAT math scores over 700: 2%; SAT writing scores over 700: 2%; ACT scores over 30: 4%.

Faculty *Total:* 516, 38% full-time, 49% with terminal degrees. *Student/faculty ratio:* 13:1.

Majors Accounting; American studies; anthropology; architecture; art; art history, criticism and conservation; biology/biological sciences; business administration and management; chemistry; communication and media related; computer science; construction management; creative writing; criminal justice/law enforcement administration; dance; dramatic/theater arts; elementary education; English; environmental science; finance; financial planning and services; foreign languages and literatures; graphic design; health/health care administration; historic preservation and conservation; history; international business/trade/commerce; legal assistant/paralegal; legal professions and studies related; liberal arts and sciences/liberal studies; management information systems; manufacturing technology; marine biology and biological oceanography; marketing/marketing management; mathematics; multi-/interdisciplinary studies related; philosophy; political science and government; pre-dentistry studies; pre-medical studies; pre-veterinary studies; psychology; public administration; secondary education; social sciences; sociology; visual and performing arts.

Academics *Calendar:* semesters. *Degrees:* certificates, associate, bachelor's, master's, first professional, and postbachelor's certificates. *Special study options:* adult/continuing education programs, advanced placement credit, cooperative education, distance learning, double majors, English as a second language, external degree program, freshman honors college, honors programs, independent study, internships, part-time degree program, services for LD students, student-designed majors, study abroad, summer session for credit. *ROTC:* Army (c).

Computers on Campus 410 computers/terminals are available on campus for general student use. Students can access the following: computer help desk, free student e-mail accounts, online (class) grades, online (class) registration, online (class) schedules. Campuswide network is available.

Student Life *Housing options:* coed, disabled students. Campus housing is university owned and leased by the school. Freshman campus housing is guaranteed. *Activities and organizations:* drama/theater group, student-run newspaper, radio station, choral group, Entertainment Network, Student Senate, American Institute of Architects, John Jay Society, residence hall councils. *Campus security:* 24-hour emergency response devices and patrols, student patrols, late-night transport/escort service, controlled dormitory access. *Student services:* health clinic, personal/psychological counseling, women's center.

Athletics Member NCAA. All Division III. *Intercollegiate sports:* baseball M, basketball M/W, cheerleading W (c), crew M (c)/W (c), cross-country running M/W (c), equestrian sports M/W, lacrosse M/W, rugby M (c), sailing M/W, soccer M/W, softball W, swimming and diving M/W, tennis M/W, track and field M (c)/W (c), volleyball M/W, wrestling M. *Intramural sports:* badminton M/W, basketball M/W, field hockey M/W, football M/W, golf M/W, lacrosse M/W, racquetball M/W, soccer M/W, softball M/W, squash M/W, swimming and diving M/W, table tennis M/W, tennis M/W, ultimate Frisbee M/W, volleyball M/W.

Standardized Tests *Required:* SAT or ACT (for admission).

Costs (2007–08) *Comprehensive fee:* $37,432 includes full-time tuition ($24,312), mandatory fees ($1630), and room and board ($11,490). Part-time tuition: $1013 per credit. *College room only:* $5990.

Financial Aid Of all full-time matriculated undergraduates who enrolled in 2006, 2,513 applied for aid, 2,247 were judged to have need, 333 had their need fully met. 715 Federal Work-Study jobs (averaging $1813). 490 state and other part-time jobs (averaging $1693). In 2006, 319 non-need-based awards were made. *Average percent of need met:* 90%. *Average financial aid package:* $17,604. *Average need-based loan:* $5698. *Average need-based gift aid:* $9929. *Average non-need-based aid:* $6352. *Average indebtedness upon graduation:* $31,400. *Financial aid deadline:* 2/1.

Applying *Options:* electronic application, early decision, deferred entrance. *Application fee:* $50. *Required:* essay or personal statement, high school transcript, minimum 2.0 GPA, letters of recommendation. *Required for some:* portfolio/audition. *Application deadlines:* 2/1 (freshmen), rolling (transfers), 11/15 (early action). *Early decision deadline:* 11/1. *Notification:* 3/15 (freshmen), continuous (transfers), 12/15 (early decision), 1/15 (early action).

Freshman Application Contact Mr. Didier Bouvet, Director of Freshman Admission, Roger Williams University, 1 Old Ferry Road, Bristol, RI 02809. *Phone:* 401-254-3500. *Toll-free phone:* 800-458-7144. *Fax:* 401-254-3557. *E-mail:* admit@rwu.edu.

See page 2368 for the College Close-Up.

SALVE REGINA UNIVERSITY

Newport, Rhode Island **www.salve.edu/**

- **Independent Roman Catholic** comprehensive, founded 1934
- **Suburban** 70-acre campus with easy access to Boston and Providence
- **Endowment** $41.1 million
- **Coed** 2,125 undergraduate students, 96% full-time, 69% women, 31% men
- **Moderately difficult** entrance level, 54% of applicants were admitted

Undergraduates 2,042 full-time, 83 part-time. Students come from 30 states and territories, 8 other countries, 85% are from out of state, 2% African American, 1% Asian American or Pacific Islander, 3% Hispanic American, 0.4% Native American, 2% international, 99% transferred in, 60% live on campus. *Retention:* 82% of 2006 full-time freshmen returned.

Freshmen *Admission:* 5,801 applied, 3,107 admitted, 555 enrolled. *Average high school GPA:* 3.32. *Test scores:* SAT critical reading scores over 500: 84%; SAT math scores over 500: 83%; SAT writing scores over 500: 80%; ACT scores over 18: 100%; SAT critical reading scores over 600: 26%; SAT math scores over 600: 24%; SAT writing scores over 600: 30%; ACT scores over 24: 47%; SAT critical reading scores over 700: 2%; SAT math scores over 700: 3%; SAT writing scores over 700: 3%; ACT scores over 30: 2%.

Faculty *Total:* 263, 46% full-time, 53% with terminal degrees. *Student/faculty ratio:* 14:1.

Majors Accounting; American studies; anthropology; art history, criticism and conservation; biology/biological sciences; biology teacher education; business administration and management; ceramic arts and ceramics; chemistry; clinical laboratory science/medical technology; communications technology; criminal justice/law enforcement administration; cytotechnology; drama and dance teacher education; dramatic/theater arts; early childhood education; economics; elementary education; English; English/language arts teacher education; finance; fine/studio arts; French; French language teacher education; graphic design; historic preservation and conservation; history; history teacher education; information science/studies; liberal arts and sciences/liberal studies; mathematics; mathematics teacher education; music; music teacher education; nursing (registered nurse training); painting; philosophy; photography; political science and government; psychology; religious studies; secondary education; social work; sociology; Spanish; Spanish language teacher education; special education.

Academics *Calendar:* semesters. *Degrees:* certificates, associate, bachelor's, master's, doctoral, post-master's, and postbachelor's certificates. *Special study options:* accelerated degree program, adult/continuing education programs, advanced placement credit, distance learning, double majors, English as a second language, honors programs, independent study, internships, part-time degree program, services for LD students, study abroad, summer session for credit. *ROTC:* Army (c). *Unusual degree programs:* 3-2 business administration; international relations, rehabilitation counseling.

Computers on Campus 163 computers/terminals are available on campus for general student use. Students can access the following: campus intranet, computer help desk, free student e-mail accounts, online (class) grades, online (class) registration, online (class) schedules. Campuswide network is available. 100% of college-owned or -operated housing units are wired for high-speed Internet access. Wireless service is available via entire campus.

Student Life *Housing:* on-campus residence required through sophomore year. *Options:* coed, men-only, women-only, disabled students. Campus housing is university owned and leased by the school. Freshman campus housing is guaranteed. *Activities and organizations:* drama/theater group, student-run newspaper, radio station, choral group, Orpheus Musical Society, Student Government Association, Student Outdoor Adventures, Student Nurse Organization, Stagefright Theatre Company. *Campus security:* 24-hour emergency response devices and patrols, late-night transport/escort service, controlled dormitory access. *Student services:* health clinic, personal/psychological counseling.

Athletics Member NCAA. All Division III. *Intercollegiate sports:* baseball M, basketball M/W, cross-country running M/W, equestrian sports M (c)/W (c), field hockey W, football M, ice hockey M/W, lacrosse M/W, rugby M (c), sailing M/W, soccer M/W, softball W, tennis M/W, track and field W, volleyball W. *Intramural sports:* baseball M, basketball M/W, cheerleading W, field hockey W, football M/W, soccer M/W, softball M/W, tennis M/W, track and field W, volleyball M/W, weight lifting M/W.

Standardized Tests *Required:* SAT or ACT (for admission).
Costs (2007–08) *One-time required fee:* $2250. *Comprehensive fee:* $37,150 includes full-time tuition ($26,750), mandatory fees ($200), and room and board ($10,200). Part-time tuition: $892 per credit. Part-time tuition and fees vary according to course load. *Required fees:* $40 per term part-time. *Room and board:* Room and board charges vary according to board plan and housing facility. *Payment plan:* installment. *Waivers:* employees or children of employees.
Financial Aid Of all full-time matriculated undergraduates who enrolled in 2007, 1,637 applied for aid, 1,429 were judged to have need, 236 had their need fully met. 425 Federal Work-Study jobs (averaging $908). 280 state and other part-time jobs (averaging $1690). In 2007, 314 non-need-based awards were made. *Average percent of need met:* 69%. *Average financial aid package:* $19,291. *Average need-based loan:* $5529. *Average need-based gift aid:* $14,111. *Average indebtedness upon graduation:* $25,588.
Applying *Options:* electronic application, early action, deferred entrance. *Application fee:* $40. *Required:* essay or personal statement, high school transcript, 2 letters of recommendation. *Recommended:* minimum 2.7 GPA. *Application deadlines:* 3/1 (freshmen), rolling (transfers), 11/1 (early action). *Notification:* continuous (freshmen), continuous (transfers), 12/15 (early action).
Freshman Application Contact Ms. Colleen Emerson, Dean of Undergraduate Admissions, Salve Regina University, 100 Ochre Point Avenue, Newport, RI 02840-4192. *Phone:* 401-341-2109. *Toll-free phone:* 888-GO SALVE. *Fax:* 401-848-2823. *E-mail:* sruadmis@salve.edu.

See page 2370 for the College Close-Up.

University of Rhode Island

Kingston, Rhode Island **www.uri.edu**

- **State-supported** university, founded 1892, part of Rhode Island State System of Higher Education
- **Small-town** 1200-acre campus
- **Endowment** $68.0 million
- **Coed** 12,516 undergraduate students, 87% full-time, 56% women, 44% men
- **Moderately difficult** entrance level, 79% of applicants were admitted

Undergraduates 10,861 full-time, 1,655 part-time. Students come from 38 states and territories, 39% are from out of state, 5% African American, 2% Asian American or Pacific Islander, 5% Hispanic American, 0.5% Native American, 0.3% international, 5% transferred in, 45% live on campus. *Retention:* 81% of 2006 full-time freshmen returned.
Freshmen *Admission:* 14,272 applied, 11,300 admitted, 3,027 enrolled. *Test scores:* SAT critical reading scores over 500: 70%; SAT math scores over 500: 75%; SAT critical reading scores over 600: 26%; SAT math scores over 600: 28%; SAT critical reading scores over 700: 2%; SAT math scores over 700: 4%.
Faculty *Total:* 732, 96% full-time, 88% with terminal degrees. *Student/faculty ratio:* 19:1.
Majors Accounting; animal sciences; anthropology; apparel and accessories marketing; apparel and textiles; applied economics; art; art history, criticism and conservation; biology/biological sciences; biomedical/medical engineering; business administration and management; chemical engineering; chemistry; civil engineering; classics and languages, literatures and linguistics; clinical laboratory science/medical technology; communication disorders; communication/speech communication and rhetoric; comparative literature; computer and information sciences; computer engineering; consumer economics; dental hygiene; dietetics; econometrics and quantitative economics; economics; electrical, electronics and communications engineering; elementary education; English; environmental studies; finance; fishing and fisheries sciences and management; foods, nutrition, and wellness; French; geology/earth science; German; health/health care administration; history; human development and family studies; human services; industrial engineering; interdisciplinary studies; international business/trade/commerce; Italian; journalism; landscape architecture; Latin American studies; liberal arts and sciences/liberal studies; management information systems; marine biology and biological oceanography; marketing/marketing management; mathematics; mechanical engineering; medical microbiology and bacteriology; music; music performance; music teacher education; music theory and composition; natural resources/conservation; natural resources management and policy; nursing (registered nurse training); ocean engineering; pharmacy; philosophy; physical education teaching and coaching; physics; political science and government; psychology; public policy analysis; secondary education; sociology; Spanish; turf and turfgrass management; wildlife and wildlands science and management; women's studies; zoology/animal biology.
Academics *Calendar:* semesters. *Degrees:* bachelor's, master's, doctoral, first professional, and postbachelor's certificates. *Special study options:* academic remediation for entering students, adult/continuing education programs, advanced placement credit, cooperative education, distance learning, double majors, honors programs, independent study, internships, off-campus study, part-time degree program, services for LD students, study abroad, summer session for credit. *ROTC:* Army (b). *Unusual degree programs:* 3-2 physical therapy, speech pathology, audiology.
Computers on Campus 552 computers/terminals are available on campus for general student use. Campuswide network is available.
Student Life *Housing options:* coed, disabled students. *Activities and organizations:* drama/theater group, student-run newspaper, radio and television station, choral group, marching band, Student Entertainment Committee, student radio station, intramural sport clubs, Student Alumni Association, student newspaper, national fraternities, national sororities. *Campus security:* 24-hour emergency response devices and patrols, student patrols, late-night transport/escort service, controlled dormitory access. *Student services:* health clinic, personal/psychological counseling, women's center.
Athletics Member NCAA. All Division I except football (Division I-AA). *Intercollegiate sports:* baseball M (s), basketball M (s)/W (s), crew M (c)/W, cross-country running M (s)/W (s), equestrian sports M (c)/W (c), fencing M (c)/W (c), field hockey W (s), golf M (s), gymnastics W (s), ice hockey M (c), lacrosse M (c)/W (c), rugby M (c)/W (c), sailing M (c)/W (c), skiing (downhill) M (c)/W (c), soccer M (s)/W (s), softball W (s), swimming and diving M (s)/W (s), tennis M/W (s), track and field M (s)/W (s), volleyball M (c)/W (s), water polo M (c). *Intramural sports:* badminton M/W, basketball M/W, football M/W, golf M/W, soccer M/W, softball M/W, swimming and diving M/W, tennis M/W, volleyball M/W, water polo M/W.
Standardized Tests *Required:* SAT or ACT (for admission).
Costs (2007–08) *Tuition:* state resident $6440 full-time, $268 per credit part-time; nonresident $21,294 full-time, $887 per credit part-time. Full-time tuition and fees vary according to reciprocity agreements. Part-time tuition and fees vary according to reciprocity agreements. *Required fees:* $1744 full-time, $49 per credit part-time, $48 per credit part-time. *Room and board:* $8732; room only: $5016. Room and board charges vary according to board plan and housing facility. *Payment plan:* installment. *Waivers:* minority students, senior citizens, and employees or children of employees.
Financial Aid Of all full-time matriculated undergraduates who enrolled in 2007, 9,278 applied for aid, 7,766 were judged to have need, 4,026 had their need fully met. In 2007, 475 non-need-based awards were made. *Average percent of need met:* 63%. *Average financial aid package:* $13,343. *Average need-based loan:* $7369. *Average need-based gift aid:* $6826. *Average non-need-based aid:* $5701. *Average indebtedness upon graduation:* $21,125.
Applying *Options:* electronic application, early admission, early action. *Application fee:* $50. *Required:* high school transcript. *Required for some:* minimum 3.0 GPA. *Recommended:* minimum 3.0 GPA, letters of recommendation, interview. *Application deadlines:* 2/1 (freshmen), 5/1 (transfers), 12/15 (early action). *Notification:* continuous (freshmen), continuous (transfers), 1/15 (early action).
Freshman Application Contact Ms. Joanne Hood, Assistant Dean of Admissions, University of Rhode Island, 8 Ranger Road, Suite 1, Kingston, RI 02881-2020. *Phone:* 401-874-7110. *Fax:* 401-874-5523. *E-mail:* jhood@uri.edu.

See page 2372 for the College Close-Up.

Zion Bible College

Barrington, Rhode Island

BROWN UNIVERSITY

PROVIDENCE, RHODE ISLAND

The University

The history of Brown University reaches back over more than two centuries and tells of a university constantly undergoing change. Brown was established with a charter from the Colony's General Assembly in 1764, and the first men registered at the college in 1765. The first women were admitted in 1891, when the establishment of the Women's College in Brown University marked the beginning of eighty years of a coordinate structure for educating women within the University. Brown is now a coeducational institution, drawing men and women from all over the United States and many other countries to participate in the academic and extracurricular life of an Ivy League university. There are more than 7,000 students at Brown, of whom 5,700 are undergraduates.

A profile of the average Brown student is practically impossible to create. Here, the typical student is atypical and happy to be so. The diversity of Brown's student body is, in fact, one of the characteristics in which the University takes most pride. Given this diversity, however, there are still some generalizations that might apply to the Brown student body as a whole. One of them is that students have a deep concern for both the process and the quality of education. Another is the students' willingness, even eagerness, to become involved. Finally, it can be said that Brown students are highly motivated to seek advanced study after their undergraduate years.

Brown students feel a commitment to learn—and live—outside of the classroom. More than 200 clubs and activities thrive on the Brown campus. These range from athletic and recreational programs to community-service organizations and environmental-action groups; music, drama, and theater groups; literary publications; political organizations; clubs for vocational interests; and the nation's first college radio station. Specific activities vary from year to year according to student interest.

Brown's Graduate School and Medical School offer courses leading to the degrees of Master of Arts, Master of Science, Master of Arts in Teaching, Master of Medical Science, Master of Fine Arts, Master of Public Health, Doctor of Medicine, and Doctor of Philosophy.

Location

Providence, by virtue of its size, location, and diversity, offers many advantages to the college student. A city large enough to support a convention center and a large, active Civic Center that draws top entertainment and sports events, Providence is still small enough to offer involvement in local politics, community service, and cultural activities. Providence also offers an excellent repertory company and a major performing arts center as well as museums, concert halls, and a good commercial transportation system. It does not overwhelm the newcomer.

Majors and Degrees

Brown University offers the following degree programs for undergraduates: the Bachelor of Arts (A.B.), the Bachelor of Science (Sc.B.), a five-year program leading to the combined Bachelor of Science and Bachelor of Arts (Sc.B. and A.B.), and the Program in Liberal Medical Education, leading to a Bachelor of Arts or Bachelor of Science at the end of four years and an M.D. degree four years later (from the Brown Medical School). In addition, a five-year dual-degree program is offered in conjunction with Rhode Island School of Design where a student earns both a Bachelor of Arts and a Bachelor of Fine Arts degree.

Within a degree program, Brown students elect a concentration that is the focus of their undergraduate work. Standardized concentrations are available in the following areas: Africana studies, American civilization, ancient studies, anthropology, anthropology–linguistics, applied mathematics (applied mathematics–biology, applied mathematics–computer science, and applied mathematics–economics), architectural studies, art (applied art and art history), art–semiotics, biological and medical sciences (biochemistry, biology, biophysics, human biology, marine biology, molecular biology, and neuroscience), chemical physics, chemistry (biochemistry, geology–chemistry), classics (classics and Sanskrit, Greek, Greek and Latin, and Latin), cognitive neuroscience, cognitive science, commerce/organizations/and entrepreneurship, community health, comparative literature, computational biology, computer science, computer science–economics, development studies, East Asian studies, economics (economics and mathematics), education studies, Egyptology (Egyptian civilization, Egyptian history, and Egyptian language and literature), engineering (biomedical, chemical, civil, computer, electrical, materials, and mechanical engineering), engineering and economics, engineering and physics, English and American literature, environmental studies, ethnic studies, French studies, gender studies, geological sciences (geology–biology, geology–chemistry, and geology–physics/mathematics), German studies, Hispanic studies, history, history of art and architecture, institute for archaeology and the ancient world, international relations, Italian studies, Judaic studies, late antique cultures, Latin American studies, linguistics, literary arts, literatures and cultures in English, mathematics (mathematical economics, mathematics–computer science, and mathematics–physics), medieval cultures, Middle East studies, modern culture and media (modern culture and media–German and modern culture and media–Italian), music, neuroscience, Old World archaeology and art, philosophy (ethics and political philosophy, logic and philosophy of science), physics, political science, Portuguese and Brazilian studies, psychology, public policy/American institutions, religious studies, Renaissance and Early Modern studies, science and society, semiotics–French, sexuality and society, Slavic studies, sociology, South Asian studies, statistics, theater arts, urban studies, and visual art. In addition, each student at Brown may pursue study in any academic area through either independent study or an independent concentration program of the student's design.

Academic Programs

Brown's philosophy of education, promoted by students and endorsed by the faculty, can be simply stated: students will get more out of their education, and it will serve them better, if it is tailored to their individual needs and goals. Because Brown's curriculum has no distribution requirements, students have both the latitude and the responsibility to create an academic program that will reflect genuine and enduring personal accomplishment.

A student may register for and complete a maximum of forty semester courses; a minimum of thirty semester courses must be completed satisfactorily to earn a diploma. Course work can be evaluated by one of two grading systems at Brown: the ABC/No Credit option or the Satisfactory/No Credit option. Work that is judged by the instructor to be unsatisfactory receives no credit, and the student's registration in the class never appears on a formal transcript. A written analysis of the student's work, in the form of a Course Performance Report, may be requested. The student must complete a concentration in order to graduate. This ensures an in-depth study that is centered on the unit provided by a discipline or disciplines, a problem, a theme, or a broad question.

Advanced Placement credit is available, as are opportunities for independent or honors work. Brown operates on a two-semester calendar. The first term begins in early September and continues through mid-December, while the second term runs from late January until mid-May.

Off-Campus Programs

Brown students can enroll in as many as four courses at the Rhode Island School of Design (Brown's neighbor on College Hill). Many students choose to study abroad for a semester or a year; Brown directly sponsors more than fifty programs in fifteen countries.

Academic Facilities

The main campus of Brown University occupies an area of approximately 140 acres. More than fifty buildings are devoted to classroom, laboratory, research, library, office, and conference use by departments of instruction. The University Library, containing more than 5 million items, includes the John D. Rockefeller Jr. Library, the John Hay Library, the Sciences Library, the Orwig Music Library, the John Carter Brown Library, and the Ann Mary Brown Library. The University provides extensive modern laboratory and computer facilities designed for undergraduate and graduate instruction as well as research. The Performing Arts Complex, the Catherine Bryan Dill Center for the Performing Arts, includes the Leeds Theater, the Stuart Theater, and the Ashamu Dance Studio.

Costs

Tuition for the 2007–08 year was $35,584. The cost of room and board was $9606. Fees totaled $758. Books and personal expenses were estimated at $2712.

Financial Aid

Brown practices a need-blind admission policy. For applicants applying for financial assistance, the Financial Aid Office makes all awards on the basis of the candidate's need, as determined from the Financial Aid PROFILE analysis of the College Scholarship Service. A three-part package of aid is awarded, consisting of a scholarship, a loan, and a campus job (first-year students who are eligible for a University scholarship are not required to work). The University participates in the federally funded Federal Work-Study, Federal Supplemental Educational Opportunity Grant (FSEOG), and Federal Perkins Loan programs. Candidates should file the PROFILE application and the Free Application for Federal Student Aid (FAFSA) by February 1 and are notified of their award in April. Approximately 40 percent of students in each entering class receive University scholarship aid.

Faculty

Brown's faculty consists of 661 full-time and 139 visiting and adjunct teaching professors. Faculty members teach both graduate and undergraduate students, and each professor must teach an undergraduate class every year. The student-faculty ratio is 9:1, allowing for extensive counseling of students by the faculty. All professors have weekly office hours during which they are available to students. Faculty members and students serve jointly on approximately a dozen University committees concerning student affairs. While faculty members usually do not live in student dormitories, some members serve as dormitory liaisons, and the majority live close to the campus.

Student Government

The Brown Undergraduate Council of Students, a group of elected representatives, has primary responsibility for the disbursement of more than $500,000 in student monies. These funds are distributed among the more than 200 clubs, organizations, and activities that form the basis of extracurricular life at Brown. In addition, Brown undergraduates participate actively with faculty and administration on a host of campus committees concerned with University policies.

Admission Requirements

Individuals are considered for admission to Brown on the basis of academic and personal qualities. A strong scholastic background and the intellectual ability to meet the demands of a rigorous academic program are required. Secondary school records, teacher and counselor evaluations, and the results of standardized tests are all important factors in a decision. To obtain a diverse student body, Brown also reviews each candidate's credentials in light of the individual's strengths. Special interests, talents, and qualities are important; the Board of Admission is concerned with the extent to which each applicant might contribute in his or her own way to the total life of the University.

Application and Information

Students may apply to Brown by submitting an application for admission (Forms 1 and 1A) and the subsequent Forms 2 through 4, which include a personal statement, secondary school reports, and teacher references. The SAT Reasoning Test and two SAT Subject Tests of the College Board or the ACT (with the Writing Test) of the American College Testing Service must be taken. No interview is necessary. The application deadline for all forms is January 1. Notification is in early April. A fall notification plan, early decision, offers candidates the opportunity to apply in November (with a deadline of November 1 for all forms) and receive an admission notification in mid-December. Early decision is a binding early program for applicants who have selected Brown as their first-choice college and who will attend Brown if admitted as an early decision candidate.

Information and application materials may be obtained by contacting:

The College Admission Office
Brown University
Box 1876
Providence, Rhode Island 02912
Phone: 401-863-2378
E-mail: admission_undergraduate@brown.edu
Web site: http://www.brown.edu

BRYANT UNIVERSITY

SMITHFIELD, RHODE ISLAND

The University

Founded in 1863, Bryant is a four-year, private university in New England where students build knowledge, develop character, and achieve success—as *they* define it.

Throughout its 144-year history, Bryant has empowered students to achieve their personal best in life and their chosen careers. The University is the choice for individuals seeking the best integration of business and liberal arts and state-of-the-art technology. Its cross-disciplinary approach provides a well-rounded education that teaches students the creative problem-solving and communication skills they need to successfully compete in a complex, global environment.

Bryant's 3,268 full-time undergraduate students represent thirty-two states and thirty-four countries. They enjoy all the advantages of small classes and the close relationships among students, faculty members, and administrators. In this environment, students come to understand the interaction between various academic disciplines and their practical applications in the global community.

Sports and recreation play an integral role at Bryant. Students can balance their academic pursuits with overall well-being at the Elizabeth and Malcolm Chace Wellness and Athletic Center. This impressive facility features a fully equipped fitness center, a six-lane swimming pool, circuit-training equipment and free weights, and a group exercise room. Students can participate in any of Bryant's twenty-two intercollegiate varsity sports teams, which will begin competing at the Division I level in 2012. In addition, students can participate in club and intramural sports throughout the academic year. Teams play on a variety of well-maintained athletic fields, and spectators can watch from the 4,000-seat Bulldog Stadium.

Bryant has close to eighty student clubs and organizations that benefit many social causes, provide recreational enjoyment, promote intellectual exploration, and offer opportunities to develop new talents and passions. The Student Programming Board, the Intercultural Center, the Arts and Culture Club, the Marketing Association, and the Student Senate are just a few of the organizations where students can get involved in campus life. There are many places on and off campus for students to gather and enjoy music, comedy, and other kinds of entertainment.

Bryant's rigorous academic programs are accredited by the New England Association of Schools and Colleges (NEASC). The University's College of Business is accredited by AACSB International–The Association to Advance Collegiate Schools of Business, a distinction earned by only 10 percent of universities worldwide.

Bryant's Graduate School of Business offers a Master of Business Administration (M.B.A.), a Master of Science in Taxation (M.S.T.), and a Master of Professional Accountancy (M.P.Ac.).

Location

Bryant University is situated on a beautiful 420-acre campus in Smithfield, Rhode Island. The campus is only 15 minutes from the state capital, Providence; 45 minutes from Boston; and 3 hours from New York City. Students can enjoy an array of activities on and off campus as well as excellent restaurants and sports events in the area.

Students are able to take advantage of internship and employment opportunities at many small and large businesses, Fortune 500 companies, and not-for-profit organizations within driving distance of the Bryant campus. All students, including freshmen, may have a car on campus. Additional transportation includes a train station in Providence and airports in nearby Warwick and Boston.

Majors and Degrees

Bryant's College of Arts and Sciences offers degrees in actuarial mathematics, applied economics, applied mathematics and statistics, applied psychology, communication, global studies, history, liberal arts, literary and cultural studies, politics and law, and sociology. The College of Business offers degrees in business administration with concentrations in accounting, computer information systems, finance, financial services, management, and marketing; information technology; and international business with concentrations in computer information systems, finance, management, and marketing.

Bryant offers twenty-seven minors in business and liberal arts. To view the additional eighty areas of study, students should visit http://www.bryant.edu/areasofstudy.

Academic Programs

Academic programs focus on the intellectual and professional development of each student, in preparation for leadership positions in a wide range of careers.

Students must complete a core curriculum that integrates business, liberal arts, and technology. Graduation requirements include a minimum of 123 semester hours, and Bryant University operates on a semester plan.

Entering students may receive credit through the Advanced Placement (AP) Program or the College-Level Examination Program (CLEP) administered by the College Board. Credit is also awarded for International Baccalaureate (IB) higher-level exams. The Honors Program is an excellent vehicle for highly motivated students to stretch their intellectual limits and experience stimulating academic challenges.

Bryant also participates in the Army ROTC Program.

Off-Campus Programs

The Amica Center for Career Education, recently named one of the top 10 university career and job placement services in the country by the Princeton Review, offers students opportunities to expand their learning beyond the classroom. Through relationships with more than 350 companies, the center helps students secure practical internships at organizations such as Fidelity Investments, PricewaterhouseCoopers, Walt Disney World, the New England Patriots, Textron, media outlets, and a variety of non-profit organizations. The Amica Center for Career Education also helps graduating seniors identify and pursue job opportunities.

In addition, the John H. Chafee Center for International Business links Bryant students directly to regional businesses that operate globally. Students can gain practical global business experiences through internships and assistantships with the Chafee Center.

Qualifying students may participate in Bryant's Study Abroad Program, where they can choose to study in one of forty-three partner countries. The University also offers a Sophomore International Experience, where students spend two weeks overseas to learn about other cultures and how businesses operate globally.

Academic Facilities

Bryant's modern campus is anchored by the Unistructure, the center of academic and social activity. The Bryant Center houses the bookstore, student organization offices, a dining hall, and a food court. The Koffler Center and the Communications Complex feature several computer labs, a state-of-the-art digital television studio and editing suites, and Bryant's student-run radio station.

The George E. Bello Center for Information and Technology has thousands of wired and wireless data ports and banks of high-speed computers. The C.V. Starr Financial Markets Center receives real-time data via live feeds through Reuters 3000, the same system used by top international financial institutions. The Bello Center also houses the state-of-the-art Douglas and Judith Krupp Library. It holds more than 150,000 items and thousands of reference databases and online resources, making it one of the most comprehensive business library collections in the region.

As part of their tuition, all freshmen receive Thinkpad® notebook computers that are network ready and fully loaded with software. Students can work on their laptops virtually anywhere on Bryant's wireless campus. Prior to the beginning of junior year, students exchange this laptop for a new model, which they may keep upon graduation. Every three years, instructional computers in the classrooms are upgraded or replaced.

Costs

For 2007–08, tuition was $27,639, which includes personal use of a Thinkpad® notebook computer for entering students. Residence hall room and board fees were $10,715. Tuition and fees are subject to change. Eighty-seven percent of students live on campus. There are a variety of housing arrangements, including the first-year complex, suite-style residence halls, and the town houses for seniors. There are special fees for summer and winter sessions.

Financial Aid

Bryant has a comprehensive program of merit- and need-based financial aid. More than $63 million in financial aid to cover educational expenses was processed for Bryant students in 2007–08. The majority of freshmen receive financial aid through a combination of scholarships, loans, grants, and part-time jobs. Students interested in applying for financial assistance in the form of need-based grants, work-study, and education loans need to file a Free Application for Federal Student Aid (FAFSA). The FAFSA can be found online at http://www.fafsa.ed.gov. The paper version of the FAFSA is available in high school guidance offices. The FAFSA can be submitted as early as January 1, and February 15 is the deadline. For more information, students should contact the Director of Financial Aid.

Faculty

Bryant faculty members are dedicated to helping students develop their intellectual potential. They continuously engage in research, publishing, consulting, community service, and practical experience. With a 16:1 student-faculty ratio, each student can develop relationships with faculty members for guidance and support. Among the faculty members at Bryant are a practicing clinical psychologist, a nationally respected expert in advertising effectiveness and public policy, and the former state poet laureate of Rhode Island.

Student Government

The Student Senate, the student governing body, serves as a channel of communication between students and faculty and administrators.

Admission Requirements

Bryant University seeks students who are motivated learners and have a history of academic achievement. Minimum entrance requirements include 4 years each of English and preparatory mathematics, including a year beyond algebra II (with a preference for precalculus or calculus in the senior year), and 2 years each of history or social science, a laboratory science, and a foreign language. Remaining secondary course work should be in a foreign language, mathematics, science, and social studies. Entering students may receive credit through the Advanced Placement (AP) Program or the College-Level Examination Program (CLEP) administered by the College Board. Credit is also awarded for International Baccalaureate (IB) higher-level exams.

SAT or ACT scores must be submitted. The Admission Committee considers recommendations from the secondary school guidance office and faculty members concerning character and personal qualifications that are not in the academic record. Interviews, though not required, may be scheduled in advance of a campus visit.

Application and Information

Applications must be submitted to the Office of Admission with a nonrefundable fee of $50 by November 15 (early decision) or February 1 (regular decision). It is the responsibility of the applicant to request that the secondary school guidance office send a copy of the student's school record directly to Bryant and also have SAT or ACT scores sent. International applicants must also submit TOEFL scores and a completed Certification of Finances form.

For admission information:
Director of Admission
Bryant University
1150 Douglas Pike
Smithfield, Rhode Island 02917-1285
Phone: 401-232-6100
800-622-7001 (toll-free)
Fax: 401-232-6741
E-mail: admission@bryant.edu
Web site: http://admission.bryant.edu

For financial aid information:
Director of Financial Aid
Phone: 401-232-6020
800-248-4036 (toll-free)
Fax: 401-232-6319
E-mail: finaid@bryant.edu
Web site: http://admission.bryant.edu

Bryant offers a comprehensive education that integrates business and liberal arts, using state-of-the-art technology.

JOHNSON & WALES UNIVERSITY

PROVIDENCE, RHODE ISLAND

The University

Founded in Providence in 1914, Johnson & Wales University (JWU) is a private, not-for-profit, career-oriented institution offering programs that are geared to the success of a range of students. The University's 16,095 students attend classes at campuses in Providence, Rhode Island; North Miami, Florida; Denver, Colorado; and Charlotte, North Carolina. Most students are recent graduates of high school business, college-preparatory, and vocational/technical programs, representing fifty states and eighty-nine countries. The academic focus of the University is on degree programs in business, culinary arts, food service, hospitality, and technology. M.B.A. programs include global business leadership (with concentrations in accounting, financial management, international trade, organizational leadership, or marketing) and hospitality and tourism global business leadership (with concentrations in finance and marketing). M.A. programs in teaching (with or without certification) include business, food service, and special education. The Graduate School also offers the Certificate of Advanced Graduate Study (CAGS) in finance, human resources management, and hospitality. There is also a Certificate in Corporate Security available to candidates holding a bachelor's degree. The University also offers a doctoral program in educational leadership.

Students are involved in a variety of extracurricular activities. Nearly 20 percent of the University's population are members of national student organizations such as Business Professionals of America; DECA (Delta Epsilon Chi), Future Business Leaders of America (Phi Beta Lambda); Family, Career, Community Leaders of America (FCCLA); National FFA; Junior Achievement; SkillsUSA; and Technology Association of America. The Student Activities Office and fraternities and sororities are among the many groups that schedule social functions throughout the academic year. Sports and fitness programs include aerobics, baseball, basketball, golf, ice hockey, sailing, soccer, tennis, volleyball, and wrestling.

The University maintains twenty-four residence halls throughout its four campuses. In addition, City View Towers, which is independently owned and operated, offers housing near the Charlotte campus for upperclassmen. Student services include academic counseling and testing, a tutorial center, and health services. The University's Career Development Office provides extensive career planning and placement services. Within sixty days of graduation, 98 percent of JWU students from the fifty states have jobs in their chosen career field.

Johnson & Wales is accredited by the New England Association of Schools and Colleges. The hospitality programs in Providence are accredited by the Accreditation Commission for Programs in Hospitality Administration.

Location

The location of each of the University's campuses enables students to take advantage of internship and part-time work activities offered by many nearby businesses, community groups, and government agencies. All of Johnson & Wales' city campuses retain a small-town feel and easy accessibility to students. The urban setting of the Providence, Rhode Island, campus provides students proximity to the city's many cultural and recreational facilities. In North Miami, Florida, the JWU campus is a short trip from the sun and fun of Fort Lauderdale and the culture and diversity of Miami. Denver, Colorado, offers students great opportunities as the nation's sixth-leading tourist destination and *Fortune* magazine's "second best city in America to work and live." The Charlotte, North Carolina, campus is located in a vibrant urban setting that combines commercial and residential life. More than 300 Fortune 500 companies have offices in Charlotte, which is known as the second-largest financial center in the U.S.

Majors and Degrees

The degree programs described in this section were for the 2007–08 academic year and are subject to change. Students may pursue concentrations related to their program of study to further tailor their degrees to their specific interests and career goals. They also have the opportunity to take concentrations through the School of Arts and Sciences.

Johnson & Wales University's Providence campus offers degree programs in accounting; advertising and marketing communications; baking and pastry arts; business administration; business/information systems analysis; computer graphics and new media; criminal justice; culinary arts; culinary arts and food service management; culinary nutrition; electronics engineering; engineering design and configuration management; entrepreneurship; equine business management; equine business management/riding; fashion merchandising and retail marketing; financial services management; food marketing; food service entrepreneurship; hotel and lodging management; international business; international hotel and tourism management; management; marketing; network engineering; pastry arts and food service management; restaurant, food, and beverage management; software engineering; sports/entertainment/event management; technology services management; travel, tourism, and hospitality management; Web management and Internet commerce; and Web site development.

In its Continuing Education division, Johnson & Wales' Providence campus offers associate and bachelor's degrees in business, culinary arts, hospitality, and technology. JWU also offers diploma programs in baking and pastry arts and culinary arts; certificate programs are offered in computer-aided drafting, legal nurse studies, and paralegal studies.

The North Miami, Florida, campus offers degree programs in baking and pastry arts; business administration; criminal justice; culinary arts; culinary arts and food service management; fashion merchandising and retail marketing; hotel and lodging management; management; marketing; pastry arts and food service management; restaurant, food, and beverage management; sports/entertainment/event management; and travel, tourism, and hospitality management.

The Denver, Colorado, campus offers degree programs in advertising and marketing communications; baking and pastry arts; business administration; criminal justice; culinary arts; culinary arts and food service management; culinary nutrition; entrepreneurship; fashion merchandising and retail marketing; hotel and lodging management; international business; management; marketing; pastry arts and food service management; restaurant, food, and beverage management; and sports/entertainment/event management.

The Charlotte, North Carolina, campus offers degree programs in accounting; baking and pastry arts; business administration; culinary arts; culinary arts and food service management; fashion merchandising and retail marketing; hotel and lodging management; international hotel and tourism management; management; marketing; pastry arts and food service management; restaurant, food, and beverage management; and sports/entertainment/event management.

Academic Programs

Johnson & Wales University offers programs in business, culinary arts, food service, hospitality, and technology within an academic structure of three 11-week terms. The "upside-down" curriculum of the University provides immediate concentration in the student's chosen major.

Learning by doing is an important part of career training at JWU, and many programs include laboratory studies as well as formal internship requirements. Special advanced-placement programs are featured for high school seniors with exceptional skills in culinary arts or baking and pastry arts. In addition, the University awards credit for certain courses based on the successful completion of Challenge, CLEP, or Portfolio Assessments. All degree candidates must successfully complete the required number of courses and/or quarter credit hours, as prescribed in the various curricula, with a minimum average of 2.0 or higher, depending on the program.

Off-Campus Programs

Learning at Johnson & Wales is not limited to the classroom. Many of the majors offer internships at University-owned facilities. The hotel-restaurant management program features an internship at the Johnson & Wales Inn, Radisson Airport Hotel, Bay Harbor Inn and Suites, or DoubleTree Hotel; all are full-service hotel complexes that are owned and/or operated by the University (the Radisson and DoubleTree are corporate franchises). For all majors, optional selective career co-ops are available with cooperating businesses throughout the U.S. and worldwide, such as Marriott International, Compass Group NAD, Foxwoods Resort and Casino, and Putnam Investments. Most internships and co-ops are one term in duration and carry 13.5 quarter hours of credit. International exchange and term-abroad programs are also offered.

Academic Facilities

The facilities of the Providence campus are located throughout the intimate state of Rhode Island and in nearby Massachusetts. The downtown Providence campus is home to the University's College of Business, the Hospitality College, and the School of Technology. A number of academic and residential facilities are located at this campus, as are several training facilities. The Harborside campus, also in Providence but located a short distance away, houses the University's College of Culinary Arts. This campus has five student residence halls as well as specialized classrooms and laboratories, production kitchens, bakeshops, dining rooms, a storeroom, and meat-cutting facilities. This campus is also home to the Alan Shawn Feinstein Graduate School, the School of Education, the University Recreation and Athletic Center, a student activities office, a bookstore, a gymnasium, a dining center, a snack bar, and an arcade.

In North Miami, Florida, the campus is located in the heart of North Miami, between Miami and Fort Lauderdale. Facilities include academic classrooms, production/demonstration kitchens, a bakeshop, residence halls, and a specially designed conference center.

The Denver, Colorado, campus, which is located in the Park Hill neighborhood, combines old-world charm with the latest technological resources, including stately turn-of-the-century buildings and newer student centers in a quiet park landscape. The traditional residential campus is fully wired, with computers in every classroom and laboratory.

The Charlotte, North Carolina, campus is located in the heart of Gateway Village in Uptown Charlotte. The academic center is home to a 200-seat auditorium, a production kitchen, state-of-the-art culinary laboratories, classrooms, seminar rooms, and computer labs.

Costs

Tuition at all campuses for 2007–08 was $20,478. Room and board plans ranged from $7650 to $9600. Each student was also charged a general fee of $984, and there was an orientation fee of $255 for new students. Books and supplies were estimated at $700 to $900 per year, depending on the program. A weekend meal plan was also available for $987 per year.

Room and board fees vary at each campus. Students should consult the respective campus catalogs for further details.

Financial Aid

Johnson & Wales students are eligible to apply for a variety of financial aid programs, including the Federal Pell Grant, Federal Supplemental Educational Opportunity Grant, Federal Work-Study, and Federal Perkins Loan programs. They are also eligible for University-based student scholarship programs and state-supported grants and scholarships. In the past, approximately 90 percent of the University's entering students have received some sort of financial assistance. Students must submit the Free Application for Federal Student Aid (FAFSA) to the Federal Student Aid Processor to be considered for financial aid. Early application is strongly suggested for full consideration.

Faculty

The University's 472 full-time and 202 part-time faculty members (all campuses) are oriented toward instruction rather than research. Many are chosen for their professional experience in business, culinary arts, hospitality services, or technology. The student-faculty ratio is 31:1.

Student Government

Student Government Association (SGA) is the voice of students on campus and serves as the governing student organization on campus. Students are elected to major leadership positions in the spring, and senator positions are available to any interested student in the fall. SGA is responsible for allocating student funds, recognizing new organizations, and addressing student concerns on campus.

Admission Requirements

Johnson & Wales University seeks students who are career-focused and have a true desire to succeed. Academic qualifications are important, but an applicant's motivation and interest in doing well are given special consideration. Graduation from high school or the equivalent credentials are required for admission. It is recommended that students applying for admission into the culinary arts and baking and pastry arts programs have some prior education or experience in food service. A bachelor's degree is required for acceptance into the paralegal studies certificate program, and a student must be a registered nurse and hold an associate degree for acceptance into the legal nurse certificate program. Although tests are not required for most programs, all applicants are encouraged to submit scores from the SAT or ACT. Students who wish to apply for the honors program must have either a score of at least 500 math and 500 critical reading on the SAT or a score of at least 21 math and 21 verbal on the ACT. High school juniors may apply for early admission under the Early Enrollment Program (EEP). Transfer students are required to submit official high school and college transcripts and to have a minimum GPA of 2.0. Credits to be transferred from other institutions are evaluated on the basis of their equivalent at Johnson & Wales.

Application and Information

Johnson & Wales does not require an application fee. After submitting the application, the student is responsible for requesting that appropriate transcripts be forwarded to the Admissions Office of the University. While there is no deadline, students are advised to apply as early as possible before the intended date of enrollment to ensure full consideration of their application. Applications are accepted for terms beginning in September, December, and March and for the summer sessions (for most programs).

Inquiries and applications should be addressed to:

Kenneth DiSaia
Vice President of Enrollment Management
Johnson & Wales University
8 Abbott Park Place
Providence, Rhode Island 02903
Phone: 401-598-1000
800-DIAL-JWU (toll-free)
Fax: 401-598-4901
E-mail: jwu@admissions.jwu.edu
Web site: http://www.jwu.edu

PROVIDENCE COLLEGE

PROVIDENCE, RHODE ISLAND

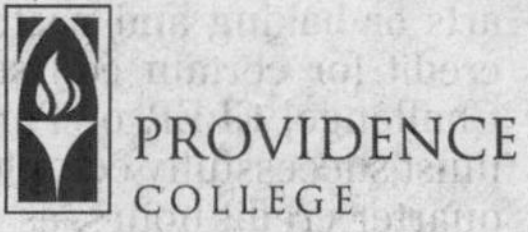

The College

Under the auspices of the Order of Preachers of the Province of St. Joseph, commonly known as the Dominicans, Providence College (PC) was established in 1917. Originally a college for men, it became coeducational in 1971. The College's full-time undergraduate enrollment is 3,850 students. Approximately 1,800 students live in nine residential halls and a suite-style residence facility, and an additional 900 upperclass students are housed in one of the five College apartment complexes. The remainder of the students live in apartments directly off campus or commute from home. At the graduate level, the College offers M.A., M.S., M.Ed., M.B.A., and Ph.D. degree programs.

The Slavin Center, as the nucleus of student, social, cultural, and recreational activity, provides numerous facilities. They include lounges; McPhail's Entertainment Facility; a newly renovated dining facility; club offices; an ATM machine; a bookstore/gift shop; the Student Activities, Involvement, and Leadership Office (SAIL); and offices for the Student Congress, the Board of Programmers, student publications, and the Career Services Office.

The Concannon Fitness Center, a 23,000-square-foot, two-level, state-of-the-art facility, opened in September 2007. Emphasizing the College's commitment to health and fitness, the center offers 62 cardiovascular machines—all but six are equipped with cable TV. There are eight types of cardiovascular machines, including eighteen treadmills, twelve cross-trainers, twelve arc-trainers, six upright bikes, and six recumbent bikes. The center also offers fitness options from selectorized strength pieces and cable motion pieces to numerous workout benches and free weights.

The Peterson Recreation Center is the site of intramural athletic activities on campus, which has one of the highest participation rates in the country. The center has five convertible basketball, tennis, and volleyball courts; a 220-yard track; three racquetball courts; a 25-meter pool; and an aerobics room. Providence College has a fine tradition of competition in intercollegiate athletics, and it continues to play an active role through its membership in the NCAA, ECAC, Hockey East Conference, Big East Conference, and Metro Atlantic Athletic Conference. Additional on-campus sports facilities include Alumni Hall, Schneider Arena, three large fields and recreational areas, and a new artificial-turf field for varsity, club, and intramural sports.

Location

The College is situated on a 105-acre campus in the city of Providence, Rhode Island. It has the advantages of an atmosphere that is far removed from the traffic and commerce of the metropolitan area but is also conveniently located near the many cultural attractions of a vibrant city that is not only the capital of a historic state but also the center of a variety of institutions of higher learning. Providence College has an established relationship with the Tony Award–winning Trinity Square Repertory Company, which is located in downtown Providence. Trinity provides special discount rates for students for the full spectrum of its programs. The Providence Performing Arts Center, which was originally a movie palace, has been restored to its former baroque splendor and now serves as the site of symphony concerts, opera, ballet, and road shows of Broadway musicals. In addition, the Dunkin' Donuts Civic Center attracts well-known performers and rock groups, trade shows, and sports events. The center is also the home court of the Friars, PC's basketball team. A Providence College ID enables students to travel free on any RIPTA bus route throughout Rhode Island.

Majors and Degrees

Providence College offers the B.A. degree, with major programs of study in American studies, art and art history, biology, business economics, chemistry, economics, education (elementary/special and secondary), English, global studies, history, humanities, mathematics, modern languages, music/music education (K–12), philosophy, political science, psychology, public and community service studies, social science, social work, sociology, theater arts, and theology. The B.S. degree is offered, with major programs of study in accountancy, applied physics, biochemistry, biology, chemistry, combined biology/optometry (3+4 program), computer science, engineering (3+2 program), finance, health policy and management, management, and marketing. The College also offers a 4+1 B.A./B.S./M.B.A. program for qualified students.

Academic Programs

The primary objective of Providence College is to further the intellectual development of its students through the disciplines of the sciences and the humanities. The liberal education provided by the College gives students the chance to increase their ability to formulate their thoughts and communicate them to others, evaluate their varied experiences, and achieve insight into the past, present, and future of civilization. The College is concerned about preparing students to become intelligent, productive, and responsible citizens in a democratic society. To this end, it endeavors not only to develop the students' capacity for disciplined thinking and critical exactness but also to give them opportunities for healthy physical development and a wide range of activities that foster a sense of social responsibility. The College's programs are also designed to help students discover their particular aptitude and prepare them to undertake specialized studies leading to careers.

Students are required to complete a minimum of 116 semester hours in the core curriculum, a selected major, and electives. The core curriculum is built around a broad range of disciplines, and 20 semester hours are allotted to study of the development of Western civilization, 6 to social science, 6 to philosophy, 6 to religion, 6 to natural science, 3 to mathematics, and 3 to the fine arts. All undergraduates must demonstrate proficiency in writing by the end of the sophomore year as part of the College's core-curriculum requirements. Special academic programs are offered to enhance the educational experience and allow for a variety of interests, including double majors, individualized programs, nondepartmental courses, liberal arts honors, preprofessional medical and legal programs, the Early Identification Program (offered to Rhode Island residents in cooperation with Brown University Medical School), and Army ROTC.

The College participates in the Advanced Placement Program, which is administered by the College Board. Students who demonstrate superior performance (a score of 4 or 5) on any of the Advanced Placement examinations are considered for advanced placement and standing in the area of study in which they qualify.

Providence College recognizes credit earned through the International Baccalaureate (I.B.), an internationally recognized curriculum and examination program. The College recognizes the Higher Level examinations when a score of 5, 6, or 7 has been achieved. Each examination that is successfully passed in the Higher Level of the I.B. program earns 3 credits.

PC operates on a two-semester calendar. Fall-semester classes begin in early September and spring-semester classes begin in mid-January.

Off-Campus Programs

Providence College recognizes that a liberal arts education can be enriched through diverse intellectual and social experiences and encourages all of its students to study abroad. With a new Center for International Studies, there is renewed energy in the opportunities available for students to gain an international academic experience. Providence College is one of the few institutions to have study-abroad arrangements with both Oxford University and Cambridge University in England. Students may also study in Africa, Asia, Australia, New Zealand, Central and Latin America, Europe, and Russia. A few of the countries that are most popular among PC students are Spain, Italy, Ireland, and England. The Washington Semester is also an option for students, allowing them to enrich their education by spending one semester of academic study and experiential learning at American University in Washington, D.C.

Academic Facilities

The Phillips Memorial Library, which has received two national architectural awards for its design, is the center of intellectual activity at the College. PC's library is an electronic resource complete with radio-frequency technology, a wireless network, electronic classrooms, and the second-largest electronic database access in the state. The library has current holdings of 366,000 volumes in open stacks and seating accommodations for 750 students. Phillips Library also houses various faculty offices, reading and rare-book rooms, archives, the Department of English, and the Office of Academic Services. The library is a member of the Consortium of Rhode Island Academic and Research Libraries, through which the resources of most of the libraries in the state are accessible to Providence College students. Located in Accino Hall and Koffler Hall are the College's academic microcomputer laboratories, which serve the computer instruction and research needs of faculty members and students. The College's state-of-the-art science laboratories, computer workstations, and research facilities are located in the Albertus Magnus–Sowa–Hickey Science Complex. The Feinstein Academic Center is a newly renovated academic facility that is the home of the Feinstein Institute for Public Service Program, the Liberal Arts Honors Program, and the Center for Teaching Excellence. The comprehensive new Smith Center for the Arts features a theater, a concert hall, a dance studio, a black-box theater, music practice rooms, and scenery and costume shops.

Costs

The total costs for the 2007–08 academic year were tuition, $28,920; room, $5785; and board, $4550 (seven-day plan). Books, travel, and personal supplies are estimated to cost $1500.

Financial Aid

Providence College's financial aid is distributed on the basis of demonstrated need and the student's ability to benefit from the educational opportunity the assistance offers. To apply for financial aid, candidates who are applying for Early Action must submit a College Scholarship Service PROFILE application by December 1 and the Free Application for Federal Student Aid (FAFSA) by February 1. Students applying for Regular Decision must submit both the College Scholarship Service PROFILE application and the FAFSA by February 1. Upon final determination of students' need, the Office of Financial Aid constructs aid packages consisting of work, loan, and grant assistance in accordance with federal regulations, the availability of funds, and institutional policy, as approved by the College's Financial Aid Advisory Committee. Sources of financial aid include Federal Work-Study Program awards, Federal Perkins Loans, Federal Pell Grants, Federal Supplemental Educational Opportunity Grants (FSEOG), Providence College grants-in-aid, Providence College Achievement Scholarships, and Merit Scholarships for highly qualified students who are invited into the Liberal Arts Honors Program.

Faculty

The faculty consists of 295 full-time and 75 visiting and adjunct professors, approximately 10 percent of whom are Dominican fathers and sisters. The majority of PC instructors teach both undergraduate- and graduate-level courses; no graduate students or student assistants teach at either level. About 91 percent of the faculty members hold terminal degrees. All professors devote their time primarily to teaching and advising undergraduates; all students are assigned a faculty adviser in their major area. The student-faculty ratio is 12:1.

Student Government

The Student Congress represents the students in its emphasis upon lifestyles and student prerogatives. Its officers are elected annually by the entire student community, and representatives are elected by each class. The Student Congress has created the Providence College Bill of Rights, the most significant of its legislative actions. Student representatives are appointed annually by the Student Congress to all standing committees of the College. The Student Congress has primary responsibility for the allocation of $125,500 in student activity funds to support most student-run organizations.

Admission Requirements

The admission committee gives recognition to students with various talents, backgrounds, and geographic origins. Admission decisions are made without regard to race, color, sex, handicap, age, or national or ethnic origin. An estimate of the applicant's character and accomplishments by his or her college adviser in secondary school and an official transcript of the secondary school record should be sent to the College no later than November 1 for Early Action and January 15 for Regular Decision. The secondary school transcript should consist of courses of a substantially college-preparatory nature. Although individual cases may vary, the College highly recommends that a student complete 4 years of English, 4 of mathematics, 3 of one foreign language, at least 2 of laboratory sciences, and 2 of social sciences. However, students who have been most competitive for admission in recent years have taken 4 years in all academic subject areas, taking advantage of honors or advanced-level courses that are available at their high school. Applicants are encouraged to submit letters of recommendation and evaluation from their secondary school teachers, especially from English teachers. Letters of recommendation from people who know the applicant personally and who have been involved in his or her scholastic development are most valuable.

Submission of standardized test scores is optional for students applying for admission. The academic review for admission at Providence College has always focused on each student's high school performance rather than standardized test results. This policy change allows each student to decide whether they wish to have their standardized test results considered as part of their application for admission. Students who choose not to submit SAT or ACT test scores will not be penalized in the review for admission. Additional details about the test-optional policy can be found online at http://www.providence.edu/testoptionalpolicy.

Application and Information

Providence College accepts the Common Application. The deadline for receiving freshman applications for the September term is November 1 for Early Action and January 15 for Regular Decision. The deadline for receiving transfer applications is April 1 for the fall term and December 1 for the spring term. Further information may be obtained by contacting:

Providence College
549 River Avenue
Providence, Rhode Island 02918-0001
Phone: 401-865-2535
800-721-6444 (toll-free)
Fax: 401-865-2826
E-mail: pcadmiss@providence.edu
Web site: http://www.providence.edu

Harkins Hall, the administration building at Providence College.

ROGER WILLIAMS UNIVERSITY

BRISTOL, RHODE ISLAND

The University

Roger Williams University (RWU), which has been ranked in the top tier of Best Comprehensive Colleges in its region and category by *U.S. News & World Report*'s "America's Best Colleges," has experienced tremendous growth with new facilities and an increasingly diverse and vigorous academic curriculum. During the last decade, Roger Williams has moved ahead by expanding undergraduate programs and creating master's degree programs to meet students' needs. As a leading liberal arts university, Roger Williams exemplifies core values that represent higher education at its best: a love for learning, preparation for the future, applied research, service to others and the community as a whole, a global perspective, and respect for the individual. Accredited by the New England Association of Schools and Colleges, Roger Williams University is an independent, coeducational university offering liberal arts and selected professional programs. The University enrolls approximately 3,775 full-time undergraduate students in thirty-eight majors, instructed by a full-time faculty of 192 professors in a medium-sized residential campus setting. The School of Law, the first and only law school in Rhode Island and a member of the Association of American Law Schools (AALS), offers the Juris Doctor degree and enrolls approximately 600 students. Master's programs in architecture, criminal justice, forensic psychology, literacy education, public administration, and teaching enroll approximately 250 students. Roger Williams University's strong teaching orientation and dedicated faculty members, who are noted experts in their fields, take a genuine interest in students, ensuring an engaging learning environment.

The main campus, overlooking beautiful Mt. Hope Bay in Bristol, Rhode Island, opened in 1969 and features modern academic and recreational facilities, including a waterfront Marine and Natural Sciences Building; the 150,000-square-foot School of Law and Law Library; an $8-million Main Library; the award-winning Architecture Building and Architecture Library; and the Performing Arts Center. In 2003, the University opened a multimillion-dollar addition to the Campus Recreation Center. The addition includes an eight-lane swimming pool, racquetball courts, and a state-of-the-art workout facility. In 2006, the University opened a dining commons, with dining facilities and a campus bookstore as well as comfortable lounges and meeting space. The University values the importance of continuing to upgrade facilities for an ideal living, learning, and wellness environment for students. Outdoor recreational facilities include softball and baseball diamonds, three rugby/lacrosse/soccer fields, six tennis courts, and a jogging track. Roger Williams University teams compete in Division III of the National Collegiate Athletic Association (NCAA), the Eastern College Athletic Conference (ECAC), and the Commonwealth Coast Conference (CCC); the University sponsors eighteen varsity sports for men and women as well as clubs in men's and women's rugby, coed crew, and coed track and field. In addition, an extensive program of intramural and recreational activities is offered all year long, with drop-in recreational activities available to the student body.

Many student residences claim impressive, sweeping waterfront views of spectacular Mt. Hope Bay. One of the most modern residence halls, Stonewall Terrace, is a wonderful addition to students' housing options. The four 3-story complexes house upperclass residents in single and double rooms in a suite-style arrangement. Each room is carpeted and fully air-conditioned. Spacious common areas provide additional meeting, study, and programming space for residents. A variety of other comfortable residences located on the main campus offer students a choice of residential living in facilities directly on Mt. Hope Bay. The Bayside Courts offers town-house-style accommodations overlooking the water. There also is an apartment complex, which is managed by the University, 2 miles from the campus. Residential units include 24-hour quiet areas for study and some specialized living/learning units grouped by major or areas of interest, including honors and wellness initiatives.

The University sponsors many athletic, social, cultural, and academic activities. Students may choose from a variety of structured and informal activities, including Socrates Café, which is held in the Mary Tefft White Cultural Center; the Alive! Arts Series; Main Season theater and dance productions; Penny Arcade Film Series; visiting speakers forum; and lectures by distinguished speakers, visiting novelists, and poets. The student radio station, WQRI, provides opportunities to gain broadcasting experience; students gain journalism and publishing experience working on the yearbook, newspaper, literary magazine, and new weekly produced news media program, *The Feed.* Additional opportunities include participation in campus and community choruses, service projects both on and off campus through the Volunteer Center and Community Service Association, numerous student clubs and organizations, and student government. Also of note are national honor societies, Alpha Chi and Beta Gamma Sigma; numerous departmental honor societies; continuing education opportunities; and a strong Career Services department.

In addition to its undergraduate degrees, the University awards the Master of Arts in Teaching (elementary education), Master of Arts in forensic psychology and literacy education, Master of Science in criminal justice, Master of Architecture, and Master of Public Administration.

Location

The University is located in Bristol, Rhode Island, a historic seacoast community with a small-town, residential character. A half-hour's drive from the campus, the Rhode Island cities of Newport, the city by the sea, and Providence, America's Renaissance City, feature restored historic buildings, shops, museums, theaters, and numerous cultural, educational, and recreational attractions. Boston is approximately 1 hour away by car or bus, and New York City can be reached in under 4 hours. A bus stop is located directly in front of the campus.

Majors and Degrees

At the undergraduate level, RWU awards the Bachelor of Science, Bachelor of Arts, and Bachelor of Fine Arts degrees. In addition, the University also awards a combined Bachelor of Science/Master of Architecture degree. Academic programs are offered through one college and five professional schools that combine traditional liberal arts education with professional studies. Professional programs are offered through the School of Architecture, Art and Historic Preservation; the Gabelli School of Business, accredited by the prestigious AACSB International–The Association to Advance Collegiate Schools of Business; the School of Engineering, Computing and Construction Management; and the School of Justice Studies. Liberal arts majors are offered through the Feinstein College of Arts and Sciences and the School of Education. Continuing education opportunities are available through the School of Continuing Studies.

All students complete an interdisciplinary core program, a major, and a core concentration or minor. Students select their majors and minors from the following disciplines: accounting, American studies, anthropology/sociology, architecture, art and architectural history, biology, business management, chemistry, communications, computer information systems, computer science, construction management, creative writing, criminal justice, dance performance studies, economics, education (elementary and secondary education), engineering, English literature, environmental science, financial services, foreign languages, graphic design communications, historic preservation, history, international business, legal studies, marine biology, marketing, mathematics, philosophy, political science, psychology, theater, and visual arts studies. Other programs include an undergraduate honors program, prelaw, premedicine, pre-veterinary science, and a 3-3 program (combining both bachelor's and Juris Doctor degrees in six years). Students can also study English as a second language.

Academic Programs

The fall semester begins in September and ends in December; the spring semester begins in late January and ends in May. During the month of January, special on- and off-campus intersession programs, including opportunities for travel and service, are open to students at other institutions of higher learning. During the summer, undergraduate day and evening classes are available in Bristol. Additional classes are available at the University's Providence Center. The University Honors Program invites applicants who have demonstrated academic excellence.

Off-Campus Programs

Honors, cooperative education, internship, study-abroad, and community service programs enhance undergraduate studies. University career-planning counselors work one-on-one with students and alumni, providing career development guidance, assessment, employment-search skills, and placement assistance. Students are encouraged to participate in off-campus opportunities or study-abroad programs in Australia, Greece, Ireland, Italy, Mexico, Scotland, and more than thirty additional destinations worldwide.

Academic Facilities

Two undergraduate libraries with a total of more than 168,000 volumes are open 92 hours a week to students, faculty members, and community residents. The 54,000-square-foot main library houses 1,225 periodical titles, seating and quiet study/reading areas for students, computerized databases, and an online catalog. The main library also houses special collections and the University archives. A computerized system allows students to utilize library services of four additional Rhode Island institutions.

The University maintains a fully staffed, state-of-the-art computer facility, where all students have access to servers and the Internet, CD-ROM capability, color scanners, and laser printers.

The Marine and Natural Sciences Building, housing science and mathematics departments, features a wet laboratory with flowing seawater, research space, and modern physics, chemistry, and biology laboratories. The Engineering Building supports modern lab facilities equipped for computing; drafting; electronics; surveying; soil, fluid, and materials mechanics; and digital and environmental systems. The Performing Arts Center houses art and sculpting studios, an art gallery, photography labs, a theater, a dance studio, rehearsal rooms, and scene and costume shops that support fine arts studies. The award-winning School of Architecture, Art, and Historic Preservation Building includes design studios, review and seminar rooms, a library, a photography studio and darkroom, a model shop, computer labs, and an exhibition gallery.

Costs

For the 2007–08 academic year, full-time tuition was $25,942 for 12 to 17 credit hours ($29,014 for architecture majors). Room and board charges for on-campus housing (double occupancy) averaged $11,490 annually.

Financial Aid

The University offers merit scholarships, which are awarded regardless of financial need, to recognize students with superior academic achievement. Merit scholarship recipients are determined by high school or prior college record, grade point average (GPA), and SAT or ACT scores. These scholarships are renewable yearly, provided that recipients maintain a designated GPA while enrolled full-time at the University. There is no separate application for these scholarships. Each applicant's record is examined to determine eligibility as part of the routine admission process.

The vast majority of the funds and programs administered by the Office of Student Financial Aid and Financial Planning at the University require the demonstration of financial need as an essential consideration. Those not based on need determination include Federal Direct Unsubsidized Loans, PLUS loans, alternative loan programs, and various external scholarships (where the selection of the recipient is made by the donor or organization). With few exceptions, all other programs require that financial need be evaluated and determined by the Office of Student Financial Aid and Financial Planning. The University requires the submission of the Free Application for Federal Student Aid (FAFSA) and the CSS Financial Aid PROFILE to the respective processors by January 1. The Roger Williams University Title IV Federal Code Number is 003410. The FAFSA must be received at the federal processor no later than February 1 to be considered for maximum financial aid.

Faculty

The University's undergraduate program employs nearly 200 full-time faculty members. Teaching is central to the undergraduate mission of the University, as is academic advisement. The University does not utilize teaching assistants, and all faculty members devote much time to working with students both in and outside the classroom. The University faculty members also reflect distinguished scholarship and applied research.

Student Government

Leadership opportunities are available to students through the Student Government Association. Students may serve in elected positions on the Student Senate, which carries out the executive and legislative functions of the association.

Admission Requirements

The University encourages applications from motivated students who have completed college-preparatory courses. In determining admissibility, the Office of Undergraduate Admission considers the student's application along with high school courses and grades, SAT or ACT scores, letter(s) of recommendation, and additional information (such as required audition or portfolio). The University offers three admission programs, early decision, early action, and regular decision.

Application and Information

The deadline for early decision is November 1; for early action, November 15; and for regular decision, February 1. A nonrefundable fee of $50 must accompany the application.

Application forms and admission information may be obtained by contacting:

Office of Undergraduate Admission
Roger Williams University
One Old Ferry Road
Bristol, Rhode Island 02809-2921
Phone: 401-254-3500
800-458-7144 Ext. 3500 (toll-free outside Rhode Island)
E-mail: admit@rwu.edu
Web site: http://www.rwu.edu

Roger Williams University is located on 140 scenic acres overlooking Mt. Hope Bay.

SALVE REGINA UNIVERSITY

NEWPORT, RHODE ISLAND

The University

Salve Regina is a private, coeducational university of distinction that offers a comprehensive undergraduate program in the arts and sciences. The University is accredited by the New England Association of Schools and Colleges, and the Salve Regina campus is composed of a number of historic estates that were built at the turn of the century against the backdrop of the Atlantic Ocean in the world-famous resort city of Newport. Chartered in 1934 by the state of Rhode Island and founded in 1947 by the Religious Sisters of Mercy, Salve Regina has positioned itself for academic excellence in the new millennium.

Today, more than 2,100 undergraduate and 500 graduate students from forty-six states and twenty-six countries are enrolled in thirty undergraduate majors and twelve graduate programs, including a Ph.D. in humanities. Nearly 15,000 alumni have distinguished themselves in public service as professionals and community leaders.

On-campus residence is an integral component of the Salve Regina educational experience—a living and learning environment that is like no other. Many of the University's residence halls are buildings of historical significance.

The University offers a wide spectrum of extracurricular activities, including student government, honor societies, art, theater and music programs, community outreach activities, and a full athletics program. A member of the Eastern Collegiate Athletic Conference, the New England Football Conference, and the Commonwealth Coast Conference, Salve Regina offers eighteen varsity sports at the NCAA Division III level for men and women. Varsity sports offered for both men and women are basketball, cross-country, ice hockey, lacrosse, soccer, and tennis. Sports offered for women only are field hockey, softball, track and field, and volleyball. Sports offered for men only are baseball and football. The University also sponsors a nationally ranked coed sailing program. The 69,000-square-foot recreation center meets the athletic and recreational needs of Salve Regina students and faculty and staff members. The Student Activities Program draws inspiration from the University's mission of service to others, and it includes many service clubs and organizations. Through the Feinstein Enriching America Program, students participate in an array of community enrichment projects and activities that broaden their classroom education. Students serve as volunteers and interns at local hospitals, schools, museums, libraries, human service agencies, and other institutions. The campus is also home to the Pell Center for International Relations and Public Policy, where international dialogue is enhanced in an effort to achieve world peace.

Location

With the good fortune to be located in the historic city of Newport, Rhode Island, Salve Regina has a unique campus situated in a recognized National Historic District, with a landscape befitting a national park. Against the backdrop of the Atlantic Ocean and Newport's famous Cliff Walk, the University campus contains twenty historic and significant buildings constructed at or near the turn of the century. These former "summer cottages" and estate buildings have been adapted by Salve Regina for academic, administrative, and residential uses. They have been augmented by the construction of modern residence halls and academic buildings that fit in with the historic flavor and distinctive landscape of the campus, which includes century-old shade trees imported from Europe and the Far East and beautifully sculpted gardens. Nearby Newport's world-famous harbor and beautifully preserved architecture reflect its colonial seaport heritage, yet the city maintains a modern resort personality. Cobbled streets and brick sidewalks in downtown Newport, just a short walk from the Salve Regina campus, connect historic homes to the city's museums, art galleries, quaint shops, world-class restaurants, and recreational areas. Just minutes from the campus, students can find beautiful beaches, nature trails, and the famous 10-mile Ocean Drive, which is ideal for hiking and biking. Newport is centrally located less than a 90-minute drive from Boston, 45 minutes from Providence, and 3½ hours from New York. Train and air connections are available less than an hour from the Salve Regina campus, and a University shuttle provides regular transportation between the campus and the surrounding community. Students receive a free statewide RIPTA bus pass.

Majors and Degrees

The University offers a selection of undergraduate degrees, including Bachelor of Arts (B.A.), Bachelor of Science (B.S.), and Bachelor of Arts and Science (B.A.S.). Academic programs include accounting, administration of justice, American studies, anthropology, art history, biology, business administration, chemistry, cultural and historic preservation, dance, early childhood education, East Asian studies, economics, elementary education, English, English communication, English literature, environmental science, French, global business, graphic design, history, human services, information systems management, interactive communications technology, management, marketing, mathematics, medical technology, music, nursing, philosophy, politics, prelaw, premedicine, psychology, religious studies, secondary education, social work, sociology, Spanish, special education, sports management, studio art, theater arts, and women's studies. Five-year programs offer students the opportunity to complete both a bachelor's and a master's degree within five academic years. Five-year combined degrees are offered in administration of justice, business administration, international relations, management, and rehabilitation counseling (5½ years).

Academic Programs

Students receiving an associate degree must complete a minimum of 64 semester hours. A bachelor's degree requires a minimum of 128 semester hours. Departments may require additional semester hours of course work in particular concentrations. General education requirements comprise approximately 40 percent of course work leading to a degree. Usually completed by the end of the sophomore year, the general education course work is linked to the theme of world citizenship. The undergraduate program operates on a two-semester calendar, with fall classes beginning in September and ending in December and spring classes beginning in mid-January and running through mid-May.

Off-Campus Programs

Salve Regina has built strong relationships with public and private agencies and businesses that provide numerous internship opportunities for students as well as expanded professional activities that enhance academic programs. Students in accounting, administration of justice, information systems science, management, medical technology, nursing, and social work all benefit from hands-on experience at professional agencies and organizations. Internships in all fields can be pursued both on and off campus to augment classroom learning with experience in a professional setting. Students seeking internships for academic credit must receive approval from the appropriate department chair and the academic dean. Salve Regina also offers students the opportunity to study abroad as a way of increasing global awareness. Programs are available in Australia, Mexico, the U.K., Japan, and Italy, among other locations. The University also encourages full-year and summer study-abroad programs in affiliation with other institutions. Several short-term study trips are available to destinations such as London, Italy, Mexico, and France.

Academic Facilities

With a modern library serving as a hub of University academic activity, Salve Regina combines modern facilities with historic structures in its academic setting. The McKillop Library, in fact, was designed to reflect the architectural lines of nearby turn-of-the-century buildings, but its functional interior includes state-of-the-art information technology that provides educational resources to meet any research needs. Students and faculty members have direct access to an array of international research databases and other online tools from workstations throughout the building, and the library's circulation and internal procedures are fully automated. Salve Regina is a member of the Rhode Island HELIN library consortium. Salve Regina's academic facilities are influenced by tradition and architectural history, with a number of nineteenth-century estate buildings serving as classrooms, visual and performing arts studio spaces, and faculty offices. Other academic facilities have been built to accommodate the specialized requirements of science laboratories, computer laboratories, and lecture halls for large audiences.

Costs

Tuition and fees for the 2007–08 academic year were $26,950. Room and board costs were $10,200.

Financial Aid

Salve Regina University is strongly committed to helping students obtain a private education. Approximately 75 percent of Salve Regina students receive financial aid through a combination of scholarships, loans, grants, and work-study employment. The University requires the Free Application for Federal Student Aid (FAFSA) and the College Scholarship Service PROFILE. These forms must be filed no later than March 1.

Faculty

During the 2006–07 academic year, there were 252 faculty members. Approximately 40 percent of the full-time faculty members are tenured, and 80 percent have earned a doctoral or terminal degree. Faculty members are committed to excellence in teaching and to the development of the academic potential of each student.

Student Government

Students have the opportunity to offer input into University activities and policies by participating in Student Government and the Activities Funding Board. In addition, students serve as elected class officers.

Admission Requirements

The qualifications of each applicant are evaluated by a committee on admission, which focuses on academic ability, intellectual curiosity, strength of character, motivation, and promise for personal growth and development. The committee reviews applicants without regard to age, race, sex, creed, national or ethnic origin, or handicap. While secondary school preparation varies, the University strongly recommends that students accomplish the following 16 units: 4 in English, 3 in mathematics, 2 in laboratory science, 2 in foreign language, 1 in history, and 4 in electives. Salve Regina's application deadline is February 1. Transfer students should follow the procedure for regular application to the University. Applicants to the Nursing Program are also evaluated by a Nursing Review Committee. Students with superior academic credentials may be considered for a number of academic scholarship programs provided by the University.

Application and Information

Candidates for admission must furnish evidence of completion or anticipated completion of a level of education equivalent to four years of high school or submit results of the GED test. All candidates must furnish a completed application with a nonrefundable fee of $40 (unless a waiver is obtained from the director of admissions), an official transcript of high school work and class rank, results of the SAT or ACT, and two letters of recommendation. Early action candidates should file an application before November 1, and notification of acceptance under this plan is sent on December 15.

Applications for admission and further information may be obtained by contacting:

Admissions Office
Salve Regina University
100 Ochre Point Avenue
Newport, Rhode Island 02840-4192
Phone: 401-341-2908
888-GO-SALVE (toll-free)
Fax: 401-848-2823
E-mail: sruadmis@salve.edu
Web site: http://explore.salve.edu
http://www.salve.edu

Ochre Court is one of many historic buildings on campus that make the learning environment at Salve Regina like no other.

UNIVERSITY OF RHODE ISLAND

KINGSTON, RHODE ISLAND

The University

As a land-grant college since its founding in 1892, the University of Rhode Island provides its students with an outstanding education and prepares them for responsible citizenship. The University also fosters significant research and takes its expertise to the community through a variety of extension and outreach programs. The current undergraduate enrollment is about 11,600 men and women. The center of the spacious country campus is a quadrangle of handsome, old granite buildings surrounded by other, newer academic buildings, student residence halls, and fraternity and sorority houses. On the plain below Kingston Hill are gymnasiums, athletic fields, tennis courts, a freshwater pond, agricultural fields, greenhouses, and a large convocation center. There are twenty-one residence halls on campus, offering a variety of living accommodations, including a new residence hall and apartment building for upperclass students. A variety of dining centers and meal plans are offered to all students. There are approximately 1,000 fraternity and sorority members living in nationally affiliated houses that are privately owned by alumni corporations. Some students commute from home, and about 3,000 students commute from houses or apartments in the local and surrounding beach communities. Approximately 50 percent of the undergraduate students come from outside Rhode Island.

Lectures, art programs, music and dance concerts, film programs, and theater presentations are available. An extensive program of intercollegiate and intramural athletics is offered and is sufficiently varied to provide an opportunity for every student to participate. The Mackal Field house, Tootell Physical Education Center and the Keaney Gymnasium provide excellent facilities, including three pools, four gymnasiums, weight-training rooms, a dance studio, and a modern athletic training room. The Mackal Fieldhouse provides gymnasium space for a variety of recreational uses as well as an indoor track. In addition to a football stadium, there are twelve tennis courts, two softball diamonds, a baseball field, a lighted lacrosse/soccer field, a hockey field, and numerous practice fields for recreation and competition. The 8,000-seat Ryan Center opened in 2002 and houses the men's and women's basketball programs, in addition to concerts and other large events. The Boss Ice Arena also opened in 2002. A sailing pavilion and rowing facility are located off campus. The Memorial Union Building houses a wide variety of educational, social, cultural, and recreational services, including lounges, study rooms, a radio station, the campus newspaper, a game room, dining facilities, a bookstore, a snack bar, a restaurant, a ballroom, and a special events room.

Location

The University's 1,200-acre campus is located in the historic village of Kingston, 30 miles south of Providence. Bus transportation is available from the campus to most locations in the area, including Wakefield, where the nearest shopping facilities are located. The Kingston Amtrak train station is 1 mile from campus, and the T. F. Greene Airport in Warwick, Rhode Island, is only 25 miles from campus. The campus is 6 miles from the ocean, and weekend ski trips to the mountains are easily managed in the winter season.

Majors and Degrees

The College of Arts and Sciences offers the Bachelor of Arts, Bachelor of Science, Bachelor of Fine Arts, and Bachelor of Music degrees. The Bachelor of Arts degree is offered in African and African American studies, anthropology, art history, art studio, chemistry, classical studies, communication studies, comparative literature, computer science, economics, English, film media, French, German, history, Italian, journalism, Latin American studies, mathematics, music, music history, philosophy, physics, political science, psychology, public relations, sociology, Spanish, women's studies, and writing and rhetoric. The Bachelor of Science degree is available in applied sociology, chemistry, chemistry and chemical oceanography, computer science, economics, mathematics, physics, and physics and physical oceanography. The Bachelor of Fine Arts degree is offered in art and theater, and the Bachelor of Music degree is available in music education and music theory, performance, and composition.

The College of Business Administration offers the Bachelor of Science degree in accounting, entrepreneurship management, finance, general business administration, international business, marketing, and supply chain management. Business degree programs are accredited by the Association to Advance Collegiate Schools of Business.

The College of Engineering offers the Bachelor of Science degree in biomedical, chemical, chemical and ocean, civil, computer, electrical, industrial, mechanical, and ocean engineering. A five-year International Engineering Program is also offered. Engineering degree programs are accredited by the Accreditation Board for Engineering and Technology, Inc.

The College of the Environment and Life Sciences offers the Bachelor of Science degree in animal science and technology, aquaculture and fishery technology, biological sciences, biology, clinical laboratory science, environmental economics and management, environmental horticulture and turfgrass management, environmental science and management, geology and geological oceanography, geosciences, marine affairs, marine biology, microbiology, nutrition and dietetics, resource economics and commerce, and wildlife and conservation biology. The Bachelor of Landscape Architecture degree is awarded in landscape architecture and is accredited by the American Society of Landscape Architects.

The College of Human Science and Services offers the Bachelor of Science degree in communicative disorders, elementary and secondary education, human development and family studies, kinesiology, textile marketing, and textiles, fashion merchandising, and design.

The College of Nursing offers the Bachelor of Science degree in nursing, which is approved by the Commission on Collegiate Nursing Education and the Rhode Island Board of Nurse Registration and Nursing Education.

The College of Pharmacy offers a six-year Doctor of Pharmacy degree, which is accredited by the American Council on Pharmaceutical Education.

Preprofessional preparation is available in dentistry, law, medicine, physical therapy, and veterinary studies.

Academic Programs

All programs of study aim for a balance of the natural and social sciences, the humanities, and professional subjects. All freshmen who enter the University to earn a bachelor's degree are first enrolled in University College; its advising program helps students choose a concentration and appropriate courses. A student must meet the curricular requirements of the college in which the degree is to be earned. As a general rule, 120 credits are required for a Bachelor of Arts degree and 130 for a Bachelor of Science degree, including the specified general education requirements. The University of Rhode Island operates on a two-semester calendar, with semesters beginning in September and January. Two 5-week summer sessions are also available. Credit is granted to students who have passed a College Board Advanced Placement examination with a grade of 3 or better. In addition, credit may be given for satisfactory scores on departmental proficiency examinations or College-Level Examination Program (CLEP) subject examinations. The University Honors Program offers academically talented students opportunities to broaden their intellectual development and to strengthen their preparation in their major fields of study.

Off-Campus Programs

The Office of Internships and Experiential Education offers internships for academic credit, including one-semester and one-year programs. Additionally, the University has exchange agreements with universities in England, France, Germany, Japan, and Spain. Other off-campus study and exchange programs are also available.

Academic Facilities

The University library has more than 1 million bound volumes and 1.5 million titles available electronically. Active research programs are carried on in all seven colleges. The Graduate School of Oceanography, located on the Narragansett Bay Campus, provides undergraduates with a living research lab for science-related courses. The University houses a large collection of American historic textiles, a center for robotics research, a planetarium, the Watson House Museum, and two animal science farms.

Costs

The comprehensive cost for 2007–08 was estimated at $32,788 for out-of-state students and $17,934 for Rhode Islanders. This covered tuition, fees, and room and board. Books, travel, and personal expenses are not included in these figures. Laboratory fees are extra. The University participates in the cooperative plan of the New England Board of Higher Education, whereby students from other New England states are able to enroll in certain degree programs that are not offered in their own states and pay reduced tuition.

Financial Aid

To be considered for financial aid at the University, students must submit the Free Application for Federal Student Aid (FAFSA). Although there is no deadline for applying, priority is given to applications received by March 1. Most students receive notification of admission decisions on or about April 1. Merit scholarships are available to incoming freshmen with superior academic credentials. Consideration for these scholarships is given to freshmen who apply by the December 17, 2007, early action deadline. For 2007–08, 75 percent of new students who completed applications were awarded some form of aid. In addition, students have opportunities for employment through work-study programs that use federal, state, and institutional funds.

Faculty

The faculty consists of 648 full-time and 17 part-time members, or 1 professor for every 18 students. Approximately 88 percent of the full-time faculty members hold doctoral degrees. Faculty members serve both the graduate and undergraduate populations and have wide-ranging interests and responsibilities. In addition to teaching and research, they serve as student advisers.

Student Government

The Student Senate is a legislative body that represents the students to the administration and faculty and supervises extracurricular activities. It also distributes the activities funds among the various student organizations through its funding committee. Individual residence halls form their own governments. The Interfraternity Council supervises fraternity affairs, and the Panhellenic Association governs sorority life. The Commuter Association provides social and other assistance to commuter students.

Admission Requirements

Admission to the University is competitive. Applicants are given individual consideration, but it is expected that all candidates have completed at least 18 units of college-preparatory work; specific unit requirements vary for each of the seven colleges of the University. Academic achievement in a challenging high school program receives the strongest consideration in the review of an applicant's credentials. An audition is required for the Bachelor of Music degree. All freshman candidates must submit a high school transcript and scores on the SAT or the ACT examination, which should be taken no later than January 1 of the senior year. International students for whom English is not the primary language must take the Test of English as a Foreign Language (TOEFL) or the International English Language Testing Systems (IELTS) exam. Scores on equivalency examinations may be presented by applicants who have not been able to complete formal high school studies. Transfer students may enter in either semester (although some degree programs admit students only in the fall semester) and must submit transcripts of all previous work at both the high school and college levels. Early admission is available to high school juniors with superior records.

Students are selected primarily on the basis of academic competence and without regard to age, race, religion, color, sex, creed, national origin, handicap, or sexual orientation.

Application and Information

Visits to the campus are encouraged. Information sessions and tours are scheduled daily during the week and on many Saturdays throughout the year. Students should visit the Admission Web site for details about these sessions as well as open house programs and directions to the campus. Admission representatives attend college fairs in Rhode Island and throughout the Northeast during the academic year.

Students are encouraged to submit applications early in their final year of high school, as the University subscribes to a rolling admission policy and reviews folders as they are complete. The early action deadline is December 17, 2007, and students receive notification by January 31, 2008. The regular deadline for fall term freshman applications is February 1, 2008, and the deadline for transfer applications is May 1, 2008. Most decisions are reported in March. The closing date for spring-term applications is November 1, 2007. Requests for application forms and further information should be directed to:

Office of Admission
University of Rhode Island
14 Upper College Road
Kingston, Rhode Island 02881
Phone: 401-874-7000
E-mail: admission@uri.edu
Web site: http://www.uri.edu/admission

are required for a Bachelor of Arts degree and 50% for a Bachelor of [illegible] degree, including the specified general education requirements. The University of Rhode Island operates on a two-semester calendar, with semesters beginning in September and January. Two [illegible] summer sessions are also available. Credit is granted to students who have passed a College Board Advanced Placement examination with a grade of 3 or better. In addition, credit may be given for satisfactory scores on appropriate [illegible] examinations or College-Level Examination Program (CLEP) subject examinations. The University Honors Program offers academically talented students opportunities to broaden their intellectual development and to strengthen their preparation in their major field of study.

Off-Campus Programs

The Office of Internships and Experiential Education offers opportunities for academic credit, including one-semester and one-year programs and [illegible]. The University has exchange agreements with universities in England, France, Germany, Japan, and Spain. Other [illegible] and exchange programs are also available.

Academic Facilities

The University library has more than [illegible] million volumes and [illegible] available electronically. [illegible] research programs are [illegible] in all seven colleges. The Graduate School of Oceanography, located on the Narragansett Bay campus, provides [illegible] with a [illegible] and [illegible] courses. The University houses a large collection of American historic textiles, a center for robotics research, a planetarium, the Watson House Museum, and two [illegible] [illegible].

Costs

The comprehensive cost for 2007–08 was estimated at $[illegible] for out-of-state students and $[illegible] for Rhode Islanders. This covered tuition, fees, and room and board. Books, supplies, and personal expenses are not included in these figures. [illegible] [illegible]. The University participates in the cooperative plan of the New England Board of Higher Education, whereby students from other New England states are able to enroll in certain degree programs that are not offered in their own states and pay reduced tuition.

Financial Aid

To be considered for financial aid at the University, students must submit the Free Application for Federal Student Aid (FAFSA). Although there is no deadline for applying, priority is given to applicants received by March 1. Most students are informed of [illegible] decisions on or about April 1. [illegible] scholarships are available to incoming freshmen with superior academic credentials. Consideration for these scholarships is given to freshmen who apply by the December [illegible], 2007, early action deadline. For 2007, [illegible] percent of new students who completed applications [illegible] some form of aid. In addition, students have opportunities for employment through work-study programs and [illegible] federal, state, and institutional funds.

Faculty

The faculty consists of [illegible] full-time and [illegible] part-time members or 1 professor for every [illegible] students. Approximately [illegible] percent of the full-time faculty members hold doctoral degrees. Faculty members serve both the graduate and undergraduate populations and have wide-ranging [illegible] responsibilities. In addition to teaching and research, they serve as student advisers.

Student Government

The Student Senate is a legislative body that represents the students in the administration and faculty and supervises student government activities. It also distributes activities funds among the various student organizations through its funding committees. Individual residence halls have their own governments. The Interfraternity Council supervises fraternity affairs, and the Panhellenic Association governs sorority life. The Commuter Association provides social and other assistance to commuter students.

Admission Requirements

Admission to the University is competitive. Applicants are given individual consideration, but it is expected that all candidates have completed at least 18 units of college-preparatory work. Specific unit requirements vary for each of the seven colleges of the University. Academic achievement in a challenging high school program receives the greatest consideration in the review of an applicant's credentials. An audition is required for the Bachelor of Music degree. All freshman candidates must submit a high school transcript and scores on the SAT or the ACT examination, which should be taken no later than January of the senior year. International students for whom English is not the primary language must submit the Test of English as a Foreign Language (TOEFL) or the International English Language Testing System (IELTS) examination scores. [illegible] examinations may be presented by applicants who have not been able to complete formal high school study. Transfer students may enter in either semester (although some degree programs admit students only in the fall semester) and must submit transcripts of all previous work at both the high school and college level. Early admission is available to high school juniors with superior records.

Students are selected primarily on the basis of academic competence and without regard to race, religion, color, sex, age, national origin, and [illegible] or sexual orientation.

Application and Information

Visits to the campus are encouraged. Information sessions and tours are scheduled daily during the week and on many Saturdays throughout the year. Students should visit the Admission Web site for details about these sessions as well as open house programs and directions to the campus. Admission representatives attend college fairs in Rhode Island and throughout the Northeast during the academic year.

Students are encouraged to submit applications early in their final year of high school, as the University subscribes to a rolling admission policy and reviews folders as they are completed. The early action deadline is December 1, 2007, and students receive notification by January 31, 2008. The regular deadline for fall semester freshman applications is February 1, 2008, and the deadline for transfer applications is May 1, 2008. Most decisions are reported in March. The closing date for spring-term applications is November 1, 2007. Requests for application forms and further information should be directed to:

Office of Admission
University of Rhode Island
14 Upper College Road
Kingston, Rhode Island 02881
Phone: 401-874-[illegible]
E-mail: admission@uri.edu
Web site: http://www.uri.edu/admission

SOUTH CAROLINA

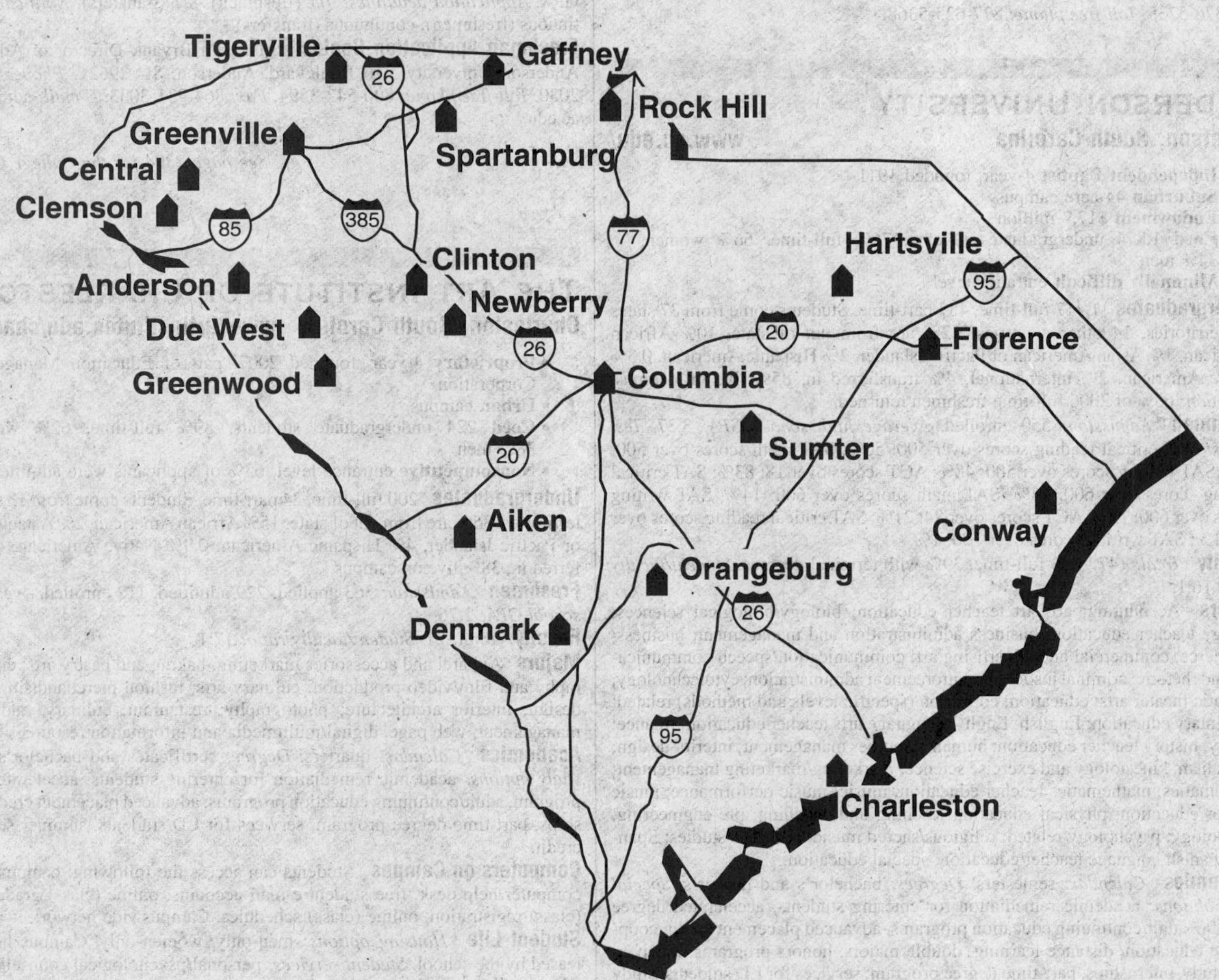

ALLEN UNIVERSITY

Columbia, South Carolina **www.allenuniversity.edu/**

Freshman Application Contact Ms. Constants Adams, Admissions Representative, Allen University, 1530 Harden Street, Columbia, SC 29204-1085. *Phone:* 803-376-5735. *Toll-free phone:* 877-625-5368.

ANDERSON UNIVERSITY

Anderson, South Carolina **www.ac.edu/**

- **Independent Baptist** 4-year, founded 1911
- **Suburban** 44-acre campus
- **Endowment** $17.7 million
- **Coed** 1,874 undergraduate students, 76% full-time, 66% women, 34% men
- **Minimally difficult** entrance level

Undergraduates 1,417 full-time, 457 part-time. Students come from 37 states and territories, 14 other countries, 12% are from out of state, 10% African American, 1% Asian American or Pacific Islander, 2% Hispanic American, 0.3% Native American, 2% international, 4% transferred in, 85% live on campus. *Retention:* 65% of 2006 full-time freshmen returned.

Freshmen *Admission:* 550 enrolled. *Average high school GPA:* 3.37. *Test scores:* SAT critical reading scores over 500: 50%; SAT math scores over 500: 52%; SAT writing scores over 500: 48%; ACT scores over 18: 83%; SAT critical reading scores over 600: 14%; SAT math scores over 600: 14%; SAT writing scores over 600: 12%; ACT scores over 24: 21%; SAT critical reading scores over 700: 1%; SAT writing scores over 700: 1%.

Faculty *Total:* 147, 49% full-time, 39% with terminal degrees. *Student/faculty ratio:* 16:1.

Majors Accounting; art; art teacher education; biology/biological sciences; biology teacher education; business administration and management; business/commerce; commercial and advertising art; communication/speech communication and rhetoric; criminal justice/law enforcement administration; cytotechnology; dramatic/theater arts; education; education (specific levels and methods) related; elementary education; English; English/language arts teacher education; finance; history; history teacher education; human resources management; interior design; journalism; kinesiology and exercise science; marketing/marketing management; mathematics; mathematics teacher education; music; music performance; music teacher education; physical education teaching and coaching; pre-engineering; psychology; psychology related; religious/sacred music; religious studies; Spanish; Spanish language teacher education; special education.

Academics *Calendar:* semesters. *Degrees:* bachelor's and master's. *Special study options:* academic remediation for entering students, accelerated degree program, adult/continuing education programs, advanced placement credit, cooperative education, distance learning, double majors, honors programs, independent study, internships, part-time degree program, services for LD students, study abroad, summer session for credit. *ROTC:* Army (c), Air Force (c).

Computers on Campus 192 computers/terminals are available on campus for general student use. Campuswide network is available. 100% of college-owned or -operated housing units are wired for high-speed Internet access. Wireless service is available via entire campus.

Student Life *Housing:* on-campus residence required through sophomore year. *Options:* men-only, women-only. Campus housing is university owned. *Activities and organizations:* drama/theater group, student-run newspaper, choral group, Baptist Campus Ministries, Fellowship of Christian Athletes, Student Government Association, Gamma Beta Phi, Student Alumni Council. *Campus security:* 24-hour emergency response devices and patrols, late-night transport/escort service, controlled dormitory access. *Student services:* health clinic, personal/psychological counseling.

Athletics Member NCAA. All Division II. *Intercollegiate sports:* baseball M (s), basketball M (s)/W (s), cheerleading W (s), cross-country running M (s)/W (s), equestrian sports M/W, golf M (s)/W (s), soccer M (s)/W (s), softball W (s), tennis M (s)/W (s), track and field M (s)/W (s), volleyball W (s), wrestling M (s). *Intramural sports:* basketball M/W, football M/W, racquetball M/W, softball M/W, table tennis M/W, ultimate Frisbee M/W, volleyball M/W, weight lifting M.

Standardized Tests *Required:* SAT or ACT (for admission).

Costs (2008–09) *Comprehensive fee:* $24,450 includes full-time tuition ($17,400) and room and board ($7050). Part-time tuition: $440 per credit hour. *College room only:* $3600.

Financial Aid Of all full-time matriculated undergraduates who enrolled in 2006, 1,205 applied for aid, 957 were judged to have need, 863 had their need fully met. 127 Federal Work-Study jobs (averaging $1662). In 2006, 1329 non-need-based awards were made. *Average percent of need met:* 90%. *Average financial aid package:* $17,200. *Average need-based loan:* $3650. *Average need-based gift aid:* $8700. *Average non-need-based aid:* $7810. *Average indebtedness upon graduation:* $15,125. *Financial aid deadline:* 7/30.

Applying *Options:* electronic application, deferred entrance. *Application fee:* $25. *Required:* high school transcript. *Required for some:* essay or personal statement, 2 letters of recommendation, interview. *Recommended:* minimum 2.5 GPA. *Application deadlines:* 7/1 (freshmen), 8/1 (transfers). *Notification:* continuous (freshmen), continuous (transfers).

Freshman Application Contact Ms. Pam Bryant, Director of Admissions, Anderson University, 316 Boulevard, Anderson, SC 29621. *Phone:* 864-231-2030. *Toll-free phone:* 800-542-3594. *Fax:* 864-231-3033. *E-mail:* admissions@ac.edu.

See page 2394 for the College Close-Up.

THE ART INSTITUTE OF CHARLESTON

Charleston, South Carolina **www.artinstitutes.edu/charleston/**

- **Proprietary** 4-year, founded 2007, part of Education Management Corporation
- **Urban** campus
- **Coed** 224 undergraduate students, 89% full-time, 62% women, 38% men
- **Noncompetitive** entrance level, 63% of applicants were admitted

Undergraduates 200 full-time, 24 part-time. Students come from 13 states and territories, 35% are from out of state, 15% African American, 2% Asian American or Pacific Islander, 4% Hispanic American, 0.9% Native American, 4% transferred in, 38% live on campus.

Freshmen *Admission:* 363 applied, 229 admitted, 112 enrolled. *Average high school GPA:* 2.76.

Faculty *Total:* 21. *Student/faculty ratio:* 17:1.

Majors Apparel and accessories marketing; baking and pastry arts; cinematography and film/video production; culinary arts; fashion merchandising; graphic design; interior architecture; photography; restaurant, culinary, and catering management; web page, digital/multimedia and information resources design.

Academics *Calendar:* quarters. *Degree:* certificates and bachelor's. *Special study options:* academic remediation for entering students, accelerated degree program, adult/continuing education programs, advanced placement credit, internships, part-time degree program, services for LD students, summer session for credit.

Computers on Campus Students can access the following: campus intranet, computer help desk, free student e-mail accounts, online (class) grades, online (class) registration, online (class) schedules. Campuswide network is available.

Student Life *Housing options:* men-only, women-only. Campus housing is leased by the school. *Student services:* personal/psychological counseling.

Standardized Tests *Recommended:* SAT and SAT Subject Tests or ACT (for admission).

Costs (2007–08) *Tuition:* tuition cost varies by program. Prospective students should contact the school for current tuition costs. Other charges include a starting kit for all first-quarter students. Kits vary in price depending on the program of study.

Applying *Options:* electronic application. *Application fee:* $50. *Required:* essay or personal statement, high school transcript, interview.

Director of Admissions Mr. Brian Stanley, The Art Institute of Charleston, The Carroll Building, 24 North Market Street, Charleston, SC 29401. *Phone:* 843-727-3500 Ext. 3442. *Toll-free phone:* 866-211-0107. *Fax:* 843-727-3440. *E-mail:* mdearsman@aii.edu.

See page 2396 for the College Close-Up.

BENEDICT COLLEGE

Columbia, South Carolina **www.benedict.edu/**

Freshman Application Contact Mr. Gary Knight, Vice President, Institutional Effectiveness, Benedict College, PO Box 98, Columbia, SC 29204. *Phone:* 803-253-5275. *Toll-free phone:* 800-868-6598. *Fax:* 803-253-5215.

BOB JONES UNIVERSITY

Greenville, South Carolina www.bju.edu/

- **Independent religious** university, founded 1927
- **Urban** 225-acre campus
- **Coed** 3,670 undergraduate students, 99% full-time, 54% women, 46% men
- **Minimally difficult** entrance level

Undergraduates 3,618 full-time, 52 part-time. Students come from 55 states and territories, 41 other countries, 75% are from out of state, 7% transferred in, 77% live on campus. *Retention:* 77% of 2006 full-time freshmen returned.

Freshmen *Admission:* 1,698 applied, 1,291 enrolled. *Average high school GPA:* 3.15. *Test scores:* ACT scores over 18: 90%; ACT scores over 24: 47%; ACT scores over 30: 7%.

Faculty *Total:* 366, 64% full-time. *Student/faculty ratio:* 15:1.

Majors Accounting; actuarial science; apparel and textiles; art; art teacher education; aviation/airway management; biblical studies; biology/biological sciences; biophysics; broadcast journalism; building/construction site management; business administration and management; carpentry; chemistry; cinematography and film/video production; commercial and advertising art; communication disorders; communication/speech communication and rhetoric; computer and information sciences; computer engineering; computer technology/computer systems technology; corrections and criminal justice related; cosmetology; counseling psychology; creative writing; dramatic/theater arts; early childhood education; electrical, electronics and communications engineering; elementary education; engineering science; English; English/language arts teacher education; family and consumer economics related; finance; foods, nutrition, and wellness; French; German; health and physical education; health/medical preparatory programs related; history; housing and human environments related; humanities; human resources management; international relations and affairs; journalism related; marketing/marketing management; mathematics; mathematics teacher education; middle school education; music performance; music related; music teacher education; nursing (registered nurse training); office management; office occupations and clerical services; operations research; physics; piano and organ; political science and government; pre-law studies; pre-medical studies; pre-veterinary studies; radio and television; religious education; restaurant, culinary, and catering management; science teacher education; social studies teacher education; Spanish; Spanish language teacher education; special education; speech and rhetoric; speech-language pathology; technical and business writing.

Academics *Calendar:* semesters. *Degrees:* certificates, associate, bachelor's, master's, doctoral, and first professional. *Special study options:* adult/continuing education programs, advanced placement credit, distance learning, English as a second language, internships, off-campus study, part-time degree program, services for LD students, summer session for credit.

Computers on Campus 450 computers/terminals and 500 ports are available on campus for general student use. Students can access the following: campus intranet, computer help desk, free student e-mail accounts, online (class) grades, online (class) registration, online (class) schedules. Campuswide network is available. 100% of college-owned or -operated housing units are wired for high-speed Internet access. Wireless service is available via classrooms, computer labs, libraries, student centers.

Student Life *Housing:* on-campus residence required through senior year. *Options:* men-only, women-only, disabled students. Campus housing is university owned. *Activities and organizations:* drama/theater group, student-run newspaper, radio and television station, choral group, Community Relations Council, Extension Ministries, Societies, Mission Prayer Band, University Business Association. *Campus security:* 24-hour patrols, student patrols, late-night transport/escort service, controlled dormitory access, 24/7 emergency dispatcher. *Student services:* health clinic.

Athletics *Intramural sports:* badminton M/W, basketball M/W, cheerleading M, racquetball M, soccer M/W, softball M/W, table tennis M/W, tennis M/W, volleyball M/W.

Standardized Tests *Required:* ACT (for admission).

Costs (2008–09) *Comprehensive fee:* $16,830 includes full-time tuition ($11,120), mandatory fees ($610), and room and board ($5100). Part-time tuition: $556 per credit hour. *Required fees:* $153 per term part-time.

Applying *Options:* electronic application. *Application fee:* $45. *Required:* high school transcript, 3 letters of recommendation. *Application deadlines:* 8/1 (freshmen), 8/1 (transfers).

Freshman Application Contact Mr. Gary Deedrick, Director of Admissions, Bob Jones University, Greenville, SC 29614. *Phone:* 864-242-5100. *Toll-free phone:* 800-BJANDME. *Fax:* 800-232-9258. *E-mail:* admissions@bju.edu.

CHARLESTON SOUTHERN UNIVERSITY

Charleston, South Carolina www.charlestonsouthern.edu/

- **Independent Baptist** comprehensive, founded 1964
- **Suburban** 500-acre campus
- **Endowment** $14.4 million
- **Coed**
- **Moderately difficult** entrance level

Located in one of the Southeast's most beautiful regions, Charleston Southern University (CSU) is a fully accredited, private university in South Carolina. Its mission is to provide academic excellence in a Christian environment for students of all faiths. CSU's enrollment has grown to more than 3,000 students. It offers both a traditional liberal arts curriculum and a comprehensive professional program. CSU encourages interested students to apply online at http://www.charlestonsouthern.edu or call 800-947-7474 (toll-free) to schedule a campus visit.

Faculty *Student/faculty ratio:* 18:1.

Academics *Calendar:* 4-4-1. *Degrees:* bachelor's and master's.

Student Life *Campus security:* 24-hour emergency response devices and patrols, late-night transport/escort service.

Athletics Member NCAA. All Division I except football (Division I-AA).

Standardized Tests *Required:* SAT or ACT (for admission).

Costs (2007–08) *Comprehensive fee:* $24,392 includes full-time tuition ($17,620) and room and board ($6772).

Financial Aid Of all full-time matriculated undergraduates who enrolled in 2007, 1,968 applied for aid, 1,749 were judged to have need, 421 had their need fully met. 614 Federal Work-Study jobs (averaging $1406). In 2007, 306 non-need-based awards were made. *Average percent of need met:* 73. *Average financial aid package:* $15,036. *Average need-based loan:* $4804. *Average need-based gift aid:* $11,008. *Average non-need-based aid:* $10,832. *Average indebtedness upon graduation:* $20,252.

Applying *Application fee:* $30. *Required:* high school transcript, minimum 2.0 GPA. *Required for some:* essay or personal statement, 1 letter of recommendation, interview.

Freshman Application Contact Ms. Kathryn LaCross, Director of Enrollment Management, Charleston Southern University, PO Box 118087, 9200 University Boulevard, Charleston, SC 19423-8087. *Phone:* 843-863-7050. *Toll-free phone:* 800-947-7474. *E-mail:* enroll@csuniv.edu.

See page 2398 for the College Close-Up.

THE CITADEL, THE MILITARY COLLEGE OF SOUTH CAROLINA

Charleston, South Carolina www.citadel.edu

- **State-supported** comprehensive, founded 1842
- **Urban** 130-acre campus
- **Endowment** $51.3 million
- **Coed** 2,248 undergraduate students, 95% full-time, 8% women, 92% men
- **Moderately difficult** entrance level, 78% of applicants were admitted

The Citadel, the Military College of South Carolina, is a coeducational, comprehensive, state-assisted, four-year institution that prepares students for principled leadership through a challenging curriculum of twenty majors. Graduates participate in all walks of life, from graduate study to private-sector and military careers. New barracks and a first-class campuswide computer network are recent features. The College actively seeks qualified students regardless of gender or ethnicity.

Undergraduates 2,125 full-time, 123 part-time. Students come from 47 states and territories, 26 other countries, 53% are from out of state, 7% African American, 3% Asian American or Pacific Islander, 5% Hispanic American, 0.5% Native American, 2% international, 2% transferred in, 100% live on campus. *Retention:* 81% of 2006 full-time freshmen returned.

Freshmen *Admission:* 2,081 applied, 1,629 admitted, 621 enrolled. *Average high school GPA:* 3.32. *Test scores:* SAT critical reading scores over 500: 71%; SAT math scores over 500: 79%; ACT scores over 18: 100%; SAT critical reading scores over 600: 22%; SAT math scores over 600: 26%; ACT scores over 24: 33%; SAT critical reading scores over 700: 2%; SAT math scores over 700: 4%; ACT scores over 30: 3%.

Faculty *Total:* 247, 68% full-time, 77% with terminal degrees. *Student/faculty ratio:* 15:1.

Majors Biology/biological sciences; business administration and management; chemistry; civil engineering; computer science; criminal justice/law enforcement administration; electrical, electronics and communications engineering; English; foreign languages and literatures; history; mathematics; physical education teaching and coaching; physics; political science and government; psychology; secondary education.

Academics *Calendar:* semesters. *Degrees:* bachelor's, master's, and post-master's certificates. *Special study options:* double majors, English as a second language, independent study, internships, off-campus study, services for LD students, summer session for credit. *ROTC:* Army (b), Navy (b), Air Force (b).

Computers on Campus 350 computers/terminals are available on campus for general student use. Students can access the following: campus intranet, computer help desk, free student e-mail accounts, online (class) registration, online (class) schedules. Campuswide network is available.

Student Life *Housing:* on-campus residence required through senior year. *Options:* coed. Campus housing is university owned. Freshman campus housing is guaranteed. *Activities and organizations:* drama/theater group, student-run newspaper, choral group, marching band. *Campus security:* 24-hour patrols, student patrols, late-night transport/escort service. *Student services:* health clinic, personal/psychological counseling.

Athletics Member NCAA. All Division I. *Intercollegiate sports:* baseball M (s), basketball M (s), cross-country running M (s)/W (s), football M (s), golf W (s), ice hockey M (c)/W (c), lacrosse M (c)/W (c), riflery M (s)/W (s), rugby M (c)/W (c), sailing M (c)/W (c), soccer W (s), tennis M (s), track and field M (s)/W (s), volleyball W (s), weight lifting M (c)/W (c), wrestling M (s). *Intramural sports:* badminton M/W, basketball M/W, football M/W, racquetball M/W, riflery M/W, soccer M/W, softball M/W, swimming and diving M/W, table tennis M/W, tennis M/W, track and field M/W, ultimate Frisbee M/W, volleyball M/W, weight lifting M/W, wrestling M/W.

Standardized Tests *Required:* SAT or ACT (for admission).

Costs (2007–08) *Tuition:* state resident $7735 full-time, $239 per credit hour part-time; nonresident $19,291 full-time, $458 per credit hour part-time. for students in the Corps of Cadets, freshmen pay a $5,470 deposit and upperclassmen pay $1,630 deposit for uniforms, books, and supplies. *Required fees:* $1000 full-time, $15 per term part-time. *Room and board:* $5390. *Waivers:* senior citizens and employees or children of employees.

Financial Aid Of all full-time matriculated undergraduates who enrolled in 2007, 1,352 applied for aid, 1,041 were judged to have need, 380 had their need fully met. 32 Federal Work-Study jobs (averaging $1496). In 2007, 244 non-need-based awards were made. *Average percent of need met:* 67%. *Average financial aid package:* $11,210. *Average need-based loan:* $4173. *Average need-based gift aid:* $12,135. *Average non-need-based aid:* $7319. *Average indebtedness upon graduation:* $20,089.

Applying *Options:* electronic application, early decision. *Application fee:* $40. *Required:* high school transcript. *Recommended:* letters of recommendation, interview. *Application deadlines:* rolling (freshmen), rolling (transfers). *Early decision deadline:* 10/26. *Notification:* 7/15 (freshmen).

Freshman Application Contact Lt. Col. John Powell, Director of Admissions, The Citadel, The Military College of South Carolina, 171 Moultrie Street, Charleston, SC 29409. *Phone:* 843-953-5230. *Toll-free phone:* 800-868-1842. *Fax:* 843-953-7036. *E-mail:* admissions@citadel.edu.

See page 2400 for the College Close-Up.

CLAFLIN UNIVERSITY

Orangeburg, South Carolina **www.claflin.edu/**

- **Independent United Methodist** comprehensive, founded 1869
- **Small-town** 32-acre campus with easy access to Columbia
- **Endowment** $18.0 million
- **Coed** 1,679 undergraduate students, 94% full-time, 68% women, 32% men
- **Minimally difficult** entrance level, 45% of applicants were admitted

Undergraduates 1,581 full-time, 98 part-time. Students come from 24 states and territories, 13 other countries, 13% are from out of state, 94% African American, 0.2% Asian American or Pacific Islander, 0.2% Hispanic American, 0.1% Native American, 4% international, 7% transferred in, 60% live on campus. *Retention:* 70% of 2006 full-time freshmen returned.

Freshmen *Admission:* 2,857 applied, 1,294 admitted, 390 enrolled. *Average high school GPA:* 3.0. *Test scores:* SAT critical reading scores over 500: 37%; SAT math scores over 500: 32%; SAT critical reading scores over 600: 7%; SAT math scores over 600: 9%; SAT critical reading scores over 700: 1%; SAT math scores over 700: 1%.

Faculty *Total:* 133, 72% full-time, 64% with terminal degrees. *Student/faculty ratio:* 13:1.

Majors African-American/Black studies; American studies; art; art teacher education; biochemistry; bioinformatics; biology/biological sciences; business administration and management; business, management, and marketing related; chemistry; computer science; computer software engineering; criminal justice/law enforcement administration; early childhood education; elementary education; English; environmental science; health and physical education; history; management information systems; marketing/marketing management; mass communication/media; mathematics; mathematics teacher education; middle school education; music; music teacher education; organizational behavior; philosophy and religious studies related; sociology; sport and fitness administration/management.

Academics *Calendar:* semesters. *Degrees:* bachelor's and master's. *Special study options:* academic remediation for entering students, adult/continuing education programs, advanced placement credit, cooperative education, freshman honors college, honors programs, independent study, internships, off-campus study, part-time degree program, study abroad, summer session for credit. *ROTC:* Army (c). *Unusual degree programs:* 3-2 engineering with South Carolina State University, Clemson University; chiropractic medicine at Sherman College of Straight Chiropractic.

Computers on Campus 500 computers/terminals are available on campus for general student use. Students can access the following: campus intranet, computer help desk, free student e-mail accounts, online (class) grades, online (class) registration, online (class) schedules. Campuswide network is available. 100% of college-owned or -operated housing units are wired for high-speed Internet access. Wireless service is available via classrooms, computer labs, libraries.

Student Life *Housing options:* men-only, women-only. Campus housing is university owned. *Activities and organizations:* drama/theater group, student-run newspaper, radio and television station, choral group, national fraternities, national sororities. *Campus security:* 24-hour emergency response devices and patrols, student patrols, controlled dormitory access. *Student services:* health clinic, personal/psychological counseling.

Athletics Member NCAA. All Division II. *Intercollegiate sports:* baseball M, basketball M (s)/W (s), cross-country running M/W, softball W, tennis M/W, track and field M/W, volleyball W. *Intramural sports:* basketball M/W, table tennis M/W, tennis M/W, volleyball M/W.

Standardized Tests *Required:* SAT or ACT (for admission). *Recommended:* SAT Subject Tests (for admission).

Costs (2007–08) *Comprehensive fee:* $18,998 includes full-time tuition ($10,368), mandatory fees ($1990), and room and board ($6640). Part-time tuition: $432 per credit hour. *Required fees:* $71 per credit hour part-time. *College room only:* $2960. Room and board charges vary according to housing facility. *Payment plan:* installment. *Waivers:* employees or children of employees.

Financial Aid Of all full-time matriculated undergraduates who enrolled in 2006, 1,517 applied for aid, 1,475 were judged to have need, 144 had their need fully met. In 2006, 300 non-need-based awards were made. *Average percent of need met:* 56%. *Average financial aid package:* $10,917. *Average need-based loan:* $3734. *Average need-based gift aid:* $8220. *Average non-need-based aid:* $17,712. *Average indebtedness upon graduation:* $19,993.

Applying *Options:* electronic application, deferred entrance. *Application fee:* $20. *Required:* essay or personal statement, high school transcript, minimum 2.0 GPA. *Recommended:* letters of recommendation. *Application deadlines:* rolling (freshmen), rolling (transfers). *Notification:* continuous (freshmen), continuous (transfers).

Freshman Application Contact Mr. Michael Zeigler, Director of Admissions, Claflin University, 400 Magnolia Street, Orangeburg, SC 29115. *Phone:* 803-535-5747. *Toll-free phone:* 800-922-1276. *Fax:* 803-535-5387. *E-mail:* mzeigler@claflin.edu.

CLEMSON UNIVERSITY

Clemson, South Carolina **www.clemson.edu/**

- **State-supported** university, founded 1889
- **Small-town** 1400-acre campus
- **Endowment** $301.2 million
- **Coed** 14,096 undergraduate students, 94% full-time, 46% women, 54% men
- **Moderately difficult** entrance level, 50% of applicants were admitted

Undergraduates 13,257 full-time, 839 part-time. Students come from 53 states and territories, 84 other countries, 32% are from out of state, 7% African American, 2% Asian American or Pacific Islander, 1% Hispanic American, 0.4% Native American, 0.8% international, 5% transferred in, 47% live on campus. *Retention:* 91% of 2006 full-time freshmen returned.

Freshmen *Admission:* 14,254 applied, 7,154 admitted, 2,903 enrolled. *Average high school GPA:* 4.06. *Test scores:* SAT critical reading scores over 500: 93%;

SAT math scores over 500: 96%; ACT scores over 18: 99%; SAT critical reading scores over 600: 54%; SAT math scores over 600: 69%; ACT scores over 24: 81%; SAT critical reading scores over 700: 9%; SAT math scores over 700: 15%; ACT scores over 30: 20%.

Faculty *Total:* 1,178, 86% full-time, 80% with terminal degrees. *Student/faculty ratio:* 14:1.

Majors Accounting; agricultural/biological engineering and bioengineering; agricultural business and management; agricultural economics; agricultural mechanization; agricultural teacher education; animal sciences; architecture; biochemistry; biology/biological sciences; biomedical/medical engineering; business administration and management; business, management, and marketing related; ceramic sciences and engineering; chemical engineering; chemistry; civil engineering; communication and journalism related; computer and information sciences; computer engineering; computer programming; computer science; construction management; counselor education/school counseling and guidance; early childhood education; economics; electrical, electronics and communications engineering; elementary education; engineering/industrial management; engineering mechanics; English; finance; fishing and fisheries sciences and management; food science; forest/forest resources management; genetics; geology/earth science; graphic communications; health professions related; health science; history; horticultural science; human resources development; industrial design; industrial engineering; information science/studies; international business/trade/commerce; international public health; landscape architecture; management information systems; marketing/marketing management; mass communications; materials engineering; mathematics; mathematics teacher education; mechanical engineering; microbiology; modern languages; natural resources/conservation; nursing (registered nurse training); parks, recreation and leisure facilities management; philosophy; physics; political science and government; polymer chemistry; psychology; science teacher education; science technologies related; secondary education; sociology; special education; speech and rhetoric; textile sciences and engineering; turf and turfgrass management; visual and performing arts; visual and performing arts related; wildlife biology.

Academics *Calendar:* semesters. *Degrees:* bachelor's, master's, and doctoral. *Special study options:* academic remediation for entering students, accelerated degree program, advanced placement credit, cooperative education, distance learning, double majors, honors programs, internships, part-time degree program, services for LD students, study abroad, summer session for credit. *ROTC:* Army (b), Air Force (b).

Computers on Campus 1,250 computers/terminals are available on campus for general student use. Students can access the following: online (class) registration. Campuswide network is available. 100% of college-owned or -operated housing units are wired for high-speed Internet access. Wireless service is available via entire campus.

Student Life *Housing:* on-campus residence required for freshman year. *Options:* coed, men-only, women-only. Campus housing is university owned. Freshman campus housing is guaranteed. *Activities and organizations:* drama/theater group, student-run newspaper, radio and television station, choral group, marching band, Student government, Fellowship of Christian Athletes, Tiger Band, national fraternities, national sororities. *Campus security:* 24-hour emergency response devices and patrols, late-night transport/escort service, controlled dormitory access. *Student services:* health clinic, personal/psychological counseling, legal services.

Athletics Member NCAA. All Division I except football (Division I-A). *Intercollegiate sports:* baseball M, basketball M (s)/W (s), bowling M (c)/W (c), cheerleading M/W, crew M (c)/W (s), cross-country running M (s)/W (s), equestrian sports M (c)/W (c), fencing M (c)/W (c), field hockey M (c)/W (c), golf M (s), ice hockey M (c)/W (c), lacrosse M (c)/W (c), riflery M (c)/W (c), rugby M (c)/W (c), sailing M (c)/W (c), soccer M (s)/W (s), softball W (c), swimming and diving M (s)/W (s), tennis M (s)/W (s), track and field M (s)/W (s), ultimate Frisbee M (c)/W (c), volleyball M (c)/W (s), weight lifting M (c)/W (c), wrestling M (c). *Intramural sports:* basketball M/W, golf M/W, racquetball M/W, soccer M/W, softball M/W, swimming and diving M (c)/W (c), table tennis M/W, tennis M (c)/W (c), volleyball M/W, water polo M/W.

Standardized Tests *Required:* SAT or ACT (for admission).

Costs (2007–08) *Tuition:* state resident $10,370 full-time; nonresident $22,300 full-time. *Room and board:* $6170; room only: $3678.

Financial Aid Of all full-time matriculated undergraduates who enrolled in 2007, 7,042 applied for aid, 5,202 were judged to have need, 1,383 had their need fully met. 628 Federal Work-Study jobs (averaging $2147). 3,000 state and other part-time jobs (averaging $1700). In 2007, 2426 non-need-based awards were made. *Average percent of need met:* 61%. *Average financial aid package:* $10,057. *Average need-based loan:* $4364. *Average need-based gift aid:* $4903. *Average non-need-based aid:* $2363.

Applying *Options:* electronic application. *Application fee:* $50. *Required:* high school transcript. *Recommended:* essay or personal statement, letters of recommendation. *Application deadlines:* 5/1 (freshmen), 8/1 (transfers), 12/1 (early action). *Notification:* continuous (freshmen), continuous (transfers), 2/15 (early action).

Freshman Application Contact Ms. Audrey R. Bodell, Associate Director of Admissions, Clemson University, 105 Sikes Hall, PO Box 345124, Clemson, SC 29634. *Phone:* 864-656-2287. *Fax:* 864-656-2464. *E-mail:* cuadmissions@clemson.edu.

See page 2402 for the College Close-Up.

COASTAL CAROLINA UNIVERSITY

Conway, South Carolina **www.coastal.edu/**

- **State-supported** comprehensive, founded 1954
- **Suburban** 302-acre campus
- **Endowment** $27.9 million
- **Coed** 7,070 undergraduate students, 91% full-time, 53% women, 47% men
- **Moderately difficult** entrance level, 68% of applicants were admitted

Undergraduates 6,452 full-time, 618 part-time. Students come from 44 states and territories, 37 other countries, 48% are from out of state, 12% African American, 1% Asian American or Pacific Islander, 2% Hispanic American, 0.5% Native American, 1% international, 9% transferred in, 32% live on campus. *Retention:* 71% of 2006 full-time freshmen returned.

Freshmen *Admission:* 6,618 applied, 4,524 admitted, 1,652 enrolled. *Average high school GPA:* 3.32. *Test scores:* SAT critical reading scores over 500: 56%; SAT math scores over 500: 66%; ACT scores over 18: 97%; SAT critical reading scores over 600: 10%; SAT math scores over 600: 16%; ACT scores over 24: 15%; SAT math scores over 700: 1%.

Faculty *Total:* 508, 52% full-time, 53% with terminal degrees. *Student/faculty ratio:* 18:1.

Majors Accounting; applied mathematics; biology/biological sciences; business administration and management; chemistry; communication/speech communication and rhetoric; computer and information sciences; dramatic/theater arts; dramatic/theater arts and stagecraft related; early childhood education; economics; elementary education; English; finance; fine/studio arts; history; liberal arts and sciences/liberal studies; marine biology and biological oceanography; marketing/marketing management; middle school education; music; philosophy; physical education teaching and coaching; physics; political science and government; psychology; public health education and promotion; resort management; sociology; Spanish; special education; sport and fitness administration/management.

Academics *Calendar:* semesters. *Degrees:* bachelor's, master's, and post-bachelor's certificates. *Special study options:* accelerated degree program, adult/continuing education programs, advanced placement credit, cooperative education, distance learning, double majors, honors programs, independent study, internships, part-time degree program, services for LD students, student-designed majors, study abroad, summer session for credit. *Unusual degree programs:* 3-2 engineering with Clemson University.

Computers on Campus 600 computers/terminals are available on campus for general student use. Students can access the following: computer help desk, free student e-mail accounts, online (class) grades, online (class) registration, online (class) schedules. Campuswide network is available. Wireless service is available via classrooms, computer centers, computer labs, dorm rooms, learning centers, libraries, student centers.

Student Life *Housing options:* coed, disabled students. Campus housing is university owned. Freshman applicants given priority for college housing. *Activities and organizations:* drama/theater group, student-run newspaper, choral group, marching band, Student Government Association, Coastal Productions Board, STAR (Students Taking Active Responsibility), FCA (Fellowship of Christian Athletes), Diversity of Programming, national fraternities, national sororities. *Campus security:* 24-hour emergency response devices and patrols, late-night transport/escort service. *Student services:* health clinic, personal/psychological counseling, women's center.

Athletics Member NCAA. All Division I. *Intercollegiate sports:* baseball M (s), basketball M (s)/W (s), cheerleading M (c)/W (c), cross-country running M (s)/W (s), football M (s), golf M (s)/W (s), soccer M (s)/W (s), softball W (s), tennis M (s)/W (s), track and field M (s)/W (s), volleyball W (s). *Intramural sports:* badminton M/W, basketball M/W, bowling M/W, football M/W, golf M/W, lacrosse M/W, racquetball M/W, rock climbing M, soccer M/W, softball M/W, swimming and diving M/W, table tennis M/W, tennis M/W, track and field M/W, volleyball M/W, water polo M/W, weight lifting M/W.

Standardized Tests *Required:* SAT or ACT (for admission).

Costs (2007–08) *Tuition:* state resident $7520 full-time, $317 per credit hour part-time; nonresident $16,510 full-time, $691 per credit hour part-time. Full-time tuition and fees vary according to course load. Part-time tuition and fees vary according to course load. *Required fees:* $80 full-time. *Room and board:* $6680; room only: $4380. Room and board charges vary according to board plan and housing facility. *Payment plans:* installment, deferred payment. *Waivers:* senior citizens and employees or children of employees.

Financial Aid Of all full-time matriculated undergraduates who enrolled in 2006, 4,536 applied for aid, 3,429 were judged to have need, 413 had their need fully met. 152 Federal Work-Study jobs (averaging $1300). 761 state and other part-time jobs (averaging $1760). In 2006, 1301 non-need-based awards were made. *Average percent of need met:* 52%. *Average financial aid package:* $7822. *Average need-based loan:* $6946. *Average need-based gift aid:* $3533. *Average non-need-based aid:* $9761. *Average indebtedness upon graduation:* $22,470.

Applying *Options:* electronic application, deferred entrance. *Application fee:* $45. *Required:* high school transcript, minimum 2.0 GPA. *Recommended:* essay or personal statement, 1 letter of recommendation, interview. *Application deadlines:* 8/15 (freshmen), 8/15 (transfers). *Notification:* continuous until 9/15 (freshmen), continuous until 8/15 (transfers).

Freshman Application Contact Dr. Judy Vogt, Vice President, Enrollment Services, Coastal Carolina University, PO Box 261954, Kingston Hall, Room 119, Conway, SC 29528. *Phone:* 843-349-2037. *Toll-free phone:* 800-277-7000. *Fax:* 843-349-2127. *E-mail:* admissions@coastal.edu.

COKER COLLEGE

Hartsville, South Carolina www.coker.edu/

- **Independent** 4-year, founded 1908
- **Small-town** 30-acre campus with easy access to Charlotte
- **Coed** 634 undergraduate students, 98% full-time, 61% women, 39% men
- **Moderately difficult** entrance level, 55% of applicants were admitted

Undergraduates 624 full-time, 10 part-time. Students come from 28 states and territories, 6 other countries, 20% are from out of state, 21% African American, 1% Asian American or Pacific Islander, 2% Hispanic American, 0.2% Native American, 2% international, 7% transferred in, 68% live on campus. *Retention:* 74% of 2006 full-time freshmen returned.

Freshmen *Admission:* 1,304 applied, 713 admitted, 200 enrolled. *Average high school GPA:* 3.4. *Test scores:* SAT critical reading scores over 500: 40%; SAT math scores over 500: 42%; ACT scores over 18: 79%; SAT critical reading scores over 600: 10%; SAT math scores over 600: 8%; ACT scores over 24: 21%; SAT critical reading scores over 700: 1%.

Faculty *Total:* 64, 89% full-time, 84% with terminal degrees. *Student/faculty ratio:* 10:1.

Majors Acting; art teacher education; biology/biological sciences; biology teacher education; business administration and management; chemistry; chemistry teacher education; clinical laboratory science/medical technology; communication/speech communication and rhetoric; computer science; corrections; corrections and criminal justice related; counseling psychology; criminal justice/law enforcement administration; criminology; dance related; dramatic/theater arts; early childhood education; education; elementary education; English; English/language arts teacher education; fine/studio arts; French; graphic design; health and physical education related; history; history teacher education; kinesiology and exercise science; mathematics; mathematics teacher education; music related; music teacher education; parks, recreation, and leisure related; photography; physical education teaching and coaching; piano and organ; political science and government; psychology; social work; sociology; sport and fitness administration/management; technical and business writing; theater design and technology; therapeutic recreation; voice and opera.

Academics *Calendar:* semesters. *Degrees:* bachelor's (also offers evening program with significant enrollment not reflected in profile). *Special study options:* academic remediation for entering students, adult/continuing education programs, advanced placement credit, cooperative education, double majors, English as a second language, honors programs, independent study, internships, part-time degree program, student-designed majors, study abroad, summer session for credit.

Computers on Campus 40 computers/terminals are available on campus for general student use. Campuswide network is available.

Student Life *Housing:* on-campus residence required through junior year. *Options:* coed, men-only, women-only. Campus housing is university owned. Freshman campus housing is guaranteed. *Activities and organizations:* drama/theater group, student-run newspaper, choral group, Coker College Union, student government, Pan-African American Sisterhood Association, Sigma Alpha Chi, Commissioners. *Campus security:* 24-hour patrols, late-night transport/escort service, controlled dormitory access. *Student services:* health clinic, personal/psychological counseling.

Athletics Member NCAA. All Division II. *Intercollegiate sports:* baseball M (s), basketball M (s)/W (s), cross-country running M (s)/W (s), golf M (s), soccer M (s)/W (s), softball W (s), tennis M (s)/W (s), volleyball W (s). *Intramural sports:* basketball M/W, football M/W, table tennis M/W, track and field M/W, volleyball M/W, weight lifting M/W.

Standardized Tests *Required:* SAT or ACT (for admission).

Costs (2007–08) *Comprehensive fee:* $24,522 includes full-time tuition ($18,072), mandatory fees ($530), and room and board ($5920). Part-time tuition: $753 per semester hour. *Required fees:* $3 per semester hour part-time, $107 per term part-time. *College room only:* $3070. *Payment plan:* installment. *Waivers:* employees or children of employees.

Financial Aid Of all full-time matriculated undergraduates who enrolled in 2003, 434 applied for aid, 398 were judged to have need, 158 had their need fully met. 157 Federal Work-Study jobs (averaging $1078). In 2003, 75 non-need-based awards were made. *Average percent of need met:* 97%. *Average financial aid package:* $16,531. *Average need-based loan:* $3775. *Average need-based gift aid:* $5885. *Average non-need-based aid:* $5269. *Average indebtedness upon graduation:* $17,093. *Financial aid deadline:* 6/1.

Applying *Options:* electronic application, early admission, deferred entrance. *Application fee:* $15. *Required:* high school transcript. *Required for some:* essay or personal statement. *Application deadlines:* 8/1 (freshmen), rolling (transfers). *Notification:* 9/1 (freshmen).

Freshman Application Contact Mrs. Perry Wilson, Director of Admissions, Coker College, 300 East College Avenue, Hartsville, SC 29550. *Phone:* 843-383-8050. *Toll-free phone:* 800-950-1908. *Fax:* 843-383-8056. *E-mail:* admissions@coker.edu.

COLLEGE OF CHARLESTON

Charleston, South Carolina www.cofc.edu/

- **State-supported** comprehensive, founded 1770
- **Urban** 52-acre campus
- **Endowment** $48.8 million
- **Coed** 9,923 undergraduate students, 91% full-time, 64% women, 36% men
- **Moderately difficult** entrance level, 65% of applicants were admitted

Undergraduates 9,034 full-time, 889 part-time. Students come from 51 states and territories, 69 other countries, 36% are from out of state, 6% African American, 2% Asian American or Pacific Islander, 2% Hispanic American, 0.3% Native American, 2% international, 7% transferred in, 34% live on campus. *Retention:* 82% of 2006 full-time freshmen returned.

Freshmen *Admission:* 8,941 applied, 5,775 admitted, 2,064 enrolled. *Average high school GPA:* 3.82. *Test scores:* SAT critical reading scores over 500: 98%; SAT math scores over 500: 98%; ACT scores over 18: 100%; SAT critical reading scores over 600: 48%; SAT math scores over 600: 57%; ACT scores over 24: 64%; SAT critical reading scores over 700: 10%; SAT math scores over 700: 6%; ACT scores over 30: 3%.

Faculty *Total:* 899, 58% full-time, 66% with terminal degrees. *Student/faculty ratio:* 13:1.

Majors Accounting; anthropology; art history, criticism and conservation; arts management; astronomy and astrophysics related; athletic training; biochemistry; biology/biological sciences; business administration and management; chemistry; classics and languages, literatures and linguistics; communication/speech communication and rhetoric; computer and information sciences; dramatic/theater arts; early childhood education; economics; elementary education; English; fine/studio arts; French; geology/earth science; German; historic preservation and conservation; history; hospitality administration; information science/studies; international business/trade/commerce; Latin American studies; marine biology and biological oceanography; mathematics; middle school education; music; philosophy; physical education teaching and coaching; physics; political science and government; pre-dentistry studies; pre-medical studies; psychology; religious studies; sociology; Spanish; special education; urban studies/affairs.

Academics *Calendar:* semesters. *Degrees:* bachelor's and master's (also offers graduate degree programs through University of Charleston, South Carolina). *Special study options:* accelerated degree program, adult/continuing education programs, advanced placement credit, cooperative education, distance learning, double majors, English as a second language, honors programs, independent study, internships, off-campus study, part-time degree program, services for LD students, study abroad, summer session for credit. *ROTC:* Air Force (c). *Unusual degree programs:* 3-2 engineering with Case Western Reserve University, Clemson University, Georgia Institute of Technology, University of South Carolina; biometry with Medical University of South Carolina, marine engineering with University of Michigan.

Computers on Campus 578 computers/terminals are available on campus for general student use. Students can access the following: online (class) registration. Campuswide network is available.

Student Life *Housing options:* coed, men-only, women-only, disabled students. Campus housing is university owned. Freshman campus housing is guaranteed. *Activities and organizations:* drama/theater group, student-run newspaper, radio station, choral group, Student Government Association, Cougar Productions, intramural basketball, Black Student Union, national fraternities, national sororities. *Campus security:* 24-hour emergency response devices and patrols, student patrols, late-night transport/escort service, controlled dormitory access. *Student services:* health clinic, personal/psychological counseling, women's center, legal services.

Athletics Member NCAA. All Division I. *Intercollegiate sports:* baseball M (s), basketball M (s)/W (s), cross-country running M (s)/W (s), equestrian sports W, golf M (s)/W (s), sailing M/W, soccer M (s)/W (s), softball W (s), swimming and diving M (s)/W (s), tennis M (s)/W (s), volleyball W (s). *Intramural sports:* badminton M/W, basketball M/W, crew M/W, equestrian sports W, fencing M/W, football M/W, racquetball M/W, rugby W, soccer M/W, softball M/W, tennis M/W, volleyball M/W, weight lifting M/W.

Standardized Tests *Required:* SAT or ACT (for admission).

Costs (2007–08) *Tuition:* state resident $7778 full-time, $324 per semester hour part-time; nonresident $18,732 full-time, $781 per semester hour part-time. Part-time tuition and fees vary according to course load. *Room and board:* $8495; room only: $5885. Room and board charges vary according to board plan and housing facility. *Payment plan:* installment. *Waivers:* senior citizens.

Financial Aid Of all full-time matriculated undergraduates who enrolled in 2007, 4,663 applied for aid, 3,402 were judged to have need, 992 had their need fully met. In 2007, 1030 non-need-based awards were made. *Average percent of need met:* 66%. *Average financial aid package:* $11,492. *Average need-based loan:* $4424. *Average need-based gift aid:* $2873. *Average non-need-based aid:* $10,529. *Average indebtedness upon graduation:* $17,118.

Applying *Options:* electronic application, early action, deferred entrance. *Application fee:* $45. *Required:* essay or personal statement, high school transcript. *Recommended:* interview. *Application deadlines:* 4/1 (freshmen), 4/1 (transfers), 11/1 (early action). *Notification:* 5/15 (freshmen), continuous (transfers), 12/15 (early action).

Freshman Application Contact Ms. Suzette Stille, Director of Undergraduate Admissions, College of Charleston, 66 George Street, Charleston, SC 29424-0001. *Phone:* 843-953-5670. *Toll-free phone:* 843-953-5670. *Fax:* 843-953-6322. *E-mail:* admissions@cofc.edu.

COLUMBIA COLLEGE

Columbia, South Carolina **www.columbiacollegesc.edu/**

- **Independent United Methodist** comprehensive, founded 1854
- **Suburban** 33-acre campus
- **Endowment** $26.0 million
- **Undergraduate: women only; graduate: coed** 1,238 undergraduate students, 79% full-time, 98% women, 2% men
- **Moderately difficult** entrance level, 71% of applicants were admitted

Undergraduates 984 full-time, 254 part-time. Students come from 21 states and territories, 14 other countries, 8% are from out of state, 44% African American, 1% Asian American or Pacific Islander, 2% Hispanic American, 0.5% Native American, 1% international, 10% transferred in, 47% live on campus. *Retention:* 68% of 2006 full-time freshmen returned.

Freshmen *Admission:* 1,075 applied, 763 admitted, 273 enrolled. *Average high school GPA:* 3.47. *Test scores:* SAT critical reading scores over 500: 52%; SAT math scores over 500: 42%; SAT writing scores over 500: 39%; ACT scores over 18: 82%; SAT critical reading scores over 600: 13%; SAT math scores over 600: 11%; SAT writing scores over 600: 14%; ACT scores over 24: 20%; SAT critical reading scores over 700: 5%; SAT math scores over 700: 1%; SAT writing scores over 700: 2%; ACT scores over 30: 2%.

Faculty *Total:* 162, 46% full-time, 55% with terminal degrees. *Student/faculty ratio:* 12:1.

Majors Accounting; applied art; behavioral sciences; biology/biological sciences; business administration and management; chemistry; communication and journalism related; communication/speech communication and rhetoric; computer and information sciences and support services related; dance; drama and dance teacher education; elementary education; English; English language and literature related; fine/studio arts; French; history; human development and family studies related; journalism; journalism related; kindergarten/preschool education; liberal arts and sciences/liberal studies; mathematics; middle school education; music; music performance; music teacher education; piano and organ; political science and government; psychology; public administration and social service professions related: public relations/image management; religious education; religious studies; social sciences; social work; Spanish; special education; speech-language pathology; voice and opera.

Academics *Calendar:* semesters. *Degrees:* bachelor's and master's. *Special study options:* academic remediation for entering students, adult/continuing education programs, advanced placement credit, distance learning, double majors, honors programs, independent study, internships, off-campus study, part-time degree program, student-designed majors, study abroad, summer session for credit. *ROTC:* Army (c), Navy (c), Air Force (c).

Computers on Campus 150 computers/terminals are available on campus for general student use. Students can access the following: campus intranet, computer help desk, free student e-mail accounts, online (class) grades, online (class) registration, online (class) schedules. Campuswide network is available. 100% of college-owned or -operated housing units are wired for high-speed Internet access. Wireless service is available via student centers.

Student Life *Housing:* on-campus residence required through sophomore year. *Options:* women-only. Campus housing is university owned. Freshman campus housing is guaranteed. *Activities and organizations:* drama/theater group, student-run newspaper, choral group, Student Government Association, African-American Student Association, Columbia College Activities Board, Heavenly Creations Gospel Choir, Student Christian Association. *Campus security:* 24-hour emergency response devices and patrols, late-night transport/escort service, controlled dormitory access. *Student services:* health clinic, personal/psychological counseling, women's center.

Athletics Member NAIA. *Intercollegiate sports:* basketball W (s), soccer W (s), tennis W (s), volleyball W (s).

Standardized Tests *Required:* SAT or ACT (for admission).

Costs (2007–08) *Comprehensive fee:* $27,882 includes full-time tuition ($21,200), mandatory fees ($450), and room and board ($6232). Full-time tuition and fees vary according to class time. Part-time tuition: $570 per semester hour. Part-time tuition and fees vary according to course load. *Room and board:* Room and board charges vary according to board plan and housing facility. *Payment plan:* installment. *Waivers:* employees or children of employees.

Financial Aid Of all full-time matriculated undergraduates who enrolled in 2005, 794 applied for aid, 698 were judged to have need, 310 had their need fully met. 200 Federal Work-Study jobs (averaging $1000). In 2005, 152 non-need-based awards were made. *Average percent of need met:* 70%. *Average financial aid package:* $20,052. *Average need-based loan:* $3810. *Average need-based gift aid:* $8495. *Average non-need-based aid:* $7775. *Average indebtedness upon graduation:* $25,333.

Applying *Options:* electronic application. *Application fee:* $25. *Required:* high school transcript, minimum 2.0 GPA, 1 letter of recommendation. *Required for some:* interview. *Recommended:* essay or personal statement. *Application deadlines:* 8/1 (freshmen), 8/1 (transfers).

Freshman Application Contact Ms. Julie King, Director of Admissions, Columbia College, 1301 Columbia College Drive, Columbia, SC 29203. *Phone:* 803-786-3765. *Toll-free phone:* 800-277-1301. *Fax:* 803-786-3674. *E-mail:* admissions@colacoll.edu.

COLUMBIA INTERNATIONAL UNIVERSITY

Columbia, South Carolina **www.ciu.edu/**

- **Independent nondenominational** comprehensive, founded 1923
- **Suburban** 450-acre campus
- **Endowment** $3.5 million
- **Coed**
- **Minimally difficult** entrance level

Faculty *Student/faculty ratio:* 17:1.

Academics *Calendar:* semesters. *Degrees:* certificates, associate, bachelor's, master's, doctoral, first professional, and postbachelor's certificates.

Student Life *Campus security:* 24-hour emergency response devices and patrols, late-night transport/escort service.

Standardized Tests *Required:* SAT or ACT (for admission).

Costs (2007–08) *Comprehensive fee:* $21,174 includes full-time tuition ($15,360) and room and board ($5814). Full-time tuition and fees vary according to course load. Part-time tuition: $640 per semester hour. Part-time tuition and fees vary according to course load. *Room and board:* Room and board charges vary according to board plan.

Financial Aid Of all full-time matriculated undergraduates who enrolled in 2005, 397 applied for aid, 331 were judged to have need, 36 had their need fully met. 76 Federal Work-Study jobs (averaging $1223). *Average percent of need met:* 69. *Average financial aid package:* $9671. *Average need-based loan:* $3725. *Average need-based gift aid:* $3796. *Average indebtedness upon graduation:* $21,678.

Applying *Options:* electronic application, deferred entrance. *Application fee:* $45. *Required:* essay or personal statement, minimum 2.0 GPA, 4 letters of recommendation. *Required for some:* high school transcript, interview.

Freshman Application Contact Ms. Michelle MacGregor, Director of College Admissions, Columbia International University, PO Box 3122, Columbia, SC 29230-3122. *Phone:* 803-754-4100 Ext. 3024. *Toll-free phone:* 800-777-2227 Ext. 3024. *Fax:* 803-786-4041. *E-mail:* yesciu@ciu.edu.

CONVERSE COLLEGE

Spartanburg, South Carolina www.converse.edu/

- **Independent** comprehensive, founded 1889
- **Urban** 70-acre campus
- **Endowment** $64.6 million
- **Undergraduate: women only; graduate: coed** 737 undergraduate students, 86% full-time, 99% women, 1% men
- **Moderately difficult** entrance level, 47% of applicants were admitted

Undergraduates 637 full-time, 100 part-time. Students come from 30 states and territories, 8 other countries, 24% are from out of state, 12% African American, 1% Asian American or Pacific Islander, 2% Hispanic American, 0.7% Native American, 3% international, 2% transferred in, 90% live on campus. *Retention:* 72% of 2006 full-time freshmen returned.

Freshmen *Admission:* 1,361 applied, 643 admitted, 156 enrolled. *Average high school GPA:* 3.85. *Test scores:* SAT critical reading scores over 500: 74%; SAT math scores over 500: 74%; SAT writing scores over 500: 68%; ACT scores over 18: 95%; SAT critical reading scores over 600: 26%; SAT math scores over 600: 22%; SAT writing scores over 600: 19%; ACT scores over 24: 40%; SAT critical reading scores over 700: 6%; SAT math scores over 700: 1%; ACT scores over 30: 2%.

Faculty *Total:* 92, 95% full-time, 87% with terminal degrees.

Majors Accounting; applied art; art; art history, criticism and conservation; art teacher education; art therapy; biochemistry; biology/biological sciences; business administration and management; chemistry; computer science; dramatic/theater arts; economics; education; elementary education; English; fine/studio arts; French; history; interior design; international business/trade/commerce; kindergarten/preschool education; marketing/marketing management; mathematics; modern languages; music; music history, literature, and theory; music teacher education; music therapy; piano and organ; political science and government; psychology; religious studies; secondary education; sign language interpretation and translation; sociology; Spanish; special education; violin, viola, guitar and other stringed instruments; voice and opera.

Academics *Calendar:* 4-1-4. *Degrees:* bachelor's, master's, and post-master's certificates. *Special study options:* adult/continuing education programs, advanced placement credit, cooperative education, distance learning, double majors, English as a second language, honors programs, independent study, internships, off-campus study, part-time degree program, services for LD students, student-designed majors, study abroad, summer session for credit. *ROTC:* Army (c).

Computers on Campus 72 computers/terminals are available on campus for general student use. Students can access the following: online (class) registration. Campuswide network is available.

Student Life *Housing:* on-campus residence required through senior year. *Options:* women-only. Campus housing is university owned. Freshman campus housing is guaranteed. *Activities and organizations:* drama/theater group, student-run newspaper, choral group, student government, student volunteer services, Student Christian Organization, Student Activities Committee, Athletic Association. *Campus security:* 24-hour emergency response devices and patrols, late-night transport/escort service, controlled dormitory access. *Student services:* health clinic, personal/psychological counseling, women's center.

Athletics Member NCAA. All Division II. *Intercollegiate sports:* basketball W (s), cheerleading W, cross-country running W (s), soccer W (s), tennis W (s), volleyball W (s). *Intramural sports:* archery W, basketball W, bowling W, equestrian sports W, fencing W, field hockey W, gymnastics W, soccer W, softball W, swimming and diving W, tennis W, volleyball W, weight lifting W.

Standardized Tests *Required:* SAT or ACT (for admission).

Costs (2008–09) *Comprehensive fee:* $32,050 includes full-time tuition ($24,500) and room and board ($7550).

Financial Aid Of all full-time matriculated undergraduates who enrolled in 2006, 446 applied for aid, 395 were judged to have need, 155 had their need fully met. 141 Federal Work-Study jobs (averaging $1446). 60 state and other part-time jobs (averaging $1000). In 2006, 176 non-need-based awards were made. *Average percent of need met:* 87%. *Average financial aid package:* $19,427. *Average need-based loan:* $4190. *Average need-based gift aid:* $16,419. *Average non-need-based aid:* $18,143. *Average indebtedness upon graduation:* $20,861.

Applying *Options:* electronic application, early admission, early decision, early action, deferred entrance. *Application fee:* $40. *Required:* high school transcript, 1 letter of recommendation. *Recommended:* essay or personal statement, minimum 3.0 GPA, interview. *Application deadline:* 7/1 (transfers). *Notification:* continuous until 5/1 (freshmen), continuous until 8/15 (transfers).

Freshman Application Contact Mr. Aaron Meis, Dean of Admission, Converse College, 580 East Main Street, Spartanburg, SC 29302. *Phone:* 864-596-9040 Ext. 9746. *Toll-free phone:* 800-766-1125. *Fax:* 864-596-9225. *E-mail:* admissions@converse.edu.

ERSKINE COLLEGE

Due West, South Carolina www.erskine.edu/

- **Independent** 4-year, founded 1839, affiliated with Associate Reformed Presbyterian Church, administratively affiliated with Erskine Theological Seminary
- **Rural** 85-acre campus
- **Endowment** $51.5 million
- **Coed** 571 undergraduate students, 98% full-time, 56% women, 44% men
- **Moderately difficult** entrance level, 66% of applicants were admitted

Undergraduates 557 full-time, 14 part-time. Students come from 15 states and territories, 4 other countries, 27% are from out of state, 7% African American, 0.5% Asian American or Pacific Islander, 1% Hispanic American, 0.9% international, 2% transferred in, 89% live on campus. *Retention:* 78% of 2006 full-time freshmen returned.

Freshmen *Admission:* 874 applied, 573 admitted, 165 enrolled. *Average high school GPA:* 3.28. *Test scores:* SAT critical reading scores over 500: 72%; SAT math scores over 500: 74%; SAT writing scores over 500: 68%; ACT scores over 18: 91%; SAT critical reading scores over 600: 29%; SAT math scores over 600: 25%; SAT writing scores over 600: 22%; ACT scores over 24: 41%; SAT critical reading scores over 700: 4%; SAT math scores over 700: 4%; SAT writing scores over 700: 3%; ACT scores over 30: 6%.

Faculty *Total:* 67, 60% full-time, 63% with terminal degrees. *Student/faculty ratio:* 12:1.

Majors American studies; art; athletic training; behavioral sciences; biblical studies; biological and physical sciences; biology/biological sciences; business administration and management; chemistry; clinical laboratory science/medical technology; elementary education; English; French; history; kindergarten/preschool education; mathematics; music; natural sciences; philosophy; physical education teaching and coaching; physics; psychology; religious education; religious/sacred music; religious studies; social studies teacher education; Spanish; special education; sport and fitness administration/management.

Academics *Calendar:* 4-1-4. *Degrees:* bachelor's, master's, doctoral, and first professional. *Special study options:* advanced placement credit, double majors, independent study, internships, off-campus study, part-time degree program, study abroad, summer session for credit. *Unusual degree programs:* 3-2 engineering with Clemson University, University of Tennessee, Knoxville; allied health programs with Medical University of South Carolina.

Computers on Campus Campuswide network is available. Wireless service is available via classrooms, dorm rooms, libraries, student centers.

Student Life *Housing:* on-campus residence required through senior year. *Options:* men-only, women-only. Campus housing is university owned. Freshman campus housing is guaranteed. *Activities and organizations:* drama/theater group, student-run newspaper, radio station, choral group, literary societies, religious organizations, Student Government Organization, publications, honor societies. *Campus security:* 24-hour patrols, late-night transport/escort service, controlled dormitory access. *Student services:* health clinic, personal/psychological counseling.

Athletics Member NCAA. All Division II. *Intercollegiate sports:* baseball M (s), basketball M (s)/W (s), cross-country running M (s)/W (s), equestrian sports M (c)/W (c), lacrosse W (s), soccer M (s)/W (s), softball W (s), tennis M (s)/W (s). *Intramural sports:* basketball M/W, football M/W, racquetball M/W, soccer M/W, softball M/W, tennis M/W, volleyball M/W.

Standardized Tests *Required:* SAT or ACT (for admission).

Costs (2007–08) *Comprehensive fee:* $29,106 includes full-time tuition ($20,185), mandatory fees ($1495), and room and board ($7426). Part-time tuition: $748 per semester hour. *Room and board:* Room and board charges vary according to board plan and housing facility. *Payment plan:* installment. *Waivers:* children of alumni and employees or children of employees.

Financial Aid Of all full-time matriculated undergraduates who enrolled in 2005, 543 applied for aid, 498 were judged to have need, 258 had their need fully met. 211 Federal Work-Study jobs (averaging $950). 110 state and other part-time jobs (averaging $1220). In 2005, 132 non-need-based awards were made. *Average*

percent of need met: 87%. *Average financial aid package:* $19,100. *Average need-based loan:* $3760. *Average need-based gift aid:* $10,000. *Average non-need-based aid:* $10,210. *Average indebtedness upon graduation:* $16,940.

Applying *Options:* electronic application. *Application fee:* $25. *Required:* essay or personal statement, high school transcript, 1 letter of recommendation. *Required for some:* interview. *Recommended:* interview. *Application deadlines:* rolling (freshmen), rolling (transfers). *Notification:* continuous (freshmen), continuous (transfers).

Freshman Application Contact Mr. Bart Walker, Director of Admissions, Erskine College, PO Box 176, Due West, SC 29639. *Phone:* 864-379-8830. *Toll-free phone:* 800-241-8721. *Fax:* 864-379-8759. *E-mail:* admissions@erskine.edu.

FRANCIS MARION UNIVERSITY

Florence, South Carolina **www.fmarion.edu/**

- **State-supported** comprehensive, founded 1970
- **Rural** 309-acre campus
- **Endowment** $16.4 million
- **Coed** 3,436 undergraduate students, 90% full-time, 67% women, 33% men
- **Moderately difficult** entrance level, 65% of applicants were admitted

Undergraduates 3,084 full-time, 352 part-time. Students come from 31 states and territories, 15 other countries, 4% are from out of state, 43% African American, 0.7% Asian American or Pacific Islander, 1% Hispanic American, 0.6% Native American, 1% international, 6% transferred in, 44% live on campus. *Retention:* 68% of 2006 full-time freshmen returned.

Freshmen *Admission:* 2,725 applied, 1,760 admitted, 779 enrolled. *Average high school GPA:* 3.46. *Test scores:* SAT critical reading scores over 500: 36%; SAT math scores over 500: 42%; SAT writing scores over 500: 27%; ACT scores over 18: 81%; SAT critical reading scores over 600: 8%; SAT math scores over 600: 9%; SAT writing scores over 600: 4%; ACT scores over 24: 14%; SAT critical reading scores over 700: 1%.

Faculty *Total:* 284, 71% full-time, 65% with terminal degrees. *Student/faculty ratio:* 15:1.

Majors Accounting; art; art teacher education; biology/biological sciences; business administration and management; chemistry; computer and information sciences; dramatic/theater arts; early childhood education; economics; elementary education; English; finance; foreign languages and literatures; French; geography; history; international relations and affairs; liberal arts and sciences/liberal studies; management information systems; marketing/marketing management; mass communication/media; mathematics; nursing (registered nurse training); physics; political science and government; pre-law studies; psychology; sociology; Spanish.

Academics *Calendar:* semesters. *Degrees:* bachelor's and master's. *Special study options:* accelerated degree program, adult/continuing education programs, advanced placement credit, distance learning, double majors, honors programs, independent study, internships, off-campus study, part-time degree program, services for LD students, study abroad, summer session for credit. *Unusual degree programs:* 3-2 engineering with Clemson University; forestry with Clemson University.

Computers on Campus 551 computers/terminals are available on campus for general student use. Students can access the following: computer help desk, online (class) registration, Blackboard. Campuswide network is available. 100% of college-owned or -operated housing units are wired for high-speed Internet access. Wireless service is available via classrooms, computer labs, dorm rooms, libraries.

Student Life *Housing options:* men-only, women-only, disabled students. Campus housing is provided by a third party. Freshman applicants given priority for college housing. *Activities and organizations:* drama/theater group, student-run newspaper, choral group, Baptist Campus Ministries, University Programming Board, Wesley Foundation, Student Alumni Association, Gamma Sigma Sigma (Service Sorority), national fraternities, national sororities. *Campus security:* 24-hour emergency response devices and patrols, late-night transport/escort service, controlled dormitory access. *Student services:* health clinic, personal/psychological counseling.

Athletics Member NCAA. All Division II except golf (Division I), soccer (Division I). *Intercollegiate sports:* baseball M (s), basketball M (s)/W (s), cross-country running M (s)/W (s), golf M (s), soccer M (s)/W (s), softball W (s), tennis M (s)/W (s), track and field M/W, volleyball W (s). *Intramural sports:* basketball M/W, bowling M/W, cheerleading M (c)/W (c), football M/W, golf M/W, racquetball M/W, soccer M/W, softball M/W, table tennis M/W, tennis M/W, track and field M/W, ultimate Frisbee M/W, volleyball M/W.

Standardized Tests *Required:* SAT or ACT (for admission).

Costs (2007–08) *Tuition:* state resident $6803 full-time, $340 per credit hour part-time; nonresident $13,606 full-time, $680 per credit hour part-time. Part-time tuition and fees vary according to course load. *Required fees:* $235 full-time, $7 per credit hour part-time. *Room and board:* $5860; room only: $3260. Room and board charges vary according to board plan and housing facility. *Payment plan:* installment. *Waivers:* senior citizens and employees or children of employees.

Financial Aid Of all full-time matriculated undergraduates who enrolled in 2005, 2,876 applied for aid, 2,615 were judged to have need. 142 Federal Work-Study jobs (averaging $1447). 145 state and other part-time jobs. In 2005, 150 non-need-based awards were made. *Average indebtedness upon graduation:* $20,640.

Applying *Options:* electronic application, early admission, deferred entrance. *Application fee:* $30. *Required:* high school transcript, minimum 2.0 GPA. *Application deadlines:* rolling (freshmen), rolling (transfers). *Notification:* continuous (freshmen).

Freshman Application Contact Mr. James Schlimmer, Director of Admissions, Francis Marion University, PO Box 100547, Florence, SC 29501-0547. *Phone:* 843-661-1231. *Toll-free phone:* 800-368-7551. *Fax:* 843-661-4635. *E-mail:* admission@fmarion.edu.

FURMAN UNIVERSITY

Greenville, South Carolina **www.furman.edu/**

- **Independent** comprehensive, founded 1826
- **Suburban** 750-acre campus
- **Endowment** $544.6 million
- **Coed** 2,774 undergraduate students, 95% full-time, 56% women, 44% men
- **Very difficult** entrance level, 56% of applicants were admitted

Undergraduates 2,633 full-time, 141 part-time. Students come from 47 states and territories, 46 other countries, 70% are from out of state, 7% African American, 2% Asian American or Pacific Islander, 1% Hispanic American, 0.2% Native American, 2% international, 2% transferred in, 90% live on campus. *Retention:* 90% of 2006 full-time freshmen returned.

Freshmen *Admission:* 3,879 applied, 2,159 admitted, 700 enrolled. *Average high school GPA:* 3.54. *Test scores:* SAT critical reading scores over 500: 96%; SAT math scores over 500: 97%; ACT scores over 18: 100%; SAT critical reading scores over 600: 67%; SAT math scores over 600: 67%; ACT scores over 24: 86%; SAT critical reading scores over 700: 22%; SAT math scores over 700: 18%; ACT scores over 30: 29%.

Faculty *Total:* 281, 84% full-time, 87% with terminal degrees. *Student/faculty ratio:* 11:1.

Majors Accounting; art; art history, criticism and conservation; Asian studies; biochemistry; biology/biological sciences; business administration and management; chemistry; classics; communication/speech communication and rhetoric; computer science; dramatic/theater arts; economics; education; elementary education; English; environmental studies; fine/studio arts; French; geology/earth science; German; history; information technology; kindergarten/preschool education; kinesiology and exercise science; Latin; mathematics; modern Greek; music; music teacher education; neuroscience; philosophy; physics; piano and organ; political science and government; pre-dentistry studies; pre-law studies; premedical studies; pre-veterinary studies; psychology; religious/sacred music; religious studies; secondary education; sociology; Spanish; special education; urban studies/affairs; voice and opera.

Academics *Calendar:* 3-2-3. *Degrees:* bachelor's, master's, and postbachelor's certificates. *Special study options:* accelerated degree program, adult/continuing education programs, advanced placement credit, double majors, independent study, internships, part-time degree program, services for LD students, student-designed majors, study abroad, summer session for credit. *ROTC:* Army (b). *Unusual degree programs:* 3-2 engineering with Georgia Institute of Technology, Clemson University, Auburn University, North Carolina State University, Washington University in St. Louis; forestry with Duke University.

Computers on Campus 340 computers/terminals and 3,000 ports are available on campus for general student use. Students can access the following: campus intranet, computer help desk, free student e-mail accounts, online (class) grades, online (class) registration, online (class) schedules. Campuswide network is available. 100% of college-owned or -operated housing units are wired for high-speed Internet access. Wireless service is available via classrooms, computer centers, computer labs, learning centers, libraries, student centers.

Student Life *Housing:* on-campus residence required through senior year. *Options:* coed, men-only, women-only. Campus housing is university owned. Freshman campus housing is guaranteed. *Activities and organizations:* drama/theater group, student-run newspaper, radio and television station, choral group, marching band, Collegiate Educational Service Corps, Fellowship of Christian

Athletes, Baptist Student Union, Student Activities Board, Furman Singers, national fraternities, national sororities. *Campus security:* 24-hour emergency response devices and patrols, student patrols, late-night transport/escort service, controlled dormitory access. *Student services:* health clinic, personal/psychological counseling.

Athletics Member NCAA. All Division I except football (Division I-AA). *Intercollegiate sports:* baseball M (s), basketball M (s)/W (s), cheerleading M/W, crew M (c)/W (c), cross-country running M (s)/W (s), equestrian sports W (c), fencing M (c)/W (c), golf M (s)/W (s), ice hockey M (c), lacrosse M (c)/W (c), rugby M (c)/W (c), soccer M (s)/W (s), softball W (s), swimming and diving M (c)/W (c), tennis M (s)/W (s), track and field M (s)/W (s), ultimate Frisbee M (c)/W (c), volleyball W (s), weight lifting M (c)/W (c), wrestling M (c). *Intramural sports:* basketball M/W, bowling M/W, cross-country running M/W, football M/W, golf M/W, racquetball M/W, soccer M/W, softball M/W, swimming and diving M/W, tennis M/W, track and field M/W, volleyball M/W.

Standardized Tests *Recommended:* SAT or ACT (for admission).

Costs (2007–08) *Comprehensive fee:* $39,624 includes full-time tuition ($31,040), mandatory fees ($520), and room and board ($8064). Part-time tuition: $970 per credit hour. Part-time tuition and fees vary according to course load. *College room only:* $4256. Room and board charges vary according to board plan and housing facility. *Payment plan:* installment. *Waivers:* employees or children of employees.

Financial Aid Of all full-time matriculated undergraduates who enrolled in 2007, 1,305 applied for aid, 1,080 were judged to have need, 426 had their need fully met. 392 Federal Work-Study jobs (averaging $1435). In 2007, 732 non-need-based awards were made. *Average percent of need met:* 85%. *Average financial aid package:* $24,109. *Average need-based loan:* $5469. *Average need-based gift aid:* $20,245. *Average non-need-based aid:* $15,806. *Average indebtedness upon graduation:* $24,512. *Financial aid deadline:* 1/15.

Applying *Options:* electronic application, early admission, early decision. *Required:* essay or personal statement, high school transcript. *Required for some:* interview. *Application deadlines:* 1/15 (freshmen), 6/1 (transfers). *Early decision deadline:* 11/15. *Notification:* 3/15 (freshmen), 6/15 (transfers), 12/15 (early decision).

Freshman Application Contact Mr. David R. O'Cain, Director of Admissions, Furman University, 3300 Poinsett Highway, Greenville, SC 29613. *Phone:* 864-294-2034. *Fax:* 864-294-2018. *E-mail:* admissions@furman.edu.

ITT Technical Institute

Greenville, South Carolina **www.itt-tech.edu/**

- **Proprietary** primarily 2-year, founded 1992, part of ITT Educational Services, Inc
- **Coed**
- **Minimally difficult** entrance level

Academics *Calendar:* quarters. *Degrees:* associate and bachelor's.

Standardized Tests *Required:* Wonderlic aptitude test (for admission).

Financial Aid Of all full-time matriculated undergraduates who enrolled in 2006, 3 Federal Work-Study jobs.

Applying *Options:* deferred entrance. *Application fee:* $100. *Required:* high school transcript, interview. *Recommended:* letters of recommendation.

Freshman Application Contact Ms. Lynette Stucka, Director of Recruitment, ITT Technical Institute, Independence Corporate Park, Six Independence Point, Greenville, SC 29615. *Phone:* 864-288-0777. *Toll-free phone:* 800-932-4488.

Lander University

Greenwood, South Carolina **www.lander.edu/**

- **State-supported** comprehensive, founded 1872, part of South Carolina Commission on Higher Education
- **Small-town** 100-acre campus
- **Coed, primarily women** 2,360 undergraduate students, 89% full-time, 66% women, 34% men
- **Moderately difficult** entrance level, 42% of applicants were admitted

Undergraduates 2,093 full-time, 267 part-time. Students come from 23 states and territories, 21 other countries, 3% are from out of state, 24% African American, 0.7% Asian American or Pacific Islander, 1% Hispanic American, 0.7% Native American, 3% international, 8% transferred in, 33% live on campus. *Retention:* 59% of 2006 full-time freshmen returned.

Freshmen *Admission:* 2,230 applied, 946 admitted, 433 enrolled. *Average high school GPA:* 3.65. *Test scores:* SAT critical reading scores over 500: 33%; SAT math scores over 500: 43%; ACT scores over 18: 66%; SAT critical reading scores over 600: 7%; SAT math scores over 600: 11%; ACT scores over 24: 8%; SAT math scores over 700: 1%.

Faculty *Total:* 200, 67% full-time, 56% with terminal degrees. *Student/faculty ratio:* 14:1.

Majors Art; athletic training; biology/biological sciences; business administration and management; chemistry; computer and information sciences; early childhood education; elementary education; English; environmental science; history; interdisciplinary studies; kinesiology and exercise science; liberal arts and sciences/liberal studies; mathematics; music; nursing (registered nurse training); nursing science; physical education teaching and coaching; political science and government; psychology; secondary education; sociology; Spanish; special education.

Academics *Calendar:* semesters plus 3 summer sessions. *Degrees:* certificates, bachelor's, and master's. *Special study options:* academic remediation for entering students, accelerated degree program, adult/continuing education programs, advanced placement credit, cooperative education, distance learning, double majors, honors programs, independent study, internships, off-campus study, part-time degree program, services for LD students, student-designed majors, study abroad, summer session for credit. *ROTC:* Army (b). *Unusual degree programs:* 3-2 engineering with Clemson University.

Computers on Campus 300 computers/terminals are available on campus for general student use. Students can access the following: campus intranet, computer help desk, free student e-mail accounts, online (class) grades, online (class) registration, online (class) schedules. Campuswide network is available. 100% of college-owned or -operated housing units are wired for high-speed Internet access. Wireless service is available via entire campus.

Student Life *Housing options:* coed, women-only. Campus housing is university owned. Freshman applicants given priority for college housing. *Activities and organizations:* drama/theater group, student-run newspaper, choral group, Students Promoting Intelligent Choices and Experiences (S.P.I.C.E.), Lander Association of Biological Science, national fraternities, national sororities. *Campus security:* 24-hour emergency response devices and patrols, late-night transport/escort service, controlled dormitory access. *Student services:* health clinic, personal/psychological counseling.

Athletics Member NCAA. All Division II. *Intercollegiate sports:* baseball M (s), basketball M (s)/W (s), cross-country running W (s), golf M (s), soccer M (s)/W (s), softball W (s), tennis M (s)/W (s), volleyball W (s). *Intramural sports:* basketball M/W, bowling M/W, equestrian sports M/W, football M/W, golf M/W, soccer M/W, softball M/W, Ultimate Frisbee M/W, volleyball M/W.

Standardized Tests *Required:* SAT or ACT (for admission).

Costs (2007–08) *Tuition:* state resident $7728 full-time, $322 per semester hour part-time; nonresident $14,616 full-time, $609 per semester hour part-time. Full-time tuition and fees vary according to course load and degree level. Part-time tuition and fees vary according to course load and degree level. *Required fees:* $550 full-time. *Room and board:* $5940; room only: $3650. Room and board charges vary according to board plan and housing facility. *Payment plan:* installment. *Waivers:* senior citizens and employees or children of employees.

Financial Aid Of all full-time matriculated undergraduates who enrolled in 2002, 1,548 applied for aid, 929 were judged to have need, 481 had their need fully met. 189 Federal Work-Study jobs (averaging $1529). 348 state and other part-time jobs (averaging $2021). In 2002, 419 non-need-based awards were made. *Average percent of need met:* 68%. *Average financial aid package:* $5105. *Average need-based loan:* $3870. *Average need-based gift aid:* $1903. *Average non-need-based aid:* $3417. *Average indebtedness upon graduation:* $16,450.

Applying *Options:* electronic application, early admission, deferred entrance. *Application fee:* $35. *Required:* high school transcript, minimum 2.0 GPA, 1 letter of recommendation. *Recommended:* interview. *Application deadlines:* 8/1 (freshmen), rolling (transfers). *Notification:* continuous (freshmen), continuous (transfers).

Freshman Application Contact Dr. Bettie R. Horne, Director of Admissions, Lander University, Greenwood, SC 29649. *Phone:* 864-388-8307. *Toll-free phone:* 888-452-6337. *Fax:* 864-388-8125. *E-mail:* admissions@lander.edu.

Limestone College

Gaffney, South Carolina **www.limestone.edu/**

- **Independent** 4-year, founded 1845
- **Suburban** 115-acre campus with easy access to Charlotte
- **Endowment** $10.1 million
- **Coed** 780 undergraduate students, 98% full-time, 43% women, 57% men
- **Moderately difficult** entrance level, 59% of applicants were admitted

Founded in 1845, Limestone is a private, coeducational liberal arts college that features a small student body and well-qualified faculty members, creating an atmosphere that ensures the intellectual, social, ethical, and physical development of students. With a student-faculty ratio of 12:1, Limestone provides the individual attention that larger institutions often lack.

Undergraduates 761 full-time, 19 part-time. Students come from 22 states and territories, 20 other countries, 44% are from out of state, 15% African American, 0.4% Asian American or Pacific Islander, 2% Hispanic American, 0.3% Native American, 6% international, 10% transferred in, 44% live on campus. *Retention:* 78% of 2006 full-time freshmen returned.

Freshmen *Admission:* 1,021 applied, 604 admitted, 190 enrolled. *Average high school GPA:* 3.34. *Test scores:* SAT critical reading scores over 500: 39%; SAT math scores over 500: 59%; ACT scores over 18: 79%; SAT critical reading scores over 600: 8%; SAT math scores over 600: 9%; ACT scores over 24: 22%; ACT scores over 30: 2%.

Faculty *Total:* 65, 85% full-time, 68% with terminal degrees. *Student/faculty ratio:* 13:1.

Majors Accounting; art teacher education; athletic training; biology/biological sciences; biology teacher education; business administration and management; business/commerce; business/managerial economics; chemistry; computer programming; computer science; corrections; corrections and criminal justice related; criminal justice/safety; dramatic/theater arts; education; elementary education; English; English/language arts teacher education; fine/studio arts; graphic design; health and physical education related; history; human resources development; information science/studies; jazz/jazz studies; liberal arts and sciences/liberal studies; marketing/marketing management; marriage and family therapy/counseling; mathematics; mathematics teacher education; music; music teacher education; physical education teaching and coaching; pre-dentistry studies; pre-law studies; pre-medical studies; pre-nursing studies; pre-pharmacy studies; pre-veterinary studies; psychology; social studies teacher education; social work; sport and fitness administration/management; web/multimedia management and webmaster.

Academics *Calendar:* semesters. *Degrees:* associate and bachelor's. *Special study options:* academic remediation for entering students, accelerated degree program, adult/continuing education programs, advanced placement credit, distance learning, double majors, honors programs, independent study, internships, part-time degree program, services for LD students, student-designed majors, summer session for credit. *ROTC:* Army (c).

Computers on Campus 102 computers/terminals are available on campus for general student use. Students can access the following: computer help desk, free student e-mail accounts, online (class) grades, online (class) registration for internet classes only. Campuswide network is available. 100% of college-owned or -operated housing units are wired for high-speed Internet access. Wireless service is available via classrooms, learning centers, libraries, student centers.

Student Life *Housing:* on-campus residence required through junior year. *Options:* men-only, women-only. Campus housing is university owned and leased by the school. Freshman applicants given priority for college housing. *Activities and organizations:* drama/theater group, choral group, Fellowship of Christian Athletes, Student Government Association, Student Alumni Leadership Council, Students in Free Enterprise, Limestone Activities Board. *Campus security:* 24-hour emergency response devices and patrols, late-night transport/escort service, controlled dormitory access. *Student services:* health clinic, personal/psychological counseling.

Athletics Member NCAA. All Division II. *Intercollegiate sports:* baseball M (s), basketball M (s)/W (s), cross-country running M (s)/W (s), golf M (s)/W (s), lacrosse M (s)/W (s), soccer M (s)/W (s), softball W (s), swimming and diving M (s)/W (s), tennis M (s)/W (s), track and field M (s)/W (s), volleyball W (s), wrestling M (s). *Intramural sports:* basketball M/W, bowling M/W, cheerleading M/W, softball M/W, table tennis M/W, tennis M/W, volleyball M/W.

Standardized Tests *Required:* SAT or ACT (for admission).

Costs (2008–09) *Comprehensive fee:* $23,700 includes full-time tuition ($17,300) and room and board ($6400). Part-time tuition: $720 per credit hour. *College room only:* $3200.

Financial Aid Of all full-time matriculated undergraduates who enrolled in 2006, 595 applied for aid, 559 were judged to have need, 73 had their need fully met. 128 Federal Work-Study jobs (averaging $1379). 36 state and other part-time jobs (averaging $958). In 2006, 41 non-need-based awards were made. *Average percent of need met:* 56%. *Average financial aid package:* $11,233. *Average need-based loan:* $3598. *Average need-based gift aid:* $9487. *Average non-need-based aid:* $706. *Average indebtedness upon graduation:* $21,349.

Applying *Options:* electronic application. *Application fee:* $25. *Required:* high school transcript, minimum 2.0 GPA. *Recommended:* 2 letters of recommendation, interview. *Application deadlines:* rolling (freshmen), rolling (transfers). *Notification:* continuous (freshmen), continuous (transfers).

Freshman Application Contact Ms. Sharon Chery, Admissions Office Manager, Limestone College, 1115 College Drive, Gaffney, SC 29340-3799. *Phone:* 864-488-4554. *Toll-free phone:* 800-795-7151 Ext. 554. *Fax:* 864-487-8706. *E-mail:* cphenicie@limestone.edu.

See page 2404 for the College Close-Up.

MEDICAL UNIVERSITY OF SOUTH CAROLINA

Charleston, South Carolina **www.musc.edu/**

Director of Admissions Mr. George W. Ohlandt, Director of Admissions, Medical University of South Carolina, PO Box 250203, Charleston, SC 29425. *Phone:* 843-792-3813.

MORRIS COLLEGE

Sumter, South Carolina **www.morris.edu/**

- **Independent** 4-year, founded 1908, affiliated with Baptist Educational and Missionary Convention of South Carolina
- **Small-town** 34-acre campus
- **Endowment** $8.5 million
- **Coed** 871 undergraduate students, 97% full-time, 57% women, 43% men
- **Noncompetitive** entrance level, 90% of applicants were admitted

Undergraduates 845 full-time, 26 part-time. Students come from 19 states and territories, 11% are from out of state, 100% African American, 5% transferred in, 75% live on campus. *Retention:* 60% of 2006 full-time freshmen returned.

Freshmen *Admission:* 1,457 applied, 1,311 admitted, 295 enrolled. *Average high school GPA:* 2.45.

Faculty *Total:* 65, 72% full-time, 55% with terminal degrees. *Student/faculty ratio:* 16:1.

Majors Biology/biological sciences; biology teacher education; business administration and management; business administration, management and operations related; community health services counseling; criminal justice/law enforcement administration; early childhood education; elementary education; English; English/language arts teacher education; history; liberal arts and sciences/liberal studies; mass communication/media; mathematics; mathematics teacher education; parks, recreation and leisure; political science and government; religious education; social studies teacher education; sociology; theology.

Academics *Calendar:* semesters. *Degree:* bachelor's. *Special study options:* academic remediation for entering students, accelerated degree program, adult/continuing education programs, advanced placement credit, cooperative education, double majors, honors programs, internships, summer session for credit. *ROTC:* Army (b). *Unusual degree programs:* 3-2 engineering with North Carolina Agricultural and Technical University.

Computers on Campus 285 computers/terminals are available on campus for general student use. Students can access the following: free student e-mail accounts. Campuswide network is available. 100% of college-owned or -operated housing units are wired for high-speed Internet access. Wireless service is available via learning centers, student centers.

Student Life *Housing options:* men-only, women-only. Campus housing is university owned. Freshman applicants given priority for college housing. *Activities and organizations:* drama/theater group, student-run newspaper, radio station, choral group, Student Government Association, New Emphasis on Nontraditional Students, Block "M" Club, Pre Alumni Council, Baptist Student Union, national fraternities, national sororities. *Campus security:* 24-hour patrols, controlled dormitory access. *Student services:* health clinic, personal/psychological counseling.

Athletics Member NAIA. *Intercollegiate sports:* baseball M (s), basketball M (s)/W (s), cross-country running M (s)/W (s), golf M (s), softball W (s), tennis M (s)/W (s), track and field M (s)/W (s), volleyball W (s). *Intramural sports:* basketball M/W, football M/W, golf M, softball M/W, table tennis M/W, tennis M/W, volleyball M/W.

Costs (2007–08) *Comprehensive fee:* $13,384 includes full-time tuition ($8990), mandatory fees ($260), and room and board ($4134). Part-time tuition: $375 per credit hour. *Required fees:* $55 per term part-time. *Payment plan:* installment.

Financial Aid Of all full-time matriculated undergraduates who enrolled in 2006, 887 applied for aid, 859 were judged to have need, 10 had their need fully met. 300 Federal Work-Study jobs (averaging $818). *Average percent of need met:* 85%. *Average financial aid package:* $12,100. *Average need-based loan:* $3900. *Average need-based gift aid:* $7400. *Average indebtedness upon graduation:* $17,125.

Applying *Options:* deferred entrance. *Application fee:* $20. *Required:* high school transcript, minimum 2.0 GPA, medical examination. *Required for some:* interview. *Application deadlines:* rolling (freshmen), rolling (transfers). *Notification:* continuous (freshmen), continuous (transfers).

Freshman Application Contact Ms. Deborah C. Calhoun, Director of Admissions and Records, Morris College, 100 West College Street, Sumter, SC 29150-3599. *Phone:* 803-934-3225. *Toll-free phone:* 866-853-1345. *Fax:* 803-773-8241. *E-mail:* dcalhoun@morris.edu.

NEWBERRY COLLEGE

Newberry, South Carolina **www.newberry.edu/**

- **Independent Evangelical Lutheran** 4-year, founded 1856
- **Small-town** 60-acre campus
- **Endowment** $16.5 million
- **Coed**
- **Moderately difficult** entrance level

Faculty *Student/faculty ratio:* 13:1.

Academics *Calendar:* semesters. *Degree:* bachelor's.

Student Life *Campus security:* 24-hour patrols.

Athletics Member NCAA. All Division II.

Standardized Tests *Required:* SAT or ACT (for admission).

Costs (2007–08) *Comprehensive fee:* $27,821 includes full-time tuition ($19,900), mandatory fees ($991), and room and board ($6930). Part-time tuition: $400 per hour. *Required fees:* $100 per term part-time. *College room only:* $3390.

Financial Aid Of all full-time matriculated undergraduates who enrolled in 2005, 658 applied for aid, 591 were judged to have need, 188 had their need fully met. 52 Federal Work-Study jobs (averaging $804). 45 state and other part-time jobs (averaging $518). In 2005, 104 non-need-based awards were made. *Average percent of need met:* 79. *Average financial aid package:* $13,886. *Average need-based loan:* $3866. *Average need-based gift aid:* $10,899. *Average non-need-based aid:* $11,851. *Average indebtedness upon graduation:* $13,477.

Applying *Options:* electronic application, early admission, deferred entrance. *Application fee:* $30. *Required:* high school transcript, minimum 2.0 GPA. *Required for some:* essay or personal statement. *Recommended:* 1 letter of recommendation, interview.

Freshman Application Contact Mr. Michael Robbins, Director of Admissions, Newberry College, 2100 College Street, Holland Hall, Newberry, SC 29108. *Phone:* 803-321-5129. *Toll-free phone:* 800-845-4955 Ext. 5127. *Fax:* 803-321-5138. *E-mail:* admissions@newberry.edu.

See page 2406 for the College Close-Up.

NORTH GREENVILLE UNIVERSITY

Tigerville, South Carolina **www.ngu.edu/**

- **Independent Southern Baptist** comprehensive, founded 1892
- **Rural** 500-acre campus with easy access to Greenville
- **Endowment** $16.0 million
- **Coed** 1,993 undergraduate students, 88% full-time, 51% women, 49% men
- **Minimally difficult** entrance level, 37% of applicants were admitted

Undergraduates 1,762 full-time, 231 part-time. Students come from 36 states and territories, 14 other countries, 27% are from out of state, 5% African American, 0.2% Asian American or Pacific Islander, 0.6% Hispanic American, 0.2% Native American, 0.8% international, 5% transferred in, 70% live on campus. *Retention:* 68% of 2006 full-time freshmen returned.

Freshmen *Admission:* 1,373 applied, 512 admitted, 512 enrolled. *Average high school GPA:* 3.79. *Test scores:* SAT critical reading scores over 500: 55%; SAT math scores over 500: 54%; ACT scores over 18: 80%; SAT critical reading scores over 600: 20%; SAT math scores over 600: 15%; ACT scores over 24: 27%; SAT critical reading scores over 700: 2%; SAT math scores over 700: 1%; ACT scores over 30: 3%.

Faculty *Total:* 145, 69% full-time, 50% with terminal degrees. *Student/faculty ratio:* 16:1.

Majors Accounting; biblical studies; biology/biological sciences; biology teacher education; business administration and management; dramatic/theater arts and stagecraft related; elementary education; English; English/language arts teacher education; fine/studio arts; history; humanities; interdisciplinary studies; international business/trade/commerce; journalism; kindergarten/preschool education; liberal arts and sciences/liberal studies; marketing/marketing management; mass communication/media; missionary studies and missiology; multi-/interdisciplinary studies related; music; music history, literature, and theory; music teacher education; pastoral studies/counseling; piano and organ; psychology; religious education; religious/sacred music; religious studies; sport and fitness administration/management; theology; voice and opera; youth ministry.

Academics *Calendar:* semesters. *Degrees:* associate, bachelor's, and master's. *Special study options:* academic remediation for entering students, accelerated degree program, advanced placement credit, double majors, English as a second language, external degree program, freshman honors college, honors programs, independent study, internships, part-time degree program, services for LD students, student-designed majors, summer session for credit. *ROTC:* Army (c).

Computers on Campus 78 computers/terminals and 10 ports are available on campus for general student use. Students can access the following: campus intranet, computer help desk, free student e-mail accounts, online (class) grades, online (class) schedules. Campuswide network is available. 100% of college-owned or -operated housing units are wired for high-speed Internet access. Wireless service is available via classrooms, student centers.

Student Life *Housing:* on-campus residence required through sophomore year. *Options:* men-only, women-only. Campus housing is university owned. Freshman campus housing is guaranteed. *Activities and organizations:* drama/theater group, student-run newspaper, radio station, choral group, Baptist Student Union, Fellowship of Christians in Service, Fellowship of Christian Athletes, Black Student Fellowship, Education Club. *Campus security:* 24-hour emergency response devices and patrols, controlled dormitory access. *Student services:* health clinic, personal/psychological counseling.

Athletics Member NCAA, NCCAA. All NCAA Division II. *Intercollegiate sports:* baseball M (s), basketball M (s)/W (s), cheerleading M (s)/W (s), cross-country running M (s)/W (s), football M (s), golf M (s), soccer M (s)/W (s), softball W (s), tennis M (s)/W (s), volleyball W (s). *Intramural sports:* basketball M/W, bowling M/W, football M, golf M/W, skiing (downhill) M/W, softball M/W, table tennis M/W, tennis M/W, volleyball W, weight lifting M/W.

Standardized Tests *Required:* SAT or ACT (for admission). *Required for some:* CPT. *Recommended:* CPT.

Costs (2008–09) *Comprehensive fee:* $18,400 includes full-time tuition ($11,680) and room and board ($6720). Part-time tuition: $200 per credit hour. *College room only:* $3040.

Financial Aid Of all full-time matriculated undergraduates who enrolled in 2006, 164 Federal Work-Study jobs (averaging $1000). 138 state and other part-time jobs (averaging $1000).

Applying *Options:* electronic application, early admission, deferred entrance. *Application fee:* $25. *Required:* high school transcript. *Required for some:* interview. *Recommended:* minimum 2.0 GPA. *Application deadlines:* 8/18 (freshmen), 8/21 (transfers). *Notification:* continuous (freshmen), continuous until 8/21 (transfers).

Director of Admissions Ms. Keli Sewell, Vice President of Admissions and Financial Aid, North Greenville University, PO Box 1872, Tigerville, SC 29688. *Phone:* 864-977-7052. *Toll-free phone:* 800-468-6642 Ext. 7001. *E-mail:* ksewell@ngu.edu.

PRESBYTERIAN COLLEGE

Clinton, South Carolina **www.presby.edu/**

- **Independent** 4-year, founded 1880, affiliated with Presbyterian Church (U.S.A.)
- **Small-town** 215-acre campus with easy access to Greenville—Spartanburg
- **Endowment** $99.5 million
- **Coed** 1,181 undergraduate students, 95% full-time, 51% women, 49% men
- **Very difficult** entrance level, 71% of applicants were admitted

Undergraduates 1,126 full-time, 55 part-time. Students come from 26 states and territories, 10 other countries, 35% are from out of state, 7% African American, 0.9% Asian American or Pacific Islander, 1% Hispanic American, 0.3% Native American, 2% transferred in, 94% live on campus. *Retention:* 83% of 2006 full-time freshmen returned.

Freshmen *Admission:* 1,138 applied, 807 admitted, 290 enrolled. *Average high school GPA:* 3.39. *Test scores:* SAT critical reading scores over 500: 78%; SAT math scores over 500: 86%; ACT scores over 18: 98%; SAT critical reading scores over 600: 31%; SAT math scores over 600: 41%; ACT scores over 24: 63%; SAT critical reading scores over 700: 5%; SAT math scores over 700: 4%; ACT scores over 30: 7%.

Faculty *Total:* 121, 70% full-time, 76% with terminal degrees. *Student/faculty ratio:* 12:1.

Majors Accounting and business/management; art; art history, criticism and conservation; biology/biological sciences; business administration and management; business/managerial economics; chemistry; computer science; dramatic/theater arts; early childhood education; economics; education; English; fine arts related; fine/studio arts; foreign languages and literatures; French; German; history; mathematics; middle school education; modern languages; music; music performance; music teacher education; philosophy; physics; physics related; political science and government; psychology; religious/sacred music; religious studies; sociology; Spanish; special education.

Academics *Calendar:* semesters. *Degree:* bachelor's. *Special study options:* accelerated degree program, advanced placement credit, double majors, honors programs, independent study, internships, off-campus study, services for LD students, study abroad, summer session for credit. *ROTC:* Army (b). *Unusual degree programs:* 3-2 engineering with Auburn University, Clemson University, Mercer University, Vanderbilt University; forestry with Duke University.

Computers on Campus 130 computers/terminals and 275 ports are available on campus for general student use. Students can access the following: free student e-mail accounts, online (class) grades, online (class) registration, online (class) schedules. Campuswide network is available. 100% of college-owned or -operated housing units are wired for high-speed Internet access. Wireless service is available via classrooms, computer centers, computer labs, dorm rooms, libraries.

Student Life *Housing:* on-campus residence required through senior year. *Options:* coed, men-only, women-only, disabled students. Campus housing is university owned. Freshman campus housing is guaranteed. *Activities and organizations:* drama/theater group, student-run newspaper, radio station, choral group, Student Volunteer Services, Intramurals, Student Union Board, Fellowship of Christian Athletes, Student Government Association, national fraternities, national sororities. *Campus security:* 24-hour emergency response devices and patrols, late-night transport/escort service, controlled dormitory access. *Student services:* health clinic, personal/psychological counseling.

Athletics Member NCAA. All Division I. *Intercollegiate sports:* baseball M (s), basketball M (s)/W (s), cheerleading M/W, cross-country running M (s)/W (s), football M (s), golf M (s)/W (s), lacrosse M (s)/W (s), soccer M (s)/W (s), softball W (s), tennis M (s)/W (s), volleyball W (s). *Intramural sports:* basketball M/W, football M/W, golf M/W, rock climbing M/W, skiing (cross-country) M/W, soccer M/W, softball M/W, swimming and diving M/W, table tennis M/W, tennis M/W, ultimate Frisbee M/W, volleyball M/W.

Standardized Tests *Required:* SAT or ACT (for admission).

Costs (2008–09) *Comprehensive fee:* $35,966 includes full-time tuition ($25,472), mandatory fees ($2430), and room and board ($8064). Part-time tuition: $1060 per credit hour. *Required fees:* $16 per credit hour part-time, $21 per term part-time.

Financial Aid Of all full-time matriculated undergraduates who enrolled in 2006, 823 applied for aid, 707 were judged to have need, 227 had their need fully met. 206 Federal Work-Study jobs (averaging $910). 200 state and other part-time jobs (averaging $750). In 2006, 408 non-need-based awards were made. *Average percent of need met:* 83%. *Average financial aid package:* $19,217. *Average need-based loan:* $3800. *Average need-based gift aid:* $16,206. *Average non-need-based aid:* $10,178. *Average indebtedness upon graduation:* $14,018.

Applying *Options:* electronic application, early admission, early decision, early action, deferred entrance. *Application fee:* $40. *Required:* essay or personal statement, high school transcript, 1 letter of recommendation. *Recommended:* interview. *Application deadlines:* 6/1 (freshmen), 7/1 (transfers), 11/15 (early action). *Early decision deadline:* 11/1. *Notification:* continuous until 7/15 (freshmen), 12/1 (early decision), 12/15 (early action).

Freshman Application Contact Mrs. Leni Patterson, Dean of Admissions and Financial Aid, Presbyterian College, South Broad Street, Clinton, SC 29325. *Phone:* 864-833-8229. *Toll-free phone:* 800-476-7272. *Fax:* 864-833-8481. *E-mail:* lpatters@presby.edu.

See page 2408 for the College Close-Up.

SOUTH CAROLINA STATE UNIVERSITY

Orangeburg, South Carolina **www.scsu.edu/**

- **State-supported** comprehensive, founded 1896, part of South Carolina Commission on Higher Education
- **Small-town** 160-acre campus
- **Endowment** $796,988
- **Coed** 4,323 undergraduate students, 93% full-time, 55% women, 45% men
- **Minimally difficult** entrance level, 88% of applicants were admitted

Undergraduates 4,033 full-time, 290 part-time. Students come from 36 states and territories, 18% are from out of state, 97% African American, 0.3% Asian American or Pacific Islander, 0.3% Hispanic American, 5% transferred in, 60% live on campus. *Retention:* 65% of 2006 full-time freshmen returned.

Freshmen *Admission:* 3,866 applied, 3,403 admitted, 1,318 enrolled. *Average high school GPA:* 2.85. *Test scores:* SAT critical reading scores over 500: 10%; SAT math scores over 500: 12%; ACT scores over 18: 28%; SAT critical reading scores over 600: 2%; SAT math scores over 600: 3%; ACT scores over 24: 3%; SAT critical reading scores over 700: 1%; SAT math scores over 700: 1%.

Faculty *Total:* 293, 78% full-time, 76% with terminal degrees. *Student/faculty ratio:* 18:1.

Majors Accounting; agricultural business and management; art teacher education; audiology and speech-language pathology; biology/biological sciences; business administration and management; business/managerial economics; business teacher education; chemistry; civil engineering technology; computer science; criminal justice/law enforcement administration; dramatic/theater arts; early childhood education; electrical, electronic and communications engineering technology; elementary education; English; family and consumer sciences/home economics teacher education; family and consumer sciences/human sciences; fine/studio arts; foods, nutrition, and wellness; foreign languages and literatures; health teacher education; history; industrial technology; marketing/marketing management; mathematics; mechanical engineering/mechanical technology; middle school education; music management and merchandising; music teacher education; nuclear engineering; nursing (registered nurse training); physical education teaching and coaching; physics; political science and government; psychology; social sciences; social work; sociology; Spanish; special education; trade and industrial teacher education.

Academics *Calendar:* semesters. *Degrees:* bachelor's, master's, doctoral, post-master's, and postbachelor's certificates. *Special study options:* academic remediation for entering students, adult/continuing education programs, advanced placement credit, cooperative education, distance learning, honors programs, independent study, internships, off-campus study, part-time degree program, study abroad, summer session for credit. *ROTC:* Army (b), Air Force (c).

Computers on Campus 300 computers/terminals are available on campus for general student use. Campuswide network is available.

Student Life *Housing:* on-campus residence required for freshman year. *Options:* coed, men-only, women-only, disabled students. Campus housing is university owned, leased by the school and is provided by a third party. Freshman applicants given priority for college housing. *Activities and organizations:* drama/theater group, student-run newspaper, choral group, marching band, Student government, Student Union Board, NAACP, national fraternities, national sororities. *Campus security:* 24-hour emergency response devices and patrols, late-night transport/escort service, controlled dormitory access. *Student services:* health clinic, personal/psychological counseling.

Athletics Member NCAA. All Division I except football (Division I-AA). *Intercollegiate sports:* basketball M (s)/W (s), cross-country running M (s)/W (s), golf M (s), softball W (s), tennis M (s)/W (s), track and field M (s)/W (s), volleyball W (s).

Standardized Tests *Required:* SAT or ACT (for admission). *Recommended:* SAT Subject Tests (for admission).

Costs (2007–08) *Tuition:* state resident $7318 full-time, $305 per credit hour part-time; nonresident $14,362 full-time, $598 per credit hour part-time. *Room and board:* $8040; room only: $5460. Room and board charges vary according to housing facility. *Payment plans:* installment, deferred payment. *Waivers:* senior citizens and employees or children of employees.

Financial Aid Of all full-time matriculated undergraduates who enrolled in 2004, 343 Federal Work-Study jobs (averaging $1048). 360 state and other part-time jobs (averaging $2050). *Average indebtedness upon graduation:* $23,580.

Applying *Options:* electronic application, deferred entrance. *Application fee:* $25. *Required:* high school transcript, minimum 2.0 GPA. *Application deadlines:* 7/31 (freshmen), 7/31 (transfers). *Notification:* continuous (freshmen), continuous (transfers).

Freshman Application Contact Mr. Antonio Boyle, Assistant Vice President of Enrollment Management, South Carolina State University, 300 College Street Northeast, Orangeburg, SC 29117-0001. *Phone:* 803-536-7186. *Toll-free phone:* 800-260-5956. *Fax.* 803-536-8990. *E-mail:* admissions@scsu.edu.

SOUTHERN METHODIST COLLEGE

Orangeburg, South Carolina **www.smcollege.edu/**

Freshman Application Contact Ms. Juanta Webb, Recruitment Officer, Southern Methodist College, PO Box 1027, 541 Broughton Street, Orangeburg, SC 29116-1027. *Phone:* 803-268-1322. *Toll-free phone:* 800-360-1503. *Fax:* 803-534-7827. *E-mail:* jwebb@smcollege.edu.

SOUTHERN WESLEYAN UNIVERSITY

Central, South Carolina **www.swu.edu/**

- **Independent** comprehensive, founded 1906, affiliated with Wesleyan Church
- **Small-town** 230-acre campus
- **Endowment** $2.9 million
- **Coed** 1,745 undergraduate students, 98% full-time, 63% women, 37% men
- **Minimally difficult** entrance level, 95% of applicants were admitted

Undergraduates 1,714 full-time, 31 part-time. Students come from 28 states and territories, 13 other countries, 17% are from out of state, 30% African American, 0.5% Asian American or Pacific Islander, 2% Hispanic American, 0.3% Native American, 1% international, 5% transferred in, 61% live on campus. *Retention:* 76% of 2006 full-time freshmen returned.

Freshmen *Admission:* 317 applied, 301 admitted, 158 enrolled. *Average high school GPA:* 3.4. *Test scores:* SAT critical reading scores over 500: 39%; SAT math scores over 500: 51%; SAT writing scores over 500: 37%; ACT scores over 18: 79%; SAT critical reading scores over 600: 14%; SAT math scores over 600: 14%; SAT writing scores over 600: 11%; ACT scores over 24: 14%; SAT critical reading scores over 700: 2%; SAT math scores over 700: 1%; SAT writing scores over 700: 2%.

Faculty *Total:* 246, 20% full-time, 42% with terminal degrees. *Student/faculty ratio:* 24:1.

Majors Accounting; biology/biological sciences; chemistry; clinical laboratory science/medical technology; computer and information sciences; divinity/ministry; education; elementary education; English; health and physical education; history; human resources management; kindergarten/preschool education; mathematics; mathematics teacher education; music; music teacher education; parks, recreation and leisure; parks, recreation, and leisure related; physical education teaching and coaching; pre-medical studies; psychology; religious/sacred music; religious studies; science teacher education; social sciences; special education; special education (emotionally disturbed); special education (mentally retarded); special education (specific learning disabilities); sport and fitness administration/management; theology.

Academics *Calendar:* semesters. *Degrees:* associate, bachelor's, and master's. *Special study options:* academic remediation for entering students, accelerated degree program, adult/continuing education programs, advanced placement credit, distance learning, double majors, English as a second language, freshman honors college, honors programs, independent study, internships, off-campus study, services for LD students, student-designed majors, study abroad, summer session for credit. *ROTC:* Army (c), Air Force (c).

Computers on Campus 85 computers/terminals are available on campus for general student use. Students can access the following: campus intranet, computer help desk, free student e-mail accounts, online (class) grades, online (class) registration, online (class) schedules. Campuswide network is available. 100% of college-owned or -operated housing units are wired for high-speed Internet access. Wireless service is available via entire campus.

Student Life *Housing:* on-campus residence required through senior year. *Options:* coed, women-only, disabled students. Campus housing is university owned. Freshman campus housing is guaranteed. *Activities and organizations:* drama/theater group, choral group, Student Government Association, Student Missions Fellowship, Ministry Teams, Music Club, Council for Exceptional Children. *Campus security:* 24-hour emergency response devices, late night security patrols until 2:00 a.m., restricted access to campus after midnight. *Student services:* health clinic, personal/psychological counseling.

Athletics Member NAIA, NCCAA. *Intercollegiate sports:* baseball M (s), basketball M (s)/W (s), cross-country running M (s)/W (s), golf M (s), soccer M (s)/W (s), softball W (s), volleyball W (s). *Intramural sports:* basketball M/W, football M/W, softball M/W, table tennis M/W, tennis M/W, ultimate Frisbee M/W, volleyball M/W.

Standardized Tests *Required:* SAT or ACT (for admission).

Costs (2007–08) *Comprehensive fee:* $23,400 includes full-time tuition ($16,700), mandatory fees ($500), and room and board ($6200). Full-time tuition and fees vary according to course load and degree level. Part-time tuition and fees vary according to course load, degree level, and location. *College room only:* $2250. Room and board charges vary according to board plan and housing facility. *Payment plan:* installment. *Waivers:* senior citizens and employees or children of employees.

Financial Aid Of all full-time matriculated undergraduates who enrolled in 2006, 437 applied for aid, 387 were judged to have need, 128 had their need fully met. 158 Federal Work-Study jobs (averaging $1150). 73 state and other part-time jobs (averaging $1150). In 2006, 90 non-need-based awards were made. *Average percent of need met:* 78%. *Average financial aid package:* $14,094. *Average need-based loan:* $4844. *Average need-based gift aid:* $9962. *Average non-need-based aid:* $9196. *Average indebtedness upon graduation:* $25,971.

Applying *Options:* electronic application, early admission, deferred entrance. *Application fee:* $25. *Required:* high school transcript, minimum 2.3 GPA. *Required for some:* interview, lifestyle statement. *Application deadlines:* 8/1 (freshmen), 8/1 (transfers). *Notification:* continuous (freshmen), continuous (transfers).

Freshman Application Contact Mrs. Beth Roe, Director of First Year Experience, Southern Wesleyan University, PO Box 1020, 907 Wesleyan Drive, Central, SC 29630-1020. *Phone:* 864-644-5149. *Toll-free phone:* 800-289-1292 Ext. 5550. *Fax:* 864-644-5901. *E-mail:* broe@swu.edu.

SOUTH UNIVERSITY

Columbia, South Carolina **www.southuniversity.edu/**

- **Proprietary** comprehensive, founded 1935, part of South University-Savannah
- **Urban** 2-acre campus
- **Coed**

Majors Business administration and management; criminal justice/law enforcement administration; graphic design; health/health care administration; information technology; legal studies; nursing.

Academics *Calendar:* quarters. *Degrees:* certificates, associate, bachelor's, and master's.

Freshman Application Contact South University, 9 Science Court, Columbia, SC 29203. *Phone:* 803-935-4299. *Toll-free phone:* 866-688-0932. *Fax:* 803-935-4382.

See page 2410 for the College Close-Up.

UNIVERSITY OF SOUTH CAROLINA

Columbia, South Carolina **www.sc.edu/**

- **State-supported** university, founded 1801, part of University of South Carolina System
- **Urban** 315-acre campus
- **Coed** 18,827 undergraduate students, 92% full-time, 55% women, 45% men
- **Moderately difficult** entrance level, 59% of applicants were admitted

Undergraduates 17,247 full-time, 1,580 part-time. Students come from 56 states and territories, 71 other countries, 24% are from out of state, 12% African American, 3% Asian American or Pacific Islander, 2% Hispanic American, 0.4% Native American, 0.9% international, 7% transferred in, 40% live on campus. *Retention:* 87% of 2006 full-time freshmen returned.

Freshmen *Admission:* 14,994 applied, 8,908 admitted, 3,719 enrolled. *Average high school GPA:* 3.87. *Test scores:* SAT critical reading scores over 500: 89%; SAT math scores over 500: 94%; ACT scores over 18: 99%; SAT critical reading scores over 600: 41%; SAT math scores over 600: 53%; ACT scores over 24: 73%; SAT critical reading scores over 700: 8%; SAT math scores over 700: 8%; ACT scores over 30: 14%.

Faculty *Total:* 1,765, 71% full-time, 61% with terminal degrees. *Student/faculty ratio:* 16:1.

Majors Accounting; advertising; African-American/Black studies; anthropology; aquatic biology/limnology; art history, criticism and conservation; art teacher education; biology/biological sciences; broadcast journalism; business administration and management; business/managerial economics; chemical engineering; chemistry; civil engineering; classics and languages, literatures and linguistics; computer and information sciences; computer engineering; criminal justice/law enforcement administration; dramatic/theater arts; economics; electrical, electronics and communications engineering; English; European studies; experimental psychology; finance; fine/studio arts; French; general retailing/wholesaling; geography; geology/earth science; geophysics and seismology; German; history; hospitality administration; insurance; international relations and affairs; Italian; journalism; kinesiology and exercise science; Latin American studies; liberal arts and sciences/liberal studies; management science; marine biology; marine biology and biological oceanography; marine science/merchant marine officer; marketing/marketing management; mathematics; mechanical engineering; music; music teacher education; nursing (registered nurse training); oceanography; office management; philosophy; physical education teaching and coaching; physics; political science and government; public relations/image management; real estate; religious studies; sociology; Spanish; sport and fitness administration/management; statistics; women's studies.

Academics *Calendar:* semesters. *Degrees:* bachelor's, master's, doctoral, first professional, post-master's, and postbachelor's certificates. *Special study options:* accelerated degree program, adult/continuing education programs, advanced placement credit, cooperative education, distance learning, double majors, English as a second language, external degree program, freshman honors college, honors programs, independent study, internships, part-time degree program, services for LD students, student-designed majors, study abroad, summer session for credit. *ROTC:* Army (b), Navy (b), Air Force (b).

Computers on Campus 2,800 computers/terminals are available on campus for general student use. Students can access the following: computer help desk, free student e-mail accounts, online (class) grades, online (class) registration, online (class) schedules. Campuswide network is available. 100% of college-owned or -operated housing units are wired for high-speed Internet access. Wireless service is available via entire campus.

Student Life *Housing:* on-campus residence required for freshman year. *Options:* coed, women-only, disabled students. Campus housing is university owned. Freshman campus housing is guaranteed. *Activities and organizations:* drama/theater group, student-run newspaper, radio station, choral group, marching band, Fellowship of Christian Athletes, Association of African-American Students, Baptist Collegiate Ministry, Garnet Circle/Student Alumni, Fraternity and Sorority Council, national fraternities, national sororities. *Campus security:* 24-hour emergency response devices and patrols, student patrols, late-night transport/escort service, controlled dormitory access. *Student services:* health clinic, personal/psychological counseling, women's center.

Athletics Member NCAA. All Division I except football (Division I-A). *Intercollegiate sports:* baseball M (s), basketball M (s)/W (s), cross-country running W (s), equestrian sports W (s), golf M (s)/W (s), soccer M (s)/W (s), softball W (s), swimming and diving M (s)/W (s), tennis M (s)/W (s), track and field M (s)/W (s), volleyball W (s). *Intramural sports:* badminton M/W, basketball M/W, bowling M/W, equestrian sports M (c)/W (c), football M/W, golf M/W, racquetball M/W, rock climbing M (c)/W (c), soccer M/W, softball M/W, swimming and diving M/W, table tennis M/W, tennis M/W, ultimate Frisbee M (c)/W (c), volleyball M/W, weight lifting M (c)/W (c), wrestling M (c).

Standardized Tests *Required:* SAT or ACT (for admission).

Costs (2008–09) *Tuition:* state resident $7946 full-time, $372 per credit hour part-time; nonresident $21,232 full-time, $970 per credit hour part-time. *Required fees:* $400 full-time. *Room and board:* $6946; room only: $4376.

Financial Aid Of all full-time matriculated undergraduates who enrolled in 2006, 10,240 applied for aid, 7,632 were judged to have need, 2,095 had their need fully met. 643 Federal Work-Study jobs (averaging $2535). In 2006, 5410 non-need-based awards were made. *Average percent of need met:* 73%. *Average financial aid package:* $9840. *Average need-based loan:* $3552. *Average need-based gift aid:* $3445. *Average non-need-based aid:* $5940. *Average indebtedness upon graduation:* $19,360.

Applying *Options:* electronic application, early action. *Application fee:* $50. *Required:* high school transcript, minimum 2.0 GPA. *Application deadlines:* 12/1 (freshmen), 6/1 (transfers). *Notification:* continuous (transfers).

Freshman Application Contact Mr. Scott Verzyl, Director of Undergraduate Admissions, University of South Carolina, Columbia, SC 29208. *Phone:* 803-777-7700. *Toll-free phone:* 800-868-5872. *Fax:* 803-777-0101. *E-mail:* admissions-ugrad@sc.edu.

See page 2412 for the College Close-Up.

UNIVERSITY OF SOUTH CAROLINA AIKEN

Aiken, South Carolina **www.usca.edu/**

- **State-supported** comprehensive, founded 1961, part of University of South Carolina System
- **Suburban** 453-acre campus with easy access to Columbia
- **Endowment** $16.1 million
- **Coed** 3,153 undergraduate students, 74% full-time, 66% women, 34% men
- **Moderately difficult** entrance level, 51% of applicants were admitted

Undergraduates 2,333 full-time, 820 part-time. Students come from 31 states and territories, 23 other countries, 10% are from out of state, 27% African American, 1% Asian American or Pacific Islander, 2% Hispanic American, 0.2% Native American, 2% international, 8% transferred in, 22% live on campus. *Retention:* 67% of 2006 full-time freshmen returned.

Freshmen *Admission:* 1,849 applied, 944 admitted, 628 enrolled. *Average high school GPA:* 2.91. *Test scores:* SAT critical reading scores over 500: 43%; SAT math scores over 500: 51%; SAT writing scores over 500: 36%; ACT scores over 18: 78%; SAT critical reading scores over 600: 11%; SAT math scores over 600: 14%; SAT writing scores over 600: 6%; ACT scores over 24: 17%; SAT critical reading scores over 700: 1%; SAT math scores over 700: 1%.

Faculty *Total:* 259, 57% full-time, 51% with terminal degrees. *Student/faculty ratio:* 14:1.

Majors Applied mathematics; biology/biological sciences; business administration and management; chemistry; communication/speech communication and rhetoric; computer science; early childhood education; elementary education; English; fine/studio arts; history; kindergarten/preschool education; kinesiology and exercise science; liberal arts and sciences/liberal studies; music teacher education; nursing (registered nurse training); political science and government; psychology; secondary education; sociology; special education.

Academics *Calendar:* semesters. *Degrees:* bachelor's and master's. *Special study options:* accelerated degree program, adult/continuing education programs, advanced placement credit, cooperative education, distance learning, double majors, honors programs, independent study, internships, off-campus study, part-time degree program, services for LD students, study abroad, summer session for credit.

Computers on Campus 450 computers/terminals are available on campus for general student use. Students can access the following: online (class) registration, student e-mail. Campuswide network is available.

Student Life *Housing options:* coed, disabled students. Campus housing is university owned. *Activities and organizations:* drama/theater group, student-run newspaper, choral group, student government, Pacesetters, Student Alumni Ambassadors, African-American Student Alliance, Pacer Union Board, national fraternities, national sororities. *Campus security:* 24-hour emergency response devices and patrols, late-night transport/escort service, controlled dormitory access. *Student services:* health clinic, personal/psychological counseling.

Athletics Member NCAA. All Division II. *Intercollegiate sports:* baseball M (s), basketball M (s)/W (s), cheerleading M (s)/W (s), cross-country running W (s), golf M (s), soccer M (s)/W (s), softball W (s), tennis M (s)/W (s), volleyball W (s). *Intramural sports:* basketball M/W, football M/W, softball M/W, table tennis M/W, tennis M/W, weight lifting M.

Standardized Tests *Required:* SAT or ACT (for admission), minimum SAT of 800 or ACT of 17 (for admission).

Costs (2007–08) *Tuition:* state resident $6806 full-time, $590 per credit hour part-time; nonresident $13,722 full-time, $1180 per credit hour part-time. Full-time tuition and fees vary according to reciprocity agreements. Part-time tuition and fees vary according to course load and reciprocity agreements. *Required fees:* $230 full-time. *Room and board:* $5870; room only: $4050. Room and board charges vary according to board plan and housing facility. *Payment plan:* deferred payment. *Waivers:* senior citizens and employees or children of employees.

Applying *Options:* electronic application, early admission, deferred entrance. *Application fee:* $45. *Required:* high school transcript. *Application deadlines:* 8/1 (freshmen), 8/1 (out-of-state freshmen), 8/1 (transfers). *Notification:* continuous (freshmen), continuous (out-of-state freshmen), continuous (transfers).

Freshman Application Contact Mr. Andrew Hendrix, Director of Admissions, University of South Carolina Aiken, 471 University Parkway, Aiken, SC 29801-6309. *Phone:* 803-648-6851 Ext. 3366. *Toll-free phone:* 888-WOW-USCA. *Fax:* 803-641-3727. *E-mail:* admit@usca.edu.

UNIVERSITY OF SOUTH CAROLINA BEAUFORT

Beaufort, South Carolina **www.sc.edu/beaufort/**

- **State-supported** 4-year, founded 1959, part of University of South Carolina System
- **Small-town** 5-acre campus
- **Endowment** $873,784
- **Coed** 1,461 undergraduate students, 62% full-time, 61% women, 39% men
- **Minimally difficult** entrance level, 61% of applicants were admitted

Undergraduates 902 full-time, 559 part-time. Students come from 44 states and territories, 20 other countries, 14% are from out of state, 17% African American, 1% Asian American or Pacific Islander, 3% Hispanic American, 0.8% Native American, 1% international, 12% transferred in, 18% live on campus. *Retention:* 55% of 2006 full-time freshmen returned.

Freshmen *Admission:* 765 applied, 469 admitted, 288 enrolled.

Faculty *Total:* 10[illegible], 45% full-time, 57% with terminal degrees. *Student/faculty ratio:* 15:1.

Majors Biology/biological sciences; business administration and management; education; English; foreign languages and literatures; history; hospitality administration; liberal arts and sciences/liberal studies; psychology; social sciences.

Academics *Calendar:* semesters. *Degrees:* certificates, associate, and bachelor's. *Special study options:* adult/continuing education programs, advanced placement credit, distance learning, double majors, independent study, internships, off-campus study, part-time degree program, services for LD students, study abroad, summer session for credit.

Computers on Campus 85 computers/terminals are available on campus for general student use. Students can access the following: online (class) grades, online (class) registration, online (class) schedules. Campuswide network is available.

Student Life *Housing:* on-campus residence required for freshman year. *Activities and organizations:* drama/theater group, student-run newspaper, Student Government Association, Gamma Beta Phi, Black Student Organization, Business Club, Environmental Awareness Club. *Campus security:* 24-hour emergency response devices, evening security service. *Student services:* personal/psychological counseling.

Athletics Member NAIA.

Standardized Tests *Required:* SAT or ACT (for admission).

Costs (2007–08) *Tuition:* state resident $5924 full-time, $247 per credit hour part-time; nonresident $13,606 full-time, $567 per credit hour part-time. Full-time tuition and fees vary according to reciprocity agreements. Part-time tuition and fees vary according to reciprocity agreements. *Required fees:* $416 full-time, $14 per credit hour part-time, $40 per semester part-time. *Room only:* $5176. *Waivers:* senior citizens and employees or children of employees.

Financial Aid Of all full-time matriculated undergraduates who enrolled in 2003, 30 Federal Work-Study jobs (averaging $3000).

Applying *Options:* electronic application, deferred entrance. *Application fee:* $40. *Required:* high school transcript. *Recommended:* minimum 2.0 GPA. *Application deadlines:* rolling (freshmen), rolling (transfers). *Notification:* continuous (freshmen).

Freshman Application Contact Ms. Monica Williams, University of South Carolina Beaufort, 801 Carteret Street, Beaufort, SC 29902. *Phone:* 843-208-8112. *Fax:* 843-208-8015. *E-mail:* mrwilli5@gwm.sc.edu.

UNIVERSITY OF SOUTH CAROLINA UPSTATE

Spartanburg, South Carolina **www.uscupstate.edu/**

- **State-supported** comprehensive, founded 1967, part of University of South Carolina System
- **Urban** 300-acre campus with easy access to Charlotte
- **Endowment** $2.7 million
- **Coed** 4,871 undergraduate students, 82% full-time, 65% women, 35% men
- **Moderately difficult** entrance level, 54% of applicants were admitted

Undergraduates 4,010 full-time, 861 part-time. Students come from 34 states and territories, 32 other countries, 4% are from out of state, 25% African American, 2% Asian American or Pacific Islander, 2% Hispanic American, 0.4% Native American, 2% international, 13% transferred in, 15% live on campus. *Retention:* 62% of 2006 full-time freshmen returned.

Freshmen *Admission:* 2,761 applied, 1,492 admitted, 824 enrolled. *Average high school GPA:* 3.5. *Test scores:* SAT critical reading scores over 500: 41%; SAT math scores over 500: 47%; SAT writing scores over 500: 39%; ACT scores over 18: 90%; SAT critical reading scores over 600: 8%; SAT math scores over 600: 9%; SAT writing scores over 600: 7%; ACT scores over 24: 17%; SAT critical reading scores over 700: 1%; SAT math scores over 700: 1%; SAT writing scores over 700: 1%; ACT scores over 30: 1%.

Faculty *Total:* 388, 61% full-time, 47% with terminal degrees. *Student/faculty ratio:* 17:1.

Majors Art teacher education; biology/biological sciences; business administration and management; chemistry; communication/speech communication and rhetoric; computer and information sciences; criminal justice/law enforcement administration; early childhood education; elementary education; engineering technology; English; fine/studio arts; history; information science/studies; interdisciplinary studies; kindergarten/preschool education; mathematics; middle school education; nursing (registered nurse training); physical education teaching and coaching; political science and government; psychology; secondary education; sociology; Spanish; special education (specific learning disabilities).

Academics *Calendar:* semesters. *Degrees:* bachelor's, master's, and post-bachelor's certificates. *Special study options:* academic remediation for entering students, accelerated degree program, adult/continuing education programs, advanced placement credit, cooperative education, distance learning, double majors, English as a second language, honors programs, independent study, internships, off-campus study, part-time degree program, services for LD students, student-designed majors, study abroad, summer session for credit. *ROTC:* Army (c).

Computers on Campus 400 computers/terminals are available on campus for general student use. Students can access the following: computer help desk, free student e-mail accounts, online (class) grades, online (class) registration. Campuswide network is available. Wireless service is available via classrooms, computer centers, computer labs, dorm rooms, libraries, student centers.

Student Life *Housing options:* coed, disabled students. Campus housing is university owned. Freshman applicants given priority for college housing. *Activities and organizations:* drama/theater group, student-run newspaper, choral group, African-American Association, Campus Activity Board, Student Nurses Association, Student Government Association, Association for the Education of Young Children, national fraternities, national sororities. *Campus security:* 24-hour emergency response devices and patrols, late-night transport/escort service, campus security cameras. *Student services:* health clinic, personal/psychological counseling, women's center.

Athletics Member NCAA. All Division I. *Intercollegiate sports:* baseball M (s), basketball M (s)/W (s), cross-country running M (s)/W (s), golf M (s)/W (s), soccer M (s)/W (s), softball W (s), tennis M (s)/W (s), track and field M (s)/W (s), volleyball W (s). *Intramural sports:* basketball M/W, football M/W, golf M/W, soccer M/W, softball M/W, table tennis M/W, tennis M/W, track and field M/W, volleyball M/W.

Standardized Tests *Required:* SAT or ACT (for admission).

Costs (2007–08) *Tuition:* state resident $7480 full-time, $293 per semester hour part-time; nonresident $15,476 full-time, $603 per semester hour part-time. Full-time tuition and fees vary according to course load. Part-time tuition and fees vary according to course load. *Required fees:* $420 full-time. *Room and board:* $6000; room only: $3400. Room and board charges vary according to board plan and housing facility. *Payment plan:* deferred payment. *Waivers:* senior citizens.

Financial Aid Of all full-time matriculated undergraduates who enrolled in 2007, 3,142 applied for aid, 2,621 were judged to have need, 412 had their need fully met. 131 Federal Work-Study jobs (averaging $1392). 317 state and other part-time jobs (averaging $1049). In 2007, 85 non-need-based awards were made. *Average percent of need met:* 49%. *Average financial aid package:* $8188. *Average need-based loan:* $3987. *Average need-based gift aid:* $3839. *Average non-need-based aid:* $2067. *Average indebtedness upon graduation:* $19,299.

Applying *Options:* electronic application, deferred entrance. *Application fee:* $40. *Required:* high school transcript, minimum 2.0 GPA, college prep courses. *Notification:* continuous (freshmen), continuous (transfers).

Freshman Application Contact Ms. Donette Stewart, Assistant Vice Chancellor for Enrollment Services, University of South Carolina Upstate, 800 University Way, Spartanburg, SC 29303. *Phone:* 864-503-5280. *Toll-free phone:* 800-277-8727. *Fax:* 864-503-5727. *E-mail:* dstewart@uscupstate.edu.

VOORHEES COLLEGE

Denmark, South Carolina **www.voorhees.edu/**

- **Independent Episcopal** 4-year, founded 1897
- **Rural** 350-acre campus
- **Endowment** $5.0 million
- **Coed** 587 undergraduate students, 95% full-time, 60% women, 40% men
- **Moderately difficult** entrance level, 89% of applicants were admitted

Undergraduates 556 full-time, 31 part-time. Students come from 9 states and territories, 8 other countries, 2% are from out of state, 99% African American, 0.7% international, 6% transferred in, 85% live on campus. *Retention:* 55% of 2006 full-time freshmen returned.

Freshmen *Admission:* 517 applied, 461 admitted, 111 enrolled. *Average high school GPA:* 2.0. *Test scores:* SAT critical reading scores over 500: 16%; SAT math scores over 500: 13%.

Faculty *Total:* 55, 64% full-time. *Student/faculty ratio:* 11:1.

Majors Accounting; biology/biological sciences; business administration and management; chemistry; computer science; criminal justice/law enforcement administration; education; elementary education; English; kindergarten/preschool education; kinesiology and exercise science; mathematics; physical education teaching and coaching; political science and government; sociology; therapeutic recreation.

Academics *Calendar:* semesters. *Degree:* bachelor's. *Special study options:* academic remediation for entering students, adult/continuing education programs, advanced placement credit, cooperative education, double majors, honors programs, internships, part-time degree program, summer session for credit. *ROTC:* Army (c).

Computers on Campus 300 computers/terminals and 300 ports are available on campus for general student use. Students can access the following: campus intranet, computer help desk, free student e-mail accounts, online (class) grades, online (class) registration, online (class) schedules. Campuswide network is

available. 100% of college-owned or -operated housing units are wired for high-speed Internet access. Wireless service is available via entire campus.

Student Life *Housing options:* coed, men-only, women-only. Campus housing is university owned. Freshman campus housing is guaranteed. *Activities and organizations:* drama/theater group, student-run newspaper, radio station, choral group, national fraternities, national sororities. *Campus security:* 24-hour emergency response devices and patrols, student patrols, late-night transport/escort service. *Student services:* health clinic, personal/psychological counseling.

Athletics Member NAIA. *Intercollegiate sports:* baseball M (s), basketball M (s)/W (s), cross-country running M (s)/W (s), softball W (s), track and field M (s)/W (s), volleyball W (s). *Intramural sports:* basketball M/W, table tennis M/W, volleyball M/W.

Standardized Tests *Recommended:* SAT or ACT (for admission).

Costs (2007–08) *Comprehensive fee:* $14,326 includes full-time tuition ($8734), mandatory fees ($250), and room and board ($5342). Part-time tuition: $273 per credit hour. *College room only:* $2400. Room and board charges vary according to housing facility. *Payment plan:* installment. *Waivers:* employees or children of employees.

Financial Aid Of all full-time matriculated undergraduates who enrolled in 2004, 813 applied for aid, 791 were judged to have need, 61 had their need fully met. 223 Federal Work-Study jobs (averaging $2000). In 2004, 65 non-need-based awards were made. *Average percent of need met:* 51%. *Average financial aid package:* $7449. *Average need-based loan:* $2840. *Average need-based gift aid:* $4805. *Average non-need-based aid:* $9582. *Average indebtedness upon graduation:* $13,383.

Applying *Options:* electronic application, deferred entrance. *Application fee:* $25. *Required:* high school transcript, minimum 2.0 GPA, secondary school GPA. *Required for some:* high school transcript, interview. *Application deadlines:* rolling (freshmen), rolling (transfers).

Freshman Application Contact Dr. Willie Jefferson, Dean of Enrollment Management, Voorhees College, Halmi Hall, PO Box 678, Denmark, SC 29042. *Phone:* 803-703-1049. *Toll-free phone:* 866-685-9904. *E-mail:* williej@voorhees.edu.

WINTHROP UNIVERSITY

Rock Hill, South Carolina **www.winthrop.edu/**

- **State-supported** comprehensive, founded 1886, part of South Carolina Commission on Higher Education
- **Suburban** 418-acre campus with easy access to Charlotte
- **Endowment** $869,822
- **Coed** 5,012 undergraduate students, 89% full-time, 69% women, 31% men
- **Moderately difficult** entrance level, 70% of applicants were admitted

Undergraduates 4,470 full-time, 542 part-time. Students come from 44 states and territories, 39 other countries, 13% are from out of state, 27% African American, 2% Asian American or Pacific Islander, 2% Hispanic American, 0.4% Native American, 2% international, 6% transferred in, 42% live on campus. *Retention:* 72% of 2006 full-time freshmen returned.

Freshmen *Admission:* 3,996 applied, 2,781 admitted, 1,074 enrolled. *Average high school GPA:* 3.59. *Test scores:* SAT critical reading scores over 500: 60%; SAT math scores over 500: 65%; ACT scores over 18: 99%; SAT critical reading scores over 600: 19%; SAT math scores over 600: 16%; ACT scores over 24: 35%; SAT critical reading scores over 700: 3%; SAT math scores over 700: 1%; ACT scores over 30: 2%.

Faculty *Total:* 559, 50% full-time, 51% with terminal degrees. *Student/faculty ratio:* 14:1.

Majors Art; art history, criticism and conservation; biology/biological sciences; business administration and management; business teacher education; chemistry; clinical laboratory science/medical technology; communication disorders; computer science; dance; dramatic/theater arts; e-commerce; elementary education; English; family and consumer sciences/home economics teacher education; foods, nutrition, and wellness; history; kindergarten/preschool education; mass communication/media; mathematics; modern languages; music; music teacher education; philosophy; physical education teaching and coaching; political science and government; psychology; religious studies; social work; sociology; special education; sport and fitness administration/management; technical and business writing.

Academics *Calendar:* semesters. *Degrees:* bachelor's and master's. *Special study options:* adult/continuing education programs, advanced placement credit, cooperative education, distance learning, double majors, honors programs, independent study, internships, off-campus study, part-time degree program, services for LD students, study abroad, summer session for credit. *ROTC:* Army (c).

Computers on Campus 250 computers/terminals are available on campus for general student use. Students can access the following: campus intranet, computer help desk, free student e-mail accounts, online (class) grades, online (class) registration, online (class) schedules. Campuswide network is available. 100% of college-owned or -operated housing units are wired for high-speed Internet access. Wireless service is available via entire campus.

Student Life *Housing:* on-campus residence required for freshman year. *Options:* coed, men-only, women-only. Campus housing is university owned. Freshman campus housing is guaranteed. *Activities and organizations:* drama/theater group, student-run newspaper, radio station, choral group, Ebonites, campus ministries, Student Government Association, Dinkins Student Union, national fraternities, national sororities. *Campus security:* 24-hour emergency response devices and patrols, late-night transport/escort service, controlled dormitory access. *Student services:* health clinic, personal/psychological counseling.

Athletics Member NCAA. All Division I. *Intercollegiate sports:* baseball M (s), basketball M (s)/W (s), cheerleading M (c)/W (c), cross-country running M (s)/W (s), fencing M (c)/W (c), golf M (s)/W (s), lacrosse M (c)/W (c), rugby M (c), soccer M (s), softball W (s), tennis M (s)/W (s), track and field M (s)/W (s), volleyball W (s). *Intramural sports:* badminton M/W, basketball M/W, cross-country running M/W, equestrian sports M (c)/W (c), football M/W, golf M/W, racquetball M/W, soccer M/W, softball M/W, swimming and diving M/W, table tennis M/W, tennis M/W, ultimate Frisbee M/W, volleyball M/W, water polo M/W, weight lifting M/W.

Standardized Tests *Required:* SAT or ACT (for admission).

Costs (2007–08) *Tuition:* state resident $10,210 full-time, $426 per semester hour part-time; nonresident $19,034 full-time, $794 per semester hour part-time. Full-time tuition and fees vary according to degree level. Part-time tuition and fees vary according to degree level. *Room and board:* $5800; room only: $3670. Room and board charges vary according to board plan and housing facility. *Payment plan:* installment. *Waivers:* senior citizens and employees or children of employees.

Financial Aid Of all full-time matriculated undergraduates who enrolled in 2007, 3,292 applied for aid, 2,664 were judged to have need, 546 had their need fully met. 304 Federal Work-Study jobs (averaging $823). In 2007, 222 non-need-based awards were made. *Average percent of need met:* 64%. *Average financial aid package:* $9232. *Average need-based loan:* $3982. *Average need-based gift aid:* $7063. *Average non-need-based aid:* $4460. *Average indebtedness upon graduation:* $22,578.

Applying *Options:* electronic application, deferred entrance. *Application fee:* $40. *Required:* high school transcript, 1 letter of recommendation. *Recommended:* essay or personal statement. *Application deadline:* 5/1 (freshmen). *Notification:* continuous (freshmen), continuous (transfers).

Freshman Application Contact Winthrop University, Stewart House, Rock Hill, SC 29733. *Phone:* 803-323-2191. *Toll-free phone:* 800-763-0230.

WOFFORD COLLEGE

Spartanburg, South Carolina **www.wofford.edu/**

- **Independent** 4-year, founded 1854, affiliated with United Methodist Church
- **Urban** 200-acre campus with easy access to Charlotte
- **Endowment** $168.0 million
- **Coed** 1,327 undergraduate students, 98% full-time, 47% women, 53% men
- **Very difficult** entrance level, 53% of applicants were admitted

Undergraduates 1,305 full-time, 22 part-time. Students come from 25 states and territories, 10 other countries, 30% are from out of state, 6% African American, 2% Asian American or Pacific Islander, 2% Hispanic American, 0.3% Native American, 0.8% international, 1% transferred in, 92% live on campus. *Retention:* 93% of 2006 full-time freshmen returned.

Freshmen *Admission:* 2,354 applied, 1,256 admitted, 385 enrolled. *Average high school GPA:* 4.0. *Test scores:* SAT critical reading scores over 500: 96%; SAT math scores over 500: 95%; SAT writing scores over 500: 93%; ACT scores over 18: 99%; SAT critical reading scores over 600: 63%; SAT math scores over 600: 63%; SAT writing scores over 600: 57%; ACT scores over 24: 63%; SAT critical reading scores over 700: 19%; SAT math scores over 700: 17%; SAT writing scores over 700: 13%; ACT scores over 30: 5%.

Faculty *Total:* 132, 80% full-time, 86% with terminal degrees. *Student/faculty ratio:* 11:1.

Majors Accounting; art history, criticism and conservation; biology/biological sciences; business/managerial economics; chemistry; Chinese; computer science; creative writing; dramatic/theater arts; economics; English; finance; French; German; history; humanities; international business/trade/commerce; international relations and affairs; mathematics; neuroscience; philosophy; physics; political science and government; pre-dentistry studies; pre-law studies; premedical studies; pre-veterinary studies; psychology; religious studies; sociology; Spanish.

Academics *Calendar:* 4-1-4. *Degree:* bachelor's. *Special study options:* accelerated degree program, advanced placement credit, double majors, independent study, internships, off-campus study, part-time degree program, student-designed majors, study abroad, summer session for credit. *ROTC:* Army (b). *Unusual degree programs:* 3-2 engineering with Clemson University, Columbia University.

Computers on Campus 250 computers/terminals are available on campus for general student use. Students can access the following: campus intranet, computer help desk, free student e-mail accounts, online (class) grades, online (class) registration, online (class) schedules. Campuswide network is available. 100% of college-owned or -operated housing units are wired for high-speed Internet access. Wireless service is available via classrooms, computer centers, computer labs, libraries, student centers.

Student Life *Housing:* on-campus residence required through senior year. *Options:* coed. Campus housing is university owned. Freshman applicants given priority for college housing. *Activities and organizations:* drama/theater group, student-run newspaper, choral group, performing arts groups, Twin Towers student volunteers, Non-denominational religious fellowships, national fraternities, national sororities. *Campus security:* 24-hour emergency response devices and patrols, late-night transport/escort service, controlled dormitory access. *Student services:* health clinic, personal/psychological counseling.

Athletics Member NCAA. All Division I except football (Division I-AA). *Intercollegiate sports:* baseball M (s), basketball M (s)/W (s), cross-country running M (s)/W (s), fencing M (c)/W (c), golf M (s)/W (s), riflery M/W, soccer M (s)/W (s), tennis M (s)/W (s), track and field M (s)/W (s), volleyball W (s). *Intramural sports:* basketball M/W, bowling M/W, football M/W, racquetball M/W, soccer M/W, softball M/W, tennis M/W, ultimate Frisbee M/W, volleyball M/W, weight lifting M/W.

Standardized Tests *Required:* SAT or ACT (for admission).

Costs (2007–08) *Comprehensive fee:* $35,535 includes full-time tuition ($27,830) and room and board ($7705). Part-time tuition: $1010 per hour. *Payment plan:* installment. *Waivers:* employees or children of employees.

Financial Aid Of all full-time matriculated undergraduates who enrolled in 2005, 746 applied for aid, 599 were judged to have need, 338 had their need fully met. In 2005, 291 non-need-based awards were made. *Average percent of need met:* 89%. *Average financial aid package:* $22,401. *Average need-based loan:* $4391. *Average need-based gift aid:* $16,648. *Average non-need-based aid:* $9884. *Average indebtedness upon graduation:* $10,242.

Applying *Options:* electronic application, early admission, early decision, deferred entrance. *Application fee:* $50. *Required:* essay or personal statement, high school transcript. *Recommended:* 2 letters of recommendation, interview. *Application deadlines:* 2/1 (freshmen), rolling (transfers). *Early decision deadline:* 11/15. *Notification:* 3/15 (freshmen), continuous (transfers), 12/1 (early decision).

Freshman Application Contact Ms. Jennifer B. Page, Director of Admissions, Wofford College, 429 North Church Street, Spartanburg, SC 29303-3663. *Phone:* 864-597-4130. *Fax:* 864-597-4147. *E-mail:* admission@wofford.edu.

ANDERSON UNIVERSITY

ANDERSON, SOUTH CAROLINA

The University

Anderson University, founded in 1911, is a private, coeducational, comprehensive university providing a challenging education grounded in the liberal arts and enhanced by professional and graduate programs and a cocurricular focus on the development of character, servant leadership, and cultural engagement. The University emphasizes exceptional teaching of undergraduate students.

Anderson enrolls approximately 1,800 students, 76 percent of whom attend full-time. In addition, about 75 percent of the full-time student population lives on campus. Typically, the University enrolls students from more than twenty-eight states and over twenty countries. The student body consists primarily of traditional-age students; however, some are nontraditional-age students enrolled in the University's evening college. Campus housing is available to international students.

A comprehensive program of student activities is provided, including varsity and intramural athletics, Christian ministry opportunities, theater, clubs and organizations, student government, and student-sponsored social activities. Intercollegiate sports programs for men include baseball, basketball, cross-country, golf, soccer, tennis, track, and wrestling. Intercollegiate sports programs for women include basketball, cross-country, golf, soccer, softball, tennis, track, and volleyball. The University also offers club sports in cheerleading and dance, which comes under the umbrella of athletics. Anderson University is a member of NCAA Division II and of Conference Carolinas.

Anderson University began offering a Master of Education degree program in January 2006, which has enrolled approximately 40 students. The University is scheduled to begin offering a Master of Business Administration degree program in August 2008.

Location

The University is located in beautiful northwestern South Carolina in the thriving city of Anderson, halfway between Charlotte, North Carolina, and Atlanta, Georgia. The campus, which includes a small wooded park, athletic facilities, and student housing, occupies a 60-acre area in an elegant, historical, urban neighborhood. The city serves as a commercial hub for a large area of northwestern South Carolina and northeastern Georgia. Anderson is served by Interstate 85 and the Greenville/Spartanburg Airport (GSP). Atlanta and Charlotte are within a 2-hour drive; Charleston, South Carolina, and other beaches are within 4 hours; Asheville, North Carolina, and other mountain destinations are within 1 to 2 hours.

Majors and Degrees

Anderson University offers almost fifty areas of study. Bachelor of Arts degrees can be earned, with majors in art (art education, ceramics, graphic design, painting/drawing), Christian ministry, church music, communications (mass media, public relations/advertising, writing), English, history, interior design, music, psychology, religion, Spanish, and theater.

The Bachelor of Science degree is awarded in biology, business (accounting, computer information services, finance/economics, human resource management, management), education (early childhood, elementary, secondary, special education), kinesiology (exercise science, physical education), and mathematics.

The University offers additional degree programs in music, including the Bachelor of Music degree, with concentrations in instrumental performance, keyboard performance, and vocal performance, and the Bachelor of Music Education degree, with concentrations in instrumental or vocal/choral music.

Teacher certification is offered in art education (K–12), elementary/early childhood education (K–8), music education (K–12), physical education (K–12), special education, and secondary education (7–12) in English, mathematics, and social studies.

There are five degrees that may be obtained through the adult accelerated evening college: the Bachelor of Business Administration, Bachelor of Business Administration with a concentration in computer information systems or health services management, Bachelor of Human Services and Resources, Bachelor of Criminal Justice, and Bachelor of Science in elementary education/early childhood.

Academic Programs

The University follows the semester calendar and offers two summer sessions. A minimum of 128 credit hours is required for the bachelor's degree for traditional students.

In order to graduate from any degree program, a student must complete a general education component and a major studies component and must satisfy competence requirements in reading, writing, mathematics, and speaking. The ethical dimension of life is emphasized in all programs. Students have the opportunity to participate in internship experiences, study-travel, and overseas study.

A special relationship with the Washington Center for Internships and Seminars provides Anderson students access to some of the most prestigious internships in the nation's capital.

Academic Facilities

Anderson's Callie Stringer Rainey Fine Arts Center provides the finest facility in the upstate of South Carolina for art, theatrical, musical, and community functions and houses chapel services and other campus events. The Watkins Teaching Center contains most of the classrooms, a computer laboratory, conference rooms, and faculty offices. Other academic facilities include the new Thrift Library, a 50,000-square-foot facility completed in January 2007; Merritt Administration Building; Merritt Auditorium; and Vandiver Hall. The new library houses a 24-hour computer center, an art gallery, and Java City, a coffee and dessert bar.

Costs

Charges for 2008–09 are $12,875 per semester, including tuition, fees, room, and board. For commuting students, the cost is $9350 per semester for tuition and fees. Books and supplies cost approximately $600 per semester. Charges for international students are the same as for regular boarding students. Personal expenses for transportation, recreation, and miscellaneous needs vary with the individual student. Students may have cars on campus; there is a $35 parking-permit fee.

Financial Aid

It is the intent of Anderson University to provide financial assistance to all accepted students who, without such aid, would be unable to attend. Institutional aid for the incoming freshman class of 2007 (boarding) averaged $6750 per year. There are additional sources of financial aid available to qualified students. It is best to complete and mail all required forms as soon as possible, since most aid is awarded on a first-come, first-served basis for qualified applicants. The first award deadline is March 1. The Financial Aid Office awards aid regardless of race, religion, place of national origin, gender, physical handicap, or ethnicity.

Faculty

A faculty of 136 full-time and part-time professors brings the student-faculty ratio to 13:1, allowing for small classes and easy accessibility to professors and instructors. Sixty-five percent of the University's faculty members have a Ph.D. or other equivalent terminal degree.

Student Government

The entire student body is represented in the Student Government Association by elected officers. These positions consist of President, Vice President, Secretary, class presidents, and 6 senators from each class. The student body is also represented through various committees: Campus Safety, Food Service, Commuter Students, and Accelerated Students. The Student Government Association leadership works with the students as well as the administration to provide activities for social, educational, spiritual, and physical enrichment.

Admission Requirements

Anderson seeks to admit those who show promise of academic and social success at the University. Each applicant's record is examined for evidence reflecting potential for intellectual and social maturity, strength of character, and seriousness of purpose. The major factors considered in admission include graduation from high school, high school grades in college-preparatory courses, high school curriculum, and SAT or ACT scores. In addition, the University may choose to examine further any applicant by use of personal interviews or tests.

TOEFL scores are required of international applicants. A minimum score of 550 is recommended. The SAT is not required of nonnative English-speaking students. An I-20 (student visa) can normally be issued within two weeks of receipt of all required admission materials and tuition funds.

Anderson admits students without regard to race, age, religion, color, gender, physical handicap, national origin, or ethnicity.

Application and Information

Qualified students are encouraged to apply as early as possible during their final year of high school. The Admissions Office processes applications on a rolling basis, which enables the University to notify a candidate of the admission decision within two weeks after all credentials have been received. Interested students are encouraged to visit the campus.

For further information and application materials, students should contact:

Director of Admissions
Anderson University
316 Boulevard
Anderson, South Carolina 29621
Phone: 864-231-2030
800-542-3594 (toll-free)
Fax: 864-231-2033
Web site: http://www.andersonuniversity.edu

The Watkins Teaching Center on the campus of Anderson University.

THE ART INSTITUTE OF CHARLESTON

CHARLESTON, SOUTH CAROLINA

The Institute

The Art Institute of Charleston provides students with an educational environment and dedicated faculty members who are committed to preparing students for entry-level positions in the creative arts. Under the guidance of industry professionals, students learn by doing the types of tasks they are likely to encounter in the workplace. In addition, assistance is available to help students with resume writing, networking, and keeping aware of what employers are looking for in job candidates. The school offers six bachelor's degree programs, four associate degree programs, and two certificate programs.

The school offers assistance in helping students to secure housing.

The student population includes recent high school graduates, transfer students, and those who have left a previous employment situation to study and train for a new career. Students are creative, competitive, and open to new ideas. They place great value on an education that prepares them for an exciting entry-level position in the arts.

The Art Institute of Charleston places a high value on the quality of student life—both in and out of the classroom. Students participate in a wide variety of activities, including clubs and organizations, community service, and various committees designed to enhance the quality of student life.

The Art Institute of Charleston is accredited by the Commission on Colleges of the Southern Association of Colleges and Schools (SACS; 1866 Southern Lane, Decatur, Georgia 30033-4097; phone: 404-679-4500; http://www.sacs.org) to award Bachelor of Fine Arts, Bachelor of Science, and Associate of Arts degrees.

Location

The school's Market Street location is close to arts, historical, and cultural organizations, allowing students to experience all that Charleston has to offer.

Majors and Degrees

Bachelor's degree programs are offered in culinary arts management, fashion and retail management, graphic design, interior design, photographic imaging, and Web design and interactive media. Associate degrees are offered in culinary arts, culinary arts with a concentration in baking and pastry, graphic design, and Web and interactive media. Certificate programs are available in commercial photography and culinary arts: skills.

Academic Programs

The Art Institute of Charleston operates on a year-round, four-quarter system.

Academic Facilities

The Art Institute of Charleston contains classrooms, Mac and PC computer labs, and a library for student use. There is also a bookstore.

Costs

Tuition cost varies by program. Prospective students should contact the school for current tuition costs. Other charges include a starting kit for all first quarter students. Kits vary in price depending on the program of study.

Financial Aid

Financial aid is available for those who qualify. Students who require financial assistance should first complete and submit a Free Application for Federal Student Aid (FAFSA) and meet with a financial aid officer. The officer determines the level of need based on a required federal formula, the cost of education, and other factors. Gift aid is available in the form of Federal Pell Grants, Federal Supplemental Educational Opportunity Grants, and veterans' benefits. Loans include Federal Stafford Loans, Federal PLUS Loans, and alternative loans. Other scholarships are available from the school and private sources. Application deadlines and eligibility requirements vary by program.

Faculty

Faculty members at The Art Institute of Charleston have professional knowledge that they bring into the classroom. The school's faculty members provide their students with a real-world, relevant educational experience.

Admission Requirements

Applicants must provide proof of high school graduation or achievement of a General Educational Development (GED) certificate as a prerequisite for admission. In lieu of documenting high school graduation or a GED certificate, applicants may provide proof of attaining an associate degree or higher from an accredited institution. An official transcript indicating date of high school graduation, GED certificate (including test scores), or date of college graduation (including degree granted) is required as proof.

All individuals seeking admission to The Art Institute of Charleston are interviewed in person or by phone by an assistant director of admissions, and each applicant must create an original essay of at least 150 words stating how an education at The Art Institute of Charleston would help the student to achieve career goals. There is a $50 application fee.

Application and Information

To obtain an application, make arrangements for an interview, or tour the school, students should contact:

The Art Institute of Charleston
24 North Market Street
Charleston, South Carolina 29401-2623
Phone: 843-727-3500
866-211-0107 (toll-free)
Fax: 843-727-3440
Web site: http://www.artinstitutes.edu/charleston

The Art Institute of Atlanta®, GA; The Art Institute of Atlanta®–Decatur, GA; The Art Institute of Austin[SM], TX; The Art Institute of California[SM]–Inland Empire; The Art Institute of California[SM]–Los Angeles; The Art Institute of California[SM]–Orange County; The Art Institute of California[SM]–Sacramento; The Art Institute of California[SM]–San Diego; The Art Institute of California[SM]–San Francisco; The Art Institute of California[SM]–Sunnyvale; The Art Institute of Charleston[SM], SC, A branch of The Art Institute of Atlanta, GA; The Art Institute of Charlotte®, NC; The Art Institute of Colorado® (Denver); The Art Institute of Dallas®, TX; The Art Institute of Fort Lauderdale®, FL; The Art Institute of Houston®, TX; The Art Institute of Indianapolis[SM], IN*; The Art Institute of Jacksonville[SM], FL, A branch of Miami International University of Art & Design; The Art Institute of Las Vegas®, NV; The Art Institute of Michigan[SM] (Detroit); The Art Institute of New York City®, NY; The Art Institute of Ohio[SM]–Cincinnati**; The Art Institute of Philadelphia®, PA; The Art Institute of Phoenix®, AZ; The Art Institute of Pittsburgh®, PA; The Art Institute of Pittsburgh®–Online Division; The Art Institute of Portland®, OR; The Art Institute of Salt Lake City[SM], UT; The Art Institute of Seattle®, WA; The Art Institute of Tampa[SM], FL, A branch of Miami International University of Art & Design; The Art Institute of Tennessee[SM]–Nashville, A branch of The Art Institute of Atlanta, GA; The Art Institute of Tucson[SM], AZ; The Art Institute of Washington® (Arlington, VA), A branch of The Art Institute of Atlanta, GA; The Art Institute of York–Pennsylvania[SM]; The Art Institutes International Minnesota[SM] (Minneapolis); California Design College[SM] (Los Angeles–Wilshire Blvd.); The Illinois Institute of Art®–Chicago; The Illinois Institute of Art®–Schaumburg; Miami International University of Art & Design[SM], FL; The New England Institute of Art® (Boston, MA).

*The Art Institute of Indianapolis is licensed by the Indiana Commission on Proprietary Education, 302 West Washington Street, Room E201, Indianapolis, IN 46204, AC-0080.

**The Art Institute of Ohio–Cincinnati, 8845 Governors Hill Drive, Suite 100, Cincinnati, OH 45249-3317, Reg. #04-01-1698B.

CHARLESTON SOUTHERN UNIVERSITY

CHARLESTON, SOUTH CAROLINA

The University

Charleston Southern University (CSU) is a fully accredited four-year liberal arts university. Its mission is to promote academic excellence in a Christian environment for students of all faiths. Charleston Southern is listed as one of *America's Best Christian Colleges*, identifying CSU as a school that provides students with the highest quality education in a Christian environment.

A coeducational university, Charleston Southern University's enrollment has grown from 500 students to more than 3,000 students in over forty years and continues to change to meet the needs of a fast-paced society. CSU is affiliated with the South Carolina Baptist Convention.

Charleston Southern University seeks to develop the total person emotionally, intellectually, and spiritually. Programs are designed to prepare students for a successful and fulfilling life. Each major program is combined with a comprehensive liberal arts foundation. Courses in the humanities, the fine arts, natural science, and social science are included in this foundation. These subjects are designed to develop problem-solving skills and the ability to communicate effectively. A special career counseling center is designed to help students plan for the future.

Men's and women's athletic teams compete in the NCAA Division I Big South Conference. The University fields teams in baseball, basketball, cross-country, golf, soccer (women), softball, tennis, track and field, and volleyball as well as an NCAA Division I-AA football team. For outdoor recreation, there are NCAA-quality tennis courts, putting greens, and athletic fields; nature trails; and a lake for fishing.

The Graduate Studies Program offers Master of Education degrees in elementary education, secondary education, and school administration. In addition, there is a Master of Science in criminal justice, and a Master of Business Administration, with emphases in accounting, finance, health-care administration, management information systems, and organizational development.

Students are informed of campus activities through the University's online newspaper, *Buc in Print,* published by students under staff member supervision. In addition, the University yearbook, *Cutlass,* and the University literary magazine, *The Sefer,* are published by students under faculty and staff supervision.

Location

Situated on 300 acres, Charleston Southern University is strategically located near Charleston, South Carolina, in the center of the modern growth patterns of North Charleston. Students take advantage of the cultural, historical, and recreational opportunities the city offers. Nearby Interstate 26, with access to Interstate 95, is conveniently located to the campus. Seven airlines serve the Charleston area. Mild winters and long summers allow many opportunities for outdoor recreation. Charleston is a city famous for its well-preserved colonial houses, famous gardens and plantations, miles of wide sandy beaches, and major fine arts events, including the Spoleto Festival USA—a kaleidoscope of opera, dance, music, theater, and visual arts.

Majors and Degrees

Charleston Southern University awards the Bachelor of Arts degree with majors in business, communications and theater, English, English education, humanities and fine arts, music (with emphases in church music and vocal performance), music education (with emphases in choral and instrumental), music therapy, religion, Spanish, Spanish education, and youth ministry. The Bachelor of Science degree is offered with majors in applied math, athletic training, biochemistry, biology, business administration (with emphases in accounting, finance, management, management information systems, and marketing), chemistry, computer science/mathematics, criminal justice, early childhood education, economics, elementary education, health promotions, history, mathematics, mathematics education, natural science, nursing, physical education, political science, psychology, science education, social science, social studies education, and sociology. Minors are offered in most of the above areas and are also offered in aerospace studies (AFROTC), art, Christian leadership, and French. The School of Education offers a secondary education minor for several majors to meet teacher certification requirements. The Bachelor of Technology degree is offered to students who have completed an associate degree in a technical field prior to entry.

Preprofessional programs are offered in allied health science, dentistry, engineering, law, medicine, pharmacy, and seminary. Some of these programs require a four-year degree from CSU while others require two or three years of study at CSU before the student transfers to a professional school.

The Bachelor of Management Arts (B.M.A.) is a new program of study for adult learners in the Evening College. Students in this program can graduate in as little as twenty months after requirements are met.

Academic Programs

The purpose of Charleston Southern University is to help students to develop intellectually, socially, culturally, and spiritually. This is accomplished by ensuring that students receive a well-rounded education. The University requires all students to complete a core of liberal arts courses. The comprehensive course of study is subdivided into general education courses, including courses in English, the fine arts, history, mathematics, computer literacy, foreign language, natural science, religion and philosophy, and the social sciences. In addition, students are offered an opportunity to pursue a field of study in a major and minor area. Elective credits may also be taken to complete the minimum graduation requirements of at least 125 semester hours.

The academic-year calendar operates on a 4-4-1 system. The fall term begins in mid-August and ends in December, and the spring term begins in January and ends in early May. May is set aside as a one-month Maymester during which students may enroll in one course. Students also have the option of attending two 5-week summer sessions.

An award-winning Air Force ROTC program is available on campus.

Advanced placement credits are given for successful scores on approved tests of the Educational Testing Service. Credit may also be granted for successful scores on the College-Level Examination Program (CLEP) tests, the Defense Activity for Non-Traditional Education Support (DANTES), military experience, CSU challenge exams, AP credit, and IB credit.

Academic Facilities

The University has a modern library that contains more than 200,000 volumes, a modern chapel-auditorium with impressive fine arts facilities, and a multipurpose gymnasium. The Brewer Center, the wellness and activities building, houses state-of-the-art exercise equipment, social areas, an intramural gym, and meeting rooms for clubs and organizations. The music facility, Whittington Hall, includes a large music rehearsal hall, practice suites, a technology lab, and classrooms.

CSU's newest addition is the 54,000-square-foot science building. It has eight research laboratories, eleven major teaching laboratories, additional classrooms, and faculty offices. The facility contains advanced technology with multiple wireless capabilities.

Costs

Tuition for the 2007–08 academic year was $17,620, and room and board were $6772 per year. Tuition and fees are subject to change.

Financial Aid

A comprehensive financial aid program, consisting of scholarships, grants, loans, and employment, has been established at Charleston Southern. Approximately 95 percent of the student body receives some type of financial assistance. The University participates in the Federal Pell Grant, Federal Supplemental Educational Opportunity Grant (FSEOG), and Federal Work-Study programs. Assistance is also available through Federal Perkins Loans and Federal Stafford Loans. Endowed or donated funds are available for many students; such awards are administered according to the provisions of the contributing agency or person. The South Carolina Tuition Grant, Palmetto Fellow Award, and South Carolina HOPE/LIFE scholarship are available to eligible South Carolina residents.

Students may also be eligible to receive institutional scholarships and grants based on academic merit, special talent, or financial need.

At Charleston Southern University, it is understood that financial concerns can often play a major role in the decision on which university to attend. The purpose of the financial aid program is to remove cost from the student's decision and allow the student to decide based on the academic and social environment offered at CSU.

Faculty

Charleston Southern University has a well-qualified and dedicated faculty. Faculty members combine teaching ability and scholarship with a concern for students. The majority hold doctoral degrees. Professors work directly with students in many phases of University life, including academic advising. Once the student selects a major course of study, he or she is assigned a faculty adviser in that major area. CSU offers small class sizes, which allow for individual attention and facilitates the pursuit of academic excellence.

The University encourages advanced study and research. Excellence in teaching is also recognized through an annual award.

Student Government

All full-time students become members of the Student Government Association upon enrollment. This organization enables students to develop leadership skills while achieving the goals the University has set for them.

Admission Requirements

The Enrollment Services staff works diligently to maintain a socially, economically, and culturally diverse student body. The University is a private, church-supported educational institution and is committed to a policy of nondiscrimination on the basis of race, sex, color, religion, national origin, or handicap.

Students may be admitted as first-time freshmen or as transfer students with acceptable credit. New freshmen must have official transcripts sent from their high schools and official SAT or ACT scores sent from the appropriate testing service. Transfer students must have official transcripts sent from all colleges previously attended. Interviews are not required, but students are encouraged to visit the campus. Arrangements may be made by calling the Office of Enrollment Services.

Application and Information

Candidates for freshman admission are encouraged to submit applications in the fall of their senior year in secondary school. Transfer students are welcome to apply anytime during the academic year. Applications can be completed online at http://www.charlestonsouthern.edu. A nonrefundable application processing fee ($40 paper, $20 online) must be submitted with an application. The University uses a rolling admission system, and students are notified of the admission decision as soon as all application materials have been received and evaluated.

Application forms and other information about Charleston Southern University may be obtained by contacting:

Office of Enrollment Services
Charleston Southern University
9200 University Boulevard
P.O. Box 118087
Charleston, South Carolina 29423-8087
Phone: 843-863-7050
800-947-7474 (toll-free)
Web site: http://www.charlestonsouthern.edu

THE CITADEL, THE MILITARY COLLEGE OF SOUTH CAROLINA

CHARLESTON, SOUTH CAROLINA

The College

The Citadel, founded in 1842, has a rich and storied history. Though it has been greatly expanded and modernized, it is basically the same distinctive institution it was when founded. The College's mission is to educate and prepare graduates to become principled leaders in all walks of life by instilling core values—academics, duty, honor, morality, discipline, diversity—in a challenging intellectual environment. The Citadel remains a stronghold of duty, self-discipline, and high ideals in a changing American society.

As a classic military college, The Citadel emphasizes the value of a strict indoctrination for first-year students, who are called knobs. The disciplined lifestyle that begins in the knob year binds cadets into a lifelong, close-knit camaraderie that is one of the strongest forces in their lives after graduation.

Citadel graduates have fought in every American conflict since the Mexican War. Cadets from The Citadel fired the first shots of the Civil War. The Corps flag displays nine battle streamers earned in that war. Citadel graduates continue to serve their country with distinction in all branches of the armed services.

The Corps of Cadets numbers approximately 2,000 young men and women and represents nearly every state in the U.S. and many other countries. All cadets are required to reside in barracks. An ultramodern physical education center provides splendid facilities for physical education and individual and team sports unrelated to varsity events. The student activities building, named for General Mark W. Clark, the late president emeritus, houses the Honor Court room, reception lounge, Office of Cadet Activities, photograph darkroom, student publication offices, canteen, barber shop, auditorium, billiard room, gift shop, and post office. The beautiful Summerall Chapel, which is a shrine of religion, patriotism, and remembrance, is flexibly designed for use by major denominational groups.

The Citadel, a member of NCAA Division I (football division I-AA) and the Southern Conference, fields fourteen men's and women's intercollegiate athletic teams. Cadets take part in the almost fifty club and intramural sports programs, which include bicycling, bowling, boxing, crew, fencing, gymnastics, ice hockey, judo, karate, lacrosse, pistol, rugby, sailing, scuba diving, skydiving, volleyball, and waterskiing. The Citadel has its own boating center with canoes, power boats, and sailboats available for cadets' use.

Location

The Citadel is located in one of America's most historic cities, Charleston, South Carolina. The beautiful 100-acre campus is bordered by the Ashley River and historic Hampton Park. The climate is ideal, with an average temperature of 67 degrees. Many excellent ocean beaches are nearby. The Citadel's very own beach house is located just a few minutes away on the lush Isle of Palms. Charleston is famous for its pre-Revolutionary houses and gardens, outstanding restaurants, golf courses, and cultural centers. Entertainment and nightlife abound.

Charleston is served by Amtrak, an international airport, two bus lines, seven taxi companies, a limousine service, and fifteen rental-car firms. The city's transit system stops at The Citadel's main entrance. The campus is readily accessible via Interstate 26 or U.S. Highway 17.

Majors and Degrees

Organized into five schools, The Citadel offers twenty majors and twenty-six minor areas of academic concentration. This provides cadets with academic opportunities normally expected only at a university, combined with the personalized attention afforded by a small college. Bachelor of Arts degrees are available in chemistry, criminal justice, English, history, mathematics, modern languages (French, German, and Spanish), political science, and psychology. Bachelor of Science degrees are offered in biology, business administration, chemistry, civil engineering, computer science, education, electrical engineering, mathematics, physical education, and physics.

Academic Programs

The Citadel provides a sound education reinforced by the best features of a disciplined environment.

All cadets participate in one of the Reserve Officers' Training Corps programs—Army, Air Force, or Naval/Marine Corps. These programs do not require students to accept a commission or be committed to active duty.

The educational requirements of all majors ensure that The Citadel graduate is conversant with literature, history, and the natural and social sciences. Cadets learn to think critically by confronting issues raised in challenging courses.

The Citadel Honors Program is a specially designed educational experience that meets the needs of students with an outstanding record of academic achievement and a sense of intellectual adventure. While pursuing any one of the twenty degree programs offered by The Citadel, Honors students take a series of general education Honors courses concentrated in their first two years and an Honors seminar in their third and fourth years.

The Citadel—a fully accredited, four-year, coeducational, comprehensive senior college—is a member of the Southern Association of Colleges and Schools, the American Council on Education, the American Association of Colleges for Teacher Education, and the Association of American Colleges. The business administration department is accredited by AACSB International–The Association to Advance Collegiate Schools of Business. The civil and environmental engineering and electrical and computer engineering departments are accredited by the Accreditation Board for Engineering and Technology. The chemistry department is accredited by the American Chemical Society. The education department is accredited by the National Council for Accreditation of Teacher Education and the National Association of State Directors of Teacher Education and Certification.

Off-Campus Programs

The Citadel's Office of International Studies provides a variety of study-abroad and internship opportunities for cadets who are interested in a semester or year abroad.

Academic Facilities

Twenty-four major buildings are efficiently grouped around a huge parade ground to provide maximum convenience for students. Among the College's academic facilities are the Daniel Library, two engineering buildings, multimedia classrooms, and computer facilities located in all academic areas. The entire campus is linked to a fiber-optic network. Through a consortium arrangement, other local college libraries and facilities are available to cadets. Cadet barracks provide computer connections to the campus wide network and the Internet for each cadet in every room.

Costs

The Citadel's extremely competitive fee structure includes uniforms, room, board, books, dry cleaning, laundry, athletic events, student publications, infirmary care, and haircuts. The total annual fees for 2007–08 by residence and by class: for residents of South Carolina, fees for first-year students were $19,595, and for sophomores, juniors, and seniors, $15,755. For out-of-state students, fees for first-year students were $31,151, and for sophomores, juniors, and seniors, $27,311.

Financial Aid

The Citadel offers two types of financial assistance: financial aid, which consists of loans and grants awarded on the basis of need, and scholarships, which are awarded on the basis of merit. In 2007, more than 76 percent of the Cadet Corps received financial aid and 49 percent received scholarships, ranging from several hundred dollars a year to complete expenses for four years. To be considered for financial aid or scholarships, students must submit an application for admission; a separate scholarship application for new students is not required. The deadline for applying for need-based financial aid is February 28 of the senior year in high school.

Faculty

All courses at The Citadel are taught by dedicated faculty members, more than 95 percent of whom hold doctoral degrees. The student-faculty ratio is 15:1. All faculty members are required to set aside time for counseling and assisting cadets with their studies.

Student Government

Cadets form a regiment, composed of a band and bagpipe unit, a ceremonial artillery unit, and four battalions of four to five companies each. Student authority is entrusted to the chain of command and the elected class officials.

A principal aspect of student government is the honor code. Under that code, a cadet does not lie, cheat, steal, or tolerate those who do. An Honor Committee elected by cadets administers the code.

Admission Requirements

Applicants must be unmarried, between 17 and 23 years of age, physically qualified for enrollment in ROTC, and graduates of an accredited secondary school or have satisfactorily completed the General Educational Development examination. The required high school subjects are 4 units of English; 3 units of mathematics (algebra I, algebra II, and geometry); 3 years of laboratory science (biology, chemistry, and a third unit that must have biology or chemistry as a prerequisite); 2 years of the same foreign language; 2 units of social science; 4 units of electives; 1 unit of U.S. history; and 1 unit of physical education or ROTC. Additional course work in mathematics and foreign language is recommended. Other considerations include the applicant's rank in class, academic performance, and scores on either the SAT or ACT. Extracurricular activities are viewed as indications of leadership and desirable character traits. All factors are weighed in the final determination of the applicant's qualifications. The Citadel actively seeks and encourages applications for admission without regard to gender, race, or ability to pay. Applicants are encouraged to apply upon completion of their junior year in high school.

Application and Information

Applications may be made at the end of the junior year in secondary school. Prospective cadets should arrange to have their SAT or ACT scores forwarded to The Citadel. While applicants are welcome to visit the campus at any time, special programs are arranged on a designated schedule, during which the accepted applicants reside in barracks. Inquiries should be addressed to:

Office of Admissions
The Citadel, The Military College of South Carolina
171 Moultrie Street
Charleston, South Carolina 29409
Phone: 800-868-1842 (toll-free)
E-mail: admissions@citadel.edu
Web site: http://www.citadel.edu

Members of the Corps of Cadets stand in formation on the quadrangle within one of The Citadel's four battalions.

CLEMSON UNIVERSITY

CLEMSON, SOUTH CAROLINA

The University

One of the country's most selective public research universities, Clemson was founded in 1889 with a mission to be a "high seminary of learning" dedicated to teaching, research, and service. Today, these three concepts remain at the heart of the University and provide the framework for an exceptional educational experience.

At Clemson University, professors take the time to get to know students and to explore innovative ways of teaching. Exceptional teaching is one reason Clemson's retention and graduation rates rank among the highest in the country among public universities.

Exceptional teaching is also why Clemson continues to attract an increasingly talented student body. In 2007, over half of the entering freshmen were ranked in the top 10 percent of their high school classes, and the freshman class averaged 1221 on the critical reading and math sections of the SAT—one of the highest averages among the nation's public research universities.

Clemson is committed to world-class research. With more than $140 million in sponsored research support annually, Clemson is one of the National Science Foundation's top-100 research universities. Undergraduates have the opportunity to work closely with faculty members on exciting and challenging research projects.

The University also encourages faculty members to engage their classes through service-learning. One example of this is the Clemson Elementary Outdoors project, in which more than 750 Clemson students from a broad range of disciplines helped research and design outdoor learning areas for the city's elementary school. Clemson has received national recognition for its innovative Communication-Across-the-Curriculum (CAC) program, in which professors focus on providing students with real-life challenges that require them to think and communicate effectively. At Clemson, CAC has become a standard teaching method used in nearly every department.

From cheering the Tigers at a football game to socializing at the Hendrix Student Center, Clemson students can participate in a wide variety of activities outside the classroom. The more than 300 campus clubs and organizations include fraternities and sororities, honoraries, international, military, performing arts, political, professional, religious, service, social interest, special interest, sports and fitness, student media, and union programs and activities.

With 19 intercollegiate sports, Clemson offers exciting spectator sports all year long. Clemson is a charter member of the Atlantic Coast Conference (ACC) and is an NCAA Division I school. Admission to regular-season events played at Clemson is included in University fees for full-time students.

Clemson University is accredited by the Commission on Colleges of the Southern Association of Colleges and Schools (1866 Southern Lane, Decatur, Georgia 30033-4097; phone: 404-679-4501) to award bachelor's, master's, specialist, and doctoral degrees.

Location

Approximately midway between Charlotte, North Carolina, and Atlanta, Georgia, Clemson University is located on 1,400 acres of beautiful rolling hills within the foothills of the Blue Ridge Mountains and along the shores of Lake Hartwell. Great weather and proximity to natural wonders and large cities offer year-round recreational opportunities.

The University's enrollment of just over 17,000 undergraduate and graduate students makes it a defining presence in Clemson, South Carolina, a town of about 12,000. Most students live on campus in one of the twenty-one residence halls and four apartment complexes, which are within a 10-minute walk to class or downtown.

Majors and Degrees

Clemson offers more than seventy undergraduate and approximately 100 graduate degree programs through five academic colleges: Agriculture, Forestry, and Life Sciences; Architecture, Arts, and Humanities; Business and Behavioral Science; Engineering and Science; and Health, Education, and Human Development. Students can earn Bachelor of Arts, Bachelor of Science, or preprofessional degrees in accounting; agricultural and applied economics; agricultural education; agricultural mechanization and business; animal and veterinary sciences; wildlife and fisheries biology; architecture; biochemistry; biological sciences; biosystems engineering; ceramic and materials engineering; chemical engineering; chemistry; civil engineering; communication studies; computer engineering; computer information systems; computer science; construction science and management; early childhood education; economics; electrical engineering; elementary education; English; environmental and natural resources; financial management; fine arts; food science; forest resource management; genetics; geology; graphic communications; health science; history; horticulture; industrial engineering; industrial management; landscape architecture; language and international health; language and international trade; management; marketing; mathematical sciences; mathematics teaching; mechanical engineering; microbiology; modern languages; nursing; packaging science; parks, recreation, and tourism management; philosophy; physics; political science; polymer and textile chemistry; preprofessional health studies; pre–rehabilitation sciences; pre–veterinary medicine; production studies in performing arts; psychology; science teaching; secondary education; sociology; special education; technology and human resource development; textile management; and turfgrass.

Academic Programs

Clemson's academic year is divided into two semesters. The fall semester begins in mid-August, the spring semester in early January. Two summer sessions and one Maymester are also available. Students average 16 credit hours per semester. Clemson requires all students to complete some general education classes specified by the University before graduation. The number of completed credit hours required for graduation varies, depending on the major.

Calhoun Honors College is a University-wide program with roughly 1,000 students, including approximately 260 freshmen each year. Calhoun Scholars have two distinctly different tracks within the Honors College, and they may also choose to pursue departmental honors within their specific academic discipline. In addition, EUREKA! (Experiences in Undergraduate Research, Exploration, and Knowledge Advancement) is a unique and exciting program that enables honors students to pursue research and scholarly activities with faculty members across all disciplines. The advantages of membership include priority registration, extended library loan privileges, honors research grants, and honors housing.

The National Scholars Program is a highly selective program for exceptional students who strive to meet their highest intellectual potential. One of its goals is to develop the interests and talents students need to compete for Rhodes, Marshall, and Truman scholarships; Fulbright Grants; National Science Foundation Graduate Fellowships; and other prestigious international fellowships.

Clemson's nationally recognized Programs for Educational Enrichment and Retention (PEER) is committed to improving academic performance of underrepresented students in engineering and science. Today, thanks in large part to PEER, the six-year graduation rate for African American first-time freshmen is above the national average.

The Women in Science and Engineering (WISE) program focuses on recruiting women into science and engineering and helping them succeed in college and their careers. WISE offers support activities such as mentoring programs, career planning, and study groups.

Tutoring, supplemental instruction, academic skills workshops, and academic counseling are also available free to all Clemson students through the Academic Support Center.

Off-Campus Programs

Clemson's study-abroad and off-campus programs give students the opportunity to study almost anywhere in the world. The International Student Exchange Program and the Clemson Exchange Program allow students to enroll for a summer, semester or full academic year at one of over 100 universities throughout the world. In addition, many departments sponsor their own programs, including architecture in Italy and engineering in Germany.

Clemson undergraduates have worked at more than 360 companies through Cooperative Education. Participating students alternate periods of academic study with periods of related work in a business, industry, agency, or organization.

Academic Facilities

The Clemson campus is home to a blend of historic buildings and advanced research facilities surrounded by stately trees and lush greenery.

The Libraries and the Division of Computing and Information Technology are committed to providing students and faculty members with the latest ways to access information. Clemson's main library, the Robert M. Cooper Library, is located at the center of campus and provides students with a variety of services and up-to-date collections. The University's wireless networking capability lets students communicate with professors and classmates, read online course materials, check e-mail, and conduct research, all from their own laptops. Students are required to complete an electronic portfolio prior to graduation, allowing them the opportunity to present themselves through a creative venue to prospective employers and graduate schools.

The campus offers an array of facilities and programs designed to enhance a student's entire educational experience. These include the Pearce Center for Professional Communication, Class of 1941 Studio for Student Communication, Rutland Center for Ethics, and Academic Support Center.

Clemson real estate holdings also include more than 32,000 acres of forestry and agricultural lands throughout the state, the majority of which are dedicated to the University's research and service missions.

Costs

For the 2007–08 academic year, undergraduate tuition and fees were $10,370 for South Carolina residents and $22,300 for out-of-state residents. Room and board costs were approximately $6170, and books and supplies were about $925. The one-time laptop computer cost was about $1500.

Financial Aid

Financial aid is usually awarded on the basis of need to supplement the amount students and their parents can contribute to college expenses. The University also awards some scholarships based entirely on academic merit. Clemson offers financial aid in the form of grants, scholarships, loans, and part-time employment.

Entering freshmen are evaluated on a competitive basis for scholarships using the admission application. There is no separate scholarship application. For Academic Recruiting Scholarships, students are ranked based on test scores, high school rank-in-class, and other academic factors. In past years, students offered one of these merit scholarships normally had a minimum SAT score of 1350 (combined score from critical reading and mathematics sections), or an ACT of at least 30, and were ranked no lower than the top 10 percent of their senior class. Stipends for in-state residents range from $500 per year to the full cost of attendance. Merit scholarships for out-of-state students range from $2500 per year to the full cost of attendance. Academic Recruiting Scholarships are available only to entering freshmen and are renewable for three additional years provided that the minimum standards are maintained. The application for admission is the first step for prospective freshmen to be considered for merit awards.

General University Scholarships are awarded to both entering freshmen and upperclassmen. To be considered for scholarships, upperclassmen must have a minimum cumulative GPR of at least 2.5. These scholarships may have special criteria set up by the donor, such as a certain residency, major, or career interest. Because of the restrictions on many of these scholarships, it is impossible to predict the recipients. However, the scholarship selection process is very competitive. Stipends range from $250 to $7500.

Faculty

Clemson has over 1,000 full-time faculty members, of whom 86 percent hold a Ph.D. or terminal degree in their fields. In addition, the University has over 150 part-time faculty members. Faculty honors include the Fulbright Scholarship, Guggenheim Fellowship, National Science Foundation CAREER Award, National Institutes of Health Senior Scientist Award, and American Academy of Arts and Sciences membership. The average class size is 29, and the student-to-faculty ratio is 15:1.

Admission Requirements

Each year, the University receives over 14,000 applications for a fall freshman class of 2,800. Transfer applications are received from about 1,500 students, of whom Clemson enrolls 800. Undergraduate applications are available online at http://www.clemson.edu/admission, and are preferred over applications submitted on paper. Nonetheless, paper applications are available for printout at the above Web address.

For freshman applicants, the following factors are considered: class standing, standardized test scores (SAT or ACT), high school curriculum, grades, and choice of major. All entering freshmen must have completed 4 credits of English, 3 credits of mathematics, 3 credits of laboratory science, 3 credits of a foreign language (in the same language), 3 credits of social sciences, 2 credits in other areas, and 1 credit of physical education.

To be considered for transfer admission, candidates must have completed a full year of college study (30 semester hours or 45 quarter hours of transferable work), earned a cumulative grade point average of at least 2.5 on a 4.0 scale (3.0 preferred), and completed all freshman-level courses in English, science, and mathematics for their intended major at Clemson.

Application and Information

Application deadlines for freshman admissions are December 1 (priority date for fall enrollment), May 1 (fall semester deadline), and December 15 (for the spring semester). For transfer admissions, the application deadlines are July 1 (for the fall semester) and December 15 (for the spring semester).

Office of Admissions
Clemson University
105 Sikes Hall, Box 345124
Clemson, South Carolina 29634-5124

Phone: 864-656-2287
Fax: 864-656-2464
E-mail: cuadmissions@clemson.edu
Web site: http://www.clemson.edu

LIMESTONE COLLEGE

GAFFNEY, SOUTH CAROLINA

The College

Founded in 1845, Limestone is a fully accredited, private, coeducational liberal arts college. The College maintains a small student body and a well-qualified faculty in order to create an atmosphere in which each student develops intellectually, physically, and socially. The College endeavors to help students prepare for a satisfying, useful life through effective communication skills, responsible decision-making abilities, meaningful leisure-time activities, and lifelong aspirations. In addition to its programs on campus, Limestone offers several of its academic majors in an accelerated format called The Block Program at several locations throughout South Carolina. These programs are intended primarily for working adults. The College also has an impressive Virtual Campus Program on the Internet with many majors offered. The two programs were combined in 2005 to be the Extended Campus.

Extracurricular activities play a vital part in the development of all students at Limestone College. Among these activities are intercollegiate athletics in men's baseball, basketball, cross-country, golf, lacrosse, soccer, swimming, tennis, track and field, and wrestling and in women's basketball, cross-country, golf, lacrosse, soccer, softball, swimming, tennis, track and field, and volleyball. Students who are interested in music have the opportunity to participate in several instrumental and choral ensembles. A theater program is also available.

The 115-acre Limestone campus is well laid out for pleasant college living. The classrooms, library, laboratories, auditorium, bookstore, post office, and administrative offices are housed in buildings that border the central and circular drives, making each easily accessible to the others. The back campus has a plaza of four dormitories, and a dining hall is located nearby. The Timken LYFE Center is a physical education complex that houses the gymnasium, an AAU-size swimming pool, and athletic training facilities. The Limestone Physical Education Center, completed in 2005, offers three classrooms, nine offices, locker rooms, athletic training and education facilities, a state-of-the-art fitness center, and a wrestling practice facility. The College also has eight lighted tennis courts, a baseball field, a softball field, a soccer/lacrosse field, and several practice fields.

Location

Gaffney, a small city with a population of 25,000, provides an ideal setting for a college campus. Whereas the distractions associated with a large city are absent from daily life, the cultural programs and services offered in Charlotte, North Carolina, and Spartanburg and Greenville, South Carolina, are all within a 50-mile radius of the campus. All are connected to Gaffney by Interstate 85.

The climate is free from extreme heat or cold. The well-known resort areas of the Blue Ridge Mountains, the Great Smoky Mountains, and the beaches of the Atlantic Coast are accessible for weekend visits. In the immediate area, facilities are available for all water sports, horseback riding, golf, tennis, and skiing.

Majors and Degrees

Limestone College offers the Bachelor of Arts, Bachelor of Science, and Bachelor of Social Work degrees with majors in art (concentrations in studio art and graphic design), athletic training, biology, business administration (concentrations in accounting, computer science, e-business, economics, general business, management, and marketing), chemistry, computer science (concentrations in Internet management, management information systems, and programming), criminal justice, English, history, liberal studies, mathematics, music, physical education (concentrations in athletic training and strength/conditioning), prelaw, psychology, social work, sports management, and theater. Majors approved for South Carolina teacher certification are elementary education, English education, mathematics education, music education, physical education, and secondary education.

The Associate of Arts degree is offered with majors in business administration (concentrations in general business), computer science (majors in Internet management, management information systems, and programming), and liberal studies.

Academic Programs

The course of study leading to the B.A., B.S., B.S.W., or A.A. degree consists of four elements: requirements in communication and quantitative skills; a general liberal arts program, involving five different subject groups; courses in the major; and appropriate electives. The baccalaureate degree programs require the completion of a minimum of 123 semester hours. The associate degree programs require the completion of a minimum of 62 semester hours.

Advanced placement and credit are given for scores of 3 or higher on the Advanced Placement examinations of the College Board.

An Honors Program involving special courses, seminars, and lectures is available for exceptional students. Admission to this program is contingent upon outstanding high school grades and scores on the SAT of the College Board, the completion of a special application, and an interview. Almost 10 percent of all Limestone students are enrolled in this rigorous academic program.

A Program for Alternative Learning Styles (PALS) is available for qualified students with certified learning disabilities who might not otherwise succeed at the college level.

Academic Facilities

Limestone has outstanding computer facilities, including free e-mail accounts for all main campus students, residence hall high-speed Internet connections, and several well-equipped, state-of-the-art computer labs. There are also well-equipped science labs. The modern A. J. Eastwood Library houses approximately 112,976 volumes and is fully computerized, including student Internet access. Fullerton Auditorium, with a seating capacity of 975, serves for drama and musical productions and is one of the finest such facilities in the state of South Carolina.

Costs

The direct cost for a student at Limestone College for the 2008–09 school year is $23,700; the tuition is $17,300, and room and board costs are $6400. In addition, the cost of books, supplies, laundry, travel, and personal expenses is estimated at $4000 per year.

Financial Aid

Limestone College, one of the least costly private colleges in South Carolina, endeavors to meet the financial need of any qualified student through scholarships, grants, loans, work-study opportunities, or a combination of these. Limestone offers merit scholarships to students with outstanding academic, leadership, or athletic abilities as well as to those who have exceptional talents in such areas as art, music, and theater.

More than 90 percent of Limestone College day students receive some type of financial aid. Because institutional financial aid is limited, students are urged to submit their applications for admission and financial aid as early as possible.

Faculty

Personal attention to students and high-quality instruction characterize the faculty at Limestone College. Three quarters of the faculty members hold Ph.D.'s or other terminal degrees in their fields. The student-faculty ratio is 12:1. Students and instructors work closely together in both learning and counseling situations. Each student has an assigned faculty adviser for assistance in course selection and for personal counseling.

Student Government

The Student Government Association exemplifies the College's democratic tradition and the principles of honor and individual responsibility. It is every student's privilege to participate in the government of the learning community of which he or she is a member. The more highly organized activities, including student organizations and social events, are coordinated through the Student Government Association. The College also has a literary magazine and a yearbook.

Admission Requirements

Limestone College does not discriminate on the basis of race, color, creed, national origin, financial need, or physical handicap. Each candidate for admission is evaluated as an individual. The College recommends that applicants have the following high school preparation: English, 4 units; social science, 3 units; mathematics, 3 units; and science, 2 units.

Applicants must submit an official transcript of the secondary school record, scores on the SAT, and a nonrefundable $25 application fee. The application fee is waived if the student applies online at the College's Web site. Transfer applications are encouraged.

Application and Information

Completed application forms for admission and for financial aid should be sent to the Office of Admissions at Limestone College. It is recommended that applications be submitted by May 1. Any admission applications received after that date are considered on a space-available basis. The College practices a rolling admissions policy. As soon as the application, high school transcript, and test scores have been received, the applicant is notified of his or her status. Upon acceptance, a student is required to submit a $100 tuition deposit.

Vice President of Enrollment Services
Limestone College
1115 College Drive
Gaffney, South Carolina 29340-3799
Phone: 864-488-4554
Fax: 864-488-8206
E-mail: admiss@limestone.edu
Web site: http://www.limestone.edu

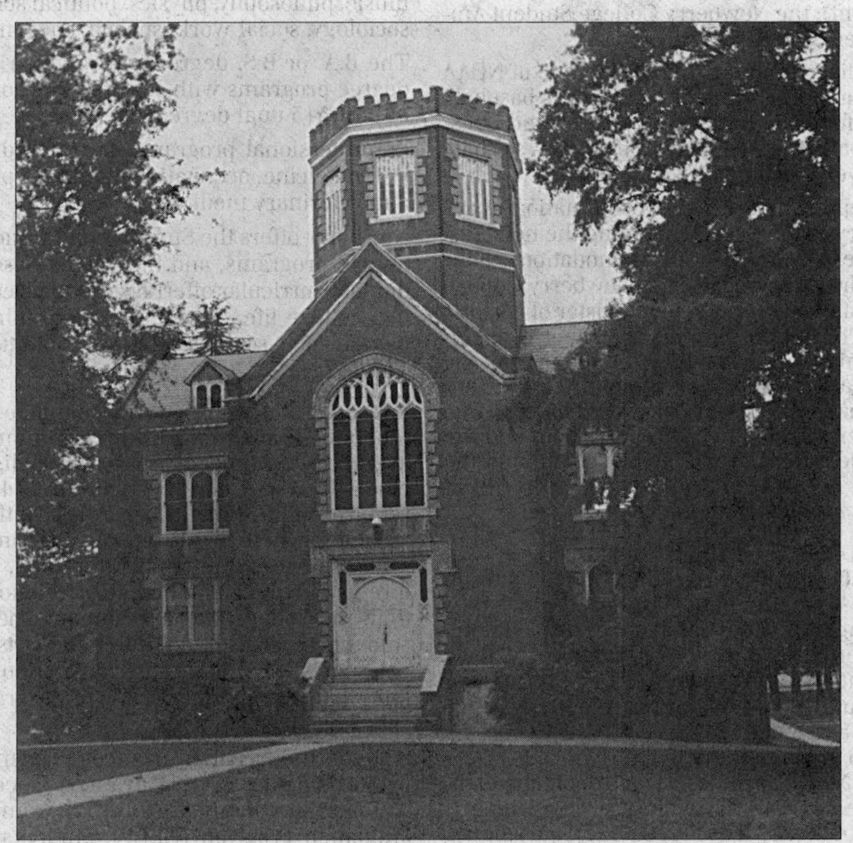

The Winnie Davis Hall of History, named in honor of the daughter of Jefferson Davis, was completed about 1904 and is listed on the National Register of Historic Places.

NEWBERRY COLLEGE

NEWBERRY, SOUTH CAROLINA

The College

A private undergraduate liberal arts institution established in 1856, Newberry College is affiliated with the Evangelical Lutheran Church in America. With a mission focused on educating the whole person, Newberry epitomizes the small-college amenities of personal attention, easy rapport between students and faculty members, and a supportive environment for academic, personal, and social development.

Newberry College's student body is made up of about 840 men and women from twenty-eight states and twelve foreign countries. About 40 percent are women. Seventy percent of the students live in College residence halls; others live off campus or commute from home.

Students participate in a variety of College-sponsored activities, including five national fraternities and four national sororities; eight music-related organizations; three campus publications; musical theater and drama productions; intramural sports; ethnic, political, and religious organizations; honor, service, and leadership societies; the Newberry College Student Government Association (student government); the Newberry College Student Ambassadors; and special interest groups.

The Newberry College Indians maintain a full schedule of NCAA Division II intercollegiate athletic competition in men's baseball, basketball, cross-country, football, golf, soccer, tennis, and wrestling and women's basketball, cross-country, golf, soccer, softball, tennis, and volleyball as well as competitive cheering.

The College's buildings represent a pleasant combination of antebellum and contemporary architecture, including the new East Residence Hall with modern suite-style accommodations. Four buildings around the quadrangle make up the Newberry College Historic District and are listed on the National Register of Historic Places. Wiles Chapel, which contains the College Theatre, exemplifies modern Gothic architecture with some influence from the Prairie school. The physical education and athletic complex, including the 1,600-seat Eleazer Arena, was completed in 1982. The O. L. Casey Student Center adjoins the swimming pool and the Physical Education Complex, the Casey Meeting Room, and the Presidential Dining Room. The Student Center houses the Physical Education Faculty and Athletic Staff offices.

Location

Listed as one of the best 100 small towns in the United States in which to live and the safest city in South Carolina, Newberry is situated in the gently rolling hills of the South Carolina Piedmont, with average winter temperatures ranging from highs of 56 to 63 degrees. Newberry is home to approximately 10,000 permanent residents. The city was founded in 1794 and is replete with historically significant homes and buildings. It is easily accessible via three exits on Interstate 26 and lies at the juncture of U.S. 76 and South Carolina 34 and 121. Newberry's closest metropolitan neighbor is Columbia, the state capital and its largest city, which is approximately 40 miles southeast. The Greenville/Spartanburg metropolitan area is 1 hour northwest of Newberry. Other points of interest within easy driving distance are Myrtle Beach and the Grand Strand (3 hours); Charleston (2½ hours); Hilton Head (3½ hours); Charlotte, North Carolina (1½ hours); the Great Smoky Mountains (2 hours); and Atlanta, Georgia (3½ hours).

Majors and Degrees

The Bachelor of Arts (B.A.) degree is offered with a major in one of the following fields: art (graphic design, studio art), church leadership (Christian education, church administration, music ministry, youth ministry), communications (electronic media, journalism, public relations), English, history, music (applied music: instrument, organ, piano, or voice; church music; music theory), political science, psychology, religion and philosophy, sociology, and theater (acting, directing, technical production).

The Bachelor of Music degree is awarded in performance. The Bachelor of Music Education degree is offered in choral or in instrumental music education.

The Bachelor of Science (B.S.) degree is available with a major in biology, business administration, chemistry, chemistry (forensic science concentration), early childhood education, elementary education, mathematics, and physical education (leisure services, sport management, and teacher certification). In partnership with Lexington Medical Center, a nursing program is available leading to the B.S.N. degree.

Minors are offered in art, biology, business administration, chemistry, church leadership, church music, coaching, communications, computer science, creative writing, criminal justice, English, environmental science, history, jazz studies, mathematics, music, philosophy, physics, political science, psychology, religion, sociology, social work, speech, sport management, and theater.

The B.A. or B.S. degree is also given through cooperative dual-degree programs with select institutions, e.g., Charleston School of Law 3+3 dual degree.

Preprofessional programs are offered in seven fields: dentistry, law, medicine, occupational therapy, pharmacy, physical therapy, and veterinary medicine.

Newberry offers the Summerland Honors Program, departmental honors programs, and the Values Based Learning Program. Additional curricular offerings (nondegree) are available in accounting, college life, economics, geography, Greek studies, humanities, science, social science, and military science.

Academic Programs

A student must satisfactorily complete a minimum of 126 semester hours of course work with a minimum cumulative grade point average of 2.0 (on a 4.0 scale) to be eligible for a Newberry bachelor's degree. A core curriculum of 43 to 50 semester hours is required of all students regardless of their declared major(s) and includes course work in the following disciplines: history and social sciences, humanities/fine arts, natural sciences, English, foreign language, mathematics, religion, speech, physical education, and College Life, a freshman experience course. In addition, students must also fulfill three fine arts and lecture requirements per semester. The Summerland Honors Community program, a four-year interdisciplinary core program, is offered to academically advanced students.

Students may receive Advanced Placement (AP) and college credit by participating in the Advanced Placement Program, the International Baccalaureate (I.B.) Program, or the College-Level Examination Program (CLEP). Students should consult the latest edition of the Newberry College catalog or contact the Office of Admissions for exact requirements.

The College operates on the two-semester calendar, consisting of a fall semester and a spring semester, each lasting sixteen weeks. The fall semester begins in late August and ends in mid-December; the spring semester begins in early January and ends in early May, with a one-week spring break in March. The College's summer session consists of two 5-week terms. During the fall and spring semesters, the normal class load ranges from 15 to 19 hours; for the summer session, two courses per term is normal.

Off-Campus Programs

Newberry's international studies program for sophomores and juniors gives qualified students the opportunity to study for a summer, a semester, or a full academic year in selected international colleges and universities as part of Newberry's regular academic program. Although this program is open to students in all majors, some proficiency in the language spoken in the host country is required.

Academic Facilities

Langford Communications Center contains state-of-the-art equipment and resources for the student of radio and television communications. As an Internet node with its own World Wide Web site, the College can extend free in-room Ethernet access for students using the Internet. Another modern building is dedicated to the study of music. Wessels Library contains nearly 100,000 books, sound and video recordings, CD-ROMs, and online electronic resources. Complete facilities for the use of audiovisual materials are provided. The library also subscribes to more than 450 magazines, newspapers, and scholarly journals. The College Archives are also displayed in the library. In addition to Wessels, students may use a smaller library that is housed in the Alumni Music Center's Music Department.

Costs

In 2007–08, tuition and fees are $19,900 and room and board is $6930. The total cost for a residential student electing a double-occupancy room is $27,821. The College estimates annual personal expenses (including books, supplies, automobile registration, and other costs) to be $4430. Once they are accepted for admission, students are requested to submit a $175 deposit, which is refundable through May 1 for fall semester admission and December 1 for spring semester admission.

Financial Aid

More than 95 percent of students at Newberry receive some form of financial assistance. Counselors are available to work with students and families to design financial aid packages that make a Newberry education affordable. Assistance is available in the form of scholarships, grants, loans, and campus employment based on need or merit. Newberry College awards many types of scholarships annually, including the prestigious Trustee, Founders, Presidential, Newberry Scholar, and Leader Scholarship awards. Talent-based awards in areas such as music and athletics are also available for men and women. Residents of South Carolina may qualify for a South Carolina Tuition Grant. Communing members of a Lutheran church may receive a scholarship from the Lutheran Scholarship Program. To apply for student aid, students should complete the Free Application for Federal Student Aid (FAFSA), which is available online at http://www.fafsa.ed.gov.

Faculty

The student-faculty ratio is 13:1. Classes are small, and the easy interchange of ideas is a constant stimulus to both student and teacher. Seventy-four percent of the full-time faculty members have earned doctorates or terminal degrees. No classes are taught by graduate students.

Student Government

The Newberry College Student Government Association (NCSGA) is composed of students elected to the Newberry Student Senate. Through its committee assignments, it assists in the formulation and implementation of College policies. The NCSGA officers are selected through campuswide elections, and senators and other representatives are elected by the various campus constituencies.

Admission Requirements

In determining the admission status of all applicants to Newberry College, the following factors are taken into consideration: grade point average on academic courses, SAT or ACT scores, high school rank, type of course work pursued, cocurricular activities, and other relevant factors such as part-time employment, community service, and volunteerism. Students whose academic records fall slightly below acceptable standards may be considered for conditional admission into the Foundations Program upon approval of the Director of Admissions.

Admissions decisions are made within two days of receiving academic transcripts and supporting documentation. Acceptance of the applicant is always contingent upon successful completion of course work in progress. Following high school graduation, an additional official final transcript bearing the date of graduation is required.

Application and Information

The College operates on a rolling admission basis, notifying most applicants of their status within three weeks after the application is complete. The application for admission (paper), along with a $30 nonrefundable fee ($25 for the online application; the fee is waived when submitted during a campus visit), should be accompanied by official high school and/or college transcripts, SAT and/or ACT scores, letters of recommendation, and other supporting materials that may be required by the Director of Admissions.

Campus visits can be scheduled online via the admissions section of the Newberry College Web site or by calling the Office of Admissions. Although walk-in visitors are welcome, a visitor's special needs and desires can best be met if he or she makes an appointment. Selected Saturday morning visits are available. Dates are listed at the admissions section of the Newberry College Web site (students should call to verify and select dates). In addition, the Office of Admissions hosts open-house functions each year for the benefit of prospective students and parents.

Students are encouraged to apply for admission online and may do so at the College's Web site.

For additional information, students should contact:

Office of Admissions and Financial Aid
Newberry College
2100 College Street
Newberry, South Carolina 29108
Phone: 803-321-5127
800-845-4955 Ext. 5127 (toll-free in the U.S.)
E-mail: admissions@newberry.edu
Web site: http://www.newberry.edu

Newberry College's Holland Hall (Admissions and Financial Aid Office).

COLLEGE DATA CENTER • SOUTH CAROLINA

PRESBYTERIAN COLLEGE

CLINTON, SOUTH CAROLINA

The College

Founded in 1880, Presbyterian College (PC) is a fully accredited Carnegie I, private four-year college of liberal arts and sciences. The College is widely known for its excellent academic program and congenial, friendly atmosphere. Thirty states and ten countries are represented in the student body of 1,188 men and women. PC is associated with the Presbyterian Church USA, and approximately 30 percent of the students are members of the Presbyterian Church. The College welcomes students of all faiths.

Extracurricular activities are an extensive and vital part of the development of all students. There are intercollegiate athletic teams competing in NCAA Division I (FCS) for men in baseball, basketball, cheerleading, cross-country, football, golf, lacrosse, soccer, and tennis and for women in basketball, cheerleading, cross-country, golf, lacrosse, soccer, softball, tennis, and volleyball. The College also offers team handball and soccer as club sports for men and women. An extensive intramural program provides exercise and entertainment in a variety of sports for both men and women. The Student Union Board provides a series of concerts, comedians, films, and special events. Students may also participate in a variety of fine arts, Greek, honorary, political, preprofessional, and religious organizations. More than 60 percent of PC students volunteer for community service. The College sponsors thirty-eight service projects, including tutoring, adult literacy, Big Brother/Big Sister, Habitat for Humanity, and Special Olympics.

The 240-acre campus has thirty major buildings of classical Jeffersonian architecture. These buildings are grouped around three plazas. Facilities include a 1,200-seat auditorium, a 342-seat recital hall, a science center with a new state-of-the-art $12-million biology addition, a library, an art gallery, a drama theater, eleven residence halls (including a newly constructed international house, an apartment complex, and a town-house development), six major classroom buildings, a dining hall, a health center, a student center, a gymnasium, a six-house fraternity court, and a 31-acre intramural park.

Students may keep automobiles on campus. Ninety-five percent of students live in a College residence hall. All single students are required to live on campus. Housing within the community is available for married students and some seniors. All residence halls are wired for Internet access, and some areas are wireless.

Location

Clinton, with a population of 10,000, is a college town located in the heart of the South Carolina Piedmont. Interstates 26 and 385 meet outside of Clinton and provide easy access from the metropolitan areas of Greenville, Spartanburg, and Columbia. It is a short drive from Clinton to the ski slopes of western North Carolina, the coast of South Carolina, and professional athletic events in Charlotte, North Carolina.

Majors and Degrees

Presbyterian College offers the Bachelor of Arts and the Bachelor of Science degrees, with majors in art, biology, business/accounting, business/management, chemistry, computer science, early childhood education, economics, English, fine arts (concentrations in art, drama/speech, and music), French, German, history, mathematics, medical physics, middle school education, modern foreign languages, music, music education, philosophy, physics, political science, psychology, religion, religion–Christian education, sacred music, social science, sociology, Spanish, special education, and theater arts.

Students may minor in African American studies, arts administration, athletic coaching, Chinese studies, Christian youth work, international studies, journalism, Latin American studies, media studies, physical education, prelaw studies, secondary education teacher certification, Southern studies, women's studies, and each of the major areas.

Preprofessional programs are offered in allied health sciences, Army ROTC, dentistry, law, medicine, ministry, pharmacy, physician's assistant studies, and veterinary medicine. The College offers dual-degree programs in engineering with Auburn, Clemson, and Vanderbilt Universities. A dual-degree program in forestry and environmental science is available with Duke University.

Academic Programs

All Presbyterian College students gain a comprehension of the liberal arts through a general education in English, fine arts, history, mathematics, modern foreign language, physical education, religion, science, and social science. To graduate, students must complete the required general education courses, fulfill the requirements of a major, attend forty cultural enrichment events, and pass 122 semester hours with a minimum cumulative average of 2.0. Students are also required to have an internship or intercultural experience, as well as a Capstone Research Experience.

The College operates on a semester system. The fall semester extends from late August to mid-December, and the spring semester runs from mid-January through early May. Classes meet Monday through Friday. An optional May fleximester enables students to travel and study with other PC students and staff members. Two 5-week summer sessions are also offered.

Directed study, honors seminars, honors research, summer research, internships, and independent research are offered through academic departments.

Students may earn credit by submitting scores from the College Board's Advanced Placement subject examinations. CLEP credit is granted for successful scores on the subject exams only. Credit is awarded to students in an International Baccalaureate program who have earned grades of 5 or better on higher-level subject tests.

An Army ROTC program is available with generous scholarship opportunities.

Off-Campus Programs

Presbyterian College offers a variety of programs for students who are interested in spending a semester, summer, or academic year studying abroad. The College is associated with fifty programs in Australia, Austria, China, England, Finland, France, Honduras, Ireland, Italy, Japan, Korea, Mexico, the Netherlands, New Zealand, Scotland, Spain, and Wales. Students may also study for a semester in Washington, D.C. All credits that are earned through these programs count toward graduation from Presbyterian College. Other study-abroad programs may be developed by the student and his or her adviser to ensure credit toward graduation.

Special courses are available for students during PC's optional May fleximester. These for-credit courses provide students with off-campus educational experiences in Africa and Australia and such areas as the Caribbean, Europe, the Galapagos Islands, and southwestern United States.

Students have the opportunity to participate in a summer program at Oxford University's Corpus Christi College in England. This three-week course includes study of two subjects in addition to travel and field trips in England.

Presbyterian College is affiliated with the Gulf Coast Research Laboratory and Duke University's marine research center. Students may enroll in marine science courses during the academic year or summer.

Academic Facilities

The new $12-million biology wing, which opened in 2008, supports the College's growing premed program and increases research opportunities. Harrington-Peachtree Hall, PC's mathematics and social science building, contains psychology labs, classrooms with state-of-the-art audiovisual technology, and a computer lab. The Harper Center houses an art gallery and flexible theater. Other academic facilities include Richardson Science Hall, Neville Hall for the humanities, and Jacobs Hall for economics and military science. Thomason Library contains 165,000 volumes, provides extensive reference sources, and features a media learning center. Computer facilities are available in all major academic buildings, with more than 100 computer terminals available for students. Through the College, all students may have free access to the Internet and a Web-based e-mail system. Wireless Internet is available as well.

Costs

For the 2007–08 school year, the cost of tuition was $24,030. Fees were $2290. Room was $3720, and board was $3890 with the seventeen-meal plan. The cost of books, supplies, travel, and personal expenses is estimated at an additional $2500 per year.

Financial Aid

Presbyterian College endeavors to meet the financial need of all accepted students through scholarships, grants, loans, work-study, or a combination of these. The College may award academic, athletic, leadership, and music grants-in-aid to students with superior talent or achievement. Approximately 90 percent of the students receive some financial assistance each year. The Free Application for Federal Student Aid (FAFSA) and an institutional form are required of all financial aid applicants. For priority consideration, all financial aid information should be submitted by March 1 of a student's senior year. For further information, students should contact the Financial Aid Office at the College.

Faculty

Presbyterian College has a full-time faculty of 84 members. Ninety-five percent of the faculty members hold doctoral or terminal degrees in their field. The student-faculty ratio is 13:1. Students and instructors work closely together in both learning and counseling situations. All faculty members teach lower-division and freshman classes as well as upper-division courses. No graduate students serve as instructors at PC. Each student has an assigned faculty adviser for assistance in course selection and personal counseling.

Student Government

All Presbyterian College students are encouraged to fully participate in campus government. The Student Senate is composed of an executive council, the class representatives, and the organizational representatives. The duly elected Student Senate regulates the affairs of the student body, oversees the Student Union Board and student publications, and approves Honor Council membership.

The Honor Council enforces the College's Honor Code. All students pledge to enforce the honor system and to not lie, steal, cheat, or plagiarize. The honor system fosters a great deal of trust among students and faculty members. Professors may give unsupervised exams; students may leave possessions unattended. Representatives from the student body serve on administrative, faculty, and trustee committees.

Admission Requirements

Presbyterian College normally requires for entrance the completion of a four-year high school course of study, including 4 units of English, 3 units of math, and 2 or more units each of foreign language, history, laboratory science, and social science. It is strongly suggested that students take as many honors, AP, and IB courses as available.

Admission is very selective. Once a student applies, the admissions committee carefully reviews the application, essay, high school transcript, recommendation from a high school official, and scores from the SAT or the ACT. The College admits students based on the applicant's academic and personal qualifications. An interview is not required, but interested students are encouraged to visit the campus. Presbyterian College strives to recruit a diverse student body. The College does not discriminate against applicants or students on the basis of handicap, national origin, race, religion, or sex.

Transfer students must submit a transfer application, an essay, college and high school transcripts, board scores, and clearance forms. To be considered for admission, a transfer student must have a minimum overall C average in college work.

Application and Information

The paper application fee is $40, and the online application fee is $25; both are nonrefundable. Application deadlines are as follows: Early Decision (binding) candidates must apply by November 1, are notified by November 15, and must commit to PC by January 15 by submitting a nonrefundable $400 deposit; Early Action (nonbinding) candidates must apply by November 15, are notified by December 15, and must submit a nonrefundable $400 deposit by May 1; Regular Decision deadline is February 1 and notification on March 15, with commitment by May 1 by submitting the $400 nonrefundable deposit. There are ten spaces held for Late Decision applicants who apply by June 1.

Students may apply electronically at the College's Web site or through the Common Application Web site at https://www.commonapp.org.

For further information, students should contact:

Presbyterian College
503 South Broad Street
Clinton, South Carolina 29325
Phone: 864-833-8230
800-960-7583 (toll-free)
Fax: 864-833-8195
E-mail: admissions@presby.edu
Web site: http://www.presby.edu

The fountain plaza behind Neville Hall at dusk.

SOUTH UNIVERSITY

COLUMBIA, SOUTH CAROLINA

SouthUniversity℠

The University

Established in 1899, South University is a private academic institution dedicated to providing educational opportunities for the intellectual, social, and professional development of a diverse student population. The Columbia, South Carolina, campus offers focused and balanced curricula at the associate and bachelor's degree levels in the areas of business, graphic design, health sciences, information technology, and legal studies. South University in Columbia also offers a Master of Arts in professional counseling, a Master of Business Administration, and a Master of Business Administration in health-care administration.

In addition, the Columbia campus offers students flexible scheduling with the choice of pursuing many of its courses on campus, online, or a combination of both through South University's unique Plus+ program. Combining campus and online classes provides students with maximum flexibility, allowing them to organize their college education around their work and/or family commitments.

The Columbia campus has a rich heritage in the Midlands area of South Carolina. Originally established in 1935, the institution was previously known as Columbia Junior College. In recent years, the campus has continued to grow through the addition of several new bachelor's and master's degree programs. Enrollment has increased steadily, and graduates have been recruited by law firms, businesses, and medical institutions.

Along with classrooms and offices, the campus includes a bookstore, student lounge, and career services center. Most students live within driving distance of the campus, but the Admissions Office does maintain information on various housing options should students relocate to the Columbia area for their education.

South University has a diverse student body enrolled in day, evening, and weekend classes. A sizeable portion of students have experience in the workforce and are pursing an education that will prepare them to expand on their current career or take them in a new professional direction.

South University is accredited by the Commission on Colleges of the Southern Association of Colleges and Schools (SACS, 1866 Southern Lane, Decatur, Georgia 30033-4097; 404-679-4501) to award associate, bachelor's, master's, and doctoral degrees. South University in Columbia is licensed by the South Carolina Commission on Higher Education (1333 Main Street, Suite 200, Columbia, South Carolina 29201; 803-737-2260) to award associate, bachelor's, and master's degrees and certificates. The Columbia campus is also chartered by the state of South Carolina and approved by the South Carolina Commission on Higher Education (Veterans' Education Section) for the training of veterans and other eligible persons.

Certain programs offered at South University in Columbia have earned programmatic accreditation. The Associate of Science in medical assisting program is accredited by the Commission on Accreditation of Allied Health Education Programs (CAAHEP, 1361 Park Street, Clearwater, Florida 33756; 727-210-2350) on recommendation of the Committee on Accreditation for Medical Assisting Education. The Bachelor of Science in legal studies and Associate of Science in paralegal studies are both approved by the American Bar Association (321 North Clark Street, Chicago, Illinois 60610; 312-988-5617).

Location

Just minutes from downtown, the new campus is conveniently located in the Carolina Research Park off I-77 at Farrow Road and Park Lane.

The campus surroundings are highlighted by a natural wooded landscape and vast green space featuring a tranquil campus courtyard. Convenient to malls, shopping, and the growing northeast side of Columbia, the new campus location provides easier access to students from throughout the greater Columbia area.

Majors and Degrees

South University in Columbia awards the following two-year degrees: Associate of Science in business administration, Associate of Science in graphic design, Associate of Science in information technology, Associate of Science in medical assisting, and Associate of Science in paralegal studies.

The following four-year bachelor's degrees are awarded: Bachelor of Business Administration, Bachelor of Science in criminal justice, Bachelor of Science in graphic design, Bachelor of Science in health-care management, Bachelor of Science in information technology, Bachelor of Science in legal studies, Bachelor of Science in Nursing (RN to B.S.N. degree completion), and Bachelor of Arts in psychology.

Academic Programs

South University in Columbia offers degree programs that are designed to meet the needs and objectives of students. Some curricula combine didactic and practical educational experiences that provide students with the academic background needed to pursue the professions of their choice. In addition, faculty members strive to instill the value not only of education and professionalism but also of contribution and commitment to the advancement of community.

Each University quarter comprises twelve weeks. Associate degree programs require a minimum of eight quarters to complete, and bachelor's degree programs require a minimum of twelve quarters to complete. Programs are offered on a year-round basis, providing students with the ability to work uninterrupted toward their degrees.

Academic Facilities

South University's new multimillion-dollar Columbia campus provides ample classroom and student service areas and features several smart classrooms with audiovisual technology. The campus also contains a tiered lecture hall with videoconferencing capability, a fully equipped medical lab, multiple computer labs featuring PC and Mac computers, and more.

The library houses a large collection that includes an extensive legal library. Students may retrieve periodicals in paper or electronic form. Students may also access several commercial online services, including Westlaw, the computerized legal research service; LIRN; SearchBank; Infotract; UMI ProQuest; and the Electronic Library. Internet access is available on all computers throughout the campus.

Costs

Information about tuition and fees can be obtained by contacting the South University Admissions Office.

Financial Aid

South University's Office of Student Financial Services helps qualified students secure financial assistance to complete their studies. The University participates in several student aid programs. Forms of financial aid available to qualified students through federal resources include the Federal Pell Grant Program, Federal Supplemental Educational Opportunity Grant (FSEOG) Program, Federal Work-Study Program, Federal Perkins Loan Program, Federal Stafford Student Loan Program (subsidized and unsubsidized), and Federal PLUS Loan Program. South University employs the Federal Need Analysis Methodology, approved by the U.S. Department of Education, as a fair and equitable means of determining a family's ability to contribute to the student's educational expenses, as well as eligibility for other financial aid programs. Qualified students may apply for the South Carolina HOPE Scholarship, LIFE Scholarship, and veterans' educational benefits. Students also are encouraged to investigate the availability of grants and scholarships through community resources.

Faculty

The South University faculty includes individuals of high academic distinction. Of the more than 50 instructors on the campus, 46 percent hold terminal degrees in their fields of expertise. In addition to teaching, faculty members strive to help students develop the requisites to appreciate knowledge and understand how experiences in the classroom and laboratory relate to professional performance in the workplace. The average student-faculty ratio per class is 14:1. Each student is assigned a faculty adviser, who oversees the student's progress and can answer questions about academic and career concerns. Students are encouraged to discuss program-related issues with and seek academic and career advice from their faculty adviser.

Admission Requirements

To be admitted to South University, prospective students must be high school graduates or hold a GED certificate and submit SAT or ACT scores or achieve a satisfactory score on the University-administered admissions examination. Students who wish to transfer must meet the criteria established for acceptance as a transfer student.

All applicants to South University in Columbia must demonstrate English as a first language through submission of a diploma from a secondary school (or above) in which English is the official language of instruction. Applicants whose first language is not English must submit a Test of English as a Foreign Language (TOEFL) score. Applicants should contact the Admissions Office to determine other examinations/scores that are acceptable as an alternative to the TOEFL.

Application and Information

Applicants must complete and submit an application form, along with the general application fee, and official transcripts from all high schools and colleges attended. Applicants must also complete all tests administered by the University or submit their SAT or ACT scores to the Registrar's Office. Applications are accepted on a rolling basis and should be made as far in advance as possible.

All international (nonimmigrant) applicants to South University must meet the same admissions standards as all other students. In addition, international applicants must have official education records prepared in English, verify sufficient funds to cover the cost of the educational program, and meet certain other immigration-mandated criteria. South University in Columbia is authorized under federal law to admit nonimmigrant students.

Admissions officers are available weekdays, Saturdays, and by appointment. An appointment for an admissions interview or a tour of the campus should be made in advance. For additional information, all prospective students should contact:

Director of Admissions
South University
9 Science Court
Columbia, South Carolina 29203-6443
Phone: 803-799-9082
866-629-3031 (toll-free)
Fax: 803-935-4382
E-mail: twade@southuniversity.edu
Web site: http://www.southuniversity.edu

South University is located on the fast-growing northeast side of Columbia, South Carolina.

UNIVERSITY OF SOUTH CAROLINA

COLUMBIA, SOUTH CAROLINA

The University

The University of South Carolina–Columbia is a flagship institution serving a diverse population of more than 27,000 undergraduate, graduate, and professional students. Approximately 80 percent of the student body is composed of South Carolina residents. Nonresident students represent all fifty states and more than 100 countries. The University of South Carolina (USC) is a state-funded coeducational institution and is a major research center for the state. Situated in the state's capital city, USC's campus location is ideal for students participating in internships related to their majors or seeking part-time employment. In addition, Columbia offers a wide variety of restaurants, entertainment, and shopping, all within walking distance of the campus. Columbia also is the home of a philharmonic orchestra, a symphony, ballet and dance companies, and theaters and galleries. Described as one of the most beautiful college campuses in America, the historic original campus is surrounded by restored nineteenth-century buildings and shaded by ancient oaks. Spreading out from the Horseshoe for more than thirty-eight city blocks, the rest of the campus is composed of contemporary facilities in landscaped settings. Regularly scheduled or self-guided campus tours may be arranged through the University's Visitor Center (http://www.sc.edu/visitorcenter/).

South Carolina is a comprehensive university that offers more than 350 degree programs and nearly eighty undergraduate majors. USC also has a graduate school, schools of law and medicine, and advanced professional degree programs. The University is fully accredited by the Southern Association of Colleges and Schools to award baccalaureate, master's, and doctoral degrees. Though the campus is a major research institution, it manages to keep its class sizes surprisingly small. The average class size for introductory lecture courses is fewer than 30 students, 65 percent of courses taken by freshmen have 25 or fewer students, and only 2.9 percent of courses taken by freshmen have more than 100 students.

USC provides an abundance of amenities to enhance the living and learning environment of its student body. On-campus housing offers a variety of residence halls, including honors housing, health and wellness-focused housing, international housing, and a residential college with live-in faculty members. There are more than twenty places to eat on campus, ranging from full-service cafeterias to salad bars and sandwich shops. A variety of meal plans may be purchased. All students are encouraged to participate in at least one of the more than 300 student organizations on campus. On the recreational side, there are more than twenty-five intramural leagues, tournaments, and events, which collectively accommodate over 1,000 individual teams. The University's varsity athletic teams, the Gamecocks and Lady Gamecocks, compete in Division I of the NCAA and play national schedules as part of the Southeastern Conference (SEC).

Location

The University's main campus is located in downtown Columbia, a Sun Belt city with a population of nearly 600,000. Columbia is in the center of the state, a 3-hour drive from the scenic Blue Ridge Mountains or Myrtle Beach and the Grand Strand.

Majors and Degrees

Of the University of South Carolina's fifteen degree-granting colleges and schools, eleven offer the undergraduate degree.

The College of Arts and Sciences offers the Bachelor of Arts degree or, in some instances, the Bachelor of Science degree, in the following liberal arts programs: African-American studies, anthropology, art education, art history, art studio, classics, comparative literature, criminology and criminal justice, dance, economics, English, European studies, film studies, French, geography, German, history, international studies, Italian, Latin American studies, media arts, philosophy, political science, psychology, religious studies, Russian, sociology, Spanish, theater, and women's studies. The College of Arts and Sciences awards the Bachelor of Science degree in the following science programs: biological sciences, cardiovascular technology, chemistry, geology, geophysics, marine science, mathematics, physics, and statistics.

The Moore School of Business awards the Bachelor of Science in Business Administration degree in accounting, business economics, finance, insurance and risk management, international business, management, management science, marketing, and real estate.

The College of Education's undergraduate program awards the Bachelor of Arts degree in early childhood education, elementary education, and middle-level education; the Bachelor of Science degree in physical education is also offered. All other teacher-preparation degrees are a combination of the baccalaureate and master's degrees, culminating in teacher certification.

The College of Engineering and Information Technology offers the Bachelor of Science degree in biomedical engineering, chemical engineering, civil engineering, computer engineering, computer information systems, computer science, electrical engineering, and mechanical engineering.

The School of the Environment provides an interdisciplinary curriculum and offers the environmental studies minor.

The College of Hospitality, Retail, and Sport Management offers the Bachelor of Science degree in business and technology education; hotel, restaurant, and tourism management; interdisciplinary studies; retailing (with an emphasis in retail management or fashion merchandising); sport and entertainment management; and technology, support, and training management. It offers the Bachelor of Arts degree or the Bachelor of Science degree with a major in interdisciplinary studies.

The College of Mass Communications and Information Studies awards the Bachelor of Arts degree in journalism and mass communications in advertising, broadcast journalism, print journalism, public relations, and visual communications.

The School of Music awards the Bachelor of Arts degree and the Bachelor of Music degree in music performance, pedagogy, and composition; music theory and history; and music education.

The College of Nursing offers the Bachelor of Science in Nursing degree.

The College of Pharmacy offers a six-year program to undergraduates that culminates in the Doctor of Pharmacy (Pharm.D.) degree.

The Arnold School of Public Health offers the Bachelor of Science degree in exercise science.

The South Carolina Honors College awards the *Baccalaureus Artium et Scientiae* degree, which allows honors students to pursue advanced study in several disciplines rather than in a single major. Students completing the Honors College's requirements, regardless of their chosen majors, are awarded their degrees "with honors from South Carolina Honors College."

Academic Programs

Many of USC's academic programs are ranked in the top twenty-five nationally. Highly motivated exceptional students find a distinctive educational niche in the University's South Carolina Honors College—recognized as one of the best in the United States. Also of note is the University 101 program, which is designed to acquaint new students with the University and its academic resources. South Carolina's program is recognized as a model for other colleges and universities both in the United States and abroad. In fact, it is designated as one of the country's top "Programs to Look For" by *U.S. News & World Report.* The periodical also ranks USC number 1 for its undergraduate international business degree. Criteria for rankings include acceptance and graduation rates, retention, class size, faculty resources, SAT scores, and alumni giving.

Off-Campus Programs

The University has study-abroad programs with more than fifty institutions in Europe, Africa, the Middle East, South America, and the Far East. Study for a semester or a year at another American university is also available. The National Student Exchange program allows students to study at any one of more than seventy-five U.S. college campuses for up to two semesters.

Academic Facilities

Computer laboratories, computerized learning centers, and/or research laboratories abound in classroom buildings and residence halls across the campus. USC has an outdoor wireless network established throughout its grounds, and all residence halls have Internet access. Classroom and computer lab space is located on-site in some of the newer residence halls. Thomas Cooper Library, the University's largest library (ranked in the top fifty in the country), has holdings in excess of 8 million titles. The card catalog is accessible on the Internet. A state-of-the-art $40-million, 192,000-square-foot fitness center features indoor and outdoor pools, an indoor track, ball courts, a 52-foot climbing wall, an 18,000-square-foot strength and conditioning area, food service, wireless Internet access, a pro shop, and a whirlpool sauna. Carolina Center, USC's 18,000-seat arena, features nationally touring concerts and family shows and also serves as home to USC men's and women's SEC basketball teams. Other campus facilities include two theater stages, Williams-Brice Stadium, and Carolina Coliseum. The University's Koger Center for the Arts attracts nationally and internationally known performing artists.

Costs

For 2007–08, in-state expenses, including tuition, fees, room and board, and books and supplies, totaled approximately $15,000, whereas out-of-state expenses totaled approximately $28,000. All full-time students living on campus incur these expenses, but most receive financial aid, which offsets these costs. Students have additional expenses for personal and miscellaneous items. Tuition and fees are determined annually by the University Board of Trustees and are subject to change at any time.

Financial Aid

More than 90 percent of the University's students receive some type of financial assistance, including financial aid, loans, work-study opportunities, and/or scholarships. Applicants must complete the Free Application for Federal Student Aid (FAFSA) before they may be considered for financial aid. The priority deadline for submitting the FAFSA is April 1. Generally, students considered for scholarships have excellent grades and score 1300 or better on the SAT. Scholarships based upon merit and strong academic potential are available, with awards ranging from $500 to $15,000 per year. Some of the University's departments also award scholarships to outstanding entering freshmen.

Faculty

There are more than 1,000 full-time faculty members at the University, all of whom hold a Ph.D. or other terminal degree. Faculty members are engaged in teaching, research, student advising, and working with student organizations.

Student Government

The University's Student Government Association is large, with more than 500 students currently holding positions. There are 5 executive officers, an executive staff, a legislative branch, and a judicial system.

Admission Requirements

A combination of high school records and SAT (critical reading and math scores combined) or ACT scores determine freshman admission. The following college-preparatory high school courses are required for admission to the University: 4 units of English (at least 2 with strong grammar and composition components, at least 1 in English literature, and at least 1 in American literature, but completion of college-preparatory English I, II, III, and IV meets this criterion); 3 units of mathematics (including algebra I and II and geometry, but applied mathematics I and II may count together as a substitute for algebra I if a student successfully completes algebra II), and a higher-level mathematics course is strongly recommended (e.g., algebra III, trigonometry, precalculus, or calculus); 3 units of laboratory science* (2 units must be taken in two different fields, selected from among biology, chemistry, or physics, and the third unit may be from the same field as 1 of the first 2 units or from any laboratory science for which biology and/or chemistry is a prerequisite); 3 units of social studies (including 1 unit of U.S. history, although ½ unit of economics and ½ unit of government are strongly recommended); 2 units of the same foreign language; 4 units of academic electives (at least three different fields, selected from computer science, English, fine arts, foreign languages, humanities, laboratory science, mathematics above algebra II, or social studies); and 1 unit of physical education or ROTC.

*Courses in earth science, general environmental science, general physical science, or other introductory science courses for which biology and/or chemistry are not prerequisites do not meet the laboratory science or academic electives requirements. Furthermore, it is strongly recommended that students take physical science as a prerequisite to the 3 required units of laboratory science.

Core course requirements are scheduled to change effective fall 2011, at which time students must have taken four math courses, one fine arts elective, and one additional academic elective.

Application and Information

High school seniors applying for admission should do so during the fall of their senior year. The priority application deadline is December 1. Transfer students are advised to apply at least three months prior to the semester in which they plan to enter. The application fee is $50.

Admission requirements, deadlines, and fees are subject to change. For the most current information, students should visit http://www.sc.edu/admissions.

For additional information about the University, students may contact:

Office of Undergraduate Admissions
University of South Carolina
Columbia, South Carolina 29208
Phone: 803-777-7700
800-868-5USC (toll-free)
E-mail: admissions-ugrad@sc.edu
Web site: http://www.sc.edu/admissions

SOUTH DAKOTA

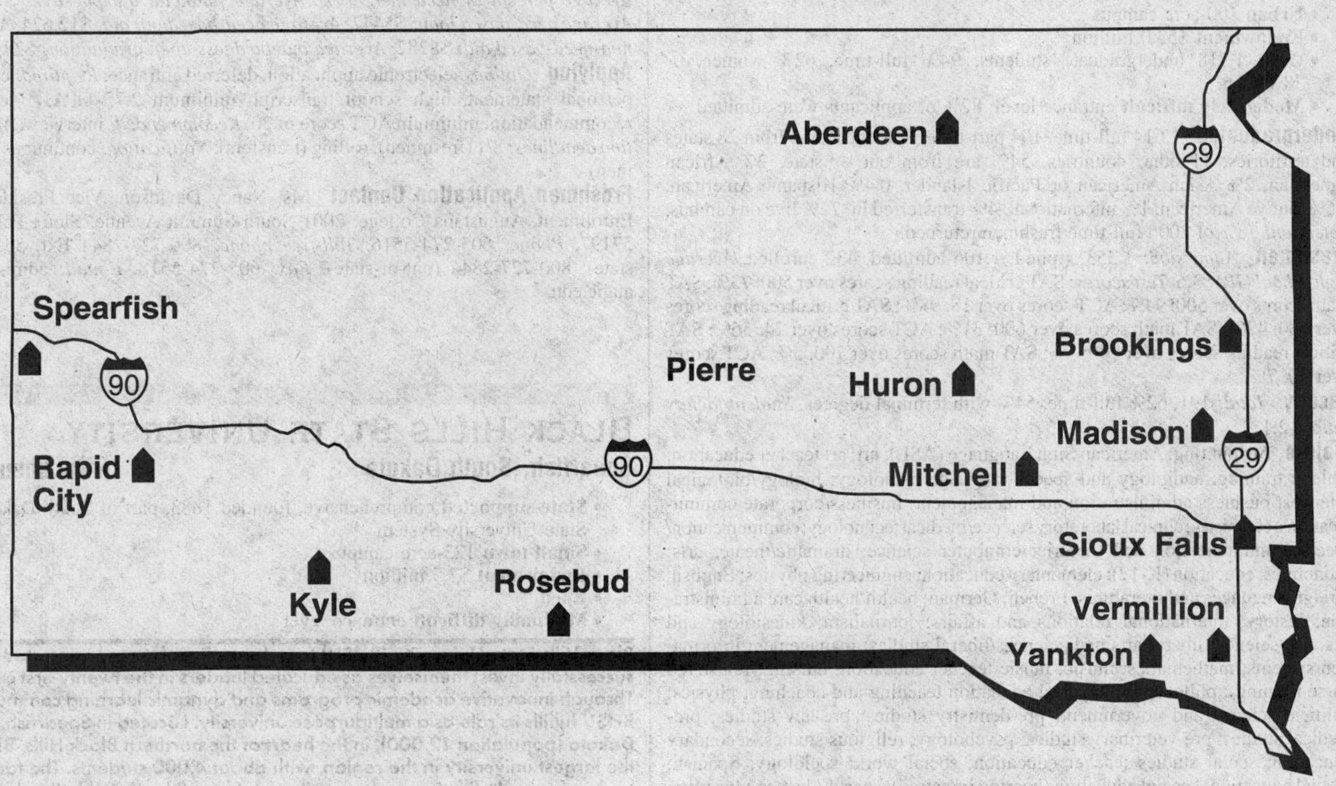

AUGUSTANA COLLEGE

Sioux Falls, South Dakota **www.augie.edu/**

- **Independent** comprehensive, founded 1860, affiliated with Evangelical Lutheran Church in America
- **Urban** 100-acre campus
- **Endowment** $53.0 million
- **Coed** 1,718 undergraduate students, 94% full-time, 62% women, 38% men
- **Moderately difficult** entrance level, 82% of applicants were admitted

Undergraduates 1,614 full-time, 104 part-time. Students come from 28 states and territories, 11 other countries, 54% are from out of state, 2% African American, 2% Asian American or Pacific Islander, 0.4% Hispanic American, 0.5% Native American, 1% international, 4% transferred in, 72% live on campus. *Retention:* 78% of 2006 full-time freshmen returned.

Freshmen *Admission:* 1,353 applied, 1,106 admitted, 432 enrolled. *Average high school GPA:* 3.6. *Test scores:* SAT critical reading scores over 500: 73%; SAT math scores over 500: 94%; ACT scores over 18: 98%; SAT critical reading scores over 600: 47%; SAT math scores over 600: 31%; ACT scores over 24: 56%; SAT critical reading scores over 700: 5%; SAT math scores over 700: 5%; ACT scores over 30: 7%.

Faculty *Total:* 191, 62% full-time, 54% with terminal degrees. *Student/faculty ratio:* 12:1.

Majors Accounting; American Sign Language (ASL); art; art teacher education; athletic training; audiology and speech-language pathology; biology/biological sciences; business administration and management; business/corporate communications; chemistry; clinical laboratory science/medical technology; communication/speech communication and rhetoric; computer science; dramatic/theater arts; economics; education (K-12); elementary education; engineering physics; English; foreign languages and literatures; French; German; health/health care administration; history; international relations and affairs; journalism; kinesiology and exercise science; liberal arts and sciences/liberal studies; management information systems; mathematics; music; music teacher education; nursing (registered nurse training); philosophy; physical education teaching and coaching; physics; political science and government; pre-dentistry studies; pre-law studies; pre-medical studies; pre-veterinary studies; psychology; religious studies; secondary education; social studies teacher education; social work; sociology; Spanish; special education; special education (hearing impaired); speech/theater education; sport and fitness administration/management.

Academics *Calendar:* 4-1-4. *Degrees:* bachelor's and master's. *Special study options:* academic remediation for entering students, accelerated degree program, advanced placement credit, cooperative education, double majors, freshman honors college, honors programs, independent study, internships, off-campus study, part-time degree program, services for LD students, student-designed majors, study abroad, summer session for credit. *Unusual degree programs:* 3-2 engineering with Columbia University, Washington University in St. Louis, University of Minnesota; occupational therapy with Washington University in St. Louis.

Computers on Campus 275 computers/terminals are available on campus for general student use. Students can access the following: computer help desk, free student e-mail accounts, online (class) grades, online (class) registration, online (class) schedules. Campuswide network is available. 100% of college-owned or -operated housing units are wired for high-speed Internet access. Wireless service is available via learning centers, libraries, student centers.

Student Life *Housing:* on-campus residence required through junior year. *Options:* coed, disabled students. Campus housing is university owned. Freshman campus housing is guaranteed. *Activities and organizations:* drama/theater group, student-run newspaper, radio station, choral group, Fellowship of Christian Athletes, Circle K, Intramurals, Habitat for Humanity, Spanish Club. *Campus security:* 24-hour emergency response devices and patrols, late-night transport/escort service, controlled dormitory access. *Student services:* health clinic, personal/psychological counseling, legal services.

Athletics Member NCAA. All Division II. *Intercollegiate sports:* baseball M (s), basketball M (s)/W (s), cheerleading W, cross-country running M (s)/W (s), football M (s), golf M/W, soccer W (s), softball W (s), tennis M/W (s), track and field M (s)/W (s), volleyball W (s), wrestling M (s). *Intramural sports:* basketball M/W, bowling M/W, cross-country running M/W, football M, golf M/W, racquetball M/W, soccer M/W, softball M/W, swimming and diving M/W, table tennis M/W, tennis M/W, ultimate Frisbee M/W, volleyball M/W.

Standardized Tests *Required:* SAT or ACT (for admission).

Costs (2007–08) *Comprehensive fee:* $26,822 includes full-time tuition ($20,932), mandatory fees ($250), and room and board ($5640). Full-time tuition and fees vary according to course load. Part-time tuition: $305 per credit. Part-time tuition and fees vary according to course load. *College room only:* $2780. Room and board charges vary according to board plan and housing facility. *Payment plan:* installment. *Waivers:* adult students, senior citizens, and employees or children of employees.

Financial Aid Of all full-time matriculated undergraduates who enrolled in 2007, 1,292 applied for aid, 1,076 were judged to have need, 235 had their need fully met. 398 Federal Work-Study jobs (averaging $1306). 436 state and other part-time jobs (averaging $866). In 2007, 507 non-need-based awards were made. *Average percent of need met:* 91%. *Average financial aid package:* $17,439. *Average need-based loan:* $5447. *Average need-based gift aid:* $12,624. *Average non-need-based aid:* $8282. *Average indebtedness upon graduation:* $28,000.

Applying *Options:* electronic application, deferred entrance. *Required:* essay or personal statement, high school transcript, minimum 2.75 GPA, 1 letter of recommendation, minimum ACT score of 20. *Recommended:* interview. *Application deadlines:* 8/1 (freshmen), rolling (transfers). *Notification:* continuous (freshmen).

Freshman Application Contact Ms. Nancy Davidson, Vice President for Enrollment, Augustana College, 2001 South Summit Avenue, Sioux Falls, SD 57197. *Phone:* 605-274-5516. *Toll-free phone:* 800-727-2844 Ext. 5516 (in-state); 800-727-2844 (out-of-state). *Fax:* 605-274-5518. *E-mail:* admission@augie.edu.

BLACK HILLS STATE UNIVERSITY

Spearfish, South Dakota **www.bhsu.edu/**

- **State-supported** comprehensive, founded 1883, part of South Dakota State University System
- **Small-town** 123-acre campus
- **Endowment** $7.5 million
- **Coed**
- **Minimally difficult** entrance level

Black Hills State University (BHSU) transforms lives by preparing students to successfully invest themselves as educated leaders in the twenty-first century. Through innovative academic programs and dynamic learning communities, BHSU fulfills its role as a multipurpose university. Located in Spearfish, South Dakota (population 12,000), in the heart of the northern Black Hills, BHSU is the largest university in the region, with about 4,000 students. The faculty is known for its dedication and commitment. In addition to athletics, there are more than seventy campus groups that provide students opportunities to develop leadership and teamwork skills. Students work with faculty mentors in hands-on research projects. BHSU takes an active role in many initiatives, including innovative changes in education, development of a world-class science lab, and emerging technology-related business. BHSU offers associate, bachelor's, and master's programs, with more than eighty bachelor's-level majors and minors and three M.S. programs in business services, curriculum and instruction, and integrative genomics. (800-ALL-BHSU (toll-free); http://www.bhsu.edu)

Faculty *Student/faculty ratio:* 21:1.

Academics *Calendar:* semesters. *Degrees:* associate, bachelor's, master's, post-master's, and postbachelor's certificates.

Student Life *Campus security:* 24-hour patrols, late-night transport/escort service, controlled dormitory access.

Athletics Member NAIA.

Standardized Tests *Required:* SAT or ACT (for admission).

Costs (2007–08) *Tuition:* state resident $2643 full-time, $83 per credit part-time; nonresident $3963 full-time, $124 per credit part-time. Full-time tuition and fees vary according to course load and reciprocity agreements. Part-time tuition and fees vary according to course load and reciprocity agreements. *Required fees:* $3160 full-time, $99 per credit part-time. *Room and board:* $4381; room only: $2308. Room and board charges vary according to board plan and housing facility. *Payment plans:* installment, deferred payment.

Financial Aid Of all full-time matriculated undergraduates who enrolled in 2006, 254 Federal Work-Study jobs (averaging $1197). 366 state and other part-time jobs (averaging $1724). *Average financial aid package:* $4993. *Average indebtedness upon graduation:* $22,328.

Applying *Options:* electronic application. *Application fee:* $20. *Required:* high school transcript, minimum 2.0 high school GPA in core curriculum.

Freshman Application Contact Ms. Lisa Jenner, Black Hills State University, University Street Box 9502, Spearfish, SD 57799-9502. *Phone:* 605-642-6343. *Toll-free phone:* 800-255-2478. *Fax:* 605-642-6254. *E-mail:* admissions@bhsu.edu.

COLORADO TECHNICAL UNIVERSITY—SIOUX FALLS

Sioux Falls, South Dakota **www.ctu-siouxfalls.com/**

- **Proprietary** comprehensive, founded 1965, administratively affiliated with Colorado Technical University
- **Urban** 3-acre campus
- **Coed**
- **Minimally difficult** entrance level

Majors Accounting; accounting and finance; business administration and management; computer engineering; computer science; computer software technology; computer systems analysis; computer technology/computer systems technology; criminal justice/law enforcement administration; e-commerce; electrical, electronic and communications engineering technology; electrical, electronics and communications engineering; finance; general studies; graphic design; health/health care administration; health information/medical records technology; human resources management; information science/studies; information technology; management information systems; marketing/marketing management; massage therapy; medical/clinical assistant; medical radiologic technology; surgical technology.

Academics *Calendar:* quarters. *Degrees:* diplomas, associate, bachelor's, and master's. *Special study options:* accelerated degree program, adult/continuing education programs, cooperative education, distance learning, double majors, internships, part-time degree program, summer session for credit. *ROTC:* Army (c).

Computers on Campus Campuswide network is available. Wireless service is available via classrooms, computer centers, computer labs, learning centers, libraries, student centers.

Student Life *Housing:* college housing not available.

Costs (2008–09) *Tuition:* Contact campus for cost.

Financial Aid Of all full-time matriculated undergraduates who enrolled in 2000, 280 applied for aid, 280 were judged to have need. *Average percent of need met:* 45%. *Average financial aid package:* $3500. *Average need-based loan:* $4648. *Average need-based gift aid:* $3300.

Applying *Options:* electronic application, deferred entrance. *Application fee:* $50. *Required:* interview. *Application deadlines:* rolling (freshmen), rolling (transfers). *Notification:* continuous (freshmen), continuous (transfers).

Freshman Application Contact Colorado Technical University—Sioux Falls, 3901 West 59th Street, Sioux Falls, SD 57108. *Phone:* 605-361-0200.

DAKOTA STATE UNIVERSITY

Madison, South Dakota **www.dsu.edu/**

- **State-supported** comprehensive, founded 1881, part of South Dakota Board of Regents
- **Rural** 40-acre campus with easy access to Sioux Falls
- **Endowment** $5.9 million
- **Coed** 2,206 undergraduate students, 51% full-time, 56% women, 44% men
- **Minimally difficult** entrance level, 97% of applicants were admitted

Undergraduates 1,120 full-time, 1,086 part-time. Students come from 17 states and territories, 14 other countries, 20% are from out of state, 1% African American, 1% Asian American or Pacific Islander, 1% Hispanic American, 1% Native American, 0.9% international, 8% transferred in, 37% live on campus. *Retention.* 71% of 2006 full-time freshmen returned.

Freshmen *Admission:* 472 applied, 457 admitted, 256 enrolled. *Average high school GPA:* 3.16. *Test scores:* ACT scores over 18: 86%; ACT scores over 24: 31%; ACT scores over 30: 4%.

Faculty *Total:* 114, 78% full-time, 61% with terminal degrees. *Student/faculty ratio:* 15:1.

Majors Accounting; biology/biological sciences; biology teacher education; business teacher education; chemical technology; computer and information sciences; computer and information systems security; computer graphics; computer programming; computer teacher education; elementary education; English language and literature related; English/language arts teacher education; finance; general studies; health information/medical records administration; health information/medical records technology; information technology; kinesiology and exercise science; marketing/marketing management; mathematics and statistics related; mathematics teacher education; office management; physical education teaching and coaching; physical sciences; special education; web page, digital/multimedia and information resources design.

Academics *Calendar:* semesters. *Degrees:* certificates, associate, bachelor's, master's, and doctoral. *Special study options:* academic remediation for entering students, adult/continuing education programs, advanced placement credit, cooperative education, distance learning, double majors, English as a second language, honors programs, independent study, internships, off-campus study, part-time degree program, services for LD students, summer session for credit. *ROTC:* Army (b), Air Force (c).

Computers on Campus 150 computers/terminals are available on campus for general student use. Students can access the following: computer help desk, free student e-mail accounts, online (class) grades, online (class) registration, online (class) schedules, wireless computing initiative placed 860 devices in the hands of full-time freshmen and sophomores. Campuswide network is available. 100% of college-owned or -operated housing units are wired for high-speed Internet access.

Student Life *Housing:* on-campus residence required through sophomore year. *Options:* coed, men-only, women-only. Campus housing is university owned and leased by the school. Freshman campus housing is guaranteed. *Activities and organizations:* drama/theater group, student-run newspaper, radio station, choral group, marching band, Business Club, band, Computer Club. *Campus security:* late-night transport/escort service, controlled dormitory access, night watchman. *Student services:* health clinic, personal/psychological counseling.

Athletics Member NAIA. *Intercollegiate sports:* baseball M, basketball M (s)/W (s), cheerleading M/W, cross-country running M (s)/W (s), football M (s), softball W, track and field M (s)/W (s), volleyball W (s). *Intramural sports:* badminton M/W, basketball M/W, bowling M/W, softball M/W, volleyball M/W, weight lifting M/W.

Standardized Tests *Required:* SAT or ACT (for admission).

Costs (2007–08) *Tuition:* state resident $2478 full-time, $83 per credit hour part-time; nonresident $3716 full-time, $124 per credit hour part-time. Full-time tuition and fees vary according to location and reciprocity agreements. Part-time tuition and fees vary according to location and reciprocity agreements. *Required fees:* $3567 full-time, $97 per credit hour part-time. *Room and board:* $4308; room only: $2297. Room and board charges vary according to board plan and housing facility. *Payment plans:* installment, deferred payment. *Waivers:* senior citizens and employees or children of employees.

Financial Aid Of all full-time matriculated undergraduates who enrolled in 2005, 1,061 applied for aid, 780 were judged to have need, 172 had their need fully met. 164 Federal Work-Study jobs (averaging $1983). 16 state and other part-time jobs (averaging $4365). In 2005, 261 non-need-based awards were made. *Average percent of need met:* 85%. *Average financial aid package:* $6360. *Average need-based loan:* $4745. *Average need-based gift aid:* $3189. *Average non-need-based aid:* $5817. *Average indebtedness upon graduation:* $23,250.

Applying *Options:* electronic application, deferred entrance. *Application fee:* $20. *Required:* high school transcript, minimum 2.7 GPA, rank in upper two-thirds of high school class. *Application deadlines:* rolling (freshmen), rolling (transfers). *Notification:* continuous (freshmen), continuous (transfers).

Freshman Application Contact Ms. Dana Hoff, Admissions Secretary, Dakota State University, 820 North Washington, Madison, SD 57042-1799. *Phone:* 605-256-5139. *Toll-free phone:* 888-DSU-9988. *Fax:* 605-256-5020. *E-mail:* yourfuture@dsu.edu.

DAKOTA WESLEYAN UNIVERSITY

Mitchell, South Dakota **www.dwu.edu/**

- **Independent United Methodist** comprehensive, founded 1885
- **Small-town** 50-acre campus
- **Endowment** $23.1 million
- **Coed** 756 undergraduate students, 96% full-time, 56% women, 44% men
- **Moderately difficult** entrance level, 68% of applicants were admitted

Undergraduates 728 full-time, 28 part-time. Students come from 27 states and territories, 3 other countries, 31% are from out of state, 4% African American, 1% Asian American or Pacific Islander, 4% Hispanic American, 3% Native American, 1% international, 17% transferred in, 40% live on campus. *Retention:* 68% of 2006 full-time freshmen returned.

Freshmen *Admission:* 564 applied, 385 admitted, 156 enrolled. *Average high school GPA:* 3.1. *Test scores:* ACT scores over 18: 88%; ACT scores over 24: 26%.

Faculty *Total:* 96, 53% full-time, 39% with terminal degrees. *Student/faculty ratio:* 13:1.

Majors Accounting; adult and continuing education; art; art teacher education; athletic training; behavioral sciences; biochemistry; biology/biological sciences; biology teacher education; business administration and management; business teacher education; computer software and media applications related; criminal justice/law enforcement administration; dramatic/theater arts; education; education (multiple levels); elementary education; English; English/language arts teacher education; finance; history; history teacher education; human services; liberal arts and sciences/liberal studies; marketing/marketing management; mathematics; mathematics teacher education; middle school education; music; music teacher education; nursing (registered nurse training); philosophy; physical education teaching and coaching; psychology; religious studies; science teacher education; secondary education; social studies teacher education; sociology; Spanish; special education; theology; wildlife and wildlands science and management.

Academics *Calendar:* semesters. *Degrees:* associate, bachelor's, and master's. *Special study options:* academic remediation for entering students, adult/continuing education programs, advanced placement credit, distance learning, double majors, honors programs, independent study, internships, off-campus study, part-time degree program, services for LD students, student-designed majors, study abroad, summer session for credit.

Computers on Campus 100 computers/terminals are available on campus for general student use. Students can access the following: online (class) registration, portal, course management system. Campuswide network is available.

Student Life *Housing:* on-campus residence required through sophomore year. *Options:* coed, men-only, women-only. Campus housing is university owned and leased by the school. Freshman campus housing is guaranteed. *Activities and organizations:* drama/theater group, student-run newspaper, choral group, Future Teachers Organization, Student Nurses Association, Multi-Culture Club, Human Services Club, Student Ministry Council. *Campus security:* 24-hour emergency response devices, student patrols, late-night transport/escort service, controlled dormitory access, campus patrol from 2am to 6am by special request only. *Student services:* health clinic, personal/psychological counseling.

Athletics Member NAIA. *Intercollegiate sports:* baseball M (s), basketball M (s)/W (s), cheerleading M (s)/W (s), cross-country running M (s)/W (s), football M (s), golf M (s)/W (s), softball W (s), track and field M (s)/W (s), volleyball W (s), wrestling M (s). *Intramural sports:* basketball M/W, softball M/W, volleyball M/W, weight lifting M/W.

Standardized Tests *Required:* SAT or ACT (for admission).

Costs (2007–08) *Comprehensive fee:* $23,000 includes full-time tuition ($17,500), mandatory fees ($100), and room and board ($5400). Full-time tuition and fees vary according to location and program. Part-time tuition: $375 per credit. Part-time tuition and fees vary according to course load and program. *College room only:* $2200. Room and board charges vary according to board plan, housing facility, and student level. *Payment plan:* installment. *Waivers:* senior citizens and employees or children of employees.

Financial Aid Of all full-time matriculated undergraduates who enrolled in 2006, 695 applied for aid, 664 were judged to have need, 50 had their need fully met. 178 Federal Work-Study jobs (averaging $1400). 6 state and other part-time jobs (averaging $1200). *Average percent of need met:* 60%. *Average financial aid package:* $12,000. *Average need-based loan:* $3726. *Average need-based gift aid:* $8400. *Average indebtedness upon graduation:* $24,000.

Applying *Options:* electronic application. *Application fee:* $25. *Required:* high school transcript. *Recommended:* minimum 2.0 GPA. *Application deadlines:* 8/27 (freshmen), 8/27 (transfers). *Notification:* continuous (freshmen), continuous (transfers).

Freshman Application Contact Mrs. Amy Novak, Vice President for Enrollment Management, Dakota Wesleyan University, 1200 West University Avenue, Mitchell, SD 57301-4398. *Phone:* 605-995-2600 Ext. 2661. *Toll-free phone:* 800-333-8506. *Fax:* 605-995-2699. *E-mail:* admissions@dwu.edu.

MOUNT MARTY COLLEGE

Yankton, South Dakota **www.mtmc.edu/**

- **Independent Roman Catholic** comprehensive, founded 1936
- **Small-town** 80-acre campus
- **Endowment** $15.9 million
- **Coed** 1,090 undergraduate students, 57% full-time, 63% women, 37% men
- **Minimally difficult** entrance level, 68% of applicants were admitted

Undergraduates 620 full-time, 470 part-time. Students come from 13 states and territories, 4 other countries, 28% are from out of state, 1% African American, 0.8% Asian American or Pacific Islander, 2% Hispanic American, 2% Native American, 0.3% international, 6% transferred in, 35% live on campus. *Retention:* 78% of 2006 full-time freshmen returned.

Freshmen *Admission:* 505 applied, 343 admitted, 128 enrolled. *Average high school GPA:* 3.31. *Test scores:* ACT scores over 18: 93%; ACT scores over 24: 33%; ACT scores over 30: 5%.

Faculty *Total:* 80, 59% full-time, 39% with terminal degrees. *Student/faculty ratio:* 11:1.

Majors Accounting; biology/biological sciences; business administration and management; chemistry; chemistry teacher education; clinical laboratory science/medical technology; computer science; criminal justice/safety; digital communication and media/multimedia; dramatic/theater arts; education; elementary education; English; English/language arts teacher education; forensic science and technology; general studies; history; history teacher education; human services; information technology; liberal arts and sciences/liberal studies; mathematics; mathematics teacher education; medical radiologic technology; music; music teacher education; nursing (registered nurse training); parks, recreation and leisure facilities management; psychology; religious studies; secondary education; special education.

Academics *Calendar:* semesters. *Degrees:* certificates, associate, bachelor's, and master's. *Special study options:* academic remediation for entering students, accelerated degree program, adult/continuing education programs, advanced placement credit, cooperative education, distance learning, double majors, honors programs, independent study, internships, off-campus study, part-time degree program, services for LD students, student-designed majors, summer session for credit. *ROTC:* Army (c).

Computers on Campus 25 computers/terminals are available on campus for general student use. Students can access the following: campus intranet, computer help desk, free student e-mail accounts, online (class) grades, online (class) registration, online (class) schedules. Campuswide network is available. 100% of college-owned or -operated housing units are wired for high-speed Internet access. Wireless service is available via entire campus.

Student Life *Housing:* on-campus residence required through senior year. *Options:* men-only, women-only. Campus housing is university owned. Freshman campus housing is guaranteed. *Activities and organizations:* drama/theater group, student-run newspaper, choral group, Campus ministry, Student Government Association, Nursing Club, Education Club, Theater Club or SIFE (Students in Free Enterprise). *Campus security:* 24-hour emergency response devices and patrols, controlled dormitory access. *Student services:* health clinic, personal/psychological counseling.

Athletics Member NAIA. *Intercollegiate sports:* baseball M (s), basketball M (s)/W (s), cross-country running M (s)/W (s), soccer M (s)/W (s), softball W (s), track and field M (s)/W (s), volleyball W (s). *Intramural sports:* basketball M/W, soccer M/W, softball W, tennis M/W, volleyball M/W.

Standardized Tests *Required:* SAT or ACT (for admission).

Costs (2007–08) *Comprehensive fee:* $22,526 includes full-time tuition ($15,638), mandatory fees ($1830), and room and board ($5058). Full-time tuition and fees vary according to course load and location. Part-time tuition: $253 per credit hour. Part-time tuition and fees vary according to course load and location. *Required fees:* $25 per credit hour part-time. *Payment plan:* installment.

Financial Aid Of all full-time matriculated undergraduates who enrolled in 2007, 486 applied for aid, 470 were judged to have need, 50 had their need fully met. 240 Federal Work-Study jobs (averaging $1200). 65 state and other part-time jobs (averaging $1200). In 2007, 24 non-need-based awards were made. *Average percent of need met:* 73%. *Average financial aid package:* $15,073. *Average need-based loan:* $6704. *Average need-based gift aid:* $7169. *Average non-need-based aid:* $8598. *Average indebtedness upon graduation:* $26,250.

Applying *Options:* electronic application, early admission, deferred entrance. *Application fee:* $35. *Required:* high school transcript, minimum 2.0 GPA. *Required for some:* letters of recommendation. *Recommended:* interview. *Application deadlines:* rolling (freshmen), rolling (transfers). *Notification:* continuous (freshmen), continuous (transfers).

Freshman Application Contact Ms. Brandi DeFries, Vice President for Enrollment Management, Mount Marty College, 1105 West 8th Street, Yankton, SD 57078. *Phone:* 605-668-1545. *Toll-free phone:* 800-658-4552. *Fax:* 605-668-1607. *E-mail:* mmcadmit@mtmc.edu.

NATIONAL AMERICAN UNIVERSITY

Rapid City, South Dakota **www.rapid.national.edu/**

- **Proprietary** comprehensive, founded 1941, part of National College
- **Urban** 8-acre campus
- **Endowment** $30,000
- **Coed** 481 undergraduate students, 73% full-time, 64% women, 36% men
- **Noncompetitive** entrance level

Undergraduates 350 full-time, 131 part-time. Students come from 22 states and territories, 6 other countries, 15% are from out of state, 2% African American, 5% Asian American or Pacific Islander, 2% Hispanic American, 8% Native American, 10% transferred in, 21% live on campus. *Retention:* 52% of 2006 full-time freshmen returned.

Freshmen *Admission:* 30 enrolled. *Average high school GPA:* 3.1.

Faculty *Total:* 47, 28% full-time, 17% with terminal degrees. *Student/faculty ratio:* 26:1.
Majors Athletic training; computer engineering technology; computer management; finance; international business/trade/commerce; legal assistant/paralegal; liberal arts and sciences/liberal studies; marketing/marketing management; operations management; pre-law studies; system, networking, and LAN/WAN management; veterinary technology.
Academics *Calendar:* quarters. *Degrees:* associate, bachelor's, and master's. *Special study options:* academic remediation for entering students, accelerated degree program, adult/continuing education programs, advanced placement credit, cooperative education, distance learning, English as a second language, external degree program, independent study, internships, part-time degree program, services for LD students, summer session for credit. *ROTC:* Army (c).
Computers on Campus 50 computers/terminals are available on campus for general student use. Campuswide network is available.
Student Life *Housing:* on-campus residence required through sophomore year. *Options:* coed. Campus housing is university owned. Freshman campus housing is guaranteed. *Activities and organizations:* Student Senate, Phi Beta Lambda, Dormitory Council, Student Association of Legal Assistants, President's Advisory Council. *Campus security:* 24-hour emergency response devices, controlled dormitory access, part-time security personnel. *Student services:* personal/psychological counseling.
Athletics Member NAIA. *Intercollegiate sports:* equestrian sports M (s)/W (s), ultimate Frisbee M (s)/W (s), volleyball M (s)/W (s). *Intramural sports:* basketball M/W, bowling M/W, skiing (cross-country) M/W, skiing (downhill) M (c)/W (c), softball M/W, ultimate Frisbee M/W, volleyball M/W.
Standardized Tests *Recommended:* ACT (for admission).
Costs (2007–08) *Required fees:* $480 full-time. *Room and board:* $4230; room only: $1995.
Applying *Options:* electronic application, early admission, deferred entrance. *Application fee:* $25. *Required for some:* high school transcript. *Recommended:* interview. *Application deadlines:* rolling (freshmen), rolling (transfers). *Notification:* continuous (freshmen), continuous (transfers).
Freshman Application Contact Ms. Angela Beck, Director of Enrollment Management, National American University, 321 Kansas City Street, Rapid City, SD 57701. *Phone:* 605-394-4902. *Toll-free phone:* 800-843-8892. *Fax:* 605-394-4871. *E-mail:* abeck@national.edu.

See page 2424 for the College Close-Up.

National American University–Sioux Falls Branch

Sioux Falls, South Dakota **www.national.edu/**

- **Proprietary** 4-year, founded 1941, part of National College
- **Urban** campus
- **Coed** 375 undergraduate students
- **Noncompetitive** entrance level, 100% of applicants were admitted

Undergraduates Students come from 6 states and territories, 0.5% African American, 0.5% Native American. *Retention:* 70% of 2006 full-time freshmen returned.
Freshmen *Admission:* 9 applied, 9 admitted.
Faculty *Total:* 35.
Majors Accounting; business administration and management; computer programming; computer programming (vendor/product certification); customer service support/call center/teleservice operation; information science/studies; information technology; legal assistant/paralegal; management information systems; massage therapy; medical/clinical assistant; web page, digital/multimedia and information resources design.
Academics *Calendar:* quarters. *Degrees:* certificates, diplomas, associate, bachelor's, and master's. *Special study options:* academic remediation for entering students, accelerated degree program, adult/continuing education programs, advanced placement credit, cooperative education, distance learning, double majors, English as a second language, internships, part-time degree program, summer session for credit.
Computers on Campus 60 computers/terminals are available on campus for general student use. Campuswide network is available.
Student Life *Housing:* college housing not available. *Campus security:* 24-hour emergency response devices.
Applying *Options:* electronic application, deferred entrance. *Application fee:* $25. *Required:* high school transcript, interview. *Application deadlines:* rolling (freshmen), rolling (transfers). *Notification:* continuous (freshmen), continuous (transfers).
Freshman Application Contact Ms. Lisa Houtsma, Director of Admissions, National American University–Sioux Falls Branch, 2801 South Kiwanis Avenue, Suite 100, Sioux Falls, SD 57105. *Phone:* 605-336-4600. *Toll-free phone:* 800-388-5430. *Fax:* 605-336-4605. *E-mail:* lhoutsma@national.edu.

Northern State University

Aberdeen, South Dakota **www.northern.edu/**

- **State-supported** comprehensive, founded 1901, part of South Dakota Board of Regents
- **Small-town** 52-acre campus
- **Endowment** $12.1 million
- **Coed** 2,219 undergraduate students, 68% full-time, 59% women, 41% men
- **Minimally difficult** entrance level, 89% of applicants were admitted

Undergraduates 1,500 full-time, 719 part-time. Students come from 32 states and territories, 15 other countries, 21% are from out of state, 8% transferred in. *Retention:* 65% of 2006 full-time freshmen returned.
Freshmen *Admission:* 914 applied, 818 admitted, 347 enrolled. *Average high school GPA:* 3.2. *Test scores:* ACT scores over 18: 89%; ACT scores over 24: 34%; ACT scores over 30: 2%.
Faculty *Total:* 104, 88% full-time, 75% with terminal degrees. *Student/faculty ratio:* 19:1.
Majors Accounting; art; art teacher education; audiology and speech-language pathology; biological and physical sciences; biology/biological sciences; business/managerial economics; business teacher education; chemistry; clinical laboratory science/medical technology; clinical/medical laboratory technology; commercial and advertising art; community organization and advocacy; criminal justice/police science; data processing and data processing technology; dramatic/theater arts; economics; education; elementary education; English; environmental studies; finance; French; German; health teacher education; history; industrial arts; international business/trade/commerce; liberal arts and sciences/liberal studies; management information systems; marketing/marketing management; mathematics; music; music teacher education; physical education teaching and coaching; political science and government; pre-dentistry studies; pre-engineering; pre-law studies; pre-medical studies; psychology; public administration; secondary education; social work; sociology; Spanish; special education; speech and rhetoric; voice and opera.
Academics *Calendar:* semesters. *Degrees:* certificates, diplomas, associate, bachelor's, master's, and postbachelor's certificates. *Special study options:* academic remediation for entering students, accelerated degree program, adult/continuing education programs, advanced placement credit, cooperative education, distance learning, English as a second language, honors programs, internships, off-campus study, part-time degree program, services for LD students, student-designed majors, study abroad, summer session for credit.
Computers on Campus 900 computers/terminals are available on campus for general student use. Students can access the following: online (class) registration. Campuswide network is available.
Student Life *Housing:* on-campus residence required through sophomore year. *Options:* coed. Campus housing is university owned. *Activities and organizations:* drama/theater group, student-run newspaper, television station, choral group, marching band, Student Ambassadors, Choices, honor society, Native American Student Association. *Campus security:* 24-hour emergency response devices, controlled dormitory access, evening patrols. *Student services:* health clinic, personal/psychological counseling, women's center, legal services.
Athletics Member NCAA. All Division II. *Intercollegiate sports:* baseball M, basketball M (s)/W (s), cross-country running M (s)/W (s), football M (s), golf M/W (s), soccer W (s), softball W (s), tennis M/W (s), track and field M (s)/W (s), volleyball W (s), wrestling M (s). *Intramural sports:* archery M/W, badminton M/W, basketball M/W, cross-country running M/W, football M, golf M/W, ice hockey M (c), racquetball M/W, softball M/W, swimming and diving M/W, table tennis M/W, tennis M/W, track and field M/W, volleyball M/W, weight lifting M/W, wrestling M.
Standardized Tests *Required:* SAT or ACT (for admission).
Costs (2007–08) *Tuition:* state resident $2478 full-time, $83 per credit hour part-time; nonresident $7872 full-time, $262 per credit hour part-time. Full-time tuition and fees vary according to course level, course load, and reciprocity agreements. Part-time tuition and fees vary according to course level, course load, and reciprocity agreements. *Required fees:* $2802 full-time, $93 per credit hour part-time. *Room and board:* $4499; room only: $2378. Room and board charges vary according to board plan. *Payment plan:* installment.
Financial Aid Of all full-time matriculated undergraduates who enrolled in 2007, 1,124 applied for aid, 889 were judged to have need, 881 had their need fully met. 325 Federal Work-Study jobs (averaging $1506). 400 state and other

part-time jobs (averaging $1284). In 2007, 115 non-need-based awards were made. *Average percent of need met:* 100%. *Average financial aid package:* $6110. *Average need-based loan:* $3839. *Average need-based gift aid:* $2579. *Average non-need-based aid:* $2274.

Applying *Options:* early admission, deferred entrance. *Application fee:* $20. *Required:* high school transcript, minimum 2.6 GPA. *Required for some:* letters of recommendation. *Application deadlines:* 9/1 (freshmen), 9/1 (transfers). *Notification:* continuous (freshmen), continuous (transfers).

Freshman Application Contact Mr. Allan Vogel, Director of Admissions-Campus, Northern State University, 1200 South Jay Street, Aberdeen, SD 57401. *Phone:* 605-626-2544. *Toll-free phone:* 800-678-5330. *Fax:* 605-626-2587. *E-mail:* admissions1@northern.edu.

OGLALA LAKOTA COLLEGE

Kyle, South Dakota **www.olc.edu/**

- **State and locally supported** comprehensive, founded 1970
- **Rural** campus
- **Coed**

Academics *Calendar:* semesters. *Degree:* associate.

Applying *Options:* early admission.

Director of Admissions Director of Admissions, Oglala Lakota College, 490 Piya Wiconi Road, Kyle, SD 57752-0490. *Phone:* 605-455-2321 Ext. 236. *E-mail:* lmeseteth@olc.edu.

PRESENTATION COLLEGE

Aberdeen, South Dakota **www.presentation.edu/**

- **Independent Roman Catholic** 4-year, founded 1951
- **Small-town** 100-acre campus
- **Endowment** $15.0 million
- **Coed, primarily women** 773 undergraduate students, 64% full-time, 81% women, 19% men
- **Noncompetitive** entrance level, 32% of applicants were admitted

Undergraduates 494 full-time, 279 part-time. Students come from 21 states and territories, 2 other countries, 40% are from out of state, 1% African American, 0.4% Asian American or Pacific Islander, 0.7% Hispanic American, 8% Native American, 0.3% international, 15% transferred in, 12% live on campus. *Retention:* 65% of 2006 full-time freshmen returned.

Freshmen *Admission:* 283 applied, 90 admitted, 87 enrolled. *Average high school GPA:* 3.09. *Test scores:* ACT scores over 18: 68%; ACT scores over 24: 18%.

Faculty *Total:* 97, 46% full-time, 22% with terminal degrees. *Student/faculty ratio:* 9:1.

Majors Biology/biological sciences; business administration and management; chemistry; clinical/medical laboratory technology; communication/speech communication and rhetoric; early childhood education; English; general studies; medical/clinical assistant; medical office management; medical radiologic technology; medical transcription; nursing (registered nurse training); parks, recreation and leisure; religious studies; social work; surgical technology.

Academics *Calendar:* semesters. *Degrees:* certificates, associate, and bachelor's. *Special study options:* academic remediation for entering students, accelerated degree program, adult/continuing education programs, advanced placement credit, cooperative education, distance learning, double majors, external degree program, internships, part-time degree program, summer session for credit.

Computers on Campus 39 computers/terminals are available on campus for general student use. Students can access the following: computer help desk, free student e-mail accounts, online (class) grades, online (class) registration, online (class) schedules. Campuswide network is available. 100% of college-owned or -operated housing units are wired for high-speed Internet access. Wireless service is available via entire campus.

Student Life *Housing:* on-campus residence required through sophomore year. *Options:* men-only, women-only, disabled students. Campus housing is university owned. Freshman campus housing is guaranteed. *Activities and organizations:* drama/theater group, student-run newspaper, choral group, Wellness/athletics, National Student Nursing Association, Social Work Organization, Theatre Group, Student Ambassadors. *Campus security:* 24-hour emergency response devices and patrols, late-night transport/escort service, controlled dormitory access. *Student services:* health clinic, personal/psychological counseling.

Athletics Member NCAA. All Division III. *Intercollegiate sports:* baseball M, basketball M/W, cross-country running M/W, golf M/W, soccer M/W, softball W, volleyball W.

Standardized Tests *Required:* SAT or ACT (for admission).

Costs (2007–08) *Comprehensive fee:* $18,025 includes full-time tuition ($13,150) and room and board ($4875). Full-time tuition and fees vary according to course load, location, and program. Part-time tuition: $475 per credit. Part-time tuition and fees vary according to course load, location, and program. *College room only:* $3975. Room and board charges vary according to board plan, housing facility, and student level. *Payment plan:* installment. *Waivers:* senior citizens and employees or children of employees.

Financial Aid Of all full-time matriculated undergraduates who enrolled in 2006, 454 applied for aid, 441 were judged to have need, 66 had their need fully met. 64 Federal Work-Study jobs (averaging $1750). 25 state and other part-time jobs (averaging $1750). In 2006, 23 non-need-based awards were made. *Average percent of need met:* 43%. *Average financial aid package:* $8737. *Average need-based loan:* $3741. *Average need-based gift aid:* $3769. *Average non-need-based aid:* $2814. *Average indebtedness upon graduation:* $27,430.

Applying *Options:* electronic application. *Required:* high school transcript. *Required for some:* 2 letters of recommendation, ACT scores, college transcripts. *Recommended:* minimum 2.0 GPA. *Application deadlines:* rolling (freshmen), rolling (transfers). *Notification:* continuous (freshmen), continuous (transfers).

Freshman Application Contact Ms. Jo Ellen Lindner, Vice President for Enrollment and Student Retention, Presentation College, 1500 North Main Street, Aberdeen, SD 57401. *Phone:* 605-229-8492. *Toll-free phone:* 800-437-6060. *Fax:* 605-229-8425. *E-mail:* admit@presentation.edu.

SINTE GLESKA UNIVERSITY

Mission, South Dakota **www.sintegleska.edu/**

Director of Admissions Mr. Jack Herman, Registrar and Director of Admissions, Sinte Gleska University, PO Box 105, Mission, SD 57555-0105. *Phone:* 605-856-8100 Ext. 8479.

SOUTH DAKOTA SCHOOL OF MINES AND TECHNOLOGY

Rapid City, South Dakota **www.sdsmt.edu/**

- **State-supported** university, founded 1885, part of South Dakota State University System
- **Suburban** 120-acre campus
- **Endowment** $37.4 million
- **Coed, primarily men** 1,834 undergraduate students, 78% full-time, 29% women, 71% men
- **Moderately difficult** entrance level, 88% of applicants were admitted

Undergraduates 1,429 full-time, 405 part-time. Students come from 36 states and territories, 14 other countries, 36% are from out of state, 0.6% African American, 1% Asian American or Pacific Islander, 1% Hispanic American, 3% Native American, 1% international, 5% transferred in, 34% live on campus. *Retention:* 76% of 2006 full-time freshmen returned.

Freshmen *Admission:* 814 applied, 720 admitted, 353 enrolled. *Average high school GPA:* 3.50. *Test scores:* SAT critical reading scores over 500: 61%; SAT math scores over 500: 90%; ACT scores over 18: 99%; SAT critical reading scores over 600: 32%; SAT math scores over 600: 41%; ACT scores over 24: 73%; SAT critical reading scores over 700: 8%; SAT math scores over 700: 10%; ACT scores over 30: 14%.

Faculty *Total:* 134, 87% full-time, 81% with terminal degrees. *Student/faculty ratio:* 14:1.

Majors Chemical engineering; chemistry; civil engineering; computer engineering; computer science; electrical, electronics and communications engineering; engineering/industrial management; environmental/environmental health engineering; general studies; geological/geophysical engineering; geology/earth science; industrial engineering; interdisciplinary studies; mathematics; mechanical engineering; metallurgical engineering; mining and mineral engineering; physics.

Academics *Calendar:* semesters. *Degrees:* associate, bachelor's, master's, and doctoral. *Special study options:* academic remediation for entering students, adult/continuing education programs, advanced placement credit, cooperative education, distance learning, double majors, English as a second language, independent study, internships, part-time degree program, services for LD students, study abroad, summer session for credit. *ROTC:* Army (b).

Computers on Campus 105 computers/terminals are available on campus for general student use. Students can access the following: campus intranet, computer help desk, free student e-mail accounts, online (class) grades, online (class) registration, online (class) schedules, laptop rental/purchase. Campuswide network is available. 100% of college-owned or -operated housing units are wired for high-speed Internet access. Wireless service is available via entire campus.

Student Life *Housing:* on-campus residence required for freshman year. *Options:* coed, men-only, women-only. Campus housing is university owned and leased by the school. Freshman campus housing is guaranteed. *Activities and organizations:* drama/theater group, student-run newspaper, radio station, choral group, TAP (Tech Activities and Programming), SADD (Students Against Drunk Driving), ASCE (American Society of Civil Engineers), ASME (American Society of Mechanical Engineers), Ski Club, national fraternities, national sororities. *Campus security:* 24-hour emergency response devices and patrols, student patrols, late-night transport/escort service, controlled dormitory access. *Student services:* health clinic, personal/psychological counseling.

Athletics Member NAIA. *Intercollegiate sports:* basketball M (s)/W (s), cross-country running M (s)/W (s), football M (s), golf M/W, tennis M, track and field M (s)/W (s), volleyball W (s). *Intramural sports:* archery M, basketball M/W, bowling M/W, football M/W, racquetball M/W, skiing (cross-country) M/W, soccer M/W, softball M/W, squash M/W, swimming and diving M/W, tennis M/W, track and field M/W, volleyball M/W, weight lifting M/W.

Standardized Tests *Required for some:* SAT or ACT (for admission). *Recommended:* SAT or ACT (for admission).

Costs (2007–08) *Tuition:* state resident $2480 full-time, $83 per credit hour part-time; nonresident $3720 full-time, $124 per credit hour part-time. Full-time tuition and fees vary according to course load, program, and reciprocity agreements. Part-time tuition and fees vary according to course load, program, and reciprocity agreements. *Required fees:* $3190 full-time, $106 per credit hour part-time, $1595 per term part-time. *Room and board:* $4600. Room and board charges vary according to board plan and housing facility. *Payment plan:* installment. *Waivers:* senior citizens.

Financial Aid Of all full-time matriculated undergraduates who enrolled in 2004, 1,344 applied for aid, 810 were judged to have need, 222 had their need fully met. In 2004, 236 non-need-based awards were made. *Average percent of need met:* 70%. *Average financial aid package:* $6899. *Average need-based loan:* $3816. *Average need-based gift aid:* $3458. *Average non-need-based aid:* $2620. *Average indebtedness upon graduation:* $1623.

Applying *Options:* electronic application. *Application fee:* $20. *Required:* high school transcript. *Recommended:* minimum 2.75 GPA. *Application deadlines:* rolling (freshmen), rolling (transfers). *Notification:* continuous (freshmen), continuous (transfers).

Freshman Application Contact Mr. Tex Claymore, Director of Admissions, South Dakota School of Mines and Technology, 501 East Saint Joseph, Rapid City, SD 57701-3995. *Phone:* 605-394-2414 Ext. 1266. *Toll-free phone:* 800-544-8162 Ext. 2414. *Fax:* 605-394-1268. *E-mail:* admissions@sdsmt.edu.

SOUTH DAKOTA STATE UNIVERSITY

Brookings, South Dakota www.sdstate.edu/

- **State-supported** university, founded 1881, part of South Dakota Board of Regents
- **Small-town** 272-acre campus
- **Endowment** $60.0 million
- **Coed** 10,257 undergraduate students, 80% full-time, 52% women, 48% men
- **Minimally difficult** entrance level, 94% of applicants were admitted

South Dakota State University (SDSU) is ranked by the Carnegie Foundation as the number 1 research institution in South Dakota. As the state's largest university, SDSU offers more academic programs and extracurricular activities than any other university in the state, providing students with a wide variety of options to choose from. Majors are available in pharmacy, nursing, engineering, arts and science, family and consumer sciences, education, agriculture and biological sciences, and general studies.

Undergraduates 8,175 full-time, 2,082 part-time. Students come from 36 states and territories, 25 other countries, 33% are from out of state, 1% African American, 0.9% Asian American or Pacific Islander, 0.8% Hispanic American, 2% Native American, 0.6% international, 8% transferred in, 33% live on campus. *Retention:* 77% of 2006 full-time freshmen returned.

Freshmen *Admission:* 3,738 applied, 3,519 admitted, 2,014 enrolled. *Average high school GPA:* 3.31. *Test scores:* ACT scores over 18: 94%; ACT scores over 24: 47%; ACT scores over 30: 5%.

Faculty *Total:* 671, 73% full-time, 63% with terminal degrees. *Student/faculty ratio:* 17:1.

Majors Aeronautics/aviation/aerospace science and technology; agribusiness; agricultural/biological engineering and bioengineering; agricultural economics; agricultural mechanization; agriculture; agronomy and crop science; animal sciences; apparel and textile marketing management; applied horticulture; athletic training; aviation/airway management; biochemistry; biology/biological sciences; chemistry; civil engineering; clinical laboratory science/medical technology; computer and information sciences; computer software engineering; construction engineering technology; consumer economics; dairy science; early childhood education; economics; electrical, electronic and communications engineering technology; electrical, electronics and communications engineering; engineering/industrial management; engineering physics; English; environmental/environmental health engineering; family resource management; flight instruction; foods, nutrition, and wellness; French; general studies; geography; geography related; German; graphic design; health and physical education; health and physical education related; history; hotel/motel administration; human development and family studies; industrial safety technology; interior design; international/global studies; journalism; landscaping and groundskeeping; liberal arts and sciences/liberal studies; manufacturing technology; mathematics; mechanical engineering; medical pharmacology and pharmaceutical sciences; microbiology; music; music management and merchandising; music teacher education; natural resources management and policy; nursing (registered nurse training); parks, recreation and leisure facilities management; pharmacy; physics; political science and government; pre-law studies; psychology; range science and management; sociology; Spanish; speech and rhetoric; technical teacher education; visual and performing arts; wildlife and wildlands science and management.

Academics *Calendar:* semesters. *Degrees:* associate, bachelor's, master's, doctoral, first professional, post-master's, and postbachelor's certificates. *Special study options:* academic remediation for entering students, accelerated degree program, adult/continuing education programs, advanced placement credit, cooperative education, distance learning, double majors, English as a second language, freshman honors college, honors programs, independent study, internships, off-campus study, part-time degree program, services for LD students, study abroad, summer session for credit. *ROTC:* Army (b), Air Force (b). *Unusual degree programs:* 3-2 economics.

Computers on Campus 728 computers/terminals are available on campus for general student use. Students can access the following: computer help desk, free student e-mail accounts, online (class) grades, online (class) registration. Campus-wide network is available. Wireless service is available via classrooms, dorm rooms, libraries, student centers.

Student Life *Housing:* on-campus residence required through sophomore year. *Options:* coed. Campus housing is university owned. Freshman campus housing is guaranteed. *Activities and organizations:* drama/theater group, student-run newspaper, radio station, choral group, marching band, Student Association, University Programming Council, Block and Bridle Club, national fraternities, national sororities. *Campus security:* 24-hour emergency response devices and patrols, student patrols, late-night transport/escort service. *Student services:* health clinic, personal/psychological counseling, women's center, legal services.

Athletics Member NCAA. All Division I. *Intercollegiate sports:* baseball M (s), basketball M (s)/W (s), bowling M (c)/W (c), cheerleading M (c)/W (c), cross-country running M (s)/W (s), equestrian sports W, football M (s), golf M (s)/W (s), ice hockey M (c)/W (c), rugby M (c)/W (c), soccer M (c)/W (s), softball W (s), swimming and diving M (s)/W (s), tennis M (s)/W (s), track and field M (s)/W (s), volleyball W (s), wrestling M (s). *Intramural sports:* badminton M/W, basketball M/W, football M/W, golf M/W, racquetball M/W, soccer W, softball M/W, swimming and diving M/W, table tennis M/W, track and field M/W, volleyball M/W, wrestling M.

Standardized Tests *Required:* SAT or ACT (for admission).

Costs (2007–08) *Tuition:* state resident $2478 full-time, $83 per credit part-time; nonresident $3716 full-time, $124 per credit part-time. Full-time tuition and fees vary according to course load, location, program, and reciprocity agreements. Part-time tuition and fees vary according to course load, location, program, and reciprocity agreements. *Required fees:* $2895 full-time, $97 per credit part-time. *Room and board:* $5240; room only: $2348. Room and board charges vary according to board plan and housing facility. *Payment plans:* installment, deferred payment. *Waivers:* children of alumni, senior citizens, and employees or children of employees.

Financial Aid Of all full-time matriculated undergraduates who enrolled in 2007, 7,132 applied for aid, 6,417 were judged to have need, 5,541 had their need fully met. 670 Federal Work-Study jobs (averaging $1015). 2,193 state and other part-time jobs (averaging $1368). In 2007, 1231 non-need-based awards were made. *Average percent of need met:* 83%. *Average financial aid package:* $8051. *Average need-based loan:* $4768. *Average need-based gift aid:* $3844. *Average non-need-based aid:* $1496. *Average indebtedness upon graduation:* $21,061.

Applying *Options:* electronic application, deferred entrance. *Application fee:* $20. *Required:* high school transcript, minimum 2.6 GPA, minimum ACT score of 18. *Application deadlines:* rolling (freshmen), rolling (transfers). *Notification:* continuous (transfers).

Freshman Application Contact Ms. Michelle Kuebler, Assistant Director of Admissions, South Dakota State University, Box 2201, Brookings, SD 57007.

Phone: 605-688-4121. *Toll-free phone:* 800-952-3541. *Fax:* 605-688-6891. *E-mail:* sdsu.admissions@sdstate.edu.

UNIVERSITY OF SIOUX FALLS

Sioux Falls, South Dakota **www.usiouxfalls.edu/**

- **Independent American Baptist Churches in the USA** comprehensive, founded 1883
- **Suburban** 22-acre campus
- **Endowment** $17.2 million
- **Coed** 1,261 undergraduate students, 82% full-time, 53% women, 47% men
- **Moderately difficult** entrance level, 97% of applicants were admitted

Undergraduates 1,032 full-time, 229 part-time. Students come from 29 states and territories, 5 other countries, 32% are from out of state, 3% African American, 0.2% Asian American or Pacific Islander, 1% Hispanic American, 0.4% Native American, 0.5% international, 7% transferred in, 53% live on campus. *Retention:* 68% of 2006 full-time freshmen returned.

Freshmen *Admission:* 642 applied, 624 admitted, 263 enrolled. *Average high school GPA:* 3.52. *Test scores:* ACT scores over 18: 92%; ACT scores over 24: 41%; SAT critical reading scores over 700: 22%; SAT math scores over 700: 11%; ACT scores over 30: 5%.

Faculty *Total:* 140, 43% full-time. *Student/faculty ratio:* 15:1.

Majors Accounting; applied mathematics; art; art teacher education; biology/biological sciences; business administration and management; chemistry; clinical laboratory science/medical technology; commercial and advertising art; communication/speech communication and rhetoric; computer and information sciences; computer science; education; elementary education; emergency medical technology (EMT paramedic); English; history; kinesiology and exercise science; liberal arts and sciences/liberal studies; mass communication/media; mathematics; medical radiologic technology; middle school education; music; music teacher education; philosophy; political science and government; pre-dentistry studies; pre-law studies; pre-medical studies; pre-veterinary studies; psychology; radio and television; science teacher education; secondary education; social sciences; social work; sociology; speech and rhetoric; youth ministry.

Academics *Calendar:* 4-1-4. *Degrees:* associate, bachelor's, master's, and doctoral. *Special study options:* academic remediation for entering students, accelerated degree program, adult/continuing education programs, advanced placement credit, distance learning, double majors, honors programs, independent study, internships, off-campus study, part-time degree program, services for LD students, student-designed majors, study abroad, summer session for credit. *Unusual degree programs:* 3-2 engineering with South Dakota State University, Washington University (St. Louis); theology and philosophy with North American Baptist Seminary.

Computers on Campus 150 computers/terminals are available on campus for general student use. Students can access the following: campus intranet, computer help desk, free student e-mail accounts, online (class) grades, online (class) registration, online (class) schedules. Campuswide network is available. 100% of college-owned or -operated housing units are wired for high-speed Internet access.

Student Life *Housing:* on-campus residence required through sophomore year. *Options:* coed, men-only, women-only. Campus housing is university owned and leased by the school. Freshman applicants given priority for college housing. *Activities and organizations:* drama/theater group, student-run newspaper, radio and television station, choral group, Fellowship of Christian Athletes, Campus Ministry Outreach, Student Senate, Social Work Club, Phi Theta Kappa. *Campus security:* 24-hour patrols, student patrols, late-night transport/escort service, controlled dormitory access. *Student services:* personal/psychological counseling, women's center.

Athletics Member NAIA. *Intercollegiate sports:* baseball M (s), basketball M (s)/W (s), cheerleading W (s), cross-country running M (s)/W (s), football M (s), golf M (s)/W (s), soccer M (s)/W (s), softball W (s), tennis M (s)/W (s), track and field M (s)/W (s), volleyball W (s). *Intramural sports:* basketball M/W, football M/W, ice hockey M/W, table tennis M/W, ultimate Frisbee M/W, volleyball M/W.

Standardized Tests *Required:* SAT or ACT (for admission).

Costs (2008–09) *Comprehensive fee:* $24,966 includes full-time tuition ($18,926), mandatory fees ($400), and room and board ($5640). Part-time tuition: $280 per semester hour. *Required fees:* $150 per year part-time. *College room only:* $2640.

Financial Aid Of all full-time matriculated undergraduates who enrolled in 2004, 130 Federal Work-Study jobs (averaging $1200).

Applying *Options:* electronic application, early admission, deferred entrance. *Application fee:* $25. *Required:* high school transcript. *Required for some:* 2 letters of recommendation, interview. *Recommended:* essay or personal statement, minimum 2.5 GPA. *Application deadlines:* rolling (freshmen), rolling (transfers). *Notification:* continuous (freshmen), continuous (transfers).

Freshman Application Contact Ms. Amanda Anderson, Director of Recruitment and Retention, University of Sioux Falls, 1101 West 22nd Street, Sioux Falls, SD 57105. *Phone:* 605-331-6600. *Toll-free phone:* 800-888-1047. *Fax:* 605-331-6615. *E-mail:* admissions@usioux falls.edu.

THE UNIVERSITY OF SOUTH DAKOTA

Vermillion, South Dakota **www.usd.edu/**

- **State-supported** university, founded 1862
- **Small-town** 216-acre campus
- **Endowment** $119.4 million
- **Coed** 6,844 undergraduate students, 65% full-time, 63% women, 37% men
- **Moderately difficult** entrance level, 80% of applicants were admitted

Undergraduates 4,453 full-time, 2,391 part-time. Students come from 44 states and territories, 32 other countries, 26% are from out of state, 1% African American, 1% Asian American or Pacific Islander, 1% Hispanic American, 2% Native American, 0.5% international, 14% transferred in, 31% live on campus. *Retention:* 72% of 2006 full-time freshmen returned.

Freshmen *Admission:* 3,517 applied, 2,805 admitted, 1,184 enrolled. *Average high school GPA:* 3.26. *Test scores:* SAT critical reading scores over 500: 47%; SAT math scores over 500: 60%; ACT scores over 18: 94%; SAT critical reading scores over 600: 20%; SAT math scores over 600: 27%; ACT scores over 24: 43%; SAT critical reading scores over 700: 7%; ACT scores over 30: 6%.

Faculty *Total:* 388, 94% full-time, 80% with terminal degrees. *Student/faculty ratio:* 17:1.

Majors Accounting; American Indian/Native American studies; anthropology; art; art teacher education; biology/biological sciences; biology teacher education; business administration and management; business/managerial economics; chemistry; classics and languages, literatures and linguistics; communication disorders; computer and information sciences; criminal justice/law enforcement administration; curriculum and instruction; drama and dance teacher education; dramatic/theater arts; economics; education; elementary education; English; English/language arts teacher education; finance; foreign language teacher education; French; French language teacher education; general studies; geology/earth science; German; German language teacher education; health teacher education; history; history teacher education; hospital and health care facilities administration; liberal arts and sciences/liberal studies; marketing/marketing management; mass communication/media; mathematics; mathematics teacher education; middle school education; music; music teacher education; nursing (registered nurse training); parks, recreation and leisure; philosophy; physical education teaching and coaching; physics; physics teacher education; political science and government; psychology; science teacher education; secondary education; social science teacher education; social work; sociology; Spanish; Spanish language teacher education; special education; speech teacher education; substance abuse/addiction counseling.

Academics *Calendar:* semesters. *Degrees:* associate, bachelor's, master's, doctoral, first professional, post-master's, and postbachelor's certificates. *Special study options:* academic remediation for entering students, advanced placement credit, distance learning, double majors, English as a second language, honors programs, independent study, internships, off-campus study, part-time degree program, services for LD students, study abroad, summer session for credit. *ROTC:* Army (b). *Unusual degree programs:* 3-2 business administration; social work; accounting, public administration.

Computers on Campus 877 computers/terminals are available on campus for general student use. Students can access the following: campus intranet, computer help desk, free student e-mail accounts, online (class) grades, online (class) registration, online (class) schedules. Campuswide network is available. Wireless service is available via entire campus.

Student Life *Housing:* on-campus residence required through sophomore year. *Options:* coed, men-only, women-only. Campus housing is university owned. Freshman campus housing is guaranteed. *Activities and organizations:* drama/theater group, student-run newspaper, radio station, choral group, marching band, Program Council, Residence Hall Association, Student Ambassadors, Delta Sigma Pi, national fraternities, national sororities. *Campus security:* 24-hour emergency response devices and patrols, student patrols, late-night transport/escort service, controlled dormitory access. *Student services:* health clinic, personal/psychological counseling, legal services.

Athletics Member NCAA. All Division II. *Intercollegiate sports:* baseball M (s), basketball M (s)/W (s), cross-country running M (s)/W (s), football M (s), softball W (s), swimming and diving M (s)/W, tennis M (s)/W (s), track and field M (s)/W (s), volleyball W (s). *Intramural sports:* badminton M/W, basketball M (c)/W (c), bowling M/W, cross-country running M/W, fencing M (c)/W (c), football M (c)/W (c), golf M/W, ice hockey M (c), racquetball M (c)/W (c), riflery M/W, rock climbing M (c), soccer M (c)/W (c), softball M (c)/W (c), swimming and diving M/W, table tennis M/W, tennis M/W, track and field M/W, volleyball M/W, water polo M/W.

Standardized Tests *Required:* SAT or ACT (for admission).

Costs (2007–08) *Tuition:* state resident $2478 full-time, $83 per credit hour part-time; nonresident $7872 full-time, $262 per credit hour part-time. Full-time tuition and fees vary according to course load and reciprocity agreements. Part-time tuition and fees vary according to course load and reciprocity agreements. *Required fees:* $2915 full-time, $98 per credit hour part-time. *Room and board:* $5174; room only: $2503. Room and board charges vary according to board plan and housing facility. *Payment plan:* deferred payment. *Waivers:* children of alumni, senior citizens, and employees or children of employees.

Financial Aid Of all full-time matriculated undergraduates who enrolled in 2005, 3,693 applied for aid, 2,802 were judged to have need, 1,891 had their need fully met. 603 Federal Work-Study jobs (averaging $1267). 750 state and other part-time jobs (averaging $1624). In 2005, 801 non-need-based awards were made. *Average percent of need met:* 73%. *Average financial aid package:* $5500. *Average need-based loan:* $3772. *Average need-based gift aid:* $3086. *Average non-need-based aid:* $3062. *Average indebtedness upon graduation:* $20,163.

Applying *Options:* electronic application, early admission, deferred entrance. *Application fee:* $20. *Required:* high school transcript. *Required for some:* letters of recommendation. *Recommended:* minimum 2.0 GPA. *Application deadlines:* rolling (freshmen), rolling (transfers). *Notification:* continuous (freshmen), continuous (transfers).

Freshman Application Contact Ms. Stephanie Moser, Director of Admissions, The University of South Dakota, 414 East Clark Street, Vermillion, SD 57069. *Phone:* 605-677-5434. *Toll-free phone:* 877-269-6837. *Fax:* 605-677-6753. *E-mail:* admiss@usd.edu.

NATIONAL AMERICAN UNIVERSITY

RAPID CITY, SOUTH DAKOTA

The University

The mission of National American University (NAU) is to provide career education to students of diverse backgrounds, interests, and abilities. NAU is a private, multicampus institution of higher education that is committed to building a learning partnership with students by creating a challenging and effective educational environment. National American University offers educational programs that are responsive to the career interests and objectives of its students and to the needs of employers, government, and society.

The first campus of National American University was established in Rapid City, South Dakota, in 1941. The curriculum was focused on business administration. Since then, the curriculum has expanded to include a variety of high-demand career choices, such as athletic training, equine management, information technology, legal studies, and veterinary technology. NAU, which was originally known as National College, changed names in 1997 as just one indication of the development and growth of the institution and its programs. National American University is accredited by the Higher Learning Commission of the North Central Association of Colleges and Schools.

Today, more than 400 students are enrolled at the Rapid City Campus. The diverse student body consists of students from across the U.S. and around the world. National American University is about giving students the tools they need to pursue their dreams. Whether a student's career path leads to business administration or equine management, NAU prepares students to excel in today's competitive marketplace. Nearly every degree program requires an internship prior to graduation, and employment during college within a student's career choice is strongly encouraged and supported by faculty and staff members. Students also have the advantage of classes in their major during their freshman year.

In addition to its undergraduate offerings, NAU also offers graduate degrees in both business administration and business management.

Campus life revolves around student organizations, intramural sports, and varsity athletics. The National American University Mavericks are members of the National Association of Intercollegiate Athletics (NAIA) and the National Intercollegiate Rodeo Association (NIRA). Intercollegiate athletics include men's and women's rodeo and women's volleyball.

Location

National American University is located in a Midwestern community with a population of about 60,000 residents. Rapid City is a retail hub for several Midwestern states. Rapid City's shops, entertainment facilities, and wide array of dining establishments offer a big-city feel without the crime, pollution, and overcrowding. A strong Rapid City economy provides many part-time employment opportunities for college students.

Just 20 minutes away lies one of the most popular tourist areas in the world—Mount Rushmore. Nestled in the majestic Black Hills, Rapid City offers everything from the Rushmore Mall and the Dahl Fine Arts Center to wilderness activities such as mountain biking and snow skiing. Rapid City offers the social and cultural diversity that students desire.

Majors and Degrees

At the Rapid City Campus, bachelor's and associate degrees are offered in accounting, applied management, athletic training, business administration (with emphases in accounting, financial management, information technology, international business, management, marketing, and prelaw), equine management, equine science, general education studies, health-care management, Internet systems development, legal studies (prelaw), management information systems, network management, paralegal studies, software development, and veterinary technology. NAU also offers a veterinary assisting diploma.

Academic Programs

In order to obtain a Bachelor of Science degree, students are required to complete all capstone courses with a minimum grade of C, finish with a minimum 2.0 grade point average overall in the major core, and complete 187 quarter hours of credit, with the final 48 coming in residence at NAU.

National American University accepts credits earned through the College-Level Examination Program (CLEP), the Defense Activity for Non-Traditional Education Support (DANTES), and ACT PEP. NAU also has its own credit-by-examination program.

National American University offers a strong English as a second language (ESL) program for international students.

Select Internet courses are available to students, allowing them to take classes from around the globe online.

Academic Facilities

National American University's on-campus library provides students with up-to-date business and legal resources. The computer laboratory gives students a state-of-the-art study aid with computerized library search capabilities and Internet access.

Costs

Tuition for the 2007–08 academic year was $11,952 for full-time students (based on 16 credit hours per quarter for three quarters). The residence hall charge was $1995 and board was $2235.

Financial Aid

NAU understands that financing higher education is a concern, and the financial aid staff works with students on affordability options. The University provides assistance in the form of grants, scholarships, work-study, and low-interest loan programs through federal, state, and local sources. When students apply for federal student aid, the information reported is used in a formula that has been established by the U.S. Congress that calculates the Expected Family Contribution (EFC). This is an amount that students and their families are expected to contribute toward education. The EFC determines the student's eligibility for federal financial aid programs.

Merit-based academic and athletic scholarships are also available to qualified new and continuing students. In addition, many NAU students work part-time while attending the University.

Faculty

A 15:1 student-faculty ratio promotes individual attention in the classroom. Instructors are individuals with experience in their fields, providing real-world experience with textbook knowledge. Instructors also serve as academic advisers and student organization sponsors, providing invaluable interaction with students. In addition, free tutoring is available for all Rapid City Campus students.

Student Government

The Student Senate provides funding for various campus student groups as well as school functions throughout the year.

Admission Requirements

It is recommended that applicants and their families visit National American University to become acquainted with the faculty, staff, and facilities of the University. A personal interview should be scheduled with a member of the admissions staff. The applicant is encouraged to contact the Admissions Department in advance so that necessary arrangements can be made.

Graduation from high school is a requirement for regular admission to NAU for applicants who are seeking a diploma or degree. Those who have satisfied graduation requirements through the General Educational Development (GED) test are also eligible for regular admission.

If a student chooses not to attend full-time, a schedule may be arranged for one or more courses. Credits earned may be applied to degree or diploma programs.

A special student is one who is not enrolled in a diploma or degree program. Special students are not eligible for receipt of financial aid.

Students who have successfully completed course work at other accredited postsecondary institutions may apply for admission to NAU.

The international student admissions procedure requires that the student complete and submit an admission application along with a $45 application fee. International applicants must obtain official transcripts and diplomas, if earned, from all high schools and colleges attended (non-English documents must be accompanied by certified English translations). They must also present an official copy of one of the following: the Test of English as a Foreign Language (TOEFL) report with a minimum score of 500, an ESL Language Center score of 107 or above, or other comparable demonstration of English proficiency (students who have not yet taken the TOEFL or do not have an ESL proficiency are recommended to attend the ESL Center at the Rapid City Campus). International applicants must also provide a certified bank statement, an annual statement of earnings, and a letter of financial commitment that indicates the ability to meet financial obligations (students under contracted agreement or written verification of full sponsorship may be exempt from a portion of the above financial certification requirements). They must also provide proof of status with the Immigration and Naturalization Services if currently living in the United States.

National American University may be in contact with respective embassies in helping students maintain proper immigration status.

Application and Information

In order for students to apply for admission, an application for admission must be completed and mailed or personally delivered to the Rapid City Campus Admissions Department. Application materials may be obtained and arrangements may be made for visiting the University through the Admissions Office. Students may also apply online at the University's Web site (http://www.rapid.national.edu).

The application for admission must be submitted along with a $25 application fee. A letter of acceptance is mailed as soon as possible. If the applicant is not accepted, the application fee is refunded. Early application is encouraged, especially if campus housing (at the Rapid City location), financial aid, and/or part-time employment are desired.

For applications or more information, students should contact:

Director of Admissions
National American University
321 Kansas City Street
Rapid City, South Dakota 57701
Phone: 605-394-4827
800-209-0490 (toll-free)
Web site: http://www.rapid.national.edu

National American University Rapid City Campus graduates compare their faces to the original "four faces" of Mount Rushmore, which is located in the Black Hills of South Dakota.

TENNESSEE

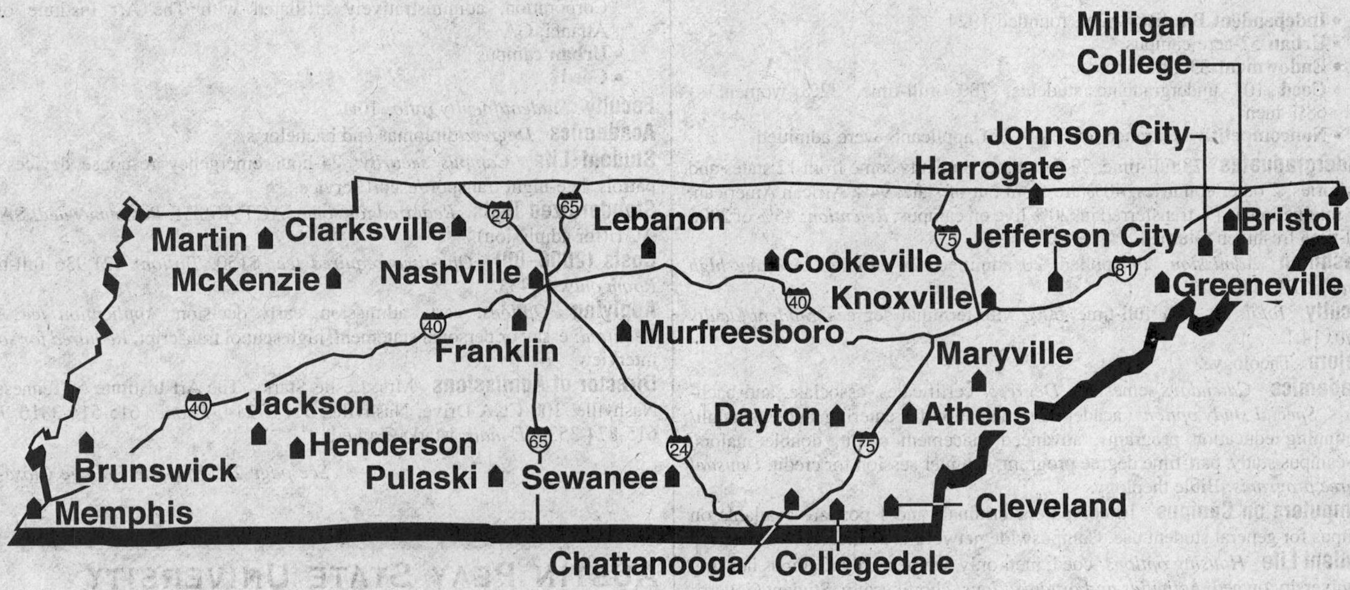
Milligan College
Johnson City
Harrogate
Bristol
Jefferson City
Greeneville
Cookeville
Knoxville
Lebanon
Clarksville
Martin
McKenzie
Nashville
Murfreesboro
Franklin
Maryville
Jackson
Henderson
Dayton
Athens
Brunswick
Pulaski
Sewanee
Memphis
Cleveland
Chattanooga
Collegedale
24
65
75
81
40
40
40
65
24
75

AMERICAN BAPTIST COLLEGE OF AMERICAN BAPTIST THEOLOGICAL SEMINARY

Nashville, Tennessee **www.abcnash.edu/**

- **Independent Baptist** 4-year, founded 1924
- **Urban** 52-acre campus
- **Endowment** $3.2 million
- **Coed** 107 undergraduate students, 73% full-time, 32% women, 68% men
- **Noncompetitive** entrance level, 69% of applicants were admitted

Undergraduates 78 full-time, 29 part-time. Students come from 12 states and territories, 2 other countries, 40% are from out of state, 94% African American, 5% international, 4% transferred in, 20% live on campus. *Retention:* 85% of 2006 full-time freshmen returned.

Freshmen *Admission:* 29 applied, 20 admitted, 20 enrolled. *Average high school GPA:* 2.95.

Faculty *Total:* 10, 40% full-time, 50% with terminal degrees. *Student/faculty ratio:* 14:1.

Majors Theology.

Academics *Calendar:* semesters. *Degrees:* certificates, associate, and bachelor's. *Special study options:* academic remediation for entering students, adult/continuing education programs, advanced placement credit, double majors, off-campus study, part-time degree program, summer session for credit. *Unusual degree programs:* Bible theology.

Computers on Campus 10 computers/terminals and 1 port are available on campus for general student use. Campuswide network is available.

Student Life *Housing options:* coed, men-only, women-only. Campus housing is university owned. *Activities and organizations:* choral group, Student Government Association, Vespers Service, national fraternities. *Campus security:* student patrols, security patrols from 10 p.m. to 7 a.m.

Athletics *Intramural sports:* basketball M, football M, golf M.

Costs (2008–09) *Comprehensive fee:* $8000 includes full-time tuition ($4560), mandatory fees ($140), and room and board ($3300). Part-time tuition: $190 per credit hour. *Required fees:* $140 per term part-time. *College room only:* $1800.

Financial Aid Of all full-time matriculated undergraduates who enrolled in 2006, 52 applied for aid, 51 were judged to have need, 12 had their need fully met. 1 Federal Work-Study job (averaging $3400). *Average financial aid package:* $2155. *Average need-based gift aid:* $1161. *Financial aid deadline:* 7/23.

Applying *Options:* deferred entrance. *Application fee:* $20. *Required:* essay or personal statement, high school transcript, minimum 2.0 GPA, 3 letters of recommendation, interview. *Application deadlines:* 7/12 (freshmen), 7/12 (transfers). *Notification:* 8/15 (freshmen), 8/15 (transfers).

Freshman Application Contact Ms. Marcella Lockhart, Director of Enrollment Management, American Baptist College of American Baptist Theological Seminary, 1800 Baptist World Center Drive, Nashville, TN 37207. *Phone:* 615-256-1463. *Fax:* 615-226-7855. *E-mail:* mlockhart@abcnash.edu.

AQUINAS COLLEGE

Nashville, Tennessee **www.aquinascollege.edu/**

Freshman Application Contact Ms. Diane LeJeune, Director of Admission, Aquinas College, 4210 Harding Road, Nashville, TN 37205-2005. *Phone:* 615-297-7545 Ext. 428. *Toll-free phone:* 800-649-9956. *Fax:* 615-279-3893.

ARGOSY UNIVERSITY, NASHVILLE

Nashville, Tennessee **www.argosy.edu/locations/nashville/**

- **Proprietary** university, founded 2001
- **Coed**

Majors Business administration and management; criminal justice/law enforcement administration; finance; health/health care administration; international business/trade/commerce; marketing/marketing management; psychology; substance abuse/addiction counseling.

Academics *Calendar:* semesters.

Admissions Office Contact Argosy University, Nashville, 100 Centerview Drive, Suite 225, Nashville, TN 37214.

See page 2452 for the College Close-Up.

THE ART INSTITUTE OF TENNESSEE–NASHVILLE

Nashville, Tennessee **www.artinstitutes.edu/nashville/**

- **Proprietary** 4-year, founded 2006, part of Education Management Corporation, administratively affiliated with The Art Institute of Atlanta, GA
- **Urban** campus
- **Coed**

Faculty *Student/faculty ratio:* 10:1.

Academics *Degree:* diplomas and bachelor's.

Student Life *Campus security:* 24-hour emergency response devices and patrols, late-night transport/escort service.

Standardized Tests *Required for some:* ACT ASSET. *Recommended:* SAT or ACT (for admission).

Costs (2008–09) *One-time required fee:* $150. *Tuition:* $21,936 full-time. *Room only:* $5433.

Applying *Options:* early admission, early decision. *Application fee:* $50. *Required:* essay or personal statement, high school transcript. *Required for some:* interview.

Director of Admissions Mrs. Leslie Starks, The Art Institute of Tennessee–Nashville, 100 CNA Drive, Nashville, TN 37214. *Phone:* 615-514-3816. *Fax:* 615-874-3530. *E-mail:* lstarks@aii.edu.

See page 2454 for the College Close-Up.

AUSTIN PEAY STATE UNIVERSITY

Clarksville, Tennessee **www.apsu.edu/**

- **State-supported** comprehensive, founded 1927, part of Tennessee Board of Regents
- **Suburban** 200-acre campus with easy access to Nashville
- **Endowment** $6.5 million
- **Coed** 8,341 undergraduate students, 72% full-time, 62% women, 38% men
- **Moderately difficult** entrance level, 91% of applicants were admitted

Undergraduates 6,046 full-time, 2,295 part-time. Students come from 38 states and territories, 4 other countries, 14% are from out of state, 16% African American, 2% Asian American or Pacific Islander, 4% Hispanic American, 0.7% Native American, 2% international, 12% transferred in, 14% live on campus. *Retention:* 66% of 2006 full-time freshmen returned.

Freshmen *Admission:* 2,575 applied, 2,340 admitted, 1,412 enrolled. *Average high school GPA:* 3.09. *Test scores:* ACT scores over 18: 91%; ACT scores over 24: 27%; ACT scores over 30: 2%.

Faculty *Total:* 510, 56% full-time. *Student/faculty ratio:* 20:1.

Majors Agriculture; art; biology/biological sciences; business administration and management; business automation/technology/data entry; chemistry; clinical laboratory science/medical technology; computer and information sciences; criminal justice/law enforcement administration; engineering technology; English; environmental studies; foreign languages and literatures; general studies; geology/earth science; health and physical education; health teacher education; history; industrial arts; interdisciplinary studies; liberal arts and sciences/liberal studies; mass communication/media; mathematics; music; non-profit management; nursing (registered nurse training); philosophy; physics; political science and government; psychology; radiologic technology/science; social work; sociology; Spanish; special education.

Academics *Calendar:* semesters. *Degrees:* certificates, associate, bachelor's, master's, post-master's, and postbachelor's certificates. *Special study options:* academic remediation for entering students, accelerated degree program, adult/continuing education programs, advanced placement credit, cooperative education, distance learning, double majors, English as a second language, honors programs, independent study, internships, part-time degree program, services for LD students, study abroad, summer session for credit. *ROTC:* Army (b), Air Force (c).

Computers on Campus 760 computers/terminals are available on campus for general student use. Students can access the following: campus intranet, computer help desk, free student e-mail accounts, online (class) grades, online (class) registration, online (class) schedules. Campuswide network is available. Wireless service is available via entire campus.

Student Life *Housing:* on-campus residence required for freshman year. *Options:* coed, men-only, women-only, disabled students. Campus housing is university owned. Freshman campus housing is guaranteed. *Activities and orga-*

nizations: drama/theater group, student-run newspaper, radio and television station, choral group, marching band, national fraternities, national sororities. *Campus security:* 24-hour patrols, late-night transport/escort service, controlled dormitory access. *Student services:* health clinic, personal/psychological counseling.

Athletics Member NCAA. All Division I. *Intercollegiate sports:* baseball M (s), basketball M (s)/W (s), cheerleading M (s)/W (s), cross-country running M (s)/W (s), football M (s), golf M (s)/W (s), riflery W (s), soccer W (s), softball W (s), tennis M (s)/W (s), track and field W (s), volleyball W (s). *Intramural sports:* badminton M/W, basketball M/W, football M/W, golf M/W, ice hockey M/W, racquetball M/W, soccer M/W, softball M/W, ultimate Frisbee M/W, volleyball M/W.

Standardized Tests *Required for some:* SAT or ACT (for admission).

Costs (2007–08) *Tuition:* state resident $4058 full-time, $178 per credit hour part-time; nonresident $14,334 full-time, $624 per credit hour part-time. Full-time tuition and fees vary according to location and program. Part-time tuition and fees vary according to location and program. *Required fees:* $1180 full-time, $56 per credit hour part-time, $15 per credit hour part-time. *Room and board:* $5510; room only: $3400. Room and board charges vary according to board plan and housing facility. *Payment plan:* installment. *Waivers:* senior citizens and employees or children of employees.

Financial Aid Of all full-time matriculated undergraduates who enrolled in 2006, 5,388 applied for aid, 4,705 were judged to have need. 163 Federal Work-Study jobs (averaging $1569). 323 state and other part-time jobs (averaging $1865). In 2006, 479 non-need-based awards were made. *Average financial aid package:* $6679. *Average need-based gift aid:* $3790. *Average non-need-based aid:* $4879.

Applying *Options:* electronic application, early admission, deferred entrance. *Application fee:* $15. *Required:* high school transcript. *Required for some:* 2.75 high school GPA, minimum ACT composite score of 19. *Application deadlines:* 7/25 (freshmen), rolling (transfers). *Notification:* continuous (freshmen), continuous (transfers).

Freshman Application Contact Mr. Ryan Forsythe, Director of Admissions, Austin Peay State University, PO Box 4548, Clarksville, TN 37044-4548. *Phone:* 931-221-7661. *Toll-free phone:* 800-844-2778. *Fax:* 931-221-6168. *E-mail:* admissions@apsu.apsu.edu.

BAPTIST COLLEGE OF HEALTH SCIENCES

Memphis, Tennessee www.bchs.edu/

- **Independent Southern Baptist** 4-year, founded 1994, administratively affiliated with Baptist Memorial Health Care Corporation
- **Urban** campus
- **Coed, primarily women** 925 undergraduate students, 68% full-time, 88% women, 12% men
- **Moderately difficult** entrance level, 38% of applicants were admitted

Undergraduates 627 full-time, 298 part-time. Students come from 10 states and territories, 29% are from out of state, 30% African American, 2% Asian American or Pacific Islander, 2% Hispanic American, 0.3% Native American, 93% transferred in, 10% live on campus. *Retention:* 83% of 2006 full-time freshmen returned.

Freshmen *Admission:* 187 applied, 71 admitted, 49 enrolled. *Average high school GPA:* 3.79.

Faculty *Total:* 97, 62% full-time, 19% with terminal degrees.

Majors Diagnostic medical sonography and ultrasound technology; health/health care administration; health services/allied health/health sciences; medical radiologic technology; nuclear medical technology; nursing (registered nurse training); radiologic technology/science; respiratory care therapy.

Academics *Calendar:* semesters. *Degree:* bachelor's. *Special study options:* advanced placement credit, cooperative education.

Computers on Campus 64 computers/terminals and 64 ports are available on campus for general student use. Students can access the following: computer help desk, free student e-mail accounts, online (class) grades, online (class) registration, online (class) schedules. Campuswide network is available. 100% of college-owned or -operated housing units are wired for high-speed Internet access. Wireless service is available via entire campus.

Student Life *Housing options:* coed. Campus housing is university owned. *Activities and organizations:* Student Government Association, Student Nursing Association, Allied Health Organization. *Campus security:* 24-hour emergency response devices, late-night transport/escort service, controlled dormitory access, 16 to 20-hour trained security personnel. *Student services:* health clinic, personal/psychological counseling.

Standardized Tests *Required:* ACT (for admission), Health Occupations Basic Entrance Test (for admission).

Costs (2007–08) *Tuition:* $7350 full-time, $245 per credit hour part-time. *Required fees:* $800 full-time, $25 per credit hour part-time. *Room only:* $2700.

Applying *Options:* electronic application, early admission. *Application fee:* $25. *Required:* high school transcript, minimum 2.75 GPA, 3 letters of recommendation, immunizations, health physical. *Required for some:* essay or personal statement, interview. *Application deadlines:* 6/1 (freshmen), 6/1 (transfers).

Director of Admissions Ms. Lissa Morgan, Manager of Admissions/Retention, Baptist College of Health Sciences, 1003 Monroe Avenue, Memphis, TN 38104. *Phone:* 901-572-2441. *Toll-free phone:* 866-575-2247. *E-mail:* Lissa.Morgan@bchs.edu.

BELHAVEN COLLEGE

Memphis, Tennessee

BELMONT UNIVERSITY

Nashville, Tennessee www.belmont.edu/

- **Independent Baptist** comprehensive, founded 1951
- **Urban** 34-acre campus
- **Endowment** $62.3 million
- **Coed** 4,028 undergraduate students, 91% full-time, 59% women, 41% men
- **Moderately difficult** entrance level, 62% of applicants were admitted

Undergraduates 3,677 full-time, 351 part-time. Students come from 48 states and territories, 27 other countries, 56% are from out of state, 4% African American, 2% Asian American or Pacific Islander, 2% Hispanic American, 0.4% Native American, 1% international, 10% transferred in, 45% live on campus. *Retention:* 80% of 2006 full-time freshmen returned.

Freshmen *Admission:* 2,766 applied, 1,712 admitted, 804 enrolled. *Average high school GPA:* 3.5. *Test scores:* SAT critical reading scores over 500: 92%; SAT math scores over 500: 90%; ACT scores over 18: 100%; SAT critical reading scores over 600: 37%; SAT math scores over 600: 38%; ACT scores over 24: 71%; SAT critical reading scores over 700: 5%; SAT math scores over 700: 6%; ACT scores over 30: 13%.

Faculty *Total:* 537, 45% full-time, 49% with terminal degrees. *Student/faculty ratio:* 12:1.

Majors Accounting; advertising; ancient Near Eastern and biblical languages; applied mathematics; art; art teacher education; biblical studies; bilingual and multilingual education; biochemistry; biological and physical sciences; biology/biological sciences; broadcast journalism; business administration and management; business/managerial economics; business teacher education; chemistry; clinical laboratory science/medical technology; computer management; computer programming; computer science; consumer merchandising/retailing management; counselor education/school counseling and guidance; developmental and child psychology; divinity/ministry; dramatic/theater arts; economics; education; elementary education; engineering science; English; entrepreneurship; finance; fine/studio arts; health and physical education; health/health care administration; health teacher education; history; information science/studies; international business/trade/commerce; journalism; marketing/marketing management; mass communication/media; mathematics; modern Greek; music; music history, literature, and theory; music management and merchandising; music teacher education; nursing (registered nurse training); parks, recreation and leisure; pastoral studies/counseling; philosophy; physical education teaching and coaching; physics; piano and organ; political science and government; psychology; public relations, advertising, and applied communication related; radio and television; religious/sacred music; social work; sociology; Spanish; special education; speech and rhetoric; voice and opera; western civilization.

Academics *Calendar:* semesters. *Degrees:* bachelor's, master's, doctoral, and post-master's certificates. *Special study options:* accelerated degree program, adult/continuing education programs, advanced placement credit, cooperative education, distance learning, double majors, honors programs, independent study, internships, off-campus study, part-time degree program, student-designed majors, study abroad, summer session for credit. *ROTC:* Army (c), Navy (c). *Unusual degree programs:* 3-2 engineering with Auburn University, Georgia Institute of Technology, University of Tennessee.

Computers on Campus 400 computers/terminals are available on campus for general student use. Students can access the following: campus intranet, free student e-mail accounts, online (class) grades, online (class) registration, online (class) schedules, individual student information via BANNER Web. Campuswide network is available. 100% of college-owned or -operated housing units are wired for high-speed Internet access. Wireless service is available via entire campus.

Student Life *Housing:* on-campus residence required through sophomore year. *Options:* men-only, women-only. Campus housing is university owned. Freshman applicants given priority for college housing. *Activities and organizations:* drama/theater group, student-run newspaper, radio and television station, choral group, marching band, national fraternities, national sororities. *Campus security:* 24-hour emergency response devices and patrols, late-night transport/escort service, controlled dormitory access, bicycle patrol. *Student services:* health clinic, personal/psychological counseling, women's center.

Athletics Member NCAA. All Division I. *Intercollegiate sports:* baseball M (s), basketball M (s)/W (s), cross-country running M (s)/W (s), golf M (s)/W (s), soccer M (s)/W (s), softball W (s), tennis M (s)/W (s), track and field M (s)/W (s), volleyball W (s). *Intramural sports:* basketball M/W, bowling M/W, football M, golf M, racquetball M/W, table tennis M/W, tennis M/W, volleyball M/W.

Standardized Tests *Required:* SAT or ACT (for admission).

Costs (2008–09) *Comprehensive fee:* $31,110 includes full-time tuition ($20,070), mandatory fees ($1040), and room and board ($10,000). Part-time tuition: $770 per credit hour. *Required fees:* $350 per term part-time. *College room only:* $6300.

Financial Aid Of all full-time matriculated undergraduates who enrolled in 2007, 2,930 applied for aid, 1,735 were judged to have need, 370 had their need fully met. 263 Federal Work-Study jobs (averaging $1386). In 2007, 1028 non-need-based awards were made. *Average percent of need met:* 79%. *Average financial aid package:* $7474. *Average need-based loan:* $4474. *Average need-based gift aid:* $4820. *Average non-need-based aid:* $6395. *Average indebtedness upon graduation:* $18,851.

Applying *Options:* early admission, deferred entrance. *Application fee:* $35. *Required:* essay or personal statement, high school transcript, minimum 3.0 GPA, letters of recommendation, resume of activities. *Required for some:* interview. *Application deadlines:* 8/1 (freshmen), 8/1 (transfers). *Notification:* continuous (freshmen), continuous (transfers).

Freshman Application Contact Dr. Kathryn Baugher, Dean of Enrollment Services, Belmont University, 1900 Belmont Boulevard, Nashville, TN 37212-3757. *Phone:* 615-460-6785. *Toll-free phone:* 800-56E-NROL. *Fax:* 615-460-5434. *E-mail:* buadmission@mail.belmont.edu.

See page 2456 for the College Close-Up.

BETHEL COLLEGE

McKenzie, Tennessee www.bethel-college.edu/

- **Independent Cumberland Presbyterian** comprehensive, founded 1842
- **Small-town** 100-acre campus
- **Endowment** $6.5 million
- **Coed** 1,995 undergraduate students, 79% full-time, 59% women, 41% men
- **Minimally difficult** entrance level, 57% of applicants were admitted

Undergraduates 1,584 full-time, 411 part-time. Students come from 27 states and territories, 16 other countries, 7% are from out of state, 29% African American, 0.5% Asian American or Pacific Islander, 2% Hispanic American, 0.4% Native American, 2% international, 3% transferred in, 29% live on campus. *Retention:* 58% of 2006 full-time freshmen returned.

Freshmen *Admission:* 771 applied, 438 admitted, 253 enrolled. *Average high school GPA:* 2.9. *Test scores:* SAT critical reading scores over 500: 36%; SAT math scores over 500: 83%; ACT scores over 18: 73%; SAT math scores over 600: 50%; ACT scores over 24: 14%; ACT scores over 30: 1%.

Faculty *Total:* 228, 37% full-time. *Student/faculty ratio:* 15:1.

Majors Accounting and business/management; biology/biological sciences; business administration and management; business administration, management and operations related; chemistry; Christian studies; elementary education; English; health and physical education; history; human services; management information systems; mathematics; multi-/interdisciplinary studies related; music; music teacher education; nursing (registered nurse training); physician assistant; pre-engineering; pre-pharmacy studies; psychology; religious/sacred music; sociology; special education.

Academics *Calendar:* semesters. *Degrees:* bachelor's, master's, and first professional. *Special study options:* academic remediation for entering students, accelerated degree program, adult/continuing education programs, advanced placement credit, double majors, honors programs, internships, off-campus study, part-time degree program, services for LD students, student-designed majors, summer session for credit. *Unusual degree programs:* 3-2 engineering with Tennessee Technological University; pharmacy with University of Memphis.

Computers on Campus 8 computers/terminals and 600 ports are available on campus for general student use. Students can access the following: campus intranet, computer help desk, free student e-mail accounts, online (class) grades, online (class) registration, online (class) schedules. Campuswide network is available. 100% of college-owned or -operated housing units are wired for high-speed Internet access. Wireless service is available via classrooms, student centers.

Student Life *Housing:* on-campus residence required through junior year. *Options:* coed, men-only, women-only, disabled students. Campus housing is university owned and leased by the school. Freshman applicants given priority for college housing. *Activities and organizations:* drama/theater group, choral group, marching band, Campus Crusade for Christ, STEA (Education), SGA, SIFE, Arete. *Campus security:* night patrols by trained security personnel. *Student services:* personal/psychological counseling.

Athletics Member NAIA. *Intercollegiate sports:* baseball M (s), basketball M (s)/W (s), cheerleading M (s)/W (s), cross-country running M (s)/W (s), football M (s), golf M (s)/W (s), soccer M (s)/W (s), softball W (s), tennis M (s)/W (s), track and field M (s)/W (s), volleyball W (s). *Intramural sports:* basketball M/W, football M, golf M/W, soccer M/W, softball M/W, table tennis M/W, tennis M/W, volleyball M/W, weight lifting M/W.

Standardized Tests *Required:* SAT or ACT (for admission).

Costs (2008–09) *Comprehensive fee:* $19,168 includes full-time tuition ($11,592), mandatory fees ($650), and room and board ($6926). Part-time tuition: $358 per credit hour.

Applying *Options:* electronic application, early admission, deferred entrance. *Application fee:* $30. *Required:* high school transcript, minimum 2.25 GPA. *Required for some:* essay or personal statement, 1 letter of recommendation, interview. *Application deadlines:* rolling (freshmen), rolling (transfers). *Notification:* continuous (freshmen), continuous (transfers).

Director of Admissions Mrs. Tina Hodges, Director of Admissions and Marketing, Bethel College, 325 Cherry Avenue, McKenzie, TN 38201. *Phone:* 731-352-4030. *Fax:* 731-352-4069. *E-mail:* hodgest@bethel-college.edu.

BRYAN COLLEGE

Dayton, Tennessee www.bryan.edu/

- **Independent interdenominational** 4-year, founded 1930
- **Small-town** 100-acre campus
- **Coed** 1,020 undergraduate students, 94% full-time, 52% women, 48% men
- **Moderately difficult** entrance level, 71% of applicants were admitted

Undergraduates 959 full-time, 61 part-time. Students come from 33 states and territories, 7 other countries, 61% are from out of state, 4% African American, 0.5% Asian American or Pacific Islander, 1% Hispanic American, 0.3% Native American, 1% international, 74% live on campus. *Retention:* 74% of 2006 full-time freshmen returned.

Freshmen *Admission:* 542 applied, 387 admitted. *Average high school GPA:* 3.6.

Faculty *Total:* 70, 50% full-time, 53% with terminal degrees. *Student/faculty ratio:* 13:1.

Majors Athletic training/sports medicine; biblical studies; biology/biological sciences; business administration and management; business/corporate communications; Christian studies; communication/speech communication and rhetoric; computer science; education; elementary education; English; English/language arts teacher education; health and physical education; history; history teacher education; kindergarten/preschool education; kinesiology and exercise science; liberal arts and sciences/liberal studies; literature; mathematics; mathematics and computer science; mathematics teacher education; middle school education; music; music management and merchandising; music pedagogy; music performance; music teacher education; nursing science; physical education teaching and coaching; piano and organ; political science and government; pre-medical studies; psychology; religious education; religious/sacred music; science teacher education; secondary education; Spanish; voice and opera; wind/percussion instruments; youth ministry.

Academics *Calendar:* semesters. *Degrees:* associate, bachelor's, and master's. *Special study options:* academic remediation for entering students, adult/continuing education programs, advanced placement credit, distance learning, double majors, honors programs, independent study, internships, part-time degree program, study abroad, summer session for credit. *Unusual degree programs:* 3-2 nursing with Vanderbilt University.

Computers on Campus 74 computers/terminals are available on campus for general student use. Students can access the following: campus intranet, computer help desk, free student e-mail accounts, online (class) grades, online (class) schedules. Campuswide network is available.

Student Life *Housing:* on-campus residence required through senior year. *Options:* men-only, women-only. Campus housing is university owned. Freshman campus housing is guaranteed. *Activities and organizations:* drama/theater group, student-run newspaper, choral group, Practical Christian Involvement, Student Government Association, Fellowship of Christian Athletes, Hilltop Players, Chorale. *Campus security:* student patrols, late-night transport/escort service, controlled dormitory access, police patrols. *Student services:* health clinic, personal/psychological counseling.

Athletics Member NAIA, NCCAA. *Intercollegiate sports:* baseball M (s), basketball M (s)/W (s), cross-country running M (s)/W (s), soccer M (s)/W (s), volleyball W (s). *Intramural sports:* basketball M/W, football M/W, golf M, soccer M/W, softball M/W, table tennis M/W, tennis M/W, volleyball M/W.

Standardized Tests *Required:* SAT or ACT (for admission).

Costs (2008–09) *Comprehensive fee:* $22,115 includes full-time tuition ($16,900), mandatory fees ($120), and room and board ($5095). Part-time tuition: $725 per credit.

Financial Aid Of all full-time matriculated undergraduates who enrolled in 2007, 687 applied for aid, 687 were judged to have need, 233 had their need fully met. 183 Federal Work-Study jobs (averaging $1500). In 2007, 109 non-need-based awards were made. *Average percent of need met:* 67%. *Average financial aid package:* $12,203. *Average need-based loan:* $4183. *Average need-based gift aid:* $4052. *Average non-need-based aid:* $7356. *Average indebtedness upon graduation:* $12,588.

Applying *Options:* electronic application, early admission, deferred entrance. *Application fee:* $30. *Required:* essay or personal statement, high school transcript, minimum 2.0 GPA, 3 letters of recommendation. *Required for some:* interview. *Application deadlines:* rolling (freshmen), rolling (transfers).

Freshman Application Contact Michael Sapienza, Director of Admissions, Bryan College, PO Box 7000, Dayton, TN 37321-7000. *Phone:* 423-775-2041. *Toll-free phone:* 800-277-9522. *Fax:* 423-775-7199. *E-mail:* admissions@bryan.edu.

CARSON-NEWMAN COLLEGE

Jefferson City, Tennessee — www.cn.edu/

- **Independent Southern Baptist** comprehensive, founded 1851
- **Small-town** 90-acre campus with easy access to Knoxville
- **Endowment** $48.1 million
- **Coed** 1,834 undergraduate students, 95% full-time, 58% women, 42% men
- **Moderately difficult** entrance level, 62% of applicants were admitted

Undergraduates 1,735 full-time, 99 part-time. Students come from 37 states and territories, 22 other countries, 31% are from out of state, 9% African American, 0.7% Asian American or Pacific Islander, 1% Hispanic American, 0.5% Native American, 3% international, 8% transferred in, 51% live on campus. *Retention:* 69% of 2006 full-time freshmen returned.

Freshmen *Admission:* 3,298 applied, 2,037 admitted, 436 enrolled. *Average high school GPA:* 3.35. *Test scores:* ACT scores over 18: 91%; ACT scores over 24: 36%; ACT scores over 30: 6%.

Faculty *Total:* 212, 59% full-time, 33% with terminal degrees. *Student/faculty ratio:* 13:1.

Majors Accounting; ancient Near Eastern and biblical languages; art; art teacher education; athletic training; biblical studies; biology/biological sciences; broadcast journalism; business administration and management; business/managerial economics; business teacher education; chemistry; child development; clinical laboratory science/medical technology; commercial and advertising art; computer science; consumer services and advocacy; creative writing; developmental and child psychology; dietetics; divinity/ministry; dramatic/theater arts; drawing; economics; education; elementary education; English; family and consumer economics related; family and consumer sciences/home economics teacher education; family and consumer sciences/human sciences; fashion merchandising; film/cinema studies; foods, nutrition, and wellness; French; history; hospital and health care facilities administration; human services; information science/studies; interdisciplinary studies; interior design; international economics; journalism; kindergarten/preschool education; kinesiology and exercise science; liberal arts and sciences/liberal studies; literature; management information systems; marketing/marketing management; mass communication/media; mathematics; music; music teacher education; music theory and composition; nursing (registered nurse training); parks, recreation and leisure; philosophy; photography; physical education teaching and coaching; physics; physics related; piano and organ; political science and government; psychology; religious studies; secondary education; small business administration; sociology; Spanish; special education; speech and rhetoric; voice and opera.

Academics *Calendar:* semesters. *Degrees:* associate, bachelor's, and master's. *Special study options:* academic remediation for entering students, accelerated degree program, adult/continuing education programs, advanced placement credit, English as a second language, honors programs, internships, off-campus study, part-time degree program, services for LD students, student-designed majors, study abroad, summer session for credit. *ROTC:* Army (b), Air Force (c). *Unusual degree programs:* 3-2 engineering with Georgia Institute of Technology, University of Tennessee, Tennessee Technological University; pharmacy with Campbell University, Mercer University, University of Georgia.

Computers on Campus 200 computers/terminals are available on campus for general student use. Campuswide network is available.

Student Life *Housing:* on-campus residence required through junior year. *Options:* men-only, women-only. Freshman campus housing is guaranteed. *Activities and organizations:* drama/theater group, student-run newspaper, choral group, marching band, Baptist Student Union, Fellowship of Christian Athletes, Student Government Association, Student Ambassadors Association, Columbians, national fraternities, national sororities. *Campus security:* 24-hour emergency response devices and patrols, late-night transport/escort service, controlled dormitory access. *Student services:* health clinic, personal/psychological counseling.

Athletics Member NCAA. All Division II. *Intercollegiate sports:* baseball M (s), basketball M (s)/W (s), cross-country running M (s)/W (s), football M (s), golf M (s), soccer M (s)/W (s), softball W (s), tennis M (s)/W (s), track and field M (s)/W (s), volleyball W (s), wrestling M (s). *Intramural sports:* badminton M/W, baseball M/W, basketball M/W, football M/W, golf M/W, racquetball M/W, skiing (downhill) M/W, soccer M/W, softball M/W, table tennis M/W, tennis M/W, volleyball M/W.

Standardized Tests *Required:* SAT or ACT (for admission).

Costs (2007–08) *Comprehensive fee:* $22,340 includes full-time tuition ($16,200), mandatory fees ($780), and room and board ($5360). Full-time tuition and fees vary according to class time and course load. Part-time tuition: $675 per semester hour. *College room only:* $2320. Room and board charges vary according to board plan, gender, and housing facility. *Payment plans:* installment, deferred payment. *Waivers:* senior citizens and employees or children of employees.

Financial Aid Of all full-time matriculated undergraduates who enrolled in 2006, 1,557 applied for aid, 1,274 were judged to have need, 387 had their need fully met. In 2006, 379 non-need-based awards were made. *Average percent of need met:* 80%. *Average financial aid package:* $14,894. *Average need-based loan:* $3178. *Average need-based gift aid:* $10,493. *Average non-need-based aid:* $6344. *Average indebtedness upon graduation:* $15,838.

Applying *Options:* electronic application, deferred entrance. *Application fee:* $25. *Required:* high school transcript, minimum 2.25 GPA, medical history. *Required for some:* essay or personal statement, letters of recommendation, interview. *Recommended:* interview. *Application deadlines:* 8/1 (freshmen), 8/1 (transfers). *Notification:* continuous (freshmen), continuous (transfers).

Freshman Application Contact Mr. Tom Huebner, Dean of Admissions, Carson-Newman College, PO Box 72025, Jefferson City, TN 37760. *Phone:* 865-471-3223. *Toll-free phone:* 800-678-9061. *Fax:* 865-471-3502. *E-mail:* cnadmiss@cn.edu.

See page 2458 for the College Close-Up.

CHRISTIAN BROTHERS UNIVERSITY

Memphis, Tennessee — www.cbu.edu/

- **Independent Roman Catholic** comprehensive, founded 1871
- **Urban** 75-acre campus
- **Endowment** $30.6 million
- **Coed** 1,462 undergraduate students, 83% full-time, 55% women, 45% men
- **Moderately difficult** entrance level, 69% of applicants were admitted

Undergraduates 1,215 full-time, 247 part-time. Students come from 27 states and territories, 15 other countries, 20% are from out of state, 33% African American, 5% Asian American or Pacific Islander, 2% Hispanic American, 2% international, 7% transferred in, 35% live on campus. *Retention:* 80% of 2006 full-time freshmen returned.

Freshmen *Admission:* 1,360 applied, 942 admitted, 321 enrolled. *Average high school GPA:* 3.34. *Test scores:* SAT critical reading scores over 500: 68%; SAT math scores over 500: 69%; ACT scores over 18: 98%; SAT critical reading scores over 600: 30%; SAT math scores over 600: 36%; ACT scores over 24: 47%; SAT critical reading scores over 700: 6%; SAT math scores over 700: 4%; ACT scores over 30: 7%.

Faculty *Total:* 158, 59% full-time, 74% with terminal degrees. *Student/faculty ratio:* 14:1.

Majors Biology teacher education; biomedical sciences; business administration and management; chemical engineering; chemistry; chemistry teacher education; civil engineering; computer science; education; electrical, electronics and communications engineering; elementary education; engineering physics; English; English/language arts teacher education; environmental/environmental health engineering; fine/studio arts; history; history teacher education; liberal arts and sciences/liberal studies; mathematics; mathematics teacher education; mechanical engineering; natural sciences; philosophy; physics; physics teacher education; psychology; public relations; religious studies.

Academics *Calendar:* semesters. *Degrees:* bachelor's and master's. *Special study options:* accelerated degree program, advanced placement credit, distance learning, double majors, external degree program, honors programs, independent study, internships, off-campus study, part-time degree program, services for LD students, study abroad, summer session for credit. *ROTC:* Army (c), Navy (c), Air Force (c).

Computers on Campus 300 computers/terminals are available on campus for general student use. Students can access the following: online (class) registration, online class listings, e-mail, course assignments. Campuswide network is available. Wireless service is available via classrooms, computer centers, computer labs, libraries.

Student Life *Housing:* on-campus residence required through sophomore year. *Options:* men-only, women-only. Campus housing is university owned. Freshman applicants given priority for college housing. *Activities and organizations:* drama/theater group, choral group, Black Student Association, BACCHUS Alcohol Awareness Group, Intercultural Club, The Chosen Generation, Lasallian Collegians, national fraternities, national sororities. *Campus security:* 24-hour emergency response devices and patrols, student patrols, late-night transport/escort service, controlled dormitory access. *Student services:* health clinic, personal/psychological counseling.

Athletics Member NCAA. All Division II. *Intercollegiate sports:* baseball M (s), basketball M (s)/W (s), cross-country running M/W, golf M/W, soccer M (s)/W (s), softball W (s), tennis M/W, volleyball W (s). *Intramural sports:* basketball M/W, bowling M/W, cross-country running M/W, football M/W, golf M, lacrosse W, racquetball M/W, soccer M/W, softball M/W, swimming and diving M/W, table tennis M/W, tennis M/W, volleyball M/W, weight lifting M.

Standardized Tests *Required:* SAT or ACT (for admission).

Costs (2008–09) *Comprehensive fee:* $28,480 includes full-time tuition ($22,080), mandatory fees ($520), and room and board ($5880). Part-time tuition: $690 per credit hour. *College room only:* $2700.

Financial Aid Of all full-time matriculated undergraduates who enrolled in 2006, 1,066 applied for aid, 846 were judged to have need, 226 had their need fully met. 182 Federal Work-Study jobs (averaging $1281). 146 state and other part-time jobs (averaging $997). In 2006, 284 non-need-based awards were made. *Average percent of need met:* 84%. *Average financial aid package:* $17,365. *Average need-based loan:* $4345. *Average need-based gift aid:* $6307. *Average non-need-based aid:* $8595. *Average indebtedness upon graduation:* $28,340.

Applying *Options:* electronic application, early admission, deferred entrance. *Application fee:* $25. *Required:* essay or personal statement, high school transcript, minimum 2.5 GPA. *Required for some:* letters of recommendation. *Recommended:* interview. *Application deadlines:* 8/1 (freshmen), 8/23 (transfers). *Notification:* 12/1 (freshmen), continuous (transfers).

Freshman Application Contact Ms. Tracey Dysart-Ford, Dean of Admissions, Christian Brothers University, 650 East Parkway South, Memphis, TN 38104. *Phone:* 901-321-3205. *Toll-free phone:* 800-288-7576. *Fax:* 901-321-3202. *E-mail:* admissions@cbu.edu.

See page 2460 for the College Close-Up.

CRICHTON COLLEGE

Memphis, Tennessee **www.crichton.edu/**

- **Independent** 4-year, founded 1941
- **Urban** 7-acre campus
- **Coed**
- **Minimally difficult** entrance level

Faculty *Student/faculty ratio:* 14:1.

Academics *Calendar:* semesters. *Degrees:* certificates, bachelor's, and post-bachelor's certificates.

Student Life *Campus security:* 24-hour patrols, controlled dormitory access, security alarms in campus apartments.

Athletics Member NAIA, NCCAA.

Standardized Tests *Required:* SAT or ACT (for admission).

Costs (2007–08) *Comprehensive fee:* $19,238 includes full-time tuition ($10,680), mandatory fees ($576), and room and board ($7982). Full-time tuition and fees vary according to course load. Part-time tuition: $445 per credit hour. *Required fees:* $19 per credit hour part-time. *College room only:* $3950. Room and board charges vary according to board plan and housing facility.

Financial Aid Of all full-time matriculated undergraduates who enrolled in 2002, 304 applied for aid, 246 were judged to have need, 16 had their need fully met. 38 Federal Work-Study jobs (averaging $1839). In 2002, 34 non-need-based awards were made. *Average percent of need met:* 53. *Average financial aid package:* $8381. *Average need-based loan:* $4031. *Average need-based gift aid:* $5240. *Average non-need-based aid:* $6173. *Average indebtedness upon graduation:* $22,514.

Applying *Options:* electronic application, deferred entrance. *Application fee:* $25. *Required:* essay or personal statement, high school transcript, minimum 2.0 GPA, 3 letters of recommendation, minimum ACT score of 18. *Recommended:* interview.

Freshman Application Contact Mrs. Shelly Luttrell, Dean of Day Admissions, Crichton College, 255 North Highland, Memphis, TN 38111-1375. *Phone:* 901-320-9797. *Toll-free phone:* 800-960-9777. *Fax:* 901-320-9791. *E-mail:* info@crichton.edu.

CUMBERLAND UNIVERSITY

Lebanon, Tennessee **www.cumberland.edu/**

- **Independent** comprehensive, founded 1842
- **Small-town** 44-acre campus with easy access to Nashville
- **Endowment** $9.2 million
- **Coed**
- **Moderately difficult** entrance level

Faculty *Student/faculty ratio:* 16:1.

Academics *Calendar:* semesters. *Degrees:* associate, bachelor's, and master's.

Student Life *Campus security:* 24-hour patrols.

Athletics Member NAIA.

Standardized Tests *Required:* SAT or ACT (for admission). *Recommended:* SAT (for admission).

Costs (2008–09) *Comprehensive fee:* $22,790 includes full-time tuition ($15,820), mandatory fees ($900), and room and board ($6070). Part-time tuition: $660 per hour. *Required fees:* $275 per term part-time.

Financial Aid Of all full-time matriculated undergraduates who enrolled in 2007, 837 applied for aid, 713 were judged to have need, 135 had their need fully met. 120 Federal Work-Study jobs (averaging $750). 16 state and other part-time jobs (averaging $750). In 2007, 125 non-need-based awards were made. *Average percent of need met:* 54. *Average financial aid package:* $12,176. *Average need-based loan:* $4073. *Average need-based gift aid:* $5669. *Average non-need-based aid:* $8069. *Average indebtedness upon graduation:* $21,562.

Applying *Options:* electronic application, deferred entrance. *Application fee:* $25. *Required:* high school transcript. *Required for some:* 3 letters of recommendation. *Recommended:* essay or personal statement, minimum 2.5 GPA.

Freshman Application Contact Mr. Jason A. Brewer, Assistant Dean of Students, Cumberland University, One Cumberland Square, Lebanon, TN 37087. *Phone:* 615-547-1280. *Toll-free phone:* 800-467-0562. *Fax:* 615-444-2569. *E-mail:* admissions@cumberland.edu.

DEVRY UNIVERSITY

Memphis, Tennessee
www.devry.edu/locations/campuses/loc_memphis.jsp

- **Proprietary** comprehensive, founded 2007
- **Coed** 39 undergraduate students, 56% full-time, 69% women, 31% men

Undergraduates 22 full-time, 17 part-time. 21% are from out of state, 79% African American, 3% Asian American or Pacific Islander, 33% transferred in.

Freshmen *Admission:* 10 enrolled.

Faculty *Total:* 1.

Majors Business administration and management; business administration, management and operations related; computer systems networking and telecommunications.

Academics *Degrees:* associate, bachelor's, and master's.

Costs (2008–09) *Tuition:* $13,810 full-time, $515 per credit hour part-time. *Required fees:* $80 full-time.

Applying *Options:* early admission, deferred entrance: *Application fee:* $50. *Application deadlines:* rolling (freshmen), rolling (transfers). *Notification:* continuous (freshmen), continuous (transfers).

Admissions Office Contact DeVry University, 6401 Poplar Avenue, Suite 600, Memphis, TN 38119. *Toll-free phone:* 888-563-3879.

EAST TENNESSEE STATE UNIVERSITY

Johnson City, Tennessee **www.etsu.edu/**

- **State-supported** university, founded 1911, part of State University and Community College System of Tennessee
- **Small-town** 366-acre campus
- **Endowment** $74.3 million
- **Coed** 10,665 undergraduate students, 84% full-time, 57% women, 43% men
- **Moderately difficult** entrance level, 97% of applicants were admitted

East Tennessee State University serves 12,000 students in the beautiful mountain and lake region of northeast Tennessee. Programs are offered in arts and sciences, business and technology, medicine, pharmacy, education, public and allied health, and nursing. Extensive graduate study provides programs leading to the Ph.D., Ed.D., Ed.S., M.D., Pharm.D., and master's degrees. Unique programs include bluegrass music, Appalachian studies, storytelling, and computer animation.

Undergraduates 8,907 full-time, 1,758 part-time. Students come from 38 states and territories, 42 other countries, 10% are from out of state, 4% African American, 2% Asian American or Pacific Islander, 1% Hispanic American, 0.5% Native American, 2% international, 10% transferred in, 20% live on campus. *Retention:* 68% of 2006 full-time freshmen returned.

Freshmen *Admission:* 2,428 applied, 2,366 admitted, 1,939 enrolled. *Average high school GPA:* 3.30. *Test scores:* SAT critical reading scores over 500: 51%; SAT math scores over 500: 56%; SAT writing scores over 500: 48%; ACT scores over 18: 91%; SAT critical reading scores over 600: 15%; SAT math scores over 600: 15%; SAT writing scores over 600: 10%; ACT scores over 24: 37%; SAT critical reading scores over 700: 1%; SAT math scores over 700: 1%; SAT writing scores over 700: 1%; ACT scores over 30: 5%.

Faculty *Total:* 784, 63% full-time, 53% with terminal degrees. *Student/faculty ratio:* 18:1.

Majors Accounting; art; biology/biological sciences; business administration and management; business/managerial economics; chemistry; child development; computer and information sciences; criminal justice/law enforcement administration; dental hygiene; economics; engineering technology; English; environmental health; family and consumer sciences/human sciences; finance; foreign languages and literatures; general studies; geography; health and physical education; health professions related; history; marketing/marketing management; mass communication/media; mathematics; multi-/interdisciplinary studies related; music; nursing (registered nurse training); philosophy; physics; political science and government; psychology; public health; social work; sociology; special education; speech and rhetoric; survey technology.

Academics *Calendar:* semesters. *Degrees:* bachelor's, master's, doctoral, first professional, post-master's, and postbachelor's certificates. *Special study options:* accelerated degree program, adult/continuing education programs, advanced placement credit, cooperative education, distance learning, double majors, freshman honors college, honors programs, independent study, internships, off-campus study, part-time degree program, services for LD students, study abroad, summer session for credit. *ROTC:* Army (b).

Computers on Campus 1,400 computers/terminals are available on campus for general student use. Students can access the following: computer help desk, free student e-mail accounts, online (class) grades, online (class) registration, online (class) schedules. Campuswide network is available. Wireless service is available via entire campus.

Student Life *Housing options:* coed, men-only, women-only, disabled students. Campus housing is university owned. *Activities and organizations:* drama/theater group, student-run newspaper, radio and television station, choral group, honor societies, Volunteer ETSU, religious groups, residence hall councils, national fraternities, national sororities. *Campus security:* 24-hour emergency response devices and patrols, student patrols, late-night transport/escort service, controlled dormitory access. *Student services:* health clinic, personal/psychological counseling, women's center.

Athletics Member NCAA. All Division I. *Intercollegiate sports:* baseball M (s), basketball M (s)/W (s), cross-country running M (s)/W (s), golf M (s)/W (s), soccer M (s)/W (s), softball W (s), tennis M (s)/W (s), track and field M (s)/W (s), volleyball W (s). *Intramural sports:* basketball M/W, cross-country running M/W, football M/W, golf M/W, racquetball M/W, softball M/W, tennis M/W, volleyball W, weight lifting M.

Standardized Tests *Required:* SAT or ACT (for admission).

Costs (2007–08) *Tuition:* state resident $4058 full-time, $178 per hour part-time; nonresident $14,334 full-time, $624 per hour part-time. Full-time tuition and fees vary according to course load and program. Part-time tuition and fees vary according to course load and program. *Required fees:* $829 full-time, $80 per hour part-time. *Room and board:* $5166; room only: $2568. Room and board charges vary according to board plan and housing facility. *Payment plans:* installment, deferred payment. *Waivers:* senior citizens and employees or children of employees.

Financial Aid Of all full-time matriculated undergraduates who enrolled in 2007, 7,479 applied for aid, 5,392 were judged to have need, 2,581 had their need fully met. 1,674 Federal Work-Study jobs (averaging $1272). 412 state and other part-time jobs (averaging $1189). In 2007, 1083 non-need-based awards were made. *Average percent of need met:* 78%. *Average financial aid package:* $4648. *Average need-based loan:* $3232. *Average need-based gift aid:* $3189. *Average non-need-based aid:* $3299. *Average indebtedness upon graduation:* $19,707.

Applying *Options:* electronic application, early admission. *Application fee:* $15. *Required:* high school transcript, minimum 2.3 GPA. *Notification:* continuous (freshmen), continuous (transfers).

Freshman Application Contact Mr. Mike Pitts, Director of Admissions, East Tennessee State University, Box 70731, Johnson City, TN 37614-0731. *Phone:* 423-439-4213. *Toll-free phone:* 800-462-3878. *Fax:* 423-439-4630. *E-mail:* go2etsu@etsu.edu.

FISK UNIVERSITY

Nashville, Tennessee **www.fisk.edu/**

Freshman Application Contact Director of Admissions, Fisk University, 1000 17th Avenue North, Nashville, TN 37208-3051. *Phone:* 615-329-8665. *Toll-free phone:* 800-443-FISK. *Fax:* 615-329-8774. *E-mail:* admit@fisk.edu.

FOUNTAINHEAD COLLEGE OF TECHNOLOGY

Knoxville, Tennessee **www.fountainheadcollege.edu/**

- **Proprietary** primarily 2-year, founded 1947
- **Suburban** 1-acre campus
- **Coed**
- **Noncompetitive** entrance level

Faculty *Student/faculty ratio:* 13:1.

Academics *Calendar:* semesters. *Degrees:* associate and bachelor's.

Student Life *Campus security:* 24-hour emergency response devices.

Costs (2007–08) *One-time required fee:* $100. *Tuition:* $13,050 full-time, $435 per credit hour part-time. No tuition increase for student's term of enrollment. *Required fees:* $200 full-time.

Applying *Application fee:* $100. *Recommended:* high school transcript.

Freshman Application Contact Mr. Todd Hill, Director of Administration, Fountainhead College of Technology, 3203 Tazewell Pike, Knoxville, TN 37918-2530. *Phone:* 865-688-9422. *Toll-free phone:* 888-218-7335. *Fax:* 865-688-2419.

FREED-HARDEMAN UNIVERSITY

Henderson, Tennessee **www.fhu.edu/**

- **Independent** comprehensive, founded 1869, affiliated with Church of Christ
- **Small-town** 96-acre campus
- **Coed** 1,479 undergraduate students, 92% full-time, 55% women, 45% men
- **Moderately difficult** entrance level, 55% of applicants were admitted

Undergraduates 1,366 full-time, 113 part-time. Students come from 35 states and territories, 18 other countries, 4% African American, 0.4% Asian American or Pacific Islander, 0.6% Hispanic American, 0.5% Native American, 3% international, 4% transferred in, 75% live on campus. *Retention:* 74% of 2006 full-time freshmen returned.

Freshmen *Admission:* 1,326 applied, 727 admitted, 386 enrolled. *Average high school GPA:* 3.37. *Test scores:* SAT critical reading scores over 500: 74%; SAT math scores over 500: 66%; ACT scores over 18: 92%; SAT critical reading scores over 600: 45%; SAT math scores over 600: 32%; ACT scores over 24: 44%; SAT critical reading scores over 700: 10%; SAT math scores over 700: 5%; ACT scores over 30: 8%.

Faculty *Total:* 148, 73% full-time, 63% with terminal degrees. *Student/faculty ratio:* 14:1.

Majors Accounting; agricultural business and management; apparel and textiles; art; art teacher education; behavioral sciences; biblical studies; biochemistry; biological and physical sciences; biology/biological sciences; biology teacher education; biophysics; business administration and management; business/managerial economics; chemistry; child development; commercial and advertising art; computer and information sciences; computer science; dramatic/theater arts; education; elementary education; English; English/language arts teacher education; family and consumer sciences/human sciences; fashion merchandising; finance; health and physical education; health services administration; health teacher education; history; humanities; human resources management; information science/studies; interdisciplinary studies; liberal arts and sciences/liberal studies; marketing/marketing management; mathematics; mathematics teacher education; missionary studies and missiology; music; music teacher education; philosophy; physical education teaching and coaching; physical sciences; psychology; public relations/image management; radio and television; science teacher education; secondary education; social sciences; social work; special education.

Academics *Calendar:* semesters. *Degrees:* associate, bachelor's, master's, first professional, post-master's, and postbachelor's certificates. *Special study options:* academic remediation for entering students, accelerated degree program, advanced placement credit, cooperative education, distance learning, double majors, honors programs, independent study, internships, off-campus study, part-time degree program, services for LD students, student-designed majors, study abroad, summer session for credit. *Unusual degree programs:* 3-2 engineering with Tennessee Technological University, Auburn University, Vanderbilt University, University of Tennessee, Oklahoma Christian University, The University of Memphis.

Computers on Campus 250 computers/terminals are available on campus for general student use. Students can access the following: online (class) registration. Campuswide network is available.

Student Life *Housing:* on-campus residence required through senior year. *Options:* men-only, women-only. Campus housing is university owned. Freshman campus housing is guaranteed. *Activities and organizations:* drama/theater group, student-run newspaper, radio and television station, choral group, Student Alumni Association, University Program Council, University Student Ambassadors, Evangelism Forum. *Campus security:* 24-hour emergency response devices and patrols, late-night transport/escort service, controlled dormitory access. *Student services:* health clinic, personal/psychological counseling.

Athletics Member NAIA. *Intercollegiate sports:* baseball M (s), basketball M (s)/W (s), cheerleading M/W (s), soccer M (s)/W (s), softball W (s), tennis M (s)/W (s), volleyball W (s). *Intramural sports:* basketball M/W, football M/W, racquetball M/W, softball M/W, table tennis M/W, tennis M/W, volleyball M/W.

Standardized Tests *Required:* SAT or ACT (for admission).

Costs (2008–09) *Comprehensive fee:* $20,830 includes full-time tuition ($11,700), mandatory fees ($2160), and room and board ($6970). Part-time tuition: $390 per semester hour. *College room only:* $3980.

Financial Aid Of all full-time matriculated undergraduates who enrolled in 2007, 1,072 applied for aid, 900 were judged to have need, 221 had their need fully met. In 2007, 260 non-need-based awards were made. *Average percent of need met:* 66%. *Average financial aid package:* $11,577. *Average need-based loan:* $3838. *Average need-based gift aid:* $8772. *Average non-need-based aid:* $11,894. *Average indebtedness upon graduation:* $34,216.

Applying *Options:* early admission, deferred entrance. *Required:* high school transcript, minimum 2.25 GPA. *Required for some:* interview. *Recommended:* essay or personal statement. *Application deadlines:* rolling (freshmen), rolling (transfers). *Notification:* continuous (freshmen), continuous until 9/1 (transfers).

Freshman Application Contact Dr. Belinda Anderson, Director of Admissions, Freed-Hardeman University, 158 East Main Street, Henderson, TN 38340. *Phone:* 731-989-6651. *Toll-free phone:* 800-630-3480. *Fax:* 731-989-6047. *E-mail:* admissions@fhu.edu.

FREE WILL BAPTIST BIBLE COLLEGE

Nashville, Tennessee **www.fwbbc.edu/**

- **Independent Free Will Baptist** 4-year, founded 1942
- **Urban** 10-acre campus
- **Endowment** $834,731
- **Coed** 324 undergraduate students, 74% full-time, 51% women, 49% men
- **Noncompetitive** entrance level, 75% of applicants were admitted

Undergraduates 241 full-time, 83 part-time. Students come from 25 states and territories, 2 other countries, 67% are from out of state, 3% African American, 0.3% Asian American or Pacific Islander, 0.6% international, 3% transferred in, 71% live on campus. *Retention:* 59% of 2006 full-time freshmen returned.

Freshmen *Admission:* 127 applied, 95 admitted, 62 enrolled. *Average high school GPA:* 3.33. *Test scores:* ACT scores over 18: 75%; ACT scores over 24: 23%; ACT scores over 30: 3%.

Faculty *Total:* 46, 46% full-time, 37% with terminal degrees. *Student/faculty ratio:* 11:1.

Majors Administrative assistant and secretarial science; athletic training; biblical studies; business administration and management; education; elementary education; English; music teacher education; physical education teaching and coaching; religious education; religious/sacred music; secondary education.

Academics *Calendar:* semesters. *Degrees:* associate and bachelor's. *Special study options:* academic remediation for entering students, advanced placement credit, distance learning, double majors, internships, part-time degree program, student-designed majors, summer session for credit. *ROTC:* Army (c), Air Force (c). *Unusual degree programs:* nursing.

Computers on Campus 39 computers/terminals are available on campus for general student use. Students can access the following: computer help desk, free student e-mail accounts. Campuswide network is available. Wireless service is available via computer centers, computer labs, libraries, student centers.

Student Life *Housing:* on-campus residence required through senior year. *Options:* men-only, women-only. Campus housing is university owned. Freshman campus housing is guaranteed. *Activities and organizations:* drama/theater group, choral group, GMF-Global Missions Fellowship, Four Women's Societies-Social and Community Service-LMA's, Brontes, Sonnets, Rossetties, Four Men's Societies-Social and Community Service-Bryans, Pi Gama Chi, Bunyans, Alpha Chi. *Campus security:* 24-hour emergency response devices, student patrols, late-night transport/escort service, controlled dormitory access. *Student services:* personal/psychological counseling.

Athletics Member NCCAA. *Intercollegiate sports:* baseball M, basketball M/W. *Intramural sports:* basketball M/W, soccer M, tennis M/W, volleyball M/W.

Standardized Tests *Required:* ACT (for admission).

Costs (2007–08) *Comprehensive fee:* $17,248 includes full-time tuition ($11,610), mandatory fees ($772), and room and board ($4866). Part-time tuition: $387 per semester hour. *Room and board:* Room and board charges vary according to board plan. *Payment plans:* installment, deferred payment.

Financial Aid Of all full-time matriculated undergraduates who enrolled in 2006, 16 Federal Work-Study jobs (averaging $1397). 90 state and other part-time jobs (averaging $1447). *Average indebtedness upon graduation:* $11,477.

Applying *Options:* electronic application, early admission, deferred entrance. *Application fee:* $35. *Required:* essay or personal statement, high school transcript, 3 letters of recommendation, medical history. *Application deadline:* rolling (freshmen).

Freshman Application Contact Mr. Heath Hubbard, Director of Recruitment, Free Will Baptist Bible College, 3606 West End Avenue, Nashville, TN 37205. *Phone:* 615-844-5197. *Toll-free phone:* 800-763-9222. *Fax:* 615-269-6028. *E-mail:* hhubbard@fwbbc.edu.

HUNTINGTON COLLEGE OF HEALTH SCIENCES

Knoxville, Tennessee **www.hchs.edu/**

- **Proprietary** comprehensive, founded 1984
- **Suburban** campus
- **Coed, primarily women** 400 undergraduate students, 100% full-time, 64% women, 36% men
- **Noncompetitive** entrance level, 100% of applicants were admitted

Undergraduates 400 full-time. Students come from 49 states and territories, 15 other countries, 98% are from out of state, 46% transferred in. *Retention:* 10% of 2006 full-time freshmen returned.

Freshmen *Admission:* 33 applied, 33 admitted, 25 enrolled.

Faculty *Total:* 20, 15% full-time, 35% with terminal degrees. *Student/faculty ratio:* 29:1.

Majors Foods, nutrition, and wellness; nutrition sciences.

Academics *Calendar:* continuous. *Degrees:* certificates, diplomas, associate, bachelor's, master's, and postbachelor's certificates (offers only external degree programs conducted through home study). *Special study options:* academic remediation for entering students, adult/continuing education programs, distance learning, external degree program, independent study, part-time degree program, student-designed majors, summer session for credit.

Costs (2008–09) *Tuition:* $165 per semester hour part-time.

Applying *Options:* electronic application, deferred entrance. *Required for some:* high school transcript, interview. *Recommended:* minimum 2.0 GPA. *Application deadlines:* rolling (freshmen), rolling (transfers). *Notification:* continuous (freshmen), continuous (transfers).

Freshman Application Contact Ms. Cheryl Freeman, Director/Registrar, Huntington College of Health Sciences, 1204-D Kenesaw Avenue, Knoxville, TN 37919.. *Phone:* 800-290-4226. *Toll-free phone:* 800-290-4226. *Fax:* 865-524-8339. *E-mail:* cfreeman@hchs.edu.

ITT Technical Institute

Cordova, Tennessee www.itt-tech.edu/

- **Proprietary** primarily 2-year, founded 1994, part of ITT Educational Services, Inc
- **Suburban** 1-acre campus
- **Coed**
- **Minimally difficult** entrance level

Academics *Calendar:* quarters. *Degrees:* associate and bachelor's.
Standardized Tests *Required:* Wonderlic aptitude test (for admission).
Applying *Options:* deferred entrance. *Application fee:* $100. *Required:* high school transcript, interview. *Recommended:* letters of recommendation.
Freshman Application Contact Ms. Sharon Johnson, Director of Recruitment, ITT Technical Institute, 7260 Goodlett Farms Parkway, Cordova, TN 38016. *Phone:* 901-381-0200. *Toll-free phone:* 866-444-5141.

ITT Technical Institute

Knoxville, Tennessee www.itt-tech.edu/

- **Proprietary** primarily 2-year, founded 1988, part of ITT Educational Services, Inc
- **Suburban** 5-acre campus
- **Coed**
- **Minimally difficult** entrance level

Academics *Calendar:* quarters. *Degrees:* associate and bachelor's.
Standardized Tests *Required:* Wonderlic aptitude test (for admission).
Applying *Options:* deferred entrance. *Application fee:* $100. *Required:* high school transcript, interview. *Recommended:* letters of recommendation.
Freshman Application Contact Mr. Dan Deck, Director of Recruitment, ITT Technical Institute, 10208 Technology Drive, Knoxville, TN 37932. *Phone:* 865-671-2800. *Toll-free phone:* 800-671-2801.

ITT Technical Institute

Nashville, Tennessee www.itt-tech.edu/

- **Proprietary** primarily 2-year, founded 1984, part of ITT Educational Services, Inc
- **Urban** 21-acre campus
- **Coed**
- **Minimally difficult** entrance level

Academics *Calendar:* quarters. *Degrees:* associate and bachelor's.
Standardized Tests *Required:* Wonderlic aptitude test (for admission).
Applying *Options:* deferred entrance. *Application fee:* $100. *Required:* high school transcript, interview. *Recommended:* letters of recommendation.
Freshman Application Contact Mr. Glenn Wallace, Director of Recruitment, ITT Technical Institute, 2845 Elm Hill Pike, Nashville, TN 37214. *Phone:* 615-889-8700. *Toll-free phone:* 800-331-8386.

Johnson Bible College

Knoxville, Tennessee www.jbc.edu/

- **Independent** comprehensive, founded 1893, affiliated with Christian Churches and Churches of Christ
- **Rural** 75-acre campus
- **Coed** 757 undergraduate students, 97% full-time, 51% women, 49% men
- **Moderately difficult** entrance level, 85% of applicants were admitted

Undergraduates 734 full-time, 23 part-time. Students come from 29 states and territories, 8 other countries, 66% are from out of state, 8% transferred in, 88% live on campus. *Retention:* 75% of 2006 full-time freshmen returned.
Freshmen *Admission:* 342 applied, 289 admitted, 166 enrolled. *Average high school GPA:* 3.25. *Test scores:* SAT critical reading scores over 500: 61%; SAT math scores over 500: 68%; ACT scores over 18: 86%; SAT critical reading scores over 600: 22%; SAT math scores over 600: 23%; ACT scores over 24: 39%; SAT math scores over 700: 1%; ACT scores over 30: 5%.
Faculty *Total:* 58, 45% full-time, 38% with terminal degrees. *Student/faculty ratio:* 17:1.
Majors Biblical studies; elementary education; mass communication/media; middle school education; religious/sacred music; teacher assistant/aide.
Academics *Calendar:* semesters. *Degrees:* certificates, associate, bachelor's, and master's. *Special study options:* academic remediation for entering students, accelerated degree program, adult/continuing education programs, advanced placement credit, cooperative education, distance learning, double majors, English as a second language, honors programs, independent study, internships, part-time degree program, services for LD students, summer session for credit.
Computers on Campus 34 computers/terminals are available on campus for general student use. Students can access the following: campus intranet, computer help desk, free student e-mail accounts, online (class) grades, online (class) registration, online (class) schedules. Campuswide network is available. 100% of college-owned or -operated housing units are wired for high-speed Internet access. Wireless service is available via classrooms.
Student Life *Housing:* on-campus residence required through senior year. *Options:* men-only, women-only. Campus housing is university owned. *Activities and organizations:* student-run radio station, choral group, Quest, Timothy Club, International Harvesters. *Campus security:* 24-hour emergency response devices, student patrols, controlled dormitory access. *Student services:* health clinic, personal/psychological counseling.
Athletics Member NCCAA. *Intercollegiate sports:* baseball M, basketball M/W, cheerleading M/W, soccer M/W, volleyball W. *Intramural sports:* basketball M, tennis M/W, ultimate Frisbee M/W, volleyball M/W.
Standardized Tests *Required:* SAT or ACT (for admission). *Required for some:* ACT (for admission).
Costs (2007–08) *Comprehensive fee:* $12,070 includes full-time tuition ($6410), mandatory fees ($770), and room and board ($4890). Part-time tuition: $267 per semester hour. Part-time tuition and fees vary according to course load. *College room only:* $2250. Room and board charges vary according to board plan and housing facility. *Payment plan:* installment. *Waivers:* employees or children of employees.
Financial Aid Of all full-time matriculated undergraduates who enrolled in 2007, 701 applied for aid, 585 were judged to have need. 141 Federal Work-Study jobs (averaging $734). *Average percent of need met:* 69%. *Average financial aid package:* $6247. *Average need-based loan:* $2640. *Average need-based gift aid:* $3091. *Average indebtedness upon graduation:* $17,487.
Applying *Options:* deferred entrance. *Application fee:* $35. *Required:* essay or personal statement, high school transcript, 3 letters of recommendation. *Required for some:* interview. *Application deadlines:* 7/1 (freshmen), 7/1 (transfers). *Notification:* continuous (freshmen), continuous (transfers).
Freshman Application Contact Mr. Tim Wingfield, Director of Admissions, Johnson Bible College, 7900 Johnson Drive, Knoxville, TN 37998. *Phone:* 865-251-2346. *Toll-free phone:* 800-827-2122. *Fax:* 865-251-2336. *E-mail:* twingfield@jbc.edu.

King College

Bristol, Tennessee www.king.edu/

- **Independent** comprehensive, founded 1867, affiliated with Presbyterian Church (U.S.A.), part of Southern Association of Colleges and Schools (SACS)
- **Suburban** 135-acre campus
- **Endowment** $29.7 million
- **Coed** 1,266 undergraduate students, 93% full-time, 63% women, 37% men
- **Moderately difficult** entrance level, 22% of applicants were admitted

Undergraduates 1,179 full-time, 87 part-time. Students come from 27 states and territories, 20 other countries, 55% are from out of state, 2% African American, 0.6% Asian American or Pacific Islander, 2% Hispanic American, 0.2% Native American, 3% international, 8% transferred in, 58% live on campus. *Retention:* 71% of 2006 full-time freshmen returned.
Freshmen *Admission:* 856 applied, 186 admitted, 184 enrolled. *Average high school GPA:* 3.38. *Test scores:* SAT critical reading scores over 500: 53%; SAT math scores over 500: 64%; ACT scores over 18: 94%; SAT critical reading scores over 600: 6%; SAT math scores over 600: 13%; ACT scores over 24: 47%; SAT math scores over 700: 1%; ACT scores over 30: 4%.
Faculty *Total:* 121, 48% full-time, 80% with terminal degrees. *Student/faculty ratio:* 14:1.
Majors Accounting; American studies; applied mathematics; athletic training; biblical studies; biochemistry; biological and physical sciences; biological specializations related; biology/biological sciences; biology teacher education; biophysics; business administration and management; chemistry; chemistry teacher education; clinical laboratory science/medical technology; computer science; e-commerce; economics; education; engineering; English; English/language arts

teacher education; finance; forensic science and technology; French; French language teacher education; health professions related; history; history teacher education; information science/studies; interdisciplinary studies; international business/trade/commerce; kindergarten/preschool education; management information systems; mathematics; mathematics teacher education; medicinal/pharmaceutical chemistry; middle school education; modern languages; music; neuroscience; nursing (registered nurse training); physics; physics teacher education; political science and government; pre-law studies; pre-medical studies; pre-pharmacy studies; pre-veterinary studies; psychology; religious studies; Spanish; Spanish language teacher education; speech/theater education; sport and fitness administration/management; technical and business writing; visual and performing arts; youth ministry.

Academics *Calendar:* semesters. *Degrees:* bachelor's and master's. *Special study options:* adult/continuing education programs, advanced placement credit, cooperative education, double majors, English as a second language, freshman honors college, honors programs, independent study, internships, off-campus study, part-time degree program, services for LD students, student-designed majors, study abroad, summer session for credit. *Unusual degree programs:* 3-2 engineering with University of Tennessee, Vanderbilt University.

Computers on Campus 90 computers/terminals and 500 ports are available on campus for general student use. Students can access the following: campus intranet, computer help desk, free student e-mail accounts, online (class) grades, online (class) registration, online (class) schedules. Campuswide network is available. 100% of college-owned or -operated housing units are wired for high-speed Internet access. Wireless service is available via classrooms, computer centers, computer labs, learning centers, libraries, student centers.

Student Life *Housing:* on-campus residence required through junior year. *Options:* men-only, women-only, disabled students. Campus housing is university owned. Freshman campus housing is guaranteed. *Activities and organizations:* drama/theater group, student-run newspaper, choral group, Student Government Association, Campus Life Committee, World Christian Fellowship, Fellowship of Christian Athletes, Drama Club. *Campus security:* late-night transport/escort service, controlled dormitory access. *Student services:* personal/psychological counseling.

Athletics Member NAIA. *Intercollegiate sports:* baseball M (s), basketball M (s)/W (s), cheerleading M (s)/W (s), cross-country running M (s)/W (s), golf M (s)/W (s), soccer M (s)/W (s), softball W (s), swimming and diving M (s)/W (s), tennis M (s)/W (s), track and field M (s)/W (s), volleyball W (s), wrestling M (s). *Intramural sports:* badminton M/W, basketball M/W, soccer M/W, softball M/W, table tennis M/W, tennis M/W, ultimate Frisbee M/W, volleyball M/W, weight lifting M.

Standardized Tests *Required:* SAT or ACT (for admission).

Costs (2008–09) *Comprehensive fee:* $27,482 includes full-time tuition ($19,426), mandatory fees ($1156), and room and board ($6900). Part-time tuition: $600 per credit hour. *College room only:* $3450.

Financial Aid Of all full-time matriculated undergraduates who enrolled in 2007, 962 applied for aid, 841 were judged to have need, 189 had their need fully met. 75 Federal Work-Study jobs (averaging $980). In 2007, 212 non-need-based awards were made. *Average percent of need met:* 73%. *Average financial aid package:* $13,892. *Average need-based loan:* $5052. *Average need-based gift aid:* $11,474. *Average non-need-based aid:* $8862. *Average indebtedness upon graduation:* $10,591.

Applying *Options:* electronic application, early admission, deferred entrance. *Application fee:* $20. *Required:* high school transcript, minimum 2.4 GPA, minimum ACT score of 19 or SAT score of 980. *Required for some:* essay or personal statement. *Recommended:* interview. *Application deadlines:* rolling (freshmen), rolling (transfers). *Notification:* continuous (freshmen), continuous (transfers).

Freshman Application Contact Ms. Mandy Butterworth, Director of Recruitment, King College, 1350 King College Road, Bristol, TN 37620-2699. *Phone:* 423-652-4861. *Toll-free phone:* 800-362-0014. *Fax:* 423-652-4727. *E-mail:* admissions@king.edu.

LAMBUTH UNIVERSITY

Jackson, Tennessee **www.lambuth.edu/**

- **Independent United Methodist** 4-year, founded 1843
- **Urban** 50-acre campus with easy access to Memphis
- **Endowment** $5.2 million
- **Coed** 751 undergraduate students, 94% full-time, 52% women, 48% men
- **Moderately difficult** entrance level, 49% of applicants were admitted

Undergraduates 707 full-time, 44 part-time. Students come from 29 states and territories, 12 other countries, 22% are from out of state, 19% African American, 2% Asian American or Pacific Islander, 2% Hispanic American, 0.1% Native American, 3% international, 13% transferred in, 57% live on campus. *Retention:* 60% of 2006 full-time freshmen returned.

Freshmen *Admission:* 826 applied, 407 admitted, 172 enrolled. *Average high school GPA:* 3.17. *Test scores:* SAT critical reading scores over 500: 60%; SAT math scores over 500: 52%; ACT scores over 18: 93%; SAT critical reading scores over 600: 19%; SAT math scores over 600: 14%; ACT scores over 24: 36%; SAT critical reading scores over 700: 3%; SAT math scores over 700: 3%; ACT scores over 30: 6%.

Faculty *Total:* 97, 69% full-time, 52% with terminal degrees. *Student/faculty ratio:* 9:1.

Majors Accounting; art; art history, criticism and conservation; art teacher education; audiology and speech-language pathology; biology/biological sciences; biology teacher education; business administration and management; business teacher education; chemistry; chemistry teacher education; computer and information sciences; criminal justice/law enforcement administration; design and visual communications; dramatic/theater arts; economics; education; education (K-12); elementary education; English; English/language arts teacher education; environmental science; environmental studies; family and consumer sciences/human sciences; fashion merchandising; fine/studio arts; foods, nutrition, and wellness; foreign languages and literatures; health and physical education related; health teacher education; history; history teacher education; interior design; international relations and affairs; liberal arts and sciences and humanities related; marketing/marketing management; mass communication/media; mathematics; mathematics teacher education; middle school education; multi-/interdisciplinary studies related; music; music performance; music teacher education; parks, recreation, and leisure related; philosophy and religious studies related; physical education teaching and coaching; political science and government; pre-dentistry studies; pre-law studies; pre-medical studies; pre-pharmacy studies; pre-theology/pre-ministerial studies; pre-veterinary studies; psychology; public relations, advertising, and applied communication related; religious/sacred music; religious studies; secondary education; sociology; Spanish; special education; special education (hearing impaired); sport and fitness administration/management; visual and performing arts.

Academics *Calendar:* semesters. *Degree:* bachelor's. *Special study options:* academic remediation for entering students, accelerated degree program, adult/continuing education programs, advanced placement credit, double majors, English as a second language, honors programs, independent study, internships, off-campus study, part-time degree program, services for LD students, student-designed majors, study abroad, summer session for credit.

Computers on Campus 100 computers/terminals are available on campus for general student use. Students can access the following: free student e-mail accounts. Campuswide network is available. 100% of college-owned or -operated housing units are wired for high-speed Internet access. Wireless service is available via classrooms, computer centers, computer labs, libraries, student centers.

Student Life *Housing:* on-campus residence required through senior year. *Options:* coed, men-only, women-only. Campus housing is university owned. Freshman campus housing is guaranteed. *Activities and organizations:* drama/theater group, student-run newspaper, choral group, Student Government, Student Activities Committee, Black Student Union, Religious Life Council, International Students Organization, national fraternities, national sororities. *Campus security:* 24-hour emergency response devices and patrols, late-night transport/escort service, controlled dormitory access. *Student services:* health clinic, personal/psychological counseling.

Athletics Member NAIA. *Intercollegiate sports:* baseball M (s), basketball M (s)/W (s), cheerleading M (s)/W (s), cross-country running M (s)/W (s), football M (s), golf M (s), soccer M (s)/W (s), softball W (s), swimming and diving M (s)/W (s), tennis M (s)/W (s), volleyball W (s). *Intramural sports:* basketball M/W, football M/W, softball M/W.

Standardized Tests *Required:* SAT or ACT (for admission).

Costs (2007–08) *Comprehensive fee:* $24,560 includes full-time tuition ($17,000), mandatory fees ($400), and room and board ($7160). Part-time tuition: $710 per credit hour. *Required fees:* $200 per term part-time. *College room only:* $3410. Room and board charges vary according to housing facility. *Payment plan:* installment. *Waivers:* employees or children of employees.

Financial Aid Of all full-time matriculated undergraduates who enrolled in 2007, 654 applied for aid, 542 were judged to have need, 203 had their need fully met. 102 Federal Work-Study jobs (averaging $1000). 31 state and other part-time jobs (averaging $1006). In 2007, 103 non-need-based awards were made. *Average percent of need met:* 94%. *Average financial aid package:* $17,000. *Average need-based loan:* $5596. *Average need-based gift aid:* $13,909. *Average non-need-based aid:* $12,304. *Average indebtedness upon graduation:* $19,947.

Applying *Options:* electronic application, early admission, deferred entrance. *Application fee:* $25. *Required:* essay or personal statement, high school transcript, minimum 2.0 GPA. *Required for some:* 3 letters of recommendation.

Recommended: interview. *Application deadlines:* rolling (freshmen), rolling (transfers). *Notification:* continuous (freshmen), continuous (transfers).

Freshman Application Contact Ms. Melissa Boyd, Director of Financial Aid, Lambuth University, 705 Lambuth Boulevard, Jackson, TN 38301. *Phone:* 731-425-3332. *Toll-free phone:* 800-526-2884. *Fax:* 731-425-3496. *E-mail:* boyd-m@lambuth.edu.

LANE COLLEGE

Jackson, Tennessee **www.lanecollege.edu/**

- **Independent** 4-year, founded 1882, affiliated with Christian Methodist Episcopal Church
- **Suburban** 25-acre campus with easy access to Memphis
- **Endowment** $2.8 million
- **Coed**
- **Minimally difficult** entrance level

Faculty *Student/faculty ratio:* 24:1.

Academics *Calendar:* semesters. *Degrees:* bachelor's and postbachelor's certificates.

Student Life *Campus security:* 24-hour emergency response devices and patrols, surveillance cameras, lighted parking areas.

Athletics Member NCAA. All Division II.

Standardized Tests *Required:* SAT or ACT (for admission).

Costs (2007–08) *Comprehensive fee:* $12,620 includes full-time tuition ($6970), mandatory fees ($650), and room and board ($5000). Part-time tuition: $310 per hour. *Required fees:* $325 per term part-time.

Financial Aid Of all full-time matriculated undergraduates who enrolled in 2003, 924 applied for aid, 897 were judged to have need, 238 had their need fully met. 378 Federal Work-Study jobs (averaging $781). *Average percent of need met:* 79. *Average financial aid package:* $8052. *Average need-based loan:* $2850. *Average need-based gift aid:* $4792. *Average indebtedness upon graduation:* $19,681.

Applying *Options:* electronic application, early admission, early decision. *Required:* high school transcript, minimum 2.0 GPA, 2 letters of recommendation.

Freshman Application Contact Ms. Sherrill Berry Scott, Vice President for Student Affairs, Lane College, 545 Lane Avenue, Bray Administration Building 2nd Floor, Jackson, TN 38301-4598. *Phone:* 731-426-7533. *Toll-free phone:* 800-960-7533. *E-mail:* sbscott@lanecollege.edu.

LEE UNIVERSITY

Cleveland, Tennessee **www.leeuniversity.edu/**

- **Independent** comprehensive, founded 1918, affiliated with Church of God
- **Small-town** 115-acre campus
- **Endowment** $8.8 million
- **Coed** 3,770 undergraduate students, 88% full-time, 56% women, 44% men
- **Minimally difficult** entrance level, 51% of applicants were admitted

Undergraduates 3,316 full-time, 454 part-time. Students come from 47 states and territories, 41 other countries, 62% are from out of state, 4% African American, 0.8% Asian American or Pacific Islander, 3% Hispanic American, 0.5% Native American, 6% international, 7% transferred in, 50% live on campus. *Retention:* 71% of 2006 full-time freshmen returned.

Freshmen *Admission:* 1,601 applied, 823 admitted, 792 enrolled. *Average high school GPA:* 3.38. *Test scores:* SAT critical reading scores over 500: 66%; SAT math scores over 500: 64%; ACT scores over 18: 88%; SAT critical reading scores over 600: 36%; SAT math scores over 600: 31%; ACT scores over 24: 52%; SAT critical reading scores over 700: 6%; SAT math scores over 700: 7%; ACT scores over 30: 10%.

Faculty *Total:* 329, 49% full-time, 49% with terminal degrees. *Student/faculty ratio:* 16:1.

Majors Accounting; anthropology; athletic training; biblical studies; biochemistry; biological and physical sciences; biology/biological sciences; business administration and management; business teacher education; chemistry; clinical laboratory science/medical technology; education; elementary education; English; health teacher education; history; human development and family studies; information science/studies; interdisciplinary studies; international relations and affairs; mass communication/media; mathematics; modern languages; music; music teacher education; natural sciences; pastoral studies/counseling; physical education teaching and coaching; piano and organ; psychology; religious education; secondary education; sociology; special education; theology; voice and opera.

Academics *Calendar:* semesters. *Degrees:* bachelor's and master's. *Special study options:* academic remediation for entering students, adult/continuing education programs, advanced placement credit, distance learning, double majors, English as a second language, external degree program, honors programs, independent study, internships, part-time degree program, services for LD students, study abroad, summer session for credit.

Computers on Campus 430 computers/terminals and 430 ports are available on campus for general student use. Students can access the following: campus intranet, computer help desk, free student e-mail accounts, online (class) grades, online (class) registration, online (class) schedules. Campuswide network is available. 95% of college-owned or -operated housing units are wired for high-speed Internet access. Wireless service is available via entire campus.

Student Life *Housing:* on-campus residence required through sophomore year. *Options:* men-only, women-only. Campus housing is university owned. Freshman campus housing is guaranteed. *Activities and organizations:* drama/theater group, student-run newspaper, choral group, Student Leadership Council, Pioneers for Christ, International Student Fellowship, Starlite Ministries, Back Yard Ministry. *Campus security:* 24-hour emergency response devices and patrols, late-night transport/escort service. *Student services:* health clinic, personal/psychological counseling.

Athletics Member NAIA, NCCAA. *Intercollegiate sports:* baseball M (s), basketball M (s)/W (s), cross-country running M (s)/W (s), golf M (s), rock climbing M (c)/W (c), soccer M (s)/W (s), softball W (s), tennis M (s)/W (s), volleyball W (s). *Intramural sports:* badminton M/W, basketball M/W, bowling M/W, football M/W, racquetball M/W, soccer M/W, softball M/W, table tennis M/W, tennis M/W, ultimate Frisbee M/W, volleyball M/W, wrestling M.

Standardized Tests *Required:* SAT or ACT (for admission).

Costs (2007–08) *Comprehensive fee:* $16,058 includes full-time tuition ($10,392), mandatory fees ($390), and room and board ($5276). Part-time tuition: $433 per credit hour. *College room only:* $2556. Room and board charges vary according to board plan and housing facility. *Payment plan:* deferred payment. *Waivers:* employees or children of employees.

Financial Aid Of all full-time matriculated undergraduates who enrolled in 2007, 2,161 applied for aid, 1,759 were judged to have need, 347 had their need fully met. 205 Federal Work-Study jobs (averaging $1485). 350 state and other part-time jobs (averaging $1714). In 2007, 725 non-need-based awards were made. *Average percent of need met:* 57%. *Average financial aid package:* $8973. *Average need-based loan:* $4256. *Average need-based gift aid:* $6770. *Average non-need-based aid:* $8172. *Average indebtedness upon graduation:* $25,990.

Applying *Options:* electronic application, early admission, deferred entrance. *Application fee:* $25. *Required:* high school transcript, minimum 2.0 GPA, MMR immunization record; minimum test score of 17 for ACT or 860 for SAT. *Required for some:* 3 letters of recommendation. *Application deadlines:* 9/1 (freshmen), 9/1 (transfers). *Notification:* continuous (freshmen), continuous (transfers).

Freshman Application Contact Mr. Phillip Cook, Assistant Vice President for Enrollment, Lee University, PO Box 3450, Cleveland, TN 37320-3450. *Phone:* 423-614-8500. *Toll-free phone:* 800-533-9930. *Fax:* 423-614-8533. *E-mail:* admissions@leeuniversity.edu.

LEMOYNE-OWEN COLLEGE

Memphis, Tennessee **www.loc.edu/**

- **Independent** 4-year, founded 1862, affiliated with United Church of Christ
- **Urban** 15-acre campus
- **Endowment** $15.1 million
- **Coed** 592 undergraduate students, 85% full-time, 65% women, 35% men
- **Minimally difficult** entrance level, 51% of applicants were admitted

Undergraduates 501 full-time, 91 part-time. Students come from 12 states and territories, 4 other countries, 12% are from out of state, 98% African American, 0.2% Hispanic American, 1% international, 30% transferred in, 20% live on campus. *Retention:* 43% of 2006 full-time freshmen returned.

Freshmen *Admission:* 673 applied, 342 admitted, 85 enrolled. *Average high school GPA:* 2.5. *Test scores:* ACT scores over 18: 15%; ACT scores over 24: 3%.

Faculty *Total:* 88, 63% full-time, 42% with terminal degrees. *Student/faculty ratio:* 8:1.

Majors Art; biology/biological sciences; business administration and management; chemistry; computer science; criminal justice/law enforcement administration; early childhood education; English; English/language arts teacher education; history; humanities; information technology; mathematics; mathematics teacher education; music; political science and government; science teacher education; social sciences; social studies teacher education; social work; sociology; special education.

Academics *Calendar:* semesters. *Degrees:* bachelor's and postbachelor's certificates. *Special study options:* academic remediation for entering students, accelerated degree program, adult/continuing education programs, advanced placement credit, cooperative education, double majors, honors programs, independent study, internships, off-campus study, part-time degree program, services for LD students, study abroad, summer session for credit. *ROTC:* Army (c), Air Force (c). *Unusual degree programs:* 3-2 engineering with Christian Brothers University, Tuskegee University, Tennessee State University; nursing with University of Tennessee at Memphis; mass communications with Rust College, pharmacy with Xavier University of Louisiana.

Computers on Campus 223 computers/terminals are available on campus for general student use. Students can access the following: computer help desk, free student e-mail accounts. Campuswide network is available. 100% of college-owned or -operated housing units are wired for high-speed Internet access. Wireless service is available via classrooms, computer centers, computer labs, dorm rooms, learning centers, libraries.

Student Life *Housing options:* men-only, women-only. Campus housing is university owned. *Activities and organizations:* drama/theater group, student-run newspaper, choral group, Greek Fraternities and Sororities, Students in Free Enterprise, National Black Student Accountant Club, Gospel Choir, Pre-alumni organization, national fraternities, national sororities. *Campus security:* 24-hour patrols, late-night transport/escort service, controlled dormitory access. *Student services:* health clinic, personal/psychological counseling.

Athletics Member NCAA, NAIA. All NCAA Division I except baseball (Division II), men's and women's basketball (Division II), men's and women's cross-country running (Division II), men's and women's golf (Division II), softball (Division II), men's and women's tennis (Division II). *Intercollegiate sports:* baseball M (s), basketball M (s)/W (s), cross-country running M (s)/W (s), golf M (s)/W (s), softball W (s), tennis M (s)/W (s), volleyball W (s).

Standardized Tests *Required:* SAT or ACT (for admission).

Costs (2007–08) *Comprehensive fee:* $15,170 includes full-time tuition ($10,098), mandatory fees ($220), and room and board ($4852). Part-time tuition: $421 per credit hour. *Payment plan:* installment. *Waivers:* employees or children of employees.

Financial Aid Of all full-time matriculated undergraduates who enrolled in 2005, 581 applied for aid, 557 were judged to have need, 35 had their need fully met. 205 Federal Work-Study jobs (averaging $1294). In 2005, 38 non-need-based awards were made. *Average percent of need met:* 55%. *Average financial aid package:* $9309. *Average need-based loan:* $3090. *Average need-based gift aid:* $6792. *Average non-need-based aid:* $8050. *Average indebtedness upon graduation:* $13,354.

Applying *Options:* electronic application. *Application fee:* $25. *Required:* essay or personal statement, high school transcript, minimum 2.0 GPA, 2 letters of recommendation, interview. *Application deadlines:* 4/1 (freshmen), rolling (transfers).

Freshman Application Contact LeMoyne-Owen College, 807 Walker Avenue, Memphis, TN 38126. *Phone:* 901-435-1500.

LINCOLN MEMORIAL UNIVERSITY

Harrogate, Tennessee **www.lmunet.edu/**

- **Independent** comprehensive, founded 1897
- **Small-town** 1000-acre campus
- **Endowment** $26.2 million
- **Coed**
- **Moderately difficult** entrance level

Faculty *Student/faculty ratio:* 14:1.

Academics *Calendar:* semesters. *Degrees:* associate, bachelor's, master's, and post-master's certificates.

Student Life *Campus security:* 24-hour emergency response devices and patrols.

Athletics Member NCAA. All Division II.

Standardized Tests *Required:* SAT or ACT (for admission).

Costs (2007–08) *Tuition:* $14,400 full-time, $600 per credit part-time.

Financial Aid Of all full-time matriculated undergraduates who enrolled in 2006, 841 applied for aid, 563 were judged to have need, 493 had their need fully met. 146 Federal Work-Study jobs (averaging $1600). In 2006, 137 non-need-based awards were made. *Average percent of need met:* 90. *Average financial aid package:* $9800. *Average need-based loan:* $3000. *Average need-based gift aid:* $5620. *Average non-need-based aid:* $5725. *Average indebtedness upon graduation:* $11,500.

Applying *Application fee:* $25. *Required:* high school transcript, minimum 2.3 GPA. *Required for some:* essay or personal statement. *Recommended:* interview.

Freshman Application Contact Mr. Conrad Daniels, Dean of Admissions and Recruitment, Lincoln Memorial University, 6965 Cumberland Gap Parkway, Harrogate, TN 37752-1901. *Phone:* 423-869-6280. *Toll-free phone:* 800-325-0900. *Fax:* 423-869-6444. *E-mail:* admissions@lmunet.edu.

See page 2462 for the College Close-Up.

LIPSCOMB UNIVERSITY

Nashville, Tennessee **www.lipscomb.edu/**

- **Independent** comprehensive, founded 1891, affiliated with Church of Christ
- **Suburban** 65-acre campus
- **Endowment** $81.5 million
- **Coed** 2,363 undergraduate students, 90% full-time, 57% women, 43% men
- **Moderately difficult** entrance level, 57% of applicants were admitted

Undergraduates 2,131 full-time, 232 part-time. Students come from 38 states and territories, 26 other countries, 31% are from out of state, 5% African American, 2% Asian American or Pacific Islander, 2% Hispanic American, 0.5% Native American, 1% international, 5% transferred in, 56% live on campus. *Retention:* 76% of 2006 full-time freshmen returned.

Freshmen *Admission:* 2,240 applied, 1,274 admitted, 576 enrolled. *Average high school GPA:* 3.49. *Test scores:* SAT critical reading scores over 500: 78%; SAT math scores over 500: 72%; SAT writing scores over 500: 69%; ACT scores over 18: 96%; SAT critical reading scores over 600: 35%; SAT math scores over 600: 32%; SAT writing scores over 600: 25%; ACT scores over 24: 54%; SAT critical reading scores over 700: 5%; SAT math scores over 700: 4%; SAT writing scores over 700: 3%; ACT scores over 30: 12%.

Faculty *Total:* 284, 38% full-time, 62% with terminal degrees. *Student/faculty ratio:* 15:1.

Majors Accounting; American studies; apparel and textiles; architecture related; art teacher education; athletic training; biblical languages/literatures; biblical studies; biochemistry; biology/biological sciences; biology teacher education; business administration and management; business/managerial economics; chemistry; chemistry teacher education; commercial and advertising art; computer engineering; computer science; dietetics; drama and dance teacher education; dramatic/theater arts; education; elementary education; engineering mechanics; engineering related; engineering science; English; English as a second/foreign language (teaching); English/language arts teacher education; environmental studies; family and consumer sciences/human sciences; family systems; fashion merchandising; fine/studio arts; foodservice systems administration; French; French language teacher education; general studies; German; health/medical preparatory programs related; history; history teacher education; human resources management; information science/studies; information technology; international business/trade/commerce; journalism; kinesiology and exercise science; legal studies; management information systems; marketing/marketing management; mass communication/media; mathematics; mathematics teacher education; mechanical engineering; missionary studies and missiology; music performance; music teacher education; music theory and composition; nursing (registered nurse training); organizational communication; pastoral counseling and specialized ministries related; pharmacy; philosophy; physical education teaching and coaching; physics; physics teacher education; piano and organ; political science and government; pre-dentistry studies; pre-law studies; pre-medical studies; pre-nursing studies; pre-pharmacy studies; pre-veterinary studies; psychology; public administration; public relations/image management; social work; Spanish; Spanish language teacher education; speech and rhetoric; urban studies/affairs; voice and opera; youth ministry.

Academics *Calendar:* semesters. *Degrees:* bachelor's, master's, first professional, and postbachelor's certificates. *Special study options:* academic remediation for entering students, accelerated degree program, adult/continuing education programs, advanced placement credit, distance learning, double majors, honors programs, independent study, internships, part-time degree program, services for LD students, study abroad, summer session for credit. *ROTC:* Army (c), Air Force (c). *Unusual degree programs:* 3-2 engineering with Auburn University, Vanderbilt University, Tennessee Technical University, University of Tennessee; nursing with Vanderbilt University, Belmont University.

Computers on Campus 245 computers/terminals are available on campus for general student use. Students can access the following: online (class) registration. Campuswide network is available. Wireless service is available via entire campus.

Student Life *Housing:* on-campus residence required through junior year. *Options:* men-only, women-only. Campus housing is university owned. Freshman applicants given priority for college housing. *Activities and organizations:* drama/theater group, student-run newspaper, radio station, choral group, social clubs, Sigma Pi Beta, Circle K, business fraternities, intramural program. *Campus* *security:* 24-hour emergency response devices and patrols, late-night transport/escort service, controlled dormitory access. *Student services:* health clinic, personal/psychological counseling.

Athletics Member NCAA. All Division I. *Intercollegiate sports:* baseball M (s), basketball M (s)/W (s), cross-country running M (s)/W (s), golf M (s)/W (s), soccer M (s)/W (s), softball W (s), tennis M (s)/W (s), volleyball W (s). *Intramural sports:* basketball M/W, football M/W, racquetball M/W, soccer M/W, softball M/W, table tennis M/W, tennis M/W, volleyball M/W.

Standardized Tests *Required:* SAT or ACT (for admission).

Costs (2007–08) *Comprehensive fee:* $23,881 includes full-time tuition ($15,986), mandatory fees ($825), and room and board ($7070). Full-time tuition and fees vary according to class time and degree level. Part-time tuition: $625 per hour. Part-time tuition and fees vary according to class time and degree level. *Required fees:* $825 per year part-time. *Room and board:* Room and board charges vary according to board plan and housing facility. *Payment plans:* installment, deferred payment. *Waivers:* minority students and employees or children of employees.

Financial Aid Of all full-time matriculated undergraduates who enrolled in 2007, 1,981 applied for aid, 1,220 were judged to have need, 803 had their need fully met. In 2007, 525 non-need-based awards were made. *Average percent of need met:* 68%. *Average financial aid package:* $15,765. *Average need-based loan:* $6176. *Average need-based gift aid:* $6173. *Average non-need-based aid:* $8183. *Average indebtedness upon graduation:* $15,939.

Applying *Options:* electronic application, early admission, deferred entrance. *Application fee:* $25. *Required:* high school transcript, minimum 2.25 GPA, 2 letters of recommendation, TOEFL for students whose first language is not English. *Recommended:* essay or personal statement, interview. *Application deadlines:* rolling (freshmen), rolling (transfers). *Notification:* continuous (freshmen), continuous (transfers).

Freshman Application Contact Corey Patterson, Senior Director of Enrollment, Lipscomb University, 3901 Granny White Pike, Nashville, TN 37204-3951. *Phone:* 615-966-1000. *Toll-free phone:* 877-582-4766. *Fax:* 615-966-1804. *E-mail:* admissions@lipscomb.edu.

See page 2464 for the College Close-Up.

MARTIN METHODIST COLLEGE

Pulaski, Tennessee **www.martinmethodist.edu/**

Freshman Application Contact Michael Kelley, Director of Admissions, Martin Methodist College, 433 West Madison Street, Pulaski, TN 38478-2716. *Phone:* 931-363-9804. *Toll-free phone:* 800-467-1273. *Fax:* 931-363-9818. *E-mail:* admissions@martinmethodist.edu.

MARYVILLE COLLEGE

Maryville, Tennessee **www.maryvillecollege.edu/**

- **Independent Presbyterian** 4-year, founded 1819
- **Suburban** 350-acre campus with easy access to Knoxville
- **Endowment** $40.5 million
- **Coed** 1,176 undergraduate students, 99% full-time, 55% women, 45% men
- **Moderately difficult** entrance level, 76% of applicants were admitted

Undergraduates 1,162 full-time, 14 part-time. Students come from 32 states and territories, 20 other countries, 22% are from out of state, 6% African American, 1% Asian American or Pacific Islander, 2% Hispanic American, 0.5% Native American, 4% international, 6% transferred in, 70% live on campus. *Retention:* 72% of 2006 full-time freshmen returned.

Freshmen *Admission:* 1,584 applied, 1,203 admitted, 317 enrolled. *Average high school GPA:* 3.51. *Test scores:* SAT critical reading scores over 500: 66%; SAT math scores over 500: 67%; SAT writing scores over 500: 65%; ACT scores over 18: 97%; SAT critical reading scores over 600: 32%; SAT math scores over 600: 25%; SAT writing scores over 600: 28%; ACT scores over 24: 54%; SAT critical reading scores over 700: 8%; SAT math scores over 700: 2%; SAT writing scores over 700: 4%; ACT scores over 30: 10%.

Faculty *Total:* 119, 66% full-time, 64% with terminal degrees. *Student/faculty ratio:* 12:1.

Majors American Sign Language (ASL); art history, criticism and conservation; art teacher education; atomic/molecular physics; biochemistry; biology/biological sciences; biology teacher education; business administration and management; chemistry; chemistry teacher education; computer and information sciences related; computer science; developmental and child psychology; dramatic/theater arts; economics; education; engineering; English; English as a second/foreign language (teaching); English/language arts teacher education; environmental studies; fine/studio arts; health and physical education; health teacher education; history; history teacher education; international business/trade/commerce; international relations and affairs; mathematics; mathematics and computer science; mathematics teacher education; multi-/interdisciplinary studies related; music performance; music teacher education; nursing (registered nurse training); parks, recreation and leisure; physical education teaching and coaching; physics teacher education; piano and organ; political science and government; psychology; religious studies; sign language interpretation and translation; social studies teacher education; sociology; Spanish; Spanish language teacher education; technical and business writing; voice and opera; wind/percussion instruments.

Academics *Calendar:* 4-1-4. *Degree:* bachelor's. *Special study options:* adult/continuing education programs, advanced placement credit, double majors, English as a second language, honors programs, independent study, internships, off-campus study, part-time degree program, services for LD students, student-designed majors, study abroad, summer session for credit. *Unusual degree programs:* 3-2 engineering with Vanderbilt University, Washington University in St. Louis, Auburn University, Tennessee Technological University; nursing with Vanderbilt University.

Computers on Campus 265 computers/terminals are available on campus for general student use. Students can access the following: campus intranet, computer help desk, free student e-mail accounts, online (class) registration. Campuswide network is available. 100% of college-owned or -operated housing units are wired for high-speed Internet access. Wireless service is available via classrooms, computer centers, computer labs, dorm rooms, learning centers, libraries, student centers.

Student Life *Housing:* on-campus residence required through senior year. *Options:* coed, men-only, women-only, disabled students. Campus housing is university owned. Freshman campus housing is guaranteed. *Activities and organizations:* drama/theater group, student-run newspaper, choral group, Voices of Praise, student government, Student Programming Board, Equestrian Club, peer mentors. *Campus security:* 24-hour emergency response devices and patrols, late-night transport/escort service, controlled dormitory access. *Student services:* health clinic, personal/psychological counseling.

Athletics Member NCAA. All Division III. *Intercollegiate sports:* baseball M, basketball M/W, cheerleading M/W, cross-country running M/W, equestrian sports M/W, football M, soccer M/W, softball W, tennis M/W, volleyball W, wrestling M. *Intramural sports:* badminton M/W, baseball M, basketball M/W, bowling M/W, football M/W, golf M/W, racquetball M/W, soccer M/W, softball M/W, swimming and diving M/W, table tennis M/W, tennis M/W, track and field M/W, ultimate Frisbee M/W, volleyball M/W, water polo M/W, weight lifting M/W.

Standardized Tests *Required:* SAT or ACT (for admission).

Costs (2007–08) *Comprehensive fee:* $33,150 includes full-time tuition ($24,675), mandatory fees ($675), and room and board ($7800). Full-time tuition and fees vary according to course load. Part-time tuition: $1028 per hour. Part-time tuition and fees vary according to course load. *College room only:* $3900. Room and board charges vary according to board plan, housing facility, and location. *Payment plan:* installment. *Waivers:* employees or children of employees.

Financial Aid Of all full-time matriculated undergraduates who enrolled in 2005, 1,120 applied for aid, 859 were judged to have need, 477 had their need fully met. 441 Federal Work-Study jobs (averaging $1464). 162 state and other part-time jobs (averaging $1768). In 2005, 246 non-need-based awards were made. *Average percent of need met:* 92%. *Average financial aid package:* $20,380. *Average need-based loan:* $5086. *Average need-based gift aid:* $13,670. *Average non-need-based aid:* $1535. *Average indebtedness upon graduation:* $18,473.

Applying *Options:* electronic application, early admission, early decision, early action, deferred entrance. *Required:* high school transcript, minimum 2.5 GPA. *Required for some:* essay or personal statement, letters of recommendation, interview. *Recommended:* minimum 3.0 GPA. *Application deadlines:* 3/1 (freshmen), rolling (transfers), 10/1 (early action). *Early decision deadline:* 11/15. *Notification:* 4/1 (freshmen), 8/15 (transfers), 12/1 (early decision), 10/15 (early action).

Freshman Application Contact Ms. Linda L. Moore, Administrative Assistant of Admissions, Maryville College, 502 East Lamar Alexander Parkway, Maryville, TN 37804-5907. *Phone:* 865-981-8092. *Toll-free phone:* 800-597-2687. *Fax:* 865-981-8005. *E-mail:* admissions@maryvillecollege.edu.

See page 2466 for the College Close-Up.

MEMPHIS COLLEGE OF ART

Memphis, Tennessee www.mca.edu/

- **Independent** comprehensive, founded 1936
- **Urban** 200-acre campus
- **Endowment** $5.3 million
- **Coed** 286 undergraduate students, 90% full-time, 55% women, 45% men
- **Moderately difficult** entrance level, 46% of applicants were admitted

Memphis College of Art (MCA) is a professional center of art and design education dedicated to preparing individuals for lives of creating, problem solving, and critical thinking. Small by choice and purpose, MCA is a cultural wellspring of creativity, nurturing and educating artists of all levels since 1936. Located within 340-acre Overton Park, MCA offers state-of-the-art facilities, excellent faculty members, interdisciplinary programs, and cutting-edge exhibitions to the public and those pursuing B.F.A., M.F.A., M.A.Art.Ed., and M.A.T. degrees. For more information, students should visit http://www.mca.edu.

Undergraduates 256 full-time, 30 part-time. Students come from 25 states and territories, 4 other countries, 46% are from out of state, 16% African American, 2% Asian American or Pacific Islander, 2% Hispanic American, 2% international, 12% transferred in, 34% live on campus. *Retention:* 56% of 2006 full-time freshmen returned.

Freshmen *Admission:* 474 applied, 219 admitted, 73 enrolled. *Average high school GPA:* 3.19. *Test scores:* ACT scores over 18: 91%; ACT scores over 24: 38%; ACT scores over 30: 3%.

Faculty *Total:* 45, 47% full-time, 67% with terminal degrees. *Student/faculty ratio:* 10:1.

Majors Advertising; applied art; art; ceramic arts and ceramics; commercial and advertising art; commercial photography; computer graphics; design and visual communications; drawing; fine arts related; fine/studio arts; graphic communications; graphic design; illustration; intermedia/multimedia; metal and jewelry arts; painting; photography; printmaking; sculpture.

Academics *Calendar:* semesters. *Degrees:* bachelor's and master's. *Special study options:* academic remediation for entering students, adult/continuing education programs, advanced placement credit, double majors, independent study, internships, off-campus study, part-time degree program, study abroad, summer session for credit.

Computers on Campus 70 computers/terminals are available on campus for general student use. Students can access the following: free student e-mail accounts, online (class) schedules. 100% of college-owned or -operated housing units are wired for high-speed Internet access. Wireless service is available via entire campus.

Student Life *Housing:* on-campus residence required for freshman year. *Options:* coed. Campus housing is university owned. Freshman campus housing is guaranteed. *Activities and organizations:* student-run newspaper, Student government, Photography Club. *Campus security:* 24-hour emergency response devices and patrols, late-night transport/escort service, controlled dormitory access, late night security patrols by trained personnel. *Student services:* personal/psychological counseling.

Standardized Tests *Required:* SAT or ACT (for admission).

Costs (2008–09) *Tuition:* $21,000 full-time, $2750 per course part-time. *Required fees:* $560 full-time, $280 per semester part-time. *Room only:* $5760.

Financial Aid Of all full-time matriculated undergraduates who enrolled in 2006, 222 applied for aid, 180 were judged to have need, 36 had their need fully met. 115 Federal Work-Study jobs (averaging $592). 40 state and other part-time jobs (averaging $625). In 2006, 63 non-need-based awards were made. *Average percent of need met:* 75%. *Average financial aid package:* $12,092. *Average need-based loan:* $5000. *Average need-based gift aid:* $3567. *Average non-need-based aid:* $4150. *Average indebtedness upon graduation:* $25,183.

Applying *Options:* electronic application, early admission, deferred entrance. *Application fee:* $25. *Required:* high school transcript, minimum 2.0 GPA, portfolio. *Recommended:* essay or personal statement, interview. *Application deadlines:* rolling (freshmen), rolling (transfers). *Notification:* continuous (freshmen), continuous (transfers).

Freshman Application Contact Ms. Annette Moore, Director of Admission, Memphis College of Art, 1930 Poplar Avenue, Memphis, TN 38104. *Phone:* 901-272-5151. *Toll-free phone:* 800-727-1088. *Fax:* 901-272-5158. *E-mail:* info@mca.edu.

MIDDLE TENNESSEE STATE UNIVERSITY

Murfreesboro, Tennessee www.mtsu.edu/

- **State-supported** university, founded 1911, part of Tennessee Board of Regents
- **Urban** 500-acre campus with easy access to Nashville
- **Endowment** $35.9 million
- **Coed** 20,883 undergraduate students, 85% full-time, 53% women, 47% men
- **Moderately difficult** entrance level, 39% of applicants were admitted

Undergraduates 17,760 full-time, 3,123 part-time. Students come from 47 states and territories, 6% are from out of state, 14% African American, 3% Asian American or Pacific Islander, 2% Hispanic American, 0.5% Native American, 10% transferred in, 20% live on campus.

Freshmen *Admission:* 14,182 applied, 5,559 admitted, 3,576 enrolled. *Test scores:* SAT critical reading scores over 500: 64%; SAT math scores over 500: 57%; ACT scores over 18: 94%; SAT critical reading scores over 600: 31%; SAT math scores over 600: 21%; ACT scores over 24: 33%; SAT critical reading scores over 700: 4%; SAT math scores over 700: 2%; ACT scores over 30: 3%.

Faculty *Total:* 1,267, 73% full-time. *Student/faculty ratio:* 21:1.

Majors Accounting; aeronautics/aviation/aerospace science and technology; agribusiness; animal sciences; anthropology; apparel and textiles; art; art teacher education; athletic training; biological and physical sciences; biology/biological sciences; business administration and management; business/managerial economics; business teacher education; chemistry; computer science; criminal justice/law enforcement administration; criminal justice/police science; dramatic/theater arts; economics; engineering/industrial management; engineering technology; English; environmental engineering technology; family resource management; finance; foods, nutrition, and wellness; foreign languages and literatures; geology/earth science; health and physical education; health teacher education; history; industrial and organizational psychology; industrial technology; interdisciplinary studies; interior design; international relations and affairs; kindergarten/preschool education; liberal arts and sciences/liberal studies; management information systems; marketing/marketing management; mass communication/media; mathematics; multi-/interdisciplinary studies related; music; music management and merchandising; nursing (registered nurse training); office management; parks, recreation and leisure facilities management; philosophy; physics; plant sciences; political science and government; psychology; public relations/image management; sales and marketing/marketing and distribution teacher education; sales, distribution and marketing; social work; sociology; special education; technology/industrial arts teacher education.

Academics *Calendar:* semesters. *Degrees:* bachelor's, master's, doctoral, post-master's, and postbachelor's certificates. *Special study options:* academic remediation for entering students, accelerated degree program, adult/continuing education programs, advanced placement credit, cooperative education, distance learning, double majors, English as a second language, freshman honors college, honors programs, independent study, internships, off-campus study, part-time degree program, services for LD students, student-designed majors, study abroad, summer session for credit. *ROTC:* Army (b), Air Force (c). *Unusual degree programs:* 3-2 engineering with University of Tennessee, Knoxville; Georgia Institute of Technology; Tennessee Technological University; The University of Memphis; Tennessee State University; Vanderbilt University.

Computers on Campus 2,400 computers/terminals are available on campus for general student use. Students can access the following: online (class) registration. Campuswide network is available.

Student Life *Housing options:* men-only, women-only. Campus housing is university owned. *Activities and organizations:* drama/theater group, student-run newspaper, radio and television station, choral group, marching band, African-American Student Association, Student Tennessee Education Association, Gamma Beta Phi, Golden Key National Honor Society, national fraternities, national sororities. *Campus security:* 24-hour emergency response devices and patrols, student patrols, late-night transport/escort service, controlled dormitory access. *Student services:* health clinic, personal/psychological counseling, women's center, legal services.

Athletics Member NCAA. All Division I except football (Division I-A). *Intercollegiate sports:* baseball M (s), basketball M (s)/W (s), cheerleading M (s)/W (s), cross-country running M (s)/W (s), equestrian sports M/W, golf M (s), soccer W (s), softball W (s), tennis M (s)/W (s), track and field M (s)/W (s), volleyball W (s). *Intramural sports:* basketball M/W, bowling M (c)/W (c), fencing M (c)/W (c), field hockey M (c)/W (c), football M, lacrosse M (c)/W (c), racquetball M (c)/W (c), riflery M, rugby M (c)/W (c), soccer M (c)/W, softball M/W, swimming and diving M/W, tennis M/W, ultimate Frisbee M (c)/W (c), volleyball M (c)/W (c), wrestling M (c)/W (c).

Standardized Tests *Required:* SAT or ACT (for admission).
Costs (2007–08) *Tuition:* state resident $4058 full-time, $178 per semester hour part-time; nonresident $14,334 full-time, $624 per semester hour part-time. Part-time tuition and fees vary according to course load. *Required fees:* $1220 full-time, $52 per semester hour part-time. *Room and board:* $6204; room only: $3726. Room and board charges vary according to board plan and housing facility. *Payment plan:* deferred payment. *Waivers:* senior citizens and employees or children of employees.
Financial Aid Of all full-time matriculated undergraduates who enrolled in 2006, 14,437 applied for aid, 8,938 were judged to have need, 5,675 had their need fully met. 249 Federal Work-Study jobs (averaging $1102). In 2006, 4000 non-need-based awards were made. *Average percent of need met:* 79%. *Average financial aid package:* $4118. *Average need-based loan:* $4370. *Average need-based gift aid:* $2033. *Average non-need-based aid:* $3358. *Average indebtedness upon graduation:* $21,301.
Applying *Options:* electronic application, deferred entrance. *Application fee:* $25. *Required:* high school transcript, minimum 3.0 GPA. *Required for some:* essay or personal statement. *Application deadlines:* 7/1 (freshmen), rolling (transfers). *Notification:* continuous (freshmen), continuous (transfers).
Freshman Application Contact Ms. Lynn Palmer, Director of Admissions, Middle Tennessee State University, 1301 East Main Street, MTSU-CAB 208, Murfreesboro, TN 37132. *Phone:* 615-898-2111. *Toll-free phone:* 800-331-MTSU (in-state); 800-433-MTSU (out-of-state). *Fax:* 615-898-5478. *E-mail:* admissions@mtsu.edu.

MILLIGAN COLLEGE

Milligan College, Tennessee **www.milligan.edu/**

- **Independent Christian** comprehensive, founded 1866
- **Suburban** 181-acre campus
- **Endowment** $11.2 million
- **Coed** 775 undergraduate students, 95% full-time, 61% women, 39% men
- **Moderately difficult** entrance level, 78% of applicants were admitted

Undergraduates 735 full-time, 40 part-time. Students come from 37 states and territories, 13 other countries, 54% are from out of state, 3% African American, 1% Asian American or Pacific Islander, 2% Hispanic American, 0.3% Native American, 3% international, 11% transferred in, 74% live on campus. *Retention:* 74% of 2006 full-time freshmen returned.
Freshmen *Admission:* 552 applied, 428 admitted, 197 enrolled. *Average high school GPA:* 3.49. *Test scores:* SAT critical reading scores over 500: 64%; SAT math scores over 500: 64%; SAT writing scores over 500: 64%; ACT scores over 18: 92%; SAT critical reading scores over 600: 29%; SAT math scores over 600: 28%; SAT writing scores over 600: 27%; ACT scores over 24: 43%; SAT critical reading scores over 700: 7%; SAT math scores over 700: 2%; SAT writing scores over 700: 3%; ACT scores over 30: 5%.
Faculty *Total:* 114, 62% full-time, 57% with terminal degrees. *Student/faculty ratio:* 11:1.
Majors Accounting; biblical studies; biology/biological sciences; business administration and management; chemistry; communication and media related; computer and information sciences; computer science; early childhood education; education; English; English language and literature related; fine/studio arts; health and physical education; health science; history; humanities; mathematics; music; music related; music teacher education; nursing (registered nurse training); pastoral studies/counseling; psychology; public administration and social service professions related; sociology.
Academics *Calendar:* semesters. *Degrees:* bachelor's and master's. *Special study options:* academic remediation for entering students, adult/continuing education programs, advanced placement credit, cooperative education, double majors, independent study, internships, off-campus study, part-time degree program, study abroad, summer session for credit. *ROTC:* Army (c).
Computers on Campus 97 computers/terminals are available on campus for general student use. Students can access the following: campus intranet, computer help desk, free student e-mail accounts, online (class) grades, online (class) registration, online (class) schedules. Campuswide network is available. 100% of college-owned or -operated housing units are wired for high-speed Internet access. Wireless service is available via classrooms, computer centers, computer labs, dorm rooms, libraries, student centers.
Student Life *Housing:* on-campus residence required through senior year. *Options:* men-only, women-only. Campus housing is university owned. Freshman campus housing is guaranteed. *Activities and organizations:* drama/theater group, student-run newspaper, radio station, choral group, Social Affairs Committee, Buffalo Ramblers, Concert Council, Volunteer Milligan, Students for Life. *Campus security:* 24-hour patrols, late-night transport/escort service. *Student services:* health clinic, personal/psychological counseling.
Athletics Member NAIA. *Intercollegiate sports:* baseball M (s), basketball M (s)/W (s), cross-country running M (s)/W (s), golf M (s), soccer M (s)/W (s), softball W (s), swimming and diving M/W, tennis M (s)/W (s), volleyball W (s). *Intramural sports:* basketball M/W, football M/W, softball M/W, swimming and diving M/W, table tennis M/W, tennis M/W, ultimate Frisbee M/W, volleyball M/W, weight lifting M/W.
Standardized Tests *Required:* SAT or ACT (for admission).
Costs (2007–08) *Comprehensive fee:* $24,860 includes full-time tuition ($18,900), mandatory fees ($610), and room and board ($5350). Full-time tuition and fees vary according to course load. Part-time tuition: $320 per credit. Part-time tuition and fees vary according to course load. *Required fees:* $255 per term part-time. *College room only:* $2550. Room and board charges vary according to housing facility. *Payment plan:* installment. *Waivers:* employees or children of employees.
Financial Aid* Of all full-time matriculated undergraduates who enrolled in 2003, 618 applied for aid, 560 were judged to have need, 291 had their need fully met. 148 Federal Work-Study jobs (averaging $741). 194 state and other part-time jobs (averaging $783). In 2003, 99 non-need-based awards were made. *Average percent of need met:* 55%. *Average financial aid package:* $13,266. *Average need-based loan:* $4351. *Average need-based gift aid:* $3836. *Average non-need-based aid:* $5756. *Average indebtedness upon graduation:* $11,617.
Applying *Options:* electronic application, deferred entrance. *Application fee:* $30. *Required:* essay or personal statement, high school transcript, minimum 2.0 GPA, 2 letters of recommendation. *Required for some:* interview. *Recommended:* minimum 3.0 GPA. *Application deadlines:* 8/1 (freshmen), rolling (transfers). *Notification:* continuous (freshmen), continuous (transfers).
Freshman Application Contact Ms. Tracy Brinn, Director of Enrollment Management, Milligan College, PO Box 210, Milligan College, TN 37682. *Phone:* 423-461-8730. *Toll-free phone:* 800-262-8337. *Fax:* 423-461-8982. *E-mail:* admissions@milligan.edu.

See page 2468 for the College Close-Up.

O'MORE COLLEGE OF DESIGN

Franklin, Tennessee **www.omorecollege.edu/**

- **Independent** 4-year, founded 1970
- **Small-town** 6-acre campus with easy access to Nashville
- **Coed, primarily women**
- **Moderately difficult** entrance level

Faculty *Student/faculty ratio:* 8:1.
Academics *Calendar:* semesters. *Degree:* bachelor's.
Student Life *Campus security:* 24-hour emergency response devices.
Standardized Tests *Required:* SAT or ACT (for admission).
Costs (2007–08) *Tuition:* $14,424 full-time, $601 per semester hour part-time. Full-time tuition and fees vary according to course load and program. Part-time tuition and fees vary according to course load and program. *Required fees:* $460 full-time.
Applying *Options:* deferred entrance. *Application fee:* $50. *Required:* essay or personal statement, high school transcript, minimum 2.25 GPA. *Required for some:* essay or personal statement, interview, portfolio.
Freshman Application Contact Mr. Chris Lee, Dean of Enrollment, O'More College of Design, 423 South Margin Street, Franklin, TN 37064-2816. *Phone:* 615-794-4254 Ext. 232. *Fax:* 615-790-1662. *E-mail:* dee@omorecollege.edu.

REMINGTON COLLEGE–MEMPHIS CAMPUS

Memphis, Tennessee **www.remingtoncollege.edu/**

- **Proprietary** primarily 2-year

Majors Business administration and management; computer systems networking and telecommunications; criminal justice/law enforcement administration; electrical, electronics and communications engineering; operations management.
Academics *Calendar:* quarters. *Degrees:* associate and bachelor's.
Director of Admissions Randal Hayes, Director of Recruitment, Remington College–Memphis Campus, 2731 Nonconnah Boulevard, Memphis, TN 38132-2131. *Phone:* 901-345-1000. *Fax:* 901-396-8310. *E-mail:* randal.hayes@remingtoncollege.edu.

RHODES COLLEGE

Memphis, Tennessee **www.rhodes.edu/**

- **Independent Presbyterian** comprehensive, founded 1848
- **Suburban** 100-acre campus
- **Endowment** $222.9 million
- **Coed** 1,685 undergraduate students, 99% full-time, 58% women, 42% men
- **Very difficult** entrance level, 51% of applicants were admitted

Undergraduates 1,662 full-time, 23 part-time. Students come from 44 states and territories, 11 other countries, 73% are from out of state, 6% African American, 5% Asian American or Pacific Islander, 2% Hispanic American, 0.2% Native American, 0.5% international, 1% transferred in, 76% live on campus. *Retention:* 88% of 2006 full-time freshmen returned.

Freshmen *Admission:* 3,709 applied, 1,887 admitted, 454 enrolled. *Average high school GPA:* 3.81. *Test scores:* SAT critical reading scores over 500: 99%; SAT math scores over 500: 99%; ACT scores over 18: 100%; SAT critical reading scores over 600: 72%; SAT math scores over 600: 72%; ACT scores over 24: 96%; SAT critical reading scores over 700: 21%; SAT math scores over 700: 21%; ACT scores over 30: 35%.

Faculty *Total:* 167, 82% full-time, 88% with terminal degrees. *Student/faculty ratio:* 11:1.

Majors Anthropology; art; art history, criticism and conservation; biochemistry; biology/biological sciences; business administration and management; chemistry; classics and languages, literatures and linguistics; computer science; dramatic/theater arts; economics; English; fine/studio arts; French; German; history; interdisciplinary studies; international business/trade/commerce; international economics; international relations and affairs; Latin; mathematics; modern Greek; music; philosophy; physics; political science and government; psychology; religious studies; Russian studies; sociology; Spanish; urban studies/affairs.

Academics *Calendar:* semesters. *Degrees:* bachelor's and master's (master's degree in accounting only). *Special study options:* advanced placement credit, double majors, honors programs, independent study, internships, off-campus study, part-time degree program, services for LD students, student-designed majors, study abroad. *ROTC:* Army (c), Air Force (c). *Unusual degree programs:* 3-2 engineering with Washington University in St. Louis.

Computers on Campus 220 computers/terminals are available on campus for general student use. Students can access the following: online (class) registration. Campuswide network is available.

Student Life *Housing:* on-campus residence required through sophomore year. *Options:* coed, men-only, women-only. Campus housing is university owned. Freshman campus housing is guaranteed. *Activities and organizations:* drama/theater group, student-run newspaper, radio and television station, choral group, Kinney Volunteer Program, Habitat for Humanity, Adopt A Friend, Foster, national fraternities, national sororities. *Campus security:* 24-hour emergency response devices and patrols, student patrols, late-night transport/escort service, 24-hour monitored security cameras in parking areas, fenced campus with monitored access at night. *Student services:* health clinic, personal/psychological counseling.

Athletics Member NCAA. All Division III. *Intercollegiate sports:* baseball M, basketball M/W, cheerleading W (c), cross-country running M/W, field hockey W, football M, golf M/W, lacrosse M (c)/W (c), rugby M (c), soccer M/W, softball W, swimming and diving M/W, tennis M/W, track and field M/W, volleyball W. *Intramural sports:* basketball M/W, football M/W, racquetball M/W, soccer M/W, softball M/W, squash M, volleyball M/W.

Standardized Tests *Required:* SAT or ACT (for admission).

Costs (2007–08) *Comprehensive fee:* $38,120 includes full-time tuition ($30,342), mandatory fees ($310), and room and board ($7468). Part-time tuition: $1275 per credit. *Payment plan:* installment. *Waivers:* employees or children of employees.

Financial Aid Of all full-time matriculated undergraduates who enrolled in 2007, 900 applied for aid, 663 were judged to have need, 291 had their need fully met. 204 Federal Work-Study jobs (averaging $1501). 263 state and other part-time jobs (averaging $1340). In 2007, 713 non-need-based awards were made. *Average percent of need met:* 82%. *Average financial aid package:* $22,891. *Average need-based loan:* $5233. *Average need-based gift aid:* $18,148. *Average non-need-based aid:* $11,145. *Average indebtedness upon graduation:* $21,035. *Financial aid deadline:* 3/1.

Applying *Options:* electronic application, early admission, early decision, deferred entrance. *Application fee:* $45. *Required:* essay or personal statement, high school transcript, 2 letters of recommendation. *Recommended:* interview. *Application deadlines:* 1/15 (freshmen), 1/15 (transfers). *Early decision deadline:* 11/1 (for plan 1), 1/1 (for plan 2). *Notification:* 4/1 (freshmen), 4/1 (transfers), 12/1 (early decision plan 1), 2/1 (early decision plan 2).

Director of Admissions Mr. David J. Wottle, Dean of Admissions and Financial Aid, Rhodes College, 2000 North Parkway, Memphis, TN 38112. *Phone:* 901-843-3700. *Toll-free phone:* 800-844-5969. *Fax:* 901-843-3631. *E-mail:* adminfo@rhodes.edu.

See page 2470 for the College Close-Up.

SEWANEE: THE UNIVERSITY OF THE SOUTH

Sewanee, Tennessee **www.sewanee.edu/**

- **Independent Episcopal** comprehensive, founded 1857
- **Small-town** 10,000-acre campus
- **Endowment** $314.9 million
- **Coed** 1,475 undergraduate students, 99% full-time, 53% women, 47% men
- **Very difficult** entrance level, 64% of applicants were admitted

Undergraduates 1,461 full-time, 14 part-time. Students come from 41 states and territories, 22 other countries, 78% are from out of state, 4% African American, 2% Asian American or Pacific Islander, 2% Hispanic American, 0.7% Native American, 2% international, 0.7% transferred in. *Retention:* 87% of 2006 full-time freshmen returned.

Freshmen *Admission:* 2,424 applied, 1,542 admitted, 402 enrolled. *Average high school GPA:* 3.49. *Test scores:* SAT critical reading scores over 500: 97%; SAT math scores over 500: 95%; SAT writing scores over 500: 96%; ACT scores over 18: 100%; SAT critical reading scores over 600: 67%; SAT math scores over 600: 57%; SAT writing scores over 600: 65%; ACT scores over 24: 86%; SAT critical reading scores over 700: 21%; SAT math scores over 700: 10%; SAT writing scores over 700: 16%; ACT scores over 30: 32%.

Faculty *Total:* 179, 78% full-time, 89% with terminal degrees. *Student/faculty ratio:* 11:1.

Majors American studies; anthropology; applied art; art; art history, criticism and conservation; Asian studies; biology/biological sciences; chemistry; classics and languages, literatures and linguistics; comparative literature; computer science; dramatic/theater arts; drawing; economics; English; environmental studies; European studies; fine/studio arts; forestry; French; geology/earth science; German; history; international relations and affairs; Latin; literature; mathematics; medieval and Renaissance studies; modern Greek; music; music history, literature, and theory; natural resources management and policy; philosophy; physics; political science and government; psychology; religious studies; Russian; Russian studies; social sciences; Spanish.

Academics *Calendar:* semesters. *Degrees:* bachelor's, master's, doctoral, first professional, post-master's, postbachelor's, and first professional certificates. *Special study options:* advanced placement credit, double majors, independent study, internships, services for LD students, student-designed majors, study abroad, summer session for credit. *Unusual degree programs:* 3-2 engineering with Georgia Institute of Technology, Washington University in St. Louis, Vanderbilt University, Rensselaer Polytechnic Institute, Columbia University; forestry with Duke University, Yale University.

Computers on Campus 340 computers/terminals are available on campus for general student use. Students can access the following: campus intranet, computer help desk, free student e-mail accounts, online (class) grades, online (class) registration, online (class) schedules. Campuswide network is available. 100% of college-owned or -operated housing units are wired for high-speed Internet access. Wireless service is available via entire campus.

Student Life *Housing:* on-campus residence required through senior year. *Options:* coed, men-only, women-only, disabled students. Campus housing is university owned. Freshman campus housing is guaranteed. *Activities and organizations:* drama/theater group, student-run newspaper, radio station, choral group, Sewanee Outing Program, Community Service Council, Student Activities Programming Board, student radio station, BACCHUS (alcohol and drug education), national fraternities. *Campus security:* 24-hour emergency response devices and patrols, late-night transport/escort service, controlled dormitory access, security lighting. *Student services:* health clinic, personal/psychological counseling, women's center, legal services.

Athletics Member NCAA. All Division III. *Intercollegiate sports:* baseball M, basketball M/W, crew M (c)/W (c), cross-country running M/W, equestrian sports M (c)/W (c), fencing M (c)/W (c), field hockey W, football M, golf M/W, lacrosse M (c)/W (c), rugby M (c), soccer M/W, softball W (c), swimming and diving M/W, tennis M/W, track and field M/W, volleyball W. *Intramural sports:* basketball M/W, cross-country running M/W, football M, golf M/W, racquetball M/W, soccer M/W, softball M/W, swimming and diving M/W, table tennis M/W, tennis M/W, track and field M/W, volleyball M/W.

Standardized Tests *Required:* SAT or ACT (for admission).

Costs (2007–08) *Comprehensive fee:* $39,440 includes full-time tuition ($30,438), mandatory fees ($222), and room and board ($8780). Part-time tuition: $1105 per hour. *College room only:* $4560. *Payment plans:* installment, deferred payment. *Waivers:* employees or children of employees.

Financial Aid Of all full-time matriculated undergraduates who enrolled in 2007, 720 applied for aid, 686 were judged to have need, 563 had their need fully met. 316 Federal Work-Study jobs (averaging $1092). 77 state and other part-time jobs (averaging $1177). In 2007, 311 non-need-based awards were made. *Average percent of need met:* 95%. *Average financial aid package:* $22,471. *Average need-based loan:* $3929. *Average need-based gift aid:* $18,565. *Average non-need-based aid:* $13,124. *Average indebtedness upon graduation:* $17,958.

Applying *Options:* electronic application, early admission, early decision, deferred entrance. *Application fee:* $45. *Required:* essay or personal statement, high school transcript, 2 letters of recommendation. *Recommended:* interview. *Application deadlines:* 2/1 (freshmen), 4/1 (transfers). *Early decision deadline:* 11/15. *Notification:* 4/1 (freshmen), continuous (transfers), 12/17 (early decision).

Freshman Application Contact Mr. David Lesesne, Dean of Admission, Sewanee: The University of the South, 735 University Avenue, Sewanee, TN 37383-1000. *Phone:* 931-598-1238. *Toll-free phone:* 800-522-2234. *Fax:* 931-598-3248. *E-mail:* admiss@sewanee.edu.

SOUTH COLLEGE

Knoxville, Tennessee **www.southcollegetn.edu/**

Director of Admissions Mr. Walter Hosea, Director of Admissions, South College, 720 North Fifth Avenue, Knoxville, TN 37917. *Phone:* 865-524-3043 Ext. 1825.

SOUTHERN ADVENTIST UNIVERSITY

Collegedale, Tennessee **www.southern.edu/**

- **Independent Seventh-day Adventist** comprehensive, founded 1892
- **Small-town** 1000-acre campus with easy access to Chattanooga
- **Endowment** $26.0 million
- **Coed** 2,477 undergraduate students, 86% full-time, 55% women, 45% men
- **Moderately difficult** entrance level, 68% of applicants were admitted

Undergraduates 2,126 full-time, 351 part-time. 70% are from out of state, 11% African American, 5% Asian American or Pacific Islander, 13% Hispanic American, 0.5% Native American, 6% international, 7% transferred in, 59% live on campus. *Retention:* 69% of 2006 full-time freshmen returned.

Freshmen *Admission:* 1,540 applied, 1,054 admitted, 535 enrolled. *Average high school GPA:* 3.41. *Test scores:* ACT scores over 18: 90%; ACT scores over 24: 37%; ACT scores over 30: 5%.

Faculty *Total:* 216, 62% full-time, 56% with terminal degrees. *Student/faculty ratio:* 16:1.

Majors Actuarial science; advertising; animation, interactive technology, video graphics and special effects; archeology; art; automobile/automotive mechanics technology; biochemistry; biology/biological sciences; broadcast journalism; business administration and management; chemistry; clinical laboratory science/medical technology; computer graphics; dental hygiene; elementary education; engineering; English; English/language arts teacher education; family systems; foods, nutrition, and wellness; foreign languages and literatures; French; general studies; graphic design; health/health care administration; history; international business/trade/commerce; journalism; kindergarten/preschool education; kinesiology and exercise science; management information systems; management science; marketing/marketing management; mass communication/media; mathematics; music; music performance; music teacher education; music theory and composition; non-profit management; nursing (registered nurse training); nursing science; occupational therapy; photography; physical education teaching and coaching; physical therapy; physician assistant; physics; psychology; public relations/image management; radio and television broadcasting technology; religious education; religious studies; respiratory care therapy; social work; Spanish; speech-language pathology; sport and fitness administration/management; theology.

Academics *Calendar:* semesters. *Degrees:* certificates, associate, bachelor's, master's, and post-master's certificates. *Special study options:* advanced placement credit, double majors, English as a second language, honors programs, independent study, internships, off-campus study, services for LD students, study abroad, summer session for credit.

Computers on Campus 200 computers/terminals are available on campus for general student use. Students can access the following: campus intranet, computer help desk, free student e-mail accounts, online (class) grades, online (class) registration, online (class) schedules. Campuswide network is available. Wireless service is available via classrooms, computer centers, computer labs, libraries, student centers.

Student Life *Housing:* on-campus residence required through junior year. *Options:* men-only, women-only. Campus housing is university owned. Freshman campus housing is guaranteed. *Activities and organizations:* drama/theater group, student-run newspaper, radio and television station, choral group, Student Association, Black Christian Union, Campus Ministries. *Campus security:* 24-hour patrols, late-night transport/escort service, controlled dormitory access. *Student services:* health clinic, personal/psychological counseling.

Standardized Tests *Required:* SAT or ACT (for admission).

Costs (2008–09) *Comprehensive fee:* $21,460 includes full-time tuition ($15,820), mandatory fees ($740), and room and board ($4900). Part-time tuition: $669 per semester hour. *Required fees:* $370 per year part-time. *College room only:* $2900.

Financial Aid Of all full-time matriculated undergraduates who enrolled in 2007, 1,292 applied for aid, 838 were judged to have need, 735 had their need fully met. In 2007, 440 non-need-based awards were made. *Average percent of need met:* 75%. *Average financial aid package:* $18,162. *Average need-based loan:* $4509. *Average need-based gift aid:* $8703. *Average non-need-based aid:* $5697. *Average indebtedness upon graduation:* $18,018.

Applying *Options:* deferred entrance. *Application fee:* $25. *Required:* high school transcript, minimum 2.0 GPA. *Required for some:* essay or personal statement. *Application deadlines:* rolling (freshmen), rolling (transfers). *Notification:* continuous (freshmen), continuous (transfers).

Freshman Application Contact Mr. Marc Grundy, Associate Vice President, Marketing and Enrollment Services, Southern Adventist University, PO Box 370, Collegedale, TN 37315-0370. *Phone:* 423-236-2844. *Toll-free phone:* 800-768-8437. *Fax:* 423-236-1844. *E-mail:* admissions@southern.edu.

TENNESSEE STATE UNIVERSITY

Nashville, Tennessee **www.tnstate.edu/**

- **State-supported** comprehensive, founded 1912, part of Tennessee Board of Regents
- **Urban** 450-acre campus
- **Coed** 7,132 undergraduate students, 81% full-time, 64% women, 36% men
- **Minimally difficult** entrance level, 80% of applicants were admitted

Undergraduates 5,754 full-time, 1,378 part-time. Students come from 42 states and territories, 30 other countries, 26% are from out of state, 80% African American, 1% Asian American or Pacific Islander, 1% Hispanic American, 0.1% Native American, 0.6% international, 10% transferred in, 39% live on campus. *Retention:* 70% of 2006 full-time freshmen returned.

Freshmen *Admission:* 6,528 applied, 5,213 admitted, 1,228 enrolled. *Average high school GPA:* 2.89. *Test scores:* SAT critical reading scores over 500: 22%; SAT math scores over 500: 19%; ACT scores over 18: 54%; SAT critical reading scores over 600: 1%; SAT math scores over 600: 3%; ACT scores over 24: 6%.

Faculty *Total:* 637, 70% full-time. *Student/faculty ratio:* 14:1.

Majors Accounting; administrative assistant and secretarial science; adult and continuing education; African studies; agriculture; animal sciences; architectural engineering; art; audiology and speech-language pathology; biology/biological sciences; business administration and management; business/managerial economics; business teacher education; chemistry; civil engineering; clinical laboratory science/medical technology; clinical psychology; computer science; consumer services and advocacy; criminal justice/law enforcement administration; dental hygiene; education; educational leadership and administration; electrical, electronics and communications engineering; elementary education; engineering; English; family and consumer economics related; food services technology; French; health/health care administration; health information/medical records administration; health teacher education; history; humanities; industrial arts; industrial engineering; industrial technology; kindergarten/preschool education; liberal arts and sciences/liberal studies; mass communication/media; mathematics; mechanical engineering; music; nursing (registered nurse training); parks, recreation and leisure; physical education teaching and coaching; physical therapy; physics; political science and government; psychology; public administration; reading teacher education; respiratory care therapy; social work; sociology; Spanish; special education; transportation technology.

Academics *Calendar:* semesters. *Degrees:* associate, bachelor's, master's, and doctoral. *Special study options:* academic remediation for entering students, accelerated degree program, adult/continuing education programs, cooperative education, external degree program, freshman honors college, honors programs, independent study, internships, off-campus study, part-time degree program, services for LD students, summer session for credit. *ROTC:* Army (c), Navy (c), Air Force (b).

Computers on Campus 1,025 computers/terminals are available on campus for general student use. Students can access the following: campus intranet, computer help desk, free student e-mail accounts, online (class) grades, online (class) registration, online (class) schedules. Campuswide network is available. Wireless service is available via entire campus.

Student Life *Housing options:* coed, men-only, women-only. Campus housing is university owned. Freshman applicants given priority for college housing. *Activities and organizations:* drama/theater group, student-run newspaper, radio and television station, choral group, marching band, Honda Civic Bowl, Jazz Ensemble, national fraternities, national sororities. *Campus security:* 24-hour patrols, controlled dormitory access. *Student services:* health clinic, personal/psychological counseling, women's center.

Athletics Member NCAA. All Division I except football (Division I-AA). *Intercollegiate sports:* basketball M (s)/W (s), cross-country running M (s)/W (s), golf M (s), softball W, tennis M (s)/W (s), track and field M (s)/W (s), volleyball W. *Intramural sports:* baseball M, basketball M/W, cheerleading M/W, football M, softball W, track and field M/W, volleyball M/W.

Standardized Tests *Required:* SAT or ACT (for admission).

Costs (2007–08) *Tuition:* state resident $4886 full-time, $178 per hour part-time; nonresident $15,162 full-time, $624 per hour part-time. Full-time tuition and fees vary according to course load. Part-time tuition and fees vary according to course load and program. *Required fees:* $20 per hour part-time, $168 per term part-time. *Room and board:* $5202; room only: $2982. Room and board charges vary according to board plan and housing facility. *Waivers:* minority students, senior citizens, and employees or children of employees.

Financial Aid Of all full-time matriculated undergraduates who enrolled in 2006, 5,199 applied for aid, 4,477 were judged to have need, 2,563 had their need fully met. 880 Federal Work-Study jobs (averaging $1734). In 2006, 538 non-need-based awards were made. *Average percent of need met:* 84%. *Average financial aid package:* $2869. *Average need-based gift aid:* $1208. *Average non-need-based aid:* $7092.

Applying *Options:* electronic application. *Application fee:* $25. *Required:* high school transcript. *Required for some:* 3 letters of recommendation. *Application deadlines:* 8/1 (freshmen), 8/1 (transfers). *Notification:* continuous until 8/15 (freshmen), continuous until 8/15 (transfers).

Freshman Application Contact Ms. Vernella Smith, Admissions Coordinator, Tennessee State University, 3500 John A Merritt Boulevard, Nashville, TN 37209-1561. *Phone:* 615-963-5104. *Fax:* 615-963-5108. *E-mail:* vsmith@tnstate.edu.

See page 2472 for the College Close-Up.

TENNESSEE TECHNOLOGICAL UNIVERSITY

Cookeville, Tennessee www.tntech.edu/

- **State-supported** university, founded 1915, part of Tennessee Board of Regents
- **Small-town** 235-acre campus
- **Endowment** $59.0 million
- **Coed** 8,060 undergraduate students, 89% full-time, 46% women, 54% men
- **Moderately difficult** entrance level, 88% of applicants were admitted

Undergraduates 7,171 full-time, 889 part-time. Students come from 40 states and territories, 40 other countries, 4% are from out of state, 4% African American, 1% Asian American or Pacific Islander, 1% Hispanic American, 0.3% Native American, 2% international, 9% transferred in, 35% live on campus. *Retention:* 73% of 2006 full-time freshmen returned.

Freshmen *Admission:* 3,790 applied, 3,329 admitted, 1,661 enrolled. *Average high school GPA:* 3.24. *Test scores:* SAT critical reading scores over 500: 62%; SAT math scores over 500: 74%; ACT scores over 18: 96%; SAT critical reading scores over 600: 32%; SAT math scores over 600: 36%; ACT scores over 24: 40%; SAT critical reading scores over 700: 4%; SAT math scores over 700: 30%; ACT scores over 30: 6%.

Faculty *Total:* 620, 63% full-time, 60% with terminal degrees. *Student/faculty ratio:* 18:1.

Majors Accounting; agricultural/biological engineering and bioengineering; agricultural business and management; agricultural teacher education; agronomy and crop science; animal sciences; art; art teacher education; biochemistry; biology/biological sciences; business administration and management; chemical engineering; chemistry; child development; civil engineering; clothing/textiles; computer engineering; computer science; dietetics; economics; education; electrical, electronics and communications engineering; elementary education; English; family and consumer sciences/home economics teacher education; family and consumer sciences/human sciences; fashion merchandising; finance; foods, nutrition, and wellness; French; geology/earth science; German; health teacher education; history; horticultural science; industrial engineering; industrial technology; information science/studies; information technology; interdisciplinary studies; international business/trade/commerce; journalism; kindergarten/preschool education; labor and industrial relations; landscaping and groundskeeping; marketing/marketing management; mathematics; mechanical engineering; music; music teacher education; nursing (registered nurse training); operations management; physical education teaching and coaching; physics; political science and government; pre-dentistry studies; pre-law studies; pre-medical studies; pre-veterinary studies; psychology; secondary education; social work; sociology; Spanish; special education; technical and business writing; turf and turfgrass management; web page, digital/multimedia and information resources design; wildlife and wildlands science and management.

Academics *Calendar:* semesters. *Degrees:* bachelor's, master's, doctoral, and postbachelor's certificates. *Special study options:* academic remediation for entering students, accelerated degree program, adult/continuing education programs, advanced placement credit, cooperative education, distance learning, double majors, English as a second language, honors programs, independent study, internships, off-campus study, part-time degree program, services for LD students, study abroad, summer session for credit. *ROTC:* Army (b), Air Force (c).

Computers on Campus 800 computers/terminals are available on campus for general student use. Students can access the following: online (class) registration. Campuswide network is available. 100% of college-owned or -operated housing units are wired for high-speed Internet access. Wireless service is available via entire campus.

Student Life *Housing:* on-campus residence required through sophomore year. *Options:* coed, men-only, women-only. Campus housing is university owned. Freshman campus housing is guaranteed. *Activities and organizations:* drama/theater group, student-run newspaper, radio station, choral group, marching band, Baptist Collegiate Center, Fellowship of Christian Athletes, University Christian Student Center, Residence Hall Association, national fraternities, national sororities. *Campus security:* 24-hour emergency response devices and patrols, late-night transport/escort service, student safety organization, lighted pathways. *Student services:* health clinic, personal/psychological counseling, women's center.

Athletics Member NCAA. All Division I except football (Division I-AA). *Intercollegiate sports:* baseball M (s), basketball M (s)/W (s), cheerleading M (s)/W (s), cross-country running M (s)/W (s), golf M (s)/W (s), riflery M (s)/W (s), soccer W (s), softball W (s), tennis M (s)/W (s), track and field W (s), volleyball W (s). *Intramural sports:* basketball M/W, bowling M/W, fencing M (c)/W (c), football M/W, golf M/W, racquetball M/W, rugby M (c)/W (c), soccer M/W, softball M/W, tennis M/W, ultimate Frisbee M/W, volleyball M/W, wrestling M.

Standardized Tests *Required:* SAT or ACT (for admission). *Recommended:* ACT (for admission).

Costs (2007–08) *Tuition:* state resident $4980 full-time, $178 per hour part-time; nonresident $15,256 full-time, $624 per hour part-time. Part-time tuition and fees vary according to course load. *Required fees:* $62 per hour part-time. *Room and board:* $6330; room only: $3210. Room and board charges vary according to board plan and housing facility. *Payment plan:* installment. *Waivers:* employees or children of employees.

Financial Aid Of all full-time matriculated undergraduates who enrolled in 2007, 5,706 applied for aid, 3,577 were judged to have need, 1,143 had their need fully met. 333 Federal Work-Study jobs (averaging $1184). 507 state and other part-time jobs (averaging $1786). In 2007, 1655 non-need-based awards were made. *Average percent of need met:* 83%. *Average financial aid package:* $3401. *Average need-based loan:* $2998. *Average need-based gift aid:* $2981. *Average non-need-based aid:* $4398. *Average indebtedness upon graduation:* $14,400.

Applying *Options:* electronic application, early admission, deferred entrance. *Application fee:* $15. *Required:* high school transcript, minimum 2.5 GPA, ACT composite score of 19. *Recommended:* interview. *Application deadlines:* 8/1 (freshmen), 8/1 (transfers). *Notification:* continuous (freshmen), continuous (transfers).

Freshman Application Contact Ms. Vanessa Palmer, Interim Director of Admissions, Tennessee Technological University, TTU Box 5006, Cookeville, TN 38505. *Phone:* 931-372-3888. *Toll-free phone:* 800-255-8881. *Fax:* 931-372-6250. *E-mail:* admissions@tntech.edu.

TENNESSEE TEMPLE UNIVERSITY

Chattanooga, Tennessee **www.tntemple.edu/**

Director of Admissions Mr. Chris Dooley, Director of Enrollment Services, Tennessee Temple University, 1815 Union Avenue, Chattanooga, TN 37404-3587. *Phone:* 423-493-4371. *Toll-free phone:* 800-553-4050.

TENNESSEE WESLEYAN COLLEGE

Athens, Tennessee **www.twcnet.edu/**

- **Independent United Methodist** 4-year, founded 1857
- **Small-town** 40-acre campus with easy access to Knoxville and Chattanooga
- **Coed** 861 undergraduate students, 86% full-time, 63% women, 37% men
- **Minimally difficult** entrance level, 79% of applicants were admitted

Undergraduates 737 full-time, 124 part-time. Students come from 22 states and territories, 11 other countries, 8% are from out of state, 3% African American, 0.5% Asian American or Pacific Islander, 2% Hispanic American, 0.1% Native American, 2% international, 17% transferred in, 29% live on campus. *Retention:* 62% of 2006 full-time freshmen returned.

Freshmen *Admission:* 463 applied, 366 admitted, 153 enrolled. *Average high school GPA:* 3.23. *Test scores:* SAT critical reading scores over 500: 47%; SAT math scores over 500: 60%; ACT scores over 18: 95%; SAT critical reading scores over 600: 20%; SAT math scores over 600: 7%; ACT scores over 24: 31%; ACT scores over 30: 4%.

Faculty *Total:* 88, 57% full-time, 50% with terminal degrees. *Student/faculty ratio:* 12:1.

Majors Accounting; allied health diagnostic, intervention, and treatment professions related; American studies; behavioral sciences; biology/biological sciences; business administration and management; chemistry; Christian studies; computer and information sciences; dramatic/theater arts; early childhood education; education; education (K-12); education (multiple levels); elementary education; English; environmental studies; finance; French; health and physical education; health science; history; human resources management; human services; interdisciplinary studies; international/global studies; kinesiology and exercise science; mathematics; multi-/interdisciplinary studies related; music; nursing (registered nurse training); ophthalmic and optometric support services and allied professions related; pre-nursing studies; pre-theology/pre-ministerial studies; psychology; religious studies; secondary education; Spanish; sport and fitness administration/management.

Academics *Calendar:* semesters. *Degrees:* bachelor's (profile includes information for both the main and branch campuses). *Special study options:* academic remediation for entering students, accelerated degree program, adult/continuing education programs, advanced placement credit, cooperative education, double majors, honors programs, independent study, internships, off-campus study, part-time degree program, services for LD students, student-designed majors, study abroad, summer session for credit.

Computers on Campus 150 computers/terminals are available on campus for general student use. Students can access the following: campus intranet, computer help desk, online (class) schedules. Campuswide network is available. 100% of college-owned or -operated housing units are wired for high-speed Internet access. Wireless service is available via classrooms, dorm rooms, libraries.

Student Life *Housing:* on-campus residence required through senior year. *Options:* coed, men-only, women-only. Campus housing is university owned. Freshman campus housing is guaranteed. *Activities and organizations:* drama/theater group, student-run newspaper, choral group, Fellowship of Christian Athletes, Business Club, Baptist Collegiate Ministries, Student Government Association, Concert Choir, national sororities. *Campus security:* 24-hour patrols, late-night transport/escort service, controlled dormitory access, night patrols by trained security personnel. *Student services:* health clinic, personal/psychological counseling.

Athletics Member NAIA. *Intercollegiate sports:* baseball M (s), basketball M (s)/W (s), cheerleading M (s)/W (s), cross-country running M (s)/W (s), golf M (s)/W (s), lacrosse M (s), soccer M (s)/W (s), softball W (s), tennis M (s)/W (s), volleyball W (s).

Standardized Tests *Required:* SAT or ACT (for admission).

Costs (2008–09) *Comprehensive fee:* $22,880 includes full-time tuition ($16,500), mandatory fees ($550), and room and board ($5830). Part-time tuition: $455 per credit hour. *Required fees:* $10 per credit hour part-time.

Financial Aid Of all full-time matriculated undergraduates who enrolled in 2006, 695 applied for aid, 588 were judged to have need, 125 had their need fully met. 88 Federal Work-Study jobs (averaging $848). 33 state and other part-time jobs (averaging $766). In 2006, 124 non-need-based awards were made. *Average percent of need met:* 67%. *Average financial aid package:* $12,158. *Average need-based loan:* $3932. *Average need-based gift aid:* $9431. *Average non-need-based aid:* $8679. *Average indebtedness upon graduation:* $16,490.

Applying *Options:* electronic application, deferred entrance. *Application fee:* $25. *Required:* high school transcript, minimum 2.25 GPA, 1 letter of recommendation. *Required for some:* interview. *Recommended:* essay or personal statement. *Application deadlines:* 8/31 (freshmen), 8/31 (transfers). *Notification:* continuous (freshmen), continuous (transfers).

Freshman Application Contact Stan Harrison, Vice President of Enrollment Services and Director of Athletics, Tennessee Wesleyan College, PO Box 40, Athens, TN 37371-0040. *Phone:* 423-746-7504 Ext. 5310. *Toll-free phone:* 800-PICK-TWC. *Fax:* 423-745-9335. *E-mail:* sharrison@twcnet.edu.

TREVECCA NAZARENE UNIVERSITY

Nashville, Tennessee **www.trevecca.edu/**

- **Independent Nazarene** comprehensive, founded 1901
- **Urban** 65-acre campus
- **Endowment** $17.8 million
- **Coed** 1,270 undergraduate students, 87% full-time, 56% women, 44% men
- **Moderately difficult** entrance level, 68% of applicants were admitted

Undergraduates 1,103 full-time, 167 part-time. Students come from 36 states and territories, 10 other countries, 60% are from out of state, 8% African American, 1% Asian American or Pacific Islander, 1% Hispanic American, 0.6% Native American, 2% international, 7% transferred in, 56% live on campus. *Retention:* 74% of 2006 full-time freshmen returned.

Freshmen *Admission:* 821 applied, 560 admitted, 239 enrolled. *Average high school GPA:* 3.12. *Test scores:* SAT critical reading scores over 500: 63%; SAT math scores over 500: 63%; ACT scores over 18: 87%; SAT critical reading scores over 600: 30%; SAT math scores over 600: 24%; ACT scores over 24: 34%; SAT critical reading scores over 700: 9%; SAT math scores over 700: 6%; ACT scores over 30: 5%.

Faculty *Total:* 210, 36% full-time, 58% with terminal degrees. *Student/faculty ratio:* 17:1.

Majors Accounting; behavioral sciences; biological and physical sciences; biology/biological sciences; biology teacher education; broadcast journalism; business administration and management; chemistry; chemistry teacher education; child development; clinical laboratory science/medical technology; communication/speech communication and rhetoric; dramatic/theater arts; education (K-12); English; English/language arts teacher education; general studies; history; history teacher education; kinesiology and exercise science; marketing/marketing management; mass communication/media; mathematics; mathematics teacher education; music; music management and merchandising; music teacher education; physical education teaching and coaching; physics; psychology; radio and television broadcasting technology; religious/sacred music; religious studies; secondary education; social sciences.

Academics *Calendar:* semesters. *Degrees:* associate, bachelor's, master's, doctoral, and post-master's certificates. *Special study options:* academic remediation for entering students, adult/continuing education programs, advanced placement credit, double majors, internships, services for LD students, study abroad, summer session for credit. *ROTC:* Army (c).

Computers on Campus 200 computers/terminals are available on campus for general student use. Students can access the following: campus intranet, computer help desk, free student e-mail accounts, online (class) grades, online (class) schedules. Campuswide network is available. Wireless service is available via entire campus.

Student Life *Housing:* on-campus residence required through senior year. *Options:* men-only, women-only. Campus housing is university owned. *Activities and organizations:* drama/theater group, student-run newspaper, radio station, choral group, marching band. *Campus security:* 24-hour patrols, student patrols, late-night transport/escort service. *Student services:* health clinic, personal/psychological counseling.

Athletics Member NAIA. *Intercollegiate sports:* baseball M (s), basketball M (s)/W (s), golf M (s)/W (s), soccer M (s)/W (s), softball W (s), volleyball W (s). *Intramural sports:* badminton M/W, basketball M/W, football M/W, golf M/W, racquetball M/W, softball M/W, table tennis M/W, track and field M/W, volleyball M/W.

Standardized Tests *Required:* SAT or ACT (for admission).

Costs (2007–08) *Comprehensive fee:* $22,386 includes full-time tuition ($15,512) and room and board ($6874). Full-time tuition and fees vary according to course load. Part-time tuition and fees vary according to course load. *College* *room only:* $3066. Room and board charges vary according to board plan. *Payment plan:* installment. *Waivers:* senior citizens and employees or children of employees.

Applying *Options:* electronic application, early admission, deferred entrance. *Application fee:* $25. *Required:* high school transcript, minimum 2.5 GPA, medical history and immunization records. *Recommended:* letters of recommendation. *Application deadlines:* 4/1 (freshmen), rolling (transfers). *Notification:* continuous (freshmen), continuous (transfers).

Freshman Application Contact Mr. Michael, Director of Undergraduate Admissions, Trevecca Nazarene University, 333 Murfreesboro Road, Nashville, TN 37210-2834. *Phone:* 615-248-1320. *Toll-free phone:* 888-210-4TNU. *Fax:* 615-248-7406. *E-mail:* admissions_und@trevecca.edu.

TUSCULUM COLLEGE

Greeneville, Tennessee **www.tusculum.edu/**

- **Independent Presbyterian** comprehensive, founded 1794
- **Small-town** 140-acre campus
- **Endowment** $13.8 million
- **Coed** 2,445 undergraduate students, 97% full-time, 61% women, 39% men
- **Moderately difficult** entrance level, 68% of applicants were admitted

Undergraduates 2,368 full-time, 77 part-time. Students come from 31 states and territories, 22 other countries, 46% are from out of state, 11% African American, 0.3% Asian American or Pacific Islander, 2% Hispanic American, 0.1% Native American, 2% international, 2% transferred in, 65% live on campus. *Retention:* 58% of 2006 full-time freshmen returned.

Freshmen *Admission:* 1,672 applied, 1,139 admitted, 360 enrolled. *Average high school GPA:* 3.1. *Test scores:* SAT critical reading scores over 500: 32%; SAT math scores over 500: 44%; ACT scores over 18: 89%; SAT critical reading scores over 600: 7%; SAT math scores over 600: 6%; ACT scores over 24: 28%; SAT critical reading scores over 700: 1%; ACT scores over 30: 1%.

Faculty *Total:* 199, 32% full-time. *Student/faculty ratio:* 16:1.

Majors Art teacher education; athletic training; biology/biological sciences; biology/biotechnology laboratory technician; biology teacher education; business administration and management; business teacher education; early childhood education; education (specific subject areas) related; elementary education; English; English/language arts teacher education; environmental studies; health and physical education; health and physical education related; health/medical preparatory programs related; history; history teacher education; kinesiology and exercise science; mathematics; mathematics and computer science; mathematics teacher education; middle school education; multi-/interdisciplinary studies related; museum studies; natural resources/conservation; physical education teaching and coaching; pre-law studies; pre-medical studies; pre-pharmacy studies; pre-veterinary studies; psychology; psychology teacher education; secondary education; special education; sport and fitness administration/management; visual and performing arts.

Academics *Calendar:* semesters. *Degrees:* bachelor's and master's. *Special study options:* academic remediation for entering students, adult/continuing education programs, advanced placement credit, double majors, English as a second language, honors programs, independent study, internships, part-time degree program, student-designed majors, study abroad, summer session for credit.

Computers on Campus 200 computers/terminals are available on campus for general student use. Students can access the following: campus intranet, computer help desk, free student e-mail accounts. Campuswide network is available. Wireless service is available via classrooms, computer labs, learning centers, libraries, student centers.

Student Life *Housing:* on-campus residence required through junior year. *Options:* coed, men-only, women-only. Campus housing is university owned. Freshman campus housing is guaranteed. *Activities and organizations:* drama/theater group, student-run newspaper, radio and television station, choral group, Pioneer Newspaper, Bonwondi, Campus Activities Board, Fellowship of Christian Athletes, "Tusculana" (yearbook). *Campus security:* 24-hour emergency response devices and patrols, student patrols, late-night transport/escort service, controlled dormitory access, trained security personnel on duty. *Student services:* health clinic, personal/psychological counseling, women's center.

Athletics Member NCAA. All Division II. *Intercollegiate sports:* baseball M (s), basketball M (s)/W (s), cheerleading W (s), cross-country running M (s)/W (s), football M (s), golf M (s)/W, soccer M (s)/W (s), softball W (s), tennis M (s)/W (s), volleyball W (s). *Intramural sports:* baseball M, basketball M/W, football M, softball M, tennis M/W, volleyball M/W.

Standardized Tests *Required:* SAT or ACT (for admission).

Costs (2007–08) *Comprehensive fee:* $24,295 includes full-time tuition ($17,385) and room and board ($6910). Full-time tuition and fees vary according to degree level and reciprocity agreements. Part-time tuition: $800 per semester hour. Part-time tuition and fees vary according to degree level and reciprocity agreements. *Room and board:* Room and board charges vary according to housing facility. *Payment plan:* installment. *Waivers:* employees or children of employees.

Financial Aid Of all full-time matriculated undergraduates who enrolled in 2006, 1,770 were judged to have need. 157 Federal Work-Study jobs (averaging $1035). 48 state and other part-time jobs (averaging $1603). *Average financial aid package:* $10,110. *Average indebtedness upon graduation:* $7078.

Applying *Options:* electronic application, early admission, deferred entrance. *Required:* essay or personal statement, high school transcript, minimum 2.0 GPA. *Required for some:* letters of recommendation. *Recommended:* interview. *Application deadlines:* rolling (freshmen), rolling (transfers).

Freshman Application Contact Ms. Melissa Ripley, Director of Operations, Tusculum College, PO Box 5047, Greeneville, TN 37743-9997. *Phone:* 423-636-7300 Ext. 5374. *Toll-free phone:* 800-729-0256. *Fax:* 423-798-1622. *E-mail:* admissions@tusculum.edu.

UNION UNIVERSITY

Jackson, Tennessee **www.uu.edu/**

- **Independent Southern Baptist** comprehensive, founded 1823
- **Small-town** 290-acre campus with easy access to Memphis
- **Endowment** $25.9 million
- **Coed** 2,310 undergraduate students, 80% full-time, 60% women, 40% men
- **Moderately difficult** entrance level, 81% of applicants were admitted

Undergraduates 1,837 full-time, 473 part-time. Students come from 44 states and territories, 36 other countries, 30% are from out of state, 11% African American, 1% Asian American or Pacific Islander, 2% Hispanic American, 0.2% Native American, 2% international, 6% transferred in, 52% live on campus. *Retention:* 84% of 2006 full-time freshmen returned.

Freshmen *Admission:* 1,140 applied, 918 admitted, 467 enrolled. *Average high school GPA:* 3.52. *Test scores:* SAT critical reading scores over 500: 85%; SAT math scores over 500: 82%; ACT scores over 18: 96%; SAT critical reading scores over 600: 50%; SAT math scores over 600: 41%; ACT scores over 24: 60%; SAT critical reading scores over 700: 19%; SAT math scores over 700: 8%; ACT scores over 30: 16%.

Faculty *Total:* 261, 67% full-time, 63% with terminal degrees. *Student/faculty ratio:* 12:1.

Majors Accounting; advertising; ancient Near Eastern and biblical languages; art; art teacher education; athletic training; biblical studies; biological and physical sciences; biology/biological sciences; broadcast journalism; business administration and management; business/managerial economics; business teacher education; chemistry; clinical laboratory science/medical technology; computer science; dramatic/theater arts; economics; education; elementary education; English; English as a second/foreign language (teaching); family and community services; finance; foreign languages and literatures; French; history; information science/studies; journalism; kindergarten/preschool education; kinesiology and exercise science; marketing/marketing management; mass communication/media; mathematics; music; music management and merchandising; music performance; music teacher education; nursing (registered nurse training); parks, recreation and leisure facilities management; philosophy; philosophy and religious studies related; physical education teaching and coaching; physics; piano and organ; political science and government; pre-dentistry studies; pre-law studies; pre-medical studies; pre-pharmacy studies; psychology; public relations/image management; radio and television; religious/sacred music; religious studies; science teacher education; secondary education; social work; sociology; Spanish; special education; speech and rhetoric; sport and fitness administration/management; theology; theology and religious vocations related; voice and opera.

Academics *Calendar:* 4-1-4. *Degrees:* certificates, diplomas, associate, bachelor's, master's, doctoral, and post-master's certificates. *Special study options:* academic remediation for entering students, accelerated degree program, adult/continuing education programs, advanced placement credit, cooperative education, distance learning, double majors, English as a second language, honors programs, independent study, internships, off-campus study, part-time degree program, services for LD students, study abroad, summer session for credit.

Computers on Campus 236 computers/terminals are available on campus for general student use. Students can access the following: campus intranet, computer help desk, free student e-mail accounts, online (class) grades, online (class) registration, online (class) schedules. Campuswide network is available. 100% of college-owned or -operated housing units are wired for high-speed Internet access. Wireless service is available via entire campus.

Student Life *Housing:* on-campus residence required through junior year. *Options:* men-only, women-only, disabled students. Campus housing is university owned. Freshman applicants given priority for college housing. *Activities and* *organizations:* drama/theater group, student-run newspaper, choral group, Campus Ministries, Student Government Association, Student Activities Council, SIFE, national fraternities, national sororities. *Campus security:* 24-hour emergency response devices and patrols, student patrols, late-night transport/escort service. *Student services:* health clinic, personal/psychological counseling.

Athletics Member NAIA, NCCAA. *Intercollegiate sports:* baseball M (s), basketball M (s)/W (s), cheerleading W (s), cross-country running M/W (s), golf M (s), soccer M (s)/W (s), softball W (s), track and field M/W, volleyball W (s). *Intramural sports:* basketball M/W, bowling M/W, cross-country running M/W, football M/W, golf M/W, racquetball M/W, soccer W, softball M/W, swimming and diving M/W, table tennis M/W, track and field M/W, ultimate Frisbee M/W, volleyball M/W.

Standardized Tests *Required:* SAT or ACT (for admission). *Recommended:* SAT Subject Tests (for admission).

Costs (2007–08) *Comprehensive fee:* $25,120 includes full-time tuition ($17,990), mandatory fees ($630), and room and board ($6500). Full-time tuition and fees vary according to course load. Part-time tuition: $620 per credit hour. *Room and board:* Room and board charges vary according to board plan and location. *Payment plans:* installment, deferred payment. *Waivers:* employees or children of employees.

Financial Aid Of all full-time matriculated undergraduates who enrolled in 2007, 1,467 applied for aid, 1,237 were judged to have need, 68 had their need fully met. 118 Federal Work-Study jobs (averaging $1573). 273 state and other part-time jobs (averaging $865). In 2007, 355 non-need-based awards were made. *Average financial aid package:* $17,421. *Average need-based loan:* $4738. *Average need-based gift aid:* $5179. *Average non-need-based aid:* $11,866. *Average indebtedness upon graduation:* $21,543.

Applying *Options:* electronic application, early admission, early action, deferred entrance. *Application fee:* $35. *Required:* high school transcript, minimum 2.5 GPA. *Required for some:* letters of recommendation. *Recommended:* essay or personal statement, interview. *Application deadlines:* rolling (freshmen), rolling (transfers), 12/1 (early action). *Notification:* continuous until 8/1 (freshmen), continuous until 8/15 (transfers), 12/15 (early action).

Freshman Application Contact Mr. Robbie Graves, Director of Enrollment Services, Union University, 1050 Union University Drive, Jackson, TN 38305-3697. *Phone:* 731-661-5590. *Toll-free phone:* 800-33-UNION. *Fax:* 731-661-5017. *E-mail:* cgraves@uu.edu.

See page 2474 for the College Close-Up.

UNIVERSITY OF MEMPHIS

Memphis, Tennessee **www.memphis.edu/**

- **State-supported** university, founded 1912, part of Tennessee Board of Regents
- **Urban** 1100-acre campus
- **Endowment** $207.0 million
- **Coed** 15,802 undergraduate students, 74% full-time, 62% women, 38% men
- **Moderately difficult** entrance level, 66% of applicants were admitted

Undergraduates 11,675 full-time, 4,127 part-time. Students come from 44 states and territories, 89 other countries, 6% are from out of state, 38% African American, 2% Asian American or Pacific Islander, 2% Hispanic American, 0.3% Native American, 2% international, 8% transferred in, 15% live on campus. *Retention:* 73% of 2006 full-time freshmen returned.

Freshmen *Admission:* 6,025 applied, 3,986 admitted, 2,017 enrolled. *Test scores:* ACT scores over 18: 88%; ACT scores over 24: 34%; ACT scores over 30: 3%.

Faculty *Total:* 1,367, 61% full-time, 77% with terminal degrees. *Student/faculty ratio:* 20:1.

Majors Accounting; African-American/Black studies; anthropology; architecture; art; art history, criticism and conservation; biochemistry/biophysics and molecular biology; biology/biological sciences; biomedical/medical engineering; business/managerial economics; chemistry; civil engineering; communication/speech communication and rhetoric; computer engineering; computer engineering technology; computer science; consumer merchandising/retailing management; criminal justice/law enforcement administration; criminology; dramatic/theater arts; economics; education (multiple levels); electrical, electronic and communications engineering technology; electrical, electronics and communications engineering; English; finance; foreign languages and literatures; general studies; geography; geology/earth science; history; hospitality administration; human development and family studies; insurance; interdisciplinary studies; international business/trade/commerce; international relations and affairs; journalism; kinesiology and exercise science; legal assistant/paralegal; liberal arts and sciences/liberal studies; management information systems; management science; manufacturing technology; marketing/marketing management; mathematics; mechanical engineering; microbiology; molecular biology; multi-/interdisciplinary studies related; music; music management and merchandising; nursing (registered nurse training); philosophy; physical education teaching and coaching; physics; political science and government; professional studies; psychology; real estate; sales, distribution and marketing; social work; sociology; special education; sport and fitness administration/management; systems engineering.

Academics *Calendar:* semesters. *Degrees:* certificates, bachelor's, master's, doctoral, first professional, post-master's, postbachelor's, and first professional certificates. *Special study options:* academic remediation for entering students, accelerated degree program, adult/continuing education programs, advanced placement credit, cooperative education, distance learning, double majors, English as a second language, external degree program, honors programs, independent study, internships, off-campus study, part-time degree program, services for LD students, student-designed majors, study abroad, summer session for credit. *ROTC:* Army (b), Navy (b), Air Force (b).

Computers on Campus 2,000 computers/terminals are available on campus for general student use. Students can access the following: campus intranet, computer help desk, free student e-mail accounts, online (class) grades, online (class) registration, online (class) schedules. Campuswide network is available. Wireless service is available via entire campus.

Student Life *Housing options:* coed, men-only, women-only, disabled students. Campus housing is university owned. *Activities and organizations:* drama/theater group, student-run newspaper, radio station, choral group, marching band, Black Student Association, Pan Hellenic Council, Honor Student Council, Campus Crusade for Christ, Blue Crew, national fraternities, national sororities. *Campus security:* 24-hour emergency response devices and patrols, student patrols, late-night transport/escort service. *Student services:* health clinic, personal/psychological counseling, women's center.

Athletics Member NCAA. All Division I except football (Division I-A). *Intercollegiate sports:* baseball M (s), basketball M (s)/W (s), cheerleading M (s)/W (s), cross-country running M (s)/W (s), golf M (s)/W (s), racquetball M (c)/W (c), riflery M (s)/W (s), soccer M (s)/W (s), softball W, swimming and diving M (c)/W (c), tennis M (s)/W (s), track and field M (s)/W (s), volleyball W (s). *Intramural sports:* archery M/W, badminton M/W, basketball M/W, bowling M/W, fencing M, golf M/W, rugby M/W, soccer M, softball M/W, swimming and diving M/W, table tennis M/W, tennis M/W, track and field M/W, volleyball M/W.

Standardized Tests *Required:* SAT or ACT (for admission).

Costs (2008–09) *Tuition:* state resident $4652 full-time, $196 per credit part-time; nonresident $15,480 full-time, $649 per credit part-time. *Required fees:* $1150 full-time, $77 per credit part-time. *Room and board:* $5433.

Financial Aid Of all full-time matriculated undergraduates who enrolled in 2007, 9,679 applied for aid, 7,306 were judged to have need, 1,117 had their need fully met. 235 Federal Work-Study jobs (averaging $2246). In 2007, 447 non-need-based awards were made. *Average percent of need met:* 73%. *Average financial aid package:* $7730. *Average need-based loan:* $3372. *Average need-based gift aid:* $3837. *Average non-need-based aid:* $4528. *Average indebtedness upon graduation:* $20,601.

Applying *Options:* electronic application, early admission. *Application fee:* $25. *Required:* high school transcript. *Required for some:* minimum 2.0 GPA, 2 letters of recommendation, interview. *Application deadlines:* 7/1 (freshmen), 7/1 (transfers). *Notification:* continuous (freshmen), continuous (transfers).

Freshman Application Contact Mr. David Wallace, Director of Admissions, University of Memphis, Memphis, TN 38152. *Phone:* 901-678-2101. *Toll-free phone:* 800-669-2678. *Fax:* 901-678-3053. *E-mail:* dwallace@memphis.edu.

See page 2476 for the College Close-Up.

UNIVERSITY OF PHOENIX–NASHVILLE CAMPUS

Nashville, Tennessee **www.phoenix.edu/**

- **Proprietary** comprehensive, founded 2003
- **Urban** campus
- **Coed**
- **Noncompetitive** entrance level

Faculty *Student/faculty ratio:* 7:1.

Academics *Calendar:* continuous. *Degrees:* bachelor's and master's.

Student Life *Campus security:* late-night transport/escort service.

Costs (2007–08) *Tuition:* $10,560 full-time, $352 per credit part-time. Full-time tuition and fees vary according to course level.

Financial Aid *Average financial aid package:* $3865. *Average need-based gift aid:* $2047.

Applying *Options:* deferred entrance. *Application fee:* $45. *Required:* 1 letter of recommendation. *Required for some:* high school transcript.

Freshman Application Contact Ms. Beth Barilla, Associate Vice President, Student Admissions and Services, University of Phoenix–Nashville Campus, 4615 East Elwood Street, Mail Stop AA-K101, Phoenix, AZ 85040-1958. *Phone:* 480-317-6000. *Toll-free phone:* 800-776-4867 (in-state); 800-228-7240 (out-of-state). *Fax:* 480-894-1758. *E-mail:* beth.barilla@phoenix.edu.

THE UNIVERSITY OF TENNESSEE

Knoxville, Tennessee **www.tennessee.edu/**

- **State-supported** university, founded 1794, part of University of Tennessee System
- **Urban** 533-acre campus
- **Endowment** $742.5 million
- **Coed** 21,369 undergraduate students, 93% full-time, 51% women, 49% men
- **Moderately difficult** entrance level, 71% of applicants were admitted

Undergraduates 19,893 full-time, 1,476 part-time. Students come from 49 states and territories, 76 other countries, 13% are from out of state, 9% African American, 3% Asian American or Pacific Islander, 2% Hispanic American, 0.3% Native American, 1% international, 6% transferred in, 32% live on campus. *Retention:* 84% of 2006 full-time freshmen returned.

Freshmen *Admission:* 12,824 applied, 9,136 admitted, 4,351 enrolled. *Average high school GPA:* 3.61. *Test scores:* SAT critical reading scores over 500: 85%; SAT math scores over 500: 86%; ACT scores over 18: 100%; SAT critical reading scores over 600: 37%; SAT math scores over 600: 42%; ACT scores over 24: 75%; SAT critical reading scores over 700: 6%; SAT math scores over 700: 7%; ACT scores over 30: 17%.

Faculty *Total:* 1,666, 93% full-time, 81% with terminal degrees. *Student/faculty ratio:* 15:1.

Majors Accounting; advertising; aerospace, aeronautical and astronautical engineering; agricultural/biological engineering and bioengineering; agricultural business and management related; agricultural economics; agricultural teacher education; animal sciences; anthropology; architecture; area, ethnic, cultural, and gender studies related; art history, criticism and conservation; art teacher education; audiology and hearing sciences; biochemistry; biology/biological sciences; botany/plant biology; business administration and management; business/commerce; business/managerial economics; business teacher education; chemical engineering; chemistry; civil engineering; classics and languages, literatures and linguistics; clinical laboratory science/medical technology; commercial and advertising art; computer engineering; computer science; consumer economics; cultural studies; dramatic/theater arts; ecology; economics; electrical, electronics and communications engineering; engineering physics; engineering science; English; family and consumer sciences/home economics teacher education; family systems; finance; fine/studio arts; food science; foods, nutrition, and wellness; forestry; French; geography; geology/earth science; German; health teacher education; history; hotel/motel administration; human development and family studies; industrial engineering; interior design; Italian; journalism; kinesiology and exercise science; logistics and materials management; marketing/marketing management; materials engineering; mathematics; mechanical engineering; medical microbiology and bacteriology; multi-/interdisciplinary studies related; music; music teacher education; nuclear engineering; nursing (registered nurse training); ornamental horticulture; parks, recreation and leisure facilities management; philosophy; physics; plant protection and integrated pest management; plant sciences; political science and government; psychology; public administration; radio and television; religious studies; Russian; social work; sociology; Spanish; special education; speech and rhetoric; speech-language pathology; sport and fitness administration/management; statistics; technical teacher education; wildlife and wildlands science and management; zoology/animal biology.

Academics *Calendar:* semesters. *Degrees:* bachelor's, master's, doctoral, first professional, post-master's, postbachelor's, and first professional certificates. *Special study options:* accelerated degree program, adult/continuing education programs, advanced placement credit, cooperative education, distance learning, double majors, English as a second language, external degree program, freshman honors college, honors programs, independent study, internships, off-campus study, part-time degree program, services for LD students, student-designed majors, study abroad, summer session for credit. *ROTC:* Army (b), Air Force (b).

Computers on Campus 600 computers/terminals are available on campus for general student use. Students can access the following: campus intranet, computer help desk, free student e-mail accounts, online (class) grades, online (class) registration, online (class) schedules, Blackboard Course Management System. Campuswide network is available. 100% of college-owned or -operated housing units are wired for high-speed Internet access. Wireless service is available via entire campus.

Student Life *Housing:* on-campus residence required for freshman year. *Options:* coed, men-only, women-only, disabled students. Campus housing is university owned and leased by the school. Freshman campus housing is guaranteed. *Activities and organizations:* drama/theater group, student-run newspaper, radio and television station, choral group, marching band, Central Program Council, religious organizations, Volunteer Outreach for Leadership and Service, Student Government Association, Black Cultural Program, national fraternities, national sororities. *Campus security:* 24-hour emergency response devices and patrols, late-night transport/escort service. *Student services:* health clinic, personal/psychological counseling, women's center, legal services.

Athletics Member NCAA. All Division I except football (Division I-A). *Intercollegiate sports:* baseball M (s), basketball M (s)/W (s), cheerleading M (s)/W (s), crew W (s), cross-country running M (s)/W (s), golf M (s)/W (s), soccer W (s), softball W (s), swimming and diving M (s)/W (s), tennis M (s)/W (s), track and field M (s)/W (s), volleyball W (s). *Intramural sports:* badminton M/W, basketball M/W, bowling M/W, crew M (c)/W (c), cross-country running M/W, equestrian sports M (c)/W (c), fencing M (c)/W (c), field hockey M/W, football M/W, golf M/W, gymnastics M (c)/W (c), ice hockey M (c)/W (c), lacrosse M (c)/W (c), racquetball M/W, riflery M (c)/W (c), rugby M (c)/W (c), sailing M (c)/W (c), skiing (downhill) M (c)/W (c), soccer M/W, softball M/W, swimming and diving M/W, table tennis M/W, tennis M/W, track and field M/W, volleyball M (c)/W, water polo M/W, weight lifting M (c)/W (c).

Standardized Tests *Required:* SAT or ACT (for admission).

Costs (2008–09) *Tuition:* state resident $5376 full-time, $225 per hour part-time; nonresident $18,216 full-time, $748 per hour part-time. *Required fees:* $812 full-time, $36 per hour part-time. *Room and board:* $6676; room only: $3516.

Financial Aid Of all full-time matriculated undergraduates who enrolled in 2007, 16,150 applied for aid, 8,976 were judged to have need, 2,898 had their need fully met. In 2007, 2796 non-need-based awards were made. *Average percent of need met:* 73%. *Average financial aid package:* $9357. *Average need-based loan:* $4145. *Average need-based gift aid:* $2818. *Average non-need-based aid:* $3060. *Average indebtedness upon graduation:* $19,341.

Applying *Options:* electronic application, early admission, early action, deferred entrance. *Application fee:* $30. *Required:* essay or personal statement, high school transcript, minimum 2.0 GPA, specific high school units. *Application deadlines:* 2/1 (freshmen), 6/1 (transfers), 11/1 (early action). *Notification:* continuous (freshmen), continuous (transfers), 12/15 (early action).

Freshman Application Contact Mr. Richard Bayer, Dean of Admissions, The University of Tennessee, 320 Student Services Building, Knoxville, TN 37996-0230. *Phone:* 865-974-2184. *Toll-free phone:* 800-221-8657. *Fax:* 865-974-6341. *E-mail:* admissions@tennessee.edu.

THE UNIVERSITY OF TENNESSEE AT CHATTANOOGA

Chattanooga, Tennessee **www.utc.edu/**

- **State-supported** comprehensive, founded 1886, part of University of Tennessee System
- **Urban** 120-acre campus with easy access to Atlanta
- **Endowment** $126.1 million
- **Coed** 8,194 undergraduate students, 87% full-time, 56% women, 44% men
- **Moderately difficult** entrance level, 83% of applicants were admitted

The University of Tennessee at Chattanooga (UTC) is a comprehensive, state-supported, coeducational institution. With an enrollment of more than 9,500 students, UTC offers a diverse educational and extracurricular experience. UTC offers more than seventy undergraduate and thirty-five master's programs within four distinct schools and colleges. Located in scenic downtown Chattanooga, students can learn, work, and play within walking distance of premiere apartment-style residence hall facilities. Merit scholarships and need-based aid are available.

Undergraduates 7,105 full-time, 1,089 part-time. Students come from 43 states and territories, 46 other countries, 24% are from out of state, 19% African American, 2% Asian American or Pacific Islander, 2% Hispanic American, 0.4% Native American, 0.7% international, 8% transferred in, 32% live on campus. *Retention:* 64% of 2006 full-time freshmen returned.

Freshmen *Admission:* 5,210 applied, 4,328 admitted, 1,947 enrolled. *Average high school GPA:* 3.18. *Test scores:* ACT scores over 18: 92%; ACT scores over 24: 28%; ACT scores over 30: 4%.

Faculty *Total:* 696, 57% full-time, 49% with terminal degrees. *Student/faculty ratio:* 17:1.

Majors Applied mathematics; art; art teacher education; biology/biological sciences; business administration and management; chemistry; clinical laboratory science/medical technology; computer science; criminal justice/law enforcement administration; criminal justice/police science; dramatic/theater arts; economics; engineering; engineering/industrial management; English; environmental studies; fine/studio arts; French; geology/earth science; history; human ecology; humanities; human services; kinesiology and exercise science; Latin; legal assistant/paralegal; mass communication/media; mathematics; middle school education; modern Greek; music; nursing (registered nurse training); parks, recreation and leisure; philosophy and religious studies related; physical therapy; physics; political science and government; psychology; science teacher education; secondary education; social work; sociology; Spanish; special education.

Academics *Calendar:* semesters. *Degrees:* bachelor's, master's, doctoral, first professional, post-master's, and postbachelor's certificates. *Special study options:* academic remediation for entering students, adult/continuing education programs, advanced placement credit, cooperative education, distance learning, double majors, English as a second language, honors programs, independent study, internships, off-campus study, part-time degree program, services for LD students, study abroad, summer session for credit. *Unusual degree programs:* 3-2 engineering with Georgia Institute of Technology, University of Tennessee, Knoxville.

Computers on Campus 300 computers/terminals are available on campus for general student use. Students can access the following: campus intranet, computer help desk, free student e-mail accounts, online (class) grades, online (class) registration, online (class) schedules. Campuswide network is available. Wireless service is available via classrooms, computer labs, libraries.

Student Life *Housing options:* coed. Campus housing is university owned and is provided by a third party. Freshman applicants given priority for college housing. *Activities and organizations:* drama/theater group, student-run newspaper, radio station, choral group, marching band, Student Government Association, Black Student Association, Association for Campus Entertainment, International Student Association, Baptist Student Union, national fraternities, national sororities. *Campus security:* 24-hour emergency response devices and patrols, late-night transport/escort service, controlled dormitory access. *Student services:* health clinic, personal/psychological counseling.

Athletics Member NCAA. All Division I except football (Division I-AA). *Intercollegiate sports:* basketball M (s)/W (s), crew M/W, cross-country running M (s)/W (s), golf M (s)/W, soccer M (s)/W (s), softball W (s), tennis M (s)/W (s), track and field M/W, volleyball W (s), wrestling M (s). *Intramural sports:* badminton M/W, basketball M/W, bowling M/W, cross-country running M/W, fencing M, football M, golf M, racquetball M/W, swimming and diving M/W, tennis M/W, volleyball W, weight lifting M, wrestling M.

Standardized Tests *Required:* SAT or ACT (for admission).

Costs (2007–08) *Tuition:* state resident $3972 full-time, $166 per hour part-time; nonresident $9962 full-time, $415 per hour part-time. *Required fees:* $1090 full-time, $128 per hour part-time. *Room and board:* $7555; room only: $5055. Room and board charges vary according to board plan and housing facility. *Payment plan:* deferred payment. *Waivers:* senior citizens and employees or children of employees.

Financial Aid Of all full-time matriculated undergraduates who enrolled in 2004, 4,620 applied for aid, 3,987 were judged to have need, 576 had their need fully met. 220 Federal Work-Study jobs (averaging $1795). 400 state and other part-time jobs (averaging $1875). In 2004, 825 non-need-based awards were made. *Average percent of need met:* 80%. *Average financial aid package:* $8450. *Average need-based loan:* $4450. *Average need-based gift aid:* $3600. *Average non-need-based aid:* $3400. *Average indebtedness upon graduation:* $14,750.

Applying *Options:* electronic application, deferred entrance. *Application fee:* $30. *Required:* high school transcript, 1 letter of recommendation. *Recommended:* essay or personal statement. *Notification:* continuous (freshmen), continuous (transfers).

Freshman Application Contact Mr. Yancy Freeman, Director, Admissions and Recruitment, The University of Tennessee at Chattanooga, 131 Hooper Hall, Chattanooga, TN 37403. *Phone:* 423-755-4597. *Toll-free phone:* 800-UTC-MOCS. *Fax:* 423-425-4157. *E-mail:* yancy-freeman@utc.edu.

THE UNIVERSITY OF TENNESSEE AT MARTIN

Martin, Tennessee **www.utm.edu/**

- **State-supported** comprehensive, founded 1900, part of University of Tennessee System
- **Small-town** 250-acre campus
- **Endowment** $23.7 million
- **Coed** 6,717 undergraduate students, 78% full-time, 57% women, 43% men
- **Moderately difficult** entrance level, 77% of applicants were admitted

Undergraduates 5,264 full-time, 1,453 part-time. Students come from 39 states and territories, 24 other countries, 5% are from out of state, 16% African American, 0.5% Asian American or Pacific Islander, 1% Hispanic American, 0.3% Native American, 2% international, 6% transferred in, 35% live on campus. *Retention:* 71% of 2006 full-time freshmen returned.

Freshmen *Admission:* 3,010 applied, 2,318 admitted, 1,311 enrolled. *Average high school GPA:* 3.37. *Test scores:* ACT scores over 18: 90%; ACT scores over 24: 31%; ACT scores over 30: 3%.

Faculty *Total:* 500, 52% full-time, 48% with terminal degrees. *Student/faculty ratio:* 18:1.

Majors Accounting; agricultural business and management; agricultural sciences; agricultural teacher education; agriculture; agronomy and crop science; animal sciences; athletic training; biology/biological sciences; biology teacher education; business administration and management; business/managerial economics; business teacher education; cell and molecular biology; chemistry; chemistry teacher education; child development; computer science; criminal justice/law enforcement administration; design and visual communications; dietetics; dramatic/theater arts; economics; education (K-12); elementary education; engineering; English; English/language arts teacher education; environmental biology; environmental studies; family and consumer sciences/home economics teacher education; family and consumer sciences/human sciences; fashion merchandising; finance; fishing and fisheries sciences and management; French; French language teacher education; general studies; geography; geography teacher education; geology/earth science; German language teacher education; graphic design; health and physical education; health science; history; history teacher education; human resources management; industrial and organizational psychology; interdisciplinary studies; interior design; international business/trade/commerce; international relations and affairs; kindergarten/preschool education; management information systems; management science; marketing/marketing management; mathematics; mathematics teacher education; music; music pedagogy; music performance; music teacher education; natural resources management; natural resources management and policy; nursing (registered nurse training); philosophy; piano and organ; political science and government; pre-dentistry studies; pre-medical studies; pre-pharmacy studies; pre-veterinary studies; psychology; public administration; science teacher education; social work; sociology; soil conservation; Spanish; Spanish language teacher education; special education; statistics; visual and performing arts; voice and opera; wildlife and wildlands science and management.

Academics *Calendar:* semesters. *Degrees:* bachelor's and master's. *Special study options:* accelerated degree program, adult/continuing education programs, advanced placement credit, cooperative education, distance learning, double majors, English as a second language, honors programs, independent study, internships, off-campus study, part-time degree program, services for LD students, student-designed majors, study abroad, summer session for credit. *ROTC:* Army (b).

Computers on Campus 710 computers/terminals and 2,490 ports are available on campus for general student use. Students can access the following: campus intranet, computer help desk, free student e-mail accounts, online (class) grades, online (class) registration, online (class) schedules, online fee payments, degree progress, financial aid data, housing applications, transcripts. Campuswide network is available. 100% of college-owned or -operated housing units are wired for high-speed Internet access. Wireless service is available via entire campus.

Student Life *Housing:* on-campus residence required for freshman year. *Options:* men-only, women-only, disabled students. Campus housing is university owned. Freshman applicants given priority for college housing. *Activities and organizations:* drama/theater group, student-run newspaper, radio and television station, choral group, marching band, Student Government Association, Student Activities Council, International Honors Society of Nurses, Gamma Beta Phi, Collegiate Future Farmers of America, national fraternities, national sororities. *Campus security:* 24-hour emergency response devices and patrols, student patrols, controlled dormitory access. *Student services:* health clinic, personal/psychological counseling.

Athletics Member NCAA. All Division I except football (Division I-AA). *Intercollegiate sports:* baseball M (s), basketball M (s)/W (s), cheerleading W, cross-country running M (s)/W (s), equestrian sports W (s), golf M (s), riflery M (s)/W (s), soccer W (s), softball W (s), tennis M (s)/W (s), volleyball W (s). *Intramural sports:* basketball M/W, cross-country running M/W, football M/W, golf M/W, rock climbing M/W, soccer M/W, softball M/W, swimming and diving M/W, table tennis M/W, tennis M/W, ultimate Frisbee M/W, volleyball M/W, water polo M/W.

Standardized Tests *Required:* SAT or ACT (for admission).

Costs (2007–08) *Tuition:* state resident $4150 full-time, $173 per credit hour part-time; nonresident $14,190 full-time, $591 per credit hour part-time. Part-time tuition and fees vary according to course load. *Required fees:* $855 full-time, $37 per credit hour part-time. *Room and board:* $4446; room only: $2160. Room and board charges vary according to board plan and housing facility. *Payment plan:* deferred payment. *Waivers:* senior citizens and employees or children of employees.

Financial Aid Of all full-time matriculated undergraduates who enrolled in 2007, 4,867 applied for aid, 3,388 were judged to have need, 1,288 had their need fully met. 307 Federal Work-Study jobs (averaging $2000). In 2007, 1121 non-need-based awards were made. *Average percent of need met:* 76%. *Average financial aid package:* $9685. *Average need-based loan:* $4109. *Average need-based gift aid:* $5055. *Average non-need-based aid:* $5138. *Average indebtedness upon graduation:* $22,528.

Applying *Options:* electronic application, early admission, deferred entrance. *Application fee:* $30. *Required:* high school transcript, minimum 2.4 GPA. *Application deadlines:* rolling (freshmen), rolling (transfers). *Notification:* continuous until 8/1 (freshmen), continuous until 8/1 (transfers).

Freshman Application Contact Ms. Judy Rayburn, Director of Admissions, The University of Tennessee at Martin, 200 Hall-Moody Administration Building, Martin, TN 38238. *Phone:* 731-881-7032. *Toll-free phone:* 800-829-8861. *Fax:* 731-881-7029. *E-mail:* jrayburn@utm.edu.

VANDERBILT UNIVERSITY

Nashville, Tennessee **www.vanderbilt.edu/**

- **Independent** university, founded 1873
- **Urban** 330-acre campus
- **Endowment** $2.6 billion
- **Coed** 6,532 undergraduate students, 99% full-time, 53% women, 47% men
- **Very difficult** entrance level, 33% of applicants were admitted

Undergraduates 6,463 full-time, 69 part-time. Students come from 54 states and territories, 36 other countries, 83% are from out of state, 9% African American, 7% Asian American or Pacific Islander, 6% Hispanic American, 0.3% Native American, 3% international, 2% transferred in, 89% live on campus. *Retention:* 96% of 2006 full-time freshmen returned.

Freshmen *Admission:* 12,911 applied, 4,238 admitted, 1,673 enrolled. *Average high school GPA:* 3.67. *Test scores:* SAT critical reading scores over 500: 98%; SAT math scores over 500: 99%; SAT writing scores over 500: 99%; ACT scores over 18: 100%; SAT critical reading scores over 600: 91%; SAT math scores over 600: 92%; SAT writing scores over 600: 90%; ACT scores over 24: 97%; SAT critical reading scores over 700: 46%; SAT math scores over 700: 54%; SAT writing scores over 700: 43%; ACT scores over 30: 70%.

Majors African-American/Black studies; African studies; American studies; anthropology; art; Asian studies (East); astronomy; biology/biological sciences; biomedical/medical engineering; chemical engineering; chemistry; civil engineering; classics and languages, literatures and linguistics; cognitive psychology and psycholinguistics; computer engineering; computer science; dramatic/theater arts; ecology; economics; education; electrical, electronics and communications engineering; elementary education; engineering; engineering science; English; European studies; French; geology/earth science; German; history; human development and family studies; human resources management; interdisciplinary studies; kindergarten/preschool education; Latin American studies; mass communication/media; mathematics; mechanical engineering; molecular biology; music; philosophy; physics; piano and organ; political science and government; Portuguese; psychology; religious studies; Russian; secondary education; sociology; Spanish; special education; urban studies/affairs; violin, viola, guitar and other stringed instruments; voice and opera; wind/percussion instruments.

Academics *Calendar:* semesters. *Degrees:* bachelor's, master's, doctoral, and first professional. *Special study options:* accelerated degree program, advanced placement credit, cooperative education, distance learning, double majors, English as a second language, honors programs, independent study, internships, off-campus study, services for LD students, student-designed majors, study abroad, summer session for credit. *ROTC:* Army (b), Navy (b), Air Force (c). *Unusual degree programs:* 3-2 business administration; engineering.

Computers on Campus 400 computers/terminals are available on campus for general student use. Students can access the following: productivity and educational software. Campuswide network is available.

Student Life *Housing:* on-campus residence required through senior year. *Options:* coed, men-only, women-only, disabled students. *Activities and organizations:* drama/theater group, student-run newspaper, radio station, choral group, marching band, national fraternities, national sororities. *Campus security:* 24-hour emergency response devices and patrols, student patrols, late-night transport/escort service, controlled dormitory access. *Student services:* health clinic, personal/psychological counseling, women's center.

Athletics Member NCAA. All Division I except football (Division I-A). *Intercollegiate sports:* baseball M (s), basketball M (s)/W (s), crew M (c)/W (c), cross-country running M (s)/W (s), equestrian sports M (c)/W (c), fencing M (c)/W (c), field hockey M (c)/W (c), golf M (s)/W (s), ice hockey M (c)/W (c), lacrosse M (c)/W (s), rugby M (c)/W (c), sailing M (c)/W (c), soccer M (s)/W (s), squash M (c)/W (c), tennis M (s)/W (s), track and field M (c)/W (s), volleyball M (c)/W (c), water polo M (c)/W (c), wrestling M (c)/W (c). *Intramural sports:* badminton M/W, baseball M, basketball M/W, bowling M/W, football M/W, golf M/W, racquetball M/W, soccer M/W, softball M/W, squash M/W, swimming and diving M/W, table tennis M/W, tennis M/W, volleyball M/W, water polo M/W, weight lifting M/W.

Standardized Tests *Required:* SAT or ACT (for admission). *Recommended:* SAT Subject Tests (for admission).

Costs (2007–08) *Comprehensive fee:* $46,722 includes full-time tuition ($34,414), mandatory fees ($862), and room and board ($11,446). Part-time tuition: $1434 per hour. *College room only:* $7456. Room and board charges vary according to board plan. *Payment plans:* tuition prepayment, installment. *Waivers:* employees or children of employees.

Financial Aid Of all full-time matriculated undergraduates who enrolled in 2007, 2,899 applied for aid, 2,689 were judged to have need, 2,516 had their need fully met. In 2007, 820 non-need-based awards were made. *Average percent of need met:* 99%. *Average financial aid package:* $35,853. *Average need-based loan:* $4060. *Average need-based gift aid:* $28,402. *Average non-need-based aid:* $17,851. *Average indebtedness upon graduation:* $20,755.

Applying *Options:* electronic application, early decision, deferred entrance. *Application fee:* $50. *Required:* essay or personal statement, high school transcript, 2 letters of recommendation. *Application deadlines:* 1/3 (freshmen), 3/1 (transfers). *Early decision deadline:* 11/1 (for plan 1), 1/3 (for plan 2). *Notification:* 4/1 (freshmen), 4/1 (transfers), 12/15 (early decision plan 1), 2/15 (early decision plan 2).

Director of Admissions Mr. Douglas Christiansen, Dean of Undergraduate Admissions, Vanderbilt University, 2305 West End Avenue, Nashville, TN 37203. *Toll-free phone:* 800-288-0432. *Fax:* 615-343-7765. *E-mail:* admissions@vanderbilt.edu.

See page 2478 for the College Close-Up.

WATKINS COLLEGE OF ART AND DESIGN

Nashville, Tennessee **www.watkins.edu/**

- **Independent** 4-year, founded 1885
- **Urban** 13-acre campus
- **Endowment** $1.1 million
- **Coed** 375 undergraduate students, 57% full-time, 63% women, 37% men
- **Moderately difficult** entrance level, 79% of applicants were admitted

Undergraduates 214 full-time, 161 part-time. Students come from 42 states and territories, 3 other countries, 15% are from out of state, 5% African American, 2% Asian American or Pacific Islander, 3% Hispanic American, 9% international, 19% transferred in, 25% live on campus. *Retention:* 58% of 2006 full-time freshmen returned.

Freshmen *Admission:* 160 applied, 127 admitted, 40 enrolled. *Average high school GPA:* 2.8.

Faculty *Total:* 47, 38% full-time, 77% with terminal degrees. *Student/faculty ratio:* 10:1.

Majors Art; film/cinema studies; fine/studio arts; graphic design; interior design; photography.

Academics *Calendar:* semesters. *Degree:* certificates and bachelor's. *Special study options:* adult/continuing education programs, advanced placement credit, cooperative education, double majors, independent study, internships, part-time degree program, services for LD students, study abroad, summer session for credit.

Computers on Campus 106 ports are available on campus for general student use. Students can access the following: campus intranet, online (class) registration, online (class) schedules. 100% of college-owned or -operated housing units are wired for high-speed Internet access. Wireless service is available via entire campus.

Student Life *Housing:* on-campus residence required for freshman year. *Options:* coed, men-only, women-only, disabled students. Campus housing is university owned. Freshman applicants given priority for college housing. *Activities and organizations:* student-run newspaper, ASID, IIGA, AIGA, PAL, Student Government. *Campus security:* 24-hour patrols, late-night transport/escort service, controlled dormitory access. *Student services:* personal/psychological counseling.

Standardized Tests *Required:* SAT or ACT (for admission).

Costs (2008–09) *Tuition:* $13,200 full-time, $550 per hour part-time. *Required fees:* $960 full-time, $40 per hour part-time. *Room only:* $6000.

Financial Aid Of all full-time matriculated undergraduates who enrolled in 2006, 198 applied for aid, 198 were judged to have need. 15 Federal Work-Study jobs (averaging $1500). 15 state and other part-time jobs (averaging $1500). In 2006, 1 non-need-based awards were made. *Average percent of need met:* 60%. *Average financial aid package:* $9000. *Average need-based loan:* $4000. *Average need-based gift aid:* $1500. *Average non-need-based aid:* $2000. *Average indebtedness upon graduation:* $18,000.

Applying *Options:* deferred entrance. *Application fee:* $50. *Required:* essay or personal statement, high school transcript, minimum 2.0 GPA, letters of recommendation, statement of good standing from prior institutions; portfolio and home exercises. *Required for some:* statement of good standing from prior institutions; portfolio and home exercises. *Application deadlines:* 6/1 (freshmen), 6/1 (transfers). *Notification:* 7/15 (freshmen), 7/15 (transfers).

Freshman Application Contact Ms. Jenna Maurice, Recruitment Officer, Watkins College of Art and Design, 2298 Metro Center Boulevard, Nashville, TN 37228. *Phone:* 615-383-4848. *Fax:* 615-383-4849. *E-mail:* admissions@watkins.edu.

WILLIAMSON CHRISTIAN COLLEGE

Franklin, Tennessee **www.williamsoncc.edu/**

- **Independent interdenominational** 4-year, founded 1997
- **Suburban** 1-acre campus with easy access to Nashville
- **Coed** 64 undergraduate students, 86% full-time, 58% women, 42% men
- **Noncompetitive** entrance level

Undergraduates 55 full-time, 9 part-time. Students come from 2 states and territories, 11% African American, 3% Hispanic American, 14% transferred in. *Retention:* 100% of 2006 full-time freshmen returned.

Freshmen *Admission:* 1 enrolled.

Faculty *Total:* 17, 29% full-time, 153% with terminal degrees. *Student/faculty ratio:* 5:1.

Majors Biblical studies; pre-theology/pre-ministerial studies; theological and ministerial studies related; theology and religious vocations related.

Academics *Calendar:* semesters. *Degrees:* associate and bachelor's. *Special study options:* accelerated degree program, adult/continuing education programs, distance learning, double majors, external degree program, independent study, internships, part-time degree program.

Computers on Campus 3 computers/terminals are available on campus for general student use. Wireless service is available via entire campus.

Student Life *Housing:* college housing not available. *Student services:* health clinic, personal/psychological counseling.

Standardized Tests *Required for some:* SAT or ACT (for admission).

Costs (2008–09) *Tuition:* $8505 full-time, $315 per credit part-time. *Required fees:* $100 full-time, $15 per course part-time.

Financial Aid Of all full-time matriculated undergraduates who enrolled in 2003, 11 applied for aid, 10 were judged to have need, 1 had their need fully met. 2 Federal Work-Study jobs (averaging $2000). *Average percent of need met:* 50%. *Average financial aid package:* $4858. *Average need-based gift aid:* $2556.

Applying *Options:* early admission, deferred entrance. *Application fee:* $25. *Required:* high school transcript. *Required for some:* interview. *Application deadlines:* 9/1 (freshmen), 9/1 (transfers). *Notification:* continuous until 10/1 (freshmen), continuous until 10/1 (transfers).

Freshman Application Contact Ms. Mary Newby, Recruiter, Williamson Christian College, 200 Seaboard Lane, Franklin, TN 37067. *Phone:* 615-771-7821. *Fax:* 615-771-7810. *E-mail:* mary@williamsoncc.edu.

ARGOSY UNIVERSITY

ARGOSY UNIVERSITY

The University

Argosy University is a leading institution offering a variety of degree programs that focus on the human side of success alongside professional competence. For students looking for a more personal approach to education, Argosy University may just be the answer. With forty-eight graduate and undergraduate programs, across nineteen campuses and twelve states, Argosy University emphasizes interpersonal skills as well as academic learning. All of its programs are taught by practicing professionals who bring real-world experience into the classroom. So students graduate with both a solid foundation of knowledge and the power to put it to work. To accommodate busy working adults, many programs at Argosy University are structured flexibly—with both campus and online learning and evening, weekend, and daytime classes. There is also a wide range of financial aid options for students who qualify.

Argosy University is a private institution of higher education dedicated to providing high-quality professional education programs at the doctoral, master's, bachelor's, and associate degree levels as well as continuing education to individuals who seek to advance their professional and personal lives. The University emphasizes programs in the behavioral sciences (psychology and counseling), business, education, and the health-care professions. A limited number of preprofessional programs and general education offerings are provided to permit students to prepare for entry into these professional fields. The programs of Argosy University are designed to instill the knowledge, skills, and ethical values of professional practice and to foster values of social responsibility in a supportive, learning-centered environment of mutual respect and professional excellence.

With nineteen campuses nationwide, Argosy University provides students with a network of resources found at larger universities, including a career resources office, an academic resources center, and extensive information access for research. The University's innovative programs feature dynamic, relevant, and practical curricula delivered in flexible class formats. Students enjoy scheduling options that make it easier to fit school into their busy lives. They can choose from day and evening courses, on campus or online. Many students find a combination of both to be an ideal way of continuing their education while meeting family and professional demands.

Most students are full-time working professionals who live within driving distance of the campus. The University does not offer or operate student housing.

Argosy University is accredited by The Higher Learning Commission of the North Central Association (30 North LaSalle Street, Suite 2400, Chicago, Illinois 60602; 800-621-7440; http://ncahlc.org).

Location

Argosy University operates nineteen locations across the U.S. and offers a variety of degree programs online (http://www.argosy.edu). Campus locations include the following:

Atlanta, 980 Hammond Drive, Suite 100, Atlanta, Georgia 30328; phone: 770-671-1200 or 888-671-4777 (toll-free)

Chicago, 225 North Michigan Avenue, Suite 1300, Chicago, Illinois 60601; phone: 312-777-7600 or 800-626-4123 (toll-free)

Dallas, 8080 Park Lane, Suite 400A, Dallas, Texas 75231; phone: 214-890-9900 or 866-954-9900 (toll-free)

Denver, 1200 Lincoln Street, Denver, Colorado 80203; phone: 303-248-2700 or 866-431-5981 (toll-free)

Hawai'i, 400 ASB Tower, 1001 Bishop Street, Honolulu, Hawaii 96813; phone: 808-536-5555 or 888-323-2777 (toll-free)

Inland Empire, 636 East Brier Drive, Suite 235, San Bernardino, California 92408; phone: 909-915-3800 or 866-217-9075 (toll-free)

Nashville, 100 Centerview Drive, Suite 225, Nashville, Tennessee 37214; phone: 615-525-2800 or 866-833-6598 (toll-free)

Orange County, 3501 West Sunflower Avenue, Suite 110, Santa Ana, California 92704; phone: 714-338-6200 or 800-716-9598 (toll-free)

Phoenix, 2233 West Dunlap Avenue, Phoenix, Arizona 85021; phone: 602-216-2600 or 866-216-2777 (toll-free)

Salt Lake City, 121 West Election Road, Suite 300, Draper, Utah 84020; phone: 888-639-4756 (toll-free)

San Diego, 7650 Mission Valley Road, San Diego, California 92108; phone: 858-598-1900 or 866-505-0333 (toll-free)

San Francisco Bay Area, 1005 Atlantic Avenue, Alameda, California 94501; phone: 510-217-4700 or 866-215-2777 (toll-free)

Santa Monica, 2950 31st Street, Santa Monica, California 90405; phone: 310-866-4000 or 866-505-0332 (toll-free)

Sarasota, 5250 17th Street, Sarasota, Florida 34235; phone: 941-379-0404 or 800-331-5995 (toll-free)

Schaumburg, 999 North Plaza Drive, Suite 111, Schaumburg, Illinois 60173-5403; phone: 847-969-4900 or 866-290-2777 (toll-free)

Seattle, 2601-A Elliott Avenue, Seattle, Washington 98121; phone: 206-283-4500 or 888-283-2777 (toll-free)

Tampa, Parkside at Tampa Bay Park, 4401 North Hines Avenue, Suite 150, Tampa, Florida 33614; phone: 813-393-5290 or 800-850-6488 (toll-free)

Twin Cities, 1515 Central Parkway, Eagan, Minnesota 55121; phone: 651-846-2882 or 888-844-2004 (toll-free)

Washington DC, 1550 Wilson Boulevard, Suite 600, Arlington, Virginia 22209; phone: 703-526-5800 or 866-703-2777 (toll-free)

Majors and Degrees

Argosy University's College of Business offers a Bachelor of Science (B.S.) in Business Administration program. Argosy University's College of Psychology and Behavioral Sciences offers the Bachelor of Arts (B.A.) in Psychology degree program.

Academic Programs

The B.S. in Business Administration program prepares students for entry- to mid-level positions within the public or private sector. The curriculum is structured to help students develop competencies in oral and written communication, leadership, team skills, solutions-focused learning, and the analysis and execution of solutions in various business situations. Students may choose one of five optional concentrations: customized professional concentration, finance, health-care management, international business, or marketing.

The B.A. in Psychology program is designed to help students begin human services careers in such capacities as entry-level counselor, case manager, or human resources administrator and

in management and business services roles. The program also lays the foundation for graduate study. Students may choose an optional concentration from the following three options: criminal justice, organizational psychology, or substance abuse. This dynamic program is built around a flexible class approach.

Argosy University's bachelor's degree programs are open to students and working professionals with no college experience, plus those who have already earned college credit at a community college, junior college, or other university.

Academic Facilities

Argosy University libraries provide curriculum support and educational resources including current text materials, diagnostic training documents, reference materials and databases, journals and dissertations, and major and current titles in program areas. There is an online public-access catalog of library resources available throughout the Argosy University system. Students enjoy full remote access to their campus library database, enabling them to study and conduct research at home. Academic databases offer dissertation abstracts, academic journals, and professional periodicals. All library computers are Internet accessible. Software applications include Word, Excel, PowerPoint, SPSS, and various test-scoring programs.

Costs

Tuition varies by program. Students should contact the Argosy University campus of their choice for tuition information.

Financial Aid

A wide range of financial aid options is available to students who qualify. Argosy University offers access to federal and state aid programs, merit-based awards, grants, loans, and a work-study program. As a first step, students should complete the Free Application for Federal Student Aid (FAFSA). Prospective students can apply electronically at http://www.fafsa.ed.gov or at the campus. To receive consideration for financial aid and ensure timely receipt of funds, it is best to submit an application promptly.

Faculty

The Argosy University faculty is composed of working professionals who have a passion to help students succeed. Members bring real-world experience and the latest practice innovations to the academic setting. The diverse faculty is widely recognized for contributions to the field. Most hold doctoral degrees. They provide a substantive education that combines comprehensive knowledge with critical skills and practical workplace relevance. Above all, faculty members are committed to their students' personal and professional development.

Student Government

Argosy University campuses offer unique opportunities for student involvement beyond individual programs of study. Most faculty committees include a student representative. In addition, a student group meets with faculty members and administrators regularly to discuss pertinent campus-related issues.

Admission Requirements

Admission requirements differ depending on the number of college credits completed prior to application.

Students who have earned 12 or fewer semester college credits must provide proof of high school graduation or GED and meet one of the following conditions for admission: ACT composite score of 18 or above, or a combined math and verbal SAT score of 870, or minimum ACCUPLACER scores of 86 in sentence skills and 53 in algebra. Applicants who do not meet any of the above conditions for admission will be admitted with academic support if they provide proof of high school graduation or GED and meet one of the following: ACT composite score of 14 to 17, or a combined math and verbal SAT score of 660 to 869, or minimum ACCUPLACER scores of 54 in sentence skills and 36 in arithmetic.

Applicants who have earned 13 or more semester college credits must provide proof of high school graduation or GED and meet one of the following conditions for admission: cumulative college GPA of 2.0 or above or minimum ACCUPLACER scores of 86 for sentence skills and 53 in algebra. Students who do not meet either of the above criteria will be admitted with academic support if they provide proof of high school graduation or GED and meet the following condition: minimum ACCUPLACER scores of 54 in reading and 36 in arithmetic.

Students admitted with academic support are limited to 12 credit hours of study during their first semester (6 credit hours per session). Students admitted with academic support will be required to complete developmental English and/or math courses unless they meet the following conditions: Writing Review (ENG099)—must meet one of the following: a minimum ACCUPLACER score of 86 in sentence skills, or a minimum ACT verbal score of 18, or a minimum SAT verbal score of 425, or completion of a college-level English composition course with a grade of C or above; Mathematics Review I (MAT096)—must meet one of the following: a minimum ACCUPLACER score of 53 in algebra, or a minimum ACT math score of 18, or a minimum SAT math score of 440, or completion of a college-level English composition course with a grade of C or above.

Other admission requirements may include credit hours of qualified transfer credit with a grade of C- or better from a regionally accredited institution or a nationally accredited institution approved and documented by the faculty and dean of the College of Business, or the College of Professional Psychology, at Argosy University or completion of an Associate of Arts or Associate of Science degree from a regionally accredited institution. A maximum of 78 lower-division or 90 total credit hours may be transferred. A minimum written TOEFL score of 500 (paper-based test), 173 (computer-based test), or 61 (Internet-based test) is required for all applicants whose native language is not English or who have not graduated from an institution in which English is the language of instruction.

Official transcripts from approved postsecondary institutions must include a minimum grade point average of 2.0 (on a scale of 4.0) for all academic work completed. Exceptions may be made for extenuating circumstances. All applications must include a completed application form, proof of high school graduation or successful completion of the GED test, official postsecondary transcripts, and a nonrefundable (except in California) application fee. Additional materials are required prior to matriculation. Some programs have additional application requirements or include exceptions to admission requirements. An admissions representative can provide further information.

Application and Information

Argosy University accepts students on a rolling admissions basis year-round, depending on availability of required courses. Applications for admission are available online at http://www.argosy.edu or by contacting one of the campus locations.

Argosy University
205 North Michigan Avenue, Suite 1300
Chicago, Illinois 60601-2250
Phone: 312-899-9900
800-377-0617 (toll-free)
E-mail: auadmissions@argosy.edu
Web site: http://www.argosy.edu

THE ART INSTITUTE OF TENNESSEE–NASHVILLE

NASHVILLE, TENNESSEE

The Institute

The Art Institute of Tennessee–Nashville helps students to cultivate and refine the talents and skills that are needed for entry-level positions in the creative arts. Classes are taught in an environment that encourages learning, leadership, and creativity.

Faculty and staff members strive to foster development and cultivate artistic growth. Students are given opportunities to develop leadership skills and build relationships. In addition, assistance is available to help students with resume writing, networking, and keeping abreast of what employers are looking for in job candidates.

The Art Institute of Tennessee–Nashville places a high value on the quality of student life both in and out of the classroom. Students participate in a wide variety of activities, including clubs and organizations, community service opportunities, and various committees designed to enhance the quality of student life.

The school provides information on independent housing options to all enrolled students requesting such assistance.

Students come to The Art Institute of Tennessee–Nashville from throughout the United States. The student population includes recent high school graduates, transfer students, and those who have left a previous employment situation to study and train for a new career. Students are creative, competitive, and open to new ideas.

The Art Institute of Tennessee–Nashville is accredited as a branch of The Art Institute of Atlanta by the Commission on Colleges of the Southern Association of Colleges and Schools (SACS; 1866 Southern Lane, Decatur, Georgia 30033-4907; phone: 404-679-4500; http://www.sacs.org), to award Associate in Arts, Bachelor of Arts, Bachelor of Science, and Bachelor of Fine Arts degrees.

Location

The Art Institute of Tennessee–Nashville is located close to downtown, providing students with ease of access, opportunities to volunteer for civic organizations, and the ability to enjoy all the culture and excitement that the city of Nashville has to offer.

Majors and Degrees

The Art Institute of Tennessee–Nashville offers bachelor's and associate degrees. Bachelor's degrees are offered in audio production, culinary arts management, digital filmmaking and video production, fashion and retail management, graphic design, interior design, photographic imaging, and Web design and interactive media. Students may also pursue associate degrees in audio production, culinary arts, graphic design, video production, and Web design and interactive media. Diploma programs are offered in culinary arts–baking and pastry and culinary arts–culinary skills.

Academic Programs

The academic year is divided into four quarters, beginning in January, April, July, and October. Each program is offered on a year-round basis, allowing students to continue to work uninterrupted toward their degrees.

Academic Facilities

The Art Institute of Tennessee–Nashville has a bookstore, Mac and PC computer labs, and classrooms.

Costs

Tuition cost varies by program. Prospective students should contact the school for current tuition costs. Other charges include a starting kit for all first-quarter students. Kits vary in price, depending on the program of study.

Financial Aid

Financial aid is available for those who qualify. Students who require financial assistance should first complete and submit a Free Application for Federal Student Aid (FAFSA) and meet with a financial aid officer. The officer determines the level of need based on a required federal formula, the cost of education, and other factors. Gift aid is available in the form of Federal Pell Grants, Federal Supplemental Educational Opportunity Grants, and veterans' benefits. Loans include Federal Stafford Loans, Federal PLUS loans, and alternative loans. Other scholarships are available from the school and private sources. Application deadlines and eligibility requirements vary by program.

Student Government

The Student Federation is responsible for student government and acts as a liaison between the student body and faculty and staff members.

Admission Requirements

Applicants must provide proof of high school graduation or achievement of a General Educational Development (GED) certificate as a prerequisite for admission. In lieu of documenting high school graduation or a GED certificate, applicants may provide proof of receiving an associate degree or higher from an accredited institution. An official transcript indicating date of high school graduation, receipt of a GED certificate (including test scores), or date of college graduation (including degree granted) is required as proof.

All individuals seeking admission to The Art Institute of Tennessee–Nashville are interviewed in person or by phone by an assistant director of admissions, and each applicant must write an original essay of at least 150 words stating how an education at the school would help the student achieve career goals. There is a $50 application fee.

Application and Information

To obtain an application, make arrangements for an interview, or tour the school, students should contact:

The Art Institute of Tennessee–Nashville
100 Centerview Drive, Suite 250
Nashville, Tennessee 37214-3439
Phone: 615-874-1067
866-747-5770 (toll-free)
Fax: 615-874-3530
Web site: http://www.artinstitutes.edu/nashville

The Art Institute of Atlanta®, GA; The Art Institute of Atlanta®–Decatur, GA; The Art Institute of Austin℠, TX; The Art Institute of California℠–Inland Empire; The Art Institute of California℠–Los Angeles; The Art Institute of California℠–Orange County; The Art Institute of California℠–Sacramento; The Art Institute of California℠–San Diego; The Art Institute of California℠–San Francisco; The Art Institute of California℠–Sunnyvale; The Art Institute of Charleston℠, SC, A branch of The Art Institute of Atlanta, GA; The Art Institute of Charlotte®, NC; The Art Institute of Colorado® (Denver); The Art Institute of Dallas®, TX; The Art Institute of Fort Lauderdale®, FL; The Art Institute of Houston®, TX; The Art Institute of Indianapolis℠, IN*; The Art Institute of Jacksonville℠, FL, A branch of Miami International University of Art & Design; The Art Institute of Las Vegas®, NV; The Art Institute of Michigan℠ (Detroit); The Art Institute of New York City®, NY; The Art Institute of Ohio℠–Cincinnati**; The Art Institute of Philadelphia®, PA; The Art Institute of Phoenix®, AZ; The Art Institute of Pittsburgh®, PA; The Art Institute of Pittsburgh®–Online Division; The Art Institute of Portland®, OR; The Art Institute of Salt Lake City℠, UT; The Art Institute of Seattle®, WA; The Art Institute of Tampa℠, FL, A branch of Miami International University of Art & Design; The Art Institute of Tennessee℠–Nashville, A branch of The Art Institute of Atlanta, GA; The Art Institute of Tucson℠, AZ; The Art Institute of Washington® (Arlington, VA), A branch of The Art Institute of Atlanta, GA; The Art Institute of York–Pennsylvania℠; The Art Institutes International Minnesota℠ (Minneapolis); California Design College℠ (Los Angeles–Wilshire Blvd.); The Illinois Institute of Art®–Chicago; The Illinois Institute of Art®–Schaumburg; Miami International University of Art & Design℠, FL; The New England Institute of Art® (Boston, MA).

*The Art Institute of Indianapolis is licensed by the Indiana Commission on Proprietary Education, 302 West Washington Street, Room E201, Indianapolis, IN 46204, AC-0080.

**The Art Institute of Ohio–Cincinnati, 8845 Governors Hill Drive, Suite 100, Cincinnati, OH 45249-3317, Reg. #04-01-1698B.

BELMONT UNIVERSITY

NASHVILLE, TENNESSEE

The University

Nationally recognized programs thrive on the Belmont University campus, which is located in the heart of the state capital, known both as Music City, U.S.A., and the Athens of the South (for its many educational institutions). Nashville offers big-city advantages with small-town charm.

Belmont's vision is to be a leader among teaching universities, bringing together the best of liberal arts and professional education in a Christian community of learning and service. Central to the fulfillment of that vision are faculty members who have a passion for teaching and the belief that premier teaching is interactive, technology-supported, motivational, creative, and exciting.

With an enrollment of approximately 4,700 students, Belmont is the second-largest of Tennessee's private colleges and universities.

In addition to the twenty-five international countries represented in the student body, Belmont University attracts students from almost every state in the United States. The culturally diverse institution is committed to listening and learning from everyone. Students of today are helping shape the way students of tomorrow will be educated.

Belmont's beautiful, antebellum campus reflects a long, rich history that dates back to the nineteenth century, when the grounds were Adelicia Acklen's Belle Monte estate. University buildings that were erected over the past 110 years flank the Italianate mansion, which is still used by the campus. On the way to classes that prepare them for the twenty-first century, students enjoy Victorian gardens, statuary, and gazebos that recall a treasured past.

Two prestigious women's schools preceded the comprehensive liberal arts institution: the original Belmont College (1890–1913) and Ward-Belmont (1913–1951). In 1951, the Tennessee Baptist Convention founded the second Belmont College (1951–1991), with an initial coeducational enrollment of 136 students. Soon after celebrating 100 years of education on the same campus, the institution became a university in 1991, culminating a decade of dramatic growth and progress.

In addition to seven baccalaureate degrees, Belmont University offers twelve graduate degrees: the Master of Accountancy, the Master of Arts in Teaching, the Master of Business Administration, the Master of Sport Administration, the Master of English, the Master of Music, the Master of Education, the Master of Science in Nursing, the Master of Science in Occupational Therapy, the Doctor of Occupational Therapy, the Doctor of Pharmacy, and the Doctor of Physical Therapy.

Location

Belmont University occupies a 72-acre campus in southeast Nashville. With more than 500,000 residents, Nashville is a cultural, educational, health-care, commercial, and financial center in the mid-South. Practical educational opportunities, offered through diverse curriculums, provide students with the hands-on experience they need in preparation for a meaningful career. The city's location halfway between the northern and southern boundaries of the United States, with three intersecting interstate highways and an international airport, makes it accessible to students from across the country.

Majors and Degrees

Belmont University is accredited by the Commission on Colleges of the Southern Association of Colleges and Schools to award baccalaureate, master's, and doctoral degrees. Belmont grants seven undergraduate degrees: the Bachelor of Arts, the Bachelor of Business Administration, the Bachelor of Fine Arts, the Bachelor of Music, the Bachelor of Science, the Bachelor of Science in Nursing, and the Bachelor of Social Work. Majors or concentrations are offered in accounting, applied discrete mathematics, art (art education, design communications, and studio art), audio and video production, audio engineering technology, biblical languages, biblical studies, biochemistry and molecular biology, biology, business administration, chemistry, Christian ethics, Christian leadership, classics, communication studies, computer science, early childhood education, economics, engineering physics, English, entertainment industry studies, entrepreneurship, environmental studies, European studies, exercise science and health promotion, finance, French, German, health, history, information systems management, international business, international economics, international politics, journalism, management, marketing, mass communication, mathematics, medical imaging technology, medical physics, medical technology, middle school education, music (church music, commercial music, music composition, music education, music with an outside minor, musical theater, music performance, piano pedagogy, music theory), music business, neuroscience, nursing, organizational and corporate communications, pharmaceutical studies, philosophy, physical education, physics, political economy, politics and public law, political science, pre-professional programs, psychology, public relations, religion and the arts, religious studies, science and engineering management, social work, sociology, songwriting, Spanish, and theater and drama, and Web programming and development.

Academic Programs

Uniquely positioned to provide the best of liberal arts and professional education, Belmont University offers celebrated professional programs structured to provide an academically well-rounded education. Belmont University operates on a two-semester schedule with classes beginning in late August and ending in early May. Two summer sessions are also offered. The academic program is arranged by school: the College of Arts and Sciences, the College of Business Administration, the Gordon E. Inman College of Health Sciences and Nursing, the College of Visual and Performing Arts, the Mike Curb College of Entertainment and Music Business, and the School of Religion.

In addition to the degrees offered through the schools, Belmont University offers an honors program, which was created to provide an enrichment opportunity for students who have potential for superior academic performance and who seek added challenge and breadth to their studies. Students enrolled in the honors program are led in designing and working through a flexible, individual curriculum and interdisciplinary general education curriculum by a private tutor who is an honors faculty member.

The University's advancements in undergraduate research are credited to a faculty committed to helping students practice their disciplines. The annual Belmont Undergraduate Research Symposium puts Belmont at the forefront of this national movement by providing a public forum for in-depth research at the undergraduate level.

Off-Campus Programs

Belmont University has contracts for dual-degree programs with Auburn University and University of Tennessee, Knoxville. These programs require three years of study at Belmont University followed by approximately two years of study at one of the above institutions. The course of study at Belmont must be mathematics, physics, or chemistry. Following completion of the academic requirements at both institutions, a student is awarded a Bachelor of Science degree from Belmont University and the appropriate degree from the second institution.

Several programs at Belmont have agreements with area organizations to provide students practical training. Nursing students gain clinical experience at all fourteen local area hospitals and other clinical agencies. Education students gain classroom experience in Metro-Davidson County Schools. Music business students gain real-world experience through internships in the Nashville music industry and in Los Angeles and New York City through the Belmont West and East (respectively) programs of study and internships.

Through a wide variety of international study programs on the six populated continents, Belmont offers students the opportunity to broaden and deepen their education while earning credit hours toward their degrees. These programs, which range in duration from two weeks to a year, are available in Australia, the Bahamas, China, Costa Rica, England, France, Germany, Hong Kong, Ireland, Italy, Mexico, New Zealand, Russia, Scotland, South Africa, and Spain.

Academic Facilities

Belmont offers a quiet, secluded environment, and classes are held in nine buildings with the library and other facilities located in proximity to those classrooms.

The Lila D. Bunch Library includes a microcomputer center, multimedia room, and group study rooms. Adjacent to it is the 3,000-square-foot Leu Art Gallery. Located next to the library is the Leu Center for the Visual Arts, featuring state-of-the-art studios with natural lighting and spacious work areas.

The Sam A. Wilson School of Music Building houses classrooms, a resource room, seminar rooms, studio/offices, music practice rooms, a piano lab, and a music technology lab.

The Jack C. Massey Business Center provides classrooms, office space, study lounges, seminar and conference rooms, a copy center, a post office, and a convenience store. A state-of-the-art learning center includes five computer labs. In addition, Massey Business Center houses the 9,000-square-foot Center for Music Business, which provides classrooms, an academic resource center, two state-of-the-art recording studios and control rooms, four isolation booths, a MIDI pre–postproduction room, and an engineering repair shop.

The recently opened Gordon Inman Center for Health Sciences and Nursing will house Belmont's nursing, social work, and occupational therapy programs. Students train in state-of-the-art labs and classrooms that include lift equipment to teach student safety, simulated mannequins that respond to basic stimuli, and apartments to teach social work students how to work with clients with special needs.

Costs

Belmont's tuition and fees were $18,420 per academic year in 2006–07. Room and board in campus residence halls was $7570.

Financial Aid

More than 75 percent of Belmont's students receive some type of financial assistance. The financial aid program at Belmont combines merit-based assistance with need-based assistance to make the University program affordable. Institutional merit awards range from full tuition Presidential Scholarships to performance scholarships. Also included are many levels of academic merit awards. Belmont University also administers traditional state and federal programs, including the Federal Pell Grant, Federal Stafford Student Loan, Federal Perkins Loan, Federal PLUS loan, and Tennessee Student Assistance Grants and Scholarships. Campus employment is available. Parents may arrange monthly tuition payments through an outside vendor. To apply for assistance, the student must complete the Free Application for Federal Student Aid (FAFSA).

Faculty

A highly competent faculty is the paramount attribute of a strong institution of higher education. Belmont University has faculty members who are dedicated to their profession and to the University. Of the more than 200 full-time faculty members, 65 percent hold terminal degrees. Another 30 percent of faculty members have completed formal studies beyond the master's degree.

The influence of the Belmont University faculty is felt beyond the campus. Faculty members are active in church, civic, professional, and academic associations; frequently speak to various groups; and often write for denominational and secular publications. Most faculty members have traveled extensively and many have experienced life in other regions of the United States and abroad.

Student Government

A liaison between the University and student body, the Student Government Association seeks to address educational, social, and spiritual needs of students. As a service organization for the student body, it offers opportunity for campus involvement, acts as the coordinating body for all student organizations, serves as a resource for the campus community, and represents student interests to the faculty and administration.

Admission Requirements

Applicants are considered based on the total picture a student's credentials present. High school students are considered competitive for admission if they present a rigorous course of college-preparatory academic studies. Students should have an above-average academic and cumulative grade point average and rank in the top half of their graduating class. Any college-level work is also expected to be at the above-average level. A strong correlation between high school grades and entrance examination scores is expected. The personal supplement information, a resume of activities, and recommendations are also strongly considered as positive indicators of success at Belmont. Additional requirements, such as portfolios or auditions, are considered in conjunction with the academic credentials for those programs that require them. Each application is considered on an individual basis. No two applicants present the same credentials or the same degree of "fit" with the University. The University desires to work with each student to determine the likelihood for that student to enroll, graduate, and benefit from the Belmont educational experience.

Application and Information

Further information and application materials may be obtained by contacting:

Office of Admissions
Belmont University
1900 Belmont Boulevard
Nashville, Tennessee 37212
Phone: 615-460-6785
800-56ENROLL (toll-free)
Fax: 615-460-5434
E-mail: buadmission@mail.belmont.edu
Web site: http://www.belmont.edu

Belmont University students enjoy a beautiful antebellum campus located in thriving metropolitan Nashville.

CARSON-NEWMAN COLLEGE

JEFFERSON CITY, TENNESSEE

The College

Founded in 1851 by Tennessee Baptists, Carson-Newman (C-N) is a private, coeducational, Christian liberal arts college. The College has an enrollment of approximately 2,000 undergraduate and over 150 graduate students. The average class size is 16 students, and the male-female ratio is 1:1. Each fall, Carson-Newman enrolls approximately 420 freshmen and 160 transfers. While Carson-Newman students come primarily from the Southeastern states, forty-four states are represented.

In addition to its outstanding academics, C-N also provides many opportunities for student involvement in various clubs and organizations, nationally recognized varsity athletics, intramural athletics, music and drama groups, an award-winning forensics team, and many other extracurricular activities. The majority of C-N students live on campus in one of the two men's and three women's residence halls.

Carson–Newman also offers graduate programs. Programs in education are available leading to Master of Arts in Teaching (M.A.T.) degrees in curriculum and instruction and in English as a second language and Master of Education (M.Ed.) degrees in curriculum and instruction, educational leadership, and school counseling. A Master of Science in Nursing (M.S.N.) degree is also offered.

Location

C-N is conveniently located in eastern Tennessee, just 30 miles from Knoxville, which has a population of 450,000, and 45 miles from Gatlinburg, a gateway to the Great Smoky Mountains. Students appreciate the diverse opportunities available in the city and in the outdoor areas. Shopping, dining, and entertainment opportunities are available near the College.

Majors and Degrees

The nine academic divisions of the College are Business, Education, Family and Consumer Sciences, Fine Arts, Humanities, Natural Sciences and Mathematics, Nursing, Religion, and Social Sciences. C-N awards Bachelor of Arts, Bachelor of Music, Bachelor of Science, and Bachelor of Science in Nursing degrees. In addition, an Associate of Arts in Christian Ministries degree is also offered.

Majors are available in art (art, photography), athletic training, business (accounting, business administration, family business, financial economics, general business, health-care administration, management), church recreation, communication studies and theater (advertising/public relations, journalism, media ministry, radio/television/film, speech), computer information systems (computer studies, data processing), computer science, education (athletic coaching, elementary education, physical education/health, secondary certification, special education), English (creative writing, literature), family and consumer sciences (child and family studies, consumer services, foods and nutrition, interior design and retail), early childhood education, foreign language (biblical languages, French, Spanish), general studies, history, human services, individual directions, mathematics, military science/U.S. Army ROTC or U.S. Air Force ROTC, music (church music, music composition, music education, music theory, music with an outside field, piano and organ performance, vocal performance), natural and physical science (biochemistry, biology, chemistry, physics), nursing, philosophy (philosophy, philosophy/religion), political science, psychology (applied psychology, social entrepreneurship), religion, sociology, and sport science (leisure services, exercise science).

The College offers extremely strong curricula in preprofessional programs and health professions. Preprofessional programs are offered in dentistry, engineering, health information management, law, medicine, occupational therapy, optometry, physical therapy, and veterinary medicine. In cooperation with several other institutions, C-N offers binary degrees (2-3 and 3-2 programs) in engineering, medical technology, pharmacy, and physician assistant studies.

Academic Programs

The College operates on a traditional semester system. May term is a three-week intensive period of study giving students the opportunity to earn 3 credit hours. Summer term is offered as a six-week program of study.

All baccalaureate degrees require completion of 128 semester hours. Students must complete 51 semester hours in general education requirements and a total of 36 semester hours at junior/senior level. Specific course requirements vary depending on major and degree program. Honors courses, independent study, and internships are available to students who qualify. Advanced credit is available for students who achieve required scores on AP exams, CLEP tests, and C-N departmental examinations.

New students are assigned a faculty adviser who assists with course selection and student concerns. Career planning services are also available. The College's exceptionally high placement rate in professional programs in medicine, law, business, and theological study is testimony to the excellence of its rigorous academic program.

Off-Campus Programs

Students have the opportunity to spend an entire semester abroad by participating in the London Semester and other study-abroad opportunities. C-N, along with International Enrichment, Inc., provides all academic and nonacademic support services.

The Washington Semester is available as an internship program primarily for political science and prelaw majors. Through the program, students earn credit for work in the nation's capital. Art and foreign language majors may earn credit while studying and traveling throughout Europe during the three-week May term.

Academic Facilities

C-N offers the facilities and resources necessary for the enrichment of each student's education. Facilities include numerous computer labs; a campuswide computer network; a media service center; two theaters for drama production; Thomas Recital Hall, which is in one of the finest music facilities in the Southeast; two art galleries and twenty-three individual art studios; the Stephens-Burnette Library, with more than 500,000 volumes; and an award-winning 96,000-square-foot Student Activities Center.

Costs

The annual cost at Carson-Newman, including room, board, and tuition, is well below the national average for four-year private colleges. Tuition for 2007–08 was $16,200, room was $2300, board was $3040, the student activity fee was $390, and the technology fee was $390. Total direct charges were $22,320. Students should allow approximately $800 for books per year.

Financial Aid

Carson-Newman allocates thousands of dollars each year to help supplement the resources of families. Financial aid awards are tailored to meet students' economic needs. Carson-Newman participates in all state and federal aid programs and awards aid based on demonstrated need as documented by a need analysis form, such as the Free Application for Federal Student Aid (FAFSA). Carson-Newman also awards academic scholarships based on achievement. Priority deadline for filing financial assistance forms is March 1.

Faculty

Carson-Newman has 122 full-time and 65 part-time faculty members. Of these, 68 percent hold the Ph.D. The student-faculty ratio is 13:1. Faculty members are involved in scholarly pursuits such as authoring books, leading national scholastic organizations, and research, but their primary focus is teaching.

Student Government

The Student Government Association (SGA) represents the entire student body by voicing student concerns in campus affairs. The purpose of SGA is to promote the welfare of every student through justice, to protect individual rights and freedoms, to encourage high standards of conduct, and to train students in the general principles of self-government.

Admission Requirements

Carson-Newman College seeks applicants who demonstrate academic preparation and who possess an appreciation of and sensitivity to a Christian education and a liberal arts curriculum. Carson-Newman accepts applications for freshman and transfer admission for each term of enrollment (fall, spring, and summer). Freshman candidates must have a GPA of 2.25 or higher in the core curriculum and a minimum score of 900 on the SAT (450 critical reading and 450 math) or 19 on the ACT; they must also rank in the top half of their high school graduating class. Transfer applicants must have a minimum cumulative GPA of 2.0 in courses that transfer to Carson-Newman.

Application and Information

Applicants must submit an application for admission, official transcripts, test scores, and a nonrefundable $25 application fee. Admission decisions are made on a rolling basis, and students are notified within two weeks of receipt of all required documents. Application deadline is May 1 for fall semester, December 1 for spring semester. Applicants who wish to be considered for merit scholarships should apply by December 31.

For additional information, students should contact the Office of Undergraduate Admissions or visit http://www.cn.edu.

Office of Undergraduate Admissions
Carson-Newman College
Jefferson City, Tennessee 37760
Phone: 865-471-3223
800-678-9061 (toll-free)
E-mail: admitme@cn.edu
Web site: http://www.cn.edu

Students on the Carson-Newman campus.

CHRISTIAN BROTHERS UNIVERSITY

MEMPHIS, TENNESSEE

The University

Students from all over the country and the world come to Christian Brothers University (CBU) in midtown Memphis for a vibrant and involved education that delivers the tools for success after graduation. CBU is academically rigorous, exciting, and diverse. CBU students are passionate about this extraordinary environment, which prepares them for the real world by pushing them to step up, ask questions, and get involved.

CBU's students, faculty, administration, and alumni are part of a much larger Catholic educational network. The University was founded in 1871 by the Brothers of the Christian Schools and is part of the Lasallian Community active in eighty-one countries of the world and in more than 1,000 educational institutions. In the United States, CBU is one of only seven Lasallian colleges and universities. Excellence in teaching and individualized attention are hallmarks of the University. CBU prepares students for professional careers and advanced study in the arts, sciences, engineering, and business and for lives of moral responsibility and constructive community involvement.

There are more than 1,700 students from thirty-one states and fourteen countries enrolled at CBU. Eighty percent of the students ranked in the top half of their high school classes; 31 percent ranked in the top 10 percent. Twenty-five different faiths are represented in the student body; 22 percent of the students are Catholic. Religious observances are not required, but students are encouraged to practice their faith openly and actively.

Approximately 65 percent of all first-year students live on the campus in traditional residence halls. All residence halls are networked, providing free e-mail and Internet access. In addition, each room is wired for free local telephone service and cable television. A wireless network is available in most major buildings across the campus, as well as outdoors in the Buckman Quad. Students also have access to hundreds of PCs across the campus in University-maintained labs.

CBU provides broad cocurricular and coeducational activity programs. A wide range of organizations, events, and other activities exist for the benefit and fulfillment of students. These include various social, cultural, and developmental events. The Thomas Center provides much of the space for these programs and activities and contains facilities for student recreation, a cafeteria and snack bar, a student fitness center, the mailroom, and various student services offices. Some of the more than forty clubs and organizations in which a student may participate include student government, individual class leadership, social and service fraternities, sororities, professional groups, men's and women's organizations, and support groups. There are also clubs that assist students in their major field of study. Opportunities are available for student participation in University theater, art, music, and publications.

The last five years have seen changes at CBU. Millions of dollars have been invested, and the University has completed major renovations to the Sabbatini Lounge in the student center; the athletic facility, including the Canale Arena; and the University Theater. During summer 2007, improvements were made to CBU residence halls, the portico of St. Joseph Hall was renovated, and the bells in the University's landmark bell tower were restored. The Cooper-Wilson Center for Life Sciences is currently under construction just south of the present Science Center, which will be renovated after the Cooper-Wilson Center is complete.

CBU competes in the NCAA Division II Gulf South Conference in women's basketball, cross-country, golf, soccer, softball, tennis and volleyball and men's baseball, basketball, cross-country, golf, soccer, and tennis. In 2002, the Lady Buccaneer soccer team captured the NCAA Division II National Championship. The 190 student athletes at CBU combined for one of the best academic years in the program's history for the year ended in May 2007. Thirteen players were named Academic All-Gulf South Conference (GSC) and 91 were named to the GSC Academic Honor Roll. CBU's 91 GSC Academic Honor Roll selections ranks fifth in the GSC and second among schools that do not play football. In addition to these teams, CBU offers men's lacrosse as a club sport and has an active intramural sports program. There are fitness and recreational facilities on campus, including an outdoor basketball court, tennis courts, a sand volleyball court, and a swimming pool.

Christian Brothers University is accredited by the Commission on Colleges of the Southern Association of Colleges and Schools to award the bachelor's and master's degrees. Programs at the graduate level include master's degree programs in business administration, education, educational leadership, and engineering management.

Location

CBU is located on a 75-acre wooded campus in the heart of midtown Memphis. The city is the eighteenth largest in the United States and offers a world of opportunity and adventure for CBU students. Wonderful internship possibilities are available with companies such as FedEx, International Paper, AutoZone, Morgan Keegan, St. Jude Children's Research Hospital, and Buckman Laboratories. Volunteer opportunities abound at nonprofit organizations, religious communities, and multicultural centers. The annual Memphis in May features the Beale Street Music Festival, bringing a long list of great shows and entertainment, and the Barbeque Festival provides competition and great food. Memphis is home to several sporting events, including the AutoZone Liberty Bowl Football Classic and Memphis Grizzlies NBA competitions. Nationally noted restaurants, a resurgence of the downtown entertainment district, and acres of lush, green parks help to round out the entertainment options in Memphis.

Majors and Degrees

The University awards both Bachelor of Arts (B.A.) and Bachelor of Science (B.S.) degrees. Majors include applied psychology, biology, biomedical science, business administration (with concentrations in accounting, finance, information technology management, management, and marketing), chemical and biochemical engineering, chemistry, civil engineering, computer science, cultural studies (licensure, 4-8), electrical and computer engineering, engineering management (packaging concentration available), engineering physics, English, English for corporate communications, history, liberal studies (licensure, K-6), mathematics, mechanical engineering, natural science, physics, prelaw, preprofessional health programs, psychology, religion and philosophy, and studio arts.

Academic Programs

With majors in the arts, business, engineering, and science, CBU offers excellent educational options while focusing on individualized attention. CBU's top-notch faculty teaches all classes and labs, encouraging CBU students to achieve above and beyond their potential and expectations. CBU's academically rigorous education also focuses on moral responsibility and community involvement and embraces diversity. Internships, onsite seminars, and the latest state-of-the-art software and research equipment give students the chance to actively participate in their own education.

The School of Arts is the heart of the educational experience at CBU. A liberal arts education is as much about living as it is about working. The goal of this school is to inspire students' intellect, clarify values, celebrate cultural diversity, and encourage compassion for others. From 2003 to 2006, 70 percent of CBU's history graduates have been accepted to graduate or law schools. Within the first year after completion of the teaching licensure requirements, 95 percent of CBU-prepared candidates are employed in the local and regional public and private schools. CBU's newest degree is the Bachelor of Fine Arts in studio arts, with concentrations in drawing, painting, printmaking, and sculpture.

The School of Business has a long tradition of educating leaders who possess real-world experience, analytical abilities, critical-thinking skills, global awareness, a technology background, and an ethical foundation. The business faculty possesses real-world experience, and CBU graduates include a circuit court judge, a Hollywood entertainment executive, a high-tech company vice-president, and a member of the New York Stock Exchange.

The School of Engineering recently celebrated fifty years of graduating engineers in Memphis. This nationally recognized, ABET-accredited program blends small classes, unrivaled equipment, tremendous internships, and flexible curricula to prepare graduates for entry directly into the engineering profession or into graduate school. Engineering graduates also have an excellent foundation for professional careers in law, medicine, business, education, and science.

Exciting things are happening in the School of Science at CBU. In May of 2007, the University broke ground on the Cooper-Wilson Center for Life Sciences, which will add about 27,000 square feet to the current science facility. The Center is designed to allow for maximum flexibility to integrate new technologies as they emerge. New labs will be designated specifically for natural science and physics, and all labs will be outfitted with new and updated instrumentation. Space will be dedicated for pre-health students who currently enjoy outstanding professional school acceptance rates of 91 percent to medical schools, 100 percent to nursing schools, and 87 percent to pharmacy schools.

A degree from CBU deals with the subject matter of a specific major, but also helps the graduate find a unique place in society and the world. The educational experience at CBU creates graduates who have the ability to think clearly, confidently, and creatively. CBU graduates are people who can turn challenges into opportunities, problems into solutions, and questions into answers.

Off-Campus Programs

Several opportunities exist for CBU students to engage in travel and study abroad. These include the Spain Study Trip at Fall Break, the December Holiday Break in Paris, and the May Session: Rome and Assisi. Students can also spend an entire semester or a summer session abroad or conduct research in Brazil or Uganda. More information is available online at http://www.cbu.edu/Academics/studyabroad/.

Academic Facilities

Plough Memorial Library is housed in a three-story building centrally located on campus and contains more than 154,000 volumes and 532 current periodical subscriptions. Access to the library's collections is provided through an online catalog and automated circulation system. The library cooperates with Memphis-area academic libraries to provide reciprocal borrowing privileges for students and faculty and staff members. Materials can be borrowed from other libraries around the country through the interlibrary loan service. Additional collections are available in the Brother I. Leo O'Donnell Archives, which traces the 130-year history of the University and includes the Leslie H. Kuehner Napoleon Collection, the Higgins Collection on the history of Bolivia, and the De La Salle Christian Brothers Midwest Province Archival Record and Museum Collections. The Beverly and Sam Ross Gallery offers students the opportunity for an enjoyable educational experience through regularly scheduled art exhibits.

Costs

Tuition for the 2006–07 academic year was $20,840. Room and board, books, and fees averaged $7956.

Financial Aid

The Christian Brothers founded their schools on the principle that an education should be available to anyone, regardless of socioeconomic status. Still true to that mission, CBU provides generous scholarship and financial aid packages, along with individualized advice on finding and obtaining any and all financial resources that might be available. Ninety-one percent of the current CBU students receive some sort of financial assistance based on need and/or merit. More information is available from the Student Financial Assistance Office at 901-321-3305 or 877-255-0032 (toll-free) or via e-mail at finaid@cbu.edu.

Faculty

Christian Brothers University has 92 full-time faculty members, all of whom hold at least a master's degree; 88 percent hold doctorates or the highest degrees in their field. No courses are taught by teaching assistants. The student-faculty ratio is 13:1.

Student Government

Programs aimed at the cultural, educational, and entertainment interests of the student body are arranged and conducted with the advice and assistance of the Student Government Programming Council, which serves as a voice for the student body. The Programming Council, along with the Director of Student Activities, plans, coordinates, and implements a variety of student activities that are publicized on campus bulletin boards, in various campus publications, and through special-events posters on campus.

Admission Requirements

Students must have graduated from an approved secondary school, have a scholastic average of at least a C, rank in the upper two thirds of their graduating class, and achieve satisfactory scores on the ACT or SAT. Applicants should submit the completed application form, the $25 application fee, an official high school transcript, official ACT or SAT scores, an essay or personal statement, and the completed health form. Transfer students should also submit official transcripts from all colleges attended. International students must also send in official TOEFL exam scores and a declaration of finances.

Application and Information

Admission is selective, and students are encouraged to apply as early as possible. The preferred application date is May 1 for the fall semester and January 1 for the spring semester. Students who apply after these dates are considered for admission on a space-available basis. Applications are reviewed on a rolling-admissions basis. Applicants are encouraged to submit complete admission credentials for the Early Scholars Program by December 1 for earlier notification of scholarship awards. The early action admissions program is nonbinding.

Office of Admissions
Christian Brothers University
650 East Parkway South
Memphis, Tennessee 38104
Phone: 901-321-3205
800-288-7576 (toll-free)
E-mail: admissions@cbu.edu
Web site: http://www.cbu.edu

LINCOLN MEMORIAL UNIVERSITY

HARROGATE, TENNESSEE

The University

Lincoln Memorial University (LMU) grew out of love and respect for Abraham Lincoln and his desire to provide the people of central Appalachia an opportunity to improve their lives through education. The University, a private, independent liberal arts school, today honors his name, values, and spirit. While the University has undergone rapid growth and change since its founding as a living memorial to Abraham Lincoln in 1897, it has retained its original mission of providing exceptional educational opportunities not only to deserving students from Appalachia but also to students from across the country and around the world.

The 1,000-acre LMU campus—its grounds, buildings, equipment, and human resources—is one of the most strikingly beautiful and functional in the country.

Lincoln Memorial University is a values-based learning community dedicated to providing educational experiences in the liberal arts and professional studies. The University believes that one of the major cornerstones of meaningful existence is service to humanity. By making educational and research opportunities available to students where they live and through various recreational and cultural events open to the community, Lincoln Memorial University seeks to advance life in the Cumberland Gap area and throughout the region.

In addition to the undergraduate programs available, the LMU College of Graduate Studies offers master's degrees in business administration (M.B.A.), education (M.Ed.), and nursing (M.S.N.) and the Educational Specialist (Ed.S.) degree. These programs are specifically designed for working adults, with classes offered in the evenings. In December 2006, the University was elevated to Level V status, clearing the way to open the DeBusk College of Osteopathic Medicine (LMU-DCOM), which opened its doors to its inaugural class in August 2007. The DeBusk College awards the Doctor of Osteopathic Medicine (D.O.). The Caylor School of Nursing awards the Master of Science in Nursing with a family nurse practitioner studies (FNP) concentration.

There are approximately 3,255 undergraduate and graduate students enrolled at LMU's Harrogate and extended-campus sites, representing eighteen countries and twenty-two states. The student body is slightly more than 70 percent women and slightly less than 30 percent men. LMU affords many opportunities for student involvement in campus life, including social fraternities and sororities, honorary societies, religious organizations, academic groups, and other clubs supported through the Student Organization Council.

Academic organizations include Alpha Chi (academic honor society for juniors and seniors), the Alpha Gamma Sigma Chapter of Sigma Tau Delta (English honor society), Phi Alpha Theta (history honor society), Phi Beta Lambda (business honor society), Psi Chi (national honor society in psychology), Psychology Club, Student Athletic Trainers Association, Student Nurses Association, Student Wildlife Society, and Veterinary Technology Club.

Social organizations include Alpha Lambda Zeta fraternity, Delta Theta Sigma sorority, Gamma Lambda Sigma fraternity, Kappa Pi Omega sorority, Zeta Tau Kappa sorority, and Sigma Pi Beta fraternity.

Other organizations include Baptist Collegiate Ministries, Fellowship of Christian Athletes, First Priority, Inter-Greek Council, International Student Union, *Railsplitter* yearbook staff, Student Affairs Advisory Board, Student Alumni Association, Student Government Association, Student Organization Council, and Wesley Foundation.

LMU competes at the NCAA Division II level and is a member of the South Atlantic Conference. Sports offered as part of the intercollegiate program include baseball, basketball, cross-country, golf, soccer, softball, tennis, and volleyball.

On-campus residency options are numerous and varied to meet the particular needs of single students and those with families. From individual rooms to shared rooms and small apartments, LMU's nine residential facilities offer the resident student opportunities for learning through living on campus. The opportunity for meeting new people takes on a decidedly international flair by virtue of LMU's long-standing friendship with the Kanto International High School of Tokyo. Each fall and spring, a new group of Japanese students comes to the LMU campus to study English and other college skills and to share their remarkable culture. In addition to LMU's Japanese students, Lincoln Memorial University draws more than 50 other international students each year.

Location

Lincoln Memorial University's beautiful, historic 1,000-acre wooded campus has thirty-six academic, administrative, and residential buildings on the grounds. It is located on U.S. Highway 25E in Harrogate, Tennessee, in the heart of Appalachia, where Tennessee, Kentucky, and Virginia merge at the Cumberland Gap. It is adjacent to Cumberland Gap National Historical Park. The campus and the park create a natural recreational area for enjoying nature. Hiking, mountain climbing, and camping in the surrounding environs are activities available for all to enjoy.

Nearby Middlesboro, Kentucky, offers a shopping mall, movie theaters, restaurants, and other businesses and amenities. Harrogate offers several banks, restaurants, a variety and drug store, grocery stores, and physicians' and dentists' offices all within walking distance of the campus. For those desiring big-city entertainment, Knoxville, Tennessee, is approximately 55 miles south of the campus.

Majors and Degrees

LMU's Paul V. Hamilton School of Arts and Sciences awards the Bachelor of Arts or Bachelor of Science degree in American studies, Appalachian studies, art, biology, chemistry, communication arts, English, environmental science, history, humanities, mathematics, music, social studies, and wildlife and fisheries management.

The Carter and Moyers School of Education awards the Bachelor of Science in Interdisciplinary Studies in human learning and development, psychology, and social work. Courses offered by the Department of Teacher Education lead to teacher licensure in Tennessee in elementary, secondary, and K–12 education. For licensure in secondary or K–12 education, students may select an accompanying major program.

The School of Business awards the Bachelor of Business Administration (B.B.A.), with concentration areas in accounting, computer information systems, economics, financial economics, general business, management, and marketing. The Bachelor of Arts degree is also awarded in general business. In 2005, a degree completion program in management leadership studies was introduced.

The Caylor School of Nursing awards the Bachelor of Science in Nursing (B.S.N.). The School of Allied Health awards the Bachelor of Science in athletic training, health, kinesiology, medical technology, and veterinary science.

Associate degrees are awarded in applied science (veterinary technology), business administration (A.B.A.), and nursing (A.S.N.).

Academic Programs

The academic year consists of two semesters. Summer courses are available. A minimum of 128 semester credit hours are required for the baccalaureate degree. A student must complete the required semester hours in a major as well as the general study requirements. The University's curriculum and commitment to high-quality instruction at every level are based on the beliefs that graduates must be able to communicate clearly and effectively in an era of rapidly and continuously expanding communication technology, have an appreciable depth of learning in a field of knowledge, appreciate and understand the various ways by which they come to know themselves and the world around them, and be able to exercise informed judgments. Lincoln Memorial University is accredited by the Commission on Colleges of the Southern Association of Colleges and Schools to award associate, baccalaureate, master's, educational specialist, and doctoral degrees.

Off-Campus Programs

LMU offers courses at extended-campus sites. The nursing program is offered in Knoxville, Madisonville, and Blount County, Tennessee, and in Corbin, Kentucky. Business and education classes are offered in Knoxville and at Walters State Community College in Morristown, Tennessee, and at Southeast Community College in Cumberland, Kentucky. Graduate studies are offered in Cleveland, Kingsport, Knoxville, Maryville, and Ducktown, Tennessee.

Academic Facilities

The Harold M. Finley Learning Resources Center houses collections totaling more than 200,000 volumes. It also provides expanded library services through subscriptions to approximately 50 electronic databases and more than 33,000 electronic books. On-site technology facilities provide access for students to the Internet.

The Abraham Lincoln Library and Museum is home to a nationally recognized Lincoln and Civil War collection. This center for history, research, and public interest contains one of the nation's largest collections of Lincoln and Civil War artifacts. Scholars from every region of the globe have visited the library and museum to study the life and thoughts of the nation's sixteenth president.

The Student Center houses the campus dining hall, snack bar (Splitters Lounge), and University Bookstore. The Office of the President, the division of student services, and the Office of Admissions are all located in this facility.

The Sigmon Communications Center is home to radio stations WLMU-FM and WRWB-AM and television station LMU-TV. The facility provides laboratory and classroom space to support the communication arts curriculum and production areas that allow student productions to be broadcast to the local community.

The 5,009-seat Tex Turner Arena is a state-of-the-art facility for intercollegiate basketball and for major concerts and special events. The multipurpose Mars Gymnasium provides classrooms, indoor swimming, and basketball courts. Outdoor athletic facilities include the Lamar Hennon Baseball Field, Gibbs Soccer Field, Neely Softball Field, Annan Tennis Courts, and walking trails.

Costs

The cost to attend LMU is substantially below the national average for private colleges and universities. Tuition and fees at LMU for 2007–08 were $14,400 for the year. Room and board costs ranged from $5380 to $8040 for the year, depending on accommodations.

Financial Aid

Ninety-seven percent of LMU undergraduate students apply for and receive some type of financial assistance through a combination of scholarships and need-based financial aid. For many, the individual cost to attend Lincoln Memorial University is less than the cost associated with state-supported institutions. The University participates in the following federally sponsored aid programs: the Federal Perkins Loan, Federal Pell Grant, Federal Supplemental Educational Opportunity Grant, Federal Work-Study, Federal Stafford Student Loan (subsidized and unsubsidized), and Federal PLUS loan programs. All financial aid applicants are required to submit the Free Application for Federal Student Aid (FAFSA). Academic scholarships are competitive and renewable. Students are strongly urged to apply for academic scholarships by the March 1 priority deadline.

Faculty

At Lincoln Memorial University, the faculty is dedicated to helping students succeed. Every effort is made to assist the individual student to accelerate a program of study or to master the developmental skills necessary for success. The average class size is 15. More than 70 percent of full-time faculty members teaching in bachelor's degree programs hold the doctorate or the highest degree available in the field.

Student Government

The Student Government Association (SGA) is the principal means for student participation in University governance and is dedicated to the well-being of the students. SGA is a student-based organization, composed of elected representatives from campus dormitories, social and academic organizations, and commuter students. LMU students serve on numerous University committees.

Admission Requirements

Application for general admission should be made as early as possible in the senior year of high school. Tentative acceptance is made during the senior year, but final acceptance is made only after receipt of the academic transcript confirming the high school diploma.

Transfer students in good academic standing are invited to apply to LMU. Transfer students must submit transcripts from their high school and each college attended.

Application and Information

All applicants must submit the following to the Office of Admissions: a completed application form (also available online at http://www.lmunet.edu) with a nonrefundable $25 application fee, an official copy of the applicant's high school transcript or GED scores (upon graduation, the student must forward a final transcript of his or her high school records), and a copy of the applicant's ACT scores (code 3982) or SAT scores (code 1408). Once these items are on file and reviewed, applicants receive prompt notification of the University's decision. Students are strongly encouraged to apply by the March 1 academic scholarship priority deadline.

For an application and additional information, students may contact:

Office of Admissions
Lincoln Memorial University
6965 Cumberland Gap Parkway
Harrogate, Tennessee 37752
Phone: 423-869-6280
800-325-0900 (toll-free)
E-mail: admissions@lmunet.edu
Web site: http://www.lmunet.edu

LIPSCOMB UNIVERSITY

NASHVILLE, TENNESSEE

The University

Lipscomb University delivers a complete education characterized by a distinctive integration of Christian faith and practice with academic excellence. The curriculum, which includes liberal arts studies and professional preparation, reflects Lipscomb's commitment to the comprehensive development of students—spiritually, intellectually, socially, and physically—to prepare them for life and eternity. Lipscomb is committed to teach truth as revealed in God's word through daily Bible classes and chapel, encouraging each student to explore scripture, to know Jesus Christ, and to grow in His image. "Faith-informed" learning encourages students to understand that all knowledge and skills are to be used to the glory of God in every pursuit. Because of its strong association with the churches of Christ, Lipscomb adheres to central doctrinal interpretations that characterize these churches while creating an inclusive environment that respects and welcomes all who seek an excellent education in a Christian context. Lipscomb also welcomes those for whom an awareness of the spiritual self is unexplored or recently awakened and who are willing to pursue a Christian education.

Lipscomb strives to be a nationally recognized Christian university with an excellent academic program, encouraging the highest level of performance and service among employees and students. Academic programs prepare graduates for roles of superior leadership and service in their chosen professions and an enthusiasm for lifelong learning. These programs help students develop a sense of world citizenship through a geographically and ethnically diverse student body, wide-ranging cultural and professional growth opportunities afforded by the city of Nashville, study-abroad curricula, and international mission programs. A vibrant, well-rounded campus life includes social, service, and spiritually oriented organizations and activities that encourage students to form lasting friendships and to become involved in service to others. Lipscomb offers more than seventy student organizations, including service and social clubs, musical groups, intramural sports, academic groups, student government, missions teams, performance groups, and student publications. Classes and a broad program of intramural and intercollegiate athletics encourage the awareness of physical health and growth and the concepts of leadership, teamwork, sportsmanship, and selflessness. A member of the NCAA Division I Atlantic Sun Conference, the Lipscomb Bisons field teams in baseball, men's and women's basketball, men's and women's cross-country, men's and women's golf, men's and women's indoor track, softball, men's and women's tennis, and men's and women's track. The majority of students live on campus in safe, comfortable residence halls. As part of the University's five-year plan, Lipscomb 2010, $54 million is being spent on capital improvements and academic enhancements. Included are a renovated student center featuring a full-service Starbucks, a new residence hall, a new learning center, a new music and arts center, and much more.

Nearly 90 percent of Lipscomb students who apply to medical school are accepted—more than double the national acceptance rate. Acceptance rates of Lipscomb students to graduate schools and professional programs are significantly above the national average.

Location

Lipscomb's beautiful 65-acre campus sits in the Green Hills area of Nashville, Tennessee, just 4 miles from downtown. Nashville is one of the nation's most exhilarating cities and is located within one day's drive of 75 percent of the nation's population.

Majors and Degrees

Lipscomb University offers the Bachelor of Arts (B.A.), the Bachelor of Business Administration (B.B.A.), the Bachelor of Music in Music Education (B.M.Ed.), the Bachelor of Science (B.S.), the Bachelor of Science in Nursing (B.S.N.), and the Bachelor of Social Work (B.S.W.) degrees. Majors are offered in accounting, American studies, art (graphic, studio, or art teaching), athletic training, Bible (biblical languages, children's ministry, interdisciplinary worship ministry, missions, preaching, or youth ministry), biochemistry, biochemistry (applied), biology, biology teaching, chemistry (applied, professional, or teaching), communication (journalism, mass communication, oral communication, or public relations), computer engineering, computer science, engineering science (with an industrial distribution option), English, English teaching, environmental science (technology and field studies, ethics and public policy, or environmental management), exercise science, family and consumer sciences (consumer sciences, dietetics, family relations, fashion merchandising, food systems management, or textiles and apparel), finance and economics, French, French teaching, general studies (interdisciplinary teaching or nonteaching), German, German teaching, government and public administration, health and physical education teaching, history, history communication, history teaching, human resources, information systems (application or management), management, marketing, mathematics, mathematics teaching, mechanical engineering, music (instrumental performance, piano performance, theory/composition, or vocal performance), music education (instrumental or vocal/general music), nursing, organizational communication, philosophy, physics, physics teaching, political science (communication), premedical studies, professional accountancy, psychology, social work, Spanish, Spanish teaching, theater, theater teaching, and urban studies.

Academic Programs

The University is dedicated to providing a challenging and sound liberal arts program. There are five essential parts to the academic program—the daily Bible requirement, the general education requirement, the major area of study, the minor area of study, and electives. Every regular student must be enrolled in a Bible course and University Bible each school day and also attend chapel. The general education program is designed to provide students with a significant and broad educational foundation in a Christian setting. The program is designed to equip students with core competencies (writing, communication, mathematics, and physical education) and introductions to major disciplines (the sciences, the social sciences, history, and the fine arts). Students pursuing the Bachelor of Arts degree are required to complete additional hours in a foreign language; those pursuing the Bachelor of Science degree must complete additional hours in mathematics and/or science. A minimum of 132 hours is required to graduate.

Off-Campus Programs

One of Lipscomb University's objectives is to help students develop an awareness and knowledge of diverse cultures. To this end, the University provides students two opportunities to study abroad under the guidance of Lipscomb faculty members—a fall semester in Vienna, Austria, and a summer term in London, England. Other study-abroad opportunities are currently under review. More information is available from the director of international programs.

Academic Facilities

The Beaman Library provides a wide range of information services. The library features an online catalog, CATACOMB, with links to the Internet. Comfortable study and reading areas are available for individual and group study. The library's holdings total more than 240,000 items, including books, periodicals, microforms, and nonprint materials. Special collections include the Restoration Collection, the Dorris Collection, the Lindsley Collection, the Goodpasture Collection, the Bailey Hymnology Collection, and archival materials. Other special collections include books by Lipscomb faculty members, the Lipscomb Collection, the Fanning Collection, and student honors theses. There are three computer classrooms in the computer center office area on the lower level of the library building. Each contains twenty-five Intel-based computers running Microsoft Windows. The Swang Center and the science building each have a computer classroom with PCs running Windows. A computer classroom containing twenty-five Macintosh computers running System X is located in the Burton Bible Building. As an additional convenience for students, each residence hall contains a small Windows PC lab next to the lobby.

Costs

A typical undergraduate boarding student taking 12–18 hours per semester can meet all regular expenses of tuition, fees, room, and meals for $23,881 for the school year. A nonboarding student can meet expenses of tuition and fees for $16,811.

Financial Aid

The University strives to make the Lipscomb education available to every student. To that end, more than 97 percent of undergraduate students receive financial assistance in the form of scholarships, grants, loans, and/or work-study programs. The Financial Aid Office coordinates the awarding of all financial assistance.

Faculty

Students are taught by highly qualified faculty members who represent the range of perspectives that exist among churches of Christ; they combine the highest academic preparation with ongoing practical experience and scholarship. Class sizes encourage faculty members and students to create relationships that are constructive, beneficial, and personal and to maintain these relationships throughout life.

Of the total 260 faculty members, 42 percent are full-time. Eighty-three percent of faculty members hold the highest degree in their fields of expertise. Students benefit from the 15:1 student-faculty ratio.

Student Government

The Student Government Association (SGA) is composed of 32 members. Five senators are elected from each class and 6 from the student body at large. The 4 executive officers complete the senate. The purposes of the SGA are to promote all phases of student life and to ensure a collaboration between students and the administration. Freshmen choose their senators early in the fall semester.

Admission Requirements

In general, applicants are expected to have followed a college-preparatory course of study in high school. This track includes at least 4 units of English, 2 units of mathematics (preferably algebra I and II), 2 units of natural sciences, 2 units of history/social sciences, 2 units in the same foreign language, and two academic electives (selected from natural sciences, mathematics, foreign languages, or social sciences). Lipscomb University admits men and women who demonstrate ability to succeed academically and who possess good moral character. A student desiring to enter must apply and furnish evidence of intellectual capacity and moral character. Applicants 18 years and older may be admitted with a GED certificate.

Students must submit the completed application, the $25 application fee, official high school transcripts, SAT or ACT scores, and a letter of reference. A personal interview, either in person or over the phone, must be scheduled. In addition, international students must send in official TOEFL scores. Applicants who present an ACT composite score of 21 or higher (or the SAT equivalent), a high school GPA of 2.5 or better, a personal statement on the application, and strong educational and personal references are generally admitted without conditions.

Application and Information

Students are usually notified of an admissions decision about two weeks after the completed application is received.

Corey Patterson, Director of Admissions
Lipscomb University
3901 Granny White Pike
Nashville, Tennessee 37204-3951
Phone: 615-966-1000
877-582-4766 (toll-free)
Fax: 615-269-1804
Web site: http://www.lipscomb.edu

MARYVILLE COLLEGE

MARYVILLE, TENNESSEE

Maryville College
Be successful. Make a difference.

The College

Founded in 1819, Maryville College is among the fifty oldest institutions of higher education in the United States and the twelfth oldest in the South. Affiliated with the Presbyterian Church (USA), the College welcomes students of all faiths. Current enrollment is 1,176 men and women; students come from thirty-one states, one territory, and fifteen other countries. Maryville College is a place where students learn the skills and are given the opportunities to be successful and to make a difference in the world.

Facilities include twenty-six structures, of which ten are residence halls. Centrally located on the beautiful 320-acre campus is the Cooper Athletic Center, which contains three full-size gymnasiums, an indoor pool, racquetball courts, a weight room, and athletic training facilities. The College is a member of NCAA Division III. It fields men's varsity teams in baseball, basketball, cheerleading, cross-country, football, soccer, and tennis. Women's varsity sports are basketball, cheerleading, cross-country, soccer, softball, tennis, and volleyball. The College offers equestrian competition through its membership in the Intercollegiate Horse Show Association (IHSA). Dance team and Ultimate Frisbee are also available as competitive club sports. A wide range of team and individual intramural sports are supported, and the College provides sixty-three social and special-interest organizations.

Maryville College's Mountain Challenge Program is among the finest outdoor programs in the nation. On-campus facilities include a low-ropes course and a climbing tower that is accessible to persons with disabilities. Equipment is available to students for rock climbing, hiking, camping, canoeing, biking, and whitewater rafting in the neighboring Great Smoky Mountains National Park.

Location

Maryville offers the best of both worlds—access to the city and to the mountains. The city of Maryville is part of the metropolitan Knoxville area in eastern Tennessee. Maryville and Alcoa are side-by-side communities with a combined population of more than 30,000. The campus is 15 minutes south of Knoxville, a community of nearly 400,000 people and the home of the University of Tennessee. Twenty minutes east of the campus are the Great Smoky Mountains, which provide ample opportunities for hiking, camping, snow skiing, and sightseeing.

Majors and Degrees

Maryville College awards the Bachelor of Arts and Bachelor of Music degrees. Areas of study are American Sign Language and deaf studies, art, art history, biochemistry, biology, business and organization management, chemical physics, chemistry, child development and learning, computer science/business, computer science/mathematics, economics, education, engineering, English, environmental studies, health care (nursing), history, international business, international studies, mathematics, music, music education, music theory/composition, music performance, outdoor recreation, philosophy, physical education, political science, psychology, religion, sign-language interpreting, sociology, Spanish, teaching English as a second language, theater studies, and writing/communication. Students may also design individualized programs that combine two or more disciplines. Education certification is available in both elementary and a variety of secondary education disciplines. Maryville College is one of very few colleges in the United States to offer four-year majors in American Sign Language and sign-language interpreting.

Minors are offered in most major areas as well as areas in which majors are not available. These include accounting, American studies, Appalachian studies, computer science, French, German, medieval studies, physics, and statistics.

Preprofessional study is offered in business administration, dentistry, law, medicine, pharmacy, physical therapy, theology/ministry, and veterinary medicine. The College offers dual-degree programs in engineering in association with several regional universities. A dual-degree program is also offered in nursing with Vanderbilt University (B.A. in health care and M.S. in nursing).

Academic Programs

Course requirements for the baccalaureate degrees may be completed in four years. Maryville operates on a semester-hour system, with a minimum of 128 hours required for graduation. Students must satisfy general education requirements, which account for about half the total number of courses. Each major has specific course requirements, which vary according to the program. Faculty academic advisers are assigned to all incoming students.

Maryville College is one of few U.S. colleges to provide every student with the opportunity for a major undergraduate research project or Senior Study. Internships and practicums are available and supported in conjunction with all majors. All students must pass an English proficiency examination in their sophomore year and a comprehensive examination in their major in the senior year.

Credit by examination is available through CLEP tests, AP tests, I.B. courses, and institutional examinations.

The College calendar includes two traditional semesters and a three-week January term.

Off-Campus Programs

Affordable study abroad is available through sister-school tuition arrangements in England, France, Germany, Japan, Korea, Mexico, Northern Ireland, Puerto Rico, South Africa, and Venezuela and through cooperative arrangements in Europe and Africa. As a member of the International Student Exchange Program (ISEP), students also have access to more than forty nations and over 100 additional institutions in Africa, Asia, Australia, Canada, Europe, Latin America, South America, and the South Pacific. The College also offers short-term study-abroad opportunities during the January term. The January term travel-study affords students alternate study environments, international experiences, and exposure to diverse cultures while earning credit toward their degree. Programs and destinations vary from year to year, and there are options to suit most areas of study.

The College is a member of Oak Ridge Associated Universities (ORAU), which affords multiple opportunities for research and study. The Great Smoky Mountains and the lakes of east Tennessee provide students with Appalachian history, biology, and natural history field study opportunities. Internships and summer programs are available at such sites as the Woods Hole Oceanographic Institution in Massachusetts, the Savannah River Ecological Station in South Carolina, and several national laboratories, such as Argonne, Brookhaven, Lawrence Livermore, and Los Alamos, Pacific Northwest. Student interns also study in Washington, D.C., at the Washington Center for Learning Alternatives; in Nashville in the Tennessee State Legislative Intern Program; and with several international corporations in the United States and abroad. The International Programming Committee and the student's major department assist in arranging study abroad, internships, and other off-campus experiences.

Academic Facilities

The Sutton Science Center is a modern, well-designed, and well-equipped facility for the sciences, computer science, mathematics, and psychology. Private study and research carrels are available to many students in the sciences. Other classroom facilities are located in a mixture of historic and modern buildings, including more than thirty smart classrooms and fifteen computer labs. All campus buildings offer complete wireless connectivity. The Lamar Memorial Library is fully automated, with an online catalog and access to libraries throughout the world as well as numerous electronic databases.

Costs

For 2007–08, tuition was $24,675, room and board costs were $3900 each, and the student activity and technology fees totaled $675, for a total of $33,150. The College estimates a cost of $2550 annually for books, supplies, transportation, and personal expenses.

Financial Aid

More than 90 percent of Maryville's students receive financial assistance through scholarships, grants, loans, or employment. The Presidential Scholarships are the College's most prestigious merit awards; these renewable awards range from $15,000 up to full tuition. Other scholarships of specific interest include the Isaac Anderson Fellowship for Church Leadership ($19,000); the Mountain Challenge Fellowship ($17,500); the Chapel Scholars (up to $17,000); the Dean's, Church and College, Art, Theatre, and Music Scholarships (up to $15,000); and the Making a Difference Scholarship (up to $12,000). Other students may qualify for merit scholarship awards ranging from $7000 to $10,000. Maryville participates in the Bonner Scholars program, which provides scholarship assistance in exchange for community service. Transfer students also have the opportunity to receive comparative scholarships, including the Phi Theta Kappa scholarship. Federal aid programs include the Federal Pell Grant, Federal Supplemental Educational Opportunity Grant, Federal Perkins Loan, and Federal Work-Study programs. Tennessee residents may qualify for the Tennessee State Grant and/or the Tennessee Education Lottery Scholarship. To apply for financial aid, students should complete the Free Application for Federal Student Aid (FAFSA) before February 1.

Faculty

The student-faculty ratio is 14:1; average class size is 16. Ninety-one percent of the 76 full-time faculty members hold doctoral or terminal degrees in their fields. Faculty members are committed to teaching in the undergraduate setting and are also involved in research and the publication of books and articles.

Student Government

The Student Government represents the entire student community and is involved in College-wide policy making, judicial issues, and student programming.

Admission Requirements

Admission to Maryville is selective. Students applying from high school are expected to have successfully completed a strong college-preparatory program. Factors evaluated in the admission decision include courses taken, grade point average, test scores (either SAT or ACT), and teachers' recommendations. Students are also required to submit an essay, either through the submission of their scores on the SAT and ACT optional writing assessment or by sending a writing sample. The majority of entering students rank within the top 25 percent of their high school graduating class. An on-campus interview is strongly recommended but is not a requirement for admission.

Application and Information

To apply to Maryville College, a student should submit the application for admission, an official high school transcript, scores on either the ACT or SAT, and an essay if a student does not take the ACT optional writing assessment. Transfer students must submit a high school transcript plus official transcripts from each college previously attended. The application deadline for early action is September 15. The application deadline for early decision is November 15. The deadline for regular admission is March 1.

Maryville College does not discriminate on the basis of race, color, gender, ethnic or national origin, religion, sexual orientation, age, disability, or political beliefs in its admission procedures and educational programs.

For further information regarding admissions, financial assistance, academic programs, and campus visits, students should contact:

Office of Admissions
Maryville College
502 East Lamar Alexander Parkway
Maryville, Tennessee 37804
Phone: 865-981-8092
800-597-2687 (toll-free)
Fax: 865-981-8005
E-mail: admissions@maryvillecollege.edu
Internet: http://www.maryvillecollege.edu

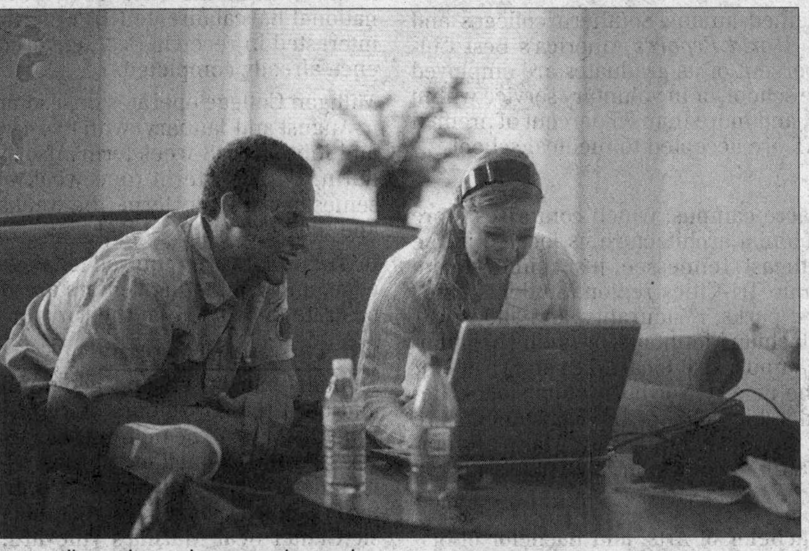

Maryville students playing in the Student Living Room.

MILLIGAN COLLEGE

MILLIGAN COLLEGE, TENNESSEE

The College

Milligan College is a four-year private Christian liberal arts college in northeast Tennessee. From its beginning in 1866, Milligan College has integrated academic excellence with a Christian worldview, and its mission is to educate men and women as Christian servant-leaders. A comprehensive humanities program and core curriculum are complemented by specialized training in more than twenty-five majors and several master's degrees. Christian perspectives are integrated throughout the curriculum and student life activities as students are prepared intellectually and spiritually to change lives and shape culture.

Milligan's student body of 900 comes from more than forty states and ten nations. Eighty percent of traditional students live on the campus in one of six residence halls. More than forty clubs and organizations provide opportunities to develop leadership skills. A wide variety of activities and campus events encourage social, cultural, and spiritual growth. Milligan College is affiliated with the Christian Churches/Churches of Christ, but the interdenominational student body is diverse.

All campus facilities are networked with fiber optics. Every residence hall room and apartment features a high-speed data connection to the campus network and the Internet as well as telephone service, voice mail, and cable TV.

Milligan is well recognized as an NAIA athletic powerhouse with a highly competitive athletic program in eighteen varsity sports. In the past ten years, Milligan has won forty-two conference titles and made forty-eight national tournament appearances. Men's varsity teams include baseball, basketball, cheerleading, cross-country, golf, soccer, swimming, tennis, and track and field. Women's varsity teams include basketball, cheerleading, cross-country, soccer, softball, swimming, tennis, track and field, and volleyball.

Milligan is accredited by the Commission on Colleges of the Southern Association of Colleges and Schools (1866 Southern Lane, Decatur, Georgia 30033-4097; phone: 404-679-4501) to award bachelor's and master's degrees. Milligan offers a Master of Education degree, a Master of Science in Occupational Therapy degree, and a Master of Business Administration degree.

Milligan continues to be named among Southern colleges and universities in *U.S. News & World Report*'s America's Best Colleges issue. More than 90 percent of its graduates are employed full-time, attending graduate school, or in voluntary service within six months after graduation, and more than 75 percent of premed students who take the MCAT are accepted to medical school.

Location

Milligan's picturesque 181-acre campus, which comprises more than twenty buildings of Colonial architecture, is located in the beautiful mountains of northeast Tennessee, just minutes from Johnson City and the dynamic Tri-Cities region. Students enjoy historical locations, theaters, parks, restaurants, and shops; explore the breathtaking Appalachian Mountains by hiking or camping in state parks near the campus; visit local lakes and rivers for outdoor recreation; or ski the nearby North Carolina slopes. Because Milligan believes leadership is about service, students are encouraged to be active in the local community. Many are employed in internships or part-time work in area businesses.

Majors and Degrees

The Bachelor of Science, Bachelor of Arts, and Bachelor of Science in Nursing degrees are offered. Undergraduate majors include applied finance and accounting, Bible (children's ministry, general studies, missions, pastoral ministry, youth ministry), biology, business administration (accounting, economics, general, health-care administration, international business, legal studies, management, marketing, sports management), chemistry, child and youth development, communications (broadcasting, digital media studies, film studies, interpersonal and public communication, journalism, public relations), computer information systems, education (professional teacher licensure), English, fine arts (art, music, photography, theater arts), history, human performance and exercise science (exercise science, fitness and wellness, physical education), humanities, language arts, mathematics, music (general music studies—applied study, jazz studies), music education (vocal, instrumental), nursing, psychology (general, preprofessional), public leadership and service, sociology, and worship leadership.

Professional teacher licensure areas include early childhood, elementary education, K–12, middle grades, and secondary education. Preprofessional programs are available in dentistry, law, medicine, occupational therapy, optometry, pharmacy, and physical therapy. An adult degree completion program allows adults who have completed 60 or more semester hours of college credit to complete a business administration or early childhood education major in about eighteen months.

Academic Programs

Milligan College offers students a liberal arts education taught from a perspective of God's activity with humanity. The College's strong core curriculum educates students toward the world in an open and constructive way. The candidate for the bachelor's degree must have completed a major and electives to total 128 semester hours of credit, with at least a 2.0 GPA. Core curriculum requirements include courses in humanities, the Bible, social sciences, ethnic studies, laboratory science, speech communication, mathematics, and health/fitness.

Realizing that not all college-level learning occurs in a college classroom, Prior Learning Assessment programs provide a method by which other modes of learning can be evaluated for college credit. The Advanced Placement (AP) program, the College-Level Examination Program (CLEP), Defense Activity for Non-Traditional Educational Support (DANTES) programs, and the International Baccalaureate (IB) program are available to all students interested in receiving college credit for studies or work experience already completed.

Milligan College operates on a semester system (semesters begin in August and January) with two 4-week summer sessions in June and July or one 8-week term. Also available are short-term classes during January term (one week before the onset of the spring semester) and May term (the weeks between the spring semester and the summer sessions).

Rising juniors are required to take a test covering general knowledge, and graduating seniors are required to take a test to demonstrate knowledge in their major field of study.

Off-Campus Programs

Students can go beyond geographical and cultural boundaries and earn up to 16 hours of credit with Milligan's Study Abroad Program or with the many off-campus learning opportunities sponsored by the Council for Christian Colleges & Universities. These include an American Studies Program in Washington, D.C.; Australia Studies Centre; China Studies Program; Contemporary Music Center near Martha's Vineyard; Latin American Studies Program in Costa Rica; Los Angeles Film Studies Center; Middle East Studies Program in Cairo; Oxford Summer Programme; Russian Studies Program; Scholars' Semester in Oxford; Summer Institute of Journalism in Washington, D.C.; and Uganda Studies Program. Through an affiliation with the International Business Institute, business majors can earn college credit through an intensive ten-week summer program in Europe. Milligan also offers a four-week summer Humanities Tour in Europe, during which students explore the origins of Western civilization. In addition, internship opportunities offer students college credit and work experience in their field of interest.

Academic Facilities

Milligan College's library has extensive holdings and online access to other major libraries and databases. Special collections within the library contain materials on the history of the College, the Restoration Movement, and the local area. The library also participates in resource-sharing agreements with Emmanuel School of Religion and East Tennessee State University. A Writing and Study Skills Center offers access to resources, instruction, and tutoring for academic success. Television and radio production studios and an FM radio station provide on-site training for communication students. A darkroom and art gallery feature works by fine arts students. Standardized laboratory facilities, including a gross anatomy lab, are available for general and advanced work in the sciences.

As part of the College's Campaign for Christian Leadership, recent on-campus projects include a new theater arts and convocation facility, a $2.5-million renovation of the College's main classroom building, the addition of a new education center, a new tennis complex, a new physical plant facility, and a 30-acre land acquisition.

Costs

Tuition for 2007–08 is $18,900. Room and board are $5390. Additional fees are approximately $610. Typical annual miscellaneous costs (books, supplies, etc.) are approximately $1000 per year. As a private institution, Milligan supplements student fees with income from endowments and gifts from alumni, friends, and churches in order to keep tuition below the national average of similar four-year private institutions.

Financial Aid

Approximately 96 percent of all students at Milligan College receive federal, state, institutional, and/or outside (such as from a church or private foundation) aid, including both academic scholarships and need-based grants. Each year, Milligan budgets more than $5 million in institutional scholarships, grants, and work-study opportunities. Financial assistance is allocated on the basis of need demonstrated by information supplied on the Free Application for Federal Student Aid (FAFSA), which should be completed by January 1 for priority consideration. Returning students must complete and submit a Milligan College Financial Aid Scholarship/Renewal Application. The Milligan College Office of Financial Aid begins mailing award letters between March 1 and March 15.

Faculty

More than 70 percent of Milligan's faculty members have earned the highest degree in their field from well-respected colleges and universities in the U.S. and abroad. Professors integrate biblical truths into their classes and are active leaders both on and off the campus. The low student-faculty ratio and small classes put the student at the center of attention and allow faculty members to cultivate special mentoring relationships with students. Professors serve as advisers to students from registration to graduation and are often instrumental in helping students find employment or gain admission to graduate school following graduation. Milligan's faculty members are mature and caring scholars who are committed to world-class scholarship, excellence in teaching, and their students.

Student Government

The Student Government Association (SGA) serves as the official representative voice of Milligan students and promotes academic, social, and spiritual activities for the campus community. SGA operates under a constitution approved and supported by the administration of the College, promotes well-ordered conduct among students, and enforces the regulations of the College. SGA leadership is provided by an executive council and representatives from throughout the campus. As a Christian college, Milligan adopts basic moral and social principles and expects students to serve Christ in an atmosphere of trust, encouragement, and respect for one another.

Admission Requirements

Character, ability, preparation, and seriousness of purpose are the qualities emphasized in considering applicants for acceptance to Milligan College. Overall excellence of performance in high school subjects as well as evidence of Christian commitment and academic potential provide the basis for admission to Milligan College. These qualities are evaluated by consideration of each applicant's academic record (based on transcripts), two personal references, ACT or SAT scores, and participation in extracurricular activities. Some majors, such as music and theater, may require auditions and interviews. All applicants should have a high school diploma or the equivalent and have completed a college-preparatory curriculum with course work in English, math, science, history and/or social sciences, foreign language, and some work in speech, music, or art in preparation for study in a liberal arts curriculum. Satisfactory scores on the ACT or SAT are required of all applicants to the freshman class. The average ACT score for the current first-year class is 24.1. Transfer students should have a grade point average of 2.5 or above and must follow the same application procedures as first-time students, with the addition of providing official transcripts of all previous college work. ACT or SAT scores and high school transcripts are not required for transfer students with at least 24 earned semester hours.

Application and Information

Applications are processed on a rolling basis, and early application is encouraged. Notification is also given on a rolling basis. An application packet, complete with detailed instructions and requirements, can be obtained from the Admissions Office.

For further information, students should contact:

Admissions Office
Milligan College
P.O. Box 210
Milligan College, Tennessee 37682
Phone: 423-461-8730
800-262-8337 (toll-free)
Fax: 423-461-8982
E-mail: admissions@milligan.edu (general)
visits@milligan.edu (visits)
Web site: http://www.milligan.edu

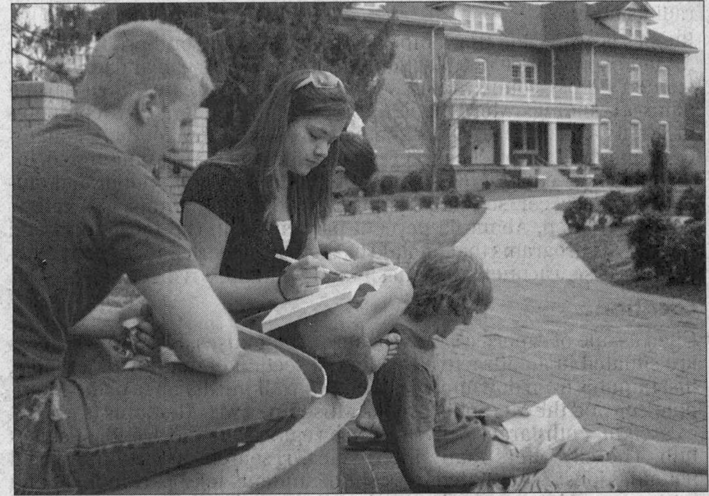

Milligan College is a Christian liberal arts college that unites humanities, sciences, and fine arts with a Christian worldview.

RHODES COLLEGE

MEMPHIS, TENNESSEE

The College

Considered by many to be one of America's premier liberal arts colleges, Rhodes brings together three major purposes of learning seldom found at a single institution: intellectual growth that is fostered by intensive interaction between students and faculty members, preparation for professional life supported by a unique internship program that draws on the city's resources, and a development of values that is part of a diverse student body that adheres to a student-run honor code.

Rhodes is listed in the top tier of America's best national liberal arts colleges, is ranked as one of the top fifty institutions in terms of quality and cost, and is one of only forty schools listed in Loren Pope's *Colleges that Change Lives*. This recognition is primarily based on the College's long and steadfast commitment to providing its students with an education that challenges them to think critically, independently, and creatively; actively engages them in research and internships; and connects them in meaningful ways to one another and to the larger Memphis community.

Rhodes is a private, coeducational college of liberal arts and sciences, founded in 1848 in Clarksville, Tennessee. The College moved to Memphis in 1925. The College is historically affiliated with the Presbyterian Church (U.S.A). In addition to the undergraduate degrees listed in this profile, Rhodes also awards the Master of Science degree in accounting.

Rhodes' 1,699 students represent forty-three states and five countries. About 75 percent of them live on campus in fourteen ivy-covered residence halls. First- and second-year students must live on campus unless they live with their family in Memphis. The East Village, an apartment-style residential complex, houses 200 juniors and seniors. Students, faculty members, and staff members enjoy the Bryan Campus Life Center, a multiuse campus gathering and recreational facility.

Residents and commuters enjoy the rich mix of extracurricular activities, from the internationally touring Rhodes Singers to the nationally ranked Mock Trial team and an active Black Student Association. Eighty-three percent of Rhodes students are active in numerous community service projects that help those in need. Rhodes sponsors more than ninety activities, clubs, and organizations, including seven national fraternities and sororities. More than 250 events each year are sponsored by the College or student organizations, including films, dances, lectures, art exhibits, service projects, concerts, and theater productions. There are several campus publications, a weekly newspaper, a literary journal, and the yearbook as well as a student-run radio station.

Rhodes is a Division III member of the NCAA and Southern Collegiate Athletic Conference (SCAC). Since 2000, the men's golf and tennis and women's cross-country, golf, soccer, and tennis teams have earned national rankings. More than 25 percent of the student body competes in varsity sports: baseball, basketball, cross-country, football, golf, indoor and outdoor track, soccer, swimming and diving, and tennis for men and basketball, cross-country, field hockey, golf, indoor and outdoor track, soccer, softball, swimming and diving, tennis, and volleyball for women. About 65 percent participate in the intramural and club sports programs that include basketball, cheerleading, crew, fencing, lacrosse, racquetball, squash, and Ultimate Frisbee.

Location

Cited as one of America's most beautiful campuses, Rhodes' 100 acres are situated in an attractive residential section of midtown Memphis, just minutes from downtown and within walking distance of the Memphis Zoo and the Memphis Brooks Museum of Art. Memphis is America's eighteenth-largest city and the region's medical and business hub. The city offers many internships, research opportunities, and potential jobs. Seventy-five percent of students take part in local and international internships by the time they graduate. The birthplace of the blues and the home of international companies, including FedEx, International Paper, and AutoZone, Memphis is a city of arts and culture, with ten local theaters, sixteen museums and art galleries, three ballet companies, visiting Broadway shows, a symphony, and an opera company, not to mention hundreds of restaurants, professional sports events, and excellent shopping facilities that round out the entertainment package.

Majors and Degrees

Rhodes grants the Bachelor of Arts or Bachelor of Science degree in thirty-three departmental and interdisciplinary areas: anthropology/sociology, art, biochemistry and molecular biology, biology, business administration, chemistry, computer science, economics, economics and business administration, economics and international studies, English, French, French and international studies, German, German and international studies, Greek and Roman studies, history, history and international studies, international studies, Latin American studies, mathematics, music, neuroscience, philosophy, physics, political science, political science and international studies, psychology, religious studies, Russian studies, Spanish, theater, and urban studies. Students may also apply for interdisciplinary majors that reflect their own interests.

Academic Programs

Students currently take a representative group of courses from the humanities, social sciences, natural sciences, and fine arts. In 2006, Rhodes implemented an academic curriculum that establishes a new approach to the study of the liberal arts and sciences at the College. The curriculum gives students greater freedom to follow their academic interests and aspirations within a framework of foundation requirements that are fundamental to the study of liberal arts. The new curriculum enhances and integrates the four components of the Rhodes education: the twelve foundation requirements, the concentration in a major, the choice of elective courses, and participation in cocurricular activities. To fulfill a humanities requirement, students must also participate in a three-term interdisciplinary course, Search for Values in the Light of Western History and Religion, or take three courses in religious studies and philosophy through the program Life: Then and Now.

The College requires one term of critical reading, thinking, and writing as well as one term of a foreign language at the intermediate level, but either can be waived by demonstrated proficiency. The academic year is divided into two semesters; students take four classes per semester.

The acceptance rate to medical schools of Rhodes graduates is approximately twice the national average, according to American Medical College Application Service (AMCAS) data. Virtually all of Rhodes' graduates either secured jobs or were accepted into graduate schools last year. Typically, nearly 100 percent of applicants to business, law, and divinity schools are accepted.

Rhodes' strong career-counseling program provides advisers in law, business, international business, finance, museum careers, psychological and social services, health professions, accounting, church professions, foreign service, music, and teaching. A research and teaching partnership with St. Jude Children's Research Hospital in Memphis allows for exciting exchanges between Rhodes students and St. Jude medical researchers. The College provides a fully staffed career development office. Students may gain additional knowledge and experience through independent research, internships, and honors programs.

Off-Campus Programs

Rhodes offers many off-campus credit-earning programs. Among them are a semester of study and travel in Europe focusing on literature, religion, art, and the humanities. Rhodes also has exchange programs at the University of Antwerp in Belgium; the University of Poitiers in France; Eberhard Karl University in Tubingen, Germany; the University of Lima in Peru; the University of Aberdeen in Scotland; Rhodes University in Grahamstown, South Africa; and the Universitas Nebrissensis in Madrid, Spain. Other Rhodes-sponsored programs are located in Buenos Aires, Argentina; Santiago, Chile; and Washington, D.C. Summer programs include British Studies at Oxford and language immersion programs in Spain, France, and Russia, as well as coral reef ecology and service-learning programs in Honduras. Domestic and international internships can be arranged through academic departments in conjunction with Career Services.

Academic Facilities

The stone and slate buildings on campus are constructed in collegiate Gothic style, and thirteen of them are listed on the National Register of Historic Places. The new $42-million Paul Barret Jr. Library opened its doors in the fall of 2005 and contains more than 278,000 bound volumes, 95,000 microform items, more than 42,000 electronic books, and more than 1,100 periodicals. A citywide library consortium put more than 1.6 million volumes at the fingertips of Rhodes students. Although the library is replete with Wi-Fi access throughout, it is also designed to facilitate personal interactions among student study groups and among students and faculty members, with twenty group study rooms.

Excellent science facilities include physics laboratories equipped for sophisticated solar emissions research and biology and chemistry laboratories with an electron microscope, a cell culture lab, and a nuclear magnetic resonance instrument. The College's computer network includes file, print, and e-mail servers and more than 200 microcomputers available primarily for student use. Rhodes is listed as one of the 100 Most Wired Colleges by *Yahoo! Internet Life* magazine. In addition to the wireless facilities in the new Barret Library, Wi-Fi access is available in numerous strategic locations on campus, including the dining hall, campus life center, coffee shop, and residence hall social rooms. Rhodes' campus network is connected to the Internet, with all residence hall rooms having an Ethernet connection for each resident.

Costs

Tuition at Rhodes for 2007–08 was $30,342, and room and board fees were $7468. There is a $310 student activity fee. Estimated expenses for books and supplies are $840. Transportation and personal expenses are additional.

Financial Aid

Rhodes invests considerable funds in need-based assistance to help make it possible for students who are admitted to the College to attend. The average need-based award for 2007–08 was more than $20,000. A large number of competitive scholarships are also available, ranging from $2000 to full tuition, fees, room, and board. Students interested in need-based financial aid must fill out the Free Application for Federal Student Aid (FAFSA) and the CSS PROFILE. Those interested in competitive scholarships must submit the application for admission by January 15. Notification of need-based awards occurs between April 1 and April 15.

Faculty

The College's 167 faculty members (137 full-time) are first and foremost teachers, but they also engage in research and creative activities, often working with students on scholarly projects. The student-faculty ratio is 10.5:1, and the average class size is 13. Ninety-six percent of full-time tenured or tenure-track faculty members hold the Ph.D. or other terminal degree in their discipline.

Student Government

Students govern their lives on campus through the Rhodes Student Government, the Honor Council, and the Social Regulations Council and through their participation on the Board of Trustees and various College committees. The honor system prevails at Rhodes; professors regularly leave the room when tests are administered.

Admission Requirements

Rhodes considers a number of criteria in the selection of its students: academic achievements, writing ability, letters of recommendation, standardized test scores, and extracurricular activities. The middle 50 percent of the freshman class who entered in fall 2007 had a combined SAT score ranging from 1200 to 1360 and a composite ACT score ranging from 25 to 30; 52 percent were in the top 10 percent of their high school class. Of the 454 first-year students, 28 were presidents of their class or student government and 41 were valedictorians or salutatorians. The College enthusiastically seeks geographic and racial diversity for its student body.

Applicants should have 16 or more high school academic units, with 4 of the units in English, 3 in mathematics (2 in algebra and 1 in geometry, or the equivalent), 2 in the same foreign language, two years of laboratory science, and two years of history or social science. Either the SAT or ACT is required. In addition to submitting the same application materials and supporting documents as all other students, home-schooled students must submit the results of two SAT Subject Tests from areas other than English or mathematics. Rhodes offers early decision, regular decision, and deferred admission. Advanced Placement credit is normally given for scores of 4 or 5 on the Advanced Placement tests and 5, 6, or 7 on International Baccalaureate Diploma higher-level exams. An interview is not required but is strongly recommended for scholarship candidates. Appointments may be scheduled from 9 to 4 Central Time, Monday through Friday, and on Saturday morning from 9 to 11:30 during the academic year. If they give notice, seniors in high school may spend the night in a residence hall between Sunday and Thursday, attend classes, and meet with faculty members and students during the week.

Application and Information

Priority is given to applications received by the January 15 deadline. Students are notified of the admission decision by April 1. Early decision candidates must file by November 1 for decision notification by December 1, or by January 1 for decision by February 1. Accompanying the application must be a $45 fee (unless applying with Rhodes online application or the Common Application online), an official high school transcript, results of the SAT or the ACT exam, a counselor's report, and a teacher's recommendation. Students may apply online free at http://apply.rhodes.edu. For further information, students should contact:

David J. Wottle, Dean of Admissions and Financial Aid
Rhodes College
2000 North Parkway
Memphis, Tennessee 38112-1690
Phone: 901-843-3700
800-844-5969 (toll-free)
E-mail: adminfo@rhodes.edu
Web site: http://www.rhodes.edu/admissions

Rhodes College has thirteen buildings named to the National Register of Historic Places for representing "one of the finest and most harmonious groupings of collegiate Gothic architecture in the nation."

COLLEGE DATA CENTER • TENNESSEE

TENNESSEE STATE UNIVERSITY

NASHVILLE, TENNESSEE

The University

Tennessee State University (TSU), founded in 1912, is a multiracial, urban, land-grant university that fulfills its mission of providing education, research, and public service for residents of central Tennessee through myriad academic, cultural, research, service, and professional activities. Students can pursue degrees during the day or in evening courses. The Center for Extended Education and Public Service offers a wide variety of off-campus credit programs, contract credit classes with local employers, noncredit courses, and seminars to serve the expanding educational needs of local business and the professional community. The University also offers graduate programs and is dedicated to providing all students with a strong academic background. The Graduate School offers programs leading to the master's, Educational Specialist, and doctoral degrees. (Information on graduate programs is available from Graduate Admissions at the address given at the end of this description.) It is hoped that students will take full advantage of the University's offerings, use the experiences to serve themselves and society, and continue the institution's tradition of excellence.

The 9,065 students (7,112 undergraduates) currently enrolled at Tennessee State University come from a variety of cultural backgrounds and geographical areas. The campus has six residence halls (three for women, two for men, and one coed), although a large percentage of students live off campus. Easily accessible public transportation facilitates the commute to either campus. Extracurricular activities include Greek fraternities and sororities, academic societies, drama and dance groups, a concert choir, and marching, jazz, and concert bands. The University has competitive intercollegiate athletic programs in football as well as men's and women's basketball, cross-country, golf, tennis, and track and women's softball and volleyball. Intramural sports are also offered. An athletic and convocation complex seats 10,000 for basketball games and assemblies; it also contains a 220-yard indoor track, dance studios, racquetball courts, and a 35-meter swimming pool. The football team won the Ohio Valley Conference Championships two consecutive years, in 1998 and 1999. In addition, the women's track team won the Ohio Valley Conference Championship in 2001–02 and 2002–03, and the women's volleyball team was co-champion of the conference in 2005–06 and champion in 2007–08.

Special student services are offered through such resources as a counseling center, reading center, health service center, and career placement center. Tennessee State University is in the midst of a $112-million capital improvement project. The capital project includes seven new buildings and a completely landscaped campus with courtyards, plazas, and a state-of-the-art utility tunnel. The three-story campus center houses student services facilities, including offices for student organizations, admissions and records, and financial aid, and a bookstore and additional recreational facilities.

Location

Nashville is the state capital and the second-largest city in Tennessee. More than 600,000 people live in this thriving center of government, business, industry, and education. Known internationally as "Music City USA," it is the hub of the nation's country music industry. The entertainment and cultural scene does not stop there, however. A performing arts center offers an active schedule of Broadway plays, community theater, films, and performances by professional dance troupes, the Nashville Symphony, and a variety of vocal and instrumental musicians. Nashville also has three professional sports teams. Night spots and restaurants cater to a variety of cultural and ethnic tastes. Nashville's 6,000 acres of public parks and recreational facilities allow for the pursuit of many sports and leisure activities. As the city's only public four-year institution, Tennessee State University occupies an important place in Nashville. Its Main Campus is located in a residential area of the city, providing students with the atmosphere of a neighborly community. The Avon Williams Campus is located in the heart of downtown Nashville, within walking distance of the capitol and the central business district. TSU students and graduates are involved in a wide variety of academic and employment activities throughout the city.

Majors and Degrees

The College of Arts and Sciences offers majors in Africana studies, art, biological sciences, chemistry, criminal justice, English, foreign languages (French and Spanish), history, mathematics, music, physics, political science, social work, sociology, and speech communications and theater. The College also offers an interdisciplinary degree with concentrations in the humanities, the sciences, and the social sciences. Teacher certification in art, biological sciences, chemistry, elementary education, English, foreign languages, history, mathematics, music, political science, and speech communications and theater is also available. The College awards Bachelor of Science degrees.

The College of Business offers majors in accounting, business administration, business information systems, and economics and finance and grants the Bachelor of Business Administration degree.

The College of Education certifies students in elementary, special, and secondary education and awards the Bachelor of Science degree to students majoring in human performance and sports sciences and in psychology.

The College of Engineering, Technology, and Computer Sciences offers Bachelor of Science degree programs in aeronautical and industrial technology, architectural engineering, civil engineering, computer science, electrical engineering, and mechanical engineering.

The College of Health Sciences offers an Associate of Applied Science degree in dental hygiene and a Bachelor of Science degree to students who major in cardiorespiratory therapy, dental hygiene, health information management, health-care administration and planning, medical technology, or speech pathology and audiology. The School of Agriculture and Consumer Sciences offers undergraduate programs leading to the Bachelor of Science degree in agricultural sciences, early childhood education, and family and consumer sciences. The Department of Agricultural Sciences offers a bachelor's degree in agricultural sciences with options in agricultural education, agricultural statistics, agronomy, animal science and pre–veterinary medicine, food technology, ornamental horticulture, and resource economics. The Department of Family and Consumer Sciences offers bachelor's degrees in early childhood education and family and consumer sciences, with options in child development and family relationships, clothing and textiles, design, fashion merchandising, foods and nutrition, and food service management. The School of Nursing grants the two-year Associate of Science and four-year Bachelor of Science degrees in nursing.

Academic Programs

Tennessee State University operates on a semester calendar and conducts two sessions during the summer. A minimum of 120 credit hours and a 2.0 or higher cumulative GPA are required for graduation. Individual departments may have additional require-

COLLEGE DATA CENTER • TENNESSEE

ments. An honors program, independent study, cooperative education, teacher certification, and the Air Force ROTC program are available. Early admission and advanced standing are offered to qualified students, and credit is given for satisfactory scores on the College-Level Examination Program tests.

The University honors program is designed to provide the challenge and opportunity for the academically superior student to achieve academic excellence. Honors courses require a higher level of achievement than those in the regular curriculum and are restricted to students in the honors program and to those with a B average who are recommended by an adviser or a teacher. Other courses from the regular curriculum may be taken for honors credit.

Off-Campus Programs

So that students can receive the practical training necessary for some professions, Tennessee State University has affiliations with several public and private institutions and agencies. The opportunities include a joint-degree program in allied health with Meharry Medical College, clinical training for nursing students through contractual arrangements with local hospitals, student teaching programs with the Metropolitan-Davidson County Public Schools, and field training programs with government agencies for students in social welfare and criminal justice. Students who participate in these programs earn credit toward their degree. The College of Arts and Sciences offers a dual degree in chemistry and pharmacy with Howard University and a dual degree in biology and medicine with Meharry Medical College, as well as co-op and internship experiences.

Academic Facilities

Tennessee State University has two campuses, the Main Campus and the Avon Williams Campus. The Main Campus, located on 450 acres, consists of sixty-five buildings, farmlands, and pastures. The Tennessee State University libraries house 463,621 volumes, 1,446 current periodical subscriptions, 78,185 bound periodicals, 816,934 microfiche, and 14,748 microfilm reels. A CD-ROM LAN serves both libraries with eleven CD databases; additional CD-ROM databases and Dialog services are also available. The Avon Williams Campus is housed in a large, modern building containing a library, a cafeteria, and ample meeting rooms. Parking facilities are adjacent to the building. A full curriculum is offered at this campus during evening hours.

A Learning Resource Center provides multimedia support for both campuses. Students pursuing programs in agriculture, engineering, biological sciences, chemistry, physics, dental hygiene, and nursing have access to fully equipped laboratories. Students also have access to advanced computer equipment and software.

Costs

Costs fall into four areas—maintenance, tuition, room and board, and special fees. In 2007–08, the maintenance fee for in-state students was $2029 (12 hours). Board plans ranged from $460 to $1110 per semester, and room rental costs ranged from $998 to $2600 per semester. The average total cost for a full-time, in-state undergraduate was $2443 per semester ($4886 per year). Out-of-state undergraduates paid tuition of $7581 per semester (including maintenance and special fees) in addition to room and board. Out-of-state students paid an average tuition of $15,162 per year. Average expenses for books, supplies, and personal items are $900 per semester ($1800 per year) for most students.

Financial Aid

The University has a strong commitment to assist students seeking financial aid. The types of aid available include grants, scholarships, loans, and employment. The University participates in the Federal Pell Grant, FSEOG, Federal Perkins Loan, Federal Stafford Student Loan, Federal PLUS loan, Federal Work-Study, and Tennessee Student Assistance Grant programs. Presidential Scholarships, Academic Work Scholarships, University Scholarships, Departmental Scholarships, and several private scholarship programs are also available. Approximately 80 percent of freshmen receive some type of financial assistance. Students who have a high school GPA of 3.0 or above (on a 4.0 scale) and an ACT score of 21 or above may apply for scholarships.

Prospective students must file the Free Application for Federal Student Aid by April 1 in order to be considered for financial aid. Students are also required to submit a processed Student Aid Report to the Financial Aid Office. All students are urged to start filing for financial aid January 1 to receive the maximum eligibility. All files must be complete by April 1 each year.

Faculty

Tennessee State University has a 434-member full-time faculty and a part-time faculty of 169, some of whom teach at both the undergraduate and graduate levels. Eighty percent of the faculty members hold doctoral degrees. The student-faculty ratio is 17:1. Some faculty members, particularly in the areas of agriculture, biological sciences, history, and psychology, are actively involved in research. Faculty members serve as advisers for students majoring in their discipline, and some also serve as advisers for student organizations.

Student Government

The Student Government Association consists of a president, a vice president, class officers, representatives-at-large, and organization representatives, all elected by student vote. The association operates under a formal constitution and is recognized by University administrators as the official voice of students.

Admission Requirements

In-state residents must pass the High School Proficiency Exam and have a high school GPA of 2.25 or better, an ACT score of at least 19, or a minimum SAT score of 900. Out-of-state residents must have a GPA of 2.5 or better, an ACT score of at least 19, or an SAT score of at least 900. In addition, students must pass fourteen State Board of Regents high school unit requirements. Scores on the TOEFL are required of international students.

Transfer applicants must submit a transcript from every college attended and must present a minimum grade point average of 2.0. Transfer students usually receive credit for grades of 2.0 and higher in Tennessee State University-equivalent courses taken at approved institutions. At least 30 hours must be completed in residence at Tennessee State University.

Application and Information

Applications should be received by July 1; the fee is $25. Additional information is available from:

Office of Admissions and Records
Tennessee State University
3500 John A. Merritt Boulevard
P.O. Box 9609
Nashville, Tennessee 37209-1561
Phone: 615-963-5052
888-463-6878 (toll-free)
Web site: http://www.tnstate.edu

UNION UNIVERSITY

JACKSON, TENNESSEE

The University

Union University is an institution of higher learning grounded in a Christian world and life view. In the words of Union President David S. Dockery, "You will find an education characterized by rigorous academic pursuit and authentic Christian commitment—an education involving head, heart and hands."

Union alumni enjoy a high acceptance rate at top graduate schools. Nearly 100 percent of faculty-recommended health science students have been accepted to medical school or professional graduate study. More than 80 percent of all graduates are accepted by graduate schools or employed, many with Fortune 500 companies, within a month of receiving their degrees. Among Union seniors, nearly 60 percent plan to complete postgraduate work.

Union has consistently received national recognition for academic excellence and value. *U.S. News & World Report* has ranked Union in the top tier of either "Baccalaureate Colleges" or, more recently, "Best Universities–Master's" each year since 1997. Independent research by *America's 100 Best College Buys* ranks Union among the nation's best for combining academic quality and affordable price.

More than 3,300 undergraduate and graduate students attend classes in Jackson and Germantown (suburban Memphis). Forty states and thirty-five countries are represented in the student body.

On its Jackson campus, the University provides each resident a private bedroom with an Internet connection. The suites are located within apartment-style complexes with gathering areas, laundry facilities, and other services. All units have kitchens.

Location

The 290-acre campus is located in suburban Jackson, Tennessee, a growing community with a population of about 100,000. Jackson is located 80 miles east of Memphis and 120 miles west of Nashville along the I-40 corridor. Students find convenient access to entertainment, shopping, and many other services. Jackson hosts many cultural, recreational, and sporting events. Daily commercial flights are available at airports in Memphis and Nashville.

Majors and Degrees

Union students choose majors from among more than 100 programs of study. Bachelor's, master's, and doctoral degrees are offered.

Majors offered in the College of Arts and Sciences include art (ceramics/sculpture, drawing/painting, graphic design, and photography), biology (cell biology, conservation biology, general biology, and zoology), broadcasting, chemical physics, chemistry, church history, church music, computer information systems, computer science, criminal justice, digital media studies (art, communication arts, and computer science), engineering (electrical and mechanical), engineering physics, English (literature and writing), film studies, French (languages and culture or literature), history, honors studies, intercultural studies, journalism, mathematics, medical technology, music, music education, music management, music marketing, music performance, music theory, physical science, physics, political science, psychology, public relations/advertising, social work, sociology and family studies, Spanish (languages and culture or literature), sport ministry, teaching English as a second language, and theater/speech.

Majors offered in the School of Christian Studies include biblical studies, biblical languages, Christian ethics, Christian studies, church history, philosophy, sport management with sport ministry emphasis, theology, and youth ministry.

Majors offered in the McAfee School of Business Administration include accounting, business administration, economics, general business, international business, management, and marketing. The McAfee School also offers a Bachelor of Science in organizational leadership.

Majors offered in the School of Education and Human Studies include athletic training, early childhood education (learning foundations pre-K–3), elementary education (learning foundations K–6), middle school education (liberal studies 4–8), modified and comprehensive special education (K–12), physical education, physical education and health/teacher licensure, sport communication, sport management, sport marketing, sport ministry, sports medicine/exercise science, and teacher licensure for secondary areas.

The School of Nursing offers a Bachelor of Science in nursing, the accelerated B.S.N., the RN-B.S.N. completion program, and the nurse anesthesia track.

The School of Pharmacy offers a Doctor of Pharmacy degree.

Preprofessional programs include chiropractry, cytotechnology, dental hygiene, dentistry, health information management, medicine, occupational therapy, optometry, pharmacy, physical therapy, physician assistant studies, podiatry, and veterinary medicine.

Academic Programs

Union University requires those seeking a bachelor's degree to complete 46 hours of general core curriculum, 18 to 21 hours of specific core curriculum, a minimum of 30 hours in the major academic program, and 18 hours in the minor academic program. The completion of the required 128 hours usually requires four years, with 32 hours per year.

For each undergraduate degree granted, at least 25 percent of the required semester hours must be earned through instruction at Union University. The last 56 semester hours of credit for a bachelor's degree must be earned at an accredited senior college.

The academic calendar is divided into fall (August to December) and spring (February to May) semesters, January term, and three summer terms. Evening accelerated courses are available each term.

Off-Campus Programs

Union offers study-abroad programs throughout the world and short-term international projects. The University affiliates with several organizations in offering numerous cross-discipline selections.

Yanbian University of Science and Technology, which ranks among China's top 100 universities, partners with Union in an exchange of students and visiting professors.

Global Outreach (GO) trips occur during school breaks. Students work in teams on mission service projects regionally, nationally, and internationally. Recently, for example, Union engineering students conducted a feasibility study on solar energy in rural North Africa.

Although students work and study all over the world, they also invest time serving the local community. Each fall, the entire campus shuts down for a day so students, faculty members, and staff members can complete service projects throughout West Tennessee. These efforts receive national recognition; Union is listed on the President's Higher Education Community Service Honor Roll.

Academic Facilities

During the past decade, Union has invested more than $62 million in campus improvements. Additions include a 64,000-square-foot science building, an athletic field house, and two other major classroom buildings. New on-campus housing and a banquet facility are under construction.

Union provides more than 300 computers for student use, with full access to e-mail and the Internet. In addition, each residential student has a port for the campus network and Internet access in their private bedroom. Wireless access is available in many areas on campus.

The Emma Waters Summar Library has immediate access to a collection of more than 150,000 books, 19,000 e-journals, and 40,000 e-books. Through its membership in cooperatives, there is easy access to the combined collections of over 41,000 libraries worldwide. The library provides knowledgeable reference service, in-depth research assistance, personalized training, and group instructional sessions to facilitate the effective use of these resources. It also maintains a safe, comfortable environment for both individual and group study.

Other academic amenities include top-quality lecture facilities, fine and performing arts practice rooms, theaters, broadcast studios, digital media labs, and science laboratories. Union is among a small group of nursing schools in the region training students with human patient simulators.

Costs

The cost for a typical student for the 2008–09 academic year is $18,980 in tuition (up to 16 hours per semester), $4900 for housing in an apartment-style residence hall, $2360 for meals (150 meals per semester), and $630 for the student services fee. These costs, excluding books, total $26,870 per academic year. Prices for housing and meals may vary slightly according to a student's preferences.

Financial Aid

More than 90 percent of Union students receive some financial aid based on need or merit. Union commits very competitive scholarships and grants to qualified students. The University helps connect students with other financial resources such as loans, student-work programs, privately funded scholarships, and a host of state and federal assistance programs.

Faculty

The faculty members at Union put a priority on classroom teaching but also join students in the pursuit of significant research, especially at the undergraduate level. Among full-time faculty members, more than 83 percent hold doctorates or the highest degree offered in their field of study. Classes at Union are small, with a student-faculty ratio of 11:1.

Faculty members also serve as student advisers. Advisers are assigned within the department of the student's major. Faculty advisers assist students in planning schedules and defining educational and career goals. The student and adviser meet at least once each semester.

Student Government

Union's Student Government Association (SGA), composed of all students enrolled in Union University, functions through its executive, legislative, and judicial branches. Its elected officers and representatives serve as the official voice of the students in institutional affairs. The SGA seeks to foster University unity, promote student welfare, and provide students with programs, activities, and services designed to meet their needs and interests.

Admission Requirements

Applicants must graduate from an accredited high school with at least 20 units in the areas of English, foreign language, mathematics, social and natural sciences, and approved electives. In addition, students who qualify for unconditional admission must meet or exceed two of the following three admissions criteria: a 2.5 core GPA, a composite score of 22 on the ACT or 1020 (math and critical reading combined) on the SAT, and a ranking in the top 50 percent of their high school class. Union also actively admits home-schooled students. A state high school equivalency diploma is accepted in lieu of a high school diploma.

Transfer students who have completed at least 24 semester hours of transferable credit at an accredited college may also apply. Transfer students with less than 24 semester hours must meet freshman and transfer admission requirements. Transfer students must have at least a 2.3 cumulative GPA to qualify for unconditional admission.

Applicants must complete and return the Union University application for undergraduate admission along with the $35 application fee. All official transcripts must be requested and mailed directly to the Office of Undergraduate Admissions. Results of either the ACT or SAT must also be sent. For detailed admission requirements, students should contact the Office of Undergraduate Admissions.

Application and Information

For more information or to request an application, students should contact:

Office of Undergraduate Admissions
Union University
1050 Union University Drive
Jackson, Tennessee 38305-3697
Phone: 731-661-5100
800-33-UNION (toll-free)
E-mail: info@uu.edu
Web site: http://www.uu.edu

A night view of West Campus.

UNIVERSITY OF MEMPHIS
MEMPHIS, TENNESSEE

The University

Located on a beautifully landscaped campus in the heart of one of the South's largest and most progressive cities, the University of Memphis (U of M) is the flagship institution of the Tennessee Board of Regents System. Since its beginning in 1912, the University of Memphis has matured into a major public, metropolitan university recognized regionally and nationally for its academic, research, and athletic programs. The University offers more than 254 areas of study from which to choose.

The University campus comprises 1,160 acres at eight sites. In addition to the main campus, the Park Avenue campus contains spacious living accommodations for married students, a research park, and outstanding varsity athletic training facilities. The University of Memphis also owns the Meeman Biological Field Station, a 623-acre tract used for biological and ecological studies. The Chucalissa Archaeological Museum in southwest Memphis is frequently used as a research and training facility in archaeology and anthropology.

The University of Memphis is an Equal Opportunity/Affirmative Action institution committed to the education of a diverse student body. It has a total enrollment of 20,379 students, including 15,802 undergraduates, from almost every state and many other countries. Approximately 45 percent of University of Memphis students are between the ages of 18 and 22, and members of minority groups account for 44 percent of the enrollment.

Location

The greater Memphis area has a population of approximately 1.1 million, which makes the city the twenty-fourth largest in the country. Centrally located on the Mississippi River, Memphis is an active hub for business, agriculture, and the transportation industry. The city has the mid-South's largest medical center and offers many cultural and entertainment opportunities. Major museum exhibits, sporting events, concerts, art shows, lectures, and even barbecue contests take place throughout the year. The AAA baseball team, the Redbirds, and the NBA team, the Grizzlies, both make their homes in Memphis. With its many businesses, industries, and schools, Memphis provides students with employment opportunities in a variety of fields during and after their college careers.

Majors and Degrees

The College of Arts and Sciences offers undergraduate majors organized into three concentration groups: the humanities, the natural and mathematical sciences, and the social sciences. Three degree programs are offered: the Bachelor of Arts, the Bachelor of Science, and the Bachelor of Science in Chemistry. Majors include African and African American studies, anthropology, biology, chemistry, computer science, criminology and criminal justice, earth sciences, economics, English, foreign languages and literatures, history, international studies, mathematical sciences, philosophy, physics, political science, psychology, social work, and sociology. Minors are available in each of those areas—as well as interdisciplinary minors in aerospace studies, Asian studies, environmental studies, Judaic studies, legal thought and liberal studies, military science, naval science, nonprofit management studies, public administration, and women's studies.

The Fogelman College of Business & Economics offers programs of study leading to the Bachelor of Business Administration degree. Majors include accounting, business economics, finance, hospitality and resort management, international business, management, management information systems, marketing management, sales, and logistics/supply chain management. The programs of the College of Business & Economics are fully accredited by AACSB International–The Association to Advance Collegiate Schools of Business.

The College of Communication and Fine Arts is made up of the Departments of Art, Communication, Journalism, Theatre and Dance, and the Rudi E. Scheidt School of Music. Majors include architecture, art, art history, communication, journalism, music, music industry, and theater. The college offers three undergraduate degrees: the Bachelor of Arts, the Bachelor of Fine Arts, and the Bachelor of Music.

The leading producer of teachers in Tennessee, the College of Education at the University of Memphis is among a select few nationwide to meet, without a weakness, National Council for the Accreditation of Teacher Education standards. In addition to teacher education, the College offers accredited degree programs in health and sport sciences, health and leisure management, and dietetics. College of Education faculty members serve the community through more than 1,000 days of direct service annually and a rigorous research agenda.

The Herff College of Engineering offers undergraduate programs in biomedical, civil, computer, electrical, and mechanical engineering and in computer, electronics, and manufacturing engineering technology. High-ability students have the opportunity to work with faculty members on world-class research for global companies such as FedEx, for governmental organizations such as the U.S. Army Corp of Engineers, or for other premier organizations such as St. Jude Children's Research Hospital.

The University College offers two nontraditional degrees: the Bachelor of Liberal Studies and the Bachelor of Professional Studies, for students with experience, talents, and interests served through personally designed or multidisciplinary programs. Examples of programs that have been developed include alcohol and drug abuse services, biomedical illustration, commercial aviation, correctional administration, family and consumer studies, fashion and home furnishings merchandising, fire administration and fire prevention technology, health services administration, human services, information technology, organizational leadership, law enforcement administration, paralegal studies, preschool and child-care administration, and religion in society.

The University of Memphis also offers specialized degree programs. The Loewenberg School of Nursing offers a Bachelor of Science in Nursing degree. The program is accredited by the National League for Nursing Accrediting Commission and the Commission on Collegiate Education in Nursing. Students benefit from exceptional learning opportunities at health-care agencies in the Memphis area, including ten major hospitals.

Preprofessional training is offered for students who intend to enter law school or a college of dentistry, medicine, nursing, optometry, pharmacy, physical therapy, or veterinary medicine. The University also offers Air Force, Army, and Navy ROTC programs.

The University of Memphis has joined forty-five Tennessee Board of Regents institutions in offering Regents Online Degree Programs. The U of M offers two degree programs: the Bachelor of Professional Studies in information technology or organizational leadership and the Bachelor of Interdisciplinary Studies in general studies, liberal studies, or university studies. These degree programs are entirely online and are transferable among the participating institutions.

Academic Programs

Many freshmen are advised through the Academic Counseling Unit of the Center for Student Development in preparation for formal enrollment in one of the degree-granting colleges. In addition to meeting the requirements for a specific degree, as established by the appropriate college or department, each student initially selects courses from broad offerings in the areas of communication skills, sciences, humanities, and social sciences, thereby ensuring the acquisition of breadth as well as depth of knowledge in various fields. A University-wide Honors Program is available for academically talented students, and there is an active Emerging Leaders program. Some entering freshmen are assigned to their degree-granting college immediately for academic advising.

The academic year begins in late August and is divided into two semesters and a summer session. The fall semester ends in mid-December, and the spring semester begins in mid-January. There are also courses offered during shorter sessions within the semesters.

Off-Campus Programs

The University of Memphis participates in both the International and National Student Exchange Programs, allowing students to study in other countries as well as in other areas in the continental United States. The University also offers credit and noncredit courses at various locations throughout west Tennessee.

Academic Facilities

The University of Memphis' Ned R. McWherter Library provides one of the most electronically up-to-date information repositories within hundreds of miles. Students are able to tap into information stored in libraries around the world. Library collections contain more than 13 million items, which include monographs, periodical volumes, federal and state documents, maps, and manuscripts. The University also provides state-of-the-art computing facilities for student and faculty use, including a collaborative Learning Commons in the library with over 100 computer workstations and another sixty-plus seats in the TigerLAN Lab, both of which are open 24 hours a day, seven days a week. Fifty-five additional labs with more than 1,049 PC and Mac workstations and 210 smart classrooms complement the University's teaching and research activities. In addition, all academic buildings offer wireless Internet access.

The Department of Theatre and Dance and the Rudi E. Scheidt School of Music, in their adjoining facilities, make an appreciable contribution to campus activities with live drama and concert series, films, and programming over WUMR, the campus radio station.

Included among the many research facilities at the University of Memphis are the Benjamin L. Hooks Institute for Social Change, the Integrated Microscopy Center, the FedEx Center for Supply Chain Management, the Institute for Artificial Intelligence, the Ground Water Institute, and the Barbara K. Lipman Early Childhood School and Research Institute. The FedEx Institute of Technology, which opened in 2003, is a cutting-edge facility that brings together students, professors, researchers, and the global business community to formulate the ideas and products of tomorrow.

The state of Tennessee has designated five Centers of Excellence at the University: the Center for Applied Psychological Research, the Center for Research Initiatives and Strategies for the Communicatively Impaired, the Center for Research in Educational Policy, the Institute of Egyptian Art and Archaeology, and the Center for Earthquake Research and Information. In addition, the University houses twenty-four endowed Chairs of Excellence.

Costs

In 2007–08, in-state students paid a maintenance fee of $2326 per semester for full-time study or $196 per semester hour for part-time study. Out-of-state students were assessed fees of $7740 per semester (full-time) or $649 per semester hour (part-time). On-campus residence hall rates ranged from $2710 to $5290 for an academic year. All part-time students pay an additional program service fee of $77 per hour for part-time study or $575 per semester.

Financial Aid

Financial assistance is provided through four basic sources: scholarships, grants, loans, and employment. Scholarships are offered through the Scholarship Office as well as through various academic, performance, and athletic departments. Residents of Tennessee may be eligible for the state's HOPE Scholarship. An application for admission is required to be considered for general and distinguished academic scholarship programs. Applicants for financial aid must submit the completed Free Application for Federal Student Aid (FAFSA) to the Financial Aid Office, which places the student under consideration for all financial aid programs. More than $150 million is awarded annually. The University operates two programs of student employment: the Federal Work-Study Program and a regular work program.

Faculty

The University of Memphis has 926 ranked faculty members. In addition, many adjunct professors are hired from the community to teach in their fields of expertise.

Student Government

The Student Government Association consists of officers, a senate, a cabinet, and a judiciary elected annually by the student body. Its goals are to present the opinions of the student body to the administration, to enact legislation beneficial to the students, and to promote a broad range of student activities.

Admission Requirements

The admission of entering freshmen is based on the transcript of a four-year course of study at an approved or accredited high school that includes prescribed units of English, mathematics, natural/physical sciences, U.S. history, social studies, foreign language, and visual/performing arts. The General Educational Development test and high school equivalency diploma are accepted when applicable. An Admission Index is calculated by first multiplying the cumulative high school GPA by 30 and then adding the ACT composite score. Applicants under 21 years of age who meet all other requirements, including high school graduation and the mandated curriculum, and whose Admission Index is 95 or greater are granted admission. The admission of transfer students is based on the applicant's quality point average, academic standing at a former institution, and scores on the approved admission tests.

Application and Information

Inquiries about admission and requests for information about any undergraduate college of the University should be addressed to the Office of Admissions. Applications and supporting credentials must be submitted to the Office of Admissions before the beginning of the intended term of entry. While the established application deadlines are July 1 for the fall semester, December 1 for the spring semester, and May 1 for the summer session, early application is strongly encouraged to be considered for scholarship opportunities and to take advantage of early registration. Registration for fall classes occurs at New Student Orientation. Prospective students are encouraged to visit the University for a campus tour, which can be arranged by contacting the Office of Admissions.

Office of Admissions
Recruitment and Orientation Services
University of Memphis
101 John Wilder Tower
Memphis, Tennessee 38152-3520
Phone: 901-678-2169
800-669-2678 (toll-free)
Web site: http://www.memphis.edu

The McWherter Library.

VANDERBILT UNIVERSITY

NASHVILLE, TENNESSEE

The University

In 1873, on the heels of the Civil War, Commodore Cornelius Vanderbilt gave a million dollars to the university that now bears his name, with the hope that it would "contribute to strengthening the ties which should exist between all sections of our common country." Today, Vanderbilt enrolls America's most talented students and challenges them daily to expand their intellectual horizons and to free their imaginations. Dialogue, service, the Honor Code, the search for knowledge, and personal fulfillment are all hallmarks of a Vanderbilt education.

Vanderbilt is a medium-sized university that includes four undergraduate schools and six graduate and professional schools. Each year, 1,600 first-year students join the University, bringing the total undergraduate population to approximately 6,400 students. The total enrollment at Vanderbilt is 11,480.

Known for the Southern splendor of its 330-acre, national arboretum campus, Vanderbilt provides a variety of housing options for its undergraduates, all of whom live on campus all four years. First-year students live in The Commons, a collection of new and newly renovated residence halls, or houses, clustered along one side of campus. Each house includes faculty apartments, and a new dining center with study space, a post office, and an exercise facility sits nearby. One of Vanderbilt's unique housing options is the McTyeire International House, which is designed for students who are interested in a range of foreign languages, such as Chinese, French, German, Japanese, and Spanish. Other on-campus options include traditional dormitories, apartments, and suites.

The Sarratt Student Center houses a cinema, a pub, meeting rooms, an art gallery, craft and darkroom facilities, and an FM radio station. Facilities at the Student Recreation Center include gymnasiums, an indoor swimming pool, squash and racquetball courts, a rock climbing wall, an indoor suspended track, and a weight room. Other facilities include indoor and outdoor tennis courts, baseball and softball diamonds, and a sand volleyball court.

Location

Vanderbilt University is located in Nashville, the capital of Tennessee. Known as Music City, USA, Nashville is a vibrant city of more than 1 million residents. The greater Nashville area is home to two major-league professional sports teams, eighty-one parks, and more than 30,000 acres of lakes. Three interstate highways intersect the city, and its international airport is served by seventeen airlines.

Majors and Degrees

The B.A., B.S., B.E., or B.M. degree is offered in African American and Diaspora studies; American studies; Ancient Mediterranean studies; anthropology; art; biological sciences; biomedical engineering; chemical engineering; chemistry; child development; child studies; civil engineering; classical languages; classics; cognitive studies; communication of science and technology; communication studies; comparative literature; computer engineering; computer science; early childhood education; earth and environmental sciences; East Asian studies; ecology, evolution, and organismal biology; economics; economics and history; electrical engineering; elementary education; engineering science; English; English and history; European studies; film studies; French; French and European studies; German; German studies; history; history of art; human and organizational development; Jewish studies; Latin American and Iberian studies; mathematics; mechanical engineering; medicine, health, and society; molecular and cellular biology; musical arts; musical arts/teacher education track; music composition and theory; music performance; neuroscience; philosophy; physics and astronomy; political science; psychology; public policy studies; religious studies; Russian; Russian and European studies; Russian studies; secondary education; sociology; Spanish; Spanish and European studies; Spanish and Portuguese; Spanish, Portuguese, and European studies; special education; theater; women's and gender studies; and individually designed majors.

Academic Programs

Students apply directly to one of the four schools that offer undergraduate programs: the College of Arts and Science, the School of Engineering, Peabody College (education and human development), or the Blair School of Music. In all four schools, honors programs and opportunities for independent study and internships are available. Vanderbilt University operates on a two-semester calendar, and classes begin in late August. First-semester examinations take place prior to the winter holidays, and the second semester ends in early May. A variety of courses are offered during Maymester and two summer sessions.

The College of Arts and Science provides many opportunities to experience a wide range of academic disciplines and subjects. Within the requirements of the AXLE (Achieving eXcellence in Liberal Education) curriculum, students refine their skills in writing, mathematics, foreign language, the humanities, natural sciences, social sciences, history, and culture.

The Blair School of Music offers the Bachelor of Music degree in composition and theory, musical arts, musical arts/teacher education, and performance. Instruction is available in every instrument of the orchestra as well as piano, organ, euphonium, multiple woodwinds, saxophone, classical guitar, and voice. Unlike many schools of music, Blair has no graduate students. The curriculum combines intensive musical training with liberal arts studies. Approximately one third of a student's work is outside of music. The Blair School also offers a music minor and a wide variety of courses, private instruction, and performing organizations for nonmajors.

For more than 125 years, the School of Engineering has educated engineers for practice in industry, government, consulting, teaching, and research careers. In addition to technical courses, each student's program includes a rich complement of course work in the humanities and social sciences, resulting in a balanced foundation for future achievement and the assumption of leadership roles in their chosen fields. All programs leading to a Bachelor of Engineering degree are ABET-accredited.

Peabody College offers degree programs leading to teacher certification and to careers in other areas of education, child development, cognitive studies, and human and organizational development. The degree reflects a strong liberal arts foundation combined with a solid program of preprofessional courses and a multitude of internship and practicum opportunities. All undergraduates must complete requirements in communication, the humanities, mathematics, the natural sciences, and the social sciences. Students have an abundance of field experiences throughout their four years.

Off-Campus Programs

Study-abroad programs allow students to immerse themselves in the languages and cultures of other countries. More than sixty programs are offered in Argentina, Australia, Austria, Brazil, Chile, China, the Czech Republic, Denmark, the Dominican Republic, England, France, Germany, Ireland, Italy, Japan, Mexico, New Zealand, Russia, Scotland, South Africa, South Korea, and Spain. Vanderbilt students receive direct credit for their courses, and the cost of tuition is usually the same as for study on campus in Nashville. In addition, any scholarships, grants, or loans a student has been awarded apply to Vanderbilt study-abroad programs. Students may also participate in programs sponsored by other universities by working with their adviser.

Academic Facilities

Students and faculty members take advantage of Vanderbilt's extensive library resources, obtaining easy access to books, periodicals, documents, microforms, and reference materials. The Jean and Alexander Heard Library is supported by nine major resource centers, which include special collections, University Archives, and more than 3.2 million volumes.

Costs

The costs for 2007–08 were: tuition, $34,414; room and board, $11,446; books and supplies, $1140; and the student activities and recreation fee, $864. All costs are subject to change. They are slightly higher for students in the School of Engineering.

Financial Aid

Approximately 60 percent of the University's undergraduate students receive some type of financial aid. Need-based aid is awarded according to the evaluation of the FAFSA and the CSS/Financial Aid PROFILE. Vanderbilt provides assistance through Federal Pell Grants, Federal Supplemental Educational Opportunity Grants, state grants, University scholarships, Federal Stafford Student Loans, institutional loans, Federal Perkins Loans, and Federal Work-Study Program employment. Information on these and other programs can be obtained from the Office of Student Financial Aid, 2309 West End Avenue, Nashville, Tennessee 37203-1725. In addition, approximately 10 percent of each year's entering class is awarded an honor scholarship based on academic merit.

Faculty

Vanderbilt has 2,527 full-time faculty members and a part-time faculty of 334. All undergraduate faculty members, many of whom hold awards for distinguished scholarship, are required to teach undergraduates. A low student-faculty ratio of 9:1 provides for an intimate academic experience between students and professors who are recognized nationally and worldwide for their research. The average class size is 19.

Student Government

The Vanderbilt Student Government provides students with an opportunity to participate actively in maintaining the high quality of life on campus. It works with many of the more than 300 student organizations to bring nationally prominent speakers to the campus and provide an interesting and diverse array of programming throughout the year. A vital part of life at Vanderbilt is the honor system, which is governed entirely by students through representatives on the Honor Council. Each year, a senior is selected as a Young Alumni Trustee of the University's Board of Trust.

Admission Requirements

Vanderbilt seeks students with high standards of scholarship and character. Admission is based on a thorough review of academic and personal credentials.

Students must submit a minimum of 15 academic units at the secondary level, although most admitted students present 20 or more academic units. Applicants to the College of Arts and Science must present a minimum of 2 years of a foreign language; applicants to the School of Engineering are strongly encouraged to take both calculus and physics in high school. The Admissions Committee evaluates each student's secondary school academic record, extracurricular involvement, counselor and teacher recommendations, and personal essay. Students must also submit scores (including the writing subscore) from either the SAT Reasoning Test or the ACT. Applicants to the Blair School of Music must also audition on their primary instrument. A personal audition is preferred, but applicants may audition by videotape with permission from the Blair School of Music.

Campus visits are recommended, though student interest is not used as a measure of admissibility. Prospective students should call in advance of their visit for information about group information sessions, campus tours, and opportunities to attend classes.

Application and Information

Students whose first choice is Vanderbilt may apply under one of Vanderbilt's early decision plans. Applications and all supporting materials must be postmarked by November 1 for Early Decision I and by January 3 for Early Decision II; notification is made by December 15 for Early Decision I and by February 15 for Early Decision II. The deadline for applying under the regular decision plan is January 3. Students are informed of the admission decision by April 1. Personal auditions are scheduled in December, January, and February for students applying to the Blair School of Music. Students seeking transfer admission must submit an application and all supporting materials no later than March 1; Vanderbilt only offers fall semester entry for transfer students.

Office of Undergraduate Admissions
Vanderbilt University
2305 West End Avenue
Nashville, Tennessee 37203-1727
Phone: 615-322-2561
800-288-0432 (toll-free)
E-mail: admissions@vanderbilt.edu
Web site: http://www.vanderbilt.edu/admissions

TEXAS

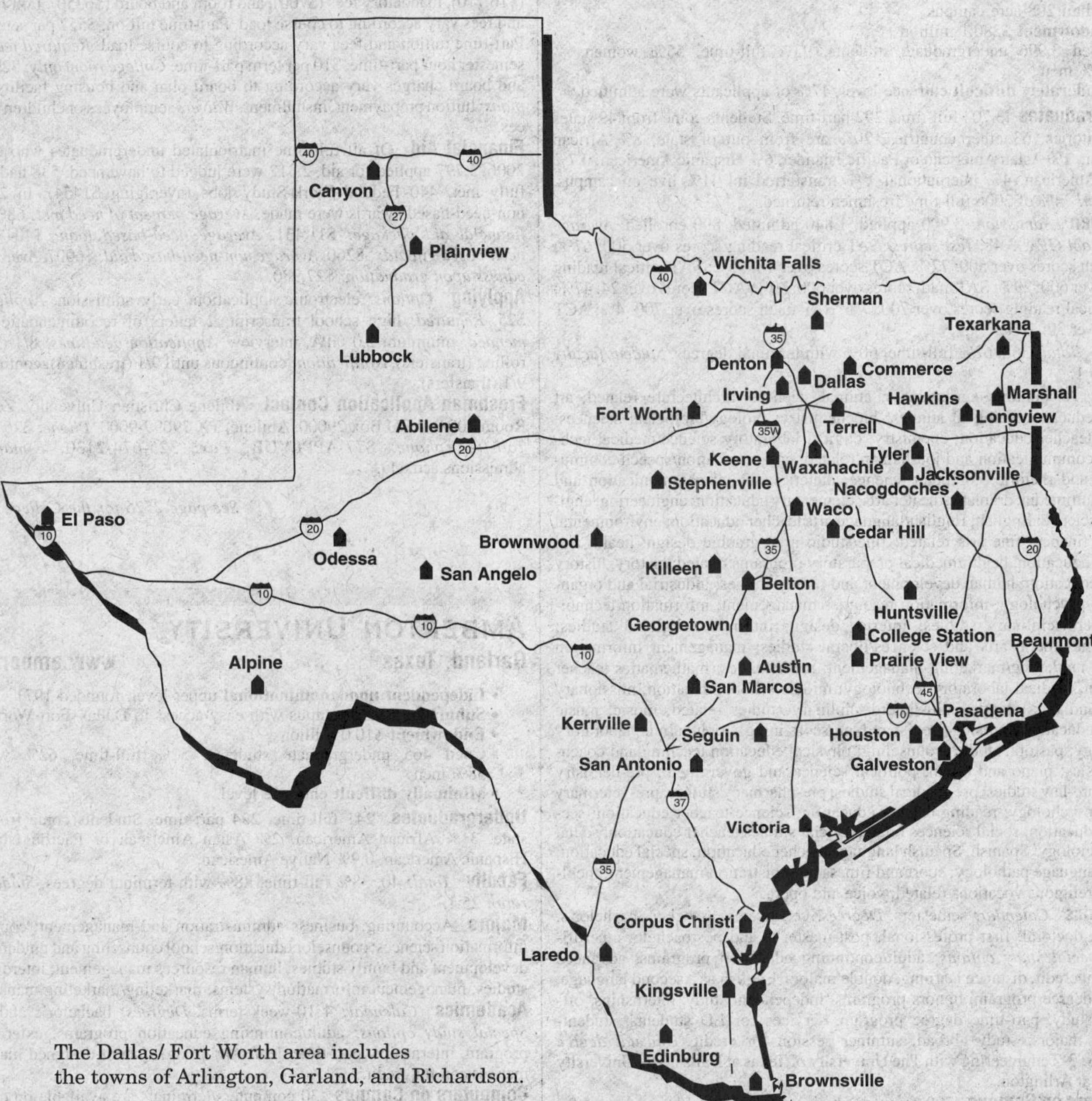

The Dallas/ Fort Worth area includes the towns of Arlington, Garland, and Richardson.

ABILENE CHRISTIAN UNIVERSITY

Abilene, Texas www.acu.edu/

- **Independent** comprehensive, founded 1906, affiliated with Church of Christ
- **Urban** 208-acre campus
- **Endowment** $280.1 million
- **Coed** 3,996 undergraduate students, 93% full-time, 55% women, 45% men
- **Moderately difficult** entrance level, 47% of applicants were admitted

Undergraduates 3,704 full-time, 292 part-time. Students come from 49 states and territories, 63 other countries, 20% are from out of state, 8% African American, 1% Asian American or Pacific Islander, 6% Hispanic American, 0.7% Native American, 4% international, 5% transferred in, 41% live on campus. *Retention:* 74% of 2006 full-time freshmen returned.

Freshmen *Admission:* 3,900 applied, 1,840 admitted, 890 enrolled. *Average high school GPA:* 3.48. *Test scores:* SAT critical reading scores over 500: 67%; SAT math scores over 500: 72%; ACT scores over 18: 95%; SAT critical reading scores over 600: 29%; SAT math scores over 600: 30%; ACT scores over 24: 47%; SAT critical reading scores over 700: 7%; SAT math scores over 700: 4%; ACT scores over 30: 11%.

Faculty *Total:* 368, 62% full-time, 60% with terminal degrees. *Student/faculty ratio:* 15:1.

Majors Accounting; agribusiness; animal sciences; architecture related; art teacher education; biblical studies; biochemistry; biology/biological sciences; biology teacher education; chemistry; clinical laboratory science/medical technology; communication and journalism related; communication/speech communication and rhetoric; computer science; dietetics; digital communication and media/multimedia; dramatic/theater arts; elementary education; engineering; engineering science; English; English/language arts teacher education; environmental science; finance; fine arts related; fine/studio arts; graphic design; health and physical education; health/medical preparatory programs related; history; history teacher education; human development and family studies; industrial and organizational psychology; information resources management; information technology; interdisciplinary studies; interior design; international/global studies; journalism; liberal arts and sciences/liberal studies; management information systems; marketing/marketing management; mathematics; mathematics teacher education; medical laboratory technology; middle school education; missionary studies and missiology; multi-/interdisciplinary studies related; music; music teacher education; nursing (registered nurse training); ophthalmic laboratory technology; pastoral studies/counseling; physical education teaching and coaching; physics; piano and organ; political science and government; pre-dentistry studies; pre-law studies; pre-medical studies; pre-pharmacy studies; pre-veterinary studies; psychology; reading teacher education; science teacher education; secondary education; social sciences related; social studies teacher education; social work; sociology; Spanish; Spanish language teacher education; special education; speech-language pathology; sport and fitness administration/management; theology and religious vocations related; voice and opera.

Academics *Calendar:* semesters. *Degrees:* certificates, associate, bachelor's, master's, doctoral, first professional, post-master's, and postbachelor's certificates. *Special study options:* adult/continuing education programs, advanced placement credit, distance learning, double majors, English as a second language, external degree program, honors programs, independent study, internships, off-campus study, part-time degree program, services for LD students, student-designed majors, study abroad, summer session for credit. *Unusual degree programs:* 3-2 engineering with The University of Texas at Dallas, The University of Texas at Arlington.

Computers on Campus 700 computers/terminals are available on campus for general student use. Students can access the following: campus intranet, computer help desk, free student e-mail accounts, online (class) grades, online (class) registration, online (class) schedules. Campuswide network is available. 97% of college-owned or -operated housing units are wired for high-speed Internet access. Wireless service is available via classrooms, computer labs, libraries.

Student Life *Housing:* on-campus residence required through sophomore year. *Options:* men-only, women-only. Campus housing is university owned. Freshman campus housing is guaranteed. *Activities and organizations:* drama/theater group, student-run newspaper, radio and television station, choral group, marching band, Student Association, Alpha Phi Omega, "W" Club, Spring Break Campaign, Student Alumni Association. *Campus security:* 24-hour emergency response devices and patrols, student patrols, late-night transport/escort service, controlled dormitory access. *Student services:* health clinic, personal/psychological counseling.

Athletics Member NCAA. All Division II. *Intercollegiate sports:* baseball M (s), basketball M (s)/W (s), cross-country running M (s)/W (s), football M (s), golf M (s), rugby M/W, soccer M (c)/W (s), softball W (s), tennis M (s)/W (s), track and field M (s)/W (s), volleyball W (s). *Intramural sports:* badminton M/W, basketball M/W, bowling M/W, cross-country running M/W, football M/W, racquetball M/W, rugby M/W, soccer M/W, softball M/W, table tennis M/W, tennis M/W, track and field M/W, volleyball M/W, water polo M.

Standardized Tests *Required:* SAT or ACT (for admission).

Costs (2007–08) *Comprehensive fee:* $23,760 includes full-time tuition ($16,710), mandatory fees ($700), and room and board ($6350). Full-time tuition and fees vary according to course load. Part-time tuition: $557 per semester hour. Part-time tuition and fees vary according to course load. *Required fees:* $34 per semester hour part-time, $10 per term part-time. *College room only:* $2950. Room and board charges vary according to board plan and housing facility. *Payment plans:* tuition prepayment, installment. *Waivers:* employees or children of employees.

Financial Aid Of all full-time matriculated undergraduates who enrolled in 2006, 3,797 applied for aid, 2,312 were judged to have need, 538 had their need fully met. 440 Federal Work-Study jobs (averaging $1454). In 2006, 1118 non-need-based awards were made. *Average percent of need met:* 68%. *Average financial aid package:* $11,431. *Average need-based loan:* $4047. *Average need-based gift aid:* $8260. *Average non-need-based aid:* $6007. *Average indebtedness upon graduation:* $27,980.

Applying *Options:* electronic application, early admission. *Application fee:* $25. *Required:* high school transcript, 2 letters of recommendation. *Recommended:* minimum 2.0 GPA, interview. *Application deadlines:* 8/1 (freshmen), rolling (transfers). *Notification:* continuous until 9/1 (freshmen), continuous until 9/1 (transfers).

Freshman Application Contact Abilene Christian University, Zellner Hall Room 200A, ACU Box 29000, Abilene, TX 79699-9000. *Phone:* 325-674-2650. *Toll-free phone:* 877-APPLYUB. *Fax:* 325-674-2130. *E-mail:* info@admissions.acu.edu.

See page 2526 for the College Close-Up.

AMBERTON UNIVERSITY

Garland, Texas www.amberton.edu/

- **Independent nondenominational** upper-level, founded 1971
- **Suburban** 5-acre campus with easy access to Dallas–Fort Worth
- **Endowment** $10.0 million
- **Coed** 465 undergraduate students, 52% full-time, 62% women, 38% men
- **Minimally difficult** entrance level

Undergraduates 241 full-time, 224 part-time. Students come from 1 other state, 31% African American, 2% Asian American or Pacific Islander, 7% Hispanic American, 0.9% Native American.

Faculty *Total:* 40, 38% full-time, 88% with terminal degrees. *Student/faculty ratio:* 25:1.

Majors Accounting; business administration and management; computer and information sciences; counselor education/school counseling and guidance; human development and family studies; human resources management; interdisciplinary studies; management information systems; marketing/marketing management.

Academics *Calendar:* 4 10-week terms. *Degrees:* bachelor's and master's. *Special study options:* adult/continuing education programs, external degree program, internships, part-time degree program, student-designed majors, summer session for credit.

Computers on Campus 30 computers/terminals are available on campus for general student use. Students can access the following: campus intranet, computer help desk, free student e-mail accounts, online (class) schedules.

Student Life *Housing:* college housing not available. *Campus security:* 24-hour emergency response devices and patrols.

Costs (2008–09) *Tuition:* $6750 full-time.

Applying *Options:* deferred entrance. *Application deadline:* rolling (transfers). *Notification:* continuous (transfers).

Application Contact Dr. Don Hebbard, Academic Dean, Amberton University, 1700 Eastgate Drive, Garland, TX 75041-5595. *Phone:* 972-279-6511. *E-mail:* advisor@amberton.edu.

AMERICAN INTERCONTINENTAL UNIVERSITY

Houston, Texas **www.aiuniv.edu/**

- **Proprietary** comprehensive, founded 2003, administratively affiliated with American InterContinental University
- **Coed**
- **Minimally difficult** entrance level

Majors Animation, interactive technology, video graphics and special effects; audiovisual communications technologies related; business administration and management; computer and information sciences; computer graphics; computer/information technology services administration related; design and visual communications; graphic design; information technology; marketing/marketing management; small business administration.

Academics *Calendar:* five 10-week terms. *Degrees:* associate, bachelor's, and master's.

Student Life *Activities and organizations:* student-run newspaper. *Student services:* personal/psychological counseling.

Costs (2008–09) *Tuition:* contact campus for information. See: www.aiuniv.edu.

Applying *Options:* electronic application, deferred entrance. *Application fee:* $50. *Required:* essay or personal statement, high school transcript, interview, TOEFL for students whose first language is not English. *Application deadlines:* rolling (freshmen), rolling (transfers). *Notification:* continuous (freshmen), continuous (transfers).

Director of Admissions Director of Admissions, American InterContinental University, 9999 Richmond Avenue, Houston, TX 77042. *Phone:* 832-201-3600. *Toll-free phone:* 888-607-9888.

ANGELO STATE UNIVERSITY

San Angelo, Texas **www.angelo.edu/**

- **State-supported** comprehensive, founded 1928, part of Texas State University System
- **Urban** 268-acre campus
- **Coed** 5,809 undergraduate students, 84% full-time, 55% women, 45% men
- **Moderately difficult** entrance level, 99% of applicants were admitted

Undergraduates 4,901 full-time, 908 part-time. Students come from 39 states and territories, 18 other countries, 3% are from out of state, 7% African American, 1% Asian American or Pacific Islander, 24% Hispanic American, 0.6% Native American, 0.9% international, 7% transferred in, 31% live on campus. *Retention:* 59% of 2006 full-time freshmen returned.

Freshmen *Admission:* 3,268 applied, 3,236 admitted, 1,475 enrolled. *Test scores:* SAT critical reading scores over 500: 36%; SAT math scores over 500: 42%; SAT writing scores over 500: 34%; ACT scores over 18: 50%; SAT critical reading scores over 600: 7%; SAT math scores over 600: 11%; SAT writing scores over 600: 6%; ACT scores over 24: 13%; SAT critical reading scores over 700: 1%; ACT scores over 30: 1%.

Faculty *Total:* 348, 69% full-time, 56% with terminal degrees. *Student/faculty ratio:* 20:1.

Majors Accounting; animal sciences; art; athletic training; biochemistry; biological and physical sciences; biology/biological sciences; business administration and management; chemistry; clinical laboratory science/medical technology; communication/speech communication and rhetoric; computer and information sciences; criminal justice/safety; dramatic/theater arts; ecology, evolution, systematics and population biology related; English; finance; fine/studio arts; French; general studies; German; health and physical education; history; interdisciplinary studies; journalism; liberal arts and sciences/liberal studies; management information systems; marketing/marketing management; mathematics; multi-/interdisciplinary studies related; music; physics; physics related; political science and government; psychology; real estate; social sciences; sociology; Spanish; visual and performing arts.

Academics *Calendar:* semesters. *Degrees:* associate, bachelor's, and master's. *Special study options:* academic remediation for entering students, advanced placement credit, distance learning, double majors, honors programs, independent study, internships, part-time degree program, study abroad, summer session for credit. *ROTC:* Air Force (b). *Unusual degree programs:* 3-2 engineering with University of Texas at El Paso, Texas A&M University; agriculture education with Texas A&M University.

Computers on Campus 700 computers/terminals are available on campus for general student use. Students can access the following: computer help desk, free student e-mail accounts, online (class) grades, online (class) registration, online (class) schedules. Campuswide network is available. 100% of college-owned or -operated housing units are wired for high-speed Internet access. Wireless service is available via classrooms, computer centers, computer labs, dorm rooms, learning centers, libraries, student centers.

Student Life *Housing:* on-campus residence required through sophomore year. *Options:* coed, women-only, disabled students. Campus housing is university owned. Freshman applicants given priority for college housing. *Activities and organizations:* drama/theater group, student-run newspaper, radio and television station, choral group, marching band, Block and Bridle Club, Baptist Student Union, Delta Sigma Pi, Air Force ROTC, Association of Mexican-American Students, national fraternities, national sororities. *Campus security:* 24-hour emergency response devices and patrols, student patrols, late-night transport/escort service, controlled dormitory access. *Student services:* health clinic, personal/psychological counseling.

Athletics Member NCAA, NAIA. All NCAA Division II. *Intercollegiate sports:* baseball M (s), basketball M (s)/W (s), cross-country running M (s)/W (s), football M (s), rock climbing M (c), soccer W (s), softball W (s), track and field M (s)/W (s), volleyball W (s). *Intramural sports:* archery M/W, badminton M/W, basketball M/W, bowling M/W, football M/W, golf M/W, racquetball M/W, rock climbing M, soccer M/W, softball M/W, swimming and diving M/W, table tennis M/W, tennis M/W, ultimate Frisbee M/W, volleyball M/W, weight lifting M/W.

Standardized Tests *Required:* SAT or ACT (for admission).

Costs (2007–08) *Tuition:* state resident $3000 full-time, $125 per credit hour part-time; nonresident $9672 full-time, $403 per credit hour part-time. Full-time tuition and fees vary according to course load. Part-time tuition and fees vary according to course load. *Required fees:* $1343 full-time, $25 per credit hour part-time, $270 per term part-time. *Room and board:* $5518; room only: $3755. Room and board charges vary according to board plan and housing facility. *Payment plan:* installment. *Waivers:* senior citizens.

Financial Aid Of all full-time matriculated undergraduates who enrolled in 2002, 4,302 applied for aid, 3,105 were judged to have need, 2,477 had their need fully met. In 2002, 202 non-need-based awards were made. *Average percent of need met:* 60%. *Average financial aid package:* $4299. *Average need-based loan:* $2500. *Average need-based gift aid:* $2193. *Average non-need-based aid:* $1872.

Applying *Options:* electronic application, early admission, deferred entrance. *Application fee:* $25. *Required:* high school transcript, high school class rank. *Application deadlines:* 8/15 (freshmen), 8/15 (transfers). *Notification:* continuous (freshmen), continuous (transfers).

Freshman Application Contact Ms. Amanda Taylor, Coordinator of Recruiting, Angelo State University, ASU Station #11014, Hardeman Building, San Angelo, TX 76909-1014. *Phone:* 325-942-2259 Ext. 233. *Toll-free phone:* 800-946-8627. *Fax:* 325-942-2128. *E-mail:* admissions@angelo.edu.

See page 2528 for the College Close-Up.

ARGOSY UNIVERSITY, DALLAS

Dallas, Texas **www.argosy.edu/locations/dallas/**

- **Proprietary** university, founded 2002, part of Argosy University System
- **Urban** campus
- **Coed**

Majors Psychology; substance abuse/addiction counseling.

Academics *Calendar:* semesters. *Degrees:* bachelor's, master's, and doctoral.

Director of Admissions Argosy University, Dallas, 8080 Parklane, Suite 400A, Dallas, TX 75231. *Phone:* 214-890-9900. *Toll-free phone:* 866-954-9900.

See page 2530 for the College Close-Up.

ARLINGTON BAPTIST COLLEGE

Arlington, Texas **www.abconline.edu/**

- **Independent Baptist** 4-year, founded 1939
- **Urban** 32-acre campus with easy access to Dallas–Fort Worth
- **Endowment** $16,195
- **Coed** 144 undergraduate students, 74% full-time, 47% women, 53% men
- **Noncompetitive** entrance level, 100% of applicants were admitted

Undergraduates 106 full-time, 38 part-time. Students come from 12 states and territories, 1 other country, 20% are from out of state, 4% African American, 3% Hispanic American, 4% international, 15% transferred in, 38% live on campus. *Retention:* 57% of 2006 full-time freshmen returned.

Freshmen *Admission:* 35 applied, 35 admitted, 19 enrolled.

Faculty *Total:* 18, 44% full-time, 11% with terminal degrees. *Student/faculty ratio:* 11:1.

Majors Biblical studies; early childhood education; education; elementary education; English/language arts teacher education; middle school education; music; music teacher education; religious studies; theology and religious vocations related.

Academics *Calendar:* semesters. *Degree:* certificates, diplomas, and bachelor's. *Special study options:* academic remediation for entering students, advanced placement credit, distance learning, double majors, independent study, internships, part-time degree program, summer session for credit.

Computers on Campus 21 computers/terminals are available on campus for general student use. Campuswide network is available. Wireless service is available via computer labs, libraries.

Student Life *Housing:* on-campus residence required through senior year. *Options:* men-only, women-only. Campus housing is university owned. Freshman campus housing is guaranteed. *Activities and organizations:* choral group, Preachers Fellowship, Student Missionary Association, L.I.F.T., International Students Association, 4-12 Group. *Campus security:* student patrols, controlled dormitory access, night security guards. *Student services:* personal/psychological counseling.

Athletics Member NCCAA. *Intramural sports:* baseball M, basketball M/W, volleyball W.

Costs (2007–08) *Comprehensive fee:* $10,190 includes full-time tuition ($5550), mandatory fees ($540), and room and board ($4100). Part-time tuition: $185 per hour.

Financial Aid Of all full-time matriculated undergraduates who enrolled in 2006, 164 applied for aid, 118 were judged to have need, 93 had their need fully met. *Average financial aid package:* $6847. *Average indebtedness upon graduation:* $4838.

Applying *Options:* early admission, deferred entrance. *Application fee:* $15. *Required:* essay or personal statement, high school transcript, 1 letter of recommendation, pastoral recommendation, medical examination. *Required for some:* interview. *Application deadlines:* rolling (freshmen), rolling (transfers). *Notification:* continuous (freshmen), continuous (transfers).

Freshman Application Contact Ms. Janie Taylor, Registrar/Admissions, Arlington Baptist College, 3001 West Division, Arlington, TX 76012-3425. *Phone:* 817-461-8741 Ext. 105. *Fax:* 817-274-1138. *E-mail:* jhall@abconline.org.

THE ART INSTITUTE OF AUSTIN

Austin, Texas **www.artinstitutes.edu/austin/**

- **Proprietary** 4-year

Majors Animation, interactive technology, video graphics and special effects; fashion merchandising; graphic design; interior design; photography; recording arts technology; retail management; Web/multimedia management and Webmaster.

Freshman Application Contact Admissions Director, The Art Institute of Austin, 101 W. Louis Henna Boulevard, Suite 100, Austin, TX 78728. *Phone:* 866-583-7952.

See page 2532 for the College Close-Up.

THE ART INSTITUTE OF DALLAS

Dallas, Texas **www.aid.edu/**

- **Proprietary** 4-year, founded 1978, part of Education Management Corporation
- **Urban** 2-acre campus
- **Coed** 1,706 undergraduate students, 67% full-time, 52% women, 48% men
- **Noncompetitive** entrance level

Undergraduates 1,136 full-time, 570 part-time. Students come from 39 states and territories, 13 other countries, 19% are from out of state, 11% African American, 3% Asian American or Pacific Islander, 15% Hispanic American, 0.6% Native American, 8% transferred in, 20% live on campus. *Retention:* 64% of 2006 full-time freshmen returned.

Freshmen *Admission:* 839 applied, 476 enrolled.

Faculty *Total:* 99, 61% full-time, 59% with terminal degrees. *Student/faculty ratio:* 17:1.

Majors Animation, interactive technology, video graphics and special effects; cinematography and film/video production; culinary arts; fashion/apparel design; fashion merchandising; graphic design; interior design; restaurant, culinary, and catering management; retail management; web page, digital/multimedia and information resources design.

Academics *Calendar:* quarters. *Degrees:* certificates, associate, and bachelor's. *Special study options:* academic remediation for entering students, advanced placement credit, distance learning, internships, part-time degree program, services for LD students, summer session for credit.

Computers on Campus 320 computers/terminals and 100 ports are available on campus for general student use. Students can access the following: computer help desk, free student e-mail accounts, online (class) grades, online (class) registration, online (class) schedules. Campuswide network is available.

Student Life *Housing options:* men-only, women-only. Campus housing is leased by the school. Freshman campus housing is guaranteed. *Activities and organizations:* drama/theater group, student-run newspaper, Young Chef Society, Multimedia Users Group, American Society of Interior Designers, Student Ambassadors, Web Girls. *Campus security:* 24-hour emergency response devices and patrols, late-night transport/escort service. *Student services:* personal/psychological counseling.

Standardized Tests *Required:* ASSET (for admission).

Costs (2008–09) *One-time required fee:* $150. *Tuition:* $26,200 full-time, $437 per credit hour part-time. *Required fees:* $325 full-time. *Room only:* $9038.

Financial Aid Of all full-time matriculated undergraduates who enrolled in 2004, 799 applied for aid, 772 were judged to have need. 33 Federal Work-Study jobs (averaging $2000). 49 state and other part-time jobs (averaging $3748). In 2004, 23 non-need-based awards were made. *Average percent of need met:* 45%. *Average financial aid package:* $6528. *Average need-based loan:* $3028. *Average need-based gift aid:* $838. *Average non-need-based aid:* $2100. *Average indebtedness upon graduation:* $23,125.

Applying *Options:* deferred entrance. *Application fee:* $50. *Required:* essay or personal statement, high school transcript, interview. *Application deadlines:* rolling (freshmen), rolling (out-of-state freshmen), rolling (transfers). *Notification:* continuous (freshmen), continuous (transfers).

Freshman Application Contact The Art Institute of Dallas, Two North Park East, 8080 Park Lane Suite 100, Dallas, TX 75231-5993. *Phone:* 214-692-8080. *Toll-free phone:* 800-275-4243. *Fax:* 214-750-9460. *E-mail:* aidadm@aii.edu.

See page 2534 for the College Close-Up.

THE ART INSTITUTE OF HOUSTON

Houston, Texas **www.aih.artinstitutes.edu/**

- **Proprietary** 4-year, founded 1978, part of Education Management Corporation
- **Urban** campus
- **Coed** 1,793 undergraduate students, 68% full-time, 58% women, 42% men
- **Moderately difficult** entrance level

Undergraduates 1,228 full-time, 565 part-time. 6% African American, 3% Asian American or Pacific Islander, 10% Hispanic American, 0.1% Native American, 0.2% transferred in, 17% live on campus. *Retention:* 74% of 2006 full-time freshmen returned.

Freshmen *Admission:* 671 admitted, 453 enrolled. *Average high school GPA:* 2.77.

Faculty *Total:* 81, 75% full-time, 7% with terminal degrees. *Student/faculty ratio:* 21:1.

Majors Animation, interactive technology, video graphics and special effects; apparel and accessories marketing; baking and pastry arts; cinematography and film/video production; culinary arts; graphic design; interior architecture; interior design; photography; restaurant, culinary, and catering management; web page, digital/multimedia and information resources design.

Academics *Calendar:* quarters. *Degrees:* diplomas, associate, and bachelor's. *Special study options:* academic remediation for entering students, adult/continuing education programs, advanced placement credit, cooperative education, distance learning, internships, off-campus study.

Computers on Campus 325 computers/terminals and 325 ports are available on campus for general student use. Students can access the following: computer help desk, free student e-mail accounts, online (class) grades, online (class) schedules. Campuswide network is available. Wireless service is available via entire campus.

Student Life *Housing options:* coed, men-only, women-only. Campus housing is leased by the school. *Activities and organizations:* American Society of Interior Designers, American Institute of Graphic Arts, Great Chef's Club, International Interior Design Association, National Technical Honor Society. *Campus security:* 24-hour emergency response devices. *Student services:* personal/psychological counseling.

Athletics *Intramural sports:* basketball M, football M/W, softball M/W, volleyball M/W.

Standardized Tests *Recommended:* SAT or ACT (for admission).

Costs (2007–08) *Comprehensive fee:* $38,020 includes full-time tuition ($26,220), mandatory fees ($200), and room and board ($11,600). Full-time tuition and fees vary according to course load. Part-time tuition: $437 per credit. No tuition increase for student's term of enrollment. tuition for the 2007—08 academic year is $25,200. Housing is $6996. Costs also include a one-time starter-kit charge for first-quarter students, which vary in cost depending on the student's program of study. Additional lab fees may apply. *Required fees:* $50 per term part-time. *College room only:* $7608. Room and board charges vary according to housing facility. *Payment plans:* tuition prepayment, installment. *Waivers:* employees or children of employees.

Applying *Options:* electronic application. *Application fee:* $50. *Required:* essay or personal statement, high school transcript, letters of recommendation. *Required for some:* minimum 2.5 GPA, portfolio. *Recommended:* minimum 2.1 GPA. *Application deadlines:* rolling (freshmen), rolling (transfers). *Notification:* continuous (freshmen), continuous (transfers).

Freshman Application Contact The Art Institute of Houston, 1900 Yorktown Street, Houston, TX 77056-4115. *Phone:* 713-966-2797. *Toll-free phone:* 800-275-4244. *E-mail:* aihadm@aih.aii.edu.

See page 2536 for the College Close-Up.

AUSTIN COLLEGE

Sherman, Texas **www.austincollege.edu/**

- **Independent Presbyterian** comprehensive, founded 1849
- **Suburban** 60-acre campus with easy access to Dallas–Fort Worth
- **Endowment** $144.7 million
- **Coed** 1,320 undergraduate students, 99% full-time, 52% women, 48% men
- **Very difficult** entrance level, 71% of applicants were admitted

Undergraduates 1,307 full-time, 13 part-time. Students come from 34 states and territories, 28 other countries, 7% are from out of state, 3% African American, 14% Asian American or Pacific Islander, 8% Hispanic American, 0.8% Native American, 1% international, 3% transferred in, 68% live on campus. *Retention:* 82% of 2006 full-time freshmen returned.

Freshmen *Admission:* 1,678 applied, 1,190 admitted, 334 enrolled. *Average high school GPA:* 3.46. *Test scores:* SAT critical reading scores over 500: 93%; SAT math scores over 500: 92%; SAT writing scores over 500: 87%; ACT scores over 18: 98%; SAT critical reading scores over 600: 61%; SAT math scores over 600: 55%; SAT writing scores over 600: 51%; ACT scores over 24: 67%; SAT critical reading scores over 700: 16%; SAT math scores over 700: 12%; SAT writing scores over 700: 13%; ACT scores over 30: 14%.

Faculty *Total:* 137, 69% full-time, 84% with terminal degrees. *Student/faculty ratio:* 12:1.

Majors Art; biochemistry; biology/biological sciences; business administration and management; chemistry; classics and classical languages related; classics and languages, literatures and linguistics; communication/speech communication and rhetoric; computer science; economics; English; French; German; history; international economics; international relations and affairs; Latin; mathematics; multi-/interdisciplinary studies related; music; philosophy; physics; political science and government; psychology; religious studies; sociology; Spanish.

Academics *Calendar:* 4-1-4. *Degrees:* bachelor's and master's. *Special study options:* adult/continuing education programs, advanced placement credit, double majors, honors programs, independent study, internships, off-campus study, part-time degree program, student-designed majors, study abroad, summer session for credit. *Unusual degree programs:* 3-2 engineering with University of Texas at Dallas; Texas A&M University; Washington University in St. Louis; Columbia University.

Computers on Campus 165 computers/terminals are available on campus for general student use. Students can access the following: campus intranet, computer help desk, free student e-mail accounts, online (class) grades, online (class) schedules. Campuswide network is available. 100% of college-owned or -operated housing units are wired for high-speed Internet access. Wireless service is available via entire campus.

Student Life *Housing:* on-campus residence required through junior year. *Options:* coed, men-only, women-only, disabled students. Campus housing is university owned. Freshman campus housing is guaranteed. *Activities and organizations:* drama/theater group, student-run newspaper, choral group, Fellowship of Christian Athletes, Campus Activity Board, Indian Cultural Association, Student Development Board, International Relations Club. *Campus security:* 24-hour emergency response devices and patrols, late-night transport/escort service, controlled dormitory access. *Student services:* health clinic, personal/psychological counseling.

Athletics Member NCAA. All Division III. *Intercollegiate sports:* baseball M, basketball M/W, cheerleading M/W, football M, soccer M/W, softball W, swimming and diving M/W, tennis M/W, volleyball W. *Intramural sports:* basketball M/W, football M/W, soccer M/W, softball M/W, table tennis M/W, ultimate Frisbee M/W, volleyball M/W.

Standardized Tests *Required:* SAT or ACT (for admission).

Costs (2008–09) *Comprehensive fee:* $34,834 includes full-time tuition ($26,370), mandatory fees ($160), and room and board ($8304). Part-time tuition: $3825 per course.

Financial Aid Of all full-time matriculated undergraduates who enrolled in 2006, 937 applied for aid, 760 were judged to have need, 760 had their need fully met. 319 Federal Work-Study jobs (averaging $1524). 216 state and other part-time jobs (averaging $1430). In 2006, 478 non-need-based awards were made. *Average percent of need met:* 99%. *Average financial aid package:* $22,532. *Average need-based loan:* $6477. *Average need-based gift aid:* $13,693. *Average non-need-based aid:* $9467.

Applying *Options:* electronic application, early admission, early decision, early action, deferred entrance. *Application fee:* $35. *Required:* essay or personal statement, high school transcript, 2 letters of recommendation. *Required for some:* interview. *Recommended:* minimum 3.0 GPA, interview. *Application deadlines:* 5/1 (freshmen), 5/1 (transfers), 1/15 (early action). *Notification:* 3/1 (early action).

Freshman Application Contact Ms. Nan Davis, Vice President for Institutional Enrollment, Austin College, 900 North Grand Avenue, Suite 6N, Sherman, TX 75090-4400. *Phone:* 903-813-3000. *Toll-free phone:* 800-442-5363. *Fax:* 903-813-3198. *E-mail:* admission@austincollege.edu.

See page 2538 for the College Close-Up.

AUSTIN GRADUATE SCHOOL OF THEOLOGY

Austin, Texas **www.austingrad.edu/**

Application Contact Celeste Scarbrough, Director of Admissions, Austin Graduate School of Theology, 1909 University Avenue, Austin, TX 78705. *Phone:* 512-476-2772. *Toll-free phone:* 866-AUS-GRAD. *Fax:* 512-476-3919. *E-mail:* registrar@austingrad.edu.

BAPTIST MISSIONARY ASSOCIATION THEOLOGICAL SEMINARY

Jacksonville, Texas **www.bmats.edu/**

Director of Admissions Dr. Philip Attebery, Dean and Registrar, Baptist Missionary Association Theological Seminary, 1530 East Pine Street, Jacksonville, TX 75766-5407. *Phone:* 903-586-2501 Ext. 229.

BAPTIST UNIVERSITY OF THE AMERICAS

San Antonio, Texas **www.bua.edu/**

Freshman Application Contact Abraham Garcia, Student Council President, Baptist University of the Americas, 8019 South Pan Am Expressway, San Antonio, TX 78224-2701. *Phone:* 210-924-4338. *Toll-free phone:* 800-721-1396. *Fax:* 210-924-2701. *E-mail:* agarcia@bua.edu.

BAYLOR UNIVERSITY

Waco, Texas **www.baylor.edu/**

- **Independent Baptist** university, founded 1845
- **Urban** 508-acre campus with easy access to Dallas–Fort Worth
- **Endowment** $1.0 billion
- **Coed** 11,902 undergraduate students, 98% full-time, 58% women, 42% men
- **Moderately difficult** entrance level, 44% of applicants were admitted

Undergraduates 11,641 full-time, 261 part-time. Students come from 51 states and territories, 71 other countries, 17% are from out of state, 8% African American, 7% Asian American or Pacific Islander, 10% Hispanic American, 0.6%

Native American, 2% international, 4% transferred in, 36% live on campus. *Retention:* 86% of 2006 full-time freshmen returned.

Freshmen *Admission:* 26,514 applied, 11,668 admitted, 2,732 enrolled. *Test scores:* SAT critical reading scores over 500: 93%; SAT math scores over 500: 96%; SAT writing scores over 500: 89%; ACT scores over 18: 99%; SAT critical reading scores over 600: 52%; SAT math scores over 600: 60%; SAT writing scores over 600: 44%; ACT scores over 24: 67%; SAT critical reading scores over 700: 12%; SAT math scores over 700: 14%; SAT writing scores over 700: 9%; ACT scores over 30: 11%.

Faculty *Total:* 1,063, 76% full-time. *Student/faculty ratio:* 15:1.

Majors Accounting; acting; airline pilot and flight crew; American studies; ancient/classical Greek; ancient Near Eastern and biblical languages; anthropology; applied mathematics; archeology; architecture; art; art history, criticism and conservation; art teacher education; Asian studies; athletic training; biochemistry; bioinformatics; biology/biological sciences; biology teacher education; business administration and management; business/commerce; business, management, and marketing related; business/managerial economics; business statistics; business teacher education; chemistry; chemistry teacher education; classics and languages, literatures and linguistics; clinical laboratory science/medical technology; communication disorders; communication/speech communication and rhetoric; computer science; computer teacher education; digital communication and media/multimedia; drama and dance teacher education; dramatic/theater arts; early childhood education; economics; education; education (specific subject areas) related; electrical, electronics and communications engineering; elementary education; engineering; English; English composition; English/language arts teacher education; entrepreneurship; environmental science; environmental studies; exercise physiology; family and consumer sciences/human sciences; fashion/apparel design; fashion merchandising; finance; financial planning and services; fine/studio arts; foreign language teacher education; forensic science and technology; forestry; French; French language teacher education; geological and earth sciences/geosciences related; geology/earth science; geophysics and seismology; German; German language teacher education; health and physical education; health/medical preparatory programs related; health occupations teacher education; health teacher education; history; human development and family studies; humanities; human nutrition; human resources management; insurance; interior design; international business/trade/commerce; international relations and affairs; journalism; kindergarten/preschool education; Latin; Latin American studies; Latin teacher education; linguistics; logistics and materials management; management information systems; marketing/marketing management; mathematics; mathematics teacher education; mechanical engineering; merchandising, sales, and marketing operations related (specialized); multi-/interdisciplinary studies related; museum studies; music; music history, literature, and theory; music pedagogy; music performance; music teacher education; music theory and composition; neuroscience; nursing (registered nurse training); operations management; philosophy; physical education teaching and coaching; physics; physics teacher education; political science and government; pre-dentistry studies; prelaw studies; pre-medical studies; pre-nursing studies; psychology; public administration; radio and television; reading teacher education; real estate; religious/sacred music; religious studies; Russian; sales, distribution and marketing; science teacher education; secondary education; Slavic studies; social science teacher education; social studies teacher education; social work; sociology; Spanish; Spanish language teacher education; special education; special education (speech or language impaired); speech teacher education; sport and fitness administration/management; statistics; theater design and technology; urban studies/affairs.

Academics *Calendar:* semesters. *Degrees:* certificates, bachelor's, master's, doctoral, first professional, and post-master's certificates. *Special study options:* accelerated degree program, advanced placement credit, double majors, honors programs, internships, part-time degree program, services for LD students, student-designed majors, study abroad, summer session for credit. *ROTC:* Air Force (b). *Unusual degree programs:* 3-2 forestry with Duke University; architecture with Washington University in St. Louis, medical technology and biology, medicine, dentistry, optometry.

Computers on Campus 1,500 computers/terminals are available on campus for general student use. Students can access the following: campus intranet, computer help desk, free student e-mail accounts, online (class) grades, online (class) registration, online (class) schedules. Campuswide network is available. 99% of college-owned or -operated housing units are wired for high-speed Internet access. Wireless service is available via entire campus.

Student Life *Housing:* on-campus residence required for freshman year. *Options:* men-only, women-only, disabled students. Campus housing is university owned. Freshman campus housing is guaranteed. *Activities and organizations:* drama/theater group, student-run newspaper, radio and television station, choral group, marching band, The Bear Pit, Baptist Student Ministries, BU Medical Ethics Discussion Society, Alpha Chi, American Medical Student Association, national fraternities, national sororities. *Campus security:* 24-hour emergency response devices and patrols, late-night transport/escort service, controlled dormitory access, bicycle patrols. *Student services:* health clinic, personal/psychological counseling, legal services.

Athletics Member NCAA. All Division I except football (Division I-A). *Intercollegiate sports:* badminton M (c)/W (c), baseball M (s), basketball M (s)/W (s), crew M (c)/W (c), cross-country running M (s)/W (s), equestrian sports W (s), fencing M (c)/W (c), golf M (s)/W (s), ice hockey M (c), lacrosse M (c)/W (c), rugby M (c)/W (c), sailing M (c)/W (c), soccer M (c)/W (s), softball W (s), tennis M (s)/W (s), track and field M (s)/W (s), volleyball M (c)/W (s), water polo M (c)/W (c). *Intramural sports:* basketball M/W, bowling M/W, cross-country running M/W, football M/W, golf M/W, racquetball M/W, soccer M/W, softball M/W, table tennis M/W, tennis M/W, ultimate Frisbee M/W, volleyball M/W, weight lifting M/W.

Standardized Tests *Required:* SAT or ACT (for admission), ACT essay (for admission).

Costs (2008–09) *Comprehensive fee:* $34,464 includes full-time tuition ($23,664), mandatory fees ($2570), and room and board ($8230). Part-time tuition: $986 per semester hour. *College room only:* $4000.

Financial Aid Of all full-time matriculated undergraduates who enrolled in 2007, 6,747 applied for aid, 5,645 were judged to have need, 897 had their need fully met. 2,870 Federal Work-Study jobs (averaging $2681). In 2007, 3879 non-need-based awards were made. *Average percent of need met:* 65%. *Average financial aid package:* $17,250. *Average need-based loan:* $2493. *Average need-based gift aid:* $12,376. *Average non-need-based aid:* $7820.

Applying *Options:* electronic application, early admission, early action. *Application fee:* $50. *Required:* high school transcript. *Required for some:* essay or personal statement, minimum 2.5 GPA, letters of recommendation. *Recommended:* interview. *Application deadlines:* 2/1 (freshmen), rolling (transfers), 11/1 (early action). *Notification:* 3/15 (freshmen), continuous (transfers), 1/15 (early action).

Freshman Application Contact Ms. Jennifer Carron, Director of Admissions, Baylor University, One Bear Place # 97056, Waco, TX 76798-7056. *Phone:* 254-710-3435. *Toll-free phone:* 800-BAYLORU. *Fax:* 254-710-3436. *E-mail:* admissions@baylor.edu.

See page 2540 for the College Close-Up.

College of Biblical Studies–Houston

Houston, Texas **www.cbshouston.edu/**

- **Independent nondenominational** 4-year, founded 1979
- **Urban** 10-acre campus
- **Coed** 1,399 students
- **Noncompetitive** entrance level

Undergraduates 47% African American, 3% Asian American or Pacific Islander, 26% Hispanic American, 0.2% Native American.

Majors Biblical studies; Christian studies.

Academics *Calendar:* semesters. *Degrees:* certificates, associate, and bachelor's. *Special study options:* academic remediation for entering students, accelerated degree program, adult/continuing education programs, English as a second language, honors programs, independent study, part-time degree program, summer session for credit.

Student Life *Campus security:* hourly patrols by trained security guards and police.

Costs (2007–08) *Tuition:* $4920 full-time, $205 per credit hour part-time. Christian Service Program Tuition is $126 per credit hour. *Required fees:* $194 full-time, $6 per credit hour part-time, $45 per term part-time.

Applying *Application fee:* $20.

Freshman Application Contact Admissions, College of Biblical Studies–Houston, 7000 Regency Square Boulevard, #110, Houston, TX 77036. *Phone:* 832-252-3377. *Fax:* 713-532-8150. *E-mail:* admissions@cbshouston.edu.

The College of Saint Thomas More

Fort Worth, Texas **www.cstm.edu/**

- **Independent** 4-year, founded 1981, affiliated with Roman Catholic Church
- **Urban** 1-acre campus with easy access to Dallas
- **Coed**
- **Moderately difficult** entrance level

Faculty *Student/faculty ratio:* 5:1.
Academics *Calendar:* semesters. *Degrees:* associate and bachelor's.
Student Life *Campus security:* 24-hour patrols, student patrols, late-night transport/escort service.
Costs (2007–08) *Tuition:* $12,150 full-time, $500 per credit part-time. *Room only:* $3690.
Financial Aid Of all full-time matriculated undergraduates who enrolled in 2005, 26 applied for aid, 18 had their need fully met. 4 state and other part-time jobs (averaging $500). In 2005, 6 non-need-based awards were made. *Average percent of need met:* 85. *Average financial aid package:* $8560. *Average need-based loan:* $4300. *Average need-based gift aid:* $3825. *Average non-need-based aid:* $1000. *Average indebtedness upon graduation:* $9250.
Applying *Options:* early admission, deferred entrance. *Application fee:* $35. *Required:* essay or personal statement, high school transcript, minimum 2.0 GPA, 1 letter of recommendation. *Recommended:* interview.
Freshman Application Contact Dr. James A. Patrick, The College of Saint Thomas More, 3020 Lubbock Avenue, Fort Worth, TX 76109-2323. *Phone:* 817-928-8459. *Toll-free phone:* 800-583-6489. *Fax:* 817-924-3206. *E-mail:* more-info@cstm.edu.

CONCORDIA UNIVERSITY TEXAS

Austin, Texas **www.concordia.edu/**

- **Independent** comprehensive, founded 1926, affiliated with Lutheran Church–Missouri Synod, part of Concordia University System
- **Urban** 20-acre campus with easy access to San Antonio
- **Endowment** $11.7 million
- **Coed** 1,156 undergraduate students, 71% full-time, 57% women, 43% men
- **Moderately difficult** entrance level, 62% of applicants were admitted

Undergraduates 823 full-time, 333 part-time. Students come from 21 states and territories, 6% are from out of state, 10% African American, 1% Asian American or Pacific Islander, 20% Hispanic American, 0.1% Native American, 0.1% international. *Retention:* 52% of 2006 full-time freshmen returned.
Freshmen *Admission:* 691 applied, 428 admitted, 165 enrolled. *Average high school GPA:* 3.19. *Test scores:* SAT critical reading scores over 500: 47%; SAT math scores over 500: 59%; SAT writing scores over 500: 49%; ACT scores over 18: 83%; SAT critical reading scores over 600: 15%; SAT math scores over 600: 15%; SAT writing scores over 600: 16%; ACT scores over 24: 39%; SAT critical reading scores over 700: 1%; SAT math scores over 700: 1%; SAT writing scores over 700: 1%; ACT scores over 30: 3%.
Faculty *Total:* 107, 42% full-time. *Student/faculty ratio:* 17:1.
Majors Biology/biological sciences; business administration and management; business/commerce; computer science; criminal justice/law enforcement administration; elementary education; English; environmental studies; general studies; history; human resources development; kinesiology and exercise science; liberal arts and sciences/liberal studies; mass communication/media; mathematics; middle school education; religious education; religious/sacred music; religious studies; secondary education; social sciences related.
Academics *Calendar:* semesters. *Degrees:* certificates, associate, bachelor's, master's, and postbachelor's certificates. *Special study options:* academic remediation for entering students, accelerated degree program, adult/continuing education programs, advanced placement credit, distance learning, double majors, external degree program, honors programs, independent study, internships, part-time degree program, services for LD students, study abroad, summer session for credit. *ROTC:* Army (c), Air Force (c).
Computers on Campus 40 computers/terminals are available on campus for general student use.
Student Life *Housing:* on-campus residence required for freshman year. *Options:* coed, men-only, women-only, disabled students. Campus housing is university owned. *Activities and organizations:* drama/theater group, student-run newspaper, choral group, student government, Education Club, Lutheran Student Fellowship, Students Active for the Environment, Accounting Club. *Campus security:* 24-hour emergency response devices, student patrols, late-night transport/escort service, controlled dormitory access. *Student services:* personal/psychological counseling.
Athletics Member NCAA. All Division III. *Intercollegiate sports:* baseball M, basketball M/W, cross-country running M/W, golf M/W, soccer M/W, softball W, tennis M/W, volleyball W. *Intramural sports:* badminton M/W, basketball M/W, football M/W, golf M/W, racquetball M/W, softball M/W, table tennis M/W, tennis M/W, volleyball M/W.
Standardized Tests *Required:* SAT or ACT (for admission).
Costs (2007–08) *Comprehensive fee:* $26,210 includes full-time tuition ($18,600), mandatory fees ($310), and room and board ($7300). Part-time tuition: $620 per hour. *College room only:* $4600.
Financial Aid Of all full-time matriculated undergraduates who enrolled in 2006, 525 applied for aid, 413 were judged to have need, 154 had their need fully met. 96 Federal Work-Study jobs (averaging $1098). 6 state and other part-time jobs (averaging $1798). In 2006, 108 non-need-based awards were made. *Average percent of need met:* 79%. *Average financial aid package:* $15,552. *Average need-based loan:* $6607. *Average need-based gift aid:* $9059. *Average non-need-based aid:* $6248. *Average indebtedness upon graduation:* $21,009.
Applying *Options:* early admission, deferred entrance. *Application fee:* $25. *Required:* high school transcript, minimum 2.5 GPA. *Required for some:* essay or personal statement, letters of recommendation, interview. *Application deadlines:* 8/15 (freshmen), rolling (transfers). *Notification:* continuous (freshmen), continuous (transfers).
Freshman Application Contact Kristi Kirk, Director of Enrollment Services, Concordia University Texas, 3400 Interstate 35 North, Austin, TX 78705. *Phone:* 512-486-2000 Ext. 1156. *Toll-free phone:* 800-285-4252. *Fax:* 512-459-8517. *E-mail:* ctxadmis@crf.cuis.edu.

THE CRISWELL COLLEGE

Dallas, Texas **www.criswell.edu/**

Director of Admissions Mr. W. Danny Blair, Vice President for Enrollment and Academic Services, The Criswell College, 4010 Gaston Avenue, Dallas, TX 75246-1537. *Phone:* 214-818-1305. *Toll-free phone:* 800-899-0012. *Fax:* 214-818-1310. *E-mail:* wdblair@criswell.edu.

DALLAS BAPTIST UNIVERSITY

Dallas, Texas **www.dbu.edu/**

- **Independent** comprehensive, founded 1965, affiliated with Baptist General Convention of Texas
- **Urban** 293-acre campus
- **Endowment** $33.0 million
- **Coed** 3,581 undergraduate students, 61% full-time, 59% women, 41% men
- **Moderately difficult** entrance level, 52% of applicants were admitted

Undergraduates 2,202 full-time, 1,379 part-time. Students come from 43 states and territories, 44 other countries, 5% are from out of state, 18% African American, 2% Asian American or Pacific Islander, 9% Hispanic American, 0.9% Native American, 8% international, 8% transferred in, 39% live on campus. *Retention:* 73% of 2006 full-time freshmen returned.
Freshmen *Admission:* 1,202 applied, 629 admitted, 329 enrolled. *Average high school GPA:* 3.58. *Test scores:* SAT critical reading scores over 500: 77%; SAT math scores over 500: 79%; ACT scores over 18: 99%; SAT critical reading scores over 600: 32%; SAT math scores over 600: 20%; ACT scores over 24: 34%; SAT critical reading scores over 700: 6%; SAT math scores over 700: 1%; ACT scores over 30: 4%.
Faculty *Total:* 504, 22% full-time, 42% with terminal degrees. *Student/faculty ratio:* 15:1.
Majors Accounting; aerospace science; Army R.O.T.C./military science; art; biblical studies; biology/biological sciences; business administration and management; business/managerial economics; Christian studies; communication/speech communication and rhetoric; computer and information sciences; computer science; criminal justice/law enforcement administration; divinity/ministry; education; elementary education; English; finance; general studies; health/health care administration; history; interdisciplinary studies; kindergarten/preschool education; liberal arts and sciences/liberal studies; management information systems; marketing/marketing management; mathematics; modern languages; multi-/interdisciplinary studies related; music; music management and merchandising; music teacher education; music theory and composition; natural sciences; pastoral studies/counseling; philosophy; physical education teaching and coaching; piano and organ; political science and government; psychology; religious education; religious/sacred music; science teacher education; secondary education; sociology.
Academics *Calendar:* 4-1-4. *Degrees:* certificates, associate, bachelor's, master's, doctoral, and postbachelor's certificates. *Special study options:* adult/continuing education programs, advanced placement credit, distance learning, double majors, English as a second language, honors programs, independent study, internships, off-campus study, part-time degree program, services for LD students, study abroad, summer session for credit. *ROTC:* Army (c), Air Force (c).

Computers on Campus 201 computers/terminals are available on campus for general student use. Students can access the following: computer help desk, free student e-mail accounts, online (class) grades, online (class) registration, online (class) schedules. Campuswide network is available. 100% of college-owned or -operated housing units are wired for high-speed Internet access. Wireless service is available via entire campus.

Student Life *Housing:* on-campus residence required through senior year. *Options:* men-only, women-only, disabled students. Campus housing is university owned and leased by the school. Freshman applicants given priority for college housing. *Activities and organizations:* drama/theater group, choral group, Student Activities Board, Baptist Student Ministry, Student Government Association, Student Education Association, International Student Organization. *Campus security:* 24-hour emergency response devices and patrols, late-night transport/escort service, controlled dormitory access. *Student services:* health clinic, personal/psychological counseling.

Athletics Member NCAA, NCCAA. All NCAA Division II. *Intercollegiate sports:* baseball M (s), basketball M (s), cross-country running M/W (s), golf M/W (s), soccer M/W (s), tennis M/W (s), track and field M/W (s), volleyball M/W (s). *Intramural sports:* basketball M/W, football M/W, golf M/W, softball M/W, table tennis M/W, tennis M/W, volleyball M/W.

Standardized Tests *Required:* SAT or ACT (for admission).

Costs (2007–08) *Comprehensive fee:* $20,088 includes full-time tuition ($14,940) and room and board ($5148). Part-time tuition: $498 per credit hour. *College room only:* $2060. Room and board charges vary according to board plan and housing facility. *Payment plan:* installment. *Waivers:* employees or children of employees.

Financial Aid Of all full-time matriculated undergraduates who enrolled in 2006, 1,807 applied for aid, 1,262 were judged to have need, 539 had their need fully met. 164 Federal Work-Study jobs (averaging $1923). 63 state and other part-time jobs (averaging $557). In 2006, 373 non-need-based awards were made. *Average percent of need met:* 75%. *Average financial aid package:* $10,172. *Average need-based loan:* $3479. *Average need-based gift aid:* $2949. *Average non-need-based aid:* $5902. *Average indebtedness upon graduation:* $19,679.

Applying *Options:* electronic application. *Application fee:* $25. *Required:* essay or personal statement, high school transcript, minimum 2.5 GPA, rank in upper 50% of high school class, minimum ACT score of 21, combined SAT score of 1,000. *Recommended:* letters of recommendation, interview. *Application deadlines:* rolling (freshmen), rolling (transfers). *Notification:* continuous (freshmen), continuous (transfers).

Freshman Application Contact Ms. Erin Dennis, Associate Director of Freshman Recruitment/Undergraduate Admissions, Dallas Baptist University, 3000 Mountain Creek Parkway, Dallas, TX 75211-9299. *Phone:* 214-333-5360. *Toll-free phone:* 800-460-1328. *Fax:* 214-333-5447. *E-mail:* admiss@dbu.edu.

DALLAS CHRISTIAN COLLEGE

Dallas, Texas — www.dallas.edu/

- **Independent** 4-year, founded 1950, affiliated with Christian Churches and Churches of Christ
- **Urban** 22-acre campus with easy access to Fort Worth
- **Endowment** $169,499
- **Coed** 334 undergraduate students, 68% full-time, 44% women, 56% men
- **Minimally difficult** entrance level, 47% of applicants were admitted

Undergraduates 227 full-time, 107 part-time. Students come from 32 states and territories, 4 other countries, 20% are from out of state, 15% African American, 2% Asian American or Pacific Islander, 11% Hispanic American, 3% Native American, 36% live on campus. *Retention:* 48% of 2006 full-time freshmen returned.

Freshmen *Admission:* 154 applied, 73 admitted, 45 enrolled. *Average high school GPA:* 3.14.

Faculty *Total:* 57, 16% full-time, 25% with terminal degrees. *Student/faculty ratio:* 16:1.

Majors Biblical studies; business administration and management; education.

Academics *Calendar:* semesters. *Degrees:* bachelor's and postbachelor's certificates. *Special study options:* academic remediation for entering students, accelerated degree program, adult/continuing education programs, advanced placement credit, distance learning, double majors, independent study, internships, part-time degree program, summer session for credit.

Computers on Campus 16 computers/terminals are available on campus for general student use. Students can access the following: free student e-mail accounts, online (class) grades, online (class) registration, online (class) schedules. Campuswide network is available. Wireless service is available via entire campus.

Student Life *Housing:* on-campus residence required through sophomore year. *Options:* men-only, women-only. Campus housing is university owned. Freshman campus housing is guaranteed. *Activities and organizations:* drama/theater group, choral group. *Campus security:* controlled dormitory access. *Student services:* personal/psychological counseling.

Athletics Member NCCAA. *Intercollegiate sports:* basketball M/W, soccer M/W, volleyball W. *Intramural sports:* volleyball M/W.

Standardized Tests *Required:* SAT or ACT (for admission).

Costs (2008–09) *Comprehensive fee:* $16,420 includes full-time tuition ($9570), mandatory fees ($600), and room and board ($6250). Part-time tuition: $319 per hour.

Financial Aid Of all full-time matriculated undergraduates who enrolled in 2005, 189 applied for aid, 132 were judged to have need. 36 Federal Work-Study jobs (averaging $1404). In 2005, 26 non-need-based awards were made. *Average percent of need met:* 43%. *Average financial aid package:* $3940. *Average need-based loan:* $3589. *Average need-based gift aid:* $1282. *Average non-need-based aid:* $3664. *Average indebtedness upon graduation:* $15,000.

Applying *Options:* electronic application, deferred entrance. *Application fee:* $40. *Required:* high school transcript, minimum 2.0 GPA, 2 letters of recommendation. *Required for some:* essay or personal statement, interview. *Application deadlines:* rolling (freshmen), rolling (transfers).

Freshman Application Contact Mr. Eric Hinton, Director of Admissions, Dallas Christian College, 2700 Christian Parkway, Dallas, TX 75234-7299. *Phone:* 972-241-3371 Ext. 149. *Fax:* 972-241-8021. *E-mail:* ehinton@dallas.edu.

DEVRY UNIVERSITY

Houston, Texas — www.devry.edu/

- **Proprietary** comprehensive
- **Coed** 927 undergraduate students, 64% full-time, 43% women, 57% men

Undergraduates 594 full-time, 333 part-time. 1% are from out of state, 35% African American, 5% Asian American or Pacific Islander, 35% Hispanic American, 0.2% Native American, 0.5% international, 18% transferred in. *Retention:* 39% of 2006 full-time freshmen returned.

Freshmen *Admission:* 221 enrolled.

Faculty *Total:* 70, 31% full-time. *Student/faculty ratio:* 21:1.

Majors Biomedical technology; business administration and management; business administration, management and operations related; computer engineering technology; computer systems analysis; computer systems networking and telecommunications; electrical, electronic and communications engineering technology; health information/medical records technology.

Academics *Calendar:* semesters. *Degrees:* associate, bachelor's, and master's. *Special study options:* academic remediation for entering students, accelerated degree program, advanced placement credit, distance learning, summer session for credit.

Costs (2008–09) *Tuition:* $13,810 full-time, $515 per credit part-time. *Required fees:* $180 full-time.

Applying *Options:* electronic application, early admission, deferred entrance. *Application fee:* $50. *Application deadlines:* rolling (freshmen), rolling (transfers). *Notification:* continuous (freshmen), continuous (transfers).

Director of Admissions Admissions Office, DeVry University, 11125 Equity Drive, Houston, TX 77041-8217. *Toll-free phone:* 866-703-3879.

DEVRY UNIVERSITY

Irving, Texas — www.devry.edu/

- **Proprietary** comprehensive, founded 1969, part of DeVry University
- **Suburban** 13-acre campus with easy access to Dallas
- **Coed** 1,454 undergraduate students, 48% full-time, 31% women, 69% men
- **Minimally difficult** entrance level

Undergraduates 692 full-time, 762 part-time. 2% are from out of state, 32% African American, 4% Asian American or Pacific Islander, 20% Hispanic American, 0.6% Native American, 0.4% international, 19% transferred in. *Retention:* 42% of 2006 full-time freshmen returned.

Freshmen *Admission:* 308 enrolled.

Faculty *Total:* 89, 44% full-time. *Student/faculty ratio:* 19:1.

Majors Biomedical technology; business administration and management; business administration, management and operations related; computer engineering technology; computer software engineering; computer systems analysis;

computer systems networking and telecommunications; electrical, electronic and communications engineering technology; health information/medical records technology.

Academics *Calendar:* semesters. *Degrees:* associate, bachelor's, and master's. *Special study options:* academic remediation for entering students, accelerated degree program, adult/continuing education programs, advanced placement credit, distance learning, part-time degree program, services for LD students, summer session for credit.

Computers on Campus 442 computers/terminals are available on campus for general student use. Students can access the following: online (class) registration. Campuswide network is available.

Student Life *Housing:* college housing not available. *Activities and organizations:* Association of Information Technology Professionals, Gamers, Business Information Systems, Toastmasters, Telecommunications Management and Associations. *Campus security:* 24-hour emergency response devices, student patrols, late-night transport/escort service, lighted pathways/sidewalks.

Athletics *Intramural sports:* basketball M, football M, golf M, softball M, volleyball M.

Costs (2008–09) *Tuition:* $13,810 full-time, $515 per credit part-time. *Required fees:* $180 full-time.

Financial Aid Of all full-time matriculated undergraduates who enrolled in 2002, 1,511 applied for aid, 1,418 were judged to have need, 32 had their need fully met. In 2002, 177 non-need-based awards were made. *Average percent of need met:* 43%. *Average financial aid package:* $8767. *Average need-based loan:* $6064. *Average need-based gift aid:* $4189. *Average non-need-based aid:* $11,101.

Applying *Options:* electronic application, early admission, deferred entrance. *Application fee:* $50. *Required:* high school transcript, interview. *Application deadlines:* rolling (freshmen), rolling (transfers). *Notification:* continuous (freshmen), continuous (transfers).

Freshman Application Contact DeVry University, 4800 Regent Boulevard, Irving, TX 75063-2439.

DeVry University
Richardson, Texas

East Texas Baptist University
Marshall, Texas www.etbu.edu/

- **Independent Baptist** 4-year, founded 1912
- **Small-town** 200-acre campus
- **Endowment** $64.7 million
- **Coed** 1,308 undergraduate students, 88% full-time, 53% women, 47% men
- **Moderately difficult** entrance level, 75% of applicants were admitted

Undergraduates 1,152 full-time, 156 part-time. Students come from 26 states and territories, 15 other countries, 11% are from out of state, 16% African American, 1% Asian American or Pacific Islander, 4% Hispanic American, 1% Native American, 1% international, 8% transferred in, 81% live on campus. *Retention:* 52% of 2006 full-time freshmen returned.

Freshmen *Admission:* 679 applied, 507 admitted, 313 enrolled. *Average high school GPA:* 3.33. *Test scores:* SAT critical reading scores over 500: 40%; SAT math scores over 500: 52%; ACT scores over 18: 77%; SAT critical reading scores over 600: 13%; SAT math scores over 600: 15%; ACT scores over 24: 24%; SAT critical reading scores over 700: 3%; SAT math scores over 700: 2%; ACT scores over 30: 2%.

Faculty *Total:* 105, 60% full-time, 53% with terminal degrees. *Student/faculty ratio:* 15:1.

Majors Accounting; athletic training; biblical studies; biology/biological sciences; biology teacher education; business/commerce; chemistry; chemistry teacher education; communication and media related; drama and dance teacher education; dramatic/theater arts; education; elementary education; English; English/language arts teacher education; health and physical education; history; history teacher education; industrial and organizational psychology; international/global studies; liberal arts and sciences/liberal studies; management information systems; mathematics; mathematics teacher education; missionary studies and missiology; multi-/interdisciplinary studies related; music; music teacher education; nursing (registered nurse training); pastoral studies/counseling; physical education teaching and coaching; piano and organ; psychology; religious education; religious/sacred music; religious studies; social studies teacher education; sociology; Spanish; Spanish language teacher education; speech and rhetoric; speech teacher education; voice and opera; youth ministry.

Academics *Calendar:* 4-4-1. *Degree:* certificates and bachelor's. *Special study options:* academic remediation for entering students, adult/continuing education programs, advanced placement credit, double majors, honors programs, independent study, internships, off-campus study, part-time degree program, study abroad, summer session for credit.

Computers on Campus 206 computers/terminals and 720 ports are available on campus for general student use. Students can access the following: campus intranet, free student e-mail accounts, online (class) grades, online (class) registration, online (class) schedules. Campuswide network is available. 100% of college-owned or -operated housing units are wired for high-speed Internet access. Wireless service is available via entire campus.

Student Life *Housing:* on-campus residence required through senior year. *Options:* men-only, women-only. Campus housing is university owned. Freshman campus housing is guaranteed. *Activities and organizations:* drama/theater group, student-run newspaper, choral group, marching band, Baptist Student Ministry, Residence Hall Councils, Student Government Association, REACT, Student Foundation Association, national fraternities. *Campus security:* 24-hour emergency response devices, controlled dormitory access.

Athletics Member NCAA. All Division III. *Intercollegiate sports:* baseball M, basketball M/W, cross-country running M/W, football M, soccer M/W, softball W, volleyball W. *Intramural sports:* basketball M/W, football M, soccer M/W, softball M/W, volleyball M/W.

Standardized Tests *Required:* SAT or ACT (for admission).

Costs (2007–08) *Comprehensive fee:* $19,343 includes full-time tuition ($14,680) and room and board ($4663). Part-time tuition: $510 per credit hour. No tuition increase for student's term of enrollment. *College room only:* $2000. Room and board charges vary according to board plan and housing facility. *Payment plan:* installment. *Waivers:* employees or children of employees.

Financial Aid Of all full-time matriculated undergraduates who enrolled in 2006, 1,101 applied for aid, 872 were judged to have need, 195 had their need fully met. 144 Federal Work-Study jobs (averaging $1108). 303 state and other part-time jobs (averaging $1099). In 2006, 130 non-need-based awards were made. *Average percent of need met:* 89%. *Average financial aid package:* $11,418. *Average need-based loan:* $3471. *Average need-based gift aid:* $6060. *Average non-need-based aid:* $7318. *Average indebtedness upon graduation:* $18,551.

Applying *Options:* electronic application, deferred entrance. *Application fee:* $25. *Required:* high school transcript, minimum 2.0 GPA. *Required for some:* interview. *Application deadlines:* 8/14 (freshmen), 8/14 (transfers). *Notification:* continuous (freshmen), continuous (transfers).

Freshman Application Contact Ms. Melissa Fitts, Director of Admissions, East Texas Baptist University, 1209 North Grove, Marshall, TX 75670-1498. *Phone:* 903-923-2000. *Toll-free phone:* 800-804-ETBU. *Fax:* 903-923-2001. *E-mail:* admissions@etbu.edu.

Hardin-Simmons University
Abilene, Texas www.hsutx.edu/

- **Independent Baptist** comprehensive, founded 1891
- **Urban** 120-acre campus
- **Endowment** $123.9 million
- **Coed** 2,030 undergraduate students, 87% full-time, 57% women, 43% men
- **Moderately difficult** entrance level, 36% of applicants were admitted

Undergraduates 1,768 full-time, 262 part-time. Students come from 27 states and territories, 19 other countries, 4% are from out of state, 5% African American, 1% Asian American or Pacific Islander, 10% Hispanic American, 0.7% Native American, 0.8% international, 8% transferred in, 44% live on campus. *Retention:* 66% of 2006 full-time freshmen returned.

Freshmen *Admission:* 1,757 applied, 635 admitted, 465 enrolled. *Average high school GPA:* 3.59. *Test scores:* SAT critical reading scores over 500: 56%; SAT math scores over 500: 63%; SAT writing scores over 500: 56%; ACT scores over 18: 87%; SAT critical reading scores over 600: 21%; SAT math scores over 600: 18%; SAT writing scores over 600: 12%; ACT scores over 24: 35%; SAT critical reading scores over 700: 2%; SAT math scores over 700: 1%; SAT writing scores over 700: 1%; ACT scores over 30: 5%.

Faculty *Total:* 200, 65% full-time, 60% with terminal degrees. *Student/faculty ratio:* 14:1.

Majors Accounting; agricultural business and management; agronomy and crop science; animal sciences; art teacher education; athletic training; audiology and speech-language pathology; biblical studies; biochemistry/biophysics and molecular biology; biology/biological sciences; broadcast journalism; business administration and management; business teacher education; chemistry; communication/speech communication and rhetoric; computer programming; computer teacher education; corrections; criminal justice/police science; drama and dance teacher education; dramatic/theater arts; early childhood education; economics; education; English; English/language arts teacher education; environmental science; finance; fine/studio arts; geology/earth science; graphic design; health and physical education; history; history teacher education; kinesiology and exercise science; management science; marketing/marketing management; mathematics; mathematics teacher education; missionary studies and missiology; music; music history, literature, and theory; music management and merchandising; music performance; music teacher education; music theory and composition; nursing (registered nurse training); philosophy; physical education teaching and coaching; physics; piano and organ; political science and government; pre-dentistry studies; pre-law studies; pre-medical studies; pre-pharmacy studies; psychology; public relations, advertising, and applied communication related; radio and television; reading teacher education; religious/sacred music; science teacher education; social studies teacher education; social work; sociology; Spanish; Spanish language teacher education; speech and rhetoric; speech teacher education; theological and ministerial studies related; theology; violin, viola, guitar and other stringed instruments; voice and opera; youth ministry.

Academics *Calendar:* semesters. *Degrees:* bachelor's, master's, doctoral, first professional, and postbachelor's certificates. *Special study options:* academic remediation for entering students, accelerated degree program, adult/continuing education programs, advanced placement credit, distance learning, double majors, honors programs, independent study, internships, off-campus study, part-time degree program, services for LD students, study abroad, summer session for credit.

Computers on Campus 217 computers/terminals and 1,000 ports are available on campus for general student use. Students can access the following: campus intranet, computer help desk, free student e-mail accounts. Campuswide network is available. 100% of college-owned or -operated housing units are wired for high-speed Internet access. Wireless service is available via entire campus.

Student Life *Housing:* on-campus residence required through sophomore year. *Options:* men-only, women-only, cooperative, disabled students. Campus housing is university owned. Freshman campus housing is guaranteed. *Activities and organizations:* drama/theater group, student-run newspaper, choral group, marching band, Baptist Student Union, Student Foundation, Student Congress, Fellowship Christian Athletes, Unity Group. *Campus security:* 24-hour emergency response devices and patrols, late-night transport/escort service, controlled dormitory access. *Student services:* health clinic, personal/psychological counseling.

Athletics Member NCAA. All Division III. *Intercollegiate sports:* baseball M, basketball M/W, cheerleading M (c)/W (c), football M, golf M/W, soccer M/W, softball W, tennis M/W, volleyball W. *Intramural sports:* badminton M/W, basketball M/W, bowling M/W, football M/W, golf M/W, gymnastics M (c)/W (c), racquetball M (c)/W (c), rugby M (c)/W (c), soccer M/W, softball M/W, tennis M (c)/W (c), ultimate Frisbee M/W, volleyball M/W.

Standardized Tests *Required:* SAT or ACT (for admission).

Costs (2008–09) *Comprehensive fee:* $23,560 includes full-time tuition ($17,400), mandatory fees ($980), and room and board ($5180). Part-time tuition: $580 per semester hour. *Required fees:* $105 per term part-time. *College room only:* $2492.

Financial Aid Of all full-time matriculated undergraduates who enrolled in 2007, 1,684 applied for aid, 1,220 were judged to have need, 996 had their need fully met. 194 Federal Work-Study jobs (averaging $1338). 307 state and other part-time jobs (averaging $1516). In 2007, 465 non-need-based awards were made. *Average percent of need met:* 72%. *Average financial aid package:* $14,838. *Average need-based loan:* $4062. *Average need-based gift aid:* $6290. *Average non-need-based aid:* $3723. *Average indebtedness upon graduation:* $31,934.

Applying *Options:* electronic application, deferred entrance. *Application fee:* $50. *Required:* high school transcript, minimum 2.0 GPA. *Recommended:* letters of recommendation. *Application deadlines:* rolling (freshmen), rolling (transfers). *Notification:* continuous (freshmen), continuous (transfers).

Freshman Application Contact Ms. Brynn Reynolds, Visitor Coordinator, Hardin-Simmons University, Box 16050, Abilene, TX 79698-6050. *Phone:* 325-670-5890. *Toll-free phone:* 877-464-7889. *Fax:* 325-671-2115. *E-mail:* breynolds@hsutx.edu.

HOUSTON BAPTIST UNIVERSITY

Houston, Texas **www.hbu.edu/**

- **Independent Baptist** comprehensive, founded 1960
- **Urban** 100-acre campus
- **Endowment** $94.0 million
- **Coed** 1,992 undergraduate students, 90% full-time, 67% women, 33% men
- **Moderately difficult** entrance level, 48% of applicants were admitted

Undergraduates 1,794 full-time, 198 part-time. Students come from 23 states and territories, 38 other countries, 3% are from out of state, 19% African American, 16% Asian American or Pacific Islander, 17% Hispanic American, 0.4% Native American, 6% international, 14% transferred in, 32% live on campus. *Retention:* 70% of 2006 full-time freshmen returned.

Freshmen *Admission:* 4,005 applied, 1,911 admitted, 456 enrolled. *Test scores:* SAT critical reading scores over 500: 63%; SAT math scores over 500: 65%; SAT writing scores over 500: 61%; ACT scores over 18: 88%; SAT critical reading scores over 600: 25%; SAT math scores over 600: 24%; SAT writing scores over 600: 21%; ACT scores over 24: 30%; SAT critical reading scores over 700: 3%; SAT math scores over 700: 2%; SAT writing scores over 700: 4%; ACT scores over 30: 3%.

Faculty *Total:* 202, 58% full-time, 54% with terminal degrees. *Student/faculty ratio:* 15:1.

Majors Accounting; art teacher education; biblical studies; bilingual and multilingual education; biology/biological sciences; biology teacher education; business administration and management; business/commerce; business/managerial economics; chemistry; child development; Christian studies; communication and media related; communication/speech communication and rhetoric; computer and information sciences; computer science; counselor education/school counseling and guidance; developmental and child psychology; early childhood education; economics; education; elementary education; engineering science; English; English/language arts teacher education; entrepreneurship; finance; fine/studio arts; foreign languages related; French; health and physical education; history; information science/studies; interdisciplinary studies; international business/trade/commerce; kindergarten/preschool education; kinesiology and exercise science; liberal arts and sciences/liberal studies; marketing/marketing management; mass communication/media; mathematics; mathematics teacher education; middle school education; molecular biology; music; music performance; music teacher education; music theory and composition; nursing (registered nurse training); physical education teaching and coaching; physics; political science and government; pre-law studies; psychology; public policy analysis; religious/sacred music; religious studies; Romance languages related; science teacher education; secondary education; social studies teacher education; sociology; Spanish; special education; speech and rhetoric.

Academics *Calendar:* quarters. *Degrees:* associate, bachelor's, master's, post-master's, and postbachelor's certificates. *Special study options:* academic remediation for entering students, accelerated degree program, adult/continuing education programs, advanced placement credit, double majors, English as a second language, honors programs, independent study, internships, part-time degree program, study abroad, summer session for credit. *ROTC:* Army (c).

Computers on Campus 95 computers/terminals are available on campus for general student use. Students can access the following: campus intranet, computer help desk, free student e-mail accounts, online (class) grades, online (class) registration, online (class) schedules. Campuswide network is available. Wireless service is available via entire campus.

Student Life *Housing:* on-campus residence required for freshman year. *Options:* men-only, women-only, disabled students. Campus housing is university owned. Freshman campus housing is guaranteed. *Activities and organizations:* drama/theater group, student-run newspaper, television station, choral group, Alpha Epsilon Delta, Alpha Phi Omega, Association of Student Educators, Alpha Kappa Psi, Phi Mu, national fraternities, national sororities. *Campus security:* 24-hour emergency response devices and patrols, late-night transport/escort service. *Student services:* health clinic, personal/psychological counseling.

Athletics Member NCAA. All Division I. *Intercollegiate sports:* baseball M (s), basketball M (s)/W (s), cheerleading M (s)/W (s), cross-country running M (s)/W (s), golf M (s)/W (s), soccer M (s)/W (s), softball W (s), track and field M (s)/W (s), volleyball W (s). *Intramural sports:* badminton M/W, basketball M/W, bowling M/W, football M/W, golf M/W, soccer M/W, softball M/W, table tennis M/W, tennis M/W, ultimate Frisbee M/W, volleyball M/W.

Standardized Tests *Required:* SAT or ACT (for admission).

Costs (2008–09) *Comprehensive fee:* $23,815 includes full-time tuition ($18,820) and room and board ($4995). Part-time tuition: $700 per credit hour.

Financial Aid Of all full-time matriculated undergraduates who enrolled in 2007, 1,157 applied for aid, 482 were judged to have need, 78 had their need fully met. 161 Federal Work-Study jobs (averaging $685). In 2007, 916 non-need-based awards were made. *Average percent of need met:* 64%. *Average financial aid package:* $14,970. *Average need-based loan:* $3533. *Average need-based gift aid:* $8844. *Average non-need-based aid:* $7096. *Average indebtedness upon graduation:* $4331. *Financial aid deadline:* 4/15.

Applying *Options:* early admission, deferred entrance. *Application fee:* $25. *Required:* essay or personal statement, high school transcript, 2 letters of recommendation. *Recommended:* interview. *Application deadlines:* rolling (freshmen), rolling (transfers). *Notification:* continuous (freshmen), continuous (transfers).

Freshman Application Contact Eduardo Borges, Director of Admissions, Houston Baptist University, 7502 Fondren Road, Houston, TX 77074-3298. *Phone:* 281-649-3299. *Toll-free phone:* 800-696-3210. *Fax:* 281-649-3217. *E-mail:* eborges@hbu.edu.

HOWARD PAYNE UNIVERSITY

Brownwood, Texas **www.hputx.edu/**

- **Independent** 4-year, founded 1889, affiliated with Baptist General Convention of Texas
- **Small-town** 30-acre campus
- **Endowment** $49.9 million
- **Coed** 1,370 undergraduate students, 76% full-time, 48% women, 52% men
- **Moderately difficult** entrance level, 62% of applicants were admitted

Undergraduates 1,039 full-time, 331 part-time. Students come from 19 states and territories, 4% are from out of state, 7% African American, 0.9% Asian American or Pacific Islander, 15% Hispanic American, 0.9% Native American, 0.5% international, 17% transferred in, 59% live on campus. *Retention:* 59% of 2006 full-time freshmen returned.

Freshmen *Admission:* 960 applied, 598 admitted, 260 enrolled. *Average high school GPA:* 3.40. *Test scores:* SAT critical reading scores over 500: 45%; SAT math scores over 500: 50%; ACT scores over 18: 76%; SAT critical reading scores over 600: 13%; SAT math scores over 600: 12%; ACT scores over 24: 22%; SAT critical reading scores over 700: 2%; SAT math scores over 700: 1%; ACT scores over 30: 3%.

Faculty *Total:* 156, 50% full-time, 40% with terminal degrees. *Student/faculty ratio:* 11:1.

Majors Accounting; American studies; ancient Near Eastern and biblical languages; applied art; art; art teacher education; athletic training; behavioral sciences; biblical studies; biology/biological sciences; biology teacher education; business administration and management; business/commerce; business teacher education; chemistry; communication/speech communication and rhetoric; computer science; drama and dance teacher education; dramatic/theater arts; education; education (multiple levels); elementary education; English; English as a second/foreign language (teaching); English/language arts teacher education; European studies; finance; fine/studio arts; general studies; health and physical education; health/health care administration; health professions related; health science; history; history teacher education; information science/studies; kindergarten/preschool education; kinesiology and exercise science; legal assistant/paralegal; liberal arts and sciences and humanities related; liberal arts and sciences/liberal studies; marketing/marketing management; mathematics; mathematics teacher education; modern languages; music; music performance; music teacher education; parks, recreation and leisure; philosophy; physical education teaching and coaching; piano and organ; political science and government; pre-law studies; pre-medical studies; psychology; public relations/image management; religious education; religious/sacred music; religious studies; science teacher education; secondary education; social sciences; social science teacher education; social studies teacher education; social work; sociology; Spanish; Spanish language teacher education; speech and rhetoric; speech teacher education; sport and fitness administration/management; telecommunications; theology; violin, viola, guitar and other stringed instruments; voice and opera; wind/percussion instruments.

Academics *Calendar:* semesters. *Degrees:* certificates, associate, bachelor's, and master's. *Special study options:* academic remediation for entering students, adult/continuing education programs, advanced placement credit, double majors, English as a second language, honors programs, independent study, internships, off-campus study, part-time degree program, services for LD students, study abroad, summer session for credit.

Computers on Campus 228 computers/terminals and 200 ports are available on campus for general student use. Students can access the following: campus intranet, computer help desk, free student e-mail accounts, online (class) grades, online (class) schedules. Campuswide network is available. 100% of college-owned or -operated housing units are wired for high-speed Internet access. Wireless service is available via computer centers, computer labs, libraries, student centers.

Student Life *Housing:* on-campus residence required through sophomore year. *Options:* men-only, women-only. Campus housing is university owned. Freshman campus housing is guaranteed. *Activities and organizations:* drama/theater group, student-run newspaper, radio and television station, choral group, marching band, Baptist Student Ministry, Zeta Zeta Zeta, Delta Chi Ro, Student Foundation, Iota Chi Alpha. *Campus security:* 24-hour emergency response devices and patrols, late-night transport/escort service, controlled dormitory access, 12-hour patrols by trained security personnel. *Student services:* health clinic, personal/psychological counseling.

Athletics Member NCAA. All Division III. *Intercollegiate sports:* baseball M, basketball M/W, cross-country running M/W, football M, soccer M/W, softball W, tennis M/W, track and field M/W, volleyball W. *Intramural sports:* basketball M/W, football M, soccer M/W, softball W, tennis M/W, volleyball W.

Standardized Tests *Required:* SAT or ACT (for admission).

Costs (2008–09) *Comprehensive fee:* $21,860 includes full-time tuition ($16,350), mandatory fees ($1050), and room and board ($4460). Part-time tuition: $485 per credit hour. *College room only:* $1980.

Financial Aid Of all full-time matriculated undergraduates who enrolled in 2004, 901 applied for aid, 790 were judged to have need, 227 had their need fully met. 118 Federal Work-Study jobs (averaging $2000). 9 state and other part-time jobs (averaging $2000). In 2004, 151 non-need-based awards were made. *Average percent of need met:* 79%. *Average financial aid package:* $10,571. *Average need-based loan:* $3486. *Average need-based gift aid:* $6888. *Average non-need-based aid:* $5155. *Average indebtedness upon graduation:* $18,960.

Applying *Options:* electronic application. *Application fee:* $25. *Required:* high school transcript, minimum 3.0 GPA. *Recommended:* letters of recommendation, interview. *Application deadlines:* 8/1 (freshmen), 8/1 (out-of-state freshmen), 8/1 (transfers). *Notification:* continuous (freshmen), continuous (out-of-state freshmen), continuous (transfers).

Freshman Application Contact Ms. Cheryl Mangrum, Associate Director of Admission, Howard Payne University, HPU Station Box 828, 1000 Fisk Avenue, Brownwood, TX 76801. *Phone:* 325-649-8020. *Toll-free phone:* 800-880-4478. *Fax:* 325-649-8901. *E-mail:* enroll@hputx.edu.

HUSTON-TILLOTSON UNIVERSITY

Austin, Texas **www.htu.edu/**

- **Independent interdenominational** 4-year, founded 1875
- **Urban** 23-acre campus
- **Endowment** $7.0 million
- **Coed** 727 undergraduate students, 94% full-time, 50% women, 50% men
- **Moderately difficult** entrance level, 41% of applicants were admitted

Undergraduates 680 full-time, 47 part-time. Students come from 24 states and territories, 10 other countries, 6% are from out of state, 76% African American, 0.8% Asian American or Pacific Islander, 12% Hispanic American, 2% international, 11% transferred in, 38% live on campus. *Retention:* 52% of 2006 full-time freshmen returned.

Freshmen *Admission:* 484 applied, 198 admitted, 194 enrolled. *Average high school GPA:* 2.8. *Test scores:* SAT critical reading scores over 500: 10%; SAT math scores over 500: 23%; ACT scores over 18: 23%; SAT critical reading scores over 600: 4%; SAT math scores over 600: 4%; ACT scores over 24: 5%; SAT critical reading scores over 700: 2%.

Faculty *Total:* 66, 52% full-time, 56% with terminal degrees. *Student/faculty ratio:* 16:1.

Majors Accounting; American government and politics; biology/biological sciences; business administration and management; chemistry; computer science; criminal justice/safety; education; elementary education; English; history; interdisciplinary studies; mathematics; music; physical education teaching and coaching; political science and government; pre-medical studies; psychology; secondary education; social studies teacher education; sociology.

Academics *Calendar:* semesters. *Degrees:* bachelor's and postbachelor's certificates. *Special study options:* academic remediation for entering students, accelerated degree program, advanced placement credit, cooperative education, double majors, English as a second language, internships, part-time degree program, services for LD students, summer session for credit. *ROTC:* Army (c), Navy (c). *Unusual degree programs:* 3-2 engineering with Prairie View A&M University.

Computers on Campus 400 computers/terminals are available on campus for general student use. Students can access the following: free student e-mail accounts, online (class) grades. Campuswide network is available. Wireless service is available via entire campus.

Student Life *Housing:* on-campus residence required for freshman year. *Options:* men-only, women-only. Campus housing is university owned. Freshman campus housing is guaranteed. *Activities and organizations:* choral group, Student Government Association, Toastmasters, Pre-Alumni Council, national fraternities, national sororities. *Campus security:* 24-hour patrols. *Student services:* health clinic, personal/psychological counseling.

Athletics Member NAIA. *Intercollegiate sports:* baseball M, basketball M/W, cross-country running W, soccer M/W, track and field M/W, volleyball W. *Intramural sports:* basketball M/W, football M, volleyball M/W.

Standardized Tests *Required:* SAT or ACT (for admission).

Costs (2007–08) *Comprehensive fee:* $15,930 includes full-time tuition ($8436), mandatory fees ($1602), and room and board ($5892). Full-time tuition and fees vary according to course load. Part-time tuition: $281 per credit hour. Part-time tuition and fees vary according to course load. *Required fees:* $92 per credit hour part-time. *College room only:* $2506. Room and board charges vary according to housing facility. *Payment plan:* deferred payment. *Waivers:* employees or children of employees.

Financial Aid Of all full-time matriculated undergraduates who enrolled in 2002, 581 applied for aid, 558 were judged to have need, 96 had their need fully met. 96 Federal Work-Study jobs (averaging $1247). 3 state and other part-time jobs (averaging $1662). *Average financial aid package:* $8471. *Average need-based loan:* $3245. *Average need-based gift aid:* $8293.

Applying *Application fee:* $25. *Required:* essay or personal statement, high school transcript, minimum 2.0 GPA. *Required for some:* interview. *Application deadlines:* 7/1 (freshmen), 7/1 (transfers).

Freshman Application Contact Mrs. Shakitha Stinson, Huston-Tillotson University, 900 Chicon Street, Austin, TX 78702. *Phone:* 512-505-3029. *Fax:* 512-505-3192. *E-mail:* slstinson@htu.edu.

JARVIS CHRISTIAN COLLEGE

Hawkins, Texas **www.jarvis.edu/**

- **Independent** 4-year, founded 1912, affiliated with Christian Church (Disciples of Christ)
- **Rural** 465-acre campus
- **Endowment** $15.0 million
- **Coed** 712 undergraduate students, 92% full-time, 50% women, 50% men
- **Minimally difficult** entrance level, 21% of applicants were admitted

Undergraduates 658 full-time, 54 part-time. Students come from 27 states and territories, 2 other countries, 21% are from out of state, 94% African American, 5% Hispanic American, 0.3% international, 14% transferred in, 83% live on campus. *Retention:* 51% of 2006 full-time freshmen returned.

Freshmen *Admission:* 589 applied, 124 admitted, 124 enrolled. *Average high school GPA:* 2.5. *Test scores:* SAT critical reading scores over 500: 39%; SAT math scores over 500: 13%; SAT writing scores over 500: 41%; ACT scores over 18: 20%; SAT critical reading scores over 600: 9%; SAT math scores over 600: 3%; SAT writing scores over 600: 11%; ACT scores over 24: 12%.

Faculty *Total:* 56, 79% full-time, 32% with terminal degrees. *Student/faculty ratio:* 13:1.

Majors Accounting; biology/biological sciences; business administration and management; business teacher education; chemistry; computer science; economics; elementary education; English; health and physical education; history; kindergarten/preschool education; marketing/marketing management; mathematics; music; music teacher education; physical education teaching and coaching; physics; reading teacher education; religious studies; secondary education; sociology; special education.

Academics *Calendar:* semesters. *Degree:* bachelor's. *Special study options:* academic remediation for entering students, adult/continuing education programs, advanced placement credit, cooperative education, distance learning, honors programs, internships, off-campus study, part-time degree program, summer session for credit. *Unusual degree programs:* 3-2 engineering with University of Texas at Arlington; nursing with University of Texas at Tyler; mass communication with University of North Texas.

Computers on Campus 318 computers/terminals are available on campus for general student use. Campuswide network is available. 100% of college-owned or -operated housing units are wired for high-speed Internet access. Wireless service is available via classrooms, computer centers, computer labs, dorm rooms, learning centers, libraries, student centers.

Student Life *Housing options:* men-only, women-only, disabled students. Campus housing is university owned. *Activities and organizations:* drama/theater group, student-run newspaper, choral group, Student Government Association, SIFE, Student Ministers' Association, SNEA, Residence Hall Councils, national fraternities, national sororities. *Campus security:* 24-hour patrols. *Student services:* health clinic, personal/psychological counseling.

Athletics Member NAIA. *Intercollegiate sports:* baseball M, basketball M/W, cheerleading W, volleyball W. *Intramural sports:* baseball M, basketball M/W, football M, golf M, soccer M, softball M/W, swimming and diving M/W, table tennis M/W, tennis M/W, volleyball M/W, water polo M/W, weight lifting M/W.

Standardized Tests *Recommended:* ACT (for admission), SAT or ACT (for admission).

Costs (2008–09) *One-time required fee:* $25. *Comprehensive fee:* $13,162 includes full-time tuition ($7416), mandatory fees ($792), and room and board ($4954). *College room only:* $2472.

Financial Aid Of all full-time matriculated undergraduates who enrolled in 2005, 591 applied for aid, 550 were judged to have need, 507 had their need fully met. 160 Federal Work-Study jobs, 4 state and other part-time jobs (averaging $4800). In 2005, 46 non-need-based awards were made. *Average percent of need met:* 94%. *Average financial aid package:* $13,600. *Average need-based loan:* $4400. *Average need-based gift aid:* $3200. *Average non-need-based aid:* $12,500. *Average indebtedness upon graduation:* $14,500.

Applying *Options:* electronic application. *Application fee:* $25. *Required:* high school transcript. *Recommended:* minimum 2.0 GPA. *Application deadlines:* 8/1 (freshmen), rolling (transfers). *Notification:* 8/15 (freshmen).

Freshman Application Contact Mr. Christopher Wooten, Admissions Counselor, Jarvis Christian College, PO Box 1470, Hawkins, TX 75765-9989. *Phone:* 903-769-5734. *Fax:* 903-769-4842. *E-mail:* chris_wooten@jarvis.edu.

LAMAR UNIVERSITY

Beaumont, Texas **www.lamar.edu/**

Freshman Application Contact Ms. Melissa Chesser, Director of Recruitment, Lamar University, PO Box 10009, Beaumont, TX 77710. *Phone:* 409-880-8888. *Fax:* 409-880-8463. *E-mail:* admissions@hal.lamar.edu.

LETOURNEAU UNIVERSITY

Longview, Texas **www.letu.edu/**

- **Independent nondenominational** comprehensive, founded 1946
- **Suburban** 162-acre campus
- **Endowment** $4.4 million
- **Coed** 3,597 undergraduate students, 87% full-time, 58% women, 42% men
- 70% of applicants were admitted

Undergraduates 3,139 full-time, 458 part-time. Students come from 50 states and territories, 27 other countries, 55% are from out of state, 22% African American, 2% Asian American or Pacific Islander, 8% Hispanic American, 0.4% Native American, 0.8% international, 2% transferred in, 76% live on campus. *Retention:* 78% of 2006 full-time freshmen returned.

Freshmen *Admission:* 938 applied, 658 admitted, 323 enrolled. *Average high school GPA:* 3.56. *Test scores:* SAT critical reading scores over 500: 78%; SAT math scores over 500: 83%; SAT writing scores over 500: 71%; ACT scores over 18: 97%; SAT critical reading scores over 600: 41%; SAT math scores over 600: 47%; SAT writing scores over 600: 31%; ACT scores over 24: 60%; SAT critical reading scores over 700: 11%; SAT math scores over 700: 11%; SAT writing scores over 700: 5%; ACT scores over 30: 17%.

Faculty *Total:* 361, 20% full-time, 48% with terminal degrees. *Student/faculty ratio:* 19:1.

Majors Accounting; airframe mechanics and aircraft maintenance technology; airline pilot and flight crew; avionics maintenance technology; biblical studies; biology/biological sciences; biomedical/medical engineering; business administration and management; chemistry; computer engineering; computer engineering technology; computer science; drafting and design technology; electrical, electronic and communications engineering technology; electrical, electronics and communications engineering; elementary education; engineering; engineering technology; English; finance; history; information science/studies; interdisciplinary studies; international business/trade/commerce; management information systems; marketing/marketing management; mathematics; mechanical engineering; mechanical engineering/mechanical technology; missionary studies and missiology; natural sciences; physical education teaching and coaching; predentistry studies; pre-law studies; pre-medical studies; pre-veterinary studies; psychology; religious studies; secondary education; sport and fitness administration/management; welding technology.

Academics *Calendar:* semesters. *Degrees:* associate, bachelor's, and master's. *Special study options:* academic remediation for entering students, accelerated degree program, adult/continuing education programs, advanced placement credit, cooperative education, distance learning, double majors, honors programs, independent study, internships, off-campus study, part-time degree program, services for LD students, study abroad, summer session for credit.

Computers on Campus 191 computers/terminals are available on campus for general student use. Students can access the following: online (class) registration. Campuswide network is available.

Student Life *Housing:* on-campus residence required through junior year. *Options:* men-only, women-only, disabled students. Campus housing is university owned. Freshman campus housing is guaranteed. *Activities and organizations:* drama/theater group, student-run newspaper, choral group, student ministries,

Themelios, Student Foundation, Student Senate, Roller Hockey Club. *Campus security:* 24-hour emergency response devices and patrols, late-night transport/escort service, controlled dormitory access. *Student services:* health clinic, personal/psychological counseling.

Athletics Member NCAA, NCCAA. All NCAA Division III. *Intercollegiate sports:* baseball M, basketball M/W, cross-country running M/W, golf M/W, soccer M/W, softball W, tennis M/W, volleyball W. *Intramural sports:* badminton M/W, basketball M/W, bowling M/W, cross-country running M/W, football M/W, golf M/W, racquetball M/W, soccer M/W, softball M/W, swimming and diving M/W, table tennis M/W, tennis M/W, volleyball M/W.

Standardized Tests *Required:* SAT or ACT (for admission).

Costs (2007–08) *Comprehensive fee:* $24,860 includes full-time tuition ($17,710), mandatory fees ($200), and room and board ($6950). Part-time tuition: $322 per hour. Part-time tuition and fees vary according to course load. *Room and board:* Room and board charges vary according to board plan. *Payment plan:* installment. *Waivers:* employees or children of employees.

Financial Aid Of all full-time matriculated undergraduates who enrolled in 2005, 1,066 applied for aid, 901 were judged to have need, 147 had their need fully met. In 2005, 233 non-need-based awards were made. *Average percent of need met:* 69%. *Average financial aid package:* $11,386. *Average need-based loan:* $3981. *Average need-based gift aid:* $7816. *Average non-need-based aid:* $4102.

Applying *Options:* electronic application, deferred entrance. *Application fee:* $25. *Application deadlines:* 8/1 (freshmen), 8/1 (transfers). *Notification:* continuous (freshmen), continuous (transfers).

Freshman Application Contact Mr. James Townsend, Director of Admissions, LeTourneau University, PO Box 7001, 2100 South Mobberly Avenue, Longview, TX 75607-7001. *Phone:* 903-233-3400. *Toll-free phone:* 800-759-8811. *Fax:* 903-233-3411. *E-mail:* admissions@letu.edu.

LUBBOCK CHRISTIAN UNIVERSITY

Lubbock, Texas **www.lcu.edu/**

- **Independent** comprehensive, founded 1957, affiliated with Church of Christ
- **Suburban** 120-acre campus
- **Endowment** $10.9 million
- **Coed** 1,718 undergraduate students, 81% full-time, 57% women, 43% men
- **Moderately difficult** entrance level, 73% of applicants were admitted

Undergraduates 1,397 full-time, 321 part-time. Students come from 33 states and territories, 7 other countries, 10% are from out of state, 5% African American, 0.6% Asian American or Pacific Islander, 16% Hispanic American, 0.2% Native American, 0.6% international, 15% transferred in, 28% live on campus. *Retention:* 65% of 2006 full-time freshmen returned.

Freshmen *Admission:* 948 applied, 692 admitted, 305 enrolled. *Average high school GPA:* 3.42. *Test scores:* SAT critical reading scores over 500: 43%; SAT math scores over 500: 50%; ACT scores over 18: 82%; SAT critical reading scores over 600: 17%; SAT math scores over 600: 13%; ACT scores over 24: 27%; SAT critical reading scores over 700: 5%; SAT math scores over 700: 1%; ACT scores over 30: 3%.

Faculty *Total:* 170, 50% full-time, 46% with terminal degrees. *Student/faculty ratio:* 14:1.

Majors Accounting; agricultural business and management; agriculture; ancient Near Eastern and biblical languages; animal sciences; applied art; art teacher education; biblical studies; biology/biological sciences; business administration and management; chemistry; clinical laboratory science/medical technology; computer and information sciences; computer science; criminal justice/safety; design and visual communications; early childhood education; education; elementary education; engineering; family and community services; finance; health and physical education; humanities; kinesiology and exercise science; marketing/marketing management; mass communication/media; mathematics; middle school education; missionary studies and missiology; music; music teacher education; nursing related; physical education teaching and coaching; plant protection and integrated pest management; plant sciences; pre-law studies; psychology; secondary education; social work; special education; sport and fitness administration/management; theology and religious vocations related; youth ministry.

Academics *Calendar:* semesters. *Degrees:* bachelor's, master's, and first professional. *Special study options:* academic remediation for entering students, accelerated degree program, adult/continuing education programs, advanced placement credit, distance learning, double majors, honors programs, internships, part-time degree program, services for LD students, student-designed majors, study abroad, summer session for credit. *ROTC:* Army (c), Air Force (c). *Unusual degree programs:* 3-2 engineering with Texas Tech University.

Computers on Campus 159 computers/terminals are available on campus for general student use. Students can access the following: computer help desk, free student e-mail accounts, online (class) registration. Campuswide network is available. 100% of college-owned or -operated housing units are wired for high-speed Internet access. Wireless service is available via entire campus.

Student Life *Housing:* on-campus residence required through sophomore year. *Options:* men-only, women-only, disabled students. Campus housing is university owned. Freshman campus housing is guaranteed. *Activities and organizations:* drama/theater group, student-run newspaper, choral group. *Campus security:* 24-hour patrols. *Student services:* health clinic, personal/psychological counseling.

Athletics Member NAIA. *Intercollegiate sports:* baseball M (s), basketball M (s)/W (s), cheerleading M/W, cross-country running M/W, golf M/W, track and field M/W, volleyball W (s). *Intramural sports:* badminton M/W, basketball M/W, bowling M/W, cross-country running M/W, football M/W, golf M/W, racquetball M/W, soccer M/W, softball M/W, table tennis M/W, tennis M/W, track and field M/W, volleyball M/W.

Standardized Tests *Required:* SAT or ACT (for admission).

Costs (2007–08) *Comprehensive fee:* $19,040 includes full-time tuition ($13,134), mandatory fees ($1156), and room and board ($4750). Part-time tuition: $421 per semester hour. *Required fees:* $431 per term part-time.

Financial Aid Of all full-time matriculated undergraduates who enrolled in 2007, 1,005 applied for aid, 877 were judged to have need, 89 had their need fully met. 871 Federal Work-Study jobs (averaging $1631). 98 state and other part-time jobs (averaging $245). In 2007, 207 non-need-based awards were made. *Average percent of need met:* 71%. *Average financial aid package:* $11,608. *Average need-based loan:* $4029. *Average need-based gift aid:* $7584. *Average non-need-based aid:* $10,935. *Average indebtedness upon graduation:* $25,352.

Applying *Options:* electronic application. *Application fee:* $25. *Required:* high school transcript. *Application deadlines:* 8/1 (freshmen), rolling (transfers). *Notification:* continuous (freshmen), continuous (transfers).

Freshman Application Contact Mr. Mondy Brewer, Director of Admissions, Lubbock Christian University, 5601 19th Street, Lubbock, TX 79407. *Phone:* 806-720-7151. *Toll-free phone:* 800-933-7601. *Fax:* 806-720-7162. *E-mail:* admissions@lcu.edu.

MCMURRY UNIVERSITY

Abilene, Texas **www.mcm.edu/**

- **Independent United Methodist** 4-year, founded 1923
- **Urban** 41-acre campus
- **Endowment** $62.9 million
- **Coed** 1,462 undergraduate students, 81% full-time, 50% women, 50% men
- **Moderately difficult** entrance level, 53% of applicants were admitted

Undergraduates 1,183 full-time, 279 part-time. Students come from 23 states and territories, 8 other countries, 4% are from out of state, 14% African American, 1% Asian American or Pacific Islander, 16% Hispanic American, 0.9% Native American, 1% international, 12% transferred in, 45% live on campus. *Retention:* 61% of 2006 full-time freshmen returned.

Freshmen *Admission:* 1,537 applied, 811 admitted, 311 enrolled. *Average high school GPA:* 3.4. *Test scores:* SAT critical reading scores over 500: 35%; SAT math scores over 500: 53%; ACT scores over 18: 74%; SAT critical reading scores over 600: 10%; SAT math scores over 600: 15%; ACT scores over 24: 18%; SAT critical reading scores over 700: 1%; SAT math scores over 700: 1%; ACT scores over 30: 2%.

Faculty *Total:* 129, 58% full-time, 50% with terminal degrees. *Student/faculty ratio:* 14:1.

Majors Accounting; art teacher education; athletic training; biochemistry; biology/biological sciences; business administration and management; business/commerce; chemistry; computer and information sciences; creative writing; design and applied arts related; dramatic/theater arts; elementary education; English; finance; fine/studio arts; history; management information systems; marketing/marketing management; mathematics; middle school education; music; nursing (registered nurse training); physical education teaching and coaching; physics; political science and government; psychology; religious studies; secondary education; sociology; Spanish.

Academics *Calendar:* semesters plus May term. *Degree:* bachelor's. *Special study options:* academic remediation for entering students, accelerated degree program, adult/continuing education programs, advanced placement credit, double majors, honors programs, independent study, internships, part-time degree program, services for LD students, study abroad, summer session for credit. *ROTC:* Air Force (c).

Computers on Campus 236 computers/terminals and 693 ports are available on campus for general student use. Students can access the following: computer help desk, free student e-mail accounts, online (class) grades, online (class) schedules, Blackboard. Campuswide network is available. 100% of college-owned or -operated housing units are wired for high-speed Internet access. Wireless service is available via entire campus.

Student Life *Housing:* on-campus residence required through junior year. *Options:* coed, men-only, women-only. Campus housing is university owned and is provided by a third party. Freshman campus housing is guaranteed. *Activities and organizations:* drama/theater group, student-run newspaper, choral group, marching band, Alpha Phi Omega (APO), Religious Life Council (RLC), McMurry Student Government (MSG), Campus Activity Board (CAB), Servant Leadership. *Campus security:* 24-hour emergency response devices and patrols, late-night transport/escort service, controlled dormitory access. *Student services:* health clinic, personal/psychological counseling.

Athletics Member NCAA. All Division III. *Intercollegiate sports:* baseball M, basketball M/W, cross-country running M/W, football M, golf M/W, soccer M/W, swimming and diving M/W, tennis M/W, track and field M/W, volleyball W. *Intramural sports:* basketball M/W, football M/W, golf M/W, racquetball M/W, soccer M/W, softball M/W, tennis M/W, ultimate Frisbee M/W, volleyball M/W.

Standardized Tests *Required:* SAT or ACT (for admission).

Costs (2008–09) *One-time required fee:* $150. *Comprehensive fee:* $24,864 includes full-time tuition ($17,225), mandatory fees ($950), and room and board ($6689). Part-time tuition: $535 per semester hour. *College room only:* $3216.

Financial Aid Of all full-time matriculated undergraduates who enrolled in 2007, 1,071 applied for aid, 959 were judged to have need, 215 had their need fully met. 289 Federal Work-Study jobs (averaging $1308). 103 state and other part-time jobs (averaging $1518). In 2007, 106 non-need-based awards were made. *Average percent of need met:* 90%. *Average financial aid package:* $15,971. *Average need-based loan:* $4393. *Average need-based gift aid:* $8795. *Average non-need-based aid:* $4285. *Average indebtedness upon graduation:* $23,050.

Applying *Options:* electronic application, deferred entrance. *Application fee:* $20. *Required:* essay or personal statement, high school transcript, minimum 2.0 GPA. *Required for some:* 3 letters of recommendation. *Application deadlines:* 8/15 (freshmen), 8/15 (transfers). *Notification:* continuous (freshmen), continuous (transfers).

Freshman Application Contact Mr. Scott Smiley, Director of Admissions, McMurry University, McMurry Station 278, Abilene, TX 79697. *Phone:* 325-793-4705. *Toll-free phone:* 800-477-0077. *Fax:* 325-793-4701. *E-mail:* admissions@mcm.edu.

MIDLAND COLLEGE

Midland, Texas **www.midland.edu/**

Freshman Application Contact Mr. Trey Wetendorf, Admissions Director, Midland College, 3600 North Garfield, Midland, TX 79705-6399. *Phone:* 432-685-5502. *Toll-free phone:* 432-685-5502. *Fax:* 432-685-6401. *E-mail:* twetendorf@midland.edu.

MIDWESTERN STATE UNIVERSITY

Wichita Falls, Texas **www.mwsu.edu/**

- **State-supported** comprehensive, founded 1922
- **Urban** 255-acre campus
- **Endowment** $34.6 million
- **Coed** 5,350 undergraduate students, 73% full-time, 58% women, 42% men
- **Minimally difficult** entrance level, 69% of applicants were admitted

Undergraduates 3,884 full-time, 1,466 part-time. Students come from 44 states and territories, 30 other countries, 6% are from out of state, 13% African American, 4% Asian American or Pacific Islander, 9% Hispanic American, 0.7% Native American, 5% international, 13% transferred in, 20% live on campus. *Retention:* 72% of 2006 full-time freshmen returned.

Freshmen *Admission:* 1,538 applied, 1,054 admitted, 762 enrolled. *Average high school GPA:* 3.26. *Test scores:* SAT critical reading scores over 500: 47%; SAT math scores over 500: 55%; SAT writing scores over 500: 45%; ACT scores over 18: 91%; SAT critical reading scores over 600: 13%; SAT math scores over 600: 14%; SAT writing scores over 600: 6%; ACT scores over 24: 21%; SAT critical reading scores over 700: 1%; SAT math scores over 700: 1%; ACT scores over 30: 1%.

Faculty *Total:* 309, 68% full-time, 55% with terminal degrees. *Student/faculty ratio:* 19:1.

Majors Accounting; applied art; art; athletic training; biology/biological sciences; business administration and management; business/commerce; business/managerial economics; chemistry; clinical laboratory science/medical technology; computer engineering; criminal justice/law enforcement administration; dental hygiene; dramatic/theater arts; early childhood education; economics; engineering technology; English; environmental science; finance; geology/earth science; health and physical education related; history; humanities; information science/studies; interdisciplinary studies; international business/trade/commerce; international/global studies; kinesiology and exercise science; liberal arts and sciences/liberal studies; management information systems and services related; manufacturing technology; marketing/marketing management; mass communication/media; mathematics; mechanical engineering/mechanical technology; multi-/interdisciplinary studies related; music; music performance; music teacher education; nursing (registered nurse training); physics; political science and government; pre-dentistry studies; pre-engineering; pre-law studies; pre-medical studies; pre-pharmacy studies; pre-veterinary studies; psychology; radiologic technology/science; respiratory care therapy; secondary education; social sciences related; social work; sociology; Spanish; sport and fitness administration/management.

Academics *Calendar:* semesters. *Degrees:* associate, bachelor's, master's, and postbachelor's certificates. *Special study options:* academic remediation for entering students, adult/continuing education programs, advanced placement credit, distance learning, double majors, English as a second language, honors programs, independent study, internships, part-time degree program, services for LD students, study abroad, summer session for credit. *ROTC:* Air Force (c). *Unusual degree programs:* 3-2 business administration.

Computers on Campus 402 computers/terminals are available on campus for general student use. Students can access the following: online (class) registration. Campuswide network is available.

Student Life *Housing:* on-campus residence required through sophomore year. *Options:* coed, men-only, women-only, disabled students. Campus housing is university owned and leased by the school. Freshman applicants given priority for college housing. *Activities and organizations:* drama/theater group, student-run newspaper, television station, choral group, marching band, honor societies, political groups, national fraternities, national sororities. *Campus security:* 24-hour emergency response devices and patrols, controlled dormitory access. *Student services:* health clinic, personal/psychological counseling.

Athletics Member NCAA. All Division II. *Intercollegiate sports:* basketball M (s)/W (s), cheerleading M (s) (c)/W (s) (c), fencing M (c)/W (c), football M (s), soccer M (s)/W (s), softball W (s), tennis M (s)/W (s), volleyball W (s). *Intramural sports:* archery M/W, badminton M/W, basketball M/W, bowling M/W, football M/W, golf M/W, rugby M (c), soccer M/W, softball M/W, table tennis M/W, tennis M/W, volleyball M/W, weight lifting M/W.

Standardized Tests *Required:* SAT or ACT (for admission).

Costs (2007–08) *Tuition:* state resident $1500 full-time, $50 per credit hour part-time; nonresident $2400 full-time, $80 per credit hour part-time. *Required fees:* $3216 full-time, $232 per credit hour part-time. *Room and board:* $5220; room only: $2660.

Financial Aid Of all full-time matriculated undergraduates who enrolled in 2007, 2,408 applied for aid, 1,875 were judged to have need, 418 had their need fully met. In 2007, 697 non-need-based awards were made. *Average percent of need met:* 73%. *Average financial aid package:* $7650. *Average need-based loan:* $4384. *Average need-based gift aid:* $4372. *Average non-need-based aid:* $1638. *Average indebtedness upon graduation:* $16,627.

Applying *Application fee:* $25. *Required:* high school transcript. *Application deadlines:* 8/7 (freshmen), 8/7 (transfers). *Notification:* continuous (freshmen), continuous (transfers).

Freshman Application Contact Ms. Barbara Merkle, Director of Admissions, Midwestern State University, Wichita Falls, TX 76308. *Phone:* 940-397-4334. *Toll-free phone:* 800-842-1922. *Fax:* 940-397-4672. *E-mail:* admissions@mwsu.edu.

NORTHWOOD UNIVERSITY, TEXAS CAMPUS

Cedar Hill, Texas **www.northwood.edu/**

- **Independent** 4-year, founded 1966, administratively affiliated with Northwood University (MI)
- **Small-town** 360-acre campus with easy access to Dallas
- **Endowment** $31.1 million
- **Coed** 526 undergraduate students, 95% full-time, 48% women, 52% men
- **Moderately difficult** entrance level, 60% of applicants were admitted

Undergraduates 502 full-time, 24 part-time. Students come from 17 states and territories, 20 other countries, 6% are from out of state, 15% African American, 4% Asian American or Pacific Islander, 30% Hispanic American, 1% Native

American, 6% international, 8% transferred in, 27% live on campus. *Retention:* 78% of 2006 full-time freshmen returned.

Freshmen *Admission:* 581 applied, 350 admitted, 124 enrolled. *Average high school GPA:* 3.2. *Test scores:* SAT critical reading scores over 500: 24%; SAT math scores over 500: 37%; SAT writing scores over 500: 25%; ACT scores over 18: 81%; SAT math scores over 600: 3%; SAT writing scores over 600: 1%; ACT scores over 24: 14%; ACT scores over 30: 2%.

Faculty *Total:* 31, 77% full-time, 23% with terminal degrees. *Student/faculty ratio:* 20:1.

Majors Accounting; marketing/marketing management; vehicle and vehicle parts and accessories marketing.

Academics *Calendar:* quarters. *Degree:* bachelor's. *Special study options:* academic remediation for entering students, accelerated degree program, adult/continuing education programs, advanced placement credit, distance learning, double majors, external degree program, honors programs, independent study, internships, off-campus study, part-time degree program, study abroad, summer session for credit.

Computers on Campus 73 computers/terminals are available on campus for general student use. Students can access the following: campus intranet, computer help desk, free student e-mail accounts, online (class) grades, online (class) registration, online (class) schedules. Campuswide network is available. 100% of college-owned or -operated housing units are wired for high-speed Internet access. Wireless service is available via entire campus.

Student Life *Housing:* on-campus residence required for freshman year. *Options:* men-only, women-only. Campus housing is university owned. Freshman campus housing is guaranteed. *Activities and organizations:* drama/theater group, student-run newspaper, choral group, Association of Entertainment and Sports Management, In-Line Hockey Club, Alpha Nu Omega, Alpha Omega, Delta Epsilon Chi. *Campus security:* 24-hour patrols, student patrols, late-night transport/escort service, controlled dormitory access. *Student services:* health clinic, personal/psychological counseling.

Athletics Member NAIA. *Intercollegiate sports:* baseball M (s), cross-country running M (s)/W (s), golf M (s)/W (s), soccer M (s)/W (s), softball W (s), track and field M (s)/W (s). *Intramural sports:* basketball M/W, soccer M/W, volleyball M/W.

Standardized Tests *Required:* SAT or ACT (for admission).

Costs (2007–08) *Comprehensive fee:* $23,343 includes full-time tuition ($15,825), mandatory fees ($630), and room and board ($6888). Part-time tuition: $330 per credit hour. *College room only:* $3720.

Financial Aid Of all full-time matriculated undergraduates who enrolled in 2007, 401 applied for aid, 352 were judged to have need, 62 had their need fully met. 180 Federal Work-Study jobs (averaging $2065). In 2007, 81 non-need-based awards were made. *Average percent of need met:* 58%. *Average financial aid package:* $15,423. *Average need-based loan:* $4299. *Average need-based gift aid:* $5212. *Average non-need-based aid:* $5235. *Average indebtedness upon graduation:* $20,170.

Applying *Options:* electronic application, early admission, deferred entrance. *Application fee:* $25. *Required:* essay or personal statement, high school transcript. *Recommended:* minimum 2.0 GPA, 1 letter of recommendation, interview. *Application deadlines:* rolling (freshmen), rolling (transfers). *Notification:* continuous (freshmen), continuous (transfers).

Freshman Application Contact Ms. Sylvia Correa, Director of Admissions, Northwood University, Texas Campus, 1114 West FM 1382, Cedar Hill, TX 75104. *Phone:* 972-293-5400. *Toll-free phone:* 800-927-9663. *Fax:* 972-291-3824. *E-mail:* txadmit@northwood.edu.

OUR LADY OF THE LAKE UNIVERSITY OF SAN ANTONIO

San Antonio, Texas **www.ollusa.edu/**

- **Independent Roman Catholic** comprehensive, founded 1895
- **Urban** 75-acre campus
- **Endowment** $26.8 million
- **Coed**
- **Moderately difficult** entrance level

Faculty *Student/faculty ratio:* 13:1.

Academics *Calendar:* semesters plus 2 summer sessions. *Degrees:* bachelor's, master's, and doctoral.

Student Life *Campus security:* 24-hour emergency response devices and patrols, late-night transport/escort service, controlled dormitory access.

Standardized Tests *Required:* SAT or ACT (for admission).

Costs (2007–08) *Comprehensive fee:* $24,954 includes full-time tuition ($18,616), mandatory fees ($500), and room and board ($5838). Full-time tuition and fees vary according to class time and degree level. Part-time tuition: $610 per hour. Part-time tuition and fees vary according to class time and degree level. *Required fees:* $12 per credit hour part-time, $48 per term part-time. *College room only:* $3538. Room and board charges vary according to board plan. *Payment plans:* installment, deferred payment.

Financial Aid Of all full-time matriculated undergraduates who enrolled in 2003, 1,236 applied for aid, 1,183 were judged to have need, 173 had their need fully met. 312 Federal Work-Study jobs (averaging $1437). 64 state and other part-time jobs (averaging $1508). In 2003, 65 non-need-based awards were made. *Average percent of need met:* 87. *Average financial aid package:* $12,944. *Average need-based loan:* $3857. *Average need-based gift aid:* $3032. *Average non-need-based aid:* $7256. *Average indebtedness upon graduation:* $17,650.

Applying *Options:* electronic application, deferred entrance. *Application fee:* $25. *Required:* high school transcript. *Required for some:* interview.

Freshman Application Contact Ms. Rhonda Moses, Retention Office, Our Lady of the Lake University of San Antonio, 411 Southwest 24th Street, San Antonio, TX 78207-4689. *Phone:* 210-434-6711 Ext. 314. *Toll-free phone:* 800-436-6558. *Fax:* 210-431-4036. *E-mail:* admission@lake.ollusa.edu.

PAUL QUINN COLLEGE

Dallas, Texas **www.pqc.edu/**

- **Independent African Methodist Episcopal** 4-year, founded 1872
- **Suburban** 132-acre campus
- **Endowment** $6.2 million
- **Coed**
- **Moderately difficult** entrance level

Faculty *Student/faculty ratio:* 5:1.

Academics *Calendar:* semesters. *Degree:* bachelor's.

Student Life *Campus security:* 24-hour patrols.

Athletics Member NAIA, NSCAA.

Standardized Tests *Required:* SAT or ACT (for admission).

Costs (2007–08) *Comprehensive fee:* $12,550 includes full-time tuition ($7800) and room and board ($4750). Part-time tuition: $325 per credit hour.

Financial Aid Of all full-time matriculated undergraduates who enrolled in 2003, 743 applied for aid, 735 were judged to have need, 611 had their need fully met. 149 Federal Work-Study jobs (averaging $826). 16 state and other part-time jobs (averaging $607). *Average percent of need met:* 83. *Average financial aid package:* $9900. *Average need-based loan:* $3875. *Average need-based gift aid:* $2954. *Average indebtedness upon graduation:* $2375.

Applying *Options:* electronic application. *Application fee:* $35. *Required:* essay or personal statement, high school transcript, minimum 2.5 GPA, medical history. *Required for some:* interview. *Recommended:* letters of recommendation, interview.

Director of Admissions Ms. Nena Taylor-Richey, Director of Admissions and Recruitment, Paul Quinn College, 3837 Simpson-Stuart Road, Dallas, TX 75241-4331. *Phone:* 214-302-3575. *Toll-free phone:* 800-237-2648.

PRAIRIE VIEW A&M UNIVERSITY

Prairie View, Texas **www.pvamu.edu/**

- **State-supported** comprehensive, founded 1878, part of Texas A&M University System
- **Small-town** 1440-acre campus with easy access to Houston
- **Endowment** $50.5 million
- **Coed** 6,118 undergraduate students, 89% full-time, 57% women, 43% men
- **Moderately difficult** entrance level, 40% of applicants were admitted

Prairie View A&M University (PVAMU) is the second-oldest public institution of higher education in Texas, originating in the Texas Constitution of 1876. The University opened in 1878 as the Agricultural and Mechanical College of Texas for Colored Youth, with 8 students and 2 faculty members. PVAMU is a historically black university (HBCU) and was founded by the Texas legislature as the first state-supported college for African Americans. Today, the University enrolls more than 8,300 students and offers fifty undergraduate and thirty-seven graduate degrees, including four doctoral degrees. Its most prominent programs are in accounting, computer science, criminal justice, education, engineering, nursing, and premedicine. Major academic units include the College of Agriculture and Human Sciences, the School of Architecture, the College of Arts and Sciences, the College of Business, the College of Education, the College of Engineering, the College of Juvenile Justice, the College of Nursing, and the Graduate School. The University is fully accredited by the

Southern Association of Colleges and Schools and has specialized accreditation in several areas, including computer science, education, engineering, nursing, nutrition, and social work.

Undergraduates 5,466 full-time, 652 part-time. Students come from 37 states and territories, 40 other countries, 7% are from out of state, 90% African American, 2% Asian American or Pacific Islander, 4% Hispanic American, 0.1% Native American, 2% international, 5% transferred in, 53% live on campus. *Retention:* 76% of 2006 full-time freshmen returned.

Freshmen *Admission:* 5,899 applied, 2,385 admitted, 1,322 enrolled. *Average high school GPA:* 2.93. *Test scores:* SAT critical reading scores over 500: 15%; SAT math scores over 500: 18%; ACT scores over 18: 40%; SAT critical reading scores over 600: 1%; SAT math scores over 600: 2%; ACT scores over 24: 4%.

Faculty *Total:* 487, 74% full-time. *Student/faculty ratio:* 17:1.

Majors Accounting; agricultural teacher education; agriculture; architecture; biology/biological sciences; business administration and management; chemical engineering; chemistry; civil engineering; clinical laboratory science/medical technology; community health services counseling; computer science; computer technology/computer systems technology; criminal justice/safety; drafting and design technology; dramatic/theater arts; electrical, electronic and communications engineering technology; electrical, electronics and communications engineering; engineering technology; English; family and community services; finance; foods, nutrition, and wellness; history; industrial technology; interdisciplinary studies; marketing/marketing management; mathematics; mechanical engineering; music; nursing (registered nurse training); physics; piano and organ; political science and government; psychology; social work; sociology; Spanish; trade and industrial teacher education; voice and opera; wind/percussion instruments.

Academics *Calendar:* semesters. *Degrees:* bachelor's, master's, and doctoral. *Special study options:* academic remediation for entering students, accelerated degree program, advanced placement credit, cooperative education, distance learning, double majors, English as a second language, honors programs, independent study, internships, off-campus study, part-time degree program, services for LD students, study abroad, summer session for credit. *ROTC:* Army (b), Navy (b).

Computers on Campus 3,000 computers/terminals and 3,000 ports are available on campus for general student use. Students can access the following: campus intranet, computer help desk, free student e-mail accounts, online (class) grades, online (class) registration, online (class) schedules. Campuswide network is available. 100% of college-owned or -operated housing units are wired for high-speed Internet access. Wireless service is available via entire campus.

Student Life *Housing:* on-campus residence required for freshman year. *Options:* coed, men-only, women-only. Campus housing is provided by a third party. Freshman campus housing is guaranteed. *Activities and organizations:* drama/theater group, student-run newspaper, radio station, choral group, marching band, National Society of Black Engineers, National Association of Black Accountants, National Organization of Black Chemists and Chemical Engineers, Toastmasters International, Baptist Student Movement, national fraternities, national sororities. *Campus security:* 24-hour emergency response devices and patrols. *Student services:* health clinic, personal/psychological counseling.

Athletics Member NCAA. All Division I except football (Division I-AA). *Intercollegiate sports:* baseball M (s), basketball M (s)/W (s), cross-country running M (s)/W (s), golf M (s)/W (s), soccer W (s), softball W (s), tennis M (s)/W (s), track and field M (s)/W (s), volleyball W (s). *Intramural sports:* baseball M, basketball M/W, bowling W, cross-country running M/W, golf M/W, soccer W, softball W, tennis M/W, track and field M/W, volleyball M/W.

Standardized Tests *Required:* SAT or ACT (for admission).

Costs (2007–08) *Tuition:* area resident $4350 full-time; nonresident $12,690 full-time. *Required fees:* $1696 full-time. *Room and board:* $6477; room only: $4206. Room and board charges vary according to board plan. *Payment plan:* installment. *Waivers:* employees or children of employees.

Financial Aid Of all full-time matriculated undergraduates who enrolled in 2002, 4,622 applied for aid, 4,311 were judged to have need. 732 Federal Work-Study jobs (averaging $1934). 328 state and other part-time jobs (averaging $1146). In 2002, 271 non-need-based awards were made. *Average percent of need met:* 75%. *Average financial aid package:* $6920. *Average need-based loan:* $4000. *Average need-based gift aid:* $3300. *Average non-need-based aid:* $1400. *Average indebtedness upon graduation:* $11,000.

Applying *Options:* electronic application, deferred entrance. *Application fee:* $25. *Required:* high school transcript, minimum 2.5 GPA, letters of recommendation. *Application deadlines:* 6/1 (freshmen), 6/1 (transfers). *Notification:* continuous (freshmen), continuous (transfers).

Freshman Application Contact Ms. Mary Gooch, Director of Admissions, Prairie View A&M University, PO Box 3089, Prairie View, TX 77446-0188. *Phone:* 936-261-1066. *Fax:* 936-857-2699. *E-mail:* megooch@pvamu.edu.

See page 2542 for the College Close-Up.

RICE UNIVERSITY

Houston, Texas **www.rice.edu/**

- **Independent** university, founded 1912
- **Urban** 300-acre campus
- **Endowment** $4.7 billion
- **Coed** 3,051 undergraduate students, 98% full-time, 48% women, 52% men
- **Most difficult** entrance level, 25% of applicants were admitted

Undergraduates 2,988 full-time, 63 part-time. Students come from 57 states and territories, 44 other countries, 45% are from out of state, 7% African American, 19% Asian American or Pacific Islander, 12% Hispanic American, 0.5% Native American, 5% international, 2% transferred in, 68% live on campus. *Retention:* 97% of 2006 full-time freshmen returned.

Freshmen *Admission:* 8,968 applied, 2,251 admitted, 742 enrolled. *Test scores:* SAT critical reading scores over 500: 96%; SAT math scores over 500: 100%; SAT writing scores over 500: 96%; ACT scores over 18: 100%; SAT critical reading scores over 600: 88%; SAT math scores over 600: 92%; SAT writing scores over 600: 84%; ACT scores over 24: 96%; SAT critical reading scores over 700: 53%; SAT math scores over 700: 64%; SAT writing scores over 700: 48%; ACT scores over 30: 71%.

Faculty *Student/faculty ratio:* 5:1.

Majors Ancient/classical Greek; anthropology; applied mathematics; architecture; art; art history, criticism and conservation; Asian studies; astronomy; astrophysics; biochemistry; biology/biological sciences; biomedical/medical engineering; business administration and management; chemical engineering; chemistry; civil engineering; classics and languages, literatures and linguistics; computer and information sciences; computer engineering; ecology; economics; electrical, electronics and communications engineering; English; environmental/environmental health engineering; evolutionary biology; fine/studio arts; French; geology/earth science; geophysics and seismology; German; history; kinesiology and exercise science; Latin; Latin American studies; linguistics; materials engineering; materials science; mathematics; mechanical engineering; multi-/interdisciplinary studies related; music; music history, literature, and theory; music performance; music theory and composition; neuroscience; philosophy; physical and theoretical chemistry; physics; political science and government; psychology; public policy analysis; religious studies; Russian; Russian studies; sociology; Spanish; statistics; visual and performing arts related; women's studies.

Academics *Calendar:* semesters. *Degrees:* bachelor's, master's, and doctoral. *Special study options:* accelerated degree program, advanced placement credit, double majors, English as a second language, honors programs, independent study, internships, off-campus study, services for LD students, student-designed majors, study abroad, summer session for credit. *ROTC:* Army (c), Navy (b), Air Force (c).

Computers on Campus 523 computers/terminals are available on campus for general student use. Students can access the following: online (class) registration. Campuswide network is available.

Student Life *Housing options:* coed. Campus housing is university owned. Freshman campus housing is guaranteed. *Activities and organizations:* drama/theater group, student-run newspaper, radio and television station, choral group, marching band, Drama Club, volunteer program, intramural sports, college government, Marching Owl Band. *Campus security:* 24-hour emergency response devices and patrols, late-night transport/escort service, controlled dormitory access. *Student services:* health clinic, personal/psychological counseling, women's center.

Athletics Member NCAA. All Division I except football (Division I-A). *Intercollegiate sports:* badminton M (c)/W (c), baseball M (s), basketball M (s)/W (s), cheerleading M (c)/W (c), crew M (c)/W (c), cross-country running M (s)/W (s), fencing M (c)/W (c), field hockey W (c), golf M (s), lacrosse M (c)/W (c), rugby M (c)/W (c), sailing M (c)/W (c), soccer M (c)/W (s), softball W (c), swimming and diving W (s), tennis M (s)/W (s), track and field M (s)/W (s), ultimate Frisbee M (c)/W (c), volleyball M (c)/W (s), water polo M (c)/W (c). *Intramural sports:* badminton M/W, basketball M/W, football M/W, racquetball M/W, soccer M/W, softball M/W, swimming and diving M/W, table tennis M/W, tennis M/W, track and field M/W, volleyball M/W.

Standardized Tests *Required:* SAT and SAT Subject Tests or ACT (for admission).

Costs (2008–09) *Comprehensive fee:* $41,229 includes full-time tuition ($29,960), mandatory fees ($519), and room and board ($10,750). Part-time tuition: $1249 per credit hour. *College room only:* $7150.

Financial Aid Of all full-time matriculated undergraduates who enrolled in 2007, 2,353 applied for aid, 1,008 were judged to have need, 1,008 had their need fully met. In 2007, 594 non-need-based awards were made. *Average percent of* *need met:* 100%. *Average financial aid package:* $23,529. *Average need-based loan:* $1708. *Average need-based gift aid:* $20,721. *Average non-need-based aid:* $7178. *Average indebtedness upon graduation:* $12,249.

Applying *Options:* electronic application, early decision, deferred entrance. *Application fee:* $60. *Required:* essay or personal statement, high school transcript, 2 letters of recommendation. *Required for some:* portfolio required for architecture students; audition required for music students. *Recommended:* interview. *Application deadlines:* 1/2 (freshmen), 3/15 (transfers). *Early decision deadline:* 11/1. *Notification:* 4/1 (freshmen), 5/15 (transfers), 12/15 (early decision).

Freshman Application Contact Office of Admission, Rice University, Office of Admission, PO Box 1892, MS 17, Houston, TX 77251-1892. *Phone:* 713-348-RICE. *Toll-free phone:* 800-527-OWLS. *E-mail:* admi@rice.edu.

See page 2544 for the College Close-Up.

St. Edward's University

Austin, Texas **www.stedwards.edu/**

- **Independent Roman Catholic** comprehensive, founded 1885
- **Urban** 160-acre campus
- **Endowment** $63.0 million
- **Coed** 4,340 undergraduate students, 77% full-time, 60% women, 40% men
- **Moderately difficult** entrance level, 65% of applicants were admitted

Undergraduates 3,341 full-time, 999 part-time. Students come from 39 states and territories, 39 other countries, 6% are from out of state, 5% African American, 2% Asian American or Pacific Islander, 31% Hispanic American, 0.8% Native American, 2% international, 6% transferred in, 36% live on campus. *Retention:* 85% of 2006 full-time freshmen returned.

Freshmen *Admission:* 2,372 applied, 1,544 admitted, 733 enrolled. *Test scores:* SAT critical reading scores over 500: 86%; SAT math scores over 500: 85%; SAT writing scores over 500: 82%; ACT scores over 18: 95%; SAT critical reading scores over 600: 37%; SAT math scores over 600: 28%; SAT writing scores over 600: 29%; ACT scores over 24: 56%; SAT critical reading scores over 700: 5%; SAT math scores over 700: 3%; SAT writing scores over 700: 4%; ACT scores over 30: 5%.

Faculty *Total:* 486, 37% full-time, 64% with terminal degrees. *Student/faculty ratio:* 15:1.

Majors Accounting; art; art teacher education; biochemistry; bioinformatics; biology/biological sciences; biology teacher education; business administration and management; chemistry; chemistry related; communication and media related; computer and information sciences; computer science; criminal justice/safety; criminology; drama and dance teacher education; dramatic/theater arts; economics; education (specific subject areas) related; English; English composition; entrepreneurship; finance; forensic science and technology; graphic design; history; history teacher education; international business/trade/commerce; international relations and affairs; kinesiology and exercise science; Latin American studies; liberal arts and sciences/liberal studies; marketing/marketing management; mathematics; mathematics teacher education; multi-/interdisciplinary studies related; parks, recreation, and leisure related; philosophy; photography; physical education teaching and coaching; political science and government; psychology; religious education; social studies teacher education; social work; sociology; Spanish; Spanish language teacher education; theology and religious vocations related.

Academics *Calendar:* semesters. *Degrees:* bachelor's, master's, and post-bachelor's certificates. *Special study options:* academic remediation for entering students, adult/continuing education programs, advanced placement credit, double majors, honors programs, internships, part-time degree program, services for LD students, study abroad, summer session for credit. *ROTC:* Army (c), Air Force (c).

Computers on Campus 642 computers/terminals and 7,200 ports are available on campus for general student use. Students can access the following: computer help desk, free student e-mail accounts, online (class) grades, online (class) registration, online (class) schedules. Campuswide network is available. 100% of college-owned or -operated housing units are wired for high-speed Internet access. Wireless service is available via classrooms, computer centers, computer labs, dorm rooms, learning centers, libraries, student centers.

Student Life *Housing:* on-campus residence required for freshman year. *Options:* coed, women-only, disabled students. Campus housing is university owned. Freshman campus housing is guaranteed. *Activities and organizations:* drama/theater group, student-run newspaper, choral group, Student Government Association, Residence Hall Association, Delta Sigma Pi Business Fraternity, Alpha Phi Omega, American Medical Student Association. *Campus security:* 24-hour emergency response devices and patrols, late-night transport/escort service, controlled dormitory access, self-defense education, informal discussions, pamphlets, posters, films, lighted pathways and sidewalks. *Student services:* health clinic, personal/psychological counseling.

Athletics Member NCAA. All Division II. *Intercollegiate sports:* baseball M (s), basketball M (s)/W (s), cross-country running M (s)/W (s), golf M (s)/W (s), soccer M (s)/W (s), softball W (s), tennis M (s)/W (s), volleyball W (s). *Intramural sports:* basketball M/W, crew M (c)/W (c), lacrosse M (c)/W (c), soccer M/W, volleyball M/W.

Standardized Tests *Required:* SAT or ACT (for admission).

Costs (2008–09) *Comprehensive fee:* $30,308 includes full-time tuition ($22,150) and room and board ($8158). Part-time tuition: $738 per credit hour. *College room only:* $4958.

Financial Aid Of all full-time matriculated undergraduates who enrolled in 2007, 2,408 applied for aid, 1,932 were judged to have need, 640 had their need fully met. 235 Federal Work-Study jobs (averaging $1826). 13 state and other part-time jobs (averaging $2077). In 2007, 375 non-need-based awards were made. *Average percent of need met:* 75%. *Average financial aid package:* $15,238. *Average need-based loan:* $5151. *Average need-based gift aid:* $10,137. *Average non-need-based aid:* $6692. *Average indebtedness upon graduation:* $25,832.

Applying *Options:* electronic application, deferred entrance. *Application fee:* $45. *Required:* essay or personal statement, high school transcript. *Recommended:* 2 letters of recommendation, interview. *Application deadlines:* 5/1 (freshmen), 7/1 (transfers). *Notification:* continuous (freshmen), continuous (transfers).

Freshman Application Contact Ms. Karen Gregg, Inquiry Coordinator, St. Edward's University, 3001 South Congress Avenue, Austin, TX 78704. *Phone:* 512-448-8580. *Toll-free phone:* 800-555-0164. *Fax:* 512-464-8877. *E-mail:* seu.admit@stedwards.edu.

See page 2546 for the College Close-Up.

St. Mary's University

San Antonio, Texas **www.stmarytx.edu/**

- **Independent Roman Catholic** comprehensive, founded 1852
- **Urban** 135-acre campus
- **Endowment** $154.3 million
- **Coed** 2,426 undergraduate students, 92% full-time, 59% women, 41% men
- **Moderately difficult** entrance level, 62% of applicants were admitted

Undergraduates 2,232 full-time, 194 part-time. Students come from 33 states and territories, 31 other countries, 4% are from out of state, 4% African American, 3% Asian American or Pacific Islander, 70% Hispanic American, 0.1% Native American, 3% international, 6% transferred in, 45% live on campus. *Retention:* 79% of 2006 full-time freshmen returned.

Freshmen *Admission:* 2,400 applied, 1,488 admitted, 566 enrolled. *Average high school GPA:* 3.4. *Test scores:* SAT critical reading scores over 500: 58%; SAT math scores over 500: 68%; ACT scores over 18: 95%; SAT critical reading scores over 600: 18%; SAT math scores over 600: 22%; ACT scores over 24: 43%; SAT critical reading scores over 700: 1%; SAT math scores over 700: 1%; ACT scores over 30: 4%.

Faculty *Total:* 322, 58% full-time, 75% with terminal degrees. *Student/faculty ratio:* 13:1.

Majors Accounting; art teacher education; biochemistry; biology/biological sciences; business administration and management; business teacher education; chemistry; communication/speech communication and rhetoric; computer engineering; computer management; computer science; criminal justice/law enforcement administration; criminology; economics; education; electrical, electronics and communications engineering; engineering; engineering science; English; finance; French; geology/earth science; health and physical education; history; human resources management; industrial engineering; information science/studies; international business/trade/commerce; kinesiology and exercise science; marketing/marketing management; mass communication/media; mathematics; music; philosophy; physics; political science and government; pre-dentistry studies; psychology; reading teacher education; sales, distribution and marketing; social studies teacher education; sociology; Spanish; speech and rhetoric; statistics; theology.

Academics *Calendar:* semesters. *Degrees:* bachelor's, master's, doctoral, and first professional. *Special study options:* academic remediation for entering students, adult/continuing education programs, advanced placement credit, cooperative education, distance learning, double majors, English as a second language, honors programs, independent study, internships, off-campus study, part-time degree program, study abroad, summer session for credit. *ROTC:* Army (b), Air Force (c).

Computers on Campus 100 computers/terminals are available on campus for general student use. Students can access the following: campus intranet, computer help desk, free student e-mail accounts, online (class) grades, online (class) registration, online (class) schedules. Campuswide network is available. 100% of college-owned or -operated housing units are wired for high-speed Internet access. Wireless service is available via entire campus.

Student Life *Housing:* on-campus residence required for freshman year. *Options:* coed, men-only, women-only, disabled students. Campus housing is university owned. Freshman applicants given priority for college housing. *Activities and organizations:* drama/theater group, student-run newspaper, choral group, Beta Beta Beta Biology Society, St. Mary's University Society of Honor Scholars, American Chemical Society of Students, Mexican Student Organization, Delta Zeta, national fraternities, national sororities. *Campus security:* 24-hour emergency response devices and patrols, late-night transport/escort service, controlled dormitory access. *Student services:* health clinic, personal/psychological counseling.

Athletics Member NCAA. All Division II. *Intercollegiate sports:* baseball M (s), basketball M (s)/W (s), golf M (s), rugby M (c), soccer M (s)/W (s), softball W, tennis M (s)/W (s), volleyball W (s). *Intramural sports:* badminton M/W, basketball M/W, bowling M/W, cross-country running M/W, football M/W, softball M/W, table tennis M/W, tennis M/W, volleyball M/W, water polo M/W.

Standardized Tests *Required:* SAT or ACT (for admission).

Costs (2007–08) *Comprehensive fee:* $28,486 includes full-time tuition ($20,300), mandatory fees ($1200), and room and board ($6986). Full-time tuition and fees vary according to course load. Part-time tuition: $609 per credit hour. Part-time tuition and fees vary according to course load. *Required fees:* $250 per term part-time. *College room only:* $4020. Room and board charges vary according to board plan, housing facility, and student level. *Payment plan:* installment. *Waivers:* employees or children of employees.

Financial Aid Of all full-time matriculated undergraduates who enrolled in 2004, 1,830 applied for aid, 1,674 were judged to have need, 398 had their need fully met. 535 Federal Work-Study jobs (averaging $2822). 184 state and other part-time jobs (averaging $2099). In 2004, 147 non-need-based awards were made. *Average percent of need met:* 69%. *Average financial aid package:* $14,188. *Average need-based loan:* $4952. *Average need-based gift aid:* $7972. *Average non-need-based aid:* $9464. *Average indebtedness upon graduation:* $23,447.

Applying *Options:* early admission, deferred entrance. *Application fee:* $30. *Required:* essay or personal statement, high school transcript. *Required for some:* letters of recommendation. *Recommended:* interview. *Application deadlines:* rolling (freshmen), rolling (transfers). *Notification:* continuous (freshmen), continuous (transfers).

Freshman Application Contact Mr. Chad Bridwell, Director of Undergraduate Admission, St. Mary's University, 1 Camino Santa Maria, San Antonio, TX 78228-8503. *Phone:* 210-436-3126. *Toll-free phone:* 800-FOR-STMU. *Fax:* 210-431-6742. *E-mail:* uadm@stmarytx.edu.

See page 2548 for the College Close-Up.

SAM HOUSTON STATE UNIVERSITY

Huntsville, Texas **www.shsu.edu/**

- **State-supported** university, founded 1879, part of The Texas State University System
- **Small-town** 1256-acre campus with easy access to Houston
- **Endowment** $30.0 million
- **Coed** 14,150 undergraduate students, 84% full-time, 57% women, 43% men
- **Moderately difficult** entrance level, 61% of applicants were admitted

Undergraduates 11,881 full-time, 2,269 part-time. Students come from 41 states and territories, 45 other countries, 1% are from out of state, 15% African American, 1% Asian American or Pacific Islander, 12% Hispanic American, 0.7% Native American, 0.8% international, 12% transferred in, 27% live on campus. *Retention:* 70% of 2006 full-time freshmen returned.

Freshmen *Admission:* 7,752 applied, 4,756 admitted, 2,263 enrolled. *Test scores:* SAT critical reading scores over 500: 51%; SAT math scores over 500: 55%; ACT scores over 18: 84%; SAT critical reading scores over 600: 11%; SAT math scores over 600: 12%; ACT scores over 24: 18%; SAT critical reading scores over 700: 1%; SAT math scores over 700: 1%.

Faculty *Total:* 942, 68% full-time, 53% with terminal degrees. *Student/faculty ratio:* 20:1.

Majors Accounting; advertising; agribusiness; agricultural business and management; agricultural mechanization; agricultural teacher education; agriculture; animal sciences; art; art teacher education; biological and physical sciences; biology/biological sciences; business administration and management; business/commerce; business/managerial economics; business teacher education; chemistry; clinical laboratory science/medical technology; clinical psychology; commercial and advertising art; community health services counseling; computer and information sciences; conducting; construction engineering technology; construction management; corrections; corrections and criminal justice related; counseling psychology; counselor education/school counseling and guidance; criminal justice/law enforcement administration; criminal justice/police science; criminal justice/safety; curriculum and instruction; dance; digital communication and media/multimedia; drafting and design technology; dramatic/theater arts; education; electrical, electronic and communications engineering technology; English; English/language arts teacher education; environmental studies; family and consumer sciences/home economics teacher education; family and consumer sciences/human sciences; fashion merchandising; finance; fine/studio arts; foods, nutrition, and wellness; foreign language teacher education; forensic psychology; forensic science and technology; French; geography; geology/earth science; German; health and physical education related; health teacher education; history; horticultural science; human resources management; industrial technology; interior design; international business/trade/commerce; journalism; kinesiology and exercise science; marketing/marketing management; mathematics; mathematics teacher education; multi-/interdisciplinary studies related; music; music performance; music teacher education; music therapy; operations management; painting; philosophy; photography; physical education teaching and coaching; physician assistant; physics; political science and government; pre-dentistry studies; pre-law studies; pre-medical studies; pre-nursing studies; pre-pharmacy studies; psychology; public relations/image management; radio and television; reading teacher education; respiratory care therapy; sociology; Spanish; speech and rhetoric; statistics; technology/industrial arts teacher education.

Academics *Calendar:* semesters. *Degrees:* bachelor's, master's, and doctoral. *Special study options:* academic remediation for entering students, adult/continuing education programs, advanced placement credit, distance learning, double majors, English as a second language, honors programs, independent study, internships, off-campus study, part-time degree program, services for LD students, study abroad, summer session for credit. *ROTC:* Army (b).

Computers on Campus 552 computers/terminals are available on campus for general student use. Students can access the following: online (class) registration. Campuswide network is available.

Student Life *Housing:* on-campus residence required for freshman year. *Options:* coed, men-only, women-only. Campus housing is university owned and is provided by a third party. Freshman campus housing is guaranteed. *Activities and organizations:* drama/theater group, student-run newspaper, radio and television station, choral group, marching band, Residence Hall Association, NAACP, Baptist Student Ministry, national fraternities, national sororities. *Campus security:* 24-hour emergency response devices and patrols, student patrols, late-night transport/escort service. *Student services:* health clinic, personal/psychological counseling, legal services.

Athletics Member NCAA. All Division I except football (Division I-AA). *Intercollegiate sports:* baseball M (s), basketball M (s)/W (s), cross-country running M (s)/W (s), equestrian sports M/W, golf M (s)/W (s), lacrosse M (c), riflery M (c)/W (c), rugby M (c), soccer M (c)/W (s), softball M (s)/W (s), tennis M (s)/W (s), track and field M (s)/W (s), volleyball W (s). *Intramural sports:* basketball M/W, bowling M/W, football M, gymnastics W (c), racquetball M/W, soccer M/W, softball M/W, swimming and diving M/W, tennis M/W, volleyball M/W, water polo M/W.

Standardized Tests *Required:* SAT or ACT (for admission).

Costs (2007–08) *Tuition:* state resident $4170 full-time; nonresident $12,510 full-time. Full-time tuition and fees vary according to course load. Part-time tuition and fees vary according to course load. *Required fees:* $1396 full-time. *Room and board:* $6046; room only: $3460. Room and board charges vary according to board plan and housing facility. *Payment plan:* installment. *Waivers:* employees or children of employees.

Financial Aid Of all full-time matriculated undergraduates who enrolled in 2005, 7,441 applied for aid, 6,418 were judged to have need, 406 had their need fully met. 211 Federal Work-Study jobs (averaging $1364). 156 state and other part-time jobs (averaging $558). In 2005, 767 non-need-based awards were made. *Average percent of need met:* 50%. *Average financial aid package:* $6116. *Average need-based loan:* $3515. *Average need-based gift aid:* $3495. *Average non-need-based aid:* $1862. *Average indebtedness upon graduation:* $16,948.

Applying *Options:* early admission. *Application fee:* $35. *Required:* high school transcript, minimum 2.0 GPA. *Application deadlines:* 8/1 (freshmen), rolling (transfers). *Notification:* continuous (freshmen), continuous (transfers).

Freshman Application Contact Mr. Trevor B. Thorn, Director of Admissions and Recruitment, Sam Houston State University, PO Box 2418, Huntsville, TX 77341. *Phone:* 936-294-1828. *Toll-free phone:* 866-232-7528 Ext. 1828. *Fax:* 936-294-3758. *E-mail:* admissions@shsu.edu.

SCHREINER UNIVERSITY

Kerrville, Texas **www.schreiner.edu/**

- **Independent Presbyterian** comprehensive, founded 1923
- **Small-town** 175-acre campus with easy access to San Antonio and Austin
- **Endowment** $46.3 million
- **Coed** 942 undergraduate students, 93% full-time, 57% women, 43% men
- **Moderately difficult** entrance level, 58% of applicants were admitted

Undergraduates 880 full-time, 62 part-time. 2% are from out of state, 3% African American, 1% Asian American or Pacific Islander, 20% Hispanic American, 1% Native American, 0.5% international, 8% transferred in, 68% live on campus. *Retention:* 64% of 2006 full-time freshmen returned.

Freshmen *Admission:* 973 applied, 563 admitted, 265 enrolled. *Average high school GPA:* 3.55. *Test scores:* SAT critical reading scores over 500: 43%; SAT math scores over 500: 53%; ACT scores over 18: 77%; SAT critical reading scores over 600: 16%; SAT math scores over 600: 13%; ACT scores over 24: 21%; SAT critical reading scores over 700: 2%; SAT math scores over 700: 1%; ACT scores over 30: 1%.

Faculty *Total:* 101, 54% full-time, 54% with terminal degrees. *Student/faculty ratio:* 13:1.

Majors Accounting; biochemistry; biology/biological sciences; business/commerce; chemistry; dramatic/theater arts; early childhood education; education; education (specific subject areas) related; elementary education; engineering; English; English/language arts teacher education; graphic design; history; history teacher education; humanities; kinesiology and exercise science; legal studies; liberal arts and sciences/liberal studies; literature; management information systems; mathematics; mathematics teacher education; music; physical education teaching and coaching; political science and government; pre-dentistry studies; pre-engineering; pre-law studies; pre-medical studies; psychology; religious studies.

Academics *Calendar:* semesters. *Degrees:* certificates, bachelor's, master's, and postbachelor's certificates. *Special study options:* academic remediation for entering students, accelerated degree program, advanced placement credit, cooperative education, double majors, honors programs, independent study, internships, part-time degree program, services for LD students, student-designed majors, study abroad, summer session for credit. *Unusual degree programs:* 3-2 engineering with University of Texas at Austin, Texas A&M University.

Computers on Campus 108 computers/terminals are available on campus for general student use. Students can access the following: computer help desk, free student e-mail accounts, online (class) grades, online (class) registration, online (class) schedules. Campuswide network is available. 100% of college-owned or -operated housing units are wired for high-speed Internet access. Wireless service is available via classrooms, computer labs, dorm rooms, learning centers, libraries, student centers.

Student Life *Housing:* on-campus residence required through junior year. *Options:* coed, disabled students. Campus housing is university owned. Freshman campus housing is guaranteed. *Activities and organizations:* drama/theater group, student-run newspaper, choral group, Student Senate, Greek Life, Campus Ministry, Honor Societies, Hall Councils, national fraternities, national sororities. *Campus security:* 24-hour emergency response devices and patrols, late-night transport/escort service. *Student services:* health clinic, personal/psychological counseling.

Athletics Member NCAA. All Division III. *Intercollegiate sports:* baseball M, basketball M/W, cross-country running M/W, golf M/W, soccer M/W, softball W, tennis M/W, volleyball W. *Intramural sports:* cheerleading W.

Standardized Tests *Required:* SAT or ACT (for admission).

Costs (2007–08) *Comprehensive fee:* $24,918 includes full-time tuition ($16,408), mandatory fees ($600), and room and board ($7910). Part-time tuition: $700 per credit hour. *College room only:* $4478. Room and board charges vary according to board plan and housing facility. *Payment plan:* installment. *Waivers:* employees or children of employees.

Financial Aid Of all full-time matriculated undergraduates who enrolled in 2007, 696 applied for aid, 605 were judged to have need, 114 had their need fully met. In 2007, 189 non-need-based awards were made. *Average percent of need met:* 72%. *Average financial aid package:* $14,372. *Average need-based loan:* $3711. *Average need-based gift aid:* $10,696. *Average non-need-based aid:* $12,517. *Average indebtedness upon graduation:* $19,528. *Financial aid deadline:* 8/1.

Applying *Options:* deferred entrance. *Application fee:* $25. *Required:* high school transcript. *Required for some:* essay or personal statement, letters of recommendation. *Application deadlines:* 8/1 (freshmen), 8/1 (transfers). *Notification:* continuous (freshmen), continuous (transfers).

Freshman Application Contact Ms. Sandy Speed, Dean of Admission and Financial Aid, Schreiner University, 2100 Memorial Boulevard, Kerrville, TX 78028. *Phone:* 830-792-7217. *Toll-free phone:* 800-343-4919. *E-mail:* admissions@schreiner.edu.

SOUTHERN METHODIST UNIVERSITY

Dallas, Texas **www.smu.edu/**

- **Independent** university, founded 1911, affiliated with United Methodist Church
- **Suburban** 210-acre campus
- **Endowment** $1.3 billion
- **Coed** 6,176 undergraduate students, 95% full-time, 54% women, 46% men
- **Moderately difficult** entrance level, 50% of applicants were admitted

Undergraduates 5,851 full-time, 325 part-time. Students come from 50 states and territories, 65 other countries, 42% are from out of state, 5% African American, 6% Asian American or Pacific Islander, 8% Hispanic American, 0.7% Native American, 5% international, 5% transferred in, 40% live on campus. *Retention:* 89% of 2006 full-time freshmen returned.

Freshmen *Admission:* 8,253 applied, 4,133 admitted, 1,309 enrolled. *Average high school GPA:* 3.55. *Test scores:* SAT critical reading scores over 500: 93%; SAT math scores over 500: 96%; SAT writing scores over 500: 93%; ACT scores over 18: 99%; SAT critical reading scores over 600: 58%; SAT math scores over 600: 64%; SAT writing scores over 600: 56%; ACT scores over 24: 86%; SAT critical reading scores over 700: 13%; SAT math scores over 700: 16%; SAT writing scores over 700: 10%; ACT scores over 30: 19%.

Faculty *Total:* 983, 64% full-time, 70% with terminal degrees. *Student/faculty ratio:* 12:1.

Majors Accounting; advertising; African-American/Black studies; anthropology; applied economics; art history, criticism and conservation; biochemistry; biology/biological sciences; business administration and management; business/commerce; chemistry; civil engineering; computer engineering; computer science; creative writing; dance; dramatic/theater arts; econometrics and quantitative economics; economics; electrical, electronics and communications engineering; English; environmental/environmental health engineering; environmental studies; European studies; film/cinema studies; finance; finance and financial management services related; financial planning and services; fine/studio arts; French; geology/earth science; geophysics and seismology; German; Hispanic-American, Puerto Rican, and Mexican-American/Chicano studies; history; humanities; information science/studies; international relations and affairs; Italian; journalism; Latin American studies; liberal arts and sciences and humanities related; management science; marketing/marketing management; mathematics; mechanical engineering; medieval and Renaissance studies; multi-/interdisciplinary studies related; music; music performance; music teacher education; music theory and composition; music therapy; philosophy; physics; piano and organ; political science and government; psychology; public policy analysis; public relations; public relations/image management; religious studies; social sciences; sociology; Spanish; statistics; voice and opera.

Academics *Calendar:* semesters. *Degrees:* bachelor's, master's, doctoral, first professional, and postbachelor's certificates. *Special study options:* academic remediation for entering students, accelerated degree program, adult/continuing education programs, advanced placement credit, cooperative education, distance learning, double majors, English as a second language, honors programs, independent study, internships, part-time degree program, services for LD students, student-designed majors, study abroad, summer session for credit. *ROTC:* Army (b), Air Force (c).

Computers on Campus 758 computers/terminals are available on campus for general student use. Students can access the following: online (class) registration, online billing/payment processing. Campuswide network is available.

Student Life *Housing:* on-campus residence required for freshman year. *Options:* coed, disabled students. Campus housing is university owned. Freshman campus housing is guaranteed. *Activities and organizations:* drama/theater group, student-run newspaper, radio station, choral group, marching band, Program Council, Student Senate, Student Foundation, Residence Hall Association, SPARC (Students Promoting Awareness, Responsibility, and Citizenship), national fraternities, national sororities. *Campus security:* 24-hour emergency response devices and patrols, late-night transport/escort service, controlled dormitory access. *Student services:* health clinic, personal/psychological counseling, women's center.

Athletics Member NCAA. All Division I except football (Division I-A). *Intercollegiate sports:* baseball M (c), basketball M (s)/W (s), cheerleading M (s) (c)/W (s) (c), crew W (s), cross-country running W (s), equestrian sports W (s), fencing M (c)/W (c), golf M (s)/W (s), ice hockey M (c), lacrosse M (c), rugby M (c)/W (c), soccer M (s)/W (s), swimming and diving M (s)/W (s), tennis M (s)/W (s), track and field W, volleyball W (s), wrestling M (c). *Intramural sports:* basketball M/W, bowling M/W, football M, golf M/W, racquetball M/W, rock climbing M (c)/W (c), soccer M/W, softball M/W, swimming and diving M/W, table tennis M (c)/W (c), tennis M/W, ultimate Frisbee M/W, volleyball M/W, water polo M/W, weight lifting M (c)/W (c).

Standardized Tests *Required:* SAT or ACT (for admission). *Required for some:* SAT Subject Tests (for admission).

Costs (2008–09) *Comprehensive fee:* $45,073 includes full-time tuition ($29,430), mandatory fees ($3768), and room and board ($11,875). Part-time tuition: $1230 per credit hour. *Required fees:* $157 per credit hour part-time. *College room only:* $7655.

Financial Aid Of all full-time matriculated undergraduates who enrolled in 2006, 2,543 applied for aid, 2,073 were judged to have need, 778 had their need fully met. 1,304 Federal Work-Study jobs (averaging $2442). 46 state and other part-time jobs (averaging $2365). In 2006, 2038 non-need-based awards were made. *Average percent of need met:* 90%. *Average financial aid package:* $24,824. *Average need-based loan:* $3191. *Average need-based gift aid:* $14,892. *Average non-need-based aid:* $11,453. *Average indebtedness upon graduation:* $17,424.

Applying *Options:* electronic application, early admission, early action, deferred entrance. *Application fee:* $60. *Required:* essay or personal statement, high school transcript, 1 letter of recommendation. *Application deadlines:* 1/15 (freshmen), 7/1 (transfers), 11/1 (early action). *Notification:* continuous (freshmen), continuous (transfers), 12/31 (early action).

Freshman Application Contact Mr. Ron Moss, Director of Admission and Enrollment Management, Southern Methodist University, PO Box 750181, Dallas, TX 75275-0181. *Phone:* 214-768-3417. *Toll-free phone:* 800-323-0672. *Fax:* 214-768-0202. *E-mail:* enrol_serv@smu.edu.

See page 2550 for the College Close-Up.

SOUTH TEXAS COLLEGE

McAllen, Texas **www.southtexascollege.edu/**

- **District-supported** primarily 2-year, founded 1993
- **Suburban** 20-acre campus
- **Endowment** $222,114
- **Coed**
- **Noncompetitive** entrance level

Faculty *Student/faculty ratio:* 22:1.

Academics *Calendar:* semesters. *Degrees:* certificates, associate, and bachelor's.

Student Life *Campus security:* 24-hour emergency response devices and patrols, late-night transport/escort service.

Standardized Tests *Required for some:* THEA.

Costs (2007–08) *Tuition:* area resident $1896 full-time; state resident $2446 full-time; nonresident $6060 full-time. *Required fees:* $350 full-time.

Applying *Options:* early admission, deferred entrance. *Required:* high school transcript.

Freshman Application Contact Mr. Matthew Hebbard, Director of Enrollment Services and Registrar, South Texas College, 3201 West Pecan, McAllen, TX 78501. *Phone:* 956-872-2147. *Toll-free phone:* 800-742-7822. *E-mail:* mshebbar@southtexascollege.edu.

SOUTHWESTERN ADVENTIST UNIVERSITY

Keene, Texas **www.swau.edu/**

- **Independent Seventh-day Adventist** comprehensive, founded 1894
- **Rural** 150-acre campus with easy access to Dallas–Fort Worth
- **Endowment** $10.9 million
- **Coed** 834 undergraduate students, 84% full-time, 60% women, 40% men
- **Minimally difficult** entrance level, 48% of applicants were admitted

Undergraduates 697 full-time, 137 part-time. Students come from 24 states and territories, 34 other countries, 26% are from out of state, 13% African American, 9% Asian American or Pacific Islander, 28% Hispanic American, 1% Native American, 9% international, 31% live on campus. *Retention:* 62% of 2006 full-time freshmen returned.

Freshmen *Admission:* 632 applied, 306 admitted, 215 enrolled. *Test scores:* SAT critical reading scores over 500: 43%; SAT math scores over 500: 28%; ACT scores over 18: 79%; SAT critical reading scores over 600: 9%; SAT math scores over 600: 3%; ACT scores over 24: 18%; SAT critical reading scores over 700: 1%; ACT scores over 30: 2%.

Faculty *Total:* 92, 54% full-time, 40% with terminal degrees. *Student/faculty ratio:* 15:1.

Majors Accounting; administrative assistant and secretarial science; biology/biological sciences; broadcast journalism; business administration and management; chemistry; clinical laboratory science/medical technology; computer science; criminal justice/law enforcement administration; elementary education; English; health and physical education; health/health care administration; history; information science/studies; international business/trade/commerce; international relations and affairs; journalism; kinesiology and exercise science; mass communication/media; mathematics; music; nursing (registered nurse training); psychology; religious studies; social sciences; social work; theology.

Academics *Calendar:* semesters. *Degrees:* associate, bachelor's, and master's. *Special study options:* academic remediation for entering students, accelerated degree program, cooperative education, English as a second language, external degree program, honors programs, independent study, internships, off-campus study, part-time degree program, student-designed majors, study abroad, summer session for credit.

Computers on Campus 50 computers/terminals are available on campus for general student use. Campuswide network is available.

Student Life *Housing:* on-campus residence required for freshman year. *Options:* men-only, women-only, cooperative. *Activities and organizations:* drama/theater group, student-run newspaper, radio and television station, choral group, Student Association, SIFE, Education/Psychology Club, Theology Club, Nursing Club. *Campus security:* 24-hour emergency response devices, student patrols. *Student services:* health clinic, personal/psychological counseling.

Athletics Member NAIA. *Intercollegiate sports:* baseball M (s), basketball M (s)/W (s), soccer M (s), softball W (c), volleyball M (c)/W (s). *Intramural sports:* basketball M/W, football M/W, skiing (downhill) M (c)/W (c), soccer M/W, softball M/W, volleyball M/W.

Standardized Tests *Required:* SAT or ACT (for admission).

Costs (2007–08) *One-time required fee:* $95. *Comprehensive fee:* $20,708 includes full-time tuition ($13,944), mandatory fees ($340), and room and board ($6424). Full-time tuition and fees vary according to course load and program. Part-time tuition: $581 per credit hour. Part-time tuition and fees vary according to course load and program. *College room only:* $2632. Room and board charges vary according to board plan. *Payment plans:* installment, deferred payment. *Waivers:* employees or children of employees.

Applying *Options:* deferred entrance. *Required:* high school transcript, minimum 2.0 GPA. *Required for some:* essay or personal statement, 1 letter of recommendation, interview. *Application deadlines:* 8/31 (freshmen), 8/31 (transfers). *Notification:* 9/1 (freshmen), 9/1 (transfers).

Freshman Application Contact Ms. Charlotte Coy, Director of Admissions, Southwestern Adventist University, PO Box 567, Keene, TX 76059. *Phone:* 817-645-3921 Ext. 6252. *Toll-free phone:* 800-433-2240. *E-mail:* ccoy@swau.edu.

SOUTHWESTERN ASSEMBLIES OF GOD UNIVERSITY

Waxahachie, Texas **www.sagu.edu/**

Freshman Application Contact Mr. Pat Thompson, Admissions Counselor, Southwestern Assemblies of God University, 1200 Sycamore Street, Waxahachie, TX 75165-5735. *Phone:* 972-937-4010. *Toll-free phone:* 888-937-7248.

SOUTHWESTERN CHRISTIAN COLLEGE

Terrell, Texas **www.swcc.edu/**

Freshman Application Contact Admissions Department, Southwestern Christian College, Box 10, 200 Bowser Street, Terrell, TX 75160. *Phone:* 214-524-3341.

SOUTHWESTERN UNIVERSITY

Georgetown, Texas **www.southwestern.edu/**

- **Independent Methodist** 4-year, founded 1840
- **Suburban** 700-acre campus with easy access to Austin
- **Endowment** $314.0 million
- **Coed** 1,294 undergraduate students, 98% full-time, 61% women, 39% men

• **Very difficult** entrance level, 67% of applicants were admitted

Undergraduates 1,267 full-time, 27 part-time. Students come from 31 states and territories, 8 other countries, 5% are from out of state, 3% African American, 5% Asian American or Pacific Islander, 14% Hispanic American, 0.7% Native American, 0.1% international, 2% transferred in, 77% live on campus. *Retention:* 87% of 2006 full-time freshmen returned.

Freshmen *Admission:* 1,916 applied, 1,291 admitted, 371 enrolled. *Test scores:* SAT critical reading scores over 500: 93%; SAT math scores over 500: 93%; ACT scores over 18: 100%; SAT critical reading scores over 600: 61%; SAT math scores over 600: 57%; ACT scores over 24: 81%; SAT critical reading scores over 700: 17%; SAT math scores over 700: 13%; ACT scores over 30: 23%.

Faculty *Total:* 175, 70% full-time, 83% with terminal degrees. *Student/faculty ratio:* 10:1.

Majors Accounting; American studies; animal behavior and ethology; anthropology; art; art history, criticism and conservation; biochemistry; biology/biological sciences; business/commerce; chemistry; Chinese; classics and languages, literatures and linguistics; communication/speech communication and rhetoric; computer and information sciences; dramatic/theater arts; economics; education; elementary education; English; environmental studies; French; German; history; international relations and affairs; Latin; Latin American studies; liberal arts and sciences and humanities related; mass communication/media; mathematics; music; music history, literature, and theory; musicology and ethnomusicology; music performance; music teacher education; music theory and composition; philosophy; physical education teaching and coaching; physical sciences; physics; political science and government; psychology; religious studies; science teacher education; social studies teacher education; sociology; Spanish; visual and performing arts related; women's studies.

Academics *Calendar:* semesters. *Degree:* bachelor's. *Special study options:* advanced placement credit, double majors, independent study, internships, off-campus study, part-time degree program, services for LD students, student-designed majors, study abroad, summer session for credit. *Unusual degree programs:* 3-2 engineering with Washington University in St. Louis, Arizona State University, Texas A&M University.

Computers on Campus 410 computers/terminals are available on campus for general student use. Students can access the following: course schedule, course catalog, grades, transcripts. Campuswide network is available.

Student Life *Housing:* on-campus residence required through sophomore year. *Options:* coed, men-only, women-only. Campus housing is university owned. Freshman campus housing is guaranteed. *Activities and organizations:* drama/theater group, student-run newspaper, choral group, Alpha Phi Omega, International Club, Latinos Unidos, national fraternities, national sororities. *Campus security:* 24-hour emergency response devices and patrols, student patrols, late-night transport/escort service, controlled dormitory access. *Student services:* health clinic, personal/psychological counseling.

Athletics Member NCAA. All Division III. *Intercollegiate sports:* baseball M, basketball M/W, cross-country running M/W, golf M/W, soccer M/W, swimming and diving M/W, tennis M/W, volleyball W. *Intramural sports:* basketball M/W, bowling M/W, football M/W, golf M/W, racquetball M/W, soccer M/W, softball M/W, swimming and diving M/W, table tennis M/W, tennis M/W, ultimate Frisbee M/W, volleyball M/W.

Standardized Tests *Required:* SAT (for admission). *Required for some:* SAT and SAT Subject Tests or ACT (for admission).

Costs (2007–08) *Comprehensive fee:* $33,870 includes full-time tuition ($25,740) and room and board ($8130). Part-time tuition: $1075 per semester hour. Part-time tuition and fees vary according to course load. *College room only:* $4410. Room and board charges vary according to board plan and housing facility. *Payment plan:* installment. *Waivers:* employees or children of employees.

Financial Aid Of all full-time matriculated undergraduates who enrolled in 2007, 782 applied for aid, 630 were judged to have need, 351 had their need fully met. In 2007, 404 non-need-based awards were made. *Average percent of need met:* 86%. *Average financial aid package:* $23,310. *Average need-based loan:* $5454. *Average need-based gift aid:* $17,421. *Average non-need-based aid:* $9248. *Average indebtedness upon graduation:* $24,057. *Financial aid deadline:* 3/1.

Applying *Options:* electronic application, early decision, deferred entrance. *Application fee:* $40. *Required:* essay or personal statement, high school transcript, 1 letter of recommendation. *Required for some:* interview. *Recommended:* interview. *Application deadlines:* 2/15 (freshmen), 4/1 (transfers). *Early decision deadline:* 11/1. *Notification:* 4/1 (freshmen), continuous (transfers), 12/1 (early decision).

Freshman Application Contact Mr. Tom Oliver, Vice President for Enrollment Services, Southwestern University, 1001 East University Avenue, Georgetown, TX 78626. *Phone:* 512-863-1200. *Toll-free phone:* 800-252-3166. *Fax:* 512-863-9601. *E-mail:* admission@southwestern.edu.

STEPHEN F. AUSTIN STATE UNIVERSITY

Nacogdoches, Texas **www.sfasu.edu/**

- **State-supported** comprehensive, founded 1923
- **Small-town** 400-acre campus
- **Endowment** $59.1 million
- **Coed** 10,106 undergraduate students, 87% full-time, 59% women, 41% men
- **Moderately difficult** entrance level, 74% of applicants were admitted

Undergraduates 8,835 full-time, 1,271 part-time. Students come from 45 states and territories, 48 other countries, 2% are from out of state, 19% African American, 1% Asian American or Pacific Islander, 9% Hispanic American, 0.7% Native American, 0.9% international, 8% transferred in, 41% live on campus. *Retention:* 64% of 2006 full-time freshmen returned.

Freshmen *Admission:* 7,409 applied, 5,481 admitted, 2,182 enrolled. *Test scores:* SAT critical reading scores over 500: 45%; SAT math scores over 500: 51%; ACT scores over 18: 79%; SAT critical reading scores over 600: 12%; SAT math scores over 600: 12%; ACT scores over 24: 20%; SAT critical reading scores over 700: 1%; SAT math scores over 700: 1%; ACT scores over 30: 2%.

Faculty *Total:* 624, 73% full-time, 63% with terminal degrees. *Student/faculty ratio:* 21:1.

Majors Accounting; agribusiness; agricultural mechanization; agricultural production; agriculture; agronomy and crop science; animal sciences; applied horticulture; art; art history, criticism and conservation; audiology and hearing sciences; audiology and speech-language pathology; biology/biological sciences; business administration and management; business/commerce; business/managerial economics; chemistry; clinical laboratory science/medical technology; communication/speech communication and rhetoric; community health services counseling; computer and information sciences; corrections; criminal justice/police science; criminal justice/safety; dance; data processing and data processing technology; dramatic/theater arts; economics; English; environmental studies; family and consumer sciences/human sciences; fashion merchandising; finance; foods, nutrition, and wellness; forest/forest resources management; forestry; French; geography; geology/earth science; gerontology; health and physical education; history; horticultural science; hospitality administration; human development and family studies; humanities; information technology; interdisciplinary studies; interior architecture; international business/trade/commerce; journalism; legal assistant/paralegal; marketing/marketing management; mathematics; multi-/interdisciplinary studies related; music; music performance; music teacher education; natural resources and conservation related; nursing (registered nurse training); office management; physics; political science and government; poultry science; psychology; public administration; radio and television; rehabilitation therapy; social sciences; social work; sociology; Spanish; special products marketing; speech and rhetoric; wildlife and wildlands science and management.

Academics *Calendar:* semesters. *Degrees:* bachelor's, master's, and doctoral. *Special study options:* academic remediation for entering students, accelerated degree program, adult/continuing education programs, advanced placement credit, distance learning, double majors, freshman honors college, honors programs, independent study, internships, off-campus study, part-time degree program, services for LD students, student-designed majors, study abroad, summer session for credit. *ROTC:* Army (b). *Unusual degree programs:* 3-2 professional accountancy.

Computers on Campus 1,000 computers/terminals are available on campus for general student use. Students can access the following: campus intranet, computer help desk, free student e-mail accounts, online (class) grades, online (class) registration, online (class) schedules. Campuswide network is available. 100% of college-owned or -operated housing units are wired for high-speed Internet access. Wireless service is available via classrooms, computer centers, computer labs, dorm rooms, libraries, student centers.

Student Life *Housing:* on-campus residence required through sophomore year. *Options:* coed, men-only, women-only, disabled students. Campus housing is university owned. Freshman campus housing is guaranteed. *Activities and organizations:* drama/theater group, student-run newspaper, radio and television station, choral group, marching band, Texas Student Education Association, American Marketing Association, Baptist Student Union, national fraternities, national sororities. *Campus security:* 24-hour emergency response devices and patrols, student patrols, late-night transport/escort service, controlled dormitory access. *Student services:* health clinic, personal/psychological counseling, legal services.

Athletics Member NCAA. All Division I except football (Division I-AA). *Intercollegiate sports:* baseball M, basketball M (s)/W (s), cross-country running M (s)/W (s), equestrian sports W, golf M (s), soccer W (s), softball W (s), tennis W (s), track and field M (s)/W (s), volleyball W (s). *Intramural sports:* badminton M/W, baseball M (c), basketball M/W, cross-country running M/W, football M/W, lacrosse M (c)/W (c), racquetball M (c)/W (c), rock climbing M (c)/W (c), soccer

M (c), softball M/W, table tennis M/W, tennis M/W, volleyball M (c)/W (c), water polo M/W, wrestling M (c)/W (c).

Standardized Tests *Required:* SAT or ACT (for admission).

Costs (2007–08) *Tuition:* state resident $4410 full-time, $147 per credit hour part-time; nonresident $12,750 full-time, $425 per credit hour part-time. Full-time tuition and fees vary according to course load. Part-time tuition and fees vary according to course load. *Required fees:* $1752 full-time, $131 per credit hour part-time, $11 per term part-time. *Room and board:* $6885. Room and board charges vary according to board plan and housing facility. *Payment plan:* installment. *Waivers:* employees or children of employees.

Financial Aid Of all full-time matriculated undergraduates who enrolled in 2006, 6,558 applied for aid, 5,073 were judged to have need, 2,823 had their need fully met. 495 Federal Work-Study jobs (averaging $1345). 97 state and other part-time jobs (averaging $1004). In 2006, 397 non-need-based awards were made. *Average percent of need met:* 98%. *Average financial aid package:* $7502. *Average need-based loan:* $3546. *Average need-based gift aid:* $4000. *Average non-need-based aid:* $2950. *Average indebtedness upon graduation:* $19,772.

Applying *Options:* electronic application. *Application fee:* $35. *Required:* high school transcript. *Application deadline:* rolling (freshmen). *Notification:* continuous (freshmen), continuous (transfers).

Freshman Application Contact Ms. Beth Smith, Associate Director of Admissions, Stephen F. Austin State University, PO Box 13051, SFA Station, Nacogdoches, TX 75962. *Phone:* 936-468-2504. *Toll-free phone:* 800-731-2902. *Fax:* 936-468-3849. *E-mail:* admissions@sfasu.edu.

See page 2552 for the College Close-Up.

Sul Ross State University

Alpine, Texas **www.sulross.edu/**

- **State-supported** comprehensive, founded 1920, part of Texas State University System
- **Small-town** 640-acre campus
- **Endowment** $5.9 million
- **Coed**
- **Noncompetitive** entrance level

Faculty *Student/faculty ratio:* 16:1.

Academics *Calendar:* semesters. *Degrees:* certificates, associate, bachelor's, and master's.

Student Life *Campus security:* 24-hour patrols, late-night transport/escort service.

Athletics Member NCAA. All Division III.

Standardized Tests *Required:* SAT or ACT (for admission).

Costs (2007–08) *Tuition:* state resident $3360 full-time, $112 per semester hour part-time; nonresident $11,700 full-time, $390 per semester hour part-time. *Required fees:* $1386 full-time, $143 per semester hour part-time. *Room and board:* $5860; room only: $3470. Room and board charges vary according to board plan and housing facility.

Applying *Options:* deferred entrance. *Application fee:* $25. *Required:* high school transcript. *Recommended:* interview.

Freshman Application Contact Robert Cullins, Registrar, Sul Ross State University, Box C-2, Alpine, TX 79832. *Phone:* 432-837-8050. *Toll-free phone:* 888-722-7778. *Fax:* 432-837-8186. *E-mail:* rcullins@sulross.edu.

Tarleton State University

Stephenville, Texas **www.tarleton.edu/**

- **State-supported** comprehensive, founded 1899, part of Texas A&M University System
- **Small-town** 125-acre campus with easy access to Fort Worth
- **Endowment** $41.0 million
- **Coed** 7,804 undergraduate students, 77% full-time, 57% women, 43% men
- **Moderately difficult** entrance level, 55% of applicants were admitted

Undergraduates 6,016 full-time, 1,788 part-time. Students come from 47 states and territories, 21 other countries, 4% are from out of state, 8% African American, 1% Asian American or Pacific Islander, 9% Hispanic American, 1% Native American, 0.8% international, 12% transferred in, 42% live on campus. *Retention:* 62% of 2006 full-time freshmen returned.

Freshmen *Admission:* 3,544 applied, 1,932 admitted, 1,216 enrolled. *Test scores:* SAT critical reading scores over 500: 38%; SAT math scores over 500: 48%; SAT writing scores over 500: 33%; ACT scores over 18: 84%; SAT critical reading scores over 600: 7%; SAT math scores over 600: 9%; SAT writing scores over 600: 4%; ACT scores over 24: 20%; SAT math scores over 700: 1%; ACT scores over 30: 1%.

Faculty *Total:* 576, 55% full-time, 42% with terminal degrees. *Student/faculty ratio:* 18:1.

Majors Accounting; agricultural and domestic animals services related; agricultural economics; agricultural production related; agricultural teacher education; agriculture and agriculture operations related; agronomy and crop science; animal/livestock husbandry and production; animal sciences; art; aviation/airway management; biology/biological sciences; business administration and management; business/commerce; chemistry; clinical laboratory science/medical technology; computer and information sciences; counselor education/school counseling and guidance; criminal justice/safety; curriculum and instruction; dramatic/theater arts; economics; education; educational leadership and administration; education (multiple levels); elementary education; engineering physics; English; English as a second/foreign language (teaching); environmental science; family and consumer sciences/human sciences; farm and ranch management; finance; fine/studio arts; geology/earth science; histologic technology/histotechnologist; history; horticultural science; human nutrition; human resources management; hydrology and water resources science; industrial arts; industrial production technologies related; interdisciplinary studies; international agriculture; international business/trade/commerce; kinesiology and exercise science; liberal arts and sciences/liberal studies; management information systems; manufacturing technology; mathematics; middle school education; multi-/interdisciplinary studies related; music; music teacher education; nursing (registered nurse training); office management; ornamental horticulture; physical education teaching and coaching; physical therapy; physics; political science and government; pre-dentistry studies; pre-medical studies; pre-pharmacy studies; pre-veterinary studies; psychology; range science and management; science teacher education; secondary education; social work; sociology; Spanish; speech and rhetoric; technical and business writing; wildlife and wildlands science and management; zoology/animal biology.

Academics *Calendar:* semesters. *Degrees:* associate, bachelor's, master's, and doctoral. *Special study options:* academic remediation for entering students, accelerated degree program, adult/continuing education programs, advanced placement credit, cooperative education, distance learning, double majors, honors programs, internships, off-campus study, part-time degree program, services for LD students, study abroad, summer session for credit. *ROTC:* Army (b).

Computers on Campus 1,000 computers/terminals are available on campus for general student use. Students can access the following: campus intranet, computer help desk, free student e-mail accounts, online (class) grades, online (class) registration, online (class) schedules. Campuswide network is available. 100% of college-owned or -operated housing units are wired for high-speed Internet access. Wireless service is available via classrooms, computer centers, computer labs, learning centers, libraries, student centers.

Student Life *Housing:* on-campus residence required for freshman year. *Options:* coed, men-only, women-only. Campus housing is university owned and leased by the school. Freshman campus housing is guaranteed. *Activities and organizations:* drama/theater group, student-run newspaper, radio station, choral group, marching band, Student Government Association, Student Programming Association, Kappa Delta Rho, Delta Zeta, Chi Alpha, national fraternities, national sororities. *Campus security:* 24-hour emergency response devices and patrols, student patrols, late-night transport/escort service, controlled dormitory access. *Student services:* health clinic, personal/psychological counseling, legal services.

Athletics Member NCAA. All Division II. *Intercollegiate sports:* baseball M (s), basketball M (s)/W (s), cheerleading M (s)/W (s), cross-country running M (s)/W (s), football M (s), golf W (s), softball W (s), tennis W (s), track and field M (s)/W (s), volleyball W (s). *Intramural sports:* archery M/W, basketball M/W, football M/W, golf M/W, racquetball M/W, soccer M/W, softball M/W, table tennis M/W, tennis M/W, volleyball M/W.

Standardized Tests *Required:* SAT or ACT (for admission).

Costs (2007–08) *Tuition:* state resident $5166 full-time, $130 per semester hour part-time; nonresident $13,506 full-time, $408 per semester hour part-time. Full-time tuition and fees vary according to course load. Part-time tuition and fees vary according to course load. *Required fees:* $1326 full-time, $40 per hour part-time, $124 per term part-time. *Room and board:* $5944; room only: $3086. Room and board charges vary according to board plan and housing facility. *Payment plan:* installment. *Waivers:* senior citizens and employees or children of employees.

Financial Aid Of all full-time matriculated undergraduates who enrolled in 2005, 4,916 applied for aid, 4,702 were judged to have need, 2,441 had their need fully met. 73 Federal Work-Study jobs, 10 state and other part-time jobs (averaging $3300). In 2005, 1180 non-need-based awards were made. *Average percent of need met:* 60%. *Average financial aid package:* $8162. *Average* *need-based loan:* $3347. *Average need-based gift aid:* $3272. *Average non-need-based aid:* $3959. *Average indebtedness upon graduation:* $16,776.

Applying *Options:* electronic application, early admission, deferred entrance. *Application fee:* $25. *Required:* high school transcript. *Required for some:* interview. *Application deadlines:* 8/1 (freshmen), 7/1 (transfers), 11/30 (early action).

Freshman Application Contact Ms. Cindy Hess, Director of Undergraduate Admissions, Tarleton State University, Box T-0030, Tarleton Station, Stephenville, TX 76402. *Phone:* 254-968-9123. *Toll-free phone:* 800-687-8236. *Fax:* 254-968-9951. *E-mail:* uadm@tarleton.edu.

TEXAS A&M HEALTH SCIENCE CENTER

College Station, Texas **www.tamhsc.edu/**

- **State-supported** upper-level, founded 1999, part of Texas A&M University System Health Science Center
- **Urban** campus
- **Coed** 60 undergraduate students, 100% full-time, 100% women

Undergraduates 60 full-time. 3% are from out of state, 2% African American, 20% Asian American or Pacific Islander, 10% Hispanic American, 2% Native American, 50% transferred in.

Faculty *Total:* 255, 54% full-time.

Majors Dental hygiene.

Academics *Calendar:* semesters. *Degrees:* bachelor's, master's, doctoral, first professional, post-master's, and first professional certificates. *Special study options:* services for LD students.

Computers on Campus Students can access the following: campus intranet, computer help desk, free student e-mail accounts. Campuswide network is available.

Student Life *Housing:* college housing not available. *Campus security:* 24-hour emergency response devices and patrols, late-night transport/escort service, electronically operated building access. *Student services:* health clinic, personal/psychological counseling.

Costs (2007–08) *Tuition:* state resident $104 per hour part-time; nonresident $380 per hour part-time.

Applying *Application fee:* $35. *Application deadline:* rolling (transfers).

Application Contact Dr. Jack L. Long, Associate Dean for Student Services, Texas A&M Health Science Center, PO Box 660677, 3302 Gaston Avenue, Dallas, TX 75266-0677. *Phone:* 214-828-8232. *Fax:* 214-874-4567.

TEXAS A&M INTERNATIONAL UNIVERSITY

Laredo, Texas **www.tamiu.edu/**

- **State-supported** comprehensive, founded 1969, part of Texas A&M University System
- **Urban** 300-acre campus
- **Endowment** $22.6 million
- **Coed** 4,121 undergraduate students, 66% full-time, 63% women, 37% men
- **Moderately difficult** entrance level, 54% of applicants were admitted

Undergraduates 2,716 full-time, 1,405 part-time. Students come from 16 states and territories, 20 other countries, 3% are from out of state, 0.8% African American, 0.6% Asian American or Pacific Islander, 92% Hispanic American, 4% international, 11% transferred in, 13% live on campus. *Retention:* 59% of 2006 full-time freshmen returned.

Freshmen *Admission:* 2,183 applied, 1,180 admitted, 621 enrolled. *Average high school GPA:* 3.6. *Test scores:* SAT critical reading scores over 500: 20%; SAT math scores over 500: 29%; SAT writing scores over 500: 19%; ACT scores over 18: 51%; SAT critical reading scores over 600: 2%; SAT math scores over 600: 3%; SAT writing scores over 600: 1%; ACT scores over 24: 5%.

Faculty *Total:* 283, 54% full-time, 47% with terminal degrees. *Student/faculty ratio:* 17:1.

Majors Accounting; bilingual and multilingual education; biology/biological sciences; biology teacher education; business administration and management; business/managerial economics; chemistry; communication/speech communication and rhetoric; criminal justice/safety; English; English/language arts teacher education; finance; health and physical education; history; history teacher education; information science/studies; kindergarten/preschool education; marketing/marketing management; mathematics; mathematics teacher education; nursing (registered nurse training); perioperative/operating room and surgical nursing; physical education teaching and coaching; physical sciences; political science and government; psychology; reading teacher education; science teacher education; social sciences; social studies teacher education; sociology; Spanish; Spanish language teacher education; special education.

Academics *Calendar:* semesters. *Degrees:* bachelor's, master's, and doctoral. *Special study options:* academic remediation for entering students, advanced placement credit, distance learning, double majors, English as a second language, honors programs, independent study, internships, part-time degree program, services for LD students, study abroad, summer session for credit. *ROTC:* Army (b).

Computers on Campus 200 computers/terminals are available on campus for general student use. Students can access the following: computer help desk, free student e-mail accounts, online (class) grades, online (class) registration, online (class) schedules. Campuswide network is available. 100% of college-owned or -operated housing units are wired for high-speed Internet access. Wireless service is available via classrooms.

Student Life *Housing options:* coed. Campus housing is provided by a third party. Freshman applicants given priority for college housing. *Activities and organizations:* student-run newspaper, choral group, TAMIU Ambassadors, Electronic Commerce Association, Rainbow Education Association of Laredo, Student Finance Society, Psychology Club, national fraternities. *Campus security:* 24-hour emergency response devices and patrols, late-night transport/escort service, controlled dormitory access. *Student services:* health clinic, personal/psychological counseling.

Athletics Member NAIA. *Intercollegiate sports:* basketball M/W, golf M/W, soccer M/W, volleyball W.

Standardized Tests *Required:* SAT or ACT (for admission).

Costs (2007–08) *Tuition:* state resident $3540 full-time; nonresident $11,880 full-time. Full-time tuition and fees vary according to course load. Part-time tuition and fees vary according to course load and reciprocity agreements. *Required fees:* $1498 full-time. *Room and board:* $6630; room only: $4750. Room and board charges vary according to board plan and housing facility. *Payment plan:* installment. *Waivers:* senior citizens.

Financial Aid Of all full-time matriculated undergraduates who enrolled in 2002, 1,910 applied for aid, 1,758 were judged to have need, 467 had their need fully met. 89 Federal Work-Study jobs (averaging $1492). 7 state and other part-time jobs (averaging $1365). In 2002, 78 non-need-based awards were made. *Average percent of need met:* 84%. *Average financial aid package:* $7593. *Average need-based loan:* $3168. *Average need-based gift aid:* $5221. *Average non-need-based aid:* $3257. *Average indebtedness upon graduation:* $9872.

Applying *Options:* electronic application, early admission, deferred entrance. *Required:* high school transcript. *Application deadlines:* 7/1 (freshmen), 7/1 (transfers). *Notification:* 7/15 (freshmen), 7/15 (transfers).

Freshman Application Contact Ms. Gina Gonzalez, Director of Recruitment and School Relations, Texas A&M International University, 5201 University Boulevard, Laredo, TX 78041-1900. *Phone:* 956-326-2270. *Toll-free phone:* 888-489-2648. *E-mail:* enroll@tamiu.edu.

TEXAS A&M UNIVERSITY

College Station, Texas **www.tamu.edu/**

- **State-supported** university, founded 1876, part of Texas A&M University System
- **Suburban** 5200-acre campus with easy access to Houston
- **Endowment** $6.6 billion
- **Coed** 37,357 undergraduate students, 91% full-time, 48% women, 52% men
- **Moderately difficult** entrance level, 76% of applicants were admitted

Undergraduates 34,033 full-time, 3,324 part-time. Students come from 52 states and territories, 128 other countries, 4% are from out of state, 3% African American, 4% Asian American or Pacific Islander, 12% Hispanic American, 0.6% Native American, 1% international, 4% transferred in, 25% live on campus. *Retention:* 92% of 2006 full-time freshmen returned.

Freshmen *Admission:* 18,817 applied, 14,380 admitted, 8,094 enrolled. *Test scores:* SAT critical reading scores over 500: 83%; SAT math scores over 500: 92%; SAT writing scores over 500: 78%; ACT scores over 18: 99%; SAT critical reading scores over 600: 42%; SAT math scores over 600: 59%; SAT writing scores over 600: 32%; ACT scores over 24: 70%; SAT critical reading scores over 700: 9%; SAT math scores over 700: 13%; SAT writing scores over 700: 5%; ACT scores over 30: 16%.

Faculty *Total:* 2,608, 84% full-time, 89% with terminal degrees. *Student/faculty ratio:* 19:1.

Majors Accounting; aerospace, aeronautical and astronautical engineering; agribusiness; agricultural and food products processing; agricultural animal breeding; agricultural/biological engineering and bioengineering; agricultural business and management; agricultural economics; agricultural/farm supplies retailing and wholesaling; agricultural production; agriculture; agronomy and crop science; American studies; animal/livestock husbandry and production; animal sciences; anthropology; applied horticulture; applied mathematics; aquaculture; architecture; atmospheric sciences and meteorology; biochemistry; biology/biological sciences; biomedical/medical engineering; biomedical sciences; botany/plant biology; business administration and management; cartography; cell and molecular biology; chemical engineering; chemistry; civil engineering; community health services counseling; computer engineering; computer science; construction engineering technology; curriculum and instruction; dairy science; digital communication and media/multimedia; dramatic/theater arts; ecology; economics; electrical, electronic and communications engineering technology; electrical, electronics and communications engineering; engineering technology; English; entomology; environmental design/architecture; environmental science; environmental studies; farm and ranch management; finance; fishing and fisheries sciences and management; food science; foods, nutrition, and wellness; forest/forest resources management; forestry; French; geography; geological and earth sciences/geosciences related; geology/earth science; geophysics and seismology; German; health and physical education; history; horticultural science; industrial engineering; interdisciplinary studies; international/global studies; journalism; landscape architecture; management science; manufacturing technology; marketing/marketing management; mathematics; mechanical engineering; mechanical engineering/mechanical technology; microbiology; molecular genetics; multi-/interdisciplinary studies related; museum studies; music; natural resources/conservation; nuclear engineering; ocean engineering; ornamental horticulture; parks, recreation and leisure; parks, recreation and leisure facilities management; petroleum engineering; philosophy; physics; plant protection and integrated pest management; political science and government; poultry science; pre-veterinary studies; psychology; public relations, advertising, and applied communication related; range science and management; Russian; sales, distribution and marketing; sociology; Spanish; speech and rhetoric; tourism and travel services management; urban forestry; wildlife and wildlands science and management; zoology/animal biology.

Academics *Calendar:* semesters. *Degrees:* bachelor's, master's, doctoral, first professional, and postbachelor's certificates. *Special study options:* academic remediation for entering students, accelerated degree program, advanced placement credit, cooperative education, distance learning, double majors, English as a second language, honors programs, independent study, internships, off-campus study, part-time degree program, services for LD students, study abroad, summer session for credit. *ROTC:* Army (b), Navy (b), Air Force (b).

Computers on Campus 1,334 computers/terminals and 5,000 ports are available on campus for general student use. Students can access the following: campus intranet, computer help desk, free student e-mail accounts, online (class) grades, online (class) registration, online (class) schedules. Campuswide network is available. 100% of college-owned or -operated housing units are wired for high-speed Internet access. Wireless service is available via classrooms, computer labs, libraries.

Student Life *Housing options:* coed, men-only, women-only, disabled students. Campus housing is university owned. *Activities and organizations:* drama/theater group, student-run newspaper, radio and television station, choral group, marching band, Memorial Student Center, Corps of Cadets, Fish Camp, student government, national fraternities, national sororities. *Campus security:* 24-hour emergency response devices and patrols, late-night transport/escort service, controlled dormitory access, student escorts. *Student services:* health clinic, personal/psychological counseling, women's center, legal services.

Athletics Member NCAA. All Division I except football (Division I-A). *Intercollegiate sports:* archery W (s), baseball M (s), basketball M (s)/W (s), cross-country running M (s)/W (s), equestrian sports W (s), golf M (s)/W (s), soccer W (s), softball W (s), swimming and diving M (s)/W (s), tennis M (s)/W (s), track and field M (s)/W (s), volleyball W (s). *Intramural sports:* archery M/W, badminton M/W, basketball M/W, bowling M/W, cross-country running M/W, fencing M (c)/W (c), field hockey M (c)/W (c), football M/W, golf M/W, gymnastics M (c)/W (c), lacrosse M (c)/W (c), racquetball M (c)/W (c), riflery M/W, rugby M (c)/W (c), sailing M (c)/W (c), soccer M/W, softball M/W, squash M/W, swimming and diving M/W, table tennis M/W, tennis M/W, track and field M/W, ultimate Frisbee M (c)/W (c), volleyball M/W, water polo M/W, weight lifting M (c)/W (c), wrestling M (c).

Standardized Tests *Required:* SAT or ACT (for admission).

Costs (2007–08) *Tuition:* state resident $4680 full-time, $156 per semester hour part-time; nonresident $13,020 full-time, $434 per semester hour part-time. Full-time tuition and fees vary according to course load, location, and program. *Required fees:* $2655 full-time. *Room and board:* $7660; room only: $3804. Room and board charges vary according to board plan, housing facility, and location. *Payment plan:* installment.

Financial Aid Of all full-time matriculated undergraduates who enrolled in 2007, 17,895 applied for aid, 12,510 were judged to have need, 5,801 had their need fully met. 859 Federal Work-Study jobs (averaging $2366). 272 state and other part-time jobs (averaging $2124). In 2007, 4831 non-need-based awards were made. *Average percent of need met:* 85%. *Average financial aid package:* $13,215. *Average need-based loan:* $5571. *Average need-based gift aid:* $7933. *Average non-need-based aid:* $3027. *Average indebtedness upon graduation:* $19,940.

Applying *Options:* electronic application. *Application fee:* $60. *Required:* essay or personal statement, high school transcript. *Application deadlines:* 2/1 (freshmen), 3/15 (transfers). *Notification:* continuous (freshmen), continuous (transfers).

Freshman Application Contact Mr. Scott McDonald, Director of Admissions, Texas A&M University, 217 John J. Koldus Building, College Station, TX 77843-1265. *Phone:* 979-845-3741. *Fax:* 979-845-8737. *E-mail:* admissions@tamu.edu.

TEXAS A&M UNIVERSITY AT GALVESTON

Galveston, Texas **www.tamug.edu/**

- **State-supported** comprehensive, founded 1962, part of Texas A&M University System
- **Suburban** 122-acre campus with easy access to Houston
- **Endowment** $2.3 million
- **Coed** 1,565 undergraduate students, 93% full-time, 41% women, 59% men
- **Moderately difficult** entrance level, 78% of applicants were admitted

Undergraduates 1,455 full-time, 110 part-time. Students come from 55 states and territories, 9 other countries, 23% are from out of state, 2% African American, 1% Asian American or Pacific Islander, 11% Hispanic American, 1% Native American, 0.8% international, 7% transferred in, 54% live on campus. *Retention:* 78% of 2006 full-time freshmen returned.

Freshmen *Admission:* 1,181 applied, 926 admitted, 461 enrolled. *Test scores:* SAT critical reading scores over 500: 74%; SAT math scores over 500: 79%; ACT scores over 18: 94%; SAT critical reading scores over 600: 29%; SAT math scores over 600: 30%; ACT scores over 24: 40%; SAT critical reading scores over 700: 3%; SAT math scores over 700: 3%; ACT scores over 30: 3%.

Faculty *Total:* 170, 40% full-time, 48% with terminal degrees. *Student/faculty ratio:* 15:1.

Majors Biological and physical sciences; business administration and management; fish/game management; marine biology and biological oceanography; marine science/merchant marine officer; maritime science; multi-/interdisciplinary studies related; natural resources/conservation; naval architecture and marine engineering; ocean engineering; oceanography (chemical and physical); transportation technology.

Academics *Calendar:* semesters. *Degrees:* bachelor's and master's. *Special study options:* academic remediation for entering students, accelerated degree program, advanced placement credit, cooperative education, double majors, English as a second language, independent study, internships, part-time degree program, study abroad, summer session for credit. *ROTC:* Navy (b).

Computers on Campus 122 computers/terminals are available on campus for general student use. Students can access the following: online (class) grades, online (class) registration, degree plan progress, billing statement. Campuswide network is available. 100% of college-owned or -operated housing units are wired for high-speed Internet access.

Student Life *Housing:* on-campus residence required for freshman year. *Options:* coed, men-only, women-only, disabled students. Campus housing is university owned. Freshman applicants given priority for college housing. *Activities and organizations:* drama/theater group, student-run newspaper, choral group, Sail Club, Caving Club, Dive Club, Rowing Club, Rifle Drill Team. *Campus security:* 24-hour emergency response devices and patrols. *Student services:* health clinic, personal/psychological counseling.

Athletics *Intercollegiate sports:* crew M/W, lacrosse M, sailing M/W. *Intramural sports:* basketball M/W, bowling M/W, football M/W, racquetball M/W, soccer M/W, softball M/W, swimming and diving M/W, tennis M/W, volleyball M/W, water polo M/W.

Standardized Tests *Required:* SAT or ACT (for admission). *Recommended:* SAT Subject Tests (for admission).

Costs (2008–09) *Tuition:* state resident $4680 full-time, $156 per credit hour part-time; nonresident $13,020 full-time, $434 per credit hour part-time. *Required fees:* $1375 full-time, $640 per term part-time. *Room and board:* $5203; room only: $1958.

Financial Aid Of all full-time matriculated undergraduates who enrolled in 2007, 804 applied for aid, 714 were judged to have need, 130 had their need fully met. 6 Federal Work-Study jobs (averaging $2383). 1 state and other part-time job (averaging $500). In 2007, 40 non-need-based awards were made. *Average percent of need met:* 18%. *Average financial aid package:* $11,234. *Average need-based loan:* $3452. *Average need-based gift aid:* $5016. *Average non-need-based aid:* $5267. *Average indebtedness upon graduation:* $16,800.

Applying *Options:* electronic application, early admission, deferred entrance. *Application fee:* $45. *Required:* essay or personal statement, high school transcript. *Required for some:* interview. *Recommended:* essay or personal statement, letters of recommendation, community involvement. *Application deadlines:* rolling (freshmen), rolling (transfers). *Notification:* continuous (freshmen), continuous (transfers).

Freshman Application Contact Ms. Sarah Trombley, Associate Director of Admissions and Records, Texas A&M University at Galveston, PO Box 1675, Galveston, TX 77553-1675. *Phone:* 409-740-4448. *Toll-free phone:* 87—SEAAGGIE. *Fax:* 409-740-4731. *E-mail:* seaaggie@tamug.edu.

TEXAS A&M UNIVERSITY–COMMERCE

Commerce, Texas **www.tamu-commerce.edu/**

- **State-supported** university, founded 1889, part of Texas A&M University System
- **Small-town** 1883-acre campus with easy access to Dallas–Fort Worth
- **Endowment** $12.6 million
- **Coed** 5,166 undergraduate students, 74% full-time, 62% women, 38% men
- **Moderately difficult** entrance level, 55% of applicants were admitted

Undergraduates 3,841 full-time, 1,325 part-time. Students come from 32 states and territories, 5 other countries, 2% are from out of state, 18% African American, 2% Asian American or Pacific Islander, 10% Hispanic American, 1% Native American, 0.9% international, 26% transferred in, 24% live on campus. *Retention:* 57% of 2006 full-time freshmen returned.

Freshmen *Admission:* 1,734 applied, 954 admitted, 644 enrolled. *Test scores:* SAT critical reading scores over 500: 49%; SAT math scores over 500: 49%; ACT scores over 18: 48%; SAT critical reading scores over 600: 14%; SAT math scores over 600: 13%; ACT scores over 24: 13%; SAT critical reading scores over 700: 1%; SAT math scores over 700: 1%.

Faculty *Total:* 811, 31% full-time. *Student/faculty ratio:* 17:1.

Majors Accounting; agricultural business and management; agricultural economics; agricultural sciences; agricultural teacher education; agriculture; agronomy and crop science; animal sciences; art; art teacher education; athletic training; biology/biological sciences; business administration and management; business teacher education; chemistry; commercial and advertising art; communication/speech communication and rhetoric; computer science; construction engineering; counselor education/school counseling and guidance; criminal justice/law enforcement administration; criminal justice/police science; criminology; design and visual communications; dramatic/theater arts; early childhood education; economics; education; educational, instructional, and curriculum supervision; educational leadership and administration; educational psychology; elementary education; English; environmental science; finance; fine/studio arts; French; health and physical education; health science; health teacher education; history; human resources management; industrial arts; industrial engineering; industrial technology; information science/studies; interdisciplinary studies; journalism; kindergarten/preschool education; kinesiology and exercise science; labor and industrial relations; legal administrative assistant/secretary; liberal arts and sciences/liberal studies; library science; management information systems; marketing/marketing management; mathematics; music; music performance; music teacher education; natural resources/conservation; operations management; photography; physical education teaching and coaching; physics; piano and organ; political science and government; psychology; radio and television; reading teacher education; secondary education; social sciences; social work; sociology; Spanish; special education; trade and industrial teacher education.

Academics *Calendar:* semesters. *Degrees:* bachelor's, master's, and doctoral. *Special study options:* academic remediation for entering students, adult/continuing education programs, advanced placement credit, cooperative education, distance learning, double majors, honors programs, independent study, internships, off-campus study, part-time degree program, services for LD students, study abroad, summer session for credit. *Unusual degree programs:* 3-2 engineering with Texas A&M University.

Computers on Campus 405 computers/terminals are available on campus for general student use. Students can access the following: campus intranet, computer help desk, free student e-mail accounts, online (class) grades, online (class) registration, online (class) schedules. Campuswide network is available.

Student Life *Housing:* on-campus residence required for freshman year. *Options:* coed, men-only, women-only, disabled students. Campus housing is university owned. Freshman campus housing is guaranteed. *Activities and organizations:* drama/theater group, student-run newspaper, radio and television station, choral group, marching band, national fraternities, national sororities. *Campus security:* 24-hour emergency response devices and patrols, controlled dormitory access. *Student services:* health clinic, personal/psychological counseling, legal services.

Athletics Member NCAA. All Division II. *Intercollegiate sports:* basketball M (s)/W (s), cheerleading M (s)/W (s), cross-country running M (s)/W (s), football M (s), golf M (s)/W (s), soccer W (s), track and field M (s)/W (s), volleyball W (s). *Intramural sports:* badminton M/W, basketball M/W, cross-country running M/W, football M/W, racquetball M/W, soccer M, softball M/W, table tennis M/W, tennis M/W, track and field M/W, volleyball M/W.

Standardized Tests *Required:* SAT or ACT (for admission).

Costs (2008–09) *Tuition:* state resident $5126 full-time; nonresident $13,466 full-time. *Room and board:* $6484.

Financial Aid Of all full-time matriculated undergraduates who enrolled in 2007, 3,053 applied for aid, 2,489 were judged to have need, 490 had their need fully met. 162 Federal Work-Study jobs (averaging $2290). 28 state and other part-time jobs (averaging $2105). In 2007, 443 non-need-based awards were made. *Average percent of need met:* 66%. *Average financial aid package:* $7926. *Average need-based loan:* $3866. *Average need-based gift aid:* $5135. *Average non-need-based aid:* $2294. *Average indebtedness upon graduation:* $17,269.

Applying *Options:* electronic application, early admission. *Application fee:* $25. *Required:* high school transcript. *Application deadlines:* 8/11 (freshmen), rolling (transfers). *Notification:* continuous (freshmen), continuous (transfers).

Freshman Application Contact Hope Young, Director of Admissions, Texas A&M University–Commerce, PO Box 3011, Commerce, TX 75429. *Phone:* 903-886-5103. *Toll-free phone:* 800-331-3878. *Fax:* 903-886-5888. *E-mail:* admissions@tamu-commerce.edu.

TEXAS A&M UNIVERSITY–CORPUS CHRISTI

Corpus Christi, Texas **www.tamucc.edu/**

- **State-supported** comprehensive, founded 1947, part of Texas A&M University System
- **Suburban** 240-acre campus
- **Endowment** $2.3 million
- **Coed**
- **Moderately difficult** entrance level

Texas A&M University–Corpus Christi embraces the growing Gulf Coast region through research and degree programs that foster new technologies, develop quality lifestyles, encourage economic growth, educate the nation's youth, and ensure healthy communities. As an Islander, students can select from among many degree programs through five academic colleges: Business, Education, Liberal Arts, Nursing and Health Sciences, and Science and Technology. For more information about "The Island University," students should visit http://www.tamucc.edu.

Faculty *Student/faculty ratio:* 19:1.

Academics *Calendar:* semesters. *Degrees:* bachelor's, master's, and doctoral.

Student Life *Campus security:* 24-hour emergency response devices and patrols, late-night transport/escort service, security gate access with card after 10 p.m.

Athletics Member NCAA.

Standardized Tests *Required:* SAT or ACT (for admission). *Recommended:* SAT (for admission).

Costs (2007–08) *Tuition:* state resident $4020 full-time, $131 per credit hour part-time; nonresident $12,360 full-time, $409 per credit hour part-time. *Required fees:* $1620 full-time, $61 per credit hour part-time, $84 per term part-time. *Room and board:* $9971; room only: $7398. Room and board charges vary according to location.

Financial Aid Of all full-time matriculated undergraduates who enrolled in 2007, 3,768 applied for aid, 3,233 were judged to have need, 149 had their need fully met. 181 Federal Work-Study jobs (averaging $2760). 110 state and other part-time jobs (averaging $2684). In 2007, 664 non-need-based awards were made. *Average percent of need met:* 45. *Average financial aid package:* $7801. *Average need-based loan:* $4291. *Average need-based gift aid:* $4649. *Average non-need-based aid:* $3907. *Average indebtedness upon graduation:* $19,014.

Applying *Application fee:* $30. *Required:* high school transcript, minimum 2.0 GPA.

Director of Admissions Ms. Margaret Dechant, Director of Admissions, Texas A&M University–Corpus Christi, 6300 Ocean Drive, Corpus Christi, TX 78412-5503. *Phone:* 361-825-2414. *Toll-free phone:* 800-482-6822. *E-mail:* jmorgan@falcon.tamucc.edu.

See page 2554 for the College Close-Up.

TEXAS A&M UNIVERSITY–KINGSVILLE

Kingsville, Texas **www.tamuk.edu/**

Director of Admissions Ms. Maggie Williams, Director of Admissions, Texas A&M University–Kingsville, Campus Box 105, Kingsville, TX 78363. *Phone:* 361-593-2811. *Toll-free phone:* 800-687-6000.

TEXAS A&M UNIVERSITY–TEXARKANA

Texarkana, Texas **www.tamut.edu/**

- **State-supported** upper-level, founded 1971, part of Texas A&M University System
- **Small-town** 1-acre campus
- **Endowment** $1.9 million
- **Coed**
- **Noncompetitive** entrance level

Faculty *Student/faculty ratio:* 14:1.

Academics *Calendar:* semesters. *Degrees:* bachelor's and master's.

Student Life *Campus security:* 24-hour patrols, late-night transport/escort service.

Costs (2007–08) *Tuition:* state resident $2496 full-time; nonresident $9168 full-time. Full-time tuition and fees vary according to course level, course load, and student level. Part-time tuition and fees vary according to course level, course load, and student level. *Required fees:* $484 full-time.

Applying *Options:* electronic application.

Application Contact Mrs. Patricia Black, Director of Admissions and Registrar, Texas A&M University–Texarkana, PO Box 5518, Texarkana, TX 75505-5518. *Phone:* 903-223-3068. *Fax:* 903-223-3140. *E-mail:* admissions@tamut.edu.

TEXAS CHIROPRACTIC COLLEGE

Pasadena, Texas **www.txchiro.edu/**

- **Independent** upper-level, founded 1908
- **Suburban** 18-acre campus with easy access to Houston
- **Coed**
- **Moderately difficult** entrance level

Faculty *Student/faculty ratio:* 15:1.

Academics *Calendar:* trimesters. *Degrees:* incidental bachelor's and first professional.

Costs (2007–08) *Tuition:* $21,750 full-time.

Financial Aid Of all full-time matriculated undergraduates who enrolled in 2003, 7 applied for aid, 7 were judged to have need.

Applying *Options:* deferred entrance. *Application fee:* $50.

Application Contact Dr. Sandra Hughes, Director of Admissions, Texas Chiropractic College, 5912 Spencer Highway, Pasadena, TX 77505-1699. *Phone:* 281-998-6098. *Toll-free phone:* 800-468-6839. *Fax:* 281-991-5237. *E-mail:* shughes@txchiro.edu.

TEXAS CHRISTIAN UNIVERSITY

Fort Worth, Texas **www.tcu.edu/**

- **Independent** university, founded 1873, affiliated with Christian Church (Disciples of Christ)
- **Suburban** 260-acre campus
- **Endowment** $1.3 billion
- **Coed** 7,382 undergraduate students, 95% full-time, 59% women, 41% men
- **Moderately difficult** entrance level, 49% of applicants were admitted

TCU's mission—to educate individuals to think and act as ethical leaders and responsible citizens in the global community—influences every area of this person-centered private university. From leadership development to a top-notch study-abroad program, TCU graduates earn more than degrees that will improve their lives. They learn to change their world.

Undergraduates 7,049 full-time, 333 part-time. Students come from 50 states and territories, 75 other countries, 20% are from out of state, 5% African American, 3% Asian American or Pacific Islander, 7% Hispanic American, 0.5% Native American, 5% international, 6% transferred in, 46% live on campus. *Retention:* 86% of 2006 full-time freshmen returned.

Freshmen *Admission:* 11,888 applied, 5,812 admitted, 1,644 enrolled.

Faculty *Total:* 796, 60% full-time, 62% with terminal degrees. *Student/faculty ratio:* 14:1.

Majors Accounting; advertising; anthropology; art history, criticism and conservation; art teacher education; astronomy and astrophysics related; athletic training; ballet; bilingual and multilingual education; biochemistry; biology/biological sciences; broadcast journalism; business administration, management and operations related; chemistry; communication/speech communication and rhetoric; computer and information sciences; computer and information sciences related; counselor education/school counseling and guidance; creative writing; criminal justice/safety; dietetics; dietetics and clinical nutrition services related; dramatic/theater arts; early childhood education; e-commerce; economics; educational leadership and administration; elementary education; engineering; English; English/language arts teacher education; environmental science; farm and ranch management; fashion merchandising; finance; fine/studio arts; French; general studies; geography; geology/earth science; health and physical education; health and physical education related; health science; history; interior design; international business/trade/commerce; international economics; international finance; international marketing; international relations and affairs; journalism; Latin American studies; liberal arts and sciences/liberal studies; management science; marketing/marketing management; mass communication/media; mathematics; mathematics teacher education; military studies; movement therapy and movement education; music; music performance; music teacher education; music theory and composition; neuroscience; nursing (registered nurse training); painting; philosophy; photography; physical education teaching and coaching; physics; piano and organ; political science and government; printmaking; psychology; radio and television; real estate; religious studies; science teacher education; sculpture; secondary education; social studies teacher education; social work; sociology; Spanish; special education; special education (gifted and talented); special education (hearing impaired); speech-language pathology; technical teacher education; theater literature, history and criticism.

Academics *Calendar:* semesters. *Degrees:* certificates, bachelor's, master's, doctoral, and postbachelor's certificates. *Special study options:* accelerated degree program, adult/continuing education programs, advanced placement credit, distance learning, double majors, English as a second language, honors programs, independent study, internships, off-campus study, part-time degree program, services for LD students, study abroad, summer session for credit. *ROTC:* Army (b), Air Force (b). *Unusual degree programs:* 3-2 business administration; education.

Computers on Campus Students can access the following: campus intranet, computer help desk, free student e-mail accounts, online (class) grades, online (class) registration, online (class) schedules. Campuswide network is available. 100% of college-owned or -operated housing units are wired for high-speed Internet access. Wireless service is available via entire campus.

Student Life *Housing:* on-campus residence required through sophomore year. *Options:* coed, men-only, women-only. Campus housing is university owned. Freshman campus housing is guaranteed. *Activities and organizations:* drama/theater group, student-run newspaper, radio and television station, choral group, marching band, national fraternities, national sororities. *Campus security:* 24-hour emergency response devices and patrols, student patrols, late-night transport/escort service, controlled dormitory access, emergency call boxes, video camera surveillance in parking lots. *Student services:* health clinic, personal/psychological counseling, women's center, legal services.

Athletics Member NCAA. All Division I. *Intercollegiate sports:* baseball M (s), basketball M (s)/W (s), cross-country running M (s)/W (s), football M (s), golf M (s)/W (s), riflery W (s), soccer W (s), swimming and diving M (s)/W (s), tennis M (s)/W (s), track and field M (s)/W (s), volleyball W (s).

Standardized Tests *Required:* SAT or ACT (for admission).

Costs (2007–08) *Comprehensive fee:* $33,068 includes full-time tuition ($24,820), mandatory fees ($48), and room and board ($8200). Part-time tuition: $1050 per credit. Part-time tuition and fees vary according to course load. *Required fees:* $24 per term part-time. *College room only:* $5000. Room and board charges vary according to board plan and housing facility. *Payment plan:* installment. *Waivers:* employees or children of employees.

Financial Aid Of all full-time matriculated undergraduates who enrolled in 2007, 3,707 applied for aid, 2,883 were judged to have need, 1,834 had their need fully met. 1,140 Federal Work-Study jobs (averaging $2250). 25 state and other part-time jobs (averaging $2400). In 2007, 1620 non-need-based awards were made. *Average percent of need met:* 76%. *Average financial aid package:* $19,570. *Average need-based loan:* $10,233. *Average need-based gift aid:* $11,862. *Average non-need-based aid:* $9735. *Average indebtedness upon graduation:* $23,651. *Financial aid deadline:* 5/1.

Applying *Options:* electronic application, early action, deferred entrance. *Application fee:* $40. *Required:* essay or personal statement, high school transcript, minimum 2.0 GPA, 2 letters of recommendation. *Recommended:* minimum 3.0

GPA, interview. *Application deadlines:* 2/15 (freshmen), 4/15 (transfers), 11/15 (early action). *Notification:* 4/1 (freshmen), continuous (transfers), 1/1 (early action).

Freshman Application Contact Mr. Wes Waggoner, Director of Freshman Admissions, Texas Christian University, TCU Box 297013, Fort Worth, TX 76129-0002. *Phone:* 817-257-7490. *Toll-free phone:* 800-828-3764. *Fax:* 817-257-7268. *E-mail:* frogmail@tcu.edu.

See page 2556 for the College Close-Up.

TEXAS COLLEGE

Tyler, Texas **www.texascollege.edu/**

- **Independent** 4-year, founded 1894, affiliated with Christian Methodist Episcopal Church
- **Urban** 25-acre campus
- **Endowment** $1.4 million
- **Coed** 741 undergraduate students, 97% full-time, 42% women, 58% men
- **Noncompetitive** entrance level

Undergraduates 720 full-time, 21 part-time. Students come from 19 states and territories, 1 other country, 12% are from out of state, 87% African American, 9% Hispanic American, 22% transferred in.

Freshmen *Admission:* 218 admitted, 218 enrolled. *Average high school GPA:* 2.6.

Faculty *Total:* 51, 71% full-time, 51% with terminal degrees. *Student/faculty ratio:* 15:1.

Majors Art; biology/biological sciences; business administration and management; computer science; criminal justice/safety; early childhood education; elementary education; English; general studies; health and physical education; history; liberal arts and sciences/liberal studies; mathematics; music; political science and government; religious studies; social work; sociology.

Academics *Calendar:* semesters. *Degrees:* certificates, bachelor's, and postbachelor's certificates. *Special study options:* academic remediation for entering students, accelerated degree program, adult/continuing education programs, distance learning, external degree program, independent study, internships, summer session for credit.

Computers on Campus 200 computers/terminals are available on campus for general student use. Students can access the following: computer help desk, free student e-mail accounts. Campuswide network is available. 100% of college-owned or -operated housing units are wired for high-speed Internet access. Wireless service is available via computer centers, computer labs, learning centers, libraries.

Student Life *Housing:* on-campus residence required for freshman year. *Options:* men-only, women-only. Campus housing is university owned and leased by the school. *Activities and organizations:* choral group, marching band, Omega Psi Phi, Delta Sigma Theta, Single Parent Support System, Student Ambassadors, Pre-Alumni Council, national fraternities, national sororities. *Campus security:* 24-hour emergency response devices and patrols, late-night transport/escort service. *Student services:* health clinic, personal/psychological counseling.

Athletics Member NAIA. *Intercollegiate sports:* baseball M, basketball M/W, cheerleading M/W, football M, soccer M/W, softball W, track and field M/W, volleyball W. *Intramural sports:* basketball M/W, softball W, volleyball W.

Costs (2007–08) *One-time required fee:* $20. *Comprehensive fee:* $14,346 includes full-time tuition ($7910), mandatory fees ($836), and room and board ($5600). Part-time tuition: $330 per credit hour. *Required fees:* $418 per semester part-time. *College room only:* $3200.

Financial Aid Of all full-time matriculated undergraduates who enrolled in 2002, 671 applied for aid, 616 were judged to have need, 550 had their need fully met. 210 Federal Work-Study jobs (averaging $1200). 5 state and other part-time jobs (averaging $1200). *Average percent of need met:* 75%. *Average financial aid package:* $3500. *Average need-based loan:* $2500. *Average need-based gift aid:* $1000. *Average indebtedness upon graduation:* $2000.

Applying *Options:* early admission. *Application fee:* $20. *Required:* high school transcript. *Application deadlines:* rolling (freshmen), rolling (transfers). *Notification:* continuous (freshmen), continuous (transfers).

Freshman Application Contact Dr. Reggie Brazzle, Dean of Enrollment Services, Texas College, PO Box 4500, 2404 North Grand Avenue, Tyler, TX 75702. *Phone:* 903-593-8311 Ext. 2277. *Toll-free phone:* 800-306-6299. *Fax:* 903-596-0001. *E-mail:* rbrazzle@texascollege.edu.

TEXAS LUTHERAN UNIVERSITY

Seguin, Texas **www.tlu.edu/**

- **Independent** 4-year, founded 1891, affiliated with Evangelical Lutheran Church
- **Suburban** 196-acre campus with easy access to San Antonio
- **Endowment** $69.0 million
- **Coed** 1,375 undergraduate students, 95% full-time, 52% women, 48% men
- **Moderately difficult** entrance level, 71% of applicants were admitted

TLU is consistently recognized for excellence. The *Princeton Review* has listed TLU as one of the best colleges in the western United States every year since 2004; *U.S. News & World Report* has repeatedly recognized TLU as one of America's best comprehensive colleges. This recognition affirms the high-quality education offered at Texas Lutheran University.

Undergraduates 1,307 full-time, 68 part-time. Students come from 22 states and territories, 8 other countries, 3% are from out of state, 9% African American, 1% Asian American or Pacific Islander, 19% Hispanic American, 0.4% Native American, 0.8% international, 4% transferred in, 66% live on campus. *Retention:* 64% of 2006 full-time freshmen returned.

Freshmen *Admission:* 1,138 applied, 804 admitted, 365 enrolled. *Average high school GPA:* 3.5. *Test scores:* SAT critical reading scores over 500: 52%; SAT math scores over 500: 63%; SAT writing scores over 500: 42%; ACT scores over 18: 88%; SAT critical reading scores over 600: 15%; SAT math scores over 600: 20%; SAT writing scores over 600: 9%; ACT scores over 24: 25%; SAT critical reading scores over 700: 2%; SAT math scores over 700: 3%; SAT writing scores over 700: 1%; ACT scores over 30: 4%.

Faculty *Total:* 139, 53% full-time, 60% with terminal degrees. *Student/faculty ratio:* 14:1.

Majors Accounting; art; art teacher education; athletic training; biology/biological sciences; business administration and management; chemistry; communication/speech communication and rhetoric; computer science; dramatic/theater arts; economics; education; education (multiple levels); elementary education; English; finance; health and physical education related; history; history teacher education; information science/studies; international relations and affairs; kinesiology and exercise science; mathematics; mathematics teacher education; middle school education; molecular biology; music; music teacher education; philosophy; physical education teaching and coaching; physics; political science and government; pre-dentistry studies; pre-law studies; pre-medical studies; pre-veterinary studies; psychology; social studies teacher education; sociology; Spanish; sport and fitness administration/management; theology.

Academics *Calendar:* semesters. *Degrees:* bachelor's and postbachelor's certificates. *Special study options:* adult/continuing education programs, advanced placement credit, double majors, honors programs, independent study, internships, part-time degree program, services for LD students, study abroad, summer session for credit. *ROTC:* Army (c), Air Force (c). *Unusual degree programs:* 3-2 engineering with Texas A&M University, Texas Tech University, Texas State University.

Computers on Campus 216 computers/terminals are available on campus for general student use. Students can access the following: campus intranet, computer help desk, free student e-mail accounts, online (class) grades, online (class) registration, online (class) schedules. Campuswide network is available. 100% of college-owned or -operated housing units are wired for high-speed Internet access. Wireless service is available via classrooms, computer centers, computer labs, learning centers, libraries, student centers.

Student Life *Housing:* on-campus residence required through senior year. *Options:* coed, men-only, women-only. Campus housing is university owned. Freshman campus housing is guaranteed. *Activities and organizations:* drama/theater group, student-run newspaper, choral group, Campus Ministry, Mexican American Student Association, Student Government Association. *Campus security:* 24-hour emergency response devices and patrols, late-night transport/escort service, controlled dormitory access. *Student services:* health clinic, personal/psychological counseling, women's center.

Athletics Member NCAA. All Division III. *Intercollegiate sports:* baseball M, basketball M/W, cross-country running W, football M, golf M/W, soccer M/W, softball W, tennis M/W, track and field W, volleyball W. *Intramural sports:* basketball M/W, bowling M/W, football M, racquetball M/W, softball M/W, tennis M/W, volleyball M/W.

Standardized Tests *Required:* SAT or ACT (for admission).

Costs (2007–08) *Comprehensive fee:* $25,920 includes full-time tuition ($19,940), mandatory fees ($120), and room and board ($5860). Full-time tuition and fees vary according to course load. Part-time tuition: $670 per credit hour. Part-time tuition and fees vary according to course load. *Required fees:* $60 per term part-time. *College room only:* $2800. Room and board charges vary according to board plan, housing facility, and location. *Payment plan:* installment. *Waivers:* children of alumni and employees or children of employees.

Financial Aid Of all full-time matriculated undergraduates who enrolled in 2006, 1,189 applied for aid, 876 were judged to have need, 397 had their need fully met. 402 Federal Work-Study jobs (averaging $997). 17 state and other part-time jobs (averaging $1240). In 2006, 294 non-need-based awards were made. *Average percent of need met:* 45%. *Average financial aid package:* $14,707. *Average need-based loan:* $4269. *Average need-based gift aid:* $10,700. *Average non-need-based aid:* $6851. *Average indebtedness upon graduation:* $26,462.

Applying *Options:* electronic application, deferred entrance. *Application fee:* $25. *Required:* essay or personal statement, high school transcript, letters of recommendation. *Required for some:* minimum 2.0 GPA. *Recommended:* interview. *Application deadlines:* rolling (freshmen), rolling (transfers). *Notification:* continuous until 8/1 (freshmen), continuous until 8/1 (transfers).

Freshman Application Contact Mr. E. Jones, Vice President for Enrollment Services, Texas Lutheran University, 1000 West Court Street, Seguin, TX 78155-5999. *Phone:* 830-372-8050. *Toll-free phone:* 800-771-8521. *Fax:* 830-372-8096. *E-mail:* admissions@tlu.edu.

See page 2558 for the College Close-Up.

TEXAS SOUTHERN UNIVERSITY

Houston, Texas www.tsu.edu/

- **State-supported** university, founded 1947, part of Texas Higher Education Coordinating Board
- **Urban** 147-acre campus
- **Endowment** $28.8 million
- **Coed** 7,572 undergraduate students, 80% full-time, 59% women, 41% men
- **Noncompetitive** entrance level, 98% of applicants were admitted

Undergraduates 6,060 full-time, 1,512 part-time. Students come from 39 states and territories, 39 other countries, 14% are from out of state, 90% African American, 3% Asian American or Pacific Islander, 4% Hispanic American, 0.1% Native American, 3% international, 8% transferred in, 15% live on campus. *Retention:* 50% of 2006 full-time freshmen returned.

Freshmen *Admission:* 7,098 applied, 6,952 admitted, 1,266 enrolled. *Average high school GPA:* 3.0. *Test scores:* ACT scores over 18: 43%; ACT scores over 24: 3%.

Faculty *Total:* 533, 64% full-time. *Student/faculty ratio:* 20:1.

Majors Accounting; art; aviation/airway management; banking and financial support services; bilingual and multilingual education; biological and physical sciences; biology/biological sciences; biomedical technology; business administration and management; business teacher education; chemistry; child development; civil engineering technology; clinical laboratory science/medical technology; clothing/textiles; communication/speech communication and rhetoric; computer and information sciences; computer engineering technology; computer science; construction engineering technology; counselor education/school counseling and guidance; criminal justice/law enforcement administration; curriculum and instruction; dietetics; drafting and design technology; dramatic/theater arts; economics; education; educational leadership and administration; education related; electrical, electronic and communications engineering technology; elementary education; engineering technology; English; environmental health; environmental science; family and consumer sciences/human sciences; fashion/apparel design; fashion merchandising; finance; fine/studio arts; French; general studies; health and physical education; health/health care administration; health information/medical records administration; health science; health teacher education; history; industrial technology; insurance; interdisciplinary studies; jazz/jazz studies; journalism; journalism related; kindergarten/preschool education; liberal arts and sciences/liberal studies; marketing/marketing management; mass communication/media; mathematics; multi-/interdisciplinary studies related; music; music teacher education; nursing (registered nurse training); occupational safety and health technology; office management; operations management; pharmacy; photography; physical education teaching and coaching; physical therapy; physics; piano and organ; political science and government; pre-dentistry studies; pre-medical studies; pre-pharmacy studies; psychology; public administration; radio and television; radio, television, and digital communication related; reading teacher education; recording arts technology; respiratory care therapy; science, technology and society; secondary education; social and philosophical foundations of education; social work; sociology; Spanish; special education; speech and rhetoric; speech therapy; technology/industrial arts teacher education; telecommunications; visual and performing arts; voice and opera; wind/percussion instruments.

Academics *Calendar:* semesters. *Degrees:* bachelor's, master's, doctoral, and first professional. *Special study options:* academic remediation for entering students, accelerated degree program, adult/continuing education programs, cooperative education, distance learning, English as a second language, honors programs, internships, off-campus study, part-time degree program, services for LD students, summer session for credit. *ROTC:* Army (c), Navy (c).

Computers on Campus 500 computers/terminals are available on campus for general student use. Students can access the following: computer help desk, free student e-mail accounts, online (class) grades, online (class) registration, online (class) schedules, Blackboard Learning and Community Portal System (E-education). Campuswide network is available. Wireless service is available via classrooms, computer centers, computer labs, student centers.

Student Life *Housing options:* coed, men-only, women-only. Campus housing is university owned, leased by the school and is provided by a third party. Freshman campus housing is guaranteed. *Activities and organizations:* drama/theater group, student-run newspaper, radio station, choral group, marching band, Debate Team, University Program Council, Student Government Association, Band, national fraternities, national sororities. *Campus security:* 24-hour emergency response devices and patrols, student patrols, late-night transport/escort service. *Student services:* health clinic, personal/psychological counseling, legal services.

Athletics Member NCAA. All Division I except football (Division I-AA). *Intercollegiate sports:* baseball M (s), basketball M (s)/W (s), bowling W (s), cross-country running M (s)/W (s), golf M (s), soccer M/W (s), softball W (s), tennis M (s)/W (s), track and field M (s)/W (s), volleyball M/W (s). *Intramural sports:* softball M/W, swimming and diving M/W, tennis M/W, volleyball M/W.

Standardized Tests *Required:* SAT or ACT (for admission).

Costs (2007–08) *Tuition:* $100 per credit part-time; state resident $5428 full-time; nonresident $13,678 full-time, $325 per credit part-time. Full-time tuition and fees vary according to course load, degree level, and program. Part-time tuition and fees vary according to course load, degree level, and program. full-time tuition includes required fees. *Required fees:* $457 per credit part-time. *Room and board:* $6664. Room and board charges vary according to board plan and housing facility. *Payment plans:* installment, deferred payment. *Waivers:* minority students and senior citizens.

Financial Aid Of all full-time matriculated undergraduates who enrolled in 2005, 7,047 applied for aid, 5,708 were judged to have need, 1,600 had their need fully met. 225 Federal Work-Study jobs (averaging $4000). 29 state and other part-time jobs (averaging $4000). *Average percent of need met:* 48%. *Average financial aid package:* $14,065. *Average need-based loan:* $6625. *Average need-based gift aid:* $9050. *Average indebtedness upon graduation:* $25,310.

Applying *Options:* electronic application. *Application fee:* $42. *Required:* high school transcript. *Application deadlines:* 8/15 (freshmen), 8/13 (transfers). *Notification:* continuous until 8/28 (freshmen), continuous until 8/28 (transfers).

Freshman Application Contact Enrollment Services Customer Service Center, Texas Southern University, 3100 Cleburne Street, Houston, TX 77004-4598. *Phone:* 713-313-7071. *Fax:* 713-313-7851. *E-mail:* eservices@em.tsu.edu.

TEXAS STATE UNIVERSITY-SAN MARCOS

San Marcos, Texas www.txstate.edu/

- **State-supported** university, founded 1899, part of Texas State University System
- **Suburban** 423-acre campus with easy access to San Antonio and Austin
- **Endowment** $24.4 million
- **Coed** 24,038 undergraduate students, 82% full-time, 55% women, 45% men
- **Moderately difficult** entrance level, 71% of applicants were admitted

Undergraduates 19,713 full-time, 4,325 part-time. Students come from 45 states and territories, 41 other countries, 1% are from out of state, 5% African American, 2% Asian American or Pacific Islander, 22% Hispanic American, 0.7% Native American, 0.9% international, 13% transferred in, 26% live on campus. *Retention:* 75% of 2006 full-time freshmen returned.

Freshmen *Admission:* 10,869 applied, 7,710 admitted, 3,065 enrolled. *Test scores:* SAT critical reading scores over 500: 66%; SAT math scores over 500: 75%; ACT scores over 18: 97%; SAT critical reading scores over 600: 20%; SAT math scores over 600: 22%; ACT scores over 24: 39%; SAT critical reading scores over 700: 3%; SAT math scores over 700: 2%; ACT scores over 30: 2%.

Faculty *Total:* 1,315, 68% full-time, 57% with terminal degrees. *Student/faculty ratio:* 23:1.

Majors Accounting; advertising; agribusiness; agriculture; American studies; animal physiology; animal sciences; anthropology; applied mathematics; aquatic biology/limnology; art; Asian studies; athletic training; audiology and speech-language pathology; biochemistry; biology/biological sciences; botany/plant biology; business administration and management; business/managerial economics;

cartography; chemistry; city/urban, community and regional planning; clinical laboratory science/medical technology; computer and information sciences; construction engineering technology; corrections; criminal justice/police science; criminal justice/safety; dance; desktop publishing and digital imaging design; dramatic/theater arts; economics; engineering technology; English; environmental science; European studies; family and consumer sciences/human sciences; fashion merchandising; finance; fine/studio arts; foods, nutrition, and wellness; French; geography; German; graphic design; health and physical education; health/health care administration; health information/medical records administration; health services/allied health/health sciences; history; human development and family studies; industrial engineering; industrial technology; interior design; international/global studies; international relations and affairs; jazz/jazz studies; journalism; management information systems; manufacturing engineering; manufacturing technology; marketing/marketing management; mass communication/media; mathematics; medical radiologic technology; microbiology; multi-/interdisciplinary studies related; music; music performance; Near and Middle Eastern studies; parks, recreation and leisure facilities management; philosophy; physics; political science and government; psychology; public administration; public relations/image management; radio and television; recording arts technology; respiratory care therapy; Russian studies; social work; sociology; Spanish; speech and rhetoric; sport and fitness administration/management; water, wetlands, and marine resources management; wildlife biology; zoology/animal biology.

Academics *Calendar:* semesters. *Degrees:* bachelor's, master's, doctoral, first professional, and postbachelor's certificates. *Special study options:* academic remediation for entering students, accelerated degree program, adult/continuing education programs, advanced placement credit, distance learning, double majors, English as a second language, honors programs, independent study, internships, off-campus study, part-time degree program, services for LD students, study abroad, summer session for credit. *ROTC:* Army (b), Air Force (b). *Unusual degree programs:* 3-2 engineering with University of Texas at Austin, Texas A&M University, Texas Tech University, University of Texas at San Antonio.

Computers on Campus 1,200 computers/terminals are available on campus for general student use. Students can access the following: computer help desk, free student e-mail accounts, online (class) grades, online (class) registration, online (class) schedules. Campuswide network is available. 100% of college-owned or -operated housing units are wired for high-speed Internet access. Wireless service is available via entire campus.

Student Life *Housing:* on-campus residence required through sophomore year. *Options:* coed, men-only, women-only. Campus housing is university owned. Freshman campus housing is guaranteed. *Activities and organizations:* drama/theater group, student-run newspaper, radio station, choral group, marching band, Non-traditional Students Association, Student Association for Campus Activities, Association Student Government, national fraternities, national sororities. *Campus security:* 24-hour emergency response devices and patrols, late-night transport/escort service, controlled dormitory access. *Student services:* health clinic, personal/psychological counseling, legal services.

Athletics Member NCAA. All Division I except football (Division I-AA). *Intercollegiate sports:* baseball M (s), basketball M (s)/W (s), cheerleading M/W, cross-country running M (s)/W (s), equestrian sports M (c)/W (c), fencing M (c)/W (c), golf M (s)/W (s), gymnastics M (c)/W (c), lacrosse M (c)/W (c), rugby M (c)/W (c), soccer M (c)/W (s), softball M (c)/W (s), tennis M (c)/W (s), track and field M (s)/W (s), ultimate Frisbee M (c)/W (c), volleyball W (s), water polo M (c)/W (c), weight lifting M (c)/W (c), wrestling M (c)/W (c). *Intramural sports:* basketball M/W, bowling M/W, cross-country running M/W, football M/W, golf M/W, racquetball M/W, soccer M/W, softball M/W, tennis M/W, ultimate Frisbee M, volleyball M/W.

Standardized Tests *Required:* SAT or ACT (for admission).

Costs (2007–08) *Tuition:* state resident $4830 full-time, $161 per semester hour part-time; nonresident $13,080 full-time, $436 per semester hour part-time. Full-time tuition and fees vary according to course load. Part-time tuition and fees vary according to course load. *Required fees:* $1706 full-time, $40 per semester hour part-time, $298 per term part-time. *Room and board:* $5878; room only: $3730. Room and board charges vary according to board plan and housing facility. *Payment plan:* installment. *Waivers:* employees or children of employees.

Financial Aid Of all full-time matriculated undergraduates who enrolled in 2007, 13,539 applied for aid, 10,396 were judged to have need, 888 had their need fully met. 788 Federal Work-Study jobs (averaging $1221). 149 state and other part-time jobs (averaging $1218). In 2007, 378 non-need-based awards were made. *Average percent of need met:* 66%. *Average financial aid package:* $10,860. *Average need-based loan:* $3923. *Average need-based gift aid:* $4424. *Average non-need-based aid:* $3006. *Average indebtedness upon graduation:* $17,086.

Applying *Options:* electronic application, early admission, deferred entrance. *Application fee:* $40. *Required:* essay or personal statement, high school transcript. *Application deadlines:* 5/1 (freshmen), 7/1 (transfers). *Notification:* continuous (freshmen), continuous (transfers).

Freshman Application Contact Mrs. Christie Kangas, Director of Admissions, Texas State University-San Marcos, Admissions and Visitors Center, San Marcos, TX 78666-5709. *Phone:* 512-245-2364 Ext. 2803. *Fax:* 512-245-8044. *E-mail:* admissions@txstate.edu.

TEXAS TECH UNIVERSITY

Lubbock, Texas **www.ttu.edu/**

- **State-supported** university, founded 1923, part of Texas Tech University System
- **Urban** 1839-acre campus
- **Endowment** $409.6 million
- **Coed** 23,018 undergraduate students, 91% full-time, 44% women, 56% men
- **Moderately difficult** entrance level, 77% of applicants were admitted

Undergraduates 21,058 full-time, 1,960 part-time. Students come from 49 states and territories, 99 other countries, 4% are from out of state, 4% African American, 3% Asian American or Pacific Islander, 13% Hispanic American, 0.7% Native American, 1% international, 9% transferred in, 26% live on campus. *Retention:* 83% of 2006 full-time freshmen returned.

Freshmen *Admission:* 13,976 applied, 10,759 admitted, 4,496 enrolled. *Test scores:* SAT critical reading scores over 500: 71%; SAT math scores over 500: 82%; SAT writing scores over 500: 55%; ACT scores over 18: 99%; SAT critical reading scores over 600: 23%; SAT math scores over 600: 33%; SAT writing scores over 600: 12%; ACT scores over 24: 50%; SAT critical reading scores over 700: 2%; SAT math scores over 700: 6%; SAT writing scores over 700: 1%; ACT scores over 30: 6%.

Faculty *Total:* 1,174, 92% full-time, 83% with terminal degrees. *Student/faculty ratio:* 18:1.

Majors Accounting; acting; advertising; agricultural business and management; agricultural communication/journalism; agricultural economics; agriculture; agronomy and crop science; animal sciences; anthropology; apparel and textiles; applied horticulture; architectural engineering technology; architecture; art; art history, criticism and conservation; biochemistry; biological and physical sciences; biology/biological sciences; business administration and management; business administration, management and operations related; business/commerce; cell and molecular biology; chemical engineering; chemistry; child development; civil engineering; classics and languages, literatures and linguistics; computer and information sciences; computer engineering; dance; dietetics; dramatic/theater arts; economics; electrical, electronic and communications engineering technology; electrical, electronics and communications engineering; engineering; engineering physics; engineering technology; English; environmental/environmental health engineering; family and community services; family and consumer sciences/human sciences; family systems; fashion/apparel design; fashion merchandising; finance; fine/studio arts; fishing and fisheries sciences and management; food science; foods, nutrition, and wellness; French; general studies; geography; geology/earth science; geophysics and seismology; German; graphic design; health and physical education; health services/allied health/health sciences; history; hotel/motel administration; human development and family studies; industrial engineering; interdisciplinary studies; interior architecture; international business/trade/commerce; journalism; landscape architecture; Latin American studies; liberal arts and sciences/liberal studies; management information systems; marketing/marketing management; mathematics; mechanical engineering; mechanical engineering/mechanical technology; microbiology; multi-/interdisciplinary studies related; music; music performance; music theory and composition; natural resources/conservation; petroleum engineering; philosophy; photojournalism; physics; plant protection and integrated pest management; political science and government; psychology; public relations/image management; radio and television; range science and management; Russian studies; social work; sociology; Spanish; speech and rhetoric; theater design and technology; wildlife and wildlands science and management; work and family studies; zoology/animal biology.

Academics *Calendar:* semesters. *Degrees:* bachelor's, master's, doctoral, first professional, and postbachelor's certificates. *Special study options:* academic remediation for entering students, accelerated degree program, advanced placement credit, cooperative education, distance learning, double majors, English as a second language, external degree program, freshman honors college, honors programs, independent study, internships, off-campus study, part-time degree program, services for LD students, student-designed majors, study abroad, summer session for credit. *ROTC:* Army (b), Air Force (b). *Unusual degree programs:* 3-2 business administration; engineering; architecture, agriculture and applied economics, mathematics, computer science.

Computers on Campus 3,000 computers/terminals are available on campus for general student use. Students can access the following: computer help desk, free student e-mail accounts, online (class) grades, online (class) registration, online (class) schedules, online degree plans, accounts, transcripts, schedules. Campuswide network is available. 100% of college-owned or -operated housing units are wired for high-speed Internet access. Wireless service is available via entire campus.

Student Life *Housing:* on-campus residence required for freshman year. *Options:* coed, men-only, women-only, disabled students. Campus housing is university owned. Freshman campus housing is guaranteed. *Activities and organizations:* drama/theater group, student-run newspaper, radio station, choral group, marching band, National Society of Collegiate Scholars, Paradigm, Campus Crusade for Christ, Chi Omega, national fraternities, national sororities. *Campus security:* 24-hour emergency response devices and patrols, late-night transport/escort service, controlled dormitory access. *Student services:* health clinic, personal/psychological counseling, legal services.

Athletics Member NCAA. All Division I except football (Division I-A). *Intercollegiate sports:* baseball M (s), basketball M (s)/W (s), cross-country running M (s)/W (s), golf M (s)/W (s), soccer W (s), softball W (s), tennis M (s)/W (s), track and field M (s)/W (s), volleyball W (s). *Intramural sports:* badminton M/W, baseball M, basketball M/W, bowling M/W, equestrian sports M (c), fencing M (c)/W (c), football M/W, golf M/W, gymnastics M (c)/W (c), ice hockey M (c), lacrosse M (c)/W (c), racquetball M/W, rock climbing M (c)/W (c), rugby M (c)/W (c), soccer M/W, softball M/W, swimming and diving M/W, table tennis M/W, tennis M/W, ultimate Frisbee M (c)/W (c), volleyball M/W, water polo M (c)/W (c), weight lifting M, wrestling M (c)/W (c).

Standardized Tests *Required:* SAT or ACT (for admission).

Costs (2007–08) *Tuition:* state resident $4310 full-time, $144 per credit hour part-time; nonresident $12,650 full-time, $422 per credit hour part-time. Full-time tuition and fees vary according to course load, program, and reciprocity agreements. Part-time tuition and fees vary according to course load, program, and reciprocity agreements. *Required fees:* $2473 full-time, $71 per credit hour part-time, $359 per term part-time. *Room and board:* $7460; room only: $3980. Room and board charges vary according to board plan and housing facility. *Payment plan:* installment. *Waivers:* senior citizens and employees or children of employees.

Financial Aid Of all full-time matriculated undergraduates who enrolled in 2006, 13,163 applied for aid, 8,368 were judged to have need, 373 had their need fully met. In 2006, 624 non-need-based awards were made. *Average percent of need met:* 60%. *Average financial aid package:* $7823. *Average need-based loan:* $3930. *Average need-based gift aid:* $5103. *Average non-need-based aid:* $1783. *Average indebtedness upon graduation:* $20,916.

Applying *Options:* electronic application, early admission. *Application fee:* $50. *Required:* high school transcript. *Required for some:* essay or personal statement. *Application deadlines:* 5/1 (freshmen), rolling (transfers). *Notification:* continuous (freshmen), continuous (transfers).

Freshman Application Contact Texas Tech University, Box 45005, Lubbock, TX 79409-5005. *Phone:* 806-742-1480. *Fax:* 806-742-0062. *E-mail:* admissions@ttu.edu.

TEXAS WESLEYAN UNIVERSITY

Fort Worth, Texas **www.txwes.edu/**

- **Independent United Methodist** comprehensive, founded 1890
- **Urban** 74-acre campus
- **Endowment** $43.9 million
- **Coed**
- **Moderately difficult** entrance level

Faculty *Student/faculty ratio:* 15:1.

Academics *Calendar:* semesters. *Degrees:* bachelor's, master's, and first professional.

Student Life *Campus security:* 24-hour emergency response devices and patrols, student patrols, late-night transport/escort service, controlled dormitory access.

Athletics Member NAIA.

Standardized Tests *Required:* SAT or ACT (for admission).

Costs (2007–08) *Comprehensive fee:* $21,275 includes full-time tuition ($14,615), mandatory fees ($1160), and room and board ($5500). Full-time tuition and fees vary according to program. Part-time tuition: $493 per credit. Part-time tuition and fees vary according to program. *Required fees:* $56 per credit part-time. *College room only:* $2890. Room and board charges vary according to board plan and student level. *Payment plans:* installment, deferred payment.

Financial Aid Of all full-time matriculated undergraduates who enrolled in 2004, 974 applied for aid, 799 were judged to have need. *Average percent of need met:* 74.

Applying *Options:* deferred entrance. *Application fee:* $25. *Required:* essay or personal statement, high school transcript, minimum 2.5 GPA. *Required for some:* interview.

Freshman Application Contact Holly Kiser, Director, Admissions, Texas Wesleyan University, 1201 Wesleyan Street, Fort Worth, TX 76105-1536. *Phone:* 817-531-4422. *Toll-free phone:* 800-580-8980. *Fax:* 817-531-7515. *E-mail:* freshman@txwesleyan.edu.

TEXAS WOMAN'S UNIVERSITY

Denton, Texas **www.twu.edu/**

- **State-supported** university, founded 1901
- **Suburban** 270-acre campus with easy access to Dallas–Fort Worth
- **Endowment** $9.0 million
- **Coed, primarily women** 7,015 undergraduate students, 71% full-time, 93% women, 7% men
- **Minimally difficult** entrance level, 88% of applicants were admitted

Texas Woman's University (TWU) offers more than 100 bachelor's, master's, and doctoral degree programs to approximately 12,000 students. A teaching and research institution, TWU emphasizes the health sciences, education, the liberal arts, and the sciences. TWU welcomes women and men and traditional and nontraditional students to its campuses in Denton, Dallas, and Houston. Although it has the look and feel of a private college, TWU is a public university, making its tuition and fees more affordable.

Undergraduates 5,008 full-time, 2,007 part-time. Students come from 31 states and territories, 41 other countries, 1% are from out of state, 21% African American, 7% Asian American or Pacific Islander, 17% Hispanic American, 0.9% Native American, 2% international, 16% transferred in, 25% live on campus. *Retention:* 69% of 2006 full-time freshmen returned.

Freshmen *Admission:* 2,190 applied, 1,924 admitted, 786 enrolled. *Average high school GPA:* 3.24. *Test scores:* SAT critical reading scores over 500: 51%; SAT math scores over 500: 52%; ACT scores over 18: 84%; SAT critical reading scores over 600: 11%; SAT math scores over 600: 9%; ACT scores over 24: 27%; SAT critical reading scores over 700: 1%; SAT math scores over 700: 1%; ACT scores over 30: 2%.

Faculty *Total:* 671, 55% full-time. *Student/faculty ratio:* 14:1.

Majors Accounting; art; audiology and speech-language pathology; biochemistry; biology/biological sciences; business administration and management; chemistry; child development; clinical laboratory science/medical technology; community health liaison; computer and information sciences; criminal justice/safety; dental hygiene; dietetics; dramatic/theater arts; English; family and consumer sciences/human sciences; fashion/apparel design; fashion merchandising; finance; foods, nutrition, and wellness; general studies; health and physical education; health services/allied health/health sciences; history; human development and family studies; interdisciplinary studies; legal assistant/paralegal; marketing/marketing management; mathematics; music; music therapy; nursing (registered nurse training); nutrition sciences; political science and government; psychology; public administration; social work; sociology; zoology/animal biology.

Academics *Calendar:* semesters. *Degrees:* bachelor's, master's, doctoral, and post-master's certificates. *Special study options:* academic remediation for entering students, accelerated degree program, adult/continuing education programs, advanced placement credit, cooperative education, distance learning, double majors, honors programs, independent study, internships, off-campus study, part-time degree program, services for LD students, study abroad, summer session for credit. *ROTC:* Army (c), Air Force (c). *Unusual degree programs:* 3-2 engineering with The University of Texas at Dallas, University of North Texas; physical therapy, human biology, kinesiology, nursing.

Computers on Campus 700 computers/terminals are available on campus for general student use. Students can access the following: online (class) registration. Campuswide network is available.

Student Life *Housing:* on-campus residence required through sophomore year. *Options:* coed, women-only, disabled students. Campus housing is university owned. Freshman campus housing is guaranteed. *Activities and organizations:* drama/theater group, student-run newspaper, choral group, Helping Hands, Athenian Honor Society, Campus Activities Board, Nursing Student Organization, Graduate Library & Information Studies Association, national sororities. *Campus security:* 24-hour emergency response devices and patrols, late-night transport/escort service, controlled dormitory access. *Student services:* health clinic, personal/psychological counseling.

Athletics Member NCAA. All Division II. *Intercollegiate sports:* basketball W (s), gymnastics W (s), soccer W (s), softball W (s), volleyball W (s). *Intramural sports:* basketball M (c)/W (c), golf M (c)/W (c), soccer M (c)/W (c), softball M (c)/W (c), volleyball M (c)/W (c).

Standardized Tests *Required for some:* SAT or ACT (for admission).
Costs (2008–09) *Tuition:* state resident $4740 full-time, $143 per hour part-time; nonresident $13,080 full-time, $421 per hour part-time. *Required fees:* $1800 full-time. *Room and board:* $5846; room only: $2828.
Financial Aid Of all full-time matriculated undergraduates who enrolled in 2006, 3,550 applied for aid, 2,918 were judged to have need, 1,208 had their need fully met. 223 Federal Work-Study jobs (averaging $1781). 517 state and other part-time jobs (averaging $3651). In 2006, 967 non-need-based awards were made. *Average percent of need met:* 98%. *Average financial aid package:* $9778. *Average need-based loan:* $3673. *Average need-based gift aid:* $4445. *Average non-need-based aid:* $1852. *Average indebtedness upon graduation:* $19,409.
Applying *Options:* electronic application, early admission, deferred entrance. *Application fee:* $30. *Required:* high school transcript, minimum 2.0 GPA. *Application deadlines:* 7/1 (freshmen), 7/15 (transfers). *Notification:* continuous until 8/15 (freshmen), continuous until 8/15 (transfers).
Freshman Application Contact Ms. Erma Nieto-Brecht, Director of Admissions, Texas Woman's University, PO Box 425589, Denton, TX 76204-5589. *Phone:* 940-898-3188. *Toll-free phone:* 888-948-9984. *Fax:* 940-898-3081. *E-mail:* admissions@twu.edu.

See page 2560 for the College Close-Up.

TRINITY UNIVERSITY

San Antonio, Texas **www.trinity.edu/**

- **Independent** comprehensive, founded 1869, affiliated with Presbyterian Church
- **Urban** 113-acre campus
- **Endowment** $991.1 million
- **Coed** 2,477 undergraduate students, 99% full-time, 54% women, 46% men
- **Very difficult** entrance level, 52% of applicants were admitted

Undergraduates 2,447 full-time, 30 part-time. Students come from 49 states and territories, 38 other countries, 30% are from out of state, 4% African American, 6% Asian American or Pacific Islander, 11% Hispanic American, 1% Native American, 5% international, 1% transferred in, 73% live on campus. *Retention:* 90% of 2006 full-time freshmen returned.
Freshmen *Admission:* 4,511 applied, 2,324 admitted, 631 enrolled. *Average high school GPA:* 3.53. *Test scores:* SAT critical reading scores over 500: 99%; SAT math scores over 500: 100%; ACT scores over 18: 100%; SAT critical reading scores over 600: 77%; SAT math scores over 600: 82%; ACT scores over 24: 99%; SAT critical reading scores over 700: 23%; SAT math scores over 700: 21%; ACT scores over 30: 45%.
Faculty *Total:* 287, 77% full-time, 80% with terminal degrees. *Student/faculty ratio:* 10:1.
Majors Accounting; acting; anthropology; art; art history, criticism and conservation; Asian studies; biochemistry; biology/biological sciences; business administration and management; chemistry; Chinese; classics and languages, literatures and linguistics; communication/speech communication and rhetoric; computer and information sciences; dramatic/theater arts; economics; engineering science; English; European studies; finance; French; geology/earth science; German; history; humanities; international business/trade/commerce; Latin American studies; management science; marketing/marketing management; mathematics; music; music performance; music theory and composition; neuroscience; philosophy; physics; political science and government; pre-dentistry studies; pre-law studies; pre-medical studies; pre-veterinary studies; psychology; religious studies; Russian; sociology; Spanish; speech and rhetoric; theater design and technology; urban studies/affairs; voice and opera.
Academics *Calendar:* semesters. *Degrees:* bachelor's and master's. *Special study options:* accelerated degree program, advanced placement credit, double majors, honors programs, independent study, internships, part-time degree program, services for LD students, study abroad, summer session for credit. *ROTC:* Air Force (c).
Computers on Campus 450 computers/terminals are available on campus for general student use. Students can access the following: campus intranet, computer help desk, free student e-mail accounts, online (class) grades, online (class) registration, online (class) schedules. Campuswide network is available. 100% of college-owned or -operated housing units are wired for high-speed Internet access. Wireless service is available via entire campus.
Student Life *Housing:* on-campus residence required through junior year. *Options:* coed. Campus housing is university owned. Freshman campus housing is guaranteed. *Activities and organizations:* drama/theater group, student-run newspaper, radio and television station, choral group, Voluntary Action Center, Alpha Phi Omega, Association of Student Representatives, Activities Council, Multicultural Network. *Campus security:* 24-hour emergency response devices and patrols, late-night transport/escort service, controlled dormitory access. *Student services:* health clinic, personal/psychological counseling.
Athletics Member NCAA. All Division III. *Intercollegiate sports:* baseball M, basketball M/W, cross-country running M/W, fencing M (c), football M, golf M/W, lacrosse M (c)/W (c), riflery M (c)/W (c), soccer M/W, softball W, swimming and diving M/W, tennis M/W, track and field M/W, volleyball M (c)/W. *Intramural sports:* basketball M/W, cross-country running M/W, fencing M, football M/W, golf M/W, racquetball M/W, soccer M/W, softball M/W, swimming and diving M/W, table tennis M/W, tennis M/W, track and field M/W, ultimate Frisbee M/W, volleyball M/W, water polo M/W, wrestling M/W.
Standardized Tests *Required:* SAT or ACT (for admission).
Costs (2008–09) *Comprehensive fee:* $36,521 includes full-time tuition ($26,664), mandatory fees ($1035), and room and board ($8822). Part-time tuition: $1111 per hour. *College room only:* $5600.
Financial Aid Of all full-time matriculated undergraduates who enrolled in 2004, 1,255 applied for aid, 979 were judged to have need, 544 had their need fully met. 10 state and other part-time jobs (averaging $1435). In 2004, 959 non-need-based awards were made. *Average percent of need met:* 82%. *Average financial aid package:* $14,343. *Average need-based loan:* $3541. *Average need-based gift aid:* $10,827. *Average non-need-based aid:* $6830. *Financial aid deadline:* 4/1.
Applying *Options:* electronic application, early decision, early action, deferred entrance. *Application fee:* $50. *Required:* essay or personal statement, high school transcript, 2 letters of recommendation. *Recommended:* interview. *Application deadlines:* 2/1 (freshmen), 3/1 (transfers), 11/1 (early action). *Early decision deadline:* 11/1. *Notification:* 4/1 (freshmen), 4/1 (transfers), 12/15 (early decision), 12/15 (early action).
Freshman Application Contact Mr. Christopher Ellertson, Dean of Admissions and Financial Aid, Trinity University, One Trinity Place, San Antonio, TX 78212-7200. *Phone:* 210-999-7207. *Toll-free phone:* 800-TRINITY. *Fax:* 210-999-8164. *E-mail:* admissions@trinity.edu.

UNIVERSITY OF DALLAS

Irving, Texas **www.udallas.edu/**

- **Independent Roman Catholic** university, founded 1955
- **Suburban** 750-acre campus with easy access to Dallas–Fort Worth
- **Endowment** $48.7 million
- **Coed** 1,233 undergraduate students, 97% full-time, 54% women, 46% men
- **Moderately difficult** entrance level, 75% of applicants were admitted

Undergraduates 1,199 full-time, 34 part-time. Students come from 44 states and territories, 11 other countries, 49% are from out of state, 1% African American, 6% Asian American or Pacific Islander, 16% Hispanic American, 0.4% Native American, 1% international, 5% transferred in, 61% live on campus. *Retention:* 79% of 2006 full-time freshmen returned.
Freshmen *Admission:* 1,161 applied, 868 admitted, 363 enrolled. *Average high school GPA:* 3.6. *Test scores:* SAT critical reading scores over 500: 89%; SAT math scores over 500: 85%; SAT writing scores over 500: 86%; ACT scores over 18: 99%; SAT critical reading scores over 600: 59%; SAT math scores over 600: 44%; SAT writing scores over 600: 52%; ACT scores over 24: 76%; SAT critical reading scores over 700: 21%; SAT math scores over 700: 10%; SAT writing scores over 700: 14%; ACT scores over 30: 21%.
Faculty *Total:* 238, 53% full-time, 60% with terminal degrees. *Student/faculty ratio:* 13:1.
Majors Art; art history, criticism and conservation; biochemistry; biology/biological sciences; business administration and management; ceramic arts and ceramics; chemistry; classics and languages, literatures and linguistics; dramatic/theater arts; economics; education; elementary education; English; fine/studio arts; French; German; history; mathematics; painting; philosophy; physics; political science and government; pre-dentistry studies; pre-law studies; pre-medical studies; pre-theology/pre-ministerial studies; printmaking; psychology; sculpture; secondary education; Spanish; theology.
Academics *Calendar:* semesters. *Degrees:* bachelor's, master's, doctoral, post-master's, and postbachelor's certificates. *Special study options:* advanced placement credit, double majors, independent study, internships, off-campus study, part-time degree program, services for LD students, student-designed majors, study abroad, summer session for credit. *ROTC:* Army (c), Air Force (c). *Unusual degree programs:* 3-2 business administration; MIA or MPsy-psychology, MA philosophy.
Computers on Campus 125 computers/terminals are available on campus for general student use. Students can access the following: campus intranet, computer help desk, free student e-mail accounts, online (class) grades, online (class) registration, online (class) schedules. Campuswide network is available. 100% of college-owned or -operated housing units are wired for high-speed Internet

access. Wireless service is available via computer centers, computer labs, dorm rooms, learning centers, libraries, student centers.

Student Life *Housing:* on-campus residence required through junior year. *Options:* coed, men-only, women-only. Campus housing is university owned. Freshman campus housing is guaranteed. *Activities and organizations:* drama/theater group, student-run newspaper, radio station, choral group, SPUD (Programming Board), Residence Hall Association, student government, Best Buddies, Alpha Phi Omega. *Campus security:* 24-hour emergency response devices and patrols, late-night transport/escort service, controlled dormitory access. *Student services:* health clinic, personal/psychological counseling.

Athletics Member NCAA. All Division III. *Intercollegiate sports:* baseball M, basketball M/W, cross-country running M/W, golf M, lacrosse W, soccer M/W, softball W, tennis W, track and field M/W, volleyball W, wrestling M. *Intramural sports:* basketball M, equestrian sports M (c)/W (c), football M/W, rugby M (c)/W (c), sailing M (c)/W (c), soccer M/W, softball M/W, tennis M (c)/W (c), ultimate Frisbee M (c)/W (c), volleyball M/W.

Standardized Tests *Required:* SAT or ACT (for admission).

Costs (2008–09) *Comprehensive fee:* $32,655 includes full-time tuition ($23,250), mandatory fees ($1520), and room and board ($7885). Part-time tuition: $975 per credit hour. *Required fees:* $1520 per year part-time. *College room only:* $4350.

Financial Aid Of all full-time matriculated undergraduates who enrolled in 2006, 838 applied for aid, 695 were judged to have need, 216 had their need fully met. 250 Federal Work-Study jobs (averaging $1376). 69 state and other part-time jobs (averaging $965). In 2006, 417 non-need-based awards were made. *Average percent of need met:* 80%. *Average financial aid package:* $21,257. *Average need-based loan:* $7466. *Average need-based gift aid:* $13,887. *Average non-need-based aid:* $10,432. *Average indebtedness upon graduation:* $23,184.

Applying *Options:* electronic application, early admission, early action, deferred entrance. *Application fee:* $40. *Required:* essay or personal statement, high school transcript, 2 letters of recommendation. *Required for some:* interview. *Recommended:* interview. *Application deadlines:* 8/1 (freshmen), 7/1 (transfers), 11/1 (early action). *Notification:* continuous (freshmen), continuous (transfers), 1/15 (early action).

Freshman Application Contact Sr. Mary Brian Bole, Assistant Dean of Enrollment Management, University of Dallas, 1845 East Northgate Drive, Irving, TX 75062-4799. *Phone:* 972-721-5266. *Toll-free phone:* 800-628-6999. *Fax:* 972-721-5017. *E-mail:* ugadmis@udallas.edu.

See page 2562 for the College Close-Up.

UNIVERSITY OF HOUSTON

Houston, Texas — www.uh.edu/

- **State-supported** university, founded 1927, part of University of Houston System
- **Urban** 550-acre campus
- **Endowment** $470.4 million
- **Coed** 27,572 undergraduate students, 71% full-time, 52% women, 48% men
- **Moderately difficult** entrance level, 77% of applicants were admitted

Undergraduates 19,656 full-time, 7,916 part-time. Students come from 52 states and territories, 140 other countries, 2% are from out of state, 15% African American, 22% Asian American or Pacific Islander, 22% Hispanic American, 0.3% Native American, 4% international, 10% transferred in, 8% live on campus. *Retention:* 77% of 2006 full-time freshmen returned.

Freshmen *Admission:* 10,984 applied, 8,466 admitted, 3,508 enrolled. *Average high school GPA:* 3.34. *Test scores:* SAT critical reading scores over 500: 56%; SAT math scores over 500: 71%; ACT scores over 18: 87%; SAT critical reading scores over 600: 16%; SAT math scores over 600: 28%; ACT scores over 24: 30%; SAT critical reading scores over 700: 2%; SAT math scores over 700: 4%; ACT scores over 30: 2%.

Faculty *Total:* 1,709, 71% full-time, 72% with terminal degrees. *Student/faculty ratio:* 21:1.

Majors Accounting; anthropology; applied mathematics; architecture; architecture related; art; art history, criticism and conservation; audiology and speech-language pathology; bilingual and multilingual education; biochemistry; biology/biological sciences; biomedical/medical engineering; business administration and management; business/corporate communications; business family and consumer sciences/human sciences; business statistics; chemical engineering; chemistry; civil engineering; civil engineering technology; classics and languages, literatures and linguistics; clinical laboratory science/medical technology; communication disorders; communication/speech communication and rhetoric; community health services counseling; computer and information sciences; computer engineering; computer engineering technology; computer systems analysis; construction engineering technology; creative writing; drafting and design technology; dramatic/theater arts; economics; education; electrical, electronics and communications engineering; electromechanical technology; English; environmental design/architecture; environmental studies; European studies (Western); family and consumer sciences/human sciences; finance; fine/studio arts; foods, nutrition, and wellness; French; geology/earth science; geophysics and seismology; German; German studies; graphic communications; health and physical education; history; hotel/motel administration; human development and family studies; human nutrition; industrial engineering; industrial technology; information science/studies; information technology; interdisciplinary studies; interior architecture; interior design; Italian; journalism; kinesiology and exercise science; Latin; management information systems; marketing/marketing management; mass communication/media; mathematics; mechanical engineering; music; music performance; music theory and composition; operations management; organizational behavior; organizational communication; painting; pharmacy; philosophy; photography; physics; political science and government; pre-dentistry studies; pre-law studies; pre-medical studies; pre-veterinary studies; printmaking; psychology; public relations/image management; Russian studies; sales, distribution and marketing; sculpture; sociology; Spanish; Spanish and Iberian studies; speech and rhetoric; statistics.

Academics *Calendar:* semesters. *Degrees:* bachelor's, master's, doctoral, and first professional. *Special study options:* academic remediation for entering students, accelerated degree program, adult/continuing education programs, advanced placement credit, cooperative education, distance learning, double majors, English as a second language, freshman honors college, honors programs, independent study, internships, off-campus study, part-time degree program, services for LD students, study abroad, summer session for credit. *ROTC:* Army (b), Navy (c).

Computers on Campus 825 computers/terminals are available on campus for general student use. Students can access the following: online (class) registration. Campuswide network is available.

Student Life *Housing options:* coed. Campus housing is university owned. *Activities and organizations:* drama/theater group, student-run newspaper, radio and television station, choral group, marching band, Council of Ethnic Organizations, Frontier Fiesta Association, intramural sports, Golden Key National Honor Society, national fraternities, national sororities. *Campus security:* 24-hour emergency response devices and patrols, student patrols, late-night transport/escort service, controlled dormitory access, vehicle assistance. *Student services:* health clinic, personal/psychological counseling, women's center, legal services.

Athletics Member NCAA. All Division I except football (Division I-A). *Intercollegiate sports:* baseball M (s), basketball M (s)/W (s), cheerleading M/W, cross-country running M (s)/W (s), golf M (s), soccer W (s), softball W (s), swimming and diving W (s), tennis W (s), track and field M (s)/W (s), volleyball W (s). *Intramural sports:* badminton M/W, baseball M, basketball M/W, bowling M (c)/W (c), cheerleading M/W, cross-country running M/W, football M/W, golf M/W, lacrosse M, racquetball M/W, rock climbing M/W, rugby M, soccer M (c), swimming and diving M/W, table tennis M/W, tennis M/W, track and field M/W, ultimate Frisbee M/W, volleyball M/W, water polo M/W, weight lifting M.

Standardized Tests *Required:* SAT or ACT (for admission). *Recommended:* SAT Subject Tests (for admission).

Costs (2007–08) *Tuition:* state resident $4826 full-time, $161 per hour part-time; nonresident $13,166 full-time, $439 per hour part-time. Full-time tuition and fees vary according to course level, course load, degree level, location, program, reciprocity agreements, and student level. Part-time tuition and fees vary according to course level, course load, degree level, location, program, reciprocity agreements, and student level. *Required fees:* $2624 full-time. *Room and board:* $6651; room only: $3778. Room and board charges vary according to board plan and housing facility. *Payment plan:* installment.

Financial Aid Of all full-time matriculated undergraduates who enrolled in 2007, 12,147 applied for aid, 10,779 were judged to have need, 1,924 had their need fully met. In 2007, 313 non-need-based awards were made. *Average percent of need met:* 67%. *Average financial aid package:* $10,494. *Average need-based loan:* $5974. *Average need-based gift aid:* $5701. *Average non-need-based aid:* $4006.

Applying *Options:* electronic application, early admission, deferred entrance. *Application fee:* $50. *Required:* high school transcript, minimum 2.0 GPA. *Application deadlines:* 4/1 (freshmen), 5/1 (transfers). *Notification:* continuous (freshmen), continuous (transfers).

Freshman Application Contact Mr. Jeff Fuller, Admissions, University of Houston, Room 122, Ezekiel Cullen Building, Houston, TX 77204-2023. *Phone:* 713-743-9620. *Fax:* 713-743-9633. *E-mail:* admissions@uh.edu.

See page 2564 for the College Close-Up.

UNIVERSITY OF HOUSTON–CLEAR LAKE

Houston, Texas **www.uhcl.edu/**

- **State-supported** upper-level, founded 1971, part of University of Houston System
- **Suburban** 487-acre campus
- **Endowment** $13.1 million
- **Coed** 4,282 undergraduate students
- **Minimally difficult** entrance level, 49% of applicants were admitted

Undergraduates Students come from 84 other countries, 8% African American, 6% Asian American or Pacific Islander, 20% Hispanic American, 0.6% Native American, 2% international, 3% live on campus.

Freshmen *Admission:* 4,050 applied, 1,989 admitted.

Faculty *Total:* 610, 33% full-time. *Student/faculty ratio:* 22:1.

Majors Accounting; anthropology; art; behavioral sciences; biology/biological sciences; business administration and management; business administration, management and operations related; business/commerce; chemistry; communication/speech communication and rhetoric; computer and information sciences; computer engineering; counselor education/school counseling and guidance; criminology; English; environmental science; finance; geography; health and physical education; health/health care administration; history; humanities; information science/studies; legal assistant/paralegal; management information systems; marketing/marketing management; mathematics; multi-/interdisciplinary studies related; parks, recreation and leisure facilities management; physical sciences; political science and government; psychology; social work; sociology; women's studies.

Academics *Calendar:* semesters. *Degrees:* certificates, bachelor's, master's, and doctoral. *Special study options:* accelerated degree program, cooperative education, distance learning, double majors, English as a second language, independent study, internships, part-time degree program, services for LD students, student-designed majors, summer session for credit.

Computers on Campus 700 computers/terminals are available on campus for general student use. Students can access the following: computer help desk, free student e-mail accounts, online (class) grades, online (class) registration, online (class) schedules. Campuswide network is available. Wireless service is available via entire campus.

Student Life *Housing options:* coed. Campus housing is provided by a third party. *Activities and organizations:* student-run newspaper, Beta Alpha Psi, The Indian Student Association, The Management Association, Texas Student Education Association, Accounting Association. *Campus security:* 24-hour emergency response devices and patrols, late-night transport/escort service. *Student services:* health clinic, personal/psychological counseling, women's center.

Athletics *Intramural sports:* football M (c)/W (c), golf M (c)/W (c), rugby M (c), soccer M (c)/W (c), softball M (c)/W (c), tennis M (c)/W (c), volleyball M (c)/W (c).

Costs (2007–08) *Tuition:* state resident $4080 full-time, $136 per credit hour part-time; nonresident $12,840 full-time, $428 per credit hour part-time. Full-time tuition and fees vary according to course load and program. Part-time tuition and fees vary according to course load and program. *Required fees:* $1539 full-time, $431 per term part-time. *Room only:* $7361. Room and board charges vary according to housing facility. *Payment plans:* installment, deferred payment. *Waivers:* senior citizens and employees or children of employees.

Financial Aid Of all full-time matriculated undergraduates who enrolled in 2003, 756 applied for aid, 642 were judged to have need, 89 had their need fully met. 58 Federal Work-Study jobs, 5 state and other part-time jobs. In 2003, 350 non-need-based awards were made. *Average percent of need met:* 53%. *Average financial aid package:* $5435. *Average need-based loan:* $4397. *Average need-based gift aid:* $2760. *Average non-need-based aid:* $2064. *Average indebtedness upon graduation:* $10,728.

Applying *Options:* electronic application, early admission, deferred entrance. *Application fee:* $35. *Application deadline:* rolling (transfers). *Notification:* continuous (transfers).

Application Contact Ms. Rauchelle Jones, Director of Admissions, University of Houston–Clear Lake, 2700 Bay Area Boulevard, Box 13, Houston, TX 77058-1098. *Phone:* 281-283-2518. *Fax:* 281-283-2530. *E-mail:* admissions@uhcl.edu.

UNIVERSITY OF HOUSTON–DOWNTOWN

Houston, Texas **www.uhd.edu/**

- **State-supported** comprehensive, founded 1974, part of University of Houston System
- **Urban** 20-acre campus
- **Endowment** $17.6 million
- **Coed** 11,670 undergraduate students, 52% full-time, 59% women, 41% men
- **Noncompetitive** entrance level, 99% of applicants were admitted

Undergraduates 6,041 full-time, 5,629 part-time. Students come from 28 states and territories, 80 other countries, 1% are from out of state, 27% African American, 10% Asian American or Pacific Islander, 36% Hispanic American, 0.2% Native American, 3% international, 17% transferred in. *Retention:* 56% of 2006 full-time freshmen returned.

Freshmen *Admission:* 1,968 applied, 1,957 admitted, 1,014 enrolled.

Faculty *Total:* 563, 51% full-time, 57% with terminal degrees. *Student/faculty ratio:* 21:1.

Majors Accounting; applied mathematics; biological and physical sciences; biology/biological sciences; biotechnology; business administration and management; business/commerce; chemistry; chemistry related; civil engineering technology; computer science; criminal justice/safety; engineering related; English; finance; fire protection and safety technology; history; humanities; industrial safety technology; interdisciplinary studies; international business/trade/commerce; liberal arts and sciences/liberal studies; management information systems; marketing/marketing management; mathematics; mechanical engineering/mechanical technology; microbiology; multi-/interdisciplinary studies related; philosophy; political science and government; psychology; purchasing, procurement/acquisitions and contracts management; social sciences; sociology; Spanish; speech and rhetoric; technical and business writing.

Academics *Calendar:* semesters. *Degrees:* bachelor's and master's. *Special study options:* academic remediation for entering students, accelerated degree program, adult/continuing education programs, advanced placement credit, cooperative education, distance learning, double majors, English as a second language, honors programs, independent study, internships, off-campus study, part-time degree program, services for LD students, student-designed majors, study abroad, summer session for credit. *ROTC:* Army (c).

Computers on Campus 1,250 computers/terminals and 96 ports are available on campus for general student use. Students can access the following: free student e-mail accounts, online (class) grades, online (class) registration, online (class) schedules. Campuswide network is available. Wireless service is available via entire campus.

Student Life *Housing:* college housing not available. *Activities and organizations:* drama/theater group, student-run newspaper, Latin American Student Services Organization, Chinese Student Association, Indo-Pakistan Student Association, Professional Accounting Society, Student Government Association, national fraternities, national sororities. *Campus security:* 24-hour emergency response devices and patrols, late-night transport/escort service. *Student services:* health clinic, personal/psychological counseling.

Athletics *Intramural sports:* badminton M/W, baseball M (c), basketball M (c)/W (c), bowling M/W, soccer M (c)/W (c), softball M/W, swimming and diving M (c)/W (c), tennis M/W, volleyball M/W (c), weight lifting M/W.

Costs (2007–08) *Tuition:* area resident $4050 full-time; state resident $135 per credit hour part-time; nonresident $12,390 full-time, $413 per credit hour part-time. *Required fees:* $782 full-time.

Financial Aid Of all full-time matriculated undergraduates who enrolled in 2007, 3,709 applied for aid, 3,527 were judged to have need, 156 had their need fully met. 110 Federal Work-Study jobs (averaging $3200). 29 state and other part-time jobs (averaging $3200). In 2007, 439 non-need-based awards were made. *Average percent of need met:* 46%. *Average financial aid package:* $7114. *Average need-based loan:* $4066. *Average need-based gift aid:* $4439. *Average non-need-based aid:* $4917. *Average indebtedness upon graduation:* $18,140.

Applying *Options:* electronic application, early admission. *Application fee:* $35. *Required:* high school transcript, successful completion of high school exit exams (TAKS for Texas students). *Application deadlines:* 7/15 (freshmen), 8/1 (transfers). *Notification:* continuous until 8/22 (freshmen), continuous until 8/22 (transfers).

Freshman Application Contact Jose Cantu, Director of Admissions, University of Houston–Downtown, One Main Street, Houston, TX 77002. *Phone:* 713-221-8522. *Fax:* 713-221-8157. *E-mail:* uhdadmit@uhd.edu.

UNIVERSITY OF HOUSTON–VICTORIA

Victoria, Texas **www.uhv.edu/**

- **State-supported** upper-level, founded 1973, part of University of Houston System
- **Small-town** 20-acre campus
- **Endowment** $7.5 million
- **Coed** 1,409 undergraduate students, 36% full-time, 74% women, 26% men
- **Minimally difficult** entrance level

Undergraduates 511 full-time, 898 part-time. 9% African American, 4% Asian American or Pacific Islander, 22% Hispanic American, 0.6% Native American, 0.4% international, 98% transferred in.

Faculty *Total:* 154, 53% full-time, 73% with terminal degrees. *Student/faculty ratio:* 16:1.

Majors Accounting; biology/biological sciences; business administration and management; computer science; criminal justice/safety; education; history; humanities; marketing/marketing management; mathematics; nursing (registered nurse training); psychology; social sciences.

Academics *Calendar:* semesters. *Degrees:* bachelor's, master's, post-master's, and postbachelor's certificates. *Special study options:* adult/continuing education programs, distance learning, double majors, external degree program, independent study, internships, off-campus study, part-time degree program, services for LD students, study abroad, summer session for credit.

Computers on Campus 150 computers/terminals are available on campus for general student use. Students can access the following: campus intranet, computer help desk, free student e-mail accounts, online (class) grades, online (class) registration, online (class) schedules. Campuswide network is available. Wireless service is available via computer centers, computer labs, libraries, student centers.

Student Life *Housing:* college housing not available. *Activities and organizations:* student-run newspaper, Texas Student Education Association. *Campus security:* 24-hour emergency response devices and patrols.

Athletics Member NAIA.

Costs (2007–08) *Tuition:* state resident $3855 full-time, $129 per semester hour part-time; nonresident $12,195 full-time, $407 per semester hour part-time. Full-time tuition and fees vary according to course load. Part-time tuition and fees vary according to course load. *Required fees:* $1110 full-time, $44 per semester hour part-time. *Payment plan:* installment. *Waivers:* senior citizens.

Financial Aid Of all full-time matriculated undergraduates who enrolled in 2006, 586 applied for aid, 285 were judged to have need, 29 had their need fully met. 17 Federal Work-Study jobs (averaging $3233). 5 state and other part-time jobs (averaging $2584). In 2006, 44 non-need-based awards were made. *Average percent of need met: 52%. Average financial aid package:* $6795. *Average need-based loan:* $4125. *Average need-based gift aid:* $3545. *Average non-need-based aid:* $3849.

Applying *Application deadline:* rolling (transfers). *Notification:* continuous (transfers).

Application Contact University of Houston–Victoria, 3007 North Ben Wilson, Victoria, TX 77901-4450. *Phone:* 361-570-4290. *Toll-free phone:* 877-970-4848 Ext. 110.

UNIVERSITY OF MARY HARDIN-BAYLOR

Belton, Texas **www.umhb.edu/**

- **Independent Southern Baptist** comprehensive, founded 1845
- **Small-town** 100-acre campus with easy access to Austin
- **Endowment** $64.2 million
- **Coed** 2,494 undergraduate students, 89% full-time, 63% women, 37% men
- **Moderately difficult** entrance level, 76% of applicants were admitted

Undergraduates 2,225 full-time, 269 part-time. Students come from 20 states and territories, 13 other countries, 3% are from out of state, 12% African American, 2% Asian American or Pacific Islander, 12% Hispanic American, 0.6% Native American, 1% international, 11% transferred in, 48% live on campus. *Retention:* 60% of 2006 full-time freshmen returned.

Freshmen *Admission:* 1,258 applied, 962 admitted, 481 enrolled. *Test scores:* SAT critical reading scores over 500: 49%; SAT math scores over 500: 55%; SAT writing scores over 500: 43%; ACT scores over 18: 93%; SAT critical reading scores over 600: 13%; SAT math scores over 600: 15%; SAT writing scores over 600: 12%; ACT scores over 24: 27%; SAT critical reading scores over 700: 2%; SAT math scores over 700: 1%; SAT writing scores over 700: 1%; ACT scores over 30: 4%.

Faculty *Total:* 232, 61% full-time, 50% with terminal degrees. *Student/faculty ratio:* 14:1.

Majors Accounting; American studies; art; athletic training; biblical studies; biology/biological sciences; business administration and management; business/commerce; chemistry; chemistry teacher education; Christian studies; clinical laboratory science/medical technology; communication/speech communication and rhetoric; computer and information sciences; computer graphics; computer science; criminal justice/law enforcement administration; dramatic/theater arts; economics; education; elementary education; English; English/language arts teacher education; finance; fine/studio arts; general studies; history; information science/studies; kindergarten/preschool education; management information systems; marketing/marketing management; mass communication/media; mathematics; mathematics teacher education; middle school education; music performance; music teacher education; music theory and composition; nursing (registered nurse training); parks, recreation and leisure; pastoral studies/counseling; physical education teaching and coaching; political science and government; psychology; religious/sacred music; religious studies; science teacher education; social studies teacher education; social work; sociology; Spanish; special education; sport and fitness administration/management; theology.

Academics *Calendar:* semesters. *Degrees:* bachelor's, master's, and doctoral. *Special study options:* academic remediation for entering students, accelerated degree program, adult/continuing education programs, advanced placement credit, distance learning, double majors, English as a second language, honors programs, independent study, internships, part-time degree program, services for LD students, study abroad, summer session for credit. *ROTC:* Air Force (c). *Unusual degree programs:* 3-2 business administration.

Computers on Campus 275 computers/terminals are available on campus for general student use. Students can access the following: campus intranet, computer help desk, free student e-mail accounts, online (class) grades, online (class) registration, online (class) schedules. Campuswide network is available.

Student Life *Housing:* on-campus residence required through sophomore year. *Options:* men-only, women-only, disabled students. Campus housing is university owned. Freshman applicants given priority for college housing. *Activities and organizations:* drama/theater group, student-run newspaper, choral group, marching band, Baptist Student Ministry, Student Government Association, Residence Hall Association, Campus Activities Board, Crusaders for Christ. *Campus security:* 24-hour emergency response devices and patrols, late-night transport/escort service, controlled dormitory access, campus police force, lighted pathways and sidewalks. *Student services:* health clinic, personal/psychological counseling.

Athletics Member NCAA. All Division III. *Intercollegiate sports:* baseball M, basketball M/W, football M, golf M/W, soccer M/W, softball W, tennis M/W, volleyball W. *Intramural sports:* basketball M/W, bowling M/W, football M/W, soccer M/W, softball M/W, table tennis M/W, tennis M/W, ultimate Frisbee M/W, volleyball M/W.

Standardized Tests *Required:* SAT or ACT (for admission).

Costs (2007–08) *Comprehensive fee:* $22,460 includes full-time tuition ($15,750), mandatory fees ($2010), and room and board ($4700). Full-time tuition and fees vary according to course load. Part-time tuition: $525 per credit hour. Part-time tuition and fees vary according to course load. *Required fees:* $65 per credit hour part-time, $30 per term part-time. *Room and board:* Room and board charges vary according to board plan and housing facility. *Payment plan:* installment. *Waivers:* employees or children of employees.

Financial Aid Of all full-time matriculated undergraduates who enrolled in 2005, 2,111 applied for aid, 1,711 were judged to have need, 370 had their need fully met. 209 Federal Work-Study jobs (averaging $2300). 201 state and other part-time jobs (averaging $2300). In 2005, 512 non-need-based awards were made. *Average percent of need met:* 73%. *Average financial aid package:* $12,511. *Average need-based loan:* $4948. *Average need-based gift aid:* $5134. *Average non-need-based aid:* $3314. *Average indebtedness upon graduation:* $15,819.

Applying *Options:* electronic application, early admission, deferred entrance. *Application fee:* $35. *Required:* high school transcript. *Required for some:* essay or personal statement, letters of recommendation, interview. *Application deadlines:* rolling (freshmen), rolling (transfers). *Notification:* continuous (freshmen), continuous (transfers).

Freshman Application Contact Ms. Robbin Steen, Director of Admissions, University of Mary Hardin-Baylor, UMHB Station Box 8004, 900 College Street, Belton, TX 76513-2599. *Phone:* 254-295-4520. *Toll-free phone:* 800-727-8642. *Fax:* 254-295-5049. *E-mail:* admission@umhb.edu.

UNIVERSITY OF NORTH TEXAS

Denton, Texas **www.unt.edu/**

- **State-supported** university, founded 1890, part of University of North Texas System
- **Suburban** 744-acre campus with easy access to Dallas–Fort Worth
- **Endowment** $91.3 million
- **Coed** 27,242 undergraduate students, 79% full-time, 55% women, 45% men
- **Moderately difficult** entrance level, 65% of applicants were admitted

Undergraduates 21,433 full-time, 5,809 part-time. Students come from 49 states and territories, 122 other countries, 3% are from out of state, 13% African American, 5% Asian American or Pacific Islander, 12% Hispanic American, 0.8% Native American, 2% international, 14% transferred in, 23% live on campus. *Retention:* 75% of 2006 full-time freshmen returned.

Freshmen *Admission:* 12,387 applied, 8,099 admitted, 3,721 enrolled. *Test scores:* SAT critical reading scores over 500: 70%; SAT math scores over 500: 76%; ACT scores over 18: 98%; SAT critical reading scores over 600: 26%; SAT math scores over 600: 28%; ACT scores over 24: 40%; SAT critical reading scores over 700: 4%; SAT math scores over 700: 5%; ACT scores over 30: 4%.

Faculty *Total:* 1,663, 56% full-time, 50% with terminal degrees. *Student/faculty ratio:* 19:1.

Majors Accounting; anthropology; art; art history, criticism and conservation; audiology and speech-language pathology; banking and financial support services; behavioral sciences; biochemistry; biology/biological sciences; broadcast journalism; business/commerce; business/managerial economics; chemistry; civil engineering technology; clinical laboratory science/medical technology; commercial and advertising art; computer and information sciences; computer engineering; construction engineering technology; criminal justice/safety; cytotechnology; dance; dramatic/theater arts; e-commerce; economics; electrical, electronic and communications engineering technology; electrical, electronics and communications engineering; English; fashion/apparel design; fashion merchandising; finance; financial planning and services; fine/studio arts; French; general studies; geography; German; gerontology; health and physical education; health services/allied health/health sciences; history; hospitality administration; human development and family studies; human services; information science/studies; insurance; interdisciplinary studies; interior design; international/global studies; jazz/jazz studies; journalism; logistics and materials management; management information systems; manufacturing technology; marketing/marketing management; mathematics; mechanical engineering; mechanical engineering/mechanical technology; multi-/interdisciplinary studies related; music; music history, literature, and theory; music performance; music theory and composition; nuclear/nuclear power technology; operations management; organizational behavior; parks, recreation and leisure facilities management; philosophy; physics; physics related; political science and government; psychology; public administration; radio and television; real estate; rehabilitation and therapeutic professions related; sales, distribution and marketing; social sciences; social work; sociology; Spanish; speech and rhetoric.

Academics *Calendar:* semesters. *Degrees:* bachelor's, master's, doctoral, and postbachelor's certificates. *Special study options:* academic remediation for entering students, accelerated degree program, advanced placement credit, cooperative education, distance learning, double majors, English as a second language, external degree program, freshman honors college, honors programs, internships, part-time degree program, services for LD students, study abroad, summer session for credit. *ROTC:* Army (c), Air Force (b).

Computers on Campus 725 computers/terminals and 5,554 ports are available on campus for general student use. Students can access the following: campus intranet, computer help desk, free student e-mail accounts, online (class) grades, online (class) registration, online (class) schedules. Campuswide network is available. 100% of college-owned or -operated housing units are wired for high-speed Internet access. Wireless service is available via entire campus.

Student Life *Housing:* on-campus residence required for freshman year. *Options:* coed, women-only, disabled students. Freshman applicants given priority for college housing. *Activities and organizations:* drama/theater group, student-run newspaper, radio and television station, choral group, marching band, Student Government Association, Residence Hall Association, Panhellenic Association, Interfraternity Council, College Life, national fraternities, national sororities. *Campus security:* 24-hour emergency response devices and patrols, late-night transport/escort service, controlled dormitory access. *Student services:* health clinic, personal/psychological counseling, women's center, legal services.

Athletics Member NCAA. All Division I except football (Division I-A). *Intercollegiate sports:* baseball M (c), basketball M (s)/W (s), bowling M (c)/W (c), cross-country running M (s)/W (s), fencing M (c)/W (c), golf M (s)/W (s), ice hockey M (c), lacrosse M (c)/W (c), racquetball M (c)/W (c), rock climbing M (c), sailing M (c)/W (c), soccer M (c)/W (s), softball M (s)/W, swimming and diving M (c)/W (s), tennis M (c)/W, track and field M (s)/W (s), ultimate Frisbee M (c)/W (c), volleyball W (s). *Intramural sports:* basketball M/W, bowling M/W, football M, golf M/W, racquetball M/W, soccer M/W, softball M/W, table tennis M/W, tennis M/W, volleyball M/W.

Standardized Tests *Required:* SAT or ACT (for admission).

Costs (2007–08) *Tuition:* state resident $4390 full-time, $148 per credit hour part-time; nonresident $12,730 full-time, $426 per credit hour part-time. Full-time tuition and fees vary according to course load. Part-time tuition and fees vary according to course load. *Required fees:* $1930 full-time, $516 per term part-time. *Room and board:* $5490. Room and board charges vary according to board plan and housing facility. *Payment plan:* installment. *Waivers:* senior citizens and employees or children of employees.

Financial Aid Of all full-time matriculated undergraduates who enrolled in 2004, 11,735 applied for aid, 8,912 were judged to have need, 1,655 had their need fully met. In 2004, 1046 non-need-based awards were made. *Average percent of need met:* 65%. *Average financial aid package:* $7269. *Average need-based loan:* $3728. *Average need-based gift aid:* $3655. *Average non-need-based aid:* $1482. *Average indebtedness upon graduation:* $18,175.

Applying *Options:* electronic application, early admission, early action, deferred entrance. *Application fee:* $40. *Required:* high school transcript. *Required for some:* essay or personal statement, 3 letters of recommendation, interview. *Application deadlines:* 6/16 (freshmen), 6/16 (transfers). *Notification:* continuous (freshmen), continuous (transfers).

Freshman Application Contact Mr. Kent Marshall, Coordinator of New Student Mentoring Programs, University of North Texas, Box 311277, Denton, TX 76203-9988. *Phone:* 940-565-3190. *Toll-free phone:* 800-868-8211. *Fax:* 940-565-2408. *E-mail:* undergradadm@unt.edu.

UNIVERSITY OF PHOENIX–DALLAS CAMPUS

Dallas, Texas **www.phoenix.edu/**

- **Proprietary** comprehensive, founded 2001
- **Urban** campus
- **Coed**
- **Noncompetitive** entrance level

Faculty *Student/faculty ratio:* 11:1.

Academics *Calendar:* continuous. *Degrees:* bachelor's and master's.

Student Life *Campus security:* late-night transport/escort service.

Costs (2007–08) *Tuition:* $11,520 full-time, $384 per credit part-time. Full-time tuition and fees vary according to course level.

Financial Aid *Average financial aid package:* $4159. *Average need-based gift aid:* $2169.

Applying *Options:* deferred entrance. *Application fee:* $45. *Required:* 1 letter of recommendation. *Required for some:* high school transcript.

Freshman Application Contact Ms. Beth Barilla, Associate Vice President, Student Admissions and Services, University of Phoenix–Dallas Campus, 4615 East Elwood Street, Mail Stop AA-K101, Phoenix, AZ 85040-1958. *Phone:* 480-317-6000. *Toll-free phone:* 800-776-4867 (in-state); 800-228-7240 (out-of-state). *Fax:* 480-894-1758. *E-mail:* beth.barilla@phoenix.edu.

UNIVERSITY OF PHOENIX–HOUSTON CAMPUS

Houston, Texas **www.phoenix.edu/**

- **Proprietary** comprehensive, founded 2001
- **Urban** campus
- **Coed**
- **Noncompetitive** entrance level

Faculty *Student/faculty ratio:* 13:1.

Academics *Calendar:* continuous. *Degrees:* bachelor's and master's.

Student Life *Campus security:* late-night transport/escort service.

Financial Aid *Average financial aid package:* $4713. *Average need-based gift aid:* $2404.

Applying *Options:* deferred entrance. *Application fee:* $45. *Required:* 1 letter of recommendation. *Required for some:* high school transcript.

Freshman Application Contact Ms. Beth Barilla, Associate Vice President, Student Admissions and Services, University of Phoenix–Houston Campus, 4615 East Elwood Street, Mail Stop AA-K101, Phoenix, AZ 85040-1958. *Phone:* 480-317-6000. *Toll-free phone:* 800-776-4867 (in-state); 800-228-7240 (out-of-state). *Fax:* 480-894-1758. *E-mail:* beth.barilla@phoenix.edu.

UNIVERSITY OF ST. THOMAS

Houston, Texas **www.stthom.edu/**

- **Independent Roman Catholic** comprehensive, founded 1947
- **Urban** 21-acre campus
- **Coed** 1,708 undergraduate students, 76% full-time, 61% women, 39% men
- **Moderately difficult** entrance level, 84% of applicants were admitted

Undergraduates 1,303 full-time, 405 part-time. Students come from 30 states and territories, 57 other countries, 4% are from out of state, 5% African American, 11% Asian American or Pacific Islander, 29% Hispanic American, 0.6% Native American, 4% international, 11% transferred in, 16% live on campus. *Retention:* 68% of 2006 full-time freshmen returned.

Freshmen *Admission:* 861 applied, 720 admitted, 294 enrolled. *Average high school GPA:* 3.41. *Test scores:* SAT critical reading scores over 500: 79%; SAT math scores over 500: 84%; SAT writing scores over 500: 77%; ACT scores over 18: 96%; SAT critical reading scores over 600: 37%; SAT math scores over 600: 38%; SAT writing scores over 600: 31%; ACT scores over 24: 54%; SAT critical reading scores over 700: 8%; SAT math scores over 700: 5%; SAT writing scores over 700: 6%; ACT scores over 30: 7%.

Faculty *Total:* 275, 48% full-time, 71% with terminal degrees. *Student/faculty ratio:* 12:1.

Majors Accounting; biology/biological sciences; business administration and management; chemistry; communication/speech communication and rhetoric; dramatic/theater arts; economics; education; elementary education; English; environmental studies; finance; fine/studio arts; French; general studies; history; international relations and affairs; liberal arts and sciences/liberal studies; management information systems; marketing/marketing management; mathematics; music; music teacher education; pastoral studies/counseling; philosophy; political science and government; pre-dentistry studies; pre-law studies; pre-medical studies; pre-pharmacy studies; pre-veterinary studies; psychology; secondary education; Spanish; theology; theology and religious vocations related.

Academics *Calendar:* semesters. *Degrees:* diplomas, bachelor's, master's, doctoral, and first professional. *Special study options:* academic remediation for entering students, adult/continuing education programs, advanced placement credit, distance learning, double majors, honors programs, independent study, internships, off-campus study, part-time degree program, services for LD students, study abroad, summer session for credit. *ROTC:* Army (c). *Unusual degree programs:* 3-2 business administration; engineering with University of Notre Dame, University of Houston, Texas A&M University.

Computers on Campus Students can access the following: computer help desk, free student e-mail accounts, online (class) grades, online (class) registration, online (class) schedules. Campuswide network is available. Wireless service is available via entire campus.

Student Life *Housing options:* coed. Campus housing is university owned. Freshman applicants given priority for college housing. *Activities and organizations:* drama/theater group, student-run newspaper, choral group. *Campus security:* 24-hour emergency response devices and patrols, late-night transport/escort service, controlled dormitory access. *Student services:* personal/psychological counseling.

Athletics *Intramural sports:* baseball M (c), basketball M/W (c), fencing M (c)/W (c), golf M/W, racquetball M/W, rugby M (c), soccer M (c)/W (c), table tennis M/W, tennis M/W, volleyball M/W (c), wrestling M (c).

Standardized Tests *Required:* SAT or ACT (for admission).

Costs (2007–08) *Comprehensive fee:* $26,200 includes full-time tuition ($18,900) and room and board ($7300). Full-time tuition and fees vary according to course load. Part-time tuition: $630 per credit. Part-time tuition and fees vary according to course load. *Room and board:* Room and board charges vary according to board plan and housing facility. *Payment plans:* installment, deferred payment. *Waivers:* senior citizens and employees or children of employees.

Financial Aid Of all full-time matriculated undergraduates who enrolled in 2006, 831 applied for aid, 734 were judged to have need, 94 had their need fully met. 37 Federal Work-Study jobs (averaging $2754). 4 state and other part-time jobs (averaging $2426). In 2006, 265 non-need-based awards were made. *Average percent of need met:* 64%. *Average financial aid package:* $13,302. *Average need-based loan:* $4001. *Average need-based gift aid:* $9624. *Average non-need-based aid:* $7064. *Average indebtedness upon graduation:* $19,668.

Applying *Options:* electronic application, deferred entrance. *Application fee:* $25. *Required:* essay or personal statement, high school transcript, minimum 2.5 GPA. *Application deadline:* rolling (freshmen). *Notification:* continuous (freshmen), continuous (transfers).

Freshman Application Contact University of St. Thomas, 3800 Montrose Boulevard, Houston, TX 77006-4696. *Phone:* 713-525-3500. *Toll-free phone:* 800-856-8565. *Fax:* 713-525-3558. *E-mail:* admissions@stthom.edu.

THE UNIVERSITY OF TEXAS AT ARLINGTON

Arlington, Texas **www.uta.edu/**

- **State-supported** university, founded 1895, part of University of Texas System
- **Urban** 395-acre campus with easy access to Dallas–Fort Worth
- **Endowment** $57.4 million
- **Coed** 19,017 undergraduate students, 68% full-time, 52% women, 48% men
- **Moderately difficult** entrance level, 77% of applicants were admitted

Undergraduates 13,013 full-time, 6,004 part-time. Students come from 48 states and territories, 81 other countries, 1% are from out of state, 15% African American, 12% Asian American or Pacific Islander, 17% Hispanic American, 0.5% Native American, 4% international, 16% transferred in, 18% live on campus. *Retention:* 61% of 2006 full-time freshmen returned.

Freshmen *Admission:* 5,811 applied, 4,447 admitted, 2,162 enrolled. *Test scores:* SAT critical reading scores over 500: 59%; SAT math scores over 500: 73%; ACT scores over 18: 88%; SAT critical reading scores over 600: 18%; SAT math scores over 600: 26%; ACT scores over 24: 32%; SAT critical reading scores over 700: 3%; SAT math scores over 700: 3%; ACT scores over 30: 3%.

Faculty *Total:* 1,396, 57% full-time. *Student/faculty ratio:* 19:1.

Majors Accounting; advertising; aerospace, aeronautical and astronautical engineering; anthropology; architecture; art; art history, criticism and conservation; athletic training; banking and financial support services; biochemistry; biology/biological sciences; business administration and management; business/managerial economics; chemistry; child development; civil engineering; classics and languages, literatures and linguistics; clinical laboratory science/medical technology; computer and information sciences; computer engineering; computer science; computer software engineering; criminal justice/safety; criminology; digital communication and media/multimedia; dramatic/theater arts; economics; electrical, electronics and communications engineering; English; fine/studio arts; foreign languages and literatures; French; geology/earth science; German; health and physical education; history; industrial engineering; interdisciplinary studies; interior architecture; international business/trade/commerce; journalism; management information systems; marketing/marketing management; mathematics; mechanical engineering; microbiology; multi-/interdisciplinary studies related; music; nursing (registered nurse training); philosophy; physics; political science and government; psychology; public relations/image management; radio and television; real estate; Russian; social work; sociology; Spanish; speech and rhetoric.

Academics *Calendar:* semesters. *Degrees:* bachelor's, master's, doctoral, post-master's, and postbachelor's certificates. *Special study options:* academic remediation for entering students, adult/continuing education programs, advanced placement credit, cooperative education, distance learning, double majors, English as a second language, freshman honors college, honors programs, independent study, internships, off-campus study, part-time degree program, services for LD students, student-designed majors, study abroad, summer session for credit. *ROTC:* Army (b), Air Force (c). *Unusual degree programs:* 3-2 business administration; psychology, health care administration.

Computers on Campus 1,000 computers/terminals and 6,000 ports are available on campus for general student use. Students can access the following: campus intranet, computer help desk, free student e-mail accounts, online (class) grades, online (class) registration, online (class) schedules. Campuswide network is available. 90% of college-owned or -operated housing units are wired for high-speed Internet access. Wireless service is available via classrooms, computer centers, computer labs, learning centers, libraries, student centers.

Student Life *Housing options:* coed, men-only, women-only. Campus housing is university owned and leased by the school. *Activities and organizations:* drama/theater group, student-run newspaper, radio station, choral group, marching band, Beta Gamma Sigma, National Society of Collegiate Scholars, CSE Grad Club, Friendship Association of Chinese Students & Scholars, Fine Arts Society of India, national fraternities, national sororities. *Campus security:* 24-hour emergency response devices and patrols, late-night transport/escort service, controlled dormitory access, remote emergency telephones, bicycle patrols, crime prevention program, student shuttle service. *Student services:* health clinic, personal/psychological counseling, legal services.

Athletics Member NCAA. All Division I. *Intercollegiate sports:* baseball M (s), basketball M (s)/W (s), cross-country running M (s)/W (s), golf M (s), squash M (s), tennis M (s)/W (s), track and field M (s)/W (s), volleyball W (s). *Intramural sports:* badminton M/W, basketball M/W, bowling M/W, football M/W, golf M/W, racquetball M/W, soccer M/W, softball M/W, squash M/W, swimming and diving M/W, table tennis M/W, volleyball M/W.

Standardized Tests *Required:* SAT or ACT (for admission).

Costs (2007–08) *Tuition:* state resident $7194 full-time; nonresident $15,534 full-time. Full-time tuition and fees vary according to course level, course load, and program. Part-time tuition and fees vary according to course level, course load, and program. *Room and board:* $6180; room only: $3296. Room and board charges vary according to board plan and housing facility. *Payment plan:* installment. *Waivers:* employees or children of employees.

Financial Aid Of all full-time matriculated undergraduates who enrolled in 2006, 8,661 applied for aid, 7,765 were judged to have need, 886 had their need fully met. 691 Federal Work-Study jobs (averaging $1528). 169 state and other part-time jobs (averaging $769). In 2006, 300 non-need-based awards were made. *Average percent of need met:* 69%. *Average financial aid package:* $7569. *Average need-based loan:* $3466. *Average need-based gift aid:* $4568. *Average non-need-based aid:* $2520.

Applying *Options:* electronic application, deferred entrance. *Application fee:* $35. *Required:* high school transcript, class rank. *Application deadlines:* 6/1 (freshmen), rolling (transfers). *Notification:* continuous (freshmen), continuous (transfers).

Freshman Application Contact Dr. Hans Gatterdam, Director of Admissions and Records, The University of Texas at Arlington, PO Box 19111, 701 South Nedderman Drive, Room 110, Davis Hall, Arlington, TX 76019-0088. *Phone:* 817-272-6287. *Fax:* 817-272-3435. *E-mail:* admissions@uta.edu.

THE UNIVERSITY OF TEXAS AT AUSTIN

Austin, Texas **www.utexas.edu/**

- **State-supported** university, founded 1883, part of University of Texas System
- **Urban** 350-acre campus with easy access to San Antonio
- **Endowment** $2.8 billion
- **Coed** 37,459 undergraduate students, 92% full-time, 52% women, 48% men
- **Very difficult** entrance level, 51% of applicants were admitted

Undergraduates 34,611 full-time, 2,848 part-time. Students come from 54 states and territories, 126 other countries, 5% are from out of state, 5% African American, 17% Asian American or Pacific Islander, 18% Hispanic American, 0.4% Native American, 4% international, 6% transferred in, 20% live on campus. *Retention:* 92% of 2006 full-time freshmen returned.

Freshmen *Admission:* 27,237 applied, 13,800 admitted, 7,478 enrolled. *Test scores:* SAT critical reading scores over 500: 87%; SAT math scores over 500: 93%; SAT writing scores over 500: 87%; ACT scores over 18: 97%; SAT critical reading scores over 600: 55%; SAT math scores over 600: 68%; SAT writing scores over 600: 53%; ACT scores over 24: 74%; SAT critical reading scores over 700: 17%; SAT math scores over 700: 25%; SAT writing scores over 700: 14%; ACT scores over 30: 25%.

Faculty *Total:* 2,872, 90% full-time, 84% with terminal degrees. *Student/faculty ratio:* 18:1.

Majors Accounting; advertising; aerospace, aeronautical and astronautical engineering; American studies; ancient/classical Greek; ancient studies; anthropology; apparel and textiles; Arabic; archeology; architectural engineering; architecture; art; art history, criticism and conservation; Asian studies; astronomy; athletic training; biochemistry; biological and physical sciences; biology/biological sciences; biomedical/medical engineering; botany/plant biology; business administration and management; business administration, management and operations related; business/commerce; chemical engineering; chemistry; civil engineering; classics and languages, literatures and linguistics; clinical laboratory science/medical technology; communication disorders; communication/speech communication and rhetoric; computer and information sciences; Czech; dance; design and visual communications; dramatic/theater arts; East Asian languages; ecology; economics; electrical, electronics and communications engineering; English; English composition; ethnic, cultural minority, and gender studies related; European studies; family and consumer sciences/human sciences; finance; fine/studio arts; foods, nutrition, and wellness; foreign languages and literatures; French; geography; geological and earth sciences/geosciences related; geology/earth science; geophysics and seismology; German; health and physical education; health services/allied health/health sciences; Hebrew; history; human development and family studies; humanities; hydrology and water resources science; interior design; Iranian/Persian languages; Islamic studies; Italian; Jewish/Judaic studies; journalism; Latin; Latin American studies; liberal arts and sciences/liberal studies; linguistics; logistics and materials management; management information systems; marketing/marketing management; mathematics; mathematics and computer science; mechanical engineering; multi-/interdisciplinary studies related; music; music performance; music theory and composition; Near and Middle Eastern studies; nursing (registered nurse training); petroleum engineering; philosophy; physics; political science and government; Portuguese; psychology; public relations/image management; radio and television; religious studies; Russian; Russian studies; Scandinavian languages; Semitic languages; social work; sociology; Spanish; sport and fitness administration/management; Turkish; urban studies/affairs; visual and performing arts; women's studies.

Academics *Calendar:* semesters. *Degrees:* bachelor's, master's, doctoral, and first professional. *Special study options:* academic remediation for entering students, accelerated degree program, adult/continuing education programs, advanced placement credit, cooperative education, distance learning, double majors, English as a second language, honors programs, independent study, internships, part-time degree program, services for LD students, student-designed majors, study abroad, summer session for credit. *ROTC:* Army (b), Navy (b), Air Force (b). *Unusual degree programs:* 3-2 architecture.

Computers on Campus 4,000 computers/terminals are available on campus for general student use. Students can access the following: computer help desk, free student e-mail accounts, online (class) grades, online (class) registration, online (class) schedules. Campuswide network is available. 100% of college-owned or -operated housing units are wired for high-speed Internet access. Wireless service is available via computer centers, computer labs, libraries, student centers.

Student Life *Housing options:* coed, men-only, women-only. Campus housing is university owned. Freshman applicants given priority for college housing. *Activities and organizations:* drama/theater group, student-run newspaper, radio and television station, choral group, marching band, Alpha Phi Omega, Student Events Center, Texas Exes-Student Chapter, Longhorn Band Student Organization, Student Volunteer Board, national fraternities, national sororities. *Campus security:* 24-hour emergency response devices and patrols, student patrols, late-night transport/escort service, controlled dormitory access. *Student services:* health clinic, personal/psychological counseling, legal services.

Athletics Member NCAA. All Division I except football (Division I-A). *Intercollegiate sports:* archery M (c)/W (c), badminton M (c)/W (c), baseball M (s), basketball M (s)/W (s), crew M (c)/W (s), cross-country running M (s)/W (s), fencing M (c)/W (c), golf M (s)/W (s), gymnastics M (c)/W (c), ice hockey M (c), lacrosse M (c)/W (c), racquetball M (c)/W (c), rugby M (c)/W (c), sailing M (c)/W (c), soccer M (c)/W (s), softball W (s), squash M (c)/W (c), swimming and diving M (s)/W (s), table tennis M (c)/W (c), tennis M (s)/W (s), track and field M (s)/W (s), volleyball M (c)/W (s), water polo M (c)/W (c), weight lifting M (c)/W (c), wrestling M (c)/W (c). *Intramural sports:* basketball M/W, bowling M/W, football M/W, golf M/W, racquetball M/W, soccer M/W, softball M/W, squash M/W, swimming and diving M/W, table tennis M/W, tennis M/W, track and field M/W, ultimate Frisbee M (c)/W (c), volleyball M/W.

Standardized Tests *Required:* SAT or ACT (for admission). *Required for some:* SAT Subject Tests (for admission).

Costs (2007–08) *Tuition:* state resident $7670 full-time; nonresident $24,544 full-time. Full-time tuition and fees vary according to course load and program. Part-time tuition and fees vary according to course load and program. *Room and board:* $8576. Room and board charges vary according to board plan, housing facility, and location. *Payment plan:* installment. *Waivers:* senior citizens and employees or children of employees.

Financial Aid Of all full-time matriculated undergraduates who enrolled in 2006, 22,700 applied for aid, 18,200 were judged to have need, 15,100 had their need fully met. 1,425 Federal Work-Study jobs (averaging $1650). 245 state and other part-time jobs (averaging $1270). In 2006, 10400 non-need-based awards were made. *Average percent of need met:* 90%. *Average financial aid package:* $10,900. *Average need-based loan:* $4700. *Average need-based gift aid:* $6300. *Average non-need-based aid:* $3300. *Average indebtedness upon graduation:* $16,800.

Applying *Options:* electronic application, deferred entrance. *Application fee:* $60. *Required:* essay or personal statement, high school transcript. *Application deadlines:* 2/1 (freshmen), 3/1 (transfers). *Notification:* continuous (freshmen), continuous (transfers).

Freshman Application Contact Dr. Bruce Walker, Vice Provost and Director of Admissions, The University of Texas at Austin, Office of Admissions/Freshmen Admissions Center, PO Box 8058, Austin, TX 78713-8058. *Phone:* 512-475-7440. *Fax:* 512-475-7475.

THE UNIVERSITY OF TEXAS AT BROWNSVILLE

Brownsville, Texas **www.utb.edu/**

- **State-supported** 4-year, founded 1973, part of University of Texas System
- **Urban** 380-acre campus
- **Coed** 16,378 undergraduate students, 36% full-time, 59% women, 41% men
- **Noncompetitive** entrance level, 100% of applicants were admitted

Undergraduates 5,816 full-time, 10,562 part-time. Students come from 13 states and territories, 20 other countries, 1% are from out of state, 0.3% African American, 0.5% Asian American or Pacific Islander, 89% Hispanic American, 0.1% Native American, 5% international, 3% transferred in, 2% live on campus. *Retention:* 68% of 2006 full-time freshmen returned.

Freshmen *Admission:* 3,680 applied, 3,680 admitted, 1,662 enrolled. *Average high school GPA:* 2.66.

Faculty *Total:* 675, 52% full-time, 35% with terminal degrees. *Student/faculty ratio:* 21:1.

Majors Accounting; art; biology/biological sciences; business administration and management; chemistry; clinical/medical laboratory technology; communication/speech communication and rhetoric; computer and information sciences; corrections; criminal justice/law enforcement administration; criminal justice/safety; diagnostic medical sonography and ultrasound technology; electrical, electronic and communications engineering technology; emergency medical technology (EMT paramedic); engineering physics; English; environmental science; finance; health and physical education; health services/allied health/health sciences; history; information science/studies; marketing/marketing management; mathematics; mechanical engineering/mechanical technology; multi-/interdisciplinary studies related; music; nursing (licensed practical/vocational nurse training); nursing (registered nurse training); physics; political science and government; psychology; public administration; radiologic technology/science; respiratory care therapy; sociology; Spanish.

Academics *Calendar:* semesters. *Degrees:* certificates, associate, bachelor's, master's, and doctoral. *Special study options:* academic remediation for entering students, advanced placement credit, cooperative education, distance learning, double majors, English as a second language, independent study, internships, off-campus study, part-time degree program, services for LD students, study abroad, summer session for credit.

Computers on Campus 332 computers/terminals are available on campus for general student use. Students can access the following: computer help desk, free student e-mail accounts, online (class) grades, online (class) registration, online (class) schedules. Campuswide network is available. 100% of college-owned or -operated housing units are wired for high-speed Internet access. Wireless service is available via entire campus.

Student Life *Housing options:* coed. Campus housing is university owned. *Activities and organizations:* student-run newspaper, choral group, Alpha Chi, Anime Viewing Club, Counseling & Guidance Student Association, Gorgas Science, Alpha Chi Psi. *Campus security:* 24-hour emergency response devices and patrols, late-night transport/escort service. *Student services:* health clinic, personal/psychological counseling, legal services.

Athletics Member NAIA. *Intercollegiate sports:* baseball M (s), golf M (s)/W (s), soccer M (s)/W (s), volleyball W (s).

Costs (2007–08) *Tuition:* state resident $2784 full-time, $116 per semester hour part-time; nonresident $9456 full-time, $394 per semester hour part-time. Full-time tuition and fees vary according to class time and course load. Part-time tuition and fees vary according to class time and course load. *Required fees:* $1090 full-time. *Room only:* $2520. *Payment plan:* installment. *Waivers:* senior citizens.

Financial Aid Of all full-time matriculated undergraduates who enrolled in 2006, 3,627 applied for aid, 3,392 were judged to have need. In 2006, 43 non-need-based awards were made. *Average percent of need met:* 29%. *Average financial aid package:* $3467. *Average need-based loan:* $1900. *Average need-based gift aid:* $2564. *Average non-need-based aid:* $1855.

Applying *Options:* electronic application, early admission. *Required:* high school transcript. *Application deadlines:* 7/1 (freshmen), 8/1 (transfers). *Notification:* continuous (transfers).

Freshman Application Contact Carlo Tamayo, New Student Relations Coordinator, The University of Texas at Brownsville, 80 Fort Brown, Brownsville, TX 78520-4991. *Phone:* 956-882-8860. *Toll-free phone:* 800-850-0160. *Fax:* 956-882-8959. *E-mail:* admissions@utb.edu.

THE UNIVERSITY OF TEXAS AT DALLAS

Richardson, Texas **www.utdallas.edu/**

- **State-supported** university, founded 1969, part of University of Texas System
- **Suburban** 455-acre campus with easy access to Dallas
- **Endowment** $262.7 million
- **Coed** 9,266 undergraduate students, 73% full-time, 46% women, 54% men
- **Very difficult** entrance level, 56% of applicants were admitted

Undergraduates 6,730 full-time, 2,536 part-time. Students come from 45 states and territories, 123 other countries, 4% are from out of state, 7% African American, 20% Asian American or Pacific Islander, 11% Hispanic American, 0.6% Native American, 4% international, 16% transferred in, 18% live on campus. *Retention:* 81% of 2006 full-time freshmen returned.

Freshmen *Admission:* 4,198 applied, 2,336 admitted, 1,057 enrolled. *Average high school GPA:* 3.64. *Test scores:* SAT critical reading scores over 500: 87%; SAT math scores over 500: 96%; SAT writing scores over 500: 83%; ACT scores over 18: 97%; SAT critical reading scores over 600: 54%; SAT math scores over 600: 68%; SAT writing scores over 600: 45%; ACT scores over 24: 75%; SAT critical reading scores over 700: 17%; SAT math scores over 700: 24%; SAT writing scores over 700: 10%; ACT scores over 30: 24%.

Faculty *Total:* 696, 71% full-time, 81% with terminal degrees. *Student/faculty ratio:* 19:1.

Majors Accounting; American studies; applied mathematics; audiology and speech-language pathology; biochemistry; biology/biological sciences; business/commerce; chemistry; cognitive psychology and psycholinguistics; computer and information sciences; computer engineering; computer science; computer software engineering; criminology; economics; electrical, electronics and communications engineering; ethnic, cultural minority, and gender studies related; finance; geography; geology/earth science; history; humanities; interdisciplinary studies; international business/trade/commerce; literature; mathematics; molecular biology; neuroscience; physics; political science and government; psychology; public administration; sociology; statistics; visual and performing arts.

Academics *Calendar:* semesters. *Degrees:* bachelor's, master's, doctoral, and postbachelor's certificates. *Special study options:* academic remediation for entering students, accelerated degree program, adult/continuing education programs, advanced placement credit, cooperative education, distance learning, double majors, freshman honors college, honors programs, independent study, internships, part-time degree program, services for LD students, student-designed majors, study abroad, summer session for credit. *ROTC:* Army (c), Air Force (c). *Unusual degree programs:* 3-2 engineering with Abilene Christian University, Austin College, Paul Quinn College, Texas Woman's University.

Computers on Campus 630 computers/terminals are available on campus for general student use. Students can access the following: computer help desk, free student e-mail accounts, online (class) grades, online (class) registration, online (class) schedules. Campuswide network is available. 100% of college-owned or -operated housing units are wired for high-speed Internet access. Wireless service is available via classrooms, computer centers, dorm rooms, libraries, student centers.

Student Life *Housing options:* coed. Campus housing is university owned and is provided by a third party. Freshman applicants given priority for college housing. *Activities and organizations:* drama/theater group, student-run newspaper, radio station, Student Government Association, Golden Key National Honor Society, Muslim Students Association, Indian Student Association, Friendship Association of Chinese Students and Scholars, national fraternities, national sororities. *Campus security:* 24-hour emergency response devices and patrols, late-night transport/escort service. *Student services:* health clinic, personal/psychological counseling, women's center, legal services.

Athletics Member NCAA. All Division III. *Intercollegiate sports:* baseball M, basketball M/W, cross-country running M/W, golf M/W, soccer M/W, softball W, tennis M/W, volleyball W. *Intramural sports:* badminton M/W, basketball M/W, cheerleading M/W, cross-country running M/W, football M, golf M/W, ice hockey M, lacrosse M, racquetball M/W, rugby M, soccer M/W, softball M/W, squash M/W, swimming and diving M/W, table tennis M/W, tennis M/W, ultimate Frisbee M/W, volleyball M/W, weight lifting M/W, wrestling M.

Standardized Tests *Required:* SAT or ACT (for admission). *Required for some:* THEA.

Costs (2007–08) *Tuition:* state resident $8554 full-time; nonresident $17,854 full-time. Full-time tuition and fees vary according to course load and degree level. Part-time tuition and fees vary according to course load and degree level. No tuition increase for student's term of enrollment. *Room and board:* $6671. Room and board charges vary according to board plan and housing facility. *Payment plan:* installment. *Waivers:* senior citizens.

Financial Aid Of all full-time matriculated undergraduates who enrolled in 2006, 3,690 applied for aid, 2,978 were judged to have need, 1,052 had their need fully met. 496 Federal Work-Study jobs (averaging $4825). 10 state and other part-time jobs (averaging $4479). In 2006, 1171 non-need-based awards were made. *Average percent of need met:* 75%. *Average financial aid package:* $9819. *Average need-based loan:* $4845. *Average need-based gift aid:* $4398. *Average non-need-based aid:* $8418. *Average indebtedness upon graduation:* $16,895.

Applying *Options:* electronic application, deferred entrance. *Application fee:* $50. *Required:* essay or personal statement, high school transcript. *Required for some:* interview. *Recommended:* 3 letters of recommendation. *Application deadline:* 7/1 (freshmen). *Notification:* continuous (freshmen), continuous (transfers).

Freshman Application Contact Enrollment Services, The University of Texas at Dallas, PO Box 830688, Mail Station MC18, Richardson, TX 75083-0688. *Phone:* 972-883-2270. *Toll-free phone:* 800-889-2443. *Fax:* 972-883-2599. *E-mail:* interest@utdallas.edu.

See page 2566 for the College Close-Up.

THE UNIVERSITY OF TEXAS AT EL PASO

El Paso, Texas **www.utep.edu/**

- **State-supported** university, founded 1913
- **Urban** 360-acre campus
- **Coed** 17,025 undergraduate students, 65% full-time, 55% women, 45% men
- **Minimally difficult** entrance level, 99% of applicants were admitted

Undergraduates 11,112 full-time, 5,913 part-time. Students come from 47 states and territories, 67 other countries, 3% are from out of state, 3% African American, 1% Asian American or Pacific Islander, 76% Hispanic American, 0.2% Native American, 10% international, 9% transferred in. *Retention:* 68% of 2006 full-time freshmen returned.

Freshmen *Admission:* 5,147 applied, 5,098 admitted, 2,331 enrolled. *Average high school GPA:* 3.1. *Test scores:* SAT math scores over 500: 36%; ACT scores over 18: 56%; SAT math scores over 600: 7%; ACT scores over 24: 10%; ACT scores over 30: 1%.

Faculty *Total:* 1,097, 60% full-time. *Student/faculty ratio:* 20:1.

Majors Accounting; anthropology; applied mathematics; art teacher education; audiology and speech-language pathology; biology/biological sciences; botany/plant biology; broadcast journalism; business administration and management; ceramic arts and ceramics; chemistry; civil engineering; clinical laboratory science/medical technology; commercial and advertising art; community organization and advocacy; computer science; creative writing; criminal justice/law enforcement administration; dramatic/theater arts; drawing; economics; electrical, electronics and communications engineering; English; finance; fine/studio arts; French; geography; geology/earth science; geophysics and seismology; German; health/health care administration; health science; Hispanic-American, Puerto Rican, and Mexican-American/Chicano studies; history; industrial engineering; information science/studies; interdisciplinary studies; journalism; Latin American studies; linguistics; marketing/marketing management; mass communication/media; mathematics; mechanical engineering; medical microbiology and bacteriology; metallurgical engineering; music; nursing (registered nurse training); philosophy; physics; political science and government; printmaking; psychology; real estate; sculpture; social work; sociology; Spanish; speech and rhetoric; statistics; zoology/animal biology.

Academics *Calendar:* semesters. *Degrees:* bachelor's, master's, and doctoral. *Special study options:* academic remediation for entering students, accelerated degree program, adult/continuing education programs, advanced placement credit, cooperative education, distance learning, English as a second language, honors programs, independent study, internships, off-campus study, part-time degree program, services for LD students, summer session for credit. *ROTC:* Army (b), Air Force (b).

Computers on Campus Campuswide network is available.

Student Life *Housing options:* coed, disabled students. Campus housing is university owned. *Activities and organizations:* drama/theater group, student-run newspaper, radio station, choral group, marching band, national fraternities, national sororities. *Campus security:* 24-hour emergency response devices and patrols, late-night transport/escort service. *Student services:* health clinic, personal/psychological counseling, women's center, legal services.

Athletics Member NCAA. All Division I except football (Division I-A). *Intercollegiate sports:* basketball M (s)/W (s), cross-country running M (s)/W (s), golf M (s), riflery M/W, tennis W (s), track and field M (s)/W (s), volleyball W (s). *Intramural sports:* archery M/W, badminton M/W, basketball M/W, bowling M/W, fencing M/W, field hockey M, golf M/W, gymnastics M/W, racquetball M/W, skiing (downhill) M, soccer M/W, squash M/W, swimming and diving M/W, tennis M/W, track and field M/W, volleyball M/W, water polo M/W, weight lifting M, wrestling M/W.

Standardized Tests *Required for some:* SAT or ACT (for admission), PAA.

Costs (2007–08) *Tuition:* state resident $4311 full-time, $144 per credit hour part-time; nonresident $12,651 full-time, $422 per credit hour part-time. Full-time tuition and fees vary according to course load and degree level. Part-time tuition and fees vary according to course load and degree level. No tuition increase for student's term of enrollment. *Required fees:* $1299 full-time. *Room only:* $4410. Room and board charges vary according to housing facility. *Payment plan:* installment. *Waivers:* employees or children of employees.

Financial Aid Of all full-time matriculated undergraduates who enrolled in 2006, 7,732 applied for aid, 6,238 were judged to have need, 2,535 had their need fully met. In 2006, 943 non-need-based awards were made. *Average percent of need met:* 84%. *Average financial aid package:* $11,084. *Average need-based loan:* $5279. *Average need-based gift aid:* $5542. *Average non-need-based aid:* $1832. *Average indebtedness upon graduation:* $7230.

Applying *Options:* deferred entrance. *Required:* high school transcript. *Application deadlines:* 7/31 (freshmen), 7/31 (transfers). *Notification:* continuous (transfers).

Freshman Application Contact Director of Admissions, The University of Texas at El Paso, 500 West University Avenue, El Paso, TX 79968-0510. *Phone:* 915-747-5588. *Toll-free phone:* 877-746-4636. *Fax:* 915-747-8893. *E-mail:* futureminer@utep.edu.

THE UNIVERSITY OF TEXAS AT SAN ANTONIO

San Antonio, Texas **www.utsa.edu/**

- **State-supported** university, founded 1969, part of University of Texas System
- **Suburban** 600-acre campus with easy access to San Antonio, Texas
- **Endowment** $44.4 million
- **Coed** 24,705 undergraduate students, 76% full-time, 51% women, 49% men
- **Moderately difficult** entrance level, 93% of applicants were admitted

Undergraduates 18,779 full-time, 5,926 part-time. Students come from 51 states and territories, 70 other countries, 2% are from out of state, 8% African American, 6% Asian American or Pacific Islander, 44% Hispanic American, 0.5% Native American, 2% international, 10% transferred in, 12% live on campus. *Retention:* 59% of 2006 full-time freshmen returned.

Freshmen *Admission:* 10,929 applied, 10,163 admitted, 4,928 enrolled. *Test scores:* SAT critical reading scores over 500: 48%; SAT math scores over 500: 58%; ACT scores over 18: 81%; SAT critical reading scores over 600: 12%; SAT math scores over 600: 17%; ACT scores over 24: 23%; SAT critical reading scores over 700: 1%; SAT math scores over 700: 2%; ACT scores over 30: 1%.

Faculty *Total:* 1,096, 75% full-time, 42% with terminal degrees. *Student/faculty ratio:* 24:1.

Majors Accounting; actuarial science; American studies; anthropology; architecture; art; art history, criticism and conservation; biological and physical sciences; biology/biological sciences; business administration and management; business/commerce; business/managerial economics; chemistry; civil engineering; classics and languages, literatures and linguistics; clinical laboratory science/medical technology; communication/speech communication and rhetoric; computer engineering; criminal justice/safety; electrical, electronics and communications engineering; English; entrepreneurship; environmental science; finance; French; geography; geology/earth science; Germanic languages; health and physical education; health services/allied health/health sciences; Hispanic-American, Puerto Rican, and Mexican-American/Chicano studies; history; humanities; human resources management; interior architecture; interior design; international business/trade/commerce; management information systems; management science; marketing/marketing management; mass communication/media; mathematics; mechanical engineering; music; music management and merchandising; music performance; music theory and composition; operations management; philosophy; physics; political science and government; psychology; sociology; Spanish; statistics; tourism and travel services management.

Academics *Calendar:* semesters. *Degrees:* bachelor's, master's, and doctoral. *Special study options:* academic remediation for entering students, accelerated degree program, adult/continuing education programs, advanced placement credit, cooperative education, distance learning, double majors, English as a second language, freshman honors college, honors programs, independent study, internships, part-time degree program, services for LD students, study abroad, summer session for credit. *ROTC:* Army (b), Air Force (b).

Computers on Campus 800 computers/terminals are available on campus for general student use. Students can access the following: online (class) registration. Campuswide network is available.

Student Life *Housing options:* coed. Campus housing is university owned and is provided by a third party. *Activities and organizations:* drama/theater group, student-run newspaper, choral group, national fraternities, national sororities. *Campus security:* 24-hour emergency response devices and patrols, crime prevention program, PSA commercials on campus TV, educational programs for students, faculty, and staff; security surveys. *Student services:* health clinic, personal/psychological counseling.

Athletics Member NCAA. All Division I. *Intercollegiate sports:* baseball M (s), basketball M (s)/W (s), cross-country running M (s)/W (s), golf M (s), softball W (s), tennis M (s)/W (s), track and field M (s)/W (s), volleyball W (s). *Intramural sports:* badminton M/W, baseball M, basketball M/W, cross-country running M/W, football M/W, golf M, soccer M/W, softball M/W, table tennis M/W, tennis M/W, track and field M/W, volleyball M/W, weight lifting M/W.

Standardized Tests *Required:* SAT or ACT (for admission). *Required for some:* ACT with writing component.

Costs (2007–08) *Tuition:* state resident $4530 full-time, $151 per hour part-time; nonresident $12,780 full-time, $429 per hour part-time. Full-time tuition and fees vary according to course load. Part-time tuition and fees vary according to course load. *Required fees:* $2147 full-time, $70 per hour part-time, $721 per term part-time. *Room and board:* $8169; room only: $5616. Room and board charges vary according to board plan and housing facility. *Payment plans:* installment, deferred payment. *Waivers:* employees or children of employees.

Financial Aid Of all full-time matriculated undergraduates who enrolled in 2006, 14,068 applied for aid, 10,572 were judged to have need, 2,606 had their need fully met. 526 Federal Work-Study jobs (averaging $2274). 104 state and other part-time jobs (averaging $1707). In 2006, 682 non-need-based awards were made. *Average percent of need met:* 1%. *Average financial aid package:* $6944. *Average need-based loan:* $3677. *Average need-based gift aid:* $4229. *Average non-need-based aid:* $1840. *Average indebtedness upon graduation:* $19,237.

Applying *Options:* electronic application. *Application fee:* $40. *Required:* high school transcript. *Application deadlines:* 7/1 (freshmen), 7/1 (transfers). *Notification:* 11/1 (freshmen), continuous (transfers).

Freshman Application Contact Ms. Jennifer Ehlers, Director of Admissions, The University of Texas at San Antonio, 6900 North Loop 1604 West, San Antonio, TX 78249-0617. *Phone:* 210-458-4536. *Toll-free phone:* 800-669-0919. *Fax:* 210-458-2001. *E-mail:* prospects@utsa.edu.

THE UNIVERSITY OF TEXAS AT TYLER

Tyler, Texas **www.uttyler.edu/**

- **State-supported** comprehensive, founded 1971, part of University of Texas System
- **Urban** 200-acre campus
- **Endowment** $63.7 million
- **Coed** 4,958 undergraduate students, 78% full-time, 59% women, 41% men
- **Moderately difficult** entrance level, 80% of applicants were admitted

Undergraduates 3,876 full-time, 1,082 part-time. 3% are from out of state, 9% African American, 2% Asian American or Pacific Islander, 7% Hispanic American, 1% Native American, 0.6% international, 17% transferred in, 15% live on campus. *Retention:* 68% of 2006 full-time freshmen returned.

Freshmen *Admission:* 1,475 applied, 1,180 admitted, 624 enrolled. *Test scores:* SAT critical reading scores over 500: 59%; SAT math scores over 500: 72%; ACT scores over 18: 97%; SAT critical reading scores over 600: 20%; SAT math scores over 600: 21%; ACT scores over 24: 35%; SAT critical reading scores over 700: 2%; SAT math scores over 700: 1%; ACT scores over 30: 2%.

Faculty *Total:* 381, 66% full-time, 57% with terminal degrees. *Student/faculty ratio:* 17:1.

Majors Accounting; art; biology/biological sciences; business administration and management; chemistry; civil engineering; clinical laboratory science/medical technology; computer and information sciences; computer science; criminal justice/safety; dramatic/theater arts; economics; electrical, electronics and communications engineering; engineering technology; English; finance; foreign languages and literatures; general studies; health and physical education; health professions related; history; human resources development; industrial technology; interdisciplinary studies; journalism; kinesiology and exercise science; liberal arts and sciences/liberal studies; marketing/marketing management; mathematics; mechanical engineering; multi-/interdisciplinary studies related; music; nursing (registered nurse training); nursing science; political science and government; psychology; sociology; Spanish; speech and rhetoric.

Academics *Calendar:* semesters. *Degrees:* bachelor's, master's, and post-bachelor's certificates. *Special study options:* adult/continuing education programs, advanced placement credit, cooperative education, distance learning, double majors, English as a second language, independent study, internships, part-time degree program, services for LD students, student-designed majors, study abroad, summer session for credit.

Computers on Campus 139 computers/terminals are available on campus for general student use. Students can access the following: computer help desk, free student e-mail accounts, online (class) grades, online (class) registration. Campus-wide network is available. 100% of college-owned or -operated housing units are wired for high-speed Internet access. Wireless service is available via classrooms, computer centers, computer labs, learning centers, libraries, student centers.

Student Life *Housing:* on-campus residence required for freshman year. *Options:* coed. Campus housing is university owned and is provided by a third party. Freshman applicants given priority for college housing. *Activities and organizations:* student-run newspaper, choral group, Student Government Association, Pre-Med/Pre-Dental Club, American Chemistry Society, Press Club, Latin Club, national fraternities, national sororities. *Campus security:* 24-hour emergency response devices and patrols, late-night transport/escort service, controlled dormitory access. *Student services:* health clinic, personal/psychological counseling.

Athletics Member NCAA. All Division III. *Intercollegiate sports:* baseball M, basketball M/W, cheerleading M/W, cross-country running M/W, golf M/W, soccer M/W, tennis M/W, track and field M/W, volleyball W. *Intramural sports:* baseball M, basketball M/W, bowling M/W, football M/W, golf M/W, racquetball M/W, soccer M/W, softball M/W, swimming and diving M/W, table tennis M/W, tennis M/W, ultimate Frisbee M/W, volleyball W, wrestling M.

Standardized Tests *Required:* SAT or ACT (for admission).

Costs (2007–08) *Tuition:* state resident $4050 full-time, $50 per semester hour part-time; nonresident $12,390 full-time, $328 per semester hour part-time. Full-time tuition and fees vary according to course load and degree level. *Required fees:* $1332 full-time. *Room and board:* $7338; room only: $4802. Room and board charges vary according to board plan and housing facility. *Payment plan:* installment. *Waivers:* senior citizens and employees or children of employees.

Financial Aid Of all full-time matriculated undergraduates who enrolled in 2006, 2,448 applied for aid, 1,924 were judged to have need, 377 had their need fully met. 89 Federal Work-Study jobs (averaging $2882). 33 state and other part-time jobs (averaging $1821). In 2006, 276 non-need-based awards were made. *Average percent of need met:* 65%. *Average financial aid package:* $7470. *Average need-based loan:* $3666. *Average need-based gift aid:* $4565. *Average non-need-based aid:* $2162. *Average indebtedness upon graduation:* $13,204.

Applying *Options:* electronic application, deferred entrance. *Application fee:* $25. *Required:* high school transcript. *Application deadlines:* rolling (freshmen), rolling (transfers). *Notification:* continuous (freshmen), continuous (transfers).

Freshman Application Contact Mr. Jim Hutto, Assistant Vice President, Enrollment Management, The University of Texas at Tyler, 3900 University Boulevard, Tyler, TX 75799-0001. *Phone:* 903-566-7195. *Toll-free phone:* 800-UTTYLER. *Fax:* 903-566-7068. *E-mail:* admissions@uttyler.edu.

THE UNIVERSITY OF TEXAS HEALTH SCIENCE CENTER AT HOUSTON

Houston, Texas **www.uth.tmc.edu/**

Application Contact Mr. Robert L. Jenkins, Registrar, The University of Texas Health Science Center at Houston, 7000 Fannin, PO Box 20036, Houston, TX 77225-0036. *Phone:* 713-500-3361.

THE UNIVERSITY OF TEXAS HEALTH SCIENCE CENTER AT SAN ANTONIO

San Antonio, Texas **www.uthscsa.edu/**

Application Contact The University of Texas Health Science Center at San Antonio, 7703 Floyd Curl Drive, San Antonio, TX 78229-3900. *Phone:* 210-567-2621. *Fax:* 210-567-2685. *E-mail:* registrars@uthscsa.edu.

THE UNIVERSITY OF TEXAS MEDICAL BRANCH

Galveston, Texas **www.utmb.edu/**

- **State-supported** upper-level, founded 1891, part of University of Texas System
- **Small-town** 85-acre campus with easy access to Houston
- **Endowment** $496.9 million
- **Coed** 562 undergraduate students, 54% full-time, 80% women, 20% men
- **Very difficult** entrance level

Undergraduates 302 full-time, 260 part-time. Students come from 6 states and territories, 13 other countries, 1% are from out of state, 15% African American, 17% Asian American or Pacific Islander, 13% Hispanic American, 0.2% Native American, 2% international, 41% transferred in.

Majors Clinical laboratory science/medical technology; nursing (registered nurse training); respiratory care therapy.

Academics *Calendar:* semesters (early semester). *Degrees:* bachelor's, master's, doctoral, first professional, and post-master's certificates. *Special study options:* advanced placement credit, distance learning, independent study, internships, part-time degree program, services for LD students, summer session for credit.

Computers on Campus Students can access the following: campus intranet, computer help desk, free student e-mail accounts, online (class) grades, online (class) registration. Campuswide network is available.

Student Life *Housing options:* coed. Campus housing is university owned. *Activities and organizations:* student-run newspaper, Texas Medical Association, American Medical Student Association, American Medical Women's Association, Texas Association Latin American Medical Students, National Medical Student Association, national fraternities. *Campus security:* 24-hour emergency response devices and patrols, late-night transport/escort service. *Student services:* health clinic, personal/psychological counseling, legal services.

Athletics *Intercollegiate sports:* ultimate Frisbee M (s)/W (s), volleyball M (s)/W (s). *Intramural sports:* basketball M/W, football M/W, soccer M/W, softball M/W, ultimate Frisbee M/W, volleyball M/W.

Costs (2007–08) *Tuition:* state resident $3504 full-time, $146 per credit hour part-time; nonresident $10,176 full-time, $424 per credit hour part-time. *Required fees:* $368 full-time, $122 per term part-time, $125 per year part-time.

Financial Aid Of all full-time matriculated undergraduates who enrolled in 2005, 362 applied for aid, 345 were judged to have need, 2 had their need fully met. 27 Federal Work-Study jobs (averaging $1654). In 2005, 17 non-need-based awards were made. *Average percent of need met:* 81%. *Average financial aid package:* $7026. *Average need-based loan:* $6077. *Average need-based gift aid:* $3575. *Average non-need-based aid:* $1000. *Average indebtedness upon graduation:* $25,083.

Applying *Options:* electronic application. *Application fee:* $30. *Notification:* continuous (transfers).

Application Contact Ms. Vicki Brewer, Registrar, The University of Texas Medical Branch, 301 University Boulevard, Galveston, TX 77555-1305. *Phone:* 409-772-1215. *Fax:* 409-772-4466. *E-mail:* enrollment.services@utmb.edu.

THE UNIVERSITY OF TEXAS OF THE PERMIAN BASIN

Odessa, Texas **www.utpb.edu/**

- **State-supported** comprehensive, founded 1969, part of University of Texas System
- **Urban** 600-acre campus
- **Coed** 2,754 undergraduate students, 72% full-time, 61% women, 39% men
- **Moderately difficult** entrance level, 98% of applicants were admitted

Undergraduates 1,976 full-time, 778 part-time. Students come from 25 states and territories, 13 other countries, 3% are from out of state, 5% African American, 2% Asian American or Pacific Islander, 40% Hispanic American, 0.9% Native American, 0.4% international, 13% transferred in, 8% live on campus. *Retention:* 62% of 2006 full-time freshmen returned.

Freshmen *Admission:* 716 applied, 701 admitted, 376 enrolled. *Average high school GPA:* 3.34. *Test scores:* SAT critical reading scores over 500: 36%; SAT math scores over 500: 47%; ACT scores over 18: 80%; SAT critical reading scores over 600: 9%; SAT math scores over 600: 13%; ACT scores over 24: 13%; SAT math scores over 700: 1%; ACT scores over 30: 1%.

Faculty *Total:* 224, 46% full-time, 55% with terminal degrees. *Student/faculty ratio:* 18:1.

Majors Accounting; art; biology/biological sciences; business administration and management; chemistry; computer science; criminology; economics; English; environmental studies; finance; geology/earth science; history; humanities; interdisciplinary studies; kinesiology and exercise science; marketing/marketing management; mass communication/media; mathematics; political science and government; psychology; sociology; Spanish; speech and rhetoric.

Academics *Calendar:* semesters. *Degrees:* bachelor's and master's. *Special study options:* academic remediation for entering students, accelerated degree program, advanced placement credit, distance learning, double majors, independent study, internships, part-time degree program, summer session for credit. *Unusual degree programs:* 3-2 accounting.

Computers on Campus 170 computers/terminals are available on campus for general student use. Students can access the following: free student e-mail accounts, online (class) grades, online (class) registration, online (class) schedules. Campuswide network is available.

Student Life *Housing options:* Campus housing is university owned. *Activities and organizations:* student-run newspaper. *Campus security:* 24-hour patrols, late-night transport/escort service. *Student services:* personal/psychological counseling.

Athletics Member NCAA. All Division II. *Intercollegiate sports:* baseball M (s), basketball M (s)/W (s), cheerleading W (s), cross-country running M (s)/W (s), soccer M (s)/W (s), softball W, swimming and diving M (s)/W (s), volleyball W (s). *Intramural sports:* badminton M/W, basketball M/W, bowling M/W, football M, golf M/W, racquetball M/W, rugby M, soccer M/W, swimming and diving M/W, table tennis M/W, tennis M/W, volleyball M/W, weight lifting M/W.

Standardized Tests *Required:* SAT or ACT (for admission).

Costs (2007–08) *One-time required fee:* $55. *Tuition:* state resident $3096 full-time, $100 per semester hour part-time; nonresident $9768 full-time, $358 per semester hour part-time. *Required fees:* $806 full-time. *Room and board:* $4160.

Financial Aid Of all full-time matriculated undergraduates who enrolled in 2007, 2,399 applied for aid, 1,727 were judged to have need, 359 had their need fully met. 75 Federal Work-Study jobs (averaging $2350). 12 state and other part-time jobs (averaging $650). In 2007, 390 non-need-based awards were made. *Average percent of need met:* 48%. *Average financial aid package:* $6051. *Average need-based loan:* $5166. *Average need-based gift aid:* $3256. *Average non-need-based aid:* $931. *Average indebtedness upon graduation:* $13,121.

Applying *Options:* electronic application, deferred entrance. *Required:* high school transcript. *Required for some:* letters of recommendation, interview. *Application deadlines:* 8/15 (freshmen), rolling (transfers). *Notification:* continuous (freshmen), continuous (transfers).

Director of Admissions Trey Wetendorf, Director of Admissions, The University of Texas of the Permian Basin, 4901 East University, Odessa, TX 79762-0001. *Phone:* 432-552-2605. *Toll-free phone:* 866-552-UTPB. *E-mail:* wetendorf_t@utpb.edu.

THE UNIVERSITY OF TEXAS–PAN AMERICAN

Edinburg, Texas **www.utpa.edu/**

- **State-supported** comprehensive, founded 1927, part of University of Texas System
- **Small-town** 289-acre campus with easy access to McAllen-Edinburg-Mission MSA
- **Endowment** $67.2 million
- **Coed** 15,187 undergraduate students, 74% full-time, 58% women, 42% men
- **Noncompetitive** entrance level, 62% of applicants were admitted

Undergraduates 11,238 full-time, 3,949 part-time. Students come from 36 states and territories, 81 other countries, 1% are from out of state, 0.6% African American, 1% Asian American or Pacific Islander, 88% Hispanic American, 0.1% Native American, 5% international, 6% transferred in, 4% live on campus. *Retention:* 68% of 2006 full-time freshmen returned.

Freshmen *Admission:* 6,884 applied, 4,266 admitted, 2,626 enrolled. *Test scores:* SAT critical reading scores over 500: 33%; SAT math scores over 500: 37%; SAT writing scores over 500: 33%; ACT scores over 18: 63%; SAT critical reading scores over 600: 8%; SAT math scores over 600: 10%; SAT writing scores over 600: 7%; ACT scores over 24: 11%; SAT critical reading scores over 700: 1%; SAT math scores over 700: 1%; SAT writing scores over 700: 1%; ACT scores over 30: 1%.

Faculty *Total:* 760, 83% full-time. *Student/faculty ratio:* 20:1.

Majors Accounting; American studies; anthropology; art; audiology and speech-language pathology; biology/biological sciences; business administration and management; chemistry; clinical laboratory science/medical technology; communication/speech communication and rhetoric; computer and information sciences; computer engineering; computer science; criminal justice/law enforcement administration; dance; dietetics; dramatic/theater arts; economics; electrical, electronics and communications engineering; English; finance; fine/studio arts; French; general studies; health and physical education; health services/allied health/health sciences; Hispanic-American, Puerto Rican, and Mexican-American/Chicano studies; history; interdisciplinary studies; international business/trade/commerce; journalism; management information systems; manufacturing engineering; marketing/marketing management; mathematics; mechanical engineering; multi-/interdisciplinary studies related; music; nursing (registered nurse training); philosophy; physician assistant; physics; political science and government; psychology; rehabilitation and therapeutic professions related; social sciences; social work; sociology; Spanish; substance abuse/addiction counseling.

Academics *Calendar:* semesters. *Degrees:* bachelor's, master's, and doctoral. *Special study options:* academic remediation for entering students, adult/

continuing education programs, advanced placement credit, cooperative education, distance learning, double majors, honors programs, independent study, internships, part-time degree program, services for LD students, study abroad, summer session for credit. *ROTC:* Army (b). *Unusual degree programs:* accounting.

Computers on Campus Students can access the following: campus intranet, computer help desk, free student e-mail accounts, online (class) grades, online (class) registration, online (class) schedules. Campuswide network is available. 100% of college-owned or -operated housing units are wired for high-speed Internet access. Wireless service is available via entire campus.

Student Life *Housing options:* coed, men-only, women-only. Campus housing is university owned. *Activities and organizations:* drama/theater group, student-run newspaper, choral group, Accounting Society, American Marketing Association, Pre-Medical/Bio Medical Society, Association of Texas Professional Educators, Financial Management Association, national fraternities, national sororities. *Campus security:* 24-hour emergency response devices and patrols, late-night transport/escort service. *Student services:* health clinic, personal/psychological counseling.

Athletics Member NCAA. All Division I. *Intercollegiate sports:* baseball M (s), basketball M (s)/W (s), cross-country running M (s)/W (s), golf M (s)/W (s), tennis M (s)/W (s), track and field M (s)/W (s), volleyball W (s). *Intramural sports:* badminton M/W, basketball M/W, bowling M/W, cheerleading M/W, football M/W, racquetball M/W, soccer M/W, softball M/W, tennis M/W, volleyball M/W.

Standardized Tests *Required:* SAT or ACT (for admission).

Costs (2007–08) *Tuition:* state resident $3100 full-time, $139 per semester hour part-time; nonresident $9772 full-time, $407 per semester hour part-time. Full-time tuition and fees vary according to course load and location. Part-time tuition and fees vary according to course load and location. *Required fees:* $799 full-time, $475 per term part-time. *Room and board:* $4900; room only: $3000. Room and board charges vary according to board plan and housing facility. *Payment plan:* installment. *Waivers:* senior citizens.

Financial Aid Of all full-time matriculated undergraduates who enrolled in 2006, 8,957 applied for aid, 8,570 were judged to have need, 772 had their need fully met. 880 Federal Work-Study jobs (averaging $2064). 105 state and other part-time jobs (averaging $2246). In 2006, 531 non-need-based awards were made. *Average percent of need met:* 85%. *Average financial aid package:* $8563. *Average need-based loan:* $4121. *Average need-based gift aid:* $8662. *Average non-need-based aid:* $5689. *Average indebtedness upon graduation:* $11,995.

Applying *Options:* electronic application. *Required:* high school transcript, minimum 2.0 GPA. *Required for some:* interview. *Application deadlines:* 8/11 (freshmen), 8/11 (transfers). *Notification:* continuous (freshmen), continuous (transfers).

Freshman Application Contact Dr. Magdalena Hinojosa, Dean of Admissions and Enrollment Services, The University of Texas–Pan American, Office of Admissions and Records, 1201 West University Drive, Edinburg, TX 78541. *Phone:* 956-381-2481. *Fax:* 956-381-2321. *E-mail:* recruitment@utpa.edu.

THE UNIVERSITY OF TEXAS SOUTHWESTERN MEDICAL CENTER AT DALLAS

Dallas, Texas **www.utsouthwestern.edu/**

- **State-supported** upper-level, founded 1943, part of University of Texas System
- **Urban** 98-acre campus
- **Endowment** $1.1 billion
- **Coed** 119 undergraduate students, 87% full-time, 76% women, 24% men
- **Moderately difficult** entrance level, 43% of applicants were admitted

Undergraduates 104 full-time, 15 part-time. Students come from 5 states and territories, 12 other countries, 9% are from out of state, 15% African American, 10% Asian American or Pacific Islander, 10% Hispanic American, 0.8% Native American, 9% international, 33% transferred in.

Freshmen *Admission:* 117 applied, 50 admitted.

Faculty *Total:* 1,928, 77% full-time.

Majors Clinical laboratory science/medical technology; dietetics; orthotics/prosthetics.

Academics *Calendar:* semesters. *Degrees:* bachelor's, master's, doctoral, first professional, and postbachelor's certificates. *Special study options:* advanced placement credit, distance learning, independent study, internships.

Computers on Campus 150 computers/terminals are available on campus for general student use. Students can access the following: campus intranet, free student e-mail accounts, online (class) grades, online (class) schedules. Campuswide network is available.

Student Life *Housing:* college housing not available. *Campus security:* 24-hour patrols, late-night transport/escort service. *Student services:* health clinic.

Athletics *Intramural sports:* badminton M/W, basketball M/W, football M, golf M/W, racquetball M/W, soccer M/W, table tennis M/W, tennis M/W, volleyball M/W.

Costs (2007–08) *Tuition:* state resident $3300 full-time, $158 per credit hour part-time; nonresident $11,640 full-time, $436 per credit hour part-time.

Financial Aid Of all full-time matriculated undergraduates who enrolled in 2006, 89 applied for aid, 89 were judged to have need. 10 Federal Work-Study jobs (averaging $1933). *Average indebtedness upon graduation:* $36,000.

Applying *Options:* electronic application. *Application fee:* $10. *Application deadline:* rolling (transfers). *Notification:* continuous (transfers).

Application Contact The University of Texas Southwestern Medical Center at Dallas, 5323 Harry Hines Boulevard, Dallas, TX 75390-9096. *Phone:* 214-648-5617.

UNIVERSITY OF THE INCARNATE WORD

San Antonio, Texas **www.uiw.edu/**

- **Independent Roman Catholic** comprehensive, founded 1881
- **Urban** 200-acre campus
- **Endowment** $50.7 million
- **Coed** 4,698 undergraduate students, 62% full-time, 68% women, 32% men
- **Moderately difficult** entrance level, 80% of applicants were admitted

Undergraduates 2,899 full-time, 1,799 part-time. Students come from 39 states and territories, 31 other countries, 6% are from out of state, 7% African American, 2% Asian American or Pacific Islander, 58% Hispanic American, 0.4% Native American, 2% international, 19% live on campus. *Retention:* 67% of 2006 full-time freshmen returned.

Freshmen *Admission:* 1,982 applied, 1,589 admitted, 718 enrolled. *Average high school GPA:* 3.36. *Test scores:* SAT critical reading scores over 500: 38%; SAT math scores over 500: 37%; SAT writing scores over 500: 31%; ACT scores over 18: 58%; SAT critical reading scores over 600: 7%; SAT math scores over 600: 8%; SAT writing scores over 600: 5%; ACT scores over 24: 13%; SAT critical reading scores over 700: 1%.

Faculty *Total:* 504, 36% full-time, 27% with terminal degrees. *Student/faculty ratio:* 13:1.

Majors Area, ethnic, cultural, and gender studies related; art; athletic training; biology/biological sciences; business administration and management; business administration, management and operations related; chemistry; child development; communication/speech communication and rhetoric; computer and information sciences; design and applied arts related; dramatic/theater arts; educational administration and supervision related; elementary education; engineering related; English; environmental science; history; human resources management; interior design; kinesiology and exercise science; liberal arts and sciences/liberal studies; mathematics; meteorology; multi-/interdisciplinary studies related; music; music related; music therapy; nuclear medical technology; nursing (registered nurse training); nutrition sciences; organizational behavior; philosophy; political science and government; psychology; religious studies; sociology; Spanish.

Academics *Calendar:* semesters. *Degrees:* associate, bachelor's, master's, doctoral, first professional, and postbachelor's certificates. *Special study options:* academic remediation for entering students, accelerated degree program, adult/continuing education programs, advanced placement credit, double majors, English as a second language, external degree program, independent study, internships, off-campus study, part-time degree program, services for LD students, study abroad, summer session for credit. *ROTC:* Army (c), Air Force (c).

Computers on Campus Students can access the following: computer help desk, free student e-mail accounts, online (class) grades, online (class) registration, online (class) schedules. Campuswide network is available. Wireless service is available via entire campus.

Student Life *Housing options:* coed, men-only, women-only. Campus housing is university owned. Freshman applicants given priority for college housing. *Activities and organizations:* drama/theater group, student-run newspaper, radio station, choral group, Business Club, Pre-Pharmacy Association, Black Student Association, APhA—ASP/SNpHa, Alpha Sigma Alpha, national fraternities, national sororities. *Campus security:* 24-hour emergency response devices and patrols, late-night transport/escort service, controlled dormitory access. *Student services:* health clinic, personal/psychological counseling.

Athletics Member NCAA. All Division II. *Intercollegiate sports:* baseball M (s), basketball M (s)/W (s), cross-country running M (s)/W (s), golf M (s)/W (s), soccer M (s)/W (s), softball W (s), swimming and diving M (s)/W (s), tennis M (s)/W (s), track and field M (s)/W (s), volleyball W (s). *Intramural sports:* basketball M/W, football M/W, racquetball M/W, soccer M/W, softball M/W, swimming and diving M/W, table tennis M/W, tennis M/W, volleyball M/W.

Standardized Tests *Required:* SAT or ACT (for admission).

Costs (2008–09) *Comprehensive fee:* $27,640 includes full-time tuition ($19,400), mandatory fees ($860), and room and board ($7380). Part-time tuition: $640 per semester hour. *Required fees:* $200 per term part-time. *College room only:* $4250.

Financial Aid Of all full-time matriculated undergraduates who enrolled in 2007, 2,729 applied for aid, 2,135 were judged to have need, 532 had their need fully met. 17 Federal Work-Study jobs (averaging $1930). 440 state and other part-time jobs (averaging $1122). In 2007, 526 non-need-based awards were made. *Average percent of need met:* 58%. *Average financial aid package:* $12,116. *Average need-based loan:* $3671. *Average need-based gift aid:* $6204. *Average non-need-based aid:* $5317. *Average indebtedness upon graduation:* $30,613.

Applying *Options:* electronic application, early admission, deferred entrance. *Application fee:* $20. *Required:* high school transcript. *Required for some:* essay or personal statement, interview. *Recommended:* minimum 2.0 GPA, 1 letter of recommendation. *Application deadlines:* rolling (freshmen), rolling (transfers).

Freshman Application Contact Ms. Andrea Cyterski-Acosta, Dean of Enrollment, University of the Incarnate Word, Box 285, San Antonio, TX 78209-6397. *Phone:* 210-829-6005. *Toll-free phone:* 800-749-WORD. *Fax:* 210-829-3921. *E-mail:* admis@uiwtx.edu.

See page 2568 for the College Close-Up.

WAYLAND BAPTIST UNIVERSITY

Plainview, Texas **www.wbu.edu/**

- **Independent Baptist** comprehensive, founded 1908
- **Small-town** 80-acre campus
- **Endowment** $52.7 million
- **Coed** 1,047 undergraduate students, 79% full-time, 55% women, 45% men
- **Minimally difficult** entrance level, 75% of applicants were admitted

Undergraduates 832 full-time, 215 part-time. Students come from 20 states and territories, 14 other countries, 11% are from out of state, 4% African American, 0.8% Asian American or Pacific Islander, 24% Hispanic American, 0.7% Native American, 2% international, 6% transferred in, 53% live on campus. *Retention:* 64% of 2006 full-time freshmen returned.

Freshmen *Admission:* 334 applied, 252 admitted, 252 enrolled. *Average high school GPA:* 3.64. *Test scores:* SAT critical reading scores over 500: 35%; SAT math scores over 500: 41%; SAT writing scores over 500: 32%; ACT scores over 18: 69%; SAT critical reading scores over 600: 11%; SAT math scores over 600: 14%; SAT writing scores over 600: 10%; ACT scores over 24: 15%; SAT critical reading scores over 700: 3%; SAT math scores over 700: 2%; ACT scores over 30: 3%.

Faculty *Total:* 115, 66% full-time, 52% with terminal degrees. *Student/faculty ratio:* 11:1.

Majors Art; biology/biological sciences; business administration and management; chemistry; Christian studies; criminal justice/safety; dramatic/theater arts; education related; elementary education; English; history; human services; mass communication/media; mathematics; music; music teacher education; physical education teaching and coaching; physical sciences; political science and government; psychology; religious education; religious/sacred music; social sciences; social sciences related; Spanish; theology and religious vocations related; trade and industrial teacher education.

Academics *Calendar:* semesters. *Degrees:* associate, bachelor's, and master's (branch locations in Anchorage, AK; Amarillo, TX; Luke Airforce Base, AZ; Glorieta, NM; Aiea, HI; Lubbock, TX; San Antonio, TX; Wichita Falls, TX). *Special study options:* academic remediation for entering students, accelerated degree program, adult/continuing education programs, advanced placement credit, distance learning, double majors, external degree program, honors programs, internships, part-time degree program, summer session for credit. *ROTC:* Army (c), Air Force (c). *Unusual degree programs:* 3-2 engineering with Texas Tech University.

Computers on Campus 241 computers/terminals are available on campus for general student use. Students can access the following: computer help desk, free student e-mail accounts, online (class) grades, online (class) registration, online (class) schedules. Campuswide network is available. 100% of college-owned or -operated housing units are wired for high-speed Internet access. Wireless service is available via libraries, student centers.

Student Life *Housing:* on-campus residence required through junior year. *Options:* men-only, women-only. Campus housing is university owned. Freshman campus housing is guaranteed. *Activities and organizations:* drama/theater group, student-run newspaper, radio and television station, choral group, marching band, student government, national fraternities, national sororities. *Campus security:* 24-hour emergency response devices and patrols, security lighting. *Student services:* health clinic, personal/psychological counseling.

Athletics Member NAIA. *Intercollegiate sports:* baseball M (s), basketball M (s)/W (s), cheerleading M (s)/W (s), cross-country running M (s)/W (s), golf M (s), soccer M (s), track and field M (s)/W (s), volleyball W (s). *Intramural sports:* basketball M/W, football M/W, golf M/W, softball M/W, volleyball M/W.

Standardized Tests *Required:* SAT or ACT (for admission). *Recommended:* ACT (for admission).

Costs (2007–08) *Comprehensive fee:* $14,834 includes full-time tuition ($10,650), mandatory fees ($600), and room and board ($3584). Full-time tuition and fees vary according to course load and location. Part-time tuition: $355 per credit hour. Part-time tuition and fees vary according to course load and location. *Required fees:* $50 per term part-time. *College room only:* $1276. Room and board charges vary according to board plan and housing facility. *Payment plan:* installment. *Waivers:* employees or children of employees.

Financial Aid Of all full-time matriculated undergraduates who enrolled in 2006, 704 applied for aid, 576 were judged to have need, 115 had their need fully met. 167 Federal Work-Study jobs (averaging $1409). 356 state and other part-time jobs (averaging $1703). In 2006, 187 non-need-based awards were made. *Average percent of need met:* 68%. *Average financial aid package:* $9423. *Average need-based loan:* $2580. *Average need-based gift aid:* $6653. *Average non-need-based aid:* $9206. *Average indebtedness upon graduation:* $18,288.

Applying *Options:* electronic application. *Application fee:* $35. *Required:* high school transcript. *Recommended:* interview. *Application deadlines:* 8/1 (freshmen), rolling (transfers). *Notification:* continuous (freshmen), continuous (transfers).

Freshman Application Contact Ms. Debbie Stennett, Director of Student Admissions, Wayland Baptist University, 1900 West 7th Street, CMB #712, Plainview, TX 79072. *Phone:* 806-291-3500. *Toll-free phone:* 800-588-1928. *Fax:* 806-291-1960. *E-mail:* admityou@wbu.edu.

WEST TEXAS A&M UNIVERSITY

Canyon, Texas **www.wtamu.edu/**

- **State-supported** comprehensive, founded 1909, part of Texas A&M University System
- **Small-town** 128-acre campus
- **Endowment** $14.2 million
- **Coed** 5,849 undergraduate students, 76% full-time, 55% women, 45% men
- **Moderately difficult** entrance level, 71% of applicants were admitted

Undergraduates 4,453 full-time, 1,396 part-time. Students come from 39 states and territories, 25 other countries, 8% are from out of state, 5% African American, 2% Asian American or Pacific Islander, 18% Hispanic American, 1% Native American, 2% international, 12% transferred in, 19% live on campus. *Retention:* 63% of 2006 full-time freshmen returned.

Freshmen *Admission:* 2,340 applied, 1,660 admitted, 960 enrolled. *Test scores:* SAT critical reading scores over 500: 51%; SAT math scores over 500: 56%; ACT scores over 18: 79%; SAT critical reading scores over 600: 15%; SAT math scores over 600: 14%; ACT scores over 24: 20%; SAT critical reading scores over 700: 1%; SAT math scores over 700: 1%; ACT scores over 30: 1%.

Faculty *Total:* 310, 77% full-time, 55% with terminal degrees. *Student/faculty ratio:* 20:1.

Majors Accounting; advertising; agribusiness; agricultural business and management; agriculture; agronomy and crop science; animal sciences; art; biology/biological sciences; biotechnology; broadcast journalism; business administration and management; business/commerce; business/managerial economics; chemistry; clinical laboratory science/medical technology; commercial and advertising art; communication disorders; computer and information sciences; criminal justice/law enforcement administration; dance; dramatic/theater arts; economics; English; environmental science; equestrian studies; finance; fine/studio arts; general studies; geography; geology/earth science; health and physical education; history; industrial technology; interdisciplinary studies; journalism; management information systems; marketing/marketing management; mass communication/media; mathematics; mechanical engineering; multi-/interdisciplinary studies related; music; music performance; music theory and composition; music therapy; nursing (registered nurse training); physics; plant protection and integrated pest management; political science and government; pre-law studies; psychology;

public administration; social sciences; social work; sociology; Spanish; speech and rhetoric; wildlife and wildlands science and management.

Academics *Calendar:* semesters. *Degrees:* bachelor's, master's, and doctoral. *Special study options:* academic remediation for entering students, adult/continuing education programs, advanced placement credit, cooperative education, distance learning, double majors, English as a second language, honors programs, independent study, internships, part-time degree program, services for LD students, study abroad, summer session for credit. *Unusual degree programs:* 3-2 engineering with Texas Tech University, Texas A&M University; accounting.

Computers on Campus 1,200 computers/terminals are available on campus for general student use. Students can access the following: free student e-mail accounts, online (class) registration. Campuswide network is available. Wireless service is available via entire campus.

Student Life *Housing:* on-campus residence required through sophomore year. *Options:* coed, men-only, women-only, disabled students. Campus housing is university owned. Freshman campus housing is guaranteed. *Activities and organizations:* drama/theater group, student-run newspaper, radio station, choral group, marching band, Residence Hall Association, Student Organizations' Roundtable, Student government, Students in Free Enterprise, national fraternities, national sororities. *Campus security:* 24-hour emergency response devices and patrols, late-night transport/escort service, controlled dormitory access. *Student services:* health clinic, personal/psychological counseling.

Athletics Member NCAA. All Division II. *Intercollegiate sports:* baseball M (s), basketball M (s)/W (s), bowling M (s) (c)/W (s) (c), cross-country running M (s)/W (s), equestrian sports M (c)/W (s), football M (s), golf M (s)/W (s), soccer M (s)/W (s), softball W (s), volleyball W (s). *Intramural sports:* badminton M/W, basketball M/W, bowling M/W, football M/W, golf M/W, racquetball M/W, soccer M/W, softball M/W, swimming and diving M/W, table tennis M/W, tennis M/W, volleyball M/W, wrestling M.

Standardized Tests *Required:* SAT or ACT (for admission).

Costs (2008–09) *Room and board:* $5627.

Financial Aid Of all full-time matriculated undergraduates who enrolled in 2005, 3,049 applied for aid, 2,804 were judged to have need, 2,301 had their need fully met. 149 Federal Work-Study jobs (averaging $1288). 97 state and other part-time jobs (averaging $557). In 2005, 582 non-need-based awards were made. *Average percent of need met:* 63%. *Average financial aid package:* $6518. *Average need-based loan:* $3743. *Average need-based gift aid:* $3557. *Average non-need-based aid:* $4859. *Average indebtedness upon graduation:* $13,136.

Applying *Options:* electronic application, deferred entrance. *Application fee:* $25. *Required:* high school transcript, class rank and Texas high school curriculum or equivalent. *Application deadlines:* rolling (freshmen), rolling (transfers). *Notification:* continuous (freshmen), continuous (transfers).

Freshman Application Contact Mr. Shawn Thomas, Director of Admissions, West Texas A&M University, WT Box 60907, Canyon, TX 79016-0001. *Phone:* 806-651-2020. *Toll-free phone:* 800-99-WTAMU. *Fax:* 806-651-5285. *E-mail:* sthomas@mail.wtamu.edu.

WILEY COLLEGE

Marshall, Texas

www.wileyc.edu/

- **Independent** 4-year, founded 1873, affiliated with United Methodist Church
- **Small-town** 58-acre campus
- **Endowment** $3.9 million
- **Coed** 925 undergraduate students, 87% full-time, 59% women, 41% men
- **Minimally difficult** entrance level, 40% of applicants were admitted

Undergraduates 803 full-time, 122 part-time. Students come from 25 states and territories, 7 other countries, 45% are from out of state, 89% African American, 3% Hispanic American, 0.2% Native American, 3% international, 11% transferred in, 51% live on campus. *Retention:* 100% of 2006 full-time freshmen returned.

Freshmen *Admission:* 976 applied, 386 admitted, 221 enrolled. *Average high school GPA:* 2.53. *Test scores:* SAT critical reading scores over 500: 25%.

Faculty *Total:* 80, 64% full-time, 41% with terminal degrees. *Student/faculty ratio:* 15:1.

Majors Administrative assistant and secretarial science; biology/biological sciences; business administration and management; business teacher education; chemistry; computer and information sciences; computer science; criminal justice/safety; elementary education; English; history; hotel/motel administration; mass communication/media; mathematics; music; music teacher education; philosophy; physical education teaching and coaching; physical sciences; physics; pre-dentistry studies; pre-law studies; pre-medical studies; religious studies; social sciences; social work; sociology; special education.

Academics *Calendar:* semesters. *Degrees:* associate and bachelor's. *Special study options:* academic remediation for entering students, adult/continuing education programs, off-campus study, part-time degree program, student-designed majors, study abroad, summer session for credit.

Computers on Campus 198 computers/terminals and 30 ports are available on campus for general student use. Students can access the following: campus intranet, computer help desk, free student e-mail accounts, online (class) grades, online (class) registration, online (class) schedules. Campuswide network is available. 100% of college-owned or -operated housing units are wired for high-speed Internet access. Wireless service is available via entire campus.

Student Life *Housing:* on-campus residence required for freshman year. *Options:* men-only, women-only. Campus housing is university owned. Freshman applicants given priority for college housing. *Activities and organizations:* drama/theater group, student-run newspaper, national fraternities, national sororities. *Campus security:* 24-hour patrols, controlled dormitory access. *Student services:* health clinic, personal/psychological counseling.

Athletics Member NAIA. *Intercollegiate sports:* baseball M (s), basketball M (s)/W (s), cheerleading M/W, track and field M (s)/W (s), volleyball W (s). *Intramural sports:* basketball M/W, track and field M/W, volleyball M/W.

Standardized Tests *Recommended:* SAT or ACT (for admission).

Costs (2007–08) *Comprehensive fee:* $13,572 includes full-time tuition ($6472), mandatory fees ($1800), and room and board ($5300). Part-time tuition: $253 per hour. *Required fees:* $900 per term part-time. *College room only:* $2550.

Financial Aid Of all full-time matriculated undergraduates who enrolled in 2003, 531 applied for aid, 531 were judged to have need, 79 had their need fully met. *Average percent of need met:* 52%. *Average financial aid package:* $6061. *Average need-based loan:* $2945. *Average need-based gift aid:* $4453. *Average non-need-based aid:* $6638. *Average indebtedness upon graduation:* $12,321.

Applying *Options:* electronic application, early admission, deferred entrance. *Application fee:* $10. *Required:* high school transcript, 1 letter of recommendation. *Application deadlines:* 8/1 (freshmen), 8/1 (transfers). *Notification:* continuous until 8/10 (freshmen), continuous until 8/10 (transfers).

Director of Admissions Ms. Alvena Jones, Interim Director of Admissions/Recruitment, Wiley College, 711 Wiley Avenue, Marshall, TX 75670. *Phone:* 903-927-3222. *Toll-free phone:* 800-658-6889. *Fax:* 903-923-8878. *E-mail:* ajones@wileyc.edu.

ABILENE CHRISTIAN UNIVERSITY

ABILENE, TEXAS

The University

Abilene Christian University (ACU) offers an exceptional education in a distinctive Christian environment at an affordable price. ACU believes strongly in the dignity and worth of the individual and in academic integrity, achieving success, and enjoying life. Christian education at ACU integrates faith and hands-on learning, represented in every facet of campus life.

Founded in 1906, ACU is a selective, four-year, private Christian university with an enrollment of approximately 4,700 students. ACU is one of the largest private universities in the Southwest and is affiliated with the Churches of Christ.

Students may choose from among sixty-one bachelor's programs that include more than 100 areas of study, twenty-six master's programs, and one doctoral program. Work completed at ACU is accepted by all colleges and universities in the United States. The University is accredited by the Commission on Colleges of the Southern Association of Colleges and Schools, and the College of Business Administration is accredited by AACSB International–The Association to Advance Collegiate Schools of Business.

As a teaching institution, ACU emphasizes a dynamic personal relationship between professors and their students. Qualified faculty members, not graduate assistants, teach undergraduate students. When professors do research, undergraduates work with them. Each year, some of the nation's top companies come to campus to interview because they hold ACU graduates in high regard for their blend of creativity, technical skills, thorough training, and moral integrity. ACU students have an acceptance rate of more than 80 percent to medical and other professional schools, well above the national average. The *Optimist,* the ACU student newspaper, has been rated All-American every year since 1975.

ACU supports an environment of honesty, Christian care, and relationships that start even before classes begin. Each fall during Welcome Week, upperclass students help freshmen adjust to the social side of college life through diverse activities, including heart-to-heart discussions and possibly the world's largest game of Twister. The student body is enriched by people generally from all fifty states and about sixty countries.

The University is a member of the National Collegiate Athletic Association (NCAA) and the Lone Star Conference. ACU competes in NCAA Division II athletics, including men's baseball, football, and golf; women's soccer, softball and volleyball; and basketball, cross-country, tennis, and outdoor and indoor track and field for both men and women. About 3,000 students participate in twenty-two intramural sports and other activities. Students also can be involved in the roller hockey, men's soccer, and bike clubs.

There are more than ninety campus clubs and groups, including men's and women's social clubs, that offer students a variety of interests and opportunities for involvement. Movie nights, devotionals, intercollegiate sports, and student music and theater productions ensure that students can find great entertainment without leaving campus.

Location

Abilene, Texas, has the reputation of being a friendly city and was named an All-America City. It is located 150 miles west of Dallas and has a population of about 111,000. Its climate is relatively warm, although it occasionally snows during the winter. Residents of Abilene are served by shopping malls, major restaurant chains, specialty shops, two hospitals, and a regional airport. The city is second only to Houston in cultural events per capita in Texas, and it has one of the lowest crime rates in the state.

Majors and Degrees

The Bachelor of Arts degree is awarded in art, biblical text, biochemistry, biology, chemistry, Christian ministry, communication, communication sciences and disorders, English, graphic design/advertising, history, international studies, math-actuarial science, mathematics, ministry to children and families, missions, music, political science, Spanish, theater, vocational missions, worship ministry, and youth and family ministry.

The Bachelor of Science degree is available in agricultural business, animal science, biochemistry, biology, chemistry, communication, communication sciences and disorders, computer science, criminal justice, electronic media, engineering science, environmental science, exercise and sport science, family studies, health professions cooperative, information technology, integrated marketing communication, interior design, journalism, mathematics, nutrition, physical education, physics, psychology, social work, and sociology. Also, the Bachelor of Science degree is offered in interdisciplinary studies leading to teaching certification at four levels: age 3 through grade 4, grades 4 through 8, grades 8 through 12, and all level. A Bachelor of Science in Nursing degree is also available.

The Bachelor of Business Administration degree is offered in accounting, financial management, information systems, management, and marketing. The Bachelor of Fine Arts degree is available in art and theater, and the Bachelor of Music degree (with teacher certification) is offered in instrumental, piano, and vocal (all levels).

The Bachelor of Applied Studies offers adults the opportunity to combine previous college experience, on-the-job training, and courses at ACU to complete their degrees. Areas of emphasis include biblical and related sciences, communication, communication disorders, education gerontology, human and professional administration, industrial psychology, liberal arts, mathematics, nursing, physical education, psychology, sociology, and sociology-criminal justice.

The preprofessional programs offered by ACU are of special interest. In general, students attend ACU for one to four years and then transfer to a professional school to complete their degree. During the past decade, more than 85 percent of ACU graduates who applied to medical and dental schools were accepted, putting ACU among the top preprofessional schools in the state.

Academic Programs

A minimum of 128 semester hours is required for most baccalaureate degrees, with 30 of these hours in a major and a total of 33 hours in upper-division work. All degrees require 15 hours of Bible studies, and most require courses in communication/speech, English, exercise science, fine arts, mathematics, science, and social and behavioral science.

ACU serves a broad spectrum of students. To help challenge the exceptionally bright student, CLEP and a comprehensive honors program are available. For the underprepared, developmental programs are offered by the English and math departments. The University also offers various enriching seminars and lectures by internationally known guests such as George W. Bush, Max Lucado, James Dobson, Tony Compolo, William Bennett, John Wooden, and Ray Bradbury.

Off-Campus Programs

In the study-abroad program, students may study in Western Europe and Latin America as well as apply for any of the study-abroad opportunities offered by Cooperative Center for Study

Abroad (CCCU). All courses completed during this cultural and educational experience are counted toward the student's degree.

Academic Facilities

Resources of the Abilene Christian University library include books, microforms, audiovisual materials, government documents, and periodicals that total more than 1 million items. Online research and access to a local library consortium greatly expand student access to worldwide resources. More than thirty computer labs across campus are available to students during days and evenings—in every academic building and residence hall. There is also a medical clinic on campus.

Exercise science and athletic activities are centered in the huge exercise science complex, which contains several gymnasiums, training rooms, racquetball courts, an Olympic-size swimming pool, a coliseum, and a state-of-the-art fitness center for student athletes. The Teague Special Events Center is used for a variety of special events that occur in both the ACU and Abilene communities. The four-story science facility contains laboratories, an outstanding collection of experimental equipment, an observatory, and computer labs. A three-story communications complex houses art studios and classrooms, newspaper and yearbook workshops, a low-power VHF TV station that broadcasts on a local station and on cable, and an FM National Public Radio station.

In addition to 100-acre and 400-acre farms, the University has access to 2,500 acres of land for observation, research, and study projects. Students enrolled in agriculture, environment, biology, and ecology courses are able to study basic and applied science in an integrated setting.

Classrooms in the Mabee Business Building and Biblical Studies Building are equipped with the latest in audiovisual and computer equipment. Business students work in a lab equipped with state-of-the-art Apple Power Macs and Pentium processors. The newest academic building is Williams Performing Arts Center, which houses the music and theater departments, and offices.

Costs

The typical expenses for 2007–08 for two semesters included tuition and fees, $17,410; room and board, $5900; books and supplies, $1100; and transportation and personal expenses, $2820, for an approximate total of $27,230. All fees are subject to change.

Financial Aid

More than 90 percent of ACU students are assisted through loans, grants, scholarships, and/or employment. In 2006–07, almost $57 million in financial aid was awarded to ACU students. The number of students employed on campus was more than 1,300. Academic scholarships are awarded according to scores on standardized tests such as the SAT and ACT examinations, class rank, and leadership activities. Full tuition scholarships are offered to National Merit Finalists. All financial aid forms may be obtained through the ACU Student Financial Services Office. Applicants for aid need to complete the Free Application for Federal Student Aid (FAFSA).

Faculty

ACU has a faculty of outstanding teachers, scholars, and specialists. Ninety percent of tenure-track faculty members have a doctorate or terminal degree. Faculty members are committed to educating the whole student, academically, socially, and spiritually. A student-teacher ratio of 15:1 allows students ready access to their teachers for counseling on careers, academics, and personal issues.

Student Government

Abilene Christian University has an active, progressive Students' Association, of which every full-time student is a member. Officers of the association and the Student Senate carry out various social and community service programs. The Student Foundation promotes awareness of the purposes of ACU and maintains communication among the administration, students, and alumni.

Admission Requirements

To qualify for admission, a student must have graduated from high school and must submit information concerning SAT or ACT scores, high school class rank, and reference letters. Generally, transfer students are required to have a 2.0 grade point average or better. Abilene Christian University does not discriminate on the basis of race, color, age, or national or ethnic origin in its admissions, employment opportunities, educational programs, or activities that it sponsors.

Application and Information

Prospective students should apply online at http://www.acu.edu/admissions or call the admissions office for application forms and financial aid information, indicating their academic and social areas of interest. Applicants should submit the necessary forms with a nonrefundable $25 processing fee ($45 for international applicants) and have their academic records (SAT or ACT scores, transcript, and class rank) sent to the University. Residence hall room reservations, accompanied by a $250 advance payment, should be made early to ensure choice of a residence hall. Students are encouraged to visit the campus at any time.

Office of Admissions
Abilene Christian University
ACU, Box 29000
Abilene, Texas 79699-9000
Phone: 325-674-2650
800-460-6228 (toll-free)
E-mail: info@admissions.acu.edu
Web site: http://www.acu.edu

ACU's Biblical Studies Building features a magnificent chapel, a huge amphitheater, and the latest in instructional technology.

COLLEGE DATA CENTER • TEXAS

ANGELO STATE UNIVERSITY

SAN ANGELO, TEXAS

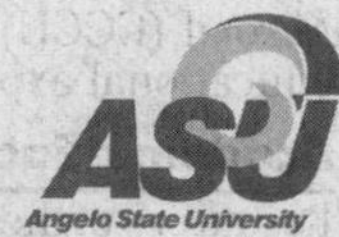

The University

Founded in 1928, Angelo State University (ASU) has been recognized as one of the United States' outstanding regional public universities. A proud member of the Texas Tech University System, ASU provides a genuine value, maintaining one of the lowest tuition and fee schedules in the state. One of the University's major goals is to create a stimulating educational climate that offers students maximum opportunities for academic achievement and personal growth both in and out of the classroom. With personal attention from a superb faculty and with numerous prospects for practical experience and internships, students enjoy an enhanced undergraduate experience. To achieve this goal, ASU maintains a distinguished student body and a superb faculty. Of the approximately 6,200 students enrolled, 5,800 are undergraduates. This diverse student population is drawn from throughout Texas, thirty-nine other states, and twenty-three countries.

Location

The 268-acre campus of Angelo State University is in San Angelo, an attractive and progressive community of 100,000 in the heart of Texas at the gateway to the scenic hill country. The attractively landscaped campus is convenient to downtown as well as to entertainment options in suburban areas. The athletic, cultural, and entertainment offerings of the campus are complemented by those of the community, including a symphony orchestra, art and historical museums, popular concerts, two professional sports teams, and a host of special events. The ASU Lake House on Lake Nasworthy, one of three recreational lakes around San Angelo, provides facilities for various university functions as well as picnicking, swimming, fishing, and other water activities.

Majors and Degrees

Angelo State University provides thirty-eight undergraduate programs leading to seven baccalaureate degrees and one associate degree.

The Bachelor of Arts degree is offered in art, communication, criminal justice, drama, English, French, German, government, history, journalism, mathematics, music, psychology, sociology, and Spanish. Programs for teacher certification at the elementary level are available as interdisciplinary programs in fine arts, language arts, and social studies. Programs for teacher certification are available in communication, drama, English language arts and reading, fine arts, French, special education, German, history, journalism, social studies, and Spanish.

The Bachelor of Business Administration degree may be earned in accounting, business, computer science, finance, finance with a financial planning option, finance with a real estate option, international business, management, management information systems, and marketing. The University's undergraduate and graduate business programs are accredited by the Association of Collegiate Business Schools and Programs. A five-year integrated undergraduate/graduate program in accounting is designed to fulfill state requirements for eligibility for the Certified Public Accountancy (CPA) examination.

The Bachelor of Music degree is offered in music, and the Bachelor of Fine Arts degree is offered in studio art. A program in teacher certification in music is available.

The Bachelor of Science degree is offered in animal science, applied physics, biochemistry, biology, chemistry, computer science, criminal justice, kinesiology, mathematics, medical technology, physics, psychology, and sociology. Programs for teacher certification are available as interdisciplinary programs in early childhood, math/science, and special learning and development and in the content areas of computer science, kinesiology, life science, mathematics, and physical science.

The University also offers a Bachelor of General Studies degree, a Bachelor of Science in Nursing degree, and an Associate in Applied Science in Nursing degree.

In addition, students may pursue courses and advising designed to help them meet entrance requirements to various professional schools, including dentistry, engineering, law, medicine, occupational therapy, pharmacy, physical therapy, and veterinary medicine.

Academic Programs

The academic requirements at ASU are designed to give the student a broad background in the liberal arts and to enhance that foundation with discipline-specific courses. Curricula are continually evaluated to ensure the best and most current educational experience possible. Baccalaureate-seeking students must file a degree plan prior to the first semester of their junior year or the completion of 70 semester hours. Faculty advisers monitor students' progress from the beginning of the academic program until completion.

Two-year and four-year aerospace studies programs for men and women are also available. Completion of these programs leads to a commission in the U.S. Air Force. ASU has one of the nation's most highly decorated detachments and can offer tremendous scholarships.

The college year consists of a long session and a summer session. The long session is divided into fall and spring semesters, each approximately sixteen weeks long. The summer session is divided into two 6-week terms.

Off-Campus Programs

The International Studies Program provides academic study and travel opportunities in Mexico and Europe. Study-abroad programs carry college credit. Other off-campus programs include professional internships in education, government, journalism, and public administration and cooperative education programs in nursing and medical technology offered in conjunction with numerous local medical centers.

ASU operates a 4,643-acre multiple-purpose agricultural production and wildlife management area called the Management, Instruction, and Research (MIR) Center. Located near O. C. Fisher Lake and San Angelo, the MIR Center is one of the most complete domestic livestock and range and wildlife management facilities in the Southwest.

Academic Facilities

Attractive and well-maintained academic buildings enable ASU students to study in some of the most pleasant and modern facilities anywhere. Classrooms range from the intimacy of seminar-oriented size to a small number of lecture halls. Specialized and general research laboratories serve many of the University's programs, including the applied sciences, nursing, communication, journalism, kinesiology, education, business, and computer science, among others. The Porter Henderson Library is the focal point of academic life at ASU. Containing more than 1 million holdings in bound volumes, government documents, and micro-

COLLEGE DATA CENTER • TEXAS

forms made accessible by an online cataloging system, the Henderson Library ranks among the finest libraries in Texas. The West Texas Collection of archival material admirably meets the genealogical and historical interests of students and faculty members desiring to learn more about the distinct West Texas heritage.

There are seven computer labs on campus that are available to all students. One of these labs is open 144 hours per week when classes are in session. The 15:1 student-to-computer ratio is extremely low. A radio/television studio, modular and proscenium theaters, a planetarium, musical rehearsal and recital halls, art studios, recreational facilities, and a Language Learning Center provide ASU students with exceptional opportunities for learning and fun outside the classroom. An extensive network of student-accessible microcomputer laboratories further complements the academic mission of the computer-intensive campus.

Costs

In 2007–08, state residents registered for a normal course load of 15 semester hours (full-time study) paid $2555 per semester for required tuition and fees. Room and board averaged $2990 per semester, depending upon the meal plans and residence hall selected. Tuition and required fees for out-of-state students were $6725 per semester. Books and supplies are estimated to cost about $500 per semester.

Financial Aid

To assist students toward meeting their financial responsibilities, the Office of Student Financial Aid administers a wide variety of programs from funds provided by the federal government and the state of Texas, including funds from the Federal Work-Study, Federal Pell Grant, Federal Supplemental Educational Opportunity Grant, Federal Perkins Loan, Federal Family Education Loan, Texas Public Educational Grant, and State Student Incentive Grant programs. In addition, numerous scholarships are awarded annually through the financial aid office in recognition of academic achievement, outstanding leadership, and exceptional promise or potential.

One of the most distinctive features of the University is the Robert G. Carr and Nona K. Carr Academic Scholarship Program. One of the largest privately endowed academic scholarship programs in the nation, this program provides scholarships ranging in value from $2000 to $6000 annually. Approximately 1,000 students enrolled at Angelo State University receive these awards. To compete favorably for one of these renewable scholarships, a student must normally rank in the top 15 percent of his or her class and present a composite score of 25 or higher on the ACT Assessment or a combined math and verbal score of 1140 or higher on the SAT.

Students interested in the University's Air Force ROTC program may also apply for scholarships awarded through the Air Force ROTC detachment. These awards are funded by an endowment established by the late Mr. and Mrs. Robert G. Carr. This unique program provides scholarships ranging in value from $500 to $1500 annually to qualified cadets enrolled in the University's ROTC program.

Faculty

Angelo State University retains a distinguished faculty. In terms of academic preparation, the faculty ranks near the top of all colleges and universities in the South. Approximately 60 percent of the faculty members hold earned doctorates in their teaching field. Faculty members are selected with great care; the University seeks to obtain the services of individuals who are prominent scholars and dedicated teachers who will merit the confidence of the students. Faculty members are associated with many of the nation's leading research universities, conduct special assignments in numerous countries, have acquired professional experience with some of the nation's leading business firms, conduct extensive applied and theoretical research, and travel internationally.

Student Government

The Student Senate is the official representative organization of the Angelo State University student body. As the primary forum for student opinion, the Student Senate provides a mutually beneficial communication link between the student body and administrative officials.

Admission Requirements

High school graduates are admitted to Angelo State University on a competitive basis. Applicants from accredited U.S. high schools must meet one of the following requirements: (1) they must satisfactorily complete the Texas Scholars Program or the Texas advanced high school program; (2) they must rank in the top half of their senior class at the time of application or graduate in the top half of their graduating class; (3) they must present a minimum composite score of 23 on the ACT Assessment or a minimum combined verbal and math score of 1030 on the SAT if ranked in the third quarter or of 30 or 1270 if ranked in the fourth quarter; or (4) they must have a 50 percent or greater probability of earning an overall C average (2.0 GPA) during the freshman year at the University as computed from their high school grades and ACT or SAT scores. Students who do not qualify for regular admission may qualify for provisional admission. Transfer students who have completed 18 or more hours of college-level work are admitted, provided they have maintained at least a 2.0 cumulative GPA. Students with less than 18 college-level hours must also meet the criteria established for high school students. The University welcomes applications from international students, who are considered on the basis of their secondary school record, their ACT or SAT scores, and their Test of English as a Foreign Language (TOEFL) scores (550 minimum).

Application and Information

High school applicants are required to submit an application for admission, results of the ACT or SAT, appropriate academic transcripts, and a $25 application fee. Requests for information and admission application forms should be made to:

Office of Admissions
Angelo State University
ASU Station #11014
San Angelo, Texas 76909-1014
Phone: 325-942-2041
800-946-8627 (toll-free)
Web site: http://www.angelo.edu

The Angelo State University Robert and Nona Carr Education–Fine Arts Building.

ARGOSY UNIVERSITY

ARGOSY UNIVERSITY

The University

Argosy University is a leading institution offering a variety of degree programs that focus on the human side of success alongside professional competence. For students looking for a more personal approach to education, Argosy University may just be the answer. With forty-eight graduate and undergraduate programs, across nineteen campuses and twelve states, Argosy University emphasizes interpersonal skills as well as academic learning. All of its programs are taught by practicing professionals who bring real-world experience into the classroom. So students graduate with both a solid foundation of knowledge and the power to put it to work. To accommodate busy working adults, many programs at Argosy University are structured flexibly—with both campus and online learning and evening, weekend, and daytime classes. There is also a wide range of financial aid options for students who qualify.

Argosy University is a private institution of higher education dedicated to providing high-quality professional education programs at the doctoral, master's, bachelor's, and associate degree levels as well as continuing education to individuals who seek to advance their professional and personal lives. The University emphasizes programs in the behavioral sciences (psychology and counseling), business, education, and the health-care professions. A limited number of preprofessional programs and general education offerings are provided to permit students to prepare for entry into these professional fields. The programs of Argosy University are designed to instill the knowledge, skills, and ethical values of professional practice and to foster values of social responsibility in a supportive, learning-centered environment of mutual respect and professional excellence.

With nineteen campuses nationwide, Argosy University provides students with a network of resources found at larger universities, including a career resources office, an academic resources center, and extensive information access for research. The University's innovative programs feature dynamic, relevant, and practical curricula delivered in flexible class formats. Students enjoy scheduling options that make it easier to fit school into their busy lives. They can choose from day and evening courses, on campus or online. Many students find a combination of both to be an ideal way of continuing their education while meeting family and professional demands.

Most students are full-time working professionals who live within driving distance of the campus. The University does not offer or operate student housing.

Argosy University is accredited by The Higher Learning Commission of the North Central Association (30 North LaSalle Street, Suite 2400, Chicago, Illinois 60602; 800-621-7440; http://ncahlc.org).

Location

Argosy University operates nineteen locations across the U.S. and offers a variety of degree programs online (http://www.argosy.edu). Campus locations include the following:

Atlanta, 980 Hammond Drive, Suite 100, Atlanta, Georgia 30328; phone: 770-671-1200 or 888-671-4777 (toll-free)

Chicago, 225 North Michigan Avenue, Suite 1300, Chicago, Illinois 60601; phone: 312-777-7600 or 800-626-4123 (toll-free)

Dallas, 8080 Park Lane, Suite 400A, Dallas, Texas 75231; phone: 214-890-9900 or 866-954-9900 (toll-free)

Denver, 1200 Lincoln Street, Denver, Colorado 80203; phone: 303-248-2700 or 866-431-5981 (toll-free)

Hawai'i, 400 ASB Tower, 1001 Bishop Street, Honolulu, Hawaii 96813; phone: 808-536-5555 or 888-323-2777 (toll-free)

Inland Empire, 636 East Brier Drive, Suite 235, San Bernardino, California 92408; phone: 909-915-3800 or 866-217-9075 (toll-free)

Nashville, 100 Centerview Drive, Suite 225, Nashville, Tennessee 37214; phone: 615-525-2800 or 866-833-6598 (toll-free)

Orange County, 3501 West Sunflower Avenue, Suite 110, Santa Ana, California 92704; phone: 714-338-6200 or 800-716-9598 (toll-free)

Phoenix, 2233 West Dunlap Avenue, Phoenix, Arizona 85021; phone: 602-216-2600 or 866-216-2777 (toll-free)

Salt Lake City, 121 West Election Road, Suite 300, Draper, Utah 84020; phone: 888-639-4756 (toll-free)

San Diego, 7650 Mission Valley Road, San Diego, California 92108; phone: 858-598-1900 or 866-505-0333 (toll-free)

San Francisco Bay Area, 1005 Atlantic Avenue, Alameda, California 94501; phone: 510-217-4700 or 866-215-2777 (toll-free)

Santa Monica, 2950 31st Street, Santa Monica, California 90405; phone: 310-866-4000 or 866-505-0332 (toll-free)

Sarasota, 5250 17th Street, Sarasota, Florida 34235; phone: 941-379-0404 or 800-331-5995 (toll-free)

Schaumburg, 999 North Plaza Drive, Suite 111, Schaumburg, Illinois 60173-5403; phone: 847-969-4900 or 866-290-2777 (toll-free)

Seattle, 2601-A Elliott Avenue, Seattle, Washington 98121; phone: 206-283-4500 or 888-283-2777 (toll-free)

Tampa, Parkside at Tampa Bay Park, 4401 North Hines Avenue, Suite 150, Tampa, Florida 33614; phone: 813-393-5290 or 800-850-6488 (toll-free)

Twin Cities, 1515 Central Parkway, Eagan, Minnesota 55121; phone: 651-846-2882 or 888-844-2004 (toll-free)

Washington DC, 1550 Wilson Boulevard, Suite 600, Arlington, Virginia 22209; phone: 703-526-5800 or 866-703-2777 (toll-free)

Majors and Degrees

Argosy University's College of Business offers a Bachelor of Science (B.S.) in Business Administration program. Argosy University's College of Psychology and Behavioral Sciences offers the Bachelor of Arts (B.A.) in Psychology degree program.

Academic Programs

The B.S. in Business Administration program prepares students for entry- to mid-level positions within the public or private sector. The curriculum is structured to help students develop competencies in oral and written communication, leadership, team skills, solutions-focused learning, and the analysis and execution of solutions in various business situations. Students may choose one of five optional concentrations: customized professional concentration, finance, health-care management, international business, or marketing.

The B.A. in Psychology program is designed to help students begin human services careers in such capacities as entry-level counselor, case manager, or human resources administrator and

in management and business services roles. The program also lays the foundation for graduate study. Students may choose an optional concentration from the following three options: criminal justice, organizational psychology, or substance abuse. This dynamic program is built around a flexible class approach.

Argosy University's bachelor's degree programs are open to students and working professionals with no college experience, plus those who have already earned college credit at a community college, junior college, or other university.

Academic Facilities

Argosy University libraries provide curriculum support and educational resources including current text materials, diagnostic training documents, reference materials and databases, journals and dissertations, and major and current titles in program areas. There is an online public-access catalog of library resources available throughout the Argosy University system. Students enjoy full remote access to their campus library database, enabling them to study and conduct research at home. Academic databases offer dissertation abstracts, academic journals, and professional periodicals. All library computers are Internet accessible. Software applications include Word, Excel, PowerPoint, SPSS, and various test-scoring programs.

Costs

Tuition varies by program. Students should contact the Argosy University campus of their choice for tuition information.

Financial Aid

A wide range of financial aid options is available to students who qualify. Argosy University offers access to federal and state aid programs, merit-based awards, grants, loans, and a work-study program. As a first step, students should complete the Free Application for Federal Student Aid (FAFSA). Prospective students can apply electronically at http://www.fafsa.ed.gov or at the campus. To receive consideration for financial aid and ensure timely receipt of funds, it is best to submit an application promptly.

Faculty

The Argosy University faculty is composed of working professionals who have a passion to help students succeed. Members bring real-world experience and the latest practice innovations to the academic setting. The diverse faculty is widely recognized for contributions to the field. Most hold doctoral degrees. They provide a substantive education that combines comprehensive knowledge with critical skills and practical workplace relevance. Above all, faculty members are committed to their students' personal and professional development.

Student Government

Argosy University campuses offer unique opportunities for student involvement beyond individual programs of study. Most faculty committees include a student representative. In addition, a student group meets with faculty members and administrators regularly to discuss pertinent campus-related issues.

Admission Requirements

Admission requirements differ depending on the number of college credits completed prior to application.

Students who have earned 12 or fewer semester college credits must provide proof of high school graduation or GED and meet one of the following conditions for admission: ACT composite score of 18 or above, or a combined math and verbal SAT score of 870, or minimum ACCUPLACER scores of 86 in sentence skills and 53 in algebra. Applicants who do not meet any of the above conditions for admission will be admitted with academic support if they provide proof of high school graduation or GED and meet one of the following: ACT composite score of 14 to 17, or a combined math and verbal SAT score of 660 to 869, or minimum ACCUPLACER scores of 54 in sentence skills and 36 in arithmetic.

Applicants who have earned 13 or more semester college credits must provide proof of high school graduation or GED and meet one of the following conditions for admission: cumulative college GPA of 2.0 or above or minimum ACCUPLACER scores of 86 for sentence skills and 53 in algebra. Students who do not meet either of the above criteria will be admitted with academic support if they provide proof of high school graduation or GED and meet the following condition: minimum ACCUPLACER scores of 54 in reading and 36 in arithmetic.

Students admitted with academic support are limited to 12 credit hours of study during their first semester (6 credit hours per session). Students admitted with academic support will be required to complete developmental English and/or math courses unless they meet the following conditions: Writing Review (ENG099)—must meet one of the following: a minimum ACCUPLACER score of 86 in sentence skills, or a minimum ACT verbal score of 18, or a minimum SAT verbal score of 425, or completion of a college-level English composition course with a grade of C or above; Mathematics Review I (MAT096)—must meet one of the following: a minimum ACCUPLACER score of 53 in algebra, or a minimum ACT math score of 18, or a minimum SAT math score of 440, or completion of a college-level English composition course with a grade of C or above.

Other admission requirements may include credit hours of qualified transfer credit with a grade of C- or better from a regionally accredited institution or a nationally accredited institution approved and documented by the faculty and dean of the College of Business, or the College of Professional Psychology, at Argosy University or completion of an Associate of Arts or Associate of Science degree from a regionally accredited institution. A maximum of 78 lower-division or 90 total credit hours may be transferred. A minimum written TOEFL score of 500 (paper-based test), 173 (computer-based test), or 61 (Internet-based test) is required for all applicants whose native language is not English or who have not graduated from an institution in which English is the language of instruction.

Official transcripts from approved postsecondary institutions must include a minimum grade point average of 2.0 (on a scale of 4.0) for all academic work completed. Exceptions may be made for extenuating circumstances. All applications must include a completed application form, proof of high school graduation or successful completion of the GED test, official postsecondary transcripts, and a nonrefundable (except in California) application fee. Additional materials are required prior to matriculation. Some programs have additional application requirements or include exceptions to admission requirements. An admissions representative can provide further information.

Application and Information

Argosy University accepts students on a rolling admissions basis year-round, depending on availability of required courses. Applications for admission are available online at http://www.argosy.edu or by contacting one of the campus locations.

Argosy University
205 North Michigan Avenue, Suite 1300
Chicago, Illinois 60601-2250
Phone: 312-899-9900
800-377-0617 (toll-free)
E-mail: auadmissions@argosy.edu
Web site: http://www.argosy.edu

THE ART INSTITUTE OF AUSTIN

AUSTIN, TEXAS

The Institute

The Art Institute of Austin provides students with an educational environment and dedicated faculty members committed to preparing students for entry-level positions in the creative arts. Under the guidance of industry professionals, students learn by doing the types of tasks they are likely to encounter in the workplace. In addition, assistance is available to help students with resume writing, networking, and keeping aware of what employers are looking for in job candidates. The school offers seven bachelor's degree programs and two associate degree programs.

The school offers assistance in helping students to secure housing.

The student population includes recent high school graduates, transfer students, and those who have left a previous employment situation to study and train for a new career. Students are creative, competitive, and open to new ideas. They place great value on an education that prepares them for an exciting entry-level position in the arts.

The Art Institute of Austin places a high value on the quality of student life—both in and out of the classroom. Students participate in a wide variety of activities, including clubs and organizations, community service, and various committees designed to enhance the quality of student life.

The Art Institute of Austin (AiAUS) is a branch of The Art Institute of Houston (AiH) through the Southern Association of Colleges and Schools (SACS) for accreditation. Final approval from the Texas Higher Education Coordinating Board (THECB) and the Southern Association of Colleges and Schools is pending.

Location

Austin is the capital of Texas and was the third-fastest-growing city in the nation from 2000 to 2006, with a population of nearly 710,000. Austin was named the number 2 Best Big City in "Best Places to Live" by *Money* magazine in 2006. It's also been called the "Greenest City in America" by MSN. The area is home to numerous cultural organizations, museums, and performing arts venues.

Majors and Degrees

The Art Institute of Austin offers bachelor's degree programs in audio production, fashion and retail management, graphic design, interior design, media arts and animation, photography, and Web design and interactive media.

Associate degrees are offered in graphic design and Web design and interactive media.

Academic Programs

The Art Institute of Austin operates on a year-round, four-quarter system.

Academic Facilities

The Art Institute of Austin contains classrooms, Mac and PC computer labs, and a library for student use. There is also a bookstore.

Costs

Tuition cost varies by program. Prospective students should contact the school for current tuition costs. Other charges include a starting kit for all first quarter students. Kits vary in price depending on the program of study.

Financial Aid

Financial aid is available for those who qualify. Students who require financial assistance should first complete and submit a Free Application for Federal Student Aid (FAFSA) and meet with a financial aid officer. The officer determines the level of need based on a required federal formula, the cost of education, and other factors. Gift aid is available in the form of Federal Pell Grants, Federal Supplemental Educational Opportunity Grants, and veterans' benefits. Loans include Federal Stafford Loans, Federal PLUS Loans, and alternative loans. Other scholarships are available from the school and private sources. Application deadlines and eligibility requirements vary by program.

Faculty

Faculty members at The Art Institute of Austin have professional knowledge that they bring into the classroom. The school's faculty members provide their students with a real-world, relevant educational experience.

Admission Requirements

Applicants must provide proof of high school graduation or achievement of a General Educational Development (GED) certificate as a prerequisite for admission. In lieu of documenting high school graduation or a GED certificate, applicants may provide proof of attaining an associate degree or higher from an accredited institution. An official transcript indicating date of high school graduation, GED certificate (including test scores), or date of college graduation (including degree granted) is required as proof.

All individuals seeking admission to The Art Institute of Austin are interviewed in person or by phone by an assistant director of admissions, and each applicant must submit an original essay of at least 150 words stating how an education at The Art Institute of Austin would help the student to achieve career goals. There is a $50 application fee.

Application and Information

To obtain an application, make arrangements for an interview, or tour the school, students should contact:

The Art Institute of Austin
100 Farmers Circle, Suite 100
Austin, Texas 78728
Phone: 512-691-1707
866-583-7952 (toll-free)
Fax: 512-691-1790
Web site: http://www.artinstitutes.edu/austin

The Art Institute of Atlanta®, GA; The Art Institute of Atlanta®–Decatur, GA; The Art Institute of Austin[SM], TX; The Art Institute of California[SM]–Inland Empire; The Art Institute of California[SM]–Los Angeles; The Art Institute of California[SM]–Orange County; The Art Institute of California[SM]–Sacramento; The Art Institute of California[SM]–San Diego; The Art Institute of California[SM]–San Francisco; The Art Institute of California[SM]–Sunnyvale; The Art Institute of Charleston[SM], SC, A branch of The Art Institute of Atlanta, GA; The Art Institute of Charlotte®, NC; The Art Institute of Colorado® (Denver); The Art Institute of Dallas®, TX; The Art Institute of Fort Lauderdale®, FL; The Art Institute of Houston®, TX; The Art Institute of Indianapolis[SM], IN*; The Art Institute of Jacksonville[SM], FL, A branch of Miami International University of Art & Design; The Art Institute of Las Vegas®, NV; The Art Institute of Michigan[SM] (Detroit); The Art Institute of New York City®, NY; The Art Institute of Ohio[SM]–Cincinnati**; The Art Institute of Philadelphia®, PA; The Art Institute of Phoenix®, AZ; The Art Institute of Pittsburgh®, PA; The Art Institute of Pittsburgh®–Online Division; The Art Institute of Portland®, OR; The Art Institute of Salt Lake City[SM], UT; The Art Institute of Seattle®, WA; The Art Institute of Tampa[SM], FL, A branch of Miami International University of Art & Design; The Art Institute of Tennessee[SM]–Nashville, A branch of The Art Institute of Atlanta, GA; The Art Institute of Tucson[SM], AZ; The Art Institute of Washington® (Arlington, VA), A branch of The Art Institute of Atlanta, GA; The Art Institute of York–Pennsylvania[SM]; The Art Institutes International Minnesota[SM] (Minneapolis); California Design College[SM] (Los Angeles–Wilshire Blvd.); The Illinois Institute of Art®–Chicago; The Illinois Institute of Art®–Schaumburg; Miami International University of Art & Design[SM], FL; The New England Institute of Art® (Boston, MA).

*The Art Institute of Indianapolis is licensed by the Indiana Commission on Proprietary Education, 302 W. Washington St., Rm. E201, Indianapolis, IN 46204, AC-0080.

**The Art Institute of Ohio–Cincinnati, 8845 Governors Hill Drive, Suite 100, Cincinnati, OH 45249-3317, OH Reg. #04-01-1698B.

THE ART INSTITUTE OF DALLAS

DALLAS, TEXAS

The Art Institute of Dallas

The Institute

The Art Institute of Dallas provides programs that help to prepare students for entry-level positions in the creative arts. Courses are taught by experienced faculty members in an environment that encourages expression, leadership, and responsible decision making. The Art Institute of Dallas offers eight bachelor's degree programs, six associate degree programs, and one certificate program.

The student population includes recent high school graduates, transfer students, and those who have left a previous employment situation to study and train for a new career. Students are creative, competitive, and open to new ideas. They place great value on an education that prepares them for an exciting entry-level position in the arts.

The Art Institute of Dallas is a truly international experience—one that is culturally diverse and creatively stimulating. Students attend the school from nearly forty countries. An international student adviser is available to assist students with their cultural adjustments and immigration matters.

The school provides students with employment assistance classes, individual employment assistance, and printed job-search information. Training includes job-search skills and interviewing techniques. Students also receive portfolio counseling from The Art Institute of Dallas staff members.

Movie nights, sports activities, and field trips are part of The Art Institute of Dallas experience. Students also get involved in the local area via community service opportunities. Through class projects and honors endeavors, students have assisted local charities in the development of their media campaigns. Numerous organizations are available for students based on special interest areas.

Many students live at The Falls at Highpoint, a controlled-access apartment complex approximately 3 miles from The Art Institute of Dallas. Students may take advantage of value-priced food at the school's Sunrise Deli.

The Art Institute of Dallas is accredited by the Commission on Colleges of the Southern Association of Colleges and Schools (SACS; 1866 Southern Lane, Decatur, Georgia 30033-4097; phone: 404-679-4500; http://www.sacs.org) to award Associate of Applied Arts, Associate of Applied Science, and Bachelor of Fine Arts degrees. The Associate of Applied Science in Culinary Arts degree program and Art of Cooking certificate program are accredited by the American Culinary Federation (ACF). The Bachelor of Fine Arts in interior design degree program is accredited by the Council for Interior Design Accreditation.

Location

The school is located in the Dallas/Fort Worth area, which has one of the lowest cost-of-living indexes of any major metropolitan area. The Dallas/Fort Worth area offers a diverse range of cultural and recreational activities, including the Dallas Symphony, Mesquite Rodeo, Six Flags, Lone Star Park, concerts in the West End, and national sports teams. Many major employers have relocated to the Dallas/Forth Worth area due to its positive economic environment.

Majors and Degrees

The Art Institute of Dallas offers bachelor's degree programs in advertising design, digital filmmaking and video production, fashion and retail management, fashion design, graphic design, interior design, media arts and animation, and Web design and interactive media. Associate degree programs include culinary arts, fashion design, graphic design, kitchen and bath design, restaurant and catering management, and video production. In addition, a certificate program is available in art of cooking.

Academic Programs

Associate degree programs can be completed in twenty-one months. Bachelor's degree programs can be completed in thirty-six months.

Academic Facilities

Computer labs offering PC and Macintosh computers are available for student use. The Art Institute of Dallas library supports the student community's information and imaging needs. In 1996, the library was officially named for its founder and first librarian, Mildred M. Kelley. The library maintains a collection of more than 20,000 books, more than 4,000 periodical titles in both print and full-text electronic versions, 1,450 videotapes, 12,500 photographic slides, and 11,000 Visual Reference Cards. In addition, it provides reference services and instruction in the use of library services and facilities, electronic database searching, and research techniques.

The Academic Improvement Center provides tutoring services in the areas of general study skills, mathematics, writing, reading, and basic computer application skills. The center is open Monday through Friday and provides academic testing (ASSET, Learning Styles Assessment) on a weekly basis.

Costs

Tuition cost varies by program. Prospective students should contact the school for current tuition costs. Other charges include a starting kit for all first quarter students. Kits vary in price depending on the program of study.

Financial Aid

Financial aid is available for those who qualify. Students who require financial assistance should first complete and submit a Free Application for Federal Student Aid (FAFSA) and meet with a financial aid officer. The officer determines the level of need based on a required federal formula, the cost of education, and other factors. Gift aid is available in the form of Federal Pell Grants, Federal Supplemental Educational Opportunity Grants, and veterans' benefits. Loans include Federal Stafford Loans,

Federal PLUS Loans, and alternative loans. Other scholarships are available from the school and private sources. Application deadlines and eligibility requirements vary by program.

Faculty

Led by an executive committee and a group of academic department directors, faculty members deliver student-centered education, and curriculum content is regularly reviewed. There are full-time and part-time faculty members.

Student Government

The Student Ambassador Organization promotes high-quality representation of the student body. The group provides a channel of communication among students, the administration, and faculty members.

Admission Requirements

Applicants are required to write a paragraph of approximately 300 words stating how The Art Institute of Dallas may help them reach their creative goals. Applicants must present proof of high school graduation or a General Educational Development (GED) certificate as well as their accomplishments and core academic courses. Successful admission depends on QPA, accomplishments, SAT or ACT scores, and a personal interview with admission representatives. Applicants who do not submit a transcript of GED scores are required to take additional testing.

To enroll, students must submit an admission application and an enrollment agreement along with a $50 application fee.

Application and Information

To obtain an application, make arrangements for an interview, or tour the school, students should contact:

The Art Institute of Dallas
8080 Park Lane, Suite 100
Dallas, Texas 75231-5993
Phone: 214-692-8080
800-275-4243 (toll-free)
Fax: 214-750-9460
Web site: http://www.artinstitutes.edu/dallas

The Art Institute of Atlanta®, GA; The Art Institute of Atlanta®–Decatur, GA; The Art Institute of Austin℠, TX; The Art Institute of California℠–Inland Empire; The Art Institute of California℠–Los Angeles; The Art Institute of California℠–Orange County; The Art Institute of California℠–Sacramento; The Art Institute of California℠–San Diego; The Art Institute of California℠–San Francisco; The Art Institute of California℠–Sunnyvale; The Art Institute of Charleston℠, SC, A branch of The Art Institute of Atlanta, GA; The Art Institute of Charlotte®, NC; The Art Institute of Colorado® (Denver); The Art Institute of Dallas®, TX; The Art Institute of Fort Lauderdale®, FL; The Art Institute of Houston®, TX; The Art Institute of Indianapolis℠, IN*; The Art Institute of Jacksonville℠, FL, A branch of Miami International University of Art & Design; The Art Institute of Las Vegas®, NV; The Art Institute of Michigan℠ (Detroit); The Art Institute of New York City®, NY; The Art Institute of Ohio℠–Cincinnati**; The Art Institute of Philadelphia®, PA; The Art Institute of Phoenix®, AZ; The Art Institute of Pittsburgh®, PA; The Art Institute of Pittsburgh®–Online Division; The Art Institute of Portland®, OR; The Art Institute of Salt Lake City℠, UT; The Art Institute of Seattle®, WA; The Art Institute of Tampa℠, FL, A branch of Miami International University of Art & Design; The Art Institute of Tennessee℠–Nashville, A branch of The Art Institute of Atlanta, GA; The Art Institute of Tucson℠, AZ; The Art Institute of Washington® (Arlington, VA), A branch of The Art Institute of Atlanta, GA; The Art Institute of York–Pennsylvania℠; The Art Institutes International Minnesota℠ (Minneapolis); California Design College℠ (Los Angeles–Wilshire Blvd.); The Illinois Institute of Art®–Chicago; The Illinois Institute of Art®–Schaumburg; Miami International University of Art & Design℠, FL; The New England Institute of Art® (Boston, MA).

*The Art Institute of Indianapolis is licensed by the Indiana Commission on Proprietary Education, 302 W. Washington St., Rm. E201, Indianapolis, IN 46204, AC-0080.

**The Art Institute of Ohio–Cincinnati, 8845 Governors Hill Drive, Suite 100, Cincinnati, OH 45249-3317, OH Reg. #04-01-1698B.

THE ART INSTITUTE OF HOUSTON

HOUSTON, TEXAS

The Art Institute of Houston®

The Institute

At The Art Institute of Houston, students develop practical skills that prepare them for entry-level positions in the creative arts. Programs incorporate traditional liberal arts and hands-on instruction. Nine bachelor's degrees and six associate degree programs are offered at the school.

Students come to The Art Institute of Houston from throughout the United States and abroad. The student population includes recent high school graduates, transfer students, and those who have left a previous employment situation to study and train for a new career. Students are creative, competitive, and open to new ideas. They place great value on an education that prepares them for an exciting entry-level position in the arts.

Students may take part in a number of clubs, social activities, and volunteer service projects in the community. Student activities include professional organizations such as the National Technical Honors Society, American Society of Interior Designers (ASID), and American Institute of Graphic Arts (AIGA). Clubs include Baking and Pastry, Great Chefs, and Poetry.

A major focus of The Art Institute of Houston involves helping students gain employment after graduation. Job search training in the classrooms, one-on-one efforts, and an on-campus job fair for potential employers assist students in achieving this goal.

Many students live in The Park at Voss, a controlled-access apartment complex located 2.8 miles from the school and one block from the Metro bus line. The most common living arrangement at this complex is a two-bedroom, two-bath apartment shared by 4 students. Double and single student-apartment options are limited and based on seniority and availability.

Academic tutoring is a service available to all students at no charge at The Art Institute of Houston. One-on-one peer tutoring is available, and many faculty members provide tutoring and workshops that are specific to the courses they instruct. Art Institute of Houston mentors devote approximately 2 hours per week to assisting new students in their adjustment to both academic life and their new surroundings. In addition, assistance is available to help students with resume writing, networking, and keeping aware of what employers are looking for in job candidates.

The Art Institute of Houston is accredited by the Commission on Colleges of the Southern Association of Colleges and Schools (SACS; 1866 Southern Lane, Decatur, Georgia 30033-4097; phone: 404-679-4500; http://www.sacs.org) to award Associate of Applied Science, Bachelor of Science, and Bachelor of Fine Arts degrees. The Associate of Applied Science in Culinary Arts degree program is accredited by the American Culinary Federation (ACF). The Bachelor of Fine Arts in Interior Design degree program is accredited by the Council for Interior Design Accreditation.

Location

The Art Institute of Houston is close to several major art museums, a premier opera, a ballet, a symphony, and live theater companies. Culturally diverse, Houston has several international ethnic communities, great restaurants, and an eclectic nightlife as well as national sports teams. The city features a mild, semitropical climate and sunny beaches in nearby Galveston and Mexico.

Majors and Degrees

The Art Institute of Houston offers bachelor's degree programs (thirty-six months) in culinary management, design and technical graphics, digital filmmaking and video production, fashion and retail management, graphic design, interior design, media arts and animation, photography, and Web design and interactive media. Associate degree programs (twenty-one months) are available in baking and pastry, culinary arts, graphic design, kitchen and bath design, restaurant and catering management, and Web design and interactive media. A diploma program (twelve months) is offered in culinary arts.

Academic Programs

The academic year is divided into four quarters of approximately eleven weeks each. Students may start their program of study in any quarter. Bachelor's degrees can be earned upon completion of 180 academic credits over twelve quarters (three years). Associate degrees are earned upon completion of 90 to 108 academic credits, depending on the program, and can take seven to eight quarters (approximately two years). Diploma programs require the completion of 61 academic credits. Online programs are offered in two sessions per academic quarter.

Academic Facilities

The Art Institute of Houston Resource Center collection consists of approximately 28,000 books, 1,700 videos, 200 journals, 4 databases, and 850 discs containing imagery files, sound files, and software tutorials. The center includes twenty-eight computer stations for patron use. PCs provide access to the online catalog, the Internet, and some Microsoft Office products. Macintosh computers provide access to the online catalog and Internet and to the software that is utilized in design classes. Complimentary scanning and printing are available.

Costs

Tuition cost varies by program. Prospective students should contact the school for current tuition costs. Other charges include a starting kit for all first-quarter students. Kits vary in price depending on the program of study.

Financial Aid

Financial aid is available for those who qualify. Students who require financial assistance should first complete and submit a Free Application for Federal Student Aid (FAFSA) and meet with a financial aid officer. The officer determines the level of need based on a required federal formula, the cost of education, and other factors. Gift aid is available in the form of Federal Pell Grants, Federal Supplemental Educational Opportunity Grants, and veterans' benefits. Loans include Federal Stafford Student Loans, Federal PLUS loans, and alternative loans. Other scholarships are available from the school and private sources. Application deadlines and eligibility requirements vary by program.

Faculty

The Art Institute of Houston faculty members have professional experience in their chosen fields, and many hold advanced degrees. There are full-time and part-time faculty members.

Student Government

The Student Government is the primary vehicle for student participation in institutional decision making. The Student Government acts as a voice on behalf of the student body and sponsors speakers, workshops, seminars, and other activities. When students seek change or have a request that affects the student body as a whole, Student Government serves as a forum for discussion and decision making. All students are eligible to belong to Student Government.

Admission Requirements

Admission to The Art Institute of Houston begins with an interview with an assistant director of admissions, either in person or by phone. Upon approval, students submit an application for admission and an enrollment agreement. Prospective students must be high school graduates, hold a General Educational Development (GED) certificate, or have earned an associate degree or higher from an accredited institution. The Art Institute of Houston considers alternative documentation from students who have completed high school or its equivalent but cannot provide the usual documentation. (The president of The Art Institute of Houston must approve all exceptions.) Evaluations are based on an applicant's previous education, background, and stated or demonstrated interest in a particular program. Portfolios are required for admission to the media arts and animation program; they are welcomed for other programs but not required. Applicants who have taken the SAT or ACT are encouraged to submit their scores for evaluation. There is a $50 application fee.

Application and Information

To obtain an application, make arrangements for an interview, or tour the school, students should contact:

The Art Institute of Houston
1900 Yorktown Street
Houston, Texas 77056-4197
Phone: 713-623-2040
800-275-4244 (toll-free)
Fax: 713-966-2797
Web site: http://www.artinstitutes.edu/houston

The Art Institute of Atlanta®, GA; The Art Institute of Atlanta®–Decatur, GA; The Art Institute of Austin[SM], TX; The Art Institute of California[SM]–Inland Empire; The Art Institute of California[SM]–Los Angeles; The Art Institute of California[SM]–Orange County; The Art Institute of California[SM]–Sacramento; The Art Institute of California[SM]–San Diego; The Art Institute of California[SM]–San Francisco; The Art Institute of California[SM]–Sunnyvale; The Art Institute of Charleston[SM], SC, A branch of The Art Institute of Atlanta, GA; The Art Institute of Charlotte®, NC; The Art Institute of Colorado® (Denver); The Art Institute of Dallas®, TX; The Art Institute of Fort Lauderdale®, FL; The Art Institute of Houston®, TX; The Art Institute of Indianapolis[SM], IN*; The Art Institute of Jacksonville[SM], FL, A branch of Miami International University of Art & Design; The Art Institute of Las Vegas®, NV; The Art Institute of Michigan[SM] (Detroit); The Art Institute of New York City®, NY; The Art Institute of Ohio[SM]–Cincinnati**; The Art Institute of Philadelphia®, PA; The Art Institute of Phoenix®, AZ; The Art Institute of Pittsburgh®, PA; The Art Institute of Pittsburgh®–Online Division; The Art Institute of Portland®, OR; The Art Institute of Salt Lake City[SM], UT; The Art Institute of Seattle®, WA; The Art Institute of Tampa[SM], FL, A branch of Miami International University of Art & Design; The Art Institute of Tennessee[SM]–Nashville, A branch of The Art Institute of Atlanta, GA; The Art Institute of Tucson[SM], AZ; The Art Institute of Washington® (Arlington, VA), A branch of The Art Institute of Atlanta, GA; The Art Institute of York–Pennsylvania[SM]; The Art Institutes International Minnesota[SM] (Minneapolis); California Design College[SM] (Los Angeles–Wilshire Blvd.); The Illinois Institute of Art®–Chicago; The Illinois Institute of Art®–Schaumburg; Miami International University of Art & Design[SM], FL; The New England Institute of Art® (Boston, MA).

*The Art Institute of Indianapolis is licensed by the Indiana Commission on Proprietary Education, 302 W. Washington St., Rm. E201, Indianapolis, IN 46204, AC-0080.

**The Art Institute of Ohio–Cincinnati, 8845 Governors Hill Drive, Suite 100, Cincinnati, OH 45249-3317, OH Reg. #04-01-1698B.

AUSTIN COLLEGE

SHERMAN, TEXAS

The College

One of the finest selective liberal arts and sciences colleges in the nation, Austin College seeks students with evidence of academic ability and achievement, an eagerness for intellectual challenge and self-exploration, and a value-centered approach to their involvement. The learning environment is well suited to students who want to be known and challenged by faculty members and peers alike. The majority of students live on campus, creating a dynamic living and learning environment. Founded in 1849, Austin College is affiliated through a covenant relationship with the Presbyterian Church (U.S.A.). The liberal arts and sciences foundation develops lifelong learning abilities, such as thinking critically, solving problems, and communicating with others, and nurtures the whole person through academic, cocurricular, and social involvement.

International education and global awareness are priorities of the College, and more than 70 percent of Austin College graduates spend at least one month in international study during their college experience.

Austin College has an enrollment of approximately 1,350 students. The students are predominantly 18–21 years old, come from thirty-four states and twenty-five countries, and represent a diversity of ethnicity, religion, and experience.

Opportunities for involvement include more than sixty student organizations, ranging from academic to special interest to local fraternities and sororities. Involvement in music, theater, and art programs is available to all students regardless of major. Intercollegiate athletics through membership in the Southern Collegiate Athletic Conference include six sports for men and six for women, and many students take part in intramural activities. The College maintains a 29-acre recreational area on Lake Texoma, about 20 minutes from the campus. All students are encouraged to participate in volunteer service and be involved in the community.

Austin College offers guidance to students through Career Services, the Academic Skills Center, and Health Services. The campus dining service offers many food options for students each day. The campus offers coed and single-sex residence halls, as well as apartments and suites that are available to upperclass students. Students of German, French, Japanese, and Spanish may choose to live in the language residence, where the target languages are spoken in common areas.

Many students continue on to graduate and professional study and enjoy successful acceptance rates at these institutions. Austin College graduates can be found around the world in exciting and successful careers, and graduates regularly earn prestigious national honors.

Location

Austin College is located in Sherman, Texas, approximately 45 miles north of the greater Dallas metroplex. Sherman is a small city of approximately 35,000 that *Money* magazine includes among the top 15 percent of the 300 "most livable small cities" in the U.S. Sherman offers students plenty of cultural, religious, and social opportunities, and nearby Lake Texoma offers many additional recreational opportunities. For those seeking "big-city" excitement, the Dallas–Fort Worth metroplex is an hour's drive south on U.S. Highway 75.

Majors and Degrees

The Bachelor of Arts degree is offered in American studies, art, Asian studies, biochemistry, biology, business administration, chemistry, classical civilization, classics, communication studies (media studies, speech and social interaction, or theater emphasis), computer science, economics, education (through the master's program), English, environmental studies, French, German, history, international economics and finance, international relations, Latin, Latin American studies, mathematics, music, philosophy, physics, political science, psychology, religious studies, sociology, and Spanish. Interdisciplinary course work allows majors in anthropology, art history, cognitive science, educational psychology, ethics, exercise and sport science, gender studies, Japanese, Southwestern and Mexican studies, and Western intellectual tradition. In addition, the Special Degree Program allows students to design an individualized major incorporating various interests.

Through the Austin Teacher Program, a special five-year teacher education program, a student earns both the Bachelor of Arts degree in a major of choice and the Master of Arts in Teaching degree.

Austin College also has excellent preprofessional programs in engineering, health sciences, law, and theology.

Academic Programs

Making connections across disciplines and discovering the "bigger picture" bring learning to life. The Austin College curriculum emphasizes both depth and breadth of study. In the fall of the freshman year, all students take a seminar course that introduces them to the inquisitive learning style that defines Austin College. Instead of requiring every student to take a prescribed list of general education courses, Austin College uses a more flexible system that gives students control over their learning experience. Students fulfill the depth dimension by completing a major in a field of specialization plus a minor (or second major) in another field. The breadth dimension offers students the opportunity to explore across the disciplines in areas of personal interest. By careful selection of a minor, students may meet the goals of the breadth dimension while achieving some depth of study in a second field.

Students seeking a nontraditional major or minor may pursue the Special Program Option, in which study is individually designed. The program is particularly adaptable to the needs of students interested in studying interdisciplinary subject areas or in preparing for unique career fields.

Austin College has a 4-1-4 calendar year. Four courses are taken in the fall and spring terms, and one course is completed during the January term. Summer courses are also available. The January term offers an opportunity for in-depth study of one academic or special interest, travel courses, internships, and individualized study.

The College also offers the four-year Posey Leadership Institute, which combines course work, international study, volunteer service, an internship, involvement with a community mentor, and interaction with national and international leaders to develop awareness of leadership skills and styles. Membership in the Posey Leadership Institute is competitive and limited in number and includes a scholarship.

Off-Campus Programs

Students have opportunities for study in England, France, Germany, Spain, Japan, and other countries through the Institute of European and Asian Studies. They participate in the Washington Semester and Washington Summer Symposium as well. Students also can become involved in field study through the social sciences laboratory or individually arranged programs.

Academic Facilities

The College's excellent facilities include the Robert J. and Mary Wright Campus Center, science classrooms and laboratories, a computer center, the new Forster Art Studio Complex, two theaters, the Robert T. Mason Athletic-Recreation Complex, and the Jordan Family Language House, which offers a residential language immersion program in French, German, Japanese, and Spanish. Abell Library Center includes more than 300,000 volumes and 900 periodicals to maximize research and learning opportunities. A campuswide fiber-optic computer network and wireless access in many campus locations provide access to on-campus resources and the Internet. Five environmental research areas are all within a short drive of the campus.

Costs

The basic tuition and fees charge for students entering in 2007–08 was $24,945 and room and board amounted to $8234, for a total of $33,179.

Financial Aid

Assistance is given in three forms: grants and/or scholarships, loans, and on-campus jobs. Students applying for need-based financial aid should request a financial aid application from Austin College and should also submit the Free Application for Federal Student Aid (FAFSA). Competitive awards, based on merit rather than on financial need, are also available. Students who wish to be considered for general scholarship awards must indicate such on the Common Application Supplement for Austin College. Separate applications are necessary for the competitive scholarships: full-tuition Presidential Scholarships, Posey Leadership Institute Scholarships, Hallam Citizen Scholarships, Center for Southwestern and Mexican Studies Scholarships, John D. Moseley Alumni Fellowships and Scholarships, Moseley Scholarships for Presbyterian Students, and fine arts scholarships in art, music, and theater. More than 90 percent of students receive some form of financial assistance.

Faculty

Of the 106 full-time faculty members, 98 percent hold terminal degrees. Faculty members holding earned doctorates teach at all levels. In addition to carrying out their academic and professional responsibilities, faculty members participate in the governance of the College and serve as students' mentors. With a student-faculty ratio of 12:1 and an average class size of 22, the emphasis at Austin College is on classroom excellence.

Student Government

Under a community-government partnership plan, in which students and members of the faculty and administration are all participants, student involvement and leadership are important aspects of College governance. The College is committed to high principles in scholarship and general behavior.

Admission Requirements

Admission is competitive, with four times the number of applicants as places in the freshman class. Transfer students are subject to the same rigorous standards required of freshman applicants. Students who cannot fulfill these requirements are considered on an individual basis. All admission credentials for fall freshman applicants must be received by the Office of Admission by one of the following deadlines: December 1 for Early Action I applicants, January 15 for Early Action II applicants (and for scholarship applicants), and March 1 for Regular Decision applicants. Students who apply for admission after March 1 are considered on a space-available basis. To reserve a place in the entering class, a $350 deposit is required by May 1. The College's early admission program allows qualified students to enroll after their junior year of high school. Admission to Austin College is on an equal basis, regardless of age, color, disability, race, sex, sexual orientation, religion, national origin, or status as a veteran.

Application and Information

Austin College exclusively accepts the Common Application. Prospective students may apply online or download a copy at http://www.commonapp.org. Students also may obtain a copy from their high school guidance counselor or by calling Austin College. The Common Application Supplement for Austin College also is required. A completed application form, including a $35 nonrefundable application fee (waived for online submission), SAT Reasoning Test or ACT with writing scores, two letters of reference, and a transcript from each high school and college attended, must be submitted to Austin College.

For more information, students should contact:

Office of Admission
Austin College
900 North Grand Avenue, Suite 6N
Sherman, Texas 75090
Phone: 903-813-3000
800-KANGAROO (526-4276, toll-free)
Fax: 903-813-3198
E-mail: admission@austincollege.edu
Web site: http://www.austincollege.edu

Austin College's tree-lined walkways and green expanses provide a backdrop for the mixture of historical and modern buildings on the campus of the more than 150-year-old college.

BAYLOR UNIVERSITY

WACO, TEXAS

BAYLOR
UNIVERSITY

The University

Baylor University was chartered by the Republic of Texas in 1845 and is the state's oldest institution of higher education in continuous operation. Baylor, affiliated with the Baptist General Convention of Texas, is an academically rigorous university based solidly on Christian values and is a renowned teaching university with an ambitious and growing research agenda. Students come to Baylor from all fifty states and more than seventy countries. Baylor has 11,902 undergraduates and a total of 14,008 men and women in attendance. More than 300 social, service, professional, religious, and honorary student organizations, including national fraternities and sororities, provide opportunities for recreation, the development of social skills, spiritual and intellectual stimulation, and the pursuit of individual interests. Cultural events on campus include numerous concerts, symposia, and lectures as well as theater and opera.

Baylor, the only private university in the Big 12 Conference, competes in eighteen NCAA sports for men and women. Beyond varsity sports, the University offers extensive intramural and club programs. The McLane Student Life Center, a comprehensive fitness facility, offers a 52-foot freestanding climbing "rock;" volleyball, racquetball, and basketball courts; an indoor track; weight and cardio training; and swimming. The health and wellness clinics also are housed at the clinic. The Baylor Marina has canoes, kayaks, and Sunfish sailboats for use on the Brazos River.

Campus Living and Learning provides on-campus housing in more than ten single-gender residential communities that enable students to live and learn together in supportive environments that address the academic, spiritual, and personal needs of each student. The North Village Residential Community, which incorporates the Engineering and Computer Science Living-Learning Center, opened in fall 2004. Brooks Village and Brooks Residential College opened in fall 2007. It is planned that the Honors College Living-Learning Center will transition to a residential college in fall 2008. Living-Learning Center and other housing options are detailed at http://www.baylor.edu/cll. All freshmen are required to live on campus. Housing applications are accepted after admission to the University and payment of the deposit fee. Priority for housing is based on the date the housing application is received in the Campus Living and Learning office. For late applicants, priority is based on the date the housing deposit is received.

In addition to 150 undergraduate degree programs, Baylor offers seventy-five masters and twenty-two doctoral degree programs. The Baylor School of Law offers the Juris Doctor degree. Graduate work is offered through the Graduate School with the College of Arts and Sciences; Hankamer School of Business; the Schools of Education, Engineering and Computer Science, Music, and Social Work; in the Louise Herrington School of Nursing at Dallas; and in the U.S. Army Academy of Health Sciences at San Antonio. The George W. Truett Theological Seminary offers the Master of Divinity and Doctor of Ministry degrees.

Location

Baylor's 735-acre campus is adjacent to the Brazos River in Waco (area population 213,000), which is halfway between Austin and Dallas/Fort Worth on I-35 and near the geographic center of Texas (affectionately called the Heart of Texas). Houston, San Antonio, and the Gulf Coast of Texas are also within easy driving distance. Among Waco's recreational options are the amazing natural green space in Cameron Park and Lake Waco, hiking and biking trails, and a revitalized warehouse district featuring restaurants and specialty shops.

Majors and Degrees

Baylor University's undergraduate programs are available in the College of Arts and Sciences; Hankamer School of Business; Louise Herrington School of Nursing; the Schools of Education, Engineering and Computer Science, Music, and Social Work; and in the Honors College. There are 150 baccalaureate degree programs.

The College of Arts and Sciences, Hankamer School of Business, Honors College, and the Schools of Education and Social Work offer departmental and intra-university programs leading to the Bachelor of Arts (B.A.), Bachelor of Science (B.S.), Bachelor of Science in Aviation Sciences (B.S.A.S.), Bachelor of Science in Education (B.S.Ed.), Bachelor of Science in Family and Consumer Sciences (B.S.F.C.S.), or Bachelor of Fine Arts (B.F.A.) degrees. Undergraduate majors in these schools and colleges include accounting; American studies; anthropology; applied mathematics; archaeology; architecture (with Washington University); art history; Asian studies; athletic training; aviation sciences; biblical and related languages; biochemistry; biology; business administration; business–arts and entertainment; business–broadcasting; business–German; business–journalism; business–Russian; business–Spanish; chemistry; child and family studies; church recreation; classics; communication sciences and disorders; communication specialist studies; community health; computer information systems; computer science; dentistry (combination program with an accredited dental school); design; distribution management and technology; earth sciences; economics; education; English; entrepreneurship; environmental science; environmental studies; exercise physiology; fashion design; fashion merchandising; finance; financial services/planning; forestry (final year at Duke University); French; general family and consumer science; general studies in health, human performance, and recreation; geography; geology; geophysics; German; great texts; Greek; health science studies; human resources management; information systems; interior design; international business; international studies; journalism; language and linguistics; Latin; Latin American studies; management; marketing; mathematics; medical humanities; medicine (combination program with an accredited medical school); museum studies; music; neuroscience; nutrition sciences; operations management; optometry (combination program with an accredited optometry school); performance; philosophy; physical education; physical science; physics; political science; professional selling; professional writing; psychology; public administration; real estate; recreation; religion; risk management and insurance; Russian (9 hours required with another Russian program); science; Slavic and East European studies; social studies; social work; sociology; Spanish; special education; speech communication; sports sponsorship and sales; statistics; studio art; teacher certification programs; telecommunication; theater arts; and University scholars. In addition, programs are available in pre–dental hygiene, predentistry, premedicine, pre–occupational therapy, preoptometry, prepharmacy, pre–physical therapy, and pre–veterinary medicine.

The School of Engineering and Computer Science offers programs of study leading to the Bachelor of Science in Engineering (B.S.E.), Bachelor of Science in Electrical and Computer Engineering (B.S.E.C.E.), and Bachelor of Science in Mechanical Engineering (B.S.M.E.) degrees with majors in electrical and computer engineering, engineering, and mechanical engineering. The school also offers programs of study leading to the Bachelor of Science in Computer Science (B.S.C.S.), including gaming and software engineering concentrations, and the Bachelor of Science in Informatics (B.S.I.).

The School of Music offers programs of study leading to the Bachelor of Music (B.M.) degree in applied music, church music, composition, history and literature, pedagogy, and theory. The Bachelor of Music Education (B.M.E.) degree is designed for prospective teachers in public schools and offers concentrations in choral and instrumental instruction.

The Louise Herrington School of Nursing combines a liberal arts curriculum and professional preparation in a four-year program leading to the Bachelor of Science in Nursing (B.S.N.) degree. Nursing majors complete their first two years on the Waco campus and then move to Dallas for two years in the professional component of the curriculum.

Academic Programs

Baylor, a Phi Beta Kappa university, operates on a two-semester academic year plus two 6-week summer sessions. In the first two years, students select courses that provide a broadly based liberal arts education. All students admitted to Baylor University as freshmen enter the College of Arts and Sciences, the School of Music, or a preprofessional program in the Hankamer School of Business, the School of

Education, School of Engineering and Computer Science, or the Louise Herrington School of Nursing. Students pursuing degrees in one of the other professional schools may apply for admission to a specific degree program during the second year. Those students admitted to the University who intend to major in music must audition to qualify for admission to the School of Music at the time they enter the University to avoid undue delay in the completion of their degree program. Many of Baylor's students enter with credit hours earned through credit by examination. A number of these students elect to join the Honors College, which includes the Baylor Interdisciplinary Core (a set of comprehensive and cohesive interdisciplinary courses that are organized around world cultures, the natural world, and the social world), the Honors Program, University Scholars, and Great Texts.

Off-Campus Programs

Students may enroll in summer, semester, or yearlong programs in more than twenty-five countries, including Argentina, Austria, Brazil, China, Costa Rica, Dominica, Egypt, England, France, Greece, Israel, Italy, Kenya, Russia, Scotland, Spain, Switzerland, Thailand, and Turkey.

Academic Facilities

Continuing the University's ongoing commitment to improve student life in the classroom and on campus, Baylor for fall 2007 opened the $42.8-million Brooks Village residential community, a nearby 800-car parking garage, and a $6-million renovation that transformed the Sid Richardson Building into the home of the Paul L. Foster Success Center, offering academic advisement, support programs, career counseling, and career services. Facilities under construction include the $34-million Highers Athletics Complex with the Simpson Athletics and Academic Center and the McMullen-Connally Faculty Center. These projects are complemented by three major projects that opened in 2004: the $103-million Baylor Sciences Building, with 500,000 square feet of multidisciplinary state-of-the-art classrooms, departmental and faculty offices, labs, and research centers; the $23-million Harry and Anna Jeanes Discovery Center, which houses the museum studies department and the centerpiece of the Mayborn Museum Complex; and the $33-million North Village Residential Community, which provides apartment-style options on campus in three houses, a community center, classrooms, in-residence faculty members, and special courses for student members of the Engineering and Computer Science Living-Learning Center. These facilities underscore the tremendous resources available to enhance students' practical and academic experiences. These resources include the central libraries, special libraries, and resource centers that provide traditional texts (more than 2.1 million bound volumes and 2.6 million microforms and government documents); high-tech resources, such as laptops for checkout and electronic resources; and study inducements, such as Java City, a café within Moody Library. Intel Corporation named Baylor as one of the nation's most unwired universities, with AirBear wireless access available almost anywhere on the campus.

Costs

The estimated direct total cost for 2008–09 is $35,472. Tuition is $23,664 (flat tuition rate for 12 hours or more, two semesters), residence hall rooms are $4564, board (sixteen meals per week) is $4674, and required fees are $2570. (Less costly room and board plans are available.) The total figure does not include the cost of books, travel, or personal expenditures. Books and supplies are estimated at $1634 per year. Travel costs and personal expenditures vary with the individual. Costs are subject to change.

Financial Aid

Four basic forms of financial aid are available and are based on merit (as shown by achievement, National Merit status, and SAT or ACT scores) and need (as determined by the FAFSA). These programs include scholarships, grants, loans, and on-campus jobs. About 84 percent of the students receive some form of assistance. Students are considered for scholarships by virtue of the application for admission. Students may obtain a FAFSA from their high school counselor, local college or university, or by going to FAFSA's Web site at http://www.fafsa.ed.gov.

Faculty

Baylor's faculty numbers 851, and 90 percent hold the highest degree offered in their fields. More than ninety-five percent of all classes are taught by faculty members. Most faculty members are actively engaged in research, several hold special chairs in their respective fields, and all are dedicated to challenging and teaching students. All faculty members work with undergraduates and serve as academic advisers to the students. The student-faculty ratio is 16:1, and a typical class numbers 29 students.

Student Government

Baylor University Student Government, whose members are elected by popular vote, is a vital and influential force in campus activities. About 300 active student organizations, numerous traditional events, special involvement programs, entertainment programs, and leadership laboratories, offer plenty of opportunities for students to get involved in campus life.

Admission Requirements

Consideration for admission to Baylor is highly competitive. Baylor seeks to enroll students with strong academic preparation who show the greatest potential to succeed. However, Baylor may use a variety of factors in determining the admissibility of any applicant, so it is not possible to identify a minimum level of achievement on each or any factor necessary to gain admission. Other applicants who do not qualify for priority admission may be considered for admission at the discretion of the Admissions Committee. Such admission may require attendance in summer school and entrance with special requirements. Required high school units are English, 4; college-preparatory mathematics, 3; laboratory science, 2; foreign language, 2; and social science, 2 (1 in history). Prospective freshmen should take the SAT or ACT examination no later than the second semester of their junior year in high school and have the results sent to Baylor by the testing company. Freshman applications can be submitted as early as the summer prior to the senior year.

Students who wish to transfer to Baylor and who have completed at least 30 semester hours must present official transcripts from each college attended verifying a minimum overall grade point average of 2.5 (on a 4.0 scale) and must be eligible to return to the last school attended. Transfer students who seek admission with fewer than 30 semester hours must meet all the admission requirements for beginning freshmen. In addition, all transfer students must meet the same minimum course requirements for admission that are required for beginning freshmen. A student may present a high school transcript or a college transcript to verify that the course requirements have been fulfilled. Transfer students should plan to apply no later than the end of their sophomore year in order to meet the Baylor residence requirement of 60 semester hours.

Application and Information

Application deadlines and notification dates are as follows: the Early Action 1 application deadline is November 1 with notification by January 15, and the regular decision application deadline is February 1 with notification by March 15. Applications received after February 1 are considered on a space-available basis.

The complete file includes a general application for admission with a $50 application fee (however, the online application is free), an official high school transcript documenting the applicant's rank in class, and official scores on the SAT or ACT. Students are encouraged to apply early in the fall to receive a decision by January 15. Requests for application forms and inquiries should be addressed to:

Admission Services
Baylor University
One Bear Place #97056
Waco, Texas 76798-7056
Phone: 254-710-3435
800-BAYLOR-U (toll-free)
E-mail: admissions@baylor.edu
Web site: http://www.baylor.edu

PRAIRIE VIEW A&M UNIVERSITY

PRAIRIE VIEW, TEXAS

The University

Prairie View A&M University (PVAMU) is dedicated to excellence in teaching, research, and service. It is committed to achieving relevance in each component of its mission by addressing issues and proposing solutions through programs and services designed to respond to the needs and aspirations of individuals, families, organizations, agencies, schools, and communities—both rural and urban. Prairie View A&M University is a state-assisted institution by legislative designation, serving a diverse ethnic and socioeconomic population, and a land-grant institution by federal statute. PVAMU is a historically black university (HBCU) and was founded by the Texas legislature as the first state-supported college for African Americans.

Having been designated by the Texas constitution as one of the three "institutions of the first class" (1984), the University is committed to preparing undergraduates in a range of careers, including (but not limited to) engineering, computer science, natural sciences, architecture, business, technology, criminal justice, the humanities, education, agricultural sciences, nursing, mathematics, and the social sciences. It is committed to advanced education through the master's degree in education, engineering, natural sciences, nursing, selected social sciences, agriculture, business, and human sciences. It is committed to expanding its advanced educational offerings to include multiple doctoral programs.

The University's public service programs, offered primarily through the Cooperative Extension Program, target both rural and urban counties in the state of Texas. The University's research foci include extending knowledge in all disciplines offered and incorporating research-based experiences in both undergraduate and graduate students' academic development.

While striving to maintain excellent instruction and a strong curriculum, the University nurtures students' academic development and intellectual curiosity by providing a stimulating physical and cultural environment. As a special-purpose university, Prairie View A&M develops special programming to identify and assist talented students who may otherwise be overlooked. The University believes it can and should help students realize the numerous possibilities of the mind and spirit so that they may become productive citizens who lead fulfilling lives.

The enrollment is nearly 8,300 students. Men account for 39 percent and women account for 61 percent of the total enrollment. Approximately 94 percent of the students are state residents. Students from other countries account for 2 percent of the total enrollment. Approximately 70 percent of the students are between the ages of 18 and 24. On-campus housing consists of an ultramodern freshman residential complex and twenty-nine apartment buildings, which collectively accommodate more than 3,000 students. Each room is equipped with a direct-line telephone, cable television services, wireless Internet access, a microwave, and a freezer/refrigerator. The apartment buildings consist of suites with two or four private bedroom units, a community living room, and a kitchenette. A limited number (about 30 percent) of the apartments have full kitchens. All housing facilities have accommodations (per ADA requirements) for the physically challenged.

Student life programs are aimed at giving students an opportunity to achieve their educational and career goals without neglecting the support, encouragement, and sense of community that foster a feeling of belonging. The student activities and leadership staff members are committed to enriching the University environment so that students can establish personal value systems and refine interpersonal and leadership skills in support of their lifetime aims and objectives. Student organizations include sororities, fraternities, honor societies, the band, choirs, religious groups, special-interest clubs, drama, the forensic team, and social clubs. The University Marching and Symphonic Bands and the Percussion Ensemble develop students' musical talents. The Prairie View Panthers sports teams for men and women compete in the Southwestern Athletic Conference in NCAA Division I baseball, basketball, bowling, football, golf, softball, tennis, track, and volleyball. Active intramural sports and recreational programs are available.

Location

The University, with its picturesque 1,509-acre campus situated on "The Hill," is located in Prairie View, Texas, on the gently rolling hills of Waller County (population 36,000) in the historic Brazos Valley known by the early Indian settlers as "the arms of God." The University's location offers the advantages of a pleasant, semirural environment, with convenient access to the excitement of a major American city. Prairie View is on the frontier of change at the Northwest Houston growth corridor. There are a variety of restaurants, shopping facilities, rodeo events, and cultural and ethnic festivals as well as access to lakes for water sports and facilities for horseback riding in the area.

The campus is located only 40 miles from the heart of Houston, the fourth-most-populous city in the U.S.; the urban environment offers students opportunities to experience its theater district, professional teams representing every major sport, and more than 500 cultural, visual, and performing arts organizations, ninety of which are devoted to multicultural and minority arts. The Prairie View College of Nursing is located in the Texas Medical Center, the largest medical center in the world. Houston is also home to eighteen Fortune 500 companies and more than 5,000 energy-related firms and is considered by many to be the energy capital of the world.

Majors and Degrees

The University offers fifty undergraduate degree programs, thirty-seven master's degrees, and four doctoral degree programs. The following undergraduate degrees are available: Bachelor of Architecture, Bachelor of Arts, Bachelor of Arts in Social Work, Bachelor of Business Administration, Bachelor of Music, and Bachelor of Science. Undergraduate degree majors include accounting, agricultural engineering, agriculture, applied music, architecture, biology, chemical engineering, chemistry, civil engineering, communications, computer-aided drafting and design technology, computer science, construction science, criminal justice, dietetics, drama, electrical engineering, electrical engineering technology, English, family and community services, finance, health, history, human development and the family, human performance, human science, interdisciplinary studies, management, management information systems, marketing, mathematics, mechanical engineering, mechanical engineering technology, merchandising and design, music, nursing, physics, political science, psychology, social work, sociology, and Spanish. Coordinate degrees are offered in biology, business, chemistry, education, engineering, human sciences, and sociology. Specializations are offered within the major areas of study in some degree programs.

Academic Programs

The requirements for a bachelor's degree at Prairie View A&M University ensure that graduates have a well-rounded educational experience. The University is committed to providing an educational environment that includes social, cultural, and service activities. Students must complete the University core course requirements in addition to the specific course and semester-hour requirements for the degree program selected. The University requires a minimum of 120 semester hours and at least a 2.0 cumulative grade point average for graduation. The University awards credit for successful scores on the Advanced Placement examinations. Highly motivated students are rewarded with an opportunity to challenge themselves academically through the accelerated courses offered by the University Scholars Program. Military science programs include Army

ROTC and Naval ROTC. Cooperative education and service-learning programs are available in some departments. Support services, tutoring, assessment testing, career exploration, precollege programs, international-student advising, undecided-major advising, multicultural programs, study-abroad and student exchange programs, crisis counseling, and placement counseling are offered.

The academic calendar is based on the semester system. In addition, three-, five-, eight-, and ten-week summer sessions are offered. The normal course load ranges from 12 semester hours to 18 semester hours during the regular academic year and up to a maximum of 12 semester hours during the summer terms.

Academic Facilities

Modern facilities include well-equipped classrooms and laboratories. Specially designed studios, theaters, and auditoriums are available for the visual and performing arts. The most modern facilities include the new architecture building, a criminal justice building, an electrical engineering building, a nursing building, a multimedia foreign-language laboratory, an engineering technology building, a chemical engineering building, and the John B. Coleman Library, which features state-of-the-art equipment, an expanded Learning Resources Center, and a laboratory for computer-assisted instruction. The library contains more than 356,000 volumes, 696,000 microforms, and several special collections. More than 25,000 electronic journals and many databases are currently available at the library. Nursing students who have fulfilled their foundation course work and who are admitted to the College of Nursing complete five semesters in a new state-of-the-art facility located in the heart of the Texas Medical Center in Houston. Other campus facilities include the Academic Computing Center and studios for Prairie View's radio station (KPVU) and cable television operations.

Costs

For 2007–08, students who were Texas residents paid $145 per semester hour. Out-of-state students paid $423 per semester hour. On-campus residence hall and University Village room rates varied according to the accommodations selected. All students who reside in University residence halls are required to participate in the University food-service plan; students have the option of seven, ten, or fourteen cafeteria-style meals per week. The approximate total cost of room and board was $4345 per academic year. Annual costs of books and supplies vary according to major and class load but typically average $600. Additional fees vary, but the minimum full-time charge was $2175 per semester for a student enrolled for 15 semester hours.

Financial Aid

Prairie View A&M University administers a wide range of programs to help students meet the cost of attending the University. Various factors are considered in determining who qualifies for financial aid. Programs available to provide financial support include academic and need-based scholarships, state and federal loans and grants, and student employment. Students are required to complete a need analysis to determine their extent of need and eligibility for aid. Approximately 88 percent of the students at Prairie View receive some form of financial assistance. For more information, students should contact the Office of Student Financial Services at 936-261-1000, prompt #1.

Faculty

The University's faculty consists of 389 full-time faculty members, 91 percent of whom have earned doctoral degrees.

Student Government

All members of the student body are members of the Student Government Association (SGA). The SGA is the official voice through which students' opinions may be expressed. Its elected student members provide effective representation and responsible participation in the overall policymaking and decision-making processes of the University. While the SGA promotes academic excellence and high-quality education, its student members have the opportunity to obtain valuable leadership and management experience. The SGA also recommends students to serve on various committees and advisory boards of the University.

Admission Requirements

Admission to Prairie View A&M University is open to qualified individuals regardless of race, color, sex, creed, age, national origin, or educationally unrelated handicap. To apply for admission, students must provide a completed application and a $25 application fee, a certified high school transcript or a GED certificate (high school equivalency diploma), and SAT or ACT scores. In addition to the admission application, transfer applicants must submit transcripts from previous colleges attended and the application fee. International students must also submit an Affidavit of Financial Support and Test of English as a Foreign Language (TOEFL) scores, along with supporting documents. Applicants should note that the Texas State Education Code requires that all students "who enter Texas public institutions of higher education in the fall of 1989 and thereafter must be tested for reading, writing, and mathematics skills." This includes all "full-time and part-time students enrolled in a certificate or degree program." Transfer students must provide Texas Higher Education Assessment (THEA) scores or proof of exemption or take the test. Students who plan to enroll must take the THEA test before enrolling in any college-level courses.

Application and Information

Office of Undergraduate Admission
Prairie View A&M University
P.O. Box 519, MS 1009
Prairie View, Texas 77446
Phone: 936-261-1000, prompt #3
Fax: 936-261-1079

Office of Recruitment and Marketing
Prairie View A&M University
P.O. Box 519, MS 1011
Prairie View, Texas 77446
Phone: 936-261-1000, prompt #2
Fax: 936-261-1094
E-mail: recruitment@pvamu.edu
Web site: http://www.pvamu.edu

The College of Nursing building.

RICE UNIVERSITY

HOUSTON, TEXAS

The University

William Marsh Rice University is a private, comprehensive, research university. Rice offers undergraduate and graduate degrees in architecture, engineering, humanities, music, social sciences, and natural sciences. The Jesse H. Jones Graduate School of Management offers graduate degrees and an undergraduate minor. The faculty-student ratio is 1:5 and the median class size is 15 students. Undergraduates choose from more than fifty different majors and find research opportunities in more than forty interdisciplinary research centers on campus. Every undergraduate has access to research, study abroad, and experiential learning opportunities.

Of the 5,243 students currently enrolled, 3,051 are undergraduates. The student body comes from all fifty states and forty-six other countries. Thirty-nine percent are members of minority groups. More than 68 percent of the entering freshmen ranked in the top 5 percent of their high school class.

Perhaps the most distinctive feature of Rice's campus life is the residential college system. All new students are randomly assigned to one of nine residential colleges. The colleges serve not only as residence halls but also as primary centers for dining, studying, playing, networking, and developing leadership skills. The residential colleges facilitate a high degree of student-faculty interaction. A faculty master and his or her family live in a house adjacent to the college. The masters and several resident associates (faculty or staff members who live in the college) assist students in various ways, from enriching intellectual life to participating in cultural and service activities to cheering on intramural teams. Approximately 20 other professors per college are nonresident associates, eating lunch in the college, serving as academic advisers, and participating in a myriad of extracurricular activities organized by the students.

Rice undergraduates pursue the highest levels of athletic competition through NCAA Division I-A sports and through club sports. As members of Conference U.S.A., Rice athletes compete in baseball, basketball, cross-country, football, golf, soccer, swimming, tennis, track and field, and volleyball. Club sports include badminton, crew, cricket, cycling, fencing, karate, lacrosse, rugby, sailing, soccer, Ultimate Frisbee, volleyball, and water polo.

Location

The fourth-largest city in the nation, Houston is a vibrant center for the arts and culture. The downtown Theater District, only 5 miles from the Rice campus, is host to permanent companies in ballet, opera, symphony, and theater. Just 3 blocks from campus is the Museum District, which is composed of eleven museums that feature outstanding collections and exhibitions of art, nature, science, medicine, and history. The district also encompasses Hermann Park, home to the Houston Zoo, an amphitheater, a public golf course, and a Japanese garden. The Texas Medical Center, the world's largest medical center, is adjacent to Hermann Park and across the street from the campus. Across the street from Rice's main entrance is a light rail stop that provides quick access to museums, shopping, professional sports, and the nation's second largest theater district. All Rice students have a Rice-sponsored "Passport to Houston," which gives free, unlimited access to the light rail, the bus system, and the museums. The campus itself covers 300 acres, shaded by almost 4,000 trees and bordered by a 3-mile jogging trail. Rice is located on the edge of one of Houston's most beautiful residential areas and in one of the safest sections of the city.

Majors and Degrees

Students interested in architecture choose between the four-year B.A. program and the six-year Bachelor of Architecture (B.Arch.) degree. Those who have been admitted to the B.Arch. program spend their fifth year in a working preceptorship with an architectural firm, returning to Rice to complete a final year of architectural study for the degree. Among the approved preceptorships are Pei, Cobb, Freed & Partners, Cesar Pelli & Associates, Michael Graves, and Renzo Piano Building Shop.

The George R. Brown School of Engineering offers majors in bioengineering, chemical engineering, civil and environmental engineering, computational and applied mathematics, computer science, electrical and computer engineering, mechanical engineering, materials science, and statistics. These programs lead to either the B.A. or the B.S. degree.

Through the School of Humanities, students may declare majors in art history, classical studies, English, French studies, German and Slavic studies, Hispanic studies, history, kinesiology, linguistics, philosophy, religious studies, and visual and dramatic arts. Interdisciplinary majors are available in ancient Mediterranean civilizations, Asian studies, medieval studies, and the study of women, gender, and sexuality.

Music students may opt for either a B.A. or a Bachelor of Music (B.Mus.) degree in composition, music history, music theory, or performance. Students who pass the qualifying examination may elect an honors program that leads to the simultaneous awarding of the B.Mus. and the Master of Music (M.Mus.) degrees after five years of study, the final two years of which are devoted to the student's particular specialization.

The Wiess School of Natural Sciences awards the B.A. degree in the field of mathematics. Students may elect either the B.A. or B.S. degree in biochemistry and cell biology, chemistry, earth science, ecology and evolutionary biology, and physics and astronomy.

The School of Social Sciences offers B.A. degrees with majors in anthropology, economics, mathematical economic analysis, political science, psychology, and sociology. In cooperation with Rice's School of Management, a business minor is also available. Interdepartmental majors include cognitive sciences, policy studies, and the study of women, gender, and sexuality.

Students at Rice enjoy very high rates of acceptance into professional and graduate schools throughout the United States

Academic Programs

Because it believes that undergraduates should become acquainted with areas of study outside their specialization, Rice has implemented a set of distribution requirements, requiring course work in three different areas of study. There is no core curriculum; rather, all students choose courses to fulfill the distribution requirements from a list that includes more than forty academic subject areas. The flexibility of the curriculum allows students the option of completing double or triple majors, interdepartmental majors, or area majors. Students are assisted in these choices by faculty advisers, who begin working with students as early as freshman orientation.

The Rice/Baylor College of Medicine Medical Scholars Program (MSP) promotes the education of students who are scientifically competent, compassionate, and socially conscious. It is the hope of Rice University and Baylor College of Medicine that these students will apply insight from the extensive study of liberal arts and other disciplines to the study of modern medical science. The MSP students explore the entire range of Rice University undergraduate programs to the extent that their interests allow. After graduation, they begin their medical education at Baylor College of Medicine. Each year, 14 incoming freshmen are admitted into the program. The scholars complete the traditional four years at Rice followed by four years at Baylor for a medical degree.

Classroom learning is enhanced by additional experiences. Each year, the number of internship opportunities posted by the Career Services Center exceeds the number of students looking for internships. In addition, a large number of undergraduates are conducting primary research. Since 1990, more than 230 undergraduates have earned graduate fellowships from the National Science Foundation.

Rice observes a two-semester calendar, and students enroll in an average of five courses per semester.

Off-Campus Programs

Recognizing the importance of a global perspective, Rice encourages students to enrich their academic experience with a summer, semester, or year of study abroad. The Office of International Programs and faculty members assist students in identifying the best programs for their individual interests and needs. Rice undergraduates have studied on every continent—including Antarctica—and earned academic credit or work experience in more than forty countries. Approximately 40 percent of Rice undergraduates study abroad. Financial assistance is available for study-abroad and exchange programs.

Academic Facilities

The Fondren Library is accessible to students 24 hours a day and is a charter member of JSTOR, an electronic archive of important journals. The library contains more than 2.4 million volumes, 3.2 million microforms, and 55,775 audiovisual materials. The library's holdings include extensive special collections, such as those in art and music and eighteenth-century British drama. Students have on-site and remote access to the library's online catalog, indexes, and full-text reference sources and direct access to the stacks, which are lined with private study carrels. PowerBooks and Macintosh and UNIX workstations are located throughout the building.

Rice students have access to some of the best computing facilities in the country. All undergraduates are eligible for an Owlnet account, which gives them free access to e-mail, word processing, spreadsheets, statistical and graphics software, and many other packages. Wireless access is available in classrooms, the library, residence halls, and the student center. Owlnet computing labs are located throughout the campus, including one in each residential college, and a network connection port for every student resident.

The Alice Pratt Brown Hall is a $22-million facility and houses the Shepherd School of Music and provides concert facilities for the Shepherd School of Music. Musical performances in its concert and recital halls enjoy outstanding acoustics and attract audiences of more than 70,000 music lovers each year. Hamman Hall provides theater space for the student drama group. The Rice University Gallery functions principally as an extension of the teaching activities of the art and art history department and sponsors major exhibits regularly. In addition, the University has extensive science and engineering laboratories, language laboratories, art studios, spacious architectural laboratories, and the Gardiner Symonds Teaching Laboratory, which facilitates interactive teaching through innovative architecture and computer technology.

Costs

Tuition at Rice is substantially less than that at comparable universities—$29,960 for the academic year 2008–09. The yearly cost, including tuition, room and board ($10,750), and fees ($519), totals $41,229.

Financial Aid

Rice offers need- and merit-based financial aid. To determine financial need, Rice requires the CSS Financial Aid PROFILE, the Free Application for Federal Student Aid (FAFSA), and a copy of the family's tax return. If need exists, Rice meets 100 percent of demonstrated need with a combination of grants, loans, and campus employment. For families with less than $60,000 in total income, Rice meets all need with grants and work-study—no loans. The University also provides merit awards. All applicants are automatically considered for merit scholarships regardless of financial status. Rice has been recognized consistently by *U.S. News & World Report, Time, The Princeton Review,* and *Money* magazine as one of the best values in higher education.

Faculty

Rice has a distinguished faculty that is devoted to teaching and research. In addition to the $71 million of sponsored research projects that are currently under way, one third of the faculty members edit or serve on editorial boards of scholarly research journals. Rice professors bring this excitement of discovery to the classroom. Ninety-one percent of undergraduate courses are taught by faculty members rather than lecturers or graduate students. Professors regularly interact with undergraduates in the classroom, as members of the residential colleges, and as academic advisers.

Student Government

All undergraduates are members of the Rice Student Association, which is governed through a Student Senate. Every student is also a member of one of nine residential colleges, each of which has its own government and judicial system. Rice also has an honor system, which is administered by an elected student Honor Council. All written examinations and assignments are conducted under the honor code.

Admission Requirements

The Admission Committee seeks students of keen intellect and diverse backgrounds who not only show potential for success at Rice, but also will contribute to the educational environment of those around them. Rice's individualized, holistic evaluation process employs many different means to identify these qualities in applicants. In the holistic review, Rice examines objective information, such as transcripts and standardized test results, as well as a wide range of subjective factors including, but not limited to, creativity, leadership, talents, community contributions, intellectual vitality, and life experiences. All applicants are required to submit an application, application fee or fee waiver, counselor and teacher recommendation, high school transcripts, and scores from the SAT or the ACT with Writing, and two SAT subject tests. Interviews are optional.

Application and Information

Two decision plans are available for freshmen. Early decision is binding; students apply by November 1 and are notified by December 15. Regular decision candidates apply by January 2 and are notified by April 1. Under regular decision, admitted students have until the national reply date of May 1 to respond. Students who have completed two full semesters of college work may apply as transfers by October 15 for midyear (January) enrollment or by March 15 for fall-term (August) enrollment. There is a $60 application fee for all applications.

Office of Admission-MS 17
Rice University
P.O. Box 1892
Houston, Texas 77251-1892
Phone: 713-348-RICE
800-527-OWLS (toll-free)
Web site: http://www.rice.edu/admission

Lovett Hall, with its trademark Sallyport, is the oldest building on the Rice campus.

ST. EDWARD'S UNIVERSITY

AUSTIN, TEXAS

The University

St. Edward's University offers students the best of both worlds—small classes and a close-knit community in the midst of one of the most exciting cities in the country. Located 10 minutes from downtown Austin, the 198-acre campus featuring hills, trees, and historic architecture offers one of the best views of the Austin skyline. But it is the University's vision, more than the view, that makes it distinctive. A St. Edward's University education combines the critical-thinking skills of a liberal arts curriculum with hands-on experience in internships, service learning, and study abroad. Its Catholic character gives students a foundation in ethics and encourages them to strive for justice.

It is an exciting time to be a student at St. Edward's. The total student population has grown to 5,220, including 3,280 undergraduates. The University has built six new buildings since 2000, including a 58,000-square-foot science building with state-of-the-art labs and a rooftop greenhouse. Next on the list is a new residence hall that will feature a dining facility, coffeehouse, and wellness resources on the ground floor. In addition to the new facilities, St. Edward's has added eleven new majors, including forensic science, graphic design, and entrepreneurship.

Founded by the Congregation of Holy Cross in 1885, the University teaches its students to think creatively and with integrity, to build a more just world, and to develop a global perspective. The St. Edward's mission statement is lived each day as students connect their education to the Austin community and the larger world. The University values diversity in all its forms—ethnic, religious, socioeconomic, geographic—and supports programs and events that help expand students' worldviews.

The most popular majors at St. Edward's are psychology, communication, biology, and business. The unique theater arts program allows students to earn points toward their Actors' Equity membership card while working with professional mentors. The new Academic Exploration Program guides students who have not chosen a major, offering a class designed to help freshmen find their strengths and interests. All students are paired with faculty advisers who assist them in planning degree programs and who provide academic counseling throughout the students' college careers.

An essential part of the academic experience at St. Edward's is preparing for life after earning an undergraduate degree. The Career Planning Office helps students explore careers, secure internship opportunities, and prepare for graduate school and employment.

Outside of class, opportunities abound for recreation and cultural enrichment. The more than seventy student organizations include intramural sports, Student Government Association, political groups, honor societies, spirit groups, and cultural organizations. Campus Ministry offers retreats, volunteer projects, interfaith dialogue, and opportunities to grow in the Catholic faith. Athletic events, theater productions, concerts, and campus traditions give students a chance to relax and have fun.

Students have many choices in on-campus housing, from apartments for upper-level students to traditional residence halls to house-style living in the Casitas. Freshmen are required to live in the residence halls unless they are living with their parents while attending the University.

St. Edward's is a member of the NCAA Division II Heartland Conference, and in the 2006–07 academic year its teams won nine conference championships. Men compete in baseball, basketball, cross-country, golf, soccer, and tennis. Women compete in basketball, cross-country, golf, soccer, softball, tennis, and volleyball.

Location

St. Edward's University is located in Austin, the capital of Texas and one of the most vibrant educational and political centers in the United States. Along with its internationally known film festival and music scene, Austin also offers local theaters, galleries, and museums. Students at St. Edward's enjoy year-round use of Austin's three major lakes and nearly 200 parks, such as nearby Zilker Park with its natural, spring-fed swimming pool, canoe rentals for use on Lady Bird Lake, a hike-and-bike trail, a botanical garden, and playing fields.

Majors and Degrees

St. Edward's University confers four undergraduate degrees—Bachelor of Arts, Bachelor of Arts in Applied Science, Bachelor of Business Administration, and Bachelor of Science—and offers more than fifty areas of study through the Schools of Behavioral and Social Sciences, Management and Business, Natural Sciences, Humanities, and Education. Majors offered are accounting, accounting information technology, art, biochemistry, bioinformatics, biology, business administration, chemistry, communication, computer information science, computer science, criminal justice, criminology, digital media, economics, English literature, English writing and rhetoric, entrepreneurship, environmental chemistry, environmental science and policy, finance, forensic chemistry, forensic science, global studies, graphic design, history, international business, kinesiology, Latin American studies, liberal studies, management, marketing, mathematics, philosophy, photocommunications, political science, psychology, religious studies, social work, sociology, Spanish, and theater arts.

The School of Education also offers teacher certification programs for early childhood–grade 4, grades 4–8, grades 8–12, early childhood–grade 12 (in art, kinesiology, and theater arts), and secondary religious education. Supplemental certification is available in bilingual education and ESL.

Many students choose to pursue a preprofessional program in conjunction with their established majors. St. Edward's offers preprofessional programs in dentistry, engineering, law, medicine and physical therapy. In addition, St. Edward's offers eight master's degrees.

Academic Programs

All students share an intensive general education requirement of 57 credit hours spanning all four years. The requirements are split into three areas: foundational skills (English writing, college math, computational skills, oral communication, and foreign language), cultural foundations (six courses including American Dilemmas, Literature and Human Experience, and Contemporary World Issues), and foundations for values and decisions (five courses including Ethics and Science in Perspective). The general education curriculum culminates with Capstone, a writing course in which students investigate a controversial issue, analyze it, and propose a resolution, both orally and in a major paper. The reasoning and communication skills and the understanding of society that these general studies develop are reinforced in each student's in-depth study of a major discipline.

Graduation is based on the successful completion of 120 semester hours of study. St. Edward's observes a two-semester academic calendar, and the University's flexible summer course schedule offers day and evening classes.

Off-Campus Programs

Hands-on experiential learning is a central component of a St. Edward's University education. Students conduct research and complete internships on and off campus, including work for businesses, nonprofit organizations, and political groups (the campus is located 10 minutes from the Texas State Capitol). In fact, students at St. Edward's logged more than 107,700 hours at internships in Austin business and service organizations in 2006–07.

St. Edward's offers study-abroad opportunities in reciprocal exchange programs with universities in Germany, Mexico, and Argentina. Students can also participate in study-abroad activities sponsored by other U.S. universities through the International Student Exchange Program and in community service programs offered by the International Partnership for Service Learning.

Academic Facilities

St. Edward's provides facilities that support every aspect of the student experience—academic, residential, and social—because learning can happen in many places and situations. Main Building, named a Texas Historic Landmark for its architectural significance, is a landmark visible from many parts of the city of Austin. Trustee Hall, the award-winning academic building, enhances the University's outstanding record as a "wired" institution. The biology and chemistry programs are housed in the new John Brooks Williams Natural Sciences Center, with state-of-the-art laboratories, classrooms, and meeting and study spaces.

The Robert and Pearle Ragsdale Center is home to everything from dining services and a coffeehouse to parties, concerts, lectures, and conferences. The Recreation and Convocation Center offers a fitness center, a swimming pool, and courts for basketball, racquetball/handball, and volleyball. Students also have access to on-campus 24-hour computer labs.

Costs

The 2008–09 fees for full-time undergraduate students are $22,150 for tuition and between $5855 and $8509 for room and board, depending on choice of residence hall and meal plan.

Financial Aid

St. Edward's has a strong track record of awarding financial assistance. In fall 2007, the average freshman grant package was $10,965, and 85 percent of freshmen received merit- or need-based grant assistance. St. Edward's University administers several financial assistance programs funded by federal, institutional, and state resources. These programs help students meet college expenses through grants, scholarships, low-interest loans, and work-study programs. To qualify for financial assistance, accepted students should submit the Free Application for Federal Student Aid (FAFSA) online at http://www.fafsa.ed.gov.

All students are automatically reviewed for academic scholar awards when they apply for admission. The priority deadline for fall semester applications is February 1, and students are strongly encouraged to apply by this date. The regular admission deadline for fall is May 1.

Faculty

Faculty members at St. Edward's do much more than teach students. From working together in service projects and research projects, students get to know faculty members inside and outside the classroom, often forming lifelong friendships. The University's 14:1 student–faculty ratio fosters collaboration between students and faculty members.

Student Government

The Student Government Association (SGA), composed of elected student officers, has campuswide representation. The executive board and senate meet weekly to plan and direct activities that involve the entire St. Edward's community. In addition, the SGA president acts as the voice of the student body and regularly attends Board of Trustees meetings and the Austin mayor's Council on Student Affairs.

Admission Requirements

Students who apply for admission to St. Edward's are evaluated individually on the basis of their academic performance in high school; rank in class; essay; SAT or ACT scores, including the writing section; and level of high school curriculum. To be considered for admission, qualified applicants should rank in the top half of their class and have test scores at or above the national average for college-bound students. The average SAT score for the fall 2007 freshman class was 1134 on the combined critical reading and math sections.

Application and Information

St. Edward's University employs a rolling admission policy. The Admission Committee makes decisions on applications shortly after a student's file becomes complete. A completed file consists of an application, an essay, a $45 nonrefundable application fee, SAT or ACT scores, and official high school transcripts.

All admission credentials should be mailed to:

Office of Undergraduate Admission
St. Edward's University
3001 South Congress Avenue
Austin, Texas 78704-6489
Phone: 512-448-8500
800-555-0164 (toll-free)
Fax: 512-464-8877
E-mail: seu.admit@stedwards.edu
Web site: http://www.gotostedwards.com

Main Building, designated a Texas Historic Landmark in 1973, is the center of the St. Edward's community.

ST. MARY'S UNIVERSITY

SAN ANTONIO, TEXAS

The University

Founded in 1852, St. Mary's University is a private, Catholic coeducational institution of higher education administered by the Society of Mary (Marianists). The high degree of personal attention given to students is a major strength, but it is the combination of interpersonal relationships, academic excellence, and global perspective that results in a community of scholars that crosses generations and cultures. The core curriculum integrates course work in the arts, humanities, social sciences, and natural sciences into each student's degree plan and helps develop creativity, analytical skills, and an understanding of the human condition. St. Mary's challenges students to greater academic excellence and personal integrity, while educating them for possibilities of greatness in career and community. The University maintains a 135-acre campus in northwest San Antonio, 10 minutes from downtown, where modern and historic buildings provide students with state-of-the-art learning facilities and comfortable living areas.

In fall 2007, St. Mary's enrolled 1,494 students in the Graduate School and School of Law and 2,426 undergraduates in the Bill Greehey School of Business and the Schools of Humanities and Social Sciences and Science, Engineering, and Technology. Dynamic student organizations include sororities and fraternities, the Student Government Association, an award-winning campus newspaper, honor societies, ethnic and cultural organizations, civic engagement and leadership organizations, professional clubs, and the International Student Association. There is an active University Ministry that serves St. Mary's by encouraging and promoting personal development, growth in the community, lived faith values, leadership, and service to the University and the world.

Beyond the undergraduate level, St. Mary's offers the Master of Arts degree in clinical psychology, communication studies, community counseling, education, educational school leadership, English literature and language, international relations, marriage and family therapy, pastoral administration, political science, public administration, reading, and theology; the Master of Science in clinical psychology, computer information systems, computer science, engineering (electrical and industrial), engineering systems management, and software engineering; the Master of Accounting; and the Master of Business Administration with concentrations in finance, information technology, international entrepreneurship, and investment analysis. Students may earn the bachelor's and master's degrees through eleven 5-year combined programs. St. Mary's also offers the Doctor of Philosophy in counseling and the Doctor of Jurisprudence.

St. Mary's is accredited by the Southern Association of Colleges and Schools, the Association of Texas Colleges and Universities, and the Texas Education Agency. Degree programs in electrical and industrial engineering are accredited by the Accreditation Board for Engineering and Technology (ABET). The Bill Greehey School of Business is accredited by AACSB International–The Association to Advance Collegiate Schools of Business. St. Mary's also holds membership in the American Association of University Women, the National Catholic Educational Association, the Association of American Colleges, the American Council on Education, and the Association of American Law Schools. It is an associate member of the National Association of Schools of Music. St. Mary's University is an equal opportunity institution and an Affirmative Action employer.

Location

Quite possibly one of the friendliest big cities, San Antonio, the seventh-largest city in the United States, offers boundless opportunities for internships and recreation. San Antonio's attractions include the Alamo and other historic Spanish missions, professional sporting events, malls and outlets, Six Flags Fiesta Texas and Sea World of Texas theme parks, art museums and galleries, and the beautiful Paseo del Rio (River Walk)—a collection of shops, restaurants, and outdoor cafés along the San Antonio River. The city is also home to eleven colleges and universities, eight hospitals, biomedical research facilities, military bases, a symphony orchestra, an opera company, and numerous cultural festivals. The VIA Transit System provides St. Mary's students with access to all parts of San Antonio.

Majors and Degrees

A Bachelor of Arts degree is offered in computer information systems, criminal justice, criminology, economics, English, English–communication arts, exercise and sport science, French, history, international relations, multinational organization studies, music (vocal and instrumental), philosophy, political science, psychology, sociology, Spanish, speech communication, teacher education, and theology.

A Bachelor of Science degree is offered in biochemistry, biology, biophysics, chemistry, computer engineering, computer science, electrical engineering, engineering management, engineering science, industrial engineering, mathematics, physics and applied physics, and software engineering/computer applications.

A Bachelor of Business Administration degree is offered in accounting, corporate finance, entrepreneurial studies, financial services/risk management, general business, human resources, information systems management, international business, and marketing.

Approved teacher preparation in elementary or secondary education leads to a Bachelor of Arts degree.

Preprofessional preparation is offered in dentistry, law, medicine, pharmacy, nursing, and allied-health professions. Students may also obtain Texas elementary and secondary teacher certification or earn a commission through the Army ROTC program.

Academic Programs

The University operates on a semester calendar. For the Bachelor of Arts degree, 128 hours of prescribed courses and electives must be completed. Requirements include English, natural science, mathematics, computer science, social science, theology, philosophy, foreign language, speech communication, and fine arts. Forty-five hours of study in residence are required, 12 of which should be in the major. Students seeking a Bachelor of Science degree are required to complete the same residence and core requirements as those for the Bachelor of Arts program, plus additional hours in their field of study. The Bachelor of Business Administration requires completion of 129 hours (132 hours for accounting); 45 hours must be completed in residence, and 12 of these must be in the major. Requirements include philosophy, English, social science, mathematics, natural science, economics, accounting, speech, fine arts, and theology. In addition to a liberal arts core of 66 hours, requirements for the Bachelor of Business Administration include 36 hours of a common body of business knowledge and 18 to 24 hours of upper-division course work in the major.

The curriculum for St. Mary's honors program spans eight courses, beginning and ending with philosophy and including courses in the social and natural sciences, aesthetics, and theology. As a capstone project, each honors scholar undertakes a senior thesis, demonstrating the ability to conduct original research at an advanced level. Beyond the curriculum, students find a stimulating variety of activities ranging from plays and concerts to community service projects and social events, often in collaboration with the student organization, the St. Mary's University Society of Honors Scholars. The majority of honors program graduates go on to pursue further studies in medicine, law, and other professions.

Off-Campus Programs

Study-abroad programs encourage a global consciousness on the part of both faculty members and students. St. Mary's conducts semester programs in London and Spain and summer study-abroad programs in Asia, the Bible lands of the Middle East, Innsbruck (law students), Innsbruck (graduate and undergraduate business students), Mexico, Southern Cone in Brazil and Chile, and numerous summer immersion trips that combine cultural immersion and community service. The University also is a member of a consortium of U.S. colleges and universities that participate in American University's Washington Semester Program. Partnerships and institutional agreements with institutions in Guadalajara, Mexico; Madrid, Spain; Rome, Italy; and Viña del Mar, Chile; also take academic and service experiences to new levels.

Academic Facilities

The Louis J. Blume Library and the Sarita Kenedy East Law Library house approximately 900,000 catalogued items, the curriculum collection for teacher education, and an extensive collection of audiovisual aids. The Learning Resources Center contains fully equipped studios for audio, video, photographic, and graphic arts production. The Academic Imaging and Media Center transforms students into multimedia experts who can manipulate video clips, take high-quality digital photographs, design effective presentation templates, and create stimulating interactive electronic portfolios. The Center for Legal and Social Justice provides a location for pro bono community service. St. Mary's has state-of-the-art laboratories for physics, engineering, biology, and geology that house equipment for X-ray diffraction and laser research, a metallurgical microscope, and a 150-keV accelerator. All freshman students purchase Dell notebook computers, and the University's one "port per pillow" ratio of network connections in residence halls, wired classrooms and libraries, and wireless networks ensure students of convenient Internet access. The Blackboard Learning System software supplements the personal classroom experience with the power of online interaction.

Costs

Tuition for the 2007–08 academic year is $20,300, less than the average for four-year private colleges. Typical room and board charges are $6308. Specific prices can be found at http://www.stmarytx.edu/businessoffice.

Financial Aid

More than 80 percent of all St. Mary's students receive financial aid funds. Assistance is available in the form of nonrepayable grants, educational loans, and part-time employment. Need-based financial aid is awarded based on financial need, as determined by an analysis of the Free Application for Federal Student Aid (FAFSA), which is available online at http://www.fafsa.ed.gov. Students are strongly encouraged to submit the FAFSA by February 15 to ensure the processed document is on file in the Office of Financial Assistance by March 31, the financial aid priority deadline.

The academic scholarship program at St. Mary's University was designed to recognize the achievements of applicants to the University. All qualified applicants are considered for an academic scholarship award, based on the Undergraduate Admission and Scholarship Application, but there is an application priority date of January 15. Students must be admitted to St. Mary's before an official award may be offered. Awards are made on the basis of high school academic performance and SAT or ACT scores. Athletic scholarships are available in men's intercollegiate baseball, basketball, golf, soccer, and tennis as well as in women's intercollegiate basketball, cross-country, golf, soccer, softball, tennis, and volleyball. Athletic scholarship eligibility is determined by the coaching staff. A limited number of music talent awards are available, with recipients selected by the department faculty.

Faculty

St. Mary's student-faculty ratio of 13:1 and average class size of 19 ensure personal attention designed to help students excel in their chosen fields. Faculty members take an active interest in students outside the classroom, with many serving as club moderators. Their concern for the individual student is matched by their professional accomplishment—92 percent of the faculty members have earned the Ph.D. or the highest degree in their field. No courses are taught by graduate assistants.

Student Government

The University has increasingly allowed students to administer certain funds and to be represented on, or to advise, bodies governing all student and some University activities. The Student Government Association president sits on the Student Development Council, and students are represented on all University standing committees dealing with student personnel service areas (athletic, rules and discipline, religious activities, student financial aid, and publications). The bylaws of the Board of Trustees provide for representatives of the Student Government Association to sit on the committees of the board. Students are represented in some departmental staff meetings and sit on committees that prepare budgets and administer funds collected from the student activity fee.

Admission Requirements

Students who possess the capability and motivation to succeed at St. Mary's are encouraged to apply for admission. Balanced consideration is given to all aspects of students' demonstrated preparation, including selection of college-preparatory courses, grade point average and grade pattern throughout high school, class rank, standardized test scores, and record of leadership and service. International students must also submit an official TOEFL score. A minimum score of 213 on the computer-based test, 550 on the paper-based test, or 79 on the Internet-based test is required for admission. Advanced placement and/or credit may be granted to students who have scored 3 or higher on the appropriate College Board Advanced Placement (AP) examination. Up to 30 credit hours may be granted through the general examinations of the College-Level Examination Program (CLEP) or specific University-administered departmental exams.

Transfer students must have a minimum 2.5 grade point average (on a 4.0 scale) in all academic work attempted and be in good academic standing at their former college to be considered for admission. Applicants presenting a grade point average between 2.0 and 2.49 may be considered for probationary admission. Transcripts must be submitted from every college previously attended. Transfer students who have completed fewer than 30 hours of college work must also submit high school transcripts and ACT or SAT scores. Each application is considered in its entirety. Original transcripts become the property of St. Mary's University.

Application and Information

St. Mary's operates on a rolling admission policy; however, there is a priority deadline of January 15. Students may apply at any time, but they are encouraged to apply early for priority consideration. For an application to be complete, the University must receive in addition to the application form an official high school transcript, official SAT or ACT scores, and a recommendation from the high school counselor. After all records are on file, the Admission Committee notifies the applicant of the decision.

For an application form and more information, students should contact:

Office of Admission
St. Mary's University
One Camino Santa Maria
San Antonio, Texas 78228-8503
Phone: 210-436-3126
800-367-7868 (toll-free)
Fax: 210-431-6742
E-mail: uadm@stmarytx.edu
Web site: http://www.stmarytx.edu

On campus at St. Mary's University of San Antonio.

COLLEGE DATA CENTER • TEXAS

SOUTHERN METHODIST UNIVERSITY

DALLAS, TEXAS

The University

Southern Methodist University (SMU) is a small, caring academic community in the heart of a vibrant city, where excellence is the standard and the goal is helping students succeed. SMU prepares students for life and leadership in the twenty-first century by educating them to meet the challenges of a rapidly changing world, intellectually equipping them for lifelong learning, and preparing them for successful careers. The broad-based curriculum provides a strong foundation in the humanities and sciences. SMU's four undergraduate schools offer nearly eighty majors in business, engineering, the arts, and humanities and sciences. Learning at SMU includes opportunities for mentoring relationships, internships, leadership development, research experience, international study, and community service.

Founded in 1911, SMU welcomes students of every religion, race, color, ethnic origin, and economic status. Students come from all fifty states and more than ninety countries. Total University enrollment is 10,901; 6,208 are undergraduates. Sixty percent of all undergraduate lecture sections have fewer than 25 students. Academically promising students are invited into the University Honors Program.

The life of a student's education is enriched at SMU, where there are nearly 200 student activities and organizations. From debate club to intramural sports, campus events to marching band, academic interests to community service, students have many options. There are also a large number of academic honorary societies.

SMU hosts more than 400 public arts events each year. The world-renowned Willis M. Tate Distinguished Lecture Series brings guests, such as Secretary of State Colin Powell, actor Julie Andrews, and former President George Bush to campus. SMU is a member of the National Collegiate Athletic Association and participates in Conference USA, Division I-A. Seventeen Division I-A teams include basketball, football, golf, soccer, swimming/diving, and tennis and women's cross-country, equestrian, rowing, track and field, and volleyball.

SMU offers fourteen residence halls and living communities, including an honors hall, a fine arts community, and a service-learning house. First-year students are required to live on campus, except in special circumstances. Residence halls have local phone service, voice mail, Ethernet computer connections, Internet and e-mail, air conditioning, and community computer and lounge areas.

Location

SMU's parklike campus, located north of downtown Dallas in a traditional and upscale residential neighborhood, features Georgian-style architecture and enjoys a pleasant Sun Belt climate. Dallas, often ranked as one of the world's most livable cities, is home to more than 6,000 corporate headquarters and offers outstanding opportunities for internships and future employment. A convenient light rail and bus system is located near the campus.

Majors and Degrees

SMU offers nearly eighty degrees through its four undergraduate schools, with flexible options such as double majors, minors, and dual degrees. Dedman College offers a Bachelor of Arts (B.A.) degree with a major in a department of the College and a Bachelor of Science (B.S.) degree with a major in mathematics, a natural science, or selected social sciences. The College also offers two part-time multidisciplinary evening degrees: the Bachelor of Humanities (B.Hum.) and the Bachelor of Social Science (B.Soc.Sci.). The Cox School of Business awards the Bachelor of Business Administration (B.B.A.) degree. The Meadows School of Arts awards the Bachelor of Fine Arts (B.F.A.) in art, art history, dance, and theater; the Bachelor of Arts (B.A.) in advertising, art history, cinema-television, journalism, music, corporate communications and public affairs; and the Bachelor of Music (B.M.) degrees. The School of Engineering offers the Bachelor of Arts (B.A.) degree in computer science and the Bachelor of Science (B.S.) degree in the fields of computer engineering, computer science, electrical engineering, environmental engineering, management science, and mechanical engineering, with specializations and biomedical and premed options.

Academic Programs

All undergraduates enter SMU through Dedman College. The College provides the University's general education curriculum, which is designed to help students develop analytical and communication skills, the ability to explore ethical issues, and a broad understanding of the world. The curriculum includes courses in such categories as cultural formation, perspectives, human diversity, and information technology. Students who know their career interest can select courses in their planned major while in Dedman College. Students majoring in the humanities, mathematics, the natural sciences, and the social or behavioral sciences remain in Dedman College. Requirements for graduation vary according to the major program.

SMU grants both credit and advanced placement for satisfactory completion of Advanced Placement (AP) courses in high school. Credit up to 6 semester hours is given for each course in which a score of 4 or 5 was earned; 12 to 14 hours of credit can be granted for foreign languages with a score of 4 or 5. SMU also gives credit for departmental examination. Credit also is awarded for scores from 5 to 7 on higher-level exams in transferable subjects for the International Baccalaureate. Credit is not awarded for subsidiary-level exams. High school students may earn dual credit by attending off-campus colleges. A maximum of 32 advanced credits can be awarded. The academic year at SMU is composed of two semesters, plus an optional summer session that comprises two 5-week terms. A May term is also available.

Off-Campus Programs

SMU Study Abroad offers twenty-six programs in Australia, China, Denmark, Egypt, France, Germany, Great Britain, Italy, Japan, Mexico, Russia, South Africa, Southeast Asia, Spain, and Taiwan. SMU-in-Taos is the University's summer campus in northern New Mexico.

Academic Facilities

Newer facilities include the Meadows Museum of Art, which houses one of the world's largest collections of Spanish art; an addition to the Fondren Library Center; the Dedman Life Sciences Building; the Lindsey Embrey Engineering Building; and the Gerald R. Ford Stadium and Paul B. Loyd Jr. All-Sports Center. SMU's Dedman Center for Lifetime Sports recently expanded to offer students more new and renovated indoor and outdoor facilities.

SMU libraries contain more than 3 million volumes. Fondren Library contains a catalog of all holdings and major works of a general nature. Other collections are located in the Science Information Center, the Underwood Law Library, the Bridwell Library (a component of Perkins School of Theology), Hamon Arts Library, DeGolyer Library, and the Business Information Center. The Altshuler Learning Enhancement Center, known as the A-LEC, offers students individual tutoring, study groups, and techniques to enhance study and time management skills and test-taking strategies.

SMU has high-quality facilities campuswide, including specialized laboratories in the Dallas Seismological Observatory and the electron microscopy laboratory. The Institute for the Study of Earth and Man houses specialized laboratories for archeology, ethnology, geology, and physical anthropology. The Dedman Life Sciences Building and the Junkins Electrical Engineering Building feature state-of-the-art research, teaching, and computer labs.

Costs

The comprehensive fee for full-time undergraduate students for the 2007–08 academic year was $41,705. This amount included tuition and fees totaling $27,400 and a room and board charge of $10,825. SMU offers a monthly payment plan and other resources and plans to help students manage their investment in a college education.

Financial Aid

About 78 percent of first-year students receive some form of financial assistance. The SMU financial aid program includes University, state, and federal scholarships; merit- and need-based scholarships; grants; part-time jobs; payment plans; and/or low-interest loans. Most students who demonstrate financial need are awarded an aid package that combines SMU funds with government resources. The University assists all qualified students who cannot afford an SMU education. Financial aid decisions are based on academic performance and financial need. Accepted students interested in federal or state financial aid must file the Free Application for Federal Student Aid (FAFSA). SMU's code is 003136. Students may file online at http://www.fafsa.ed.gov. Students should complete the FAFSA by February 15 to receive primary consideration.

Students who also wish to be considered for SMU need-based assistance must complete the College Scholarship Service Financial Aid PROFILE (CSS PROFILE) in addition to the FAFSA. The PROFILE is available online at http://profileonline.collegeboard.com.

Financial aid, such as grants, low-interest loans, and campus employment, is also available to transfer students who demonstrate financial need based on the FAFSA and the CSS PROFILE, both of which should be filed each year. SMU offers transfer students a range of merit scholarships. For details, students should contact a transfer admission counselor at the phone number listed in this description.

SMU's merit-based scholarships have been named among the best in the United States by *America's Best College Scholarships 2001*. SMU's most prestigious scholarship programs include the President's Scholars, the Nancy Ann and Ray L. Hunt Leadership Scholars, Dean's Scholars, SMU Distinguished Scholars, and University Scholars. National Merit Scholarships are available only to finalists who name SMU as their first college choice. Students must apply for merit scholarships by January 15.

Faculty

The undergraduate student-faculty ratio is 12:1, which allows students to interact closely with faculty members. Sixty percent of all undergraduate lecture sections have fewer than 25 students. Almost 90 percent of the full-time faculty members hold a Ph.D. or the highest degrees in their field. Regular, full-time faculty members teach most undergraduate classes (74 percent). SMU has more than 500 full-time faculty members.

Student Government

The SMU Student Senate is a comprehensive governing body that meets weekly to initiate and facilitate action on student affairs. The Senate is composed of 4 student body officers, 40 senators, and ten committees.

Admission Requirements

The Office of Admission bases selection of applicants on several criteria: the strength of the high school program and the grades received, SAT or ACT scores, teacher and counselor recommendations, an essay, and optional input from parents and peers. Applicants should present a college-preparatory program and are expected to complete a minimum of 4 years of English, 3 of mathematics (including algebra I and II and plane geometry), 3 of a natural science (including two lab sciences), 3 of social studies, and 2 of a foreign language. SMU places value on personal accomplishment, and an attempt is made to get to know the individual and the academic record beyond standardized scores.

Although the average GPA of successful transfer applicants who have completed 30 or more transferable hours is considerably higher than a 2.7 GPA (on a 4.0 scale), applicants with a GPA below this threshold are not typically successful in gaining admission. Candidates with a transferable GPA below 2.0 are not admitted to the University. For all candidates who have completed 30 or more college hours, the Admission Committee considers the rigorous nature of the courses attempted; in particular, applicants should have completed at least one course in English composition, a lab science, a math course beyond college algebra, and a course pertaining to the intended major. The committee weighs overall academic performance as well as evidence of recent improvement. For some applicants, the high school performance is also a factor. Candidates with fewer than 30 hours are considered on an individual basis and may be required to submit additional information, including high school records.

As a privately endowed institution, SMU has no limits on enrollment based solely on geography, and it makes no distinctions in tuition, fees, or other costs based on the home state of the student. Southern Methodist University does not discriminate on the basis of race, color, religion, national origin, sex, age, disability, or veteran status. SMU's commitment to equal opportunity includes nondiscrimination on the basis of sexual orientation.

Application and Information

Students should apply soon after completing the junior year of high school. Online applications are available at http://www.smu.edu/apply. The nonbinding early action deadline is November 1, with notification by December 31. For regular decision and priority merit scholarship application consideration, the deadline is January 15, with notification by March 15. SMU offers a spring decision deadline of March 15 on a space-available basis.

Transfer application deadlines are April 1 for the summer term entry, June 1 for fall term and merit scholarship consideration, and November 1 for spring term (including scholarship applicants).

For admission information, students should contact:

Division of Enrollment Services
Southern Methodist University
P.O. Box 750181
Dallas, Texas 75275-0181
Phone: 214-768-2058
800-323-0672 (toll-free)
E-mail: ugadmission@smu.edu
Web site: http://www.smu.edu/admission/

Dallas Hall is the landmark building of SMU, reflecting the neo-Georgian architecture of the campus.

STEPHEN F. AUSTIN STATE UNIVERSITY

NACOGDOCHES, TEXAS

The University

Stephen F. Austin State University (SFA) is a public four-year university located in the piney woods of East Texas, only a few hours' drive from Houston or Dallas. Established as a teachers' college that first held classes in 1923, the University today is perfectly sized. Enrolling more than 11,000 students, SFA offers a wide variety of high-quality academic programs with the personalization one would expect to find at a private college.

SFA offers an array of strong undergraduate and graduate programs through its six colleges: Business, Education, Fine Arts, Forestry and Agriculture, Liberal and Applied Arts, and Sciences and Mathematics. Students can choose from eighty-three undergraduate majors, more than 120 study areas, and nearly fifty graduate degrees, including two doctoral programs. SFA is accredited by the Commission on Colleges of the Southern Association of Colleges and Schools (1866 Southern Lane, Decatur, Georgia 30033-4097; phone: 404-679-4501) to award degrees at the bachelor's, master's, and doctoral levels.

Students study, live, and thrive on SFA's beautiful campus, with an impressive setting among towering pines that has led many groups to name it one of the most beautiful in the state. In fact, Kaplan Publishing has called SFA a "hidden treasure." The main campus encompasses 360 acres, part of the original homestead of Thomas J. Rusk, early Texas patriot and United States senator. In addition, SFA maintains a 642-acre agricultural research center that includes beef, poultry, and swine production and an equine center; an experimental forest; and a forestry field station on Lake Sam Rayburn.

Because living on campus is one of the best and most memorable experiences of one's college career, the campus offers numerous residence halls and apartments. Students with fewer than 60 semester hours or who are younger than 21 live on campus and have the opportunity to live the full college experience.

Recent progress at the University has been marked and continues at an unprecedented pace. Construction recently completed or in progress totals more than $168 million. In April 2007, the University completed a $30-million student center renovation and expansion that features a three-story atrium, a movie theater, a food court, retail shops, and more.

Lumberjack Lodge, a four-story apartment-style facility that houses approximately 315 students, opened in January 2006. A 550-space detached parking garage accommodates students living in the new residential facility. Lumberjack Village, a 610-bed, four-building student housing complex, and a 750-space parking garage also opened in 2006.

In September 2007 the University opened a $24-million student recreation center, which features a large cardio-fitness and weight area, an indoor elevated walking and jogging track, aerobics and dance rooms, a climbing rock, leisure pool and spa, glass-backed racquetball courts, outdoor adventure center, wood-floor basketball courts, outdoor sand volleyball and basketball courts, and a picnic area.

Outside of class, students have numerous opportunities to make friends or develop leadership skills through SFA's thriving Greek community or one of the more than 200 student organizations. The University competes in intercollegiate varsity sports offering men's baseball, basketball, cross-country, football, golf, and track and women's basketball, cross-country, equestrian, soccer, softball, tennis, track, and volleyball. With campus activities from movies to mattress wrestling tournaments to intramurals, there is never a reason to be bored.

Location

SFA is located in Nacogdoches, the oldest town in Texas. With a population of approximately 30,000, Nacogdoches offers the friendliness and hospitality of a small town with the conveniences of a city. A popular tourist destination, Nacogdoches entices visitors with its old brick streets of downtown and its many antique shops and dining opportunities. The city is steeped in history and offers a number of museums, including the Stone Fort Museum on the SFA campus. Recreational opportunities, including water skiing and fishing at Lake Nacogdoches, abound. Nacogdoches is 140 miles from Houston; 180 miles from Dallas; 80 miles from Shreveport, Louisiana; and 260 miles from Austin.

Majors and Degrees

The University offers more than 1,600 undergraduate courses as part of its curriculum. Bachelor's degrees are offered in accounting, agribusiness, agricultural machinery, agriculture development, agronomy, animal science, applied arts and sciences, art, art history, biochemistry, biology, business economics, chemistry, child development and family living, communication (journalism, radio/television), communication disorders, communication studies, computer information systems, computer science, creative writing, criminal justice (corrections, law enforcement, legal assistant studies), dance, deaf and hard-of-hearing studies, economics, elementary education, English, environmental science, family and consumer sciences, fashion merchandising, finance, foods and nutrition/dietetics, forestry (management, recreation, wildlife), French, general agriculture, general business, geography, geology, gerontology, health science, history, horticulture, hospitality administration, interdisciplinary studies (teacher education), interior design, interior merchandising, international business, kinesiology, liberal studies, management, marketing, mathematics, military science, music, nursing, orientation and mobility, philosophy, physics, political science, poultry science, psychology, public administration, rehabilitation services, social work, sociology, Spanish, and theater.

Preprofessional programs include predentistry, pre-engineering, prelaw, premedicine, pre–occupational therapy, preoptometry, prepharmacy, pre–physical therapy, pre–physician's assistant studies, and pre–veterinary medicine.

The five most popular areas of study at the University are interdisciplinary studies (teacher education), nursing, kinesiology, psychology, and music. Other popular majors include biology, business, and communication studies.

Academic Programs

At SFA, career preparation is a top priority. In addition to the academic education one should expect to receive in college, internships, hands-on study, and research opportunities are an important part of preparing students for rewarding careers and fulfilling lives. Through opportunities like these, SFA's students hone critical-thinking and communication skills and discover their calling, their world, and their future.

Students in the Nelson Rusche College of Business recently traveled to Washington, D.C.; New York; China; and Singapore to evaluate established government regulatory systems, financial markets, and global business enterprises. The James I. Perkins College of Education is one of the largest, most comprehensive producers of Texas educators and routinely achieves one of the highest educator certification pass rates in the state. The College of Fine Arts has embraced increased societal globalization by developing international initiatives, including School of Art summer course offerings in Italy; School of Music performance tours to England, Austria, and Italy; and School of Theatre academic exchanges with institutions in London and Singapore. The Arthur Temple College of Forestry and Agriculture fulfills vital Texas needs through rural economic development and enhanced educational research opportunities with unique programs such as the Columbia Geospatial Service Center, the Pharmaceutical Crops Center, and the Poultry Science Center. The College of Liberal and Applied Arts provides a solid, diverse educational foundation by teaching nearly half of all core curriculum courses and developing study-abroad opportunities in Spain, Costa Rica, and Ireland. The Richard and Lucille Dewitt School of Nursing achieves one of the highest licensure pass rates (94 percent) and graduation/persistence rates (94 percent) in Texas. The College of Sciences and Mathematics is also home to the second-largest observatory in the Central Time Zone and the William W. Gibson Entomarium, one of the largest public insect collections in the state.

The School of Honors provides exceptional intellectual challenge and stimulation for academically talented students. All qualified students, regardless of their major, are eligible to apply for admission to the program, which offers scholarships, specialized classes, and access to laptop computers.

Off-Campus Programs

The Office of International Studies and Programs coordinates international enrollment and exchanges at SFA. Since the creation of the office, study groups have traveled to Austria, China, Costa Rica, England, Germany, Ireland, Italy, Mexico, Spain, and a number of other places. Students may choose to study abroad for a single semester or longer, depending on the number of credits desired and the availability of appropriate courses. SFA recently became a member of the International Student Exchange Program, which allows SFA students to study abroad at the University's tuition and fee cost.

Academic Facilities

The University has twenty-eight major instructional buildings with modern classrooms and laboratories. State-of-the-art facilities include a $16.6-million Human Services Building that opened in 2004. The building contains classrooms with the latest technology and excellent clinics and research facilities, including a groundbreaking Human Neuroscience Laboratory. Also in 2004, SFA built a facility that provides academic space for its athletic training program. Other recent construction has included four new broiler houses operated by the University's respected Center for Applied Poultry Studies and Research.

The Ralph W. Steen Library is one of the largest academic library facilities in the state. The library contains extensive electronic resources that are available to students both in-house and from remote locations. Three general-purpose student microlabs collectively house approximately 200 public-access workstations. Campus computing and instructional technology services are supported by three main offices and by laboratories and technology centers in various departments and colleges, with twenty computer labs and approximately 800 workstations.

The library houses the award-winning Academic Assistance and Resource Center, which provides one-on-one peer tutoring and student-led study groups to improve intellectual development and ensure student success. It is the only learning center in the nation to achieve distinguished certification from the National Association for Developmental Education. The Texas Higher Education Coordinating Board has recognized the center's success and its contribution to higher education with a Star Award.

Costs

SFA is a tremendous value in education, in comparison with other state universities and with private institutions. Tuition and room and board fees are competitive with other Texas public universities. Annual tuition and fees for 2007–08 for full-time undergraduates were $5064 for Texas residents and $11,736 for out-of-state residents. Room and board were estimated at $7266 for an academic year.

Financial Aid

SFA awarded an estimated $89.4 million in scholarships, grants, work-study, educational loans, waivers, and exemptions during 2006–07. Financial aid programs in which the University participates include the Federal Pell Grant, Federal Supplemental Educational Opportunity Grant, B-on-Time Loan, Texas Grant Program, Texas Public Educational Grant, Federal Work-Study Program, Federal Perkins Loan, Federal Family Educational Loan Program (Stafford Loan), and Hinson-Hazelwood Student Loan Program.

SFA has hundreds of scholarships available to new and returning students. Scholarships are based on need, merit, or athletic and special skills. Selection criteria may include, but are not limited to, an applicant's academic record, degree goals, financial status, and performance on a standardized test. Prospective students can search scholarships at http://www.sfascholarships.sfasu.edu. The application deadline for most is February 1 for the fall semester. Included are scholarships offered by Office of Admissions, Office of Student Financial Assistance, Alumni Foundation, SFASU Foundation, Intercollegiate Athletics, and various academic departments and organizations. Amounts vary, with some as much as $10,000 per year.

Faculty

In fall 2006, the faculty numbered 696 members, of whom 457 were full-time. Nearly 85 percent of professors and instructors hold the highest degrees in their field. SFA has a student-faculty ratio of 19:1 and an average class size of 28.

Student Government

The Student Government Association serves as the representative voice of the student body to the faculty and administration. Concerns and issues that are important to students can be made known through legislation passed by the SGA. A three-branch system, consisting of the executive, legislative, and judicial, is used.

Admission Requirements

Applicants for admission must meet the following high school class rank and minimum test scores: first quarter, no minimum score; second quarter, 850 SAT/18 ACT; third quarter, 1050 SAT/23 ACT; fourth quarter, 1250 SAT/28 ACT. First-time freshman applicants are required to have completed the Recommended High School Program or the Distinguished Achievement Program or demonstrate they have completed a high school curriculum more rigorous than what is required of the Minimum Graduation Plan.

Application and Information

All new undergraduate applicants for admission must complete the Texas Common Application and submit it with a $35 nonrefundable application fee. For additional information, prospective students should contact:

Office of Admissions
Stephen F. Austin State University
P.O. Box 13051, SFA Station
Nacogdoches, Texas 75962-3051
Phone: 936-468-2504
E-mail: admissions@sfasu.edu
Web site: http://www.gosfa.com

On the campus of Stephen F. Austin State University.

TEXAS A&M UNIVERSITY–CORPUS CHRISTI

CORPUS CHRISTI, TEXAS

The University

Texas A&M University–Corpus Christi, a public institution of higher education, awards bachelor's, master's, and doctoral degrees. Situated on a coastal island along Corpus Christi Bay, Texas A&M–Corpus Christi's modern campus serves a diverse, growing student population of more than 8,600 students. The University is a member of the Texas A&M University system. Texas A&M University–Corpus Christi is accredited by the Commission on Colleges of the Southern Association of Colleges and Schools.

The University is driven by a desire to achieve. The Texas A&M University System Board of Regents has called Texas A&M University–Corpus Christi "the gem of the A&M System." *U.S. News & World Report* has included the University many times in its list of best colleges and universities, and the University is the only senior-level institution to twice receive the prestigious Texas Higher Education Coordinating Board Star Award.

On-campus housing provides students with the opportunity to develop friendships, participate in group activities, and enjoy the unique island setting of the University. Camden Miramar apartments and residence halls have several floor plans available, accommodating 1, 2, or 4 residents. The University hosts a broad array of academic, community service, cultural, Greek, honors, religious, and special-interest organizations. And, as an NCAA Division I institution, the "Islanders" provide top-flight game action. On campus, the University offers intramural sports, fitness and wellness classes, informal recreation, sport clubs, outdoor adventure, and special events.

New Student Orientation is an action-packed and informative program designed especially for incoming freshman students. This two-day program reflects the University's collective effort to provide care and instruction to students to facilitate their transition into Texas A&M–Corpus Christi. In addition, New Student Orientation prepares students for the University's educational opportunities, builds awareness about student services, familiarizes students with their environment, and helps students form friendships that may last a lifetime. At New Student Orientation, students register for classes for the upcoming semester, meet representatives from the academic colleges, discuss the multitude of services and resources available, learn about opportunities to become involved in on-campus student activities and organizations, tour on-campus classroom buildings and housing facilities, and interact with other new and current students.

In 2006, more than 6,500 undergraduates attended Texas A&M University–Corpus Christi, 61 percent of who were women. International students came from more than twenty countries.

Location

Texas A&M University–Corpus Christi is a unique campus. Not only is it located on its own island, but it has its own beach and easy access to miles of Gulf Coast beachfront. Students have the benefit of being able to take advantage of one of Texas' top tourist destinations. Corpus Christi, a vibrant community of more than 300,000 people, is festive, with seasonal events such as Bayfest, Buccaneer Days, Velocity Games, the Texas Jazz Festival, C-Sculptures, weekly sailing regattas, powerboat races, parades, and fireworks celebrations. The city also has a thriving downtown, with art studios, restaurants, and shops as well as an active nightlife.

Majors and Degrees

The University offers the Bachelor of Arts, the Bachelor of Business Administration, the Bachelor of Fine Arts, the Bachelor of Music, the Bachelor of Science, and the Bachelor of Science in Nursing. Programs of study are accounting, art, athletic training, biology, biomedical sciences, business, business–general, chemistry, clinical laboratory science, coastal and marine system science, communication, computer science, counseling, counselor education, criminal justice, curriculum and instruction, early childhood education, economics, educational administration, educational leadership, educational technology, electrical engineering technology, elementary education, English, environmental science, finance, geographic information science, geology, geomatics, health sciences, history, interdisciplinary studies, kinesiology, management, management information systems, mariculture, marketing, mathematics, mechanical engineering technology, music, nursing, occupational training and development, political science, psychology, public administration, reading, secondary education, sociology, Spanish, special education, studio art, teacher education, and theater. Preprofessional programs are offered in dental, medical, optometry, and veterinary medicine. Teacher certification is available through the College of Education.

Academic Programs

For the bachelor's degree, students must complete 120 semester hours, at least 45 of which must be upper-division course work. The University core curriculum is a 45- to 48-semester-hour program of study that is required of undergraduates to provide them with a foundation for further study and learning. Students are involved with core curriculum course work through the junior year. A broad range of disciplines are covered, including English composition, U.S. history, political science, natural science, mathematics, public speaking, social science, literature, fine arts, and philosophy.

In each of their first two semesters, full-time students are expected to enroll in specially selected groups of three or four classes known as Triads and Tetrads. The students and teachers within each Triad or Tetrad form a learning community; they take all the classes within a given Triad or Tetrad together and have many opportunities to collaborate, get to know each other, and learn. The teachers in each learning community work with each other to develop connections among the classes. All Triads and Tetrads include the First-Year Seminar (FYS) and the First-Year Writing class, both of which have 25 or fewer students. FYS immerses students in an active learning environment to help them develop their ability to learn through study, discussion, cooperation, and collaboration. FYS teachers attend the large Triad/Tetrad lecture classes with their students and help them explore the interconnections among the Triad/Tetrad courses, develop their critical thinking and information literacy skills, and clarify their personal values and goals.

Off-Campus Programs

Study-abroad and local internship programs are available. Students should contact Career Services for more information (telephone: 361-825-2628).

Academic Facilities

The Mary and Jeff Bell Library is the University's major resource for research and study. The library houses a collection of approximately 1.1 million books, bound periodicals, microforms, and government publications and maintains subscriptions to more than 2,800 serials and research sets in paper and microform formats. In addition, the library provides electronic access to thousands of electronic journals, newspapers, and other resources. Strong media collections and significant collections of South Texas books and archival materials provide unique resources for scholars. The Special Collections and Archives Department houses a collection of rare books and archives dealing primarily with the life, history, and culture of Corpus Christi and South Texas as well as other books and manuscripts that require special housing and handling. Another specialized collection, the State Adopted Textbook Collection, includes curriculum guides and serves as a laboratory facility for students in the teacher education program. The library is also an authorized depository for both federal and state publications. Through the statewide TexShare cooperative library program, students and faculty members have borrowing privileges at many other academic and public libraries in Texas.

Student computing facilities are part of the campus network. Computer laboratories available for student use are located in the library and several other buildings. Many personal computers, full-page scanners, laser printers, and graphics stations make up the laboratory hardware. Most computer laboratories are open more than 85 hours per week and are staffed with lab assistants who provide support for various programs. The laboratories are equipped with a wide range of software applications, such as word processors, spreadsheets, graphics programs, programming languages, and specialized applications that support individual classes. Internet access and e-mail are available for University students either on- or off-campus. Wireless access is available. Remote access to the network is provided through dial-in facilities and the World Wide Web. Students are afforded assistance by training classes, computer help sheets, and a help desk.

Costs

In 2007–08, tuition and fees for 18 credits totaled $2890 for Texas residents and $7894 for nonresidents. Housing ranged between $520 and $935 per month, depending on accommodations selected.

Financial Aid

Programs to assist students and parents in financing an education at Texas A&M University–Corpus Christi are administered by the Office of Student Financial Assistance. Students may apply for financial assistance through scholarship, grant, work-study, and loan programs. Academically competitive scholarships are offered through the University. Academic Achievement Scholarships are $2000 per year for four academic years. The President's Council Scholarship, the most prestigious scholarship award offered by the University, provides $6000 per year for four years to an outstanding individual. Application forms and detailed instructions on applying for financial aid are available through the Office of Student Financial Assistance and at http://www.tamucc.edu/~faoweb.

Faculty

The student-faculty ratio is 19:1.

Student Government

The Student Government Association (SGA) is composed of the Executive Branch, class senators, college senators, and the Judicial Branch. Officers and senators are elected in the spring semester for one year. Elections for freshman senators are held in September. The Judicial Branch is appointed by the SGA President and approved by the Student Senate.

Admission Requirements

High school students should have completed 4 credits in English; 3 credits in laboratory science, 1 of which must be in biology, chemistry, or physics; 3 credits in mathematics, algebra and higher; 3 credits in social studies; and 2 credits in another language. Transfer students should have completed a minimum of 30 credits with a GPA of at least 2.0 Prospective students should complete and submit the application, either online or on paper, the $25 application fee, official transcripts, and SAT or ACT scores. In addition, international students must submit TOEFL scores and an Affidavit of Support; the application fee for international students is $50.

Application and Information

Completed applications for first-time freshmen are processed as they are received, and applicants are usually informed of their admission status within three to four weeks. Applications are due July 1, November 1, and April 1 for the fall, spring, and summer semesters, respectively. The deadlines for international applications are May 1, September 1, and February 1 for the fall, spring, and summer semesters, respectively.

Office of Admissions and Records
Texas A&M University–Corpus Christi
6300 Ocean Drive
Corpus Christi, Texas 78412
Phone: 361-825-2624
800-4TAMUCC (toll-free)
Fax: 361-825-5887
E-mail: admiss@tamucc.edu
Web site: http://www.tamucc.edu

On the campus of Texas A&M University–Corpus Christi.

TEXAS CHRISTIAN UNIVERSITY

FORT WORTH, TEXAS

The University

The mission of Texas Christian University (TCU) is to educate individuals to think and act as ethical leaders and responsible citizens in the global community, an idea that influences every area of the University.

Founded in 1873, TCU defied the American frontier status quo and offered an education grounded in values, innovation, and creativity. It was the first college in the Southwest to educate both men and women.

Today, TCU is a major teaching and research institution balanced by student-centered warmth typical of a smaller liberal arts college. The University rolls across some 269 picturesque tree-lined acres and within sixty buildings, from the traditional yellow-bricked neo-Georgians to a few angular ultramodern creations. Students find a diverse learning community offering over 100 undergraduate areas of study across seven colleges: business, communication, education, fine arts, health and human sciences, humanities and social sciences, and science and engineering. Approximately ninety percent of TCU's professors hold the highest degrees in their fields. It is also common to find qualified undergraduates assisting professors in the latest research activities.

TCU enrolls about 7,380 full-time undergraduate men and women from nearly every state and over eighty countries. The University competes in the nation's top collegiate athletics tier, Division I-A, offering more than twenty sports. TCU is also a member of leading education organizations such as Phi Beta Kappa, Sigma Xi, and Mortar Board. Research-oriented Ph.D. programs are offered in chemistry, divinity, education, English, history, physics, and psychology. Facilities and services include nineteen residence halls, each with telephone, cable, and high-speed Internet connections. Upperclassmen have the option of living in fully furnished apartments complete with full kitchens. Sophomores may live in fully furnished, newly built lofts. Other campus amenities include nine campus cafeterias, a bistro in the library, a campus store, a post office, thirty-one tennis courts, and a University Recreation Center with five basketball courts, a climbing wall, six racquetball courts, an elevated running track, pool and game tables, video arcade, outdoor pool and patio, and a floor full of the latest in cardio-fitness equipment. Students publish an award-winning newspaper and magazine and operate a top Dallas–Fort Worth radio station featuring alternative music and campus sports coverage.

Location

Fort Worth is home to some of the finest museums in the Southwest, including the Kimbell Art Museum. In fact, its cultural district also includes Casa Mañana, the Amon Carter Museum, the Modern Art Museum of Fort Worth, and the Fort Worth Museum of Science and Natural History. Downtown, one finds the Texas Ballet Theater, the Fort Worth Opera, the Fort Worth Symphony, and the world-class Bass Performance Hall, called one of the top ten opera houses in the world by *Travel and Leisure* magazine.

While the TCU Horned Frogs are considered the home team of Fort Worth, other nearby sports teams include the Texas Rangers, Dallas Cowboys, Dallas Stars, and Dallas Mavericks. The Texas Motor Speedway, which features NASCAR auto racing, is located north of Fort Worth. Those looking for other entertainment won't be disappointed, either. The Fort Worth Zoo is 1 minute from the campus, and the world-famous Stockyards are just a bit farther. Six Flags Over Texas is only a short drive away, as is Hurricane Harbor.

Fort Worth is also home to some of America's greatest corporations, including RadioShack, Bell Helicopter-Textron, American Airlines, Pier 1 Imports, and Lockheed Martin. Other companies that look to TCU for employees are BankOne, Accenture, Intel, Frito-Lay, and Electronic Data Systems.

Majors and Degrees

Programs lead to bachelor's degrees in more than eighty major areas: advertising/public relations, allied-health professions (athletic training, pre–occupational therapy*, pre–physical therapy*, and pre–physician assistant studies*), anthropology, art (art education, art history, and studio, with concentrations in ceramics, painting, photography, and sculpture), astronomy, ballet, ballet and modern dance, biochemistry, biology, broadcast journalism, business (with concentrations in accounting, electronic business, finance, finance/real estate, entrepreneurial management, marketing, and supply and value chain management, all of which are available with an international emphasis), chemistry, communication sciences and disorders (speech-language pathology and habilitation of the deaf), communication studies, computer information science, computer science, coordinated program in dietetics, criminal justice, design, dietetics, economics, education (early childhood, exceptional children, middle school, secondary, all-level certification, and endorsement in English as a second language), engineering (electrical and mechanical), English, environmental earth resources, environmental sciences, fashion merchandising (fashion merchandising, merchandising and textiles), food management, foreign languages, general studies, geography, geology, graphic design, habilitation of the deaf, health and fitness, history, interior design, international communications (emphasizing advertising/public relations and news), international economics, international relations, journalism (broadcast and news-editorial), liberal studies, lighting (minor), mathematics, modern dance, modern languages and literature (major in Spanish and minors in French, German, Japanese, and Portuguese), movement science, music (church music, music education, music history, performance, piano pedagogy, and theory/composition), neuroscience, nursing, nutritional sciences, philosophy, physical education, physics, political science, pre–health professions (dentistry, medicine, optometry, and veterinary), prelaw, psychology, psychosocial kinesiology, radio-TV-film (criticism, industry, and production), ranch management, religion, Reserve Officers' Training Corps (ROTC; aerospace studies or military science), social work, sociology, Spanish (fluency and teaching), speech-language pathology, theater (performance, production, and education), and women's studies (minor). Programs that are indicated by an asterisk (*) begin at TCU and finish elsewhere.

Preprofessional programs are available in dentistry, law, and medicine. A certificate in ranch management is available; other certificate programs are offered by the Office of Extended Education.

Academic Programs

TCU specializes in a liberal arts and sciences education that strives to expose students to the world around them. Within the University core curriculum requirements, students have wide choices in the humanities, natural sciences, social sciences, fine arts, religion, and communication. Emphasis is placed on writing skills and critical and evaluative thinking. Freshmen are also given the opportunity to take part in Freshman Seminars, which are small classes taught by top professors.

The Center for Academic Services provides full-time advisers for students who choose to postpone the choice of a major. During the first four semesters of study, such students can satisfy University requirements while investigating potential majors. The Writing Center, also provided by the Center for Academic Services, is available to all students and faculty members who wish to refine or improve their writing skills. A full-time professional writing staff conducts individual consultation and group workshops.

Most TCU programs include internships, practicums, or other field experiences with organizations in the Dallas–Fort Worth area.

In addition, TCU's honors program challenges students to pursue high intellectual goals. It joins interdisciplinary colloquiums and independent research with dedicated faculty members and motivated students in all fields of study.

Off-Campus Programs

Nationally recognized for the international experiences available to students, TCU's offerings include the TCU London Centre, which offers fall, spring, and summer courses in a variety of disciplines. Other study-abroad programs include those in Germany, Hungary, Japan, Mexico, Spain, and the United Kingdom. In addition, annual summer-study tours with faculty-led seminars are conducted in a variety of fields, such as language, art, and international business.

Academic Facilities

The library houses more than 2 million volumes, as well as an Internet collection that links students to hundreds of thousands of other periodicals and resources. It also has special collections in music, theology, government documents, and rare books. More than fifteen spacious computer labs are open to fit students' schedules, with a few open 24 hours a day. Of two concert halls, one is rated among the nation's best acoustically. The Neeley School of Business, geared toward e-business and entrepreneurship, is equipped with a trading room with stock market quote machines and newswire services, presentation rooms with videotape equipment, board rooms, a staffed computer resource center, and classrooms with a computer at every desk. Theater students enjoy the Walsh Center for Performing Arts, which includes the Pepsico Recital Hall, a theater, an all-Steinway piano wing, and two large rehearsal rooms.

Costs

For 2007–08, tuition and fees were $12,410 per semester, or $24,820 per academic year. Residence hall costs averaged $4600 per academic year. Board fees, which averaged $2800 per academic year, cover the cost of most meals in campus cafeterias or snack bars. Books and supplies averaged $850 per year. Student government fees were $48. Total annual costs for resident students were about $30,940.

Financial Aid

Approximately 78 percent of last year's freshman class received aid. Academic scholarships are based on the student's SAT or ACT scores, rank in class, and overall application. Awards range from $5500 to full tuition and include the Chancellor, Dean, Faculty, and TCU Scholarships. National Merit Finalists who name TCU as their first choice receive a basic scholarship of $2000 and may be eligible for higher awards. Students with demonstrated financial need are eligible for federal-, state-, and University-funded awards, which include grants, loans, and work-study programs.

Faculty

The 465 full-time faculty members hold their highest degrees from more than 125 different institutions; 90 percent have the Ph.D. or other appropriate terminal degree. The University has kept classes comparatively small, with fewer than 4 percent of all classes having more than 50 students. Most instructors have an open-door policy for students, and all instructors post regular office hours. Some departments enlist part-time faculty members from the Dallas–Fort Worth professional community to augment their programs.

Student Government

The Student Government Association, composed of elected members, serves as the basis for student government. Its officers and programming council direct a varied program of entertainment, speakers, films, and social and cultural events. The House of Student Representatives makes many of its own policies within broad University guidelines. Residence halls form student councils to recommend policies and to provide activities for the hall. Students are voting members of all University-wide committees that recommend policy changes.

Admission Requirements

TCU evaluates applications by using broad criteria. Emphasis is placed on both test scores and on individual character. While academic credentials are most important, TCU also looks for talent, leadership potential, and personal determination to make a difference. Admitted students show above-average academic ability. Applicants are expected to have completed a college-preparatory curriculum during high school. A campus visit and interview are recommended before a decision is reached; admitted students are required to take part in an orientation session on campus before enrolling officially. Qualified students are admitted without regard to race, color, creed, age, sex, or ethnic or national origin, in accordance with Title IX and other government regulations.

Application and Information

Information about application deadlines and notification dates may be obtained from:

Raymond A. Brown
Dean of Admission
TCU Box 297013
Texas Christian University
2800 South University Drive, #112
Fort Worth, Texas 76129
Phone: 817-257-7490
800-TCU-FROG (828-3764; toll-free)
Fax: 817-257-7268
E-mail: frogmail@tcu.edu
Web site: http://www.tcu.edu

TCU graduates earn more than degrees that will improve their lives. They learn to change their world.

COLLEGE DATA CENTER • TEXAS

TEXAS LUTHERAN UNIVERSITY

SEGUIN, TEXAS

The University

Founded in 1891, Texas Lutheran University (TLU) is a private, exclusively undergraduate university of the liberal arts, sciences, and professional studies. The mission of the University is to prepare undergraduates academically, spiritually, and socially for fulfilling lives of leadership and service.

The hallmark of TLU's academic program is small classes that average just 18 students. Nearly one fourth of the classes in fall 2006 had 9 or fewer students. This creates a highly personalized teaching and learning environment that promotes class participation and enables professors to know, challenge, and support their students as individuals, not as anonymous faces in a crowd or identification numbers. The University also offers several life-enriching experiential opportunities, including internships, international study, and Washington Semester.

The high-quality education that TLU provides its students has been recognized repeatedly in *U.S News & World Report*'s annual ranking of America's Best Colleges and by the *Princeton Review*, which has named TLU to its "Best Western Colleges" list for four consecutive years.

TLU is a residential campus, with nearly two thirds of the 1,400 students living on campus. The University offers a broad array of cocurricular activities, including social and service organizations, choir and band, student publications, political groups, and fourteen NCAA Division III intercollegiate sports.

Affiliated with the Evangelical Lutheran Church in America, TLU welcomes students of all faiths. Approximately 28 percent of the students identify themselves as Lutheran. Ninety-four percent of the students are from Texas, with more than twenty states and several other countries also represented in the student body. Ethnic minority and international students comprise 30 percent of the student body.

Location

Seguin, a city of 25,000 people, is 35 miles east of San Antonio, the nation's eighth-largest city, and 50 miles south of Austin, the state capital. This proximity makes it easy for students to take advantage of these cities' cultural, social, and artistic attractions. Facilities for outdoor sports such as fishing, waterskiing, scuba diving, rafting, and sailing are readily available on the rivers and lakes of the surrounding Texas Hill Country. In addition, the sun, sand, and surf of the Texas Gulf Coast are only a 2½-hour drive away.

Majors and Degrees

Texas Lutheran University grants the Bachelor of Arts (B.A.), Bachelor of Business Administration (B.B.A.), Bachelor of Science (B.S.), and Bachelor of Music (B.M.) degrees. Bachelor of Arts degrees are offered in art, biology, chemistry, communication studies, computer science, dramatic media, economics, English studies, history, kinesiology, mathematics, multidisciplinary studies, music, philosophy, physics, political science, psychology, sociology, Spanish, and theology. The Bachelor of Business Administration degree is offered in business administration, with specializations in accounting, economics, finance, international business, management, and marketing. Bachelor of Science degrees are available in athletic training, biology, computer science, chemistry, information systems, kinesiology, mathematics, and psychology. A collateral major is offered in international studies. The Bachelor of Music degree is offered in all-level music education (vocal or instrumental emphasis), church music, instrumental performance, and vocal performance.

Specializations are also available in certain majors: criminal justice, environmental biology, exercise science, literature, molecular biology, pre–actuarial science, preseminary, public policy and administration, sport and fitness management, teaching/coaching all-level, and writing. Thirty minors are also offered.

Professional preparation is offered in athletic training and education (certification at elementary, secondary, and all levels). Preprofessional preparation is available in dentistry, law, medicine, nursing, occupational therapy, optometry, pharmacy, physical therapy, physician assistant studies, professional lay ministry, and veterinary science. A dual-degree engineering program is also available, with a major in applied science.

Academic Programs

The academic program at Texas Lutheran University is designed to provide an education in the liberal arts, sciences, and professional studies that makes life more exciting and satisfying. TLU students pursue a broad and general education while following programs of study that prepare them for employment directly after graduation or for further academic work at graduate or specialized professional schools.

Texas Lutheran uses a 4-4 academic calendar. The fall semester of four months begins in late August, and final examinations are completed before the Christmas vacation begins. The spring semester of four months starts in mid-January and ends in May.

Special academic programs offered include the Alternative Teacher Certification Program, bilingual teacher certification, international education, Languages Across the Curriculum, the Leadership Certificate, the Honors Program, independent study, off-campus semester programs, Mexican-American studies, the International Student Exchange Program, the Center for Women's Studies, and the Krost Life Enrichment Program. The Krost Symposium annually brings scholars, journalists, and government officials to the campus to discuss issues of relevance and importance to the community at large. Emphasis is placed on the TLU Internship Program. These valuable career experiences, in conjunction with the efforts of the Career Services Center, have resulted in 95 percent of the alumni being placed in graduate school or professional careers within six months of graduation.

To graduate with a bachelor's degree, students must complete a minimum of 124 semester hours with a cumulative grade point average of at least 2.0. Each student attending TLU is required to complete a general education curriculum in addition to a major area of study.

Off-Campus Programs

Students may participate in a variety of off-campus programs, all of which carry academic credit. The Washington Semester Program allows students with an interest in economics, journalism, history, or political science to enroll in a 12-semester-hour curriculum at the American University in Washington, D.C. The curriculum involves research, seminars, and lectures and is open to juniors and seniors who have taken a basic course in American government. Study-abroad opportunities are available through the International Student Exchange Program, Center for Global Education, Central College Abroad, Kansai Gaidai Exchange, and Ecuador Exchange. These programs bring students from various countries to Texas Lutheran as well as placing TLU students in universities across the globe.

Academic Facilities

Tschoepe Hall, home of the College of Professional Studies, opened for classes in fall 2005 and houses modern classrooms, offices, and conference space with state-of-the-art instructional technology.

The O. G. Beck College Center houses administrative offices, a classroom, and meeting rooms. The Jesse H. Jones Physical Education Complex incorporates a 2,200-seat gym, fitness center, Kinesiology Annex (Kiefer Lab), auxiliary activity center, faculty offices, classroom, handball/racquetball courts, and eight-lane heated aquatic center. The Blumberg Memorial Library houses more than 260,000 items of library materials and subscribes to 720 journal titles. The Yolanda Schuech Fine Arts Center is a multipurpose facility that includes a 200-seat theater, recital hall, music studios, band hall, art labs, and art gallery. The Chapel of the Abiding Presence is the campus worship center, seating 400 and containing a tracker-action Schlicker organ. Moody Science Building provides classrooms, laboratories, and student research space. In 1995, an additional 10,000-square-foot Krost Center was added to include seminar rooms, classrooms, student labs, offices, and equipment for the Krost fitness tests. The 1,100-seat John and Katie Jackson Auditorium is the site of student productions, fine art presentations, and major lectures and serves as home for the Mid-Texas Symphony. Langner Hall contains the Mexican American Studies Center, Fiedler Memorial Museum, and various size and style classrooms and professor offices.

Costs

For 2007–08, the comprehensive fee was $25,920, which included room, board, tuition, phone service, and the activities fee. Parking fees are $80 per year. Private music lessons (one lesson per week) cost $225 per semester. Most students spend $2700 for books, entertainment, travel, clothing, and other expenses.

Financial Aid

More than 95 percent of the students at Texas Lutheran University receive some type of need-based or merit-based financial support. In 2006–07, more than $19 million in financial aid was given to TLU students; the average financial aid package was $15,035. Campus employment and work-study awards are readily available. A variety of merit and competitive scholarships are also offered.

Faculty

In 2006–07, Texas Lutheran employed 77 full-time and 50 part-time faculty members. Eighty percent of the faculty members have doctorates or terminal degrees in their fields. The student-faculty ratio is 14:1, which allows the students' names to be known, their faces recognized, and their futures brought into focus with the professors' supportive guidance.

Student Government

All full-time students are members of the Student Government Association, a comprehensive student government structure. The president and vice president of the student body, together with a representative Student Government Association, work with the faculty and staff in achieving University goals and in providing an open forum for student opinion and action. Students appointed by the student-body president represent student opinion on most faculty committees that are concerned with academic matters as well as with certain aspects of the cocurricular program.

Admission Requirements

Each candidate is considered individually by the Admissions Committee, which evaluates the student's probable success at TLU based on courses taken in secondary school, test scores (either ACT or SAT), grade point average, essay, letters of recommendation, and activities. Although not required, a personal interview is recommended. Eighty-one percent of the freshmen rank in the top half of their high school graduating class. Fifty-one percent of the freshmen have a minimum SAT critical reading score of 500, and 60 percent have a minimum SAT math score of 500. Fifty-four percent of the freshmen have a minimum ACT score of 21.

Transfer applicants must submit a transcript from each college previously attended and may be asked to submit their high school records. A minimum 2.25 grade point average on previous college work is required for admission consideration.

Application and Information

A completed application form, SAT or ACT scores, the essay, two letters of recommendation, and an official transcript are required for admission. Admission decisions are announced on a rolling basis.

For more information about TLU, students should contact:

Norm Jones
Vice President for Enrollment Services
Texas Lutheran University
1000 West Court Street
Seguin, Texas 78155
Phone: 830-372-8050
800-771-8521 (toll-free)
E-mail: admissions@tlu.edu
Web site: http://www.tlu.edu

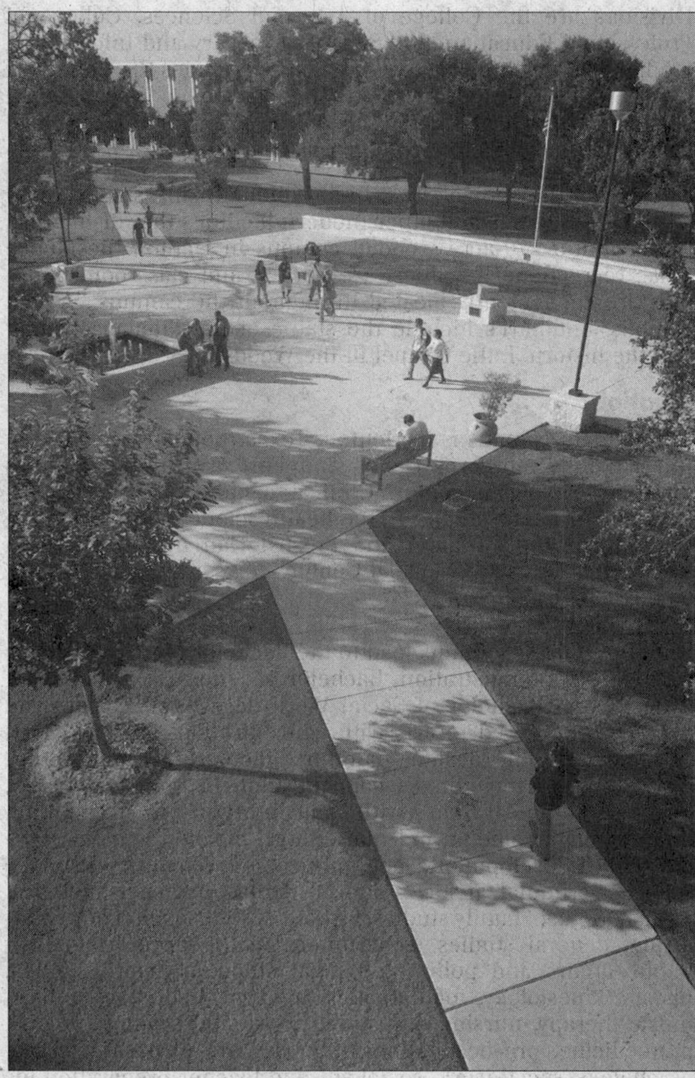

Texas Lutheran University's spacious, parklike campus provides an attractive setting for academic, social, and cocurricular activities.

TEXAS WOMAN'S UNIVERSITY

DENTON, TEXAS

The University

Texas Woman's University (TWU) is a public university offering bachelor's, master's, and doctoral degree programs. A teaching and research institution, TWU emphasizes the health sciences, education, and the liberal arts. With an enrollment of more than 12,000 students in fall 2007, the University enrolls 8 percent men and welcomes all qualified students.

Established in 1901 by the Texas Legislature, Texas Woman's University is organized into three major academic divisions: the University General Divisions, the Institute of Health Sciences, and the Graduate School. Included in the University General Divisions are the College of Arts and Sciences, College of Professional Education, and School of Library and Information Studies. The Institute of Health Sciences includes the College of Health Sciences, College of Nursing, School of Occupational Therapy, and School of Physical Therapy. The Graduate School coordinates advanced degree programs across the University.

Old Main, the University's first building, still stands amid high-rise buildings and other modern facilities that distinguish the beautiful 270-acre wooded campus in Denton. Residence halls, recreational facilities, the library, and classroom buildings are conveniently located throughout the campus. Special campus landmarks include the statue of the Pioneer Woman and the historic Little Chapel in the Woods.

Location

TWU's main campus is in Denton, Texas (population 80,000+), just 35 miles north of Dallas and Fort Worth—the nation's ninth-largest urban center. Clinical centers, offering upper-level and graduate studies in the health sciences, are located in Dallas near the Parkland and Presbyterian hospitals and in Houston in the Texas Medical Center.

Majors and Degrees

Undergraduate programs lead to the Bachelor of Arts, Bachelor of Business Administration, Bachelor of Fine Arts, Bachelor of Science, and Bachelor of Social Work degrees. Baccalaureate degrees are offered in art (with concentrations in art history, ceramics, graphic design, painting, photography, and sculpture), biology (including a concentration in human biology), business administration (with concentrations in accounting, finance, management, and marketing), biochemistry, chemistry, child development, communication science, computer science, criminal justice, dance, dental hygiene, dietetics, drama, English, family studies, fashion design, fashion merchandising, general studies, government (with concentrations in public affairs and policy and legal studies), health studies, history, kinesiology, mathematics, medical technology, music, music therapy, nursing, nutrition, pre–dental science, prelaw, premedicine, pre–occupational therapy, pre–physical therapy, psychology, social work, sociology, and teacher preparation for elementary, reading and bilingual, secondary, and special education.

Academic Programs

TWU is accredited by the Commission on Colleges of the Southern Association of Colleges and Schools to award bachelor's, master's, and doctoral degrees. Various programs are also accredited by appropriate state, regional, and national agencies. The University emphasizes the importance of a liberal arts education and specialized or professional study, especially in the health sciences.

The University's requirement for all bachelor's degrees includes the successful completion of a minimum of 120 credit hours, with at least 42 semester credit hours of core curriculum requirements plus additional hours specified for each degree. The University calendar consists of two semesters of approximately four months each, one minimester, two summer terms of five weeks each, and one summer session of ten weeks. Most degree programs are designed to allow students who carry a normal course load to complete degree requirements in eight semesters.

In accordance with the Texas Success Initiative, all undergraduate students must prove academic readiness prior to enrollment in a college or university by passing the Texas Higher Education Assessment (THEA). Students are exempt from taking the THEA if a qualifying score has been met on the TAKS, the SAT, or the ACT; there are other exemptions as well. More information about the THEA and the Texas Success Initiative can be found at http://www.thecb.state.tx.us.

Off-Campus Programs

Programs in each of the University's colleges and schools include clinical and practicum experiences that give students access to outstanding facilities of major health-care, business, and other institutions located in major metropolitan centers. Programs are offered annually to provide study-travel opportunities in the United States and abroad. A diverse cooperative education program integrates classroom study with planned and supervised work experience in educational activities outside the formal classroom.

Academic Facilities

The University library has holdings of 515,181 print volumes and 100,000 e-book volumes, 2,470 current periodical and serial publications, 1,588,563 microforms, and 87,740 audiovisual titles to support all major areas of study at TWU. In addition to the standard printed bibliographies, indexes, and abstracts, the library offers Web-based and local access to literature searches from 174 computer databases with access to 26,754 electronic journals. Special resources include the Woman's Collection, the largest depository in the South and Southwest of research materials about women. Other materials include a rare book collection as well as a departmental children's library in the School of Library and Information Studies.

Students have access to Texas academic and public library collections through TexShare, and, through membership in Amigos Library Services (the OCLC regional network), the TWU Library has access to collections in libraries throughout the United States. The Dallas Center maintains a special collection for students in the health sciences. Through a consortia membership, the students at the Houston Center have access to printed and online database collections and full library services in the Houston Academy of Medicine–Texas Medical Center Library as well as to an in-house TWU librarian for assistance with accessing and using all TWU Library resources.

Numerous classroom and laboratory buildings, including an undergraduate science laboratory building, are conveniently located on the Denton campus to meet specific needs of the individual components of the University. Special facilities on the Denton campus include honors and international programs with special housing facilities, Margo Jones Performance Hall, a theater, an auditorium, dance studios, a television studio, numerous art and music studios and practice rooms, science laboratories, a computer center and several computer laboratories, a writing laboratory, laboratory facilities for programs related to therapy, and the Institute for Women's Health. Clinics are provided for speech and hearing, dental hygiene, occupational therapy, and reading. Also included are tennis courts, a golf course, an indoor track, indoor and outdoor pools, a Wellness Center and fitness room, and other facilities that support programs in physical education and human movement. Residence hall rooms are linked to the campus computer network.

The Dallas Center includes a campus in the Parkland Memorial Hospital complex and a campus adjacent to Presbyterian Hospital of Dallas. The Houston Center is located at the entrance of the Texas Medical Center. Both centers offer outstanding instructional facilities, including excellent library holdings, clinical learning resources, simulation and research laboratories, laboratories for occupational and physical therapy, and anatomy laboratories. The Dallas Center has renovated nursing skills laboratories, and the new Houston Center, opened in 2006, has research laboratories in biochemistry and nutrition.

Costs

The average cost for in-state resident students in 2007–08 for one semester of 15 semester hours was $2145 plus course fees and $948 for books and supplies. For out-of-state residents, the average cost of tuition for 15 semester hours was $6270. Residence hall rates, meals, and personal expenses vary. All rates are subject to change. Scholarship programs for honors students, class valedictorians from Texas, new freshmen, new transfer students, and international students are available.

Financial Aid

More than 60 percent of TWU's students receive financial aid in the form of scholarships, grants, loans, or on-campus employment. In addition to offering numerous scholarships and grants funded by the state and by friends of the University, TWU participates in many federally funded programs. Federal Pell Grants, Federal Supplemental Educational Opportunity Grants, Federal Perkins Loans, Federal Nursing Student Loans, Federal Stafford Loans, Federal Parent Loans, and Federal Work-Study Program awards are available. Suggested filing dates for financial aid applicants are April 1 for the fall and spring terms and March 1 for summer sessions. Applications for academic scholarships for both the fall and spring semesters should be made by March 1.

Faculty

A faculty of approximately 500 guides the academic program at TWU and gives careful attention to student needs. Faculty members hold the doctoral degree or another terminal or graduate degree in their field.

Student Government

All students are members of the United Student Association, which enables them to participate in a wide variety of activities. Students work with the faculty and administrators to develop University policies and programs of special interest and concern to the student body. Students also serve on various University committees. Leadership development is a special focus.

Admission Requirements

First-time freshman applicants are assured admission to Texas Woman's University if they have graduated from a regionally accredited high school in Texas within the last two years and have a class ranking that places them in the top 25 percent of their high school graduating class. Regular admission to the University is based on graduation from an accredited high school, a grade point average of at least 2.0 on a 4.0 scale, a score of at least 1000 (verbal and math combined) on the SAT or a composite score of at least 21 on the ACT, and completion of at least 22 academic credits of the new recommended Texas high school graduation program. Transfer students must submit an official transcript from each college previously attended. They must have obtained a GPA of 2.0 or higher on a 4.0 scale when transferring to the University. Students holding an Associate of Arts or Associate of Science degree are assured admission.

Application and Information

Applicants should submit a completed application for admission and their official transcripts to the Office of Admissions. The fall and spring priority deadlines are June 30 and November 1, respectively. There is a $30 application fee for all new students ($50 for international students).

Additional information about the University and its programs is available from:

Office of Admissions
Texas Woman's University
P.O. Box 425589
Denton, Texas 76204-5589
Phone: 940-898-3188
866-809-6130 (toll-free)
E-mail: admissions@twu.edu
Web site: http://www.twu.edu

TWU welcomes women and men and traditional and nontraditional students to its campuses in Denton, Dallas, and Houston. TWU offers more than 100 degree programs and awards bachelor's, master's, and doctoral degrees.

UNIVERSITY OF DALLAS

IRVING, TEXAS, AND ROME, ITALY

The University

In 1955, the Roman Catholic Diocese of Dallas/Fort Worth purchased land for a university on a 1,000-acre tract of rolling hills northwest of Dallas, and in 1956, the University of Dallas (UD) opened. His Excellency Bishop Thomas K. Gorman, Chancellor of the new university, announced that it would be a coeducational institution, welcoming students of all faiths and ethnic backgrounds. Headed by a lay president and a lay academic dean, the faculty was composed of laymen, diocesan and Cistercian priests, and sisters of the Order of St. Mary of Namur.

Current undergraduate enrollment is about 1,200 men and women. Undergraduates come from all fifty states and thirty-three other countries. Although approximately 71 percent are Catholic, twenty faiths are represented on campus.

The University of Dallas was the first Catholic institution to have a board of trustees made up of both lay and religious members. Since its founding, many other universities and colleges have followed its example. The first class, a group of individuals who won significant honors, such as Fulbright and Woodrow Wilson fellowships, graduated in 1960. There is a Phi Beta Kappa chapter on campus.

Through a $6-million endowment provided by the Blakley-Braniff Foundation, the Braniff Graduate School was established in 1966. Twelve graduate programs are now in existence, including doctoral programs in philosophy, politics, and literature and the M.F.A. program in art. The College of Business houses the Graduate School of Management, which is distinguished by its practice-oriented education, close ties with leading companies and professionals, and a global student body. In addition to its undergraduate programs, the College of Business offers Master of Business Administration (M.B.A.) and Master of Management degrees. The M.B.A. includes sixteen concentrations in the areas of finance, health care, information technology, management, marketing, and telecommunications.

The University of Dallas is a center of learning, and the experience on campus is intensive and highly directed. People choose to come to the University because they are serious students. While they engage in a full complement of extracurricular activities and independent study, it is the act of learning in association with their professors that shapes their college years. Because the undergraduate college is small and largely residential, it forms a close-knit community. The University sponsors a number of lectures, concerts, and art exhibits, ranging from the old masters to the UD international printmaking invitational. The Student Government sponsors weekly events and current and classic films. The *University News* has consistently won awards for excellence in writing and design. Collegium Cantorum, the a cappella liturgical choir, performs both nationally and internationally. Intercollegiate NCAA Division III sports include baseball, basketball, cross-country, golf, lacrosse, soccer, softball, tennis, track, and volleyball. Rugby is very popular at the club level. Eighty-five percent of the on-campus students are involved in intramurals: basketball, flag football, soccer, softball, paintball, and other sports. Traditional events include coffeehouses featuring student entertainment, Charity Week, Mallapalooza, Oktoberfest, Spring Olympics, and Groundhog.

For Catholic students, daily and weekly Mass, Reconciliation, and rosary are held in the 500-seat Church of the Incarnation. Transportation is arranged for students of other faiths to attend services nearby. Campus Ministry provides numerous volunteer opportunities, including annual service projects in Appalachia and Ecuador.

Location

Irving, Texas, a city of 195,000 on the northwest side of the city of Dallas, is about 15 minutes from downtown Dallas, 10 minutes from Love Field airport, and 15 minutes from DFW airport. The Dallas–Fort Worth Metroplex offers a diverse mix of cultural and entertainment attractions, including the Dallas Museum of Modern Art, the new Nasher Sculpture Center, and the Kimbell Museum in Fort Worth. The Dallas Theater Center and Stage One have built reputations as top-notch theaters and as proving grounds for Broadway-bound productions. Texas Stadium, home of the Dallas Cowboys, is just three blocks from the University. Dallas is home to professional sports teams in hockey, soccer, and basketball. Nearby Arlington is home to the Texas Rangers.

Majors and Degrees

The Constantin College of Liberal Arts offers programs leading to the Bachelor of Arts (B.A.) degree in art and art history, biology, business, chemistry, classics, computer science, drama, economics, economics and finance, education, English, history, mathematics, modern languages (French, German, and Spanish), philosophy, physics, politics, psychology, and theology. The Bachelor of Science degree is awarded in biochemistry, biology, chemistry, mathematics, and physics.

The College of Business offers Bachelor of Arts degrees in business leadership.

The University offers twenty-seven concentrations, or minors, including applied math, applied physics, art history, business, Christian contemplative studies, computer science, entrepreneurship, environmental science, international studies, journalism, math, medieval and Renaissance studies, modern language, music, and pure math.

Preprofessional programs in architecture, business, dentistry, engineering, law, medicine, and physical therapy are carefully integrated with the undergraduate Core Curriculum. The rate of acceptance and enrollment of the college's students by professional schools is exceptional. More than 80 percent eventually go on to graduate school, and the rate of acceptance for medical and law school applicants is more than 90 percent.

A five-year, dual-degree program allows students to combine any undergraduate major with the graduate program in business management. Upon completion of the program, a student will have earned both the B.A. and M.B.A. degrees.

Academic Programs

The undergraduate Core Curriculum is a shared series of specific courses that outline the development of Western thought and culture from classical to modern times. Every student becomes familiar with the same works of literature and the same great books and concepts, fostering a natural understanding and exchange of ideas. All students then go on to pursue their chosen major discipline, reaching a level of maturity and competence in the discipline that they could not have attained in the absence of a strong foundation shared among all students entering the major. The student body has an active and personal involvement with the Core Curriculum.

The University observes a two-semester calendar, with the semester examinations occurring before the monthlong Christmas break. An interterm session and three summer sessions are also offered.

Off-Campus Programs

All undergraduates, regardless of major, are encouraged to spend one semester on the University's campus in Rome. While not compulsory, the Rome experience is an important part of the undergraduate education; to seek one's heritage in the liberal arts and to be a student of the Western world is, in a sense, to be a citizen of Rome. Courses offered in Rome are from the Core Curriculum and are taught by professors from the Texas campus. The Rome campus is located just outside of downtown Rome. Transfer students who need courses offered on the Rome campus may participate after one semester on the main campus. The cost for tuition, room, and board for all participants is roughly equivalent to that on the main campus. More than 80 percent of University of Dallas graduates have participated in the Rome program.

Academic Facilities

The Science Center, a $6-million, state-of-the-art facility, houses some of the most advanced tools for scientific research available, including a working observatory. The Haggerty Arts Village has established the University as a leading center for ceramics and fine arts in the Southwest. Drama productions are staged in the Margaret Jonsson Theater. Blakely Library holds more than 275,000 volumes, including the personal library of the late political philosopher Wilmoore Kendall.

Costs

Annual tuition and fees for 2007–08 are $23,222; room and board costs average $7615. Costs are the same for in-state and out-of-state students.

Financial Aid

Tuition, fees, room, and board are substantially lower at the University of Dallas than at many other nationally recognized universities. In addition, all high school seniors who apply for admission by the freshman scholarship priority deadline of January 15 receive priority consideration for all of the University's achievement-based awards. The University currently offers three types of achievement-based awards: academic achievements, community achievements, and special talents. Talent areas that are currently recognized include art, chemistry, classics (Latin and Greek), German, French, math, physics, and Spanish. Students who apply for admission between January 16 and March 1 receive regular consideration for achievement-based awards. Those who apply for admission after March 1 are considered for achievement-based awards dependent on the availability of funding.

All students who submit a Free Application for Federal Student Aid (FAFSA) are considered for all forms of financial assistance based on their family's finances. These forms of assistance include scholarships, grants, loans, and work-study programs. Priority is given to applicants whose FAFSA is received by the University of Dallas on or before March 1. The school code for sending a FAFSA to the University of Dallas is 003651.

Faculty

The University prides itself on its teaching faculty. Ninety-two percent hold terminal degrees. With a faculty-student ratio of 1:12, extensive consultation and direction are possible. The average class size is 19. The faculty is characterized by authority in the various disciplines, and its members have published more than 1,000 books and articles and secured major research grants.

Student Government

The Student Government Association and various departmental and special clubs, such as the social, film, lecture, and fine arts committees, encourage an extracurricular life created by the students themselves.

Admission Requirements

Although no rigid cutoff point is adhered to in admission, 52 percent of the students who enter as freshmen rank in the top 10 percent of their high school class. General admission requirements include SAT or ACT scores, rank in the upper third of the high school class, and 16 college-preparatory units, including 4 in English, 3 in mathematics, 2 in the same foreign language, 2 in social science, and 2 in a laboratory science. Interviews are not required but are strongly recommended. Through the Office of Undergraduate Admission, counseling appointments, tours, and overnight accommodations on campus may be arranged. Transfer students are welcome.

Application and Information

A transcript, official rank in class, and SAT or ACT scores must be submitted along with a letter of recommendation and a completed application form, which is obtainable online or via mail or phone from the Office of Admission. Transfer students should submit all transcripts from colleges previously attended. A $40 application fee should accompany the application; the other material may follow as ready. The Early Action I deadline is November 1; the Early Action II deadline is December 1. The freshman priority scholarship deadline is January 15. The regular admission deadline is March 1. Rolling admission is March 2–August 1.

Transfer students should apply by December 1 for spring entry and by July 1 for fall entry.

For applications or further information, students should contact:

Office of Undergraduate Admission and Financial Aid
University of Dallas
1845 East Northgate Drive
Irving, Texas 75062
Phone: 972-721-5266
800-628-6999 (toll-free)
Web site: http://www.udallas.edu

University of Dallas students learning on-site at Sicily, Italy.

UNIVERSITY OF HOUSTON

HOUSTON, TEXAS

The University

The University of Houston's (UH) main campus, a leading institution in the state-assisted system of higher education in Texas, stands on the forefront of education, research, and service. The largest and most comprehensive component of the University of Houston System, the UH main campus serves more than 35,000 students in twelve colleges and the Honors College, offering more than 300 undergraduate, graduate, and special professional degrees.

UH conducts research in each academic department, operating more than forty research centers and institutes on campus. Through these facilities, the University maintains creative partnerships with government and private industry. The research conducted breaks new ground in such vital areas as superconductivity, space commercialization, chemical engineering, economics, and education. The University's advanced professional programs include architecture, law, pharmacy, and optometry.

In 2007, sponsored research was at $86 million, an increase of 10 percent over the previous year. Considering its commitment to excellence, the University anticipates continued support and growth in grants and awards.

Outstanding faculty members and facilities draw students from 126 nations. As a result, UH is characterized by a rich mix of cultural backgrounds in a student body that is 37.5 percent white, 19.6 percent Asian/Pacific Islander, 19.4 percent Hispanic, 13.2 percent African American, 68.1 percent international students who represent countries across the globe, and .3 percent Native American.

University of Houston public service and community activities, such as cultural offerings, clinical services, policy studies, and small-business initiatives, serve a diverse metropolitan population. Likewise, the resources of the Gulf Coast region complement and enrich the University's academic programs, providing students with professional expertise, practical experience, and career opportunities and allowing them to secure career-level jobs soon after graduation.

Location

Located just minutes from downtown Houston on Interstate 45, the University is set on 557 acres of parks, fountains, plazas, sculptures, and recreational fields surrounding more than ninety modern facilities. This offers students a comfortable and well-equipped setting for academic pursuits and proximity to the resources of the nation's fourth-largest city. Gulf Coast beaches, Texas hill country, and piney woods are equally accessible from Houston, and a warm climate permits outdoor activity throughout the year.

Majors and Degrees

UH awards Bachelor of Arts and Bachelor of Science degrees, with majors in accounting, anthropology, applied music, architecture, art, art history, biochemical/biophysical sciences, biology, biomedical engineering, business management, chemical engineering, chemistry, civil engineering, classical studies, communication, communication science and disorders, computer engineering, computer engineering technology, computer science, computer science–business, computer science–systems, construction management surveying and mapping, construction management technology, consumer science and merchandising, creative writing, dance, earth science, economics, education, electrical engineering, electrical power technology, electrical technology–control systems, engineering, English, entrepreneurship, environmental design, exercise science, finance, French, geology, geophysics, German, German area studies, graphic communications, health, history, hotel and restaurant management, human development and family studies, human nutrition and foods, industrial design, industrial engineering, information systems, information systems technology, interdisciplinary studies, interdisciplinary science, interpersonal communication, Italian studies, journalism, kinesiology, leadership and supervision-occupational technology, logistics technology, management, marketing, mathematics, mechanical engineering, mechanical technology, media policy/studies, media production, medical technology, movement and sports studies, music, music composition, music theory, operations management, organizational/corporate communication, painting, pharmacy, philosophy, photography/digital media, physics, physics-geophysics, political science, pre-optometry, preprofessional English studies, printmaking, psychology, public relations/advertising, Russian studies, sculpture, sociology, Spanish, sports administration, studio art, theater, and training/human resources.

Academic Programs

UH offers an undergraduate curriculum that provides students with a broad base in the liberal arts complemented by in-depth studies in disciplines of their choice, affording students a foundation for lifelong learning. UH enrolls a substantial number of National Merit Scholars each year, and the quality of UH students is further reflected in the growing enrollment in the Honors College. Created to serve the intellectual needs of gifted undergraduates in more than 100 fields of study, the Honors College provides the careful guidance, flexibility, and personal instruction that nurture individual excellence. The Honors College offers all the advantages of a small college without sacrificing the wealth of resources and the rich diversity of a large university.

UH's nationally ranked programs include Clinical Psychology (20), Creative Writing (2), Health Law (2), Intellectual Property Law (4), Kinesiology Ph.D. (15), and M.B.A. (17).

Off-Campus Programs

The College of Liberal Arts and Social Sciences and the College of Business Administration offer fall and spring semesters in London, during which students can earn 15 hours of credit. Courses are taught by UH professors, faculty members from other Texas universities, and the University of London faculty. The Department of Modern and Classical Languages sponsors two summer programs in Puebla, Mexico, and Madrid, Spain. The Department of French has a summer program in Bourges, France, and the College of Architecture sponsors two summer programs in Saintes and Paris, France. In addition, UH has a wide variety of courses and programs that are offered through distance education and study abroad.

Academic Facilities

The newly renovated, $49-million M. D. Anderson Library and other libraries at UH provide abundant resources for research, with total collective holdings of more than 2 million volumes, 3.8 million microfilm units, 15,152 research journal subscriptions, and various other research materials. A computerized catalog system links all four UH System libraries and the specialized libraries in architecture, law, music, optometry, and pharmacy at UH. The University's computer-intensive environment enhances both teaching and research. A computer network links more than 4,000 workstations across the campus, and UH is connected to several wide area networks, providing access to more than 1,100 universities, research institutions, and corporations worldwide.

Costs

The estimated average total cost for 30 credit hours for the 2006–07 academic year was $6084 for Texas residents and $12,756 for nonresidents. These totals include tuition and fees. Costs are subject to change. Prospective students should visit the Student Financial Services Web site at http://www.uh.edu/sfs/ for updated tuition information.

Financial Aid

Several types of student financial assistance are offered, including scholarships, which are generally based on measures of academic performance such as GPA, class rank, and SAT or ACT scores, and need-based (as determined from the Free Application for Federal Student Aid) assistance, which includes loans, grants, and part-time employment. Applicants are encouraged to apply online at http://www.fafsa.ed.gov/. For additional information, students should call 713-743-1010 or visit http://www.uh.edu/enroll/sfa.

Faculty

Ranked faculty members number more than 900. The number of lecturers, teaching fellows, and visiting and adjunct faculty members is more than 900. Faculty members include Nobel Peace Prize, National Medal of Science, Tony Award, and Pulitzer Prize winners. Students also benefit from instruction at an urban institution where more than 1,000 business and community leaders bring their expertise and experience to the classroom.

Student Government

The Student Government is the University's student government and official student representative organization. It works to improve the quality of education and campus life and participates in policymaking decisions. The association participates in student disciplinary cases and works to preserve student rights.

Admission Requirements

Freshmen should submit their high school transcript, including class rank and GPA plus SAT or ACT test scores. Applicants who rank in the top 20 percent of their high school are automatically accepted regardless of SAT/ACT. Applicants who rank in the 21–50 percent range of their high school class are admitted if they score at least 1000 on the SAT (Critical Reading and Math only) or at least 21 composite on the ACT. Applicants not meeting these requirements are holistically reviewed. Applicants should have taken 4 years of English and 3 years each of math and science in high school; 2 years of foreign language are recommended. Transfers should have 15 or more hours of transferable college credit and a minimum GPA of 2.5; some majors require a higher GPA. The TOEFL is required for international students. Prospective students should refer to the University's Web site for more details.

Application and Information

Notifications of acceptance are based on a review of an applicant's complete file and continue on a rolling admission basis. An application fee of $50 is required. Students are urged to apply early. Deadlines for summer and fall are April 1 for freshmen and May 1 for transfer/postbaccalaureate students; for spring, applications should be received by December 1 for both freshman and transfer/postbaccalaureate students.

Applicants are strongly encouraged to apply for admission using the Texas Common Application at http://www.applytexas.org and are reminded to select the University of Houston main campus as the receiving institution.

For additional information, students should visit http://www.uh.edu/beacougar or contact:

Office of Admissions
122 E. Cullen Building
University of Houston
Houston, Texas 77204-2023
Phone: 713-743-1010
Web site: http://www.uh.edu/admissions

Houston: The city and its university.

COLLEGE DATA CENTER • TEXAS

THE UNIVERSITY OF TEXAS AT DALLAS

RICHARDSON, TEXAS

The University

The University of Texas at Dallas (UT Dallas) attracts an extraordinary combination of student and faculty resources to the vibrant, dynamic, and globally connected Dallas/Fort Worth area. Students seeking the close-knit community of a liberal arts college and the reputation and resources of a research university find the perfect balance at UT Dallas.

UT Dallas provides a high-quality education. Students enjoy many benefits, including apartment-style living and easy access to a first-rate faculty and research team that has included Nobel laureates and members of the National Academies of Sciences and Engineering. The cultural and recreational opportunities of the Dallas metropolitan area provide many advantages. Students enjoy unique academic opportunities with UT Dallas's emphasis on innovative, multidisciplinary degree programs. Collegium V—the UT Dallas honors program—features an enriched curriculum, special seminars, and research opportunities with faculty.

UT Dallas students excel in national and international competitions of the mind. Its chess team is ranked one of the top intercollegiate chess teams in the nation, and its debate team has qualified for the National Debate Tournament for the past three years. Other mind-game endeavors include creative problem solving (formerly Odyssey of the Mind), medical computation, moot court, legal mediation, model United Nations, college bowl, and world-level computer programming competitions.

UT Dallas consistently ranks among the top 100 colleges and universities in the United States in number of freshmen National Merit Scholars. The average SAT score of incoming freshmen, usually above 1200, is among the highest of any public university in the state. Students who take a college-prep high school curriculum and graduate in good standing and who possess an SAT score of 1200 or greater or an ACT score of at least 26 or rank within the top 15 percent of their high school graduating class in an accredited high school are typically admitted.

Also of interest is the fact that 50 percent of UT Dallas undergrads are transfer students. Special programs for transfers include the Comet Connection, a program offering transfer students from select community colleges the opportunity to lock in a money-saving fixed tuition rate by declaring their intention to attend UT Dallas early in their community college careers.

UT Dallas has more than 100 degree programs and has a national, and in some cases an international, reputation in such areas as audiology, telecommunications, arts and technology, brain health, digital forensics and cybercrime prevention, nanotechnology, sickle-cell disease research, and space science. UT Dallas launched the first accredited telecommunications engineering degree in the United States, and it is one of only a handful of institutions that offers a software engineering degree.

Exciting research in next-generation technology and biotechnology is at the crux of many collaborative efforts at such UT Dallas centers as NanoTech Institute, Digital Forensics and Emergency Preparedness Institute, Callier Center for Communications Disorders, Center for BrainHealth, and the Institute for Interactive Arts and Engineering. The University provides outstanding education and research programs from the freshman through Ph.D. levels. Qualified undergraduates benefit from having access to research opportunities with faculty members, employment at the many nearby companies, and participation in fast-track academic programs offering the option of a dual bachelor's and master's degree in five years, depending on the discipline. UT Dallas graduates are routinely recruited by major corporations, continue their studies at top-ranked graduate schools, and are admitted to medical and law schools at rates far higher than the national averages.

UT Dallas offers an outstanding quality of life. Students live in convenient apartments featuring wireless Internet access. The apartments provide students with their own living areas, kitchens, swimming pools, volleyball courts, and clubhouses. The Activities Center houses basketball courts, a 25-meter pool, a fitness/weight room, racquetball and squash courts, locker rooms, and an auxiliary gym for indoor soccer. The more than 100 organizations on campus present students with opportunities to pursue extracurricular interests in professional organizations; ethnic and honor societies; Greek letter fraternities and sororities; political, religious, and service groups; student government; and club sports. Students also have opportunities to pursue music, theater, debate, and varsity sports (Division III). There is also a strong tradition of creating new organizations.

Location

Located on 500 acres in the Dallas suburb of Richardson, UT Dallas is next door to one of the largest concentrations of corporate headquarters in the nation. Many alumni work in the area, and the University actively maintains relationships with corporate partners through alumni groups and by working with companies to provide employment opportunities, internships, and co-op programs for UT Dallas students.

While the rolling, creek-lined campus offers a quiet setting for study, the nearby attractions of the Dallas/Fort Worth area include everything anyone would expect in a major metropolitan city, including movies, restaurants, numerous museums, theater productions, the symphony, theme parks, and professional sports teams.

Majors and Degrees

UT Dallas offers Bachelor of Arts and Bachelor of Science degrees in a wide range of academic programs. Majors include accounting and information management, American studies, applied mathematics, art and performance, arts and humanities, arts and technology, biochemistry, biology, biology–business, biology–criminology, biology–premedicine, business administration, chemistry, cognitive science, computer science, computer engineering, criminology, early childhood development, economics, electrical engineering, finance, gender studies, geography, geosciences, historical studies, interdisciplinary studies, international political economy, literary studies, mathematical sciences, molecular biology, neuroscience, physics, political science, pre-health programs, psychology, public administration, sociology, software engineering, speech-language pathology and audiology, statistics, teacher certification (secondary and elementary), and telecommunications engineering. Many offer the option of a master's degree through a five-year program.

Academic Programs

Undergraduate education at UT Dallas is designed to provide students with a breadth of knowledge in natural sciences, mathematics, arts, humanities, and social and behavioral sciences through a general education core of 42 semester credit hours in addition to depth in a major field of study. A total of at least 120 semester credit hours are required for graduation, with at least 51 junior- and senior-level semester credit hours.

UT Dallas students have an impressive 56 percent graduation rate, which ranks above the national average. Transfer students who join UT Dallas after two years of college elsewhere have a graduation rate of nearly 60 percent, which ranks The University of Texas at Dallas as one of the top three public universities in Texas in terms of graduation rates for transfer students.

Academic Facilities

UT Dallas has a well-equipped, modern campus with extensive research facilities, including student labs in natural sciences, engineering, computer science, and rhetoric.

The Natural Science and Engineering Research Laboratory—one of the most revolutionary research facilities in the nation—is a four-story 192,000-square-foot facility that supports interdisciplinary collaborations among researchers in disciplines as diverse as chemistry, biology, physics, electrical engineering, and materials science.

The Eugene McDermott Library houses a collection of 1 million volumes and 1.65 million units of microform and provides access to a wide range of journals and newspapers through its Electronic Reference Center.

Costs

UT Dallas' Guaranteed Tuition Plan guarantees fixed tuition and mandatory fees for four full years. As a further financial incentive, all courses beyond 15 credit hours incur no additional basic tuition or mandatory fee charges. The following costs are what students might expect to pay for one year at UT Dallas, taking 15 semester-credit-hours in fall and spring semesters for a total of 30 semester credit hours. Texas residents can expect total costs of approximately $20,499. This total includes $8554 for guaranteed fixed tuition and mandatory fees, $1200 for books, and—though the cost-of-living expense varies from student to student—typical students can estimate $6671 for housing and meals, $1885 in miscellaneous expenses, and $2189 in transportation costs. Nonresidents who earn a merit-based competitive scholarship of $1000 or more may be granted a waiver of nonresident tuition for the period of time covered by the scholarship, not to exceed twelve months.

Financial Aid

Every student who applies to UT Dallas is considered an applicant to the Academic Excellence Scholarship (AES) program. This merit-based program offers a variety of generous awards to outstanding students. Scholarship programs range from $1000 per semester (for eight semesters) to cash awards, tuition, fees, and housing allowance for up to four years. Last year, more than 50 percent of first-time-in-college freshmen received AES scholarships. In addition, UT Dallas is a sponsor of the National Merit Scholarship program.

The Financial Aid Office provides a comprehensive program of need-based grants and scholarships, loans, and job opportunities. To apply for need-based financial aid, students should complete the Free Application for Federal Student Aid (FAFSA). The FAFSA is available from high school counselors and online. Students can visit the Financial Aid Office Web site at http://financial-aid.utdallas.edu, select Applying for Financial Aid, and access the FAFSA. To receive priority consideration for the fall semester, students should submit all financial aid application materials prior to March 31.

Faculty

UT Dallas has a world-class faculty and one of the best research faculties in the Southwest. Since most of the undergraduate courses are taught by full-time faculty members, students learn from leaders in their fields. Students regularly praise the availability of faculty members to answer questions, give advice, and provide mentoring.

Student Government

Students play a critical role in shaping UT Dallas. Student Government Association leaders are instrumental in advocacy for policy changes and facility expansion. The University administration seeks student input on a wide range of issues, including sports, recreation, entertainment, and other University programs affecting students.

Admission Requirements

Students who take a college-prep high school curriculum and graduate in good standing and who possess an SAT score of 1200 or greater or an ACT score of at least 26 or rank within the top 15 percent of their high school graduating class in an accredited high school are typically admitted. Entering freshmen should have successfully completed a full, college-track high school curriculum, including language arts (4 units), mathematics (3.5 units), science (3 units of laboratory science, excluding physical science), social sciences (3 units), foreign language (2 units in a single foreign language), and fine arts (.5 unit in music, art, or drama). In addition, students must demonstrate strong general verbal/quantitative aptitudes as measured on national standardized tests (ACT or SAT).

All students who do not meet the assured admission criteria are reviewed by the UT Dallas Admissions Committee. The UT Dallas Admissions Committee considers the applicant's achievements in work experiences, community service, extracurricular activities, and surmounting obstacles to pursue higher education. Letters of reference from high school teachers, counselors, supervisors, and activity leaders are appropriate in such instances. Students seeking such consideration should respond to essay topic C on the Texas Common Application. Students may refer to the UT Dallas catalog on the University's Web site at http://www.utdallas.edu/student/catalog/ or contact a UT Dallas admissions counselor for further clarification.

Application and Information

To apply for admission to UT Dallas, students should submit a completed application; one current high school transcript sent directly in a sealed school envelope (one official final high school transcript that reflects graduation date, class rank, and national test scores must be sent upon graduation from high school); SAT or ACT scores (if test scores are not on the high school transcript, they must be submitted by the testing agency); and a $50 nonrefundable application fee. Students should use the electronic application available at http://www.applytexas.org.

Permanent residents and United States citizens should submit applications, including all necessary supporting documents, prior to the following dates to ensure timely processing: fall semester, July 1; spring semester, November 1; and summer semester, April 1. Application deadlines for international students are: fall semester, May 1; spring semester, September 1; and summer semester, March 1. International applicants must also submit a financial affidavit of support, TOEFL scores (550 paper-based test or 213 computer-based test), and an additional $50 fee for evaluation of international documents.

For further information, students should contact:

Office of Enrollment Services
The University of Texas at Dallas
P.O. Box 830688, HH10
Richardson, Texas 75083-0688
Phone: 972-883-2270
800-889-2443 (toll-free)
E-mail: interest@utdallas.edu
Web site: http://www.utdallas.edu

UT Dallas students.

UNIVERSITY OF THE INCARNATE WORD

SAN ANTONIO, TEXAS

The University

Consistently rated among the top liberal arts universities in the Southwest, the University of the Incarnate Word (UIW) welcomes the interest of prospective students seeking a challenging and diverse Catholic university atmosphere. The University seeks students who value small classes, interaction with faculty members, and dynamic learning experiences. Founded in 1881 as Incarnate Word College by the Sisters of Charity of the Incarnate Word, the school achieved university status in 1996. The University has a population of just over 6,000 students, with more than 5,000 students seeking baccalaureate degrees in more than forty undergraduate programs and more than 800 students seeking degrees in more than fifteen graduate programs. The student body at the University of the Incarnate Word reflects the rich cultural diversity of south Texas—52 percent of students are Hispanic American, 25 percent are European American, 7 percent are African American, and 6 percent are international. Students at the University come from twenty-nine states and Puerto Rico as well as thirty-seven other countries. More than fifty percent of students reside on campus with housing options that include traditional dormitories, suites, and apartments. There are two dining facilities on campus, including a full-service cafeteria, a Chick-fil-A, and two Starbucks. There are more than thirty different clubs and organizations on campus, including fraternities and sororities, honors organizations, *The Logos* campus newspaper, and theater and musical ensembles.

The School of Graduate Studies offers a Master of Arts (M.A.) in communication arts, education, mathematics teaching, multidisciplinary sciences, multidisciplinary studies, and religious studies; the Master of Arts in Administration (M.A.A.); the Master of Arts in Teaching (M.A.T.); the Master of Business Administration (M.B.A.); the Master of Education (M.Ed.); the Master of Science in Nursing (M.S.N.); and the Master of Science (M.S.) in biology, health informatics, kinesiology, mathematics, nutrition, and sport management. The Graduate School also offers a joint master's program in nursing and business (M.S.N./M.B.A.). In 1998, the University initiated its first doctoral programs in education, with concentrations in organizational leadership, mathematics education, and international education and entrepreneurship. A Doctor of Pharmacy (Pharm.D.) program was launched in 2006.

The University of the Incarnate Word is fully accredited by the Southern Association of Colleges and Schools, Texas Education Agency, Council of Baccalaureate and Higher Degree Programs of the National League for Nursing, Committee on Accreditation of Allied Health Education (CAAHE), American Dietetic Association, Joint Review Committee on Educational Programs in Nuclear Medicine, Joint Review Committee on Education Programs in Athletic Training, American Association for Music Therapy, National Association of Schools of Theatre, Board of Nurse Examiners for the State of Texas, and Commission for Collegiate Nursing Education. The University is affiliated with the American Association of Colleges for Teacher Education, Association of Collegiate Business Schools and Programs, Association of Texas Colleges and Universities, Association of Texas Graduate Schools, and National Catholic Education Association.

The University of the Incarnate Word is an equal opportunity institution and an Affirmative Action employer.

Location

The University of the Incarnate Word is located in the Alamo Heights area of San Antonio—an area replete with artisans, studios, specialty shops, cafés, and coffeehouses. The 115-acre campus of rolling hills is filled with live oak and pecan trees and many varieties of blooming trees and flowers. In addition, the waters of the San Antonio River flow through the campus, originating from natural springs located nearby. Within easy walking distance are the Witte Museum, San Antonio Zoo, Brackenridge Park, Sunken Garden Theatre, and San Antonio Botanical Gardens. San Antonio, the "City of Fiesta" and America's eighth-largest city, boasts an international reputation for beauty and excitement—the Alamo, Paseo del Rio (Riverwalk), historic missions, Market Square, Institute of Texan Cultures, Sea World of Texas, and Six Flags Fiesta Texas are among its largest attractions. San Antonio is also home to four military bases, numerous cultural and civic groups, a symphony orchestra, the San Antonio Spurs (NBA), major concerts, and many festivals and celebrations. San Antonio International Airport and downtown San Antonio are just 10 minutes from the University and easily accessed via public transportation.

Majors and Degrees

The Bachelor of Arts (B.A.) degree is offered in art, communication arts, computer graphic arts, computer information systems, cultural studies, English, fashion management, history, interdisciplinary studies, interior environmental design, mathematics, music, music industry studies, Native American studies, philosophy, political science, psychology, religious studies, sociology, Spanish, and theater arts.

The Bachelor of Business Administration (B.B.A.) degree is offered in accounting, banking and finance, general business, information systems, international business, management, marketing, merchandising management, organizational administration, and sports management.

The Bachelor of Music (B.M.) is offered in accompanying, applied music, music education, music therapy, and performance.

The Bachelor of Science (B.S.) is offered in athletic training, biology, chemistry, engineering management, kinesiology, nuclear medicine science, and nutrition. The Bachelor of Science in Nursing (B.S.N.) is also offered.

The University offers teacher certification and preprofessional programs, such as predentistry, pre-engineering, prelaw, premedicine, pre-optometry, prepharmacy, and pre–veterinary science.

Academic Programs

To receive any degree from the University of the Incarnate Word, a student must fulfill the requirements of the University's core curriculum in addition to course work specific to the major. The University of the Incarnate Word recognizes the core curriculum as the heart of the institution. Its mission of producing critical thinkers, effective communicators, ethical leaders, responsible citizens, and caring individuals is well demonstrated in the many successful graduates of the University. The core is composed of approximately 53 hours of course work in rhetoric, literature and arts, foreign language, wellness development, mathematics and natural science, and computer literacy. Students must complete 45 hours of community service to receive their diploma.

The Bachelor of Arts degree entails 128 hours of specified course work; the Bachelor of Business Administration requires 133 hours; the Bachelor of Music specifies 137 hours; the Bachelor of Science in Nursing requires 136 hours; and the Bachelor of Science specifies 133 hours. Individual programs may vary in graduation requirements depending on the minor sought, teacher certification requirements, clinical requirements, and credits transferred.

Academic credit is granted to students who achieve a score of 3 or higher on the College Board Advanced Placement examination. The University routinely administers examinations in the College-Level Examination Program (CLEP) for credit purposes. The University operates on semester calendar with two summer sessions.

Off-Campus Programs

The School of Extended Studies operates education sites at several locations: Alamo Heights, Northeast, Del Mar College in Corpus Christi, and Santa Rosa. The School's burgeoning Adult Degree Completion Program (ADCaP) assists working adults with college credit who seek to complete their bachelor's degree. The University Online program offers Internet-based courses, allowing students with busy or varied schedules to pursue an associate, bachelor's or master's degree at UIW from anywhere in the world. Consortium agreements allow UIW students access to libraries at eight local colleges and universities. In addition, students may cross-register with three of these institutions for course work if necessary. The University of the Incarnate Word recognizes the importance of providing opportunities for students to gain employment experience in their major field before graduation. As a result UIW students are involved in numerous challenging and rewarding internship and cooperative education ventures. With a diverse student body, UIW is a leader in international education with more than ninety sister schools around the world. UIW is also the first North American university with a campus in the People's Republic of China. The University also operates a campus in Mexico City, Miguel Angel–Incarnate Word, which is one of the first schools to offer degrees that are accredited both in the U.S. and in Mexico.

Academic Facilities

The library at the University houses 235,000 volumes and 3,048 periodical titles. Information systems currently available to students include CINAHL and HaPI for nursing majors; ERIC for education students; ABI/INFORM for business majors; and OCLC online system, Info Trac, National Newspaper and Dissertation Abstract, Books in Print, Dynix, and the Internet for general student use. All housing units are computer accessible. The Learning Assistance Center (LAC) underscores the University's commitment to student achievement. Study groups, tutors, and special services are coordinated through the LAC as well. The University's fine arts complex is among the most impressive in south Texas; it includes three theaters (including a downstage), art and music studios, and the Semmes Art Gallery. A new math, science, and engineering complex was completed in 2006. The commitment to technology extends beyond classrooms and dormitories. UIW offers Gateway laptops to all students.

Costs

For the 2007–08 academic year, full-time resident students paid $25,180 for tuition, room and board, books, and fees. Full-time students who commute to campus paid $18,400 for tuition.

Financial Aid

More than 80 percent of all students at the University receive some type of financial assistance, and more than $57 million is spent annually in scholarships, work-study, loans, and grants. The University awards Presidential/Academic, performance/visual arts, and athletic scholarships, none of which are need-based. Presidential/Academic scholarships are awarded based on high school grade point average and SAT/ACT test scores. All other forms of financial assistance are awarded based on financial need as determined by the Free Application for Federal Student Aid (FAFSA). Other federal/state/institutional financial assistance awarded includes the Federal Pell Grant, Federal Supplemental Educational Opportunity Grant, Texas Equalization Grant, UIW Grant, Federal Perkins Loan, Federal Subsidized and Unsubsidized Stafford Loans, Federal Parent Loan, Texas College Access Loan, Federal Work-Study, Texas Work-Study, and Institutional Employment.

Faculty

The University of the Incarnate Word prides itself on its 125-year tradition of teaching excellence. The University's 341 faculty members (131 full-time and 210 part-time) include scholars with a variety of backgrounds and experiences. Eighty-five percent of the full-time faculty members possess either a doctorate or terminal degree. Faculty members at the University insist on playing an active role in the students' learning process. Small class sizes facilitate the dialogue and interaction that faculty members and students enjoy most.

Student Government

The Student Government Association (SGA) has a long and productive history at the University. Student representatives are included on every policymaking body, including the Board of Trustees. SGA initiatives include a number of forums each year on issues of student concern and workshops/seminars on events of significance (Black History Month, Women's History Month, Earth Day, and the annual Golden Harvest). SGA also approves funding allocations for student clubs and organizations. Elections are held in April of each year for president and executive officers and in September for individual representatives.

Admission Requirements

The University of the Incarnate Word actively recruits students who can enrich and be enriched by a small private selective Catholic liberal arts atmosphere. Applicants are evaluated using a number of criteria—GPA, course difficulty, class rank, SAT and/or ACT scores, letters of recommendation, and extracurricular activities (including part-time work). Prospective students are strongly encouraged to visit the campus and meet with an admissions counselor. Applicants with nontraditional or disadvantaged backgrounds are encouraged to apply. Prospective freshmen are advised to complete a minimum of 16 Carnegie units of work in high school, including 4 units of English, 2 units of mathematics, 2 units of natural science, 2 units of language, and 1 unit of the fine arts. Favorable consideration is given to students who enroll in courses at the honors or advanced placement (AP) level. High school graduates within less than two years of the entrance date must submit either SAT or ACT test scores. Applicants must submit an official transcript of high school work completed or General Educational Development (GED) test scores. Transfer students must submit official transcripts of all college-level work attempted. Those with fewer than 24 college credits completed must submit official high school transcripts and ACT or SAT scores as well. The University requires a minimum 2.5 cumulative GPA for consideration as a transfer student. It is recommended that international students apply no later than three months prior to the beginning of the intended semester of attendance. The Test of English as a Foreign Language (TOEFL) is required of international students. An intensive English program, which is administered by the Berlitz Company, is available on campus.

Application and Information

Applications for admission are accepted on a rolling basis. February 1, 2008, is the early application deadline. If any student applies for the fall 2008 semester on or before February 1, 2008, the application fee is waived. April 1 is the priority deadline for financial assistance. A complete application file is processed within two weeks.

Office of Admissions
University of the Incarnate Word
4301 Broadway
San Antonio, Texas 78209
Phone: 210-829-6005
800-749-WORD (toll-free)
Fax: 210-829-3921
E-mail: admis@uiwtx.edu
Web site: http://www.uiw.edu

Blue skies and warm temperatures make for the ideal college campus.

UTAH

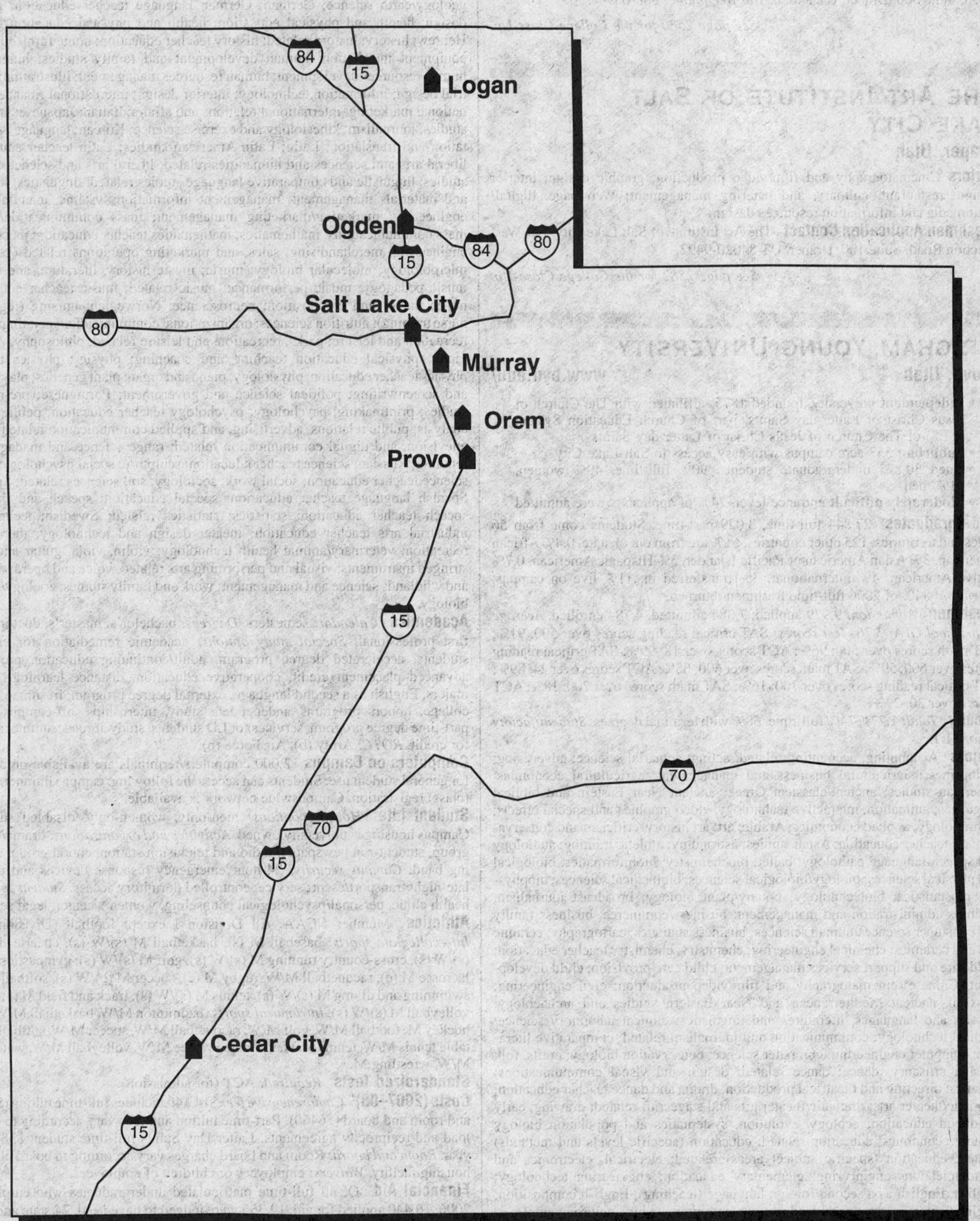
84
15
Logan
Ogden
84
80
15
Salt Lake City
80
Murray
Orem
Provo
15
70
70
15
Cedar City
15

ARGOSY UNIVERSITY, SALT LAKE CITY

Draper, Utah

Director of Admissions Argosy University, Salt Lake City, 121 West Election Road, Suite 300, Draper, UT 84020. *Toll-free phone:* 888-639-4756.

See page 2580 for the College Close-Up.

THE ART INSTITUTE OF SALT LAKE CITY

Draper, Utah

Majors Cinematography and film/video production; graphic design; interior design; restaurant, culinary, and catering management; Web page, digital/ multimedia and information resources design.

Freshman Application Contact The Art Institute of Salt Lake City, 121 West Election Road, Suite 100, Draper, UT 84020-9492.

See page 2582 for the College Close-Up.

BRIGHAM YOUNG UNIVERSITY

Provo, Utah **www.byu.edu/**

- **Independent** university, founded 1875, affiliated with The Church of Jesus Christ of Latter-day Saints, part of Church Education System (CES) of The Church of Jesus Christ of Latter-day Saints
- **Suburban** 557-acre campus with easy access to Salt Lake City
- **Coed** 30,873 undergraduate students, 90% full-time, 49% women, 51% men
- **Moderately difficult** entrance level, 74% of applicants were admitted

Undergraduates 27,844 full-time, 3,029 part-time. Students come from 56 states and territories, 125 other countries, 61% are from out of state, 0.4% African American, 3% Asian American or Pacific Islander, 3% Hispanic American, 0.7% Native American, 4% international, 3% transferred in, 11% live on campus. *Retention:* 84% of 2006 full-time freshmen returned.

Freshmen *Admission:* 9,979 applied, 7,384 admitted, 4,784 enrolled. *Average high school GPA:* 3.76. *Test scores:* SAT critical reading scores over 500: 91%; SAT math scores over 500: 96%; ACT scores over 18: 99%; SAT critical reading scores over 600: 59%; SAT math scores over 600: 65%; ACT scores over 24: 89%; SAT critical reading scores over 700: 16%; SAT math scores over 700: 18%; ACT scores over 30: 29%.

Faculty *Total:* 1,771, 74% full-time, 68% with terminal degrees. *Student/faculty ratio:* 21:1.

Majors Accounting; accounting related; acting; actuarial science; advertising; agribusiness; agricultural business and management; agricultural economics; American studies; ancient/classical Greek; ancient Near Eastern and biblical languages; animation, interactive technology, video graphics and special effects; anthropology; applied economics; Arabic; art; art history, criticism and conservation; art teacher education; Asian studies; astronomy; athletic training; audiology and speech-language pathology; ballet; biochemistry; bioinformatics; biological and physical sciences; biology/biological sciences; biomedical sciences; biophysics; biostatistics; biotechnology; botany/plant biology; broadcast journalism; business administration and management; business/commerce; business family and consumer sciences/human sciences; business statistics; cartography; ceramic arts and ceramics; chemical engineering; chemistry; chemistry teacher education; child care and support services management; child care provision; child development; Chinese; cinematography and film/video production; civil engineering; classical, ancient Mediterranean and Near Eastern studies and archaeology; classics and languages, literatures and linguistics; clinical laboratory science/ medical technology; communication and journalism related; comparative literature; computer engineering; computer science; conservation biology; crafts, folk art and artisanry; dance; dance related; design and visual communications; dietetics; directing and theatrical production; drama and dance teacher education; dramatic/theater arts; dramatic/theater arts and stagecraft related; drawing; early childhood education; ecology, evolution, systematics and population biology related; economics; education related; education (specific levels and methods) related; education (specific subject areas) related; electrical, electronics and communications engineering; elementary education; engineering technology; English; English as a second/foreign language (teaching); English composition; English/language arts teacher education; entrepreneurship; environmental science; European studies (Central and Eastern); family and consumer economics related; family and consumer sciences/home economics teacher education; family and consumer sciences/human sciences; family and consumer sciences/human sciences business services related; family resource management; family systems; film/cinema studies; film/video and photographic arts related; financial planning and services; fine/studio arts; food science; food technology and processing; foreign language teacher education; French; French language teacher education; geography; geography related; geological and earth sciences/geosciences related; geology/earth science; German; German language teacher education; graphic design; health and physical education; health and physical education related; Hebrew; history; history related; history teacher education; home furnishings and equipment installation; human development and family studies; humanities; human resources development; human resources management; illustration; industrial design; information technology; interior design; international finance; international marketing; international relations and affairs; Italian; Japanese; jazz/jazz studies; journalism; kinesiology and exercise science; Korean; language interpretation and translation; Latin; Latin American studies; Latin teacher education; liberal arts and sciences and humanities related; liberal arts and sciences/liberal studies; linguistic and comparative language studies related; linguistics; logistics and materials management; management information systems; manufacturing engineering; marketing/marketing management; mass communication/media; mass communications; mathematics; mathematics teacher education; mechanical engineering; merchandising, sales, and marketing operations related (general); microbiology; molecular biology; music; music history, literature, and theory; music pedagogy; music performance; music related; music teacher education; music theory and composition; neuroscience; Norwegian; nursing (registered nurse training); nutrition sciences; organizational communication; painting; parks, recreation and leisure; parks, recreation, and leisure related; philosophy; photography; physical education teaching and coaching; physics; physics related; physics teacher education; physiology; piano and organ; plant genetics; playwriting and screenwriting; political science and government; Portuguese; pre-nursing studies; printmaking; psychology; psychology teacher education; public policy analysis; public relations, advertising, and applied communication related; radio, television, and digital communication related; range science and management; retailing; Russian; science teacher education; sculpture; social psychology; social science teacher education; social work; sociology; soil sciences related; Spanish; Spanish language teacher education; special education; speech and rhetoric; speech teacher education; statistics; statistics related; Swedish; technology/ industrial arts teacher education; theater design and technology; therapeutic recreation; veterinary/animal health technology; violin, viola, guitar and other stringed instruments; visual and performing arts related; voice and opera; wildlife and wildlands science and management; work and family studies; zoology/animal biology.

Academics *Calendar:* semesters. *Degrees:* bachelor's, master's, doctoral, and first professional. *Special study options:* academic remediation for entering students, accelerated degree program, adult/continuing education programs, advanced placement credit, cooperative education, distance learning, double majors, English as a second language, external degree program, freshman honors college, honors programs, independent study, internships, off-campus study, part-time degree program, services for LD students, study abroad, summer session for credit. *ROTC:* Army (b), Air Force (b).

Computers on Campus 2,000 computers/terminals are available on campus for general student use. Students can access the following: campus intranet, online (class) registration. Campuswide network is available.

Student Life *Housing options:* men-only, women-only, disabled students. Campus housing is university owned. *Activities and organizations:* drama/theater group, student-run newspaper, radio and television station, choral group, marching band. *Campus security:* 24-hour emergency response devices and patrols, late-night transport/escort service, controlled dormitory access. *Student services:* health clinic, personal/psychological counseling, women's center, legal services.

Athletics Member NCAA. All Division I except football (Division I-A). *Intercollegiate sports:* baseball M (s), basketball M (s)/W (s), cheerleading M (s)/W (s), cross-country running M (s)/W (s), golf M (s)/W (s), gymnastics W (s), lacrosse M (c), racquetball M/W, rugby M (c), soccer M (c)/W (s), softball W (s), swimming and diving M (s)/W (s), tennis M (s)/W (s), track and field M (s)/W (s), volleyball M (s)/W (s). *Intramural sports:* badminton M/W, basketball M/W, field hockey M, football M/W, golf M/W, racquetball M/W, soccer M/W, softball M/W, table tennis M/W, tennis M/W, ultimate Frisbee M/W, volleyball M/W, water polo M/W, wrestling M.

Standardized Tests *Required:* ACT (for admission).

Costs (2007–08) *Comprehensive fee:* $14,140 includes full-time tuition ($7680) and room and board ($6460). Part-time tuition and fees vary according to course load and reciprocity agreements. Latter Day Saints full-time student $3840 per year. *Room and board:* Room and board charges vary according to board plan and housing facility. *Waivers:* employees or children of employees.

Financial Aid Of all full-time matriculated undergraduates who enrolled in 2006, 16,440 applied for aid, 12,355 were judged to have need. 74 state and other part-time jobs (averaging $2400). In 2006, 9968 non-need-based awards were made. *Average percent of need met:* 34%. *Average financial aid package:* $4464. *Average need-based loan:* $1616. *Average need-based gift aid:* $2848. *Average non-need-based aid:* $3210. *Average indebtedness upon graduation:* $13,714.

Applying *Options:* electronic application, early admission, deferred entrance. *Application fee:* $30. *Required:* essay or personal statement, high school transcript, 1 letter of recommendation, interview. *Application deadlines:* 2/1 (freshmen), 3/1 (transfers). *Notification:* continuous (freshmen), continuous (transfers).

Freshman Application Contact Mr. Tom Gourley, Dean of Admissions and Records, Brigham Young University, A-153 Abraham Smoot Building, Provo, UT 84602. *Phone:* 801-422-2507. *Fax:* 801-422-0005. *E-mail:* admissions@byu.edu.

DEVRY UNIVERSITY

Sandy, Utah

www.devry.edu/keller/locations/centers/loc_sandy.jsp

- **Proprietary** comprehensive
- **Coed** 39 undergraduate students, 23% full-time, 44% women, 56% men

Undergraduates 9 full-time, 30 part-time. 3% African American, 10% Hispanic American, 31% transferred in.

Freshmen *Admission:* 2 enrolled.

Faculty *Total:* 11. *Student/faculty ratio:* 8:1.

Majors Business administration and management; business administration, management and operations related.

Academics *Degrees:* bachelor's and master's.

Costs (2008–09) *Tuition:* $13,810 full-time, $515 per credit hour part-time. *Required fees:* $80 full-time.

Applying *Options:* electronic application, early admission, deferred entrance. *Application fee:* $50. *Application deadlines:* rolling (freshmen), rolling (transfers). *Notification:* continuous (freshmen), continuous (transfers).

Director of Admissions Admissions Office, DeVry University, 150 S. 150 East, Suite 420, Sandy, UT 84070.

DIXIE STATE COLLEGE OF UTAH

St. George, Utah **www.dixie.edu/**

- **State-supported** 4-year, founded 1911, part of Utah System of Higher Education
- **Small-town** 117-acre campus
- **Endowment** $10.9 million
- **Coed** 5,598 undergraduate students, 56% full-time, 54% women, 46% men
- **Noncompetitive** entrance level, 72% of applicants were admitted

Undergraduates 3,149 full-time, 2,449 part-time. Students come from 44 states and territories, 11 other countries, 14% are from out of state, 5% transferred in, 8% live on campus. *Retention:* 53% of 2006 full-time freshmen returned.

Freshmen *Admission:* 2,777 applied, 1,995 admitted, 1,249 enrolled. *Average high school GPA:* 3.24. *Test scores:* SAT critical reading scores over 500: 44%; SAT math scores over 500: 46%; SAT writing scores over 500: 25%; ACT scores over 18: 78%; SAT critical reading scores over 600: 10%; SAT math scores over 600: 4%; SAT writing scores over 600: 2%; ACT scores over 24: 20%; SAT critical reading scores over 700: 2%; ACT scores over 30: 1%.

Faculty *Total:* 319, 35% full-time, 27% with terminal degrees. *Student/faculty ratio:* 22:1.

Majors Accounting; automobile/automotive mechanics technology; biology/biological sciences; business administration and management; business/commerce; communication/speech communication and rhetoric; computer and information sciences; criminal justice/safety; dental hygiene; early childhood education; elementary education; emergency medical technology (EMT paramedic); engineering; English; graphic and printing equipment operation/production; liberal arts and sciences/liberal studies; multi-/interdisciplinary studies related; nursing (registered nurse training); radiologic technology/science.

Academics *Calendar:* semesters. *Degrees:* certificates, diplomas, associate, and bachelor's. *Special study options:* academic remediation for entering students, adult/continuing education programs, advanced placement credit, cooperative education, distance learning, English as a second language, honors programs, independent study, off-campus study, part-time degree program, services for LD students, summer session for credit.

Computers on Campus 400 computers/terminals are available on campus for general student use. Students can access the following: free student e-mail accounts, online (class) grades, online (class) registration, online (class) schedules. Campuswide network is available. 100% of college-owned or -operated housing units are wired for high-speed Internet access. Wireless service is available via classrooms, computer labs, dorm rooms, libraries, student centers.

Student Life *Housing options:* coed, men-only. Campus housing is university owned. *Activities and organizations:* drama/theater group, student-run newspaper, radio and television station, choral group, Dixie Spirit, Outdoor Club, Association of Women Students. *Campus security:* 24-hour emergency response devices and patrols. *Student services:* health clinic, personal/psychological counseling.

Athletics Member NCAA. except baseball (Division II), men's and women's basketball (Division II), men's and women's cross-country running (Division II), football (Division II), golf (Division II), men's and women's soccer (Division II), softball (Division II), tennis (Division II), ultimate Frisbee (Division II), volleyball (Division II) *Intercollegiate sports:* baseball M (s), basketball M (s)/W (s), cross-country running M (s)/W (s), football M (s), golf M (s), soccer M (s)/W (s), softball W (s), tennis W, ultimate Frisbee W (s), volleyball W (s). *Intramural sports:* basketball M/W, football M, golf M/W, racquetball M/W, soccer M/W, softball M/W, swimming and diving M/W, tennis M/W, ultimate Frisbee M/W, volleyball M/W, water polo M/W, weight lifting M/W.

Standardized Tests *Recommended:* SAT or ACT (for admission).

Costs (2008–09) *Tuition:* state resident $2442 full-time, $102 per credit part-time; nonresident $9612 full-time, $401 per credit part-time. *Required fees:* $451 full-time. *Room and board:* $3498; room only: $1500.

Financial Aid Of all full-time matriculated undergraduates who enrolled in 2006, 100 Federal Work-Study jobs (averaging $2700). 20 state and other part-time jobs (averaging $2700).

Applying *Options:* electronic application, deferred entrance. *Application fee:* $35. *Required:* high school transcript. *Application deadline:* rolling (freshmen). *Notification:* continuous (transfers).

Freshman Application Contact Ms. Darla Rollins, Admissions Coordinator, Dixie State College of Utah, 225 South 700 East Street, St. George, UT 84770-3876. *Phone:* 435-652-7702. *Toll-free phone:* 888-GO2DIXIE. *Fax:* 435-656-4005. *E-mail:* rollins@dixie.edu.

INDEPENDENCE UNIVERSITY

Salt Lake City, Utah **www.independence.edu/**

Freshman Application Contact Ms. Deborah Hopkins, Enrollment Manager, Independence University, 239 Main Street Suite 201, Dickson City, PA 18519. *Toll-free phone:* 800-791-7353.

ITT TECHNICAL INSTITUTE

Murray, Utah **www.itt-tech.edu/**

- **Proprietary** primarily 2-year, founded 1984, part of ITT Educational Services, Inc
- **Suburban** 3-acre campus with easy access to Salt Lake City
- **Coed**
- **Minimally difficult** entrance level

Academics *Calendar:* quarters. *Degrees:* associate and bachelor's.

Standardized Tests *Required:* Wonderlic aptitude test (for admission).

Applying *Options:* deferred entrance. *Application fee:* $100. *Required:* high school transcript, interview. *Recommended:* letters of recommendation.

Freshman Application Contact Gabrielle Roh, Director of Recruitment, ITT Technical Institute, 920 West Levoy Drive, Murray, UT 84123. *Phone:* 801-263-3313. *Toll-free phone:* 800-365-2136.

MIDWIVES COLLEGE OF UTAH

Orem, Utah **www.midwifery.edu/**

- **Independent** comprehensive, founded 1980
- **Urban** campus
- **Women only** 66 undergraduate students
- **Noncompetitive** entrance level, 76% of applicants were admitted

Undergraduates 66 part-time. *Retention:* 93% of 2006 full-time freshmen returned.

Freshmen *Admission:* 25 applied, 19 admitted. *Average high school GPA:* 3.2.

Faculty *Total:* 8, 88% with terminal degrees.

Majors Direct entry midwifery.

Academics *Calendar:* semesters. *Degrees:* certificates, diplomas, associate, bachelor's, and master's.

Computers on Campus Wireless service is available via entire campus.
Student Life *Housing:* college housing not available.
Athletics *Intercollegiate sports:* ultimate Frisbee M (s)/W (s), volleyball M (s)/W (s). *Intramural sports:* ultimate Frisbee M/W, volleyball M/W.
Costs (2008–09) *Tuition:* tuition varies by program. Contact school for details.
Applying *Options:* electronic application. *Application fee:* $35. *Required:* essay or personal statement, high school transcript, letters of recommendation, interview. *Application deadline:* 7/29 (freshmen). *Notification:* 8/8 (freshmen).
Freshman Application Contact Kristy Ridd-Young, President, Midwives College of Utah, 560 South State Street, Suite B2, Orem, UT 84058. *Phone:* 801-649-5230. *Toll-free phone:* 866-764-9068. *Fax:* 866-207-2024. *E-mail:* office@midwifery.edu.

NEUMONT UNIVERSITY

South Jordan, Utah **www.neumont.edu/**

- **Proprietary** 4-year, founded 2002, administratively affiliated with Morrison University
- **Suburban** campus
- **Coed, primarily men** 259 undergraduate students, 100% full-time, 7% women, 93% men
- **Moderately difficult** entrance level, 59% of applicants were admitted

Undergraduates 259 full-time. Students come from 40 states and territories, 10 other countries, 31% are from out of state, 30% live on campus. *Retention:* 96% of 2006 full-time freshmen returned.
Freshmen *Admission:* 94 applied, 55 admitted.
Faculty *Total:* 33, 55% full-time, 18% with terminal degrees. *Student/faculty ratio:* 9:1.
Majors Computer and information sciences; computer and information sciences related; computer programming; computer programming related; computer programming (specific applications); computer programming (vendor/product certification); computer science; computer software and media applications related; data modeling/warehousing and database administration; information technology; web page, digital/multimedia and information resources design.
Academics *Calendar:* quarters. *Degrees:* bachelor's and master's. *Special study options:* accelerated degree program.
Computers on Campus Students can access the following: campus intranet, computer help desk, free student e-mail accounts, online (class) grades, online (class) registration, online (class) schedules. Campuswide network is available. Wireless service is available via entire campus.
Student Life *Housing options:* men-only, women-only, disabled students. Campus housing is leased by the school and is provided by a third party. Freshman campus housing is guaranteed. *Activities and organizations:* Unified Student Government, Neumont Chapter of the Society of Women Engineers, Robotics and Science Club, Rhythm-based Game Lovers Association, Athletic Club. *Student services:* health clinic, personal/psychological counseling.
Athletics *Intramural sports:* basketball M, soccer M.
Standardized Tests *Required:* SAT or ACT (for admission).
Costs (2007–08) *One-time required fee:* $100. *Tuition:* $36,000 full-time, $495 per quarter hour part-time. *Room only:* Room and board charges vary according to housing facility and location. *Payment plans:* tuition prepayment, installment. *Waivers:* employees or children of employees.
Applying *Options:* electronic application. *Application fee:* $35. *Required:* essay or personal statement, high school transcript, 2 letters of recommendation, interview. *Application deadlines:* rolling (freshmen), rolling (transfers).
Freshman Application Contact Charlie Parker, Director of Admissions, Neumont University, 10701 South Riverfront Parkway, Suite 300, South Jordain, UT 84095. *Phone:* 801-302-2800. *Toll-free phone:* 866-622-3448. *Fax:* 801-302-2811. *E-mail:* charlie.parker@neumont.edu.

SOUTHERN UTAH UNIVERSITY

Cedar City, Utah **www.suu.edu/**

- **State-supported** comprehensive, founded 1897, part of Utah System of Higher Education
- **Small-town** 113-acre campus
- **Endowment** $5.1 million
- **Coed** 6,489 undergraduate students, 77% full-time, 56% women, 44% men
- **Moderately difficult** entrance level, 84% of applicants were admitted

Undergraduates 5,002 full-time, 1,487 part-time. Students come from 40 states and territories, 14 other countries, 12% are from out of state, 1% African American, 2% Asian American or Pacific Islander, 4% Hispanic American, 2% Native American, 1% international, 7% transferred in, 13% live on campus. *Retention:* 66% of 2006 full-time freshmen returned.
Freshmen *Admission:* 2,774 applied, 2,336 admitted, 1,214 enrolled. *Average high school GPA:* 3.44. *Test scores:* SAT critical reading scores over 500: 43%; SAT math scores over 500: 46%; ACT scores over 18: 84%; SAT critical reading scores over 600: 14%; SAT math scores over 600: 13%; ACT scores over 24: 29%; SAT critical reading scores over 700: 2%; SAT math scores over 700: 1%; ACT scores over 30: 3%.
Faculty *Total:* 316, 70% full-time, 61% with terminal degrees. *Student/faculty ratio:* 23:1.
Majors Accounting; agriculture; art; art teacher education; automobile/automotive mechanics technology; biology/biological sciences; botany/plant biology; business administration and management; business teacher education; carpentry; chemistry; child development; computer science; construction engineering technology; criminal justice/law enforcement administration; dance; drafting and design technology; dramatic/theater arts; economics; education; electrical, electronic and communications engineering technology; elementary education; English; family and community services; family and consumer sciences/home economics teacher education; family and consumer sciences/human sciences; French; geology/earth science; German; history; industrial arts; information science/studies; interior design; mass communication/media; mathematics; music; music teacher education; physical education teaching and coaching; physical sciences; political science and government; pre-engineering; psychology; secondary education; social sciences; sociology; Spanish; special education; speech and rhetoric; zoology/animal biology.
Academics *Calendar:* semesters. *Degrees:* certificates, diplomas, associate, bachelor's, and master's. *Special study options:* academic remediation for entering students, adult/continuing education programs, advanced placement credit, cooperative education, distance learning, double majors, English as a second language, honors programs, independent study, internships, part-time degree program, services for LD students, summer session for credit. *ROTC:* Army (b).
Computers on Campus 300 computers/terminals are available on campus for general student use. Campuswide network is available.
Student Life *Housing options:* coed, men-only, women-only, disabled students. *Activities and organizations:* drama/theater group, student-run newspaper, radio and television station, choral group, marching band, Outdoor Club, Intertribal Club, Latter Day Saints Student Association, Ski Club, Residence Halls Association, national fraternities, national sororities. *Campus security:* 24-hour emergency response devices, student patrols, late-night transport/escort service, controlled dormitory access. *Student services:* health clinic, personal/psychological counseling, women's center.
Athletics Member NCAA. All Division I except football (Division I-AA). *Intercollegiate sports:* baseball M (s), basketball M (s)/W (s), cross-country running M/W, golf M (s), gymnastics W (s), softball W (s), tennis W (s), track and field M (s)/W (s). *Intramural sports:* basketball M/W, football M, golf M/W, soccer M/W, tennis M/W, track and field M/W, volleyball M/W.
Standardized Tests *Required:* SAT or ACT (for admission).
Costs (2007–08) *Tuition:* state resident $3274 full-time, $160 per credit hour part-time; nonresident $10,804 full-time, $528 per credit hour part-time. Part-time tuition and fees vary according to course load. *Required fees:* $522 full-time. *Room only:* $1820. Room and board charges vary according to board plan and housing facility. *Payment plan:* installment. *Waivers:* employees or children of employees.
Financial Aid Of all full-time matriculated undergraduates who enrolled in 2006, 3,132 applied for aid, 2,770 were judged to have need, 1,599 had their need fully met. In 2006, 1614 non-need-based awards were made. *Average percent of need met:* 77%. *Average financial aid package:* $5947. *Average need-based loan:* $3816. *Average need-based gift aid:* $4136. *Average non-need-based aid:* $4534. *Average indebtedness upon graduation:* $8311.
Applying *Options:* electronic application, early admission, deferred entrance. *Application fee:* $40. *Required:* high school transcript, minimum 2.0 GPA. *Application deadlines:* 8/1 (freshmen), rolling (transfers). *Notification:* continuous (freshmen), continuous (transfers).
Director of Admissions Mr. Dale S. Orton, Director of Admissions, Southern Utah University, 351 West University Boulevard, Cedar City, UT 84720. *Phone:* 801-586-7740. *E-mail:* adminfo@suu.edu.

See page 2584 for the College Close-Up.

STEVENS-HENAGER COLLEGE

West Haven, Utah **www.stevenshenager.edu/**

Freshman Application Contact Admissions Office, Stevens-Henager College, PO Box 9428, Ogden, UT 84409. *Phone:* 801-394-7791. *Toll-free phone:* 800-622-2640.

UNIVERSITY OF PHOENIX–UTAH CAMPUS

Salt Lake City, Utah **www.phoenix.edu/**

- **Proprietary** comprehensive, founded 1984
- **Urban** campus
- **Coed**
- **Noncompetitive** entrance level

Faculty *Student/faculty ratio:* 10:1.

Academics *Calendar:* continuous. *Degrees:* bachelor's and master's.

Student Life *Campus security:* late-night transport/escort service.

Costs (2007–08) *Tuition:* $10,440 full-time, $348 per credit part-time. Full-time tuition and fees vary according to course level.

Financial Aid *Average financial aid package:* $4810. *Average need-based gift aid:* $2249.

Applying *Options:* deferred entrance. *Application fee:* $45. *Required for some:* high school transcript.

Freshman Application Contact Ms. Beth Barilla, Associate Vice President, Student Admissions and Services, University of Phoenix–Utah Campus, 4615 East Elwood Street, Mail Stop AA-K101, Phoenix, AZ 85040-1958. *Phone:* 480-317-6000. *Toll-free phone:* 800-776-4867 (in-state); 800-228-7240 (out-of-state). *Fax:* 480-894-1758. *E-mail:* beth.barilla@phoenix.edu.

UNIVERSITY OF UTAH

Salt Lake City, Utah **www.utah.edu/**

- **State-supported** university, founded 1850, part of Utah System of Higher Education
- **Urban** 1500-acre campus
- **Endowment** $468.0 million
- **Coed** 21,421 undergraduate students, 68% full-time, 45% women, 55% men
- **Moderately difficult** entrance level, 82% of applicants were admitted

Undergraduates 14,515 full-time, 6,906 part-time. Students come from 55 states and territories, 104 other countries, 17% are from out of state, 0.9% African American, 5% Asian American or Pacific Islander, 5% Hispanic American, 0.7% Native American, 3% international, 8% transferred in, 7% live on campus. *Retention:* 80% of 2006 full-time freshmen returned.

Freshmen *Admission:* 7,123 applied, 5,833 admitted, 2,743 enrolled. *Average high school GPA:* 3.53. *Test scores:* SAT critical reading scores over 500: 74%; SAT math scores over 500: 75%; ACT scores over 18: 97%; SAT critical reading scores over 600: 36%; SAT math scores over 600: 36%; ACT scores over 24: 52%; SAT critical reading scores over 700: 8%; SAT math scores over 700: 8%; ACT scores over 30: 12%.

Faculty *Total:* 1,870, 67% full-time, 71% with terminal degrees. *Student/faculty ratio:* 13:1.

Majors Accounting; anthropology; Arabic; architecture; architecture related; art; art history, criticism and conservation; Asian studies; audiology and speech-language pathology; ballet; biology/biological sciences; biomedical/medical engineering; business administration and management; business/commerce; business, management, and marketing related; cell biology and histology; chemical engineering; chemistry; Chinese; civil engineering; classics and languages, literatures and linguistics; communication/speech communication and rhetoric; computer engineering; computer science; consumer economics; dance; developmental and child psychology; dramatic/theater arts; economics; education; electrical, electronics and communications engineering; elementary education; engineering; English; environmental studies; family and consumer economics related; family resource management; film/cinema studies; finance; French; geography; geological and earth sciences/geosciences related; geological/geophysical engineering; geology/earth science; geophysics and seismology; German; health and physical education; health services/allied health/health sciences; history; human development and family studies; humanities; international/global studies; Japanese; kinesiology and exercise science; linguistics; management information systems; marketing/marketing management; mass communication/media; materials engineering; mathematics; mechanical engineering; metallurgical engineering; meteorology; mining and mineral engineering; music; Near and Middle Eastern studies; nursing (registered nurse training); occupational therapy; parks, recreation and leisure; pharmacy; philosophy; physical sciences; physical therapy; physics; political science and government; pre-pharmacy studies; psychology; public relations/image management; radio and television; Russian; secondary education; social sciences; social work; sociology; Spanish; special education; speech and rhetoric; urban studies/affairs; visual and performing arts; women's studies.

Academics *Calendar:* semesters. *Degrees:* bachelor's, master's, doctoral, first professional, post-master's, and postbachelor's certificates. *Special study options:* academic remediation for entering students, accelerated degree program, advanced placement credit, cooperative education, distance learning, double majors, English as a second language, freshman honors college, honors programs, independent study, internships, off-campus study, part-time degree program, services for LD students, student-designed majors, study abroad, summer session for credit. *ROTC:* Army (b), Navy (b), Air Force (b). *Unusual degree programs:* 3-2 physical therapy, occupational therapy.

Computers on Campus 8,000 computers/terminals are available on campus for general student use. Students can access the following: campus intranet, computer help desk, free student e-mail accounts, online (class) grades, online (class) registration, online (class) schedules, online classes. Campuswide network is available. Wireless service is available via entire campus.

Student Life *Housing options:* coed. Campus housing is university owned. *Activities and organizations:* drama/theater group, student-run newspaper, radio and television station, choral group, marching band, Bennion Center, Latter-Day Saints Student Association, Newman Center, Center for Ethnic Student Affairs, national fraternities, national sororities. *Campus security:* 24-hour emergency response devices and patrols, student patrols, late-night transport/escort service, controlled dormitory access. *Student services:* health clinic, personal/psychological counseling, women's center, legal services.

Athletics Member NCAA. All Division I. *Intercollegiate sports:* baseball M (s), basketball M (s), cheerleading M (s)/W (s), cross-country running W (s), football M (s), golf M (s), gymnastics W (s), rugby M (c), skiing (cross-country) M (s)/W (s), skiing (downhill) M (s)/W (s), soccer W (s), softball W (s), swimming and diving M (s)/W (s), table tennis M (c)/W (c), tennis M (s)/W (s), track and field W (s), volleyball W (s). *Intramural sports:* crew M/W, fencing M/W, riflery M/W, rugby M/W, soccer M/W, softball W, track and field M, ultimate Frisbee M/W, volleyball M/W.

Standardized Tests *Required:* SAT or ACT (for admission).

Costs (2007–08) *Tuition:* state resident $4269 full-time, $120 per credit hour part-time; nonresident $14,945 full-time, $412 per credit hour part-time. Full-time tuition and fees vary according to course level, course load, degree level, program, reciprocity agreements, and student level. Part-time tuition and fees vary according to course level, course load, degree level, program, reciprocity agreements, and student level. contact university directly for part-time tuition costs. *Required fees:* $717 full-time. *Room and board:* $5778; room only: $2890. Room and board charges vary according to board plan and housing facility. *Payment plan:* installment. *Waivers:* senior citizens and employees or children of employees.

Financial Aid Of all full-time matriculated undergraduates who enrolled in 2007, 8,104 applied for aid, 5,476 were judged to have need, 648 had their need fully met. 373 Federal Work-Study jobs (averaging $4745). In 2007, 423 non-need-based awards were made. *Average percent of need met:* 58%. *Average financial aid package:* $8974. *Average need-based loan:* $4878. *Average need-based gift aid:* $4488. *Average non-need-based aid:* $3644. *Average indebtedness upon graduation:* $13,994.

Applying *Options:* electronic application, early admission. *Application fee:* $35. *Required:* high school transcript, minimum 2.6 GPA. *Required for some:* essay or personal statement, letters of recommendation. *Recommended:* minimum 3.0 GPA. *Application deadlines:* 4/1 (freshmen), 4/1 (transfers).

Freshman Application Contact Mateo Remsburg, Director of High School Services, University of Utah, 250 South Student Services Building, 201 South, 460 E Room 205, Salt Lake City, UT 84112. *Phone:* 801-581-8761. *Toll-free phone:* 800-444-8638. *Fax:* 801-585-3257. *E-mail:* mremsburg@sa.utah.edu.

UTAH STATE UNIVERSITY

Logan, Utah **www.usu.edu/**

- **State-supported** university, founded 1888, part of Utah System of Higher Education
- **Urban** 456-acre campus
- **Endowment** $110.3 million
- **Coed** 13,179 undergraduate students, 84% full-time, 49% women, 51% men
- **Moderately difficult** entrance level, 98% of applicants were admitted

Undergraduates 11,108 full-time, 2,071 part-time. Students come from 53 states and territories, 52 other countries, 23% are from out of state, 0.8% African American, 1% Asian American or Pacific Islander, 2% Hispanic American, 0.5% Native American, 4% international, 8% transferred in. *Retention:* 74% of 2006 full-time freshmen returned.

Freshmen *Admission:* 6,045 applied, 5,907 admitted, 2,842 enrolled. *Average high school GPA:* 3.52. *Test scores:* ACT scores over 18: 95%; ACT scores over 24: 49%; ACT scores over 30: 9%.

Faculty *Total:* 918, 78% full-time. *Student/faculty ratio:* 17:1.

Majors Accounting; aeronautical/aerospace engineering technology; aerospace, aeronautical and astronautical engineering; agricultural/biological engineering and bioengineering; agricultural business and management; agricultural business and management related; agricultural economics; agricultural teacher education; agriculture; agronomy and crop science; American studies; animal physiology; animal sciences; anthropology; area studies related; art; Asian studies; audiology and speech-language pathology; biological specializations related; biology/biological sciences; biology teacher education; botany/plant biology; business administration and management; business/commerce; business teacher education; chemistry; chemistry teacher education; civil engineering; clinical laboratory science/medical technology; computer and information sciences; computer and information sciences and support services related; computer engineering; computer engineering technology; curriculum and instruction; dairy science; dance; drafting and design technology; dramatic/theater arts; ecology; economics; education (multiple levels); education (specific subject areas) related; electrical, electronics and communications engineering; elementary education; English; entomology; environmental/environmental health engineering; family and consumer economics related; family and consumer sciences/home economics teacher education; fashion merchandising; finance; foods and nutrition related; forestry; forestry related; French; general studies; geography; geology/earth science; German; health teacher education; history; horticultural science; housing and human environments; human development and family studies; human development and family studies related; human resources management; industrial production technologies related; information science/studies; interior design; international agriculture; journalism; kindergarten/preschool education; landscape architecture; liberal arts and sciences/liberal studies; marketing/marketing management; mathematics; mathematics teacher education; mechanical engineering; medical microbiology and bacteriology; multi-/interdisciplinary studies related; music; music teacher education; music therapy; natural resources and conservation related; occupational safety and health technology; operations management; parks, recreation and leisure; parks, recreation, and leisure related; philosophy; physical education teaching and coaching; physics; physics teacher education; plant sciences; plant sciences related; political science and government; pre-dentistry studies; pre-law studies; pre-medical studies; pre-veterinary studies; psychology; public health related; range science and management; sales and marketing/marketing and distribution teacher education; science teacher education; secondary education; social studies teacher education; social work; sociology; soil science and agronomy; Spanish; special education; speech and rhetoric; statistics; technical teacher education; technology/industrial arts teacher education; tool and die technology; wildlife and wildlands science and management; zoology/animal biology.

Academics *Calendar:* semesters. *Degrees:* certificates, associate, bachelor's, master's, doctoral, post-master's, and postbachelor's certificates. *Special study options:* academic remediation for entering students, accelerated degree program, adult/continuing education programs, advanced placement credit, cooperative education, distance learning, double majors, English as a second language, freshman honors college, honors programs, independent study, internships, off-campus study, part-time degree program, services for LD students, student-designed majors, study abroad, summer session for credit. *ROTC:* Army (b), Air Force (b).

Computers on Campus 880 computers/terminals are available on campus for general student use. Students can access the following: computer help desk, free student e-mail accounts, online (class) grades, online (class) registration, online (class) schedules. Campuswide network is available. 96% of college-owned or -operated housing units are wired for high-speed Internet access.

Student Life *Housing options:* coed, men-only, women-only, disabled students. Campus housing is university owned. *Activities and organizations:* drama/theater group, student-run newspaper, choral group, marching band, Latter-Day Saints Student Association, multicultural clubs, volunteer groups, college councils, national fraternities, national sororities. *Campus security:* 24-hour emergency response devices and patrols, student patrols, late-night transport/escort service, video monitors in pedestrian tunnels. *Student services:* health clinic, personal/psychological counseling, women's center, legal services.

Athletics Member NCAA. All Division I except football (Division I-A). *Intercollegiate sports:* baseball M (c), basketball M (s)/W (s), cross-country running M (s)/W (s), equestrian sports M (c)/W (c), golf M (s), gymnastics W (s), ice hockey M (c), rugby M (c)/W (c), soccer M (c)/W (s), softball W (s), tennis M (s)/W (s), track and field M (s)/W (s), volleyball M (c)/W (s). *Intramural sports:* badminton M/W, basketball M/W, cross-country running M/W, fencing M (c)/W (c), football M/W, golf M/W, ice hockey W (c), lacrosse M (c), racquetball M (c)/W (c), skiing (cross-country) M (c)/W (c), skiing (downhill) M (c)/W (c), soccer M/W, softball M/W, squash M/W, swimming and diving M/W, table tennis M/W, tennis M/W, ultimate Frisbee M (c)/W (c), volleyball M/W, water polo M (c)/W (c).

Standardized Tests *Required:* SAT or ACT (for admission).

Costs (2007–08) *Tuition:* state resident $3615 full-time; nonresident $11,640 full-time. Full-time tuition and fees vary according to course load and student level. Part-time tuition and fees vary according to course load and student level. *Required fees:* $585 full-time. *Room and board:* $4580; room only: $1600. Room and board charges vary according to board plan and housing facility. *Payment plan:* deferred payment. *Waivers:* minority students, children of alumni, adult students, senior citizens, and employees or children of employees.

Financial Aid Of all full-time matriculated undergraduates who enrolled in 2007, 5,971 applied for aid, 5,127 were judged to have need, 719 had their need fully met. 475 Federal Work-Study jobs (averaging $3380). 88 state and other part-time jobs (averaging $3380). In 2007, 241 non-need-based awards were made. *Average percent of need met:* 63%. *Average financial aid package:* $7608. *Average need-based loan:* $4307. *Average need-based gift aid:* $3876. *Average non-need-based aid:* $2381.

Applying *Options:* electronic application, early admission, deferred entrance. *Application fee:* $40. *Required:* high school transcript. *Recommended:* minimum 2.75 GPA. *Application deadlines:* rolling (freshmen), rolling (transfers). *Notification:* continuous (freshmen), continuous (transfers).

Freshman Application Contact Ms. Jenn Putnam, Director, Admissions Office, Utah State University, 0160 Old Main Hill, Logan, UT 84322-0160. *Phone:* 435-797-1079. *Toll-free phone:* 800-488-8108. *Fax:* 435-797-3708. *E-mail:* admit@usu.edu.

UTAH VALLEY STATE COLLEGE

Orem, Utah **www.uvsc.edu/**

- **State-supported** 4-year, founded 1941, part of Utah System of Higher Education
- **Suburban** 200-acre campus with easy access to Salt Lake City
- **Endowment** $10.4 million
- **Coed** 23,840 undergraduate students, 9% full-time, 7% women, 8% men
- **Noncompetitive** entrance level, 100% of applicants were admitted

Undergraduates 2,145 full-time, 1,364 part-time. Students come from 50 states and territories, 55 other countries, 14% are from out of state, 45% transferred in. *Retention:* 49% of 2006 full-time freshmen returned.

Freshmen *Admission:* 4,715 applied, 4,715 admitted, 3,509 enrolled. *Average high school GPA:* 3.22. *Test scores:* SAT math scores over 500: 45%; ACT scores over 18: 77%; SAT math scores over 600: 9%; ACT scores over 24: 21%; SAT math scores over 700: 1%; ACT scores over 30: 1%.

Faculty *Total:* 1,497, 30% full-time. *Student/faculty ratio:* 20:1.

Majors Accounting; airline pilot and flight crew; American Sign Language (ASL); autobody/collision and repair technology; automobile/automotive mechanics technology; banking and financial support services; biology/biological sciences; biology teacher education; biotechnology; building/construction site management; building/home/construction inspection; building/property maintenance and management; business administration and management; business automation/technology/data entry; business teacher education; cabinetmaking and millwork; chemistry; chemistry teacher education; commercial and advertising art; communication/speech communication and rhetoric; community health and preventive medicine; computer and information sciences; computer and information sciences and support services related; computer science; computer software engineering; construction trades; construction trades related; criminal justice/law enforcement administration; culinary arts; dance; dance related; data processing and data processing technology; dental hygiene; design and visual communications; diesel mechanics technology; drafting and design technology; drama and dance teacher education; dramatic/theater arts; early childhood education; economics; electrical, electronic and communications engineering technology; electromechanical technology; elementary education; engineering; engineering technologies related; English; English/language arts teacher education; environmental control technologies related; fire science; fire services administration; forensic science and technology; general studies; geological and earth sciences/geosciences related; health and physical education; health teacher education; heating, air conditioning, ventilation and refrigeration maintenance technology; history; history teacher education; hospitality administration; humanities; information science/studies; international business/trade/commerce; kindergarten/preschool education; legal assistant/paralegal; lineworker; mathematics; mathematics teacher education; mechanics and repair; multi-/interdisciplinary studies related; music; music teacher education; nursing (registered nurse training); operations management; philosophy; physical education teaching and coaching; physical sciences; physics; political science and government; psychology; science teacher education; secondary education; Spanish; Spanish language teacher education; special education (hearing impaired); web page, digital/multimedia and information resources design; welding technology.

Academics *Calendar:* semesters. *Degrees:* certificates, diplomas, associate, and bachelor's. *Special study options:* academic remediation for entering students, accelerated degree program, advanced placement credit, cooperative education, distance learning, double majors, English as a second language, honors programs, independent study, internships, off-campus study, part-time degree program, services for LD students, student-designed majors, study abroad, summer session for credit. *ROTC:* Army (b), Air Force (c).

Computers on Campus 1,000 computers/terminals are available on campus for general student use. Students can access the following: campus intranet, computer help desk, free student e-mail accounts, online (class) grades, online (class) registration, online (class) schedules. Campuswide network is available. Wireless service is available via entire campus.

Student Life *Housing:* college housing not available. *Activities and organizations:* drama/theater group, student-run newspaper, television station, choral group. *Campus security:* 24-hour patrols. *Student services:* health clinic, personal/psychological counseling, women's center, legal services.

Athletics Member NCAA. All Division I. *Intercollegiate sports:* baseball M (s), basketball M (s)/W (s), cross-country running M (s)/W (s), golf M (s)/W (s), soccer W (s), softball W (s), track and field M (s)/W (s), volleyball W (s), wrestling M (s). *Intramural sports:* basketball M/W, bowling M/W, football M/W, golf M/W, racquetball M/W, rock climbing M/W, soccer M/W, softball M/W, tennis M/W, ultimate Frisbee M/W, volleyball W.

Standardized Tests *Required for some:* SAT or ACT (for admission).

Costs (2007–08) *Tuition:* state resident $3000 full-time, $100 per credit part-time; nonresident $10,500 full-time, $350 per credit part-time. Full-time tuition and fees vary according to course load. Part-time tuition and fees vary according to course load. *Required fees:* $528 full-time, $264 per term part-time. *Room and board:* $6212; room only: $4142. Room and board charges vary according to housing facility. *Payment plans:* installment, deferred payment. *Waivers:* employees or children of employees.

Financial Aid Of all full-time matriculated undergraduates who enrolled in 2006, 6,289 applied for aid, 5,761 were judged to have need, 1,102 had their need fully met. In 2006, 536 non-need-based awards were made. *Average percent of need met:* 66%. *Average financial aid package:* $6477. *Average need-based loan:* $1965. *Average need-based gift aid:* $2278. *Average non-need-based aid:* $1603. *Average indebtedness upon graduation:* $6273.

Applying *Options:* electronic application, deferred entrance. *Application fee:* $35. *Recommended:* high school transcript. *Application deadlines:* rolling (freshmen), rolling (transfers). *Notification:* continuous (freshmen), continuous (transfers).

Freshman Application Contact Mrs. Liz Childs, Senior Director of Admissions, Utah Valley State College, 800 West University Parkway, Orem, UT 84058-5999. *Phone:* 801-863-8460. *Fax:* 801-225-4677. *E-mail:* info@uvsc.edu.

WEBER STATE UNIVERSITY

Ogden, Utah — weber.edu/

- **State-supported** comprehensive, founded 1889, part of Utah System of Higher Education
- **Urban** 526-acre campus with easy access to Salt Lake City
- **Endowment** $60.6 million
- **Coed** 17,617 undergraduate students, 54% full-time, 51% women, 49% men
- **Noncompetitive** entrance level, 100% of applicants were admitted

Undergraduates 9,439 full-time, 8,178 part-time. Students come from 50 states and territories, 35 other countries, 8% are from out of state, 1% African American, 2% Asian American or Pacific Islander, 4% Hispanic American, 0.6% Native American, 0.8% international, 6% transferred in, 4% live on campus. *Retention:* 67% of 2006 full-time freshmen returned.

Freshmen *Admission:* 4,221 applied, 4,221 admitted, 2,186 enrolled. *Average high school GPA:* 3.49. *Test scores:* ACT scores over 18: 83%; ACT scores over 24: 28%; ACT scores over 30: 2%.

Faculty *Total:* 907, 51% full-time, 44% with terminal degrees. *Student/faculty ratio:* 22:1.

Majors Accounting; aerospace, aeronautical and astronautical engineering; Air Force R.O.T.C./air science; applied mathematics; archeology; art; art teacher education; athletic training; autobody/collision and repair technology; automotive engineering technology; bilingual and multilingual education; biology/biotechnology laboratory technician; biology teacher education; botany/plant biology; business administration and management; business/managerial economics; business teacher education; chemical technology; chemistry; chemistry teacher education; child care and support services management; commercial and advertising art; computer engineering technology; computer systems networking and telecommunications; dance; design and visual communications; diagnostic medical sonography and ultrasound technology; diesel mechanics technology; drafting and design technology; drama and dance teacher education; dramatic/theater arts; economics; elementary education; emergency medical technology (EMT paramedic); English; English/language arts teacher education; family systems; fashion merchandising; finance; French; French language teacher education; geography; geology/earth science; German; German language teacher education; gerontology; health and physical education; health/health care administration; health information/medical records technology; history; history teacher education; human resources management; industrial arts; interior design; journalism; kindergarten/preschool education; kinesiology and exercise science; logistics and materials management; machine tool technology; mathematics; medical microbiology and bacteriology; music; music performance; music teacher education; nuclear medical technology; office management; photography; physical education teaching and coaching; physics; physics teacher education; piano and organ; political science and government; psychology; public relations/image management; radio and television; science teacher education; secondary education; social science teacher education; social studies teacher education; social work; sociology; Spanish; Spanish language teacher education; technical and business writing; zoology/animal biology.

Academics *Calendar:* semesters. *Degrees:* certificates, associate, bachelor's, master's, and postbachelor's certificates. *Special study options:* academic remediation for entering students, accelerated degree program, adult/continuing education programs, advanced placement credit, cooperative education, distance learning, double majors, English as a second language, external degree program, freshman honors college, honors programs, independent study, internships, off-campus study, part-time degree program, services for LD students, student-designed majors, study abroad, summer session for credit. *ROTC:* Army (b), Navy (b), Air Force (b).

Computers on Campus 558 computers/terminals are available on campus for general student use. Students can access the following: campus intranet, computer help desk, free student e-mail accounts, online (class) grades, online (class) registration, online (class) schedules. Campuswide network is available.

Student Life *Housing options:* men-only, women-only, cooperative, disabled students. Campus housing is university owned and is provided by a third party. *Activities and organizations:* drama/theater group, student-run newspaper, radio and television station, choral group, marching band, LDSSA, Mountaineering Club, Rodeo Club, Beta Alpha Psi, student nurses organization, national fraternities, national sororities. *Campus security:* 24-hour emergency response devices and patrols, student patrols, late-night transport/escort service, controlled dormitory access. *Student services:* health clinic, personal/psychological counseling, women's center, legal services.

Athletics Member NCAA. All Division I except football (Division I-AA). *Intercollegiate sports:* baseball M (c), basketball M (s)/W (s), bowling M (c)/W (c), cheerleading M (s)/W (s), cross-country running M (s)/W (s), fencing M (c)/W (c), golf M (s)/W (s), ice hockey M (c), lacrosse M (c)/W (c), racquetball M (c)/W (c), rugby M (c)/W (c), skiing (downhill) M (c)/W (c), soccer M (c)/W (s), softball W (c), swimming and diving M (c)/W (c), tennis M (s)/W (s), track and field M (s)/W (s), volleyball W (s), water polo M (c)/W (c). *Intramural sports:* baseball M/W, basketball M/W, bowling M/W, cross-country running M/W, football M/W, golf M/W, racquetball M/W, soccer M/W, softball M/W, tennis M/W, volleyball M/W.

Standardized Tests *Recommended:* SAT or ACT (for admission).

Costs (2007–08) *Tuition:* state resident $2988 full-time, $123 per credit hour part-time; nonresident $10,459 full-time, $429 per credit hour part-time. Part-time tuition and fees vary according to course load. *Required fees:* $675 full-time. *Room and board:* $5328; room only: $2142. Room and board charges vary according to board plan and housing facility. *Payment plans:* installment, deferred payment. *Waivers:* senior citizens and employees or children of employees.

Financial Aid Of all full-time matriculated undergraduates who enrolled in 2001, 8,410 applied for aid, 7,401 were judged to have need, 5,462 had their need fully met. In 2001, 2470 non-need-based awards were made. *Average percent of need met:* 87%. *Average financial aid package:* $5300. *Average need-based loan:* $2620. *Average need-based gift aid:* $3750. *Average non-need-based aid:* $1420. *Average indebtedness upon graduation:* $10,500.

Applying *Options:* electronic application, early admission, deferred entrance. *Application fee:* $30. *Required:* high school transcript. *Application deadlines:* 8/22 (freshmen), rolling (transfers). *Notification:* continuous (freshmen), continuous (transfers).

Freshman Application Contact Mr. Mark Simpson, Admissions Advisor, Weber State University, 1137 University Circle, 3750 Harrison Boulevard, Ogden, UT 84408-1137. *Phone:* 801-626-6047. *Toll-free phone:* 800-634-6568 (in-state); 800-848-7770 (out-of-state). *Fax:* 801-626-6744. *E-mail:* admissions@weber.edu.

WESTERN GOVERNORS UNIVERSITY

Salt Lake City, Utah **www.wgu.edu/**

Freshman Application Contact Chris Mallett, Director of Enrollment, Western Governors University, 2040 East Murray Holladay Road, Suite 106, Salt Lake City, UT 84117. *Phone:* 801-274-3280. *Toll-free phone:* 877-435-7948. *Fax:* 801-274-3305. *E-mail:* info@wgu.edu.

WESTMINSTER COLLEGE

Salt Lake City, Utah **www.westminstercollege.edu/**

- **Independent** comprehensive, founded 1875
- **Suburban** 27-acre campus
- **Endowment** $63.5 million
- **Coed** 2,048 undergraduate students, 89% full-time, 58% women, 42% men
- **Moderately difficult** entrance level, 86% of applicants were admitted

Undergraduates 1,819 full-time, 229 part-time. Students come from 41 states and territories, 19 other countries, 18% are from out of state, 0.9% African American, 3% Asian American or Pacific Islander, 6% Hispanic American, 0.8% Native American, 2% international, 11% transferred in, 27% live on campus. *Retention:* 77% of 2006 full-time freshmen returned.

Freshmen *Admission:* 1,146 applied, 987 admitted, 452 enrolled. *Average high school GPA:* 3.52. *Test scores:* SAT critical reading scores over 500: 71%; SAT math scores over 500: 67%; ACT scores over 18: 96%; SAT critical reading scores over 600: 38%; SAT math scores over 600: 29%; ACT scores over 24: 51%; SAT critical reading scores over 700: 10%; SAT math scores over 700: 4%; ACT scores over 30: 5%.

Faculty *Total:* 286, 45% full-time, 62% with terminal degrees. *Student/faculty ratio:* 10:1.

Majors Accounting; airline pilot and flight crew; art; arts management; aviation/airway management; biology/biological sciences; biology teacher education; business administration and management; business/commerce; business/managerial economics; chemistry; chemistry teacher education; communication/speech communication and rhetoric; computer science; economics; elementary education; English; environmental studies; finance; financial planning and services; history; international business/trade/commerce; management information systems and services related; marketing/marketing management; mathematics; neuroscience; nursing (registered nurse training); philosophy; physics; political science and government; psychology; social sciences; social science teacher education; sociology.

Academics *Calendar:* 4-4-1. *Degrees:* bachelor's, master's, and postbachelor's certificates. *Special study options:* academic remediation for entering students, accelerated degree program, advanced placement credit, cooperative education, double majors, external degree program, honors programs, independent study, internships, part-time degree program, services for LD students, student-designed majors, study abroad, summer session for credit. *ROTC:* Army (c), Navy (c), Air Force (c). *Unusual degree programs:* 3-2 engineering with University of Southern California, Washington University in St. Louis.

Computers on Campus 400 computers/terminals and 650 ports are available on campus for general student use. Students can access the following: campus intranet, computer help desk, free student e-mail accounts, online (class) grades, online (class) registration, online (class) schedules. Campuswide network is available. 100% of college-owned or -operated housing units are wired for high-speed Internet access. Wireless service is available via classrooms, computer centers, computer labs, learning centers, libraries, student centers.

Student Life *Housing:* on-campus residence required for freshman year. *Options:* coed. Campus housing is university owned. Freshman campus housing is guaranteed. *Activities and organizations:* drama/theater group, student-run newspaper, choral group, Student Nurses of Westminster (SNOW), Latter Day Saints Student Association, Aero Club, Pierced (Non-denominational Christian Club), Finance Club. *Campus security:* 24-hour emergency response devices and patrols, student patrols, late-night transport/escort service, controlled dormitory access. *Student services:* health clinic, personal/psychological counseling.

Athletics Member NAIA. *Intercollegiate sports:* basketball M (s)/W (s), cross-country running M/W, golf M/W, lacrosse M, soccer M (s), volleyball W (s). *Intramural sports:* basketball M/W, football M/W, table tennis M/W, volleyball M/W.

Standardized Tests *Required:* SAT or ACT (for admission).

Costs (2007–08) *Comprehensive fee:* $28,728 includes full-time tuition ($21,984), mandatory fees ($390), and room and board ($6354). Full-time tuition and fees vary according to course load. Part-time tuition: $916 per credit hour. *Required fees:* $110 per term part-time. *Room and board:* Room and board charges vary according to board plan. *Payment plans:* installment, deferred payment. *Waivers:* employees or children of employees.

Financial Aid Of all full-time matriculated undergraduates who enrolled in 2005, 1,323 applied for aid, 1,182 were judged to have need, 546 had their need fully met. 248 Federal Work-Study jobs (averaging $2050). In 2005, 479 non-need-based awards were made. *Average percent of need met:* 88%. *Average financial aid package:* $15,651. *Average need-based loan:* $4122. *Average need-based gift aid:* $9154. *Average non-need-based aid:* $6998. *Average indebtedness upon graduation:* $16,450.

Applying *Options:* electronic application, deferred entrance. *Application fee:* $40. *Required:* essay or personal statement, high school transcript, minimum 2.5 GPA, 1 letter of recommendation. *Recommended:* interview. *Application deadlines:* rolling (freshmen), rolling (out-of-state freshmen), rolling (transfers). *Notification:* continuous (freshmen), continuous (out-of-state freshmen), continuous (transfers).

Freshman Application Contact Christina Twelves, Interim Director of Undergraduate Admissions, Westminster College, 1840 South 1300 East, Salt Lake City, UT 84105-3697. *Phone:* 801-832-2200. *Toll-free phone:* 800-748-4753. *Fax:* 801-832-3101. *E-mail:* admission@westminstercollege.edu.

See page 2586 for the College Close-Up.

ARGOSY UNIVERSITY

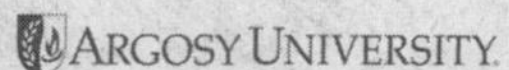

The University

Argosy University is a leading institution offering a variety of degree programs that focus on the human side of success alongside professional competence. For students looking for a more personal approach to education, Argosy University may just be the answer. With forty-eight graduate and undergraduate programs, across nineteen campuses and twelve states, Argosy University emphasizes interpersonal skills as well as academic learning. All of its programs are taught by practicing professionals who bring real-world experience into the classroom. So students graduate with both a solid foundation of knowledge and the power to put it to work. To accommodate busy working adults, many programs at Argosy University are structured flexibly—with both campus and online learning and evening, weekend, and daytime classes. There is also a wide range of financial aid options for students who qualify.

Argosy University is a private institution of higher education dedicated to providing high-quality professional education programs at the doctoral, master's, bachelor's, and associate degree levels as well as continuing education to individuals who seek to advance their professional and personal lives. The University emphasizes programs in the behavioral sciences (psychology and counseling), business, education, and the health-care professions. A limited number of preprofessional programs and general education offerings are provided to permit students to prepare for entry into these professional fields. The programs of Argosy University are designed to instill the knowledge, skills, and ethical values of professional practice and to foster values of social responsibility in a supportive, learning-centered environment of mutual respect and professional excellence.

With nineteen campuses nationwide, Argosy University provides students with a network of resources found at larger universities, including a career resources office, an academic resources center, and extensive information access for research. The University's innovative programs feature dynamic, relevant, and practical curricula delivered in flexible class formats. Students enjoy scheduling options that make it easier to fit school into their busy lives. They can choose from day and evening courses, on campus or online. Many students find a combination of both to be an ideal way of continuing their education while meeting family and professional demands.

Most students are full-time working professionals who live within driving distance of the campus. The University does not offer or operate student housing.

Argosy University is accredited by The Higher Learning Commission of the North Central Association (30 North LaSalle Street, Suite 2400, Chicago, Illinois 60602; 800-621-7440; http://ncahlc.org).

Location

Argosy University operates nineteen locations across the U.S. and offers a variety of degree programs online (http://www.argosy.edu). Campus locations include the following:

Atlanta, 980 Hammond Drive, Suite 100, Atlanta, Georgia 30328; phone: 770-671-1200 or 888-671-4777 (toll-free)

Chicago, 225 North Michigan Avenue, Suite 1300, Chicago, Illinois 60601; phone: 312-777-7600 or 800-626-4123 (toll-free)

Dallas, 8080 Park Lane, Suite 400A, Dallas, Texas 75231; phone: 214-890-9900 or 866-954-9900 (toll-free)

Denver, 1200 Lincoln Street, Denver, Colorado 80203; phone: 303-248-2700 or 866-431-5981 (toll-free)

Hawai'i, 400 ASB Tower, 1001 Bishop Street, Honolulu, Hawaii 96813; phone: 808-536-5555 or 888-323-2777 (toll-free)

Inland Empire, 636 East Brier Drive, Suite 235, San Bernardino, California 92408; phone: 909-915-3800 or 866-217-9075 (toll-free)

Nashville, 100 Centerview Drive, Suite 225, Nashville, Tennessee 37214; phone: 615-525-2800 or 866-833-6598 (toll-free)

Orange County, 3501 West Sunflower Avenue, Suite 110, Santa Ana, California 92704; phone: 714-338-6200 or 800-716-9598 (toll-free)

Phoenix, 2233 West Dunlap Avenue, Phoenix, Arizona 85021; phone: 602-216-2600 or 866-216-2777 (toll-free)

Salt Lake City, 121 West Election Road, Suite 300, Draper, Utah 84020; phone: 888-639-4756 (toll-free)

San Diego, 7650 Mission Valley Road, San Diego, California 92108; phone: 858-598-1900 or 866-505-0333 (toll-free)

San Francisco Bay Area, 1005 Atlantic Avenue, Alameda, California 94501; phone: 510-217-4700 or 866-215-2777 (toll-free)

Santa Monica, 2950 31st Street, Santa Monica, California 90405; phone: 310-866-4000 or 866-505-0332 (toll-free)

Sarasota, 5250 17th Street, Sarasota, Florida 34235; phone: 941-379-0404 or 800-331-5995 (toll-free)

Schaumburg, 999 North Plaza Drive, Suite 111, Schaumburg, Illinois 60173-5403; phone: 847-969-4900 or 866-290-2777 (toll-free)

Seattle, 2601-A Elliott Avenue, Seattle, Washington 98121; phone: 206-283-4500 or 888-283-2777 (toll-free)

Tampa, Parkside at Tampa Bay Park, 4401 North Hines Avenue, Suite 150, Tampa, Florida 33614; phone: 813-393-5290 or 800-850-6488 (toll-free)

Twin Cities, 1515 Central Parkway, Eagan, Minnesota 55121; phone: 651-846-2882 or 888-844-2004 (toll-free)

Washington DC, 1550 Wilson Boulevard, Suite 600, Arlington, Virginia 22209; phone: 703-526-5800 or 866-703-2777 (toll-free)

Majors and Degrees

Argosy University's College of Business offers a Bachelor of Science (B.S.) in Business Administration program. Argosy University's College of Psychology and Behavioral Sciences offers the Bachelor of Arts (B.A.) in Psychology degree program.

Academic Programs

The B.S. in Business Administration program prepares students for entry- to mid-level positions within the public or private sector. The curriculum is structured to help students develop competencies in oral and written communication, leadership, team skills, solutions-focused learning, and the analysis and execution of solutions in various business situations. Students may choose one of five optional concentrations: customized professional concentration, finance, health-care management, international business, or marketing.

The B.A. in Psychology program is designed to help students begin human services careers in such capacities as entry-level counselor, case manager, or human resources administrator and

in management and business services roles. The program also lays the foundation for graduate study. Students may choose an optional concentration from the following three options: criminal justice, organizational psychology, or substance abuse. This dynamic program is built around a flexible class approach.

Argosy University's bachelor's degree programs are open to students and working professionals with no college experience, plus those who have already earned college credit at a community college, junior college, or other university.

Academic Facilities

Argosy University libraries provide curriculum support and educational resources including current text materials, diagnostic training documents, reference materials and databases, journals and dissertations, and major and current titles in program areas. There is an online public-access catalog of library resources available throughout the Argosy University system. Students enjoy full remote access to their campus library database, enabling them to study and conduct research at home. Academic databases offer dissertation abstracts, academic journals, and professional periodicals. All library computers are Internet accessible. Software applications include Word, Excel, PowerPoint, SPSS, and various test-scoring programs.

Costs

Tuition varies by program. Students should contact the Argosy University campus of their choice for tuition information.

Financial Aid

A wide range of financial aid options is available to students who qualify. Argosy University offers access to federal and state aid programs, merit-based awards, grants, loans, and a work-study program. As a first step, students should complete the Free Application for Federal Student Aid (FAFSA). Prospective students can apply electronically at http://www.fafsa.ed.gov or at the campus. To receive consideration for financial aid and ensure timely receipt of funds, it is best to submit an application promptly.

Faculty

The Argosy University faculty is composed of working professionals who have a passion to help students succeed. Members bring real-world experience and the latest practice innovations to the academic setting. The diverse faculty is widely recognized for contributions to the field. Most hold doctoral degrees. They provide a substantive education that combines comprehensive knowledge with critical skills and practical workplace relevance. Above all, faculty members are committed to their students' personal and professional development.

Student Government

Argosy University campuses offer unique opportunities for student involvement beyond individual programs of study. Most faculty committees include a student representative. In addition, a student group meets with faculty members and administrators regularly to discuss pertinent campus-related issues.

Admission Requirements

Admission requirements differ depending on the number of college credits completed prior to application.

Students who have earned 12 or fewer semester college credits must provide proof of high school graduation or GED and meet one of the following conditions for admission: ACT composite score of 18 or above, or a combined math and verbal SAT score of 870, or minimum ACCUPLACER scores of 86 in sentence skills and 53 in algebra. Applicants who do not meet any of the above conditions for admission will be admitted with academic support if they provide proof of high school graduation or GED and meet one of the following: ACT composite score of 14 to 17, or a combined math and verbal SAT score of 660 to 869, or minimum ACCUPLACER scores of 54 in sentence skills and 36 in arithmetic.

Applicants who have earned 13 or more semester college credits must provide proof of high school graduation or GED and meet one of the following conditions for admission: cumulative college GPA of 2.0 or above or minimum ACCUPLACER scores of 86 for sentence skills and 53 in algebra. Students who do not meet either of the above criteria will be admitted with academic support if they provide proof of high school graduation or GED and meet the following condition: minimum ACCUPLACER scores of 54 in reading and 36 in arithmetic.

Students admitted with academic support are limited to 12 credit hours of study during their first semester (6 credit hours per session). Students admitted with academic support will be required to complete developmental English and/or math courses unless they meet the following conditions: Writing Review (ENG099)—must meet one of the following: a minimum ACCUPLACER score of 86 in sentence skills, or a minimum ACT verbal score of 18, or a minimum SAT verbal score of 425, or completion of a college-level English composition course with a grade of C or above; Mathematics Review I (MAT096)—must meet one of the following: a minimum ACCUPLACER score of 53 in algebra, or a minimum ACT math score of 18, or a minimum SAT math score of 440, or completion of a college-level English composition course with a grade of C or above.

Other admission requirements may include credit hours of qualified transfer credit with a grade of C- or better from a regionally accredited institution or a nationally accredited institution approved and documented by the faculty and dean of the College of Business, or the College of Professional Psychology, at Argosy University or completion of an Associate of Arts or Associate of Science degree from a regionally accredited institution. A maximum of 78 lower-division or 90 total credit hours may be transferred. A minimum written TOEFL score of 500 (paper-based test), 173 (computer-based test), or 61 (Internet-based test) is required for all applicants whose native language is not English or who have not graduated from an institution in which English is the language of instruction.

Official transcripts from approved postsecondary institutions must include a minimum grade point average of 2.0 (on a scale of 4.0) for all academic work completed. Exceptions may be made for extenuating circumstances. All applications must include a completed application form, proof of high school graduation or successful completion of the GED test, official postsecondary transcripts, and a nonrefundable (except in California) application fee. Additional materials are required prior to matriculation. Some programs have additional application requirements or include exceptions to admission requirements. An admissions representative can provide further information.

Application and Information

Argosy University accepts students on a rolling admissions basis year-round, depending on availability of required courses. Applications for admission are available online at http://www.argosy.edu or by contacting one of the campus locations.

Argosy University
205 North Michigan Avenue, Suite 1300
Chicago, Illinois 60601-2250
Phone: 312-899-9900
800-377-0617 (toll-free)
E-mail: auadmissions@argosy.edu
Web site: http://www.argosy.edu

THE ART INSTITUTE OF SALT LAKE CITY

DRAPER, UTAH

The Art Institute of Salt Lake City™

The Institute

The Art Institute of Salt Lake City provides students with an educational environment and dedicated faculty members who are committed to preparing students for entry-level positions in the creative arts. Under the guidance of industry professionals, students learn by doing the types of tasks they are likely to encounter in the workplace. In addition, assistance is available to help students with resume writing, networking, and keeping aware of what employers are looking for in job candidates. The school offers five bachelor's degree programs, three associate degree programs, and two diploma programs.

The school offers assistance in helping students to secure housing.

The student population includes recent high school graduates, transfer students, and those who have left a previous employment situation to study and train for a new career. Students are creative, competitive, and open to new ideas. They place great value on an education that prepares them for an exciting entry-level position in the arts.

The Art Institute of Salt Lake City places a high value on the quality of student life—both in and out of the classroom. Students participate in a wide variety of activities, including clubs and organizations, community service, and various committees designed to enhance the quality of student life.

The Art Institute of Salt Lake City is accredited by the Accrediting Commission of Career Schools and Colleges of Technology (ACCSCT) as a branch of The Art Institute of Las Vegas.

Location

Draper is located in the Wasatch Mountains at the south end of the Salt Lake Valley. The city has long been known as a premier hang-gliding destination with breathtaking views. Draper is fast becoming a hub for new development in the Salt Lake and Utah Valleys.

Majors and Degrees

Bachelor's degree programs are offered in culinary management, digital filmmaking and video production, graphic design, interior design, and Web design and interactive media.

Associate degrees are offered in baking and pastry, culinary arts, graphic design, and Web design and interactive media.

Diploma programs are available in baking and pastry and the art of cooking.

Academic Programs

The Art Institute of Salt Lake City operates on a year-round, four-quarter system.

Academic Facilities

The Art Institute of Salt Lake City contains classrooms, Macintosh and PC computer labs, and a library for student use. There is also a bookstore.

Costs

Tuition cost varies by program. Prospective students should contact the school for current tuition costs. Other charges include a starting kit for all first-quarter students. Kits vary in price depending on the program of study.

Financial Aid

Financial aid is available for those who qualify. Students who require financial assistance should first complete and submit a Free Application for Federal Student Aid (FAFSA) and meet with a financial aid officer. The officer determines the level of need based on a required federal formula, the cost of education, and other factors. Gift aid is available in the form of Federal Pell Grants, Federal Supplemental Educational Opportunity Grants, and veterans' benefits. Loans include Federal Stafford Student Loans, Federal PLUS loans, and alternative loans. Other scholarships are available from the school and private sources. Application deadlines and eligibility requirements vary by program.

Faculty

Faculty members at The Art Institute of Salt Lake City have professional knowledge that they bring into the classroom. The school's faculty members provide their students with a real-world, relevant educational experience.

Admission Requirements

Applicants must provide proof of high school graduation or achievement of a General Educational Development (GED) certificate as a prerequisite for admission. In lieu of documenting high school graduation or a GED certificate, applicants may provide proof of attaining an associate degree or higher from an accredited institution. An official transcript indicating date of high school graduation, receipt of a GED certificate (including test scores), or date of college graduation (including degree granted) is required as proof.

All individuals seeking admission to The Art Institute of Salt Lake City are interviewed in person or by phone by an assistant director of admissions, and each applicant must create an original essay of at least 150 words stating how an education at The Art Institute of Salt Lake City would help the student to achieve career goals. There is a $50 application fee.

Application and Information

To obtain an application, make arrangements for an interview, or tour the school, students should contact:

The Art Institute of Salt Lake City
121 West Election Road, Suite 100
Draper, Utah 84020-9492
Phone: 801-601-4700
800-978-0096 (toll-free)
Fax: 801-601-4724
Web site: http://www.artinstitutes.edu/saltlakecity

The Art Institute of Atlanta®, GA; The Art Institute of Atlanta®–Decatur, GA; The Art Institute of Austin℠, TX; The Art Institute of California℠–Inland Empire; The Art Institute of California℠–Los Angeles; The Art Institute of California℠–Orange County; The Art Institute of California℠–Sacramento; The Art Institute of California℠–San Diego; The Art Institute of California℠–San Francisco; The Art Institute of California℠–Sunnyvale; The Art Institute of Charleston℠, SC, A branch of The Art Institute of Atlanta, GA; The Art Institute of Charlotte®, NC; The Art Institute of Colorado® (Denver); The Art Institute of Dallas®, TX; The Art Institute of Fort Lauderdale®, FL; The Art Institute of Houston®, TX; The Art Institute of Indianapolis℠, IN*; The Art Institute of Jacksonville℠, FL, A branch of Miami International University of Art & Design; The Art Institute of Las Vegas®, NV; The Art Institute of Michigan℠ (Detroit); The Art Institute of New York City®, NY; The Art Institute of Ohio℠–Cincinnati**; The Art Institute of Philadelphia®, PA; The Art Institute of Phoenix®, AZ; The Art Institute of Pittsburgh®, PA; The Art Institute of Pittsburgh®–Online Division; The Art Institute of Portland®, OR; The Art Institute of Salt Lake City℠, UT; The Art Institute of Seattle®, WA; The Art Institute of Tampa℠, FL, A branch of Miami International University of Art & Design; The Art Institute of Tennessee℠–Nashville, A branch of The Art Institute of Atlanta, GA; The Art Institute of Tucson℠, AZ; The Art Institute of Washington® (Arlington, VA), A branch of The Art Institute of Atlanta, GA; The Art Institute of York–Pennsylvania℠; The Art Institutes International Minnesota℠ (Minneapolis); California Design College℠ (Los Angeles–Wilshire Blvd.); The Illinois Institute of Art®–Chicago; The Illinois Institute of Art®–Schaumburg; Miami International University of Art & Design℠, FL; The New England Institute of Art® (Boston, MA).

*The Art Institute of Indianapolis is licensed by the Indiana Commission on Proprietary Education, 302 W. Washington St., Rm. E201, Indianapolis, IN 46204, AC-0080.

**The Art Institute of Ohio–Cincinnati, 8845 Governors Hill Drive, Suite 100, Cincinnati, OH 45249-3317, OH Reg. #04-01-1698B.

SOUTHERN UTAH UNIVERSITY

CEDAR CITY, UTAH

The University

Southern Utah University (SUU) is a comprehensive regional institution offering graduate, baccalaureate, associate, and technical programs. Throughout its 110-year history, SUU has been committed to providing an excellent education through a diverse, dynamic, and personalized learning environment, educating students to be critical thinkers, effective communicators, lifelong learners, and individuals who demonstrate integrity and empathy in the pursuit of their life's ambitions. People throughout the region look to the University for skill development, academic specialties, outreach services, cultural and athletic activities, and economic and business development. The University is fully accredited by the Northwest Commission on Colleges and Universities.

SUU was established in 1897 as a state teacher training school. The first class met in September 1897, and the first building was erected a year later, made from the trees that grew nearby. Over the decades, SUU has expanded to include undergraduate and graduate programs plus specialized programs for members of the community, including disadvantaged youth, nontraditional students, and youth with disabilities. Each semester, the University enrolls 7,000 students in more than seventy undergraduate and eight graduate programs offered by its seven schools and colleges. Students come from all twenty-nine counties in Utah, fifty states, and fifty-five other countries. Of the total enrollment, 57 percent are women, and 43 percent are men.

About 70 percent of all students live on campus or in apartments near the campus, giving them easy access to all that SUU has to offer. In 2006, 140 clubs and organizations were operating on the SUU campus, comprising a wide range of activities and interests. In addition, students have ample opportunity to participate in sports activities, whether they want to play intramural sports at the physical education facility or on one of thirteen NCAA Division I sports teams, including basketball, baseball, football, and soccer.

The Fitness Center has some of the finest state-of-the-art equipment available, including stair climbers, treadmills, elliptical machines, and stationary bikes. The large assortment of free weights and single-station exercise equipment gives students the opportunity to manage weight, build muscle mass, and relieve stress. The Outdoor Recreation Center is the campus resource for adventure education seminars and rental equipment. A variety of trips, such as backpacking, cross-country skiing, and kayaking, are available. The center also sponsors workshops that help teach outdoor fundamentals, such as climbing techniques, clothing and equipment, and outdoor cooking.

Location

Located in southwestern Utah, Cedar City is renowned for its arts and entertainment, natural beauty, and outdoor recreation. The Tony Award–winning Utah Shakespeare Festival attracts thousands of theater lovers every summer, and the Heritage Center presents an assortment of plays, symphonies, ballets, and art shows. The historic downtown shopping district offers unique restaurants, antique stores, arts and craft shops, and live music. Moreover, Cedar City's business-friendly environment has attracted national industrial and manufacturing businesses.

Because it is surrounded by national parks and monuments, Cedar City is ideal for rock climbing, mountain biking, golfing, four-wheeling, fishing, skiing, and snowboarding. Three Peaks provides picnic areas, miles of mountain bike and ATV trails, and unique rock formations. Navajo Lake on Cedar Mountain is a perfect spot for snowboarding in the winter and hiking in the summer. Zion National Park, Utah's oldest national park, is also nearby. For those who want to explore the region, Cedar City is 2½ hours north of Las Vegas and 3½ hours south of Salt Lake City.

Majors and Degrees

Bachelor's degrees are available in the following fields: accounting; agriculture science and industries; art composite; art education; art history; athletic training; biology; chemistry; communication; computer science; construction management; criminal justice; dance education; dance performance; economics; elementary education; engineering technology; English; family life and human development; finance; French; French education; geology; German; German education; graphic design; history; history education; hotel, resort, and hospitality management; human nutrition; information systems; integrated engineering; management; marketing; mathematics; mathematics education; music education composite; music performance composite; nursing; outdoor recreation in parks and tourism; physical education; political science; psychology; secondary education; sociology; Spanish; Spanish education; special education; studio art; theater arts; and theater arts education.

Academic Programs

The academic year is divided into three semesters. The fall semester begins in late August and ends in mid-December. Following a three-week winter break, the spring semester begins in early January and ends in early May. The summer semester comprises three sessions: a "Maymester" session of three weeks and two summer sessions of five weeks each.

In order to complete the bachelor's degree, students must complete a minimum of 120 credits with a GPA of 2.0 or higher. Of these, at least 40 credits must be earned in upper-division courses. Minimum general education requirements are as follows: 6 credits in writing and composition, 3 credits in mathematics, 3 credits in computer applications, 3 credits in social science, 1 credit each in information literacy and a first-year seminar; and 19 credits in fine arts, interdisciplinary studies, humanities, social and behavioral sciences, life sciences, and physical sciences. The remaining credits are earned in electives and the major/minor program of study. Students earning a Bachelor of Arts degree must complete at least 16 credits in a foreign language or American Sign Language or demonstrate proficiency in a language. Bachelor of Science students must complete 12 or more credits in mathematics or laboratory science. Electives or required courses in the major or minor may satisfy this requirement.

A total of 30 credits can be achieved by a combination of special course examinations, credit by portfolio, or individual study. Some general education requirements may be satisfied by successfully completing selected CLEP exams. Credit by portfolio is designed specifically for people who have experience manifested by a portfolio and documented as their personal work by records or letters from those aware of the activity. The portfolio should already exist as a result of previous work and should not be something created for the purpose of gaining credit. In addition, up to 8 credits are granted for a composite grade of 5, 4, or 3 on any Advanced Placement examination. The University may grant credit to current students who have served in the armed forces.

Off-Campus Programs

Study-abroad programs afford the opportunity to spend a summer or a semester earning college credit while visiting some of the world's most beautiful and exciting areas. Current programs include studying English literature in London, learning the German language and culture in Austria, and spending an entire semester in Germany, Sweden, Mexico, or France. The Office of Off-Campus Degree Programs delivers courses and degree programs throughout southern Utah. Courses are primarily offered at the University Center at Snow College South in Richfield and at Dixie State College in St. George. Delivery methods include faculty members traveling to these sites as well as technology-mediated courses via the EdNet system, satellite, and the Internet.

Academic Facilities

The Gerald R. Sherratt Library provides high-quality resources and responsive services to the SUU community. The library houses more than 1,200 computer workstations and study rooms. Special sections are devoted to materials that are rare, expensive, or in need of special handling; materials about SUU and southern Utah; materials in opera, drama, literature, and language; and materials about the Paiute Indians and southern Utah. The Media/Curriculum Collection includes videotapes, DVDs, computer programs, recordings, pictures, CDs, books on tape, charts, maps, models, and current public school curriculum materials. Moreover, an optical-fiber network connects the library to approximately 22,700 periodicals that complement the in-house periodical collection of 1,000 titles.

Costs

In 2007–08, full-time tuition was $1637 per semester for residents and $5402 for nonresidents, plus $261 in miscellaneous fees. Part-time tuition was $160 per credit for residents and $528 for nonresidents, plus fees of $25 per credit. Students can expect to spend between $300 and $500 per semester for books and supplies plus additional costs for transportation and other miscellaneous expenses.

Housing rates range from $910 per semester for a shared bedroom in a traditional residence hall to $1750 for a private room in an apartment-style hall. These charges include utilities, phone service, Internet service, and parking. Meal plans range from $757 for five meals per week to $1551 for nineteen meals per week. All plans include flexible spending funds.

Financial Aid

Admissions applicants are automatically considered for academic scholarships. New students are generally awarded scholarships in amounts of $1000 to $3000 per year, from one to four years; out-of-state students may receive between $3000 and $10,000 per year. Leadership scholarships are awarded to students with outstanding leadership ability who have excelled in student government, community service, and other cocurricular activities. Awards generally range from one to four years. A minimum GPA of 3.0 is required for scholarship consideration. Other scholarships are awarded by the University and private foundations on the basis of military service, athletic participation, academic excellence, ethnicity, or intended program of study. Award amounts and eligibility requirements vary.

Students may borrow additional funds under a number of loan programs, including the Federal Perkins Loan, Federal Stafford Loan, and Parent Loan for Undergraduate Students (PLUS). The Federal Work-Study program pays students in exchange for working up to 20 hours per week; jobs may be on or off campus.

Faculty

The University attracts faculty members who are dedicated to excellence in teaching, creative in generating new knowledge, and generous in using their expertise to solve society's problems. High-quality teaching is their primary goal, giving students the opportunity to work with some of the finest and most caring professors in the state. In addition to helping students learn, faculty members assist business, industry, educational institutions, government agencies, and professional groups with educational programs to upgrade the knowledge and skills of employees. More than 300 professors teach at the University every year, most of whom hold the terminal degree in their field of study.

Student Government

The Southern Utah University Student Association (SUUSA) provides opportunities for student involvement, leadership development, and planning and implementing successful activities that meet the social and academic needs of students. Members work with the Office of Student Involvement under the advisement of the Director of Student Leadership to enhance campus life and the collegiate experience.

The leadership is separated into three branches: executive, legislative, and judicial. Under the direction of the student body president, the executive council sponsors social activities and provides other services, including cultural awareness, internship opportunities, and support of student organizations. The Senate, which is composed of 18 elected senators, 3 from each college or school, approves all allocations of student fees. The Judicial Council consists of a Chief Justice and four Associate Justices. Its jurisdiction extends to all cases regarding the SUUSA constitution, such as election bylaws and parking appeals.

Admission Requirements

Prospective students must submit a completed application form, official high school transcripts, official SAT/ACT scores, and a nonrefundable $40 application fee. All students are evaluated against the Admissions Index, which is a score based on GPA and SAT/ACT scores. Students with an Admission Index score of 85 or higher are admitted; those with a score below 85 may be admitted through the College Connections Program. Most students have a GPA of 2.0 or higher and SAT scores of at least 900 or ACT scores of 19 or higher.

Application and Information

To be considered for University scholarships, prospective students should submit their applications by February 1 (March 1 for transfer students). Additional information may be requested from:

Admissions Office
Sharwan Smith Center 166
Southern Utah University
351 West University Boulevard
Cedar City, Utah 84720
Phone: 435-586-7740
Fax: 435-865-8225
E-mail: admissions@truman.edu
Web site: http://www.suu.edu/

WESTMINSTER COLLEGE
SALT LAKE CITY, UTAH

The College

Westminster College offers students a unique environment for learning. A Westminster education is characterized by three features: active and engaged learning, a vibrant community, and a record of success.

In traditional educational models, colleges focus on what is taught and measure student success by the time they spend in classes and the grades they earn. Westminster focuses on outcomes—what students actually learn and what they can do with that knowledge. Students are active participants in their own learning; faculty members are directly involved in mentoring and guiding their development through experiences that are active, experiential, collaborative, and cross-disciplinary; and learning goes beyond mastery of subject-specific skills to College-wide learning goals that integrate the skills and attributes that are critical to success in a rapidly changing world.

Westminster knows that learning takes place out of the classroom as well as within it, so it offers a full range of activities on campus: fifty clubs, health and wellness programming, plays, concerts, lectures, and the like. The College also enjoys the benefits of a diverse and vibrant city that serves as a center of state government, banking, and high technology—all of which students experience through internships, a campus concierge, and classes that expose students to the Salt Lake City's resources, challenges, and opportunities. In addition, Westminster is located near the Rocky Mountains and provides an outdoor recreation program that can get students to world-class ski resorts within 20 minutes or the solitude of forests or the wonders of national parks.

The College has been recognized by *U.S. News & World Report,* the Princeton Review, and Kaplan/*Newsweek.* Its goal is to add value to each student's experience at Westminster. After graduation, some students have gone to work at firms such as General Electric, American Express, and Hewlett-Packard; others have continued their education at schools such as Columbia, Georgetown, Berkeley, and the University of London.

Westminster is tucked into the quaint and eclectic Sugar House neighborhood of Salt Lake City and provides a welcome academic haven for learners. Distinguished by old-growth trees, a small creek, and a graceful blend of old and new architecture, the urban College campus still provides plenty of green space to enjoy in the midst of the city. The College's on-campus housing, which accommodates 500 students, includes new apartment-style suites featuring entertainment systems and cooking facilities. Off-campus rental housing is readily available in the neighborhood.

The current enrollment is approximately 2,600. Undergraduates make up 75 percent of the student body, with graduate students making up 25 percent. Students come to Westminster from thirty-seven states and twenty-four countries. The average undergraduate student age is 24, and the undergraduate ratio of men to women is 41:59.

Westminster College offers intercollegiate basketball, cross-country, golf, lacrosse, and soccer for men and basketball, cross-country, golf, soccer, and volleyball for women. Teams compete in the Frontier Conference (NAIA). The College is in the process of creating a ski team as well.

Student services include academic advising, career planning and placement, internships, personal counseling, tutoring, and testing.

Residential students are required to participate in a meal plan. Daily selections include a burger bar, a pizza station, a Mexican buffet, a fruit and salad bar, and daily specials.

Location

Salt Lake City, the home of the 2002 Winter Olympics and the Sundance Film Festival, is a metropolitan area of approximately 1.3 million people. Downtown Salt Lake is 10 minutes from the campus by bus, car, or bicycle. Attractions include professional sports events, ballet, theater, concerts, and shopping to suit all tastes. A new campus concierge program facilitates student access to cultural events, recreational and entertainment options, student discounts, and volunteer opportunities. Salt Lake and the surrounding areas have four distinct seasons, with limited amounts of rain and snow in the valley and moderate temperatures. However, the Wasatch Mountains, a section of the Rockies that borders the Salt Lake Valley on the east, are famous for the "greatest snow on earth." With approximately 500 inches of annual snowfall, these mountains are ideal for winter sports enthusiasts as well as for those who enjoy summer hiking, biking, and camping. Ten world-class ski and snowboard resorts lie within an hour's drive of the campus, and sixteen national parks and recreational areas are within a day's drive or less. Golf, backpacking, mountain biking, kayaking, wakeboarding, mountain climbing, canyoneering, spelunking, and rafting are all within easy reach of the campus.

Majors and Degrees

Westminster College offers more than seventy academic programs through its four schools: the Bill and Vieve Gore School of Business, the School of Nursing and Health Sciences, the School of Education, and the School of Arts and Sciences. Bachelor of Arts and Bachelor of Science degrees are offered in the following areas: art (including a Bachelor of Fine Arts), arts administration, aviation (flight operations and aviation management), biology, business (including an emphasis in accounting, economics, economics prelaw, financial services, finance, international business, management, or marketing), chemistry, communication, computer science, education (early childhood or elementary), English, environmental studies, history, justice studies, mathematics, neuroscience, nursing, philosophy, physics, political studies, psychology, social science, sociology, and preprofessional programs (dentistry, law, medicine, veterinary medicine, and 3-2 engineering). In addition to the above-listed majors, the College offers minors in many of those program areas plus the following areas: anthropology, film studies, French, gender studies, music, paleontology, political science, religious studies, Spanish, special education, and theater arts. Special programs include Honors, Chinese, and Japanese.

Academic Programs

By integrating a liberal arts foundation with professional education, Westminster exhibits features of both a liberal arts college and a comprehensive university. Students are challenged to experiment with ideas, raise questions, critically examine alternatives, and make informed decisions. Students are also encouraged to accept responsibility for their own learning, to discover and pursue their passions, and to act with responsibility.

Each student must complete at least 124 semester hours to receive a bachelor's degree, of which approximately 40 hours consist of liberal arts education core requirements that are common to all students regardless of major. Semester-hour requirements vary among majors, but all students are exposed to liberal arts concepts as well as practical, career-oriented experiences. Credit is awarded for successful scores on Advanced Placement and CLEP examinations.

Students can participate in the U.S. Air Force Reserve Officer Training Corps program, the U.S. Army Reserve Officers' Training Corps program, and the U.S. Naval Reserve Officers' Training Corps program through cooperative programs at the University of Utah.

The College has a 4-4-1 calendar, consisting of two 15-week semesters followed by a one-month May term, as well as a summer session. Students who attend full-time during fall and spring semesters earn free May-term tuition.

Off-Campus Programs

Westminster students may participate in travel/study trips (for credit) during May term and the summer session. Students can also make individual arrangements for international study by advisement from the College's International Studies Chair and the Career Resource Center and through a cooperative agreement with the Foreign Study Office at the University of Utah.

Students are encouraged to participate in service-learning activities through the Center for Civic Engagement, to take advantage of internships and other opportunities offered by the Career Resource Center, and to consider work-study opportunities on campus that are designed to be integrated with their more traditional academic activities.

Westminster is also a member of the Utah Asian Studies Consortium, which promotes connections between faculty members and students in Utah and businesses and schools in Asia, offering May-term trips, internships, semester study-abroad programs, and other opportunities in several Asian countries.

Academic Facilities

Classes are never more than a 5-minute walk away on the pristine, tree-filled 27-acre campus. The careful blend of architecture is illustrated by the Emma Eccles Jones Conservatory of Music and Theatre. The Gore School of Business, Aviation, and Entrepreneurship, one of the most technologically advanced business education facilities in the nation, integrates innovative, new laboratories and state-of-the-art classroom facilities with the Center for Financial Analysis, offering real-time access to world market data, a behavioral simulation lab, and a flight simulation and testing center.

The Flight Operations Center, which includes a state-of-the-art hangar, flight simulators, and thirteen new aircraft, is located at Salt Lake International Airport. The Dolores Doré Eccles Health, Wellness, and Athletic Center includes a lap pool, exercise facilities, and a climbing wall and also houses the School of Nursing and Health Sciences. Westminster plans to begin construction of a new Science Center in spring 2008. The building, which will meet exacting environmental standards established by the United States Green Building Council, is designed to encourage interaction between various scientific disciplines and allow students to work with state-of-the-art equipment as part of their classroom activity and Westminster's extensive undergraduate research program. Current facilities include major classroom buildings, multiple computer and presentation classrooms, a unique bi-level athletic field/parking garage structure, an award-winning library, a ceramics studio, and a nursing laboratory.

All students have Internet access and e-mail accounts, using a high-speed gigabit network. A secure student Web portal consolidates online e-mail, course, and registration services. Network connections abound in all classrooms and every residence-hall room and library seat. Eighty percent of classrooms are set up for multimedia presentations. Technical support is available to students and faculty and staff members seven days a week.

Costs

Tuition and fees for 2007–08 were $22,374 for the academic year for a full-time student (12 to 16 semester hours). This figure includes costs for the fall semester, spring semester, and May term. Room and board costs were $6354 for the same period. Books and supplies were estimated at $1000 per year.

Financial Aid

More than 95 percent of freshmen at Westminster receive some form of financial aid, averaging $17,773 each year per student. Aid programs include need-based institutional grants and need-based federal aid programs such as grants, loans, and employment (Federal Work-Study Program). The Free Application for Federal Student Aid (FAFSA) is the only form required for new students seeking financial aid. Students wishing to apply for federal aid programs should plan to submit applications by early April. Merit-based scholarships are available to incoming freshmen and transfer students as well as to continuing students through a generous endowment and institutional aid programs. Every full-time student is automatically considered for merit-based scholarships awarded by the College. The scholarships are based on their GPA from previous academic course work.

Faculty

Full-time faculty members number 130. The student-faculty ratio is 10:1. All faculty members teach; no full-time research faculty positions exist and no graduate students teach. Many full-time faculty members are actively involved as advisers and sponsors of campus-based student activities. Approximately 94 percent of the faculty members hold a Ph.D. or the highest degree available in their fields.

Student Government

The official student governing body is the Associated Students of Westminster College (ASWC), which sponsors all student activities and organizations and provides funding and authorization for them. The ASWC is made up of three branches: the executive cabinet, the legislative assembly, and the judiciary branch. The three branches function in a similar fashion to the federal government system. The president of the ASWC is considered the primary spokesperson for the student body and has access to all senior administrators of the College.

Admission Requirements

Individual applications are reviewed based on a student's potential for success at Westminster and their potential to add vibrancy to the classroom environment. Academic preparation, which includes both course work and grades, is most important. Also important to the review committee are items such as entrance exams (ACT or SAT), recommendations, and extracurricular activities. A campus visit to meet with an academic counselor is highly recommended, as it helps complete the picture for both the prospective student and the College.

Transfer students must have earned at least a 2.5 cumulative GPA in previous college work. In addition to all other admissions criteria, international students must have at least a 3.0 GPA in non-U.S. high school or college work and a Test of English as a Foreign Language (TOEFL) score of at least 550 (or equivalent).

Application and Information

To apply for admission, a student must submit an application for admission, an application fee, and official transcripts of previous high school and/or college class work. Freshman applicants must submit ACT or SAT scores. Applicants are notified of their admission status within two weeks of receipt of all required materials. Westminster operates on a rolling admissions basis, so it's best to send applications in as soon as possible. To preserve the faculty-student ratio, classes are limited. Westminster College reserves the right to close the class earlier than the dates specified if enrollment goals are met before those dates. New applicants are accepted for the start of all sessions. For application forms and additional information, students should contact:

Office of Admissions
Westminster College
1840 South 1300 East
Salt Lake City, Utah 84105
Phone: 801-832-2200
800-748-4753 (toll-free)
Web site: http://www.westminstercollege.edu

Westminster College offers high-quality education in one of the most unique learning environments in the country.

VERMONT

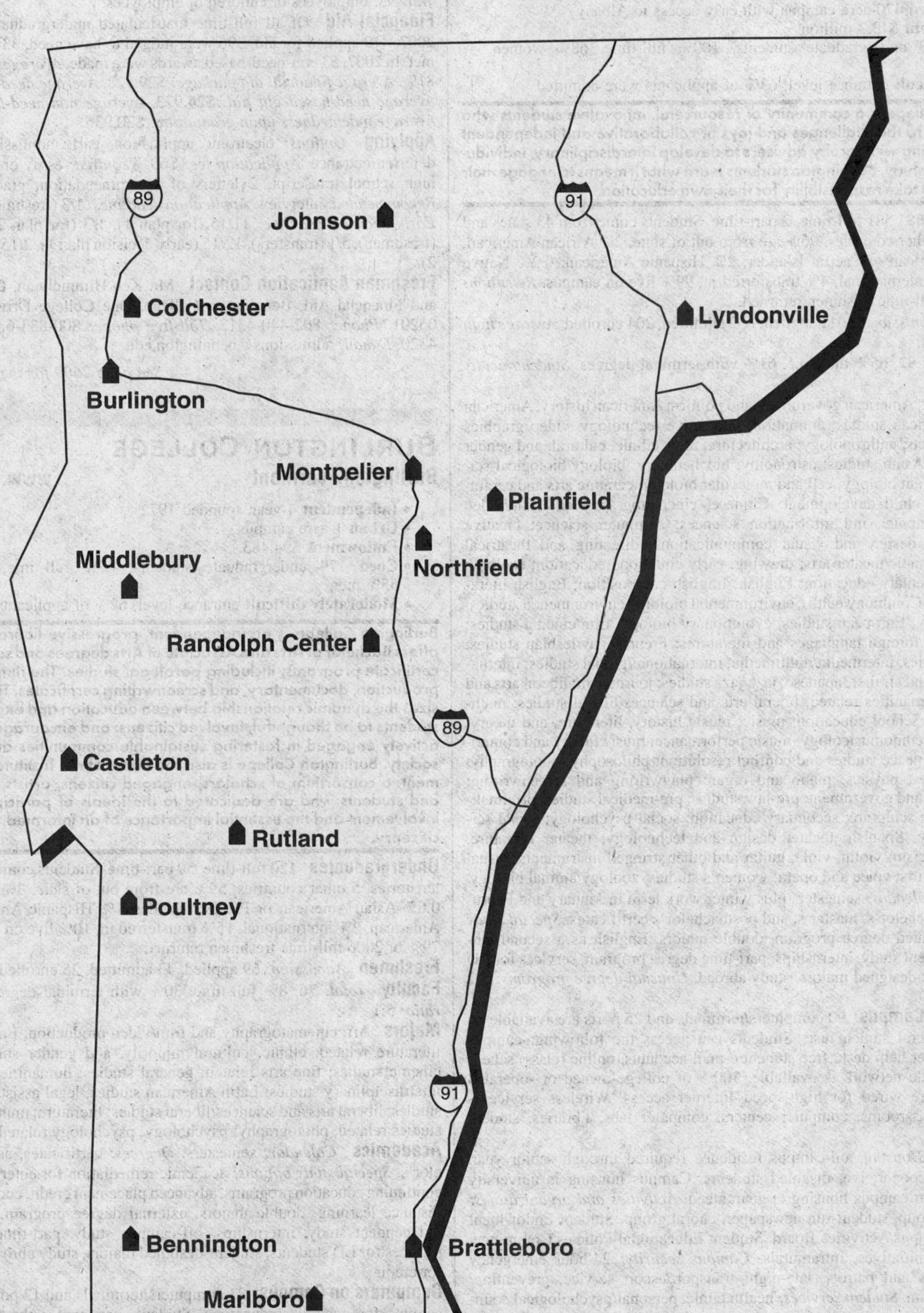

89
Johnson
91
Colchester
Lyndonville
Burlington
Montpelier
Plainfield
Middlebury
Northfield
Randolph Center
89
Castleton
Rutland
Poultney
91
Bennington
Brattleboro
Marlboro

BENNINGTON COLLEGE

Bennington, Vermont **www.bennington.edu/**

- **Independent** comprehensive, founded 1932
- **Small-town** 470-acre campus with easy access to Albany
- **Endowment** $13.2 million
- **Coed** 583 undergraduate students, 100% full-time, 68% women, 32% men
- **Very difficult** entrance level, 63% of applicants were admitted

Bennington College is a community of resourceful, innovative students who are committed to the challenges and joys of collaborative and independent work. By working with faculty advisers to develop interdisciplinary, individualized plans of study, Bennington students learn what it means to engage their curiosity and to take responsibility for their own education.

Undergraduates 581 full-time, 2 part-time. Students come from 43 states and territories, 13 other countries, 96% are from out of state, 2% African American, 2% Asian American or Pacific Islander, 2% Hispanic American, 0.2% Native American, 3% international, 4% transferred in, 99% live on campus. *Retention:* 81% of 2006 full-time freshmen returned.

Freshmen *Admission:* 1,011 applied, 632 admitted, 204 enrolled. *Average high school GPA:* 3.4.

Faculty *Total:* 92, 65% full-time, 61% with terminal degrees. *Student/faculty ratio:* 8:1.

Majors Acting; American government and politics; American history; American literature; American studies; animation, interactive technology, video graphics and special effects; anthropology; architecture; area, ethnic, cultural, and gender studies related; Asian studies; astronomy; biochemistry; biology/biological sciences; botany/plant biology; cell and molecular biology; ceramic arts and ceramics; chemistry; child development; Chinese; cinematography and film/video production; computer and information sciences; computer science; creative writing; dance; design and visual communications; directing and theatrical production; dramatic/theater arts; drawing; early childhood education; ecology; education; elementary education; English; English composition; English literature (British and Commonwealth); environmental biology; environmental studies; European history; European studies; evolutionary biology; film/cinema studies; fine/studio arts; foreign languages and literatures; French; gay/lesbian studies; history; humanities; intermedia/multimedia; international/global studies; international relations and affairs; Japanese; jazz/jazz studies; journalism; liberal arts and sciences and humanities related; liberal arts and sciences/liberal studies; mathematics; middle school education; music; music history, literature, and theory; musicology and ethnomusicology; music performance; music theory and composition; painting; peace studies and conflict resolution; philosophy; photography; physical sciences; physics; piano and organ; playwriting and screenwriting; political science and government; pre-law studies; pre-medical studies; printmaking; psychology; sculpture; secondary education; social psychology; social sciences; sociology; Spanish; theater design and technology; theater literature, history and criticism; violin, viola, guitar and other stringed instruments; visual and performing arts; voice and opera; women's studies; zoology/animal biology.

Academics *Calendar:* semesters plus winter work term in January and February. *Degrees:* bachelor's, master's, and postbachelor's certificates. *Special study options:* accelerated degree program, double majors, English as a second language, independent study, internships, part-time degree program, services for LD students, student-designed majors, study abroad. *Unusual degree programs:* 3-2 education.

Computers on Campus 90 computers/terminals and 25 ports are available on campus for general student use. Students can access the following: campus intranet, computer help desk, free student e-mail accounts, online (class) schedules. Campuswide network is available. 100% of college-owned or -operated housing units are wired for high-speed Internet access. Wireless service is available via classrooms, computer centers, computer labs, libraries, student centers.

Student Life *Housing:* on-campus residence required through senior year. *Options:* coed, cooperative, disabled students. Campus housing is university owned. Freshman campus housing is guaranteed. *Activities and organizations:* drama/theater group, student-run newspaper, choral group, Student Endowment for the Arts, Campus Activities Board, Student Educational Policies Committee, Environmental Initiatives, Intramurals. *Campus security:* 24-hour emergency response devices and patrols, late-night transport/escort service, prevention/awareness program. *Student services:* health clinic, personal/psychological counseling.

Athletics *Intercollegiate sports:* soccer M (c)/W (c). *Intramural sports:* badminton M/W, basketball M/W, bowling M/W, skiing (cross-country) M/W, skiing (downhill) M/W, soccer M/W, softball M (c)/W (c), table tennis M/W, tennis M/W, volleyball M/W.

Standardized Tests *Required for some:* TOEFL (minimum score—577 paper-based; 233 computer-based; 90-91 internet-based).

Costs (2007–08) *Comprehensive fee:* $46,180 includes full-time tuition ($35,850), mandatory fees ($950), and room and board ($9380). Part-time tuition: $1120 per credit hour. *College room only:* $5030. *Payment plan:* installment. *Waivers:* employees or children of employees.

Financial Aid Of all full-time matriculated undergraduates who enrolled in 2007, 419 applied for aid, 396 were judged to have need, 33 had their need fully met. In 2007, 53 non-need-based awards were made. *Average percent of need met:* 81%. *Average financial aid package:* $29,528. *Average need-based loan:* $4030. *Average need-based gift aid:* $24,973. *Average non-need-based aid:* $17,786. *Average indebtedness upon graduation:* $20,936.

Applying *Options:* electronic application, early admission, early decision, deferred entrance. *Application fee:* $60. *Required:* essay or personal statement, high school transcript, 2 letters of recommendation, graded analytic paper. *Recommended:* interview. *Application deadlines:* 1/3 (freshmen), 3/15 (transfers). *Early decision deadline:* 11/15 (for plan 1), 1/3 (for plan 2). *Notification:* 4/1 (freshmen), 5/1 (transfers), 12/15 (early decision plan 1), 2/15 (early decision plan 2).

Freshman Application Contact Mr. Ken Himmelman, Dean of Admissions and Financial Aid, Bennington College, One College Drive, Bennington, VT 05201. *Phone:* 802-440-4312. *Toll-free phone:* 800-833-6845. *Fax:* 802-440-4320. *E-mail:* admissions@bennington.edu.

See page 2600 for the College Close-Up.

BURLINGTON COLLEGE

Burlington, Vermont **www.burlington.edu/**

- **Independent** 4-year, founded 1972
- **Urban** 1-acre campus
- **Endowment** $94,483
- **Coed** 179 undergraduate students, 67% full-time, 45% women, 55% men
- **Moderately difficult** entrance level, 62% of applicants were admitted

Burlington College is an independent, progressive liberal arts college that offers Bachelor of Arts and Associate of Arts degrees and several professional certificate programs, including paralegal studies. The film school offers film production, documentary, and screenwriting certificates. The College emphasizes the dynamic relationship between education and experience; prepares students to be thoughtful, involved citizens; and encourages them to become actively engaged in fostering sustainable communities and a just, humane society. Burlington College is also the home of the Institute for Civic Engagement, a consortium of scholars, engaged citizens, artists, scientists, writers, and students who are dedicated to the ideals of participatory community involvement and the essential importance of an informed, critical, and active citizenry.

Undergraduates 120 full-time, 59 part-time. Students come from 22 states and territories, 5 other countries, 59% are from out of state, 3% African American, 0.6% Asian American or Pacific Islander, 1% Hispanic American, 2% Native American, 2% international, 15% transferred in, 10% live on campus. *Retention:* 79% of 2006 full-time freshmen returned.

Freshmen *Admission:* 69 applied, 43 admitted, 25 enrolled.

Faculty *Total:* 76, 8% full-time, 30% with terminal degrees. *Student/faculty ratio:* 5:1.

Majors Art; cinematography and film/video production; English language and literature related; ethnic, cultural minority, and gender studies related; film/cinema studies; fine arts related; general studies; humanities; human services; interdisciplinary studies; Latin American studies; legal assistant/paralegal; legal studies; liberal arts and sciences/liberal studies; literature; multi-/interdisciplinary studies related; photography; psychology; psychology related; women's studies.

Academics *Calendar:* semesters. *Degrees:* certificates, associate, and bachelor's. *Special study options:* academic remediation for entering students, adult/continuing education programs, advanced placement credit, cooperative education, distance learning, double majors, external degree program, honors programs, independent study, internships, off-campus study, part-time degree program, services for LD students, student-designed majors, study abroad, summer session for credit.

Computers on Campus 21 computers/terminals and 12 ports are available on campus for general student use. Students can access the following: campus intranet, computer help desk, free student e-mail accounts. Campuswide network is available. 100% of college-owned or -operated housing units are wired for high-speed Internet access. Wireless service is available via entire campus.

Student Life *Housing options:* cooperative. Campus housing is university owned and leased by the school. Freshman applicants given priority for college housing. *Activities and organizations:* drama/theater group, student-run newspaper, Student Association, Community Garden, The Recon Soiree, The Institute for Civic Engagement. *Campus security:* 24-hour emergency response devices. *Student services:* personal/psychological counseling, legal services.

Athletics *Intercollegiate sports:* ultimate Frisbee M/W, volleyball M/W. *Intramural sports:* ultimate Frisbee M/W, volleyball M/W.

Costs (2008–09) *One-time required fee:* $150. *Tuition:* $19,640 full-time, $650 per credit hour part-time. *Room only:* $6095.

Financial Aid Of all full-time matriculated undergraduates who enrolled in 2006, 77 applied for aid, 72 were judged to have need, 4 had their need fully met. 50 Federal Work-Study jobs (averaging $1247). In 2006, 5 non-need-based awards were made. *Average percent of need met:* 48%. *Average financial aid package:* $10,029. *Average need-based loan:* $5590. *Average need-based gift aid:* $5640. *Average non-need-based aid:* $3570. *Average indebtedness upon graduation:* $40,153.

Applying *Options:* electronic application, early action, deferred entrance. *Application fee:* $50. *Required:* essay or personal statement, high school transcript, 2 letters of recommendation, interview. *Notification:* continuous (freshmen), continuous (transfers).

Freshman Application Contact Admissions, Burlington College, 95 North Avenue, Burlington, VT 05401-2998. *Phone:* 802-862-9616 Ext. 104. *Toll-free phone:* 800-862-9616. *Fax:* 802-660-4331. *E-mail:* admissions@burlington.edu.

CASTLETON STATE COLLEGE

Castleton, Vermont **www.castleton.edu/**

- **State-supported** comprehensive, founded 1787, part of Vermont State Colleges System
- **Rural** 160-acre campus
- **Endowment** $5.2 million
- **Coed** 1,935 undergraduate students, 87% full-time, 55% women, 45% men
- **Moderately difficult** entrance level, 71% of applicants were admitted

Located in southern Vermont, close to the best snowboarding and skiing in New England, Castleton is small enough to be a community where every student matters yet large enough to offer thirty academic programs, nineteen intercollegiate sports, and more than forty clubs and student organizations. Castleton stresses community service and internships and provides exceptional programs for first-year students.

Undergraduates 1,690 full-time, 245 part-time. Students come from 29 states and territories, 1 other country, 34% are from out of state, 0.7% African American, 0.9% Asian American or Pacific Islander, 2% Hispanic American, 0.7% Native American, 0.3% international, 9% transferred in, 50% live on campus. *Retention:* 66% of 2006 full-time freshmen returned.

Freshmen *Admission:* 1,828 applied, 1,303 admitted, 408 enrolled. *Average high school GPA:* 2.9. *Test scores:* SAT critical reading scores over 500: 43%; SAT math scores over 500: 44%; SAT writing scores over 500: 36%; ACT scores over 18: 77%; SAT critical reading scores over 600: 9%; SAT math scores over 600: 8%; SAT writing scores over 600: 5%; ACT scores over 24: 15%; SAT critical reading scores over 700: 1%; SAT math scores over 700: 1%.

Faculty *Total:* 208, 42% full-time, 54% with terminal degrees. *Student/faculty ratio:* 14:1.

Majors Accounting; American literature; art; athletic training; biological and physical sciences; biology/biological sciences; business administration and management; business/commerce; chemistry; computer and information sciences; computer programming; criminal justice/law enforcement administration; criminology; developmental and child psychology; dramatic/theater arts; environmental studies; finance; general studies; geology/earth science; health and physical education; health science; history; journalism; kinesiology and exercise science; literature; marketing/marketing management; mathematics; mathematics teacher education; music; music teacher education; natural sciences; nursing (registered nurse training); physical education teaching and coaching; psychology; public relations/image management; radio and television; science teacher education; social sciences; social studies teacher education; social work; sociology; Spanish.

Academics *Calendar:* semesters. *Degrees:* associate, bachelor's, master's, and post-master's certificates. *Special study options:* academic remediation for entering students, advanced placement credit, cooperative education, double majors, honors programs, independent study, internships, off-campus study, part-time degree program, services for LD students, student-designed majors, study abroad, summer session for credit. *ROTC:* Army (c).

Computers on Campus 225 computers/terminals are available on campus for general student use. Students can access the following: campus intranet, computer help desk, free student e-mail accounts, online (class) grades. Campuswide network is available. Wireless service is available via classrooms, dorm rooms, libraries.

Student Life *Housing:* on-campus residence required for freshman year. *Options:* coed. Campus housing is university owned. Freshman campus housing is guaranteed. *Activities and organizations:* drama/theater group, student-run newspaper, radio station, choral group, Community service, Student radio station, Women's issues organization, Rugby, Outing Club. *Campus security:* 24-hour emergency response devices and patrols, student patrols, late-night transport/escort service, controlled dormitory access. *Student services:* health clinic, personal/psychological counseling.

Athletics Member NCAA. All Division III. *Intercollegiate sports:* baseball M, basketball M/W, cheerleading M (c)/W (c), cross-country running M/W, equestrian sports M (c)/W (c), field hockey W, golf M, ice hockey M/W, lacrosse M/W, rugby M (c)/W (c), skiing (downhill) M/W, soccer M/W, softball W, tennis M/W, volleyball W. *Intramural sports:* basketball M/W, football M/W, racquetball M/W, rock climbing M/W, soccer M/W, softball M/W, table tennis M/W, tennis M/W, volleyball M/W, water polo M/W.

Standardized Tests *Required:* SAT or ACT (for admission).

Costs (2008–09) *One-time required fee:* $195. *Tuition:* state resident $7488 full-time, $312 per credit part-time; nonresident $16,152 full-time, $673 per credit part-time. *Required fees:* $796 full-time. *Room and board:* $7509.

Financial Aid Of all full-time matriculated undergraduates who enrolled in 2006, 1,471 applied for aid, 1,174 were judged to have need, 371 had their need fully met. 360 Federal Work-Study jobs (averaging $1000). In 2006, 40 non-need-based awards were made. *Average percent of need met:* 72%. *Average financial aid package:* $9213. *Average need-based loan:* $3715. *Average need-based gift aid:* $4307. *Average non-need-based aid:* $3247. *Average indebtedness upon graduation:* $25,474.

Applying *Options:* electronic application, deferred entrance. *Application fee:* $35. *Required:* essay or personal statement, high school transcript, minimum 2.5 GPA, letters of recommendation. *Recommended:* interview. *Application deadlines:* rolling (freshmen), rolling (transfers). *Notification:* continuous (freshmen), continuous (transfers).

Freshman Application Contact Mr. Maurice Ouimet, Admissions Director, Castleton State College, Seminary Street, Castleton, VT 05735. *Phone:* 802-468-1213. *Toll-free phone:* 800-639-8521. *Fax:* 802-468-1476. *E-mail:* info@castleton.edu.

See page 2602 for the College Close-Up.

CHAMPLAIN COLLEGE

Burlington, Vermont **www.champlain.edu/**

- **Independent** comprehensive, founded 1878
- **Suburban** 21-acre campus with easy access to Montreal, Canada
- **Endowment** $7.0 million
- **Coed**
- **Moderately difficult** entrance level

Champlain College is known for professionally focused programs balanced by an interdisciplinary core curriculum, delivered in small, engaging classes. Built-in internships, study-abroad campuses, and classes in their major during the freshman year contribute to students' success. Burlington, a quintessential college town, is energized with music, arts, and world-class outdoor recreation.

Faculty *Student/faculty ratio:* 16:1.

Academics *Calendar:* semesters. *Degrees:* certificates, associate, bachelor's, and master's.

Student Life *Campus security:* 24-hour emergency response devices and patrols, late-night transport/escort service, controlled dormitory access.

Standardized Tests *Required:* SAT or ACT (for admission). *Required for some:* SAT Subject Tests (for admission).

Costs (2007–08) *Comprehensive fee:* $33,460 includes full-time tuition ($22,550) and room and board ($10,910). Full-time tuition and fees vary according to course load. Part-time tuition: $940 per credit. Part-time tuition and fees vary according to course level, course load, and degree level. *College room only:* $6510. Room and board charges vary according to board plan and housing facility.

Financial Aid Of all full-time matriculated undergraduates who enrolled in 2007, 1,438 applied for aid, 1,251 were judged to have need, 49 had their need fully met. 230 Federal Work-Study jobs (averaging $2495). In 2007, 615 non-need-based awards were made. *Average percent of need met:* 60. *Average financial aid package:* $13,850. *Average need-based loan:* $4597. *Average need-based gift aid:* $3840. *Average non-need-based aid:* $4602.

Applying *Options:* electronic application. *Application fee:* $40. *Required:* essay or personal statement, high school transcript. *Recommended:* minimum 2.0 GPA, 1 letter of recommendation, interview.

Freshman Application Contact Dr. Laryn Runco, Director of Admissions, Champlain College, 163 South Willard Street, Burlington, VT 05401. *Phone:* 802-860-2727. *Toll-free phone:* 800-570-5858. *Fax:* 802-860-2767. *E-mail:* admission@champlain.edu.

COLLEGE OF ST. JOSEPH

Rutland, Vermont **www.csj.edu/**

- **Independent Roman Catholic** comprehensive, founded 1950
- **Small-town** 90-acre campus
- **Endowment** $3.1 million
- **Coed** 261 undergraduate students, 62% full-time, 56% women, 44% men
- **Minimally difficult** entrance level, 88% of applicants were admitted

Undergraduates 161 full-time, 100 part-time. Students come from 13 states and territories, 1 other country, 34% are from out of state, 3% African American, 0.8% Asian American or Pacific Islander, 4% Hispanic American, 0.8% Native American, 6% transferred in, 31% live on campus. *Retention:* 83% of 2006 full-time freshmen returned.

Freshmen *Admission:* 101 applied, 89 admitted, 33 enrolled. *Average high school GPA:* 2.8. *Test scores:* SAT critical reading scores over 500: 33%; SAT math scores over 500: 22%; ACT scores over 18: 50%; SAT critical reading scores over 600: 7%; SAT math scores over 600: 4%.

Faculty *Total:* 64, 22% full-time, 25% with terminal degrees. *Student/faculty ratio:* 11:1.

Majors Accounting; business administration and management; criminal justice/law enforcement administration; elementary education; English; history; human services; liberal arts and sciences/liberal studies; professional studies; psychology; radiologic technology/science; secondary education; substance abuse/addiction counseling.

Academics *Calendar:* semesters. *Degrees:* associate, bachelor's, master's, and postbachelor's certificates. *Special study options:* academic remediation for entering students, accelerated degree program, adult/continuing education programs, advanced placement credit, double majors, English as a second language, internships, part-time degree program, services for LD students, study abroad, summer session for credit.

Computers on Campus 30 computers/terminals are available on campus for general student use. Students can access the following: campus intranet, free student e-mail accounts, online (class) schedules. Campuswide network is available. 100% of college-owned or -operated housing units are wired for high-speed Internet access. Wireless service is available via libraries, student centers.

Student Life *Housing:* on-campus residence required through sophomore year. *Options:* men-only, women-only. Campus housing is university owned. Freshman campus housing is guaranteed. *Activities and organizations:* choral group, Business Club, Human Services Club, Psi Chi, Orientation Leaders, chorus. *Campus security:* 24-hour emergency response devices. *Student services:* personal/psychological counseling.

Athletics Member NAIA. *Intercollegiate sports:* baseball M, basketball M/W, soccer M/W, softball W. *Intramural sports:* baseball M, basketball M/W, bowling M/W, racquetball M/W, soccer M/W, softball M/W.

Standardized Tests *Required:* SAT or ACT (for admission).

Costs (2008–09) *Comprehensive fee:* $24,890 includes full-time tuition ($16,450), mandatory fees ($290), and room and board ($8150). Part-time tuition: $250 per credit. *Required fees:* $45 per credit part-time.

Financial Aid Of all full-time matriculated undergraduates who enrolled in 2006, 176 applied for aid, 158 were judged to have need, 19 had their need fully met. 38 Federal Work-Study jobs (averaging $980). 77 state and other part-time jobs (averaging $945). In 2006, 15 non-need-based awards were made. *Average percent of need met:* 66%. *Average financial aid package:* $12,702. *Average need-based loan:* $4548. *Average need-based gift aid:* $7722. *Average non-need-based aid:* $4238. *Average indebtedness upon graduation:* $28,522.

Applying *Options:* electronic application, early admission, deferred entrance. *Application fee:* $25. *Required:* essay or personal statement, high school transcript, minimum 2.0 GPA, 2 letters of recommendation. *Recommended:* interview. *Application deadlines:* rolling (freshmen), rolling (transfers). *Notification:* continuous (freshmen), continuous (transfers).

Freshman Application Contact Mrs. Tracy Gallipo, College of St. Joseph, 71 Clement Road, Rutland, VT 05701-3899. *Phone:* 802-773-5900 Ext. 3236. *Toll-free phone:* 877-270-9998. *Fax:* 802-776-5258. *E-mail:* admissions@csj.edu.

GODDARD COLLEGE

Plainfield, Vermont **www.goddard.edu/**

- **Independent** comprehensive, founded 1938
- **Rural** 250-acre campus
- **Endowment** $932,377
- **Coed** 255 undergraduate students, 98% full-time, 71% women, 29% men
- **Moderately difficult** entrance level, 100% of applicants were admitted

Undergraduates 250 full-time, 5 part-time. Students come from 33 states and territories, 82% are from out of state, 4% African American, 2% Asian American or Pacific Islander, 4% Hispanic American, 2% Native American, 19% transferred in.

Freshmen *Admission:* 8 applied, 8 admitted, 8 enrolled.

Faculty *Total:* 83, 6% full-time. *Student/faculty ratio:* 11:1.

Majors Botany/plant biology; foods, nutrition, and wellness; interdisciplinary studies; liberal arts and sciences and humanities related; nutrition sciences.

Academics *Calendar:* semesters. *Degrees:* bachelor's and master's. *Special study options:* adult/continuing education programs, advanced placement credit, distance learning, double majors, external degree program, independent study, internships, off-campus study, services for LD students, student-designed majors.

Computers on Campus 55 computers/terminals are available on campus for general student use. Students can access the following: campus intranet, computer help desk, free student e-mail accounts, online (class) schedules, library services. Campuswide network is available. 80% of college-owned or -operated housing units are wired for high-speed Internet access. Wireless service is available via entire campus.

Student Life *Housing options:* coed, women-only, disabled students. Campus housing is university owned. *Campus security:* 24-hour patrols, patrols by trained security personnel 9 p.m. to 6 a.m. *Student services:* personal/psychological counseling.

Costs (2008–09) *One-time required fee:* $125. *Comprehensive fee:* $12,752 includes full-time tuition ($11,504), mandatory fees ($160), and room and board ($1088).

Financial Aid Of all full-time matriculated undergraduates who enrolled in 2007, 259 applied for aid, 227 were judged to have need, 8 had their need fully met. In 2007, 10 non-need-based awards were made. *Average percent of need met:* 38%. *Average financial aid package:* $6492. *Average need-based loan:* $4249. *Average need-based gift aid:* $3921. *Average non-need-based aid:* $8241. *Average indebtedness upon graduation:* $23,054.

Applying *Options:* electronic application, deferred entrance. *Application fee:* $40. *Required:* essay or personal statement, high school transcript, 2 letters of recommendation, interview. *Application deadlines:* rolling (freshmen), rolling (transfers). *Notification:* continuous (freshmen), continuous (transfers).

Freshman Application Contact Rachel Keach, Admissions Counselor, Goddard College, 123 Pitkin Road, King, Plainfield, VT 05667-9432. *Phone:* 802-454-8311 Ext. 262. *Toll-free phone:* 800-906-8312 Ext. 243. *Fax:* 802-454-1029. *E-mail:* admissions@goddard.edu.

GREEN MOUNTAIN COLLEGE

Poultney, Vermont **www.greenmtn.edu/**

- **Independent** comprehensive, founded 1834
- **Small-town** 155-acre campus
- **Endowment** $3.6 million
- **Coed** 770 undergraduate students, 98% full-time, 49% women, 51% men
- **Moderately difficult** entrance level, 79% of applicants were admitted

Undergraduates 752 full-time, 18 part-time. Students come from 34 states and territories, 10 other countries, 85% are from out of state, 3% African American, 0.9% Asian American or Pacific Islander, 2% Hispanic American, 1% Native American, 0.3% international, 6% transferred in, 80% live on campus. *Retention:* 62% of 2006 full-time freshmen returned.

Freshmen *Admission:* 1,290 applied, 1,018 admitted, 255 enrolled. *Average high school GPA:* 3.0. *Test scores:* ACT scores over 18: 78%; ACT scores over 24: 38%.

Faculty *Total:* 73, 62% full-time, 59% with terminal degrees. *Student/faculty ratio:* 14:1.

Majors Anthropology; art; biology/biological sciences; business/managerial economics; communication and media related; creative writing; elementary education; English; environmental studies; fine/studio arts; history; liberal arts and sciences/liberal studies; natural resources management; parks, recreation and leisure; philosophy; psychology; resort management; secondary education; sociology; special education.

Academics *Calendar:* semesters. *Degrees:* bachelor's and master's. *Special study options:* accelerated degree program, adult/continuing education programs, advanced placement credit, cooperative education, double majors, English as a second language, honors programs, independent study, internships, off-campus study, part-time degree program, services for LD students, student-designed majors, study abroad, summer session for credit.

Computers on Campus 86 computers/terminals are available on campus for general student use. Students can access the following: campus intranet, computer help desk, free student e-mail accounts, online (class) grades, online (class) registration, online (class) schedules, personal network folders, electronic course folders. Campuswide network is available. 100% of college-owned or -operated housing units are wired for high-speed Internet access.

Student Life *Housing:* on-campus residence required through senior year. *Options:* coed. Campus housing is university owned. Freshman campus housing is guaranteed. *Activities and organizations:* drama/theater group, student-run newspaper, choral group, Student Government Association, Green Mountain College Ultimate Frisbee, Divercity, College Programming Board, International Awareness Club. *Campus security:* 24-hour emergency response devices and patrols, student patrols, late-night transport/escort service, controlled dormitory access. *Student services:* health clinic, personal/psychological counseling.

Athletics Member NAIA. *Intercollegiate sports:* basketball M/W, cross-country running M/W, golf M, lacrosse M/W, skiing (downhill) M/W, soccer M/W, softball W, tennis M, volleyball W. *Intramural sports:* tennis W (c), track and field M (c)/W (c), ultimate Frisbee M (c)/W (c), volleyball M (c)/W (c).

Standardized Tests *Recommended:* SAT or ACT (for admission).

Costs (2007–08) *One-time required fee:* $150. *Comprehensive fee:* $33,629 includes full-time tuition ($23,772), mandatory fees ($793), and room and board ($9064). Full-time tuition and fees vary according to course load. Part-time tuition: $792 per credit hour. Part-time tuition and fees vary according to course load. *Required fees:* $793 per year part-time. *College room only:* $5380. Room and board charges vary according to housing facility. *Payment plan:* installment. *Waivers:* employees or children of employees.

Financial Aid Of all full-time matriculated undergraduates who enrolled in 2006, 671 applied for aid, 613 were judged to have need, 139 had their need fully met. 166 Federal Work-Study jobs (averaging $1500). 153 state and other part-time jobs (averaging $1500). In 2006, 68 non-need-based awards were made. *Average percent of need met:* 73%. *Average financial aid package:* $19,825. *Average need-based loan:* $6056. *Average need-based gift aid:* $14,291. *Average non-need-based aid:* $15,683. *Average indebtedness upon graduation:* $34,260.

Applying *Options:* electronic application, deferred entrance. *Application fee:* $30. *Required:* essay or personal statement, high school transcript, 1 letter of recommendation. *Required for some:* interview. *Recommended:* minimum 2.5 GPA, interview. *Application deadlines:* rolling (freshmen), rolling (transfers). *Notification:* continuous until 8/1 (freshmen), continuous until 8/1 (transfers).

Freshman Application Contact Ms. Anne Lundquist, Dean of Student Life, Green Mountain College, One College Circle, Poultney, VT 05764. *Phone:* 802-287-8377. *Toll-free phone:* 800-776-6675. *Fax:* 802-287-8098. *E-mail:* lundquista@greenmtn.edu.

JOHNSON STATE COLLEGE

Johnson, Vermont **www.johnsonstatecollege.edu/**

- **State-supported** comprehensive, founded 1828, part of Vermont State Colleges System
- **Rural** 350-acre campus with easy access to Montreal
- **Endowment** $1.6 million
- **Coed** 1,601 undergraduate students, 66% full-time, 60% women, 40% men
- **Moderately difficult** entrance level, 80% of applicants were admitted

Undergraduates 1,055 full-time, 546 part-time. Students come from 12 states and territories, 2 other countries, 36% are from out of state, 2% African American, 0.6% Asian American or Pacific Islander, 2% Hispanic American, 0.8% Native American, 0.2% international, 5% transferred in, 57% live on campus. *Retention:* 65% of 2006 full-time freshmen returned.

Freshmen *Admission:* 1,245 applied, 997 admitted, 281 enrolled. *Average high school GPA:* 3.4. *Test scores:* SAT critical reading scores over 500: 45%; SAT math scores over 500: 36%; SAT critical reading scores over 600: 11%; SAT math scores over 600: 6%; SAT critical reading scores over 700: 1%.

Faculty *Total:* 143, 39% full-time, 38% with terminal degrees. *Student/faculty ratio:* 17:1.

Majors Accounting; acting; alternative and complementary medicine related; anthropology; art; art teacher education; athletic training; biology/biological sciences; biology teacher education; business administration and management; business/commerce; creative writing; dance; drama and dance teacher education; dramatic/theater arts; education; elementary education; English; English/language arts teacher education; environmental education; environmental studies; fine/studio arts; general studies; health and physical education; health science; history; history teacher education; hospitality administration; humanities; information science/studies; jazz/jazz studies; journalism; kinesiology and exercise science; liberal arts and sciences/liberal studies; literature; management information systems; marketing/marketing management; mathematics; mathematics teacher education; middle school education; music; music management and merchandising; music performance; music teacher education; natural resources management and policy; parks, recreation and leisure; physical education teaching and coaching; political science and government; pre-medical studies; psychology; secondary education; social science teacher education; social studies teacher education; sociology; sport and fitness administration/management; theater design and technology; tourism and travel services management; visual and performing arts.

Academics *Calendar:* semesters. *Degrees:* certificates, associate, bachelor's, and master's. *Special study options:* accelerated degree program, advanced placement credit, cooperative education, distance learning, double majors, English as a second language, external degree program, honors programs, independent study, internships, off-campus study, part-time degree program, services for LD students, summer session for credit. *ROTC:* Army (c).

Computers on Campus 131 computers/terminals are available on campus for general student use. Students can access the following: campus intranet, computer help desk, free student e-mail accounts, online (class) grades, online (class) registration, online (class) schedules. Campuswide network is available. Wireless service is available via libraries, student centers.

Student Life *Housing:* on-campus residence required through sophomore year. *Options:* coed. Campus housing is university owned. *Activities and organizations:* drama/theater group, student-run newspaper, radio station, choral group, SERVE (Break Away, Habitat for Humanity), Outing Club, snowboarding, Earth Action Club, Gay-Straight Alliance. *Campus security:* 24-hour emergency response devices and patrols, student patrols, late-night transport/escort service, controlled dormitory access. *Student services:* health clinic, personal/psychological counseling, women's center.

Athletics Member NCAA. All Division III. *Intercollegiate sports:* basketball M/W, cross-country running M/W, golf M, lacrosse W, soccer M/W, softball W, tennis M/W, volleyball W. *Intramural sports:* badminton M/W, basketball M/W, cross-country running M/W, golf M (c)/W (c), ice hockey M (c)/W (c), lacrosse M (c)/W, racquetball M/W, rock climbing M (c)/W (c), soccer M/W, softball M/W, swimming and diving M (c)/W (c), table tennis M/W, tennis M/W, volleyball M/W, water polo M/W, weight lifting M/W.

Standardized Tests *Required:* SAT (for admission).

Costs (2008–09) *Tuition:* state resident $7500 full-time; nonresident $16,000 full-time. *Required fees:* $500 full-time. *Room and board:* $7581; room only: $4500.

Financial Aid *Average percent of need met:* 80%. *Average financial aid package:* $7835. *Average indebtedness upon graduation:* $16,910.

Applying *Options:* electronic application, deferred entrance. *Application fee:* $35. *Required:* essay or personal statement, high school transcript, minimum 2.0 GPA, 1 letter of recommendation. *Recommended:* minimum 2.5 GPA, interview. *Application deadlines:* rolling (freshmen), rolling (transfers). *Notification:* continuous (freshmen), continuous (transfers).

Freshman Application Contact Patrick Rogers, Assistant Director of Admissions, Johnson State College, 337 College Hill, Johnson, VT 05656-9405. *Phone:* 802-635-1219. *Toll-free phone:* 800-635-2356. *Fax:* 802-635-1230. *E-mail:* jscadmissions@jsc.edu.

See page 2604 for the College Close-Up.

LYNDON STATE COLLEGE

Lyndonville, Vermont **www.lyndonstate.edu/**

- **State-supported** comprehensive, founded 1911, part of Vermont State Colleges System
- **Rural** 175-acre campus
- **Endowment** $2.3 million
- **Coed** 1,371 undergraduate students, 88% full-time, 47% women, 53% men
- **Moderately difficult** entrance level, 89% of applicants were admitted

Undergraduates 1,206 full-time, 165 part-time. Students come from 11 states and territories, 49% are from out of state, 2% African American, 1% Asian American or Pacific Islander, 1% Hispanic American, 1% Native American, 0.2% international, 7% transferred in, 50% live on campus. *Retention:* 53% of 2006 full-time freshmen returned.

Freshmen *Admission:* 1,171 applied, 1,039 admitted, 388 enrolled. *Average high school GPA:* 2.5. *Test scores:* SAT critical reading scores over 500: 34%; SAT math scores over 500: 29%; SAT critical reading scores over 600: 7%; SAT math scores over 600: 3%; SAT critical reading scores over 700: 1%.

Faculty *Total:* 167, 35% full-time, 60% with terminal degrees. *Student/faculty ratio:* 17:1.

Majors Accounting; athletic training; atmospheric sciences and meteorology; biological and physical sciences; commercial and advertising art; communication/speech communication and rhetoric; computer science; elementary education; English; English/language arts teacher education; health and physical education; journalism; mathematics; mathematics teacher education; parks, recreation and leisure; parks, recreation and leisure facilities management; physical education teaching and coaching; physical sciences; psychology; radio and television; radio and television broadcasting technology; reading teacher education; science teacher education; social sciences; social science teacher education; special education; sport and fitness administration/management.

Academics *Calendar:* semesters. *Degrees:* associate, bachelor's, and master's. *Special study options:* academic remediation for entering students, accelerated degree program, adult/continuing education programs, advanced placement credit, cooperative education, double majors, honors programs, independent study, internships, part-time degree program, services for LD students, student-designed majors, study abroad, summer session for credit. *ROTC:* Air Force (c).

Computers on Campus 125 computers/terminals are available on campus for general student use. Students can access the following: computer help desk, free student e-mail accounts, online (class) grades. Campuswide network is available.

Student Life *Housing:* on-campus residence required through sophomore year. *Options:* coed, women-only, disabled students. Campus housing is university owned and leased by the school. Freshman applicants given priority for college housing. *Activities and organizations:* drama/theater group, student-run newspaper, radio and television station, choral group, American Meteorological Society, ASSIST (A Society of Students in Service Together), Student Senate, Campus Activities Board, Outing Club. *Campus security:* 24-hour emergency response devices, student patrols, late-night transport/escort service, controlled dormitory access. *Student services:* health clinic, personal/psychological counseling.

Athletics Member NCAA. All Division III. *Intercollegiate sports:* baseball M, basketball M/W, cross-country running M/W, lacrosse M, soccer M/W, softball W, tennis M/W, volleyball W. *Intramural sports:* badminton M/W, basketball M/W, bowling M/W, cross-country running M/W, field hockey M/W, football M/W, golf M/W, ice hockey M/W, racquetball M/W, rock climbing M/W, skiing (cross-country) M/W, skiing (downhill) M/W, softball M/W, squash M/W, swimming and diving M/W, table tennis M/W, tennis M/W, track and field M/W, volleyball M/W, water polo M/W, weight lifting M/W.

Standardized Tests *Required:* SAT or ACT (for admission).

Costs (2007–08) *Tuition:* state resident $7056 full-time, $294 per credit hour part-time; nonresident $15,240 full-time, $635 per credit hour part-time. Full-time tuition and fees vary according to course load. Part-time tuition and fees vary according to course load. *Required fees:* $188 full-time, $8 per credit hour part-time. *Room and board:* $7220; room only: $4300. Room and board charges vary according to board plan and housing facility. *Payment plan:* installment. *Waivers:* employees or children of employees.

Applying *Options:* electronic application, early admission, deferred entrance. *Application fee:* $36. *Required:* high school transcript, minimum 2.0 GPA, 1 letter of recommendation. *Required for some:* essay or personal statement, minimum 3.0 GPA. *Recommended:* minimum 3.0 GPA, interview. *Application deadlines:* rolling (freshmen), rolling (transfers). *Notification:* continuous (freshmen), continuous (transfers).

Freshman Application Contact Ms. Donna "Dee" Gile, Admissions Assistant, Lyndon State College, 1001 College Road, PO Box 919, Lyndonville, VT 05851. *Phone:* 802-626-6413. *Toll-free phone:* 800-225-1998. *Fax:* 802-626-6335. *E-mail:* admissions@lyndonstate.edu.

See page 2606 for the College Close-Up.

MARLBORO COLLEGE

Marlboro, Vermont **www.marlboro.edu/**

- **Independent** comprehensive, founded 1946
- **Rural** 350-acre campus
- **Endowment** $31.5 million
- **Coed** 323 undergraduate students, 98% full-time, 51% women, 49% men
- **Moderately difficult** entrance level, 44% of applicants were admitted

Undergraduates 316 full-time, 7 part-time. Students come from 36 states and territories, 5 other countries, 80% are from out of state, 1% African American, 4% Asian American or Pacific Islander, 3% Hispanic American, 0.3% Native American, 1% international, 6% transferred in, 82% live on campus.

Freshmen *Admission:* 420 applied, 185 admitted, 65 enrolled. *Average high school GPA:* 3.3. *Test scores:* SAT critical reading scores over 500: 94%; SAT math scores over 500: 70%; ACT scores over 18: 100%; SAT critical reading scores over 600: 74%; SAT math scores over 600: 34%; ACT scores over 24: 62%; SAT critical reading scores over 700: 32%; SAT math scores over 700: 8%; ACT scores over 30: 24%.

Faculty *Total:* 53, 75% full-time, 74% with terminal degrees. *Student/faculty ratio:* 8:1.

Majors African studies; American studies; anthropology; applied mathematics; art; art history, criticism and conservation; Asian studies; Asian studies (East); astronomy; astrophysics; behavioral sciences; biblical studies; biochemistry; biology/biological sciences; botany/plant biology; cell biology and histology; ceramic arts and ceramics; chemistry; classics and languages, literatures and linguistics; comparative literature; computer science; creative writing; cultural studies; dance; developmental and child psychology; dramatic/theater arts; drawing; ecology; economics; English; environmental biology; environmental studies; European studies; European studies (Central and Eastern); experimental psychology; film/cinema studies; fine/studio arts; folklore; French; German; history; history of philosophy; humanities; interdisciplinary studies; international economics; international relations and affairs; Italian; Latin; Latin American studies; linguistics; literature; mathematics; medieval and Renaissance studies; modern Greek; modern languages; molecular biology; music; music history, literature, and theory; natural resources/conservation; natural sciences; philosophy; photography; physics; political science and government; Portuguese; pre-law studies; pre-medical studies; pre-veterinary studies; psychology; religious studies; Romance languages; Russian studies; sculpture; social sciences; sociology; Spanish; women's studies.

Academics *Calendar:* semesters. *Degrees:* bachelor's, master's, and first professional. *Special study options:* accelerated degree program, advanced placement credit, double majors, independent study, internships, off-campus study, part-time degree program, services for LD students, student-designed majors, study abroad.

Computers on Campus 47 computers/terminals are available on campus for general student use. Students can access the following: campus intranet, computer help desk, free student e-mail accounts. Campuswide network is available. Wireless service is available via classrooms, computer centers, computer labs, learning centers, libraries, student centers.

Student Life *Housing options:* coed, women-only, cooperative. Campus housing is university owned. Freshman campus housing is guaranteed. *Activities and organizations:* drama/theater group, student-run newspaper, radio station, choral group, outdoor program, theater, farm program, Gay/Lesbian/Bisexual Alliance, madricgal and acappella groups. *Campus security:* 24-hour emergency response devices. *Student services:* health clinic, personal/psychological counseling.

Athletics *Intercollegiate sports:* rock climbing M/W, soccer M/W. *Intramural sports:* basketball M/W, fencing M/W, ice hockey M/W, rock climbing M/W, skiing (cross-country) M/W, skiing (downhill) M/W, soccer M/W, softball M/W, table tennis M/W, volleyball M/W, weight lifting M/W.

Standardized Tests *Required:* SAT or ACT (for admission).

Costs (2007–08) *Comprehensive fee:* $39,540 includes full-time tuition ($29,700), mandatory fees ($980), and room and board ($8860). Part-time tuition: $990 per credit. *College room only:* $4880.

Financial Aid Of all full-time matriculated undergraduates who enrolled in 2005, 263 applied for aid, 244 were judged to have need. 244 Federal Work-Study jobs (averaging $2050). 2 state and other part-time jobs (averaging $2000). In 2005, 25 non-need-based awards were made. *Average percent of need met:* 80%. *Average need-based loan:* $3728. *Average need-based gift aid:* $7621. *Average non-need-based aid:* $7621. *Average indebtedness upon graduation:* $18,404. *Financial aid deadline:* 3/1.

Applying *Options:* electronic application, early admission, early decision, early action, deferred entrance. *Application fee:* $50. *Required:* essay or personal statement, high school transcript, 2 letters of recommendation, expository essay. *Required for some:* interview. *Recommended:* interview. *Application deadlines:* 3/1 (freshmen), 4/15 (transfers), 2/1 (early action). *Early decision deadline:* 12/1. *Notification:* 4/1 (freshmen), 4/25 (transfers), 12/15 (early decision), 2/1 (early action).

Freshman Application Contact Ms. Amy VanTassel, Associate Director of Admission, Marlboro College, PO Box A, South Road, Marlboro, VT 05344-0300. *Toll-free phone:* 800-343-0049. *Fax:* 800-451-7555. *E-mail:* admissions@marlboro.edu.

See page 2608 for the College Close-Up.

MIDDLEBURY COLLEGE

Middlebury, Vermont **www.middlebury.edu/**

- **Independent** comprehensive, founded 1800
- **Small-town** 350-acre campus
- **Endowment** $936.4 million
- **Coed** 2,500 undergraduate students, 99% full-time, 51% women, 49% men
- **Most difficult** entrance level, 21% of applicants were admitted

Undergraduates 2,475 full-time, 25 part-time. Students come from 52 states and territories, 75 other countries, 93% are from out of state, 3% African American, 8% Asian American or Pacific Islander, 6% Hispanic American, 0.5% Native American, 10% international, 0.6% transferred in, 97% live on campus.

Freshmen *Admission:* 7,180 applied, 1,479 admitted, 644 enrolled.

Faculty *Total:* 305, 82% full-time, 93% with terminal degrees. *Student/faculty ratio:* 9:1.

Majors American literature; American studies; art history, criticism and conservation; Asian studies (East); biochemistry; biology/biological sciences; chemistry; Chinese; cinematography and film/video production; classics and languages, literatures and linguistics; computer science; dance; dramatic/theater arts; economics; English; environmental studies; European studies; European studies (Central and Eastern); fine/studio arts; French; geography; geology/earth science; German; history; international relations and affairs; Italian; Japanese; Latin American studies; liberal arts and sciences/liberal studies; mathematics; modern languages; molecular biology; music; neuroscience; philosophy; physics; political science and government; psychology; religious studies; Russian; Russian studies; sociology; Spanish; women's studies.

Academics *Calendar:* 4-1-4. *Degrees:* bachelor's, master's, and doctoral. *Special study options:* accelerated degree program, advanced placement credit, double majors, honors programs, independent study, internships, off-campus study, services for LD students, student-designed majors, study abroad, summer session for credit. *ROTC:* Army (c). *Unusual degree programs:* 3-2 business administration with University of Chicago; New York University; Rutgers, The State University of New Jersey, Graduate School of Management; University of Rochester; Columbia University; Boston University; Dartmouth College; engineering with Columbia University, Rensselaer Polytechnic Institute, University of Rochester; forestry with Duke University; nursing with Columbia University.

Computers on Campus 494 computers/terminals are available on campus for general student use. Students can access the following: computer help desk, free student e-mail accounts, online (class) registration, online (class) schedules, help-line, personal Web pages, file servers. Campuswide network is available. Wireless service is available via entire campus.

Student Life *Housing:* on-campus residence required through junior year. *Options:* coed, disabled students. Campus housing is university owned. Freshman campus housing is guaranteed. *Activities and organizations:* drama/theater group, student-run newspaper, radio station, choral group, Volunteer Service Organization, International Students Organization, Mountain Club, Activities Board, WRMC radio. *Campus security:* 24-hour patrols, student patrols, late-night transport/escort service, controlled dormitory access. *Student services:* health clinic, personal/psychological counseling, women's center.

Athletics Member NCAA. All Division III. *Intercollegiate sports:* baseball M, basketball M/W, cross-country running M/W, field hockey W, football M, golf M/W, ice hockey M/W, lacrosse M/W, skiing (cross-country) M/W, skiing (downhill) M/W, soccer M/W, softball W, squash W, swimming and diving M/W, tennis M/W, track and field M/W, volleyball W. *Intramural sports:* badminton M/W, basketball M/W, crew M (c)/W (c), cross-country running M/W, equestrian sports M (c)/W (c), football M/W, golf M/W, ice hockey M/W, rock climbing M (c)/W (c), rugby M (c)/W (c), sailing M (c)/W (c), skiing (cross-country) M/W, skiing (downhill) M/W, soccer M/W, softball M/W, squash M (c)/W, swimming and diving M/W, table tennis M/W, tennis M/W, ultimate Frisbee M (c)/W (c), volleyball M/W, water polo M (c)/W (c).

Standardized Tests *Required:* three tests to include: a writing test, a quantitative test, and an area of the applicant's choice (for admission).

Costs (2007–08) *Comprehensive fee:* $46,910. *Payment plan:* tuition prepayment. *Waivers:* employees or children of employees.

Financial Aid Of all full-time matriculated undergraduates who enrolled in 2006, 1,125 applied for aid, 967 were judged to have need, 967 had their need fully met. *Average percent of need met:* 100%. *Average financial aid package:* $30,439. *Average need-based loan:* $3395. *Average need-based gift aid:* $27,323. *Average indebtedness upon graduation:* $20,808. *Financial aid deadline:* 1/1.

Applying *Options:* electronic application, early admission, early decision, deferred entrance. *Application fee:* $65. *Required:* essay or personal statement, high school transcript, 3 letters of recommendation. *Recommended:* interview. *Application deadlines:* 1/1 (freshmen), 3/1 (transfers). *Early decision deadline:* 11/1. *Notification:* 4/1 (freshmen), 4/10 (transfers), 12/15 (early decision).

Freshman Application Contact Mr. Robert Clagett, Dean of Admissions, Middlebury College, Emma Willard House, Middlebury, VT 05753-6002. *Phone:* 802-443-3000. *Fax:* 802-443-2056. *E-mail:* admissions@middlebury.edu.

NEW ENGLAND CULINARY INSTITUTE

Montpelier, Vermont **www.neci.edu/**

- **Proprietary** primarily 2-year, founded 1980
- **Small-town** campus
- **Endowment** $291,550
- **Coed**
- **Moderately difficult** entrance level

Faculty *Student/faculty ratio:* 8:1.

Academics *Calendar:* quarters. *Degrees:* certificates, associate, and bachelor's.

Student Life *Campus security:* 24-hour emergency response devices, student patrols, Mod patrols in the evening.

Costs (2007–08) *Comprehensive fee:* $32,481 includes full-time tuition ($24,788), mandatory fees ($865), and room and board ($6828). Full-time tuition and fees vary according to course level, program, and student level.

Financial Aid Of all full-time matriculated undergraduates who enrolled in 2006, 320 Federal Work-Study jobs (averaging $1000).

Applying *Options:* electronic application, early admission, deferred entrance. *Required:* essay or personal statement, high school transcript, 1 letter of recommendation, minimum TOEFL scores for foreign students. *Required for some:* letters of recommendation, interview.

Freshman Application Contact Jan Knutsen, Vice President of Enrollment, New England Culinary Institute, 250 Main Street, Montpelier, VT 05602. *Toll-free phone:* 877-223-6324. *Fax:* 802-225-3280. *E-mail:* janknutsen@neci.edu.

NEW ENGLAND CULINARY INSTITUTE AT ESSEX

Essex Junction, Vermont **www.neci.edu/**

Freshman Application Contact Sherri Gilmore, Director of Admissions, New England Culinary Institute at Essex, 48½ Park Street, Essex Junction, VT 05452. *Phone:* 802-223-6324. *Fax:* 802-225-3280. *E-mail:* sherrigilmore@neci.edu.

NORWICH UNIVERSITY

Northfield, Vermont **www.norwich.edu/**

- **Independent** comprehensive, founded 1819
- **Small-town** 1125-acre campus with easy access to Burlington
- **Endowment** $173.5 million
- **Coed, primarily men** 1,958 undergraduate students, 96% full-time, 27% women, 73% men
- **Moderately difficult** entrance level, 59% of applicants were admitted

Undergraduates 1,889 full-time, 69 part-time. Students come from 30 states and territories, 8 other countries, 85% are from out of state, 3% African American, 2% Asian American or Pacific Islander, 4% Hispanic American, 0.2% Native American, 3% transferred in, 82% live on campus. *Retention:* 77% of 2006 full-time freshmen returned.

Freshmen *Admission:* 2,701 applied, 1,594 admitted, 519 enrolled. *Average high school GPA:* 3.18.

Faculty *Total:* 311, 39% full-time. *Student/faculty ratio:* 14:1.

Majors Accounting; architecture; athletic training; biochemical technology; biology/biological sciences; business administration and management; chemistry; civil engineering; communication/speech communication and rhetoric; computer engineering; computer science; criminal justice/law enforcement administration; economics; electrical, electronics and communications engineering; English; environmental studies; geology/earth science; health science; history; international relations and affairs; mathematics; mechanical engineering; nursing (registered nurse training); peace studies and conflict resolution; physical education teaching and coaching; physics; political science and government; psychology.

Academics *Calendar:* semesters. *Degrees:* bachelor's, master's, and post-bachelor's certificates. *Special study options:* academic remediation for entering students, adult/continuing education programs, advanced placement credit, cooperative education, distance learning, double majors, English as a second language, external degree program, independent study, internships, part-time degree program, services for LD students, study abroad, summer session for credit. *ROTC:* Army (b), Navy (b), Air Force (b).

Computers on Campus 200 computers/terminals are available on campus for general student use. Students can access the following: campus intranet, computer help desk, free student e-mail accounts, online (class) grades, online (class) schedules. Campuswide network is available. 100% of college-owned or -operated housing units are wired for high-speed Internet access. Wireless service is available via entire campus.

Student Life *Housing:* on-campus residence required through senior year. *Options:* coed. Campus housing is university owned. Freshman campus housing is guaranteed. *Activities and organizations:* drama/theater group, student-run newspaper, radio station, choral group, marching band, DREAM, NUEMS, IEEE, CJSA, Politeia/Model UN. *Campus security:* 24-hour emergency response devices and patrols, late-night transport/escort service. *Student services:* health clinic, personal/psychological counseling.

Athletics Member NCAA. All Division III. *Intercollegiate sports:* baseball M, basketball M/W, cross-country running M/W, fencing M (c)/W (c), football M, ice hockey M/W (c), lacrosse M, riflery M/W, rugby M (c)/W (c), sailing M (c)/W (c), skiing (cross-country) M (c)/W (c), skiing (downhill) M (c)/W (c), soccer M/W, softball W, swimming and diving M/W, tennis M/W (c), track and field M/W, volleyball M (c)/W (c), weight lifting M (c)/W (c), wrestling M. *Intramural sports:* basketball M/W, cross-country running M/W, football M, golf M/W, ice hockey M/W, lacrosse M/W, racquetball M/W, rugby M/W, soccer M/W, softball W, swimming and diving M/W, tennis M/W, track and field M/W, volleyball M/W, water polo M/W, weight lifting M/W, wrestling M.

Standardized Tests *Required:* SAT or ACT (for admission).

Costs (2007–08) *Comprehensive fee:* $32,952 includes full-time tuition ($23,214), mandatory fees ($1216), and room and board ($8522). Full-time tuition and fees vary according to program. Part-time tuition: $578 per credit. Part-time tuition and fees vary according to course load. *Payment plan:* installment. *Waivers:* employees or children of employees.

Applying *Options:* electronic application. *Application fee:* $35. *Required:* essay or personal statement, high school transcript. *Required for some:* portfolio. *Recommended:* minimum 2.0 GPA, 2 letters of recommendation, interview. *Application deadlines:* rolling (freshmen), rolling (transfers). *Notification:* continuous (freshmen), continuous (transfers).

Director of Admissions Ms. Shelby Wallace, Director of Admissions, Norwich University, 27 I.D. White Avenue, Northfield, VT 05663. *Phone:* 802-485-2658. *Toll-free phone:* 800-468-6679. *E-mail:* nuadm@norwich.edu.

See page 2610 for the College Close-Up.

SAINT MICHAEL'S COLLEGE

Colchester, Vermont **www.smcvt.edu/**

- **Independent Roman Catholic** comprehensive, founded 1904
- **Suburban** 440-acre campus with easy access to Montreal
- **Endowment** $77.4 million
- **Coed** 2,008 undergraduate students, 98% full-time, 53% women, 47% men
- **Moderately difficult** entrance level, 69% of applicants were admitted

Undergraduates 1,968 full-time, 40 part-time. Students come from 38 states and territories, 12 other countries, 80% are from out of state, 0.7% African American, 1% Asian American or Pacific Islander, 1% Hispanic American, 0.4% Native American, 1% international, 1% transferred in, 99% live on campus. *Retention:* 90% of 2006 full-time freshmen returned.

Freshmen *Admission:* 3,504 applied, 2,423 admitted, 524 enrolled. *Average high school GPA:* 3.4. *Test scores:* SAT critical reading scores over 500: 84%; SAT math scores over 500: 84%; SAT writing scores over 500: 84%; ACT scores over 18: 97%; SAT critical reading scores over 600: 36%; SAT math scores over 600: 32%; SAT writing scores over 600: 36%; ACT scores over 24: 62%; SAT critical reading scores over 700: 4%; SAT math scores over 700: 3%; SAT writing scores over 700: 5%; ACT scores over 30: 6%.

Faculty *Total:* 212, 73% full-time, 72% with terminal degrees. *Student/faculty ratio:* 13:1.

Majors Accounting; American studies; art; art teacher education; biochemistry; biology/biological sciences; business administration and management; chemistry; classics and languages, literatures and linguistics; computer science; dramatic/theater arts; economics; education; elementary education; English; environmental science; French; history; information science/studies; journalism; mathematics; modern languages; music; philosophy; physical sciences; physics; political science and government; pre-dentistry studies; pre-law studies; pre-medical studies; pre-veterinary studies; psychology; religious studies; secondary education; sociology; Spanish; women's studies.

Academics *Calendar:* semesters. *Degrees:* bachelor's, master's, post-master's, and postbachelor's certificates. *Special study options:* advanced placement credit, double majors, English as a second language, honors programs, independent study, internships, off-campus study, part-time degree program, student-designed majors, study abroad, summer session for credit. *ROTC:* Army (c), Air Force (c). *Unusual degree programs:* 3-2 business administration with (4+1) MBA Program with Clarkson University; engineering with University of Vermont, and Clarkson University.

Computers on Campus 233 computers/terminals and 5,000 ports are available on campus for general student use. Students can access the following: computer help desk, free student e-mail accounts, online (class) grades, online (class) registration, online (class) schedules. Campuswide network is available. 100% of college-owned or -operated housing units are wired for high-speed Internet access. Wireless service is available via classrooms, libraries, student centers.

Student Life *Housing:* on-campus residence required through senior year. *Options:* coed, men-only, women-only, disabled students. Campus housing is university owned. Freshman campus housing is guaranteed. *Activities and organizations:* drama/theater group, student-run newspaper, radio station, choral group, Student Association, Mobilization of Volunteer Efforts (MOVE), Student radio station (WPPV-FM), Wilderness Program, Student Newspaper. *Campus security:* 24-hour emergency response devices and patrols, student patrols, late-night transport/escort service, bicycle patrols. *Student services:* health clinic, personal/psychological counseling, women's center.

Athletics Member NCAA. All Division II. *Intercollegiate sports:* baseball M, basketball M (s)/W (s), cheerleading M (c)/W (c), cross-country running M/W, field hockey W, golf M, ice hockey M/W, lacrosse M/W, rugby M (c)/W (c), skiing (cross-country) M/W, skiing (downhill) M/W, soccer M/W, softball W, swimming and diving M/W, tennis M/W, volleyball W. *Intramural sports:* basketball M/W, cross-country running M/W, golf M/W, ice hockey M/W, racquetball M/W, rock climbing M/W, skiing (cross-country) M/W, skiing (downhill) M/W, soccer M/W, softball M/W, swimming and diving M/W, table tennis M/W, tennis M/W, track and field M (c)/W (c), volleyball M/W.

Standardized Tests *Required:* SAT or ACT (for admission).

Costs (2007–08) *Comprehensive fee:* $37,405 includes full-time tuition ($29,695), mandatory fees ($250), and room and board ($7460). Part-time tuition: $990 per credit hour. *Room and board:* Room and board charges vary according to housing facility. *Payment plan:* installment. *Waivers:* employees or children of employees.

Financial Aid Of all full-time matriculated undergraduates who enrolled in 2006, 1,438 applied for aid, 1,253 were judged to have need, 290 had their need fully met. 489 Federal Work-Study jobs (averaging $833). 499 state and other part-time jobs (averaging $750). In 2006, 377 non-need-based awards were made. *Average percent of need met:* 79%. *Average financial aid package:* $21,672. *Average need-based loan:* $4488. *Average need-based gift aid:* $14,884. *Average non-need-based aid:* $6050. *Average indebtedness upon graduation:* $22,264.

Applying *Options:* electronic application, early action, deferred entrance. *Application fee:* $50. *Required:* essay or personal statement, high school transcript. *Recommended:* minimum 3.0 GPA, 3 letters of recommendation, interview. *Application deadlines:* 2/1 (freshmen), 3/15 (transfers), 11/1 (early action). *Notification:* 4/1 (freshmen), 4/15 (transfers), 1/1 (early action).

Freshman Application Contact Ms. Jacqueline Murphy, Director of Admission, Saint Michael's College, One Winooski Park, Colchester, VT 05439. *Phone:* 802-654-3000. *Toll-free phone:* 800-762-8000. *Fax:* 802-654-2906. *E-mail:* admission@smcvt.edu.

See page 2612 for the College Close-Up.

SOUTHERN VERMONT COLLEGE

Bennington, Vermont **www.svc.edu/**

- **Independent** 4-year, founded 1926
- **Small-town** 371-acre campus with easy access to Albany
- **Endowment** $1.2 million
- **Coed** 450 undergraduate students
- **Minimally difficult** entrance level, 94% of applicants were admitted

Undergraduates Students come from 24 states and territories, 5 other countries, 72% are from out of state, 6% African American, 1% Asian American or Pacific Islander, 2% Hispanic American, 0.5% Native American, 1% international, 50% live on campus. *Retention:* 58% of 2006 full-time freshmen returned.

Freshmen *Admission:* 530 applied, 499 admitted. *Average high school GPA:* 2.7. *Test scores:* SAT critical reading scores over 500: 32%; SAT math scores over 500: 19%; SAT writing scores over 500: 22%; ACT scores over 18: 45%; SAT critical reading scores over 600: 9%; SAT math scores over 600: 4%; SAT writing scores over 600: 7%; SAT critical reading scores over 700: 2%.

Faculty *Total:* 40, 43% full-time, 10% with terminal degrees. *Student/faculty ratio:* 17:1.

Majors Business administration and management; communication/speech communication and rhetoric; creative writing; criminal justice/law enforcement administration; English; environmental studies; history; human services; liberal arts and sciences/liberal studies; management science; mass communication/media; medical radiologic technology; non-profit management; nursing (registered nurse training); political science and government related; pre-law studies; professional studies; psychology.

Academics *Calendar:* semesters. *Degrees:* associate and bachelor's. *Special study options:* academic remediation for entering students, accelerated degree program, adult/continuing education programs, advanced placement credit, cooperative education, distance learning, double majors, external degree program, honors programs, independent study, internships, part-time degree program, services for LD students, student-designed majors, study abroad, summer session for credit.

Computers on Campus 43 computers/terminals are available on campus for general student use. Students can access the following: campus intranet, free student e-mail accounts. Campuswide network is available.

Student Life *Housing:* on-campus residence required through sophomore year. *Options:* coed. Campus housing is university owned. Freshman campus housing is guaranteed. *Activities and organizations:* drama/theater group, student-run newspaper, Student Government Association, Summit Yearbook, Student Newspaper/The Mountain Press, Diversity Club, Mad Hatter's Drama Club. *Campus security:* 24-hour patrols, late-night transport/escort service, controlled dormitory access. *Student services:* health clinic, personal/psychological counseling.

Athletics Member NCAA. All Division III. *Intercollegiate sports:* baseball M, basketball M/W, cross-country running M/W, rugby M/W, soccer M/W, softball W, track and field M/W, volleyball M/W, wrestling M. *Intramural sports:* baseball M/W, basketball M/W, cheerleading W (c), football M/W, golf M/W, lacrosse M (c), rugby M (c)/W (c), skiing (cross-country) M (c)/W (c), skiing (downhill) M (c)/W (c), soccer M/W, softball M/W, tennis M/W, volleyball M/W.

Standardized Tests *Required:* SAT or ACT (for admission).

Costs (2007–08) *Comprehensive fee:* $24,900 includes full-time tuition ($16,800) and room and board ($8100). Part-time tuition: $575 per credit. *College room only:* $4000. Room and board charges vary according to board plan. *Payment plan:* installment. *Waivers:* employees or children of employees.

Financial Aid Of all full-time matriculated undergraduates who enrolled in 2006, 287 applied for aid, 262 were judged to have need, 32 had their need fully met. 71 Federal Work-Study jobs (averaging $1200). In 2006, 18 non-need-based awards were made. *Average percent of need met:* 65%. *Average financial aid package:* $12,689. *Average need-based loan:* $4231. *Average need-based gift aid:* $9088. *Average non-need-based aid:* $3461. *Average indebtedness upon graduation:* $20,244.

Applying *Options:* electronic application, early admission, deferred entrance. *Application fee:* $30. *Required:* essay or personal statement, high school transcript, 2 letters of recommendation. *Required for some:* interview. *Recommended:* minimum 2.0 GPA, interview. *Application deadlines:* rolling (freshmen), rolling (transfers). *Notification:* continuous (freshmen), continuous (transfers).

Freshman Application Contact Southern Vermont College, 982 Mansion Drive, Bennington, VT 05201. *Phone:* 802-447-6304. *Toll-free phone:* 800-378-2782. *Fax:* 802-447-4695. *E-mail:* admis@svc.edu.

STERLING COLLEGE

Craftsbury Common, Vermont **www.sterlingcollege.edu/**

- **Independent** 4-year, founded 1958
- **Rural** 430-acre campus
- **Endowment** $920,272
- **Coed** 105 undergraduate students, 98% full-time, 45% women, 55% men
- **Moderately difficult** entrance level, 76% of applicants were admitted

Sterling College offers an environmentally focused liberal arts curriculum combining traditional and experiential academics. Internships and global field studies provide travel-study opportunities. Self-designed studies focus on human ecology, outdoor leadership, sustainability, northern communities, agriculture, and more. Students earn money toward tuition through Sterling's Work-Learning-Service Program. Financial aid and scholarships are available.

Undergraduates 103 full-time, 2 part-time. Students come from 22 states and territories, 77% are from out of state, 2% Hispanic American, 13% transferred in, 77% live on campus. *Retention:* 67% of 2006 full-time freshmen returned.

Freshmen *Admission:* 97 applied, 74 admitted, 30 enrolled. *Average high school GPA:* 2.99.

Faculty *Total:* 33, 42% full-time, 30% with terminal degrees. *Student/faculty ratio:* 5:1.

Majors Agricultural and domestic animals services related; agricultural and horticultural plant breeding; agricultural animal breeding; agricultural business and management; agricultural business and management related; agricultural communication/journalism; agricultural production related; agricultural public services related; agricultural teacher education; agriculture; agriculture and agriculture operations related; animal health; animal/livestock husbandry and production; animal nutrition; animal sciences; animal sciences related; animal training; applied horticulture; area, ethnic, cultural, and gender studies related; biological and physical sciences; Canadian studies; conservation biology; crop production; cultural resource management and policy analysis; dairy husbandry and production; ecology; ecology, evolution, systematics and population biology related; educational, instructional, and curriculum supervision; educational leadership and administration; education related; energy management and systems technology; environmental biology; environmental design/architecture; environmental studies; ethnic, cultural minority, and gender studies related; farm and ranch management; fishing and fisheries sciences and management; forest/forest resources management; forest resources production and management; forestry; forestry related; forest sciences and biology; greenhouse management; horse husbandry/equine science and management; horticultural science; human ecology; international agriculture; international/global studies; land use planning and management; liberal arts and sciences/liberal studies; livestock management; multi-/interdisciplinary studies related; natural resources and conservation related; natural resources/conservation; natural resources/conservation related; natural resources management; natural resources management and policy; natural sciences; parks, recreation and leisure; parks, recreation and leisure facilities management; plant protection and integrated pest management; plant sciences; plant sciences related; range science and management; Scandinavian studies; soil science and agronomy; soil sciences related; solar energy technology; water, wetlands, and marine resources management; wildlife and wildlands science and management; wildlife biology.

Academics *Calendar:* semesters. *Degree:* bachelor's. *Special study options:* advanced placement credit, independent study, internships, off-campus study, part-time degree program, services for LD students, student-designed majors, study abroad, summer session for credit.

Computers on Campus 15 computers/terminals are available on campus for general student use. Students can access the following: campus intranet, computer help desk, free student e-mail accounts. Campuswide network is available. 100% of college-owned or -operated housing units are wired for high-speed Internet access. Wireless service is available via entire campus.

Student Life *Housing:* on-campus residence required for freshman year. *Options:* coed. Campus housing is university owned. Freshman campus housing is guaranteed. *Activities and organizations:* Outing Club, Timbersports Team, Student Union (government), Art Club, Musical Groups. *Campus security:* student patrols. *Student services:* health clinic, personal/psychological counseling.

Athletics *Intramural sports:* baseball M/W, basketball M/W, cross-country running M/W, rock climbing M/W, skiing (cross-country) M/W, skiing (downhill) M/W, soccer M/W, softball M/W, table tennis M/W, ultimate Frisbee M/W, volleyball M/W.

Costs (2008–09) *Comprehensive fee:* $28,847 includes full-time tuition ($21,280), mandatory fees ($375), and room and board ($7192). Part-time tuition: $650 per credit.

Financial Aid Of all full-time matriculated undergraduates who enrolled in 2006, 79 applied for aid, 71 were judged to have need, 7 had their need fully met. 33 Federal Work-Study jobs (averaging $457). 98 state and other part-time jobs (averaging $1751). In 2006, 5 non-need-based awards were made. *Average percent of need met:* 86%. *Average financial aid package:* $17,710. *Average need-based loan:* $4241. *Average need-based gift aid:* $10,189. *Average non-need-based aid:* $1200. *Average indebtedness upon graduation:* $15,880.

Applying *Options:* electronic application, early admission, early action, deferred entrance. *Application fee:* $35. *Required:* essay or personal statement, high school transcript, 2 letters of recommendation. *Recommended:* minimum 2.0 GPA, interview. *Application deadlines:* 2/15 (freshmen), rolling (transfers), 12/15 (early action). *Notification:* 4/1 (freshmen), 8/30 (transfers), 1/15 (early action).

Freshman Application Contact Gwyn Harris, Director of Admissions, Sterling College, PO Box 72, Craftsbury Common, VT 05827. *Phone:* 802-586-7711 Ext. 100. *Toll-free phone:* 800-648-3591 Ext. 100. *Fax:* 802-586-2596. *E-mail:* admissions@sterlingcollege.edu.

UNIVERSITY OF VERMONT

Burlington, Vermont www.uvm.edu/

- **State-supported** university, founded 1791
- **Suburban** 425-acre campus
- **Endowment** $337.6 million
- **Coed** 10,504 undergraduate students, 89% full-time, 55% women, 45% men
- **Moderately difficult** entrance level, 70% of applicants were admitted

Undergraduates 9,299 full-time, 1,205 part-time. Students come from 50 states and territories, 25 other countries, 65% are from out of state, 1% African American, 2% Asian American or Pacific Islander, 2% Hispanic American, 0.3% Native American, 0.9% international, 4% transferred in, 54% live on campus. *Retention:* 86% of 2006 full-time freshmen returned.

Freshmen *Admission:* 18,814 applied, 13,079 admitted, 2,450 enrolled. *Test scores:* SAT critical reading scores over 500: 89%; SAT math scores over 500: 89%; SAT writing scores over 500: 90%; ACT scores over 18: 99%; SAT critical reading scores over 600: 45%; SAT math scores over 600: 45%; SAT writing scores over 600: 44%; ACT scores over 24: 69%; SAT critical reading scores over 700: 8%; SAT math scores over 700: 6%; SAT writing scores over 700: 7%; ACT scores over 30: 10%.

Faculty *Total:* 769, 76% full-time, 73% with terminal degrees. *Student/faculty ratio:* 16:1.

Majors Agriculture; agronomy and crop science; ancient/classical Greek; animal sciences; anthropology; art history, criticism and conservation; art teacher education; Asian studies; athletic training; biochemistry; biology/biological sciences; botany/plant biology; business administration and management; Canadian studies; chemistry; Chinese; civil engineering; classics and languages, literatures and linguistics; clinical laboratory science/medical technology; communication disorders; computer and information sciences; computer science; computer systems analysis; dairy husbandry and production; development economics and international development; dietetics; dramatic/theater arts; early childhood education; economics; education; electrical, electronics and communications engineering; elementary education; engineering/industrial management; English; English/language arts teacher education; entrepreneurship; environmental/environmental health engineering; environmental science; environmental studies; European studies; family and consumer sciences/home economics teacher education; film/cinema studies; fine/studio arts; foreign language teacher education; forestry; French; geography; geology/earth science; history; horticultural science; human development and family studies; industrial engineering; information science/studies; interdisciplinary studies; Italian studies; Japanese; kindergarten/preschool education; kinesiology and exercise science; Latin; Latin American studies; liberal arts and sciences/liberal studies; mathematics; mathematics teacher education; mechanical engineering; medical microbiology and bacteriology; medical radiologic technology; microbiology; middle school education; molecular biology; molecular genetics; movement therapy and movement education; music; music history, literature, and theory; music performance; music teacher education; natural resources/conservation; nuclear medical technology; nursing (registered nurse training); nutrition sciences; parks, recreation and leisure facilities management; philosophy; physical education teaching and coaching; physics; plant sciences; political science and government; psychology; public relations, advertising, and applied communication related; religious studies; Russian; Russian studies; science teacher education; secondary education; social studies teacher education; social work; sociology; Spanish; special education (early childhood); statistics; wildlife biology; women's studies; zoology/animal biology.

Academics *Calendar:* semesters. *Degrees:* bachelor's, master's, doctoral, first professional, post-master's, and postbachelor's certificates. *Special study options:* advanced placement credit, cooperative education, distance learning, double majors, English as a second language, freshman honors college, honors programs, independent study, internships, off-campus study, part-time degree program, services for LD students, student-designed majors, study abroad, summer session for credit. *ROTC:* Army (b). *Unusual degree programs:* 3-2 computer science.

Computers on Campus 538 computers/terminals and 99 ports are available on campus for general student use. Students can access the following: campus intranet, computer help desk, free student e-mail accounts, online (class) grades, online (class) registration, online (class) schedules, Web pages, on-line course support. Campuswide network is available. 100% of college-owned or -operated housing units are wired for high-speed Internet access. Wireless service is available via classrooms, computer centers, computer labs, learning centers, libraries, student centers.

Student Life *Housing:* on-campus residence required through sophomore year. *Options:* coed. Campus housing is university owned. Freshman campus housing is guaranteed. *Activities and organizations:* drama/theater group, student-run newspaper, radio and television station, choral group, Volunteers in Action, Outing Club, Ski & Snowboard Club, national fraternities, national sororities. *Campus security:* 24-hour emergency response devices and patrols, late-night transport/escort service, controlled dormitory access. *Student services:* health clinic, personal/psychological counseling, women's center, legal services.

Athletics Member NCAA. All Division I. *Intercollegiate sports:* baseball M (s), basketball M (s)/W (s), cheerleading M (c)/W (c), crew M (c)/W (c), cross-country running M (s)/W (s), equestrian sports M (c)/W (c), fencing M (c)/W (c), field hockey W (s), gymnastics M (c)/W (c), ice hockey M (s)/W (s), lacrosse M (s)/W (s), rugby M (c)/W (c), sailing M (c)/W (c), skiing (cross-country) M (s)/W (s), skiing (downhill) M (s)/W (s), soccer M (s)/W (s), softball W (s), swimming and diving W (s), table tennis M (c)/W (c), track and field M (s)/W (s), ultimate Frisbee M (c)/W (c), volleyball M (c)/W (c), water polo M (c)/W (c). *Intramural sports:* basketball M/W, bowling M/W, football M/W, ice hockey M/W, lacrosse M/W, racquetball M/W, soccer M/W, softball M/W, tennis M/W, volleyball M/W, water polo M/W.

Standardized Tests *Required:* SAT or ACT (for admission).

Costs (2007–08) *Tuition:* state resident $10,422 full-time, $434 per credit part-time; nonresident $26,306 full-time, $1096 per credit part-time. Part-time tuition and fees vary according to course load. *Required fees:* $1632 full-time. *Room and board:* $8024; room only: $5426. Room and board charges vary according to board plan and housing facility. *Payment plans:* installment, deferred payment. *Waivers:* senior citizens and employees or children of employees.

Financial Aid Of all full-time matriculated undergraduates who enrolled in 2007, 6,042 applied for aid, 4,894 were judged to have need, 1,185 had their need fully met. 1,945 Federal Work-Study jobs (averaging $1454). In 2007, 1719 non-need-based awards were made. *Average percent of need met:* 76%. *Average financial aid package:* $16,809. *Average need-based loan:* $6013. *Average need-based gift aid:* $11,733. *Average non-need-based aid:* $2180. *Average indebtedness upon graduation:* $25,036.

Applying *Options:* electronic application, early action, deferred entrance. *Application fee:* $45. *Required:* essay or personal statement, high school transcript, 1 letter of recommendation. *Recommended:* 2 letters of recommendation. *Application deadlines:* 1/15 (freshmen), 4/1 (transfers), 11/1 (early action). *Notification:* 3/31 (freshmen), continuous (transfers), 12/15 (early action).

Freshman Application Contact Susan Wertheimer, Interim Dean of Admissions, University of Vermont, Office of Admissions, 194 South Prospect Street, Burlington, VT 05401-3596. *Phone:* 802-656-3370. *Fax:* 802-656-8611. *E-mail:* admissions@uvm.edu.

See page 2614 for the College Close-Up.

VERMONT TECHNICAL COLLEGE

Randolph Center, Vermont www.vtc.edu/

- **State-supported** 4-year, founded 1866, part of Vermont State Colleges System
- **Rural** 544-acre campus
- **Endowment** $4.8 million
- **Coed** 1,556 undergraduate students, 75% full-time, 41% women, 59% men
- **Moderately difficult** entrance level, 58% of applicants were admitted

Undergraduates 1,160 full-time, 396 part-time. Students come from 14 states and territories, 3 other countries, 13% are from out of state, 0.8% African American, 2% Asian American or Pacific Islander, 1% Hispanic American, 0.7% Native American, 0.1% international, 21% transferred in, 35% live on campus. *Retention:* 65% of 2006 full-time freshmen returned.

Freshmen *Admission:* 920 applied, 529 admitted, 284 enrolled. *Average high school GPA:* 2.9. *Test scores:* SAT critical reading scores over 500: 36%; SAT math scores over 500: 49%; SAT writing scores over 500: 67%; ACT scores over 18: 67%; SAT critical reading scores over 600: 7%; SAT math scores over 600: 13%; SAT writing scores over 600: 20%; ACT scores over 24: 24%; SAT critical reading scores over 700: 1%; SAT math scores over 700: 2%; SAT writing scores over 700: 2%.

Faculty *Total:* 156, 51% full-time, 69% with terminal degrees. *Student/faculty ratio:* 12:1.

Majors Aeronautical/aerospace engineering technology; agribusiness; architectural engineering technology; automotive engineering technology; business administration and management; civil engineering technology; computer engineering technology; computer software engineering; construction engineering technology; construction management; dairy science; dental hygiene; diesel mechanics technology; electrical, electronic and communications engineering technology; electromechanical technology; horse husbandry/equine science and management; information technology; landscaping and groundskeeping; mechanical engineering/mechanical technology; nursing (licensed practical/vocational nurse training); nursing (registered nurse training); ornamental horticulture; respiratory care therapy; telecommunications technology; veterinary technology.

Academics *Calendar:* semesters. *Degrees:* certificates, associate, and bachelor's. *Special study options:* academic remediation for entering students, accelerated degree program, advanced placement credit, cooperative education, distance learning, double majors, English as a second language, honors programs, independent study, internships, part-time degree program, services for LD students, summer session for credit. *ROTC:* Army (c).

Computers on Campus 350 computers/terminals are available on campus for general student use. Students can access the following: campus intranet, computer help desk, free student e-mail accounts, online (class) grades, online (class) registration, online (class) schedules. Campuswide network is available. 100% of college-owned or -operated housing units are wired for high-speed Internet access. Wireless service is available via entire campus.

Student Life *Housing:* on-campus residence required through sophomore year. *Options:* coed. Campus housing is university owned. *Activities and organizations:* student-run radio and television station, ASVTC (student government), Hockey Club, student radio station, American Institute of Architecture Students, Golf Club. *Campus security:* 24-hour emergency response devices and patrols, late-night transport/escort service, controlled dormitory access. *Student services:* health clinic, personal/psychological counseling.

Athletics Member NAIA, NSCAA. *Intercollegiate sports:* baseball M, basketball M/W, golf M/W, soccer M/W, volleyball M/W. *Intramural sports:* basketball M/W, bowling M (c)/W (c), cross-country running M/W, fencing M (c)/W (c), football M/W, golf M (c)/W (c), ice hockey M (c)/W (c), racquetball M/W, riflery M (c)/W (c), rock climbing M (c)/W (c), skiing (cross-country) M (c)/W (c), skiing (downhill) M (c)/W (c), soccer M/W, softball M/W, swimming and diving M/W, table tennis M/W, tennis M/W, volleyball M/W, water polo M/W, weight lifting M (c)/W (c).

Standardized Tests *Required for some:* SAT or ACT (for admission).

Costs (2007–08) *Tuition:* area resident $8760 full-time; state resident $13,128 full-time, $365 per credit part-time; nonresident $16,704 full-time, $696 per credit part-time. Full-time tuition and fees vary according to course load and program. Part-time tuition and fees vary according to program. *Required fees:* $638 full-time. *Room and board:* $7220; room only: $4300. Room and board charges vary according to board plan. *Payment plan:* installment. *Waivers:* employees or children of employees.

Financial Aid Of all full-time matriculated undergraduates who enrolled in 2006, 942 applied for aid, 809 were judged to have need, 174 had their need fully met. 167 Federal Work-Study jobs (averaging $1150). In 2006, 19 non-need-based awards were made. *Average percent of need met:* 64%. *Average financial aid package:* $9000. *Average need-based loan:* $3436. *Average need-based gift aid:* $5188. *Average non-need-based aid:* $3343. *Average indebtedness upon graduation:* $25,600.

Applying *Options:* electronic application. *Application fee:* $36. *Required:* high school transcript. *Required for some:* essay or personal statement, 2 letters of recommendation, interview. *Recommended:* minimum 3.0 GPA, 2 letters of recommendation, interview. *Application deadlines:* rolling (freshmen), rolling (transfers). *Notification:* continuous until 9/1 (freshmen), continuous until 9/1 (transfers).

Freshman Application Contact Mr. Dwight A. Cross, Assistant Dean of Enrollment, Vermont Technical College, PO Box 500, Randolph Center, VT 05061. *Phone:* 802-728-1244. *Toll-free phone:* 800-442-VTC1. *Fax:* 802-728-1390. *E-mail:* admissions@vtc.edu.

See page 2616 for the College Close-Up.

WOODBURY COLLEGE

Montpelier, Vermont **www.woodbury-college.edu/**

- **Independent** 4-year, founded 1975
- **Small-town** 8-acre campus
- **Endowment** $315,574
- **Coed** 70 undergraduate students, 76% full-time, 96% women, 4% men
- **Noncompetitive** entrance level, 40% of applicants were admitted

Undergraduates 53 full-time, 17 part-time. 7% are from out of state, 3% Asian American or Pacific Islander, 1% Hispanic American, 19% transferred in. *Retention:* 96% of 2006 full-time freshmen returned.

Freshmen *Admission:* 10 applied, 4 admitted, 4 enrolled.

Faculty *Total:* 32, 13% full-time. *Student/faculty ratio:* 7:1.

Majors Community organization and advocacy; legal assistant/paralegal; multi-/interdisciplinary studies related.

Academics *Calendar:* trimesters. *Degrees:* certificates, associate, bachelor's, master's, and postbachelor's certificates. *Special study options:* academic remediation for entering students, adult/continuing education programs, distance learning, double majors, independent study, internships, part-time degree program, services for LD students, student-designed majors.

Computers on Campus 22 computers/terminals and 1 port are available on campus for general student use. Students can access the following: campus intranet, computer help desk, free student e-mail accounts, online (class) schedules. Wireless service is available via entire campus.

Student Life *Housing:* college housing not available. *Student services:* personal/psychological counseling.

Costs (2007–08) *Tuition:* $15,900 full-time, $663 per credit part-time. *Required fees:* $150 full-time, $50 per term part-time. *Payment plan:* installment. *Waivers:* employees or children of employees.

Financial Aid Of all full-time matriculated undergraduates who enrolled in 2005, 81 applied for aid, 74 were judged to have need, 6 had their need fully met. In 2005, 3 non-need-based awards were made. *Average percent of need met:* 52%. *Average financial aid package:* $8436. *Average need-based loan:* $3631. *Average need-based gift aid:* $5603. *Average non-need-based aid:* $2897. *Average indebtedness upon graduation:* $21,879.

Applying *Options:* electronic application. *Application fee:* $30. *Required:* essay or personal statement, interview. *Required for some:* high school transcript. *Application deadlines:* rolling (freshmen), rolling (transfers).

Freshman Application Contact Admissions Office, Woodbury College, 660 Elm Street, Montpelier, VT 05602. *Phone:* 802-229-0516. *Toll-free phone:* 800-639-6039. *Fax:* 802-229-2141. *E-mail:* admiss@woodbury-college.edu.

BENNINGTON COLLEGE

BENNINGTON, VERMONT

The College

A Bennington education is characterized by cross-disciplinary learning, the close working relationship between student and teacher, the self-direction of its academic planning process, and the connection to the world through its winter internship term. The principle of learning by practice underlies every major feature of a Bennington education. Under the thoughtful guidance of faculty advisers, Bennington students learn what it means to take increasing responsibility for their own education, their own work, and their own lives. Bennington is grounded in the conviction that as a college education develops students' professional capacities, it should also prepare them to be deeply thoughtful and actively engaged citizens of the world.

A coeducational liberal arts college, Bennington confers Bachelor of Arts degrees, Master of Fine Arts degrees in the performing arts and writing, a Master of Arts degree in teaching, and a postbaccalaureate certificate in premedical and allied health sciences.

Location

Bennington, Vermont, is located in the southwestern corner of the state, just 160 miles from New York City, 150 miles from Boston, and 40 miles from Saratoga and Albany, New York. The internationally distinguished Sterling and Francine Clark Art Institute, the Tony Award–winning Williamstown Theatre Festival, and the Massachusetts Museum of Contemporary Art (MASS MoCA), the largest center for contemporary art in the country, are just down the road. Also nearby is the renowned performance space of the Boston Symphony Orchestra, Tanglewood Music Center, as is Jacob's Pillow, the site of America's first and longest-running dance festival. Designer shopping outlets, six ski resorts, and the recreational opportunities of the Appalachian Trail attract visitors from across the Northeast.

The Bennington College campus is nestled on 470 rolling acres at the foot of the Green Mountains. Original buildings from the 1930s and small student houses preserve the heritage of New England village architecture, with modern additions such as the 10,000-square-foot Student Center, featuring a café and stage.

Majors and Degrees

Bennington offers programs of study in all of the traditional liberal arts disciplines within the humanities, sciences, social sciences, and visual and performing arts. These include anthropology, architecture, biology, ceramics, chemistry, Chinese, composition (music), dance, democracy, drama, drawing, film and video, French, history, instrumental study, Italian, Japanese, literature and creative writing, mathematics, media arts, music, painting, philosophy, photography, physics, politics and international relations, prelaw, pre–medical studies, printmaking, psychology, sculpture, sound design and recording, Spanish, teaching, and voice.

In addition, Bennington offers a five-year Bachelor of Arts/Master of Arts degree in teaching. Graduates of this program are certified in early childhood, elementary, or secondary education and earn a license to teach in the state of Vermont. Reciprocity exists for all states except Iowa and Minnesota. Students may apply to this program after their freshman year.

Academic Programs

Students work with faculty members to design their own rigorous course of study, which may focus on a single discipline or combine disciplines. The Plan Process is the structure Bennington students use to design and evaluate this course of study. In one-on-one advising sessions, in conversation with faculty review panels, and in a series of both prospective and retrospective essays throughout their years at Bennington, students learn to articulate what they want to study and how they intend to study it. They identify not only the classes they wish to take but also how those classes relate to each other and the rest of their Bennington experience.

By working through short-lived passions and discovering abiding ones, cultivating abilities and finding resources (whether in the form of a teacher, a method, a craft, or discipline), and forming significant questions, Bennington students forge the shape of their education.

Off-Campus Programs

Each academic year includes a seven-week winter term of fieldwork off campus. During Field Work Term, students take their interests to the world beyond the College, where they work at jobs or internships in fields that complement their studies, clarify their interests, and open possibilities for their future. After spending four terms at work in the world, each student graduates with a resume as well as a diploma.

Bennington offers students a range of options for study abroad that carry academic credit. The College has relationships with several study-abroad programs but also allows students to research new programs and propose them for study-abroad possibilities. Among its affiliations are the School for Field Studies (SFS), which coordinates programs in field biology on five continents and provides students with a hands-on educational experience that addresses some of the world's most critical environmental issues, and the Winchester School of Art in England, which offers an opportunity for a term-long immersion in the fine arts.

Academic Facilities

Most of the classrooms at Bennington are arranged for seminar-style discussions, and all of the academic buildings are equipped with "smart" classrooms. Faculty members have offices throughout the campus, where they meet regularly with students to discuss their work outside of class. The Dickinson Science Building includes fully equipped science labs, and the Stickney Observatory offers opportunities for explorations of night skies. The 120,000-square-foot visual and performing arts center (VAPA) contains two state-of-the-art professional theaters, a 10,000-square-foot dance theater with one of the world's largest sprung wood floors, the Usdan Art Gallery, a forty-eight-seat film and video theater and studio, and studios for music, dance, and the visual arts.

The College's Computer Center includes two media labs, which are equipped with high-end audio and video digitizing and processing capabilities, a range of multimedia software, and a service and support unit. The Kaplan Center for Languages and Cultures hosts a Language Media Lab for interactive language study, and the Jennings Music Building houses a fully equipped electronic music studio.

Costs

For undergraduates in 2007–08, total charges were $46,180, including tuition, room, board, activities, and health services fees.

Financial Aid

Approximately 75–80 percent of Bennington students receive some form of financial assistance. Bennington offers need-based grants and loans as well as merit scholarships, and it participates in federal work-study programs. In addition to the Bennington financial aid application, the College requires the PROFILE and FAFSA.

Faculty

Bennington faculty members are all teacher-practitioners doing ongoing work that engages the world outside the classroom. The many ways in which faculty members create new work and pose new questions make them models for students, who in turn and over time create work and pose questions of their own, with the faculty members now as mentors.

The average class size is 12, and the overall student-faculty ratio is 8:1. All faculty members teach first-year as well as advanced students.

Student Government

The responsibility students assume in planning a course of study extends to life outside the classroom. Bennington treats the idea and the ideals of self-governance very seriously. Students are expected to discover the balance between freedom and responsibility and to do so by meeting the challenges of self-governance in their academic and nonacademic lives.

Admission Requirements

Bennington admits students who have demonstrated a passion for learning and academic excellence. The College requires the Common Application and the Bennington Supplement (an essay, a graded analytic paper, and the option to submit supplementary materials). Submission of standardized test scores is optional. The College hopes to learn as much about each applicant as possible and interviews the majority of applicants in person or by phone.

Application and Information

The deadline for freshman applications is January 3; for transfer applications, the deadlines are November 1 for the spring term and March 15 for the fall term. Early decision deadlines are November 15 and January 3, with notifications by mid-December and early February, respectively. Financial aid applicants should file the CSS PROFILE and Bennington's Financial Aid Supplement as soon as possible and no later than January 3; the FAFSA is due by March 1.

For more information about Bennington College, students should contact:

Office of Admissions
Bennington College
One College Drive
Bennington, Vermont 05201-6003
Phone: 802-440-4312
800-833-6845 (toll-free)
Fax: 802-440-4320
E-mail: admissions@bennington.edu
Web site: http://www.bennington.edu

Bennington students work within and across disciplines to discover the often-startling connections at the heart of things.

COLLEGE DATA CENTER • VERMONT

CASTLETON STATE COLLEGE

CASTLETON, VERMONT

The College

Castleton State College was founded in 1787; it was the first institution of higher learning in Vermont and the eighteenth in the United States. The 165-acre campus is located in Castleton, a historic Vermont village. Sixty-five percent of the 1,750 full-time undergraduate students at the College are Vermonters; the balance of the student population comes from New England and the Middle Atlantic states.

Castleton is committed to providing an undergraduate education in which the liberal arts and career preparation complement each other. Through an innovative program called Soundings, freshmen earn academic credit by attending a series of special events that include theater, music, dance, film, debate, and opinion from influential people. New students also participate in the First-Year Seminar, giving them the opportunity to develop the skills of a successful college student. First-year students may apply for the College's Honors Program. Community service and internships play an important role in a Castleton education.

There are ten major residence halls. Together, the residences accommodate nearly 900 students. Each residence hall room is equipped with at least two Internet hookups and wireless access, which give each student the opportunity to access the Web and e-mail using their own personal computer. There is no additional charge for this service. Each room is also equipped with cable TV connections and individual telephone lines. Off-campus housing is available in the Castleton, Fair Haven, and Rutland areas. Students who live on campus eat in Huden Dining Hall. All students are allowed to have automobiles on campus.

More than forty clubs and organizations provide a wide variety of student activities that include club sports, an FM radio station, the student newspaper, and an active outing club. Other clubs relate to college majors and future careers; still others serve the College or local community. Castleton is a member of the North Atlantic Conference of NCAA Division III. There are nineteen intercollegiate sports. Men compete in baseball, basketball, cross-country running, golf, ice hockey, lacrosse, skiing, soccer, and tennis; women compete in basketball, cross-country running, field hockey, ice hockey, lacrosse, skiing, soccer, softball, tennis, and volleyball. A majority of Castleton's students are involved in the intramural and recreational sports program.

Location

The campus is 12 miles west of Rutland, one of Vermont's largest cities. Montreal, Boston, Hartford, Albany, and New York City are all within easy driving distance and are accessible by public transportation from Rutland. Killington and Pico ski areas, Lake Bomoseen, and the Green Mountains provide excellent recreational opportunities and an exceptional living and learning environment.

Majors and Degrees

Castleton State College offers B.A. or B.S. degrees in more than thirty areas of study: accounting, American literature, art, athletic training, biology, children's literature, computer information systems, communication, criminal justice, digital media, elementary education, environmental science, exercise science, forensic psychology, geology, health science, history, journalism, management, marketing, mass media, mathematics, music, music education, natural science, physical education, psychology, public relations, secondary education, social work, sociology, Spanish, special education, sports administration, theater arts, and world literature. Associate degrees can be earned in business, communication, computer programming, criminal justice, general studies, or nursing.

Academic Programs

The Castleton curriculum is designed to provide the student with a strong liberal arts background plus the opportunity for career preparation in a specific area. All four-year students are required to complete a core of general education requirements during the four-year degree program. The first year of study can be used by the undecided student to explore various areas of interest. The student with a specific career interest may begin study in the major field as a freshman, although four-year students are not required to formally declare their major until the end of the sophomore year.

Castleton students typically enroll in five courses each semester. The academic calendar consists of two 15-week semesters and three 4-week summer sessions. Grading is traditional, and a pass/no-pass option is available. Internships and field experiences complement many of the academic programs at Castleton and are required in the communication, criminal justice, social work, and education programs.

Students may transfer internally from two-year to four-year programs in business, communication, computer information systems, criminal justice, and general studies. Students who transfer to Castleton after graduating from an accredited two-year college are granted full transfer credit for all academic work up to 64 credits or the number required for the associate degree.

Freshman students achieving at least a 3.5 grade point average in their first year at Castleton are recognized by the Castleton Chapter of Phi Eta Sigma, a national honor society that recognizes freshman scholastic achievement in colleges throughout the country. Outstanding junior and senior scholars are recognized by the Castleton Chapter of Alpha Chi. Pinnacle, the honor society for nontraditional students, honors qualified candidates. There are honor societies in theater arts, education, psychology, and Spanish. Students who have achieved a 4.0 grade point average are named to the President's List of Outstanding Students and those with a 3.5 grade point average or better to the Dean's List.

Academic Facilities

The Calvin Coolidge Library houses a collection of more than 500,000 books, periodicals, microforms, and nonprint media. Access to Castleton's library resources and outside scholarly sources is made possible through numerous online and CD databases; a sophisticated, networked electronic library system; the Internet; and strong consortial relationships within the state of Vermont. An audiovisual media facility provides a wide range of audiovisual equipment, including digital video editing, digital cameras, and presentation equipment.

Castleton's Stafford Academic Center houses the Computing Center, a high-tech multimedia lecture hall, distance learning classrooms, and the Departments of Education, Mathematics, and Nursing.

Glenbrook Gymnasium houses the athletic training room, the Human Performance Center, the swimming pool, two racquetball courts, a new fitness center, and a large indoor activity area.

The Fine Arts Center contains a 500-seat auditorium; facilities for art, drama, dance, and music; and television studios.

The Jeffords Center for Science, which was renovated and expanded in the spring and summer of 2007, houses general classrooms and laboratories, a state-of-the-art auditorium, laboratories for faculty and student research projects, a greenhouse, a computing center, and an astronomical observatory.

There are more than 225 personal computers designated for student use located in labs across the campus.

Costs

Costs for 2007–08 were as follows: tuition for Vermont residents, $7056, and for nonresidents, $15,240. Room and board expenses totaled $6942. There was a student activity fee of $188. The orientation and registration for new students was $195.

Financial Aid

Eighty percent of Castleton's full-time undergraduate students receive financial assistance from federal, state, College, or other sources. Grants, loans, and work-study jobs are available for qualified students. Applicants for financial aid should file the Free Application for Federal Student Aid (FAFSA) form by February 15 of the senior year in high school. All financial aid awards are based on need.

Most Castleton scholarships are awarded as part of the College's Honors Scholarship Program. Amounts range from $1000 to $5000 per year. First-year students who have a combined critical reading and math SAT score of at least 1100 and have a GPA of at least 3.3 on a 4.0 scale are eligible for one of these scholarships. Additional scholarships are available to new students based on certain academic credentials, service to their community, and financial need. There are also special scholarships for students wishing to study music or Spanish.

Faculty

The full-time faculty at Castleton consists of 90 men and women, 94 percent of whom hold terminal degrees in their field. Adjunct faculty members, many of them local businesspeople and members of the professions, complement the efforts of the full-time faculty. The student-faculty ratio is 14:1. Each student has a faculty member as an adviser.

Student Government

The Student Association is the chief vehicle of student government. All students who are registered for 8 or more credit hours are members. Elected representatives hold membership on most College committees, including the Curriculum and Cultural Affairs Committees. Students are also able to develop leadership qualities by participating in the various clubs and other organizations on campus.

Admission Requirements

Applicants are evaluated on the basis of their secondary school records, standardized test scores, and recommendations. Admission is granted to those applicants who have demonstrated their ability and potential to meet the challenges of a postsecondary learning experience.

Application and Information

Students may apply for admission through the Castleton Web site. Under Castleton's rolling admission policy, applications are processed throughout the year, and candidates are notified of the admission decision as soon as their folders are complete. Students are admitted in the fall and spring semesters.

For more information about Castleton State College or to arrange a campus visit, students should contact:

Director of Admissions
Castleton State College
Castleton, Vermont 05735
Phone: 802-468-1213
800-639-8521 (toll-free)
Fax: 802-468-1476
E-mail: info@castleton.edu
Web site: http://www.castleton.edu

Between classes, students gather on the patio near historic Woodruff Hall.

JOHNSON STATE COLLEGE
JOHNSON, VERMONT

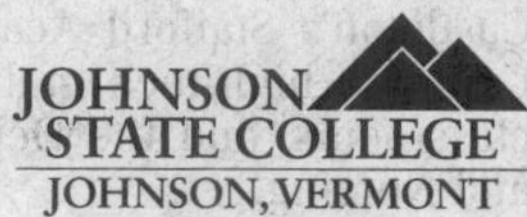

The College

Founded in 1828, Johnson State College (JSC) served as a school for the training of teachers until the 1960s, when it expanded into the liberal arts and the sciences. The current enrollment is more than 1,930 men and women. Sixty-five percent of the College's students are Vermonters; 35 percent are out-of-state and come from more than twenty-three states and ten other countries. The campus has modern facilities, including a state-of-the-art Library and Learning Center, Dewey Campus Center, the beautiful Dibden Center for the Fine and Performing Arts, a visual arts building, an excellent science facility, a health/athletics complex, an on-campus snowboard park, and renovated residence halls. The College is surrounded by 350 acres of meadowland and forest. Located on a hill overlooking the village of Johnson, the campus commands a breathtaking view of the Green Mountains. The College is accredited by the New England Association of Schools and Colleges and is approved by the Vermont State Board of Higher Education.

At the graduate level, the College offers the Master of Arts in Education degree with specializations in applied behavior analysis, curriculum instruction, elementary licensure, gifted and talented, middle school licensure, secondary licensure, and special education. The curriculum instruction track allows students to choose from several strands: content specialist, early childhood, and literacy, as well as individually designed strands that can be negotiated by the student with a faculty adviser. JSC also offers the Master of Arts in counseling and the Master of Fine Arts in studio arts, in conjunction with the Vermont Studio Center.

More than thirty clubs and organizations provide a variety of student activities. These include *Basement Medicine* (the student newspaper), the Dance Ensemble, the radio station (WJSC-FM), and the Outing, Rugby, Snowboarding, Theater, and Writers' Clubs. Varsity athletic competition is available for women in basketball, cross-country running, soccer, softball, tennis, and volleyball and for men in basketball, cross-country running, golf, lacrosse, soccer, and tennis. Many intramural and club sports, including arena flag football, bicycle racing, dodge ball, indoor soccer, rugby, swimming, and Ultimate Frisbee, are also available. Johnson State College's health education/sports complex includes two weight-lifting areas, racquetball courts, a basketball court, gymnasium, swimming pool, training room, climbing wall, and human performance lab. Also on campus are outdoor tennis courts, cross-country running and ski trails, a snowboard park, and large playing fields. The gymnasium and outdoor athletic facilities also provide recreational outlets for many individuals in the campus community. Stearns Hall is currently housing the post office, the Summit Book Store, and a spacious dining room. Johnson State College is planning to renovate Stearns Hall to make it a true 24-hour student center. The College has a Counseling and Health Center. The Dewey Campus Center houses the Dewey Commons Snack Bar, the Advising Center, and a Career Resource Center.

Location

The College is just 20 minutes from Stowe, the ski capital of the East; 45 minutes from Burlington, Vermont's largest city; and 90 minutes from Montreal, Canada. Other attractions near the College are Smugglers' Notch ski area, Jay Peak ski area, Ben & Jerry's Ice Cream Factory, and Lake Champlain. The College can be reached by rail (Amtrak) or air (Burlington International Airport).

Majors and Degrees

Johnson State College offers major academic programs leading to the Bachelor of Arts or Bachelor of Science degree in anthropology/sociology, art, biology: field naturalist, business management, drama and theater, English, environmental sciences/natural resources, health sciences, history, hospitality and tourism management, integrated environmental science, journalism, liberal arts, mathematics, music, musical theater, outdoor education, political science, psychology, and wellness and alternative medicine. The Bachelor of Fine Arts degree is offered in creative writing and studio arts.

The Bachelor of Arts or Bachelor of Science degree leading to state teacher certification is offered in art education (K–12), dance secondary education, elementary education, English secondary education, life sciences (biology) secondary education, mathematics secondary education, music education (K–12), physical education (K–12), physical sciences (chemistry) secondary education, social studies secondary education, and theater arts secondary education.

Associate of Arts or Associate of Science degrees are offered in general studies, management, and technical theater.

Certificate programs leading to business certification in nonprofit management and small business management are offered as well.

Minors are available in adventure education, anthropology/sociology, arts management, biology, business, chemistry, creative writing, dance, environmental education, French, gender studies, history, journalism, literature, mathematics, music, natural resources, political science, prelaw, psychology, Spanish, studio arts, and theater.

Academic Programs

The Johnson State curriculum provides students with a general liberal arts background and the opportunity for career preparation in a specific area. All students in four-year programs are required to complete at least 120 credit hours in the selected program of study. Those studying for the associate degree must complete at least 60 semester hours of credit in the selected program of study. Students may transfer internally from two-year to four-year programs.

Transfer credit is awarded for college courses in which a grade of C– or above was earned. Accepted transfer students receive a credit evaluation.

The academic year consists of fall and spring semesters of fifteen weeks each and a six-week summer session. The College offers courses in the evening and on weekends through the External Degree Program.

Off-Campus Programs

Johnson State College provides internship opportunities in all degree programs, including two semesters of student teaching experience for education majors.

Johnson State College encourages students to experience a global education through study abroad. Opportunities are available through the National Student Exchange and a variety of study-abroad programs. In addition, many JSC programs and faculty members sponsor short-term, international study tours; field research projects; and service-learning opportunities.

Academic Facilities

The 350-acre, hilltop campus houses modern, well-equipped buildings. College facilities include an art gallery, art studios, dance studios, the Visual Arts Center, three computer centers, a library, a student center, the Child Development Center, and the Dibden Center for the Fine and Performing Arts, which contains a theater. The Library and Learning Center contains more than 109,000 volumes, an audiovisual department, microfilm and microfiche units, government documents, periodicals, journals, records, the Vermont Room, the Art Room, the Ellsworth International Room, and the Children's Library. The Babcock Nature Preserve, a 1,000-acre tract of forests and ponds, serves as an outdoor laboratory for scientific and educational research.

Costs

Estimated tuition and fees for the academic year 2008–09 for Vermont residents are $7500 and for nonresidents, $16,000. Room and board expenses are $7581.

Financial Aid

Seventy-six percent of Johnson's students receive financial assistance from federal, state, College, or other sources. Grants, loans, and work-study jobs are available for qualified students. Applicants for financial aid should file the Free Application for Federal Student Aid (FAFSA) by March 1 of the year preceding anticipated enrollment. All financial aid awards are based on need. The College offers renewable academic scholarships for both freshmen and transfers. Special scholarships are also available.

Faculty

The full-time faculty at Johnson consists of 56 men and women, 75 percent of whom hold a Ph.D. or equivalent degree. Adjunct faculty members, many of whom are local professionals, complement the full-time faculty. The student-faculty ratio is 17:1. Each student has a faculty member serving as an academic adviser.

Student Government

The Johnson State College Student Government Association is a vital and active organization that has a strong voice in College affairs. Student representatives are elected to the association, which helps plan curriculum and program developments. The association coordinates student social and cultural activities, including concerts, dances, and numerous clubs.

Admission Requirements

Admission to Johnson State College is granted to applicants who have demonstrated the potential to succeed at the college level. They are evaluated on the basis of their high school transcripts, letters of recommendation, standardized test scores (SAT or ACT), and class rank. The College emphasizes course selection, grades, and participation in extracurricular activities in reviewing applications.

All candidates should successfully complete a college-preparatory program that includes 4 years of high school English, 2 years of mathematics (3 years is recommended), 3 years of social science, and 2 years of science (one course with a laboratory). Applicants who do not qualify for regular admission may receive acceptance to the Transition Year Experience. A campus visit and an interview are strongly recommended.

Application and Information

The College has a rolling admission policy and processes applications throughout the year. However, high school students seeking fall enrollment are encouraged to apply early in their senior year. The College admits first-year and transfer students regardless of their state of residence. Notification dates are also rolling. Students may enter at the beginning of the fall or spring semester.

The student's application file is complete when the following items have been received: a completed application form, a $35 nonrefundable application fee, a transcript from the high school and any colleges previously attended, a writing sample, standardized test scores, and a reference from a teacher, a college adviser, or an employer. Application fees are waived for online applicants. An enrollment deposit of $200 and a $100 housing deposit are required by May 1 or within two weeks of notification of acceptance if the applicant applies after May 1.

For application forms and further information, students should contact:

Penny P. Howrigan
Associate Dean of Enrollment Services
Johnson State College
337 College Hill
Johnson, Vermont 05656
Phone: 802-635-1219
800-635-2356 (toll-free)
Fax: 802-635-1230
E-mail: jscadmissions@jsc.vsc.edu
Web site: http://www.jsc.edu

Mount Mansfield.

LYNDON STATE COLLEGE

LYNDONVILLE, VERMONT

The College

Lyndon State College (LSC), established in 1911 as a one-room teacher-training college, has grown to a fully accredited, comprehensive four-year college, serving more than 1,400 students in liberal arts and professional programs. Fifty-five percent of the 1,400 students at Lyndon are Vermonters; the remainder of the student population is from New England and states throughout the U.S. as well as fifteen countries. The 174-acre campus is located in Lyndonville, Vermont, the heart of the Northeast Kingdom; few campuses in the country can match the sheer beauty of Lyndon State's location.

Lyndon provides two- and four-year degree programs that prepare students for a wide variety of careers and graduate study. The hallmark of a Lyndon education is experience. Lyndon's dedicated faculty members have developed programs that offer a unique blend of experiential, hands-on learning with the traditionally structured lecture/discussion courses to give students optimum career preparation. New students participate in the First-Year Experience, a one- or two-day field trip that serves as an introduction to their major. The students are accompanied by faculty members and upperclassmen from their major and visit sites related to their major. This trip is the students' first of many hands-on, real-life experiences.

LSC is accredited by the New England Association of Schools and Colleges. Lyndon's three degree programs in recreation and ski resort management are accredited by the National Recreation and Park Association.

There are ten residences halls, including the new Rita L. Bole Complex, a 132 apartment-style hall for upperclassmen. Together, the residence halls accommodate more than 730 students. Each residence hall room is equipped with Internet connections, giving each student access to the Web, e-mail, and the Vermont State College network through his or her own personal computer. Also, each room is equipped with cable TV connections and telephone lines. Students who live on campus eat at the Stevens Dining Hall and the Hornet's Nest Snack Bar. All students are allowed to have vehicles on campus.

The dedicated staff provides endless, high-quality support to students. Lyndon's Academic Support Center, Career Planning and Placement Office, Financial Aid Office, Student Life, and Health Services are a few of the key offices that serve the needs and promote the well-being of students.

More than twenty-five clubs and organizations provide a wide variety of student activities that include the campus radio station (91.5 FM The Impulse), the student newspaper (*The Critic*), sports clubs, and numerous social and academic clubs. Lyndon State is in its second year of provisional membership status with NCAA Division III. There are eleven intercollegiate sports. Men compete in baseball, basketball, cross-country, soccer, and tennis; women compete in basketball, cross-country, lacrosse (starting spring 2008), soccer, softball, tennis, and volleyball. Intercollege competitive hockey, rugby, and Nordic and Alpine skiing for men and women are club teams. Lyndon's intramural program attracts the majority of the student body. Lyndon also has a new 6,700-square-foot fitness center, which is available to students and faculty and staff members.

Location

Lyndon State College is situated high on a hillside overlooking magnificent Burke Mountain and the picturesque Passumpsic Valley in the heart of Vermont's scenic Northeast Kingdom. It is located 1 mile west of Lyndonville and 9 miles north of St. Johnsbury and is easily accessible from all points by Interstate 91. The College is a 3-hour drive from Boston and Springfield, Massachusetts, and 2 hours from Montreal.

Facilities for such recreational sports as Alpine and cross-country skiing, snowboarding, hiking, fishing, mountain biking, and swimming are available within minutes of the College.

Majors and Degrees

Lyndon State College offers the Bachelor of Arts or Bachelor of Science degree in interdisciplinary studies (an individually designed program). The Bachelor of Arts degree is offered in digital media, English (journalism and creative writing, literature and cultural studies, secondary education), global studies, graphic design, liberal studies, mathematics (applied mathematics, pure mathematics, secondary education 7–12), psychology, and social sciences (secondary education 7–12). The Bachelor of Science degree is offered in accounting, business administration (computer information systems, e-business), computer information systems (business, meteorology), education (early childhood education, elementary education, secondary education, special education), environmental science, exercise science (athletic training [4+2], physical therapy [3+3], sports management, self-designed), human services, meteorology (American Meteorological Society/graduate school, broadcasting, global information systems, National Weather Service/military, private industry), natural science (secondary education 7–12), physical education K–12, recreation resource and ski resort management (adventure-based program planning/outdoor education, natural resources/GIS mapping and planning, ski resort management), small-business management and entrepreneurship, and television studies/broadcast journalism (broadcast news, broadcast design and production). The Associate of Science degree is offered in business administration, computer science, digital media, geographic information systems/global positioning systems, geographic information systems/meteorology, graphic design, nursing (offered jointly with Castleton State College), television production, and television studies. The Associate of Arts degree is available in general studies.

Lyndon has added a new bachelor's program, music business and industry, for the 2007–08 academic year.

Academic Programs

Lyndon operates on a two-semester calendar and a six-week summer-session schedule. To graduate with a bachelor's degree, a student must complete 122 semester hours of credit and meet College and program requirements. Sixty-two semester hours are required for an associate degree. Each student is tested for competence in writing and mathematics at entry to the College; any deficiencies noted must be made up in noncredit classes during the first two semesters. The College has a general education (distribution) requirement of 42 semester hours.

For two-year programs, students are accepted into a concentration upon admission; for four-year programs, in the fourth semester. Academic departments are responsible for advising and for planning the student's core courses within the concentration. In bachelor's degree programs, most concentrations require at least 42 credits of junior- and senior-level course work. The College requires that 30 of the last 39 hours toward any degree be spent in residence. Leaves of absence are granted to students in good academic standing.

Lyndon recognizes learning acquired from previous experience through an assessment course that documents nontraditional learning. The College offers fieldwork and practicums in most academic programs through the Cooperative Education Office.

Off-Campus Programs

A key component of a Lyndon State education is the variety of opportunities for off-campus study for credit, on either a full-time or part-time basis. Students can apply professional theories and principles through practicums and internships in all majors. For example, students in elementary education participate in a sophomore-year exploratory field experience (a full semester of work blending on-campus study and off-campus experience), a junior-year field experience (two half-days a week), and a full semester of student teaching. Students majoring in psychology or human services complete required fieldwork related to their particular studies at least twice during their upperclass years.

Lyndon grants credit for study in other countries through an approved program such as the Experiment in International Living or the American Institute for Foreign Study.

Academic Facilities

Lyndon State College's Academic Center—located atop the Samuel Read Hall Library—features state-of-the-art academic and computer classrooms and laboratories, including a fully equipped computer laboratory that is linked to the College's expanding computer information network.

The library maintains a collection of more than 110,000 circulating volumes as well as periodicals, audio and video materials, and microfiche collections. The library also participates in the Inter-Library Loan System, which allows students more extensive access to reference materials. The library's electronic catalog allows access to the collections of many other Vermont colleges, the Vermont Department of Libraries, and the University of Vermont. The language and science laboratories, the computer center and laboratories, and the music rooms are available to students for study, experimentation, and practice.

The state-of-the-art meteorology laboratory, staffed by a technician, prepares weather information and forecast information that is broadcast over Vermont radio and television stations. Meteorology students also operate a 24-hour weather-reporting telephone line.

Operated daily by students, LSCTV/News 7 is a noncommercial, public-service television facility that provides local news and educational, cultural, and public-service programs. Radio station WWLR 91.5 FM, The Impulse, is staffed by student volunteers who provide local communities with programs of news, music, and interviews.

Costs

The 2007–08 tuition for Vermont residents was $7056 per year; for nonresidents, it was $15,240. Room and board (twenty-one-meal plan) for one academic year were $7220. Required College fees, including health and accident insurance, totaled $1445. Total expenses for a Vermont resident living on campus were $15,721; for a nonresident, $23,905. Miscellaneous expenses were estimated at $1100. The estimate for these expenses is included in the financial aid budget.

Financial Aid

Financial aid is available in the form of loans, grants, and campus employment under the Federal Work-Study Program. Approximately 80 percent of the student population receives some type of financial aid from institutional and outside sources. Approximately 35 percent of the students are employed by either the Federal Work-Study Program or the College dining hall.

Applicants for aid are required to complete the Free Application for Federal Student Aid (FAFSA). In addition to filing the FAFSA, transfer students are required to have a financial aid transcript completed by the financial aid officer of each college they attended. For a student to be considered an on-time applicant, the FAFSA should be filed in early February in order to reach the College's Financial Aid Office by the March 15 deadline.

Faculty

Lyndon's excellent faculty consists of 59 full-time members and 95 part-time members. The student-faculty ratio is 13:1. The faculty is dedicated fully to undergraduate teaching. Full-time faculty members serve as academic advisers to students and as advisers to student organizations. Student evaluation of teaching is a formal process and is used in personnel decisions. Faculty members participate in dramatic, musical, and intramural athletic activities on campus and in many civic and community organizations.

Student Government

Students play an important role in Lyndon's internal organization. Students actively represent Lyndon on the Vermont State Colleges' Board of Trustees, in the Vermont State Colleges' Student Association, and on many campus committees.

The Student Senate heads the student organizations. It has jurisdiction over all student affairs and is responsible for addressing student issues and concerns, evaluating all campus clubs and organizations, and allocating Student Activities moneys.

Admission Requirements

Each application for admission is evaluated on its individual merits. Applicants for admission are expected to successfully complete a college-preparatory program and rank in at least the upper 50 percent of their graduating class. Recommended secondary school preparation includes 4 years of English and 2 to 3 years each of mathematics, science, and history. Admission decisions for first-year students are determined on the basis of the student's application, a copy of the secondary school transcript, the recommendation of a secondary school guidance counselor or teacher, performance on the ACT or the SAT, and, if possible, a personal interview. Although applicants' scores on the ACT or the SAT are reviewed, more emphasis is placed on transcripts, class rank, and recommendations than on test scores.

Applicants who have completed examinations taken through the College Board's Advanced Placement Program with a grade of 3 or higher are granted both advanced placement and course credit after evaluation by the Registrar's Office. Advanced standing is awarded for successful performance on the tests of the College-Level Examination Program. Lyndon grants up to 60 college credits for scores above the 40th percentile on the five general examinations in English composition, humanities, mathematics, natural science, and social science/history and for scores at or above the minimum score established by the College Board for a wide variety of subject examinations.

Transfer students are encouraged to apply. A minimum 2.0 cumulative grade point average is recommended for consideration. Admission requirements for transfer students are the same as those for freshman applicants, but an official transcript must also be obtained from each college-level institution that the applicant has attended. Transcripts are required even if no credit is being transferred from a particular institution. Transfer credit may be given at Lyndon for courses completed with the equivalent of a grade of C or better at accredited or officially approved institutions.

The College may permit candidates to defer their enrollment for a period of two semesters.

Application and Information

A nonrefundable $36 fee must accompany each application. Lyndon uses a rolling admission system, and applicants may apply and be accepted throughout the year. All applications are given prompt attention, and applicants may expect a decision within two weeks of the date the application process has been completed.

For further information, students should contact:

Bernard Hartshorn
Associate Director of Admissions
Lyndon State College
P.O. Box 919
Lyndonville, Vermont 05851
Phone: 802-626-6413
800-225-1998 (toll-free in New England)
Fax: 802-626-6335
E-mail: admissions@lyndonstate.edu
Web site: http://www.lyndonstate.edu

MARLBORO COLLEGE

MARLBORO, VERMONT

The College

Students come to Marlboro College with a passion for learning and a desire to create a course of study tailored to their own interests. Tucked away in the foothills of Vermont's Green Mountains, Marlboro offers a rigorous liberal arts curriculum that is taught in small classes and advanced one-to-one instruction, called tutorials. Marlboro's goal is to teach students to think clearly and learn independently, develop a command of concise and correct writing, and aspire to academic excellence, all while participating responsibly in a self-governing community. The College's 8:1 student-faculty ratio sparks dynamic exchanges between students and faculty members both in and out of the classroom and fosters a close-knit community in which asking the right questions is more important than knowing the right answers. Two thirds of all Marlboro students go on to graduate study.

Marlboro opened in fall 1947. The campus was originally a cluster of barns and other farm buildings that the first students converted into classrooms and dormitories. The fields and woodlands that make up its rural 350-acre campus are ideal for cross-country skiing and other outdoor activities. The Outdoor Program offers instruction and equipment for canoeing, kayaking, rock climbing, backpacking, and other sports that bring students in touch with the surrounding environment. The soccer team competes with other colleges, and more impromptu volleyball, basketball, softball, and Ultimate Frisbee teams compete intramurally. In addition, Marlboro's broomball (a game akin to hockey) tournament takes place each winter, with prizes for the winning teams and those with the best costumes. Campus committees organize many events both on and off campus, including concerts, lectures, poetry and fiction readings, art shows, and trips to Boston, Montreal, and New York for museum visits, shopping, and baseball games. Other activities that enrich campus life include parties, dances, plays, and film screenings.

Marlboro is—and intends to remain—one of the nation's smallest liberal arts colleges, with some 330 students. Students come from nearly forty states and approximately six other countries. Transfer students—who make up one quarter of each incoming class—bring an important perspective to the campus community. More than 80 percent of all students live in campus housing, which consists of small dormitories (both single-sex and coed), several four-bedroom cottages, and a renovated country inn.

Location

The village of Marlboro, which is 2 miles from the College, consists of a post office, a town clerk's office, and an inn. About 1,200 residents live within the 36-square-mile township. During the summer, the village swells to accommodate the famous Marlboro Music Festival. The town of Brattleboro, 12 miles away, is a lively cultural and commercial center located on the first Vermont exit off Interstate 91. The College is 2 hours by car from Boston and 4 hours from New York City and Montreal.

Majors and Degrees

Marlboro confers the Bachelor of Arts and Bachelor of Science degrees in more than thirty areas of study, which can be combined in an almost limitless number of ways. Students have the license to design their own majors, which allows them to make interdisciplinary connections and pursue individualized research. The College also offers Bachelor of Arts and Bachelor of Science degrees in international studies through its World Studies Program (WSP).

Areas of study offered at Marlboro include American studies, anthropology, art history, Asian studies, astronomy, biochemistry, biology, ceramics, chemistry, classics, computer science, cultural history, dance, development studies (in the WSP), economics, environmental studies, film/video studies, history, international studies, languages, literature, mathematics, music, painting, philosophy, photography, physics, political science, psychology, religion, sculpture, sociology, theater, visual arts, and writing.

Academic Programs

In the first two years, Marlboro students study broadly, discover new interests, and begin to see the connections that lead many to pursue interdisciplinary work. Each new student is paired with a faculty adviser and joins an advising group of sophomores, juniors, and seniors as well as freshmen. Students learn from each other at Marlboro in seminar-style classes.

Marlboro believes that clear writing both reflects and engenders clear thinking. The College, therefore, requires each new student to pass a Clear Writing Requirement within three semesters of enrolling at the College. Designated writing courses, faculty advisers, and student writing tutors all help new students meet the requirement.

Marlboro's Plan of Concentration, more than any other academic component, sets the College apart from other undergraduate programs. Undertaken by all Marlboro students in their junior and senior years, the plan is the collection of related projects and papers that form the final product of the student's academic work at Marlboro. It is an individualized program of classes, research, experiences, one-to-one study, and original thought, driven by the student's interests and academic goals and designed in close collaboration with faculty sponsors. Final evaluation of the student's plan is conducted by her or his faculty advisers and an outside examiner who is a recognized expert in the student's field.

Off-Campus Programs

Students working on the Plan of Concentration often travel abroad or attend other institutions for a period of time to augment their academic work. Marlboro faculty members may help plan these pursuits and frequently aid students in securing internships in academic fields. The College sponsors multiple academic, adventure, and humanitarian trips each year, ranging from community service work in South Carolina and Costa Rica to interdisciplinary research in Cuba, Vietnam, and China.

The World Studies Program is a four-year program leading to a Bachelor of Arts or Bachelor of Science degree in international studies. The program involves intensive study on campus as well as a six- to eight-month internship abroad. In addition, WSP sponsors regular International Nights, which generally include a themed dinner, music from other countries, and lectures or films.

Academic Facilities

Marlboro's academic facilities offer small classrooms and oversized faculty offices for students to meet in small groups and individually with their professors. Facilities are open 24 hours a day, supporting student research and creative explorations include a DNA lab, a state-of-the-art black-and-white/digital darkroom, a digital film-editing studio, two pottery studios, and an astronomical observatory. In the last five years, Marlboro's ongoing campus renewal project has doubled the size of the library and added a suite-style dorm. The new Rudolf and Irene Serkin Performing Arts Center has been added to offer more than 10,000 square feet for music, dance, and drama rehearsals and performances. In 2008, the campus will add a new Total Health Center to provide additional space for medical and psychological counseling services and a fitness room. Renovations on one of the original farmhouses will also be completed to provide more student housing.

Costs

Tuition and fees at Marlboro were $29,700 for the 2007–08 academic year. Room and board costs were $8860.

Financial Aid

No one should refrain from applying to Marlboro because of perceived inability to meet costs. More than 80 percent of all Marlboro students receive financial help. The College is committed to helping any student who qualifies for admission assemble the financial resources necessary to attend, and need is not a factor in the admission decision. Merit scholarships are also available.

Faculty

Marlboro's 40 full-time faculty members are committed first and foremost to teaching, rather than to publishing or research. The lively exchange of ideas between teachers and students is the cornerstone of the Marlboro curriculum.

Student Government

All students and faculty and staff members are equal members of the College Town Meeting. Since the opening of the College in 1947, the community has come together every few weeks to debate and decide budget initiatives, College policies, and other issues. A board of Selectpersons, elected by the College community, serves the College's interests and is responsible for drafting Town Meeting rules and regulations. Students serve with faculty and staff members on more than thirty College committees, including those that make admissions and faculty-hiring decisions. Other important committees include the social committee and the Community Court, which is responsible for enforcing campus regulations.

Admission Requirements

The Admissions Committee seeks students with intellectual promise; a high degree of motivation, self-discipline, personal stability, and social concern; and the ability and desire to contribute to the College community. All applicants are considered without regard to race, creed, sex, sexual orientation, national or ethnic origin, age, or disability. Transfers and older or returning students are encouraged to apply.

Like most colleges, Marlboro requires students to submit a variety of documentation, from high school transcripts to teacher recommendations. Unlike most colleges, however, Marlboro's review process is conducted by an Admissions Committee composed of students and faculty and staff members. This committee evaluates each applicant as a unique individual who possesses qualities that are not necessarily quantifiable.

A campus visit is strongly recommended for all applicants, and interviews are encouraged. Many campus interviews are conducted by faculty members in the applicant's area of interest. Marlboro does not use a formulaic approach in making admission decisions. Applicants are encouraged to demonstrate their particular strengths; the goal is a successful match between the student and the College.

Application and Information

New students and transfers are admitted for either the spring or fall semester. Applicants for the fall semester have a choice of three admission plans. The early decision plan is for those students who have thoroughly researched Marlboro and for whom Marlboro is the first choice. Applicants should be aware that early decision is binding. The deadline for submitting application materials is December 1, and applicants are notified by December 15. Early action, a nonbinding plan, has a deadline of February 1. These applicants are notified of a decision on February 15. The recommended regular admission deadline is March 1.

An application for admission must include a completed Common Application form and a Marlboro College Supplement Form with Marlboro-specific essay, a $50 fee, complete transcripts from all secondary schools and colleges, SAT or ACT scores, an analytical writing sample, a "Why Marlboro?" personal statement, and two recommendations. The Admissions Committee welcomes applications from homeschooled students. In lieu of a high school transcript, homeschooled students must submit a detailed description of their curriculum.

Office of Admissions
Marlboro College
2582 South Road
Marlboro, Vermont 05344-0300
Phone: 802-257-4333
800-343-0049 (toll-free)
Fax: 802-451-7555
E-mail: admissions@marlboro.edu
Web site: http://www.marlboro.edu

The center of the campus at Marlboro College.

NORWICH UNIVERSITY

NORTHFIELD, VERMONT

The University

Norwich University was established in 1819 as the first private military college in America. It was at Norwich that the idea of the citizen-soldier developed and eventually evolved into the Reserve Officer Training Corps (ROTC) program. Norwich was the first private college to offer civil engineering, and many University alumni were involved in the construction of the nation's continental railway system. In 1974, Norwich became one of the first military colleges to admit women into its Corps of Cadets, preceding the Federal Academies.

Norwich University offers a diverse blend of disciplines, teaching styles, and viewpoints. Students enrolled in the Corps of Cadets have a more disciplined, challenging, and structured path through college, while their civilian student classmates lead a more traditional collegiate lifestyle. However, both groups are coeducational and attend classes and participate in sports and other activities together.

In keeping with its mission, Norwich provides opportunities for all of its students to develop leadership skills with a strong commitment to community service. Both groups gain skills such as leadership, honor, and integrity, which are required to be successful in today's job market. These two diverse groups of students are very different and yet have much in common—they are Norwich.

Norwich University has an enrollment of 2,000 students from more than forty states and twenty countries. The University's minority enrollment is consistently higher (by percentage) than that of any other Vermont university or college.

The athletic facilities at Norwich are comparable to the best at any of New England's Division III universities. The main athletic complex, Andrews Hall, features a gymnasium, a modernized athletic training room, an equipment room, laundry facilities, five racquetball courts, and locker rooms. Kreitzberg Arena is a multipurpose facility with a seating capacity of 1,500 and a fully equipped weight room. It was here that the University's men's hockey team won the Division III National Championship in 2003. Plumley Armory has a huge gym as well as an indoor track, weight and aerobics rooms, a wrestling room, and an indoor swimming pool. Shapiro Field House has 50,000 square feet of floor space and includes a 200-meter indoor track, tennis courts, a climbing wall, and a high-ropes course. The 1,200-acre campus includes numerous playing fields for baseball, football, rugby, soccer, and softball. Norwich also has a paintball course, a rappel tower, an obstacle and confidence course, and an indoor rifle range.

Norwich has the only professional five-year Master of Architecture program in northern New England. The University also offers online graduate degrees in business administration, diplomacy, information security assurance, and justice administration.

Location

Norwich University is located in the heart of the Green Mountains of Vermont, right in the middle of ski country. Some of the nation's most popular resorts, such as Stowe, Sugarbush, and Killington, are located within an hour's drive. Vermont is world renowned as one of America's most beautiful states. Nature's playground is just outside the dorm room—skiing, snowboarding, telemark skiing, cross-country skiing, snowshoeing, rock climbing, hiking, mountain biking, canoeing, kayaking, and more are available.

The University campus is located in the small town of Northfield, Vermont. Northfield is 10 miles south of the state capital of Montpelier and is 50 miles from Burlington, the largest city in Vermont. Both Montpelier and Burlington are cultural centers for the arts. Burlington International Airport is within an hour's drive. In addition, the cities of Boston and Montreal are only a 3-hour drive from the campus.

Majors and Degrees

Norwich offers students more than thirty academic majors from which to choose. The Bachelor of Arts degree is awarded in communications; criminal justice; English; history; international studies; peace, war, and diplomacy studies; political science; and psychology. The Bachelor of Science degree is awarded in accounting, athletic training, architecture, biochemistry, biology, chemistry, civil/environmental engineering, communications, computer engineering, computer information systems, computer science, computer security and information assurance, economics, electrical engineering, engineering management, environmental science, geology, international studies, management, mathematics, mechanical engineering, physical education, physics, sports medicine, and studies in war and peace. Teacher licensure, prelaw, premedical, and dental programs are also available.

Academic Programs

Norwich University is dedicated to the discovery, preservation, and dissemination of knowledge and the search for truth. Norwich is distinctive in that it maintains a strong emphasis on the development of leadership in both military and civilian pursuits and in providing for the educational needs of students. The University's mission is to foster in each student the growth of self-discipline, personal integrity, social responsibility, physical fitness, respect for law, and intellectual ability essential for full and effective participation in a free society.

For students enrolling in the Corps of Cadets, six semesters of Reserve Officer Training Corps are required. Norwich is considered the birthplace of ROTC; therefore, all four service branches can be found on campus. Prior to their junior year, cadets may elect to contract with their ROTC program and be considered upon graduation for a commission as officers in the Army, Navy, Air Force, or Marine Corps. Cadets not on an ROTC scholarship are not required to join the military.

Students typically take an average of five classes per semester. Each semester is sixteen weeks long, with holiday breaks at Thanksgiving, Christmas, and New Year's and in March during spring break. The academic year normally begins the last week in August and ends after the first week in May.

Academic Facilities

The academic facilities at Norwich are among the finest in New England. Completed in 1997, the math and science building was designed to keep classes small. Its labs hold no more than 16 students, and all of the classrooms are hard-wired to allow for multimedia presentations. Students can find numerous computer labs across the campus, and the Kreitzberg Library offers students plenty of resources, space, and technology. Students may research Norwich's facilities on the University's Web site.

Costs

For 2007–08, tuition and fees were $11,607 per semester. The cost of room and board was $4261 per semester. Books and personal expenses averaged $900 per semester. Cadets paid a one-time uniform fee of $1440.

Financial Aid

Most families assume they cannot afford a private college education and fall victim to "sticker shock," but a Norwich education is often as affordable as a local state college. Last year, 92 percent of Norwich students, with an average family income of $44,000, shared in more than $35 million of financial aid from all sources, including ROTC scholarships. This included an aggressive need-based financial aid program that enabled deserving students to secure a private education at Norwich.

Norwich awards academic scholarships on a competitive basis to students who are placed in the top 10 or 20 percent of their high school class. These scholarships can pay from 33 to 50 percent of the student's tuition for four years. Students are required to maintain a specified GPA in order to renew the scholarship each year. Students whose high schools do not rank should contact the University admissions office and ask to speak with a counselor.

Norwich also offers a vast array of leadership and merit scholarships based on a student's record of demonstrated leadership as well as their participation in sports, community and school organizations, employment, volunteer work, and other extracurricular activities. Students who bring a three- or four-year ROTC scholarship to Norwich are eligible for the General I. D. White Scholarship, which covers the cost of room and board. Students who are interested in applying for an ROTC scholarship should visit the individual ROTC detachment's Web page on the Norwich University Web site.

Faculty

The student-faculty ratio is 14:1. Faculty members are full-time instructors with advanced degrees; 80 percent hold a doctorate. Small classes help promote a close relationship between faculty members and students. Students are assigned faculty advisers within each academic division.

Student Government

The Norwich University Corps of Cadets is a military organization made up of and led by cadets under the supervision of the Commandant of Cadets. Members of the Corps and student body preside over the University Honor Council. The University's honor code binds all Norwich students. Members of the Corps and student body also participate on the Student Affairs Committee, whose members include the Dean of Students, members of the faculty, and the Senior Vice President and Commandant of Cadets. This committee serves as the voice of the Norwich community and provides a channel of communication for change.

Admission Requirements

Admission to Norwich is based on a review of the applicant's academic record, personal essay, letters of recommendation, and extracurricular activities. Students at Norwich are heavily involved in community service and leadership development activities. Applicants should be able to demonstrate participation in activities both inside and outside of their high school.

Norwich is looking for students who want to become leaders, serve others, and give back to their communities. While the admissions office uses a rolling admissions system (meaning applications may be submitted at any time), there is a priority deadline of March 1. Students applying for admission or financial aid after March 1 are admitted on a space-available basis.

Application and Information

Students can visit the University's Web site or contact the University for more information.

Dean of Enrollment Management
Norwich University
27 I. D. White Avenue
Northfield, Vermont 05663
Phone: 800-468-6679 (toll-free)
Fax: 802-485-2032
E-mail: nuadm@norwich.edu
Web site: http://www.norwich.edu

A view of Norwich University's campus.

COLLEGE DATA CENTER • VERMONT

SAINT MICHAEL'S COLLEGE

COLCHESTER, VERMONT

The College

Saint Michael's College is a residential, Catholic liberal arts college in Vermont where 2,000 undergraduates learn to make the world a better place.

Saint Michael's is among the elite ranks of only 270 colleges and universities nationwide allowed to host a prestigious Phi Beta Kappa chapter on campus. The superb faculty members are committed first and foremost to teaching and are known for challenging students to reach higher than they ever thought possible. With a student-faculty ratio of just 12:1, students are ensured personal attention from their professors both in class (lively First-Year Seminars set the interactive tone) and out of class. Because of the holistic approach, Saint Michael's graduates are the beneficiaries of an education that prepares them not only for their first jobs, but also for entire careers.

Service to the community and to all humankind is a vibrant part of student life, reflecting the heritage of service of the Edmundite priests who founded Saint Michael's—the one and only Edmundite college in the world—in 1904. Today, more than 70 percent of the student body actively pursues community service projects through Mobilization of Volunteer Efforts (M.O.V.E.), reflecting a unique passion for social justice issues on campus. In the classroom, ethical and moral considerations always complement intellectual discourse. Also, students can find spiritual engagement through the extensive programming offered by the Office of Edmundite Campus Ministry.

With nearly 100 percent of the students living on campus (with guaranteed housing for four years), the 24/7 living and learning environment means that exceptional teaching extends beyond the classroom, building lifelong bonds among the College's students and faculty and staff members. The remarkable sense of community on campus is fueled by the size of the student body and the supportive learning environment, which compels students to get involved in campus organizations, take risks, and think differently. Global perspectives enrich the atmosphere through the thriving study-abroad programs and the presence of the Applied Linguistics Department, one of the nation's oldest English language institutes.

Location

Saint Michael's is situated less than 3 miles from Burlington, Vermont's largest city and a vibrant college town that is home to the 14,000 students enrolled in five local colleges and universities. In addition to the shops, restaurants, and cafés of the Church Street Marketplace and a lively local music scene, Burlington offers great opportunities for hands-on learning through internships. Vermont, known for its natural beauty, environmentalism, and year-round recreational activities, inspires many students to take advantage of some of the best skiing in the East through a relationship with Smugglers' Notch ski resort—a program that provides an all-access season pass to any Saint Michael's student in good academic standing—and through the College's renowned Wilderness Program.

Saint Michael's enjoys a uniquely accessible location. Burlington International Airport is only a 10-minute drive from the campus. In addition, an Amtrak station is in nearby Essex Junction and a Greyhound bus station is in Burlington; both are within a 15-minute drive of the campus.

Majors and Degrees

Saint Michael's College offers bachelor's degrees in the following areas: accounting, American studies, art, biochemistry, biology, business administration, chemistry, classics, computer science, economics, elementary education, engineering, English, environmental science, French, gender/women's studies, history, information systems, journalism, mathematics, music, philosophy, physical science, physics, political science, psychology, religious studies, sociology, Spanish, and theater. In addition, advising programs for premedicine, prelaw, predentistry, and pre–veterinary studies are available. Secondary education licensure is also available in several subject areas.

A special 3+2 engineering program is offered in conjunction with Clarkson University (Potsdam, New York) and the University of Vermont (Burlington, Vermont) for students interested in combining a liberal arts background with engineering. A 4+1 M.B.A. program is offered in conjunction with Clarkson University. An English as a second language program is available for international students. Saint Michael's also offers minors in many subject areas, some of which are interdisciplinary. Environmental studies, global studies, marketing, and peace and justice are just some of the minors offered.

Academic Programs

Saint Michael's academic year consists of two semesters and a summer session. The College's focus is on undergraduate instruction, and its small classes support this primary emphasis. All students must complete a liberal studies core curriculum, which includes course work in the following areas: social sciences, organizational studies, natural and mathematical sciences, humanities, religious studies, philosophy, and an artistic experience. Students must also demonstrate writing and foreign language proficiency. In addition to fulfilling these requirements, students must complete the degree requirements for one of the majors listed above or for an approved combination of those majors.

Off-Campus Programs

Many students enhance their academic work with an internship related to their career goals and major. Internships are available both locally and in other selected areas around the U.S. and abroad. Sites have included scientific research laboratories, brokerage houses, hospitals, schools, newspapers, and accounting firms.

Study-abroad programs are available to students in most majors. Programs and locations are selected by the student in consultation with the Director of Study Abroad.

Unique Saint Michael's programs include study-abroad experiences at University of the Americas, Mexico; College of Ripon and York St. John, England; Kansai Gaidai University, Japan; and a Washington, D.C., semester program. In recent years, many students have studied abroad in locations such as Australia, Botswana, China, France, Ghana, Ireland, Italy, Nepal, Samoa, and Spain.

Academic Facilities

The Jeremiah Durick Library holds 227,000 volumes, 110 research databases, access to articles from more than 25,000 online journals, and 10,000 electronic books, maps, videos, and other items. Students in all majors are able to take short courses in computer applications. Although most students bring their own computers, students have access to more than 120 computers connected to the College's campuswide information technology network. This network provides access to PC applications, including Microsoft Windows XP Professional, the Internet, e-mail, and the College library. Computer hookups are available in all residence hall rooms. Wireless access is available in the Durick Library, Alliot Student Center, and select academic buildings.

Cheray Science Center has facilities for the study of biochemistry, biology, chemistry, environmental science, and physics. Generous grants in recent years have provided state-of-the-art research equipment that is always available to undergraduates.

Saint Edmund's Hall, an impressive academic complex, includes media labs, psychology labs, computer facilities, and language labs, in addition to traditional classroom and lecture hall space.

Costs

The 2007–08 tuition and residence fee was $37,405. The residence fee includes housing and meals and is based on a standard double room and a standard meal plan. Housing options on campus include traditional residence halls, apartment-style housing, theme housing, and suite-style housing. Some science, journalism, language, and art courses require laboratory fees. Book, personal, and travel expenses vary according to course selection and individual needs.

Financial Aid

Approximately 90 percent of admitted students receive financial aid in the form of loans, grants, and work-study dollars. Students must file the FAFSA by February 15 for fall-semester enrollment.

Faculty

The undergraduate faculty at Saint Michael's consists of 150 full-time professors. Ninety-four percent of tenured and tenure-track faculty members have the doctoral or terminal degree in their field, and many have been recipients of grants, awards, and honors in recent years. While undergraduate instruction is the focus of the College, faculty members are encouraged to remain abreast of developments in their field through research and publication, often facilitated through sabbaticals.

Student Government

The Student Association (SA), an active and important part of campus life, is an elected body of students that authorizes and funds most other student activities and organizations. Representatives from the SA sit on many campuswide committees, including the Curriculum Committee and various committees of the Board of Trustees.

Admission Requirements

Successful applicants to Saint Michael's typically rank in the top 25 percent of their high school class and have a strong college-preparatory background. Students should have completed 16 units of courses in English, foreign language, mathematics, science, and social science. SAT or ACT scores are required. For reference, the average SAT score last year ranged between 1590 and 1890, and the average ACT score ranged between 25 and 26. In addition, students should submit a counselor recommendation and any teacher recommendations they choose. Transfer applicants must submit transcripts of all college work in addition to the information required of first-year applicants.

Application and Information

Saint Michael's offers an Early Action admission program deadline of either November 1 or December 1, as well as a Regular Action deadline of February 1. Students should consult the Web site for application deadlines and information. Candidates for the fall semester are notified of their admission decision on or before April 1. A limited number of students may be admitted to the spring semester and should have their applications in by November 1. The College adheres to the Candidates Reply Date of May 1 for the fall semester.

For further information, students should contact:

Office of Admission
Saint Michael's College
One Winooski Park, Box 7
Colchester, Vermont 05439
Phone: 800-762-8000 (toll-free)
Fax: 802-654-2906
E-mail: admission@smcvt.edu
Web site: http://www.smcvt.edu

Students enjoy a sunny day on campus, with the Durick Library in the background.

UNIVERSITY OF VERMONT
BURLINGTON, VERMONT

The University

The University of Vermont, or UVM (from the Latin name Universitas Viridis Montis, which means University of the Green Mountains), is in its third century of educational excellence.

Founded in 1791, the University of Vermont is the fifth-oldest university in New England (after Harvard, Yale, Dartmouth, and Brown) and among the twenty oldest institutions of higher learning in the nation. UVM was one of the first universities to earn a chapter of Phi Beta Kappa and, in 1875 and 1877, became the first to admit women and African Americans, respectively, to this national honor society.

A doctoral-degree-granting research university, UVM enrolls students from a variety of geographical, social, economic, ethnic, and personal backgrounds. The University of Vermont deliberately seeks students with such diverse backgrounds, with approximately 36 percent of the student population coming from Vermont and 64 percent drawn from throughout the United States and around the world. Each of the 9,040 undergraduate students contributes his or her unique experiences to enrich this diverse campus community.

UVM is composed of seven undergraduate colleges and schools: the College of Agriculture and Life Sciences, the College of Arts and Sciences, the College of Education and Social Services, the College of Engineering and Mathematical Sciences, the College of Nursing and Health Sciences, the School of Business Administration, and The Rubenstein School of Environment and Natural Resources. In addition, there are the Graduate College, Honors College, and the College of Medicine. The Graduate College offers seventy master's degree programs and twenty doctoral programs in a variety of fields, including agriculture, business, education, engineering, foreign languages, health sciences, natural resources, physical and biological sciences, psychology, and social sciences. A Doctor of Medicine is also offered.

In the first two years, students are required to live in one of the thirty-six residence halls, with options including small and large housing complexes and historic older buildings as well as modern residence halls. Many students opt for theme-based housing.

More than 100 student organizations are currently recognized by the Student Government Association. These include a broad range of academic, media-based, and recreational options as well as arts, religious, cultural, and political organizations.

UVM fields nine men's and eleven women's NCAA Division I athletic teams. More than fifty intramural and club sports are available to all UVM undergraduates.

Location

UVM is located in Burlington, Vermont, within a county of approximately 146,000. The University's main campus sits on a hill overlooking the city, Lake Champlain, and the Green Mountains. Because of the natural beauty of its surrounding area and its many sporting and entertainment opportunities, Burlington has been named one of the nation's "Big Ten" college towns by Edward B. Fiske in his book *The Best Buys in College Education.*

Majors and Degrees

The University of Vermont offers ninety undergraduate majors leading to Bachelor of Arts and Bachelor of Science degrees.

The College of Agriculture and Life Sciences offers the following majors: animal science, biochemistry, biological sciences, community and international development, community entrepreneurship, dietetics, ecological agriculture, environmental sciences, environmental studies, microbiology, molecular genetics, nutrition and food sciences, plant biology (B.A. and B.S. options), public communication, self-designed, sustainable landscape horticulture, and undeclared.

The College of Arts and Sciences offers the following majors: anthropology, art history, art studio, Asian studies, biochemistry, biological sciences, biology (B.A. option), Canadian studies, chemistry (B.A. and B.S. options), classical civilization, communication science, computer science, economics, English, environmental sciences, environmental studies, European studies, film and television studies, French, geography, geology (B.A. and B.S. options), German, Greek, history, individually designed, Italian studies, Latin, Latin American studies, mathematics, music (B.A. and B.Mus. options), philosophy, physics (B.A. and B.S. options), plant biology (B.A. and B.S. options), political science, psychology (B.A. and B.S. options), religion, Russian, Russian and Eastern European studies, sociology, Spanish, theater, undeclared, women's and gender studies, and zoology (B.A. and B.S. options).

The College of Education and Social Services offers the following majors: art (B.S.A.E.), early childhood education (P–3 and preschool; P–3 leads to the B.S.E.D.), early childhood special education, elementary education (K–6 and reading options leading to the B.S.E.D.), family and consumer sciences, human development and family studies, middle-level education, music education (B.S.M.S.), physical education, secondary education (English, language, mathematics, science, and social science options leading to the B.S.E.D.), self-designed majors, social work, and undeclared.

The College of Engineering and Mathematics offers the following majors: civil engineering (B.S.C.E.), computer science (B.S.C.S.), computer science information systems (B.S.), electrical engineering (B.S.E.E.), engineering management (B.S.E.M.), environmental engineering (B.S.), mathematics (B.S.M.), mechanical engineering (B.S.M.E.), statistics (B.S.M.), and undeclared.

The School of Business Administration offers the business administration major (B.S.B.A.). During their senior year, business administration majors must complete one of the following concentrations: accounting, entrepreneurship, finance, human resource management, international management, management and the environment, management information systems, marketing, production and operations management, or a self-designed concentration.

The Rubenstein School of Environment and Natural Resources offers the following majors leading to the B.S. degree: environmental sciences, environmental studies, forestry, natural resources, recreation management, undeclared, and wildlife and fisheries biology.

The College of Nursing and Health Sciences offers the following Bachelor of Science degree majors: athletic training, exercise and movement science, medical laboratory science, nuclear medicine technology, nursing, and radiation therapy. Graduates of this Bachelor of Science degree program are eligible for registered nurse (RN) licensure.

An accelerated B.S./D.V.M. program with Tufts School of Veterinary Medicine is available. There are also 3+3 and 4+3 programs offered for guaranteed admission to the doctoral program in physical therapy for entering first-year students. The University also offers curricula and advising for predental, prelaw, premedical, and preveterinary students.

Academic Programs

The University's academic calendar consists of two semesters (fall and spring), with extensive summer courses also available. Students are classified based on progress toward meeting degree requirements in terms of credit hours earned as follows: first year, fewer than 27 credit hours; sophomore, 27 to fewer than 57 credit hours; junior, 57 to fewer than 87 credit hours; senior, 87 or more credit hours. A total of 122 credit hours are needed for graduation for most bachelor's programs at UVM. The number varies, however; some programs, such as those in the College of Engineering and Mathematics, require as many as 130 credit hours.

General requirements are designed by the specific departments within the colleges and schools. In addition to the course requirements of the particular curriculum, students entering in the fall 2008 semester must also fulfill the general requirements of 2 credits in physical education and two courses (6 credits) in race and culture. Academic advising is facilitated through faculty members who are assigned to incoming students. These faculty members assist the student with academic planning and course registration. A student remains under the guidance of this adviser until a major has been selected, at which time a department adviser is assigned.

Off-Campus Programs

The University offers an array of study-abroad programs in Africa, Asia, Canada, Central and South America, Eastern and Western Europe, and Oceania through its Office of International Education as well as in conjunction with other colleges and universities.

Academic Facilities

Facilities at the University of Vermont include state-of-the-art laboratories serving the biological, health, physical, natural, and engineering sciences; a major medical center/teaching hospital on campus; a premier lakeside research center and vessel dedicated to aquatic studies; four research farms serving veterinary/animal, horticultural, and food production sciences; nine University-managed natural areas (including the summit of Mr. Mansfield) engaging students in natural resource and environment-related studies; Royall Tyler Theatre, Redstone Music Recital Hall, and Ira Allen Chapel, serving vibrant campus performing arts programs; and the Robert Hull Fleming museum, featuring rotating exhibitions and a superb collection of classic and contemporary works of art and ethnographic materials.

The main campus, where most classes are taught, features the stately brick and stone buildings and classic architecture of a historic New England university. The "Redstone" and "East/Athletic" sections of campus have a more contemporary feel, with modern buildings and views of the mountains and Lake Champlain. Many residential complexes and athletic facilities are located in these areas of campus.

UVM libraries include Bailey/Howe, the largest library in Vermont; Dana Medical Library; and Cook Physical Sciences Library. Holdings include more than 1.39 million texts and serial files, 1.1 million government documents, 20,000 serial subscriptions, 1.9 million microforms, significant manuscripts and archival materials, and graphic, cartographic, audio, and film materials. Library users also have access to 240 online databases and full-text resources and access to more than 800 e-journals.

Costs

Tuition and fees for the 2007–08 school year were $26,306 for out-of-state students and $10,422 for Vermont residents. Room and board average approximately $8000. Miscellaneous personal expenses, including books and supplies, are in addition to these costs.

Financial Aid

More than half of UVM's students receive financial aid. Awards are based on need as determined by the Free Application for Federal Student Aid (FAFSA). An applicant's financial aid award may include University and federal grant funds, on-campus employment, and student loans. More than one third of admitted students are offered merit scholarship assistance.

Financial assistance has no bearing on admission to the University.

Faculty

The University's student-faculty ratio of 15:1 enables faculty members to be accessible to students. UVM's faculty is composed of very distinguished scholars, 88 percent of whom hold a terminal degree in their specific field of interest.

Student Government

The Student Government Association, the primary student governing organization, assumes responsibility for voicing student concerns and interest in the political activities of the University community. It recognizes and funds more than 100 student organizations.

Admission Requirements

Prospective first-year students must present at least 16 high school units, including a minimum of 4 years of English, 3 years of mathematics up to Algebra 2, 3 years of social sciences, 2 years of the same foreign language, and 2 years of natural or physical science, including at least 1 year of lab science; most successful applicants present above this minimum. Some areas of study have additional requirements. In addition to the required and recommended courses, the overall strength and challenge of a student's course load is evaluated.

Qualification for admission is determined on the basis of secondary school record, rank in graduating class, recommendations, writing ability, strength of preparation in the area chosen as a major, and scores on the SAT or ACT.

Admission is competitive. Thirty-five percent of admitted students rank in the top 10 percent of their graduating class; 72 percent rank in the top quarter.

Transfer students must meet all entrance requirements mentioned above. Candidates must send an official transcript from each postsecondary school attended. SAT and ACT results are not required for transfers.

Application and Information

Applications and supporting materials for first-year fall admission should be completed and on file by January 15 (November 1 for early action). Transfer students seeking fall admission should apply by April 1. First-year and transfer students seeking admission for the spring semester should apply by November 1. The nonrefundable application fee is $45. The Common Application is the primary application form and must be submitted with the UVM Supplement.

The University welcomes applications from all interested students regardless of race, color, religion, sexual orientation, age, disability, nationality, or sex. Prospective first-year and transfer students interested in applying for admission in either January or September can receive application forms by contacting:

Admissions Office
University of Vermont
194 South Prospect Street
Burlington, Vermont 05401-3596
Phone: 802-656-3370
Fax: 802-656-8611
E-mail: admissions@uvm.edu
Web site: http://www.uvm.edu/admissions/undergraduate

VERMONT TECHNICAL COLLEGE

RANDOLPH CENTER, VERMONT

The College

Founded in 1866, Vermont Technical College's (VTC) main campus is situated on a hilltop in Randolph Center, Vermont, in the heart of the Green Mountains. The College also has campuses in Williston, Bennington, and Brattleboro, Vermont—plus a network of extended nursing campuses statewide. Vermont Technical College is the only technical college in the Vermont State Colleges system. Most of the 1,453 students enrolled come from Vermont and the other New England states.

Through its bachelor, associate, and certificate programs, the College provides students with a broad-based practical education. As a result, Vermont Tech graduates are prepared to work effectively in a variety of positions that support the activities of engineers, scientists, and other professionals. Degrees offered in such allied health fields as nursing, dental hygiene, and respiratory therapy prepare students to assume medical positions operating on the frontline of patient care.

There are twenty-two major buildings on the 544-acre main campus, including a Student Health and Physical Education (SHAPE) facility with a double-court gymnasium, a six-lane indoor pool, and two racquetball courts. A major addition to the SHAPE facility is now underway. A Campus Center addition is planned to include expanded fitness and weight rooms, a new dining area, and a large student lounge. The addition is set to open in August 2007. The four residence halls can house 567 students. Every student room has connections for direct access to the campuswide computer network, telephone service, and cable TV lines.

Campus life at Vermont Tech includes sports, recreation, social events, and community-service learning opportunities. The Student Life Office arranges weekly activities and social events and provides students with support and counseling. There are many student clubs, from the student-run radio station WVTC-FM to student chapters of professional organizations. There is also an on-campus ski hill where students can snowboard and ski after classes conclude for the day.

Students enthusiastically participate in the College's nine varsity and twenty-five intramural sports for men and women. Fall varsity sports include men's baseball; men's and women's cross-country, golf, and soccer; and women's volleyball. In the winter, the men's and women's basketball teams take the court. In the spring, the baseball and golf teams swing into action for their "second season," and the men's volleyball team plays its schedule. Varsity athletic programs are certainly on the rise at Vermont Tech. The College has expanded from six to nine varsity athletic programs over the past two years. Additional programs under consideration are varsity tennis, softball, and Nordic skiing.

Vermont Tech maintains national affiliations with the National Association of Intercollegiate Athletics (NAIA) and the United States Collegiate Athletic Association (USCAA), thereby offering its athletes two opportunities for postseason national championship competition. Vermont Tech athletes compete in the Sunrise Conference (NAIA) and the Yankee Small College Conference (YSCC). The College has a rich history of athletic success with many conference championships in various sports to its credit. The men's basketball team has earned a coveted spot in the USCAA's Elite Eight national basketball championship tournament in each of the past two years. Both the men's and women's basketball teams achieved top ten USCAA national ranking during the 2005–06 and 2006–07 seasons.

The College is accredited by the New England Association of Schools and Colleges. In addition, the following degree programs are accredited by the Technology Accreditation Commission of the Accreditation Board for Engineering and Technology, Inc. (TAC of ABET): architectural and building engineering technology, architectural engineering technology, civil and environmental engineering technology, computer engineering technology, electrical engineering technology, electromechanical engineering technology, and mechanical engineering technology. The veterinary technology program is accredited by the American Veterinary Medical Association as a program for educating veterinary technicians. Practical nursing programs are approved by the Vermont Board of Nursing and accredited by the National League for Nursing Accrediting Commission (NLNAC). The associate degree program in nursing is approved by the Vermont Board of Nursing. The dental hygiene program is accredited by the American Dental Association Commission on Dental Accreditation (CODA), and the respiratory therapy program is accredited by the Committee on Accreditation of Respiratory Care Programs (CoARC).

Location

Vermont Tech's location is rural, but far from isolated—exit 4 of Interstate 89 is just 1 mile away. For day-to-day needs, the nearby village of Randolph offers a variety of shops and restaurants as well as a movie theater, a bowling alley, and the Chandler Music Hall. For special shopping and events, Burlington and Montpelier, Vermont, and Hanover, New Hampshire, are within an hour's drive. Boston and Montreal are just 3 hours away. There is convenient bus service from Randolph, and Amtrak's Vermonter stops in Randolph twice daily.

Students enjoy the variety of recreational activities available to them in Vermont. Some of the top ski resorts in the East are less than an hour from the campus. Students can also hike on the Appalachian Trail, canoe on numerous lakes and rivers, camp in the Green Mountain National Forest, and bike on the miles of country roads.

Majors and Degrees

Vermont Technical College offers a Bachelor of Science degree in architectural engineering technology, business technology and management, computer engineering technology, dental hygiene, electromechanical engineering technology, equine studies, information technology, software engineering, and sustainable design and technology.

Vermont Tech offers five programs leading to the Associate in Engineering degree: aeronautical engineering technology, civil and environmental engineering technology, computer engineering technology, electrical engineering technology, and mechanical engineering technology.

Programs leading to the Associate in Applied Science degree are agribusiness management technology, architectural and building engineering technology, automotive technology, business technology and management, construction practice and management, dairy farm management technology, diesel power technology, fire science, general engineering technology, landscape development and ornamental horticulture, telecommunications technology, and veterinary technology.

Programs leading to the Associate in Science degree are dental hygiene, information technology, nursing, respiratory therapy, and software engineering. The nursing programs (certificate and associate degree) offered by Vermont Tech are located in Bennington, Brattleboro, or Williston, Vermont, and on the College's residential main campus in Randolph Center. Other locations are available for part-time study in collaboration with the Community College of Vermont.

The College also offers a certificate program in practical nursing and three-year options in selected associate degree programs for those students whose math, science, or English skills need some strengthening.

Academic Programs

Whether preparing for an associate or a bachelor's degree, Vermont Tech students receive a rigorous broad-based education centered on a core curriculum that includes both technical and general education electives. The number of credits required for graduation ranges from 65 to 72 for the associate degree and from 130 to 139 for the bachelor's degree, depending on the program. Honors courses are offered in all engineering technology programs. Most degree programs also offer project courses in which students work as teams on real-world applications in their fields of study.

Academic Facilities

Vermont Tech students learn in modern laboratories with state-of-the-art equipment. Hartness Library is the on-campus library, serving about 3,000 on-campus, extended-campus, and distance education students of Vermont Tech and the Community College of Vermont. Open more than 80 hours per week during the academic year, Hartness houses an extensive collection of material and offers professional staff assistance with library research and information literacy skills. A library Web site (http://www.vctclib.org) gives access to thousands of full-text periodicals and reference databases. Students can request books 24 hours per day.

Facilities housed in the major academic buildings include four computer-aided drafting and design labs (one 13-station, one 19-station, and two 22-one-station); four 21-station general academic computing labs; an 8-station electrical/electronics lab; recently renovated mechanical labs that include computer numerically controlled equipment and computer-aided manufacturing software; state-of-the-art veterinary technology facilities, including a 12-station lab area, a radiography suite and darkroom, and a surgery suite; a biotechnology lab with instrumentation typical of the most modern research labs; a nursing lab with a dedicated computer room and nursing station; two civil engineering labs; architectural drafting studios; a campuswide microcomputer network with Internet access; four instrumented electronics labs; and a fully equipped automotive technology center with the latest in computerized diagnostics. Facilities at the College's Williston campus include an 8,400-square-foot dental hygiene clinic that features twenty-two dental operatories, four radiographic units, a dedicated classroom, faculty offices, and a patient reception area.

Agriculture students gain practical experience at the College's dairy facility, where a main free-stall barn houses a milking herd of 80 registered Holsteins. Students have the opportunity to participate in all aspects of the farm's management. Veterinary technology students work with several species of domestic animals in the livestock facility on the farm. Conant Hall houses most of the College's academic support services. Students visit the support services offices to sign up for tutoring, meet with counselors to discuss personal or academic issues, or visit the career/transfer center to update their resumes and explore career options and internship opportunities. Disabilities Services, where students with a disability can find out about classroom accommodations or assistive technology, is also located in Conant Hall, as is the College's Learning Center. At the Learning Center students may take advantage of drop-in and scheduled tutoring, supplemental instruction, study groups, and review sessions; The General Education Department's Writing and Communication Center is on the same floor and provides students with help in reading, writing, oral presentations, study skills, and assistive-technology training.

Costs

Tuition for 2006–07 was $8184 per year for Vermont residents and $15,600 for out-of-state students. The yearly room rate was $4134, and the annual meal plan was $2808. Other required annual fees totaled $330. An additional $1235 health insurance fee was required of students not covered by another medical plan. New students also are assessed a $190 orientation fee. Many of Vermont Tech's programs are available at reduced tuition to New England students through the New England Regional Student Program, sponsored by the New England Board of Higher Education.

Financial Aid

About 80 percent of Vermont Tech students receive financial aid from federal, state, and campus-based sources. There are a growing number of institutional scholarships available, including the Vermont Technical College Scholars Program, as well as work-study opportunities. Prospective students seeking aid must file the Free Application for Federal Student Aid (FAFSA). Some state agencies may require additional information. Students are urged to apply for financial aid by the March 1 priority deadline so awards can be announced by May. However, applications are reviewed on a rolling basis after March 1 until available funds are exhausted. The Vermont Tech Web site provides more financial aid information.

Faculty

The College's excellence in instruction is a direct result of the quality of the faculty at Vermont Tech. More than 140 full- and part-time faculty members bring a special blend of industrial experience and teaching expertise to the College. Almost all have advanced degrees. Students are assured individual attention as a result of the 10:1 student-faculty ratio.

Admission Requirements

Each applicant receives individual consideration for admission based on receipt and review of the official secondary school transcript, letters of recommendation, proof of high school graduation or a high school equivalency diploma, and SAT scores. A personal interview is strongly recommended for all applicants. Because of the technical nature of the curriculum, applicants should have a strong math and science aptitude.

Application and Information

Vermont Technical College follows a rolling admission policy, but timely application is recommended. Applicants are notified of their status within two weeks of receipt of their completed application and supporting documents. For more information on Vermont Technical College, students should contact:

Office of Admissions
Vermont Technical College
P.O. Box 500
Randolph Center, Vermont 05061
Phone: 802-728-1000
800-442-VTC-1 (admissions; toll-free)
Fax: 802-728-1390
E-mail: admissions@vtc.edu
Web site: http://www.vtc.edu

The high-tech campus of Vermont Technical College is situated in a scenic New England village in the heart of Vermont.

The College also offers a certificate program in practical nursing and three-year options in selected associate degree programs for those students whose math, science, or English skills need some strengthening.

Academic Programs

Whether preparing for an associate or a bachelor's degree, Vermont Tech students receive a rigorous broad-based education centered on a core curriculum that includes both technical and general education electives. The number of credits required for graduation ranges from 65 to 72 for the associate degree and from 130 to 139 for the bachelor's degrees, depending on the program. Honors courses are offered in all engineering technology programs. Most degree programs also offer practical courses in which students work on teams on real-world applications in their fields of study.

Academic Facilities

Vermont Tech students learn in modern laboratories with state-of-the-art equipment. Hartness Library is the on-campus library serving about 5,000 on-campus, extended campus, and distance education students of Vermont Tech and the Community College of Vermont. Open more than 90 hours per week during the academic year, Hartness houses an extensive collection of material and offers professional staff assistance with library research and information literacy skills. A library Web site (http://www.vtc.edu/library) gives access to thousands of full-text periodicals and reference databases. Students can request books 24 hours per day.

Facilities housed in the major academic buildings include four computer aided drafting and design labs (one 15-station, one 16-station, and two 22-station); four 24-station general academic computing labs; an 8-station electrical/electronics lab; recently renovated mechanical labs that include computer numerically controlled equipment and computer aided manufacturing software; state-of-the-art veterinary technology facilities, including a 14-station lab, an x-ray radiography suite and darkroom, and a surgery suite; a biotechnology lab with instrumentation typical in the most modern research labs; a nursing lab with a dedicated computer lab and nursing station; two civil engineering labs; a geographic mapping studio; a campuswide microcomputer network with Internet access; four instrumented electronics labs; and a fully equipped automotive technology center with the latest in computerized diagnostics. Facilities at the College's Williston campus include an 8,400-square-foot dental hygiene clinic that features twenty-two dental operatories, four radiography units, a dedicated classroom, faculty offices, and a patient reception area.

Agriculture students gain practical experience at the College's dairy facility, where a modern free-stall barn houses a milking herd of 40 registered Holsteins; students have the opportunity to participate in all aspects of the farm's management. Veterinary technology students work with several species of domestic animals in the livestock facility on the farm. Conant Hall houses most of the College's academic support services. Students visit the support services offices to sign up for tutoring, meet with counselors to discuss personal or academic issues, or visit the career development center to update their résumés and explore career options and internship opportunities. Disability Services, where students with a disability can find out about classroom accommodations or assistive technology, is also located in Conant Hall, as is the College's Learning Center. At the Learning Center, students may take advantage of drop-in and scheduled tutoring, supplemental instruction, study groups, and review sessions. The General Education Department's Writing and Communication Center is on the same floor and provides students with help in reading, writing, oral presentations, study skills, and assistive technology training.

Costs

Tuition for 2006–07 was $8184 per year for Vermont residents and $15,360 for out-of-state students. The yearly room rate was $4104 and the minimum meal plan was $2398. Other required fees totaled $650. An additional $1445 health insurance fee was required of students not covered by another insurance plan. New students also are assessed a $150 orientation fee. Many of Vermont Tech's programs are identifiable or include tuition by New England students through the New England Regional Student Program, sponsored by the New England Board of Higher Education.

Financial Aid

About 80 percent of Vermont Tech students receive financial aid through federal, state, and campus-based sources. There are a growing number of institutional scholarships available, including the Vermont Technical College Scholars Program, as well as work study opportunities. Prospective students seeking aid must file the Free Application for Federal Student Aid (FAFSA). Some financial aid may require additional information. Students are urged to apply for financial aid by the March 1 priority deadline so awards can be announced by May. However, applications are reviewed on a rolling basis after March 1 until available funds are exhausted. The Vermont Tech Web site provides financial aid information.

Faculty

The College's excellence in instruction is a direct result of the quality of the faculty at Vermont Tech. More than 130 full- and part-time faculty members bring a special blend of industrial experience and teaching expertise to the College. Almost all have advanced degrees. Students are assured individual attention as a result of the 10:1 student-faculty ratio.

Admission Requirements

Each applicant receives individual consideration for admission based on a thorough review of the official secondary school transcript, letters of recommendation, and official high school graduation or high school equivalency diploma and SAT scores. A personal interview is strongly recommended for all applicants. Because of the technical nature of the curriculum, applicants should have a strong math and science aptitude.

Application and Information

Vermont Technical College follows a rolling admission policy, but timely application is recommended. Applicants are notified of their status within two weeks of receipt of their completed application and supporting documents. For more information on Vermont Technical College, students should contact:

Office of Admissions
Vermont Technical College
P.O. Box 500
Randolph Center, Vermont 05061
Phone: 802-728-1000
800-442-VTC1 (admissions; toll-free)
Fax: 802-728-1390
E-mail: admissions@vtc.edu
Web site: http://www.vtc.edu

VIRGINIA

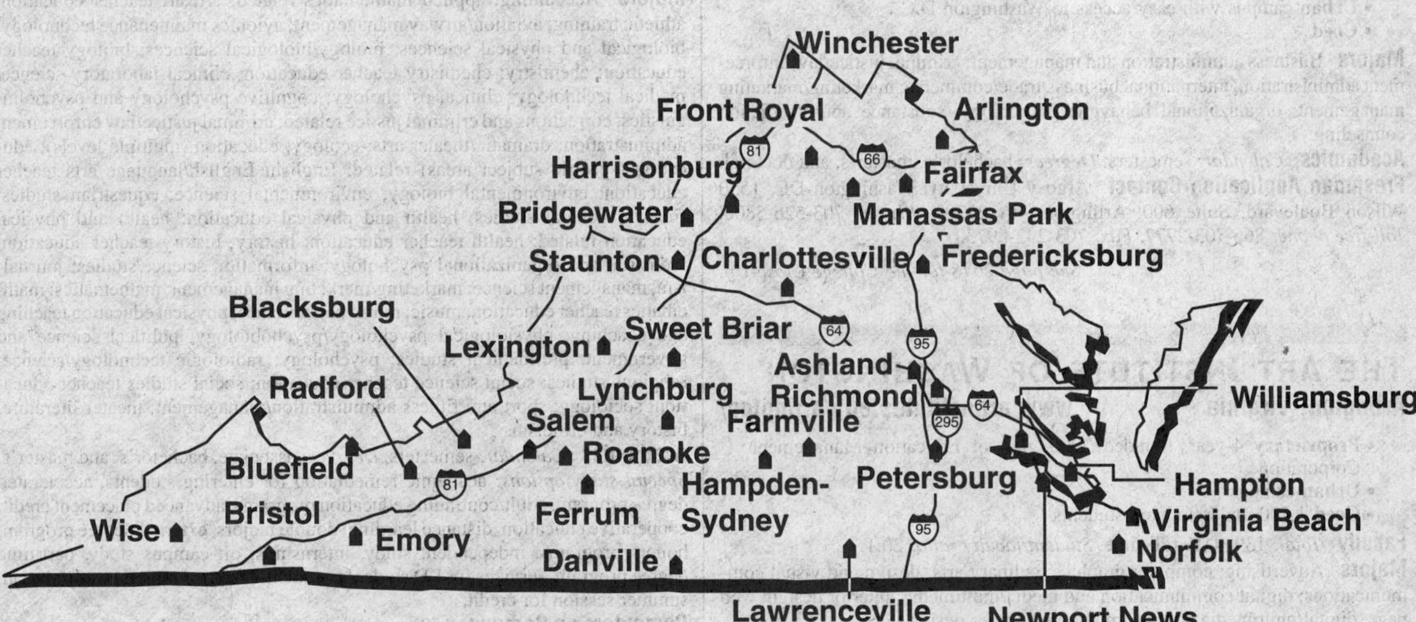
Winchester
Front Royal
Arlington
Harrisonburg
Fairfax
Bridgewater
Manassas Park
Staunton
Charlottesville
Fredericksburg
Blacksburg
Sweet Briar
Lexington
Ashland
Radford
Lynchburg
Richmond
Williamsburg
Salem
Farmville
Roanoke
Bluefield
Hampden-Sydney
Petersburg
Hampton
Bristol
Ferrum
Virginia Beach
Wise
Emory
Norfolk
Danville
Lawrenceville
Newport News
81
66
64
95
295

ARGOSY UNIVERSITY, WASHINGTON DC

Arlington, Virginia **www.argosy.edu/locations/washington-dc/**

- **Proprietary** university, founded 1994, part of Argosy Education Group
- **Urban** campus with easy access to Washington D.C.
- **Coed**

Majors Business administration and management; criminal justice/law enforcement administration; international business/trade/commerce; marketing/marketing management; organizational behavior; psychology; substance abuse/addiction counseling.

Academics *Calendar:* semesters. *Degrees:* bachelor's, master's, and doctoral.

Freshman Application Contact Argosy University, Washington DC, 1550 Wilson Boulevard, Suite 600, Arlington, VA 22209. *Phone:* 703-526-5800. *Toll-free phone:* 866-703-2777. *Fax:* 703-243-8973.

See page 2648 for the College Close-Up.

THE ART INSTITUTE OF WASHINGTON

Arlington, Virginia **www.artinstitutes.edu/arlington/**

- **Proprietary** 4-year, founded 2000, part of Education Management Corporation
- **Urban** campus
- **Coed** 1,700 undergraduate students

Faculty *Total:* 139, 41% full-time. *Student/faculty ratio:* 20:1.

Majors Advertising; computer graphics; culinary arts; design and visual communications; digital communication and media/multimedia; interior design; web page, digital/multimedia and information resources design.

Academics *Calendar:* quarters. *Degrees:* diplomas, associate, and bachelor's. *Special study options:* academic remediation for entering students, accelerated degree program, advanced placement credit, cooperative education, distance learning, honors programs, independent study, internships, part-time degree program, services for LD students, study abroad.

Computers on Campus 375 computers/terminals are available on campus for general student use. Students can access the following: computer help desk, free student e-mail accounts, online (class) grades, online (class) registration, online (class) schedules. 100% of college-owned or -operated housing units are wired for high-speed Internet access. Wireless service is available via entire campus.

Student Life *Housing options:* coed. Campus housing is leased by the school. *Campus security:* AM & PM trained security officers and cameras and devices around campus. *Student services:* personal/psychological counseling.

Costs (2008–09) *Tuition:* $20,880 full-time, $435 per credit part-time. *Room only:* $8385.

Applying *Options:* electronic application. *Application fee:* $50. *Required:* essay or personal statement, high school transcript, interview. *Application deadlines:* rolling (freshmen), rolling (transfers). *Notification:* continuous (freshmen), continuous (transfers).

Freshman Application Contact Ms. Sara Cruley, Director of Admissions, The Art Institute of Washington, 1820 North Fort Myer Drive, Arlington, VA 22209. *Phone:* 703-358-9550. *Toll-free phone:* 877-303-3771. *Fax:* 703-358-9759. *E-mail:* aiw_admin@aii.edu.

See page 2650 for the College Close-Up.

AVERETT UNIVERSITY

Danville, Virginia **www.averett.edu/**

- **Independent** comprehensive, founded 1859, affiliated with Baptist General Association of Virginia
- **Small-town** 19-acre campus with easy access to Greensboro and Raleigh
- **Endowment** $23.8 million
- **Coed** 799 undergraduate students, 95% full-time, 45% women, 55% men
- **Moderately difficult** entrance level, 90% of applicants were admitted

Undergraduates 757 full-time, 42 part-time. Students come from 30 states and territories, 10 other countries, 38% are from out of state, 28% African American, 0.8% Asian American or Pacific Islander, 4% Hispanic American, 0.6% Native American, 2% international, 9% transferred in, 57% live on campus. *Retention:* 56% of 2006 full-time freshmen returned.

Freshmen *Admission:* 1,173 applied, 1,052 admitted, 238 enrolled. *Average high school GPA:* 2.93. *Test scores:* SAT critical reading scores over 500: 23%; SAT math scores over 500: 31%; ACT scores over 18: 66%; SAT critical reading scores over 600: 3%; SAT math scores over 600: 1%; ACT scores over 24: 3%.

Faculty *Total:* 107, 50% full-time, 54% with terminal degrees. *Student/faculty ratio:* 11:1.

Majors Accounting; applied mathematics related; art; art teacher education; athletic training; aviation/airway management; avionics maintenance technology; biological and physical sciences; biology/biological sciences; biology teacher education; chemistry; chemistry teacher education; clinical laboratory science/medical technology; clinical psychology; cognitive psychology and psycholinguistics; corrections and criminal justice related; criminal justice/law enforcement administration; dramatic/theater arts; ecology; education (multiple levels); education (specific subject areas) related; English; English/language arts teacher education; environmental biology; environmental science; equestrian studies; finance; general studies; health and physical education; health and physical education related; health teacher education; history; history teacher education; industrial and organizational psychology; information science/studies; journalism; management science; marketing/marketing management; mathematics; mathematics teacher education; music; music performance; physical education teaching and coaching; physiological psychology/psychobiology; political science and government; pre-medical studies; psychology; radiologic technology/science; religious studies; social science teacher education; social studies teacher education; sociology; sport and fitness administration/management; theater literature, history and criticism.

Academics *Calendar:* semesters. *Degrees:* associate, bachelor's, and master's. *Special study options:* academic remediation for entering students, accelerated degree program, adult/continuing education programs, advanced placement credit, cooperative education, distance learning, double majors, external degree program, honors programs, independent study, internships, off-campus study, part-time degree program, services for LD students, student-designed majors, study abroad, summer session for credit.

Computers on Campus 150 computers/terminals are available on campus for general student use. Students can access the following: computer help desk, free student e-mail accounts, online (class) grades, online (class) registration, online (class) schedules. Campuswide network is available. 75% of college-owned or -operated housing units are wired for high-speed Internet access. Wireless service is available via entire campus.

Student Life *Housing:* on-campus residence required through junior year. *Options:* coed, men-only, women-only. Campus housing is university owned. Freshman campus housing is guaranteed. *Activities and organizations:* drama/theater group, student-run newspaper, choral group, Student Government Association, Campus Activities Board, Christian Student Union, Averett Gospel Choir, Averett Anime Association, national fraternities, national sororities. *Campus security:* 24-hour emergency response devices and patrols, late-night transport/escort service, controlled dormitory access. *Student services:* personal/psychological counseling.

Athletics Member NCAA. All Division III. *Intercollegiate sports:* baseball M, basketball M/W, cross-country running M/W, equestrian sports M/W, football M, golf M, lacrosse W, soccer M/W, softball W, tennis M/W, volleyball W. *Intramural sports:* basketball M/W, cheerleading M/W, football M/W, golf M/W, racquetball M/W, soccer M/W, softball M/W, table tennis M/W, tennis M/W, volleyball M/W.

Standardized Tests *Required:* SAT or ACT (for admission).

Costs (2007–08) *Comprehensive fee:* $27,612 includes full-time tuition ($19,512), mandatory fees ($1000), and room and board ($7100). Part-time tuition: $330 per credit. *Required fees:* $250 per term part-time. *College room only:* $4700.

Financial Aid Of all full-time matriculated undergraduates who enrolled in 2007, 691 applied for aid, 634 were judged to have need, 131 had their need fully met. 151 Federal Work-Study jobs (averaging $953). In 2007, 144 non-need-based awards were made. *Average percent of need met:* 78%. *Average financial aid package:* $15,155. *Average need-based loan:* $4678. *Average need-based gift aid:* $11,203. *Average non-need-based aid:* $13,088. *Average indebtedness upon graduation:* $24,360.

Applying *Options:* electronic application, deferred entrance. *Required:* high school transcript, minimum 2.2 GPA, college prep curriculum. *Recommended:* essay or personal statement, 1 letter of recommendation, interview. *Application deadlines:* 7/15 (freshmen), 8/15 (transfers). *Notification:* continuous (freshmen), continuous (transfers).

Freshman Application Contact Mr. Jerry McCombs, Director of Admissions, Averett University, Admissions Office, Danville, VA 24541. *Phone:* 434-791-5664. *Toll-free phone:* 800-AVERETT. *Fax:* 434-797-2784. *E-mail:* jerry.mccombs@averett.edu.

See page 2652 for the College Close-Up.

BLUEFIELD COLLEGE

Bluefield, Virginia www.bluefield.edu/

- **Independent Southern Baptist** 4-year, founded 1922
- **Small-town** 85-acre campus
- **Endowment** $5.6 million
- **Coed** 793 undergraduate students, 81% full-time, 60% women, 40% men
- **Minimally difficult** entrance level, 52% of applicants were admitted

Undergraduates 641 full-time, 152 part-time. Students come from 20 states and territories, 9 other countries, 17% are from out of state, 19% African American, 0.3% Asian American or Pacific Islander, 1% Hispanic American, 0.1% Native American, 21% transferred in, 41% live on campus. *Retention:* 64% of 2006 full-time freshmen returned.

Freshmen *Admission:* 556 applied, 288 admitted, 90 enrolled. *Average high school GPA:* 3.1. *Test scores:* SAT critical reading scores over 500: 45%; SAT math scores over 500: 36%; ACT scores over 18: 75%; SAT critical reading scores over 600: 13%; SAT math scores over 600: 3%; ACT scores over 24: 13%; SAT critical reading scores over 700: 3%.

Faculty *Total:* 104, 33% full-time, 47% with terminal degrees. *Student/faculty ratio:* 12:1.

Majors Accounting; art; biblical studies; biology/biological sciences; biology teacher education; business administration and management; business teacher education; chemistry; chemistry teacher education; computer science; criminal justice/law enforcement administration; divinity/ministry; dramatic/theater arts; education; elementary education; English; English/language arts teacher education; health teacher education; history; history teacher education; information technology; interdisciplinary studies; kindergarten/preschool education; kinesiology and exercise science; liberal arts and sciences/liberal studies; mass communication/media; mathematics; mathematics teacher education; middle school education; music; music teacher education; physical education teaching and coaching; psychology; religious/sacred music; religious studies; science teacher education; secondary education; social sciences; social studies teacher education; theology.

Academics *Calendar:* semesters. *Degree:* bachelor's. *Special study options:* academic remediation for entering students, accelerated degree program, adult/continuing education programs, advanced placement credit, distance learning, double majors, external degree program, honors programs, internships, off-campus study, part-time degree program, study abroad, summer session for credit.

Computers on Campus 100 computers/terminals are available on campus for general student use. Students can access the following: free student e-mail accounts, online (class) grades, online (class) registration, online (class) schedules, Blackboard, COWL, career assessment tests, library database. Campuswide network is available. 100% of college-owned or -operated housing units are wired for high-speed Internet access. Wireless service is available via libraries, student centers.

Student Life *Housing:* on-campus residence required through junior year. *Options:* coed, men-only, women-only. Campus housing is university owned. Freshman applicants given priority for college housing. *Activities and organizations:* drama/theater group, student-run newspaper, choral group, Baptist Student Union, Fellowship of Christian Athletes, Student Union Board, Student Government Association, Bluefield Singers. *Campus security:* controlled dormitory access, night security patrols. *Student services:* health clinic, personal/psychological counseling.

Athletics Member NAIA. *Intercollegiate sports:* baseball M (s), basketball M (s)/W (s), cross-country running M (s)/W (s), golf M (s), soccer M (s)/W (s), softball W (s), tennis M (s)/W (s), volleyball W (s). *Intramural sports:* badminton M/W, baseball M, basketball M/W, bowling M/W, football M/W, softball M/W, table tennis M/W, tennis M/W, volleyball M/W.

Standardized Tests *Required:* SAT or ACT (for admission).

Costs (2008–09) *Comprehensive fee:* $22,214 includes full-time tuition ($15,000), mandatory fees ($630), and room and board ($6584). Part-time tuition: $488 per hour. *Required fees:* $160 per term part-time.

Financial Aid Of all full-time matriculated undergraduates who enrolled in 2003, 606 applied for aid, 543 were judged to have need, 128 had their need fully met. 98 Federal Work-Study jobs (averaging $800). In 2003, 137 non-need-based awards were made. *Average percent of need met:* 68%. *Average financial aid package:* $8957. *Average need-based loan:* $4430. *Average need-based gift aid:* $5403. *Average non-need-based aid:* $6464. *Average indebtedness upon graduation:* $12,177.

Applying *Options:* electronic application, deferred entrance. *Application fee:* $30. *Required:* high school transcript, minimum 2.0 GPA. *Required for some:* letters of recommendation, interview. *Recommended:* interview. *Application deadlines:* rolling (freshmen), rolling (transfers). *Notification:* continuous (freshmen), continuous (transfers).

Freshman Application Contact Mr. George Campbell, Bluefield College, 3000 College Drive, Bluefield, VA 24605-1799. *Phone:* 276-326-4602. *Toll-free phone:* 800-872-0175. *Fax:* 276-326-4395. *E-mail:* admissions@bluefield.edu.

BRIDGEWATER COLLEGE

Bridgewater, Virginia www.bridgewater.edu/

- **Independent** 4-year, founded 1880, affiliated with Church of the Brethren
- **Small-town** 190-acre campus
- **Endowment** $61.5 million
- **Coed** 1,541 undergraduate students, 99% full-time, 57% women, 43% men
- **Moderately difficult** entrance level, 84% of applicants were admitted

At Bridgewater College, the liberal arts and sciences curriculum emphasizes scholarly pursuits while nurturing the skills and maturity necessary for a lifetime of learning. Through the Personal Development Portfolio (PDP) Program, students may explore their full potential by combining academic quests and cocurricular activities that foster intellectual, emotional, physical, and spiritual growth. In doing so, students discover their potential as leaders, equipped to live ethical and productive lives that contribute to the local and global communities.

Undergraduates 1,529 full-time, 12 part-time. Students come from 26 states and territories, 8 other countries, 21% are from out of state, 7% African American, 0.9% Asian American or Pacific Islander, 2% Hispanic American, 0.5% Native American, 0.5% international, 4% transferred in, 83% live on campus. *Retention:* 76% of 2006 full-time freshmen returned.

Freshmen *Admission:* 1,537 applied, 1,290 admitted, 445 enrolled. *Average high school GPA:* 3.4. *Test scores:* SAT critical reading scores over 500: 51%; SAT math scores over 500: 61%; ACT scores over 18: 78%; SAT critical reading scores over 600: 13%; SAT math scores over 600: 16%; ACT scores over 24: 20%; SAT critical reading scores over 700: 2%; SAT math scores over 700: 1%; ACT scores over 30: 2%.

Faculty *Total:* 127, 76% full-time, 69% with terminal degrees. *Student/faculty ratio:* 14:1.

Majors Athletic training; biology/biological sciences; business administration and management; chemistry; chemistry teacher education; clinical laboratory science/medical technology; computer science; computer teacher education; economics; elementary education; English; English/language arts teacher education; environmental science; family and consumer sciences/home economics teacher education; family and consumer sciences/human sciences; fine/studio arts; foods, nutrition, and wellness; French; French language teacher education; health and physical education; history; history related; history teacher education; international relations and affairs; kinesiology and exercise science; liberal arts and sciences/liberal studies; management information systems; mass communication/media; mathematics; mathematics teacher education; music history, literature, and theory; music teacher education; philosophy and religious studies related; physical education teaching and coaching; physics; physics related; physics teacher education; political science and government; psychology; social science teacher education; sociology; Spanish; Spanish language teacher education.

Academics *Calendar:* 4-1-4. *Degree:* bachelor's. *Special study options:* adult/continuing education programs, advanced placement credit, double majors, honors programs, independent study, internships, off-campus study, part-time degree program, services for LD students, study abroad, summer session for credit. *Unusual degree programs:* 3-2 engineering with George Washington University, Virginia Tech; forestry with Duke University; nursing with Vanderbilt University; physical therapy with George Washington University, Shenandoah University, veterinary science with Virginia Tech.

Computers on Campus 187 computers/terminals are available on campus for general student use. Students can access the following: campus intranet, computer help desk, free student e-mail accounts, online (class) grades, online (class) registration, online (class) schedules. Campuswide network is available. 100% of college-owned or -operated housing units are wired for high-speed Internet access. Wireless service is available via classrooms, libraries, student centers.

Student Life *Housing:* on-campus residence required through senior year. *Options:* coed, men-only, women-only, disabled students. Campus housing is university owned. Freshman campus housing is guaranteed. *Activities and organizations:* drama/theater group, student-run newspaper, radio station, choral group, Eagle Productions (program board), Pep band, Oratorio Choir, Baptist Student Union, Brethren Student Fellowship. *Campus security:* 24-hour emergency response devices and patrols, controlled dormitory access. *Student services:* health clinic, personal/psychological counseling.

Athletics Member NCAA. All Division III. *Intercollegiate sports:* baseball M, basketball M/W, cheerleading M (c)/W (c), cross-country running M/W, equestrian sports M/W, field hockey W, football M, golf M, lacrosse W, soccer M/W, softball W, swimming and diving W, tennis M/W, track and field M/W, volleyball W. *Intramural sports:* badminton M/W, basketball M/W, bowling M/W, football M/W, golf M/W, racquetball M/W, soccer M/W, softball M/W, table tennis M/W, tennis M/W, ultimate Frisbee M/W, volleyball M/W.

Standardized Tests *Required:* SAT or ACT (for admission).

Costs (2008–09) *Comprehensive fee:* $32,990 includes full-time tuition ($23,090) and room and board ($9900). Part-time tuition: $775 per credit hour. *Required fees:* $30 per term part-time. *College room only:* $4960.

Financial Aid Of all full-time matriculated undergraduates who enrolled in 2007, 1,242 applied for aid, 1,057 were judged to have need, 255 had their need fully met. 318 Federal Work-Study jobs (averaging $1144). 88 state and other part-time jobs (averaging $1031). In 2007, 463 non-need-based awards were made. *Average percent of need met:* 83%. *Average financial aid package:* $18,884. *Average need-based loan:* $5294. *Average need-based gift aid:* $4900. *Average non-need-based aid:* $8767. *Average indebtedness upon graduation:* $29,050.

Applying *Options:* electronic application, deferred entrance. *Application fee:* $30. *Required:* high school transcript, minimum 2.5 GPA, 2 letters of recommendation. *Required for some:* interview. *Recommended:* minimum 3.0 GPA, interview. *Application deadlines:* rolling (freshmen), rolling (transfers). *Notification:* continuous (freshmen), continuous (transfers).

Freshman Application Contact Ms. Linda Stout, Director of Enrollment Operations, Bridgewater College, 402 East College Street, Bridgewater, VA 22812-1599. *Phone:* 540-828-5375. *Toll-free phone:* 800-759-8328. *Fax:* 540-828-5481. *E-mail:* admissions@bridgewater.edu.

See page 2654 for the College Close-Up.

BRYANT AND STRATTON COLLEGE, RICHMOND CAMPUS

Richmond, Virginia **www.bryantstratton.edu/**

Freshman Application Contact Mr. David K. Mayle, Director of Admissions, Bryant and Stratton College, Richmond Campus, 8141 Hull Street Road, Richmond, VA 23235-6411. *Phone:* 804-745-2444. *Fax:* 804-745-6884. *E-mail:* tlawson@bryanstratton.edu.

BRYANT AND STRATTON COLLEGE, VIRGINIA BEACH

Virginia Beach, Virginia **www.bryantstratton.edu/**

Director of Admissions Mr. Greg Smith, Director of Admissions, Bryant and Stratton College, Virginia Beach, 301 Centre Pointe Drive, Virginia Beach, VA 23462-4417. *Phone:* 757-499-7900.

CHRISTENDOM COLLEGE

Front Royal, Virginia **www.christendom.edu/**

- **Independent Roman Catholic** comprehensive, founded 1977
- **Rural** 100-acre campus with easy access to Washington, DC
- **Endowment** $3.1 million
- **Coed** 397 undergraduate students, 98% full-time, 54% women, 46% men
- **Very difficult** entrance level, 81% of applicants were admitted

Undergraduates 389 full-time, 8 part-time. Students come from 43 states and territories, 2 other countries, 75% are from out of state, 2% Asian American or Pacific Islander, 3% Hispanic American, 0.3% Native American, 3% international, 4% transferred in, 95% live on campus. *Retention:* 88% of 2006 full-time freshmen returned.

Freshmen *Admission:* 254 applied, 206 admitted, 93 enrolled. *Average high school GPA:* 3.6. *Test scores:* SAT critical reading scores over 500: 94%; SAT math scores over 500: 78%; SAT writing scores over 500: 96%; SAT critical reading scores over 600: 60%; SAT math scores over 600: 43%; SAT writing scores over 600: 53%; SAT critical reading scores over 700: 25%; SAT math scores over 700: 6%; SAT writing scores over 700: 16%.

Faculty *Total:* 41, 49% full-time, 46% with terminal degrees. *Student/faculty ratio:* 14:1.

Majors Classics and languages, literatures and linguistics; history; liberal arts and sciences/liberal studies; literature; philosophy; political science and government; theology.

Academics *Calendar:* semesters. *Degrees:* associate, bachelor's, and master's. *Special study options:* academic remediation for entering students, accelerated degree program, advanced placement credit, cooperative education, double majors, independent study, internships, services for LD students, study abroad, summer session for credit.

Computers on Campus 60 computers/terminals are available on campus for general student use. Students can access the following: computer help desk, free student e-mail accounts. Wireless service is available via student centers.

Student Life *Housing options:* men-only, women-only. Campus housing is university owned. Freshman campus housing is guaranteed. *Activities and organizations:* drama/theater group, student-run newspaper, choral group, drama, choir, Shield of Roses, Legion of Mary, debate team. *Campus security:* 24-hour emergency response devices, late-night transport/escort service, night patrols by trained security personnel. *Student services:* health clinic, personal/psychological counseling.

Athletics Member NCCAA. *Intercollegiate sports:* baseball M, basketball M/W, soccer M/W, volleyball W. *Intramural sports:* basketball M/W, fencing M/W, football M/W, golf M/W, racquetball M/W, soccer M/W, softball M/W, table tennis M/W, tennis M/W, volleyball M/W.

Standardized Tests *Required:* SAT or ACT (for admission).

Costs (2008–09) *Comprehensive fee:* $25,444 includes full-time tuition ($18,306), mandatory fees ($450), and room and board ($6688).

Financial Aid Of all full-time matriculated undergraduates who enrolled in 2006, 230 applied for aid, 187 were judged to have need, 187 had their need fully met. 145 state and other part-time jobs (averaging $1944). In 2006, 25 non-need-based awards were made. *Average percent of need met:* 90%. *Average financial aid package:* $14,235. *Average need-based loan:* $5000. *Average need-based gift aid:* $7065. *Average non-need-based aid:* $5015. *Average indebtedness upon graduation:* $19,170.

Applying *Options:* electronic application, early admission, early action. *Application fee:* $25. *Required:* essay or personal statement, high school transcript, 2 letters of recommendation. *Recommended:* minimum 3.0 GPA, interview. *Application deadlines:* 3/1 (freshmen), 3/1 (transfers), 12/1 (early action). *Notification:* 4/1 (freshmen), continuous until 4/1 (transfers), 12/15 (early action).

Freshman Application Contact Mr. Tom McFadden, Director of Admissions, Christendom College, 134 Christendom Drive, Front Royal, VA 22630-5103. *Phone:* 540-636-2900. *Toll-free phone:* 800-877-5456 Ext. 290. *Fax:* 540-636-1655. *E-mail:* tmcfadden@christendom.edu.

CHRISTOPHER NEWPORT UNIVERSITY

Newport News, Virginia **www.cnu.edu/**

- **State-supported** comprehensive, founded 1960
- **Suburban** 175-acre campus with easy access to Norfolk
- **Endowment** $12.1 million
- **Coed** 4,691 undergraduate students, 95% full-time, 55% women, 45% men
- 54% of applicants were admitted

Undergraduates 4,459 full-time, 232 part-time. Students come from 29 states and territories, 30 other countries, 3% are from out of state, 7% African American, 3% Asian American or Pacific Islander, 3% Hispanic American, 0.7% Native American, 0.2% international, 3% transferred in, 64% live on campus. *Retention:* 82% of 2006 full-time freshmen returned.

Freshmen *Admission:* 6,694 applied, 3,639 admitted, 1,242 enrolled. *Average high school GPA:* 3.5. *Test scores:* SAT critical reading scores over 500: 94%; SAT math scores over 500: 93%; ACT scores over 18: 99%; SAT critical reading scores over 600: 44%; SAT math scores over 600: 39%; ACT scores over 24: 51%; SAT critical reading scores over 700: 6%; SAT math scores over 700: 4%; ACT scores over 30: 4%.

Faculty *Total:* 362, 62% full-time, 62% with terminal degrees. *Student/faculty ratio:* 17:1.

Majors Accounting; biology/biological sciences; business administration and management; business/managerial economics; chemistry; communication/speech communication and rhetoric; computer and information sciences; computer engineering; computer science; dramatic/theater arts; economics; education; English; environmental studies; finance; fine/studio arts; French; German; history; horticultural science; information science/studies; interdisciplinary studies; international business/trade/commerce; legal studies; literature; marketing/marketing management; mathematics; middle school education; music; music history, literature, and theory; music theory and composition; philosophy; physics; political science and government; pre-law studies; social work; sociology; Spanish.

Academics *Calendar:* semesters. *Degrees:* bachelor's and master's. *Special study options:* accelerated degree program, advanced placement credit, coopera-

COLLEGE DATA CENTER • VIRGINIA

tive education, distance learning, double majors, honors programs, independent study, internships, off-campus study, services for LD students, student-designed majors, study abroad, summer session for credit. *ROTC:* Army (b).

Computers on Campus 325 computers/terminals are available on campus for general student use. Students can access the following: campus intranet, computer help desk, free student e-mail accounts, online (class) grades, online (class) registration, online (class) schedules. Campuswide network is available. 100% of college-owned or -operated housing units are wired for high-speed Internet access. Wireless service is available via classrooms, computer centers, computer labs, libraries, student centers.

Student Life *Housing:* on-campus residence required for freshman year. *Options:* coed, disabled students. Campus housing is university owned and leased by the school. Freshman campus housing is guaranteed. *Activities and organizations:* drama/theater group, student-run newspaper, radio station, choral group, marching band, Campus Activities Board, Student Government Association, Multicultural Association, national fraternities, national sororities. *Campus security:* 24-hour emergency response devices and patrols, late-night transport/escort service, controlled dormitory access, campus police. *Student services:* health clinic, personal/psychological counseling.

Athletics Member NCAA. All Division III. *Intercollegiate sports:* baseball M, basketball M/W, cheerleading M/W, cross-country running M/W, equestrian sports M (c)/W (c), field hockey W, football M, golf M, lacrosse M (c)/W (c), rock climbing M (c), sailing M/W, soccer M/W, softball W, tennis M/W, track and field M/W, volleyball W. *Intramural sports:* badminton M/W, basketball M/W, bowling M (c)/W (c), football M/W, golf M/W, soccer M/W, softball M/W, table tennis M/W, tennis M/W, volleyball M/W, weight lifting M/W.

Standardized Tests *Required:* SAT or ACT (for admission).

Costs (2007–08) *Tuition:* state resident $7050 full-time, $294 per credit hour part-time; nonresident $14,150 full-time, $591 per credit hour part-time. Full-time tuition and fees vary according to course load and degree level. Part-time tuition and fees vary according to course load and degree level. *Required fees:* $3088 full-time, $128 per credit hour part-time. *Room and board:* $8500. Room and board charges vary according to board plan and housing facility. *Payment plan:* installment. *Waivers:* senior citizens and employees or children of employees.

Financial Aid Of all full-time matriculated undergraduates who enrolled in 2006, 2,878 applied for aid, 1,727 were judged to have need, 400 had their need fully met. 67 Federal Work-Study jobs (averaging $1232). 975 state and other part-time jobs (averaging $1578). In 2006, 314 non-need-based awards were made. *Average percent of need met:* 75%. *Average financial aid package:* $6599. *Average need-based loan:* $3322. *Average need-based gift aid:* $4440. *Average non-need-based aid:* $1379. *Average indebtedness upon graduation:* $16,139.

Applying *Options:* electronic application, early admission, early action, deferred entrance. *Application fee:* $45. *Required:* high school transcript, minimum 3.0 GPA. *Required for some:* essay or personal statement, 3 letters of recommendation, interview. *Application deadlines:* 3/1 (freshmen), 3/1 (transfers), 12/1 (early action). *Notification:* continuous (freshmen), 5/21 (transfers), 1/11 (early action).

Freshman Application Contact Mr. Curtis Davidson, Senior Associate Director of Admissions, Christopher Newport University, 1 University Place, Newport News, VA 23606-2998. *Phone:* 757-594-7015. *Toll-free phone:* 800-333-4268. *Fax:* 757-594-7333. *E-mail:* admit@cnu.edu.

See page 2656 for the College Close-Up.

THE COLLEGE OF WILLIAM AND MARY

Williamsburg, Virginia **www.wm.edu/**

- **State-supported** university, founded 1693
- **Small-town** 1200-acre campus with easy access to Richmond
- **Endowment** $585.9 million
- **Coed** 5,792 undergraduate students, 98% full-time, 54% women, 46% men
- **Very difficult** entrance level, 34% of applicants were admitted

Undergraduates 5,703 full-time, 89 part-time. Students come from 47 states and territories, 54 other countries, 31% are from out of state, 7% African American, 7% Asian American or Pacific Islander, 6% Hispanic American, 0.7% Native American, 2% international, 3% transferred in, 75% live on campus. *Retention:* 95% of 2006 full-time freshmen returned.

Freshmen *Admission:* 10,853 applied, 3,655 admitted, 1,346 enrolled. *Average high school GPA:* 4.0. *Test scores:* SAT critical reading scores over 500: 98%; SAT math scores over 500: 98%; SAT writing scores over 500: 98%; ACT scores over 18: 100%; SAT critical reading scores over 600: 85%; SAT math scores over 600: 84%; SAT writing scores over 600: 83%; ACT scores over 24: 93%; SAT critical reading scores over 700: 45%; SAT math scores over 700: 32%; SAT writing scores over 700: 36%; ACT scores over 30: 46%.

Faculty *Total:* 797, 78% full-time, 77% with terminal degrees. *Student/faculty ratio:* 11:1.

Majors African-American/Black studies; American studies; anthropology; art; art history, criticism and conservation; Asian studies (East); biology/biological sciences; biopsychology; business administration and management; chemistry; classics and languages, literatures and linguistics; computer and information sciences; cultural studies; dramatic/theater arts; economics; English; environmental studies; European studies; French; geology/earth science; German; history; interdisciplinary studies; international relations and affairs; Latin; Latin American studies; linguistics; mathematics; medieval and Renaissance studies; modern Greek; modern languages; multi-/interdisciplinary studies related; music; philosophy; physical education teaching and coaching; physics; political science and government; psychology; public policy analysis; religious studies; Russian studies; sociology; Spanish; women's studies.

Academics *Calendar:* semesters. *Degrees:* bachelor's, master's, doctoral, first professional, and post-master's certificates. *Special study options:* accelerated degree program, advanced placement credit, double majors, honors programs, independent study, services for LD students, student-designed majors, study abroad, summer session for credit. *ROTC:* Army (b). *Unusual degree programs:* 3-2 engineering with Columbia University, Washington University in St. Louis, Rensselaer Polytechnic Institute, Case Western Reserve University, University of Virginia; forestry with Duke University.

Computers on Campus 400 computers/terminals and 6,000 ports are available on campus for general student use. Students can access the following: campus intranet, computer help desk, free student e-mail accounts, online (class) grades, online (class) registration, online (class) schedules. Campuswide network is available. 100% of college-owned or -operated housing units are wired for high-speed Internet access. Wireless service is available via entire campus.

Student Life *Housing:* on-campus residence required for freshman year. *Options:* coed, women-only. Campus housing is university owned and leased by the school. Freshman campus housing is guaranteed. *Activities and organizations:* drama/theater group, student-run newspaper, radio and television station, choral group, Alpha Phi Omega, College Partnership for Kids, student assembly, Flat Hat (student newspaper), Resident Housing Association, national fraternities, national sororities. *Campus security:* 24-hour emergency response devices and patrols, student patrols, late-night transport/escort service, controlled dormitory access. *Student services:* health clinic, personal/psychological counseling, legal services.

Athletics Member NCAA. All Division I except football (Division I-AA). *Intercollegiate sports:* baseball M (s), basketball M (s)/W (s), cross-country running M (s)/W (s), field hockey W (s), golf M/W, gymnastics M (s)/W (s), lacrosse W (s), soccer M (s)/W (s), swimming and diving M (s)/W, tennis M (s)/W (s), track and field M (s)/W (s), volleyball W (s). *Intramural sports:* badminton M (c)/W (c), baseball M (c), basketball M/W, bowling M/W, crew M (c)/W (c), cross-country running M (c)/W (c), equestrian sports M (c)/W (c), fencing M (c)/W (c), field hockey W (c), football M/W, golf M/W, gymnastics M (c)/W (c), ice hockey M (c), lacrosse M (c)/W (c), racquetball M (c)/W (c), rugby M (c)/W (c), sailing M (c)/W (c), soccer M (c)/W (c), softball M (c)/W, swimming and diving M (c)/W (c), table tennis M/W, tennis M (c)/W (c), ultimate Frisbee M/W, volleyball M (c)/W (c), weight lifting M (c)/W (c), wrestling M.

Standardized Tests *Required:* SAT or ACT (for admission). *Recommended:* SAT Subject Tests (for admission).

Costs (2007–08) *Tuition:* state resident $5549 full-time, $196 per credit hour part-time; nonresident $23,110 full-time, $750 per credit hour part-time. Full-time tuition and fees vary according to program. Part-time tuition and fees vary according to program. *Required fees:* $3615 full-time. *Room and board:* $7385; room only: $4527. Room and board charges vary according to board plan and housing facility. *Payment plan:* installment. *Waivers:* senior citizens and employees or children of employees.

Financial Aid Of all full-time matriculated undergraduates who enrolled in 2007, 2,670 applied for aid, 1,588 were judged to have need, 748 had their need fully met. 145 state and other part-time jobs (averaging $1188). In 2007, 259 non-need-based awards were made. *Average percent of need met:* 86%. *Average financial aid package:* $13,302. *Average need-based loan:* $2830. *Average need-based gift aid:* $12,884. *Average non-need-based aid:* $5403. *Average indebtedness upon graduation:* $15,602.

Applying *Options:* electronic application, early admission, early decision, deferred entrance. *Application fee:* $60. *Required:* essay or personal statement, high school transcript. *Recommended:* 1 letter of recommendation. *Application deadlines:* 1/1 (freshmen), 2/15 (transfers). *Early decision deadline:* 11/1. *Notification:* 4/1 (freshmen), 4/15 (transfers), 12/1 (early decision).

Freshman Application Contact Henry Broaddus, Dean of Admissions, The College of William and Mary, PO Box 8795, Williamsburg, VA 23187-8795. *Phone:* 757-221-4223. *Fax:* 757-221-1242. *E-mail:* admiss@wm.edu.

DeVry University

Arlington, Virginia

www.devry.edu/

- **Proprietary** comprehensive, founded 2001, part of DeVry University
- **Coed** 552 undergraduate students, 60% full-time, 27% women, 73% men
- **Minimally difficult** entrance level

Undergraduates 331 full-time, 221 part-time. 61% are from out of state, 48% African American, 4% Asian American or Pacific Islander, 10% Hispanic American, 0.5% Native American, 1% international, 13% transferred in. *Retention:* 51% of 2006 full-time freshmen returned.

Freshmen *Admission:* 177 enrolled.

Faculty *Total:* 33, 58% full-time. *Student/faculty ratio:* 20:1.

Majors Business administration and management; business administration, management and operations related; computer engineering technology; computer software engineering; computer systems analysis; computer systems networking and telecommunications; electrical, electronic and communications engineering technology.

Academics *Calendar:* semesters. *Degrees:* associate, bachelor's, and master's. *Special study options:* academic remediation for entering students, accelerated degree program, adult/continuing education programs, advanced placement credit, distance learning, part-time degree program, services for LD students, summer session for credit.

Computers on Campus 380 computers/terminals are available on campus for general student use. Students can access the following: online (class) registration. Campuswide network is available.

Student Life *Housing:* college housing not available.

Costs (2008–09) *Tuition:* $14,070 full-time, $525 per credit part-time. *Required fees:* $180 full-time.

Financial Aid Of all full-time matriculated undergraduates who enrolled in 2002, 350 applied for aid, 325 were judged to have need, 4 had their need fully met. In 2002, 46 non-need-based awards were made. *Average percent of need met:* 31%. *Average financial aid package:* $6344. *Average need-based loan:* $4422. *Average need-based gift aid:* $3585. *Average non-need-based aid:* $8612.

Applying *Options:* electronic application, early admission, deferred entrance. *Application fee:* $50. *Required:* high school transcript, interview. *Application deadlines:* rolling (freshmen), rolling (transfers). *Notification:* continuous (freshmen), continuous (transfers).

Freshman Application Contact DeVry University, 2450 Crystal Drive, Arlington, VA 22202-3843.

DeVry University

McLean, Virginia

Eastern Mennonite University

Harrisonburg, Virginia

www.emu.edu/

- **Independent Mennonite** comprehensive, founded 1917
- **Small-town** 93-acre campus
- **Endowment** $20.2 million
- **Coed** 970 undergraduate students, 97% full-time, 62% women, 38% men
- **Moderately difficult** entrance level, 71% of applicants were admitted

Eastern Mennonite University (EMU) envisions a learning community marked by academic excellence, creative process, professional competence, and passionate Christian faith—offering healing and hope in today's diverse world. To this end, the University commits itself to do justice, love, and mercy and walk humbly with God. EMU students complete a cross-cultural requirement for graduation; for many, it is a life-changing learning experience. Whatever a student's major—liberal arts or business, premed, visual arts—EMU offers the opportunity to study in an environment where personal relationships with professors are the norm, ethics and justice issues are emphasized, and varied opinions and perspectives are welcomed. With some fifty majors and minors, dozens of international students, and cross-cultural experiences, EMU offers students the world within a warm and supportive community.

Undergraduates 942 full-time, 28 part-time. Students come from 36 states and territories, 21 other countries, 56% are from out of state, 8% African American, 1% Asian American or Pacific Islander, 3% Hispanic American, 0.2% Native American, 4% international, 8% transferred in, 58% live on campus. *Retention:* 76% of 2006 full-time freshmen returned.

Freshmen *Admission:* 740 applied, 525 admitted, 203 enrolled. *Average high school GPA:* 3.45. *Test scores:* SAT critical reading scores over 500: 62%; SAT math scores over 500: 62%; SAT writing scores over 500: 77%; ACT scores over 18: 88%; SAT critical reading scores over 600: 29%; SAT math scores over 600: 27%; SAT writing scores over 600: 30%; ACT scores over 24: 53%; SAT critical reading scores over 700: 9%; SAT math scores over 700: 4%; SAT writing scores over 700: 5%; ACT scores over 30: 15%.

Faculty *Total:* 157, 75% full-time, 56% with terminal degrees. *Student/faculty ratio:* 10:1.

Majors Accounting; art; art teacher education; biblical studies; biochemistry; biology/biological sciences; biology teacher education; business administration and management; chemistry; chemistry teacher education; clinical laboratory science/medical technology; communication/speech communication and rhetoric; computer science; digital communication and media/multimedia; dramatic/theater arts; early childhood education; economics; elementary education; English; English as a second/foreign language (teaching); English/language arts teacher education; environmental science; French; French language teacher education; general studies; health teacher education; history; international business/trade/commerce; kindergarten/preschool education; liberal arts and sciences/liberal studies; mathematics; mathematics teacher education; middle school education; multi-/interdisciplinary studies related; music; music teacher education; nursing (registered nurse training); organizational behavior; peace studies and conflict resolution; philosophy and religious studies related; photography; physical education teaching and coaching; physics teacher education; pre-dentistry studies; pre-engineering; pre-law studies; pre-medical studies; pre-nursing studies; pre-theology/pre-ministerial studies; pre-veterinary studies; psychology; secondary education; social sciences; social science teacher education; social work; sociology; Spanish; Spanish language teacher education; special education (emotionally disturbed); special education (mentally retarded); special education (specific learning disabilities); sport and fitness administration/management; teacher assistant/aide; theology; youth ministry.

Academics *Calendar:* semesters. *Degrees:* certificates, associate, bachelor's, master's, first professional, and postbachelor's certificates. *Special study options:* academic remediation for entering students, adult/continuing education programs, advanced placement credit, distance learning, double majors, English as a second language, honors programs, independent study, internships, off-campus study, part-time degree program, services for LD students, study abroad, summer session for credit.

Computers on Campus 152 computers/terminals and 10 ports are available on campus for general student use. Students can access the following: campus intranet, computer help desk, free student e-mail accounts, online (class) grades, online (class) registration, online (class) schedules. Campuswide network is available. 98% of college-owned or -operated housing units are wired for high-speed Internet access. Wireless service is available via learning centers, libraries, student centers.

Student Life *Housing:* on-campus residence required through junior year. *Options:* coed, men-only, women-only, disabled students. Campus housing is university owned. Freshman campus housing is guaranteed. *Activities and organizations:* drama/theater group, student-run newspaper, choral group, YPCA, Student Government Association, Student Education Association, Black Student Union, International Student Organization. *Campus security:* 24-hour emergency response devices, controlled dormitory access, night watchman. *Student services:* health clinic, personal/psychological counseling.

Athletics Member NCAA. All Division III. *Intercollegiate sports:* baseball M, basketball M/W, cross-country running M/W, field hockey W, soccer M/W, softball W, track and field M/W, volleyball M/W. *Intramural sports:* basketball M/W, golf M/W, lacrosse M/W, rock climbing M/W, soccer M/W, softball M/W, table tennis M/W, tennis M/W, volleyball M/W.

Standardized Tests *Required:* SAT or ACT (for admission).

Costs (2007–08) *Comprehensive fee:* $28,860 includes full-time tuition ($21,960) and room and board ($6900). Part-time tuition: $915 per credit hour. Part-time tuition and fees vary according to course load. *Required fees:* $3 per credit hour part-time. *College room only:* $3800. Room and board charges vary according to board plan, housing facility, and student level. *Payment plan:* installment. *Waivers:* employees or children of employees.

Financial Aid Of all full-time matriculated undergraduates who enrolled in 2003, 735 applied for aid, 652 were judged to have need, 246 had their need fully met. 326 Federal Work-Study jobs (averaging $1787). In 2003, 82 non-need-based awards were made. *Average percent of need met:* 87%. *Average financial aid package:* $15,530. *Average need-based loan:* $5665. *Average need-based gift aid:* $5520. *Average non-need-based aid:* $7765. *Average indebtedness upon graduation:* $18,208.

Applying *Options:* electronic application, deferred entrance. *Application fee:* $25. *Required:* high school transcript, minimum 2.2 GPA, statement of commitment. *Required for some:* 2 letters of recommendation. *Recommended:* interview.

Application deadlines: rolling (freshmen), 8/15 (transfers). *Notification:* continuous (freshmen), continuous (transfers).

Freshman Application Contact Mrs. Stephanie C. Shafer, Director of Admissions, Eastern Mennonite University, 1200 Park Road, Harrisonburg, VA 22802-2462. *Phone:* 540-432-4118. *Toll-free phone:* 800-368-2665. *Fax:* 540-432-4444. *E-mail:* admiss@emu.edu.

ECPI College of Technology

Virginia Beach, Virginia **www.ecpi.edu/**

- **Proprietary** primarily 2-year, founded 1966
- **Suburban** 8-acre campus
- **Coed**
- **Moderately difficult** entrance level

Faculty *Student/faculty ratio:* 15:1.

Academics *Calendar:* trimesters. *Degrees:* certificates, diplomas, associate, and bachelor's.

Student Life *Campus security:* building and parking lot security.

Standardized Tests *Recommended:* SAT or ACT (for admission), SAT Subject Tests (for admission).

Financial Aid Of all full-time matriculated undergraduates who enrolled in 2006, 120 Federal Work-Study jobs (averaging $2000).

Applying *Options:* electronic application, deferred entrance. *Application fee:* $100. *Required:* high school transcript, interview.

Freshman Application Contact Mr. Ronald Ballance, Vice President, ECPI College of Technology, 5555 Greenwich Road, Suite 100, Virginia Beach, VA 23462. *Phone:* 757-671-7171. *Toll-free phone:* 800-986-1200. *Fax:* 757-671-8661. *E-mail:* rballance@ecpi.edu.

ECPI Technical College

Richmond, Virginia **www.ecpitech.edu/**

- **Proprietary** primarily 2-year, founded 1966
- **Urban** campus
- **Coed**
- **Moderately difficult** entrance level

Faculty *Student/faculty ratio:* 18:1.

Academics *Calendar:* semesters. *Degrees:* certificates, diplomas, associate, and bachelor's.

Student Life *Campus security:* building and parking lot security.

Standardized Tests *Recommended:* SAT (for admission), SAT Subject Tests (for admission).

Financial Aid Of all full-time matriculated undergraduates who enrolled in 2006, 40 Federal Work-Study jobs (averaging $2000).

Applying *Options:* deferred entrance. *Application fee:* $100. *Required:* high school transcript, interview.

Freshman Application Contact Director, ECPI Technical College, 800 Moorefield Park Drive, Richmond, VA 23236. *Phone:* 804-330-5533. *Toll-free phone:* 800-986-1200. *Fax:* 804-330-5577. *E-mail:* agerard@ecpi.edu.

ECPI Technical College

Roanoke, Virginia **www.ecpi.net/**

- **Proprietary** primarily 2-year, founded 1966
- **Suburban** 3-acre campus
- **Coed**
- **Moderately difficult** entrance level

Faculty *Student/faculty ratio:* 15:1.

Academics *Calendar:* semesters. *Degrees:* certificates, diplomas, associate, and bachelor's.

Student Life *Campus security:* building and parking lot security.

Standardized Tests *Recommended:* SAT (for admission), SAT Subject Tests (for admission).

Financial Aid Of all full-time matriculated undergraduates who enrolled in 2006, 20 Federal Work-Study jobs (averaging $2000).

Applying *Options:* electronic application, deferred entrance. *Application fee:* $100. *Required:* high school transcript, interview.

Freshman Application Contact Ms. Carol Rouch, Director, ECPI Technical College, 5234 Airport Road, Roanoke, VA 24012. *Phone:* 540-563-8080. *Toll-free phone:* 800-986-1200. *Fax:* 540-362-5400. *E-mail:* crouch@ecpi.edu.

Emory & Henry College

Emory, Virginia **www.ehc.edu/**

- **Independent United Methodist** comprehensive, founded 1836
- **Rural** 331-acre campus
- **Endowment** $91.3 million
- **Coed** 977 undergraduate students, 95% full-time, 49% women, 51% men
- **Moderately difficult** entrance level, 72% of applicants were admitted

Undergraduates 925 full-time, 52 part-time. Students come from 26 states and territories, 8 other countries, 31% are from out of state, 6% African American, 1% Asian American or Pacific Islander, 0.7% Hispanic American, 0.4% Native American, 1% international, 4% transferred in, 72% live on campus. *Retention:* 68% of 2006 full-time freshmen returned.

Freshmen *Admission:* 1,455 applied, 1,048 admitted, 257 enrolled. *Average high school GPA:* 3.25. *Test scores:* SAT critical reading scores over 500: 55%; SAT math scores over 500: 54%; SAT writing scores over 500: 12%; ACT scores over 18: 94%; SAT critical reading scores over 600: 21%; SAT math scores over 600: 14%; SAT writing scores over 600: 1%; ACT scores over 24: 37%; SAT critical reading scores over 700: 2%; SAT math scores over 700: 1%; ACT scores over 30: 4%.

Faculty *Total:* 121, 62% full-time, 57% with terminal degrees. *Student/faculty ratio:* 10:1.

Majors Accounting; applied mathematics; art; Asian studies (East); biology/biological sciences; business administration and management; chemistry; clinical laboratory science/medical technology; community organization and advocacy; computer science; creative writing; dramatic/theater arts; economics; English; environmental studies; European studies; French; geography; health and physical education; history; interdisciplinary studies; international relations and affairs; mass communication/media; mathematics; music; Near and Middle Eastern studies; philosophy; physics; political science and government; pre-dentistry studies; pre-law studies; pre-medical studies; pre-veterinary studies; psychology; religious studies; sociology; Spanish.

Academics *Calendar:* semesters. *Degrees:* bachelor's and master's. *Special study options:* advanced placement credit, cooperative education, double majors, honors programs, independent study, internships, services for LD students, student-designed majors, study abroad, summer session for credit.

Computers on Campus 202 computers/terminals are available on campus for general student use. Students can access the following: computer help desk, free student e-mail accounts, online (class) grades, online (class) registration, online (class) schedules. Campuswide network is available. Wireless service is available via entire campus.

Student Life *Housing:* on-campus residence required for freshman year. *Options:* coed, men-only, women-only, disabled students. Campus housing is university owned. Freshman campus housing is guaranteed. *Activities and organizations:* drama/theater group, student-run newspaper, radio station, choral group, Alpha Phi Omega, Intramurals, Campus Christian Fellowship, Psychology Club, Student Radio Station. *Campus security:* 24-hour emergency response devices and patrols, late-night transport/escort service, controlled dormitory access. *Student services:* health clinic, personal/psychological counseling.

Athletics Member NCAA. All Division III. *Intercollegiate sports:* baseball M, basketball M/W, cross-country running M/W, football M, golf M, soccer M/W, softball W, tennis M/W, volleyball W. *Intramural sports:* basketball M/W, football M/W, golf M/W, racquetball M/W, skiing (cross-country) M (c)/W (c), skiing (downhill) M (c), soccer M/W, softball M/W, table tennis M/W, tennis M/W, ultimate Frisbee M/W, volleyball M/W, water polo M/W, weight lifting M/W.

Standardized Tests *Required:* SAT or ACT (for admission).

Costs (2008–09) *Comprehensive fee:* $31,840 includes full-time tuition ($23,860) and room and board ($7980). *College room only:* $3930.

Financial Aid Of all full-time matriculated undergraduates who enrolled in 2007, 865 applied for aid, 755 were judged to have need, 217 had their need fully met. 362 Federal Work-Study jobs (averaging $1752). In 2007, 72 non-need-based awards were made. *Average percent of need met:* 85%. *Average financial aid package:* $17,557. *Average need-based loan:* $4090. *Average need-based gift aid:* $14,793. *Average non-need-based aid:* $7456. *Average indebtedness upon graduation:* $11,577.

Applying *Options:* electronic application, early action, deferred entrance. *Application fee:* $30. *Required:* high school transcript, letters of recommendation. *Recommended:* essay or personal statement, interview. *Application deadlines:* rolling (freshmen), rolling (transfers), 12/1 (early action). *Notification:* continuous (freshmen), continuous (transfers), 1/1 (early action).

Freshman Application Contact Ms. Liz Daniels, Dean of Admissions and Financial Aid, Emory & Henry College, 30479 Armbrister Drive, PO Box 10, Emory, VA 24327. *Phone:* 276-944-6133. *Toll-free phone:* 800-848-5493. *Fax:* 276-944-6935. *E-mail:* ehadmiss@ehc.edu.

See page 2658 for the College Close-Up.

FERRUM COLLEGE

Ferrum, Virginia

www.ferrum.edu/

- **Independent United Methodist** 4-year, founded 1913
- **Rural** 720-acre campus
- **Endowment** $47.1 million
- **Coed** 1,240 undergraduate students, 98% full-time, 44% women, 56% men
- **Minimally difficult** entrance level, 78% of applicants were admitted

Undergraduates 1,214 full-time, 26 part-time. Students come from 24 states and territories, 7 other countries, 15% are from out of state, 27% African American, 1% Asian American or Pacific Islander, 2% Hispanic American, 0.8% Native American, 0.8% international, 4% transferred in, 83% live on campus. *Retention:* 60% of 2006 full-time freshmen returned.

Freshmen *Admission:* 2,009 applied, 1,570 admitted, 525 enrolled. *Average high school GPA:* 2.73. *Test scores:* SAT critical reading scores over 500: 25%; SAT math scores over 500: 25%; SAT writing scores over 500: 20%; ACT scores over 18: 53%; SAT critical reading scores over 600: 6%; SAT math scores over 600: 3%; SAT writing scores over 600: 2%; ACT scores over 24: 9%; SAT critical reading scores over 700: 1%; SAT math scores over 700: 1%.

Faculty *Total:* 114, 61% full-time, 45% with terminal degrees. *Student/faculty ratio:* 15:1.

Majors Accounting; agriculture; applied horticulture; art; biology/biological sciences; business administration and management; chemistry; clinical laboratory science/medical technology; computer science; criminal justice/safety; dramatic/theater arts; education; English; environmental studies; fine/studio arts; history; horticultural science; information science/studies; international relations and affairs; liberal arts and sciences/liberal studies; mathematics; parks, recreation and leisure; philosophy; physical education teaching and coaching; political science and government; psychology; religious studies; Russian; social work; sociology; Spanish; sport and fitness administration/management; tourism and travel services management.

Academics *Calendar:* semesters. *Degree:* bachelor's. *Special study options:* academic remediation for entering students, adult/continuing education programs, advanced placement credit, cooperative education, double majors, honors programs, independent study, internships, services for LD students, student-designed majors, study abroad, summer session for credit. *Unusual degree programs:* 3-2 forestry with Shenandoah University; Sherman College of Straight Chiropractic.

Computers on Campus 470 computers/terminals and 550 ports are available on campus for general student use. Students can access the following: campus intranet, computer help desk, free student e-mail accounts, online (class) grades, online (class) schedules. Campuswide network is available. 100% of college-owned or -operated housing units are wired for high-speed Internet access. Wireless service is available via entire campus.

Student Life *Housing:* on-campus residence required through senior year. *Options:* coed, men-only, women-only, disabled students. Campus housing is university owned. Freshman campus housing is guaranteed. *Activities and organizations:* drama/theater group, student-run newspaper, radio station, choral group, Student Government Association, Agriculture Club, BACCHUS, Panther Productions, African American Student Association, Students in Free Enterprise. *Campus security:* 24-hour emergency response devices and patrols, student patrols, late-night transport/escort service, controlled dormitory access. *Student services:* health clinic, personal/psychological counseling.

Athletics Member NCAA. All Division III. *Intercollegiate sports:* baseball M, basketball M/W, cheerleading M/W, cross-country running M/W, football M, golf M, lacrosse W, soccer M/W, softball W, tennis M/W, volleyball W. *Intramural sports:* basketball M/W, football M/W, racquetball M/W, softball M/W, tennis M/W.

Standardized Tests *Required:* SAT or ACT (for admission).

Costs (2007–08) *Comprehensive fee:* $27,785 includes full-time tuition ($20,840), mandatory fees ($45), and room and board ($6900). Part-time tuition: $420 per credit hour.

Financial Aid Of all full-time matriculated undergraduates who enrolled in 2006, 1,113 applied for aid, 1,024 were judged to have need, 5 had their need fully met. 504 Federal Work-Study jobs (averaging $844). 46 state and other part-time jobs (averaging $768). In 2006, 76 non-need-based awards were made. *Average percent of need met:* 81%. *Average financial aid package:* $20,016. *Average need-based loan:* $4584. *Average need-based gift aid:* $4667. *Average non-need-based aid:* $4301. *Average indebtedness upon graduation:* $8520.

Applying *Options:* electronic application, early admission, deferred entrance. *Application fee:* $25. *Required:* high school transcript. *Required for some:* interview. *Recommended:* essay or personal statement, minimum 2.0 GPA, 2 letters of recommendation, interview. *Application deadlines:* rolling (freshmen), rolling (transfers). *Notification:* continuous (freshmen), continuous (transfers).

Freshman Application Contact Ms. Gilda Q. Woods, Director of Admissions, Ferrum College, Spilman-Daniel House, PO Box 1000, Ferrum, VA 24088-9001. *Phone:* 540-365-4290. *Toll-free phone:* 800-868-9797. *Fax:* 540-365-4266. *E-mail:* admissions@ferrum.edu.

GEORGE MASON UNIVERSITY

Fairfax, Virginia

www.gmu.edu/

- **State-supported** university, founded 1957
- **Suburban** 677-acre campus with easy access to Washington, DC
- **Endowment** $54.7 million
- **Coed** 18,589 undergraduate students, 75% full-time, 53% women, 47% men
- **Moderately difficult** entrance level, 56% of applicants were admitted

Undergraduates 13,948 full-time, 4,641 part-time. Students come from 47 states and territories, 125 other countries, 11% are from out of state, 8% African American, 16% Asian American or Pacific Islander, 7% Hispanic American, 0.3% Native American, 4% international, 12% transferred in, 23% live on campus. *Retention:* 85% of 2006 full-time freshmen returned.

Freshmen *Admission:* 13,327 applied, 7,436 admitted, 2,229 enrolled. *Average high school GPA:* 3.46. *Test scores:* SAT critical reading scores over 500: 78%; SAT math scores over 500: 82%; SAT writing scores over 500: 76%; ACT scores over 18: 96%; SAT critical reading scores over 600: 29%; SAT math scores over 600: 31%; SAT writing scores over 600: 25%; ACT scores over 24: 44%; SAT critical reading scores over 700: 5%; SAT math scores over 700: 3%; SAT writing scores over 700: 2%; ACT scores over 30: 3%.

Faculty *Total:* 2,067, 53% full-time. *Student/faculty ratio:* 15:1.

Majors Accounting; anthropology; art; art history, criticism and conservation; astronomy; athletic training/sports medicine; biology/biological sciences; business administration and management; business, management, and marketing related; chemistry; civil engineering related; clinical laboratory science/medical technology; computer and information sciences; computer and information sciences related; computer engineering; criminal justice/police science; dance; dramatic/theater arts; economics; electrical, electronics and communications engineering; engineering related; English; finance; fine/studio arts; foreign languages and literatures; geography; geology/earth science; health professions related; health teacher education; history; interdisciplinary studies; international relations and affairs; Latin American studies; liberal arts and sciences and humanities related; liberal arts and sciences/liberal studies; management sciences and quantitative methods related; marketing/marketing management; mathematics; mathematics and computer science; music performance; nursing (registered nurse training); peace studies and conflict resolution; philosophy; physical education teaching and coaching; physical sciences related; physics; political science and government; psychology; public administration; religious studies; Russian studies; social work; sociology; speech and rhetoric; systems engineering; visual and performing arts.

Academics *Calendar:* semesters. *Degrees:* bachelor's, master's, doctoral, first professional, post-master's, and postbachelor's certificates. *Special study options:* accelerated degree program, adult/continuing education programs, advanced placement credit, cooperative education, distance learning, double majors, English as a second language, external degree program, honors programs, independent study, internships, off-campus study, part-time degree program, services for LD students, student-designed majors, study abroad, summer session for credit. *ROTC:* Army (b), Navy (c), Air Force (c).

Computers on Campus 1,545 computers/terminals are available on campus for general student use. Students can access the following: campus intranet, computer help desk, free student e-mail accounts, online (class) grades, online (class) registration, online (class) schedules. Campuswide network is available. 100% of college-owned or -operated housing units are wired for high-speed Internet access. Wireless service is available via entire campus.

Student Life *Housing options:* coed, men-only, women-only, disabled students. Campus housing is university owned and leased by the school. Freshman campus housing is guaranteed. *Activities and organizations:* drama/theater group, student-run newspaper, radio and television station, choral group, intramurals, student government, club sports, volunteer and community service, national fraternities, national sororities. *Campus security:* 24-hour emergency response devices and patrols, student patrols, late-night transport/escort service, controlled dormitory access. *Student services:* health clinic, personal/psychological counseling, women's center.

Athletics Member NCAA. All Division I. *Intercollegiate sports:* baseball M (s), basketball M (s)/W (s), cheerleading M/W, crew W, cross-country running M (s)/W (s), golf M (s), lacrosse W (s), soccer M (s)/W (s), softball W (s), swimming and diving M (s)/W (s), tennis M (s)/W (s), track and field M (s)/W (s), volleyball M (s)/W (s), wrestling M (s). *Intramural sports:* crew M, equestrian sports M/W, field hockey W, football M, ice hockey M/W, lacrosse M, rugby M, ultimate Frisbee M/W.

Standardized Tests *Required for some:* SAT or ACT (for admission). *Recommended:* SAT and SAT Subject Tests or ACT (for admission).

Costs (2007–08) *Tuition:* state resident $5035 full-time, $210 per credit part-time; nonresident $17,923 full-time, $747 per credit part-time. Full-time tuition and fees vary according to course load. Part-time tuition and fees vary according to course load. *Required fees:* $1805 full-time. *Room and board:* $7020; room only: $4000. Room and board charges vary according to board plan and housing facility. *Payment plans:* installment, deferred payment. *Waivers:* senior citizens and employees or children of employees.

Financial Aid Of all full-time matriculated undergraduates who enrolled in 2007, 7,398 applied for aid, 5,429 were judged to have need, 821 had their need fully met. 1,006 Federal Work-Study jobs (averaging $2048). In 2007, 347 non-need-based awards were made. *Average percent of need met:* 66%. *Average financial aid package:* $9260. *Average need-based loan:* $4307. *Average need-based gift aid:* $5344. *Average non-need-based aid:* $5414. *Average indebtedness upon graduation:* $16,705.

Applying *Options:* electronic application, early action, deferred entrance. *Application fee:* $70. *Required:* essay or personal statement, high school transcript, minimum 2.0 GPA, interview. *Recommended:* minimum 3.0 GPA. *Application deadlines:* 1/15 (freshmen), 4/1 (transfers), 11/1 (early action). *Notification:* 4/1 (freshmen), continuous (transfers), 12/20 (early action).

Freshman Application Contact Mr. Eddie Tallent, Assistant Dean, Executive Director Undergraduate Admissions, George Mason University, 4400 University Drive, MSN 3A4, Fairfax, VA 22030-4444. *Phone:* 703-993-2398. *E-mail:* etallent@gmu.edu.

HAMPDEN-SYDNEY COLLEGE

Hampden-Sydney, Virginia **www.hsc.edu/**

- **Independent** 4-year, founded 1776, affiliated with Presbyterian Church (U.S.A.)
- **Rural** 1200-acre campus with easy access to Richmond
- **Endowment** $142.4 million
- **Men only** 1,122 undergraduate students, 100% full-time
- **Moderately difficult** entrance level, 67% of applicants were admitted

Undergraduates 1,122 full-time. Students come from 40 states and territories, 18 other countries, 34% are from out of state, 5% African American, 0.8% Asian American or Pacific Islander, 1% Hispanic American, 0.2% Native American, 2% international, 2% transferred in, 95% live on campus. *Retention:* 77% of 2006 full-time freshmen returned.

Freshmen *Admission:* 1,470 applied, 984 admitted, 334 enrolled. *Average high school GPA:* 3.26. *Test scores:* SAT critical reading scores over 500: 78%; SAT math scores over 500: 81%; SAT critical reading scores over 600: 29%; SAT math scores over 600: 35%; SAT critical reading scores over 700: 2%; SAT math scores over 700: 2%.

Faculty *Total:* 124, 78% full-time, 49% with terminal degrees. *Student/faculty ratio:* 10:1.

Majors Ancient/classical Greek; applied mathematics; biochemistry; biology/biological sciences; biophysics; business/managerial economics; chemistry; classics and languages, literatures and linguistics; computer science; econometrics and quantitative economics; economics; English; fine/studio arts; French; German; history; humanities; international relations and affairs; Latin; mathematics; mathematics and computer science; philosophy; physics; physics related; political science and government; psychology; religious studies; Spanish.

Academics *Calendar:* semesters. *Degree:* bachelor's. *Special study options:* academic remediation for entering students, accelerated degree program, advanced placement credit, double majors, honors programs, independent study, internships, off-campus study, study abroad, summer session for credit. *ROTC:* Army (c). *Unusual degree programs:* 3-2 engineering with University of Virginia.

Computers on Campus 140 computers/terminals are available on campus for general student use. Students can access the following: campus intranet, computer help desk, free student e-mail accounts, online (class) grades, online (class) registration, online (class) schedules. Campuswide network is available. 100% of college-owned or -operated housing units are wired for high-speed Internet access.

Student Life *Housing:* on-campus residence required through senior year. *Options:* men-only. Campus housing is university owned. Freshman campus housing is guaranteed. *Activities and organizations:* drama/theater group, student-run newspaper, radio station, choral group, Republican Society, Pre-Health Society, Outsiders Club, Tiger Athletic Club, Pre-Law Society, national fraternities. *Campus security:* 24-hour emergency response devices and patrols. *Student services:* health clinic, personal/psychological counseling.

Athletics Member NCAA. All Division III. *Intercollegiate sports:* baseball M, basketball M, crew M (c), cross-country running M, fencing M (c), football M, golf M, lacrosse M, riflery M (c), rugby M (c), soccer M, tennis M, ultimate Frisbee M (c). *Intramural sports:* basketball M, football M, soccer M, softball M, volleyball M.

Standardized Tests *Required:* SAT or ACT (for admission). *Recommended:* SAT Subject Tests (for admission).

Costs (2008–09) *One-time required fee:* $250. *Comprehensive fee:* $38,402 includes full-time tuition ($28,144), mandatory fees ($1110), and room and board ($9148). Part-time tuition: $904 per credit hour.

Financial Aid Of all full-time matriculated undergraduates who enrolled in 2006, 688 applied for aid, 539 were judged to have need, 175 had their need fully met. 206 Federal Work-Study jobs (averaging $1540). In 2006, 576 non-need-based awards were made. *Average percent of need met:* 85%. *Average financial aid package:* $20,484. *Average need-based loan:* $4720. *Average need-based gift aid:* $16,067. *Average non-need-based aid:* $16,880. *Average indebtedness upon graduation:* $16,472.

Applying *Options:* electronic application, early admission, early decision, early action. *Application fee:* $30. *Required:* essay or personal statement, high school transcript, minimum 2.0 GPA, 2 letters of recommendation. *Recommended:* minimum 3.0 GPA, interview. *Application deadlines:* 3/1 (freshmen), 7/1 (transfers), 1/15 (early action). *Early decision deadline:* 11/15. *Notification:* continuous until 4/15 (freshmen), 12/15 (early decision), 2/15 (early action).

Freshman Application Contact Ms. Anita H. Garland, Dean of Admissions, Hampden-Sydney College, PO Box 667, Hampden-Sydney, VA 23943-0667. *Phone:* 434-223-6120. *Toll-free phone:* 800-755-0733. *Fax:* 434-223-6346. *E-mail:* hsapp@hsc.edu.

See page 2660 for the College Close-Up.

HAMPTON UNIVERSITY

Hampton, Virginia **www.hamptonu.edu/**

- **Independent** university, founded 1868
- **Urban** 210-acre campus with easy access to Norfolk
- **Endowment** $185.8 million
- **Coed** 4,886 undergraduate students, 94% full-time, 64% women, 36% men
- **Moderately difficult** entrance level, 45% of applicants were admitted

Undergraduates 4,603 full-time, 283 part-time. Students come from 41 states and territories, 20 other countries, 70% are from out of state, 95% African American, 0.6% Asian American or Pacific Islander, 0.9% Hispanic American, 0.3% Native American, 0.8% international, 4% transferred in, 59% live on campus. *Retention:* 85% of 2006 full-time freshmen returned.

Freshmen *Admission:* 5,401 applied, 2,433 admitted, 1,202 enrolled. *Average high school GPA:* 3.2. *Test scores:* SAT critical reading scores over 500: 66%; SAT math scores over 500: 53%; ACT scores over 18: 64%; SAT critical reading scores over 600: 19%; SAT math scores over 600: 7%; ACT scores over 24: 4%; SAT critical reading scores over 700: 1%; SAT math scores over 700: 1%; ACT scores over 30: 1%.

Faculty *Total:* 447, 72% full-time. *Student/faculty ratio:* 16:1.

Majors Accounting; advertising; air traffic control; architecture; Army R.O.T.C./military science; art; art teacher education; audiology and speech-language pathology; aviation/airway management; biology/biological sciences; broadcast journalism; business administration and management; business teacher education; ceramic arts and ceramics; chemical engineering; chemistry; child development; commercial and advertising art; computer science; construction engineering technology; construction management; criminal justice/law enforcement administration; developmental and child psychology; dramatic/theater arts; drawing; economics; education; electrical, electronic and communications engineering technology; electrical, electronics and communications engineering; elementary education; English; environmental studies; family and consumer sciences/home economics teacher education; fashion/apparel design; fashion merchandising; finance; fire science; general studies; health teacher education; history; hotel/motel administration; information science/studies; interior design; jazz/jazz studies; journalism; kindergarten/preschool education; legal assistant/paralegal; marine biology and biological oceanography; marine science/merchant marine officer; marketing/marketing management; mass communication/media; mathematics;

middle school education; modern languages; molecular biology; music; music related; music teacher education; Navy/Marine Corps R.O.T.C./naval science; nursing (registered nurse training); photography; physical education teaching and coaching; physical sciences; physical therapy; physics; political science and government; pre-dentistry studies; pre-law studies; pre-medical studies; pre-veterinary studies; psychology; public relations/image management; religious studies; sales, distribution and marketing; secondary education; social sciences; social work; sociology; special education; speech therapy; sport and fitness administration/management; therapeutic recreation.

Academics *Calendar:* semesters. *Degrees:* certificates, associate, bachelor's, master's, doctoral, and first professional. *Special study options:* academic remediation for entering students, accelerated degree program, adult/continuing education programs, advanced placement credit, cooperative education, distance learning, double majors, honors programs, independent study, internships, off-campus study, part-time degree program, services for LD students, study abroad, summer session for credit. *ROTC:* Army (b), Navy (b).

Computers on Campus 1,300 computers/terminals are available on campus for general student use. Students can access the following: online (class) registration. Campuswide network is available.

Student Life *Housing options:* coed, men-only, women-only. Campus housing is university owned. Freshman applicants given priority for college housing. *Activities and organizations:* drama/theater group, student-run newspaper, radio station, choral group, marching band, student government, student leaders, Student Union Board, student recruitment team, resident assistants, national fraternities, national sororities. *Campus security:* 24-hour emergency response devices and patrols, controlled dormitory access, emergency call boxes. *Student services:* health clinic, personal/psychological counseling, women's center.

Athletics Member NCAA. All Division I. *Intercollegiate sports:* basketball M (s)/W (s), bowling W (s), cross-country running M (s)/W (s), football M (s), golf M (s)/W (s), sailing M (s)/W (s), softball W (s), tennis M (s)/W (s), track and field M (s)/W (s), volleyball W (s). *Intramural sports:* basketball M/W, bowling W, football M, sailing M/W, soccer M/W, softball M/W, volleyball W.

Standardized Tests *Required:* SAT or ACT (for admission).

Costs (2007–08) *Comprehensive fee:* \$22,694 includes full-time tuition (\$14,026), mandatory fees (\$1584), and room and board (\$7084). Full-time tuition and fees vary according to course load, degree level, and program. Part-time tuition: \$350 per credit. *College room only:* \$3684. Room and board charges vary according to board plan and housing facility. *Payment plan:* deferred payment. *Waivers:* employees or children of employees.

Financial Aid Of all full-time matriculated undergraduates who enrolled in 2005, 4,053 applied for aid, 3,783 were judged to have need, 2,918 had their need fully met. 378 Federal Work-Study jobs (averaging \$1800). In 2005, 320 non-need-based awards were made. *Average percent of need met:* 46%. *Average financial aid package:* \$3220. *Average need-based loan:* \$2892. *Average need-based gift aid:* \$2058. *Average non-need-based aid:* \$7474. *Average indebtedness upon graduation:* \$3645. *Financial aid deadline:* 3/1.

Applying *Options:* electronic application, early admission, deferred entrance. *Application fee:* \$35. *Required:* essay or personal statement, high school transcript, minimum 2.0 GPA, 1 letter of recommendation. *Application deadline:* 3/1 (freshmen). *Early decision deadline:* 12/1. *Notification:* continuous until 7/31 (freshmen), 12/15 (early decision).

Freshman Application Contact Mrs. Barbara Inman, Assistant Vice President of Student Affairs, Hampton University, Hampton, VA 23668. *Phone:* 757-727-5495. *Toll-free phone:* 800-624-3328. *Fax:* 757-727-5095. *E-mail:* barbara.inman@hamptonu.edu.

HOLLINS UNIVERSITY

Roanoke, Virginia **www.hollins.edu/**

- **Independent** comprehensive, founded 1842
- **Suburban** 475-acre campus
- **Endowment** \$126.7 million
- **Undergraduate: women only; graduate: coed** 783 undergraduate students, 96% full-time, 100% women
- **Moderately difficult** entrance level, 88% of applicants were admitted

Undergraduates 755 full-time, 28 part-time. Students come from 43 states and territories, 11 other countries, 46% are from out of state, 8% African American, 2% Asian American or Pacific Islander, 3% Hispanic American, 0.6% Native American, 3% international, 4% transferred in, 89% live on campus. *Retention:* 68% of 2006 full-time freshmen returned.

Freshmen *Admission:* 632 applied, 559 admitted, 205 enrolled. *Average high school GPA:* 3.5. *Test scores:* SAT critical reading scores over 500: 86%; SAT math scores over 500: 67%; SAT writing scores over 500: 85%; ACT scores over 18: 89%; SAT critical reading scores over 600: 46%; SAT math scores over 600: 20%; SAT writing scores over 600: 36%; ACT scores over 24: 55%; SAT critical reading scores over 700: 12%; SAT math scores over 700: 1%; SAT writing scores over 700: 5%; ACT scores over 30: 7%.

Faculty *Total:* 108, 67% full-time, 77% with terminal degrees. *Student/faculty ratio:* 9:1.

Majors Art; art history, criticism and conservation; arts management; biology/biological sciences; business/commerce; chemistry; classics and languages, literatures and linguistics; creative writing; dance; dramatic/theater arts; economics; education; English; film/video and photographic arts related; French; German; history; interdisciplinary studies; international relations and affairs; mass communication/media; mathematics; music; philosophy; physics; political science and government; psychology; religious studies; sociology; Spanish; women's studies.

Academics *Calendar:* 4-1-4. *Degrees:* bachelor's, master's, and post-master's certificates. *Special study options:* accelerated degree program, adult/continuing education programs, advanced placement credit, double majors, independent study, internships, off-campus study, part-time degree program, student-designed majors, study abroad. *Unusual degree programs:* 3-2 engineering with Washington University in St. Louis.

Computers on Campus 100 computers/terminals are available on campus for general student use. Students can access the following: campus intranet, computer help desk, free student e-mail accounts, online (class) grades, online (class) registration, online (class) schedules, applications software. Campuswide network is available. 100% of college-owned or -operated housing units are wired for high-speed Internet access. Wireless service is available via entire campus.

Student Life *Housing:* on-campus residence required through senior year. *Options:* women-only. Campus housing is university owned. Freshman campus housing is guaranteed. *Activities and organizations:* drama/theater group, student-run newspaper, television station, choral group, Student Government Association, SHARE (volunteer group), Religious Life Association, Student Athletic Association, campus political organizations. *Campus security:* 24-hour emergency response devices and patrols, late-night transport/escort service, controlled dormitory access, emergency call boxes. *Student services:* health clinic, personal/psychological counseling, women's center.

Athletics Member NCAA. All Division III. *Intercollegiate sports:* basketball W, equestrian sports W, fencing W (c), golf W, lacrosse W, soccer W, swimming and diving W, tennis W.

Standardized Tests *Required:* SAT or ACT (for admission).

Costs (2008–09) *Comprehensive fee:* \$36,705 includes full-time tuition (\$26,500), mandatory fees (\$555), and room and board (\$9650). Part-time tuition: \$830 per credit.

Financial Aid Of all full-time matriculated undergraduates who enrolled in 2005, 744 applied for aid, 474 were judged to have need, 101 had their need fully met. 278 Federal Work-Study jobs (averaging \$2111). 86 state and other part-time jobs (averaging \$1948). In 2005, 190 non-need-based awards were made. *Average percent of need met:* 75%. *Average financial aid package:* \$17,913. *Average need-based loan:* \$4761. *Average need-based gift aid:* \$14,983. *Average non-need-based aid:* \$9830. *Average indebtedness upon graduation:* \$16,853. *Financial aid deadline:* 2/15.

Applying *Options:* electronic application, early admission, early decision, deferred entrance. *Application fee:* \$35. *Required:* essay or personal statement, high school transcript, 3 letters of recommendation. *Recommended:* interview. *Application deadline:* rolling (freshmen). *Early decision deadline:* 11/15. *Notification:* continuous (freshmen), 12/15 (early decision).

Freshman Application Contact Ms. Rebecca Eckstein, Dean of Admissions, Hollins University, PO Box 9707, Roanoke, VA 24020-1707. *Phone:* 540-362-6401. *Toll-free phone:* 800-456-9595. *Fax:* 540-362-6218. *E-mail:* huadm@hollins.edu.

See page 2662 for the College Close-Up.

ITT TECHNICAL INSTITUTE

Chantilly, Virginia **www.itt-tech.edu/**

- **Proprietary** primarily 2-year, founded 2002, part of ITT Educational Services, Inc
- **Coed**
- **Minimally difficult** entrance level

Academics *Calendar:* quarters. *Degrees:* associate and bachelor's.

Standardized Tests *Required:* (for admission).

Applying *Options:* deferred entrance. *Application fee:* \$100. *Required:* high school transcript, interview. *Recommended:* letters of recommendation.

Freshman Application Contact Ms. Peggy T. Payne, Director of Recruitment, ITT Technical Institute, 14420 Albemarle Point Place, Chantilly, VA 20151. *Phone:* 703-263-2541. *Toll-free phone:* 888-895-8324.

ITT TECHNICAL INSTITUTE

Norfolk, Virginia www.itt-tech.edu/

- **Proprietary** primarily 2-year, founded 1988, part of ITT Educational Services, Inc
- **Suburban** 2-acre campus
- **Coed**
- **Minimally difficult** entrance level

Academics *Calendar:* quarters. *Degrees:* associate and bachelor's.

Standardized Tests *Required:* Wonderlic aptitude test (for admission).

Financial Aid Of all full-time matriculated undergraduates who enrolled in 2006, 3 Federal Work-Study jobs (averaging $5000).

Applying *Options:* deferred entrance. *Application fee:* $100. *Required:* high school transcript, interview. *Recommended:* letters of recommendation.

Freshman Application Contact Mr. Jack Keesee, Director of Recruitment, ITT Technical Institute, 863 Glenrock Road, Norfolk, VA 23502. *Phone:* 757-466-1260. *Toll-free phone:* 888-253-8324.

ITT TECHNICAL INSTITUTE

Richmond, Virginia www.itt-tech.edu/

- **Proprietary** primarily 2-year, founded 1999, part of ITT Educational Services, Inc
- **Coed**
- **Minimally difficult** entrance level

Academics *Calendar:* quarters. *Degrees:* associate and bachelor's.

Standardized Tests *Required:* Wonderlic aptitude test (for admission).

Applying *Options:* deferred entrance. *Application fee:* $100. *Required:* high school transcript, interview. *Recommended:* letters of recommendation.

Freshman Application Contact Director of Recruitment, ITT Technical Institute, 300 Gateway Centre Parkway, Richmond, VA 23235. *Phone:* 804-330-4992. *Toll-free phone:* 888-330-4888.

ITT TECHNICAL INSTITUTE

Springfield, Virginia www.itt-tech.edu/

- **Proprietary** primarily 2-year, founded 2002, part of ITT Educational Services, Inc
- **Coed**
- **Minimally difficult** entrance level

Academics *Calendar:* quarters. *Degrees:* associate and bachelor's.

Standardized Tests *Required:* Wonderlic aptitude test (for admission).

Applying *Options:* deferred entrance. *Application fee:* $100. *Required:* high school transcript, interview. *Recommended:* letters of recommendation.

Freshman Application Contact Ms. Cheryl Painter, Director of Recruitment, ITT Technical Institute, 7300 Boston Boulevard, Springfield, VA 22153. *Phone:* 703-440-9535. *Toll-free phone:* 866-817-8324.

JAMES MADISON UNIVERSITY

Harrisonburg, Virginia www.jmu.edu/

- **State-supported** comprehensive, founded 1908
- **Small-town** 655-acre campus
- **Endowment** $35.9 million
- **Coed** 16,414 undergraduate students, 95% full-time, 60% women, 40% men
- **Very difficult** entrance level, 64% of applicants were admitted

Undergraduates 15,651 full-time, 763 part-time. Students come from 45 states and territories, 50 other countries, 30% are from out of state, 4% African American, 5% Asian American or Pacific Islander, 2% Hispanic American, 0.3% Native American, 0.9% international, 4% transferred in, 36% live on campus. *Retention:* 91% of 2006 full-time freshmen returned.

Freshmen *Admission:* 18,352 applied, 11,660 admitted, 3,867 enrolled. *Average high school GPA:* 3.71. *Test scores:* SAT critical reading scores over 500: 81%; SAT math scores over 500: 85%; ACT scores over 18: 98%; SAT critical reading scores over 600: 27%; SAT math scores over 600: 33%; ACT scores over 24: 55%; SAT critical reading scores over 700: 3%; SAT math scores over 700: 3%; ACT scores over 30: 3%.

Faculty *Total:* 1,252, 68% full-time, 63% with terminal degrees. *Student/faculty ratio:* 16:1.

Majors Accounting; anthropology; art; art history, criticism and conservation; athletic training; biology/biological sciences; business administration and management; business/managerial economics; chemistry; community health services counseling; computer and information sciences; dramatic/theater arts; economics; engineering; English; finance; finance and financial management services related; foods, nutrition, and wellness; foreign languages and literatures; geography; geology/earth science; health and physical education; health/health care administration; history; hospitality administration; information science/studies; international business/trade/commerce; international relations and affairs; liberal arts and sciences/liberal studies; marketing/marketing management; mathematics; music performance; nursing (registered nurse training); philosophy and religious studies related; physics; political science and government; psychology; public administration; science, technology and society; social sciences; social work; sociology; speech-language pathology; systems science and theory; technical and business writing.

Academics *Calendar:* semesters. *Degrees:* bachelor's, master's, doctoral, and post-master's certificates (also offers specialist in education degree). *Special study options:* accelerated degree program, adult/continuing education programs, advanced placement credit, distance learning, double majors, freshman honors college, honors programs, independent study, internships, part-time degree program, services for LD students, study abroad, summer session for credit. *ROTC:* Army (b), Air Force (c). *Unusual degree programs:* 3-2 engineering with University of Virginia; forestry with Virginia Tech.

Computers on Campus 600 computers/terminals and 7,000 ports are available on campus for general student use. Students can access the following: campus intranet, computer help desk, free student e-mail accounts, online (class) grades, online (class) registration, online (class) schedules. Campuswide network is available. 100% of college-owned or -operated housing units are wired for high-speed Internet access. Wireless service is available via classrooms, learning centers, libraries, student centers.

Student Life *Housing:* on-campus residence required for freshman year. *Options:* coed. Campus housing is university owned and leased by the school. Freshman campus housing is guaranteed. *Activities and organizations:* drama/theater group, student-run newspaper, radio station, choral group, marching band, Student Ambassadors, Student Duke Club, Campus Crusades for Christ, Intervarsity Christian Fellowship, Catholic Campus Ministry, national fraternities, national sororities. *Campus security:* 24-hour emergency response devices and patrols, student patrols, late-night transport/escort service, controlled dormitory access, lighted pathways. *Student services:* health clinic, personal/psychological counseling, women's center.

Athletics Member NCAA. All Division I except football (Division I-AA). *Intercollegiate sports:* baseball M (s), basketball M (s)/W (s), cheerleading M/W, cross-country running W (s), field hockey W (s), golf M (s)/W (s), lacrosse W (s), soccer M (s)/W (s), softball W (s), swimming and diving W (s), tennis M (s)/W (s), track and field W (s), volleyball W (s). *Intramural sports:* archery M (c)/W (c), baseball M (c), basketball M/W, bowling M/W, cheerleading W (c), cross-country running M (c)/W (c), equestrian sports M (c)/W (c), fencing M (c)/W (c), field hockey W (c), football M, golf M/W, gymnastics M (c)/W (c), lacrosse M (c)/W (c), racquetball M/W, rugby M (c)/W (c), skiing (downhill) M (c)/W (c), soccer M/W, softball M/W, swimming and diving M (c)/W (c), table tennis M/W, tennis M/W, track and field M (c)/W (c), ultimate Frisbee M/W, volleyball M/W, water polo M (c)/W (c), wrestling M (c).

Standardized Tests *Required:* SAT or ACT (for admission).

Costs (2007–08) *Tuition:* state resident $3420 full-time, $222 per credit hour part-time; nonresident $14,140 full-time, $579 per credit hour part-time. Part-time tuition and fees vary according to course load. *Required fees:* $3246 full-time. *Room and board:* $7108; room only: $3712. Room and board charges vary according to board plan and housing facility. *Payment plan:* installment. *Waivers:* senior citizens and employees or children of employees.

Financial Aid Of all full-time matriculated undergraduates who enrolled in 2007, 12,214 applied for aid, 5,504 were judged to have need, 2,781 had their need fully met. 1,940 Federal Work-Study jobs (averaging $1809). 2,405 state and other part-time jobs (averaging $1966). In 2007, 288 non-need-based awards were made. *Average percent of need met:* 50%. *Average financial aid package:* $8116. *Average need-based loan:* $4180. *Average need-based gift aid:* $6419. *Average non-need-based aid:* $2039. *Average indebtedness upon graduation:* $16,546.

Applying *Options:* electronic application, early action, deferred entrance. *Application fee:* $40. *Required:* high school transcript. *Recommended:* minimum 3.0 GPA. *Application deadlines:* 1/15 (freshmen), 3/1 (transfers), 11/1 (early action). *Notification:* 4/1 (freshmen), 4/15 (transfers), 1/15 (early action).

Freshman Application Contact Mr. Michael D. Walsh, Director of Admission, James Madison University, Office of Admission, Sonner Hall MSC 0101, Harrisonburg, VA 22807. *Phone:* 540-568-5681. *Fax:* 540-568-3332. *E-mail:* admissions@jmu.edu.

JEFFERSON COLLEGE OF HEALTH SCIENCES

Roanoke, Virginia **www.jchs.edu/**

- **Independent** comprehensive, founded 1982
- **Urban** 1-acre campus
- **Endowment** $2.2 million
- **Coed** 939 undergraduate students, 70% full-time, 83% women, 17% men
- **Moderately difficult** entrance level, 43% of applicants were admitted

Undergraduates 660 full-time, 279 part-time. Students come from 16 states and territories, 2 other countries, 5% are from out of state, 13% African American, 1% Asian American or Pacific Islander, 0.6% Hispanic American, 0.3% Native American, 0.4% international, 28% transferred in, 5% live on campus. *Retention:* 67% of 2006 full-time freshmen returned.

Freshmen *Admission:* 554 applied, 237 admitted, 91 enrolled. *Average high school GPA:* 3.07. *Test scores:* SAT critical reading scores over 500: 31%; SAT writing scores over 500: 20%; ACT scores over 18: 80%; SAT critical reading scores over 600: 6%; SAT writing scores over 600: 4%; ACT scores over 24: 5%; ACT scores over 30: 5%.

Faculty *Total:* 100, 62% full-time, 23% with terminal degrees. *Student/faculty ratio:* 11:1.

Majors Athletic training; biological and physical sciences; biomedical sciences; emergency medical technology (EMT paramedic); fire protection and safety technology; health/health care administration; health/medical psychology; kinesiology and exercise science; nursing (registered nurse training); occupational therapist assistant; physical therapist assistant; physician assistant; radiologic technology/science; respiratory care therapy.

Academics *Calendar:* semesters. *Degrees:* certificates, associate, bachelor's, and master's. *Special study options:* academic remediation for entering students, accelerated degree program, adult/continuing education programs, advanced placement credit, distance learning, internships, part-time degree program, services for LD students, summer session for credit.

Computers on Campus 56 computers/terminals are available on campus for general student use. Students can access the following: computer help desk, free student e-mail accounts, online (class) grades, online (class) registration, online (class) schedules. Campuswide network is available. 100% of college-owned or -operated housing units are wired for high-speed Internet access.

Student Life *Housing options:* coed. Campus housing is university owned. *Activities and organizations:* student-run newspaper, choral group, Jefferson Activities Group (JAG), Student Ambassadors, Hands of Healing, American Medical Students Association (AMSA), Crossroads. *Campus security:* 24-hour emergency response devices and patrols, late-night transport/escort service, controlled dormitory access. *Student services:* health clinic, personal/psychological counseling.

Athletics *Intercollegiate sports:* basketball M (c), cross-country running M (c)/W (c), softball M (c)/W (c), volleyball M (c)/W (c). *Intramural sports:* table tennis M (c)/W (c).

Standardized Tests *Required:* SAT or ACT (for admission). *Recommended:* SAT (for admission).

Costs (2007–08) *Comprehensive fee:* $21,810 includes full-time tuition ($15,500) and room and board ($6310). Full-time tuition and fees vary according to program. Part-time tuition: $445 per credit hour. *Payment plan:* installment. *Waivers:* employees or children of employees.

Financial Aid Of all full-time matriculated undergraduates who enrolled in 2005, 894 applied for aid, 518 were judged to have need, 35 had their need fully met. 185 Federal Work-Study jobs (averaging $1414). In 2005, 98 non-need-based awards were made. *Average percent of need met:* 47%. *Average financial aid package:* $10,391. *Average need-based loan:* $4409. *Average need-based gift aid:* $6270. *Average non-need-based aid:* $9164. *Average indebtedness upon graduation:* $20,780.

Applying *Options:* electronic application, deferred entrance. *Application fee:* $35. *Required:* high school transcript, minimum 2.0 GPA. *Required for some:* letters of recommendation, interview, volunteer experience. *Application deadline:* rolling (freshmen). *Notification:* continuous (freshmen).

Freshman Application Contact Jefferson College of Health Sciences, PO Box 13186, Roanoke, VA 24031-3186. *Phone:* 540-985-9083. *Toll-free phone:* 888-985-8483.

LIBERTY UNIVERSITY

Lynchburg, Virginia **www.liberty.edu/**

- **Independent nondenominational** comprehensive, founded 1971
- **Suburban** 4400-acre campus
- **Endowment** $6.2 million
- **Coed** 18,597 undergraduate students, 70% full-time, 52% women, 48% men
- **Minimally difficult** entrance level, 95% of applicants were admitted

Undergraduates 12,947 full-time, 5,650 part-time. Students come from 52 states and territories, 72 other countries, 69% are from out of state, 12% African American, 1% Asian American or Pacific Islander, 4% Hispanic American, 0.6% Native American, 3% international, 15% transferred in, 33% live on campus. *Retention:* 70% of 2006 full-time freshmen returned.

Freshmen *Admission:* 6,583 applied, 6,258 admitted, 3,394 enrolled. *Average high school GPA:* 3.17. *Test scores:* SAT critical reading scores over 500: 49%; SAT math scores over 500: 42%; ACT scores over 18: 78%; SAT critical reading scores over 600: 14%; SAT math scores over 600: 10%; ACT scores over 24: 26%; SAT critical reading scores over 700: 2%; SAT math scores over 700: 1%; ACT scores over 30: 2%.

Faculty *Total:* 825, 41% full-time. *Student/faculty ratio:* 24:1.

Majors Accounting; aeronautics/aviation/aerospace science and technology; apparel and textiles; athletic training; biochemistry/biophysics and molecular biology; biology/biological sciences; biology teacher education; business administration and management; business/commerce; business teacher education; communication/speech communication and rhetoric; computer and information sciences; computer engineering; computer software engineering; computer teacher education; criminal justice/law enforcement administration; design and visual communications; developmental and child psychology; economics; education (multiple levels); elementary education; engineering; English; English as a second/foreign language (teaching); English/language arts teacher education; family and consumer sciences/home economics teacher education; family and consumer sciences/human sciences; fashion merchandising; health and physical education; health services/allied health/health sciences; health teacher education; history; history teacher education; human development and family studies; industrial engineering; interdisciplinary studies; journalism; kinesiology and exercise science; linguistics; management information systems; mathematics; mathematics teacher education; multi-/interdisciplinary studies related; music; music teacher education; nursing (registered nurse training); philosophy; physical education teaching and coaching; political science and government; psychology; public health education and promotion; religious/sacred music; religious studies; social sciences; social science teacher education; Spanish; Spanish language teacher education; special education; sport and fitness administration/management; web page, digital/multimedia and information resources design.

Academics *Calendar:* semesters. *Degrees:* certificates, associate, bachelor's, master's, doctoral, first professional, and post-master's certificates (also offers external degree program with significant enrollment not reflected in profile). *Special study options:* academic remediation for entering students, accelerated degree program, advanced placement credit, cooperative education, distance learning, double majors, English as a second language, external degree program, honors programs, independent study, internships, part-time degree program, services for LD students, student-designed majors, summer session for credit. *ROTC:* Army (b), Air Force (c).

Computers on Campus 406 computers/terminals are available on campus for general student use. Students can access the following: online (class) registration. Campuswide network is available.

Student Life *Housing:* on-campus residence required through junior year. *Options:* men-only, women-only, disabled students. Campus housing is university owned and leased by the school. Freshman campus housing is guaranteed. *Activities and organizations:* drama/theater group, student-run newspaper, radio station, choral group, marching band, College Republicans, Youthquest, Circle K. *Campus security:* 24-hour patrols, late-night transport/escort service, 24-hour emergency dispatch. *Student services:* health clinic, personal/psychological counseling.

Athletics Member NCAA. All Division I except football (Division I-AA). *Intercollegiate sports:* baseball M (s), basketball M (s)/W (s), cheerleading M (s)/W (s), cross-country running M (s)/W (s), field hockey W (c), golf M (s), ice hockey M (c), lacrosse M (c), soccer M (s)/W (s), softball W (s), tennis M (s)/W (s), track and field M (s)/W (s), volleyball W (s). *Intramural sports:* basketball M/W, football M/W, soccer M/W, softball M/W, tennis M/W, volleyball M/W.

Standardized Tests *Required:* SAT or ACT (for admission).

Costs (2007–08) *Comprehensive fee:* $21,200 includes full-time tuition ($14,850), mandatory fees ($950), and room and board ($5400). Part-time tuition: $495 per hour.

Financial Aid Of all full-time matriculated undergraduates who enrolled in 2004, 7,440 applied for aid, 6,259 were judged to have need, 1,004 had their need fully met. 2,712 Federal Work-Study jobs (averaging $1170). In 2004, 1207 non-need-based awards were made. *Average percent of need met:* 69%. *Average financial aid package:* $10,538. *Average need-based loan:* $4055. *Average need-based gift aid:* $1652. *Average non-need-based aid:* $5305. *Average indebtedness upon graduation:* $18,078.

Applying *Options:* electronic application, early admission, deferred entrance. *Application fee:* $50. *Required:* essay or personal statement, high school transcript. *Required for some:* letters of recommendation, interview. *Recommended:* minimum 2.0 GPA, letters of recommendation. *Application deadline:* 6/30 (freshmen). *Notification:* continuous until 8/15 (freshmen).

Freshman Application Contact Mr. Richmond Plyter, Director of Admissions, Liberty University, 1971 University Boulevard, Lynchburg, VA 24502. *Phone:* 434-592-3072. *Toll-free phone:* 800-543-5317. *Fax:* 800-542-2311. *E-mail:* admissions@liberty.edu.

See page 2664 for the College Close-Up.

LONGWOOD UNIVERSITY

Farmville, Virginia www.longwood.edu/

- **State-supported** comprehensive, founded 1839, part of The State Council of Higher Education for Virginia
- **Small-town** 160-acre campus with easy access to Richmond
- **Coed** 3,986 undergraduate students, 96% full-time, 65% women, 35% men
- **Moderately difficult** entrance level, 66% of applicants were admitted

Undergraduates 3,832 full-time, 154 part-time. Students come from 25 states and territories, 11 other countries, 10% are from out of state, 6% African American, 2% Asian American or Pacific Islander, 2% Hispanic American, 0.4% Native American, 1% international, 5% transferred in, 71% live on campus. *Retention:* 79% of 2006 full-time freshmen returned.

Freshmen *Admission:* 4,352 applied, 2,872 admitted, 988 enrolled. *Average high school GPA:* 3.32. *Test scores:* SAT critical reading scores over 500: 68%; SAT math scores over 500: 64%; SAT writing scores over 500: 59%; ACT scores over 18: 99%; SAT critical reading scores over 600: 15%; SAT math scores over 600: 14%; SAT writing scores over 600: 10%; ACT scores over 24: 35%; SAT critical reading scores over 700: 1%; SAT math scores over 700: 1%; SAT writing scores over 700: 1%; ACT scores over 30: 2%.

Faculty *Total:* 247, 84% full-time. *Student/faculty ratio:* 20:1.

Majors Accounting; anthropology; applied mathematics; Army R.O.T.C./military science; art; art history, criticism and conservation; art teacher education; athletic training; biology/biological sciences; biophysics; business administration and management; business/managerial economics; chemistry; clinical laboratory science/medical technology; clinical/medical laboratory technology; commercial and advertising art; communication disorders; communication/speech communication and rhetoric; community health services counseling; computer science; criminal justice/law enforcement administration; developmental and child psychology; dramatic/theater arts; drawing; economics; education; elementary education; English; environmental studies; experimental psychology; finance; fine/studio arts; French; geography; geology/earth science; German; health science; health teacher education; history; interior design; international economics; international relations and affairs; journalism; kindergarten/preschool education; kinesiology and exercise science; liberal arts and sciences/liberal studies; library science; management information systems; marketing/marketing management; mathematics; modern languages; music; music teacher education; natural sciences; physical education teaching and coaching; physics; political science and government; pre-dentistry studies; pre-law studies; pre-medical studies; pre-pharmacy studies; pre-veterinary studies; printmaking; psychology; reading teacher education; science teacher education; sculpture; secondary education; social work; sociology; Spanish; special education; sport and fitness administration/management; therapeutic recreation.

Academics *Calendar:* semesters. *Degrees:* bachelor's and master's. *Special study options:* accelerated degree program, advanced placement credit, distance learning, double majors, honors programs, independent study, internships, off-campus study, part-time degree program, services for LD students, study abroad, summer session for credit. *ROTC:* Army (b). *Unusual degree programs:* 3-2 engineering with University of Virginia, Old Dominion University, University of Tennessee, Virginia Polytechnic Institute and University, Christopher Newport University.

Computers on Campus 270 computers/terminals are available on campus for general student use. Students can access the following: online (class) registration. Campuswide network is available. 100% of college-owned or -operated housing units are wired for high-speed Internet access. Wireless service is available via classrooms, computer centers, computer labs, libraries, student centers.

Student Life *Housing:* on-campus residence required through junior year. *Options:* coed, women-only, disabled students. Campus housing is university owned. Freshman campus housing is guaranteed. *Activities and organizations:* drama/theater group, student-run newspaper, radio station, choral group, Student Government Association, Alpha Phi Omega, Inter-Varsity Christian Fellowship, Longwood Ambassadors, Wellness Advocates, national fraternities, national sororities. *Campus security:* 24-hour emergency response devices and patrols, late-night transport/escort service, controlled dormitory access, security lighting. *Student services:* health clinic, personal/psychological counseling.

Athletics Member NCAA. All Division I. *Intercollegiate sports:* baseball M (s), basketball M (s)/W (s), cross-country running M (s)/W (s), equestrian sports M (c)/W (c), field hockey W (s), golf M (s)/W (s), lacrosse W (s), rugby M (c)/W (c), soccer M (s)/W (s), softball W (s), swimming and diving M (c)/W (c), tennis M (s)/W (s), track and field M (c)/W (c), volleyball M (c)/W (c), wrestling M (c). *Intramural sports:* badminton M/W, basketball W, bowling M/W, cheerleading M/W, football M/W, golf M/W, racquetball M/W, soccer M/W, softball M/W, table tennis M/W, tennis M/W, ultimate Frisbee M/W, volleyball M/W.

Standardized Tests *Required:* SAT or ACT (for admission).

Costs (2007–08) *Tuition:* state resident $4249 full-time, $281 per credit hour part-time; nonresident $12,450 full-time, $609 per credit hour part-time. Full-time tuition and fees vary according to course load. Part-time tuition and fees vary according to course load. *Required fees:* $3809 full-time. *Room and board:* $6740; room only: $3840. Room and board charges vary according to board plan, housing facility, and location. *Payment plan:* installment. *Waivers:* senior citizens.

Financial Aid Of all full-time matriculated undergraduates who enrolled in 2006, 2,335 applied for aid, 1,547 were judged to have need, 656 had their need fully met. In 2006, 999 non-need-based awards were made. *Average percent of need met:* 83%. *Average financial aid package:* $8502. *Average need-based loan:* $4068. *Average need-based gift aid:* $4935. *Average non-need-based aid:* $5777.

Applying *Options:* electronic application, early admission, early action, deferred entrance. *Application fee:* $40. *Required:* essay or personal statement, high school transcript. *Required for some:* letters of recommendation. *Recommended:* minimum 2.7 GPA, interview. *Application deadlines:* 3/1 (freshmen), 3/1 (transfers), 12/1 (early action). *Notification:* continuous until 6/1 (freshmen), continuous until 6/1 (transfers), 1/1 (early action).

Freshman Application Contact Mr. Robert J. Chonko, Dean of Admissions, Longwood University, 201 High Street, Farmville, VA 23909. *Phone:* 434-395-2060. *Toll-free phone:* 800-281-4677. *Fax:* 434-395-2332. *E-mail:* admissions@longwood.edu.

See page 2666 for the College Close-Up.

LYNCHBURG COLLEGE

Lynchburg, Virginia www.lynchburg.edu/

- **Independent** comprehensive, founded 1903, affiliated with Christian Church (Disciples of Christ)
- **Suburban** 214-acre campus
- **Endowment** $84.6 million
- **Coed** 2,113 undergraduate students, 95% full-time, 59% women, 41% men
- **Moderately difficult** entrance level, 69% of applicants were admitted

Undergraduates 1,999 full-time, 114 part-time. Students come from 34 states and territories, 6 other countries, 35% are from out of state, 7% African American, 2% Asian American or Pacific Islander, 2% Hispanic American, 0.5% Native American, 0.9% international, 5% transferred in, 80% live on campus. *Retention:* 73% of 2006 full-time freshmen returned.

Freshmen *Admission:* 4,248 applied, 2,934 admitted, 601 enrolled. *Average high school GPA:* 3.11. *Test scores:* SAT critical reading scores over 500: 58%; SAT math scores over 500: 57%; ACT scores over 18: 78%; SAT critical reading scores over 600: 15%; SAT math scores over 600: 15%; ACT scores over 24: 17%; SAT critical reading scores over 700: 2%; SAT math scores over 700: 1%; ACT scores over 30: 1%.

Faculty *Total:* 214, 73% full-time, 67% with terminal degrees. *Student/faculty ratio:* 12:1.

Majors Accounting; art; athletic training; biological and biomedical sciences related; biology/biological sciences; business administration and management; chemistry; communication/speech communication and rhetoric; computer science; creative writing; dramatic/theater arts; economics; education; elementary education; English; environmental studies; French; health teacher education; history; international relations and affairs; journalism; kindergarten/preschool education; kinesiology and exercise science; marketing/marketing management; mass communication/media; mathematics; music; music performance; music theory and composition; nursing (registered nurse training); organizational com-

COLLEGE DATA CENTER • VIRGINIA

munication; philosophy; physical education teaching and coaching; physics; political science and government; pre-dentistry studies; pre-law studies; pre-medical studies; pre-veterinary studies; psychology; religious studies; secondary education; sociology; Spanish; special education; speech and rhetoric; sport and fitness administration/management.

Academics *Calendar:* semesters. *Degrees:* bachelor's and master's. *Special study options:* accelerated degree program, adult/continuing education programs, advanced placement credit, double majors, honors programs, independent study, internships, off-campus study, part-time degree program, services for LD students, study abroad, summer session for credit. *Unusual degree programs:* 3-2 engineering with Old Dominion University, University of Virginia.

Computers on Campus 300 computers/terminals are available on campus for general student use. Students can access the following: campus intranet, computer help desk, free student e-mail accounts, online (class) grades, online (class) registration, online (class) schedules. Campuswide network is available. Wireless service is available via classrooms, learning centers, libraries, student centers.

Student Life *Housing:* on-campus residence required through junior year. *Options:* coed, disabled students. Campus housing is university owned. Freshman campus housing is guaranteed. *Activities and organizations:* drama/theater group, student-run newspaper, choral group, Association of Commuter Students, Omicron Delta Kappa, Ski and Snowboarding Club, Kappa Delta, Baptist Student Union, national fraternities, national sororities. *Campus security:* 24-hour emergency response devices and patrols, late-night transport/escort service, controlled dormitory access. *Student services:* health clinic, personal/psychological counseling.

Athletics Member NCAA. All Division III. *Intercollegiate sports:* baseball M, basketball M/W, cheerleading M/W, cross-country running M/W, equestrian sports W, field hockey W, golf M, lacrosse M/W, soccer M/W, softball W, tennis M/W, track and field M/W, volleyball W. *Intramural sports:* badminton M/W, baseball M, basketball M/W, bowling M/W, equestrian sports W, football M, golf M, racquetball M/W, rugby M/W, soccer M/W, softball W, tennis M/W, track and field M/W, volleyball M/W.

Standardized Tests *Required:* SAT or ACT (for admission).

Costs (2007–08) *Comprehensive fee:* $34,135 includes full-time tuition ($26,360), mandatory fees ($405), and room and board ($7370). Part-time tuition: $350 per credit hour. Part-time tuition and fees vary according to course load. *Required fees:* $4 per credit hour part-time. *College room only:* $3660. Room and board charges vary according to board plan and housing facility. *Payment plans:* tuition prepayment, installment. *Waivers:* senior citizens and employees or children of employees.

Financial Aid Of all full-time matriculated undergraduates who enrolled in 2005, 1,491 applied for aid, 1,226 were judged to have need, 421 had their need fully met. 352 Federal Work-Study jobs (averaging $1088). 465 state and other part-time jobs (averaging $1373). In 2005, 702 non-need-based awards were made. *Average percent of need met:* 87%. *Average financial aid package:* $18,221. *Average need-based loan:* $4000. *Average need-based gift aid:* $13,610. *Average non-need-based aid:* $8196. *Average indebtedness upon graduation:* $18,517.

Applying *Options:* electronic application, early admission, early decision, deferred entrance. *Application fee:* $30. *Required:* high school transcript. *Recommended:* essay or personal statement, 2 letters of recommendation, interview. *Application deadlines:* rolling (freshmen), rolling (transfers). *Early decision deadline:* 11/15. *Notification:* continuous (freshmen), continuous (transfers), 12/15 (early decision).

Freshman Application Contact Ms. Sharon Walters-Bower, Director of Admissions, Lynchburg College, 1501 Lakeside Drive, Lynchburg, VA 24501-3199. *Phone:* 434-544-8300. *Toll-free phone:* 800-426-8101. *Fax:* 434-544-8653. *E-mail:* admissions@lynchburg.edu.

See page 2668 for the College Close-Up.

MARY BALDWIN COLLEGE

Staunton, Virginia **www.mbc.edu/**

- **Independent** comprehensive, founded 1842
- **Small-town** 54-acre campus
- **Endowment** $40.4 million
- **Coed** 1,515 undergraduate students, 69% full-time, 94% women, 6% men
- **Moderately difficult** entrance level, 74% of applicants were admitted

Undergraduates 1,050 full-time, 465 part-time. Students come from 33 states and territories, 4 other countries, 36% are from out of state, 18% African American, 2% Asian American or Pacific Islander, 4% Hispanic American, 0.5% Native American, 1% international, 2% transferred in, 83% live on campus. *Retention:* 64% of 2006 full-time freshmen returned.

Freshmen *Admission:* 1,474 applied, 1,098 admitted, 276 enrolled. *Average high school GPA:* 3.29. *Test scores:* SAT critical reading scores over 500: 60%; SAT math scores over 500: 50%; ACT scores over 18: 90%; SAT critical reading scores over 600: 20%; SAT math scores over 600: 12%; ACT scores over 24: 45%; SAT critical reading scores over 700: 3%; SAT math scores over 700: 1%; ACT scores over 30: 4%.

Faculty *Total:* 144, 51% full-time. *Student/faculty ratio:* 10:1.

Majors Applied mathematics; art; arts management; Asian studies; biochemistry; biology/biological sciences; business administration and management; chemistry; clinical laboratory science/medical technology; communication and journalism related; communication/speech communication and rhetoric; computer and information sciences; dramatic/theater arts; economics; English; French; health/health care administration; history; international relations and affairs; mathematics; music; philosophy; physics; political science and government; psychology; religious studies; social work; sociology; Spanish.

Academics *Calendar:* 4-4-1. *Degrees:* certificates, bachelor's, and master's. *Special study options:* academic remediation for entering students, accelerated degree program, adult/continuing education programs, advanced placement credit, double majors, English as a second language, external degree program, freshman honors college, honors programs, independent study, internships, off-campus study, part-time degree program, services for LD students, student-designed majors, study abroad. *ROTC:* Army (b), Navy (c), Air Force (c). *Unusual degree programs:* 3-2 engineering with University of Virginia; nursing with Vanderbilt University.

Computers on Campus 244 computers/terminals are available on campus for general student use. Students can access the following: computer help desk, free student e-mail accounts, online (class) grades, online (class) registration, online (class) schedules. Campuswide network is available. 100% of college-owned or -operated housing units are wired for high-speed Internet access. Wireless service is available via entire campus.

Student Life *Housing:* on-campus residence required through senior year. *Options:* women-only. Campus housing is university owned. Freshman campus housing is guaranteed. *Activities and organizations:* drama/theater group, student-run newspaper, radio station, choral group, marching band, Student Senate, Baldwin Program Board, President's Society, Black Student Alliance, Stars. *Campus security:* 24-hour emergency response devices and patrols, late-night transport/escort service, controlled dormitory access. *Student services:* health clinic, personal/psychological counseling.

Athletics Member NCAA. All Division III. *Intercollegiate sports:* basketball W, cross-country running W (c), field hockey W (c), soccer W, softball W, swimming and diving W, tennis W, volleyball W.

Standardized Tests *Required:* SAT or ACT (for admission).

Costs (2007–08) *Comprehensive fee:* $29,200 includes full-time tuition ($22,530), mandatory fees ($200), and room and board ($6470). Full-time tuition and fees vary according to degree level. Part-time tuition: $380 per semester hour. Part-time tuition and fees vary according to degree level. *Required fees:* $380 per semester hour part-time. *College room only:* $4127. Room and board charges vary according to housing facility. *Payment plan:* installment. *Waivers:* employees or children of employees.

Financial Aid Of all full-time matriculated undergraduates who enrolled in 2006, 894 applied for aid, 793 were judged to have need, 404 had their need fully met. 310 Federal Work-Study jobs (averaging $1782). 85 state and other part-time jobs (averaging $1283). In 2006, 221 non-need-based awards were made. *Average percent of need met:* 89%. *Average financial aid package:* $20,510. *Average need-based loan:* $3313. *Average need-based gift aid:* $9521. *Average non-need-based aid:* $12,866. *Average indebtedness upon graduation:* $23,598. *Financial aid deadline:* 4/15.

Applying *Options:* electronic application, early admission, early decision, deferred entrance. *Application fee:* $35. *Required:* high school transcript, minimum 2.0 GPA, 1 letter of recommendation. *Recommended:* interview. *Application deadlines:* rolling (freshmen), rolling (transfers). *Early decision deadline:* 11/15. *Notification:* continuous (freshmen), continuous (transfers), 12/1 (early decision).

Freshman Application Contact Ms. Lisa Branson, Associate Vice President for Enrollment Management, Mary Baldwin College, Frederick and New Streets, Staunton, VA 24401. *Phone:* 540-887-7260. *Toll-free phone:* 800-468-2262. *Fax:* 540-887-7229. *E-mail:* lbranson@mbc.edu.

MARYMOUNT UNIVERSITY

Arlington, Virginia **www.marymount.edu/**

- **Independent** comprehensive, founded 1950, affiliated with Roman Catholic Church
- **Suburban** 21-acre campus with easy access to Washington, DC
- **Endowment** $24.0 million

• **Coed** 2,238 undergraduate students, 86% full-time, 75% women, 25% men
• **Moderately difficult** entrance level, 81% of applicants were admitted

Undergraduates 1,928 full-time, 310 part-time. Students come from 34 states and territories, 54 other countries, 42% are from out of state, 15% African American, 8% Asian American or Pacific Islander, 12% Hispanic American, 0.6% Native American, 6% international, 12% transferred in, 34% live on campus. *Retention:* 71% of 2006 full-time freshmen returned.

Freshmen *Admission:* 1,904 applied, 1,541 admitted, 400 enrolled. *Average high school GPA:* 3.14. *Test scores:* SAT critical reading scores over 500: 54%; SAT math scores over 500: 48%; SAT writing scores over 500: 52%; ACT scores over 18: 80%; SAT critical reading scores over 600: 14%; SAT math scores over 600: 12%; SAT writing scores over 600: 13%; ACT scores over 24: 31%; SAT critical reading scores over 700: 1%; SAT math scores over 700: 1%; SAT writing scores over 700: 1%.

Faculty *Total:* 321, 43% full-time, 68% with terminal degrees. *Student/faculty ratio:* 14:1.

Majors Biology/biological sciences; business administration and management; communication/speech communication and rhetoric; criminal justice/safety; criminology; economics; economics related; English; fashion/apparel design; fashion merchandising; fine/studio arts; graphic design; history; information science/studies; interior design; kinesiology and exercise science; liberal arts and sciences/liberal studies; mathematics; nursing (registered nurse training); philosophy; political science and government; psychology; religious studies; sociology; sport and fitness administration/management.

Academics *Calendar:* semesters plus 2 summer terms. *Degrees:* certificates, bachelor's, master's, doctoral, post-master's, and postbachelor's certificates (Associate). *Special study options:* academic remediation for entering students, advanced placement credit, double majors, English as a second language, honors programs, independent study, internships, off-campus study, part-time degree program, services for LD students, student-designed majors, study abroad, summer session for credit. *ROTC:* Army (c).

Computers on Campus 260 computers/terminals are available on campus for general student use. Students can access the following: computer help desk, free student e-mail accounts, online (class) grades, online (class) registration, online (class) schedules, online drive space. Campuswide network is available. 100% of college-owned or -operated housing units are wired for high-speed Internet access. Wireless service is available via classrooms, computer centers, learning centers, libraries, student centers.

Student Life *Housing:* on-campus residence required through sophomore year. *Options:* coed, men-only, women-only. Campus housing is university owned and leased by the school. Freshman applicants given priority for college housing. *Activities and organizations:* drama/theater group, student-run newspaper, choral group, American Society of Interior Design, Student Nurses Association, Fashion Club, International Club, One 2 One (drama club). *Campus security:* 24-hour emergency response devices and patrols, late-night transport/escort service, controlled dormitory access. *Student services:* health clinic, personal/psychological counseling.

Athletics Member NCAA. All Division III. *Intercollegiate sports:* basketball M/W, cross-country running M/W, golf M, lacrosse M/W, soccer M/W, swimming and diving M/W, volleyball W. *Intramural sports:* basketball M/W, cheerleading W, football M/W, golf M, soccer M/W, softball M/W.

Standardized Tests *Required:* SAT or ACT (for admission).

Costs (2007–08) *Comprehensive fee:* $29,115 includes full-time tuition ($20,190), mandatory fees ($220), and room and board ($8705). Part-time tuition: $655 per credit hour. *Required fees:* $7 per credit hour part-time. *Payment plan:* installment. *Waivers:* children of alumni, senior citizens, and employees or children of employees.

Financial Aid Of all full-time matriculated undergraduates who enrolled in 2006, 1,352 applied for aid, 1,141 were judged to have need, 166 had their need fully met. 273 Federal Work-Study jobs (averaging $1682). In 2006, 342 non-need-based awards were made. *Average percent of need met:* 71%. *Average financial aid package:* $13,510. *Average need-based loan:* $4209. *Average need-based gift aid:* $6813. *Average non-need-based aid:* $9152. *Average indebtedness upon graduation:* $20,686.

Applying *Options:* electronic application, deferred entrance. *Application fee:* $40. *Required:* high school transcript, minimum 2.5 GPA, 1 letter of recommendation. *Recommended:* essay or personal statement, interview. *Application deadlines:* rolling (freshmen), rolling (transfers). *Notification:* continuous (freshmen), continuous (transfers).

Freshman Application Contact Mr. Mike Canfield, Associate Director of Undergraduate Admissions, Marymount University, 2807 North Glebe Road, Arlington, VA 22207-4299. *Phone:* 703-284-1500. *Toll-free phone:* 800-548-7638. *Fax:* 703-522-0349. *E-mail:* admissions@marymount.edu.

See page 2670 for the College Close-Up.

NATIONAL COLLEGE

Salem, Virginia **www.national-college.edu/**

Freshman Application Contact Ms. Bunnie Hancock, Admissions Representative, National College, PO Box 6400, Roanoke, VA 24017. *Phone:* 540-986-1800. *Toll-free phone:* 800-664-1886.

NORFOLK STATE UNIVERSITY

Norfolk, Virginia **www.nsu.edu/**

• **State-supported** comprehensive, founded 1935, part of State Council of Higher Education for Virginia
• **Urban** 134-acre campus
• **Coed**

Academics *Calendar:* semesters.

Costs (2007–08) *Tuition:* state resident $2700 full-time, $235 per hour part-time; nonresident $13,620 full-time, $599 per hour part-time. Full-time tuition and fees vary according to course load. Part-time tuition and fees vary according to course load. *Required fees:* $2622 full-time, $145 per hour part-time. *Room and board:* $6909; room only: $4402. Room and board charges vary according to board plan and housing facility.

Financial Aid Of all full-time matriculated undergraduates who enrolled in 2006, 3,938 applied for aid, 3,466 were judged to have need, 293 had their need fully met. *Average percent of need met:* 87. *Average financial aid package:* $8884. *Average need-based loan:* $3977. *Average need-based gift aid:* $5020. *Average indebtedness upon graduation:* $15,467. *Financial aid deadline:* 5/31.

Applying *Options:* electronic application, deferred entrance.

Freshman Application Contact Ms. Michelle Marable, Director of Admissions, Norfolk State University, 700 Park Avenue, Norfolk, VA 23504. *Phone:* 757-823-8396. *Fax:* 757-823-2078. *E-mail:* admissions@nsu.edu.

OLD DOMINION UNIVERSITY

Norfolk, Virginia **www.odu.edu/**

• **State-supported** university, founded 1930
• **Urban** 188-acre campus with easy access to Virginia Beach
• **Endowment** $183.5 million
• **Coed** 16,066 undergraduate students, 73% full-time, 58% women, 42% men
• 74% of applicants were admitted

Undergraduates 11,680 full-time, 4,386 part-time. Students come from 50 states and territories, 76 other countries, 10% are from out of state, 22% African American, 6% Asian American or Pacific Islander, 4% Hispanic American, 0.6% Native American, 2% international, 13% transferred in, 29% live on campus. *Retention:* 73% of 2006 full-time freshmen returned.

Freshmen *Admission:* 8,504 applied, 6,321 admitted, 2,571 enrolled. *Average high school GPA:* 3.37. *Test scores:* SAT critical reading scores over 500: 63%; SAT math scores over 500: 67%; SAT writing scores over 500: 57%; ACT scores over 18: 79%; SAT critical reading scores over 600: 17%; SAT math scores over 600: 20%; SAT writing scores over 600: 12%; ACT scores over 24: 16%; SAT critical reading scores over 700: 2%; SAT math scores over 700: 2%; SAT writing scores over 700: 1%; ACT scores over 30: 1%.

Faculty *Total:* 1,103, 62% full-time.

Majors Accounting; acting; art; art history, criticism and conservation; art teacher education; Asian studies; audiology and speech-language pathology; biochemistry; biology/biological sciences; biology teacher education; business administration and management; business/managerial economics; chemistry; chemistry teacher education; civil engineering; civil engineering technology; clinical laboratory science/medical technology; communication and journalism related; computer and information sciences; computer engineering; computer engineering technologies related; criminology; cytotechnology; dance; dental hygiene; drama and dance teacher education; dramatic/theater arts; economics; education (specific subject areas) related; electrical and electronic engineering technologies related; electrical, electronics and communications engineering; engineering technologies related; English; English language and literature related; English/language arts teacher education; environmental/environmental health engineering; environmental health; finance; fine/studio arts; foreign languages and literatures; foreign language teacher education; French; French language teacher education; geography; geography teacher education; geology/earth science; German; German language teacher education; graphic design; health

COLLEGE DATA CENTER • VIRGINIA

services/allied health/health sciences; history; history teacher education; international business/trade/commerce; international relations and affairs; kinesiology and exercise science; management information systems; marine biology and biological oceanography; marketing/marketing management; mathematics; mathematics teacher education; mechanical engineering; mechanical engineering technologies related; mental and social health services and allied professions related; multi-/interdisciplinary studies related; music; music performance; music teacher education; nuclear engineering technology; nuclear medical technology; nursing (registered nurse training); oceanography (chemical and physical); ophthalmic technology; parks, recreation and leisure facilities management; philosophy; physical education teaching and coaching; physics; physics teacher education; political science and government; psychology; sales and marketing/marketing and distribution teacher education; sociology; Spanish; Spanish language teacher education; speech and rhetoric; sport and fitness administration/management; women's studies.

Academics *Calendar:* semesters. *Degrees:* bachelor's, master's, doctoral, and post-master's certificates. *Special study options:* accelerated degree program, adult/continuing education programs, advanced placement credit, cooperative education, distance learning, double majors, English as a second language, freshman honors college, honors programs, independent study, internships, off-campus study, part-time degree program, services for LD students, student-designed majors, study abroad, summer session for credit. *ROTC:* Army (b), Navy (b). *Unusual degree programs:* 3-2 business administration; engineering; nursing; international studies, dental hygiene, communications/humanities, English, English/applied linguistics, history, interdisciplinary studies/humanities, health science/community health, computer science.

Computers on Campus 2,035 computers/terminals and 100 ports are available on campus for general student use. Students can access the following: campus intranet, computer help desk, free student e-mail accounts, online (class) grades, online (class) registration, online (class) schedules, online courses. Campuswide network is available. 100% of college-owned or -operated housing units are wired for high-speed Internet access. Wireless service is available via classrooms, computer centers, computer labs, dorm rooms, learning centers, libraries, student centers.

Student Life *Housing options:* coed, disabled students. Campus housing is university owned. *Activities and organizations:* drama/theater group, student-run newspaper, radio and television station, choral group, marching band, Black Student Alliance, Student Government Association, Student Activities Council, Fraternities and Sororities, Filipino-American Student Association, national fraternities, national sororities. *Campus security:* 24-hour emergency response devices and patrols, late-night transport/escort service, controlled dormitory access. *Student services:* health clinic, personal/psychological counseling, women's center.

Athletics Member NCAA. All Division I. *Intercollegiate sports:* baseball M (s), basketball M (s)/W (s), crew M (c)/W (c), cross-country running M (c)/W (c), fencing M (c)/W (c), field hockey W (s), football M (s), golf M (s)/W (s), ice hockey M (c)/W (c), lacrosse W (s), rock climbing M (c), sailing M/W, soccer M (s)/W (s), softball W (c), swimming and diving M (s)/W (s), tennis M (s)/W (s), wrestling M (s). *Intramural sports:* badminton M/W, basketball M/W, bowling M/W, cross-country running M/W, golf M/W, sailing M/W, soccer M/W, softball M/W, table tennis M/W, tennis M/W, ultimate Frisbee M/W, volleyball M/W, water polo M/W.

Standardized Tests *Required:* SAT or ACT (for admission).

Costs (2008–09) *Tuition:* state resident $211 per credit hour part-time; nonresident $585 per credit hour part-time. *Required fees:* $39 per term part-time.

Financial Aid Of all full-time matriculated undergraduates who enrolled in 2004, 7,221 applied for aid, 6,050 were judged to have need, 2,722 had their need fully met. In 2004, 458 non-need-based awards were made. *Average percent of need met:* 69%. *Average financial aid package:* $6313. *Average need-based loan:* $3721. *Average need-based gift aid:* $3676. *Average non-need-based aid:* $3296. *Average indebtedness upon graduation:* $16,775. *Financial aid deadline:* 3/15.

Applying *Options:* electronic application, early admission, early action, deferred entrance. *Application fee:* $40. *Required:* essay or personal statement, high school transcript, minimum 2.7 GPA, 1 letter of recommendation, test scores. *Required for some:* interview. *Application deadlines:* 3/15 (freshmen), 5/1 (transfers), 12/1 (early action). *Notification:* continuous (freshmen), continuous (transfers), 1/15 (early action).

Freshman Application Contact Ms. Alice McAdory, Director of Admissions, Old Dominion University, 108 Rollins Hall, Norfolk, VA 23529-0050. *Phone:* 757-683-3648. *Toll-free phone:* 800-348-7926. *Fax:* 757-683-3255. *E-mail:* admissions@odu.edu.

See page 2672 for the College Close-Up.

PATRICK HENRY COLLEGE

Purcellville, Virginia **www.phc.edu/**

- **Independent nondenominational** 4-year, founded 1999
- **Small-town** 106-acre campus with easy access to Washington, DC
- **Coed** 461 undergraduate students, 70% full-time, 48% women, 52% men
- **Very difficult** entrance level, 56% of applicants were admitted

Undergraduates 322 full-time, 139 part-time. Students come from 44 states and territories, 87% are from out of state, 80% live on campus. *Retention:* 86% of 2006 full-time freshmen returned.

Freshmen *Admission:* 150 applied, 84 admitted. *Average high school GPA:* 3.79. *Test scores:* SAT critical reading scores over 500: 98%; SAT math scores over 500: 94%; SAT writing scores over 500: 100%; ACT scores over 18: 100%; SAT critical reading scores over 600: 87%; SAT math scores over 600: 62%; SAT writing scores over 600: 78%; ACT scores over 24: 100%; SAT critical reading scores over 700: 36%; SAT math scores over 700: 11%; SAT writing scores over 700: 24%; ACT scores over 30: 35%.

Faculty *Total:* 33, 48% full-time, 73% with terminal degrees. *Student/faculty ratio:* 17:1.

Majors English language and literature related; history; journalism; liberal arts and sciences/liberal studies; political science and government.

Academics *Calendar:* semesters. *Degree:* bachelor's. *Special study options:* double majors, independent study, internships. *ROTC:* Army (c).

Computers on Campus Students can access the following: campus intranet, computer help desk, free student e-mail accounts, online (class) grades, online (class) registration, online (class) schedules. Campuswide network is available. 100% of college-owned or -operated housing units are wired for high-speed Internet access. Wireless service is available via entire campus.

Student Life *Housing:* on-campus residence required through sophomore year. *Options:* men-only, women-only, disabled students. Campus housing is university owned. Freshman applicants given priority for college housing. *Activities and organizations:* drama/theater group, student-run newspaper, choral group, Intercollegiate Forensics (debate and moot court), Student Government, Eden Troupe (drama club), Chorale, College Republicans. *Campus security:* 24-hour emergency response devices, student patrols, late-night transport/escort service, controlled dormitory access, after hours patrols by trained security personnel. *Student services:* personal/psychological counseling.

Athletics *Intercollegiate sports:* basketball M/W, soccer M/W. *Intramural sports:* basketball M/W, fencing M/W, soccer M/W, softball M/W, table tennis M/W, ultimate Frisbee M/W.

Standardized Tests *Required:* SAT or ACT (for admission).

Costs (2008–09) *Comprehensive fee:* $25,100 includes full-time tuition ($18,500) and room and board ($6600). Part-time tuition: $565 per credit hour.

Applying *Options:* electronic application, deferred entrance. *Application fee:* $40. *Required:* essay or personal statement, high school transcript, 2 letters of recommendation, interview, faith and purpose essay; educational samples (2); issue analysis essay; literature list.

Freshman Application Contact Ms. Rebekah A. Knable, Director of Admissions, Patrick Henry College, PO Box 1776, One Patrick Henry Circle, Purcellville, VA 20134. *Phone:* 540-338-1776. *Fax:* 540-338-9808. *E-mail:* admissions@phc.edu.

RADFORD UNIVERSITY

Radford, Virginia **www.radford.edu/**

- **State-supported** comprehensive, founded 1910
- **Small-town** 177-acre campus
- **Endowment** $58.6 million
- **Coed** 8,023 undergraduate students, 95% full-time, 58% women, 42% men
- **Moderately difficult** entrance level, 78% of applicants were admitted

Undergraduates 7,645 full-time, 378 part-time. Students come from 36 states and territories, 25 other countries, 7% are from out of state, 6% African American, 2% Asian American or Pacific Islander, 2% Hispanic American, 0.3% Native American, 0.6% international, 7% transferred in, 37% live on campus. *Retention:* 77% of 2006 full-time freshmen returned.

Freshmen *Admission:* 7,046 applied, 5,466 admitted, 1,841 enrolled. *Average high school GPA:* 3.15. *Test scores:* SAT critical reading scores over 500: 50%; SAT math scores over 500: 57%; ACT scores over 18: 98%; SAT critical reading scores over 600: 11%; SAT math scores over 600: 11%; ACT scores over 24: 30%; SAT critical reading scores over 700: 1%; SAT math scores over 700: 1%; ACT scores over 30: 2%.

Faculty *Total:* 625, 64% full-time, 62% with terminal degrees. *Student/faculty ratio:* 18:1.

Majors Accounting; anthropology; art; biology/biological sciences; business administration and management; chemistry; clinical laboratory science/medical technology; communication disorders; communication/speech communication and rhetoric; computer science; criminal justice/law enforcement administration; dance; design and visual communications; dramatic/theater arts; economics; English; finance; foods, nutrition, and wellness; foreign languages and literatures; general studies; geography; geology/earth science; history; information science/studies; journalism; marketing/marketing management; mathematics; multi-/interdisciplinary studies related; music; nursing (registered nurse training); parks, recreation and leisure; philosophy and religious studies related; physical education teaching and coaching; physics; political science and government; psychology; social sciences; social work; sociology.

Academics *Calendar:* semesters. *Degrees:* bachelor's, master's, doctoral, and post-master's certificates. *Special study options:* accelerated degree program, advanced placement credit, distance learning, double majors, English as a second language, honors programs, independent study, internships, off-campus study, part-time degree program, services for LD students, student-designed majors, study abroad, summer session for credit. *ROTC:* Army (b).

Computers on Campus 708 computers/terminals are available on campus for general student use. Students can access the following: campus intranet, computer help desk, free student e-mail accounts, online (class) grades, online (class) registration, online (class) schedules, online financial aid status and student accounts payable. Campuswide network is available. 100% of college-owned or -operated housing units are wired for high-speed Internet access. Wireless service is available via entire campus.

Student Life *Housing:* on-campus residence required through sophomore year. *Options:* coed, disabled students. Campus housing is university owned and leased by the school. Freshman campus housing is guaranteed. *Activities and organizations:* drama/theater group, student-run newspaper, radio and television station, choral group, Student Government Association, Student Education Association, International Club, Ski Club, Student Life Committee, national fraternities, national sororities. *Campus security:* 24-hour emergency response devices and patrols, late-night transport/escort service, controlled dormitory access. *Student services:* health clinic, personal/psychological counseling.

Athletics Member NCAA. All Division I. *Intercollegiate sports:* baseball M (s), basketball M (s)/W (s), cross-country running M (s)/W (s), field hockey W (s), golf M (s)/W (s), soccer M (s)/W (s), softball W (s), swimming and diving W (s), tennis M (s)/W (s), track and field M (s)/W (s), volleyball W (s). *Intramural sports:* baseball M (c), basketball M/W, bowling M/W, cross-country running M/W, equestrian sports M (c)/W (c), football M/W, ice hockey M (c), racquetball M/W, rock climbing M/W, rugby M (c)/W (c), soccer M/W, softball M/W, tennis M/W, ultimate Frisbee M (c)/W (c), volleyball M/W, weight lifting M/W, wrestling M/W.

Standardized Tests *Required:* SAT or ACT (for admission).

Costs (2007–08) *Tuition:* state resident $4026 full-time, $168 per credit hour part-time; nonresident $12,360 full-time, $515 per credit hour part-time. *Required fees:* $2150 full-time, $90 per credit hour part-time. *Room and board:* $6490; room only: $3452. Room and board charges vary according to board plan and housing facility. *Payment plan:* installment. *Waivers:* senior citizens and employees or children of employees.

Financial Aid Of all full-time matriculated undergraduates who enrolled in 2006, 4,534 applied for aid, 3,032 were judged to have need, 1,352 had their need fully met. 461 Federal Work-Study jobs (averaging $1258). 720 state and other part-time jobs (averaging $2241). In 2006, 253 non-need-based awards were made. *Average percent of need met:* 77%. *Average financial aid package:* $7768. *Average need-based loan:* $3764. *Average need-based gift aid:* $5187. *Average non-need-based aid:* $3244. *Average indebtedness upon graduation:* $14,729.

Applying *Options:* electronic application, early admission, early action, deferred entrance. *Application fee:* $50. *Required:* high school transcript. *Recommended:* essay or personal statement, letters of recommendation, interview. *Application deadlines:* 2/1 (freshmen), 6/1 (transfers), 12/15 (early action). *Notification:* 3/20 (freshmen), continuous (transfers), 1/9 (early action).

Freshman Application Contact Mr. David W. Kraus, Director of Admissions, Radford University, PO Box 6903, RU Station, Radford, VA 24142. *Phone:* 540-831-5371. *Toll-free phone:* 800-890-4265. *Fax:* 540-831-5038. *E-mail:* ruadmiss@radford.edu.

See page 2674 for the College Close-Up.

RANDOLPH COLLEGE

Lynchburg, Virginia **www.randolphcollege.edu/**

- **Independent Methodist** 4-year, founded 1891
- **Suburban** 100-acre campus
- **Endowment** $155.6 million
- **Coed** 649 undergraduate students, 96% full-time, 88% women, 12% men
- **Moderately difficult** entrance level, 83% of applicants were admitted

Undergraduates 623 full-time, 26 part-time. Students come from 44 states and territories, 44 other countries, 52% are from out of state, 9% African American, 3% Asian American or Pacific Islander, 6% Hispanic American, 0.6% Native American, 12% international, 3% transferred in, 89% live on campus. *Retention:* 78% of 2006 full-time freshmen returned.

Freshmen *Admission:* 1,222 applied, 1,018 admitted, 178 enrolled. *Average high school GPA:* 3.4. *Test scores:* SAT critical reading scores over 500: 77%; SAT math scores over 500: 69%; SAT critical reading scores over 600: 40%; SAT math scores over 600: 29%; SAT critical reading scores over 700: 8%; SAT math scores over 700: 5%.

Faculty *Total:* 93, 81% full-time, 82% with terminal degrees. *Student/faculty ratio:* 8:1.

Majors Ancient/classical Greek; art; art history, criticism and conservation; biology/biological sciences; business/commerce; chemistry; classics and languages, literatures and linguistics; communication/speech communication and rhetoric; creative writing; dance; dramatic/theater arts; economics; elementary education; engineering physics; English; environmental studies; fine/studio arts; French; German; health professions related; history; international relations and affairs; Latin; liberal arts and sciences/liberal studies; mathematics; museum studies; music history, literature, and theory; music performance; music theory and composition; philosophy; physics; political science and government; psychology; religious studies; sociology; Spanish.

Academics *Calendar:* semesters. *Degrees:* bachelor's and master's. *Special study options:* accelerated degree program, adult/continuing education programs, advanced placement credit, double majors, honors programs, independent study, internships, off-campus study, part-time degree program, services for LD students, student-designed majors, study abroad. *Unusual degree programs:* 3-2 engineering with University of Virginia, Vanderbilt University, Washington University, Virginia Commonwealth University; nursing with Johns Hopkins University.

Computers on Campus 154 computers/terminals and 10 ports are available on campus for general student use. Students can access the following: campus intranet, computer help desk, free student e-mail accounts, online (class) grades, online (class) registration, online (class) schedules. Campuswide network is available. 100% of college-owned or -operated housing units are wired for high-speed Internet access. Wireless service is available via classrooms, computer centers, learning centers, libraries, student centers.

Student Life *Housing:* on-campus residence required through senior year. *Options:* coed, women-only. Campus housing is university owned. Freshman campus housing is guaranteed. *Activities and organizations:* drama/theater group, student-run newspaper, radio station, choral group, Pan World Club, Macon Activities Council, Model United Nations, BIONIC (Believe It or Not, I Care volunteer organization), Black Students Alliance. *Campus security:* 24-hour emergency response devices and patrols, late-night transport/escort service. *Student services:* health clinic, personal/psychological counseling.

Athletics Member NCAA. All Division III. *Intercollegiate sports:* basketball M/W, cross-country running M/W, equestrian sports M/W, lacrosse M/W, soccer M/W, softball W, swimming and diving W, tennis M/W, volleyball W.

Standardized Tests *Required:* SAT or ACT (for admission).

Costs (2007–08) *One-time required fee:* $125. *Comprehensive fee:* $34,860 includes full-time tuition ($25,350), mandatory fees ($510), and room and board ($9000). Part-time tuition: $1060 per semester hour. Part-time tuition and fees vary according to course load. *Required fees:* $53 per term part-time. *Payment plan:* installment. *Waivers:* adult students and employees or children of employees.

Financial Aid Of all full-time matriculated undergraduates who enrolled in 2007, 458 applied for aid, 404 were judged to have need, 155 had their need fully met. 78 Federal Work-Study jobs (averaging $1860). 290 state and other part-time jobs (averaging $1070). In 2007, 205 non-need-based awards were made. *Average percent of need met:* 88%. *Average financial aid package:* $23,600. *Average need-based loan:* $6659. *Average need-based gift aid:* $17,261. *Average non-need-based aid:* $15,458. *Average indebtedness upon graduation:* $28,218.

Applying *Options:* electronic application, early admission, early decision, deferred entrance. *Application fee:* $35. *Required:* essay or personal statement, high school transcript, 2 letters of recommendation. *Recommended:* interview.

Application deadlines: 3/1 (freshmen), 6/1 (transfers). *Early decision deadline:* 11/15. *Notification:* continuous (freshmen), continuous (transfers), 12/15 (early decision).

Freshman Application Contact Mr. Jim Duffy, Senior Associate Director of Admissions, Randolph College, 2500 Rivermont Avenue, Lynchburg, VA 24503-1526. *Phone:* 434-947-8100. *Toll-free phone:* 800-745-7692. *Fax:* 434-947-8996. *E-mail:* admissions@randolphcollege.edu.

See page 2676 for the College Close-Up.

RANDOLPH-MACON COLLEGE

Ashland, Virginia **www.rmc.edu/**

- **Independent United Methodist** 4-year, founded 1830
- **Suburban** 120-acre campus with easy access to Richmond
- **Endowment** $128.1 million
- **Coed** 1,176 undergraduate students, 98% full-time, 54% women, 46% men
- **Moderately difficult** entrance level, 61% of applicants were admitted

Undergraduates 1,152 full-time, 24 part-time. Students come from 29 states and territories, 15 other countries, 31% are from out of state, 9% African American, 2% Asian American or Pacific Islander, 2% Hispanic American, 0.7% Native American, 2% international, 1% transferred in, 87% live on campus. *Retention:* 72% of 2006 full-time freshmen returned.

Freshmen *Admission:* 3,177 applied, 1,953 admitted, 392 enrolled. *Average high school GPA:* 3.3. *Test scores:* SAT critical reading scores over 500: 73%; SAT math scores over 500: 76%; SAT writing scores over 500: 69%; SAT critical reading scores over 600: 20%; SAT math scores over 600: 24%; SAT writing scores over 600: 15%; SAT critical reading scores over 700: 2%; SAT math scores over 700: 2%; SAT writing scores over 700: 3%.

Faculty *Total:* 159, 57% full-time, 67% with terminal degrees. *Student/faculty ratio:* 11:1.

Majors Accounting; ancient/classical Greek; arts management; biology/biological sciences; business/managerial economics; chemistry; computer science; dramatic/theater arts; economics; English; environmental studies; fine/studio arts; French; German; history; international/global studies; Latin; mathematics; music; philosophy; physics; political science and government; psychology; religious studies; sociology; Spanish; women's studies.

Academics *Calendar:* 4-1-4. *Degree:* bachelor's. *Special study options:* academic remediation for entering students, accelerated degree program, advanced placement credit, double majors, honors programs, independent study, internships, off-campus study, part-time degree program, services for LD students, study abroad, summer session for credit. *ROTC:* Army (c). *Unusual degree programs:* 3-2 business administration with Union College; engineering with Columbia University, University of Virginia; forestry with Duke University.

Computers on Campus 350 computers/terminals and 1,500 ports are available on campus for general student use. Students can access the following: campus intranet, computer help desk, free student e-mail accounts, online (class) grades, online (class) registration, online (class) schedules. Campuswide network is available. 100% of college-owned or -operated housing units are wired for high-speed Internet access. Wireless service is available via classrooms, computer labs, dorm rooms, libraries, student centers.

Student Life *Housing:* on-campus residence required through junior year. *Options:* coed, men-only, women-only, disabled students. Campus housing is university owned. Freshman campus housing is guaranteed. *Activities and organizations:* drama/theater group, student-run newspaper, radio and television station, choral group, Macon Outdoors Club, Campus Activities Board/Student Government Association, Drama Guild, Student Honors Association, national fraternities, national sororities. *Campus security:* 24-hour emergency response devices and patrols, late-night transport/escort service, controlled dormitory access. *Student services:* health clinic, personal/psychological counseling, women's center.

Athletics Member NCAA. All Division III. *Intercollegiate sports:* baseball M, basketball M/W, field hockey W, football M, golf M, lacrosse M/W, soccer M/W, softball W, swimming and diving W, tennis M/W, volleyball W. *Intramural sports:* basketball M/W, cheerleading M/W, cross-country running M/W, football M/W, lacrosse M/W, racquetball M/W, rugby M/W, soccer M/W, softball M/W, swimming and diving M, table tennis M/W, tennis M/W, ultimate Frisbee M/W, volleyball M/W.

Standardized Tests *Required:* SAT or ACT (for admission). *Recommended:* SAT Subject Tests (for admission), SAT Subject Tests (for placement).

Costs (2007–08) *One-time required fee:* $100. *Comprehensive fee:* $35,010 includes full-time tuition ($26,195), mandatory fees ($635), and room and board ($8180). Full-time tuition and fees vary according to reciprocity agreements. Part-time tuition: $970 per credit. *College room only:* $4495. Room and board charges vary according to housing facility. *Payment plan:* installment. *Waivers:* employees or children of employees.

Financial Aid Of all full-time matriculated undergraduates who enrolled in 2007, 790 applied for aid, 651 were judged to have need, 152 had their need fully met. 214 Federal Work-Study jobs (averaging $1981). In 2007, 478 non-need-based awards were made. *Average percent of need met:* 84%. *Average financial aid package:* $21,028. *Average need-based loan:* $5510. *Average need-based gift aid:* $15,683. *Average non-need-based aid:* $15,230. *Average indebtedness upon graduation:* $22,725.

Applying *Options:* electronic application, early admission, early action, deferred entrance. *Application fee:* $30. *Required:* essay or personal statement, high school transcript, minimum 2.0 GPA, 1 letter of recommendation. *Recommended:* interview. *Application deadlines:* 3/1 (freshmen), 4/1 (transfers), 11/15 (early action). *Notification:* 4/1 (freshmen), 5/1 (transfers), 1/1 (early action).

Freshman Application Contact Dr. Steven W. Nape, Dean of Admissions and Financial Aid, Randolph-Macon College, PO Box 5005, Ashland, VA 23005-5505. *Phone:* 804-752-7305. *Toll-free phone:* 800-888-1762. *Fax:* 804-752-4707. *E-mail:* admissions@rmc.edu.

See page 2678 for the College Close-Up.

REGENT UNIVERSITY

Virginia Beach, Virginia **www.regent.edu/**

- **Independent** comprehensive, founded 1977
- **Suburban** campus
- **Endowment** $277.6 million
- **Coed** 1,236 undergraduate students, 47% full-time, 69% women, 31% men
- **Minimally difficult** entrance level, 53% of applicants were admitted

Undergraduates 578 full-time, 658 part-time. Students come from 49 states and territories, 14 other countries, 53% are from out of state, 25% African American, 2% Asian American or Pacific Islander, 5% Hispanic American, 0.6% Native American, 1% international, 29% transferred in, 5% live on campus. *Retention:* 67% of 2006 full-time freshmen returned.

Freshmen *Admission:* 1,256 applied, 670 admitted, 380 enrolled. *Average high school GPA:* 3.16. *Test scores:* SAT critical reading scores over 500: 68%; SAT math scores over 500: 56%; SAT writing scores over 500: 63%; ACT scores over 18: 93%; SAT critical reading scores over 600: 31%; SAT math scores over 600: 15%; SAT writing scores over 600: 2%; ACT scores over 24: 32%; SAT critical reading scores over 700: 5%; ACT scores over 30: 2%.

Faculty *Total:* 629, 29% full-time. *Student/faculty ratio:* 10:1.

Majors Communication/speech communication and rhetoric; divinity/ministry; education; international business/trade/commerce; organizational behavior; political science and government; psychology.

Academics *Calendar:* trimesters. *Degrees:* bachelor's, master's, doctoral, first professional, and post-master's certificates. *Special study options:* adult/continuing education programs, distance learning, external degree program, off-campus study, part-time degree program, study abroad, summer session for credit.

Computers on Campus 200 computers/terminals and 1,500 ports are available on campus for general student use. Students can access the following: campus intranet, computer help desk, free student e-mail accounts, online (class) grades, online (class) registration, online (class) schedules. Campuswide network is available. 50% of college-owned or -operated housing units are wired for high-speed Internet access. Wireless service is available via entire campus.

Student Life *Housing options:* Campus housing is university owned. *Activities and organizations:* Regent Undergraduate Council (RUC), Students in Free Enterprise, Psychology Club, Student Alumni Ambassadors, Toastmasters International Club. *Campus security:* 24-hour emergency response devices and patrols. *Student services:* personal/psychological counseling.

Standardized Tests *Required for some:* SAT or ACT (for admission).

Costs (2007–08) *Tuition:* $12,450 full-time, $420 per credit hour part-time. *Required fees:* $300 full-time, $150 per term part-time. *Payment plan:* installment. *Waivers:* employees or children of employees.

Applying *Options:* electronic application. *Application fee:* $50. *Required:* essay or personal statement. *Required for some:* high school transcript, minimum 3.0 GPA. *Application deadlines:* 8/1 (freshmen), 8/1 (transfers).

Freshman Application Contact Mr. Ken Baker, Director of Admissions, Regent University, 1000 Regent University Drive, Virginia Beach, VA 23464. *Phone:* 757-226-4845. *Toll-free phone:* 800-373-5504. *Fax:* 757-226-4509. *E-mail:* kbaker@regent.edu.

ROANOKE COLLEGE

Salem, Virginia **www.roanoke.edu/**

- **Independent** 4-year, founded 1842, affiliated with Evangelical Lutheran Church in America
- **Suburban** 68-acre campus
- **Endowment** $124.6 million
- **Coed** 2,006 undergraduate students, 95% full-time, 57% women, 43% men
- **Moderately difficult** entrance level, 73% of applicants were admitted

Undergraduates 1,915 full-time, 91 part-time. Students come from 27 states and territories, 17 other countries, 43% are from out of state, 3% African American, 1% Asian American or Pacific Islander, 2% Hispanic American, 0.4% Native American, 0.7% international, 4% transferred in, 64% live on campus. *Retention:* 74% of 2006 full-time freshmen returned.

Freshmen *Admission:* 3,258 applied, 2,385 admitted, 566 enrolled. *Average high school GPA:* 3.27. *Test scores:* SAT critical reading scores over 500: 78%; SAT math scores over 500: 76%; SAT writing scores over 500: 65%; SAT critical reading scores over 600: 26%; SAT math scores over 600: 24%; SAT writing scores over 600: 18%; SAT critical reading scores over 700: 4%; SAT math scores over 700: 3%; SAT writing scores over 700: 2%.

Faculty *Total:* 190, 83% full-time, 68% with terminal degrees. *Student/faculty ratio:* 14:1.

Majors Art; art history, criticism and conservation; athletic training; biochemistry; biology/biological sciences; business administration and management; chemistry; clinical laboratory science/medical technology; computer science; criminal justice/safety; dramatic/theater arts; economics; English; environmental science; French; health and physical education; history; information science/studies; international relations and affairs; mathematics; music; natural resources management and policy; philosophy; physics; political science and government; psychology; religious studies; sociology; Spanish; theology.

Academics *Calendar:* semesters. *Degree:* bachelor's. *Special study options:* accelerated degree program, adult/continuing education programs, advanced placement credit, double majors, English as a second language, honors programs, independent study, internships, off-campus study, part-time degree program, services for LD students, study abroad, summer session for credit. *Unusual degree programs:* 3-2 engineering with Washington University in St. Louis, Virginia Polytechnic Institute and State University, University of Tennessee-Knoxville.

Computers on Campus 175 computers/terminals are available on campus for general student use. Students can access the following: campus intranet, computer help desk, free student e-mail accounts, online (class) grades, online (class) registration, online (class) schedules. Campuswide network is available. 100% of college-owned or -operated housing units are wired for high-speed Internet access. Wireless service is available via entire campus.

Student Life *Housing options:* coed, men-only, women-only. Campus housing is university owned and leased by the school. Freshman campus housing is guaranteed. *Activities and organizations:* drama/theater group, student-run newspaper, radio station, choral group, Outdoor Adventures, Habitat for Humanity, Honors Association, Campus Activities Board, Inter-Varsity Christian Fellowship, national fraternities, national sororities. *Campus security:* 24-hour emergency response devices and patrols, late-night transport/escort service, controlled dormitory access. *Student services:* health clinic, personal/psychological counseling.

Athletics Member NCAA. All Division III. *Intercollegiate sports:* baseball M, basketball M/W, cross-country running M/W, field hockey W, golf M/W (c), ice hockey M (c), lacrosse M/W, soccer M/W, softball W, tennis M/W, track and field M/W, volleyball M (c)/W. *Intramural sports:* badminton M/W, basketball M/W, cheerleading M/W, field hockey W, football M/W, ice hockey M, lacrosse M, racquetball M/W, soccer M/W, softball M/W, table tennis M/W, tennis M/W, volleyball M/W, water polo M/W.

Standardized Tests *Required:* SAT or ACT (for admission).

Costs (2008–09) *Comprehensive fee:* $37,220 includes full-time tuition ($27,210), mandatory fees ($725), and room and board ($9285). Part-time tuition: $1300 per course. *College room only:* $4340.

Financial Aid Of all full-time matriculated undergraduates who enrolled in 2007, 1,485 applied for aid, 1,160 were judged to have need, 420 had their need fully met. In 2007, 672 non-need-based awards were made. *Average percent of need met:* 86%. *Average financial aid package:* $21,387. *Average need-based loan:* $4677. *Average need-based gift aid:* $17,304. *Average non-need-based aid:* $9306. *Average indebtedness upon graduation:* $21,807.

Applying *Options:* electronic application, early admission, early decision, deferred entrance. *Application fee:* $30. *Required:* high school transcript. *Recommended:* essay or personal statement, 3 letters of recommendation, interview. *Application deadlines:* 3/15 (freshmen), 8/1 (transfers). *Early decision deadline:* 12/1. *Notification:* 4/1 (freshmen), 8/15 (transfers), 12/15 (early decision).

Freshman Application Contact Roanoke College, 221 College Lane, Salem, VA 24153. *Phone:* 540-375-2270. *Toll-free phone:* 800-388-2276.

See page 2680 for the College Close-Up.

SAINT PAUL'S COLLEGE

Lawrenceville, Virginia **www.saintpauls.edu/**

Director of Admissions Mrs. Rosemary Lewis, Vice President for Student Affairs, Saint Paul's College, 115 College Drive, Lawrenceville, VA 23868. *Phone:* 434-848-6493. *Toll-free phone:* 800-678-7071. *Fax:* 434-848-0229. *E-mail:* rlewis@saintpauls.edu.

SHENANDOAH UNIVERSITY

Winchester, Virginia **www.su.edu/**

- **Independent United Methodist** comprehensive, founded 1875
- **Small-town** 100-acre campus with easy access to Baltimore and Washington, DC
- **Endowment** $50.5 million
- **Coed** 1,658 undergraduate students, 92% full-time, 57% women, 43% men
- **Moderately difficult** entrance level, 88% of applicants were admitted

Undergraduates 1,521 full-time, 137 part-time. Students come from 38 states and territories, 45 other countries, 36% are from out of state, 7% African American, 2% Asian American or Pacific Islander, 1% Hispanic American, 0.3% Native American, 3% international, 11% transferred in, 45% live on campus. *Retention:* 65% of 2006 full-time freshmen returned.

Freshmen *Admission:* 1,281 applied, 1,132 admitted, 398 enrolled. *Average high school GPA:* 3.22. *Test scores:* SAT critical reading scores over 500: 52%; SAT math scores over 500: 55%; SAT writing scores over 500: 50%; ACT scores over 18: 67%; SAT critical reading scores over 600: 15%; SAT math scores over 600: 14%; SAT writing scores over 600: 14%; ACT scores over 24: 19%; SAT critical reading scores over 700: 1%; SAT math scores over 700: 2%; SAT writing scores over 700: 1%; ACT scores over 30: 4%.

Faculty *Total:* 285, 49% full-time, 47% with terminal degrees. *Student/faculty ratio:* 8:1.

Majors Acting; American studies; arts management; biology/biological sciences; business administration and management; chemistry; communication/speech communication and rhetoric; criminal justice/law enforcement administration; dance; drama and dance teacher education; dramatic/theater arts; dramatic/theater arts and stagecraft related; educational psychology; English; environmental studies; history; kinesiology and exercise science; liberal arts and sciences/liberal studies; mathematics; music; music performance; music related; music teacher education; music theory and composition; music therapy; nursing (registered nurse training); physical education teaching and coaching; piano and organ; political science and government; psychology; public administration; religious studies; respiratory care therapy; sociology; Spanish; theater design and technology; visual and performing arts.

Academics *Calendar:* semesters. *Degrees:* certificates, diplomas, associate, bachelor's, master's, doctoral, first professional, post-master's, and postbachelor's certificates. *Special study options:* accelerated degree program, adult/continuing education programs, advanced placement credit, cooperative education, distance learning, double majors, English as a second language, independent study, internships, off-campus study, part-time degree program, services for LD students, student-designed majors, study abroad, summer session for credit.

Computers on Campus 175 computers/terminals and 50 ports are available on campus for general student use. Students can access the following: campus intranet, computer help desk, free student e-mail accounts, online (class) grades, online (class) registration, online (class) schedules, online student account information. Campuswide network is available. 100% of college-owned or -operated housing units are wired for high-speed Internet access. Wireless service is available via entire campus.

Student Life *Housing:* on-campus residence required through sophomore year. *Options:* coed, disabled students. Campus housing is university owned and is provided by a third party. Freshman campus housing is guaranteed. *Activities and organizations:* drama/theater group, student-run newspaper, radio and television station, choral group, Psychology Club, Scar Higher, Political Science Society, Campus Crusade for Christ, Colleges against Cancer, national fraternities, national sororities. *Campus security:* 24-hour emergency response devices and patrols, late-night transport/escort service, controlled dormitory access, side door alarms, guard gate house, bike patrols. *Student services:* health clinic, personal/psychological counseling.

Athletics Member NCAA. All Division III. *Intercollegiate sports:* baseball M, basketball M/W, cross-country running M/W, field hockey W, football M, golf M, lacrosse M/W, soccer M/W, softball W, tennis M/W, volleyball W. *Intramural sports:* basketball M/W, cheerleading M/W, soccer M/W, softball M/W, tennis M/W, track and field M/W, volleyball M/W.

Standardized Tests *Required:* SAT or ACT (for admission).

Costs (2008–09) *Comprehensive fee:* $31,690 includes full-time tuition ($23,040), mandatory fees ($300), and room and board ($8350). Part-time tuition: $670 per credit hour.

Financial Aid Of all full-time matriculated undergraduates who enrolled in 2006, 948 applied for aid, 948 were judged to have need, 176 had their need fully met. 364 Federal Work-Study jobs (averaging $1500). 215 state and other part-time jobs (averaging $1500). In 2006, 172 non-need-based awards were made. *Average percent of need met:* 92%. *Average financial aid package:* $15,545. *Average need-based loan:* $6898. *Average need-based gift aid:* $7604. *Average non-need-based aid:* $4200. *Average indebtedness upon graduation:* $19,518.

Applying *Options:* electronic application, deferred entrance. *Application fee:* $30. *Required:* high school transcript. *Required for some:* essay or personal statement, interview, audition. *Recommended:* minimum 2.4 GPA. *Application deadlines:* rolling (freshmen), rolling (transfers). *Notification:* continuous (freshmen), continuous (transfers).

Freshman Application Contact Mr. David Anthony, Dean of Admissions, Shenandoah University, 1460 University Drive, Winchester, VA 22601-5195. *Phone:* 540-665-4581. *Toll-free phone:* 800-432-2266. *Fax:* 540-665-4627. *E-mail:* admit@su.edu.

See page 2682 for the College Close-Up.

SOUTHERN VIRGINIA UNIVERSITY

Buena Vista, Virginia **svu.edu/**

- **Independent Latter-day Saints** 4-year, founded 1867
- **Small-town** 155-acre campus
- **Endowment** $1.0 million
- **Coed**
- **Moderately difficult** entrance level

Faculty *Student/faculty ratio:* 16:1.

Academics *Calendar:* semesters. *Degree:* bachelor's.

Student Life *Campus security:* 24-hour emergency response devices and patrols.

Athletics Member NAIA.

Standardized Tests *Required:* SAT or ACT (for admission).

Costs (2007–08) *Comprehensive fee:* $21,400 includes full-time tuition ($16,500) and room and board ($4900). Part-time tuition: $585 per hour. Part-time tuition and fees vary according to course load. *College room only:* $2900. Room and board charges vary according to housing facility and location.

Financial Aid Of all full-time matriculated undergraduates who enrolled in 2007, 545 applied for aid, 477 were judged to have need, 62 had their need fully met. 164 Federal Work-Study jobs (averaging $1000). 19 state and other part-time jobs (averaging $2168). In 2007, 102 non-need-based awards were made. *Average percent of need met:* 60. *Average financial aid package:* $11,719. *Average need-based loan:* $3993. *Average need-based gift aid:* $8756. *Average non-need-based aid:* $6489. *Average indebtedness upon graduation:* $15,444. *Financial aid deadline:* 5/1.

Applying *Application fee:* $35. *Required:* high school transcript, ecclesiastical endorsement. *Required for some:* essay or personal statement, interview. *Recommended:* minimum 2.0 GPA.

Freshman Application Contact Mr. Tony Caputo, Dean of Admissions, Southern Virginia University, One University Hill Drive, Buena Vista, VA 24416. *Phone:* 540-261-2756. *Toll-free phone:* 800-229-8420. *Fax:* 540-261-8559. *E-mail:* admissions@southernvirginia.edu.

See page 2684 for the College Close-Up.

STRATFORD UNIVERSITY

Falls Church, Virginia **www.stratford.edu/**

Freshman Application Contact Kelly Martin, Director of High School Program, Stratford University, 7777 Leesburg Pike, Falls Church, VA 22043. *Phone:* 703-821-8570. *Toll-free phone:* 800-444-0804. *Fax:* 703-734-5339. *E-mail:* kmartin@stratford.edu.

See page 2686 for the College Close-Up.

SWEET BRIAR COLLEGE

Sweet Briar, Virginia **www.sbc.edu/**

- **Independent** comprehensive, founded 1901
- **Rural** 3250-acre campus
- **Endowment** $103.1 million
- **Women only** 800 undergraduate students, 94% full-time
- **Moderately difficult** entrance level, 81% of applicants were admitted

Undergraduates 751 full-time, 49 part-time. Students come from 39 states and territories, 4 other countries, 46% are from out of state, 3% African American, 1% Asian American or Pacific Islander, 3% Hispanic American, 0.8% Native American, 0.8% international, 2% transferred in, 90% live on campus. *Retention:* 75% of 2006 full-time freshmen returned.

Freshmen *Admission:* 619 applied, 504 admitted, 202 enrolled. *Average high school GPA:* 3.4. *Test scores:* SAT critical reading scores over 500: 81%; SAT math scores over 500: 69%; ACT scores over 18: 94%; SAT critical reading scores over 600: 35%; SAT math scores over 600: 24%; ACT scores over 24: 39%; SAT critical reading scores over 700: 9%; SAT math scores over 700: 2%; ACT scores over 30: 4%.

Faculty *Total:* 108, 56% full-time, 69% with terminal degrees. *Student/faculty ratio:* 9:1.

Majors Anthropology; archeology; art history, criticism and conservation; biochemistry, biophysics and molecular biology related; biology/biological sciences; business, management, and marketing related; chemistry; classics and languages, literatures and linguistics; computer science; creative writing; dance; dramatic/theater arts; economics; engineering science; English; environmental science; environmental studies; fine/studio arts; foreign languages and literatures; French; German; German studies; history; interdisciplinary studies; international relations and affairs; Italian; Italian studies; liberal arts and sciences/liberal studies; mathematics; music; philosophy; physics; political science and government; psychology; religious studies; sociology; Spanish; theoretical and mathematical physics.

Academics *Calendar:* semesters. *Degrees:* bachelor's and master's. *Special study options:* accelerated degree program, adult/continuing education programs, advanced placement credit, double majors, honors programs, independent study, internships, off-campus study, part-time degree program, services for LD students, student-designed majors, study abroad, summer session for credit. *Unusual degree programs:* 3-2 engineering with Virginia Polytechnic Institute and State University, University of Virginia, Columbia University, Washington University in St. Louis.

Computers on Campus 123 computers/terminals and 3,018 ports are available on campus for general student use. Students can access the following: campus intranet, computer help desk, free student e-mail accounts, online (class) grades, online (class) registration, online (class) schedules. Campuswide network is available. 80% of college-owned or -operated housing units are wired for high-speed Internet access. Wireless service is available via classrooms, dorm rooms, learning centers, libraries, student centers.

Student Life *Housing:* on-campus residence required through senior year. *Options:* women-only. Campus housing is university owned. Freshman campus housing is guaranteed. *Activities and organizations:* drama/theater group, student-run newspaper, radio and television station, choral group, Alpha Lambda Delta, Golf Club, Young Democrats, Business Club, Vixen Inklings. *Campus security:* 24-hour emergency response devices and patrols, late-night transport/escort service, controlled dormitory access, front gate security. *Student services:* health clinic, personal/psychological counseling.

Athletics Member NCAA. All Division III. *Intercollegiate sports:* equestrian sports W (c), fencing W (c), field hockey W, lacrosse W, soccer W, softball W, swimming and diving W, tennis W, volleyball W.

Standardized Tests *Required:* SAT or ACT (for admission).

Costs (2008–09) *Comprehensive fee:* $37,155 includes full-time tuition ($26,720), mandatory fees ($275), and room and board ($10,160). *College room only:* $4150.

Financial Aid Of all full-time matriculated undergraduates who enrolled in 2006, 359 applied for aid, 359 were judged to have need. 59 Federal Work-Study jobs (averaging $877). 88 state and other part-time jobs (averaging $919). In 2006, 279 non-need-based awards were made. *Average percent of need met:* 83%. *Average financial aid package:* $15,150. *Average need-based loan:* $4382. *Average need-based gift aid:* $14,467. *Average non-need-based aid:* $11,150. *Average indebtedness upon graduation:* $5496.

Applying *Options:* electronic application, early admission, early decision, deferred entrance. *Application fee:* $40. *Required:* essay or personal statement, high school transcript, 2 letters of recommendation. *Required for some:* portfolio with courses taken, list of texts covered, essay about homeschooling, campus visit, interview for homeschooled applicants. *Recommended:* interview. *Application deadlines:* 2/1 (freshmen), 5/1 (transfers). *Early decision deadline:* 12/1. *Notification:* 3/1 (freshmen), 5/15 (transfers), 12/15 (early decision).

Freshman Application Contact Mr. Ken Huus, Director of Admissions, Sweet Briar College, PO Box B, Sweet Briar, VA 24595. *Phone:* 434-381-6142. *Toll-free phone:* 800-381-6142. *Fax:* 434-381-6152. *E-mail:* admissions@sbc.edu.

See page 2688 for the College Close-Up.

UNIVERSITY OF MANAGEMENT AND TECHNOLOGY

Arlington, Virginia **www.umtweb.edu/**

- **Proprietary** comprehensive, founded 1998
- **Urban** campus with easy access to Washington, D.C.
- **Coed**

Majors Business administration and management; computer science; computer software engineering; general studies; information science/studies.

Academics *Calendar:* continuous. *Degrees:* certificates, associate, bachelor's, master's, doctoral, post-master's, and postbachelor's certificates.

Computers on Campus Students can access the following: campus intranet, online (class) grades, online (class) registration, online (class) schedules. Campuswide network is available.

Student Life *Housing:* college housing not available.

Costs (2007–08) *Tuition:* $10,800 full-time, $390 per credit hour part-time. No tuition increase for student's term of enrollment. *Required fees:* $90 full-time, $30 per term part-time. *Payment plans:* tuition prepayment, installment.

Freshman Application Contact Dr. C. Kirkland, Vice President, University of Management and Technology, 1901 North Fort Meyers Drive, Suite 700, Arlington, VA 22209. *Phone:* 703-516-0035. *Toll-free phone:* 800-924-4885. *Fax:* 703-516-0985. *E-mail:* admissions@umtweb.edu.

UNIVERSITY OF MARY WASHINGTON

Fredericksburg, Virginia **www.umw.edu/**

- **State-supported** comprehensive, founded 1908
- **Small-town** 176-acre campus with easy access to Richmond and Washington, DC
- **Endowment** $38.4 million
- **Coed** 4,271 undergraduate students, 86% full-time, 66% women, 34% men
- **Very difficult** entrance level, 71% of applicants were admitted

Undergraduates 3,670 full-time, 601 part-time. Students come from 43 states and territories, 16 other countries, 22% are from out of state, 3% African American, 4% Asian American or Pacific Islander, 3% Hispanic American, 0.5% Native American, 0.5% international, 5% transferred in, 70% live on campus. *Retention:* 87% of 2006 full-time freshmen returned.

Freshmen *Admission:* 4,475 applied, 3,187 admitted, 966 enrolled. *Average high school GPA:* 3.67. *Test scores:* SAT critical reading scores over 500: 93%; SAT math scores over 500: 90%; SAT writing scores over 500: 92%; SAT critical reading scores over 600: 58%; SAT math scores over 600: 43%; SAT writing scores over 600: 52%; SAT critical reading scores over 700: 13%; SAT math scores over 700: 6%; SAT writing scores over 700: 8%.

Faculty *Total:* 353, 71% full-time. *Student/faculty ratio:* 15:1.

Majors American studies; art; art history, criticism and conservation; biology/biological sciences; business administration and management; chemistry; classics and languages, literatures and linguistics; computer science; dramatic/theater arts; economics; elementary education; English; environmental studies; fine/studio arts; French; geography; geology/earth science; German; historic preservation and conservation; history; interdisciplinary studies; international relations and affairs; Latin; liberal arts and sciences/liberal studies; mathematics; modern languages; music; music teacher education; philosophy; physics; political science and government; pre-dentistry studies; pre-law studies; pre-medical studies; pre-veterinary studies; psychology; religious studies; secondary education; sociology; Spanish.

Academics *Calendar:* semesters. *Degrees:* bachelor's, master's, and postbachelor's certificates. *Special study options:* accelerated degree program, adult/continuing education programs, advanced placement credit, cooperative education, double majors, independent study, internships, part-time degree program, services for LD students, student-designed majors, study abroad, summer session for credit. *Unusual degree programs:* 3-2 education.

Computers on Campus 306 computers/terminals are available on campus for general student use. Students can access the following: computer help desk, free student e-mail accounts, online (class) registration. Campuswide network is available.

Student Life *Housing options:* coed, men-only, women-only, disabled students. Campus housing is university owned. Freshman campus housing is guaranteed. *Activities and organizations:* drama/theater group, student-run newspaper, radio station, choral group, Student Senate, Debate Team, Trek Club, Entertainment Committee, Class Council. *Campus security:* 24-hour emergency response devices and patrols, student patrols, late-night transport/escort service, controlled dormitory access, self-defense and safety classes. *Student services:* health clinic, personal/psychological counseling, women's center.

Athletics Member NCAA. All Division III. *Intercollegiate sports:* baseball M, basketball M/W, cheerleading M (c)/W (c), crew M/W, cross-country running M/W, equestrian sports M/W, field hockey W, lacrosse M/W, rugby M (c)/W (c), soccer M/W, softball W, swimming and diving M/W, tennis M/W, track and field M/W, volleyball M (c)/W. *Intramural sports:* baseball M/W, basketball M/W, fencing M/W, football M/W, golf M/W, ice hockey M (c), soccer M/W, softball M/W, table tennis M/W, tennis M/W, ultimate Frisbee M/W, volleyball M/W, water polo M/W.

Standardized Tests *Required:* SAT or ACT (for admission). *Recommended:* SAT Subject Tests (for admission).

Costs (2008–09) *Tuition:* state resident $250 per credit hour part-time; nonresident $700 per credit hour part-time.

Financial Aid Of all full-time matriculated undergraduates who enrolled in 2006, 1,770 applied for aid, 960 were judged to have need, 160 had their need fully met. 45 Federal Work-Study jobs (averaging $1600). 751 state and other part-time jobs (averaging $1480). In 2006, 294 non-need-based awards were made. *Average percent of need met:* 56%. *Average financial aid package:* $6600. *Average need-based loan:* $3900. *Average need-based gift aid:* $5000. *Average non-need-based aid:* $2095. *Average indebtedness upon graduation:* $12,665.

Applying *Options:* electronic application, deferred entrance. *Application fee:* $45. *Required:* essay or personal statement, high school transcript. *Application deadlines:* 2/1 (freshmen), 3/1 (transfers), 1/15 (early action). *Notification:* 4/1 (freshmen), 5/1 (transfers).

Freshman Application Contact Dr. Martin Wilder, Vice President for Enrollment and Communications, University of Mary Washington, 1301 College Avenue, Fredericksburg, VA 22401. *Phone:* 540-654-2000. *Toll-free phone:* 800-468-5614. *Fax:* 540-654-1857. *E-mail:* admit@umw.edu.

UNIVERSITY OF NORTHERN VIRGINIA

Manassas, Virginia **www.unva.edu/**

Director of Admissions Mr. Robert Frantz, Director of Admissions, University of Northern Virginia, 10021 Balls Ford Road, Manassas, VA 20109. *Phone:* 703-392-0771 Ext. 2402. *E-mail:* bfrantz@unva.edu.

UNIVERSITY OF PHOENIX–NORTHERN VIRGINIA CAMPUS

Reston, Virginia **www.phoenix.edu/**

- **Proprietary** comprehensive
- **Urban** campus
- **Coed**
- **Noncompetitive** entrance level

Faculty *Student/faculty ratio:* 7:1.

Academics *Degrees:* bachelor's and master's.

Student Life *Campus security:* late-night transport/escort service.

Costs (2007–08) *Tuition:* $12,180 full-time, $406 per credit part-time. Full-time tuition and fees vary according to course level.

Financial Aid *Average financial aid package:* $3562.

Applying *Options:* deferred entrance. *Application fee:* $45. *Required:* 1 letter of recommendation. *Required for some:* high school transcript.

Freshman Application Contact Ms. Beth Barilla, Associate Vice President, Student Admissions and Services, University of Phoenix–Northern Virginia Campus, 4615 East Elwood Street, Mail Stop AA-K101, Phoenix, AZ 85040-1958. *Phone:* 480-317-6000. *Toll-free phone:* 800-776-4867 (in-state); 800-228-7240 (out-of-state). *Fax:* 480-894-1758. *E-mail:* beth.barilla@phoenix.edu.

UNIVERSITY OF PHOENIX–RICHMOND CAMPUS

Richmond, Virginia **www.phoenix.edu/**

- **Proprietary** comprehensive
- **Urban** campus
- **Coed**
- **Noncompetitive** entrance level

Faculty *Student/faculty ratio:* 6:1.

Academics *Degrees:* bachelor's and master's.

Student Life *Campus security:* late-night transport/escort service.

Costs (2007–08) *Tuition:* $12,180 full-time, $406 per credit part-time. Full-time tuition and fees vary according to course level.

Financial Aid *Average financial aid package:* $3228. *Average need-based gift aid:* $1756.

Applying *Options:* deferred entrance. *Application fee:* $45. *Required:* 1 letter of recommendation. *Required for some:* high school transcript.

Freshman Application Contact Ms. Beth Barilla, Associate Vice President, Student Admissions and Services, University of Phoenix–Richmond Campus, 4615 East Elwood Street, Phoenix, AZ 85040-1958. *Phone:* 480-317-6000. *Toll-free phone:* 800-776-4867 (in-state); 800-228-7240 (out-of-state). *Fax:* 480-894-1758. *E-mail:* beth.barilla@phoenix.edu.

UNIVERSITY OF RICHMOND

Richmond, Virginia **www.richmond.edu/**

- **Independent** comprehensive, founded 1830
- **Suburban** 350-acre campus
- **Endowment** $1.7 billion
- **Coed** 2,795 undergraduate students, 99% full-time, 49% women, 51% men
- **Very difficult** entrance level, 40% of applicants were admitted

Undergraduates 2,767 full-time, 28 part-time. Students come from 45 states and territories, 72 other countries, 83% are from out of state, 6% African American, 4% Asian American or Pacific Islander, 3% Hispanic American, 0.3% Native American, 7% international, 1% transferred in, 92% live on campus. *Retention:* 91% of 2006 full-time freshmen returned.

Freshmen *Admission:* 6,649 applied, 2,654 admitted, 801 enrolled. *Test scores:* SAT critical reading scores over 500: 97%; SAT math scores over 500: 98%; SAT writing scores over 500: 96%; ACT scores over 18: 100%; SAT critical reading scores over 600: 71%; SAT math scores over 600: 80%; SAT writing scores over 600: 75%; ACT scores over 24: 95%; SAT critical reading scores over 700: 21%; SAT math scores over 700: 24%; SAT writing scores over 700: 23%; ACT scores over 30: 52%.

Faculty *Total:* 361, 79% full-time, 86% with terminal degrees. *Student/faculty ratio:* 9:1.

Majors Accounting; American studies; art; art history, criticism and conservation; art teacher education; biology/biological sciences; business administration and management; business/managerial economics; chemistry; classics and languages, literatures and linguistics; computer science; criminal justice/law enforcement administration; dramatic/theater arts; economics; English; environmental studies; European studies; European studies (Central and Eastern); finance; fine/studio arts; French; German; health teacher education; history; human resources management; interdisciplinary studies; international business/trade/commerce; international economics; international relations and affairs; journalism; Latin; Latin American studies; legal administrative assistant/secretary; management information systems; marketing/marketing management; mathematics; middle school education; modern Greek; molecular biology; music; music history, literature, and theory; philosophy; physical education teaching and coaching; physics; political science and government; psychology; religious studies; secondary education; sociology; Spanish; speech and rhetoric; urban studies/affairs; women's studies.

Academics *Calendar:* semesters. *Degrees:* certificates, diplomas, associate, bachelor's, master's, first professional, and postbachelor's certificates. *Special study options:* accelerated degree program, adult/continuing education programs, advanced placement credit, cooperative education, distance learning, double majors, English as a second language, honors programs, independent study, internships, off-campus study, part-time degree program, services for LD students, student-designed majors, study abroad, summer session for credit. *ROTC:* Army (b). *Unusual degree programs:* 3-2 engineering with Columbia University, George Washington University, University of Virginia, Virginia Commonwealth University, Virginia Polytechnic Institute and State University.

Computers on Campus 700 computers/terminals are available on campus for general student use. Students can access the following: campus intranet, computer help desk, free student e-mail accounts, online (class) registration, online (class) schedules. Campuswide network is available. 100% of college-owned or -operated housing units are wired for high-speed Internet access. Wireless service is available via entire campus.

Student Life *Housing options:* coed, men-only, women-only, disabled students. Campus housing is university owned. Freshman applicants given priority for college housing. *Activities and organizations:* drama/theater group, student-run newspaper, radio station, choral group, Volunteer Action Council, Student Government Association, Campus Activities Board, Multicultural Student Union, intramurals, national fraternities, national sororities. *Campus security:* 24-hour emergency response devices and patrols, late-night transport/escort service, controlled dormitory access, campus police. *Student services:* health clinic, personal/psychological counseling, women's center.

Athletics Member NCAA. All Division I except football (Division I-AA). *Intercollegiate sports:* baseball M (s), basketball M (s)/W (s), cheerleading M/W, crew M (c)/W (c), cross-country running M/W (s), fencing M (c)/W (c), field hockey W (s), golf M (s)/W (s), lacrosse M (c)/W (s), rugby M (c)/W (c), soccer M (s)/W (s), swimming and diving M (c)/W (s), tennis M (s)/W (s), track and field M/W (s), ultimate Frisbee M (c)/W (c), volleyball M (c)/W (c), water polo M (c)/W (c), wrestling M (c). *Intramural sports:* archery M/W, badminton M/W, baseball M (c), basketball M/W, field hockey W (c), football M/W, golf M/W, lacrosse W (c), racquetball M/W, soccer M (c)/W (c), softball M/W, squash M/W, swimming and diving M/W, table tennis M/W, tennis M/W, volleyball M/W, water polo M, wrestling M.

Standardized Tests *Required:* SAT or ACT (for admission).

Costs (2008–09) *Comprehensive fee:* $47,050 includes full-time tuition ($38,850) and room and board ($8200). *College room only:* $3680.

Financial Aid Of all full-time matriculated undergraduates who enrolled in 2007, 1,396 applied for aid, 1,132 were judged to have need, 1,068 had their need fully met. 282 Federal Work-Study jobs (averaging $1470). In 2007, 421 non-need-based awards were made. *Average percent of need met:* 100%. *Average financial aid package:* $30,646. *Average need-based loan:* $3041. *Average need-based gift aid:* $27,556. *Average non-need-based aid:* $17,717. *Average indebtedness upon graduation:* $19,214. *Financial aid deadline:* 2/15.

Applying *Options:* electronic application, early admission, early decision, deferred entrance. *Application fee:* $50. *Required:* essay or personal statement, high school transcript, minimum 2.0 GPA, 1 letter of recommendation, signed character statement. *Application deadlines:* 1/15 (freshmen), 2/15 (transfers). *Early decision deadline:* 11/15. *Notification:* 4/1 (freshmen), 4/15 (transfers), 12/15 (early decision).

Freshman Application Contact Ms. Pamela Spence, Dean of Admission, University of Richmond, 28 Westhampton Way, University of Richmond, VA 23173. *Phone:* 804-289-8640. *Toll-free phone:* 800-700-1662. *Fax:* 804-287-6003. *E-mail:* admissions@richmond.edu.

UNIVERSITY OF VIRGINIA

Charlottesville, Virginia **www.virginia.edu/**

- **State-supported** university, founded 1819
- **Suburban** 1160-acre campus with easy access to Richmond
- **Endowment** $4.4 billion
- **Coed** 15,078 undergraduate students, 95% full-time, 56% women, 44% men
- **Very difficult** entrance level, 35% of applicants were admitted

Undergraduates 14,262 full-time, 816 part-time. Students come from 52 states and territories, 113 other countries, 28% are from out of state, 9% African American, 11% Asian American or Pacific Islander, 4% Hispanic American, 0.2% Native American, 5% international, 4% transferred in, 43% live on campus. *Retention:* 97% of 2006 full-time freshmen returned.

Freshmen *Admission:* 17,798 applied, 6,273 admitted, 3,248 enrolled. *Average high school GPA:* 4.0. *Test scores:* SAT critical reading scores over 500: 96%; SAT math scores over 500: 97%; SAT writing scores over 500: 97%; SAT critical reading scores over 600: 75%; SAT math scores over 600: 80%; SAT writing scores over 600: 78%; SAT critical reading scores over 700: 29%; SAT math scores over 700: 37%; SAT writing scores over 700: 30%.

Faculty *Total:* 1,340, 94% full-time, 89% with terminal degrees. *Student/faculty ratio:* 15:1.

Majors Aerospace, aeronautical and astronautical engineering; African-American/Black studies; anthropology; architectural history and criticism; architecture; area studies related; art; astronomy; audiology and speech-language pathology; biology/biological sciences; biomedical/medical engineering; business/commerce; chemical engineering; chemistry; city/urban, community and regional planning; civil engineering; classics and languages, literatures and linguistics; comparative literature; computer and information sciences; computer engineering; cultural studies; dramatic/theater arts; economics; electrical, electronics and communications engineering; engineering; English; environmental science; French; German; history; international relations and affairs; Italian; liberal arts and sciences/liberal studies; mathematics; mechanical engineering; multi-/interdisciplinary studies related; music; nursing (registered nurse training); philosophy; physical education teaching and coaching; physics; political science and government; psychology; religious studies; Slavic languages; sociology; Spanish; systems engineering.

Academics *Calendar:* semesters. *Degrees:* bachelor's, master's, doctoral, first professional, and post-master's certificates. *Special study options:* accelerated degree program, adult/continuing education programs, advanced placement credit, cooperative education, double majors, English as a second language, honors programs, independent study, internships, part-time degree program, services for LD students, student-designed majors, study abroad, summer session for credit. *ROTC:* Army (b), Navy (b), Air Force (b). *Unusual degree programs:* 3-2 joint BA in College of Arts and Sciences and MT in Education. 5 year degree program with graduate work interspersed throughout 5 years.

Computers on Campus Students can access the following: campus intranet, computer help desk, free student e-mail accounts, online (class) grades, online (class) registration, online (class) schedules, online course management tool. Campuswide network is available. Wireless service is available via classrooms, computer centers, computer labs, dorm rooms, learning centers, libraries, student centers.

Student Life *Housing:* on-campus residence required for freshman year. *Options:* coed. Campus housing is university owned. Freshman campus housing is guaranteed. *Activities and organizations:* drama/theater group, student-run newspaper, radio and television station, choral group, marching band, Madison House, student government, university guides, University Union, The Cavalier Daily, national fraternities, national sororities. *Campus security:* 24-hour emergency response devices and patrols, late-night transport/escort service, controlled dormitory access. *Student services:* health clinic, personal/psychological counseling, women's center, legal services.

Athletics Member NCAA. All Division I except football (Division I-A). *Intercollegiate sports:* baseball M (s), basketball M (s)/W (s), crew W (s), cross-country running M (s)/W (s), field hockey W (s), golf M (s)/W (s), lacrosse M (s)/W (s), soccer M (s)/W (s), softball W (s), swimming and diving M (s)/W (s), tennis M (s)/W (s), track and field M (s)/W (s), volleyball W (s), wrestling M (s). *Intramural sports:* archery M (c)/W (c), badminton M (c)/W (c), baseball M (c), basketball M (c)/W (c), cheerleading M (c)/W (c), crew M (c)/W, cross-country running M (c)/W (c), equestrian sports M/W, fencing M (c)/W (c), field hockey W (c), football M/W, golf M (c)/W (c), gymnastics M (c)/W (c), ice hockey M (c)/W (c), lacrosse M (c)/W (c), riflery M (c)/W (c), rugby M (c)/W (c), sailing M (c)/W (c), skiing (downhill) M (c)/W (c), soccer M (c)/W (c), softball M/W, squash M (c)/W (c), swimming and diving M (c)/W (c), tennis M (c)/W (c), ultimate Frisbee M (c)/W (c), volleyball M (c)/W (c), water polo M (c)/W (c), weight lifting M (c)/W (c), wrestling M.

Standardized Tests *Required:* SAT (for admission), SAT or ACT (for admission). *Recommended:* either SAT or ACT plus optional ACT writing test (ACT alone does not satisfy requirement); two SAT subject tests (student's choice).

Costs (2007–08) *Tuition:* state resident $6628 full-time; nonresident $25,878 full-time. Part-time tuition and fees vary according to course load. *Required fees:* $1872 full-time. *Room and board:* $7435; room only: $4015. Room and board charges vary according to board plan and housing facility. *Payment plan:* installment. *Waivers:* senior citizens and employees or children of employees.

Financial Aid Of all full-time matriculated undergraduates who enrolled in 2007, 5,522 applied for aid, 3,446 were judged to have need, 3,446 had their need fully met. 559 Federal Work-Study jobs (averaging $2176). In 2007, 1686 non-need-based awards were made. *Average percent of need met:* 100%. *Average financial aid package:* $17,192. *Average need-based loan:* $4500. *Average need-based gift aid:* $14,176. *Average non-need-based aid:* $7959. *Average indebtedness upon graduation:* $16,847.

Applying *Options:* electronic application, deferred entrance. *Application fee:* $60. *Required:* essay or personal statement, high school transcript, 1 letter of recommendation. *Application deadlines:* 1/2 (freshmen), 3/1 (transfers). *Notification:* 4/1 (freshmen), 4/15 (transfers).

Freshman Application Contact Mr. John A. Blackburn, Dean of Admission, University of Virginia, PO Box 400160, Charlottesville, VA 22904-4160. *Phone:* 434-982-3200. *Fax:* 434-954-3587. *E-mail:* undergrad-admission@virginia.edu.

THE UNIVERSITY OF VIRGINIA'S COLLEGE AT WISE

Wise, Virginia **www.uvawise.edu/**

- **State-supported** 4-year, founded 1954, part of University of Virginia
- **Small-town** 396-acre campus
- **Endowment** $30.5 million
- **Coed** 1,803 undergraduate students, 84% full-time, 52% women, 48% men
- **Moderately difficult** entrance level, 80% of applicants were admitted

Undergraduates 1,509 full-time, 294 part-time. Students come from 7 states and territories, 8 other countries, 5% are from out of state, 7% African American, 0.9% Asian American or Pacific Islander, 2% Hispanic American, 0.3% Native American, 0.9% international, 7% transferred in, 30% live on campus. *Retention:* 72% of 2006 full-time freshmen returned.

Freshmen *Admission:* 1,121 applied, 893 admitted, 401 enrolled. *Average high school GPA:* 3.2. *Test scores:* SAT critical reading scores over 500: 39%; SAT math scores over 500: 42%; SAT writing scores over 500: 32%; ACT scores over 18: 71%; SAT critical reading scores over 600: 9%; SAT math scores over 600: 7%; SAT writing scores over 600: 6%; ACT scores over 24: 17%; SAT critical reading scores over 700: 2%; ACT scores over 30: 1%.

Faculty *Total:* 161, 59% full-time, 47% with terminal degrees. *Student/faculty ratio:* 17:1.

Majors Accounting; art; biology/biological sciences; business administration and management; chemistry; clinical laboratory science/medical technology; communication/speech communication and rhetoric; computer and information sciences; criminal justice/safety; dramatic/theater arts; economics; English; environmental studies; family practice nursing/nurse practitioner; foreign languages and literatures; French; history; interdisciplinary studies; liberal arts and sciences/liberal studies; mathematics; political science and government; psychology; sociology; Spanish.

Academics *Calendar:* semesters. *Degrees:* bachelor's and postbachelor's certificates. *Special study options:* academic remediation for entering students, accelerated degree program, adult/continuing education programs, advanced placement credit, cooperative education, distance learning, double majors, honors programs, independent study, internships, part-time degree program, services for LD students, student-designed majors, study abroad, summer session for credit.

Computers on Campus 130 computers/terminals are available on campus for general student use. Students can access the following: campus intranet, computer help desk, free student e-mail accounts, online (class) grades, online (class) registration, online (class) schedules. Campuswide network is available. 100% of college-owned or -operated housing units are wired for high-speed Internet access. Wireless service is available via learning centers, libraries, student centers.

Student Life *Housing options:* coed, men-only, women-only. Campus housing is university owned. *Activities and organizations:* drama/theater group, student-run newspaper, radio and television station, choral group, student government, Student Activities Board, Multicultural Association, Residence Hall Association, national fraternities, national sororities. *Campus security:* 24-hour emergency response devices and patrols, student patrols, late-night transport/escort service, self-defense, informal discussions, pamphlets/posters/films, and crime prevention office. *Student services:* health clinic, personal/psychological counseling.

Athletics Member NAIA. *Intercollegiate sports:* baseball M (s), basketball M (s)/W (s), cross-country running M (s)/W (s), football M (s), golf M/W, softball W (s), tennis M (s)/W (s), track and field M/W, volleyball W (s). *Intramural sports:* badminton M/W, basketball M/W, football M/W, golf M/W, racquetball M/W, soccer M/W, softball M/W, table tennis M/W, tennis M/W, ultimate Frisbee M/W, volleyball M/W, water polo M/W.

Standardized Tests *Required:* SAT or ACT (for admission).

Costs (2008–09) *Tuition:* state resident $3482 full-time, $149 per semester hour part-time; nonresident $15,256 full-time, $634 per semester hour part-time. *Required fees:* $2957 full-time, $76 per semester hour part-time, $841 per semester part-time. *Room and board:* $6912; room only: $3944.

Financial Aid Of all full-time matriculated undergraduates who enrolled in 2006, 1,303 applied for aid, 1,003 were judged to have need, 952 had their need fully met. 191 Federal Work-Study jobs (averaging $1353). In 2006, 257 non-need-based awards were made. *Average percent of need met:* 95%. *Average financial aid package:* $5807. *Average need-based loan:* $2852. *Average need-based gift aid:* $3609. *Average non-need-based aid:* $1899. *Average indebtedness upon graduation:* $8385.

Applying *Options:* early admission, early action. *Application fee:* $25. *Required:* high school transcript, minimum 2.3 GPA. *Required for some:* interview. *Recommended:* 2 letters of recommendation. *Application deadlines:* 8/1 (freshmen), 8/15 (transfers), 2/1 (early action). *Notification:* continuous until 8/20 (freshmen), continuous until 8/20 (transfers), 2/15 (early action).

Freshman Application Contact Mr. Russell D. Necessary, Vice Chancellor for Enrollment Management, The University of Virginia's College at Wise, 1 College Avenue, Wise, VA 24293. *Phone:* 276-328-0322. *Toll-free phone:* 888-282-9324. *Fax:* 276-328-0251. *E-mail:* admissions@uvawise.edu.

VIRGINIA COMMONWEALTH UNIVERSITY

Richmond, Virginia **www.vcu.edu/**

- **State-supported** university, founded 1838
- **Urban** 140-acre campus
- **Endowment** $329.2 million
- **Coed** 22,163 undergraduate students, 80% full-time, 59% women, 41% men
- 62% of applicants were admitted

Undergraduates 17,673 full-time, 4,490 part-time. Students come from 47 states and territories, 84 other countries, 9% are from out of state, 21% African American, 11% Asian American or Pacific Islander, 4% Hispanic American, 0.6% Native American, 3% international, 8% transferred in. *Retention:* 82% of 2006 full-time freshmen returned.

Freshmen *Admission:* 15,160 applied, 9,331 admitted, 3,882 enrolled. *Average high school GPA:* 3.27. *Test scores:* SAT critical reading scores over 500: 65%; SAT math scores over 500: 65%; SAT writing scores over 500: 60%; ACT scores over 18: 85%; SAT critical reading scores over 600: 24%; SAT math scores over 600: 20%; SAT writing scores over 600: 17%; ACT scores over 24: 28%; SAT critical reading scores over 700: 4%; SAT math scores over 700: 3%; SAT writing scores over 700: 2%; ACT scores over 30: 5%.

Faculty *Total:* 2,989, 63% full-time. *Student/faculty ratio:* 18:1.

Majors Accounting; African-American/Black studies; anthropology; area studies related; art history, criticism and conservation; art teacher education; bioinformatics; biological and physical sciences; biology/biological sciences; biomedical/medical engineering; business administration and management; business/managerial economics; chemical engineering; chemistry; cinematography and film/video production; clinical laboratory science/medical technology; computer and information sciences; computer engineering; crafts, folk art and artisanry; criminal justice/law enforcement administration; dance; dental hygiene; design and applied arts related; design and visual communications; dramatic/theater arts; electrical, electronics and communications engineering; English; environmental studies; fashion/apparel design; finance and financial management services related; fine arts related; foreign languages and literatures; forensic science and technology; graphic design; health teacher education; history; illustration; information science/studies; interior design; international business/trade/commerce; marketing/marketing management; mass communication/media; mathematics; mechanical engineering; multi-/interdisciplinary studies related; music performance; nursing (registered nurse training); painting; parks, recreation and leisure; philosophy; photography; physics; political science and government; psychology; radiologic technology/science; religious studies; sculpture; security and protective services related; social work; sociology; urban studies/affairs; women's studies.

Academics *Calendar:* semesters. *Degrees:* certificates, bachelor's, master's, doctoral, first professional, post-master's, postbachelor's, and first professional certificates. *Special study options:* academic remediation for entering students, accelerated degree program, adult/continuing education programs, advanced placement credit, cooperative education, distance learning, double majors, English as a second language, honors programs, independent study, internships, off-campus study, part-time degree program, services for LD students, student-designed majors, study abroad, summer session for credit. *ROTC:* Army (c).

Computers on Campus 2,000 computers/terminals and 15,700 ports are available on campus for general student use. Students can access the following: computer help desk, free student e-mail accounts, online (class) registration, online (class) schedules. Campuswide network is available. 98% of college-owned or -operated housing units are wired for high-speed Internet access. Wireless service is available via classrooms, computer labs, dorm rooms, libraries.

Student Life *Housing options:* coed, disabled students. Campus housing is university owned. *Activities and organizations:* drama/theater group, student-run newspaper, radio station, choral group, marching band, Student Government Organization, Activities Programming Board, Muslim Student Association, Black Caucus, national fraternities, national sororities. *Campus security:* 24-hour emergency response devices and patrols, student patrols, late-night transport/escort service, controlled dormitory access, security personnel in residence halls. *Student services:* health clinic, personal/psychological counseling.

Athletics Member NCAA. All Division I. *Intercollegiate sports:* baseball M (s), basketball M (s)/W (s), crew M, cross-country running M (s)/W (s), field hockey W (s), golf M (s), ice hockey M, lacrosse M/W, rugby M/W, soccer M (s)/W (s), swimming and diving M/W, tennis M (s)/W (s), track and field M (s)/W (s), volleyball W (s). *Intramural sports:* badminton M/W, basketball M/W, cheerleading M/W, fencing M (c)/W (c), golf M (c)/W (c), ice hockey M (c), lacrosse M (c)/W (c), racquetball M/W, rugby M (c)/W (c), soccer M/W, softball M/W (c), swimming and diving M (c)/W (c), table tennis M/W, tennis M (c)/W (c), volleyball M/W, water polo M/W, weight lifting M (c)/W (c), wrestling M (c)/W (c).

Standardized Tests *Required:* SAT or ACT (for admission).

Costs (2007–08) *Tuition:* state resident $4482 full-time, $187 per credit part-time; nonresident $16,858 full-time, $703 per credit part-time. *Required fees:* $1714 full-time, $71 per credit part-time. *Room and board:* $7567; room only: $4497. Room and board charges vary according to board plan. *Payment plan:* installment. *Waivers:* senior citizens and employees or children of employees.

Financial Aid Of all full-time matriculated undergraduates who enrolled in 2007, 10,376 applied for aid, 8,162 were judged to have need, 1,792 had their need fully met. 1,152 Federal Work-Study jobs (averaging $2129). In 2007, 931 non-need-based awards were made. *Average percent of need met:* 70%. *Average financial aid package:* $13,806. *Average need-based loan:* $4186. *Average need-based gift aid:* $4367. *Average non-need-based aid:* $5398. *Average indebtedness upon graduation:* $20,468.

Applying *Options:* electronic application, early admission, deferred entrance. *Application fee:* $40. *Required:* high school transcript. *Notification:* continuous until 11/1 (freshmen).

Freshman Application Contact Ms. Sybil Halloran, Director of Undergraduate Admissions, Virginia Commonwealth University, 821 West Franklin Street, Box 842526, Richmond, VA 23284-2526. *Phone:* 804-828-6125. *Toll-free phone:* 800-841-3638. *Fax:* 804-828-1899. *E-mail:* ugrad@vcu.edu.

See page 2690 for the College Close-Up.

VIRGINIA INTERMONT COLLEGE

Bristol, Virginia **www.vic.edu/**

- **Independent** 4-year, founded 1884, affiliated with Baptist Church
- **Small-town** 13-acre campus
- **Endowment** $5.8 million
- **Coed** 635 undergraduate students, 83% full-time, 74% women, 26% men
- **Minimally difficult** entrance level, 69% of applicants were admitted

Undergraduates 527 full-time, 108 part-time. Students come from 36 states and territories, 8 other countries, 51% are from out of state, 5% African American, 0.3% Asian American or Pacific Islander, 0.9% Hispanic American, 0.3% Native American, 2% international, 5% transferred in, 55% live on campus. *Retention:* 64% of 2006 full-time freshmen returned.

Freshmen *Admission:* 672 applied, 466 admitted, 66 enrolled. *Average high school GPA:* 3.27. *Test scores:* SAT critical reading scores over 500: 54%; SAT math scores over 500: 48%; ACT scores over 18: 90%; SAT critical reading scores over 600: 21%; SAT math scores over 600: 18%; ACT scores over 24: 37%; SAT critical reading scores over 700: 1%; SAT math scores over 700: 1%; ACT scores over 30: 5%.

Faculty *Total:* 81, 48% full-time, 59% with terminal degrees. *Student/faculty ratio:* 10:1.

Majors Art; art teacher education; biology/biological sciences; biology teacher education; business administration and management; commercial and advertising art; computer and information sciences; criminal justice/law enforcement administration; dance; dramatic/theater arts; education; elementary education; English; English/language arts teacher education; environmental studies; equestrian studies; general studies; health and physical education; history; interdisciplinary studies; international business/trade/commerce; legal assistant/paralegal; legal studies; liberal arts and sciences and humanities related; marketing/marketing management; photography; physical education teaching and coaching; political science and government; pre-law studies; pre-medical studies; pre-veterinary studies; psychology; public administration; religious studies; restaurant, culinary, and catering management; secondary education; social studies teacher education; social work; sport and fitness administration/management.

Academics *Calendar:* semesters. *Degrees:* associate and bachelor's. *Special study options:* academic remediation for entering students, accelerated degree program, adult/continuing education programs, advanced placement credit, double majors, English as a second language, honors programs, independent study, internships, off-campus study, part-time degree program, services for LD students, study abroad, summer session for credit.

Computers on Campus 80 computers/terminals are available on campus for general student use. Students can access the following: campus intranet, computer help desk, free student e-mail accounts, online (class) grades, online (class) schedules. Campuswide network is available. 100% of college-owned or -operated housing units are wired for high-speed Internet access. Wireless service is available via student centers.

Student Life *Housing:* on-campus residence required through junior year. *Options:* coed, men-only, women-only. Campus housing is university owned. Freshman campus housing is guaranteed. *Activities and organizations:* drama/theater group, choral group, Student Activities Committee, Social Work Club, Student Government Association, Equestrian Club, Business Organization for Student Success. *Campus security:* 24-hour patrols, late-night transport/escort service. *Student services:* health clinic, personal/psychological counseling, women's center.

Athletics Member NAIA. *Intercollegiate sports:* baseball M (s), basketball M (s)/W (s), equestrian sports M (s)/W (s), golf M (s), softball W (s), tennis M (s)/W (s), volleyball W (s). *Intramural sports:* basketball M/W, bowling M/W, football M/W, golf M/W, skiing (downhill) M/W, softball M/W, swimming and diving M/W, table tennis M/W, tennis M/W, volleyball M/W, weight lifting M/W.

Standardized Tests *Required:* SAT or ACT (for admission).

Costs (2007–08) *Comprehensive fee:* $28,645 includes full-time tuition ($21,200), mandatory fees ($950), and room and board ($6495). Full-time tuition and fees vary according to class time and program. Part-time tuition: $220 per credit. Part-time tuition and fees vary according to class time, course level, course load, and program. *Required fees:* $50 per credit part-time. *College room only:* $3100. Room and board charges vary according to housing facility. *Payment plan:* installment. *Waivers:* senior citizens and employees or children of employees.

Financial Aid Of all full-time matriculated undergraduates who enrolled in 2006, 592 applied for aid, 539 were judged to have need, 62 had their need fully met. 85 Federal Work-Study jobs (averaging $2000). In 2006, 158 non-need-based awards were made. *Average percent of need met:* 57%. *Average financial aid package:* $11,776. *Average need-based loan:* $3868. *Average need-based gift aid:* $8225. *Average non-need-based aid:* $7072. *Average indebtedness upon graduation:* $19,217. *Financial aid deadline:* 6/1.

Applying *Options:* electronic application, early admission, early action, deferred entrance. *Application fee:* $25. *Required:* essay or personal statement, high school transcript, minimum 2.0 GPA. *Required for some:* interview. *Application deadlines:* rolling (freshmen), rolling (transfers). *Notification:* continuous (freshmen), continuous (transfers).

Freshman Application Contact Mr. Tony England, Director of Admissions, Virginia Intermont College, 1013 Moore Street, Campus Box D-460, Bristol, VA 24201. *Phone:* 276-466-7856. *Toll-free phone:* 800-451-1842. *Fax:* 276-466-7885. *E-mail:* viadmit@vic.edu.

VIRGINIA MILITARY INSTITUTE

Lexington, Virginia **www.vmi.edu/**

- **State-supported** 4-year, founded 1839
- **Small-town** 134-acre campus
- **Endowment** $373.9 million
- **Coed, primarily men** 1,378 undergraduate students, 100% full-time, 8% women, 92% men
- **Moderately difficult** entrance level, 54% of applicants were admitted

Undergraduates 1,378 full-time. Students come from 45 states and territories, 9 other countries, 42% are from out of state, 6% African American, 4% Asian American or Pacific Islander, 3% Hispanic American, 0.4% Native American, 2% international, 2% transferred in, 100% live on campus. *Retention:* 80% of 2006 full-time freshmen returned.

Freshmen *Admission:* 1,704 applied, 926 admitted, 410 enrolled. *Average high school GPA:* 3.37. *Test scores:* SAT critical reading scores over 500: 80%; SAT math scores over 500: 87%; SAT writing scores over 500: 70%; ACT scores over 18: 98%; SAT critical reading scores over 600: 31%; SAT math scores over 600: 31%; SAT writing scores over 600: 20%; ACT scores over 24: 42%; SAT critical reading scores over 700: 3%; SAT math scores over 700: 3%; SAT writing scores over 700: 1%; ACT scores over 30: 4%.

Faculty *Total:* 166, 70% full-time, 81% with terminal degrees. *Student/faculty ratio:* 10:1.

Majors Biology/biological sciences; chemistry; civil engineering; computer science; economics; electrical, electronics and communications engineering; English; history; international relations and affairs; mathematics; mechanical engineering; modern languages; physics; psychology.

Academics *Calendar:* semesters. *Degree:* bachelor's. *Special study options:* accelerated degree program, advanced placement credit, double majors, honors programs, independent study, internships, services for LD students, study abroad, summer session for credit. *ROTC:* Army (b), Navy (b), Air Force (b).

Computers on Campus 200 computers/terminals are available on campus for general student use. Campuswide network is available.

Student Life *Housing:* on-campus residence required through senior year. *Options:* coed. Campus housing is university owned. Freshman campus housing is guaranteed. *Activities and organizations:* drama/theater group, student-run newspaper, choral group, marching band, Newman Club, Officers Christian Fellowship, strength and fitness organizations, Promaji, Pre-Law Society. *Campus security:* 24-hour emergency response devices and patrols, student patrols. *Student services:* health clinic, personal/psychological counseling.

Athletics Member NCAA. All Division I except football (Division I-AA). *Intercollegiate sports:* baseball M (s), basketball M (s), cross-country running M (s)/W (s), fencing M (c)/W (c), golf M (s), ice hockey M (c), lacrosse M (s), racquetball M (c)/W (c), riflery M (s)/W (s), rugby M (c)/W (c), soccer M (s), swimming and diving M (s)/W, tennis M (s), track and field M (s)/W (s), volleyball M (c)/W (c), water polo M (c)/W (c), weight lifting M (c)/W (c), wrestling M (s). *Intramural sports:* basketball M/W, football M/W, soccer M/W, softball M/W.

Standardized Tests *Required:* SAT or ACT (for admission).

Costs (2007–08) *One-time required fee:* $2005. *Tuition:* state resident $5062 full-time; nonresident $20,906 full-time. *Required fees:* $2981 full-time. *Room and board:* $6108. *Payment plan:* installment.

Financial Aid Of all full-time matriculated undergraduates who enrolled in 2005, 769 applied for aid, 586 were judged to have need, 318 had their need fully met. 42 Federal Work-Study jobs (averaging $873). In 2005, 285 non-need-based awards were made. *Average percent of need met:* 90%. *Average financial aid package:* $13,960. *Average need-based loan:* $3676. *Average need-based gift aid:* $16,821. *Average non-need-based aid:* $4667. *Average indebtedness upon graduation:* $11,754.

Applying *Options:* electronic application, early admission, early decision. *Application fee:* $35. *Required:* high school transcript. *Recommended:* essay or personal statement, 2 letters of recommendation, interview. *Application deadlines:* 3/1 (freshmen), 2/15 (transfers). *Early decision deadline:* 11/15. *Notification:* continuous (freshmen), continuous until 5/1 (transfers), 12/15 (early decision).

Freshman Application Contact Lt. Col. Tom Mortenson, Associate Director of Admissions, Virginia Military Institute, 309 Letcher Avenue, Lexington, VA 24450. *Phone:* 540-464-7211. *Toll-free phone:* 800-767-4207. *Fax:* 540-464-7746. *E-mail:* admissions@vmi.edu.

See page 2692 for the College Close-Up.

VIRGINIA POLYTECHNIC INSTITUTE AND STATE UNIVERSITY

Blacksburg, Virginia **www.vt.edu/**

- **State-supported** university, founded 1872
- **Small-town** 2600-acre campus
- **Endowment** $524.7 million
- **Coed** 23,041 undergraduate students, 98% full-time, 42% women, 58% men
- **Moderately difficult** entrance level, 67% of applicants were admitted

Undergraduates 22,506 full-time, 535 part-time. Students come from 49 states and territories, 77 other countries, 24% are from out of state, 4% African American, 7% Asian American or Pacific Islander, 3% Hispanic American, 0.3% Native American, 2% international, 4% transferred in, 40% live on campus. *Retention:* 89% of 2006 full-time freshmen returned.

Freshmen *Admission:* 19,429 applied, 13,031 admitted, 5,122 enrolled. *Average high school GPA:* 3.76. *Test scores:* SAT critical reading scores over 500: 91%; SAT math scores over 500: 96%; SAT writing scores over 500: 89%; SAT critical reading scores over 600: 44%; SAT math scores over 600: 62%; SAT writing scores over 600: 43%; SAT critical reading scores over 700: 8%; SAT math scores over 700: 13%; SAT writing scores over 700: 5%.

Faculty *Total:* 1,602, 86% full-time. *Student/faculty ratio:* 17:1.

Majors Accounting; aerospace, aeronautical and astronautical engineering; agricultural economics; agronomy and crop science; animal sciences; architecture; art; biochemistry; biology/biological sciences; business administration and management; business family and consumer sciences/human sciences; business/managerial economics; chemical engineering; chemistry; civil engineering; clothing/textiles; communication/speech communication and rhetoric; computer and information sciences; computer engineering; computer science; construction management; consumer/homemaking education; dairy science; dramatic/theater arts; economics; electrical, electronics and communications engineering; engineering mechanics; English; environmental studies; finance; food science; foods, nutrition, and wellness; forestry; French; geography; geology/earth science; German; history; horticultural science; hotel/motel administration; human development and family studies; industrial design; industrial engineering; information science/studies; interdisciplinary studies; interior design; international relations and affairs; landscape architecture; management science; marketing/marketing management; materials engineering; mathematics; mechanical engineering; mining and mineral engineering; music; ocean engineering; philosophy; physics; political science and government; poultry science; psychology; public policy analysis; secondary education; sociology; Spanish; statistics.

Academics *Calendar:* semesters. *Degrees:* associate, bachelor's, master's, doctoral, and first professional. *Special study options:* accelerated degree program, adult/continuing education programs, advanced placement credit, cooperative education, distance learning, double majors, English as a second language, honors programs, independent study, internships, part-time degree program, services for LD students, study abroad, summer session for credit. *ROTC:* Army (b), Navy (b), Air Force (b).

Computers on Campus 8,000 computers/terminals are available on campus for general student use. Students can access the following: campus intranet, computer help desk, free student e-mail accounts, online (class) grades, online (class) registration, online (class) schedules. Campuswide network is available. Wireless service is available via entire campus.

Student Life *Housing:* on-campus residence required for freshman year. *Options:* coed, men-only, women-only. Campus housing is university owned. Freshman campus housing is guaranteed. *Activities and organizations:* drama/theater group, student-run newspaper, radio and television station, choral group, marching band, Virginia Tech Union, Student Government Association, international student organizations, national fraternities, national sororities. *Campus security:* 24-hour emergency response devices and patrols, student patrols, late-night transport/escort service, controlled dormitory access. *Student services:* health clinic, personal/psychological counseling, women's center, legal services.

Athletics Member NCAA. All Division I except football (Division I-A). *Intercollegiate sports:* baseball M, basketball M, cross-country running M/W, golf M (s), lacrosse W (s), soccer M (s)/W (s), swimming and diving M (s)/W (s), tennis M (s)/W (s), track and field M (s)/W (s), ultimate Frisbee M/W, volleyball W. *Intramural sports:* baseball M (c), basketball M, bowling M/W, crew M (c)/W (c), cross-country running M/W, equestrian sports M (c)/W (c), fencing M (c)/W (c), field hockey M (c)/W (c), football M/W, golf M/W, gymnastics M (c)/W (c), ice hockey M/W, lacrosse M (c)/W (c), racquetball M/W, riflery M (c)/W (c), rugby M (c)/W (c), soccer M/W, softball M/W, swimming and diving M/W, table tennis M/W, tennis M/W, volleyball M/W, water polo M/W.

Standardized Tests *Required:* SAT or ACT (for admission). *Required for some:* SAT and SAT Subject Tests or ACT (for admission).

Costs (2007–08) *Tuition:* state resident $5772 full-time, $241 per credit hour part-time; nonresident $17,980 full-time, $749 per credit hour part-time. Full-time tuition and fees vary according to program. Part-time tuition and fees vary according to program. *Required fees:* $1625 full-time, $276 per term part-time. *Room and board:* $5106. Room and board charges vary according to board plan and location. *Payment plan:* installment. *Waivers:* senior citizens.

Financial Aid Of all full-time matriculated undergraduates who enrolled in 2006, 13,293 applied for aid, 8,128 were judged to have need, 1,664 had their need fully met. 837 Federal Work-Study jobs (averaging $1023). 4,255 state and other part-time jobs (averaging $1578). In 2006, 1991 non-need-based awards were made. *Average percent of need met:* 69%. *Average financial aid package:* $10,013. *Average need-based loan:* $4063. *Average need-based gift aid:* $4851. *Average non-need-based aid:* $2407. *Average indebtedness upon graduation:* $20,209.

Applying *Options:* electronic application, early admission, early decision, deferred entrance. *Application fee:* $50. *Required:* high school transcript. *Recommended:* minimum 3.0 GPA. *Application deadlines:* 1/15 (freshmen), 2/15 (transfers). *Early decision deadline:* 11/1. *Notification:* 4/1 (freshmen), 5/1 (transfers), 12/15 (early decision).

Freshman Application Contact Ms. Mildred Johnson, Senior Associate Director for Undergraduate Admissions, Virginia Polytechnic Institute and State University, 201 Burruss Hall, Blacksburg, VA 24061. *Phone:* 540-231-6267. *Fax:* 540-231-3242. *E-mail:* vtadmiss@vt.edu.

VIRGINIA STATE UNIVERSITY

Petersburg, Virginia **www.vsu.edu/**

- **State-supported** comprehensive, founded 1882, part of State Council of Higher Education for Virginia
- **Suburban** 236-acre campus with easy access to Richmond
- **Endowment** $14.8 million
- **Coed** 4,231 undergraduate students, 93% full-time, 61% women, 39% men
- **Minimally difficult** entrance level, 58% of applicants were admitted

Undergraduates 3,933 full-time, 298 part-time. Students come from 42 states and territories, 31% are from out of state, 95% African American, 0.3% Asian American or Pacific Islander, 0.7% Hispanic American, 0.1% Native American, 6% transferred in, 53% live on campus. *Retention:* 74% of 2006 full-time freshmen returned.

Freshmen *Admission:* 4,481 applied, 2,590 admitted, 1,044 enrolled. *Average high school GPA:* 2.8. *Test scores:* SAT critical reading scores over 500: 16%; SAT math scores over 500: 14%; SAT writing scores over 500: 11%; SAT critical reading scores over 600: 1%; SAT math scores over 600: 1%.

Faculty *Total:* 388, 68% full-time. *Student/faculty ratio:* 14:1.

Majors Accounting; agriculture; biology/biological sciences; business administration and management; business/managerial economics; business teacher education; chemistry; computer engineering; computer science; criminal justice/safety; electrical and electronic engineering technologies related; English; family and consumer economics related; history; hospitality administration; information technology; interdisciplinary studies; liberal arts and sciences/liberal studies; manufacturing engineering; marketing/marketing management; mass communication/media; mathematics; mechanical engineering/mechanical technology; music; nursing (licensed practical/vocational nurse training); physical education teaching and coaching; physics; political science and government; psychology; public administration; public relations, advertising, and applied communication related; social work; sociology; trade and industrial teacher education; visual and performing arts.

Academics *Calendar:* semesters. *Degrees:* associate, bachelor's, master's, doctoral, post-master's, and postbachelor's certificates. *Special study options:* adult/continuing education programs, advanced placement credit, cooperative education, double majors, honors programs, independent study, internships, part-time degree program, services for LD students, student-designed majors, summer session for credit. *ROTC:* Army (b). *Unusual degree programs:* 3-2 engineering with Old Dominion University.

Computers on Campus 750 computers/terminals are available on campus for general student use. Students can access the following: computer help desk, free student e-mail accounts, online (class) grades, online (class) registration, online (class) schedules. Campuswide network is available.

Student Life *Housing:* on-campus residence required for freshman year. *Options:* coed, men-only, women-only. Campus housing is university owned. Freshman applicants given priority for college housing. *Activities and organizations:* drama/theater group, student-run newspaper, choral group, marching band, NAACP, Betterment of Brothers/Sisters, Student Government Association, dormitory cabinets, pre-alumni associations, national fraternities, national sororities. *Campus security:* 24-hour emergency response devices and patrols, late-night transport/escort service. *Student services:* health clinic, personal/psychological counseling.

Athletics Member NCAA. All Division II. *Intercollegiate sports:* baseball M (s), basketball M (s)/W (s), bowling W (s), cheerleading M/W, cross-country running M (s)/W (s), football M (s), golf M (s)/W (s), softball W (s), tennis M (s)/W (s), track and field M (s)/W (s), volleyball W (s). *Intramural sports:* basketball M/W, football M, tennis M/W, track and field M/W, volleyball W.

Standardized Tests *Required:* SAT or ACT (for admission).

Costs (2007–08) *Tuition:* state resident $3186 full-time, $189 per credit hour part-time; nonresident $10,716 full-time, $444 per credit hour part-time. Full-time tuition and fees vary according to course load. Part-time tuition and fees vary according to course load. *Required fees:* $2469 full-time. *Room and board:* $7340; room only: $4249. Room and board charges vary according to board plan and housing facility. *Payment plan:* installment. *Waivers:* senior citizens.

Financial Aid Of all full-time matriculated undergraduates who enrolled in 2005, 4,048 applied for aid, 3,643 were judged to have need, 546 had their need fully met. 400 Federal Work-Study jobs (averaging $2000). In 2005, 430 non-need-based awards were made. *Average percent of need met:* 68%. *Average financial aid package:* $9678. *Average need-based loan:* $5925. *Average need-based gift aid:* $4500. *Average indebtedness upon graduation:* $28,250.

Applying *Options:* electronic application. *Application fee:* $25. *Required:* high school transcript, minimum 2.2 GPA, 2 letters of recommendation. *Application deadlines:* 5/1 (freshmen), 5/1 (transfers). *Notification:* continuous (freshmen), continuous (transfers).

Freshman Application Contact Mrs. Irene Logan, Director of Admissions, Virginia State University, PO Box 9018, Petersburg, VA 23806-2096. *Phone:* 804-524-5902. *Toll-free phone:* 800-871-7611. *Fax:* 804-524-5055. *E-mail:* ilogan@vsu.edu.

VIRGINIA UNION UNIVERSITY

Richmond, Virginia **www.vuu.edu/**

Freshman Application Contact Mr. Gil Powell, Director of Admissions, Virginia Union University, 1500 North Lombardy Street, Richmond, VA 23220-1170. *Phone:* 804-257-5881. *Toll-free phone:* 800-368-3227. *Fax:* 804-329-8477. *E-mail:* gpowell@vuu.edu.

VIRGINIA UNIVERSITY OF LYNCHBURG

Lynchburg, Virginia **www.vul.edu/**

- **Independent religious** comprehensive, founded 1886
- **Urban** campus
- **Coed** 128 undergraduate students, 31% full-time, 61% women, 39% men
- **Noncompetitive** entrance level, 100% of applicants were admitted

Undergraduates 40 full-time, 88 part-time. Students come from 10 states and territories, 1 other country, 3% are from out of state, 96% African American, 0.8% Asian American or Pacific Islander, 0.8% international, 16% transferred in, 4% live on campus. *Retention:* 87% of 2006 full-time freshmen returned.

Freshmen *Admission:* 9 applied, 9 admitted, 9 enrolled.

Faculty *Total:* 82, 11% full-time, 22% with terminal degrees. *Student/faculty ratio:* 7:1.

Majors Business administration and management; liberal arts and sciences/liberal studies; religious studies; sociology.

Academics *Calendar:* semesters. *Degrees:* certificates, associate, bachelor's, master's, doctoral, and first professional. *Special study options:* academic remediation for entering students, adult/continuing education programs, advanced placement credit, distance learning, external degree program, independent study, part-time degree program, summer session for credit.

Computers on Campus 10 computers/terminals are available on campus for general student use. Students can access the following: computer help desk, free student e-mail accounts. Campuswide network is available. 100% of college-owned or -operated housing units are wired for high-speed Internet access. Wireless service is available via entire campus.

Student Life *Housing options:* coed. Campus housing is university owned. Freshman applicants given priority for college housing. *Activities and organizations:* choral group, Choir, Community Service. *Campus security:* 24-hour emergency response devices. *Student services:* personal/psychological counseling.

Costs (2008–09) *Comprehensive fee:* $300 includes full-time tuition ($5000), mandatory fees ($300), and room and board ($3600). Part-time tuition: $167 per credit. *Required fees:* $167 per credit part-time.

Applying *Application fee:* $25. *Required:* high school transcript. *Required for some:* essay or personal statement. *Application deadline:* rolling (freshmen). *Notification:* continuous (freshmen).

Director of Admissions Ms. Debbie Smith, Registrar, Virginia University of Lynchburg, 2058 Garfield Avenue, Lynchburg, VA 24501-6417. *Phone:* 434-528-5276. *Fax:* 434-528-2705. *E-mail:* dsmith@vul.edu.

VIRGINIA WESLEYAN COLLEGE

Norfolk, Virginia **www.vwc.edu/**

- **Independent United Methodist** 4-year, founded 1961
- **Urban** 300-acre campus with easy access to Norfolk/Virginia Beach
- **Endowment** $53.0 million
- **Coed** 1,444 undergraduate students, 83% full-time, 63% women, 37% men
- **Moderately difficult** entrance level, 90% of applicants were admitted

Undergraduates 1,195 full-time, 249 part-time. Students come from 29 states and territories, 2 other countries, 23% are from out of state, 19% African American, 2% Asian American or Pacific Islander, 4% Hispanic American, 0.1% Native American, 0.1% international, 5% transferred in, 67% live on campus. *Retention:* 71% of 2006 full-time freshmen returned.

Freshmen *Admission:* 1,502 applied, 1,359 admitted, 362 enrolled. *Average high school GPA:* 3.09. *Test scores:* SAT critical reading scores over 500: 45%; SAT math scores over 500: 47%; ACT scores over 18: 68%; SAT critical reading scores over 600: 10%; SAT math scores over 600: 10%; ACT scores over 24: 13%; SAT critical reading scores over 700: 2%; SAT math scores over 700: 1%.

Faculty *Total:* 129, 66% full-time. *Student/faculty ratio:* 13:1.

Majors American studies; art; art teacher education; biology/biological sciences; business administration and management; chemistry; classics; communication and media related; computer science; criminology; dramatic/theater arts; education (K-12); elementary education; English; environmental studies; foreign languages and literatures; foreign language teacher education; French; geology/earth science; German; history; humanities; human services; interdisciplinary studies; international relations and affairs; liberal arts and sciences/liberal studies; mathematics; middle school education; music; natural sciences; parks, recreation and leisure; philosophy; political science and government; pre-dentistry studies; pre-law studies; pre-medical studies; pre-veterinary studies; psychology; religious studies; secondary education; social sciences; social studies teacher education; sociology; Spanish; women's studies.

Academics *Calendar:* 4-1-4. *Degree:* bachelor's. *Special study options:* academic remediation for entering students, adult/continuing education programs, advanced placement credit, distance learning, double majors, freshman honors college, honors programs, independent study, internships, off-campus study, part-time degree program, services for LD students, student-designed majors, study abroad, summer session for credit. *ROTC:* Army (c).

Computers on Campus 100 computers/terminals are available on campus for general student use. Students can access the following: campus intranet, computer help desk, free student e-mail accounts, online (class) grades, online (class) schedules, grades, class materials and family schedules. Campuswide network is available. 100% of college-owned or -operated housing units are wired for high-speed Internet access. Wireless service is available via classrooms, computer centers, computer labs, learning centers, libraries, student centers.

Student Life *Housing:* on-campus residence required through senior year. *Options:* coed. Campus housing is university owned. Freshman campus housing is guaranteed. *Activities and organizations:* drama/theater group, student-run newspaper, radio station, choral group, Wesleyan Activities Council, Community Service, Student Government Association, student newspaper, Black Student Union, national fraternities, national sororities. *Campus security:* 24-hour emergency response devices and patrols, late-night transport/escort service, controlled dormitory access, well-lit pathways. *Student services:* health clinic, personal/psychological counseling, women's center.

Athletics Member NCAA. All Division III. *Intercollegiate sports:* baseball M, basketball M/W, cheerleading W, cross-country running M/W, field hockey W, golf M, lacrosse M/W, soccer M/W, softball W, tennis M/W, track and field M/W, volleyball W. *Intramural sports:* basketball M/W, field hockey W, football M/W, soccer M/W, softball M/W, table tennis M/W, volleyball M/W.

Standardized Tests *Required:* SAT or ACT (for admission).

Costs (2008–09) *Comprehensive fee:* $33,538 includes full-time tuition ($25,938), mandatory fees ($500), and room and board ($7100). Part-time tuition: $1080 per hour.

Financial Aid Of all full-time matriculated undergraduates who enrolled in 2006, 732 applied for aid, 731 were judged to have need, 40 had their need fully met. 142 Federal Work-Study jobs (averaging $1500). In 2006, 299 non-need-based awards were made. *Average percent of need met:* 68%. *Average financial aid package:* $16,496. *Average need-based loan:* $3912. *Average need-based gift aid:* $1856. *Average non-need-based aid:* $7151. *Average indebtedness upon graduation:* $18,604.

Applying *Options:* electronic application. *Application fee:* $40. *Required:* essay or personal statement, high school transcript, minimum 2.5 GPA. *Required for some:* interview. *Application deadlines:* rolling (freshmen), rolling (transfers). *Notification:* continuous (freshmen), continuous (transfers).

Freshman Application Contact Mrs. Sara Gastler, Director of Admissions, Virginia Wesleyan College, 1584 Wesleyan Drive, Norfolk, VA 23502-5599. *Phone:* 757-455-3208. *Toll-free phone:* 800-737-8684. *Fax:* 757-461-5238. *E-mail:* admissions@vwc.edu.

WASHINGTON AND LEE UNIVERSITY

Lexington, Virginia **www.wlu.edu/**

- **Independent** comprehensive, founded 1749
- **Small-town** 322-acre campus
- **Endowment** $1.5 billion
- **Coed** 1,778 undergraduate students, 100% full-time, 50% women, 50% men
- **Most difficult** entrance level, 27% of applicants were admitted

Undergraduates 1,775 full-time, 3 part-time. Students come from 49 states and territories, 42 other countries, 85% are from out of state, 4% African American, 3% Asian American or Pacific Islander, 1% Hispanic American, 0.3% Native American, 4% international, 0.6% transferred in, 60% live on campus. *Retention:* 95% of 2006 full-time freshmen returned.

Freshmen *Admission:* 4,215 applied, 1,158 admitted, 463 enrolled. *Test scores:* SAT critical reading scores over 500: 100%; SAT math scores over 500: 100%; ACT scores over 18: 100%; SAT critical reading scores over 600: 95%; SAT math scores over 600: 97%; ACT scores over 24: 100%; SAT critical reading scores over 700: 47%; SAT math scores over 700: 48%; ACT scores over 30: 53%.

Faculty *Total:* 214, 99% full-time, 94% with terminal degrees. *Student/faculty ratio:* 10:1.

Majors Accounting; anthropology; archeology; art history, criticism and conservation; Asian studies (East); biochemistry; biology/biological sciences; business administration and management; chemical engineering; chemistry; classics; computer and information sciences; computer science; dramatic/theater arts;

economics; engineering physics; English; fine/studio arts; foreign languages and literatures; French; geological and earth sciences/geosciences related; geology/earth science; German; history; journalism; mathematics; medieval and Renaissance studies; multi-/interdisciplinary studies related; music; neuroscience; philosophy; physics; political science and government; psychology; public policy analysis; religious studies; Russian studies; sociology; Spanish.

Academics *Calendar:* 4-4-2. *Degrees:* bachelor's, master's, and first professional. *Special study options:* advanced placement credit, double majors, honors programs, independent study, internships, off-campus study, services for LD students, student-designed majors, study abroad. *ROTC:* Army (c). *Unusual degree programs:* 3-2 engineering with Rensselaer Polytechnic Institute and Columbia University.

Computers on Campus 297 computers/terminals are available on campus for general student use. Students can access the following: online (class) registration. Campuswide network is available. 100% of college-owned or -operated housing units are wired for high-speed Internet access. Wireless service is available via entire campus.

Student Life *Housing:* on-campus residence required through sophomore year. *Options:* coed, men-only, women-only. Campus housing is university owned. Freshman campus housing is guaranteed. *Activities and organizations:* drama/theater group, student-run newspaper, radio and television station, choral group, Outing Club, Student Activities Board, Nabors Service League, Mock Convention, College Republicans, national fraternities, national sororities. *Campus security:* 24-hour emergency response devices and patrols, late-night transport/escort service, controlled dormitory access. *Student services:* health clinic, personal/psychological counseling, women's center.

Athletics Member NCAA. All Division III. *Intercollegiate sports:* baseball M, basketball M/W, cross-country running M/W, equestrian sports M/W, fencing M (c)/W (c), field hockey W, football M, golf M, ice hockey M (c)/W (c), lacrosse M (c)/W (c), rock climbing M (c), skiing (cross-country) M (c)/W (c), soccer M/W, softball W (c), swimming and diving M/W, tennis M/W, track and field M/W, ultimate Frisbee M (c)/W (c), volleyball M (c)/W, wrestling M. *Intramural sports:* basketball M/W, bowling M/W, cross-country running M/W, football M, golf M/W, racquetball M/W, skiing (downhill) M (c)/W (c), soccer M/W, softball M/W, squash M (c)/W (c), swimming and diving M/W, table tennis M, tennis M/W, track and field M/W, ultimate Frisbee M/W, volleyball M/W, wrestling M.

Standardized Tests *Required:* SAT or ACT (for admission), 2 unrelated SAT Subject Tests (for admission).

Costs (2007–08) *Comprehensive fee:* $44,170 includes full-time tuition ($34,650), mandatory fees ($795), and room and board ($8725). Part-time tuition: $1155 per credit hour. *College room only:* $4030. Room and board charges vary according to housing facility and student level. *Waivers:* employees or children of employees.

Financial Aid Of all full-time matriculated undergraduates who enrolled in 2007, 747 applied for aid, 633 were judged to have need, 570 had their need fully met. 139 Federal Work-Study jobs (averaging $1394). 363 state and other part-time jobs (averaging $1349). In 2007, 155 non-need-based awards were made. *Average percent of need met:* 99%. *Average financial aid package:* $30,933. *Average need-based loan:* $4400. *Average need-based gift aid:* $26,021. *Average non-need-based aid:* $20,540. *Average indebtedness upon graduation:* $16,784. *Financial aid deadline:* 3/3.

Applying *Options:* electronic application, early decision, deferred entrance. *Application fee:* $50. *Required:* high school transcript, 3 letters of recommendation. *Recommended:* essay or personal statement, interview. *Application deadlines:* 1/15 (freshmen), 4/1 (transfers). *Early decision deadline:* 11/15. *Notification:* 4/1 (freshmen), continuous (transfers), 12/22 (early decision).

Freshman Application Contact Mr. William M. Hartog, Dean of Admissions and Financial Aid, Washington and Lee University, Lexington, VA 24450-0303. *Phone:* 540-458-8710. *Fax:* 540-458-8062. *E-mail:* admissions@wlu.edu.

WESTWOOD COLLEGE–ANNANDALE CAMPUS

Annandale, Virginia

www.westwood.edu/locations/virginia-colleges/annandale-college.asp

- **Proprietary** 4-year, part of Westwood Colleges, Inc
- **Suburban** campus
- **Coed**
- **Noncompetitive** entrance level

Faculty *Student/faculty ratio:* 12:1.

Academics *Degrees:* associate and bachelor's.

Costs (2007–08) *Tuition:* $12,900 full-time.

Freshman Application Contact Ms. Amy McPherson, Westwood College–Annandale Campus, 7619 Little River Turnpike, Suite 500, Annandale, VA 22003. *Phone:* 703-462-6550. *Toll-free phone:* 800-281-2978. *Fax:* 703-642-3772. *E-mail:* amcpherson@westwood.edu.

WESTWOOD COLLEGE–ARLINGTON BALLSTON CAMPUS

Arlington, Virginia **www.westwood.edu/**

- **Proprietary** 4-year, part of Westwood Colleges, Inc
- **Urban** campus
- **Coed**
- **Minimally difficult** entrance level

Academics *Degrees:* associate and bachelor's.

Applying *Application fee:* $100. *Required:* interview, Accuplacer Test.

Freshman Application Contact Shebony Corbin, Westwood College–Arlington Ballston Campus, 1901 North Ft. Myer Drive, Arlington, VA 22209. *Phone:* 703-243-3900. *Fax:* 703-243-3992. *E-mail:* scorbin@westwood.edu.

WORLD COLLEGE

Virginia Beach, Virginia **www.worldcollege.edu/**

- **Proprietary** 4-year, founded 1992
- **Suburban** campus
- **Coed** 445 undergraduate students
- **Noncompetitive** entrance level

Undergraduates Students come from 50 states and territories, 25 other countries.

Faculty *Total:* 7, 57% full-time.

Majors Computer and information systems security; electrical, electronic and communications engineering technology.

Academics *Calendar:* semesters. *Degrees:* bachelor's (offers only external degree programs). *Special study options:* academic remediation for entering students, accelerated degree program, adult/continuing education programs, distance learning, external degree program, part-time degree program.

Student Life *Housing:* college housing not available.

Costs (2008–09) *Tuition:* $3540 full-time.

Applying *Options:* early admission. *Required:* high school transcript. *Application deadline:* rolling (freshmen). *Notification:* continuous (freshmen).

Freshman Application Contact Mrs. Audre Piratsky, Admissions Counselor, World College, 5193 Shore Drive, Suite 105, Virginia Beach, VA 23455. *Phone:* 757-464-4600. *Toll-free phone:* 800-696-7532. *Fax:* 757-464-3687. *E-mail:* instruct@cie-wc.edu.

ARGOSY UNIVERSITY

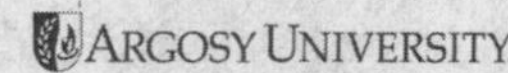

The University

Argosy University is a leading institution offering a variety of degree programs that focus on the human side of success alongside professional competence. For students looking for a more personal approach to education, Argosy University may just be the answer. With forty-eight graduate and undergraduate programs, across nineteen campuses and twelve states, Argosy University emphasizes interpersonal skills as well as academic learning. All of its programs are taught by practicing professionals who bring real-world experience into the classroom. So students graduate with both a solid foundation of knowledge and the power to put it to work. To accommodate busy working adults, many programs at Argosy University are structured flexibly—with both campus and online learning and evening, weekend, and daytime classes. There is also a wide range of financial aid options for students who qualify.

Argosy University is a private institution of higher education dedicated to providing high-quality professional education programs at the doctoral, master's, bachelor's, and associate degree levels as well as continuing education to individuals who seek to advance their professional and personal lives. The University emphasizes programs in the behavioral sciences (psychology and counseling), business, education, and the health-care professions. A limited number of preprofessional programs and general education offerings are provided to permit students to prepare for entry into these professional fields. The programs of Argosy University are designed to instill the knowledge, skills, and ethical values of professional practice and to foster values of social responsibility in a supportive, learning-centered environment of mutual respect and professional excellence.

With nineteen campuses nationwide, Argosy University provides students with a network of resources found at larger universities, including a career resources office, an academic resources center, and extensive information access for research. The University's innovative programs feature dynamic, relevant, and practical curricula delivered in flexible class formats. Students enjoy scheduling options that make it easier to fit school into their busy lives. They can choose from day and evening courses, on campus or online. Many students find a combination of both to be an ideal way of continuing their education while meeting family and professional demands.

Most students are full-time working professionals who live within driving distance of the campus. The University does not offer or operate student housing.

Argosy University is accredited by The Higher Learning Commission of the North Central Association (30 North LaSalle Street, Suite 2400, Chicago, Illinois 60602; 800-621-7440; http://ncahlc.org).

Location

Argosy University operates nineteen locations across the U.S. and offers a variety of degree programs online (http://www.argosy.edu). Campus locations include the following:

Atlanta, 980 Hammond Drive, Suite 100, Atlanta, Georgia 30328; phone: 770-671-1200 or 888-671-4777 (toll-free)

Chicago, 225 North Michigan Avenue, Suite 1300, Chicago, Illinois 60601; phone: 312-777-7600 or 800-626-4123 (toll-free)

Dallas, 8080 Park Lane, Suite 400A, Dallas, Texas 75231; phone: 214-890-9900 or 866-954-9900 (toll-free)

Denver, 1200 Lincoln Street, Denver, Colorado 80203; phone: 303-248-2700 or 866-431-5981 (toll-free)

Hawai'i, 400 ASB Tower, 1001 Bishop Street, Honolulu, Hawaii 96813; phone: 808-536-5555 or 888-323-2777 (toll-free)

Inland Empire, 636 East Brier Drive, Suite 235, San Bernardino, California 92408; phone: 909-915-3800 or 866-217-9075 (toll-free)

Nashville, 100 Centerview Drive, Suite 225, Nashville, Tennessee 37214; phone: 615-525-2800 or 866-833-6598 (toll-free)

Orange County, 3501 West Sunflower Avenue, Suite 110, Santa Ana, California 92704; phone: 714-338-6200 or 800-716-9598 (toll-free)

Phoenix, 2233 West Dunlap Avenue, Phoenix, Arizona 85021; phone: 602-216-2600 or 866-216-2777 (toll-free)

Salt Lake City, 121 West Election Road, Suite 300, Draper, Utah 84020; phone: 888-639-4756 (toll-free)

San Diego, 7650 Mission Valley Road, San Diego, California 92108; phone: 858-598-1900 or 866-505-0333 (toll-free)

San Francisco Bay Area, 1005 Atlantic Avenue, Alameda, California 94501; phone: 510-217-4700 or 866-215-2777 (toll-free)

Santa Monica, 2950 31st Street, Santa Monica, California 90405; phone: 310-866-4000 or 866-505-0332 (toll-free)

Sarasota, 5250 17th Street, Sarasota, Florida 34235; phone: 941-379-0404 or 800-331-5995 (toll-free)

Schaumburg, 999 North Plaza Drive, Suite 111, Schaumburg, Illinois 60173-5403; phone: 847-969-4900 or 866-290-2777 (toll-free)

Seattle, 2601-A Elliott Avenue, Seattle, Washington 98121; phone: 206-283-4500 or 888-283-2777 (toll-free)

Tampa, Parkside at Tampa Bay Park, 4401 North Hines Avenue, Suite 150, Tampa, Florida 33614; phone: 813-393-5290 or 800-850-6488 (toll-free)

Twin Cities, 1515 Central Parkway, Eagan, Minnesota 55121; phone: 651-846-2882 or 888-844-2004 (toll-free)

Washington DC, 1550 Wilson Boulevard, Suite 600, Arlington, Virginia 22209; phone: 703-526-5800 or 866-703-2777 (toll-free)

Majors and Degrees

Argosy University's College of Business offers a Bachelor of Science (B.S.) in Business Administration program. Argosy University's College of Psychology and Behavioral Sciences offers the Bachelor of Arts (B.A.) in Psychology degree program.

Academic Programs

The B.S. in Business Administration program prepares students for entry- to mid-level positions within the public or private sector. The curriculum is structured to help students develop competencies in oral and written communication, leadership, team skills, solutions-focused learning, and the analysis and execution of solutions in various business situations. Students may choose one of five optional concentrations: customized professional concentration, finance, health-care management, international business, or marketing.

The B.A. in Psychology program is designed to help students begin human services careers in such capacities as entry-level counselor, case manager, or human resources administrator and

in management and business services roles. The program also lays the foundation for graduate study. Students may choose an optional concentration from the following three options: criminal justice, organizational psychology, or substance abuse. This dynamic program is built around a flexible class approach.

Argosy University's bachelor's degree programs are open to students and working professionals with no college experience, plus those who have already earned college credit at a community college, junior college, or other university.

Academic Facilities

Argosy University libraries provide curriculum support and educational resources including current text materials, diagnostic training documents, reference materials and databases, journals and dissertations, and major and current titles in program areas. There is an online public-access catalog of library resources available throughout the Argosy University system. Students enjoy full remote access to their campus library database, enabling them to study and conduct research at home. Academic databases offer dissertation abstracts, academic journals, and professional periodicals. All library computers are Internet accessible. Software applications include Word, Excel, PowerPoint, SPSS, and various test-scoring programs.

Costs

Tuition varies by program. Students should contact the Argosy University campus of their choice for tuition information.

Financial Aid

A wide range of financial aid options is available to students who qualify. Argosy University offers access to federal and state aid programs, merit-based awards, grants, loans, and a work-study program. As a first step, students should complete the Free Application for Federal Student Aid (FAFSA). Prospective students can apply electronically at http://www.fafsa.ed.gov or at the campus. To receive consideration for financial aid and ensure timely receipt of funds, it is best to submit an application promptly.

Faculty

The Argosy University faculty is composed of working professionals who have a passion to help students succeed. Members bring real-world experience and the latest practice innovations to the academic setting. The diverse faculty is widely recognized for contributions to the field. Most hold doctoral degrees. They provide a substantive education that combines comprehensive knowledge with critical skills and practical workplace relevance. Above all, faculty members are committed to their students' personal and professional development.

Student Government

Argosy University campuses offer unique opportunities for student involvement beyond individual programs of study. Most faculty committees include a student representative. In addition, a student group meets with faculty members and administrators regularly to discuss pertinent campus-related issues.

Admission Requirements

Admission requirements differ depending on the number of college credits completed prior to application.

Students who have earned 12 or fewer semester college credits must provide proof of high school graduation or GED and meet one of the following conditions for admission: ACT composite score of 18 or above, or a combined math and verbal SAT score of 870, or minimum ACCUPLACER scores of 86 in sentence skills and 53 in algebra. Applicants who do not meet any of the above conditions for admission will be admitted with academic support if they provide proof of high school graduation or GED and meet one of the following: ACT composite score of 14 to 17, or a combined math and verbal SAT score of 660 to 869, or minimum ACCUPLACER scores of 54 in sentence skills and 36 in arithmetic.

Applicants who have earned 13 or more semester college credits must provide proof of high school graduation or GED and meet one of the following conditions for admission: cumulative college GPA of 2.0 or above or minimum ACCUPLACER scores of 86 for sentence skills and 53 in algebra. Students who do not meet either of the above criteria will be admitted with academic support if they provide proof of high school graduation or GED and meet the following condition: minimum ACCUPLACER scores of 54 in reading and 36 in arithmetic.

Students admitted with academic support are limited to 12 credit hours of study during their first semester (6 credit hours per session). Students admitted with academic support will be required to complete developmental English and/or math courses unless they meet the following conditions: Writing Review (ENG099)—must meet one of the following: a minimum ACCUPLACER score of 86 in sentence skills, or a minimum ACT verbal score of 18, or a minimum SAT verbal score of 425, or completion of a college-level English composition course with a grade of C or above; Mathematics Review I (MAT096)—must meet one of the following: a minimum ACCUPLACER score of 53 in algebra, or a minimum ACT math score of 18, or a minimum SAT math score of 440, or completion of a college-level English composition course with a grade of C or above.

Other admission requirements may include credit hours of qualified transfer credit with a grade of C- or better from a regionally accredited institution or a nationally accredited institution approved and documented by the faculty and dean of the College of Business, or the College of Professional Psychology, at Argosy University or completion of an Associate of Arts or Associate of Science degree from a regionally accredited institution. A maximum of 78 lower-division or 90 total credit hours may be transferred. A minimum written TOEFL score of 500 (paper-based test), 173 (computer-based test), or 61 (Internet-based test) is required for all applicants whose native language is not English or who have not graduated from an institution in which English is the language of instruction.

Official transcripts from approved postsecondary institutions must include a minimum grade point average of 2.0 (on a scale of 4.0) for all academic work completed. Exceptions may be made for extenuating circumstances. All applications must include a completed application form, proof of high school graduation or successful completion of the GED test, official postsecondary transcripts, and a nonrefundable (except in California) application fee. Additional materials are required prior to matriculation. Some programs have additional application requirements or include exceptions to admission requirements. An admissions representative can provide further information.

Application and Information

Argosy University accepts students on a rolling admissions basis year-round, depending on availability of required courses. Applications for admission are available online at http://www.argosy.edu or by contacting one of the campus locations.

Argosy University
205 North Michigan Avenue, Suite 1300
Chicago, Illinois 60601-2250

Phone: 312-899-9900
800-377-0617 (toll-free)
E-mail: auadmissions@argosy.edu
Web site: http://www.argosy.edu

THE ART INSTITUTE OF WASHINGTON

ARLINGTON, VIRGINIA

The Institute

The Art Institute of Washington prepares students for entry-level careers in the creative arts. Programs of study are carefully designed with the support and contributions of the professional community. The curricula are reviewed periodically to help ensure that students are trained to meet the needs of a changing marketplace. The Art Institute of Washington offers fourteen bachelor's degree programs and seven associate degree programs.

The student population includes recent high school graduates, transfer students, and those who have left a previous employment situation to study and train for a new career. Students are creative, competitive, and open to new ideas. They place great value on an education that prepares them for an exciting entry-level position in the arts.

The school's blend of theoretical study and practical skill building gives graduates a foundation on which to build creative goals. Students who attend The Art Institute of Washington are given opportunities to develop leadership skills and build relationships within their fields.

Services are available to assist students with resume writing, networking, and keeping abreast of what employers are looking for in job applicants. The student-faculty ratio is 20:1.

Getting involved and becoming an active participant in the school is an important part of a student's educational experience. Many activities take place each quarter that provide opportunities for students to connect with peers, members of the staff and faculty, and members of the local community. Student ambassadors assist new students in their adjustment to the college and serve as hosts to important visitors. Students may also join student clubs, get involved in student leadership functions, and participate in social events, including student art shows. Art Institute of Washington students also volunteer for local charities.

Residential communities provide a living-learning environment that is conducive to study, relaxation, and entertainment. The Art Institute of Washington provides housing in the Rosslyn neighborhood of Arlington. Apartments are carpeted and fully furnished and include a washer and dryer. Residence life advisers live on-site to assist students with academic and personal matters and to organize a wide variety of social and educational programs.

The Art Institute of Washington is accredited as a branch of The Art Institute of Atlanta by the Commission on Colleges of the Southern Association of Colleges and Schools (SACS; 1866 Southern Lane, Decatur, Georgia 30033-4097; phone: 404-679-4500; http://www.sacs.org) to award Associate in Arts, Bachelor of Arts, Bachelor of Science, and Bachelor of Fine Arts degrees. The Associate in Arts in Culinary Arts program is accredited by the American Culinary Federation (ACF).

Location

Located in Arlington, Virginia, directly across the Potomac River from Washington, D.C., The Art Institute of Washington occupies the ground floor and the ninth through twelfth floors of the Ames Center. The area is home to a variety of activities, including professional sports, first-rate theatrical and musical entertainment, beautiful parks, and cultural events. Some of the most popular places to visit are the Washington Monument, Lincoln Memorial, Vietnam and Korean War Memorials, Arlington National Cemetery, Smithsonian Institution and Museums, and Capitol Building. The Arlington community is home to the Fashion Center at Pentagon City, with its more than 150 stores, and the Crystal City Underground and Plaza Shops, which hosts more than 120 retail shops. In addition, Arlington has more than 170 county parks and playgrounds, including over 80 miles of bicycle routes and jogging trails.

Majors and Degrees

Bachelor's degrees are available in advertising, audio production, culinary arts management, digital filmmaking and video production, fashion and retail management, food and beverage management, game art and design, graphic design, interior design, media arts and animation, photographic imaging, visual and game programming, visual effects and motion graphics, and Web design and interactive media. Associate degrees are offered in audio production, culinary arts, graphic design, photographic imaging, video production, Web design and interactive media, and wine, spirits, and beverage management. Diploma programs are available in advertising design, commercial photography, culinary arts–baking and pastry, culinary arts–culinary skills, digital design, video skills, and Web design.

Academic Programs

The academic year is divided into four quarters, beginning in January, April, July, and October. Students may begin their program of study during any quarter. Bachelor's degrees require the completion of 192 credit hours (thirty-six months), and associate degree programs require completion of 96 to 112 credit hours (eighteen to twenty-one months, depending on the program of study).

Academic Facilities

The school's setting in the Ames Center consists of classrooms, studios, computer labs, a student lounge, administrative offices for staff and faculty members, and a Learning Resource Center with a library and reference materials. The building also houses the student counseling center, the tutoring center, teaching kitchens and dining lab, an art supply store, and an exhibition gallery, as well as a television studio and sound stage.

Costs

Tuition cost varies by program. Prospective students should contact the school for current tuition costs. Other charges include a starting kit for all first-quarter students. Kits vary in price, depending on the program of study.

Financial Aid

Financial aid is available for those who qualify. Students who require financial assistance should first complete and submit a Free Application for Federal Student Aid (FAFSA) and meet with a financial aid officer. The officer determines the level of need based on a required federal formula, the cost of education, and other factors. Gift aid is available in the form of Federal Pell Grants, Federal Supplemental Educational Opportunity Grants, and veterans' benefits. Loans include Federal Stafford Student Loans, Federal PLUS loans, and alternative loans. Other scholarships are available from the school and private sources. Application deadlines and eligibility requirements vary by program.

Faculty

The Art Institute of Washington faculty consists of full-time and part-time members, many of whom have professional experience in their industries. The faculty prides itself on building close personal relationships with the students. Faculty and staff members maintain an informal, open-door policy and are available for student questions and suggestions.

Admission Requirements

Prospective students must interview, either by telephone or in person, with a member of the admissions staff in order to explore the student's background and interests and how they relate to The Art Institute of Washington's programs. To apply, students must submit a completed application for admission, including an essay, high school transcripts or General Educational Development (GED) test scores, SAT or ACT scores, and a $50 nonrefundable application fee. Prospective students may apply at any time of the year. Applications may be submitted online or mailed to the school.

Application and Information

To obtain an application, make arrangements for an interview, or tour the school, students should contact:

The Art Institute of Washington
1820 North Fort Myer Drive
Arlington, Virginia 22209-1802
Phone: 703-358-9550
877-303-3771 (toll-free)
Fax: 703-358-9759
Web site: http://www.artinstitutes.edu/arlington

The Art Institute of Atlanta®, GA; The Art Institute of Atlanta®–Decatur, GA; The Art Institute of Austin℠, TX; The Art Institute of California℠–Inland Empire; The Art Institute of California℠–Los Angeles; The Art Institute of California℠–Orange County; The Art Institute of California℠–Sacramento; The Art Institute of California℠–San Diego; The Art Institute of California℠–San Francisco; The Art Institute of California℠–Sunnyvale; The Art Institute of Charleston℠, SC, A branch of The Art Institute of Atlanta, GA; The Art Institute of Charlotte®, NC; The Art Institute of Colorado® (Denver); The Art Institute of Dallas®, TX; The Art Institute of Fort Lauderdale®, FL; The Art Institute of Houston®, TX; The Art Institute of Indianapolis℠, IN*; The Art Institute of Jacksonville℠, FL, A branch of Miami International University of Art & Design; The Art Institute of Las Vegas®, NV; The Art Institute of Michigan℠ (Detroit); The Art Institute of New York City®, NY; The Art Institute of Ohio℠–Cincinnati**; The Art Institute of Philadelphia®, PA; The Art Institute of Phoenix®, AZ; The Art Institute of Pittsburgh®, PA; The Art Institute of Pittsburgh®–Online Division; The Art Institute of Portland®, OR; The Art Institute of Salt Lake City℠, UT; The Art Institute of Seattle®, WA; The Art Institute of Tampa℠, FL, A branch of Miami International University of Art & Design; The Art Institute of Tennessee℠–Nashville, A branch of The Art Institute of Atlanta, GA; The Art Institute of Tucson℠, AZ; The Art Institute of Washington® (Arlington, VA), A branch of The Art Institute of Atlanta, GA; The Art Institute of York–Pennsylvania℠; The Art Institutes International Minnesota℠ (Minneapolis); California Design College℠ (Los Angeles–Wilshire Blvd.); The Illinois Institute of Art®–Chicago; The Illinois Institute of Art®–Schaumburg; Miami International University of Art & Design℠, FL; The New England Institute of Art® (Boston, MA).

*The Art Institute of Indianapolis is licensed by the Indiana Commission on Proprietary Education, 302 W. Washington St., Rm. E201, Indianapolis, IN 46204, AC-0080.

**The Art Institute of Ohio–Cincinnati, 8845 Governors Hill Drive, Suite 100, Cincinnati, OH 45249-3317, OH Reg. #04-01-1698B.

AVERETT UNIVERSITY

DANVILLE, VIRGINIA

The University

Students who want to learn in a traditional campus setting, and those who are working professionals who need convenience and flexibility, find that Averett has a degree program to fit their lives.

Founded in 1859, Averett University's main campus is situated on 19-acres in a beautiful residential section of Danville, Virginia. Students can choose from more than thirty undergraduate degree options and two master's degree programs.

No matter their stage in life, Averett provides the education students need to succeed. Averett is a place that honors its Christian heritage, emphasizing both academic and religious freedom. Just like in the "real world," Averett's students encounter a diversity of people and ideas. They not only learn how to form and defend their own opinions, but also how to thoughtfully evaluate the opinions of others. Averett's graduates communicate clearly, think critically, and function effectively in today's rapidly changing and globally oriented information age. The University recognizes its unique responsibilities to the Danville region and promotes higher education, provides cultural opportunities, and serves as a resource for the community.

Students from more than thirty-one states and fifteen other countries make Averett their university of choice, and *U.S. News & World Report* has acknowledged the University for its diverse student body. The University's total enrollment is more than 2,400, of which 38 percent are minority students and 27 percent are undergraduates. More than 800 students study on the main campus in the traditional program, and over 1,749 working professionals study accelerated business and education programs in Averett's statewide Graduate and Professional Studies (GPS) Program.

Averett's 19-acre main campus has eight residence halls that offer traditional residence-hall-style accommodations as well as suites and apartment-style living. Six tennis courts and a gymnasium are also available. Life on campus is enhanced by Averett's new student center, which is equipped for wireless computing. Complete with a specialty dining hall, café, game room, Career Services Center, comfortable areas for students to relax and chat, offices for clubs, and computer lab, the center has plenty of space for students to gather.

The 70-acre North Campus, a 10-minute drive from the main campus (shuttle-van service is available during class hours), offers the E. Stuart James Grant Center, one of the finest athletic facilities in the athletic conference. The center, which seats more than 1,600 for athletic events, includes three basketball courts, a training room, fitness facility, classrooms, and locker rooms. Surrounding the center are baseball and softball fields, two practice fields, and Cougar Stadium, where football, soccer, and lacrosse teams compete.

Averett's scenic 100-acre equestrian center is located 15 minutes from the main campus. It features an indoor arena, forty stalls with removable partitions, three tack rooms, a wash room, offices, and a laboratory. The outdoor facilities include a round pen, riding ring, jumping area, pastures, and cross-country trails.

The Averett Flight Center is located at the Danville Regional Airport, only 4 miles from campus. Averett's facility houses aircraft, areas for ground instruction, a simulator room, a technology center, and offices. Averett's aeronautics students can train in the uncrowded skies above the airport or use the flight simulators for situational training and training in bad weather.

Averett students enjoy a variety of campus activities, from concerts to lectures to trips, sponsored by the Campus Activities Board. In addition, an active Student Government Association and clubs, organizations, honor societies, and Greek life add to the campus. An annual Concert-Lecture Series brings plays, concerts, and guest lecturers to campus, while the Averett Theatre Players, the Averett Singers, and the handbell choir perform throughout the year, adding to the cultural offerings.

Students participate in a variety of intramural sports, and more than 280 Cougar student athletes represent the University on the University's NCAA Division III athletic teams in the USA South Athletic Conference. Averett fields teams in men's baseball, football, golf, and softball; women's lacrosse; and men's and women's basketball, cross-country, soccer, tennis, and volleyball. Averett has 18 athletes who have been recognized nationally as Division III All Americans. Equestrian has been added as an intercollegiate sport.

Averett University is accredited by the Commission on Colleges of the Southern Association of Colleges and Schools (SACS) (1866 Southern Lane, Decatur, Georgia 30033-4097; telephone: 404-679-4501) to award associate, baccalaureate, and master's degrees.

Location

Averett's main campus sits in the historic city of Danville, Virginia. Danville, with a population of 53,000, is just 3 miles from the Virginia–North Carolina border and is convenient to airports in both states. The campus is in a residential neighborhood adjacent to Danville's famed Millionaire's Row, a collection of vast Victorian homes recognized by historians for their architectural splendor. Within walking distance are a variety of churches, several restaurants, a movie theater, and Ballou Park, a 107-acre park and shopping center. Piedmont Mall, other shopping outlets, and a selection of chain and family-owned restaurants are just a short drive across the Dan River. Averett is also conveniently located down the street from Danville Regional Medical Center and other medical service providers. In addition to the tennis courts, playing fields, fitness center, and basketball courts available at Averett, the city offers recreational facilities, including the 150-acre Dan Daniel Park, home of the Danville Braves, Atlanta's Rookie Class minor league baseball team. Dan Daniel Park also features trails for hiking and biking. Averett is within walking distance of both YWCA and YMCA facilities, which offer swimming, racquetball, and other fitness activities. The city also maintains a popular 3.2-mile paved walk along the Dan River.

Majors and Degrees

Degrees offered include the Associate of Arts (A.A.), Associate of Science in Business (A.S.B.), Bachelor of Applied Science (B.A.S.), Bachelor of Arts (B.A.), Bachelor of Business Administration (B.B.A.), and the Bachelor of Science (B.S.). Majors are accounting; aerospace management (aviation business, aviation maintenance operations (transfer students only), aviation technical systems, flight operations); aerospace management/criminal justice; art; art education (PK–12); athletic training; biology (biomedical science-predental, biomedical science-premed, ecology/environmental biology); biology/chemistry; business administration (finance, global marketing management, management science); chemistry; computer information systems; computer science; education (elementary education or secondary education or PK–12 teacher licensure); English; English/theater; environmental sciences; equestrian studies (dressage instruction, equine management, eventing instruction); history; journalism; liberal studies; mathematical decision science; mathematics; medical technology; music (church music, performance); physical education, wellness, and sport science (health and physical education and driver's education–teacher licensure (PK–12), health and physical education–teacher licensure (PK–12), physical education, sport management, wellness/sport medicine); political science; prelaw; premed; psychology (biological psychology, cognitive science, counseling and clinical, industrial/organizational); 2+2 radiologic technology (transfer students only); religion; sociology; sociology/criminal justice; and theater. Minors are available in most program areas in addition to those in church ministries, coaching, French, leadership studies, Spanish, and special education.

Academic Programs

Under the general education curriculum, all students are required to take at least 9 semester hours of English, 6 in the fine arts, 15 in history and social sciences, and 6 in religion and philosophy. Those enrolled in the A.A. or B.A. programs must take an additional 3 semester hours in mathematics, 4 in natural sciences, and 6 to 14 in a foreign language. Students in the B.A.S. or B.S. programs must take an additional 6 semester hours in mathematics and 8 in natural science. Students may take classes during two semesters and two optional summer terms. Students may elect to double major or complete their baccalaureate degree in three years by enrolling in several of the optional summer terms.

Averett offers students an Honors program and the Human-Computer Interaction program. Honors program students explore in-depth, selected areas of academics, with approximately 20 percent of all course work carrying honors credit. The program culminates with a senior honors project. The Human-Computer Interaction program exposes students to the principles of design, human behavior, and computer science. Students major in art, computer science, computer information systems, or psychology and combine their study with a program in Human-Computer Interaction. Graduates of this program are prepared for a variety of careers in the fast-growing technology field.

Off-Campus Programs

Study-abroad and travel programs are available in business, science and the humanities. Internships are available to students in all majors.

Academic Facilities

Main campus facilities include academic buildings, an art building and pottery area, a 630-seat auditorium, a music center, and a library. The Blount Library supports research and reading interests with print and electronic books and journals, databases, subject guides, and 24-hour remote access. The library offers a quiet place to study and collaborate on team projects, a computer lab, a wireless hub, and DVD, CD-RW, and media production equipment. Library staff members offer research classes and consultations.

Costs

Estimated annual costs in the 2007–08 academic year were $19,512 in tuition, $7100 in room and board, and $1000 in general fees. Specific lab fees are assigned per course.

Financial Aid

Averett disburses more than $16.8 million in financial assistance to eligible students each year. Academic scholarships, Perkins loans, Pell grants, Supplemental Educational Opportunity Grants, Virginia Tuition Assistance Grants, on- and off-campus employment opportunities, ample private scholarships, and low-interest loans are available. The Free Application for Federal Student Aid (FAFSA) is required for determining eligibility for federal and state aid and need-based scholarships, and should be submitted prior to April 1.

Faculty

Averett faculty members are scholars, teachers, authors, and experts in their field. Seventy-eight percent hold doctorates or terminal degrees. Members of the faculty take a personal interest in the success of their students. With a student-faculty ratio of 14:1, there are many opportunities for students and faculty members to work together on projects, solve problems, or just sit and talk. Each student is assigned a faculty adviser in his or her major area of study who assists with class selection and is available to guide students through their academic study.

Student Government

The mission of the Student Government Association (SGA) of Averett University is to serve as a voice for student concerns and ideas and to increase student involvement in clubs and activities on the campus.

Admission Requirements

Students are required to take the SAT or ACT and to have graduated from high school with 16 acceptable units in grades 9–12: 4 in English, 3 in college-prep mathematics, 3 in lab sciences, 3 in history and social sciences, and 3 in electives. Advanced Placement (AP) and/or University credit may be granted for AP, IB, and CLEP tests. Students who have completed the GED may be considered for admission.

Applicants should submit a completed application, SAT or ACT scores, and transcripts of credits completed (or in progress) from high school. A letter of recommendation from a guidance counselor, teacher, employer, or principal is recommended but not required. Transfer students must also include a transcript of credits completed (or in progress) from all previously attended colleges, be in good standing with their previous university, and have a cumulative GPA of at least 2.0 (on a 4.0 scale). International students must also take the TOEFL and achieve a score of at least 500 on the paper version or 173 on the computer version.

Application and Information

Averett operates on the rolling admissions system. When all necessary supporting documents arrive at the University, the Admissions Committee reviews the application and promptly informs the applicant of its decision.

Dean of Admissions
Averett University
420 West Main Street
Danville, Virginia 24541
Phone: 434-791-4996
800-AVERETT (283-7388) (toll-free)
E-mail: admit@averett.edu
Web site: http://www.averett.edu

BRIDGEWATER COLLEGE

BRIDGEWATER, VIRGINIA

The College

Since 1880 Bridgewater College's mission has been to "Educate and develop the whole person." At Bridgewater it is believed that exceptional scholarship and academic excellence must be combined with a focus on the formation of values, character, and leadership ability. This educational vision is made unique by its application. Learning and growth at Bridgewater focuses on each individual's personal development, recognizing and developing each person's gifts and potential.

On-campus housing is guaranteed at Bridgewater, and the close interaction among peers contributes to a thriving spirit of community, where students and faculty and staff members demonstrate respect and care for one another. More than 1,550 students are enrolled representing a variety of backgrounds and religious affiliations. Students come from twenty-six states and eight countries, with the majority from Virginia and the mid-Atlantic states.

An apartment-style residence hall, seven traditional residence halls, ten College-owned houses, and ten apartments are located on the campus for residential students. New students are assigned to a residence hall room with another new student of compatible interests through a nonautomated housing-selection process.

More than seventy clubs, societies, and organizations exist on the campus to meet students' needs and interests. Health and physical education facilities include a large gymnasium, a 25-meter indoor pool, playing fields, and an all-weather track. The Funkhouser Center for Health and Wellness provides facilities for intramural and recreational activities, including basketball, racquetball courts, and volleyball; a cardiac and weight-training center; an indoor track; and a multipurpose room for aerobics, dance, and wrestling. A complete schedule of intercollegiate sports for men and women is offered during each session, and an extensive intramural sports program, open to all students, promotes sportsmanship, leadership, physical health, and team play. The College is a member of the Old Dominion Athletic Conference (ODAC) and the NCAA Division III.

Special services available to assist students with academic and personal needs include a writing center, tutors, academic support workshops, career services, counseling services, and a chaplain. Reasonable and appropriate accommodations are provided to enrolled students with documented disabilities to ensure equal access to the academic program and College-administered activities.

Bridgewater College is accredited by the Commission on Colleges of the Southern Association of Colleges and Schools (1866 Southern Lane, Decatur, Georgia, 30033-4097; telephone: 404-679-4501) to award baccalaureate degrees.

Location

Bridgewater College (BC) is located in the town of Bridgewater in the scenic and historic Shenandoah Valley. Facilities for boarding horses are adjacent to the campus, and also five miles south at the Bridgewater College Equestrian Center. Bridgewater is located 7 miles south of the city of Harrisonburg and is convenient to the urban areas of Washington, D.C.; Richmond; and Roanoke. Air transportation is available at Shenandoah Valley Regional Airport, 13 miles from the campus. The valley area is rich in the history of the early United States and the Civil War. The College conducts an Outdoor Program to provide students with opportunities to participate in outdoor activities, such as climbing, hiking, skiing, and whitewater rafting and the BC Outdoor Center provides supplies for camping and canoeing.

Majors and Degrees

Bridgewater College offers majors in allied health science, applied physics (tracks in engineering physics, physical science, physics and technology), art (tracks in digital media/graphics design, digital media/photography, traditional studio media), athletic training, biology, business administration, chemistry, communication studies, computer science, economics, English (tracks in language and literature, literary studies, writing), environmental science, family and consumer sciences, French, health and exercise science, health and physical education, history, history and political science, information systems management, international studies, liberal studies (available only to students in the elementary programs), mathematics, medical technology, music, nutrition and wellness, philosophy and religion, physics, physics and mathematics, political science, psychology, sociology, and Spanish.

The College offers four-year curricula leading to the bachelor's degree and a state-approved program of teacher preparation at the PK–6 and 6–12 levels. The elementary education program prepares the student to teach in PK through grade 6. The secondary education program prepares students to teach in the content areas in grades 6–12. Art, music (vocal and instrumental), health and physical education, foreign language, and English as a second language (ESL) endorsements prepare students to teach in grades PK through 12. Students who complete Bridgewater's teacher education program may be certified to teach in other states.

Minors may be earned in art (tracks in art history and criticism, digital media, traditional media), biology, business administration, chemistry, coaching, communication studies, computer information systems, computer science, crime and justice, economics, English, equine studies, family and consumer sciences, French, German, history, international studies, mathematics, music, neuroscience, nutrition and wellness, peace studies, philosophy and religion, physics, political science, psychology, social work, sociology, Spanish, and theater.

Concentrations and specializations are available in accounting, church music, comparative cultural analysis, family and consumer sciences education, fashion merchandising, finance, interior design, international commerce, marketing, media studies (communications), organization management, public relations, and U.S. history.

Dual-degree programs are offered in engineering with George Washington University and Virginia Tech, forestry with Duke University, nursing with Vanderbilt University, veterinary science with Virginia Tech, and physical therapy with Shenandoah University and George Washington University. Bridgewater is also associated with American University for internships/research opportunities in their Washington Semester and World Capitals program. Preprofessional programs are offered in dentistry, engineering, law, medicine, ministry, occupational therapy, pharmacy, physical therapy, and veterinary science.

Academic Programs

Bridgewater's emphasis on the liberal arts reflects a commitment to writing, public speaking, analytical and critical thinking, and global awareness and understanding. The general education curriculum enhances the depth of knowledge gained through academic major courses, which ultimately prepare students for work after graduation, or for graduate or professional studies. Through the Personal Development Portfolio (PDP) program, students document their participation in scholarly activities and cocurricular pursuits that foster intellectual, emotional, physical, and spiritual growth. In doing so, students are challenged not only to develop their talents but also to venture beyond their chosen disciplines to discover new interests. In addition, a focus on service learning and an emphasis on ethical development round out the educational experience.

Students may also add to their curriculum by completing minor field requirements. Flexibility is added to the academic program through an internship program, honors projects, independent study, and the Honors Program. Bridgewater's academic calendar provides a January interterm experience, when many of the courses offered provide opportunities to travel in the United States and abroad. Students may be exempted from certain course requirements by demonstrating proficiency in written expression, quantitative reasoning, or foreign languages. Credit and advanced placement are awarded to students on the basis of scores on Advanced Placement tests of the College Board. In order to be considered for unassigned credit, course credit, and/or exemption from certain requirements, students must earn scores of 3 or higher (varies by department) on Advanced Placement tests or a 5, 6, or 7 on the International Baccalaureate examination.

Off-Campus Programs

The Brethren Colleges Abroad program gives students the opportunity to study in Australia, Belgium, China, Ecuador, England, France, Germany, Greece, India, Ireland, Northern Ireland, Italy, Japan, Mexico, New Zealand, and Spain. The program provides a firsthand knowledge of a foreign language and culture and an opportunity to become an active participant in the challenging task of creating a climate of mutual respect and understanding among the nations of the world.

Academic Facilities

Bridgewater has outstanding classroom and scientific laboratory facilities. Each classroom building has computer laboratories with Internet and campus network access for student use. The Cole Hall auditorium seats approximately 650 people and is equipped with a stage, dressing rooms, a stage lighting system, two artist grand pianos, and a fifty-one-rank Möller pipe organ. The Carter Center for Worship and Music includes a recital hall, a chapel, ten soundproof practice rooms, a Steinway concert grand piano, two Reuter pipe organs, and twenty-three pianos for practice and instruction. Special library collections include the Church of the Brethren Collection, Genealogy, and Virginiana. The Reuel B. Pritchett Museum contains more than 10,000 items of historical, cultural, and religious interest.

Costs

The cost for residential students for 2008–09 is $32,990. Accounts are payable by the semester or through a monthly payment plan arranged through an external agency.

Financial Aid

Scholarships, grants, loans, and on-campus jobs are available for qualified students through federal, state, institutional, and outside sources and are awarded in individualized financial aid packages. All applicants for need-based financial aid must submit the Free Application for Federal Student Aid (FAFSA) by March 1. A work-study program provides jobs for qualified students, and early application is advised. Academic scholarships up to full tuition are awarded based on a student's GPA, SAT scores, and academic achievement. To be considered for an academic scholarship a student must apply and be accepted. No additional application is necessary.

Faculty

The Bridgewater faculty consists of 96 full-time members. Faculty members serve as faculty advisers, major professors, and sponsors of student organizations and activities. With a student-faculty ratio of 14:1, the small class sizes allow for one-to-one interaction with faculty members who model scholarship. Many professors at Bridgewater become mentors for their students, developing close working relationships as they take personal interest in each student's academic progress, oversee student research projects, and advise students in career preparations. Students also have numerous opportunities throughout the academic year to interact with faculty members outside of the classroom at campus events such as recitals, theater productions, and athletic events.

Student Government

The Student Government acts as a representative of the student body by presenting student opinions and ideas to the faculty and administration and by interpreting the policies and standards of the College to the students. Through its own structure as well as the appointment of students to serve on College committees, the Student Government involves students in many aspects of the operation of the College. The student body president, vice president, and senators are elected by the students. The College Honor System is administered by the Honor Council, a judicial body composed of 9 students appointed by the student body president and with faculty members serving as advisers.

Admission Requirements

Bridgewater College seeks students with above-average preparation who demonstrate a serious attitude toward studies. Admissions decisions are made based on careful consideration of a student's academic achievement, including GPA, standardized test scores (SAT or ACT), curriculum, and letters of recommendation. The admissions policy for transfers is similar to that of freshman applicants. The College seeks to enroll qualified students regardless of sex, race, color, creed, handicap, religion, or national or ethnic origin.

Application and Information

Information relating to Bridgewater College, including an online application, can be accessed through the College's Web site. It is recommended that applications be submitted between completion of the junior year and March of the year of enrollment. Under the College's rolling admissions policy, students can expect notification of the admission decision within thirty days of the College's receipt of all records and credentials.

Linda F. Stout
Director of Enrollment Operations
Bridgewater College
402 East College Street
Bridgewater, Virginia 22812
Phone: 540-828-5375
800-759-8328 (toll-free)
E-mail: admissions@bridgewater.edu
Web site: http://www.bridgewater.edu

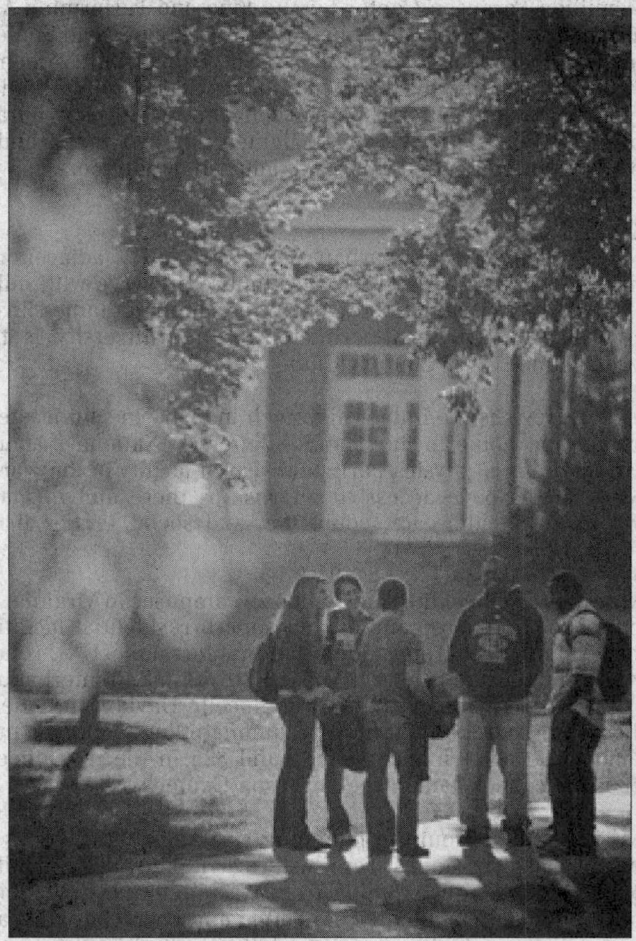

Bridgewater College is located in the beautiful Shenandoah Valley of Virginia.

CHRISTOPHER NEWPORT UNIVERSITY

NEWPORT NEWS, VIRGINIA

The University

Christopher Newport University (CNU) was founded in 1960 and currently enrolls 4,800 students in more than seventy areas of study (including three 5-year master's degree programs). The University takes pride in its "student-first, teaching-first" community. Small classes taught by veteran faculty members, a beautiful and safe campus, and one of the nation's finest sports programs make CNU a distinctive choice among Virginia's public universities.

State-of-the-art residence halls and upperclass apartments accommodate 3,000 students on campus. CNU is home to the $16-million Freeman Sports and Convocation Center, the $64-million Ferguson Center for the Fine and Performing Arts (designed by I. M. Pei), and the new $35-million David Student Union. The dazzling Paul and Rosemary Trible Library opened in 2007 with more than 100,000 square feet for information technology and traditional library collections. The new library features a fourteen-story tower, lighted day and night, and a 1,600-square-foot coffee shop with adjacent study rooms.

Location

CNU is located in suburban Newport News, adjacent to Mariner's Park, a pristine 600-acre nature preserve with miles of jogging trails around Lake Maury and along the James River. Bordering the southern perimeter of the University is the elegant James River Country Club.

Newport News is the hub of high-tech industry in southeastern Virginia and home to the Thomas Jefferson National Laboratory, the premier physics/particle research facility in the world. CNU students have access to internships there and in many local media, health-care, education, and social service firms and agencies.

CNU ranks as one of the safest midsize campuses in Virginia. Its picturesque 250-acre campus and superb residential facilities receive high praise from students and visitors alike. CNU is host to the annual Ella Fitzgerald Music Festival and to internationally known performers like Andrea Bocelli, David Copperfield, Whoopi Goldberg, and B. B. King, among others. Students may attend these performances for $5 and $25 in the magnificent 1,700-seat concert hall of the Ferguson Center.

CNU is 35 miles from the pounding surf and rolling dunes of Virginia Beach, 25 miles from historic Williamsburg, 75 miles from Richmond, and 150 miles from Washington, D.C. Students enjoy the moderate climate year-round and appreciate the easy driving distance to the beach and the region's many recreational opportunities.

Majors and Degrees

The College of Liberal Arts and Sciences offers the Bachelor of Arts degree in communication studies, English (concentrations in creative writing, journalism, language arts, literature, and technical writing), fine arts (concentrations in art history and studio art), foreign language (majors in French, German, and Spanish), history (interdisciplinary prelaw program available), interdisciplinary studies, philosophy (concentrations in critical thinking, Indic studies, preseminary studies, religious studies, and values and the professions), political science, psychology, social work, and sociology (concentrations in anthropology and criminology).

Students may choose the Bachelor of Music degree (concentrations in history/literature, performance, and theory/composition and emphases in choral music and instrumental music) or the Bachelor of Science degree in interdisciplinary studies. A Bachelor of Arts in Theater is offered (concentrations in acting, arts administration, design/technical, directing and dramatic literature, and music theater/dance).

Minors are available in anthropology, art, childhood studies, English, film studies, French, geography, German, gerontology, government and public affairs, history, leadership studies, music, philosophy, professional writing, psychology, sociology, speech communication, Spanish, theater arts, and women's and gender studies.

A special curriculum is offered in jazz studies.

Also offered in the sciences are the Bachelor of Arts degree in applied physics, biology, interdisciplinary studies, and mathematics and the Bachelor of Science degree in applied physics (concentrations in computation, instrumentation, and solid state/optics), biology (preprofessional programs in dental, medical, and veterinary studies), chemistry, computer engineering, computer science, environmental science, information science, interdisciplinary studies, mathematics (concentrations in computer science, mathematics education, and physics), and ornamental horticulture. Minors are available in applied physics, biology, business administration, chemistry, computer science, economics, finance, mathematics, and physics.

The Joseph W. Luter III School of Business, accredited by AACSB International–The Association to Advance Collegiate Schools of Business, offers the Bachelor of Science in Business Administration degree, with majors in accounting, economics, finance, management, and marketing and minors in business administration and economics.

Academic Programs

To be eligible for an undergraduate degree, students must successfully complete 120 academic semester hours. The last 45 semester hours of credit must be taken in residence.

The first two years of all students' academic programs require successful completion of the Liberal Learning Core requirements in such areas as English (writing), foreign language, humanities, laboratory science, mathematics, social science, and various areas of inquiry. New, innovative freshman seminars allow students to explore unique interdisciplinary courses.

Off-Campus Programs

Christopher Newport University actively supports study abroad for all its students and sponsors a variety of international study programs each year. CNU students have recently participated with faculty members in study-abroad programs in Belgium, China, England, France, Germany, Holland, Ireland, Italy, Kenya, Morocco, and Spain. CNU operates its own study center in Prague and offers top freshmen the opportunity to study at Oxford University each summer. CNU provides up to $5000 for international study to students who participate in the President's Leadership Program. Students may also travel to Europe with the CNU Chamber Singers or worldwide with CNU's award-winning Model U.N. Club.

Academic Facilities

In 2008, CNU is scheduled to break ground on a multimillion-dollar center for the study of humanities. Ratcliffe Hall, now home to the departments of English and political science, offers an airy atrium entrance with quiet lounge space for study and discussion.

CNU's academic buildings contain a variety of small classrooms and auditoriums, computer laboratories, specialty laboratories, an instructional technology center, and a greenhouse/herbarium. The Ferguson Center for the Arts houses a 1,700-seat concert hall; an art museum; practice and performance rooms for theater, music, and dance; an experimental black-box theater; and the 450-seat Music and Theater Hall. Both the Concert Hall and the Music and Theater Hall feature perfect natural acoustics.

CNU provides 1,200 computer workstations on campus as well as e-mail and Internet access in its residential facilities. Wireless access is available in all public areas of the campus.

CNU has completed $500 million in new facilities over the past seven years, creating an impressive and appealing "home" for its students and faculty. The dazzling rotunda in the Trible Library and its many elegant study spaces have created an outstanding academic home for study.

Costs

In-state tuition for full-time students for the 2007–08 academic year was $7050; nonresident tuition for full-time students was $14,150. Books and supplies average $750–$1000 per year. The room and board rate for the 2007–08 academic year was $8500.

Financial Aid

The University's financial aid programs serve about 50 percent of the student body. CNU offers every form of federally funded financial aid and a variety of renewable merit scholarships for freshmen, ranging from $1000 per year to full tuition. The President's Leadership Program offers a minor in leadership studies and up to $5000 per year for academically superior students, regardless of need.

Faculty

Nearly 90 percent of CNU faculty members hold the highest degree in their professional field. Faculty members are chosen at CNU only if teaching is their top priority. They are advisers, mentors, and friends to the students. It is a common occurrence at CNU for students to publish a paper or research with their professors. Professors place great emphasis on undergraduate research and students' preparation for graduate school.

Student Government

The University encourages students to participate in the formulation of rules, regulations, and policies directly affecting student life. Students may get involved with the Student Government Association (SGA) and University committees and councils. SGA awards support monies to many of the more than 100 active campus clubs and organizations each year. CNU is a community of honor, and all freshmen take an Honors Pledge during their Welcome Week orientation activities.

Admission Requirements

CNU welcomes applications from Virginia residents and out-of-state students whose education includes a strong college-preparatory curriculum and a record of success. Of the students accepted into the freshman class, the midrange (middle 50 percent) SAT score was 1080 to 1250 (critical reading and math) and the GPA range was 3.3 to 4.0. CNU applicants may also submit the ACT exam, with or without the writing sample. Superior students with a GPA of 3.5 or better may apply to the University without submitting an SAT or ACT score.

Application and Information

Applications, viewbooks, and additional information may be obtained from the University's Web site or by contacting:

Admissions Office
Christopher Newport University
1 University Place
Newport News, Virginia 23606-2998
Phone: 757-594-7015
757-594-7938 (TDD)
800-333-4CNU (toll-free)
E-mail: admit@cnu.edu
Web site: http://www.cnu.edu

EMORY & HENRY COLLEGE

EMORY, VIRGINIA

The College

Founded in 1836, Emory & Henry College has enjoyed a solid reputation for inspiring students from all walks of life and guiding them toward personal success and lifelong achievement. Located on a pristine, historic campus in southwest Virginia, Emory & Henry enrolls approximately 1,000 students, who represent a diverse group and come from rural areas, urban centers, twenty-five states, and ten countries.

The College provides a wide array of academic programs, including prelaw, premedicine, visual and performing arts, international studies, business, education, environmental studies, and public policy and community service—just to name a few. With a global perspective and an emphasis on service, excellence, and action, Emory & Henry encourages students to envision the world in which they would like to live and then challenges them to create it. The College is named for two men who symbolize this dual emphasis on thought and action—Bishop John Emory, an eminent Methodist church leader at the time the College was founded, and Patrick Henry, a famous orator of the American Revolution and Virginia's first governor.

Emory & Henry graduates have found tremendous personal success, which they have used to improve the world around them. Through its comprehensive, four-year liberal arts education, Emory & Henry has produced leading scientific researchers, NASA engineers, well-known writers, and successful physicians, ministers, lawyers, educators, and businesspeople. Emory & Henry provides innovative programs in public policy and community service as well as international studies and environmental science.

Students have opportunities for involvement in a variety of campus activities: service clubs, Christian fellowship, fraternities, sororities, sports clubs, honor groups, and multicultural groups. Student staffs produce a yearbook, an online magazine, and a literary magazine; others operate an educational FM radio station. Musically talented students have opportunities to participate in a choral program and a pep band. The prestigious Concert Choir has toured throughout the United States and in parts of Europe. The Barter Theatre, a professional theater in nearby Abingdon, works with Emory & Henry College to provide a theater education program that integrates college-level drama study with the benefits of experience on a professional stage. The Appalachian Center for Community Service is available for students committed to community service and integrates service learning into many classes. The King Health and Physical Education Center includes a state-of-the-art fitness center and enhances the College athletics program. Varsity sports for men are baseball, basketball, cross-country, football, golf, soccer, and tennis; women compete in basketball, cross-country, soccer, softball, swimming, tennis, and volleyball. Several sports are also played on either a club or an intramural basis.

Location

Emory & Henry is located in Emory, Virginia, which is approximately 25 miles north of Bristol, a city that offers large shopping areas, movies, and restaurants. The area surrounding Emory is known for its scenic beauty, recreational opportunities, and talented craftsmen. Within an hour's drive are slopes for snow skiing, lakes for waterskiing, the Appalachian Trail for hiking, and locations for horseback riding, canoeing, and many other sports. The historic town of Abingdon, Virginia, which lies just 7 miles south of Emory, is the home of the renowned Barter Theatre, the oldest professional theater in the United States. Abingdon's downtown district includes shopping areas, movie theaters, restaurants, and museums. The town also hosts the annual Virginia Highlands Festival, bringing together musicians, artists, and craftsmen for exhibitions and competition.

Majors and Degrees

Emory & Henry College offers programs of study in art, athletic training, biology, business administration, chemistry, computer information management, economics, education (early childhood through high school, including many subject-area options), English, environmental studies, geography, history, international studies (East Asia, European community, or Middle Eastern and Islamic studies), languages, mass communications, mathematics, music, philosophy, physical education, physics, political science, psychology, public policy and community service, religion, sociology, and theater. Preprofessional preparation in dentistry, law, medicine, and veterinary medicine may be completed within several of the programs.

The Bachelor of Arts degree is awarded in all programs of study and the Bachelor of Science degree in selected areas. Individualized programs of study may be developed in consultation with a faculty adviser.

Academic Programs

Emory & Henry offers a liberal arts program with an emphasis on writing, reasoning, value inquiry, and knowledge of global concerns, as well as a broad introduction to liberal arts subjects. All students complete a core curriculum, which includes a yearlong, interdisciplinary Western Tradition course and a writing course for all first-year students. Sophomores complete an ambitious Great Books program, and upperclass students take courses related to value inquiry and global studies. Along with the core curriculum, each student completes a major and a minor or a combined program referred to as an area of concentration. Students also have the opportunity to choose elective courses and to participate in international exchange programs.

Undergraduate programs of study include art, athletic training, biology, business administration, chemistry, computer information management, economics, education, English, geography, history, languages, mass communications, mathematics, music, philosophy, physical education, physics, political science, psychology, religion, sociology, and theater. Special and interdisciplinary programs of study offered are environmental studies, international studies, pre-engineering, prelaw, premedicine, and public policy and community service.

Emory & Henry operates on a semester calendar from late August to mid-December and from mid-January to mid-May. Two summer sessions run from late May to early July. First-year students typically carry a four-course load of 13 to 14 credit hours per semester, including the yearlong course on Western Tradition. Upperclass students carrying a full load complete five courses (14 to 15 credit hours) each semester. Classes meet on Monday-Wednesday-Friday or Tuesday-Thursday schedules.

One important feature of the Emory & Henry curriculum is the College's orientation in helping students achieve a smooth transition from high school to college. The Powell Resource Center provides academic support, advising, career services, and personal counseling. The Writing Center helps students in every department to use writing for effective communication.

Off-Campus Programs

Many faculty members encourage students to get involved in community projects or research that benefit the region. Internship opportunities are available for students in most of the College's programs, providing academic credit for off-campus work in community agencies and businesses. Many students have completed internships in the surrounding communities, while others have opted for internships outside the region, including several in Washington, D.C., in positions related to the Congress or the federal government.

Emory & Henry students participate in a wide variety of study-abroad programs. From Rome to Beijing and from Eastern Europe to East Asia, Emory & Henry students experience cultures and people in a way that enriches their perspective on their studies, their lives, and their futures. Emory & Henry helps students prepare for these experiences through language study, including Arabic, and with courses offered through a comprehensive international studies program and an international studies and business program. The College has exchange agreements with colleges and universities in Asia, Europe, and Central and South America. Students who desire other types of travel/study are assisted by faculty and staff members in locating suitable programs.

Academic Facilities

McGlothlin-Street Hall is a 70,000-square-foot academic center that houses the Departments of Biology, Business, Chemistry, Education, Environmental Studies, Geography, International Studies, and Psychology, along with a 104-seat auditorium and a tiered sixty-seat auditorium. Classrooms and laboratories in McGlothlin-Street Hall are equipped with the most current technological equipment. Miller Hall contains computerized classrooms used for instruction in such fields as accounting and computer science. Another computerized classroom in Byars Hall is used for instruction in writing, desktop publishing, and related fields. Science departments located in Miller and McGlothlin-Street Halls feature a variety of equipment, such as a microcomputer-based laboratory for physics students, computerized chromatography for chemistry students, a DNA sequencer in the biology department, and biofeedback equipment. Art students have access to studios, an exhibition area, and printing equipment, and music students make use of practice rooms and a recital hall.

As part of the College's changing campus, Byars Hall, the College's fine arts building, is currently undergoing massive renovations and updates. A spring 2008 reopening is planned. In addition to planned updates to the College's main administrative building (Wiley Hall), Emory & Henry is also involved with two major fund-raising projects that will increase and enhance student involvement within fine arts and athletics.

Costs

For 2007–08, resident students paid a comprehensive fee of $29,990, which included tuition, room, and board.

Financial Aid

Forms of aid include need-based and non-need-based scholarships, loans, and part-time jobs. A Bonner Scholars program provides substantial scholarships for selected students who do volunteer work in the surrounding region. Virginia residents are eligible for a special residency grant. Merit-based scholarships are awarded based on academic performance, and many can be renewed based on continued academic success. The average first-year student received an aid package (grants and scholarships) worth $15,547. The priority application deadline for financial aid is April 1.

Faculty

Emory & Henry professors are among the best in the nation. Over the last seventeen years, Emory & Henry has received the Carnegie Foundation Virginia Professor of the Year Award six times—more than any other college or university in Virginia. Emory & Henry has 75 full-time faculty members, and the current faculty-student ratio is 1:10. The majority of the faculty members hold terminal degrees. Every student is provided with a faculty adviser, who assists in the selection of courses. While the faculty members are encouraged to continue study and research, their primary function is teaching. Many professors live near the campus, and they make their homes open to students for special events, informal class meetings, or other activities.

Student Government

Students at Emory & Henry are encouraged to take part in campus decision making. They have voting representatives on nearly every faculty committee and on the Board of Trustees. The central body in campus government is the Student Senate, which brings together representatives of the student body, faculty, and administration.

Admission Requirements

Admission to Emory & Henry is determined on the basis of both academic achievement and personal qualifications. An applicant's secondary school preparation must include the following: 4 years of English, 3 years of mathematics (algebra I, algebra II, and geometry), 2 years of laboratory sciences, 2 years of a single foreign language, and 2 years of social studies. Strong emphasis is also placed on involvement and leadership in extracurricular and community activities, in addition to consistency and improvement surrounding academic progress.

Application and Information

To apply for admission, students should submit the basic application form, a copy of the high school transcript, scores from either the SAT or the ACT, at least one recommendation letter, and a nonrefundable $30 application fee. While not required, an essay/personal statement is strongly recommended.

Transfer applicants must submit an application and a transcript from any college previously attended, along with a completed Dean's Certificate for Transfer Students. A rolling admissions policy allows notification of a decision within two to four weeks after a file has been completed.

In addition to its rolling admissions policy, Emory & Henry College also welcomes interested applicants under the Early Application program. This program offers a nonbinding decision made on completed applications and aforementioned materials received by December 1. Not only does the College guarantee a decision by December 15, but a tentative financial aid package (with necessary materials) is offered to these students prior to January 1. Like rolling admissions decisions, students receiving acceptance under Early Application have until May 1 to make their final decision.

Application forms and other information may be obtained by contacting:

Office of Admissions
Emory & Henry College
P.O. Box 10
Emory, Virginia 24327-0947
Phone: 276-944-6133
800-848-5493 (toll-free)
Fax: 276-944-6935
E-mail: ehadmiss@ehc.edu
Web site: http://www.ehc.edu

Wiley Hall.

COLLEGE DATA CENTER • VIRGINIA

HAMPDEN-SYDNEY COLLEGE

HAMPDEN-SYDNEY, VIRGINIA

The College

Hampden-Sydney, a four-year liberal arts college for men, has been in continuous operation since November 1775, eight months before Jefferson wrote the Declaration of Independence. The tenth-oldest college in the country, Hampden-Sydney was formed with the guidance of such men as James Madison and Patrick Henry, who were members of the first Board of Trustees. The College was modeled after the Presbyterian College of New Jersey (now Princeton), and the same curriculum was chosen, except that at Hampden-Sydney there was to be a "greater emphasis on the cultivation of the English language." Throughout its history, Hampden-Sydney College's mission has been "to form good men and good citizens."

Today, the College has a total enrollment of 1,100 students, representing thirty-two states and seventeen other countries. Students enjoy a complete and diverse campus life, with an active student government and honor court. Interest clubs, literary organizations, and performing societies, as well as intellectual and social gatherings, enhance the extracurricular offerings. Hampden-Sydney's Union-Philanthropic Society is the second-oldest active debate club in the country. Approximately 30 percent of the students belong to the ten social fraternities. Eight varsity teams enjoy spirited NCAA Division III competition as members of the Old Dominion Athletic Conference, while club and intramural teams draw strong participation.

As a wholly undergraduate institution, Hampden-Sydney is committed to the belief that liberal education provides the best foundation not only for a professional career but also for the challenges of life. Nearly half of the graduating seniors enter graduate or professional school within five years. Basic to the College's program and success are the professors, 78 percent of whom hold earned doctoral or terminal degrees in their fields. The student-faculty ratio is 10:1, and the average class size is 15. It is in this setting that the true value of the Hampden-Sydney education shines through. Students work closely with professors, learning to think critically and analytically, to assimilate and interpret information, and to express themselves cogently and coherently. Beyond the classroom, faculty-student relationships flourish as well. Faculty members and students jointly contribute to the community in a wide variety of service activities and share social and enrichment opportunities.

Hampden-Sydney faculty members are nationally recognized as inspired teachers and productive scholars in such diverse fields as NASA-sponsored gamma ray research, environmental economics, and cetacean (whale and dolphin) evolution.

Hampden-Sydney is fully accredited by the Southern Association of Colleges and Schools and is a member of the Association of Virginia Colleges, the Association of American Colleges, the Southern University Conference, the College Entrance Examination Board, the American Chemical Society, and the College Scholarship Service.

Location

Hampden-Sydney is an hour from Richmond, Charlottesville, and Lynchburg. Its stately Federal-style buildings have earned designation as a National Historic Preservation Zone. Southern Virginia's rolling countryside and temperate climate are delightful year-round and especially in the spring and fall. The College's rural setting and tree-studded campus provide miles of jogging and bicycling trails and excellent fishing. Hampden-Sydney has a picture-perfect 1,240-acre campus, with a wonderful feel of community.

Majors and Degrees

Students may choose one of twenty-seven established majors, plus custom programs, which lead to the degree of Bachelor of Arts or Bachelor of Science: applied computational physics, applied mathematics, biochemistry, biology, chemistry, classical studies, computer science, economics, economics and commerce, English, fine arts (with concentrations in music, theater, or visual arts), French, German, Greek, Greek and Latin, history, humanities, Latin, mathematical economics, mathematics, philosophy, physics, political science, psychology, religion, religion and philosophy, and Spanish, plus double majors, minors, and customized programs.

Academic Programs

The curriculum is divided into three principal areas of study: humanities, social sciences, and natural sciences (including mathematics). The study of the humanities allows students to gain an understanding of the intellectual and literary influences that have shaped culture. Exposure to the humanities also increases students' appreciation of the importance of ideas and expands their ability to communicate. Studying the social sciences gives insight into human behavior and institutions and is central to the liberal arts education. The world's increasing reliance on scientific and technological advances—and the practical and ethical problems that accompany them—makes a general understanding of natural science indispensable.

To ensure that individual programs are broadly based, students are required to study in each division. Students take at least two semesters of English composition and rhetoric and study a foreign language through the second-year level. The College requires that students complete 120 semester hours for graduation.

In addition to the curriculum offerings, students may profit from one of Hampden-Sydney's special academic options, such as the honors program, study-abroad program, or business internship programs. Students may take courses at six other private colleges in Virginia; pursue a public service, military leadership, or national security concentration; apply for a B.S./M.D. joint program with The George Washington University or Eastern Virginia Medical School; pursue a dual-degree program in engineering with the University of Virginia; study foreign policy in Washington; or engage in international studies at Oxford University. Faculty advisers help develop programs suited to individual interests.

Academic Facilities

Hampden-Sydney is committed to providing state-of-the-art facilities. The J. B. Fuqua Computing Center contains a variety of computer systems for student use. Students can access the campus network and the Internet with their own computers from their dormitory rooms or by using one of the computing laboratories located in Bagby Hall, Wilson-Mottley Library, Gilmer Hall, Morton Hall, and the Computing Center.

The new state-of-the-art Wilson-Mottley Library is one of the College's most valuable academic resources; its collection was specifically selected to support Hampden-Sydney's liberal arts curriculum. The Wilson-Mottley Library contains 246,500 volumes, 18,000 periodical titles, an electronic catalog, microform, and government documents arranged in open stacks or computerized for ease of use. Ten group study rooms are available for use by groups of 4 to 10 students. Individual study carrels are located throughout the library and many may be reserved for individual use for a semester. Computers are conveniently located throughout the library, and laptops may be checked out at the main circulation desk for intra-library use. Also located in Wilson-Mottley Library, the Fuqua International Communications Center houses the newest electronic equipment to support learning. It maintains a collection of more than 10,640 videodiscs, videotapes, compact discs, sound recordings, and computer software programs. Viewing-listening rooms hold a variety of hardware for individual and group use. A coffee bar serving cold drinks and a variety of coffees is located on the main floor of the building with easy access to comfortable reading spots or the reading porch.

Costs

Tuition for the 2007–08 academic year was $26,676. Other required College fees were a telecommunications fee of $696 and a student activities fee of $360. Room and board came to $8672. Books and miscellaneous expenses were estimated at $2200.

Financial Aid

Hampden-Sydney College offers financial aid to students who can make the most of the education that the College offers. Both academic achievement and promise, as well as financial need, are considered in the initial award of College funds. Similarly, financial aid for returning students is based on both academic performance and demonstrated need. Approximately 97 percent of students receive financial aid based on academic scholarship and need. The average need-based award of $20,700 includes scholarships, loans, and work-study appointments. Financial aid in 2006–07 totaled nearly $22 million, including all federal aid awarded.

Entering students who wish to be considered for financial aid must complete two forms—the Free Application for Federal Student Aid (FAFSA), which determines eligibility for federal programs, and the CSS PROFILE, which is used for consideration for College funds. These forms may be obtained from high school guidance offices, online, or by contacting Hampden-Sydney and must be submitted between November 1 (for early decision) and March 1 of the senior year.

Faculty

Hampden-Sydney has 112 faculty members (93 full-time and 19 part-time). While the College places primary emphasis on teaching skills, faculty research is encouraged as an aid to improving the quality of teaching. Seventy-eight percent of faculty members have doctoral or terminal degrees, and 90 percent are involved in academic advising. With 75 percent living on or within 10 miles of campus, faculty members are involved with students in a full range of academic, social, and recreational activities.

Student Government

Hampden-Sydney has a long tradition of student involvement in College affairs. Students serve as members of the faculty's Academic Affairs, Student Affairs, Lectures and Programs, and Athletic Committees. In addition, students are often named to various task forces, ad hoc committees, and search committees seeking key College officials. The Student Court, elected by classes, is the judicial arm of Student Government. The court tries cases arising from breaches of the Code of Student Conduct and Honor Code, assisted by a corps of student investigators and advisers. The College Activities Committee keeps an active calendar of events, planning dances, concerts, movies, and other activities for students.

Admission Requirements

Prospective students are expected to have mastered a solid, demanding college-preparatory program, including at least 4 units of English, 2 units of one foreign language, 3 units of mathematics, 2 units of natural science (one of which must be a laboratory course), and 1 unit of social science. In addition, a third unit of foreign language and a fourth unit of mathematics are recommended. Hampden-Sydney also considers SAT or ACT scores and looks closely at recommendations from guidance counselors, teachers, and other people who know the applicant well. The records of successful applicants often include examples of impressive school and community extracurricular contributions in addition to their academic preparation.

There are three admission plans. If Hampden-Sydney is the student's first-choice college, he should apply under the early decision plan by November 15. The deadline for the early action plan is January 15. The deadline for the regular decision program is March 1. Application forms are available on request from the Admissions Office. Hampden-Sydney also accepts the Common Application in lieu of its own form and gives equal consideration to both.

Students may apply electronically using the Hampden-Sydney Web site, the Common Application, or XAP. Though not a requirement, the College encourages campus visits as the one true way to witness the spirit and community of Hampden-Sydney.

The College also welcomes armed service veterans and students who wish to transfer from another college or university. Students must be in good standing, with a C average or above.

Hampden-Sydney College, while exempted from Subpart C of the Title IX regulation with respect to its admissions and recruitment activities, does not discriminate on the basis of race, color, sex, religion, age, national origin, handicap, or veteran status in its educational programs and with respect to employment.

Application and Information

Completed applications for admission should be submitted to the Dean of Admissions before the noted deadlines for each admission plan. Notification for early decision candidates is mailed on December 15. Notification for early action candidates is mailed on January 15. Regular decision notification begins on February 1 and continues through April 15. The candidate's reply date is May 1.

For further information or to request application forms, students should contact:

Dean of Admissions
Hampden-Sydney College
Hampden-Sydney, Virginia 23943
Phone: 800-755-0733 (toll-free)
Fax: 434-223-6346
Web site: http://www.hsc.edu

Hampden-Sydney's campus has 1,240 wooded acres. Near several big cities, the campus is quiet, safe, and busy, with lots of room in which to work and play.

COLLEGE DATA CENTER • VIRGINIA

HOLLINS UNIVERSITY

ROANOKE, VIRGINIA

The University

Hollins University was founded in 1842 as Virginia's first chartered women's college. Today, Hollins is an independent arts and sciences university that enrolls approximately 1,100 students in its undergraduate programs for women and its coed graduate programs. Hollins is proud of its creative writing program, career internships, leadership opportunities, small class size, and study-abroad opportunities. Hollins prepares its students for career excellence in the social sciences, sciences, humanities, fine arts, and business. A 10:1 student-faculty ratio enables students to work closely with their professors both inside and outside the classroom. In addition to the Bachelor of Arts degree in twenty-seven major fields, Hollins awards a Master of Arts degree in children's literature, liberal studies, screenwriting and film studies, and teaching and a Master of Fine Arts degree in creative writing, children's literature, dance, playwriting, and screenwriting. Hollins' coeducational graduate creative writing program has long been acknowledged as one of the best of its size in the country.

Hollins structures the academic year to give students the month of January to focus on an internship, innovative course work, senior thesis, independent study, or travel/study abroad.

Hollins' internship program gives students a head start on their careers while they earn academic credit. Eighty-two percent of Hollins students do at least one internship before graduation. Students have interned at the New York Stock Exchange; CNBC in London; Centers for Disease Control; ABC News; National Geographic Society; Time, Inc.; the *London Times*; National Zoological Park; the Metropolitan Museum of Art; and the Peace Corps, to name a few.

Hollins' Batten Leadership Institute, open to all students, offers a combination of classes, skills-building groups, and hands-on projects, culminating in a Certificate of Leadership Studies.

Situated on a 475-acre campus in the Shenandoah Valley of the Blue Ridge Mountains, Hollins is a quiet campus for the serious student looking to broaden her mind through a rigorous academic program. Students come to Hollins from forty-six states and nine countries and bring with them cultural and ethnic diversity. Women returning to college can earn a bachelor's degree in the Horizon Program.

Because approximately 89 percent of Hollins women live on campus in dormitories, language houses, or University apartments, a large family of friends develops in the first year and replaces the need for sororities. For those interested in group activities, there are more than thirty-five clubs and organizations, including a multicultural club, Black Student Alliance, literary societies, and political, environmental, women's, and volunteer organizations. Each year, many students volunteer in social service agencies locally and internationally, including a Hollins-directed Jamaica service project. The Wyndham Robertson Library features state-of-the-art technology and is a National Literary Landmark. The well-equipped athletic complex enables Hollins to compete and train its athletes effectively for NCAA Division III competition in basketball, golf, lacrosse, riding, soccer, swimming, and tennis. Hollins' strong riding program offers top facilities, including stables where collegiate riders may board their horses. The academic program is enriched by guest lectures, dance and theater productions, and the annual Literary Festival.

Location

Hollins is located on the outskirts of Roanoke, a cosmopolitan center with a population of approximately 236,000. Roanoke has its own opera, ballet, and orchestra. Mill Mountain Theatre, the Science Museum, the Art Museum of Western Virginia, and the Center in the Square cultural center provide entertainment for the area. The historic downtown market, with fresh flower and fruit stands and specialty shops, is a favorite spot on the weekends. Hollins is a 3½-hour drive from both Washington, D.C., and Richmond; 5 hours from Virginia Beach; and within easy driving distance of more than a dozen other colleges. The Roanoke Regional Airport is a 10-minute drive from the campus. The campus has been described as "achingly picturesque." The Front Quadrangle is listed on the National Register of Historic Places. The Blue Ridge Mountains are minutes from campus and ideal for hiking the Appalachian Trail, camping, caving, and skiing.

Majors and Degrees

Hollins grants the Bachelor of Arts degree in art history, biology, business, chemistry, classical studies, communication studies, dance, economics, English, English and creative writing, environmental studies, film and photography, French, history, interdisciplinary studies, international studies, mathematics, music, philosophy, physics, political science, psychology, religious studies, sociology, Spanish, studio art, theater, and women's studies. Hollins grants the B.A./B.F.A. degree in dance and the B.S. degree in biology, chemistry, mathematics, and psychology. Minors are offered in most major areas, and preprofessional programs are offered in education, law, medicine, and veterinary science. The Rubin Writing Semester offers women from other colleges and universities an opportunity to become visiting student writers.

Hollins has an agreement with Monterey Institute of International Studies that streamlines entry in their M.B.A, M.P.A., translation and interpretation, and policy studies programs.

Academic Programs

Candidates for the Bachelor of Arts degree normally follow a four-year program. They are required to complete 128 credits of academic work and 16 January Short Term credits.

Candidates for the degree of Bachelor of Arts and Bachelor of Fine Arts normally follow a four-year program. They are required to complete a minimum of 158 semester credits of academic work, four Short Term activities (16 Short Term credits), and two physical education courses. Included in the 158 credits are 90 credits in dance and general education skills and perspectives.

Candidates for the degree of Bachelor of Science normally follow a four-year program. They are required to complete a minimum of 140 semester credits of academic work, four Short Term activities (16 Short Term credits), and two physical education courses. Included in the 140 credits are 60 credits in the major (biology, chemistry, mathematics, or psychology) and general education skills and perspectives.

First-year students are required to take a seminar on campus during Short Term. Students may spend subsequent Short Terms pursuing career internships, independent study, study-abroad experiences, or service projects. Instead of a standard general education program, Hollins has ESP: Education through Skills and Perspectives. Students choose from a wide variety of classes that reinforce the basics of a liberal arts education. In addition, two regular terms of physical education or varsity sport participation are required.

Students must choose a major by the end of their sophomore year and complete a minimum of 32 credits in the major field prior to graduation. Each first-year student must meet a writing requirement. Hollins grants 4 academic credits for Advanced Placement examination scores of 4 or 5 and in some cases for a score of 3. Hollins grants 8 academic credits for International Baccalaureate scores between 5 and 7 and up to 32 credits for an I.B. diploma with a score of 30 or higher.

Off-Campus Programs

In 1955, Hollins was one of the nation's first colleges to establish a program that enabled students to study overseas. For semester or full-year study, Hollins has its own programs in England and France and affiliated programs in Argentina, Ghana, Greece, Ireland, Italy, Japan, Mexico, South Africa, and Spain as well as with the School for Field Studies. About half of Hollins students have an international learning experience before graduation. Domestic exchange programs are possible with members of the six-college exchange.

Academic Facilities

Opened in spring 1999, the Wyndham Robertson Library, a national literary landmark, houses a collection that consists of more than half a million items, including books, print periodicals, e-texts, musical scores, recordings, videos, screenplays, incunabula, rare books, and manuscripts. The library offers extensive media facilities, including a forty-seat screening room, a television studio, and a video-editing suite featuring nonlinear editing stations. Hollins houses a notable selection of children's books, including items from the personal collections of Francelia Butler, former editor-in-chief of *Children's Literature,* the field's leading scholarly journal, and former poet laureate William Jay Smith. The University's Archives and Special Collections includes books and manuscripts from many famous faculty members and alumnae/alumni of Hollins, including Richard Dillard, George Garrett, Eudora Welty, Margaret Wise Brown, Lee Smith, and Annie Dillard. Through a Web-based catalog shared with Roanoke College, readers are offered access to the combined materials in both collections.

Windows XP/Professional– and Macintosh-based computers are available in dedicated computer labs as well as various common areas around the university—many open 24 hours a day. Wireless access is abundant on campus.

The Dana Science Building houses accessible labs and research facilities for computerized recording and analysis of physiological and behavioral data, plant and animal tissue culture, animal learning laboratories, photomicroscopy, biochemistry and molecular biology, chromatography, spectrophotometry, electrochemistry, gas kinetics, centrifugation, and EEG and biofeedback equipment.

The Richard Wetherill Visual Arts Center, which opened in fall 2004, houses the Eleanor D. Wilson Museum, which has been named a Museum Partner by the Virginia Museum of Fine Arts (VMFA), a designation that helps bring world-class exhibitions and other arts programming to the campus.

Hollins also has a career center, writing center, theater, dance studio, and health and counseling center.

Costs

The 2007–08 costs were $25,110 for tuition and $9140 for room and board, which includes telephone, cable television, and computer network connections for each student's room. The Student Government Association fee is $275, and the student technology support fee is $260. The University estimates a budget of $1000 for books, $800 for transportation, and $1000 for other expenses.

Financial Aid

Financial aid is awarded on the basis of both academic merit and need. Seventy percent receive need-based aid in the form of grants, merit scholarships, low-interest loans, and campus jobs. The average award in 2007 was $20,581. The types of scholarships and grants available to undergraduates are Federal Pell Grants, Federal Supplemental Educational Opportunity Grants (FSEOG), state grants, University scholarships and grants, private scholarships and grants, academic merit scholarships, and aid for undergraduate students who are members of a minority group. Federal Perkins Loans, Federal PLUS loans, and Federal Stafford Student Loans are also available, as well as a tuition payment plan with Sallie Mae. A financial aid form should be filed with the financial aid office by February 15. Notification of awards is on a rolling basis.

Faculty

Faculty members are committed to teaching and are dedicated to their students. Although scholarly research and writing are emphasized, primary attention is placed on education. Currently, there are 67 full-time and 34 part-time faculty members, of whom 56 percent are women; 97 percent of the full-time faculty members hold the doctoral or corresponding terminal degree in their fields. With a student-faculty ratio of 10:1, students have considerable opportunity for personal attention. A few courses are taught by graduate assistants.

Student Government

Each year, students sign the honor code, pledging not to lie, cheat, or steal. Hollins is thereby able to conduct daily operations with a great deal of trust. Final exams are freely scheduled and administered by students under the Independent Exam System. The campus judicial system is run by the students. Students who are elected to the Student Government Association have the authority to administer all student-related activities. Weekly Senate meetings are open to the entire campus. Students are represented on policymaking faculty committees and the Board of Trustees.

Admission Requirements

To be considered for admission, a student must have completed a minimum of 16 secondary school units in English, mathematics, science, social studies, and foreign language. All students must take the SAT or the ACT. In addition to standardized test scores, the Admissions Committee takes into account an applicant's secondary school record, class rank, essay, recommendation, and personal interview. Transfer students are accepted in both semesters. International applicants can submit TOEFL scores in place of the SAT or ACT.

At Hollins, the application process is very personal. The admissions officers go to great lengths to ensure that Hollins and the applicant are a good match.

Application and Information

Hollins has a formal early decision plan. The early decision application deadline is December 1; the deadline is February 15 for regular admission. Notification of admission is on a rolling basis beginning December 15 for early decision candidates and late January for regular admission candidates. The application fee is $35. A $400 tuition deposit must be made by early January for early decision, May 1 for others. For more information, students should contact:

Office of Admissions
Hollins University
P.O. Box 9707
Roanoke, Virginia 24020
Phone: 540-362-6401
800-456-9595 (toll-free)
E-mail: huadm@hollins.edu
Web site: http://www.hollins.edu

Students in Hollins' historic Front Quadrangle.

LIBERTY UNIVERSITY

LYNCHBURG, VIRGINIA

The University

Founded in 1971 by Dr. Jerry Falwell, Liberty University (LU) provides a Christian, comprehensive, coeducational environment committed to serious education at the undergraduate and graduate levels. The University is situated on a 5,000-acre campus with complete classroom, residence, study, leisure, and recreational facilities. Liberty University is approved by the State Council of Higher Education for Virginia and is accredited by the Commission on Colleges of the Southern Association of Colleges and Schools to award associate, bachelor's, master's, and doctoral degrees. There are more than 9,558 undergraduate and graduate students in the traditional resident program. The student body represents all fifty states and more than eighty other countries, with 21 percent of the student population representing minorities and international students.

Liberty's facilities include the 4,000-seat Earl H. Schilling Center; the 12,000-seat A. L. Williams Stadium (football); the 10,000-seat Vines Center (men's and women's basketball and volleyball and convocation services); the Matthes-Hopkins Track Complex, a superb outdoor-track facility; the Tolsma Indoor Track Center; Worthington Stadium, the baseball field; the new LaHaye Ice Center; the state-of-the-art, 83,968-square-foot LaHaye Student Center that includes a lounge, five full-length basketball courts, cardio and weight rooms, a cafe, multipurpose rooms, an aerobic room, and a 25-yard swimming pool and two spas; and the brand new Williams Football Operations Center, situated at the north end of Williams Stadium.

Intercollegiate athletic competition is in NCAA Division I. Men compete in baseball, basketball, cross-country, football, golf, indoor track, soccer, tennis, track and field, and wrestling. Women compete in basketball, cross-country, soccer, softball, tennis, track and field, and volleyball. Other sports programs at the club level include ice hockey, lacrosse, and volleyball for men and lacrosse and ice hockey for women. Intramural competition is offered for both men and women in various sports, including Ultimate Frisbee and men's and women's flag football.

Residence halls include traditional-style hall housing, quad-living residences, and new apartment-style living within walking distance of main campus. These new apartments include full furnishings, a kitchen, laundry facilities, and the Campus East Clubhouse, which offers billiards, PlayStation, Xbox, satellite TV, a theater, a computer lounge, the Campus East Market, and a pool.

Liberty offers several majors in a wide variety of degrees on the graduate level, in addition to its baccalaureate and associate degree programs. The Master of Arts degree is offered in counseling and religious studies. Students who are interested in education can pursue a Master of Education and a Doctor of Education through Liberty. The Teacher Licensure Option is available at the graduate level in early childhood (NK–3), elementary (K–6), and secondary (7–12) education; administration/supervision; gifted education; reading; school counseling; and special education. In addition, a Master of Nursing degree and a Ph.D. program in professional counseling and pastoral care are also offered.

Through the Liberty Baptist Theological Seminary, the University offers the following graduate degrees: Master of Arts in Religion, Master of Religious Education, Master of Divinity, Master of Theology, and Doctor of Ministry.

Liberty University's School of Law opened in August 2004 and graduated its first class in May 2007. The American Bar Association (ABA) has granted provisional accreditation to Liberty University School of Law, which is housed in 122,000 square feet of allocated space in the University's Campus North facility—all advantageously located on the same level. At present, the law school comprises 79,100 square feet of the allocated space. The facility houses seven classrooms that are equipped with multimedia technology and wireless Internet access, two seminar rooms, a mock trial courtroom, the Ehrhorn Law Library, a study center with 24-hour student access, law review offices, seven professional skills rooms, an administrative suite, a faculty suite, and an academic support suite.

For international students, Liberty offers the English Language Institute (ELI). English grammar, comprehension, and reading are taught for international students with little or no English skills. An English Language Institute certification is awarded, and students are invited to enroll as a student at Liberty University once completed or while enrolled in the institute. For more information, students should contact the University.

Location

The University is located in the heart of Virginia in Lynchburg (population 68,000), with the scenic Blue Ridge Mountains as a backdrop. The city is more than 200 years old and is noted for its culture, beauty, and educational advantages. Nearby are such sites as Thomas Jefferson's Poplar Forest; Appomattox Court House; Natural Bridge; historic Lexington; Washington, D.C.; and other places of interest.

The city of Lynchburg offers a wide variety of activities for recreation and entertainment. Excellent sports facilities and programs, cultural events at the Lynchburg Fine Arts Center, beautiful lakes and streams, and many other local attractions enhance the lives of Lynchburg residents. Lynchburg also has more than 2,000 hotel rooms, numerous outlets and malls, and a number of restaurants that serve a wide variety of cuisines. Lynchburg is accessible by air, train, and bus.

Majors and Degrees

The Bachelor of Science degree is offered in accounting, athletic training, aviation (commercial/corporate, military, and missions), biochemistry and molecular biology, biology (environmental science, general, molecular biology, and premed), business (economics, finance, international business, management, and marketing), communication studies (advertising/public relations, broadcasting, graphic design, journalism, and speech communication), computer engineering, computer science, criminal justice, electrical engineering, English, family and child development, family and consumer sciences (FACS), fashion merchandising and interiors, general studies, government (administration of justice, politics and policy, prelaw, and international relations), health promotion (CHES and clinical tracks), history (international studies), integrated studies (elementary, middle, and special education), industrial and systems engineering, interdisciplinary studies, kinesiology (exercise science, fitness science, and health and physical education), management information systems, mathematics, nursing, psychology (adult development, child/adolescent development, clinical/experimental, human services counseling, and industrial/organization), religion (biblical studies, children's ministries, cross-cultural studies, pastoral leadership, women's ministries, and youth ministries), social sciences, software engineering, sport management, visual communication arts, Web technology and design, and worship and music studies (biblical studies, business, cross-cultural studies, drama ministries, pastoral leadership, women's ministry, worship leadership, and worship technology). Secondary teaching licensure is available in several degree programs.

The Bachelor of Arts degree is offered in English, general studies, history (international studies), interdisciplinary studies, pastoral leadership and biblical exposition, philosophy and religion (biblical studies and philosophy), Spanish, teaching English as a second/foreign language (TESL), and theater arts (acting, drama ministry, musical theater, and production).

The Bachelor of Music degree is offered in choral music and instrumental music.

The Associate of Arts (A.A.) degree is available in criminal justice, general studies, and religion.

Minors are available in accounting, aviation, biblical Greek, biblical studies, biology, business, chemistry, coaching, communication studies (advertising/public relations, journalism, and speech), computer science, criminal justice, cross-cultural studies, English, enterprise data analysis, family and consumer sciences (clothing and textiles, general, family and child development, and foods and nutrition), French, government, health promotion, history, kinesiology, management information systems, mathematics, music (brass, percussion, and woodwind), music (church ministries and liberal arts), music (keyboard, strings, and voice), philosophy, psychology, sociology, Spanish, special education, sport management, theater arts, theology, women's ministries, and youth ministries.

The Teacher Licensure Option is available at the elementary (K–6), middle school (6–8), and secondary (7–12) levels in biology, business, computer science, English, history/social sciences, mathematics, and work and family studies and at the comprehensive (K–12) level in teaching English as a second language, health/physical education, music (choral or instrumental), and special education.

Academic Programs

A minimum of 120 semester hours is required for the B.S., while a minimum of 123 semester hours is necessary for the B.A. In addition to the major, the student must complete general education courses in humanities, natural sciences and mathematics, social sciences, physical education, and religion. The A.A. requires a minimum of 64 semester hours.

Liberty is on the early semester calendar. During the summer, there are several one- and two-week modular classes offered. Winter modulars are also offered between semesters.

The University also offers higher education degrees for the adult learner through home study. Liberty's Distance Learning Program (DLP) is accredited by the Commission on Colleges of the Southern Association of Colleges and Schools to award associate, bachelor's, master's, and doctoral degrees. For more information, students should call 800-424-9595 (toll-free) or visit the Web site at http://www.liberty.edu/distancelearning.

Academic Facilities

The Arthur S. DeMoss Learning Center, the academic hub of the campus, is a 500,000-square-foot Jeffersonian-style building that encompasses nearly all academic aspects of the University. All academic rooms are wired for Internet access, with large computer screens installed for interactive learning. This impressive facility is one of the largest academic buildings in central Virginia and houses the campus library, which currently contains 283,000 bound or microfilmed volumes. Students may find employment or volunteer their services in the University's 50,000-watt FM radio station or student-run radio and TV stations. The Fine Arts Hall houses the Lloyd Auditorium, which has a seating capacity of 315 as well as a recital hall and several practice rooms.

Ehrhorn Law Library currently occupies more than 34,000 square feet of the Law School's facility. Features include a forty-seat computer lab, an online legal research instructional room with sixteen computer stations, four group-study rooms, a faculty reading room, two special collections rooms, and a large reference-reading area that serves as the physical center of the law library.

The computer structure of the campus allows each student to reach professors, various campus offices, and the Internet from residence hall rooms. Liberty also offers wireless capabilities in each academic building. The plan to make the campus completely wireless is in progress, and quite a few residence halls already have wireless access.

Costs

Tuition, room, board (twenty-six meals per week), and activity/student center fees for 2007–08 were $21,200 for 12 to 18 credit hours per semester. The estimated cost for books per semester was $450. A technology fee of $250 per semester provides each student with an e-mail address and high-speed Internet access in the residence hall. It also gives the student unlimited access to the many computer labs around the campus. The average student paid $14,000, based on Liberty University's generous scholarships.

Additional fees, such as lab fees, are required for specific classes and are listed in the class registration book. Automobiles are permitted if they are registered and a fee of $150 per semester has been paid. The student activity fee of $225 per semester (included in the yearly cost above as a total amount of $450), gives students unlimited access to the LaHaye Student Center, workout facilities, Christian concerts, and much more.

Financial Aid

A variety of grants, scholarships, and on-campus jobs are available at Liberty. All federally funded student financial aid programs, except the Federal Perkins Loan Program, are available. Athletic, academic, merit, talent, Association of Christian Schools International (ACSI), National Merit, and other Liberty University assistance grants are also available for qualified candidates. Students are required to submit a Free Application for Federal Student Aid (FAFSA) to the U.S. Department of Education and include Liberty University's school code (010392) on that application. This is the student's application for all financial aid. Approximately 90 percent of the student body received some type of aid last year.

Liberty offers generous scholarships, grants, and other financial aid to all students. Students should contact the University about financial aid opportunities. Liberty also partners with many Christian ministries around the world, offering scholarships to participating students.

Faculty

About 300 different colleges and universities worldwide are represented in the education of the Liberty faculty. The average Liberty faculty member has more than thirteen years of teaching experience. Courses are taught by faculty members.

Student Government

Students elect representatives to serve on the Student Senate. This group provides recommendations and suggestions to the student development staff. Student Senate members also organize and direct activities and civic programs.

Admission Requirements

All applicants should be familiar with Liberty's philosophy and expectations before applying. Applicants to the A.A., B.A., and B.S. programs must be high school graduates and must submit two official copies of the high school transcript, indicating graduation date (or GED test scores, if applicable). Applicants must also submit either ACT or SAT scores, which are used for academic counseling and placement. High school transcripts and SAT/ACT requirements are waived if the student transfers 60 hours or holds an associate degree. Test scores are also waived if the applicant is 22 years of age or older. The applicant must demonstrate the ability to do college work. Three personal references may be requested if needed. Although interviews are not required, prospective students are encouraged to visit the campus. Four "College For A Weekend" events are available each year, giving prospective students an opportunity to participate in classes, attend social and athletic events, experience residence hall life, and interact with students and faculty members.

Application and Information

Admissions decisions are made on a rolling basis, however June 30 is the preferred deadline for fall enrollment. Applicants are encouraged to complete the application process by January 1 to be considered for maximum scholarship opportunities. Applicants for the spring term should complete the process by November 30, although early October is preferred.

To learn more about Liberty University, students should contact:

Office of Admissions
Liberty University
1971 University Boulevard
Lynchburg, Virginia 24502
Phone: 800-543-5317 (toll-free)
Fax: 800-542-2311 (toll-free)
E-mail: ljamason@liberty.edu
Web site: http://www.liberty.edu (Advantage Code 00043)
http://www.libertyu.com

An aerial view of Liberty University.

LONGWOOD UNIVERSITY

FARMVILLE, VIRGINIA

The University

"Discover the Power in You" is not just a tagline—it is a call to action for every Longwood University student. Longwood empowers students to discover interests and talents, turn them into real-world pursuits, and pursue them with knowledge and determination. Building upon its strong foundation in the liberal arts and sciences, Longwood provides an environment in which exceptional teaching fosters student learning, scholarship, and achievement.

Longwood graduates start careers in business, chemistry, geology, law, medicine, physics, education, theater, and hundreds of other disciplines every year because they are well prepared. Strong academics, a faculty devoted to teaching, and required internships prime Longwood students to tackle the real world. Longwood's job placement rate is more than 90 percent. Longwood is consistently ranked by *U.S. News & World Report*. The University was listed "Best in the Southeast" in the *Princeton Review*'s 2007 report of the "Best 361 Colleges." It was also ranked in *Kiplinger's* personal finance magazine as one of the "100 Best Values in Public Colleges," a report based on the combination of top-flight academics and an affordable cost. Longwood was also recognized in *USA Today* as one of twenty colleges nationwide that foster student success.

Of the University's 3,986 undergraduate students, 65 percent are women, and 15 percent are transfer students. Longwood is a destination for students from all over the country and the world. More than twenty-five states and sixteen countries are represented on campus. The majority of out-of-state students come from Maryland, New Jersey, Pennsylvania, New York, and Connecticut.

Approximately 70 percent of undergraduates live in University-managed housing. Longwood Landings, a new residence hall adjacent to Longwood's 60-acre campus, offers apartment-style living above ground-floor bookstores and coffee shops. University-managed, apartment-style living is also available in two other off-campus locations. Game rooms, theaters, and an outdoor pool add appeal for upper-class students. Access to the Internet is available from each residence hall room as well as from all campus buildings. For additional information on housing and residential life, prospective students should visit the Web site at http://www.longwood.edu/rcl/.

More than 125 clubs, organizations, and special-interest groups, in addition to student-run festivals and a thriving live-music scene, offer something for every student. Through these organizations, students work closely with faculty members and other campus leaders to create an unusually well-coordinated academic and student-affairs program that has a strong impact on the Longwood environment. About 17 percent of students are in social fraternities or sororities.

Longwood University is a member of NCAA Division I. Men's and women's intercollegiate teams include basketball, cross-country, golf, soccer, and tennis. In addition, the University fields a men's baseball team and women's field hockey, lacrosse, and softball teams. Club and intramural sports are available for basketball, bicycling, equestrian, flag football, golf, racquetball, rugby, soccer, swimming, ultimate Frisbee, and volleyball, among others.

In addition to its undergraduate degrees, Longwood also offers graduate degree programs in business, communication sciences and disorders, education, English and modern languages, and sociology.

Location

Farmville is a dynamic two-college town with all of the best features of a small community—beautiful scenery, quaint shops, and a rich history. Students appreciate the lower cost of living and the ease of travel in and out of town. They also enjoy key features, such as trendy restaurants and nightspots, an eight-screen multiplex cinema, and three golf courses. Farmville also is less than 30 minutes from three of Virginia's state parks and approximately an hour away from Richmond and Charlottesville—perfect for day trips. Theme parks, skiing, the Atlantic Ocean, and even the nation's capital also are short drives away.

Majors and Degrees

Longwood University offers the Bachelor of Arts (B.A.), the Bachelor of Fine Arts (B.F.A.), the Bachelor of Music (B.M.), the Bachelor of Science (B.S.), and the Bachelor of Science in Business Administration (B.S.B.A.) degrees.

Majors are anthropology, art (education, graphic design, history, painting, photography), biology, business administration (accounting, business education, computer information systems, economics, finance, management, marketing, real estate, retailing), chemistry, communication sciences and disorders, communication studies (mass media, organizational and strategic communication), computer science, criminology/criminal justice, economics (business economics, international economics, public policy), English, French, German, history, kinesiology (athletic training, exercise science, K–12 teaching), liberal studies (with licensure in elementary, middle, and special education), mathematics, music (education, performance, piano pedagogy), physics, political science (prelaw), preprofessional medical, psychology, secondary education certification, social work, sociology, Spanish, theater, and therapeutic recreation.

Academic Programs

The purpose of the General Education Program at Longwood is the development of disciplined, informed, and creative minds. General education is the foundation upon which all other learning is built and is therefore the central component of a Longwood education. The General Education Program comprises fifteen goals, most of which are addressed by a variety of core courses from which students may choose. A total of 41 hours of core courses are required.

The Longwood Seminar is a 1-credit course required of all freshmen. It is designed to promote critical thinking and analysis in all aspects of the students' lives and develop the knowledge and skills that lead to college success. This is accomplished by establishing a network that fosters a positive transition to college. Freshmen normally carry 15 to 17 credits per semester.

The Longwood Honors program is a special opportunity for incoming students who have been high achievers in high school and desire continued academic challenges in college. For additional information, students should visit the Web site at http://www.longwood.edu/honors/.

Longwood participates in cooperative programs in engineering with the University of Virginia, Virginia Tech, Virginia Commonwealth University, Old Dominion University, Christopher Newport University, Georgia Institute of Technology, and the University of Tennessee. The University's preprofessional program in the medical sciences prepares students for admission to schools of medicine, dentistry, veterinary medicine, medical technology, dental hygiene, physical therapy, occupational therapy, and pharmacy.

Off-Campus Programs

Longwood requires all students to participate in an internship or a directed research experience. Students gain hands-on real-world experience at a wide range of organizations. The study-abroad program offers exchanges in such places as Australia, Belize, China, England, France, Ireland, and Spain. Other destinations are offered through affiliated programs.

Academic Facilities

The Greenwood Library, conveniently located near the center of the campus, offers 250,000 cataloged titles and currently subscribes to 1,600 journals. Some 700,000 microform units and sound and video recordings supplement the book and journal collections. The library also provides access to the holdings of other libraries through its interlibrary loan service. Students can access the library from the campus network or the Internet. The library's information center, with forty-eight workstations, provides Internet access and a variety of reference services. Small group meeting rooms facilitate learning, and students enjoy an onsite coffee shop.

A new, four-story Science Center opened in December 2005. The 70,822-square-foot facility includes classrooms, laboratories, faculty offices, and additional research space for both undergraduate and graduate research projects. The building features a state-of-the-art, climate-controlled environment, with safety ventilation systems and hazardous materials safeguards, along with a high-tech infrastructure for classrooms, laboratories, and distance learning facilities. A greenhouse and herbarium, housing the world's largest collection of Virginia plant specimens, are located on the roof.

The health and physical education complex has a pool, dance studio, human-performance lab, and a 3,000-seat gymnasium. In addition, the complex offers eight tennis courts. A nine-hole golf course is several blocks from campus. A new Health and Fitness Center, opened in 2007, features a rock-climbing wall, a track, basketball and racquetball courts, and the newest weight machines.

A new Communication Studies and Theatre facility, currently under construction, is planned to house high-tech classrooms, media labs, studios, and black box theaters.

Costs

For the 2007–08 academic year, tuition, room, board, and fees were approximately $14,420 for Virginia residents and $22,654 for nonresidents who were enrolled full-time (at least 30 credit hours per year) and purchased a meal plan of fourteen meals per week.

Financial Aid

Longwood makes every effort to provide qualified students with the opportunity to attend college. Scholarships, grants, loans, and work-study programs are available. Students who submit completed applications by January 15 are considered for scholarships ranging from $500 to full tuition, but competition is steep. The University's financial aid Web site (http://www.longwood.edu/financialaid/) has additional information.

Faculty

At Longwood, students receive personal attention from faculty members who really get to know them—not just their names. There are 247 faculty members, 84 percent of whom are full-time; of these, 80 percent hold a doctorate or terminal degree in their field. The student-faculty ratio is 19:1. The average class has 25 students, but one quarter of all classes have 10 or fewer students.

Student Government

The Student Government Association of Longwood University consists of a 34-member Senate, which includes a 6-member Executive Council. In accordance with the guidelines set forth by the Student Government Association Constitution, all students of Longwood University "shall be members of this association." Thus, every student is considered to be represented by the Senate—but only the Senate may vote on an issue.

Admission Requirements

Admission decisions are competitive and based on a student's academic performance in high school, grade point average, types of courses, class standing, and SAT or ACT scores. Additional information in support of the application is reviewed by the Admissions Committee. The average GPA for fall 2007 freshmen was 3.32; the SAT midrange was between 1010 and 1200. Students should have completed at least 4 years of English; 3 years of math (algebra I, algebra II, and geometry); 3 years of science (biology, chemistry, physics, physical science, or earth science), and 2 units must include a lab; 3 years of history or social studies; 2 years of a foreign language (additional years of one language are strongly recommended); 2 years of health and/or physical education; and 1 year of fine or practical arts.

Students applying to transfer from another college must have a cumulative GPA of at least 2.5 and at least 30 transferable credits, including course work in English, math, science, and history to be competitive. The average transfer GPA for fall 2007 was 3.1.

Applicants must submit the completed application, the $40 nonrefundable application fee, official high school (and college, if applicable) transcripts, and SAT or ACT scores.

Application and Information

Applications are available at the University Web site, and students are encouraged to apply online. The deadline for early action (nonbinding) admission is December 1. The deadline for scholarship consideration is January 15. The deadlines for regular admission are March 1 for the fall semester and October 15 for the spring. Although Longwood has a rolling admission policy, the University recommends that students apply early. Admission decisions for the fall semester are mailed beginning in mid-January.

For more information, students should contact:

Robert J. Chonko, Dean of Admissions
Longwood University
201 High Street
Farmville, Virginia 23909
Phone: 434-395-2060
800-281-4677 (toll-free)
E-mail: admissions@longwood.edu
Internet: http://whylongwood.com

COLLEGE DATA CENTER • VIRGINIA

LYNCHBURG COLLEGE

LYNCHBURG, VIRGINIA

The College

Lynchburg College is a fully accredited, coeducational, nonsectarian liberal arts college related to the Christian Church (Disciples of Christ). It offers undergraduate programs in the liberal arts, sciences, and professional disciplines (including business, communications, education, and nursing) and graduate programs in business, education, and English. The College is committed to the principle that every individual is of infinite worth, and it endeavors to provide a program of liberal education consistent with the needs of contemporary society. It draws its undergraduate student body of approximately 2,100 men and women from thirty-one states and six countries. The College community is largely residential, with approximately 87 percent of the full-time undergraduate student body living on campus. Approximately 45 percent of the undergraduates are from out of state.

The 214-acre campus has long been considered one of the most beautiful in the South. Thirty-seven buildings of mostly Georgian Colonial design have the majestic Blue Ridge Mountains as a backdrop. The Claytor Nature Student Center, a 470-acre farm in nearby Bedford County, is utilized for environmental and educational purposes as a learning laboratory to promote the property as a model of environmental management in cooperation with various organizations locally and nationally. This year, the College added an astronomical observatory to the grounds, including a 20-inch telescope that will be put to use by students and faculty members.

A wide variety of activities are available in the Lynchburg College community: service and honor organizations, including the national Bonnor Leader Program; more than seventy clubs and organizations; five fraternities; and five sororities as well as opportunities to participate in dramatic productions, student publications, religious activities, and musical performances. New Horizons provides adventure-based leadership and team-building opportunities for individuals and groups. Community service is a distinguishing feature of the Lynchburg College students, who annually contribute more than 30,000 volunteer hours to the community through such projects as Habitat for Humanity, Camp Jaycees, Special Olympics, and other programs.

The varsity athletic program is diverse and includes baseball, basketball, cheerleading, cross-country, equestrian sports, golf, indoor and outdoor track and field, lacrosse, soccer, and tennis for men and basketball, cheerleading, cross-country, equestrian sports, field hockey, lacrosse, soccer, softball, tennis, track, and volleyball for women. The College participates in NCAA Division III and is a charter member of the Old Dominion Athletic Conference, which includes Bridgewater, Eastern Mennonite, Emory & Henry, Guilford, Hampden-Sydney, Hollins, Lynchburg, Randolph-Macon, Randolph, Roanoke, Sweet Briar, Virginia Wesleyan, and Washington and Lee. In addition, the College supports several club sports, including men's lacrosse, women's soccer, cycling, skiing and snowboarding, shotokan karate, and a ballroom dance. An intramural program exists for interested men and women as well. In 2001 and 2002, the College won the Commissioner's Cup for having the best athletic program in its conference. The Turner Athletic Facility includes state-of-the-art exercise and fitness areas, a dance studio, and one of the top exercise physiology labs in Virginia. The gymnasium seats 1,500.

The College's Shellenberger Field has been newly renovated to include artificial turf, a new stadium, a resurfaced track, and lights for night use. Also included are Moon Field upgrades—a permanent softball outfield fence and new areas for the track and field events of javelin, hammer, shot put, and discus. These improvements allow students to enjoy many more recreational opportunities in varsity, intramural, and club sports and general activities.

Location

Lynchburg College is located in central Virginia, 100 miles from Richmond, 180 miles southwest of Washington, D.C., and 50 miles east of Roanoke. Greater Lynchburg is a growing business and industrial center with a population of more than 240,000. The city is noted for its climate, culture, and historic landmarks. It is within an easy drive of the Blue Ridge Mountains, where many popular lakes and resorts are located. Air, bus, and railroad transportation place Lynchburg within easy reach of any urban center.

Majors and Degrees

Lynchburg College offers the Bachelor of Arts in the following fields: accounting, art (graphic design or studio art), business administration, communication studies (journalism or speech communication), economics (financial or general), English (literature or writing), French, history, international relations, management, marketing, music, philosophy, political science, religious studies, sociology (criminology or general), Spanish, sports management, and theater. The degree of Bachelor of Science is offered in the following fields: applied physical science, athletic training, biology, biomedical science, chemistry (professional or technical), computer science, environmental science, exercise physiology, health and movement science, health promotion, human development and learning (elementary education or special education), mathematics, nursing, physics, and psychology.

A candidate for a B.A. degree may elect to take a joint major in foreign language–business management, philosophy–political science, philosophy–religious studies, psychology–special education, religious studies–sociology, or religious studies and another major. Double majors and minors may also be taken in many areas of study. Advanced undergraduates may also take some graduate courses.

Preprofessional and professional courses are available for students who want preparation for careers in art therapy, dentistry, forestry and wildlife management, law, library science, medicine, ministry and ministry-related occupations, museum studies, occupational therapy, optometry, pharmacy, physical therapy, and veterinary medicine.

Academic Programs

To be eligible for a degree, a student must complete at least 124 semester hours of college-level academic work. In addition, a degree candidate must have a grade point average of at least 2.0 on all work undertaken, plus an average of at least 2.0 on all work undertaken in the major field.

The curriculum at Lynchburg College is divided into two general areas; some additional hours are available for students to explore course work in free elective areas of their choice. The first of the two areas of study consists of General Education Requirements (GERs) selected from the broad disciplines of world literature, fine arts, philosophy, religious studies, mathematics, history, social science, laboratory science, foreign languages, and health and movement science. All students are exposed to each of these academic areas. The second of the two general areas is the major. The College offers thirty-six majors, ranging from education and business to the sciences and the humanities, as well as thirteen preprofessional programs. This curriculum offers students breadth (GERs) as well as depth (the major). Students may devote their free elective hours to one of forty-three minor programs to further enhance their education.

Outstanding students may be selected to participate in the College's Westover Honors Program, the purpose of which is to attract, stimulate, challenge, and fulfill academically gifted students. The program offers a challenging curriculum that promotes intellectual curiosity and independent thinking and places strong emphasis on creative problem solving.

The College operates on an early semester calendar. The first semester begins in late August and ends before Christmas, and the second semester runs from mid-January to early May. An optional three-week winter term is also offered. An Advanced Placement Scholars Program permits some students to enter with advanced standing, credit, or both. Credit is also awarded on the basis of satisfactory scores on the CLEP subject exams. Early admission is available for the talented student. Eligible students who want to accelerate their program may meet degree requirements in three years.

Lynchburg offers entry-level computer courses to all students, and students are strongly encouraged to become computer literate. New students may bring a computer of their own or utilize one of the many available on campus. All students are assigned an e-mail account and have access to the Internet. In addition, all students are allowed to develop their own home pages on the World Wide Web, which they have access to through the computer resources provided by the College. All residence hall rooms are wired for network access and the Intranet, which serves the College community. Wireless Internet access is available in most areas of the campus.

Off-Campus Programs

Various agency and intercollegiate exchange programs are available for interested students. Language students may engage in foreign-study programs and are encouraged to do so. In addition, any student who wishes to study abroad may do so as part of the College's study-abroad program.

Internships, organized through the Academic and Career Services Office, are available locally, nationally, and internationally. More than 1,000 internships are already established, and new sites are developed each year. Specific guidelines for these programs are set forth by each department. In addition, Lynchburg College, Randolph College, and Sweet Briar College, as members of the Tri-College Consortium of Virginia, maintain cooperative relationships for the sharing of facilities and offerings. Students at each of the colleges have access to the libraries of the other two and may enroll in a course on either of the other campuses without payment of additional tuition.

Academic Facilities

The Hobbs Science Center provides an outstanding learning environment for students pursuing studies in biology, chemistry, physics, biomedical sciences, environmental science, psychology, mathematics, and computer science. In addition to state-of-the-art research labs, including a cadaver lab, students studying environmental science can utilize the online weather station, GIS and remote sensing software, and digitizer. This modern facility is also used during the summer by the Virginia Governor's School for Math and Science to provide programming for selected high school students. Extending over 470 acres, the Claytor Nature Study Center is a hands-on learning environment with natural woodlands, grasslands, two lakes, wetlands, and a mile-long stretch of the Big Otter River, and an 8,000-square-foot education/research facility.

Schewel Hall is Lynchburg College's state-of-the-art, $12-million classroom and laboratory facility, which houses the School of Business and Economics, the Communication Studies program, foreign languages, performing arts, and multiple venues for students to congregate and study. This 67,000-square-foot facility includes technology-based classrooms, computer laboratories, and specialized teaching-learning settings, including a model stock exchange room, a digital darkroom, and a multimedia development center with television and recording studios.

The regional community can also enjoy a variety of special events in the 250-seat Sydnor Performance Hall.

The Daura Art Gallery is the major repository of more than 1,000 works of the Catalan-American artist, Pierre Daura. The expansion of this facility makes the Daura Gallery the largest visual art exhibit center in the city of Lynchburg. Each year, it is the site for the Senior Art Show in which chosen student works are exhibited.

Costs

For resident students who enter in the 2007–08 session, total charges are $33,785; this includes $26,360 for tuition, $6570 for room and board, and $855 for student fees.

Financial Aid

Lynchburg College administers a financial aid program of more than $27 million. These resources are awarded to students as a result of meritorious achievement and/or demonstrated need. Lynchburg College offers academic and achievement scholarships that range from $3000 to $12,000 and are based on performance and accomplishments at the high school or community college level. These awards are renewable each year until the student graduates, as long as the recipient maintains a qualifying minimum academic average each year. Students are identified to receive these scholarships through the admission application; no separate application is necessary. Free early aid estimates are available for students. More than 95 percent of last year's entering class received academic and/or need-based financial aid. The average amount of aid received was $16,000.

To determine eligibility for need-based financial aid, the student should complete the Free Application for Federal Student Aid (FAFSA), which may be obtained at most high schools and at Lynchburg College. The FAFSA results determine the student's eligibility for federally funded grants and loans and other support such as work-study opportunities. In addition, students from Virginia are eligible to apply for the Virginia Tuition Assistance grant.

Faculty

The Lynchburg College faculty has 135 full-time members, 80 percent of whom hold the doctorate or terminal degree in their field. The student-faculty ratio is 12:1. While many faculty members are involved in research projects, it is a College policy that the faculty's top priorities must be in the classroom.

Student Government

The student government of Lynchburg College is regulated by agreements determined by the students, faculty, and administration. It is felt that the College should not be run by the faculty alone, nor by students alone, but through the cooperative interest of all. Campus government is vested in the Student Government Association, the Judicial Boards, the Campus Life Policies Committee, and the Office of the Dean of Student Development. The Student Government Association is also responsible for the Academic Honor Code, a prominent part of campus life.

Admission Requirements

A candidate for admission to Lynchburg College should be a graduate of an approved secondary school with a minimum of 16 academic units or the equivalent, as shown by examination. It is required that the academic work include major emphases in the areas of English, foreign language, social science, natural sciences, and mathematics. An applicant must demonstrate above-average academic ability in all areas of study, as admission is competitive. In support of the record, a student must present satisfactory scores on the SAT (critical reading and math scores are used to determine admission decisions and merit scholarship awards) or ACT. It is recommended that all students have a personal interview and visit the campus beginning the spring semester of their junior year or during their senior year. Enrollment Office hours during the academic year are 9 to 5 Monday through Friday and 9 to noon on Saturday during the academic year.

Application and Information

Early decision admission applications must be received by November 15; notification of acceptance is made by December 15. All other applications are processed on a rolling admissions basis. Applicants are notified of the status of their application usually within two to four weeks of the date their application file is completed.

For information, students should contact:

Sharon Walters-Bower, Director of Admissions
Lynchburg College
1501 Lakeside Drive
Lynchburg, Virginia 24501
Phone: 434-544-8300
800-426-8101 (toll-free)
Fax: 434-544-8653
E-mail: admissions@lynchburg.edu
Web site: http://www.lynchburg.edu

MARYMOUNT UNIVERSITY

ARLINGTON, VIRGINIA

The University

Marymount University is a comprehensive, coeducational Catholic university. Located just 6 miles from the nation's capital, it serves a diverse student body of approximately 2,200 undergraduates and 1,400 graduate students, who represent forty-five states and seventy countries. The University offers a wide range of majors and graduate degree programs through the Schools of Arts and Sciences, Business Administration, Education and Human Services, and Health Professions. Marymount is accredited by the Commission on Colleges of the Southern Association of Colleges and Schools.

The University takes full advantage of the resources in and around Washington, D.C. Government, business, and professional leaders are frequent visitors to the campus, enriching the learning experience. In addition, many students have internships with federal agencies, international businesses, and technology companies. The State Department, Smithsonian museums, and Congressional offices are popular internship sites. The blending of academics with hands-on, practical experience serves as a cornerstone of a well-rounded Marymount education. The University emphasizes excellence in teaching, attention to the individual, and values and ethics across the curriculum.

Students enjoy NCAA Division III sports, an active student government, a strong campus ministry group, more than thirty clubs, and a wide range of service opportunities. The Activities Programming Board plans activities both on and off campus, including comedy nights, concerts, movies, and theater evenings in D.C. It also gets tickets to local sporting events and schedules outings to ski and beach destinations.

The Lee Center serves as the hub of campus life. The center has a 1,000-seat sports arena, café, bookstore, pool, recreational gym, fitness center, dance studio, meeting rooms, and lounges.

Living on campus is an important aspect of college life. Students who are under 21 and whose families do not live within commuting distance are required to live on campus for the first two years. Four residence halls house approximately 670 students. The rooms are wired with fiber-optic cable for Internet, phone, and cable TV access. The campus also has wireless-access areas.

Location

With Marymount's proximity to the nation's capital, students enjoy the cultural and educational advantages of Washington, D.C. Museums, galleries, theaters, the Capitol, the Library of Congress, and the National Archives are all easily accessible. Marymount shuttle buses provide service to the Metro system. Union Station and Reagan National Airport are also within easy reach. The resources of Washington, whether for research, recreation, or internships, are right next door, while students enjoy the benefits of a suburban, 21-acre campus.

Majors and Degrees

The University awards the undergraduate degrees of Bachelor of Arts (B.A.), Bachelor of Business Administration (B.B.A.), Bachelor of Science (B.S.), and Bachelor of Science in Nursing (B.S.N.).

The Bachelor of Arts degree may be earned in art, communications, criminal justice, economics in society, English, fashion design, fashion merchandising, graphic design, history, interior design, liberal studies, philosophy, politics, psychology, sociology, and theology and religious studies. A Bachelor of Science degree may be earned in biology, criminal justice/forensic science, health sciences, information technology, and mathematics. Bachelor of Business Administration specialties include accounting, business law and paralegal studies, finance, general business, international business, management, and marketing. A Bachelor of Science program is offered in nursing.

Education licensure programs in the areas of elementary education (pre-K–6), secondary education (7–12), English as a second language, learning disabilities, and art education (K–12) are available to degree-seeking undergraduates who complete course work for education programs in addition to the courses required for the major discipline.

Marymount also offers preprofessional programs for law, medicine, and physical therapy.

Academic Programs

Marymount is dedicated to educating the whole person—to helping students develop every aspect of their potential. The college years are years of transformation. They are a time to explore interests and to grow in knowledge and understanding. Marymount is committed to preparing students intellectually and morally for the tasks ahead, enabling them to achieve success and make a positive impact on the world.

Marymount students study a liberal arts core curriculum and the required elements of their chosen disciplines. Requirements for earning a degree include a cumulative GPA of 2.0 or better and a minimum of 36 credits as a student at Marymount. The total number of credits required varies by program. Marymount operates on a semester system. Small classes and personal attention help ensure student success and a strong sense of community. An honor system guides academic and social conduct. The cultural and educational resources of the nation's capital add to the curriculum through off-campus activities.

Marymount's honors program is for students who are seeking significant challenges and rewards. New, current, and transfer students of all disciplines may apply. The honors program experience culminates in the completion and defense of an honors thesis. Admission is competitive and limited to 20 new students each year. Students in the honors program receive substantial scholarship support, priority registration, special courses and opportunities, one-on-one faculty mentoring, direct involvement with program governance, travel support for professional conferences, and recognition at graduation and on the diploma and transcripts.

Off-Campus Programs

Undergraduate degrees require completion of an internship in the chosen field, in addition to all necessary course work in the major and liberal arts core courses. Marymount students intern regularly in Congressional offices, the State Department, Smithsonian museums, technology and biotechnology companies, media organizations, and international businesses, just to name a few of the choices available. For many students, internships lead to full-time employment after graduation.

Through the University's study-abroad program, Marymount offers semester-long programs in Africa, Australia, Austria, Central and South America, China, England, France, Ireland, Italy, Japan, Spain, and other locations.

Academic Facilities

The Main Campus has classrooms, computer labs and wireless-access areas, science labs, seminar rooms, language labs, nursing auto-tutorials, and studios for fine and graphic arts, fashion design, and interior design. The Emerson G. Reinsch Library is also located on the Main Campus. It houses more than 194,000 volumes and over 950 journals, with access to more than 10,000 journals through electronic resources and over seventy online information resources. Students have access to member libraries of the Washington Research Library Consortium and the Consortium for Continuing Higher Education in Northern Virginia.

The Learning Resource Center (LRC), located in the Reinsch complex, is a year-round academic counseling and learning center designed to support and enhance Marymount's instructional programs. Staffed by full-time learning specialists and by graduate and undergraduate peer tutors, the LRC provides tutoring assistance in writing, science, mathematics, and study skills for a broad range of courses. The Barry Art Gallery, also located in the Reinsch Library building, features a variety of exhibitions throughout the year.

The Ballston Center, an eight-story building just minutes from the Main Campus by free shuttle bus, also houses classrooms, seminar rooms, and computer labs and wireless-access areas as well as physical therapy labs, the Truland Auditorium, the Electronic Learning Center, and the recently opened Verizon Information Security Lab. The lab provides students with hands-on experience to prepare them for current and future cybersecurity challenges.

Marymount's recently opened Reston Center serves an adult learner population and offers graduate programs in business and education as well as two undergraduate options. The Bachelor of Business Administration is offered for returning students who have earned significant college business credits and who now wish to complete their degree. An online nursing program is also facilitated through the Reston Center for registered nurses who wish to earn the Bachelor of Science in Nursing.

Costs

The undergraduate tuition for 2007–08 was $20,190 per academic year. Room and board for 2007–08 were $8705 per academic year for double occupancy; there was an additional fee of $827.50 per semester for single occupancy.

Financial Aid

Marymount has an extensive scholarship and grant program and participates in all federal and state aid programs. To be considered for aid, students must file the Free Application for Federal Student Aid (FAFSA) with the College Scholarship Service. In fall 2007, 77 percent of full-time, degree-seeking undergraduate students received financial aid. The financial aid includes scholarships, grants, loans, work-study awards, and on-campus employment.

Faculty

At Marymount, faculty members are committed to the success of each student. They make themselves readily available to discuss course work or career plans or to simply chat. The University has 143 full-time faculty members and a number of highly qualified adjunct faculty members. In addition, business and professional leaders often visit as lecturers. The undergraduate student-faculty ratio is 13:1. Marymount classes are small, so students and professors really get to know each other.

Student Government

The student government acts as the official liaison between students, faculty members, and the administration. It may make policy recommendations related to student issues. The Activities Programming Board plans and implements a variety of student events.

Admission Requirements

The Admissions team reviews the strength of an applicant's academic record, national test scores, breadth of academic preparation, and letters of recommendation. Applicants to the freshman class are considered if a student's high school grade point average in academic courses is 2.5 or better on a 4.0 scale, the combined SAT score is within 100 points of the national average or better, and the student's academic preparation, recommendations, and character indicate that he or she is qualified to undertake Marymount programs. It is recommended that students have at least 4 years of English; 3 years of a foreign language, mathematics, and the social sciences; and 2 years of science.

A campus interview is not required but is strongly recommended. It gives students a chance to see if Marymount would be a good fit. The University holds Campus Visit Days in the fall and spring. Visitors are welcome at any time, and appointments with Admissions staff members may be made in advance.

Application and Information

High school students seeking admission are advised to apply early during their senior year. They should submit an application (which can be completed online), a nonrefundable fee of $40, a high school transcript, SAT or ACT scores, evidence of expected graduation from an accredited high school, and a recommendation from a high school counselor or an appropriate school official. Those who have attended another college or university must also submit transcripts of college-level study and a recommendation from the Dean of Students at the previous institution. The University has a rolling admission policy and notifies applicants soon after the application process is completed and a decision on admission has been made.

For more information, prospective students should contact:

Chris Domes
Vice President of Enrollment and Student Services
Marymount University
2807 North Glebe Road
Arlington, Virginia 22207-4299
Phone: 703-284-1500
800-548-7638 (toll-free)
E-mail: admissions@marymount.edu
Web site: http://www.marymount.edu

Marymount University's historic 21-acre campus is only 10 minutes from Washington, D.C.

OLD DOMINION UNIVERSITY

NORFOLK, VIRGINIA

The University

Old Dominion University (ODU) began its tradition of excellence when it was founded in 1930 as the Norfolk Division of the College of William & Mary, the second-oldest university in the United States. The two-year school rapidly evolved into a full four-year college and was granted independence in 1962. Proud of its past, Old Dominion constantly looks to the future and prides itself on its constantly expanding research and teaching programs. The four-year college has grown over the years and is now one of only 101 public universities with the Carnegie Foundation's RU/H: Research University (high research activity) distinction. Old Dominion is an agent of change for its students, for the region, and for the nation it serves.

Old Dominion enrolls about 15,000 undergraduates and 6,000 graduate students, who hail from all fifty states and U.S. territories as well as 108 countries. Old Dominion offers sixty-eight bachelor's degree programs, sixty master's degree programs, two education specialist's programs, and thirty-five doctoral degree programs and is accredited by the Commission on Colleges of the Southern Association of Colleges and Schools. Each degree program is housed within one of the University's six colleges: Education, Engineering and Technology, Arts and Letters, Business and Public Administration, Health Sciences, and Sciences. Through the Career Advantage Program, ODU is the only doctoral degree–granting university in the United States to guarantee each of its students an internship in their field of study.

Old Dominion offers a wide variety of activities, creating a dynamic, energetic campus environment. The 1,400 international students and the 200 student organizations reflect the diversity that exists. As a member of the Colonial Athletic Association, ODU has sixteen intercollegiate Division I athletic teams and has won twenty-eight team and four individual national titles.

Location

Located in a residential section of historic Norfolk, Virginia, the 188 acres of the Old Dominion University campus stretch from the Elizabeth River to the Lafayette River. The University offers a small-college look and feel, with tree-lined walkways, a mix of old and new buildings, and colorful gardens and ponds. Norfolk is one of the seven cities that comprise what is known as Hampton Roads, Virginia's most populated region, at approximately 1.5 million. Norfolk is well known as a major cultural center for its abundance of museums, historic sites, sporting venues, festivals, concerts, shops, and restaurants. Norfolk is ideally situated, as the Virginia Beach oceanfront is within a 20-minute drive and historic places such as Colonial Williamsburg, Jamestown, and Yorktown are within a 40-minute drive. Richmond and Washington, D.C., are near enough for weekend visits.

Majors and Degrees

The College of Arts and Letters confers B.A. and B.S. degrees for students in the following majors: African American and African studies, art education, art history, art studio, Asian studies, communication, criminal justice, English, foreign languages, geography, history, interdisciplinary studies, international studies, music, philosophy, political science, professional writing, sociology, theater and dance, and women's studies. In addition, the College of Arts and Letters awards a Bachelor of Fine Arts in acting and fine arts as well as a Bachelor of Music in composition, music education, and performance.

The College of Business and Public Administration confers a B.A in economics and a B.S. in e-commerce systems as well as a B.S. in business administration in the following majors: accounting, decision sciences, economics, finance, information systems and technology, international business, management, maritime, and supply chain management and marketing.

The Darden College of Education awards B.S. degrees to students in the following majors: human services, occupational and technical studies, physical education, recreation and tourism studies, and speech-language pathology and audiology.

The Frank Batten College of Engineering and Technology confers B.S. degrees to students in the following majors: civil engineering, civil engineering technology, computer engineering, electrical engineering, electrical engineering technology, engineering, environmental engineering, mechanical engineering, and mechanical engineering technology.

The College of Health Sciences awards B.S. degrees to students in the following majors: dental hygiene, environmental health, health sciences, medical technology, nuclear medicine technology, and nursing.

The College of Sciences confers B.S. degrees to students in the following majors: biochemistry, biology, chemistry, computer science, mathematics, ocean and earth sciences, physics, and psychology.

Academic Programs

Old Dominion provides each student with a broad liberal arts core curriculum that ensures that students have a well-rounded foundation before they move into their upper-level classes within their chosen majors. Old Dominion has a traditional semester calendar with numerous summer sessions. The Honors College is open to exceptional students from all majors, and accepted students must maintain a minimum 3.0 GPA in their course work. With some of the largest military installations in the United States located in the region, Old Dominion is a prime choice for students who are interested in an Army or Navy ROTC program.

ODU also offers various accelerated programs in which students can attain both a bachelor's and a master's degree in a condensed period of time. Students may choose from the following programs: B.A./M.A. in applied linguistics; B.A./M.A. in English; B.A./M.A. in history; B.A./M.A. in international studies; B.A. or B.S. in communication/M.A. in humanities; B.A. or B.S. in individualized interdisciplinary studies/M.A. in humanities; B.A. or B.S. in women's studies/M.A. in humanities; B.S./M.S. in engineering; B.S./Ph.D. in engineering; B.A. or B.S./M.B.A. (business administration); B.S. in dental hygiene/M.S. in dental hygiene; B.S.N. postlicensure/M.S.N. (nursing); B.S. in health sciences/M.S. in community health; bachelor's/M.S. programs in biology, chemistry, and oceanography; and a bachelor's-to-M.D. program (with Eastern Virginia Medical School).

Old Dominion University offers regular degree programs at numerous locations away from its Norfolk campus. In Virginia, students may attend classes at the Peninsula Higher Education Center in Hampton, the Virginia Beach Higher Education Center, the Northern Virginia Center in Sterling, and the Tri-Cities Center in Suffolk. Old Dominion offers regular degree programs to students in every region of the commonwealth and to students in various states across the U.S. via distance learning. Students may take classes that are broadcast from the ODU Norfolk campus to locations in their respective communities (often a local community college). Currently, Old Dominion broadcasts courses to nearly fifty locations throughout Virginia; to sites in Arizona, North Carolina, Georgia, Washington State, and Indiana; and to U.S. Navy ships and submarines deployed around the globe. In addition, Old Dominion offers classes that are streamed in real time over the Internet, allowing students to take classes from their home computers.

Off-Campus Programs

The Old Dominion Study Abroad Program allows students to spend a semester of study at one of many overseas locations.

Academic Facilities

The University's seventy-fifth anniversary in 2005 found an impressive array of cutting-edge facilities that have created a campus ideal for the pursuit of a diverse number of majors. Among these are the fully automated Perry Library, with more than 2.8 million items; state-of-the-art laboratories in the sciences and engineering; and the new Engineering and Computational Sciences Building. There are eight computer labs on campus that are free and accessible to all students, and free high-speed wireless connectivity is provided throughout the campus, including in dorm rooms.

The following resources are available for individuals with specific needs: Disability Services, Writing Center, Testing Center, Advising Services, Center for Professional Training and Development, International Center, and Career Management Center.

Other academic facilities are the University Theater, Experimental Theater, Diehn Fine Arts Center, Nuclear and Particle Physics Facility, Benthic Ecology Lab, Engineering Learning Center, Applied Research Center, Center for Advanced Engineering Environments, Langley Full-Scale Wind Tunnel, Technology Applications Center, Virginia Modeling Analysis and Simulation Center, and Virginia Space Flight Center at Wallops Island.

Costs

Tuition and fees for average full-time undergraduates in 2006–07 were $5910 for in-state students and $16,470 for out-of-state students. Room and board were $6640.

Financial Aid

Nearly 55 percent of Old Dominion students receive financial aid in the form of grants, loans, work-study, and academic merit-based scholarships. Students often find it easy to attain part-time employment on campus or in the local area. Old Dominion offers more than $6.5 million in scholarships. All incoming freshmen who submit their applications and credentials by the December 1 early action deadline and transfer students who submit their applications and credentials by March 15 are automatically considered for merit-based scholarships. All students are encouraged to submit the Free Application for Federal Student Aid (FAFSA). The FAFSA should be submitted to the Department of Education by February 15.

Faculty

Approximately 640 full-time and 500 part-time faculty members bring a wealth of talent to their classrooms each day. Their lively, provocative teaching, research, and applied experience, along with their commitment to academic excellence, combine to make the Old Dominion experience a rewarding one for students. The student-faculty ratio is 18:1, and 86 percent of the faculty members have attained the terminal degree in their field. The average class size is 25. Old Dominion faculty members are largely responsible for the $50 million in research grants that the University receives each year. All faculty members are required to keep office hours, which makes professors readily available to meet out-of-class student needs. Faculty members also serve as academic advisers and supervisors of independent-study programs and counsel students in their educational and professional endeavors.

Student Government

The Student Senate is the primary body of student governance at Old Dominion. The Student Senate consists of 24 senators, who are chosen by the student body as representatives. Student senators are assigned to committees and must attend meetings. The student body elects 3 senators as Executive Officers, including the Student Body President. The Senate was designed to assist the University in its effort to increase the quality of student life at Old Dominion.

Admission Requirements

Old Dominion University is a selective university that reviews applications on an individual basis. Each application is read and reviewed by the admissions staff. While academic performance is a vital factor in the decision-making process, Old Dominion also takes into account any athletic, student organization, or community service involvement. Admitted students are those who have a zest for higher education and career development. The average freshman admitted to Old Dominion ranks in the top third of his or her graduating class; earned a minimum of 16 high school academic units in English, math, science, foreign language, and social studies; and is actively involved in school- and/or community-based clubs, organizations, and athletics. Approximately 50 percent of the transfer students have earned an associate degree or have completed 60 semester hours at another institution prior to enrolling at Old Dominion.

Application and Information

For students who wish to apply for the fall semester, the deadline for application is March 15. A completed application includes a completed official application, a $40 nonrefundable application fee, official high school transcripts, SAT or ACT scores, a student activity resume, an essay, and a letter of recommendation. The deadline for transfer applications is May 1.

Requests for additional information and application forms should be sent to:

Office of Admissions
108 Rollins Hall
Old Dominion University
Norfolk, Virginia 23529-0050
Phone: 757-683-3685
E-mail: admit@odu.edu
Internet: http://www.odu.edu

A view of Old Dominion's campus.

RADFORD UNIVERSITY

RADFORD, VIRGINIA

The University

Radford University is a comprehensive, residential university committed to individualized instruction in medium-sized classes, high academic standards, and excellence in teaching. Established in 1910, Radford's enrollment has grown to more than 9,200, of whom 88 percent are undergraduates. The state-supported University offers 106 undergraduate and thirty-eight graduate program options through the College of Humanities and Behavioral Sciences, the College of Business and Economics, the College of Education and Human Development, the College of Science and Technology, the College of Visual and Performing Arts, the Waldron College of Health and Human Services, and the College of Graduate and Extended Studies.

At the graduate level, Radford University awards M.S., M.A., M.B.A., M.F.A., M.S.N., M.S.W., and Ed.S. degrees.

Fifteen residence halls, housing from 120 to 950 students each, offer a variety of options to the 3,150 students who live on campus. All residence halls are in suite arrangements, with two rooms sharing one bathroom. Freshmen are required to live on campus and can choose one of several learning/residential communities. Most off-campus students reside in rental housing within four to five blocks of the campus. Members of the Radford community come from all over Virginia as well as from forty-five other states and forty-seven countries. Radford provides many opportunities for students to participate in exchange and study-abroad programs.

Radford University offers guest speakers, theatrical productions, concerts, films, social fraternities and sororities, student publications, WVRU radio station and television station, intramural sports, and other cultural, social, and leisure opportunities. In all, there are more than 200 clubs and organizations on campus. The new Bonnie Hurlburt Student Center has lounge, study, and meeting areas as well as a bowling alley, movie theater, and three additional eateries. Dalton Hall, the student services building, houses the food court, dining hall, bookstore, and post office. The Dedmon Center, a $10.8-million sports and recreation complex, provides complete sports and fitness facilities, including an Olympic-size swimming pool and Cupp Stadium, a new track and soccer complex. Radford University's teams participate in seventeen intercollegiate sports and are members of NCAA Division I.

Location

Radford, a city of 16,200 people, is located approximately 36 miles southwest of Roanoke in the Blue Ridge Mountains in scenic western Virginia. The Blue Ridge Parkway, Appalachian Trail, New River, and Claytor Lake, which has more than 100 miles of shoreline, offer many outdoor activities in a region noted for its natural beauty. Students can ski, hike, canoe, bicycle, and enjoy other seasonal activities.

The local community offers opportunities for dining, socializing, shopping, and off-campus living. The University's campus is near I-81 and is located about 45 minutes from the Roanoke airport.

Majors and Degrees

Radford University awards B.A., B.S., B.F.A., B.M., B.B.A., B.S.N., and B.S.W. degrees in the areas of accounting; anthropology; art; biology; chemistry; communication; communication sciences and disorders; computer science and technology; criminal justice; dance; economics; English; exercise, sport, and health education; fashion; finance; foods and nutrition; foreign languages (French, German, Spanish); geography; geology; history; information science and systems; interdisciplinary studies (education); interior design; management; marketing; mathematics and statistics; media studies; medical technology; music; nursing; philosophy and religious studies; physics; political science; psychology; recreation, parks, and tourism; social science; social work; sociology; and theater.

Radford also offers preprofessional programs in law, medicine, pharmacy, and physical therapy.

Academic Programs

To be eligible for an undergraduate degree, students must complete at least 120 semester hours of college-level academic work, including 50 semester hours of general education courses. Honors courses are available to students enrolled in the Honors Academy and to any qualified student. The Office of New Student Programs coordinates several programs designed to ease the transition from high school to college. The University 100 class and Success Starts Here are programs that help first-year students become active and successful college students. Quest, Radford's summer orientation program, allows incoming students to acclimate themselves to campus, receive advising, register for classes, and make friends before coming to school in the fall. An Army ROTC program is also available to interested and qualified students.

The University year consists of two semesters, August to December (fall) and January to May (spring), and summer sessions.

Academic Facilities

The McConnell Library offers students access to textual material, periodicals, and information recorded on film, microfilm, records, compact audio discs, and tapes. Services include interlibrary loans, computer-assisted bibliographical searches, multimedia classes, and the use of multimedia equipment.

RU's newest academic facilities include Waldron Hall and a newly renovated Peters Hall. Waldron Hall serves as the home for the Waldron College of Health and Human Services and is one of the country's most comprehensive and technologically sophisticated educational environments. Academic divisions include the Schools of Nursing and Social Work and the Departments of Communication Sciences and Disorders, Foods and Nutrition, and Recreation, Parks, and Tourism. An on-site clinical simulation center provides students with practical experience in their chosen fields. Peters Hall houses the entire College of Education and Human Development under one roof. This academic facility has numerous state-of-the-art classrooms with "smart boards," a Teaching Resource Center, and new studios for the Dance Department.

Costs

The basic expenses for the 2007–08 academic year (August–May) are $6176 for tuition and fees for in-state undergraduate students ($14,510 for out-of-state students), $6398 for room and board, and an average of $800 for books and supplies.

Financial Aid

The University provides financial aid awards, based on demonstrated financial need, and scholarships, based on leadership, character, and academic achievement. Financial aid at Radford University is provided through loans, work-study awards, and grants from the federal and state governments and from private funds established through the Radford University Foundation. In addition, some departments have special fellowship funds for undergraduates. Students seeking financial aid should submit the Free Application for Federal Student Aid (FAFSA) to Federal Student Aid Programs by March 1. Transfer students who have attended summer school or who transfer for the spring semester must also request a completed Financial Aid Transcript from colleges and universities previously attended, even if financial aid was not received.

The Radford University Foundation sponsors an annual scholarship competition for qualified freshman students. For students to be eligible to compete, completed admissions applications must be received by the Office of Admissions no later than December 15. Students chosen to compete for scholarships are those who have excelled academically during their high school career. Several full scholarships, which include the equivalent of in-state tuition and fees, room and board, and a book stipend, are available. Partial scholarships, which are applied to tuition and fees as well as room and board, are also available.

Faculty

More than 80 percent of Radford University's faculty members hold terminal degrees in their fields of study. With a student-faculty ratio of 21:1, Radford is committed to interaction between faculty members and students both in and out of the classroom. In addition to their primary responsibilities of teaching and advising students, faculty members are engaged in research, publication, and other professional activities. Fewer than 5 percent of Radford's undergraduate classes are taught by graduate instructors.

Student Government

Radford University's Student Government Association enables students to participate in the administration of their own affairs and provides representation on behalf of students. Every undergraduate student is automatically a member of the Student Government Association. Students can participate in various councils, including the senate, international student affairs council, and diversity promotions council.

Admission Requirements

Admission to Radford University is based on a review of each applicant's academic qualifications. The University admits students whose ability, preparation, and character indicate potential for success in the programs of study offered. Admission is not based on race, gender, handicap, age, veteran status, national origin, religious or political affiliation, or sexual preference. Applicants for admission are considered on the basis of high school records (course of study, grade point average, and rank in class), SAT or ACT scores, and evidence of interest and motivation. Most successful applicants have taken 4 units of English, 4 units of college-preparatory math, 4 units of lab science, 4 units of social science, and 3–4 units of foreign language. All applicants need to have completed at least Algebra 1, Geometry, and Algebra 2 in order to meet the University's minimum math requirement. Students planning to major in nursing should complete units in both biology and chemistry. Students who wish to visit the campus are encouraged to call for an appointment between 8 and 5, Monday through Friday. Tours of the campus are conducted at 10 a.m., noon, and 2 p.m., Monday and Friday; 10 and 2, Tuesday through Thursday, and at 10, 11, and noon on most Saturdays during the academic year.

Application and Information

A complete application consists of an application form returned with a nonrefundable application fee, an official transcript of high school work completed, and official SAT or ACT results. Essays and letters of recommendation are also strongly encouraged. Students wishing to transfer to Radford University from an accredited college or university should send an application form and official transcripts of work attempted at all colleges attended. Applications for fall admission should be received by December 15 for Early Action and February 1 for Regular Decision for new freshmen and June 1 for new transfer students. Applications received after these dates are reviewed on a space-available basis.

For more information, students should contact:

Office of Admissions
Radford University
Radford, Virginia 24142-6903
Phone: 540-831-5371
540-831-5128 (V/TDD)
800-890-4265 (toll-free)
Fax: 540-831-5038
E-mail: ruadmiss@radford.edu
Web site: http://www.radford.edu

Whitt Hall at Radford University.

COLLEGE DATA CENTER • VIRGINIA

RANDOLPH COLLEGE

LYNCHBURG, VIRGINIA

The College

Randolph College, founded as Randolph-Macon Woman's College in 1891, was the first women's college to be accredited by the Southern Association of Colleges and Schools and the first southern women's college to be granted a Phi Beta Kappa charter. Academic excellence through the liberal arts and an emphasis on individual learning continue to be the College's top priorities, and its enduring commitment to education has fostered strong programs in career development and career networking. The College began enrolling men beginning fall 2007.

The current enrollment is about 715 students. Students come from forty-seven states and forty-five countries. Surveys show that many choose the College for its academic reputation and for its warm, friendly atmosphere. There are six residence halls on the 100-acre campus, housing 90 percent of the students. The College's location near the Blue Ridge Mountains provides ample recreational opportunities, and proximity to neighboring colleges and major universities enhances the social life on and off campus. Most students are involved in at least one of the many clubs or organizations and activities, which include campus publications, Chorale and Songshine, the Dance Group, political organizations, language clubs, theater, religious and volunteer organizations, an outdoor club, and a nationally ranked riding program. Intercollegiate sports for men include basketball, cross-country, lacrosse, riding, soccer, and tennis. Women's sports include basketball, cross-country, lacrosse, riding, soccer, softball, swimming, tennis, and volleyball. Courses are also offered in a variety of activities and sports, including aerobics, fitness walking, golf, kickboxing, weight training, and yoga.

The academic program is enhanced throughout the year by visiting speakers, performers, and artists. In recent years, these have included Jehan Sadat of Egypt, advocate for women's rights and peace; Maya Lin, architect of the Vietnam Veteran's Memorial; Katha Pollitt, essayist and contributing editor of *The Nation;* Sister Helen Prejean, author of *Dead Man Walking;* and Barry Lopez, acclaimed naturalist writer and winner of the National Book Award. In addition, the College sponsors numerous plays, awards, and exhibitions.

Location

Randolph College is located in a beautiful residential area of Lynchburg, a city of 70,000 people in the foothills of the Blue Ridge Mountains. Shopping areas are convenient to the campus, and public transportation is readily available. Lynchburg is within easy driving distance of Washington, D.C., and Richmond, Virginia.

Majors and Degrees

Randolph College offers more than sixty majors, concentrations (minors), and programs of study leading to a Bachelor of Arts (B.A.), Bachelor of Science (B.S.), or Bachelor of Fine Arts (B.F.A.) degree. Majors are art (history, museum studies, and studio), biology (environmental, molecular and cell, and organismal), chemistry, classics (archaeology, classical civilization, and classical languages), communication studies, dance, economics, engineering physics, English (creative writing and literature), environmental studies, French, history, international studies, mathematics, music (history, performance, and theory), philosophy, physics, politics, psychology, religion, sociology, Spanish, and theater. The double major is a popular option, and there is also the opportunity to devise a special major such as comparative literature or mathematical biology. In addition, there is the education program, which offers courses that meet the requirements for primary and secondary education certification. Travel/study opportunities and visiting scholar programs augment the international curriculum.

Every student has the option of selecting up to two minors in addition to the major. Minors are offered in all of the major fields as well as the interdisciplinary areas of American arts, Asian studies, British history and literature, the classical tradition, French civilization, French for commerce, human services, journalism, Renaissance studies, sport and exercise studies, symbol and myth, and women's studies. Students declare majors and concentrations in the spring of the sophomore year.

Randolph has 3-2 programs in engineering and nursing and preprofessional programs in law, medicine, and veterinary studies.

Academic Programs

The academic program is structured to develop the student as a whole person. The curriculum is designed to ensure that students acquire a broad range of knowledge and depth in their chosen field while they are prepared for meaningful careers. Randolph College trains students to think critically and independently and speak and write effectively. The College's graduation requirement is 124 hours of credit with a quality point ratio of 2.0.

Students also use the Randolph Plan, an individualized, systematic plan that helps them define their personal, educational, and professional goals. Working with faculty and staff members, students move through a series of steps to identify the many courses, internships, study-abroad opportunities, and clubs and activities that constitute a coherent plan to meet their goals.

The College operates on a traditional semester system, with self-scheduled exams given before the December vacation and at the end of the second semester in May. Most classes meet either two or three times a week. Randolph College provides maximum opportunity for independent study and research.

The Writing Program includes formal evaluation of student writing skills in all courses at the end of every semester. There are elective courses in intermediate composition and in academic writing as well as writing-intensive sections across the curriculum. First-year students may be granted exemption from the English composition degree requirement on the basis of their entering record (usually Advanced Placement examination scores).

Sixty-five percent of graduates continue their studies beyond the undergraduate level within five years of graduation. Special advisers at the College counsel students who are preparing for medical, veterinary, or law school or other specialized graduate study. Research is encouraged in the various areas of academic concentration, and in the senior year students may pursue honors work involving the presentation and defense of a thesis under the supervision of a faculty member. Sixty-seven percent of all seniors had their education broadened through internships or special summer experiences for academic credit.

Off-Campus Programs

Internships provide an exciting opportunity for students to gain valuable work experience in area hospitals, veterinary clinics, schools, law firms, industries, courts, social service agencies, and radio and television stations. The College maintains a listing of nearly 1,000 internship opportunities through which students may earn up to 6 hours of credit toward the degree.

More than one fourth of the juniors study abroad. Students have studied recently in Argentina, Australia, the Czech Republic, England, France, Japan, Russia, Scotland, and Spain. Other students participate in programs sponsored by other colleges. Students of the classics may spend a summer working at an archaeological dig in Carthage, Tunisia. Other summer research and travel opportunities are available.

Programs in this country include the Washington Semester at American University. Randolph College participates in the seven-college consortium of colleges in Virginia, along with Hampden-Sydney College, Hollins College, Mary Baldwin College, Randolph-Macon College, Sweet Briar College, and Washington and Lee University. The local Tri-College Consortium of Randolph College, Lynchburg College, and Sweet Briar College increases the diversity of courses open to students.

The College's spring semester American Culture Program offers an interdisciplinary immersion into the study of American culture both on campus and at key locations in Virginia and across the nation. The program capitalizes on the College's central location in historic Virginia as well as its own outstanding Maier Museum of Art's collection of American art. This one-semester program is open to students from Randolph College as well as to undergraduate students, both men and women, from other institutions.

The Susan F. Davenport Global Leadership Program is a four-year program focused on the skills and global perspectives students need to become leaders in the world today.

Academic Facilities

The Lipscomb Library contains more than 200,000 volumes, 860 current periodical titles, and more than 6,000 electronic periodical subscriptions. The Martin Science Building has been completely renovated to incorporate state-of-the-art laboratory design and instrumentation, enhanced facilities for student-faculty research, and multimedia instructional centers. Equipment and resources readily available for student use include an FT-NMR and computer-driven IR and UV spectrometers, exceptional herbarium and fossil collections, a greenhouse, and nature preserves. The Winfree Observatory houses a 14-inch pier-mounted telescope equipped with a computer-operated CCD camera for variable star research to support instruction in physics and astronomy. The Ethyl Science and Mathematics Resource Center in Martin offers a networked computer cluster with specific software for science and math applications and library, study, and lounge facilities. A satellite telecommunications program with the University of Virginia has been established to broaden learning opportunities.

The College's Maier Museum of Art houses an outstanding collection of nineteenth- and twentieth-century American paintings, while Presser Hall, the music building, has a concert auditorium, studios, and practice rooms. The Learning Resources Center and the Writing Lab offer academic support and tutorial services related to study skills, word processing, and the writing program.

Many facilities exist to integrate technology into teaching and learning. Virtually all of the classrooms on campus provide multimedia display capabilities, and several classrooms are equipped with student computer workstations for hands-on instruction in discipline-specific software and for general purpose technology workshops. The campus also has a number of rooms equipped with special purpose technology, including SMART Boards, a small theater with computer/video display and surround sound, a media center/language lab where students can work on language drills and exercises as well as edit digital video, and a digital darkroom for high-end digital, still picture editing.

Macintosh and PC-compatible computers are provided in numerous labs on campus for student use 24 hours a day, seven days a week. Laser printers and scanners are also available in all computer labs. Web-based information resources allow students to view their student records, class schedules, and grades.

All computer labs and residence hall rooms have access to the Internet and to the College's extensive Web site. The Web site provides comprehensive information about the College and a variety of services to prospective students and their parents. Students enjoy the campus portal system and the College's numerous locations for wireless connection to the network.

Costs

The 2007–08 comprehensive fee for room, board, and tuition was $34,350. The College recommends a budget of $1800 for books, supplies, fees, and personal expenses, excluding travel costs.

Financial Aid

Randolph College administers almost $14 million in aid each year through a comprehensive program of financial assistance, which includes academic-based scholarships, need-based grants, low-interest student loans, and campus employment. All students are encouraged to apply for financial aid, even those who assume that they are ineligible for assistance due to family income level. Academic scholarships, which range from $6000 per year to full comprehensive fees, are renewable for four years. The student's application for admission serves as the application for all academic scholarships. More than 95 percent of the College's students receive financial assistance of some kind. The average need-based financial aid package is $19,000. To apply for need-based aid, students are encouraged to submit the Free Application for Federal Student Aid (FAFSA) by March 1. International students are eligible for merit scholarships, which range from $6000 to $15,000 per year.

Faculty

Approximately 92 percent of the full-time teaching faculty members hold a Ph.D. degree or terminal degree. The faculty-student ratio of 1:9 encourages individual rapport between faculty members and students and contributes to the close community that typifies Randolph College. Faculty members are dedicated primarily to teaching, with secondary emphasis on research and publication.

Student Government

The honor system is a vital part of college life and allows students to live and study in an atmosphere of integrity and trust. Each student is a member of the Student Government, which voices student opinion, oversees student activities, and makes policy through the elected representatives. Students serve on almost all College committees.

Admission Requirements

A minimum of 16 academic high school units is recommended and should be distributed as follows: 4 units of English, 3 units of mathematics, 3–4 units of a foreign language, 2 units of laboratory science, 2 units of social studies, and sufficient electives from these areas to make up the recommended total. Because of the flexible nature of the College's curriculum, favorable consideration may be given to students whose high school preparation departs from the recommendations outlined above. Each applicant must have maintained a good academic record and must submit scores on the SAT or ACT. Randolph College readily accepts the Common Application. An online application is available at http://www.RandolphCollege.edu.

Application and Information

Early decision candidates should apply by November 15 of the senior year in secondary school and will receive notification from the College about December 15. Candidates for general admission must apply by March 1 in order to receive preferential consideration; they will receive notification at the time their files are complete, beginning in late January. A $35 application fee must accompany the application for admission, but this fee may be waived in cases of hardship at the request of the student and the recommendation of her high school counselor. Randolph College also participates in the College Board test fee waiver program.

For more information, students should contact:

Director of Admissions
Randolph College
2500 Rivermont Avenue
Lynchburg, Virginia 24503
Phone: 434-947-8100
800-745-7692 (toll-free)
E-mail: admissions@randolphcollege.edu
Web site: http://www.randolphcollege.edu

RANDOLPH-MACON COLLEGE

ASHLAND, VIRGINIA

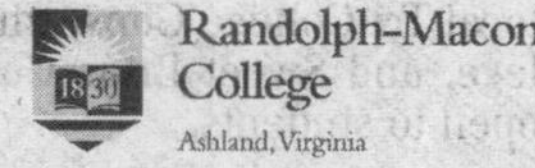

The College

Randolph-Macon is an independent liberal arts college for men and women founded in 1830. With fewer than 1,200 students, the College has deliberately maintained a limited enrollment so that it can give its students the opportunity for dialogue and more personal relationships that only a midsize college can provide. Randolph-Macon is fully accredited by the Southern Association of Colleges and Schools and is historically affiliated with the United Methodist Church.

Students come mostly from Virginia and nearby mid-Atlantic states, but usually about thirty states, the District of Columbia, and fifteen countries are represented in the student body. There is diversity among the students, and an atmosphere of informality and friendliness is evident. Students indicate that they are attracted to the College primarily because of its size, the quality of its academic program, the strong connections between students and faculty, and its supportive, unpretentious atmosphere.

The campus, situated on 110 wooded acres in the town of Ashland, is both convenient and spacious. Most students live in residence halls, fraternity houses, sorority houses, town-house apartments, and special interest houses.

The Frank E. Brown Campus Center provides centralized facilities for a wide variety of student activities, including student government and the literary staffs, and also houses the bookstore, game room, post office, and coffeehouse.

The 73,000-square-foot Brock Sports and Recreation Center contains a field house for badminton, basketball, volleyball, and other activities; a six-lane, 25-yard pool; three racquetball courts; one squash court; a 4,000-square-foot fitness room; an indoor track; an aerobics room; a climbing wall; and a sauna and locker room for students and faculty members.

A performing arts center was recently completed, as was the new Birdsong Peaks of Excellence Center, which includes three central student academic service departments. The Center for Career and Counseling Services offers personal, career, and academic counseling for students. The Bassett Internship Program works individually with students to help them find internship opportunities within their majors. The Higgins Academic Center offers academic tutoring and mentoring, disability support services, a writing center, and a speech center.

Other noteworthy facilities include the McGraw-Page Library; the spacious Estes Dining Hall; the Crenshaw Gymnasium; the Center for Counseling and Career Planning; the Keeble Observatory, with its 12-inch reflecting telescope and 3-meter radio telescope; and several historic buildings, including the beautifully renovated Washington-Franklin Hall.

Location

Ashland, the home of Randolph-Macon for more than a century, is a pleasant residential town with a population of 6,000. Two shopping centers three blocks from campus offer a variety of stores. Daily Amtrak service is available just one block from the edge of campus. Ashland is 15 miles north of Richmond, the capital of Virginia, and 90 miles south of Washington, D.C. This proximity allows access to excellent facilities, such as the Smithsonian Institution, the Library of Congress, the Virginia Museum of Fine Arts, the Virginia State Library, and other educational resources. These nearby cities are also popular sites for the College's fast-growing internship program. Midway between the Atlantic Ocean and the Blue Ridge Mountains, the College also provides students with diverse recreational opportunities.

Majors and Degrees

The B.A. and B.S. degrees are offered in the following fields: accounting, art history, arts management, biology, chemistry, classical studies (Greek and Latin), computer science, drama, economics, economics-business, English, environmental studies, French, German, Greek, history, international studies, Latin, mathematics, music, philosophy, physics, political science, psychology, religious studies, sociology, Spanish, studio art, and women's studies. In addition, students may formally select a minor field from the above areas. Additional minors are offered in Asian studies, black studies, astrophysics, communication studies, elementary and secondary education, and ethics.

The College offers preprofessional studies for such fields as business, dentistry, law, medicine, the ministry, and teaching, as well as preparation for graduate school in other major fields of study. A state-approved teacher education program leads to certification for teaching both in elementary and secondary schools. Dual-degree programs in engineering and forestry enable students to spend the first three years at Randolph-Macon and the final two years at a recognized college of engineering or forestry. In addition, students who follow a prescribed course of study at Randolph-Macon can obtain a master's degree in accounting at Virginia Commonwealth University in one year instead of the usual two years.

Academic Programs

The College offers a liberal arts curriculum that is designed to allow students considerable freedom in planning their own program, while assuring them that they will acquire not only the breadth of knowledge traditionally emphasized in a liberal education but also a sound foundation in a particular field. There is a flexible system of collegiate requirements in English, mathematics, a foreign language, and physical education. In addition, all students take courses in literature, the natural sciences, the social sciences, the fine arts, philosophy or religion, history, computer literacy, and oral communication. In addition, all freshmen participate in the College's innovative interdisciplinary First Year Experience (FYE) Program. The College offers the most comprehensive liberal arts core curriculum of any college in Virginia.

The academic calendar is on the 4-1-4 plan, featuring a one-course term in January. During the January term, students may take special-topic courses, traditional and interdisciplinary courses, and travel-study courses in the United States and abroad, or they may participate in off-campus internships and field-study programs. Internships and other field-study experiences enable students to test classroom theory in practical situations. Internships are offered in Richmond; Washington, D.C.; New York City; and other locations both domestic and abroad. Independent study and senior project options are also available.

Off-Campus Programs

International study opportunities are offered in over forty countries around the world through Randolph-Macon programs and the College's participation in the International Student Exchange Programs (ISEP). The College is a member of a consortium composed of seven private colleges in Virginia. Students may apply to spend a term at one of the other participating institutions, taking advantage of special programs or courses offered at these colleges. The other colleges in the consortium are Washington and Lee, Hampden-Sydney, Mary Baldwin, Hollins, Sweet Briar, and Randolph College.

Academic Facilities

The multimillion-dollar Copley Science Center houses classrooms, study rooms, research and teaching laboratory facilities for all of the sciences, and an expanded computer center, including the technology hub for the College. Technology on campus is supported by a total of twenty-eight servers, 12 miles of fiber-optic cabling, and high-speed connections to all academic buildings, administrative facilities, and student residence halls on campus. In addition, students have access to more than 400 computers in computer centers throughout campus. Most of the academic buildings and residence halls have wireless Internet service. McGraw-Page Library, the College's main library and principal research center, has the capacity for 240,000 volumes, subscribes to more than 1,000 periodicals, and has wireless Internet capability. Open stacks are maintained except in the special collections. The library also provides an audiovisual center, a personal computer lab, and access to computerized information sources, including the Virtual Library of Virginia.

Costs

College fees for 2007–08 totaled $35,010. This includes tuition, fees, and room and board. Students should expect to pay about $1000 per year for books if he or she buys them new. Transportation and personal expenses of up to $1000 should also be anticipated. Members of fraternities and sororities must pay initiation fees as well as monthly dues.

Financial Aid

The College administers a diversified program of scholarships, grants, loans, student employment, and other forms of aid. Financial aid comes from a variety of sources, including federal (Federal Pell Grants, Federal Supplemental Educational Opportunity Grants, Federal Perkins Loans, and Federal Work-Study awards), state, College, and private funds. Academic scholarships of $7500 to $20,000 are offered to outstanding students through the Presidential Scholars Program, and additional grants and scholarships are awarded on the basis of achievement and special talents. However, most financial aid is awarded on the basis of demonstrated need. Applicants should file the Free Application for Federal Student Aid no later than February 1. All Virginia residents attending Randolph-Macon are eligible to receive the Virginia Tuition Assistance Grant (TAG), which was $3200 for 2007–08. There are numerous opportunities for students to work on campus. The Financial Aid Office also provides a student referral service for part-time jobs with employers within walking distance of the College. Inquiries regarding financial aid should be addressed to the director of financial aid.

Faculty

As an undergraduate institution, Randolph-Macon offers students full access to its teaching faculty. Ninety-three percent of the faculty members have earned the doctorate or highest appropriate degree in their field. The student-faculty ratio is 11:1. Almost all professors teach classes at all levels. Thus, a freshman is as likely as a senior to encounter the most distinguished and experienced members of the faculty.

Student Government

At Randolph-Macon the principal governing and coordinating agency for students is the Student Government Association (SGA). It represents student interests on College committees that deal with the curriculum, academic policies, orientation, and college life. In addition, the SGA charters and allocates funds for student organizations and activities. Together with the Committee on Assemblies and Special Events, SGA plans and sponsors social, cultural, and educational events throughout the year for the entire College community.

Admission Requirements

The Admissions Committee places primary emphasis on the applicant's secondary school record, scores on the SAT or the ACT, the secondary school counselor's recommendation, personal characteristics, and evidence of leadership and involvement in extracurricular activities. Students who take the ACT are encouraged to take the writing section.

The College does not discriminate on the basis of ethnicity, gender, disability, sexual orientation, or age in its admissions, financial aid, athletics, employment, or educational programs.

Application and Information

Applications should be received by March 1. Applications received after that date are considered as long as space is available. Students who have applied by March 1 are informed of the admission decision no later than April 1. The College also offers a nonbinding Early Action Plan with an application deadline of November 15 and an admission notification of January 1. Students may apply online at the College's Web site, or they can apply using the Common Application. For more information, prospective students should contact:

Dean of Admissions
Randolph-Macon College
P.O. Box 5005
Ashland, Virginia 23005-5005
Phone: 804-752-7305
800-888-1762 (toll-free)
E-mail: admissions@rmc.edu
Web site: http://www.rmc.edu

Randolph-Macon's 110-acre campus has been planned to complement the educational program and enhance student life.

ROANOKE COLLEGE

SALEM, VIRGINIA

The College

Roanoke College, the country's second-oldest Lutheran-related college, is an independent, coeducational, four-year liberal arts college. Located in Salem, Virginia, just a few miles from the Appalachian Trail, the College offers a picturesque and safe historic campus for 2,000 students from around the country and around the world. Roanoke College is accredited by the Commission on Colleges of the Southern Association of Colleges and Schools and is affiliated with the Evangelical Lutheran Church in America.

Roanoke College was founded as the Virginia Institute in 1842 in Staunton by two Lutheran pastors as a preparatory school for boys who wished to enroll in Gettysburg College and, hopefully, the seminary. In 1845, the school was moved to its current home in Salem, and in 1853 it was renamed Roanoke College.

Today, Roanoke College is a center of learning offering programs in the arts, science, and business as well as a number of preprofessional programs. *Princeton Review* names it as "one of the best in the Southeast." *U.S. News & World Report* named Roanoke among the top 10 regional liberal arts colleges in the South in its annual Best Colleges Guide and places it in the competitive Best National Liberal Arts Colleges category. Also, the College was ranked the "nineteenth fittest college in America" by *Men's Fitness* magazine.

Approximately 2,000 students are enrolled in Roanoke College each year. Sixty percent come from Virginia, and the other 40 percent represent forty-one other states and twenty-two foreign countries. Two thirds of all students live on campus, ensuring that campus life is robust. More than 100 clubs and organizations, including fraternities and sororities and a variety of ethnic and religious organizations, operate on campus. Community service and campus ministry are vital to campus life. During freshman orientation, students work together to construct a Habitat for Humanity house that is built on campus, then moved across town where it is presented to its recipient. The Dean of the Chapel is an ordained Lutheran pastor who directs a variety of religious life programs, including weekly worship, Bible studies, and fellowship activities. Although the College is associated with the Evangelical Lutheran Church in America, more than a dozen religious and ethnic groups are represented on campus.

The Colket Center, the community hub of the college, serves students, faculty, staff, alumni, and guests. The Colket Center sponsors late-night programming, such as open mic nights, box office hit movie showings, and student performances, as well as billiards, Ping Pong, and air hockey tournaments.

Roanoke has excellent facilities to support every phase of a well-rounded athletic program. The brand-new Donald J. Kerr Stadium, home to men's and women's soccer, field hockey, and men's and women's lacrosse, features all-weather artificial turf, seating for approximately 1,000, and nonglare lights. There are an additional six athletic fields, an all-weather track, and tennis courts. The physical education and recreation center includes two basketball courts, a state-of-the-art fitness center, classrooms, an athletic training room, offices, and locker rooms.

The College is a member of the NCAA Division III and the Old Dominion Athletic Conference. Men compete in baseball, basketball, cross-country, golf, lacrosse, soccer, tennis, and indoor and outdoor track and field. Women's varsity sports include basketball, cross-country, field hockey, lacrosse, soccer, softball, tennis, indoor and outdoor track and field, and volleyball. In addition, the College has twelve intramural programs and an extensive outdoor adventures program.

Location

Located in the Roanoke Valley of southwest Virginia, between the scenic Allegheny and Blue Ridge Mountains, the area is home to approximately 250,000 people. The Roanoke Valley serves as the region's cultural, economic, education, and entertainment center. Roanoke College resides in the small city of Salem, which has several community parks, tennis courts, and golf courses. Nearby, Jefferson National Forest and the Appalachian Trail provide excellent opportunities for outdoor recreation. Salem Civic Center hosts concerts and spectator sports. A variety of festivals are held throughout the year, including Olde Salem Days, which includes one of the largest antique cars shows on the East Coast, and Floydfest, a world music and arts festival. The Center in the Square, 8 miles away in downtown Roanoke, houses numerous art museums. Other attractions include the Virginia Museum of Transportation and Mill Mountain Zoo. Salem is just a few hours' drive from Richmond or Washington, D.C. From Roanoke Regional Airport, New York, Atlanta, and Charlotte are less than an hour's flight.

Majors and Degrees

Bachelor of Arts degrees are available in art, art history, biology, chemistry, criminal justice, economics, English, environmental policy, French, history, international relations, music, philosophy, physics, political science, psychology, religion, sociology, Spanish, theater, and theology.

Bachelor of Science degrees are available in athletic training, biochemistry, biology, chemistry, computer information systems, computer science, environmental science, health and human performance, mathematics, medical technology, physics, and psychology.

Students interested in business can earn a Bachelor of Business Administration degree.

Students may also enroll in preprofessional programs in engineering, the health professions, law, and ministry.

Academic Programs

To earn a bachelor's degree, students must pass a minimum of 33 academic units, including general education requirements, courses in the student's major program of study, at least one intensive-learning experience, two ¼-unit physical education activities, one ¼-unit cocurricular requirement, and elective courses. A minimum GPA of 2.0 is required to complete the degree.

The academic year is divided into three semesters. The fall term begins in late August and ends in early December. Following a four-week winter break, the spring term begins in mid-January and ends in mid-April. A three-week Intensive Learning Term takes place in May, and is intended for students to take a single, nontraditional course such as Tropical Marine Biology, History of Hawaii, or Forensic Chemistry. Many courses involve domestic or international travel. This is followed by two summer sessions, one in June and one in July.

The general education requirements include 2 units in critical writing and reading; 2 units in the humanities; 1 unit in values; 2 units in foreign languages; 3 units in mathematics, science, and computer science; 3 units in scientific reasoning; 2 units in social sciences; a course in health and human performance; and a symposium to be taken during the senior year. The major requirements vary from program to program. In addition, students may elect a minor program of study, a second major, or an area of concentration.

Off-Campus Programs

The Summer Scholar Program enables students to conduct independent research for 8 to 12 weeks during the summer. Each student works with a faculty mentor and presents finished work through oral presentations, poster sessions, and research exhibits. A one-semester program in Washington, D.C., through the Lutheran College Washington Consortium, allows students to live and work in the nation's capital, completing an internship in a field of interest to the student, whether in government, nonprofit, or the arts.

More than ten study-abroad programs allow students to earn academic credit while pursuing summer, semester, or academic-year opportunities outside the U.S. Programs are available at prestigious universities in Canada, China, England, Italy, Japan, Northern Ireland, and Norway. Through the Virginia Summer Program at Oxford University in England, students may spend six weeks studying literature and history with Oxford dons. Even the Intensive Learning Program in May offers highly focused study-abroad programs in cities like Athens, Florence, Kyoto, Lima, Madrid, and Paris.

Academic Facilities

The Fintel Library has a collection containing over 218,000 volumes, 710 journal subscriptions, and 326,200 microfilm/fiche, DVD, VHS, and audiovisual items. In addition, the library has access to more than 23,000 full-text and online periodicals and newspapers. More than 3,000 new items are added to the library's collection annually. In addition, the library houses the Roanoke College Archives as well as historical records relating to the College. Roanoke is a selective depository library for United States government documents.

Eleven computer labs comprise a total of 178 workstations, all equipped with Microsoft Office, Mathematica, Minitab, SPSS, Microcase, and Netscape. Linux is available on fifty workstations in Trexler Hall.

Costs

In 2007–08, full-time tuition was $25,550 per academic year. Students living on campus expected to spend $4076 per year for room and $4650 for a nineteen-meal dining plan. Other mandatory fees included a student activity fee of $250, a technology fee of $450, a telecommunications fee of $250, and an orientation fee of $125. Depending on their circumstances, students also expected to spend approximately $1000 per year on books and supplies, $1250 for transportation, and $1000 on miscellaneous costs.

Financial Aid

Roanoke College makes every effort to see that no student is denied an opportunity to attend because of financial circumstances. Eighty-five percent of full-time students receive financial assistance of some kind, with an average award of $20,200. In order to be considered for financial assistance, students must submit the Free Application for Federal Student Aid (FAFSA) to the financial aid office.

Incoming freshmen are eligible for a number of scholarships, ranging from $1000 to full tuition plus room and board. Other scholarships may be available from private sources. The Virginia Tuition Assistance Grant (VTAG) Program awards grants to Virginia residents who are enrolled full-time in a participating Virginia private college or university. Assistance is also available in the form of loans and part-time employment. Students may borrow up to $23,000 under the Stafford Loan Program or up to $1500 annually under the Federal Perkins Loan Program. Other loans may be available through the Roanoke College Student Loan Fund or from private lenders. Under the Federal Work-Study Program, students may earn money by working up to 20 hours per week, either on or off campus.

Faculty

About 120 tenured professors teach at the College; 95 percent of these professors hold the highest degrees in their fields. Students consider the faculty to be open to questions in class, giving them a 4.6 rating on a 1–5 scale in one survey. The large number of faculty members means that class sizes are small. Class sizes range from 3 to 41 students, with an average class size of 18 and a student-faculty ratio of 14:1.

Student Government

Participation in the Student Government Association helps students develop the discipline and sound judgment necessary to put education to the wisest possible use. Responsibility for certain areas of campus life is delegated to the students by the President of the College. As a result, students serve on numerous bodies involved in college life, academic integrity, student conduct, and resources and planning.

The Executive Committee consists of a president, vice president, secretary, and treasurer. The president of the student body is invited as a student observer to meetings of the Board of Trustees and of the faculty. Each class also elects a president, vice president, and secretary/treasurer, and 2 students serve as commuter representatives.

Admission Requirements

Because of the College's challenging liberal arts and sciences curriculum, prospective students must have substantial preparation in a broad range of academic subjects, including English, social studies, foreign languages, mathematics, and laboratory sciences. While the Admissions Committee places primary emphasis on the applicant's secondary school record, other factors, such as SAT or ACT scores, class rank, and courses taken are considered. More than 90 percent of accepted students rank in the upper half of their graduating class.

When applying for admission, prospective students must submit a completed application form, an official copy of their high school transcripts, official results of either the SAT or the ACT, and the $33 application fee. A visit to the College is strongly recommended; visitors are able to talk with a member of the admissions staff, tour the campus with a student guide, attend classes, and dine in the Commons as guests of the College.

Application and Information

Applications are accepted throughout the fall on a rolling basis. Students who wish to apply early decision must submit their applications by December 1; they are notified of the College's decision by December 15. All other students must apply before November 15 and are notified of a decision within one month of applying.

Requests for applications and all other inquiries may be sent to:

Office of Admissions
Roanoke College
221 College Lane
Salem, Virginia 24153-3794
Phone: 800-388-2276 (toll-free)
Fax: 540-375-2267
E-mail: admissions@roanoke.edu
Web site: http://www.roanoke.edu

On the campus at Roanoke College.

COLLEGE DATA CENTER • VIRGINIA

SHENANDOAH UNIVERSITY

WINCHESTER, VIRGINIA

The University

Shenandoah University was founded at Dayton, Virginia, in 1875. Although the institution was established to provide "classical" and music studies, by 1888 an unusual blend of educational opportunities had been formulated that included arts, sciences, music, medical arts, and business management. These programs, on a much more sophisticated basis, are found at Shenandoah today. In 1960, Shenandoah moved to a 62-acre campus in Winchester, Virginia. The main campus now covers more than 100 acres, with nineteen buildings, including six residence halls. Of these six facilities for boarding students, one is for women and five are coeducational. There are five additional buildings at off-campus locations. Shenandoah's historical relationship with the United Methodist Church does not place sectarian obligations on any student.

Shenandoah's students have the distinct advantage of being on a small campus near large metropolitan cultural centers. Such student organizations as academic fraternities, service and honor organizations, and various departmental clubs provide opportunities for leadership and recreation. Students come to Shenandoah because they want an educational experience of superior quality and believe that the facilities of a small campus, with a personal atmosphere, are the most conducive to achieving this experience. Fifty-one percent of the 3,000 students are from Virginia; the remaining 49 percent represent forty-five states and forty-one countries.

Graduate study is also available at Shenandoah. Programs are offered in athletic training, business administration, dance, education, music, nursing, occupational therapy, pharmacy, physical therapy, and physician assistant studies. Further information about graduate study may be obtained by writing to the Dean of Admissions.

Shenandoah University is accredited by the Commission on Colleges of the Southern Association of Colleges and Schools (1866 Southern Lane, Decatur, Georgia 30033-4097; phone: 404-679-4501) to award associate, bachelor's, master's, and doctoral degrees. Shenandoah holds membership in a number of professional organizations.

Location

The Shenandoah campus, which is adjacent to Interstate 81, is located 72 miles west of Washington, D.C., in the historic Shenandoah Valley of Virginia. The University is located on the southeast edge of the city of Winchester, Virginia. Winchester/Frederick County, rich in history, is a vigorous community of approximately 70,000 people. The region has a moderate, healthful climate; cultural groups; park and recreation areas; resorts; fishing; hunting; winter sports; modern retail centers; and major medical facilities.

Majors and Degrees

Shenandoah University offers seven undergraduate degrees: the Bachelor of Arts, the Bachelor of Business Administration, the Bachelor of Fine Arts, the Bachelor of Music, the Bachelor of Music Therapy, the Bachelor of Science, and the Associate in Science and several certificate programs. Programs of study that are available include administration of justice, arts management (dance, music, and theater), arts studies, athletic training, biology, business education, business administration (accounting, banking and finance, information systems and computer technology, international business, management, and marketing), business studies, chemistry, Christian leadership, church music, commercial music, composition, dance, dance education, educational psychology, elementary education, English, environmental studies, health-care management, history, information systems and computer technology, jazz studies, kinesiology (exercise science, physical education and health, and sports administration), mass communications, mathematics, middle school education, music education, music theater, music theater accompanying, music therapy, music with elective studies, nursing (LPN to B.S.N. and RN to B.S.N.), pedagogy (guitar or piano), performance (opera and pedagogy), piano accompanying, professional studies/teacher education, psychology, public administration/political science, purchasing management, religion, respiratory care (both two- and four-year degree programs), secondary education, sociology, Spanish, Spanish interpreting, teaching English to speakers of other languages, theater (acting, costume design, directing, and scenic and lighting design), theater for youth, university studies, and women's studies. Selected programs of study may result in double majors for students who wish to concentrate on more than one area of study. Preprofessional programs of study are available in athletic training, dentistry, law, medicine, occupational therapy, pharmacy, physical therapy, physician assistant studies, and veterinary medicine.

Academic Programs

Shenandoah's academic calendar is divided into fall and spring semesters. Summer terms, ranging in length from two to eleven weeks, are also available. Each academic division (arts and sciences, business, conservatory, and health professions) offers diversified programs, with specific courses required by the various accreditation agencies. Credit is available through the tests of the College-Level Examination Program (CLEP), Proficiency Examination Program (PEP), Advanced Placement (AP) program, and International Baccalaureate and through various departmental challenge examinations.

Off-Campus Programs

Clinical practice, internships, and student-teaching opportunities are arranged with local businesses, hospitals, clinics, nursing homes, mental-health-care centers, and elementary, middle, and secondary schools in the Winchester area. Students are given the opportunity to enrich their educational experience through travel and study-abroad programs.

Academic Facilities

Three new facilities, the Brandt Student Center, Halpin-Harrison Hall (the new home of the Harry F. Byrd, Jr. School of Business), and the History and Tourism Center, are scheduled to be added in the 2007–08 academic year. The Alson H. Smith, Jr. Library contains approximately 123,000 volumes, 134,169 microforms, 17,823 records and CDs, and 16,200 music scores and subscribes to 1,150 periodicals. The media center contains visual and audio materials and equipment and preview and listening rooms. The Gregory Building contains laboratories for biology, chemistry, environmental studies, modern languages, and physics; a digital radio station; and multimedia classrooms. A digital television station is on campus. Henkel Hall contains a 200-seat lecture hall, a student computer laboratory, and a teaching computer laboratory for business and arts and sciences students. The Health Professions Building contains a health professions library, computer laboratories, multimedia classrooms, research laboratories, and interactive video and computer laboratories that simulate clinical practice realities for nursing, pharmacy, and respiratory-care students. Physician assistant studies program facilities include laboratories and multimedia classrooms. The Cork Street Center contains multimedia classrooms, computer laboratories, the Center for Clinical Research, and the Clinical Skills Laboratory for occupational therapy and physical therapy students. Conservatory facilities include the Ohrstrom-Bryant Theatre, which seats 632 people and includes a scene shop, a costume shop, and the Glaize Studio Theatre; Goodson Chapel–Recital Hall, with a Möller tracker-action organ; Ruebush Hall, with a fully equipped twenty-four-track professional recording studio, practice rooms, and music education and music therapy laboratories; the Shingleton Building, with two dance studios; and Armstrong Hall, with a 700-seat concert hall. The Shingleton Building contains a gymnasium, a fitness room, and athletic training laboratories. Athletic facilities include practice fields, Aikens Stadium, and the new 2,500-seat Shentel Stadium. The Athletic Center contains a weight room and athletic training laboratories.

The Shenandoah University Network (SUnet) structure provides a high-speed fiber backbone that supports numerous networked Windows and Macintosh workstations. The campus has four IBM-platform labs and a Macintosh-platform lab for general use. All workstations in the labs have full Internet and e-mail access, and all Shenandoah University students have Internet and e-mail accounts. Wireless Internet access is available in some buildings and will be expanded to the entire campus. The campus is also equipped with e-mail stations. Remote access is available for faculty, staff, and student use.

Costs

The 2007–08 comprehensive annual fee (two semesters) for resident full-time undergraduate students was $29,690, which included tuition and room and board. The comprehensive annual tuition (two semesters) for commuting (day) full-time undergraduate students was $21,090. Undergraduate part-time tuition was $610 per credit hour. Private applied music lessons for music students cost an additional $500 per year for major study (1 hour per week) and $250 per year for minor study (½ hour per week). Such incidentals as transportation, personal expenses, and laundry vary in cost; textbook costs, however, can be estimated at $1000 per year. There is no difference in the cost of tuition and fees for out-of-state students. The Board of Trustees reserves the right to alter charges at any time.

Financial Aid

Shenandoah makes every effort to assist students in finding resources to finance their education. Approximately 91 percent of the University's students receive some type of financial aid. Shenandoah annually awards more than $28 million in aid to students in the form of grants, loans, scholarships, and employment on the campus. Previous financial aid packages have averaged approximately $14,000 per undergraduate student per year. To qualify for scholarships and financial aid, students must submit the Free Application for Federal Student Aid (FAFSA). Aid is awarded on a first-come, first-served basis, as funds are available. A student must be accepted for admission to a degree program before a financial aid offer is made. Specific information regarding financial aid should be requested from the Director of Financial Aid.

Faculty

Shenandoah has 212 full-time faculty members and 199 part-time faculty members. The faculty-student ratio is approximately 1:8. The size of the student body encourages excellent communication and rapport among students and faculty members. Members of the faculty advise students and plan activities that concern the student body as a whole. Shenandoah faculty members have a strong commitment to teaching and counseling students.

Student Government

The Student Government Association (SGA) is the main student organization on campus. In addition to promoting activities of varied interest, the SGA provides a means of communication and understanding among students, faculty members, and administrators. Students are encouraged to participate in the governing of Shenandoah and are represented on all faculty and administrative committees.

Admission Requirements

Admission to Shenandoah is competitive; applicants are selected based on their likelihood of being successful in the university environment. Applicants are evaluated on the basis of their high school record, SAT or ACT scores, recommendations, and extracurricular activities. Students applying for degree programs in music, dance, or theater must successfully complete an audition or portfolio interview. Shenandoah does not discriminate on the basis of sex, race, color, religion, national or ethnic origin, age, or physical disability. Although interviews are not required, students are encouraged to visit the campus.

Application and Information

To apply, a student must submit an application with a $30 nonrefundable application fee, SAT or ACT scores, and an official high school transcript. Transfer students must submit an official college transcript for all postsecondary course work in addition to meeting the freshman score and transcript requirements. Applicants are notified of the admission decision after receipt of all credentials. An application, financial aid information, and other materials may be obtained by contacting:

Dean of Admissions
Shenandoah University
1460 University Drive
Winchester, Virginia 22601
Phone: 540-665-4581
800-432-2266 (toll-free)
Fax: 540-665-4627
E-mail: admit@su.edu

SOUTHERN VIRGINIA UNIVERSITY

BUENA VISTA, VIRGINIA

The University

Southern Virginia University (SVU) is a private, nonprofit, coeducational four-year university operated by a board of trustees predominantly made up of members of the Church of Jesus Christ of Latter-day Saints (LDS). Although SVU is not owned or operated by the Church, its primary purpose is to provide a high-quality education in an environment that is supportive of LDS values and standards.

Southern Virginia University began in 1867 as Bowling Green Female Seminary, an institution of higher education for women. (At that time, a seminary often referred to an institution of secondary or higher education.) In 1894, the school moved to a resort hotel in Buena Vista and changed its name to Southern Seminary. The hotel, which was built in 1890, is now Main Hall and is listed on the National Register as a National Historic Landmark. From 1922 to 1996, the school operated as a junior college, until declining enrollment and financial instability threatened to close its doors. In 1996, a group of Latter-day Saint educators and business leaders assumed responsibility for the college, converting it into a four-year liberal arts college. That fall, the new Southern Virginia College enrolled 74 students. It has since grown dramatically, enrolling 700 students in fall 2007. In 2001, the name was changed to Southern Virginia University to reflect growth of the curriculum and the rapidly increasing size of the student body.

Southern Virginia University offers thirteen majors and seventeen minors and is fully accredited by the American Academy for Liberal Education. There are twenty-one intercollegiate sports, a student government association, a student orchestra, a chamber choir, a theater guild, and other various campus groups and activities. SVU's intercollegiate sports include men's and women's basketball, cheerleading, cross-country, golf, lacrosse (club), soccer, tennis (club), and track and field; men's baseball, football, and wrestling; and women's softball and volleyball. The Church of Jesus Christ of Latter-day Saints operates an Institute of Religion on campus and five student wards.

Location

Buena Vista, Virginia, a town of nearly 7,000 residents, is located by the scenic Blue Ridge Mountains in the heart of the Shenandoah Valley. Buena Vista is close to Interstate 81 and is approximately 6 miles east of historic Lexington, a popular tourist destination. Nearby cities include Roanoke (50 miles south), Charlottesville (55 miles northeast), and Washington, D.C. (165 miles northeast). Air service to SVU is available from the Roanoke Airport, which is less than an hour's drive from Buena Vista.

The Blue Ridge Parkway, Appalachian Trail, and Blue Ridge Mountains offer many opportunities for hiking, skiing, biking, camping, and other outdoor activities. Many American historical sites are also nearby, including Monticello, Appomattox, Williamsburg, and Yorktown. The Virginia Military Institute and Washington and Lee University, which are located in the neighboring town of Lexington, offer many additional services to students.

Majors and Degrees

The State Council of Higher Education for Virginia (SCHEV) has granted Southern Virginia University approval to confer Bachelor of Arts degrees. SVU offers majors in the following areas: art, biology, business management and leadership, computer science, English, family and child development, history, liberal arts, music, philosophy, politics, Spanish, and theater.

Academic Programs

To be eligible for a baccalaureate degree, students must complete a minimum of 120 credit hours of study; at least 60 of the credit hours or at least the last two full-time semesters before graduation must be completed at SVU. No more than 9 credit hours are granted for internship courses. In addition, students must complete all general education requirements (typically 61 hours), a minimum of 36 credit hours in upper-division (300- and 400-level) courses, and all the requirements of at least one major. Students must earn a minimum grade point average of 2.0 on all course work taken at the University, and they must comply with all University standards, regulations, and procedures from the date of matriculation through the date of final graduation.

The academic year consists of two semesters (fall, August to December; spring, January to April) and one term each in May and June.

Academic Facilities

The Von Canon Library offers students access to a collection of 123,000 titles, 18,200 periodicals, 4,800 reference materials, 4,000 audiovisual materials, and an on-campus computer lab. Durham Hall is the main academic building on campus, housing biology, chemistry, and geology lecture rooms and labs on the lower level. Classrooms for the social sciences, math, English, and business are located throughout the building, as are faculty offices. Other academic buildings include Landrum House, Chandler Hall, Tucson Art Building, the Knight Sports Arena, Main Hall, and the Student Union Building.

Costs

Southern Virginia University is a private, nonprofit institution. Tuition and other fees are maintained at a minimum consistent with high academic standards and efficiency of operation. The basic expenses for a full-time student for the 2007–08 academic year (excluding summer school) were $16,500 for tuition and fees and $4900 for room and board (breakfast, lunch, and dinner).

Financial Aid

Through its financial aid program, Southern Virginia University attempts to keep education costs as affordable as possible by providing assistance to many students through various scholarships and grants. SVU facilitates financing of educational expenses by offering financial aid from four general sources: federal, state, private, and institutional. A financial aid package often includes more than one type of aid.

To ensure that every student receives the maximum assistance for which they are eligible, every student is encouraged to complete the Free Application for Federal Student Aid (FAFSA) (http://www.fafsa.ed.gov). The U.S. Department of Education uses a standard formula, which was established by Congress, to evaluate the information reported on the FAFSA to determine a student's eligibility.

SVU offers a number of institutional scholarships, grants, and employment opportunities to both incoming and returning students. Scholarships and grants are awarded only to full-time students and are applicable only to tuition. Students may receive additional funds from federal, state, and private sources other than SVU. Most SVU scholarships and grants are awarded for an academic year (meaning that they are good for both the fall and spring semesters) and are awarded half in the fall and half in the spring, unless otherwise stipulated. Institutional work-study and tuition installment plans are also offered by the University to assist in financing educational expenses.

Faculty

Eighty percent of all full-time faculty members at SVU hold terminal degrees in their fields of study. Including part-time professors, the SVU faculty is made up of 69 professors. With a student-faculty ratio of 16:1, SVU offers an interactive course setting where faculty members and students have a close mentor relationship. Faculty members also serve as academic advisers to all students enrolled.

Student Government

The SVU Student Association (SVUSA) provides students with a means to carry out programs, activities, and events that enhance student life and promote within students the qualities of service, integrity, leadership, academic excellence, fellowship, and moral conduct. Student leaders are elected by students and are advised through the Office of the Dean of Students. SVUSA also acts as a mediator and advocate with the administration for student needs.

Admission Requirements

Each applicant is evaluated individually on academic performance, ACT or SAT scores, class rank, extracurricular activities, demonstrated leadership, exemplary standards of conduct, maturity, service, and a commitment to the pursuit of a college degree. An applicant's high school course of study should include at least 14 units of core academic classes in English, foreign language, mathematics, science, social science, and history and at least 4 units of elective classes. Although the University does not require specific courses for admission, successful applicants usually have completed at least 4 years of English, 2 years of foreign language, 2 years of college-preparatory mathematics, 2 years of laboratory science, and elective credits in subjects such as art, music, drama, and physical education. Transfer students with fewer than 24 semester credit hours are evaluated according to the same admission criteria used for incoming freshmen, except that their college transcripts are also considered. Transfer students with 24 semester credit hours or more are evaluated academically according to their previous college work. Transfer students should have at least a 2.0 GPA for all previous college work.

Application and Information

A complete application consists of an official application form returned with a nonrefundable application fee of $35, official transcripts of completed high school course work, official SAT or ACT results, and an ecclesiastical endorsement from a bishop or branch president for LDS applicants or a clergyman or other spiritual leader for applicants of other faiths. As part of the application, students must pledge to abide by the Principles of Honor and Conduct, which include standards of honesty, conduct, dress, and grooming. Visits to the campus are always welcomed.

For more information, students should contact:

Office of Admissions
Southern Virginia University
One University Hill Drive
Buena Vista, Virginia 24416
Phone: 540-261-8421
800-229-8420 (toll-free)
Fax: 540-261-8559
E-mail: admissions@svu.edu
Web site: http://www.svu.edu

STRATFORD UNIVERSITY

FALLS CHURCH AND WOODBRIDGE, VIRGINIA

The University

Stratford University was founded in 1976 and has undergone constant changes as it has continued to expand and adapt to changing employer demands. Stratford is a small, private institution with a personalized approach to student needs. The Stratford community includes two campuses in northern Virginia just a short distance from Washington, D.C. The Stratford philosophy is to provide professional competencies that satisfy employer needs, utilizing a teaching method that accommodates a variety of different learning styles.

Stratford enrolls more than 1,500 students in its programs, offering small classes to ensure personal attention to each student. Stratford students represent a diverse population, from recent high school graduates to adult learners seeking to make a career change. The friendly and supportive environment at Stratford University ensures that students feel comfortable and well supported.

The University offers programs in technology, business, allied health, hospitality, and culinary arts at both the undergraduate and graduate levels. The University is located in the heart of Fairfax County, Virginia, home of the Internet and numerous businesses that support the Internet, telecommunications, and information. User groups, national societies, and various technology councils provide networking avenues for Stratford students. Hospitality-related businesses abound in the Washington area, from world-class restaurants to boutique hotels; career opportunities are numerous. In addition, the business of government provides varied career paths for Stratford graduates.

The University provides a full array of career development and placement services. Students attend workshops on academic planning, resume writing, and effective interviewing skills. Career Services strives to help students make the contacts that lead to internships or permanent positions.

Stratford University partners with Collegiate Housing Services to offer comfortable and affordable dormitory-style apartments near both campuses. The typical housing configuration is a furnished, two-bedroom, two-bathroom apartment shared by up to 4 Stratford students of the same gender.

Location

Stratford University has two campuses in the greater Washington, D.C., region. Washington has much to offer. From politics to urban events, culture to recreation, the capital region is a great place to live, work, and study. Local sights include Mount Vernon, Old Town Alexandria, the White House, Capitol Hill, the Mall, and the Smithsonian Institute. Most of the sights are easily accessible by public transportation.

The prosperous D.C. job market is a draw for Stratford students. For both working students looking to upgrade skills and full-time students concerned with finding a job quickly after graduation, the region offers a wealth of jobs for graduates of all of Stratford's programs. As the nation's capital and a major tourist center, the metropolitan Washington area is a center for business, finance, industry, and entertainment.

Majors and Degrees

The School of Business Administration offers Associate of Applied Science (A.A.S.) and Bachelor of Science (B.S.) degrees in business administration. The School of Computer Information Systems offers A.A.S. degrees in digital design and in network management and security and a B.S. degree in information technology. The School of Culinary Arts and Hospitality confers A.A.S. degrees in advanced culinary arts, baking and pastry arts, and hotel and restaurant management; and a B.A. degree in hospitality management. The School of Allied Health confers an A.A.S. degree in allied health with a concentration in medical assisting. The business administration, hotel and restaurant management, and hospitality management programs are also offered online.

Academic Programs

Stratford University delivers competency-based educational programs that prepare individuals for employment in specific career areas. These competencies are employer centered. The curriculum in each program is designed to ensure that students have the required competencies demanded in their fields of endeavor. The instructional techniques at Stratford are student centered. At the beginning of each program, students are tested for both learning styles and learning modes, and instruction in all classes is individualized based on the results of this assessment. This dual emphasis results in student academic success, without lowering required employer-based standards. As a result, students who graduate enjoy a high placement rate.

The A.A.S. and the B.S. degree programs include core requirements, elective requirements, and general education requirements. The total requirement is 90 quarter credits for the A.A.S. programs, and they normally take sixty weeks to complete. The total requirement for the B.S. degree programs is 180 quarter credits. The first 90 quarter credits are completed prior to beginning the 90 credits of junior- or senior-level courses. The B.S. programs take 120 weeks to complete.

The diploma programs include core and elective requirements. The total requirement for these programs is 60 quarter credits, and they normally take fifty weeks to complete.

Students may receive transfer credit for courses transferred from accredited institutions. Also, certain training received from prior military schools, military service, or prior work experiences may be awarded as transfer credit. Stratford is approved for the training of veterans.

The course calendar is divided into five sessions, each of which is ten weeks in length. With start dates in January, March, May, August, and October, Stratford's flexible scheduling accommodates its busy students.

Academic Facilities

Stratford's libraries are located at the Falls Church and Woodbridge campuses, but all 2,400 titles are available online. In addition, the library subscribes to OCLC FirstSearch, a collection of more than 50 databases, and EBSCO Research Host database.

The campus has state-of-the-art facilities equipped with the latest technology and resources. All information systems classrooms are equipped with one computer for every student, and Stratford's networking students work with state-of-the-art Cisco routers and switches. Students may also access one of several computers for general use in the library. Culinary arts students are trained in one of six fully equipped professional kitchens.

Costs

Tuition is $325 per credit hour plus laboratory fees where applicable.

Financial Aid

Financial aid officers at Stratford are trained to guide students through the financial aid process to ensure that all available financial aid has been explored. Federal loans and grants (including PLUS, PELL, FSEOG, FWS) are applicable toward tuition at Stratford. The University is also approved for Veterans Association benefits, Vocational Rehabilitation benefits, and private institutional financing.

Stratford offers the Graduating High School Senior Scholarship Program and the Culinary Scholarship Programs. Stratford University also accepts private scholarships from foundations, service clubs, and other organizations.

Faculty

Stratford University's faculty members have been hand-chosen for their teaching ability, personality traits, and experience in their fields. The entire Stratford University staff works as a team to help students succeed.

Admission Requirements

Graduation from a secondary school or equivalent education as certified by the state department of education is normally required for admission.

Stratford is approved to offer I-20 certification for F1 visas for international students. Students for whom English is a second language are required to demonstrate English proficiency through a TOEFL score.

Application and Information

Students must submit a completed application for admission and a $50 nonrefundable application fee. Applicants must also schedule an interview with admissions to complete the assessment instrument. Students may bring or have the registrar from their high school, college, or state GED office forward a copy of their transcripts to Stratford University. Student-issued copies of transcripts or diplomas can be submitted directly to the University.

Students interested in applying should contact:

Stratford University
7777 Leesburg Pike
Falls Church, Virginia 22043
Phone: 703-821-8570
800-444-0804 (toll-free)
Fax: 703-734-5339

Stratford University
13576 Minnieville Road
Woodbridge, Virginia 22192
Phone: 703-897-1982
888-546-1250 (toll-free)
E-mail: admissions@stratford.edu
Web site: http://www.stratford.edu

SWEET BRIAR COLLEGE

SWEET BRIAR, VIRGINIA

The College

Deeply committed to the education of women since its founding in 1901, Sweet Briar College is consistently ranked as one of the top national liberal arts and sciences colleges in the country. Its excellent academic reputation, beautiful campus, and attention to the individual attract ambitious, intellectually self-confident women who want to excel. Students can expect their Sweet Briar experience to allow them to fulfill their promise as scholars and leaders, while enjoying the close-knit friendships and camaraderie that come with a personal, residential community.

A Sweet Briar education sets in motion the conviction that any goal is achievable. Small classes (averaging 12 students per class) and a student-faculty ratio of 9:1 ensure personal attention and academic interaction. Students work one-on-one with faculty members who are committed to each student's academic success. The College has a wide geographic, ethnic, and socioeconomic representation. About 675 women from more than forty states and nineteen countries are enrolled at Sweet Briar's Virginia campus; another 130 students are enrolled in Sweet Briar's coed Junior Year in France and Junior Year in Spain programs. Any student may have a car.

Students who derive the most from the Sweet Briar experience are those who participate in and contribute to community life, striking a good balance between academic work and the rest of life. They recognize that one of the advantages of the College is the unlimited opportunities for women to participate and assume leadership roles in many types of organizations and activities. More than fifty campus organizations are available, including honor societies, a literary journal, community service groups, a multicultural club, political groups, a student newspaper, drama and dance clubs, a radio station, and singing groups. Students plan and participate in an extensive array of concerts, films, and dance and theater productions as well as workshops and master classes by visiting scholars and performers. Recent speakers on campus include the author Salman Rushdie, environmental attorney Robert F. Kennedy Jr., Olympic swimmer Maddy Crippen, *USA Today* sports columnist Christine Brennan, and civil rights pioneer Elaine Jones.

Twenty-one campus buildings, the work of renowned American architect Ralph Adams Cram, are on the National Register of Historic Places. In 2006, Sweet Briar opened a beautiful new studio arts facility. Sweet Briar is the only college in the United States with a residential artists' colony on its campus. Known as the Virginia Center for the Creative Arts, the colony is a working retreat for international writers, visual artists, and composers. The on-campus equestrian center, one of the largest and best college facilities in the country, attracts both competitive and recreational riders. Sweet Briar's equestrian program, both competitive and instructional, has consistently garnered national recognition. The 100-acre Rogers Riding Center has a 120-foot by 300-foot indoor arena with Perma-Flex footing, well-appointed stables for approximately. 90 horses, several outdoor rings, numerous paddocks, and miles of hacking trails—all within walking distance of the main campus.

A fiber-optic backbone allows high-speed Ethernet communication among all academic and administrative buildings, as well as in residence hall rooms, with more than 1,000 terminal and network connections campuswide. Many of the academic buildings and student common spaces are equipped for wireless connection to the campus network.

In 2004, Sweet Briar launched two graduate degree programs: the Master of Arts in Teaching and the Master of Education. These programs are rooted in the teaching philosophy of differentiated curriculum and instruction. Sweet Briar also established a new degree program in engineering, only the second such undergraduate program at a women's college.

Varsity athletes compete in NCAA Division III field hockey, lacrosse, soccer, softball, swimming, tennis, and volleyball. Club sports include cross-country, fencing, and riding.

Location

Sweet Briar's 3,250-acre campus in the foothills of the Blue Ridge Mountains includes hiking, biking, and riding trails and two lakes that provide spectacular venues for outdoor recreational activities. The College is centrally located on the outskirts of Lynchburg, Virginia, southwest of Washington, D.C., and Charlottesville. Students also enjoy activities in nearby Roanoke and Richmond.

Majors and Degrees

Sweet Briar awards the Bachelor of Arts, Bachelor of Science, and Bachelor of Fine Arts degrees. The College offers thirty-seven majors: anthropology, archaeology, art history, biochemistry and molecular biology, biology, business management, chemistry, classics, computer science, dance, economics, education, engineering and management, engineering science, English, English and creative writing, environmental science, environmental studies, French, German, German studies, government, history, international affairs, Italian studies, mathematics, mathematics-physics, modern languages and literatures, music, philosophy, physics, psychology, religion, sociology, Spanish, studio art, and theater.

Additional area studies, minors, and certificate programs include arts management, equine studies, engineering (3-2 dual degree), film studies, Italian, Latin American studies, law and society, musical theater, prelaw, premed, pre–veterinary science, and women and gender studies. Students may design an interdisciplinary major focused on a topic of special interest or may construct personalized majors.

Academic Programs

Sweet Briar's mission is to prepare women to be active, responsible members of a world community. Underscoring every one of the thirty-seven major fields of study is the idea that the best way to learn about the world is to experience it. The curriculum emphasizes hands-on learning, comprehensive understanding, analysis, reflection, creativity, and communication across disciplines. The academic programs are nationally celebrated. To add to this, the College recently launched the Sweet Briar Promise, a distinctive program that provides six guarantees to ensure every student has the opportunity for an academic experience that prepares her for a lifetime of success. Every qualified student is guaranteed an internship, study-abroad experience, and leadership and research opportunities. The Sweet Briar Promise also allows students who have an interest in an area not covered by one of the thirty-seven majors, or who would like to focus on more than one area, the opportunity to create, with the help of a faculty mentor, a personalized program of study. The final component of the Sweet Briar Promise goes a step further than most and makes a team of advisers, including alumnae, staff members, and professors, available to assist every student with academic and career planning.

The general education program has four components—English 104, skills requirements, experiences requirements, and knowledge areas requirements—that work together to ensure the development of strong communication and quantitative reasoning skills. Independent studies and seminars are included in most majors, with a culminating senior course or exercise required in most majors. Sweet Briar has a chapter of Phi Beta Kappa and was the first women's college to establish a chapter of the prelaw honorary society Phi Alpha Delta. It also has a four-year honors program that is nationally recognized for its innovative partnering of interdisciplinary academic and cocurricular programs. Honors students may take special tutorials and seminars as well as complete a yearlong research project culminating in an honors thesis on an original topic.

Sweet Briar's two-semester calendar allows students to participate in intensive courses, independent research projects, or internships on campus or throughout the world.

Off-Campus Programs

By the time they graduate, more than a third of Sweet Briar students have studied abroad. The Sweet Briar Junior Year in France, the first program in Paris for American students, is considered the most academically rigorous program available today. Students from 258 colleges and universities have participated in the coed program. The successful Junior Year in Spain is recognized as the premier program in Seville. The College has special relationships with the University of St. Andrews in Scotland, Heidelberg University in Germany, Doshisha Women's College in Japan, and the University of Urbino in Italy. In recent years, Sweet Briar students have also chosen the following destinations for study abroad: Australia, China, the Czech Republic, Denmark, Greece, Holland, Ireland, Jamaica, Korea, Mongolia, Morocco, New Zealand, and Thailand. Off-campus study may also include an Environmental Junior Year, the Washington Semester at American University, and summer programs at St. Anne's College in Oxford, England. In addition, summer programs are offered in Australia; Central America, including Costa Rica; Münster, Germany; Rome and Urbino, Italy; Nepal; and Spain.

Sweet Briar participates in the Tri-College Consortium, which also includes Randolph College and Lynchburg College. In addition to taking courses at the other colleges, students can participate in combined social and cultural activities on those campuses.

Academic Facilities

Sweet Briar has the largest private undergraduate library collection in the state of Virginia, with resources of more than 240,000 volumes, 1,000 journal subscriptions, 430,000 microforms, 6,800 audiovisual materials, and special libraries in art, music, and the sciences. Some of the notable special holdings include Virginia Woolf, T. E. Lawrence, George Meredith, W. H. Auden, and a rare collection of twentieth-century Chinese works. Three computer labs with Macintosh and Windows/Intel Pentium computers are open free of charge 24 hours a day. The student-computer ratio is 6:1. A lab for Sweet Briar's new engineering department includes a 5-Kip-capacity Universal Test Machine; a United Tru-Blue Rockwell hardness tester; a set of gauged beams and test fixtures for mechanics experiments; eight new computers, each with NI ELVIS and Labview with Protoboards; and a well-equipped machine shop. Students studying science use state-of-the-art equipment that enhances faculty-student collaborative research. Biology equipment includes a scanning electron microscope with digital imaging system, equipment for plant and animal tissue culture, and DNA sequencing equipment. Chemistry students have access to two nuclear magnetic resonance spectrometers (NMR; 400 MHz and 60 MHz), an atomic absorption spectrometer (AAS), a diode array UV/Vis spectrometer, a Fourier-transform infrared spectrometer (FT-IR), a modular LASER laboratory, a gas chromatograph/mass spectrograph (GC/MS), a high-pressure liquid chromatograph (HPLC), and a differential scanning calorimeter (DSC). Physics equipment includes a scanning tunneling microscope, an X-ray crystallography system, a 10-inch-diameter reflecting telescope, and holographic instrumentation.

The environmental studies program occupies two sites. A renovated train station provides classroom and laboratory space equipped with a Rigaku Miniflex powder X-ray diffraction system for mineralogical analysis, a Rocklabs bench-top ring mill for grinding rock and soil samples, a drying oven and a high-temperature muffle furnace, and much more. An adjacent caboose car provides office space for faculty members. A water treatment plant was also converted to an environmental education/nature center and environmental lab; equipment includes water, soil, wastewater, and sediment sampling instrumentation, including N-Con composite samplers, macroinvertebrate samplers, and specialized water-collection devices.

The Babcock Fine Arts Center includes individual practice rooms, an electronic piano lab, dance studios, theaters, and Murchison Lane Auditorium for lectures and performing arts. Two former dairy barns were recently renovated for classroom and office space to house studio arts, including a ceramics and sculpture studio; four large studios for painting, drawing, and printmaking; and a photo studio and darkroom.

The Academic Resource Center (ARC) provides free of charge to all students academic support services that include assistance with papers and study strategies, a personalized time management system, stress management advice, tutoring information, and one-on-one peer mentoring. The ARC also provides support and learning strategies for students with diagnosed learning differences.

Costs

For 2007–08, tuition and fees were $25,015 and room and board totaled $10,040. Books and supplies are estimated to be $1500. Personal expenses average $1000.

Financial Aid

A family's financial circumstance does not limit a student's choices at Sweet Briar because of the College's generous financial aid program. More than 90 percent of enrolling students receive financial assistance from the College, including merit scholarships, need-based grants, loans, and work-study awards. Scholarships for international students are also available on a competitive basis.

Faculty

Sweet Briar's faculty members have been commended by numerous regional and national educational groups for their excellence in teaching. Faculty members are actively engaged in teaching, research, publication, and other forms of creative activity. More than 95 percent of full-time faculty members have a doctorate or the highest professional degree in his or her field. All classes are taught by a faculty member. About half of the faculty members are women.

Student Government

The Student Government Association (SGA) is founded upon a highly developed concept of honor and student ownership and involvement. The Honor System applies to all phases of academic and social life. Each entering student becomes a full member of the Student Government Association upon taking the Honor Pledge, which states that Sweet Briar women do not lie, cheat, steal, or violate the rights of others. Students participate in the governance of the College through the many offices and committee positions of the Student Government Association. SGA and its committees are largely responsible for the self-governance of the student body.

Admission Requirements

Sweet Briar seeks talented women who are adventurous, are enthusiastic about learning, and want to take an active part in their education. The Admissions Committee looks for qualities such as independent thinking, ethical principles, assertiveness, and an appreciation of diversity. Sweet Briar welcomes students of all economic, ethnic, geographic, religious, and social backgrounds.

Requirements normally include a minimum of 4 units in English, 3 in mathematics, 3 in social studies, 2 sequential years in a foreign language, and 3 units in science, as well as additional units in these subjects to total 16. Most candidates have 20 such academic units. Special attention is given to the difficulty of the applicant's curriculum and her academic achievement in the classroom; scores on the SAT or ACT are required. An interview at the College is strongly encouraged but not required. Candidates who are unable to visit the campus are invited to meet with staff members or to talk with alumnae in their hometowns.

Application and Information

Early decision applications are due by December 1 of the senior year, and notifications are sent December 15. The enrollment deposit is due January 15. Regular decision applications are due by February 1, and notifications are mailed by March 15. Students who are regular decision applicants have until the National Candidate's Reply Date of May 1 to submit the enrollment deposit. Transfer applications are due by May 1 for the fall semester and by November 1 for the spring semester. A completed application includes a transcript of the candidate's academic work, scores on the required test, recommendations from the guidance counselor and a teacher, and an essay written by the candidate. There is a $40 application fee, which may be waived at the request of the student's guidance counselor if it is deemed to be a financial burden. Sweet Briar also accepts the Common Application (paper or online; a supplement is required). All materials should be sent to the admissions office at the address listed in this description. Information may be requested from the same office.

Dean of Admissions
Sweet Briar College
P.O. Box B
Sweet Briar, Virginia 24595
Phone: 434-381-6142
800-381-6142 (toll-free)
Fax: 434-381-6152
E-mail: admissions@sbc.edu
Web site: http://www.sbc.edu

VIRGINIA COMMONWEALTH UNIVERSITY

RICHMOND, VIRGINIA

The University

Virginia Commonwealth University (VCU) was created in 1968 by an act of the Virginia General Assembly that combined the Richmond Professional Institute and the Medical College of Virginia (MCV). However, VCU uses the founding date of 1838, the year in which the Medical College of Virginia was created. VCU is one of three comprehensive universities in Virginia. On the graduate level, the University offers the M.A., M.Acc., M.B.A., M.F.A., M.A.E., M.Ed., M.H.A., M.M., M.M.Ed., M.P.A., M.P.H., M.S., M.S.N.A., M.S.O.T., M.S.W., M.T., M.Tax., M.I.S., M.U.R.P., D.D.S., M.D., Pharm.D., D.M.D., D.H.A., D.B.A., D.P.T., and Ph.D. degrees. Undergraduate and graduate programs are offered in more than 190 fields.

VCU is a diverse metropolitan university that has a major educational, cultural, and economic impact on the Richmond community. VCU is administratively and structurally composed of two campuses, the Monroe Park Campus (west) and the MCV Campus (east), operating as one institution. The two campuses provide distinct locations for learning. The Monroe Park Campus, located in the historic Fan District, combines hand-paved streets and Victorian town houses with spacious, contemporary classroom facilities. It houses the following colleges and schools: Arts, Business, Education, Engineering, Government and Public Affairs, Humanities and Sciences, Mass Communications, Social Work, World Studies, the School of Graduate Studies, the University College, and the Division of External Relations. The MCV Campus is located in the business section of Richmond, 1½ miles east of the Monroe Park Campus. On this campus are the schools of Allied Health Professions, Dentistry, Medicine, Nursing, Pharmacy, and Public Health. Each campus has several buildings listed on either the Virginia or National Historic Landmarks registers. Free shuttle service between the campuses is provided by the University.

Of the 31,907 men and women at VCU, 22,163 are undergraduates. Seventy-four percent of the 3,882 freshmen reside in University residence facilities, which include modern high-rise buildings and stylish town houses. Nearly 300 student organizations exist on campus, reflecting the diverse social, political, religious, and academic interests of the student body. Campus life is active, and there are numerous social and athletic events scheduled through these groups.

VCU offers postbaccalaureate certificate programs in accounting, aging studies, applied social research, business administration, computer science, criminal justice, environmental studies, gender violence intervention (social work), geographic information systems, health sciences, historic preservation planning, homeland security and emergency preparedness, human resource management, information systems, instructional technology, marketing, mathematical sciences, nonprofit management, patient counseling, planning information systems, premedical basic health sciences (anatomy, biochemistry and molecular biophysics, human genetics, microbiology and immunology, neurobiology, pharmacology and toxicology, and physiology), public management, public safety, real estate and land development, statistics, teaching, and urban revitalization.

Location

VCU is located in the city of Richmond, the state capital and focal point for Virginia's political, cultural, and social events. It is within a 1-hour drive of Williamsburg and within a 2-hour drive of the Blue Ridge Mountains, Virginia Beach, and Washington, D.C. Founded in 1607, Richmond is home to many historic sites. It also offers theater, concerts, symphony performances, ballet, art museums, shopping, athletics, and recreational opportunities. The University extends into the life of the city, and students participate in many activities in the University and Richmond communities.

Majors and Degrees

Virginia Commonwealth University awards B.A., B.F.A., B.I.S., B.M., B.M.Ed., B.S., and B.S.W. degrees. The undergraduate majors are accounting, advertising (business and creative), African American studies, anthropology, art, art education, art history (architectural history and art historical), bioinformatics (biology/genomics, computational science bioinformatics, and quantitative/statistical bioinformatics), biology, broadcast journalism, business administration and management, business law and marketing, chemistry, clinical laboratory sciences, clinical radiation sciences, communication arts, computer science, craft and material studies (ceramics, fabric design, fiberwork, furniture design, glassworking, jewelry, metalsmithing, and woodworking), criminal justice (forensic crime scene investigation and justice), dance and choreography, dental hygiene, economics, education (art, early childhood, elementary, health and physical, middle school, music, secondary, special, and theater), engineering (biomedical, chemical and life science, computer, electrical, and mechanical), English, environmental studies, exercise science (community health education, exercise science, and teacher education), fashion design, fashion merchandising, finance, financial technology, forensic science, French, German, graphic design, history, home fashions merchandising, homeland security and emergency preparedness, human resource management/industrial relations, illustration, information systems, interior design, interdisciplinary studies, international studies, journalism (broadcast and print), kinetic imaging, management, marketing, mass communications (advertising, journalism, and public relations), mathematical sciences (applied mathematics, computing science, mathematics, operations research, secondary mathematics teacher preparation, and statistics), music (performance/jazz studies and composition), nontraditional studies, nursing, occupational therapy, painting and printmaking, pharmacy, philosophy, photography and film, physical education, physical therapy, physics, political science, predentistry studies, prelaw studies, premedicine studies, preoptometry studies, preveterinary studies, print journalism, psychology, public relations, radiological sciences (nuclear medicine, radiation therapy, and radiological technology), real estate and urban land development, religious studies, science, sculpture, social work, sociology and anthropology, Spanish, theater (performance and design/technical), urban and regional planning, urban studies and geography, and women's studies.

Selected study plans resulting in double majors and/or minors are available to students who wish to intensify their academic backgrounds in more than one area of study. A number of major programs offer students an opportunity to specialize within their major. Extensive pre–health sciences programs are also offered.

Several undergraduate programs serve as preparatory programs for graduate and professional programs. Undergraduate studies in early childhood/elementary, middle, secondary, and special education are part of a five-year program culminating in a B.A., B.I.S., or B.S. and a Master of Teaching. Students must apply to the upper-division graduate program once they have junior status. Undergraduate study in the pre–health sciences prepares students to apply for the professional or graduate portion of the program. Acceptance to a preparatory program does not guarantee admission to the professional or graduate program.

Academic Programs

The numerous schools that exist within the University allow students to take courses in many different disciplines. The requirements for a bachelor's degree vary from 120 to 135 semester hours, according to the major program. Advanced placement, early admission, early decision, honors programs, and credit by examination are available. An eight-year medical program, an eight-year dental program, and guaranteed admission to graduate and professional programs in basic health sciences and programs in business (four-year programs leading to the master's degree) are available to superior freshmen. VCU operates on a traditional semester calendar with a winter intersession and numerous summer sessions. Cooperative education and internships are available in most majors.

Off-Campus Programs

VCU sponsors various travel/study-abroad programs and opportunities for students interested in gaining exposure to other cultures and languages.

Academic Facilities

A large number of support facilities and programs supplement the various academic offerings at VCU. These include animal laboratories and a workshop; class 1000 clean-room space for the fabrication of microelectronic chips, biochips, and microelectromechanical systems; a greenhouse and aquatics laboratory; math tutorial labs; well-equipped labs for the sciences; language labs; the Foreign Language Bank for those needing translating services; the Center for Psychological Services Development; the Center for Teacher Leadership; the Management Center; the Computer Center; the Center for Public Policy; the Correctional Training and Evaluation Center; the Training and Technical Assistance Center; the University Child Study Center; the Cancer Center; the Poison Control Center; four teaching hospitals; two theaters; a music center; a ceramics and sculpture workshop; art studios; a graphics lab; an audiovisual lab; a campus learning center and writing center; and a photography studio with complete darkroom facilities. The Anderson Gallery, a University-owned art museum, is located on the Monroe Park Campus. The University is also the location of Virginia's Highway Safety Training Center and a Biotechnology Research Park.

Costs

Academic-year expenses for undergraduate students in 2007–08 were $6196 for in-state tuition and fees and $18,740 for nonresident tuition and fees. Room and board were estimated at $7567.

Financial Aid

University financial aid programs serve approximately 67 percent of the student body. The University participates in all federal and state grant, loan, and work-study programs. The University also sponsors a major academic scholarship program whose awards are based upon academic merit rather than need. Normally, students encounter few problems finding part-time employment on campus or in the community. To apply for assistance, students are required to complete the Free Application for Federal Student Aid (FAFSA). The FAFSA must be mailed before March 1 to meet the University deadline. Further information may be obtained by contacting the VCU Office of Financial Aid at 901 West Franklin Street, P.O. Box 843537, Richmond, Virginia 23284-2527.

Faculty

Eighty-nine percent of VCU faculty members hold the highest degree in their professional field. Faculty members work with students in developing academic programs, supervise independent study programs, and assist with academic advising.

Student Government

The student government at Virginia Commonwealth University consists of a body of 33 senators representing both schools. Each of the senators serves on at least one of seven subcommittees. Elections are held during spring preregistration. The student government provides programs and services to the University community and gives students the opportunity to get involved with the governance of the institution.

Admission Requirements

Admission to programs on the Monroe Park Campus requires graduation from an accredited secondary school (or a high school equivalency diploma) with a minimum of 20 units, which must include 4 units in English; 3 units in history, social sciences, or government; 3 units in mathematics (including at least 2 units in algebra I, geometry, and algebra II); and 3 units in science (including 1 unit in a laboratory science). Two units of foreign language are strongly recommended. Additional units in mathematics and other academically challenging areas of study are also recommended. The Advanced Studies diploma is preferred. Applicants are evaluated on the basis of their academic record in high school, class standing, SAT or ACT scores, extracurricular activities, and suitability of preparation for the intended major. Transfer students with at least 30 semester hours or 45 quarter hours of undergraduate credit are admitted on the basis of their accumulated college credits.

Admission to programs on the MCV Campus requires from two to four years of undergraduate study. Each school and program has specified academic requirements.

VCU is an Equal Opportunity/Affirmative Action institution providing access to education and employment without regard to age, race, color, national origin, gender, religion, sexual orientation, veteran's status, political affiliation, or disability.

Application and Information

The processing of applications for the spring and fall semesters begins in October. Applicants are considered when all necessary documents have been received, and applicants are notified by April 1 if the application file is complete by February 1. Applicants interested in being considered for scholarships should apply by January 5. Applicants interested in the School of Medicine's Guaranteed Admission Program must apply by November 15; this program requires that a separate application packet be submitted in addition to the application for undergraduate admission. The Guaranteed Admission Program application is available on the VCU Honors College Web site. The necessary materials for admission consideration to the University include the official application form; a $55 nonrefundable application fee for undergraduate programs in the School of the Arts for students who are applying using the paper application or a $30 nonrefundable application fee if applying online; a $40 nonrefundable application fee for programs other than those in the School of the Arts for students who are applying using the paper application or a $30 nonrefundable application fee if applying online; official high school transcripts, indicating class rank and grade point average; and scores on the SAT (the VCU code number is 475570) or ACT (the VCU code number is 474379). Those applying to visual arts programs in the School of the Arts must submit a portfolio, and those intending to major in theater, dance, or music must audition or interview. Transfer applicants who have earned fewer than 30 semester hours or 45 quarter hours of credit must also meet freshman guidelines and submit those documents required of freshmen (including SAT or ACT scores if the candidates are under 22 years of age) in addition to official transcripts from all institutions attended. The transfer application deadline is June 1 but may vary for health science programs and programs in the School of the Arts.

Applications and additional information may be obtained by contacting:

Office of Undergraduate Admissions
Virginia Commonwealth University
821 West Franklin Street
P.O. Box 842526
Richmond, Virginia 23284-2526
Phone: 804-828-1222
800-841-3638 (toll-free)
E-mail: ugrad@vcu.edu
Web site: http://www.ugrad.vcu.edu

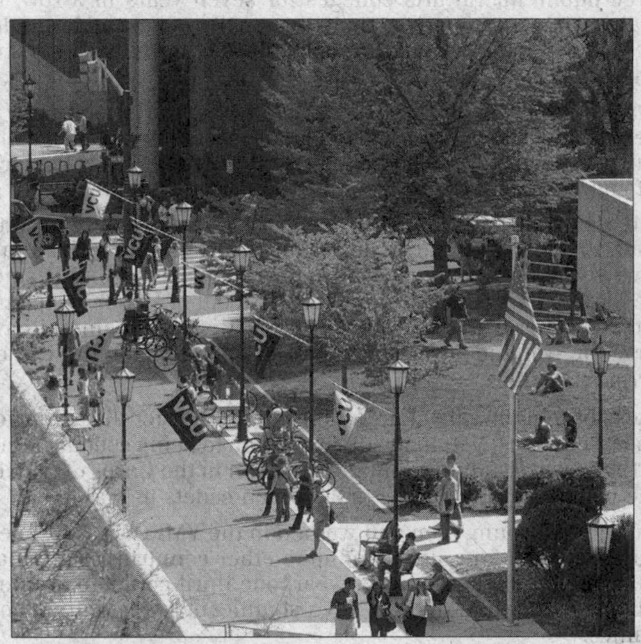

VCU offers many excellent academic programs and a diverse faculty and student body.

VIRGINIA MILITARY INSTITUTE

LEXINGTON, VIRGINIA

The Institute

The Virginia Military Institute (VMI) is the nation's oldest state-supported military college, founded in 1839 in Lexington, Virginia, and located at the southern end of the Shenandoah Valley. VMI offers qualified young men and women a demanding combination of academic study and rigorous military training that exists nowhere else, and grants B.A. and B.S. degrees in fourteen disciplines within the general fields of engineering, science, and liberal arts. The Institute's emphasis on qualities of honor, integrity, and responsibility contributes to its unique educational philosophy. Professional leadership training is provided to all cadets through the Reserve Officers' Training Corps (ROTC) programs, maintained at VMI by the Department of Defense. Cadets may pursue commissions in the U.S. Army, Air Force, Navy, or Marine Corps.

In every field of endeavor, whether it is leadership in business, industry, public service, education, the professions, or careers in the military, success comes early to a high number of VMI graduates. In an independent survey of college graduates seeking employment, armed forces commission, or admission to graduate or professional school following graduation, 95 percent of VMI graduates met their goal by the following October.

VMI's breadth is diverse. The curricula for the selected major begin in the first year. More than 20 percent of cadets major in civil, electrical, or mechanical engineering, and more than 50 percent of cadets major in liberal arts fields. The two most popular fields are economics/business and history.

The academic excellence of VMI and its stature among institutions of higher education are highlighted by the fact that *U.S. News & World Report* has named VMI among the nation's top three public liberal arts colleges for seven years in a row. Its engineering programs remain in the top tier of best undergraduate accredited programs at schools offering only bachelor's or master's degrees.

VMI's alumni support is unparalleled in many ways, especially in their financial support. The National Association of College and University Business Officers has reported that VMI has the largest endowment per student of any public institution.

VMI alumni include Nobel Peace Prize winner George C. Marshall, 10 Rhodes scholars, and 39 college presidents. VMI alumni have distinguished themselves in every American conflict since the Mexican War, and they include 7 Medal of Honor recipients and 265 general and flag officers. More than 1,000 alumni have served in war zones and in support of operations in the war on terror since 2001.

After nearly 160 years of preparing young men for distinguished leadership roles, VMI made the transition to being coeducational in 1997, successfully assimilating women in the Corps of Cadets. The Institute graduated its first women cadets in May 1999.

Today, 1,370 young men and women in the VMI Corps of Cadets represent forty-four states and nine other countries. More than 100 cadets study abroad each year, one third compete in intercollegiate athletics, and all have significant leadership opportunities.

All cadets reside in Barracks, at the centerpiece of the VMI Post. The original structure was built in 1850 and is a National Historic Landmark. An additional wing was added in 1949. A third section of the Barracks is under construction, to be followed by renovation of the existing Barracks structures. When completed, the new Barracks will also house facilities such as the bookstore, a cadet visitor's center and lounge, and other cadet-oriented functions. All cadet rooms are equipped for computer technology.

VMI cadets uphold an honor system as old as the Institute. An oath of honor is taken by each cadet, "not to lie, cheat, or steal, nor tolerate those who do," and the oath is practiced in daily life. As it is basic to cadet life, it is ingrained and builds strong character. Honor is at the cornerstone of every cadet's lifelong commitment to integrity, duty, self-discipline, and self-reliance.

One of the oldest VMI traditions is the orientation and instruction provided to new cadets by older cadets. Regardless of background or prior training, every cadet in the first year at VMI is a Rat, and each is a Brother Rat to the other. They live under the Rat System until Break Out in late winter, and their bonds formed by this experience last a lifetime.

VMI places great emphasis on physical fitness and training programs, whether cadets participate in athletics, ROTC training, or physical education programs. VMI offers fifteen intercollegiate athletics programs at the NCAA Division I level and supports numerous club sports and intramural activities. The VMI "Keydet" Club is one of the oldest and most productive athletic foundations in the country, raising more than $1 million annually for athletic scholarships and grants-in-aid to 185 cadets in all fifteen sports. Athletic grounds and facilities are within easy access to the Post.

A member of the Southern Conference since 1924, VMI recently made the decision to move to the Big South conference.

Location

Lexington is in Rockbridge County, Virginia, an area rich in history and natural beauty. VMI adjoins the campus of Washington and Lee University, the nation's ninth-oldest institution of higher learning. Both colleges are within walking distance to historic downtown Lexington, a popular tourist destination. Interstate Highways 81 and 64 intersect only minutes from VMI, north of Lexington's downtown area. U.S. Highways 11 (north-south) and 60 (east-west), the area's crossroads for two centuries, intersect in downtown Lexington. Air service to VMI is available from Roanoke Regional Airport, less than an hour's drive from Lexington.

Majors and Degrees

VMI offers the baccalaureate degree in fourteen curricula. The B.S. is awarded in chemistry, civil engineering, computer science, electrical engineering, mechanical engineering, and physics. The B.A. is conferred in economics and business, English, history, international studies, modern languages, and psychology. A B.S. or B.A. can be earned in biology and applied mathematics. A course of study leading to a B.S. or B.A. is chosen upon entering VMI, but a transfer from one major field of study to another is permitted.

Academic Programs

VMI's demanding academic program reflects established needs and emerging trends of an ever-changing, global society. A newly funded undergraduate research initiative extends through summer, affording cadets and faculty members financial incentives and continuous support for a wide range of investigative projects. The Institute's international programs include faculty and student exchanges with more than a dozen international academies and universities, seven international internships, and numerous study-abroad programs each semester and during the summer.

VMI is accredited by the Southern Association of Colleges and Schools and is a member of American Council on Education, the Association of American Colleges, the College Entrance Examination Board, and the Association of Virginia Colleges. VMI's engineering and computer science programs are ABET-accredited; the chemistry program is accredited by ACS.

Academic Facilities

The VMI Post covers 134 acres, of which 12 acres are designated a National Historic District. VMI's academic facilities, Superintendent's quarters, library, alumni hall, and other administrative buildings, along with Barracks, encircle a 12-acre parade ground used for marching drills, weekly parades, training exercises, and social gatherings. The physics department has X-ray and nuclear physics laboratories and operates both an observatory and planetarium. The George C. Marshall Research Museum and the VMI Museum are located on Post.

Costs

Charges at VMI are based on a cadet's classification as a Virginia or out-of-state resident. Total charges cover most direct expenses, including tuition, room, board (twenty-one meals per week), fees, uniforms, laundry, routine medical care, and barber services. As an example, in 2007–08 total costs were $16,156 for Virginia residents and $32,000 for non-Virginia residents. (Books and transportation are additional.) ROTC pay and allowances to qualified cadets total up to $10,000 over four years, and should be considered in net costs at VMI.

Financial Aid

Although aid is generally awarded on the basis of financial need, numerous scholarships are awarded for academic and athletic excellence and as room and board supplements to ROTC scholarship recipients. Students interested in financial assistance should write to VMI's Director of Financial Aid.

Faculty

All VMI faculty members teach in the classroom, and 97 percent of full-time faculty members hold doctoral or terminal degrees. The cadet-faculty ratio is 12:1, permitting a close, mentor relationship between a cadet and instructor. Faculty research is conducted in partnership with cadets. ROTC instructors are experienced military officers and make an outstanding contribution to cadet leadership training.

Student Government

VMI has two systems of student government. The regimental system oversees cadet accountability for conduct, appearance, military training, and all ceremonial functions. The regiment of the Corps is divided into two battalions of four companies each, plus a band company.

Although Institute regulations govern the discipline of cadets, a large measure of supervision resides in each of the four closely knit classes within the Corps. The class system administers the Corps' standards and the privileges accorded each class and governs with the regimental system to oversee cadet appearance and conduct.

Representatives to the Honor Court are elected from the Corps, by the Corps, to enforce the rules of the honor system and prosecute Honor Court cases.

Admission Requirements

Applicants must be unmarried, 16 to 22 years of age (a one-year age waiver may be granted for an applicant who has served in active duty in the armed forces or in certain other circumstances), physically fit for enrollment in ROTC, and graduated from an accredited secondary school with 16 or more academic units. Recommended course credits include 4 English, 3 social studies, 3 laboratory sciences, 3 foreign language, 3 mathematics (including 2 years of algebra and 1 of geometry), and 2 electives. The average GPA of incoming freshmen is approximately 3.3. Other qualifications include rank in the upper 50 percent of the senior class (significance of rank depends on class size and other factors), above-average scores on SAT or ACT, and satisfactory character recommendations. Extracurricular activities are viewed as favorable indicators of leadership and character traits. Transfer students are accepted, but two years of residency at VMI are required. Admissions standards are applied without regard to gender, race, nationality, or religion, and all factors are weighed in the final determination of the applicant's qualifications.

Application and Information

An application may be submitted anytime between September 1 and February 15 of the senior year in high school and should be accompanied by a nonrefundable $35 application fee, a transcript of the school record for grade 9 through the last completed semester, and SAT or ACT scores. Visits to the Institute are highly recommended. Open House visits are held throughout the academic year.

Interested students should contact:

Director of Admissions
Virginia Military Institute
Lexington, Virginia 24450
Phone: 540-464-7211
800-767-4207 (toll-free)
Fax: 540-464-7746
E-mail: admissions@vmi.edu
Web site: http://www.vmi.edu

VMI Barracks, a National Historic Landmark and home to the VMI Corps of Cadets.

VIRGIN ISLANDS

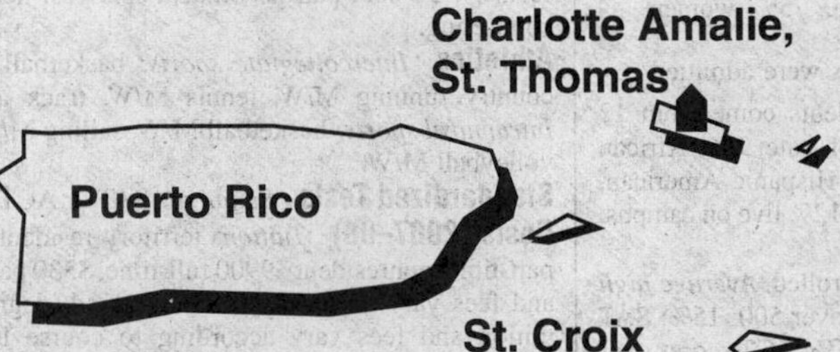

UNIVERSITY OF THE VIRGIN ISLANDS

Saint Thomas, Virgin Islands **www.uvi.edu/**

- **Territory-supported** comprehensive, founded 1962
- **Small-town** 518-acre campus
- **Endowment** $27.8 million
- **Coed** 2,300 undergraduate students, 55% full-time, 75% women, 25% men
- **Minimally difficult** entrance level, 97% of applicants were admitted

Undergraduates 1,258 full-time, 1,042 part-time. Students come from 12 states and territories, 13 other countries, 9% are from out of state, 76% African American, 0.7% Asian American or Pacific Islander, 6% Hispanic American, 0.2% Native American, 6% international, 4% transferred in, 12% live on campus. *Retention:* 79% of 2006 full-time freshmen returned.

Freshmen *Admission:* 913 applied, 884 admitted, 417 enrolled. *Average high school GPA:* 2.74. *Test scores:* SAT critical reading scores over 500: 15%; SAT math scores over 500: 10%; SAT writing scores over 500: 17%; ACT scores over 18: 49%; SAT critical reading scores over 600: 2%; SAT math scores over 600: 1%; SAT writing scores over 600: 1%; ACT scores over 24: 3%.

Faculty *Total:* 225, 44% full-time, 38% with terminal degrees. *Student/faculty ratio:* 17:1.

Majors Accounting; administrative assistant and secretarial science; biology/biological sciences; business administration and management; chemistry; computer science; criminal justice/police science; data processing and data processing technology; dramatic/theater arts; elementary education; English; hotel/motel administration; humanities; marine biology and biological oceanography; mathematics; music teacher education; nursing (registered nurse training); physics; psychology; social sciences; social work; speech and rhetoric; trade and industrial teacher education.

Academics *Calendar:* semesters. *Degrees:* associate, bachelor's, and master's. *Special study options:* academic remediation for entering students, adult/continuing education programs, advanced placement credit, distance learning, external degree program, independent study, internships, off-campus study, part-time degree program, summer session for credit. *ROTC:* Army (b).

Computers on Campus 100 computers/terminals are available on campus for general student use. Students can access the following: online (class) registration. Campuswide network is available.

Student Life *Housing options:* men-only, women-only. Campus housing is university owned. *Activities and organizations:* drama/theater group, student-run newspaper, choral group, The Squad, Predators, Golden Key Honor Society, National Student Exchange Club, St. Kitts and Nevis, national sororities. *Campus security:* 24-hour patrols. *Student services:* health clinic, personal/psychological counseling.

Athletics *Intercollegiate sports:* basketball M/W, cheerleading M/W, cross-country running M/W, tennis M/W, track and field M/W, volleyball M/W. *Intramural sports:* basketball M/W, sailing M/W, table tennis M/W, tennis M/W, volleyball M/W.

Standardized Tests *Required:* SAT or ACT (for admission).

Costs (2007–08) *Tuition:* territory resident $3300 full-time, $110 per credit part-time; nonresident $9900 full-time, $330 per credit part-time. Full-time tuition and fees vary according to course load, degree level, and program. Part-time tuition and fees vary according to course load, degree level, and program. *Required fees:* $500 full-time, $316 per year part-time. *Room and board:* $8100; room only: $2750. Room and board charges vary according to board plan and housing facility. *Waivers:* senior citizens and employees or children of employees.

Financial Aid Of all full-time matriculated undergraduates who enrolled in 2006, 1,204 applied for aid, 1,079 were judged to have need, 24 had their need fully met. 38 Federal Work-Study jobs (averaging $1720). 32 state and other part-time jobs (averaging $1639). In 2006, 27 non-need-based awards were made. *Average financial aid package:* $4419. *Average need-based loan:* $2768. *Average need-based gift aid:* $3191. *Average non-need-based aid:* $6460. *Average indebtedness upon graduation:* $9922.

Applying *Options:* early admission, early action, deferred entrance. *Application fee:* $30. *Required:* essay or personal statement, high school transcript, 2 letters of recommendation. *Application deadlines:* 4/30 (freshmen), 4/30 (transfers). *Notification:* continuous (freshmen), 6/15 (transfers).

Freshman Application Contact University of the Virgin Islands, No. 2 John Brewers Bay, St. Thomas, VI 00802. *Phone:* 340-693-1224.

WASHINGTON

The Seattle area includes the towns of Bothell, Bellevue, Edmonds, Everett, Issaquah, Kirkland, and Poulsbo.

ANTIOCH UNIVERSITY SEATTLE

Seattle, Washington www.antiochsea.edu/

Application Contact Ms. Vickie Lopez, Admissions Associate, Antioch University Seattle, 2326 Sixth Avenue, Seattle, WA 98121-1814. *Phone:* 206-441-5352. *E-mail:* admissions@antiochsea.edu.

ARGOSY UNIVERSITY, SEATTLE

Seattle, Washington www.argosy.edu/locations/seattle/

- **Proprietary** university, founded 1995
- **Urban** campus with easy access to Seattle
- **Coed**

Majors Business administration and management; finance; health/health care administration; international business/trade/commerce; marketing/marketing management; organizational behavior; psychology; substance abuse/addiction counseling.

Academics *Calendar:* semesters. *Degrees:* bachelor's, master's, and doctoral.

Director of Admissions Argosy University, Seattle, 2601-A Elliot Avenue, Seattle, WA 98121. *Phone:* 206-283-4500. *Toll-free phone:* 866-283-2777. *Fax:* 206-283-5777.

See page 2712 for the College Close-Up.

THE ART INSTITUTE OF SEATTLE

Seattle, Washington www.ais.artinstitutes.edu/

- **Proprietary** 4-year, founded 1982, part of Education Management Corporation
- **Urban** campus
- **Coed** 2,352 undergraduate students, 65% full-time, 51% women, 49% men
- **Moderately difficult** entrance level, 94% of applicants were admitted

Undergraduates 1,535 full-time, 817 part-time. Students come from 46 states and territories, 28 other countries, 17% are from out of state, 4% African American, 12% Asian American or Pacific Islander, 6% Hispanic American, 2% Native American, 6% international, 18% transferred in, 19% live on campus. *Retention:* 62% of 2006 full-time freshmen returned.

Freshmen *Admission:* 577 applied, 542 admitted, 452 enrolled. *Average high school GPA:* 2.42.

Faculty *Total:* 144, 44% full-time, 1% with terminal degrees. *Student/faculty ratio:* 20:1.

Majors Animation, interactive technology, video graphics and special effects; baking and pastry arts; cinematography and film/video production; culinary arts; fashion/apparel design; fashion merchandising; graphic design; industrial design; interior design; photography; recording arts technology; web page, digital/multimedia and information resources design.

Academics *Calendar:* quarters. *Degrees:* diplomas, associate, and bachelor's. *Special study options:* academic remediation for entering students, adult/continuing education programs, advanced placement credit, distance learning, honors programs, internships, part-time degree program, services for LD students, study abroad, summer session for credit.

Computers on Campus 494 computers/terminals are available on campus for general student use. Students can access the following: free student e-mail accounts, online (class) grades, online (class) schedules. Campuswide network is available. Wireless service is available via libraries.

Student Life *Housing options:* coed. Campus housing is leased by the school. Freshman campus housing is guaranteed. *Activities and organizations:* Multicultural Affairs Organization, American Society of Interior Designers, DECA, Student Advisory Board, Student Council. *Campus security:* 24-hour emergency response devices, late-night transport/escort service, controlled dormitory access, patrols by trained security personnel for 17 hours. *Student services:* personal/psychological counseling.

Athletics *Intramural sports:* soccer M/W, softball M/W.

Standardized Tests *Recommended:* SAT (for admission), ACT (for admission), ACT COMPASS, ACCUPLACER.

Costs (2007–08) *Comprehensive fee:* $30,652 includes full-time tuition ($19,968) and room and board ($10,684). Part-time tuition: $435 per credit. tuition cost varies by program. Prospective students should contact the school for current tuition costs. Other charges include a starting kit for all first-quarter students. Kits vary in price depending on the program of study.

Financial Aid Of all full-time matriculated undergraduates who enrolled in 2006, 18 Federal Work-Study jobs (averaging $1795).

Applying *Options:* electronic application, deferred entrance. *Application fee:* $50. *Required:* essay or personal statement, high school transcript, minimum 2.0 GPA, interview. *Required for some:* 2.5 GPA required for Bachelor degree applicants. *Recommended:* 3 letters of recommendation. *Application deadlines:* rolling (freshmen), rolling (transfers). *Notification:* continuous (freshmen), continuous (transfers).

Freshman Application Contact Mr. Michael Reese, Registrar, The Art Institute of Seattle, 2323 Elliott Avenue, Seattle, WA 98121-1622. *Phone:* 206-239-2284. *Toll-free phone:* 800-275-2471. *E-mail:* mreese@aii.edu.

See page 2714 for the College Close-Up.

BASTYR UNIVERSITY

Kenmore, Washington www.bastyr.edu/

- **Independent** upper-level, founded 1978
- **Suburban** 50-acre campus with easy access to Seattle
- **Coed** 218 undergraduate students, 91% full-time, 83% women, 17% men
- 77% of applicants were admitted

Undergraduates 198 full-time, 20 part-time. Students come from 7 states and territories, 8 other countries, 50% are from out of state, 0.5% African American, 6% Asian American or Pacific Islander, 5% Hispanic American, 2% Native American, 6% international, 43% transferred in, 7% live on campus.

Freshmen *Admission:* 188 applied, 145 admitted.

Faculty *Total:* 132, 38% full-time. *Student/faculty ratio:* 13:1.

Majors Dietetics; foods, nutrition, and wellness; health science; herbalism; kinesiology and exercise science; psychology.

Academics *Calendar:* quarters. *Degrees:* bachelor's, master's, doctoral, first professional, post-master's, postbachelor's, and first professional certificates. *Special study options:* cooperative education, double majors, independent study, internships, part-time degree program, summer session for credit.

Computers on Campus 53 computers/terminals are available on campus for general student use. Campuswide network is available. 100% of college-owned or -operated housing units are wired for high-speed Internet access. Wireless service is available via entire campus.

Student Life *Housing options:* coed. Campus housing is university owned. *Activities and organizations:* Parent Resource Center, Nature Club, Spirituality in Focus, Environmental Action Team, Toastmasters. *Campus security:* student patrols, late-night transport/escort service, controlled dormitory access. *Student services:* health clinic, personal/psychological counseling.

Athletics *Intramural sports:* basketball M, soccer M/W, ultimate Frisbee M/W, volleyball M/W.

Costs (2007–08) *Tuition:* $17,040 full-time, $340 per credit part-time. Full-time tuition and fees vary according to course load and program. Part-time tuition and fees vary according to course load and program. *Required fees:* $1740 full-time. *Room only:* $4100. Room and board charges vary according to board plan and housing facility. *Waivers:* employees or children of employees.

Financial Aid Of all full-time matriculated undergraduates who enrolled in 2006, 220 applied for aid, 195 were judged to have need. 40 Federal Work-Study jobs (averaging $3000). 31 state and other part-time jobs (averaging $3000). *Average percent of need met:* 50%. *Average financial aid package:* $17,600. *Average need-based loan:* $5500. *Average need-based gift aid:* $8750. *Average indebtedness upon graduation:* $30,000.

Applying *Options:* electronic application, deferred entrance. *Application fee:* $60. *Application deadline:* 3/15 (transfers). *Notification:* continuous until 9/1 (transfers).

Application Contact Mr. Ted Olsen, Director of Admissions, Bastyr University, 14500 Juanita Drive NE, Kenmore, WA 98028-4966. *Phone:* 425-602-3101. *Fax:* 425-602-3090. *E-mail:* admissions@bastyr.edu.

See page 2716 for the College Close-Up.

CENTRAL WASHINGTON UNIVERSITY

Ellensburg, Washington www.cwu.edu/

- **State-supported** comprehensive, founded 1891
- **Small-town** 380-acre campus
- **Endowment** $9.7 million
- **Coed** 9,979 undergraduate students, 87% full-time, 53% women, 47% men

• **Moderately difficult** entrance level, 80% of applicants were admitted

Undergraduates 8,684 full-time, 1,295 part-time. Students come from 35 states and territories, 46 other countries, 2% are from out of state, 3% African American, 7% Asian American or Pacific Islander, 8% Hispanic American, 2% Native American, 2% international, 11% transferred in, 34% live on campus. *Retention:* 77% of 2006 full-time freshmen returned.

Freshmen *Admission:* 4,602 applied, 3,688 admitted, 1,483 enrolled. *Average high school GPA:* 3.2. *Test scores:* SAT critical reading scores over 500: 47%; SAT math scores over 500: 51%; ACT scores over 18: 82%; SAT critical reading scores over 600: 11%; SAT math scores over 600: 12%; ACT scores over 24: 22%; SAT critical reading scores over 700: 1%; SAT math scores over 700: 1%.

Faculty *Total:* 578, 69% full-time. *Student/faculty ratio:* 21:1.

Majors Accounting; aeronautics/aviation/aerospace science and technology; anthropology; art; art teacher education; Asian studies; biology/biological sciences; biology teacher education; business administration and management; business teacher education; chemistry; chemistry teacher education; community health services counseling; computer and information sciences; criminal justice/law enforcement administration; drama and dance teacher education; dramatic/theater arts; early childhood education; economics; electrical, electronic and communications engineering technology; elementary education; emergency medical technology (EMT paramedic); English; English/language arts teacher education; family and consumer sciences/human sciences; fashion merchandising; foods, nutrition, and wellness; foreign languages and literatures; French language teacher education; geography; geology/earth science; German language teacher education; gerontology; health teacher education; history; history teacher education; industrial technology; journalism; kindergarten/preschool education; kinesiology and exercise science; mass communication/media; mathematics; mathematics teacher education; mechanical engineering/mechanical technology; music; music management and merchandising; music teacher education; music theory and composition; natural resources management; occupational safety and health technology; office management; operations management; parks, recreation and leisure; philosophy; physical education teaching and coaching; physics; piano and organ; political science and government; psychology; public policy analysis; public relations/image management; radio and television; religious studies; science teacher education; social science teacher education; sociology; Spanish language teacher education; special education; sport and fitness administration/management; technology/industrial arts teacher education; trade and industrial teacher education; voice and opera.

Academics *Calendar:* quarters. *Degrees:* bachelor's, master's, and postbachelor's certificates. *Special study options:* academic remediation for entering students, adult/continuing education programs, advanced placement credit, cooperative education, distance learning, double majors, English as a second language, honors programs, independent study, internships, off-campus study, part-time degree program, services for LD students, student-designed majors, study abroad, summer session for credit. *ROTC:* Army (b), Air Force (b). *Unusual degree programs:* 3-2 engineering with University of Washington, Washington State University.

Computers on Campus 720 computers/terminals are available on campus for general student use. Students can access the following: campus intranet, computer help desk, free student e-mail accounts, online (class) grades, online (class) registration, online (class) schedules. Campuswide network is available. 100% of college-owned or -operated housing units are wired for high-speed Internet access. Wireless service is available via learning centers, libraries, student centers.

Student Life *Housing:* on-campus residence required for freshman year. *Options:* coed, women-only, disabled students. Campus housing is university owned. Freshman campus housing is guaranteed. *Activities and organizations:* drama/theater group, student-run newspaper, radio and television station, choral group, marching band, International Business Club, Marketing Club, Associated Students of CWU. *Campus security:* 24-hour emergency response devices and patrols, late-night transport/escort service, controlled dormitory access. *Student services:* health clinic, personal/psychological counseling.

Athletics Member NCAA. All Division II. *Intercollegiate sports:* baseball M (s), basketball M (s)/W (s), bowling M (c)/W (c), cheerleading M/W, cross-country running M (s)/W (s), fencing M (c)/W (c), football M (s), golf M (c)/W (c), ice hockey M (c)/W (c), rugby M (c)/W (c), soccer M (c)/W (s), softball W (s), track and field M (s)/W (s), volleyball W (s), water polo M (c)/W (c). *Intramural sports:* badminton M/W, basketball M/W, football M/W, golf M/W, racquetball M/W, soccer M/W, softball M/W, tennis M/W, ultimate Frisbee M/W, volleyball M/W.

Standardized Tests *Required:* SAT or ACT (for admission).

Costs (2007–08) *Tuition:* state resident $4611 full-time, $154 per credit part-time; nonresident $14,013 full-time, $467 per credit part-time. Part-time tuition and fees vary according to course load. *Required fees:* $846 full-time. *Room and board:* $7842. Room and board charges vary according to board plan and housing facility. *Payment plan:* installment. *Waivers:* senior citizens and employees or children of employees.

Financial Aid Of all full-time matriculated undergraduates who enrolled in 2005, 5,822 applied for aid, 4,319 were judged to have need, 789 had their need fully met. 290 Federal Work-Study jobs (averaging $2288). 262 state and other part-time jobs (averaging $3319). In 2005, 9 non-need-based awards were made. *Average percent of need met:* 69%. *Average financial aid package:* $7775. *Average need-based loan:* $3890. *Average need-based gift aid:* $5369. *Average non-need-based aid:* $452. *Average indebtedness upon graduation:* $14,591.

Applying *Options:* electronic application. *Application fee:* $50. *Required:* high school transcript, minimum 2.0 GPA. *Required for some:* essay or personal statement, letters of recommendation, interview. *Application deadlines:* 4/1 (freshmen), 4/1 (transfers). *Notification:* continuous (freshmen), continuous (transfers).

Freshman Application Contact Ms. Lisa Garcia-Hanson, Director of Admissions, Central Washington University, 400 East University Way, Ellensburg, WA 98926-7463. *Phone:* 509-963-1211. *Toll-free phone:* 866-298-4968. *Fax:* 509-963-3022. *E-mail:* cwuadmis@cwu.edu.

CITY UNIVERSITY OF SEATTLE

Bellevue, Washington **www.cityu.edu/**

- **Independent** comprehensive, founded 1973
- **Suburban** campus with easy access to Seattle
- **Coed** 1,444 undergraduate students, 56% full-time, 61% women, 39% men
- **Noncompetitive** entrance level

Undergraduates 805 full-time, 639 part-time. Students come from 47 states and territories, 33 other countries, 11% are from out of state, 3% African American, 5% Asian American or Pacific Islander, 3% Hispanic American, 1% Native American, 7% international.

Freshmen *Admission:* 16 enrolled.

Faculty *Total:* 1,241, 4% full-time, 20% with terminal degrees. *Student/faculty ratio:* 7:1.

Majors Accounting; business administration and management; computer and information sciences and support services related; computer programming; elementary education; general studies; international business/trade/commerce; mass communication/media; psychology; special education.

Academics *Calendar:* quarters. *Degrees:* certificates, diplomas, associate, bachelor's, master's, and postbachelor's certificates. *Special study options:* accelerated degree program, adult/continuing education programs, advanced placement credit, distance learning, double majors, English as a second language, external degree program, internships, part-time degree program, services for LD students, student-designed majors, summer session for credit.

Computers on Campus 145 computers/terminals are available on campus for general student use. Students can access the following: campus intranet, computer help desk, free student e-mail accounts, online (class) grades, online (class) registration, online (class) schedules. Campuswide network is available. Wireless service is available via classrooms, computer centers, computer labs, libraries.

Student Life *Housing:* college housing not available. *Campus security:* 24-hour emergency response devices. *Student services:* personal/psychological counseling.

Costs (2007–08) *Tuition:* $13,275 full-time, $295 per credit hour part-time. *Payment plan:* installment. *Waivers:* employees or children of employees.

Financial Aid Of all full-time matriculated undergraduates who enrolled in 2003, 824 applied for aid, 721 were judged to have need. 1 Federal Work-Study job (averaging $1300). In 2003, 18 non-need-based awards were made. *Average percent of need met:* 15%. *Average financial aid package:* $4943. *Average need-based loan:* $4353. *Average need-based gift aid:* $2344. *Average non-need-based aid:* $3738. *Average indebtedness upon graduation:* $16,369.

Applying *Options:* electronic application, deferred entrance. *Application fee:* $50. *Recommended:* high school transcript. *Application deadlines:* rolling (freshmen), rolling (transfers). *Notification:* continuous (freshmen).

Freshman Application Contact Student Services Center, City University of Seattle, 11900 NE First Street, Bellevue, WA 98005. *Phone:* 888-422-4898. *Toll-free phone:* 888-42-CITYU. *Fax:* 425-709-5361. *E-mail:* info@cityu.edu.

See page 2718 for the College Close-Up.

CORNISH COLLEGE OF THE ARTS

Seattle, Washington **www.cornish.edu/**

Freshman Application Contact Ms. Sharron Starling, Associate Director of Admissions, Cornish College of the Arts, 1000 Lenora Street, Seattle, WA 98121.

Phone: 206-726-5017. *Toll-free phone:* 800-726-ARTS. *Fax:* 206-720-1011. *E-mail:* admissions@cornish.edu.

DeVry University
Bellevue, Washington

DeVry University
Federal Way, Washington www.devry.edu/

- **Proprietary** comprehensive, founded 2001, part of DeVry University
- **Suburban** 12-acre campus
- **Coed** 662 undergraduate students, 68% full-time, 27% women, 73% men
- **Minimally difficult** entrance level

Undergraduates 451 full-time, 211 part-time. 5% are from out of state, 9% African American, 11% Asian American or Pacific Islander, 7% Hispanic American, 1% Native American, 0.5% international, 14% transferred in. *Retention:* 50% of 2006 full-time freshmen returned.

Freshmen *Admission:* 119 enrolled.

Faculty *Total:* 53, 43% full-time. *Student/faculty ratio:* 17:1.

Majors Accounting; biomedical technology; business administration and management; business administration, management and operations related; computer engineering technology; computer software engineering; computer systems analysis; computer systems networking and telecommunications; electrical, electronic and communications engineering technology.

Academics *Calendar:* semesters. *Degrees:* associate, bachelor's, and master's. *Special study options:* academic remediation for entering students, accelerated degree program, adult/continuing education programs, advanced placement credit, distance learning, part-time degree program, services for LD students, summer session for credit.

Computers on Campus 150 computers/terminals are available on campus for general student use. Students can access the following: online (class) registration. Campuswide network is available.

Student Life *Housing:* college housing not available. *Activities and organizations:* Associated Student Body (ASB), Ski Club, Computer Information Club, Basketball Club. *Campus security:* 24-hour emergency response devices and patrols, lighted pathways, emergency response team.

Athletics *Intramural sports:* basketball M/W, golf M/W, soccer M/W.

Costs (2008–09) *Tuition:* $14,480 full-time, $540 per credit part-time. *Required fees:* $180 full-time.

Financial Aid Of all full-time matriculated undergraduates who enrolled in 2002, 684 applied for aid, 657 were judged to have need, 15 had their need fully met. In 2002, 40 non-need-based awards were made. *Average percent of need met:* 33%. *Average financial aid package:* $7190. *Average need-based loan:* $5153. *Average need-based gift aid:* $3856. *Average non-need-based aid:* $11,520.

Applying *Options:* electronic application, early admission, deferred entrance. *Application fee:* $50. *Required:* high school transcript, interview. *Application deadlines:* rolling (freshmen), rolling (transfers). *Notification:* continuous (freshmen), continuous (transfers).

Freshman Application Contact DeVry University, 3600 South 344th Way, Federal Way, WA 98001-9558.

DigiPen Institute of Technology
Redmond, Washington www.digipen.edu/

- **Proprietary** comprehensive, founded 1988
- **Suburban** 1-acre campus
- **Coed** 821 undergraduate students
- **Moderately difficult** entrance level, 36% of applicants were admitted

Freshmen *Admission:* 509 applied, 181 admitted.

Faculty *Total:* 61, 66% full-time. *Student/faculty ratio:* 14:1.

Majors Computer and information sciences related; computer engineering related.

Academics *Calendar:* semesters. *Degrees:* bachelor's and master's. *Special study options:* academic remediation for entering students, advanced placement credit, independent study, internships, services for LD students, summer session for credit.

Computers on Campus Students can access the following: campus intranet, computer help desk, free student e-mail accounts, online (class) grades, online (class) registration, online (class) schedules. Campuswide network is available. Wireless service is available via entire campus.

Student Life *Housing:* college housing not available. *Options:* Campus housing is provided by a third party. *Activities and organizations:* Student Association, Music Club, Women In Games and Entertainment, Board Games Club. *Student services:* personal/psychological counseling.

Standardized Tests *Required:* SAT or ACT (for admission).

Costs (2008–09) *One-time required fee:* $150. *Tuition:* $19,040 full-time, $476 per credit part-time. *Required fees:* $160 full-time, $80 per term part-time.

Applying *Options:* electronic application, deferred entrance. *Application fee:* $75. *Required:* essay or personal statement, high school transcript, minimum 2.5 GPA, 2 letters of recommendation. *Required for some:* art portfolio. *Recommended:* art portfolio. *Application deadlines:* rolling (freshmen), rolling (out-of-state freshmen), rolling (transfers).

Freshman Application Contact Ms. Angela Kugler, Admissions Director, DigiPen Institute of Technology, 5001 150th Avenue, NE, Redmond, WA 98052. *Phone:* 425-895-4438. *Fax:* 425-558-0378. *E-mail:* akugler@digipen.edu.

Eastern Washington University
Cheney, Washington www.ewu.edu/

- **State-supported** comprehensive, founded 1882
- **Small-town** 335-acre campus
- **Endowment** $4.5 million
- **Coed**
- **Moderately difficult** entrance level

Faculty *Student/faculty ratio:* 20:1.

Academics *Calendar:* quarters. *Degrees:* bachelor's, master's, and doctoral.

Student Life *Campus security:* 24-hour emergency response devices and patrols, student patrols, late-night transport/escort service, controlled dormitory access, emergency call boxes.

Athletics Member NCAA. All Division I except football (Division I-AA).

Standardized Tests *Required:* SAT or ACT (for admission).

Costs (2007–08) *Tuition:* state resident $4485 full-time, $150 per credit part-time; nonresident $13,350 full-time, $445 per credit part-time. Full-time tuition and fees vary according to course load and program. Part-time tuition and fees vary according to course load and program. *Required fees:* $291 full-time, $97 per term part-time. *Room and board:* $6459. Room and board charges vary according to board plan and housing facility.

Financial Aid Of all full-time matriculated undergraduates who enrolled in 2004, 5,725 applied for aid, 4,753 were judged to have need, 693 had their need fully met. 261 Federal Work-Study jobs (averaging $1817). 503 state and other part-time jobs (averaging $2061). In 2004, 114 non-need-based awards were made. *Average percent of need met:* 38. *Average financial aid package:* $10,381. *Average need-based loan:* $3684. *Average need-based gift aid:* $4627. *Average non-need-based aid:* $3136. *Average indebtedness upon graduation:* $18,097.

Applying *Options:* electronic application, early admission, deferred entrance. *Application fee:* $50. *Required:* high school transcript, minimum 2.0 GPA. *Required for some:* essay or personal statement, letters of recommendation, interview. *Recommended:* minimum 3.0 GPA.

Freshman Application Contact Ms. Shannon Carr, Director of Admissions, Eastern Washington University, 526 Fifth Street, SUT 101, Cheney, WA 99004-2447. *Phone:* 509-359-6582. *Fax:* 509-359-6692. *E-mail:* admissions@mail.ewu.edu.

See page 2720 for the College Close-Up.

The Evergreen State College
Olympia, Washington www.evergreen.edu/

- **State-supported** comprehensive, founded 1967, part of Washington State Public Baccalarueate Institution
- **Rural** 1000-acre campus with easy access to Seattle
- **Endowment** $2.5 million
- **Coed** 4,282 undergraduate students, 89% full-time, 56% women, 44% men
- **Moderately difficult** entrance level, 97% of applicants were admitted

Undergraduates 3,802 full-time, 480 part-time. Students come from 51 states and territories, 11 other countries, 24% are from out of state, 4% African American, 5% Asian American or Pacific Islander, 5% Hispanic American, 4% Native American, 0.4% international, 20% transferred in, 22% live on campus. *Retention:* 68% of 2006 full-time freshmen returned.

Freshmen *Admission:* 1,806 applied, 1,750 admitted, 686 enrolled. *Average high school GPA:* 3.06. *Test scores:* SAT critical reading scores over 500: 83%; SAT math scores over 500: 64%; ACT scores over 18: 95%; SAT critical reading scores over 600: 42%; SAT math scores over 600: 24%; ACT scores over 24: 53%; SAT critical reading scores over 700: 9%; SAT math scores over 700: 2%; ACT scores over 30: 8%.

Faculty *Total:* 242, 65% full-time, 73% with terminal degrees. *Student/faculty ratio:* 23:1.

Majors American Indian/Native American studies; area, ethnic, cultural, and gender studies related; art; biological and physical sciences; biology/biological sciences; business administration and management; cinematography and film/video production; classics and languages, literatures and linguistics; communication and journalism related; communication/speech communication and rhetoric; computer and information sciences; dramatic/theater arts; English; environmental science; environmental studies; film/cinema studies; fine/studio arts; foreign languages related; health professions related; humanities; intercultural/multicultural and diversity studies; intermedia/multimedia; international/global studies; liberal arts and sciences/liberal studies; mathematics and statistics related; multi-/interdisciplinary studies related; natural resources/conservation; natural sciences; physical sciences; political science and government; psychology related; social sciences; visual and performing arts.

Academics *Calendar:* quarters. *Degrees:* bachelor's and master's. *Special study options:* accelerated degree program, advanced placement credit, cooperative education, double majors, independent study, internships, off-campus study, part-time degree program, services for LD students, student-designed majors, study abroad, summer session for credit.

Computers on Campus 375 computers/terminals are available on campus for general student use. Students can access the following: campus intranet, computer help desk, free student e-mail accounts, online (class) grades, online (class) registration, online (class) schedules, online payment and student accounts history. Campuswide network is available. Wireless service is available via entire campus.

Student Life *Housing options:* coed, disabled students. Campus housing is university owned. Freshman campus housing is guaranteed. *Activities and organizations:* drama/theater group, student-run newspaper, radio and television station, choral group, Environmental Resource Center, Women's Resource Center, Evergreen Queer Alliance, Evergreen Political Information Center, Students Educating Students about the Middle East (SESAME). *Campus security:* 24-hour emergency response devices and patrols, student patrols, late-night transport/escort service, controlled dormitory access. *Student services:* health clinic, personal/psychological counseling, women's center.

Athletics Member NAIA. *Intercollegiate sports:* basketball M (s)/W (s), crew M (c)/W (c), cross-country running M (s)/W (s), soccer M (s)/W (s), track and field M (s)/W (s), volleyball W (s). *Intramural sports:* badminton M/W, baseball M (c), basketball M/W, racquetball M/W, soccer M/W, softball M/W (c), tennis M/W, ultimate Frisbee M/W, volleyball M/W.

Standardized Tests *Required:* SAT or ACT (for admission).

Costs (2007–08) *Tuition:* state resident $4590 full-time, $153 per quarter hour part-time; nonresident $14,934 full-time, $498 per quarter hour part-time. Full-time tuition and fees vary according to course load, degree level, and location. Part-time tuition and fees vary according to course load, degree level, and location. *Required fees:* $537 full-time, $10 per quarter hour part-time, $47 per term part-time. *Room and board:* $7842; room only: $5310. Room and board charges vary according to board plan, housing facility, and student level. *Payment plan:* installment. *Waivers:* employees or children of employees.

Financial Aid Of all full-time matriculated undergraduates who enrolled in 2006, 2,906 applied for aid, 2,182 were judged to have need, 877 had their need fully met. 196 Federal Work-Study jobs (averaging $1988). 154 state and other part-time jobs (averaging $2253). In 2006, 14 non-need-based awards were made. *Average percent of need met:* 81%. *Average financial aid package:* $11,066. *Average need-based loan:* $4871. *Average need-based gift aid:* $5672. *Average non-need-based aid:* $3793. *Average indebtedness upon graduation:* $13,818.

Applying *Options:* electronic application. *Application fee:* $50. *Required:* high school transcript, minimum 2.0 GPA. *Recommended:* essay or personal statement. *Application deadlines:* rolling (freshmen), rolling (transfers). *Notification:* 12/1 (freshmen), 4/1 (transfers).

Freshman Application Contact Mr. Doug Scrima, Director of Admissions, The Evergreen State College, 2700 Evergreen Parkway NW, Admissions, Olympia, WA 98505. *Phone:* 360-867-6170. *Fax:* 360-867-5114. *E-mail:* admissions@evergreen.edu.

GONZAGA UNIVERSITY

Spokane, Washington **www.gonzaga.edu/**

- **Independent Roman Catholic** comprehensive, founded 1887
- **Urban** 94-acre campus
- **Endowment** $151.6 million
- **Coed** 4,385 undergraduate students, 97% full-time, 53% women, 47% men
- **Moderately difficult** entrance level, 69% of applicants were admitted

Gonzaga University's nationally dominant debate team, excellent preparation for graduate and professional schools, and CPA examination pass rates exemplify its commitment to academic excellence. A 37,000-square-foot addition to Hughes Hall Life Sciences Building adds new opportunities for study in environmental biology. In addition, the new 23,000-square-foot wing of the Jepson Center for Business Administration allows for expansion of the Hogan Entrepreneurial Leadership and Scholarship Program. The Martin Athletic Center houses a 13,000-square-foot modern fitness center. Scheduled to open in 2008, the PACCAR Center for Applied Science will house a transmission and distribution power engineering lab, a robotics lab, a computer science lab with high-speed cluster computer array, classrooms, and research space.

Undergraduates 4,240 full-time, 145 part-time. Students come from 53 states and territories, 40 other countries, 54% are from out of state, 1% African American, 5% Asian American or Pacific Islander, 4% Hispanic American, 1% Native American, 2% international, 4% transferred in, 51% live on campus. *Retention:* 91% of 2006 full-time freshmen returned.

Freshmen *Admission:* 5,744 applied, 3,961 admitted, 1,036 enrolled. *Average high school GPA:* 3.69. *Test scores:* SAT critical reading scores over 500: 90%; SAT math scores over 500: 91%; ACT scores over 18: 100%; SAT critical reading scores over 600: 44%; SAT math scores over 600: 50%; ACT scores over 24: 81%; SAT critical reading scores over 700: 9%; SAT math scores over 700: 9%; ACT scores over 30: 19%.

Faculty *Total:* 694, 51% full-time. *Student/faculty ratio:* 11:1.

Majors Accounting; art; Asian studies; biochemistry; biology/biological sciences; broadcast journalism; business administration and management; business/managerial economics; chemistry; civil engineering; computer engineering; computer science; criminal justice/law enforcement administration; dramatic/theater arts; economics; electrical, electronics and communications engineering; elementary education; engineering; English; finance; French; German; history; information science/studies; international business/trade/commerce; international relations and affairs; Italian; journalism; kinesiology and exercise science; liberal arts and sciences/liberal studies; literature; marketing/marketing management; mass communication/media; mathematics; mechanical engineering; music; music teacher education; nursing (registered nurse training); philosophy; physical education teaching and coaching; physics; political science and government; psychology; public relations/image management; religious studies; secondary education; sociology; Spanish; special education; speech and rhetoric; sport and fitness administration/management.

Academics *Calendar:* semesters. *Degrees:* bachelor's, master's, doctoral, first professional, and post-master's certificates. *Special study options:* accelerated degree program, adult/continuing education programs, advanced placement credit, double majors, English as a second language, honors programs, independent study, internships, off-campus study, part-time degree program, services for LD students, study abroad, summer session for credit. *ROTC:* Army (b). *Unusual degree programs:* 3-2 nursing with Gonzaga RN to MSN program.

Computers on Campus 625 computers/terminals are available on campus for general student use. Students can access the following: computer help desk, free student e-mail accounts, online (class) grades, online (class) registration, online (class) schedules. Campuswide network is available. Wireless service is available via classrooms, computer centers, computer labs, dorm rooms, libraries, student centers.

Student Life *Housing:* on-campus residence required through sophomore year. *Options:* coed, men-only, women-only, disabled students. Campus housing is university owned and leased by the school. Freshman campus housing is guaranteed. *Activities and organizations:* drama/theater group, student-run newspaper, radio and television station, choral group, Student Body Association, Search, Circle K, Encore, Knights and Setons. *Campus security:* 24-hour emergency response devices and patrols, late-night transport/escort service, controlled dormitory access. *Student services:* health clinic, personal/psychological counseling.

Athletics Member NCAA. All Division I. *Intercollegiate sports:* baseball M (s), basketball M (s)/W (s), crew M (c)/W (c), cross-country running M/W, golf M/W, skiing (cross-country) M (c)/W (c), skiing (downhill) M (c)/W (c), soccer M (s)/W (s), tennis M (s)/W (s), track and field M/W, volleyball W (s). *Intramural sports:* basketball M (c)/W (c), football M (c)/W (c), racquetball M (c)/W (c), softball M (c)/W (c), volleyball M (c)/W (c).

Standardized Tests *Required:* SAT or ACT (for admission).
Costs (2008–09) *Comprehensive fee:* $36,122 includes full-time tuition ($27,820), mandatory fees ($442), and room and board ($7860). Part-time tuition: $810 per credit. *Required fees:* $50 per term part-time. *College room only:* $3880.
Financial Aid Of all full-time matriculated undergraduates who enrolled in 2006, 3,072 applied for aid, 2,405 were judged to have need, 767 had their need fully met. 447 Federal Work-Study jobs (averaging $3560). 369 state and other part-time jobs (averaging $4845). In 2006, 1465 non-need-based awards were made. *Average percent of need met:* 84%. *Average financial aid package:* $19,207. *Average need-based loan:* $5687. *Average need-based gift aid:* $13,529. *Average non-need-based aid:* $8070. *Average indebtedness upon graduation:* $23,971.
Applying *Options:* electronic application, early action, deferred entrance. *Application fee:* $45. *Required:* essay or personal statement, high school transcript, minimum 3.0 GPA, 1 letter of recommendation. *Recommended:* interview. *Application deadlines:* 2/1 (freshmen), 6/1 (transfers), 11/15 (early action). *Notification:* 3/15 (freshmen), continuous (transfers), 1/15 (early action).
Freshman Application Contact Ms. Julie McCulloh, Dean of Admission, Gonzaga University, 502 East Boone Avenue, Spokane, WA 99258-0102. *Phone:* 509-323-6591. *Toll-free phone:* 800-322-2584 Ext. 6572. *Fax:* 509-323-5780. *E-mail:* admissions@gonzaga.edu.

See page 2722 for the College Close-Up.

HERITAGE UNIVERSITY
Toppenish, Washington — www.heritage.edu/

Freshman Application Contact Ms. Leticia Garcia, Director of Admissions and Recruitment, Heritage University, 3240 Fort Road, Toppenish, WA 98948-9599. *Phone:* 509-865-8508. *Toll-free phone:* 888-272-6190. *Fax:* 509-865-4469. *E-mail:* garcia_1@heritage.edu.

ITT TECHNICAL INSTITUTE
Bothell, Washington — www.itt-tech.edu/

- **Proprietary** primarily 2-year, founded 1993, part of ITT Educational Services, Inc
- **Coed**
- **Minimally difficult** entrance level

Academics *Calendar:* quarters. *Degrees:* associate and bachelor's.
Standardized Tests *Required:* Wonderlic aptitude test (for admission).
Applying *Options:* deferred entrance. *Application fee:* $100. *Required:* high school transcript, interview. *Recommended:* letters of recommendation.
Freshman Application Contact Mr. Brad Tmavsky, Director of Recruitment, ITT Technical Institute, 1615 75th Street SW, Everett, WA 98203. *Phone:* 425-583-0200. *Toll-free phone:* 800-272-3791.

ITT TECHNICAL INSTITUTE
Seattle, Washington — www.itt-tech.edu/

- **Proprietary** primarily 2-year, founded 1932, part of ITT Educational Services, Inc
- **Urban** campus
- **Coed**
- **Minimally difficult** entrance level

Academics *Calendar:* quarters. *Degrees:* associate and bachelor's.
Standardized Tests *Required:* Wonderlic aptitude test (for admission).
Applying *Options:* deferred entrance. *Application fee:* $100. *Required:* high school transcript, interview. *Recommended:* letters of recommendation.
Freshman Application Contact Mr. David Thompson, Director of Recruitment, ITT Technical Institute, 12720 Gateway Drive, Seattle, WA 98168. *Phone:* 206-244-3300. *Toll-free phone:* 800-422-2029.

ITT TECHNICAL INSTITUTE
Spokane, Washington — www.itt-tech.edu/

- **Proprietary** primarily 2-year, founded 1985, part of ITT Educational Services, Inc
- **Suburban** 3-acre campus
- **Coed**
- **Minimally difficult** entrance level

Academics *Calendar:* quarters. *Degrees:* associate and bachelor's.
Standardized Tests *Required:* Wonderlic aptitude test (for admission).
Financial Aid Of all full-time matriculated undergraduates who enrolled in 2006, 9 Federal Work-Study jobs (averaging $4000).
Applying *Options:* deferred entrance. *Application fee:* $100. *Required:* high school transcript, interview. *Recommended:* letters of recommendation.
Freshman Application Contact Mr. Gregory L. Alexander, Director of Recruitment, ITT Technical Institute, 13518 East Indiana Avenue, Spokane Valley, WA 99216. *Phone:* 509-926-2900. *Toll-free phone:* 800-777-8324.

NORTHWEST COLLEGE OF ART
Poulsbo, Washington — www.nca.edu/

- **Proprietary** 4-year, founded 1982
- **Small-town** 26-acre campus with easy access to Seattle
- **Coed**
- **Moderately difficult** entrance level

Academics *Calendar:* semesters. *Degree:* bachelor's.
Costs (2007–08) *Tuition:* $14,300 full-time, $625 per credit part-time. Full-time tuition and fees vary according to course load. Part-time tuition and fees vary according to course load. *Required fees:* $100 full-time, $100 per year part-time.
Financial Aid *Financial aid deadline:* 5/1.
Applying *Options:* deferred entrance. *Application fee:* $50. *Required:* essay or personal statement, high school transcript, minimum 2.5 GPA, 3 letters of recommendation, interview, portfolio.
Freshman Application Contact Mr. Mark Stoddard, Admissions, Northwest College of Art, 16464 State Highway 305, Poulsbo, WA 98370. *Phone:* 360-779-9993. *Toll-free phone:* 800-769-ARTS. *E-mail:* mstoddard@nca.edu.

NORTHWEST UNIVERSITY
Kirkland, Washington — www.northwestu.edu/

- **Independent** comprehensive, founded 1934, affiliated with Assemblies of God
- **Suburban** 56-acre campus with easy access to Seattle
- **Endowment** $8.9 million
- **Coed**
- **Moderately difficult** entrance level

Faculty *Student/faculty ratio:* 17:1.
Academics *Calendar:* semesters. *Degrees:* certificates, diplomas, associate, bachelor's, and master's.
Student Life *Campus security:* 24-hour emergency response devices and patrols, late-night transport/escort service, controlled dormitory access.
Athletics Member NAIA.
Standardized Tests *Required:* SAT or ACT (for admission).
Costs (2008–09) *Comprehensive fee:* $27,368 includes full-time tuition ($20,520), mandatory fees ($270), and room and board ($6578). Part-time tuition: $855 per credit.
Financial Aid Of all full-time matriculated undergraduates who enrolled in 2007, 833 applied for aid, 732 were judged to have need, 135 had their need fully met. 72 Federal Work-Study jobs (averaging $2338). 32 state and other part-time jobs (averaging $3412). In 2007, 164 non-need-based awards were made. *Average percent of need met:* 66. *Average financial aid package:* $13,681. *Average need-based loan:* $4078. *Average need-based gift aid:* $9465. *Average non-need-based aid:* $9971. *Average indebtedness upon graduation:* $20,050. *Financial aid deadline:* 8/1.
Applying *Options:* electronic application, deferred entrance. *Application fee:* $30. *Required:* essay or personal statement, high school transcript, minimum 2.3 GPA, 2 letters of recommendation. *Required for some:* interview.
Freshman Application Contact Mr. Ben Thomas, Director of Admissions, Northwest University, PO Box 579, Kirkland, WA 98083-0579. *Phone:* 425-889-5212. *Toll-free phone:* 800-669-3781. *Fax:* 425-889-5224. *E-mail:* admissions@northwestu.edu.

PACIFIC LUTHERAN UNIVERSITY

Tacoma, Washington **www.plu.edu/**

- **Independent** comprehensive, founded 1890, affiliated with Evangelical Lutheran Church in America
- **Suburban** 126-acre campus with easy access to Seattle
- **Endowment** $69.2 million
- **Coed** 3,349 undergraduate students, 93% full-time, 63% women, 37% men
- **Moderately difficult** entrance level, 76% of applicants were admitted

Success is measured differently for every student at Pacific Lutheran University (PLU). It springs from academic challenge in a community where everyone has high expectations for one another. It is developed when every member of the PLU community supports each other in meeting challenges and helps students define success in a way that best fits their goals and abilities.

Undergraduates 3,110 full-time, 239 part-time. Students come from 40 states and territories, 21 other countries, 21% are from out of state, 2% African American, 7% Asian American or Pacific Islander, 2% Hispanic American, 1% Native American, 6% international, 7% transferred in, 50% live on campus. *Retention:* 84% of 2006 full-time freshmen returned.

Freshmen *Admission:* 2,236 applied, 1,707 admitted, 715 enrolled. *Average high school GPA:* 3.61. *Test scores:* SAT critical reading scores over 500: 75%; SAT math scores over 500: 71%; SAT writing scores over 500: 69%; ACT scores over 18: 98%; SAT critical reading scores over 600: 36%; SAT math scores over 600: 30%; SAT writing scores over 600: 26%; ACT scores over 24: 62%; SAT critical reading scores over 700: 6%; SAT math scores over 700: 4%; SAT writing scores over 700: 4%; ACT scores over 30: 16%.

Faculty *Total:* 255, 94% full-time, 82% with terminal degrees. *Student/faculty ratio:* 14:1.

Majors Anthropology; art; biology/biological sciences; business administration and management; chemistry; Chinese; Chinese studies; classics and languages, literatures and linguistics; computer science; economics; education; engineering; English; environmental studies; fine/studio arts; French; geological and earth sciences/geosciences related; geology/earth science; German; history; international/global studies; mathematics; military studies; movement therapy and movement education; music; music teacher education; Norwegian; nursing (registered nurse training); philosophy; physics; political science and government; pre-law; pre-medical studies; psychology; religious studies; Scandinavian studies; social work; sociology; Spanish; theology; women's studies.

Academics *Calendar:* 4-1-4. *Degrees:* bachelor's, master's, post-master's, and postbachelor's certificates. *Special study options:* adult/continuing education programs, advanced placement credit, cooperative education, double majors, English as a second language, independent study, internships, part-time degree program, services for LD students, student-designed majors, study abroad, summer session for credit. *ROTC:* Army (b). *Unusual degree programs:* 3-2 engineering with Columbia University, Washington University in St. Louis.

Computers on Campus 390 computers/terminals and 1,200 ports are available on campus for general student use. Students can access the following: campus intranet, computer help desk, free student e-mail accounts, online (class) grades, online (class) registration, online (class) schedules. Campuswide network is available. 100% of college-owned or -operated housing units are wired for high-speed Internet access.

Student Life *Housing:* on-campus residence required through sophomore year. *Options:* coed, women-only. Campus housing is university owned. Freshman campus housing is guaranteed. *Activities and organizations:* drama/theater group, student-run newspaper, radio and television station, choral group, Ignite, Circle K, Adult Students Club, Residence Hall Government, Inter-Varsity Fellowship. *Campus security:* 24-hour emergency response devices and patrols, student patrols, late-night transport/escort service. *Student services:* health clinic, personal/psychological counseling, women's center.

Athletics Member NCAA. All Division III. *Intercollegiate sports:* baseball M, basketball M/W, cheerleading M/W, crew M/W, cross-country running M/W, football M, golf M/W, lacrosse M (c)/W (c), soccer M/W, softball W, swimming and diving M/W, tennis M/W, track and field M/W, ultimate Frisbee M (c)/W (c), volleyball M (c)/W. *Intramural sports:* badminton M/W, basketball M/W, cross-country running M/W, football M/W, racquetball M/W, soccer M/W, softball W, squash M/W, volleyball M/W.

Standardized Tests *Required:* SAT or ACT (for admission).

Costs (2007–08) *Comprehensive fee:* $32,800 includes full-time tuition ($25,088) and room and board ($7712). Full-time tuition and fees vary according to course load. Part-time tuition and fees vary according to course load. *College room only:* $3720. Room and board charges vary according to board plan and housing facility. *Payment plan:* installment. *Waivers:* employees or children of employees.

Financial Aid Of all full-time matriculated undergraduates who enrolled in 2006, 2,512 applied for aid, 2,127 were judged to have need, 651 had their need fully met. 590 Federal Work-Study jobs (averaging $1864). 255 state and other part-time jobs (averaging $5098). In 2006, 794 non-need-based awards were made. *Average percent of need met:* 86%. *Average financial aid package:* $24,551. *Average need-based loan:* $8063. *Average need-based gift aid:* $13,524. *Average non-need-based aid:* $10,033. *Average indebtedness upon graduation:* $23,348.

Applying *Options:* electronic application, early admission, deferred entrance. *Application fee:* $40. *Required:* essay or personal statement, high school transcript, 1 letter of recommendation. *Required for some:* interview. *Recommended:* minimum 2.5 GPA. *Application deadlines:* rolling (freshmen), rolling (transfers). *Notification:* continuous (freshmen), continuous (transfers).

Freshman Application Contact Dr. Laura Majovski, Vice President for Admissions and Student Life, Pacific Lutheran University, Tacoma, WA 98447. *Phone:* 253-535-7151. *Toll-free phone:* 800-274-6758. *Fax:* 253-536-5136. *E-mail:* admission@plu.edu.

SAINT MARTIN'S UNIVERSITY

Lacey, Washington **www.stmartin.edu/**

- **Independent Roman Catholic** comprehensive, founded 1895
- **Suburban** 300-acre campus with easy access to Tacoma
- **Endowment** $13.9 million
- **Coed** 1,334 undergraduate students, 81% full-time, 54% women, 46% men
- **Moderately difficult** entrance level, 93% of applicants were admitted

Undergraduates 1,077 full-time, 257 part-time. Students come from 34 states and territories, 11 other countries, 12% are from out of state, 7% African American, 10% Asian American or Pacific Islander, 6% Hispanic American, 2% Native American, 5% international, 13% transferred in, 29% live on campus. *Retention:* 77% of 2006 full-time freshmen returned.

Freshmen *Admission:* 657 applied, 611 admitted, 241 enrolled. *Average high school GPA:* 0. *Test scores:* SAT critical reading scores over 500: 55%; SAT math scores over 500: 54%; ACT scores over 18: 77%; SAT critical reading scores over 600: 22%; SAT math scores over 600: 17%; ACT scores over 24: 22%; SAT critical reading scores over 700: 4%; ACT scores over 30: 5%.

Faculty *Total:* 189, 37% full-time, 38% with terminal degrees. *Student/faculty ratio:* 11:1.

Majors Accounting; biology/biological sciences; business administration and management; chemistry; civil engineering; community organization and advocacy; computer science; criminal justice/law enforcement administration; dramatic/theater arts; economics; education; elementary education; English; finance; history; humanities; information science/studies; management information systems; marketing/marketing management; mathematics; mechanical engineering; political science and government; pre-dentistry studies; pre-law studies; premedical studies; pre-pharmacy studies; pre-veterinary studies; psychology; religious studies; secondary education; special education.

Academics *Calendar:* semesters. *Degrees:* bachelor's, master's, post-master's, and postbachelor's certificates. *Special study options:* academic remediation for entering students, accelerated degree program, adult/continuing education programs, advanced placement credit, cooperative education, double majors, English as a second language, independent study, internships, off-campus study, part-time degree program, services for LD students, study abroad, summer session for credit. *ROTC:* Army (c).

Computers on Campus 153 computers/terminals and 130 ports are available on campus for general student use. Students can access the following: campus intranet, computer help desk, free student e-mail accounts, online (class) grades, online (class) registration, online (class) schedules. Campuswide network is available. 100% of college-owned or -operated housing units are wired for high-speed Internet access. Wireless service is available via entire campus.

Student Life *Housing:* on-campus residence required through sophomore year. *Options:* coed. Campus housing is university owned and leased by the school. Freshman campus housing is guaranteed. *Activities and organizations:* drama/theater group, student-run newspaper, choral group, Mexico Service Club, Education Club, Hands of Campus Ministry, Society of Women Engineering, Soccer Club. *Campus security:* 24-hour emergency response devices and patrols, late-night transport/escort service, night patrols by security personnel. *Student services:* personal/psychological counseling.

Athletics Member NCAA. All Division II. *Intercollegiate sports:* baseball M (s), basketball M (s)/W (s), cross-country running M (s)/W (s), golf M (s)/W (s), softball W (s), track and field M (s)/W (s), volleyball W (s). *Intramural sports:* basketball M/W, golf M/W, soccer M/W, softball W, tennis M/W, ultimate Frisbee M/W, volleyball M/W.

Standardized Tests *Required:* SAT or ACT (for admission).

Costs (2008–09) *Comprehensive fee:* $31,850 includes full-time tuition ($23,810) and room and board ($8040). Part-time tuition: $794 per credit.

Financial Aid Of all full-time matriculated undergraduates who enrolled in 2005, 750 applied for aid, 681 were judged to have need, 232 had their need fully met. 191 Federal Work-Study jobs (averaging $1875). 175 state and other part-time jobs (averaging $1893). In 2005, 112 non-need-based awards were made. *Average percent of need met:* 85%. *Average financial aid package:* $17,572. *Average need-based loan:* $5197. *Average need-based gift aid:* $11,679. *Average non-need-based aid:* $9545. *Average indebtedness upon graduation:* $27,846.

Applying *Options:* electronic application. *Application fee:* $35. *Required:* essay or personal statement, high school transcript, minimum 2.5 GPA, 1 letter of recommendation, minimum combined score of 900 in SAT. *Required for some:* interview. *Application deadline:* 8/1 (transfers). *Notification:* continuous until 8/15 (freshmen), continuous until 8/15 (transfers).

Freshman Application Contact Mr. Eric Pedersen, Dean of Enrollment, Saint Martin's University, 5300 Pacific Avenue, SE, Lacey, WA 98503. *Phone:* 360-438-4590. *Toll-free phone:* 800-368-8803. *Fax:* 360-412-6189. *E-mail:* admissions@stmartin.edu.

SEATTLE PACIFIC UNIVERSITY

Seattle, Washington **www.spu.edu/**

- **Independent Free Methodist** comprehensive, founded 1891
- **Urban** 35-acre campus
- **Endowment** $43.4 million
- **Coed** 3,038 undergraduate students, 95% full-time, 67% women, 33% men
- **Moderately difficult** entrance level, 85% of applicants were admitted

Founded in 1891, Seattle Pacific University (SPU) is a premier Christian university that equips people to engage the culture and change the world. Its comprehensive academic program serves more than 3,800 undergraduate and graduate students. Known for both their competence and character, SPU graduates are bringing about positive change in communities around the globe.

Undergraduates 2,893 full-time, 145 part-time. Students come from 46 states and territories, 24 other countries, 38% are from out of state, 2% African American, 7% Asian American or Pacific Islander, 3% Hispanic American, 1% Native American, 0.7% international, 7% transferred in, 56% live on campus. *Retention:* 86% of 2006 full-time freshmen returned.

Freshmen *Admission:* 2,055 applied, 1,756 admitted, 716 enrolled. *Average high school GPA:* 3.59. *Test scores:* SAT critical reading scores over 500: 85%; SAT math scores over 500: 80%; SAT writing scores over 500: 80%; ACT scores over 18: 98%; SAT critical reading scores over 600: 41%; SAT math scores over 600: 34%; SAT writing scores over 600: 35%; ACT scores over 24: 60%; SAT critical reading scores over 700: 11%; SAT math scores over 700: 5%; SAT writing scores over 700: 6%; ACT scores over 30: 13%.

Faculty *Total:* 324, 57% full-time, 54% with terminal degrees. *Student/faculty ratio:* 14:1.

Majors Accounting; apparel and textiles; art; art teacher education; biochemistry; biology/biological sciences; biology teacher education; business administration and management; chemistry; classics and languages, literatures and linguistics; communication/speech communication and rhetoric; computer/information technology services administration related; computer science; computer systems analysis; dramatic/theater arts; economics; electrical, electronics and communications engineering; engineering science; English; English/language arts teacher education; European studies; family and consumer economics related; family and consumer sciences/home economics teacher education; foods, nutrition, and wellness; French; general studies; German; history; kinesiology and exercise science; Latin; Latin American studies; liberal arts and sciences/liberal studies; mathematics; mathematics and statistics related; mathematics teacher education; music; music teacher education; nursing (registered nurse training); philosophy; physical education teaching and coaching; physics; political science and government; pre-dentistry studies; pre-law studies; pre-medical studies; psychology; religious education; Russian; science teacher education; social science teacher education; sociology; Spanish; special education; theology.

Academics *Calendar:* quarters. *Degrees:* diplomas, bachelor's, master's, doctoral, and post-master's certificates. *Special study options:* academic remediation for entering students, adult/continuing education programs, advanced placement credit, cooperative education, distance learning, double majors, English as a second language, external degree program, honors programs, independent study, internships, off-campus study, part-time degree program, services for LD students, student-designed majors, study abroad, summer session for credit. *ROTC:* Army (c), Navy (c), Air Force (c).

Computers on Campus 150 computers/terminals are available on campus for general student use. Students can access the following: online (class) registration. Campuswide network is available.

Student Life *Housing:* on-campus residence required through senior year. *Options:* coed. Campus housing is university owned. Freshman campus housing is guaranteed. *Activities and organizations:* drama/theater group, student-run newspaper, radio station, choral group, Centurions, Falconettes, forensics organization, Amnesty International, University Players. *Campus security:* 24-hour emergency response devices and patrols, student patrols, late-night transport/escort service, closed-circuit TV monitors. *Student services:* health clinic, personal/psychological counseling.

Athletics Member NCAA. All Division II. *Intercollegiate sports:* basketball M (s)/W (s), crew M/W, cross-country running M (s)/W (s), gymnastics W (s), soccer M (s)/W, track and field M (s)/W (s), volleyball W (s). *Intramural sports:* badminton M/W, basketball M/W, bowling M/W, cross-country running M/W, football M/W, golf M/W, skiing (cross-country) M (c)/W (c), skiing (downhill) M (c)/W (c), soccer M/W (c), softball M/W, swimming and diving M/W, table tennis M/W, tennis M/W, track and field M/W, volleyball M (c)/W (c), weight lifting M/W, wrestling M.

Standardized Tests *Required:* SAT or ACT (for admission).

Costs (2007–08) *Comprehensive fee:* $33,210 includes full-time tuition ($24,783), mandatory fees ($345), and room and board ($8082). Part-time tuition: $689 per credit. Part-time tuition and fees vary according to course load. *College room only:* $4368. Room and board charges vary according to board plan and housing facility. *Payment plan:* installment. *Waivers:* senior citizens and employees or children of employees.

Financial Aid Of all full-time matriculated undergraduates who enrolled in 2007, 2,115 applied for aid, 1,756 were judged to have need, 249 had their need fully met. 375 Federal Work-Study jobs (averaging $1442). 413 state and other part-time jobs (averaging $1923). In 2007, 808 non-need-based awards were made. *Average percent of need met:* 82%. *Average financial aid package:* $20,988. *Average need-based loan:* $5872. *Average need-based gift aid:* $16,834. *Average non-need-based aid:* $11,696. *Average indebtedness upon graduation:* $23,738.

Applying *Options:* electronic application, early admission, early action. *Application fee:* $45. *Required:* essay or personal statement, high school transcript, minimum 2.5 GPA, 2 letters of recommendation. *Application deadlines:* 2/1 (freshmen), 8/1 (transfers), 11/15 (early action). *Notification:* continuous until 3/1 (freshmen), continuous (transfers), 1/5 (early action).

Freshman Application Contact Mr. Jobe Nice, Acting Director of Admissions, Seattle Pacific University, 3307 Third Avenue West, Seattle, WA 98119-1997. *Phone:* 206-281-2021. *Toll-free phone:* 800-366-3344. *Fax:* 206-281-2669. *E-mail:* admissions@spu.edu.

See page 2724 for the College Close-Up.

SEATTLE UNIVERSITY

Seattle, Washington **www.seattleu.edu/**

- **Independent Roman Catholic** comprehensive, founded 1891
- **Urban** 46-acre campus
- **Endowment** $184.7 million
- **Coed** 4,253 undergraduate students, 93% full-time, 61% women, 39% men
- **Moderately difficult** entrance level, 64% of applicants were admitted

Undergraduates 3,951 full-time, 302 part-time. Students come from 47 states and territories, 76 other countries, 55% are from out of state, 5% African American, 20% Asian American or Pacific Islander, 7% Hispanic American, 1% Native American, 8% international, 9% transferred in, 39% live on campus. *Retention:* 86% of 2006 full-time freshmen returned.

Freshmen *Admission:* 4,918 applied, 3,131 admitted, 768 enrolled. *Average high school GPA:* 3.55. *Test scores:* SAT critical reading scores over 500: 84%; SAT math scores over 500: 87%; SAT writing scores over 500: 81%; ACT scores over 18: 99%; SAT critical reading scores over 600: 43%; SAT math scores over 600: 41%; SAT writing scores over 600: 36%; ACT scores over 24: 68%; SAT critical reading scores over 700: 11%; SAT math scores over 700: 6%; SAT writing scores over 700: 6%; ACT scores over 30: 11%.

Faculty *Total:* 645, 66% full-time, 76% with terminal degrees. *Student/faculty ratio:* 13:1.

Majors Accounting; applied mathematics; art; art history, criticism and conservation; Asian studies (East); biochemistry; biological and physical sciences; biology/biological sciences; business administration and management; business/managerial economics; chemistry; civil engineering; clinical laboratory science/medical technology; computer science; creative writing; criminal justice/law enforcement administration; diagnostic medical sonography and ultrasound technology; dramatic/theater arts; economics; electrical, electronics and communications engineering; English; environmental/environmental health engineering; environmental studies; European studies (Western); finance; fine/studio arts; forensic science and technology; French; German; history; humanities; industrial engineering; insurance; international business/trade/commerce; international economics; international relations and affairs; journalism; liberal arts and sciences/liberal studies; management information systems; marketing/marketing management; mass communication/media; mathematics; mechanical engineering; nursing (registered nurse training); operations management; philosophy; photography; physics; political science and government; psychology; public administration; public relations/image management; religious studies; social work; sociology; Spanish.

Academics *Calendar:* quarters. *Degrees:* bachelor's, master's, doctoral, first professional, post-master's, postbachelor's, and first professional certificates. *Special study options:* accelerated degree program, adult/continuing education programs, advanced placement credit, double majors, English as a second language, freshman honors college, honors programs, independent study, internships, off-campus study, part-time degree program, services for LD students, student-designed majors, study abroad, summer session for credit. *ROTC:* Army (b), Air Force (c).

Computers on Campus 401 computers/terminals are available on campus for general student use. Students can access the following: online (class) registration. Campuswide network is available.

Student Life *Housing:* on-campus residence required through sophomore year. *Options:* coed, men-only. Campus housing is university owned. Freshman campus housing is guaranteed. *Activities and organizations:* drama/theater group, student-run newspaper, radio station, choral group, student government, Volunteer Center, Hawaiian Club, International Student Club. *Campus security:* 24-hour emergency response devices and patrols, late-night transport/escort service, controlled dormitory access, bicycle patrols. *Student services:* health clinic, personal/psychological counseling, women's center.

Athletics Member NCAA, NAIA. All NCAA Division II. *Intercollegiate sports:* archery M (c)/W (c), baseball M (c)/W (c), basketball M (s)/W (s), cheerleading M (c)/W (c), crew M (c)/W (c), cross-country running M (s)/W (s), golf M (c)/W (c), riflery M (c)/W (c), skiing (downhill) M (c)/W (c), soccer M (s)/W (s), softball W (s), swimming and diving M (s)/W (s), track and field M (s)/W (s), volleyball M (c)/W, water polo M (c)/W (c). *Intramural sports:* basketball M/W, field hockey M/W, football M/W, soccer M/W, softball M/W, tennis M/W, ultimate Frisbee M/W, volleyball M/W.

Standardized Tests *Required:* SAT or ACT (for admission).

Costs (2008–09) *Comprehensive fee:* $36,600 includes full-time tuition ($28,260) and room and board ($8340). Part-time tuition: $628 per credit. *College room only:* $5265.

Financial Aid Of all full-time matriculated undergraduates who enrolled in 2007, 3,156 applied for aid, 2,527 were judged to have need, 220 had their need fully met. In 2007, 179 non-need-based awards were made. *Average percent of need met:* 71%. *Average financial aid package:* $24,468. *Average need-based loan:* $4098. *Average need-based gift aid:* $5442. *Average non-need-based aid:* $9308. *Average indebtedness upon graduation:* $20,067.

Applying *Options:* electronic application, early action, deferred entrance. *Application fee:* $45. *Required:* essay or personal statement, high school transcript, minimum 2.5 GPA, 2 letters of recommendation. *Application deadlines:* rolling (freshmen), 8/15 (transfers), 11/15 (early action). *Notification:* continuous (freshmen), continuous (transfers), 12/22 (early action).

Freshman Application Contact Mr. Michael K. McKeon, Dean of Admissions, Seattle University, 901 12th Avenue, PO Box 222000, Seattle, WA 98122-1090. *Phone:* 206-296-2000. *Toll-free phone:* 800-542-0833 (in-state); 800-426-7123 (out-of-state). *Fax:* 206-296-5656. *E-mail:* admissions@seattleu.edu.

See page 2726 for the College Close-Up.

TRINITY LUTHERAN COLLEGE

Issaquah, Washington **www.tlc.edu/**

- **Independent Lutheran** 4-year, founded 1944
- **Suburban** 46-acre campus with easy access to Seattle
- **Coed** 115 undergraduate students
- **Minimally difficult** entrance level, 51% of applicants were admitted

Undergraduates Students come from 13 states and territories, 6 other countries, 10% are from out of state.

Freshmen *Admission:* 113 applied, 58 admitted. *Average high school GPA:* 3.1.

Faculty *Total:* 28, 46% full-time.

Majors Business administration and management; communication/speech communication and rhetoric; early childhood education; elementary education; intercultural/multicultural and diversity studies; psychology; religious/sacred music; social work.

Academics *Calendar:* quarters. *Degrees:* associate, bachelor's, and postbachelor's certificates. *Special study options:* academic remediation for entering students, advanced placement credit, double majors, English as a second language, independent study, internships, off-campus study, part-time degree program, services for LD students, study abroad.

Computers on Campus 15 computers/terminals are available on campus for general student use.

Student Life *Housing options:* coed. Campus housing is university owned. Freshman campus housing is guaranteed. *Activities and organizations:* drama/theater group, choral group, Environmental Commission, Student government, Worship Commission, Global Concerns, Activities Commission. *Campus security:* 24-hour emergency response devices, student patrols, controlled dormitory access. *Student services:* health clinic, personal/psychological counseling.

Athletics *Intramural sports:* basketball M/W, softball M/W, tennis M/W, volleyball M/W.

Standardized Tests *Required:* SAT or ACT (for admission).

Costs (2007–08) *Comprehensive fee:* $20,248 includes full-time tuition ($13,720), mandatory fees ($450), and room and board ($6078). Part-time tuition: $490 per credit hour. Part-time tuition and fees vary according to course load. *Required fees:* $10 per credit hour part-time, $150 per term part-time. *Room and board:* Room and board charges vary according to board plan and housing facility. *Payment plan:* installment. *Waivers:* senior citizens.

Financial Aid Of all full-time matriculated undergraduates who enrolled in 2006, 33 Federal Work-Study jobs (averaging $1014).

Applying *Options:* early admission, deferred entrance. *Application fee:* $30. *Required:* high school transcript, minimum 2.0 GPA, 2 letters of recommendation. *Required for some:* interview. *Application deadlines:* 9/15 (freshmen), 9/15 (transfers).

Director of Admissions Mr. Sean Lacy, Director of Admissions, Trinity Lutheran College, 4221 228th Avenue, SE, Issaquah, WA 98029-9299. *Phone:* 425-961-5512. *Toll-free phone:* 800-843-5659. *Fax:* 425-392-0404. *E-mail:* admissn@lbi.edu.

UNIVERSITY OF PHOENIX–EASTERN WASHINGTON CAMPUS

Spokane Valley, Washington **www.phoenix.edu/**

- **Proprietary** comprehensive, founded 2003
- **Urban** campus
- **Coed**
- **Noncompetitive** entrance level

Faculty *Student/faculty ratio:* 4:1.

Academics *Calendar:* continuous. *Degrees:* bachelor's and master's.

Student Life *Campus security:* late-night transport/escort service.

Costs (2007–08) *Tuition:* $10,530 full-time, $351 per credit part-time. Full-time tuition and fees vary according to course level.

Financial Aid *Average financial aid package:* $4005. *Average need-based gift aid:* $2184.

Applying *Options:* deferred entrance. *Application fee:* $45. *Required:* 1 letter of recommendation. *Required for some:* high school transcript.

Freshman Application Contact Ms. Beth Barilla, Associate Vice President, Student Admissions and Services, University of Phoenix–Eastern Washington Campus, 4615 East Elwood Street, Mail Stop AA-K101, Phoenix, AZ 85040-1958. *Phone:* 480-894-1758. *Toll-free phone:* 800-697-8223 (in-state); 800-228-7240 (out-of-state). *E-mail:* beth.barilla@phoenix.edu.

UNIVERSITY OF PHOENIX–WASHINGTON CAMPUS

Seattle, Washington **www.phoenix.edu/**

- **Proprietary** comprehensive, founded 1997
- **Urban** campus
- **Coed**
- **Noncompetitive** entrance level

Faculty *Student/faculty ratio:* 9:1.

Academics *Calendar:* continuous. *Degrees:* bachelor's and master's.

Student Life *Campus security:* late-night transport/escort service.
Costs (2007–08) *Tuition:* $11,520 full-time, $384 per credit part-time. Full-time tuition and fees vary according to course level.
Financial Aid *Average financial aid package:* $3681. *Average need-based gift aid:* $2035.
Applying *Options:* deferred entrance. *Application fee:* $45. *Required:* 1 letter of recommendation. *Required for some:* high school transcript.
Freshman Application Contact Ms. Beth Barilla, Associate Vice President, Student Admissions and Services, University of Phoenix–Washington Campus, 4615 East Elwood Street, Mail Stop AA-K101, Phoenix, AZ 85040-1958. *Phone:* 480-317-6000. *Toll-free phone:* 800-776-4867 (in-state); 800-228-7240 (out-of-state). *Fax:* 480-894-1758. *E-mail:* beth.barilla@phoenix.edu.

UNIVERSITY OF PUGET SOUND

Tacoma, Washington **www.ups.edu/**

- **Independent** comprehensive, founded 1888
- **Suburban** 97-acre campus with easy access to Seattle
- **Endowment** $259.3 million
- **Coed** 2,539 undergraduate students, 98% full-time, 59% women, 41% men
- **Moderately difficult** entrance level, 66% of applicants were admitted

Undergraduates 2,499 full-time, 40 part-time. Students come from 47 states and territories, 19 other countries, 71% are from out of state, 3% African American, 9% Asian American or Pacific Islander, 4% Hispanic American, 1% Native American, 0.3% international, 3% transferred in, 59% live on campus. *Retention:* 86% of 2006 full-time freshmen returned.
Freshmen *Admission:* 5,273 applied, 3,502 admitted, 644 enrolled. *Average high school GPA:* 3.54. *Test scores:* SAT critical reading scores over 500: 94%; SAT math scores over 500: 92%; SAT writing scores over 500: 93%; ACT scores over 18: 100%; SAT critical reading scores over 600: 64%; SAT math scores over 600: 58%; SAT writing scores over 600: 58%; ACT scores over 24: 86%; SAT critical reading scores over 700: 21%; SAT math scores over 700: 11%; SAT writing scores over 700: 12%; ACT scores over 30: 25%.
Faculty *Total:* 279, 80% full-time, 76% with terminal degrees. *Student/faculty ratio:* 11:1.
Majors Art; Asian studies; biochemistry; biology/biological sciences; business/commerce; chemistry; classics and languages, literatures and linguistics; communication/speech communication and rhetoric; computer programming (specific applications); computer science; creative writing; developmental biology and embryology; dramatic/theater arts; economics; English; French; geology/earth science; German; history; interdisciplinary studies; international business/trade/commerce; international economics; international relations and affairs; kinesiology and exercise science; mathematics; molecular biology; music; music management and merchandising; music performance; music teacher education; natural sciences; philosophy; physics; political science and government; pre-dentistry studies; pre-law studies; pre-medical studies; pre-veterinary studies; psychology; religious studies; science, technology and society; sociology; Spanish.
Academics *Calendar:* semesters. *Degrees:* bachelor's, master's, first professional, and post-master's certificates. *Special study options:* advanced placement credit, cooperative education, double majors, honors programs, independent study, internships, part-time degree program, student-designed majors, study abroad, summer session for credit. *ROTC:* Army (c). *Unusual degree programs:* 3-2 engineering with Washington University in St. Louis, Columbia University, Duke University, Boston University, University of Southern California.
Computers on Campus 314 computers/terminals and 5,000 ports are available on campus for general student use. Students can access the following: campus intranet, computer help desk, free student e-mail accounts, online (class) grades, online (class) registration, online (class) schedules, financial aid, admission, student employment, library. Campuswide network is available. 100% of college-owned or -operated housing units are wired for high-speed Internet access. Wireless service is available via entire campus.
Student Life *Housing options:* coed, women-only, disabled students. Campus housing is university owned. Freshman applicants given priority for college housing. *Activities and organizations:* drama/theater group, student-run newspaper, radio station, choral group, Hui-O-Hawaii, Repertory Dance Group, Film and Theatre Society, outdoor programs, Lighthouse, national fraternities, national sororities. *Campus security:* 24-hour emergency response devices and patrols, student patrols, late-night transport/escort service, controlled dormitory access, 24-hour locked residence hall entrances. *Student services:* health clinic, personal/psychological counseling, legal services.
Athletics Member NCAA. All Division III. *Intercollegiate sports:* baseball M, basketball M/W, cheerleading M/W, crew M/W, cross-country running M/W, football M, golf M/W, ice hockey M (c), lacrosse M (c)/W, rugby M (c), sailing M (c)/W (c), skiing (downhill) M (c)/W (c), soccer M/W, softball W, swimming and diving M/W, tennis M/W, track and field M/W, volleyball W. *Intramural sports:* archery M (c)/W (c), basketball M/W, fencing M (c)/W (c), football M/W, racquetball M/W, soccer M/W, softball M/W, tennis M/W, ultimate Frisbee M/W, volleyball M/W.
Standardized Tests *Required:* SAT or ACT (for admission).
Costs (2007–08) *Comprehensive fee:* $40,160 includes full-time tuition ($31,700), mandatory fees ($195), and room and board ($8265). Full-time tuition and fees vary according to course load. Part-time tuition: $4000 per unit. Part-time tuition and fees vary according to course load. *College room only:* $4610. Room and board charges vary according to board plan and housing facility. *Payment plans:* installment, deferred payment. *Waivers:* employees or children of employees.
Financial Aid Of all full-time matriculated undergraduates who enrolled in 2007, 1,683 applied for aid, 1,487 were judged to have need, 419 had their need fully met. 447 Federal Work-Study jobs (averaging $3000). 929 state and other part-time jobs (averaging $2500). In 2007, 653 non-need-based awards were made. *Average percent of need met:* 83%. *Average financial aid package:* $25,089. *Average need-based loan:* $6106. *Average need-based gift aid:* $19,374. *Average non-need-based aid:* $6649. *Average indebtedness upon graduation:* $27,648.
Applying *Options:* electronic application, early admission, early decision, deferred entrance. *Application fee:* $40. *Required:* essay or personal statement, high school transcript, 2 letters of recommendation, school report. *Recommended:* minimum 3.0 GPA, interview. *Application deadlines:* 2/1 (freshmen), 7/1 (transfers). *Early decision deadline:* 11/15 (for plan 1), 12/15 (for plan 2). *Notification:* 4/1 (freshmen), continuous (transfers), 12/15 (early decision plan 1), 1/15 (early decision plan 2).
Freshman Application Contact Dr. George Mills, Vice President for Enrollment, University of Puget Sound, 1500 North Warner Street, Tacoma, WA 98416-1062. *Phone:* 253-879-3211. *Toll-free phone:* 800-396-7191. *Fax:* 253-879-3993. *E-mail:* admission@ups.edu.

See page 2728 for the College Close-Up.

UNIVERSITY OF WASHINGTON

Seattle, Washington **www.washington.edu/**

- **State-supported** comprehensive, founded 1861
- **Urban** 703-acre campus
- **Endowment** $2.1 billion
- **Coed**
- **Moderately difficult** entrance level

Faculty *Student/faculty ratio:* 12:1.
Academics *Calendar:* quarters. *Degrees:* bachelor's, master's, doctoral, first professional, and first professional certificates.
Student Life *Campus security:* 24-hour emergency response devices and patrols, late-night transport/escort service, controlled dormitory access.
Athletics Member NCAA. All Division I except football (Division I-A).
Standardized Tests *Required:* SAT or ACT (for admission).
Costs (2007–08) *Tuition:* state resident $6385 full-time; nonresident $22,131 full-time. Full-time tuition and fees vary according to course load. Part-time tuition and fees vary according to course load. *Room and board:* $8337. Room and board charges vary according to board plan and housing facility.
Financial Aid Of all full-time matriculated undergraduates who enrolled in 2006, 15,700 applied for aid, 11,500 were judged to have need, 5,100 had their need fully met. 855 Federal Work-Study jobs (averaging $2690). 156 state and other part-time jobs (averaging $3000). In 2006, 500 non-need-based awards were made. *Average percent of need met:* 86. *Average financial aid package:* $12,000. *Average need-based loan:* $4200. *Average need-based gift aid:* $8500. *Average non-need-based aid:* $4500. *Average indebtedness upon graduation:* $15,900.
Applying *Options:* electronic application, early admission. *Application fee:* $50. *Required:* essay or personal statement, minimum 2.0 GPA. *Required for some:* high school transcript.
Freshman Application Contact Admissions Office, University of Washington, 1410 NE Campus Parkway, Box 355852, Seattle, WA 98195-5852. *Phone:* 206-543-9686. *Fax:* 206-685-3655.

UNIVERSITY OF WASHINGTON, BOTHELL

Bothell, Washington **www.uwb.edu**

- **State-supported** upper-level, founded 1990, part of University of Washington
- **Suburban** 128-acre campus
- **Endowment** $2.3 million
- **Coed** 1,583 undergraduate students, 63% full-time, 57% women, 43% men
- **Moderately difficult** entrance level, 73% of applicants were admitted

Undergraduates 992 full-time, 591 part-time. Students come from 5 states and territories, 10 other countries, 2% are from out of state, 3% African American, 17% Asian American or Pacific Islander, 5% Hispanic American, 1% Native American, 1% international, 24% transferred in.

Freshmen *Admission:* 560 applied, 406 admitted.

Faculty *Total:* 103, 71% full-time, 92% with terminal degrees. *Student/faculty ratio:* 14:1.

Majors Business administration and management; computer and information sciences; education; environmental science; multi-/interdisciplinary studies related; nursing (registered nurse training).

Academics *Degrees:* diplomas, bachelor's, and master's. *Special study options:* adult/continuing education programs, advanced placement credit, cooperative education, double majors, honors programs, independent study, internships, part-time degree program, services for LD students, study abroad, summer session for credit. *ROTC:* Army (c), Air Force (c).

Computers on Campus 110 computers/terminals and 275 ports are available on campus for general student use. Students can access the following: campus intranet, computer help desk, free student e-mail accounts, online (class) grades, online (class) registration, online (class) schedules, electronic reserves, online course management system. Campuswide network is available. Wireless service is available via entire campus.

Student Life *Housing:* college housing not available. *Activities and organizations:* Entrepreneur's Network, Snowboard Club, Delta Epsilon Chi (Marketing Fraternity), MBA Association, UW Bothell Soccer Club. *Campus security:* 24-hour emergency response devices and patrols, student patrols, late-night transport/escort service. *Student services:* personal/psychological counseling.

Standardized Tests *Required:* SAT or ACT (for admission).

Costs (2007–08) *Tuition:* state resident $6247 full-time, $208 per credit part-time; nonresident $21,993 full-time, $733 per credit part-time. *Payment plan:* installment. *Waivers:* employees or children of employees.

Applying *Options:* electronic application, early admission, early decision, deferred entrance. *Application fee:* $50. *Early decision deadline:* 12/1. *Notification:* 12/15 (early decision).

Application Contact Lindsey Kattenhorn, Assistant Director of Admissions, University of Washington, Bothell, 18115 Campus Way NE, Bothell, WA 98011-8246. *Phone:* 425-352-5000. *Fax:* 425-352-5455. *E-mail:* freshmen@uwb.edu.

UNIVERSITY OF WASHINGTON, TACOMA

Tacoma, Washington **www.tacoma.washington.edu/**

- **State-supported** upper-level, founded 1990, part of University of Washington
- **Urban** 46-acre campus
- **Endowment** $24.0 million
- **Coed** 2,181 undergraduate students, 69% full-time, 59% women, 41% men
- **Minimally difficult** entrance level, 82% of applicants were admitted

Undergraduates 1,514 full-time, 667 part-time. Students come from 9 states and territories, 3 other countries, 2% are from out of state, 6% African American, 16% Asian American or Pacific Islander, 6% Hispanic American, 1% Native American, 0.2% international, 33% transferred in.

Freshmen *Admission:* 520 applied, 427 admitted.

Faculty *Total:* 192, 71% full-time. *Student/faculty ratio:* 15:1.

Majors Business administration and management; computer and information sciences; education; environmental science; multi-/interdisciplinary studies related; nursing (registered nurse training); social work; urban studies/affairs.

Academics *Calendar:* quarters. *Degrees:* certificates, bachelor's, master's, first professional, and postbachelor's certificates. *Special study options:* academic remediation for entering students, accelerated degree program, adult/continuing education programs, advanced placement credit, cooperative education, distance learning, double majors, honors programs, independent study, internships, part-time degree program, services for LD students, study abroad, summer session for credit. *ROTC:* Army (c), Navy (c), Air Force (c).

Computers on Campus 138 computers/terminals and 20 ports are available on campus for general student use. Students can access the following: computer help desk, free student e-mail accounts, online (class) grades, online (class) registration, online (class) schedules, (online courseware-Blackboard). Campuswide network is available. Wireless service is available via entire campus.

Student Life *Housing:* college housing not available. *Activities and organizations:* student-run newspaper, Association of Student Accountants, Black Student Union, Grey Hat Group, Finnce Society, CIVITAS. *Campus security:* 24-hour emergency response devices and patrols, late-night transport/escort service, key card access to buildings after hours. *Student services:* personal/psychological counseling.

Standardized Tests *Required:* SAT or ACT (for admission).

Costs (2008–09) *Tuition:* $1051 per course part-time; state resident $1051 per course part-time; nonresident $3674 per course part-time.

Applying *Options:* electronic application, deferred entrance. *Application fee:* $50.

Application Contact Fiona Johnson, Admissions Advising and Outreach, University of Washington, Tacoma, 1900 Commerce Street, Tacoma, WA 98402-3100. *Phone:* 253-692-4742. *Toll-free phone:* 800-736-7750. *Fax:* 253-692-4788.

WALLA WALLA UNIVERSITY

College Place, Washington **www.wallawalla.edu/**

- **Independent Seventh-day Adventist** comprehensive, founded 1892
- **Small-town** 77-acre campus
- **Endowment** $16.1 million
- **Coed** 1,611 undergraduate students, 93% full-time, 48% women, 52% men
- **Moderately difficult** entrance level, 93% of applicants were admitted

Undergraduates 1,501 full-time, 110 part-time. Students come from 41 states and territories, 19 other countries, 40% are from out of state, 4% African American, 6% Asian American or Pacific Islander, 9% Hispanic American, 1% Native American, 1% international, 8% transferred in. *Retention:* 73% of 2006 full-time freshmen returned.

Freshmen *Admission:* 374 applied, 349 admitted, 346 enrolled. *Test scores:* SAT math scores over 500: 62%; ACT scores over 18: 87%; SAT math scores over 600: 26%; ACT scores over 24: 41%; SAT math scores over 700: 3%; ACT scores over 30: 7%.

Faculty *Total:* 204, 57% full-time, 45% with terminal degrees. *Student/faculty ratio:* 8:1.

Majors Accounting; ancient Near Eastern and biblical languages; art; art teacher education; biology/biological sciences; biomedical/medical engineering; biomedical technology; biophysics; business teacher education; chemistry; civil engineering; clinical laboratory science/medical technology; computer programming; computer science; economics; education (K-12); electrical, electronics and communications engineering; electromechanical technology; elementary education; engineering; engineering technology; English; environmental studies; French; German; health and physical education; health science; history; humanities; industrial arts; journalism; kinesiology and exercise science; management information systems; marketing/marketing management; mass communication/media; mathematics; mechanical engineering; modern languages; music; music teacher education; nursing (registered nurse training); philosophy; physical education teaching and coaching; physics; piano and organ; pre-dentistry studies; pre-law studies; pre-medical studies; pre-veterinary studies; psychology; public health education and promotion; public relations/image management; radio and television; religious studies; social work; sociology; Spanish; speech and rhetoric; theology; voice and opera.

Academics *Calendar:* quarters. *Degrees:* associate, bachelor's, and master's. *Special study options:* academic remediation for entering students, advanced placement credit, cooperative education, double majors, English as a second language, freshman honors college, honors programs, independent study, internships, part-time degree program, services for LD students, study abroad, summer session for credit.

Computers on Campus 118 computers/terminals are available on campus for general student use. Students can access the following: campus intranet, free student e-mail accounts, online (class) grades, online (class) registration, online (class) schedules. Campuswide network is available.

Student Life *Housing:* on-campus residence required through junior year. *Options:* men-only, women-only, disabled students. Campus housing is university owned and leased by the school. Freshman campus housing is guaranteed. *Activities and organizations:* drama/theater group, student-run newspaper, radio and television station, choral group, Associated Students of Walla Walla College, Village Singles' Club, Aleph Gimel Ain (women's club), Amnesty International, Omicron Pi Sigma (men's club). *Campus security:* 24-hour emergency response devices and patrols, student patrols, late-night transport/escort service, controlled dormitory access. *Student services:* health clinic, personal/psychological counseling.

Athletics Member NCCAA. *Intercollegiate sports:* basketball M/W, golf M, ice hockey M, soccer M, softball W, volleyball M/W. *Intramural sports:* basketball M/W, football M/W, gymnastics M/W, ice hockey M, racquetball M/W, softball M/W, table tennis M/W, tennis M/W, volleyball M/W.

Standardized Tests *Required:* SAT or ACT (for admission). *Recommended:* ACT (for admission).

Costs (2007–08) *Comprehensive fee:* $27,000 includes full-time tuition ($21,735), mandatory fees ($210), and room and board ($5055). Full-time tuition and fees vary according to course load and degree level. Part-time tuition: $569 per credit. Part-time tuition and fees vary according to degree level. *College room only:* $2655. Room and board charges vary according to housing facility and location. *Payment plans:* installment, deferred payment.

Financial Aid Of all full-time matriculated undergraduates who enrolled in 2006, 1,262 applied for aid, 935 were judged to have need, 187 had their need fully met. 624 Federal Work-Study jobs (averaging $2670). 64 state and other part-time jobs (averaging $3105). In 2006, 248 non-need-based awards were made. *Average percent of need met:* 88%. *Average financial aid package:* $18,550. *Average need-based loan:* $6505. *Average need-based gift aid:* $6952. *Average non-need-based aid:* $3777. *Average indebtedness upon graduation:* $28,482.

Applying *Options:* electronic application, early decision, deferred entrance. *Application fee:* $40. *Required:* high school transcript, minimum 2.0 GPA. *Application deadlines:* rolling (freshmen), rolling (out-of-state freshmen), rolling (transfers). *Notification:* continuous (freshmen), continuous (out-of-state freshmen), continuous (transfers).

Freshman Application Contact Mr. Dallas Weis, Interim Vice President for Admissions and Marketing, Walla Walla University, 204 South College Avenue, College Place, WA 99324. *Phone:* 509-527-2327. *Toll-free phone:* 800-541-8900. *Fax:* 509-527-2397. *E-mail:* info@wwc.edu.

WASHINGTON STATE UNIVERSITY

Pullman, Washington **www.wsu.edu/**

- **State-supported** university, founded 1890
- **Rural** 620-acre campus
- **Endowment** $650.9 million
- **Coed** 20,282 undergraduate students, 85% full-time, 52% women, 48% men
- **Moderately difficult** entrance level, 76% of applicants were admitted

Undergraduates 17,323 full-time, 2,959 part-time. Students come from 49 states and territories, 60 other countries, 10% are from out of state, 2% African American, 6% Asian American or Pacific Islander, 5% Hispanic American, 1% Native American, 3% international, 13% transferred in, 35% live on campus. *Retention:* 84% of 2006 full-time freshmen returned.

Freshmen *Admission:* 10,853 applied, 8,240 admitted, 3,477 enrolled. *Average high school GPA:* 3.42. *Test scores:* SAT critical reading scores over 500: 72%; SAT math scores over 500: 80%; SAT writing scores over 500: 64%; ACT scores over 18: 96%; SAT critical reading scores over 600: 26%; SAT math scores over 600: 32%; SAT writing scores over 600: 18%; ACT scores over 24: 49%; SAT critical reading scores over 700: 4%; SAT math scores over 700: 4%; SAT writing scores over 700: 2%; ACT scores over 30: 6%.

Faculty *Total:* 1,652, 71% full-time, 78% with terminal degrees. *Student/faculty ratio:* 14:1.

Majors Accounting; accounting related; agricultural business and management; agricultural communication/journalism; agricultural economics; agricultural mechanization; agricultural teacher education; agriculture; agronomy and crop science; American studies; animal sciences; anthropology; apparel and textiles; architecture; art history, criticism and conservation; Asian studies; athletic training; audiology and speech-language pathology; bilingual and multilingual education; biochemistry; biology/biological sciences; biology teacher education; biotechnology; business administration and management; business/commerce; business/managerial economics; chemical engineering; chemistry; chemistry teacher education; civil engineering; communication/speech communication and rhetoric; computer engineering; computer science; criminal justice/law enforcement administration; crop production; digital communication and media/multimedia; dramatic/theater arts; early childhood education; ecology; e-commerce; economics; education; electrical, electronics and communications engineering; elementary education; English; English as a second/foreign language (teaching); English/language arts teacher education; entomology; entrepreneurship; environmental science; ethnic, cultural minority, and gender studies related; family and consumer sciences/home economics teacher education; finance; fine/studio arts; food science; foreign languages and literatures; foreign language teacher education; forestry; French; French language teacher education; genetics; geology/earth science; German; German language teacher education; health and physical education; health teacher education; history; history teacher education; horticultural science; hospitality administration; human development and family studies; humanities; human nutrition; human resources management; insurance; interior design; international business/trade/commerce; kindergarten/preschool education; kinesiology and exercise science; landscape architecture; linguistics; management information systems; management science; marketing/marketing management; materials engineering; materials science; mathematics; mathematics teacher education; mechanical engineering; microbiology; music; music performance; music teacher education; music theory and composition; natural resources/conservation; neuroscience; nursing (registered nurse training); nutrition science; operations management; pharmacology and toxicology; philosophy; physical education teaching and coaching; physical sciences; physics; plant protection and integrated pest management; political science and government; sociology; sport and fitness administration/management; women's studies.

Academics *Calendar:* semesters. *Degrees:* certificates, bachelor's, master's, doctoral, first professional, post-master's, and postbachelor's certificates. *Special study options:* accelerated degree program, advanced placement credit, distance learning, double majors, English as a second language, external degree program, honors programs, independent study, internships, off-campus study, part-time degree program, services for LD students, student-designed majors, study abroad, summer session for credit. *ROTC:* Army (b), Navy (c), Air Force (b). *Unusual degree programs:* 3-2 business administration; architecture, doctor of veterinary medicine, doctor of pharmacy.

Computers on Campus 2,500 computers/terminals are available on campus for general student use. Students can access the following: campus intranet, computer help desk, free student e-mail accounts, online (class) grades, online (class) registration, online (class) schedules. Campuswide network is available. 100% of college-owned or -operated housing units are wired for high-speed Internet access. Wireless service is available via classrooms, computer labs, dorm rooms, libraries, student centers.

Student Life *Housing:* on-campus residence required for freshman year. *Options:* coed, men-only, women-only. Campus housing is university owned. Freshman campus housing is guaranteed. *Activities and organizations:* drama/theater group, student-run newspaper, radio station, choral group, marching band, Panhellenic Association, Interfraternity Council, College Republicans, International Students Council, Chilastal (Chicana/o Latina/o Student Alliance, national fraternities, national sororities. *Campus security:* 24-hour emergency response devices and patrols, student patrols, late-night transport/escort service, controlled dormitory access. *Student services:* health clinic, personal/psychological counseling, women's center, legal services.

Athletics Member NCAA. All Division I except football (Division I-A). *Intercollegiate sports:* baseball M (s), basketball M (s)/W (s), bowling M (c)/W (c), crew M (c)/W (s), cross-country running M (s)/W (s), equestrian sports M (c)/W (c), golf M (s)/W (s), ice hockey M (c)/W (c), lacrosse M (c)/W (c), rugby M (c)/W (c), sailing M (c)/W (c), skiing (cross-country) M (c)/W (c), skiing (downhill) M (c)/W (c), soccer M (c)/W (s), softball W (c), swimming and diving W (s), tennis M (c)/W (s), track and field M (s)/W (s), ultimate Frisbee M (c), volleyball M (c)/W (s), water polo M (c)/W (c). *Intramural sports:* badminton M/W, basketball M/W, bowling M/W, cheerleading M/W, cross-country running M/W, fencing M (c)/W (c), football M/W, golf M/W, gymnastics M (c)/W (c), racquetball M/W, soccer M/W, softball M/W, table tennis M/W, tennis M/W, track and field M/W, volleyball M/W.

Standardized Tests *Required:* SAT or ACT (for admission).

Costs (2007–08) *Tuition:* state resident $5812 full-time, $315 per credit part-time; nonresident $16,126 full-time, $830 per credit part-time. Full-time tuition and fees vary according to location and reciprocity agreements. Part-time tuition and fees vary according to course load and reciprocity agreements. *Required fees:* $1054 full-time. *Room and board:* $7316; room only: $3556. Room and board charges vary according to board plan, housing facility, and location. *Waivers:* children of alumni and employees or children of employees.

Financial Aid Of all full-time matriculated undergraduates who enrolled in 2006, 12,256 applied for aid, 7,925 were judged to have need, 2,976 had their need fully met. 487 Federal Work-Study jobs (averaging $1640). 1,147 state and other part-time jobs (averaging $1740). In 2006, 971 non-need-based awards were made. *Average percent of need met:* 86%. *Average financial aid package:* $10,915. *Average need-based loan:* $4593. *Average need-based gift aid:* $6689. *Average non-need-based aid:* $2072.

Applying *Options:* electronic application. *Application fee:* $50. *Required:* essay or personal statement, high school transcript, minimum 2.0 GPA. *Notification:* 12/1 (freshmen), 12/1 (transfers).

Freshman Application Contact Ms. Wendy Peterson, Director of Admissions, Washington State University, PO Box 641067, Pullman, WA 99164-1067. *Phone:* 509-335-5586. *Toll-free phone:* 888-468-6978. *Fax:* 509-335-4902. *E-mail:* admiss2@wsu.edu.

WESTERN WASHINGTON UNIVERSITY

Bellingham, Washington **www.wwu.edu/**

- **State-supported** comprehensive, founded 1893
- **Small-town** 223-acre campus with easy access to Seattle and Vancouver
- **Endowment** $29.4 million
- **Coed** 13,099 undergraduate students, 92% full-time, 55% women, 45% men
- **Moderately difficult** entrance level, 73% of applicants were admitted

A vibrant campus in a spectacular location, Western Washington University is recognized for excellence in undergraduate education. Student satisfaction, graduation rates, job placement, graduate school admission, and *U.S. News & World Report* rankings are among the highest in the Pacific Northwest. Leadership development, global awareness, civic engagement, and sustainability are core values inside and outside the classroom.

Undergraduates 11,986 full-time, 1,113 part-time. Students come from 46 states and territories, 31 other countries, 6% are from out of state, 3% African American, 9% Asian American or Pacific Islander, 4% Hispanic American, 2% Native American, 0.5% international, 7% transferred in, 30% live on campus. *Retention:* 84% of 2006 full-time freshmen returned.

Freshmen *Admission:* 8,850 applied, 6,447 admitted, 2,586 enrolled. *Average high school GPA:* 3.5. *Test scores:* SAT critical reading scores over 500: 75%; SAT math scores over 500: 76%; ACT scores over 18: 96%; SAT critical reading scores over 600: 32%; SAT math scores over 600: 30%; ACT scores over 24: 52%; SAT critical reading scores over 700: 6%; SAT math scores over 700: 3%; ACT scores over 30: 7%.

Faculty *Total:* 737, 69% full-time, 69% with terminal degrees. *Student/faculty ratio:* 19:1.

Majors Accounting; accounting and computer science; American studies; anthropology; archeology; art; art history, criticism and conservation; art teacher education; Asian studies; Asian studies (East); audiology and speech-language pathology; biochemistry; biological and physical sciences; biology/biological sciences; business administration and management; Canadian studies; cell and molecular biology; cell biology and histology; ceramic arts and ceramics; chemistry; chemistry teacher education; classics and languages, literatures and linguistics; communication/speech communication and rhetoric; community health services counseling; computer science; counselor education/school counseling and guidance; creative writing; cultural studies; design and visual communications; developmental and child psychology; dramatic/theater arts; drawing; economics; education; educational leadership and administration; education (multiple levels); electrical, electronic and communications engineering technology; elementary education; engineering related; engineering technology; English; environmental biology; environmental education; environmental science; environmental studies; fiber, textile and weaving arts; finance; fine/studio arts; French; general studies; geography; geology/earth science; geophysics and seismology; German; graphic design; health teacher education; history; humanities; human resources management; human services; industrial design; industrial technology; interdisciplinary studies; intermedia/multimedia; international business/trade/commerce; jazz/jazz studies; journalism; kindergarten/preschool education; kinesiology and exercise science; Latin American studies; liberal arts and sciences/liberal studies; linguistics; literature; management information systems; manufacturing technology; marine biology and biological oceanography; marketing/marketing management; mathematics; music; music history, literature, and theory; music teacher education; operations management; painting; parks, recreation and leisure; philosophy; physical education teaching and coaching; physics; plastics engineering technology; political science and government; printmaking; psychology; science teacher education; sculpture; secondary education; sociology; Spanish; special education; visual and performing arts; women's studies.

Academics *Calendar:* quarters. *Degrees:* certificates, bachelor's, master's, and postbachelor's certificates. *Special study options:* accelerated degree program, advanced placement credit, cooperative education, distance learning, double majors, English as a second language, honors programs, independent study, internships, off-campus study, services for LD students, student-designed majors, study abroad, summer session for credit.

Computers on Campus 2,408 computers/terminals are available on campus for general student use. Students can access the following: online (class) registration. Campuswide network is available. 99% of college-owned or -operated housing units are wired for high-speed Internet access. Wireless service is available via classrooms, computer centers, computer labs, dorm rooms, learning centers, libraries, student centers.

Student Life *Housing options:* coed, disabled students. Campus housing is university owned and leased by the school. Freshman campus housing is guaranteed. *Activities and organizations:* drama/theater group, student-run newspaper, radio and television station, choral group, intramurals, Residence Hall Association, Associated Students, Outdoor Center, Ethnic Student Center. *Campus security:* 24-hour emergency response devices and patrols, student patrols, late-night transport/escort service, controlled dormitory access. *Student services:* health clinic, personal/psychological counseling, women's center, legal services.

Athletics Member NCAA. All Division II. *Intercollegiate sports:* basketball M (s)/W (s), cheerleading M/W, crew M (s)/W (s), cross-country running M (s)/W (s), football M (s), golf M (s)/W (s), soccer M (s)/W (s), softball W (s), track and field M (s)/W (s), volleyball W (s). *Intramural sports:* badminton M/W, baseball M, basketball M/W, ice hockey M, lacrosse M/W, racquetball M/W, rock climbing M/W, sailing M/W, skiing (downhill) M/W, soccer M/W, softball M/W, swimming and diving M/W, table tennis M/W, tennis M/W, volleyball M/W, water polo M/W, wrestling M.

Standardized Tests *Required:* SAT or ACT (for admission), TOEFL for International Students (for admission).

Costs (2007–08) *Tuition:* state resident $5291 full-time; nonresident $16,365 full-time. Full-time tuition and fees vary according to location. Part-time tuition and fees vary according to location. *Room and board:* $7090. Room and board charges vary according to board plan and housing facility. *Payment plan:* installment. *Waivers:* employees or children of employees.

Financial Aid Of all full-time matriculated undergraduates who enrolled in 2006, 6,783 applied for aid, 4,462 were judged to have need, 1,535 had their need fully met. 221 Federal Work-Study jobs (averaging $2876). 443 state and other part-time jobs (averaging $2963). In 2006, 240 non-need-based awards were made. *Average percent of need met:* 88%. *Average financial aid package:* $9709. *Average need-based loan:* $4109. *Average need-based gift aid:* $6914. *Average non-need-based aid:* $1525. *Average indebtedness upon graduation:* $15,280.

Applying *Options:* electronic application, deferred entrance. *Application fee:* $50. *Required:* high school transcript. *Recommended:* essay or personal statement. *Application deadlines:* 3/1 (freshmen), 4/1 (transfers). *Notification:* continuous until 4/15 (freshmen), continuous until 6/1 (transfers).

Freshman Application Contact Ms. Karen Copetas, Director of Admissions, Western Washington University, 516 High Street, Bellingham, WA 98225-9009. *Phone:* 360-650-3440. *Fax:* 360-650-7369. *E-mail:* admit@wwu.edu.

WHITMAN COLLEGE

Walla Walla, Washington **www.whitman.edu/**

- **Independent** 4-year, founded 1859
- **Small-town** 117-acre campus
- **Endowment** $391.4 million
- **Coed** 1,489 undergraduate students, 98% full-time, 56% women, 44% men
- **Very difficult** entrance level, 49% of applicants were admitted

Whitman College, one of the nation's leading liberal arts colleges, develops students' capacities to engage, analyze, interpret, critique, and communicate. Residential living, academic support systems, and cocurricular opportunities foster social development as well as self-development. It is a place where both the individual and the collective are celebrated. Whitman students' intellectual vitality, confidence, leadership, and flexibility make it possible to adapt to and impact an ever-changing multicultural and global world. Located in historic Walla Walla, Washington, the College offers an ideal setting for rigorous academics, an active campus life, a strong sense of community, and wonderful outdoor recreational opportunities in the Pacific Northwest.

Undergraduates 1,452 full-time, 37 part-time. Students come from 41 states and territories, 34 other countries, 60% are from out of state, 2% African American, 10% Asian American or Pacific Islander, 5% Hispanic American, 1% Native American, 4% international, 1% transferred in, 62% live on campus. *Retention:* 94% of 2006 full-time freshmen returned.

Freshmen *Admission:* 2,882 applied, 1,398 admitted, 400 enrolled. *Average high school GPA:* 3.77. *Test scores:* SAT critical reading scores over 500: 98%; SAT math scores over 500: 98%; SAT writing scores over 500: 96%; ACT scores over 18: 100%; SAT critical reading scores over 600: 86%; SAT math scores over 600: 82%; SAT writing scores over 600: 80%; ACT scores over 24: 93%; SAT critical reading scores over 700: 39%; SAT math scores over 700: 32%; SAT writing scores over 700: 28%; ACT scores over 30: 53%.

Faculty *Total:* 183, 69% full-time, 80% with terminal degrees. *Student/faculty ratio:* 10:1.

Majors Anthropology; art; art history, criticism and conservation; Asian studies; astronomy; astrophysics; biochemistry; biochemistry/biophysics and molecular biology; biology/biological sciences; biophysics; chemistry; chemistry related; classics and languages, literatures and linguistics; communication/speech communication and rhetoric; dramatic/theater arts; economics; English; ethnic, cultural minority, and gender studies related; film/cinema studies; French; geological and earth sciences/geosciences related; geology/earth science; German; history; mathematics; mathematics and computer science; molecular biology; music; music history, literature, and theory; music performance; music theory and composition; philosophy; physics; physics related; political science and government; political science and government related; psychology; religious studies; social sciences related; sociology; Spanish.

Academics *Calendar:* semesters. *Degree:* bachelor's. *Special study options:* accelerated degree program, advanced placement credit, cooperative education, double majors, honors programs, independent study, off-campus study, services for LD students, student-designed majors, study abroad. *Unusual degree programs:* 3-2 engineering with California Institute of Technology, Columbia University, Duke University, University of Washington, Washington University in St. Louis; forestry with Duke University; international studies with Monterey Institute of International Studies, oceanography with University of Washington, teacher education with Bank Street College of Education, law with Columbia University.

Computers on Campus 397 computers/terminals are available on campus for general student use. Students can access the following: computer help desk, free student e-mail accounts, online (class) grades, online (class) registration, online (class) schedules, course registration information. Campuswide network is available. 100% of college-owned or -operated housing units are wired for high-speed Internet access. Wireless service is available via classrooms, computer centers, computer labs, dorm rooms, learning centers, libraries, student centers.

Student Life *Housing:* on-campus residence required through sophomore year. *Options:* coed, women-only. Campus housing is university owned. Freshman campus housing is guaranteed. *Activities and organizations:* drama/theater group, student-run newspaper, radio station, choral group, Associated Students, Outdoor Program, Center for Community Service, Intramural Sports, national fraternities, national sororities. *Campus security:* 24-hour emergency response devices and patrols, student patrols, late-night transport/escort service, controlled dormitory access. *Student services:* health clinic, personal/psychological counseling, women's center.

Athletics Member NCAA. All Division III except men's and women's skiing (cross-country) (Division I), men's and women's skiing (downhill) (Division I). *Intercollegiate sports:* baseball M, basketball M/W, cross-country running M/W, fencing M (c)/W (c), golf M/W, ice hockey M (c), lacrosse M (c)/W (c), rugby M (c)/W (c), skiing (cross-country) M/W, skiing (downhill) M/W, soccer M/W, softball M (c)/W (c), swimming and diving M/W, tennis M/W, track and field M (c)/W (c), ultimate Frisbee M (c)/W (c), volleyball M (c)/W. *Intramural sports:* basketball M/W, bowling M/W, football M/W, soccer M/W, softball M/W, tennis M/W, ultimate Frisbee M/W, volleyball M/W.

Standardized Tests *Required:* SAT or ACT (for admission).

Costs (2007–08) *Comprehensive fee:* $41,290 includes full-time tuition ($32,670), mandatory fees ($310), and room and board ($8310). Part-time tuition: $1370 per credit hour. *College room only:* $3820. Room and board charges vary according to board plan and housing facility. *Payment plan:* deferred payment. *Waivers:* employees or children of employees.

Financial Aid Of all full-time matriculated undergraduates who enrolled in 2007, 704 applied for aid, 641 were judged to have need, 473 had their need fully met. 510 Federal Work-Study jobs (averaging $2110). 174 state and other part-time jobs (averaging $1559). In 2007, 434 non-need-based awards were made. *Average percent of need met:* 98%. *Average financial aid package:* $28,779. *Average need-based loan:* $2619. *Average need-based gift aid:* $21,316. *Average non-need-based aid:* $6155. *Average indebtedness upon graduation:* $16,108. *Financial aid deadline:* 2/1.

Applying *Options:* electronic application, early decision, deferred entrance. *Application fee:* $45. *Required:* essay or personal statement, high school transcript, 1 letter of recommendation. *Recommended:* interview. *Application deadlines:* 1/15 (freshmen), 3/1 (transfers). *Early decision deadline:* 11/15. *Notification:* 4/1 (freshmen), 4/15 (transfers), 12/21 (early decision).

Freshman Application Contact Mr. Tony Cabasco, Dean of Admission and Financial Aid, Whitman College, 515 Boyer Avenue, Walla Walla, WA 99362-2083. *Phone:* 509-527-5176. *Toll-free phone:* 877-462-9448. *Fax:* 509-527-4967. *E-mail:* admission@whitman.edu.

See page 2730 for the College Close-Up.

WHITWORTH UNIVERSITY

Spokane, Washington **www.whitworth.edu/**

- **Independent Presbyterian** comprehensive, founded 1890
- **Suburban** 200-acre campus
- **Endowment** $87.2 million
- **Coed** 2,331 undergraduate students, 88% full-time, 59% women, 41% men
- **Very difficult** entrance level, 49% of applicants were admitted

Undergraduates 2,048 full-time, 283 part-time. Students come from 30 states and territories, 18 other countries, 36% are from out of state, 2% African American, 3% Asian American or Pacific Islander, 3% Hispanic American, 1% Native American, 1% international, 4% transferred in, 63% live on campus. *Retention:* 87% of 2006 full-time freshmen returned.

Freshmen *Admission:* 5,062 applied, 2,490 admitted, 533 enrolled. *Average high school GPA:* 3.69. *Test scores:* SAT critical reading scores over 500: 90%; SAT math scores over 500: 91%; SAT writing scores over 500: 90%; ACT scores over 18: 99%; SAT critical reading scores over 600: 54%; SAT math scores over 600: 57%; SAT writing scores over 600: 46%; ACT scores over 24: 84%; SAT critical reading scores over 700: 12%; SAT math scores over 700: 9%; SAT writing scores over 700: 7%; ACT scores over 30: 20%.

Faculty *Total:* 294, 42% full-time. *Student/faculty ratio:* 13:1.

Majors Accounting; American studies; art; arts management; art teacher education; athletic training; biology/biological sciences; business administration and management; chemistry; computer science; dramatic/theater arts; economics; elementary education; English; fine/studio arts; French; history; international business/trade/commerce; international relations and affairs; journalism; mass communication/media; mathematics; music; music teacher education; nursing (registered nurse training); peace studies and conflict resolution; philosophy; physical education teaching and coaching; physics; piano and organ; political science and government; pre-dentistry studies; pre-law studies; pre-medical studies; pre-veterinary studies; psychology; religious studies; secondary education; sociology; Spanish; special education; speech and rhetoric; voice and opera.

Academics *Calendar:* 4-1-4. *Degrees:* bachelor's and master's. *Special study options:* adult/continuing education programs, advanced placement credit, cooperative education, double majors, English as a second language, independent study, internships, off-campus study, part-time degree program, services for LD students, student-designed majors, study abroad, summer session for credit. *ROTC:* Army (c). *Unusual degree programs:* 3-2 engineering with Seattle Pacific University, University of Southern California, Washington University in St. Louis, Columbia University; nursing with Intercollegiate Center for Nursing.

Computers on Campus 300 computers/terminals are available on campus for general student use. Students can access the following: campus intranet, computer help desk, free student e-mail accounts, online (class) grades, online (class) registration, online (class) schedules. Campuswide network is available. Wireless service is available via classrooms, computer centers, computer labs, libraries, student centers.

Student Life *Housing:* on-campus residence required through sophomore year. *Options:* coed, men-only, women-only. Campus housing is university owned. Freshman campus housing is guaranteed. *Activities and organizations:* drama/theater group, student-run newspaper, radio station, choral group, International Club, Young Life, En Christo, Hawaiian Club, intramural sports. *Campus security:* 24-hour emergency response devices and patrols, late-night transport/escort service. *Student services:* health clinic, personal/psychological counseling.

Athletics Member NCAA. All Division III. *Intercollegiate sports:* baseball M, basketball M/W, cross-country running M/W, football M, golf M/W, soccer M/W, softball W, swimming and diving M/W, tennis M/W, track and field M/W, volleyball W. *Intramural sports:* basketball M/W, football M/W, rugby M/W, skiing (cross-country) M/W, skiing (downhill) M/W, soccer M/W, ultimate Frisbee M/W, volleyball M/W, water polo M/W.

Standardized Tests *Required for some:* SAT or ACT (for admission).

Costs (2007–08) *Comprehensive fee:* $32,986 includes full-time tuition ($25,382), mandatory fees ($310), and room and board ($7294). Part-time tuition: $1060 per credit. Part-time tuition and fees vary according to class time. *Room and board:* Room and board charges vary according to board plan and housing facility. *Payment plan:* installment. *Waivers:* employees or children of employees.

Financial Aid Of all full-time matriculated undergraduates who enrolled in 2007, 1,495 applied for aid, 1,278 were judged to have need, 285 had their need fully met. 502 Federal Work-Study jobs (averaging $2301). 234 state and other part-time jobs (averaging $2810). In 2007, 580 non-need-based awards were made. *Average percent of need met:* 81%. *Average financial aid package:* $18,549. *Average need-based loan:* $5018. *Average need-based gift aid:* $13,298. *Average non-need-based aid:* $9976. *Average indebtedness upon graduation:* $18,543.

Applying *Options:* electronic application, early admission, early action, deferred entrance. *Required:* essay or personal statement, high school transcript, letters of recommendation. *Required for some:* interview. *Application deadlines:* 3/1 (freshmen), 7/1 (transfers), 11/30 (early action). *Notification:* 12/20 (early action).

Freshman Application Contact Ms. Marianne Hansen, Director of Admission, Whitworth University, 300 West, Hawthorne Road, Spokane, WA 99251. *Phone:* 509-777-4348. *Toll-free phone:* 800-533-4668. *Fax:* 509-777-3758. *E-mail:* admission@whitworth.edu.

See page 2732 for the College Close-Up.

ARGOSY UNIVERSITY

ARGOSY UNIVERSITY

The University

Argosy University is a leading institution offering a variety of degree programs that focus on the human side of success alongside professional competence. For students looking for a more personal approach to education, Argosy University may just be the answer. With forty-eight graduate and undergraduate programs, across nineteen campuses and twelve states, Argosy University emphasizes interpersonal skills as well as academic learning. All of its programs are taught by practicing professionals who bring real-world experience into the classroom. So students graduate with both a solid foundation of knowledge and the power to put it to work. To accommodate busy working adults, many programs at Argosy University are structured flexibly—with both campus and online learning and evening, weekend, and daytime classes. There is also a wide range of financial aid options for students who qualify.

Argosy University is a private institution of higher education dedicated to providing high-quality professional education programs at the doctoral, master's, bachelor's, and associate degree levels as well as continuing education to individuals who seek to advance their professional and personal lives. The University emphasizes programs in the behavioral sciences (psychology and counseling), business, education, and the health-care professions. A limited number of preprofessional programs and general education offerings are provided to permit students to prepare for entry into these professional fields. The programs of Argosy University are designed to instill the knowledge, skills, and ethical values of professional practice and to foster values of social responsibility in a supportive, learning-centered environment of mutual respect and professional excellence.

With nineteen campuses nationwide, Argosy University provides students with a network of resources found at larger universities, including a career resources office, an academic resources center, and extensive information access for research. The University's innovative programs feature dynamic, relevant, and practical curricula delivered in flexible class formats. Students enjoy scheduling options that make it easier to fit school into their busy lives. They can choose from day and evening courses, on campus or online. Many students find a combination of both to be an ideal way of continuing their education while meeting family and professional demands.

Most students are full-time working professionals who live within driving distance of the campus. The University does not offer or operate student housing.

Argosy University is accredited by The Higher Learning Commission of the North Central Association (30 North LaSalle Street, Suite 2400, Chicago, Illinois 60602; 800-621-7440; http://ncahlc.org).

Location

Argosy University operates nineteen locations across the U.S. and offers a variety of degree programs online (http://www.argosy.edu). Campus locations include the following:

Atlanta, 980 Hammond Drive, Suite 100, Atlanta, Georgia 30328; phone: 770-671-1200 or 888-671-4777 (toll-free)

Chicago, 225 North Michigan Avenue, Suite 1300, Chicago, Illinois 60601; phone: 312-777-7600 or 800-626-4123 (toll-free)

Dallas, 8080 Park Lane, Suite 400A, Dallas, Texas 75231; phone: 214-890-9900 or 866-954-9900 (toll-free)

Denver, 1200 Lincoln Street, Denver, Colorado 80203; phone: 303-248-2700 or 866-431-5981 (toll-free)

Hawai'i, 400 ASB Tower, 1001 Bishop Street, Honolulu, Hawaii 96813; phone: 808-536-5555 or 888-323-2777 (toll-free)

Inland Empire, 636 East Brier Drive, Suite 235, San Bernardino, California 92408; phone: 909-915-3800 or 866-217-9075 (toll-free)

Nashville, 100 Centerview Drive, Suite 225, Nashville, Tennessee 37214; phone: 615-525-2800 or 866-833-6598 (toll-free)

Orange County, 3501 West Sunflower Avenue, Suite 110, Santa Ana, California 92704; phone: 714-338-6200 or 800-716-9598 (toll-free)

Phoenix, 2233 West Dunlap Avenue, Phoenix, Arizona 85021; phone: 602-216-2600 or 866-216-2777 (toll-free)

Salt Lake City, 121 West Election Road, Suite 300, Draper, Utah 84020; phone: 888-639-4756 (toll-free)

San Diego, 7650 Mission Valley Road, San Diego, California 92108; phone: 858-598-1900 or 866-505-0333 (toll-free)

San Francisco Bay Area, 1005 Atlantic Avenue, Alameda, California 94501; phone: 510-217-4700 or 866-215-2777 (toll-free)

Santa Monica, 2950 31st Street, Santa Monica, California 90405; phone: 310-866-4000 or 866-505-0332 (toll-free)

Sarasota, 5250 17th Street, Sarasota, Florida 34235; phone: 941-379-0404 or 800-331-5995 (toll-free)

Schaumburg, 999 North Plaza Drive, Suite 111, Schaumburg, Illinois 60173-5403; phone: 847-969-4900 or 866-290-2777 (toll-free)

Seattle, 2601-A Elliott Avenue, Seattle, Washington 98121; phone: 206-283-4500 or 888-283-2777 (toll-free)

Tampa, Parkside at Tampa Bay Park, 4401 North Hines Avenue, Suite 150, Tampa, Florida 33614; phone: 813-393-5290 or 800-850-6488 (toll-free)

Twin Cities, 1515 Central Parkway, Eagan, Minnesota 55121; phone: 651-846-2882 or 888-844-2004 (toll-free)

Washington DC, 1550 Wilson Boulevard, Suite 600, Arlington, Virginia 22209; phone: 703-526-5800 or 866-703-2777 (toll-free)

Majors and Degrees

Argosy University's College of Business offers a Bachelor of Science (B.S.) in Business Administration program. Argosy University's College of Psychology and Behavioral Sciences offers the Bachelor of Arts (B.A.) in Psychology degree program.

Academic Programs

The B.S. in Business Administration program prepares students for entry- to mid-level positions within the public or private sector. The curriculum is structured to help students develop competencies in oral and written communication, leadership, team skills, solutions-focused learning, and the analysis and execution of solutions in various business situations. Students may choose one of five optional concentrations: customized professional concentration, finance, health-care management, international business, or marketing.

The B.A. in Psychology program is designed to help students begin human services careers in such capacities as entry-level counselor, case manager, or human resources administrator and

in management and business services roles. The program also lays the foundation for graduate study. Students may choose an optional concentration from the following three options: criminal justice, organizational psychology, or substance abuse. This dynamic program is built around a flexible class approach.

Argosy University's bachelor's degree programs are open to students and working professionals with no college experience, plus those who have already earned college credit at a community college, junior college, or other university.

Academic Facilities

Argosy University libraries provide curriculum support and educational resources including current text materials, diagnostic training documents, reference materials and databases, journals and dissertations, and major and current titles in program areas. There is an online public-access catalog of library resources available throughout the Argosy University system. Students enjoy full remote access to their campus library database, enabling them to study and conduct research at home. Academic databases offer dissertation abstracts, academic journals, and professional periodicals. All library computers are Internet accessible. Software applications include Word, Excel, PowerPoint, SPSS, and various test-scoring programs.

Costs

Tuition varies by program. Students should contact the Argosy University campus of their choice for tuition information.

Financial Aid

A wide range of financial aid options is available to students who qualify. Argosy University offers access to federal and state aid programs, merit-based awards, grants, loans, and a work-study program. As a first step, students should complete the Free Application for Federal Student Aid (FAFSA). Prospective students can apply electronically at http://www.fafsa.ed.gov or at the campus. To receive consideration for financial aid and ensure timely receipt of funds, it is best to submit an application promptly.

Faculty

The Argosy University faculty is composed of working professionals who have a passion to help students succeed. Members bring real-world experience and the latest practice innovations to the academic setting. The diverse faculty is widely recognized for contributions to the field. Most hold doctoral degrees. They provide a substantive education that combines comprehensive knowledge with critical skills and practical workplace relevance. Above all, faculty members are committed to their students' personal and professional development.

Student Government

Argosy University campuses offer unique opportunities for student involvement beyond individual programs of study. Most faculty committees include a student representative. In addition, a student group meets with faculty members and administrators regularly to discuss pertinent campus-related issues.

Admission Requirements

Admission requirements differ depending on the number of college credits completed prior to application.

Students who have earned 12 or fewer semester college credits must provide proof of high school graduation or GED and meet one of the following conditions for admission: ACT composite score of 18 or above, or a combined math and verbal SAT score of 870, or minimum ACCUPLACER scores of 86 in sentence skills and 53 in algebra. Applicants who do not meet any of the above conditions for admission will be admitted with academic support if they provide proof of high school graduation or GED and meet one of the following: ACT composite score of 14 to 17, or a combined math and verbal SAT score of 660 to 869, or minimum ACCUPLACER scores of 54 in sentence skills and 36 in arithmetic.

Applicants who have earned 13 or more semester college credits must provide proof of high school graduation or GED and meet one of the following conditions for admission: cumulative college GPA of 2.0 or above or minimum ACCUPLACER scores of 86 for sentence skills and 53 in algebra. Students who do not meet either of the above criteria will be admitted with academic support if they provide proof of high school graduation or GED and meet the following condition: minimum ACCUPLACER scores of 54 in reading and 36 in arithmetic.

Students admitted with academic support are limited to 12 credit hours of study during their first semester (6 credit hours per session). Students admitted with academic support will be required to complete developmental English and/or math courses unless they meet the following conditions: Writing Review (ENG099)—must meet one of the following: a minimum ACCUPLACER score of 86 in sentence skills, or a minimum ACT verbal score of 18, or a minimum SAT verbal score of 425, or completion of a college-level English composition course with a grade of C or above; Mathematics Review I (MAT096)—must meet one of the following: a minimum ACCUPLACER score of 53 in algebra, or a minimum ACT math score of 18, or a minimum SAT math score of 440, or completion of a college-level English composition course with a grade of C or above.

Other admission requirements may include credit hours of qualified transfer credit with a grade of C- or better from a regionally accredited institution or a nationally accredited institution approved and documented by the faculty and dean of the College of Business, or the College of Professional Psychology, at Argosy University or completion of an Associate of Arts or Associate of Science degree from a regionally accredited institution. A maximum of 78 lower-division or 90 total credit hours may be transferred. A minimum written TOEFL score of 500 (paper-based test), 173 (computer-based test), or 61 (Internet-based test) is required for all applicants whose native language is not English or who have not graduated from an institution in which English is the language of instruction.

Official transcripts from approved postsecondary institutions must include a minimum grade point average of 2.0 (on a scale of 4.0) for all academic work completed. Exceptions may be made for extenuating circumstances. All applications must include a completed application form, proof of high school graduation or successful completion of the GED test, official postsecondary transcripts, and a nonrefundable (except in California) application fee. Additional materials are required prior to matriculation. Some programs have additional application requirements or include exceptions to admission requirements. An admissions representative can provide further information.

Application and Information

Argosy University accepts students on a rolling admissions basis year-round, depending on availability of required courses. Applications for admission are available online at http://www.argosy.edu or by contacting one of the campus locations.

Argosy University
205 North Michigan Avenue, Suite 1300
Chicago, Illinois 60601-2250
Phone: 312-899-9900
800-377-0617 (toll-free)
E-mail: auadmissions@argosy.edu
Web site: http://www.argosy.edu

THE ART INSTITUTE OF SEATTLE

SEATTLE, WASHINGTON

The Institute

The Art Institute of Seattle provides programs that prepare graduates for entry-level employment in the creative arts. Programs are developed with and taught by experienced educators. The Art Institute of Seattle has a proud history both as a part of the Seattle community and as a contributor to the Northwest's creative industries.

The Art Institute of Seattle offers nine bachelor's degree programs and twelve associate degree programs.

The Career Services Department works with students to refine their presentations to potential employers. The department also helps provide student advisers with insight into each student's specialized skills and interests. Specific career advising occurs during the last two quarters of a student's education. Interviewing techniques and resume-writing skills are developed, and students receive portfolio advising from faculty members.

Students come to The Art Institute of Seattle from throughout the United States and abroad. The student population includes recent high school graduates, transfer students, and those who have left a previous employment situation to study and train for a new career. Students are creative, competitive, and open to new ideas. They place great value on an education that prepares them for an exciting entry-level position in the arts.

The Art Institute of Seattle places high importance on student life, both inside and outside the classroom. The school provides an environment that encourages involvement in a wide variety of activities, including clubs and organizations, community service opportunities, and various committees designed to enhance the quality of student life. Numerous all-school programs and events are planned throughout the year to meet students' needs.

The Student Affairs Department offers a variety of services to students to help them make the most of their educational experience. These services include both school-sponsored and independent housing options.

The Art Institute of Seattle is accredited by the Northwest Commission on Colleges and Universities (NWCCU), an institutional accrediting body recognized by the United States Department of Education. The Associate of Applied Arts in Culinary Arts degree program is accredited by the American Culinary Federation (ACF).

Location

The Art Institute of Seattle is located in the city's Belltown district. Founded by Native Americans and traders, the city has retained respect for its different cultures and customs. People from all over the world come to study, work, and live in this city that is known for its friendly people and beautiful natural surroundings.

World-class companies, such as Microsoft, Boeing, Starbucks, Amazon.com, and Nordstrom, make their global headquarters in Seattle. As a gateway to the Pacific Rim, Seattle is a crossroads where creativity, technology, and business meet.

Majors and Degrees

Bachelor's degree programs are available in digital filmmaking and video production, fashion design, fashion marketing, game art and design, graphic design, interior design, media arts and animation, photography, and Web design and interactive media.

Associate degrees are available in animation art and design, audio production, baking and pastry, culinary arts, fashion design, fashion marketing, graphic design, industrial design technology, interior design, photography, video production, and Web design and interactive media.

Diploma programs are offered in baking and pastry, digital design, residential design, and the art of cooking.

Academic Programs

The Art Institute of Seattle operates on a year-round, quarterly basis. Each quarter totals eleven weeks. Bachelor's degree programs are twelve quarters in length.

Academic Facilities

The Art Institute of Seattle is an urban campus that comprises three facilities. The school houses classrooms, audio and video studios, a student store, student lounges, copy centers, a gallery, a woodshop, a sculpture room, fashion display windows, a resource center, a technology center, and culinary facilities. The Art Institute of Seattle is also home to a public restaurant.

Costs

Tuition cost varies by program. Prospective students should contact the school for current tuition costs. Other charges include a starting kit for all first quarter students. Kits vary in price depending on the program of study.

Financial Aid

Financial aid is available for those who qualify. The school's student financial aid officers take a holistic approach to developing a financial plan to assist the students in meeting projected education costs.

Eligible students may apply for financial assistance under various federal and state programs, including the Federal Pell Grant, Federal Supplemental Educational Opportunity Grant (FSEOG), Federal Academic Competitiveness Grant, Federal SMART Grant, Federal Perkins Loan, Federal Stafford Student Loan (subsidized and unsubsidized), Federal Work Study Program (FWS), Alaska State Student Loan, Federal PLUS Loan (for parents), Washington State Need Grant, Vocational Rehabilitation Assistance, Veterans Administration benefits, and Bureau of Indian Affairs awards. Awards are based on individual need, the availability of funds, and the individual student's eligibility.

The Art Institute of Seattle offers scholarships based on merit, motivation, and financial need. Scholarship awards and programs include the Advantage Grant Program, The Art Institute of Seattle Excellence Award, The Art Institute of Seattle Scholarship Competition, The Art Institute of Seattle Culinary Scholarship Competition, the National Art Honor Society Scholarship, the Evelyn Keedy Memorial Scholarship, VICA Skills USA Championship, Scholastic Arts Competition, HERO, IACP Foundation, C-Cap, ProStart, Technology Student Association Competition, and New York City Public Schools Scholarship Competition. Application deadlines and eligibility requirements vary.

Faculty

Faculty members at The Art Institute of Seattle are experienced professionals, many of whom bring real-world knowledge into the classroom. There are full-time and part-time faculty members.

Admission Requirements

A student seeking admission to The Art Institute of Seattle is required to interview with an admissions representative (in person or over the phone). Applicants are required to have a high school diploma or a General Educational Development (GED) certificate and to submit an admissions application and an essay describing how an education at The Art Institute of Seattle may help the student to achieve career goals. For advanced placement, additional information, including college transcripts, letters of recommendation, or portfolio work, may be required. Students may apply for admission online.

The Art Institute of Seattle follows a rolling admissions schedule. Students are encouraged to apply for their chosen quarter early so that they may take advantage of orientation activities. Students may also apply until the actual start date for any given quarter, depending on space availability. There is a $50 application fee.

Application and Information

To obtain an application, make arrangements for an interview, or tour the school, students should contact:

The Art Institute of Seattle
2323 Elliott Avenue
Seattle, Washington 98121-1642
Phone: 206-448-6600
800-275-2471 (toll-free)
Fax: 206-269-0275
Web site: http://www.artinstitutes.edu/seattle

The Art Institute of Atlanta®, GA; The Art Institute of Atlanta®–Decatur, GA; The Art Institute of Austin℠, TX; The Art Institute of California℠–Inland Empire; The Art Institute of California℠–Los Angeles; The Art Institute of California℠–Orange County; The Art Institute of California℠–Sacramento; The Art Institute of California℠–San Diego; The Art Institute of California℠–San Francisco; The Art Institute of California℠–Sunnyvale; The Art Institute of Charleston℠, SC, A branch of The Art Institute of Atlanta, GA; The Art Institute of Charlotte®, NC; The Art Institute of Colorado® (Denver); The Art Institute of Dallas®, TX; The Art Institute of Fort Lauderdale®, FL; The Art Institute of Houston®, TX; The Art Institute of Indianapolis℠, IN*; The Art Institute of Jacksonville℠, FL, A branch of Miami International University of Art & Design; The Art Institute of Las Vegas®, NV; The Art Institute of Michigan℠ (Detroit); The Art Institute of New York City®, NY; The Art Institute of Ohio℠–Cincinnati**; The Art Institute of Philadelphia®, PA; The Art Institute of Phoenix®, AZ; The Art Institute of Pittsburgh®, PA; The Art Institute of Pittsburgh®–Online Division; The Art Institute of Portland®, OR; The Art Institute of Salt Lake City℠, UT; The Art Institute of Seattle®, WA; The Art Institute of Tampa℠, FL, A branch of Miami International University of Art & Design; The Art Institute of Tennessee℠–Nashville, A branch of The Art Institute of Atlanta, GA; The Art Institute of Tucson℠, AZ; The Art Institute of Washington® (Arlington, VA), A branch of The Art Institute of Atlanta, GA; The Art Institute of York–Pennsylvania℠; The Art Institutes International Minnesota℠ (Minneapolis); California Design College℠ (Los Angeles–Wilshire Blvd.); The Illinois Institute of Art®–Chicago; The Illinois Institute of Art®–Schaumburg; Miami International University of Art & Design℠, FL; The New England Institute of Art® (Boston, MA).

*The Art Institute of Indianapolis is licensed by the Indiana Commission on Proprietary Education, 302 W. Washington St., Rm. E201, Indianapolis, IN 46204, AC-0080.

**The Art Institute of Ohio–Cincinnati, 8845 Governors Hill Drive, Suite 100, Cincinnati, OH 45249-3317, OH Reg. #04-01-1698B.

BASTYR UNIVERSITY

SEATTLE, WASHINGTON

BASTYR UNIVERSITY

The University

An undergraduate education at Bastyr University is the first step on a path leading to a richly rewarding future in the dynamic field of natural health. Founded as a naturopathic medical college in 1978, Bastyr has since expanded its offerings to become a multidisciplinary university with a wide range of graduate and undergraduate educational opportunities. As a leader in natural medicine education, the foundation of Bastyr University's entire curriculum rests on the integration of modern science with traditional healing methods.

As a small independent university, Bastyr offers students a strong sense of community with abundant academic and personal support. Undergraduate students enjoy a collegial relationship with graduate students as well as with faculty and staff members.

Bastyr undergraduate students are goal-oriented individuals who bring a passionate interest and intense focus to their areas of study. They thrive on diversity and individual expression, and they continually seek out opportunities to grow both intellectually and personally.

The Bastyr University Research Center is devoted to the evaluation of natural medicine practices and the exploration of natural therapies for serious chronic diseases. Participation in research projects is available to a limited number of students.

The University's teaching clinic in Seattle, Bastyr Center for Natural Health, is the largest natural health clinic in the Northwest and provides the main venue for graduate students' clinical training.

Bastyr University is accredited by the Northwest Commission on Colleges and Universities.

In addition to its undergraduate programs, the University offers graduate programs in nutrition and in acupuncture as well as doctoral programs in naturopathic medicine and in acupuncture and Oriental medicine.

Location

The Bastyr University campus is located in Kenmore, Washington, just north of Seattle, in the heart of the picturesque Pacific Northwest. Bastyr's inviting campus environment is a strong attraction for students, who find it uniquely suited to the study of healing practices. Adjacent to the University's 51 acres of fields and gardens are miles of wooded trails winding through the 316-acre St. Edward State Park on the northeast shore of Lake Washington. The park also features a public swimming pool, outdoor volleyball courts, tennis courts, and playfields, which are available to Bastyr students.

Seattle is one of the most attractive cities in the Pacific Northwest and has easy access to mountains, ocean beaches, lakes, and numerous national, state, and city parks. Several ski areas are within an hour's drive, and there are plentiful opportunities for hiking, camping, and other outdoor recreation. The city offers a full range of museums, theaters, fine restaurants, a major opera company, a symphony orchestra, major-league sports, and outdoor activities.

Majors and Degrees

Bastyr University offers several two-year, upper-division programs that lead to Bachelor of Science degrees. Undergraduates may choose majors in exercise science and wellness, health psychology, herbal sciences, or nutrition or a combined B.S./M.S. program in acupuncture and Oriental medicine (AOM) that is designed to meet the requirements for national licensure in acupuncture.

Academic Programs

In each degree program at Bastyr, students learn to integrate the pursuit of physical health with the mental, spiritual, and environmental factors involved in wellness.

The Bachelor of Science with a major in nutrition provides a whole-foods, science-based nutrition education that explores how food affects the human body and how food choices impact the environment. This B.S. degree program can be combined with the Didactic Program in Dietetics for those interested in becoming registered dieticians (RD). Bastyr University's Didactic Program in Dietetics has been approved by the American Dietetic Association Council on Education.

The Bachelor of Science with a major in exercise science and wellness combines a rigorous, in-depth study of the body's physiology and mechanics with a focus on nutrition, stress management, and holistic wellness. Graduates possess the educational requirements needed to achieve exercise certification from the American College of Sports Medicine and other professional exercise affiliates.

The Bachelor of Science with a major in health psychology offers a solid foundation in core psychology with a progressive focus on the relationship between health and the body, mind and spirit. Students learn the tools to improve people's quality of life and to address systemic problems in society and social institutions. Students may enroll in one of two tracks: health psychology or psychology and human biology (psychology premed).

The Bachelor of Science with a major in herbal sciences provides a thorough and scientifically rigorous introduction to herbal medicine, including plant identification and pharmacology. The program also imparts real-world skills and expertise in the herbal products industry and introduces the student to concepts of disease prevention and health maintenance using medicinal herbs.

Bastyr's unique program combines the ancient wisdom and time-honored traditions of Oriental medicine with the rigors of contemporary medical science. The combined B.S./M.S. option in acupuncture and Oriental medicine is generally a 3.5 year program. A certificate program for additional study in Chinese herbal medicine is also offered. The University's acupuncture and Oriental medicine programs are accredited by the ACAOM and meet the requirements of the national certification exam.

Academic Facilities

The University's 186,000-square-foot facility houses a wealth of resources dedicated to student success, including a comprehensive bookstore, numerous scientific laboratories, a whole-foods nutrition kitchen, research facilities, a gourmet vegetarian cafeteria, a cooperative childcare center and parent resource center, dormitory space, and conference and seminar space, as well as wireless Internet access and computer labs.

The University also maintains a medical library with extensive resources for conventional and natural medicine. These include more than 19,000 volumes; 250 journal subscriptions; special collections in the areas of nutrition, herbal sciences, psychology, and exercise science; and access to many health and natural medicine databases. Students at Bastyr University are also eligible to use the Health Sciences Library at the University of Washington.

Costs

Tuition for the 2007–08 academic year was $370 per credit for 1 to 11 credits and $340 per credit for 12–16 credits; the cost for each additional credit over 16 is $282. The total cost of tuition and fees for a full-time student for the academic year was $17,040 ($21,425 for the combined B.S./M.S. AOM program), depending on the number of credits needed to complete a program. Students can expect to spend approximately $1125 per year on books and supplies ($1625 for the combined B.S./M.S. program).

The University has limited dormitory space. Many students live in shared housing facilities off campus; the average rent per person ranges from $500 to $900 per month. The Student Services Office maintains listings of available housing. The Washington Financial Aid Association estimates that living expenses for nine months, including transportation and personal expenses, average $1359 per month.

Financial Aid

Students are eligible to participate in state and federal financial aid programs, including the Washington State Need Grant, Washington State Education Opportunity Grant, Federal Pell Grant, Federal Supplemental Educational Opportunity Grant (FSEOG), Federal Stafford Student Loan, Federal Perkins Loan, and the Federal Work-Study Program. Applicants seeking financial aid should complete the application process by May 15. Financial aid information is provided by the University on request.

Faculty

Bastyr University students enjoy a 13:1 student-faculty ratio with professors who are approachable and accessible. There are 51 core and 91 adjunct faculty members, many of whom teach in both the undergraduate and graduate programs. More than 80 percent hold advanced or doctoral degrees. All faculty members are involved in teaching and are dedicated to providing students with a program of the highest quality.

Student Government

The University relies upon the participation of students to create a more effective learning environment. The Student Council makes decisions focusing on social activities as well as policies and budget items affecting students. Each class and program is represented. Students also serve on the Curriculum Review, Library, and Resident Selection committees; the Appeals Board; and ad hoc committees.

Admission Requirements

Admission is based on academic achievement, personal and social development, and demonstrated humanistic qualities. Credentials to be submitted include all official transcripts, a completed application form, and a $60 application fee. The minimum prerequisite for the bachelor's programs is two years of college-level general education (90 quarter or 60 semester credits), including those distribution and course requirements described below. Students must take the following distribution of general education courses, which are not counted toward any other requirements: arts and humanities, 15 quarter credits; social sciences, 15 quarter credits; and natural sciences and mathematics, 12 quarter credits. In addition, specific required courses include 9 credits of English composition and/or literature, 4 credits of college-level algebra, 4 credits of general biology, 3 credits of general psychology, and 3 credits of public speaking. Nutrition majors are required to have taken 5 credits of introductory nutrition. Herbal sciences majors are required to have 3 credits of botany. A minimum 2.25 overall GPA and a C or better in all required courses are needed.

Application and Information

Applications should be submitted to the University by March 15 for priority consideration for fall admission. Late applications are considered if space is available. Application may be made by submitting the Bastyr University undergraduate application with a $60 nonrefundable fee and all official transcripts. Online applications are also available and can be accessed at http://www.bastyr.edu/admissions.

Prospective students are encouraged to visit the campus or attend recruiting events in their region. For further information, students should contact:

Admissions Office
Bastyr University
14500 Juanita Drive NE
Kenmore, Washington 98028
Phone: 425-602-3330
E-mail: admissions@bastyr.edu
Web site: http://www.bastyr.edu/sub/adtrack.asp?adid=pe01

Students on the Bastyr Kenmore campus.

COLLEGE DATA CENTER • WASHINGTON

CITY UNIVERSITY OF SEATTLE

BELLEVUE, WASHINGTON

The University

City University of Seattle opened its doors in 1973 with one primary purpose: to provide educational opportunities for those segments of the population not being fully served through traditional means. City University believes that education is a lifelong process, and it is a pioneer in the concept of education unhindered by time, format, or location. City University is a private, not-for-profit institution of higher learning, open to anyone with the desire to achieve. Classes are offered in the day, evening, on weekends, or online in order to meet student needs without interrupting established lifestyles and associations.

City University's students are primarily working adults, drawn from all walks of life. In the 2006–07 school year, the University enrolled more than 4,000 undergraduate students worldwide. Of those, more than 56 percent were women and, for those reporting, 11 percent were members of minority groups. Although the majority of students attend classes near their homes in the Pacific Northwest, many live and study at locations around the globe. Often programs are available at the student's workplace through cooperative arrangements with progressive employers or professional associations.

City University of Seattle is accredited by the Northwest Commission on Colleges and Universities. Graduate programs leading to the Master of Arts in counseling and psychology, the Master of Science in business administration, the Master of Science in computer systems, the Master of Science in project management, the Master of Education, and the Master in Teaching are also offered.

Most City University students are already established in either a job or career and have chosen a path they are preparing to follow. As alumni, they are able to realize their career goals in business, in public administration, or in one of several professions.

Location

The University's mission statement specifies a commitment to education that is affordable, accessible, and relevant as well as academically sound. Accordingly, the University owns or leases classroom space in metropolitan centers, smaller cities, military installations, or any other space that is convenient for students. Eight locations serve the Greater Seattle/Puget Sound area. Classes are also held in Bellevue, Renton, Everett, North Seattle, Bellingham, Tacoma, Centralia, and Vancouver in Washington; and Vancouver and Victoria, British Columbia and Calgary and Edmonton, Alberta in Canada. Classes are also offered around the globe through distance learning and from sites in Europe and China.

Majors and Degrees

City University of Seattle offers a range of programs leading to Associate of Science, Associate of Arts, Bachelor of Science, and Bachelor of Arts degrees. Students are given a vast array of options and may choose the course of study best suited to their experience, prior learning, and the realization of their personal and professional goals.

The Associate of Science degree is offered in general studies.

City University offers the Bachelor of Science degree with a range of possible emphases. These include accounting, business administration, computer systems, general studies, and communications.

The Bachelor of Arts degree in applied psychology or education is also offered.

Undergraduate certificate programs offer professional credentials for those whose immediate needs do not require the completion of a degree. Various preparation classes for industry certifications are available as part of the Bachelor of Science in database technology, information systems/technology, individualized study, and project management. Students can choose among classes geared toward accounting, Programming in C++, human resource management, marketing, networking/telecommunications, Web languages, and Web design. City University also offers Professional Human Resource/Senior Professional Human Resource Management (PHR/SPHR) preparation.

Students who live in other areas may complete a degree program through City University's online distance learning format, which serves students worldwide. Distance learning makes completing an education possible anywhere via the World Wide Web. These courses are on the traditional quarterly schedule.

Academic Programs

Candidates for the bachelor's degree must complete 180 hours of credit by completing regular or distance learning classes or through recognized transfer credits or prior learning experience. Lower-division requirements total 90 credits, including a total of 55 general education credits in the broad areas of writing, mathematics, humanities, natural sciences/mathematics, and social sciences. For most bachelor's degree programs, upper-division course work consists of a series of common core courses respective to their degrees, followed by a series of elective courses. Most undergraduate programs are designed to allow students to satisfy certain general education requirements through upper-division course work.

For the Associate of Science degree, students complete 90 credit hours, 35 of which are in general education. Each of these programs is wholly compatible with and transferable to baccalaureate degree study. Depending on the particular choice of program, students can complete an undergraduate certificate program with 24 to 45 credits.

The academic year is divided into four quarters. City University offers day, evening, weekend, and distance learning courses.

Academic Facilities

City University's library serves students throughout the Seattle area with a schedule of service that extends more than 68 hours per week. Extensive reference resources, indexes, journals, and online databases are made available by a professional staff at the main library in Bellevue. Reference and interlibrary loan services are offered to all students. For those residing outside the Seattle area, access is facilitated by the library's 800 telephone number and through e-mail. Most online databases are available 24 hours per day through the University's Web site. Student and faculty research is also supported by cooperative agreements with many libraries in the United States and Canada.

Costs

For 2006–07, tuition was $240 to $268 per undergraduate credit hour, depending on program of study, and $337 to $458 per graduate credit hour, depending on program of study. Additional fees apply for certificate completion, graduation application, course registration and various tests or examinations that the student may request. Textbooks and other instructional materials are additional. All initial applicants to certificate or degree programs pay a nonrefundable application fee of $80. Tuition and fees are subject to annual review on July 1.

Financial Aid

To help qualified students achieve their educational and professional goals, City University participates in several financial aid programs. Federal Pell Grants, Federal Supplemental Educational Opportunity Grants, Federal Stafford Student Loans, Federal PLUS loans, and Federal Work-Study are available.

In addition, the University awards scholarships on the basis of financial need, demonstrated academic ability, and other criteria. Employer reimbursement programs and military tuition assistance programs are also recognized, and all programs are approved for veterans' education benefits.

Students interested in financial aid should contact City University's Financial Aid Office at the toll-free number listed below for more information.

Faculty

The University's senior administration and faculty have a University-wide role in quality assurance, academic policies and standards, curricular development, and instructional quality. City University's faculty is composed of distinguished practitioners in the fields of business, education, and government and in civic and research organizations and the legal community. They unite strong academic preparation with active professional careers in the fields in which they teach. Some of the University's approximately 147 full-time faculty members worldwide also serve as senior faculty members in charge of various academic disciplines. They oversee more than 800 teaching faculty members instructing in both classroom theory and actual practice at more than a dozen locations around the world. The University draws on this faculty pool to achieve an average class size of 18 students.

Student Government

The philosophy and structure of City University of Seattle do not lend themselves to the traditional student organization activities revolving around life on a fixed campus. The Student Code of Conduct creates an atmosphere conducive to an uninhibited, scholastically honest learning environment. City University encourages and responds to current and prospective students' comments in an effort to help maintain currency and relevance in its academic offerings.

Admission Requirements

Undergraduate degree programs are generally open to applicants over the age of 18 who hold a high school or GED diploma, who can benefit from postsecondary education. Students who began but did not complete academic careers at other postsecondary institutions are welcome to continue their education at City University. Course work completed at other recognized institutions is evaluated to determine its applicability to the selected degree and major objective.

To gain general admission to the University, students must begin by contacting or meeting with an admissions adviser to select an educational objective and to complete initial enrollment. An application form must be filled out and an application fee submitted. Transcripts and other documentation may be required. International students and veterans find that additional requirements apply.

In addition to general admission requirements, program-specific admissions criteria may apply to select programs and must be met prior to beginning study.

A rolling admissions policy governs most City University programs. That is, the University accepts applications and announces admissions decisions continuously throughout the year. Most degree programs may be commenced at the start of the fall, winter, spring, or summer quarters.

Application and Information

Because of City University's rolling admissions policy, applications for admission may be submitted at any time.

For application forms or other information, prospective students may contact:

Office of Admissions and Student Services
City University of Seattle
11900 NE First Street
Bellevue, Washington 98005
Phone: 888-42-CITYU (24898) (toll-free)
425-450-4660 (TTY)
Fax: 425-709-5361
E-mail: info@cityu.edu
Web site: http://www.cityu.edu

EASTERN WASHINGTON UNIVERSITY

CHENEY, WASHINGTON

The University

Established in 1882 as the Benjamin P. Cheney Academy, Eastern Washington University (EWU) has grown from a premier teachers' college into a comprehensive state university providing an excellent student-centered learning environment; professionally accomplished faculty members who are strongly committed to student learning; high-quality, integrated, interdependent academic programs; and exceptional student support services, resources, and facilities. The University retains the charm and personality of its founding on the parklike campus in Cheney. It also exhibits the distinctive marks of the modern comprehensive university in its newer facilities and the expansion of higher educational opportunities into downtown Spokane. Eastern is fully accredited by the Northwest Association of Schools and Colleges and by numerous professional accreditation agencies in specific disciplines. In addition to the undergraduate degrees that are listed, Eastern offers master's degrees in the arts and sciences, business administration, creative writing, education, nursing, public administration, social work, and urban and regional planning. Eastern also offers a doctorate in physical therapy.

Eastern's 10,000 students come from more than forty states and twenty-four countries. Nonwhite students make up 17 percent of the student body, and international students make up 4 percent. About 58 percent of Eastern's students are women. Educational and support services are available through the American Indian Studies, Chicano Education, African American Education, and Women's Studies Programs; the English Language Institute; and the Academic Support Center. Seven residence halls can accommodate 2,086 students on campus. Additional housing is available for married students and students with children. Fraternity and sorority housing, as well as off-campus housing within walking distance in Cheney, affords a variety of housing options. All residence halls are smoke free. Students and the University community enjoy one of the Northwest's premier sports and recreation centers. The PHASE complex includes a 5,500-seat pavilion, an indoor aquatics center, a field house with indoor track and tennis, and the main PHASE building, which houses indoor courts for basketball, volleyball, and racquetball; dance studios; a fitness center; and a large, multisurfaced rock for climbing practice. These facilities, totaling 100,000 square feet, and Woodward Field are the venues for the NCAA Division I Eagles, who compete in the Big Sky Conference.

Location

The University's main campus is located in Cheney, a comfortable and compact city of more than 10,000, where students may find a variety of services, facilities, and shopping while enjoying the pleasant, secure feel of a small town. Spokane, one of the state's largest cities and a regional hub for manufacturing, business, transportation, and health services for more than 450,000 residents, is just 17 miles away and offers a full range of social, cultural, recreational, and consumer opportunities. The Inland Northwest region offers virtually unlimited scenic and recreational attractions in a four-season climate. More than seventy-five lakes lie within 50 miles of the campus, and the mountains and many rivers are easily accessible. Other outdoor activities include excellent skiing within a short drive in nearly every direction. The University sits amid fascinating geological and geographic diversity, with the arid high country to the west, the rich Palouse farming area to the south, and the fir-covered mountains climbing from Spokane into Idaho and Montana. The Spokane International Airport, rail and bus service, and interstate access serve the region.

Majors and Degrees

EWU is responding to the needs of the state as defined by the Washington Council of the American Electronics Association by offering a new degree program in electrical engineering. A comprehensive university, Eastern offers the following majors: anthropology; art; biology (including biochemistry/biotechnology, predental, premedicine, and pre–veterinary medicine); business administration (including accounting, economics, finance, general management, human resource management, international business, management information systems, marketing, operations management, and pre-M.B.A.); chemistry and biochemistry (including forensic science); communication disorders; communication studies (including interpersonal, organizational, public communication, and public relations); computer science (including computer information systems and multimedia programming and development); counseling, developmental, and educational psychology; criminal justice; dental hygiene; earth science; economics; education (including elementary and secondary options); electronic media and filmic arts; engineering and design (including computer engineering technology, construction design, electronics, manufacturing, mechanical engineering technology, and visual communication design); English (including creative writing, literary studies, and technical communication); environmental science; geography; geology (including environmental); government (including prelaw); health services administration; history; humanities; interdisciplinary studies; international affairs; journalism (including news editorial, public relations, and technology); mathematics (including computer science, economics, and statistics); military science; modern languages and literature (including French, German, and Spanish); music (including instrumental performance, liberal arts, music composition, piano performance, and vocal performance); natural science; nursing; occupational therapy; physical education, health, and recreation (including athletic training, coaching, community health education, exercise science, health, health and fitness/elementary or secondary education, health education, health promotion and wellness, outdoor recreation, recreation management, and therapeutic recreation); physics; psychology; social work; sociology; theater; and urban and regional planning.

Academic Programs

Eastern's mission is to prepare broadly educated, technologically proficient, and highly productive citizens to attain meaningful careers, to enjoy enriched lives, and to contribute to a culturally diverse society. Graduates must have well-developed skills in critical thinking and the ability to express themselves in oral, written, and quantitative forms of communication. The liberal arts core curriculum extends throughout the student's four-year program and includes both breadth and depth requirements as well as writing instruction and assessment in all areas of the curriculum. Small classes, a student-faculty ratio of 24:1, and facilities like the Writers' Center offer the student the resources to meet high expectations. Eastern's unique core curriculum and liberal arts goals were designed as a direct response to input from Eastern alumni, employers, and students. Minors are available in many areas of study, and teacher certification requirements and specific endorsements are available in conjunction with academic disciplines. The prestigious University Honors Program offers motivated students the opportunity to challenge their limits through special honors courses that are part of the core curriculum. University and departmental honor societies continue to provide these opportunities in the major fields. Career preparation is a focus during each student's entire program. Internships and career exploration opportunities for freshmen and sophomores assist in early career and major selection, enhanced employment skills, and locating professional internships as upper-division students.

Off-Campus Programs

Study-abroad opportunities are available for Eastern students as well as for students from other campuses. Programs are available in more than twenty-five countries. In addition, internships are available for students in the Inland Northwest, across the United States, and internationally. These programs provide countless training and research opportunities for graduate and undergraduate students.

Academic Facilities

Eastern's campus includes more than 300 acres in Cheney. The University also maintains classroom, office, and laboratory/clinic facilities in downtown Spokane and shares facilities at the Riverpoint Higher Education Center, also in downtown Spokane. The University libraries include the Kennedy Library on the Cheney campus, with more than 800,000 items, online catalogs, and computer search capabilities covering Eastern as well as other Washington State libraries. Eastern and Washington State University jointly support a downtown library facility. Student computer labs, including a multimedia lab, are located throughout the campus. The Pence Union Building houses the main computer lab, with Macintosh and IBM-compatible systems, on-site assistance, DEC mainframe access with faculty sponsorship, and Internet access. The residence halls are wired for both voice and data communications. Additional facilities for learning and teaching include the planetarium, the Robert Reid Laboratory School (an elementary school directly on campus that includes observation facilities), a speech and hearing clinic, and the Turnbull Laboratory for Ecological Studies.

Costs

Annual undergraduate tuition and fees for 2006–07 were $4695 for Washington State residents and $13,725 for nonresidents. Students participating in the Western Undergraduate Exchange Program paid $6609 for tuition and fees. Typical on-campus room and board cost about $6549.

Financial Aid

The Financial Aid and Scholarship Office assists students in identifying the most appropriate sources of funding for their college education. Students who are admitted to the University may apply for federal, state, and University funds by using the Free Application for Federal Student Aid and by applying before the priority deadline of February 15. Although most financial aid is based on need, a number of scholarships are available for students who meet competitive academic criteria. Academic scholarships also reward outstanding performance by continuing students at Eastern. The University scholarship application must be submitted for consideration by February 1. A reduction of the nonresident tuition is available to qualified students from Idaho, Montana, Nevada, New Mexico, North Dakota, Oregon, South Dakota, Utah, and Wyoming through the Western Undergraduate Exchange Program. Applicants interested in need-based financial aid and academic scholarships should contact the Financial Aid and Scholarship Office, 102 Sutton Hall, Eastern Washington University, Cheney, Washington 99004.

Faculty

More than 600 faculty members provide highly personalized instruction to undergraduates at Eastern. Faculty members are committed to keeping class sizes small and to helping students graduate in a timely manner. Eastern's faculty members are teachers and take pride in innovative curricula, in maintaining close relationships with the community and with professionals outside of the University for the benefit of their students, and in their research, which brings new information and methods into the classroom.

Student Government

All students are members of the Associated Students of Eastern Washington University. A president, executive officers, and a 12-member council are elected annually. The 12 council members represent the students' interest in every facet of student life at Eastern. The student government is responsible for budgeting and managing student fees collected from all students. These funds are used for the operation of the student union, the Pence Union Building; athletic and intramural programs; and the more than seventy-five clubs and organizations that provide opportunities for involvement of students both on campus and in the community.

Admission Requirements

Freshman applicants are admitted based on their high school GPA and test scores on the SAT or the ACT with writing. Applicants also must meet the following core requirements in high school (having extra core classes is highly encouraged): English, 4; math, 3 (algebra I and II and geometry); social science, 3; science, 2 (including 1 lab science); foreign language, 2 (same language); and fine arts (or elective from above subject areas), 1. Transfer students with fewer than 40 transferable credits must meet the high school core and admissions index requirements and have a minimum 2.0 cumulative GPA. Transfer students with more than 40 transferable credits must have a cumulative GPA of at least 2.0 and completed a minimum of precollege-level English and intermediate algebra with a 2.0 or better. Students who do not meet the academic criteria for admission may be considered on the basis of additional evidence of potential presented to the Office of Admissions. Many majors require considerably higher grade point averages for entry into the major field. Transfer students should consult the University catalog or contact the department for specific program requirements.

Application and Information

All freshman applicants should submit an application, complete high school (and any college) transcripts, SAT or ACT with writing scores, and a personal statement to the Office of Admissions. Decisions for fall freshmen are made on December 1 and on a rolling basis thereafter. Transfer students should submit an application, an official high school transcript (if applicable), and official transcripts from all colleges and universities attended. A nonrefundable application fee of $50 is required of all applicants. A campus visit or participation in an overnight on-campus program is the best way to learn more about Eastern. Students should contact the Office of Admissions to find out more about these and other programs designed to provide an opportunity to explore Eastern Washington University. For additional information, students should contact:

Office of Admissions
101 Sutton Hall
Eastern Washington University
Cheney, Washington 99004
Phone: 509-359-2397
Fax: 509-359-6692
E-mail: admissions@mail.ewu.edu
Web site: http://www.ewu.edu

The state-of-the-art John F. Kennedy Library has 50 different databases available, 500 study carrels, wireless laptops that may be checked out, and more.

GONZAGA UNIVERSITY

SPOKANE, WASHINGTON

The University

Founded in 1887, Gonzaga is an independent, comprehensive university with a distinguished background in the Catholic, Jesuit, and humanistic tradition. Gonzaga emphasizes the moral and ethical implications of learning, living, and working in today's global society. As a testament to this educational approach, Gonzaga's first-to-second-year retention rate tops 90 percent. Through the University Core Curriculum, each student develops a strong liberal arts foundation, which many alumni cite as a most valuable asset. In addition, students specialize in any of more than seventy-five academic areas of study.

Gonzaga's 110-acre campus is characterized by sprawling green lawns and majestic evergreen trees. Towering above the campus are the stately spires of St. Aloysius Church, the well-recognized landmark featured in the University logo.

Because personal growth is as important as intellectual development, Gonzaga places great emphasis on student life outside of class. Ranging in population size from 35 to 361 students and offering both coed and single-sex living, Gonzaga's seventeen residence halls and seven apartment complexes offer an intimate atmosphere and a lively campus experience. Each hall has one or more Residence Assistants and a chaplain or a resident Jesuit. While freshmen and sophomores are required to live on campus, 40 percent of the upperclass students also reside in Gonzaga's halls and apartments. Campus-based activities ranging from residence hall government to current affairs symposiums to intramural sports keep students informed and entertained. Students in all academic majors integrate with the Spokane community through a variety of activities, such as volunteer opportunities and internships at numerous businesses and agencies. Gonzaga provides both career and counseling centers.

Gonzaga enrolls approximately 6,600 students, of whom about 4,275 are undergraduates. About 45 percent of the students come from Washington State, with forty-three other states and forty-two other countries also represented. In addition to its undergraduate colleges and schools, Gonzaga University offers about twenty master's programs, a doctoral program in leadership studies, and a School of Law.

Location

Located along the banks of the Spokane River in a quiet, turn-of-the-century neighborhood, Gonzaga University is just a 15-minute walk from downtown Spokane, a city with a metropolitan-area population of 446,700. Spokane's beautiful 100-acre Riverfront Park, in the heart of downtown, lies near the INB Performing Arts Center, Spokane Convention Center, and Spokane Arena. Fine restaurants, a twenty-screen AMC movie theater, and an assortment of shops and department stores, many of which can be reached through a convenient, weatherproof skywalk system, are also in the city's core. For mall shoppers, the Northtown Mall is a 10-minute drive from the campus. Easily accessible outdoor recreation activities, such as skiing, golfing, hiking, biking, camping, and rock climbing, add excitement for the avid outdoorsperson.

Majors and Degrees

Gonzaga's undergraduate school awards the B.A., B.B.A., B.E., B.Ed., B.G.S., B.S., B.S.C.E., B.S.Cp.E., B.S.G.E., B.S.E.E., B.S.M.E., and B.S.N. degrees. Majors offered in the College of Arts and Sciences are applied communication studies, art, biology, broadcast and electronic media studies, chemistry (biochemistry option), classical civilizations, criminal justice, economics, English, French, history, integrated studies, international studies (including international relations and Asian, European, and Latin American studies), Italian studies, journalism, mathematics, mathematics/computer science, music (including composition, education, literature, liturgical, and performance), philosophy, physics, political science, psychology, public relations, religious studies, sociology, Spanish, and theater arts.

The School of Business Administration, which is accredited by AACSB International–The Association to Advance Collegiate Schools of Business, offers a Bachelor of Business Administration degree with a major in accounting or a major in business administration, with concentrations in economics, entrepreneurship, finance, human resource management, individualized study, international business, law and public policy, management information systems, marketing, and operations and supply chain management.

As well as granting teacher certification on both the elementary and secondary levels, the School of Education offers degrees in physical education, special education, and sport management.

The School of Engineering and Applied Science awards Bachelor of Science degrees in civil, computer, electrical, general, and mechanical engineering and computer science. The general engineering program includes numerous business courses and also allows attainment of the M.B.A. in five years of study. The civil, computer, electrical, and mechanical programs are accredited by the Engineering Accreditation Commission of the Accreditation Board for Engineering and Technology, Inc. (EAC/ABET).

The School of Professional Studies offers degrees in exercise science, general studies, and nursing.

Academic Programs

Gonzaga University believes that all students, regardless of their chosen major or profession, benefit from attaining an education that goes beyond specialization. Therefore, all students receive a strong liberal arts background as well as depth in their majors. The Core Curriculum is a very important component of the minimum 128 semester units a student must earn for graduation.

The Honors Program challenges exceptional students with an integrated curriculum that is compatible with any major and most double majors. Motivated and imaginative students in all majors create new ventures and seek to make a difference in the world through the Hogan Entrepreneurial Leadership Program. The Comprehensive Leadership Program, which is also open to students from all majors, allows students to fine-tune their leadership skills and knowledge while completing an academic leadership concentration. All three programs require separate applications. Gonzaga University Summer Term (GUST) offers motivated high school students intensive course work in a variety of academic disciplines. Academic and cocurricular activities are included in the six-week session.

Credits earned through the Washington State Running Start Program or International Baccalaureate (I.B.) program are accepted on a class-by-class basis. College credit is given for certain test scores in most Advanced Placement (AP) subjects. The academic year follows a two-semester system, beginning in late August. Two summer sessions are also available.

Off-Campus Programs

Gonzaga University offers qualified students the opportunity to study abroad through programs in Australia, Benin, Brazil, British West Indies, China, Costa Rica, El Salvador, England, France, Ireland, Italy, Japan, Mexico, the Netherlands, Spain, and Zambia. As the largest and most popular program, Gonzaga-in-Florence allows approximately 100 students the opportunity to live in Italy for a year or a summer and to travel to many other countries and continents.

Academic Facilities

Gonzaga's "library of the future," the Ralph E. and Helen Higgins Foley Center, is a $20-million window to worldwide information resources. The library features more than 300 specialized databases, satellite capabilities, an advanced computer-controlled video editing system, a rare book room, computerized retrieval services, a wireless Internet connection, and beautiful views.

Foley Center holdings include 782,000 volumes and microform titles, with two special collections of materials that are especially rich in the areas of philosophy and classical civilization. The Foley Center also has the nation's most extensive collection of works by the famous Jesuit poet Gerard Manley Hopkins. The School of Law maintains its own library of 130,000 volumes. The historic Administration Building houses Russell Theatre, the computer center, a 24-hour computer lab, the University chapel, and the main administrative offices and classrooms. A student-operated FM radio station, a state-of-the-art television broadcasting studio, and the offices of the *Bulletin*, a weekly student-published newspaper, reside in the newly renovated Communications Building.

Campus computing services include more than 250 PC and Macintosh computers and Sun workstations dispersed throughout a dozen computer labs. An HP9000/K100 minicomputer provides central academic services and student electronic mail. Students have sculpted T-3 cable access to the Internet, library, and central academic services from their dorm rooms and other University facilities. Almost all buildings on campus and some open spaces are wireless-accessible. The Herak Center for Engineering houses a CAD/CAE center, general-purpose computer facilities, electronics and mechanical calibration rooms, and laboratories for physics, electronics, digital electronics/circuits, microprocessors, communications/controls, computer analysis, automation and embedded systems, power, mechanical design, mechanical engineering, materials testing, manufacturing engineering, rapid prototyping, water/wastewater, geotechnical engineering, and hydrology/hydraulics. The center also contains a large Fabrication Facility and extensive areas for the design and construction of student projects.

The 2003 addition to the Hughes Hall Life Sciences building adds lab and classroom space for a program that is especially rich in environmental biology opportunities. The Martin Athletic Centre provides a 13,000-square-foot fitness center, and the 6,000-seat McCarthey Athletic Center hosts basketball games and concerts. In addition, the new home of Gonzaga baseball, Patterson Baseball Complex and Washington Trust Field, opened in March 2007. On the west side of the campus, a 23,000-square-foot addition to the Jepson Center for Business Administration houses additional classrooms, computer labs, the Ethics Institute, the Hogan Entrepreneurial Leadership Program, and a student lounge and café.

Costs

Tuition for the 2007–08 academic year is $26,120. Average room and board costs are $7520 for the year.

Financial Aid

Gonzaga University offers many different types of financial aid to qualified students, including scholarships, Federal Pell Grants, Federal Supplemental Educational Opportunity Grants, work-study jobs, Federal Perkins Loans, Federal Stafford Student Loans, and on- and off-campus employment. In order to apply for financial aid awards, a student must first be accepted by the University and must submit the Free Application for Federal Student Aid (FAFSA) by February 1. After this date, awards are made on a funds-available basis. Approximately 95 percent of the students at Gonzaga receive financial assistance, and the average award for this group is $19,181 (includes all types of aid).

Faculty

The student-faculty ratio is 12:1, and the average class size is 25, allowing close, mentoring relationships to develop. All classes at Gonzaga are taught by faculty members, and faculty members also serve as academic advisers. Eight percent of the faculty members are Jesuits, and 83 percent of the 335 full-time faculty members hold the highest degree in their fields.

Student Government

The Gonzaga Student Body Association provides the means for students to participate in making decisions about student life at Gonzaga. The 5-member Executive Council, an elected board of students that administers and initiates programs, also serves as a liaison between the administration and the students. The Student Senate, a legislative body consisting of 24 senators, is responsible for sounding out the needs of the student body and directing this information to the Executive Council. Students also serve on the Board of Regents, search committees, the budget committee, and many other University committees.

Admission Requirements

Gonzaga expects freshman applicants to have taken a challenging college-preparatory curriculum and to submit strong test scores on the ACT or SAT. Transfer students who have earned at least 30 semester credits or 45 quarter credits do not need to submit a high school transcript or test scores. The admission process is selective, and applicants are considered through a pooling process. The Admissions Committee seeks motivated, well-rounded students and considers the rigor of academic study in high school, in addition to grades and test scores, as well as personal characteristics, awards and activities, and an essay.

Application and Information

Gonzaga University's nonbinding Early Action deadline for admission applications is November 15. Students who meet this deadline with a complete application are notified of an admission decision by January 15. The final deadline for freshmen to apply for admission under Regular Decision is February 1. Regular Decision applicants receive an admission decision by the middle of March. Transfer students are admitted on a rolling admission basis. Transfer students seeking financial aid are encouraged to apply for admission by March 1. Otherwise, to ensure a smooth transition to Gonzaga, transfer students should apply by June 1. After June 1, the University accepts transfer applicants only if space is available. Students may apply by using the Common Application, APPLY!, CollegeLink, and the Catholic College Common Application. For priority financial aid, all students are encouraged to submit the FAFSA by February 1.

All requests for further information or materials should be addressed to:

Julie McCulloh
Dean of Admission
Gonzaga University
Spokane, Washington 99258-0102
Phone: 800-322-2584 (toll-free)
E-mail: admissions@gonzaga.edu
Web site: http://www.gonzaga.edu

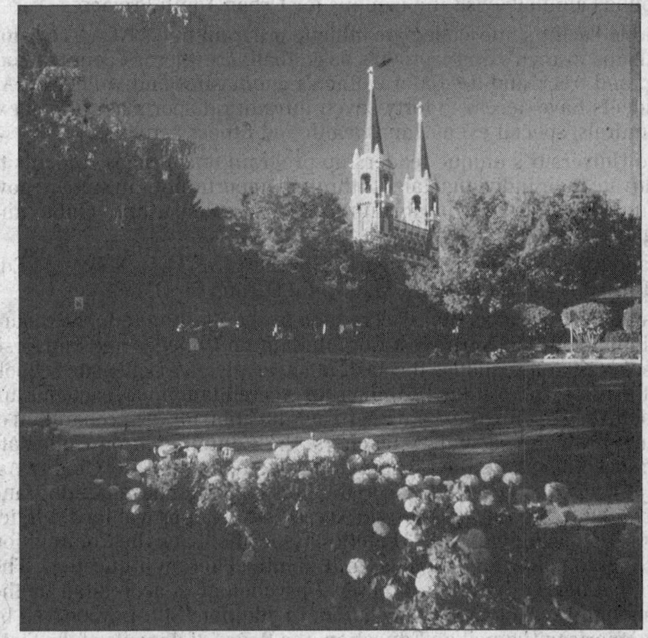

Gonzaga University: Education for the mind, body, and spirit.

SEATTLE PACIFIC UNIVERSITY

SEATTLE, WASHINGTON

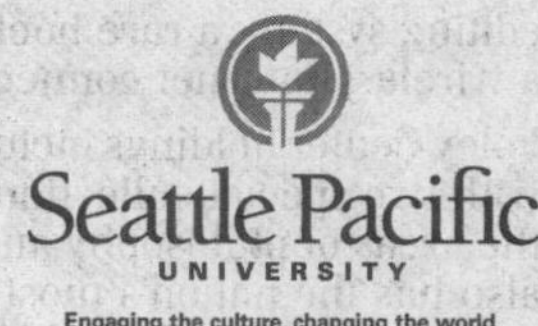

Seattle Pacific
UNIVERSITY
Engaging the culture, changing the world.

The University

With a long and distinguished history in Christian higher education, Seattle Pacific University (SPU) entered the new century positioned to engage the culture and influence the world for good. At a time when the legacy of the secularized modern university is under scrutiny, Seattle Pacific provides more than 3,800 students with a high-quality, comprehensive education grounded on the gospel of Jesus Christ. This combination of vital scholarship and thoughtful faith is a powerful one that brings about lasting change in the lives of graduates and in the people and communities they serve.

Founded in 1891, SPU has been designated one of "America's Best Colleges" by *U.S. News & World Report* and has been acknowledged as one of the country's character-building institutions. Located just minutes from downtown Seattle, the leading urban center in the Pacific Northwest, SPU is committed to engaging and serving in the modern city, cultivating a global consciousness, supporting the church, and addressing the crisis of meaning in modern culture. SPU believes these are some of the Christian university's most important contributions in this century.

SPU students come from forty-four states and twenty-four countries, representing more than forty-two different Christian denominations. More than half of Seattle Pacific's undergraduate students live on the campus in four residence halls and several apartment complexes. All Seattle Pacific residence facilities are wired to allow students dedicated online connections to e-mail, the Internet, and the campus computer network.

Seattle Pacific University celebrates diversity and learning to live together in Christian community. In 2004, civil rights leader John Perkins and SPU President Philip Eaton founded the John Perkins Center on campus. The first of its kind in the nation, the Perkins Center helps SPU become a more diverse campus, practice reconciliation, build new relationships in the city, and bring about positive change in the world. The Ames Minority Leadership Scholarships support high school graduates who come from minority groups and have leadership potential. Prospective students from urban areas and diverse backgrounds annually visit the campus for Urban Youth Preview.

Seattle Pacific's intercollegiate athletic program fields NCAA Division II teams in men's and women's basketball, crew, cross-country, soccer, and track and field and women's gymnastics and volleyball. All students have access to forty-seven intramural sports as well as extramurals, special events, and health and fitness activities.

The University's unique leadership program encourages students to cultivate their individual talents through opportunities in student government, ministries, performing groups, publications, clubs, and organizations.

In addition to its bachelor's degrees, SPU awards M.A., M.B.A., M.Ed., M.F.A., M.S., M.A. (TESOL), M.S.N., Ed.D., and Ph.D. degrees.

Seattle Pacific University is accredited by the Washington State Board of Education, the Northwest Commission on Colleges and Universities, AACSB International–the Association to Advance Collegiate Schools of Business, the National Council for Accreditation of Teacher Education, the Washington State Board of Education for the preparation of elementary and secondary teachers, the Commission on Collegiate Nursing Education, the Washington State Nursing Care Quality Assurance Commission, the Accreditation Board for Engineering and Technology, the Commission on Accreditation/Approval for Dietetics Education of the American Dietetics Association, and the Commission on Accreditation for Marriage and Family Therapy Education. The doctoral degree program in clinical psychology is accredited by the American Psychological Association. In addition, SPU is approved by the American Council on Education, the Board of Regents of the State of New York, the Commission on Christian Education of the Free Methodist Church for preparation of ministers and missionaries, and the Department of Christian Education of the Free Methodist Church.

SPU is a member of the Christian College Consortium, the Council for Christian Colleges and Universities, the American Association of Colleges for Teacher Education, and the National Association of Schools of Music.

Location

Seattle Pacific's beautiful 43-acre, tree-lined city campus lies in a residential area just 10 minutes from downtown Seattle, the business and cultural heart of the Pacific Northwest. A gateway to Canada and the Pacific Rim, Seattle offers easy access to a wide variety of outdoor recreation such as sailing, skiing, hiking, and camping. The city also offers world-class fine arts, including opera, theater, symphony, and ballet. Seattle Pacific takes advantage of its urban setting by providing hundreds of internship and service experiences in the city's hospitals, schools, businesses, and churches.

Majors and Degrees

An array of academic options in the arts, sciences, and professions allows Seattle Pacific students to specialize in one discipline while exploring many others. The University awards B.A. and B.S. degrees and offers fifty-six undergraduate majors.

The College of Arts and Sciences offers the following undergraduate majors: art; biochemistry; biology; biology education; biotechnology; chemistry; classics; communication; computational mathematics; computer engineering; computer science; electrical engineering; engineering and applied science; English; European studies (Europe, French, German, Latin, Russian, and Spanish); exercise science; family and consumer sciences; fine and applied arts education; food and nutritional sciences; general studies; history; language arts education; Latin American studies (Spanish); mathematics; mathematics education; music; music education; philosophy; physical education; physics; political science; science education; social science education; sociology; textiles, clothing, and interiors; theater; and visual communication.

The School of Business and Economics offers undergraduate majors in accounting, business administration, and economics. The School of Education offers elementary certification with any major of the University, secondary certification with endorsements in most Washington state–approved areas, and a major in special education. The School of Health Sciences offers an undergraduate nursing degree. The School of Psychology, Family, and Community offers undergraduate majors in organizational behavior and psychology. The School of Theology offers undergraduate majors in Christian theology, Christian scriptures, educational ministries, global and urban ministry, and youth ministry. Preprofessional programs are available in dentistry, law, medicine, optometry, pharmacy, and physical therapy.

Academic Programs

Seattle Pacific's academic disciplines set high standards for students. Undergraduate students are taught not by graduate assistants but by experienced professors who are recognized locally and nationally for the quality of their scholarship. Small classes mean students actively participate in their own education, gaining the confidence to achieve their goals. In addition, SPU's clear Christian commitment gives depth and perspective to classroom learning, balancing knowledge with values.

The Common Curriculum, which includes seven required courses spread out over four years, is at the heart of an undergraduate liberal arts education at Seattle Pacific. Only 5 percent of four-year institutions in the United States, most of them very small and homogenous, offer such a curriculum. Very few comprehensive universities in an urban setting with an equal mix of residential and commuter students require participation in common learning over four years.

SPU students begin in the first quarter of their freshman year with University Seminar, a focused exploration of a special interdisciplinary topic. The fewer than 25 students enrolled in each course form a "cohort" and attend other freshman classes in the Common Curriculum together, with their University Seminar professor serving as their academic adviser. In their freshman, sophomore, and junior years, students participate in two parallel sequences of required courses that address key human questions from the perspective of various disciplines and the foundations of Christian faith. Cumulative and developmental in nature, these classes are designed to support and enhance students' learning in the majors.

Off-Campus Programs

Seattle Pacific students have many opportunities to enhance their education with off-campus study. The Pacific Northwest itself provides a living laboratory for academic pursuits in all disciplines. SPU's own campuses on Whidbey Island and Blakely Island in Puget Sound are ideal for research and field study in areas such as marine biology and environmental science.

From summer 2006 to summer 2007, 135 Seattle Pacific students participated in overseas study programs: European Quarter, the Normandy (France) Studies Program, and the Salamanca (Spain) Program. Biennially, 30 to 35 students travel and study in Britain during British Isles Quarter. During quarter and summer breaks, students have the opportunity to join Seattle Pacific Reachout International (SPRINT) teams that travel to countries such as Northern Ireland, Russia, Nicaragua, Uganda, and Romania for a short-term mission experience.

The University maintains exchange agreements with institutions in Kenya, Japan, and Korea. Students may apply to take one or two quarters of study at one of the twelve other Christian College Consortium campuses, or they may enroll in programs sponsored by the Council for Christian Colleges and Universities, including American Studies in Washington, D.C.; Latin American Studies in Costa Rica; Film Studies in Los Angeles; Australian Center in Sydney; Contemporary Music Center in Martha's Vineyard; Middle East Studies; Russian Studies; China Studies; Oxford Program in Oxford, United Kingdom; or Journalism in Washington, D.C.

Academic Facilities

At the heart of the Seattle Pacific campus is the 62,000-square-foot library. This spacious, four-level facility serves as the center for academic endeavors outside the classroom. It provides learning resource services, the latest technology, space for study and research, and approximately 200,000 volumes. The library also has seventy networked computers, and the building is one of the University "hotspots" for wireless connections. Students also have access to 31 million items held in twenty-six Washington and Oregon academic libraries through the Orbis Cascade Alliance and Summit. SPU's Center for Scholarship and Faculty Development is located in the library, and it includes Instructional Technology Services, which offers media production, satellite downlink, and duplication services.

Other educational facilities at SPU include a new $24-million science facility for biology, chemistry, and related sciences. Otto Miller Hall, which houses computer science, electrical engineering, mathematics, and physics, has undergone a $5.4-million renovation. The University's flexible-forestage performing arts facility, E. E. Bach Theatre, is one of the city's finest, and the Royal Brougham Pavilion is one of the premier sports and recreation arenas in the Puget Sound area.

Costs

Tuition and fees for the 2007–08 academic year are $24,783; annual room and board are $8082 (based on 2 people in a room, full meal plan). Individualized meal plans are available. Book costs and personal expenses vary, depending on personal needs.

Financial Aid

Seattle Pacific expects to award nearly $60 million in scholarships and financial aid in 2008–09. Need-based financial aid is available in the form of scholarships, grants, loans, and employment. To be considered for maximum aid, students must submit the Free Application for Federal Student Aid (FAFSA) as soon as possible after January 1 and be admitted to the University by March 1. SPU participates in various federal aid programs, including the Federal Pell Grant, Federal Supplemental Educational Opportunity Grant, Federal Perkins Loan, Federal Work-Study Program, and Federal Stafford Student Loan.

Merit-based University scholarships are given annually to students who exhibit academic excellence and exemplify the ideals of the institution. Merit scholarships are available in amounts ranging from $1500 to full tuition. The Division of Fine Arts offers renewable scholarships (up to $3000) regardless of major. The Athletic Department awards scholarship aid to qualified athletes.

Faculty

The faculty at Seattle Pacific is composed of 175 full-time faculty members and 171 adjunct and other faculty members, who are committed to the highest academic standards. Eighty-six percent of SPU's full-time faculty members hold the Ph.D. or an equivalent terminal degree. Seattle Pacific professors are experts in their fields; they publish, speak, and conduct research throughout the world. Their first priority, however, is teaching. SPU faculty members also make themselves available to students outside the classroom and act as models of compassionate, educated Christians.

Student Government

All full-time students are members of the Associated Students of Seattle Pacific (ASSP). Each spring, students elect 5 ASSP executive officers, along with representatives to the ASSP Senate, the student governing body. ASSP provides services to students in the areas of campus activities, campus ministries, leadership development, and student publications.

Admission Requirements

Admission to Seattle Pacific is offered on the basis of academic credentials and personal qualifications. SPU selects those students who will benefit most from a Christian university education. Factors in the admission decision include high school or college grades, academic and personal recommendations, the application essays, and scores on the SAT or ACT. An applicant is also evaluated in terms of leadership potential, church and community activities, special talents, and personal responsibility. Prospective students are encouraged to visit the campus at any time.

Application and Information

Prospective students may visit the Seattle Pacific University Web site to apply online or request application materials. High school students should request these materials early in their senior year. While applications for autumn quarter are accepted until June 1, prospective students must be admitted by March 1 to be considered for scholarships and the best financial aid, housing, and course registration opportunities.

Applications are reviewed in the order they are received in the Office of Undergraduate Admissions. Beginning December 1, decisions regarding admission are announced after all application materials have been received. If an interview is required, students are contacted by telephone.

Forms may be requested from:

Jobe Nice, Director of Undergraduate Admissions
Seattle Pacific University
3307 Third Avenue West, Suite 115
Seattle, Washington 98119-1922
Phone: 206-281-2021
800-366-3344 (toll-free)
E-mail: admissions@spu.edu
Web site: http://www.spu.edu

Alexander Hall, built in 1904, was Seattle Pacific University's first building.

SEATTLE UNIVERSITY

SEATTLE, WASHINGTON

The University

Seattle University (SU) provides an ideal environment for motivated students interested in self-reliance, awareness of different cultures, social justice, and the fulfillment that comes from making a difference in the world. Its location in the center of one of the nation's most diverse and progressive cities attracts a varied student body, faculty, and staff. Its urban setting promotes the development of leadership skills and independence and provides a variety of opportunities for students to apply what they learn through internships, clinical experiences, and volunteer work.

As a Jesuit institution, Seattle University is part of a network of twenty-eight colleges and universities and forty-six high schools across the United States noted for academic strength. Academic offerings are designed to provide leadership opportunities, develop global awareness, and enable graduates to serve society through a demanding liberal arts and sciences foundation. In the Jesuit educational tradition, students are taught how to think, not what to think. Professional undergraduate offerings include highly respected Colleges of Business, Nursing, and Science and Engineering and career-oriented liberal arts programs such as communication, criminal justice, journalism, public affairs, and social work. The University's Colleges of Education, Law, and Theology and Ministry offer graduate-level opportunities.

Seattle University is noted for its focus on the individual through small, faculty-taught classes and excellent student services. The result is graduates who go on to lead personally fulfilling and economically successful lives. SU is recognized as one of the leading institutions in the Pacific Northwest in producing Truman and Wilson scholars.

The Seattle University campus has undergone $176 million in recent improvements. Although its First Hill location is in the heart of the city, the 48-acre campus has been designated by the state as an official Backyard Wildlife Sanctuary for its distinctive landscaping and environmentally conscious practices.

Fall quarter 2006 had a freshman class of 787, with 50 percent coming from outside Washington State. The ethnic breakdown for the class was 52 white, 21 percent Asian American, and 15 percent African American, Latino, and American Indian. The 4,160 undergraduate students represent forty-seven states and seventy-six nations. International students make up approximately 6 percent of the student body.

There is a wide variety of on-campus housing, including an apartment complex, that accommodates 1,600 students; 88 percent of freshmen live on campus. There is a two-year on-campus residence requirement for noncommuting students.

Seattle University has more than eighty-five extracurricular clubs and organizations and has five varsity teams for men (basketball, cross-country, soccer, swimming, and track) and seven for women (basketball, cross-country, soccer, softball, swimming, track, and volleyball). SU is in NCAA Division II. The student life program includes sixty extracurricular clubs and organizations, including the Hawaiian Club, Associated Students of African Descent, Hiyu Coulee Hiking Club, Beta Alpha Psi (national accounting honorary), and other professional honoraries and clubs.

The Connolly Athletic Center serves as the major facility for varsity and intramural athletics and recreation. It features two swimming pools, two full-size gymnasiums, and locker room saunas. A 6-acre complex provides fields for outdoor sports.

Seattle University receives the highest professional accreditation from the Accreditation Board for Engineering and Technology, AACSB International–The Association to Advance Collegiate Schools of Business, American Bar Association, American Chemical Society, Association of Theological Schools, Commission on Accreditation of Allied Health Education Programs, National Association of Schools of Public Affairs and Administration, National Council for Accreditation of Teacher Education, Commission on Collegiate Nursing Education, Council on Social Work Education, and Northwest Commission on Colleges and Universities.

Location

Nestled between two mountain ranges, containing three lakes, and situated along Puget Sound, Seattle is a magnificent setting for a university. The city pulses with light and life: music, art, and culture. Because Seattle is the Pacific Northwest's center for the legal, medical, business, and high-tech industries, SU students are close to pacesetters in these fields. Students find connections to their studies through mentors, internships, volunteer projects, and meeting alumni in their fields.

Seattle's residents love the outdoors, and areas for skiing, hiking, backpacking, and climbing are within an hour of campus. Biking, walking, and jogging are also popular, with paths and trails throughout the city.

Seattle's sights and sounds, rich ethnic diversity, celebrated restaurants, first-run entertainment, major-league athletics, theater, opera, and ballet are within walking distance and enhance campus life.

Majors and Degrees

Seattle University offers the following undergraduate degrees: Bachelor of Arts, Bachelor of Fine Arts, Bachelor of Science, Bachelor of Science in Nursing, Bachelor of Social Work, Bachelor of Criminal Justice, Bachelor of Public Affairs, and the Bachelor of Arts in Business Administration.

The University offers programs in six major academic units. The Albers School of Business and Economics awards degrees in accounting, business administration, business economics, e-commerce/information systems, finance, international business, management, and marketing. The College of Arts and Sciences grants degrees in art history, Asian studies, communication studies, criminal justice, cultural anthropology, drama, environmental studies, economics, English, fine arts, French, German, history, international studies, journalism, liberal studies, military science/ROTC, philosophy, photography, political science, psychology, public affairs, social work, sociology, Spanish, strategic communication, theology/religious studies, visual art, and women's studies. The College of Nursing offers a Bachelor of Science in Nursing degree. Matteo Ricci College awards degrees in humanities and humanities for teaching. The College of Science and Engineering offers degree programs in biochemistry, biology, chemistry, civil engineering, clinical laboratory science, computer engineering, computer science, diagnostic ultrasound, electrical engineering, environmental engineering, environmental science, general science, mechanical engineering, mathematics, and physics. Preprofessional programs include dentistry, law, medicine, optometry, and veterinary medicine.

Academic Programs

The Core Curriculum is known for its strength and has several distinguishing characteristics in keeping with the Jesuit tradition: it provides an integrated freshman year; it gives order and sequence to student learning; it provides experience in the methods and content of the range of liberal arts, sciences, philosophy, and theology; it calls for active learning in all classes, for practice in writing and thinking, and for an awareness of values; and it fosters a global perspective and a sense of social and personal responsibility.

Seattle University offers two honors program options for students seeking the greatest possible challenge. The University Honors Program is a small, select two-year-long learning community. It is humanities focused, and its fully integrated curriculum examines the most significant texts and ideas of Western culture. The Core Honors Program involves seminar sections of nine required courses in English, history, philosophy, social science, and theology/religious studies. This option is particularly suited to students in profession-oriented majors for whom participation in University Honors is less feasible due to specific major requirements and scheduling conflicts.

SU operates on a quarter calendar. The fall quarter begins in mid-September; the winter quarter in early January; the spring quarter in late March; and the summer quarter in mid-June. Undergraduates typically take 15 credit hours per quarter for the fall, winter, and spring quarters.

Off-Campus Programs

SU offers international study programs—one for French in France, one for Latin American studies in Mexico, one for Chinese in China, and two reciprocal exchange programs with the University of Graz in Austria and Sophia University in Japan. These programs are open to all students in all majors and emphasize language and culture through total immersion. Other programs include Campus Ministry missions in Nicaragua and Belize and Albers School of Business and Economics tours in Mexico, Italy, Hong Kong, and Vietnam. The Calcutta Club offers an intense volunteer opportunity with Mother Teresa's ministry in India. Additional study-abroad programs in other nations, in conjunction with other colleges' overseas programs, are also offered. Arrangements are made through SU's Study Abroad Office.

Academic Facilities

Twelve academic buildings house classrooms, thirty-four instructional laboratories, twenty-five specialized laboratories, computer facilities, and other instructional equipment providing state-of-the-art instruction.

The Lemieux Library has nearly 300,000 volumes and 2,700 current serial subscriptions, 1,300 online databases, and microforms periodicals. Study carrels enable quiet study while lounges accommodate study groups.

The Albers School of Business and Economics features classrooms designed to enhance student interaction and access to high-tech teaching equipment.

The College of Nursing's new 20,000-square-foot clinical performance laboratory is among the most technically advanced clinical laboratories in the country. It joins two clinical practice rooms and suite of laboratories.

The new Lee Center for the Arts is a showcase for theater and musical performances. The modern building seats 135 and includes a prop room, dressing room, costume shop, and professional lighting and sound booths that give students career-building technical skills.

The Chapel of St. Ignatius is the University's spiritual center. This award-winning structure is marking its tenth anniversary as a place of beauty, contemplation, and worship.

Costs

In 2007–08, tuition is $26,325; room and meals are $7860. The estimate for books, fees, and personal expenses is $3393. Costs are subject to change.

Financial Aid

Seattle University awarded $7.4 million in its own financial aid to fall 2006 freshmen, including 240 scholarships ranging from $9000 to $32,118. Sixty-eight percent of freshmen received University aid. Students are required to apply for financial aid by February 1, as awards are made early each spring for the following fall quarter. Applications received after this deadline are evaluated in order received for any remaining aid. Students must submit the Free Application for Federal Student Aid (FAFSA) and be accepted for admission to be considered for financial assistance. A number of scholarships for freshmen are awarded on the basis of academic achievement, extracurricular involvement, and community service. Similar transfer scholarships are determined primarily on the basis of course selection and cumulative grade point average.

Faculty

There are 594 faculty members; 80 percent of full-time faculty members possess doctoral or terminal degrees. Like the University, the mission of faculty members who choose Seattle University is teaching. Most classes average 20; the faculty-student ratio is 1:13. All classes are taught by faculty members. Faculty members are available to provide extra assistance, to help students with their research, and to assist in the arranging of internships. Faculty advisers provide guidance, direction, and encouragement throughout the year. New students are assigned faculty advisers according to their major prior to registration.

Student Government

All undergraduates belong to the Associated Students of Seattle University (ASSU). This is the central student organization on campus. ASSU is organized around an elected president, an executive vice president, and an activities vice president. In addition, a 12-member representative council oversees every facet of the student body and is responsible for policymaking. Its primary responsibility is to provide a diverse activities program to meet the needs of SU's diverse student body. In addition, ASSU communicates student needs to the administration and faculty. ASSU oversees eighty-five clubs and organizations.

Admission Requirements

Freshman applicants are required to have completed a college-preparatory program upon high school graduation, including 4 years of English, 3 years of social studies/history, 3 years of mathematics, 2 years of laboratory science, and 2 years of a foreign language. Applicants to the College of Science and Engineering must complete 4 units of college-preparatory mathematics for admission to any of its specific majors; applicants to the nursing major must complete laboratory biology and chemistry to be considered for admission.

ACT or SAT scores, an official high school transcript, two recommendations, and an essay are also required for admission consideration. The middle 50 percent of 2006 freshman had GPAs between 3.3 and 3.8 on a 4.0 scale and ACT scores between 22 and 27 or SAT scores between 530 and 640 (critical reading) and 520 and 630 (math).

College credit is awarded to those who have successfully completed Advanced Placement or International Baccalaureate examinations. Qualifying scores can be obtained by contacting the Office of the Registrar.

Seattle University is an exclusive Common Application institution and requires its completion for admission consideration. A SU Supplemental Application is also required. The Common Application's personal essay and SU Supplemental Application's personal statement are carefully considered during application review.

Application and Information

Application can be made online at http://www.commonapp.org, or the forms can be downloaded at the Seattle University Web site (http://www.seattleu.edu) or requested by contacting the Admissions Office.

Secondary school students who have completed at least six semesters are encouraged to apply by January of their senior year. Transfer students must submit official transcripts from all postsecondary institutions attended, regardless of whether course work was completed. For fall admission, freshmen should complete the process by February 1 to receive consideration for scholarships and priority consideration for other Seattle University financial aid; the recommended admissions deadline for transfers is March 1. Please note that applications will be accepted after these dates on a space available basis, but funds for financial aid may no longer be available.

Campus visits can be scheduled Monday through Friday and many Saturdays. With two weeks' notice, visitors can be scheduled to attend a class, meet with a faculty adviser, participate in a campus tour, and speak individually with a representative from the Admissions Office. For additional information students should contact:

Michael K. McKeon, Dean
Admissions Office
Seattle University
901 12th Avenue
Seattle, Washington 98122-1090
Phone: 206-296-2000
800-426-7123 (toll-free)
E-mail: admissions@seattleu.edu
Web site: http://www.seattleu.edu

UNIVERSITY OF PUGET SOUND

TACOMA, WASHINGTON

The University

Founded in 1888, the University of Puget Sound is an independent university committed to the liberal arts and sciences, superb teaching, and the recognition of each student as an individual. A nationally acclaimed teaching faculty, well-planned facilities, and a limited enrollment ensure excellence in education.

Puget Sound, the only national liberal arts college in western Washington, is one of only two independent colleges in Washington State to be granted a chapter by Phi Beta Kappa. A record number of Puget Sound graduates have received undergraduate and postgraduate honors, including Rhodes, National Science Foundation, Fulbright, Rotary, Watson, Phi Kappa Phi, Truman, Goldwater, Hertz, and National Endowment for the Humanities fellowships and scholarships. Equally impressive, among national colleges and universities with fewer than 5,000 undergraduate students, Puget Sound is in the top five for number of alumni currently serving as Peace Corps volunteers worldwide.

The University enrolls 2,600 students, with 75 percent coming to Puget Sound from outside the state of Washington. In addition, forty-seven states and fourteen other countries are represented in the student body. Puget Sound is a 24-hour-a-day, seven-day-a-week residential community. Students live in eleven residence halls, eight Greek-letter-society residences, and more than fifty University-owned houses on campus. Special theme houses and halls are available for students with common interests. The neighboring residential community provides many facilities for those who wish to live off campus. Approximately 25 percent of students belong to Greek letter organizations. State-of-the-art athletic facilities include Memorial Fieldhouse and Pamplin Fitness Center, Wallace Pool, Peyton Field at Baker Stadium, an indoor climbing wall, and numerous varsity and intramural athletic fields.

Students find that participating in activities sponsored by the student government is an excellent way to learn outside the classroom and improve leadership abilities. Athletics include twenty-three varsity teams, various club teams, and numerous intramural teams. In addition, students are involved in a variety of clubs and associations, such as forensics, theater, music, FM radio station, art and literary magazine, weekly newspaper, yearbook, Student Senate, religious groups, a variety of faculty and trustee committees, Black Student Union, Hui-O-Hawaii, Earth Activists, B-GLAD (Bisexuals, Gays, Lesbians, and Allies for Diversity), Asian Pacific American Student Union, Community for Hispanic Awareness, and Habitat for Humanity. Seventy-five percent of students participate in community service activities, one of the highest participation rates in the country.

Graduate degrees offered at the University of Puget Sound include the Master of Occupational Therapy, Doctor of Physical Therapy, Master of Arts in Teaching, and Master of Education.

Location

The campus is located in a quiet residential neighborhood in the historic North End of Tacoma. Thirty-five miles south of Seattle and easily accessible from Interstate 5, Tacoma is a dynamic city of 200,000 people. It was recently ranked by *Money* magazine as one of the most livable medium-sized cities in the country. The University occupies thirty-nine buildings on a 97-acre parklike campus. The architecture is Tudor Gothic, with its distinctive red-brick pattern arches and porticoes. Located close to the shores of Puget Sound and a short distance from ski slopes and the Pacific Ocean, the University is also the center of much of Tacoma's cultural life. Tacoma also features Point Defiance Zoo and Aquarium, many parks, a public library system, museums, new convention center, and hospitals.

Majors and Degrees

The University of Puget Sound offers more than forty-five majors leading to the Bachelor of Arts, Bachelor of Science, and Bachelor of Music degrees. Academic programs are art, Asian studies (interdisciplinary emphasis), biochemistry, biology, business, chemistry, classics, communication, comparative sociology, computer science, computer science in business, economics, English, exercise science, foreign languages and literature (majors in French, German, international affairs, and Spanish; course offerings in Chinese, Greek, Japanese, and Latin), geology, history, international political economy, mathematics, molecular and cellular biology, music, natural science, philosophy, physics, politics and government, psychology, religion, and theater arts. Latin American studies, African-American studies, environmental studies, and gender studies are minor-only programs. The introduction of a special interdisciplinary major allows exceptional students the opportunity to pursue a degree in a recognized interdisciplinary or emergent field.

The University offers a dual-degree program in engineering, leading to a joint Bachelor of Arts/Bachelor of Science degree in engineering. Students in this program complete prerequisites in chemistry, mathematics/computer science, and physics, then transfer to an accredited engineering school for course work in chemical, civil, electrical, environmental, mechanical, or petroleum engineering, among others. Affiliated schools are Washington University in St. Louis, Columbia University, Duke University, and the University of Southern California.

Academic Programs

At the heart of the academic program is the core curriculum—eight course groupings around which major and elective studies are arranged over a four-year period. The emphasis throughout a student's undergraduate education is on the acquisition of intellectual skills: the ability to express oneself clearly, both orally and in writing; the ability to reason quantitatively; and the ability to think logically, critically, and independently. By mastering the literature and techniques of a specific academic major, the student learns to cultivate the unique power of his or her own mind and to respond vigorously, but humanely, to important social, moral, and intellectual challenges.

A particularly well-designed curriculum for the freshman year and a model program of academic advising and career counseling enable each student to develop his or her own skills and interests in preparation for a lifetime of creative work and leisure. Puget Sound's highly successful and award-winning student orientation process—Prelude, Passages and Perspectives—is a nine-day program that allows new students to become involved in writing and thinking seminars, academic workshops, community service, and a three-day excursion to the nearby Olympic Peninsula.

The academic year is divided into two semesters, beginning in late August and mid-January, and a thirteen-week summer session (two miniterms). A normal academic load is 4 units (typically four courses) per semester. Each unit of credit is equivalent to 6 quarter hours or 4 semester hours. Thirty-two units are required for graduation.

Off-Campus Programs

The University of Puget Sound offers an outstanding selection of international opportunities for its students and operates or offers programs in more than fifty countries, including Australia, England, Scotland, Spain, France, Germany, Italy, Austria, China, Japan, Taiwan, Argentina, and Chile, among others. The Pacific Rim/Asia Study-Travel Program offers students an intense year of study and travel in six to eight Asian countries. A summer archaeological excavation in Greece rounds out the international opportunities at Puget Sound.

Puget Sound's location in one of the fastest-growing regions of the country places its internship program at the forefront of national liberal arts colleges. In fact, Tacoma was named the number one midsized city in the nation for entrepreneurship by *Entrepreneur* magazine. Opportunities for student research abound, as students may apply for summer research grants in the sciences, social sciences, humanities, and the arts.

Academic Facilities

Collins Memorial Library contains more than 550,000 volumes of books and periodicals plus a sizable collection of federal and Washington State government publications, maps, microforms, videotapes, cassettes, compact discs, and other media materials. These resources are strengthened through participation in the Orbis Cascade Alliance, a consortium of twenty-seven public and private institutions of higher education in Oregon and Washington, with combined holdings of more than 22 million volumes. Other major academic facilities include Thompson Science Complex, Kittredge Art Gallery, Schneebeck Concert Hall, Norton Clapp Theatre, Gordon D. Alcorn Arboretum, Lowry Wyatt Hall, and Slater Museum of Natural History. Harned Hall, a 51,000-square-foot addition to the newly remodeled Thompson Science Complex, opened in 2006.

Puget Sound, as a natural resource, provides students of environmental science and marine biology with a superb outdoor laboratory. A working relationship with Point Defiance Zoo and Aquarium, just minutes north of the campus, offers teaching and research opportunities in marine and biological sciences. Equipment and facilities in the Thompson Science Complex include a modern greenhouse; an observatory; an aquarium with a tidal cycle; a state-of-the-art genetics laboratory; a scanning electron microscope and a transmission electron microscope; ultraviolet, visible, fluorescence, infrared, and nuclear magnetic resonance spectrophotometric equipment; and a seismograph. Students also have access to human cadavers as learning tools. The University has special facilities for students of occupational and physical therapy, education, counseling, foreign languages, and psychology. The music building has twenty-two individual practice rooms.

All University residence halls and Greek houses are wired to provide students with instant access to the Internet and e-mail accounts. In addition, numerous wireless hotspots and on-campus computer labs offer 24-hour access to these services.

Costs

Tuition and required student fees were $31,700 and $360, respectively, for the 2007–08 academic year. Room and board were $8265. It is estimated that an additional $3300 per year is adequate for books, laundry, and other essentials, including travel to and from home.

Financial Aid

Ninety percent of the University's students receive financial aid in one or a combination of the following forms: scholarships, grants, low-interest loans, and part-time employment. Most financial aid is awarded on the basis of demonstrated financial need, as determined through analysis of the Free Application for Federal Student Aid (FAFSA). In addition, the University's Financial Aid Office administers a scholarship program based solely on academic merit: the Trustee ($12,000), President's ($9000), and Dean's ($3000) Scholarships. Each award is renewable annually. In November 2007, the University announced the Lillis Scholarship, a renewable award that covers tuition, room, and board for 2 selected students. Twenty-five students from the University applicant pool will be invited to apply. Many other talent awards are available in the arts, selected academic areas, forensics, and leadership. Admission decisions are made independent of financial need, and all students, regardless of family income, are encouraged to apply for financial aid.

Faculty

Members of the faculty work closely with individual students both in the classroom and in student-originated research projects within and across the disciplines. Ninety-three percent of the faculty members teach full-time; 98 percent of tenured faculty members hold a Ph.D. or an equivalent terminal degree. In agreement with Ted Taranovski, Professor of History, faculty members feel that the University of Puget Sound is "an institution geared to human beings—small enough to give one a sense of community and yet large enough to provide an excellent academic curriculum; it is not an impersonal machine where people become cogs." In recent years, professors at the University have been recognized for their academic and teaching achievements through awards and distinctions, including the Graves Award in the Humanities and fellowships from various organizations, including the National Endowment for the Humanities, the American Council of Learned Societies, and the Danforth Foundation. In 2007, the Carnegie Foundation for the Advancement of Teaching named history professor Nancy Bristow the Washington State Professor of the Year.

Admission Requirements

Each applicant to the University of Puget Sound is considered individually and is admitted on the basis of his or her qualifications and achievements. In considering applicants for freshman admission, the Admission Committee evaluates the following: high school course selection, high school grade point average, rank in graduating class (if available), SAT or ACT scores, a counselor's and an academic teacher's recommendations, an essay, a recommended interview, and extracurricular activities. College credit is awarded to students who have earned scores of 4 or higher on Advanced Placement examinations. Credit for a score of 3 is available for selected examinations only. Credit is also available for a score of 5, 6, or 7 on the International Baccalaureate higher-level examinations.

Application and Information

Prospective freshmen may apply for admission anytime after the beginning of the senior year in high school. Admission decisions are generally mailed on or before March 15. The application preference deadline is February 1. Students who have decided that Puget Sound is their first-choice college may choose one of two early decision plans. Early decision I has a November 15 application deadline, with admission and tentative financial aid notification by December 15. Early decision II has a December 15 application deadline, with admission and tentative financial aid notification by January 15. Transfer students are admitted in both semesters. Students applying for transfer admission should submit the *Application for Transfer Admission.*

For more information about the University or for application materials, students should contact:

Office of Admission
University of Puget Sound
1500 North Warner Street, #1062
Tacoma, Washington 98416-1062
Phone: 253-879-3211
800-396-7191 (toll-free)
E-mail: admission@ups.edu
Web site: http://www.ups.edu

WHITMAN COLLEGE

WALLA WALLA, WASHINGTON

The College

Challenging its students to excel in sciences, humanities, art, and social sciences, Whitman College is one of the nation's leading liberal arts colleges. It combines the educational prestige of the best liberal arts colleges of the East with the outdoor values and vitality of the Pacific Northwest. Since 1882, men and women have chosen this private, independent college because of its commitment to undergraduate education. With just 1,450 students and an average class size of 15, Whitman encourages its students to be active participants in their own education. In 1913, the College led the nation by requiring all students to successfully complete a comprehensive oral examination in their major field of study upon graduation. The installation of a chapter of Phi Beta Kappa in 1919 marked the general recognition of the high quality of Whitman's curriculum and the standards of teaching and learning that distinguish the College. Nearly 60 percent of Whitman graduates enroll in a graduate program of some type within five years of earning their undergraduate degree.

Current enrollment includes students from forty-five states and thirty countries. As a residential college, Whitman has approximately 75 percent of its students living on campus. A variety of residence hall living options are available, including coeducational housing, apartment-style living, eleven special-interest houses, four fraternity houses, and an all-women's residence hall that houses, among others, the members of three national sororities. First-year students and sophomores are required to live on the campus. Whitman has an extremely active student body. They participate in more than 130 interest groups, clubs, and organizations, ranking first in the country in combined policy and parliamentary debate. In 2004, Jim Hanson was named the National Parliamentary Debate Coach of the Year. The highly acclaimed theater department produces eight to ten shows during the academic year, while the music department supports more than two dozen different musical groups on campus. The College fields eighteen varsity teams (nine for men and nine for women) and offers twelve club sports and sixteen intramural activities. In 2006, Whitman's club cycling team defended its national championship for all schools with fewer than 15,000 students.

Location

Whitman is located in Walla Walla, a historic community of 30,000 nestled in the foothills of the Blue Mountains of southeastern Washington. The Walla Walla Valley has four distinct seasons and enjoys 300 days of sunshine a year. With rich natural terrain at its doorstep, outdoor activities abound. These include cross-country and downhill skiing, backpacking, hiking, kayaking, rafting, and rock climbing. Whitman imports a wide array of cultural activities to the campus, including concerts, art exhibits, environmental forums, internationally renowned speakers and performers, and cinema arts films. Students also perform with the community symphony, browse in the area's seventeen art galleries, and act in the community theater.

Majors and Degrees

Whitman College confers the Bachelor of Arts (B.A.) degree, with departmental majors in anthropology; art (history, studio, and visual culture studies); Asian studies; biochemistry, biophysics, and molecular biology (BBMB); biology; chemistry; classics; economics; English; foreign languages and literatures (French, German studies, or Spanish); gender studies; geology; history; Latin American studies; mathematics; music; philosophy; physics; politics; psychology; race and ethnic studies; religion; rhetoric and film studies; sociology; and theater. Combined or interdepartmental major study programs are offered in Asian studies, astronomy-geology, biology-geology, chemistry-geology, economics-mathematics, environmental studies (emphasis in biology, chemistry, economics, geology, physics, politics, or sociology), geology-physics, mathematics-physics, and physics-astronomy. Minor study options are available in each of the departmental programs, as well as Chinese, computer science, educational studies, Japanese, Latin American and Caribbean literature, sports studies/recreation and athletics, and world literature. Students with special interests may develop combined or interdepartmental major programs, subject to faculty approval. Whitman offers outstanding cooperative programs in engineering with Caltech, Columbia, Duke, the University of Washington, and Washington University in St. Louis; in environmental management or forestry with Duke; in law with Columbia School of Law; in international studies and international business with the Monterey Institute of International Studies; in education with the University of Puget Sound and Whitworth College; and in computer science or oceanography with the University of Washington.

Academic Programs

Whitman's primary goal is to provide an atmosphere in which students can learn how to learn. At the heart of Whitman's academic curriculum is the general studies program. Through this program, students develop skills such as intellectual reasoning, critical analysis of major works, effective writing, solid understanding of humanity's cultural and historic roots, valid bases for judgment of values, and confident abilities to ask tough questions and lead others. The required general studies program consists of a first-year core curriculum and certain distribution requirements. The first-year core is a two-semester course focusing on the foundations and reshaping of Western culture, involving extensive reading, writing, and discussion. To satisfy distribution requirements, students must complete at least 6 semester credits in fine arts, humanities, science, and social sciences; take two courses dealing with alternative voices; and take at least one course in quantitative analysis. Every candidate for a bachelor's degree must complete at least 124 credits in appropriate course work with acceptable grades and a senior assessment. Honors programs are available for qualified students. Whitman helps fund student research and internships, and approximately 125 students present professional-level research at the Annual Whitman Undergraduate Conference. Scores of 4 and 5 on the College Board's Advanced Placement tests are accepted for credit (the economics, English, and history departments accept only a score of 5). Whitman observes a two-semester calendar with a weeklong break for Thanksgiving, a month off over the winter holiday, and two weeks for spring break.

Off-Campus Programs

Whitman is noted for its strong study-abroad and domestic off-campus study programs. Each year, nearly half of the junior class studies abroad. There are 180 different programs available, spanning six of the seven continents (excluding Antarctica). In addition to academic course work, many students pursue internships and research opportunities. The College is formally affiliated with the Institute for the International Education of Students, which has programs in Australia, Austria, China, England, France, Germany, and Italy. The school for field studies has opportunities in Australia, the Caribbean, Costa Rica, Kenya, and Mexico. Students may also study at the Universities of East Anglia and York in England; St. Andrews University in Scotland; Doshisha University in Kyoto, Japan; and the University of Otago in Dunedin, New Zealand, and at programs in Argentina, Botswana, China, Costa Rica, Egypt, Greece, India, Ireland, Italy, Japan, Mexico, Spain, Sri Lanka, and Taiwan. Each year, 4 Whitman graduates are selected to teach English to university students in Kunming or Xi'an in the People's Republic of China. The College offers urban-semester study and internships in Chicago, Philadelphia, and Washington, D.C. Students may participate in one of more than 300 science research internships available through the College.

Academic Facilities

To enhance Whitman's learning environment, students have access to exceptional facilities and technological and cultural resources. The recently expanded, 24-hour Penrose Memorial Library houses more than 350,000 volumes, 550,000 government documents, and 2,000 subscriptions. In addition, the ORBIS Cascade Alliance provides access to approximately 3.5 million volumes that can be delivered to Whitman in less than 72 hours. A $13-million, 51,000-square-foot campus center featuring a ballroom, a cyber lounge, coffeehouse performance space, and flexible dining and meeting facilities opened in January 2002. Olin Hall of Humanities and Fine Arts features an audiovisual center, extensive art studios, a foreign language learning lab, and the Donald Sheehan Art Gallery. A newer addition to Olin now houses the computing equipment and is the center for the campuswide fiber-optic network. The student-computer ratio on campus is 5:1. Maxey Hall, which houses the social sciences, includes a natural history and anthropology museum, a 350-seat auditorium, and animal demonstration labs. The Hall of Science, which was renovated and expanded in 2003, houses a sophisticated physics lecture/demonstration hall and laboratory, expanded chemistry work stations, the Clise Planetarium, and support facilities for two electron microscopes. It also contains laboratories for botany, ecology, vertebrate biology, physiology and developmental biology, and biochemistry and genetics; preparation and display cases for the herbarium and the preserved animal collections; a seismograph; and large, well-equipped student research laboratories. Some of the newest features include organic chemistry and geology labs, computer stations, and new greenhouse spaces. The 105,000-square-foot Hall of Science has a wireless network for Internet access, more student-faculty research labs, and enhanced classroom space. The total cost of the project was $17 million. Off campus, Whitman operates an observatory as well as the Johnston Wilderness Center—a 27-acre mountain property serving as an environmental studies field station. The Hall of Music houses an acoustically perfect performance hall and twenty-seven practice rooms that are open 24 hours a day. The theater department in Harper Joy Theater consists of two main stages. Cordiner Hall is a 1,500-seat auditorium featuring a 3,000-pipe Holtkamp organ.

Costs

Tuition and fees for 2007–08 were $32,670. Room and board cost $8310. The estimated cost of books, supplies, and incidentals is $1400. Associated student body fees are $310.

Financial Aid

Financial aid offers are usually a combination of scholarships, student employment opportunities, and low-interest loans. In 2006–07, Whitman provided more than $15 million in scholarships. Forty-seven percent of Whitman students qualified for need-based aid. Roughly 50 percent of the students are employed on campus. Whitman also has an extensive achievement scholarship program that rewards students who have demonstrated excellence in academics. Merit scholarships range from $6000 to $10,000 and are renewable for four years, given academic eligibility. Special awards are also available for students who demonstrate exceptional talent in art, music, debate, theater, and leadership. To apply for financial aid, students must submit the Free Application for Federal Student Aid (FAFSA) and the CSS PROFILE. Early decision candidates should apply for financial aid by January 1; regular decision and transfer candidates must apply by February 1. Spring-semester candidates need to complete their forms no later than December 1.

Faculty

Whitman College's faculty is composed of men and women selected, retained, and promoted for their demonstrated effectiveness as teachers as well as for leadership within their chosen fields. Ninety-four percent of the faculty members hold a doctoral degree or terminal degree in their field, and all serve as academic advisers. The student-faculty ratio is 10:1. Recognized nationally for faculty accessibility, Whitman offers personal attention outside the classroom, setting it apart from peer institutions. At Whitman, students collaborate with professors on research projects, compete with them on athletic fields, serve with them on College committees, and dine with them in their homes. In the past five years, Whitman faculty members have distinguished themselves by receiving awards, honors, and fellowships from the National Institute of Mental Health, National Endowment for the Humanities, Battelle Research Institute, Washington State Arts Commission, Burlington Northern Foundation, Department of Health and Human Services, and Department of Energy.

Student Government

The College encourages its students to participate and take leadership roles in self-governing campus organizations. The largest of these organizations is the Associated Students of Whitman College (ASWC), in which every student is a member. ASWC acts through an elected student congress and executive council and is responsible for the *Whitman Pioneer* (a weekly student newspaper), choral contest, Renaissance Faire, campus radio station KWCW (90.5 FM), and a multitude of all-campus concerts, speakers, films, and social events.

Admission Requirements

Whitman is a highly selective college that seeks academic excellence and diversity within its student body. Competition for admission is keen; about 60 percent of entering first-year students ranked in the top 10 percent of their high school class. Ninety percent were in the top quarter. The Admission Committee looks for evidence of demonstrated intellectual achievement, motivation, creativity, responsibility, and maturity. The middle 50 percent of the class of 2010 scored in the following ranges on the SAT: 620–720 critical reasoning, 620–690 math, and 610–700 reading. The minimum TOEFL scores for international students were 220 on the computer-based test and 560 on the paper test. The following pattern of high school subjects is highly recommended: 4 years of English, mathematics, science, and history or social sciences; at least 2 years of a foreign language; and 1 year of an art elective. Students who have decided early in their senior year that Whitman is their first-choice school are encouraged to apply for admission through early decision.

Application and Information

The application deadlines and notification dates for admission to Whitman are as follows: early decision candidates apply by November 15 or January 1 and receive notification of admission by December 15 or February 1; regular decision applicants for the fall semester apply by January 15 and letters are postmarked by April 1; transfer students apply by March 1 and receive notification by April 15; and spring-semester candidates apply by November 15 and receive notification by December 15. First-year candidates are required to submit the following credentials: the Common Application (for selective colleges), including the School Report Form; secondary school transcript; one teacher recommendation; and an application fee of $40. Whitman also requires test scores (SAT or ACT) and a Personal Supplement (Whitman's own analytical writing requirement). International applicants must also submit a TOEFL score and the College Board's International Student Financial Aid Application and Certification. For more information, students should contact:

Office of Admission
Whitman College
345 Boyer Avenue
Walla Walla, Washington 99362-2046
Phone: 509-527-5176
877-462-9448 (toll-free)
Fax: 509-527-4967
E-mail: admission@whitman.edu
Web site: http://www.whitman.edu

Students on the Whitman College campus.

WHITWORTH UNIVERSITY

SPOKANE, WASHINGTON

The University

Whitworth, founded in 1890, is among a select group of educational institutions known for both academic rigor and Christian commitment. The Whitworth faculty is committed to encouraging open intellectual inquiry as well as respect for diverse points of view. The University's community of scholars is also dedicated to the challenging task of integrating faith perspectives into all aspects of life and learning. This dual commitment distinguishes Whitworth among Christian colleges and universities.

The campus has thirty-eight buildings, mostly of red brick, that border the parklike Loop, including the Harriet Cheney Cowles Memorial Library, Cowles Memorial Auditorium, Hixson Union Building, Dixon Hall, and the Seeley Mudd Chapel. The Whitworth Fieldhouse is home to the Scotford Fitness and Aquatic Center, which has a 25-meter, six-lane pool with a movable bulkhead and a 15-foot diving pool. The Hixson Union Building houses the bookstore, post office, snack bar, student media and student government offices, and a 450-seat dining hall.

The University's 2,100 full-time undergraduate students come from thirty-one states and twenty-five countries. Nearly 70 percent of the full-time undergraduate students live on campus in ten residential areas that range from suites and traditional dorms to cottage-size apartments and theme houses. Residence life is considered an essential part of a student's growth process, and living groups are encouraged, with the help of trained residence staff, to design their own living environments. Peer leaders in each residence hall include resident assistants, health coordinators, ministry coordinators, and cultural diversity advocates.

Also serving the personal development of each student are the Office of the Chaplain and Student Life Department. The Christian environment on campus is centered on midweek chapel and Hosanna, a late-evening student-led service. Small discussion groups and opportunities for service also originate in the Office of the Chaplain. The Student Life Program assists all students in adjusting to college life and defining individual goals by providing counseling, tutoring, services for international students and members of minority groups, job placement, career planning, and aptitude testing.

Whitworth University holds membership in the NCAA Division III and is a member of the Northwest Conference. Varsity teams for men compete in baseball, basketball, cross-country, football, golf, soccer, swimming, tennis, and track and field. Women's teams compete in basketball, cross-country, fast-pitch softball, golf, soccer, swimming, tennis, track and field, and volleyball. Twelve Whitworth teams have won conference championships in the past three years, and four teams have led the nation in team GPA for their sports in NCAA Division III. A broad intramural program, as well as club sports, offers athletic competition to everyone on campus, including faculty and staff members, and fitness evaluation services in the Scotford Fitness Center are available to all. Whitworth believes that physical development is an essential element in each student's pursuit of personal wholeness.

Location

Whitworth University is located just 10 minutes from downtown Spokane on a scenic, wooded 200-acre site, surrounded by quiet suburban residential areas. Spokane, a metropolitan area with a population of 414,500, is surrounded by an extraordinary outdoor recreation area containing thousands of acres of state and national forests, four major ski resorts, and more than seventy-five lakes within an hour's drive. The city is the commercial and cultural center for more than a million people, and the size of this market area is reflected in the excellence of Spokane's many cultural and entertainment opportunities, restaurants, shopping centers, and transportation.

Majors and Degrees

Whitworth awards Bachelor of Arts and Bachelor of Science degrees. Programs and majors are available in accounting, American studies, art, arts administration, athletic training, biology, business management, chemistry, communication, computer science, cross-cultural studies, economics, education (elementary and secondary certification programs, with academic department emphases), English, environmental studies, French, German, history, international business, international studies, journalism and mass communications, kinesiology, leadership studies, liberal studies, marketing, mathematics, modern languages, music, organizational management, peace studies, philosophy, physical education, physics, political studies, pre-ministry, psychology, quantitative analysis, religion, sociology, Spanish, speech communication, theater, and women's studies.

Preprofessional programs are offered in dentistry, engineering (3-2), law, medical technology, medicine, occupational therapy, pharmacy, physical therapy, and veterinary medicine.

Academic Programs

The University is dedicated to academic excellence as expressed through its core of liberal arts and sciences and through rigorous disciplinary and interdisciplinary study. A Whitworth education is designed to broaden students' understanding of their cultural heritage, to promote critical thinking, to prepare students for productive work, and to stimulate creativity in responding to the challenges of life. As a Christian institution, Whitworth takes seriously its responsibility to help students understand and respond compassionately to the needs of the world. Recognizing that contemporary society is globally interdependent and increasingly multicultural, Whitworth seeks to foster in its students an attitude of curiosity and respect for diverse cultures.

The University's 4-1-4 calendar provides time for intensive study in a single subject during the month of January, often in an off-campus setting.

Off-Campus Programs

January terms and full semesters of off-campus study are available to encourage students to relate their education to real-life environments. Urban studies in San Francisco; international studies in Europe, Latin America, South Africa, Thailand, and the Middle East; music studies in Rome and Munich; and rural studies in various locales are offered to augment classroom learning. Students are not traveling as tourists; they are accompanied by faculty members who guide their research and studies and join them in experiencing the culture to the greatest degree possible.

Exchange-student arrangements are available through the International Student Exchange Program (ISEP). This program offers placements in any of the 150 member universities in Africa, Asia, Australia, Canada, Europe, or Latin America.

Cooperative education/internship opportunities are available for Whitworth students in Spokane or in almost any area of the country. For instance, political studies majors routinely intern in Washington, D.C. The co-op/internship program enables students to gain actual experience and build contacts in a chosen field prior to graduation. A January-term internship often leads to declaring a major, a modification of a career goal, or, just as often, a job opportunity.

Academic Facilities

With its state-of-the-art information retrieval technology and a capacity exceeding 250,000 volumes, the Harriet Cheney Cowles Memorial Library provides students and faculty members with a superb research facility. The library's computerized card catalogs and databases also provide access to the holdings of other libraries in the region and across the country. In addition, the library is home to three computer labs, six group study rooms, climate-controlled archives, a music library, a curriculum lab for teacher education, audiovisual services, and a Writing Center.

The Whitworth Music Building has the most advanced facilities available for music education. Laboratories for chemistry, physics, and biology are maintained in the Eric Johnston Science Center. A generous grant from the National Science Foundation provided funds to upgrade these laboratories. The Fine Arts Building contains studios for drawing, painting, and pottery and houses the John Koehler Gallery, which is used for student shows. The Dr. James P. Evans Sports Medicine Center includes a complete hydrotherapy center, ultrasound equipment, and a variety of ergometers and isokinetic machines.

Costs

For the 2007–08 academic year, tuition was $25,382 and room and board were $7284. Additional costs for books, fees, and personal expenses vary.

Financial Aid

More than 90 percent of Whitworth's students receive financial aid, with the average freshman scholarship and grant award exceeding $10,000. The Free Application for Federal Student Aid (FAFSA) is used to determine a student's financial need for awarding grants, scholarships, loans, and work-study. Academic scholarships and fine arts, pre-engineering, and science and journalism talent awards are available to exceptional students regardless of their demonstrated need. Student employment, under the Federal Work-Study Program, is available on campus for up to 20 hours per week through the Student Employment Office, which provides placement assistance for off-campus jobs as well. The following non-need-based federal loan programs are available to Whitworth students and their families: the Federal Unsubsidized Stafford Loan and the Federal PLUS loan for parents. Whitworth also recently joined The Tuition Plan program, offering tuition discounts and prepayment options to lock in tuition costs.

Faculty

The Whitworth faculty is made up of 120 full-time professors, most of whom have earned either a Ph.D. or the terminal degree in their field. These dedicated Christian scholars conduct important research, perform in demanding musical venues, write critically acclaimed books, and earn recognition in their fields. But their primary commitment is to teaching—sharing their knowledge, their faith journeys, and their friendship with students inside and outside the classroom.

Student Government

A full-time student activities coordinator works with the elected members of the Associated Students of Whitworth University (ASWU) and the appointed student managers to plan and carry out University activities, which range from Homecoming festivities to mountain climbs to political lobbying. Student government is responsible for the continuing involvement of students in the community, organizing outreach ministry opportunities on- and off-campus, and meeting the academic, social, and spiritual needs of the campus community. Individual students are full-fledged members, along with faculty members, of various councils that formulate major campus policies.

Admission Requirements

Whitworth selects its students from those applicants who, by reason of their academic achievement, measured aptitudes, and academic interests, demonstrate their ability to succeed at a rigorous Christian liberal arts college. Generally, 4 years of English; 3 years each of history, science (including lab science), and mathematics; and 2 years of a foreign language constitute a competitive college-preparatory program for a high school applicant. Transfer students are also welcome to apply; Whitworth grants junior standing and a waiver of most general graduation requirements to students who have earned an approved Associate of Arts degree at any Washington community college as well as North Idaho College.

Application and Information

High-achieving students who have decided that Whitworth University is their first or second choice are eligible to apply for early action. The early action application deadline is November 30. For regular admission, the deadline is March 1. Campus visits and admission interviews are welcome at any time throughout the calendar year but are recommended from the week after Labor Day in September through mid-May while classes are in session.

Application for admission may be made by submitting a completed Whitworth application form, a personal statement, an evaluation by the student's high school counselor or principal, a current transcript of high school work, and ACT or SAT scores.

For information and application forms, students should contact:

Office of Admissions
Whitworth University
West 300 Hawthorne Road
Spokane, Washington 99251-0106
Phone: 509-777-3212
800-533-4668 (toll-free)
E-mail: admission@whitworth.edu
Web site: http://www.whitworth.edu

Whitworth students represent thirty-one states and twenty-five countries.

WEST VIRGINIA

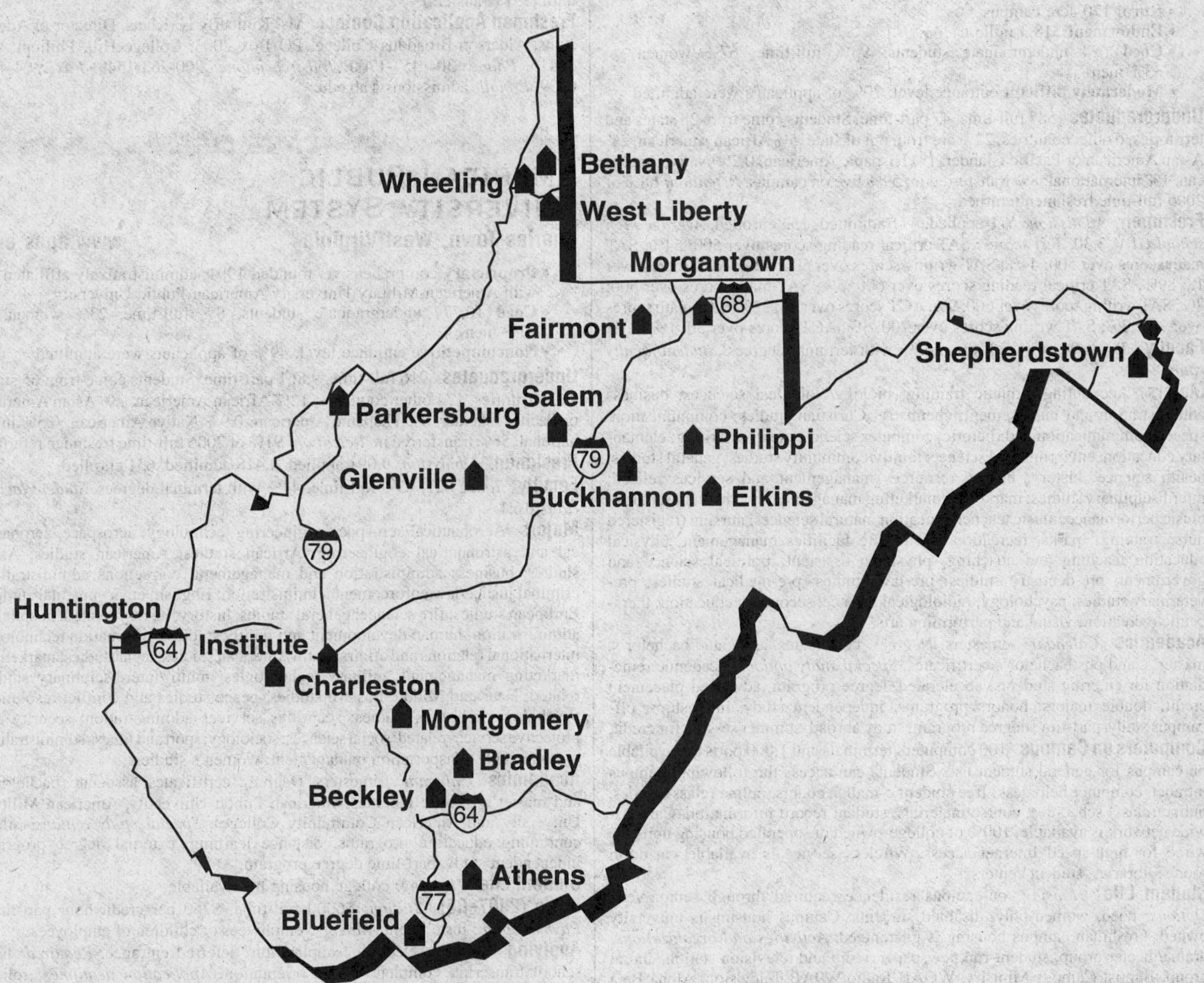

ALDERSON-BROADDUS COLLEGE

Philippi, West Virginia **www.ab.edu/**

- **Independent** comprehensive, founded 1871, affiliated with American Baptist Churches in the U.S.A.
- **Rural** 170-acre campus
- **Endowment** $18.3 million
- **Coed** 634 undergraduate students, 93% full-time, 67% women, 33% men
- **Moderately difficult** entrance level, 70% of applicants were admitted

Undergraduates 587 full-time, 47 part-time. Students come from 28 states and territories, 6 other countries, 22% are from out of state, 5% African American, 2% Asian American or Pacific Islander, 1% Hispanic American, 0.2% Native American, 1% international, 8% transferred in, 59% live on campus. *Retention:* 68% of 2006 full-time freshmen returned.

Freshmen *Admission:* 671 applied, 471 admitted, 153 enrolled. *Average high school GPA:* 3.30. *Test scores:* SAT critical reading scores over 500: 54%; SAT math scores over 500: 44%; SAT writing scores over 500: 42%; ACT scores over 18: 89%; SAT critical reading scores over 600: 5%; SAT math scores over 600: 8%; SAT writing scores over 600: 9%; ACT scores over 24: 22%; SAT math scores over 700: 3%; SAT writing scores over 700: 3%; ACT scores over 30: 1%.

Faculty *Total:* 96, 60% full-time, 43% with terminal degrees. *Student/faculty ratio:* 10:1.

Majors Accounting; athletic training; biology/biological sciences; business administration and management; chemistry; Christian studies; communication/speech communication and rhetoric; computer science; creative writing; elementary education; environmental science; family/community studies; general studies; health science; history; human resources management and services related; interdisciplinary studies; marketing/marketing management; mathematics; music; music performance; music teacher education; natural sciences; nursing (registered nurse training); parks, recreation and leisure facilities management; physical education teaching and coaching; physician assistant; political science and government; pre-dentistry studies; pre-law studies; pre-medical studies; pre-veterinary studies; psychology; radiological science; secondary education; therapeutic recreation; visual and performing arts.

Academics *Calendar:* semesters. *Degrees:* certificates, associate, bachelor's, master's, and postbachelor's certificates. *Special study options:* academic remediation for entering students, accelerated degree program, advanced placement credit, double majors, honors programs, independent study, internships, off-campus study, part-time degree program, study abroad, summer session for credit.

Computers on Campus 100 computers/terminals and 1,000 ports are available on campus for general student use. Students can access the following: campus intranet, computer help desk, free student e-mail accounts, online (class) grades, online (class) schedules, course materials, student record information. Campus-wide network is available. 100% of college-owned or -operated housing units are wired for high-speed Internet access. Wireless service is available via dorm rooms, libraries, student centers.

Student Life *Housing:* on-campus residence required through senior year. *Options:* coed, women-only, disabled students. Campus housing is university owned. Freshman campus housing is guaranteed. *Activities and organizations:* drama/theater group, student-run newspaper, radio and television station, choral group, Baptist Campus Ministry, WQAB Radio/W9AB Television, Alpha Beta Nu (Student Nurses), Student Government Association, AB Student Mission Team. *Campus security:* 24-hour patrols, late-night transport/escort service, controlled dormitory access. *Student services:* health clinic, personal/psychological counseling.

Athletics Member NCAA. All Division II. *Intercollegiate sports:* baseball M (s), basketball M (s)/W (s), cross-country running M (s)/W (s), soccer M (s), softball W (s), volleyball W (s). *Intramural sports:* basketball M/W, football M/W, gymnastics M/W, racquetball M/W, soccer M/W, softball W, tennis M/W, track and field M/W, ultimate Frisbee M/W, volleyball M/W.

Standardized Tests *Required:* SAT and SAT Subject Tests or ACT (for admission).

Costs (2007–08) *Comprehensive fee:* $26,500 includes full-time tuition ($19,830), mandatory fees ($200), and room and board ($6470). Full-time tuition and fees vary according to program and student level. Part-time tuition: $660 per credit hour. Part-time tuition and fees vary according to program and student level. *Required fees:* $50 per term part-time. *College room only:* $3150. Room and board charges vary according to housing facility. *Payment plan:* installment. *Waivers:* employees or children of employees.

Financial Aid Of all full-time matriculated undergraduates who enrolled in 2007, 574 applied for aid, 547 were judged to have need, 133 had their need fully met. 324 Federal Work-Study jobs (averaging $1400). 157 state and other part-time jobs (averaging $1400). In 2007, 28 non-need-based awards were made. *Average percent of need met:* 82%. *Average financial aid package:* $18,707. *Average need-based loan:* $4972. *Average need-based gift aid:* $13,792. *Average non-need-based aid:* $7302. *Average indebtedness upon graduation:* $27,852.

Applying *Options:* electronic application, deferred entrance. *Application fee:* $25. *Required:* high school transcript, minimum 2.0 GPA. *Required for some:* 3 letters of recommendation, interview. *Application deadlines:* rolling (freshmen), rolling (transfers). *Notification:* continuous until 8/31 (freshmen), continuous until 8/31 (transfers).

Freshman Application Contact Ms. Kimberly N. Klaus, Director of Admissions, Alderson-Broaddus College, PO Box 2003, College Hill, Philippi, WV 26416. *Phone:* 304-457-1700. *Toll-free phone:* 800-263-1549. *Fax:* 304-457-6239. *E-mail:* admissions@ab.edu.

AMERICAN PUBLIC UNIVERSITY SYSTEM

Charles Town, West Virginia **www.apus.edu/**

- **Proprietary** comprehensive, founded 1991, administratively affiliated with American Military University/American Public University
- **Coed** 10,777 undergraduate students, 8% full-time, 23% women, 77% men
- **Noncompetitive** entrance level, 49% of applicants were admitted

Undergraduates 916 full-time, 9,861 part-time. Students come from 65 states and territories, 174 other countries, 12% African American, 2% Asian American or Pacific Islander, 8% Hispanic American, 0.9% Native American, 0.5% international, 56% transferred in. *Retention:* 91% of 2006 full-time freshmen returned.

Freshmen *Admission:* 9,091 applied, 4,418 admitted, 651 enrolled.

Faculty *Total:* 627, 15% full-time, 44% with terminal degrees. *Student/faculty ratio:* 16:1.

Majors Aeronautical/aerospace engineering technology; aerospace, aeronautical and astronautical engineering; African studies; American studies; Asian studies; business administration and management; corrections administration; criminal justice/law enforcement administration; English; environmental studies; European studies; fire science; general studies; history; history related; hospitality administration; human development and family studies; information technology; international relations and affairs; Latin American studies; legal studies; marketing/marketing management; military technologies; multi-/interdisciplinary studies related; Near and Middle Eastern studies; peace studies and conflict resolution; psychology; religious studies; securities services administration; security and protective services related; social sciences; sociology; sport and fitness administration/management; transportation management; women's studies.

Academics *Calendar:* trimesters. *Degrees:* certificates, associate, bachelor's, and master's (profile includes American Public University, American Military University and American Community College). *Special study options:* adult/continuing education programs, distance learning, external degree program, independent study, part-time degree program.

Student Life *Housing:* college housing not available.

Costs (2007–08) *Tuition:* $6000 full-time, $250 per credit hour part-time. *Payment plan:* installment. *Waivers:* employees or children of employees.

Applying *Options:* electronic application, deferred entrance. *Required:* high school transcript, complete no-fee orientation. *Application deadlines:* rolling (freshmen), rolling (transfers).

Freshman Application Contact Student Advisor, American Public University System, 322-C West Washington Street, Charles Town, WV 25414. *Phone:* 703-330-5398. *Toll-free phone:* 877-468-6268. *Fax:* 304-724-3788. *E-mail:* admissions@apus.edu.

APPALACHIAN BIBLE COLLEGE

Bradley, West Virginia **www.abc.edu/**

- **Independent nondenominational** 4-year, founded 1950
- **Small-town** 110-acre campus
- **Endowment** $316,677
- **Coed** 258 undergraduate students, 81% full-time, 47% women, 53% men
- **Noncompetitive** entrance level, 62% of applicants were admitted

Undergraduates 209 full-time, 49 part-time. Students come from 36 states and territories, 10 other countries, 10% transferred in, 95% live on campus. *Retention:* 71% of 2006 full-time freshmen returned.

Freshmen *Admission:* 117 applied, 73 admitted, 58 enrolled. *Test scores:* SAT critical reading scores over 500: 63%; SAT math scores over 500: 46%; ACT scores over 18: 86%; SAT critical reading scores over 600: 25%; SAT math scores over 600: 21%; ACT scores over 24: 40%; SAT critical reading scores over 700: 8%; ACT scores over 30: 2%.

Faculty *Total:* 18, 61% full-time, 28% with terminal degrees. *Student/faculty ratio:* 17:1.

Majors Biblical studies; theology.

Academics *Calendar:* semesters. *Degrees:* certificates, associate, bachelor's, and master's. *Special study options:* academic remediation for entering students, adult/continuing education programs, advanced placement credit, honors programs, independent study, internships, part-time degree program, summer session for credit.

Computers on Campus 30 computers/terminals are available on campus for general student use. Students can access the following: campus intranet, computer help desk, free student e-mail accounts. Campuswide network is available. 100% of college-owned or -operated housing units are wired for high-speed Internet access. Wireless service is available via computer labs, libraries, student centers.

Student Life *Housing:* on-campus residence required through senior year. *Options:* men-only, women-only. Campus housing is university owned. Freshman campus housing is guaranteed. *Activities and organizations:* drama/theater group, choral group. *Campus security:* 24-hour emergency response devices, patrols by trained security personnel. *Student services:* health clinic, personal/psychological counseling.

Athletics Member NCCAA. *Intercollegiate sports:* basketball M/W, soccer M, volleyball W.

Standardized Tests *Required:* SAT or ACT (for admission).

Costs (2007–08) *Comprehensive fee:* $14,190 includes full-time tuition ($7880), mandatory fees ($1390), and room and board ($4920). Part-time tuition: $328 per hour. *Required fees:* $35 per hour part-time.

Financial Aid Of all full-time matriculated undergraduates who enrolled in 2006, 229 applied for aid, 216 were judged to have need, 12 had their need fully met. 34 Federal Work-Study jobs (averaging $490). *Average percent of need met:* 54%. *Average financial aid package:* $6525. *Average need-based loan:* $2510. *Average need-based gift aid:* $5139. *Financial aid deadline:* 6/15.

Applying *Options:* electronic application. *Application fee:* $20. *Required:* essay or personal statement, high school transcript, 3 letters of recommendation. *Recommended:* minimum 2.5 GPA, interview. *Application deadlines:* rolling (freshmen), rolling (transfers).

Freshman Application Contact Miss Ashley Siders, Admissions Assistant, Appalachian Bible College, PO Box ABC, Bradley, WV 25818. *Phone:* 304-877-6428 Ext. 3213. *Toll-free phone:* 800-678-9ABC Ext. 3213. *Fax:* 304-877-5082. *E-mail:* admissions2@abc.edu.

BETHANY COLLEGE

Bethany, West Virginia **www.bethanywv.edu/**

- **Independent** 4-year, founded 1840, affiliated with Christian Church (Disciples of Christ)
- **Rural** 1600-acre campus with easy access to Pittsburgh
- **Endowment** $47.4 million
- **Coed** 815 undergraduate students, 99% full-time, 54% women, 46% men
- **Moderately difficult** entrance level, 60% of applicants were admitted

Undergraduates 805 full-time, 10 part-time. Students come from 37 states and territories, 6 other countries, 76% are from out of state, 4% African American, 0.7% Asian American or Pacific Islander, 1% Hispanic American, 0.6% Native American, 2% international, 4% transferred in, 92% live on campus. *Retention:* 66% of 2006 full-time freshmen returned.

Freshmen *Admission:* 1,328 applied, 802 admitted, 288 enrolled. *Average high school GPA:* 3.20. *Test scores:* SAT critical reading scores over 500: 50%; SAT math scores over 500: 52%; ACT scores over 18: 82%; SAT critical reading scores over 600: 18%; SAT math scores over 600: 12%; ACT scores over 24: 26%; SAT critical reading scores over 700: 2%; SAT math scores over 700: 1%; ACT scores over 30: 3%.

Faculty *Total:* 90, 57% full-time, 47% with terminal degrees. *Student/faculty ratio:* 14:1.

Majors Accounting; art; biology/biological sciences; business/managerial economics; chemistry; communication/speech communication and rhetoric; computer science; dramatic/theater arts; economics; education; English; environmental studies; fine/studio arts; French; German; history; horse husbandry/equine science and management; interdisciplinary studies; international relations and affairs; mathematics; music; physical education teaching and coaching; physics; political science and government; pre-dentistry studies; pre-law studies; pre-medical studies; pre-veterinary studies; psychology; religious studies; social work; Spanish; sport and fitness administration/management.

Academics *Calendar:* 4-1-4. *Degree:* bachelor's. *Special study options:* academic remediation for entering students, advanced placement credit, double majors, independent study, internships, off-campus study, part-time degree program, services for LD students, student-designed majors, study abroad. *Unusual degree programs:* 3-2 engineering with Columbia University, Washington University in St. Louis, Case Western Reserve University.

Computers on Campus 136 computers/terminals are available on campus for general student use. Students can access the following: computer help desk, free student e-mail accounts. Campuswide network is available. 100% of college-owned or -operated housing units are wired for high-speed Internet access. Wireless service is available via classrooms, computer centers, computer labs, learning centers, libraries, student centers.

Student Life *Housing:* on-campus residence required through senior year. *Options:* coed, men-only, women-only, disabled students. Campus housing is university owned. Freshman campus housing is guaranteed. *Activities and organizations:* drama/theater group, student-run newspaper, radio and television station, choral group, Student Board of Governors, Outdoor Club, Model United Nations, Public Relations Society, International Student Association, national fraternities, national sororities. *Campus security:* 24-hour emergency response devices and patrols, late-night transport/escort service, controlled dormitory access. *Student services:* health clinic, personal/psychological counseling.

Athletics Member NCAA. All Division III.

Standardized Tests *Required:* SAT or ACT (for admission).

Costs (2007–08) *Comprehensive fee:* $25,975 includes full-time tuition ($18,205) and room and board ($7770). *College room only:* $4000.

Financial Aid Of all full-time matriculated undergraduates who enrolled in 2007, 715 applied for aid, 632 were judged to have need. *Average need-based loan:* $4597.

Applying *Options:* electronic application, deferred entrance. *Application fee:* $25. *Required:* essay or personal statement, high school transcript, minimum 2.5 GPA, 1 letter of recommendation, documentation of student involvement. *Required for some:* interview. *Recommended:* interview. *Application deadlines:* rolling (freshmen), rolling (transfers). *Notification:* continuous until 8/15 (freshmen), continuous until 8/15 (transfers).

Freshman Application Contact Mr. Kevin Wilson, Director of Admission, Bethany College, Office of Admission, Bethany, WV 26032. *Phone:* 304-829-7611. *Toll-free phone:* 800-922-7611. *Fax:* 304-829-7142. *E-mail:* admission@bethanywv.edu.

BLUEFIELD STATE COLLEGE

Bluefield, West Virginia **www.bluefieldstate.edu/**

- **State-supported** 4-year, founded 1895, part of Higher Education Policy Commission System
- **Small-town** 45-acre campus
- **Endowment** $8.0 million
- **Coed** 1,804 undergraduate students, 81% full-time, 59% women, 41% men
- **Noncompetitive** entrance level, 91% of applicants were admitted

Undergraduates 1,453 full-time, 351 part-time. Students come from 17 states and territories, 16 other countries, 10% are from out of state, 12% African American, 0.5% Asian American or Pacific Islander, 0.4% Hispanic American, 0.3% Native American, 1% international, 13% transferred in. *Retention:* 62% of 2006 full-time freshmen returned.

Freshmen *Admission:* 445 applied, 404 admitted, 228 enrolled. *Average high school GPA:* 3.27. *Test scores:* SAT critical reading scores over 500: 32%; SAT math scores over 500: 41%; ACT scores over 18: 61%; SAT critical reading scores over 600: 3%; SAT math scores over 600: 5%; ACT scores over 24: 10%.

Faculty *Total:* 131, 59% full-time. *Student/faculty ratio:* 14:1.

Majors Accounting; administrative assistant and secretarial science; architectural engineering technology; biological and physical sciences; business administration and management; business/commerce; civil engineering technology; communications technology; computer and information sciences; corrections; criminal justice/police science; criminal justice/safety; electrical, electronic and communications engineering technology; elementary education; general studies; hotel/motel administration; humanities; interdisciplinary studies; legal assistant/paralegal; liberal arts and sciences/liberal studies; marketing/marketing management; mechanical engineering/mechanical technology; medical/clinical assistant; medical radiologic technology; mining technology; nursing (registered nurse training); psychology; social sciences.

Academics *Calendar:* semesters. *Degrees:* associate and bachelor's. *Special study options:* academic remediation for entering students, adult/continuing education programs, advanced placement credit, distance learning, double majors, external degree program, honors programs, internships, part-time degree program, student-designed majors, summer session for credit.

Computers on Campus 358 computers/terminals are available on campus for general student use. Students can access the following: online (class) registration. Campuswide network is available.

Student Life *Housing:* college housing not available. *Activities and organizations:* drama/theater group, student-run newspaper, radio station, choral group, Phi Eta Sigma, Student Nurses Association, Student Government Association, Minorities on the Move, national fraternities, national sororities. *Campus security:* 24-hour emergency response devices and patrols, student patrols. *Student services:* health clinic, personal/psychological counseling.

Athletics Member NCAA. All Division II. *Intercollegiate sports:* baseball M (s), basketball M (s)/W (s), cheerleading W, cross-country running M (s)/W (s), golf M (s), softball W (s), tennis M (s)/W (s). *Intramural sports:* badminton M/W, basketball M/W, football M, soccer M, swimming and diving M/W, table tennis M/W, volleyball M/W, water polo M/W.

Standardized Tests *Required:* SAT or ACT (for admission).

Costs (2007–08) *Tuition:* state resident $3984 full-time, $166 per credit hour part-time; nonresident $8160 full-time, $340 per credit hour part-time. *Payment plan:* installment. *Waivers:* adult students and senior citizens.

Financial Aid Of all full-time matriculated undergraduates who enrolled in 2007, 1,260 applied for aid, 1,060 were judged to have need, 430 had their need fully met. 102 Federal Work-Study jobs (averaging $1900). 110 state and other part-time jobs (averaging $2600). In 2007, 410 non-need-based awards were made. *Average percent of need met:* 70%. *Average financial aid package:* $6000. *Average need-based loan:* $3500. *Average need-based gift aid:* $3400. *Average non-need-based aid:* $1375. *Average indebtedness upon graduation:* $19,200.

Applying *Options:* electronic application, early admission, deferred entrance. *Required:* high school transcript, minimum 2.0 GPA. *Application deadlines:* rolling (freshmen), rolling (transfers). *Notification:* continuous (freshmen), continuous (transfers).

Freshman Application Contact Mr. Kenneth Mandeville, Director of Student Recruitment, Bluefield State College, 219 Rock Street, Bluefield, WV 24701-2198. *Phone:* 304-327-4067. *Toll-free phone:* 800-344-8892 Ext. 4065 (in-state); 800-654-7798 Ext. 4065 (out-of-state). *Fax:* 304-325-7747. *E-mail:* bscadmit@bluefieldstate.edu.

CONCORD UNIVERSITY

Athens, West Virginia **www.concord.edu/**

- **State-supported** 4-year, founded 1872, part of State College System of West Virginia
- **Rural** 100-acre campus
- **Endowment** $24.3 million
- **Coed** 2,729 undergraduate students, 82% full-time, 59% women, 41% men
- **Minimally difficult** entrance level, 69% of applicants were admitted

Undergraduates 2,229 full-time, 500 part-time. Students come from 24 states and territories, 16 other countries, 16% are from out of state, 6% African American, 1% Asian American or Pacific Islander, 0.8% Hispanic American, 0.1% Native American, 4% transferred in, 39% live on campus. *Retention:* 63% of 2006 full-time freshmen returned.

Freshmen *Admission:* 1,975 applied, 1,359 admitted, 628 enrolled. *Average high school GPA:* 3.25. *Test scores:* SAT critical reading scores over 500: 43%; SAT math scores over 500: 42%; ACT scores over 18: 83%; SAT critical reading scores over 600: 12%; SAT math scores over 600: 9%; ACT scores over 24: 29%; SAT critical reading scores over 700: 2%; SAT math scores over 700: 3%; ACT scores over 30: 2%.

Faculty *Total:* 192, 54% full-time, 40% with terminal degrees. *Student/faculty ratio:* 20:1.

Majors Accounting; art teacher education; biology/biological sciences; business administration and management; business teacher education; ceramic arts and ceramics; chemistry; clinical laboratory science/medical technology; commercial and advertising art; computer science; education; elementary education; English; geography; health teacher education; history; hospitality administration; hotel/motel administration; information science/studies; kindergarten/preschool education; library science; mass communication/media; mathematics; music teacher education; parks, recreation and leisure facilities management; physical education teaching and coaching; political science and government; pre-medical studies; pre-veterinary studies; psychology; secondary education; social work; sociology; special education; special products marketing; tourism and travel services management.

Academics *Calendar:* semesters. *Degrees:* associate, bachelor's, and master's. *Special study options:* academic remediation for entering students, accelerated degree program, advanced placement credit, distance learning, double majors, English as a second language, external degree program, honors programs, independent study, internships, off-campus study, part-time degree program, services for LD students, student-designed majors, study abroad, summer session for credit.

Computers on Campus 250 computers/terminals are available on campus for general student use. Campuswide network is available. Wireless service is available via classrooms, computer centers, computer labs, libraries, student centers.

Student Life *Housing:* on-campus residence required through senior year. *Options:* coed, men-only, women-only. Campus housing is university owned. Freshman campus housing is guaranteed. *Activities and organizations:* drama/theater group, student-run newspaper, radio and television station, choral group, Student Board, Student government, Student-run publications, Music groups, Student union activities board, national fraternities, national sororities. *Campus security:* 24-hour emergency response devices and patrols, student patrols, late-night transport/escort service, controlled dormitory access. *Student services:* health clinic.

Athletics Member NCAA. All Division II. *Intercollegiate sports:* baseball M (s), basketball M (s)/W (s), cheerleading M/W, cross-country running M (s)/W (s), football M (s), golf M (s), soccer W (s), tennis M (s)/W (s), track and field M (s)/W (s), volleyball W (s). *Intramural sports:* basketball M/W, bowling M/W, football M, golf M/W, lacrosse M, racquetball M/W, soccer M/W, tennis M/W, volleyball M/W, water polo M/W, weight lifting M/W, wrestling M.

Standardized Tests *Required:* SAT or ACT (for admission). *Recommended:* ACT (for admission).

Costs (2007–08) *Tuition:* state resident $4414 full-time, $184 per credit hour part-time; nonresident $9806 full-time, $409 per credit hour part-time. Full-time tuition and fees vary according to course load. Part-time tuition and fees vary according to course load. *Room and board:* $6280; room only: $3214. *Payment plan:* installment. *Waivers:* adult students and senior citizens.

Financial Aid Of all full-time matriculated undergraduates who enrolled in 2007, 1,929 applied for aid, 1,505 were judged to have need, 629 had their need fully met. 368 Federal Work-Study jobs (averaging $1242). 284 state and other part-time jobs (averaging $1090). In 2007, 189 non-need-based awards were made. *Average percent of need met:* 97%. *Average financial aid package:* $8310. *Average need-based loan:* $3655. *Average need-based gift aid:* $4675. *Average non-need-based aid:* $3075. *Average indebtedness upon graduation:* $11,559.

Applying *Options:* electronic application, early admission, early decision. *Required:* high school transcript, minimum 2.0 GPA. *Required for some:* essay or personal statement, interview. *Recommended:* interview. *Application deadlines:* rolling (freshmen), 1/15 (out-of-state freshmen), rolling (transfers). *Notification:* continuous (freshmen), continuous (transfers).

Freshman Application Contact Mr. Michael Curry, Vice President of Admissions and Financial Aid, Concord University, 1000 Vermillion Street, Athens, WV 24712. *Phone:* 304-384-5248. *Toll-free phone:* 888-384-5249. *Fax:* 304-384-9044. *E-mail:* admissions@concord.edu.

DAVIS & ELKINS COLLEGE

Elkins, West Virginia **www.davisandelkins.edu/**

- **Independent Presbyterian** 4-year, founded 1904
- **Small-town** 170-acre campus
- **Endowment** $22.7 million
- **Coed** 640 undergraduate students, 89% full-time, 65% women, 35% men
- **Moderately difficult** entrance level, 75% of applicants were admitted

Undergraduates 568 full-time, 72 part-time. Students come from 19 states and territories, 21 other countries, 34% are from out of state, 4% African American, 0.5% Asian American or Pacific Islander, 2% Hispanic American, 0.8% Native American, 6% international, 10% transferred in, 49% live on campus. *Retention:* 66% of 2006 full-time freshmen returned.

Freshmen *Admission:* 351 applied, 264 admitted, 117 enrolled. *Average high school GPA:* 2.9. *Test scores:* SAT critical reading scores over 500: 37%; SAT math scores over 500: 30%; SAT writing scores over 500: 34%; ACT scores over 18: 67%; SAT critical reading scores over 600: 8%; SAT math scores over 600: 8%; SAT writing scores over 600: 2%; ACT scores over 24: 19%.

Faculty *Total:* 64, 69% full-time, 59% with terminal degrees. *Student/faculty ratio:* 10:1.

Majors Accounting; accounting technology and bookkeeping; art; art teacher education; biological and biomedical sciences related; business administration and management; business teacher education; chemistry; communication/speech communication and rhetoric; computer science; criminology; dramatic/theater arts; economics; elementary education; English; environmental control technologies related; forestry related; history; hospitality administration related; information science/studies; international business/trade/commerce; international marketing; kinesiology and exercise science; management information systems; management information systems and services related; marketing/marketing management; mathematics; mathematics teacher education; music; music teacher education; nursing (registered nurse training); parks, recreation and leisure; physical education teaching and coaching; political science and government; pre-dentistry studies; pre-law studies; pre-medical studies; pre-veterinary studies; psychology; religious education; religious studies; social sciences; sociology; Spanish; sport and fitness administration/management; theater design and technology.

Academics *Calendar:* 4-1-4. *Degrees:* associate and bachelor's. *Special study options:* accelerated degree program, adult/continuing education programs, advanced placement credit, cooperative education, double majors, English as a second language, external degree program, honors programs, independent study, internships, part-time degree program, services for LD students, student-designed majors, study abroad, summer session for credit. *Unusual degree programs:* 3-2 forestry with State University of New York College of Environmental Science and Forestry (Syracuse).

Computers on Campus 80 computers/terminals and 3 ports are available on campus for general student use. Students can access the following: campus intranet, computer help desk, free student e-mail accounts, online (class) grades, online (class) schedules. Campuswide network is available. Wireless service is available via classrooms, computer labs, libraries, student centers.

Student Life *Housing:* on-campus residence required through senior year. *Options:* coed, men-only, women-only, disabled students. Campus housing is university owned. Freshman campus housing is guaranteed. *Activities and organizations:* drama/theater group, student-run newspaper, radio station, choral group, Beta Alpha Beta, campus radio station, Student Nurses Association, Student Education Association, International Student Organization, national fraternities, national sororities. *Campus security:* 24-hour emergency response devices, late-night transport/escort service, controlled dormitory access, late night security personnel. *Student services:* health clinic, personal/psychological counseling.

Athletics Member NCAA, NAIA, NCCAA. All NCAA Division II. *Intercollegiate sports:* baseball M (s), basketball M (s)/W (s), cross-country running M (s)/W (s), golf M (s), skiing (downhill) M (s)/W (s), soccer M (s)/W (s), softball W (s), volleyball W (s). *Intramural sports:* basketball M/W, football M/W, lacrosse M (c), skiing (cross-country) M/W, skiing (downhill) M/W, soccer M/W, softball M/W, swimming and diving M/W, table tennis M/W, tennis M/W, track and field M/W, ultimate Frisbee M/W, volleyball M/W (c), water polo M/W.

Standardized Tests *Required:* SAT or ACT (for admission).

Costs (2007–08) *Comprehensive fee:* $25,096 includes full-time tuition ($18,226), mandatory fees ($520), and room and board ($6350). Full-time tuition and fees vary according to course load. Part-time tuition: $560 per credit hour. Part-time tuition and fees vary according to course load. *Room and board:* Room and board charges vary according to board plan. *Payment plan:* installment. *Waivers:* senior citizens and employees or children of employees.

Financial Aid Of all full-time matriculated undergraduates who enrolled in 2006, 473 applied for aid, 422 were judged to have need, 92 had their need fully met. 184 Federal Work-Study jobs (averaging $770). 49 state and other part-time jobs (averaging $1200). In 2006, 120 non-need-based awards were made. *Average percent of need met:* 70%. *Average financial aid package:* $12,635. *Average need-based loan:* $4432. *Average need-based gift aid:* $4516. *Average non-need-based aid:* $5840. *Average indebtedness upon graduation:* $23,973.

Applying *Options:* electronic application, early admission, deferred entrance. *Application fee:* $35. *Required:* high school transcript, minimum 2.0 GPA. *Required for some:* essay or personal statement, 2 letters of recommendation, interview. *Recommended:* essay or personal statement, interview. *Application deadlines:* rolling (freshmen), rolling (transfers). *Notification:* continuous (freshmen), continuous (transfers).

Freshman Application Contact Ms. Reneé Heckel, Director of Enrollment Management, Davis & Elkins College, 100 Campus Drive, Elkins, WV 26241. *Phone:* 304-637-1974. *Toll-free phone:* 800-624-3157 Ext. 1230. *Fax:* 304-637-1800. *E-mail:* admiss@davisandelkins.edu.

See page 2748 for the College Close-Up.

FAIRMONT STATE UNIVERSITY

Fairmont, West Virginia **www.fairmontstate.edu/**

- **State-supported** comprehensive, founded 1865, part of State College System of West Virginia
- **Small-town** 80-acre campus
- **Endowment** $11.9 million
- **Coed** 6,942 undergraduate students, 74% full-time, 57% women, 43% men
- **Minimally difficult** entrance level, 79% of applicants were admitted

Undergraduates 5,140 full-time, 1,802 part-time. Students come from 25 states and territories, 19 other countries, 5% are from out of state, 4% African American, 0.5% Asian American or Pacific Islander, 0.7% Hispanic American, 0.3% Native American, 0.8% international, 5% transferred in, 35% live on campus. *Retention:* 70% of 2006 full-time freshmen returned.

Freshmen *Admission:* 3,400 applied, 2,692 admitted, 1,220 enrolled. *Average high school GPA:* 3.0. *Test scores:* SAT critical reading scores over 500: 28%; SAT math scores over 500: 28%; ACT scores over 18: 68%; SAT critical reading scores over 600: 8%; SAT math scores over 600: 5%; ACT scores over 24: 14%.

Faculty *Total:* 495, 47% full-time, 38% with terminal degrees. *Student/faculty ratio:* 18:1.

Majors Accounting; administrative assistant and secretarial science; art teacher education; aviation/airway management; avionics maintenance technology; biology/biological sciences; business administration and management; business teacher education; chemistry; child development; civil engineering technology; clinical/medical laboratory technology; commercial and advertising art; community organization and advocacy; computer science; construction engineering technology; consumer merchandising/retailing management; criminal justice/police science; drafting and design technology; dramatic/theater arts; economics; education; electrical, electronic and communications engineering technology; elementary education; engineering technology; English; family and consumer economics related; family and consumer sciences/home economics teacher education; family and consumer sciences/human sciences; fashion merchandising; finance; French; graphic and printing equipment operation/production; health information/medical records administration; health science; history; human services; industrial arts; industrial technology; information science/studies; institutional food workers; interior design; liberal arts and sciences/liberal studies; mathematics; mechanical engineering/mechanical technology; music teacher education; nursing (registered nurse training); occupational safety and health technology; physical education teaching and coaching; physical therapy; political science and government; psychology; real estate; science teacher education; secondary education; sign language interpretation and translation; sociology; special education; speech and rhetoric; veterinary technology.

Academics *Calendar:* semesters. *Degrees:* certificates, associate, bachelor's, and master's. *Special study options:* academic remediation for entering students, accelerated degree program, adult/continuing education programs, advanced placement credit, double majors, English as a second language, honors programs, internships, part-time degree program, services for LD students, summer session for credit. *ROTC:* Army (b).

Computers on Campus 1,200 computers/terminals are available on campus for general student use. Students can access the following: campus intranet, computer help desk, free student e-mail accounts, online (class) grades, online (class) registration, online (class) schedules. Campuswide network is available. Wireless service is available via entire campus.

Student Life *Housing:* on-campus residence required through sophomore year. *Options:* coed, men-only, women-only. Campus housing is university owned. Freshman campus housing is guaranteed. *Activities and organizations:* drama/theater group, student-run newspaper, choral group, marching band, Alpha Phi Omega, Circle K, Society for Non-traditional Students, Criminal Justice Club, Honors Association, national fraternities, national sororities. *Campus security:* 24-hour emergency response devices and patrols, student patrols, controlled dormitory access. *Student services:* health clinic, personal/psychological counseling, legal services.

Athletics Member NCAA. All Division II. *Intercollegiate sports:* baseball M, basketball M (s)/W (s), cross-country running M/W, football M (s), golf M (s)/W, softball W, swimming and diving M (s)/W (s), tennis M (s)/W (s), volleyball W. *Intramural sports:* archery M/W, basketball M/W, bowling M/W, cross-country running M/W, football M, golf M/W, swimming and diving M/W, table tennis M/W, tennis M/W, volleyball M/W, wrestling M.

Standardized Tests *Required:* SAT or ACT (for admission).

Costs (2007–08) *Tuition:* state resident $4656 full-time, $188 per credit part-time; nonresident $9956 full-time, $393 per credit part-time. Full-time tuition and fees vary according to degree level and location. Part-time tuition and fees vary according to course load, degree level, and location. *Required fees:* $200 full-time. *Room and board:* $5990; room only: $2990. Room and board charges vary according to board plan and housing facility. *Payment plan:* installment.

Financial Aid Of all full-time matriculated undergraduates who enrolled in 2004, 4,868 applied for aid, 4,218 were judged to have need, 299 had their need fully met. 292 Federal Work-Study jobs (averaging $1164). 396 state and other part-time jobs (averaging $1037). In 2004, 473 non-need-based awards were made. *Average percent of need met:* 67%. *Average financial aid package:* $5676. *Average need-based loan:* $2997. *Average need-based gift aid:* $8077. *Average non-need-based aid:* $946. *Average indebtedness upon graduation:* $17,500. *Financial aid deadline:* 2/1.

Applying *Options:* electronic application. *Required:* high school transcript. *Recommended:* minimum 2.0 GPA. *Application deadlines:* 6/15 (freshmen), 6/15 (transfers).

Freshman Application Contact Mr. Steve Leadman, Director of Admissions and Recruiting, Fairmont State University, 1201 Locust Avenue, Fairmont, WV 26554. *Phone:* 304-367-4892. *Toll-free phone:* 800-641-5678. *Fax:* 304-367-4789. *E-mail:* admit@fairmontstate.edu.

See page 2750 for the College Close-Up.

GLENVILLE STATE COLLEGE

Glenville, West Virginia **www.glenville.edu/**

- **State-supported** 4-year, founded 1872, part of West Virginia Higher Education Policy Commission
- **Rural** 331-acre campus
- **Endowment** $6.1 million
- **Coed** 1,441 undergraduate students, 75% full-time, 49% women, 51% men
- **Noncompetitive** entrance level, 100% of applicants were admitted

Undergraduates 1,078 full-time, 363 part-time. Students come from 26 states and territories, 3 other countries, 12% are from out of state, 13% African American, 0.3% Asian American or Pacific Islander, 1% Hispanic American, 0.3% Native American, 5% transferred in, 30% live on campus. *Retention:* 59% of 2006 full-time freshmen returned.

Freshmen *Admission:* 1,143 applied, 1,143 admitted, 291 enrolled. *Average high school GPA:* 2.96. *Test scores:* SAT critical reading scores over 500: 15%; SAT math scores over 500: 19%; ACT scores over 18: 65%; SAT critical reading scores over 600: 2%; SAT math scores over 600: 2%; ACT scores over 24: 15%; SAT critical reading scores over 700: 2%; ACT scores over 30: 1%.

Faculty *Total:* 85, 67% full-time, 47% with terminal degrees. *Student/faculty ratio:* 19:1.

Majors Behavioral sciences; biology/biological sciences; biology teacher education; business administration and management; business/commerce; business teacher education; chemistry; chemistry teacher education; computer science; criminal justice/law enforcement administration; education; elementary education; English; English/language arts teacher education; forestry technology; history; information science/studies; kindergarten/preschool education; liberal arts and sciences/liberal studies; mathematics teacher education; multi-/interdisciplinary studies related; music performance; music teacher education; natural resources management; nursing (registered nurse training); physical education teaching and coaching; science teacher education; secondary education; social studies teacher education; special education; sport and fitness administration/management; survey technology.

Academics *Calendar:* semesters. *Degrees:* certificates, associate, and bachelor's. *Special study options:* academic remediation for entering students, accelerated degree program, adult/continuing education programs, advanced placement credit, cooperative education, distance learning, double majors, English as a second language, internships, off-campus study, part-time degree program, services for LD students, student-designed majors, summer session for credit.

Computers on Campus 232 computers/terminals and 599 ports are available on campus for general student use. Students can access the following: campus intranet, computer help desk, free student e-mail accounts, online (class) grades, online (class) registration, online (class) schedules, WebVista. Campuswide network is available. 100% of college-owned or -operated housing units are wired for high-speed Internet access. Wireless service is available via entire campus.

Student Life *Housing:* on-campus residence required through sophomore year. *Options:* coed, men-only, women-only, disabled students. Campus housing is university owned. Freshman campus housing is guaranteed. *Activities and organizations:* drama/theater group, student-run newspaper, choral group, marching band, Student Government Association, American Chemical Society, Student Education Association, Kappa Delta Pi, Fellowship of Christian Athletes, national fraternities. *Campus security:* 24-hour emergency response devices and patrols, student patrols, late-night transport/escort service, controlled dormitory access. *Student services:* health clinic, personal/psychological counseling.

Athletics Member NCAA. All Division II. *Intercollegiate sports:* basketball M (s)/W (s), cross-country running M (s)/W (s), football M (s), golf M (s)/W (s), softball W (s), track and field M (s)/W (s), volleyball W (s). *Intramural sports:* basketball M/W, softball M/W, swimming and diving M/W, table tennis M/W, tennis M/W, volleyball M/W, wrestling M/W.

Standardized Tests *Required:* SAT or ACT (for admission).

Costs (2007–08) *Tuition:* state resident $4174 full-time, $174 per credit hour part-time; nonresident $9990 full-time, $416 per credit hour part-time. Full-time tuition and fees vary according to location and program. Part-time tuition and fees vary according to course load, location, and program. *Room and board:* $5800; room only: $2800. Room and board charges vary according to housing facility. *Payment plan:* installment. *Waivers:* senior citizens.

Financial Aid Of all full-time matriculated undergraduates who enrolled in 2007, 962 applied for aid, 864 were judged to have need, 215 had their need fully met. 107 Federal Work-Study jobs (averaging $1280). 269 state and other part-time jobs (averaging $1284). In 2007, 63 non-need-based awards were made. *Average percent of need met:* 75%. *Average financial aid package:* $9653. *Average need-based loan:* $3870. *Average need-based gift aid:* $4982. *Average non-need-based aid:* $1837. *Average indebtedness upon graduation:* $15,931.

Applying *Options:* electronic application, deferred entrance. *Application fee:* $10. *Required:* high school transcript, minimum 2.0 GPA, completion of college-preparatory program. *Application deadlines:* rolling (freshmen), 8/27 (transfers). *Notification:* continuous (freshmen), 8/27 (transfers).

Freshman Application Contact Lucinda Patrick, Glenville State College, 200 High Street, Glenville, WV 26351-1200. *Phone:* 304-462-4128. *Toll-free phone:* 800-924-2010. *Fax:* 304-462-8619. *E-mail:* admissions@glenville.edu.

MARSHALL UNIVERSITY

Huntington, West Virginia **www.marshall.edu/**

- **State-supported** university, founded 1837, part of University System of West Virginia
- **Urban** 70-acre campus
- **Endowment** $66.2 million
- **Coed** 9,586 undergraduate students, 82% full-time, 56% women, 44% men
- **Moderately difficult** entrance level, 86% of applicants were admitted

Undergraduates 7,902 full-time, 1,684 part-time. Students come from 41 states and territories, 29 other countries, 20% are from out of state, 5% African American, 0.9% Asian American or Pacific Islander, 1% Hispanic American, 0.4% Native American, 1% international, 7% transferred in. *Retention:* 71% of 2006 full-time freshmen returned.

Freshmen *Admission:* 2,405 applied, 2,059 admitted, 1,688 enrolled. *Average high school GPA:* 3.33. *Test scores:* SAT critical reading scores over 500: 55%; SAT math scores over 500: 56%; ACT scores over 18: 94%; SAT critical reading scores over 600: 19%; SAT math scores over 600: 16%; ACT scores over 24: 37%; SAT critical reading scores over 700: 4%; SAT math scores over 700: 3%; ACT scores over 30: 4%.

Faculty *Total:* 702, 66% full-time, 56% with terminal degrees. *Student/faculty ratio:* 20:1.

Majors Accounting; adult and continuing education administration; art; biology/biological sciences; business administration and management; business/managerial economics; chemistry; clinical laboratory science/medical technology; clinical/medical laboratory technology; computer and information sciences; computer engineering technology; counselor education/school counseling and guidance; criminal justice/safety; cytotechnology; dietetics; economics; elementary education; engineering; English; environmental science; family and consumer sciences/human sciences; fashion/apparel design; finance; foreign languages and literatures; general studies; geography; geology/earth science; history; humanities; international relations and affairs; journalism; liberal arts and sciences and humanities related; marketing/marketing management; mathematics; multi-/interdisciplinary studies related; nursing (registered nurse training); occupational safety and health technology; parks, recreation and leisure facilities management; physical education teaching and coaching; physics; political science and government; psychology; rehabilitation and therapeutic professions related; respiratory care therapy; secondary education; social work; sociology; speech and rhetoric; speech-language pathology; systems science and theory.

Academics *Calendar:* semesters. *Degrees:* associate, bachelor's, master's, doctoral, first professional, and post-master's certificates. *Special study options:* academic remediation for entering students, accelerated degree program, adult/continuing education programs, advanced placement credit, cooperative education, distance learning, double majors, English as a second language, honors programs, independent study, internships, off-campus study, part-time degree program, services for LD students, study abroad, summer session for credit. *ROTC:* Army (b). *Unusual degree programs:* 3-2 forestry with Duke University.

Computers on Campus 1,461 computers/terminals are available on campus for general student use. Students can access the following: computer help desk, free student e-mail accounts, online (class) grades, online (class) registration, online (class) schedules. Campuswide network is available. Wireless service is available via computer centers, computer labs, libraries, student centers.

Student Life *Housing:* on-campus residence required through sophomore year. *Options:* coed, men-only, women-only, disabled students. Campus housing is university owned. Freshman campus housing is guaranteed. *Activities and organizations:* drama/theater group, student-run newspaper, radio and television station, choral group, marching band, Campus Crusade for Christ, Gamma Beta

Phi, The International Students' Organization, Newman Association, Phi Alpha Theta, national fraternities, national sororities. *Campus security:* 24-hour emergency response devices and patrols, student patrols, late-night transport/escort service, controlled dormitory access. *Student services:* health clinic, personal/psychological counseling, women's center, legal services.

Athletics Member NCAA. All Division I except football (Division I-A). *Intercollegiate sports:* baseball M (s), basketball M (s)/W (s), cross-country running M (s)/W (s), golf M (s)/W (s), lacrosse M (c), rugby M (c)/W (c), soccer M (s)/W (s), softball W (s), swimming and diving W (s), tennis W (s), track and field M (s)/W (s), volleyball W (s). *Intramural sports:* basketball M/W, bowling M/W, football M/W, golf M/W, racquetball M/W, soccer M/W, softball M/W, swimming and diving M/W, tennis M/W, track and field M/W, volleyball M/W.

Standardized Tests *Required:* SAT or ACT (for admission).

Costs (2007–08) *Tuition:* state resident $4360 full-time, $170 per credit hour part-time; nonresident $11,264 full-time, $457 per credit hour part-time. Full-time tuition and fees vary according to degree level, location, program, and reciprocity agreements. Part-time tuition and fees vary according to course load, degree level, location, program, and reciprocity agreements. *Required fees:* $200 full-time. *Room and board:* $6818; room only: $3944. Room and board charges vary according to board plan and housing facility. *Payment plan:* installment. *Waivers:* senior citizens and employees or children of employees.

Financial Aid Of all full-time matriculated undergraduates who enrolled in 2007, 5,387 applied for aid, 4,007 were judged to have need, 1,620 had their need fully met. 359 Federal Work-Study jobs (averaging $1761). 58 state and other part-time jobs (averaging $6030). In 2007, 1468 non-need-based awards were made. *Average percent of need met:* 60%. *Average financial aid package:* $8080. *Average need-based loan:* $5350. *Average need-based gift aid:* $4916. *Average non-need-based aid:* $5442. *Average indebtedness upon graduation:* $16,342.

Applying *Options:* electronic application, early admission, deferred entrance. *Application fee:* $30. *Required:* minimum 2.0 GPA. *Required for some:* high school transcript. *Application deadlines:* rolling (freshmen), rolling (transfers). *Notification:* continuous (freshmen), continuous (transfers).

Freshman Application Contact Dr. Tammy Johnson, Director of Admissions, Marshall University, 1 John Marshall Drive, Huntington, WV 25755. *Phone:* 800-642-3499. *Toll-free phone:* 800-642-3499. *Fax:* 304-696-3135. *E-mail:* admissions@marshall.edu.

See page 2752 for the College Close-Up.

MOUNTAIN STATE UNIVERSITY

Beckley, West Virginia **www.mountainstate.edu/**

- **Independent** comprehensive, founded 1933
- **Small-town** 24-acre campus
- **Endowment** $8.6 million
- **Coed** 4,169 undergraduate students, 73% full-time, 64% women, 36% men
- **Noncompetitive** entrance level, 100% of applicants were admitted

Undergraduates 3,030 full-time, 1,139 part-time. Students come from 43 states and territories, 45 other countries, 29% are from out of state, 8% African American, 3% Asian American or Pacific Islander, 2% Hispanic American, 0.6% Native American, 3% international, 17% transferred in, 3% live on campus. *Retention:* 52% of 2006 full-time freshmen returned.

Freshmen *Admission:* 1,652 applied, 1,652 admitted, 540 enrolled. *Average high school GPA:* 3.21. *Test scores:* SAT critical reading scores over 500: 34%; SAT math scores over 500: 34%; SAT writing scores over 500: 34%; ACT scores over 18: 50%; SAT critical reading scores over 600: 17%; SAT math scores over 600: 17%; SAT writing scores over 600: 17%; SAT critical reading scores over 700: 17%; SAT math scores over 700: 17%; SAT writing scores over 700: 17%.

Faculty *Total:* 364, 26% full-time, 25% with terminal degrees. *Student/faculty ratio:* 22:1.

Majors Accounting; administrative assistant and secretarial science; aviation/airway management; banking and financial support services; behavioral sciences; business administration and management; business/commerce; computer science; computer systems networking and telecommunications; criminal justice/law enforcement administration; criminal justice/safety; culinary arts; diagnostic medical sonography and ultrasound technology; e-commerce; elementary education; emergency medical technology (EMT paramedic); engineering; English; entrepreneurship; environmental studies; fire science; forensic science and technology; health/health care administration; hospitality administration; hospitality administration related; hospitality/recreation marketing; humanities; human resources management and services related; information science/studies; information technology; interdisciplinary studies; legal assistant/paralegal; legal studies; liberal arts and sciences/liberal studies; library science; logistics and materials management; management science; marketing/marketing management; mass communication/media; mathematics and computer science; medical/clinical assistant; medical radiologic technology; natural resources/conservation; non-profit management; nursing (registered nurse training); occupational health and industrial hygiene; occupational therapist assistant; office management; organizational behavior; physical sciences; physical therapist assistant; pre-medical studies; psychology; public health education and promotion; radiologic technology/science; respiratory care therapy; secondary education; social work; tourism and travel services management; tourism/travel marketing; web page, digital/multimedia and information resources design.

Academics *Calendar:* semesters. *Degrees:* certificates, associate, bachelor's, master's, post-master's, and postbachelor's certificates. *Special study options:* academic remediation for entering students, accelerated degree program, adult/continuing education programs, advanced placement credit, cooperative education, distance learning, double majors, English as a second language, external degree program, independent study, internships, part-time degree program, student-designed majors, summer session for credit.

Computers on Campus 185 computers/terminals are available on campus for general student use. Students can access the following: campus intranet, computer help desk, online (class) grades, online (class) registration, online (class) schedules. Campuswide network is available. 100% of college-owned or -operated housing units are wired for high-speed Internet access. Wireless service is available via entire campus.

Student Life *Housing:* on-campus residence required through sophomore year. *Options:* coed. Campus housing is university owned. *Activities and organizations:* drama/theater group, student-run newspaper, choral group, FIA-Forensics Investigation Association, SNA-Student Nursing Association, MSU-Culinarians, MSU-Ambassadors, Student Government Association. *Campus security:* 24-hour emergency response devices and patrols, late-night transport/escort service, controlled dormitory access. *Student services:* health clinic.

Athletics Member NAIA. *Intercollegiate sports:* basketball M (s), softball W (s), volleyball W. *Intramural sports:* basketball M/W, cheerleading M/W, soccer M/W, table tennis M/W, volleyball M/W.

Standardized Tests *Required for some:* SAT or ACT (for admission). *Recommended:* SAT Subject Tests (for admission).

Costs (2007–08) *Comprehensive fee:* $13,954 includes full-time tuition ($6150), mandatory fees ($1950), and room and board ($5854). Full-time tuition and fees vary according to course load and program. Part-time tuition: $205 per credit. Part-time tuition and fees vary according to course load and program. *Required fees:* $65 per credit hour part-time. *College room only:* $2954. Room and board charges vary according to board plan. *Payment plan:* installment. *Waivers:* senior citizens and employees or children of employees.

Financial Aid Of all full-time matriculated undergraduates who enrolled in 2006, 2,699 applied for aid, 1,820 were judged to have need, 33 had their need fully met. 197 Federal Work-Study jobs (averaging $1248). In 2006, 11 non-need-based awards were made. *Average percent of need met:* 44%. *Average financial aid package:* $6107. *Average need-based loan:* $4075. *Average need-based gift aid:* $3664. *Average non-need-based aid:* $5857. *Average indebtedness upon graduation:* $27,903.

Applying *Options:* electronic application, early admission, deferred entrance. *Application fee:* $25. *Required:* high school transcript. *Required for some:* essay or personal statement, letters of recommendation, interview. *Application deadlines:* rolling (freshmen), rolling (transfers).

Freshman Application Contact Ms. Darlene Brown, Administrative Assistant for Recruiting Services, Mountain State University, PO Box 9003, Beckley, WV 25802-9003. *Phone:* 304-929-1433. *Toll-free phone:* 800-766-6067 Ext. 1433. *Fax:* 304-253-5072. *E-mail:* gomsu@mountainstate.edu.

See page 2754 for the College Close-Up.

OHIO VALLEY UNIVERSITY

Vienna, West Virginia **www.ovu.edu/**

- **Independent** 4-year, founded 1960, affiliated with Church of Christ
- **Small-town** 299-acre campus
- **Endowment** $1.0 million
- **Coed** 546 undergraduate students, 93% full-time, 54% women, 46% men
- **Minimally difficult** entrance level, 56% of applicants were admitted

Undergraduates 509 full-time, 37 part-time. Students come from 30 states and territories, 9 other countries, 57% are from out of state, 6% African American, 0.2% Asian American or Pacific Islander, 3% Hispanic American, 0.4% Native American, 7% international, 10% transferred in, 60% live on campus. *Retention:* 57% of 2006 full-time freshmen returned.

Freshmen *Admission:* 493 applied, 277 admitted, 108 enrolled. *Average high school GPA:* 3.0. *Test scores:* SAT critical reading scores over 500: 52%; SAT

math scores over 500: 46%; SAT writing scores over 500: 43%; ACT scores over 18: 71%; SAT critical reading scores over 600: 13%; SAT math scores over 600: 14%; SAT writing scores over 600: 14%; ACT scores over 24: 21%; SAT critical reading scores over 700: 2%; SAT math scores over 700: 2%; SAT writing scores over 700: 2%; ACT scores over 30: 2%.

Faculty *Total:* 71, 42% full-time, 28% with terminal degrees. *Student/faculty ratio:* 12:1.

Majors Accounting; adult and continuing education; biblical studies; business administration and management; business/commerce; health/medical preparatory programs related; human resources management; liberal arts and sciences/liberal studies; mathematics teacher education; physical education teaching and coaching; psychology; religious studies; science technologies related; secondary education.

Academics *Calendar:* semesters. *Degrees:* associate and bachelor's. *Special study options:* academic remediation for entering students, adult/continuing education programs, advanced placement credit, double majors, English as a second language, external degree program, honors programs, internships, part-time degree program, study abroad, summer session for credit. *ROTC:* Air Force (c).

Computers on Campus 60 computers/terminals are available on campus for general student use. Students can access the following: campus intranet, computer help desk, free student e-mail accounts, online (class) grades, online (class) registration, online (class) schedules. Campuswide network is available.

Student Life *Housing:* on-campus residence required through sophomore year. *Options:* men-only, women-only. Campus housing is university owned. Freshman campus housing is guaranteed. *Activities and organizations:* drama/theater group, student-run newspaper, choral group, Alpha Chi Honor Society, SNEA, SIFE, Ambassadors for Christ, Timothy Club. *Campus security:* 24-hour emergency response devices, controlled dormitory access. *Student services:* health clinic, personal/psychological counseling.

Athletics Member NCAA. All Division II. *Intercollegiate sports:* baseball M (s), basketball M (s)/W (s), cross-country running M (s)/W (s), golf M (s)/W (s), soccer M (s)/W (s), softball W (s), volleyball W (s). *Intramural sports:* basketball M/W, bowling M/W, football M/W, golf M/W, soccer M/W, softball M/W, volleyball M/W.

Standardized Tests *Required:* SAT or ACT (for admission).

Costs (2008–09) *Comprehensive fee:* $19,650 includes full-time tuition ($11,998), mandatory fees ($1512), and room and board ($6140). Part-time tuition: $500 per credit hour. *Required fees:* $63 per credit hour part-time. *College room only:* $3200.

Financial Aid Of all full-time matriculated undergraduates who enrolled in 2006, 436 applied for aid, 381 were judged to have need, 55 had their need fully met. 120 Federal Work-Study jobs (averaging $1000). 78 state and other part-time jobs (averaging $1000). In 2006, 107 non-need-based awards were made. *Average percent of need met:* 64%. *Average financial aid package:* $9618. *Average need-based loan:* $3559. *Average need-based gift aid:* $6743. *Average non-need-based aid:* $7401. *Average indebtedness upon graduation:* $9300.

Applying *Options:* electronic application, early admission, early action, deferred entrance. *Application fee:* $20. *Required:* high school transcript. *Required for some:* essay or personal statement, interview. *Recommended:* letters of recommendation. *Application deadlines:* 8/15 (freshmen), rolling (transfers), 9/1 (early action). *Notification:* continuous (freshmen), continuous (transfers), 10/1 (early action).

Freshman Application Contact Mrs. Valerie Wright, Admissions Office Manager, Ohio Valley University, 1 Campus View Drive, Vienna, WV 26105. *Phone:* 304-865-6200. *Toll-free phone:* 877-446-8668 Ext. 6200. *Fax:* 304-865-6001. *E-mail:* admissions@ovu.edu.

SALEM INTERNATIONAL UNIVERSITY

Salem, West Virginia **www.salemu.edu/**

- **Independent** comprehensive, founded 1888
- **Rural** 300-acre campus
- **Coed**
- **Minimally difficult** entrance level

Undergraduates Students come from 16 states and territories, 11 other countries, 34% are from out of state, 70% live on campus.

Faculty *Total:* 16, 81% full-time, 44% with terminal degrees. *Student/faculty ratio:* 13:1.

Majors Biology/biological sciences; business administration and management; computer science; criminal justice/law enforcement administration; education; education (K-12); international business/trade/commerce; liberal arts and sciences/liberal studies; mass communication/media; mathematics; physical education teaching and coaching; radio and television; secondary education; sport and fitness administration/management; telecommunications.

Academics *Calendar:* modular. *Degrees:* associate, bachelor's, and master's. *Special study options:* academic remediation for entering students, accelerated degree program, advanced placement credit, distance learning, double majors, English as a second language, independent study, internships, off-campus study, part-time degree program, services for LD students, study abroad.

Computers on Campus 104 computers/terminals are available on campus for general student use. Students can access the following: campus intranet, computer help desk, free student e-mail accounts, online (class) grades, online (class) registration, online (class) schedules. Campuswide network is available. 100% of college-owned or -operated housing units are wired for high-speed Internet access. Wireless service is available via entire campus.

Student Life *Housing options:* coed, men-only, women-only. Campus housing is university owned. Freshman campus housing is guaranteed. *Activities and organizations:* Student Government, Xi Rho Zeta, Gamma Beta Phi, Zi Theta Phi, Rainbow Alliance, national fraternities, national sororities. *Campus security:* 24-hour emergency response devices and patrols. *Student services:* personal/psychological counseling.

Athletics Member NCAA. All Division II. *Intercollegiate sports:* baseball M (s), basketball M (s)/W (s), cheerleading M/W, golf M, gymnastics W (s), ice hockey M (s), soccer M (s)/W (s), softball W (s), swimming and diving M (s)/W (s), tennis M (s), volleyball W (s), water polo M (s)/W (s). *Intramural sports:* badminton M/W, basketball M/W, racquetball M/W, skiing (downhill) M/W, soccer M/W, softball M/W, swimming and diving M/W, table tennis M/W, tennis W, water polo M/W, weight lifting M/W.

Standardized Tests *Required:* SAT or ACT (for admission).

Costs (2008–09) *Tuition:* $12,750 full-time.

Financial Aid Of all full-time matriculated undergraduates who enrolled in 2006, 230 applied for aid, 200 were judged to have need, 120 had their need fully met. 106 Federal Work-Study jobs (averaging $650). 25 state and other part-time jobs (averaging $911). In 2006, 230 non-need-based awards were made. *Average percent of need met:* 100%. *Average financial aid package:* $18,110. *Average need-based loan:* $5500. *Average need-based gift aid:* $5400. *Average non-need-based aid:* $7860. *Average indebtedness upon graduation:* $15,794.

Applying *Options:* electronic application, deferred entrance. *Application fee:* $25. *Required:* high school transcript, minimum 2.0 GPA. *Required for some:* interview. *Recommended:* essay or personal statement, interview. *Application deadlines:* rolling (freshmen), rolling (transfers).

Freshman Application Contact Ms. Gina Cossey, Vice President, Recruiting and Admissions, Salem International University, PO Box 500, Salem, WV 26426-0500. *Phone:* 304-326-1359. *Toll-free phone:* 800-283-4562. *Fax:* 304-326-1592. *E-mail:* admissions@salemiu.edu.

SHEPHERD UNIVERSITY

Shepherdstown, West Virginia **www.shepherd.edu/**

- **State-supported** comprehensive, founded 1871, part of West Virginia Higher Education Policy Commission
- **Small-town** 320-acre campus with easy access to Washington, DC
- **Endowment** $23.0 million
- **Coed** 3,965 undergraduate students, 79% full-time, 58% women, 42% men
- **Moderately difficult** entrance level, 88% of applicants were admitted

Shepherd University, a West Virginia public liberal arts university, is a diverse community of learners and a gateway to the world of opportunities and ideas. Shepherd is the regional center for academic, cultural, and economic opportunity. The University's mission of service succeeds because it is dedicated to its core values: learning, engagement, integrity, accessibility, and community. The University was listed in *Princeton Review* as a Best Southeastern College for 2007. In addition, Shepherd was named to the 2007 edition of the *Princeton Review*'s "America's Best Value Colleges."

Undergraduates 3,123 full-time, 842 part-time. Students come from 50 states and territories, 16 other countries, 40% are from out of state, 6% African American, 1% Asian American or Pacific Islander, 3% Hispanic American, 0.3% Native American, 0.6% international, 9% transferred in, 33% live on campus. *Retention:* 67% of 2006 full-time freshmen returned.

Freshmen *Admission:* 1,611 applied, 1,418 admitted, 706 enrolled. *Average high school GPA:* 3.07. *Test scores:* SAT critical reading scores over 500: 53%; SAT math scores over 500: 53%; ACT scores over 18: 96%; SAT critical reading scores over 600: 14%; SAT math scores over 600: 10%; ACT scores over 24: 29%; SAT critical reading scores over 700: 1%; SAT math scores over 700: 1%; ACT scores over 30: 1%.

Faculty *Total:* 314, 37% full-time, 44% with terminal degrees. *Student/faculty ratio:* 19:1.

Majors Accounting; art; biology/biological sciences; business administration and management; chemistry; communication/speech communication and rhetoric; computer and information sciences; economics; elementary education; English; environmental studies; family and consumer sciences/human sciences; general studies; history; mathematics; music; nursing (registered nurse training); parks, recreation and leisure; political science and government; psychology; secondary education; social work; sociology; Spanish.

Academics *Calendar:* semesters. *Degrees:* bachelor's and master's. *Special study options:* academic remediation for entering students, accelerated degree program, adult/continuing education programs, advanced placement credit, cooperative education, double majors, honors programs, independent study, internships, part-time degree program, services for LD students, study abroad, summer session for credit. *ROTC:* Air Force (c).

Computers on Campus 350 computers/terminals and 150 ports are available on campus for general student use. Students can access the following: campus intranet, computer help desk, free student e-mail accounts, online (class) grades, online (class) registration, online (class) schedules, personal Web pages. Campuswide network is available. 100% of college-owned or -operated housing units are wired for high-speed Internet access. Wireless service is available via classrooms, computer labs, libraries, student centers.

Student Life *Housing:* on-campus residence required through senior year. *Options:* coed. Campus housing is university owned. Freshman applicants given priority for college housing. *Activities and organizations:* drama/theater group, student-run newspaper, radio station, choral group, marching band, Shepherd University Games and Anime Guild, Sigma Sigma Sigma, Lambda Chi Alpha, Common Ground, Cross Country/Track and Field Club, national fraternities, national sororities. *Campus security:* 24-hour emergency response devices and patrols, late-night transport/escort service, controlled dormitory access. *Student services:* health clinic, personal/psychological counseling.

Athletics Member NCAA. All Division II. *Intercollegiate sports:* baseball M (s), basketball M (s)/W (s), football M (s), golf M, lacrosse W (s), soccer M (s)/W (s), softball W (s), tennis M (s)/W (s), volleyball W (s). *Intramural sports:* basketball M/W, bowling M/W, football M/W, racquetball M/W, soccer M/W, softball M/W, swimming and diving M/W, tennis M/W, ultimate Frisbee M/W, volleyball M/W, water polo M/W, weight lifting M/W, wrestling M/W.

Standardized Tests *Required:* SAT or ACT (for admission).

Costs (2007–08) *Tuition:* state resident $4564 full-time, $186 per credit hour part-time; nonresident $12,036 full-time, $497 per credit hour part-time. Full-time tuition and fees vary according to program and reciprocity agreements. Part-time tuition and fees vary according to program. *Room and board:* $6714. Room and board charges vary according to board plan and housing facility. *Payment plan:* installment. *Waivers:* minority students and senior citizens.

Financial Aid Of all full-time matriculated undergraduates who enrolled in 2007, 2,551 applied for aid, 1,596 were judged to have need, 279 had their need fully met. 187 Federal Work-Study jobs (averaging $1387). 358 state and other part-time jobs (averaging $2310). In 2007, 641 non-need-based awards were made. *Average percent of need met:* 74%. *Average financial aid package:* $9609. *Average need-based loan:* $3986. *Average need-based gift aid:* $4290. *Average non-need-based aid:* $7853. *Average indebtedness upon graduation:* $18,994.

Applying *Options:* electronic application, early admission, early action, deferred entrance. *Application fee:* $35. *Required:* high school transcript, minimum 2.0 GPA. *Recommended:* essay or personal statement, minimum 3.0 GPA, 3 letters of recommendation. *Application deadlines:* rolling (freshmen), rolling (transfers), 11/15 (early action). *Notification:* continuous until 8/15 (freshmen), continuous until 8/15 (transfers), 12/15 (early action).

Freshman Application Contact Mr. Randall Friend, Acting Director of Admissions, Shepherd University, PO Box 3210, Shepherdstown, WV 25443-3210. *Phone:* 304-876-5212. *Toll-free phone:* 800-344-5231. *Fax:* 304-876-5165. *E-mail:* admissions@shepherd.edu.

See page 2756 for the College Close-Up.

UNIVERSITY OF CHARLESTON

Charleston, West Virginia **www.ucwv.edu/**

- **Independent** comprehensive, founded 1888
- **Urban** 40-acre campus
- **Endowment** $35.5 million
- **Coed** 1,171 undergraduate students, 93% full-time, 60% women, 40% men
- **Moderately difficult** entrance level, 67% of applicants were admitted

Undergraduates 1,090 full-time, 81 part-time. Students come from 35 states and territories, 17 other countries, 31% are from out of state, 5% African American, 0.8% Asian American or Pacific Islander, 0.9% Hispanic American, 0.2% Native American, 9% international, 8% transferred in, 55% live on campus. *Retention:* 70% of 2006 full-time freshmen returned.

Freshmen *Admission:* 1,451 applied, 966 admitted, 328 enrolled. *Average high school GPA:* 3.45. *Test scores:* SAT critical reading scores over 500: 42%; SAT math scores over 500: 53%; ACT scores over 18: 91%; SAT critical reading scores over 600: 12%; SAT math scores over 600: 14%; ACT scores over 24: 42%; SAT critical reading scores over 700: 1%; ACT scores over 30: 4%.

Faculty *Total:* 143, 62% full-time, 41% with terminal degrees. *Student/faculty ratio:* 13:1.

Majors Accounting; art; athletic training; biology/biological sciences; biology teacher education; business administration and management; business administration, management and operations related; chemistry; computer and information sciences; education; elementary education; environmental biology; environmental science; finance; general studies; health professions related; health teacher education; history; information science/studies; marketing/marketing management; music teacher education; nursing (registered nurse training); pre-pharmacy studies; psychology; public policy analysis; radiologic technology/science; science teacher education; social studies teacher education.

Academics *Calendar:* semesters. *Degrees:* associate, bachelor's, master's, and doctoral. *Special study options:* academic remediation for entering students, accelerated degree program, adult/continuing education programs, advanced placement credit, distance learning, double majors, English as a second language, independent study, internships, part-time degree program, services for LD students, student-designed majors, study abroad, summer session for credit. *ROTC:* Army (b).

Computers on Campus 200 computers/terminals are available on campus for general student use. Students can access the following: campus intranet, computer help desk, free student e-mail accounts, online (class) grades, online (class) registration, online (class) schedules. Campuswide network is available. 100% of college-owned or -operated housing units are wired for high-speed Internet access. Wireless service is available via classrooms, computer centers, computer labs, libraries, student centers.

Student Life *Housing:* on-campus residence required through sophomore year. *Options:* coed, disabled students. Campus housing is university owned. Freshman campus housing is guaranteed. *Activities and organizations:* drama/theater group, student-run newspaper, choral group, Student Activities Board, American Society of Interior Designers, Student Government Association, Capitol Association of Nursing Students, International Student Organization, national fraternities. *Campus security:* 24-hour emergency response devices and patrols, student patrols, late-night transport/escort service, controlled dormitory access, radio connection to city police and ambulance. *Student services:* health clinic, personal/psychological counseling.

Athletics Member NCAA. All Division II. *Intercollegiate sports:* baseball M (s), basketball M (s)/W (s), cheerleading W (s), crew M (s)/W (s), cross-country running M (s)/W (s), football M (s), golf M (s), soccer M (s)/W (s), softball W (s), swimming and diving M (s)/W (s), tennis M (s)/W (s), track and field M (s)/W (s), volleyball W (s). *Intramural sports:* basketball M/W, bowling M/W, football M/W, tennis M/W, volleyball M/W, water polo M/W.

Standardized Tests *Required:* SAT or ACT (for admission).

Costs (2007–08) *Comprehensive fee:* $29,980 includes full-time tuition ($22,050) and room and board ($7930). Part-time tuition: $400 per credit. Part-time tuition and fees vary according to program. *Required fees:* $75 per term part-time. *College room only:* $4334. Room and board charges vary according to board plan and housing facility. *Payment plan:* installment. *Waivers:* senior citizens and employees or children of employees.

Financial Aid Of all full-time matriculated undergraduates who enrolled in 2007, 943 applied for aid, 848 were judged to have need, 695 had their need fully met. 110 Federal Work-Study jobs (averaging $975). 25 state and other part-time jobs (averaging $850). In 2007, 210 non-need-based awards were made. *Average percent of need met:* 85%. *Average financial aid package:* $20,030. *Average need-based loan:* $5785. *Average need-based gift aid:* $3198. *Average non-need-based aid:* $13,750. *Average indebtedness upon graduation:* $27,305.

Applying *Options:* electronic application, early admission, deferred entrance. *Application fee:* $25. *Required:* high school transcript, minimum 2.25 GPA, minimum scores ACT 19; SAT 900. *Required for some:* interview. *Recommended:* essay or personal statement, letters of recommendation. *Application deadlines:* rolling (freshmen), rolling (transfers). *Notification:* continuous (freshmen), continuous (transfers).

Freshman Application Contact Mr. Brad Parrish, Vice President for Enrollment, University of Charleston, 2300 MacCorkle Avenue, SE, Charleston, WV 25304. *Phone:* 304-357-4750. *Toll-free phone:* 800-995-GOUC. *Fax:* 304-357-4781. *E-mail:* admissions@ucwv.edu.

See page 2758 for the College Close-Up.

WEST LIBERTY STATE COLLEGE

West Liberty, West Virginia **www.westliberty.edu/**

- **State-supported** 4-year, founded 1837, part of West Virginia Higher Education Policy Commission
- **Rural** 290-acre campus with easy access to Pittsburgh
- **Endowment** $14.6 million
- **Coed** 2,402 undergraduate students, 86% full-time, 57% women, 43% men
- **Minimally difficult** entrance level, 83% of applicants were admitted

Undergraduates 2,068 full-time, 334 part-time. Students come from 24 states and territories, 4 other countries, 30% are from out of state, 4% African American, 0.5% Asian American or Pacific Islander, 0.9% Hispanic American, 0.2% Native American, 0.2% international, 11% transferred in, 45% live on campus. *Retention:* 65% of 2006 full-time freshmen returned.

Freshmen *Admission:* 1,524 applied, 1,262 admitted, 503 enrolled. *Average high school GPA:* 3.12. *Test scores:* SAT critical reading scores over 500: 36%; SAT math scores over 500: 36%; ACT scores over 18: 70%; SAT critical reading scores over 600: 4%; SAT math scores over 600: 3%; ACT scores over 24: 15%; SAT critical reading scores over 700: 1%; ACT scores over 30: 1%.

Faculty *Total:* 163, 61% full-time, 36% with terminal degrees. *Student/faculty ratio:* 18:1.

Majors Accounting; art teacher education; banking and financial support services; biology/biological sciences; business administration and management; business/managerial economics; chemistry; clinical laboratory science/medical technology; commercial and advertising art; criminal justice/law enforcement administration; dental hygiene; education; elementary education; English; health science; health teacher education; history; information science/studies; interdisciplinary studies; kindergarten/preschool education; kinesiology and exercise science; marketing/marketing management; mass communication/media; mathematics; music teacher education; nursing (registered nurse training); physical education teaching and coaching; political science and government; pre-dentistry studies; pre-law studies; pre-medical studies; psychology; secondary education; social sciences; sociology.

Academics *Calendar:* semesters. *Degrees:* associate and bachelor's. *Special study options:* academic remediation for entering students, accelerated degree program, adult/continuing education programs, advanced placement credit, double majors, external degree program, honors programs, independent study, internships, off-campus study, part-time degree program, student-designed majors, summer session for credit.

Computers on Campus 400 computers/terminals are available on campus for general student use. Students can access the following: campus intranet, computer help desk, free student e-mail accounts, online (class) grades, online (class) registration, online (class) schedules. Campuswide network is available. 100% of college-owned or -operated housing units are wired for high-speed Internet access. Wireless service is available via classrooms, computer labs, dorm rooms, learning centers, libraries, student centers.

Student Life *Housing options:* coed, men-only, women-only, disabled students. Campus housing is university owned. *Activities and organizations:* drama/theater group, student-run newspaper, radio and television station, choral group, marching band, Delta Sigma Pi, Student Senate, Drama Club, Students in Free Enterprise, national fraternities, national sororities. *Campus security:* 24-hour emergency response devices and patrols, late-night transport/escort service. *Student services:* health clinic, personal/psychological counseling.

Athletics Member NCAA. All Division II. *Intercollegiate sports:* baseball M (s), basketball M (s)/W (s), cross-country running M (s)/W (s), football M (s), golf M (s)/W (s), softball W (s), tennis M (s)/W (s), track and field M (s)/W (s), volleyball W (s), wrestling M (s). *Intramural sports:* basketball M/W, golf M/W, racquetball M/W, softball M/W, table tennis M/W, tennis M/W, volleyball M/W.

Standardized Tests *Required:* SAT or ACT (for admission).

Costs (2007–08) *One-time required fee:* $50. *Tuition:* state resident $4242 full-time, $174 per credit hour part-time; nonresident $10,260 full-time, $425 per credit hour part-time. *Required fees:* $70 full-time. *Room and board:* $5984; room only: $3420. Room and board charges vary according to board plan and housing facility. *Payment plans:* installment, deferred payment. *Waivers:* senior citizens and employees or children of employees.

Financial Aid Of all full-time matriculated undergraduates who enrolled in 2007, 1,918 applied for aid, 1,335 were judged to have need. 139 Federal Work-Study jobs (averaging $952). 55 state and other part-time jobs (averaging $3993). *Average financial aid package:* $7431. *Average need-based loan:* $4023. *Average need-based gift aid:* $3787. *Average indebtedness upon graduation:* $13,800.

Applying *Options:* electronic application. *Required:* high school transcript, minimum 2.0 GPA. *Recommended:* interview. *Notification:* continuous (freshmen), continuous (transfers).

Freshman Application Contact Ms. Stephanie North, Admissions Counselor, West Liberty State College, PO Box 295, West Liberty, WV 26074. *Phone:* 304-336-8078. *Toll-free phone:* 800-732-6204 Ext. 8076. *Fax:* 304-336-8403. *E-mail:* wladmsn1@westliberty.edu.

WEST VIRGINIA STATE UNIVERSITY

Institute, West Virginia **www.wvstateu.edu/**

- **State-supported** comprehensive, founded 1891, part of State College System of West Virginia
- **Suburban** 98-acre campus
- **Coed**
- **Minimally difficult** entrance level

Faculty *Student/faculty ratio:* 19:1.

Academics *Calendar:* semesters. *Degrees:* bachelor's and master's.

Student Life *Campus security:* 24-hour emergency response devices and patrols, late-night transport/escort service.

Athletics Member NCAA. All Division II.

Standardized Tests *Required:* SAT or ACT (for placement). *Required for some:* SAT or ACT (for admission). *Recommended:* SAT (for admission).

Costs (2007–08) *Tuition:* state resident $4136 full-time, $172 per credit hour part-time; nonresident $9718 full-time, $405 per credit hour part-time. Full-time tuition and fees vary according to program. Part-time tuition and fees vary according to course load and program. *Room and board:* $5550; room only: $2500. Room and board charges vary according to board plan and housing facility.

Financial Aid *Financial aid deadline:* 6/15.

Applying *Options:* electronic application, early admission. *Required:* high school transcript.

Freshman Application Contact Ms. Trina Sweeney, Admission Assistant, West Virginia State University, Campus Box 197, PO Box 1000, Ferrell Hall, Room 106, Institute, WV 25112-1000. *Phone:* 304-766-3032. *Toll-free phone:* 800-987-2112. *Fax:* 304-766-4158. *E-mail:* sweeneyt@wvstateu.edu.

WEST VIRGINIA UNIVERSITY

Morgantown, West Virginia **www.wvu.edu/**

- **State-supported** university, founded 1867, part of West Virginia Higher Education Policy Commission (NCA)
- **Small-town** 913-acre campus with easy access to Pittsburgh
- **Endowment** $491.1 million
- **Coed** 21,145 undergraduate students, 93% full-time, 46% women, 54% men
- **Moderately difficult** entrance level, 89% of applicants were admitted

Undergraduates 19,748 full-time, 1,397 part-time. Students come from 52 states and territories, 68 other countries, 42% are from out of state, 3% African American, 2% Asian American or Pacific Islander, 2% Hispanic American, 0.4% Native American, 2% international, 4% transferred in, 25% live on campus. *Retention:* 7% of 2006 full-time freshmen returned.

Freshmen *Admission:* 13,634 applied, 12,200 admitted, 4,731 enrolled. *Average high school GPA:* 3.3. *Test scores:* SAT critical reading scores over 500: 60%; SAT math scores over 500: 71%; ACT scores over 18: 96%; SAT critical reading scores over 600: 14%; SAT math scores over 600: 24%; ACT scores over 24: 48%; SAT critical reading scores over 700: 2%; SAT math scores over 700: 3%; ACT scores over 30: 7%.

Faculty *Total:* 1,152, 70% full-time, 64% with terminal degrees. *Student/faculty ratio:* 23:1.

Majors Accounting; advertising; aerospace, aeronautical and astronautical engineering; agricultural economics; agricultural teacher education; animal sciences; anthropology; art; art history, criticism and conservation; audiology and speech-language pathology; biology/biological sciences; business administration and management; business/managerial economics; chemical engineering; chemistry; child development; civil engineering; clinical laboratory science/medical technology; communication and journalism related; computer and information sciences and support services related; computer and information sciences related; computer engineering; computer science; criminalistics and criminal science; dental hygiene; dramatic/theater arts; economics; electrical, electronics and communications engineering; elementary education; English; environmental studies; exercise physiology; family and consumer sciences/human sciences; finance; fish/game management; foreign languages and literatures; forensic science and technology; forest/forest resources management; forestry; general studies; geography; geology/earth science; health and physical education; history; industrial engineering; interdisciplinary studies; international relations and affairs; journalism; kinesiology and exercise science; landscape architecture; liberal arts and sciences/liberal studies; management information systems; marketing/marketing management; mass communication/media; mathematics; mechanical engineering; mining and mineral engineering; music; music related; natural resources management and policy; nursing (registered nurse training); occupational therapy; parks, recreation and leisure; parks, recreation and leisure facilities management; petroleum engineering; philosophy; physical education teaching and coaching; physical therapy; physics; plant sciences related; political science and government; psychology; secondary education; social work; sociology; sport and fitness administration/management; theater literature, history and criticism; wildlife and wildlands science and management; wood science and wood products/pulp and paper technology.

Academics *Calendar:* semesters. *Degrees:* bachelor's, master's, doctoral, and first professional. *Special study options:* academic remediation for entering students, accelerated degree program, adult/continuing education programs, advanced placement credit, distance learning, double majors, English as a second language, external degree program, honors programs, independent study, internships, off-campus study, part-time degree program, services for LD students, student-designed majors, study abroad, summer session for credit. *ROTC:* Army (b), Air Force (b). *Unusual degree programs:* 3-2 education, business/foreign language, occupational therapy, physical therapy, social work.

Computers on Campus 2,500 computers/terminals are available on campus for general student use. Students can access the following: campus intranet, computer help desk, free student e-mail accounts, online (class) grades, online (class) registration, online (class) schedules. Campuswide network is available. 100% of college-owned or -operated housing units are wired for high-speed Internet access. Wireless service is available via classrooms, libraries, student centers.

Student Life *Housing:* on-campus residence required for freshman year. *Options:* coed, men-only, women-only, cooperative, disabled students. Campus housing is university owned and leased by the school. Freshman campus housing is guaranteed. *Activities and organizations:* drama/theater group, student-run newspaper, radio station, choral group, marching band, Residential Hall Association, Alpha Phi Omega Service Fraternity, WVU Greek System, Mountaineer Maniacs, Campus Crusade for Christ, national fraternities, national sororities. *Campus security:* 24-hour emergency response devices and patrols, student patrols, late-night transport/escort service, patrol officers just for housing. *Student services:* health clinic, personal/psychological counseling, women's center, legal services.

Athletics Member NCAA. All Division I except football (Division I-A). *Intercollegiate sports:* baseball M (s), basketball M (s)/W (s), cheerleading M (s)/W (s), crew W (s), cross-country running W (s), gymnastics W (s), riflery M (s)/W (s), soccer M (s)/W (s), swimming and diving M (s)/W (s), tennis W (s), track and field W (s), volleyball W (s), wrestling M (s). *Intramural sports:* basketball M (c)/W (c), crew M (c)/W (c), equestrian sports M (c)/W (c), fencing M (c)/W (c), field hockey W (c), football M, golf M (c)/W (c), ice hockey M (c), lacrosse M (c)/W (c), racquetball M/W, riflery M/W, rugby M (c)/W (c), skiing (cross-country) M (c)/W (c), skiing (downhill) M (c)/W (c), soccer M/W (c), softball W (c), swimming and diving M/W, tennis M (c)/W (c), track and field W, ultimate Frisbee M (c)/W (c), volleyball M (c)/W, wrestling M (c).

Standardized Tests *Required:* SAT or ACT (for admission).

Costs (2007–08) *Tuition:* state resident $4722 full-time, $197 per credit hour part-time; nonresident $14,600 full-time, $608 per credit hour part-time. Full-time tuition and fees vary according to location, program, and reciprocity agreements. Part-time tuition and fees vary according to course load, location, program, and reciprocity agreements. *Room and board:* $7046. Room and board charges vary according to board plan, housing facility, and location. *Payment plan:* installment. *Waivers:* senior citizens and employees or children of employees.

Financial Aid Of all full-time matriculated undergraduates who enrolled in 2007, 14,113 applied for aid, 13,802 were judged to have need, 2,814 had their need fully met. 1,402 Federal Work-Study jobs (averaging $1002). 1,200 state and other part-time jobs (averaging $1078). In 2007, 5282 non-need-based awards were made. *Average percent of need met:* 76%. *Average financial aid package:* $5870. *Average need-based loan:* $4146. *Average need-based gift aid:* $3742. *Average non-need-based aid:* $1922. *Financial aid deadline:* 3/1.

Applying *Options:* early admission, deferred entrance. *Application fee:* $25. *Required:* high school transcript, minimum 2.0 GPA. *Required for some:* essay or personal statement, minimum 2.25 GPA. *Application deadlines:* 8/1 (freshmen), 8/1 (transfers). *Notification:* continuous (transfers).

Freshman Application Contact Ms. Kim Guynn, Admissions Supervisor, West Virginia University, PO Box 6009, Morgantown, WV 26506-6009. *Phone:* 304-293-2124. *Toll-free phone:* 800-344-9881. *Fax:* 304-293-3080. *E-mail:* go2wvu@mail.wvu.edu.

WEST VIRGINIA UNIVERSITY AT PARKERSBURG

Parkersburg, West Virginia **www.wvup.edu/**

- **State-supported** primarily 2-year, founded 1961, administratively affiliated with West Virginia University
- **Small-town** 120-acre campus
- **Coed**
- **Noncompetitive** entrance level

Faculty *Student/faculty ratio:* 20:1.

Academics *Calendar:* semesters. *Degrees:* certificates, associate, and bachelor's.

Costs (2007–08) *Tuition:* state resident $1825 full-time, $76 per credit hour part-time; nonresident $6460 full-time, $269 per credit hour part-time. Full-time tuition and fees vary according to degree level and reciprocity agreements. Part-time tuition and fees vary according to degree level and reciprocity agreements.

Applying *Options:* electronic application, early admission, deferred entrance. *Required for some:* high school transcript.

Freshman Application Contact Ms. Violet Mosser, Senior Admissions Counselor, West Virginia University at Parkersburg, 300 Campus Drive, Parkersburg, WV 26101. *Phone:* 304-424-8223 Ext. 223. *Toll-free phone:* 800-WVA-WVUP. *Fax:* 304-424-8332. *E-mail:* violet.mosser@mail.wvu.edu.

WEST VIRGINIA UNIVERSITY INSTITUTE OF TECHNOLOGY

Montgomery, West Virginia **www.wvutech.edu/**

West Virginia University Institute of Technology and the Community and Technical College's home is in scenic, wild-and-wonderful West Virginia, with opportunities for snow skiing and white-water rafting nearby. Tech offers more than thirty-five majors, including engineering, engineering technologies, business, computer science, criminal justice, social sciences, nursing, dental hygiene, health service administration, psychology, and printing. In addition, Tech offers an optional five-year program in cooperative education and a practicum experience in social science. The low student-faculty ratio (16:1) ensures a personalized education for Tech students.

Freshman Application Contact Ms. Lisa Graham, Director of Admissions, West Virginia University Institute of Technology, Box 10, Old Main, Montgomery, WV 25136. *Phone:* 304-442-3167. *Toll-free phone:* 888-554-8324. *E-mail:* wvutech@wvit.wvnet.edu.

See page 2760 for the College Close-Up.

WEST VIRGINIA WESLEYAN COLLEGE

Buckhannon, West Virginia **www.wvwc.edu/**

- **Independent** comprehensive, founded 1890, affiliated with United Methodist Church
- **Small-town** 80-acre campus
- **Endowment** $45.3 million
- **Coed** 1,234 undergraduate students, 97% full-time, 54% women, 46% men
- **Moderately difficult** entrance level, 77% of applicants were admitted

Undergraduates 1,202 full-time, 32 part-time. Students come from 35 states and territories, 13 other countries, 41% are from out of state, 3% African American, 0.5% Asian American or Pacific Islander, 1% Hispanic American, 0.1% Native American, 4% international, 4% transferred in, 76% live on campus. *Retention:* 75% of 2006 full-time freshmen returned.

Freshmen *Admission:* 1,388 applied, 1,065 admitted, 402 enrolled. *Average high school GPA:* 3.32. *Test scores:* SAT critical reading scores over 500: 50%; SAT math scores over 500: 43%; SAT writing scores over 500: 44%; ACT scores over 18: 94%; SAT critical reading scores over 600: 13%; SAT math scores over 600: 10%; SAT writing scores over 600: 11%; ACT scores over 24: 48%; SAT critical reading scores over 700: 1%; ACT scores over 30: 4%.

Faculty *Total:* 138, 50% full-time, 43% with terminal degrees. *Student/faculty ratio:* 13:1.

Majors Accounting; art; art history, criticism and conservation; art teacher education; athletic training; biology/biological sciences; business administration and management; business/managerial economics; ceramic arts and ceramics; chemistry; commercial and advertising art; communication/speech communication and rhetoric; computer and information sciences; computer science; creative writing; criminal justice/law enforcement administration; dramatic/theater arts; drawing; economics; education; education (K-12); elementary education; engineering physics; English; English/language arts teacher education; environmental science; finance; fine/studio arts; health and physical education; health teacher education; history; information science/studies; international relations and affairs; kindergarten/preschool education; kinesiology and exercise science; literature; marketing/marketing management; mathematics; mathematics teacher education; middle school education; music; music teacher education; nursing (registered nurse training); painting; philosophy; philosophy and religious studies related; physical education teaching and coaching; physics; political science and government; pre-dentistry studies; pre-law studies; pre-medical studies; pre-pharmacy studies; pre-veterinary studies; psychology; public relations/image management; religious education; religious studies; secondary education; sociology; special education; special education (specific learning disabilities); speech and rhetoric; sport and fitness administration/management.

Academics *Calendar:* semesters. *Degrees:* bachelor's and master's. *Special study options:* academic remediation for entering students, adult/continuing education programs, advanced placement credit, double majors, English as a second language, honors programs, independent study, internships, off-campus study, part-time degree program, services for LD students, student-designed majors, study abroad, summer session for credit. *Unusual degree programs:* 3-2 engineering with University of Virginia, West Virginia University.

Computers on Campus Students can access the following: laptop computer required of all students. Campuswide network is available.

Student Life *Housing:* on-campus residence required through senior year. *Options:* coed, men-only, women-only, disabled students. Campus housing is university owned. Freshman campus housing is guaranteed. *Activities and organizations:* drama/theater group, student-run newspaper, radio station, choral group, Campus Activities Board, Environmental Club, American Marketing Club, Wesleyan Ambassadors, national fraternities, national sororities. *Campus security:* 24-hour emergency response devices and patrols, student patrols, late-night transport/escort service, controlled dormitory access. *Student services:* health clinic, personal/psychological counseling.

Athletics Member NCAA. All Division II. *Intercollegiate sports:* baseball M (s), basketball M (s)/W (s), cheerleading M/W, cross-country running M (s)/W (s), football M (s), golf M (s)/W (s), lacrosse M (c)/W (c), soccer M (s)/W (s), softball W (s), swimming and diving M (s)/W (s), tennis M (s)/W (s), track and field M (s)/W (s), volleyball W (s). *Intramural sports:* basketball M/W, bowling M/W, football M/W, golf M/W, racquetball M/W, soccer M/W, softball M/W, table tennis M/W, volleyball M/W, water polo M/W.

Standardized Tests *Required:* SAT or ACT (for admission). *Required for some:* SAT Subject Tests (for admission), SAT or ACT (for placement).

Costs (2007–08) *Comprehensive fee:* $27,140 includes full-time tuition ($20,980) and room and board ($6160).

Financial Aid Of all full-time matriculated undergraduates who enrolled in 2007, 986 applied for aid, 889 were judged to have need, 216 had their need fully met. In 2007, 239 non-need-based awards were made. *Average percent of need met:* 81%. *Average financial aid package:* $21,821. *Average need-based loan:* $4340. *Average need-based gift aid:* $18,704. *Average non-need-based aid:* $10,787. *Average indebtedness upon graduation:* $20,501.

Applying *Options:* electronic application, early decision, early action, deferred entrance. *Application fee:* $35. *Required:* high school transcript. *Recommended:* essay or personal statement, letters of recommendation, interview. *Notification:* continuous (freshmen), continuous (transfers).

Freshman Application Contact Director of Admission, West Virginia Wesleyan College, 59 College Avenue, Buckhannon, WV 26201. *Phone:* 304-473-8510. *Toll-free phone:* 800-722-9933. *Fax:* 304-473-8108. *E-mail:* admissions@wvwc.edu.

WHEELING JESUIT UNIVERSITY

Wheeling, West Virginia **www.wju.edu/**

- **Independent Roman Catholic (Jesuit)** comprehensive, founded 1954
- **Suburban** 65-acre campus with easy access to Pittsburgh, PA
- **Endowment** $21.9 million
- **Coed** 1,199 undergraduate students, 80% full-time, 62% women, 38% men
- **Moderately difficult** entrance level, 69% of applicants were admitted

The 2008 edition of *U.S. News & World Report*'s "America's Best Colleges" ranks Wheeling Jesuit University number 18 in the "Best Universities–Master's Category" in the South, making it the highest-ranked college or university in West Virginia for eleven consecutive years. The University moved up in its ranking from last year by three spots. WJU is home to the National Technology Transfer Center, the Center for Educational Technologies, a Challenger Learning Center, a $1.5-million soccer/track and field complex, a 100,000-square-foot recreation center, and a new $10-million science center.

Undergraduates 964 full-time, 235 part-time. Students come from 24 states and territories, 14 other countries, 63% are from out of state, 2% African American, 1% Asian American or Pacific Islander, 1% Hispanic American, 0.2% Native American, 3% international, 4% transferred in, 78% live on campus. *Retention:* 76% of 2006 full-time freshmen returned.

Freshmen *Admission:* 1,370 applied, 950 admitted, 240 enrolled. *Average high school GPA:* 3.4. *Test scores:* SAT critical reading scores over 500: 59%; SAT math scores over 500: 64%; ACT scores over 18: 96%; SAT critical reading scores over 600: 19%; SAT math scores over 600: 19%; ACT scores over 24: 40%; SAT critical reading scores over 700: 2%; SAT math scores over 700: 2%; ACT scores over 30: 2%.

Faculty *Total:* 138, 57% full-time, 51% with terminal degrees. *Student/faculty ratio:* 12:1.

Majors Accounting; athletic training; biology/biological sciences; biology teacher education; business administration and management; chemistry; chemistry teacher education; communication and journalism related; computer programming; computer science; criminal justice/law enforcement administration; digital communication and media/multimedia; education; elementary education; English; English/language arts teacher education; environmental studies; foreign language teacher education; French; French language teacher education; health/health care administration; history; history teacher education; international business/trade/commerce; international relations and affairs; journalism; liberal arts and sciences/liberal studies; management science; marketing/marketing management; mathematics; mathematics teacher education; middle school education; nuclear medical technology; nursing administration; nursing (registered nurse training); philosophy; physical therapy; physics; physics teacher education; political science and government; pre-dentistry studies; pre-law studies; pre-medical studies; pre-veterinary studies; psychology; public relations/image management; religious studies; respiratory care therapy; science teacher education; secondary education; social studies teacher education; Spanish; Spanish language teacher education; special education (specific learning disabilities); theology.

Academics *Calendar:* semesters. *Degrees:* bachelor's, master's, and doctoral. *Special study options:* academic remediation for entering students, accelerated degree program, adult/continuing education programs, advanced placement credit, distance learning, double majors, English as a second language, external degree program, honors programs, independent study, internships, off-campus study, part-time degree program, services for LD students, student-designed majors, study abroad, summer session for credit. *Unusual degree programs:* 3-2 engineering with Case Western Reserve University.

Computers on Campus 243 computers/terminals are available on campus for general student use. Students can access the following: campus intranet, computer help desk, free student e-mail accounts, online (class) grades, online (class) registration, online (class) schedules. Campuswide network is available. 100% of college-owned or -operated housing units are wired for high-speed Internet access. Wireless service is available via entire campus.

Student Life *Housing:* on-campus residence required for freshman year. *Options:* coed, men-only, women-only, disabled students. Campus housing is university owned. Freshman campus housing is guaranteed. *Activities and organizations:* drama/theater group, student-run newspaper, choral group, Student Government, Student Senate, Campus Activity Board, Inter Hall Council, Campus Ministry. *Campus security:* 24-hour emergency response devices and patrols, student patrols, late-night transport/escort service, controlled dormitory access. *Student services:* health clinic, personal/psychological counseling, women's center.

Athletics Member NCAA. All Division II. *Intercollegiate sports:* baseball M (s), basketball M (s)/W (s), cheerleading M/W, cross-country running M (s)/W (s), golf M (s)/W (s), lacrosse M (s), soccer M (s)/W (s), softball W (s), swimming and diving M (s)/W (s), track and field M (s)/W (s), volleyball W (s). *Intramural sports:* basketball M/W, cross-country running M/W, football M, ice hockey M (c), soccer M/W, softball M/W, tennis M/W, ultimate Frisbee M/W, volleyball M/W.

Standardized Tests *Required:* SAT or ACT (for admission).

Costs (2008–09) *Comprehensive fee:* $33,030 includes full-time tuition ($23,590), mandatory fees ($800), and room and board ($8640). Part-time tuition: $556 per credit hour. *College room only:* $3980.

Financial Aid Of all full-time matriculated undergraduates who enrolled in 2006, 903 applied for aid, 795 were judged to have need, 270 had their need fully met. 154 Federal Work-Study jobs (averaging $1556). 177 state and other part-time jobs (averaging $1511). In 2006, 121 non-need-based awards were made. *Average percent of need met:* 85%. *Average financial aid package:*

$19,168. *Average need-based loan:* $3980. *Average need-based gift aid:* $5709. *Average non-need-based aid:* $9608. *Average indebtedness upon graduation:* $23,218.

Applying *Options:* electronic application, deferred entrance. *Application fee:* $25. *Required:* high school transcript. *Required for some:* interview. *Recommended:* essay or personal statement, minimum 2.5 GPA, 2 letters of recommendation, interview. *Application deadlines:* rolling (freshmen), rolling (transfers). *Notification:* continuous (freshmen), continuous (transfers).

Director of Admissions Mr. Denny Bardos, Dean of Enrollment, Wheeling Jesuit University, 316 Washington Avenue, Wheeling, WV 26003. *Phone:* 304-243-2359. *Toll-free phone:* 800-624-6992 Ext. 2359. *Fax:* 304-243-2397. *E-mail:* dbardos@wju.edu.

See page 2762 for the College Close-Up.

DAVIS & ELKINS COLLEGE
ELKINS, WEST VIRGINIA

The College

A comprehensive liberal arts and sciences education is the hallmark of Davis & Elkins College. Educational programs range from the highly professional, in nursing and teaching, to the innovative, in hospitality management and tourism management, to the traditional, in the liberal arts and sciences.

There are two fraternities and sororities active on campus and a wide variety of extracurricular organizations, including the concert choir, jazz choir, radio station, theater, newspaper, yearbook, and literary magazine.

An extensive schedule of intramural and club athletics is offered for men and women in addition to a sound program of varsity sports. Intercollegiate athletics for women include basketball, cross-country, soccer, softball, and volleyball. Teams for men include baseball, basketball, cross-country, golf, and soccer. The College holds membership in the NCAA Division II and WVIAC and provides the opportunity to be part of a USCS coed ski team.

Location

The College is located in Elkins, West Virginia, rated among the top thirty small towns in America. Elkins is situated at the entrance to the Monongahela National Forest in the center of one of the nation's most prosperous and fastest-growing outdoor recreation areas. Three nearby resorts provide a variety of recreational opportunities, including camping, golfing, hiking, fishing, tennis, and cross-country and downhill skiing.

Majors and Degrees

Davis & Elkins College offers programs of study leading to bachelor's degrees in accounting, art, art education, biology, chemistry, communication, computer science, criminology, elementary education, English, environmental science, exercise science, health education, history, hospitality and tourism management, management, management information systems, marketing, mathematics, music, nursing, physical education, political science, psychology and human services, recreation management and tourism, religion and philosophy, religious education, secondary education, sociology, Spanish, sports management, theater arts, and theater education.

Preprofessional programs prepare students for admission to schools of medicine, veterinary science, dentistry, church ministry, pharmacy, and law. An additional area of study is available in forestry (3-2 bachelor's-master's programs offered by special arrangement with the State University of New York College of Environmental Science and Forestry at Syracuse).

Associate degrees are available in accounting, business, computer business systems, criminal justice, hospitality, and nursing.

Academic Programs

Davis & Elkins College emphasizes a strong liberal arts and sciences foundation for all students. The Contract Degree Program provides opportunities to design individual programs of study under close faculty supervision. An honors program challenges the more advanced students. The William James Career, Academic and Personal Services (CAPS) Center provides academic, personal, and career support for all students. Included in the CAPS Center is the Supported Learning Program for students with documented learning disabilities.

Off-Campus Programs

Off-campus and independent experiences include cultural studies of the Caribbean, England, Italy, Scotland, and Spain; marine biology courses in Florida; and internships and practicums at several sites throughout Maryland, New Jersey, New York, Pennsylvania, Virginia, West Virginia, and Washington, D.C.

Academic Facilities

An arts center/auditorium complex has a 1,300-seat auditorium for concerts, plays, and other cultural events. The complex also houses the music, art, and theater departments, a swimming pool, and the fitness center. A science center accommodates the business and natural science divisions. The center also contains a planetarium, rooftop greenhouse, computer center, and several microcomputer laboratories. The Booth Library opened in 1992 with a capacity of 300,000 volumes. The library includes a fully equipped media center with computer capabilities and an online computer catalog. One-day calls for materials can be made to three other Mountain State Association of Colleges libraries. Students may also use the resources of the West Virginia University library in Morgantown, West Virginia.

Costs

The comprehensive tuition and fees charge for 2007–08 was $18,746, and room and board costs were $6350. The tuition and fees cover the full cost of student publications, health service, laboratory classes, the Student Union, and athletic contests.

Financial Aid

Scholarships, grants, loans, and campus employment are offered to help students meet financial obligations; a student may be given one award or a combination of several awards. Most financial aid is based on need, but academic, honors, athletic, and performance scholarships are also available; 93 percent of the student body receives some form of financial assistance. Students applying for financial assistance should complete the Free Application for Federal Student Aid before March 1. Forms may be obtained from the Office of Financial Planning.

Faculty

The College has 45 full-time faculty members, of whom 82 percent hold terminal degrees. They include distinguished Fulbright scholars, authors, and lecturers. A student-faculty ratio of 12:1 provides students with ongoing opportunities to interact with instructors on a personal level.

Student Government

Davis & Elkins recognizes through its special governance system the value of student involvement in developing the academic and social policies of the College. Students work alongside members of the faculty and administration in planning and deciding policies in all basic areas of decision making (with the exception of finances) that affect students. Students participating in this process are elected to the Student Assembly by their classmates.

Admission Requirements

Davis & Elkins College seeks to enroll students with academic and personal qualities that indicate potential for intellectual, social, and spiritual growth. A basic premise of the admissions policy is that all applicants are reviewed individually to determine if they are capable of successfully meeting their responsibilities as a Davis & Elkins student and benefiting from the personalized educational experience the College provides. The Enrollment Management Committee establishes guidelines for admission that reflect the College's desire to identify academically capable students who demonstrate potential for further achievement; who are active at school and in the community, with a record of service; and who represent diverse cultures and backgrounds. Freshman applicants are required to submit scores from either the ACT or SAT and an official high school transcript that demonstrates a solid preparation for college-level work. Transfer applicants are also required to submit official transcripts from all colleges and universities attended. Exceptions may be made to high school unit requirements, with the provision that the student complete specific college-level course work. High school students must achieve a minimum GPA of 2.3 (ninth through twelfth grade) to be admitted to Davis & Elkins College. Students who submit a transcript with a cumulative GPA between 2.0 and 2.3 are considered for conditional admission to the College. High school and transfer students with a cumulative GPA below 2.0 are not admitted except under unusual circumstances and then are only admitted under an academic contract.

Davis & Elkins admits students regardless of race, color, sex, handicap, religious affiliation, or national or ethnic origin.

Application and Information

Along with the College application form, prospective students must submit a complete transcript of college-preparatory studies. SAT or ACT scores are also required. In addition to regular freshman admission, early and deferred admission plans are available. Transfers may be admitted during both the August and January terms. They must have maintained a minimum overall average of C at all colleges attended and must submit satisfactory personal credentials.

Davis & Elkins follows a system of rolling admission (not applicable to international student applicants). Candidates whose files are completed during the early part of their senior year receive decisions first. Financial aid candidates are requested to complete the application process as early in the calendar year as possible. Admitted students have until May 1 or two weeks after admission (whichever is later) to present the required advance payment deposit that holds their place in the entering freshman class.

For further information, students should contact:

Office of Admissions
Davis & Elkins College
100 Campus Drive
Elkins, West Virginia 26241-3996
Phone: 304-637-1230
800-624-3157 Ext. 1230 (toll-free)
E-mail: admiss@davisandelkins.edu
Web site: http://www.davisandelkins.edu

Discover and excel at Davis & Elkins College.

FAIRMONT STATE UNIVERSITY

FAIRMONT, WEST VIRGINIA

The University

Fairmont State University (FSU) has an enrollment of approximately 4,000 students. Founded as a private school in 1865, the University is located in Fairmont, West Virginia.

The mission of FSU is to provide opportunities for individuals to achieve their professional and personal goals and discover roles for responsible citizenship that promote the common good. FSU includes Pierpont Community and Technical College, which has a mission to provide opportunities for learning, teaching, training, and further education that enrich the lives of individuals and promote the economic growth of its service region and the state. FSU offers more than ninety baccalaureate programs/concentrations as well as graduate programs. Graduate programs are available in education, criminal justice, and nursing.

The main campus features twenty-two buildings on more than 90 acres. From the historic administration building, Hardway Hall, to the brand-new Bryant Place residence hall, the facilities are a blend of tradition and technology. Facilities also include the Robert C. Byrd National Aerospace Education Center in Bridgeport, West Virginia, and the Gaston Caperton Center in Clarksburg, West Virginia.

The student center, called the Falcon Center, features 7,000 square feet of fitness equipment; five versatile courts for indoor sports; space for fitness classes; four-lane pool with a whirlpool, sauna, and outdoor sunning deck; four-lane cushioned jogging/walking track; game rooms; dining facilities; and more.

Fairmont State is a member of the NCAA Division II and the West Virginia Intercollegiate Athletic Conference. Varsity programs for men are offered in football, basketball, baseball, cross-country, golf, tennis, and swimming. The intercollegiate athletic programs for women include tennis, golf, basketball, volleyball, swimming, softball, and cross-country.

Fairmont State offers more than eighty clubs, organizations, student publications, honoraries, sororities, and fraternities, as well as wide range of intramural sports. Many fine arts performances and exhibits are planned each semester. Nationally prominent speakers are invited to the campus.

Location

Fairmont, a city of more than 19,000 in North-Central West Virginia, is the county seat of Marion County. Located along Interstate 79 approximately 90 miles south of Pittsburgh, Fairmont and the University are easily accessible to all travelers. Shopping malls, restaurants, cultural entertainment, and nightlife are easily found throughout the area.

West Virginia's natural treasures—mountains, rivers, waterfalls, wildlife, wildflowers, clean air, and vast tracts of national forest—are all close at hand. In and near Fairmont are popular trails for hiking and biking, rivers for white-water rafting, excellent spots for rock and mountain climbing, camping, fishing, and some of the best skiing in the East.

Majors and Degrees

FSU offers more than ninety baccalaureate programs/concentrations. For a complete list of majors offered, students should visit the University's Web site (http://www.fairmontstate.edu).

FSU offers more than ninety baccalaureate as well as grad

Academic Programs

Programs are offered in the following areas: business, education, health, fine arts, health careers, language, science, mathematics, social science, and technology.

The Honors Program encourages and instructs highly motivated students through general honors classes, advanced seminars, and an interdisciplinary colloquium. Students conduct independent scholarship, research assignments, internships, and creative projects. Students have the opportunity for field trips, lectures, and cultural events.

Academic Facilities

The Ruth Ann Musick Library has a collection of more than 200,000 books and more than 15,000 bound periodicals, microfilms, and other materials, including a large collection of audiotapes and videotapes. The library also has sites at the Caperton Center and the National Aerospace Education Center.

FSU's state-of-the-art technology infrastructure includes thirty computer labs and high-speed network connections that are accessible from the library, classrooms, and every residence hall room, as well as the most up-to-date teaching software.

FSU is also home to the Frank and Jane Gabor West Virginia Folklife Center, which is dedicated to the identification, preservation, and perpetuation of the region's rich cultural heritage through academic studies, educational programs, festivals, performances, and publications. The center is part of the FSU Department of Language and Literature.

Costs

For the 2007–08 academic year, in-state students at Fairmont State paid $2328 in tuition and fees, $2995 for room and board, and $450 for books and supplies, for a total of $5773 each semester. For out-of-state students, tuition and fees were $4978, room and board were $2995, and books and supplies were $450, for a total of $8423 each semester.

Financial Aid

About 86 percent of Fairmont State students receive some form of aid. Guidelines and forms for West Virginia and out-of-state residents are available from high school guidance counselors or the Fairmont State Financial Aid Office. Fairmont State awards more than $36 million in financial assistance each year.

Faculty

FSU employs more than 200 full-time faculty members, ensuring a student-teacher ratio of 17:1. Dedicated academic advisers and faculty members work one-on-one with students to meet their individual needs.

Student Government

Student Government actively seeks to supplement the academic atmosphere with intellectual, cultural, and social activities. Student Government members are involved in all aspects of life on campus and work cooperatively with the administration.

Admission Requirements

First-time freshmen who wish to apply for admission to Fairmont State University must submit an application for admission; an official high school transcript or GED certificate (sent by the high school or the Department of Education), with a GPA of 2.0 or higher; ACT or SAT scores (at least 18 on the ACT or 870 on the SAT); a college transcript (if college credit was earned during high school); immunization records (if the applicant was born after January 1, 1957); and a statement of activities (if the applicant has been out of high school more than six months). Students applying for transfer admission must submit an application for admission; a college transcript from accredited institutions, showing a minimum GPA of 2.0; an official high school transcript and ACT/SAT scores if there are fewer than 24 earned credit hours being transferred; immunization records (if the applicant was born after January 1, 1957); and a statement of activities. Postbaccalaureate students who are seeking another degree must submit an application for admission, official college transcripts, a statement of activities, and immunization records (if the applicant was born after January 1, 1957).

Transient students (students enrolled at another school and returning to that institution) must submit an application for admission and a course approval form (from their Registrar's office).

Application and Information

On a Saturday each spring and fall, Fairmont State schedules a Campus Visitation Day so potential students and their family members and friends can visit the campus and attend information sessions on admissions, financial aid, and living on campus. An Academic Fair is also scheduled so students can meet with faculty members about the academic schools and departments.

Campus tours through the Office of Admissions are available Mondays through Fridays. To set up a tour, students should call 800-641-5678 Ext. 2 (toll-free) or 304-367-4892. Tours can also be scheduled online at the University's Web site (http://www.fairmontstate.edu).

For further information, students may contact:

Office of Admissions
Fairmont State University
1201 Locust Avenue
Fairmont, West Virginia 26554
Phone: 304-367-4892 (admissions)
800-641-5678 (toll-free)
304-367-4213 (financial aid)
304-367-4216 (residence life)
304-367-4000 (campus operator)
304-367-4026 (Gaston Caperton Center)
304-842-8300 (Robert C. Byrd National Aerospace Education Center)
304-367-4200 (TDD)
Fax: 304-367-4789
E-mail: admit@fairmontstate.edu
Web site: http://www.fairmontstate.edu

The Falcon Center, centrally located on FSU's main campus. provides an environment where students and faculty and staff members can comfortably interact while enjoying a variety of fitness and wellness programs, eating areas, and places to take a break between classes. The campus bookstore, Aladdin food services, the Nickel (a convenience store and fast food restaurant), and game room are available. The building also features a pool and sauna, a large fitness area, an indoor track, and a conference center.

COLLEGE DATA CENTER • WEST VIRGINIA

MARSHALL UNIVERSITY

HUNTINGTON, WEST VIRGINIA

The University

Marshall University is a public institution, established as Marshall Academy in 1837 and granted university status in 1961. Assigned a major role as an urban-oriented university by the West Virginia Higher Education Policy Commission, it is devoted to offering both undergraduate and graduate courses of study to accommodate both full-time students and employed persons who wish to pursue studies on a part-time basis. The health-care expertise of the medical staff and faculty has given rise to a concentration of undergraduate programs in allied health technologies and sciences. The school has been recognized as a "best value" based on academic quality and moderate cost.

The Graduate School offers various master's degree programs, a Ph.D. in biomedical sciences, and a Psy.D. in psychology; the M.D. is available at the Marshall University School of Medicine. Marshall offers a master's degree in adult and technical education; art; biological sciences; biomedical sciences; business administration; chemistry; communication disorders; communication studies; counseling; criminal justice; early childhood, elementary, or secondary education; educational specialist studies; engineering; English; environmental science; exercise science; family and consumer science; forensic science; geography; health and physical education; health-care administration; history; humanities; industrial and employee relations; information systems; journalism; leadership studies; mathematics; music; nursing; physical science; political science; psychology; reading education; safety; sociology; special education; teaching; and technology management.

Marshall also offers the Ed.D. degree in educational leadership. The Ed.D. degree in curriculum and instruction is offered in cooperation with West Virginia University. A master's degree in forestry and in environmental management is offered in cooperation with Duke University.

All of the University's academic programs are highly regarded by professional schools and educators and by business, industry, and government. The University is fully accredited by the North Central Association of Colleges and Schools. AACSB International–The Association to Advance Collegiate Schools of Business accredits the Lewis College of Business.

Eighty percent of Marshall's students are residents of West Virginia. Approximately 2,200 live in campus housing. The informal and relaxed atmosphere of ten traditional and suite residence halls, single sex and coed, contributes an important focus to life at Marshall. The University offers more than 180 student organizations that provide excellent opportunities for extracurricular involvement. Twelve national fraternities and seven national sororities represent social organizations, with the majority having houses. Clubs, organizations, intramural athletics, theater, musical ensembles, student government, religious groups, and Black United Students provide many cultural and social activities. The University also offers a cooperative work-study program, remediation services, academic assistance, counseling, and job placement. Marshall is a member of the NCAA IA Conference USA. Intercollegiate sports include men's baseball, basketball, cheerleading, cross-country, football, golf, soccer, and track and field and women's basketball, cheerleading, cross-country, golf, soccer, softball, swimming and diving, tennis, track and field, and volleyball.

Location

Huntington, with a population of 55,000, is the second-largest urban center in West Virginia. It is located on the banks of the Ohio River in the Tri-State region, bordering eastern Kentucky and southern Ohio. The area has many good shopping centers, theaters, parks, swimming pools, golf courses, churches, and art galleries. Huntington's Big Sandy Superstore Arena is host to some of the top names in entertainment. Many of these activities are within walking distance of the Marshall University campus. The city and the University work effectively together to provide the best educational and cultural opportunities possible. A regional airport, Amtrak, and Greyhound Bus Line provide transportation to and from the city.

Majors and Degrees

The Bachelor of Arts (B.A.) degree is offered in basic humanities, classical or modern languages (French, German, Latin, and Spanish), communication disorders, communication studies, counseling, criminal justice, economics, education (elementary and secondary), English, family and consumer science, geography, geology, history, international affairs, journalism and mass communications, multidisciplinary studies, physical education, political science, psychology, and sociology. The B.A. degree is also available through the Board of Regents External Degree Program. The Bachelor of Science (B.S.) degree is offered in biological science, botany, chemistry, computer science, cytotechnology, dietetics, environmental biology, geography, geology, integrated science and technology, mathematics, microbiology, park resources and leisure services, physics, physiology/molecular biology, safety technology, and zoology. The Bachelor of Business Administration (B.B.A.) degree is awarded in accounting, economics, finance, management, management information systems, and marketing. The Bachelor of Fine Arts (B.F.A.) is offered in music, theater, and visual arts. The Bachelor of Science in Medical Technology (B.S.M.T.), the Bachelor of Science in Nursing (B.S.N.), and the Bachelor of Social Work (B.S.W.) degrees are also offered.

Academic Programs

Each undergraduate division specifies its own sequence of requirements, but all baccalaureate degree students must complete a minimum of 128 credit hours with an overall GPA of at least 2.0. All students must complete general requirements in humanities, mathematics, science, and social sciences. To qualify as full-time, the undergraduate student must carry at least 12 credit hours per semester. Permission from the academic dean is required for students who wish to enroll for 19 hours or more in one semester.

Students may receive credit through Advanced Placement or College-Level Examination Program tests. Marshall University also offers the U.S. Army Reserve Officers' Training Corps (ROTC) program and an honors program.

The Marshall Plan for Quality Undergraduate Education went into effect in 1995. Designed to provide Marshall graduates with a competitive advantage, it includes science/computer literacy, global studies, intensified writing courses, and a capstone experience for all baccalaureate students entering at that time and later.

Off-Campus Programs

Marshall University participates in the following special programs: Public Service Internship, Semester Abroad Program, National Student Exchange, and Academic Common Market.

Academic Facilities

Facilities on the Marshall University campus include the Center for Academic Excellence; the Center for the Fine and Performing Arts; the Birke Art Gallery; the H.E.L.P. Center, for those with learning disabilities; the Center for International Programs; the Psychology Clinic; the Fitness and Wellness Center; the Speech and Hearing Clinic; the Writing Center; the Learning Resource Center; language, mathematics, chemistry, and physics laboratories; WPBY-TV and WMUL-FM studios; and the Center for Academic Support. The John Deaver Drinko Library, an ultramodern library and information center that opened in 1998, provides 390 computer stations, group-study rooms, a reading lab, a 24-hour computer lab, and a café among its many features.

Costs

Tuition and fees for the 2007–08 academic year were $4360 for West Virginia residents, $7592 for Metro students (residents of the counties adjacent to Huntington, West Virginia), and $11,264 for out-of-state students. Room and board were $6818, and books averaged $1000.

Financial Aid

Approximately 60 percent of the student body receives some type of financial assistance. Students who are admitted by February 1 and submit the application for financial aid by March 1 are considered for some form of assistance. Marshall University participates in the following programs: Federal Pell Grant, Federal Supplemental Educational Opportunity Grant, West Virginia Higher Education Grant, Federal Work-Study Program, Federal Stafford Student Loans, Federal Perkins Loans, and Federal PLUS Program. Scholarships of $500 are guaranteed to students with a minimum ACT composite score of 20 (or an SAT composite score of at least 930) and a minimum 3.2 GPA. Scholarships of $750 are awarded to freshmen with either a 3.2–3.49 GPA and a minimum ACT composite score of 25 (or an SAT composite score of at least 1130) or a minimum 3.5 GPA with a minimum ACT composite score of 23 (or an SAT composite score of at least 1050). Scholarships of $1250 are guaranteed to students with a minimum ACT composite score of 25 (or an SAT composite score of at least 1140) and a minimum 3.5 GPA; a tuition waiver and $1250 are guaranteed to students with a minimum ACT composite score of 30 (or an SAT composite score of at least 1340) and a minimum 3.5 GPA. There is no separate application for scholarships at the University; however, a student's application for admission must be received in the Office of Admissions by January 31 to be eligible for an academic scholarship.

Faculty

Marshall University has 666 full-time faculty members; 79 percent hold a doctorate or terminal degree in their field. The student-faculty ratio is approximately 17:1.

Student Government

Marshall University sponsors the Student Government Association (SGA), a student-oriented organization that ensures practical and creative interaction among those students interested in administration and campus politics. The SGA mimics the federal government with three branches containing representatives from all academic colleges. All officers and representatives serve from the spring of their election year until the following spring. The executive members receive a small monthly salary. Only full-time students with an overall GPA of 2.25 or higher are eligible for office. The goal of the SGA is to provide students with a number of important services, including off-campus housing assistance, a student consumer liaison, and various entertainment opportunities. The SGA appoints students in the University community to various planning and organizational positions and committees on campus. The SGA also accepts requests for special project funding from recognized groups or clubs throughout the year. The SGA is active and viable at Marshall University, helping students and the University to grow together.

Admission Requirements

The average ACT and SAT scores of entering freshmen at Marshall University are 22.8 and 990, respectively, and the average cumulative high school GPA is 3.39. Students seeking a baccalaureate degree must have the following high school preparation: 4 years of English, 3 years of social studies, 3 years of science (2 years must be in a laboratory science), and 3 years of mathematics (including algebra I and one higher-level course). In addition, they must graduate from an approved high school with either a minimum GPA of 2.0 and a minimum composite score on the ACT of 19 (a minimum combined score of 910 on the SAT). Applications from transfer students and nontraditional or returning students are welcome. Transfer applicants are required to have earned a cumulative GPA of at least 2.0 (C) on all previous college work. Academically superior high school juniors or seniors may be admitted to Marshall University on a part-time basis, provided they have a GPA of at least 3.0 (B) and the recommendation of a high school counselor or principal. Campus visits for prospective students are conducted through the Welcome Center by appointment, Monday through Friday at 10 a.m. and on some Saturdays. Students may call the Welcome Center at 304-696-6833 or Marshall's toll-free number to make arrangements.

Admission to the University is not necessarily admission to a particular college or curriculum within the University. Applicants for the nursing program should apply a year in advance and show satisfactory scores on the ACT; an interview is required. Entry into the music program requires an audition.

Application and Information

Applicants to the freshman class should submit the Undergraduate Application for Admission and have their high school counselor or principal forward a transcript of grades to the Office of Admissions. Scores on the ACT/SAT should be forwarded to Marshall (code number 4526 on the ACT form, code 5396 on the SAT form). High school students who have not been admitted to Marshall and who have their ACT/SAT scores forwarded to the Office of Admissions are sent an application. The student should complete the application and take it to the high school counselor, who should then certify the student's GPA and return the form to Marshall. Transfer applicants should submit an application and request that official transcripts from each college previously attended be forwarded to the Office of Admissions. Prospective students are notified as soon as action is taken on their application. For more information, students should contact:

Office of Recruitment
Marshall University
One John Marshall Drive
Huntington, West Virginia 25755-2026-1

Phone: 304-696-6833
1-877-GOHERD1 (464-3731; toll-free)
Fax: 304-696-6858
E-mail: recruitment@marshall.edu
Web site: http://www.marshall.edu

Drinko Library.

COLLEGE DATA CENTER • WEST VIRGINIA

MOUNTAIN STATE UNIVERSITY

BECKLEY, WEST VIRGINIA

The University

Mountain State University (MSU) is a private not-for-profit university located in the scenic highlands of southern West Virginia. MSU is dedicated to providing students with an outstanding professionally oriented education, firmly rooted in the liberal arts, in a relaxed environment that promotes academic excellence, self-esteem, personal growth, cultural enrichment, and aesthetic awareness. Mountain State University serves more than 5,000 students a year from across the United States and around the world, with degree programs offered at the associate, bachelor's, and master's levels. It is accredited by the Higher Learning Commission of the North Central Association of Colleges and Schools (telephone: 312-263-0456; World Wide Web: http://www.ncahigherlearningcommission.org).

The School of Arts and Sciences offers degrees in a wide range of professional fields, including criminal justice, forensic investigation, and social work. It also offers individualized degrees in general studies and liberal studies.

The School of Business and Technology prepares students for careers in traditional areas of business administration and accounting and in specialized fields, including computer science and information technology, culinary arts, legal studies, office administration, and paralegal studies. These programs help students develop the managerial and technical skills they need to identify and respond to complex challenges in business.

The School of Health Sciences prepares students for a wide range of health-care professions, including nursing, occupational therapy assistant studies, physical therapist assistant studies, and health studies. A prerequisite physician assistant studies curriculum prepares undergraduate students for the University's entry-level master's program. These health sciences programs prepare students to apply for certifications and licensures required for clinical practice and qualify them to pursue more advanced degrees in their specific field or a related discipline.

The School of Leadership and Professional Development offers a bachelor's degree completion program in organizational leadership and a master's degree program in strategic leadership. Both are available in a format that requires one evening a week in a classroom or online meeting, with individual assignments and group projects between meetings. Optional undergraduate concentrations in criminal justice leadership and hospitality leadership are available.

At the graduate level, MSU offers degree programs in criminal justice administration, health science, interdisciplinary studies, nursing, and physician assistant studies in addition to the previously discussed strategic leadership program. Some graduate programs provide for flexible study and distance learning with no residency requirement.

Student services include orientation, academic counseling, and a tutoring center. A variety of student organizations and activities are based on campus, and a student union is centrally located on campus.

All Mountain State University students receive a complimentary membership to the Beckley–Raleigh County YMCA, located within easy walking distance of the campus, which provides an indoor pool and track, racquetball and basketball courts, a well-equipped fitness center with Nautilis and free weight areas, and a variety of classes, including spinning and Pilates. The University fields intercollegiate teams in NAIA Division I men's basketball and soccer and women's soccer, softball, and volleyball; the basketball team regularly appears in tournament play and won the 2004 national championship.

Hogan Hall, a 192-bed residence hall, provides two-bedroom suites and apartment-style living in a central campus location. Renovated Hogan Hall's accommodations include high-speed Internet connections, lounges, study rooms, and laundry facilities. Meal plans are available for students to take advantage of campus dining facilities.

Location

Mountain State University is located in Beckley, West Virginia, a small metropolitan area in the heart of the southern West Virginia highlands. The campus is within walking distance of downtown restaurants, retail stores, and services. Beckley is about an hour away by car from the state capital of Charleston; most major cities in the eastern United States are within a day's drive.

City, state, and national parks provide breathtaking panoramas as well as perfect settings for outdoor activities that range from mountain biking and rock climbing to hiking, picnicking, and swimming. In season, outdoor enthusiasts enjoy white-water rafting on the famed Gauley and New Rivers or hit the slopes of nearby ski areas. All are within a 20-minute drive of the campus.

Selected degree programs and courses are available through MSU's branch campuses, located in Martinsburg, West Virginia (greater D.C. area); Center Township, Pennsylvania (greater Pittsburgh area); and Orlando, Florida. Selected programs and courses are also available at the Hickory Metro Higher Education Center in Hickory, North Carolina.

Majors and Degrees

Bachelor's and associate degrees are offered in accounting; applied technology, aviation; biology; business administration (concentrations in finance, hospitality, management, and marketing); business studies; computer networking; computer science; criminal justice (concentrations in corrections management, homeland security, and police science); culinary arts; diagnostic medical sonography; elementary and secondary teacher preparation; emergency medical services; environmental studies; fire science; forensic investigation; general engineering; general studies; health science education; health studies; human resource management; information technology; information technology/Web site design; legal studies; legal studies/paralegal; liberal studies; mining/environmental engineering; medical assisting; nursing; occupational therapy assistant studies; office administration (medical and secretarial concentrations); organizational leadership (optional concentrations in criminal justice leadership and hospitality leadership); physical therapist assistant studies; psychology; psychology of early childhood development; radiologic technology; religious studies; respiratory care; social work; and wildlife management.

Academic Programs

To earn a bachelor's degree, students must complete a minimum of 120 semester hours, including 36 hours of general studies, and meet all program requirements. Degree requirements vary on some branch campuses in compliance with state regulations. Many programs include an internship or practicum that provides hands-on experience and employment credentials.

Students in associate degree programs must complete a minimum of 64 hours, including 24 hours of general studies, and meet all program requirements.

MSU grants credit for nontraditional course work and demonstrated college-level learning. Students gain credit through transfer, Internet, and independent study courses; proficiency examinations, including the College-Level Examination Program (CLEP) and Advanced Placement exams; demonstration of prior experiential learning; and independent study. Degree completion programs allow adult students who have already earned at least 40 credit hours to earn a bachelor's degree on a compressed schedule, and the Spectrum program of integrated general education helps students complete general education requirements conveniently.

Academic Facilities

Mountain State University's rapidly growing main campus currently encompasses ten main structures and four smaller buildings. The newest, Wisemen Hall, opened in fall 2007 and houses health sciences classrooms and lab space in addition to the University's testing center.

Academic facilities housed within the University's Robert C. Byrd Learning Resource Center, or LRC, include a library and media center. The library has holdings of more than 95,500 titles and networked access to more than one million titles. The core collection is supported by an online catalog and supplemented by electronic resources that include ProQuest, Cumulative Index to Nursing and Allied Health Literature (CINAHL), Social Issues Resources Index (SIRS), EBSCOhost, Westlaw, Wilson Web, NewsBank, and MEDLINE.

Computer stations include current software and broadband Internet access. Specialized learning resources include multimedia classrooms, a video lab, computer-assisted instruction, and science laboratories.

Costs

Mountain State University provides the educational advantages of a private institution at a financially accessible cost. Full-time tuition and fees for the 2007–08 academic year were $8100, or $270 for each credit hour. Tuition varies for some programs, and additional laboratory and clinical fees are sometimes required.

Financial Aid

Eligible students receive Federal Pell Grants, Federal Supplemental Educational Opportunity Grants, West Virginia Higher Education Grants, Federal Work-Study, and Federal Stafford Student Loans. Students must submit the Free Application for Federal Student Aid (FAFSA) for determination of eligibility. A number of scholarships based on academic merit and/or financial need are available to students. Available state loan programs vary for branch campus students outside West Virginia.

Faculty

More than 350 full- and part-time faculty members provide students with personalized, high-quality instruction. Approximately one third of the University's full-time faculty members hold earned doctorates or other terminal degrees.

Student Government

The Student Government Association (SGA) links students with the University's administration and faculty. Governed by student-elected officers, the SGA works to improve the quality of student life, develops leadership skills in students, and provides representation of student views and opinions on University issues.

Admission Requirements

The University's overall admissions policy is open, although some programs have more competitive requirements. Prospective students who have graduated from an accredited high school or received a General Educational Development (GED) certificate are eligible to apply. Applications are welcome from all qualified students regardless of age, sex, religion, race, color, creed, national origin, or disability.

Application and Information

Students apply for undergraduate admission by submitting an application; an official high school transcript, home schooling document, or GED certificate; and a housing application or exemption form with the $25 application fee. Transfer applicants must also submit official transcripts for previous college-level course work. Applications are accepted on a rolling basis, and applicants are notified of their acceptance status as soon as the application process is completed. ACT or SAT scores are not required for University admission but are recommended for placement purposes. Competitive programs or courses may have minimum ACT or SAT scores, placement tests, recommended application dates, or other requirements.

Mountain State University encourages prospective students and their families to arrange a campus visit. Campus tours and individual meetings are available.

For an application or more information, students should contact:

Mountain State University Information Center
Box 9003
Beckley, West Virginia 25802-9003
Phone: 304-929-INFO (4636)
866-FOR-MSU1 (866-766-6067) (toll-free)
Web site: http://www.mountainstate.edu

SHEPHERD UNIVERSITY

SHEPHERDSTOWN, WEST VIRGINIA

The University

Shepherd University, founded in 1871, is a competitive, four-year, state-supported institution offering more than seventy undergraduate fields of study in the liberal arts and sciences, business, and teacher education. Graduate programs are offered in ten fields. Shepherd is one of the fastest-growing institutions in West Virginia. There are approximately 4,100 students on the 323-acre campus; 56 percent come from West Virginia, and the remaining 44 percent represent forty-nine other states and sixteen countries.

The University prides itself on its friendly and helpful atmosphere and the individual contact the students receive as a result of small classes. On campus there are over seventy organizations, ranging from national fraternities and sororities to community service groups, from professional organizations to student government. Students are encouraged to join and interact with all of the groups that interest them.

Shepherd University also offers both men's and women's intercollegiate sports. The men's program consists of baseball, basketball, football, golf, soccer, and tennis. The women's sports program consists of basketball, cheerleading, soccer, softball, tennis, and volleyball. Men and women compete in the NCAA Division II program and the West Virginia Intercollegiate Athletic Conference. An NCLC club lacrosse program for both men and women and a men's wrestling club are available. For students who are not interested in playing intercollegiate sports, an extensive intramural and recreation program is also available.

Students are housed on campus in fourteen residence halls. Seven offer suite arrangements, with 4 students sharing two bedrooms, a living room, and a bath. Five buildings house students in traditional 2-student dorm rooms. All buildings are coeducational. Two apartment buildings are available for upperclass and graduate students.

Location

Shepherd University is located in historic Shepherdstown (founded in 1730), a small community on the banks of the Potomac River with a population of approximately 7,000. Shepherdstown is the oldest town in West Virginia and the site of the launching of the first successful steamboat in 1787 by James Rumsey. Shepherdstown hosted the Syrian-Israeli Peace Talks in January 2000. Other historic landmarks located within 8 miles of the campus include the Antietam National Battlefield Park, Harpers Ferry National Historical Park, and the Chesapeake and Ohio Canal Historical Park and Trail. The area is rural, and fishing, horseback riding, hunting, snow skiing, and waterskiing are available for recreation. Communication and cooperation between the community and the University are very good, and many cultural events are sponsored jointly.

The University is a 10-minute drive from Martinsburg, West Virginia; 15 minutes from Charles Town and Harpers Ferry, West Virginia; 25 minutes from Hagerstown and Frederick, Maryland; 45 minutes from Leesburg and Winchester, Virginia; and 70 minutes from Washington, D.C., and Baltimore, Maryland.

Majors and Degrees

Shepherd University offers the Bachelor of Arts, Bachelor of Fine Arts, and Bachelor of Science degrees in accounting, art (graphic design, painting, photography, printmaking, and sculpture), biology (traditional and ecological science), business administration (entrepreneurship and small-business management, financial planning, general business, human resources, management, and marketing), chemistry (biochemistry, environmental chemistry, and traditional), computer and information sciences (computer programming and information systems, computer science, and networking and data communications), economics, elementary education, English, environmental studies (aquatic science, environmental engineering, environmental science, historic preservation, and resource management), family and consumer science, history (Civil War and nineteenth-century American history, public history, and traditional), mass communication, mathematics (engineering, industrial, and traditional), middle school education (English 5–9, math 5–9, and social studies 5–9), music (music theater, performance, piano pedagogy, and theory/composition), political science (traditional and international concentration), psychology, recreation and leisure studies (athletic coaching/officiating, commercial recreation/tourism, fitness/exercise science, sport communication, sport and event management, and therapeutic recreation), secondary education (art, biology, chemistry, English, family and consumer science, general science, health, mathematics, music, physical education, social studies, and Spanish), and Spanish. Also offered are the Bachelor of Science in Nursing, Bachelor of Science in Social Work, and Regents Bachelor of Arts.

Preprofessional programs are available in the fields of dentistry, law, medicine, pharmacy, and veterinary science.

An early acceptance to the medical, dental, and pharmacy school programs with the West Virginia University School of Health Sciences is available predominantly to West Virginia and occasionally to non–West Virginia preprofessional students.

Academic Programs

All candidates for the baccalaureate degree must complete a minimum of 128 semester hours of course work with a minimum 2.0 overall average and a minimum 2.0 average in their major. Students in teacher education must have a minimum 2.5 average in their elementary education or secondary education field. The 128 semester hours include a general studies core, consisting of 19 hours in the humanities, 11 hours in science and mathematics, 15 hours in social sciences, and 2 hours in physical education.

Student internships and practicums are required or recommended in the following areas of study: education, graphic design, mass communications, nursing, photography, psychology, recreation and leisure services, and social work. Biology and chemistry majors may utilize such nearby research facilities as the U.S. Fish and Wildlife Service National Education Training Center, the National Cancer Research Center at Fort Dietrick, the National Fisheries Center at Leetown, and the Appalachian Fruit Research Center at Bardane for their directed research projects. CIS majors may do their internships with the IRS National Computer Center, the ATF Firearms Identification Center, or the Coast Guard Vessel Identification Center located in Martinsburg. The Washington Gateway and Washington Semester programs provide formal internships in Washington, D.C. Co-op programs may be arranged in most major fields.

Academic Facilities

Academic facilities on the Shepherd University campus include an open-stack library with a collection of 500,000 materials; nine academic buildings housing classrooms and laboratories; a new center for contemporary arts; a new nursing education center that features specialized classrooms, labs, and conference areas;

and a comprehensive health, physical education, and athletic complex. The nearby libraries, museums, and cultural and research centers of the Washington, D.C., metropolitan area are also available for research and study.

Costs

For 2007–08, tuition and fees were $4564 per year for West Virginia residents and $12,036 per year for out-of-state students. Average room and board charges are $6714 per year. Books and supplies are about $1000 per year. Additional expenses vary, depending on a student's personal tastes, but are estimated to be between $40 and $80 per week.

Financial Aid

The University offers financial aid through the Federal Pell Grant, Federal Supplemental Educational Opportunity Grant, Federal Perkins Loan, Federal Stafford Student Loan, and Federal Work-Study Programs. Federally insured student loans (arranged in cooperation with the student's local bank) are also available. The University offers academic, athletic, and talent scholarships based on merit.

Faculty

Of the University's 116 full-time faculty members, 81 percent have earned doctorates or terminal degrees; all other faculty members have completed advanced work beyond the master's level, and many are doctoral candidates. All teaching is done by faculty members. The student-faculty ratio is 20:1. Faculty members serve as advisers to students in their respective disciplines, and they work with and participate in extracurricular organizations and activities on campus.

Student Government

The Shepherd University Student Government Association (SGA) consists of a policymaking body, the Executive Council, which is composed of the student body president and the cabinet, and an advisory and regulatory body, the Senate, which is composed of student representatives. Also affiliated with the SGA are 3 students who are elected to serve on the Student Affairs Committee, the central decision-making body on the campus concerned with student-life policies. The SGA sanctions student organizations and activities and controls the student activity fees and their disbursement among the various units of the University. Student representatives are members of all policymaking and program committees on campus.

Admission Requirements

Applicants must be graduates of accredited high schools. Shepherd University requires academic units to be in the following areas: English, 4 units (years); mathematics, 4 units (3 units must be algebra I and higher); science, 3 units (biology, chemistry, physics, and other courses with a strong laboratory science orientation); social studies, 3 units (including U.S. history); foreign language, 2 units (must be 2 units of the same foreign language); and art, 1 unit. Electives should be selected from the academic core or subjects such as computer science, fine arts, humanities, and keyboarding. Art applicants must submit a portfolio, and music majors must audition for admission to the program.

Applicants wishing full consideration for admission should have at least a 2.0 academic grade point average in high school and a minimum combined SAT score of 910 or a minimum composite ACT score of 19. Students who have achieved at least a 3.0 academic GPA may have a minimum combined SAT score of 820 or a minimum composite ACT score of 17 and be fully admitted. Students are encouraged to take honors or Advanced Placement Program courses in high school. College credit is given for most Advanced Placement test scores of 3 and above. Admission interviews are not required, but campus visits are strongly advised.

Transfer students should have a minimum cumulative grade point average of 2.0 and at least 26 college credits from their previous institution. Shepherd University does not admit transfer students who are on academic probation or suspension at any other institution.

Application and Information

Applications are accepted on a rolling basis; however, there are some academic programs with additional deadlines. Admission to Shepherd University does not guarantee admission to a specific major or academic program. Shepherd University offers early decision to students whose first college choice is Shepherd. Under early decision, qualified applicants who have submitted all required documents for admission by November 15 receive notice of the admission decision within ten business days. Students applying for regular admission are notified of their admission status on a rolling basis. Students are strongly encouraged to call the admissions office to schedule an admissions interview and a tour of the campus.

For information about admission and programs, prospective students should contact:

Office of Admissions
Shepherd University
P.O. Box 3210
Shepherdstown, West Virginia 25443-3210
Phone: 304-876-5212
800-344-5231 (toll-free)
Fax: 304-876-5165
E-mail: admissions@shepherd.edu
Internet: http://unexpected.shepherd.edu

McMurran Hall, which was built in 1859, is named for Shepherd's first principal, Professor Joseph McMurran.

COLLEGE DATA CENTER • WEST VIRGINIA

UNIVERSITY OF CHARLESTON

CHARLESTON, WEST VIRGINIA

The University

The University of Charleston (UC) strives to educate each student for a life of productive work, enlightened living, and community involvement. The University is very serious about its responsibility to provide students with the knowledge, abilities, and character necessary for them to have successful careers and to be productive and active citizens.

Founded in 1888 and formerly known as Morris Harvey College, the University of Charleston acquired its new name in 1979 to signify its importance as the leading higher education opportunity in the capital. Today, UC proudly represents the capital city of Charleston and the surrounding Kanawha Valley. Currently, approximately 1,400 students representing thirty-five states and twenty countries enjoy the University's 40-acre riverfront campus overlooking the State Capitol Complex and the beautiful city of Charleston.

The University has received numerous national accolades for its outstanding quality and educational approach. In September 2007, the University of Charleston was recognized as the national leader in outcomes-based learning and student assessment by the *New York Times Magazine.* The University also was ranked number 1 in the nation for 2007 by the Collegiate Learning Assessment (CLA), which also showed that UC students show the largest learning gain from freshman to sophomore year among all schools in the CLA report. The University of Charleston has been recognized as a national model for the Freshman-Year Experience, which includes faculty mentoring, university transitions, and living/learning communities. In addition, *U.S. News & World Report* placed UC in the top 20 in the Baccalaureate Colleges in the South category and as the Top Ranked Comprehensive College in West Virginia in its "Best Colleges for 2007" rankings. Students at UC also score among the highest in the country on the National Survey of Student Engagement.

The UC educational program focuses on "Learning Your Way." Students are the focus at UC. The academic program allows them to demonstrate what they have learned in order to earn the credits necessary for graduation. Students are expected to demonstrate knowledge and skills in the areas of communication, critical thinking, citizenship, ethical practice, science, and creativity. These attributes are integrated with knowledge and skills in a chosen field of study. Future employers and graduate schools consistently seek and employ college graduates with these abilities, and it is imperative that all University graduates have a strong foundation in these skills. Therefore, the University of Charleston has designed this program to help students master the knowledge and skills that are necessary for success.

Students are also encouraged to demonstrate mastery and earn credits at their own pace. Many students earn more than the traditional 15–18 credits per semester and graduate within three years, double major, or earn a master's degree quicker than at other schools.

Housing facilities for residential students are very modern and student friendly. Brotherton Hall was built in 2000 and houses 220 students; New Hall, built in 2003, houses 183 students; and Middle Hall, built in 2005 and 2006, houses 240 students. An expansion was completed for Middle Hall in August 2006 to accommodate increased student housing numbers, allowing the campus to house approximately 700 students.

Because the University believes that students learn from their involvement in community and campus activities, students are strongly encouraged to participate in one or more of the forty cocurricular organizations found at the University. There are academic clubs, publications, fraternities, sororities, religious organizations, intramural sports, honorary societies, drama clubs, cheerleading, chorus and band programs, and many student leadership organizations. The new Morrison Fitness Center opened in January 2007 and houses modern exercise equipment, weight systems, and classrooms for dance, yoga, Tae Kwon Do, or other activities. The University's Welch Colleague program integrates student involvement, the academic curriculum, community service, and leadership. The Community Service program provides opportunities for students to participate both on campus and in the Charleston area through opportunities like Habitat for Humanity. In addition, there are numerous civic, political, social, and charitable organizations easily accessible in the community.

The varsity sports program for men and women has become one of the University's most valuable assets. Men and women may participate in basketball, cheerleading, soccer, and tennis. Men may also participate in baseball, football, and golf and women in crew, cross-country, softball, track and field, and volleyball. The University's athletic teams compete in Division II of the NCAA. In recent years, men's and women's teams have been contenders in the WVIAC tournaments, with several teams winning conference championships and attending national championship tournaments. The women's basketball team participated in the Elite 8 in 2005 and 2006, and the men's football team had the largest one-season turnaround in conference history in 2005. UC athletics won the President's and Commissioner's Cups in 2006–07, signifying the top athletic teams in the WVIAC Conference.

The University of Charleston is accredited by the North Central Association of Colleges and Schools, National Council for Accreditation of Teacher Education, National Athletic Trainers Association, Commission on the Accreditation of Allied Health Education Programs–Athletic Training, Joint Review Committee on Education in Radiological Technology, and the National League for Nursing Accrediting Commission. The University holds a variety of professional recognitions, approvals, and memberships, including the International Assembly of Collegiate Business Education, West Virginia Academy of Sciences, Interior Design Educator's Council, and the American Council on Education.

The University offers master's degrees in business administration: an Executive M.B.A. and a plus-one M.B.A. for full-time study, one year beyond the bachelor's degree. A new Graduate School of Business is scheduled to open in fall 2008 with an emphasis on experiential learning and an enhanced master's program for outstanding students. The University of Charleston School of Pharmacy, which offers the University's first doctoral-level program, opened in fall 2006.

Location

Charleston, West Virginia's vibrant state capital, is a cultural, social, political, and economic hub. Located in the Kanawha Valley near the foothills of the Appalachian Mountains, it offers scenic tranquility as well as the convenience and excitement of a modern city. With a metropolitan population of 200,000, Charleston has grown to be West Virginia's finest city. Accessibility to the city is quite easy via plane, car, bus, and train. A large civic center, historic sites, libraries, movie theaters, shopping malls, and a symphony orchestra are all highlights of the Charleston business district. The rapport between the University and the community is excellent, and many events are cosponsored annually.

Downtown Charleston, just a short ride from the campus by campus shuttle or city bus, offers the kind of social and cultural opportunities that can be found only in a large city. In addition, fishing, hunting, horseback riding, waterskiing, snow skiing, mountain biking, and white-water rafting are just a few of the many recreational activities to be found within a short distance of the campus.

Majors and Degrees

The University of Charleston offers undergraduate degree programs through its various divisions: the Morris Harvey Division of Arts and Sciences, the Herbert Jones Division of Business, and the Bert Bradford Division of Health Sciences.

The Morris Harvey Division of Arts and Sciences offers the Bachelor of Arts degree with the following majors: art, communications, education (various certifications), general studies, interior design, political science, and psychology. The Bachelor of Science degree is offered with majors in biology, chemistry, and a biology/chemistry preprofessional program focused on the health sciences. The Division of Arts and Sciences is also home to the popular Pre-Pharmacy program. This program is segmented into the Pre-Pharmacy Scholars track and the Traditional Pre-Pharmacy track. Students who excel in this unique program have preferential entry into the Pharm.D. program.

The Jones Division of Business offers Bachelor of Science degree programs in accounting, sports administration, business administration, and finance.

The Division of Health Sciences offers the Bachelor of Science degree in athletic training, nursing, and radiologic science. An Associate of Arts degree in nursing is also offered at the University.

Students may pursue directed independent study and internships in most majors. Army ROTC is offered to interested men and women.

Academic Programs

Candidates for a bachelor's degree from UC are required to complete a minimum of 120 semester hours and have a cumulative grade point average of at least 2.0 on all college work attempted. This must include 30 hours in upper division courses; demonstration of learning in the required outcomes of communication, critical thinking, ethical practice, creativity, science, and citizenship; and advanced work leading to a major in a department or a division. The minimum requirement for an associate degree is 60 semester hours and a cumulative grade point average of at least a 2.0 on all college work attempted, including completion of a prescribed program of general education and specialized work in a department.

The University follows a semester academic calendar and offers summer terms for students who wish to accelerate their college program.

Academic Facilities

A large number of support facilities and programs supplement the various academic opportunities at the University of Charleston. The Schoenbaum Library serves as the center of the learning experience. Located in the technologically advanced Clay Tower Building, the library has a collection of more than 120,000 books, 200,000 microforms, and 3,600 audiovisual items. More than 8,000 journal titles are available either in print or electronically and are accessible from any Web-enabled computer, on or off campus. In addition, numerous specialized collections, CD-ROM-based electronic indexes, and online electronic search services are at the students' disposal for specialized research and study. The library also offers wireless technology and laptop computer check-out.

The University has numerous computer labs for student and faculty use: the Cabot Apple Lab, the IBM-PC combination classroom labs, an IBM-PC network lab, and an IBM-PC open lab. Wireless access is also available on much of the campus, including the scenic riverbank. The Learning Support Center provides a variety of services and classes to help students achieve academic, personal, and professional success. The Communication Resource Center provides support for students and faculty members through consultation services, workshops, and electronic access to a variety of writing resources.

The Clay Tower Building houses state-of-the-art science, technology, and information resource facilities. Riggleman Hall, the main college building, houses classrooms, a 976-seat auditorium and stage, education and language laboratories, the Carleton Varney Department of Art and Design, and administrative offices.

Costs

For the 2007–08 academic year, tuition was $22,050, and room (double occupancy) and board were $7930, for a total of $29,980. This does not include the cost of books, supplies, or other incidental charges.

Financial Aid

The University of Charleston provides generous financial assistance that may include a combination of scholarships, grants, loans, and work-study. In 2007–08, more than 90 percent of full-time students received some form of financial aid. Special academic scholarships and grants are awarded to outstanding full-time students. The University also offers grants to qualified athletes and to students who are involved in leadership, community service, band, school newspaper, or vocal music.

Faculty

The University has 61 full-time and 38 part-time undergraduate faculty members. At the University of Charleston, faculty members provide academic, career, and in some cases, personal advice to students. They encourage active learning through collaborative projects and faculty/student research. Small classes through a 13:1 faculty-student ratio allow for individual attention for students.

Student Government

The Student Government Association is a policymaking body composed of students representing most campus organizations and student classes. Both the Student Government Association and the University believe that students should have the privilege, along with the faculty and administration, of participating in the governance of the University.

Admission Requirements

Admission to the University of Charleston is based on the academic records and potential for leadership and involvement. A qualified applicant's credentials must strongly suggest ability and motivation to succeed in higher education and in the University community. Candidates for admission must present a transcript of work from an accredited secondary school showing at least 16 academic units, grades indicating intellectual ability and promise, and proof of graduation or a GED. The pattern of courses should show purpose and continuity and furnish a background for the liberal learning outcomes curriculum offered by the University.

Since the unique and student-friendly curriculum emphasizes communication, critical thinking, and citizenship, secondary school courses should emphasize courses in English, mathematics, sciences, and social sciences. Candidates are also required to submit scores on the ACT or SAT. Students must have an above-average academic profile that includes a minimum 2.25 academic grade point average and a minimum ACT composite score of 19 or SAT score (combined math and critical reading) of 900. Applicants for admission are considered on an individual basis without regard to race, religion, geographic origin, or handicap. Letters of recommendation and a personal visit to the campus scheduled with the Office of Admissions are highly recommended.

Application and Information

For more information, interested students should contact:

Office of Admissions
University of Charleston
2300 MacCorkle Avenue, SE
Charleston, West Virginia 25304
Phone: 304-357-4750
800-995-GO UC (4682) (toll-free)
Fax: 304-357-4781
E-mail: admissions@ucwv.edu
Web site: http://www.ucwv.edu

The Clay Tower Building houses state-of-the-art science facilities and a library with lounges overlooking the Kanawha River. The campus is directly across the river from the State Capitol.

WEST VIRGINIA UNIVERSITY INSTITUTE OF TECHNOLOGY

MONTGOMERY, WEST VIRGINIA

The University

West Virginia University Institute of Technology (WVU Tech) and the Community and Technical College at WVU Tech (CTC @ WVU Tech), co-located in Montgomery, West Virginia, offer students programs with strong reputations that provide a high value for their investment. The institution has experienced a number of significant changes since it began as a preparatory school extension of West Virginia University in 1895. It began offering bachelor's degrees in engineering in 1952 and added community and technical education in 1966.

WVU Tech and the CTC @ WVU Tech give students a family-like campus atmosphere. There are numerous social, athletic, and cultural activities on campus through which students can satisfy personal interests. Five national social fraternities and two sororities have chapters at WVU Tech. A master's degree program in control systems engineering is also available.

Location

Montgomery, West Virginia, is a small town of about 2,500 residents, just 28 miles southeast of Charleston, the state capital. Interstate Highways 64, 77, and 79 all run within 30 miles of the campus, and U.S. Route 60, a major east-west artery, runs immediately adjacent to the campus. Bus services are available through Greyhound Lines as well as the Kanawha Rapid Transit (KRT) and Mountain Transit Authority (MTA). Both the KRT and the MTA run regular schedules to Montgomery with destination points in Charleston, West Virginia, and many Kanawha Valley communities.

Another major asset to WVU Tech is the Amtrak service located across from the campus. With stops such as Chicago, Cincinnati, New York City, and Washington, D.C., and the railway provides a convenient method of transportation for many students living in the continental United States. With Yeager Airport only 30 minutes away, WVU Tech is just a flight away from any destination in the world.

WVU Tech's campus is also convenient to many tourist attractions and thrill-seekers' adventures. Hawks Nest State Park, with its aerial tram to the bottom of the New River canyon, is located 30 miles from the campus. The New River, considered by many authoritative geologists to be the second-oldest river in the world, is a challenge to enthusiasts of white-water rafting, and the New River Gorge Bridge is the largest arch bridge east of the Mississippi. WVU Tech is also close to three popular skiing areas, including Snowshoe Mountain, Silver Creek, and Winter Place Ski Lodge.

Majors and Degrees

Tech offers the Bachelor of Arts, Bachelor of Science, Associate in Science, and Associate of Applied Science degrees. The Bachelor of Arts degree is available in government and history. Bachelor of Science degrees are offered in accounting; aerospace engineering (2+2 program); athletic coaching education; biology; business management; chemical, civil, computer, electrical, and mechanical engineering; chemistry; computer science; criminal justice; electronic, industrial, and engineering technology; health-services administration; industrial relations and human resources; interdisciplinary studies; management information systems; mathematics; nursing; predental; prelaw; premedicine; prepharmacy; printing management; psychology; public service administration; sport management; and technology management. For more information on any degree programs, students should visit the WVU Tech Web site at http://www.wvutech.edu.

The CTC @ WVU Tech provides both two-year degrees and one-year certificates. Two-year Associate in Science degrees are offered in business technology (emphases in accounting, business supervision, and computer information systems), computer and information technology, computer science, construction technology, dental hygiene, diesel technology, engineering technologies (civil, drafting and design, electrical, and mechanical), general studies, occupational development (emphasis in corrections and culinary apprentice), office technology management (emphases in computer applications specialist, computer specialist, executive, medical assistant, medical facilities management, and medical office assistant studies), online medical transcription, printing technology, and respiratory-care technology.

A two-year Associate of Applied Science degree is offered in automotive service technology and technical studies in information technology.

A one-year certificate program is offered in claims processing, digital imaging, electrical computer network specialist, electrical mining specialist, electromechanical mining specialist, entrepreneurship, general studies–health science, help desk, internetworking security administrator specialist, manufacturing specialist, mechanical mining specialist, medical transcription, network security administrator specialist, pre-engineering, prepress technology, press technology, and press control specialist. For more information, students should visit the CTC @ WVU Tech Web site at http://www.ctc.wvutech.edu.

Academic Programs

WVU Tech, a four-year institution of higher learning, offers a variety of bachelor degree programs in areas ranging from business, science, and technology to engineering. WVU Tech has always sustained a high reputation for its accredited and nationally recognized degree programs in engineering. In addition, WVU Tech has many unique programs and newly added programs. For a full listing of available programs, students should visit the WVU Tech Web site at http://www.wvutech.edu.

The CTC @ WVU Tech provides a vast array of one-year certificate programs and two-year associate degrees. With a focus on technology and the needs of tomorrow's workforce, the CTC @ WVU Tech offers an inclusive learning environment that services the campus, community, and distance learning. The CTC @ WVU Tech continues to expand their offerings each year with new additions. For a full listing of available programs, students should visit the CTC @ WVU Tech's Web site at http://www.ctc.wvutech.edu.

To earn a bachelor's degree, students must complete a minimum of 128 semester hours. To earn an associate degree, students must complete a minimum of 64 semester hours.

Tech operates on a two-semester calendar year. The first semester begins in August and ends in December; the second begins in January and ends in May. Summer courses are also available.

Off-Campus Programs

WVU Tech offers a unique "earn while you learn" approach through the Cooperative Education Program, which combines an organized curriculum that integrated practical industrial experience. Students participate in the three-semester industry rotation that is interwoven among on-campus classroom instruction. WVU Tech also has academic centers in Beckley, Charleston, and Huntington, with various offerings at each location.

Academic Facilities

The Montgomery campus consists of nineteen academic, administrative, and residential buildings situated on 200 acres. Many of the facilities are equipped for classroom instruction, auditorium lectures, and hands-on laboratories for majors such as (but not limited to) biology, chemistry, nursing, engineering, art, engineering technology, and computer science. WVU Tech also features a theater facility for seasonal productions and special performances.

Costs

For 2007–08, costs for tuition and fees per academic year were $4598 for West Virginia residents and $11,808 for nonresidents. Additional student fees can apply for specific majors. Room costs were approximately $4000 per semester (single occupancy—double rooms cost less); board costs totaled $2600. Students should expect to spend approximately $2924 each semester for books and supplies. Tuition and fees for CTC @ WVU Tech for the 2007–08 academic year were $3266 for West Virginia residents and $11,208 for nonresidents.

Financial Aid

WVU Tech offers a wide range of financial aid resources, including institutional scholarships, privately and federally funded loans, Federal Pell Grants, Federal Supplemental Educational Opportunity Grants, the National Science and Mathematics Access to Retain Talent grant (SMART), the Academic Competitiveness Grant (ACG) , Federal Work-Study Program awards, privately funded scholarships for both academic and special talent, and West Virginia Higher Education Grant Program awards. The student's parents or guardians are required to submit the Free Application for Federal Student Aid (http://www.fafsa.ed.gov) for determination of eligibility. Applications for financial aid, both from incoming freshmen and from enrolled students, should be submitted to WVU Tech's Office of Student Financial Aid by April 1 in order to receive consideration for the next academic year.

Faculty

Faculty members at WVU Tech and the CTC @ WVU Tech are well prepared both academically and professionally to teach the institution's career-oriented curricula. Faculty members come from all over the United States and from several other countries, and most have had considerable practical experience in their field. In the Leonard C. Nelson College of Engineering alone, nearly 90 percent of the faculty members have earned doctorates. The student-faculty ratio is 16:1. Faculty members work with students in developing academic programs, and they assist in personal counseling, although WVU Tech also has professional counselors on staff to help students with problems.

Student Government

The Student Government Association (SGA) consists of students elected in campuswide referendums that are held each fall and spring. One of the SGA's most important functions is to develop a budget on which to base the student activity fees that fund the many diverse student activities and organizations on campus.

Admission Requirements

Applicants who are residents of West Virginia must graduate from an accredited high school or pass the GED test and must take the ACT and have test scores sent to the Institute directly from American College Testing, Inc. Out-of-state residents must graduate from an accredited high school or pass the GED test, rank in the upper three fourths of their graduating class or attain a standard composite score of at least 18 on the ACT (SAT combined score of at least 870), and have their scores sent to the Institute directly from American College Testing, Inc., or the Educational Testing Service. Scores are used for placement and counseling purposes, and no other test may be substituted.

Admission to the college does not necessarily admit a student to all programs. Prerequisites apply for admission to certain curricula, as follows: for engineering, 2 units of algebra, 1 unit of plane geometry, 1 unit of advanced math, a minimum 3.0 GPA, and a math ACT score of at least 19 or SAT score of at least 460; for engineering technology, 1 unit of algebra, 1 unit of plane geometry, and ½ unit of trigonometry. Students lacking one or more of these prerequisites are given an opportunity to enroll in pretechnology mathematics courses. Allied health–nursing candidates need 2 units of algebra and 2 units of laboratory science, 1 unit of which must be in chemistry. Dental hygiene candidates need 1 unit of algebra, 1 unit of biology, and 1 unit of chemistry. Because of the limited enrollment in allied health programs, candidates for these areas are selected by a special committee. Students with high school averages of B or better and/or ACT composite scores of 23 (SAT combined score of 950) or higher are given priority by the admission committee.

Application and Information

Students are encouraged to apply by January, however, applications are processed on a rolling decision basis. Students with a B average or better are notified of the admission decision upon receipt of their sixth-semester high school transcript and ACT or SAT scores. All other students are notified upon receipt of their seventh-semester or final transcript and ACT or SAT scores.

Applications for admission and requests for further information should be addressed to:

Director of Admissions
West Virginia University Institute of Technology
Montgomery, West Virginia 25136
Phone: 888-554-TECH (toll-free)
Web site: http://www.wvutech.edu

Old Main.

COLLEGE DATA CENTER • WEST VIRGINIA

WHEELING JESUIT UNIVERSITY

WHEELING, WEST VIRGINIA

The University

Wheeling Jesuit University (WJU), which was founded in 1954, is the youngest of America's twenty-eight Jesuit colleges and the only one that has been coeducational from the beginning. The University's mission is to educate men and women for life, leadership, and service with and among others. Students have the advantage of a world-recognized Jesuit education on a scale where personal student-faculty interaction occurs daily. Although Catholic in affiliation, Wheeling Jesuit University welcomes students of all faiths. Of the approximately 1,200 undergraduate students, approximately 60 percent are Catholic. Students come from thirty-two states, with the majority from the East and Midwest. International students come from eleven different countries.

Wheeling Jesuit University is accredited by the North Central Association of Colleges and Schools, and its programs in the respective areas are accredited by the Commission on Collegiate Nursing Education, the Commission on Accreditation in Physical Therapy Education, and the AMA Committee on Allied Health Education and Accreditation.

In addition to the undergraduate programs, the University offers master's degrees in accountancy, business administration, nursing, and organizational leadership. A six-year program leading to a doctoral degree in physical therapy is also offered.

The campus has fifteen modern buildings spread out over 65 acres of rolling hillside. Residential housing is available to all students who wish to live on campus, and 75 percent of the students enrolled take advantage of this. The dining hall and snack bar are operated by Parkhurst Dining Services, and the Rathskeller is operated by the students. Student organizations and clubs offer an array of cultural and social activities, including dramatics, a University newspaper and magazine, cinema, concerts, and community services. Intercollegiate sports include men's and women's basketball, cross-country, golf, soccer, swimming, and track and field; men's lacrosse and baseball; and women's volleyball and softball. Club and intramural sports include basketball, football, ice hockey, lacrosse, rugby, softball, tennis, and volleyball. The Health and Recreation Center features a 2,200-seat gymnasium, a jogging track, racquetball courts, and a six-lane swimming pool.

Location

Wheeling, one of the country's most livable and safe small cities, has a population of approximately 50,000 and is easily accessible via interstate highways. The University is a 1-hour drive from the international airport in Pittsburgh, Pennsylvania, and a 2-hour drive from Columbus, Ohio. Many recreational and cultural facilities are available, including 1,500-acre Oglebay Park and 250-acre Wheeling Park. Excellent local recreational areas provide opportunities for camping, golf, hiking, skiing, swimming, and other activities.

Majors and Degrees

Bachelor's degrees are offered in accountancy, athletic training, biology, business (management, marketing, and sports management), chemistry, computer science, criminal justice, education (elementary and secondary education and special education certification), engineering (3/2), English, French, general science (biology and physics), global studies, history, mathematics, nuclear medicine technology, nursing, philosophy, physics, political and economic philosophy, political science, professional communications (audio/visual, graphic design, new media, and print), psychology, respiratory therapy, romance languages, Spanish, and theology and religious studies. Preprofessional programs include dentistry, forensics, law, medicine, pharmacy, physical therapy, and veterinary medicine.

Academic Programs

Wheeling Jesuit University combines preprofessional majors with those in traditional arts and sciences. A strong background in the liberal arts is provided to all students through a required general studies core curriculum. A minimum of 120 credit hours completed with an average of 2.0 or better is required for graduation. The Laut Honors Program for students of exceptional ability is a sequence of honors courses, an independent project or thesis, and a special senior seminar.

Off-Campus Programs

Wheeling Jesuit University students have a wide range of study-abroad opportunities, ranging from short study tours to semester or yearlong programs overseas. WJU offers semester and yearlong programs in France; England; Macerata, Italy; Vienna, Austria; Segovia, Spain; and Beijing, China. Summer programs are available in France, Segovia, and Dublin. Students can also participate in a number of short study trips led by WJU faculty members to such locations as Vietnam, Dominica, France, and Ireland. In addition to the programs outlined above, students can avail themselves to a host of other programs throughout the world through WJU's membership in various consortia and ties with other Jesuit universities.

Academic Facilities

Wheeling Jesuit University's campus has a quality and depth of facilities unprecedented for an institution its size. There are fifteen modern and spacious buildings, including a $10-million science center, a state-of-the-art health and recreation facility, a $1.5-million soccer and track complex, new and renovated residence halls, and a 153,000-volume library with 28 online databases. The campus is linked by a fiber-optic network, and both students and faculty members have unlimited access to the resources of the Robert C. Byrd National Technology Transfer Center, the Erma Ora Byrd Center for Educational Technologies, and the NASA-sponsored Classroom of the Future.

Costs

Tuition and fees for 2008–09 are approximately $24,390. Room and board fees are approximately $8360. Books and supplies cost approximately $300 to $600, and personal expenses average $600 per year.

Financial Aid

Wheeling Jesuit University assists students who have financial need with financial award packages that include loans, grants, work-study jobs, and scholarships. In 2007–08, more than 95 percent of full-day students received some form of aid. The average assistance level to those receiving aid was more than $23,000, including working loans. Federal aid includes Federal Perkins Loans, Federal Pell Grants, Federal Work-Study Program awards, Federal Supplemental Educational Opportunity Grants, and Federal Stafford Student Loans. West Virginia, Pennsylvania, Rhode Island, and Vermont state grants can be used at Wheeling Jesuit University by eligible students. The University also provides need-based grants from institutional funds.

Scholarships based solely on academic ability are also awarded by the University. These scholarships range from $12,000 to $13,000 per year. Two full-tuition scholarships are awarded on a competitive basis to entering Laut Honors Program students. All academic scholarships are renewable for four years if the specified cumulative grade point average is maintained. Athletic scholarships are awarded to men and women in various intercollegiate sports. Athletic awards are determined by the Athletic Department.

For further information on scholarships or financial aid, applicants should contact the Financial Aid Office (phone: 800-624-6992 (toll-free); e-mail: finaid@wju.edu). The FAFSA should be filed before March 1.

Faculty

An energetic, diversified faculty (84 percent of whose members have doctoral or other terminal degrees) has a strong voice in the policies of the institution through a faculty council and other standing committees. All 75 full-time faculty members are professional teachers; no teaching is done by graduate assistants. About 5 percent of the faculty members are Jesuits. Faculty members and students interact outside the classroom through activities, dining, intramural sports, and informal gatherings. The student-faculty ratio is 14:1. Academic advising is done by the faculty.

Student Government

Students participate fully in formulating the policies of the University through the Student Government and residence hall governments and as voting or auditing participants on virtually all faculty-administration committees of the University. Students plan and control the entire student activity budget.

Admission Requirements

Wheeling Jesuit University is a democratic institution where all students are accepted on the same basis regardless of race, color, gender, creed, sexual orientation, religion, national origin, age, marital status, or disability. The Committee on Admissions selects the students who are best qualified to complete the required program of studies. Applicants are considered for admission if they have successfully completed a high school course of study and have achieved reasonable success on either the SAT or the ACT. For transfer students, transcripts are required from colleges previously attended.

Application and Information

There is a rolling admissions policy. Students receive notification of the admissions decision shortly after all their academic credentials have been received by the Admissions Office.

For more information, students should contact:

Office of Admissions
Wheeling Jesuit University
Wheeling, West Virginia 26003
Phone: 304-243-2359
800-624-6992 (toll-free)
Fax: 304-243-2397
E-mail: admiss@wju.edu
Web site: http://www.wju.edu

Students on the campus of Wheeling Jesuit University.

WISCONSIN

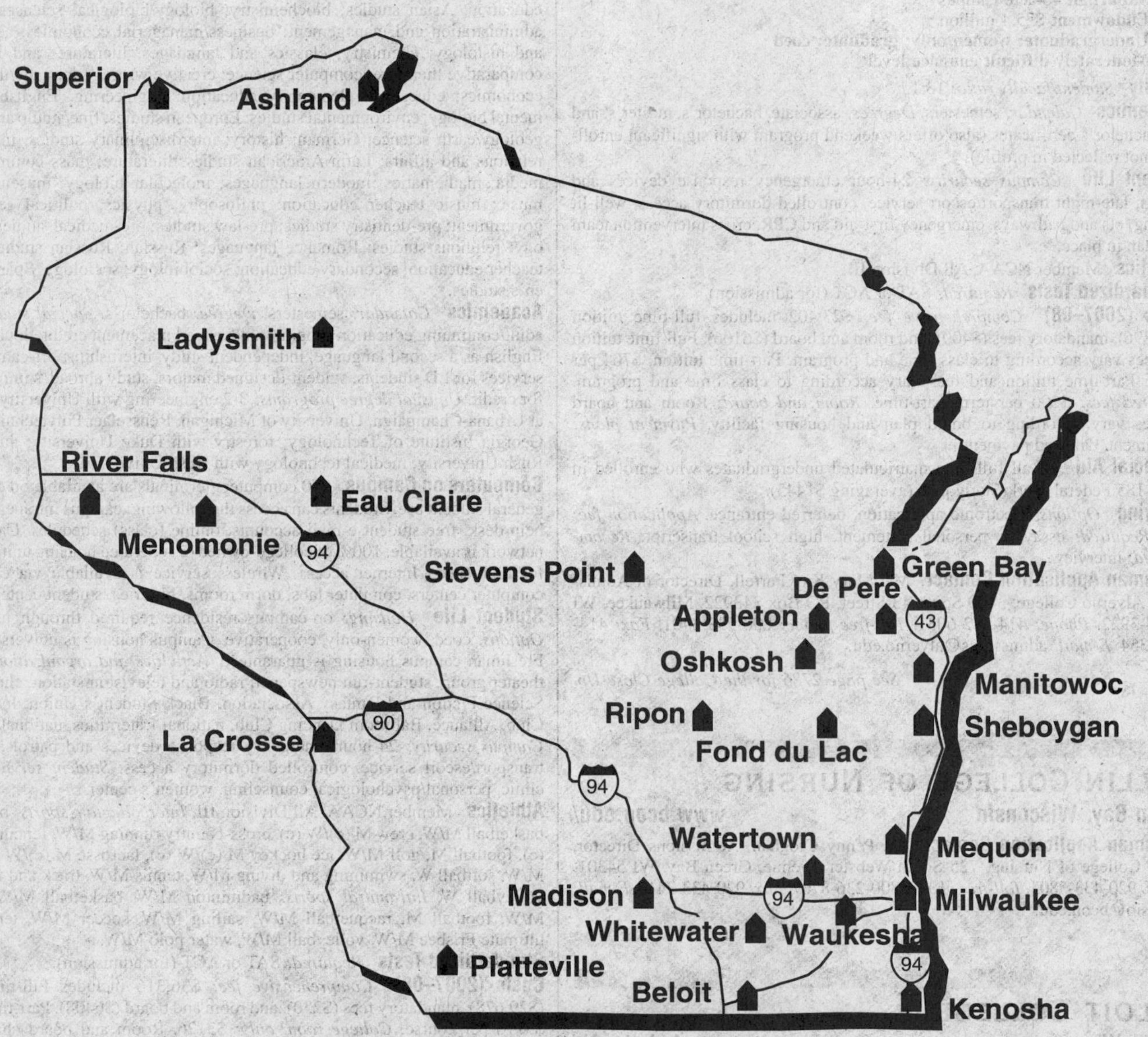
Superior
Ashland
Ladysmith
River Falls
Eau Claire
Menomonie
94
Stevens Point
Green Bay
De Pere
Appleton
43
Oshkosh
Manitowoc
Ripon
Sheboygan
Fond du Lac
90
La Crosse
94
Watertown
Mequon
Madison
94
Milwaukee
Whitewater
Waukesha
Platteville
94
Beloit
Kenosha

ALVERNO COLLEGE

Milwaukee, Wisconsin **www.alverno.edu/**

- **Independent Roman Catholic** comprehensive, founded 1887
- **Suburban** 46-acre campus
- **Endowment** $25.4 million
- **Undergraduate: women only; graduate: coed**
- **Moderately difficult** entrance level

Faculty *Student/faculty ratio:* 13:1.

Academics *Calendar:* semesters. *Degrees:* associate, bachelor's, master's, and postbachelor's certificates (also offers weekend program with significant enrollment not reflected in profile).

Student Life *Campus security:* 24-hour emergency response devices and patrols, late-night transport/escort service, controlled dormitory access, well-lit parking lots and pathways, emergency first-aid and CPR, crisis intervention team and plan in place.

Athletics Member NCAA. All Division III.

Standardized Tests *Required:* SAT or ACT (for admission).

Costs (2007–08) *Comprehensive fee:* $23,402 includes full-time tuition ($16,896), mandatory fees ($400), and room and board ($6106). Full-time tuition and fees vary according to class time and program. Part-time tuition: $704 per credit. Part-time tuition and fees vary according to class time and program. *Required fees:* $200 per term part-time. *Room and board:* Room and board charges vary according to board plan and housing facility. *Payment plans:* installment, deferred payment.

Financial Aid Of all full-time matriculated undergraduates who enrolled in 2005, 185 Federal Work-Study jobs (averaging $1445).

Applying *Options:* electronic application, deferred entrance. *Application fee:* $20. *Required:* essay or personal statement, high school transcript. *Recommended:* interview.

Freshman Application Contact Ms. Mary Kay Farrell, Director of Admissions, Alverno College, 3400 South 43 Street, PO Box 343922, Milwaukee, WI 53234-3922. *Phone:* 414-382-6031. *Toll-free phone:* 800-933-3401. *Fax:* 414-382-6354. *E-mail:* admissions@alverno.edu.

See page 2786 for the College Close-Up.

BELLIN COLLEGE OF NURSING

Green Bay, Wisconsin **www.bcon.edu/**

Freshman Application Contact Dr. Penny Croghan, Admissions Director, Bellin College of Nursing, 725 South Webster Avenue, Green Bay, WI 54301. *Phone:* 920-433-5803. *Toll-free phone:* 800-236-8707. *Fax:* 920-433-7416. *E-mail:* admissio@bcon.edu.

BELOIT COLLEGE

Beloit, Wisconsin **www.beloit.edu/**

- **Independent** 4-year, founded 1846
- **Small-town** 65-acre campus with easy access to Chicago and Milwaukee
- **Endowment** $134.6 million
- **Coed** 1,352 undergraduate students, 97% full-time, 58% women, 42% men
- **Very difficult** entrance level, 60% of applicants were admitted

Experiential learning, interdisciplinary thought, and global understanding have been the hallmarks of a Beloit education since the College's founding more than 150 years ago. Beloit students, who come from nearly every state and more than forty countries, combine rigorous academics with internships, research, service, and a global perspective. The approximate full-time enrollment is 1,250.

Undergraduates 1,308 full-time, 44 part-time. Students come from 47 states and territories, 43 other countries, 77% are from out of state, 3% African American, 4% Asian American or Pacific Islander, 3% Hispanic American, 0.5% Native American, 6% international, 2% transferred in, 92% live on campus. *Retention:* 89% of 2006 full-time freshmen returned.

Freshmen *Admission:* 2,157 applied, 1,304 admitted, 325 enrolled. *Average high school GPA:* 3.4. *Test scores:* SAT critical reading scores over 500: 95%; SAT math scores over 500: 94%; ACT scores over 18: 98%; SAT critical reading scores over 600: 82%; SAT math scores over 600: 71%; ACT scores over 24: 84%; SAT critical reading scores over 700: 34%; SAT math scores over 700: 13%; ACT scores over 30: 24%.

Faculty *Total:* 130, 92% full-time, 93% with terminal degrees. *Student/faculty ratio:* 11:1.

Majors Anthropology; art history, criticism and conservation; art teacher education; Asian studies; biochemistry; biology/biological sciences; business administration and management; business/managerial economics; cell biology and histology; chemistry; classics and languages, literatures and linguistics; comparative literature; computer science; creative writing; dramatic/theater arts; economics; education; elementary education; engineering; English; environmental biology; environmental studies; European studies; fine/studio arts; French; geology/earth science; German; history; interdisciplinary studies; international relations and affairs; Latin American studies; literature; mass communication/media; mathematics; modern languages; molecular biology; museum studies; music; music teacher education; philosophy; physics; political science and government; pre-dentistry studies; pre-law studies; pre-medical studies; psychology; religious studies; Romance languages; Russian; Russian studies; science teacher education; secondary education; sociobiology; sociology; Spanish; women's studies.

Academics *Calendar:* semesters. *Degree:* bachelor's. *Special study options:* adult/continuing education programs, advanced placement credit, double majors, English as a second language, independent study, internships, off-campus study, services for LD students, student-designed majors, study abroad, summer session for credit. *Unusual degree programs:* 3-2 engineering with University of Illinois at Urbana-Champaign, University of Michigan, Rensselaer Polytechnic Institute, Georgia Institute of Technology; forestry with Duke University; nursing with Rush University; medical technology with Rush University.

Computers on Campus 270 computers/terminals are available on campus for general student use. Students can access the following: campus intranet, computer help desk, free student e-mail accounts, online (class) schedules. Campuswide network is available. 100% of college-owned or -operated housing units are wired for high-speed Internet access. Wireless service is available via classrooms, computer centers, computer labs, dorm rooms, libraries, student centers.

Student Life *Housing:* on-campus residence required through junior year. *Options:* coed, women-only, cooperative. Campus housing is university owned. Freshman campus housing is guaranteed. *Activities and organizations:* drama/theater group, student-run newspaper, radio and television station, choral group, Science Fiction and Fantasy Association, Black Student's Union, International Club, Alliance, Ballroom Dancing Club, national fraternities, national sororities. *Campus security:* 24-hour emergency response devices and patrols, late-night transport/escort service, controlled dormitory access. *Student services:* health clinic, personal/psychological counseling, women's center.

Athletics Member NCAA. All Division III. *Intercollegiate sports:* baseball M, basketball M/W, crew M (c)/W (c), cross-country running M/W, fencing M (c)/W (c), football M, golf M/W, ice hockey M (c)/W (c), lacrosse M (c)/W (c), soccer M/W, softball W, swimming and diving M/W, tennis M/W, track and field M/W, volleyball W. *Intramural sports:* badminton M/W, basketball M/W, bowling M/W, football M, racquetball M/W, sailing M/W, soccer M/W, tennis M/W, ultimate Frisbee M/W, volleyball M/W, water polo M/W.

Standardized Tests *Required:* SAT or ACT (for admission).

Costs (2007–08) *Comprehensive fee:* $36,316 includes full-time tuition ($29,678), mandatory fees ($230), and room and board ($6408). Part-time tuition: $3710 per course. *College room only:* $3126. Room and board charges vary according to board plan. *Payment plan:* installment. *Waivers:* employees or children of employees.

Financial Aid Of all full-time matriculated undergraduates who enrolled in 2007, 1,002 applied for aid, 838 were judged to have need, 602 had their need fully met. 516 Federal Work-Study jobs (averaging $1694). 546 state and other part-time jobs (averaging $1231). In 2007, 323 non-need-based awards were made. *Average percent of need met:* 96%. *Average financial aid package:* $24,506. *Average need-based loan:* $5177. *Average need-based gift aid:* $17,819. *Average non-need-based aid:* $11,946. *Average indebtedness upon graduation:* $23,214.

Applying *Options:* electronic application, early admission, early action, deferred entrance. *Application fee:* $35. *Required:* essay or personal statement, high school transcript, 1 letter of recommendation. *Required for some:* interview. *Recommended:* interview. *Application deadlines:* 1/15 (freshmen), rolling (transfers), 12/15 (early action). *Notification:* 4/1 (freshmen), continuous (transfers), 1/15 (early action).

Freshman Application Contact Mr. James S. Zielinski, Director of Admissions, Beloit College, 700 College Street, Beloit, WI 53511-5596. *Phone:* 608-363-2500. *Toll-free phone:* 800-9-BELOIT. *Fax:* 608-363-2075. *E-mail:* admiss@beloit.edu.

See page 2788 for the College Close-Up.

BRYANT AND STRATTON COLLEGE

Milwaukee, Wisconsin **www.bryantstratton.edu/**

Freshman Application Contact Ms. Kathryn Cotey, Director of Admissions, Bryant and Stratton College, 310 West Wisconsin Avenue, Milwaukee, WI 53203-2214. *Phone:* 414-276-5200.

BRYANT AND STRATTON COLLEGE, WAUWATOSA CAMPUS

Wauwatosa, Wisconsin **www.bryantstratton.edu/**

Director of Admissions Mr. Cori Prohaska, Campus Director, Bryant and Stratton College, Wauwatosa Campus, 10950 W. Potter Road, Wauwatosa, WI 53226. *Phone:* 414-302-7000.

CARDINAL STRITCH UNIVERSITY

Milwaukee, Wisconsin **www.stritch.edu/**

- **Independent Roman Catholic** comprehensive, founded 1937
- **Suburban** 40-acre campus
- **Endowment** $19.9 million
- **Coed**
- **Moderately difficult** entrance level

Cardinal Stritch University is a Catholic, coeducational institution rooted in the liberal arts. Stritch provides all of the resources associated with a large university yet offers the benefits of personal attention and one-on-one instruction associated with a smaller institution. Graduate and undergraduate programs, offered in traditional and nontraditional formats, range from business and education to nursing and art.

Faculty *Student/faculty ratio:* 16:1.

Academics *Calendar:* semesters. *Degrees:* certificates, associate, bachelor's, master's, doctoral, and postbachelor's certificates.

Student Life *Campus security:* 24-hour emergency response devices and patrols, late-night transport/escort service.

Athletics Member NAIA.

Standardized Tests *Required:* SAT or ACT (for admission).

Costs (2007–08) *Comprehensive fee:* $24,924 includes full-time tuition ($18,624), mandatory fees ($450), and room and board ($5850). Full-time tuition and fees vary according to course load. Part-time tuition: $582 per credit. Part-time tuition and fees vary according to course load. *Required fees:* $175 per term part-time. *Room and board:* Room and board charges vary according to board plan. *Payment plans:* installment, deferred payment.

Financial Aid Of all full-time matriculated undergraduates who enrolled in 2002, 2,176 applied for aid, 2,037 were judged to have need, 188 had their need fully met. In 2002, 234 non-need-based awards were made. *Average percent of need met:* 43. *Average financial aid package:* $7843. *Average need-based loan:* $3575. *Average need-based gift aid:* $5634. *Average non-need-based aid:* $9402.

Applying *Options:* electronic application, deferred entrance. *Application fee:* $25. *Required:* essay or personal statement, high school transcript, minimum 2.0 GPA. *Required for some:* letters of recommendation. *Recommended:* interview.

Freshman Application Contact Kristine Bueno, Director of Admissions, Cardinal Stritch University, 6801 North Yates Road, Milwaukee, WI 53217. *Phone:* 414-410-4040. *Toll-free phone:* 800-347-8822 Ext. 4040. *Fax:* 414-410-4058. *E-mail:* admityou@stritch.edu.

See page 2790 for the College Close-Up.

CARROLL COLLEGE

Waukesha, Wisconsin **www.cc.edu/**

- **Independent Presbyterian** comprehensive, founded 1846
- **Suburban** 52-acre campus with easy access to Milwaukee
- **Endowment** $43.1 million
- **Coed** 3,060 undergraduate students, 82% full-time, 68% women, 32% men
- **Moderately difficult** entrance level, 72% of applicants were admitted

Carroll College gives its students the support they need to learn and grow. Small classes and individual attention provide a high-quality educational experience at Wisconsin's oldest college. Students are encouraged to explore the world around them by studying in other countries or participating in internships. An honors program is available to academically talented students.

Undergraduates 2,498 full-time, 562 part-time. Students come from 23 states and territories, 25 other countries, 20% are from out of state, 2% African American, 1% Asian American or Pacific Islander, 3% Hispanic American, 0.4% Native American, 2% international, 7% transferred in, 51% live on campus. *Retention:* 74% of 2006 full-time freshmen returned.

Freshmen *Admission:* 2,728 applied, 1,975 admitted, 657 enrolled. *Average high school GPA:* 3.3. *Test scores:* ACT scores over 18: 96%; ACT scores over 24: 44%; ACT scores over 30: 3%.

Faculty *Total:* 289, 42% full-time, 36% with terminal degrees. *Student/faculty ratio:* 16:1.

Majors Accounting; actuarial science; animal behavior and ethology; applied mathematics; applied mathematics related; art; art teacher education; athletic training; biochemistry; biology/biological sciences; biology teacher education; business administration and management; chemistry; chemistry teacher education; clinical laboratory science/medical technology; commercial and advertising art; communication/speech communication and rhetoric; computer and information sciences; computer software engineering; creative writing; dramatic/theater arts; early childhood education; education; elementary education; engineering physics; English; English/language arts teacher education; environmental science; European studies; finance; fine/studio arts; foreign language teacher education; forensic science and technology; graphic communications; health and physical education; health teacher education; history; history teacher education; human resources management; information science/studies; international relations and affairs; journalism; kinesiology and exercise science; management information systems; marketing/marketing management; mathematics; mathematics teacher education; middle school education; music; music teacher education; natural resources/conservation; nursing (registered nurse training); organizational behavior; organizational communication; photography; physical education teaching and coaching; political science and government; pre-dentistry studies; premedical studies; pre-pharmacy studies; pre-veterinary studies; printing management; psychology; psychology teacher education; public relations, advertising, and applied communication related; public relations/image management; religious studies; science teacher education; small business administration; social science teacher education; social studies teacher education; sociology; Spanish; Spanish language teacher education; trade and industrial teacher education.

Academics *Calendar:* semesters. *Degrees:* bachelor's, master's, and doctoral. *Special study options:* academic remediation for entering students, adult/continuing education programs, advanced placement credit, distance learning, double majors, honors programs, independent study, internships, part-time degree program, services for LD students, student-designed majors, study abroad, summer session for credit. *ROTC:* Army (c), Air Force (c). *Unusual degree programs:* 3-2 physical therapy.

Computers on Campus 250 computers/terminals are available on campus for general student use. Students can access the following: online (class) registration. Campuswide network is available. 95% of college-owned or -operated housing units are wired for high-speed Internet access. Wireless service is available via classrooms, computer centers, computer labs, libraries.

Student Life *Housing:* on-campus residence required for freshman year. *Options:* coed, women-only. Campus housing is university owned. Freshman campus housing is guaranteed. *Activities and organizations:* drama/theater group, student-run newspaper, radio station, choral group, College Activities Board, Student Senate, Black Student Union, Carroll College Christian Fellowship, Residence Hall Association, national sororities. *Campus security:* 24-hour emergency response devices and patrols, student patrols, late-night transport/escort service, controlled dormitory access. *Student services:* health clinic, personal/psychological counseling.

Athletics Member NCAA. All Division III. *Intercollegiate sports:* baseball M, basketball M/W, cross-country running M/W, football M, golf M/W, soccer M/W, swimming and diving M/W, track and field M/W, volleyball W. *Intramural sports:* basketball M/W, bowling M/W, cheerleading M/W, football M/W, soccer M/W, tennis M/W, ultimate Frisbee M/W, volleyball M/W.

Standardized Tests *Required:* SAT or ACT (for admission). *Recommended:* ACT (for admission).

Costs (2008–09) *Comprehensive fee:* $27,180 includes full-time tuition ($20,400), mandatory fees ($430), and room and board ($6350). Part-time tuition: $260 per credit. *College room only:* $3450.

Financial Aid Of all full-time matriculated undergraduates who enrolled in 2007, 2,223 applied for aid, 1,667 were judged to have need, 1,317 had their need fully met. 626 Federal Work-Study jobs (averaging $1806). 710 state and other part-time jobs (averaging $1714). In 2007, 831 non-need-based awards were made. *Average percent of need met:* 100%. *Average financial aid package:*

$16,047. *Average need-based loan:* $3324. *Average need-based gift aid:* $10,664. *Average non-need-based aid:* $7854. *Average indebtedness upon graduation:* $21,794.

Applying *Options:* electronic application, deferred entrance. *Required:* high school transcript, minimum 2.0 GPA, 1 letter of recommendation. *Required for some:* essay or personal statement. *Recommended:* interview. *Application deadlines:* rolling (freshmen), rolling (transfers). *Notification:* continuous until 8/20 (freshmen), continuous until 8/20 (transfers).

Freshman Application Contact Mr. James Wiseman, Vice President of Enrollment, Carroll College, 100 North East Avenue, Waukesha, WI 53186-5593. *Phone:* 262-524-7221. *Toll-free phone:* 800-CARROLL. *Fax:* 262-524-7139. *E-mail:* cc.info@ccadmin.cc.edu.

See page 2792 for the College Close-Up.

CARTHAGE COLLEGE

Kenosha, Wisconsin **www.carthage.edu/**

Freshman Application Contact Carthage College, Kenosha, WI 53140. *Phone:* 262-551-6000. *Toll-free phone:* 800-351-4058.

COLUMBIA COLLEGE OF NURSING

Milwaukee, Wisconsin **www.ccon.edu/**

- **Independent** 4-year, founded 1901
- **Urban** campus
- **Endowment** $900,000
- **Coed** 260 undergraduate students, 93% full-time, 97% women, 3% men
- **Moderately difficult** entrance level, 46% of applicants were admitted

Undergraduates 243 full-time, 17 part-time. Students come from 2 states and territories, 5% are from out of state, 13% African American, 3% Asian American or Pacific Islander, 2% Hispanic American, 2% live on campus. *Retention:* 63% of 2006 full-time freshmen returned.

Freshmen *Admission:* 123 applied, 56 admitted, 30 enrolled. *Average high school GPA:* 2.5. *Test scores:* ACT scores over 18: 96%; ACT scores over 24: 34%.

Faculty *Total:* 18, 72% full-time, 11% with terminal degrees. *Student/faculty ratio:* 15:1.

Majors Nursing (registered nurse training).

Academics *Calendar:* semesters. *Degrees:* bachelor's (nursing degree is awarded in conjunction with Mount Mary College). *Special study options:* advanced placement credit, double majors, honors programs, independent study, off-campus study, part-time degree program, summer session for credit.

Computers on Campus 18 computers/terminals are available on campus for general student use. Campuswide network is available.

Student Life *Housing options:* coed. Campus housing is university owned. *Activities and organizations:* Student Senate, Student Nurses Association. *Campus security:* 24-hour emergency response devices and patrols, student patrols, late-night transport/escort service, controlled dormitory access. *Student services:* health clinic, personal/psychological counseling.

Standardized Tests *Required:* SAT or ACT (for admission).

Costs (2007–08) *Comprehensive fee:* $24,395 includes full-time tuition ($18,995), mandatory fees ($1200), and room and board ($4200). Part-time tuition: $510 per credit. Part-time tuition and fees vary according to program. *College room only:* $3200. Room and board charges vary according to board plan, housing facility, location, and student level. *Payment plan:* installment. *Waivers:* employees or children of employees.

Financial Aid Of all full-time matriculated undergraduates who enrolled in 2000, 1,782 applied for aid, 1,336 were judged to have need, 1,336 had their need fully met. In 2000, 426 non-need-based awards were made. *Average percent of need met:* 100%. *Average financial aid package:* $13,219. *Average need-based loan:* $3186. *Average need-based gift aid:* $9050. *Average non-need-based aid:* $7051. *Average indebtedness upon graduation:* $16,000.

Applying *Options:* electronic application. *Application fee:* $25. *Required:* high school transcript. *Required for some:* essay or personal statement. *Recommended:* essay or personal statement, 1 letter of recommendation, interview. *Application deadlines:* 8/1 (freshmen), rolling (transfers).

Freshman Application Contact Ms. Amy Dobson, Dean of Admissions, Columbia College of Nursing, 2900 North Menomonee River Parkway, Milwaukee, WI 53222-4597. *Phone:* 414-256-1219. *Toll-free phone:* 800-321-6265. *Fax:* 414-256-0180. *E-mail:* admiss@mtmary.edu.

CONCORDIA UNIVERSITY WISCONSIN

Mequon, Wisconsin **www.cuw.edu/**

- **Independent** comprehensive, founded 1881, affiliated with Lutheran Church–Missouri Synod, part of Concordia University System
- **Suburban** 192-acre campus with easy access to Milwaukee
- **Endowment** $41.9 million
- **Coed** 3,636 undergraduate students, 55% full-time, 62% women, 38% men
- **Moderately difficult** entrance level, 66% of applicants were admitted

Undergraduates 1,994 full-time, 1,642 part-time. Students come from 41 states and territories, 23 other countries, 30% are from out of state, 12% African American, 0.7% Asian American or Pacific Islander, 2% Hispanic American, 0.9% Native American, 0.8% international, 3% transferred in, 60% live on campus. *Retention:* 77% of 2006 full-time freshmen returned.

Freshmen *Admission:* 2,112 applied, 1,397 admitted, 425 enrolled. *Average high school GPA:* 3.32. *Test scores:* ACT scores over 18: 91%; ACT scores over 24: 35%; ACT scores over 30: 5%.

Faculty *Total:* 231, 42% full-time, 39% with terminal degrees. *Student/faculty ratio:* 13:1.

Majors Accounting; ancient Near Eastern and biblical languages; art; art teacher education; athletic training; biology/biological sciences; business administration and management; business teacher education; commercial and advertising art; computer science; criminal justice/law enforcement administration; economics; education; education (multiple levels); elementary education; English; English as a second/foreign language (teaching); exercise physiology; general studies; German; German language teacher education; graphic design; health and physical education; health and physical education related; health/health care administration; Hebrew; history; history teacher education; humanities; industrial radiologic technology; interior design; kindergarten/preschool education; legal assistant/paralegal; liberal arts and sciences/liberal studies; marketing/marketing management; mass communication/media; mathematics; medical office assistant; middle school education; missionary studies and missiology; modern Greek; music; music teacher education; nursing (registered nurse training); occupational therapy; pastoral studies/counseling; physical education teaching and coaching; physical therapy; pre-dentistry studies; pre-law studies; pre-medical studies; pre-nursing studies; psychology; religious studies; science teacher education; secondary education; social work; Spanish; Spanish language teacher education; sport and fitness administration/management; theology; youth ministry.

Academics *Calendar:* 4-1-4. *Degrees:* certificates, associate, bachelor's, master's, doctoral, and postbachelor's certificates. *Special study options:* academic remediation for entering students, accelerated degree program, adult/continuing education programs, advanced placement credit, distance learning, double majors, English as a second language, honors programs, independent study, internships, off-campus study, part-time degree program, services for LD students, student-designed majors, study abroad, summer session for credit.

Computers on Campus 100 computers/terminals are available on campus for general student use. Campuswide network is available.

Student Life *Housing options:* men-only, women-only. Campus housing is university owned. Freshman applicants given priority for college housing. *Activities and organizations:* drama/theater group, student-run newspaper, radio station, choral group, Fellowship of Christian Athletes, Kammerchor, Youth Ministry, band. *Campus security:* student patrols, controlled dormitory access. *Student services:* health clinic, personal/psychological counseling.

Athletics Member NCAA. All Division III. *Intercollegiate sports:* baseball M, basketball M/W, cross-country running M/W, football M, golf M/W, soccer M/W, softball W, tennis M/W, track and field M/W, volleyball W, wrestling M. *Intramural sports:* basketball M/W, softball M/W, volleyball M/W.

Standardized Tests *Required:* ACT (for admission).

Costs (2007–08) *Comprehensive fee:* $26,240 includes full-time tuition ($18,950), mandatory fees ($90), and room and board ($7200). Full-time tuition and fees vary according to program. Part-time tuition: $790 per credit hour. Part-time tuition and fees vary according to class time and program. No tuition increase for student's term of enrollment. *Room and board:* Room and board charges vary according to board plan. *Payment plans:* installment, deferred payment. *Waivers:* employees or children of employees.

Financial Aid Of all full-time matriculated undergraduates who enrolled in 2007, 1,590 applied for aid, 1,363 were judged to have need, 457 had their need fully met. 82 Federal Work-Study jobs (averaging $1700). 75 state and other part-time jobs (averaging $500). In 2007, 276 non-need-based awards were made. *Average percent of need met:* 75%. *Average financial aid package:* $18,475. *Average need-based loan:* $6203. *Average need-based gift aid:* $9553. *Average non-need-based aid:* $8037. *Average indebtedness upon graduation:* $22,020.

Applying *Application fee:* $35. *Required:* high school transcript, minimum 2.0 GPA. *Required for some:* essay or personal statement, minimum 3.0 GPA, 3 letters of recommendation. *Recommended:* interview. *Application deadlines:* 8/15 (freshmen), rolling (transfers). *Notification:* continuous (freshmen), continuous (transfers).

Freshman Application Contact Ms. Julie Schroeder, Concordia University Wisconsin, 12800 North Lake Shore Drive, Mequon, WI 53097. *Phone:* 262-243-4305 Ext. 4305. *Toll-free phone:* 888-628-9472. *E-mail:* admission@cuw.edu.

DeVry University

Milwaukee, Wisconsin **www.devry.edu/**

- **Proprietary** comprehensive, part of DeVry University
- **Coed** 108 undergraduate students, 39% full-time, 65% women, 35% men
- **Minimally difficult** entrance level

Undergraduates 42 full-time, 66 part-time. 3% are from out of state, 48% African American, 3% Asian American or Pacific Islander, 10% Hispanic American, 18% transferred in. *Retention:* 43% of 2006 full-time freshmen returned.

Freshmen *Admission:* 20 enrolled.

Faculty *Total:* 4. *Student/faculty ratio:* 79:1.

Majors Business administration and management; business administration, management and operations related; computer systems analysis.

Academics *Calendar:* semesters. *Degrees:* bachelor's and master's. *Special study options:* academic remediation for entering students, accelerated degree program, adult/continuing education programs, advanced placement credit, distance learning, part-time degree program, services for LD students, summer session for credit.

Computers on Campus Students can access the following: online (class) registration. Campuswide network is available.

Student Life *Housing:* college housing not available.

Costs (2008–09) *Tuition:* $13,810 full-time, $515 per credit part-time. *Required fees:* $80 full-time.

Applying *Options:* electronic application, early admission, deferred entrance. *Application fee:* $50. *Required:* high school transcript, interview. *Application deadlines:* rolling (freshmen), rolling (transfers). *Notification:* continuous (freshmen), continuous (transfers).

Director of Admissions Admissions Office, DeVry University, 100 East Wisconsin Avenue, Suite 2550, Milwaukee, WI 53202-4107.

DeVry University

Waukesha, Wisconsin

Edgewood College

Madison, Wisconsin **www.edgewood.edu/**

- **Independent Roman Catholic** comprehensive, founded 1927
- **Urban** 55-acre campus
- **Endowment** $15.4 million
- **Coed**
- **Moderately difficult** entrance level

Faculty *Student/faculty ratio:* 12:1.

Academics *Calendar:* 4-1-4. *Degrees:* associate, bachelor's, master's, and doctoral.

Student Life *Campus security:* 24-hour emergency response devices and patrols, student patrols, late-night transport/escort service, controlled dormitory access.

Athletics Member NCAA. All Division III.

Standardized Tests *Required:* SAT and SAT Subject Tests or ACT (for admission).

Costs (2008–09) *Comprehensive fee:* $26,866 includes full-time tuition ($20,040) and room and board ($6826). Part-time tuition: $630 per credit. *College room only:* $3466.

Financial Aid Of all full-time matriculated undergraduates who enrolled in 2005, 1,164 applied for aid, 988 were judged to have need, 178 had their need fully met. 334 Federal Work-Study jobs (averaging $1676). 656 state and other part-time jobs (averaging $1667). In 2005, 300 non-need-based awards were made. *Average percent of need met:* 72. *Average financial aid package:* $12,859. *Average need-based loan:* $4360. *Average need-based gift aid:* $8043. *Average non-need-based aid:* $9742. *Average indebtedness upon graduation:* $24,727.

Applying *Options:* deferred entrance. *Application fee:* $25. *Required:* high school transcript, minimum 2.5 GPA. *Required for some:* essay or personal statement, 2 letters of recommendation, interview. *Recommended:* interview.

Freshman Application Contact Ms. Christine Benedict, Director of Admission, Edgewood College, 1000 Edgewood College Drive, Madison, WI 53711-1997. *Phone:* 608-663-2328. *Toll-free phone:* 800-444-4861 Ext. 2294. *Fax:* 608-663-2214. *E-mail:* admissions@edgewood.edu.

See page 2794 for the College Close-Up.

Herzing College

Madison, Wisconsin **www.herzing.edu/madison**

- **Proprietary** primarily 2-year, founded 1948, part of Herzing Institutes, Inc
- **Suburban** campus with easy access to Milwaukee
- **Coed, primarily men**
- **Moderately difficult** entrance level

Faculty *Student/faculty ratio:* 13:1.

Academics *Calendar:* semesters. *Degrees:* diplomas, associate, and bachelor's.

Student Life *Campus security:* 24-hour emergency response devices.

Costs (2007–08) *Tuition:* $10,050 full-time, $335 per credit hour part-time. Full-time tuition and fees vary according to course load, location, and program. Part-time tuition and fees vary according to course load, location, and program. *Required fees:* $48 full-time.

Financial Aid *Financial aid deadline:* 6/30.

Applying *Options:* electronic application, early admission. *Required:* high school transcript, interview.

Freshman Application Contact Ms. Rebecca M. Abrams, Admissions Director, Herzing College, 5218 East Terrace Drive, Madison, WI 53718. *Phone:* 608-663-0804. *Toll-free phone:* 800-582-1227. *Fax:* 608-249-8593. *E-mail:* info@msn.herzing.edu.

ITT Technical Institute

Green Bay, Wisconsin **www.itt-tech.edu/**

- **Proprietary** primarily 2-year, founded 2000, part of ITT Educational Services, Inc
- **Coed**
- **Minimally difficult** entrance level

Academics *Calendar:* quarters. *Degrees:* associate and bachelor's.

Standardized Tests *Required:* Wonderlic aptitude test (for admission).

Applying *Options:* deferred entrance. *Application fee:* $100. *Required:* high school transcript, interview. *Recommended:* letters of recommendation.

Freshman Application Contact Ms. Marnie Glanner, Director of Recruitment, ITT Technical Institute, 470 Security Boulevard, Green Bay, WI 54313. *Phone:* 920-662-9000. *Toll-free phone:* 888-884-3626. *Fax:* 920-662-9384.

ITT Technical Institute

Greenfield, Wisconsin **www.itt-tech.edu/**

- **Proprietary** primarily 2-year, founded 1968, part of ITT Educational Services, Inc
- **Suburban** campus with easy access to Milwaukee
- **Coed**
- **Minimally difficult** entrance level

Academics *Calendar:* quarters. *Degrees:* associate and bachelor's.

Standardized Tests *Required:* Wonderlic aptitude test (for admission).

Applying *Options:* deferred entrance. *Application fee:* $100. *Required:* high school transcript, interview. *Recommended:* letters of recommendation.

Freshman Application Contact Ms. Geraldine Purcell, Director of Recruitment, ITT Technical Institute, 6300 West Layton Avenue, Greenfield, WI 53220. *Phone:* 414-282-9494.

Lakeland College

Sheboygan, Wisconsin **www.lakeland.edu/**

- **Independent** comprehensive, founded 1862, affiliated with United Church of Christ
- **Rural** 240-acre campus with easy access to Milwaukee
- **Endowment** $11.1 million
- **Coed**
- **Minimally difficult** entrance level

Faculty *Student/faculty ratio:* 17:1.

Academics *Calendar:* 4-4-1. *Degrees:* bachelor's and master's.

Student Life *Campus security:* 24-hour emergency response devices, student patrols, late-night transport/escort service, controlled dormitory access.

Athletics Member NCAA. All Division III.

Standardized Tests *Required:* SAT or ACT (for admission).

Costs (2007–08) *Comprehensive fee:* $23,740 includes full-time tuition ($16,845), mandatory fees ($750), and room and board ($6145). Part-time tuition: $1686 per course.

Financial Aid Of all full-time matriculated undergraduates who enrolled in 2006, 1,180 applied for aid, 998 were judged to have need, 237 had their need fully met. 200 Federal Work-Study jobs (averaging $1650). 160 state and other part-time jobs (averaging $1650). In 2006, 224 non-need-based awards were made. *Average percent of need met:* 71. *Average financial aid package:* $11,728. *Average need-based loan:* $4198. *Average need-based gift aid:* $8474. *Average non-need-based aid:* $8747. *Financial aid deadline:* 7/1.

Applying *Options:* electronic application, deferred entrance. *Application fee:* $20. *Required:* essay or personal statement, high school transcript, minimum 2.0 GPA. *Required for some:* interview. *Recommended:* letters of recommendation.

Freshman Application Contact Mr. Nathan Dehne, Director of Admissions, Lakeland College, PO Box 359, Nash Visitors Center, Sheboygan, WI 53082-0359. *Phone:* 920-565-1588. *Toll-free phone:* 800-242-3347. *Fax:* 920-565-1206. *E-mail:* admissions@lakeland.edu.

Lawrence University

Appleton, Wisconsin **www.lawrence.edu/**

- **Independent** 4-year, founded 1847
- **Small-town** 84-acre campus
- **Endowment** $231.7 million
- **Coed** 1,451 undergraduate students, 96% full-time, 54% women, 46% men
- **Very difficult** entrance level, 56% of applicants were admitted

Lawrence University is committed to the development of intellect and talent, the acquisition of knowledge and understanding, and the cultivation of judgment and values. Research opportunities and independent study with faculty members, an academic honor code, a conservatory of music, a freshman seminar that focuses on developing communication and analysis skills, and weekend retreats to the college's 425-acre estate on Lake Michigan are among the various aspects that contribute to "The Lawrence Difference."

Undergraduates 1,388 full-time, 63 part-time. Students come from 43 states and territories, 50 other countries, 61% are from out of state, 2% African American, 3% Asian American or Pacific Islander, 2% Hispanic American, 0.2% Native American, 7% international, 1% transferred in, 95% live on campus. *Retention:* 88% of 2006 full-time freshmen returned.

Freshmen *Admission:* 2,599 applied, 1,445 admitted, 353 enrolled. *Average high school GPA:* 3.59. *Test scores:* SAT critical reading scores over 500: 96%; SAT math scores over 500: 96%; SAT writing scores over 500: 96%; ACT scores over 18: 100%; SAT critical reading scores over 600: 82%; SAT math scores over 600: 71%; SAT writing scores over 600: 76%; ACT scores over 24: 96%; SAT critical reading scores over 700: 35%; SAT math scores over 700: 30%; SAT writing scores over 700: 23%; ACT scores over 30: 43%.

Faculty *Total:* 190, 81% full-time, 84% with terminal degrees. *Student/faculty ratio:* 9:1.

Majors Ancient/classical Greek; anthropology; archeology; art history, criticism and conservation; art teacher education; Asian studies (East); biochemistry; biology/biological sciences; chemistry; Chinese; classics and classical languages related; classics and languages, literatures and linguistics; cognitive psychology and psycholinguistics; cognitive science; computer science; dramatic/theater arts; ecology; economics; English; environmental studies; ethnic, cultural minority, and gender studies related; fine/studio arts; French; geology/earth science; German; history; international economics; international relations and affairs; Japanese; Latin; linguistics; mathematics; mathematics and computer science; music; music pedagogy; music performance; music teacher education; music theory and composition; neuroscience; philosophy; physics; piano and organ; political science and government; pre-dentistry studies; pre-law studies; pre-medical studies; pre-veterinary studies; psychology; religious studies; Russian; Russian studies; secondary education; Slavic studies; social psychology; Spanish; violin, viola, guitar and other stringed instruments; voice and opera; wind/percussion instruments.

Academics *Calendar:* trimesters. *Degree:* bachelor's. *Special study options:* advanced placement credit, double majors, independent study, internships, off-campus study, services for LD students, student-designed majors, study abroad. *Unusual degree programs:* 3-2 engineering with Rensselaer Polytechnic Institute, Washington University in St. Louis, Columbia University; forestry with Duke University; nursing with Rush University; medical technology with Rush University, occupational therapy with Washington University.

Computers on Campus 354 computers/terminals and 1,055 ports are available on campus for general student use. Students can access the following: campus intranet, computer help desk, free student e-mail accounts, online (class) grades, online (class) registration, online (class) schedules, online transcripts, financial aid, financial account information. Campuswide network is available. 100% of college-owned or -operated housing units are wired for high-speed Internet access. Wireless service is available via classrooms, computer labs, learning centers, libraries.

Student Life *Housing:* on-campus residence required through senior year. *Options:* coed, men-only, women-only, cooperative. Campus housing is university owned. Freshman campus housing is guaranteed. *Activities and organizations:* drama/theater group, student-run newspaper, radio station, choral group, Lawrence Swing Dancers, Lawrence International, Outdoor Recreation Club, Lawrence Christian Fellowship, Greenfire, national fraternities, national sororities. *Campus security:* 24-hour emergency response devices, student patrols, late-night transport/escort service, controlled dormitory access, evening patrols by trained security personnel. *Student services:* health clinic, personal/psychological counseling.

Athletics Member NCAA. All Division III. *Intercollegiate sports:* baseball M, basketball M/W, crew M (c)/W (c), cross-country running M/W, fencing M/W, football M, golf M, ice hockey M/W (c), soccer M/W, softball W, swimming and diving M/W, tennis M/W, track and field M/W, ultimate Frisbee M (c)/W (c), volleyball M (c)/W, wrestling M. *Intramural sports:* badminton M/W, basketball M/W, bowling M/W, cheerleading W, cross-country running M/W, equestrian sports M/W, fencing M/W, golf M/W, racquetball M/W, squash M/W, swimming and diving M/W, table tennis M/W, tennis M/W, track and field M/W, volleyball M/W, water polo M/W, weight lifting M/W.

Costs (2007–08) *Comprehensive fee:* $37,770 includes full-time tuition ($30,846), mandatory fees ($234), and room and board ($6690). *College room only:* $3081. Room and board charges vary according to board plan. *Payment plans:* tuition prepayment, installment. *Waivers:* employees or children of employees.

Financial Aid Of all full-time matriculated undergraduates who enrolled in 2007, 1,012 applied for aid, 831 were judged to have need, 715 had their need fully met. 598 Federal Work-Study jobs (averaging $2350). 309 state and other part-time jobs (averaging $2400). In 2007, 298 non-need-based awards were made. *Average percent of need met:* 94%. *Average financial aid package:* $25,800. *Average need-based loan:* $5500. *Average need-based gift aid:* $18,000. *Average non-need-based aid:* $10,690. *Average indebtedness upon graduation:* $25,374.

Applying *Options:* electronic application, early admission, early decision, early action, deferred entrance. *Application fee:* $40. *Required:* essay or personal statement, high school transcript, 2 letters of recommendation, audition for music program. *Recommended:* minimum 3.0 GPA, interview. *Application deadlines:* 1/15 (freshmen), 5/1 (transfers), 12/1 (early action). *Early decision deadline:* 11/15. *Notification:* 4/1 (freshmen), 12/1 (early decision), 1/15 (early action).

Freshman Application Contact Mr. Steven T. Syverson, Vice President for Enrollment Management, Lawrence University, PO Box 599, Appleton, WI 54912-0599. *Phone:* 920-832-6500. *Toll-free phone:* 800-227-0982. *Fax:* 920-832-6782. *E-mail:* excel@lawrence.edu.

See page 2796 for the College Close-Up.

Maranatha Baptist Bible College

Watertown, Wisconsin **www.mbbc.edu/**

- **Independent Baptist** comprehensive, founded 1968
- **Small-town** 60-acre campus with easy access to Milwaukee
- **Endowment** $251,547
- **Coed** 848 undergraduate students, 93% full-time, 55% women, 45% men
- **Noncompetitive** entrance level, 63% of applicants were admitted

Undergraduates 791 full-time, 57 part-time. Students come from 44 states and territories, 10 other countries, 69% are from out of state, 1% African American, 1% Asian American or Pacific Islander, 1% Hispanic American, 0.6% international, 6% transferred in, 72% live on campus. *Retention:* 78% of 2006 full-time freshmen returned.

Freshmen *Admission:* 350 applied, 222 admitted, 222 enrolled. *Test scores:* ACT scores over 18: 92%; ACT scores over 24: 45%; ACT scores over 30: 8%.

Faculty *Total:* 72, 60% full-time, 22% with terminal degrees. *Student/faculty ratio:* 16:1.

Majors Accounting and business/management; administrative assistant and secretarial science; biblical studies; biology/biological sciences; business administration and management; business teacher education; early childhood education; education; elementary education; English; English/language arts teacher education; history teacher education; humanities; kindergarten/preschool education; management information systems; marketing/marketing management; mathematics teacher education; missionary studies and missiology; music; music pedagogy; music performance; music teacher education; nursing (registered nurse training); office management; pastoral studies/counseling; physical education teaching and coaching; piano and organ; religious education; religious/sacred music; religious studies; science teacher education; secondary education; social studies teacher education; youth ministry.

Academics *Calendar:* semesters. *Degrees:* certificates, associate, bachelor's, and master's. *Special study options:* academic remediation for entering students, accelerated degree program, distance learning, double majors, independent study, internships, off-campus study, part-time degree program, summer session for credit. *ROTC:* Army (b).

Computers on Campus 120 computers/terminals are available on campus for general student use. Students can access the following: campus intranet, computer help desk, free student e-mail accounts. Campuswide network is available.

Student Life *Housing:* on-campus residence required through senior year. *Options:* men-only, women-only. Campus housing is university owned. Freshman campus housing is guaranteed. *Activities and organizations:* drama/theater group, choral group. *Campus security:* student patrols, late-night transport/escort service, controlled dormitory access. *Student services:* health clinic, personal/psychological counseling.

Athletics Member NCAA, NCCAA. All NCAA Division III. *Intercollegiate sports:* baseball M, basketball M/W, cross-country running M/W, football M, soccer M/W, softball W, volleyball W, wrestling M. *Intramural sports:* basketball M/W, softball M.

Standardized Tests *Required:* ACT (for admission), ACT (for placement).

Costs (2007–08) *Comprehensive fee:* $14,986 includes full-time tuition ($8576), mandatory fees ($910), and room and board ($5500). Part-time tuition: $268 per semester hour. *Payment plan:* installment. *Waivers:* employees or children of employees.

Financial Aid Of all full-time matriculated undergraduates who enrolled in 2006, 631 applied for aid, 569 were judged to have need, 44 had their need fully met. In 2006, 22 non-need-based awards were made. *Average percent of need met:* 46%. *Average financial aid package:* $5071. *Average need-based loan:* $3482. *Average need-based gift aid:* $3044. *Average non-need-based aid:* $1040. *Average indebtedness upon graduation:* $17,733.

Applying *Options:* electronic application, early admission, deferred entrance. *Application fee:* $50. *Required:* essay or personal statement, high school transcript, 4 letters of recommendation. *Application deadlines:* rolling (freshmen), rolling (transfers).

Freshman Application Contact Dr. James Harrison, Director of Admissions, Maranatha Baptist Bible College, 745 West Main Street, Watertown, WI 53094. *Phone:* 920-206-2327. *Toll-free phone:* 800-622-2947. *E-mail:* admissions@mbbc.edu.

MARIAN COLLEGE OF FOND DU LAC

Fond du Lac, Wisconsin **www.mariancollege.edu/**

- **Independent Roman Catholic** comprehensive, founded 1936
- **Small-town** 77-acre campus with easy access to Milwaukee
- **Endowment** $6.9 million
- **Coed** 2,065 undergraduate students, 70% full-time, 74% women, 26% men
- **Moderately difficult** entrance level, 85% of applicants were admitted

Undergraduates 1,439 full-time, 626 part-time. Students come from 13 states and territories, 5 other countries, 5% are from out of state, 3% African American, 1% Asian American or Pacific Islander, 2% Hispanic American, 0.7% Native American, 1% international, 7% transferred in, 34% live on campus. *Retention:* 76% of 2006 full-time freshmen returned.

Freshmen *Admission:* 747 applied, 633 admitted, 267 enrolled. *Average high school GPA:* 3.00. *Test scores:* ACT scores over 18: 78%; ACT scores over 24: 17%.

Faculty *Total:* 269, 32% full-time, 34% with terminal degrees. *Student/faculty ratio:* 12:1.

Majors Accounting; art teacher education; art therapy; biology/biological sciences; biology teacher education; business administration and management; business/commerce; business/managerial economics; chemistry; chemistry teacher education; clinical laboratory science/medical technology; communication/speech communication and rhetoric; criminal justice/law enforcement administration; cytotechnology; education; elementary education; English; English composition; English/language arts teacher education; English literature (British and Commonwealth); finance; fine/studio arts; foreign languages and literatures; graphic design; history; history teacher education; human resources management; information technology; kindergarten/preschool education; liberal arts and sciences/liberal studies; marketing/marketing management; mathematics; mathematics teacher education; medical radiologic technology; middle school education; multi-/interdisciplinary studies related; music; music management and merchandising; music teacher education; nursing (registered nurse training); operations management; organizational communication; political science and government; psychology; radiologic technology/science; science teacher education; secondary education; social work; sociology; Spanish; Spanish language teacher education; sport and fitness administration/management.

Academics *Calendar:* semesters. *Degrees:* bachelor's, master's, and doctoral. *Special study options:* academic remediation for entering students, accelerated degree program, adult/continuing education programs, advanced placement credit, cooperative education, distance learning, double majors, English as a second language, external degree program, honors programs, independent study, internships, part-time degree program, services for LD students, student-designed majors, study abroad, summer session for credit. *ROTC:* Army (b).

Computers on Campus 315 computers/terminals are available on campus for general student use. Students can access the following: campus intranet, computer help desk, free student e-mail accounts, online (class) grades, online (class) registration, online (class) schedules. Campuswide network is available. 100% of college-owned or -operated housing units are wired for high-speed Internet access. Wireless service is available via entire campus.

Student Life *Housing:* on-campus residence required through sophomore year. *Options:* coed, disabled students. Campus housing is university owned. Freshman campus housing is guaranteed. *Activities and organizations:* drama/theater group, student-run newspaper, choral group, Student Senate, Student Nurses Association, Student Education Association, Arts and Humanities Club, Music Performance Organization, national fraternities, national sororities. *Campus security:* 24-hour emergency response devices and patrols, student patrols, late-night transport/escort service, controlled dormitory access. *Student services:* health clinic, personal/psychological counseling.

Athletics Member NCAA. All Division III. *Intercollegiate sports:* baseball M, basketball M/W, cross-country running M/W, golf M/W, ice hockey M, soccer M/W, softball W, tennis M/W, volleyball W. *Intramural sports:* basketball M/W, bowling M/W, football M, skiing (downhill) M/W, tennis M/W, volleyball M/W.

Standardized Tests *Required:* SAT or ACT (for admission).

Costs (2007–08) *One-time required fee:* $100. *Comprehensive fee:* $23,900 includes full-time tuition ($18,330), mandatory fees ($350), and room and board ($5220). Full-time tuition and fees vary according to class time, course load, and program. Part-time tuition: $300 per credit. Part-time tuition and fees vary according to class time, course load, and program. *Required fees:* $80 per term part-time. *College room only:* $3620. Room and board charges vary according to board plan and housing facility. *Payment plan:* installment. *Waivers:* senior citizens and employees or children of employees.

Financial Aid Of all full-time matriculated undergraduates who enrolled in 2006, 1,307 applied for aid, 1,111 were judged to have need, 452 had their need fully met. 682 Federal Work-Study jobs (averaging $1878). 378 state and other part-time jobs (averaging $800). In 2006, 196 non-need-based awards were made. *Average percent of need met:* 90%. *Average financial aid package:* $17,973. *Average need-based loan:* $5079. *Average need-based gift aid:* $9656. *Average non-need-based aid:* $4311. *Average indebtedness upon graduation:* $21,500.

Applying *Options:* electronic application, deferred entrance. *Application fee:* $20. *Required:* high school transcript. *Required for some:* interview. *Recommended:* minimum 2.0 GPA, letters of recommendation. *Application deadlines:* rolling (freshmen), rolling (transfers). *Notification:* continuous until 8/15 (freshmen), continuous until 8/15 (transfers).

Freshman Application Contact Marian College of Fond du Lac, 45 South National Avenue, Fond du Lac, WI 54935. *Phone:* 800-262-7426. *Toll-free phone:* 800-2-MARIAN Ext. 7652. *Fax:* 920-923-8755. *E-mail:* admit@mariancollege.edu.

MARQUETTE UNIVERSITY

Milwaukee, Wisconsin **www.marquette.edu/**

- **Independent Roman Catholic (Jesuit)** university, founded 1881
- **Urban** 80-acre campus
- **Endowment** $360.3 million
- **Coed** 7,955 undergraduate students, 94% full-time, 54% women, 46% men
- **Moderately difficult** entrance level, 67% of applicants were admitted

Undergraduates 7,511 full-time, 444 part-time. Students come from 51 states and territories, 47 other countries, 53% are from out of state, 5% African American, 5% Asian American or Pacific Islander, 5% Hispanic American, 0.3% Native American, 2% international, 2% transferred in, 51% live on campus. *Retention:* 89% of 2006 full-time freshmen returned.

Freshmen *Admission:* 13,375 applied, 9,005 admitted, 1,820 enrolled. *Test scores:* SAT critical reading scores over 500: 91%; SAT math scores over 500: 93%; SAT writing scores over 500: 89%; ACT scores over 18: 100%; SAT critical reading scores over 600: 44%; SAT math scores over 600: 60%; SAT writing scores over 600: 45%; ACT scores over 24: 78%; SAT critical reading scores over 700: 9%; SAT math scores over 700: 12%; SAT writing scores over 700: 8%; ACT scores over 30: 20%.

Faculty *Total:* 1,076, 57% full-time, 71% with terminal degrees. *Student/faculty ratio:* 15:1.

Majors Accounting; advertising; African-American/Black studies; anthropology; athletic training; audiology and speech-language pathology; biochemistry; biology/biological sciences; biomedical/medical engineering; biomedical sciences; broadcast journalism; business administration and management; business/managerial economics; chemistry; civil engineering; classics and languages, literatures and linguistics; clinical/medical laboratory technology; communication and journalism related; communication/speech communication and rhetoric; computational mathematics; computer engineering; computer science; creative writing; criminology; dental hygiene; dramatic/theater arts; economics; education; education (specific subject areas) related; electrical, electronics and communications engineering; elementary education; engineering; engineering related; English; English/language arts teacher education; environmental/environmental health engineering; finance; foreign languages related; foreign language teacher education; French; German; history; history of philosophy; history related; human resources management; industrial engineering; information science/studies; intercultural/multicultural and diversity studies; interdisciplinary studies; international business/trade/commerce; international/global studies; international relations and affairs; journalism; kinesiology and exercise science; management information systems; marketing/marketing management; mass communication/media; mathematics; mathematics teacher education; mechanical engineering; middle school education; molecular biology; multi-/interdisciplinary studies related; nursing (registered nurse training); philosophy; physical therapy; physician assistant; physics; political science and government; pre-dentistry studies; pre-law studies; pre-medical studies; psychology; public relations/image management; religious studies; science teacher education; secondary education; social science teacher education; social studies teacher education; social work; sociology; Spanish; speech and rhetoric; statistics; women's studies.

Academics *Calendar:* semesters. *Degrees:* bachelor's, master's, doctoral, first professional, and post-master's certificates. *Special study options:* adult/continuing education programs, advanced placement credit, cooperative education, double majors, English as a second language, honors programs, internships, off-campus study, part-time degree program, services for LD students, study abroad, summer session for credit. *ROTC:* Army (b), Navy (b), Air Force (b).

Computers on Campus 1,200 computers/terminals and 500 ports are available on campus for general student use. Students can access the following: campus intranet, computer help desk, free student e-mail accounts, online (class) grades, online (class) registration, online (class) schedules. Campuswide network is available. 100% of college-owned or -operated housing units are wired for high-speed Internet access. Wireless service is available via classrooms, computer centers, computer labs, dorm rooms, learning centers, libraries, student centers.

Student Life *Housing:* on-campus residence required through sophomore year. *Options:* coed, men-only, women-only, disabled students. Campus housing is university owned. Freshman campus housing is guaranteed. *Activities and organizations:* drama/theater group, student-run newspaper, radio and television station, choral group, student government, club sports, community service organizations, band/jazz/orchestra, Residence Hall Association, national fraternities, national sororities. *Campus security:* 24-hour emergency response devices and patrols, student patrols, late-night transport/escort service, 24-hour desk attendants in residence halls. *Student services:* health clinic, personal/psychological counseling.

Athletics Member NCAA. All Division I. *Intercollegiate sports:* baseball M (c), basketball M (s)/W (s), cheerleading M/W, crew M (c)/W (c), cross-country running M (s)/W (s), fencing M (c)/W (c), football M (c), golf M (s), lacrosse M (c), rugby M (c)/W (c), skiing (downhill) M (c)/W (c), soccer M (s)/W (s), softball W (c), swimming and diving M (c)/W (c), tennis M (s)/W (s), track and field M (s)/W (s), volleyball M (c)/W (s). *Intramural sports:* badminton M/W, basketball M/W, football W, golf M/W, racquetball M/W, soccer M/W, softball M/W, squash M/W, tennis M/W, track and field M/W, ultimate Frisbee M/W, volleyball M/W, water polo M/W, weight lifting M/W.

Standardized Tests *Required:* SAT or ACT (for admission).

Costs (2008–09) *Tuition:* $27,720 full-time, $810 per credit part-time. *Required fees:* $408 full-time.

Financial Aid Of all full-time matriculated undergraduates who enrolled in 2006, 5,476 applied for aid, 4,558 were judged to have need, 1,569 had their need fully met. 894 Federal Work-Study jobs (averaging $2500). In 2006, 540 non-need-based awards were made. *Average percent of need met:* 77%. *Average financial aid package:* $18,248. *Average need-based loan:* $5367. *Average need-based gift aid:* $11,619. *Average non-need-based aid:* $8242. *Average indebtedness upon graduation:* $25,753.

Applying *Options:* electronic application, deferred entrance. *Application fee:* $30. *Required:* essay or personal statement, high school transcript, minimum 2.5 GPA, 1 letter of recommendation. *Recommended:* minimum 3.4 GPA. *Application deadlines:* 12/1 (freshmen), 12/1 (transfers). *Notification:* 1/31 (freshmen), 1/31 (transfers).

Freshman Application Contact Mr. Robert Blust, Dean of Undergraduate Admissions, Marquette University, PO Box 1881, Milwaukee, WI 53201-1881. *Phone:* 414-288-7004. *Toll-free phone:* 800-222-6544. *Fax:* 414-288-3764. *E-mail:* admissions@marquette.edu.

MILWAUKEE INSTITUTE OF ART AND DESIGN

Milwaukee, Wisconsin **www.miad.edu/**

Freshman Application Contact Mr. Mark Fetherston, Director of Admissions, Milwaukee Institute of Art and Design, 273 East Erie Street, Milwaukee, WI 53202. *Phone:* 414-847-3259. *Toll-free phone:* 888-749-MIAD. *Fax:* 414-291-8077. *E-mail:* admissions@miad.edu.

MILWAUKEE SCHOOL OF ENGINEERING

Milwaukee, Wisconsin **www.msoe.edu/**

- **Independent** comprehensive, founded 1903
- **Urban** 15-acre campus
- **Endowment** $51.7 million
- **Coed, primarily men** 2,317 undergraduate students, 89% full-time, 19% women, 81% men
- **Moderately difficult** entrance level, 65% of applicants were admitted

Undergraduates 2,066 full-time, 251 part-time. Students come from 36 states and territories, 16 other countries, 34% are from out of state, 4% African American, 3% Asian American or Pacific Islander, 3% Hispanic American, 0.6% Native American, 2% international, 7% transferred in, 44% live on campus. *Retention:* 73% of 2006 full-time freshmen returned.

Freshmen *Admission:* 2,732 applied, 1,767 admitted, 575 enrolled. *Average high school GPA:* 3.5. *Test scores:* SAT critical reading scores over 500: 85%; SAT math scores over 500: 100%; SAT writing scores over 500: 89%; ACT scores over 18: 100%; SAT critical reading scores over 600: 47%; SAT math scores over 600: 81%; SAT writing scores over 600: 39%; ACT scores over 24: 70%; SAT critical reading scores over 700: 2%; SAT math scores over 700: 26%; SAT writing scores over 700: 14%; ACT scores over 30: 13%.

Faculty *Total:* 235, 51% full-time, 49% with terminal degrees. *Student/faculty ratio:* 14:1.

Majors Architectural engineering; biomedical/medical engineering; business administration and management; business/commerce; communication and journalism related; computer engineering; computer software engineering; construction management; electrical, electronic and communications engineering technology; electrical, electronics and communications engineering; engineering; industrial engineering; international business/trade/commerce; management information systems; mechanical engineering; mechanical engineering/mechanical technology; nursing (registered nurse training).

Academics *Calendar:* quarters. *Degrees:* bachelor's and master's. *Special study options:* academic remediation for entering students, adult/continuing education programs, advanced placement credit, distance learning, double majors, English as a second language, independent study, internships, part-time degree program, services for LD students, study abroad, summer session for credit. *ROTC:* Army (c), Navy (c), Air Force (c).

Computers on Campus 125 computers/terminals and 2,000 ports are available on campus for general student use. Students can access the following: campus intranet, computer help desk, free student e-mail accounts, online (class) grades, online (class) registration, online (class) schedules. Campuswide network is available. 100% of college-owned or -operated housing units are wired for high-speed Internet access. Wireless service is available via entire campus.

Student Life *Housing:* on-campus residence required through sophomore year. *Options:* coed, disabled students. Campus housing is university owned. Freshman campus housing is guaranteed. *Activities and organizations:* drama/theater group, student-run radio station, choral group, Architectural Engineering and Construction Management Societies, Student Athletic Advisory Committee, MAGE, Student Government, Student Union Board, national fraternities, national sororities. *Campus security:* 24-hour emergency response devices and patrols, late-night transport/escort service, controlled dormitory access. *Student services:* health clinic, personal/psychological counseling.

Athletics Member NCAA. All Division III. *Intercollegiate sports:* baseball M, basketball M/W, cheerleading M/W, cross-country running M/W, golf M/W, ice hockey M, soccer M/W, softball W, tennis M/W, track and field M/W, volleyball M/W, wrestling M. *Intramural sports:* basketball M/W, bowling M (c)/W (c), cross-country running M (c)/W (c), fencing M (c)/W (c), football M/W, gymnastics M (c)/W (c), lacrosse M (c)/W (c), rugby M (c), soccer M/W, softball M/W, volleyball M/W, weight lifting M (c)/W (c).

Standardized Tests *Required:* SAT or ACT (for admission).

Costs (2007–08) *Comprehensive fee:* $32,481 includes full-time tuition ($25,980) and room and board ($6501). Part-time tuition: $450 per quarter hour. Part-time tuition and fees vary according to course load. *College room only:* $4170. Room and board charges vary according to board plan and housing facility. *Payment plan:* installment. *Waivers:* employees or children of employees.

Financial Aid Of all full-time matriculated undergraduates who enrolled in 2006, 1,594 applied for aid, 1,435 were judged to have need, 253 had their need fully met. 208 Federal Work-Study jobs (averaging $1300). In 2006, 290 non-need-based awards were made. *Average percent of need met:* 72%. *Average financial aid package:* $16,915. *Average need-based loan:* $3951. *Average need-based gift aid:* $13,221. *Average non-need-based aid:* $14,159. *Average indebtedness upon graduation:* $34,862.

Applying *Options:* electronic application, deferred entrance. *Application fee:* $25. *Required:* high school transcript, minimum 2.5 GPA. *Required for some:* essay or personal statement, interview. *Application deadlines:* rolling (freshmen), rolling (out-of-state freshmen), rolling (transfers). *Notification:* continuous (freshmen), continuous (out-of-state freshmen), continuous (transfers).

Freshman Application Contact Paul Borens, Director of Admissions, Milwaukee School of Engineering, 1025 North Broadway, Milwaukee, WI 53202-3109. *Phone:* 414-277-6765. *Toll-free phone:* 800-332-6763. *Fax:* 414-277-7475. *E-mail:* borens@msoe.edu.

See page 2798 for the College Close-Up.

MOUNT MARY COLLEGE

Milwaukee, Wisconsin **www.mtmary.edu/**

- **Independent Roman Catholic** comprehensive, founded 1913
- **Urban** 80-acre campus
- **Endowment** $10.1 million
- **Undergraduate: women only; graduate: coed** 1,369 undergraduate students, 60% full-time, 97% women, 3% men
- **Moderately difficult** entrance level, 59% of applicants were admitted

Undergraduates 816 full-time, 553 part-time. Students come from 9 states and territories, 9 other countries, 7% are from out of state, 19% African American, 4% Asian American or Pacific Islander, 6% Hispanic American, 2% Native American, 1% international, 9% transferred in, 12% live on campus. *Retention:* 68% of 2006 full-time freshmen returned.

Freshmen *Admission:* 482 applied, 285 admitted, 129 enrolled. *Average high school GPA:* 3.03.

Faculty *Total:* 203, 33% full-time, 37% with terminal degrees. *Student/faculty ratio:* 9:1.

Majors Accounting; art; art teacher education; art therapy; behavioral sciences; bilingual and multilingual education; biology/biological sciences; biology teacher education; business administration and management; business teacher education; chemistry; chemistry teacher education; commercial and advertising art; communication/speech communication and rhetoric; computer science; corrections and criminal justice related; dietetics; education; elementary education; English; English/language arts teacher education; fashion/apparel design; fashion merchandising; French; French language teacher education; graphic design; history; history teacher education; interior design; international relations and affairs; kindergarten/preschool education; liberal arts and sciences/liberal studies; marketing/marketing management; mathematics; mathematics teacher education; music; music teacher education; nursing (registered nurse training); occupational therapy; philosophy; pre-dentistry studies; pre-law studies; pre-medical studies; pre-veterinary studies; psychology; public relations/image management; religious education; religious studies; secondary education; social work; Spanish; Spanish language teacher education; technical and business writing.

Academics *Calendar:* semesters. *Degrees:* bachelor's, master's, and post-bachelor's certificates. *Special study options:* academic remediation for entering students, accelerated degree program, advanced placement credit, distance learning, double majors, honors programs, independent study, internships, part-time degree program, services for LD students, student-designed majors, study abroad, summer session for credit. *ROTC:* Army (c).

Computers on Campus 170 computers/terminals are available on campus for general student use. Campuswide network is available.

Student Life *Housing:* on-campus residence required for freshman year. *Options:* women-only. Campus housing is university owned. Freshman campus housing is guaranteed. *Activities and organizations:* drama/theater group, student-run newspaper, choral group, department-affiliated clubs, Campus Ministry, student athletics, student government. *Campus security:* 24-hour patrols, late-night transport/escort service, controlled dormitory access. *Student services:* health clinic, personal/psychological counseling, women's center.

Athletics Member NCAA. *Intercollegiate sports:* basketball W, soccer W, softball W, tennis W, volleyball W. *Intramural sports:* basketball W, bowling W, golf W, skiing (cross-country) W, soccer W, swimming and diving W, tennis W, track and field W, volleyball W.

Standardized Tests *Required:* SAT or ACT (for admission).

Costs (2008–09) *Comprehensive fee:* $27,344 includes full-time tuition ($20,350) and room and board ($6994). Part-time tuition: $575 per credit.

Financial Aid Of all full-time matriculated undergraduates who enrolled in 2007, 666 applied for aid, 594 were judged to have need, 107 had their need fully met. 150 Federal Work-Study jobs (averaging $1391). 50 state and other part-time jobs (averaging $1171). In 2007, 100 non-need-based awards were made. *Average percent of need met:* 67%. *Average financial aid package:* $13,245. *Average need-based loan:* $4565. *Average need-based gift aid:* $8481. *Average non-need-based aid:* $9993. *Average indebtedness upon graduation:* $22,590.

Applying *Options:* electronic application, deferred entrance. *Application fee:* $25. *Required:* high school transcript, minimum 2.5 GPA. *Required for some:* essay or personal statement, 2 letters of recommendation. *Recommended:* interview. *Application deadlines:* rolling (freshmen), rolling (transfers). *Notification:* continuous (freshmen), continuous (transfers).

Freshman Application Contact Ms. Mary Ellen Stepanski, Admission Counselor Assistant/Receptionist, Mount Mary College, 2900 North Menomonee River Parkway, Milwaukee, WI 53222-4597. *Phone:* 414-258-4810 Ext. 219. *Fax:* 414-256-0180. *E-mail:* admiss@mtmary.edu.

See page 2800 for the College Close-Up.

NORTHLAND COLLEGE

Ashland, Wisconsin **www.northland.edu/**

- **Independent** 4-year, founded 1892, affiliated with United Church of Christ
- **Small-town** 130-acre campus
- **Endowment** $21.3 million
- **Coed** 676 undergraduate students, 91% full-time, 55% women, 45% men
- **Moderately difficult** entrance level, 71% of applicants were admitted

Undergraduates 618 full-time, 58 part-time. Students come from 43 states and territories, 6 other countries, 44% are from out of state, 1% African American, 1% Asian American or Pacific Islander, 3% Hispanic American, 2% Native American, 2% international, 7% transferred in, 65% live on campus. *Retention:* 71% of 2006 full-time freshmen returned.

Freshmen *Admission:* 1,243 applied, 883 admitted, 152 enrolled. *Average high school GPA:* 3.33. *Test scores:* SAT critical reading scores over 500: 83%; SAT math scores over 500: 66%; ACT scores over 18: 98%; SAT critical reading scores over 600: 48%; SAT math scores over 600: 38%; ACT scores over 24: 57%; SAT critical reading scores over 700: 3%; ACT scores over 30: 8%.

Faculty *Total:* 96, 40% full-time, 47% with terminal degrees. *Student/faculty ratio:* 15:1.

Majors American Indian/Native American studies; applied mathematics; art; art teacher education; atmospheric sciences and meteorology; biological and physical sciences; biology/biological sciences; business administration and management; business/managerial economics; chemistry; creative writing; ecology; economics; education; elementary education; English; environmental biology; environmental education; environmental studies; fine/studio arts; fish/game management; forestry; geology/earth science; history; hydrology and water resources science; information science/studies; interdisciplinary studies; land use planning and management; mathematics; middle school education; music; music teacher education; natural resources/conservation; natural resources management and policy; natural sciences; parks, recreation and leisure; parks, recreation and leisure facilities management; peace studies and conflict resolution; philosophy; pre-dentistry studies; pre-law studies; pre-medical studies; pre-veterinary studies; psychology; religious studies; science teacher education; secondary education; social sciences; sociology; therapeutic recreation; veterinary sciences; wildlife and wildlands science and management; wildlife biology; zoology/animal biology.

Academics *Calendar:* 4-4-1. *Degree:* bachelor's. *Special study options:* accelerated degree program, adult/continuing education programs, advanced placement credit, cooperative education, distance learning, double majors, honors programs, independent study, internships, off-campus study, part-time degree program, services for LD students, student-designed majors, study abroad, summer session for credit. *Unusual degree programs:* 3-2 engineering with Michigan Technological University, Washington University in St. Louis; forestry with Michigan Technological University.

Computers on Campus 120 computers/terminals are available on campus for general student use. Students can access the following: computer help desk, free student e-mail accounts, online (class) grades, online (class) registration, online (class) schedules. Campuswide network is available. 100% of college-owned or -operated housing units are wired for high-speed Internet access. Wireless service is available via entire campus.

Student Life *Housing:* on-campus residence required through sophomore year. *Options:* coed, men-only, women-only, cooperative. Campus housing is university owned. Freshman campus housing is guaranteed. *Activities and organizations:* drama/theater group, student-run newspaper, radio station, choral group, Psi Chi, the National Honor Society in Psychology, Northland College Student Association, Native American Student Association, Northland Greens, "N" Club. *Campus security:* 24-hour emergency response devices and patrols, late-night transport/escort service, controlled dormitory access. *Student services:* health clinic, personal/psychological counseling, women's center.

Athletics Member NCAA, NAIA. All NCAA Division III. *Intercollegiate sports:* baseball M, basketball M/W, cross-country running M/W, ice hockey M, soccer M/W, softball W, volleyball W. *Intramural sports:* archery M/W, badminton M/W, basketball M/W, cross-country running M/W, football M/W, golf M/W, ice hockey M/W, lacrosse M, racquetball M/W, rock climbing M (c)/W (c), skiing (cross-country) M (c)/W (c), skiing (downhill) M (c)/W (c), soccer M/W, softball M/W, swimming and diving M/W, table tennis M/W, tennis M/W, volleyball M/W, water polo M/W, weight lifting M/W.

Standardized Tests *Required:* SAT or ACT (for admission).

Costs (2008–09) *Comprehensive fee:* $29,541 includes full-time tuition ($22,500), mandatory fees ($601), and room and board ($6440). *College room only:* $2600.

Financial Aid Of all full-time matriculated undergraduates who enrolled in 2007, 578 applied for aid, 523 were judged to have need, 76 had their need fully met. 322 Federal Work-Study jobs (averaging $1481). 217 state and other part-time jobs (averaging $1427). In 2007, 88 non-need-based awards were made. *Average percent of need met:* 82%. *Average financial aid package:* $18,081. *Average need-based loan:* $4296. *Average need-based gift aid:* $12,618. *Average non-need-based aid:* $8318. *Average indebtedness upon graduation:* $23,630.

Applying *Options:* electronic application, deferred entrance. *Application fee:* $25. *Required:* essay or personal statement, high school transcript, 1 letter of recommendation. *Recommended:* minimum 2.0 GPA, interview. *Application deadlines:* 5/1 (freshmen), 5/1 (transfers). *Notification:* continuous (freshmen), continuous (transfers).

Freshman Application Contact Susan Greenwald, Director of Admission, Northland College, 1411 Ellis Avenue, Ashland, WI 54806. *Phone:* 715-682-1224. *Toll-free phone:* 800-753-1840 (in-state); 800-753-1040 (out-of-state). *Fax:* 715-682-1258. *E-mail:* admit@northland.edu.

RIPON COLLEGE

Ripon, Wisconsin — www.ripon.edu/

- **Independent** 4-year, founded 1851
- **Small-town** 250-acre campus with easy access to Milwaukee
- **Endowment** $59.4 million
- **Coed** 1,000 undergraduate students, 98% full-time, 53% women, 48% men
- **Moderately difficult** entrance level, 80% of applicants were admitted

Undergraduates 984 full-time, 16 part-time. Students come from 31 states and territories, 13 other countries, 24% are from out of state, 2% African American, 1% Asian American or Pacific Islander, 3% Hispanic American, 0.6% Native American, 1% international, 3% transferred in, 87% live on campus. *Retention:* 86% of 2006 full-time freshmen returned.

Freshmen *Admission:* 974 applied, 775 admitted, 262 enrolled. *Average high school GPA:* 3.38. *Test scores:* SAT critical reading scores over 500: 58%; SAT math scores over 500: 71%; SAT writing scores over 500: 98%; ACT scores over 18: 98%; SAT critical reading scores over 600: 29%; SAT math scores over 600: 35%; SAT writing scores over 600: 52%; ACT scores over 24: 52%; SAT math scores over 700: 14%; SAT writing scores over 700: 9%; ACT scores over 30: 9%.

Faculty *Total:* 90, 58% full-time, 79% with terminal degrees. *Student/faculty ratio:* 15:1.

Majors Anthropology; art; biochemistry; biology/biological sciences; business administration and management; chemistry; communication/speech communication and rhetoric; computer science; dramatic/theater arts; early childhood education; economics; education; elementary education; English; environmental studies; French; German; history; interdisciplinary studies; Latin American studies; mathematics; music; music teacher education; philosophy; physical education teaching and coaching; physical sciences; physiological psychology/psychobiology; political science and government; pre-dentistry studies; pre-law studies; pre-medical studies; pre-veterinary studies; psychology; religious studies; Romance languages; secondary education; sociology; Spanish.

Academics *Calendar:* semesters. *Degree:* bachelor's. *Special study options:* accelerated degree program, advanced placement credit, double majors, internships, off-campus study, part-time degree program, services for LD students, student-designed majors, study abroad. *ROTC:* Army (b). *Unusual degree programs:* 3-2 engineering with Rensselaer Polytechnic Institute, Washington University in St. Louis, University of Wisconsin-Madison; forestry with Duke University; nursing with Rush University; environmental studies with Duke University.

Computers on Campus 150 computers/terminals are available on campus for general student use. Students can access the following: campus intranet, computer help desk, free student e-mail accounts. Campuswide network is available.

Student Life *Housing:* on-campus residence required through senior year. *Options:* coed, men-only, women-only. Campus housing is university owned. Freshman campus housing is guaranteed. *Activities and organizations:* drama/theater group, student-run newspaper, radio station, choral group, Environmental Group, Student Senate, Community Service Coalition, SMAC (Student Media and Activities Committee), national fraternities, national sororities. *Campus security:* 24-hour emergency response devices and patrols, student patrols, late-night transport/escort service, controlled dormitory access. *Student services:* health clinic, personal/psychological counseling.

Athletics Member NCAA. All Division III. *Intercollegiate sports:* baseball M, basketball M/W, cheerleading M (c)/W, cross-country running M/W, football M, golf M/W, rugby M (c)/W (c), soccer M/W, softball W, swimming and diving M/W, tennis M/W, track and field M/W, volleyball W. *Intramural sports:* basketball M/W, bowling M/W, fencing M/W, football M/W, golf M/W, racquetball M/W, soccer M/W, softball M/W, table tennis M/W, tennis M/W, ultimate Frisbee M/W, volleyball M/W.

Standardized Tests *Required:* SAT or ACT (for admission).

Costs (2007–08) *Comprehensive fee:* $29,708 includes full-time tuition ($23,048), mandatory fees ($250), and room and board ($6410). Part-time tuition: $890 per credit. No tuition increase for student's term of enrollment. *College room only:* $3280. *Payment plan:* installment. *Waivers:* children of alumni and employees or children of employees.

Financial Aid Of all full-time matriculated undergraduates who enrolled in 2007, 842 applied for aid, 750 were judged to have need, 368 had their need fully met. 348 Federal Work-Study jobs (averaging $1492). 345 state and other part-time jobs (averaging $1727). In 2007, 219 non-need-based awards were made. *Average percent of need met:* 93%. *Average financial aid package:* $20,438. *Average need-based loan:* $5167. *Average need-based gift aid:* $15,544. *Average non-need-based aid:* $16,813. *Average indebtedness upon graduation:* $19,929.

Applying *Options:* electronic application, deferred entrance. *Application fee:* $30. *Required:* essay or personal statement, high school transcript, minimum 2.0 GPA, 1 letter of recommendation. *Required for some:* interview. *Recommended:* interview. *Application deadlines:* rolling (freshmen), rolling (transfers). *Notification:* continuous (freshmen), continuous (transfers).

Freshman Application Contact Office of Admission, Ripon College, 300 Seward Street, PO Box 248, Ripon, WI 54971. *Phone:* 920-748-8114. *Toll-free phone:* 800-947-4766. *Fax:* 920-748-8335. *E-mail:* adminfo@ripon.edu.

See page 2802 for the College Close-Up.

ST. NORBERT COLLEGE

De Pere, Wisconsin **www.snc.edu/**

- **Independent Roman Catholic** comprehensive, founded 1898
- **Suburban** 92-acre campus
- **Endowment** $71.1 million
- **Coed** 2,086 undergraduate students, 97% full-time, 57% women, 43% men
- **Moderately difficult** entrance level, 87% of applicants were admitted

Undergraduates 2,032 full-time, 54 part-time. Students come from 26 states and territories, 29 other countries, 28% are from out of state, 0.9% African American, 1% Asian American or Pacific Islander, 3% Hispanic American, 1% Native American, 3% international, 3% transferred in, 74% live on campus. *Retention:* 85% of 2006 full-time freshmen returned.

Freshmen *Admission:* 1,789 applied, 1,562 admitted, 543 enrolled. *Average high school GPA:* 3.52. *Test scores:* ACT scores over 18: 98%; ACT scores over 24: 55%; ACT scores over 30: 6%.

Faculty *Total:* 176, 62% full-time, 76% with terminal degrees. *Student/faculty ratio:* 14:1.

Majors Accounting; art; biological and physical sciences; biology/biological sciences; business administration and management; chemistry; commercial and advertising art; communication/speech communication and rhetoric; computer and information sciences; economics; elementary education; English; environmental science; environmental studies; French; geology/earth science; German; history; humanities; international business/trade/commerce; international relations and affairs; mathematics; music; music teacher education; philosophy; physics; political science and government; psychology; religious studies; sociology; Spanish.

Academics *Calendar:* semesters. *Degrees:* bachelor's and master's. *Special study options:* academic remediation for entering students, advanced placement credit, double majors, English as a second language, honors programs, independent study, internships, off-campus study, part-time degree program, services for LD students, student-designed majors, study abroad, summer session for credit. *ROTC:* Army (b).

Computers on Campus 221 computers/terminals are available on campus for general student use. Students can access the following: campus intranet, computer help desk, free student e-mail accounts, online (class) grades, online (class) registration, online (class) schedules. Campuswide network is available. 100% of college-owned or -operated housing units are wired for high-speed Internet access. Wireless service is available via classrooms, libraries.

Student Life *Housing:* on-campus residence required through senior year. *Options:* coed, women-only, disabled students. Campus housing is university owned. Freshman campus housing is guaranteed. *Activities and organizations:* drama/theater group, student-run newspaper, radio and television station, choral group, CC Hams (Women's Social Group), Habitat for Humanity, Student Education Association, Beta Beta Beta (Biology Club), Knight Theatre, national fraternities, national sororities. *Campus security:* 24-hour emergency response devices and patrols, student patrols, late-night transport/escort service, controlled dormitory access, crime prevention programs. *Student services:* health clinic, personal/psychological counseling, women's center.

Athletics Member NCAA. All Division III. *Intercollegiate sports:* baseball M, basketball M/W, cross-country running M/W, football M, golf M/W, ice hockey M, soccer M/W, softball W, swimming and diving W, tennis M/W, track and field M/W, volleyball W. *Intramural sports:* basketball M/W, cheerleading M (c)/W (c), crew M (c)/W (c), football M/W, lacrosse M, rugby W (c), skiing (downhill) M (c)/W (c), soccer M/W, softball M/W, volleyball M/W.

Standardized Tests *Required:* SAT or ACT (for admission).

Costs (2007–08) *Comprehensive fee:* $31,232 includes full-time tuition ($24,253), mandatory fees ($400), and room and board ($6579). Full-time tuition and fees vary according to course load. Part-time tuition: $758 per credit. Part-time tuition and fees vary according to course load. *College room only:* $3449. Room and board charges vary according to board plan, housing facility, and student level. *Payment plans:* installment, deferred payment. *Waivers:* employees or children of employees.

Financial Aid Of all full-time matriculated undergraduates who enrolled in 2006, 1,522 applied for aid, 1,251 were judged to have need, 436 had their need fully met. 247 Federal Work-Study jobs (averaging $1489). 595 state and other part-time jobs (averaging $1891). In 2006, 600 non-need-based awards were made. *Average percent of need met:* 88%. *Average financial aid package:* $17,025. *Average need-based loan:* $4712. *Average need-based gift aid:* $12,349. *Average non-need-based aid:* $7343.

Applying *Options:* electronic application, early admission, deferred entrance. *Application fee:* $25. *Required:* high school transcript, 1 letter of recommendation. *Required for some:* interview. *Recommended:* essay or personal statement. *Application deadlines:* rolling (freshmen), rolling (transfers). *Early decision deadline:* 12/1. *Notification:* continuous (freshmen), continuous (transfers), 12/15 (early decision).

Freshman Application Contact Ms. Bridget O'Connor, Interim Vice President for Enrollment Management and Communications, St. Norbert College, 100 Grant Street, De Pere, WI 54115-2099. *Phone:* 920-403-3005. *Toll-free phone:* 800-236-4878. *Fax:* 920-403-4072. *E-mail:* admit@snc.edu.

See page 2804 for the College Close-Up.

SILVER LAKE COLLEGE

Manitowoc, Wisconsin **www.sl.edu/**

- **Independent Roman Catholic** comprehensive, founded 1869
- **Rural** 30-acre campus with easy access to Milwaukee
- **Endowment** $5.3 million
- **Coed**
- **Minimally difficult** entrance level

In a recent survey of Silver Lake College (SLC) graduates, 92 percent of those responding indicated that they are satisfied with the commitment to academic excellence on campus. For information about the College's outstanding programs of study, students should contact the admissions office at 800-236-4SLC Ext. 175 (toll-free) or visit the College's Web site at http://www.sl.edu.

Faculty *Student/faculty ratio:* 5:1.

Academics *Calendar:* semesters. *Degrees:* certificates, associate, bachelor's, master's, and postbachelor's certificates.

Student Life *Campus security:* 24-hour emergency response devices.

Athletics Member NSCAA.

Standardized Tests *Required:* SAT or ACT (for admission).

Costs (2008–09) *Comprehensive fee:* $24,644 includes full-time tuition ($19,194) and room and board ($5450). Part-time tuition: $595 per credit. *College room only:* $4900.

Financial Aid Of all full-time matriculated undergraduates who enrolled in 2007, 148 applied for aid, 139 were judged to have need, 24 had their need fully met. 73 Federal Work-Study jobs (averaging $2031). In 2007, 12 non-need-based awards were made. *Average percent of need met:* 68. *Average financial aid package:* $14,756. *Average need-based loan:* $4578. *Average need-based gift aid:* $10,233. *Average non-need-based aid:* $5726. *Average indebtedness upon graduation:* $24,029.

Applying *Options:* electronic application, early admission, deferred entrance. *Application fee:* $35. *Required:* high school transcript, minimum 2.0 GPA. *Required for some:* interview, audition.

Freshman Application Contact Matthew Thielen, Student Life and Dean of Students, Silver Lake College, 2406 South Alverno Road, Manitowoc, WI 54220. *Phone:* 920-686-6199 Ext. 199. *Toll-free phone:* 800-236-4752 Ext. 175. *Fax:* 920-684-7082. *E-mail:* admslc@silver.sl.edu.

UNIVERSITY OF PHOENIX–WISCONSIN CAMPUS

Brookfield, Wisconsin **www.phoenix.edu/**

- **Proprietary** comprehensive, founded 2001
- **Urban** campus
- **Coed**
- **Noncompetitive** entrance level

Faculty *Student/faculty ratio:* 6:1.

Academics *Calendar:* continuous. *Degrees:* bachelor's and master's.

Student Life *Campus security:* late-night transport/escort service.

Costs (2007–08) *Tuition:* $11,430 full-time, $381 per credit part-time. Full-time tuition and fees vary according to course level.

Financial Aid *Average financial aid package:* $3918. *Average need-based gift aid:* $2230.

Applying *Options:* deferred entrance. *Application fee:* $45. *Required:* 1 letter of recommendation. *Required for some:* high school transcript.

Freshman Application Contact Ms. Beth Barilla, Associate Vice President, Student Admissions and Services, University of Phoenix–Wisconsin Campus, 4615 East Elwood Street, Mail Stop AA-K101, Phoenix, AZ 85040-1958. *Phone:* 480-317-6000. *Toll-free phone:* 800-776-4867 (in-state); 800-228-7240 (out-of-state). *Fax:* 480-894-1758. *E-mail:* beth.barilla@phoenix.edu.

UNIVERSITY OF WISCONSIN–EAU CLAIRE

Eau Claire, Wisconsin **www.uwec.edu/**

- **State-supported** comprehensive, founded 1916, part of University of Wisconsin System
- **Urban** 333-acre campus
- **Endowment** $29.7 million
- **Coed** 10,096 undergraduate students, 93% full-time, 59% women, 41% men
- **Moderately difficult** entrance level, 69% of applicants were admitted

Undergraduates 9,427 full-time, 669 part-time. Students come from 35 states and territories, 39 other countries, 22% are from out of state, 0.5% African American, 3% Asian American or Pacific Islander, 1% Hispanic American, 0.6% Native American, 1% international, 6% transferred in, 37% live on campus. *Retention:* 81% of 2006 full-time freshmen returned.

Freshmen *Admission:* 7,446 applied, 5,142 admitted, 2,034 enrolled. *Test scores:* SAT critical reading scores over 500: 90%; SAT math scores over 500: 90%; SAT writing scores over 500: 81%; ACT scores over 18: 100%; SAT critical reading scores over 600: 52%; SAT math scores over 600: 60%; SAT writing scores over 600: 38%; ACT scores over 24: 60%; SAT critical reading scores over 700: 17%; SAT math scores over 700: 19%; SAT writing scores over 700: 10%; ACT scores over 30: 5%.

Faculty *Total:* 530, 78% full-time, 72% with terminal degrees. *Student/faculty ratio:* 19:1.

Majors Accounting; American Indian/Native American studies; art; athletic training; biomedical sciences; business administration and management; chemistry; chemistry related; communication disorders; communication/speech communication and rhetoric; computer and information sciences; criminal justice/safety; dramatic/theater arts; economics; education (specific subject areas) related; elementary education; English; environmental health; finance; French; geography; geology/earth science; Germanic languages; health/health care administration; history; information resources management; journalism; kinesiology and exercise science; Latin American studies; liberal arts and sciences/liberal studies; marketing/marketing management; mass communication/media; mathematics; molecular biology; music; music therapy; nursing (registered nurse training); philosophy; physics; political science and government; psychology; religious studies; science teacher education; social studies teacher education; social work; sociology; Spanish; special education.

Academics *Calendar:* semesters. *Degrees:* certificates, associate, bachelor's, master's, post-master's, and postbachelor's certificates. *Special study options:* academic remediation for entering students, adult/continuing education programs, advanced placement credit, cooperative education, distance learning, double majors, English as a second language, honors programs, independent study, internships, off-campus study, part-time degree program, services for LD students, study abroad, summer session for credit.

Computers on Campus 1,150 computers/terminals are available on campus for general student use. Students can access the following: online (class) registration. Campuswide network is available. 100% of college-owned or -operated housing units are wired for high-speed Internet access.

Student Life *Housing:* on-campus residence required for freshman year. *Options:* coed, men-only, women-only. Campus housing is university owned. Freshman campus housing is guaranteed. *Activities and organizations:* drama/theater group, student-run newspaper, radio and television station, choral group, marching band, American Marketing Association, Beta Upsilon Sigma, International Greek Association, Student Information Management Society, Hobnailers, national fraternities, national sororities. *Campus security:* 24-hour emergency response devices and patrols, late-night transport/escort service, controlled dormitory access. *Student services:* health clinic, personal/psychological counseling, legal services.

Athletics Member NCAA. All Division III. *Intercollegiate sports:* basketball M/W, cross-country running M/W, football M, golf M/W, gymnastics W, ice hockey M/W, soccer W, softball W, swimming and diving M/W, tennis M/W, track and field M/W, volleyball W, wrestling M. *Intramural sports:* archery M (c)/W (c), baseball M (c), basketball M/W, bowling M (c)/W (c), cheerleading M (c)/W (c), equestrian sports M (c)/W (c), football M/W, lacrosse M (c)/W (c), racquetball M/W, rock climbing M (c)/W (c), skiing (cross-country) M (c)/W (c), skiing (downhill) M (c)/W (c), soccer M (c)/W, softball M/W, tennis M/W, ultimate Frisbee M (c)/W (c), volleyball M (c)/W, water polo M.

Standardized Tests *Required:* SAT or ACT (for admission).

Costs (2007–08) *Tuition:* state resident $4968 full-time, $207 per credit part-time; nonresident $12,541 full-time, $523 per credit part-time. Full-time tuition and fees vary according to reciprocity agreements. Part-time tuition and fees vary according to reciprocity agreements. *Required fees:* $877 full-time, $36 per credit part-time, $2 per term part-time. *Room and board:* $5150; room only: $2670. Room and board charges vary according to board plan. *Payment plan:* installment. *Waivers:* minority students.

Financial Aid Of all full-time matriculated undergraduates who enrolled in 2006, 6,334 applied for aid, 4,022 were judged to have need, 2,961 had their need fully met. 1,956 Federal Work-Study jobs (averaging $1694). 1,894 state and other part-time jobs (averaging $1243). In 2006, 919 non-need-based awards were made. *Average percent of need met:* 93%. *Average financial aid package:* $7576. *Average need-based loan:* $4456. *Average need-based gift aid:* $4837. *Average non-need-based aid:* $1720. *Average indebtedness upon graduation:* $18,466.

Applying *Options:* electronic application, early admission. *Application fee:* $35. *Required:* high school transcript, rank in upper 50% of high school class. *Application deadlines:* rolling (freshmen), 7/1 (transfers). *Notification:* continuous (freshmen), continuous (transfers).

Freshman Application Contact Ms. Kristina Anderson, Executive Director of Enrollment Management and Director of Admissions, University of Wisconsin–Eau Claire, PO Box 4004, Eau Claire, WI 54702-4004. *Phone:* 715-836-5415. *Fax:* 715-836-2409. *E-mail:* admissions@uwec.edu.

UNIVERSITY OF WISCONSIN–GREEN BAY

Green Bay, Wisconsin **www.uwgb.edu/**

- **State-supported** comprehensive, founded 1968, part of University of Wisconsin System
- **Suburban** 700-acre campus
- **Endowment** $11.5 million
- **Coed** 5,882 undergraduate students, 79% full-time, 65% women, 35% men
- **Moderately difficult** entrance level, 71% of applicants were admitted

Undergraduates 4,632 full-time, 1,250 part-time. Students come from 37 states and territories, 25 other countries, 5% are from out of state, 0.7% African American, 3% Asian American or Pacific Islander, 1% Hispanic American, 2% Native American, 0.7% international, 12% transferred in, 33% live on campus. *Retention:* 75% of 2006 full-time freshmen returned.

Freshmen *Admission:* 3,452 applied, 2,461 admitted, 1,000 enrolled. *Average high school GPA:* 3.27. *Test scores:* ACT scores over 18: 96%; ACT scores over 24: 36%; ACT scores over 30: 2%.

Faculty *Total:* 283, 64% full-time. *Student/faculty ratio:* 24:1.

Majors Accounting; American Indian/Native American studies; art; biology/biological sciences; biomedical sciences; business administration and management; chemistry; communication and journalism related; computer science; developmental and child psychology; dramatic/theater arts; economics; education; English; environmental science; environmental studies; French; geology/earth science; Germanic languages; history; humanities; interdisciplinary studies; liberal arts and sciences and humanities related; liberal arts and sciences/liberal studies; management information systems; mathematics; music; nursing (registered nurse training); philosophy; political science and government; psychology; public administration; social sciences related; social work; Spanish; urban studies/affairs; visual and performing arts related.

Academics *Calendar:* semesters. *Degrees:* associate, bachelor's, master's, and postbachelor's certificates. *Special study options:* academic remediation for entering students, adult/continuing education programs, advanced placement credit, distance learning, double majors, external degree program, independent study, internships, off-campus study, part-time degree program, services for LD students, student-designed majors, study abroad, summer session for credit. *ROTC:* Army (c). *Unusual degree programs:* 3-2 engineering with University of Wisconsin-Milwaukee.

Computers on Campus 550 computers/terminals are available on campus for general student use. Students can access the following: computer help desk, free student e-mail accounts, online (class) grades, online (class) registration, online (class) schedules, online degree progress, online financial records and bill paying. Campuswide network is available. 100% of college-owned or -operated housing units are wired for high-speed Internet access. Wireless service is available via entire campus.

Student Life *Housing options:* coed. Campus housing is university owned and is provided by a third party. Freshman applicants given priority for college housing. *Activities and organizations:* drama/theater group, student-run newspaper, radio station, choral group, marching band, Good Times, Psychology and Human Development Club, Ambassadors, Residence Hall Apartment Association, Student Government Association, national fraternities, national sororities. *Campus security:* 24-hour emergency response devices and patrols, late-night transport/escort service, controlled dormitory access. *Student services:* health clinic, personal/psychological counseling.

Athletics Member NCAA. All Division I. *Intercollegiate sports:* basketball M (s)/W (s), cross-country running M (s)/W (s), golf M (s)/W (s), skiing (cross-country) M (s)/W (s), soccer M (s)/W (s), softball W (s), swimming and diving M (s)/W (s), tennis M (s)/W (s), volleyball W (s). *Intramural sports:* basketball M/W, bowling M/W, cheerleading M/W, football M/W, golf M/W, racquetball M/W, sailing M/W, skiing (cross-country) M/W, soccer M/W, softball M/W, swimming and diving M/W, tennis M/W, ultimate Frisbee M/W, volleyball M/W, weight lifting M/W.

Standardized Tests *Required:* SAT or ACT (for admission).

Costs (2007–08) *Tuition:* state resident $4819 full-time, $201 per credit part-time; nonresident $12,392 full-time, $516 per credit part-time. Full-time tuition and fees vary according to reciprocity agreements. *Required fees:* $1140 full-time, $48 per credit part-time. *Room and board:* $5200; room only: $3200. Room and board charges vary according to housing facility. *Payment plan:* installment.

Financial Aid Of all full-time matriculated undergraduates who enrolled in 2007, 3,644 applied for aid, 2,733 were judged to have need, 1,220 had their need fully met. 190 Federal Work-Study jobs (averaging $2000). In 2007, 58 non-need-based awards were made. *Average percent of need met:* 82%. *Average financial aid package:* $8462. *Average need-based loan:* $4281. *Average need-based gift aid:* $5004. *Average non-need-based aid:* $2421. *Average indebtedness upon graduation:* $16,114.

Applying *Options:* electronic application, deferred entrance. *Application fee:* $44. *Required:* essay or personal statement, high school transcript. *Required for some:* letters of recommendation, interview. *Notification:* continuous until 8/15 (freshmen), continuous until 8/15 (transfers).

Freshman Application Contact Ms. Pam Harvey-Jacobs, Director of Admissions, University of Wisconsin–Green Bay, 2420 Nicolet Drive, Green Bay, WI 54311-7001. *Phone:* 920-465-2111. *Toll-free phone:* 888-367-8942. *Fax:* 920-465-5754. *E-mail:* uwgb@uwgb.edu.

University of Wisconsin–La Crosse

La Crosse, Wisconsin **www.uwlax.edu/**

- **State-supported** comprehensive, founded 1909, part of University of Wisconsin System
- **Suburban** 121-acre campus
- **Endowment** $11.0 million
- **Coed** 8,521 undergraduate students, 95% full-time, 58% women, 42% men
- **Moderately difficult** entrance level, 65% of applicants were admitted

Undergraduates 8,116 full-time, 405 part-time. Students come from 38 states and territories, 37 other countries, 16% are from out of state, 1% African American, 3% Asian American or Pacific Islander, 1% Hispanic American, 0.7% Native American, 2% international, 4% transferred in, 35% live on campus. *Retention:* 87% of 2006 full-time freshmen returned.

Freshmen *Admission:* 6,777 applied, 4,411 admitted, 1,753 enrolled. *Test scores:* SAT critical reading scores over 500: 77%; SAT math scores over 500: 77%; ACT scores over 18: 99%; SAT critical reading scores over 600: 27%; SAT math scores over 600: 23%; ACT scores over 24: 66%; SAT critical reading scores over 700: 8%; SAT math scores over 700: 8%; ACT scores over 30: 5%.

Faculty *Total:* 446, 78% full-time, 60% with terminal degrees. *Student/faculty ratio:* 23:1.

Majors Accounting; archeology; art; athletic training; biology/biological sciences; business administration and management; chemistry; clinical laboratory science/medical technology; communication/speech communication and rhetoric; computer and information sciences; dramatic/theater arts; economics; elementary education; English; finance; French; general studies; geography; German; health teacher education; history; international business/trade/commerce; kinesiology and exercise science; management information systems; marketing/marketing management; mathematics; microbiology; music; nuclear medical technology; parks, recreation and leisure facilities management; philosophy; physical therapy; physician assistant; physics; political science and government; psychology; rehabilitation and therapeutic professions related; science teacher education; social studies teacher education; sociology; Spanish; therapeutic recreation.

Academics *Calendar:* semesters. *Degrees:* associate, bachelor's, master's, and postbachelor's certificates. *Special study options:* academic remediation for entering students, adult/continuing education programs, advanced placement credit, cooperative education, distance learning, double majors, English as a second language, freshman honors college, honors programs, internships, off-campus study, part-time degree program, services for LD students, study abroad, summer session for credit. *ROTC:* Army (b). *Unusual degree programs:* 3-2 engineering with University of Wisconsin-Madison, University of Wisconsin-Milwaukee, University of Wisconsin- Platteville, University of Minnesota; physical therapy and physics, physical therapy and biology, occupational therapy and psychology.

Computers on Campus 600 computers/terminals and 100 ports are available on campus for general student use. Students can access the following: campus intranet, computer help desk, free student e-mail accounts, online (class) grades, online (class) registration, online (class) schedules. Campuswide network is available. 100% of college-owned or -operated housing units are wired for high-speed Internet access. Wireless service is available via classrooms, computer centers, computer labs, dorm rooms, learning centers, libraries, student centers.

Student Life *Housing options:* coed, women-only, disabled students. Campus housing is university owned. Freshman applicants given priority for college housing. *Activities and organizations:* drama/theater group, student-run newspaper, radio and television station, choral group, marching band, Sports and Activities Club, Residential Hall Council, Religious/Spiritual Organizations, Human Diversity Organizations, national fraternities, national sororities. *Campus security:* 24-hour emergency response devices and patrols, late-night transport/escort service, controlled dormitory access. *Student services:* health clinic, personal/psychological counseling, women's center, legal services.

Athletics Member NCAA. All Division III. *Intercollegiate sports:* baseball M, basketball M/W, cheerleading M/W, cross-country running M/W, football M, gymnastics W, soccer W, softball W, swimming and diving M/W, tennis M/W, track and field M/W, volleyball W, weight lifting M/W, wrestling M. *Intramural sports:* badminton M/W, football M/W, golf M, ice hockey W (c), lacrosse M (c), racquetball M/W, rugby M (c)/W (c), sailing M (c)/W (c), skiing (downhill) M (c)/W (c), soccer M (c)/W, softball W, tennis M/W, volleyball M/W, wrestling M (c).

Standardized Tests *Required:* SAT or ACT (for admission). *Recommended:* ACT (for admission).

Costs (2007–08) *Tuition:* state resident $4876 full-time, $203 per credit hour part-time; nonresident $12,448 full-time, $519 per credit hour part-time. Full-time tuition and fees vary according to program and reciprocity agreements. Part-time tuition and fees vary according to course load, program, and reciprocity agreements. *Room and board:* $5130; room only: $2930. Room and board charges vary according to board plan. *Payment plan:* installment. *Waivers:* minority students.

Financial Aid Of all full-time matriculated undergraduates who enrolled in 2006, 5,070 applied for aid, 3,273 were judged to have need, 661 had their need fully met. 350 Federal Work-Study jobs (averaging $1500). 1,647 state and other part-time jobs (averaging $1030). In 2006, 154 non-need-based awards were made. *Average percent of need met:* 74%. *Average financial aid package:* $4491. *Average need-based loan:* $3549. *Average need-based gift aid:* $4617. *Average non-need-based aid:* $1202. *Average indebtedness upon graduation:* $12,145.

Applying *Options:* electronic application, early admission. *Application fee:* $35. *Required:* high school transcript. *Required for some:* interview. *Recommended:* essay or personal statement. *Application deadlines:* rolling (freshmen), rolling (out-of-state freshmen), rolling (transfers). *Notification:* continuous (freshmen), continuous (out-of-state freshmen), continuous (transfers).

Freshman Application Contact Ms. Kathryn Kiefer, Director of Admissions, University of Wisconsin–La Crosse, 1725 State Street, LaCrosse, WI 54601. *Phone:* 608-785-8939. *Fax:* 608-785-8940. *E-mail:* admissions@uwlax.edu.

University of Wisconsin–Madison

Madison, Wisconsin **www.wisc.edu/**

- **State-supported** university, founded 1848, part of University of Wisconsin System
- **Urban** 1050-acre campus with easy access to Milwaukee
- **Endowment** $1.5 billion
- **Coed** 30,618 undergraduate students, 91% full-time, 53% women, 47% men
- **Very difficult** entrance level, 56% of applicants were admitted

Undergraduates 27,879 full-time, 2,739 part-time. Students come from 53 states and territories, 101 other countries, 32% are from out of state, 3% African American, 6% Asian American or Pacific Islander, 3% Hispanic American, 0.7% Native American, 4% international, 4% transferred in, 24% live on campus. *Retention:* 93% of 2006 full-time freshmen returned.

Freshmen *Admission:* 24,870 applied, 13,977 admitted, 5,996 enrolled. *Average high school GPA:* 3.77. *Test scores:* SAT critical reading scores over 500: 89%; SAT math scores over 500: 97%; SAT writing scores over 500: 93%; ACT scores over 18: 100%; SAT critical reading scores over 600: 59%; SAT math scores over 600: 82%; SAT writing scores over 600: 64%; ACT scores over 24: 92%; SAT critical reading scores over 700: 17%; SAT math scores over 700: 32%; SAT writing scores over 700: 16%; ACT scores over 30: 31%.

Faculty *Total:* 2,871, 83% full-time, 87% with terminal degrees. *Student/faculty ratio:* 13:1.

Majors Accounting; actuarial science; advertising; African-American/Black studies; African languages; African studies; agricultural/biological engineering and bioengineering; agricultural business and management; agricultural economics; agricultural teacher education; agriculture; agronomy and crop science; American studies; animal genetics; animal sciences; anthropology; applied art; applied mathematics; art; art history, criticism and conservation; art teacher education; Asian studies; Asian studies (Southeast); astronomy; biochemistry; biology/biological sciences; biomedical/medical engineering; botany/plant biology; broadcast journalism; business administration and management; cartography; cell biology and histology; chemical engineering; chemistry; child development; Chinese; civil engineering; classics and languages, literatures and linguistics; clinical laboratory science/medical technology; clothing/textiles; comparative literature; computer engineering; computer science; construction management; consumer services and advocacy; dairy science; developmental and child psychology; dietetics; dramatic/theater arts; electrical, electronics and communications engineering; elementary education; engineering; engineering mechanics; engineering physics; English; entomology; environmental/environmental health engineering; experimental psychology; family and consumer economics related; family and consumer sciences/home economics teacher education; family and consumer sciences/human sciences; farm and ranch management; fashion merchandising; finance; food science; foods, nutrition, and wellness; forestry; French; geography; geology/earth science; geophysics and seismology; German; Hebrew; Hispanic-American, Puerto Rican, and Mexican-American/Chicano studies; history; history and philosophy of science and technology; horticultural science; hydrology and water resources science; industrial engineering; insurance; interior design; international relations and affairs; Italian; Japanese; journalism; kindergarten/preschool education; labor and industrial relations; landscape architecture; Latin; Latin American studies; linguistics; mass communication/media; mathematics; mechanical engineering; medical microbiology and bacteriology; metallurgical engineering; mining and mineral engineering; modern Greek; molecular biology; music; music teacher education; natural resources management and policy; nuclear engineering; nursing (registered nurse training); occupational therapy; parks, recreation and leisure; pharmacology; pharmacy; philosophy; physical education teaching and coaching; physician assistant; political science and government; Portuguese; poultry science; psychology; public relations/image management; radio and television; real estate; Russian; Scandinavian languages; science teacher education; secondary education; Slavic languages; social sciences; social work; sociology; Spanish; special education; speech therapy; statistics; survey technology; toxicology; urban studies/affairs; wildlife and wildlands science and management; women's studies; zoology/animal biology.

Academics *Calendar:* semesters. *Degrees:* bachelor's, master's, doctoral, first professional, post-master's, and first professional certificates. *Special study options:* accelerated degree program, adult/continuing education programs, advanced placement credit, cooperative education, distance learning, double majors, English as a second language, honors programs, independent study, internships, part-time degree program, services for LD students, student-designed majors, study abroad, summer session for credit. *ROTC:* Army (b), Navy (b), Air Force (b). *Unusual degree programs:* 3-2 accounting, pharmacy.

Computers on Campus Students can access the following: computer help desk, free student e-mail accounts, online (class) grades, online (class) registration, online (class) schedules. Campuswide network is available. 100% of college-owned or -operated housing units are wired for high-speed Internet access. Wireless service is available via entire campus.

Student Life *Housing options:* coed, men-only, women-only, cooperative. Campus housing is university owned. Freshman applicants given priority for college housing. *Activities and organizations:* drama/theater group, student-run newspaper, radio station, choral group, marching band, national fraternities, national sororities. *Campus security:* 24-hour emergency response devices and patrols, late-night transport/escort service, controlled dormitory access, free cab rides throughout the city. *Student services:* health clinic, personal/psychological counseling, women's center.

Athletics Member NCAA. All Division I except football (Division I-A). *Intercollegiate sports:* basketball M (s)/W (s), cheerleading M/W, cross-country running M (s)/W (s), golf M (s)/W (s), ice hockey M (s)/W (s), sailing M (c)/W (c), soccer M (s)/W (s), softball W (s), swimming and diving M (s)/W (s), tennis M (s)/W (s), track and field M (s)/W (s), ultimate Frisbee M (c)/W (c), volleyball W (s), water polo M (c)/W (c), wrestling M (s).

Standardized Tests *Required:* SAT or ACT (for admission).

Costs (2007–08) *Tuition:* state resident $7188 full-time; nonresident $21,440 full-time. Full-time tuition and fees vary according to degree level, program, and reciprocity agreements. Part-time tuition and fees vary according to course load, degree level, program, and reciprocity agreements. *Required fees:* $859 full-time. *Room and board:* Room and board charges vary according to board plan, housing facility, and location.

Financial Aid Of all full-time matriculated undergraduates who enrolled in 2006, 12,833 applied for aid, 8,926 were judged to have need, 2,530 had their need fully met. In 2006, 2964 non-need-based awards were made. *Average percent of need met:* 84%. *Average financial aid package:* $10,005. *Average need-based loan:* $5346. *Average need-based gift aid:* $3319. *Average non-need-based aid:* $2533. *Average indebtedness upon graduation:* $21,018.

Applying *Options:* electronic application, deferred entrance. *Application fee:* $44. *Required:* essay or personal statement, high school transcript. *Application deadlines:* 2/1 (freshmen), 2/1 (transfers). *Notification:* continuous (freshmen), continuous (transfers).

Freshman Application Contact Office of Undergraduate Admissions, University of Wisconsin–Madison, 716 Langdon Street, Madison, WI 53706-1481. *Phone:* 608-262-3961. *Fax:* 608-262-7706. *E-mail:* onwisconsin@admissions.wisc.edu.

UNIVERSITY OF WISCONSIN–MILWAUKEE

Milwaukee, Wisconsin **www.uwm.edu/**

- **State-supported** university, founded 1956, part of University of Wisconsin System
- **Urban** 90-acre campus
- **Coed** 24,395 undergraduate students, 83% full-time, 52% women, 48% men
- **Moderately difficult** entrance level, 83% of applicants were admitted

Undergraduates 20,190 full-time, 4,205 part-time. Students come from 53 states and territories, 41 other countries, 3% are from out of state, 7% African American, 4% Asian American or Pacific Islander, 4% Hispanic American, 0.8% Native American, 0.9% international, 6% transferred in, 12% live on campus. *Retention:* 72% of 2006 full-time freshmen returned.

Freshmen *Admission:* 12,555 applied, 10,385 admitted, 4,598 enrolled. *Average high school GPA:* 3.04. *Test scores:* SAT critical reading scores over 500: 70%; SAT math scores over 500: 78%; ACT scores over 18: 90%; SAT critical reading scores over 600: 33%; SAT math scores over 600: 35%; ACT scores over 24: 33%; SAT critical reading scores over 700: 6%; SAT math scores over 700: 5%; ACT scores over 30: 3%.

Faculty *Total:* 797, 93% full-time. *Student/faculty ratio:* 33:1.

Majors Accounting; African-American/Black studies; American Indian/Native American studies; anthropology; applied mathematics; architecture; art; art history, criticism and conservation; art teacher education; atmospheric sciences and meteorology; audiology and speech-language pathology; bilingual and multilingual education; biochemistry; biology/biological sciences; broadcast journalism; business administration and management; ceramic arts and ceramics; chemistry; civil engineering; classics and languages, literatures and linguistics; clinical laboratory science/medical technology; comparative literature; computer science; criminal justice/law enforcement administration; criminal justice/police science; cultural studies; dance; dramatic/theater arts; ecology; economics; education; electrical, electronics and communications engineering; elementary education; engineering; English; fiber, textile and weaving arts; film/cinema studies; finance; fine/studio arts; forestry; French; geography; geology/earth science; German; health/health care administration; health information/medical records administration; health science; Hebrew; history; human resources management; industrial engineering; interdisciplinary studies; international relations and affairs; Italian; journalism; kindergarten/preschool education; labor and industrial relations; Latin; Latin American studies; linguistics; literature; management information systems; marketing/marketing management; mass communication/media; materials engineering; mathematics; mechanical engineering; metal and jewelry arts; modern Greek; music; music history, literature, and theory; music teacher education; music therapy; natural resources/conservation; nursing (registered nurse training); occupational therapy; parks, recreation and leisure; peace studies and conflict resolution; philosophy; physical therapy; physics; political science and government; pre-dentistry studies; pre-law studies; pre-medical studies; psychology; real estate; religious studies; Russian; Russian studies; sculpture; secondary education; Slavic languages; social work; sociology; Spanish; special education; statistics; therapeutic recreation; urban studies/affairs; violin, viola, guitar and other stringed instruments; voice and opera; wind/percussion instruments; women's studies; zoology/animal biology.

Academics *Calendar:* semesters. *Degrees:* certificates, bachelor's, master's, doctoral, post-master's, and postbachelor's certificates. *Special study options:* academic remediation for entering students, accelerated degree program, adult/continuing education programs, advanced placement credit, cooperative education, distance learning, double majors, English as a second language, honors programs, independent study, internships, off-campus study, part-time degree program, services for LD students, student-designed majors, study abroad, summer session for credit. *ROTC:* Army (c), Air Force (c).

Computers on Campus 1,000 computers/terminals and 3,200 ports are available on campus for general student use. Students can access the following: campus intranet, computer help desk, free student e-mail accounts, online (class) grades, online (class) registration, online (class) schedules. Campuswide network is available. 100% of college-owned or -operated housing units are wired for high-speed Internet access. Wireless service is available via entire campus.

Student Life *Housing options:* coed, disabled students. *Activities and organizations:* drama/theater group, student-run newspaper, radio station, choral group, marching band, national fraternities, national sororities. *Campus security:* 24-hour emergency response devices, late-night transport/escort service. *Student services:* health clinic, personal/psychological counseling, women's center, legal services.

Athletics Member NCAA. All Division I. *Intercollegiate sports:* baseball M, basketball M (s)/W (s), cross-country running M (s)/W (s), soccer M (s)/W (s), swimming and diving M (s)/W (s), tennis M (s)/W (s), track and field M (s)/W (s), volleyball M/W (s). *Intramural sports:* badminton M/W, basketball M/W, bowling M (c)/W (c), fencing M (c)/W (c), field hockey M/W, football M, golf M/W, racquetball M/W, riflery M (c)/W (c), rugby M (c)/W (c), sailing M (c)/W (c), skiing (downhill) M (c)/W (c), soccer M/W, swimming and diving M/W, tennis M/W, volleyball M/W, water polo M/W, weight lifting M/W, wrestling M.

Standardized Tests *Required:* SAT or ACT (for admission), ACT for state residents (for admission).

Costs (2007–08) *Tuition:* state resident $6960 full-time, $277 per credit part-time; nonresident $16,686 full-time, $683 per credit part-time. Full-time tuition and fees vary according to location, program, and reciprocity agreements. Part-time tuition and fees vary according to course load, location, program, and reciprocity agreements. *Required fees:* $767 full-time. *Room only:* $3620. Room and board charges vary according to board plan and housing facility. *Payment plan:* installment. *Waivers:* senior citizens.

Financial Aid Of all full-time matriculated undergraduates who enrolled in 2006, 16,319 applied for aid, 13,263 were judged to have need, 2,969 had their need fully met. In 2006, 65 non-need-based awards were made. *Average percent of need met:* 58%. *Average financial aid package:* $6266. *Average need-based loan:* $3926. *Average need-based gift aid:* $5107. *Average non-need-based aid:* $2628. *Average indebtedness upon graduation:* $16,683.

Applying *Options:* electronic application, deferred entrance. *Application fee:* $35. *Required:* high school transcript. *Recommended:* essay or personal statement. *Application deadlines:* 7/1 (freshmen), 8/1 (transfers). *Notification:* continuous (freshmen).

Freshman Application Contact Ms. Jan Ford, Director, Recruitment and Outreach, University of Wisconsin–Milwaukee, PO Box 749, Milwaukee, WI 53201. *Phone:* 414-229-4397. *Fax:* 414-229-6940. *E-mail:* uwmlook@uwm.edu.

UNIVERSITY OF WISCONSIN–OSHKOSH

Oshkosh, Wisconsin **www.uwosh.edu/**

- **State-supported** comprehensive, founded 1871, part of University of Wisconsin System
- **Suburban** 192-acre campus with easy access to Milwaukee
- **Endowment** $350,000
- **Coed** 11,091 undergraduate students, 79% full-time, 59% women, 41% men
- **Moderately difficult** entrance level, 79% of applicants were admitted

Undergraduates 8,724 full-time, 2,367 part-time. Students come from 30 states and territories, 32 other countries, 2% are from out of state, 1% African American, 3% Asian American or Pacific Islander, 2% Hispanic American, 1% Native American, 0.7% international, 8% transferred in, 34% live on campus. *Retention:* 73% of 2006 full-time freshmen returned.

Freshmen *Admission:* 5,056 applied, 4,017 admitted, 1,763 enrolled. *Average high school GPA:* 3.29. *Test scores:* ACT scores over 18: 95%; ACT scores over 24: 33%; ACT scores over 30: 2%.

Faculty *Total:* 567, 67% full-time, 61% with terminal degrees. *Student/faculty ratio:* 22:1.

Majors Accounting; anthropology; art; art teacher education; audiology and speech-language pathology; biology/biological sciences; broadcast journalism; business administration and management; chemistry; clinical laboratory science/medical technology; computer science; criminal justice/law enforcement administration; dramatic/theater arts; economics; education; elementary education; English; English as a second/foreign language (teaching); finance; fine/studio arts; French; geography; geology/earth science; German; history; human services; international relations and affairs; journalism; kindergarten/preschool education; liberal arts and sciences/liberal studies; management information systems; marketing/marketing management; mass communication/media; mathematics; medical microbiology and bacteriology; music; music teacher education; music therapy; nursing (registered nurse training); philosophy; physical education teaching and coaching; physics; political science and government; pre-dentistry studies; pre-law studies; pre-medical studies; pre-veterinary studies; psychology; radio and television; religious studies; secondary education; social work; sociology; Spanish; special education; urban studies/affairs.

Academics *Calendar:* semesters. *Degrees:* certificates, associate, bachelor's, master's, and postbachelor's certificates. *Special study options:* academic remediation for entering students, accelerated degree program, adult/continuing education programs, advanced placement credit, cooperative education, distance learning, double majors, English as a second language, honors programs, independent study, internships, part-time degree program, services for LD students, student-designed majors, study abroad, summer session for credit. *ROTC:* Army (b).

Computers on Campus 475 computers/terminals and 10 ports are available on campus for general student use. Students can access the following: campus intranet, computer help desk, free student e-mail accounts, online (class) grades, online (class) registration, online (class) schedules. Campuswide network is available. 100% of college-owned or -operated housing units are wired for high-speed Internet access. Wireless service is available via entire campus.

Student Life *Housing:* on-campus residence required through sophomore year. *Options:* coed, women-only. Campus housing is university owned. Freshman campus housing is guaranteed. *Activities and organizations:* drama/theater group, student-run newspaper, radio and television station, choral group, USRH, Model UN, Pi Sigma Epsilon, Human Services Organization, national fraternities, national sororities. *Campus security:* 24-hour emergency response devices and patrols, student patrols, late-night transport/escort service, controlled dormitory access. *Student services:* health clinic, personal/psychological counseling, women's center, legal services.

Athletics Member NCAA. All Division III. *Intercollegiate sports:* baseball M, basketball M/W, cross-country running M/W, football M, golf W, gymnastics W, riflery M/W, soccer M/W, softball W, swimming and diving M/W, tennis M/W, track and field M/W, volleyball W, wrestling M. *Intramural sports:* basketball M/W, bowling M (c)/W (c), cross-country running M/W, football M/W, golf M/W, gymnastics M (c), ice hockey M (c), lacrosse M (c)/W (c), racquetball M/W, skiing (downhill) M/W, soccer M/W, softball M/W, tennis M/W, volleyball M (c)/W, wrestling M.

Standardized Tests *Required:* SAT or ACT (for admission), ACT required for state residents (for admission).

Costs (2007–08) *Tuition:* state resident $5693 full-time, $239 per credit hour part-time; nonresident $13,266 full-time, $555 per credit hour part-time. *Room and board:* $5746; room only: $3162. *Payment plan:* installment.

Financial Aid Of all full-time matriculated undergraduates who enrolled in 2003, 6,864 applied for aid, 5,148 were judged to have need, 2,986 had their need fully met. In 2003, 60 non-need-based awards were made. *Average percent of need met:* 53%. *Average financial aid package:* $3080. *Average need-based loan:* $3500. *Average need-based gift aid:* $2000. *Average non-need-based aid:* $3333. *Average indebtedness upon graduation:* $14,000.

Applying *Options:* electronic application, deferred entrance. *Application fee:* $35. *Required:* high school transcript, rank in upper 50% of high school class or ACT composite score of 23 or above. *Recommended:* essay or personal statement. *Application deadlines:* rolling (freshmen), rolling (transfers). *Notification:* continuous (freshmen), continuous (transfers).

Freshman Application Contact Mr. Richard Hillman, Associate Director of Admissions, University of Wisconsin–Oshkosh, Oshkosh, WI 54901-8602. *Phone:* 920-424-0202. *E-mail:* oshadmuw@uwosh.edu.

UNIVERSITY OF WISCONSIN–PARKSIDE

Kenosha, Wisconsin **www.uwp.edu/**

- **State-supported** comprehensive, founded 1968, part of University of Wisconsin System
- **Suburban** 700-acre campus with easy access to Chicago and Milwaukee
- **Endowment** $2.5 million
- **Coed** 4,893 undergraduate students, 73% full-time, 55% women, 45% men
- **Moderately difficult** entrance level, 76% of applicants were admitted

Undergraduates 3,563 full-time, 1,330 part-time. Students come from 26 states and territories, 10 other countries, 9% are from out of state, 11% African American, 3% Asian American or Pacific Islander, 7% Hispanic American, 0.7% Native American, 1% international, 8% transferred in, 17% live on campus. *Retention:* 60% of 2006 full-time freshmen returned.

Freshmen *Admission:* 2,493 applied, 1,902 admitted, 949 enrolled. *Test scores:* ACT scores over 18: 76%; ACT scores over 24: 19%; ACT scores over 30: 1%.

Faculty *Total:* 274, 64% full-time, 54% with terminal degrees. *Student/faculty ratio:* 20:1.

Majors Accounting; art; biological and biomedical sciences related; business administration and management; chemistry; communication/speech communication and rhetoric; computer science; creative writing; criminal justice/law enforcement administration; dramatic/theater arts; economics; English; finance; French; geography; geology/earth science; German; history; humanities; interdisciplinary studies; international relations and affairs; mathematics; molecular biology; music; nursing (registered nurse training); philosophy; physics; political science and government; pre-dentistry studies; pre-law studies; pre-medical studies; pre-pharmacy studies; pre-veterinary studies; psychology; sociology; Spanish; sport and fitness administration/management.

Academics *Calendar:* semesters. *Degrees:* certificates, bachelor's, and master's. *Special study options:* academic remediation for entering students, accelerated degree program, advanced placement credit, distance learning, double majors, English as a second language, external degree program, honors programs, independent study, internships, off-campus study, part-time degree program, services for LD students, study abroad, summer session for credit. *ROTC:* Army (c). *Unusual degree programs:* 3-2 molecular biology.

Computers on Campus 259 computers/terminals are available on campus for general student use. Students can access the following: computer help desk, free student e-mail accounts, online (class) grades, online (class) registration, online (class) schedules. Campuswide network is available. 100% of college-owned or -operated housing units are wired for high-speed Internet access. Wireless service is available via dorm rooms, libraries, student centers.

Student Life *Housing options:* coed, disabled students. Campus housing is university owned. *Activities and organizations:* drama/theater group, student-run newspaper, radio station, choral group, Black Student Union, Latinos Unidos, Parkside Student Government Association, Asian-American Club, Parkside Adult Student Alliance, national fraternities, national sororities. *Campus security:* 24-hour emergency response devices and patrols, late-night transport/escort service, controlled dormitory access. *Student services:* health clinic, personal/psychological counseling, women's center.

Athletics Member NCAA. All Division II. *Intercollegiate sports:* baseball M (s), basketball M (s)/W (s), cross-country running M (s)/W (s), golf M (s), soccer M (s)/W (s), softball W (s), track and field M (s)/W (s), volleyball W (s), wrestling M (s). *Intramural sports:* basketball M/W, cheerleading M (c)/W (c), football M (c)/W (c), racquetball M/W, rock climbing M (c), soccer M/W, softball M/W, table tennis M/W, tennis M/W, volleyball M/W.

Standardized Tests *Required for some:* SAT or ACT (for admission).

Costs (2008–09) *Tuition:* area resident $4819 full-time, $201 per credit hour part-time; nonresident $12,392 full-time, $516 per credit hour part-time. *Required fees:* $940 full-time. *Room and board:* $5610; room only: $2360.

Financial Aid Of all full-time matriculated undergraduates who enrolled in 2005, 2,509 applied for aid, 2,509 were judged to have need, 449 had their need fully met. *Average percent of need met:* 77%. *Average financial aid package:* $8377. *Average need-based loan:* $3509. *Average need-based gift aid:* $4631.

Applying *Options:* electronic application, deferred entrance. *Application fee:* $35. *Required:* high school transcript, minimum of 17 high school units distributed as specified in the UW-Parkside catalog. *Application deadlines:* 8/1 (freshmen), 8/1 (transfers). *Notification:* continuous (freshmen), continuous (transfers).

Freshman Application Contact Mr. Matthew Jensen, Director of Admissions, University of Wisconsin–Parkside, PO Box 2000, 900 Wood Road, Kenosha, WI 53141-2000. *Phone:* 262-595-2784. *Fax:* 262-595-2008. *E-mail:* matthew.jensen@uwp.edu.

UNIVERSITY OF WISCONSIN–PLATTEVILLE

Platteville, Wisconsin **www.uwplatt.edu/**

- **State-supported** comprehensive, founded 1866, part of University of Wisconsin System
- **Small-town** 380-acre campus
- **Endowment** $2.7 million
- **Coed** 6,353 undergraduate students, 90% full-time, 36% women, 64% men
- **Moderately difficult** entrance level, 85% of applicants were admitted

Undergraduates 5,692 full-time, 661 part-time. Students come from 15 states and territories, 13 other countries, 16% are from out of state, 2% African American, 1% Asian American or Pacific Islander, 1% Hispanic American, 0.5% Native American, 0.3% international, 5% transferred in, 43% live on campus. *Retention:* 75% of 2006 full-time freshmen returned.

Freshmen *Admission:* 3,519 applied, 2,978 admitted, 1,467 enrolled. *Test scores:* ACT scores over 18: 92%; ACT scores over 24: 35%; ACT scores over 30: 3%.

Faculty *Total:* 367, 78% full-time, 66% with terminal degrees. *Student/faculty ratio:* 20:1.

Majors Accounting; agricultural business and management; agricultural teacher education; agronomy and crop science; animal sciences; art; biological and physical sciences; biology/biological sciences; broadcast journalism; business administration and management; business/managerial economics; cartography; civil engineering; commercial and advertising art; computer science; computer software engineering; construction management; criminal justice/law enforcement administration; economics; education; electrical, electronics and communications engineering; elementary education; English; environmental/environmental health engineering; geology/earth science; German; history; industrial arts; industrial design; industrial engineering; industrial technology; international relations and affairs; kindergarten/preschool education; land use planning and management; liberal arts and sciences/liberal studies; mass communication/media; mathematics; mechanical engineering; middle school education; music; ornamental horticulture; philosophy; political science and government; psychology; science teacher education; secondary education; social sciences; Spanish; speech and rhetoric; telecommunications.

Academics *Calendar:* semesters. *Degrees:* associate, bachelor's, master's, and postbachelor's certificates. *Special study options:* academic remediation for entering students, adult/continuing education programs, advanced placement credit, cooperative education, distance learning, double majors, English as a second language, external degree program, honors programs, independent study, internships, off-campus study, part-time degree program, services for LD students, student-designed majors, study abroad, summer session for credit. *ROTC:* Army (c).

Computers on Campus 1,200 computers/terminals and 1,000 ports are available on campus for general student use. Students can access the following: campus intranet, computer help desk, free student e-mail accounts, online (class) grades, online (class) registration, online (class) schedules. Campuswide network is available. 100% of college-owned or -operated housing units are wired for high-speed Internet access. Wireless service is available via classrooms, libraries, student centers.

Student Life *Housing:* on-campus residence required through sophomore year. *Options:* coed, men-only, women-only, disabled students. Campus housing is university owned. Freshman campus housing is guaranteed. *Activities and organizations:* drama/theater group, student-run newspaper, radio and television station, choral group, marching band, Intervarsity Christian Fellowship, Student Senate, Greek Life, Paintball Club, CPR, national fraternities, national sororities. *Campus security:* 24-hour emergency response devices and patrols, student patrols, late-night transport/escort service. *Student services:* health clinic, personal/psychological counseling, women's center.

Athletics Member NCAA. All Division III. *Intercollegiate sports:* baseball M, basketball M/W, bowling M (c)/W (c), cheerleading M/W, cross-country running M/W, football M, golf W, ice hockey M (c)/W (c), lacrosse M (c)/W (c), rugby M (c)/W (c), soccer M/W, softball W, track and field M/W, ultimate Frisbee M (c)/W (c), volleyball M (c)/W, wrestling M. *Intramural sports:* badminton M/W, basketball M/W, bowling M/W, cheerleading M (c)/W (c), football M/W, racquetball M/W, soccer M/W, softball M/W, tennis M/W, volleyball M/W, water polo M/W.

Standardized Tests *Required:* SAT or ACT (for admission). *Required for some:* SAT Subject Tests (for admission).

Costs (2008–09) *Tuition:* state resident $5572 full-time, $212 per credit part-time; nonresident $13,557 full-time, $544 per credit part-time. *Required fees:* $493 full-time. *Room and board:* $5440; room only: $2940.

Financial Aid Of all full-time matriculated undergraduates who enrolled in 2002, 3,289 applied for aid, 2,468 were judged to have need. 382 Federal Work-Study jobs (averaging $1392). In 2002, 652 non-need-based awards were made. *Average financial aid package:* $6161. *Average need-based loan:* $3499. *Average need-based gift aid:* $3599. *Average non-need-based aid:* $1427. *Average indebtedness upon graduation:* $15,785.

Applying *Options:* electronic application. *Application fee:* $35. *Required:* high school transcript. *Required for some:* letters of recommendation, interview. *Recommended:* essay or personal statement. *Application deadlines:* rolling (freshmen), rolling (transfers). *Notification:* continuous (transfers).

Freshman Application Contact Ms. Angela Udelhofen, Director of Admissions and Enrollment Management, University of Wisconsin–Platteville, 1 University Plaza, 120 Brigham Hall, Platteville, WI 53818-3099. *Phone:* 608-342-1125. *Toll-free phone:* 800-362-5515. *Fax:* 608-342-1122. *E-mail:* admit@uwplatt.edu.

UNIVERSITY OF WISCONSIN–RIVER FALLS

River Falls, Wisconsin www.uwrf.edu/

- **State-supported** comprehensive, founded 1874, part of University of Wisconsin System
- **Suburban** 225-acre campus with easy access to Minneapolis–St. Paul
- **Coed**
- **Moderately difficult** entrance level

Faculty *Student/faculty ratio:* 17:1.

Academics *Calendar:* semesters. *Degrees:* certificates, bachelor's, master's, and post-master's certificates.

Student Life *Campus security:* 24-hour emergency response devices and patrols, student patrols, late-night transport/escort service, controlled dormitory access.

Athletics Member NCAA. All Division III.

Standardized Tests *Required:* ACT (for admission).

Costs (2007–08) *Tuition:* area resident $5886 full-time, $314 per credit part-time; state resident $6356 full-time, $333 per credit part-time; nonresident $13,458 full-time, $629 per credit part-time. Full-time tuition and fees vary according to course load and reciprocity agreements. Part-time tuition and fees vary according to course load and reciprocity agreements. *Room and board:* $5244; room only: $2974. Room and board charges vary according to board plan and housing facility.

Financial Aid Of all full-time matriculated undergraduates who enrolled in 2003, 3,631 applied for aid, 2,727 were judged to have need, 1,240 had their need fully met. *Average percent of need met:* 77. *Average financial aid package:* $4429. *Average need-based loan:* $2353. *Average need-based gift aid:* $1652. *Average non-need-based aid:* $3738. *Average indebtedness upon graduation:* $12,500.

Applying *Options:* electronic application, deferred entrance. *Application fee:* $35. *Required:* high school transcript. *Recommended:* rank in upper 40% of high school class.

Director of Admissions Dr. Alan Tuchtenhagen, Director of Admissions, University of Wisconsin–River Falls, 410 South Third Street, 112 South Hall, River Falls, WI 54022-5001. *Phone:* 715-425-3500. *Fax:* 715-425-0676. *E-mail:* alan.j.tuchtenhagen@uwrf.edu.

UNIVERSITY OF WISCONSIN–STEVENS POINT

Stevens Point, Wisconsin www.uwsp.edu/

- **State-supported** comprehensive, founded 1894, part of University of Wisconsin System
- **Small-town** 335-acre campus
- **Endowment** $15.6 million
- **Coed** 8,642 undergraduate students, 93% full-time, 53% women, 47% men
- **Moderately difficult** entrance level, 74% of applicants were admitted

Undergraduates 8,072 full-time, 570 part-time. Students come from 27 states and territories, 23 other countries, 6% are from out of state, 1% African American, 2% Asian American or Pacific Islander, 1% Hispanic American, 0.7% Native American, 2% international, 8% transferred in, 37% live on campus. *Retention:* 76% of 2006 full-time freshmen returned.

Freshmen *Admission:* 5,123 applied, 3,779 admitted, 1,618 enrolled. *Average high school GPA:* 3.40. *Test scores:* ACT scores over 18: 98%; ACT scores over 24: 37%; ACT scores over 30: 3%.

Faculty *Total:* 480, 83% full-time, 69% with terminal degrees. *Student/faculty ratio:* 21:1.

Majors Accounting; actuarial science; arts management; athletic training; audiology and speech-language pathology; biology/biological sciences; business administration and management; chemistry; clinical laboratory science/medical technology; commercial and advertising art; communication/speech communication and rhetoric; computer and information sciences; dance; dietetics; dramatic/theater arts; economics; education; elementary education; English; family and consumer economics related; family and consumer sciences/home economics teacher education; fine/studio arts; forestry; French; general studies; geography; German; health and physical education; history; hydrology and water resources science; interior design; international relations and affairs; kindergarten/preschool education; liberal arts and sciences/liberal studies; mathematics; music; music teacher education; natural resources/conservation; natural resources management and policy; natural sciences; philosophy; physical education teaching and coaching; physics; political science and government; polymer chemistry; psychology; public administration; secondary education; social sciences; sociology; soil conservation; Spanish; web page, digital/multimedia and information resources design; wildlife and wildlands science and management; wood science and wood products/pulp and paper technology.

Academics *Calendar:* semesters. *Degrees:* associate, bachelor's, master's, and doctoral. *Special study options:* academic remediation for entering students, accelerated degree program, adult/continuing education programs, advanced placement credit, distance learning, double majors, English as a second language, independent study, internships, off-campus study, part-time degree program, services for LD students, student-designed majors, study abroad, summer session for credit. *ROTC:* Army (b).

Computers on Campus 634 computers/terminals are available on campus for general student use. Students can access the following: free student e-mail accounts, online (class) grades, online (class) registration, online (class) schedules. Campuswide network is available. Wireless service is available via entire campus.

Student Life *Housing:* on-campus residence required through sophomore year. *Options:* coed, men-only, women-only. Campus housing is university owned. Freshman campus housing is guaranteed. *Activities and organizations:* drama/theater group, student-run newspaper, radio and television station, choral group, national fraternities, national sororities. *Campus security:* 24-hour emergency response devices and patrols, student patrols, late-night transport/escort service, controlled dormitory access. *Student services:* health clinic, personal/psychological counseling.

Athletics Member NCAA. All Division III. *Intercollegiate sports:* baseball M, basketball M/W, cross-country running M/W, football M, golf W, ice hockey M/W, soccer W, softball W, swimming and diving M/W, tennis W, track and field M/W, volleyball W, wrestling M. *Intramural sports:* badminton M/W, basketball M/W, football M/W, golf M/W, ice hockey M/W, racquetball M/W, soccer M/W, softball M/W, table tennis M/W, tennis M/W, volleyball M/W, wrestling M/W.

Standardized Tests *Required:* SAT or ACT (for admission).

Costs (2007–08) *Tuition:* state resident $4819 full-time, $201 per credit part-time; nonresident $12,392 full-time, $516 per credit part-time. Full-time tuition and fees vary according to course load and reciprocity agreements. Part-time tuition and fees vary according to course load and reciprocity agreements. *Required fees:* $1015 full-time, $89 per credit part-time. *Room and board:* $4832; room only: $2944. *Payment plan:* installment. *Waivers:* children of alumni and senior citizens.

Financial Aid Of all full-time matriculated undergraduates who enrolled in 2005, 7,131 applied for aid, 4,004 were judged to have need, 2,865 had their need fully met. 945 Federal Work-Study jobs (averaging $1310). In 2005, 479 non-need-based awards were made. *Average percent of need met:* 96%. *Average financial aid package:* $6887. *Average need-based loan:* $4235. *Average need-based gift aid:* $4489. *Average non-need-based aid:* $1987. *Average indebtedness upon graduation:* $17,025.

Applying *Options:* electronic application, deferred entrance. *Application fee:* $35. *Required:* high school transcript. *Recommended:* essay or personal statement, letters of recommendation. *Application deadlines:* rolling (freshmen), rolling (out-of-state freshmen), rolling (transfers). *Notification:* continuous (freshmen), continuous (out-of-state freshmen), continuous (transfers).

Freshman Application Contact Ms. Catherine Glennon, Director of Admissions, University of Wisconsin–Stevens Point, 2100 Main Street, Stevens Point, WI 54481. *Phone:* 715-346-2441. *Fax:* 715-346-3296. *E-mail:* admiss@uwsp.edu.

UNIVERSITY OF WISCONSIN–STOUT

Menomonie, Wisconsin www.uwstout.edu/

- **State-supported** comprehensive, founded 1891, part of University of Wisconsin System
- **Small-town** 120-acre campus with easy access to Minneapolis–St. Paul
- **Coed**
- **Moderately difficult** entrance level

Faculty *Student/faculty ratio:* 19:1.

Academics *Calendar:* 4-1-4. *Degrees:* certificates, bachelor's, master's, and post-master's certificates.

Student Life *Campus security:* 24-hour patrols, student patrols, controlled dormitory access.

Athletics Member NCAA. All Division III.

Standardized Tests *Required:* SAT or ACT (for admission).

Costs (2007–08) *Tuition:* state resident $5367 full-time, $179 per credit part-time; nonresident $13,113 full-time, $437 per credit part-time. Full-time tuition and fees vary according to reciprocity agreements. Part-time tuition and fees vary according to reciprocity agreements. *Required fees:* $1905 full-time, $64 per credit part-time. *Room and board:* $4994; room only: $3100. Room and board charges vary according to board plan and housing facility.

Financial Aid Of all full-time matriculated undergraduates who enrolled in 2007, 4,865 applied for aid, 3,364 were judged to have need, 1,729 had their need fully met. 1,199 Federal Work-Study jobs (averaging $1671). In 2007, 117 non-need-based awards were made. *Average percent of need met:* 86. *Average financial aid package:* $8297. *Average need-based loan:* $4586. *Average need-based gift aid:* $5030. *Average non-need-based aid:* $1356. *Average indebtedness upon graduation:* $23,825.

Applying *Options:* electronic application. *Application fee:* $35. *Required:* high school transcript. *Required for some:* minimum 2.75 GPA. *Recommended:* minimum 2.5 GPA.

Freshman Application Contact Dr. Cynthia S. Gilberts, Executive Director of Enrollment Services, University of Wisconsin–Stout, Admissions UW-Stout, Bowman Hall, Menomonie, WI 54751. *Phone:* 715-232-2639. *Toll-free phone:* 800-HI-STOUT. *Fax:* 715-232-2639. *E-mail:* admissions@uwstout.edu.

UNIVERSITY OF WISCONSIN–SUPERIOR

Superior, Wisconsin **www.uwsuper.edu/**

- **State-supported** comprehensive, founded 1893, part of University of Wisconsin System
- **Suburban** 230-acre campus
- **Endowment** $7.7 million
- **Coed** 2,497 undergraduate students, 82% full-time, 57% women, 43% men
- **Moderately difficult** entrance level, 74% of applicants were admitted

Undergraduates 2,043 full-time, 454 part-time. Students come from 26 states and territories, 28 other countries, 46% are from out of state, 2% African American, 1% Asian American or Pacific Islander, 0.7% Hispanic American, 3% Native American, 4% international, 13% transferred in, 24% live on campus. *Retention:* 63% of 2006 full-time freshmen returned.

Freshmen *Admission:* 919 applied, 679 admitted, 350 enrolled. *Test scores:* ACT scores over 18: 92%; ACT scores over 24: 30%; ACT scores over 30: 3%.

Faculty *Total:* 175, 66% full-time, 62% with terminal degrees. *Student/faculty ratio:* 17:1.

Majors Accounting; art history, criticism and conservation; art teacher education; art therapy; biological and physical sciences; biology/biological sciences; biology teacher education; broadcast journalism; business administration and management; business/managerial economics; business teacher education; chemistry; chemistry teacher education; computer and information sciences; computer science; criminal justice/police science; criminal justice/safety; dramatic/theater arts; economics; education; educational leadership and administration; elementary education; English; English/language arts teacher education; finance; fine/studio arts; general studies; health and physical education; health and physical education related; history; history teacher education; information science/studies; international relations and affairs; journalism; kinesiology and exercise science; legal studies; liberal arts and sciences/liberal studies; marketing/marketing management; mass communication/media; mathematics; mathematics teacher education; multi-/interdisciplinary studies related; music; music performance; music teacher education; peace studies and conflict resolution; physical education teaching and coaching; physical sciences; political science and government; pre-law studies; psychology; radio and television; reading teacher education; sales, distribution and marketing; science teacher education; social psychology; social sciences; social science teacher education; social studies teacher education; social work; sociology; special education; speech and rhetoric; transportation management; visual and performing arts.

Academics *Calendar:* semesters. *Degrees:* certificates, bachelor's, and master's (associate, educational specialist). *Special study options:* academic remediation for entering students, adult/continuing education programs, advanced placement credit, cooperative education, distance learning, double majors, English as a second language, external degree program, freshman honors college, honors programs, independent study, internships, off-campus study, part-time degree program, services for LD students, student-designed majors, study abroad, summer session for credit. *ROTC:* Air Force (c). *Unusual degree programs:* 3-2 engineering with Michigan Technological University, University of Wisconsin-Madison; forestry with Michigan Technological University.

Computers on Campus 200 computers/terminals are available on campus for general student use. Students can access the following: campus intranet, computer help desk, free student e-mail accounts, online (class) grades, online (class) registration, online (class) schedules. Campuswide network is available. 100% of college-owned or -operated housing units are wired for high-speed Internet access. Wireless service is available via entire campus.

Student Life *Housing:* on-campus residence required for freshman year. *Options:* coed, women-only, disabled students. Campus housing is university owned. Freshman campus housing is guaranteed. *Activities and organizations:* drama/theater group, student-run newspaper, radio and television station, choral group, Student Senate, Student Activities Board, Residence Hall Association, Inter-Varsity Christian Fellowship, World Student Association. *Campus security:* 24-hour emergency response devices and patrols, student patrols, late-night transport/escort service, controlled dormitory access. *Student services:* health clinic, personal/psychological counseling, women's center.

Athletics Member NCAA. All Division III. *Intercollegiate sports:* baseball M, basketball M/W, cheerleading M/W, cross-country running M/W, golf W, ice hockey M/W, soccer M/W, softball W, track and field M/W, volleyball W. *Intramural sports:* badminton M/W, baseball M/W, basketball M/W, bowling M/W, cross-country running M/W, football M/W, golf M/W, ice hockey M, racquetball M/W, riflery M/W, rock climbing M/W, rugby M, skiing (cross-country) M/W, skiing (downhill) M/W, soccer M/W, softball M/W, table tennis M/W, tennis M/W, volleyball M/W.

Standardized Tests *Required:* SAT or ACT (for admission).

Costs (2007–08) *Tuition:* $361 per semester hour part-time; state resident $4969 full-time, $361 per semester hour part-time; nonresident $12,572 full-time, $676 per semester hour part-time. Full-time tuition and fees vary according to reciprocity agreements. Part-time tuition and fees vary according to reciprocity agreements. *Required fees:* $938 full-time. *Room and board:* $4720; room only: $2770. Room and board charges vary according to board plan and housing facility. *Payment plan:* installment.

Financial Aid Of all full-time matriculated undergraduates who enrolled in 2007, 1,457 applied for aid, 1,185 were judged to have need, 326 had their need fully met. 536 Federal Work-Study jobs (averaging $1430). In 2007, 47 non-need-based awards were made. *Average financial aid package:* $7049. *Average need-based loan:* $3838. *Average need-based gift aid:* $5116. *Average non-need-based aid:* $2720.

Applying *Options:* electronic application, early admission, deferred entrance. *Application fee:* $35. *Required:* high school transcript. *Required for some:* essay or personal statement, letters of recommendation. *Recommended:* interview. *Application deadlines:* rolling (freshmen), rolling (transfers). *Notification:* continuous (freshmen), continuous (transfers).

Freshman Application Contact Lee Parker, Admissions Advisor, University of Wisconsin–Superior, Belknap and Catlin, PO Box 2000, Superior, WI 54880-4500. *Phone:* 715-394-8217. *Toll-free phone:* 715-394-8230. *Fax:* 715-394-8407. *E-mail:* admissions@uwsuper.edu.

UNIVERSITY OF WISCONSIN–WHITEWATER

Whitewater, Wisconsin **www.uww.edu/**

- **State-supported** comprehensive, founded 1868, part of University of Wisconsin System
- **Small-town** 385-acre campus with easy access to Milwaukee
- **Endowment** $14.3 million
- **Coed** 9,408 undergraduate students, 92% full-time, 50% women, 50% men
- **Moderately difficult** entrance level, 75% of applicants were admitted

Undergraduates 8,660 full-time, 748 part-time. Students come from 24 states and territories, 27 other countries, 6% are from out of state, 5% African American, 2% Asian American or Pacific Islander, 3% Hispanic American, 0.5% Native American, 0.7% international, 6% transferred in, 40% live on campus. *Retention:* 76% of 2006 full-time freshmen returned.

Freshmen *Admission:* 6,211 applied, 4,667 admitted, 2,063 enrolled. *Average high school GPA:* 3.25. *Test scores:* SAT critical reading scores over 500: 69%; SAT math scores over 500: 69%; ACT scores over 18: 92%; SAT critical reading scores over 600: 30%; SAT math scores over 600: 30%; ACT scores over 24: 32%; SAT critical reading scores over 700: 2%; SAT math scores over 700: 3%; ACT scores over 30: 2%.

Faculty *Total:* 501, 78% full-time, 74% with terminal degrees. *Student/faculty ratio:* 22:1.

Majors Accounting; art; art history, criticism and conservation; art teacher education; biological and physical sciences; biology/biological sciences; business administration and management; business/commerce; business/managerial economics; business teacher education; chemistry; chemistry related; communication/speech communication and rhetoric; computer and information sciences; dramatic/theater arts; early childhood education; economics; education; elementary education; English; environmental engineering technology; finance; French; geography; German; history; human resources management; information technology; international/global studies; international relations and affairs; journalism;

liberal arts and sciences and humanities related; liberal arts and sciences/liberal studies; management information systems; marketing/marketing management; mathematics; music; music teacher education; occupational safety and health technology; operations management; physical education teaching and coaching; physics; political science and government; psychology; public administration; public policy analysis; science teacher education; secondary education; social sciences; social work; sociology; Spanish; special education; speech and rhetoric; speech-language pathology; women's studies.

Academics *Calendar:* semesters. *Degrees:* associate, bachelor's, and master's. *Special study options:* academic remediation for entering students, accelerated degree program, adult/continuing education programs, advanced placement credit, cooperative education, distance learning, double majors, English as a second language, external degree program, honors programs, independent study, internships, part-time degree program, services for LD students, student-designed majors, study abroad, summer session for credit. *ROTC:* Army (b), Air Force (b).

Computers on Campus 1,300 computers/terminals are available on campus for general student use. Students can access the following: campus intranet, computer help desk, free student e-mail accounts, online (class) grades, online (class) registration, online (class) schedules. Campuswide network is available. 100% of college-owned or -operated housing units are wired for high-speed Internet access. Wireless service is available via entire campus.

Student Life *Housing:* on-campus residence required through sophomore year. *Options:* coed, women-only. Campus housing is university owned. Freshman campus housing is guaranteed. *Activities and organizations:* drama/theater group, student-run newspaper, radio and television station, choral group, marching band, Finance Association, American Marketing Association, Black Student Union, Golden Key, Wisconsin Education Association, national fraternities, national sororities. *Campus security:* 24-hour emergency response devices, late-night transport/escort service, controlled dormitory access. *Student services:* health clinic, personal/psychological counseling, women's center, legal services.

Athletics Member NCAA. All Division III. *Intercollegiate sports:* baseball M, basketball M/W, bowling M (c)/W, cheerleading M (c)/W (c), cross-country running M/W, football M, golf W, gymnastics W, ice hockey M (c)/W (c), lacrosse M (c), rugby M (c)/W (c), soccer M/W, softball W, swimming and diving M/W, tennis M/W, track and field M/W, volleyball M (c)/W, weight lifting M (c), wrestling M. *Intramural sports:* basketball M/W, football M/W, golf M/W, racquetball M/W, rock climbing M (c)/W (c), skiing (downhill) M (c)/W (c), soccer M, softball M/W, table tennis M/W, tennis M/W, ultimate Frisbee M (c)/W (c), volleyball M/W, water polo M/W.

Standardized Tests *Required for some:* ACT (for admission), SAT or ACT (for admission). *Recommended:* SAT or ACT (for admission).

Costs (2007–08) *Tuition:* state resident $5859 full-time, $244 per credit part-time; nonresident $13,432 full-time, $560 per credit part-time. Full-time tuition and fees vary according to degree level and reciprocity agreements. *Required fees:* $871 full-time, $36 per credit part-time. *Room and board:* $4474; room only: $2768. Room and board charges vary according to board plan. *Payment plan:* installment. *Waivers:* children of alumni and senior citizens.

Financial Aid Of all full-time matriculated undergraduates who enrolled in 2007, 6,153 applied for aid, 4,139 were judged to have need, 2,226 had their need fully met. 590 Federal Work-Study jobs (averaging $1106). 1,691 state and other part-time jobs (averaging $1502). In 2007, 390 non-need-based awards were made. *Average percent of need met:* 79%. *Average financial aid package:* $7006. *Average need-based loan:* $3997. *Average need-based gift aid:* $5208. *Average non-need-based aid:* $1954. *Average indebtedness upon graduation:* $18,838.

Applying *Options:* electronic application, early admission, deferred entrance. *Application fee:* $35. *Required:* high school transcript. *Required for some:* letters of recommendation. *Application deadlines:* rolling (freshmen), rolling (transfers). *Notification:* 9/15 (freshmen), continuous (transfers).

Freshman Application Contact Mr. Stephen J. McKellips, Director of Admissions, University of Wisconsin–Whitewater, 800 West Main Street, Whitewater, WI 53190-1790. *Phone:* 262-472-1440 Ext. 1512. *Fax:* 262-472-1515. *E-mail:* uwwadmit@uww.edu.

VITERBO UNIVERSITY

La Crosse, Wisconsin — www.viterbo.edu/

- **Independent Roman Catholic** comprehensive, founded 1890
- **Suburban** 72-acre campus
- **Endowment** $23.9 million
- **Coed** 2,019 undergraduate students, 75% full-time, 71% women, 29% men
- **Moderately difficult** entrance level, 88% of applicants were admitted

Established in 1890, Viterbo University, located in La Crosse, Wisconsin, is western Wisconsin's premier private university. Viterbo offers undergraduate and graduate degrees through five undergraduate schools and the School of Extended Learning, which allows students to select from thirty-eight majors and twenty-seven minors. Viterbo's nursing, fine arts, and education programs have earned outstanding reputations for exceptional quality. Some 2,100 students are formally enrolled. The student-faculty ratio is 16:1. More than 95 percent of all Viterbo graduates have been placed. A total of 70 percent of the students are women; 30 percent are men. Named a character-building college by the prestigious Templeton Foundation, Viterbo is housed on 21 acres in a residential area and has recently opened a new $11-million science center and a new $7.5-million athletic complex.

Undergraduates 1,508 full-time, 511 part-time. Students come from 19 states and territories, 16 other countries, 22% are from out of state, 1% African American, 1% Asian American or Pacific Islander, 0.9% Hispanic American, 1% Native American, 1% international, 14% transferred in, 29% live on campus. *Retention:* 74% of 2006 full-time freshmen returned.

Freshmen *Admission:* 1,148 applied, 1,013 admitted, 368 enrolled. *Average high school GPA:* 3.30. *Test scores:* ACT scores over 18: 96%; ACT scores over 24: 33%; ACT scores over 30: 2%.

Faculty *Total:* 225, 48% full-time, 43% with terminal degrees. *Student/faculty ratio:* 12:1.

Majors Accounting; art; arts management; art teacher education; biochemistry; biology/biological sciences; biology teacher education; biopsychology; business administration and management; business administration, management and operations related; business teacher education; chemistry; chemistry teacher education; computer and information sciences; criminal justice/safety; design and visual communications; dietetics; divinity/ministry; drama and dance teacher education; dramatic/theater arts; elementary education; English; English language and literature related; English/language arts teacher education; general studies; graphic design; liberal arts and sciences/liberal studies; management information systems; marketing/marketing management; mathematics; mathematics teacher education; multi-/interdisciplinary studies related; music; music pedagogy; music performance; music teacher education; natural sciences; nursing (registered nurse training); philosophy and religious studies related; psychology; religious studies; science teacher education; social sciences; social studies teacher education; social work; sociology; Spanish; Spanish language teacher education; speech/theater education; technology/industrial arts teacher education; visual and performing arts.

Academics *Calendar:* semesters. *Degrees:* associate, bachelor's, master's, and postbachelor's certificates. *Special study options:* academic remediation for entering students, accelerated degree program, adult/continuing education programs, advanced placement credit, distance learning, double majors, honors programs, independent study, internships, off-campus study, part-time degree program, services for LD students, student-designed majors, study abroad, summer session for credit. *ROTC:* Army (c).

Computers on Campus 314 computers/terminals are available on campus for general student use. Students can access the following: campus intranet, computer help desk, free student e-mail accounts, online (class) grades, online (class) registration, online (class) schedules, Blackboard courses. Campuswide network is available. 100% of college-owned or -operated housing units are wired for high-speed Internet access. Wireless service is available via entire campus.

Student Life *Housing:* on-campus residence required through sophomore year. *Options:* coed, men-only, women-only. Campus housing is university owned. Freshman campus housing is guaranteed. *Activities and organizations:* drama/theater group, student-run newspaper, choral group, Viterbo Student Nurses Association, Campus Ministry (volunteer services and service trips), Rugby, Student Government Association, Residence Hall Council. *Campus security:* 24-hour emergency response devices, late-night transport/escort service, controlled dormitory access, security officers on campus 5:00 p.m. to 7:00 a.m, lighted pathways, emergency evacuation plan, self-defense education programs. *Student services:* health clinic, personal/psychological counseling.

Athletics Member NAIA. *Intercollegiate sports:* baseball M (s), basketball M (s)/W (s), cross-country running M (s)/W (s), golf M (s)/W (s), soccer M (s)/W (s), softball W (s), volleyball W (s). *Intramural sports:* badminton M/W, basketball M/W, bowling M/W, cross-country running M/W, golf M/W, racquetball M/W, rugby M/W, skiing (cross-country) M/W, skiing (downhill) M/W, soccer M/W, softball M/W, swimming and diving M/W, table tennis M/W, tennis M/W, ultimate Frisbee M/W, volleyball M/W.

Standardized Tests *Required:* ACT (for admission).

Costs (2008–09) *Comprehensive fee:* $25,870 includes full-time tuition ($19,000), mandatory fees ($490), and room and board ($6380). Part-time tuition: $560 per credit. *Required fees:* $15 per credit part-time, $45 per term part-time. *College room only:* $2910.

Financial Aid Of all full-time matriculated undergraduates who enrolled in 2003, 1,311 applied for aid, 1,208 were judged to have need, 309 had their need fully met. 387 Federal Work-Study jobs (averaging $1680). 19 state and other part-time jobs (averaging $1615). In 2003, 223 non-need-based awards were made. *Average percent of need met:* 71%. *Average financial aid package:* $13,534. *Average need-based loan:* $4317. *Average need-based gift aid:* $8859. *Average non-need-based aid:* $5629. *Average indebtedness upon graduation:* $16,619.

Applying *Options:* electronic application, deferred entrance. *Application fee:* $25. *Required:* high school transcript, minimum 2.0 GPA. *Required for some:* essay or personal statement, 1 letter of recommendation, interview, audition for theater and music; portfolio for art. *Application deadlines:* rolling (freshmen), rolling (out-of-state freshmen), rolling (transfers). *Notification:* continuous until 8/15 (freshmen), continuous until 8/15 (out-of-state freshmen), continuous until 8/15 (transfers).

Freshman Application Contact Mr. Wayne Wojciechowski, Assistant Academic Vice President, Viterbo University, 900 Viterbo Drive, LaCrosse, WI 54601. *Phone:* 608-796-3085. *Toll-free phone:* 800-VITERBO Ext. 3010. *Fax:* 608-796-3020. *E-mail:* admission@viterbo.edu.

WISCONSIN LUTHERAN COLLEGE

Milwaukee, Wisconsin **www.wlc.edu/**

- **Independent** 4-year, founded 1973, affiliated with Wisconsin Evangelical Lutheran Synod
- **Suburban** 48-acre campus
- **Endowment** $20.4 million
- **Coed**
- **Moderately difficult** entrance level

Faculty *Student/faculty ratio:* 10:1.

Academics *Calendar:* semesters. *Degree:* bachelor's.

Student Life *Campus security:* 24-hour emergency response devices and patrols, late-night transport/escort service, controlled dormitory access, closed-circuit TV monitors.

Athletics Member NCAA. All Division III.

Standardized Tests *Required:* SAT or ACT (for admission).

Costs (2007–08) *Comprehensive fee:* $26,474 includes full-time tuition ($19,430), mandatory fees ($134), and room and board ($6910). *College room only:* $3680.

Financial Aid Of all full-time matriculated undergraduates who enrolled in 2006, 578 applied for aid, 524 were judged to have need, 155 had their need fully met. 255 Federal Work-Study jobs (averaging $1699). 25 state and other part-time jobs (averaging $5200). In 2006, 152 non-need-based awards were made. *Average percent of need met:* 84. *Average financial aid package:* $14,709. *Average need-based loan:* $3618. *Average need-based gift aid:* $10,604. *Average non-need-based aid:* $11,600. *Average indebtedness upon graduation:* $14,028.

Applying *Options:* electronic application. *Application fee:* $20. *Required:* high school transcript, minimum 2.7 GPA, minimum ACT score of 21. *Required for some:* interview. *Recommended:* 1 letter of recommendation.

Freshman Application Contact Ms. Amanda Delaney, Wisconsin Lutheran College, 8800 West Bluemound Road, Milwaukee, WI 53226-9942. *Phone:* 414-443-8726. *Toll-free phone:* 888-WIS LUTH. *Fax:* 414-443-8514. *E-mail:* amanda.delaney@wlc.edu.

ALVERNO COLLEGE
MILWAUKEE, WISCONSIN

The College

Alverno College is a college like no other. Its creative hands-on learning style has gained national and worldwide praise and emulation. Hundreds of educators representing more than 200 institutions from the United States and abroad visit Alverno each year to study Alverno's teaching methods. The College's unique approach to evaluation and assessment provides students with a comprehensive education that takes them from the classroom to the community to a career where they can make their mark. Students receive individual attention and demonstrate what they have learned through assessments, not traditional examinations. Classes are small, and projects are student centered.

Internationally known for its innovative, abilities-based, assessment-as-learning approach to education, Alverno College is an award-winning, four-year, independent liberal arts college for women. Founded in 1887 by the School Sisters of St. Francis, Alverno has one of the most diverse student bodies in the nation. Currently, there are more than 2,480 students enrolled. The College offers bachelor's degree programs in weekday and weekend time frames, initial teacher certification programs for postgraduates, a Master of Arts in Education for teachers and business professionals, a Master of Science in Nursing, and a Master of Business Administration. Alverno also offers educational licensure programs and a licensure-to-master's program.

Alverno College is accredited by the Higher Learning Commission of the North Central Association of Colleges and Schools, National Council for Accreditation of Teacher Education, Wisconsin Department of Public Instruction, Wisconsin Board of Nursing, Commission on Collegiate Nursing Education, and National Association of Schools of Music. In *U.S. News & World Report*'s 2007 edition of *America's Best Colleges,* Alverno ranked in six of eight categories within the "Programs to Look For" section. Alverno also ranked in the top tier–Midwest Region and ranked second in the Midwest for campus diversity among Comprehensive Colleges–Bachelor's.

Alverno's mission is to promote the personal and professional development of women through four areas: creating a community of learning, creating a curriculum, creating ties to the community, and creating relationships with higher education. Alverno accomplishes this by remaining focused on the student and higher education.

The hallmark of an Alverno education is to prepare students for real life, not just for finals. Faculty members develop curricula that meet today's challenges.

In every class, students learn to analyze issues from a variety of perspectives, make value decisions, engage in meaningful discussion, and apply creative solutions in problem solving—abilities needed in today's changing world.

Students are able to follow their own progress through Alverno's patented Diagnostic Digital Portfolio (DDP), the first-of-its-kind Web-based system that enables each student to access feedback from faculty members, external assessors, and peers.

Each student is required to complete one off-campus professional internship. These internships complement the classroom experience and expose each student to real-life work situations by providing insight into career options. Local organizations and businesses that regularly participate include Harley-Davidson, Miller Brewing, Milwaukee Art Museum, the mayor's office, and scores of others.

Alverno's Career Education Center is fully integrated into the learning process, providing students with numerous services, resources, training opportunities, and tools to assist them with their career planning. Nearly 90 percent of Alverno graduates report that they are working in their chosen fields within six months of graduation.

Students take advantage of a wide variety of athletic, social, cultural, and cocurricular academic activities on and off campus. There are more than thirty student organizations, including service, professional, musical, cultural, and other interest groups.

The College's NCAA Division III athletics program provides students with five competitive sports: basketball, cross-country, soccer, softball, and volleyball. Intramural sports are also available. Alverno Presents is one of the longest-running performing arts series in the Midwest, offering such top-notch performers as Dianne Reeves, Stefon Harris, Wynton Marsalis, The Roches, McCoy Tyner, David Neumann, and others. Austin Hall, the main residence hall, features the Mug, a coffeehouse run by students for students as a place to relax and study and enjoy live music, lively discussions, large-screen TVs, and movie nights. Each room in the residence hall features high-speed Internet access and cable television capability.

Alverno College features several extracurricular and cocurricular facilities on campus. Pitman Theatre is a beautiful art deco–style theater with seating for 930. The theater is home to Alverno Presents and numerous concerts and special events each season, including the Schwartz Live@Alverno author series. Wehr Hall, with seating for 375, is a state-of-the-art presentation hall designed for multimedia presentations as well as smaller performances. Alverno's Conference Center can accommodate seated dinners for up to 300 and is host to countless alumnae weddings and other celebrations each year.

Location

Alverno's 46-acre campus is nestled in the residential Jackson Park neighborhood in Milwaukee, just minutes from downtown and the beautiful Lake Michigan shoreline. Students are only minutes from the world-famous Milwaukee Art Museum and its Calatrava addition, the Marcus Center for the Performing Arts, the lakefront festival grounds, the gallery and theater districts, and Miller Park, the home of the Milwaukee Brewers. In addition, the city offers a mix of trendy nightspots and chic coffee bars and has a highly eclectic dining scene.

Majors and Degrees

Alverno College is a fully accredited four-year baccalaureate institution conferring Bachelor of Arts, Bachelor of Science, Master of Arts, Master of Business Administration, and Master of Science in Nursing degrees.

The College has more than sixty majors and minors, including accounting, art, art education/art therapy, biology, business, chemistry, computing and information technology, education, English, environmental science, global studies, history, international business, liberal studies, management, marketing, mathematics, music therapy, nursing, philosophy, political science, professional communication, psychology, religious studies, sociology, Spanish, a host of preprofessional training programs, and many other areas of study.

Academic Programs

Alverno's learning process prepares students for success. The curriculum includes academic course work as well as external experiences and develops the student's abilities in eight specific core areas: communication, analysis, problem solving, valuing in decision making, social interaction, developing a global perspective, effective citizenship, and aesthetic engagement. Each student acquires the knowledge that is needed to demonstrate learning in each of these areas, tying her studies to her personal and professional goals.

Alverno is home to Wisconsin's original Weekend College program, one of the first in the nation. The program, which began in 1977, allows students to earn their degrees in professional communication, communication management and technology, community leadership and development, international business, management, management accounting, marketing management, and nursing (RN to B.S.N.) by attending classes on alternate weekends.

Off-Campus Programs

The travel-abroad program provides students with the opportunity to study for a semester or a shorter term in such places as England, France, Japan, Mexico, Northern Ireland, and South Korea. International internship programs are continually being developed to accommodate Alverno's diverse student body. Travel courses that culminate in a trip are also available.

Academic Facilities

Alverno College remains one of the most technologically advanced campuses in the region. The Teaching, Learning and Technology Center (TLTC) is a 73,000-square-foot facility that features cutting-edge science labs, computer and multimedia centers, and an on-campus digital production facility. The center features a state-of-the-art Media Hub, a videoconferencing center that allows for long-distance learning, and multiple computer labs and smart classrooms. These classrooms are equipped with a computer, TV, VCR, DVD player, document camera, overhead projector, and electronic projector screen. Portable equipment is also available.

The TLTC is also home to hundreds of networked high-tech computers plus writing devices, the latest software, digital cameras, scanners, laptops, and more. The production facility houses nonlinear digital editing equipment that allows students to produce and edit their own projects. All of these service areas are staff supported to assist students.

Alverno's library provides on-site and remote access to its print, audiovisual, and electronic collection of more than 250,000 items, as well as access to worldwide resources available through technology. The library's resources and services are further enhanced through a consortium of seven local college and university libraries.

The Nursing Education Building provides resources dedicated to meeting the needs of nursing students, including a library and a clinical nursing resource center. The center allows students to practice their nursing therapeutic skills and to participate in simulated clinical experiences. Computers are equipped with interactive nursing software, and registered nurses serve as mentors and assessors.

Costs

For 2007–08, the tuition is $16,896–$17,640 per year, and the room and board rate is $6106 per year. Books vary by course load but average $300 per semester for full-time students. Personal expenses vary greatly by student.

Financial Aid

Financial aid is readily available based on student need, academic performance, and other criteria. Aid can take the form of scholarships, grants, loans, and campus work-study programs. Approximately 87 percent of Alverno students receive some form of financial assistance, with an average award of $11,415 per student per year. More than 100 Alverno-sponsored scholarships are available.

Faculty

Alverno's coed faculty is made up of 107 full-time members, 90 percent of whom have earned the highest degree available in their field. Faculty members also serve as academic advisers to students in their major areas of concentration. Class sizes average 20 to 25 students, and the student-faculty ratio is 13:1.

Admission Requirements

Candidates applying for admission to Alverno College directly after high school must have completed at least 17 academic units. These units should include at least 4 units in English, with the rest distributed among foreign languages, history and the social sciences, mathematics, and natural sciences. All students must have satisfactory scores on the ACT or SAT and complete an evaluation of their abilities through the Communication Placement Assessment before beginning classes.

Application and Information

Students who wish to apply for admission can apply online, or they can write, call, or e-mail the Admissions Office for the necessary forms. An application is considered complete upon receipt of the application form, the application fee (waived if students apply online), a high school transcript, and SAT or ACT scores. Students may submit any additional evidence that they believe might help the College determine their capacity to benefit from an Alverno education. Alverno's admission policy permits notification of acceptance within three weeks of receipt of all credentials. Acceptance is contingent upon satisfactory completion of the secondary school courses.

For more information about Alverno College, interested students should contact:

Admissions Office
Alverno College
3400 South 43rd Street
P.O. Box 343922
Milwaukee, Wisconsin 53234-3922
Phone: 414-382-6100
800-933-3401 (toll-free)
E-mail: admissions@alverno.edu
Web site: http://www.alverno.edu

Students demonstrate panel discussion skills.

BELOIT COLLEGE

BELOIT, WISCONSIN

The College

Beloit College is an independent, national college of liberal arts and sciences that engages the intelligence, imagination, and curiosity of its students. Beloit's focus is on teaching and on the close collaboration that takes place among students and faculty members in small classroom and lab settings. Undergraduates learn to approach the complex problems of the world ethically and thoughtfully in an academic community that values and emphasizes international and interdisciplinary perspectives and the integration of knowledge with experience.

Beloit is Wisconsin's first college, founded in 1846 to serve a frontier society. Today, a geographically diverse population of 1,250 students is drawn to Beloit's residential campus from nearly all North American states and more than forty countries. Seven percent come from countries outside the United States, 15 percent of U.S. students are non-Caucasian, and a variety of religious orientations and socioeconomic backgrounds are represented on campus. Beloit students are equally diverse in their academic choices. No more than 10 percent of the seniors are represented in any one of more than fifty majors available.

Beloit students are informed and experienced in political and social issues, and they place a premium on individual expression. The range of student activities reflects the spectrum of their interests and involvement. Beloit students serve on College governance committees, establish organizations, manage an annual music festival, and host their own radio and cable TV shows. In a given week, students may have the choice of attending (or organizing) a lecture series, a movie, music performances, a poetry reading, or an environmental debate. Seventy percent of Beloit's students participate in club, intramural, or varsity athletics and use the College's athletic complex adjacent to the residential side of campus. Those who live on campus (and nearly all do) may choose to live in residence halls, on quiet floors or substance-free floors, in one of three fraternity houses or three sorority houses, or in one of the special-interest houses, which include houses that form around students' interests, such as particular languages, gay and lesbian issues, anthropology, the arts, black student issues, faith and spirituality, music, the environment, peace and justice issues, science fiction and fantasy, Latino student issues, and women's issues. Two new town-house complexes have been constructed in the past five years and offer roomy, apartment-style living for juniors and seniors. Meals, served in two dining halls on campus, are offered on a twenty-meal weekly plan and include organic, vegetarian, and vegan meal options.

New students quickly become part of this active and diverse environment through First-Year Initiatives (FYI), an innovative program that places new students in interdisciplinary seminars taught by experienced professors and staff members. These seminars begin the first day students arrive on campus and provide an academic grounding and a social base. They also begin two years of advising by faculty members, which is designed to assist students in their adjustment to Beloit and to bolster campus involvement. FYI leads students into a curriculum that is open and collaborative.

Location

Beloit's 40-acre campus is located on the border between Wisconsin and Illinois, 90 miles northwest of Chicago, 50 miles south of Madison, and 70 miles southwest of Milwaukee, in a small city that Margaret Mead once called "American society in a microcosm." Students may take advantage of the resources of the three major metropolitan areas, and Beloit's hospital, clinics, manufacturers, and various civic and service organizations provide numerous internship, job shadowing, enrichment, and community outreach opportunities. The academic buildings of Beloit College cluster around lawns dotted with ancient North American Indian mounds, while across the campus, newly renovated residence halls encourage interaction among resident students. A 25-acre athletic field and Strong Memorial Stadium are located a few blocks east of the main campus.

Majors and Degrees

Beloit awards Bachelor of Arts and Bachelor of Science degrees in nineteen departments and more than fifty fields of study. In the natural sciences and mathematics division, students may choose majors from the departments of biology, biochemistry, chemistry, environmental studies, geology, mathematics and computer science, and physics and astronomy. In the social sciences division, students may choose majors from the departments of anthropology, economics and management, education and youth studies, political science and international relations, psychology, and sociology. In the arts and humanities division, majors are offered in the departments of art and art history, classics, English, history, modern languages and literatures, music, philosophy and religious studies, theater arts, and women's and gender studies. Students are also encouraged to create a unique interdisciplinary major. The College offers departmental minors in anthropology, biology and society, chemistry, computer science, English, geology, history, integrative biology, international economics, management, mathematics, music, philosophy, physics, political economy, political science, and religious studies. Permanent interdisciplinary minors include African studies, American studies, ancient Mediterranean studies, Asian studies, computational visualization and modeling, environmental studies, European studies, health and society, journalism, Latin American studies, legal studies, medieval studies, museum studies, peace and justice studies, performing arts, Russian studies, and women's and gender studies.

Beloit offers 3-2 cooperative programs for students interested in engineering and environmental management and forestry; preprofessional programs in dentistry, law, and medicine; and a cooperative program that guarantees qualified graduates entry into a master's degree program in nursing. These programs, which have strong advisory and internship components, complement a major in an appropriate discipline. Beloit students may also earn teaching certification.

Academic Programs

Beloit's academic calendar consists of two 14-week semesters with one-week midterm breaks. At the end of the sophomore year, students are required to declare a major and may choose to add a second major, a minor, or teaching certification. Sophomore students work with faculty advisers to define academic and personal goals, including completion of graduation requirements and the declaration of majors, and develop a plan—which may include internships, independent research, or study abroad—for accomplishing them. A structured program called My Academic Plan (MAP) allows students to shape their time at Beloit to ensure they will reach their goals. In addition, Beloit's open curriculum requires two classes from each of the three academic divisions plus an interdisciplinary course, three writing-intensive courses, and significant contact with a culture not one's own. Thirty-one units are required for graduation, each unit representing the equivalent of a course of study involving 4 hours of class time a week per semester.

Off-Campus Programs

Beloit has a century-old tradition of domestic and international off-campus study opportunities, and more than half of new Beloit graduates will have studied and/or conducted research in such a program. Domestic programs include an opportunity to study at the Marine Biological Laboratory at Woods Hole in Massachusetts; a science semester at the Oak Ridge National Laboratory in Knoxville, Tennessee; a semester in the arts, an urban studies program, and a Newberry Library semester in the humanities, all in Chicago; and a Washington Semester at American University in Washington, D.C. Internships, field terms, and summer employment opportunities are arranged through the Office of Field and Career Services. Anthropology field training programs and geology field expeditions take students to domestic and international locations, and additional experiential opportunities exist through Beloit's membership in the Keck Consortium in Geology and the Pew Midstates Science and Mathematics Consortium.

At Beloit College, study abroad is more of an expectation than a luxury. Whether through Beloit's own extensive programs or the Associated

Colleges of the Midwest (ACM) and independent programs, Beloit students have studied in more than forty countries worldwide, from Australia to Zimbabwe.

Academic Facilities

Beloit's library collection is in excess of half a million holdings, which include books, periodicals, government documents, an international center, a science library, and other special collections. There are individual and group study areas, a computer lab, and an extensive listening and viewing area for use of audiovisual materials. The library is connected to a statewide interlibrary loan system, and Beloit students have access to the University of Wisconsin–Madison libraries. The Logan Museum of Anthropology and the Wright Museum of Art are world-class museums, which offer students excellent resources for research and work experience. The Neese Performing Arts Theatre complex features a large thrust stage theater, a black-box theater, a scenic design studio, and a complete costume shop. The World Affairs Center Language Lab includes eighteen student stations and an enclosed area for viewing international videotapes, TV programs, and newscasts taken from the lab's satellite antenna. More than 900 student-accessible microcomputers and workstations are located throughout the campus, and every residence hall room, classroom, and office has access to the Internet through the campuswide fiber-optic network. A 6,000-square-foot center for entrepreneurship in downtown Beloit provides physical space, office resources, and a recording studio where students can put venture plans of their own design into action. Beloit's current science center offers privileges and technology normally reserved for graduate students. A new Center for the Sciences is scheduled to be open for classes in fall 2008. This state-of-the-art teaching facility will set new standards for environmental responsibility and efficiency.

Costs

Tuition for the 2007–08 academic year is $29,678, fees are $230, a double room is $3126, and board (twenty-meal plan) is $3282, for a total comprehensive fee of $36,316. While the cost of books and incidental expenses varies, it is about $1300.

Financial Aid

Beloit College has a need-blind admissions policy and is committed to making the Beloit experience affordable to all qualified students. The financial aid program recognizes two criteria—scholastic ability and financial need—that may qualify students for awards. During the 2006–07 academic year, about 91 percent of first-year students received financial assistance through grants, loans, or work-study. The College also awards merit scholarships.

In 2006, new students from families with incomes below $40,000 received an average grant of $24,500; qualifying students from families with incomes above $100,000 received an average grant of $12,000. Beloit's attention to providing students high value has won the College recognition in the *Fiske Guide to Colleges, The Princeton Review*, and *U.S. News & World Report* as among the nation's "best buys" in top colleges.

Faculty

The focus of Beloit's faculty is great teaching. Beloit professors are drawn to work in a setting that emphasizes discussion and collaborative learning in small classes. Of the 103 full-time faculty members, 96 percent hold the highest academic degree in their field. All classes are taught by professors. In classrooms, it is easy for students and faculty members to become immersed in their work, since the student-faculty ratio is 11:1 and the average class size is 15 students. All Beloit professors are also academic advisers who are involved in students' academic concerns as well as their adjustment to life at the College. Discussions begun in the classroom are often continued in an informal setting, such as at a basketball game or over dinner at a professor's house.

Student Government

Students at Beloit are actively involved in the governance of the College. The Beloit Student Congress is the College's student government. Its committees (Governance Committee, Publicity Committee, Food Committee, Organization Task Force, and Programming Board) allow the Congress to focus on representing the student body and meeting its goals. In addition to this entirely student-run governing body, students are elected to the College's Academic Senate and serve as voting members of major College committees. Students also sit on all academic search committees.

Admission Requirements

Admission to Beloit is selective. Beloit seeks applicants with special qualities and talents, as well as those from diverse ethnic, geographic, and economic backgrounds. When reviewing applications, the transcript is the most important element. Beloit has no absolute secondary school requirements but recommends a rigorous college-preparatory program. This includes 4 years of English, 4 years of college-preparatory mathematics, 4 years of laboratory science, 4 years of history or social science, and 4 years of a foreign language. Seventh-semester grades may be required. A counselor recommendation is a required part of the application. One teacher recommendation is also required. The essay component of Beloit's application is critical. There is no required topic, so students should write about a topic they believe will represent them well. Either SAT or ACT test scores are required, but they are the least important part of the application. Beloit does not consider the SAT or ACT writing exam for purposes of admission. Interviews are not required for admission but are encouraged. Off-campus alumni interviews can be arranged if a student would like to interview but cannot travel to the campus. Transfer applications are considered for August or January entrance. Applicants must hold at least a B- average at an accredited college or university.

Application and Information

Beloit has modified rolling admissions, so students may apply at any time. For priority consideration, both in admissions and in financial aid, however, students should file their applications by January 15. Students who apply by this date are mailed notification by early March. Early Action applications are due December 1, with notification January 15. Transfer applications for the fall term are due by March 15 and for the spring term, by November 1. Notification for transfer applications is rolling. For more information, students should contact:

Admissions Office
Beloit College
700 College Street
Beloit, Wisconsin 53511
Phone: 608-363-2500
800-9-BELOIT (toll-free)
Fax: 608-363-2075
E-mail: admiss@beloit.edu
Web site: http://www.beloit.edu

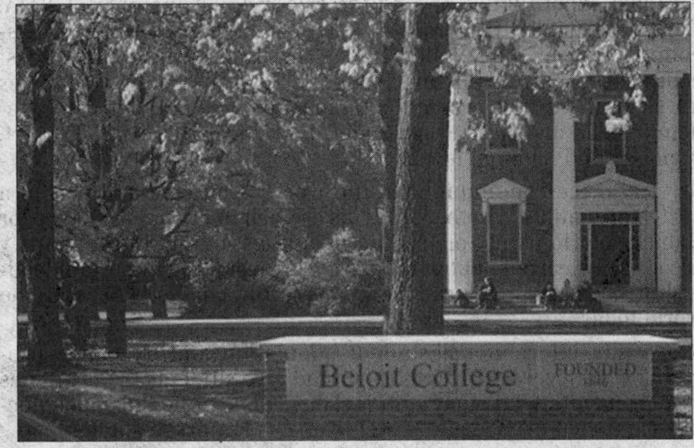

Middle College, which houses the Admissions Office, is at the center of Beloit's New England–style campus.

CARDINAL STRITCH UNIVERSITY

MILWAUKEE, WISCONSIN

The University

Cardinal Stritch University is a comprehensive, coeducational institution rooted in the liberal arts and established in the Catholic tradition. Since its founding in 1937 by the Sisters of St. Francis of Assisi, Stritch has emerged as the largest Franciscan institution of higher education in North America and the second-largest private university in Wisconsin.

With a total population of more than 7,600 students on two campuses and at numerous off-site locations in Wisconsin and Minnesota, Stritch's size can be deceiving. While Stritch provides all of the resources associated with large universities, it still offers the benefits of personal attention and one-on-one instruction associated with smaller institutions. The University keeps current with technological trends yet remains committed to maintaining the high-quality, value-centered education that has defined Stritch's history and continues to attract its diverse student body. At Stritch, a student-faculty ratio of 17:1 allows students easy access to faculty members, who give students the personal attention needed to realize their full potential. A selection of more than sixty fields of study means students can choose from a wide variety of majors to prepare themselves for future endeavors. For students who seek to continue their education after earning their undergraduate degree, the University offers eighteen master's degrees in a variety of specialty areas, including art, business, education, history, music, nursing, psychology, and religious studies. In addition to a robust traditional program offering, Stritch was among the first institutions of higher learning in the state to offer both undergraduate and graduate degrees geared to meet the needs of working adults. These programs meet once a week and are taught at an accelerated pace, with students taking one class at a time and progressing through their programs as a group. The University also offers a doctorate in leadership for the advancement of learning and service in an accelerated weekend/evening format.

With ten athletic teams, more than twenty student clubs and organizations, and the chance to create new campus organizations to suit their own interests, students discover social, cultural, and professional opportunities beyond the classroom. A member of NAIA, Cardinal Stritch University offers baseball, basketball, cross-country, soccer, and volleyball for men and basketball, cross-country, soccer, softball, and volleyball for women. Stritch athletes have a distinguished reputation for balancing their athletic and academic skills and have represented the University at the district, regional, and national levels.

Service to the community and the world is an essential part of a Stritch education. Whether students are helping to build a house for Habitat for Humanity or leading health lessons in Tanzania, they are actively learning about themselves, developing important leadership skills, and exploring solutions to the challenges facing the world today.

A growing international student population and exchange programs with several universities abroad give students opportunities to meet people from other cultures, develop a more global perspective of current events, and travel overseas to pursue studies.

The main campus houses a three-story residence hall, which is connected to several academic buildings and allows residents easy and climate-controlled access to many of the University's facilities. The student union, field house, bookstore, and auditorium are anchored by the Alfred S. Kliebhan Great Hall, where students study, visit with friends, or simply relax. Serra Dining Hall provides buffet-style meals with numerous menu selections. The student union includes fast-food choices as well as a student-run coffee shop. The chapel facilitates group worship at regular services and opportunities for personal reflection and individual prayer.

Location

Cardinal Stritch University's 40-acre, parklike main campus is situated in a quiet suburban neighborhood just north of Milwaukee. Downtown Milwaukee is a 15-minute drive from the campus, while access to Lake Michigan is available within several blocks. The campus is conveniently accessible from Interstate 43, which offers a direct route to Mitchell International Airport, the downtown Amtrak train station, and the Greyhound bus depot. The Milwaukee County Transit System provides students with a public transportation option when they are involved in off-campus pursuits. Interstate 43 also is a link to downtown Milwaukee, which is home to numerous ethnic and American restaurants, specialty retailers, a downtown mall, the Milwaukee Art Museum, the Milwaukee Public Museum, several conference and performance centers, and cultural and sports entertainment.

Majors and Degrees

Cardinal Stritch University offers a wide variety of undergraduate degrees and encourages students to personalize their experience by creating a unique double major or minor to fit their specific career and educational goals. Personal advisers lead students through the process of choosing a major by answering questions and providing individual guidance. The College of Arts and Sciences offers Associate of Arts degrees in art, general studies, and women's studies and bachelor's degree programs in accounting, art (studio), art education, biology, business, chemistry, communication, computer science, English, environmental chemistry, graphic design, history, interactive media development, international business, jazz studies, management information systems, mathematics, music education, music performance, photography, political science, preprofessional programs in both premed and prelaw, psychology, religious studies, social studies, sociology, Spanish, sport management, theater, and writing.

The College of Education and Leadership offers bachelor's degrees in elementary, secondary, and special education.

The College of Business offers undergraduate degree programs that are exclusively designed to meet the special needs of working adults at on- and off-campus locations. Certificate programs and associate and bachelor's degrees are available.

The College of Nursing offers an associate degree in nursing for entry into nursing practice. Once completed, graduates of the program can take the exam to become a registered nurse and begin working in the field. The bachelor's degree in nursing is geared toward working nurses and is offered in a nontraditional format.

Academic Programs

The University strives to help students develop skills needed for a successful career as well as a personal code of ethics by which to live. Each degree program is based upon a foundation of liberal arts courses combined with a concentration in a major area of study. Courses in the general areas of communication, humanities, social and behavioral sciences, mathematics, and the natural sciences are common to all of the programs. The Associate of Arts degree is granted upon completion of 64 credits. The Associate of Science degree in nursing is granted upon completion of 70 credits, and the Associate of Science degree in business requires completion of 64 credits. The Bachelor of Arts degree, the Bachelor of Fine Arts degree, the Bachelor of Science degrees in business administration and management, and the Bachelor of Science in Nursing degree all require 128 credits.

A dual-advising system for the undergraduate degree programs in the Colleges of Arts and Sciences and Education and Leadership helps to ensure that students graduate in four years. Students work closely with a faculty adviser from the start of their Stritch education to determine required courses and electives. Advisers in the One-Stop Enrollment Services Center help students select liberal arts core and elective courses.

Off-Campus Programs

Opportunities to study abroad and participate in international service projects are available. Stritch students have studied in or traveled to such countries as England, India, Italy, Mexico, South Korea, and Spain as well as the continents of Africa and Australia.

Academic Facilities

An exceptional resource, the library is easily accessible and contains a wealth of information necessary to complete in-depth research. Its holdings change daily and now include more than 122,000 items in a variety of formats, as well as 1,300 periodical titles in paper, micro, and online formats. The library offers the resources of eight college libraries through its collaborative Southeastern Wisconsin Information Technology Exchange (SWITCH) consortium and Topcat, a combined online public-access catalog. Students can access an array of electronic resources and interactive research services, which are available both on-site and from wherever learning takes place. The library's resources also include a number of laptop computers that are available for checkout for up to seven days at a time, an Instructional Materials Center containing children's literary materials for educators, and the Franciscan Center, which is a library of materials devoted to Franciscan studies.

The Information Technology Department gives students a competitive edge in today's computerized society. There are open computer labs, public spaces with computers and network connections for laptops/personal computers, wireless access to the Internet in public spaces, and discipline-specific computer labs. The student computing areas are equipped with laser printers and scanners and house PC and Macintosh computers.

The Career Services Center provides internship and job-search services and resources to all Stritch students and alumni. Individual counseling is available, and workshops offered throughout the year include career choices, job-search techniques, resume writing, interviewing, and choosing a major.

Other academic facilities include a 400-seat teaching theater, a spacious art gallery, photo labs, a dance studio, metal and woodworking shops, a graphic arts computer laboratory, state-of-the-art biology and chemistry laboratories, and a newly renovated nursing resource laboratory.

Costs

Full-time tuition for 2007–08 is $18,624; room and board are $5750. Part-time tuition is $582 per credit for all undergraduate programs except nursing, which is subject to additional fees.

Financial Aid

As one of the least expensive private colleges in Wisconsin, Cardinal Stritch University is quite affordable. Approximately 93 percent of Stritch students receive some type of financial aid. On average, Stritch students get half of their tuition paid by grants and scholarships. A wide range of financial aid options is available at Cardinal Stritch University, including government-subsidized loan and grant programs as well as University scholarships, on-campus employment opportunities, and off-campus internships. Eligibility for need-based grant and loan programs is determined after filing the Free Application for Federal Student Aid (FAFSA). Candidates for financial aid should complete and mail the FAFSA by April 15 to receive full consideration for all University scholarships and grants.

Faculty

Cardinal Stritch University faculty members play an active role in every student's life. Faculty members teach their own classes, so students can benefit directly from their knowledge, expertise, and open-door policy. As a result of the small class sizes, students can benefit from the personal attention of individual faculty members, can take advantage of opportunities to participate fully in class discussions, and are challenged to interact with and learn from their peers.

Through their research, writing, and presentations, faculty members keep abreast of the most current trends and continually update the subject matter and teaching techniques of the courses. Many keep connected to the community and expand their areas of expertise through professional partnerships with local schools, nonprofit organizations, and community agencies.

Student Government

All undergraduate students are members of the Student Government Association (SGA) and are represented by a 30-member governing body. Student representatives, who are appointed by the SGA, sit on University academic committees and have a voice in issues related to educational policy and campus life.

Admission Requirements

The average student at Cardinal Stritch University graduated from high school with a B average, achieved a composite score of 23 on the ACT, and ranked in the top 40 percent of his or her high school class. The University considers for acceptance those students who achieve an ACT score of 20 or above or a combined SAT score of 940 or above; rank in the top 50 percent of their high school graduating class; graduate from high school with at least a 2.0 cumulative grade point average (on a 4.0 scale); and complete 16 high school academic units, broken down as follows: 4 years of English, 2 years of mathematics, 2 years of science, 2 years of social studies, and 6 units of academic electives. When applying for admission, students should send the completed application form, $25 application fee, high school transcripts, and ACT and/or SAT scores. Students are encouraged to apply online at the University's Web site. On-campus interviews are not required but are recommended.

Transfer students who have more than 12 credits from another institution of higher education must submit their transcripts from all previous college course work. International students are welcome to apply. In addition to the application form and $25 fee, international students should also send evaluated copies of all high school and college transcripts, verification of a minimum score of 213 on the computer-based Test of English as a Foreign Language (TOEFL) or a minimum score of 79 on the Internet-based TOEFL, the International Student Financial Aid Application, and proof of financial viability.

Application and Information

The Admissions Office at Cardinal Stritch University accepts applications on a rolling admission basis, with the exception of the College of Nursing, which has an application deadline. Applicants are notified of the decision two weeks after all records are complete.

Inquiries and application materials should be directed to:

Kirk Messer
Director of Admissions
Cardinal Stritch University
6801 North Yates Road
Milwaukee, Wisconsin 53217-3985

Phone: 414-410-4040
800-347-8822 Ext. 4040 (toll-free)
E-mail: admityou@stritch.edu
Web site: http://www.stritch.edu

A student taps into the library's extensive resources.

CARROLL COLLEGE

WAUKESHA, WISCONSIN

The College

Carroll College was chartered by the territorial legislature of Wisconsin in 1846. Carroll College is affiliated with the Presbyterian Church (U.S.A.) but is nonsectarian and ecumenical.

The College realizes that personalized education is the special province of a small college and recognizes the variety of students' individual needs and preferences. Carroll's student body is diverse, with representation from thirty-two states and twenty-seven countries. The campus has more than 2,300 full-time men and women, as well as more than 700 part-time students. In addition, there are more than 250 graduate students on the Carroll campus.

Many opportunities exist for cocurricular involvement. Three fraternities and four sororities draw participation from about 13 percent of the students. A broad variety of special interest organizations provide a full program of campus activities in addition to the all-campus social, intellectual, and athletic events that are scheduled throughout the year. The College's facilities for recreation and athletics include the Van Male Fieldhouse, which has a basketball court; an indoor track; indoor facilities for badminton, tennis, and volleyball; and a pool. The adjacent Ganfield Gymnasium provides additional space for athletics and recreation. A football field, a soccer field, and a softball diamond are also available.

In addition to the bachelor's degrees Carroll offers, the College also grants the master's degree in education and software engineering as well as a clinical doctorate in physical therapy.

Location

The College is located in the city of Waukesha, a residential community of 68,000 people, which is 18 miles west of Milwaukee and 100 miles north of Chicago. The College's proximity to these two major urban centers and to the settings associated with Wisconsin's famous outdoor sports and leisure activities provides Carroll students with numerous opportunities for recreation, entertainment, and enrichment.

Majors and Degrees

Carroll College grants the B.A., B.S., and B.S.N. degrees. Areas of study include accounting, actuarial science, art, athletic training, biochemistry, biology, business administration (finance, human resources, management, management information systems, marketing, small-business management), chemistry, communication, computer science (information systems, Internet software development, software engineering), criminal justice, education (adaptive, early childhood, elementary, secondary), English, environmental science, European studies, exercise science, forensic science, graphic communication, history, human biology, international relations, journalism, marine biology, mathematics, music, nursing, oceanography, organizational leadership, photography, physical education, physical therapy, politics, print management, psychology, public relations, recreation management, religious studies, self-designed major, sociology, Spanish, theater arts, and writing.

Academic Programs

The College currently operates on a semester calendar. All students must complete 128 credits with a C average or better. A major, generally consisting of 40 credits, must be completed. General education requirements include the First Year Seminar, English, liberal studies distribution courses, and a capstone experience. B.A. students must take two years of a modern language or the equivalent. B.S. students must take mathematics and either a computer science or logic course. Students may also select a second major or they may select a minor, which generally requires 16 to 28 credits. The honors program offers intensive sections of courses in the arts and sciences for academically talented students.

Advanced placement or credit may be granted to students who have completed the appropriate College Board Advanced Placement examinations. Credit may be granted for a score at or above the 75th percentile on the humanities, natural science, or social science general examination of the College-Level Examination Program (CLEP). Scores on CLEP subject examinations may also qualify to be approved for credit. A total of not more than 48 credit hours may be awarded through CLEP general and subject examinations.

Off-Campus Programs

The New Cultural Experiences Program gives all Carroll students the opportunity to study in a different cultural setting. Students may plan an individual program or participate in a planned group experience involving other students and Carroll faculty members. Group experiences are offered in locations such as Australia, Belize, England, and Japan and countries in Europe and Africa. Other off-campus programs include the Washington Semester, the United Nations Semester, and the Junior Year Abroad. In addition, career internships are provided in the Milwaukee-Waukesha area for students interested in gaining practical work experience in their proposed career field. All of these programs carry degree credit; the amount depends upon the nature and duration of the experience.

Academic Facilities

The College library houses more than 150,000 volumes, 18,000 microforms, and 400 periodicals. The Department of Education is in the Barstow Building with the Modern Language and Communication Departments. Rankin Hall houses the Departments of Biology, Psychology, and Religious Studies, as well as the psychology laboratories. Maxon Hall houses the Departments of Geography and Mathematics. It also contains the laboratories for advanced chemistry; the geography laboratory, with independent-study booths and audiovisual instruments; a darkroom; a cartography laboratory; a map library; and a National Weather Service observation station. The chemistry and physics laboratories are in Lowry Hall. All science laboratories are provided with up-to-date equipment. The newly renovated Main Hall houses classrooms for all academic areas. MacAllister Hall is home to the Departments of English, History, Politics, and Philosophy and houses the Norman FitzGerald Civil War Collection.

The Shattuck Music Center houses a recital hall that seats 150, an auditorium that seats 1,350, and a Schantz seventy-two-stop pipe organ. The Department of Music has a large band-practice room, teaching studios, a multisensing room, a computerized music laboratory, and classrooms. The Humphrey Building houses the Art Department and Humphrey Memorial Chapel. The College's physical therapy program is located adjacent to the College's athletic complex. A new, state-of-the-art nursing lab is found in the lower level of the Theatre Arts Building.

Costs

For 2007–08, the tuition was approximately $20,400 and room and board were $6350.

Financial Aid

Approximately 98 percent of Carroll's students receive some form of financial aid. Aid is based on need, as determined by the U.S. Department of Education's Free Application for Federal Student Aid (FAFSA), as well as on scholastic ability and achievement. Generally, students receive a package consisting of a scholarship, a grant, a loan, and/or campus employment.

Various merit scholarships are available to students. Merit scholarships range from $24,000 to $44,000 over four years and are determined by a student's ACT or SAT scores and class rank. Students who attend high schools that do not rank are not excluded from consideration for any academic scholarships. Additional scholarships are awarded to qualified students who are interested in music, theater, history, art, math, or the sciences. Students should contact the Office of Admission for details.

Faculty

The student-faculty ratio at Carroll is approximately 16:1. More than 85 percent of faculty members hold a doctorate in their specialized area of study. There are more than 100 full-time faculty members at Carroll.

Student Government

Through election to the Student Senate and College Activities Board, students have responsibility for nonacademic matters affecting their lives at the College. In addition, there is voting student representation on all College committees, and there are student observers on the Board of Trustees.

Admission Requirements

Carroll's admission procedure is intended to ensure academic and personal success for accepted students. Each candidate is evaluated individually; evidence of the interest in and ability to do college-level work is important. The College exercises careful selection, but no candidate is disqualified because of race, color, religion, sex, national origin, age, disability, sexual orientation, or veteran status.

Application and Information

To be considered, each candidate for freshman admission must submit the following materials: a completed application for admission, a transcript from an accredited high school showing progress toward or completion of 15 units of work and graduation, a satisfactory personal evaluation from the high school, and scores on the SAT or ACT. Transfer students must submit a transcript from every college attended previously and a statement of good standing. Admission decisions are made on a rolling basis until the class is filled. There are no deadlines, but early application is recommended.

Admission to the College may be granted following the completion of three years of high school work, provided that the high school indicates that this is in the applicant's best interest. The candidate may or may not have completed the course work required for high school graduation at the time of admission, but he or she must show unusual promise and achievement.

For more information about Carroll College, prospective students should contact:

Admission Office
Carroll College
100 North East Avenue
Waukesha, Wisconsin 53186
Phone: 262-524-7220
800-CARROLL (toll-free)
E-mail: ccinfo@cc.edu
Web site: http://www.cc.edu

EDGEWOOD COLLEGE

MADISON, WISCONSIN

The College

With a meaningful and challenging curriculum, Edgewood College offers the advantages of a small private college in a larger university-oriented city. The result is a stimulating learning environment rich in academic and recreational resources.

Edgewood's 55-acre wooded campus is situated on the shore of Lake Wingra in a residential neighborhood of Madison near parks and an arboretum. The College has four residence halls and three apartment buildings for students, a student center/union, the state-of-the-art Sonderegger Science Center, a library, classrooms, athletic facilities, a chapel, and a theater. Campus organizations include the student newspaper, student government, professional groups, and a variety of clubs to meet personal interests. There are intramural athletics and intercollegiate teams in men's baseball, basketball, cross-country, track, golf, and soccer and women's basketball, cross-country, golf, soccer, softball, tennis, track, and volleyball.

Edgewood College has completed a major building program that has added several campus improvements, including the Sonderegger Science Center and the Henry J. Predolin Humanities Center. The Sonderegger Science Center was designed to be a national model for science education and collaboration. The Henry J. Predolin Humanities Center consists of state-of-the-art classrooms, offices, and a student center/union.

Edgewood College collaborates with the University of Wisconsin–Madison, located only a few blocks away, in a program of shared resources that gives students opportunities that are not usually available at a liberal arts college. Edgewood College students may enroll in one university class per semester and have access to the university's library system and art museum. Guest lecturers, concerts, athletic events, and special programs are all readily available on a regular basis.

The current full-time undergraduate student population is approximately 1,500. The student body includes both residents and commuters. Although the majority of students come from the Midwest, about 15 percent are from states other than Wisconsin or from countries outside the United States.

Open to students from all religious backgrounds, Edgewood College is a Catholic college in the Dominican tradition, committed to the values of truth, justice, compassion, partnership, and community. The College is accredited by the North Central Association of Colleges and Schools. The nursing program is approved by the Wisconsin State Board of Nursing and the American Association of Colleges of Nursing.

Location

Madison is a growing and exciting community, with a colorful assortment of art fairs, outdoor markets, festivals, sporting events, and concerts taking place throughout the year. As Wisconsin's state capital, Madison is home to a vigorous state legislature and a politically active community at all levels. The city has a stable economy driven by a broad base of educational, medical, and financial institutions as well as light industry. While Madison is renowned for its scenic beauty, it is also the gateway to hundreds of vacation, park, and lake areas in northern and central Wisconsin. Many students take advantage of the Madison community by gaining valuable work experience, participating in volunteer opportunities, and becoming involved in internships.

Majors and Degrees

Edgewood College offers baccalaureate degrees with majors in accounting, art, art therapy, biology, broad-field social studies (concentration in economics, history, political science, or sociology/anthropology), business (concentration in finance, management, or marketing), chemistry, child life, computer information systems, criminal justice, cytotechnology, early childhood–exceptional needs, economics, elementary education, English (writing or literature), French, graphic design, history, international relations, mathematics, music, natural science and mathematics, nursing, performing arts, psychology, public policy and administration, religious studies, sociology, and Spanish. Preprofessional programs are available in dentistry, engineering, law, medicine, pharmacy, and social work. Individualized majors and minors may also be arranged. Minors include many traditional areas, plus computer science, environmental studies, philosophy, secondary education, and women's studies.

Many people also attend classes for personal enrichment or professional development or participate in a separate continuing education program of noncredit short courses.

Academic Programs

The goal of an Edgewood College education is to prepare students for a meaningful personal and professional life, ethical leadership, service, and a lifelong search for truth. The curriculum includes a foundation for all students in composition, logic, mathematics, speech, foreign language, arts, and sciences, with an advanced sequence designed for honors students. Departmental course requirements for majors and minors are added to the above. The Human Issues project, a multidisciplinary study or activity, requires every student to apply knowledge and experience to the examination of a selected aspect of the human condition and the values involved.

Students are encouraged to participate in field experiences, internships, and independent studies, regardless of major. Education students begin classroom observation and practice as early as the freshman year. Nursing, medical technology, and cytotechnology students engage in clinicals in hospitals and laboratories as juniors and seniors.

The College is on a 4-1-4 calendar that consists of four months of classwork each semester and the Winterim, an optional educational and cultural program held each January between semesters, during which credit may be earned or independent pursuits followed. Two 8-week summer sessions are also available.

Edgewood College offers alternative routes to credit for its degrees through the College-Level Examination Program (CLEP), the College Board's Advanced Placement (AP), the ACT Program's Proficiency Examination Program (PEP), locally administered programs of retroactive credit for foreign language proficiency, and credit for work experience that closely matches the content of a course.

Off-Campus Programs

Collaboration with the University of Wisconsin–Madison enables Edgewood College students to take one course per semester at the university under the College's tuition. This relationship greatly broadens the scope of courses, libraries, museums, and faculty members available to students of the College.

Edgewood College encourages students to take advantage of community resources. Arrangements with a children's hospital, a local nursing home, a school for exceptional children, and a school for juvenile offenders provide education, psychology, and sociology majors with opportunities for off-campus experiences. Volunteer service at community meal programs, local correctional facilities, shelters, centers for at-risk children, and public health agencies is also encouraged.

Qualified students may plan for special one- or two-week courses abroad or for a semester or year at an international institution of higher learning.

Academic Facilities

The Edgewood College library is a comfortable facility with a reading atrium and group study rooms. Its collection includes books, periodicals, DVDs and videotapes, audio recordings, and online databases for several fields, including business. In addition, video equipment and digital editing equipment are available for student and faculty use. The library offers direct computerized access to the catalog of the University of Wisconsin libraries and to other library catalogs through the Internet. An interlibrary-loan delivery service connects hundreds of libraries in the state.

Computer labs on campus have both Mac and PC equipment that connects to a local access network. Student rooms in the residence halls are also joined to the network. Wireless Internet service is available in several locations on campus. The foreign language lab has audio and videotape equipment and receives international programs via satellite.

Costs

Edgewood College's tuition and fees are $19,080 per year for 2008–09. The complete cost of room and board for a campus residence is approximately $6200 per year. Other expenses, including books, travel, and supplies, average $2000.

Financial Aid

Edgewood College's financial aid program combines innovative merit-based assistance with traditional need-based assistance to make the Edgewood College experience affordable. Institutional merit awards are available based on academic, leadership, science, and fine arts skills. More than 90 percent of freshman aid applicants receive some form of grant or scholarship. The College administers traditional federal and state programs, including the Federal Pell Grant and the Wisconsin Tuition Grant. Campus employment is available along with Federal Stafford Student Loans, Federal Perkins Loans, and supplemental loans. To apply for assistance, students must complete the Free Application for Federal Student Aid (FAFSA). Students may arrange with the College to pay tuition in monthly installments. Early aid eligibility estimates are available upon request.

Faculty

The College currently has a teaching faculty of more than 120 full-time professors, of whom 80 percent have doctoral or terminal degrees in their fields. All classes and labs are taught by the primary professor and not by graduate students. The favorable student-faculty ratio of 13:1 allows good rapport between professors and students. Faculty members take a keen interest in their students, serving as academic advisers and becoming involved in student activities. The full-time faculty is supported by a cadre of part-time instructors who bring added expertise to the classroom.

Student Government

Through their participation in various committees and organizations and through the Student Government Association, students have the opportunity to take part in determining scholastic, intellectual, recreational, social, and cultural activities both on and off campus. Students have a voice and vote on commencement, curriculum and education policy, library policies, student affairs, and teacher education programs.

Admission Requirements

Edgewood College accepts applicants on the basis of the amount and kind of ability a student possesses, as reflected in scholastic standards that have been met, high school and community activities, and employment. Candidates for admission to Edgewood College must submit 16 units of high school study, including 12 units in English, speech, mathematics, history, natural science, social science, and foreign language. High school grade point average, rank in class, ACT or SAT scores, and recommendations are considered in determining the applicant's potential to do college work. Applicants from nontraditional high schools are welcome to apply.

Transfer students are evaluated on the college-level work they have done as well as on the standard criteria for admission. Each department determines transferability of credits, but a minimum of 32 hours must be completed in residence, including the major requirements.

Application and Information

Office of Admissions
Edgewood College
1000 Edgewood College Drive
Madison, Wisconsin 53713
Phone: 608-663-4861
800-444-4861 (toll-free)
E-mail: admissions@edgewood.edu
Web site: http://www.edgewood.edu

Edgewood College students enjoy catching up after class as they walk through the campus on a sunny fall afternoon.

COLLEGE DATA CENTER • WISCONSIN

LAWRENCE UNIVERSITY

APPLETON, WISCONSIN

The University

Lawrence University offers a distinguished education in the liberal arts and sciences that blends study in the traditional disciplines with programs that address contemporary issues. Its 1,400 undergraduate men and women, from nearly every state and fifty other countries, participate in a curriculum that not only promotes in-depth study within a single area but also invites exploration of the connections among different academic fields. Bright, motivated students are attracted to Lawrence by the exceptional level of student-faculty interaction both inside and outside the classroom.

Lawrence offers a number of meaningful differences that set it apart from other colleges. Among the most important are Freshman Studies, a two-term seminar-style course that, through major works of literature, art, and music, develops the ability to think critically, write cogently, and argue persuasively; Individualized Study, which encourages and requires intellectual maturity and self-direction and emphasizes the application of knowledge over the simple rote learning of facts; and the Honor Code, which ensures academic integrity, promotes mutual trust and respect, and values cooperation and collaboration over competition in all aspects of campus life. Additional features include Bjorklunden, Lawrence's 425-acre estate on the shore of Lake Michigan, where groups of students and faculty members gather every weekend of the academic year for relaxed yet focused discussions on issues and ideas covering a wide range of topics, and the Conservatory of Music, which not only provides intensive training in performance, theory-composition, and music education but also provides musical opportunities to all Lawrence students and supports performances of a quality and frequency not found in other colleges of similar size.

Lawrence offers an active social life and a full range of recreational and athletic opportunities. Seven residence halls on campus offer living arrangements from single and double rooms to 4-person suites. Upperclass students may also choose from theme houses, apartment-style living, and small residences that accommodate 7 to 27 students each. Twenty percent of Lawrence's students belong to five national fraternities and three national sororities. Approximately 100 student clubs and organizations provide a wide variety of activities, ranging from performances by major music ensembles and an international film series to the annual Trivia Weekend (the longest-running and most notorious trivia contest in the country), crew on the Fox River, and winter camping along Lake Michigan. The Buchanan Kiewit Recreation Center offers an indoor track, swimming pool, weight/exercise room, dance room, racquetball, gymnasium, and saunas. Alexander Gymnasium, Whiting Field, and the Banta Bowl (a 5,300-seat football stadium) house most of the twenty-three varsity (NCAA Division III) teams. The spirit of volunteerism flourishes at Lawrence, with campus organizations devoted to tutoring local school-age children, building with Habitat for Humanity, serving as Big Brothers/Sisters, and volunteering for other activities. A staffed volunteer bureau assists students in finding volunteer opportunities.

Location

Lawrence is in Appleton, a city of 70,000 people, located on the banks of the historic Fox River in northeast Wisconsin. The Fox Cities area (population 250,000), of which Appleton is the center, has been considered one of the three best medium-sized metropolitan areas in the United States, based on "quality of life" indicators and has been cited as among the safest cities of its size. The 84-acre Lawrence campus overlooks the river and is situated adjacent to the city's downtown area. Appleton is accessible by car, bus, and plane and offers the commercial/retail advantages of a larger urban area and the recreational opportunities and safety of a Midwestern town.

Majors and Degrees

Lawrence awards the Bachelor of Arts (B.A.), the Bachelor of Music (B.Mus.), and the five-year B.A./B.Mus. The more than thirty areas of study include anthropology, art history, biology, biomedical ethics, chemistry, Chinese, classics, cognitive science, computer science, East Asian studies, economics, education, English, environmental studies, ethnic studies, French, gender studies, geology, German, government, history, international studies, Japanese, linguistics, mathematics, mathematics–computer science, mathematics–economics, music, music education, music performance, music theory–composition, natural sciences, neuroscience, philosophy, physics, psychology, religious studies, Russian, Spanish, studio art, and theater arts. Preprofessional study is available in business, education, law, and medicine. Cooperative degree programs are available in engineering, environmental management, forestry, medical technology, nursing, and occupational therapy.

Academic Programs

The academic program not only emphasizes in-depth work within a single discipline but also encourages breadth by exposure to many fields of inquiry. Distribution requirements for both B.A. and B.Mus. candidates promote exposure to all areas of the arts and sciences. Working with their faculty advisers, students are encouraged to take initiative and responsibility for selecting a course of study best suited to them. More than 90 percent of Lawrence's students take advantage of tutorials and independent study, working one-on-one with faculty members. The Honors in Independent Study Program culminates in a written thesis or piece of work in the creative or performing arts and an oral examination.

Lawrence operates on a three-term calendar, with students taking three courses in each ten-week term. The academic year begins in late September and ends in mid-June.

Off-Campus Programs

Approximately one half of all Lawrence students take advantage of a wide variety of both domestic and international off-campus study opportunities. The value of participating in off-campus opportunities is supported by the faculty through a resolution encouraging all students to do so. Many choose to attend Lawrence's program with its own campus in London, which operates all three terms of each academic year. Others choose from fifty-five programs in cities such as Beijing, Florence, Melbourne, Rome, and Tokyo; areas and countries such as the British West Indies, Costa Rica, the Czech Republic, France, India, Russia, Senegal, Spain, and Tanzania; and domestic programs in Chicago; Washington, D.C.; Woods Hole, Massachusetts; and Oak Ridge, Tennessee. Need-based financial aid is available to assist students with the additional costs of attending an off-campus program sponsored by or endorsed by Lawrence.

Academic Facilities

Seeley G. Mudd Library has 390,000 volumes, 336,000 government documents, 1,500 current periodical subscriptions, 14,000 recordings and videotapes, and more than 104,000 microform items. In addition to the online catalog, the library can access national computerized bibliographic databases. The library houses the Media Center, with its listening facilities, audiovisual equipment, and video studio, and the Career Center. There are more than 250 terminals and PC and Macintosh computers located across the campus, providing round-the-clock access to the campuswide computing system. Fiber-optic cabling interconnects all principal stations and residence halls by room and all halls have central computer lounges available around the clock.

Science facilities include twenty-three general laboratories for student use; twenty-five special laboratories for research, including a laser physics lab; a graphics and computational physics lab; four environmentally controlled rooms; animal rooms for psychology and biology; a greenhouse; multiple electron microscopes; a variety of spectroscopic instruments (nuclear magnetic resonance, infrared, UV-visible, atomic absorbance), atomic force microscope, scanning tunneling microscope, a MALDI-TOF mass spectrometer, and an X-ray diffractometer.

Briggs Hall, the facility for the social sciences and math, opened in 1997. Science Hall opened in 2000, with a complete renovation of Youngchild Hall following in 2001. Main Hall, which was recently updated, houses humanities classrooms, seminar rooms, a computer text laboratory, a language acquisition center, and the Hiram A. Jones Latin Library.

The Music-Drama Center and the Shattuck Hall of Music house private practice studios, classrooms, a recital hall, large and small ensemble rehearsal halls, a digital recording studio, and performance facilities for the Theatre Arts Department. Lawrence has two theaters: the first, with a proscenium stage, seats 500 people; the second is an experimental theater, adaptable to arena- or thrust-stage productions. The Memorial Chapel seats 1,250 people and is the primary venue for convocations, performances by Lawrence's large ensembles, and other public events and concerts. The Wriston Art Center offers a first-rate facility for the studio art and art history programs. It includes an outdoor amphitheater, three galleries, and two- and three-dimensional art studios and houses the University's outstanding permanent collection.

Costs

For 2007–08, annual tuition was $30,846, room and board averaged $6690, and the activity fee was $234. Books, travel, and living expenses were estimated at $1900 per year.

Financial Aid

Lawrence adheres to a need-blind admission policy. For U.S. citizens and permanent residents, the Financial Aid Office makes awards on the basis of the candidate's need, as determined from the Free Application for Federal Student Aid (FAFSA) and the Lawrence University Application for Financial Aid. Lawrence strives to make it financially viable for all admitted domestic students to enroll. More than 90 percent of Lawrence's students receive need-based and/or merit-based financial aid. For 2006–07, the average aid package was about $23,000. To apply for financial aid, students must submit the FAFSA, the Lawrence Application for Financial Aid, and student and parent tax forms. Non-need-based scholarships and conservatory performance awards ranging from $7000 to $15,000 per year are available.

Faculty

Lawrence has more than 130 full-time faculty members; 99 percent hold a Ph.D. or the highest degree in their field; 32 percent are women. The student-faculty ratio is 9:1, and the median class size is 15. The faculty plays a central role in guiding students' experiences. Active scholars and artists, the faculty members encourage students to join with them in academic pursuits, many of which have led to collaborative faculty-student published works. Lawrence was recently ranked fifth nationally among 205 small, private undergraduate institutions in the total amount of awards received from the Research Corporation's Cottrell College Science Program for faculty and student participatory research. Members of the Lawrence faculty have received seven National Endowment for the Humanities fellowships in the past several years.

Student Government

The Lawrence University Community Council governs most non-academic matters. It has a student president, vice president, and treasurer; 12 student representatives; and 4 faculty representatives.

Admission Requirements

The admission staff considers the strength of an applicant's course of study (16 units of English, math, history, social studies, physical sciences, and foreign languages are recommended), grades, recommendations, and extracurricular activities. Lawrence is test optional, so neither SAT nor ACT scores are needed for admission or for consideration for scholarships. In addition, candidates for the B.Mus. degree are judged on musicianship, performance potential, recommendations of teachers, and general academic ability. All music applicants must audition. Roughly half of Lawrence's students graduated in the top 10 percent of their high school class. A personal interview is not required, but a campus visit is strongly recommended.

Application and Information

One early decision plan (deadline November 15, notification December 1) as well as a nonbinding early action application plan (deadline December 1, notification January 15) and a regular decision plan (deadline January 15, notification April 1) are available for high school seniors. International students or students interested in music should apply under the regular decision plan. A $200 nonrefundable enrollment deposit is due four weeks after notification of admission under the early decision option; it is due on or before the candidates reply date of May 1 under the early action or regular application procedures. A completed application consists of the Common Application and the Lawrence Supplement, the secondary school report form and official transcript, the teacher's report form, and the application fee of $40. ACT and SAT score reports are optional. In addition, music applicants must complete the music portion of the Lawrence Supplement, submit a music teacher evaluation, and audition on campus or at a regional site. Transfer applicants are considered for each of the three terms and should submit high school and college transcripts.

For more information, students should contact:

Office of Admissions
Lawrence University
P.O. Box 599
Appleton, Wisconsin 54912-0599
Phone: 920-832-6500
800-227-0982 (toll-free)
E-mail: excel@lawrence.edu
Web site: http://www.lawrence.edu

MILWAUKEE SCHOOL OF ENGINEERING

MILWAUKEE, WISCONSIN

The School

Ambitious students who want personal and professional success find a home at Milwaukee School of Engineering (MSOE). For more than 105 years, top students choose a rigorous and collaborative education and the supportive guidance of expert faculty members who are dedicated to student success. The university is fully dedicated to every student who is willing to be challenged and work hard to become a better person as a successful MSOE graduate. The campus has a close community feel, being nestled in a vibrant downtown Milwaukee neighborhood, and offers students an engaging learning and living environment.

Advancing beyond acquisition to the highly sophisticated application of knowledge is the foundation of MSOE's educational philosophy. This approach, the university's educational niche, produces graduates who are well-rounded, technologically experienced, and highly productive professionals and leaders. Graduates begin their careers as work-ready problem solvers and develop into leaders: creating new products, starting or heading companies, and working to better their communities.

MSOE has a 98 percent graduate placement rate. Representatives from hundreds of firms from throughout the country, including representatives from Fortune 500 companies, visit MSOE during the academic year to interview graduating students for employment and discuss career opportunities. MSOE's longstanding ties with business, industry, and health care are represented by the Board of Regents, with more than 50 members, and the MSOE Corporation, with more than 200 members, who are elected from leaders in business and industry nationwide.

The student body of more than 2,500 men and women comes from throughout the United States and numerous countries. Since its founding, the university has encouraged the enrollment of students of any race, color, creed, or gender. Approximately half of the full-time students live in three high-rise residence halls.

MSOE's Counseling Services Office provides individual assistance for students with educational, personal, or vocational concerns. Free on-campus tutoring is provided by the Learning Resource Center and Tau Omega Mu, an honorary fraternity founded in 1953 for the purpose of aiding students who need extra help with their studies.

The Student Life and Campus Center provides on-campus recreational activities. This facility houses student activity rooms, student organization offices, a TV viewing area, a marketplace eatery, and a game room. Additional recreation areas can be found in the residence halls. The Kern Center is a 210,000-square-foot health, wellness, and fitness facility that houses a 1,600-seat ice arena, a fitness center, a 1,200-seat basketball arena, a field house, a recreational running track, and a wrestling area.

More than seventy professional societies, fraternities, and other special-interest groups serve the campus. MSOE's students tend to be participants, so many participate in intramural sports programs. MSOE is a member of the National Collegiate Athletic Association (NCAA) Division III and the Northern Athletics Conference (NAC). The Athletic Department sponsors NCAA varsity teams in men's baseball, basketball, cross-country, golf, ice hockey, indoor and outdoor track and field, rowing, soccer, tennis, volleyball, and wrestling and women's basketball, cross-country, golf, indoor and outdoor track and field, soccer, softball, tennis, and volleyball that compete with teams from other private colleges and universities in the Midwest.

MSOE's (and Milwaukee's) newest attraction and home to the world's most comprehensive art collection dedicated to the evolution of human work opened in October 2007. The Grohmann Museum welcomes visitors to three floors of galleries where the Eckhart G. Grohmann Collection "Man at Work" is housed. The collection comprises 700 paintings and sculptures from 1580 to today, reflecting a variety of artistic styles and subjects that depict organized work from farming to mining to trades to more unusual occupations such as seaweed gathering.

In addition to its seventeen undergraduate degree programs in the fields of engineering, architectural engineering and building construction, engineering technology, computers, business, and health-related areas, MSOE offers eleven Master of Science degree programs: cardiovascular studies, engineering, engineering management (accelerated option available), environmental engineering, marketing and export management, medical informatics (jointly offered with the Medical College of Wisconsin), new-product management, nursing–clinical nurse leadership, perfusion, and structural engineering.

Milwaukee School of Engineering (MSOE) is a member of, and accredited by, the North Central Association of Colleges and Schools. Program-specific accrediting agencies are identified in the MSOE academic catalogs.

Location

The MSOE campus is located in the vibrant neighborhood of East Town in downtown Milwaukee. Nearby are the Bradley Center sports arena, the Midwest Airlines Center, the Marcus Center for the Performing Arts, the theater district, churches of most denominations, major hotels and office buildings, restaurants, and department stores. Famous for its friendly atmosphere, Milwaukee offers students many opportunities for educational, cultural, and professional growth as well as ample employment opportunities. The metropolitan area has more than 15,000 acres of parks and river parkways and miles of bike trails. A few blocks east of the MSOE campus is Lake Michigan, a place of year-round natural beauty. MSOE also offers classes in other locations in Wisconsin for students who wish to pursue select programs in the evening on a part-time basis.

Majors and Degrees

Four-year programs are offered that lead to Bachelor of Science degrees in business, construction management, engineering, and specific areas of engineering (architectural, biomedical, computer, electrical, industrial, mechanical, and software), engineering technology—transfer programs only (electrical and mechanical), international business, management, management information systems, and nursing. A Bachelor of Science or Bachelor of Arts degree is offered in technical communication. A five-year, double-major option is available in a combination of business, construction management, engineering, and technical communication programs. An engineering/environmental or structural engineering dual degree (B.S./M.S. combination) also is available. An RN-to-B.S.N. program is available through the MSOE School of Nursing. Study-abroad opportunities and many double majors also exist.

Academic Programs

MSOE guarantees that the classes needed to graduate in four years will be available for full-time undergraduate students who start and stay on track and meet academic requirements.

The degree programs at MSOE combine study in degree specialty courses with basic study in sciences, communication, mathematics, and humanities in a high-technology, applications-oriented atmosphere. Students who are admitted with advanced credit to a program leading to a bachelor's degree must complete at least 50 percent of the curriculum in residence at MSOE. MSOE operates on a quarter system. Students average between 16 and 19 credits per quarter, which represent a combination of lecture and laboratory courses. Undergraduate students average 600 hours of laboratory experience.

MSOE offers students the opportunity to participate in the Air Force Reserve Officer Training Corps (AFROTC) program, the Army ROTC program, or the Navy ROTC program.

Academic Facilities

The Fred Loock Engineering Center adjoins the Allen-Bradley Hall of Science, forming a prime technical education and applied research complex. Rosenberg Hall houses the Rader School of Business faculty and technology-integrated classrooms.

The Walter Schroeder Library houses more than 60,000 volumes, with collections that represent the specialized curricula of the university. The library offers Web-based access to more than 40,000 e-journals, 25,000 e-books, hundreds of specialized databases, unique collections, government agencies, and other sources of information throughout the world.

All students participate in a Technology Package program that includes a notebook computer and affiliated services. A full range of software is available on these systems and via the local area network linked by a fiber-optic ring around the campus. Most areas also have wireless capability for laptop use. State-of-the-art architectural, computer, electrical, mechanical, industrial nursing, and software laboratories complement the respective areas of study.

The Applied Technology Center™ (ATC) utilizes faculty and student expertise to solve technological problems confronting business and industry. The ATC is heavily involved in the transferring of new technologies into real business practice through the Rapid Prototyping Center (MSOE is the only university in the world to possess the five leading rapid prototyping technologies), the Fluid Power Institute™, the NanoEngineering Laboratory, the Photonics and Applied Optics Center, the Construction Science and Engineering Center, and the Center for BioMolecular Modeling.

There are more laboratories than classrooms at MSOE, many with industrial sponsorship from such companies as Johnson Controls, Harley-Davidson, Rockwell Automation/Allen-Bradley, Master Lock, Snap-On, General Electric and Outboard Marine Corp. Undergraduates average an amazing 600 hours of laboratory experience.

Costs

For 2007–08, tuition was $25,980 per year plus $1140 for the Technology Package (notebook computer, software, insurance, maintenance, Internet access, and user services). The cost of room and board in the residence halls was approximately $6500 per year. Books and supplies average $400 per quarter but may be somewhat higher for the first quarter.

Financial Aid

Qualified students are assisted by a comprehensive financial aid program, including MSOE and industry-supported scholarships, student loans, and part-time employment; Federal Perkins Loan, Federal Stafford Student Loan, Federal Work-Study, Federal Pell Grant, and Federal Supplemental Educational Opportunity Grant Programs; and state-supported grant programs. Students can also visit MSOE's Web site for a financial aid estimate.

Faculty

MSOE faculty members engage and challenge students, with individual attention and practical perspectives gained from an average of seven years of professional employment experience in their area of expertise. They are at MSOE because they love to teach—there is no "publish or perish" tenure system. There are more than 200 men and women on the MSOE faculty (full-time and part-time). Many are registered professional engineers, architects, and/or nurses. They and their colleagues in nontechnical academic areas are active in related professional societies. The student-faculty ratio is 12:1. MSOE does not use teaching assistants.

Student Government

The MSOE Student Government Association (SGA) represents clubs and fraternities as well as residence halls and commuting students. SGA appoints representatives to the Campus Security and Disciplinary Hearing committees, the Executive Educational Council, and the Alumni Association's Board of Directors.

Admission Requirements

Each applicant to MSOE is reviewed individually on the basis of potential for success as determined by academic preparation. Admission may be gained by submitting an application for admission and the appropriate transcripts. High school students are encouraged to complete math through precalculus (including algebra and geometry), chemistry, biology (nursing), physics, and four years of English. All entering freshmen are also required to provide results from the ACT or the SAT.

Transfer opportunities exist into the junior year of the Bachelor of Science in electrical engineering technology, management, mechanical engineering technology, and technical communication programs with the appropriate associate degree or equivalent credits.

Application and Information

Classes start in September, November, March, and late May. Freshmen and transfer students may enter at the beginning of any quarter; however, entry in the fall quarter is recommended. An application for admission may be obtained by contacting the address below or by visiting MSOE's Web site. Applicants are encouraged to visit MSOE and have a preadmission counseling interview. Transfer students are required to submit transcripts from all prior institutions attended. An applicant's prior course work is reviewed to determine eligibility for admission. Required course work varies depending on the desired course of study.

Admission Office
Milwaukee School of Engineering
1025 North Broadway
Milwaukee, Wisconsin 53202-3109
Phone: 414-277-6763
800-332-6763 (toll-free)
E-mail: explore@msoe.edu
Web site: http://www.msoe.edu

MSOE's undergraduate students average 600 hours of laboratory experience—just one more advantage to an MSOE education.

MOUNT MARY COLLEGE

MILWAUKEE, WISCONSIN

The College

Mount Mary College, Wisconsin's first Catholic college for women, was founded at Prairie du Chien on the Mississippi River in 1913 and moved to Milwaukee in 1929. Mount Mary is sponsored by the School Sisters of Notre Dame, traditionally recognized as excellent educators. More than 1,600 undergraduate and graduate students from a variety of backgrounds attend Mount Mary. Students at Mount Mary are fully engaged in the classroom, learning not just the subject matter but also how to express opinions and develop leadership skills. Students are inspired, challenged, and motivated by excellent teaching. Through exciting internships, club activities, community service, and campus ministry programs, students explore their interests and discover their skills. Special and professional interests are served by affiliates of national societies.

The College is situated on a beautiful 80-acre wooded campus with stately stone buildings. Caroline Hall, the student residence hall, provides accommodations for private occupancy and single and double suites. Every floor in Caroline Hall has a kitchen and a mini–computer lab with laser printers. All residence halls are wired for cable, telephone, and Internet connections.

Physical fitness and an interest in athletics are fostered through various activities, fitness programs, health and dance courses, and intramural and intercollegiate athletics. Mount Mary College is a provisional member of the NCAA Division III. The Blue Angels compete in basketball, cross-country, soccer, softball, tennis, and volleyball. Facilities on campus and in the Bloechl Recreation Center, which opened in 2006, include a gymnasium, an indoor swimming pool, outdoor soccer fields, a fitness center, and a sand volleyball court. Bordering the campus is a large parkway for biking, jogging, cross-country skiing, and much more.

Mount Mary College sponsors many social activities, including performances by musicians and comedians, dances, and all-campus picnics. These events are sponsored by the Mount Mary Programming and Activities Council (MMPAC), Student Government, Residence Hall Association, and other groups on campus. Other events include films, concerts, and lectures. Mount Mary students also attend social functions at area colleges and universities and invite students from those institutions to Mount Mary events.

Academic and professional student services are available to all Mount Mary students, including tutoring and assistance with tests through the Academic Resource Center, advising, resume writing, career planning through the Advising and Career Development Center, and personal counseling through the Counseling Center.

In addition to undergraduate programs, Mount Mary College offers graduate programs in art therapy, business administration (M.B.A.), community counseling, dietetics, English (writing concentration), and occupational therapy.

Location

Mount Mary College is located in a residential area in northwestern Milwaukee, just 15 minutes from downtown and less than 5 minutes from a major shopping mall. Students can access public transportation right in front of the campus. Milwaukee offers a symphony, well-respected dance and theater companies, a beautiful lakefront, a newly expanded art museum, and a well-known zoo. Numerous professional and collegiate sports teams are based in Milwaukee.

Majors and Degrees

Mount Mary offers nearly thirty undergraduate degree programs leading to bachelor's degrees in accounting, art, art therapy, behavioral science, biology, business administration, business/professional communication, chemistry, communication, dietetics, English, English professional writing, fashion: apparel product development, fashion: merchandise management, French, graphic design, history, interior design, international studies, justice, liberal studies, mathematics, occupational therapy, philosophy, psychology/behavioral science, public relations, social work, Spanish, student designed, teacher education, and theology. Columbia College of Nursing and Mount Mary College jointly offer a Bachelor of Science in Nursing (B.S.N.) degree. Special services for undeclared students help them find and focus on a major suited to their interests and talents.

Academic Programs

Mount Mary's curriculum integrates leadership skills into each student's educational experience, developing leaders who take individual responsibility for social justice. The curriculum and cocurricular activities promote self-knowledge and competence, an entrepreneurial sense of vision, effective oral and written communication skills, and the ability to strengthen leadership in others. In their professions, churches, and communities, Mount Mary students model collaborative leadership, enabling them to work effectively both in leadership positions and as supportive team members.

Mount Mary faculty members incorporate technology into the classroom through group projects and presentations. Students have access to the latest software and hardware in classrooms, labs, and the residence hall. Internet access is available throughout the campus.

The core curriculum consists of studies in five areas of the liberal arts: synoptics (12 credits in theology and philosophy), symbolics (8 credits in communication arts and mathematics), esthetics (12 credits in fine art), humanistics (12 credits in history and behavioral or social science), and empirics (4 credits of science). To qualify for graduation, baccalaureate degree students must complete a minimum of 128 credits that consist of 48 in core courses (a minimum of 24 in the major) and electives, with a minimum grade point average (GPA) of 2.0. Each academic department establishes its own requirements for the major and GPA needed for graduation.

Two signature courses at Mount Mary College are Leadership Seminar and Search for Meaning. Leadership Seminar is a 3-credit course designed to introduce students to Mount Mary's mission and the College's leadership model. This interactive and reflective course focuses on leadership and issues of social justice and includes a justice-in-action component. The course emphasizes critical thinking, reading, writing, and speaking skills and provides both a context for subsequent courses and a foundation for Search for Meaning. Search for Meaning, a 4-credit course offering 2 credits in theology and 2 credits in philosophy, includes reading and discussion of classical and contemporary authors from philosophical and theological viewpoints and reflection on such elemental human concern as the possible sources of happiness, the role of conscience in personal integrity, the meaning of suffering and death, and the transcendent dimension of reality.

Many academic programs at Mount Mary College offer internships, which allow students to relate theory to practice and interact with professionals while learning life skills. The process encourages students to reflect on the skills and knowledge they hope to gain and allows them to tailor their practical experience to the career goals they have set for the future. Many of the programs incorporate a work experience into the curriculum. Work experience includes student teaching, clinicals, fieldwork, practicum, and internships.

Mount Mary College is committed to the academic success of each student and strives to meet all adult students' needs, whether they are first-time college students or returning to complete or enhance a college degree.

Off-Campus Programs

Mount Mary encourages its students to take advantage of a variety of study abroad opportunities. Accordingly, Mount Mary College sponsors trips to China, England, France, Guatemala, Ireland, Italy, Nicaragua, and Peru. In addition to these study-abroad programs, the College maintains affiliate relationships with numerous international colleges and universities, including the American College, Dublin, Ireland; the American Intercontinental University, London and Dubai; Nanzan College, Japan; Universidad Cathólica de Santa Maria (UCSM), Arequipa, Peru; and Notre Dame College, Kyoto, Japan. Mount Mary College is part of a consortium directed by the Wisconsin Association of Independent Colleges and Universities that enables member institutions to share study-abroad opportunities.

The Office of International Studies also aids students in finding an accredited program that meets their individual needs.

Academic Facilities

Located on 80 beautiful acres, Mount Mary offers students unlimited space to grow. Facilities include the Marian Art Gallery, the Walter and Olive Stiemke Memorial Hall and Conference Center, Macintosh computer laboratories, two chapels, a fitness center, and an 800-seat theater. The Patrick and Beatrice Haggerty Library collection includes more than 110,000 volumes and 500 subscription periodical titles, along with a significant collection of audio-visual materials. As a member of the SWITCH library consortium, Haggerty Library is connected to six college and university libraries in the greater Milwaukee area. The consortium shares a common catalog, with complete exchange privileges for students and faculty members of member institutions; comprehensive subscription databases are available as well. The Web-based online catalog and an interactive library Web site provide services on and off campus.

Costs

For the 2007–08 academic year, undergraduate tuition was $18,995 for full-time students and $510 per credit for part-time students. The undergraduate fee (including matriculation, student activities, library, computer lab, parking, and health services) for full-time students was $210 per year; part-time students paid $105 per year. Room and board costs averaged $6195. All costs are subject to change.

Financial Aid

The financial aid office at Mount Mary College develops a financial package on an individual basis for all qualified students. More than 90 percent of Mount Mary's full-time students receive some form of financial assistance. Students filing for financial aid should complete the Free Application for Federal Student Aid (FAFSA) and an early financial aid estimate, both available through the Financial Aid Office. Additional information on numerous merit-based scholarships, grants, and work-study opportunities are available for first-year students as well as transfer students.

Faculty

Faculty members holding advanced degrees do all the teaching; no classes are taught by teaching assistants. Faculty members are available to provide academic counseling. Mount Mary has 70 full-time and 90 part-time faculty members. With a total enrollment of over 1,600, Mount Mary offers a low faculty-to-student ratio.

Student Government

Students are encouraged to participate in the governance of the College. Student Government makes recommendations about College policies and other matters of importance to students and serves as a liaison to the Mount Mary administration, faculty, and staff.

Admission Requirements

Candidates for admission are considered on the basis of academic preparation, scholarship, and evidence of the ability to do college work and benefit from it. Sixteen secondary school units are required; of these, 11 must be academic (3 in English, 2 in college-preparatory mathematics, 2 in science, 4 in history, language, or social science) and 4 in electives. Students must have achieved a minimum composite score of 18 on the ACT (870 on the SAT) and rank in the top 40 percent of their high school graduating class or have a minimum GPA of 2.5 (on a 4.0 scale). Students who do not meet the admission requirements are reviewed by an admission committee. International students must take the Test of English as a Foreign Language (TOEFL) and achieve a minimum score of 500. Mount Mary does not discriminate against any individual for reasons of race, color, religion, age, national or ethnic origin, or disability.

Application and Information

Mount Mary has a rolling admission policy. Early acceptance is available, and advanced placement is honored. An admission decision is sent as soon as all required materials, including a $25 application fee, have been received and reviewed by the Admission Office. After notification of acceptance, students wishing to enroll need to submit the $200 nonrefundable tuition deposit.

For further information, students should contact:

The Admission Office
Mount Mary College
2900 North Menomonee River Parkway
Milwaukee, Wisconsin 53222-4597
Phone: 414-256-1219
800-321-6265 (toll-free)
Fax: 414-256-0180
E-mail: admiss@mtmary.edu
Web site: http://www.mtmary.edu

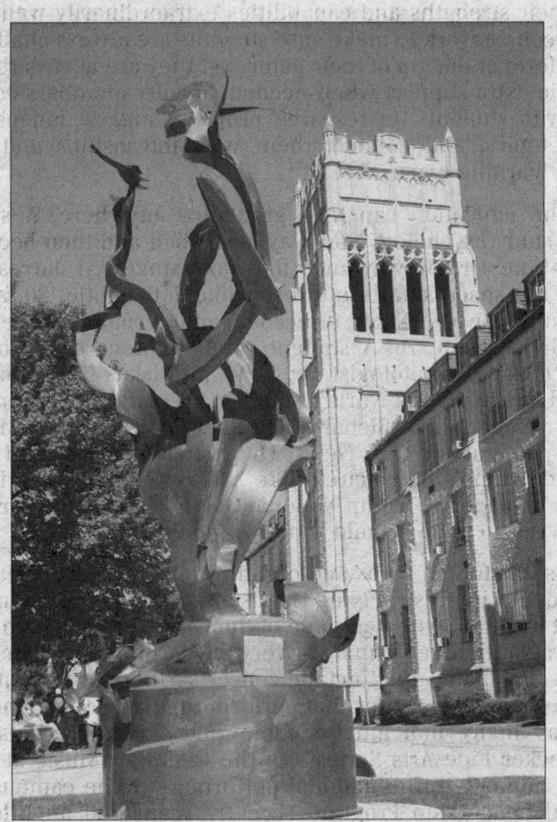

Mount Mary College is located on 80 acres in a convenient Milwaukee neighborhood. Students have a safe, secure environment in which to live and learn.

RIPON COLLEGE

RIPON, WISCONSIN

The College

Together with the other members of its tightly knit learning community, Ripon students often feel as if they learn more deeply, live more fully, and achieve more success. There are more opportunities to be involved, lead, speak out, make a difference, explore new interests than at many colleges many times its size. Through collaborative learning, group living, teamwork, and networking, students tap into the power of a community where all work together to ensure their success, at Ripon and beyond. The best residential liberal arts colleges strive to be true learning communities like Ripon. Ripon succeeds better than most, because the enrollment of 1,000 students is perfect for fostering connections inside and outside the classroom. Students flourish in this environment of mutual respect, where shared values are elevated and diverse ideas are valued. Students who are seeking academic challenge and want to benefit from an environment of personal attention and support should take a closer look at Ripon. In classes that average 20 students, professors are able to know the students and their strengths and capabilities extraordinarily well. They tailor course work to make sure students are always challenged to perform at the top of their game, yet they are always ready to provide extra support when needed. Faculty members collaborate with students on research projects, suggest independent study topics, and connect them with internships and other active learning experiences.

A Ripon education can take graduates anywhere. A student could study psychology and play basketball and then become a seven-time Grammy winner like jazz singer Al Jarreau '62; guide the space shuttle into orbit like Jeff Bantle '80, a chief flight director with NASA; or become an international opera star like Gail Dobish '76. A student could set records in medical science like neonatologist Dr. John Muraskas '78, who is on record for saving the world's smallest premature baby, or cover world events, like Richard Threlkeld '59, former Moscow correspondent for CBS News. Or a student might end up in Donald Trump's inner circle like Ashley Cooper '82, a former senior manager of Trump National Golf Club, who has served as an adviser to "The Donald" on *The Apprentice.*

The list of student clubs and organizations is as ever-changing as students' interests. Flying Hands, the sign language club, is a recent addition, whereas some of the Greek organizations have celebrated their centennials. Every day at Ripon is packed with a host of activities that include concerts—there are seven vocal and instrumental groups that perform regularly on campus—as well as many individual student and faculty recitals. The Caestecker Fine Arts Series and the Chamber Music at Ripon Series annually bring national performers to the campus. The Ethical Leadership Program recently sponsored an Ethics in Sports conference, which included nationally known personalities Bud Selig and Myles Brand. The Theater Department sponsors two major productions annually, plus a series of student-directed one-acts. The most recent Ripon Film Festival, an annual showcase for independent films from around the country, included the premiere of a feature-length horror film written, directed, and starred in by the same Ripon student.

Ripon's NCAA Division III intercollegiate teams compete in the Midwest Conference. Men's varsity sports include baseball, basketball, cross-country, football, golf, indoor and outdoor track and field, soccer, swimming and diving, and tennis. Women's varsity sports include basketball, cross-country, dance, golf, indoor and outdoor track and field, soccer, softball, swimming and diving, and tennis.

Location

Located on 250 tree-lined, rolling acres adjacent to downtown Ripon, the campus looks and feels like a college should. Ripon's twenty-six first-rate buildings are a striking combination of historic (ten campus structures listed on the National Register of Historic Places) and modern architecture.

Majors and Degrees

Majors and degrees include anthropology, art, art history, biology, business administration, chemistry, chemistry/biology, communication, computer science, economics, educational studies, English, environmental sciences, exercise science, foreign languages, French, German, global studies, history, Latin American area studies, mathematics, music, philosophy, physics, politics and government, psychobiology, psychology, religion, sociology/anthropology, Spanish, and theater. Programs are also available in leadership studies, sports medicine/athletic training, and women's studies.

Preprofessional programs include dentistry, journalism, law and government, library and information science, medicine, ministry, optometry, physical therapy, veterinary medicine.

Dual-degree programs include engineering, forestry, nursing and allied health sciences/medical technology, and social welfare.

Certification programs include education certification, early childhood, elementary, elementary/middle school, secondary, secondary/middle, music K–12, and physical education K–12.

Academic Programs

Ripon's liberal arts curriculum is designed to introduce students to a wide variety of disciplines. About 40 percent of the students complete double or triple majors, whereas some create special self-designed majors. Excellent communications skills—written and oral—as well as critical-thinking and problem-solving skills are the hallmark of a Ripon education, regardless of major. In addition, the leadership studies program and the newly established ethical leadership program provide a strong foundation for leadership skills. An Army ROTC program is also available.

Off-Campus Programs

Ripon offers more than forty different programs to choose from, each one officially sanctioned by and affiliated with Ripon. Although most programs are connected with a major or minor program, all are open to every Ripon student, regardless of major. U.S. programs include the Fisk University–Ripon Exchange Program, Newberry Seminar in the Humanities, Oak Ridge Science Semester, Urban Education (Chicago), Urban Studies (Chicago), Washington Semester, and Woods Hole Marine Biology. International programs include the Budapest Semester; Central European Studies Program in the Czech Republic; Cost Rica; Florence Program; France and Spain; Bonn, Germany Program; Global Studies Program in Turkey; India Studies; Japan Study; London and Florence Program in the Arts;

Madrid Program; Montpellier, France; Paris, France; Ripon and York St. John Exchange; Russia Program; Sea Semester at Woods Hole; Swansea Program; Tanzania; Toledo, Spain; University of Wales in Bangor; and Sea Education Association (marine biology abroad).

Academic Facilities

Constant additions and improvements, like a recent multimillion-dollar apartment-style residence hall, the renovation and classroom expansion of Todd Wehr Hall, and upgrades to upperclass residence halls, the library, the bookstore, dining facilities, and a coffee shop, maintain Ripon's ability to meet the needs of today and tomorrow. Technology services include high-speed Internet and e-mail, telephone, and video communication. Intranet and Internet services are accessible from systems located throughout the College. The campuswide network provides access from every room, and several wireless hot spots in key areas let students access the world without being tied down.

The library staff provides friendly efficient circulation, reference, instruction, and interlibrary loan services that aid in research. The library also houses the College archives, a computer lab, and more than a dozen online databases. Library holdings include 164,000 volumes, 800 current periodicals, and microfilms.

The C. J. Rodman Center for the Arts is home to a theater with a state-of-the-art computerized lighting system, a recital hall with one of only fifty existing Bedient organs, an art gallery, and a sculpture garden.

The J. M. Storzer Center includes an Olympic-size pool, a first-class gymnasium, tennis and racquetball courts, a dance studio, training facilities, and a weight room. The outdoor playing fields and courts are among the best in their class. In addition, a large, modern exercise facility was recently added in the main student residence area.

Costs

Tuition is $23,048, room and board are $6410, and fees are $275, for a total cost of $29,733.

Financial Aid

Ripon is one of just eighty-one colleges and universities in the country recognized as a best value by the Princeton Review in the 2006 edition of *America's Best Value Colleges,* which noted, "Best of all, Ripon strives to provide aid in a form that reduces your long-term debt." More than 90 percent of Ripon students receive some form of merit-based scholarship and/or need-based grants and loans.

Ripon recognizes and rewards students' success in high school with its institutionally funded scholarships, based not only on academic merit, but also on special achievements in other areas, such as the creative arts. The scholarships range from $1000 to full tuition. Ripon participates in all federal and state need-based financial aid programs. The financial aid counselors work individually with students and their families to investigate every possible financial resource for which they are eligible.

Faculty

Ripon has 50 full-time and 25 part-time faculty members. Ninety percent of the full-time faculty members have Ph.D.'s.

Admission Requirements

Ripon enrolls students who are expected to contribute to and benefit from the academic and residential programs provided. Ripon does not discriminate on the basis of gender, sexual orientation, race, color, age, religion, national and ethnic origin, or disability in the administration of its educational policies, admission practices, scholarship and loan programs, and athletic and other College-administered programs.

Application and Information

The faculty committee on academic standards establishes the criteria for admission. The school considers a variety of factors, including secondary school record, standardized test scores (SAT or ACT), recommendations, a written essay, and extracurricular or community service activities. Ripon's admission process reflects the personal attention students can expect to receive during their college careers, and applicants are encouraged to provide any additional information they consider helpful.

For further information, students should contact:

Steven M. Schuetz
Dean of Admission
Ripon College
300 Seward Street
P.O. Box 248
Ripon, Wisconsin 54971-0248
Phone: 800-947-4766 (toll-free)
E-mail: adminfo@ripon.edu
Web site: http://www.ripon.edu

Ripon College students and their families celebrate commencement on the lawn of Harwood Memorial Union.

ST. NORBERT COLLEGE

DE PERE, WISCONSIN

The College

St. Norbert College (SNC) is the only college in the world sponsored by the Norbertines, a Catholic order devoted to community, education, and serving the needs of others. Father Bernard Pennings, a Norbertine priest, founded St. Norbert College in 1898 with the mission of providing a superior education that provides academic, social, and spiritual nourishment. St. Norbert prides itself in sustaining an environment that encourages students from all religions to develop their full potential inside as well as outside the classroom.

The student body is made up of 2,100 students, hailing from twenty-eight states and thirty-one countries; more than half of the population comes from distances of more than 100 miles. Ninety percent of the students are between the ages of 18 and 22 years. Nearly all of the students live on or near the campus, which creates a strong sense of community and a wide range of opportunities for involvement.

About sixty student activities and organizations—academic honor societies, independent social organizations, community service organizations, academic clubs, local and national fraternities and sororities, and special-interest activities—await the St. Norbert student. Students who want to write for a newspaper, get involved in community service, work for political candidates, or gain other leadership experiences find them at St. Norbert. Students who like physical activities should know that St. Norbert maintains membership in the Midwest Conference for men and women, offers NCAA Division III teams in twenty sports, and is a member of the Northern Collegiate Hockey Association. Successful men's and women's teams have acquired fifty-five conference championships since St. Norbert joined the Midwest Conference in 1983–84. An extensive intramural program, including club teams in crew, lacrosse, and rugby, complements the activities program and helps guarantee that St. Norbert does not become a suitcase college.

An innovative Career Services Office provides four years of service to help students toward a lifetime of productive, satisfying employment. Counseling, aptitude and interest assessments, career shadowing, career exploration workshops, resume-writing workshops, on-campus recruitment interviews, and job-search strategies are among the services available. St. Norbert pioneered the Career Network, in which professionals—many of whom are alumni of the College—conduct interviews with St. Norbert students. Students learn about their chosen profession from people in the field and develop leads to future employment. Extensive on- and off-campus internships complement classroom learning and ease the transition to the professional world. The goal is to achieve near-perfect placement for St. Norbert graduates. Twenty-seven percent of a typical graduating class immediately attends graduate or professional schools; seventy-two percent of new graduates seeking employment are employed within six months following graduation.

Location

The St. Norbert campus—approximately 86 acres—is located on the banks of the Fox River in De Pere, Wisconsin, just minutes south of Green Bay, a metropolitan area of about 250,000 people and home to the world-famous Green Bay Packers football team. Wisconsin's oldest community, today De Pere is a charming blend of old and new. The community of 20,000 has recently redeveloped its business district, which is within walking distance of the campus. Motels of the major chains are within a few miles, and Door County, Wisconsin's favorite vacation spot, is less than an hour away. Greater Green Bay serves St. Norbert students as an internship laboratory. Students are found in financial, industrial, and retail organizations and as reporters and writers at newspapers and television stations within the community.

Majors and Degrees

St. Norbert offers programs leading to the Bachelor of Arts, Bachelor of Science, Bachelor of Music, and Bachelor of Business Administration degrees. The Bachelor of Arts can be earned in art; communication, media, and theater; economics; education; English; graphic communication; history; international economics; international studies; mathematics; modern foreign languages (French, German, and Spanish); music education; philosophy; political science; psychology; religious studies; and sociology.

Bachelor of Science degrees are conferred in biology, chemistry, computer information systems, computer science, environmental policy, environmental science, geology, natural sciences, and physics. In addition, a Bachelor of Science in natural sciences is awarded to students bound for professional schools (dentistry, medicine, and veterinary medicine). The Bachelor of Music is awarded in applied music. The Bachelor of Business Administration degree is offered to majors in accounting, business administration, and international business and language area studies.

In 2007, St. Norbert College entered into a collaborative agreement with the Bellin College of Nursing. The St. Norbert College and Bellin College of Nursing partnership provides more choices and more opportunities for students interested in health sciences, especially those who value a liberal arts foundation and a residential environment. Nursing students live and take half of their classes on St. Norbert college's beautiful, riverfront campus; have labs and clinicals in local hospitals, community health centers, and outpatient settings; and earn a Bellin College of Nursing Bachelor of Science in Nursing degree within four years. This unique arrangement brings an added advantage for nursing students seeking to make a difference.

Academic Programs

Degrees are awarded upon the successful completion of thirty-two courses (128 semester hours) that include an approved major sequence, course work in general education, and either an academic minor or electives. Academic majors can be begun as early as the first semester of the freshman year. Early selection of a major is encouraged but not required in most majors. Students are not required to officially declare a major until the end of the sophomore year. The College offers a four-year graduation guarantee in all but two academic programs.

The General Education Program spans nine areas. The goal is to educate students broadly, regardless of major. Competence in writing and quantitative skills is required of all graduates. Other areas include study of philosophy, religion, the sciences, fine arts, American heritage, international heritage, and social science areas, e.g., sociology and psychology. The academic minor option provides flexibility for students planning graduate or professional study or those who seek career-related course work prior to entering the job market. An Honors Program offers additional challenge in areas of general education to those of superior ability, and an honors degree is awarded to those who successfully complete the program.

The accounting program is accredited by the Wisconsin Accounting Examination Board. The education programs lead to certification at elementary and secondary levels. A nursery school option is included in the elementary program. Student teaching can be completed in the greater Green Bay area or in Australia, Belize, England, Kenya, New Zealand, Scotland, Ireland, the Virgin Islands, and Wales. A program leading to certification for K–12 teaching in music is also available.

Army ROTC is available at St. Norbert through a collaborative program with the University of Wisconsin–Oshkosh. Several SNC students are recipients of full Army ROTC scholarships each year. Among the College's alumni are 11 Army generals who completed ROTC at the College—the highest total of any college (with the exception of West Point).

Off-Campus Programs

St. Norbert students, regardless of major, can spend a summer, a semester, or a year abroad. Students completing liberal arts majors are encouraged to spend at least a semester abroad. An international study component is a part of majors in French, Spanish, and German and both the international business program and the international studies major. All approved international study carries regular academic credit. St. Norbert scholarship assistance and other financial aid are available to students studying overseas. Study-abroad opportunities include a Third World science field trip; exchange programs in Australia, France, Japan, Germany, the Philippines, Spain, and Ukraine; student teaching in Europe, Africa, Australia, and Latin America; and other study sites throughout Europe, South America, and Egypt. Programs run by the International Center help students, faculty members, and others discover new and exciting ways to explore and broaden their global horizons. St. Norbert's international curriculum, taught by a faculty committed to global learning, prepares students to live in a global society. The international experience that St. Norbert considers vital to today's graduates is a key component of the College's educational mission. A Washington semester is also available through American University.

Academic Facilities

The John Minahan Science Hall houses the science programs and thirty-eight laboratories, including the Center for Adaptive Education. Austin E. Cofrin Hall houses the business administration, computer science, mathematics, and economics programs. It also contains computing resources for the campus, which include minicomputers and 350 microcomputers. The Todd Wehr Library's open concept provides easy access to the College's 274,000 books, periodicals, and manuscripts. The College's archives are located in the library. The College's art collection can be viewed throughout the campus. The F. K. Bemis International Center provides students with opportunities to prepare for careers with greater international emphasis. It is also a culture and language resource to K–12 schools and Wisconsin businesses. Campus improvements in the past six years include the $6.8-million Bush Family Art Center, which was dedicated in 2002. Funding is currently under way for a new $23-million library and an extensive renovation of athletic and science facilities. Global links via multifaceted telecommunications technology, including compressed video, two-way interactive video, and satellite downlinks, bring world news to student residence halls, classrooms, and conference and seminar rooms. Seven computer labs are available for student use at no charge.

Costs

For 2007–08, tuition and required fees for full-time students total $24,253. Room costs average $3200 per year, and the average meal plan for full-time students costs $3200 per year.

Financial Aid

Students share in more than $21 million of financial aid each year, including scholarships and grants, campus jobs, and educational loans. SNC awards $14 million of its own scholarships and grants annually. Awards are based on need and merit. No-need scholarships available for freshmen include the Trustees Distinguished Scholarship (special consideration for National Merit and National Achievement commended students, semifinalists, and winners), the Presidential Scholarship, and the John F. Kennedy Scholarship.

Wisconsin residents who show need can qualify for assistance provided by the state through the Wisconsin Tuition Grant Program, which pays up to $2700 of tuition each year. Students also utilize Federal Pell Grants and Federal Stafford Student Loans. The College participates in the Federal Supplemental Educational Opportunity Grant, Federal Perkins Loan, and Federal Work-Study programs. Each year, nearly 1,300 SNC students are employed on campus. The typical job involves about 10 hours of work per week and produces about $1600 in annual wages. A number of students are hired through the College's own $1.7-million-per-year employment program. Qualified students, regardless of financial need, fill positions.

Need-based awards are made on the basis of the Free Application for Federal Student Aid (FAFSA) and the St. Norbert College institutional application for financial aid. Freshman applicants should submit these forms by March of their senior year of high school.

Faculty

The St. Norbert faculty is composed of 170 men and women, 126 of whom are full-time. Ninety-two percent of the full-time faculty members hold the doctoral or other terminal degree in their field. The faculty-student ratio is approximately 1:14. Faculty members work closely with students in their major area of study, help students prepare for graduate school, and work with those who seek independent study and research opportunities. Faculty members also work with Career Services in its professional practice program.

Student Government

Leadership is a key component of community life at St. Norbert. As one of the few institutions to offer a leadership studies minor, St. Norbert includes cocurricular involvement in its description of a rewarding college experience. Students may take advantage of numerous opportunities, including Emerging Leaders, a program providing guidance for students interested in leadership roles on campus.

The Office of Leadership, Service, and Involvement coordinates a variety of clubs and service organizations, adventure trip programming, and recreation tournaments. A student-elected Campus Ministry Council sponsors various community outreach activities, both local and in the inner-city areas of major cities. Other social action activities are offered through the Peace and Justice Center, and students with an interest in College government can contribute through such activities as serving on the student-run College Activities Board, being a student representative on College Committees, and taking a decision-making role on the Residence Hall Association.

Living and learning are linked at St. Norbert through programs in the residence halls. Some residence halls focus on community service or feature campus programs, such as the Women's Center in Sensenbrenner Hall or Freshman Seminar in Bergstrom Hall. Many halls have chapels for students to use to reflect and pray.

Admission Requirements

The student's high school record is the single most important element in the admission decision. Students who have taken an academic or college-preparatory program are considered best qualified. Nearly 80 percent of the freshman class ranked in the top two fifths of their high school senior class. The middle 50 percent of ACT composite scores range from 22 to 27. Students with superior scores and grades may enroll in the honors program.

The College seeks a diversified student body. Because St. Norbert is residential in nature, emphasis in admission decisions is placed on how a student used his or her spare time during the high school years. The College seeks students who have participated in, or are interested in participating in, a variety of athletic, social, cultural, and intellectual activities. Transfer students are encouraged to apply. The minimum acceptable GPA for transfers is 2.0 (C) on a 4.0 scale.

Application and Information

Early application for the freshman class is encouraged in order for students to benefit from the College's practice of registering students and assigning housing in the order in which they enroll. Notification of the admission decision is made on a rolling basis beginning in late September. A $350 deposit is required to confirm enrollment. For more information about St. Norbert, students should contact:

Director of Admission
St. Norbert College
100 Grant Street
De Pere, Wisconsin 54115
Phone: 920-403-3005
800-236-4878 (toll-free)
Web site: http://www.snc.edu

WYOMING

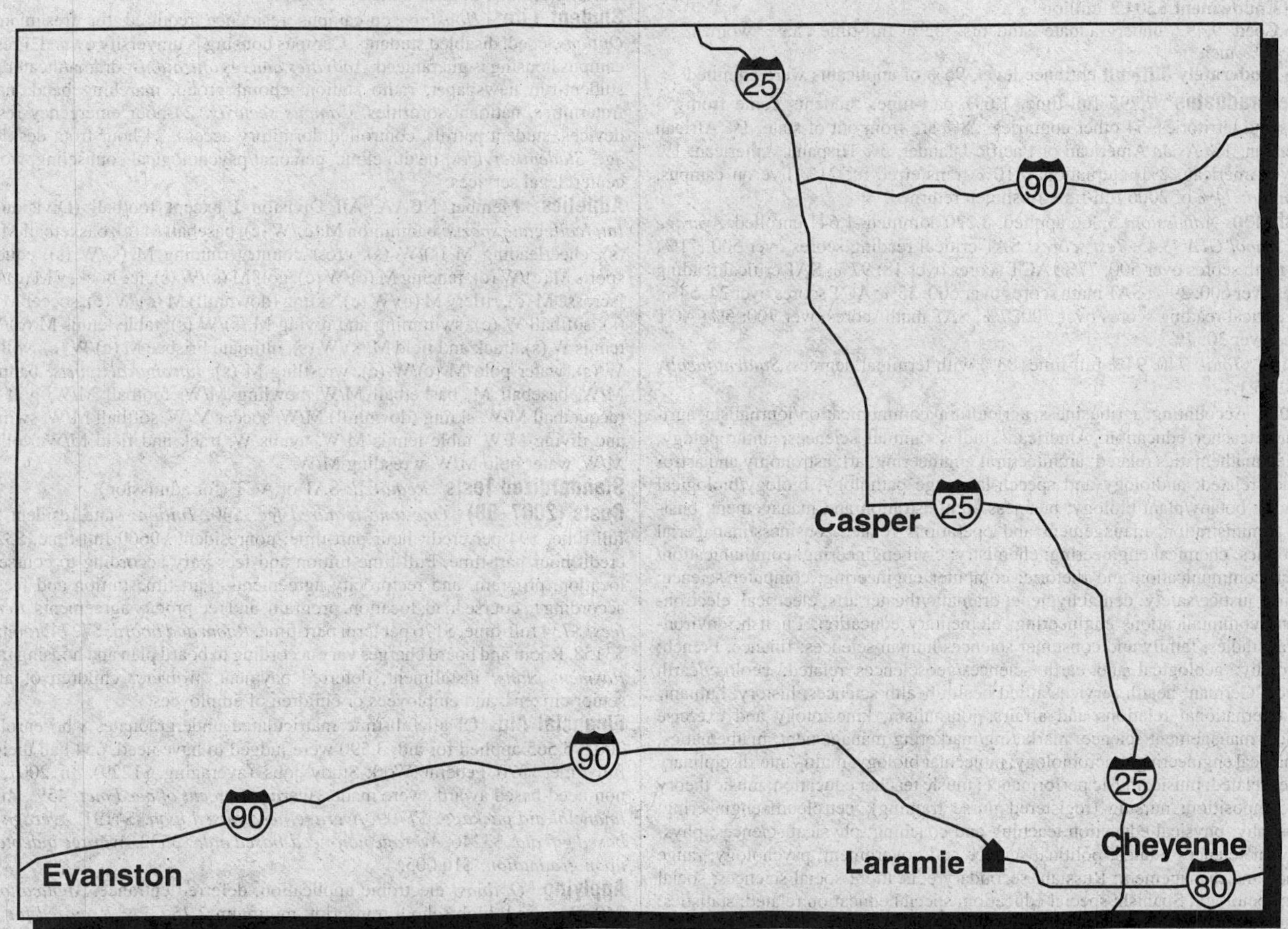

UNIVERSITY OF WYOMING

Laramie, Wyoming **www.uwyo.edu/**

- **State-supported** university, founded 1886
- **Small-town** 785-acre campus
- **Endowment** $304.2 million
- **Coed** 9,492 undergraduate students, 82% full-time, 53% women, 47% men
- **Moderately difficult** entrance level, 96% of applicants were admitted

Undergraduates 7,795 full-time, 1,697 part-time. Students come from 53 states and territories, 54 other countries, 28% are from out of state, 1% African American, 1% Asian American or Pacific Islander, 3% Hispanic American, 1% Native American, 2% international, 10% transferred in, 21% live on campus. *Retention:* 74% of 2006 full-time freshmen returned.

Freshmen *Admission:* 3,366 applied, 3,220 admitted, 1,641 enrolled. *Average high school GPA:* 3.45. *Test scores:* SAT critical reading scores over 500: 71%; SAT math scores over 500: 77%; ACT scores over 18: 97%; SAT critical reading scores over 600: 29%; SAT math scores over 600: 35%; ACT scores over 24: 54%; SAT critical reading scores over 700: 7%; SAT math scores over 700: 5%; ACT scores over 30: 7%.

Faculty *Total:* 740, 94% full-time, 83% with terminal degrees. *Student/faculty ratio:* 15:1.

Majors Accounting; agribusiness; agricultural communication/journalism; agricultural teacher education; American studies; animal sciences; anthropology; applied mathematics related; architectural engineering; art; astronomy and astrophysics related; audiology and speech-language pathology; biology/biological sciences; botany/plant biology; business administration and management; business administration, management and operations related; business/managerial economics; chemical engineering; chemistry; civil engineering; communication/speech communication and rhetoric; computer engineering; computer science; criminal justice/safety; dental hygiene; dramatic/theater arts; electrical, electronics and communications engineering; elementary education; English; environmental studies; family and consumer sciences/human sciences; finance; French; geography; geological and earth sciences/geosciences related; geology/earth science; German; health services/allied health/health sciences; history; humanities; international relations and affairs; journalism; kinesiology and exercise science; management science; marketing/marketing management; mathematics; mechanical engineering; microbiology; molecular biology; multi-/interdisciplinary studies related; music; music performance; music teacher education; music theory and composition; nursing (registered nurse training); petroleum engineering; philosophy; physical education teaching and coaching; physical sciences; physics; plant sciences related; political science and government; psychology; range science and management; Russian; secondary education; social sciences; social work; sociology; Spanish; special education; special education related; statistics; technology/industrial arts teacher education; trade and industrial teacher education; wildlife biology; women's studies; zoology/animal biology.

Academics *Calendar:* semesters. *Degrees:* certificates, bachelor's, master's, doctoral, first professional, post-master's, and postbachelor's certificates. *Special study options:* accelerated degree program, advanced placement credit, distance learning, double majors, English as a second language, external degree program, honors programs, independent study, internships, off-campus study, part-time degree program, services for LD students, student-designed majors, study abroad, summer session for credit. *ROTC:* Army (b), Air Force (b).

Computers on Campus 1,269 computers/terminals are available on campus for general student use. Students can access the following: computer help desk, free student e-mail accounts, online (class) grades, online (class) registration, online (class) schedules. Campuswide network is available. 100% of college-owned or -operated housing units are wired for high-speed Internet access. Wireless service is available via classrooms, computer centers, computer labs, learning centers, libraries, student centers.

Student Life *Housing:* on-campus residence required for freshman year. *Options:* coed, disabled students. Campus housing is university owned. Freshman campus housing is guaranteed. *Activities and organizations:* drama/theater group, student-run newspaper, radio station, choral group, marching band, national fraternities, national sororities. *Campus security:* 24-hour emergency response devices, student patrols, controlled dormitory access, 24-hour front desk coverage. *Student services:* health clinic, personal/psychological counseling, women's center, legal services.

Athletics Member NCAA. All Division I except football (Division I-A). *Intercollegiate sports:* badminton M (c)/W (c), baseball M (c), basketball M (s)/W (s), cheerleading M (s)/W (s), cross-country running M (s)/W (s), equestrian sports M (c)/W (c), fencing M (c)/W (c), golf M (s)/W (s), ice hockey M (c)/W (c), lacrosse M (c), riflery M (c)/W (c), skiing (downhill) M (c)/W (c), soccer M (c)/W (s), softball W (c), swimming and diving M (s)/W (s), table tennis M (c)/W (c), tennis W (s), track and field M (s)/W (s), ultimate Frisbee M (c)/W (c), volleyball W (s), water polo M (c)/W (c), wrestling M (s). *Intramural sports:* badminton M/W, baseball M, basketball M/W, bowling M/W, football M/W, golf M/W, racquetball M/W, skiing (downhill) M/W, soccer M/W, softball M/W, swimming and diving M/W, table tennis M/W, tennis W, track and field M/W, volleyball M/W, water polo M/W, wrestling M/W.

Standardized Tests *Required:* SAT or ACT (for admission).

Costs (2007–08) *One-time required fee:* $40. *Tuition:* state resident $2820 full-time, $94 per credit hour part-time; nonresident $9660 full-time, $322 per credit hour part-time. Full-time tuition and fees vary according to course load, location, program, and reciprocity agreements. Part-time tuition and fees vary according to course load, location, program, and reciprocity agreements. *Required fees:* $734 full-time, $176 per term part-time. *Room and board:* $7274; room only: $3158. Room and board charges vary according to board plan and housing facility. *Payment plans:* installment, deferred payment. *Waivers:* children of alumni, senior citizens, and employees or children of employees.

Financial Aid Of all full-time matriculated undergraduates who enrolled in 2007, 5,565 applied for aid, 3,590 were judged to have need, 654 had their need fully met. 370 Federal Work-Study jobs (averaging $1229). In 2007, 1420 non-need-based awards were made. *Average percent of need met:* 45%. *Average financial aid package:* $7709. *Average need-based loan:* $4191. *Average need-based gift aid:* $3246. *Average non-need-based aid:* $3532. *Average indebtedness upon graduation:* $16,005.

Applying *Options:* electronic application, deferred entrance. *Application fee:* $40. *Required:* high school transcript, minimum 2.75 GPA. *Required for some:* minimum 3.0 GPA. *Application deadlines:* 8/10 (freshmen), 8/10 (transfers). *Notification:* continuous (freshmen), continuous (transfers).

Freshman Application Contact Aaron Appelhans, Assistant Director of Admissions, University of Wyoming, Box 3435, Laramie, WY 82071. *Phone:* 307-766-5160. *Toll-free phone:* 800-342-5996. *Fax:* 307-766-4042. *E-mail:* whywyo@uwyo.edu.

See page 2810 for the College Close-Up.

UNIVERSITY OF WYOMING

LARAMIE, WYOMING

The University

The University of Wyoming, a public land-grant institution founded in 1886, is a reflection of the global community it serves. The extensive range of academic programs offered at UW, as the school is affectionately known, inspires the development of new thinking and promotes fulfilling careers throughout the rapidly evolving world.

The research done by the professors and students of the University of Wyoming pushes the boundaries of modern science and technology, meriting UW's classification as a Carnegie Doctoral/Research University–Extensive.

It is this academic ambition that has allowed UW to provide high-quality undergraduate and graduate education, research, and service since its inception.

Wyoming, unique among the fifty states, has only one university. UW enjoys tremendous support from within its state as well as from an alumni network that spans the globe. More than 13,203 students from all parts of the U.S., and seventy-seven other countries attend UW classes in Laramie and at outreach sites around the state. The variety of students at UW enriches the educational experience for all by fostering a multicultural environment that encourages sharing and learning about those with different heritages and cultural backgrounds. It is this dialogue that continues to promote respect and appreciation for diversity.

UW offers bachelor's degree programs in six undergraduate colleges: the Colleges of Agriculture, Arts and Sciences, Business, Education, Engineering and Applied Science, and Health Sciences. Undergraduate education is a high priority at UW. More than 89 percent of the undergraduate courses are taught by professors, and the average class size is 30 students. UW also offers graduate and professional programs, including the Doctor of Pharmacy and the Juris Doctor.

There are more than 200 recognized campus clubs and organizations, including fifteen national fraternities and sororities, honor and professional societies, political and religious organizations, and special interest groups. Students have the opportunity to participate in more than sixty different intramural and club sports. UW is a Division I member of the NCAA and competes in the Mountain West Conference in seventeen men's and women's sports. Campus recreational facilities include the Wyoming Union, which recently underwent a $10-million renovation and includes the UW bookstore, eating establishments, student computers, study areas, and a variety of services and resources for students. Additional facilities on campus include Half Acre Gym, an indoor climbing wall, an eighteen-hole golf course, tennis and racquetball courts, weight rooms, two swimming pools, rifle and archery ranges, indoor and outdoor tracks, softball and baseball fields, and a hockey rink.

UW houses 2,400 students in six residence halls, and freshmen are required to live on campus during their first year. While primarily coed, the residence halls offer a number of unique living environments, including quiet/study floors, special interest floors, honors floors, single-sex floors, and other academic living environments. UW also offers fourteen different Freshman Interest Groups, which are learning communities that offer common living areas and clustered classes to students with similar academic areas of interest.

Location

UW's 785-acre campus is located at the foot of the Rocky Mountains in Laramie, a scenic town of 30,000 people in southeastern Wyoming. Many UW students enjoy the easy access to Alpine and Nordic skiing, snowboarding, snowmobiling, hiking, backpacking, camping, hunting, fishing, rock climbing, and mountain biking. Laramie—with its blue skies, clean air, and 320 days of sunshine a year—is a friendly and supportive university town, conveniently located 45 miles west of Wyoming's capital, Cheyenne, and only 130 miles northwest of Denver, Colorado.

Majors and Degrees

UW offers more than eighty undergraduate programs within its six colleges, leading to B.A., B.S., B.F.A., and B.S.N. degrees.

The College of Agriculture offers majors in agricultural business (with options in agribusiness management, farm and ranch management, and international agriculture), agricultural communications, agroecology, animal and veterinary sciences (with options in animal biology, business, communication, meat science and food technology, pre–veterinary science, production, and range livestock), family and consumer science (with options in child development, dietetics, family services, human nutrition and food, and textiles and merchandising), microbiology, molecular biology, and rangeland ecology and watershed management.

The College of Arts and Sciences offers majors in American studies, anthropology, art, astronomy/astrophysics, biology, botany, chemistry, communication, criminal justice, English, French, geography and recreation, geology (with options in earth science and environment/natural resources), German, history, humanities/fine arts, international studies, journalism, management, mathematical sciences, mathematics, music (with options in education, performance, and theory and composition), philosophy, physics, political science, psychology, Russian, social science, sociology, Spanish, statistics, theater and dance, wildlife/fisheries, women's studies, and zoology and physiology as well as the option of a self-designed major.

The College of Business offers majors in accounting, business administration, business economics, economics, finance, management, and marketing.

The College of Education offers majors in elementary education, industrial technology education, and secondary education (with options in agriculture, art, business, English, family and consumer sciences, industrial technology, mathematics, modern languages, sciences, and social studies).

The College of Engineering and Applied Science offers majors in architectural engineering, chemical engineering (with environmental and petroleum options), civil engineering, computer engineering, computer science, electrical engineering (with bioengineering and computer engineering options), management information systems (with accounting, business, and computer science options), and mechanical engineering.

The College of Health Sciences offers majors in dental hygiene, exercise and sports science, health education, health sciences, nursing, pharmacy, physical education teaching, social work, and speech-language and hearing sciences.

UW offers preprofessional programs in dentistry, forestry, law, medicine, nursing, occupational therapy, optometry, pharmacy, physical therapy, and veterinary medicine.

The School of Environment and Natural Resources also offers interdisciplinary studies that can be combined with course work in seven other fields of study, including the humanities, physical sciences, and social sciences.

Academic Programs

The UW academic calendar consists of two semesters and a complete summer session. Depending on their degree program, students are required to complete 120 to 164 credit hours for graduation. Undergraduate programs for most majors can be completed in four years. Students may choose to double major within the same college, or they may pursue majors in two separate colleges for a cross-college major. Minors are also available in many areas. All students are required to complete the University Studies Program, which is a core curriculum that assists students in developing their knowledge of oral and written communication, mathematics, science, diversity, global awareness, government, and culture.

The University honors program provides academically ambitious undergraduates innovative and intellectual learning opportunities. Award-winning faculty members, unique and challenging course work, and senior research projects are the hallmarks of this program.

Off-Campus Programs

UW has approximately 350 international students and close to 100 international researchers/scholars during any given academic year. This diverse community represents some seventy-seven countries. International Students Services provides support to this population through an extensive orientation program, the Friendship Families program, the International Neighbors program, and the International Resource Center.

International Student Services coordinates the National Student Exchange (NSE), which is a domestic student exchange consortium of more than 180 colleges and universities throughout the U.S. In addition, NSE host sites are available in Canada, Puerto Rico, the Virgin Islands, and Guam. Membership in the NSE provides UW students with access to thousands of unique academic programs, classes, and faculty members on host campuses for either a semester or an academic year.

The UW Outreach School extends the university learning experience to Wyoming and the nation through credit and noncredit programs, University of Wyoming Television, Wyoming Public Radio, and the UW/Casper College Center. Credit programs are delivered via Internet/Web-based instruction, compressed video, audio teleconferencing, flexible enrollment (correspondence study), and on-site instruction. Select programs are offered, and degree availability may be limited.

Academic Facilities

The University libraries' collections number nearly 1.3 million volumes and offer links to a variety of library service collections. The William Robertson Coe Library houses materials in the social sciences, humanities, visual and performing arts, business, education, and health sciences as well as more than 2 million federal publications and the Audio Visual Library, a collection of 4,000 video and film titles. Other libraries include the Science Library, the Brinkerhoff Earth Resources Information Center (geology library), and the Rocky Mountain Herbarium Research Collection. Additional collections are housed in the American Heritage Center and the George W. Hooper Law Library. A branch library is located at the National Park Service Research Center in Jackson, Wyoming. UW libraries participate in the Colorado Alliance of Research Libraries and in Region Four of the National Network of Libraries of Medicine. In addition, FERRET provides high-speed access to UW's online library catalogs.

Costs

UW tuition and fees for full-time undergraduates in the 2007–08 academic year were $3366 for Wyoming residents and $9750 for nonresidents (based on an average class load of 14 credit hours). Room and board (double occupancy, unlimited meal plan) costs were $7274. Estimated expenses include $1200 for books and supplies, $890 for travel costs, and $2200 for personal expenses.

Financial Aid

Nearly 80 percent of all UW students receive financial assistance. More than $76 million is available in the form of scholarships, loans, grants, and work-study opportunities. The Free Application for Federal Student Aid (FAFSA) is required for need-based assistance (loans, grants, work-study) and for many scholarships. Most scholarships at UW are based on academic merit. UW participates in the Western Undergraduate Exchange (WUE) program, which is awarded through the Peak Achievement Scholarship. The Peak Achievement Scholarship is also available to students from non-WUE states. The priority deadline for financial aid is March 1.

Faculty

More than 700 professors from the world's most respected colleges and universities have come to teach at UW. Recognized nationally and internationally as experts, almost 90 percent of the professors hold the highest degrees in their fields. UW professors are deeply committed to the success of their students. Only a small number of undergraduate courses are taught by graduate assistants, and many of the most distinguished and accomplished professors at UW teach first-year courses. UW maintains a low student-faculty ratio (15:1), which allows for individualized attention, instruction, and academic advising, as well as the inclusion of undergraduates in cutting-edge research projects.

Student Government

The Associated Students of the University of Wyoming (ASUW) is composed all students at UW. ASUW serves as the voice of the students, and its legislation impacts many aspects of student life. The ASUW Senate acts as a liaison between the student body and the administration as well as the UW Board of Trustees and local and state governments. The student body president also sits as an *ex officio* member of the UW Board of Trustees. UW encourages all students to actively participate in ASUW.

Admission Requirements

To ensure admission, high school graduates and new first-year students with fewer than 30 transferable college credit hours should have a cumulative high school GPA of 2.75 or above (Wyoming residents) or 3.0 or above (nonresidents). Students should have a composite ACT score of 20 or greater or an SAT verbal/math score of 960 or greater. In addition, all students have completed 4 units of English, 3 units of mathematics, 3 units of science (including a physical science), and 3 units of cultural context courses (behavioral or social sciences, visual arts, performing arts, humanities, or foreign languages). Admission with conditions can be granted to students who do not meet these standards but have a minimum 2.5 GPA or a 2.25 GPA with a composite ACT score of at least 20 or an SAT score of at least 960. Transfer students with 30 or more transferable semester credit hours must have a minimum cumulative college GPA of 2.0.

Application and Information

Students must submit a completed UW Application for Admission, official high school or college transcripts, ACT or SAT scores, and a $40 nonrefundable application fee. Students may apply and pay the application fee online at the Web address listed in this description. UW strongly encourages all prospective students and their parents to visit the campus.

Admissions Office
Department 3435
University of Wyoming
1000 East University Avenue
Laramie, Wyoming 82071-3435
Phone: 307-766-5160
800-DIAL-WYO (342-5996; toll-free)
E-mail: why-wyo@uwyo.edu
Web site: http://www.uwyo.edu/

Historic Old Main at the University of Wyoming was built in 1886.

COLLEGE DATA CENTER • WYOMING

CANADA

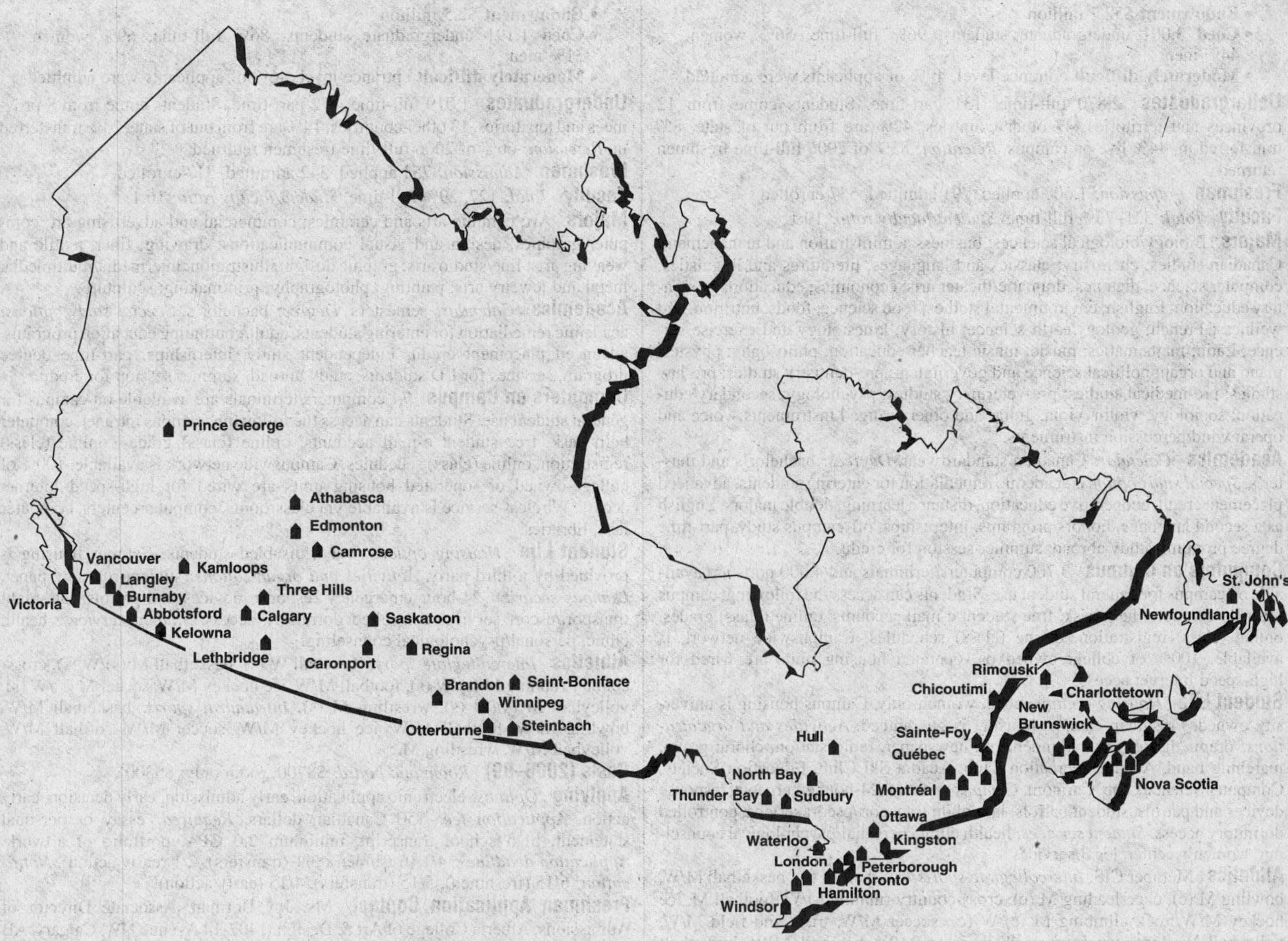

The Toronto area includes the towns of Ancaster, Cambridge, Guelph, Kitchener, Thornhill, North York, and St. Catharines.

Quebec includes the towns of Lennoxville, Rouyn-Noranda, Sherbrooke, and Trois-Riviéres.

Nova Scotia includes the towns of Antigonish, Church Point, Halifax, Sydney, Truro, and Wolfville.

The New Brunswick area includes the towns of Fredericton, Moncton, Sackville, Saint John, and Sussex.

ACADIA UNIVERSITY

Wolfville, Nova Scotia, Canada **www.acadiau.ca/**

- **Province-supported** comprehensive, founded 1838
- **Small-town** 250-acre campus
- **Endowment** $52.7 million
- **Coed** 3,001 undergraduate students, 96% full-time, 56% women, 44% men
- **Moderately difficult** entrance level, 49% of applicants were admitted

Undergraduates 2,870 full-time, 131 part-time. Students come from 12 provinces and territories, 47 other countries, 42% are from out of state, 8% transferred in, 44% live on campus. *Retention:* 83% of 2006 full-time freshmen returned.

Freshmen *Admission:* 1,600 applied, 791 admitted, 537 enrolled.

Faculty *Total:* 331, 73% full-time. *Student/faculty ratio:* 10:1.

Majors Biology/biological sciences; business administration and management; Canadian studies; chemistry; classics and languages, literatures and linguistics; computer science; dietetics; dramatic/theater arts; economics; education; elementary education; English; environmental studies; food science; foods, nutrition, and wellness; French; geology/earth science; history; kinesiology and exercise science; Latin; mathematics; music; music teacher education; philosophy; physics; piano and organ; political science and government; pre-dentistry studies; pre-law studies; pre-medical studies; pre-veterinary studies; psychology; secondary education; sociology; violin, viola, guitar and other stringed instruments; voice and opera; wind/percussion instruments.

Academics *Calendar:* Canadian standard year. *Degrees:* bachelor's and master's. *Special study options:* academic remediation for entering students, advanced placement credit, cooperative education, distance learning, double majors, English as a second language, honors programs, internships, off-campus study, part-time degree program, study abroad, summer session for credit.

Computers on Campus 3,700 computers/terminals and 4,000 ports are available on campus for general student use. Students can access the following: campus intranet, computer help desk, free student e-mail accounts, online (class) grades, online (class) registration, online (class) schedules. Campuswide network is available. 100% of college-owned or -operated housing units are wired for high-speed Internet access.

Student Life *Housing options:* coed, women-only. Campus housing is university owned. Freshman campus housing is guaranteed. *Activities and organizations:* drama/theater group, student-run newspaper, radio station, choral group, marching band, Acadia Recreation Club, Acadia Ski Club, Education Society, Computer Science Club, Caricom. *Campus security:* 24-hour emergency response devices and patrols, student patrols, late-night transport/escort service, controlled dormitory access. *Student services:* health clinic, personal/psychological counseling, women's center, legal services.

Athletics Member CIS. *Intercollegiate sports:* baseball M (c), basketball M/W, bowling M (c), cheerleading M (c), cross-country running M/W, football M, ice hockey M/W, rock climbing M (c)/W (c), soccer M/W, track and field M/W, volleyball W. *Intramural sports:* badminton M/W, baseball M/W, basketball M/W, bowling M/W, cheerleading M/W, cross-country running M/W, field hockey M/W, ice hockey M/W, racquetball M/W, rock climbing M/W, skiing (cross-country) M/W, skiing (downhill) M/W, soccer M/W, softball M/W, squash M/W, swimming and diving M/W, table tennis M/W, tennis M/W, track and field M/W, ultimate Frisbee M/W, volleyball M/W, water polo M/W, wrestling M.

Standardized Tests *Required:* SAT (for admission). *Required for some:* SAT Subject Tests (for admission).

Costs (2007–08) *Tuition:* area resident $8062 Canadian dollars full-time, $890 Canadian dollars per course part-time; nonresident $1560 Canadian dollars per course part-time. Full-time tuition and fees vary according to course level, course load, degree level, and program. Part-time tuition and fees vary according to course level, course load, degree level, and program. *Required fees:* $180 Canadian dollars full-time, $5 Canadian dollars per course part-time. *Room and board:* $8284 Canadian dollars; room only: $5107 Canadian dollars. Room and board charges vary according to board plan and housing facility. *Payment plan:* installment. *Waivers:* senior citizens and employees or children of employees.

Applying *Options:* electronic application, deferred entrance. *Application fee:* $25 Canadian dollars. *Required:* high school transcript, minimum 2.5 GPA. *Required for some:* essay or personal statement, letters of recommendation, interview. *Application deadlines:* 7/1 (freshmen), 7/1 (out-of-state freshmen), 7/1 (transfers). *Notification:* continuous (freshmen), continuous (out-of-state freshmen), continuous (transfers).

Freshman Application Contact Ms. Anne Scott, Manager of Admissions, Acadia University, Wolfville, NS B4P 2R6, Canada. *Phone:* 902-585-1016. *Fax:* 902-585-1092. *E-mail:* admissions@acadiau.ca.

ALBERTA COLLEGE OF ART & DESIGN

Calgary, Alberta, Canada **www.acad.ca/**

- **Province-supported** 4-year, founded 1926
- **Urban** 1-acre campus
- **Endowment** $2.5 million
- **Coed** 1,191 undergraduate students, 86% full-time, 69% women, 31% men
- **Moderately difficult** entrance level, 46% of applicants were admitted

Undergraduates 1,019 full-time, 172 part-time. Students come from 8 provinces and territories, 13 other countries, 14% are from out of state, 24% transferred in. *Retention:* 66% of 2006 full-time freshmen returned.

Freshmen *Admission:* 751 applied, 342 admitted, 317 enrolled.

Faculty *Total:* 127, 29% full-time. *Student/faculty ratio:* 16:1.

Majors Art; ceramic arts and ceramics; commercial and advertising art; computer graphics; design and visual communications; drawing; fiber, textile and weaving arts; fine/studio arts; graphic design; illustration; intermedia/multimedia; metal and jewelry arts; painting; photography; printmaking; sculpture.

Academics *Calendar:* semesters. *Degree:* bachelor's. *Special study options:* academic remediation for entering students, adult/continuing education programs, advanced placement credit, independent study, internships, part-time degree program, services for LD students, study abroad, summer session for credit.

Computers on Campus 74 computers/terminals are available on campus for general student use. Students can access the following: campus intranet, computer help desk, free student e-mail accounts, online (class) grades, online (class) registration, online (class) schedules. Campuswide network is available. 100% of college-owned or -operated housing units are wired for high-speed Internet access. Wireless service is available via classrooms, computer centers, computer labs, libraries.

Student Life *Housing options:* coed, disabled students. Campus housing is provided by a third party. *Activities and organizations:* student-run newspaper. *Campus security:* 24-hour emergency response devices and patrols, late-night transport/escort service, controlled dormitory access. *Student services:* health clinic, personal/psychological counseling.

Athletics *Intercollegiate sports:* baseball W (s), basketball M (s)/W (s), cross-country running M (s)/W (s), football M/W, ice hockey M/W, soccer M (s)/W (s), volleyball M (s)/W (s), wrestling M (s). *Intramural sports:* basketball M/W, bowling M/W, football M/W, ice hockey M/W, soccer M/W, softball M/W, volleyball M/W, wrestling M.

Costs (2008–09) *Room and board:* $8700; room only: $5300.

Applying *Options:* electronic application, early admission, early decision, early action. *Application fee:* $50 Canadian dollars. *Required:* essay or personal statement, high school transcript, minimum 2.0 GPA, portfolio of artwork. *Application deadlines:* 4/1 (freshmen), 3/1 (transfers), 2/1 (early action). *Notification:* 6/15 (freshmen), 5/15 (transfers), 4/15 (early action).

Freshman Application Contact Ms. Joy Borman, Associate Director of Admissions, Alberta College of Art & Design, 1407-14 Avenue NW, Calgary, AB T2N 4R3, Canada. *Phone:* 403-284-7689. *Toll-free phone:* 800-251-8290. *Fax:* 403-284-7644. *E-mail:* admissions@acad.ca.

AMBROSE UNIVERSITY COLLEGE

Calgary, Alberta, Canada **www.ambrose.edu/**

Director of Admissions Admissions Officer, Ambrose University College, 630, 833-4th Avenue SW, Calgary, AB T2P 3T5, Canada. *Toll-free phone:* 800-461-1222. *E-mail:* enrolment@auc-nuc.ca.

ATHABASCA UNIVERSITY

Athabasca, Alberta, Canada **www.athabascau.ca/**

- **Province-supported** comprehensive, founded 1970
- **Small-town** 480-acre campus
- **Endowment** $1.2 million
- **Coed** 31,233 undergraduate students
- **Noncompetitive** entrance level

Undergraduates Students come from 33 provinces and territories, 87 other countries, 47% are from out of state.

Faculty *Total:* 166.

Majors Accounting; anthropology; applied art; biological and physical sciences; business administration and management; Canadian studies; communication and media related; computer and information sciences; criminal justice/police science; English; French; general studies; history; human resources management; information science/studies; labor and industrial relations; liberal arts and sciences/ liberal studies; marketing/marketing management; nursing (registered nurse training); organizational behavior; political science and government; psychology; public administration; sociology; women's studies.

Academics *Calendar:* continuous. *Degrees:* certificates, diplomas, bachelor's, master's, and doctoral (offers only external degree programs). *Special study options:* academic remediation for entering students, accelerated degree program, adult/continuing education programs, advanced placement credit, distance learning, English as a second language, external degree program, off-campus study, part-time degree program, services for LD students, student-designed majors, study abroad, summer session for credit.

Computers on Campus 28 computers/terminals are available on campus for general student use. Students can access the following: online (class) registration. Campuswide network is available.

Student Life *Housing:* college housing not available. *Activities and organizations:* student-run newspaper. *Campus security:* 24-hour emergency response devices.

Costs (2007–08) *Tuition:* province resident $5910 Canadian dollars full-time, $591 Canadian dollars per course part-time; nonresident $6890 Canadian dollars full-time, $689 Canadian dollars per course part-time; International tuition $8840 Canadian dollars full-time. *Waivers:* employees or children of employees.

Applying *Options:* electronic application. *Application fee:* $60 Canadian dollars. *Application deadlines:* rolling (freshmen), rolling (transfers). *Notification:* continuous (freshmen), continuous (transfers).

Freshman Application Contact Information Centre, Athabasca University, 1 University Drive, Athabasca, AB T9S 3A3. *Phone:* 800-788-9041. *Toll-free phone:* 800-788-9041. *Fax:* 780-675-6437. *E-mail:* reginfo@cs.athabascau.ca.

ATLANTIC BAPTIST UNIVERSITY

Moncton, New Brunswick, Canada **www.abu.nb.ca/**

- **Independent Baptist** 4-year, founded 1949, administratively affiliated with The Council of Christian Colleges and Universities
- **Urban** 220-acre campus
- **Coed**
- **Minimally difficult** entrance level

Faculty *Student/faculty ratio:* 16:1.

Academics *Calendar:* semesters. *Degrees:* certificates, bachelor's, and post-bachelor's certificates.

Student Life *Campus security:* 24-hour emergency response devices, student patrols, controlled dormitory access.

Costs (2007–08) *Comprehensive fee:* $8660 Canadian dollars includes full-time tuition ($6460 Canadian dollars) and room and board ($2200 Canadian dollars). Full-time tuition and fees vary according to program. Part-time tuition: $700 Canadian dollars per course. Part-time tuition and fees vary according to course load. International tuition: $7460 Canadian dollars full-time. *Room and board:* Room and board charges vary according to board plan and housing facility.

Financial Aid *Financial aid deadline:* 5/15.

Applying *Options:* deferred entrance. *Application fee:* $35 Canadian dollars. *Required:* essay or personal statement, high school transcript, minimum 2.67 GPA, 3 letters of recommendation. *Required for some:* interview.

Freshman Application Contact Ms. Lorie Ward, Admissions Counselor, Atlantic Baptist University, Box 6004, Moncton, NB E1C 9L7, Canada. *Phone:* 506-858-8970. *Toll-free phone:* 888-YOU-N-ABU. *Fax:* 506-858-9694. *E-mail:* admissions@abu.nb.ca.

BETHANY BIBLE COLLEGE

Sussex, New Brunswick, Canada **www.bethany-ca.edu/**

- **Independent** 4-year, founded 1945, affiliated with Wesleyan Church
- **Small-town** 57-acre campus
- **Endowment** $94,150
- **Coed** 273 undergraduate students, 96% full-time, 55% women, 45% men
- **Moderately difficult** entrance level, 41% of applicants were admitted

Undergraduates 263 full-time, 10 part-time. Students come from 9 provinces and territories, 5 other countries, 44% are from out of state, 3% African American, 1% Asian American or Pacific Islander, 0.7% Hispanic American, 0.7% Native American, 4% transferred in, 77% live on campus. *Retention:* 79% of 2006 full-time freshmen returned.

Freshmen *Admission:* 232 applied, 96 admitted, 46 enrolled. *Average high school GPA:* 3.04. *Test scores:* SAT critical reading scores over 500: 72%; SAT math scores over 500: 29%; SAT writing scores over 500: 58%; ACT scores over 18: 100%; ACT scores over 24: 75%.

Faculty *Total:* 28, 39% full-time, 25% with terminal degrees. *Student/faculty ratio:* 17:1.

Majors Biblical studies; divinity/ministry; elementary education; music; religious education; religious studies.

Academics *Calendar:* semesters. *Degree:* certificates, diplomas, and bachelor's. *Special study options:* double majors, internships, part-time degree program, summer session for credit.

Computers on Campus 23 computers/terminals are available on campus for general student use.

Student Life *Housing:* on-campus residence required through senior year. *Options:* men-only, women-only. Campus housing is university owned. *Activities and organizations:* drama/theater group, choral group, Ministerial Association, Athletic Association, Student Mission Fellowship, Social Committee, Drama Club. *Campus security:* controlled dormitory access. *Student services:* personal/ psychological counseling.

Athletics *Intercollegiate sports:* basketball M/W, ice hockey M, soccer M/W, softball M/W, volleyball W. *Intramural sports:* basketball M/W, table tennis M/W, volleyball M/W.

Standardized Tests *Required for some:* SAT or ACT (for admission).

Costs (2008–09) *Comprehensive fee:* $13,000 Canadian dollars includes full-time tuition ($8300 Canadian dollars) and room and board ($4700 Canadian dollars). Part-time tuition: $275 Canadian dollars per credit hour.

Financial Aid *Financial aid deadline:* 10/15.

Applying *Options:* electronic application, early admission. *Application fee:* $20 Canadian dollars. *Required:* high school transcript, 2 letters of recommendation. *Recommended:* interview. *Application deadlines:* rolling (freshmen), rolling (transfers).

Freshman Application Contact Mrs. Kathy Shanks, Executive Director of Admissions, Bethany Bible College, 26 Western Street, Sussex, NB E4E 1E6, Canada. *Phone:* 506-432-4422. *Toll-free phone:* 888-432-4422. *Fax:* 506-432-4442. *E-mail:* shanksk@bbc.ca.

BISHOP'S UNIVERSITY

Sherbrooke, Quebec, Canada **www.ubishops.ca/**

- **Province-supported** comprehensive, founded 1843
- **Small-town** 500-acre campus
- **Endowment** $32.5 million
- **Coed** 2,233 undergraduate students, 81% full-time, 55% women, 45% men
- **Moderately difficult** entrance level

Undergraduates 1,808 full-time, 425 part-time. Students come from 12 provinces and territories, 40 other countries, 59% are from out of state, 30% live on campus.

Freshmen *Admission:* 589 admitted.

Faculty *Total:* 190, 66% full-time. *Student/faculty ratio:* 16:1.

Majors Accounting; art; arts management; art teacher education; biochemistry; biological and physical sciences; biology/biological sciences; biology teacher education; business administration and management; business/managerial economics; Canadian studies; chemistry; chemistry teacher education; classics and languages, literatures and linguistics; computer and information sciences; computer programming; computer science; computer teacher education; drama and dance teacher education; dramatic/theater arts; economics; education; elementary education; English; English/language arts teacher education; environmental studies; film/cinema studies; finance; fine/studio arts; French; French as a second/ foreign language (teaching); French language teacher education; geography; geography teacher education; German; gerontology; history; history teacher education; humanities; human resources management; international business/trade/ commerce; international relations and affairs; Italian; liberal arts and sciences and humanities related; liberal arts and sciences/liberal studies; literature; management information systems; marketing/marketing management; mathematics; mathematics teacher education; modern languages; music; music teacher education; natural sciences; neuroscience; philosophy; physics; physics teacher education; political science and government; psychology; religious studies; science teacher education; secondary education; social sciences; sociology; Spanish; Spanish language teacher education; Web page, digital/multimedia and information resources design; women's studies.

Academics *Calendar:* Canadian standard year. *Degrees:* certificates, bachelor's, and master's. *Special study options:* academic remediation for entering students, accelerated degree program, adult/continuing education programs, advanced placement credit, cooperative education, double majors, English as a second language, honors programs, independent study, internships, off-campus study, part-time degree program, services for LD students, student-designed majors, study abroad, summer session for credit. *Unusual degree programs:* 3-2 engineering with Universitè de Sherbrooke.

Computers on Campus 200 computers/terminals are available on campus for general student use. Students can access the following: campus intranet, computer help desk, free student e-mail accounts, online (class) registration, online (class) schedules, Web course management systems, individualized Web access. Campuswide network is available. Wireless service is available via entire campus.

Student Life *Housing options:* coed, women-only, disabled students. Campus housing is university owned. Freshman campus housing is guaranteed. *Activities and organizations:* drama/theater group, student-run newspaper, radio station, choral group, Big Buddies, The Campus, Psychology Club, Student Patrol, Inter-Varsity Christian Fellowship, national fraternities, national sororities. *Campus security:* 24-hour emergency response devices and patrols, student patrols, late-night transport/escort service, controlled dormitory access. *Student services:* health clinic, personal/psychological counseling, women's center, legal services.

Athletics Member CIS. *Intercollegiate sports:* basketball M/W, field hockey W (c), football M, golf M, ice hockey W (c), lacrosse M (c)/W (c), rock climbing M/W, skiing (downhill) M/W, soccer W, volleyball W (c). *Intramural sports:* badminton M/W, basketball M/W, cross-country running M/W, equestrian sports M (c)/W (c), football M, golf M/W, ice hockey M/W, riflery M (c)/W (c), soccer M/W, softball M/W, squash M/W, swimming and diving M/W, table tennis M/W, tennis M/W, ultimate Frisbee M/W, volleyball M/W, water polo M/W, weight lifting M/W.

Standardized Tests *Required:* SAT or ACT (for admission). *Recommended:* SAT Subject Tests (for admission).

Costs (2007–08) *Tuition:* province resident $1290 Canadian dollars full-time, $56 Canadian dollars per credit part-time; nonresident $2912 Canadian dollars full-time, $159 Canadian dollars per credit part-time; International tuition $2670 Canadian dollars full-time. *Required fees:* $811 Canadian dollars full-time. *Room and board:* $6460 Canadian dollars; room only: $4680 Canadian dollars.

Applying *Options:* electronic application. *Application fee:* $55 Canadian dollars. *Required:* high school transcript, minimum 3.0 GPA, birth certificate, copy of student visa. *Required for some:* essay or personal statement, 1 letter of recommendation. *Application deadlines:* 3/1 (freshmen), 3/1 (transfers). *Notification:* continuous until 8/31 (freshmen), continuous until 8/31 (transfers).

Freshman Application Contact Mr. Hans Rouleau, Coordinator of Liaison, Bishop's University, 2600 College Street, Sherbrooke, QC J1M 0C8, Canada. *Phone:* 819-822-9600 Ext. 2217. *Toll-free phone:* 877-822-8200. *Fax:* 819-822-9661. *E-mail:* liaison@ubishops.ca.

See page 2848 for the College Close-Up.

BRANDON UNIVERSITY

Brandon, Manitoba, Canada **www.brandonu.ca/**

Freshman Application Contact Murray Kerr, Director of Admissions, Brandon University, 270 18th Street, Brandon, MB R7A 6A9, Canada. *Phone:* 204-727-7352. *Toll-free phone:* 800-644-7644. *Fax:* 204-728-3221. *E-mail:* kerr@brandonu.ca.

BRIERCREST COLLEGE

Caronport, Saskatchewan, Canada **www.briercrest.ca/**

- **Independent interdenominational** 4-year, founded 1935, part of Briercrest Family of Schools
- **Rural** 300-acre campus
- **Endowment** $950,000
- **Coed**
- **Noncompetitive** entrance level

Faculty *Student/faculty ratio:* 16:1.

Academics *Calendar:* semesters. *Degrees:* certificates, diplomas, associate, and bachelor's.

Student Life *Campus security:* 24-hour patrols, controlled dormitory access.

Costs (2007–08) *Comprehensive fee:* $12,603 includes full-time tuition ($7360), mandatory fees ($50), and room and board ($5193). Part-time tuition: $230 per credit. *College room only:* $3009. Room and board charges vary according to board plan and housing facility.

Applying *Options:* electronic application, early admission, deferred entrance. *Application fee:* $35 Canadian dollars. *Required:* essay or personal statement, high school transcript, 2 letters of recommendation. *Required for some:* interview.

Freshman Application Contact Mr. Mike Benallick, Director of Admissions, Briercrest College, 510 College Drive, Caronport, SK S0H 0S0, Canada. *Phone:* 306-756-3200. *Toll-free phone:* 800-667-5199. *Fax:* 403-669-2024. *E-mail:* enrollment@briercrest.ca.

BRITISH COLUMBIA INSTITUTE OF TECHNOLOGY

Burnaby, British Columbia, Canada **www.bcit.ca/**

- **Province-supported** 4-year, founded 1964
- **Urban** 103-acre campus with easy access to Vancouver
- **Coed** 22,507 undergraduate students, 32% full-time, 43% women, 57% men
- **Moderately difficult** entrance level, 44% of applicants were admitted

Undergraduates 7,120 full-time, 15,387 part-time. 5% live on campus.

Freshmen *Admission:* 7,721 applied, 3,383 admitted.

Faculty *Total:* 1,359, 54% full-time.

Majors Accounting; accounting technology and bookkeeping; administrative assistant and secretarial science; aeronautical/aerospace engineering technology; aircraft powerplant technology; airframe mechanics and aircraft maintenance technology; allied health diagnostic, intervention, and treatment professions related; architectural drafting and CAD/CADD; architectural engineering technology; autobody/collision and repair technology; automobile/automotive mechanics technology; avionics maintenance technology; biology/biotechnology laboratory technician; biotechnology; business administration and management; cabinetmaking and millwork; cardiovascular technology; carpentry; chemical technology; civil drafting and CAD/CADD; civil engineering technology; clinical/medical laboratory technology; commercial and advertising art; computer science; computer systems analysis; construction engineering technology; construction management; construction trades related; critical care nursing; data processing and data processing technology; diesel mechanics technology; drafting and design technology; electrical and power transmission installation; electrical, electronic and communications engineering technology; engineering related; entrepreneurship; environmental engineering technology; environmental/environmental health engineering; environmental health; finance; finance and financial management services related; financial planning and services; fire protection and safety technology; forensic science and technology; forest/forest resources management; forestry technology; health and medical administrative services related; health/health care administration; health professions related; heating, air conditioning, ventilation and refrigeration maintenance technology; heavy equipment maintenance technology; human resources management; industrial mechanics and maintenance technology; industrial technology; information science/studies; interior design; international business/trade/commerce; machine tool technology; management science; marketing/marketing management; mechanical drafting and CAD/CADD; mechanical engineering/mechanical technology; medical administrative assistant and medical secretary; medical laboratory technology; medical radiologic technology; mining technology; naval architecture and marine engineering; nuclear medical technology; nursing administration; nursing (registered nurse training); nursing related; occupational and environmental health nursing; occupational health and industrial hygiene; operations management; pediatric nursing; perioperative/operating room and surgical nursing; petroleum technology; pipefitting and sprinkler fitting; plastics engineering technology; precision systems maintenance and repair technologies related; radio and television broadcasting technology; real estate; robotics technology; science technologies related; sheet metal technology; small engine mechanics and repair technology; survey technology; taxation; tourism and travel services management; trade and industrial teacher education; transportation and highway engineering; vehicle maintenance and repair technologies related; welding technology; wildlife and wildlands science and management.

Academics *Calendar:* quarters. *Degrees:* certificates, diplomas, associate, and bachelor's.

Computers on Campus Students can access the following: online (class) registration. Campuswide network is available.

Student Life *Housing options:* coed, men-only, women-only, disabled students. Campus housing is university owned. Freshman applicants given priority for college housing. *Activities and organizations:* student-run newspaper, radio station. *Campus security:* 24-hour emergency response devices and patrols, student patrols, late-night transport/escort service. *Student services:* health clinic, personal/psychological counseling.

Athletics *Intramural sports:* archery M (c)/W (c), basketball M/W, crew M (c)/W (c), football M/W, ice hockey M/W, rugby M (c)/W (c), soccer M/W, softball M/W, ultimate Frisbee M/W, volleyball M/W.

Costs (2007–08) *Tuition:* area resident $4567 Canadian dollars full-time; International tuition $15,491 Canadian dollars full-time. No tuition increase for student's term of enrollment. *Room only:* $3835 Canadian dollars. *Payment plan:* deferred payment.

Applying *Options:* electronic application. *Application fee:* $60 Canadian dollars. *Required:* high school transcript. *Required for some:* essay or personal statement, 2 letters of recommendation, interview.

Freshman Application Contact Ms. Anna Dosen, Supervisor of Admissions, British Columbia Institute of Technology, 3700 Willingdon Avenue, Burnaby, BC V5G 3H2, Canada. *Phone:* 604-432-8576. *Fax:* 604-431-6917.

BROCK UNIVERSITY

St. Catharines, Ontario, Canada **www.brocku.ca/**

- **Province-supported** university, founded 1964
- **Urban** 540-acre campus with easy access to Toronto
- **Coed** 15,747 undergraduate students
- **Moderately difficult** entrance level, 61% of applicants were admitted

Undergraduates Students come from 8 provinces and territories, 70 other countries, 14% live on campus.

Freshmen *Admission:* 19,742 applied, 12,000 admitted. *Average high school GPA:* 3.0.

Faculty *Total:* 577, 100% full-time. *Student/faculty ratio:* 30:1.

Majors Accounting; adult and continuing education; ancient/classical Greek; applied mathematics; archeology; art; biochemistry; biological and physical sciences; biology/biological sciences; biomedical sciences; biotechnology; business administration and management; business/commerce; business/corporate communications; business/managerial economics; Canadian studies; chemistry; communication disorders; communication/speech communication and rhetoric; computer engineering technology; computer programming; computer science; computer software engineering; dramatic/theater arts; economics; education; elementary education; English; English as a second/foreign language (teaching); film/cinema studies; finance; fine/studio arts; French; French studies; geography; geology/earth science; German; German studies; health/health care administration; health science; history; humanities; human resources management; information science/studies; interdisciplinary studies; international business/trade/commerce; international economics; Italian; Italian studies; kinesiology and exercise science; labor and industrial relations; liberal arts and sciences/liberal studies; linguistics; literature; marketing/marketing management; mass communication/media; mathematics; mathematics teacher education; movement therapy and movement education; music; music teacher education; neuroscience; nursing science; parks, recreation and leisure; philosophy; physical education teaching and coaching; physical sciences; physics; political science and government; psychology; public administration; public health; sales, distribution and marketing; science teacher education; secondary education; social sciences; sociology; Spanish; sport and fitness administration/management; statistics; tourism and travel services management; women's studies.

Academics *Calendar:* Canadian standard year. *Degrees:* certificates, bachelor's, master's, and doctoral. *Special study options:* academic remediation for entering students, accelerated degree program, adult/continuing education programs, advanced placement credit, cooperative education, double majors, English as a second language, honors programs, internships, part-time degree program, services for LD students, student-designed majors, study abroad, summer session for credit.

Computers on Campus 429 computers/terminals are available on campus for general student use. Students can access the following: computer help desk, free student e-mail accounts, online (class) grades, online (class) registration, online (class) schedules. Campuswide network is available. 100% of college-owned or -operated housing units are wired for high-speed Internet access. Wireless service is available via classrooms, computer centers, computer labs, learning centers, libraries, student centers.

Student Life *Housing options:* coed, disabled students. Campus housing is university owned and leased by the school. Freshman campus housing is guaranteed. *Activities and organizations:* drama/theater group, student-run newspaper, radio and television station, choral group, International Students Association, Brock University Student Association, Business Administration Association, Brock Christian Fellowship, Ace Brock. *Campus security:* 24-hour emergency response devices and patrols, student patrols, late-night transport/escort service, controlled dormitory access. *Student services:* health clinic, personal/psychological counseling, women's center.

Athletics Member CIS. *Intercollegiate sports:* baseball M, basketball M (s)/W (s), cheerleading M/W, crew M (s)/W (s), cross-country running M/W, fencing M/W, field hockey W (c), ice hockey M (s)/W (s), lacrosse M, rugby M/W, soccer M (s)/W (s), swimming and diving M/W, volleyball W, wrestling M (s)/W (s). *Intramural sports:* badminton M/W, basketball M/W, football M/W, ice hockey M/W, skiing (downhill) M/W, soccer M/W, softball M/W, swimming and diving M/W, ultimate Frisbee M/W, volleyball M/W, water polo M/W.

Standardized Tests *Required:* SAT or ACT (for admission).

Costs (2007–08) *Tuition:* International tuition $12,519 Canadian dollars full-time. Full-time tuition and fees vary according to course load. Part-time tuition and fees vary according to course load. *Room and board:* $7760 Canadian dollars; room only: $4120 Canadian dollars. Room and board charges vary according to board plan and housing facility. *Payment plan:* installment. *Waivers:* senior citizens and employees or children of employees.

Financial Aid Of all full-time matriculated undergraduates who enrolled in 2006, 80 state and other part-time jobs.

Applying *Options:* electronic application. *Application fee:* $115 Canadian dollars. *Required:* high school transcript, minimum 3.0 GPA, letters of recommendation. *Required for some:* essay or personal statement, audition, portfolio. *Application deadlines:* 4/1 (freshmen), 4/1 (transfers). *Notification:* continuous (freshmen), continuous (transfers).

Freshman Application Contact Mrs. Lynn Thompson-Dovi, International Admissions Officer, Brock University, 500 Glenridge Avenue, St. Catharines, ON L2S 3A1, Canada. *Phone:* 905-688-5550 Ext. 3431. *Fax:* 905-688-5488. *E-mail:* admissns@brocku.ca.

CANADIAN MENNONITE UNIVERSITY

Winnipeg, Manitoba, Canada **www.cmu.ca/**

- **Independent Mennonite** comprehensive, founded 1943
- **Urban** 44-acre campus
- **Coed** 432 undergraduate students, 81% full-time, 58% women, 42% men
- **Moderately difficult** entrance level, 95% of applicants were admitted

Undergraduates 349 full-time, 83 part-time. Students come from 7 provinces and territories, 6 other countries, 30% are from out of state, 45% live on campus. *Retention:* 65% of 2006 full-time freshmen returned.

Freshmen *Admission:* 280 applied, 265 admitted, 179 enrolled. *Average high school GPA:* 3.28.

Faculty *Total:* 30, 77% full-time, 87% with terminal degrees. *Student/faculty ratio:* 15:1.

Majors Biblical studies; biology/biological sciences; computer science; conducting; development economics and international development; divinity/ministry; economics; English; geography; history; international relations and affairs; mathematics; microbiology; missionary studies and missiology; music; music history, literature, and theory; musicology and ethnomusicology; music performance; music theory and composition; music therapy; pastoral studies/counseling; peace studies and conflict resolution; philosophy; piano and organ; political science and government; pre-nursing studies; psychology; religious education; religious studies; theology; voice and opera; youth ministry.

Academics *Calendar:* semesters. *Degree:* certificates, diplomas, and bachelor's. *Special study options:* academic remediation for entering students, adult/continuing education programs, double majors, independent study, internships, off-campus study, part-time degree program, services for LD students, study abroad.

Computers on Campus 40 computers/terminals are available on campus for general student use. Campuswide network is available.

Student Life *Housing options:* coed, men-only, women-only. Campus housing is university owned. Freshman applicants given priority for college housing. *Activities and organizations:* drama/theater group, student-run newspaper, choral group, Oratorio Choir, Fellowship Groups, Christian Emphasis Committee, Peace and Social Concerns, Witness and Service Committee. *Campus security:* student patrols, late-night transport/escort service, controlled dormitory access, combination door locks to sections of the campus. *Student services:* personal/psychological counseling.

Athletics *Intercollegiate sports:* basketball M/W, ice hockey M, soccer M/W, volleyball M/W. *Intramural sports:* badminton M/W, basketball M/W, ice hockey M/W, table tennis M/W, volleyball M/W.

Costs (2007–08) *Comprehensive fee:* $10,533 Canadian dollars includes full-time tuition ($5130 Canadian dollars), mandatory fees ($465 Canadian dollars), and room and board ($4938 Canadian dollars). Part-time tuition: $171 Canadian dollars per credit hour. International tuition: $8980 Canadian dollars full-time. *College room only:* $1694 Canadian dollars. Room and board charges vary according to board plan and housing facility. *Payment plan:* installment. *Waivers:* senior citizens and employees or children of employees.

Financial Aid *Financial aid deadline:* 9/30.

Applying *Options:* electronic application, deferred entrance. *Application fee:* $35 Canadian dollars. *Required:* high school transcript, minimum 2.0 GPA. *Required for some:* essay or personal statement, letters of recommendation. *Recommended:* letters of recommendation. *Application deadlines:* 8/28 (freshmen), 8/28 (transfers). *Notification:* continuous until 9/1 (freshmen), continuous until 9/1 (transfers).

Freshman Application Contact Mr. Abe Bergen, Director of Enrollment Services, Canadian Mennonite University, 500 Shaftesbury Boulevard, Winnipeg, MB R3P 2N2, Canada. *Phone:* 204-487-3300 Ext. 652. *Toll-free phone:* 877-231-4570. *Fax:* 204-487-3858. *E-mail:* cu@cmu.ca.

CAPE BRETON UNIVERSITY

Sydney, Nova Scotia, Canada **www.capebretonu.ca/**

- **Province-supported** comprehensive, founded 1974
- **Small-town** 57-hectare campus
- **Endowment** $15.0 million
- **Coed**
- **Moderately difficult** entrance level

Faculty *Student/faculty ratio:* 16:1.

Academics *Calendar:* Canadian standard year. *Degrees:* certificates, diplomas, bachelor's, master's, and postbachelor's certificates.

Student Life *Campus security:* 24-hour patrols, controlled dormitory access, security for social events, escort service.

Athletics Member CIS.

Costs (2007–08) *Tuition:* nonresident $5660 full-time; International tuition $11,320 full-time. Full-time tuition and fees vary according to course load and degree level. Part-time tuition and fees vary according to course load and degree level.

Applying *Options:* electronic application. *Application fee:* $35 Canadian dollars. *Required:* high school transcript. *Required for some:* essay or personal statement, 3 letters of recommendation, interview.

Freshman Application Contact Ms. Cheryl Livingstone, Admissions Officer, Cape Breton University, PO Box 5300, Sydney, NS B1P 6L2, Canada. *Phone:* 902-563-1166. *Toll-free phone:* 888-959-9995. *Fax:* 902-563-1371. *E-mail:* admissions@cbu.ca.

CARLETON UNIVERSITY

Ottawa, Ontario, Canada **www.carleton.ca/**

Freshman Application Contact Ms. Jean Mullan, Director, Undergraduate Recruitment Office, Carleton University, 1125 Colonel By Drive, Ottawa, ON K1S 5B6, Canada. *Phone:* 613-520-3663. *Toll-free phone:* 888-354-4414. *E-mail:* liaison@admissions.carleton.ca.

COLLÈGE DOMINICAIN DE PHILOSOPHIE ET DE THÉOLOGIE

Ottawa, Ontario, Canada **www.collegedominicain.ca/**

- **Independent Roman Catholic** comprehensive, founded 1909
- **Urban** campus
- **Endowment** $7.5 million
- **Coed** 174 undergraduate students, 41% full-time, 57% women, 43% men
- **Noncompetitive** entrance level, 97% of applicants were admitted

Undergraduates 71 full-time, 103 part-time. Students come from 1 other province, 12 other countries, 0.6% African American, 0.6% Asian American or Pacific Islander, 2% Hispanic American, 9% international, 4% transferred in, 12% live on campus. *Retention:* 84% of 2006 full-time freshmen returned.

Freshmen *Admission:* 60 applied, 58 admitted, 42 enrolled.

Faculty *Total:* 52, 67% full-time, 62% with terminal degrees. *Student/faculty ratio:* 4:1.

Majors Pastoral studies/counseling; philosophy; theology.

Academics *Calendar:* semesters. *Degrees:* certificates, bachelor's, master's, and doctoral. *Special study options:* accelerated degree program, part-time degree program, summer session for credit.

Computers on Campus 4 computers/terminals are available on campus for general student use. Students can access the following: online (class) schedules.

Student Life *Housing options:* men-only, disabled students. Campus housing is university owned and is provided by a third party. *Activities and organizations:* Association Etudiant College Dominicain. *Campus security:* late-night transport/escort service.

Costs (2008–09) *Comprehensive fee:* $9890 Canadian dollars includes full-time tuition ($3170 Canadian dollars), mandatory fees ($120 Canadian dollars), and room and board ($6600 Canadian dollars). Part-time tuition: $130 Canadian dollars per credit. International tuition: $7000 Canadian dollars full-time. *Required fees:* $85 Canadian dollars per term part-time.

Applying *Application fee:* $35 Canadian dollars. *Required:* high school transcript. *Required for some:* interview. *Recommended:* minimum 3.0 GPA. *Application deadlines:* 6/1 (freshmen), 3/1 (out-of-state freshmen), rolling (transfers).

Freshman Application Contact Fr. Hervé Tremblay OJ, Registrar, Collège Dominicain de Philosophie et de Théologie, 96 Empress Avenue, Ottawa, ON K1R 7G3, Canada. *Phone:* 613-233-5696 Ext. 308. *Fax:* 613-233-6064. *E-mail:* registraire@collegedominicain.ca.

COLLEGE OF EMMANUEL AND ST. CHAD

Saskatoon, Saskatchewan, Canada

www.usask.ca/stu/emmanuel/

- **Independent Episcopal** comprehensive, founded 1879
- **Urban** campus
- **Coed** 20 students
- **Noncompetitive** entrance level, 100% of applicants were admitted

Freshmen *Admission:* 4 applied, 4 admitted.

Faculty *Total:* 5, 80% full-time, 100% with terminal degrees. *Student/faculty ratio:* 8:1.

Majors Theology.

Academics *Calendar:* Canadian standard year. *Degrees:* bachelor's and master's. *Special study options:* academic remediation for entering students, adult/continuing education programs, cooperative education, distance learning, internships, off-campus study, part-time degree program, services for LD students, summer session for credit.

Student Life *Housing:* college housing not available. *Campus security:* 24-hour emergency response devices and patrols, late-night transport/escort service.

Costs (2007–08) *Tuition:* $5500 full-time, $550 per course part-time. Full-time tuition and fees vary according to course level, course load, and degree level. Part-time tuition and fees vary according to course level, course load, and degree level. *Required fees:* $600 full-time.

Applying *Application fee:* $50 Canadian dollars. *Required:* essay or personal statement, high school transcript, 3 letters of recommendation, interview. *Application deadline:* 6/30 (freshmen). *Notification:* 8/1 (freshmen).

Freshman Application Contact Ms. Colleen Walker, Registrar, College of Emmanuel and St. Chad, 1337 College Drive, Saskatoon, SK S7N0W6, Canada. *Phone:* 306-975-1558. *Fax:* 306-934-2683. *E-mail:* colleen.walker@usadk.ca.

COLLÈGE UNIVERSITAIRE DE SAINT-BONIFACE

Saint-Boniface, Manitoba, Canada

COLUMBIA BIBLE COLLEGE

Abbotsford, British Columbia, Canada **www.columbiabc.edu/**

Freshman Application Contact Ms. Esther Martens, Academic Executive Assistant, Columbia Bible College, 2940 Clearbrook Road, Abbotsford, BC V2T 2Z8. *Phone:* 604-853-3358. *Toll-free phone:* 800-283-0881. *Fax:* 604-853-3063. *E-mail:* esther.martens@columbiabc.edu.

Concordia University

Montréal, Quebec, Canada **www.concordia.ca/**

- **Province-supported** university, founded 1974, part of Province of Quebec University System
- **Urban** 52-acre campus
- **Endowment** $77.8 million
- **Coed** 27,437 undergraduate students, 62% full-time, 51% women, 49% men
- **Moderately difficult** entrance level, 67% of applicants were admitted

Undergraduates 17,133 full-time, 10,304 part-time. Students come from 13 provinces and territories, 160 other countries, 2% live on campus.

Freshmen *Admission:* 15,622 applied, 10,391 admitted, 4,947 enrolled.

Faculty *Total:* 1,966, 47% full-time. *Student/faculty ratio:* 19:1.

Majors Accounting; actuarial science; adult and continuing education; American native/native American education; ancient studies; animation, interactive technology, video graphics and special effects; anthropology; applied economics; Arabic; archeology; art history, criticism and conservation; art teacher education; Asian studies (South); Asian studies (Southeast); biology/biological sciences; business administration and management; cell and molecular biology; ceramic arts and ceramics; chemistry; Chinese; cinematography and film/video production; city/urban, community and regional planning; civil engineering; classics and languages, literatures and linguistics; communication and journalism related; communication and media related; communication/speech communication and rhetoric; computer engineering; computer science; computer software engineering; computer systems analysis; construction engineering; creative writing; cultural studies; dance; dramatic/theater arts; ecology; economics; education; electrical, electronics and communications engineering; elementary education; English; English as a second/foreign language (teaching); English literature (British and Commonwealth); environmental science; film/cinema studies; finance; fine/studio arts; French; geography; German; history; humanities; human resources management; industrial engineering; intercultural/multicultural and diversity studies; intermedia/multimedia; international business/trade/commerce; Italian; jazz/jazz studies; Jewish/Judaic studies; journalism; kindergarten/preschool education; kinesiology and exercise science; language interpretation and translation; linguistics; management information systems; marketing/marketing management; mass communication/media; mathematical statistics and probability; mathematics; mechanical engineering; music; music performance; music theory and composition; neuroscience; operations management; painting; parks, recreation and leisure; philosophy; photography; physics; playwriting and screenwriting; political science and government; printmaking; psychology; public administration; religious studies; sculpture; social sciences related; sociology; Spanish; statistics; theological and ministerial studies related; theology; therapeutic recreation; urban studies/affairs; visual and performing arts; western civilization; women's studies.

Academics *Calendar:* trimesters. *Degrees:* certificates, diplomas, bachelor's, master's, doctoral, and postbachelor's certificates. *Special study options:* academic remediation for entering students, accelerated degree program, adult/continuing education programs, advanced placement credit, cooperative education, distance learning, double majors, English as a second language, external degree program, honors programs, independent study, internships, off-campus study, part-time degree program, services for LD students, student-designed majors, study abroad, summer session for credit.

Computers on Campus 220 computers/terminals are available on campus for general student use. Students can access the following: campus intranet, computer help desk, free student e-mail accounts, online (class) grades, online (class) registration, online (class) schedules, specialized software applications. Campus-wide network is available. 67% of college-owned or -operated housing units are wired for high-speed Internet access. Wireless service is available via entire campus.

Student Life *Housing options:* coed, disabled students. Campus housing is university owned. Freshman applicants given priority for college housing. *Activities and organizations:* drama/theater group, student-run newspaper, radio and television station, choral group, ethnic clubs, student media, departmental clubs, national fraternities, national sororities. *Campus security:* 24-hour emergency response devices and patrols, student patrols, late-night transport/escort service, controlled dormitory access. *Student services:* health clinic, personal/psychological counseling, women's center, legal services.

Athletics Member CIS. *Intercollegiate sports:* baseball M (c), basketball M (s)/W (s), cross-country running M (c)/W (c), football M (s), golf M (c), ice hockey M (s)/W (s), rugby M (s)/W (s), skiing (downhill) M (c)/W (c), soccer M (s)/W (s), wrestling M (s)/W (s). *Intramural sports:* badminton M/W, basketball M/W, cross-country running M/W, ice hockey M/W, lacrosse W, soccer M/W, ultimate Frisbee M/W, volleyball M/W.

Costs (2008–09) *Tuition:* $62 per credit part-time; province resident $1868 full-time, $179 per credit part-time; nonresident $5378 full-time. *Room only:* $3968.

Financial Aid Of all full-time matriculated undergraduates who enrolled in 2006, 349 state and other part-time jobs (averaging $1286). *Financial aid deadline:* 3/31.

Applying *Options:* electronic application. *Application fee:* $75 Canadian dollars. *Required:* high school transcript, minimum 2.76 GPA. *Required for some:* essay or personal statement, 2 letters of recommendation, interview. *Application deadlines:* 3/1 (freshmen), 3/1 (transfers), 2/1 (early action). *Notification:* continuous until 9/1 (freshmen), continuous until 9/1 (transfers).

Freshman Application Contact Ms. Assunta Fargnoli, Assistant Registrar, Concordia University, Admissions Application Center, PO Box 2900, Montréal, QC H3G 2S2, Canada. *Phone:* 514-848-2424 Ext. 2628. *Fax:* 514-848-2621. *E-mail:* fargnoli@alcor.concordia.ca.

Concordia University College of Alberta

Edmonton, Alberta, Canada **www.concordia.ab.ca/**

- **Independent Lutheran** 4-year, founded 1921
- **Urban** 15-acre campus
- **Coed**
- **Moderately difficult** entrance level

Faculty *Student/faculty ratio:* 18:1.

Academics *Calendar:* semesters. *Degrees:* certificates, diplomas, bachelor's, and postbachelor's certificates.

Student Life *Campus security:* 24-hour patrols, late-night transport/escort service.

Costs (2007–08) *Comprehensive fee:* $11,048 includes full-time tuition ($5900), mandatory fees ($418), and room and board ($4730). Full-time tuition and fees vary according to class time, course load, program, and reciprocity agreements. Part-time tuition: $420 per course. Part-time tuition and fees vary according to class time, course load, program, and reciprocity agreements. International tuition: $8816 full-time. *Required fees:* $23 per credit part-time. *Room and board:* Room and board charges vary according to board plan.

Applying *Options:* electronic application, early admission. *Required:* high school transcript, minimum 2.0 GPA. *Required for some:* essay or personal statement, 2 letters of recommendation, interview.

Freshman Application Contact Admissions and Financial Aid Office, Concordia University College of Alberta, 7128 Ada Boulevard, Edmonton, AB T5B 4E4, Canada. *Phone:* 780-479-9224. *Toll-free phone:* 866-479-5200. *Fax:* 780-378-8460. *E-mail:* admits@concordia.ab.ca.

Dalhousie University

Halifax, Nova Scotia, Canada **www.dal.ca/**

- **Province-supported** university, founded 1818
- **Urban** 80-acre campus
- **Endowment** $230.3 million
- **Coed**
- **Moderately difficult** entrance level

Faculty *Student/faculty ratio:* 14:1.

Academics *Calendar:* semesters. *Degrees:* diplomas, bachelor's, master's, doctoral, first professional, and postbachelor's certificates.

Student Life *Campus security:* 24-hour emergency response devices and patrols, student patrols, late-night transport/escort service, controlled dormitory access.

Athletics Member CIS.

Standardized Tests *Required:* SAT (for admission).

Costs (2007–08) *Tuition:* province resident $6800 Canadian dollars full-time; International tuition $13,250 Canadian dollars full-time. *Required fees:* $782 Canadian dollars full-time. *Room and board:* $7575 Canadian dollars.

Applying *Options:* electronic application, early decision, deferred entrance. *Application fee:* $45 Canadian dollars. *Required:* high school transcript, minimum 3.0 GPA. *Required for some:* essay or personal statement, 1 letter of recommendation, interview, minimum 1100 comprehensive score on SAT for U.S. applicants.

Freshman Application Contact Mr. Terry Gallivan, Associate Director of Admissions and Recruitment, Dalhousie University, Office of the Registrar, Halifax, NS B3H 4H6. *Phone:* 902-494-2148. *Fax:* 902-494-1630. *E-mail:* admissions@dal.ca.

EMMANUEL BIBLE COLLEGE

Kitchener, Ontario, Canada **www.ebcollege.on.ca/**

Freshman Application Contact Mrs. Ruth Scott, Recruitment Officer, Emmanuel Bible College, 100 Fergus Avenue, Kitchener, ON N2A 2H2, Canada. *Phone:* 519-894-8900 Ext. 30.

HEC MONTREAL

Montréal, Quebec, Canada **www.hec.ca/**

- **Province-supported** comprehensive, founded 1910, part of Universite de Montreal
- **Urban** 9-acre campus
- **Coed** 9,557 undergraduate students, 49% full-time, 50% women, 50% men
- **Moderately difficult** entrance level, 57% of applicants were admitted

Undergraduates 4,677 full-time, 4,880 part-time. Students come from 7 provinces and territories, 49 other countries, 0.5% are from out of state. *Retention:* 99% of 2006 full-time freshmen returned.

Freshmen *Admission:* 2,866 applied, 1,643 admitted, 895 enrolled.

Faculty *Total:* 629, 41% full-time, 36% with terminal degrees. *Student/faculty ratio:* 22:1.

Majors Accounting; applied economics; business administration and management; business/commerce; business/managerial economics; business statistics; computer management; computer systems analysis; consumer merchandising/retailing management; entrepreneurship; finance; human resources management; information science/studies; international business/trade/commerce; international economics; international finance; management information systems; management science; marketing/marketing management; sales, distribution and marketing.

Academics *Calendar:* trimesters. *Degrees:* certificates, bachelor's, master's, doctoral, and postbachelor's certificates. *Special study options:* academic remediation for entering students, adult/continuing education programs, English as a second language, honors programs, independent study, off-campus study, student-designed majors, study abroad, summer session for credit.

Computers on Campus 250 computers/terminals are available on campus for general student use. Students can access the following: campus intranet, computer help desk, free student e-mail accounts, online (class) grades, online (class) registration, online (class) schedules, Corporate calendar. Campuswide network is available. Wireless service is available via classrooms, libraries, student centers.

Student Life *Housing options:* Campus housing is provided by a third party. *Activities and organizations:* student-run newspaper, radio station, AEMBA (MBA Students' Association), AGEMSCPHD (MSc & PhD Students' Association), AEDESS (Post—Bachelor's Certificate Students' Association), AEHEC (BBA Students' Association), AEPC (Certificate Students' Association). *Campus security:* 24-hour emergency response devices and patrols. *Student services:* health clinic, personal/psychological counseling, legal services.

Costs (2007–08) *Tuition:* province resident $1768 Canadian dollars full-time, $59 Canadian dollars per credit part-time; nonresident $5141 Canadian dollars full-time, $171 Canadian dollars per credit part-time; International tuition $12,226 Canadian dollars full-time. Full-time tuition and fees vary according to program. Part-time tuition and fees vary according to program. *Required fees:* $901 Canadian dollars full-time, $25 Canadian dollars per credit part-time, $68 Canadian dollars per term part-time. *Room only:* $2955 Canadian dollars. Room and board charges vary according to board plan and housing facility. *Waivers:* employees or children of employees.

Financial Aid Of all full-time matriculated undergraduates who enrolled in 2006, 3,001 applied for aid, 2,523 were judged to have need.

Applying *Options:* electronic application, deferred entrance. *Application fee:* $75 Canadian dollars. *Required:* high school transcript. *Required for some:* cote de rendement collégial. *Application deadlines:* 3/1 (freshmen), 2/15 (out-of-state freshmen). *Notification:* 3/30 (freshmen), 4/30 (out-of-state freshmen).

Freshman Application Contact Sylvie Deschamps, Office of the Registrar, HEC Montreal, 3000 chemin de la Côte-Sainte-Catherine, Montréal, QC H3T 2A7. *Phone:* 514-340-6151. *Fax:* 514-340-5640. *E-mail:* admission.info@hec.ca.

HERITAGE BAPTIST COLLEGE AND HERITAGE THEOLOGICAL SEMINARY

Cambridge, Ontario, Canada **www.heritage-theo.edu/**

- **Independent Baptist** comprehensive, founded 1993
- **Urban** 7-acre campus with easy access to Toronto
- **Endowment** $478.1 million
- **Coed** 211 undergraduate students, 48% full-time, 42% women, 58% men
- **Noncompetitive** entrance level, 100% of applicants were admitted

Undergraduates 101 full-time, 110 part-time. Students come from 6 provinces and territories, 6 other countries, 3% are from out of state, 14% transferred in, 37% live on campus. *Retention:* 71% of 2006 full-time freshmen returned.

Freshmen *Admission:* 48 applied, 48 admitted, 18 enrolled.

Faculty *Total:* 29, 28% full-time, 34% with terminal degrees. *Student/faculty ratio:* 13:1.

Majors Biblical studies; religious education; religious/sacred music; theology.

Academics *Calendar:* Canadian standard year. *Degrees:* certificates, diplomas, bachelor's, and master's (artist diploma). *Special study options:* advanced placement credit, distance learning, double majors, independent study, internships, off-campus study, part-time degree program, summer session for credit.

Computers on Campus 6 computers/terminals and 6 ports are available on campus for general student use. Campuswide network is available. Wireless service is available via classrooms, computer labs, libraries.

Student Life *Housing options:* men-only, women-only. Campus housing is university owned. Freshman applicants given priority for college housing. *Activities and organizations:* drama/theater group, student-run newspaper, choral group. *Campus security:* controlled dormitory access. *Student services:* health clinic, personal/psychological counseling, legal services.

Athletics *Intercollegiate sports:* basketball M/W, volleyball M/W. *Intramural sports:* ice hockey M, soccer M/W.

Costs (2007–08) *Comprehensive fee:* $11,290 includes full-time tuition ($7040), mandatory fees ($90), and room and board ($4160). Part-time tuition: $220 per credit hour. *Required fees:* $25 per term part-time. *Payment plans:* installment, deferred payment. *Waivers:* senior citizens and employees or children of employees.

Financial Aid Of all full-time matriculated undergraduates who enrolled in 2006, 12 state and other part-time jobs.

Applying *Options:* deferred entrance. *Application fee:* $50 Canadian dollars. *Required:* essay or personal statement, high school transcript, audition. *Required for some:* audition. *Application deadlines:* 9/1 (freshmen), 9/1 (transfers). *Notification:* 4/1 (transfers).

Freshman Application Contact Mr. Mark Walther, Assistant Dean of Students, Heritage Baptist College and Heritage Theological Seminary, 175 Holiday Inn Drive, Cambridge, ON N3C 3T2, Canada. *Phone:* 519-651-2869 Ext. 251. *Fax:* 519-651-2870. *E-mail:* mwalther@heritagecollege.net.

HORIZON COLLEGE & SEMINARY

Saskatoon, Saskatchewan, Canada **www.horizon.edu/**

- **Independent** 4-year, founded 1930, affiliated with Pentecostal Assemblies of Canada, administratively affiliated with University of Saskatchewan
- **Urban** 5-acre campus
- **Coed** 50 undergraduate students, 92% full-time, 28% women, 72% men
- **Minimally difficult** entrance level, 84% of applicants were admitted

Undergraduates 46 full-time, 4 part-time. Students come from 4 provinces and territories, 1 other country, 40% are from out of state, 3% African American, 3% Native American, 3% international, 2% transferred in, 57% live on campus. *Retention:* 80% of 2006 full-time freshmen returned.

Freshmen *Admission:* 19 applied, 16 admitted, 16 enrolled.

Faculty *Total:* 14, 7% full-time, 100% with terminal degrees. *Student/faculty ratio:* 10:1.

Majors Biblical studies; Christian studies; missionary studies and missiology; pastoral counseling and specialized ministries related; pastoral studies/counseling; religious/sacred music; theological and ministerial studies related; theology; theology and religious vocations related; youth ministry.

Academics *Calendar:* semesters. *Degree:* certificates, diplomas, and bachelor's. *Special study options:* academic remediation for entering students, distance learning, independent study, internships, part-time degree program, student-designed majors, study abroad.

Computers on Campus 30 computers/terminals are available on campus for general student use. Students can access the following: campus intranet, computer help desk, online (class) schedules. Campuswide network is available. 100% of college-owned or -operated housing units are wired for high-speed Internet access. Wireless service is available via entire campus.

Student Life *Housing options:* Campus housing is university owned. Freshman campus housing is guaranteed. *Activities and organizations:* drama/theater group, choral group. *Campus security:* 24-hour emergency response devices, late-night transport/escort service. *Student services:* personal/psychological counseling.

Athletics *Intramural sports:* basketball M/W, ice hockey M, soccer M/W, volleyball M/W.

Costs (2008–09) *Comprehensive fee:* $10,628 includes full-time tuition ($5440), mandatory fees ($596), and room and board ($4592). Part-time tuition: $170 per credit hour.

Applying *Options:* electronic application, deferred entrance. *Application fee:* $45 Canadian dollars. *Required:* essay or personal statement, high school transcript, 3 letters of recommendation. *Required for some:* interview. *Application deadline:* 9/15 (freshmen).

Freshman Application Contact Ms. Judy Heyer, Assistant Registrar, Horizon College & Seminary, 1303 Jackson Avenue, Saskatoon, SK S7H 2M9, Canada. *Phone:* 306-374-6655. *Toll-free phone:* 877-374.6655. *Fax:* 306-373-6968. *E-mail:* admissions@horizon.edu.

THE KING'S UNIVERSITY COLLEGE

Edmonton, Alberta, Canada **www.kingsu.ca/**

- **Independent interdenominational** 4-year, founded 1979
- **Suburban** 20-acre campus
- **Endowment** $1.5 million
- **Coed** 511 undergraduate students, 91% full-time, 59% women, 41% men
- **Moderately difficult** entrance level, 86% of applicants were admitted

Undergraduates 466 full-time, 45 part-time. Students come from 7 provinces and territories, 10 other countries, 16% are from out of state, 15% transferred in, 26% live on campus. *Retention:* 66% of 2006 full-time freshmen returned.

Freshmen *Admission:* 235 applied, 201 admitted, 119 enrolled. *Average high school GPA:* 3.3.

Faculty *Total:* 95, 35% full-time, 83% with terminal degrees. *Student/faculty ratio:* 11:1.

Majors Biology/biological sciences; business administration and management; chemistry; computer science; elementary education; English; environmental studies; history; music; philosophy; psychology; social sciences; sociology; theology.

Academics *Calendar:* Canadian standard year. *Degrees:* certificates, diplomas, bachelor's, and postbachelor's certificates. *Special study options:* adult/continuing education programs, advanced placement credit, double majors, English as a second language, independent study, internships, off-campus study, part-time degree program, services for LD students, study abroad, summer session for credit. *Unusual degree programs:* 3-2 elementary education.

Computers on Campus 69 computers/terminals are available on campus for general student use. Students can access the following: campus intranet, computer help desk, free student e-mail accounts, online (class) grades, online (class) registration, online (class) schedules. Campuswide network is available. 100% of college-owned or -operated housing units are wired for high-speed Internet access. Wireless service is available via entire campus.

Student Life *Housing options:* coed, women-only. Campus housing is university owned. Freshman applicants given priority for college housing. *Activities and organizations:* drama/theater group, student-run newspaper, choral group, Action and Awareness, The King's Players (drama club), Chamber and Concert Choirs, King's Science Society, Hockey Club. *Campus security:* 24-hour emergency response devices, student patrols, controlled dormitory access. *Student services:* personal/psychological counseling.

Athletics *Intercollegiate sports:* basketball M (s)/W (s), soccer M (s)/W (s), volleyball M (s)/W (s). *Intramural sports:* basketball M/W, ice hockey M, volleyball M/W.

Costs (2008–09) *Comprehensive fee:* $13,246 includes full-time tuition ($8091), mandatory fees ($355), and room and board ($4800). Part-time tuition: $261 per credit. International tuition: $9591 full-time. *Required fees:* $89 per term part-time. *College room only:* $2520.

Financial Aid Of all full-time matriculated undergraduates who enrolled in 2006, 70 state and other part-time jobs. *Financial aid deadline:* 3/31.

Applying *Options:* electronic application. *Application fee:* $50 Canadian dollars. *Required:* high school transcript, minimum 2.0 GPA, 1 letter of recommendation. *Required for some:* essay or personal statement, interview. *Application deadlines:* rolling (freshmen), rolling (transfers). *Notification:* 8/15 (freshmen), 8/15 (transfers).

Freshman Application Contact Mr. Glenn Keeler, Registrar/Director of Admissions, The King's University College, 9125-50 Street, Edmonton, AB T6B 2H3. *Phone:* 780-465-3500 Ext. 8035. *Toll-free phone:* 800-661-8582. *Fax:* 780-465-3534. *E-mail:* admissions@kingsu.ca.

KWANTLEN UNIVERSITY COLLEGE

Surrey, British Columbia, Canada **www.kwantlen.ca/**

- **Province-supported** 4-year, founded 1981
- **Urban** campus with easy access to Vancouver
- **Endowment** $7.3 million
- **Coed** 12,280 undergraduate students, 67% full-time, 59% women, 41% men
- 95% of applicants were admitted

Undergraduates 8,212 full-time, 4,068 part-time. Students come from 99 other countries. *Retention:* 65% of 2006 full-time freshmen returned.

Freshmen *Admission:* 9,119 applied, 8,664 admitted.

Faculty *Total:* 596. *Student/faculty ratio:* 35:1.

Majors Accounting; anthropology; community psychology; criminology; English; English composition; entrepreneurship; fashion/apparel design; geography; geological and earth sciences/geosciences related; graphic design; history; information technology; interior design; journalism; music; music theory and composition; nursing (registered nurse training); philosophy; piano and organ; political science and government; psychology; social psychology; social sciences; sociology; violin, viola, guitar and other stringed instruments; voice and opera.

Academics *Calendar:* semesters. *Degrees:* certificates, diplomas, associate, bachelor's, and postbachelor's certificates (profile includes information from Langley, Richmond, Newton and Surrey campuses). *Special study options:* academic remediation for entering students, accelerated degree program, adult/continuing education programs, advanced placement credit, cooperative education, distance learning, double majors, English as a second language, honors programs, independent study, internships, part-time degree program, services for LD students, study abroad, summer session for credit.

Computers on Campus 1,158 computers/terminals are available on campus for general student use. Students can access the following: campus intranet, computer help desk, free student e-mail accounts, online (class) grades, online (class) registration, online (class) schedules. Campuswide network is available. Wireless service is available via entire campus.

Student Life *Housing:* college housing not available. *Activities and organizations:* student-run newspaper, choral group, academic clubs, Rowing Club, Cultural Diversity Club, Buddy Language Club, Global Villagers. *Campus security:* 24-hour emergency response devices and patrols. *Student services:* health clinic, personal/psychological counseling, women's center.

Athletics *Intercollegiate sports:* badminton M/W, baseball M/W, basketball M/W, golf M/W, soccer M/W. *Intramural sports:* badminton M/W, basketball M/W, soccer M/W, volleyball M/W.

Costs (2007–08) *Tuition:* province resident $3428 Canadian dollars full-time, $114 Canadian dollars per credit part-time; International tuition $12,000 Canadian dollars full-time. Full-time tuition and fees vary according to course load and program. Part-time tuition and fees vary according to course load and program. *Required fees:* $592 Canadian dollars full-time, $6 Canadian dollars per credit part-time. *Waivers:* employees or children of employees.

Applying *Options:* electronic application, early admission, early decision, early action. *Application fee:* $40 Canadian dollars. *Required:* high school transcript. *Required for some:* essay or personal statement, minimum 2.0 GPA, letters of recommendation, interview, portfolio, external testing, certain levels of certification (i.e.—first aid). *Recommended:* high school transcript. *Application deadlines:* 6/30 (freshmen), 5/30 (out-of-state freshmen), 6/30 (transfers). *Early decision deadline:* 2/28. *Notification:* continuous until 6/30 (freshmen), 5/30 (out-of-state freshmen), 3/31 (early decision).

Freshman Application Contact Admissions, Kwantlen University College, 12666—72nd Avenue, Surrey, BC V3W 2M8, Canada. *Phone:* 604-599-2000. *Fax:* 604-599-2086. *E-mail:* admission@kwantlen.ca.

LAKEHEAD UNIVERSITY

Thunder Bay, Ontario, Canada **www.lakeheadu.ca/**

- **Province-supported** comprehensive, founded 1965
- **Suburban** 345-acre campus
- **Coed** 7,116 undergraduate students, 80% full-time, 58% women, 42% men
- **Moderately difficult** entrance level, 73% of applicants were admitted

Undergraduates 5,702 full-time, 1,414 part-time. Students come from 13 provinces and territories, 50 other countries, 17% live on campus.

Freshmen *Admission:* 7,422 applied, 5,442 admitted. *Average high school GPA:* 3.06.

Faculty *Total:* 313. *Student/faculty ratio:* 25:1.

Majors Accounting; anthropology; art; athletic training; biological and physical sciences; biology/biological sciences; business administration and management; chemical engineering; chemical engineering technology; chemistry; civil engineering; civil engineering technology; clinical psychology; computer engineering; computer science; economics; education; electrical, electronic and communications engineering technology; electrical, electronics and communications engineering; elementary education; engineering; English; environmental biology; environmental studies; finance; forestry; French; general studies; geography; geology/earth science; gerontology; history; human resources management; hydrology and water resources science; information science/studies; labor and industrial relations; liberal arts and sciences/liberal studies; management information systems; marketing/marketing management; mathematics; mechanical engineering; mechanical engineering/mechanical technology; molecular biology; music; natural sciences; nursing (registered nurse training); nursing science; parks, recreation and leisure; philosophy; physical education teaching and coaching; physics; plant sciences; political science and government; psychology; science teacher education; secondary education; social work; sociology; women's studies.

Academics *Calendar:* Canadian standard year. *Degrees:* diplomas, bachelor's, master's, and doctoral. *Special study options:* accelerated degree program, advanced placement credit, cooperative education, distance learning, double majors, external degree program, honors programs, independent study, internships, off-campus study, part-time degree program, services for LD students, student-designed majors, study abroad, summer session for credit.

Computers on Campus 700 computers/terminals are available on campus for general student use. Students can access the following: campus intranet, computer help desk, free student e-mail accounts, online (class) grades, online (class) registration, online (class) schedules. Campuswide network is available. 100% of college-owned or -operated housing units are wired for high-speed Internet access.

Student Life *Housing:* on-campus residence required through senior year. *Options:* coed, disabled students. Campus housing is university owned. Freshman campus housing is guaranteed. *Activities and organizations:* student-run newspaper, radio station, choral group, Outdoor Recreation Students Association, Engineering Students Society, Business Association, ECHO/LUFROG, Educational Students Association. *Campus security:* 24-hour emergency response devices and patrols, student patrols, late-night transport/escort service, controlled dormitory access. *Student services:* health clinic, personal/psychological counseling, women's center.

Athletics Member CIS. *Intercollegiate sports:* basketball M/W, cheerleading W, crew M/W, cross-country running M/W, ice hockey M, rock climbing M/W, skiing (cross-country) M/W, soccer M (c)/W (c), track and field M/W, volleyball M (c)/W, weight lifting M, wrestling M/W. *Intramural sports:* badminton M/W, baseball M/W, basketball M/W, bowling M/W, ice hockey M/W, soccer M/W, volleyball M/W.

Standardized Tests *Required:* SAT or ACT (for admission).

Costs (2007–08) *Tuition:* province resident $894 per course part-time; nonresident $4500 full-time; International tuition $12,000 full-time. Full-time tuition and fees vary according to location and program. Part-time tuition and fees vary according to course load, location, and program. *Required fees:* $628 full-time, $84 per course part-time. *Room and board:* $7030; room only: $5380. Room and board charges vary according to board plan, housing facility, and location. *Payment plan:* installment. *Waivers:* senior citizens and employees or children of employees.

Financial Aid *Financial aid deadline:* 6/30.

Applying *Options:* electronic application, early admission, deferred entrance. *Application fee:* $105 Canadian dollars. *Required:* Visual Arts Program requires a portfolio. Music Program requires an audition. *Required for some:* essay or personal statement. *Recommended:* minimum 3.0 GPA. *Application deadlines:* 9/19 (freshmen), 9/19 (transfers). *Notification:* continuous (transfers).

Freshman Application Contact Mr. John D. Smith, Director, Admissions and Recruitment, Lakehead University, 955 Oliver Road, Thunder Bay, ON P7B 5E1, Canada. *Phone:* 807-343-8500. *Toll-free phone:* 800-465-3959. *Fax:* 807-766-7209. *E-mail:* admissions@lakeheadu.ca.

LAURENTIAN UNIVERSITY

Sudbury, Ontario, Canada **www.laurentian.ca/**

- **Province-supported** comprehensive, founded 1960
- **Suburban** 700-acre campus
- **Endowment** $8.9 million
- **Coed** 8,147 undergraduate students
- **Minimally difficult** entrance level, 85% of applicants were admitted

Undergraduates Students come from 8 provinces and territories, 54 other countries, 22% live on campus. *Retention:* 80% of 2006 full-time freshmen returned.

Freshmen *Admission:* 6,795 applied, 5,743 admitted.

Faculty *Total:* 401, 100% full-time, 81% with terminal degrees.

Majors Adult and continuing education; American Indian/Native American studies; anthropology; astronomy; behavioral sciences; biochemistry; biology/biological sciences; biophysics; business administration and management; chemistry; classics and languages, literatures and linguistics; computer science; dramatic/theater arts; economics; education; English; film/cinema studies; folklore; French; geography; geological/geophysical engineering; geology/earth science; history; Italian; kinesiology and exercise science; language interpretation and translation; legal studies; liberal arts and sciences/liberal studies; mathematics; metallurgical engineering; mining and mineral engineering; modern languages; music; nursing (registered nurse training); philosophy; physical education teaching and coaching; physics; political science and government; psychology; public health education and promotion; religious studies; social work; sociology; Spanish; sport and fitness administration/management; women's studies.

Academics *Calendar:* Canadian standard year. *Degrees:* certificates, diplomas, bachelor's, master's, and doctoral. *Special study options:* academic remediation for entering students, accelerated degree program, adult/continuing education programs, cooperative education, external degree program, honors programs, off-campus study, part-time degree program, services for LD students, summer session for credit.

Computers on Campus 400 computers/terminals are available on campus for general student use. Students can access the following: computer help desk, free student e-mail accounts, online (class) grades, online (class) registration, online (class) schedules. Campuswide network is available. 100% of college-owned or -operated housing units are wired for high-speed Internet access. Wireless service is available via classrooms, computer labs, learning centers, libraries, student centers.

Student Life *Housing options:* coed. Campus housing is university owned. *Activities and organizations:* drama/theater group, student-run newspaper, radio station, Students General Association, Association des étudiantes et-tudiants francophones, Association of Mature and Part-time Students, Graduate Students Association. *Campus security:* 24-hour emergency response devices and patrols, late-night transport/escort service. *Student services:* health clinic, personal/psychological counseling, women's center.

Athletics Member CIS. *Intercollegiate sports:* basketball M/W, cross-country running M/W, field hockey W, ice hockey M/W, skiing (cross-country) M/W, skiing (downhill) M/W, soccer M, swimming and diving M/W, track and field M/W, volleyball M. *Intramural sports:* basketball M/W, cross-country running M/W, football M/W, golf M/W, gymnastics M/W, ice hockey M/W, skiing (cross-country) M/W, skiing (downhill) M/W, swimming and diving M/W, tennis M/W, volleyball M/W.

Costs (2007–08) *Tuition:* $4525 Canadian dollars full-time, $905 Canadian dollars per course part-time; International tuition $11,014 Canadian dollars full-time. Full-time tuition and fees vary according to program. Part-time tuition and fees vary according to course load. *Required fees:* $517 Canadian dollars full-time, $36 Canadian dollars per term part-time. *Room only:* $3250 Canadian dollars. Room and board charges vary according to housing facility. *Payment plan:* installment. *Waivers:* senior citizens and employees or children of employees.

Financial Aid Of all full-time matriculated undergraduates who enrolled in 2006, 241 state and other part-time jobs (averaging $1563).

Applying *Options:* electronic application, early admission. *Application fee:* $40 Canadian dollars. *Required:* high school transcript. *Required for some:* essay or personal statement, 2 letters of recommendation, interview. *Application deadlines:* 2/1 (freshmen), rolling (transfers).

Freshman Application Contact Mr. Ron Smith, Registrar, Laurentian University, Ramsey Lake Road, Sudbury, ON P3E 2C6, Canada. *Phone:* 705-675-1151 Ext. 3919. *Fax:* 705-675-4891. *E-mail:* admissions@laurentian.ca.

MALASPINA UNIVERSITY-COLLEGE

Nanaimo, British Columbia, Canada **www.mala.bc.ca/**

Freshman Application Contact Ms. Leslie Peterson, Admissions Manager, Malaspina University-College, 900 Fifth Street, Nanaimo, BC V9R 5S5, Canada. *Phone:* 250-740-6355. *Fax:* 250-740-6479.

MASTER'S COLLEGE AND SEMINARY

Toronto, Ontario, Canada **www.mcs.edu/**

- **Independent Pentecostal** 4-year, founded 1939
- **Urban** campus
- **Endowment** $331,456
- **Coed** 315 undergraduate students
- **Noncompetitive** entrance level, 82% of applicants were admitted

Undergraduates Students come from 7 provinces and territories, 5 other countries, 10% are from out of state. *Retention:* 67% of 2006 full-time freshmen returned.

Freshmen *Admission:* 51 applied, 42 admitted.

Faculty *Total:* 39, 13% full-time, 10% with terminal degrees. *Student/faculty ratio:* 15:1.

Majors Biblical studies; divinity/ministry; missionary studies and missiology; religious education; theology; theology and religious vocations related; youth ministry.

Academics *Calendar:* semesters. *Degree:* certificates, diplomas, and bachelor's. *Special study options:* academic remediation for entering students, accelerated degree program, distance learning, independent study, internships, off-campus study, part-time degree program, services for LD students, study abroad, summer session for credit. *Unusual degree programs:* 3-2 theology.

Computers on Campus 6 computers/terminals are available on campus for general student use. Students can access the following: free student e-mail accounts, online (class) registration, online (class) schedules. Campuswide network is available. Wireless service is available via entire campus.

Student Life *Housing:* college housing not available.

Athletics *Intercollegiate sports:* basketball W, volleyball W.

Costs (2007–08) *Tuition:* $5472 Canadian dollars full-time, $171 Canadian dollars per credit hour part-time. Full-time tuition and fees vary according to course load. Part-time tuition and fees vary according to course load. *Required fees:* $544 Canadian dollars full-time; $17 Canadian dollars per credit hour part-time. *Payment plans:* installment, deferred payment. *Waivers:* adult students and employees or children of employees.

Applying *Options:* deferred entrance. *Application fee:* $75 Canadian dollars. *Required:* essay or personal statement, high school transcript, 3 letters of recommendation, Christian commitment. *Required for some:* interview. *Recommended:* minimum 2.0 GPA. *Application deadlines:* 8/31 (freshmen), 8/31 (transfers).

Freshman Application Contact Ms. Flora Anthony, Recruitment, Master's College and Seminary, 3080 Yonge Street, Box 70, Suite 3040, Toronto, ON M4N 3N1, Canada. *Phone:* 416-482-2224. *Toll-free phone:* 800-295-6368 Ext. 243. *Fax:* 416-482-7004. *E-mail:* flora.anthony@mcs.edu.

MCGILL UNIVERSITY

Montréal, Quebec, Canada **www.mcgill.ca/**

- **Province-supported** university, founded 1821
- **Urban** 80-acre campus
- **Endowment** $913.4 million
- **Coed** 22,262 undergraduate students, 83% full-time, 59% women, 41% men
- **Very difficult** entrance level, 54% of applicants were admitted

Undergraduates 18,406 full-time, 3,856 part-time. Students come from 13 provinces and territories, 118 other countries, 36% are from out of state, 17% international, 3% transferred in, 11% live on campus. *Retention:* 92% of 2006 full-time freshmen returned.

Freshmen *Admission:* 20,391 applied, 11,082 admitted, 4,977 enrolled. *Average high school GPA:* 3.53. *Test scores:* SAT critical reading scores over 500: 99%; SAT math scores over 500: 100%; SAT writing scores over 500: 100%; ACT scores over 18: 100%; SAT critical reading scores over 600: 93%; SAT math scores over 600: 92%; SAT writing scores over 600: 93%; ACT scores over 24: 100%; SAT critical reading scores over 700: 48%; SAT math scores over 700: 41%; SAT writing scores over 700: 42%; ACT scores over 30: 55%.

Faculty *Total:* 2,539, 66% full-time, 76% with terminal degrees. *Student/faculty ratio:* 16:1.

Majors Accounting; accounting and finance; African studies; agricultural/biological engineering and bioengineering; agricultural business and management; agricultural economics; agriculture; agronomy and crop science; analytical chemistry; anatomy; animal behavior and ethology; animal sciences; anthropology; applied horticulture; applied mathematics; aquatic biology/limnology; architecture; art history, criticism and conservation; Asian history; Asian studies (East); atmospheric physics and dynamics; atmospheric sciences and meteorology; auditing; bilingual and multilingual education; biochemistry; biological and physical sciences; biology/biological sciences; biology teacher education; biomedical sciences; botany/plant biology; business/commerce; business/managerial economics; Canadian history; Canadian studies; Caribbean studies; cell biology and anatomy; cell biology and histology; chemical engineering; chemistry; chemistry teacher education; civil engineering; classics and languages, literatures and linguistics; cognitive science; computer and information sciences; computer engineering; computer science; computer software engineering; development economics and international development; dramatic/theater arts; early childhood education; East Asian languages; ecology; e-commerce; economics; education; electrical, electronics and communications engineering; elementary education; English; English as a second/foreign language (teaching); English/language arts teacher education; entrepreneurship; environmental biology; environmental science; environmental studies; European history; finance; food science; foods, nutrition, and wellness; French; French as a second/foreign language (teaching); French language teacher education; genetics; geography; geography teacher education; geology/earth science; geophysics and seismology; German; German studies; health and physical education; health teacher education; Hispanic-American, Puerto Rican, and Mexican-American/Chicano studies; history; history teacher education; humanities; human nutrition; human resources management; hydrology and water resources science; inorganic chemistry; insurance; international business/trade/commerce; international finance; Italian; Italian studies; jazz/jazz studies; Jewish/Judaic studies; kinesiology and exercise science; labor and industrial relations; language interpretation and translation; Latin American studies; legal studies; linguistics; management science; marine biology and biological oceanography; marketing/marketing management; materials engineering; mathematical statistics and probability; mathematics; mathematics and computer science; mathematics teacher education; mechanical engineering; medical microbiology and bacteriology; metallurgical engineering; microbiology; mining and mineral engineering; molecular biology; music; music history, literature, and theory; music pedagogy; music performance; music teacher education; music theory and composition; natural resources/conservation; natural resources management and policy; natural sciences; Near and Middle Eastern studies; neuroanatomy; nursing (registered nurse training); nutrition sciences; operations management; organic chemistry; organizational behavior; philosophy; physical education teaching and coaching; physics; physics teacher education; physiology; piano and organ; planetary astronomy and science; plant sciences; political science and government; psychology; regional studies; religious education; religious/sacred music; religious studies; Russian; Russian studies; science teacher education; secondary education; social science teacher education; social studies teacher education; social work; sociology; soil science and agronomy; Spanish; Spanish and Iberian studies; statistics; taxation; theology; transportation management; urban studies/affairs; violin, viola, guitar and other stringed instruments; voice and opera; wildlife and wildlands science and management; wildlife biology; women's studies; zoology/animal biology.

Academics *Calendar:* semesters. *Degrees:* certificates, diplomas, bachelor's, master's, doctoral, first professional, post-master's, and postbachelor's certificates. *Special study options:* accelerated degree program, adult/continuing education programs, advanced placement credit, cooperative education, distance learning, double majors, English as a second language, honors programs, independent study, internships, off-campus study, part-time degree program, services for LD students, study abroad, summer session for credit.

Computers on Campus 3,797 computers/terminals are available on campus for general student use. Students can access the following: campus intranet, computer help desk, free student e-mail accounts, online (class) grades, online (class) registration, online (class) schedules. Campuswide network is available. 100% of college-owned or -operated housing units are wired for high-speed Internet access. Wireless service is available via entire campus.

Student Life *Housing options:* coed, women-only, cooperative. Campus housing is university owned. Freshman campus housing is guaranteed. *Activities and organizations:* drama/theater group, student-run newspaper, radio station, choral group, Muslim Students Association, Hillel McGill, Midnight Kitchen, MISN (McGill International Students Association), Queer McGill. *Campus security:* 24-hour emergency response devices and patrols, student patrols, late-night transport/escort service, controlled dormitory access. *Student services:* health clinic, personal/psychological counseling, legal services.

Athletics Member CIS. *Intercollegiate sports:* badminton M/W, baseball M, basketball M/W, cheerleading M/W, crew M/W, cross-country running M/W, fencing M/W, field hockey W, football M, golf M/W, ice hockey M/W, lacrosse M/W, rugby M/W, sailing M/W, skiing (cross-country) M/W, skiing (downhill) M/W, soccer M/W, squash M/W, swimming and diving M/W, tennis M/W, track and field M/W, ultimate Frisbee M/W, volleyball M/W, wrestling M/W. *Intramural sports:* badminton M/W, basketball M/W, football M, ice hockey M/W, soccer M/W, squash M/W, table tennis M/W, tennis M/W, volleyball M/W.

Standardized Tests *Required for some:* SAT and SAT Subject Tests or ACT (for admission).

Costs (2007–08) *Tuition:* province resident $1768 Canadian dollars full-time; nonresident $5140 Canadian dollars full-time. Full-time tuition and fees vary according to class time, course load, degree level, location, program, and student level. Part-time tuition and fees vary according to class time, course load, degree level, location, program, and student level. *Required fees:* $1421 Canadian dollars full-time. *Room and board:* $10,400 Canadian dollars. Room and board charges vary according to board plan, gender, housing facility, and location. *Payment plan:* deferred payment. *Waivers:* senior citizens and employees or children of employees.

Financial Aid Of all full-time matriculated undergraduates who enrolled in 2007, 4,755 were judged to have need. 741 state and other part-time jobs (averaging $2235). In 2007, 1336 non-need-based awards were made. *Average financial aid package:* $3371. *Average need-based loan:* $4176. *Average need-based gift aid:* $3601. *Average non-need-based aid:* $2721. *Financial aid deadline:* 6/30.

Applying *Options:* electronic application, deferred entrance. *Application fee:* $80 Canadian dollars. *Required:* high school transcript, minimum 3.3 GPA. *Required for some:* letters of recommendation, interview, audition for music program, portfolio for architecture program. *Application deadlines:* 1/15 (freshmen), 1/15 (transfers). *Notification:* continuous until 1/15 (freshmen), continuous (transfers).

Freshman Application Contact Enrollment Services, McGill University, 845 Sherbrooke Street West, Montreal, QC H3A 2T5, Canada. *Phone:* 514-398-3910. *Fax:* 514-398-4193. *E-mail:* admissions@mcgill.ca.

McMaster University

Hamilton, Ontario, Canada **www.mcmaster.ca/**

Director of Admissions Mrs. Lynn Giordano, Associate Registrar, Admissions, McMaster University, 1280 Main Street West, Hamilton, ON L8S 4M2, Canada. *Phone:* 905-525-9140 Ext. 24034. *E-mail:* macadmit@mcmaster.ca.

Memorial University of Newfoundland

St. John's, Newfoundland and Labrador, Canada

www.mun.ca/

- **Province-supported** university, founded 1925
- **Urban** 220-acre campus
- **Endowment** $56.2 million
- **Coed** 14,789 undergraduate students, 85% full-time, 61% women, 39% men
- **Moderately difficult** entrance level

Undergraduates 12,634 full-time, 2,155 part-time. Students come from 13 provinces and territories, 79 other countries, 14% are from out of state, 10% live on campus. *Retention:* 81% of 2006 full-time freshmen returned.

Freshmen *Admission:* 2,459 enrolled.

Faculty *Total:* 1,226, 96% full-time. *Student/faculty ratio:* 14:1.

Majors Accounting; acting; adult and continuing education; anthropology; applied mathematics; archeology; area studies; art; art history, criticism and conservation; athletic training; biochemistry; biological and physical sciences; biology/biological sciences; business administration and management; Canadian studies; cartography; cell biology and histology; chemical engineering; chemistry; civil engineering; classics and languages, literatures and linguistics; computer programming; computer science; counselor education/school counseling and guidance; criminal justice/police science; criminology; dietetics; dramatic/theater arts; drawing; ecology; economics; education; electrical, electronics and communications engineering; elementary education; engineering; English; entomology; environmental biology; environmental studies; finance; folklore; food science; foods, nutrition, and wellness; forest sciences and biology; French; geography; geological/geophysical engineering; geology/earth science; geophysics and seismology; German; history; humanities; industrial engineering; information science/studies; kinesiology and exercise science; labor and industrial relations; Latin; linguistics; literature; marine biology and biological oceanography; marine science/merchant marine officer; marketing/marketing management; mathematics; mechanical engineering; medical microbiology and bacteriology; medieval and Renaissance studies; middle school education; modern Greek; music; music history, literature, and theory; music teacher education; music theory and composition; naval architecture and marine engineering; neuroscience; nursing (registered nurse training); ocean engineering; oceanography (chemical and physical); organizational behavior; painting; parks, recreation and leisure; pharmacy; philosophy; photography; physical education teaching and coaching; physics; piano and organ; political science and government; pre-medical studies; printmaking; psychology; religious studies; Russian; science teacher education; sculpture; secondary education; social sciences; social work; sociology; Spanish; special education; statistics; theater design and technology; theater literature, history and criticism; trade and industrial teacher education; violin, viola, guitar and other stringed instruments; voice and opera; wind/percussion instruments; women's studies; zoology/animal biology.

Academics *Calendar:* trimesters. *Degrees:* certificates, diplomas, bachelor's, master's, doctoral, and postbachelor's certificates. *Special study options:* academic remediation for entering students, accelerated degree program, adult/continuing education programs, advanced placement credit, cooperative education, distance learning, double majors, English as a second language, honors programs, internships, off-campus study, part-time degree program, services for LD students, study abroad, summer session for credit. *Unusual degree programs:* 3-2 forestry with University of New Brunswick.

Computers on Campus 825 computers/terminals are available on campus for general student use. Students can access the following: computer help desk, free student e-mail accounts, online (class) grades, online (class) registration, online (class) schedules. Campuswide network is available. 100% of college-owned or -operated housing units are wired for high-speed Internet access. Wireless service is available via entire campus.

Student Life *Housing options:* coed, men-only, women-only, disabled students. Campus housing is university owned. Freshman applicants given priority for college housing. *Activities and organizations:* drama/theater group, student-run newspaper, radio station, choral group, International Student Center, Students Older Than Average, Memorial's Organization for the Disabled, Biology Society, Student Parents at MUN. *Campus security:* 24-hour emergency response devices and patrols, student patrols, late-night transport/escort service. *Student services:* health clinic, personal/psychological counseling, women's center, legal services.

Athletics Member CIS. *Intercollegiate sports:* basketball M/W, cross-country running M/W, soccer M/W, swimming and diving M/W, volleyball M/W, wrestling M/W. *Intramural sports:* badminton M/W, basketball M/W, cross-country running M/W, soccer M/W, softball M/W, squash M/W, swimming and diving M/W, table tennis M/W, tennis M/W, volleyball M/W, water polo M/W, weight lifting M (c).

Costs (2008–09) *Tuition:* province resident $2550 Canadian dollars full-time, $85 Canadian dollars per credit hour part-time; International tuition $8800 Canadian dollars full-time. *Required fees:* $466 Canadian dollars full-time, $67 Canadian dollars per semester part-time. *Room and board:* $5088 Canadian dollars; room only: $2112 Canadian dollars.

Applying *Options:* electronic application, early admission, early decision, deferred entrance. *Application fee:* $40 Canadian dollars. *Required:* high school transcript. *Required for some:* essay or personal statement, 2 letters of recommendation, interview, audition, portfolio. *Application deadlines:* rolling (freshmen), 3/1 (out-of-state freshmen), 3/1 (transfers).

Freshman Application Contact Ms. Marian Abbott, Admissions Office, Memorial University of Newfoundland, Elizabeth Avenue, St. John's, NL A1C 5S7, Canada. *Phone:* 709-737-3705. *E-mail:* sturecru@morgan.ucs.mun.ca.

Mount Allison University

Sackville, New Brunswick, Canada **www.mta.ca/**

- **Province-supported** comprehensive, founded 1839
- **Small-town** 50-acre campus
- **Endowment** $65.0 million
- **Coed** 2,163 undergraduate students, 92% full-time, 58% women, 42% men
- **Moderately difficult** entrance level, 88% of applicants were admitted

Undergraduates 1,998 full-time, 165 part-time. Students come from 15 provinces and territories, 38 other countries, 60% are from out of state, 4% transferred in, 50% live on campus. *Retention:* 76% of 2006 full-time freshmen returned.

Freshmen *Admission:* 1,591 applied, 1,401 admitted, 696 enrolled. *Average high school GPA:* 3.36.

Faculty *Total:* 164, 81% full-time, 77% with terminal degrees. *Student/faculty ratio:* 15:1.

Majors Accounting; American studies; ancient/classical Greek; anthropology; applied mathematics; art history, criticism and conservation; biochemistry; biological and physical sciences; biology/biological sciences; biopsychology; business administration and management; business/commerce; business/managerial economics; Canadian studies; chemistry; classics and languages, literatures and linguistics; computer science; dramatic/theater arts; drawing; economics; English; environmental studies; fine/studio arts; French; geography; geology/earth science; German; history; humanities; interdisciplinary studies; international business/trade/commerce; international relations and affairs; Latin; liberal arts and sciences/liberal studies; literature; mathematics; mathematics and computer science; medieval and Renaissance studies; modern languages; music; music history, literature, and theory; music performance; natural sciences; philosophy; photography; physics; physiological psychology/psychobiology; piano and organ; political science and government; pre-dentistry studies; pre-law studies; pre-medical studies; pre-pharmacy studies; pre-theology/pre-ministerial studies; pre-veterinary studies; printmaking; psychology; religious studies; Romance languages; sculpture; sociology; Spanish; violin, viola, guitar and other stringed instruments; voice and opera; wind/percussion instruments.

Academics *Calendar:* Canadian standard year. *Degrees:* bachelor's and master's. *Special study options:* academic remediation for entering students, adult/continuing education programs, advanced placement credit, distance learning, double majors, honors programs, independent study, internships, off-campus study, part-time degree program, services for LD students, student-designed majors, study abroad, summer session for credit.

Computers on Campus 100 computers/terminals and 120 ports are available on campus for general student use. Students can access the following: computer help desk, free student e-mail accounts, online (class) registration, online (class) schedules, online student account/Websis. Campuswide network is available. 100% of college-owned or -operated housing units are wired for high-speed Internet access. Wireless service is available via entire campus.

Student Life *Housing options:* coed, women-only. Campus housing is university owned. Freshman campus housing is guaranteed. *Activities and organizations:* drama/theater group, student-run newspaper, radio station, choral group, Commerce Society, Windsor Theatre, President's Leadership Development Certificate, Leadership Mount Allison, Garnet and Gold Society. *Campus security:* 24-hour emergency response devices, late-night transport/escort service. *Student services:* health clinic, personal/psychological counseling.

Athletics Member CIS. *Intercollegiate sports:* basketball M/W, football M, ice hockey W, rugby M/W, soccer M/W, swimming and diving M/W. *Intramural sports:* badminton M/W, baseball M/W, basketball M/W, football M/W, golf M/W, ice hockey M/W, rugby M/W, skiing (cross-country) M/W, skiing (downhill) M/W, soccer M/W, softball M/W, tennis M/W, ultimate Frisbee M/W, volleyball M/W, weight lifting M/W.

Costs (2007–08) *Tuition:* province resident $6720 Canadian dollars full-time, $672 Canadian dollars per course part-time; nonresident $1344 Canadian dollars per course part-time; International tuition $13,440 Canadian dollars full-time. Full-time tuition and fees vary according to course load. Part-time tuition and fees vary according to course load. *Required fees:* $257 Canadian dollars full-time, $59 Canadian dollars per term part-time. *Room and board:* $6795 Canadian dollars; room only: $3530 Canadian dollars. Room and board charges vary according to board plan. *Payment plans:* installment, deferred payment. *Waivers:* senior citizens and employees or children of employees.

Applying *Options:* electronic application, deferred entrance. *Application fee:* $50 Canadian dollars. *Required:* high school transcript, minimum 3.0 GPA. *Required for some:* essay or personal statement, interview. *Recommended:* 2 letters of recommendation. *Application deadlines:* rolling (freshmen), rolling (transfers). *Notification:* continuous (freshmen), continuous (transfers).

Freshman Application Contact Mr. Matt Sheridan-Jonah, Manager of Admissions, Mount Allison University, 65 York Street, Sackville, NB E4L 1E4, Canada. *Phone:* 506-364-3294. *Fax:* 506-364-2272. *E-mail:* admissions@mta.ca.

MOUNT SAINT VINCENT UNIVERSITY

Halifax, Nova Scotia, Canada **www.msvu.ca/**

- **Province-supported** comprehensive, founded 1873
- **Suburban** 40-acre campus
- **Endowment** $19.5 million
- **Coed, primarily women** 2,856 undergraduate students
- **Moderately difficult** entrance level

Undergraduates Students come from 13 provinces and territories, 40 other countries, 10% are from out of state. *Retention:* 79% of 2006 full-time freshmen returned.

Faculty *Total:* 376, 40% full-time. *Student/faculty ratio:* 13:1.

Majors Accounting; adult development and aging; anthropology; applied mathematics; art teacher education; biological and physical sciences; biology/biological sciences; business administration and management; chemistry; child development; computer and information sciences; computer systems analysis; developmental and child psychology; dietetics; economics; education; elementary education; English; family and consumer economics related; fine/studio arts; foods, nutrition, and wellness; French; German; gerontology; history; hospitality administration; hotel/motel administration; human ecology; humanities; information science/studies; interdisciplinary studies; kindergarten/preschool education; liberal arts and sciences/liberal studies; linguistics; literature; management information systems; marketing/marketing management; marketing research; mathematics; mathematics and computer science; modern languages; nutrition sciences; peace studies and conflict resolution; philosophy; political science and government; psychology; public relations/image management; reading teacher education; religious studies; secondary education; social sciences; sociology; Spanish; special products marketing; statistics; tourism and travel services management; tourism and travel services marketing; women's studies.

Academics *Calendar:* Canadian standard year. *Degrees:* certificates, diplomas, bachelor's, master's, first professional, and postbachelor's certificates. *Special study options:* adult/continuing education programs, cooperative education, distance learning, double majors, external degree program, honors programs, independent study, internships, off-campus study, part-time degree program, study abroad, summer session for credit.

Computers on Campus Students can access the following: online (class) registration. Campuswide network is available.

Student Life *Housing options:* coed, men-only, women-only. Campus housing is university owned. Freshman applicants given priority for college housing. *Activities and organizations:* student-run newspaper, choral group, Business Society, Residence Society, Science Society, History Society. *Campus security:* 24-hour emergency response devices and patrols, late-night transport/escort service, controlled dormitory access. *Student services:* health clinic, personal/psychological counseling, women's center.

Athletics *Intercollegiate sports:* badminton M/W, basketball M/W, soccer M/W, volleyball W. *Intramural sports:* badminton M/W, basketball M/W, soccer M/W, volleyball M/W.

Costs (2007–08) *Tuition:* province resident $1110 Canadian dollars per unit part-time; nonresident $5550 Canadian dollars full-time, $1110 Canadian dollars per unit part-time; International tuition $10,845 Canadian dollars full-time. Full-time tuition and fees vary according to course level, course load, degree level, location, program, reciprocity agreements, and student level. Part-time tuition and fees vary according to course level, course load, degree level, location, program, reciprocity agreements, and student level. *Required fees:* $743 Canadian dollars full-time, $42 Canadian dollars per unit part-time, $5 Canadian dollars per year part-time. *Room and board:* $6795 Canadian dollars; room only: $4570 Canadian dollars. Room and board charges vary according to board plan and housing facility. *Payment plan:* installment. *Waivers:* senior citizens and employees or children of employees.

Financial Aid *Financial aid deadline:* 11/3.

Applying *Options:* electronic application, deferred entrance. *Application fee:* $30 Canadian dollars. *Required:* high school transcript, minimum 2.0 GPA. *Required for some:* essay or personal statement, minimum 3.0 GPA, 2 letters of recommendation, interview. *Application deadlines:* 3/15 (freshmen), 5/30 (out-of-state freshmen), 8/15 (transfers). *Notification:* continuous until 9/1 (freshmen), 1/6 (out-of-state freshmen), continuous until 9/1 (transfers).

Freshman Application Contact Mr. Karl Turner, Assistant Registrar/Admissions, Mount Saint Vincent University, 166 Bedford Highway, Halifax, NS B3M2J6, Canada. *Phone:* 902-457-6117. *Fax:* 902-457-6498. *E-mail:* admissions@msvu.ca.

NER ISRAEL YESHIVA COLLEGE OF TORONTO

Thornhill, Ontario, Canada

Director of Admissions Rabbi Y. Kravetz, Director of Admissions, Ner Israel Yeshiva College of Toronto, 8950 Bathurst Street, Thornhill, ON L4J 8A7, Canada. *Phone:* 905-731-1224.

NIPISSING UNIVERSITY

North Bay, Ontario, Canada www.nipissingu.ca/

- **Province-supported** comprehensive, founded 1992
- **Urban** 290-hectare campus
- **Endowment** $5.5 million
- **Coed**
- **Moderately difficult** entrance level

Academics *Calendar:* semesters. *Degrees:* bachelor's, master's, and post-bachelor's certificates.

Student Life *Campus security:* 24-hour emergency response devices and patrols, student patrols, late-night transport/escort service, controlled dormitory access.

Athletics Member CIS.

Standardized Tests *Required:* SAT and SAT Subject Tests or ACT (for admission).

Costs (2007–08) *Tuition:* province resident $4315 full-time, $432 per course part-time; nonresident $4315 full-time, $432 per course part-time; International tuition $10,500 full-time. Full-time tuition and fees vary according to course level, course load, degree level, location, and program. Part-time tuition and fees vary according to course level, course load, degree level, location, and program. *Required fees:* $925 full-time, $50 per course part-time. *Room only:* $4300. Room and board charges vary according to housing facility and location.

Applying *Options:* early admission. *Application fee:* $40 Canadian dollars. *Required:* high school transcript. *Required for some:* essay or personal statement, letters of recommendation.

Freshman Application Contact Ms. Heather Brown, Assistant Registrar-Liaison, Nipissing University, 100 College Drive, Box 5002, North Bay, ON P1B 8L7, Canada. *Phone:* 705-474-3461 Ext. 4518. *Fax:* 705-474-1947. *E-mail:* liaison@nipissingu.ca.

NOVA SCOTIA AGRICULTURAL COLLEGE

Truro, Nova Scotia, Canada www.nsac.ns.ca/

- **Province-supported** comprehensive, founded 1905
- **Small-town** 408-acre campus with easy access to Halifax
- **Coed** 720 undergraduate students
- **Minimally difficult** entrance level, 78% of applicants were admitted

Undergraduates Students come from 10 provinces and territories, 20 other countries, 30% are from out of state, 50% live on campus. *Retention:* 85% of 2006 full-time freshmen returned.

Freshmen *Admission:* 622 applied, 487 admitted.

Faculty *Total:* 80, 78% full-time, 76% with terminal degrees. *Student/faculty ratio:* 12:1.

Majors Agricultural business and management; agricultural economics; agricultural mechanization; agriculture; animal sciences; applied horticulture; engineering; environmental studies; plant sciences; pre-veterinary studies.

Academics *Calendar:* semesters. *Degrees:* diplomas, bachelor's, and master's. *Special study options:* academic remediation for entering students, adult/continuing education programs, advanced placement credit, cooperative education, internships, off-campus study, part-time degree program, services for LD students, study abroad, summer session for credit.

Computers on Campus 110 computers/terminals are available on campus for general student use. Students can access the following: campus intranet, computer help desk, free student e-mail accounts, online (class) grades, online (class) registration, online (class) schedules. Campuswide network is available. 100% of college-owned or -operated housing units are wired for high-speed Internet access. Wireless service is available via classrooms, computer centers, libraries, student centers.

Student Life *Housing options:* coed. Campus housing is university owned. Freshman campus housing is guaranteed. *Activities and organizations:* drama/theater group, student-run newspaper, choral group, Pre-Vet Club, Equestrian Club, Environmental Club, ACCF, Adventure Club. *Campus security:* 24-hour patrols, student patrols. *Student services:* health clinic, personal/psychological counseling.

Athletics *Intercollegiate sports:* badminton M/W, basketball M/W, equestrian sports M/W, golf M/W, rugby M/W, soccer M/W, volleyball M/W. *Intramural sports:* badminton M/W, basketball M/W, cross-country running M/W, equestrian sports M/W, golf M/W, ice hockey M/W, racquetball M/W, skiing (cross-country) M/W, skiing (downhill) M/W, soccer M/W, softball M/W, squash M/W, swimming and diving M/W, table tennis M/W, ultimate Frisbee M/W, volleyball M/W, water polo M/W.

Costs (2008–09) *Tuition:* province resident $5500 full-time, $550 per course part-time; International tuition $11,000 full-time. *Room and board:* $7618.

Applying *Options:* electronic application. *Application fee:* $25 Canadian dollars. *Required:* high school transcript. *Required for some:* essay or personal statement, 1 letter of recommendation, interview. *Application deadline:* 8/1 (freshmen).

Freshman Application Contact Ms. Elizabeth Johnson, Admissions Officer, Nova Scotia Agricultural College, PO Box 550, Truro, NS B2N 5E3, Canada. *Phone:* 902-893-8212. *Toll-free phone:* 888-700-6722. *Fax:* 902-895-5529. *E-mail:* recruit@nsac.ca.

NSCAD UNIVERSITY

Halifax, Nova Scotia, Canada www.nscad.ca/

- **Province-supported** comprehensive, founded 1887
- **Urban** 1-acre campus
- **Endowment** $1.1 million
- **Coed** 1,052 undergraduate students, 84% full-time, 68% women, 32% men
- **Very difficult** entrance level, 77% of applicants were admitted

Undergraduates 882 full-time, 170 part-time. Students come from 11 provinces and territories, 17 other countries, 7% transferred in, 10% live on campus.

Freshmen *Admission:* 300 applied, 230 admitted, 210 enrolled.

Faculty *Total:* 114, 40% full-time. *Student/faculty ratio:* 9:1.

Majors Art; art history, criticism and conservation; ceramic arts and ceramics; commercial and advertising art; crafts, folk art and artisanry; design and applied arts related; design and visual communications; drawing; fiber, textile and weaving arts; film/cinema studies; fine/studio arts; graphic design; metal and jewelry arts; painting; photography; printmaking; sculpture.

Academics *Calendar:* semesters. *Degrees:* bachelor's and master's. *Special study options:* cooperative education, double majors, external degree program, honors programs, independent study, internships, off-campus study, part-time degree program, services for LD students, student-designed majors, study abroad, summer session for credit.

Computers on Campus 60 computers/terminals are available on campus for general student use. Students can access the following: free student e-mail accounts, online (class) registration.

Student Life *Housing options:* coed. Campus housing is provided by a third party. *Campus security:* 24-hour emergency response devices, evening patrols by trained security personnel. *Student services:* personal/psychological counseling.

Costs (2007–08) *Tuition:* province resident $5500 Canadian dollars full-time, $230 Canadian dollars per credit part-time; International tuition $12,125 Canadian dollars full-time. *Required fees:* $375 Canadian dollars full-time, $33 Canadian dollars per term part-time. *Waivers:* children of alumni, senior citizens, and employees or children of employees.

Applying *Options:* deferred entrance. *Application fee:* $35 Canadian dollars. *Required:* essay or personal statement, high school transcript, portfolio. *Required for some:* 2 letters of recommendation, interview. *Recommended:* minimum 3.0 GPA. *Application deadlines:* 5/15 (freshmen), 2/15 (transfers). *Early decision deadline:* 3/15. *Notification:* continuous until 6/30 (freshmen), continuous until 6/30 (transfers).

Freshman Application Contact Mr. Terry Bailey, Director of Admissions and Enrollment Services, NSCAD University, 5163 Duke Street, Halifax, NS B3J 3J6, Canada. *Phone:* 902-494-8129. *Fax:* 902-425-2987. *E-mail:* admissions@nscad.ca.

OKANAGAN COLLEGE

Kelowna, British Columbia, Canada **www.okanagan.bc.ca/**

- **Province-supported** 4-year, founded 2005, part of Ministry of Advanced Education
- **Endowment** $6.6 million
- **Coed** 2,533 undergraduate students, 63% full-time, 61% women, 39% men
- 45% of applicants were admitted

Undergraduates 1,598 full-time, 935 part-time. Students come from 6 provinces and territories, 30 other countries, 3% are from out of state, 2% transferred in, 3% live on campus. *Retention:* 76% of 2006 full-time freshmen returned.

Freshmen *Admission:* 479 applied, 216 admitted, 120 enrolled.

Faculty *Total:* 398. *Student/faculty ratio:* 13:1.

Majors Business administration and management; computer and information sciences.

Academics *Degrees:* certificates, diplomas, associate, and bachelor's. *Special study options:* academic remediation for entering students, adult/continuing education programs, advanced placement credit, cooperative education, distance learning, English as a second language, external degree program, honors programs, internships, off-campus study, part-time degree program, services for LD students, study abroad, summer session for credit.

Computers on Campus 1,000 computers/terminals are available on campus for general student use. Students can access the following: campus intranet, free student e-mail accounts, online (class) grades, online (class) registration, online (class) schedules. Campuswide network is available. 100% of college-owned or -operated housing units are wired for high-speed Internet access. Wireless service is available via entire campus.

Student Life *Housing options:* coed. Campus housing is university owned. *Activities and organizations:* student-run newspaper, choral group. *Campus security:* 24-hour patrols, late-night transport/escort service, controlled dormitory access, 24-hour emergency phone. *Student services:* personal/psychological counseling.

Athletics *Intercollegiate sports:* basketball M (s)/W (s), soccer M (s)/W (s), volleyball M (s)/W (s). *Intramural sports:* ice hockey M/W, soccer M/W, volleyball M/W.

Costs (2007–08) *Tuition:* area resident $3018 Canadian dollars full-time, $97 Canadian dollars per credit part-time; International tuition $9000 Canadian dollars full-time. Full-time tuition and fees vary according to course load and program. Part-time tuition and fees vary according to course load and program. *Required fees:* $304 Canadian dollars full-time, $8 Canadian dollars per credit part-time, $176 Canadian dollars per term part-time. *Room only:* $3400 Canadian dollars. Room and board charges vary according to housing facility. *Payment plan:* deferred payment. *Waivers:* senior citizens and employees or children of employees.

Applying *Options:* electronic application, early admission. *Application fee:* $30 Canadian dollars. *Required for some:* essay or personal statement, high school transcript, minimum 2.0 GPA, interview.

Freshman Application Contact Mr. Paul Campo, Okanagan College, 1000 KLO Road, Kelowna, BC V1Y 4X8, Canada. *Phone:* 250-762-5445 Ext. 4332. *E-mail:* pgcampo@okanagan.bc.ca.

PRAIRIE BIBLE INSTITUTE

Three Hills, Alberta, Canada **www.pbi.ab.ca/**

Director of Admissions Mr. Kevin Kirk, Vice President Marketing and Enrollment Management, Prairie Bible Institute, 319 Sixth Avenue North, PO Box 4000, Three Hills, AB T0M 2N0, Canada. *Phone:* 403-443-5511 Ext. 3007. *Toll-free phone:* 800-661-2425.

PROVIDENCE COLLEGE AND THEOLOGICAL SEMINARY

Otterburne, Manitoba, Canada **www.prov.ca/**

Freshman Application Contact Ms. Joy Lise, Director of Environment Management, Providence College and Theological Seminary, General Delivery, Otterburne, MB R0A 1G0, Canada. *Phone:* 204-433-7488. *Toll-free phone:* 800-668-7768. *Fax:* 204-433-7158. *E-mail:* info@prov.ca.

QUEEN'S UNIVERSITY AT KINGSTON

Kingston, Ontario, Canada **www.queensu.ca/**

- **Province-supported** university, founded 1841
- **Urban** 160-acre campus
- **Endowment** $653.0 million
- **Coed** 15,891 undergraduate students, 80% full-time, 60% women, 40% men
- **Most difficult** entrance level, 44% of applicants were admitted

Undergraduates 12,786 full-time, 3,105 part-time. Students come from 13 provinces and territories, 90 other countries, 20% are from out of state, 0.7% transferred in, 32% live on campus. *Retention:* 95% of 2006 full-time freshmen returned.

Freshmen *Admission:* 26,292 applied, 11,518 admitted, 3,205 enrolled. *Test scores:* SAT critical reading scores over 500: 82%; SAT math scores over 500: 90%; SAT critical reading scores over 600: 52%; SAT math scores over 600: 64%; SAT critical reading scores over 700: 16%; SAT math scores over 700: 22%.

Faculty *Total:* 1,525, 71% full-time, 86% with terminal degrees. *Student/faculty ratio:* 15:1.

Majors American native/native American education; art history, criticism and conservation; biochemistry; biology/biological sciences; business/commerce; Canadian studies; cartography; chemical engineering; chemistry; civil engineering; cognitive science; computer engineering; computer science; dramatic/theater arts; economics; education; education (multiple levels); electrical, electronics and communications engineering; elementary education; engineering; engineering physics; engineering related; English; environmental science; film/cinema studies; French; geography; geological/geophysical engineering; geology/earth science; German; German studies; health and physical education; history; linguistics; mathematics; mechanical engineering; mining and mineral engineering; music; nursing (registered nurse training); occupational therapy; philosophy; physical education teaching and coaching; physical therapy; physics; political science and government; psychology; religious studies; science teacher education; sociology; Spanish; statistics; technical teacher education; theology; women's studies.

Academics *Calendar:* Canadian standard year. *Degrees:* bachelor's, master's, doctoral, and first professional. *Special study options:* accelerated degree program, adult/continuing education programs, advanced placement credit, cooperative education, distance learning, double majors, English as a second language, honors programs, internships, part-time degree program, services for LD students, student-designed majors, study abroad, summer session for credit.

Computers on Campus 455 computers/terminals are available on campus for general student use. Students can access the following: computer help desk, free student e-mail accounts, online (class) grades, online (class) registration, online (class) schedules. Campuswide network is available. 100% of college-owned or -operated housing units are wired for high-speed Internet access. Wireless service is available via computer centers, computer labs, learning centers, libraries, student centers.

Student Life *Housing options:* coed, men-only, women-only, cooperative, disabled students. Campus housing is university owned. Freshman campus housing is guaranteed. *Activities and organizations:* drama/theater group, student-run newspaper, radio station, choral group, marching band, Arts and Sciences Undergraduate Society, Alma Mater Society, Engineering Society, Commerce Society, Dance Club. *Campus security:* 24-hour emergency response devices and patrols, student patrols, late-night transport/escort service, controlled dormitory access. *Student services:* health clinic, personal/psychological counseling, women's center, legal services.

Athletics Member CIS. *Intercollegiate sports:* baseball M (c), basketball M/W, cheerleading M (c)/W (c), crew M/W, cross-country running M/W, fencing M/W, field hockey W, football M, golf M, gymnastics M (c)/W (c), ice hockey M/W, lacrosse M (c)/W, rock climbing M/W, sailing M (c)/W (c), skiing (cross-country) M/W, skiing (downhill) M (c)/W (c), soccer M/W, squash M/W, swimming and diving M/W, table tennis M (c)/W (c), tennis M/W, track and field M/W, ultimate Frisbee M/W, volleyball M/W, water polo M/W, wrestling M/W. *Intramural sports:* badminton M/W, basketball M/W, crew M (c)/W (c), equestrian sports M (c)/W (c), fencing M (c)/W (c), football M, golf M, ice hockey M/W, rock climbing M/W, skiing (cross-country) M (c)/W (c), soccer M/W, softball M/W, squash M/W, swimming and diving M/W, tennis M/W, ultimate Frisbee M (c)/W (c), volleyball M/W, water polo M/W.

Standardized Tests *Required:* SAT or ACT (for admission).

Costs (2008–09) *Tuition:* $457 per unit part-time; province resident $5587 full-time, $1508 per unit part-time; nonresident $5587 full-time; International tuition $15,888 full-time. *Required fees:* $802 full-time, $10 per unit part-time. *Room and board:* $9867.

Financial Aid Of all full-time matriculated undergraduates who enrolled in 2006, 477 state and other part-time jobs (averaging $1320).

Applying *Options:* deferred entrance. *Application fee:* $165 Canadian dollars. *Required:* essay or personal statement, high school transcript, minimum 2.3 GPA. *Required for some:* 1 letter of recommendation. *Application deadlines:* 2/1 (freshmen), 5/15 (transfers). *Notification:* continuous until 5/28 (freshmen), 6/15 (transfers).

Freshman Application Contact Ms. Wendy Smith, US Admission Coordinator, Queen's University at Kingston, Richardson Hall, Kingston, ON K7L 3N6, Canada. *Phone:* 613-533-2217. *Fax:* 613-533-6810. *E-mail:* admission@queensu.ca.

REDEEMER UNIVERSITY COLLEGE

Ancaster, Ontario, Canada **www.redeemer.on.ca/**

- **Independent interdenominational** 4-year, founded 1980
- **Small-town** 90-acre campus with easy access to Toronto
- **Endowment** $3.1 million
- **Coed** 885 undergraduate students, 87% full-time, 63% women, 37% men
- **Moderately difficult** entrance level, 81% of applicants were admitted

Undergraduates 767 full-time, 118 part-time. Students come from 8 provinces and territories, 5 other countries, 46% live on campus. *Retention:* 72% of 2006 full-time freshmen returned.

Freshmen *Admission:* 389 applied, 316 admitted. *Test scores:* ACT scores over 18: 100%; ACT scores over 24: 64%.

Faculty *Total:* 70, 64% full-time, 63% with terminal degrees. *Student/faculty ratio:* 17:1.

Majors Accounting; art; biblical studies; biological and physical sciences; biology/biological sciences; business administration and management; computer science; dramatic/theater arts; education; education (K-12); elementary education; English; French; health and physical education; history; humanities; human resources management; kinesiology and exercise science; liberal arts and sciences/liberal studies; mathematics; music; natural sciences; parks, recreation and leisure; philosophy; political science and government; pre-dentistry studies; pre-law studies; pre-medical studies; pre-theology/pre-ministerial studies; pre-veterinary studies; psychology; religious studies; social work; sociology; theology.

Academics *Calendar:* semesters. *Degree:* certificates and bachelor's. *Special study options:* academic remediation for entering students, cooperative education, double majors, honors programs, independent study, internships, off-campus study, part-time degree program, services for LD students, study abroad, summer session for credit. *Unusual degree programs:* chemistry with University of Guelph, education with Ridgetown College, horticulture with Ridgetown College.

Computers on Campus 35 computers/terminals are available on campus for general student use. Students can access the following: campus intranet, computer help desk, free student e-mail accounts, online (class) grades, online (class) schedules. Campuswide network is available. Wireless service is available via classrooms, libraries.

Student Life *Housing:* on-campus residence required through sophomore year. *Options:* men-only, women-only. Campus housing is university owned. Freshman campus housing is guaranteed. *Activities and organizations:* drama/theater group, student-run newspaper, choral group, Church in the Box, Mission trips, Bible study groups, Concert choir, Intramurals. *Campus security:* 24-hour emergency response devices, student patrols, late-night transport/escort service, controlled dormitory access, path lighting. *Student services:* health clinic, personal/psychological counseling.

Athletics *Intercollegiate sports:* basketball M/W, cross-country running M/W, soccer M/W, ultimate Frisbee M/W, volleyball M/W. *Intramural sports:* badminton M/W, basketball M/W, football M/W, golf M/W, ice hockey M, racquetball M/W, skiing (cross-country) M/W, skiing (downhill) M/W, soccer M/W, softball M/W, squash M/W, table tennis M/W, tennis M/W, ultimate Frisbee M/W, volleyball M/W, weight lifting M/W.

Standardized Tests *Required for some:* SAT or ACT (for admission).

Financial Aid Of all full-time matriculated undergraduates who enrolled in 2006, 272 state and other part-time jobs (averaging $1280).

Applying *Options:* deferred entrance. *Application fee:* $35 Canadian dollars. *Required:* essay or personal statement, high school transcript, minimum 2.0 GPA, 2 letters of recommendation, personal reference. *Required for some:* interview. *Application deadlines:* 5/31 (freshmen), 5/31 (transfers). *Notification:* continuous (freshmen), continuous (transfers).

Freshman Application Contact Ms. Marian Ryks-Szelekovszky, Senior Director of Admissions and Student Services, Redeemer University College, 777 Garner Road East, Ancaster, ON L9K 1J4, Canada. *Phone:* 905-648-2139 Ext. 4280. *Toll-free phone:* 800-263-6467 Ext. 4280. *Fax:* 905-648-9545. *E-mail:* adm@redeemer.on.ca.

ROCKY MOUNTAIN COLLEGE

Calgary, Alberta, Canada **www.rockymountaincollege.ca/**

Freshman Application Contact Ms. Dayna Chu, Director of Enrollment, Rocky Mountain College, 4039 Brentwood Drive NW, Calgary, AB T2L 1L1. *Phone:* 403-284-5100 Ext. 222. *E-mail:* enrolment@rockymountaincollege.ca.

ROYAL MILITARY COLLEGE OF CANADA

Kingston, Ontario, Canada **www.rmc.ca/**

- **Federally supported** comprehensive, founded 1876
- **Suburban** 90-acre campus
- **Coed** 2,170 undergraduate students
- **Most difficult** entrance level, 50% of applicants were admitted

Undergraduates Students come from 13 provinces and territories, 60% are from out of state, 90% live on campus. *Retention:* 84% of 2006 full-time freshmen returned.

Freshmen *Admission:* 1,500 applied, 750 admitted.

Faculty *Total:* 149.

Majors Astronomy; business administration and management; chemical engineering; chemistry; civil engineering; computer engineering; computer science; electrical, electronics and communications engineering; English; French; history; mechanical engineering; military technologies; physics; psychology; social sciences.

Academics *Calendar:* Canadian standard year. *Degrees:* certificates, diplomas, bachelor's, master's, and doctoral. *Special study options:* distance learning, English as a second language, honors programs, off-campus study, part-time degree program.

Computers on Campus Campuswide network is available.

Student Life *Housing:* on-campus residence required through senior year. *Options:* coed. Campus housing is provided by a third party. Freshman campus housing is guaranteed. *Activities and organizations:* drama/theater group, student-run newspaper, choral group, marching band, Band. *Campus security:* 24-hour emergency response devices and patrols. *Student services:* health clinic, personal/psychological counseling, legal services.

Athletics Member CIS. *Intercollegiate sports:* basketball M/W, fencing M/W, ice hockey M, rock climbing M, soccer M/W, volleyball M/W. *Intramural sports:* basketball M/W, crew M/W, cross-country running M/W, ice hockey M/W, riflery M/W, soccer M/W, squash M/W, swimming and diving M/W, ultimate Frisbee M/W, volleyball M/W, water polo M/W.

Costs (2007–08) *Tuition:* $4520 Canadian dollars full-time, $515 Canadian dollars per semester hour part-time. Full-time tuition and fees vary according to program. Part-time tuition and fees vary according to program. *Required fees:* $14,000 Canadian dollars full-time.

Applying *Options:* electronic application, early decision. *Required:* high school transcript, letters of recommendation, interview, medical, aptitude and physical fitness testing for full-time students; Canadian residency. *Application deadline:* 1/15 (freshmen). *Notification:* 5/15 (freshmen).

Freshman Application Contact Royal Military College of Canada, PO Box 17000, Station Forces, Kingston, ON K7K 7B4, Canada. *Phone:* 613-541-6000 Ext. 6579.

ROYAL ROADS UNIVERSITY

Victoria, British Columbia, Canada **www.royalroads.ca/**

Director of Admissions Mr. David Rees, Registrar, Royal Roads University, Office of Learner Services and Registrar, 2005 Sooke Road, Victoria, BC V9B 5Y2, Canada. *Phone:* 250-391-2511. *Toll-free phone:* 800-788-8028.

RYERSON UNIVERSITY

Toronto, Ontario, Canada **www.ryerson.ca/**

- **Province-supported** comprehensive, founded 1948
- **Urban** 20-acre campus
- **Coed**
- **Moderately difficult** entrance level

Academics *Calendar:* Canadian standard year or semesters depending on program. *Degrees:* certificates, diplomas, bachelor's, master's, and doctoral.
Student Life *Campus security:* 24-hour emergency response devices and patrols, late-night transport/escort service, controlled dormitory access, staffed access control is in place 24 hours a day, with ID checks of all persons attempting to enter.
Athletics Member CIS.
Costs (2007–08) *Tuition:* $188 Canadian dollars per hour part-time; province resident $4373 Canadian dollars full-time; International tuition $12,925 Canadian dollars full-time. Full-time tuition and fees vary according to course load, degree level, and program. Part-time tuition and fees vary according to course load, degree level, and program. *Required fees:* $548 Canadian dollars full-time. *Room and board:* $7782 Canadian dollars. Room and board charges vary according to board plan and housing facility.
Financial Aid *Financial aid deadline:* 1/15.
Applying *Options:* electronic application. *Application fee:* $100 Canadian dollars. *Required:* high school transcript. *Required for some:* essay or personal statement, letters of recommendation, interview, portfolio, audition, entrance examination.
Freshman Application Contact Mrs. Charmaine Hack, Associate Registrar and Director of Admissions, Ryerson University, 350 Victoria Street, Toronto, ON M5B 2K3, Canada. *Phone:* 416-979-5036. *Fax:* 416-979-5221. *E-mail:* inquire@ryerson.ca.

See page 2850 for the College Close-Up.

ST. FRANCIS XAVIER UNIVERSITY
Antigonish, Nova Scotia, Canada **www.stfx.ca/**

- **Independent Roman Catholic** comprehensive, founded 1853
- **Small-town** 100-acre campus
- **Endowment** $34.9 million
- **Coed** 4,495 undergraduate students, 85% full-time, 62% women, 38% men
- **Moderately difficult** entrance level, 38% of applicants were admitted

Undergraduates 3,838 full-time, 657 part-time. Students come from 12 provinces and territories, 37 other countries, 49% are from out of state, 45% live on campus. *Retention:* 88% of 2006 full-time freshmen returned.
Freshmen *Admission:* 3,200 applied, 1,200 admitted.
Faculty *Total:* 265, 84% full-time, 66% with terminal degrees. *Student/faculty ratio:* 16:1.
Majors Accounting; anthropology; biological and physical sciences; biology/biological sciences; business administration and management; Canadian studies; chemistry; classics and languages, literatures and linguistics; computer and information sciences; cultural studies; economics; education; elementary education; English; environmental studies; foods, nutrition, and wellness; French; geology/earth science; history; hydrology and water resources science; information science/studies; jazz/jazz studies; kinesiology and exercise science; liberal arts and sciences/liberal studies; management information systems; mathematics; modern languages; music; nursing (registered nurse training); nursing science; philosophy; physical education teaching and coaching; physical sciences; physics; political science and government; pre-dentistry studies; pre-law studies; pre-medical studies; pre-veterinary studies; psychology; religious studies; secondary education; sociology; women's studies.
Academics *Calendar:* Canadian standard year. *Degrees:* diplomas, bachelor's, and master's. *Special study options:* academic remediation for entering students, accelerated degree program, adult/continuing education programs, advanced placement credit, cooperative education, distance learning, double majors, English as a second language, honors programs, independent study, internships, off-campus study, part-time degree program, services for LD students, student-designed majors, study abroad, summer session for credit.
Computers on Campus 350 computers/terminals are available on campus for general student use. Students can access the following: campus intranet, computer help desk, free student e-mail accounts, online (class) grades, online (class) registration, online (class) schedules. Campuswide network is available. 100% of college-owned or -operated housing units are wired for high-speed Internet access. Wireless service is available via entire campus.
Student Life *Housing options:* coed, men-only, women-only, disabled students. Campus housing is university owned. Freshman campus housing is guaranteed. *Activities and organizations:* drama/theater group, student-run newspaper, radio station, choral group, X-Project, Walkhome Program, orientation committee, Exekoi Tutoring, Off-Campus Society. *Campus security:* 24-hour emergency response devices and patrols, student patrols, late-night transport/escort service, controlled dormitory access. *Student services:* health clinic, personal/psychological counseling, women's center.
Athletics Member CIS. *Intercollegiate sports:* basketball M/W, cheerleading M/W, cross-country running M/W, football M, ice hockey M/W, lacrosse M, rock climbing M/W, soccer M, tennis M/W, volleyball W. *Intramural sports:* badminton M/W, basketball M/W, cross-country running M/W, football M/W, golf M/W, ice hockey M/W, racquetball M/W, rock climbing M/W, soccer M/W, softball M/W, squash M/W, swimming and diving M/W, table tennis M/W, tennis M/W, track and field M/W, ultimate Frisbee M/W, volleyball M/W, water polo M/W, weight lifting M/W.
Standardized Tests *Required for some:* SAT or ACT (for admission). *Recommended:* SAT or ACT (for admission), SAT Subject Tests (for admission).
Costs (2007–08) *Comprehensive fee:* $13,845 Canadian dollars includes full-time tuition ($6205 Canadian dollars), mandatory fees ($1145 Canadian dollars), and room and board ($6495 Canadian dollars). Full-time tuition and fees vary according to course load. International tuition: $12,410 Canadian dollars full-time. *Room and board:* Room and board charges vary according to board plan and housing facility. *Waivers:* senior citizens and employees or children of employees.
Applying *Options:* electronic application, early admission, early decision, deferred entrance. *Application fee:* $40 Canadian dollars. *Required:* essay or personal statement, high school transcript, 2 letters of recommendation. *Application deadlines:* rolling (freshmen), rolling (transfers). *Notification:* continuous until 8/15 (freshmen), continuous until 8/15 (transfers).
Freshman Application Contact Ms. Sarah Murray, Admissions Officer, St. Francis Xavier University, PO Box 5000, Antigonish, NS B2G 2W5, Canada. *Phone:* 902-867-2219. *Toll-free phone:* 877-867-7839 (in-state); 877-867-STFX (out-of-state). *Fax:* 902-867-2329. *E-mail:* mbarry@stfx.ca.

SAINT MARY'S UNIVERSITY
Halifax, Nova Scotia, Canada **www.stmarys.ca/**

Director of Admissions Mr. Greg Ferguson, Director of Admissions, Saint Mary's University, Halifax, NS B3H 3C3, Canada. *Phone:* 902-420-5415. *E-mail:* greg.ferguson@smu.ca.

SAINT PAUL UNIVERSITY
Ottawa, Ontario, Canada **www.ustpaul.ca/**

Director of Admissions Claudette Dubé-Socqué, Registrar, Saint Paul University, 223 Main Street, Ottawa, ON K1S 1C4, Canada. *Phone:* 613-236-1393 Ext. 2238.

ST. THOMAS UNIVERSITY
Fredericton, New Brunswick, Canada **www.stu.ca/**

- **Independent Roman Catholic** 4-year, founded 1910
- **Small-town** 16-acre campus
- **Endowment** $30.8 million
- **Coed** 2,652 undergraduate students, 91% full-time, 66% women, 34% men
- **Moderately difficult** entrance level, 81% of applicants were admitted

Undergraduates 2,423 full-time, 229 part-time. Students come from 10 provinces and territories, 42 other countries, 27% are from out of state, 5% international, 5% transferred in, 28% live on campus. *Retention:* 69% of 2006 full-time freshmen returned.
Freshmen *Admission:* 1,345 applied, 1,085 admitted, 768 enrolled. *Average high school GPA:* 3.3.
Faculty *Total:* 203, 54% full-time, 67% with terminal degrees. *Student/faculty ratio:* 19:1.
Majors Adult development and aging; American Indian/Native American studies; anthropology; criminology; economics; education; English; French; gerontology; history; interdisciplinary studies; journalism; mathematics; philosophy; political science and government; psychology; religious studies; social work; sociology; Spanish.
Academics *Calendar:* Canadian standard year. *Degrees:* certificates, bachelor's, first professional, and postbachelor's certificates. *Special study options:*

COLLEGE DATA CENTER • CANADA

academic remediation for entering students, accelerated degree program, advanced placement credit, cooperative education, distance learning, double majors, English as a second language, honors programs, independent study, internships, off-campus study, part-time degree program, services for LD students, student-designed majors, study abroad, summer session for credit.

Computers on Campus 200 computers/terminals and 21 ports are available on campus for general student use. Students can access the following: computer help desk, free student e-mail accounts, online (class) grades, online (class) registration, online (class) schedules, WebCT. Campuswide network is available. 100% of college-owned or -operated housing units are wired for high-speed Internet access. Wireless service is available via dorm rooms, libraries, student centers.

Student Life *Housing options:* coed, women-only. Campus housing is university owned. Freshman campus housing is guaranteed. *Activities and organizations:* drama/theater group, student-run newspaper, radio station, choral group, Theatre St. Thomas, St. Thomas Student Union, Political Science Society, Economics Society, Student Help Centre. *Campus security:* 24-hour emergency response devices and patrols, student patrols, late-night transport/escort service, controlled dormitory access. *Student services:* health clinic, personal/psychological counseling, women's center.

Athletics Member CIS. *Intercollegiate sports:* basketball M/W, cross-country running M/W, golf M/W, ice hockey M (s)/W (s), rock climbing M/W, soccer M/W, volleyball M/W. *Intramural sports:* badminton M/W, basketball M/W, cheerleading M/W, cross-country running M/W, fencing M/W, football M, ice hockey M/W, racquetball M/W, skiing (cross-country) M/W, skiing (downhill) M/W, soccer M/W, softball M/W, squash M/W, swimming and diving M/W, table tennis M/W, tennis M/W, track and field M/W, ultimate Frisbee M/W, volleyball M/W, water polo M/W.

Standardized Tests *Recommended:* SAT (for admission).

Costs (2007–08) *Comprehensive fee:* $11,311 Canadian dollars includes full-time tuition ($4570 Canadian dollars), mandatory fees ($291 Canadian dollars), and room and board ($6450 Canadian dollars). Full-time tuition and fees vary according to course load, degree level, and program. Part-time tuition: $510 Canadian dollars per course. Part-time tuition and fees vary according to course load. International tuition: $9140 Canadian dollars full-time. *Required fees:* $28 Canadian dollars per course part-time. *Room and board:* Room and board charges vary according to board plan, housing facility, and location. *Payment plans:* installment, deferred payment. *Waivers:* senior citizens and employees or children of employees.

Financial Aid *Financial aid deadline:* 3/1.

Applying *Options:* electronic application, early action. *Application fee:* $35 Canadian dollars. *Required:* high school transcript, minimum 3.0 GPA. *Required for some:* essay or personal statement, interview. *Application deadlines:* 8/31 (freshmen), 8/31 (transfers), 12/7 (early action). *Notification:* continuous (freshmen), continuous (transfers).

Freshman Application Contact Ms. Kathryn Monti, Director of Admissions, St. Thomas University, Admissions and Welcome Building, St. Thomas University, Fredericton, NB E3B 5G3. *Phone:* 506-452-0532. *Fax:* 506-452-0617. *E-mail:* admissions@stu.ca.

SIMON FRASER UNIVERSITY

Burnaby, British Columbia, Canada **www.sfu.ca/**

- **Province-supported** university, founded 1965
- **Suburban** campus with easy access to Vancouver
- **Endowment** $180.8 million
- **Coed** 21,796 undergraduate students, 52% full-time, 55% women, 45% men
- **Moderately difficult** entrance level, 71% of applicants were admitted

Undergraduates 11,408 full-time, 10,388 part-time. Students come from 11 provinces and territories, 97 other countries, 5% are from out of state, 5% transferred in, 8% live on campus. *Retention:* 73% of 2006 full-time freshmen returned.

Freshmen *Admission:* 10,816 applied, 7,673 admitted, 5,386 enrolled. *Average high school GPA:* 3.2.

Faculty *Total:* 911, 100% full-time, 87% with terminal degrees. *Student/faculty ratio:* 28:1.

Majors Actuarial science; applied mathematics; archeology; art; biochemistry; biological and physical sciences; biology/biological sciences; business administration and management; Canadian studies; chemical physics; chemistry; clinical psychology; cognitive science; communication/speech communication and rhetoric; computer science; criminology; dance; dramatic/theater arts; economics; education; engineering science; English; environmental science; film/cinema studies; French; general studies; geography; geology/earth science; history; humanities; kinesiology and exercise science; liberal arts and sciences/liberal studies; linguistics; management information systems; management science; mathematics; molecular biochemistry; molecular biology; music; philosophy; physics; political science and government; psychology; social sciences related; sociology; statistics; visual and performing arts related; women's studies.

Academics *Calendar:* trimesters. *Degrees:* certificates, diplomas, bachelor's, master's, doctoral, post-master's, and postbachelor's certificates. *Special study options:* advanced placement credit, cooperative education, distance learning, double majors, honors programs, independent study, off-campus study, part-time degree program, services for LD students, student-designed majors, study abroad, summer session for credit.

Computers on Campus 900 computers/terminals are available on campus for general student use. Students can access the following: free student e-mail accounts, online (class) grades, online (class) registration, online (class) schedules. Campuswide network is available. 50% of college-owned or -operated housing units are wired for high-speed Internet access. Wireless service is available via entire campus.

Student Life *Housing options:* coed, women-only, disabled students. Campus housing is university owned. Freshman applicants given priority for college housing. *Activities and organizations:* drama/theater group, student-run newspaper, radio station, The Peak Newspaper, orientation leaders, Crisis line, Women's Centre, Simon Fraser Public Interest Research Group. *Campus security:* 24-hour emergency response devices and patrols, student patrols, late-night transport/escort service, controlled dormitory access, safe-walk stations, 24-hour safe study area. *Student services:* health clinic, personal/psychological counseling, women's center, legal services.

Athletics Member NAIA, CIS. *Intercollegiate sports:* basketball M (s)/W (s), cross-country running M (s)/W (s), field hockey W, football M (s), golf M (s), gymnastics M, soccer M (s)/W (s), softball W (s), swimming and diving M (s)/W (s), track and field M (s)/W (s), volleyball W (s), wrestling M (s). *Intramural sports:* archery M (c)/W (c), badminton M (c)/W (c), basketball M/W, cheerleading M (c)/W (c), crew M (c)/W (c), fencing M (c)/W (c), field hockey W (c), football M/W, golf W (c), gymnastics W (c), ice hockey W (c), lacrosse M (c), rugby M (c)/W (c), soccer M/W, softball M/W, squash M (c)/W (c), table tennis M (c)/W (c), tennis M/W, ultimate Frisbee M (c)/W (c), volleyball M (c)/W (c), water polo M (c)/W (c).

Standardized Tests *Required for some:* SAT or ACT (for admission).

Costs (2007–08) *Tuition:* province resident $151 Canadian dollars per credit hour part-time; nonresident $4539 Canadian dollars full-time, $484 Canadian dollars per credit hour part-time; International tuition $14,532 Canadian dollars full-time. Full-time tuition and fees vary according to degree level and program. Part-time tuition and fees vary according to degree level and program. *Required fees:* $321 Canadian dollars full-time, $99 Canadian dollars per term part-time. *Room and board:* $6818 Canadian dollars; room only: $4118 Canadian dollars. *Waivers:* senior citizens and employees or children of employees.

Financial Aid Of all full-time matriculated undergraduates who enrolled in 2006, 573 state and other part-time jobs (averaging $1105). *Financial aid deadline:* 11/15.

Applying *Options:* electronic application, early admission, early decision. *Application fee:* $100 Canadian dollars. *Required:* high school transcript, minimum 3.2 GPA. *Required for some:* essay or personal statement, letters of recommendation, interview. *Application deadlines:* 4/30 (freshmen), rolling (transfers). *Early decision deadline:* 3/1. *Notification:* 6/30 (freshmen), continuous (transfers), 4/15 (early decision).

Freshman Application Contact Ms. Donna Moore, Director of Admissions, Simon Fraser University, 8888 University Drive, Burnaby, BC V5A 1S6, Canada. *Phone:* 778-782-3224. *Fax:* 778-782-4969. *E-mail:* undergraduate-admissions@sfu.ca.

See page 2852 for the College Close-Up.

SOUTHERN ALBERTA INSTITUTE OF TECHNOLOGY

Calgary, Alberta, Canada **www.sait.ca/**

- **Province-supported** 4-year, founded 1916
- **Coed** 7,120 undergraduate students, 92% full-time, 42% women, 58% men

Undergraduates 6,550 full-time, 570 part-time.

Majors Business administration and management; business administration, management and operations related; geography related; information science/studies; petroleum engineering.

Academics *Calendar:* trimesters. *Degrees:* certificates, diplomas, bachelor's, and first professional certificates.
Computers on Campus Students can access the following: campus intranet, computer help desk, free student e-mail accounts, online (class) grades, online (class) registration, online (class) schedules. Campuswide network is available. 100% of college-owned or -operated housing units are wired for high-speed Internet access. Wireless service is available via classrooms, computer centers, computer labs, dorm rooms, learning centers, libraries, student centers.
Student Life *Housing options:* coed, disabled students. Campus housing is university owned. *Activities and organizations:* drama/theater group, student-run newspaper, radio and television station, SAIT Petroleum Society, Business Student's Association, Global Passport, Environmental Technology Students Organization, Civil Engineering Technology Concrete Tobagon. *Student services:* health clinic, personal/psychological counseling.
Athletics *Intercollegiate sports:* basketball M (s)/W (s), cross-country running M/W, ice hockey M (s)/W (s), soccer M (s)/W (s), volleyball M (s)/W (s). *Intramural sports:* basketball M/W, football M/W, ice hockey M/W, soccer M/W, softball M/W, volleyball M/W.
Applying *Options:* electronic application, early admission, early decision. *Application fee:* $25 Canadian dollars. *Required:* high school transcript. *Required for some:* essay or personal statement, letters of recommendation, interview. *Application deadline:* 2/28 (freshmen).
Director of Admissions Ms. Jennifer Bennett, Registrar/Director, Southern Alberta Institute of Technology, 1301-16 Avenue, NW, Calgary, AB T2N 3W2, Canada. *Phone:* 403-284-8857. *Toll-free phone:* 877-284-SAIT. *Fax:* 403-284-7112.

STEINBACH BIBLE COLLEGE

Steinbach, Manitoba, Canada **sbcollege.ca/**

- **Independent Mennonite** 4-year, founded 1936
- **Small-town** 16-acre campus with easy access to Winnipeg
- **Coed** 149 undergraduate students
- **Minimally difficult** entrance level, 96% of applicants were admitted

Undergraduates 12% are from out of state. *Retention:* 67% of 2006 full-time freshmen returned.
Freshmen *Admission:* 50 applied, 48 admitted.
Faculty *Total:* 18, 11% full-time, 11% with terminal degrees. *Student/faculty ratio:* 15:1.
Majors Biblical studies; music; religious studies.
Academics *Calendar:* semesters. *Degree:* certificates, diplomas, and bachelor's.
Costs (2008–09) *Comprehensive fee:* $10,015 includes full-time tuition ($5632), mandatory fees ($283), and room and board ($4100). Part-time tuition: $176 per credit hour. *Required fees:* $60 per year part-time.
Applying *Options:* electronic application. *Application fee:* $50 Canadian dollars.
Freshman Application Contact Ms. Darlene Friesen, Admissions Counselor, Steinbach Bible College, 50 PTH 12 North, Steinbach, MB R5G 1T4, Canada. *Phone:* 204-326-6451 Ext. 232. *Toll-free phone:* 800-230-8478. *Fax:* 204-326-6908. *E-mail:* info@sbcollege.ca.

SUMMIT PACIFIC COLLEGE

Abbotsford, British Columbia, Canada **www.summitpacific.ca/**

Director of Admissions Ms. Melody Deeley, Registrar, Summit Pacific College, Box 1700, Abbotsford, BC V2S 7E7, Canada. *Phone:* 604-853-7491. *Toll-free phone:* 800-976-8388.

TAYLOR UNIVERSITY COLLEGE AND SEMINARY

Edmonton, Alberta, Canada **www.taylor-edu.ca/**

- **Independent North American Baptist** comprehensive, founded 1940
- **Urban** 27-acre campus
- **Endowment** $4.5 million
- **Coed** 158 undergraduate students, 71% full-time, 54% women, 46% men
- **Minimally difficult** entrance level, 78% of applicants were admitted

Undergraduates 112 full-time, 46 part-time. Students come from 4 provinces and territories, 4 other countries, 28% are from out of state, 8% transferred in, 30% live on campus. *Retention:* 88% of 2006 full-time freshmen returned.
Freshmen *Admission:* 152 applied, 119 admitted, 22 enrolled.
Faculty *Total:* 30, 23% full-time, 60% with terminal degrees. *Student/faculty ratio:* 16:1.
Majors Biblical studies; divinity/ministry; education; English; liberal arts and sciences/liberal studies; music; religious studies.
Academics *Calendar:* semesters. *Degrees:* certificates, associate, bachelor's, and master's. *Special study options:* academic remediation for entering students, adult/continuing education programs, advanced placement credit, cooperative education, English as a second language, internships, off-campus study, part-time degree program, student-designed majors.
Computers on Campus 16 computers/terminals are available on campus for general student use. Students can access the following: campus intranet, free student e-mail accounts. Campuswide network is available. 100% of college-owned or -operated housing units are wired for high-speed Internet access.
Student Life *Housing:* on-campus residence required for freshman year. *Options:* coed. Campus housing is university owned. Freshman campus housing is guaranteed. *Activities and organizations:* drama/theater group, student-run newspaper, choral group, Choristers (choral group), Student Union, prayer groups, Sacrifice of Praise (band), Athletics. *Campus security:* evening and late night patrols by security.
Standardized Tests *Recommended:* SAT or ACT (for admission).
Costs (2007–08) *One-time required fee:* $300. *Comprehensive fee:* $11,950 includes full-time tuition ($6930), mandatory fees ($480), and room and board ($4540). Part-time tuition: $225 per credit hour. *Required fees:* $10 per credit hour part-time, $15 per term part-time. *College room only:* $2240.
Financial Aid *Financial aid deadline:* 6/1.
Applying *Options:* electronic application, deferred entrance. *Application fee:* $35 Canadian dollars. *Required:* essay or personal statement, high school transcript, 3 letters of recommendation. *Required for some:* minimum 2.0 GPA, interview. *Application deadlines:* 8/1 (freshmen), 8/1 (transfers). *Notification:* continuous until 8/31 (freshmen), continuous until 8/31 (transfers).
Freshman Application Contact Ms. Michelle Hudson, Taylor University College and Seminary, 11525 Twenty-third Avenue, AB T6J 4T3, Canada. *Phone:* 780-431-5218. *Toll-free phone:* 800-567-4988. *Fax:* 780-436-9416. *E-mail:* admissions@taylor-edu.ca.

TÉLÉ-UNIVERSITÉ

Québec, Quebec, Canada **www.teluq.uquebec.ca/**

Freshman Application Contact Ms. Louise Bertrand, Registraire, Télé-université, 455, rue de l'Église, C.P. 4800, succ. Terminus, Québec, QC G1K 9H5, Canada. *Phone:* 418-657-2262 Ext. 5307. *Toll-free phone:* 888-843-4333.

THOMPSON RIVERS UNIVERSITY

Kamloops, British Columbia, Canada **www.tru.ca**

- **Province-supported** 4-year, founded 1970, part of Ministry of Advanced Education—Government of the Province of British Columbia
- **Small-town** 100-acre campus
- **Endowment** $7.4 million
- **Coed** 7,425 undergraduate students
- 48% of applicants were admitted

Undergraduates Students come from 10 provinces and territories, 60 other countries, 7% are from out of state, 13% live on campus.
Freshmen *Admission:* 3,671 applied, 1,750 admitted.
Faculty *Total:* 731, 60% full-time. *Student/faculty ratio:* 12:1.
Majors Accounting; anesthesiologist assistant; animal/livestock husbandry and production; animal sciences; biochemistry; biology/biological sciences; business administration and management; business/commerce; Canadian studies; cardiovascular technology; carpentry; cell and molecular biology; cell biology and histology; chemistry; child care and support services management; communications systems installation and repair technology; computer and information

sciences; computer engineering related; computer graphics; computer installation and repair technology; computer programming; computer science; computer systems analysis; computer technology/computer systems technology; desktop publishing and digital imaging design; drafting and design technology; dramatic/theater arts; dramatic/theater arts and stagecraft related; early childhood education; ecology; economics; electrical, electronics and communications engineering; electrical/electronics equipment installation and repair; electrician; elementary education; engineering; English; environmental biology; executive assistant/executive secretary; finance; fine/studio arts; general studies; geography; graphic design; health science; health services/allied health/health sciences; history; hospitality administration; hospitality administration related; hospitality and recreation marketing; hotel/motel administration; human resources management; human resources management and services related; industrial electronics technology; journalism; liberal arts and sciences/liberal studies; manufacturing technology; marketing/marketing management; mathematics; molecular biology; natural resources/conservation; nursing (licensed practical/vocational nurse training); nursing (registered nurse training); nursing science; office management; perfusion technology; physics; pipefitting and sprinkler fitting; plumbing technology; political science and government; pre-dentistry studies; pre-medical studies; pre-pharmacy studies; pre-veterinary studies; psychology; public relations, advertising, and applied communication related; resort management; respiratory care therapy; respiratory therapy technician; sales, distribution and marketing; social sciences; social work; sociology; sport and fitness administration/management; system administration; system, networking, and LAN/WAN management; tourism and travel services marketing; tourism promotion; veterinary/animal health technology; visual and performing arts; visual and performing arts related; web page, digital/multimedia and information resources design; zoology/animal biology related.

Academics *Calendar:* semesters. *Degrees:* certificates, diplomas, associate, bachelor's, master's, and postbachelor's certificates. *Special study options:* academic remediation for entering students, accelerated degree program, adult/continuing education programs, advanced placement credit, cooperative education, distance learning, double majors, English as a second language, external degree program, honors programs, independent study, internships, off-campus study, part-time degree program, services for LD students, study abroad, summer session for credit.

Computers on Campus 300 computers/terminals are available on campus for general student use. Students can access the following: campus intranet, computer help desk, free student e-mail accounts, online (class) grades, online (class) registration, online (class) schedules, WebCT. Campuswide network is available. 100% of college-owned or -operated housing units are wired for high-speed Internet access. Wireless service is available via entire campus.

Student Life *Housing options:* coed. Campus housing is university owned and is provided by a third party. *Activities and organizations:* drama/theater group, student-run newspaper, radio station, choral group, national fraternities. *Campus security:* 24-hour emergency response devices and patrols, student patrols, late-night transport/escort service, controlled dormitory access. *Student services:* health clinic, personal/psychological counseling.

Athletics Member CIS. *Intercollegiate sports:* badminton M (s)/W (s), baseball M, basketball M (s)/W (s), soccer M (s)/W (s), volleyball M (s)/W (s). *Intramural sports:* crew M/W, cross-country running M/W, football M, ice hockey M, racquetball M/W, rugby M, skiing (cross-country) M/W, skiing (downhill) M/W, softball M/W, squash M/W, swimming and diving M/W, table tennis M/W, track and field M/W.

Costs (2007–08) *Tuition:* province resident $3400 Canadian dollars full-time, $113 Canadian dollars per credit part-time; nonresident $3400 Canadian dollars full-time, $113 Canadian dollars per credit part-time; International tuition $12,000 Canadian dollars full-time. *Required fees:* $710 Canadian dollars full-time, $26 Canadian dollars per credit part-time, $40 Canadian dollars per term part-time. *Room only:* $3400 Canadian dollars.

Applying *Options:* electronic application. *Application fee:* $25 Canadian dollars. *Required:* high school transcript. *Required for some:* essay or personal statement, letters of recommendation, interview. *Application deadlines:* 3/1 (freshmen), 3/1 (transfers). *Notification:* continuous until 3/1 (freshmen).

Freshman Application Contact Mr. Josh Keller, Director, Public Relations and Student Recruitment, Thompson Rivers University, PO Box 3010, 900 McGill Road, Kamloops, BC V2C 5N3, Canada. *Phone:* 250-828-5008. *Fax:* 250-828-5159. *E-mail:* jkeller@tru.ca.

TRENT UNIVERSITY

Peterborough, Ontario, Canada **www.trentu.ca/**

- **Province-supported** university, founded 1963
- **Suburban** 1400-acre campus with easy access to Toronto
- **Endowment** $3.3 million
- **Coed** 7,546 undergraduate students, 81% full-time, 66% women, 34% men
- **Moderately difficult** entrance level, 28% of applicants were admitted

Undergraduates 6,137 full-time, 1,409 part-time. Students come from 34 provinces and territories, 114 other countries, 7% transferred in, 17% live on campus. *Retention:* 86% of 2006 full-time freshmen returned.

Freshmen *Admission:* 8,699 applied, 2,433 admitted, 2,261 enrolled.

Faculty *Total:* 432, 63% full-time. *Student/faculty ratio:* 18:1.

Majors American Indian/Native American studies; anthropology; applied mathematics; biochemistry; biological and physical sciences; biology/biological sciences; business administration and management; Canadian studies; chemistry; classics and languages, literatures and linguistics; computer science; economics; education; elementary education; English; environmental studies; French; geography; German; Hispanic-American, Puerto Rican, and Mexican-American/Chicano studies; history; humanities; interdisciplinary studies; international relations and affairs; liberal arts and sciences/liberal studies; literature; mathematics; modern Greek; modern languages; natural sciences; nursing (registered nurse training); philosophy; physical sciences; physics; political science and government; psychology; secondary education; social sciences; sociology; women's studies.

Academics *Calendar:* Canadian standard year. *Degrees:* diplomas, bachelor's, master's, and doctoral. *Special study options:* academic remediation for entering students, accelerated degree program, adult/continuing education programs, advanced placement credit, double majors, honors programs, off-campus study, part-time degree program, services for LD students, student-designed majors, study abroad, summer session for credit.

Computers on Campus 264 computers/terminals and 264 ports are available on campus for general student use. Students can access the following: campus intranet, computer help desk, free student e-mail accounts, online (class) grades, online (class) registration, online (class) schedules, online tuition payment. Campuswide network is available. Wireless service is available via classrooms, computer centers, computer labs, learning centers, libraries, student centers.

Student Life *Housing options:* coed, women-only. Campus housing is university owned. *Activities and organizations:* drama/theater group, student-run newspaper, radio station, choral group, Trent Radio, Trent International Program, Trent Central Student Association, Arthur (student newspaper), Excalibur (yearbook). *Campus security:* 24-hour emergency response devices and patrols, student patrols, late-night transport/escort service. *Student services:* health clinic, personal/psychological counseling, women's center.

Athletics Member CIS. *Intercollegiate sports:* basketball M (c)/W (c), crew M/W, cross-country running M/W, fencing M/W, field hockey W, golf M/W, rugby M/W, skiing (cross-country) M/W, soccer M/W, squash M/W, swimming and diving M/W, volleyball M (c)/W (c). *Intramural sports:* badminton M/W, basketball M/W, cross-country running M/W, football M/W, ice hockey M/W, soccer M/W, softball M/W, squash M/W, swimming and diving M/W, tennis M/W, track and field M/W, volleyball M/W, water polo M/W.

Standardized Tests *Required for some:* SAT or ACT (for admission).

Costs (2007–08) *Tuition:* area resident $4569 Canadian dollars full-time; province resident $1003 Canadian dollars per course part-time; nonresident $1003 Canadian dollars per course part-time; International tuition $12,452 Canadian dollars full-time. Full-time tuition and fees vary according to location and student level. Part-time tuition and fees vary according to course load and student level. *Required fees:* $2126 Canadian dollars full-time, $9 Canadian dollars per term part-time. *Room and board:* $6402 Canadian dollars; room only: $3872 Canadian dollars. Room and board charges vary according to board plan, housing facility, and location. *Payment plans:* installment, deferred payment. *Waivers:* employees or children of employees.

Applying *Options:* early decision, deferred entrance. *Application fee:* $95 Canadian dollars. *Required:* high school transcript, minimum 2.8 GPA. *Required for some:* essay or personal statement, letters of recommendation, interview. *Application deadlines:* 6/1 (freshmen), 6/1 (transfers).

Freshman Application Contact Mr. Luis Fleming, Admissions Officer, Trent University, Office of the Registrar, Peterborough, ON K9J 7B8, Canada. *Phone:* 705-748-1215. *Fax:* 705-748-1629. *E-mail:* leaders@trentu.ca.

See page 2854 for the College Close-Up.

TRINITY WESTERN UNIVERSITY

Langley, British Columbia, Canada **www.twu.ca/**

Director of Admissions Brian Kerr, Director of Admissions, Trinity Western University, 7600 Glover Road, Langley, BC V2Y 1Y1, Canada. *Phone:* 604-888-7511 Ext. 3005. *Toll-free phone:* 888-468-6898. *E-mail:* admissions@twu.ca.

TYNDALE UNIVERSITY COLLEGE & SEMINARY

Toronto, Ontario, Canada **www.tyndale.ca/**

- **Independent interdenominational** comprehensive, founded 1894
- **Urban** 10-acre campus
- **Endowment** $2.0 million
- **Coed** 479 undergraduate students, 73% full-time, 48% women, 52% men
- **Moderately difficult** entrance level, 53% of applicants were admitted

Undergraduates 348 full-time, 131 part-time. Students come from 7 provinces and territories, 12 other countries, 30% live on campus. *Retention:* 49% of 2006 full-time freshmen returned.

Freshmen *Admission:* 368 applied, 196 admitted, 193 enrolled.

Faculty *Total:* 54. *Student/faculty ratio:* 23:1.

Majors Biblical studies; business/commerce; divinity/ministry; English; history; hospitality and recreation marketing; human services; liberal arts and sciences/liberal studies; parks, recreation and leisure; pastoral studies/counseling; philosophy; psychology; religious education.

Academics *Calendar:* semesters. *Degrees:* certificates, bachelor's, master's, and first professional. *Special study options:* academic remediation for entering students, accelerated degree program, adult/continuing education programs, honors programs, off-campus study, part-time degree program, summer session for credit.

Computers on Campus 30 computers/terminals are available on campus for general student use. Students can access the following: free student e-mail accounts, online (class) registration, online (class) schedules. Campuswide network is available. Wireless service is available via entire campus.

Student Life *Housing options:* coed. Campus housing is university owned. Freshman applicants given priority for college housing. *Activities and organizations:* drama/theater group, student-run newspaper, choral group, choir, student government, Urban Ministry Team, "Steadfast" drama team. *Campus security:* student patrols, late-night transport/escort service, controlled dormitory access. *Student services:* personal/psychological counseling.

Athletics *Intercollegiate sports:* basketball M/W, ice hockey M, ultimate Frisbee M (s)/W (s), volleyball M (s)/W (s). *Intramural sports:* badminton M (c)/W (c), basketball M (c), football M, golf M, skiing (cross-country) M (c)/W (c), skiing (downhill) M (c)/W (c), soccer M (c)/W (c), softball M/W, swimming and diving M (c)/W (c), ultimate Frisbee M/W, volleyball M/W, weight lifting M (c)/W (c).

Costs (2008–09) *Comprehensive fee:* $14,110 includes full-time tuition ($11,040), mandatory fees ($1020), and room and board ($2050). Part-time tuition: $1104 per course. *Required fees:* $102 per course part-time. *College room only:* $1050.

Applying *Options:* deferred entrance. *Application fee:* $50 Canadian dollars. *Required:* essay or personal statement, high school transcript, 2 letters of recommendation, all post-secondary transcripts. *Required for some:* interview. *Application deadlines:* 8/15 (freshmen), 8/15 (transfers). *Notification:* 9/19 (freshmen), 9/19 (transfers).

Freshman Application Contact Tricia McKenley, Admissions Office Coordinator, Tyndale University College & Seminary, 25 Ballyconnor Court, Toronto, ON M2M 4B3, Canada. *Phone:* 416-218-6757 Ext. 6738. *Toll-free phone:* 800-663-6052. *E-mail:* admissions@tydale.ca.

UNIVERSITÉ DE MONCTON

Moncton, New Brunswick, Canada **www.umoncton.ca/**

Freshman Application Contact Miss Nicole Savois, Chief Admission Officer, Université de Moncton, Moncton, NB E1A 3E9, Canada. *Phone:* 506-858-4115. *Toll-free phone:* 800-363-8336. *E-mail:* gallanrm@umoncton.ca.

UNIVERSITÉ DE MONTRÉAL

Montréal, Quebec, Canada **www.umontreal.ca/**

- **Independent** university, founded 1920, administratively affiliated with L'Ecole Polytechnique de Montrèal, HEC Montrèal
- **Urban** 150-acre campus
- **Endowment** $837.0 million
- **Coed**
- **Moderately difficult** entrance level

Academics *Calendar:* trimesters. *Degrees:* certificates, bachelor's, master's, and doctoral.

Student Life *Campus security:* 24-hour emergency response devices and patrols, student patrols, late-night transport/escort service, controlled dormitory access, cameras, alarm systems, crime prevention programs.

Athletics Member CIS.

Costs (2007–08) *Tuition:* province resident $1668 Canadian dollars full-time, $60 Canadian dollars per credit part-time; nonresident $4401 Canadian dollars full-time, $147 Canadian dollars per credit part-time; International tuition $10,878 Canadian dollars full-time. *Required fees:* $265 Canadian dollars full-time.

Financial Aid Of all full-time matriculated undergraduates who enrolled in 2006, 400 state and other part-time jobs.

Applying *Application fee:* $50 Canadian dollars. *Required:* Diploma of Collegiate Studies (and transcript) or equivalent. *Required for some:* interview.

Freshman Application Contact Mr. Pierre Chenard, Registrar, Université de Montréal, Case postale 6205, Succursale Centre-ville, 2332 boul. Édouard-Montpetit, Montréal, QC H3C 3T5, Canada. *Phone:* 514-343-2214. *Fax:* 514-343-2097. *E-mail:* pierre.chenard@umontreal.ca.

UNIVERSITÉ DE SHERBROOKE

Sherbrooke, Quebec, Canada **www.usherbrooke.ca/**

- **Independent** university, founded 1954
- **Urban** 800-acre campus with easy access to Montreal
- **Coed** 14,437 undergraduate students, 71% full-time, 55% women, 45% men
- **Moderately difficult** entrance level, 68% of applicants were admitted

Undergraduates 10,222 full-time, 4,215 part-time. Students come from 3 provinces and territories, 53 other countries, 3% are from out of state, 6% transferred in.

Freshmen *Admission:* 9,332 applied, 6,328 admitted, 2,512 enrolled.

Faculty *Total:* 1,331, 66% full-time.

Majors Accounting; athletic training; biochemistry; biology/biological sciences; business administration and management; chemical engineering; chemistry; civil engineering; communication and media related; computer and information sciences related; computer engineering; computer management; computer programming; computer science; counselor education/school counseling and guidance; ecology; education; electrical, electronics and communications engineering; elementary education; English; finance; French; history; information science/studies; information technology; interdisciplinary studies; kindergarten/preschool education; kinesiology and exercise science; legal studies; marketing/marketing management; mathematics; mechanical engineering; medical microbiology and bacteriology; nursing (registered nurse training); philosophy; physical education teaching and coaching; physics; pre-medical studies; psychology; secondary education; social work; special education.

Academics *Calendar:* Canadian standard year. *Degrees:* certificates, diplomas, bachelor's, master's, doctoral, and first professional. *Special study options:* accelerated degree program, adult/continuing education programs, cooperative education, English as a second language, internships, off-campus study, part-time degree program, services for LD students, student-designed majors, study abroad, summer session for credit.

Computers on Campus 300 computers/terminals are available on campus for general student use. Campuswide network is available.

Student Life *Housing options:* coed. *Activities and organizations:* drama/theater group, student-run newspaper, radio station. *Campus security:* 24-hour emergency response devices and patrols. *Student services:* health clinic, personal/psychological counseling, legal services.

Athletics Member CIS. *Intercollegiate sports:* badminton M/W, football M (s), soccer M (s)/W (s), swimming and diving M (s)/W (s), track and field M (s)/W (s), volleyball M (s)/W (s). *Intramural sports:* badminton M/W, basketball M/W, cheerleading M/W, cross-country running M/W, ice hockey M, racquetball M/W, skiing (cross-country) M/W, skiing (downhill) M/W, soccer M/W, softball M/W, squash M/W, swimming and diving M/W, tennis M/W, track and field M/W, ultimate Frisbee M/W, volleyball M/W.

Costs (2007–08) *Tuition:* province resident $2600 Canadian dollars full-time, $56 Canadian dollars per credit part-time; nonresident $5050 Canadian dollars full-time, $163 Canadian dollars per credit part-time; International tuition $10,020 Canadian dollars full-time. Full-time tuition and fees vary according to course load, location, and reciprocity agreements. Part-time tuition and fees vary according to course load, location, and reciprocity agreements. *Required fees:*

$382 Canadian dollars full-time, $11 Canadian dollars per credit part-time, $30 Canadian dollars per term part-time. *Room and board:* $5800 Canadian dollars; room only: $2900 Canadian dollars. Room and board charges vary according to board plan, housing facility, and student level. *Waivers:* employees or children of employees.

Financial Aid Of all full-time matriculated undergraduates who enrolled in 2006, 332 state and other part-time jobs. *Financial aid deadline:* 3/31.

Applying *Options:* electronic application, early admission. *Application fee:* $70 Canadian dollars. *Required:* high school transcript. *Required for some:* letters of recommendation, interview. *Application deadline:* 3/1 (freshmen). *Notification:* continuous until 5/15 (freshmen).

Freshman Application Contact Ms. Lisa Bedard or Valerie Bergeron, Admissions Officers, Université de Sherbrooke, 2500, boulevard de l'Université, Sherbrooke, QC J1K 2R1, Canada. *Phone:* 819-821-7687. *Toll-free phone:* 800-267-UDES.

Université du Québec à Chicoutimi

Chicoutimi, Quebec, Canada **www.uqac.uquebec.ca/**

Freshman Application Contact Mr. Claudio Zoccastello, Admissions Officer, Université du Québec à Chicoutimi, 555, boulevard de L'Université, Chicoutimi, QC G7H 2B1, Canada. *Phone:* 418-545-5005. *E-mail:* czoccast@uqac.uquebec.ca.

Université du Québec à Montréal

Montréal, Quebec, Canada **www.uqam.ca/**

Freshman Application Contact Ms. Lucille Boisselle-Roy, Admissions Officer, Université du Québec à Montréal, CP 8888, Succursale Centre-ville, Montréal, QC H2L 4S8, Canada. *Phone:* 514-987-3132. *E-mail:* admission@uqam.ca.

Université du Québec à Rimouski

Rimouski, Quebec, Canada **www.uqar.qc.ca/**

- **Province-supported** comprehensive, founded 1973, part of Université du Québec
- **Small-town** campus
- **Coed**
- **Noncompetitive** entrance level

Academics *Calendar:* trimesters. *Degrees:* bachelor's, master's, and doctoral.

Student Life *Campus security:* 24-hour emergency response devices and patrols, security cameras.

Applying *Required:* high school transcript, Diploma of Collegiate Studies or equivalent. *Required for some:* interview.

Freshman Application Contact Ms. Marie Saint Laurent, Admissions Officer, Université du Québec à Rimouski, 300, Allee des Ursulines, CP 3300, Rimouski, QC G5L 3A1, Canada. *Phone:* 418-724-1433. *E-mail:* philippe_horth@uqar.uquebec.ca.

Université du Québec à Trois-Rivières

Trois-Rivières, Quebec, Canada **www.uqtr.ca/**

- **Province-supported** university, founded 1969, part of Université du Québec
- **Urban** campus with easy access to Montreal
- **Endowment** $3.3 million
- **Coed**
- **Noncompetitive** entrance level

Academics *Calendar:* trimesters. *Degrees:* certificates, bachelor's, master's, and doctoral.

Student Life *Campus security:* 24-hour emergency response devices and patrols, late-night transport/escort service, controlled dormitory access.

Athletics Member CIS.

Applying *Application fee:* $30 Canadian dollars. *Required:* Diploma of Collegiate Studies (and transcript) or equivalent. *Required for some:* interview.

Freshman Application Contact Ms. Jean Bois, Admissions Officer, Université du Québec à Trois-Rivières, Bureau du registraire, Service des admissions, 3350 Boulevard Des Forges, Trois Rivieres, QC G9A 5H7, Canada. *Phone:* 819-376-5011. *Toll-free phone:* 800-365-0922. *Fax:* 819-376-5232. *E-mail:* registraire@uqtr.ca.

Université du Québec, École de technologie supérieure

Montréal, Quebec, Canada **www.etsmtl.ca/**

Director of Admissions Mme. Francine Gamache, Registraire, Université du Québec, École de technologie supérieure, 1100, rue Notre Dame Ouest, Montréal, QC H3C 1K3, Canada. *Phone:* 514-396-8885. *E-mail:* admission@ets.mtl.ca.

Université du Québec en Abitibi-Témiscamingue

Rouyn-Noranda, Quebec, Canada **www.uqat.ca/**

Freshman Application Contact Mrs. Monique Fay, Admissions Officer, Université du Québec en Abitibi-Témiscamingue, 445 boulevard de l'Université, Rouyn-Noranda, QC J9X 5E4, Canada. *Phone:* 819-762-0971. *E-mail:* micheline.chevalier@uqat.uquebec.ca.

Université du Québec en Outaouais

Gatineau, Quebec, Canada **www.uqo.ca/**

- **Province-supported** university, founded 1981, part of Université du Québec
- **Small-town** campus with easy access to Ottawa
- **Coed** 4,337 undergraduate students
- **Noncompetitive** entrance level

Undergraduates Students come from 32 other countries. *Retention:* 90% of 2006 full-time freshmen returned.

Majors Accounting; art; business administration and management; computer engineering; computer science; design and visual communications; education; elementary education; fine/studio arts; human resources management and services related; international business/trade/commerce; kindergarten/preschool education; labor and industrial relations; language interpretation and translation; management information systems; nursing (registered nurse training); psychology; secondary education; social sciences; social work; sociology; special education.

Academics *Calendar:* trimesters. *Degrees:* certificates, bachelor's, master's, doctoral, and postbachelor's certificates. *Special study options:* accelerated degree program, adult/continuing education programs, internships, off-campus study, part-time degree program, services for LD students, study abroad, summer session for credit.

Computers on Campus 141 computers/terminals are available on campus for general student use. Students can access the following: online (class) registration. Campuswide network is available.

Student Life *Housing:* on-campus residence required through senior year. *Options:* coed. Campus housing is university owned. *Activities and organizations:* student-run newspaper, radio station, AGE, AIESEC, AEME, REMAA. *Campus security:* 24-hour emergency response devices and patrols, late-night transport/escort service. *Student services:* personal/psychological counseling.

Athletics *Intramural sports:* badminton M/W, basketball M/W, ice hockey M, rock climbing M/W, skiing (downhill) M, soccer M/W, swimming and diving M/W, table tennis M/W, tennis M/W, volleyball M/W, water polo M/W, weight lifting M/W.

Costs (2007–08) *Tuition:* area resident $2326 Canadian dollars full-time; International tuition $12,475 Canadian dollars full-time. Full-time tuition and fees vary according to course load, degree level, program, and reciprocity agreements. Part-time tuition and fees vary according to course load, degree level, and program. *Required fees:* $2407 Canadian dollars full-time. *Room and board:* $4680 Canadian dollars. Room and board charges vary according to housing facility. *Payment plan:* installment.

Applying *Application fee:* $60 Canadian dollars. *Required:* high school transcript, Diploma of Collegiate Studies (and transcript) or equivalent. *Required for some:* interview. *Application deadline:* 3/1 (freshmen). *Notification:* 5/15 (freshmen).

Freshman Application Contact Registrar Office, Université du Québec en Outaouais, CP 1250, Succursale B, 101, rue Saint-Jean-Bosco, bureau B-0150, Gatineau, QC J8X 3X7, Canada. *Phone:* 819-595-3900. *Toll-free phone:* 800-567-1283 Ext. 1840. *Fax:* 819-773-1835. *E-mail:* registraire@uqo.ca.

Université Laval

Québec, Quebec, Canada **www.ulaval.ca/**

- **Independent** university, founded 1852
- **Urban** 465-acre campus with easy access to Quebec City
- **Endowment** $436.0 million
- **Coed**
- **Minimally difficult** entrance level

Faculty *Student/faculty ratio:* 7:1.

Academics *Calendar:* trimesters. *Degrees:* certificates, diplomas, associate, bachelor's, master's, doctoral, first professional, postbachelor's, and first professional certificates.

Student Life *Campus security:* 24-hour emergency response devices and patrols, student patrols, late-night transport/escort service, controlled dormitory access, video cameras in most buildings, underground walkways.

Athletics Member CIS.

Applying *Options:* electronic application. *Application fee:* $30 Canadian dollars. *Required:* high school transcript, general knowledge of French language. *Required for some:* essay or personal statement, interview.

Freshman Application Contact Promotion and Recruitment Division, Université Laval, C.P. 2208, succursale Terminus, Québec, QC G1K 7P4, Canada. *Phone:* 418-656-2764. *Toll-free phone:* 877-785-2825. *Fax:* 418-656-5216. *E-mail:* info@dap.ulaval.ca.

Université Sainte-Anne

Church Point, Nova Scotia, Canada **www.usainteanne.ca/**

Freshman Application Contact Mrs. Blanche Thériault, Admissions Officer, Université Sainte-Anne, Church Point, NS B0W 1M0. *Phone:* 902-769-2114 Ext. 116. *E-mail:* admission@ustanne.ednet.ns.ca.

University College of the Fraser Valley

Abbotsford, British Columbia, Canada **www.ucfv.ca/**

Freshman Application Contact Ms. Robin Smith, Admissions Coordinator, University College of the Fraser Valley, 33844 King Road, Abbotsford, BC V2S 7M8, Canada. *Phone:* 604-504-7441 Ext. 4540. *Toll-free phone:* 808-504-7441. *Fax:* 604-853-0138. *E-mail:* reginfo@ucfv.ca.

University of Alberta

Edmonton, Alberta, Canada **www.ualberta.ca/**

- **Province-supported** university, founded 1906
- **Urban** 154-acre campus
- **Endowment** $486.1 million
- **Coed**
- **Moderately difficult** entrance level

Faculty *Student/faculty ratio:* 21:1.

Academics *Calendar:* Canadian standard year. *Degrees:* bachelor's, master's, and doctoral.

Student Life *Campus security:* 24-hour emergency response devices and patrols, student patrols, late-night transport/escort service, controlled dormitory access.

Athletics Member CIS.

Standardized Tests *Required for some:* SAT and SAT Subject Tests required for United States students.

Applying *Options:* electronic application, deferred entrance. *Application fee:* $100 Canadian dollars. *Required:* high school transcript. *Required for some:* essay or personal statement, letters of recommendation, interview. *Recommended:* minimum 2.0 GPA.

Freshman Application Contact Mr. Gerry Kendal, Associate Registrar/ Director of Enrollment Management, University of Alberta, 201 Administration Building, Edmonton, AB T6G 2M7, Canada. *Phone:* 780-492-3113. *Fax:* 780-492-4380. *E-mail:* registrar@ualberta.ca.

The University of British Columbia

Vancouver, British Columbia, Canada **www.ubc.ca/**

- **Province-supported** university, founded 1915, part of Two main campuses: UBC Vancouver & UBC Okanagan
- **Urban** 1000-acre campus
- **Endowment** $1.0 billion
- **Coed** 30,170 undergraduate students, 66% full-time, 55% women, 45% men
- **Very difficult** entrance level, 60% of applicants were admitted

Undergraduates 19,941 full-time, 10,229 part-time. Students come from 40 provinces and territories, 135 other countries, 100% international, 3% transferred in, 23% live on campus. *Retention:* 92% of 2006 full-time freshmen returned.

Freshmen *Admission:* 18,773 applied, 11,343 admitted, 5,017 enrolled.

Faculty *Total:* 2,141. *Student/faculty ratio:* 15:1.

Majors Accounting; agricultural and food products processing; agricultural economics; agriculture; animal genetics; animal/livestock husbandry and production; animal sciences; anthropology; applied mathematics; archeology; art history, criticism and conservation; art teacher education; Asian studies; Asian studies (South); astronomy; atmospheric sciences and meteorology; biochemistry; biochemistry/biophysics and molecular biology; biology/biological sciences; biomedical/medical engineering; biophysics; biotechnology; business administration and management; business/commerce; business teacher education; Canadian government and politics; Canadian studies; cell biology and histology; chemical engineering; chemistry; Chinese; civil engineering; classics and languages, literatures and linguistics; clinical/medical laboratory technology; clinical psychology; cognitive science; computer engineering; computer science; counselor education/ school counseling and guidance; creative writing; cultural studies; dental hygiene; developmental and child psychology; dietetics; dramatic/theater arts; economics; education; educational leadership and administration; electrical, electronics and communications engineering; elementary education; engineering physics; engineering technologies related; English; English as a second/foreign language (teaching); environmental biology; environmental engineering technology; environmental studies; European studies; European studies (Central and Eastern); experimental psychology; family and consumer sciences/home economics teacher education; family and consumer sciences/human sciences; film/cinema studies; finance; fine/studio arts; fish/game management; foods and nutrition related; food science; food science and technology related; foods, nutrition, and wellness; forest/forest resources management; forestry; French; geography; geological/ geophysical engineering; geology/earth science; geophysics and seismology; German; history; horticultural science; human nutrition; human resources management and services related; interdisciplinary studies; international business/ trade/commerce; international relations and affairs; Italian; Japanese; kindergarten/ preschool education; kinesiology and exercise science; labor and industrial relations; landscape architecture; Latin; Latin American studies; liberal arts and sciences/liberal studies; linguistics; management information systems; marine biology and biological oceanography; marketing/marketing management; materials engineering; mathematics; mechanical engineering; mechanical engineering/ mechanical technology; medical microbiology and bacteriology; metallurgical engineering; mining and mineral engineering; music; music history, literature, and theory; music teacher education; music theory and composition; natural resources and conservation related; natural resources/conservation; natural resources management; natural resources management and policy; nursing (registered nurse training); occupational therapy; oceanography (chemical and physical); parks, recreation and leisure facilities management; pharmacology; pharmacy; philosophy; physical therapy; physics; physiology; piano and organ; political science and government; pre-dentistry studies; pre-law studies; pre-medical studies; pre-veterinary studies; psychology; reading teacher education; real estate; rehabilitation therapy; religious studies; Romance languages; Russian; Russian studies; science teacher education; secondary education; Slavic languages; social sciences; social work; sociology; soil science and agronomy; South Asian languages; Spanish; special education; speech therapy; statistics; theater/theater arts management; transportation technology; urban studies/affairs; violin, viola, guitar and other stringed instruments; visual and performing arts; voice and opera; wildlife and wildlands science and management; women's studies; wood science and wood products/pulp and paper technology; zoology/animal biology.

Academics *Calendar:* Canadian standard year. *Degrees:* certificates, diplomas, bachelor's, master's, doctoral, first professional, and postbachelor's certificates. *Special study options:* academic remediation for entering students, adult/continuing education programs, advanced placement credit, cooperative education, distance learning, double majors, English as a second language, freshman honors college, honors programs, internships, off-campus study, part-time degree program, services for LD students, study abroad, summer session for credit.

Computers on Campus 1,500 computers/terminals are available on campus for general student use. Students can access the following: free student e-mail accounts, online (class) registration. Campuswide network is available. Wireless service is available via entire campus.

Student Life *Housing options:* coed, men-only, women-only, disabled students. Campus housing is university owned. Freshman applicants given priority for college housing. *Activities and organizations:* drama/theater group, student-run newspaper, radio station, choral group, Ski and Board Club, Dance Club, AIESEC Club, UBC Film Society, Varsity Outdoors Club, national fraternities, national sororities. *Campus security:* 24-hour emergency response devices and patrols, student patrols, late-night transport/escort service, 24-hour desk attendants in residence halls. *Student services:* health clinic, personal/psychological counseling, women's center, legal services.

Athletics Member NAIA, CIS. *Intercollegiate sports:* baseball M (s), basketball M (s)/W (s), cheerleading M (c)/W (c), crew M (s)/W (s), cross-country running M (s)/W (s), fencing M (c)/W (c), field hockey M (s)/W (s), football M (s), golf M (s)/W (s), ice hockey M (s)/W (s), rock climbing M (s)/W (s), soccer M (s)/W (s), swimming and diving M (s)/W (s), track and field M (s)/W (s), volleyball M (s)/W (s). *Intramural sports:* badminton M/W, basketball M/W, cross-country running M/W, football M/W, gymnastics M/W, ice hockey M/W, racquetball M/W, rugby M/W, sailing M/W, skiing (cross-country) M/W, skiing (downhill) M/W, soccer M/W, softball M/W, squash M/W, swimming and diving M/W, table tennis M/W, tennis M/W, ultimate Frisbee M/W, volleyball M/W, water polo M/W, weight lifting M/W, wrestling M/W.

Standardized Tests *Required for some:* SAT or ACT plus writing required of applicants following US curriculum.

Costs (2008–09) *Tuition:* nonresident $644 per credit part-time; International tuition $19,334 full-time. *Required fees:* $662 full-time, $12 per credit part-time, $134 per term part-time. *Room and board:* $6650.

Financial Aid Of all full-time matriculated undergraduates who enrolled in 2006, 825 state and other part-time jobs (averaging $3000). *Financial aid deadline:* 9/15.

Applying *Options:* electronic application, early admission, deferred entrance. *Application fee:* $100 Canadian dollars. *Required:* high school transcript, minimum 2.6 GPA. *Required for some:* essay or personal statement, letters of recommendation. *Application deadlines:* 2/28 (freshmen), 2/28 (transfers). *Notification:* continuous until 8/31 (freshmen), continuous until 8/31 (transfers).

Freshman Application Contact Ms. Denise Lauritano, Acting Associate Director, Undergraduate Admissions, The University of British Columbia, 1874 East Mall, Vancouver, BC V6T 1Z1, Canada. *Phone:* 604-822-8999. *Toll-free phone:* 877-292-1422. *Fax:* 604-822-9888.

See page 2856 for the College Close-Up.

THE UNIVERSITY OF BRITISH COLUMBIA–OKANAGAN

Kelowna, British Columbia, Canada

web.ubc.ca/okanagan/welcome.html

- **Province-supported** university, founded 2005
- **Urban** 260-acre campus
- **Endowment** $1.0 billion
- **Coed** 4,407 undergraduate students, 71% full-time, 61% women, 39% men
- **Moderately difficult** entrance level, 62% of applicants were admitted

Undergraduates 3,108 full-time, 1,299 part-time. Students come from 8 provinces and territories, 41 other countries. *Retention:* 85% of 2006 full-time freshmen returned.

Freshmen *Admission:* 3,351 applied, 2,064 admitted, 1,222 enrolled.

Faculty *Total:* 257. *Student/faculty ratio:* 8:1.

Majors Accounting; anthropology; art history, criticism and conservation; biochemistry; biology/biological sciences; chemistry; civil engineering; computer science; creative writing; cultural studies; dramatic/theater arts; ecology, evolution, systematics and population biology related; economics; education; electrical, electronics and communications engineering; English; entrepreneurship; environmental science; finance; French; general studies; geography; health science; history; human resources management; information technology; international relations and affairs; kinesiology and exercise science; marketing/marketing management; mathematics; mathematics and statistics related; mechanical engineering; microbiology; molecular biology; nursing (registered nurse training); philosophy; physics; political science and government; psychology; social work; sociology; Spanish; visual and performing arts.

Academics *Degrees:* certificates, diplomas, bachelor's, master's, doctoral, and first professional. *Special study options:* academic remediation for entering students, adult/continuing education programs, advanced placement credit, cooperative education, distance learning, double majors, English as a second language, freshman honors college, honors programs, internships, off-campus study, part-time degree program, services for LD students, student-designed majors, study abroad, summer session for credit.

Computers on Campus Students can access the following: campus intranet, computer help desk, free student e-mail accounts, online (class) registration, online (class) schedules. Campuswide network is available. 100% of college-owned or -operated housing units are wired for high-speed Internet access. Wireless service is available via entire campus.

Student Life *Housing options:* coed, men-only, women-only. Campus housing is university owned. Freshman applicants given priority for college housing. *Activities and organizations:* drama/theater group, student-run newspaper, radio station. *Campus security:* 24-hour emergency response devices and patrols, controlled dormitory access, 24-hour desk attendants in residence halls. *Student services:* health clinic, personal/psychological counseling, women's center, legal services.

Athletics Member CIS. *Intercollegiate sports:* basketball M (s)/W (s), soccer M (s)/W (s), volleyball M (s)/W (s). *Intramural sports:* basketball M/W, cross-country running M/W, field hockey M/W, gymnastics M/W, ice hockey M/W, soccer M/W, tennis M/W, volleyball M/W.

Standardized Tests *Required for some:* SAT or ACT plus writing required of applicants following US curriculum.

Costs (2008–09) *Tuition:* nonresident $644 per credit part-time; International tuition $19,334 full-time. *Required fees:* $714 full-time. *Room and board:* $5700.

Applying *Options:* electronic application, early decision, deferred entrance. *Application fee:* $100 Canadian dollars. *Required:* high school transcript, minimum 2.6 GPA. *Required for some:* essay or personal statement, letters of recommendation. *Application deadlines:* 2/28 (freshmen), 2/28 (transfers). *Early decision deadline:* 2/28. *Notification:* continuous until 8/31 (freshmen), continuous until 8/31 (transfers), 5/1 (early decision).

Freshman Application Contact International Student Recruitment, The University of British Columbia–Okanagan, 3333 University Way, Kelowna, BC V1V 1V7, Canada. *Phone:* 604-822-8999. *Fax:* 604-822-9888.

UNIVERSITY OF CALGARY

Calgary, Alberta, Canada **www.ucalgary.ca/**

Director of Admissions Director of Enrollment Services, University of Calgary, Office of Admissions, Calgary, AB T2N 1N4, Canada. *Phone:* 403-220-6645.

UNIVERSITY OF GUELPH

Guelph, Ontario, Canada **www.uoguelph.ca/**

- **Province-supported** university, founded 1964
- **Urban** 817-acre campus with easy access to Toronto
- **Coed**
- **Moderately difficult** entrance level

The University of Guelph is renowned in Canada and around the world for its research-intensive and learning-centered environment and for its commitment to open learning, internationalism, and collaboration. The University offers a wide variety of academic programs, ranging from undergraduate, graduate, and postgraduate degrees to diploma and certificate programs. Courses are also offered for those seeking to upgrade their skills or develop their interests. The University is located in Guelph and Toronto and has three other regional campuses. Prospective students should visit the University Web site at http://www.uoguelph.ca.

Faculty *Student/faculty ratio:* 22:1.
Academics *Calendar:* trimesters. *Degrees:* certificates, diplomas, bachelor's, master's, doctoral, and first professional.
Student Life *Campus security:* 24-hour emergency response devices and patrols, student patrols, late-night transport/escort service, controlled dormitory access, video camera surveillance in parking lots, alarms in women's locker room.
Athletics Member CIS.
Standardized Tests *Required:* SAT or ACT (for admission).
Costs (2007–08) *One-time required fee:* $200 Canadian dollars. *Tuition:* province resident $5718 Canadian dollars full-time; nonresident $457 Canadian dollars per course part-time; International tuition $17,490 Canadian dollars full-time. Full-time tuition and fees vary according to program. Part-time tuition and fees vary according to course load and program. *Required fees:* $2186 Canadian dollars full-time, $377 Canadian dollars per term part-time. *Room and board:* $8781 Canadian dollars; room only: $5076 Canadian dollars. Room and board charges vary according to board plan and housing facility.
Applying *Options:* early admission. *Application fee:* $105 Canadian dollars. *Required:* high school transcript, minimum 3.0 GPA. *Required for some:* essay or personal statement, letters of recommendation.
Freshman Application Contact Mr. Hugh Clark, Admissions Coordinator, University of Guelph, L-3 University Centre, Guelph, ON N1G 2W1, Canada. *Phone:* 519-824-4120 Ext. 56066. *Fax:* 519-766-9481. *E-mail:* usainfo@riegistrar.uoguelph.ca.

See page 2858 for the College Close-Up.

UNIVERSITY OF KING'S COLLEGE

Halifax, Nova Scotia, Canada **www.ukings.ca/**

- **Province-supported** 4-year, founded 1789, administratively affiliated with Dalhousie University
- **Urban** 4-acre campus
- **Endowment** $33.2 million
- **Coed** 1,137 undergraduate students, 98% full-time, 57% women, 43% men
- **Moderately difficult** entrance level, 72% of applicants were admitted

Undergraduates 1,115 full-time, 22 part-time. Students come from 19 provinces and territories, 7 other countries, 53% are from out of state, 5% transferred in, 24% live on campus. *Retention:* 80% of 2006 full-time freshmen returned.
Freshmen *Admission:* 1,170 applied, 845 admitted, 291 enrolled.
Faculty *Total:* 51, 100% full-time, 71% with terminal degrees. *Student/faculty ratio:* 22:1.
Majors Anthropology; biochemistry; biology/biological sciences; chemistry; classics and languages, literatures and linguistics; computer science; development economics and international development; dramatic/theater arts; economics; English; French; geology/earth science; German; history; journalism; linguistics; marine biology and biological oceanography; mathematics; medical microbiology and bacteriology; multi-/interdisciplinary studies related; music; neuroscience; philosophy; physics; political science and government; psychology; religious studies; Russian; science, technology and society; sociology; Spanish; statistics; western civilization; women's studies.
Academics *Calendar:* Canadian standard year. *Degree:* bachelor's. *Special study options:* accelerated degree program, advanced placement credit, cooperative education, double majors, honors programs, independent study, internships, off-campus study, part-time degree program, services for LD students, student-designed majors, study abroad, summer session for credit.
Computers on Campus 18 computers/terminals are available on campus for general student use. Students can access the following: online (class) registration. Campuswide network is available. Wireless service is available via libraries, student centers.
Student Life *Housing options:* coed, men-only, women-only. Campus housing is university owned. Freshman applicants given priority for college housing. *Activities and organizations:* drama/theater group, student-run newspaper, radio station, choral group, King's Theatrical Society, student newspaper, King's College Dance Collective, St. Andrew's Missionary Society, King's Independent Film-Makers Society. *Campus security:* student patrols, late-night transport/escort service. *Student services:* health clinic, personal/psychological counseling, women's center, legal services.
Athletics *Intercollegiate sports:* badminton M/W, basketball M/W, rugby M/W, soccer M/W, volleyball M/W. *Intramural sports:* badminton M/W, basketball M/W, field hockey M/W, soccer M/W, softball M/W, tennis M/W, ultimate Frisbee M/W, volleyball M/W, water polo M/W.
Standardized Tests *Required for some:* SAT (for admission).
Costs (2007–08) *Tuition:* province resident $6418 Canadian dollars full-time, $201 Canadian dollars per credit hour part-time; nonresident $6418 Canadian dollars full-time; International tuition $14,288 Canadian dollars full-time. Full-time tuition and fees vary according to course load and program. Part-time tuition and fees vary according to course load and program. *Room and board:* $7371 Canadian dollars; room only: $4813 Canadian dollars. Room and board charges vary according to housing facility. *Payment plan:* installment. *Waivers:* senior citizens and employees or children of employees.
Financial Aid Of all full-time matriculated undergraduates who enrolled in 2006, 86 applied for aid, 83 were judged to have need. In 2006, 188 non-need-based awards were made. *Average non-need-based aid:* $1800.
Applying *Options:* electronic application, early admission, early decision, deferred entrance. *Application fee:* $45 Canadian dollars. *Required:* high school transcript, minimum 3.0 GPA. *Required for some:* essay or personal statement, writing sample. *Application deadlines:* 3/1 (freshmen), 6/1 (transfers). *Notification:* 4/15 (freshmen), continuous (transfers).
Freshman Application Contact Ms. Jill MacBeath, Admissions and Recruitment Coordinator, University of King's College, Registrar's Office, Halifax, NS B3H 2A1, Canada. *Phone:* 902-422-1271. *Fax:* 902-425-8183. *E-mail:* admissions@ukings.ns.ca.

UNIVERSITY OF LETHBRIDGE

Lethbridge, Alberta, Canada **www.uleth.ca/**

- **Province-supported** university, founded 1967
- **Urban** 576-acre campus
- **Endowment** $31.5 million
- **Coed** 7,756 undergraduate students, 90% full-time, 56% women, 44% men
- **Moderately difficult** entrance level, 42% of applicants were admitted

Undergraduates 6,961 full-time, 795 part-time. Students come from 12 provinces and territories, 88 other countries, 14% are from out of state, 10% live on campus. *Retention:* 71% of 2006 full-time freshmen returned.
Freshmen *Admission:* 2,720 applied, 1,152 admitted.
Faculty *Total:* 416, 71% with terminal degrees.
Majors Accounting; agricultural business and management; agriculture; American Indian/Native American studies; American native/native American education; American Native/Native American languages; anthropology; art; art teacher education; biochemistry; biological and physical sciences; biology/biological sciences; biotechnology; business administration and management; business teacher education; Canadian studies; chemistry; computer and information sciences related; computer science; counseling psychology; digital communication and media/multimedia; drama and dance teacher education; dramatic/theater arts; economics; education; educational leadership and administration; education (K-12); English; environmental science; finance; foreign language teacher education; French; geography; German; health teacher education; history; humanities; human resources management; international business/trade/commerce; kinesiology and exercise science; management information systems; marketing/marketing management; mathematics; mathematics teacher education; modern languages; music; music teacher education; neuroscience; nursing (registered nurse training); parks, recreation and leisure; philosophy; physical education teaching and coaching; physics; political science and government; psychology; public administration; religious studies; science teacher education; social sciences; social studies teacher education; sociology; special education; substance abuse/addiction counseling; technology/industrial arts teacher education; theater design and technology; urban studies/affairs.
Academics *Calendar:* semesters. *Degrees:* certificates, diplomas, bachelor's, master's, and doctoral. *Special study options:* academic remediation for entering students, accelerated degree program, cooperative education, distance learning, double majors, English as a second language, independent study, internships, off-campus study, part-time degree program, student-designed majors, study abroad, summer session for credit. *Unusual degree programs:* 3-2 education.
Computers on Campus 600 computers/terminals are available on campus for general student use. Students can access the following: online (class) registration. Campuswide network is available.

Student Life *Housing options:* coed. Campus housing is university owned. *Activities and organizations:* drama/theater group, student-run newspaper, radio station, choral group, Management Students Society, Inter-Varsity Christian Fellowship, Organization of Residence Students, Geography Club, Education Undergraduate Society. *Campus security:* 24-hour emergency response devices and patrols, student patrols, late-night transport/escort service, controlled dormitory access, video camera monitored entrances, hallways. *Student services:* health clinic, personal/psychological counseling, women's center.

Athletics Member CIS. *Intercollegiate sports:* cross-country running M (s)/W (s), ice hockey M (s)/W (s), soccer M (s)/W (s), swimming and diving M (s)/W (s), track and field M (s)/W (s), volleyball W. *Intramural sports:* archery M, fencing M (c)/W (c), football M/W, golf M/W, gymnastics M/W, ice hockey M/W, racquetball M/W, rugby M (c)/W (c), skiing (cross-country) M/W, skiing (downhill) M/W, soccer M/W, softball M/W, squash M/W, tennis M (c)/W (c), volleyball M/W, water polo M/W, weight lifting M/W.

Costs (2007–08) *Tuition:* nonresident $4380 full-time, $438 per course part-time; International tuition $9920 full-time. Full-time tuition and fees vary according to course load. Part-time tuition and fees vary according to course load. *Required fees:* $624 full-time, $99 per course part-time. *Room and board:* $5265; room only: $3776. Room and board charges vary according to board plan and housing facility. *Waivers:* employees or children of employees.

Applying *Options:* electronic application, early admission, early decision, deferred entrance. *Application fee:* $60 Canadian dollars. *Required:* high school transcript, minimum 2.0 GPA. *Required for some:* minimum 3.0 GPA, letters of recommendation, interview. *Application deadlines:* 6/1 (freshmen), 6/1 (transfers). *Early decision deadline:* 4/1. *Notification:* continuous (freshmen), continuous (transfers), 4/22 (early decision).

Freshman Application Contact Mr. Peter Haney, Assistant Registrar, University of Lethbridge, 4401 University Drive, Lethbridge, AB T1K 3M4. *Phone:* 403-320-5700. *Fax:* 403-329-5159. *E-mail:* inquiries@uleth.ca.

UNIVERSITY OF MANITOBA

Winnipeg, Manitoba, Canada www.umanitoba.ca/

- **Province-supported** university, founded 1877
- **Suburban** 685-acre campus
- **Coed**
- **Moderately difficult** entrance level

Academics *Calendar:* 8-month academic year plus 6-week summer session. *Degrees:* bachelor's, master's, and doctoral.

Student Life *Campus security:* 24-hour emergency response devices, student patrols, late-night transport/escort service.

Athletics Member CIS.

Costs (2007–08) *Tuition:* tuition varies by major. Contact institution directly for tuition information.

Financial Aid Of all full-time matriculated undergraduates who enrolled in 2006, 50 state and other part-time jobs (averaging $980).

Applying *Application fee:* $75 Canadian dollars. *Required:* high school transcript.

Freshman Application Contact Mr. Peter Dueck, Director of Enrollment Services, University of Manitoba, Winnipeg, MB R3T 2N2, Canada. *Phone:* 204-474-6382.

UNIVERSITY OF NEW BRUNSWICK FREDERICTON

Fredericton, New Brunswick, Canada www.unb.ca/

- **Province-supported** university, founded 1785
- **Urban** 7100-acre campus
- **Coed** 7,491 undergraduate students, 88% full-time, 52% women, 48% men
- **Moderately difficult** entrance level, 81% of applicants were admitted

Undergraduates 6,601 full-time, 890 part-time. Students come from 12 provinces and territories, 65 other countries, 20% live on campus.

Freshmen *Admission:* 2,220 applied, 1,806 admitted.

Faculty *Total:* 658, 79% full-time. *Student/faculty ratio:* 18:1.

Majors Accounting; adult and continuing education; animal physiology; anthropology; applied mathematics; art teacher education; biochemistry; biological and physical sciences; biology/biological sciences; biophysics; botany/plant biology; business administration and management; business/managerial economics; business teacher education; Canadian studies; chemical engineering; chemistry; civil engineering; classics and languages, literatures and linguistics; clinical psychology; comparative literature; computer engineering; computer science; construction engineering; counselor education/school counseling and guidance; data processing and data processing technology; developmental and child psychology; dramatic/theater arts; ecology; economics; education; electrical, electronics and communications engineering; elementary education; engineering; English; English as a second/foreign language (teaching); entomology; family and consumer sciences/home economics teacher education; finance; fire science; fish/game management; forest engineering; forestry; French; geochemistry; geological/geophysical engineering; geology/earth science; geophysics and seismology; German; health teacher education; history; human resources management; information science/studies; international business/trade/commerce; international relations and affairs; kindergarten/preschool education; kinesiology and exercise science; Latin; legal studies; liberal arts and sciences/liberal studies; linguistics; literature; marketing/marketing management; mathematics; mechanical engineering; medical microbiology and bacteriology; modern Greek; modern languages; molecular biology; music teacher education; nursing (registered nurse training); operations research; parks, recreation and leisure; philosophy; physical education teaching and coaching; physics; physiological psychology/psychobiology; political science and government; pre-dentistry studies; pre-law studies; pre-medical studies; pre-veterinary studies; psychology; Romance languages; Russian; science teacher education; secondary education; sociology; Spanish; special education; statistics; survey technology; wildlife and wildlands science and management; wildlife biology; zoology/animal biology.

Academics *Calendar:* Canadian standard year. *Degrees:* bachelor's, master's, and doctoral. *Special study options:* accelerated degree program, adult/continuing education programs, advanced placement credit, cooperative education, distance learning, double majors, English as a second language, external degree program, honors programs, independent study, internships, off-campus study, part-time degree program, services for LD students, student-designed majors, study abroad, summer session for credit.

Computers on Campus 1,142 computers/terminals are available on campus for general student use. Students can access the following: computer help desk, free student e-mail accounts, online (class) grades, online (class) registration, online (class) schedules. Campuswide network is available.

Student Life *Housing options:* coed, men-only, women-only. Campus housing is university owned. Freshman campus housing is guaranteed. *Activities and organizations:* drama/theater group, student-run newspaper, radio station, choral group. *Campus security:* late-night transport/escort service. *Student services:* health clinic, personal/psychological counseling, women's center.

Athletics Member CIS. *Intercollegiate sports:* basketball M/W, cross-country running M/W, field hockey W, ice hockey M/W, soccer M/W, swimming and diving M/W, volleyball M/W, wrestling M/W. *Intramural sports:* badminton M/W, baseball M/W, basketball M/W, cheerleading M/W, crew M/W, fencing M/W, field hockey W, ice hockey M/W, rock climbing M/W, rugby M/W, soccer M/W, swimming and diving M/W, volleyball M/W.

Standardized Tests *Required for some:* SAT (for admission).

Costs (2007–08) *Tuition:* area resident $5482 Canadian dollars full-time, $548 Canadian dollars per course part-time; International tuition $11,098 Canadian dollars full-time. Full-time tuition and fees vary according to program. Part-time tuition and fees vary according to course load. *Required fees:* $673 Canadian dollars full-time, $33 Canadian dollars per term part-time. *Room and board:* $7266 Canadian dollars. Room and board charges vary according to board plan. *Payment plan:* installment. *Waivers:* employees or children of employees.

Financial Aid Of all full-time matriculated undergraduates who enrolled in 2006, 123 state and other part-time jobs (averaging $1264). *Financial aid deadline:* 5/15.

Applying *Options:* electronic application, early admission, deferred entrance. *Application fee:* $45 Canadian dollars. *Required:* high school transcript. *Required for some:* essay or personal statement, 1 letter of recommendation, interview. *Application deadlines:* 3/31 (freshmen), 3/31 (transfers). *Notification:* continuous until 8/31 (freshmen), continuous until 8/31 (transfers).

Freshman Application Contact Mr. Mark Bishop, Assistant Registrar/Admissions, University of New Brunswick Fredericton, PO Box 4400, Sir Howard Douglas Hall, Fredericton, NB E3B 5A3, Canada. *Phone:* 506-453-4865. *Fax:* 506-453-5016. *E-mail:* chooseunb@unb.ca.

UNIVERSITY OF NEW BRUNSWICK SAINT JOHN

Saint John, New Brunswick, Canada **www.unb.ca/**

Freshman Application Contact Ms. Sue Ellis Loparco, Admissions Officer, University of New Brunswick Saint John, PO Box 5050, Tucker Park Road, Saint John, NB E2L 4L5. *Phone:* 506-648-5674. *Toll-free phone:* 800-743-4333 (in-state); 800-743-5691 (out-of-state). *E-mail:* apply@unbsj.ca.

UNIVERSITY OF NORTHERN BRITISH COLUMBIA

Prince George, British Columbia, Canada **www.unbc.ca/**

- **Province-supported** university, founded 1994
- **Suburban** 1344-acre campus
- **Endowment** $35.1 million
- **Coed**
- **Noncompetitive** entrance level

Faculty *Student/faculty ratio:* 17:1.

Academics *Calendar:* semesters. *Degrees:* certificates, diplomas, bachelor's, master's, doctoral, first professional, and postbachelor's certificates.

Student Life *Campus security:* 24-hour emergency response devices and patrols, late-night transport/escort service, controlled dormitory access.

Costs (2007–08) *Tuition:* area resident $4276 Canadian dollars full-time, $143 Canadian dollars per credit hour part-time; International tuition $14,996 Canadian dollars full-time. Full-time tuition and fees vary according to location and program. Part-time tuition and fees vary according to location and program. *Required fees:* $972 Canadian dollars full-time, $5 Canadian dollars per credit hour part-time, $176 Canadian dollars per term part-time. *Room only:* $4524 Canadian dollars. Room and board charges vary according to housing facility.

Financial Aid *Financial aid deadline:* 4/1.

Applying *Options:* early admission, early decision. *Application fee:* $25 Canadian dollars. *Required:* high school transcript, minimum 2.0 GPA. *Required for some:* essay or personal statement, letters of recommendation.

Freshman Application Contact Mr. Grant Kerr, Assistant Registrar-Admissions, University of Northern British Columbia, Office of the Registrar, 3333 University Way, Prince George, BC V2N 4Z9. *Phone:* 250-960-6347. *Fax:* 250-960-6330. *E-mail:* registrar-info@unbc.ca.

UNIVERSITY OF OTTAWA

Ottawa, Ontario, Canada **www.uottawa.ca/**

- **Province-supported** university, founded 1848
- **Urban** 105-acre campus
- **Endowment** $128.4 million
- **Coed** 30,882 undergraduate students, 82% full-time, 60% women, 40% men
- **Moderately difficult** entrance level, 61% of applicants were admitted

Undergraduates 25,462 full-time, 5,420 part-time. Students come from 13 provinces and territories, 151 other countries, 19% are from out of state, 9% live on campus. *Retention:* 88% of 2006 full-time freshmen returned.

Freshmen *Admission:* 32,680 applied, 19,960 admitted. *Average high school GPA:* 3.26.

Faculty *Total:* 2,177, 56% full-time. *Student/faculty ratio:* 22:1.

Majors Accounting; American Indian/Native American studies; anthropology; Arabic; art history, criticism and conservation; behavioral sciences; biochemistry; biological and biomedical sciences related; biology/biological sciences; biology/biotechnology laboratory technician; biomedical/medical engineering; biomedical sciences; Canadian studies; chemical engineering; chemistry; civil engineering; classical, ancient Mediterranean and Near Eastern studies and archaeology; classics and languages, literatures and linguistics; communication/speech communication and rhetoric; computer and information sciences; computer engineering; computer software engineering; criminology; development economics and international development; dramatic/theater arts; e-commerce; economics; education (specific levels and methods) related; electrical, electronics and communications engineering; engineering science; English; environmental science; environmental studies; ethics; finance; fine/studio arts; foods, nutrition, and wellness; French; geography; geological and earth sciences/geosciences related; German; health and physical education; health services/allied health/health sciences; history; humanities; human resources management; international business/trade/commerce; international/global studies; international relations and affairs; Italian; journalism; language interpretation and translation; Latin; linguistics; management information systems; marketing/marketing management; mathematics; mechanical engineering; medieval and Renaissance studies; modern languages; multi-/interdisciplinary studies related; music; nursing (registered nurse training); occupational therapy; ophthalmic laboratory technology; parks, recreation and leisure; peace studies and conflict resolution; philosophy; physical sciences; physical therapy; physics; physics related; physiology; political science and government; psychology; public administration; rehabilitation therapy; religious studies; Russian; social sciences; social work; sociology; Spanish; statistics; women's studies.

Academics *Calendar:* semesters. *Degrees:* certificates, bachelor's, master's, doctoral, first professional, and postbachelor's certificates. *Special study options:* academic remediation for entering students, accelerated degree program, adult/continuing education programs, advanced placement credit, cooperative education, distance learning, double majors, English as a second language, honors programs, internships, off-campus study, part-time degree program, services for LD students, student-designed majors, study abroad, summer session for credit. *Unusual degree programs:* 3-2 law.

Computers on Campus 1,500 computers/terminals and 150 ports are available on campus for general student use. Students can access the following: campus intranet, computer help desk, free student e-mail accounts, online (class) grades, online (class) registration, online (class) schedules. Campuswide network is available. 100% of college-owned or -operated housing units are wired for high-speed Internet access. Wireless service is available via libraries.

Student Life *Housing options:* coed, disabled students. Campus housing is university owned. Freshman campus housing is guaranteed. *Activities and organizations:* drama/theater group, student-run newspaper, radio station, choral group, Student Federation of the University of Ottawa, Graduate Student's Association, national fraternities, national sororities. *Campus security:* 24-hour emergency response devices and patrols, student patrols, late-night transport/escort service, controlled dormitory access. *Student services:* health clinic, personal/psychological counseling, women's center, legal services.

Athletics Member CIS. *Intercollegiate sports:* basketball M (s)/W (s), crew M/W, cross-country running M/W, fencing M/W, football M (s), golf M/W, ice hockey M (s)/W (s), rugby W, soccer W (s), swimming and diving M/W, volleyball W. *Intramural sports:* basketball M/W, football M, ice hockey M/W, soccer M/W, ultimate Frisbee M/W, volleyball M/W.

Standardized Tests *Required for some:* SAT or ACT required for American citizens.

Costs (2007–08) *Tuition:* nonresident $4546 Canadian dollars full-time, $180 Canadian dollars per credit part-time; International tuition $13,858 Canadian dollars full-time. Full-time tuition and fees vary according to program and student level. Part-time tuition and fees vary according to program and student level. *Required fees:* $586 Canadian dollars full-time, $98 Canadian dollars per term part-time. *Room and board:* $6468 Canadian dollars; room only: $3968 Canadian dollars. Room and board charges vary according to board plan and housing facility. *Payment plan:* deferred payment. *Waivers:* employees or children of employees.

Financial Aid Of all full-time matriculated undergraduates who enrolled in 2006, 1,056 state and other part-time jobs (averaging $3000). *Financial aid deadline:* 1/31.

Applying *Options:* electronic application, early admission. *Application fee:* $165 Canadian dollars. *Required:* high school transcript, minimum 3.0 GPA. *Required for some:* interview. *Application deadline:* 6/1 (freshmen). *Notification:* continuous until 8/30 (freshmen).

Freshman Application Contact Ms. Caroline Pharand, University of Ottawa, 550 Cumberland Street, PO Box 450, Station A, Ottawa, ON K1N 6N5, Canada. *Phone:* 613-562-5800 Ext. 1593. *Fax:* 613-562-5790. *E-mail:* cpharand@uottawa.ca.

UNIVERSITY OF PHOENIX–VANCOUVER CAMPUS

Burnaby, British Columbia, Canada **www.phoenix.edu/**

Freshman Application Contact Ms. Beth Barilla, Associate Vice President, Student Admissions and Services, University of Phoenix–Vancouver Campus, 4615 East Elwood Street, Mail Stop AA-K101, Phoenix, AZ 85040-1958. *Phone:* 480-317-6000. *Toll-free phone:* 800-776-4867 (in-state); 800-228-7240 (out-of-state). *Fax:* 480-894-1758. *E-mail:* beth.barilla@phoenix.edu.

UNIVERSITY OF PRINCE EDWARD ISLAND

Charlottetown, Prince Edward Island, Canada **www.upei.ca/**

- **Province-supported** comprehensive, founded 1834
- **Small-town** 130-acre campus
- **Endowment** $17.3 million
- **Coed** 3,449 undergraduate students, 83% full-time, 62% women, 38% men
- **Moderately difficult** entrance level, 61% of applicants were admitted

Undergraduates 2,855 full-time, 594 part-time. Students come from 12 provinces and territories, 37 other countries, 15% are from out of state, 11% live on campus. *Retention:* 74% of 2006 full-time freshmen returned.

Freshmen *Admission:* 1,044 applied, 635 admitted.

Faculty *Total:* 378, 65% full-time. *Student/faculty ratio:* 12:1.

Majors Anthropology; biology/biological sciences; business administration and management; Canadian studies; chemistry; computer science; economics; education; elementary education; English; family and consumer economics related; foods, nutrition, and wellness; French; German; history; hospitality administration; mathematics; medical radiologic technology; music; music teacher education; nursing (registered nurse training); philosophy; physics; political science and government; pre-dentistry studies; pre-medical studies; pre-veterinary studies; psychology; religious studies; secondary education; sociology; Spanish.

Academics *Calendar:* Canadian standard year. *Degrees:* certificates, diplomas, bachelor's, master's, doctoral, and first professional. *Special study options:* advanced placement credit, cooperative education, distance learning, double majors, English as a second language, honors programs, internships, part-time degree program, services for LD students, study abroad, summer session for credit.

Computers on Campus 120 computers/terminals are available on campus for general student use. Students can access the following: online (class) registration. Campuswide network is available.

Student Life *Housing options:* coed, disabled students. Campus housing is university owned. *Activities and organizations:* drama/theater group, student-run newspaper, choral group, Business Society, Biology Club, Music Society, intramurals, Theatre Society. *Campus security:* 24-hour emergency response devices and patrols, late-night transport/escort service, controlled dormitory access, late night residence hall security personnel. *Student services:* health clinic, personal/psychological counseling, women's center.

Athletics Member CIS. *Intercollegiate sports:* basketball M/W, field hockey W, golf M (c), ice hockey M/W, rugby M/W, soccer M/W, volleyball W. *Intramural sports:* badminton M/W, basketball M/W, fencing M (c)/W (c), ice hockey M, racquetball M (c)/W (c), rugby M (c)/W (c), skiing (cross-country) M (c)/W (c), skiing (downhill) M (c)/W (c), soccer M, squash M (c)/W (c), tennis M (c)/W (c), volleyball M/W, weight lifting M (c)/W (c).

Costs (2007–08) *Tuition:* province resident $4440 Canadian dollars full-time, $444 Canadian dollars per course part-time; nonresident $444 Canadian dollars per course part-time; International tuition $8760 Canadian dollars full-time. Full-time tuition and fees vary according to course load and degree level. Part-time tuition and fees vary according to course load. *Required fees:* $737 Canadian dollars full-time. *Room and board:* $8720 Canadian dollars. Room and board charges vary according to board plan and housing facility. *Waivers:* senior citizens and employees or children of employees.

Applying *Options:* electronic application, early admission. *Application fee:* $50 Canadian dollars. *Required:* high school transcript, minimum 2.5 GPA. *Required for some:* 3 letters of recommendation, interview. *Application deadlines:* 8/1 (freshmen), 8/1 (out-of-state freshmen), 8/1 (transfers). *Notification:* continuous until 8/31 (freshmen), continuous until 8/31 (out-of-state freshmen), continuous until 8/31 (transfers).

Freshman Application Contact alan Buchanan, Registrar, University of Prince Edward Island, Registrar's Office, Charlottetown, PE C1A 4D3, Canada. *Phone:* 902-566-0439. *Fax:* 902-566-0795. *E-mail:* registrar@upei.ca.

UNIVERSITY OF REGINA

Regina, Saskatchewan, Canada **www.uregina.ca/**

- **Province-supported** university, founded 1974
- **Urban** 930-hectare campus
- **Endowment** $23.6 million
- **Coed** 10,589 undergraduate students, 76% full-time, 62% women, 38% men
- **Minimally difficult** entrance level, 86% of applicants were admitted

Undergraduates 8,024 full-time, 2,565 part-time. Students come from 11 provinces and territories, 86 other countries, 4% are from out of state, 8% transferred in. *Retention:* 72% of 2006 full-time freshmen returned.

Freshmen *Admission:* 2,283 applied, 1,973 admitted, 1,282 enrolled.

Faculty *Total:* 478, 100% full-time, 82% with terminal degrees. *Student/faculty ratio:* 25:1.

Majors Accounting; acting; actuarial science; adult and continuing education; American history; American Indian/Native American studies; American native/native American education; American Native/Native American languages; anthropology; art; art history, criticism and conservation; art teacher education; Asian history; bilingual and multilingual education; biochemistry; biological and physical sciences; biology/biological sciences; biology teacher education; business administration and management; business/commerce; business teacher education; Canadian history; Canadian studies; ceramic arts and ceramics; chemical technology; chemistry; chemistry teacher education; Chinese; cinematography and film/video production; classics and languages, literatures and linguistics; clinical/medical laboratory science and allied professions related; computer science; computer software engineering; criminal justice/law enforcement administration; criminal justice/police science; criminal justice/safety; dramatic/theater arts; dramatic/theater arts and stagecraft related; drawing; early childhood education; economics; education; educational psychology; electrical, electronic and communications engineering technology; electrical, electronics and communications engineering; elementary education; engineering; English; English/language arts teacher education; environmental biology; environmental/environmental health engineering; environmental health; environmental science; environmental studies; ethnic, cultural minority, and gender studies related; European history; film/cinema studies; film/video and photographic arts related; finance; fine arts related; French; French language teacher education; general studies; geography; geology/earth science; German; health services/allied health/health sciences; history; history of philosophy; history related; humanities; industrial engineering; intermedia/multimedia; international/global studies; Japanese; journalism; kindergarten/preschool education; kinesiology and exercise science; kinesiotherapy; liberal arts and sciences/liberal studies; linguistics; marketing/marketing management; mathematics; mathematics and computer science; mathematics and statistics related; mathematics teacher education; middle school education; music; music history, literature, and theory; musicology and ethnomusicology; music performance; music teacher education; music theory and composition; nursing (registered nurse training); painting; petroleum engineering; philosophy; physical education teaching and coaching; physics; physics related; physics teacher education; political science and government; pre-dentistry studies; pre-law studies; pre-medical studies; pre-pharmacy studies; pre-veterinary studies; printmaking; psychology; public administration; religious studies; religious studies related; science teacher education; sculpture; secondary education; social sciences; social studies teacher education; social work; sociology; Spanish; sport and fitness administration/management; statistics; systems engineering; theater design and technology; trade and industrial teacher education; visual and performing arts; women's studies.

Academics *Calendar:* semesters. *Degrees:* certificates, diplomas, bachelor's, master's, and doctoral. *Special study options:* academic remediation for entering students, adult/continuing education programs, advanced placement credit, cooperative education, distance learning, double majors, English as a second language, honors programs, internships, off-campus study, part-time degree program, services for LD students, student-designed majors, study abroad, summer session for credit.

Computers on Campus 300 computers/terminals are available on campus for general student use. Students can access the following: campus intranet, computer help desk, free student e-mail accounts, online (class) registration, online (class) schedules. Campuswide network is available. 100% of college-owned or -operated housing units are wired for high-speed Internet access. Wireless service is available via entire campus.

Student Life *Housing options:* coed, disabled students. Campus housing is university owned. *Activities and organizations:* drama/theater group, student-run newspaper, television station, choral group, Administration Students' Society, Education Students' Society, Engineering Students Society, Chinese Students and Scholars Association, Luther Student Association. *Campus security:* 24-hour emergency response devices and patrols, student patrols, late-night transport/escort service, controlled dormitory access, crime prevention assistance. *Student services:* health clinic, personal/psychological counseling, women's center.

Athletics Member CIS. *Intercollegiate sports:* basketball M (s)/W (s), cross-country running M (s)/W (s), football M (s), ice hockey M (s)/W (s), soccer W (s), swimming and diving M (s)/W (s), track and field M (s)/W (s), volleyball M (s)/W (s), wrestling M (s)/W (s). *Intramural sports:* badminton M/W, basketball M/W, cheerleading M/W, football M, ice hockey M/W, soccer M/W, softball M/W, tennis M/W, ultimate Frisbee M/W, volleyball M/W, water polo M/W.

Standardized Tests *Required for some:* SAT or ACT (for admission), SAT Subject Tests (for admission).

Costs (2007–08) *Tuition:* province resident $4551 Canadian dollars full-time, $136 Canadian dollars per credit hour part-time; nonresident $136 Canadian dollars per credit hour part-time; International tuition $8627 Canadian dollars full-time. Full-time tuition and fees vary according to course load and program. Part-time tuition and fees vary according to course load and program. *Required fees:* $442 Canadian dollars full-time, $120 Canadian dollars per term part-time. *Room and board:* $6772 Canadian dollars; room only: $4272 Canadian dollars. Room and board charges vary according to board plan and housing facility. *Waivers:* senior citizens.

Applying *Options:* electronic application, early admission, early action, deferred entrance. *Application fee:* $85 Canadian dollars. *Required:* high school transcript, minimum 2.3 GPA. *Required for some:* essay or personal statement, letters of recommendation, interview. *Application deadlines:* 7/1 (freshmen), 7/1 (transfers), 6/15 (early action).

Freshman Application Contact University of Regina, AH 213, Regina, SK S4S0A2. *Phone:* 306-585-4942. *Toll-free phone:* 306-585-4591 (in-state); 800-664-4756 (out-of-state).

UNIVERSITY OF SASKATCHEWAN

Saskatoon, Saskatchewan, Canada **www.usask.ca/**

- **Province-supported** university, founded 1907
- **Urban** 2425-acre campus
- **Coed**
- **Moderately difficult** entrance level

Faculty *Student/faculty ratio:* 5:1.

Academics *Calendar:* Canadian standard year. *Degrees:* certificates, diplomas, bachelor's, master's, and doctoral.

Student Life *Campus security:* 24-hour emergency response devices and patrols, student patrols, late-night transport/escort service, controlled dormitory access.

Athletics Member CIS.

Costs (2007–08) *Tuition:* area resident $4560 Canadian dollars full-time, $152 Canadian dollars per credit part-time; nonresident $395 Canadian dollars per credit part-time; International tuition $11,850 Canadian dollars full-time. *Required fees:* $454 Canadian dollars full-time, $61 Canadian dollars per term part-time. *Room and board:* $5508 Canadian dollars; room only: $2323 Canadian dollars.

Financial Aid *Financial aid deadline:* 3/15.

Applying *Options:* electronic application, early admission, early action. *Application fee:* $90 Canadian dollars. *Required:* high school transcript. *Required for some:* essay or personal statement, 3 letters of recommendation, interview.

Freshman Application Contact Recruitment and Admissions, University of Saskatchewan, Recruitment and Admissions, 105 Administration Place, Saskatoon, SK S7N 5A2. *Phone:* 306-966-5788. *Fax:* 306-966-2115. *E-mail:* admissions@usask.ca.

UNIVERSITY OF TORONTO

Toronto, Ontario, Canada **www.utoronto.ca/uoft.html**

- **Province-supported** university, founded 1827
- **Urban** 714-hectare campus
- **Endowment** $1.8 billion
- **Coed** 47,623 undergraduate students, 88% full-time, 58% women, 42% men
- **Very difficult** entrance level, 68% of applicants were admitted

Undergraduates 42,080 full-time, 5,543 part-time. Students come from 12 provinces and territories, 165 other countries, 6% are from out of state, 2% transferred in, 15% live on campus. *Retention:* 90% of 2006 full-time freshmen returned.

Freshmen *Admission:* 62,983 applied, 43,027 admitted, 13,530 enrolled.

Faculty *Total:* 3,032, 90% full-time. *Student/faculty ratio:* 24:1.

Majors Accounting; actuarial science; aerospace, aeronautical and astronautical engineering; African studies; American Indian/Native American studies; American studies; ancient Near Eastern and biblical languages; animal behavior and ethology; animal genetics; animal physiology; anthropology; applied mathematics; Arabic; archeology; architecture; art; art history, criticism and conservation; arts management; Asian studies; Asian studies (East); Asian studies (South); astronomy; biochemistry; biological and physical sciences; biology/biological sciences; biomedical/medical engineering; biophysics; botany/plant biology; business administration and management; Canadian studies; chemical engineering; chemistry; civil engineering; classical, ancient Mediterranean and Near Eastern studies and archaeology; classics and languages, literatures and linguistics; computer engineering; computer science; computer software engineering; computer systems networking and telecommunications; criminal justice/police science; criminology; cultural studies; digital communication and media/multimedia; dramatic/theater arts; ecology; e-commerce; economics; education; electrical, electronics and communications engineering; engineering; engineering science; English; environmental studies; European studies; European studies (Central and Eastern); film/cinema studies; finance; fine/studio arts; foods, nutrition, and wellness; forensic science and technology; forest/forest resources management; forestry; French; French as a second/foreign language (teaching); French language teacher education; geography; geological engineering; geology/earth science; geophysics and seismology; German; health and physical education; health teacher education; history; history and philosophy of science and technology; history of philosophy; humanities; hydrology and water resources science; industrial engineering; international relations and affairs; Islamic studies; Italian; Jewish/Judaic studies; labor and industrial relations; Latin; Latin American studies; linguistics; literature; manufacturing engineering; mass communication/media; materials engineering; materials science; mathematics; mechanical engineering; medical microbiology and bacteriology; medieval and Renaissance studies; metallurgical engineering; microbiology; mining and mineral engineering; modern Greek; modern languages; molecular biology; music; music history, literature, and theory; music teacher education; Near and Middle Eastern studies; neuroscience; nursing midwifery; nursing (registered nurse training); operations research; paleontology; peace studies and conflict resolution; petroleum engineering; pharmacology; pharmacy; philosophy; physical sciences related; physics; political science and government; Portuguese; psychology; public administration; public relations/image management; radiological science; religious studies; Romance languages; Russian; Russian studies; science teacher education; Slavic languages; sociology; Spanish; statistics; theology; toxicology; transportation and highway engineering; urban studies/affairs; visual and performing arts; women's studies; wood science and wood products/pulp and paper technology; zoology/animal biology.

Academics *Calendar:* Canadian standard year. *Degrees:* certificates, diplomas, bachelor's, master's, doctoral, and first professional. *Special study options:* adult/continuing education programs, cooperative education, double majors, English as a second language, off-campus study, part-time degree program, services for LD students, study abroad, summer session for credit.

Computers on Campus 2,000 computers/terminals are available on campus for general student use. Campuswide network is available.

Student Life *Housing options:* coed, women-only. Campus housing is university owned and leased by the school. Freshman campus housing is guaranteed. *Activities and organizations:* drama/theater group, student-run newspaper, radio station, choral group, national fraternities, national sororities. *Campus security:* 24-hour emergency response devices and patrols, student patrols, late-night transport/escort service. *Student services:* health clinic, personal/psychological counseling, women's center, legal services.

Athletics Member CIS. *Intercollegiate sports:* archery M/W, badminton M/W, basketball M/W, crew M, cross-country running M/W, fencing M/W, field hockey W, football M, golf M, gymnastics M/W, ice hockey M/W, rugby M, skiing (cross-country) M/W, skiing (downhill) M/W, soccer M/W, squash M/W, swimming and diving M/W, tennis M/W, track and field M/W, volleyball M/W, wrestling M. *Intramural sports:* archery M/W, badminton M/W, basketball M/W, crew M, fencing M/W, field hockey W, football M/W, gymnastics M/W, ice hockey M/W, lacrosse M/W, racquetball M, rugby M, skiing (downhill) M/W, soccer M/W, squash M/W, swimming and diving M/W, tennis M/W, track and field M/W, volleyball M/W, water polo M/W.

Standardized Tests *Required:* SAT and SAT Subject Tests or ACT (for admission).

Costs (2007–08) *Tuition:* nonresident $4570 Canadian dollars full-time; International tuition $17,640 Canadian dollars full-time. Full-time tuition and fees vary according to course level, course load, and program. Part-time tuition and fees vary according to course load. *Required fees:* $900 Canadian dollars full-time. *Room and board:* $9000 Canadian dollars; room only: $5500 Canadian dollars. Room and board charges vary according to board plan, housing facility, and location. *Payment plan:* installment. *Waivers:* senior citizens and employees or children of employees.

Applying *Options:* deferred entrance. *Application fee:* $60 Canadian dollars. *Required:* high school transcript. *Required for some:* interview. *Application deadlines:* 3/1 (freshmen), 7/1 (transfers). *Notification:* continuous (freshmen), continuous (transfers).

Freshman Application Contact Ms. Karel Swift, University Registrar (Admissions and Awards), University of Toronto, Toronto, ON M5S 1A1, Canada. *Phone:* 416-978-2190. *Fax:* 416-978-7022. *E-mail:* admissions.help@utoronto.ca.

UNIVERSITY OF VICTORIA

Victoria, British Columbia, Canada **www.uvic.ca/**

- **Province-supported** university, founded 1963
- **Suburban** 380-acre campus with easy access to Vancouver
- **Coed** 16,582 undergraduate students, 65% full-time, 56% women, 44% men
- **Moderately difficult** entrance level, 75% of applicants were admitted

Undergraduates 10,716 full-time, 5,866 part-time. Students come from 13 provinces and territories, 85 other countries, 13% are from out of state, 9% transferred in, 16% live on campus.

Freshmen *Admission:* 7,721 applied, 5,782 admitted, 2,590 enrolled. *Average high school GPA:* 3.6.

Faculty *Total:* 760, 95% full-time. *Student/faculty ratio:* 26:1.

Majors Ancient/classical Greek; anthropology; art history, criticism and conservation; art teacher education; Asian studies; astronomy; atmospheric sciences and meteorology; biochemistry; biology/biological sciences; botany/plant biology; business/commerce; chemistry; child development; Chinese; classics and languages, literatures and linguistics; computer engineering; computer science; computer software engineering; creative writing; dramatic/theater arts; ecology; economics; education; electrical, electronics and communications engineering; elementary education; English; English as a second/foreign language (teaching); environmental studies; European studies (Central and Eastern); fine/studio arts; French; French studies; geography; geology/earth science; geophysics and seismology; German; German studies; health and physical education related; health/health care administration; history; hotel/motel administration; international business/trade/commerce; Italian; Italian studies; Japanese; kindergarten/preschool education; kinesiology and exercise science; Latin; liberal arts and sciences/liberal studies; linguistics; literature; marine biology and biological oceanography; mathematics; mechanical engineering; medical microbiology and bacteriology; medieval and Renaissance studies; modern languages; music; music history, literature, and theory; music teacher education; music theory and composition; nursing (registered nurse training); nursing science; oceanography (chemical and physical); Pacific area/Pacific rim studies; philosophy; physical education teaching and coaching; physics; piano and organ; political science and government; pre-dentistry studies; pre-law studies; pre-medical studies; pre-veterinary studies; psychology; public administration; Romance languages; Russian; Russian studies; secondary education; Slavic languages; social work; sociology; Spanish; special education; sport and fitness administration/management; statistics; technical and business writing; voice and opera; women's studies; zoology/animal biology.

Academics *Calendar:* Canadian standard year. *Degrees:* certificates, diplomas, bachelor's, master's, doctoral, and first professional. *Special study options:* academic remediation for entering students, adult/continuing education programs, advanced placement credit, cooperative education, distance learning, double majors, English as a second language, honors programs, independent study, internships, off-campus study, part-time degree program, services for LD students, student-designed majors, study abroad, summer session for credit.

Computers on Campus 400 computers/terminals are available on campus for general student use. Students can access the following: online (class) registration. Campuswide network is available.

Student Life *Housing options:* coed. Campus housing is university owned. Freshman campus housing is guaranteed. *Activities and organizations:* drama/theater group, student-run newspaper, radio station, choral group. *Campus security:* 24-hour emergency response devices and patrols, student patrols, late-night transport/escort service. *Student services:* health clinic, personal/psychological counseling, women's center, legal services.

Athletics Member NAIA, CIS. *Intercollegiate sports:* basketball M (s)/W (s), crew M (s)/W (s), cross-country running M (s)/W (s), field hockey W (s), golf M/W, rugby M (s)/W (s), soccer M (s)/W (s), swimming and diving M (s)/W (s). *Intramural sports:* badminton M/W, baseball W, basketball M/W, cross-country running M/W, fencing M/W, field hockey M/W, football M/W, golf M/W, ice hockey M/W, racquetball M/W, rock climbing M (c)/W (c), rugby M/W, sailing M/W, skiing (downhill) M/W, soccer M/W, softball M/W, squash M/W, swimming and diving M/W, table tennis M/W, tennis M/W, ultimate Frisbee M/W, volleyball M/W, water polo M/W, weight lifting M/W.

Costs (2007–08) *Tuition:* province resident $4491 Canadian dollars full-time, $299 Canadian dollars per unit part-time; International tuition $14,532 Canadian dollars full-time. *Required fees:* $645 Canadian dollars full-time, $645 Canadian dollars per year part-time. *Room and board:* $6300 Canadian dollars; room only: $3970 Canadian dollars. Room and board charges vary according to board plan and housing facility.

Applying *Options:* electronic application, early admission, early action, deferred entrance. *Application fee:* $100 Canadian dollars. *Required:* high school transcript, minimum 2.5 GPA. *Required for some:* essay or personal statement, minimum 3.0 GPA, interview, audition, portfolio. *Application deadlines:* 4/30 (freshmen), 4/30 (transfers), 2/28 (early action). *Notification:* continuous (freshmen), continuous (transfers), 5/1 (early action).

Freshman Application Contact Mr. Bruno Rocca, Student Recruitment Director, University of Victoria, PO Box 3025, Victoria, BC V8W 3P2. *Phone:* 250-721-8121 Ext. 8109. *Fax:* 250-721-6225. *E-mail:* admit@uvic.ca.

UNIVERSITY OF WATERLOO

Waterloo, Ontario, Canada **www.uwaterloo.ca/**

- **Province-supported** university, founded 1957
- **Suburban** 900-acre campus with easy access to Toronto
- **Coed**
- **Moderately difficult** entrance level

Faculty *Student/faculty ratio:* 22:1.

Academics *Calendar:* trimesters. *Degrees:* certificates, diplomas, bachelor's, master's, doctoral, first professional, and postbachelor's certificates.

Student Life *Campus security:* 24-hour emergency response devices and patrols, student patrols, late-night transport/escort service.

Athletics Member CIS.

Standardized Tests *Required:* SAT or ACT (for admission). *Required for some:* SAT or ACT (for admission), SAT Subject Tests (for admission).

Financial Aid Of all full-time matriculated undergraduates who enrolled in 2006, 500 state and other part-time jobs (averaging $1000).

Applying *Options:* electronic application, early admission, deferred entrance. *Application fee:* $115 Canadian dollars. *Required:* high school transcript. *Required for some:* essay or personal statement, minimum 3.0 GPA, letters of recommendation, interview.

Freshman Application Contact Ms. Nancy Weiner, Associate Registrar, Admissions, University of Waterloo, 200 University Avenue West, Waterloo, ON N2L 3G1, Canada. *Phone:* 519-888-4567 Ext. 33106. *Fax:* 519-746-2882. *E-mail:* registrar@nhladm.uwaterloo.ca.

THE UNIVERSITY OF WESTERN ONTARIO

London, Ontario, Canada **www.uwo.ca/**

- **Province-supported** university, founded 1878, administratively affiliated with Brescia University College, Huron University College, King's University College
- **Suburban** 420-acre campus
- **Coed** 26,804 undergraduate students, 86% full-time, 59% women, 41% men
- **Very difficult** entrance level, 57% of applicants were admitted

Undergraduates 22,968 full-time, 3,836 part-time. Students come from 13 provinces and territories, 125 other countries, 5% are from out of state, 2% transferred in, 15% live on campus. *Retention:* 92% of 2006 full-time freshmen returned.

Freshmen *Admission:* 33,081 applied, 18,945 admitted, 6,228 enrolled.

Faculty *Total:* 1,307, 100% full-time. *Student/faculty ratio:* 21:1.

Majors Accounting; accounting and business/management; accounting and finance; actuarial science; American Indian/Native American studies; American studies; analytical chemistry; anatomy; ancient/classical Greek; animal genetics; animal physiology; anthropology; anthropology related; applied mathematics; archeology; area, ethnic, cultural, and gender studies related; art; art history, criticism and conservation; arts management; art teacher education; Asian studies; Asian studies (East); astronomy; astrophysics; audiology and hearing sciences; audiology and speech-language pathology; aviation/airway management; biblical studies; biochemistry; biochemistry/biophysics and molecular biology; bioinformatics; biological and physical sciences; biology/biological sciences; biophysics; business administration and management; business administration, management and operations related; business/commerce; business/corporate communications; business, management, and marketing related; business/managerial economics; business teacher education; Canadian studies; cell biology and anatomy; cell biology and histology; chemical engineering; chemistry; child development; Chinese; city/urban, community and regional planning; civil engineering; classics; classics and languages, literatures and linguistics; clinical/medical social work; clinical pastoral counseling/patient counseling; communication and media related; communication disorders; communication disorders sciences and services related; community health services counseling; comparative literature; computer and information sciences; computer engineering; computer programming; computer science; computer software and media applications related; computer software engineering; conservation biology; criminology; demography and population; dietetics; digital communication and media/multimedia; divinity/ministry; earth sciences; East Asian languages; ecology; economics; education; electrical, electronics and communications engineering; elementary education; engineering science; English; English language and literature related; English/language arts teacher education; entrepreneurship; environmental/environmental health engineering; environmental science; environmental studies; ethnic, cultural minority, and gender studies related; family and consumer sciences/human sciences; family and consumer sciences/human sciences related; family practice nursing/nurse practitioner; film/cinema studies; finance; fine arts related; fine/studio arts; foods, nutrition, and wellness; French; gay/lesbian studies; genetics; geography; geology/earth science; geophysics and seismology; German; health information/medical records administration; health science; health services/allied health/health sciences; Hebrew; history; human ecology; human resources management; immunology; information science/studies; information technology; inorganic chemistry; interdisciplinary studies; international business/trade/commerce; international finance; international/global studies; international relations and affairs; Italian; Japanese; Jewish/Judaic studies; journalism related; kindergarten/preschool education; kinesiology and exercise science; Latin; Latin American studies; legal studies; liberal arts and sciences/liberal studies; linguistics; management information systems; management science; marketing/marketing management; marriage and family therapy/counseling; mass communication/media; materials engineering; mathematical statistics and probability; mathematics; mathematics teacher education; mechanical engineering; medical microbiology and bacteriology; microbiological sciences and immunology related; microbiology; middle school education; modern languages; music; music history, literature, and theory; music management and merchandising; musicology and ethnomusicology; music pedagogy; music performance; music related; music teacher education; music theory and composition; natural resources management and policy; nursing administration; nursing (licensed practical/vocational nurse training); nursing (registered nurse training); occupational therapy; organic chemistry; organizational behavior; peace studies and conflict resolution; pharmacology; pharmacology and toxicology; philosophy; physical and theoretical chemistry; physical anthropology; physical education teaching and coaching; physical therapy; physics; physics related; physiological psychology/psychobiology; piano and organ; planetary astronomy and science; plant sciences; political science and government; psychology; psychology related; public administration; public health/community nursing; public health education and promotion; radio and television; rehabilitation and therapeutic professions related; religious education; religious studies; religious studies related; secondary education; social sciences related; social work; social work related; sociology; Spanish; special education; speech-language pathology; statistics; substance abuse/addiction counseling; theology; theoretical and mathematical physics; toxicology; urban studies/affairs; violin, viola, guitar and other stringed instruments; voice and opera; women's studies; youth services.

Academics *Calendar:* Canadian standard year. *Degrees:* certificates, diplomas, bachelor's, master's, doctoral, and first professional. *Special study options:* academic remediation for entering students, accelerated degree program, adult/continuing education programs, cooperative education, distance learning, double majors, honors programs, internships, off-campus study, part-time degree program, services for LD students, student-designed majors, study abroad, summer session for credit.

Computers on Campus 351 computers/terminals are available on campus for general student use. Students can access the following: campus intranet, computer help desk, free student e-mail accounts, online (class) grades, online (class) registration, online (class) schedules. Campuswide network is available. 100% of college-owned or -operated housing units are wired for high-speed Internet access. Wireless service is available via classrooms, computer centers, computer labs, learning centers, libraries, student centers.

Student Life *Housing options:* coed, men-only, women-only. Campus housing is university owned. Freshman campus housing is guaranteed. *Activities and organizations:* drama/theater group, student-run newspaper, radio and television station, choral group, marching band, national fraternities, national sororities. *Campus security:* 24-hour emergency response devices and patrols, student patrols, late-night transport/escort service, controlled dormitory access, Elgin Hall, Essex Hall, London Hall, Perth Hall. *Student services:* health clinic, personal/psychological counseling, women's center, legal services.

Athletics Member CIS. *Intercollegiate sports:* badminton M (s)/W (s), baseball M (s)/W (c), basketball M (s)/W (s), cheerleading M/W, crew M (s)/W (s), cross-country running M (s)/W (s), fencing M (s)/W (s), field hockey W (s), football M (s), golf M (s)/W (s), ice hockey M (s)/W (s), lacrosse M (c)/W (s), rugby M (s)/W (s), skiing (cross-country) M/W, soccer M (s)/W (s), squash M (s)/W (s), swimming and diving M (s)/W (s), tennis M (s)/W (s), track and field M (s)/W (s), volleyball M (s)/W (s), water polo M (s), wrestling M (s)/W (s). *Intramural sports:* badminton M/W, basketball M/W, bowling M/W, equestrian sports M (c)/W (c), fencing M (c)/W (c), field hockey M (c)/W (c), football M/W, ice hockey M/W, racquetball M/W, riflery M (c)/W (c), rugby W, skiing (cross-country) M (c)/W (c), skiing (downhill) M (c)/W (c), soccer M/W, softball M/W, squash M (c)/W (c), swimming and diving M (c)/W (c), table tennis M (c)/W (c), tennis M/W, volleyball M/W, water polo M/W.

Standardized Tests *Required:* SAT or ACT (for admission).

Costs (2007–08) *Tuition:* province resident $904 per course part-time; nonresident $4521 full-time, $2710 per course part-time; International tuition $13,550 full-time. Full-time tuition and fees vary according to program. Part-time tuition and fees vary according to course load, location, and program. *Required fees:* $110 per course part-time. *Room and board:* $8778; room only: $4970. Room and board charges vary according to board plan and housing facility. *Payment plans:* installment, deferred payment. *Waivers:* senior citizens and employees or children of employees.

Financial Aid Of all full-time matriculated undergraduates who enrolled in 2006, 1,433 state and other part-time jobs (averaging $1621).

Applying *Options:* electronic application, deferred entrance. *Application fee:* $115 Canadian dollars. *Required:* high school transcript, minimum 3.5 GPA. *Application deadlines:* 6/1 (freshmen), 5/15 (out-of-state freshmen), 6/1 (transfers). *Notification:* continuous (freshmen), continuous (out-of-state freshmen).

Freshman Application Contact Undergraduate Recruitment and Admissions, The University of Western Ontario, 1151 Richmond Street, Suite 2, London, ON N5A 5B8, Canada. *Phone:* 519-661-2100. *Fax:* 519-661-3710. *E-mail:* reg-admissions@uwo.ca.

UNIVERSITY OF WINDSOR

Windsor, Ontario, Canada www.uwindsor.ca/

- **Province-supported** university, founded 1857
- **Urban** 125-acre campus with easy access to Detroit
- **Endowment** $56.0 million
- **Coed** 13,620 undergraduate students, 78% full-time, 55% women, 45% men
- **Moderately difficult** entrance level, 78% of applicants were admitted

The University of Windsor combines a strong and focused emphasis on the learning experience of every student with a very broad range of programs. Windsor offers more than 150 undergraduate and graduate programs across nine faculties and nine cooperative education programs. Academic disciplines range from humanities and liberal arts to science. Professional studies are offered in business, engineering, education, law, computer science, creative writing, kinesiology, nursing, social work, clinical psychology, music, dramatic art, and visual arts. The tree-lined campus of the University of Windsor is in the midst of Windsor, Ontario, Canada's southernmost city. It is considered a premier location for advanced automotive manufacturing technology and the largest agribusiness region in eastern Canada. The campus is also the only one in Canada to be located on an international border. The University has academic agreements with several major U.S. universities. The University of Windsor is Canada's most international campus—10 percent of its population comes from eighty countries outside of Canada. This sharing of international experiences helps prepare Windsor graduates for the global workforce.

Undergraduates 10,560 full-time, 3,060 part-time. Students come from 16 provinces and territories, 91 other countries, 5% transferred in, 13% live on campus. *Retention:* 82% of 2006 full-time freshmen returned.

Freshmen *Admission:* 12,180 applied, 9,469 admitted, 2,998 enrolled.

Faculty *Total:* 871, 60% full-time, 53% with terminal degrees. *Student/faculty ratio:* 21:1.

Majors Accounting; accounting and finance; acting; anthropology; applied mathematics; art; art history, criticism and conservation; artificial intelligence and robotics; arts management; art teacher education; athletic training; biochemical technology; biochemistry; bioinformatics; biological and physical sciences; biology/biological sciences; biology teacher education; biophysics; biopsychology; biotechnology; broadcast journalism; business administration and management; business/commerce; business/managerial economics; chemistry; chemistry teacher education; city/urban, community and regional planning; civil engineering; classics and languages, literatures and linguistics; clinical child psychology; clinical psychology; communication/speech communication and rhetoric; communications technologies and support services related; comparative literature; computer and information sciences; computer and information sciences related; computer engineering; computer programming (specific applications); computer science; computer software and media applications related; computer systems networking and telecommunications; counselor education/school counseling and guidance; creative writing; criminal justice/safety; criminology; developmental and child psychology; development economics and international development; drama and dance teacher education; dramatic/theater arts; drawing; economics; education; educational leadership and administration; education (K-12); electrical, electronics and communications engineering; elementary education; engineering; engineering mechanics; English; English/language arts teacher education; environmental biology; environmental/environmental health engineering; environmental science; environmental studies; family and consumer economics related; family practice nursing/nurse practitioner; film/cinema studies; finance; fine/studio arts; foreign language teacher education; forensic science and technology; French; French as a second/foreign language (teaching); French language teacher education; French studies; general studies; geography teacher education; geology/earth science; German; German language teacher education; German studies; health and physical education; health teacher education; Hispanic-American, Puerto Rican, and Mexican-American/Chicano studies; history; history teacher education; humanities; human resources management; industrial engineering; information science/studies; information technology; intermedia/multimedia; international relations and affairs; Italian; Italian studies; Japanese; journalism; kindergarten/preschool education; kinesiology and exercise science; labor and industrial relations; labor studies; Latin; legal studies; linguistics; literature; management information systems; management science; marketing/marketing management; marketing research; mass communication/media; materials engineering; mathematics; mathematics and computer science; mathematics teacher education; mechanical engineering; medical laboratory technology; medical microbiology and bacteriology; modern Greek; modern languages; music; music history, literature, and theory; music performance; music teacher education; music theory and composition; music therapy; natural resources management and policy; neuroscience; nursing administration; nursing (registered nurse training); organizational communication; painting; parks, recreation and leisure; philosophy; physical education teaching and coaching; physics; physics teacher education; political science and government; pre-dentistry studies; pre-law studies; pre-medical studies; pre-pharmacy studies; printmaking; psychology; public administration; radio and television; Romance languages; Russian; science teacher education; science, technology and society; sculpture; secondary education; Slavic languages; social sciences; social work; sociology; Spanish; special education; speech/theater education; sport and fitness administration/management; statistics; visual and performing arts; women's studies.

Academics *Calendar:* semesters. *Degrees:* certificates, bachelor's, master's, doctoral, first professional, and postbachelor's certificates. *Special study options:* academic remediation for entering students, accelerated degree program, adult/continuing education programs, advanced placement credit, cooperative education, distance learning, double majors, external degree program, honors programs, internships, off-campus study, part-time degree program, services for LD students, student-designed majors, study abroad, summer session for credit. *Unusual degree programs:* 3-2 business administration; engineering; social work; computer science.

Computers on Campus 1,225 computers/terminals are available on campus for general student use. Students can access the following: campus intranet, computer help desk, free student e-mail accounts, online (class) grades, online (class) registration, online transcripts, degree audits, grades, bursaries, grants, online applications for graduation. Campuswide network is available. 100% of college-owned or -operated housing units are wired for high-speed Internet access. Wireless service is available via entire campus.

Student Life *Housing options:* coed, men-only, women-only, disabled students. Campus housing is university owned. Freshman campus housing is guaranteed. *Activities and organizations:* drama/theater group, student-run newspaper, radio station, choral group, University of Windsor Student Alliance, Environmental Awareness Association, Social Science Society, Commerce Society, Science Society. *Campus security:* 24-hour emergency response devices and patrols, student patrols, late-night transport/escort service, controlled dormitory access. *Student services:* health clinic, personal/psychological counseling, women's center, legal services.

Athletics Member NAIA, CIS. *Intercollegiate sports:* basketball M/W, cheerleading M/W, cross-country running M/W, football M, golf M/W, ice hockey M/W, rugby M/W, soccer M/W, softball W, track and field M/W, volleyball M/W. *Intramural sports:* badminton M/W, basketball M/W, bowling M/W, football M/W, golf M/W, ice hockey M/W, rugby M/W, soccer M/W, softball M/W, swimming and diving M/W, table tennis M/W, ultimate Frisbee M/W, volleyball M/W, water polo M/W.

Standardized Tests *Required for some:* SAT or ACT (for admission), SAT and SAT Subject Tests or ACT (for admission), SAT Subject Tests (for admission).

Costs (2008–09) *Tuition:* area resident $4660 full-time; province resident $466 per course part-time; nonresident $1433 per course part-time; International tuition $14,330 full-time. *Required fees:* $733 full-time, $229 per term part-time. *Room and board:* $8290; room only: $4601.

Financial Aid *Financial aid deadline:* 6/15.

Applying *Options:* electronic application, early admission. *Application fee:* $60 Canadian dollars. *Required:* high school transcript, minimum 3.0 GPA. *Required for some:* essay or personal statement, minimum 3.3 GPA, 1 letter of recommendation, interview. *Application deadlines:* rolling (freshmen), 7/1 (out-of-state freshmen), rolling (transfers). *Notification:* continuous until 8/30 (freshmen), continuous until 8/30 (transfers).

Freshman Application Contact Ms. Charlene Yates, Manager of Undergraduate Admissions, University of Windsor, Office of the Registrar, 401 Sunset Avenue, Windsor, ON N9B 3P4, Canada. *Phone:* 519-253-3000 Ext. 3315. *Toll-free phone:* 800-864-2860. *Fax:* 519-971-3653. *E-mail:* registr@uwindsor.ca.

See page 2860 for the College Close-Up.

THE UNIVERSITY OF WINNIPEG

Winnipeg, Manitoba, Canada **www.uwinnipeg.ca/**

- **Province-supported** comprehensive, founded 1967
- **Urban** 8-acre campus
- **Endowment** $16.8 million
- **Coed** 9,006 undergraduate students, 69% full-time, 63% women, 37% men
- **Moderately difficult** entrance level, 75% of applicants were admitted

Undergraduates 6,231 full-time, 2,775 part-time. Students come from 7 provinces and territories, 32 other countries, 3% transferred in, 3% live on campus. *Retention:* 60% of 2006 full-time freshmen returned.

Freshmen *Admission:* 4,203 applied, 3,159 admitted, 2,438 enrolled. *Average high school GPA:* 3.13.

Faculty *Total:* 321, 84% full-time, 70% with terminal degrees. *Student/faculty ratio:* 35:1.

Majors Anthropology; applied mathematics; art history, criticism and conservation; biochemistry; biology/biological sciences; business administration and management; Canadian studies; chemistry; classics and languages, literatures and linguistics; criminal justice/police science; data processing and data processing technology; developmental and child psychology; development economics and international development; dramatic/theater arts; ecology; economics; education; elementary education; English; English language and literature related; environmental studies; French; French studies; geography; German; German studies; history; information science/studies; interdisciplinary studies; Italian studies; journalism; Latin; mathematics; modern Greek; molecular biology; music; peace studies and conflict resolution; philosophy; physics; political science and government; pre-dentistry studies; pre-law studies; pre-medical studies; pre-nursing studies; pre-pharmacy studies; pre-veterinary studies; psychology; religious studies; religious studies related; secondary education; sociology; Spanish and Iberian studies; statistics; theology; urban studies/affairs; women's studies.

Academics *Calendar:* Canadian standard year. *Degrees:* bachelor's and master's. *Special study options:* academic remediation for entering students, accelerated degree program, adult/continuing education programs, advanced placement credit, cooperative education, English as a second language, honors programs, internships, off-campus study, part-time degree program, services for LD students, student-designed majors, study abroad, summer session for credit.

Computers on Campus 175 computers/terminals are available on campus for general student use. Students can access the following: campus intranet, computer help desk, free student e-mail accounts. Campuswide network is available. Wireless service is available via entire campus.

Student Life *Housing options:* coed. Campus housing is university owned and leased by the school. Freshman applicants given priority for college housing. *Activities and organizations:* drama/theater group, student-run newspaper, radio station, choral group, Woman's Centre, LGBT (Lesbian Gay Bisexual Transgender), radio station, International Resource Centre, Aboriginal Student Centre, national fraternities. *Campus security:* 24-hour emergency response devices and patrols, student patrols, video controlled external access. *Student services:* health clinic, personal/psychological counseling, women's center.

Athletics Member CIS. *Intercollegiate sports:* basketball M (s)/W (s), volleyball M (s)/W (s). *Intramural sports:* basketball M/W, racquetball M/W, table tennis M/W, volleyball M/W, weight lifting M/W.

Costs (2008–09) *One-time required fee:* $100 Canadian dollars. *Tuition:* province resident $2995 Canadian dollars full-time; International tuition $7160 Canadian dollars full-time. *Required fees:* $200 Canadian dollars full-time. *Room and board:* $4800 Canadian dollars; room only: $3772 Canadian dollars.

Financial Aid Of all full-time matriculated undergraduates who enrolled in 2006, 60 state and other part-time jobs (averaging $1000). *Financial aid deadline:* 3/1.

Applying *Options:* early admission, deferred entrance. *Application fee:* $60. *Required:* minimum 2.0 GPA. *Required for some:* high school transcript, interview. *Application deadlines:* 8/9 (freshmen), 7/15 (out-of-state freshmen), 8/9 (transfers). *Notification:* continuous (freshmen), continuous (out-of-state freshmen), continuous (transfers).

Director of Admissions Mr. Colin Russell, Registrar, The University of Winnipeg, 515 Portage Avenue, Winnipeg, MB R3B 2E9, Canada. *Phone:* 204-786-9776. *Fax:* 204-786-8656. *E-mail:* admissions@uwinnipeg.ca.

VANGUARD COLLEGE

Edmonton, Alberta, Canada **www.vanguardcollege.com/**

Director of Admissions Gonam Raju, Registrar, Vanguard College, 12140-103 Street NW, Edmonton, AB T5G 2J9, Canada. *Phone:* 780-452-0808 Ext. 223. *Toll-free phone:* 866-222-0808. *Fax:* 780-452-5803.

WESTERN CHRISTIAN COLLEGE

Dauphin, Manitoba, Canada **www.westernchristian.ca/**

- **Independent** 4-year, founded 1957, affiliated with Church of Christ
- **Urban** campus
- **Coed**

Academics *Calendar:* semesters.

Costs (2007–08) *Comprehensive fee:* $12,500 Canadian dollars includes full-time tuition ($6600 Canadian dollars), mandatory fees ($1100 Canadian dollars), and room and board ($4800 Canadian dollars). Part-time tuition: $660 Canadian dollars per course. *Required fees:* $200 Canadian dollars per term part-time. *Room and board:* Room and board charges vary according to board plan.

Applying *Application fee:* $50 Canadian dollars. *Required:* essay or personal statement, high school transcript, letters of recommendation. *Required for some:* interview.

Freshman Application Contact Ms. Jennifer Kerr, Registrar, Western Christian College, 220 Whitmore Avenue West, Box 5000, Dauphin, MB R7N 2V5, Canada. *Phone:* 306-545-1515 Ext. 500. *Fax:* 306-352-2198.

WILFRID LAURIER UNIVERSITY

Waterloo, Ontario, Canada **www.wlu.ca/**

- **Province-supported** comprehensive, founded 1911
- **Urban** 40-acre campus with easy access to Toronto
- **Coed** 13,563 undergraduate students, 86% full-time, 60% women, 40% men
- **Moderately difficult** entrance level, 59% of applicants were admitted

Undergraduates 11,618 full-time, 1,945 part-time. Students come from 14 provinces and territories, 62 other countries, 21% live on campus.

Freshmen *Admission:* 25,671 applied, 15,175 admitted, 3,545 enrolled.

Faculty *Total:* 485. *Student/faculty ratio:* 23:1.

Majors Anthropology; archeology; area studies; biology/biological sciences; biotechnology; business administration and management; Canadian studies; chemistry; classics and languages, literatures and linguistics; cognitive psychology and psycholinguistics; community psychology; computer and information sciences related; computer science; criminal justice/safety; developmental and child psychology; economics; education; English; experimental psychology; film/cinema studies; French; French studies; geography; German; health science; history; intercultural/multicultural and diversity studies; international/global studies; journalism; kinesiology and exercise science; Latin; mass communication/media; mathematics; medieval and Renaissance studies; modern Greek; music; music therapy; philosophy; physical education teaching and coaching; physics; political science and government; psychology; religious studies; sociology; Spanish; statistics; women's studies.

Academics *Calendar:* Canadian standard year. *Degrees:* diplomas, bachelor's, master's, and doctoral. *Special study options:* accelerated degree program, adult/continuing education programs, advanced placement credit, cooperative education, distance learning, double majors, honors programs, internships, off-campus study, part-time degree program, services for LD students, study abroad, summer session for credit. *Unusual degree programs:* 3-2 education.

Computers on Campus 450 computers/terminals are available on campus for general student use. Students can access the following: campus intranet, computer help desk, free student e-mail accounts, online (class) grades, online (class) registration, online (class) schedules. Campuswide network is available. Wireless service is available via entire campus.

Student Life *Housing options:* coed, men-only, women-only, disabled students. Campus housing is university owned. *Activities and organizations:* drama/theater group, student-run newspaper, radio station, choral group, Water Buffaloes, TAMIAE, Ski Club, Musicians' Network, Laurier Christian Fellowship. *Campus security:* 24-hour emergency response devices and patrols, student patrols, late-night transport/escort service, controlled dormitory access. *Student services:* health clinic, personal/psychological counseling, women's center, legal services.

Athletics Member CIS. *Intercollegiate sports:* baseball M, basketball M/W, cheerleading M/W, cross-country running M/W, football M, golf M, ice hockey M/W, lacrosse W, rugby M/W, soccer M/W, swimming and diving M/W, tennis W, volleyball M/W. *Intramural sports:* badminton M/W, basketball M/W, football M/W, golf M, ice hockey M/W, lacrosse M (c), skiing (cross-country) M (c)/W (c), skiing (downhill) M (c)/W (c), soccer M/W, softball M/W, squash M/W, swimming and diving M/W, tennis M/W, ultimate Frisbee M/W, volleyball M/W, water polo M/W, weight lifting W.

Standardized Tests *Required for some:* SAT or ACT (for admission).

Costs (2007–08) *Tuition:* province resident $4568 Canadian dollars full-time; International tuition $16,300 Canadian dollars full-time. Full-time tuition and fees vary according to program. *Required fees:* $1309 Canadian dollars full-time. *Room and board:* $7334 Canadian dollars; room only: $4159 Canadian dollars. Room and board charges vary according to board plan and location. *Waivers:* senior citizens and employees or children of employees.

Applying *Application fee:* $105 Canadian dollars. *Required:* high school transcript. *Required for some:* essay or personal statement, letters of recommendation, interview, audition for music programs. *Application deadlines:* 5/1 (freshmen), 5/1 (transfers). *Notification:* continuous (freshmen).

Freshman Application Contact Ms. Lois Wood, Associate Registrar, Undergraduate Admissions, Wilfrid Laurier University, 75 University Avenue West, Waterloo, ON N2L 3C5, Canada. *Phone:* 519-884-0710. *Fax:* 519-884-8826. *E-mail:* admissions@wlu.ca.

WILLIAM AND CATHERINE BOOTH COLLEGE

Winnipeg, Manitoba, Canada **www.boothcollege.ca/**

Director of Admissions Ms. Mary Ann Austin, Registrar, William and Catherine Booth College, 447 Webb Place, Winnipeg, MB R3B 2P2, Canada. *Phone:* 204-947-6701. *Toll-free phone:* 800-781-6044.

YORK UNIVERSITY

Toronto, Ontario, Canada **www.yorku.ca/**

- **Province-supported** university, founded 1959
- **Urban** 650-acre campus
- **Endowment** $145.2 million
- **Coed** 46,233 undergraduate students, 85% full-time, 62% women, 38% men
- **Moderately difficult** entrance level, 15% of applicants were admitted

Undergraduates 39,101 full-time, 7,132 part-time. Students come from 11 provinces and territories, 173 other countries, 2% are from out of state, 6% live on campus.

Freshmen *Admission:* 39,890 applied, 6,058 admitted. *Average high school GPA:* 3.3. *Test scores:* ACT scores over 18: 100%; ACT scores over 24: 100%.

Faculty *Total:* 1,415, 91% full-time, 100% with terminal degrees. *Student/faculty ratio:* 17:1.

Majors Accounting; acting; actuarial science; aeronautics/aviation/aerospace science and technology; aerospace, aeronautical and astronautical engineering; African studies; ancient Near Eastern and biblical languages; anthropology; applied art; applied mathematics; art; art history, criticism and conservation; art teacher education; Asian studies (East); astronomy; atmospheric sciences and meteorology; behavioral sciences; bilingual and multilingual education; biological and physical sciences; biology/biological sciences; biology teacher education; biotechnology; business administration and management; business/commerce; business/managerial economics; business statistics; Canadian studies; chemistry;

chemistry teacher education; cinematography and film/video production; classics; classics and languages, literatures and linguistics; commercial and advertising art; communication/speech communication and rhetoric; computer and information sciences; computer engineering; computer hardware engineering; computer programming; computer science; computer software engineering; creative writing; cultural studies; curriculum and instruction; dance; design and visual communications; development economics and international development; drama and dance teacher education; dramatic/theater arts; drawing; ecology; economics; education; education (K-12); elementary education; engineering; engineering physics; English; English as a second/foreign language (teaching); English/language arts teacher education; entrepreneurship; environmental biology; environmental education; environmental science; environmental studies; European studies; film/cinema studies; finance; fine/studio arts; French; French studies; geography; geology/earth science; geotechnical engineering; German; German studies; gerontology; health and physical education; health science; health services/allied health/health sciences; Hebrew; history; history teacher education; hospital and health care facilities administration; humanities; human resources management; information technology; interdisciplinary studies; international business/trade/commerce; international marketing; international relations and affairs; Italian; Italian studies; Japanese; Jewish/Judaic studies; kindergarten/preschool education; labor and industrial relations; language interpretation and translation; Latin; Latin American studies; legal studies; liberal arts and sciences/liberal studies; linguistics; literature; management information systems; marketing/marketing management; mass communication/media; mathematics; mathematics and computer science; mathematics teacher education; middle school education; modern Greek; modern languages; molecular biology; music; music history, literature, and theory; musicology and ethnomusicology; music performance; music teacher education; music theory and composition; natural sciences; nursing (registered nurse training); nursing science; operations research; organizational behavior; painting; philosophy; photography; physical education teaching and coaching; physical sciences; physics; physics teacher education; piano and organ; playwriting and screenwriting; political science and government; pre-dentistry studies; pre-law studies; pre-medical studies; pre-pharmacy studies; pre-veterinary studies; printmaking; psychology; public administration; public health; public policy analysis; rehabilitation therapy; religious studies; Romance languages; Russian; Russian studies; sales, distribution and marketing; science teacher education; science, technology and society; sculpture; secondary education; sign language interpretation and translation; social sciences; social science teacher education; social studies teacher education; social work; sociology; Spanish; Spanish and Iberian studies; special education; speech/theater education; sport and fitness administration/management; statistics; technical and business writing; urban studies/affairs; visual and performing arts; voice and opera; women's studies.

Academics *Calendar:* semesters. *Degrees:* certificates, diplomas, bachelor's, master's, doctoral, first professional, post-master's, and postbachelor's certificates. *Special study options:* academic remediation for entering students, accelerated degree program, adult/continuing education programs, advanced placement credit, distance learning, double majors, English as a second language, honors programs, independent study, internships, off-campus study, part-time degree program, services for LD students, student-designed majors, study abroad, summer session for credit. *Unusual degree programs:* 3-2 social work; education.

Computers on Campus 1,900 computers/terminals are available on campus for general student use. Students can access the following: computer help desk, free student e-mail accounts, online (class) grades, online (class) registration, online (class) schedules. Campuswide network is available. Wireless service is available via entire campus.

Student Life *Housing options:* coed, disabled students. Campus housing is university owned. Freshman applicants given priority for college housing. *Activities and organizations:* drama/theater group, student-run newspaper, radio station, choral group, college student councils, York Federation of Students, Jewish Student Association, First Nations and Aboriginal Student Association, International and Exchange Students Club. *Campus security:* 24-hour emergency response devices and patrols, student patrols, late-night transport/escort service, controlled dormitory access. *Student services:* health clinic, personal/psychological counseling, women's center, legal services.

Athletics Member CIS. *Intercollegiate sports:* badminton M/W, basketball M/W, cross-country running M/W, field hockey W, football M, ice hockey M/W, rugby W, soccer M/W, swimming and diving M/W, tennis M/W, track and field M/W, volleyball M/W, water polo M/W. *Intramural sports:* badminton M/W, baseball M/W, basketball M/W, bowling M/W, cheerleading M/W, cross-country running M/W, fencing M/W, football M/W, golf M/W, ice hockey M, soccer M/W, softball M/W, squash M/W, swimming and diving M/W, tennis M/W, volleyball M/W, water polo M/W.

Standardized Tests *Required:* SAT or ACT (for admission).

Costs (2007–08) *Comprehensive fee:* $11,664 Canadian dollars includes full-time tuition ($5278 Canadian dollars) and room and board ($6386 Canadian dollars). Full-time tuition and fees vary according to course load, degree level, and program. Part-time tuition: $176 Canadian dollars per credit. Part-time tuition and fees vary according to course load and program. International tuition: $15,278 Canadian dollars full-time. *College room only:* $3986 Canadian dollars. Room and board charges vary according to board plan and housing facility. *Payment plan:* installment. *Waivers:* senior citizens and employees or children of employees.

Financial Aid Of all full-time matriculated undergraduates who enrolled in 2006, 1,280 state and other part-time jobs.

Applying *Options:* electronic application, early admission, deferred entrance. *Application fee:* $175 Canadian dollars. *Required:* high school transcript, minimum 3.0 GPA, audition/evaluation for fine arts program, supplemental applications for business. *Required for some:* essay or personal statement, 2 letters of recommendation, interview. *Application deadlines:* 2/1 (freshmen), 2/1 (transfers), 2/1 (early action). *Notification:* 6/1 (early action).

Freshman Application Contact Ms. Amber Burkett, International Recruitment Officer, York University, 4700 Keele Street, Toronto, ON M3J 1P3, Canada. *Phone:* 416-736-5825. *Fax:* 416-736-5741. *E-mail:* intlenq@yorku.ca.

See page 2862 for the College Close-Up.

BISHOP'S UNIVERSITY

SHERBROOKE, QUEBEC, CANADA

The University

Since 1843 Bishop's University has provided students from across Canada and around the world with a small and [illegible] education. Today, Bishop's offers undergraduate degrees in business, education, humanities, natural sciences, and social sciences to 2,350 students from across Canada, its provinces and several countries around the world. Although it is located in Quebec, Bishop's is an English-language university in a bilingual setting. The mission of Bishop's University is to provide a sound and broad education primarily at the undergraduate level. The goal is the education of individuals to realize their full potential in their intellectual, spiritual, social, and physical dimensions. To this end, Bishop's emphasizes excellence in teaching informed by scholarship and research. Furthermore, the University encourages frequent interaction among students and faculty members, participation in nonacademic activities, a keen sense of responsibility to others and to themselves within as well as a commitment to the Quebec, Canadian, and international communities.

In September 2007 full-time undergraduate students were enrolled at Bishop's, making it one of the smallest universities in Canada. Forty-five percent of students came from outside the province of Quebec, and 29 percent list French as their first language. The average class size in first-year courses is 40 students; in upper-level courses, the average drops to 17 students. First-year students are guaranteed housing. Half of all students reside in residence on campus. All rooms are single or double and are wired for Internet access.

Athletics plays a major role at Bishop's. Varsity sports include football and golf for men, soccer for women, and alpine skiing, basketball, and rugby for both men and women. Club sports include lacrosse and women's ice hockey. Bishop's is blessed with excellent facilities and equipment for sports and activities. The athletic complex includes [illegible] gyms, two weight rooms, an indoor pool, an indoor running track, squash courts, a dance studio, and numerous tennis courts (including six lighted courts). Bishop's has its own 18-hole golf course on campus, and 134 kilometers (47 miles) of cross-country ski trails that begin on the campus. More than fifty clubs and organizations offer a variety of student activities, including the Student Representative Council, a student-run radio station, the newspaper, the yearbook, the performing arts, and [illegible] Association.

Location

Bishop's has a picturesque residential campus in the borough of Lennoxville, just minutes away from downtown Sherbrooke, one of the largest cities in Quebec. The Eastern Townships of Quebec—a region blessed with some of the finest outdoor recreational opportunities in Canada—is also less than a day's drive from Ottawa, Toronto, Boston, and New York City, and between the dynamic cities of Montreal and Quebec City and the American border states of Vermont, New Hampshire, and Maine. Sherbrooke was recently [illegible] as one of the best places to live in Canada. Besides, the [illegible] Sherbrooke [illegible] in education, including eight post-secondary institutions, including [illegible] universities. This gives Sherbrooke one of the highest concentrations of university students in the country, and contributes a billion dollars to the local economy.

Majors and Degrees

Bishop's offers a Bachelor of Arts (B.A.), Bachelor of Business Administration (B.B.A.), Bachelor of Business and Science (B.B.Sc.), Bachelor of Education (B.Ed.), and Bachelor of Science (B.Sc.) degrees. Programs are available in biology, biochemistry, business administration, chemistry, classical studies, computer science, drama, economics, education (elementary or secondary), English, French and Quebec studies, fine arts, history, liberal arts, mathematics, modern languages, music, philosophy, physics, political studies, psychology, religion, sociology, and women's studies. Students can also enroll in interdisciplinary programs.

Academic Programs

Students are encouraged to study outside of their division and to choose majors or double majors. Many students combine diverse studies—such as double majors in business and drama, a major in biology and a minor in the fine arts, or a major in political studies and a minor in sociology.

Prospective students are encouraged to choose a specific major when applying to Bishop's. The major normally requires that a student take sixteen courses, or 48 credits, within one discipline. A wide range of complementary courses or a major or minor in another subject area may be added during the course of a student's degree and completed in conjunction with the original major. A minor requires eight courses, or 24 credits, within a single concentration and is added to a student's program during the course of a student's degree program.

The honours course of study is the most highly specialized concentration of courses within a degree. Students must normally take the majority of their courses (twenty courses, or 60 credits) in one discipline, as designated by the department concerned, while maintaining a high academic standing. An honours designation is normally declared during a student's second or third year of study and is based on academic performance. Students who intend to pursue graduate studies are strongly urged to consider an honours degree.

Off-Campus Programs

Full-time students with a 70 percent or better cumulative GPA and who are enrolled in their first degree can apply to participate in an exchange program. Bishop's University has exchange agreements with universities in several different countries, and new possibilities are added every year. Students may consider Australia, Belgium, England, Finland, France, Germany, Korea, Mexico, the Netherlands, Norway, South Africa, Spain, Sweden, New Zealand, and the United States. Most students who participate go in either the second year of a three-year Bishop's degree program or the third year of a four-year degree program. Other arrangements are possible.

Academic Facilities

Most of Bishop's classroom and laboratory facilities have recently been renovated or are scheduled to be renovated in the near future. The Core Computer Centre houses the main computer systems and wireless networks. More than 150 desktop computers and five general-purpose and departmental labs provide a 10:1 student-computer ratio. Stand-alone e-mail workstations for all students and staff and faculty members are located throughout the campus.

The Dobson-Lagassé Centre for Entrepreneurship, established to assist start-up businesses [illegible]

BISHOP'S UNIVERSITY

SHERBROOKE, QUEBEC, CANADA

The University

Since 1843 Bishop's University has provided students from across Canada and around the world with a sound and liberal education. Today, Bishop's offers undergraduate degrees in business, education, humanities, natural sciences, and social sciences to 1,850 students from every Canadian province and sixty-five countries around the world. Although it is located in Quebec, Bishop's is an English-language university in a bilingual setting. The mission of Bishop's University is to provide a sound and liberal education primarily at the undergraduate level. The goal is the education of individuals to realize their full potential in their intellectual, spiritual, social, and physical dimensions. To this end, Bishop's emphasizes excellence in teaching enriched by scholarship and research. Furthermore, the University encourages frequent interactions among students and faculty members, participation in nonacademic activities, a keen sense of responsibility to others, and an openness within as well as a commitment to the Quebec, Canadian, and international communities.

In September 2007, 1,817 full-time undergraduate students were enrolled at Bishop's, making it one of the smallest universities in Canada. Fifty-five percent of students come from outside the province of Quebec, and 29 percent list French as their first language. The average class size in first-year courses is 40 students; in upper-level courses, the average drops to 17 students. First-year students are guaranteed housing in one of seven residence halls on campus. All rooms are single or double and are wired for Internet access.

Athletics plays a major role at Bishop's. Varsity sports include football and golf for men, soccer for women, and alpine skiing, basketball, and rugby for both men and women. Club sports include lacrosse and women's ice hockey. Bishop's is blessed with excellent facilities and numerous extracurricular activities. The Athletic Complex includes two gyms, two weight rooms, an indoor pool, an indoor running track, six squash courts, an aerobics studio, and ten outdoor tennis courts (including six lighted courts). Bishop's has a nine-hole golf course on campus and 124 kilometers (77 miles) of bike trails and cross-country ski paths that begin on the campus. More than fifty clubs and organizations offer a variety of student activities, including the Student Representative Council, a student-run radio station and newspaper, the yearbook, the debating team, and the Big Buddies Association.

Location

Bishop's is a peaceful, residential campus in the borough of Lennoxville, just minutes away from downtown Sherbrooke, one of the largest cities in Quebec. The Eastern Townships of Quebec—a region blessed with some of the finest outdoor recreational opportunities in Canada—is also less than a day's drive from Ottawa, Toronto, Boston, and New York City. Nearby are the dynamism of Montreal, Quebec City, and the American-border states of Vermont, New Hampshire, and Maine. Sherbrooke topped the *Canadian Business'* sixth annual ranking of the best places to set up a business. The survey also cited Sherbrooke traffics in education, boasting eight post-secondary institutions, including two universities. "This gives Sherbrooke one of the highest concentrations of brains, students and R&D on the continent, and contributes a billion dollars to the local economy."

Majors and Degrees

Bishop's offers Bachelor of Arts (B.A.), Bachelor of Business Administration (B.B.A.), Bachelor of Business and Science (B.B.Sc.), Bachelor of Education (B.Ed.), and Bachelor of Science (B.Sc.) degrees. Programs are available in biology, biochemistry, business administration, chemistry, classical studies, computer science, drama, economics, education (elementary or secondary), English, French and Québécois studies, fine arts, history, liberal arts, mathematics, modern languages, music, philosophy, physics, political studies, psychology, religion, sociology, and women's studies. Students can also enroll in interdisciplinary programs.

Academic Programs

Students are encouraged to study outside of their division and to choose minors or double majors. Many students combine very diverse studies—such as double majors in business and drama, a major in biology and a minor in the fine arts, or a major in political studies and a minor in sociology.

Prospective students are encouraged to choose a specific major when applying to Bishop's. The major normally requires that a student take sixteen courses, or 48 credits, within one discipline. A wide range of complementary courses or a major or minor in another subject area may be added during the course of a student's degree and completed in conjunction with the original major. A minor requires eight courses, or 24 credits, within a single concentration and is added to a student's program during the course of a student's degree program.

The honors course of study is the most highly specialized concentration of courses within a degree. Students must normally take the majority of their courses (twenty courses or 60 credits) in one discipline, as designated by the department concerned, while maintaining a high academic standing. An honors degree is normally declared during a student's second or third year of study and is based on academic performance. Students who intend to pursue graduate studies are strongly urged to consider an honors degree.

Off-Campus Programs

Full-time students with a 70 percent or better cumulative GPA and who are enrolled in their first degree can apply to participate in an exchange program. Bishop's University has exchange agreements with universities in several different countries, and new possibilities are added every year. Students may consider Australia, Belgium, England, Finland, France, Germany, Korea, Mexico, Netherlands, Norway, South Africa, Spain, Sweden, Switzerland, and the United States. Most students who participate go in either the second year of a three-year Bishop's degree program or the third year of a four-year degree program. Other arrangements are possible.

Academic Facilities

Most of Bishop's classroom and laboratory facilities have recently been renovated or are scheduled to be renovated in the near future. The Cole Computer Centre houses the main computer systems and wireless connectivity. More than 650 desktop computers and five general-purpose and departmental labs provide a 10:1 student-computer ratio. Stand-up e-mail workstations for all students and staff and faculty members are located throughout the campus.

The Dobson-Lagassé Centre for Entrepreneurship, established to assist start-up businesses with rapid access to strategic information, provides assistance in writing business plans and flexible mentoring for better business performance. The Eastern Townships Research Centre was established in 1982 to foster and stimulate research on historical, cultural, and social aspects of the Eastern Townships. The Curry Wildlife Refuge, a 3-hectare wetland conservation area, acts as an on-campus laboratory.

The Foreman Art Gallery serves as a forum for the presentation and examination of the visual arts through a program of contemporary and historical exhibitions as well as a lecture series and films. The Centennial Theatre seats 575 and accommodates a variety of theatrical productions, concerts, and guest speakers as well as weekly films. There is also a multipurpose studio theater (in-the-round) with seating for 175. First constructed in 1897 and completely renovated in 1991, Bandeen Hall is a 156-seat recital hall that combines outstanding acoustics and modern equipment with the grace and charm of a nineteenth-century structure.

The John Bassett Memorial Library, with a seating capacity of 500, houses a collection of 590,577 items. The library has a computer lab with twenty-seven workstations, six laptop ports, and wireless access to the Internet. In addition to books and audio-visual materials, the collection includes subscriptions to 18,408 print and online periodical titles and twenty-six electronic products, such as abstracts, company reports, and full-text online journals.

Costs

In 2007, Quebec residents paid Can$55.61 per credit, while out-of-province Canadian residents paid Can$162.79 per credit. International students enrolled in a science, mathematics, computer science, drama, music, or fine art program paid Can$387.61 per credit, while all other disciplines cost Can$347.61 per credit. All students paid Can$455.50 in fees. The room-only portion of the residence fees during the academic year was from Can$385 per month for a double room and Can$480 per month for a single room with a semiprivate bathroom. All residents selected a meal plan, which varied in cost from Can$300 to Can$450 per month.

Financial Aid

Bishop's University invests more than $1 million each year in its students. Renewable entrance scholarships, ranging from Can$1000 to Can$4000, are guaranteed for all Canadian and CEGEP students who meet the scholarship criteria. To be eligible for an academic scholarship, students must apply to Bishop's no later than March 1, and recipients are notified no later than May 1. In addition, there are ten Can$2000 admission scholarships awarded to students from the American high school system. The University also grants a number of awards and bursaries to students in financial need who meet specific criteria. For example, students who have demonstrated outstanding records of leadership may be eligible for an APEX (Awards for Peer Excellence) of Can$1000 for one year.

Faculty

Faculty members are loyal, committed teachers who deem personal interaction with undergraduate students to be a priority. They have chosen to teach at Bishop's because it is possible to know and appreciate each of their students on an individual basis. In all divisions and schools, professors are involved in interesting and exciting research activities, ranging from complex chemical experiments to political and literature studies to the creation of new works of art and music. The student-faculty ratio is 17:1.

Student Government

The Bishop's University Students' Representative Council (SRC) is a nonprofit student-run organization to which all students automatically belong. The SRC provides students with a voice in student-related issues, not only at the University level but also at the provincial and national level. The SRC comprises a 5-member executive branch (the president, the academic vice president, the internal vice president, the external vice president, and the director of finance), which, with 5 student senators, 6 students-at-large, and 1 corporate representative, forms the 17-member Executive Council.

Admission Requirements

Bishop's invites applications from students interested in participating academically and socially in the University. Acceptance to the University is based upon a review of a student's past academic record in CEGEP, secondary, or postsecondary studies. School performance and the quality of academic work are the most important criteria used in judging the probability of an applicant's success at the university level and in determining their eligibility for admission.

CEGEP applicants must complete a DEC and enter a 93-credit (three-year) program. Canadian high school applicants must have a high school diploma and a minimum 75 percent overall average on academic courses. U.S. high school applicants must have their high school diploma and submit SAT or ACT scores. Transfer applicants are assessed on an individual basis. Adjustments in degree length may be made for International Baccalaureate or Advanced Placement courses. Students are encouraged to visit the Web site for application and program requirements (http://www.ubishops.ca).

Applicants should submit a completed application form (paper or online), an academic transcript of work completed to the end of the previous semester (student copies are accepted from CEGEP and Ontario applicants, but all others must submit an official transcript), the Can$55 application fee, and a copy of their birth certificate (and Canadian permanent resident documentation, if applicable).

Application and Information

Those planning to begin their studies at Bishop's in September must apply by March 1. The application deadline for January admission is October 15. Although late applications are considered, admission may be limited by space availability after these dates. Deadlines for students making applications based on international credentials are July 1 and November 1, respectively, with no late applications accepted. Those who apply by the deadlines should have a response within five weeks.

Hans Rouleau, Coordinator of Liaison
Liaison Office
Bishop's University
Sherbrooke, Quebec J1M 1Z7
Canada
Phone: 819-822-9600, Ext. 2681
877-822-8200 (toll-free)
Fax: 819-822-9661
E-mail: hrouleau@ubishops.ca
Web site: http://www.ubishops.ca

RYERSON UNIVERSITY

TORONTO, CANADA

The University

Founded in 1948, Ryerson University is Canada's leader in providing a high standard of professionally relevant education that combines the traditional university focus on theory with a career-oriented emphasis on professional practice and application.

Ryerson offers more than eighty undergraduate, master's, and Ph.D. programs. Undergraduate degree programs are offered through the University's five faculties: Arts; Engineering, Architecture, and Science; Community Services; Business; and Communications and Design. Known for attracting people with motivation, direction, and drive, Ryerson offers professionally targeted programs as well as contemporary arts and science degrees. Professional relevance is the essence of Ryerson, characterizing the people, curricula, and facilities that serve Ryerson's more than 23,000 undergraduate and graduate students. This special combination has earned Ryerson its reputation for excellence.

A vibrant and energetic campus community is characterized by on-campus residences, state-of-the-art athletic facilities, and numerous cultural, political, and recreational clubs. The University's location enables students to pursue their education in the financial, industrial, and cultural centre of Canada—the nation's largest city, Toronto.

Ryerson houses 840 students in three residences: Pitman Hall, O'Keefe House, and the International Living Learning Centre. Each residence has its own unique features and attributes. For more information, prospective students should visit http://www.ryerson.ca/housing.

Ryerson operates fourteen men's and women's varsity teams that continually qualify for postseason playoffs. In 2006–07, Ryerson had 16 student athletes named as all-stars and/or medalists in the Ontario University Athletics (OUA). Ryerson student athletes travel throughout Ontario, across Canada, and south to the United States to represent the University. Ryerson's intramural program is open to all students regardless of their skill level in sports and offers students the opportunity to meet people and get some exercise at the same time. More than twenty-five different leagues run throughout the academic year.

The Recreation and Athletics Centre (RAC) at Ryerson offers an extensive fitness centre with free weights and weight machines; a large cardio room with treadmills, elliptical trainers, stationary bicycles, recumbent bikes, and rowing machines; a three-lane, 160-yard, banked indoor running track; two sprung hardwood-floor dance studios; four international squash courts; six gymnasiums; a pool; spacious locker rooms with saunas; and helpful staff members.

Location

Ryerson University is located right in the heart of downtown Toronto. Named by *Fortune* magazine as one of the world's best cities in which to live, Toronto is a major cultural center and Canada's hub for business and finance, providing students with exciting learning opportunities. Ryerson's campus lies within walking distance of music, movies, theaters, and great food and shopping, and it is a short distance from professional sports complexes and international attractions. One of North America's cleanest, safest, and most ethnically diverse cities, Toronto offers many neighborhoods to explore, such as Chinatown, the Beaches, and the Danforth. Other attractions include Ontario Place, the Canadian National Exhibition (CNE), the Ontario Science Centre, and the Royal Ontario Museum (ROM).

Majors and Degrees

Ryerson offers the following undergraduate degrees: Bachelor of Arts, Bachelor of Applied Science, Bachelor of Architectural Science, Bachelor of Commerce, Bachelor of Design, Bachelor of Engineering, Bachelor of Fine Arts, Bachelor of Health Administration, Bachelor of Health Sciences, Bachelor of Interior Design, Bachelor of Journalism, Bachelor of Science, Bachelor of Science in Nursing, Bachelor of Social Work, Bachelor of Technology, and Bachelor of Urban and Regional Planning.

The full-time undergraduate programs available in Ryerson's five faculties are Arts: arts and contemporary studies, arts undeclared, criminal justice, geographic analysis, international economics and finance, politics and governance, psychology, and sociology; Business: business management (accounting, economics and management science, entrepreneurship, finance, human resource management, management, marketing management), hospitality and tourism management, information technology management, and retail management; Communications and Design: fashion (communication, design), graphic communications management, image arts (film studies, new media, photography studies), journalism, radio and television, and theatre (acting, dance, technical production); Community Services: child and youth care, early childhood education, midwifery, nursing, nutrition and food, occupational and public health, social work, and urban and regional planning; and Engineering, Architecture, and Science: architectural science, biology, chemistry, computer science, contemporary science, mathematics and its applications*, medical physics, and nine engineering programs (aerospace, biomedical*, chemical, civil, computer, electrical, industrial, mechanical, and undeclared). *Pending approval.

Academic Programs

Relevant curricula—a unique mix of professional, professionally related, and liberal studies course work—enable students to practice while they learn; students are well prepared with the skills necessary to enter their chosen career or profession upon graduation. In professional and professionally related courses, theory and practice are viewed as partners in the learning process. Lecture material is translated into practice through cooperative education and internship options, laboratory work, field trips, off-campus project work, and regular contact with business and industry. Liberal studies courses enhance the students' capacity to understand the social and cultural environment in which they will function, both as professionals and as educated citizens. With an education of this scope and rigor, graduates are uniquely adaptable to the challenges and opportunities in their professional fields.

Off-Campus Programs

Ryerson University offers a unique cooperative education program in the disciplines of applied chemistry and biology, chemical engineering, computer science, information technology management, occupational health and safety, and public health and safety. All co-op students complete four semesters, or two full years, of academic study before going out on their first work term. Internship programs are available in aerospace, electrical and computer, industrial, and mechanical engineering. All internship students must first complete six semesters, or three full years, of academic study. The period of work is twelve to sixteen months and normally begins in May.

Academic Facilities

Ryerson has recently completed a $210-million expansion, transforming the University campus with the addition of six new buildings. The new buildings include the 30,000-square-foot Heidelberg Centre–School of Graphic Communications Management and the Sally Horsfall Eaton Centre for Studies in Community Health, both adding specialized classroom and laboratory space, and the Centre for Computing and Engineering, featuring state-of-the-art lecture theatres and classrooms, high-tech labs, and specialized applied research facilities. Other new buildings include the Faculty of Business Building on Bay Street—the street that defines business in Canada—housing the Schools of Business Management, Information Technology Management, Retail Management, and Hospitality and Tourism Management.

The Ryerson Library has approximately 487,361 print titles, 24,808 print and electronic journal titles, and 11,014 audiovisual materials. The library's Ronald D. Besse Information and Learning Commons combines the expertise of student services and new technologies to equip students with the academic skills needed to access and analyze information effectively. About 1,400 computers are available on campus for general student use. A campus-wide network can be accessed from student residence rooms and from off campus. The Rogers Communications Centre (RCC) is the University's flagship building for studies in converging communications and interactive media. Over the past ten years, the Rogers Communications Centre has grown to become one of Canada's premier facilities for education in digital media communications. As an integral part of Ryerson University, the RCC houses and supports the Schools of Computer Science, Journalism, Image Arts, and Radio and Television.

Costs

Tuition for full-time international students for the 2007–08 academic year is Can$13,500 to Can$14,500. The average cost for room and board is Can$7271. Expenses vary according to the student's choice of board plan and housing facility.

Financial Aid

Various scholarships and bursaries and a dedicated series of financial-planning services are available. Every year, the University offers more than Can$10 million in scholarships, awards, and bursaries. All international students are automatically considered for an entrance merit award of Can$1000. Ryerson has been authorized by the U.S. Department of Education to administer Federal Stafford Student Loans and the Federal PLUS Program.

Faculty

Ryerson has 650 full-time faculty members. Many of Ryerson's professors are professionals who either are currently working in the industry or have worked in the industry in the past. They bring their expertise and up-to-date knowledge or even internship opportunities for students. Ryerson's relatively small class sizes enhance the learning process by maximizing student contact with faculty members.

Student Government

The Ryerson Students' Administrative Council (RyeSAC) is the student government. RyeSAC's Board of Directors is an elected representative body of full-time students. Terms for those elected begin in May and run through the next academic year, ending in April. The board comprises a number of different types of directors. As defined in the bylaws, RyeSAC empowers an executive team to be responsible for the day-to-day operations of the organization and to carry the directions of the Board of Directors. These 4 individuals act as officers of the corporation. The president and 3 vice presidents are elected annually by Ryerson's full-time students.

Admission Requirements

To be eligible for admission to a Ryerson program, students must meet Ryerson's admission requirements from the jurisdiction or country from which the student is applying and hold the prerequisites for the specific program of interest. Individual programs may stipulate specific subject prerequisites for admission, including specific courses and minimum grades. Due to competition, candidates may be required to present averages/grades above the minimum. It is essential that the required subject prerequisites and grades for specific programs form part of an applicant's academic background, especially in the last two years of secondary and/or postsecondary studies. Programs may also stipulate nonacademic requirements for admission, such as a portfolio, an admission essay, an interview, or an audition. Students are strongly encouraged to check the requirements before applying to any programs at Ryerson.

Proof of English proficiency at a satisfactory level is required from all students, except those whose first language is English or who have four years of full-time study in an English-language school in a country where the primary language is English. For more details about the English proficiency requirement, students should check the English Language Requirements page on Ryerson's Web site.

Application and Information

Ryerson programs begin only in September of each year. Ryerson generally does not grant admission in the winter (January) or spring (May) terms. Application for admission should be made as early as possible.

All students must apply to Ryerson through the Ontario Universities' Application Centre (OUAC) at http://www.ouac.on.ca. The Office of Undergraduate Admissions must receive all officially certified academic transcripts that include promotion/graduation status. The date for guaranteed consideration for fall 2008 semester for grades-plus-selective-admission programs (those that select students on the basis of grades plus auditions, interviews, portfolios, essays, etc.) is February 1 and March 1 for programs that select on the basis of grades.

General campus tours are available Monday through Friday at 10 a.m. Prospective students who are interested in scheduling a group or international tour should call 416-979-5080. Ryerson also offers Tour and Discussion Days, which offer an opportunity to tour the campus, meet professors and current students, and tour departments, studios, and labs.

Office of Undergraduate Admissions
Ryerson University
350 Victoria Street
Toronto, Ontario M5B 2K3
Canada
Phone: 416-979-5036
416-979-5080 (international applicants)
Fax: 416-979-5067
E-mail: international@ryerson.ca
Web site: http://www.ryerson.ca/undergraduate/admission/

SIMON FRASER UNIVERSITY

BRITISH COLUMBIA, CANADA

The University

Since its founding in 1965, Simon Fraser University (SFU) has earned an international reputation for innovative teaching, leading research, outstanding athletics, and global community outreach. With three distinctive campuses (in Burnaby, Vancouver, and Surrey), SFU is a community of more than 20,000 students, over 800 faculty members, and nearly 90,000 alumni worldwide. SFU is one of Canada's leading comprehensive universities. In the classroom, the laboratory, and the international arena, SFU continually sets new standards of excellence.

SFU is best known for its groundbreaking interdisciplinary approach and offers innovative programs that facilitate study across various areas of academic interest. Students may choose to engage in interdisciplinary studies within their major or pursue double-major, joint-major, joint-minor, or minor options. SFU's flexible trimester system also allows students an extraordinary range of choice in their studies, which might include participating in the Cooperative Education program (available in all academic subjects), participating in an exchange at one of more than 100 universities around the world, or going on a field school with fellow classmates. New students can enter into SFU three times a year, and more than 75 percent of course options are available in the summer semester.

In addition to world-class educational facilities, SFU has fourteen varsity sport teams that involve nearly 300 student-athletes. The Lorne Davies Complex offers a variety of aquatic, fitness, recreational, and competitive opportunities. It houses the East and West Gymnasiums, an aquatic center, Piper's Gym Fitness Centre, a weight room, a combatives' room, and seven squash and racquetball courts. SFU has also opened a new $11-million, 40,000-square-foot training centre and gym complex, along with a second multipurpose field. Recreational Services and Athletics offers access to four tennis courts, an outdoor play court, a 400-meter track, two grass fields, and a multipurpose field with lights. Recreation services include intramural programs, fitness classes/workshops, aquatic programs, noncredit instructional activity classes, and clubs. From photography to snowboarding, there are more than 100 SFU clubs to meet all interests.

More than 2,000 students now reside on campus. The Towers at SFU Burnaby are designed to meet the needs of first-year students. Complete with a meal plan, the Towers provide comfortable accommodation in about 700 fully furnished single rooms, each with its own fridge, cable service, and high-speed connection. SFU guarantees residence space to all new full-time undergraduate students.

Location

SFU's main campus, on beautiful Burnaby Mountain, is less than a half-hour's drive from downtown Vancouver. Vancouver, the third-largest city in Canada, is a progressive and cosmopolitan centre of more than 2 million people. It is a safe, clean city with a large variety of cultural and recreational pastimes, including skiing, ocean sports, hiking, mountain biking, arts, theaters, music, and dance. Vancouver is a host city for the 2010 Olympic Winter Games.

Simon Fraser's Harbour Centre campus is located in the business district of beautiful downtown Vancouver and is home to a large number of upper-level and graduate programs.

Surrey, a major suburb to the south of Vancouver, is the location of SFU's newest campus, which opened September 2005. SFU Surrey offers a range of undergraduate and graduate programs—notably, the novel School of Interactive Arts and Technology, the first of its kind in Canada.

All three SFU campuses are easily accessible by public transit.

Majors and Degrees

Innovation, interdisciplinary research, and flexibility—these are the hallmarks of SFU's progressive academic approach. SFU offers more than 100 undergraduate and graduate programs within its six faculties of Applied Sciences, Arts and Social Sciences, Business Administration, Education, Science, and Health Sciences.

Programs include actuarial science; anthropology; applied mathematics; applied physics; archaeology; archaeology and anthropology; art and culture studies; art and culture studies and sociology and/or anthropology; arts (general); Asia-Canada; biological sciences; business administration; business administration and communication, computing science, economics, geography, or psychology; Canadian studies; Canadian studies and anthropology, archaeology, business administration, communication, criminology, economics, English, geography, history, political science, or sociology; chemical physics; chemistry; cognitive science; communication; computer and electronics design; computing science; computing science and molecular biology and biochemistry; criminology; criminology and women's studies; curriculum and instruction; dance; early childhood education; earth sciences; economics; education; educational psychology; elementary school physical education; engineering science (biomedical, computer, electronics, mechatronics, physics and systems); English; English and French literatures, humanities, or women's studies; environmental chemistry; environmental education; environmental science; environmental toxicology; film; film and video studies; fine and performing arts; fine arts in interdisciplinary studies; first nations studies; French; French, history, and politics; general studies; general science; geographic information science; geography; geography and economics (environmental specialty); gerontology; history; history and humanities; humanities; humanities and French; information systems in business administration and computing science; interactive arts and technology; international studies; kinesiology; labor studies; Latin American studies; Latin American studies and archaeology, business administration, communication, economics, geography, history, political science, or sociology; learning disabilities; linguistics; management and systems science; mathematical physics; mathematics; mathematics and computing science; molecular biology and biochemistry; molecular biology and biochemistry and business administration; music; nuclear science; philosophy; philosophy and humanities; physical education; physical geography; physics; physics and physiology; political science; political science and economics or women's studies; psychology; psychology and criminology or women's studies; public administration and community services; publishing; science (general); sociology; sociology and anthropology, art and culture studies, communication, criminology, linguistics, or women's studies; statistics; theater; visual art; women's studies; and world literature.

In addition, students have the option of creating their own degree program.

Academic Programs

SFU's innovative trimester system means that students can take classes in any combination of the fall, spring, or summer semesters. This gives students the flexibility to schedule classes and co-op work terms at the times that are best for them. Many classes use a lecture/tutorial model so that concepts presented in the lecture hall can be further explored in small-group tutorial or lab sessions led by the professor or a graduate student.

SFU gives students the intellectual foundation they need to do anything they want. The University's graduates pursue successful careers in virtually every field, attend the graduate schools of their choice, or enter professional programs that include medicine, law, and architecture.

Off-Campus Programs

For students who dream of studying archaeology in Greece, contemporary European society in the Czech Republic, or performing arts in Ghana, SFU International offers a wide range of field schools, enabling them to travel with SFU students and professors around the world. Students live and study abroad, gaining a unique and unforgettable insight into the culture and society of their chosen region.

SFU International also offers exchanges to more than 100 universities around the world. This is an opportunity for immersion in a new country while pursuing one's studies. Students typically spend one or two semesters at one of SFU's partner universities; the courses students complete are normally counted toward their SFU degree. In addition, students pay SFU tuition rates when they participate in exchanges and field-school programs.

SFU has one of the largest and most diverse cooperative education programs in Canada. Co-op provides students with an opportunity to alternate degree-relevant and paid-learning experiences with academic study each January, May, and September. Accredited by the Canadian Association for Co-operative Education (CAFCE), SFU Co-op requires students to participate in cooperative curricula that focus on skills transfer, employability, and career development. In addition to the University's unique and high-quality student-preparation program, SFU's commitment to service ensures that both the student's as well as the employer's needs are recognized and addressed every step of the way. Cooperative education programs are optional for most students but mandatory for those enrolled in engineering science. Nearly 80 percent of SFU Co-op graduates are hired by their cooperative employer after graduation.

Academic Facilities

A library is located on all three SFU campuses, with Burnaby's W. A. C. Bennett Library being the largest. The Samuel and Frances Belzberg Library at Harbour Centre and the SFU Library at Surrey are branch libraries with a full range of services and timely delivery of requested materials between Bennett, Belzberg, and Surrey. All three locations have reference librarians to assist students and faculty members with their research needs. In addition to the print collections, the library provides access to many online information resources. More than $7 million is spent annually to add to the library's collections, which include more than 2.4 million volumes and more than 26,000 online and print journals. SFU students and faculty and staff members can borrow material from other Canadian university libraries as well as British Columbia University College libraries and have access to material in more than 10,000 North American libraries through interlibrary loans.

Joint research facilities at SFU include the Bamfield Marine Station on Vancouver Island, a major center for teaching and research in marine biology operated by SFU and four other universities; TRIUMF, a powerful cyclotron used in subatomic physics and chemistry research, operated by SFU and four other Canadian universities; and MITACS, the federally funded network center of excellence that brings together more than 200 researchers at twenty-six universities and seventy-five companies across Canada to address design and productivity problems in five key sectors of the economy.

Costs

Students take approximately 24 to 30 credits per academic year. In 2007–08, the cost per credit for Canadian residents is (in Canadian dollars) $201.50 for business courses, $166.20 for engineering science courses, $158.70 for computing science courses, and $151.10 for all other courses. The cost per credit for American and international students is $534.80 for business courses, $499.50 for engineering science courses, $492 for computing science courses, and $484.40 for all other courses. Included in the tuition fee at SFU is the U-Pass, which gives students unlimited public transit access for the duration of the semester. The activity fee is $61.39 for all students. The typical student away from home paying Canadian tuition spent between $4500 and $5000 for rent, food, books, supplies, and miscellaneous expenses.

Financial Aid

SFU awards more than 4,000 entrance scholarships and awards ranging between CAN$500 and CAN$34,000 to outstanding new students. All scholars must meet certain academic and registration requirements for complete disbursement of funds. Students should visit http://students.sfu.ca/fa/ for more information.

Faculty

Simon Fraser University has more than 800 faculty members. The student-faculty ratio is 30:1.

Student Government

The Simon Fraser Student Society is the students' union at SFU, representing students' interests to University administrators and the broader community. Each student enrolled at the University is a member. The Student Society is governed by the Board of Directors, all of whom are democratically elected each year by the student body. The board's main task is to set priorities and policies for the society, with input from the forum and the standing committees of the society. The Student Society also offers services, such as the Ombuds Office, the Women's Centre, free legal clinics, and the only pub on campus. SFU students stand in solidarity with more than 450,000 students across Canada as Local 23 of the Canadian Federation of Students. As such, the Student Society works collectively with more than seventy student unions across the country to ensure that student issues and concerns are represented at the provincial and national level.

Admission Requirements

In general, a high academic standing is required for admission to SFU. SFU admits students whose average in their final year of high school education is about 80 percent, or a B average. Those who have below this average are still encouraged to apply through diverse qualifications. All students whose primary language is not English must submit scores from either the Test of English as a Foreign Language (TOEFL) or the International English Language Testing System (IELTS). The required minimum TOEFL scores are 230 (CBT with minimum 4.5 essay), 88 (iBT with a minimum score of 20 in listening, speaking, writing, reading), or a minimum 6.5 IELTS.

Academic requirements vary by country; students should check the Web site at http://students.sfu.ca/is/ for more information. To apply, students must go through the Postsecondary Application Service of British Columbia (PASBC). After registering, applicants receive an e-mail from SFU that contains instructions on the next steps, including how to pay the application fee and the document evaluation fee (if applicable).

Application and Information

The deadline for early fall admission is February 28; for the fall semester, April 30; for the spring semester, September 30; and for the summer semester, January 31.

Simon Fraser University
MBC 3000
8888 University Drive
Burnaby, British Columbia V5A 1S6
Canada
Phone: 1-778-782-7690
Fax: 1-778-782-5399
E-mail: international_recruitment@sfu.ca
Web site: http://students.sfu.ca/ps/

TRENT UNIVERSITY

PETERBOROUGH, ONTARIO, CANADA

The University

Trent University is a leader. As Canada's leading undergraduate research university and with average class sizes that are among the smallest in the country, Trent is committed to excellence in the humanities, social sciences, and natural sciences and places great value on personal attention and interdisciplinary study. A vibrant international program draws gifted students from more than 110 countries around the globe. All Trent students find a welcoming community and a safe, diverse environment in which to learn.

Trent University was formally created as an independent university with full degree-granting powers by the Ontario Legislature in 1963. It is a member of the Association of Universities and Colleges of Canada and the Association of Commonwealth Universities. Trent graduates have received prestigious graduate scholarships at top Ivy League schools and have assumed leadership roles in the public and private sectors.

With 7,000 full-time students, the University has chosen to remain small and concentrate on undergraduate studies while gradually expanding its interdisciplinary graduate programs. More than 75 percent of first- and second-year classes have fewer than 25 students.

Trent's 1,400-acre Symons campus, situated on the banks of the Otonabee River amid forests, lakes, and gently rolling hills, features award-winning modern architecture. Three miles north of Peterborough's downtown core, the campus comprises the University's administrative offices, library, brand-new athletics facilities, Science Complex, and Environmental Sciences Centre and four of the five residential colleges. The fifth college, Catharine Parr Traill, is in a residential area of Peterborough, housed in historic Victorian buildings with stained-glass windows and hardwood floors. A shuttle bus makes the 10- to 20-minute trip between the Symons campus and the downtown college throughout the day. The colleges combine residential and teaching space, allowing students to live and learn in a friendly, close-knit environment. All colleges have common areas, a dining hall, study and recreation areas, and laundry facilities, as well as academic, social, and athletic activities. Early application is strongly encouraged to all international students intending to stay in residence.

Trent provides students with the support services they need to succeed, from finding a part-time job or seeing a doctor to coping with family or personal relationships. For international students, Trent's International Program Office offers counselling in areas such as health insurance, immigration information, and academic programs. To ease the transition to university, the office also publishes the *International Students Handbook* and organizes a three-day orientation camp in September and January. After the camp, all new students starting in September take part in Introductory Seminar Week, which provides social activities and an opportunity for students to choose their courses. Academic departments give introductory lectures to provide a better understanding of course content and workload, and each student is assigned an academic adviser. The Trent International Ambassadors program connects upper-year international students with incoming students from abroad.

With a variety of facilities, student clubs, and organizations, Trent offers diverse ways to spend time outside the classroom. Athletics facilities include a 25-metre pool, a gymnasium, squash courts, a flood-lit playing field, tennis courts, a rowing course, and cross-country trails for skiing, running, and biking. The University hosts the largest timed rowing regatta in Canada each fall and a triathlon each March.

Location

Trent's Symons campus lies 3 miles north of downtown Peterborough, a student city of 80,000 that is renowned for its vibrant arts scene and its eclectic shops and cafés. The city's strategic location in the Kawartha Lake district—with proximity to lakes, beaches, hiking/ski trails, and conservation areas—makes the campus a natural extension of one of Canada's great outdoor playgrounds. Students are just 90 minutes by car from Toronto, Canada's largest city; 3½ hours from Ottawa, the nation's capital city; and a quick 1-hour flight from New York, Boston, and Washington, D.C.

The city of Peterborough offers a wide range of restaurants, shops, cafés, bookstores, galleries, cinemas, and museums, as well as a comprehensive performing arts center. Trent students, faculty members, and staff members play an important role in the city's political and cultural life and are active in such projects as the Peterborough Symphony, the Peterborough Theatre Guild, and the Kawartha World Issues Center.

Majors and Degrees

The majority of Trent students pursue Honours degrees, the normal prerequisite for graduate studies. Honours and General Bachelor of Arts degrees are available in ancient history and classics, anthropology, Canadian studies, computer studies, cultural studies, economics, education, English literature, environmental and resource studies, French studies, geography, global studies, German studies, Hispanic studies, history, Indigenous environmental studies, Indigenous studies, international development studies, modern languages and literatures, museum studies, Native management and economic development, philosophy, political studies, psychology, sociology, and women's studies.

There are Honours and General Bachelor of Science degrees in anthropology, biochemistry and molecular biology, biology, chemical physics, chemistry, computer science, computing and physics, economics, environmental and resource science, environmental chemistry, forensic science, geographical information systems (GIS), geography, mathematics, nursing, physics, and psychology.

Trent also offers an Honours Bachelor of Business Administration.

Students may use the Special Emphasis option to create an integrating theme to govern their choice of courses if their academic needs cannot be met by any of the existing majors.

In the concurrent teacher education program, cosponsored by Queen's University in Kingston, Trent students graduate with a Bachelor of Arts or a Bachelor of Science from Trent and a Bachelor of Education from Queen's. Students may also choose a one-year Consecutive Bachelor of Education degree at Trent after the successful completion of an undergraduate degree.

In affiliation with Sir Sandford Fleming College, Peterborough's community college, Trent offers degree programs in geographical information systems, museum studies, nursing, and forensic science.

The University also offers diplomas in the Canadian Studies, Indigenous Environmental Studies, Native Management and Economic Development, and Native Studies Programs.

Academic Programs

The academic year consists of three sessions. The fall session is a twelve-week term that runs from September to December. The winter session is a twelve-week term that runs from January to April. The summer session runs from May to August and is made up of twelve-, eight-, and six-week terms. September and January are entry points for full-time studies. Four-year Honours degrees require successful completion of 20 course credits. Three-year general degrees consist of 15 course credits. All degrees require completion of University and program requirements.

The Academic Skills Centre offers assistance in writing, reading, and study techniques. It also offers tutoring in mathematics and French and additional help for students for whom English is a second language. The Special Needs Office assists students with physical, sensory, or learning disabilities.

Off-Campus Programs

Trent students are encouraged to spend one year of their undergraduate programs studying in another country. The Trent International Study and Exchange Program (TISEP) offers exchange and study-abroad opportunities in many countries, including Australia, England, Finland, France, Germany, Iceland, Japan, Korea, Malaysia, Mauritius, Mexico, Scotland, South Africa, Spain, the United States, and Wales. The International Development Studies programs in Ecuador and Ghana and the Native Studies Program in Thailand combine academic courses with work-placement experience. Students receive full credit for all courses successfully completed while abroad.

Academic Facilities

The bright and spacious Bata Library is electronically connected to the two in-town college libraries and the Peterborough Public Library. An extensive interlibrary loan network enables students to borrow material from all parts of North America. Three hundred fifty computers are available for general student use in the computer centre, library, classrooms, residences, and labs. They provide access to the Internet, Gopher, e-mail, Microsoft programs, and library catalogues.

Costs

Tuition fees (including ancillary fees) for Canadian citizens and permanent residents for the 2007–08 academic year were Can$5744; they were Can$14,578 for international students. A single room in residence, including various meal plans, cost between Can$6000 and Can$9300.

Financial Aid

All students are considered for entrance scholarships when admitted. Exceptional students are invited to apply for the Board of Governors' Scholarship and the two Champlain Scholarships, prestigious renewable scholarships. Upperclass students can apply for in-course scholarships based on academic performance. Bursary funds, primarily to assist in emergency situations, are available. Scholarships and bursaries are available for outstanding international students through Trent's Global Citizen scholarship program. International students also are allowed to work on campus part-time and up to two years after graduation. Also, international students, upon completion of six months of full-time studies, can apply for an off-campus work permit and, if granted, work up to 20 hours during the week and full-time during the summer.

Faculty

Much of the teaching at Trent takes place in seminars and labs. Because these are generally led by professors rather than teaching assistants, students have ample opportunity to get to know their instructors.

Student Government

There is active involvement in student politics through such groups as the Trent Central Student Association and the five residential College Cabinets. Students have a voice in the administrative affairs of the University through membership in the University Senate and the Board of Governors.

Admission Requirements

For Ontario residents, an Ontario Secondary School Diploma (OSSD); ENGL1 or ENG4U, with a grade of 70 percent or higher; and five additional OAC, Gr 12U, or Gr 12M courses are required. For Quebec residents studying CEGEP, a minimum of twelve academic courses is required. Other Canadian residents are required to have a grade 12 diploma.

Advanced credit is granted for select Advanced Placement programs with examination grades of 4 or better.

For students from the United States, a high school diploma, with a minimum average of B (3.0 GPA on a 4.0 scale), is required. A combined SAT score of at least 1650 or a composite ACT score of at least 24 is preferred. Senior students should send their midterm grades.

General Certificate of Education requirements include passes in at least five subjects, two at the advanced level with grades of C or better, or passes in four subjects, three at the advanced level with grades of C or better. Two advanced supplementary courses may be substituted for one advanced-level course. Advanced credit may be granted for A levels with a grade of C or better.

International Baccalaureate requires a minimum of 28 points. Advanced credit may be granted for higher-level subjects with a score of 5 or higher.

Students who believe that their marks do not accurately reflect their ability to succeed at university may send supporting documentation, such as references from teachers or guidance counsellors, to the Registrar's Office.

The language of instruction at Trent is English. All students must be proficient at speaking, reading, writing, and understanding English. Candidates from areas where English is not the language of instruction must provide evidence of language proficiency. Trent accepts results from a variety of tests. The more commonly used services and minimum required scores are as follows: Test of English as a Foreign Language (TOEFL), 580 on the paper-based test, 237 on the computer-based test (with a minimum TWE score of 4.5), or 86 on the Internet-based test; Michigan English Language Assessment Battery (MELAB), 85, with no part below 80; International English Language Testing System (IELTS), overall band of 6.5, with no band below 6.0; and Canadian Academic English Language Assessment (CAEL), 60. International students who meet all criteria for admission except the language requirements may be admitted to the TRENT-ESL, English for University program. Upon successful completion of this program, students continue regular degree programs.

Application and Information

Applications for admission for the 2007–08 academic year must be received by the Office of the Registrar no later than June 1, 2007. The deadline to apply for residence is June 2007. Early application is strongly encouraged. Complete applications should include official transcripts, language test scores (if needed), and notarized translation of material not in English. For information on admission and programs and for application forms, students should contact:

Office of the Registrar
Trent University
1600 West Bank Drive
Peterborough, Ontario K9J 7B8
Canada
E-mail: tip@trentu.ca
Web site: http://www.trentu.ca
http://www.trentu.ca/tip

One of the residential colleges at Trent University.

COLLEGE DATA CENTER • CANADA

THE UNIVERSITY OF BRITISH COLUMBIA

VANCOUVER AND OKANAGAN, BRITISH COLUMBIA, CANADA

The University

The University of British Columbia (UBC) is one of North America's leading universities, with an international reputation for excellence in teaching and research. Originally incorporated in 1908, the University now has two major campuses. The 1,000-acre UBC Vancouver campus is situated on the Pacific Ocean, surrounded by forest and mountains. The UBC Okanagan campus is located in lakeside Kelowna, in B.C.'s scenic interior.

Through nineteen faculties and thirteen schools, UBC provides a comprehensive range of bachelor's, graduate, and professional programs. Currently registered students number 47,711 (39,860 undergraduates). International students (5,550, 12 percent) come from the United States and over 130 other countries. UBC's International House offers a full range of reception, advising, and social services. Special-needs provision is made through the Disability Resource Centre and the Equity Office.

University residences accommodate more than 7,000 students in single-student, coed, shared, and family housing units. First-year international student (including those from the U.S.) have priority. Early application (at http://www.housing.ubc.ca) is advised.

UBC has one of Canada's most successful interuniversity athletic programs, and the student society runs more than 250 clubs of academic and social interest. Other Vancouver facilities include the Museum of Anthropology, the Botanical Gardens, the Chan Concert Hall, art gallery, Asian Centre, the Liu Centre for Global Studies, a conference centre, the aquatic centre, a fitness centre and gymnasium, tennis courts, and sports stadium.

Location

UBC's main campus, a few miles from downtown Vancouver, is situated on a forested peninsula, with spectacular views of the Pacific Ocean, the Vancouver skyline, and the snowcapped peaks of the surrounding Coastal Mountains. With 2 million inhabitants, Canada's third-largest city is ethnically diverse with a vibrant cultural life. In 2010, Vancouver will host the Winter Olympic Games. The proximity of mountains, forest, and public beaches provides outdoor recreational opportunities year-round. Vancouver enjoys mild winters, with plenteous rains from fall to spring, and pleasant dry summers. UBC Okanagan's college-size campus is located in the friendly lakeside city of Kelowna, B.C., a popular tourist destination with a gentler pace of life than Vancouver's bustling metropolis. Both campuses are close to mountain, lake, and ski resorts. Local transit is reliable, and a transit pass is included in student fees.

Majors and Degrees

The Faculty of Land and Food Systems offers a Bachelor of Science (B.Sc.) for programs in agroecology, animal studies, dietetics, food and nutritional sciences, global resource systems, horticulture, resource economics, and soil and environment.

The Faculty of Applied Sciences offers programs leading to the Bachelor of Applied Sciences (B.A.Sc.) in: chemical and biological engineering, civil engineering, computer engineering, electrical engineering, engineering physics, environmental engineering, geological engineering, integrated engineering, materials engineering, mechanical engineering, and mining engineering.

The Bachelor of Environmental Design (B.En.D.) is offered in the School of Architecture.

The Faculty of Arts programs lead to the Bachelor of Arts (B.A.) in anthropology; archaeology; art history; Asian area studies; Asian language and culture (including a broad range of Asian language options); Canadian studies; classical studies; classics; cognitive systems; computer science; drama; economics; English; family studies; film production; film studies; First Nations languages and linguistics; First Nations studies; French; geography; German; history; interdisciplinary studies; international relations; Latin American studies; linguistics; mathematics; medieval studies; modern European studies; music; myth and literature in Greece, Rome, and the Near East; philosophy; political science; psychology; religion, literature, and the arts; religious studies; Romance studies; sociology; Spanish; speech sciences; theatre studies; United States studies; and women's and gender studies. The Bachelor of Fine Arts (B.F.A.) is offered in creative writing, theatre (acting), theatre (production and design), and visual arts.

The Bachelor of Social Work (B.S.W.) is offered by the School of Social Work.

The Sauder School of Business offers programs leading to the Bachelor of Commerce (B.Com.), with specializations in accounting, business and computer science, commerce and economics, finance, general business management, human resources management, international business, management information systems, marketing, real estate, and transportation and logistics.

The Faculty of Dentistry offers the Bachelor of Dental Science (B.D.Sc.) in dental hygiene, which is competitively open to all applicants. Admission to the Doctor of Dental Medicine degree program is restricted to Canadian citizens and permanent residents.

The Faculty of Education offers a postbaccalaureate program of initial teacher education leading to the Bachelor of Education (B.Ed.) in elementary, elementary native Indian, middle-years, and secondary teacher education with a wide range of teaching concentrations.

The Faculty of Forestry offers programs toward a Bachelor of Science in Forestry (B.S.F.) in forest operations and forest resources management, and a B.Sc. in forest science, natural resources conservation, and wood products processing.

The School of Human Kinetics offers a Bachelor of Human Kinetics (B.H.K.) with specializations in human kinetics interdisciplinary studies, kinesiology and health science, and physical and health education.

The Faculty of Law offers a Bachelor of Laws (LL.B.). Entry is after a minimum completion of three years' university study.

The Faculty of Medicine medical program leads to the Doctor of Medicine (M.D.). Admission is restricted to Canadian citizens and permanent residents. Competitively open to all applicants are programs leading to the Bachelor of Medical Laboratory Science (B.L.Sc) and the Bachelor of Midwifery (B.Mw.).

The School of Music offers programs leading to the Bachelor of Music (B.Mus.) in composition, music scholarship, and performance.

The School of Nursing offers a postbaccalaureate program of study leading to the Bachelor of Science in Nursing (B.S.N.).

The Faculty of Pharmaceutical Sciences program leads to the Bachelor of Science in Pharmacy (B.Sc.Pharm.). Admission is restricted to Canadian citizens and permanent residents. Students complete the first year in required Faculty of Science courses.

The Faculty of Science offers programs leading to the B.Sc. in astronomy, atmospheric science, biochemistry, biology, biophysics, biotechnology, chemistry, cognitive systems, computer science, earth and ocean sciences, environmental sciences, general science, geography, geological sciences, geophysics, integrated sciences, mathematics, mathematical sciences, mathematics and economics, microbiology and immunology, oceanography, pharmacology, physics, physiology, psychology, and statistics.

UBC Okanagan provides a distinctive range of study options, with flexible courses to meet individual interests. The Irving K. Barber School of Arts and Sciences encourages integration of traditionally separate disciplines through novel curricula. Bachelor of Arts or

Bachelor of Science programs include anthropology, biochemistry, biology, chemistry, computer science, earth and environmental sciences, econology and evolutionary biology, economics, environmental chemistry, freshwater science, general science, general studies, geography, history, indigenous studies, international relations, mathematical sciences, mathematics, mathematics and statistics, microbiology, molecular cell and developmental biology, philosophy, philosophy/politics/economics, physics and astronomy, political science, psychology, and sociology.

The Faculty of Creative and Critical Studies programs lead to B.A. or B.F.A. degrees in art history, creative writing, cultural studies, English, French, performance/theatre, Spanish, and visual arts with a wide range of specialization options.

Faculty of Engineering programs lead to the Bachelor of Applied Science degree (B.A.Sc.) in civil engineering, electrical engineering, and mechanical engineering.

The Faculty of Health and Social Development programs in human kinetics lead to a Bachelor of Human Kinetics (B.H.K.) degree; in health studies they lead to a B.A. degree.

Programs in the Faculty of Management lead to Bachelor of Management (B.Mgt.) degrees in accounting and control; entrepreneurship and general management; finance; human resource management; information, technology, and operations; and marketing.

Academic Programs

Winter session terms are September–December and January–April. Summer session terms are May–June and July–August, but not all programs are offered during the Summer sessions. Most programs require a minimum of 120 credits for a bachelor's degree; honours programs may require 132 credits.

Off-Campus Programs

The University offers exchange programs with 155 universities in forty-two countries. Co-op (work-study) programs are available in selected programs in the Faculties of Applied Sciences, Arts, Forestry, Land and Food Systems, Science, and the Sauder School of Business at UBC Vancouver and in the Schools of Arts and Sciences and of Engineering at UBC Okanagan. Coop terms extend time to degree completion.

Academic Facilities

The University of British Columbia's library is one of the largest research libraries in Canada and has twenty-two branches. The Barber Learning Centre is a major new study and research facility equipped with the latest technology in information search and retrieval. Residences have high-speed Internet access and campus-wide wireless connectivity. Significant research centres are located on the Vancouver campus, including the Tri-University Meson Facility (TRIUMF) for research in subatomic physics.

Costs

For U.S. and international students, undergraduate tuition in most programs for the 2007–08 academic year is Can$623.28 per credit, with higher fees in business. A typical first-year course load in arts costs Can$18,698. A first-year, 35-credit course load in applied science (engineering) costs Can$21,815. For Canadian citizens and permanent residents, undergraduate program tuition for 2007–08 is Can$141.91 per credit, with higher fees in business, dentistry, law, and medicine. A typical first-year course load of 30 credits cost Can$4257. Room and board, living expenses, student fees, books, and health insurance total approximately Can$12,500.

Financial Aid

UBC offers merit-based awards for undergraduates, generally of modest sums. Needs-based aid is limited to Canadian citizens and permanent residents. For information about eligibility, application deadlines, and student loans and bursaries, students should visit Tuition, Scholarships, and Support at https://you.ubc.ca.

International students with financial need and of demonstrated leadership potential or outstanding perseverance may be nominated for the International Leader of Tomorrow or International Humanitarian Awards. More information about these awards is available on the Web site.

For U.S. citizens applying for Stafford Loans, the UBC Title IV code is G08369. Students should visit http://www.fafsa.edu.gov for details.

Faculty

More than 99 percent of UBC's 2,000 full-time faculty members hold a Ph.D. degree. Faculty members are regularly recognized with achievement awards. UBC pioneered interdisciplinary first-year programs such as Arts One, Science One, and Integrated Science. Faculties provide academic advising programs to support undergraduate achievement.

Student Government

Originally established in 1908, the Alma Mater Society (AMS) of UBC represents more than 40,000 students. The AMS is governed by a 45-member Student Council, which ensures student participation at all levels of student government, administers clubs, and represents student interests to the University and the provincial government of British Columbia.

Admission Requirements

Admission to UBC is competitive and is based on a strong academic background. Applicants must have graduated from an acceptable university preparatory curriculum with applicable program prerequisites. General admission for students from an American school system is based on 4 years of English and 3 years of math, at least three other senior-level academic subjects, and prerequisites for the intended program. Applicants schooled in the U.S. curriculum must submit SAT or ACT plus Writing Test scores. Exemptions may be granted where these tests are not available. International Baccalaureate (I.B.) students must have a completed I.B. diploma, with admission average calculated on three standard levels (including English) and three higher levels. Admission for I.B. Certificate course students is based on high school curriculum. Students applying to science-based programs must meet specific program requirements in math, chemistry, physics, and/or biology. All students must demonstrate competence in written and spoken English. Generous course credits are allowed for students achieving specified grades in enriched curricula, such as I.B., A-levels, or Advanced Placement. Well-qualified students at recognized universities and colleges may apply for transfer to second or third years at UBC. All applicants to UBC must complete the application for admission, accompanied by a non-refundable application fee. A separate application and supplemental fee is required for the Sauder School of Business. Early admission is possible for students with strong academic standing enrolled in their final year of secondary school. Further details are available at the Admissions section at https://you.ubc.ca.

Application and Information

Early application is encouraged and should be made online at https://you.ubc.ca. The application deadline for undergraduate programs is February 28.

International Student Recruitment
Room 1200, 1874 East Mall (Brock Hall)
The University of British Columbia
Vancouver, British Columbia V6T 1Z1
Canada

Phone: 604-822-8999
877-272-1422 (toll-free in the U.S. and Canada)
Fax: 604-822-9888
E-mail: petersons.youbc@ubc.ca
Internet: https://you.ubc.ca
http://askme.ubc.ca (for questions)

UNIVERSITY OF GUELPH

GUELPH, ONTARIO, CANADA

The University

The University of Guelph is a high-quality, student-focused, residential college that is committed to innovative programs, dynamic student-faculty interaction, and an integration of learning and research. It offers a wide range of undergraduate and graduate programs in the arts, humanities, social sciences, and natural sciences. Building on these core disciplines, Guelph also has a strong commitment to interdisciplinary programs, to a selected range of professional and applied programs, and to agriculture and veterinary medicine as areas of special responsibility.

Established in 1964 when three century-old founding colleges joined with a new college of arts and science, the University of Guelph is a vital community of more than 18,000 students on a campus of historical and modern buildings and redbrick walkways. By Canadian standards Guelph is of medium size, offering a wide range of academic programs while providing a safe, accommodating environment for learning. On-campus living is available for more than 5,200 students, with all new first-semester students guaranteed on-campus housing if they apply by the deadline.

Guelph features state-of-the-art athletic facilities that include a double arena with an Olympic-size ice surface, two pools, a field house and indoor track, aerobic and weight-training gymnasiums, six squash courts, and a climbing wall. Guelph offers thirty-one varsity sports teams and in recent years has fielded national and provincial championship football, hockey, and rugby teams.

With 63 percent of Guelph's undergraduate classes consisting of fewer than 25 students, Guelph ensures a personal approach to learning with a 1:22 faculty-student ratio. The Center for New Students assists new students with the transition from secondary school to university, which gives Guelph a 91.1 percent student retention and an 89.5 percent graduation rate, the highest among Canadian comprehensive universities.

The University of Guelph offers a Doctor of Veterinary Medicine degree as well as several diploma programs and more than eighty master's and doctoral degree programs. The graduate calendar is available on the Web at http://www.uoguelph.ca/GraduateStudies.

Location

The University of Guelph's main campus is located in the southwestern Ontario region the *New York Times* calls "Canada's Technology Triangle," a locale known for its high-caliber educational institutions and its innovative companies. This city of more than 115,000 features internationally recognized folk, jazz, and writers' festivals as well as a multipurpose performing arts center and a sports and entertainment center. Positioned within an hour's drive of Toronto, Canada's largest city and airline hub, Guelph offers the comfort of small-community living with the excitement of an international metropolis at its doorstep. In addition to the main campus, the University of Guelph offers degrees in Toronto at the University of Guelph–Humber and has regional campuses throughout the province of Ontario in Alfred, Kemptville, and Ridgetown.

Majors and Degrees

The University of Guelph offers a number of undergraduate degree programs. Programs followed by an asterisk (*) indicate co-op programs, which are not normally available to international students.

The University of Guelph offers Bachelor of Arts degrees in agricultural economics, anthropology, art history, classical languages, classical studies, criminal justice and public policy, economics*, English, European studies, French, geography, history, information systems and human behavior, international development, applied economics, mathematical economics, mathematics, music, philosophy, political science, psychology*, rural development sociology, sociology, Spanish, statistics, studio art, theater studies, and women's studies. In addition, a Bachelor of Arts and Sciences degree is available to students who excel in both arts/social sciences and sciences.

Bachelor of Applied Science degrees are available in applied human nutrition; child, youth, and family; and adult development, families, and well-being*.

Bachelor of Commerce degrees are available in agricultural business*, hotel and food administration*, human resources management, management economics (industry and finance)*, marketing management*, public management, real estate and housing*, and tourism management.

Bachelor of Bio-Resource Management degrees are available in environmental management and equine management. Students in these programs begin their studies in the regional campuses and finish the final two years in Guelph.

The Bachelor of Computing degree has various areas of application and is offered in a co-op format at both the general and honors levels.

Bachelor of Engineering degrees are available in biological engineering*, engineering systems and computing*, environmental engineering*, and water resources engineering*.

Bachelor of Science degrees are available in animal biology, applied mathematics and statistics*, biological chemistry, biomedical science, biomedical toxicology*, biochemistry*, biological science, biophysics*, chemical physics*, chemistry*, computing and information science*, earth surface science, ecology, environmental biology, environmental toxicology*, food science*, human kinetics, marine and freshwater biology, mathematics, microbiology*, molecular biology and genetics, nanoscience, nutritional and nutraceutical sciences, physical sciences, physics*, plant biology, plant biotechnology, psychology (brain and cognition), statistics, theoretical physics, wildlife biology, and zoology.

Bachelor of Science, Agriculture, degrees are available in agricultural economics; crop, horticulture, and turfgrass sciences; honors agricultural science; organic agriculture; and urban landscape management.

Bachelor of Science, Environmental Sciences, degrees are available in earth and atmospheric science*, ecology*, environmental economics and policy*, environmental monitoring and analysis*, environmental protection*, environmental geography*, environmetrics and modeling*, and natural resources management*.

Bachelor of Science, Technology, degrees are available in applied pharmaceutical chemistry* and physics and technology*.

The University of Guelph also offers a Bachelor of Landscape Architecture degree and a Doctor of Veterinary Medicine degree.

Guelph–Humber programs include honors degrees in business administration; applied science (early childhood services, family and community social services, justice studies, kinesiology, or psychology); and applied arts in media studies (journalism, public relations, or creative photography).

Academic Programs

The academic year is divided into three semesters: fall (September through December), winter (January through April), and summer (May through August), with the majority of students in attendance during the fall and winter semesters. Fall is the normal entry point for all students.

Four-year honors degrees require the completion of eight semesters. Three-year general degrees require the completion of six semesters. A typical full-time semester totals 2.5 credits.

Off-Campus Programs

An important part of Guelph's mission is to attract students from around the world and to develop a global perspective in its students. The campus attracts more than 700 international students from more than 100 countries and maintains fifty-six exchange programs with twenty-seven countries. In addition, approximately 500 Guelph students study overseas each year in programs in Africa, Australia, Europe, and South and Central America.

Thirty-four of the programs offered at the University of Guelph include co-op work semesters, with 90 percent of the students in these

COLLEGE DATA CENTER • CANADA

programs finding work. Guelph also offers more than 100 distance degree credit courses to nearly 8,000 Open Learning course registrants.

Academic Facilities

Guelph's two libraries are linked with libraries at two other universities in the region, providing students with access to 7.5 million items through a new, state-of-the-art automated library system. Guelph's library holdings include Canada's largest collection of theater archives, extensive Scottish study materials, and one of the best collections of postcolonial African literature in Canada.

A 30-acre research park adjacent to the campus is home to a growing number of research-intensive industries. Industry and government trust Guelph's faculty members to meet their research needs, offering approximately Can$145 million annually for research that ranges from workplace efficiency to developing better approaches to food packaging and marketing to ensuring the availability of clean water.

All students receive free central computing accounts, which allow access to the University's integrated electronic services from on or off campus. These services include e-mail, access to the Internet, computer-assisted instruction, conferencing, course selection, and high-quality laser printing. All student residences are directly connected to the Internet via the campus high-speed network. Off-campus students have dial-up access to both free and chargeable modems.

The campus also features two art galleries, a Sculpture Park, two performance stages, and a new covered field house. The 408-acre Arboretum has nearly 5 miles of jogging trails and nature paths.

Costs

Full-time tuition for the 2007 academic year ranged from Can$2284 to Can$2650 per semester for Canadian residents and from Can$7414 to Can$10,254 per semester for international students. Mandatory fees totaled approximately Can$500 per semester, with slight variations according to each college. Student health/dental fees were Can$180 per year. International students were obliged to purchase health-care coverage through the University. The cost for international students to attend Guelph for two semesters, including tuition and academic fees, housing, clothing, food, and books, totaled between Can$25,000 and Can$30,000.

Financial Aid

The University of Guelph is committed to ensuring that a university education remains an attainable goal. In total, Can$17.5 million in annual student financial aid is given in the form of scholarships, awards, bursaries, and work-study opportunities. There are scholarships (ranging from Can$500 to Can$6000) and bursaries specifically designed for international students who are allowed to work on and off campus.

Faculty

The percentage of Guelph's 760 full-time professors who hold the Ph.D. degree or its equivalent is 99.8 percent, and all strive to bring the excitement and process of research into the learning environment. More than 100 professors have been recognized for their excellence in teaching by external agencies, their peers, and students. No comparably sized university in the country has garnered more 3M awards, Canada's most prestigious university teaching honor. Guelph numbers 19 Fellows of the Royal Society of Canada among its researchers.

Student Government

Students are involved at all levels of University government, from the residence council to the Senate and the Board of Governors. The Central Student Association (CSA), which represents all undergraduate students, oversees more than fifty student clubs that range from political to recreational. In addition, there are more than fifty academic and other student-government organizations located on campus. Students also have access to a number of service groups on campus, which range from the Ontario Public Interest Research Group to a community radio station and Habitat for Humanity.

Admission Requirements

Ontario applicants must present the Ontario Secondary School Diploma (OSSD), with a minimum of 6 4U or 4M courses and specific subject requirements for the degree program desired. English 4U is required for all degree programs. For those outside the Ontario secondary school system, the secondary graduation certificate that would admit a student to a university in his or her home country is normally acceptable. Applicants must also satisfy the specific subject requirements for the program desired. Students admitted on the basis of having completed the International Baccalaureate (I.B.) are granted credit for higher-level courses with grades of 5 or better. Applicants who have completed Advanced Placement (AP) exams with a minimum grade of 4 are eligible to receive University credit to a maximum of 2 credits, which is subject to the discretion of the appropriate faculty. United States applicants are required to have a minimum grade point average of 3.0 and a combined SAT score of at least 1100 (critical reading and math components) or an ACT score of at least 24. Applicants should include specific subject requirements at the highest secondary school level offered.

Interested students should call Admission Services or refer to its Web site at http://admission.uoguelph.ca for application and deadline dates, detailed admission information, and downloadable application forms. Students interested in University of Guelph–Humber programs should contact Admission Services at admission@guelphhumber.ca and visit http://www.guelphhumber.ca.

Application and Information

For additional information about admissions, academic programs, or University visits and tours, students should contact:

Admission Services
Office of Registrarial Services
Third Floor, University Centre
University of Guelph
Guelph, Ontario N1G 2W1
Canada
Phone: 519-821-2130 or 824-4120 Ext. 58721
Fax: 519-766-9481
E-mail: internat@registrar.uoguelph.ca
admission@guelphhumber.ca
Internet: http://admission.uoguelph.ca
http://www.guelphhumber.ca

Students on the campus of the University of Guelph.

COLLEGE DATA CENTER • CANADA

UNIVERSITY OF WINDSOR

WINDSOR, ONTARIO, CANADA

The University

The University of Windsor offers a very broad range of programs—its 16,000 full- and part-time students are enrolled in some 150 bachelor, master's, and doctoral degree programs. Academic disciplines range from humanities and liberal arts to science. Professional studies are offered in business, engineering, education, law, computer science, creative writing, kinesiology, nursing, social work, clinical psychology, music, dramatic art, and visual arts.

The University has an impressive commitment to research in a richly diverse community, with a special focus on automotive-, environmental-, and social justice–oriented interdisciplinary research. It is also firmly committed to providing increased opportunities for students to participate in research at the undergraduate level.

Community and business partnerships have helped to establish research institutions at the University of Windsor that are unmatched in Canada. The University's Great Lakes Institute for Environmental Research is the world's leading institution in large lakes research, attracting top students from around the world. And the University of Windsor/DaimlerChrysler Canada Research and Development Centre, with more than half a billion dollars invested by the company, is the largest teaching and research partnership in Canada.

The University of Windsor is Canada's most international campus—10 percent of its population comes from eighty countries outside of Canada. This sharing of international experiences helps prepare Windsor graduates for the global workforce.

The University began as Assumption College in 1857, affiliated with the University of Western Ontario. In 1954, it was admitted to full membership in the National Conference of Canadian Universities and Colleges, the University Articulation Board of Ontario, and the Association of the British Commonwealth. The University became the University of Windsor in 1963, and, a year later, it became a member of the International Association of Universities. In recent years, the University has spent millions of dollars in new buildings, classroom upgrades, and lab renovations, including a new residence hall and facilities for health education and dramatic arts.

Today, the campus offers more than 150 undergraduate and graduate programs across nine faculties for 17,000 full- and part-time students. It offers nine cooperative education programs for approximately 1,100 students. Although the majority of the University's undergraduate students are in their early twenties, many other students are in their late twenties, thirties, and even forties. Most come from the Ontario region, but some come from other regions of Canada; 10 percent of students are international students. The University currently ranks second among Canadian schools in terms of value, and more than 95 percent of graduates find employment within six months.

The University operates several residences on or adjacent to the campus, offering many accommodation choices from traditional residence rooms to suite-style accommodations. All residences are coed, with some single-gender floors. Most rooms are double rooms, but some single-occupancy spaces are available throughout the residence halls. Each residence hall includes laundry rooms, common lounge areas for watching TV or relaxing, vending machines, kitchen areas, and other amenities. Residence life staff members are available at each residence hall to assist students. A variety of meal plans are available for students, allowing them to eat at one of the University's dining facilities or off campus at partnering restaurants.

Location

The tree-lined campus of the University of Windsor is in the midst of Windsor, Ontario. Windsor is Canada's southernmost city and is located just across the river from Detroit. It is considered both the premier location for advanced automotive manufacturing technology and the largest agribusiness region in eastern Canada. This has contributed to one of the highest quality workforces in Canada, earning above average wages while enjoying higher than average disposable incomes. The city is bordered by Lake Erie, Lake St. Clair, and the Detroit River. Its temperate climate makes it ideal for recreational activities, such as biking, golfing, hiking, and swimming, and it makes it possible to enjoy such outdoor attractions as Dieppe Gardens, Jackson Park, Odette Sculpture Park, and the Canada Vietnam War Memorial. Windsor also offers restaurants, shopping venues, museums, and galleries as well as performances in dance, music, and theatre, and it is home to Casino Windsor.

Majors and Degrees

Students may earn a Bachelor of Arts degree in anthropology, art history, classical civilization, classics and modern languages, communication studies, criminology, developmental psychology, diaspora studies, drama, drama and communication studies, drama in education and community, economics, English language and literature, English literature and creative writing, family and social relations, forensics and criminology, French studies, history, interdisciplinary studies (Lambton College), international relations and development studies, labour studies, language and logic, liberal and professional studies, modern languages (German, Italian, Spanish), modern languages and multicultural studies, modern languages and second language education, multicultural studies, music, philosophy, political science, psychology, social justice, sociology, sociology and criminology, visual arts, visual arts and art history, visual arts and communication studies, or women's studies.

Bachelor of Commerce degrees are available in business administration, business administration co-op, business and computer science, business and computer science co-op, business and economics, and international business.

Bachelor of Computer Science degrees are available, including computer science and computer science co-op.

The Bachelor of Education is available as a consecutive program; it is also available in concurrent programs that include the Bachelor of Arts/Bachelor of Education/Early Childhood Education Diploma; Bachelor of Arts-French/Bachelor of Education; Bachelor of Math/Bachelor of Education; Bachelor of Science/Bachelor of Education; and Bachelor of Science/Bachelor of Education/Early Childhood Education Diploma.

Bachelor's degrees in engineering can be obtained in civil; electrical; electrical, with options in communications, computer, and electronics; environmental; industrial; industrial, with options in automotive manufacturing systems and in supply chain; mechanical; and mechanical, with options in automotive, automotive (Georgian College), environmental, and materials.

Bachelor of Fine Arts degrees are available in acting and in visual arts.

Bachelor of Mathematics degrees are available in mathematics, general mathematics, mathematics and statistics, mathematics and computer science, and operations research.

The Bachelor of Music, Bachelor of Arts Honours in Music, and Bachelor of Music Therapy are available.

Bachelor of Science degrees are offered in behaviour, cognition, and neuroscience; biochemistry; biochemistry and biotechnology; biology; biology and biotechnology; chemistry; chemistry and physics; computer information systems; computer information systems co-op; computer science with software engineering specialization; computer science with software engineering specialization co-op; environmental biology (co-op); environmental geoscience (co-op); environmental science; general science; geoinformatics; geology; geology (co-op); physical geography; physics and computer science; physics and high technology; physics and high technology (co-op); and science, technology, and society. Also available is the Bachelor of Science/Medical Laboratory Science.

The Bachelor of Social Work degree is available in social work, social work and diaspora studies, and social work and women's studies.

Other degrees offered include a Bachelor of Arts and Science; Bachelor of Environmental Studies; Bachelor of Forensic Science; Bachelor of Human Kinetics; Bachelor of Laws; combined Bachelor of Laws and Doctor of Jurisprudence; Bachelor of Nursing; and Bachelor of Operations Research.

There are also many programs in Science and in Arts and Social Sciences that combine two or more majors.

Academic Programs

During each regular academic year, the fall term runs from early September to early December, and the winter term runs from early January to mid-April. In addition, the University schedules courses during a summer term, which includes Intersession (May–June) and Summer Session (July–August), each of which is approximately six weeks in duration. Some courses run from May through August (twelve weeks). Each term includes approximately thirteen weeks of classes. Bachelor's degrees typically require the completion of thirty courses, including ten to sixteen courses within the major program of study; six to eight courses in arts, languages, sciences, or social sciences; and ten to twelve courses in any area within or outside the major program of study. Honours programs of study require the completion of forty courses.

Academic Facilities

The Leddy Library, the main campus library for the University, has a collection that consists of more than 3 million items, including electronic resource holdings of more than 23,000 digital journal titles and several hundred thousand digital monographs and data sets. The Leddy Library is completely wireless capable and also has more than 350 hard-wired computer workstations that provide access to library resources and the Internet and run Microsoft, Adobe, SPSS, and other programs.

The Academic Writing Centre provides writing assistance to University students through individualized writing programs, small group workshops, and classroom presentations. The Computer Literacy Skills (CLS) program provides all members of the University community with the tools necessary to gain the confidence and experience to effectively use campus computer systems and productivity software. This is achieved through both e-learning and instructor-led workshops. Academic resource centres are available for mathematics and statistics and chemistry and physics.

Costs

For 2007–08, annual full-time tuition (in Canadian dollars) ranges from $5189 to $6559 for Canadian students and $13,106 to $17,165 for international students, depending on the program of study. Residence fees are $4419 to $4816 per year for a double room or $4715 to $6371 per year for a single room. These rates include activity fees, wireless Internet, refrigerator rental, cable TV, and laundry and telephone fees. Meal plans cost an additional $3024–$3654 per year, depending on the meal plan selected. Books and other materials typically cost approximately $800 to $1000 per year.

Financial Aid

U.S./Mexico Entrance Scholarships: For newly admitted students with U.S./Mexican citizenship or permanent resident status, an entrance scholarship is available. A renewable scholarship (for up to eight terms) valued at $3000 per term is offered to engineering, education, and nursing students. A renewable scholarship of $1500 per term is offered to students in other programs of study (except for law).

Entrance Scholarships: Outstanding Scholars Awards of $10,000 to $16,000 (over four years) are given to students entering the University directly from high school who demonstrate and maintain outstanding academic achievement. The candidate must be entering one of the selected academic programs supported by the Outstanding Scholars Award.

In-Course Scholarships and Awards: The University of Windsor also offers a variety of awards for students in their second, third, and fourth years of study through In-Course Scholarships and Awards.

For further information, students should visit the Scholarship and Bursary section of the University's Web site

Faculty

There are approximately 524 faculty members at the University, with a fairly equal number of full, associate, and assistant professors and many lecturers. The ratio of men to women faculty members is approximately 3:2. Faculty members are from around the world and have won numerous awards, earning national and international acclaim.

Student Government

The University of Windsor Student Alliance (UWSA) represents all full-time undergraduate students who pay fees to the organization on a semester basis and are considered members of the organization. The UWSA strives to enhance student life through advocacy, representation, and services, such as the used book store and the student health and dental plan, and it works to ensure that all qualified students are able to obtain a university education, regardless of their financial situation. The UWSA also provides students with an element of campus life outside of the classroom. Events are organized on and off campus, and students can get involved through clubs, committees, and all aspects of the community.

Admission Requirements

Admission is competitive for many of the University's programs. Direct entry is available to most programs within the Faculty of Arts and Social Sciences, although some require specific grade 12 U prerequisites. Auditions are required in acting and music programs. Programs within the Faculties of Science, Engineering, Human Kinetics, and Nursing and the Odette School of Business Administration require prerequisite courses at the grade 12 U level and fulfillment of minimum average requirements in these prerequisite courses. Admission to the University requires a GPA of at least 70 percent (some programs require 75 to 80 percent); specific departments may require completion of certain high school courses in English, math, and sciences for admission. Applicants from the United States must submit ACT or SAT test scores with their applications; other international students must submit certification in compliance with their country's requirements. Application requirements vary depending on the program of study.

Application and Information

Applications must be submitted online through the Ontario Universities' Application Centre (OUAC), 170 Research Lane, Guelph, Ontario N1G 5E2; http://www.ouac.on.ca.

For more information, students should contact:

Office of Liaison and Student Recruitment
University of Windsor
401 Sunset Avenue
Windsor, Ontario N9B 3P4
Canada
Phone: 519-253-3000 Ext. 7014
Fax: 519-561-1428
Internet: http://prospectives.uwindsor.ca/

YORK UNIVERSITY

TORONTO, ONTARIO, CANADA

The University

York University is the leading interdisciplinary teaching and research university in Canada. York offers a modern academic experience at the undergraduate and graduate levels in Toronto, Canada's most international city. The third-largest university in the country, York is host to a dynamic academic community of over 50,000 students and 7,000 faculty and staff members as well as more than 181,000 alumni worldwide. York's eleven faculties and twenty-four research centres conduct ambitious, groundbreaking interdisciplinary research—cutting across traditional academic boundaries. This distinctive and collaborative approach is preparing students for the future and bringing fresh insights and solutions to real-world challenges. In addition to its undergraduate programs, York's Faculty of Graduate Studies offers forty-six master's, doctoral, and professional programs.

Location

York University is located in Toronto, Canada's largest city and main financial centre. Known for its friendly people, beautiful spaces, and vibrant cities, Canada is recognized as one of the best places in the world to live. As one of the world's most multicultural cities, Toronto has theatre, music, and restaurants from all around the globe. From art galleries and museums to restaurants and major-league sports, Toronto has all the elements of a world-class city. Toronto is convenient—it is a 1-hour flight from New York City, Boston, Chicago, or Detroit and a 90-minute drive from the Canadian-U.S. border at Buffalo, New York.

Students can choose between two unique campuses. The Keele campus, located in north Toronto, is home to eight of the nine undergraduate faculties and offers extensive modern facilities, including more than forty restaurants, a shopping mall, banks, a medical/dental clinic, five libraries, art galleries, theatres, an athletic complex, the Rexall™ Tennis Centre, on-campus housing, an executive learning centre, and a wide variety of events and cultural activities. The Glendon campus, a picturesque, parklike campus minutes from the boutiques, restaurants, and nightlife of midtown Toronto, is a close-knit, bilingual liberal arts community of 2,200 students.

Majors and Degrees

York University offers more than 5,000 courses through eleven faculties: Arts, Atkinson Faculty of Liberal and Professional Studies, Education, Environmental Studies, Fine Arts, Glendon, Graduate Studies, Health, Osgoode Hall Law School, Schulich School of Business, and Science and Engineering.

The Bachelor of Arts (daytime studies, Keele campus) is offered in African studies; anthropology; applied mathematics; business and society; children's studies; classical studies/classics; cognitive science; communication studies; computer science; creative writing; criminology; East Asian studies; economics; economics and business; English; European studies; French studies; geography; German studies; global political studies; health and society; Hellenic studies; history; humanities; individualized studies; information technology; information technology and applied mathematics; information technology and communication studies; information technology and mathematics; information technology and mathematics for commerce; information technology and statistics; international development studies; Italian studies; labour studies; languages and literatures (includes courses in American Sign Language, Arabic, Chinese, Greek (modern and classical), Hebrew, Hindi, Japanese, Korean, Latin, Portuguese, and Yiddish); Latin American and Caribbean studies; law and society; linguistics; mathematics; mathematics for commerce; philosophy; political science; professional writing; public policy and administration; religious studies; race, ethnicity, and indigeneity; Russian; Russian studies; science and technology; social and political thought; sociology; South Asian studies; Spanish; statistics; translation; undecided major; urban studies; and women's studies. Joint programs with some Ontario community colleges are available in communication arts and rehabilitation services. Certificates are available in athletic therapy, coaching, fitness assessment and exercise counselling, geographic information systems and remote sensing, sport administration, and teaching English to speakers of other languages.

The Atkinson Faculty of Liberal and Professional Studies offers the following degrees: Bachelor of Administrative Studies (accounting*, business research*, finance, general management*, human resources management*, information technology, and marketing), Bachelor of Arts (business economics, Canadian studies, computer science, computer security, culture and expression, economics, English, history, humanities, individualized studies, information technology, mathematics, mathematics for commerce, philosophy, political science, public administration and justice studies, public policy and administration, public policy and management, religious studies, science and technology studies, social science, sociology, undecided major, and women's studies), Bachelor of Human Resources Management, Bachelor of Science (computer science, computer security, general science, mathematics, and psychology), and Bachelor of Social Work. Certificates are available in accounting, antiracist research and practice, biblical studies, emergency management, health administration, health informatics, human resources management, logistics, management, marketing, nurse practitioner studies, professional ethics, public-sector management, real estate, refugee and migration studies, sexuality studies, and women's studies: theory and practice. An asterisk (*) indicates that a program is available through distance education.

The Bachelor of Education offers both concurrent and consecutive education programs, which are offered in primary/junior (K–6), junior/intermediate (4–10), and intermediate/senior (7–12) levels. There are no specialization subjects in the primary/junior program. Subjects of specialization in the junior/intermediate program include dance, drama, English, French as a second language, geography, history, mathematics, music, physical and health education, religious studies, science (general), and visual arts. The intermediate/senior program asks for specialization in two of the following subjects: accounting, biology, chemistry, computer science, dance, drama, economics, English, family studies, French as a second language, geography, German, history, individual and society, information management, Italian, law, marketing and merchandising, mathematics, music, physical and health education, physics, political science, religious studies, science (general), Spanish, and visual arts. Students may also pursue the Jewish Teacher Education Program within concurrent Education.

The Bachelor of Environmental Studies degree is offered in environmental management, environmental politics, environment and culture, and urban and regional environments; certificates are offered in community arts practice, environmental landscape design, and geographic information systems and remote sensing. Joint college programs also offer ecosystem management, international project management, and urban sustainability.

The Faculty of Fine Arts offers Bachelor of Design, Bachelor of Fine Arts, and Bachelor of Arts degrees in the following programs: dance, design, film, fine arts cultural studies, music, theater, and visual arts (includes art history, drawing, media arts, painting, photography, printmaking, and sculpture). The Bachelor of Arts at the Glendon campus (courses taught in English and/or French) is offered in business economics, Canadian studies, computer science in liberal arts, drama studies, economics, English, environmental and health studies, French studies, history, individualized/multidisciplinary studies, information technology, international studies, linguistics and language studies, mathematics, mathematics for commerce, philosophy, political science, psychology, sociology, Spanish (Hispanic studies), statistics, translation, undecided major, and women's studies. Certificates are available in law and social thought, public administration and public policy, rédaction professionelle, refugee and migration studies, Spanish/English translation/Traducción ingles-español, teaching English as an international language, and technical and professional writing.

The Faculty of Health offers programs in health studies (health informatics, health management, and health policy), kinesiology and health science, nursing, and psychology.

York's Osgoode Hall Law School offers a Bachelor of Laws. The Schulich School of Business offers a Bachelor of Business Administration

COLLEGE DATA CENTER • CANADA

degree in accounting, economics, entrepreneurship and family business, finance, international business, marketing, operations management and information systems, and organizational behaviour/industrial relations. An International Bachelor of Business Administration degree is also offered.

The Bachelor of Science is offered in applied math, biochemistry, biology, biomedical science, biophysics, biotechnology, chemistry, computational mathematics, computer science, earth and atmospheric science, environmental science, geography, international B.Sc., mathematics, mathematics for education, physics and astronomy, science and technology studies, and space science. A joint program with Seneca College is available in rehabilitation services. Certificates are available in athletic therapy, coaching, fitness assessment and exercise counselling, geographic information systems and remote sensing, meteorology, and sport administration. The Bachelor of Applied Science is offered in computer engineering, computer security, geomatics engineering, and space engineering.

Academic Programs

Students can begin their studies at York in September (all programs) or, in a limited number of programs, in May or January. Students can study on a full- or part-time basis during the day or evening. All undergraduate and professional degrees have specific requirements that students must complete prior to graduating. The University calendar is organized on a semester system, including two 6-week summer sessions. Detailed information about program requirements can be found in the Calendars at http://www.registrar.yorku.ca.

Off-Campus Programs

York has more than 150 partnership agreements with universities throughout the world and offers more than 100 exchange and study-abroad opportunities in thirty-four countries. The University-wide Exchange Program has partnerships with universities in Australia, Austria, Barbados, Brazil, China, Denmark, Ecuador, England, Finland, France, Germany, Greece, Guyana, Israel, Italy, Jamaica, Japan, Latvia, Lithuania, Mexico, Mongolia, the Netherlands, Poland, Russia, Singapore, South Korea, Spain, Sweden, Thailand, Trinidad and Tobago, Turkey, the United States, Venezuela, and Wales. Qualifying students at the undergraduate level must be in an honors program, have completed two years of study, have maintained at least an overall B average, and, in some cases, have proficiency in the host country's language.

Academic Facilities

York's five libraries contain more than 6.5 million items—books, print periodicals, e-journals, theses, archival material, microforms, maps, films, and music CDs. The Osgoode Hall Law Library is the largest in the Commonwealth, housing a collection of approximately 450,000 volumes (including microform) on five floors. With twenty-four research centres, York is one of the most highly valued and sought-after research institutions. Students have access to a wide range of computer facilities, including forty-two computer labs and more than 2,500 workstations. All students receive free e-mail and Internet access. To help students succeed in their studies, there are academic tutors, advisers to help with course selection, and an extensive learning disabilities program. Students whose first language is not English can get extra help at the English as a Second Language Open Learning Centre and take ESL courses that count toward their degrees. At York, facilities include visual arts studios, three theatres, three art galleries (excluding college-based student galleries), state-of-the-art science laboratories, an astronomical observatory with two telescopes, two stadiums, four gymnasiums, five sport playing fields, four softball fields, nine outdoor tennis courts, the Rexall™ Tennis Centre, seven squash courts, three dance/aerobic studios, five NHL-sized ice rinks and one international-sized rink, two swimming pools, and a newly renovated, 11,000-square-foot fitness centre. The Accolade Project houses outstanding Faculty of Fine Arts facilities, including a 325-seat proscenium theatre, a 325-seat recital hall equipped with a recording studio, a state-of-the-art screening facility, studios, and teaching spaces.

Costs

For the 2007–08 academic year, tuition fees for a full-time student are a minimum of Can$5065 for Canadian citizens and permanent residents or Can$15,065 for international students. Room and board (double room) start at Can$3793, and a meal plan ranges from Can$1400 to Can$2400. Students living in residence must purchase a meal plan. Course materials, books, health insurance, and supplies range from Can$1200 to Can$2200. For details, prospective students should visit http://www.yorku.ca/osfs.

Financial Aid

International candidates can compete for the prestigious Global Leader of Tomorrow Award, worth Can$15,000 and renewable for up to four years of undergraduate study as long as excellent grades are maintained. An application for this award is necessary. Once at York, international students are eligible for continuing student scholarships worth up to Can$3000 based on their academic performance in York courses. U.S. citizens may be eligible to receive FAFSA funding to study at York (York's FAFSA code is G07679). All full-time international students may work part-time on campus. For full scholarship details, prospective students should visit http://www.yorku.ca/web/futurestudents/scholarships.

Faculty

York employs 4,340 professors, spread over two campuses. York's professors are mentors, known internationally for excellence and innovation in teaching and research. Excellence in research is central to York's mission and is fundamental to the University's ability to contribute to the economic, scientific, cultural, and social health of society. Research takes place in every discipline and spans the full spectrum of programs. In addition, York has renowned research strength in areas such as space science, vision science, aboriginal and indigenous studies, history, and psychology. A complete list of prestigious award recipients can be found at http://research.yorku.ca.

Student Government

There are nine student governments at York located within the residential colleges and Faculties. There is also a central government, the York Federation of Students, which represents all York students. York students have representation on the Board of Governors, Senate, Faculty Councils, Council of Masters, and other advisory committees.

Admission Requirements

York is a selective university; therefore, only those candidates who show potential for academic success are considered. Meeting minimum requirements does not guarantee admission. Some programs may require specific preparation in certain subject areas. York's TOEFL code is 0894. Academically outstanding students with a minimum SAT score of 1300 may receive early admission.

Application and Information

Applications are available online at http://www.ouac.on.ca. The deadline for international applicants interested in September admission is February 1. Students are encouraged to submit their application and supporting documentation well in advance of the deadline date. Programs such as Fine Arts and the Schulich School of Business also require supplemental application forms. For additional information about admissions, academic requirements, programs, courses, or University events and tours, students should visit http://www.yorku.ca/futurestudents.

Office of Admissions
York University
4700 Keele Street
Toronto, Ontario M3J 1P3
Canada
Phone: 416-736-5825
Fax: 416-650-8195
Web site: http://www.yorku.ca

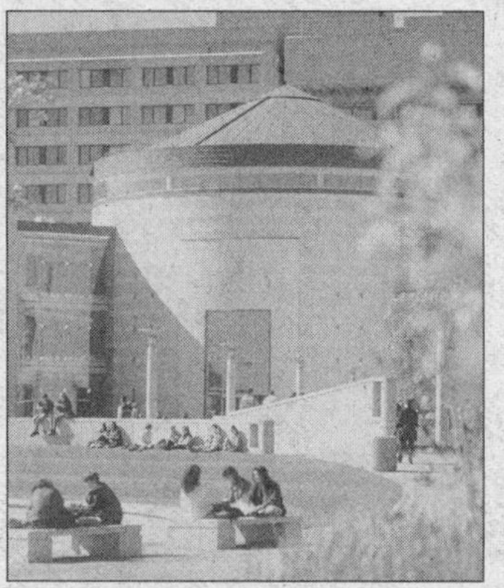

Vari Hall, the focal point of the Keele campus.

COLLEGE DATA CENTER • CANADA

INTERNATIONAL

BULGARIA

AMERICAN UNIVERSITY IN BULGARIA

Blagoevgrad, Bulgaria **www.aubg.bg/**

- **Independent** comprehensive, founded 1991
- **Small-town** campus with easy access to Sofia
- **Endowment** $2.1 million
- **Coed**
- 45% of applicants were admitted

Faculty *Student/faculty ratio:* 18:1.

Academics *Calendar:* semesters. *Degrees:* bachelor's and master's.

Student Life *Campus security:* 24-hour emergency response devices and patrols.

Standardized Tests *Required:* SAT (for admission).

Costs (2007–08) *Tuition:* $8200 full-time. Full-time tuition and fees vary according to location.

Applying *Application fee:* $25. *Required:* minimum 3.0 GPA, 3 letters of recommendation.

Director of Admissions Yordanka Melnikliyska, Director of Admissions, American University in Bulgaria, Blagoevgrad 2700, Bulgaria. *Phone:* 359-73 888 218. *Fax:* 359-73 800 174. *E-mail:* admission@aubg.bg.

CAYMAN ISLANDS

INTERNATIONAL COLLEGE OF THE CAYMAN ISLANDS

Newlands, Cayman Islands **www.icci.edu.ky/**

Freshman Application Contact Ms. Dianne Levy, Admissions Representative, International College of the Cayman Islands, PO Box 136, Savannah Post Office, Newlands, Grand Cayman, Cayman Islands. *Phone:* 345-947-1100 Ext. 301.

See page 2886 for the College Close-Up.

EGYPT

THE AMERICAN UNIVERSITY IN CAIRO

Cairo, Egypt **www.aucegypt.edu/**

- **Independent** comprehensive, founded 1919
- **Urban** 26-acre campus
- **Endowment** $492.4 million
- **Coed**
- **Very difficult** entrance level

Faculty *Student/faculty ratio:* 13:1.

Academics *Calendar:* semesters. *Degrees:* certificates, diplomas, bachelor's, and master's (majority of students are Egyptians; enrollment open to all nationalities).

Student Life *Campus security:* 24-hour emergency response devices and patrols, controlled dormitory access.

Standardized Tests *Required for some:* SAT (for admission), SAT or ACT (for admission), SAT Subject Tests (for admission).

Applying *Options:* electronic application, early decision. *Application fee:* $50. *Required:* essay or personal statement, high school transcript, minimum 2.0 GPA.

Freshman Application Contact Ms. Randa Kamel, Director of Enrollment Services, The American University in Cairo, The Office of Student Affairs, 420 Fifth Avenue, 3rd Floor, New York, NY 10018-2728. *Phone:* 202-797-5551. *E-mail:* randa_k@aucnyo.edu.

FRANCE

THE AMERICAN UNIVERSITY OF PARIS

Paris, France **www.aup.edu/**

- **Independent** comprehensive, founded 1962
- **Urban** campus
- **Endowment** $677,000
- **Coed** 994 undergraduate students, 96% full-time, 70% women, 30% men
- **Moderately difficult** entrance level, 68% of applicants were admitted

Undergraduates 956 full-time, 38 part-time. Students come from 43 states and territories, 82 other countries, 7% transferred in. *Retention:* 70% of 2006 full-time freshmen returned.

Freshmen *Admission:* 579 applied, 393 admitted, 172 enrolled.

Faculty *Total:* 134, 46% full-time, 69% with terminal degrees. *Student/faculty ratio:* 13:1.

Majors Art history, criticism and conservation; comparative literature; computer science; economics; European studies; film/cinema studies; finance; French; history; international business/trade/commerce; international economics; international relations and affairs; mass communication/media; mathematics and statistics related; psychology.

Academics *Calendar:* semesters. *Degrees:* bachelor's and master's. *Special study options:* advanced placement credit, cooperative education, double majors, honors programs, independent study, internships, off-campus study, part-time degree program, study abroad, summer session for credit.

Computers on Campus 100 computers/terminals are available on campus for general student use. Students can access the following: campus intranet, computer help desk, free student e-mail accounts, online (class) schedules, trading room. Campuswide network is available. Wireless service is available via entire campus.

Student Life *Housing:* college housing not available. *Options:* Campus housing is provided by a third party. *Activities and organizations:* drama/theater group, student-run newspaper, radio and television station, Safe Haven Aids Information, Publications Board, Student Senate, International Business Student Association, Sports Association. *Campus security:* 24-hour emergency response devices. *Student services:* personal/psychological counseling.

Athletics *Intramural sports:* basketball M/W, fencing M, football M, golf M, racquetball M/W, soccer M, squash M/W, tennis M/W, volleyball M/W.

Standardized Tests *Required for some:* SAT or ACT (for admission).

Costs (2008–09) *Comprehensive fee:* $34,084 includes full-time tuition ($23,000), mandatory fees ($1584), and room and board ($9500). *Required fees:* $770 per credit part-time.

Applying *Options:* electronic application, deferred entrance. *Application fee:* $50. *Required:* essay or personal statement, high school transcript, 2 letters of recommendation. *Recommended:* minimum 3.0 GPA, interview. *Application deadlines:* 3/15 (freshmen), 3/15 (transfers). *Notification:* continuous (freshmen), continuous (transfers).

Freshman Application Contact International Admissions Office, The American University of Paris, US Office, 950 South Cherry Street, Suite 210, Denver, CO 80246. *Phone:* 303-757-6333. *E-mail:* usoffice@aup.edu.

See page 2880 for the College Close-Up.

PARSONS PARIS

Paris, France www.parsons-paris.com/

- **Independent** 4-year
- **Urban** campus
- **Coed** 174 undergraduate students, 95% full-time, 83% women, 17% men
- **Very difficult** entrance level, 76% of applicants were admitted

Undergraduates 166 full-time, 8 part-time. Students come from 29 states and territories, 43 other countries, 100% are from out of state. *Retention:* 65% of 2006 full-time freshmen returned.

Freshmen *Admission:* 144 applied, 109 admitted, 43 enrolled.

Faculty *Total:* 75, 1% full-time, 52% with terminal degrees. *Student/faculty ratio:* 3:1.

Majors Business administration and management; fashion/apparel design; fine/studio arts.

Academics *Degrees:* bachelor's (Bachelor of Fine Arts, Bachelor of Business Administration). *Special study options:* adult/continuing education programs, advanced placement credit, independent study, study abroad, summer session for credit.

Student Life *Housing:* college housing not available.

Standardized Tests *Required for some:* SAT or ACT (for admission).

Costs (2007–08) *Tuition:* 28,534 euros full-time, 1200 euros per credit part-time. Full-time tuition and fees vary according to course load. Part-time tuition and fees vary according to course load. *Required fees:* 950 euros full-time. *Payment plan:* deferred payment. *Waivers:* employees or children of employees.

Financial Aid *Financial aid deadline:* 7/15.

Applying *Application fee:* 50 euros. *Required:* high school transcript. *Required for some:* essay or personal statement, portfolio. *Recommended:* letters of recommendation, interview. *Application deadlines:* rolling (freshmen), rolling (out-of-state freshmen).

Freshman Application Contact Sara Krauskopf, Parsons Paris, 14 rue Letellier, F-75015 Paris, France. *Phone:* 331-45 77 40 17. *Fax:* 331-45 77 44 12. *E-mail:* sara.krauskopf@parsons-paris.com.

SCHILLER INTERNATIONAL UNIVERSITY

Paris, France www.schiller.edu/

- **Independent** comprehensive, founded 1967, part of Schiller International University
- **Urban** campus
- **Coed** 44 undergraduate students, 95% full-time, 41% women, 59% men
- **Minimally difficult** entrance level

Schiller International University (SIU) is an independent American university with campuses in England, France, Germany, Spain, Switzerland, and the United States. Students can transfer from campus to campus without loss of credit. English is the language of instruction at all campuses. SIU offers undergraduate and graduate students an American education in an international setting.

Undergraduates 42 full-time, 2 part-time. Students come from 20 states and territories, 32 other countries, 5% transferred in.

Freshmen *Admission:* 14 enrolled.

Faculty *Total:* 24, 8% full-time, 46% with terminal degrees. *Student/faculty ratio:* 11:1.

Majors Business administration and management; interdisciplinary studies; international business/trade/commerce; international relations and affairs; liberal arts and sciences/liberal studies.

Academics *Calendar:* semesters. *Degrees:* associate, bachelor's, and master's. *Special study options:* accelerated degree program, adult/continuing education programs, advanced placement credit, distance learning, English as a second language, internships, part-time degree program, student-designed majors, study abroad, summer session for credit.

Computers on Campus 11 computers/terminals are available on campus for general student use. Campuswide network is available. 100% of college-owned or -operated housing units are wired for high-speed Internet access. Wireless service is available via entire campus.

Student Life *Housing:* college housing not available. *Activities and organizations:* student-run newspaper, Student government, Student newspaper, Yearbook staff. *Student services:* personal/psychological counseling.

Costs (2007–08) *Tuition:* 16,450 euros full-time, 450 euros per credit part-time. *Required fees:* 430 euros full-time. *Payment plan:* installment. *Waivers:* employees or children of employees.

Financial Aid *Financial aid deadline:* 6/1.

Applying *Options:* deferred entrance. *Application fee:* 65 euros. *Required:* essay or personal statement, high school transcript, letters of recommendation. *Recommended:* minimum 2.0 GPA. *Application deadlines:* rolling (freshmen), rolling (transfers).

Freshman Application Contact Ms. Kamala Dontamsetti, Associate Director of Admissions, Schiller International University, 9 rue d'Yvart, F-75015 Paris, France. *Phone:* 727-736-5082 Ext. 234. *Fax:* 727-734-0347. *E-mail:* kamala_dontamsetti@schiller.edu.

See page 2896 for the College Close-Up.

GERMANY

SCHILLER INTERNATIONAL UNIVERSITY

Heidelberg, Germany www.schiller.edu/

- **Independent** comprehensive, founded 1969, part of Schiller International University
- **Urban** campus with easy access to Frankfurt
- **Coed**
- **Minimally difficult** entrance level

Schiller International University (SIU) is an independent American university with campuses in England, France, Germany, Spain, Switzerland, and the United States. Students can transfer from campus to campus without loss of credit. English is the language of instruction at all campuses. SIU offers undergraduate and graduate students an American education in an international setting.

Faculty *Student/faculty ratio:* 7:1.

Academics *Calendar:* semesters. *Degrees:* associate, bachelor's, and master's.

Student Life *Campus security:* 24-hour emergency response devices.

Costs (2007–08) *Tuition:* 16,260 euros full-time, 450 euros per credit part-time. *Required fees:* 510 euros full-time. *Room only:* 3589 euros.

Financial Aid *Financial aid deadline:* 6/1.

Applying *Options:* deferred entrance. *Application fee:* 65 euros. *Required:* essay or personal statement, high school transcript. *Recommended:* minimum 2.0 GPA.

Freshman Application Contact Ms. Kamala Dontamsetti, Associate Director of Admissions, Schiller International University, Bergstrasse 106, 69121 Heidelberg, Germany. *Phone:* 727-736-5082 Ext. 234. *Fax:* 727-734-0359. *E-mail:* kamala_dontamsetti@schiller.edu.

See page 2896 for the College Close-Up.

GREECE

AMERICAN COLLEGE OF THESSALONIKI

Pylea, Greece www.act.edu/

- **Independent** comprehensive, founded 1886, administratively affiliated with Anatolia College
- **Suburban** 40-acre campus
- **Coed** 378 undergraduate students, 70% full-time, 44% women, 56% men
- **Minimally difficult** entrance level, 72% of applicants were admitted

Undergraduates 263 full-time, 115 part-time. Students come from 23 other countries, 3% transferred in, 18% live on campus. *Retention:* 85% of 2006 full-time freshmen returned.

Freshmen *Admission:* 134 applied, 97 admitted, 72 enrolled. *Average high school GPA:* 2.7.

Faculty *Total:* 47, 32% full-time, 45% with terminal degrees. *Student/faculty ratio:* 11:1.

Majors Balkans studies; business administration and management; computer science; finance; international business/trade/commerce; international relations and affairs; management information systems; marketing/marketing management.

Academics *Calendar:* semesters. *Degrees:* certificates, bachelor's, and master's. *Special study options:* academic remediation for entering students, advanced placement credit, double majors, English as a second language, independent study, internships, part-time degree program, study abroad, summer session for credit.

Computers on Campus 170 computers/terminals and 20 ports are available on campus for general student use. Students can access the following: campus intranet, computer help desk, free student e-mail accounts, online (class) grades. Campuswide network is available. 100% of college-owned or -operated housing units are wired for high-speed Internet access. Wireless service is available via computer centers, learning centers, libraries, student centers.

Student Life *Housing options:* coed. Campus housing is university owned and leased by the school. *Activities and organizations:* student-run radio station, choral group, Field Trip Club, History and International Relations Society, International Student Society, Marketing Society, radio station. *Campus security:* 24-hour patrols.

Athletics *Intercollegiate sports:* basketball M/W, soccer M, volleyball M/W. *Intramural sports:* basketball M, golf M/W, soccer M, volleyball M/W.

Costs (2007–08) *Tuition:* 7200 euros full-time, 240 euros per credit hour part-time. Full-time tuition and fees vary according to degree level and program. Part-time tuition and fees vary according to degree level and program. *Required fees:* 100 euros full-time, 50 euros per term part-time. *Room only:* 3300 euros. *Waivers:* employees or children of employees.

Applying *Options:* electronic application, deferred entrance. *Application fee:* $100. *Required:* high school transcript, proficiency in English. *Required for some:* essay or personal statement, interview. *Recommended:* minimum 2.0 GPA, letters of recommendation. *Application deadlines:* 7/4 (freshmen), 9/1 (transfers). *Notification:* 9/10 (freshmen), 9/10 (transfers).

Freshman Application Contact Ms. Roula Lebetli, Director of Admissions, American College of Thessaloniki, PO Box 21021, Pylea, Thessaloniki 55510, Greece. *Phone:* 30-2310-398239. *Fax:* 30-2310-398389. *E-mail:* admissions@act.edu.

THE AMERICAN UNIVERSITY OF ATHENS

Athens, Greece **www.aua.edu/**

- **Independent** comprehensive, founded 1982
- **Urban** campus
- **Endowment** $7.7 million
- **Coed** 1,164 undergraduate students, 80% full-time, 44% women, 56% men
- **Moderately difficult** entrance level, 77% of applicants were admitted

Undergraduates 937 full-time, 227 part-time. Students come from 15 states and territories, 40 other countries, 42% are from out of state, 7% Asian American or Pacific Islander, 7% transferred in, 19% live on campus. *Retention:* 89% of 2006 full-time freshmen returned.

Freshmen *Admission:* 566 applied, 435 admitted, 306 enrolled. *Average high school GPA:* 2.8.

Faculty *Total:* 54, 69% full-time, 56% with terminal degrees. *Student/faculty ratio:* 13:1.

Majors Accounting; advertising; archeology; architectural engineering; art history, criticism and conservation; biochemistry; biology/biological sciences; business administration and management; business/commerce; business/managerial economics; chemistry; civil engineering; computer and information sciences; computer graphics; computer science; computer systems networking and telecommunications; electrical, electronics and communications engineering; engineering science; English; English literature (British and Commonwealth); environmental design/architecture; fashion/apparel design; finance; foreign languages and literatures; graphic design; history; hospitality administration; hotel/motel administration; human resources management; industrial engineering; international business/trade/commerce; journalism; legal studies; management science; management sciences and quantitative methods related; marketing/marketing management; mathematics; mechanical engineering; molecular biology; philosophy; physics; political science and government; public relations/image management; sociology; structural engineering; tourism and travel services management; western civilization.

Academics *Calendar:* semesters. *Degrees:* bachelor's and master's. *Special study options:* accelerated degree program, adult/continuing education programs, cooperative education, double majors, English as a second language, independent study, internships, part-time degree program, study abroad, summer session for credit.

Computers on Campus 57 computers/terminals are available on campus for general student use. Students can access the following: computer help desk, free student e-mail accounts. Campuswide network is available. Wireless service is available via entire campus.

Student Life *Housing options:* coed, men-only, women-only. Campus housing is leased by the school. Freshman campus housing is guaranteed. *Activities and organizations:* drama/theater group, student-run newspaper, Poetry and Literature Society, Journalism Association, Drama Club, Political Science Association, Parliamentary Debating Society. *Campus security:* 24-hour emergency response devices and patrols, closed-circuit TV. *Student services:* personal/psychological counseling.

Athletics *Intercollegiate sports:* baseball M. *Intramural sports:* basketball M, sailing M, skiing (downhill) M/W, soccer M, swimming and diving M/W, table tennis M/W, volleyball M/W, water polo M/W.

Costs (2008–09) *Tuition:* $12,348 full-time. *Room only:* $4998.

Financial Aid Of all full-time matriculated undergraduates who enrolled in 2006, 15 state and other part-time jobs (averaging $1125).

Applying *Options:* electronic application. *Application fee:* 100 euros. *Required:* high school transcript, 2 letters of recommendation, interview. *Recommended:* essay or personal statement, letters of recommendation. *Application deadline:* 8/15 (freshmen). *Notification:* continuous (transfers).

Director of Admissions Ms. Thalia Poulos, Director of Admissions, The American University of Athens, 17 Patriarchou Ieremiou Street, Athens 11475, Greece. *Phone:* 30-210-725-9301. *E-mail:* admissions@aua.edu.

See page 2878 for the College Close-Up.

DEREE COLLEGE, THE AMERICAN COLLEGE OF GREECE

Athens, Greece **www.acg.edu/**

- **Independent** 4-year, founded 1875
- **Urban** 60-acre campus
- **Coed**
- **Moderately difficult** entrance level

Faculty *Student/faculty ratio:* 11:1.

Academics *Calendar:* 4-1-4. *Degrees:* associate and bachelor's.

Student Life *Campus security:* 24-hour emergency response devices and patrols.

Costs (2007–08) *Tuition:* $8100 full-time, $270 per credit part-time. Full-time tuition and fees vary according to course load. *Required fees:* $1107 full-time.

Financial Aid Of all full-time matriculated undergraduates who enrolled in 2006, 86 state and other part-time jobs (averaging $734). *Financial aid deadline:* 1/15.

Applying *Options:* deferred entrance. *Required:* high school transcript, minimum 2.0 GPA, 1 letter of recommendation, interview. *Required for some:* essay or personal statement. *Recommended:* medical certificate.

Freshman Application Contact Ms. Lucy Kanatsouli, Deree College, The American College of Greece, 6 Gravias Street, Aghia Paraskevi 153-42, Athens, Greece. *Phone:* 30-210-600-9800 Ext. 1322. *E-mail:* dereeadm@hol.gr.

IRELAND

INSTITUTE OF PUBLIC ADMINISTRATION

Dublin, Ireland **www.ipa.ie/**

Director of Admissions Dr. Denis O'Brien, Registrar, Institute of Public Administration, 57-61 Lansdowne Road, Dublin 4, Ireland. *Phone:* 353-1-240-3600. *Fax:* 353-1-668-9135.

ITALY

THE AMERICAN UNIVERSITY OF ROME

Rome, Italy www.aur.edu/

- **Independent** 4-year, founded 1969, administratively affiliated with The College of Staten Island
- **Urban** 1-acre campus
- **Endowment** $1.3 million
- **Coed**
- **Moderately difficult** entrance level

Faculty *Student/faculty ratio:* 15:1.

Academics *Calendar:* semesters. *Degrees:* associate and bachelor's.

Student Life *Campus security:* 24-hour emergency response devices, security guards during opening hours and 24-hour surveillance cameras.

Standardized Tests *Required:* ACT (for admission). *Required for some:* SAT or ACT (for admission).

Costs (2007–08) *Tuition:* 5960 euros full-time, 1490 euros per course part-time. Part-time tuition and fees vary according to course load. *Required fees:* 80 euros full-time, 80 euros per term part-time. *Room only:* 7500 euros. Room and board charges vary according to housing facility.

Applying *Options:* deferred entrance. *Application fee:* $35. *Required:* essay or personal statement, high school transcript, minimum 2.5 GPA, letters of recommendation, interview.

Freshman Application Contact Ms. Mara Nisdeo, Director of Admissions, The American University of Rome, Via Pietro Roselli 4, Rome 00153, Italy. *Phone:* 39-06-58330919 Ext. 206. *Toll-free phone:* 888-791-8327. *E-mail:* admissions@aur.edu.

See page 2882 for the College Close-Up.

JOHN CABOT UNIVERSITY

Rome, Italy www.johncabot.edu/

- **Independent** 4-year, founded 1972
- **Urban** campus
- **Coed**
- **Moderately difficult** entrance level

Located in Rome, Italy, John Cabot University is an accredited independent institution offering an American university education with a distinctive international character. John Cabot students come from more than sixty countries. The average class size is 20 students, and there are 100 dedicated faculty members. Scholarships and FAFSA loans are available.

Faculty *Student/faculty ratio:* 18:1.

Academics *Calendar:* semesters. *Degrees:* associate and bachelor's.

Student Life *Campus security:* 24-hour emergency response devices.

Standardized Tests *Required for some:* SAT or ACT (for admission).

Costs (2007–08) *Comprehensive fee:* $30,000 includes full-time tuition ($17,000), mandatory fees ($800), and room and board ($12,200). Full-time tuition and fees vary according to course load. Part-time tuition: $650 per credit. Part-time tuition and fees vary according to course load. *College room only:* $7800. Room and board charges vary according to board plan, housing facility, and location.

Applying *Options:* electronic application, deferred entrance. *Application fee:* $50. *Required:* essay or personal statement, high school transcript, 2 letters of recommendation. *Recommended:* minimum 2.7 GPA, interview.

Freshman Application Contact Ms. Jill Peacock, Director of Admissions, John Cabot University, Via della Lungara 233, Roma 00165, Italy. *Phone:* 39-06 6819121. *Toll-free phone:* 866-227-0112. *Fax:* 39-06 589-7429. *E-mail:* admissions@johncabot.edu.

See page 2890 for the College Close-Up.

KENYA

UNITED STATES INTERNATIONAL UNIVERSITY

Nairobi, Kenya www.usiu.ac.ke/

Director of Admissions Mr. George Lumbasi, Admissions Director, United States International University, PO Box 14634, Thika Road, Kasarani, Nairobi 00800, Kenya. *Phone:* 254-02-3606563. *E-mail:* admit@usiu.ac.ke.

LEBANON

AMERICAN UNIVERSITY OF BEIRUT

Beirut, Lebanon www.aub.edu.lb/

- **Independent** university, founded 1866
- **Urban** 313-acre campus
- **Endowment** $466.8 million
- **Coed** 6,058 undergraduate students, 97% full-time, 49% women, 51% men
- 74% of applicants were admitted

Undergraduates 5,891 full-time, 167 part-time. Students come from 68 other countries, 0.5% transferred in, 12% live on campus. *Retention:* 92% of 2006 full-time freshmen returned.

Freshmen *Admission:* 3,556 applied, 2,635 admitted, 1,708 enrolled. *Average high school GPA:* 2.74. *Test scores:* SAT critical reading scores over 500: 39%; SAT math scores over 500: 94%; SAT writing scores over 500: 45%; SAT critical reading scores over 600: 7%; SAT math scores over 600: 57%; SAT writing scores over 600: 10%; SAT math scores over 700: 14%; SAT writing scores over 700: 1%.

Faculty *Total:* 635, 64% full-time, 69% with terminal degrees. *Student/faculty ratio:* 13:1.

Majors Agriculture; anthropology; Arabic; archeology; architecture; art history, criticism and conservation; biology/biological sciences; business administration and management; chemistry; civil engineering; computer engineering; computer science; economics; electrical, electronics and communications engineering; elementary education; English; food science; geology/earth science; health science; history; landscaping and groundskeeping; mathematics; mechanical engineering; Near and Middle Eastern studies; nursing (registered nurse training); nutrition sciences; petroleum technology; philosophy; physics; political science and government; psychology; public administration; sociology; statistics; veterinary sciences.

Academics *Calendar:* semesters. *Degrees:* certificates, diplomas, bachelor's, master's, and first professional. *Special study options:* academic remediation for entering students, advanced placement credit, English as a second language, honors programs, independent study, internships, services for LD students, study abroad, summer session for credit. *Unusual degree programs:* 3-2 business administration; nursing.

Computers on Campus 885 computers/terminals and 2,000 ports are available on campus for general student use. Students can access the following: campus intranet, computer help desk, free student e-mail accounts, online (class) grades, online (class) registration, online (class) schedules. Campuswide network is available. 100% of college-owned or -operated housing units are wired for high-speed Internet access. Wireless service is available via entire campus.

Student Life *Housing options:* men-only, women-only. Campus housing is university owned. Freshman campus housing is guaranteed. *Activities and organizations:* drama/theater group, student-run newspaper, choral group, Red Cross Club, Skiing Society, Business Society, Music Society, Student Activism Club. *Campus security:* 24-hour emergency response devices and patrols, late-night transport/escort service, staff monitors entrance 24/7. *Student services:* health clinic, personal/psychological counseling, legal services.

Athletics *Intercollegiate sports:* badminton M/W, basketball M/W, cross-country running M/W, skiing (downhill) M/W, soccer M/W, squash M/W, swimming and diving M/W, table tennis M/W, tennis M/W, track and field M/W, volleyball M/W. *Intramural sports:* badminton M/W, basketball M/W, cross-country running M/W, soccer M/W, squash M/W, swimming and diving M/W, table tennis M/W, tennis M/W, volleyball M/W.
Standardized Tests *Required:* SAT (for admission). *Required for some:* SAT Subject Tests (for admission).
Costs (2008–09) *One-time required fee:* $33. *Tuition:* $11,000 full-time, $466 per credit part-time. *Required fees:* $413 full-time, $207 per term part-time. *Room only:* $2860.
Applying *Options:* electronic application, early admission, early action, deferred entrance. *Application fee:* $50. *Required:* high school transcript. *Required for some:* letters of recommendation. *Recommended:* essay or personal statement. *Application deadlines:* 1/15 (freshmen), 1/15 (out-of-state freshmen), 4/30 (transfers), 11/30 (early action). *Notification:* 4/30 (freshmen), 4/30 (out-of-state freshmen), continuous (transfers), 1/31 (early action).
Freshman Application Contact Dr. Salim Kanaan, Director of Admissions Office, American University of Beirut, PO Box 11-236, Beirut 1107 2020, Lebanon. *Phone:* 961-1-374 374 Ext. 2592. *Fax:* 961-1-750775. *E-mail:* admissions@aub.edu.lb.

LEBANESE AMERICAN UNIVERSITY

Beirut, Lebanon **www.lau.edu.lb/**

Director of Admissions Leila Saleeby Dapher, Director of Admissions, Lebanese American University, PO Box 13-5053, Beirut, Lebanon. *Phone:* 961-1 786456 Ext. 1129. *Fax:* 961-1 786454. *E-mail:* admissions.beirut@lau.edu.lb.

MEXICO

ALLIANT INTERNATIONAL UNIVERSITY–MÉXICO CITY

Mexico City, Mexico **www.alliantmexico.edu/**

- **Independent** comprehensive, founded 1970, part of Alliant International University
- **Urban** campus
- **Coed** 68 undergraduate students, 47% full-time, 44% women, 56% men
- **Moderately difficult** entrance level, 71% of applicants were admitted

Undergraduates 32 full-time, 36 part-time. Students come from 9 states and territories, 8 other countries, 52% are from out of state, 3% African American, 15% Hispanic American, 43% international, 15% transferred in. *Retention:* 75% of 2006 full-time freshmen returned.
Freshmen *Admission:* 24 applied, 17 admitted, 11 enrolled. *Average high school GPA:* 3.2.
Faculty *Total:* 24, 33% full-time, 54% with terminal degrees. *Student/faculty ratio:* 12:1.
Majors Business administration and management; international business/trade/commerce; international relations and affairs; Latin American studies; liberal arts and sciences/liberal studies; management information systems; psychology; tourism and travel services management.
Academics *Calendar:* semesters. *Degrees:* bachelor's and master's. *Special study options:* accelerated degree program, advanced placement credit, English as a second language, internships, study abroad, summer session for credit.
Computers on Campus 15 computers/terminals are available on campus for general student use.
Student Life *Housing:* college housing not available. *Activities and organizations:* student-run newspaper, International Business Club, German Club, Student Council.
Standardized Tests *Required:* SAT or ACT (for admission).
Applying *Options:* electronic application, deferred entrance. *Application fee:* 500 Mexican pesos. *Required:* essay or personal statement, high school transcript, minimum 2.0 GPA, 1 letter of recommendation. *Required for some:* interview. *Recommended:* minimum 3.0 GPA. *Application deadlines:* rolling (freshmen), rolling (transfers).
Freshman Application Contact Ms. Susan Topham, Systemwide Director of Admissions, Alliant International University–México City, 10455 Pomerado Road, San Diego, CA 92131-1799. *Phone:* 858-635-4772. *Fax:* 858-635-4355. *E-mail:* admissions@alliantmexico.edu.

INSTITUTO TECNOLÓGICO Y DE ESTUDIOS SUPERIORES DE MONTERREY, CAMPUS CENTRAL DE VERACRUZ

Córdoba, Mexico **www.ver.itesm.mx/**

Director of Admissions Ing. Luis Pablo Villareal, Registrar, Instituto Tecnológico y de Estudios Superiores de Monterrey, Campus Central de Veracruz, Avenida Eugenio Garza Sada 1, Apartado Postal 314, 94500 Córdoba, Veracruz, Mexico. *Phone:* 27-13-23-40 Ext. 123.

INSTITUTO TECNOLÓGICO Y DE ESTUDIOS SUPERIORES DE MONTERREY, CAMPUS CHIAPAS

Tuxtla Gutiérrez, Mexico **www.chs.itesm.mx/**

Director of Admissions Lic. Luis Enrique Cancino, Registrar, Instituto Tecnológico y de Estudios Superiores de Monterrey, Campus Chiapas, Carretera a Tapanatepec Km 149&746, Apartado Postal 312, 29000 Tuxtla Gutiérrez, Chiapas, Mexico. *Phone:* 96-15-1723.

INSTITUTO TECNOLÓGICO Y DE ESTUDIOS SUPERIORES DE MONTERREY, CAMPUS CHIHUAHUA

Chihuahua, Mexico **www.chi.itesm.mx/**

Director of Admissions Ing. Juan Manuel Fernandez, Registrar, Instituto Tecnológico y de Estudios Superiores de Monterrey, Campus Chihuahua, Colegio Militar 4700, Colonia Nombre de Dios, Apartado Postal 728, 31300 Chihuahua, Chihuahua, Mexico. *Phone:* 14-17-48-58 Ext. 117.

INSTITUTO TECNOLÓGICO Y DE ESTUDIOS SUPERIORES DE MONTERREY, CAMPUS CIUDAD DE MÉXICO

Ciudad de Mexico, Mexico **www.ccm.itesm.mx/**

Freshman Application Contact Admissions Office, Instituto Tecnológico y de Estudios Superiores de Monterrey, Campus Ciudad de México, Calle del Puente #222 esquina con Periférico, 14380 Colonia Huipulco, Tlalpan, MDF, Mexico. *Phone:* 5-673-6488.

INSTITUTO TECNOLÓGICO Y DE ESTUDIOS SUPERIORES DE MONTERREY, CAMPUS CIUDAD JUÁREZ

Ciudad Juárez, Mexico **www.cdj.itesm.mx/**

Director of Admissions Lic. Alberto Trejo, Registrar, Instituto Tecnológico y de Estudios Superiores de Monterrey, Campus Ciudad Juárez, Boulevard Tomas Fernandez y Avenida A J Bermudez, Apartado Postal 3105-J, 32320 Ciudad Juárez, Chihuahua, Mexico. *Phone:* 16-17-88-07 Ext. 113.

INSTITUTO TECNOLÓGICO Y DE ESTUDIOS SUPERIORES DE MONTERREY, CAMPUS CIUDAD OBREGÓN

Ciudad Obregón, Mexico **www.cob.itesm.mx/**

Director of Admissions Lic. Judith Almeida, Registrar, Instituto Tecnológico y de Estudios Superiores de Monterrey, Campus Ciudad Obregón, Dr Norman E Borlaug Km 14, Apartado Postal 662, 85000 Ciudad Obregón, Sonora, Mexico. *Phone:* 64-15-03-12.

INSTITUTO TECNOLÓGICO Y DE ESTUDIOS SUPERIORES DE MONTERREY, CAMPUS COLIMA

Colima, Mexico **www.col.itesm.mx/**

Director of Admissions Lic. Manuel Perez Rivera, Registrar, Instituto Tecnológico y de Estudios Superiores de Monterrey, Campus Colima, Prolongacion Ignacio Sandoval s/n, Fraccionamiento Jardines de Vista Hermosa, Apartado Postal 190, 28010 Colima, Colima, Mexico. *Phone:* 33-12-53-39.

INSTITUTO TECNOLÓGICO Y DE ESTUDIOS SUPERIORES DE MONTERREY, CAMPUS CUERNAVACA

Temixco, Mexico **www.mor.itesm.mx/**

Director of Admissions Lic. Miguel Angel Machua S., Registrar, Instituto Tecnológico y de Estudios Superiores de Monterrey, Campus Cuernavaca, Paseo de la Reforma 182-A, Colonia Lomas de Cuernavaca, 62000 Temixco, Morelos, Mexico. *Phone:* 73 18-49-57.

INSTITUTO TECNOLÓGICO Y DE ESTUDIOS SUPERIORES DE MONTERREY, CAMPUS ESTADO DE MÉXICO

Estado de Mexico, Mexico **www.cem.itesm.mx/**

Director of Admissions Prof. Jose de Jesus Molina, Registrar, Instituto Tecnológico y de Estudios Superiores de Monterrey, Campus Estado de México, Carretera Lago de Guadalupe Km. 3.5, Atizapan de Zaragoza, Estado de Mexico 52926, Mexico. *Phone:* 5-873-3600.

INSTITUTO TECNOLÓGICO Y DE ESTUDIOS SUPERIORES DE MONTERREY, CAMPUS GUADALAJARA

Zapopan, Mexico **www.gda.itesm.mx/**

Director of Admissions Ms. Janet Martell Sotomayor, Registration Director, Instituto Tecnológico y de Estudios Superiores de Monterrey, Campus Guadalajara, Avenida General Ramón Corona 2514, 44100 Zapopan, Jalisco, Mexico. *Phone:* 3-669-3006.

INSTITUTO TECNOLÓGICO Y DE ESTUDIOS SUPERIORES DE MONTERREY, CAMPUS HIDALGO

Pachuca, Mexico **www.hgo.itesm.mx/**

Director of Admissions Lic. Lizbet Melo, Registrar, Instituto Tecnológico y de Estudios Superiores de Monterrey, Campus Hidalgo, Boulevard Felipe Angeles, No. 2003, C.P. 42080, Pachuca, Hildago, Mexico. *Phone:* 714-25-00 Ext. 128.

INSTITUTO TECNOLÓGICO Y DE ESTUDIOS SUPERIORES DE MONTERREY, CAMPUS IRAPUATO

Irapuato, Mexico **www.ira.itesm.mx/**

Director of Admissions Ing. Marcela Beltrán, Registrar, Instituto Tecnológico y de Estudios Superiores de Monterrey, Campus Irapuato, Paseo Mirador del Valle No. 445, Col. Villas de Irapuato, Apartado Postal 568, 36660 Irapuato, Guanajuato, Mexico. *Phone:* 46-230342.

INSTITUTO TECNOLÓGICO Y DE ESTUDIOS SUPERIORES DE MONTERREY, CAMPUS LAGUNA

Torreón, Mexico **www.lag.itesm.mx/**

Director of Admissions Ing. Aroldo Camargo Soto, Registrar, Instituto Tecnológico y de Estudios Superiores de Monterrey, Campus Laguna, Paseo del Tecnologico s/n Ampliacion La Rosita, Apartado Postal 506, 27250 Torreón, Coahuila, Mexico. *Phone:* 17-20-66-61 Ext. 23.

INSTITUTO TECNOLÓGICO Y DE ESTUDIOS SUPERIORES DE MONTERREY, CAMPUS LEÓN

León, Mexico **www.leo.itesm.mx/**

Director of Admissions Lic. Eddie Villegas, Registrar, Instituto Tecnológico y de Estudios Superiores de Monterrey, Campus León, Apdo. Postal No. 872, Leon 37120, Mexico. *Phone:* 47-17-10-00 Ext. 131.

INSTITUTO TECNOLÓGICO Y DE ESTUDIOS SUPERIORES DE MONTERREY, CAMPUS MAZATLÁN

Mazatlán, Mexico **www.maz.itesm.mx/**

Director of Admissions Ing. Martin Ley Urias, Registrar, Instituto Tecnológico y de Estudios Superiores de Monterrey, Campus Mazatlán, Carretera Mazatlan-Higueras, Km 3, Camino al Conchi, Apartado Postal 799, 82000 Mazatlán, Sinaloa, Mexico. *Phone:* 69-80-1143.

INSTITUTO TECNOLÓGICO Y DE ESTUDIOS SUPERIORES DE MONTERREY, CAMPUS MONTERREY

Monterrey, Mexico **www.mty.itesm.mx/**

Director of Admissions Lic. Carlos Ordoñez, International Student Advisor, Instituto Tecnológico y de Estudios Superiores de Monterrey, Campus Monterrey, Avenue Eugenio Garza Sada, #2501 sur, Col. Tecnologico, Monterrey, Nuevo Leon 64849, Mexico. *Phone:* 52-81-83284065 Ext. 3942. *Toll-free phone:* 52-81-83284065 (in-state); 52-81-83593293 (out-of-state).

INSTITUTO TECNOLÓGICO Y DE ESTUDIOS SUPERIORES DE MONTERREY, CAMPUS QUERÉTARO

Santiago de Querétaro, Mexico **www.qro.itesm.mx/**

Director of Admissions Lic. Marco Vinicio Lopez, Registrar, Instituto Tecnológico y de Estudios Superiores de Monterrey, Campus Querétaro, Avenida Epigmenio Gonzalez #500, Fracc. San Pablo, Queretaro 76130, Mexico. *Phone:* 42-17-38-25 Ext. 156.

INSTITUTO TECNOLÓGICO Y DE ESTUDIOS SUPERIORES DE MONTERREY, CAMPUS SALTILLO

Saltillo, Mexico **www.sal.itesm.mx/**

Director of Admissions Lic. Esteban Ramos, Registrar, Instituto Tecnológico y de Estudios Superiores de Monterrey, Campus Saltillo, Prolongacion Juan de la Barrera 1241 Ote, Apartado Postal 539, 25270 Saltillo, Coahuila, Mexico. *Phone:* 84-15-06-90 Ext. 12.

INSTITUTO TECNOLÓGICO Y DE ESTUDIOS SUPERIORES DE MONTERREY, CAMPUS SAN LUIS POTOSÍ

San Luis Potosí, Mexico **www.slp.itesm.mx/**

Director of Admissions Ing. Consuelo Gonzalez, Registrar, Instituto Tecnológico y de Estudios Superiores de Monterrey, Campus San Luis Potosí, Avenida Robles 600, Colonia Jacarandas, Apartado Postal 1473 Suc E, 78140 San Luis Potosí, SLP, Mexico. *Phone:* 48-13-3441 Ext. 14.

INSTITUTO TECNOLÓGICO Y DE ESTUDIOS SUPERIORES DE MONTERREY, CAMPUS SINALOA

Culiacán, Mexico **www.sin.itesm.mx/**

Director of Admissions Lic. Hugo Guerrero, Registrar, Instituto Tecnológico y de Estudios Superiores de Monterrey, Campus Sinaloa, Boulevard Culiacán 3773, Apartado Postal 69-F, 80800 Culiacán, Sinaloa, Mexico. *Phone:* 67-14-03-69.

INSTITUTO TECNOLÓGICO Y DE ESTUDIOS SUPERIORES DE MONTERREY, CAMPUS SONORA NORTE

Hermosillo, Mexico **www.her.itesm.mx/**

Director of Admissions Ing. Victor Eduardo Perez Orozco, Library and Admissions/Registration Director, Instituto Tecnológico y de Estudios Superiores de Monterrey, Campus Sonora Norte, Carretera Hermosillo-Nogales Km 9, Apartado Postal 216, 83000 Hermosillo, Sonora, Mexico. *Phone:* 62-15-52-05 Ext. 131.

INSTITUTO TECNOLÓGICO Y DE ESTUDIOS SUPERIORES DE MONTERREY, CAMPUS TAMPICO

Altimira, Mexico **www.tam.itesm.mx/**

Director of Admissions Ing. Javier Ponce, Registrar, Instituto Tecnológico y de Estudios Superiores de Monterrey, Campus Tampico, Apdo. Postal 7, Conedor Industrial, Canekra Tampico-Mark, Altamira 89600, Mexico. *Phone:* 126-4-19-79.

INSTITUTO TECNOLÓGICO Y DE ESTUDIOS SUPERIORES DE MONTERREY, CAMPUS TOLUCA

Toluca, Mexico **www.tol.itesm.mx/**

Director of Admissions Ing. Victor M. Martinez Orta, Registrar, Instituto Tecnológico y de Estudios Superiores de Monterrey, Campus Toluca, Ex-hacienda La Pila, 100 metros al norte de San Antonio Buenavista, 50252 Toluca, Estado de Mexico, Mexico. *Phone:* 72-74-11-92.

INSTITUTO TECNOLÓGICO Y DE ESTUDIOS SUPERIORES DE MONTERREY, CAMPUS ZACATECAS

Zacatecas, Mexico **www.zac.itesm.mx/**

Director of Admissions Lic. de Lourdes Zorrilla, Business Affairs Director and Registrar, Instituto Tecnológico y de Estudios Superiores de Monterrey, Campus Zacatecas, Calzada Pedro Coronel #16, Frente al Club Bernades, Municipio de Guadalupe, 98000 Zacatecas, Zacatecas, Mexico. *Phone:* 49-23-00-40.

UNIVERSIDAD DE LAS AMERICAS, A.C.

Mexico City, Mexico

UNIVERSIDAD DE LAS AMÉRICAS–PUEBLA

Puebla, Mexico **www.pue.udlap.mx/**

Freshman Application Contact Lic. Jorge A. Varela Olivares, Chief of Admissions, Universidad de las Américas–Puebla, Cholula Apartado 359, 72820 Cholula, Mexico. *Phone:* 22-29-20-17 Ext. 4015. *E-mail:* jvarela@udlapvms.pue.udlap.mx.

UNIVERSIDAD DE MONTERREY

San Pedro Garza Garcia, Mexico

MONACO

THE INTERNATIONAL UNIVERSITY OF MONACO

Monte Carlo, Monaco **www.monaco.edu/**

Freshman Application Contact Dr. Gisele Dudognon, Director of Admissions, The International University of Monaco, 2, Avenue Albert II, MC-98000 Principality of Monaco, Monaco. *Phone:* 377-97986 994. *Fax:* 377-92052 830. *E-mail:* gdudognon@monaco.edu.

NICARAGUA

AVE MARIA COLLEGE OF THE AMERICAS

San Marcos, Nicaragua **www.avemaria.edu.ni/**

Director of Admissions Mr. Patrick Clark, Director of Admissions, Ave Maria College of the Americas, San Marcos, Carazo, Nicaragua. *Phone:* 43-22314-138. *E-mail:* pclark@avemaria.edu.ni.

NIGERIA

The Nigerian Baptist Theological Seminary

Ogbomoso, Nigeria

Director of Admissions Mr. Daniel F. Oroniran, Registrar, The Nigerian Baptist Theological Seminary, PO Box 30, Ogbomoso, Oyo, Nigeria. *Phone:* 038-710011.

SOUTH AFRICA

University of South Africa

Pretoria, South Africa

SPAIN

Saint Louis University, Madrid

Madrid, Spain **spain.slu.edu/**

- **Independent Roman Catholic (Jesuit)** comprehensive, part of Saint Louis University
- **Urban** 1-acre campus
- **Endowment** $800.0 million
- **Coed**
- **Moderately difficult** entrance level

Faculty *Student/faculty ratio:* 8:1.
Academics *Calendar:* semesters. *Degrees:* bachelor's and master's.
Student Life *Campus security:* 24-hour patrols.
Standardized Tests *Required:* SAT or ACT (for admission).
Costs (2007–08) *Comprehensive fee:* $28,200 includes full-time tuition ($19,800) and room and board ($8400).
Applying *Options:* electronic application. *Application fee:* $45. *Required:* essay or personal statement, high school transcript. *Required for some:* interview.
Freshman Application Contact Ms. Phyllis Chaney, Director, Saint Louis University, Madrid, Avda. del Valle 34, Madrid 28003, Spain. *Phone:* 34-91-554-5858. *Fax:* 34-91-554-6202. *E-mail:* chaneyp@madrid.slu.edu.

See page 2894 for the College Close-Up.

Schiller International University

Madrid, Spain **www.schillermadrid.edu/**

- **Independent** comprehensive, founded 1967, part of Schiller International University
- **Urban** campus
- **Coed**
- **Minimally difficult** entrance level

Schiller International University (SIU) is an independent American university with campuses in England, France, Germany, Spain, Switzerland, and the United States. Students can transfer from campus to campus without loss of credit. English is the language of instruction at all campuses. SIU offers undergraduate and graduate students an American education in an international setting.

Academics *Calendar:* semesters. *Degrees:* associate, bachelor's, and master's.
Standardized Tests *Required:* TOEFL for international (for admission). *Recommended:* SAT (for admission).
Costs (2007–08) *Tuition:* 14,750 euros full-time, 375 euros per credit part-time. *Required fees:* 475 euros full-time.
Financial Aid Of all full-time matriculated undergraduates who enrolled in 2006, 3 Federal Work-Study jobs (averaging $4880). *Financial aid deadline:* 4/15.
Applying *Options:* deferred entrance. *Application fee:* 60 euros. *Required:* essay or personal statement, high school transcript. *Recommended:* minimum 2.0 GPA, interview.
Freshman Application Contact Ms. Kamala Dontamsetti, Associate Director of Admissions, Schiller International University, San Bernardo 97-99, Edif. Colomina, 28015 Madrid, Spain. *Phone:* 727-736-5082 Ext. 234. *Fax:* 727-734-0359. *E-mail:* admissions@schiller.edu.

See page 2896 for the College Close-Up.

SWITZERLAND

Ecole Hôtelière de Lausanne

Lausanne, Switzerland **www.ehl.ch/**

- **Independent** 4-year, founded 1893, part of Hautes Ecoles Spécialisées de Suisse Occidentale (HES-SO) (Universityof Applied Sciences) + NEASC Commission on Institutions of Higher Education
- **Suburban** 5-acre campus
- **Coed** 1,397 undergraduate students
- **Moderately difficult** entrance level, 45% of applicants were admitted

Undergraduates 0.7% African American, 5% Asian American or Pacific Islander, 6% Hispanic American, 0.3% Native American, 20% live on campus.
Freshmen *Admission:* 516 applied, 234 admitted. *Test scores:* SAT critical reading scores over 500: 96%; SAT math scores over 500: 99%; SAT writing scores over 500: 90%; ACT scores over 18: 100%; SAT critical reading scores over 600: 30%; SAT math scores over 600: 34%; SAT writing scores over 600: 30%; ACT scores over 24: 70%; SAT critical reading scores over 700: 5%; SAT math scores over 700: 9%; SAT writing scores over 700: 5%.
Faculty *Total:* 86, 65% full-time. *Student/faculty ratio:* 13:1.
Majors Hospitality administration; hotel and restaurant management.
Academics *Degrees:* diplomas, bachelor's, and master's. *Special study options:* English as a second language.
Computers on Campus 10 computers/terminals and 2,000 ports are available on campus for general student use. Students can access the following: campus intranet, computer help desk, free student e-mail accounts, online (class) grades, online (class) registration, online (class) schedules. Campuswide network is available. 1% of college-owned or -operated housing units are wired for high-speed Internet access. Wireless service is available via entire campus.
Student Life *Housing options:* coed. Campus housing is university owned. Freshman applicants given priority for college housing. *Activities and organizations:* student-run newspaper, Student Ambassador Programme, Fête Finale Planning Committee, Career Club, Yearbook, Student Council, Student Social Space, Sailing Committee. *Campus security:* 24-hour emergency response devices and patrols, controlled dormitory access. *Student services:* health clinic, personal/psychological counseling.
Standardized Tests *Required for some:* SAT and SAT Subject Tests or ACT (for admission).
Costs (2008–09) *Tuition:* 27,229 Swiss francs full-time.
Applying *Options:* electronic application, early admission, early decision, deferred entrance. *Application fee:* 240 Swiss francs. *Required:* essay or personal statement, high school transcript, interview. *Required for some:* letters of recommendation. *Application deadline:* 4/1 (freshmen). *Early decision deadline:* 11/1. *Notification:* continuous (freshmen), 12/21 (early decision).
Freshman Application Contact Ecole Hôtelière de Lausanne, Le Chalet-a-Gobet, CH-1000 Lausanne 25, Switzerland. *Phone:* 41-21 785 1111.

FRANKLIN COLLEGE SWITZERLAND

Sorengo, Switzerland **www.fc.edu/**

- **Independent** 4-year, founded 1969
- **Suburban** 5-acre campus with easy access to Milan
- **Endowment** $476,971
- **Coed** 378 undergraduate students, 98% full-time, 64% women, 36% men
- **Moderately difficult** entrance level, 72% of applicants were admitted

Franklin College is a four-year, coeducational, residential American liberal arts college located in southern Switzerland that specializes in international studies. Students from more than fifty countries attend. Semester and year-abroad students are welcome. Summer sessions are offered May–July. Every semester, students take faculty-led academic travel trips to destinations worldwide.

Undergraduates 369 full-time, 9 part-time. Students come from 35 states and territories, 57 other countries, 100% are from out of state, 6% transferred in, 88% live on campus. *Retention:* 69% of 2006 full-time freshmen returned.

Freshmen *Admission:* 623 applied, 446 admitted, 134 enrolled. *Average high school GPA:* 3.2. *Test scores:* SAT critical reading scores over 500: 91%; SAT math scores over 500: 78%; SAT writing scores over 500: 87%; ACT scores over 18: 100%; SAT critical reading scores over 600: 52%; SAT math scores over 600: 42%; SAT writing scores over 600: 44%; ACT scores over 24: 67%; SAT critical reading scores over 700: 15%; SAT math scores over 700: 7%; SAT writing scores over 700: 9%; ACT scores over 30: 8%.

Faculty *Total:* 52, 42% full-time, 52% with terminal degrees. *Student/faculty ratio:* 10:1.

Majors Art history, criticism and conservation; communication and media related; European studies; history; international business/trade/commerce; international economics; international finance; international relations and affairs; liberal arts and sciences/liberal studies; literature; modern languages; Romance languages.

Academics *Calendar:* semesters. *Degrees:* associate and bachelor's. *Special study options:* accelerated degree program, advanced placement credit, double majors, English as a second language, honors programs, independent study, internships, part-time degree program, study abroad, summer session for credit.

Computers on Campus 57 computers/terminals are available on campus for general student use. Students can access the following: campus intranet, computer help desk, free student e-mail accounts, online (class) grades, online (class) registration, online (class) schedules. Campuswide network is available. 100% of college-owned or -operated housing units are wired for high-speed Internet access. Wireless service is available via entire campus.

Student Life *Housing:* on-campus residence required through sophomore year. *Options:* coed, women-only. Campus housing is university owned and leased by the school. Freshman campus housing is guaranteed. *Activities and organizations:* drama/theater group, student-run newspaper, Student Assembly, newspaper, Literary Society, Drama Society, Photography Club. *Campus security:* controlled dormitory access, late night patrols by trained security personnel. *Student services:* health clinic, personal/psychological counseling.

Athletics *Intramural sports:* basketball M (c)/W (c), ice hockey M (c)/W (c), sailing M (c)/W (c), skiing (cross-country) M (c)/W (c), skiing (downhill) M (c)/W (c), soccer M (c)/W (c), swimming and diving M (c)/W (c), tennis M (c)/W (c), volleyball M (c)/W (c), water polo M (c), weight lifting M (c)/W (c).

Standardized Tests *Required:* SAT or ACT (for admission). *Recommended:* SAT Subject Tests (for admission).

Costs (2007–08) *Comprehensive fee:* $41,560 includes full-time tuition ($29,500), mandatory fees ($1360), and room and board ($10,700). Part-time tuition: $2590 per course. *Required fees:* $285 per term part-time. *College room only:* $7800. Room and board charges vary according to board plan and housing facility. *Payment plan:* deferred payment. *Waivers:* employees or children of employees.

Applying *Options:* electronic application, early admission, early action, deferred entrance. *Application fee:* $85. *Required:* essay or personal statement, high school transcript, minimum 2.0 GPA, 3 letters of recommendation. *Recommended:* interview. *Application deadlines:* 3/15 (freshmen), 6/15 (transfers), 12/1 (early action). *Notification:* continuous (freshmen), continuous (transfers), 1/15 (early action).

Freshman Application Contact Ms. Karen Ballard, Director of Admissions, Franklin College Switzerland, 91-31 Queens Boulevard, Suite 411, Elmhurst, NY 11373. *Phone:* 718-335-6800. *Fax:* 718-335-6733. *E-mail:* info@fc.edu.

See page 2884 for the College Close-Up.

GLION INSTITUTE OF HIGHER EDUCATION

Glion-sur-Montreux, Switzerland

INTERNATIONAL UNIVERSITY IN GENEVA

Geneva, Switzerland **www.iun.ch/**

- **Private** comprehensive
- **Urban** campus
- **Coed** 112 undergraduate students, 100% full-time, 47% women, 53% men
- **Moderately difficult** entrance level

Undergraduates 112 full-time. Students come from 62 other countries, 6% transferred in. *Retention:* 94% of 2006 full-time freshmen returned.

Freshmen *Admission:* 29 enrolled. *Average high school GPA:* 2.5.

Faculty *Total:* 44, 18% full-time, 36% with terminal degrees. *Student/faculty ratio:* 7:1.

Majors Business administration and management; international relations and affairs; mass communication/media.

Academics *Calendar:* trimesters. *Degrees:* bachelor's and master's. *Special study options:* academic remediation for entering students, accelerated degree program, adult/continuing education programs, advanced placement credit, double majors, English as a second language, independent study, off-campus study, part-time degree program, study abroad, summer session for credit.

Computers on Campus 30 computers/terminals are available on campus for general student use. Students can access the following: campus intranet, computer help desk, free student e-mail accounts, online (class) schedules. Campuswide network is available. Wireless service is available via classrooms, student centers.

Student Life *Housing:* college housing not available. *Activities and organizations:* student-run newspaper, UNICEF, UNITED NATIONS Women Bazaar. *Student services:* personal/psychological counseling.

Athletics *Intercollegiate sports:* basketball M, tennis M/W, volleyball W.

Costs (2007–08) *Tuition:* 32,250 Swiss francs full-time.

Applying *Options:* electronic application, early decision, early action, deferred entrance. *Application fee:* 140 Swiss francs. *Required:* essay or personal statement, high school transcript, minimum 2.0 GPA, letters of recommendation, TOEFL for students whose first language is not English. *Required for some:* interview. *Application deadlines:* rolling (freshmen), rolling (transfers). *Notification:* continuous (freshmen), continuous (transfers).

Freshman Application Contact Ms. Sanela Pavlovic, Admissions Officer, International University in Geneva, International University in Geneva, ICC, Rte. de Pre-Bois 20, Geneva 1215, Switzerland. *Phone:* 41-22710-7110. *Toll-free phone:* 41-22710-7110. *Fax:* 41-22710-7111. *E-mail:* admissions@iun.ch.

See page 2888 for the College Close-Up.

LES ROCHES, SWISS HOTEL ASSOCIATION, SCHOOL OF HOTEL MANAGEMENT

Bluche, Switzerland

SCHILLER INTERNATIONAL UNIVERSITY, AMERICAN COLLEGE OF SWITZERLAND

Leysin, Switzerland **www.american-college.com/**

- **Independent** comprehensive, founded 1963, part of Schiller International University
- **Small-town** 15-acre campus with easy access to Geneva
- **Coed**
- **Minimally difficult** entrance level

Schiller International University (SIU) is an independent American university with campuses in England, France, Germany, Spain, Switzerland, and the United States. Students can transfer from campus to campus without loss of

credit. English is the language of instruction at all campuses. SIU offers undergraduate and graduate students an American education in an international setting.

Faculty *Student/faculty ratio:* 5:1.
Academics *Calendar:* semesters. *Degrees:* associate, bachelor's, and master's.
Student Life *Campus security:* 24-hour emergency response devices and patrols.
Costs (2007–08) *Comprehensive fee:* 39,830 Swiss francs includes full-time tuition (28,650 Swiss francs) and room and board (11,180 Swiss francs). Part-time tuition: 800 Swiss francs per course.
Applying *Options:* deferred entrance. *Application fee:* $60. *Required:* essay or personal statement, high school transcript, minimum 2.0 GPA, 1 letter of recommendation.
Freshman Application Contact Ms. Kamala Dontamsetti, Assistant Director of Admissions, Schiller International University, American College of Switzerland, 300 East Bay Drive, Largo, FL 33770. *Phone:* 813-736-5082. *Toll-free phone:* 800-336-4133. *Fax:* 813-734-0359. *E-mail:* admissions@schiller.edu.

See page 2896 for the College Close-Up.

TAIWAN

CHRIST'S COLLEGE
Taipei, Taiwan

UNITED ARAB EMIRATES

THE AMERICAN UNIVERSITY IN DUBAI
Dubai, United Arab Emirates **www.aud.edu**

- **Proprietary** comprehensive, founded 1995, administratively affiliated with American InterContinental University
- **Urban** campus
- **Coed**
- 56% of applicants were admitted

Faculty *Student/faculty ratio:* 25:1.
Academics *Calendar:* quarters. *Degrees:* bachelor's and master's.
Student Life *Campus security:* 24-hour patrols.
Standardized Tests *Required for some:* SAT (for admission). *Recommended:* SAT (for admission).
Applying *Options:* early admission. *Application fee:* 50 United Arab Emirates dirhams. *Required:* high school transcript, minimum 2.0 GPA, 2 letters of recommendation, TOEFL and SAT I or the English and Math Placement test to be taken at American University of Dubai. *Recommended:* essay or personal statement.
Freshman Application Contact Ms. Sarah McConnell, Admissions Coordinator, The American University in Dubai, PO Box 28282, Dubai. *Phone:* 971-4 3948889. *Fax:* 971-4 399 8899. *E-mail:* admissions@aud.edu.

AMERICAN UNIVERSITY OF SHARJAH
Sharjah, United Arab Emirates **www.aus.edu/**

Director of Admissions Ali Shuhaimy, Dean of Admissions, American University of Sharjah, PO Box 26666, Sharjah, United Arab Emirates. *Phone:* 971- 6 515-5555.

UNITED KINGDOM

AMERICAN INTERCONTINENTAL UNIVERSITY-LONDON
London, United Kingdom **www.aiuniv.edu/**

- **Proprietary** comprehensive, founded 1970, administratively affiliated with American InterContinental University
- **Urban** campus
- **Coed**
- **Minimally difficult** entrance level

Majors Animation, interactive technology, video graphics and special effects; art; audiovisual communications technologies related; computer graphics; computer/information technology services administration related; design and visual communications; fashion/apparel design; fashion merchandising; graphic design; interior design; international business/trade/commerce; marketing/marketing management.
Academics *Calendar:* five 10-week terms. *Degrees:* associate, bachelor's, and master's. *Special study options:* academic remediation for entering students, accelerated degree program, double majors, English as a second language, independent study, internships, part-time degree program, study abroad, summer session for credit.
Student Life *Activities and organizations:* student-run newspaper, Student Government Association, Drama Group, International Interior Designers Association. *Campus security:* 24-hour emergency response devices, controlled dormitory access. *Student services:* personal/psychological counseling.
Costs (2008–09) *Tuition:* contact campus for information. See: www.aiuniv.edu.
Applying *Options:* electronic application, deferred entrance. *Application fee:* $50. *Required:* essay or personal statement, high school transcript, interview. *Application deadlines:* rolling (freshmen), rolling (transfers). *Notification:* continuous (freshmen), continuous (transfers).
Director of Admissions Director of Admissions and Marketing, American InterContinental University-London, 110 Marylebone High Street, London W1U 4RY, United Kingdom. *Phone:* 44 207 467-6600. *Toll-free phone:* 888-567-5888.

BRITISH AMERICAN COLLEGE LONDON
London, United Kingdom

HURON UNIVERSITY USA IN LONDON
London, United Kingdom **www.huron.ac.uk/**

Freshman Application Contact Mr. Arvind Vepa, Director of Admissions, Huron University USA in London, 46/47 Russell Square, Bloomsbury, London WC1B 4JP, United Kingdom. *Phone:* 44-207-636-5667. *Fax:* 44-207-299-3297. *E-mail:* admissions@huron.ac.uk.

RICHMOND, THE AMERICAN INTERNATIONAL UNIVERSITY IN LONDON
Richmond, United Kingdom **www.richmond.ac.uk/**

- **Independent** comprehensive, founded 1972
- **Urban** 5-acre campus with easy access to London
- **Coed**
- **Moderately difficult** entrance level

Faculty *Student/faculty ratio:* 12:1.
Academics *Calendar:* semesters. *Degrees:* bachelor's, master's, and post-bachelor's certificates.
Student Life *Campus security:* 24-hour patrols.
Standardized Tests *Required:* SAT or ACT (for admission).
Costs (2007–08) *Comprehensive fee:* $36,000 includes full-time tuition ($25,000) and room and board ($11,000). Part-time tuition: $850 per credit.

Applying *Options:* electronic application, deferred entrance. *Application fee:* $50. *Required:* essay or personal statement, high school transcript, minimum 2.5 GPA, 1 letter of recommendation.

Freshman Application Contact Mr. Brian Davis, Director of United States Admissions, Richmond, The American International University in London, 343 Congress Street, Suite 3100, Boston, MA 02210-1214. *Phone:* 617-450-5617. *Fax:* 617-450-5601. *E-mail:* enroll@richmond.ac.uk.

See page 2892 for the College Close-Up.

SCHILLER INTERNATIONAL UNIVERSITY

London, United Kingdom **www.schiller.edu/**

- **Independent** comprehensive, founded 1970, part of Schiller International University
- **Urban** campus
- **Coed** 283 undergraduate students
- **Minimally difficult** entrance level

Schiller International University (SIU) is an independent American university with campuses in England, France, Germany, Spain, Switzerland, and the United States. Students can transfer from campus to campus without loss of credit. English is the language of instruction at all campuses. SIU offers undergraduate and graduate students an American education in an international setting.

Undergraduates Students come from 40 other countries, 81% are from out of state. *Retention:* 78% of 2006 full-time freshmen returned.

Faculty *Total:* 37, 68% full-time. *Student/faculty ratio:* 8:1.

Majors Economics; hotel/motel administration; interdisciplinary studies; international business/trade/commerce; international relations and affairs; liberal arts and sciences/liberal studies; pre-medical studies; pre-veterinary studies; psychology.

Academics *Calendar:* semesters. *Degrees:* associate, bachelor's, and master's. *Special study options:* accelerated degree program, adult/continuing education programs, advanced placement credit, double majors, English as a second language, independent study, internships, part-time degree program, student-designed majors, study abroad, summer session for credit.

Computers on Campus 39 computers/terminals are available on campus for general student use. Students can access the following: free student e-mail accounts.

Student Life *Housing options:* coed, women-only. Campus housing is university owned. *Activities and organizations:* student-run newspaper, Student council, Campus newspaper, Yearbook staff. *Campus security:* 24-hour patrols. *Student services:* personal/psychological counseling.

Athletics *Intramural sports:* archery M/W, baseball M/W, rugby M, soccer M/W, volleyball M/W.

Costs (2008–09) *Room and board:* $6700; room only: $4000.

Financial Aid Of all full-time matriculated undergraduates who enrolled in 2006, 2 Federal Work-Study jobs (averaging $4330).

Applying *Options:* deferred entrance. *Application fee:* 50 British pounds. *Required:* essay or personal statement, high school transcript. *Recommended:* minimum 2.0 GPA. *Application deadlines:* rolling (freshmen), rolling (transfers).

Freshman Application Contact Ms. Kamala Dontamsetti, Associate Director of Admissions, Schiller International University, 300 East Bay Drive, Largo, FL 33770. *Phone:* 727-736-5082 Ext. 239. *Toll-free phone:* 800-336-4133 Ext. 234. *Fax:* 727-734-0359. *E-mail:* admissions@schiller.edu.

See page 2896 for the College Close-Up.

THE AMERICAN UNIVERSITY OF ATHENS

ATHENS, GREECE

The University

Founded in 1982, the American University of Athens (AUA) is a senior college that awards bachelor's, master's, and doctoral degrees. It was recently upgraded to the status of a teaching and research institution and has an enrollment of approximately 1,000 students. Coeducational in all divisions, the University has students from the U.S., Greece, and thirty-eight other countries. Students may choose from more than forty-five undergraduate majors in the three schools and later may pursue graduate degrees in eight specializations. The small-sized classes, the use of English in instruction, the highly qualified faculty members, the curricula, and the teaching methodologies reflect the educational philosophy and structure of an American university, thus making the American University of Athens one of the most competitive institutions in Europe, especially in southeastern Europe. Major University divisions are the School of Business Administration, the School of Sciences and Engineering, and the School of Liberal Arts, as well as the Graduate School.

Location

The American University of Athens is located in the center of Athens, the ancient capital of Greece and home of the Olympic Games. The campus is very accessible to all modes of transportation. Athens is a warm and exciting city belonging to that privileged class of historic cities of antiquity that offer students a fascinating selection of cultural events. Greece has the reputation of being one of the safest and most hospitable countries in Europe.

Majors and Degrees

The University's undergraduate program in business administration is divided into three departments, all offering a bachelor's degree in business administration with various concentrations. In the Department of Accounting, Finance, and Economics, concentrations are available in accounting, economics, and finance. In the Department of Management, concentrations are available in hotel management, human resource management, management, management science and quantitative methods, shipping management, and travel and tourism management. In the Department of Marketing and General Business, concentrations are available in general business, international business, and marketing.

The School of Sciences and Engineering consists of two departments and awards Bachelor of Science degrees in various concentrations. In the Department of Computer Sciences and Engineering, concentrations are available in architectural engineering, civil engineering, computer hardware and digital electronics, computer information systems, computer science, electrical engineering, engineering science, manufacturing engineering, and mechanical engineering. In the Department of Natural Sciences and Mathematics, concentrations are available in biochemistry, biology, chemistry, mathematics, pharmacy, and physics. This department also offers a 2- or 2½-year program in premedical studies, preparing students for entrance into a school of medical or biomedical studies in the U.S.

The School of Liberal Arts has five departments, all leading to the Bachelor of Arts degree. The Department of Humanities has concentrations available in English literature and philosophy. The Department of Social Sciences has concentrations available in history, political science, psychology, and sociology. The Department of Communication has concentrations available in journalism and public relations. The Arts Department has concentrations available in art history and Byzantine studies. The Department of Applied Arts has concentrations available in fashion design and graphic design 3-D animation. The Department of Social Sciences also offers a four-year professional program in law studies in affiliation with the Institute of Legal Executives (ILEX) in the United Kingdom.

Students may select minor areas of study in art history, business, Byzantine studies, computer hardware and digital electronics, computer science, English literature, history, journalism, marketing for public relations students, philosophy, political science, psychology, public relations, and sociology.

Academic Programs

The academic year comprises two semesters. A winter intersession and two summer intersessions are also available. A minimum of 129 semester hours of appropriate academic credit is required for a Bachelor of Science degree in all business concentrations. In order to graduate, a student must maintain a minimum 2.0 cumulative grade point average as well as a minimum 2.0 grade point average for each of the major courses.

While the number of semester credit hours required for graduation varies with each concentration in the School of Sciences and Engineering, a minimum of 131 hours are required for a degree. In order to graduate, a student must maintain a minimum 2.0 cumulative grade point average as well as a minimum 2.0 grade point average for each of the major courses.

A degree in the liberal arts concentrations requires a minimum of 126 semester credit hours. In order to graduate, a student must maintain a minimum 2.0 cumulative grade point average as well as a minimum 2.0 grade point average for each of the major courses.

AUA offers a study-abroad program in the subject areas of art history, Greek literature and civilization, history, Modern Greek language, philosophy, political science, and more. A particular feature of the program is that a number of courses include visits to historical and archaeological sites, museums, and theaters. Athens, the host city of the 2004 Summer Olympics, represents a very exciting environment for a summer, semester, or year study-abroad program.

Academic Facilities

The American University of Athens students have access to the AUA library, which contains a wide variety of reference books and slides. Electronic data retrieval is also available, allowing access to the main European or American libraries and data banks. The Computer Center provides computing resources to students and offers access to computers and software programs. There are also biology, chemistry, electronics, and physics laboratories with state-of-the-art equipment.

Costs

Tuition and fees from spring to fall in 2008 are €8900 per academic year. Housing costs in the residence centers average €2900 (double room) and €3400 (single room) per academic year. Books and supplies cost about €250 per semester. Food and miscellaneous personal expenses for twelve months are approximately €2000 for a student with a conservative lifestyle. There is also a €460 insurance charge.

For the study-abroad program, tuition is €4450 per semester and housing costs €2900 for ten months.

Financial Aid

The American University of Athens offers an arrangement of financial assistance to full-time students through work-study programs. Successful candidates earn 40 percent of their semester tuition through completion of a 20-hour weekly work schedule during the fifteen-week semester.

Faculty

The faculty numbers 75 members, 85 percent of whom hold doctoral degrees. The student-faculty ratio is 6:1, and the average class size is 14 students. Academic, career, and personal counseling is available. AUA faculty members are creative, dedicated individuals who take the time to consider the welfare of their students.

Student Government

The Student Representative Council (SRC) is the governing body of the Student Association, which acts on behalf of the students, recommends changes, and refers problems to the appropriate heads. The council is made up of 8 elected members.

Admission Requirements

The American University of Athens seeks a student body that represents diverse backgrounds. A strong commitment to minority recruitment, equality of the sexes, and opportunities for the handicapped guarantee this diversity. AUA is proud of its history of providing opportunities for students from various educational and cultural backgrounds and from many geographic regions. International students are eligible to apply for admission if they have completed the equivalent of an American secondary school education (approximately twelve years of formal education starting at age 6) and have the appropriate diplomas or satisfactory results on exit examinations. It is strongly recommended, but not compulsory, that applicants submit a personal essay and two recommendation letters. Each candidate is required to have an interview. It is compulsory for freshmen who are not native speakers of English to take the AUA English Placement Test.

Transfer students in good academic standing are encouraged to apply to the American University of Athens. AUA grants transfer credits for courses to candidates with grades higher than C. Undergraduate transfer candidates are encouraged to file an application at least sixty days prior to the beginning of the semester of enrollment. Each applicant must arrange for official transcripts of all previous college records to be sent directly to AUA.

Application and Information

To be considered for admission, students are encouraged to file an application approximately sixty days prior to the beginning of the semester of enrollment. There is a €100 application fee. Subsequently, a copy of secondary school credentials must be filed with the Office of Admissions. The personal statement and recommendation letters are very important but not compulsory.

For application forms and additional information, students should contact:

Admissions Office
The American University of Athens
Kifissias Avenue and 4 Sochou Street
Athens 11525
Greece
Phone: 30210-7259301-3
Fax: 30210-7259304
E-mail: information@aua.edu
Web site: http://www.aua.edu

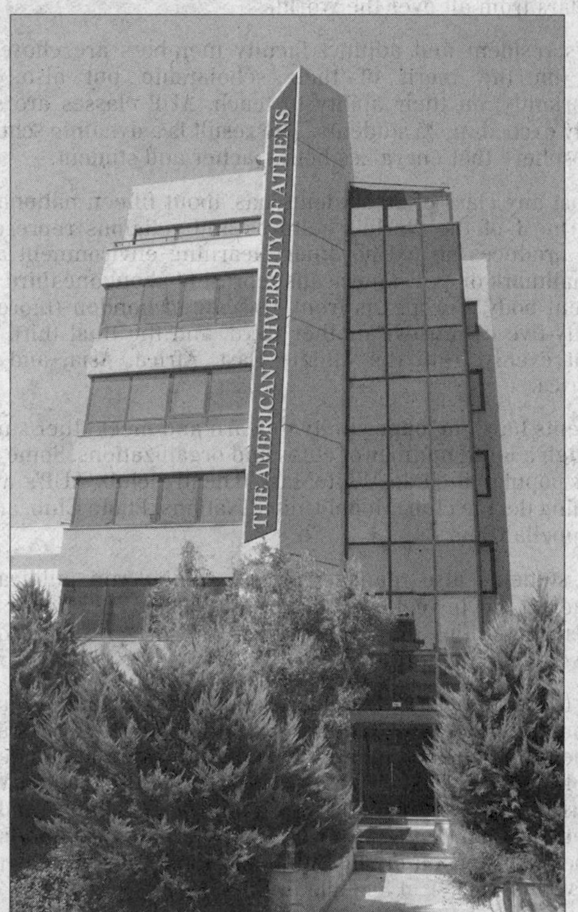

The American University of Athens.

THE AMERICAN UNIVERSITY OF PARIS

THE AMERICAN UNIVERSITY OF PARIS
knowledge, perspective, understanding

PARIS, FRANCE

The University

Founded in 1962, The American University of Paris (AUP) is among the oldest American institutions of higher education in Europe. AUP's mission is to educate generations of academic, social, political, intellectual, and business citizens of the world, and to enhance the advancement of scholarship in the arts and sciences in an international, multicultural, and plural environment.

AUP, which is accredited in the United States by the Commission on Higher Education of the Middle States Association of Colleges and Schools, is a nonprofit educational institution incorporated in the state of Delaware. The University is also recognized by the French Ministry of Education and is an institution of international higher education authorized to deliver bachelor's and master's degrees.

The American University of Paris is accredited in the U.S. by the Commission on Higher Education of the Middle States Association of Colleges and Schools.

The University enjoys a fine international faculty, representing fifteen nationalities. AUP supplements resident faculty members with a robust visiting professor program of renowned scholars from all over the world.

AUP's resident and adjunct faculty members are chosen not only on the merit of their scholarship but also, more importantly, on their ability to teach. AUP classes are small, rarely exceeding 25 students. The result is a dynamic scholastic atmosphere that energizes both teacher and student.

Almost any class of 20 students has about fifteen nationalities, with most of the world's cultures and religions represented. This produces an extraordinary learning environment and is the hallmark of AUP. Americans represent about one third of the student body, Europeans from Moscow to London (more than twenty-five countries) another third, and the final third come about evenly from the Middle East, Africa, Asia, and Latin America.

Students have the opportunity to learn and meet other students through a large number of clubs and organizations. Some of the most popular include WhiteMask Theatre club, AUP's award-winning debate club, Model United Nations, Photo Club, and the A'Cappella Choir.

AUP students also manage several student-run publications, including the biweekly student newspaper, *The Planet; Core,* AUP's humanities journal; *Scripta Politica et Economica;* and *Paris/Atlantic,* a journal of creative work.

AUP offers a liberal arts undergraduate curriculum of fourteen majors and thirty-two minors for the Bachelor of Arts and the Bachelor of Science degrees. In addition, five graduate degrees are offered: the Master of Arts in global communication; Master of Arts in international affairs, conflict resolution, and civil society development; Master of Arts in Middle East and Islamic studies; Master of Public Administration in strategic public policy; and Master of Science in finance.

The University's academic excellence, dynamic classroom experience, and genuinely international/multicultural environment have proven important advantages. Many AUP students go on to the finest graduate schools and careers in the United States, Europe, and elsewhere around the world.

AUP students live off campus, many in the beautiful Parisian neighborhoods near the University. The Housing Office helps AUP students find lodging in chambres de bonne (small private rooms generally found on the top floor of older French apartment buildings), with French hosts, or in apartments.

Location

AUP is an urban institution composed of six buildings centrally located in the seventh arrondissement of Paris, on the Left Bank, near the Eiffel Tower and the Seine. All of the landmarks of this historic city are easily reached by foot or public transportation. AUP students and professors take advantage of the urban campus's proximity to some of the world's best cultural and academic offerings.

Majors and Degrees

Undergraduate students at AUP can earn a Bachelor of Arts or a Bachelor of Science degree. Bachelor of Arts degrees are conferred in applied international finance, art history, comparative literature, computer science, European and Mediterranean cultures, film studies, French studies, history and social sciences, international business administration, international communications, international economics, international and comparative politics, psychology, and quantitative and computational methods in the social sciences.

Students may also elect to double major or minor in another field. Minors include the following: American studies, applied mathematics, applied statistics, art history, cities: architecture and urban culture, classical civilization, comparative literature, comparative European politics, comparative political communications, computer science, critical theory, development studies, European and Mediterranean cultures, film history and theory, film studies, fine arts, French studies, gender studies, global communications, global studies, history, information technology, international business administration, international economics, international journalism, international law, medieval studies, philosophy, psychology, Renaissance studies, social sciences, and theater and performance.

Academic Programs

Students plan their academic career following guidelines established in the AUP catalog and with the help of a faculty adviser. The bachelor's degree requires a minimum of 120 credit hours. Each completed course counts as 1 to 4 credits toward a degree. Every student at AUP follows a general education program that complements the student's work in the major and runs parallel to it over the course of a student's academic trajectory. The general education program, entitled Envisioning a World of Interdependence, requires students to fulfill the following requirements: FirstBridge, a freshman program of two creatively joined courses linked by a reflective seminar (7 credits); 6 credits of English writing and humanities; proficiency and the ability to engage in intellectual discourse in French; one course in natural or physical science and one course in mathematics; two courses (6 credits) in Comparing Worlds Past and Present: Historical and Cross-Cultural Understandings; and two courses (6 credits) in Mapping the World: Social Experience and Organization.

The English Foundation program was created for students whose mother tongue is not English and who need to improve their English skills, specifically in writing for academic purposes. This is a one- or two-semester curriculum designed to help students integrate into university education in English.

AUP has a fall and spring semester and one summer term.

The Dean's List, which is published at the end of each semester, includes the names of students who have achieved a distinguished level of academic performance. Chapters of the following honor societies exist at the University: Pi Delta Phi (National French Honor Society), Phi Sigma Iota (International Foreign Language Honor Society), Sigma Tau Delta (National English Honor Society), and Omicron Delta Epsilon (International Economics Honor Society).

Off-Campus Programs

AUP students are welcome to spend one or two semesters in an approved AUP study-abroad program at New York University, the University of California (Berkeley, Davis, Irvine, Los Angeles, Riverside, San Diego, Santa Barbara, or Santa Cruz), the University of Miami (Florida), or the University of Cape Town (South Africa). Individual arrangements are also possible with other universities.

Academic Facilities

The AUP Library houses more than 72,000 books and more than 6,000 print and electronic periodicals. Other databases, as well as a document delivery service, facilitate materials that are not owned by the library.

ARC@AUP (the Academic Resource Center) is a project designed to link technology to the curriculum and to supplement academic support services at AUP. On the ground floor of the Grenelle Building, ARC provides multiple services to students, including library research stations and video production equipment. Peer tutoring services, including the Writing Lab, are also available in the ARC space.

There are five student computer labs containing 100 IBM and Macintosh computers. Students have free e-mail accounts and Internet access as well as use of a variety of software, printers, projectors, and scanners.

Costs

Information on full-time tuition can be found on the Web site (http://www.aup.edu). Part-time students' tuition is determined on a per-credit basis. Students can estimate paying an additional €10,000 per academic year for housing, meals, and books, not including other discretionary spending.

Financial Aid

In keeping with AUP's mission to educate students from all over the world, AUP offers a program of University-funded scholarships and grants that are awarded on the basis of both a student's academic strength and the family's financial circumstances. Students with a good record of academic achievement are eligible for academic merit scholarships. Approximately 30 percent of students receive financial aid from the University.

A broad range of loan funds is available for students and is not restricted to American citizens. In addition to the traditional American student loan options, such as Federal Stafford Student, PLUS, and Signature loans, an International Student Loan Program now exists for non-American students.

Faculty

The ratio of students to full-time faculty members is 20:1. The faculty is dedicated to both research and teaching. There are no graduate assistants. Eighty percent of the full-time faculty members hold doctoral degrees from the world's most distinguished graduate schools. AUP faculty members represent more than fifteen nationalities; all are at least bilingual. All courses are taught by faculty members. AUP does not use teaching assistants for any of its courses.

Student Government

At the heart of AUP's student activities is the SGA, an elected body of executive officers, class officers, and departmental student representatives. Organized to deal with issues affecting the student body, AUP's strongly vocal SGA holds weekly Senate meetings, represents student needs to the administration, manages the student activities budget, and plans and promotes social events for the AUP community.

Admission Requirements

AUP evaluates applicants based on the breadth of their program of study, their academic record, the results of national examinations, and the evaluation of teachers and counselors. The applicant's written statement of purpose, as well as evidence of his or her maturity, also weighs heavily. Admission interviews, either in person or by telephone, are strongly encouraged.

Application and Information

Undergraduate candidates living in the United States, Canada, Mexico, Central and South America (except Brazil) should submit their application to the U.S. office:

U.S. Office
The American University of Paris
950 South Cherry Street, Suite 210
Denver, Colorado 80246
Phone: 303-757-6333
E-mail: usoffice@aup.edu
Web site: http://www.aup.edu

All other candidates, including undergraduates living in Brazil and graduate school applicants, should submit their applications to:

International Admissions Office
The American University of Paris
6, rue du Colonel Combes
75007 Paris
France
Phone: 33-1-40-62-07-20
E-mail: admissions@aup.edu
Web site: http://www.aup.edu

THE AMERICAN UNIVERSITY OF ROME

ROME, ITALY

The University

The American University of Rome (AUR) is a private, independent American institution of higher education in Rome, Italy, offering liberal arts studies and professional courses in an international environment that promotes cross-cultural understanding. The University offers American degree programs primarily to undergraduate students. It also serves study-abroad students, graduate students pursuing their degrees at other universities, and individuals interested in ongoing professional development and liberal arts studies.

Founded in 1969, the American University of Rome is the oldest degree-granting American university in Rome. A coeducational university, AUR offers undergraduate degrees in six disciplines to a student body of 560 students each semester. AUR is dedicated to encouraging academic achievement in its students and offers a curriculum that is designed to complement its high academic standards and to ensure an active-learning environment with a small student-faculty ratio.

The American University of Rome is accredited by the Accrediting Council for Independent Colleges and Schools (ACICS) in the United States and is licensed by the Education Licensure Commission of the District of Columbia (Washington, D.C., U.S.A.). AUR is incorporated in the District of Columbia as a nonprofit corporation.

Location

The University is located in a prestigious area of Rome, on the Janiculum, Rome's highest hill, just a few minutes' walk from the historic Trastevere district. The neighborhood surrounding AUR offers a full range of amenities, including restaurants, shops, cafés, and outdoor markets. Several bus lines connect it to the center of Rome. Located near the ancient Roman road Via Aurelia Antica and Porta San Pancrazio, AUR is just a few minutes from the heart of Rome.

Majors and Degrees

The American University of Rome offers a strong undergraduate curriculum with an international perspective. The Associate of Arts degree is offered in international business and liberal arts. The Bachelor of Arts degree is awarded in art history, communication, interdisciplinary studies, international relations, and Italian studies. A Bachelor of Science degree is awarded in business administration. All courses (except for Italian, Latin, and Greek language courses) are taught in English.

Academic Programs

All students must satisfy a general education requirement of 41 semester hours, of which 6 may be also used toward a minor. Consistent with the mission of the University, the program aims to develop important skills; address social issues of diversity, multiculturalism, and ethics; and draw on the rich resources of the city of Rome as a learning tool. All students, regardless of their major, should share a common dialogue. The objectives of the American University of Rome's general education program are to develop and strengthen basic skills that can prepare graduates for a modern working environment and that will be adaptable to a rapidly evolving economy; to cultivate an awareness of, and sensitivity to, cultural, ethnic, and social diversity and its importance in personal and professional decision making; to expand the intellectual, cultural, societal, aesthetic, and scientific horizons of students and enable them to discover not only the connections between academic disciplines but also the real-life applications of their knowledge; and, finally, to encourage active and responsible citizenship through knowledge of the forces shaping the actions of individuals and societies and through the development of critical thinking.

A student normally takes five courses (15 semester hours) each semester. A student is considered a sophomore after having completed 30 hours of credit, a junior once he or she has completed 60 hours of credit and officially declares a major field of study or enrolls in a degree program, and a senior after having completed 90 hours of course work.

One semester hour equals, at a minimum, 15 classroom contact hours of lectures, 30 hours of laboratory, and 45 hours of practicum. Internships also carry 3 semester hours and require 135 hours of practicum as well as oversight by an on-site supervisor and a faculty member as the project sponsor. An internship requires a daily log of activities. It also requires a final paper/presentation summarizing how goals were achieved and demonstrating the relationship of academic material to the work performed during the internship. The University also offers a study-abroad program for students studying at other universities.

Academic Facilities

The American University of Rome possesses a specialized library of course-related books and periodicals. The American University of Rome also provides electronic library services to its students and faculty members. These holdings are supplemented by a number of sizeable libraries in the city that are available to all students, including the Library of the British Council, the Library of the Church of Santa Susanna, and Centro Studi Americani. The University library can access a central catalog of the Italian National Library System and also participates in interlibrary loan programs.

There are two computer laboratories on campus that are available to students. All computers are IBM compatible and have access to e-mail, the Internet, and network printers. One laboratory is located in the library and is devoted principally to student research and term-paper requirements. The other computer laboratory is open for general student use.

A multimedia projector and laptop computer are available for classroom presentations using computer images and the Internet. Wireless services are available to students and faculty members from locations on and around the campus, such as the gardens and terraces of University buildings as well as a café and park near the campus.

In addition to overhead and slide projectors, an extensive slide collection, and various audio systems, the American University of Rome possesses tri-system videotape televisions for projecting films for cinema classes and other purposes. The videotape and DVD collection includes films that are essential to courses in Italian cinema and Italian opera as well as general cultural programs.

Costs

The comprehensive tuition fee at the American University of Rome for the current academic year for full-time undergraduates is €12,200. A nonrefundable tuition deposit of 500 U.S. dollars/euros is required from all new students, payable by the deadline indicated on the acceptance letter. The tuition deposit is deducted from the final tuition payment prior to the commencement of the semester. Some courses require travel or attendance at cultural events, as indicated by the course instructor. The cost of these events and travel are not included in the tuition and must be borne by the student.

Financial Aid

The American University of Rome is authorized by the U.S. Department of Education to participate in Title IV student financial assistance programs. Eligible students may apply to participate in the Federal Family Education Loan (FFEL) program. The American University of Rome is considered a foreign school and is not authorized to award federal grants. The federal financial aid that is available for United States citizens or eligible noncitizens through the FFEL program consists of subsidized and unsubsidized Federal Stafford Student Loans and parent PLUS loans.

The American University of Rome is committed to assisting students whose financial need and academic merit warrant support. The University aims to give every student the opportunity to take advantage of a high-quality AUR education and, therefore, offers scholarships. Funds that are awarded must be applied to tuition expenses. Assistance is awarded for at least one semester. The value of a single scholarship does not exceed the cost of one year's tuition.

Faculty

The American University of Rome has an international, culturally diverse faculty. Thirteen countries are represented by the full-time faculty. Nearly 75 percent of the full-time faculty members have received doctoral degrees, and all professors either work professionally in their field or are active in scholarly research. The majority are bilingual, and all faculty members act as teachers as well as advisers. The University also invites visiting professors from other universities for short-term residencies.

Student Government

Students are encouraged to take an active role in the student government as a way of contributing to the continued growth and development of the University. Elected officers of the student government meet regularly with the University administration to discuss matters of administrative and academic relevance. They also take responsibility for directing a variety of student social activities, athletic tournaments, club activities, and cultural events. The student government maintains funds for these activities, and the student officers enjoy a wide degree of autonomy in managing these financial resources.

Admission Requirements

Admission to the American University of Rome is highly selective. Candidates for admission to the University are reviewed by the Admissions Committee. Students are selected without regard to age, race, sex, creed, national or ethnic origin, or handicap. Requests for financial aid do not affect decisions on admission.

Candidates for admission must show evidence that they have completed or anticipate completing a level of education equivalent to four years of high school. Applicants for admission from high school or a secondary school are required to submit a completed application form, accompanied by a nonrefundable application fee; an official transcript of high school work; one academic recommendation from a principal, guidance counselor, teacher, or professor; and a 200- to 500-word personal statement indicating how a study experience in Rome could help further the student's career and life goals. Results of the SAT or ACT are required for students graduating from a U.S. high school system, whether in the U.S. or abroad. Face-to-face or phone interviews are required of all applicants. Transfer students must also submit official transcripts from all colleges or universities attended, as detailed below.

Each applicant is reviewed individually. Leadership, motivation, academic improvement, the level of difficulty of the high school program, involvement in activities, and potential for growth are important considerations in the application review process. Applicants whose native language is not English are required to submit scores from the TOEFL or another English language proficiency exam. The English language proficiency exam requirement may be waived for applicants who complete high school at English-speaking institutions. The American University of Rome TOEFL institutional code for reporting purposes is 0579. Information concerning the TOEFL may be obtained by going online to http://www.toefl.org.

Advanced standing may be granted for academic credits earned at institutions outside the university system of the United States. Candidates who have credentials from European lyceums, such as the Italian maturita', the International Baccalaureate, the British GCSE A-levels, and other equivalent programs, are evaluated, and advanced credits may be granted on the basis of that evaluation. In most instances, the first year of college (equivalent to 30 semester hours) may be granted. Students applying for advanced standing must submit official records of the last year of lyceum and a copy of the diploma, if granted. If the records are not written in either English or Italian, the admissions office requires a certified translation into English.

The American University of Rome welcomes transfer students. Upon submission of complete transcripts of all college and university courses previously taken, the University evaluates the credits earned and determines the number of credits to be accepted. Credit is granted only for courses completed with a grade of C or above. Transfer credits may be applied to no more than 50 percent of a student's major degree requirements. Students must complete at least 30 semester hours at the American University of Rome for an associate degree and at least 45 semester hours at the American University of Rome for a bachelor's degree. Transfer students with an equivalent of 60 semester hours of university study may seek a waiver for SAT and high school transcript requirements.

Application and Information

Applicants are notified of the admission decision two to four weeks after the application, supporting credentials, recommendation letter, and application fee are received.

Prospective students are encouraged to visit the campus. An application for admission and further information may be obtained by contacting the American University of Rome at its address in the United States or in Rome.

The American University of Rome
Via Pietro Roselli, 4
00153 Rome, Italy
Phone: 39-0658330919 (direct dial from U.S.)
Fax: 39-0658330992 (direct fax from U.S.)
E-mail: admissions@aur.edu

The American University of Rome
1730 Rhode Island Avenue, Suite 409
Washington, D.C. 20036
Phone: 202-331-8327
888-791-8327 (toll-free)
Fax: 202-296-9577
E-mail: aur.homeoffice@dc.aur.edu
Web site: http://www.aur.edu

FRANKLIN COLLEGE SWITZERLAND

LUGANO, SWITZERLAND

The College

Named for the United States' first and most illustrious ambassador to Europe, Franklin College was founded in 1969 as a nonprofit and independent postsecondary institution that takes as its cornerstone Benjamin Franklin's vigorous support of intellectual interchange between nations. An American liberal arts institution in an international environment, Franklin is fully accredited in the United States by the Commission on Higher Education of the Middle States Association of Colleges and Schools and in Switzerland by the Swiss University Conference.

Franklin College places extraordinary emphasis on cross-cultural perspectives, advocating that international studies should be an integral part of a college education, as a prelude to, and basis for, a student's commitment to a major field of study. Franklin defines higher education from its beginning as the experience of thinking internationally. Its emphasis, both academic and social, on global perspectives is designed to affect the direction and meaning of a student's college experience, life, and career.

The essence of a Franklin College education is the exposure of its students to cultures other than their own. The College's location, in a vibrant Swiss city that is part of the cultural milieu of northern Italy, ensures a constant commingling of cultures in a quadri-lingual nation. Students and faculty members, many who have a cross-cultural background, come to Franklin College from every corner of the globe, further strengthening international study and international experiences.

Approximately 60 percent of the students come from the United States; 40 percent are from Europe, Asia, Africa, South America, and the Middle East. Bringing a variety of experiences and perspectives to college life, they live in College dormitories and apartment residences on and near the campus. The apartments all have kitchens that are available, and the campus cafeterias also provide regular meal service and a meal plan. There is a residence supervisor for each of the eight buildings.

Campus activities are varied. The College Student Assembly promotes a student newspaper, a literary magazine, a theater group, language and sports clubs, and a variety of social events that take advantage of southern Switzerland's extensive recreational resources. There are competitive College sports teams in men's and women's soccer, and intermural teams include basketball, soccer, and volleyball. In addition, the Athletic Director enrolls interested students in the considerable number of local Swiss clubs and teams that welcome newcomers—especially basketball, football, ice hockey, soccer, and volleyball teams, but also clubs for crew, fencing, flying, golf, hang gliding, ice skating, judo, parachuting, riding, rock climbing, sailing, swimming, tennis, track, and windsurfing. By joining the local groups, Franklin students become part of the region's life; they are themselves essential to the cross-cultural learning the College promotes.

Location

The Franklin College campus is in the Sorengo section of the city of Lugano, southern Switzerland's principal business, banking, medical, and cultural center. Accessible from the campus either by public transportation or on foot, downtown Lugano and its surrounding lakeside villages are renowned for their scenic beauty and Mediterranean climate. Palm trees line lakefront piazzas, and an outdoor lifestyle is typical of Ticino, the Italian-speaking canton of Switzerland that best exemplifies Swiss versatility in all three of the national languages—Italian, German, and French.

Throughout the year, Lugano features outstanding cultural activities at the world-famous Thyssen art collection, the Swiss-Italian radio station with its own permanent symphony orchestra, and the International Convention Center, which attracts guest performers from around the world. Nine public museums, many art galleries, several movie houses, and a multitude of restaurants and discotheques make for a range of recreational choices normally found only in a large city. A covered ice rink, swimming pools, and a wide range of other sports facilities are maintained by local sports clubs; Lugano and the southern part of Switzerland offer access to an extraordinary variety of sports activities. In the spring and fall, Ticino's most popular recreation is hiking. In winter, skiing is available on Mount Tamaro, a 20-minute drive from the campus, or in the fabled St. Moritz, Davos, Klosters, and Zermatt.

Majors and Degrees

The Bachelor of Arts program offers majors in art history, comparative literary and cultural studies, environmental studies, European studies, history and literature, international banking and finance, international communications, international economics, international management, international relations, literature, modern languages, and visual and communication arts, with combined and double majors in two of nine subject areas. The Associate in Arts degree program provides a strong liberal arts foundation for students who usually continue their education in a baccalaureate degree program.

Academic Programs

Franklin's curricula promote international awareness and integrative thinking by being interdisciplinary in the highest tradition of liberal education. The courses of study explore the diverse disciplines that inform an educated human being. Students must complete at least 126 credit hours to be eligible for the B.A. degree (64 for the A.A. degree) and must maintain a minimum cumulative grade point average of 2.0 on a 4.0 scale.

As an integral credit-bearing part of the academic program, students participate twice a year (in mid-October and mid-March) in faculty-led academic travel-study programs to various destinations in Eastern and Western Europe, Africa, Asia, Latin America, and North America.

All degree candidates must demonstrate a foreign language proficiency equivalent to three years of university-level instruction in a language taught at Franklin. They meet this requirement, in a language other than their mother tongue, by successfully completing appropriate courses at Franklin or by passing an equivalency test administered by the language department.

In addition to their major field of study, students may add courses within another discipline to form a minor. The number of credit hours (12 to 15) and the program of courses are subject to departmental approval.

The College operates on a two-semester calendar, with classes starting in late August and mid-January; two summer sessions are also available. A required orientation program for all new students is held in August and mid-January.

Off-Campus Programs

The Academic Travel Program is a fully integrated part of the regular curriculum. Each semester, students participate in two weeks of faculty-led academic travel. More than any other program of study, it gives students an opportunity to learn the "other way"—by experience. Travel destinations for 2007–08 included Namibia; Malawi and Zambia; England; Paris and Southern France; Germany; Northern Greece and Turkey; Ireland; Morocco; Portugal; Russia; Slovenia, Croatia, and Serbia; Sicily; Slovenia; and Madrid, Barcelona, and Andalusia, Spain.

Internships are also available. Students with academic interest in any area may apply for an internship after two semesters of residence at Franklin, either by asking to be considered for one of the internships provided by the College or by arranging for an appointment themselves. The internship program is coordinated by a member of the Franklin faculty; a student may earn a maximum of 3 credit hours in an assignment.

Students in good standing who major in modern languages are eligible for study in a country where the target language is spoken; such study is limited to one semester at an approved institution.

Academic Facilities

The Franklin College Library contains 38,000 volumes and offers numerous English and foreign-language periodicals. The library also participates in the Swiss interlibrary loan system linking major Swiss university libraries. Three computer labs with Internet access are available for student use.

Costs

The comprehensive fee for the 2007–08 academic year was $41,560. This figure includes the cost of tuition, the room and board charge, academic travel, and student fees. The estimated cost of incidentals is $5000 per year. The estimated cost to fly round-trip from the United States ranges from $700 to $1500.

Financial Aid

Franklin College offers academic merit awards and need-based financial aid to qualified students. U.S. applicants for financial aid must submit the FAFSA for evaluation. Veterans' and Social Security benefits are available to eligible students. Federal Stafford Student Loans and PLUS loans may be obtained through local lenders. International students must submit the International Student Financial Aid Form. On-campus employment is available. Students interested in applying for on-campus employment should notify the campus Financial Aid Office at the beginning of each semester.

Faculty

The Franklin College faculty numbers 45 full-time and part-time teachers, approximately half of whom are American or British; the other half are of various European nationalities. The majority have advanced degrees from American universities, the others from British and Continental universities, and most have lived, studied, and taught in a variety of countries. The teaching staff represents the cross-cultural aims of the College. Faculty members are committed to the European arena of study, are familiar enough with particular countries to organize and lead academic travel, are competent in more than one language, and are dedicated to the personal, discursive style of teaching demanded by a small liberal arts college with small classes. These teachers also advise the various student activities, lead local excursions, and regularly contribute to the College's cocurricular program of lectures. In addition, each faculty member acts as academic counselor to a number of students. The faculty-conducted Academic Travel Program promotes the intellectual friendship between teacher and student essential to a liberal arts education. The student-faculty ratio is approximately 10:1.

Student Government

The student body elects the members of the Student Assembly. In addition to sponsoring interest groups and arranging social events, the Student Union appoints members to attend meetings of the College Faculty Assembly and the Appeals Board.

Admission Requirements

Franklin College seeks students who are eager to meet the challenge of studying and living in Europe, serious about undertaking college-level learning, and prepared to contribute positively to the intellectual life of the College. To identify such students, and also to ensure a diverse student population, the College Admissions Committee considers both academic and personal facts, including the student's academic record, evaluations by teachers and counselors, standardized test scores, extracurricular interests and talents, and academic distinctions. Admission to the College is limited and therefore competitive. To achieve the best match between the student and Franklin, a personal interview is strongly recommended; one can be arranged by contacting the Admissions Office in Lugano or New York. Applicants to the freshman class must submit a completed application form and a nonrefundable fee of $85; an official transcript of their secondary school record; SAT or ACT scores, either included on transcripts or forwarded by the testing service to Franklin College (CEEB code number 0922); and three letters of academic evaluation. Applicants whose first language is not English must submit their score on the Test of English as a Foreign Language (TOEFL); a score of at least 79 iBT, 217 CBT, or 550 PBT is required. Transfer applicants and institute applicants are required to submit a completed application and a nonrefundable application fee of $85, an official transcript of their college record, and one letter of academic recommendation.

Application and Information

The priority application deadline for fall entry is March 15 for applicants to the freshman class and June 15 for transfer and institute applicants. The application deadline for the spring semester is November 15. Admission decisions are made on a rolling basis. Applicants can usually expect a decision within three weeks from the time their application is completed. All inquiries and applications should be directed to the nearest Admissions Office.

U.S. Admissions Office
Franklin College Switzerland
91-31 Queens Boulevard, Suite 411
Elmhurst, New York 11373
Phone: 718-335-6800
Fax: 718-335-6733
E-mail: info@fc.edu

Karen Ballard
Director of Admissions
Franklin College Switzerland
Via Ponte Tresa, 29
6924 Sorengo/Lugano
Switzerland
Phone: 41-91-986-3613
Fax: 41-91-993-3906
E-mail: info@fc.edu
Web site: http://www.fc.edu

INTERNATIONAL COLLEGE OF THE CAYMAN ISLANDS

NEWLANDS, GRAND CAYMAN, CAYMAN ISLANDS

The College

International College of the Cayman Islands (ICCI) is situated in one of the world's premier banking and financial business centers and is ideally located to prepare students for careers in business. The College, which was founded in 1970, operates as a nonprofit, privately controlled, American-style senior college in Newlands, Grand Cayman.

The international student body is made up of about 200 men and women each quarter and usually includes representatives from other Caribbean islands as well as from countries around the world. The student body demonstrates intergenerational diversity, with students ranging in age from their late teens up to retired seniors. This diversity enhances class discussions and is an integral part of the educational goals of ICCI. ICCI offers the flexibility of allowing students to enroll for any of the four quarters.

Caribbean flavor permeates the area. The newly renovated campus provides air-conditioned classrooms in a tropical setting. The rich cultural heritage of the Cayman Islands, which is available to students through the National Museum, Heroes' Square, the Turtle Farm, Queen Elizabeth Botanic Park, the Blow Holes, the Wreck of the Ten Sails, environmental tours on land and sea, and local art and craft production of all kinds, enhances the educational experience at ICCI. No place is very far from another on this 22-mile island. The sister islands, Cayman Brac and Little Cayman, are also popular tourist destinations. The bluff on Cayman Brac has a 150-foot-high limestone formation. Bloody Bay Wall, which was ranked by *Skin Diver* magazine in May 1999 as the world's premier dive site, is located in the waters off Little Cayman.

The island abounds in recreational activities, such as running, swimming, scuba diving, golfing, volleyball, softball, netball, basketball, cricket, rugby, soccer, bicycle racing, and miniature golf. Soccer and cricket are two of the sports played professionally on the island. ICCI is less than 4 miles from Spotts Public Beach and 2½ miles from Pedro St. James Castle, the site of the "birthplace of democracy in the Cayman Islands." There are cultural events, such as plays, musicals, and concerts, at the Prospect Playhouse. The National Gallery hosts local and international exhibits. Annual festivities, such as the Agricultural Fair, the art show at the governor's mansion, Batabano Festival, and Pirates Week, are part of the island and campus life.

Students live off campus. On request, the College assists students in finding suitable accommodations.

The Accrediting Council for Independent Colleges and Schools (ACICS), Washington, D.C., accredits the College as a senior college to award associate, bachelor's, and master's degrees. In addition to its undergraduate programs, the College offers a Master of Business Administration degree program and a Master of Science degree program in management, with a human resources or education concentration.

Location

The Cayman Islands, which are located in the Caribbean Sea south of Cuba and west of Jamaica, are internationally famous for exceptional water sports. The clarity of the 80-plus-degree ocean waters makes underwater photography and fishing major attractions for the more than 1 million visitors to the Cayman Islands each year. The islands are an English-speaking British Overseas Territory and are known for the friendliness of their approximately 40,000 citizens. The temperature averages 85 degrees year-round, with sunshine and gentle trade winds.

The College, which is located in the quiet, rural village of Newlands, is a 15-minute drive from the capital, George Town, and Grand Cayman's airport, Owen Roberts International.

Majors and Degrees

The Associate of Science degree is offered in business with concentrations in accounting, banking, broadcasting, finance, hotel and tourism management, and information systems. General studies and office administration are also offered at the associate degree level.

The Bachelor of Science degree is offered in business administration, community service, liberal studies, and office administration. Several concentrations are available within these major areas, including accounting, an interdisciplinary arts/science concentration for elementary school teachers, international finance, and Dean-approved liberal studies concentrations.

For those employed in the banking industry, there is the Bachelor of Science degree in business administration with a concentration in international finance. The business administration program also has an accounting concentration.

Academic Programs

The academic year consists of four quarters—fall, winter, spring, and summer. A full academic load is 12 to 15 credits each quarter. A typical course is 5 credits.

A minimum of 180 credits is required for the Bachelor of Science degree, with no fewer than 60 credits earned in upper-division (300- and 400-level) courses and at least 55 credits in general education courses outside the major field. The specific requirements for each major vary. Credit by examination is available.

A minimum of 90 credits is required for the Associate of Science degree. No fewer than 30 credits must be earned in general education courses.

A cumulative grade point average of 2.0 or higher is required of all students in undergraduate programs at the College. To fulfill degree residence requirements, the equivalent of three quarters of full-time study must be taken at International College of the Cayman Islands.

The College also offers developmental courses in English, reading, math, and English as a second language.

Off-Campus Programs

Students who have earned at least 45 credits and meet additional criteria may participate, with approval, in internship programs with businesses and agencies and receive up to 5 credits for participation in the program. Each quarter, one or more seminars are offered over a long weekend in Miami. Two Miami seminars are required for graduation. Some of the many business and community service organizations that operate on the island are Rotary, Kiwanis, Lions Club, and Toastmasters.

Academic Facilities

Since reopening after Hurricane Ivan in 2004, the entire campus has undergone an extensive renovation. The library is still in the process of rebuilding its collection but offers students online access to thousands of periodicals, journals, and other full-text offerings. The Cayman Islands' first radio station, ICCI-FM, 101.1 MHz, is owned and operated by the College.

Costs

In 2007–08, tuition per course for an associate or bachelor's degree was $468.75. A registration fee of $62.50 and other fees of about $20 were charged each quarter. Books cost approximately $1250 for the school year. All costs are in U.S. dollars.

Financial Aid

Four kinds of financial assistance are available for students who qualify when funding permits: scholarships, grants, grants-in-aid, and loans. (Grants-in-aid include campus work assignments.) Approximately 15 percent of the students at International College of the Cayman Islands receive financial assistance.

Faculty

International College of the Cayman Islands has a full-time and adjunct faculty of 40 members. Adjunct faculty members generally work full-time in the area in which they teach, giving students the benefit of current, hands-on business experience that has been tested in the marketplace. All full-time faculty members serve as academic advisers. Guest lecturers, who are drawn to the Cayman Islands from around the world, share their expertise with students. Most classes are small, enabling the instructors to know their students by name. The student-faculty ratio was 11:1 for the 2006–07 academic year.

Student Government

The Student Activities Committee (SAC) is a dedicated core group of students who also serve as a voice in student government. All students are invited to join this organization.

Admission Requirements

Admission to the College for undergraduate studies is determined on an individual basis. Generally, a student should be at least 17 years old.

Admission to an undergraduate degree program at ICCI requires submission of a completed, paid application form and graduation from high school or its equivalent. In addition, a student must meet one of the following criteria: have a minimum SAT score of 1010 or an ACT cumulative score of at least 21; be a mature student (five or more years post–high school graduation with relevant work and/or business experience); have five General Certificate of Education (GCE), General Certificate of Secondary Education (GCSE), Caribbean Examinations Council (CXC), or other passes inclusive of English; or be a transfer student with credit(s) from an accredited, internationally recognized college or university. Transfer students must submit official transcripts. Applicants must also provide two letters of reference attesting to their intellectual and emotional readiness for college-level work. A satisfactory interview is required of local residents. In addition, a Test of English as a Foreign Language (TOEFL) score of at least 550 (paper-based) or its equivalent is required for international students whose native language is not English.

Each applicant is requested to visit the College and meet with one of the College admissions personnel or faculty members for a personal interview and to discuss plans and career goals.

Continuing education or transient students are required to provide a completed, paid application form. Overseas students should request a Student Visa Application Packet and return all completed application materials at least four months before the beginning of the quarter in which they wish to enroll. Cayman Islands immigration approval is a prerequisite for overseas students' enrollment. A one-year deposit is required.

Application and Information

The College catalog, applications, and other important forms may be found online at the College's Web site (http://www.icci.edu.ky). Applications for any quarter are considered at any time up to the opening of the quarter; however, overseas students must submit an application at least four months before the quarter in which they wish to enroll. Overseas applications must be sent via international airmail and include a nonrefundable application fee of $37.50 (U.S. dollars).

For application forms and additional information, students should contact:

Director of Admissions
International College of the Cayman Islands
P.O. Box 136
Grand Cayman KY1-1501
Cayman Islands
Phone: 345-947-1100
E-mail: icci@icci.edu.ky
Web site: http://www.icci.edu.ky

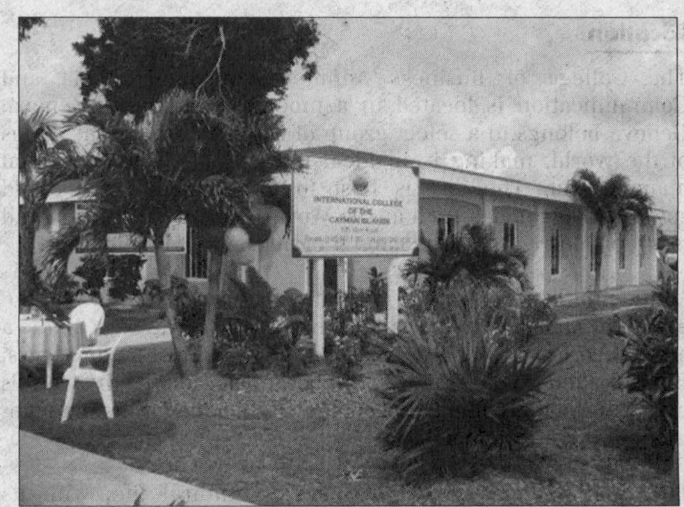

A view of ICCI's Caribbean-style campus.

INTERNATIONAL UNIVERSITY IN GENEVA

GENEVA, SWITZERLAND

The University

The International University in Geneva proposes undergraduate and graduate degrees in the areas of business administration, communication and media, and international relations. The International University in Geneva emphasizes the importance of interpersonal skills such as leadership, communication, and the ability to work in a multicultural team. These skills are encouraged through active participation and regular presentations in class.

The multicultural student body and faculty and the dynamic environment of the University contribute to the creation of a framework in which the students acquire global experience. The use of experiential learning methods such as case analysis and business simulations ensures the development of analytical skills, which are critical in today's competitive and rapidly changing world.

Students have access to several sport facilities, including basketball, volleyball, and tennis courts. Students have unlimited access to the Internet. The University provides personalized assistance for students looking for University housing or private apartments. An extensive range of student lodging is available in Geneva.

The University is accredited by the International Assembly for Collegiate Business Education (IACBE).

Location

The College of Business Administration and Media and Communication is located in a modern building in Geneva. Geneva belongs to a select group of truly "international" cities of the world, making it an ideal place to study international management. The city is host to the United Nations and specialized agencies such as the World Trade Organization and is often referred to as the capital of peace and diplomacy.

Many multinationals are located in the region due to the excellent logistical network and the central location of Geneva at the heart of Europe, only 1 hour by air from London, Paris, Brussels, and Milan. Geneva is well known as one of the world's major international financial centers, especially for the management of private capital assets.

The quality and variety of Geneva's cultural life, with its numerous theaters, museums, and international conferences, makes it the right place to obtain a global education. The city is a showcase for the most celebrated names in fashion, jewelry, and watch-making and is home to Rolex and Patek Philippe, among others. Ideally situated on the shores of Lake Leman at the foot of the Alps, Geneva offers excellent outdoor sporting activities.

Majors and Degrees

The International University in Geneva proposes five majors: finance and accounting, international relations, marketing and international business, media and communication, and, since September 2007, luxury goods management.

Academic Programs

The academic year consists of three trimesters, starting in September, January, and April. Students in the undergraduate programs must achieve a total of 129 credits in order to graduate. The total can be reduced by transfer credits or waiver examinations. As part of the academic program at the undergraduate level, students are required to take a foreign language such as French, Spanish, or Italian. With an emphasis on management and media, the curriculum helps the student to prepare for a career in business and related areas.

Off-Campus Programs

International University in Geneva has developed educational affiliation agreements with Indiana University of Pennsylvania; Monterey Institute of International Studies, California; Tulane University, New Orleans; and the University of Connecticut in the United States and with Institut Supérieur du Commerce in Paris, ESIC in Madrid, Yeditepe in Istanbul, Anahuac University in Mexico City, and the Universidad de San Ignacio de Loyola in Lima, Peru.

Academic Facilities

Most of the University's classrooms are equipped with state-of-the-art equipment, including beamers, video equipment, and Internet access. All computers have ADSL technology, allowing rapid Internet connections.

Costs

The 2008–09 tuition fees are 32,250 Swiss francs (or the equivalent in U.S. dollars) and include books. Access to the library and the computer center is free of charge. Room and board costs average 1,200 Swiss francs per trimester.

Financial Aid

Each year, International University in Geneva sponsors several assistantships. The selection criteria for the assistantships include academic achievement and the financial need of the applicant. A student can apply for an assistantship by writing a letter, which should be included with the application form. Students receiving the assistantships are required to devote 15 hours per week to the University, performing administrative duties.

Faculty

The faculty at International University in Geneva is multidisciplinary in professional training, international in experience, and practical in orientation, and its members are focused on their teaching. The full-time faculty is organized into unit coordinators, and the adjunct faculty is drawn from other educational institutions in the area and from the business community.

Student Government

The Student Council is the principal representation of student governance in the University. The Student Council is elected once a year and is organized into several subcommittees, including the Year Book Committee.

Admission Requirements

The International University in Geneva seeks a diverse student body and encourages applications from around the world. Admission to the University is competitive and emphasizes the applicant's previous academic performance and intellectual capacity. For the student's convenience, applications are considered on a rolling admission basis. The University has three starting dates throughout the academic year, in September, January, and April.

To enter the undergraduate program, the applicant must have successfully completed secondary education or high school with a minimum grade point average (GPA) of 2.3. In addition, the student is required to possess proficiency in English. The Test of English as a Foreign Language (TOEFL) is required of all applicants whose native language is not English. The minimum TOEFL score required is 80 (Internet-based test).

Application and Information

To be considered for admission, a student must submit the application form with the application fee of 150 Swiss francs (or $100); an official high school transcript should be sent by the school. An application and additional information may be obtained by downloading an electronic application form from the University's Web site or by contacting:

International University in Geneva
ICC, route de Pré-Bois 20
1215 Geneva 15
Switzerland

Phone: (+41 +22) 710 71 10
Fax: (+41 +22) 710 71 11
E-mail: info@iun.ch
Web site: http://www.iun.ch

JOHN CABOT UNIVERSITY

ROME, ITALY

The University

John Cabot University (JCU) was founded in 1972. The University concentrates on the liberal arts and social sciences using the American system, with a distinctive European and international character. It is strategically located in one of the world centers of diplomacy and international organizations. That, coupled with its unique relationship with leading multinational corporations, embassies, media, and other organizations, gives degree-seeking students the opportunity to participate in exclusive internship programs and become first-run candidates for job openings around the world. The University has a truly international student body—about a quarter of the students are Italian, half are American, and a quarter are from more than sixty other countries. The average class size is 20 students, and there are approximately 100 full- and part-time faculty members holding advanced degrees from major universities in the U.S. and Europe. Working closely with professors and classmates in a small-class setting, students receive the individual attention needed to fully develop their talents and abilities. With a student-centered approach to both education and human relationships, the University offers an active learning environment while also teaching the ethical standards that are essential in dealing with social pressures and in deciding how best to fulfill one's own goals in life.

As a four-year American university in Italy, JCU offers a wide variety of courses, taught in a truly international atmosphere. The Housing Office places students in off-campus apartments and in a residential hotel close to the University. Along with various campus activities, the Student Services and Activities Office organizes a wide variety of off-campus events, including educational travel throughout Italy.

The University is licensed by the Delaware Department of Education to award its degrees and is authorized by the Italian Ministry of Research and Instruction to operate as an institution of American higher education in Rome. John Cabot University is accredited by the Commission on Higher Education of the Middle States Association of Colleges and Schools, 3624 Market Street, Philadelphia, Pennsylvania 19104; telephone: 215-662-5606.

Location

Located in Rome, Italy, in the picturesque Trastevere neighborhood, just down the river from St. Peter's Basilica and the Vatican, John Cabot University is housed in a former convent, which consists of a central main building of three floors and an adjacent wing connected by terraces and courtyards. The original separate chapel is now the student lounge. The property offers students a tranquil atmosphere in which to study and interact, while historic, bustling Rome is just a few steps away. Surrounded by the green gardens of the Accademia dei Lincei (Galileo was an early member) and next door to the Villa Farnesina of Raphael's famous frescoes, the University is buttressed by the Aurelian Wall of the Roman Empire. John Cabot University is approached through the Porta Settimiana, which was built by Pope Alexander VI Borgia in 1498 and later restored by Pope Pius VI in 1798. However, the walls of an old convent do not confine, nor completely define, the University. Across the Tiber, in the Centro Storico (Historic Center), John Cabot also has spacious classrooms in the Sacchetti Building, overlooking the river. JCU has use of the impressive library of the Centro Studi Americani (Center for American Studies) in the beautiful Renaissance palace Palazzo Mattei. Fine arts and art history classes often meet at famous monuments such as the Colosseum and the Forum, which are within easy reach of JCU. In effect, all of Rome is John Cabot University's campus.

Majors and Degrees

John Cabot University offers the Bachelor of Arts degree in art history, business administration, communications, economics and finance, English literature, humanistic studies, international affairs, Italian studies, and political science. The University of Wales, in the United Kingdom, has validated JCU degrees in business administration, international affairs, and political science. As a result of this validation, students in these programs may work toward both an American degree from John Cabot University and a European degree (validated Honors) from the University of Wales. Students may select minors in art history, business administration, communications, computer science, economics and finance, English literature, history, international affairs, Italian studies, political science, and psychology.

John Cabot also offers the Associate of Arts degree in art history, business administration, communications, computer science, economics and finance, English literature, history, humanistic studies, international affairs, Italian studies, and political science. Each of these programs is designed to develop the characteristics of the individual student by means of a unique learning and living experience in a setting rich in history, culture, and geopolitical interaction.

Academic Programs

Unlike most European university systems, the American system of higher education encourages experimentation and breadth, particularly during the first two years of the university experience. The curricula of the University's programs are, therefore, divided into two basic categories: the general distribution requirements of the first two years of study, which give the student a broad exposure to the basic disciplines of the liberal arts educational experience, and the specified, additional requirements of each degree awarded by the University.

The general distribution and other introductory courses equip the student to select an area of specialization as a degree candidate in the junior and senior years. Within each degree program, there are specific requirements that must be met by the student who wishes to earn a degree at John Cabot. These requirements include ten to twelve core courses deemed by faculty members to be essential to the discipline of the degree and comparable to the requirements for the same degree at recognized and accredited colleges and universities in the American system of higher education. In addition to the core requirements, other requisites include electives that support the core program and offer opportunities to take courses in other discipline areas of particular interest or need.

The academic year is divided into two semesters of fifteen weeks each, beginning in September and January (students should see the academic calendar for more information). In one semester, a student normally enrolls in five courses, earning 15 credits in the semester and 30 credits in the year. A summer session of five weeks allows students to take one or two additional courses. To earn the Bachelor of Arts degree, a student must complete 120 credits (forty courses); to earn the Associate of Arts degree, a student must complete 60 credits (twenty courses).

Special programs include the Honors Program, internships, and the American Language Program (ALP).

Off-Campus Programs

Degree-seeking students also have the opportunity to study in the United States for credit for a semester or a year.

Academic Facilities

The Frohring Library, constructed in 1999, provides the latest in online access to academic journals and indexes and is the University center for research in support of the academic programs as well as a quiet place for study and pleasure reading. The computer laboratories provide a central point for students to work on computer science projects, prepare business presentations, write compositions and papers, check and send e-mail, and surf the Web. The labs contain IBM and IBM-compatible personal computers equipped with the latest software as well as high-speed printers and a full-color scanner. The Aula Magna is the largest room in the University and serves as the theater for the drama club. The Aula Magna is also used for orientation, cultural and community events, concerts, and student activities. This great hall is named in memory of Regina Occhiena of Castel Nuovo Don Bosco, who was a great-niece of Saint John Bosco and a great-grandmother of Charles Norman Secchia.

Costs

Tuition is $8850 or €6450 per semester, and the freshman student activity fee is $450 or €380. Housing costs begin at $4100 per semester.

Financial Aid

U.S. citizens attending a college or university outside the United States are eligible to apply for the Federal Family Education Loans (FFEL), including the Stafford Student Loan and PLUS loans. The Free Application for Federal Student Aid (FAFSA) form must be completed to apply for a Stafford Student Loan. Current U.S. government legislation prohibits U.S. citizens enrolled in colleges or universities outside the United States from receiving Federal Pell Grants, Federal Supplemental Educational Opportunity Grants (FSEOG), Federal Perkins Loans, and Federal Work-Study Program funds, even though they may be eligible for such assistance. Academic scholarships are awarded each year based on merit and need. John Cabot University is proud to participate in the Secchia Family Foundation's Secchia Scholars program. The four types of Secchia Scholarships are the Norman R. Peterson Scholarship, the Order Sons of Italy in America Scholarships, the Secchia–De Vos Merit Scholarships (up to nine awarded each year), and the Economic Club of Grand Rapids–Secchia Scholarship. Other institutional scholarships include the Presidential Scholarships, the Italian Merit Scholarships, and the 100/100 Italian Maturità Scholarships as well as the Maxwell Rabb Scholarship. A number of work-study assistantships are available for full-time, degree-seeking students who are interested in and capable of assisting the various administrative offices and academic departments of the University.

Faculty

The University has a distinguished faculty of approximately 100 part- and full-time professors from around the world. In addition to teaching, the faculty members take part in academic advising, the careful planning and monitoring of a student's progress through the academic program, and extracurricular activities, such as academic field trips and support of the student government.

Student Government

Student government at John Cabot University contributes significantly to the quality of student life. A Student Senate is elected each spring to coordinate activities. Three Student Government committees—the Entertainment Committee, the Cultural Affairs Committee, and the Service Committee—are open to all students for participation. During the year, the Student Government sponsors a number of programs, such as Jazz Night, Opera Night, and JCU theater productions. The Student Government works closely with the faculty adviser and the staff adviser in planning social, cultural, intellectual, and sports activities to respond to students' interests and needs.

Admission Requirements

Admission to John Cabot University is selective. Successful applicants must have maintained a scholastic record demonstrating a serious commitment to their studies and the ability to succeed at college-level work.

Each applicant is considered as an individual, and no single factor can guarantee acceptance to the University. The previous school's documentation of the applicant's academic ability, motivation, character, and contribution to school life is very important. This information should be reflected in the student's academic record and letters of recommendation. The University does not prescribe a fixed secondary school course of study but considers both the quality and breadth of the student's record. The University is open to all applicants without regard to race, national origin, religion, or gender. For applicants coming from the U.S. secondary school system, a standard college-preparatory program is expected. For applicants from other national systems, an essential requirement is successful completion of a secondary school program permitting university admission in the respective system. Students holding the Italian Diploma di Maturità, the International Baccalaureate, or other equivalent academic credentials may be granted advanced standing. Results of the SAT or the ACT are required for high school students graduating from an American secondary school. Applicants whose first language is not English or who did not attend a secondary school where classes were taught in English must demonstrate sufficient preparation in the English language. Standardized test scores, such as the Test of English as a Foreign Language (TOEFL) or the International English Language Testing System (IELTS), are useful in assessing a student's language capability. A minimum score of 550 on the TOEFL (213 on the computer-based exam or 85 on the Internet-based test), a minimum score of 6.5 on the IELTS, or an equivalent passing score on the John Cabot English Proficiency Test are accepted as evidence of sufficient preparation in the English language.

Application and Information

Admissions decisions are based on the review of official transcripts, results of standardized tests, the student's GPA, final examination results, a personal statement, and letters of recommendation from teachers or university professors. Students applying as transfer students from another university must be in good academic standing. An application form completed in its entirety must be accompanied by two recent passport-size photographs and a nonrefundable application fee of $50 or €50. Students may complete the application online or use the printable application. The University deadline is July 15 for fall admission and November 15 for the spring semester. Candidates are urged to submit their application and supporting documents as early as possible.

Students may apply online or obtain an application by contacting:

Admissions Office
John Cabot University
Via della Lungara, 233
00165 Rome
Italy
Phone: 39-06-681-9121
Fax: 39-06-683-2088
E-mail: admissions@johncabot.edu
Web site: http://www.johncabot.edu

RICHMOND, THE AMERICAN INTERNATIONAL UNIVERSITY IN LONDON

LONDON, ENGLAND

The University

Richmond, The American International University in London, prepares men and women to serve with purpose and generosity in an interdependent and multicultural world. Richmond offers a strong academic program with many choices of fields of study, an exceptional faculty, superb campus life, and fellow students from all over the world. In the United States, Richmond is accredited by the Commission on Higher Education of the Middle States Association of Colleges and Schools, a regional accrediting body recognized by the U.S. Department of Education. Richmond is accredited in the United Kingdom by the Open University and holds related degree validation. The University's undergraduate and graduate degrees are designated by the United Kingdom's Department of Education and Employment. The University is a comprehensive American liberal arts and professional university. In addition to the undergraduate degree programs described below, Richmond offers a Master of Arts in art history.

Freshmen and sophomores study and live at the Richmond campus, 7 miles from central London. Junior and senior years are spent at the Kensington campus in one of London's most beautiful residential and historic districts. As part of their four-year B.A. degree program, students may spend a semester or a year studying at one of the University's two international study centers in Florence and Rome, Italy. Richmond currently enrolls 1,000 students from more than 100 countries. Approximately 19 percent of the degree students are from Europe and the United Kingdom, 15 percent are from Pacific Rim countries, and 15 percent are from the Middle East. Fifteen percent of the student body represent the continent of Africa, and 2 percent are from Latin America. The remaining students are from North America. About 175 study-abroad U.S. students are enrolled for a semester or a year at the University.

Small classes, averaging 18 students, enable students to receive personal attention from professors in a supportive environment. The curriculum and academic advising system are structured to enable students to choose courses that provide broad knowledge, relevant skills, and an understanding of the world's many cultures and nations.

Richmond students supplement academic programs with activities that complement and balance the classroom experience. Many extracurricular and cocurricular programs are available to students, including Student Government, sports, and debate, drama, computer, Hellenic, Pan-African, and business clubs. There is also a University Honor Society.

Location

The Richmond Hill campus in the London suburb of Richmond offers a variety of entertainment, shopping, cultural, and recreational opportunities. Only yards from the University campus is Richmond Park, more than 2,200 acres of rolling hills and lush woodland, where one can ride horses, play tennis, jog, or simply relax. The journey from Richmond into Central London takes about 30 minutes.

The Kensington campus is located in the heart of London's Borough of Kensington, which has fine museums, libraries, theatres, concert halls, historic buildings, and well-known cultural and educational resources. The University takes full advantage of London's cultural and social resources through selected academic courses, work experience placements with multinational corporations, and special visits to museums, art galleries, theatres, and concert halls.

Majors and Degrees

Richmond operates its academic program on the American system. The University offers the four-year Bachelor of Arts (B.A.) and Bachelor of Science (B.S.) degrees in thirteen majors, with a further choice of seventeen minors, as well as the two-year Associate of Arts (A.A.) degree. Majors offered by the University are art, design, and media; business administration (finance, international business, marketing); communications; computing (computer systems engineering, information systems); economics; history; international relations; political science; and psychology. In addition, Richmond offers an engineering program jointly with George Washington University.

Academic Programs

In order to graduate with the dual-validated U.S. and U.K. degree [B.A./B.A. (Honors) or the B.S./B.Sc. (Honors)], students must earn a minimum of 120 credits. Usually, this means taking a full load for four years, or eight semesters. Within these 120 credits, students must complete all course requirements for their majors. Students must also meet the University's Language Proficiency and General Education requirements. In addition, valuable work experience for credit is offered through the International Internship program. Recent placements have been at the International Herald Tribune, General Electric, The House of Commons, CNN, the United Nations, Lloyds Bank, the Museum of London, and Sony Music Corporation.

Credit is also awarded for Advanced Placement tests (6 credits for each subject grade of 3, 4, or 5); a grade of A, B, or C on the "A" Level exams is awarded 9 credits (6 for D or E). Credit is also awarded for the International Baccalaureate, the Baccalauréat de l'Enseignement du Second Degré (France), the Abitur/Reifzuegnis (Germany), the Diploma di Maturità (Italy), and the School Leaving Diploma (Denmark, Finland, Norway, and Sweden).

The fall semester begins in late August and ends in mid-December. The spring semester begins in mid-January and runs through mid-May. Two sessions of summer school run from mid-May to mid-June and mid-June to mid-July.

Off-Campus Programs

Students may complement their studies in London with a semester, year, or summer at one of two international study centers. The centers, each offering intensive study of the language and culture of the country, are in Florence and Rome, Italy. The Florence Study Center emphasizes studio and fine arts. The Rome Center offers study in the Italian language and culture, art history, economics, and political science.

Academic Facilities

Information technology is integrated into the curriculum in ways that are natural to the discipline under study. Supporting this are nine student computer laboratories with 300 PCs and Macintosh computers, which connect to the Internet and are networked for student, faculty, and administrative use. Wireless network access is also available.

Richmond's libraries support the courses taught at each campus. Students may use either campus library. The libraries house 75,000 volumes and add approximately 4,000 new titles each year. In addition, the libraries have subscriptions to approximately 250 periodicals. Computers are available in both libraries for CD-ROM data searches and access to online databases through the network. Richmond students also have access to thirty-seven of the best libraries in London.

Costs

Tuition for the 2007–08 academic year was $25,000. Room and board were $11,000. Personal expenses, books and supplies, clothing, recreation, and travel costs also need to be factored in.

Financial Aid

Scholarships are awarded annually to students of high academic ability. Financial aid for U.S. citizens includes Federal Stafford Student Loans and Federal PLUS loans. All U.S. citizens must file the Free Application for Federal Student Aid (FAFSA) to qualify. Students should contact the admissions office for details regarding application procedures for scholarships and financial aid.

Faculty

The student-faculty ratio of 12:1 enables optimum interaction and individualized instructional assistance. The 105 faculty members (39 full-time, 66 part-time) have professional degrees from top European and American universities such as Harvard, Yale, the University of Michigan, Cambridge, Oxford, the London School of Economics, the Sorbonne, and the University of Bonn.

Student Government

The Richmond Student Union acts as a resource for all students, student organizations, and clubs to voice their opinions and ideas. The Student Union functions as a network between the student body and the administration. Using student ideas, it holds events and seeks to feature student talent while enhancing the overall University experience. The Student Union is ongoing in its development and thus offers possibilities for students to shape and change it. It is an organization directed by students for students and is structured to provide flexibility as well as the opportunity for all students to become involved.

Admission Requirements

Applicants are admitted on the basis of academic performance, references, intended major, and career interests. The required autobiographical essay is of paramount importance. Applicants to Richmond have usually completed a total of twelve years of primary and secondary school with a minimum grade of C+ (2.5 out of 4.0) in the American high school grading system, or its equivalent. British system students should have attained a minimum of five GCSE passes (grades of A, B, or C) in acceptable academic subjects, one of which must be mathematics or science. Equivalent qualifications gained under other educational systems are also considered for the purpose of admission.

Students must submit a completed application form, an essay, transcripts of all secondary and postsecondary school work, one letter of recommendation, and SAT or ACT scores (applies only to students graduating from the American education system). The ATP code for Richmond is 0823L. The ACT code is 5244. Evidence of proficiency in the English language is required from students whose first language is not English or who did not attendEnglish-speaking schools. Standardized test scores, such as the TOEFL or the ALIGU, or completion of recognized examinations, such as GCSE, Pitman, RSA, or lower Cambridge, are considered in assessing students' language capability.

Richmond admits students on a rolling basis, and applicants are encouraged to submit their application at the earliest opportunity. All documents in languages other than English must be accompanied by official translations. Applicants are usually notified of a decision within two to three weeks.

Application and Information

An application for admission and further information may be obtained by contacting the appropriate admissions office.

Applicants residing in the United States should contact:

Director of U.S. Admissions
U.S. Office of Admissions
Richmond, The American International University in London
343 Congress Street, Suite 3100
Boston, Massachusetts 02210-1214
Phone: 617-450-5617
Fax: 617-450-5601
E-mail: us_admissions@richmond.ac.uk
Web site: http://www.richmond.ac.uk

Applicants residing in all other countries should contact:

Director of Admissions
Office of Admissions
Richmond, The American International University in London
Queens Road, Richmond
Surrey TW10 6JP
England
Phone: 44-20-8332-9000
Fax: 44-20-8332-1596
E-mail: enroll@richmond.ac.uk
Web site: http://www.richmond.ac.uk

The Richmond Hill campus is situated near the River Thames in one of London's most attractive and secure areas. The impressive neo-Gothic structure was constructed in 1843.

SAINT LOUIS UNIVERSITY, MADRID

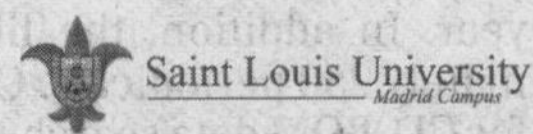

MADRID, SPAIN

The University

Founded in 1969, Saint Louis University, Madrid (SLU–Madrid), is the European campus of Saint Louis University in St. Louis, Missouri, United States, with an enrollment of approximately 650 undergraduate and 20 graduate students each academic semester. There are also about 350 undergraduate and 100 graduate students during the two summer sessions. About 25 percent of the University's students come from Spain, 45 percent from the U.S. (all fifty states), and the rest from sixty-five other countries.

Originally conceived as a home for study-abroad students, SLU–Madrid is now the only full-service American university in Spain. In addition to offering spaces to visiting students from all over the world, each year the University admits about 200 first-year students who begin their undergraduate careers on the Madrid campus. Students majoring in communications, economics, English, international business, international relations, and Spanish can complete their entire four-year degree program in Madrid. Students studying in the dual-degree International Nursing Program spend the first, second, and fourth years in Madrid; the third year is spent at the School of Nursing on the home campus in Missouri. All other degree majors transfer after two to three years to either the University's home campus or elsewhere to finish their degrees.

In addition to offering undergraduate career options for students who begin their programs in Madrid, the University also offers a master's degree in English language and literature and another in Spanish language and literature. The master's in English is a dual-degree program offered year-round with the Universidad Autónoma de Madrid and requires one 6-week summer session on the home campus. The master's in Spanish, offered on both a year-round and summer-only basis, can be completed in its entirety on the campus in Madrid.

SLU–Madrid is accredited through the North Central Association of Colleges and Secondary Schools as an integral part of the St. Louis campus. Individual schools and programs on the home campus also maintain separate accreditations (e.g., business, engineering, nursing) with their respective professional organizations.

Academic and social orientation is held at the beginning of the fall semester for all new degree-seeking students. Five-day orientation hiking trips in the Pyrenees and along the Camino de Santiago, the pilgrimage trail through northern Spain, give new students the opportunity to make friends and settle into life in Spain. A similar orientation program is offered at the beginning of each semester and summer session for visiting (study-abroad) students.

All new, first-year, degree-seeking students are required to live in University-approved housing. Students with extenuating circumstances may petition for independent housing arrangements prior to arriving in Spain. The University operates half room and board residencias in the surrounding neighborhoods. The residencias are three- to five-bedroom (single and double occupancy) fully furnished apartments. In addition, the housing department places students with Spanish host families—either single-stay or with other students. Second-, third-, and fourth-year continuing students can continue in the housing system or may make their own housing arrangements.

Visiting (study-abroad) students may choose to live with a Spanish host family or in the University-run residencias, space permitting. Most years, about 90 percent of these students live within the housing system; the rest make their own housing arrangements.

Location

The Madrid campus was the first American university program in Spain and the first free-standing campus in Europe operated by a U.S.-based university. Madrid, Spain's capital, with a population of more than 3 million, is politically, culturally, and geographically the heart of Spain. From the Prado Museum to the Palacio Real, the city's spectacular cultural offerings are surpassed only by its vibrant nightlife.

The campus is located in the prestigious university quarter of Madrid, overlooking the Sierra de Guadarrama Mountains, yet it is only 20 minutes by metro from Puerta del Sol, the center of the city. Surrounded by other private Spanish universities, the campus' location facilitates interaction between the University's Spanish, international, and American students.

Majors and Degrees

SLU–Madrid offers the first two years of more than sixty undergraduate degree programs, all of which are fully integrated with programs at the Missouri campus. Communication, economics, English, international business, international relations, and Spanish majors may choose to spend all four years of their degree program on the Madrid campus.

All students (permanent and visiting) are encouraged to participate in the Ibero-American Certificate Program. Over the course of two semesters (or one spring semester and one summer session) in residence in Madrid, the student takes courses on the arts, history, culture, economics, and politics of Iberia (Spain and Portugal) and Latin America. Participants can also opt to join a three-week seminar trip to South America at the end of the spring semester.

SLU–Madrid places a strong emphasis on language acquisition and fluency. Portuguese, Italian, German, French, and Arabic are offered apart from the obvious offerings in English and Spanish.

Further, while the language of instruction is English, students can choose to take a number of selected courses across disciplines in Spanish; an exceptional opportunity to develop fluency.

SLU–Madrid, in conjunction with the Universidad Autónoma de Madrid, offers a four-year, dual-degree program in international nursing. Participants spend two years on the Madrid campus, the third year at the School of Nursing on the home campus in St. Louis, and the final year at the Universidad Autónoma campus in Madrid. Nursing students earn two degrees: the Bachelor of Nursing from Saint Louis University and *la Diplomatura en Enfermería* from la Universidad Autónoma.

Academic Programs

The academic year consists of two semesters and two summer sessions. While the number of semester hours required for graduation varies with the program chosen, a minimum of 120 hours are required for a degree. A student must fulfill the required semester hours in a major as well as the basic requirements of the core curriculum. Students in most degree programs can complete 60–80 credit hours on the Madrid campus. The remainder must be completed on the home campus in St. Louis or at any other American university. Students pursuing the Bachelor of Arts degrees in communication, economics, English, international relations, and Spanish or the Bachelor of Business Administration degree in international business can complete all 120 credit hours on the Madrid campus.

Off-Campus Programs

As an international campus of Saint Louis University, SLU–Madrid designs courses to take advantage of its location in Europe. Select classes in each of the disciplines include mandatory trips to destinations in Europe, the Middle-East, Africa, and/or South America.

In coordination with the Association of American International Colleges and Universities, students can pursue study-abroad opportunities at partner schools in Europe, Africa, and the Middle East.

Business and engineering students with the required level of Spanish language skills are encouraged to pursue internships in the offices of multinational corporations, such as Hewlett-Packard, Kodak, and John Deere, which are all located in Madrid.

Academic Facilities

The Madrid campus comprises five buildings: Padre Rubio Hall, Padre Arrupe Hall, Loyola Hall, Manresa Hall, and Manresa Annex. Padre Arrupe Hall, a restored eighteenth-century chalet, contains administrative offices and faculty offices; three classrooms; two computer labs; and the biology, chemistry, and physics labs. Padre Rubio Hall, also dating to the eighteenth-century, houses the student life offices, Campus Ministry, faculty offices, a computer lab, and the bookstore and copy center. The University library and cafeteria are located in Loyola Hall. Manresa hall is the location of the Academic Services Department, which includes the Registrar Advising Center and Career Development offices. Manresa Annex houses the art studio.

Costs

Tuition and fees for U.S. permanent students at the Saint Louis University, Madrid campus, for 2007–08 were $9900 per semester. Non-U.S. students paid €7000 per semester. Non-U.S. status is determined by residency status outside the U.S. Room and board costs average €2900 per semester, depending on accommodations. Books and supplies cost approximately €500 per semester. Students should budget €500 per month for travel and activities. Costs are subject to change.

Financial Aid

All new degree-seeking and transfer students are automatically considered for Madrid one-year, renewable, merit-based scholarships. U.S. students also have access to all federal, state, and privately funded student aid programs by submitting the Free Application for Federal Student Aid (FAFSA).

Faculty

The Madrid campus of Saint Louis University has approximately 90 full- and part-time faculty members, the majority of whom hold the highest degrees in their fields. The average class size is 20 students, and the student-to-teacher ratio is 8:1.

Admission Requirements

The programs of SLU–Madrid, are open to all without regard to race, color, sex, age, national origin, religion, sexual orientation, disability, or veteran status. All University policies, practices, and procedures are administrated in a manner consistent with its Catholic Jesuit identity. Students who have demonstrated past academic achievement and who show promise and aptitude for successful performance in an international-university environment are encouraged to apply for admission. SLU–Madrid welcomes students from diverse school systems around the world. This diversity of secondary school experience raises the academic level on the campus.

A student's potential for success in college studies on the Madrid campus is judged by the student's high school average, rank in class, aptitude test scores (ACT and SAT), and recommendations.

Transfer students in good academic standing are invited to apply. Transfer students must submit transcripts from high school and each college attended.

Students from universities and colleges are invited to spend a semester, summer, or year on the Madrid campus. SLU–Madrid specializes in semester programs for students from academic disciplines, such as engineering and premedicine, who traditionally have a difficult time enrolling in a study-abroad program.

Admissions decisions are made on a rolling basis.

Application and Information

To be considered for admission, a student should complete the online application found at the University's Web site. Paper applications are available upon request from the Admissions Department. The application deadline for the fall semester is May 30 for freshman enrollment; however, U.S. applicants are encouraged to apply earlier to receive full consideration for financial aid.

Admissions Department
Saint Louis University, Madrid
Avenida del Valle, 34
28003 Madrid
Spain
Phone: 34-91-554-58-58
E-mail: admissions@madrid.slu.edu
Internet: http://spain.slu.edu

COLLEGE DATA CENTER • INTERNATIONAL

SCHILLER INTERNATIONAL UNIVERSITY

LARGO, FLORIDA

The University

Schiller International University (SIU) was founded in 1964. Although originally intended for American students, the University soon attracted men and women from other nations and is now an international, coeducational, four-year institution with seven locations in six countries and alumni from more than 150 countries. SIU prepares students for careers in business and management, multinational organizations, government agencies, academic institutions, and the social services as well as for further study. Through enrollment in both practical and theoretical courses and through discussions with instructors and classmates with multicultural backgrounds, students gain firsthand knowledge of business and cultural relations among the peoples of the world. In addition, SIU students have the unique opportunity to transfer between SIU campuses, without losing any credits, while continuing their chosen program of study. The language of instruction at all campuses is English. The current enrollment is 1,400 students.

SIU students are housed in University residence halls, with selected host families, or in private rooms or apartments. Residence hall accommodations are available at the London and Florida campuses and in Heidelberg, Strasbourg, and Leysin. At all campuses not requiring on-campus residence, or in the event that all residence halls are full, trained staff members assist students in securing housing in the private market or with families. Many Schiller academic programs are also available by distance learning.

SIU offers the Master of Arts degree in international hotel and tourism management and the Master of Arts degree in international relations and diplomacy with an optional specialization in international business or European studies; the Master of Arts degree in communication; the Master of Business Administration degree; the Master of Business Administration degree in financial planning, hotel and tourism management, international business, international hotel and tourism management, and IT management; and the Master of International Management in international business. SIU also offers the Master of Science degree in computer engineering on the Florida campus.

Schiller International University is an accredited member of the Accrediting Council for Independent Colleges and Schools, which is recognized by the United States Department of Education as a national institutional accrediting agency. SIU degrees correspond to the American system of university education.

Location

Schiller International University has campuses in Largo (Tampa area), Florida; central London, England; Paris and Strasbourg, France; Heidelberg, Germany; Madrid, Spain; and Leysin, Switzerland.

SIU Florida (residential), the main campus, is in the city of Largo near the Gulf of Mexico in one of America's most beautiful coastal regions, near the Tampa–St. Petersburg metropolitan area. The campus facilities, two modern buildings, face directly across the street from beautiful Largo Central Park and within eyesight of a new $22-million public library and the renowned Largo Cultural Center. World-famous entertainment centers, amusement parks, and movie production centers are within easy driving distance.

SIU London—Waterloo (central London–residential) is in the magnificent Royal Waterloo House, centrally located near the Waterloo Bridge and the South Bank cultural center.

SIU Paris (nonresidential) is centrally located in a modern building on the left bank of the Seine in the exciting Montparnasse area, with easy access to all of Paris.

SIU Strasbourg (residential) occupies the Château de Pourtalès in Robertsau at the northern edge of the city. The Château offers classroom, dormitory, and dining facilities (two restaurants and a Salon de Thé) and access to the European Community's Parliament Building and Court of Justice in Strasbourg.

SIU Heidelberg (residential) is located next to the Law School of the University of Heidelberg in the center of town. The Graduate Center and student residence are located just across the Neckar River in the beautiful Palais Friedrich.

SIU Madrid (nonresidential) is located in a modern building in the Arguelles, one of the city's most attractive districts.

SIU Leysin, American College of Switzerland (residential), is a campus of SIU located above the eastern end of Lake Geneva in the French-speaking portion of Switzerland, near Geneva and the French and Italian borders.

Majors and Degrees

Schiller International University offers the Bachelor of International Business Administration (B.B.A. in international business) degree, with concentrations in banking, financial management, management, management of information technology, and marketing. Schiller also offers the Bachelor of Business Administration degree in resort/club management and in international hotel and tourism management, with concentrations in hotel management and tourism management, and the B.B.A. in club/resort management.

The Bachelor of Arts (B.A.) degree is offered in interdepartmental studies, international economics, international relations and diplomacy, and psychology. Psychology is offered in conjunction with the New School of Psychotherapy and Counseling, located on the SIU London campus.

The Bachelor of Business Administration (B.B.A.) degree is offered in economics, IT management, and international business administration.

The associate degree in business administration (A.S.) is offered in club management and with an optional concentration in computer system management.

Schiller also offers the associate degree in business administration (A.S.) in international hotel and tourism management, with concentrations in hotel management and tourism management.

Associate of Arts (A.A.) degrees are offered in general studies, with a concentration in art and design.

Diplomas are available in hotel operational management and Swiss hotel management. The hotel operational management diploma requires two semesters of on-campus study and a six-month internship.

Academic Programs

The academic emphasis at Schiller International University is on international business, international relations and diplomacy, international hotel and tourism management, information technology, and languages.

An associate degree program requires 62 credits; a bachelor's degree program requires 124 credits. An average grade of C (2.0) or higher is required for all programs. Each credit reflects 15 academic hours of classroom work; typical courses earn 3–4 credits.

Classes run during two 15-week semesters and a seven-week summer session in a manner similar to that at most universities in the United States.

Academic Facilities

Each campus includes classrooms, computer facilities, a library, and a student lounge. The University library holdings are about 92,000 volumes. In addition, students have access to millions of publications via extensive external libraries for original research.

Costs

For 2008–09, tuition and required fees at the Florida campus are $9082 per semester. Costs at the European campuses vary by campus but are approximately $10,190 per semester for tuition and required fees. Some campuses offer room and board. Students should contact 866-748-4338 (toll-free) for details about each campus.

Financial Aid

SIU grants two kinds of financial aid: academic tuition awards and University service (work-study) grants for those who qualify. Total aid does not exceed one half of the tuition. Students are encouraged to seek assistance through private or government loan and scholarship programs before applying to the University. Eligible students may apply for a Pell Grant, Supplemental Educational Opportunity Grant, Federal Work-Study, the Federal Family Educational Loan Program, U.S. veterans' training programs (U.S. citizens or eligible noncitizens), or a Canada Student Loan (Canadian citizens only). Applications for financial aid must be received by March 31 for the following academic year.

Faculty

The faculty consists of more than 280 men and women who are academically qualified and experienced in their fields. Extensive student-faculty interaction is encouraged; the student-faculty ratio is about 16:1.

Student Government

Each campus has an elected Student Council that acts as a liaison between the students and the administration and is involved in many areas of academic and social life.

Admission Requirements

Applicants must have completed the secondary level of education in a government-recognized educational system, generally of twelve years' duration, or have the equivalent of five GCE-O-level examinations (British school system). Students who have not completed the equivalent of high school studies or five GCE-O-level examinations may be eligible to apply for special University-preparatory programs.

All nonnative English speakers must take the SIU–English Placement Test when first enrolling. Those whose English language proficiency is not adequate for University-level studies are required to take additional English language courses.

Application and Information

Applications are handled individually and without regard to race, sex, religion, national or ethnic origin, or country of citizenship. Because SIU operates on a rolling admissions system, applicants are advised of their admission status soon after all application materials (a completed application form and official transcripts of all secondary-level education and, for transfer applicants, all college-level study) and the $60 application fee have been received. For application forms or further information, students should contact the University.

Schiller International University
300 East Bay Drive
Largo, Florida 33770
Phone: 866-748-4338 (toll-free)
Fax: 727-734-0359
E-mail: admissions@schiller.edu
Web site: http://www.schiller.edu/

On the campus at Schiller International University.

NOTES

Peterson's Book Satisfaction Survey

Give Us Your Feedback

Thank you for choosing Peterson's as your source for personalized solutions for your education and career achievement. Please take a few minutes to answer the following questions. Your answers will go a long way in helping us to produce the most user-friendly and comprehensive resources to meet your individual needs.

When completed, please tear out this page and mail it to us at:

Publishing Department
Peterson's, a Nelnet company
2000 Lenox Drive
Lawrenceville, NJ 08648

You can also complete this survey online at **www.petersons.com/booksurvey.**

1. What is the ISBN of the book you have purchased? (The ISBN can be found on the book's back cover in the lower right-hand corner.) ____________________

2. Where did you purchase this book?

❑ Retailer, such as Barnes & Noble
❑ Online reseller, such as Amazon.com
❑ Petersons.com
❑ Other (please specify) ______________________________

3. If you purchased this book on Petersons.com, please rate the following aspects of your online purchasing experience on a scale of 4 to 1 (4 = Excellent and 1 = Poor).

	4	3	2	1
Comprehensiveness of Peterson's Online Bookstore page	❑	❑	❑	❑
Overall online customer experience	❑	❑	❑	❑

4. Which category best describes you?

❑ High school student
❑ Parent of high school student
❑ College student
❑ Graduate/professional student
❑ Returning adult student
❑ Teacher
❑ Counselor
❑ Working professional/military
❑ Other (please specify) ________________________

5. Rate your overall satisfaction with this book.

Extremely Satisfied	Satisfied	Not Satisfied
❑	❑	❑

6. **Rate each of the following aspects of this book on a scale of 4 to 1 (4 = Excellent and 1 = Poor).**

	4	3	2	1
Comprehensiveness of the information	❑	❑	❑	❑
Accuracy of the information	❑	❑	❑	❑
Usability	❑	❑	❑	❑
Cover design	❑	❑	❑	❑
Book layout	❑	❑	❑	❑
Special features *(e.g., CD, flashcards, charts, etc.)*	❑	❑	❑	❑
Value for the money	❑	❑	❑	❑

7. **This book was recommended by:**

❑ Guidance counselor
❑ Parent/guardian
❑ Family member/relative
❑ Friend
❑ Teacher
❑ Not recommended by anyone—I found the book on my own
❑ Other (please specify) ______________________________

8. **Would you recommend this book to others?**

Yes	Not Sure	No
❑	❑	❑

9. **Please provide any additional comments.**

____

____

____

____

____

Remember, you can tear out this page and mail it to us at:

Publishing Department
Peterson's, a Nelnet company
2000 Lenox Drive
Lawrenceville, NJ 08648

or you can complete the survey online at **www.petersons.com/booksurvey.**

Your feedback is important to us at Peterson's, and we thank you for your time!

If you would like us to keep in touch with you about new products and services, please include your e-mail address here: ______________________________